P9-DMP-225

STUDENT BIBLE

Presented To

Lisa Fahey

On this 21 day of December 94

By Jeff Pennala

The publisher wishes to acknowledge Michael Pink and Hidden Manna, Inc., for assistance with the compiling and editing of *The Rock*.

Cover Design by: Mark Herron Productions
Book Design by: Kerry Woo

ISBN: 0-8024-7599-X

Printed in the United States of America

NEW AMERICAN STANDARD BIBLE

MOODY PRESS
CHICAGO

TABLE OF CONTENTS

RELEVANCY OF GOD'S WORD

For thousands of years, people have been relying on God's Word to do everything from guide the everyday affairs of life to provide a system of laws and just government. Now it is true that not everyone puts their trust in God or His Word, but it is written in Scripture that *"Man shall not live on bread alone, but on every word that proceeds out of the mouth of God."* (Mat.4:4)

It is God's intention that everyone live according to His Word. The reason many people choose not to follow God's Word is not because they have studied it and disagree - It's because, in many cases, they haven't seen a living demonstration of it from those who do know God's Word.

The best way to discover the relevancy of God's Word is to read it for yourself, consider what it says and how it applies to your everyday life, incorporate it into your conversation and do what it says. In fact Joshua 1:8 says *"This book of the law shall not depart from your mouth, but you shall meditate on it day and night, so that you may be careful to do according to all that is written in it; for then you will make your way prosperous, and then you will have success."*

Once you know God's Word and begin to live by what it says, not only will you benefit from its wisdom, but people around you will begin to notice the difference. When others see that God has given man instructions on how to handle every area of life, not to limit him, but to help him reach his potential, many will quite naturally want to know God and how they can live by every word that proceeds from His mouth.

Yes, the Word of God is truly relevant for every situation, whether it be in times of heartbreak or happiness, at work or in the home, God's Word shines as a light to our path to show us the way of life. Indeed God is a loving Father and He has given us His Word that if we meditate in it, we will be strong, and if we obey it we will live and *"eat the best of the land."*

HOW TO USE THE ROCK STUDENT BIBLE

The Rock Student Bible has been designed especially for you. Its purpose is to assist you in getting the most out of God's Word so that you may apply it more effectively in your daily life. Throughout the Bible you will find tools written to expand your understanding of God's Word and to fill in the gaps which exist because of the enormous time span between now and the time it was written.

One of the key features of *The Rock* is its extensive use of cross references. The purpose of these cross references is to direct you to other passages in the Bible that relate to the one you are reading. By comparing passages you will gain a broader understanding of the person, place, event or concept in the passage.

To use the cross reference system follow this example. Locate John 3:16 on the next page. Notice that the letter "a" appears in superscript beside the word "loved." Now locate the letter "a" next to number 16 in the center column of the page (near the bottom). Beside the letter "a" is a reference to Romans 5:8. Turning to Romans 5:8 you'll find a verse of Scripture that expands on the concept of God's love found in John 3:16.

The concordance located at the end of the New Testament book of Revelation is a similar tool for study. Use the concordance to locate key Bible passages associated with a specific word. Let's say you were interested in knowing what the Bible says about "Love." Turn to page 53 of the concordance and find the word "Love" in bold. Following this word are the key Scriptures to look up for a better understanding of the word.

In the back of the Bible there is a section entitled "Tough Questions Facing the 90's Generation" which will be of great help to you. Included with these most-asked questions are Scripture passages providing the Bible's answers.

Special sections entitled "A Closer Look" are spread throughout the Bible text. These sections will help you better understand what life was like during Bible times. Questions have been provided to guide you in applying biblical truths and principles to today. You may use these questions in group discussion or individual study.

You will make your Bible more personal and usable by following the guidelines presented on page G1, "Creative Ways to Get More from Your Bible." Here you will find step by step suggestions, such as Note Taking, that will help you apply Scripture toeveryday life.

First Passover—Cleansing the Temple

13 And [a]the Passover of the Jews was
at hand, and Jesus [b]went up to Jerusalem.
14 [a]And He found in the temple those
who were selling oxen and sheep and
doves, and the moneychangers seated.
15 And He made a scourge of cords,
and drove *them* all out of the temple,
with the sheep and the oxen; and He
poured out the coins of the moneychangers, and overturned their tables;
16 and to those who were selling [a]the
doves He said, "Take these things away;
stop making [b]My Father's house a house
of merchandise."
17 His [a]disciples remembered that it
was written, "[b]ZEAL FOR THY HOUSE
WILL CONSUME ME."
18 [a]The Jews therefore answered and
said to Him, "[b]What sign do You show
to us, seeing that You do these things?"
19 Jesus answered and said to them,
"[a]Destroy this [1]temple, and in three
days I will raise it up."
20 [a]The Jews therefore said, "It took
[b]forty-six years to build this [1]temple,
and will You raise it up in three days?"
21 But He was speaking of [a]the [1]tem-
ple of His body.
22 When therefore He was raised from
the dead, His [a]disciples [b]remembered
that He said this; and they believed [c]the
Scripture, and the word which Jesus had
spoken.
23 Now when He was in Jerusalem at
[a]the Passover, during the feast, many
believed in His name, [b]beholding His
signs which He was doing.
24 But Jesus, on His part, was not
entrusting Himself to them, for [a]He
knew all men,
25 and because He did not need anyone to bear witness concerning man [a]for
He Himself knew what was in man.

The New Birth

3 NOW there was a man of the Pharisees, named [a]Nicodemus, a [b]ruler of
the Jews;
2 this man came to Him by night,
and said to Him, "[a]Rabbi, we know that
You have come from God *as* a teacher;
for no one can do these [1b]signs that You
do unless [c]God is with him."
3 Jesus answered and said to him,
"Truly, truly, I say to you, unless one [a]is
born [1]again, he cannot see [b]the kingdom
of God."
4 Nicodemus *said to Him, "How
can a man be born when he is old? He
cannot enter a second time into his
mother's womb and be born, can he?"
5 Jesus answered, "Truly, truly, I say
to you, unless one is born of [a]water and
the Spirit, he cannot enter into [b]the
kingdom of God.

13 [a]Deut. 16:1-6; John 5:1; 6:4; 11:55 [b]Luke 2:41; John 2:23
14 [a]John 2:14-16: *Matt. 21:12ff.; Mark 11:15, 17; Luke 19:45f.;* Mal. 3:1ff.
16 [a]Matt. 21:12 [b]Luke 2:49
17 [a]John 2:2 [b]Ps. 69:9
18 [a]John 1:19 [b]Matt. 12:38
19 [1]Or, *sanctuary* [a]Matt. 26:61; 27:40; Mark 14:58; 15:29; Acts 6:14
20 [1]Or, *sanctuary* [a]John 1:19 [b]Ezra 5:16
21 [1]Or, *sanctuary* [a]1 Cor. 6:19
22 [a]John 2:2 [b]Luke 24:8; John 2:17; 12:16; 14:26 [c]Ps. 16:10; Luke 24:26f.; John 20:9; Acts 13:33
23 [a]John 2:13 [b]John 2:11
24 [a]Acts 1:24; 15:8
25 [a]Matt. 9:4; John 1:42, 47; 6:61, 64; 13:11

1 [a]John 7:50; 19:39 [b]Luke 23:13; John 7:26, 48
2 [1]Or, *attesting miracles* [a]Matt. 23:7; John 3:26 [b]John 2:11 [c]John 9:33; 10:38; 14:10f.; Acts 2:22; 10:38
3 [1]Or, *from above* [a]2 Cor. 5:17; 1 Pet. 1:23 [b]Matt. 19:24; 21:31; Mark 9:47; 10:14f.; John 3:5
5 [a]Ezek. 36:25-27; Eph. 5:26; Titus 3:5 [b]Matt. 19:24; 21:31; Mark 9:47; 10:14f.; John 3:3
6 [a]John 1:13; 1 Cor. 15:50
7 [1]Or, *from above*
8 [a]Ps. 135:7; Eccl. 11:5; Ezek. 37:9
10 [a]Luke 2:46; 5:17; Acts 5:34
11 [a]John 1:18; 7:16f.; 8:26, 28; 12:49; 14:24 [b]John 3:32
13 [1]Later mss. add *who is in heaven* [a]Deut. 30:12; Prov. 30:4; Acts 2:34; Rom. 10:6; Eph. 4:9 [b]John 3:31; 6:38, 42 [c]Matt. 8:20
14 [a]Num. 21:9 [b]Matt. 8:20 [c]John 8:28; 12:34
15 [1]Some mss. read *believes in Him may have eternal life* [a]John 20:31; 1 John 5:11-13
16 [1]Or, *unique, only one of His kind* [a]Rom. 5:8; Eph. 2:4; 2 Thess. 2:16; 1 John 4:10; Rev. 1:5 [b]Rom. 8:32; 1 John 4:9 [c]John 1:18; 3:18; 1 John 4:9 [d]John 3:36; 6:40; 11:25f.

6 "[a]That which is born of the flesh is
flesh, and that which is born of the Spirit
is spirit.
7 "Do not marvel that I said to you,
'You must be born [1]again.'
8 "[a]The wind blows where it wishes
and you hear the sound of it, but do not
know where it comes from and where it
is going; so is everyone who is born of
the Spirit."
9 Nicodemus answered and said to
Him, "How can these things be?"
10 Jesus answered and said to him,
"Are you [a]the teacher of Israel, and do
not understand these things?
11 "Truly, truly, I say to you, [a]we speak
that which we know, and [b]bear witness
of that which we have seen; and [b]you do
not receive our witness.
12 "If I told you earthly things and you
do not believe, how shall you believe if I
tell you heavenly things?
13 "And [a]no one has ascended into
heaven, but [b]He who descended from
heaven, *even* [c]the Son of Man.[1]
14 "And as [a]Moses lifted up the serpent in the wilderness, even so must [b]the
Son of Man [c]be lifted up;
15 that whoever [1]believes may [a]in
Him have eternal life.
16 "For God so [a]loved the world, that
He [b]gave His [1c]only begotten Son, that
whoever [d]believes in Him should not
perish, but have eternal life.
17 "For God [a]did not send the Son into
the world [b]to judge the world, but that
the world should be saved through Him.
18 "[a]He who believes in Him is not
judged; he who does not believe has
been judged already, because he has not
believed in the name of [b]the [1]only begotten Son of God.
19 "And this is the judgment, that [a]the
light is come into the world, and men
loved the darkness rather than the light;
for [b]their deeds were evil.
20 "[a]For everyone who does evil hates
the light, and does not come to the light,
lest his deeds should be exposed.
21 "But he who [a]practices the truth
comes to the light, that his deeds may be
manifested as having been wrought in
God."

John's Last Testimony

22 After these things Jesus and His
[a]disciples came into the land of Judea,
and there He was spending time with
them and [b]baptizing.

17 [a]John 3:34; 5:36, 38; 6:29, 38, 57; 7:29; 8:42; 10:36; 11:42; 17:3, 8, 18, 21, 23, 25; 20:21 [b]Luke 19:10; John 8:15; 12:47; 1 John 4:14
18 [1]Or, *unique,* only one of His kind [a]Mark 16:16; John 5:24 [b]John 1:18; 1 John 4:9
19 [a]John 1:4; 8:12; 9:5; 12:46 [b]John 7:7
20 [a]John 3:20, 21; Eph. 5:11, 13
21 [a]1 John 1:6
22 [a]John 2:2 [b]John 4:1, 2

THE ROCK DAILY DEVOTIONAL

JANUARY

1 The Creation *Gen. 1*
2 Adam and Eve *Gen. 2*
3 The Fall *Gen. 3*
4 The Flood *Gen. 6-8*
5 Tower of Babel
Gen. 11:1-8, Ps. 10
6 Sodom and Gomorrah
Gen. 18-19:29
7 Israel in Captivity
Gen. 50:22-Exo. 1
8 The Plagues
Exo. 7:14 - Exo. 11
9 The Passover *Exo. 12:1-30*
10 The Exodus *Exo. 12:31-42*
11 The Firstborn *Exo. 13:1-16*
12 Crossing the Red Sea
Exo. 13:17-Exo. 14
13 The Wilderness
Exo. 16-17:7, 23:20-33
14 The Ten Commandments
Exo. 19-20
15 The Tabernacle
Exo. 2, 5, 26-28
16 The Tabernacle
Exo. 29-30, 35-36
17 The Sabbath *Exo. 31:12-18, Isa. 58:13-14*
18 The Priests *Lev. 8, 9*
19 Day of Atonement
Lev. 16, 23:26-32
20 The Golden Calf *Exo. 32-33:6*
21 Travels of Israel
Num. 10:11-36
22 Exploring Canaan *Num. 13*
23 Aaron's Staff *Num. 17, 24*
24 Water from the Rock *Num. 20*
25 Bronze Snake
Num. 21:4-9, John 13
26 Balaam's Donkey
Num. 22:21-24
27 Israel's Spies *Deut. 1:6-2:23*
28 Other gods *Deut. 13*
29 Crossing the Jordan *Josh. 3-4*
30 Jericho's Fall *Josh. 5:13-6:27*
31 Time Stands Still *Josh. 10*

FEBRUARY

1 Theft of the Ark
1 Sam. 4:1-11, 5, 7:1
2 Miracles for Elijah *1 Kings 17*
3 Miracles for Elisha *2 Kings 4*
4 A Call to Build *Hagg. 1-2*
5 Cain and Abel *Gen. 4*
6 Abram's Call
Gen. 11:31- Gen. 12:20
7 Abram and Lot *Gen. 13-14*
8 God's Covenant with Abram
Gen. 15
9 Abram's Sons
Gen. 16, 17, 21:1-20
10 Abram's Test
Gen. 22:1-9, Ps. 128
11 Isaac and Rebekah *Gen. 24*
12 Jacob and Esau *Gen. 25:19-34, Gen. 27-28*
13 Jacob and the Blessing
Gen. 28:10-31:21, 35:1-14
14 Jacob and Esau's Reunion
Gen. 32-33
15 Joseph, The Dreamer
Gen. 37, 39-41
16 Joseph and His Brothers
Gen. 42-45:24
17 Joseph and Father Reunited
Gen. 45:25- Gen. 46
18 Moses *Exo. 1:22- Exo. 2:25*
19 Holy Ground *Exo. 3-5*
20 God's Covenant with Moses
Exo. 24
21 Joshua *Josh. 1*
22 Rahab the Harlot *Josh. 2*
23 Achan and His Sin *Josh. 7*
24 Deborah *Judg. 4-5*
25 Gideon *Judg. 6-8:35*
26 Samson *Judg. 13-14*
27 The Vengeance of Samson
Judg. 15
28 Samson and Deliah
Judg. 16:1-21, Ps. 139

MARCH

1 Samson's Death *Judg. 16:22-31, Ps. 145*

2 Ruth and Naomi *Ruth 1*

3 Ruth and Boaz *Ruth 2-4*

4 Hannah *1 Sam. 1-2:11*

5 Samuel *1 Sam. 3*

6 Saul as King *1 Sam. 8-10, 11:12-15*

7 Saul's Jealousy *1 Sam. 18-19, 23:7-1 Sam. 24*

8 Saul's Death *1 Sam. 31, 2 Sam 1*

9 David Anointed *1 Sam. 16*

10 David and Goliath *1 Sam. 17*

11 Jonathan and David *1 Sam. 20*

12 David as King *2 Sam. 2:1-7, 5:1-5, Ps. 72*

13 David the Warrior *2 Sam. 5:6-25, 8:1-14, Ps. 20*

14 David and Bathsheba *2 Sam. 2*

15 David's Song of Praise *2 Sam. 22, Ps. 18*

16 Solomon *1 Kings 2*

17 Solomon's Wisdom *1 Kings 3, 4: 29-34*

18 Solomon Builds the Temple *1 Kings 6*

19 Elijah *1 Kings 18, Ps. 124*

20 Naaman *2 Kings 5*

21 Esther *Esth. 1-5*

22 Esther as Queen *Esth. 6-10*

23 Job Tested *Job 1-2:10; 42*

24 Job Hears God *Job 38-41*

25 Jeremiah *Jer. 1*

26 Jeremiah Searches His Heart *Jer. 17:5-10*

27 Jeremiah and The Potter *Jer. 18-19*

28 Ezekiel *Ezek. 1-3*

29 Nebuchadnezzar's Dream *Dan. 2, 4*

30 Writing on the Wall *Dan. 5*

31 Shadrach, Meshach, Abednego *Dan. 3*

APRIL

1 Daniel in the Lion's Den *Dan. 6*

2 Daniel's Visions *Dan. 7-8*

3 Daniel's Vision of a Man *Dan. 10*

4 Hosea's Reconciliation *Hos. 1, 3*

5 Jonah's Call *Jonah 1-2*

6 Jonah and The Whale *Jonah 3-4*

6 Obedience and Disobedience *Duet. 28*

8 Redemption Prophecy *Isa. 1:18-31*

9 The Joy of the Redeemed *Isa. 35*

10 Comfort from the Lord *Isa. 40*

11 Help from the Lord *Isa. 41*

12 Restoration in Isaiah *Isa. 54:17-55, Ps. 27*

13 The Exiles *Jer. 2 9, Ps. 137*

14 Reconciliation with God *Jer. 30-31*

15 God's Compassion *Lam. 3*

16 Glory and Favor *Isa. 60-61*

17 Decisions *Joel 1-4*

18 Complacency *Amos 6*

19 Robbing God *Mal. 3:6-18, Lev. 27:30, Luke 18:12, Ps. 105*

20 Jesus' Birth *Matt. 1:24-25, Luke 1:26-38, 2:1-20, Ps. 100*

21 Jesus in The Temple *Luke 12:41-50, Deut. 16:18, Ps. 132*

22 Jesus Baptized *Matt. 3:13-17, Mark 1:9-11, Luke 3:21-33, John 1:29-34, Ps. 120*

23 Jesus Tempted *Matt. 4:1-11, Mark 1:12-13, Luke 4:1-13*

24 Jesus and the Disciples *Matt. 10, John 1:35-51*

25 Jesus' First Miracle *John 2:1-11, 1:14, Exo. 14:31, Ps. 129*

26 Lepers Healed *Matt. 8:2, Mark 1:40, Luke 5:12, 17:11, Ps. 131*

27 Healing the Sick *Matt. 7:14, 8:5, 14, 16, 9:20, John 4:43-54*

28 Jesus Commands Nature *Matt. 8:23, 17:24, Mark 6:48, Ps. 79, Mark 11:12, Luke 5:1, 17:11, Ps. 80*
29 Demons are cast out *Matt. 8:28, 9:32, 12:22, 15:21-28, Ps. 82*
30 The Lame are Healed *Matt. 8:22, 9:2, Mark 3:1, John 5*

MAY

1 Jesus Raises the Dead *Matt. 9:18, 23, John 11*
2 Feeding the Multitudes *John 14:13-21, 15:29-31*
3 Lamp under a Basket *Matt. 5:14-16, Luke 11:33-36*
4 The Wise and The Foolish *Matt. 7:24-27, 6:47-49*
5 New and Old *Matt. 9:16-17, Mark 2:21-22, Ps.69*
6 The Sower and The Tares *Matt.13:3-30, Luke 8:4-15*
7 The Mustard Seed *Matt. 13:31-32, Heb. 11:1-6, Ps. 76*
8 The Great Treasure *Matt. 13:44-46, 2 Cor. 4 & 5*
9 The Dragnet *Matt. 13: 47-50, Matt. 8, Ps. 15*
10 The Lost Sheep *Matt. 18:12-14, 15:3-7, Ps. 97*
11 The Workers in the Vineyard *Matt. 20:1-16, Ps. 68*
12 The Two Sons and Evil Tenants *Matt. 21: 28-46, Ps. 14*
13 The Wedding Feast *Matt. 2:2-14, Luke 14:16-24, Ps. 6*
14 The Wise and Foolish Virgins *Matt. 25:1-13, 24:37-51*
15 The Fig Tree *Matt 24:32-44, Mark 13:28-32, Luke 21:29-33, Ps. 48*
16 The Talents *Matthew 25:14-30, Luke 19:12-27*
17 The Creditor and Debtors *Luke 7:41-50, Ps. 117*
18 The Good Samaritan *Luke 10:30-37, Matt. 22:34-40, Ps. 99*
19 A Friend in Need *Luke 11:5-13, Prov. 17:17, Ps. 85*
20 The Rich Fool *Luke 12:16-34, Ps. 98*
21 Faithful and Evil Servants *Luke 12:35-48, Ps. 83*
22 The Barren Fig Tree *Luke 13: 1-9, Ps. 67*
23 The Great Supper *Luke 14:16-24, Matt 22:2-14*
24 Building a Tower and a King in War *Luke 14:25-35, Ps. 66*
25 On Things Lost *Luke 15:8-32*
26 The Unjust Steward *Luke 16:1-13, Ps. 126*
27 Lazarus and the Rich Man *Luke 16:19-31, Ps. 106*
28 Unprofitable Servants *Luke 17:7-10, Ecc.9*
29 The Persistent Widow *Luke 18:1-8, James 5:13-20, Ps. 5*
30 The Absent Householder *Mark 13:33-37, Luke 12:35-40, Ps. 78*
31 The Growing Seed *Mark 4:26-29, Rev 14:15, Ps. 142*

JUNE

1 The Tax Collector *Luke 18:9-14, I Pet. 5:5-7*
2 The Pounds *Luke 19:11-27, Matt. 25:14-30*
3 Jesus Cleanses the Temple *John 2:13-22, Ps. 69:9*
4 The Transfiguration *Matt. 17:1-13, Luke 9:28-36*
5 The Triumphant Entry *Matt 21:1-9, Mark 11:1-10*
6 The Lord's Supper *Matt 26:17-29, I Co 11:23-25*
7 Jesus and Nicodemus *John 3:1-21, Num. 21:8-9*
8 Samaritan Woman *John 4:5-42, Ps. 17, 19*
9 Rich Young Ruler *Matt 19:16-29, Mark 10:17-30*
10 Zacchaeus *Luke 19:1-9, Ps. 104*
11 Casting of Stones *John 8:1-11, Rom 3:23-31*

12 Greatest Commandment *Matt. 22:34-40, Exo. 20*
13 Seven Woes *Matt. 23*
14 Sign of the End *Matt. 4:1-51, Luke 21:5-36*
15 The Unknown Hour *Luke 12:42-46, Matt. 24:36-50*
16 The Word Made Flesh *John 1:1-18, Ps. 102*
17 Bread of Life *John 6:29-59, Ps. 115*
18 The Lord's Prayer *Matt. 6:9-13, Luke 11:2-4*
19 The Beatitudes *Matt. 5:3-12, Luke 6:20-23*
20 Fulfillment of the Law *Matt. 5:17-48, Ps. 23*
21 Treasures in Heaven *Matt. 6:19-24, Luke 11:34-36, Ps. 56*
22 Do Not Worry *Matt. 6:25-33, Luke 12:22-31*
23 Ask, Seek and Knock *Matt 7:7-12, Luke 11:9-13, Ps. 93*
24 Judging *Luke 6:41-42, Matt. 7:3-5, Ps. 95*
25 The Harvest *Matt. 9:35-36, John 4:35, John 3:16, Ps. 96*
26 A Narrow Door *Luke 13:22-30, Ps.122*
27 Lamb of God *John 1:29-34, Isa.53*
28 The Shepherd and Flock *John 10: 1-21*
29 Foot Washing *John 13:1-17, Ps. 47*
30 The Holy Spirit *John 14:15-31, John 16:5-16*

JULY

1 Comfort *John 14:1-14, 15:18-27, John 17*
2 Vine and the Branches *John 15:1-17*
3 Prophecy of Jesus' Birth *Isa. 9:1-7, Luke 2:11, Ps. 141*
4 Prophecy of Jesus the Redeemer *Isa. 53, Ps 22*
5 Jesus as a Servant *Isa. 42:1-9, 43:1-13, Ps. 54*
6 Jesus Death *Matt. 26 Mark 14, Luke 22, John 18*
7 The Burial of Jesus *Matt. 27, Mark 15, Luke 23, John 18*
8 Resurrection *Matt. 28, Luke 24:1-14*
9 Great Commission *Matt 28:16-20, Mark 16:15-18*
10 The Ascension *Luke 24:50-53, Acts 1:1-10*
11 Second Coming *1 Thess. 4:13-18, 5:1-11, Ps. 81*
12 Jesus in Hebrews *Heb. 1-5, 7-10*
13 John the Baptist *Luke 1:5-25, Num 6:3, Ps. 86*
14 John's Ministry *Matt. 3:1-12, John 1:13-28*
15 John Beheaded *Matt 14:1-12, Mark 6:14-29, Ps. 90*
16 Mary the Mother of Jesus *Luke 1:26-2:56, John 19:25-27, Ps. 75*
17 Joseph *Matt. 1:16-25, Ps.109*
18 Elizabeth and Zechariah *Luke 1:5-25, 36-45, 57-80*
19 Ananias and Sapphira *Acts 5:1-11, Mal. 3:6-12, Ps. 103*
20 Stephen *Acts 6:1-8:3*
21 Simon *Acts 8*
22 The Ethiopian Eunuch *Acts 8: 26-39, Ps. 108*
23 Saul's Conversion *Acts 9:1-31*
24 Saul in Prison *Acts 16:16-40, Ps. 91*
25 Paul in Ephesus *Acts 19*
26 Paul's Travels *Acts 21:27, Acts 28*
27 Paul and His Ministry *2 Cor. 6:3-13, 9:6-15, 2 Cor. 10-13*
28 Cornelius *Acts 10-11:18*
29 Peter *Matt 26:31-35, John 21: 15-25, Acts 12*
30 Mary Magdalene *Luke 8:2, John 19:25, John 20:1, 10-18*
31 Herod *Acts 12:19-23, Gal. 6:7, Ps. 89*

AUGUST

1 The Apostles *1 Cor. 4, 9*
2 John *Acts 4:1-3, Gal 2:9, Acts 12:12-13*
3 *Ps. 148-150*
4 Andrew *Matt. 4:18-22, Mark 1:16-18*
5 Apollos *Acts 18:24-28, I Cor. 1:12, 3:4-6*
6 Priscilla and Aquila *Acts 18*
7 Silas *Acts 15:22-40, 16: 16-17:15*
8 Pentecost *Acts 2:1-47*
9 Crippled Beggar *Acts 3:1-26*
10 Healing *Acts 9:32-43*
11 Persecution *Acts 4:1-31, Acts 5:17-42*
12 The Seven Churches *Rev. 1-4*
13 End Times *Rev. 19, 20, 21, 22*
14 Righteous Judgement *Rom. 1-3*
15 Wisdom *1 Cor. 1:18-1 Cor. 2*
16 Wisdom *James 3*
17 Forgiveness *2 Cor. 2:5-11. Ps 123*
18 Forgiveness *2 Cor. 5:11-6:2*
19 Forgiveness *Gal. 3:26-4:7*
20 Forgiveness *Heb. 10:1-18*
21 Forgiveness *Gal. 6:1-10, Ps. 147*
22 Forgiveness *Eph. 1*
23 Faith *Gal. 3:1-25*
24 Faith *Heb. 11*
25 Faith *James 2:14-26, Ps. 110*
26 Faith *1 John 5*
27 Protection and Provision *Eph. 5:10-20*
28 Protection and Provision *Phil. 4:4-20*
29 Prayer *James 5:13-20, Ps. 146*
30 Life in the Spirit *Gal 5:16-26, Ps. 87*
31 Alive in Christ *Eph. 2*

SEPTEMBER

1 Glorious Riches *Eph. 3*
2 Children of Light *Eph. 4*
3 Humility *Phil. 2*
4 Supreme Authority *Col. 1:1-23, 2:2-3*
5 Christ Like *Col 2:6-23*
6 Instructions for Living *1 Th. 5:12-28*
7 High Calling *Phil. 3:12-4:1, Ps 143*
8 Living for God *1 Pet. 3:8- 1 Pet 5:14*
9 Perseverance *Heb. 10:19-39*
10 Holy Living *Col. 3:1-17*
11 Standing Firm *2 Thess. 2:13-17, Ps. 130*
12 Faithfulness *2 Tim. 1-2:13*
13 Study the Word *2 Tim. 2:14-26, Ps. 116*
14 Godliness *2 Tim 3-4*
15 Submission *Jam. 4;1-17, 1 Pet. 2:4-12*
16 Holiness *1 Pet.1:13-2:3*
17 Walk in the Light *1 John 1-2:14*
18 God's Love *1 John 4:7-21*
19 Worship *1 Cor. 11:2-16, 14:26-40, 1 Tim 2*
20 Thanksgiving *Phil. 1, Ps. 135*
21 Heaven *2 Cor. 4-5:10*
22 A New Covenant *2 Cor. 2:12- 2 Cor. 3:18*
23 Giving *2 Cor. 9:6-15*
24 Death *1 Cor. 15*
25 Death *Rom. 4-6*
26 Sins and the Law *Rom. 7-9*
27 Idols *1 Cor. 8, 1 Cor. 10:14-22*
28 Unbelievers *2 Cor. 6:14-7:1, Heb. 2:1-4, 3:7-19*
29 The Flesh *Phil. 3:1-11, Ps. 136*
30 Disobedience *2 Thess. 2:1-12, Ps. 74*

OCTOBER

1 False Teachers *1 Tim. 1:3-11, Ps. 88*
2 Love of Money *1 Tim. 6:3-21, Ps. 64*
3 Falling Away *Heb. 6:4-6, 10:26-31, Ps. 118*
4 Warnings Against Sin *Heb. 1, 13*
5 Trials and Temptations *James 1:2-27*
6 The Tongue *James 3*

7 Love of the World
1 John 2:15-3:24
8 Try the Spirits *1 John 4*
9 Church Division *1 Cor. 3*
10 One Body, Many Parts
1 Cor. 12:12-31, Ps. 114
11 Unity *Eph. 4:1-16, Ps. 133*
12 The Church *1 Tim. 3-6:2*
13 The Sabbath
Heb. 4:1-13, Ps. 138
14 Favoritism *James 2*
15 What to Teach *Titus 2*
16 Lawsuits and Believers
1 Cor. 6
17 Sexual Immorality
1 Cor. 5, 6:12-20
18 Marriage *1 Cor. 7*
19 Wives and Husbands
Eph. 5:22-33
20 Christian Homes *Col. 3:18-4:1, Eph. 5:22 -6:9*
21 Wives and Husbands
1 Pet. 3:1-7, Ps. 134
22 Children *Eph. 6: 1-4, Ps. 127*
23 The Weak and The Strong
Rom. 14, 15:1-13
24 Love *1 Cor. 13*
25 Love *Rom. 12:9-21, 13:8-14, Ps. 113*
26 Freedom
1 Cor. 10:23-11:1. Ps. 53
27 Freedom in Christ
Gal. 5:1-15, Ps. 112
28 Comfort *2 Cor. 1:3-11, Ps. 52*
29 Encouragement *2 Cor. 4*
30 Goodness
Titus 3:1-11, Ps. 144
31 Chosen People
1 Pet. 2:4-12, Ps. 50

NOVEMBER

1 Your Calling *2 Pet. 1:3-11*
2 *Prov. 1, Ecc.1*
3 *Ps. 119*
4 *Prov. 2*
5 *Ps. 49, 50*
6 *Prov. 3, Ecc 2*
7 *Ps. 7, 16*
8 *Prov. 4*
9 *Ps. 38, 40*
10 *Prov. 5, Ecc. 3*
11 *Ps. 101, 39*
12 *Prov. 6*
13 *Ps. 12, 33*
14 *Prov. 7, Ecc. 4*
15 *Ps. 34, 37*
16 *Prov. 8*
17 *Ps. 84, 111*
18 *Prov. 9, Ecc.5*
19 *Ps. 2, 121*
20 *Prov. 10*
21 *Ps. 125, 29*
22 *Prov. 11, Ecc 6*
23 *Ps. 11, 94*
24 *Prov. 12*
25 *Ps. 62, 63*
26 *Prov. 13, Ecc 7*
27 *Ps. 3, 4*
28 *Prov. 14*
29 *Ps. 8, 46*
30 *Prov. 15, Ecc. 8*

DECEMBER

1 *Ps. 9, 13*
2 *Prov. 16*
3 *Ps. 30, 55*
4 *Prov. 17, Ecc. 9*
5 *Ps. 24, 31*
6 *Prov. 18*
7 *Ps. 25, 32*
8 *Prov. 19, Ecc 10*
9 *Ps. 26, 35*
10 *Prov. 20*
11 *Ps. 21, 36*
12 *Prov. 21, Ecc. 11*
13 *Ps. 28, 70*
14 *Prov. 22*
15 *Ps. 43, 65*
16 *Prov. 23*
17 *Ps. 41, 77*
18 *Prov. 24*
19 *Ps. 59, 60*
20 *Prov. 25*
21 *Ps. 44, 107*
22 *Prov. 26*
23 *Ps. 42, 45*
24 *Prov. 27*
25 *Ps. 139, 122*
26 *Prov. 28*
27 *Ps. 57, 71*
28 *Prov. 29*
29 *Ps. 51, 73*
30 *Prov. 30, 31*
31 *Ps. 58, 61*

THE WHOLE PICTURE

From the account of creation in Genesis to the prophetic record of future events in Revelation the Bible gives us a sweeping picture of God's dealings with man. It does not record primarily what man thinks about God, but what God has to say to man—about sin and its consequences, about God's justice and mercy and love, and about His Son.

It is impossible to understand this full sweep of God's revelation without knowing the relationship between the Old Testament and the New. Each is essential to the other. The New completes and fulfills the Old (Matthew 5:17). And the Old is the foundation for the New (it is estimated that the Old Testament is quoted or alluded to over 600 times in the New).

Jesus Christ, who was with the Father before the world was, is the Book's central figure. The world was made by Him and for Him (Colossians 1:16) and world history will culminate in Him (Revelation 11:15). The Old Testament looks forward to Him. The New reveals Him as the Lamb of God (John 1:29), the one mediator between God and men (1 Timothy 2:5).

The harmony and unity of the Bible—though written by about forty authors (whose writings God superintended) over a period of some two thousand years—is a tremendous argument for the Bible's divine nature and authority.

THE OLD TESTAMENT

The Books of the Law

These first five books of the Bible, called the Pentateuch (meaning "five volumes"), were written by Moses. While the first book deals with the beginnings of all things, the last four books focus on the beginnings of Israel, the nation through which salvation by grace would be made available to the entire world.

The Books of History

These books picture the rise and fall of Israel over a thousand-year-period—Israel's settling of Canaan, her faltering under the Judges, her rise under Saul, David, and Solomon. They also tell of the divided kingdom after Solomon's death, the fall of the northern kingdom in 722 B.C. and the fall of Judah more than a century later. The last record the history of the remnant of Jews who returned from the Babylonian captivity.

The Books of Poetry

These five books are so called because they were written as

poetry rather than prose. Hebrew poetry had as its chief characteristic a "sense rhythm," or repetition of ideas. Lamentations is also poetic.

The Books of Prophecy

The Bible does not present the prophetic books in chronological order. Instead, it groups the major prophets first and then the twelve minor prophets. The prophets, official spokesmen whom God raised up to speak for Him, especially in times of unbelief and apostasy, came into special prominence during the decline and fall of Israel and Judah. The prophets proclaim judgment and future restoration for both kingdoms. After Malachi there was a four-hundred-year "silence" between the Old and New Testaments before the coming of Christ.

THE NEW TESTAMENT

The Gospels and Acts

The four gospels record the earthly life and ministry of Jesus Christ. Matthew emphasizes Him as King, Mark as Servant, Luke as the perfect Man, John as the Son of God. Yet all four accounts harmonize. The book of Acts written by Luke, records the early growth of Christianity after Jesus' ascension.

The Epistles

The twenty-one epistles contain the inspired correspondence of the apostles and those chosen by our Lord to communicate His truth to His church. The Bible does not present these in chronological order but according to authorship. Paul wrote the first thirteen. The first nine are directed to specific churches and the next four to individuals. Hebrews was written to the Jews by an unknown writer. The other seven, often known as "general epistles" because they were not directed to anyone specifically, were written by James, Peter, John, and Jude.

Prophecy

The book of Revelation, penned by John, is the climactic book of the Bible, giving us a glimpse into the future and the culmination of all history in the events surrounding the second coming of Jesus Christ.

The Bible—66 Books

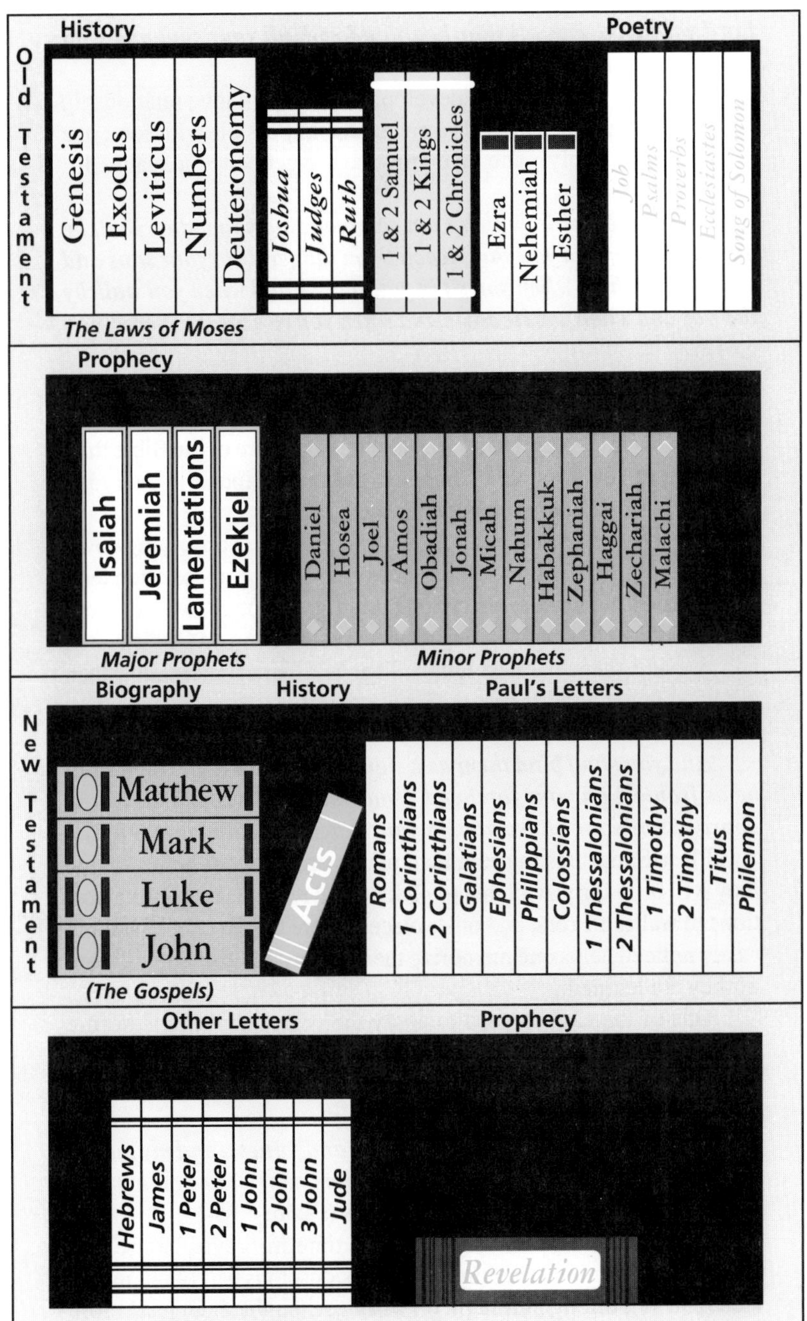

SEVEN WAYS TO MAKE TIME FOR GOD AND HIS WORD

The Lord is our God, the Lord is one! And you shall love the Lord your God with all your heart and with all your soul and with all your might. (Deuteronomy 6:4-5).

Place a high priority on developing a personal love relationship with God. We want to spend as much time as possible with someone we love very deeply. The love grows as we get better acquainted!

And these words, which I am commanding you today, shall be on your heart; and you shall teach them diligently to your sons and shall talk of them when you sit in your house and when you walk by the way and when you lie down and when you rise up. (Deuteronomy 6:6-7).

Teach God's Word to children (your own or someone else's). No one learns more than the teacher. Digging into Scripture and simplifying it to a child's level causes us to retain far more of the Bible than we might dream possible. Conversing about Scripture in everyday situations is especially effective, as well.

Use those times of day when you are sitting, walking, lying down and getting up to meditate on Scripture. Otherwise, these often tend to be wasted minutes. If we are memorizing Scripture, we can more easily use traveling and waiting times for meditating on God's words and praying them back to Him. That is a better alternative than allowing one's mind to just drift into neutral.

And you shall bind them as a sign on your hand and they shall be as frontals on your forehead. And you shall write them on the doorposts of your house and on your gates (Deuteronomy 6:8-9).

Place Scriptures in prominent places around your home so that they will be readily available to pick up and read. Taping Bible portions to walls, mirrors, and other places where they will be often and easily noticed helps one memorize them faster. Keep changing them as they are learned.

One of the easiest ways to apply the verses above is to secure Scripture portions on tape or disk that can be played while driving, relaxing, or working around the house.

My soul is satisfied as with marrow and fatness, and my mouth offers praises with joyful lips. When I remember Thee on my bed, I meditate on Thee in the night watches (Psalm 63:5-6).

Finish your day right by spending time in prayer, praise and Scripture meditation at bedtime. The subconscious part of our minds tends to dwell through the night on what we thought about just before going to sleep and will give you a good start the next day.

If because of the sabbath, you turn your foot from doing your own pleasure on My holy day, and call the sabbath a delight, the holy day of the Lord honorable, and shall honor it, desisting from your own ways, from seeking your own pleasure, and speaking your own word, then you shall take delight in the Lord, and I will make you ride on the heights of the earth (Isaiah 58:13-14).

The timeless principle here is that one day out of every seven should be God's special day. Imagine how much time there would be for God if we gave Him one-seventh of each week's waking hours. Even allowing for church attendance, fellowship, rest and ministries, there would be ample time for Bible study and prayer.

Therefore be careful how you walk, not as unwise men, but as wise, making the most of your time, because the days are evil. So then do not be foolish, but understand what the will of the Lord is. And do not get drunk with wine, for that is dissipation, but be filled with the Spirit (Ephesians 5:15-18).

Allow yourself to be continuously controlled by the Holy Spirit by presenting ;your body, mind, emotions, and will to Him regularly. Only He can give the directions and motivation for truly wise use of one's time. Seek His will in prayer for definite goals in the area of personal priorities (those areas most important to a person). Break up each goal into what must be done weekly or daily to accomplish it.

Two are better than one because they have a good return for their labor. For if either of them falls, the one will lift up his companion. But woe to the one who falls when there is not another to lift him up. Furthermore, if two lie down together they keep warm, but how can one be warm alone? And if one can overpower him who is alone, two can resist him. A cord of three strands is not quickly torn apart (Ecclesiastes 4:9-10,12).

Enlist the help of a friend or two in mutually-agreed-upon Scripture and personal development projects. Having definite, regular times for working together to advance, review and check up gives us deadlines that are harder to pass by than those we set with ourselves alone. Many find that even initial memorization of a passage comes easier and faster when doing it with a friend.

CREATIVE WAYS TO GET MORE FROM YOUR BIBLE

When most Christians pick up a Bible all they see is miracles, demons, angels, sacrifices, prophets, the flood, the creation of the world and the end of time. Then they put it back down, unable to make sense of it all in light of their present needs: school, a disintegrating family, financial pressures, dissolving relationships and different kinds of abuse.

Why is it that most Christians don't turn to the Bible for comfort and strength to grow?

Quite simply, they just don't know how.

Following are several different principles, ranging from very simple, basic methods to more complex approaches that have helped many people understand how to read the Bible and get something from it.

1. **The first and most basic step is regular Scripture intake. That means attending a church where the Scriptures are preached and taught. Attend regularly, and take a Bible.**

A conscious decision must be made to attend regularly where God's Word is taught. Like white-hot charcoals removed from a grill, believers also tend to cool when they attempt to survive as spiritual hermits. Some stop attending church because they don't see it making any difference in their lives from week to week. But people don't stop eating just because they don't completely mature in a month or a year.

A conscious decision must also be made for personal Bible study. Though some have begun with as little as one or two study times a week, the ideal is a daily time, perhaps five to thirty minutes. Most people find the best time is at the beginning of the day. The important thing, though, is to get Bible intake regularly–each day if possible. Many with varied schedules find it helpful to make an "appointment" with God for the next day.

To begin, find a quiet place to read and think, make notes, and study. Expect God's help. Pray for His guidance and trust the Holy Spirit to give understanding. One of the purposes of the indwelling Holy Spirit is to help believers understand what is in the Bible. *"For who among men knows the thoughts of a man except the spirit of the man, which is in him? Even so the thoughts of God no one knows except the Spirit of God. Now we have received, not the spirit of the world, but the Spirit who is from God, that we might know the things freely given to us by God"* (1 Corinthians 2:11-12).

Spiritual growth starts with receiving new life in Christ, who wants us to spend time developing our relationship with Him. He speaks to us through Scripture; we speak to him through prayer. thank God for revealing Himself in this special book, the Bible. Depend on

His Holy Spirit to help you understand the Bible and personally apply its truths to your life.

2. **One of the most important ways to get more from the Bible is to form the habit of taking simple notes. Take brief notes during a sermon. Make any notes of something striking during a personal time of reading or reflection.**

   It is also good to make summary notes on a notepad or in a notebook. Notes may be short and simple–the main points of a message or the two or three things you notice in a passage. Write down chapter and verse so you have a reference for each point or statement. The more you study the more notes you take, but even a few highlights will help you grasp and hold the thought.

   True, making notes means work. But that's the value. Searching out what the Bible says and putting it into your own words will double or triple what you get from listening or reading. Taking notes will help you get off those Bible water skis!

   What should you do with your notes once you have made them? Even if you throw them away in a day or two, you'll find they will be worth the trouble. But you'll probably want to keep them in a notebook or a Bible file.

   A simple but effective way of keeping notes is to use personal notebooks, such as a looseleaf notebook with at least five sections. One is for sermon notes, another for notes on personal Bible study, another for notes on Sunday school or bible class lessons, a fourth for prayer requests and answers, and fifth for miscellaneous items. When one notebook becomes filled, simply start another.

   A better way for the person who finds himself filling several notebooks is a personal Bible study file. Begin by buying one hundred letter-size folders, the kind used in offices for filing correspondence. If possible, get the third-cut kind with three possible positions for tabs across the top. The first one hundred folders should have left-hand tabs.

   Begin by labeling sixty-six of your folders with left-hand tabs with the books of the Bible, one folder for each book. Arrange these in the order of the Bible books, Genesis to Revelation. Then also have folders labeled "Bible–General," "Old Testament–General," and "New Testament–General."

   Folders can be kept in a corrugated cardboard box. A wooden box or steel or plastic file cabinet is even better.

3. **Get a Panoramic View.**

   Reading for a panoramic view is one approach to what is called synthetic Bible study. In this case synthetic does not mean "artificial," but putting parts together to form the whole. It is always good to do this kind of study before moving on to examine a book or passage in more detail.

To get a panoramic view, choose a book of the Bible and read it through quite rapidly, if possible at a single sitting. That is not difficult. Half the books of the Bible are so short they would take up less than two columns in a daily paper.

Reading once is good; reading twice is better. You'll find perhaps to your surprise, that each rereading will enrich your understanding.

The first time through a book, read to find out what it is all about. Make notes. Try to discover what the book is saying as a whole.

In a second reading you might look for the "big ideas." Jot down the major events and key people, noting the passage in which each person or event is mentioned. Ask yourself, "What really impresses me? What has left a mark on my mind as I've read the book this time?"

You may want to make a special reading in which you look for repeated items–events or people or even statements that occur again and again.

Keep in mind that you may come back to a book for panoramic readings at a later time since there are many different things to look for. At some future time you may want to reread a book to learn what you can about the author or major character–his background and family or the changes in his life that affected him, his ministry and his relationship with others.

Or you may read through a book, noting what is different at the end than at the beginning. Have the characters changed location or leadership? Have they had a change of heart toward God?

Another possibility: a reading in which you look for contrasts within the book. Often the Bible contrasts people, such as Abraham with Lot, Isaac with Ishmael, or Jacob with Esau. Look also for contrasting events, contrasts in place, or contrasts in attitudes.

As you read, jot down a list of questions you would like to answer in a more detailed study later. Your list might include people you can't readily identify and dates or customs you would like to know more about.

4. Read for Chapter Headings

Another good way to get more from your Bible is to write out personal chapter headings. That simply involves reading a given Bible book, a chapter at at time, and writing a short title or heading for each chapter.

Here are four guidelines for creating a good chapter title.

- A title should be distinctive. It should fit that chapter and not other. "God's Laws," for example, is not a good chapter title because the heading would fit too many chapters.
- A title should be original. It should be the product of your own thinking if it is to help you realize what you're reading. You

might use a good reference Bible with great chapter headings, but they would not be yours, and copying them would help you very little.

- A title should be brief, perhaps four or five words. Longer titles are hard to grasp and hard to remember.

Sometimes you'll find so many subjects in a chapter, you'll think it can't be summarized in five words or less. When you feel that way, try jotting down a title for each paragraph or subject. Then combine them to for a chapter title.

- A title should be memorable. That is, it should remind you of the chapter's major themes.

Making your own chapter headings does several things for you. First, it slows you down and makes you more reflective. You have to read more carefully, and often reread, perhaps several times.

Reading for chapter headings also reminds you that you are looking for what the Bible says. You have to think about what you are reading. You have to notice, too, what the Bible emphasizes and what it covers rather briefly.

Composing original chapter titles also gives you a way to remember the content of the Bible, and helps you relate one part of the Bible to other parts. For example, jot down the chapter headings of the book you're reading. Then when you have a little extra time you can turn them over in your mind, seeing how one chapter leads into another, or you can memorize your titles. That way, you can remember them and use a large part of what you have read.

5. Make a Survey Chart

Once you know how to write original chapter titles, you are well on the way to being able to picture entire books of the Bible by making original survey charts.

Making charts teaches you about a book as almost nothing else can. You learn by gathering material and making the chart. When it is finished, your chart also pictures what you have learned so you can refer to it easily and quickly.

A survey chart records your discoveries in an organized manner for future study and reference. Such a chart also helps you see a Bible book's component parts and how they fit together. It is invaluable if you want to share an overview of the book with others in a Bible class or other situation in which time is limited.

Making a Bible survey is not difficult. Begin by reading through the book of the Bible you have chosen and noting original chapter titles as already described.

Now, beginning about two inches from the top of the page, list the chapter numbers with the original titles you have written in a column on the left-hand side of the page. Leave three or four spaces between each entry. If the book is long, tape several sheets of paper end-to-end, so you have a long column of chapter headings. Or chart longer books by separate smaller sections.

Next, draw a series of vertical lines at the right of your list of chapter titles about one-half inch apart. This will give you several columns at the right in which you can tract the treatment of a major subject throughout the book.

For example, suppose in charting Nehemiah you have discovered that there are many prayers in the book. Label one of the vertical columns "Prayers." Then go down the column indicating chapters that contain prayers. You could also indicate what kinds of prayers appear in each chapter and the verses in which they are located.

Other spaces may be used for charting other subjects such as "Leadership," "Motivation of Others," or "Confession." Still other columns can be used to indicate contrasts and comparisons you may have noted in your reading.

In Nehemiah, for example, chapters 1-6 are concerned with physical work; chapters 7-13 deal largely with spiritual work in the lives of the people. Another column, or even two, might therefore be used to show the portion of the book that deals with physical work and another the chapters stressing work in the hearts of the people.

The subjects you trace through on your chart can be chosen on the basis or your own interest and findings. Ask yourself who is involved throughout the book, what happens to them, when it happened, where it happened, and why it happened. Your answers to such questions will lead you to discoveries about the book that can be preserved on your original chart.

Other topics foı the right-hand columns will surface through repeated readings of a Bible book. When you have finished making your chart for one Bible book over a period of time, you will be surprised at how much you have learned! When you come back to the same book later, your chart summarizes your earlier findings as a base for deeper digging.

6. Discover Who Is Responsible

Many portions of the Bible emphasize God's commands and the blessings that follow obedience. Such passages come alive when studied and analyzed in the light of what God asks us to do and what He promises to do for us. This kind of study can be carried out with great profit by discovering God's and our responsibilities in a passage. Some of God's promises have one or more conditions attached–something we must do first.

For example, consider these two familiar verses. *"Be anxious for nothing, but in everything by prayer and supplication with thanksgiving let your requests be made known to God. And the peace of God, which surpasses all comprehension, shall guard your hearts and your minds in Christ Jesus."* (Philippians 4:6-7). If we want to experience

God's peace, we must first choose prayer over anxiety.

Begin by drawing two vertical lines on a sheet of paper so that the page is divided into three columns. The columns on the left and right should be larger than the one in the center. Head the left-hand column "My Responsibility" and the right-hand column "God's Responsibility." The middle column should be labeled "Results."

The object is to read the passage in the light of what it says to you. Personalize each verse by summarizing your findings point by point in the appropriate column.

What God's Word says you should do is listed in the first column. What God promises to do for you gets summarized in the third column. In the center column goes anything that the vers says will result when God or I fulfill our stated "duties."

Let's apply this technique to a familiar verse. *"For God so loved the world, that He gave His only begotten Son, that whoever believes in Him should not perish, but have eternal life"* (John 3:16). In this verse, your responsibility is to believe in God's Son. God's responsibility is to love the world, and give His one and only Son, with the result that believers will not perish but have eternal life.

Not all verses have entries for all three columns. James 1:21, for example, contains these duties for us; Get rid of all moral filth and the evil that is so prevalent, and humbly accept the Word planted in me. As a result, the Word will save us. There is no directly-stated task for the Lord in this verse.

It takes about fifteen minutes to rewrite about eight verses in this way. Once you've made your entries, look up definitions of key words, to make sure you really understand what the Bible is talking about. A dictionary will help here or, even better, a concordance that gives biblical definitions of the words involved. Write these definitions very briefly right on the three-column analysis page wherever you can fit them in.

"But this takes careful thinking," someone may say. Exactly. That's why it works. We are listening to God, thinking about what He's saying, and thinking about how to put His words into practice.

You should also make note of any implications. For example, in Psalm 1:2, our responsibility is to delight in and meditate on God's laws. This implies that we must know what the law of the Lord says; so write in that insight. And, there may be implications to be noted in the "God's Responsibility" column.

When we see an implied principle or personal application, we are on good ground if we find that idea clearly taught in two or three different Bible passages.

But how do we find those other passages? Consulting the cross-references printed in many Bibles is a good place to start. Another good place to look is in a topical Bible (such as *Nave's Topical Bible*), which is an index to subjects in the Bible. Unlike in a concordance, the same word is not necessarily repeated, just a similar idea.

Is there some aspect of God's law you need to be pondering today? If so, write that down. After all, you're searching the Scriptures to let them change your life.

This leads to a very important step—turning all three columns into personal prayer. Items in the first column may prompt you to thank God for what you have discovered in Scripture, especially about Himself. Or you may be led to confess a sin or failure or to pray for help. Items in the "God's Responsibility" column lead to thanks for what He promises to do or prayers of expectation, trusting God to do what He has promised.

Psalm 119 is an excellent passage to study using the "Whose Responsibility" method. Its twenty-two sections of eight verses each provide ideal reading portions for twenty-two days.

HOW TO ANALYZE INDIVIDUAL BIBLE CHAPTERS

Three-step analysis is a good way to discover the nugget truths in any chapter you wish to study. The steps are (1) observation, or what does the passage say? (2) interpretation, or what does it mean? and (3) applications, or what does it mean to me? You may do a step a day or do all three steps at a single sitting. Longer chapters could be done by individual paragraphs.

1. Observation. Write out original chapter titles as explained before. For a more detailed approach, use a literal Bible version that divides the chapters into paragraphs. Write original summary title for each paragraph.

Or simply jot down a list of the important facts or ideas appearing in the chapter. Write these down the left side of a notebook page, keeping the right side of the same page free for notes about interpretation and application.

2. Interpretation. Ask and answer six basic questions: Who?; What?; When?; Where?; Why? and How? You can apply these questions to the chapter as a whole, to each paragraph in turn or to each fact of happening. Write out the answers briefly.

If you listed separate facts from a chapter, answer these six questions about them in the space remaining to the right on your page. Otherwise, list the six basic questions down the left side of a page.

Many of the answers to these questions will be clear from the Scripture context, though you may find help from cross-references in your Bible or from a Bible dictionary, Bible handbook or passages located through a Bible concordance.

The important thing is to examine every facet of the Bible chapter. Most people are surprised at what the written answers reveal. The reason: you will have forced yourself to examine, to question, and to think about what the Bible says.

A good way to see how well you understand a passage is to write out an original paraphrase, that is, restate the Bible portion in your own words, using "I" and "me" whenever possible.

3. Application. Don't forget this final important step. What do the facts you have discovered mean to you? What difference should they make in your actions?

HOW TO ANALYZE INDIVIDUAL BIBLE CHAPTERS

(Example from Jonah 1)

1. **Observation** (from the Bible only–what the chapter says)

   CHAPTER TITLE: Jonah's flight from God

   KEY VERSE: 1:10 - *"Then the men became extremely frightened and they said to him, "How could you do this?" For the men knew that he was fleeing from the presence of the Lord, because he had told them."*

   KEY WORD OR WORDS: flee, fear

2. **Interpretation** (from the Bible, Bible dictionary, and concordance)

   WHO:

- Jonah, a prophet in Israel called to carry God's message of judgement to Nineveh. At first, he fled in the opposite direction
- Sailors on ship who got converted transporting a prophet being disciplined by God
- The Lord (Jehovah, the self-existent, eternal One) who graciously pursued His sinning prophet
- Great fish prepared by God to rescue Jonah

WHEN:

- Eighth century B.C. during reign of Jeroboam II of Israel (2 Kings 14:25)

WHERE:

- Nineveh, capital of Assyria on northern headwaters of Tigris River
- Joppa, Israel's seaport 35 miles west of Jerusalem on the Mediterranean Sea. (From Jonah's home town of Gathhepher in Israel, Joppa is southwest, and Nineveh is northeast!)
- Tarshish (perhaps near Gibralter in Spain)

WHY:

- Why did Jonah try to run from God's call?
  (1) He was afraid God's mercy would win out and Nineveh would be spared (Jonah 4:2).
  (2) Pride–maybe Jonah was afraid his message of judgement would not come true.
  (3) Fear–knowing Assyria's might and cruelty in war, Jonah may

have feared God would save Assyria to judge Israel. He may have also feared for his personal safety.

- Why did God send the terrible storm and great fish?
  (1) God will not let us run from His will.
  (2) In love God pursued Jonah, not to punish but to save him from himself and bring him to a place of willing obedience.

3. **Application** (from the Bible only, answering the question, "What does this mean to me?")

   PRINCIPLES:

- I cannot run away from God, even though I may try.
- God loves all people and acts to bring them His message of salvation.
- God is in control of His universe and will use everything in it to bring a believer to a place of willing obedience.
- God will let people pay their own way into sin, but He will graciously pay their way out (though not always by the means we might choose!).
- I should obey God the first time He speaks, since I will end up doing His will anyway.

Another way of noting application is to write down answers to five basic questions. Does the passage speak of any:

- **Sin** to be forsaken?
- **Promise** to be claimed?
- **Example** to be followed?
- **Command** to be obeyed?
- **Stumbling block** or hindrance to be avoided?

As a final question, ask yourself, "what do I do now? Is there something here I should do today?"

Note that the first letters of the five key words – sin, promise, example, command, stumbling block– spell SPECS. We therefore call these the "SPECS?" questions, adding the final question mark to remind us to ask, What do I do now?

PERSONAL APPLICATION WITH "SPECS?"

(Example from Jonah 1)

Sins to Forsake:

- Disobedience in what I believe God wants me to do
- Delayed obedience; obey the Lord now
- Following my own reason instead of what God reveals

Promises to Claim:

- God's continual, inescapable, loving presence (implied)
- God in love will work out His good purpose in my life
- He will graciously pursue and discipline me for my good

Examples to Follow:

- I should be willing to make any sacrifice to spare others (as the sailors were)
- I should make commitments to God after He has dealt with me in a special way to make sure I profit

Commands to Obey:

- Jesus's great commission to make disciples of all nations is strongly implied in this chapter

Stumbling Blocks To Avoid:

- I should never let self-will stand in the way of doing God's will
- I should never let what may seem like favorable circumstances be the only test of God's will

Another way to close such an analysis is to write out a very specific first-person prayer. You can thank God for the truth or example given, ask for help in applying what God has said, or make a confession of what you have failed to do.

Once you have used this three-step approach to analyze Scripture, you will find the Bible speaking clearly to the needs of daily life.

These are, of course, but a few of the myriad methods available for personal Bible reading and study. Never forget that Bible study methods can degenerate into "mechanics." Let them always be a tool the Holy Spirit can use to a better end–fellowship with God. The Bible is not designed just to satisfy our curiosity, but to touch our emotions and move our wills to choose God's ways. We don't just study the Bible–we live it!

FOREWORD

SCRIPTURAL PROMISE

"The grass withers, the flower fades,
but the word of our God stands forever."
Isaiah 40:8

The New American Standard Bible has been produced with the conviction that the words of Scripture as originally penned in the Hebrew, Aramaic, and Greek were inspired by God. Since they are the eternal Word of God, the Holy Scriptures speak with fresh power to each generation, to give wisdom that leads to salvation, that men may serve Christ to the glory of God.

The Editorial Board had a twofold purpose in making this translation: to adhere as closely as possible to the original languages of the Holy Scriptures, and to make the translation in a fluent and readable style according to current English usage.

THE FOURFOLD AIM OF THE LOCKMAN FOUNDATION

1. These publications shall be true to the original Hebrew, Aramaic, and Greek.
2. They shall be grammatically correct.
3. They shall be understandable to the masses.
4. They shall give the Lord Jesus Christ His proper place, the place which the Word gives Him; therefore, no work will ever be personalized.

PREFACE TO THE NEW AMERICAN STANDARD BIBLE

In the history of English Bible translations, the King James Version is the most prestigious. This time-honored version of 1611, itself a revision of the Bishops' Bible of 1568, became the basis for the English Revised Version appearing in 1881 (New Testament) and 1885 (Old Testament). The American counterpart of this last work was published in 1901 as the American Standard Version. Recognizing the values of the American Standard Version, the Lockman Foundation felt an urgency to update it by incorporating recent discoveries of Hebrew and Greek textual sources and by rendering it into more current English. Therefore, in 1959 a new translation project was launched, based on the ASV. The result is the New American Standard Bible.

The American Standard Version (1901) has been highly regarded for its scholarship and accuracy. A product of both British and American scholarship, it has frequently been used as a standard for other translations. It is still recognized as a valuable tool for study of the Scriptures. The New American Standard Bible has sought to preserve these and other lasting values of the ASV.

Furthermore, in the preparation of this work numerous other translations have been consulted along with the linguistic tools and literature of biblical scholarship. Decisions about English renderings were made by consensus of a team composed of educators and pastors. Subsequently, review and evaluation by other Hebrew and Greek scholars outside the Editorial Board were sought and carefully considered.

The Editorial Board has continued to function since publication of the complete Bible in 1971. Minor revisions and refinements, recommended over the last several years, are presented in this edition.

PRINCIPLES OF TRANSLATION

MODERN ENGLISH USAGE: The attempt has been made to render the grammar and terminology in contemporary English. When it was felt that the word-for-word literalness was unacceptable to the modern reader, a change was made in the direction of a more current English idiom. In the instances where this has been done, the more literal rendering has been indicated in the notes.

ALTERNATIVE READINGS: In addition to the more literal renderings, notations have been made to include alternate translations, readings of variant manuscripts and explanatory equivalents of the text. Only such notations have been used as have been felt justified in assisting the reader's comprehension of the terms used by the original author.

HEBREW TEXT: In the present translation the latest edition of Rudolf Kittel's BIBLIA HEBRAICA has been employed together with the most recent light from lexicography, cognate languages, and the Dead Sea Scrolls.

HEBREW TENSES: Consecution of tenses in Hebrew remains a puzzling factor in translation. The translators have been guided by the requirements of a literal translation, the sequence of tenses, and the immediate and broad contexts.

THE PROPER NAME OF GOD IN THE OLD TESTAMENT: In the Scriptures, the name of God is most significant and understandably so. It is inconceivable to think of spiritual matters without a proper designation for the Supreme Deity. Thus the most common name for the Deity is God, a translation of the original Elohim. One of the titles for God is Lord, a translation of Adonai. There is yet another name which is particularly assigned to God as His special or proper name, that is, the four letters YHWH (Exodus 3:14 and Isaiah 42:8). This name has not been pronounced by the Jews because of reverence for the great sacredness of the divine name. Therefore, it has been consistently translated LORD. The only exception to this translation of YHWH is when it occurs in immediate proximity to the word Lord, that is, Adonai. In that case it is regularly translated GOD in order to avoid confusion. It is known that for many years YHWH has been transliterated as Yahweh, however no complete certainty attaches to this pronunciation.

GREEK TEXT: Consideration was given to the latest available manuscripts with a view to determining the best Greek text. In most instances the 23rd edition of Eberhard Nestle's NOVUM TESTAMENTUM GRAECE was followed.

GREEK TENSES: A careful distinction has been made in the treatment of the Greek aorist tense (usually translated as the English past, "He did") and the Greek imperfect tense (rendered either as English past progressive, "He was doing"; or, if inceptive, as "He *began* to do" or "He started to do"; or else if customary past, as "He used to do"). "Began" is italicized if it renders an imperfect tense, in order to distinguish it from the Greek verb for "begin."

On the other hand, not all aorists have been rendered as English pasts ("He did"), for some of them are clearly to be rendered as English perfects ("He has done"), or even as past perfects ("He had done"), judging from the context in which they occur. Such aorists have been rendered as perfects or past perfects in this translation.

As for the distinction between aorist and present imperatives, the translators have usually rendered these imperatives in the customary manner, rather than attempting any such fine distinction as "Begin to do!" (for the aorist imperative), or, "Continually do!" (for the present imperative).

As for sequence of tenses, the translators took care to follow English rules rather than Greek in translating Greek presents, imperfects and aorists. Thus, where English says, "We knew that he was doing," Greek puts it, "We knew that he does"; similarly, "We knew that he had done" is the Greek, "We knew that he did." Likewise, the English, "When he had come, they met him," is represented in Greek by: "When he came, they met him." In all cases a consistent transfer has been made from the Greek tense in the subordinate clause to the appropriate tense in English.

In the rendering of negative questions introduced by the particle **mē** (which always expects the answer, "No") the wording has been altered from a mere, "Will he not do this?" to a more accurate, "He will not do this, will he?"

Editorial Board, THE LOCKMAN FOUNDATION

EXPLANATION OF GENERAL FORMAT

Notes and Cross References are placed in a column adjoining the text on the page and listed under verse numbers to which they refer. Superior numbers refer to literal renderings, alternate translations, or explanations. Superior letters refer to cross references. Cross references in italics are parallel passages.

Paragraphs are designated by bold face numbers or letters.

Quotation Marks are used in the text in accordance with modern English usage.

"Thou," "Thee" and "Thy" are not used in this translation except in the language of prayer when addressing Deity.

Personal Pronouns are capitalized when pertaining to Deity.

Italics are used in the text to indicate words which are not found in the original Hebrew, Aramaic, or Greek but implied by it. Italics are used in the marginal notes to signify alternate readings for the text.

Small Caps in the New Testament are used in the text to indicate Old Testament quotations or obvious allusions to Old Testament texts. Variations of Old Testament wording are found in New Testament citations depending on whether the New Testament writer translated from a Hebrew text, used existing Greek or Aramaic translations, or paraphrased the material. It should be noted that modern rules for the indication of direct quotation were not used in biblical times thus allowing freedom for omissions or insertions without specific indication of these.

Asterisks are used to mark verbs that are historical presents in the Greek which have been translated with an English past tense in order to conform to modern usage. The translators recognized that in some contexts the present tense seems more unexpected and unjustified to the English reader than a past tense would have been. But Greek authors frequently used the present tense for the sake of heightened vividness, thereby transporting their readers in imagination to the actual scene at the time of occurrence. However, the translators felt that it would be wise to change these historical presents to English past tenses.

ABBREVIATIONS AND SPECIAL MARKINGS:

Aram.	=	Aramaic
DSS	=	Dead Sea Scrolls
Gr.	=	Greek translation of O.T. (Septuagint or LXX) or Greek text of N.T.
Heb.	=	Hebrew text, usually Masoretic
Lat.	=	Latin
M.T.	=	Masoretic text
Syr.	=	Syriac
Lit.	=	A literal translation
Or	=	An alternate translation justified by the Hebrew, Aramaic, or Greek
[ ]	=	In text, brackets indicate words probably not in the original writings
[ ]	=	In margin, brackets indicate references to a name, place or thing similar to, but not identical with that in the text.
cf.	=	compare
f., ff.	=	following verse or verses
ms., mss.	=	manuscript, manuscripts
v., vv.	=	verse, verses

BOOKS OF THE OLD TESTAMENT

BOOKS OF THE NEW TESTAMENT

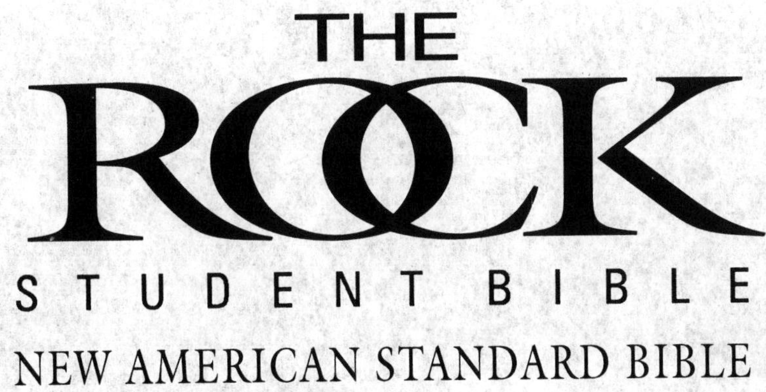

Old Testament

GENESIS

The Creation

1 [a]IN the beginning [b]God [c]created the
heavens and the earth.
2 And the earth was [1a]formless and
void, and [b]darkness was over the [2]sur-
face of the deep; and [c]the Spirit of God
[d]was [3]moving over the [2]surface of the
waters.
3 Then [a]God said, "Let there be
light"; and there was light.
4 And God saw that the light was
[a]good; and God [b]separated the light
from the darkness.
5 And [a]God called the light day, and
the darkness He called night. And [b]there
was evening and there was morning, one
day.
6 Then God said, "Let there be [1]an
[a]expanse in the midst of the waters, and
let it separate the waters from the waters."
7 And God made the [1]expanse, and
separated [a]the waters which were below
the [1]expanse from the waters [b]which
were above the [1]expanse; and it was so.
8 And God called the [1]expanse
heaven. And there was evening and there
was morning, a second day.
9 Then God said, "[a]Let the waters
below the heavens be gathered into one
place, and let [b]the dry land appear"; and
it was so.
10 And God called the dry land earth,
and the [a]gathering of the waters He
called seas; and God saw that it was
good.
11 Then God said, "Let the earth
sprout [1a]vegetation, [2]plants yielding
seed, *and* fruit trees bearing fruit after
[3]their kind, [4]with seed in them, on the
earth"; and it was so.
12 And the earth brought forth [1]vege-
tation, [2]plants yielding seed after [3]their
kind, and trees bearing fruit, [4]with seed
in them, after [3]their kind; and God saw
that it was good.
13 And there was evening and there
was morning, a third day.
14 Then God said, "Let there be
[1a]lights in the [2b]expanse of the heavens
to separate the day from the night, and
let them be for [c]signs, and for [d]seasons,
and for days and years;
15 and let them be for [1]lights in the
[2]expanse of the heavens to give light on
the earth"; and it was so.
16 And God made the two [1]great
lights, the [a]greater [2]light [3]to govern the
day, and the lesser [2]light [3]to govern the
night; *He made* [b]the stars also.
17 [a]And God placed them in the [1]ex-
panse of the heavens to give light on the
earth,
18 and [1]to [a]govern the day and the
night, and to separate the light from the
darkness; and God saw that it was good.
19 And there was evening and there
was morning, a fourth day.
20 Then God said, "Let the waters
[1]teem with swarms of living creatures,
and let birds fly above the earth [2]in the
open [3]expanse of the heavens."

1 [a]Ps. 102:25; Is. 40:21; John 1:1, 2; Heb. 1:10 [b]Ps. 89:11; 90:2; Acts 17:24; Rom. 1:20; Heb. 11:3 [c]Job 38:4; Is. 42:5; 45:18; Rev. 4:11

2 [1]Or, *a waste and emptiness* [2]Lit., *face of* [3]Or, *hovering* [a]Jer. 4:23 [b]Job 38:9 [c]Ps. 104:30; Is. 40:13, 14 [d]Deut. 32:11; Is. 31:5

3 [a]Ps. 33:6, 9; 2 Cor. 4:6

4 [a]Ps. 145:9, 10 [b]Is. 45:7

5 [a]Ps. 74:16 [b]Ps. 65:8

6 [1]Or, *a firmament* [a]Is. 40:22; Jer. 10:12; 2 Pet. 3:5

7 [1]Or, *firmament* [a]Job 38:8-11 [b]Ps. 148:4

8 [1]Or, *firmament*

9 [a]Ps. 104:6-9; Jer. 5:22; 2 Pet. 3:5 [b]Ps. 24:1, 2; 95:5

10 [a]Ps. 33:7; 95:5; 146:6

11 [1]Or, *grass* [2]Or, *herbs* [3]Lit., *its* [4]Lit., *in which is its seed* [a]Ps. 65:9-13; 104:14; Heb. 6:7

12 [1]Or, *grass* [2]Or, *herbs* [3]Lit., *its* [4]Lit., *in which is its seed*

14 [1]Or, *luminaries, light-bearers* [2]Or, *firmament* [a]Ps. 74:16; 136:7 [b]Ps. 19:1; 150:1 [c]Jer. 10:2 [d]Ps. 104:19

15 [1]Or, *luminaries, light-bearers* [2]Or, *firmament*

16 [1]Or, *luminaries, light-bearers* [2]Or, *luminary, light-bearer* [3]Lit., *for the dominion of* [a]Ps. 136:8, 9 [b]Job 38:7; Ps. 8:3; Is. 40:26

17 [1]Or, *firmament* [a]Jer. 33:20, 25

18 [1]Lit., *for the dominion of* [a]Jer. 31:35

20 [1]Or, *swarm* [2]Lit., *on the face of* [3]Or, *firmament*

21 [a]Ps. 104:25-28

24 [1]Lit., *its* [a]Gen. 2:19; 6:20; 7:14; 8:19

25 [1]Lit., *its* [a]Gen. 7:21, 22; Jer. 27:5

26 [1]Lit., *heavens* [a]Gen. 3:22; 11:7 [b]Gen. 5:1; 9:6; 1 Cor. 11:7; Eph. 4:24; James 3:9 [c]Ps. 8:6-8

27 [a]Gen. 5:1f.; 1 Cor. 11:7; Eph. 4:24; Col. 3:10 [b]Matt. 19:4; Mark 10:6

28 [1]Lit., *heavens* [2]Or, *creeps* [a]Gen. 9:1, 7; Lev. 26:9; Ps. 127:3, 5

29 [1]Lit., *face of* [2]Lit., *in which is the fruit of a tree yielding seed* [a]Ps. 104:14; 136:25

21 And God created [a]the great sea
monsters, and every living creature that
moves, with which the waters swarmed
after their kind, and every winged bird
after its kind; and God saw that it was
good.
22 And God blessed them, saying, "Be
fruitful and multiply, and fill the waters
in the seas, and let birds multiply on the
earth."
23 And there was evening and there
was morning, a fifth day.
24 [a]Then God said, "Let the earth
bring forth living creatures after [1]their
kind: cattle and creeping things and
beasts of the earth after [1]their kind";
and it was so.
25 And God made the [a]beasts of the
earth after [1]their kind, and the cattle
after [1]their kind, and everything that
creeps on the ground after its kind; and
God saw that it was good.
26 Then God said, "Let [a]Us make
[b]man in Our image, according to Our
likeness; and let them [c]rule over the fish
of the sea and over the birds of the [1]sky
and over the cattle and over all the earth,
and over every creeping thing that creeps
on the earth."
27 And God created man [a]in His own
image, in the image of God He created
him; [b]male and female He created them.
28 And God blessed them; and God
said to them, "[a]Be fruitful and multiply,
and fill the earth, and subdue it; and rule
over the fish of the sea and over the birds
of the [1]sky, and over every living thing
that [2]moves on the earth."
29 Then God said, "Behold, [a]I have
given you every plant yielding seed that
is on the [1]surface of all the earth, and
every tree [2]which has fruit yielding seed;
it shall be food for you;
30 and [a]to every beast of the earth and
to every bird of the [1]sky and to every
thing that [2]moves on the earth [3]which
has life, *I have given* every green plant
for food"; and it was so.
31 And God saw all that He had
made, and behold, it was very [a]good.
And there was evening and there was
morning, the sixth day.

The Creation of Man and Woman

2 THUS the heavens and the earth
were completed, and all [a]their hosts.
2 And by [a]the seventh day God
completed His work which He had
done; and [b]He rested on the seventh day
from all His work which He had done.
3 Then God blessed the seventh day
and sanctified it, because in it He rested
from all His work which God had created [1]and made.

30 [1]Lit., *heavens* [2]Or, *creeps* [3]Lit., *in which is a living soul* [a]Ps. 145:15, 16; 147:9

31 [a]Ps. 104:24, 28; 119:68; 1 Tim. 4:4

1 [a]Deut. 4:19; 17:3

2 [a]Ex. 20:8-11; 31:17 [b]Heb. 4:4, 10

3 [1]Lit., *to make*

4 [1a]This is the account of the heavens and the earth when they were created, in [b]the day that the LORD God made earth and heaven.

5 [a]Now no shrub of the field was yet in the earth, and no plant of the field had yet sprouted, [b]for the LORD God had not sent rain upon the earth; and there was no man to [1]cultivate the ground.

6 But a [1]mist used to rise from the earth and water the whole [2]surface of the ground.

7 Then the LORD God formed man of [a]dust from the ground, and breathed into his nostrils the breath of life; and [b]man became a living [1]being.

8 And the LORD God planted a [a]garden toward the east, in Eden; and there He placed the man whom He had formed.

9 And out of the ground the LORD God caused to grow [a]every tree that is pleasing to the sight and good for food; [b]the tree of life also in the midst of the garden, and the tree of the knowledge of good and evil.

10 Now a [a]river [1]flowed out of Eden to water the garden; and from there it divided and became four [2]rivers.

11 The name of the first is Pishon; it [1]flows around the whole land of [a]Havilah, where there is gold.

12 And the gold of that land is good; the bdellium and the onyx stone are there.

13 And the name of the second river is Gihon; it [1]flows around the whole land of Cush.

14 And the name of the third river is [1a]Tigris; it [2]flows east of Assyria. And the fourth river is the [3b]Euphrates.

15 Then the LORD God took the man and put him into the garden of Eden to cultivate it and keep it.

16 And the LORD God [a]commanded the man, saying, "From any tree of the garden you may eat freely;

17 but from the tree of the knowledge of good and evil you shall not [1]eat, for in the day that you eat from it [a]you shall surely die."

18 Then the LORD God said, "It is not good for the man to be alone; [a]I will make him a helper [1]suitable for him."

19 And [a]out of the ground the LORD God formed every beast of the field and every bird of the [1]sky, and [b]brought *them* to the man to see what he would call them; and whatever the man called a living creature, that was its name.

20 And the man gave names to all the cattle, and to the birds of the [1]sky, and to every beast of the field, but for [2]Adam there was not found [a]a helper [3]suitable for him.

21 So the LORD God caused a [a]deep sleep to fall upon the man, and he slept; then He took one of his ribs, and closed up the flesh at that place.

22 And the LORD God [1]fashioned into a woman [a]the rib which He had taken from the man, and brought her to the man.

23 And the man said,
"[a]This is now bone of my bones,
And flesh of my flesh;
[1]She shall be called [2]Woman,
Because [1]she was taken out of [3]Man."

24 [a]For this cause a man shall leave his father and his mother, and shall cleave to his wife; and they shall become one flesh.

25 [a]And the man and his wife were both naked and were not ashamed.

The Fall of Man

3 NOW [a]the serpent was more crafty than any beast of the field which the LORD God had made. And he said to the woman, "Indeed, has God said, 'You shall not eat from [1]any tree of the garden'?"

2 And the woman said to the serpent, "[a]From the fruit of the trees of the garden we may eat;

3 but from the fruit of the tree which is in the middle of the garden, God has said, 'You shall not eat from it or touch it, lest you die.'"

4 [a]And the serpent said to the woman, "You surely shall not die!

5 "For God knows that in the day you eat from it your eyes will be opened, and [a]you will be like God, knowing good and evil."

6 [a]When the woman saw that the tree was good for food, and that it was a delight to the eyes, and that the tree was desirable to make *one* wise, she took from its fruit and ate; and she gave also to her husband with her, and he ate.

7 Then the eyes of both of them were opened, and they [a]knew that they were naked; and they sewed fig leaves together and made themselves [1]loin coverings.

8 And they heard the sound of [a]the LORD God walking in the garden in the [1]cool of the day, [b]and the man and his wife hid themselves from the presence of the LORD God among the trees of the garden.

9 Then the LORD God called to the man, and said to him, "[a]Where are you?"

10 And he said, "[a]I heard the sound of Thee in the garden, and I was afraid because I was naked; so I hid myself."

11 And He said, "Who told you that you were naked? Have you eaten from the tree of which I commanded you not to eat?"

12 [a]And the man said, "The woman whom Thou gavest *to be* with me, she gave me from the tree, and I ate."

13 Then the LORD God said to the woman, "What is this you have done?" And the woman said, "[a]The serpent deceived me, and I ate."

14 And the LORD God said to the serpent,

---

4 [1]Lit., *These are the generations* [a]Job 38:4-11 [b]Gen. 1:3-31

5 [1]Lit., *work, serve* [a]Gen. 1:11 [b]Ps. 65:9, 10; Jer. 10:12, 13

6 [1]Or, *flow* [2]Lit., *face of*

7 [1]Lit., *soul* [a]Gen. 3:19 [b]1 Cor. 15:45

8 [a]Gen. 13:10; Is. 51:3; Ezek. 28:13

9 [a]Ezek. 47:12 [b]Gen. 3:22; Rev. 2:7; 22:2, 14

10 [1]Lit., *was going out* [2]Lit., *heads* [a]Ps. 46:4

11 [1]Lit., *surrounds* [a]Gen. 25:18

13 [1]Lit., *is the one surrounding*

14 [1]Heb., *Hiddekel* [2]Lit., *is the one going* [3]Heb., *Perath* [a]Dan. 10:4 [b]Gen. 15:18

16 [a]Gen. 3:2, 3

17 [1]Lit., *eat from it* [a]Deut. 30:15, 19, 20; Rom. 6:23; 1 Tim. 5:6; James 1:15

18 [1]Lit., *corresponding to* [a]1 Cor. 11:9

19 [1]Lit., *heavens* [a]Gen. 1:24 [b]Gen. 1:26

20 [1]Lit., *heavens* [2]Or, *man* [3]Lit., *corresponding to* [a]Gen. 2:18

21 [a]Gen. 15:12

22 [1]Lit., *built* [a]1 Cor. 11:8, 9

23 [1]Lit., *This one* [2]Heb., *Ishshah* [3]Heb., *Ish* [a]Gen. 29:14; Eph. 5:28, 29

24 [a]Matt. 19:5; Mark 10:7, 8; 1 Cor. 6:16; Eph. 5:31

25 [a]Gen. 3:7, 10, 11

1 [1]Or, *every* [a]2 Cor. 11:3; Rev. 12:9; 20:2

2 [a]Gen. 2:16, 17

4 [a]John 8:44; 2 Cor. 11:3

5 [a]Is. 14:14; Ezek. 28:2, 12-17

6 [a]Rom. 5:12-19; 1 Tim. 2:14; James 1:14, 15; 1 John 2:16

7 [1]Or, *girdles* [a]Is. 47:3; Lam. 1:8

8 [1]Lit., *wind, breeze* [a]Gen. 18:33; Lev. 26:12; Deut. 23:14 [b]Job 31:33; Ps. 139:1-12; Hos. 10:8; Amos 9:3; Rev. 6:15-17

9 [a]Gen. 4:9; 18:9

10 [a]Ex. 20:18, 19; Deut. 5:25

12 [a]Job 31:33; Prov. 28:13

13 [a]2 Cor. 11:3; 1 Tim. 2:14

"[a]Because you have done this,
Cursed are you more than all
cattle,
And more than every beast of the
field;
On your belly shall you go,
And [b]dust shall you eat
All the days of your life;
15 And I will put [a]enmity
Between you and the woman,
And between your seed and her
seed;
[b]He shall [1]bruise you on the head,
And you shall bruise him on the
heel."
16 To the woman He said,
"I will greatly multiply
Your pain [1]in childbirth,
In pain you shall [a]bring forth
children;
Yet your desire shall be for your
husband,
And [b]he shall rule over you."
17 Then to Adam He said, "Because
you have listened to the voice of your
wife, and have eaten from the tree about
which I commanded you, saying, 'You
shall not eat from it';
[a]Cursed is the ground because of
you;
[b]In [1]toil you shall eat of it
All the days of your life.
18 "Both thorns and thistles it shall
grow for you;
And you shall eat the [1]plants of
the field;
19 By the sweat of your face
You shall eat bread,
Till you [a]return to the ground,
Because [b]from it you were taken;
For you are dust,
And to dust you shall return."
20 Now the man called his wife's
name [1a]Eve, because she was the mother
of all *the* living.
21 And the LORD God made garments
of skin for Adam and his wife, and
clothed them.
22 Then the LORD God said, "Behold,
the man has become like one of [a]Us,
knowing good and evil; and now, lest he
stretch out his hand, and take also from
[b]the tree of life, and eat, and live forever"—
23 therefore the LORD God sent him
out from the garden of Eden, to cultivate
the ground from which he was taken.
24 So [a]He drove the man out; and at
the [b]east of the garden of Eden He
stationed the [c]cherubim, and the flaming
sword which turned every direction, to
guard the way to [d]the tree of life.

Cain and Abel

4 NOW the man [1]had relations with
his wife Eve, and she conceived and
gave birth to [2]Cain, and she said, "I have
gotten a [3]manchild with *the help of* the
LORD."
2 And again, she gave birth to his
brother Abel. And [a]Abel was [b]a keeper
of flocks, but Cain was a tiller of the
ground.
3 So it came about [1]in the course of
time that Cain brought an offering to the
LORD of the fruit of the ground.
4 And [a]Abel, on his part also
brought of the firstlings of his flock and
of their fat portions. And [b]the LORD had
regard for Abel and for his offering;
5 but [a]for Cain and for his offering
He had no regard. So [b]Cain became very
angry and his countenance fell.
6 Then the LORD said to Cain,
"[a]Why are you angry? And why has your
countenance fallen?
7 "[a]If you do well, [1]will not *your*
countenance be lifted up? [b]And if you do
not do well, sin is crouching at the door;
and its desire is for you, [c]but you must
master it."
8 And Cain [1]told Abel his brother.
And it came about when they were in the
field, that Cain rose up against Abel his
brother and [a]killed him.
9 Then the LORD said to Cain,
"[a]Where is Abel your brother?" And he
said, "I do not know. Am I my brother's
keeper?"
10 And He said, "What have you
done? [a]The voice of your brother's blood
is crying to Me from the ground.
11 "And now [a]you are cursed from the
ground, which has opened its mouth to
receive your brother's blood from your
hand.
12 "[a]When you cultivate the ground, it
shall no longer yield its strength to you;
[b]you shall be a vagrant and a wanderer
on the earth."
13 And Cain said to the LORD, "My
punishment is too great to bear!
14 "Behold, Thou hast [a]driven me this
day from the face of the ground; and
from Thy face I shall be hidden, and [b]I
shall be a vagrant and a wanderer on the
earth, and it will come about that [c]who-
ever finds me will kill me."
15 So the LORD said to him, "Therefore whoever kills Cain, vengeance will
be taken on him [a]sevenfold." And the
LORD [1b]appointed a sign for Cain, lest
anyone finding him should slay him.
16 Then Cain went out from the presence [a]of the LORD, and [1]settled in the
land of [2]Nod, east of Eden.
17 And Cain [1]had relations with his
wife and she conceived, and gave birth
to Enoch; and he built a city, and called
the name of the city Enoch, after the
name of his son.
18 Now to Enoch was born Irad; and
Irad [1]became the father of Mehujael;
and Mehujael [1]became the father of
Methushael; and Methushael [1]became
the father of Lamech.
19 And Lamech took to himself [a]two
wives: the name of the one was Adah,
and the name of the other, Zillah.
20 And Adah gave birth to Jabal; he
was the father of those who dwell in
tents and *have* livestock.
21 And his brother's name was Jubal;
he was the father of all those who play
the lyre and pipe.

14 [a]Deut. 28:15-20 [b]Is. 65:25; Mic. 7:17
15 [1]Or, *crush* [a]Rev. 12:17 [b]Rom. 16:20
16 [1]Lit., *and your pregnancy, conception* [a]John 16:21; 1 Tim. 2:15 [b]1 Cor. 14:34
17 [1]Or, *sorrow* [a]Gen. 5:29; Rom. 8:20-22; Heb. 6:8 [b]Job 5:7; 14:1; Eccl. 2:23
18 [1]Lit., *plant*
19 [a]Ps. 90:3; 104:29; Eccl. 12:7 [b]Gen. 2:7
20 [1]I.e., living; or, life [a]2 Cor. 11:3; 1 Tim. 2:13
22 [a]Gen. 1:26 [b]Gen. 2:9; Rev. 22:14
24 [a]Ezek. 31:11 [b]Gen. 2:8 [c]Ex. 25:18-22; Ps. 104:4; Ezek. 10:1-20; Heb. 1:7 [d]Gen. 2:9

1 [1]Lit., *knew* [2]I.e., gotten one [3]Or, *man, the LORD*
2 [a]Luke 11:50, 51 [b]Gen. 46:32; 47:3
3 [1]Lit., *at the end of days*
4 [a]Heb. 11:4 [b]1 Sam. 15:22
5 [a]1 Sam. 16:7 [b]Is. 3:9; Jude 11
6 [a]Jon. 4:4
7 [1]Or, *surely you will be accepted* [a]Jer. 3:12; Mic. 7:18 [b]Num. 32:23 [c]Job 11:14, 15; Rom. 6:12, 16
8 [1]Lit., *said to* [a]Matt. 23:35; Luke 11:51; 1 John 3:12-15; Jude 11
9 [a]Gen. 3:9
10 [a]Num. 35:33; Deut. 21:1-9; Heb. 12:24; Rev. 6:9, 10
11 [a]Gen. 3:14; Deut. 28:15-20; Gal. 3:10
12 [a]Deut. 28:15-24; Joel 1:10-20 [b]Lev. 26:17, 36
14 [a]Gen. 3:24; Jer. 52:3 [b]Deut. 28:64-67 [c]Num. 35:19
15 [1]Or, *set a mark on* [a]Gen. 4:24 [b]Ezek. 9:4, 6
16 [1]Lit., *dwelt* [2]I.e., wandering [a]2 Kin. 24:20; Jer. 23:39; 52:3
17 [1]Lit., *knew*
18 [1]Lit., *begot*
19 [a]Gen. 2:24

22 As for Zillah, she also gave birth to
Tubal-cain, the forger of all implements
of bronze and iron; and the sister of
Tubal-cain was Naamah.
23 And Lamech said to his wives,
"Adah and Zillah,
Listen to my voice,
You wives of Lamech,
Give heed to my speech,
[a]For I [1]have killed a man for
wounding me;
And a boy for striking me;
24 If Cain is avenged [a]sevenfold,
Then Lamech seventy-sevenfold."
25 And [a]Adam [1]had relations with his
wife again; and she gave birth to a son,
and named him [2]Seth, for, *she said,*
"God [3]has appointed me another [4]off-
spring in place of Abel; [b]for Cain killed
him."
26 And to Seth, to him also [a]a son was
born; and he called his name Enosh.
Then *men* began [b]to call [1]upon the name
of the LORD.

Descendants of Adam

5 THIS is the book of the generations
of Adam. In the day when God
created man, He made him [a]in the
likeness of God.
2 He created them [a]male and female,
and He [b]blessed them and named them
[1]Man in the day when they were created.
3 When Adam had lived one hundred and thirty years, he [1]became the
father of *a son* in his own likeness,
according to his image, and named him
Seth.
4 Then the days of Adam after he
became the father of Seth were eight
hundred years, and he had *other* sons
and daughters.
5 So all the days that Adam lived
were nine hundred and thirty years, and
he died.
6 And Seth lived one hundred and
five years, and became the father of
Enosh.
7 Then Seth lived eight hundred and
seven years after he became the father of
Enosh, and he had *other* sons and
daughters.
8 So all the days of Seth were nine
hundred and twelve years, and he died.
9 And Enosh lived ninety years, and
became the father of Kenan.
10 Then Enosh lived eight hundred
and fifteen years after he became the
father of Kenan, and he had *other* sons
and daughters.
11 So all the days of Enosh were nine
hundred and five years, and he died.
12 And Kenan lived seventy years,
and became the father of Mahalalel.
13 Then Kenan lived eight hundred
and forty years after he became the
father of Mahalalel, and he had *other*
sons and daughters.
14 So all the days of Kenan were nine
hundred and ten years, and he died.
15 And Mahalalel lived sixty-five
years, and became the father of Jared.
16 Then Mahalalel lived eight hundred and thirty years after he became the
father of Jared, and he had *other* sons
and daughters.
17 So all the days of Mahalalel were
eight hundred and ninety-five years, and
he died.
18 And Jared lived one hundred and
sixty-two years, and became the father
of Enoch.
19 Then Jared lived eight hundred
years after he became the father of
Enoch, and he had *other* sons and
daughters.
20 So all the days of Jared were nine
hundred and sixty-two years, and he
died.
21 And Enoch lived sixty-five years,
and became the father of Methuselah.
22 Then Enoch [a]walked with God
three hundred years after he became the
father of Methuselah, and he had *other*
sons and daughters.
23 So all the days of Enoch were three
hundred and sixty-five years.
24 And [a]Enoch walked with God; and
he was not, for God [b]took him.
25 And Methuselah lived one hundred
and eighty-seven years, and became the
father of Lamech.
26 Then Methuselah lived seven hundred and eighty-two years after he became the father of Lamech, and he had
other sons and daughters.
27 So all the days of Methuselah were
nine hundred and sixty-nine years, and
he died.
28 And Lamech lived one hundred
and eighty-two years, and became the
father of a son.
29 Now he called his name Noah,
saying, "This one shall [1]give us rest from
our work and from the toil of our hands
arising from [a]the ground which the
LORD has cursed."
30 Then Lamech lived five hundred
and ninety-five years after he became the
father of Noah, and he had *other* sons
and daughters.
31 So all the days of Lamech were
seven hundred and seventy-seven years,
and he died.
32 And Noah was [a]five hundred years
old, and Noah became the father of
Shem, Ham, and Japheth.

The Corruption of Mankind

6 NOW it came about, when men
began to multiply on the face of the
land, and daughters were born to them,
2 that the sons of God saw that the
daughters of men were [1]beautiful; and
they took wives for themselves, whomever they chose.
3 Then the LORD said, "[a]My Spirit
shall not [1]strive with man forever, [2][b]be-
cause he also is flesh; [3]nevertheless his
days shall be one hundred and twenty
years."
4 The [a]Nephilim were on the earth in
those days, and also afterward, when the
sons of God came in to the daughters of

23 [1]Or, *kill* [a]Ex. 20:13; Lev. 19:18; Deut. 32:35; Ps. 94:1

24 [a]Gen. 4:15

25 [1]Lit., *knew* [2]Heb., *Sheth* [3]Heb., *shath* [4]Lit., *seed* [a]Gen. 5:3 [b]Gen. 4:8

26 [1]Or, *by* [a]Luke 3:38 [b]Gen. 12:8; 26:25; 1 Kin. 18:24; Ps. 116:17; Joel 2:32; Zeph. 3:9; 1 Cor. 1:2

1 [a]Gen. 1:26, 27; Eph. 4:24; Col. 3:10

2 [1]Lit., *Adam* [a]Matt. 19:4; Mark 10:6 [b]Gen. 1:28

3 [1]Lit., *begot,* and so throughout the ch.

22 [a]Gen. 6:9; 17:1; 24:40; 48:15; Mic. 6:8; Mal. 2:6; 1 Thess. 2:12

24 [a]2 Kin. 2:11; Jude 14 [b]2 Kin. 2:10; Ps. 49:15; 73:24; Heb. 11:5

29 [1]Lit., *comfort us in* [a]Gen. 3:17-19; 4:11

32 [a]Gen. 7:6

2 [1]Lit., *good*

3 [1]Or, *rule in;* some ancient versions read *abide in* [2]Or, *in his going astray he is flesh* [3]Or, *therefore* [a]Gal. 5:16, 17; 1 Pet. 3:20 [b]Ps. 78:39

4 [a]Num. 13:33

men, and they bore *children* to them.
Those were the mighty men who *were* of
old, men of renown.
5 Then the LORD saw that the wickedness of man was great on the earth,
and that [a]every intent of the thoughts of
his heart was only evil continually.
6 And [a]the LORD was sorry that He
had made man on the earth, and He was
[b]grieved [1]in His heart.
7 And the LORD said, "[a]I will blot
out man whom I have created from the
face of the land, from man to animals to
creeping things and to birds of the [1]sky;
for [b]I am sorry that I have made them."
8 But [a]Noah [b]found favor in the eyes
of the LORD.
9 These are *the records of* the generations of Noah. Noah was a [a]righteous
man, [1b]blameless in his [2]time; Noah
[c]walked with God.
10 And Noah [1]became the father of
three sons: Shem, Ham, and Japheth.
11 Now the earth was [a]corrupt in the
sight of God, and the earth was [b]filled
with violence.
12 And God looked on the earth, and
behold, it was corrupt; for [a]all flesh had
corrupted their way upon the earth.
13 Then God said to Noah, "[a]The end
of all flesh has come before Me; for the
earth is filled with violence because of
them; and behold, I am about to destroy
them with the earth.
14 "Make for yourself an ark of gopher
wood; you shall make the ark with
rooms, and shall [1]cover it inside and out
with pitch.
15 "And this is how you shall make it:
the length of the ark three hundred
[1]cubits, its breadth fifty [1]cubits, and its
height thirty [1]cubits.
16 "You shall make a [1]window for the
ark, and finish it to a cubit from [2]the
top; and set the door of the ark in
the side of it; you shall make it with
lower, second, and third decks.
17 "And behold, [a]I, even I am bringing
the flood of water upon the earth, to
destroy all flesh in which is the breath of
life, from under heaven; everything that
is on the earth shall perish.
18 "But I will establish [a]My covenant
with you; and [b]you shall enter the ark—
you and your sons and your wife, and
your sons' wives with you.
19 "[a]And of every living thing of all
flesh, you shall bring two of every *kind*
into the ark, to keep *them* alive with you;
they shall be male and female.
20 "[a]Of the birds after their kind, and
of the animals after their kind, of every
creeping thing of the ground after its
kind, two of every *kind* shall come to
you to keep *them* alive.
21 "And as for you, take for yourself
some of all [a]food which is edible, and
gather *it* to yourself; and it shall be for
food for you and for them."
22 [a]Thus Noah did; according to all
that God had commanded him, so he
did.

5 [a]Gen. 8:21; Ps. 14:1-3; Prov. 6:18; Matt. 15:19; Rom. 1:28-32
6 [1]Lit., *to* [a]Gen. 6:7; Jer. 18:7-10 [b]Is. 63:10; Eph. 4:30
7 [1]Lit., *heavens* [a]Deut. 28:63; 29:20 [b]Gen. 6:6; Amos 7:3, 6
8 [a]Matt. 24:37; Luke 17:26; 1 Pet. 3:20 [b]Gen. 19:19; Ex. 33:17; Luke 1:30
9 [1]Lit., *complete, perfect;* or, *having integrity* [2]Lit., *generations* [a]Ps. 37:39; 2 Pet. 2:5 [b]Gen. 17:1; Deut. 18:13; Job 1:1 [c]Gen. 5:24
10 [1]Lit., *begot*
11 [a]Deut. 31:29; Judg. 2:19 [b]Ezek. 8:17
12 [a]Ps. 14:1-3
13 [a]Is. 34:1-4; Ezek. 7:2, 3; Amos 8:2; 1 Pet. 4:7
14 [1]Or, *pitch*
15 [1]I.e., One cubit equals approx. 18 in.
16 [1]Or, *roof* [2]Lit., *above*
17 [a]2 Pet. 2:5
18 [a]Gen. 9:9-16; 17:7 [b]Gen. 7:7
19 [a]Gen. 7:2, 14, 15
20 [a]Gen. 7:3
21 [a]Gen. 1:29, 30
22 [a]Gen. 7:5; Heb. 11:7

1 [1]Lit., *generation* [a]Gen. 6:9
2 [1]Lit., *to* [2]Lit., *seven seven* [a]Lev. 11:1-31; Deut. 14:3-20
3 [1]Lit., *heavens* [2]Lit., *seven seven* [3]Lit., *seed*
4 [a]Gen. 7:10 [b]Gen. 7:12, 17 [c]Gen. 6:7, 13
5 [a]Gen. 6:22
6 [1]Lit., *was* [a]Gen. 5:32
7 [a]Gen. 6:18; 7:13; Matt. 24:38f.; Luke 17:27
8 [a]Gen. 6:19, 20; 7:2, 3
9 [1]Lit., *two two*
10 [1]Lit., *were* [a]Gen. 7:4
11 [1]Or, *windows of the heavens* [a]Gen. 7:6 [b]Gen. 8:2
12 [1]Lit., *was* [a]Gen. 7:4, 17
13 [a]Gen. 6:18; 7:7
14 [1]Lit., *its* [2]Lit., *every bird, every wing*
15 [a]Gen. 6:19; 7:9
17 [1]Lit., *was* [a]Gen. 7:4
18 [1]Lit., *went* [2]Lit., *face*
19 [1]Lit., *which were under all the heavens*

The Flood

7 THEN the LORD said to Noah,
"Enter the ark, you and all your
household; for you *alone* I have seen *to*
be [a]righteous before Me in this [1]time.
2 "You shall take [1]with you of every
[a]clean animal [2]by sevens, a male and his
female; and of the animals that are not
clean two, a male and his female;
3 also of the birds of the [1]sky, [2]by
sevens, male and female, to keep [3]off-
spring alive on the face of all the earth.
4 "For after [a]seven more days, I will
send rain on the earth [b]forty days and
forty nights; and I will blot out from the
face of the land [c]every living thing that I
have made."
5 [a]And Noah did according to all
that the LORD had commanded him.
6 Now Noah was [a]six hundred years
old when the flood of water [1]came upon
the earth.
7 Then [a]Noah and his sons and his
wife and his sons' wives with him entered the ark because of the water of the
flood.
8 [a]Of clean animals and animals that
are not clean and birds and everything
that creeps on the ground,
9 there went into the ark to Noah [1]by
twos, male and female, as God had
commanded Noah.
10 And it came about after [a]the seven
days, that the water of the flood [1]came
upon the earth.
11 In the [a]six hundredth year of
Noah's life, in the second month, on the
seventeenth day of the month, on the
same day all [b]the fountains of the great
deep burst open, and the [1]floodgates of
the sky were opened.
12 And [a]the rain [1]fell upon the earth
for forty days and forty nights.
13 On the very same day [a]Noah and
Shem and Ham and Japheth, the sons of
Noah, and Noah's wife and the three
wives of his sons with them, entered the
ark,
14 they and every beast after its kind,
and all the cattle after [1]their kind, and
every creeping thing that creeps on the
earth after its kind, and every bird after
its kind, [2]all sorts of birds.
15 So they went into the ark to Noah,
[a]by twos of all flesh in which was the
breath of life.
16 And those that entered, male and
female of all flesh, entered as God had
commanded him; and the LORD closed *it*
behind him.
17 Then the flood [1]came upon the
earth for [a]forty days; and the water
increased and lifted up the ark, so that it
rose above the earth.
18 And the water prevailed and increased greatly upon the earth; and the
ark [1]floated on the [2]surface of the water.
19 And the water prevailed more and
more upon the earth, so that all the high
mountains [1]everywhere under the heavens were covered.

20 The water prevailed fifteen [1]cubits
higher, [a]and the mountains were covered.
21 [a]And all flesh that [1]moved on the
earth perished, birds and cattle and
beasts and every swarming thing that
swarms upon the earth, and all mankind;
22 of all that was on the dry land, all
[a]in whose nostrils was the breath of the
spirit of life, died.
23 Thus He blotted out [1]every living
thing that was upon the face of the land,
from man to animals to creeping things
and to birds of the [2]sky, and they were
blotted out from the earth; and only
[a]Noah was left, together with those that
were with him in the ark.
24 [a]And the water prevailed upon the
earth one hundred and fifty days.

The Flood Subsides

8 BUT [a]God remembered Noah and
all the beasts and all the cattle that
were with him in the ark; and [b]God
caused a wind to pass over the earth, and
the water subsided.
2 Also [a]the fountains of the deep and
the [1]floodgates of the sky were closed,
and [b]the rain from the sky was restrained;
3 and the water receded steadily
from the earth, and at the end [a]of one
hundred and fifty days the water decreased.
4 And in the seventh month, on the
seventeenth day of the month, [a]the ark
rested upon the mountains of Ararat.
5 And the water decreased steadily
until the tenth month; in the tenth
month, on the first day of the month, the
tops of the mountains became visible.
6 Then it came about at the end of
forty days, that Noah opened the [a]win-
dow of the ark which he had made;
7 and he sent out a raven, and it
[1]flew here and there until the water was
dried up [2]from the earth.
8 Then he sent out a dove from him,
to see if the water was abated from the
face of the land;
9 but the dove found no resting place
for the sole of her foot, so she returned
to him into the ark; for the water was on
the [1]surface of all the earth. Then he put
out his hand and took her, and brought
her into the ark to himself.
10 So he waited yet another seven
days; and again he sent out the dove
from the ark.
11 And the dove came to him toward
[1]evening; and behold, in her [2]beak was a
freshly picked olive leaf. So Noah knew
that the water was abated from the
earth.
12 Then he waited yet another seven
days, and sent out [a]the dove; but she did
not return to him again.
13 Now it came about in the [a]six
hundred and first year, in the first *month,*
on the first of the month, the water was
dried up [1]from the earth. Then Noah
removed the covering of the ark, and
looked, and behold, the [2]surface of the
ground was dried up.
14 And in the second month, on the
twenty-seventh day of the month, the
earth was dry.
15 Then God spoke to Noah, saying,
16 "Go out of the ark, you and your
wife and your sons and your sons' wives
with you.
17 "Bring out with you every living
thing of all flesh that is with you, birds
and animals and every creeping thing
that creeps on the earth, that they may
[1a]breed abundantly on the earth, and be
fruitful and multiply on the earth."
18 So Noah went out, and his sons
and his wife and his sons' wives with
him.
19 Every beast, every creeping thing,
and every bird, everything that moves on
the earth, went out [1]by their families
from the ark.
20 Then Noah built [a]an altar to the
LORD, and took of every [b]clean animal
and of every clean bird and offered
[c]burnt offerings on the altar.
21 And the LORD [a]smelled the soothing aroma; and the LORD said [1]to Himself, "I will never again [b]curse the
ground on account of man, for [c]the
[2]intent of man's heart is evil from his
youth; [d]and I will never again [3]destroy
every living thing, as I have done.
22 "While the earth remains,
Seedtime and harvest,
And cold and heat,
And [a]summer and winter,
And [b]day and night
Shall not cease."

Covenant of the Rainbow

9 AND God blessed Noah and his
sons and said to them, "[a]Be fruitful
and multiply, and fill the earth.
2 "And the fear of you and the terror
of you shall be on every beast of the
earth and on every bird of the [1]sky; with
everything that creeps on the ground,
and all the fish of the sea, into your hand
they are given.
3 "Every moving thing that is alive
shall be food for you; I give all to you,
[a]as *I gave* the green plant.
4 "Only you shall not eat flesh with its
life, *that is,* [a]its blood.
5 "And surely I will require [1a]your
lifeblood; [2b]from every beast I will
require it. And [2]from *every* man, [2]from
every man's brother I will require the life
of man.
6 "[a]Whoever sheds man's blood,
By man his blood shall be shed,
For [b]in the image of God
He made man.
7 "And as for you, [a]be fruitful and
multiply;
[1]Populate the earth abundantly
and multiply in it."
8 Then God spoke to Noah and to
his sons with him, saying,
9 "Now behold, [a]I Myself do establish
My covenant with you, and with your
[1]descendants after you;

7:20 [1]I.e., One cubit equals approx. 18 in. [a]Gen. 8:4
21 [1]Or, *crept* [a]Gen. 6:7, 13, 17; 7:4
22 [a]Gen. 2:7
23 [1]Lit., *all existence* [2]Lit., *heavens* [a]Matt. 24:38, 39; Luke 17:26, 27; Heb. 11:7; 1 Pet. 3:20; 2 Pet. 2:5
24 [a]Gen. 8:3

8:1 [a]Gen. 19:29; Ex. 2:24; 1 Sam. 1:19; Ps. 105:42 [b]Ex. 14:21; 15:10; Job 12:15; Ps. 29:10; Is. 44:27; Nah. 1:4
2 [1]Or, *windows of the heavens* [a]Gen. 7:11 [b]Gen. 7:4, 12
3 [a]Gen. 7:24
4 [a]Gen. 7:20
6 [a]Gen. 6:16
7 [1]Lit., *went out, going and returning* [2]Lit., *from upon*
9 [1]Lit., *face*
11 [1]Lit., *the time of evening* [2]Lit., *mouth*
12 [a]Jer. 48:28
13 [1]Lit., *from upon* [2]Lit., *face* [a]Gen. 7:6
17 [1]Or, *swarm* [a]Gen. 1:22, 28
19 [1]Or, *according to their kind*
20 [a]Gen. 12:7, 8; 13:18; 22:9 [b]Gen. 7:2; Lev. 11:1-47 [c]Gen. 22:2; Ex. 10:25
21 [1]Lit., *to His heart* [2]Or, *inclination* [3]Lit., *smite* [a]Ex. 29:18, 25 [b]Gen. 3:17; 6:7, 13, 17; Is. 54:9 [c]Gen. 6:5; Ps. 51:5; Jer. 17:9; Rom. 1:21; 3:23; Eph. 2:1-3 [d]Gen. 9:11, 15
22 [a]Ps. 74:17 [b]Jer. 33:20, 25

9:1 [a]Gen. 1:28; 9:7
2 [1]Lit., *heavens*
3 [a]Gen. 1:29
4 [a]Lev. 7:26f.; 17:10-16; 19:26; Deut. 12:16, 23; 15:23; 1 Sam. 14:34; Acts 15:20, 29
5 [1]Lit., *your blood of your lives* [2]Lit., *from the hand of* [a]Ex. 20:13; 21:12 [b]Ex. 21:28, 29
6 [a]Ex. 21:12-14; Lev. 24:17; Num. 35:33; Matt. 26:52 [b]Gen. 1:26, 27
7 [1]Lit., *Swarm in the earth* [a]Gen. 9:1
9 [1]Lit., *seed* [a]Gen. 6:18

10 and with every living creature that is with you, the birds, the cattle, and every beast of the earth with you; of all that comes out of the ark, even every beast of the earth.

11 "And I establish My covenant with you; and all flesh shall [a]never again be cut off by the water of the flood, [b]neither shall there again be a flood to destroy the earth."

12 And God said, "This is [a]the sign of the covenant which I am making between Me and you and every living creature that is with you, for [1]all successive generations;

13 I set My [a]bow in the cloud, and it shall be for a sign of a covenant between Me and the earth.

14 "And it shall come about, when I bring a cloud over the earth, that the bow shall be seen in the cloud,

15 and [a]I will remember My covenant, which is between Me and you and every living creature of all flesh; and [b]never again shall the water become a flood to destroy all flesh.

16 "When the bow is in the cloud, then I will look upon it, to remember the [a]everlasting covenant between God and every living creature of all flesh that is on the earth."

17 And God said to Noah, "This is the sign of the covenant which I have established between Me and all flesh that is on the earth."

18 Now the sons of Noah who came out of the ark were Shem and Ham and Japheth; and [a]Ham was the father of Canaan.

19 These three *were* the sons of Noah; and [a]from these the whole earth was [1]populated.

20 Then Noah began [1]farming and planted a vineyard.

21 And he drank of the wine and [a]became drunk, and uncovered himself inside his tent.

22 And Ham, the father of Canaan, [a]saw the nakedness of his father, and told his two brothers outside.

23 But Shem and Japheth took a garment and laid it upon both their shoulders and walked backward and covered the nakedness of their father; and their faces were [1]turned away, so that they did not see their father's nakedness.

24 When Noah awoke from his wine, he knew what his youngest son had done to him.

25 So he said,
"[a]Cursed be Canaan;
[1b]A servant of servants
He shall be to his brothers."

26 He also said,
"[a]Blessed be the LORD,
The God of Shem;
And let Canaan be [1]his servant.

27 "[a]May God enlarge Japheth,
And let him dwell in the tents of Shem;
And let Canaan be [1]his servant."

28 And Noah lived three hundred and fifty years after the flood.

29 So all the days of Noah were nine hundred and fifty years, and he died.

Descendants of Noah

10 NOW these are *the records of* the generations of Shem, Ham, and Japheth, the sons of Noah; and sons were born to them after the flood.

2 [a]The sons of Japheth *were* [b]Gomer and Magog and [c]Madai and [d]Javan and Tubal and [e]Meshech and Tiras.

3 And the sons of Gomer *were* [a]Ashkenaz and [1]Riphath and [b]Togarmah.

4 And the sons of Javan *were* Elishah and [a]Tarshish, Kittim and [1]Dodanim.

5 From these the coastlands of the nations [1]were separated into their lands, every one according to his language, according to their families, into their nations.

6 [a]And the sons of Ham *were* Cush and Mizraim and Put and Canaan.

7 And the sons of Cush *were* [a]Seba and Havilah and Sabtah and [b]Raamah and Sabteca; and the sons of Raamah *were* [b]Sheba and [c]Dedan.

8 Now Cush [1]became the father of Nimrod; he [2]became a mighty one on the earth.

9 He was a mighty hunter before the LORD; therefore it is said, "Like Nimrod a mighty hunter before the LORD."

10 And the beginning of his kingdom was [1a]Babel and Erech and Accad and Calneh, in the land of [b]Shinar.

11 From that land he went forth [a]into Assyria, and built Nineveh and Rehoboth-Ir and Calah,

12 and Resen between Nineveh and Calah; that is the great city.

13 And Mizraim [1]became the father of [a]Ludim and Anamim and Lehabim and Naphtuhim

14 and [a]Pathrusim and Casluhim (from which came the Philistines) and Caphtorim.

15 And Canaan [1]became the father of [a]Sidon, his first-born, and [b]Heth

16 and [a]the Jebusite and the Amorite and the Girgashite

17 and the Hivite and the Arkite and the Sinite

18 and the Arvadite and the Zemarite and the Hamathite; and afterward the families of the Canaanite were spread abroad.

19 And [a]the territory of the Canaanite [1]extended from Sidon as you go toward Gerar, as far as Gaza; as you go toward [b]Sodom and Gomorrah and Admah and Zeboiim, as far as Lasha.

20 These are the sons of Ham, according to their families, according to their languages, by their lands, by their nations.

21 And also to Shem, the father of all the children of Eber, *and* the [1]older brother of Japheth, children were born.

22 [a]The sons of Shem *were* [b]Elam and Asshur and [c]Arpachshad and [d]Lud and Aram.

11 [a]Gen. 8:21 [b]Is. 54:9
12 [1]Or, *everlasting generations* [a]Gen. 9:13, 17; 17:11
13 [a]Ezek. 1:28
15 [a]Lev. 26:42, 45; Deut. 7:9; Ezek. 16:60 [b]Gen. 9:11
16 [a]Gen. 17:13, 19; 2 Sam. 23:5
18 [a]Gen. 9:25-27; 10:6
19 [1]Lit., *scattered* [a]Gen. 9:1, 7; 10:32; 1 Chr. 1:4
20 [1]Lit., to be *a farmer*
21 [a]Prov. 20:1
22 [a]Hab. 2:15
23 [1]Lit., *backward*
25 [1]I.e., The lowest of servants [a]Deut. 27:16 [b]Josh. 9:23
26 [1]Or, *their* [a]Gen. 14:20; 24:27
27 [1]Or, *their* [a]Gen. 10:2-5; Is. 66:19
2 [a]1 Chr. 1:5-7 [b]Ezek. 38:2, 6 [c]2 Kin. 17:6 [d]Is. 66:19 [e]Ezek. 38:2
3 [1]I.e., In 1 Chr. 1:6, *Diphath* [a]Jer. 51:27 [b]Ezek. 27:14
4 [1]I.e., In 1 Chr. 1:7, *Rodanim* [a]Ezek. 27:12, 25
5 [1]Or, *separated themselves*
6 [a]1 Chr. 1:8-10
7 [a]Is. 43:3 [b]Ezek. 27:22 [c]Ezek. 27:15, 20
8 [1]Lit., *begot* [2]Lit., *began to be*
10 [1]Or, *Babylon* [a]Gen. 11:9 [b]Gen. 11:2; 14:1
11 [a]Mic. 5:6
13 [1]Lit., *begot* [a]Jer. 46:9
14 [a]1 Chr. 1:12
15 [1]Lit., *begot* [a]1 Chr. 1:13; Jer. 47:4 [b]Gen. 23:3
16 [a]Gen. 15:19-21
19 [1]Lit., *was* [a]Num. 34:2-12 [b]Gen. 14:2, 3
21 [1]Or, *the brother of Japheth the elder*
22 [a]1 Chr. 1:17 [b]Gen. 14:1, 9 [c]Gen. 11:10 [d]Is. 66:19

23 And the sons of Aram *were* [a]Uz
and Hul and Gether and Mash.
24 And Arpachshad [1]became the father of [a]Shelah; and Shelah [1]became the
father of Eber.
25 And [a]two sons were born to Eber;
the name of the one *was* [1]Peleg, for in his
days the earth was divided; and his
brother's name *was* Joktan.
26 And Joktan [1]became the father of
Almodad and Sheleph and Hazarmaveth
and Jerah
27 and Hadoram and Uzal and Diklah
28 and [1]Obal and Abimael and Sheba
29 and Ophir and Havilah and Jobab;
all these were the sons of Joktan.
30 Now their [1]settlement [2]extended
from Mesha as you go toward Sephar,
the hill country of the east.
31 These are the sons of Shem, according to their families, according to
their languages, by their lands, according to their nations.
32 These are the families of the sons
of Noah, according to their genealogies,
by their nations; and [a]out of these the
nations were separated on the earth after
the flood.

Universal Language, Babel, Confusion

11 NOW the whole earth [1]used the
same language and [2]the same
words.
2 And it came about as they journeyed east, that they found a plain in the
land [a]of Shinar and [1]settled there.
3 And they said to one another,
"Come, let us make bricks and burn
them thoroughly." And they used brick
for stone, and they used [a]tar for mortar.
4 And they said, "Come, let us build
for ourselves a city, and a tower whose
top [a]*will reach* into heaven, and let us
make for ourselves [b]a name; lest we [c]be
scattered abroad over the face of the
whole earth."
5 [a]And the LORD came down to see
the city and the tower which the sons of
men had built.
6 And the LORD said, "Behold, they
are one people, and they all have [1a]the
same language. And this is what they
began to do, and now nothing which
they purpose to do will be [2]impossible
for them.
7 "Come, [a]let Us go down and there
[b]confuse their [1]language, that they may
not understand one another's [1]speech."
8 So the LORD [a]scattered them
abroad from there over the face of the
whole earth; and they stopped building
the city.
9 Therefore its name was called [1a]Ba-
bel, because there the LORD confused
the [2]language of the whole earth; and
from there the LORD scattered them
abroad over the face of the whole earth.

Descendants of Shem

10 [a]These are *the records of* the generations of Shem. Shem was one hundred years old, and [1]became the father
of Arpachshad two years after the flood;
11 and Shem lived five hundred years
after he became the father of Arpachshad, and he had *other* sons and daughters.
12 And Arpachshad lived thirty-five
years, and became the father of Shelah;
13 and Arpachshad lived four hundred and three years after he became the
father of Shelah, and he had *other* sons
and daughters.
14 And Shelah lived thirty years, and
became the father of Eber;
15 and Shelah lived four hundred and
three years after he became the father of
Eber, and he had *other* sons and daughters.
16 And Eber lived thirty-four years,
and became the father of Peleg;
17 and Eber lived four hundred and
thirty years after he became the father of
Peleg, and he had *other* sons and daughters.
18 And Peleg lived thirty years, and
became the father of Reu;
19 and Peleg lived two hundred and
nine years after he became the father of
Reu, and he had *other* sons and daughters.
20 And Reu lived thirty-two years,
and became the father of Serug;
21 and Reu lived two hundred and
seven years after he became the father of
Serug, and he had *other* sons and daughters.
22 And Serug lived thirty years, and
became the father of Nahor;
23 and Serug lived two hundred years
after he became the father of Nahor, and
he had *other* sons and daughters.
24 And Nahor lived twenty-nine
years, and became the father of [a]Terah;
25 and Nahor lived one hundred and
nineteen years after he became the father
of Terah, and he had *other* sons and
daughters.
26 And Terah lived seventy years, and
became [a]the father of Abram, Nahor
and Haran.
27 Now these are *the records of* the
generations of Terah. Terah became the
father of Abram, Nahor and Haran; and
[a]Haran became the father of [b]Lot.
28 And Haran died [1]in the presence of
his father Terah in the land of his birth,
in [a]Ur of the Chaldeans.
29 And Abram and [a]Nahor took wives
for themselves. The name of Abram's
wife was [b]Sarai; and the name of Nahor's wife was [c]Milcah, the daughter of
Haran, the father of Milcah [1]and Iscah.
30 And [a]Sarai was barren; she had no
child.
31 And Terah took Abram his son,
and Lot the son of Haran, his grandson,
and Sarai his daughter-in-law, his son
Abram's wife; and they went out [1]to-
gether from [a]Ur of the Chaldeans in
order to enter the land of Canaan; and
they went as far as Haran, and [2]settled
there.

23 [a]Job 1:1; Jer. 25:20
24 [1]Lit., *begot* [a]Gen. 11:12; Luke 3:35
25 [1]I.e., division [a]1 Chr. 1:19
26 [1]Lit., *begot*
28 [1]I.e., In 1 Chr. 1:22, *Ebal*
30 [1]Lit., *dwelling* [2]Lit., *was*
32 [a]Gen. 9:19
1 [1]Lit., *was one lip* [2]Or, *few* or *one* set of *words*
2 [1]Lit., *dwelt* [a]Gen. 10:10; 14:1; Dan. 1:2
3 [a]Gen. 14:10
4 [a]Deut. 1:28; 9:1; Ps. 107:26 [b]Gen. 6:4; 2 Sam. 8:13 [c]Deut. 4:27
5 [a]Gen. 18:21; Ex. 3:8; 19:11, 18, 20
6 [1]Lit., *one lip* [2]Lit., *withheld from* [a]Gen. 11:1
7 [1]Lit., *lip* [a]Gen. 1:26 [b]Gen. 42:23; Ex. 4:11; Deut. 28:49; Is. 33:19; Jer. 5:15
8 [a]Gen. 11:4; Ps. 92:9; Luke 1:51
9 [1]Or, *Babylon;* cf. Heb., *balal,* confuse [2]Lit., *lip* [a]Gen. 10:10
10 [1]Lit., *begot,* and so throughout the ch. [a]Gen. 10:22-25
24 [a]Josh. 24:2
26 [a]Josh. 24:2
27 [a]Gen. 11:31; 12:4 [b]Gen. 13:10; 14:12; 19:1, 29
28 [1]Or, *during the lifetime of* [a]Gen. 11:31
29 [1]Lit., *and the father of* [a]Gen. 24:10 [b]Gen. 17:15; 20:12 [c]Gen. 22:20, 23; 24:15
30 [a]Gen. 16:1
31 [1]Lit., *with them* [2]Lit., *dwelt* [a]Gen. 15:7; Neh. 9:7; Acts 7:4

32 And the days of Terah were two
hundred and five years; and Terah died
in Haran.

Abram Journeys to Egypt

12 NOW [a]the LORD said to Abram,
"[1]Go forth from your country,
And from your relatives
And from your father's house,
To the land which I will show
you;
2 And [a]I will make you a great
nation,
And [b]I will bless you,
And make your name great;
And so [1c]you shall be a blessing;
3 And [a]I will bless those who bless
you,
And the one who [1]curses you I
will [2]curse.
[b]And in you all the families of the
earth shall be blessed."
4 So Abram went forth as the LORD
had spoken to him; and [a]Lot went with
him. Now Abram was seventy-five years
old when he departed from Haran.
5 And Abram took Sarai his wife and
Lot his nephew, and all their [a]possessions which they had accumulated, and
[b]the [1]persons which they had acquired in
Haran, and they [2]set out for the land of
Canaan; [c]thus they came to the land of
Canaan.
6 And Abram passed through the
land as far as the site of [a]Shechem, to the
[1]oak of Moreh. Now the Canaanite *was*
then in the land.
7 And the LORD [a]appeared to Abram
and said, "[b]To your [1]descendants I will
give this land." So he built [c]an altar
there to the LORD who had appeared to
him.
8 Then he proceeded from there to
the mountain on the east of Bethel, and
pitched his tent, with [a]Bethel on the west
and Ai on the east; and there he built an
altar to the LORD and [b]called upon the
name of the LORD.
9 And Abram journeyed on, continuing toward [a]the [1]Negev.
10 Now there was [a]a famine in the
land; so Abram went down to Egypt to
sojourn there, for the famine was [b]severe
in the land.
11 And it came about when he [1]came
near to Egypt, that he said to Sarai his
wife, "See now, I know that you are a
[2a]beautiful woman;
12 [a]and it will come about when the
Egyptians see you, that they will say,
'This is his wife'; and they will kill me,
but they will let you live.
13 "Please say that you are [a]my sister
so that it may go well with me because of
you, and that [1b]I may live on account of
you."
14 And it came about when Abram
came into Egypt, the Egyptians [1]saw
that the woman was very beautiful.
15 And Pharaoh's officials saw her
and praised her to Pharaoh; and [a]the
woman was taken into Pharaoh's house.

1 [1]Lit., *Go for yourself* [a]Gen. 15:7; Acts 7:3; Heb. 11:8
2 [1]Lit., *be a blessing* [a]Gen. 17:4-6; 18:18; 46:3; Deut. 26:5 [b]Gen. 22:17 [c]Zech. 8:13
3 [1]Or, *reviles* [2]Or, *bind under a curse* [a]Gen. 24:35; 27:29; Num. 24:9 [b]Gen. 22:18; 26:4; 28:14; Acts 3:25; Gal. 3:8
4 [a]Gen. 11:27, 31
5 [1]Lit., *souls* [2]Lit., *went forth to go to* [a]Gen. 13:6 [b]Gen. 14:14; Lev. 22:11 [c]Gen. 11:31; Heb. 11:8
6 [1]Or, *terebinth* [a]Gen. 35:4; Deut. 11:30
7 [1]Lit., *seed* [a]Gen. 17:1; 18:1 [b]Gen. 13:15; 15:18; Deut. 34:4; Ps. 105:9-12; Acts 7:5; Gal. 3:16 [c]Gen. 13:4, 18; 22:9
8 [a]Josh. 8:9, 12 [b]Gen. 4:26; 21:33
9 [1]I.e., South country [a]Gen. 13:1, 3; 20:1; 24:62
10 [a]Gen. 26:1 [b]Gen. 43:1
11 [1]Lit., *drew near to enter* [2]Lit., *woman of beautiful appearance* [a]Gen. 26:7; 29:17
12 [a]Gen. 20:11
13 [1]Lit., *my soul* [a]Gen. 20:2, 5, 12; 26:7 [b]Jer. 38:17, 20
14 [1]Lit., *saw the woman that she was*
15 [a]Gen. 20:2
16 [1]Lit., *he had* [a]Gen. 20:14 [b]Gen. 13:2
17 [a]Gen. 20:18; 1 Chr. 16:21; Ps. 105:14
18 [a]Gen. 20:9, 10; 26:10
19 [1]Or, *behold*
20 [1]Lit., *sent*

1 [1]I.e., South country [a]Gen. 12:9
2 [a]Gen. 24:35
3 [1]Lit., *by his stages* [2]I.e., South country [a]Gen. 12:8
4 [a]Gen. 12:7, 8
5 [a]Gen. 12:5
6 [1]Lit., *bear* [2]Lit., *to dwell* [a]Gen. 36:7 [b]Gen. 12:5, 16; 13:2
7 [a]Gen. 26:20 [b]Gen. 12:6; 15:20, 21
8 [a]Prov. 15:18; 20:3
10 [1]Lit., *circle* [a]Gen. 19:17-29; Deut. 34:3 [b]Gen. 19:24 [c]Gen. 2:8, 10 [d]Gen. 47:6 [e]Gen. 14:2, 8; 19:22; Deut. 34:3
11 [1]Lit., *circle*

16 Therefore [a]he treated Abram well
for her sake; and [1b]gave him sheep and
oxen and donkeys and male and female
servants and female donkeys and camels.
17 But the LORD [a]struck Pharaoh and
his house with great plagues because of
Sarai, Abram's wife.
18 Then Pharaoh called Abram and
said, "[a]What is this you have done to
me? Why did you not tell me that she
was your wife?
19 "Why did you say, 'She is my sister,'
so that I took her for my wife? Now
then, [1]here is your wife, take her and
go."
20 And Pharaoh commanded *his* men
concerning him; and they [1]escorted him
away, with his wife and all that belonged
to him.

Abram and Lot

13 SO Abram went up from Egypt
to [a]the [1]Negev, he and his wife
and all that belonged to him; and Lot
with him.
2 Now Abram was [a]very rich in
livestock, in silver and in gold.
3 And he went [1]on his journeys from
the [2]Negev as far as Bethel, to the place
where his tent had been at the beginning,
[a]between Bethel and Ai,
4 to the place of the [a]altar, which he
had made there formerly; and there
Abram called on the name of the LORD.
5 Now [a]Lot, who went with Abram,
also had flocks and herds and tents.
6 And [a]the land could not [1]sustain
them [2]while dwelling together; [b]for their
possessions were so great that they were
not able to remain together.
7 [a]And there was strife between the
herdsmen of Abram's livestock and the
herdsmen of Lot's livestock. Now
[b]the Canaanite and the Perizzite were
dwelling then in the land.
8 [a]Then Abram said to Lot, "Please
let there be no strife between you and
me, nor between my herdsmen and your
herdsmen, for we are brothers.
9 "Is not the whole land before you?
Please separate from me: if *to* the left,
then I will go to the right; or if *to* the
right, then I will go to the left."
10 And Lot lifted up his eyes and saw
all the [1a]valley of the Jordan, that it was
well watered everywhere—*this was* before the LORD [b]destroyed Sodom and
Gomorrah—like [c]the garden of the
LORD, [d]like the land of Egypt as you go
to [e]Zoar.
11 So Lot chose for himself all the
[1]valley of the Jordan; and Lot journeyed
eastward. Thus they separated from each
other.
12 Abram [1]settled in the land of Canaan, while Lot [1]settled in [a]the cities of
the [2]valley, and moved his tents as far as
Sodom.

12 [1]Lit., *dwelt* [2]Lit., *circle* [a]Gen. 14:2; 19:24, 25, 29

13 Now [a]the men of Sodom were
wicked [1]exceedingly and [b]sinners against
the LORD.
14 And the LORD said to Abram, after
Lot had separated from him, "[a]Now lift
up your eyes and look from the place
where you are, [b]northward and southward and eastward and westward;
15 [a]for all the land which you see, [b]I
will give it to you and to your [1]descend-
ants forever.
16 "And I will make your [1]descendants
[a]as the dust of the earth; so that if
anyone can number the dust of the
earth, then your [1]descendants can also
be numbered.
17 "Arise, [a]walk about the land
through its length and breadth; for [b]I
will give it to you."
18 Then Abram moved his tent and
came and dwelt by the [1a]oaks of Mamre,
which are in Hebron, and there he built
[b]an altar to the LORD.

War of the Kings

14 AND it came about in the days
of Amraphel king of [a]Shinar,
Arioch king of Ellasar, Chedorlaomer
king of [b]Elam, and Tidal king of [1]Goiim,
2 *that* they made war with Bera king
of Sodom, and with Birsha king of
Gomorrah, Shinab king of [a]Admah, and
Shemeber king of [b]Zeboiim, and the
king of Bela (that is, [c]Zoar).
3 All these [1]came as allies to [a]the
valley of Siddim (that is, [b]the Salt Sea).
4 Twelve years they had served
Chedorlaomer, but the thirteenth year
they rebelled.
5 And in the fourteenth year Chedorlaomer and the kings that were with him,
came and [1]defeated the [a]Rephaim in
[b]Ashteroth-karnaim and the Zuzim in
Ham and the Emim in [2c]Shaveh-kiriath-
aim,
6 and the [a]Horites in their Mount
Seir, as far as [b]El-paran, which is by the
wilderness.
7 Then they turned back and came to
En-mishpat (that is, [a]Kadesh), and [1]con-
quered all the country of the Amalekites,
and also the Amorites, who lived in
[b]Hazazon-tamar.
8 And the king of Sodom and the
king of Gomorrah and the king of Admah and the king of Zeboiim and the
king of Bela (that is, Zoar) came out;
and they arrayed for battle against them
in [a]the valley of Siddim,
9 against Chedorlaomer king of Elam
and Tidal king of [1]Goiim and Amraphel
king of Shinar and Arioch king of Ellasar—four kings against five.
10 Now the valley of Siddim was full
of tar pits; and [a]the kings of Sodom and
Gomorrah fled, and they fell [1]into them.
But those who survived fled to the [b]hill
country.
11 Then they took all the goods of
Sodom and Gomorrah and all their food
supply, and departed.
12 And they also took Lot, [a]Abram's
nephew, and his possessions and departed, [b]for he was living in Sodom.
13 Then [1]a fugitive came and told
Abram the [a]Hebrew. Now he was [2]living
by the [3b]oaks of Mamre the Amorite,
brother of Eshcol and brother of Aner,
and these were [4c]allies with Abram.
14 And when Abram heard that [a]his
[1]relative had been taken captive, he [2]led
out his trained men, [b]born in his house,
three hundred and eighteen, and went in
pursuit as far as [c]Dan.
15 And [a]he divided [1]his forces against
them by night, he and his servants, and
[2]defeated them, and pursued them as far
as Hobah, which is [3]north of [b]Damas-
cus.
16 And he [a]brought back all the
goods, and also brought back [b]his [1]rela-
tive Lot with his possessions, and also
the women, and the people.

God's Promise to Abram

17 Then after his return from the
[1]defeat of Chedorlaomer and the kings
who were with him, [a]the king of Sodom
went out to meet him at the valley of
Shaveh (that is, [b]the King's Valley).
18 And [a]Melchizedek king of Salem
brought out [b]bread and wine; now he
was a [c]priest of [1]God Most High.
19 And he blessed him and said,
"Blessed be Abram of [1]God Most
High,
[2a]Possessor of heaven and earth;
20 And blessed be [1]God Most High,
Who has delivered your enemies
into your hand."
[a]And he gave him a tenth of all.
21 And the king of Sodom said to
Abram, "Give the [1]people to me and
take the goods for yourself."
22 And Abram said to the king of
Sodom, "I have [1]sworn to the LORD
[2a]God Most High, [3b]possessor of heaven
and earth,
23 that [a]I will not take a thread or a
sandal thong or anything that is yours,
lest you should say, 'I have made Abram
rich.'
24 "[1]I will take nothing except what the
young men have eaten, and the share of
the men who went with me, [a]Aner,
Eshcol, and Mamre; let them take their
share."

Abram Promised a Son

15 AFTER these things [a]the word of
the LORD came to Abram in a
vision, saying,
"[b]Do not fear, Abram,
I am [c]a shield to you;
[1]Your [d]reward shall be very
great."

13 [1]Lit., *wicked and sinners exceedingly* [a]Gen. 18:20; Ezek. 16:49 [b]Gen. 39:9; Num. 32:23; 2 Pet. 2:7, 8
14 [a]Deut. 3:27; 34:1-4; Is. 49:18 [b]Gen. 28:14
15 [1]Lit., *seed* [a]Gen. 12:7 [b]Gen. 13:17; 15:7; 17:8; 2 Chr. 20:7; Acts 7:5
16 [1]Lit., *seed* [a]Gen. 16:10; 28:14; Num. 23:10
17 [a]Num. 13:17-24 [b]Gen. 13:15
18 [1]Or, *terebinths* [a]Gen. 14:13 [b]Gen. 8:20; 12:7, 8

1 [1]Or, *nations* [a]Gen. 10:10; 11:2 [b]Gen. 10:22; Is. 11:11; Dan. 8:2
2 [a]Gen. 10:19 [b]Deut. 29:23 [c]Gen. 13:10; 19:22
3 [1]Lit., *joined together* [a]Gen. 14:8, 10 [b]Num. 34:12; Deut. 3:17; Josh. 3:16
5 [1]Lit., *smote* [2]Or, *the plain of Kiriathaim* [a]Deut. 3:11, 13 [b]Deut. 1:4; Josh. 9:10 [c]Num. 32:37
6 [a]Gen. 36:20; Deut. 2:12, 22 [b]Gen. 21:21; Num. 10:12
7 [1]Lit., *smote* [a]Num. 13:26 [b]2 Chr. 20:2
8 [a]Gen. 14:3
9 [1]Or, *nations*
10 [1]Lit., *there* [a]Gen. 14:17, 21, 22 [b]Gen. 19:17
12 [a]Gen. 11:27 [b]Gen. 13:12
13 [1]Lit., *the* [2]Lit., *abiding* [3]Or, *terebinths* [4]Lit., *possessors of the covenant* [a]Gen. 40:15; Ex. 3:18 [b]Gen. 13:18; 14:24 [c]Gen. 21:27, 32
14 [1]Lit., *brother* [2]Or, *mustered* [a]Gen. 14:12 [b]Gen. 12:5; 15:3; 17:27; Eccl. 2:7 [c]Deut. 34:1; Judg. 18:29; 1 Kin. 15:20
15 [1]Lit., *himself* [2]Lit., *smote* [3]Lit., *on the left* [a]Judg. 7:16 [b]Gen. 15:2
16 [1]Lit., *brother* [a]1 Sam. 30:8, 18, 19 [b]Gen. 14:12, 14
17 [1]Lit., *smiting* [a]Gen. 14:10 [b]2 Sam. 18:18
18 [1]Heb., *El Elyon* [a]Heb. 7:1-10 [b]Ps. 104:15 [c]Ps. 110:4; Heb. 5:6, 10
19 [1]Heb., *El Elyon* [2]Or, *Creator* [a]Gen. 14:22
20 [1]Heb., *El Elyon* [a]Heb. 7:4
21 [1]Lit., *soul*
22 [1]Lit., *lifted up my hand* [2]Heb., *El Elyon* [3]Or, *Creator* [a]Gen. 14:19 [b]Ps. 24:1
23 [a]2 Kin. 5:16
24 [1]Lit., *Not to me except* [a]Gen. 14:13

1 [1]Or, *Your very great reward* [a]Gen. 15:4; 46:2; 1 Sam. 15:10 [b]Gen. 21:17; 26:24; Is. 41:10 [c]Deut. 33:29 [d]Num. 18:20; Ps. 58:11

2 And Abram said, "O Lord [1]GOD,
what wilt Thou give me, since I [2]am
childless, and the [3]heir of my house is
Eliezer of Damascus?"
3 And Abram said, "[1]Since Thou
hast given no [2]offspring to me, [3]one
[a]born in my house is my heir."
4 Then behold, the word of the LORD
came to him, saying, "This man will not
be your heir; [a]but one who shall come
forth from your own [1]body, he shall be
your heir."
5 And He took him outside and said,
"Now look toward the heavens, and
[a]count the stars, if you are able to count
them." And He said to him, "[b]So shall
your [1]descendants be."
6 [a]Then he believed in the LORD;
and He reckoned it to him as righteousness.
7 And He said to him, "I am the
LORD who brought you out of [a]Ur of the
Chaldeans, to [b]give you this land to
[1]possess it."
8 And he said, "O Lord [1]GOD, [a]how
may I know that I shall [2]possess it?"
9 So He said to him, "[1]Bring Me a
three year old heifer, and a three year
old female goat, and a three year old
ram, and a turtledove, and a young
pigeon."
10 Then he [1]brought all these to Him
and [a]cut them [2]in two, and laid each half
opposite the other; but he [b]did not cut
the birds.
11 And the birds of prey came down
upon the carcasses, and Abram drove
them away.
12 Now when the sun was going
down, [a]a deep sleep fell upon Abram;
and behold, [1]terror *and* great darkness
fell upon him.
13 And *God* said to Abram, "Know
for certain that [a]your [1]descendants will
be strangers in a land that is not theirs,
[2]where [b]they will be enslaved and oppressed [c]four hundred years.
14 "But I will also judge the nation
whom they will serve; and afterward
they will come out [a]with [1]many possessions.
15 "And as for you, [a]you shall go to
your fathers in peace; you shall be
buried at a good old age.
16 "Then in [a]the fourth generation they
shall return here, for [b]the iniquity of the
Amorite is not yet complete."
17 And it came about when the sun
had set, that it was very dark, and
behold, *there appeared* a smoking oven
and a flaming torch which [a]passed between these pieces.
18 On that day the LORD made a
covenant with Abram, saying,
"[a]To your [1]descendants I have given this land,
From [b]the river of Egypt as far as the great river, the river Euphrates:
19 [a]the Kenite and the Kenizzite and
the Kadmonite
20 and the Hittite and the Perizzite
and the Rephaim
21 and the Amorite and the Canaanite
and the Girgashite and the Jebusite."

Sarai and Hagar

16 NOW [a]Sarai, Abram's wife had
borne him no *children,* and she
had [b]an Egyptian maid whose name was
Hagar.
2 So Sarai said to Abram, "Now
behold, the LORD has prevented me
from bearing *children.* [a]Please go in to
my maid; perhaps I shall [1]obtain children through her." And Abram listened
to the voice of Sarai.
3 And after Abram had [1]lived [a]ten
years in the land of Canaan, Abram's
wife Sarai took Hagar the Egyptian, her
maid, and gave her to her husband
Abram as his wife.
4 And he went in to Hagar, and she
conceived; and when she saw that she
had conceived, her mistress was despised
in her sight.
5 And Sarai said to Abram, "[a]May
the wrong done me be upon you. I gave
my maid into your [1]arms; but when she
saw that she had conceived, I was despised in her [2]sight. [b]May the LORD
judge between [3]you and me."
6 But Abram said to Sarai, "Behold,
your maid is in your [1]power; do to her
what is good in your [2]sight." So Sarai
treated her harshly, and [a]she fled from
her presence.
7 Now [a]the angel of the LORD found
her by a spring of water in the wilderness, by the spring on the way to [b]Shur.
8 And he said, "Hagar, Sarai's maid,
[a]where have you come from and where
are you going?" And she said, "I am
fleeing from the presence of my mistress
Sarai."
9 Then the angel of the LORD said to
her, "Return to your mistress, and submit yourself [1]to her authority."
10 Moreover, the [a]angel of the LORD
said to her, "[b]I will greatly multiply your
[1]descendants so that [2]they shall be too
many to count."
11 The angel of the LORD said to her
further,
"Behold, you are with child,
And you shall bear a son;
And you shall call his name [1]Ishmael,
Because [a]the LORD [2]has given heed to your affliction.
12 "And he will be a [a]wild donkey of a man,
His hand *will be* against everyone,
And everyone's hand *will be* against him;
And he will [1]live [2b]to the east of all his brothers."
13 Then she called the name of the
LORD who spoke to her, "[1]Thou art [2]a
God who sees"; for she said, "[a]Have I
even [3]remained alive here after seeing
Him?"

2 [1]Heb., *YHWH,* usually rendered *LORD* [2]Lit., *go* [3]Lit., *son of acquisition*
3 [1]Lit., *Behold* [2]Lit., *seed* [3]Lit., *and behold, a son of* [a]Gen. 14:14
4 [1]Lit., *inward parts* [a]Gal. 4:28
5 [1]Lit., *seed* [a]Gen. 22:17; 26:4; Deut. 1:10 [b]Ex. 32:13; Rom. 4:18; Heb. 11:12
6 [a]Rom. 4:3, 20-22; Gal. 3:6; James 2:23
7 [1]Or, *inherit* [a]Gen. 11:31 [b]Gen. 13:15, 17
8 [1]Heb., *YHWH,* usually rendered *LORD* [2]Or, *inherit* [a]Judg. 6:36-40; Luke 1:18
9 [1]Lit., *Take*
10 [1]Lit., *took* [2]Lit., *in the midst* [a]Gen. 15:17 [b]Lev. 1:17
12 [1]Or, *a terror of great darkness* [a]Gen. 2:21; 28:11; Job 33:15
13 [1]Lit., *seed* [2]Lit., *and shall serve them; and they shall afflict them* [a]Acts 7:6, 17 [b]Ex. 1:11; Deut. 5:15 [c]Ex. 12:40; Gal. 3:17
14 [1]Lit., *great* [a]Ex. 12:32-38
15 [a]Gen. 25:8; 47:30
16 [a]Gen. 15:13 [b]Lev. 18:24-28
17 [a]Jer. 34:18, 19
18 [1]Lit., *seed* [a]Gen. 17:8; Josh. 21:43; Acts 7:5 [b]Ex. 23:31; Num. 34:1-15; Deut. 1:7, 8
19 [a]Ex. 3:17; 23:28; Josh. 24:11; Neh. 9:8

1 [a]Gen. 11:30 [b]Gen. 12:16
2 [1]Lit., *be built from her* [a]Gen. 30:3, 4, 9, 10
3 [1]Lit., *dwelt* [a]Gen. 12:4
5 [1]Lit., *bosom* [2]Lit., *eyes* [3]Lit., *me and you* [a]Jer. 51:35 [b]Gen. 31:53; Ex. 5:21
6 [1]Lit., *hand* [2]Lit., *eyes* [a]Gen. 16:9
7 [a]Gen. 21:17, 18; 22:11, 15; 31:11 [b]Gen. 20:1; 25:18
8 [a]Gen. 3:9; 1 Kin. 19:9, 13
9 [1]Lit., *under her hands*
10 [1]Lit., *seed* [2]Or, *it shall not be counted for multitude* [a]Gen. 22:15-18 [b]Gen. 17:20
11 [1]I.e., God hears [2]Lit., *has heard* [a]Ex. 2:23, 24; 3:7, 9
12 [1]Lit., *dwell* [2]Lit., *before the face of;* or, *in defiance of* [a]Job 24:5; 39:5-8 [b]Gen. 25:18

13 [1]Or, *Thou, God, dost see me* [2]Heb., *Elroi* [3]Lit., *seen here after the one who saw me* [a]Gen. 32:30; Ps. 139:1-12

14 Therefore the well was called [1]Beer-lahai-roi; behold, it is between [a]Kadesh and Bered.
15 So Hagar bore Abram a son; and Abram called the name of his son, whom Hagar bore, Ishmael.
16 And Abram was [a]eighty-six years old when Hagar bore Ishmael to [1]him.

Abraham and the Covenant of Circumcision

17 NOW when Abram was ninety-nine years old, [a]the LORD appeared to Abram and said to him,
"I am [1]God [b]Almighty;
Walk before Me, and be [2c]blameless.
2 "And I will [1]establish My [a]covenant between Me and you,
And I will [b]multiply you exceedingly."
3 And Abram [a]fell on his face, and God talked with him, saying,
4 "As for Me, behold, My covenant is with you,
And you shall be the father of a [a]multitude of nations.
5 "No longer shall your name be called [1]Abram,
But [a]your name shall be [2]Abraham;
For [b]I will make you the father of a multitude of nations.
6 "And I will make you exceedingly fruitful, and I will make nations of you, and [a]kings shall come forth from you.
7 "And I will establish My covenant between Me and you and your [1]descendants after you throughout their generations for an [a]everlasting covenant, [b]to be God to you and [c]to your [1]descendants after you.
8 "And [a]I will give to you and to your [1]descendants after you, the land of your sojournings, all the land of Canaan, for an everlasting possession; and [b]I will be their God."
9 God said further to Abraham, "Now as for you, [a]you shall keep My covenant, you and your [1]descendants after you throughout their generations.
10 "[a]This is My covenant, which you shall keep, between Me and you and your [1]descendants after you: every male among you shall be circumcised.
11 "And [a]you shall be circumcised in the flesh of your foreskin; and it shall be the sign of the covenant between Me and you.
12 "And every male among you who is [a]eight days old shall be circumcised throughout your generations, a *servant* who is born in the house or who is bought with money from any foreigner, who is not of your [1]descendants.
13 "A *servant* who is born in your house or [a]who is bought with your money shall surely be circumcised; thus shall My covenant be in your flesh for an everlasting covenant.
14 "But an uncircumcised male who is not circumcised in the flesh of his foreskin, that person shall be [a]cut off from his people; he has broken My covenant."
15 Then God said to Abraham, "As for Sarai your wife, you shall not call her name Sarai, but [1]Sarah *shall be* her name.
16 "And I will bless her, and indeed I will give you [a]a son by her. Then I will bless her, and she shall be *a mother of* nations; [b]kings of peoples shall [1]come from her."
17 Then Abraham [a]fell on his face and laughed, and said in his heart, "Will a child be born to a man one hundred years old? And [b]will Sarah, who is ninety years old, bear *a child?*"
18 And Abraham said to God, "Oh that Ishmael might live before Thee!"
19 But God said, "No, but Sarah your wife shall bear you [a]a son, and you shall call his name [1]Isaac; and [b]I will establish My covenant with him for an everlasting covenant for his [2]descendants after him.
20 "And as for Ishmael, I have heard you; behold, I will bless him, and [a]will make him fruitful, and will multiply him exceedingly. [b]He shall [1]become the father of twelve princes, and I will make him a [c]great nation.
21 "But My covenant I will establish with [a]Isaac, whom [b]Sarah will bear to you at this season next year."
22 And when He finished talking with him, [a]God went up from Abraham.
23 Then Abraham took Ishmael his son, and all *the servants* who were [a]born in his house and all who were bought with his money, every male among the men of Abraham's household, and circumcised the flesh of their foreskin in the very same day, [b]as God had said to him.
24 Now Abraham was ninety-nine years old when [a]he was circumcised in the flesh of his foreskin.
25 And [a]Ishmael his son was thirteen years old when he was circumcised in the flesh of his foreskin.
26 In the very same day Abraham was circumcised, and Ishmael his son.
27 And all the men of his household, who were [a]born in the house or bought with money from a foreigner, were circumcised with him.

Birth of Isaac Promised

18 NOW [a]the LORD appeared to him by the [1b]oaks of Mamre, while he was sitting at the tent door in the heat of the day.
2 And when he lifted up his eyes and looked, behold, three [a]men were standing opposite him; and when he saw *them,* he ran from the tent door to meet them, and bowed himself to the earth,
3 and said, "[1]My lord, if now I have found favor in [2]your sight, please do not [3]pass [2]your servant by.
4 "Please let a little water be brought and [a]wash your feet, and [1]rest yourselves under the tree;

14 [1]I.e., the well of the living one who sees me [a]Gen. 14:7
16 [1]Lit., *Abram* [a]Gen. 12:4; 16:3

1 [1]Heb., *El Shaddai* [2]Lit., *complete, perfect;* or, *having integrity* [a]Gen. 12:7; 18:1 [b]Gen. 28:3; 35:11 [c]Gen. 6:9; Deut. 18:13
2 [1]Lit., *give* [a]Gen. 15:18 [b]Gen. 13:16; 15:5
3 [a]Gen. 17:17; 18:2
4 [a]Gen. 35:11; 48:19
5 [1]I.e., exalted father [2]I.e., father of a multitude [a]Neh. 9:7 [b]Rom. 4:17
6 [a]Gen. 17:16; 35:11
7 [1]Lit., *seed* [a]Gen. 17:13, 19; Ps. 105:9, 10; Luke 1:55 [b]Gen. 26:24; Lev. 11:45; 26:12, 45; Heb. 11:16 [c]Gen. 28:13; Gal. 3:16
8 [1]Lit., *seed* [a]Gen. 12:7; 13:15, 17; Acts 7:5 [b]Ex. 6:7; 29:45; Lev. 26:12; Deut. 29:13; Rev. 21:7
9 [1]Lit., *seed* [a]Ex. 19:5
10 [1]Lit., *seed* [a]John 7:22; Acts 7:8; Rom. 4:11
11 [a]Ex. 12:48; Deut. 10:16; Acts 7:8; Rom. 4:11
12 [1]Lit., *seed* [a]Lev. 12:3
13 [a]Ex. 12:44
14 [a]Ex. 4:24-26
15 [1]I.e., princess
16 [1]Lit., *be* [a]Gen. 18:10 [b]Gen. 17:6; 36:31
17 [a]Gen. 17:3; 18:12; 21:6 [b]Gen. 21:7
19 [1]I.e., he laughs [2]Lit., *seed* [a]Gen. 17:16; 18:10; 21:2 [b]Gen. 26:2-5
20 [1]Lit., *beget twelve princes* [a]Gen. 16:10 [b]Gen. 25:12-16 [c]Gen. 21:18
21 [a]Gen. 17:19; 18:10, 14 [b]Gen. 21:2
22 [a]Gen. 18:33; 35:13
23 [a]Gen. 14:14 [b]Gen. 17:9-11
24 [a]Rom. 4:11
25 [a]Gen. 16:16
27 [a]Gen. 14:14

1 [1]Or, *terebinths* [a]Gen. 12:7; 17:1 [b]Gen. 13:18; 14:13
2 [a]Gen. 18:16, 22; 32:24; Josh. 5:13; Judg. 13:6-11; Heb. 13:2
3 [1]Or, *O Lord* [2]Or, *Thy* [3]Lit., *pass away from your servant*
4 [1]Lit., *support* [a]Gen. 19:2; 24:32; 43:24

5 and I will [1a]bring a piece of bread,
that you may [2]refresh yourselves; after
that you may go on, since you have
[3]visited your servant." And they said,
"So do, as you have said."
6 So Abraham hurried into the tent
to Sarah, and said, "[1]Quickly, prepare
three [2]measures of fine flour, knead *it,*
and make bread cakes."
7 Abraham also ran to the herd, and
took a tender and [1]choice calf, and gave
it to the servant; and he hurried to
prepare it.
8 And he took curds and milk and
the calf which he had prepared, and
placed *it* before them; and he was standing by them under the tree [1]as they ate.
9 Then they said to him, "Where is
Sarah your wife?" And he said, "Behold,
in the tent."
10 And he said, "[a]I will surely return
to you [1]at this time next year; and
behold, Sarah your wife shall have a
son." And Sarah was listening at the tent
door, which was behind him.
11 Now [a]Abraham and Sarah were
old, advanced in age; Sarah was [b]past
[1]childbearing.
12 And Sarah laughed [1]to herself,
saying, "[a]After I have become old, shall
I have pleasure, my [b]lord being old
also?"
13 And the LORD said to Abraham,
"Why did Sarah laugh, saying, 'Shall I
indeed [1]bear *a child,* when I am *so* old?'
14"[a]Is anything too [1]difficult for the
LORD? At the [b]appointed time I will
return to you, [2]at this time next year,
and Sarah shall have a son."
15 Sarah denied *it* however, saying, "I
did not laugh"; for she was afraid. And
He said, "No, but you did laugh."
16 Then [a]the men rose up from there,
and looked down toward Sodom; and
Abraham was walking with them to send
them off.
17 And [a]the LORD said, "Shall I hide
from Abraham [b]what I am about to do,
18 since Abraham will surely become
a great and [1]mighty nation, and in him
[a]all the nations of the earth will be
blessed?
19"For I have [1a]chosen him, in order
that he may [b]command his children and
his household after him to [c]keep the way
of the LORD by doing righteousness and
justice; in order that the LORD may
bring upon Abraham [d]what He has
spoken about him."
20 And the LORD said, "[a]The outcry
of Sodom and Gomorrah is indeed great,
and their sin is exceedingly grave.
21"I will [a]go down now, and see if they
have done entirely according to its outcry, which has come to Me; and if not, I
will know."
22 Then [a]the men turned away from
there and went toward Sodom, while
Abraham was still standing before [b]the
LORD.
23 And Abraham came near and said,
"[a]Wilt Thou indeed sweep away the
righteous with the wicked?

5 [1]Lit., *take* [2]Lit., *sustain your heart* [3]Lit., *come to* [a]Judg. 6:18, 19; 13:15, 16
6 [1]Lit., *Hasten three measures* [2]Heb., *seah;* i.e., one seah equals approx. eleven qts.
7 [1]Lit., *good*
8 [1]Lit., *and*
10 [1]Lit., *when the time revives* [a]Gen. 21:2; Rom. 9:9
11 [1]Lit., *the manner of women* [a]Gen. 17:17; Rom. 4:19 [b]Heb. 11:11
12 [1]Lit., *within* [a]Gen. 17:17; Luke 1:18 [b]1 Pet. 3:6
13 [1]Lit., *surely bear*
14 [1]Or, *wonderful* [2]Lit., *when the time revives* [a]Jer. 32:17, 27; Zech. 8:6; Matt. 19:26; Luke 1:37; Rom. 4:21 [b]Gen. 17:21; 18:10
16 [a]Gen. 18:2, 22; 19:1
17 [a]Gen. 18:22, 26, 33; Amos 3:7 [b]Gen. 18:21; 19:24
18 [1]Or, *populous* [a]Gen. 12:3; 22:18; Acts 3:25; Gal. 3:8
19 [1]Lit., *known* [a]Neh. 9:7; Amos 3:2 [b]Deut. 6:6, 7 [c]Gen. 17:9 [d]Gen. 12:2, 3
20 [a]Gen. 19:13; Ezek. 16:49, 50
21 [a]Gen. 11:5; Ex. 3:8; Ps. 14:2
22 [a]Gen. 18:16; 19:1 [b]Gen. 18:1, 17
23 [a]Ex. 23:7; Num. 16:22; 2 Sam. 24:17; Ps. 11:4-7
24 [1]Or, *forgive*
25 [1]Lit., *after this manner* [2]Lit., *do justice* [a]Deut. 1:16, 17; 32:4; Job 8:3, 20; Ps. 58:11; 94:2; Is. 3:10, 11; Rom. 3:5, 6
26 [1]Or, *forgive* [a]Jer. 5:1
27 [1]Lit., *undertaken* [a]Gen. 3:19; Job 30:19; 42:6
31 [1]Lit., *undertaken*
32 [a]Judg. 6:39
33 [a]Gen. 17:22; 35:13

1 [1]Lit., *bowed himself* [a]Gen. 18:2, 22 [b]Gen. 18:2-5
3 [a]Gen. 18:6-8
4 [1]Or, *without exception;* lit., *from every end* [a]Gen. 13:13; 18:20
5 [1]I.e., have intercourse [a]Lev. 18:22; Judg. 19:22

24"Suppose there are fifty righteous
within the city; wilt Thou indeed sweep
it away and not [1]spare the place for the
sake of the fifty righteous who are in it?
25"Far be it from Thee to do [1]such a
thing, to slay the righteous with the
wicked, so that the righteous and the
wicked are *treated* alike. Far be it from
Thee! Shall not [a]the Judge of all the
earth [2]deal justly?"
26 So the LORD said, "[a]If I find in
Sodom fifty righteous within the city,
then I will [1]spare the whole place on
their account."
27 And Abraham answered and said,
"Now behold, I have [1]ventured to speak
to the Lord, although I am *but* [a]dust and
ashes.
28"Suppose the fifty righteous are
lacking five, wilt Thou destroy the whole
city because of five?" And He said, "I
will not destroy *it* if I find forty-five
there."
29 And he spoke to Him yet again and
said, "Suppose forty are found there?"
And He said, "I will not do *it* on account
of the forty."
30 Then he said, "Oh may the Lord
not be angry, and I shall speak; suppose
thirty are found there?" And He said, "I
will not do *it* if I find thirty there."
31 And he said, "Now behold, I have
[1]ventured to speak to the Lord; suppose
twenty are found there?" And He said,
"I will not destroy *it* on account of the
twenty."
32 Then he said, "[a]Oh may the Lord
not be angry, and I shall speak only this
once; suppose ten are found there?" And
He said, "I will not destroy *it* on account
of the ten."
33 And as soon as He had finished
speaking to Abraham [a]the LORD departed; and Abraham returned to his
place.

The Doom of Sodom

19 NOW the [a]two angels came to
Sodom in the evening as Lot was
sitting in the gate of Sodom. When [b]Lot
saw *them,* he rose to meet them and
[1]bowed down *with his* face to the
ground.
2 And he said, "Now behold, my
lords, please turn aside into your servant's house, and spend the night, and
wash your feet; then you may rise early
and go on your way." They said however, "No, but we shall spend the night
in the square."
3 Yet he urged them strongly, so they
turned aside to him and entered his
house; [a]and he prepared a feast for
them, and baked unleavened bread, and
they ate.
4 Before they lay down, [a]the men of
the city, the men of Sodom, surrounded
the house, both young and old, all the
people [1]from every quarter;
5 and they called to Lot and said to
him, "[a]Where are the men who came to
you tonight? Bring them out to us that
we may [1]have relations with them."

6 But Lot went out to them at the
doorway, and shut the door behind him,
7 and said, "Please, my brothers, do
not act wickedly.
8 "Now behold, [a]I have two daughters
who have not [1]had relations with man;
please let me bring them out to you, and
do to them [2]whatever you like; only do
nothing to these men, inasmuch as they
have come under the [3]shelter of my
roof."
9 But they said, "Stand aside." Furthermore, they said, "This one came in
[1]as an alien, and already [a]he is acting
like a judge; now we will treat you worse
than them." So they pressed hard
against [2]Lot and came near to break the
door.
10 But [a]the men reached out their
[1]hands and brought Lot into the house
[2]with them, and shut the door.
11 And [a]they [1]struck the men who
were at the doorway of the house with
blindness, both small and great, so that
they wearied *themselves trying* to find the
doorway.
12 Then the men said to Lot, "Whom
else have you here? A son-in-law, and
your sons, and your daughters, and
whomever you have in the city, bring
them out of the place;
13 for we are about to destroy this
place, because [a]their outcry has become
so great before the LORD that [b]the LORD
has sent us to destroy it."
14 And Lot went out and spoke to his
sons-in-law, who [1]were to marry his
daughters, and said, "Up, [a]get out of this
place, for the LORD will destroy the
city." [b]But he appeared to his sons-in-
law [2]to be jesting.
15 And when morning dawned, the
angels urged Lot, saying, "Up, take your
wife and your two daughters, who are
here, lest you be swept away in the
[1]punishment of the city."
16 But he hesitated. So the men
[a]seized his hand and the hand of his wife
and the [1]hands of his two daughters, for
[b]the compassion of the LORD *was* upon
him; and they brought him out, and put
him outside the city.
17 And it came about when they had
brought them outside, that [1]one said,
"[a]Escape for your life! [b]Do not look
behind you, and do not stay [2]anywhere
in the [c]valley; escape to [d]the [3]mountains,
lest you be swept away."
18 But Lot said to them, "Oh no, my
lords!
19 "Now behold, your servant has
found favor in your sight, and you have
magnified your lovingkindness, which
you have shown me by saving my life;
but I cannot escape to the [1]mountains,
lest the disaster overtake me and I die;
20 now behold, this town is near
enough to flee to, and it is small. Please,
let me escape there (is it not small?)
[1]that my life may be saved."
21 And he said to him, "Behold, I
grant you this [1]request also, not to
overthrow the town of which you have
spoken.
22 "Hurry, escape there, for I cannot
do anything until you arrive there."
Therefore the name of the town was
called [1a]Zoar.
23 The sun had risen over the earth
when Lot came to Zoar.
24 Then the LORD [a]rained on Sodom
and Gomorrah brimstone and fire from
the LORD out of heaven,
25 and [a]He overthrew those cities, and
all the [1]valley, and all the inhabitants of
the cities, and what grew on the ground.
26 But his wife, from behind him,
[a]looked *back;* and she became a pillar of
salt.
27 Now Abraham arose early in the
morning *and went* to [a]the place where he
had stood before the LORD;
28 and he looked down toward Sodom
and Gomorrah, and toward all the land
of the [1]valley, and he saw, and behold,
[a]the smoke of the land ascended like the
smoke of a [2]furnace.
29 Thus it came about, when God
destroyed the cities of the [1]valley, that
[a]God remembered Abraham, and [b]sent
Lot out of the midst of the overthrow,
when He overthrew the cities in which
Lot lived.

Lot Is Debased

30 And Lot went up from Zoar, and
[1a]stayed in the [2]mountains, and his two
daughters with him; for he was afraid to
[3]stay in Zoar; and he [1]stayed in a cave,
he and his two daughters.
31 Then the first-born said to the
younger, "Our father is old, and there is
not a man [1]on earth to [a]come in to us
after the manner of the earth.
32 "Come, [a]let us make our father
drink wine, and let us lie with him, that
we may preserve [1]our family through our
father."
33 So they made their father drink
wine that night, and the first-born went
in and lay with her father; and he did
not know when she lay down or when
she arose.
34 And it came about on the morrow,
that the first-born said to the younger,
"Behold, I lay last night with my father;
let us make him drink wine tonight also;
then you go in and lie with him, that we
may preserve [1]our family through our
father."
35 So they made their father drink
wine that night also, and the younger
arose and lay with him; and he did not
know when she lay down or when she
arose.
36 Thus both the daughters of Lot
were with child by their father.
37 And the first-born bore a son, and
called his name [a]Moab; he is the father
of the Moabites to this day.
38 And as for the younger, she also
bore a son, and called his name Ben-
ammi; he is the father of the [1]sons of
[a]Ammon to this day.

8 [1]I.e., had intercourse [2]Lit., *as is good in your sight* [3]Lit., *shadow* [a]Judg. 19:24

9 [1]Lit., *to sojourn* [2]Lit., *the man, against Lot* [a]Ex. 2:14

10 [1]Lit., *hand* [2]Lit., *to* [a]Gen. 19:1

11 [1]Lit., *smote* [a]Deut. 28:28, 29; 2 Kin. 6:18; Acts 13:11

13 [a]Gen. 18:20 [b]Lev. 26:30-33; Deut. 4:26; 28:45; 1 Chr. 21:15

14 [1]Or, *had married;* lit., *were taking* [2]Lit., *like one who was jesting* [a]Num. 16:21, 45; Rev. 18:4 [b]Jer. 43:1, 2

15 [1]Or, *iniquity*

16 [1]Lit., *hand* [a]Deut. 5:15; 6:21; 7:8; 2 Pet. 2:7 [b]Ex. 34:7; Ps. 32:10; 33:18, 19

17 [1]Lit., *he* [2]Lit., *in all the circle* [3]Lit., *mountain* [a]Jer. 48:6 [b]Gen. 19:26 [c]Gen. 13:10 [d]Gen. 14:10

19 [1]Lit., *mountain*

20 [1]Lit., *and my soul will live*

21 [1]Lit., *thing*

22 [1]I.e., small [a]Gen. 13:10; 14:2

24 [a]Deut. 29:23; Ps. 11:6; Is. 13:19; Ezek. 16:49, 50; Luke 17:29; Jude 7

25 [1]Lit., *circle* [a]Deut. 29:23; Ps. 107:34; Is. 13:19; Lam. 4:6; 2 Pet. 2:6

26 [a]Gen. 19:17; Luke 17:32

27 [a]Gen. 18:22

28 [1]Lit., *circle* [2]Lit., *kiln* [a]Rev. 9:2; 18:9

29 [1]Lit., *circle* [a]Deut. 7:8; 9:5, 27 [b]2 Pet. 2:7

30 [1]Lit., *dwelt* [2]Lit., *mountain* [3]Lit., *dwell* [a]Gen. 19:17, 19

31 [1]Or, *in the land* [a]Gen. 16:2, 4; 38:8; Deut. 25:5

32 [1]Lit., *seed from our father* [a]Luke 21:34

34 [1]Lit., *seed from our father*

37 [a]Deut. 2:9

38 [1]Heb., *Bene-Ammon* [a]Deut. 2:19

Abraham's Treachery

20 NOW Abraham journeyed from
[a]there toward the land of [b]the
[1]Negev, and [2]settled between Kadesh
and Shur; then he sojourned in [c]Gerar.
2 And Abraham said of Sarah his
wife, "[a]She is my sister." So [b]Abimelech
king of Gerar sent and took Sarah.
3 [a]But God came to Abimelech in a
dream of the night, and said to him,
"Behold, [b]you are a dead man because
of the woman whom you have taken, for
she is [1]married."
4 Now Abimelech had not come near
her; and he said, "Lord, [a]wilt Thou slay
a nation, even *though* [1]blameless?
5 "Did he not himself say to me, 'She
is my sister'? And she [a]herself said, 'He
is my brother.' In [b]the integrity of my
heart and the innocence of my [1]hands I
have done this."
6 Then God said to him in the
dream, "Yes, I know that in the integrity
of your heart you have done this, and I
also [1a]kept you from sinning against Me;
therefore I did not let you touch her.
7 "Now therefore, restore the man's
wife, for [a]he is a prophet, and he will
pray for you, and you will live. But if
you do not restore *her,* know that you
shall surely die, you and all who are
yours."
8 So Abimelech arose early in the
morning and called all his servants and
told all these things in their hearing; and
the men were greatly frightened.
9 [a]Then Abimelech called Abraham
and said to him, "What have you done
to us? And [1]how have I sinned against
you, that you have brought on me and
on my kingdom [b]a great sin? You have
done to me [2]things that ought not to be
done."
10 And Abimelech said to Abraham,
"What have you [1]encountered, that you
have done this thing?"
11 And Abraham said, "Because I
thought, surely there is no [a]fear of God
in this place; and [b]they will kill me
because of my wife.
12 "Besides, she actually is my sister,
the daughter of my father, but not the
daughter of my mother, and she became
my wife;
13 and it came about, when [a]God
caused me to wander from my father's
house, that I said to her, 'This is [1]the
kindness which you will show to me:
[2]everywhere we go, [b]say of me, "He is
my brother." ' "
14 [a]Abimelech then took sheep and
oxen and male and female servants, and
gave them to Abraham, and restored his
wife Sarah to him.
15 And Abimelech said, "[a]Behold, my
land is before you; [1]settle wherever [2]you
please."
16 And to Sarah he said, "Behold, I
have given your [a]brother a thousand
pieces of silver; behold, it is [1]your
vindication before all who are with you,
and before all men you are cleared."
17 And [a]Abraham prayed to God;
and God healed Abimelech and his wife
and his maids, so that they bore *children.*
18 [a]For the LORD had closed fast all
the wombs of the household of Abimelech because of Sarah, Abraham's wife.

Isaac Is Born

21 [a]THEN the LORD took note of
Sarah as He had said, and the
LORD did for Sarah as He had [1]prom-
ised.
2 [a]So Sarah conceived and bore a son
to Abraham in his old age, at [b]the
appointed time of which God had spoken to him.
3 And Abraham called the name of
his son who was born to him, whom
Sarah bore to him, [a]Isaac.
4 Then Abraham circumcised his son
Isaac when he was [a]eight days old, as
God had commanded him.
5 Now Abraham was [a]one hundred
years old when his son Isaac was born to
him.
6 And Sarah said, "God has made
[a]laughter for me; everyone who hears
will laugh [1]with me."
7 And she said, "[a]Who would have
said to Abraham that Sarah would nurse
children? Yet I have borne him a son in
his old age."
8 And the child grew and was
weaned, and Abraham made a great
feast on the day that Isaac was weaned.

Sarah Turns against Hagar

9 Now Sarah saw [a]the son of Hagar
the Egyptian, whom she had borne to
Abraham, [1b]mocking.
10 Therefore she said to Abraham,
"[a]Drive out this maid and her son, for
the son of this maid shall not be an heir
with my son [1]Isaac."
11 [a]And the matter [1]distressed Abraham greatly because of his son.
12 But God said to Abraham, "[1]Do
not be distressed because of the lad and
your maid; whatever Sarah tells you,
listen to her, for [a]through Isaac [2]your
descendants shall be named.
13 "And of [a]the son of the maid I will
make a nation also, because he is your
[1]descendant."
14 So Abraham rose early in the
morning, and took bread and a [1]skin of
water, and gave *them* to Hagar, putting
them on her shoulder, and *gave her* the
boy, and sent her away. And she departed, and wandered about in the wilderness of Beersheba.
15 And the water in the skin was used
up, and she [1]left the boy under one of
the bushes.
16 Then she went and sat down opposite him, about a bowshot away, for she
said, "Do not let me [1]see the boy die."
And she sat opposite him, and [a]lifted up
her voice and wept.
17 And God [a]heard the lad crying;
and the angel of God called to Hagar
from heaven, and said to her, "What is
the matter with you, Hagar? [b]Do not

---

1 [1]I.e., South country [2]Lit., *dwelt* [a]Gen. 18:1 [b]Gen. 12:9 [c]Gen. 26:1, 6
2 [a]Gen. 12:11-13; 20:12; 26:7 [b]Gen. 12:15
3 [1]Lit., *married to a husband* [a]Gen. 12:17, 18 [b]Gen. 20:7
4 [1]Lit., *righteous* [a]Gen. 18:23-25
5 [1]Lit., *palms* [a]Gen. 20:13 [b]1 Kin. 9:4; Ps. 7:8; 26:6
6 [1]Lit., *restrained* [a]1 Sam. 25:26, 34
7 [a]1 Sam. 7:5; 2 Kin. 5:11; Job 42:8
9 [1]Lit., *what* [2]Lit., *deeds* [a]Gen. 12:18 [b]Gen. 39:9
10 [1]Lit., *seen*
11 [a]Neh. 5:15; Prov. 16:6 [b]Gen. 12:12; 26:7
13 [1]Lit., *your* [2]Lit., *at every place where* [a]Gen. 12:1-9 [b]Gen. 12:13; 20:5
14 [a]Gen. 12:16
15 [1]Lit., *dwell* [2]Lit., *it is good in your sight* [a]Gen. 13:9; 34:10; 47:6
16 [1]Lit., *for you a covering of the eyes* [a]Gen. 20:5
17 [a]Num. 12:13; 21:7; James 5:16
18 [a]Gen. 12:17

1 [1]Lit., *spoken* [a]Gen. 17:16, 21; 18:10, 14; Gal. 4:23
2 [a]Acts 7:8; Gal. 4:22; Heb. 11:11 [b]Gen. 17:21; 18:10, 14
3 [a]Gen. 17:19, 21
4 [a]Gen. 17:12; Acts 7:8
5 [a]Gen. 17:17
6 [1]Lit., *for* [a]Gen. 18:13; Ps. 126:2; Is. 54:1
7 [a]Gen. 18:11, 13
9 [1]Or, *playing* [a]Gen. 16:1, 4, 15 [b]Gal. 4:29
10 [1]Lit., *with Isaac* [a]Gal. 4:30
11 [1]Lit., *was very grievous in Abraham's sight* [a]Gen. 17:18
12 [1]Lit., *Do not let it be grievous in your sight* [2]Lit., *your seed will be called* [a]Rom. 9:7; Heb. 11:18
13 [1]Lit., *seed* [a]Gen. 16:10; 21:18; 25:12-18
14 [1]I.e., a skin used as a bottle
15 [1]Lit., *cast*
16 [1]Lit., *look upon the death of the child* [a]Jer. 6:26; Amos 8:10
17 [a]Ex. 3:7; Deut. 26:7; Ps. 6:8 [b]Gen. 26:24

fear, for God has heard the voice of the
lad where he is.
18 "Arise, lift up the lad, and hold him
by [1]the hand; [a]for I will make a great
nation of him."
19 Then God [a]opened her eyes and
she saw [b]a well of water; and she went
and filled the [1]skin with water, and gave
the lad a drink.
20 And [a]God was with the lad, and he
grew; and he [1]lived in the wilderness,
and became an archer.
21 And [a]he [1]lived in the wilderness of
Paran; and his mother took a wife for
him from the land of Egypt.

Covenant with Abimelech

22 Now it came about at that time,
that [a]Abimelech and Phicol, the commander of his army, spoke to Abraham,
saying, "[b]God is with you in all that you
do;
23 now therefore, [a]swear to me here
by God that you will not deal falsely
with me, or with my offspring, or with
my posterity; but according to the kindness that I have shown to you, you shall
show to me, and to the land in which
you have sojourned."
24 And Abraham said, "I swear it."
25 But Abraham [1]complained to
Abimelech because of the well of water
which the servants of Abimelech [a]had
seized.
26 And Abimelech said, "I do not
know who has done this thing; neither
did you tell me, nor did I hear of it [1]until
today."
27 And Abraham took sheep and
oxen, and gave them to Abimelech; and
[a]the two of them made a covenant.
28 Then Abraham set seven ewe
lambs of the flock by themselves.
29 And Abimelech said to Abraham,
"What do these seven ewe lambs mean,
which you have set by themselves?"
30 And he said, "You shall take these
seven ewe lambs from my hand in order
that it may be a [a]witness to me, that I
dug this well."
31 Therefore he called that place
[a]Beersheba; because there the two of
them took an oath.
32 So they made a covenant at Beersheba; and Abimelech and Phicol, the
commander of his army, arose and returned to the land of the Philistines.
33 And *Abraham* planted a tamarisk
tree at Beersheba, and there [a]he called
on the name of the LORD, the [b]Ever-
lasting God.
34 And Abraham sojourned [a]in the
land of the Philistines for many days.

The Offering of Isaac

22 NOW it came about after these
things, that [a]God tested Abraham, and said to him, "[b]Abraham!" And
he said, "Here I am."
2 And He said, "Take now [a]your son,
your only son, whom you love, Isaac,
and go to the land of [b]Moriah; and offer
him there as a [c]burnt offering on one of
the mountains of which I will tell you."
3 So Abraham rose early in the
morning and saddled his donkey, and
took two of his young men with him and
Isaac his son; and he split wood for the
burnt offering, and arose and went to the
place of which God had told him.
4 On the third day Abraham raised
his eyes and saw the place from a distance.
5 And Abraham said to his young
men, "Stay here with the donkey, and I
and the lad will go yonder; and we will
worship and return to you."
6 And Abraham took the wood of
the burnt offering and [a]laid it on Isaac
his son, and he took in his hand the fire
and the knife. So the two of them walked
on together.
7 And Isaac spoke to Abraham his
father and said, "My father!" And he
said, "Here I am, my son." And he said,
"Behold, the fire and the wood, but
where is the [a]lamb for the burnt offering?"
8 And Abraham said, "God will
[1]provide for Himself the lamb for the
burnt offering, my son." So the two of
them walked on together.
9 Then they came to [a]the place of
which God had told him; and Abraham
built [b]the altar there, and arranged the
wood, and bound his son Isaac, and
[c]laid him on the altar on top of the
wood.
10 And Abraham stretched out his
hand, and took the knife to slay his son.
11 But [a]the angel of the LORD called
to him from heaven, and said, "Abraham, Abraham!" And he said, "Here I
am."
12 And he said, "Do not stretch out
your hand against the lad, and do nothing to him; for now [a]I know that you
[1]fear God, since you have not withheld
[b]your son, your only son, from Me."
13 Then Abraham raised his eyes and
looked, and behold, behind *him* a ram
caught in the thicket by his horns; and
Abraham went and took the ram, and
offered him up for a burnt offering in the
place of his son.
14 And Abraham called the name of
that place [1]The LORD Will Provide, as it
is said to this day, "In the mount of the
LORD [a]it will [2]be provided."
15 Then the angel of the LORD called
to Abraham a second time from heaven,
16 and said, "[a]By Myself I have
sworn, declares the LORD, because you
have done this thing, and have not
withheld your son, your only son,
17 indeed I will greatly bless you, and
I will greatly [a]multiply your [1]seed as the
stars of the heavens, and as [b]the sand
which is on the seashore; and [c]your
[1]seed shall possess the gate of [2]their
enemies.
18 "And [a]in your [1]seed all the nations
of the earth shall [2]be blessed, because
you have [b]obeyed My voice."

18 [1]Lit., *your* [a]Gen. 16:10; 21:13; 25:12-16
19 [1]V. 14, note 1 [a]Num. 22:31; 2 Kin. 6:17 [b]Gen. 16:7, 14
20 [1]Lit., *dwelt* [a]Gen. 28:15; 39:2, 3, 21
21 [1]Lit., *dwelt* [a]Gen. 25:18
22 [a]Gen. 20:2, 14; 26:26 [b]Gen. 26:28; Is. 8:10
23 [a]Josh. 2:12; 1 Sam. 24:21
25 [1]Lit., *reproved* [a]Gen. 26:15, 18, 20-22
26 [1]Lit., *except*
27 [a]Gen. 26:31
30 [a]Gen. 31:48
31 [a]Gen. 21:14; 26:33
33 [a]Gen. 12:8 [b]Ex. 15:18; Deut. 32:40; Ps. 90:2; 93:2; Is. 40:28; Jer. 10:10; Hab. 1:12; Heb. 13:8
34 [a]Gen. 22:19

1 [a]Deut. 8:2, 16; Heb. 11:17; James 1:12-14 [b]Gen. 22:11
2 [a]Gen. 22:12, 16; John 3:16; 1 John 4:9 [b]2 Chr. 3:1 [c]Gen. 8:20
6 [a]John 19:17
7 [a]Ex. 29:38-42; John 1:29, 36; Rev. 13:8
8 [1]Lit., *see*
9 [a]Gen. 22:2 [b]Gen. 12:7, 8; 13:18 [c]Heb. 11:17-19; James 2:21
11 [a]Gen. 16:7-11; 21:17, 18
12 [1]Or, *reverence;* lit., *are a fearer of God* [a]James 2:21, 22 [b]Gen. 22:2, 16
14 [1]Heb., *YHWH-jireh* [2]Lit., *be seen* [a]Gen. 22:8
16 [a]Ps. 105:9; Luke 1:73; Heb. 6:13, 14
17 [1]Or, *descendants* [2]Lit., *his* [a]Gen. 15:5; 26:4; Jer. 33:22; Heb. 11:12 [b]Gen. 32:12 [c]Gen. 24:60
18 [1]Or, *descendants* [2]Or, *bless themselves* [a]Gen. 12:3; 18:18; Acts 3:25; Gal. 3:8, 16 [b]Gen. 18:19; 22:3, 10; 26:5

19 [a]So Abraham returned to his young
men, and they arose and went together
to Beersheba; and Abraham lived at
Beersheba.
20 Now it came about after these
things, that it was told Abraham, saying,
"Behold, [a]Milcah [1]also has borne children to your brother Nahor:
21 Uz his first-born and Buz his
brother and Kemuel the father of Aram
22 and Chesed and Hazo and Pildash
and Jidlaph and Bethuel."
23 And Bethuel [1]became the father of
[a]Rebekah: these eight Milcah bore to
Nahor, Abraham's brother.
24 And his concubine, whose name
was Reumah, [1]also bore Tebah and
Gaham and Tahash and Maacah.

Death and Burial of Sarah

23 NOW [1]Sarah lived one hundred
and twenty-seven years; *these*
were the years of the life of Sarah.
2 And Sarah died in [a]Kiriath-arba
(that is, Hebron) in the land of Canaan;
and Abraham [1]went in to mourn for
Sarah and to weep for her.
3 Then Abraham rose from before
his dead, and spoke to the [a]sons of Heth,
saying,
4 "I am [a]a stranger and a sojourner
among you; [b]give me [1]a [c]burial site
among you, that I may bury my dead
out of my sight."
5 And the sons of Heth answered
Abraham, saying to him,
6 "Hear us, my lord, you are a
[1a]mighty prince among us; bury your
dead in the choicest of our graves; none
of us will refuse you his grave for burying your dead."
7 So Abraham rose and bowed to the
people of the land, the sons of Heth.
8 And he spoke with them, saying,
"If it is your [1]wish *for me* to bury my
dead out of my sight, hear me, and
approach [a]Ephron the son of Zohar for
me,
9 that he may give me the cave of
Machpelah which he owns, which is at
the end of his field; for the full price let
him give it to me in [1]your presence for [2]a
burial site."
10 Now Ephron was sitting among the
sons of Heth; and Ephron the Hittite
answered Abraham in the hearing of the
sons of Heth; *even* [a]of all who went in at
the gate of his city, saying,
11 "No, my lord, hear me; [a]I give you
the field, and I give you the cave that is
in it. In the presence of the sons of my
people I give it to you; bury your dead."
12 And Abraham bowed before the
people of the land.
13 And he spoke to Ephron in the
hearing of the people of the land, saying,
"If you will only please listen to me; I
will give the price of the field, accept *it*
from me, that I may bury my dead
there."
14 Then Ephron answered Abraham,
saying to him,
15 "My lord, listen to me; a piece of
land worth four hundred [a]shekels of
silver, what is that between me and you?
So bury your dead."
16 And Abraham listened to Ephron;
and Abraham [a]weighed out for Ephron
the silver which he had named in the
[1]hearing of the sons of Heth, four hundred shekels of silver, [2]commercial standard.
17 So [a]Ephron's field, which was in
Machpelah, which faced Mamre, the
field and cave which was in it, and all the
trees which were in the field, that were
[1]within all the confines of its border,
[2]were deeded over
18 to Abraham for a possession [a]in
the presence of the sons of Heth, before
all who went in at the gate of his city.
19 And after this, Abraham buried
Sarah his wife in the cave of the field at
Machpelah facing Mamre (that is, Hebron) in the land of Canaan.
20 So the field, and the cave that is in
it, [1]were [a]deeded over to Abraham for [2]a
burial site by the sons of Heth.

A Bride for Isaac

24 NOW [a]Abraham was old, advanced in age; and the LORD had
[b]blessed Abraham in every way.
2 And Abraham said to his servant,
the oldest of his household, who had
[a]charge of all that he owned, "[b]Please
place your hand under my thigh,
3 and I will make you swear by the
LORD, [a]the God of heaven and the God
of earth, that you [b]shall not take a wife
for my son from the daughters of [c]the
Canaanites, among whom I live,
4 but you shall go to [a]my country
and to my relatives, and take a wife for
my son Isaac."
5 And the servant said to him, "Suppose the woman will not be willing to
follow me to this land; should I take
your son back to the land from where
you came?"
6 Then Abraham said to him, "[a]Be-
ware lest you take my son back there!
7 "[a]The LORD, the God of heaven,
who took me from my father's house and
from the land of my birth, and who
spoke to me, and who swore to me,
saying, '[b]To your [1]descendants I will
give this land,' He will send [c]His angel
before you, and you will take a wife for
my son from there.
8 "But if the woman is not willing to
follow you, then you will [a]be free from
this my oath; [b]only do not take my son
back there."
9 So the servant [a]placed his hand
under the thigh of Abraham his master,
and swore to him concerning this matter.
10 Then the servant took ten camels
from the camels of his master, and set
out with a variety of [a]good things of his
master's in his hand; and he arose, and
went to [1]Mesopotamia, to [b]the city of
Nahor.

19 [a]Gen. 22:5
20 [1]Lit., *she also* [a]Gen. 11:29
23 [1]Lit., *begot* [a]Gen. 24:15
24 [1]Lit., *she also*

1 [1]Lit., *the life of Sarah was*
2 [1]Or, *proceeded* [a]Josh. 14:15; 15:13; 21:11
3 [a]Gen. 10:15; 15:20
4 [1]Lit., *possession of a grave* [a]Gen. 17:8; Lev. 25:23; 1 Chr. 29:15; Ps. 39:12; 105:12; 119:19; Heb. 11:9, 13 [b]Acts 7:16 [c]Gen. 49:30
6 [1]Lit., *prince of God* [a]Gen. 14:14; 20:7
8 [1]Lit., *soul* [a]Gen. 25:9
9 [1]Lit., *the midst of you* [2]Lit., *possession of a burial place*
10 [a]Gen. 23:18; 34:20, 24; Ruth 4:1, 11
11 [a]2 Sam. 24:21-24
15 [a]Ex. 30:13; Ezek. 45:12
16 [1]Lit., *ears* [2]Lit., *current according to the merchant* [a]2 Sam. 14:26; Jer. 32:9, 10; Zech. 11:12
17 [1]Lit., *in all its border around* [2]Or, *were ratified* [a]Gen. 25:9; 49:29, 30; 50:13
18 [a]Gen. 23:10
20 [1]Or, *were ratified* [2]Lit., *possession of a burial place* [a]Jer. 32:10-14

1 [a]Gen. 18:11 [b]Gen. 12:2; 13:2; 24:35; Gal. 3:9
2 [a]Gen. 39:4-6 [b]Gen. 24:9; 47:29
3 [a]Gen. 14:19, 22 [b]Deut. 7:3; 2 Cor. 6:14-17 [c]Gen. 10:15-19; 26:34, 35; 28:1, 8
4 [a]Gen. 12:1; Heb. 11:15
6 [a]Gen. 24:8
7 [1]Lit., *seed* [a]Gen. 24:3 [b]Gen. 12:7; 13:15; 15:18; Ex. 32:13 [c]Gen. 16:7; 21:17; 22:11; Ex. 23:20, 23
8 [a]Josh. 2:17-20 [b]Gen. 24:6
9 [a]Gen. 24:2
10 [1]Heb., *Aram-naharaim, Aram of the two rivers* [a]Gen. 24:22, 53 [b]Gen. 11:31, 32

11 And he made the camels kneel down outside the city by [a]the well of water at evening time, [b]the time when women go out to draw water.

12 And he said, "[a]O LORD, the God of my master Abraham, please [1b]grant me success today, and show lovingkindness to my master Abraham.

13 "Behold, [a]I am standing by the [1]spring, and the daughters of the men of the city are coming out to draw water;

14 now may it be that the girl to whom I say, 'Please let down your jar so that I may drink,' and [1]who answers, 'Drink, and I will water your camels also';—*may* she *be the one* whom Thou hast appointed for Thy servant Isaac; and by this I shall know that Thou hast shown lovingkindness to my master."

Rebekah Is Chosen

15 And it came about [a]before he had finished speaking, that behold, [b]Rebekah who was born to Bethuel the son of [c]Milcah, the wife of Abraham's brother Nahor, came out with her jar on her shoulder.

16 And the girl was [a]very beautiful, a virgin, and no man had [1]had relations with her; and she went down to the spring and filled her jar, and came up.

17 Then the servant ran to meet her, and said, "[a]Please let me drink a little water from your jar."

18 And [a]she said, "Drink, my lord"; and she quickly lowered her jar to her hand, and gave him a drink.

19 Now when she had finished giving him a drink, [a]she said, "I will draw also for your camels until they have finished drinking."

20 So she quickly emptied her jar into the trough, and ran back to the well to draw, and she drew for all his camels.

21 [a]Meanwhile, the man was gazing at her [1]in silence, to know whether the LORD had made his journey successful or not.

22 Then it came about, when the camels had finished drinking, that the man took a [a]gold ring weighing a half-shekel and two bracelets for her [1]wrists weighing ten shekels in gold,

23 and said, "Whose daughter are you? Please tell me, is there room for us to lodge in your father's house?"

24 And she said to him, "[a]I am the daughter of Bethuel, the son of Milcah, whom she bore to Nahor."

25 Again she said to him, "We have plenty of both straw and feed, and room to lodge in."

26 Then the man [a]bowed low and worshiped the LORD.

27 And he said, "[a]Blessed be the LORD, the God of my master Abraham, who has not forsaken [b]His lovingkindness and His truth toward my master; as for me, [c]the LORD has guided me in the way to the house of my master's brothers."

28 Then [a]the girl ran and told her mother's household about these things.

29 Now Rebekah had a brother whose name was [a]Laban; and Laban ran outside to the man at the spring.

30 And it came about that when he saw the ring, and the bracelets on his sister's [1]wrists, and when he heard the words of Rebekah his sister, saying, "[2]This is what the man said to me," he went to the man; and behold, he was standing by the camels at the spring.

31 And he said, "[a]Come in, [b]blessed of the LORD! Why do you stand outside since [c]I have prepared the house, and a place for the camels?"

32 So the man entered the house. Then [1a]Laban unloaded the camels, and he gave straw and feed to the camels, and water to wash his feet and the feet of the men who were with him.

33 But when *food* was set before him to eat, he said, "I will not eat until I have told my business." And he said, "Speak on."

34 So he said, "I am [a]Abraham's servant.

35 "And the LORD has greatly [a]blessed my master, so that he has become [1]rich; and He has given him [b]flocks and herds, and silver and gold, and servants and maids, and camels and donkeys.

36 "Now [a]Sarah my master's wife bore a son to my master [1]in her old age; and [b]he has given him all that he has.

37 "[a]And my master made me swear, saying, 'You shall not take a wife for my son from the daughters of the Canaanites, in whose land I [1]live;

38 but you shall go to my father's house, and to my relatives, and take a wife for my son.'

39 "[a]And I said to my master, 'Suppose the woman does not follow me.'

40 "And he said to me, '[a]The LORD, before whom I have [b]walked, will send [c]His angel with you to make your journey successful, and you will take a wife for my son from my relatives, and from my father's house;

41 [a]then you will be free from my oath, when you come to my relatives; and if they do not give her to you, you will be free from my oath.'

42 "So [a]I came today to the spring, and said, 'O LORD, the God of my master Abraham, if now Thou wilt make my journey on which I go [b]successful;

43 behold, [a]I am standing by the [1]spring, and may it be that the maiden who comes out to draw, and to whom I say, "[b]Please let me drink a little water from your jar";

44 and she will say to me, "You drink, and I will draw for your camels also"; let her be the woman whom the LORD has appointed for my master's son.'

45 "Before I had finished [a]speaking in my heart, behold, [b]Rebekah came out with her jar on her shoulder, and went down to the spring and drew; and [c]I said to her, 'Please let me drink.'

11 [a]Gen. 24:42 [b]Ex. 2:16; 1 Sam. 9:11

12 [1]Lit., *cause to occur for me* [a]Gen. 24:27, 42, 48; 26:24; Ex. 3:6, 15 [b]Gen. 27:20

13 [1]Lit., *fountain of water* [a]Gen. 24:43

14 [1]Lit., *she will say*

15 [a]Gen. 24:45 [b]Gen. 22:20, 23 [c]Gen. 11:29

16 [1]Lit., *known* [a]Gen. 12:11; 26:7; 29:17

17 [a]John 4:7

18 [a]Gen. 24:14, 46

19 [a]Gen. 24:14

21 [1]Lit., *keeping silent* [a]Gen. 24:12-14, 27, 52

22 [1]Lit., *hands* [a]Gen. 24:47; Ex. 32:2, 3

24 [a]Gen. 24:15

26 [a]Gen. 24:48, 52; Ex. 4:31

27 [a]Gen. 24:12, 42, 48; Ex. 18:10; Ruth 4:14; 1 Sam. 25:32; 2 Sam. 18:28; Luke 1:68 [b]Gen. 32:10; Ps. 98:3 [c]Gen. 24:21, 48

28 [a]Gen. 29:12

29 [a]Gen. 29:5, 13

30 [1]Lit., *hands* [2]Lit., *Thus the man*

31 [a]Gen. 29:13 [b]Gen. 26:29; Ruth 3:10; Ps. 115:15 [c]Gen. 18:3-5; 19:2, 3

32 [1]Lit., *he* [a]Gen. 43:24; Judg. 19:21

34 [a]Gen. 24:2

35 [1]Lit., *great* [a]Gen. 24:1 [b]Gen. 13:2

36 [1]Lit., *after she was old* [a]Gen. 21:1-7 [b]Gen. 25:5

37 [1]Lit., *dwell* [a]Gen. 24:2-4

39 [a]Gen. 24:5

40 [a]Gen. 24:7 [b]Gen. 5:22, 24; 17:1 [c]Ex. 23:20

41 [a]Gen. 24:8

42 [a]Gen. 24:11, 12 [b]Neh. 1:11

43 [1]Lit., *fountain of water* [a]Gen. 24:13 [b]Gen. 24:14

45 [a]1 Sam. 1:13 [b]Gen. 24:15 [c]Gen. 24:17

46 "And she quickly lowered her jar from her *shoulder,* and said, '[a]Drink, and I will water your camels also'; so I drank, and she watered the camels also.

47 "[a]Then I asked her, and said, 'Whose daughter are you?' And she said, 'The daughter of Bethuel, Nahor's son, whom Milcah bore to him'; and I put the [b]ring on her nose, and the bracelets on her [1]wrists.

48 "And I [a]bowed low and worshiped the LORD, and blessed the LORD, the God of my master Abraham, [b]who had guided me in the right way to take the daughter of my master's [1]kinsman for his son.

49 "So now if you are going to [1a]deal kindly and truly with my master, tell me; and if not, let me know, that I may turn to the right hand or the left."

50 Then Laban and Bethuel answered and said, "[a]The matter comes from the LORD; [b]*so* we cannot speak to you bad or good.

51 "Behold, Rebekah is before you, take *her* and go, and let her be the wife of your master's son, as the LORD has spoken."

52 And it came about when Abraham's servant heard their words, that he [a]bowed himself to the ground [1]before the LORD.

53 And the servant brought out [a]articles of silver and articles of gold, and garments, and gave them to Rebekah; he also gave precious things to her brother and to her mother.

54 Then he and the men who were with him ate and drank and spent the night. When they arose in the morning, he said, "[a]Send me away to my master."

55 But her brother and her mother said, "[a]Let the girl stay with us *a few* days, say ten; afterward she may go."

56 And he said to them, "Do not delay me, since [a]the LORD has prospered my way. Send me away that I may go to my master."

57 And they said, "We will call the girl and [1]consult her wishes."

58 Then they called Rebekah and said to her, "Will you go with this man?" And she said, "I will go."

59 Thus they sent away their sister Rebekah and [a]her nurse with Abraham's servant and his men.

60 And they blessed Rebekah and said to her,

"May you, our sister,
[a]Become thousands of ten thousands,
And may [b]your [1]descendants possess
The gate of those who hate them."

Isaac Marries Rebekah

61 Then Rebekah arose with her maids, and they mounted the camels and followed the man. So the servant took Rebekah and departed.

62 Now Isaac had come from going to [a]Beer-lahai-roi; for he [1]was living in [b]the [2]Negev.

63 And Isaac went out [a]to [1]meditate in the field toward evening; and [b]he lifted up his eyes and looked, and behold, camels were coming.

64 And Rebekah lifted up her eyes, and when she saw Isaac she dismounted from the camel.

65 And she said to the servant, "Who is that man walking in the field to meet us?" And the servant said, "He is my master." Then she took her [1]veil and covered herself.

66 And the servant told Isaac all the things that he had done.

67 Then Isaac brought her into his mother Sarah's tent, and [a]he took Rebekah, and she became his wife; and [b]he loved her; thus Isaac was comforted after [c]his mother's death.

Abraham's Death

25 NOW Abraham took another wife, [1]whose name was Keturah.

2 And [a]she bore to him Zimran and Jokshan and Medan and Midian and Ishbak and Shuah.

3 And Jokshan [1]became the father of Sheba and Dedan. And the sons of Dedan were Asshurim and Letushim and Leummim.

4 And the sons of Midian *were* Ephah and Epher and Hanoch and Abida and Eldaah. All these *were* the sons of Keturah.

5 [a]Now Abraham gave all that he had to Isaac;

6 but to the sons of [1]his concubines, Abraham gave gifts while he was still living, and [a]sent them away from his son Isaac eastward, to the land of the east.

7 And these are [1]all the years of Abraham's life that he lived, [a]one hundred and seventy-five years.

8 And Abraham breathed his last and died [a]in a [1]ripe old age, an old man and satisfied *with life;* and he was [b]gathered to his people.

9 Then his sons Isaac and Ishmael buried him in [a]the cave of Machpelah, in the field of Ephron the son of Zohar the Hittite, facing Mamre,

10 [a]the field which Abraham purchased from the sons of Heth; there Abraham was buried with Sarah his wife.

11 And it came about after the death of Abraham, that [a]God blessed his son Isaac; and Isaac [1]lived by [b]Beer-lahai-roi.

Descendants of Ishmael

12 Now these are *the records of* the generations of [a]Ishmael, Abraham's son, whom Hagar the Egyptian, Sarah's maid, bore to Abraham;

13 and these are the names of [a]the sons of Ishmael, by their names, [1]in the

---

46 [a]Gen. 24:18, 19
47 [1]Lit., *hands* [a]Gen. 24:23, 24 [b]Ezek. 16:11, 12
48 [1]Lit., *brother* [a]Gen. 24:26, 52 [b]Gen. 24:27; Ps. 32:8; 48:14; Is. 48:17
49 [1]Lit., *show lovingkindness and truth* [a]Gen. 47:29; Josh. 2:14
50 [a]Ps. 118:23; Mark 12:11 [b]Gen. 31:24, 29
52 [1]Lit., *to* [a]Gen. 24:26, 48
53 [a]Gen. 24:10, 22; Ex. 3:22; 11:2; 12:35
54 [a]Gen. 24:56, 59; 30:25
55 [a]Judg. 19:4
56 [a]Gen. 24:40
57 [1]Lit., *ask her mouth*
59 [a]Gen. 35:8
60 [1]Lit., *seed* [a]Gen. 17:16 [b]Gen. 22:17
62 [1]Lit., *was dwelling* [2]I.e., South country [a]Gen. 16:14; 25:11 [b]Gen. 20:1
63 [1]Or, *stroll;* meaning uncertain [a]Josh. 1:8; Ps. 1:2; 77:12; 119:15, 27, 48; 143:5; 145:5 [b]Gen. 18:2
65 [1]Or, *shawl*
67 [a]Gen. 25:20 [b]Gen. 29:18 [c]Gen. 23:1, 2

1 [1]Lit., *and her name*
2 [a]1 Chr. 1:32, 33
3 [1]Lit., *begot*
5 [a]Gen. 24:35, 36
6 [1]Lit., *concubines which belonged to Abraham* [a]Gen. 21:14
7 [1]Lit., *the days of* [a]Gen. 12:4
8 [1]Lit., *good* [a]Gen. 15:15; 47:8, 9 [b]Gen. 25:17; 35:29; 49:29, 33
9 [a]Gen. 23:17, 18; 49:29, 30; 50:13
10 [a]Gen. 23:3-16
11 [1]Lit., *dwelt* [a]Gen. 12:2, 3; 22:17; 26:3 [b]Gen. 16:14; 24:62
12 [a]Gen. 16:15
13 [1]Lit., *in regard to their generations* [a]1 Chr. 1:29-31

order of their birth: Nebaioth, the firstborn of Ishmael, and Kedar and Adbeel and Mibsam

14 and Mishma and Dumah and Massa,

15 Hadad and Tema, Jetur, Naphish and Kedemah.

16 These are the sons of Ishmael and these are their names, by their villages, and by their camps; [a]twelve princes according to their [1]tribes.

17 And these are the years of the life of Ishmael, [a]one hundred and thirty-seven years; and he breathed his last and died, and was [b]gathered to his people.

18 And they [1]settled from [a]Havilah to [b]Shur which is [2]east of Egypt [3]as one goes toward Assyria; [c]he [4]settled in defiance of all his [5]relatives.

Isaac's Sons

19 Now these are *the records of* [a]the generations of Isaac, Abraham's son: Abraham [1]became the father of Isaac;

20 and Isaac was forty years old when he took [a]Rebekah, the [b]daughter of Bethuel the [1]Aramean of Paddan-aram, the [c]sister of Laban the [1]Aramean, to be his wife.

21 And Isaac prayed to the LORD on behalf of his wife, because she was barren; and [a]the LORD [1]answered him and Rebekah his wife [b]conceived.

22 But the children struggled together within her; and she said, "If it is so, why then am I *this way?*" So she went to [a]inquire of the LORD.

23 And the LORD said to her,
"[a]Two nations are in your womb;
[b]And two peoples shall be separated from your body;
And one people shall be stronger than the other;
And [c]the older shall serve the younger."

24 When her days to be delivered were fulfilled, behold, there were twins in her womb.

25 Now the first came forth red, [a]all over like a hairy garment; and they named him Esau.

26 And afterward his brother came forth with [a]his hand holding on to Esau's heel, so [b]his name was called [1]Jacob; and Isaac was [c]sixty years old when she gave birth to them.

27 When the boys grew up, Esau became a skillful hunter, a man of the field; but Jacob was a [1]peaceful man, [2a]living in tents.

28 Now Isaac loved Esau, because [1]he had [a]a taste for game; [b]but Rebekah loved Jacob.

29 And when Jacob had cooked [a]stew, Esau came in from the field and he was [1]famished;

30 and Esau said to Jacob, "Please let me have a swallow of [1]that red stuff there, for I am [2]famished." Therefore his name was called [3]Edom.

31 But Jacob said, "[1]First sell me your [a]birthright."

32 And Esau said, "Behold, I am about to die; so of what *use* then is the birthright to me?"

33 And Jacob said, "[1]First swear to me"; so he swore to him, and [a]sold his birthright to Jacob.

34 Then Jacob gave Esau bread and lentil stew; and he ate and drank, and rose and went on his way. Thus Esau despised his birthright.

Isaac Settles in Gerar

26 NOW there was [a]a famine in the land, besides the previous famine that had occurred in the days of Abraham. So Isaac went to Gerar, to [b]Abimelech king of the Philistines.

2 And the LORD [a]appeared to him and said, "Do not go down to Egypt; [1b]stay in the land of which I shall tell you.

3 "Sojourn in this land and [a]I will be with you and [b]bless you, for [c]to you and to your [1]descendants I will give all these lands, and I will establish [d]the oath which I swore to your father Abraham.

4 "And [a]I will multiply your [1]descendants as the stars of heaven, and will give your [1]descendants all these lands; and [b]by your [1]descendants all the nations of the earth [2]shall be blessed;

5 because Abraham [1a]obeyed Me and kept My charge, My commandments, My statutes and My laws."

6 So Isaac [1]lived in Gerar.

7 When the men of the place asked about his wife, he said, "[a]She is my sister," for he was [b]afraid to say, "my wife," *thinking,* "[1]the men of the place might kill me on account of Rebekah, for she is [c]beautiful."

8 And it came about, when he had been there a long time, that Abimelech king of the Philistines looked out through a window, and saw, and behold, Isaac was caressing his wife Rebekah.

9 Then Abimelech called Isaac and said, "Behold, certainly she is your wife! How then did you say, 'She is my sister'?" And Isaac said to him, "Because I said, 'Lest I die on account of her.' "

10 And [a]Abimelech said, "What is this you have done to us? One of the people might easily have lain with your wife, and you would have brought guilt upon us."

11 So Abimelech charged all the people, saying, "He who [a]touches this man or his wife shall surely be put to death."

12 Now Isaac sowed in that land, and [1]reaped in the same year a hundredfold. And [a]the LORD blessed him,

13 and the man [a]became rich, and continued to grow [1]richer until he became very [1]wealthy;

14 for [a]he had possessions of flocks [1]and herds and a great household, so that the Philistines envied him.

15 Now [a]all the wells which his father's servants had dug in the days of Abraham his father, the Philistines stopped up [1]by filling them with earth.

16 [1]Or, *peoples* [a]Gen. 17:20
17 [a]Gen. 16:16 [b]Gen. 25:8; 49:33
18 [1]Lit., *dwelt* [2]Lit., *before* [3]Lit., *as you go* [4]Lit., *fell over against* [5]Lit., *brothers* [a]1 Sam. 15:7 [b]Gen. 20:1 [c]Gen. 16:12
19 [1]Lit., *begot* [a]Matt. 1:2
20 [1]I.e., Syrian [a]Gen. 24:15, 29, 67 [b]Gen. 22:23 [c]Gen. 24:29
21 [1]Lit., *was entreated of him* [a]1 Sam. 1:17; 1 Chr. 5:20; 2 Chr. 33:13; Ezra 8:23; Ps. 127:3 [b]Rom. 9:10
22 [a]1 Sam. 9:9; 10:22
23 [a]Gen. 17:4-6, 16; Num. 20:14; Deut. 2:4, 8 [b]Gen. 27:29 [c]Gen. 27:40; Mal. 1:2, 3; Rom. 9:12
25 [a]Gen. 27:11
26 [1]I.e., one who takes by the heel or supplants [a]Hos. 12:3 [b]Gen. 27:36 [c]Gen. 25:20
27 [1]Lit., *complete* [2]Lit., *dwelling* [a]Heb. 11:9
28 [1]Lit., *game was in his mouth* [a]Gen. 27:19 [b]Gen. 27:6-10
29 [1]Lit., *weary* [a]2 Kin. 4:38
30 [1]Lit., *the red, this red* [2]Lit., *weary* [3]I.e., red
31 [1]Lit., *Today* [a]Deut. 21:16, 17; 1 Chr. 5:1, 2
33 [1]Lit., *Today* [a]Heb. 12:16

1 [a]Gen. 12:10 [b]Gen. 20:1, 2
2 [1]Lit., *dwell* [a]Gen. 12:7; 17:1; 18:1 [b]Gen. 12:1
3 [1]Lit., *seed* [a]Gen. 26:24; 28:15; 31:3 [b]Gen. 12:2 [c]Gen. 12:7; 13:15; 15:18 [d]Gen. 22:16-18; Ps. 105:9
4 [1]Lit., *seed* [2]Or, *bless themselves* [a]Gen. 15:5; 22:17; Ex. 32:13 [b]Gen. 22:18; Gal. 3:8
5 [1]Lit., *hearkened to My voice* [a]Gen. 22:16
6 [1]Lit., *dwelt*
7 [1]Lit., *lest . . . place* [a]Gen. 12:13; 20:2, 12 [b]Prov. 29:25 [c]Gen. 12:11; 24:16; 29:17
10 [a]Gen. 20:9
11 [a]Ps. 105:15
12 [1]Lit., *found* [a]Gen. 24:1; 26:3; Job 42:12; Prov. 10:22
13 [1]Lit., *great* [a]Prov. 10:22
14 [1]Lit., *and possessions of herds* [a]Gen. 24:35; 25:5
15 [1]Lit., *and filled them* [a]Gen. 21:25, 30

16 Then Abimelech said to Isaac, "Go away from us, for you are [1a]too powerful for us."

17 And Isaac departed from there and camped in the valley of Gerar, and [1]settled there.

Quarrel over the Wells

18 Then Isaac dug again the wells of water which [1]had been dug in the days of his father Abraham, for the Philistines had stopped them up after the death of Abraham; and he [2]gave them the same names which his father had [3]given them.

19 But when Isaac's servants dug in the valley and found there a well of [1]flowing water,

20 the herdsmen of Gerar [a]quarreled with the herdsmen of Isaac, saying, "The water is ours!" So he named the well [1]Esek, because they contended with him.

21 Then they dug another well, and they quarreled over it too, so he named it [1]Sitnah.

22 And he moved away from there and dug another well, and they did not quarrel over it; so he named it [1]Rehoboth, for he said, "[2a]At last the LORD has made [3]room for us, and we shall be [b]fruitful in the land."

23 Then he went up from there to [a]Beersheba.

24 And the LORD [a]appeared to him the same night and said,

"[b]I am the God of your father Abraham;
[c]Do not fear, for I am with you.
I [d]will bless you, and multiply your [1]descendants,
For the sake of My servant Abraham."

25 So he built an [a]altar there, and called upon the name of the LORD, and pitched his tent there; and there Isaac's servants dug a well.

Covenant with Abimelech

26 Then [a]Abimelech came to him from Gerar [1]with his adviser Ahuzzath, and Phicol the commander of his army.

27 And Isaac said to them, "[a]Why have you come to me, since you hate me, and have sent me away from you?"

28 And they said, "We see plainly [a]that the LORD has been with you; so we said, 'Let there now be an oath between us, *even* between [1]you and us, and let us make a covenant with you,

29 that you will do us no harm, just as we have not touched you [1]and have done to you nothing but good, and have sent you away in peace. You are now the [a]blessed of the LORD.'"

30 Then [a]he made them a feast, and they ate and drank.

31 And in the morning they arose early and [1a]exchanged oaths; then Isaac sent them away and they departed from him in peace.

32 Now it came about on the same day, that Isaac's servants came in and told him about the well which they had dug, and said to him, "We have found water."

33 So he called it Shibah; therefore the name of the city is [a]Beersheba to this day.

34 And when Esau was forty years old [a]he [1]married Judith the daughter of Beeri the Hittite, and Basemath the daughter of Elon the Hittite;

35 and [a]they [1]brought grief to Isaac and Rebekah.

Jacob's Deception

27 NOW it came about, when Isaac was old, and [a]his eyes were too dim to see, that he called his [b]older son Esau and said to him, "My son." And he said to him, "Here I am."

2 [a]And [1]Isaac said, "Behold now, I am old *and* I do not know the day of my death.

3 "Now then, please take your gear, your quiver and your bow, and go out to the field and [a]hunt game for me;

4 and prepare a savory dish for me such as I love, and bring it to me that I may eat, so that [a]my soul may bless you before I die."

5 And Rebekah was listening while Isaac spoke to his son Esau. So when Esau went to the field to hunt for game to bring *home,*

6 [a]Rebekah said to her son Jacob, "Behold, I heard your father speak to your brother Esau, saying,

7 'Bring me *some* game and prepare a savory dish for me, that I may eat, and bless you in the presence of the LORD before my death.'

8 "Now therefore, my son, [a]listen to [1]me [2]as I command you.

9 "Go now to the flock and [1]bring me two choice [2]kids from there, that I may prepare them *as* a savory dish for your father, such as he loves.

10 "Then you shall bring *it* to your father, that he may eat, so that he may bless you before his death."

11 And Jacob [1]answered his mother Rebekah, "Behold, Esau my brother is a [a]hairy man and I am a smooth man.

12 "[a]Perhaps my father will feel me, then I shall be as a [1]deceiver in his sight; and I shall bring upon myself a curse and not a blessing."

13 But his mother said to him, "Your curse be on me, my son; only [a]obey my voice, and go, get *them* for me."

14 So he went and got *them,* and brought *them* to his mother; and his mother made savory food such as his father loved.

15 Then Rebekah took the [1]best [a]garments of Esau her elder son, which were with her in the house, and put them on Jacob her younger son.

16 And she put the skins of the [1]kids on his hands and on the smooth part of his neck.

17 She also gave the savory food and the bread, which she had made, [1]to her son Jacob.

---

16 [1]Lit., *much mightier than we* [a]Ex. 1:9

17 [1]Lit., *dwelt*

18 [1]Lit., *they had dug* [2]Lit., *called their names as the names* [3]Lit., *called*

19 [1]Lit., *living*

20 [1]I.e., contention [a]Gen. 21:25

21 [1]I.e., enmity

22 [1]I.e., broad places [2]Lit., *Truly now* [3]Or, *broad* [a]Ps. 4:1; Is. 54:2, 3 [b]Gen. 17:6; Ex. 1:7

23 [a]Gen. 22:19

24 [1]Lit., *seed* [a]Gen. 26:2 [b]Gen. 17:7, 8; 24:12; Ex. 3:6; Acts 7:32 [c]Gen. 15:1 [d]Gen. 22:17; 26:3, 4

25 [a]Gen. 12:7, 8; 13:4, 18; Ps. 116:17

26 [1]Lit., *and his confidential friend* [a]Gen. 21:22

27 [a]Judg. 11:7

28 [1]Lit., *us and you* [a]Gen. 21:22, 23

29 [1]Lit., *and just as we* [a]Gen. 24:31; Ps. 115:15

30 [a]Gen. 19:3

31 [1]Lit., *swore one to another* [a]Gen. 21:31

33 [a]Gen. 21:31

34 [1]Lit., *took as wife* [a]Gen. 28:8; 36:2

35 [1]Lit., *were a bitterness of spirit to* [a]Gen. 27:46

1 [a]Gen. 48:10; 1 Sam. 3:2 [b]Gen. 25:25, 33, 34

2 [1]Lit., *he* [a]Gen. 47:29

3 [a]Gen. 25:28

4 [a]Gen. 27:19, 25, 31; 48:9, 15, 16; Deut. 33:1; Heb. 11:20

6 [a]Gen. 25:28

8 [1]Lit., *my voice* [2]Lit., *according to what* [a]Gen. 27:13, 43

9 [1]Lit., *take* [2]Lit., *kids of goats*

11 [1]Lit., *said to* [a]Gen. 25:25

12 [1]Lit., *mocker* [a]Gen. 27:21, 22

13 [a]Gen. 27:8

15 [1]Lit., *desirable; or, choice* [a]Gen. 27:27

16 [1]Lit., *kids of the goats*

17 [1]Lit., *into the hand of*

18 Then he came to his father and
said, "My father." And he said, "Here I
am. Who are you, my son?"
19 And Jacob said to his father, "I am
Esau your first-born; I have done as you
told me. [a]Get up, please, sit and eat of
my game, that [1b]you may bless me."
20 And Isaac said to his son, "How is
it that you have *it* so quickly, my son?"
And he said, "[a]Because the LORD your
God caused *it* to happen to me."
21 Then Isaac said to Jacob, "Please
come close, that [a]I may feel you, my son,
whether you are really my son Esau or
not."
22 So Jacob came close to Isaac his
father, and he felt him and said, "The
voice is the voice of Jacob, but the hands
are the hands of Esau."
23 And he did not recognize him,
because his hands were [a]hairy like his
brother Esau's hands; so he blessed him.
24 And he said, "Are you really my
son Esau?" And he said, "I am."
25 So he said, "Bring *it* to me, and I
will eat of my son's game, that [1a]I may
bless you." And he brought *it* to him,
and he ate; he also brought him wine
and he drank.
26 Then his father Isaac said to him,
"Please come close and kiss me, my
son."
27 So he came close and kissed him;
and when he smelled the smell of his
garments, he [a]blessed him and said,
"See, [b]the smell of my son
Is like the smell of a field [c]which
the LORD has blessed;
28 Now may [a]God give you of the
dew of heaven,
And of the [b]fatness of the earth,
And an abundance of grain and
new wine;
29 [a]May peoples serve you,
And nations bow down to you;
[b]Be master of your brothers,
[c]And may your mother's sons
bow down to you.
[d]Cursed be those who curse you,
And blessed be those who bless
you."

The Stolen Blessing

30 Now it came about, as soon as
Isaac had finished blessing Jacob, and
Jacob had hardly gone out from the
presence of Isaac his father, that Esau
his brother came in from his hunting.
31 Then he also made savory food,
and brought it to his father; and he said
to his father, "[a]Let my father arise, and
eat of his son's game, that [1b]you may
bless me."
32 And Isaac his father said to him,
"[a]Who are you?" And he said, "I am
your son, [b]your first-born, Esau."
33 Then Isaac [1]trembled violently,
and said, "[a]Who was he then that
hunted game and brought *it* to me, so
that I ate of all *of it* before you came,
and blessed him? [b]Yes, and he shall be
blessed."

19 [1]Lit., *your soul* [a]Gen. 27:31 [b]Gen. 27:4
20 [a]Gen. 24:12
21 [a]Gen. 27:12
23 [a]Gen. 27:16
25 [1]Lit., *my soul* [a]Gen. 27:4
27 [a]Heb. 11:20 [b]Song 4:11 [c]Ps. 65:10
28 [a]Gen. 27:39; Deut. 33:13, 28; Prov. 3:20; Zech. 8:12 [b]Num. 18:12
29 [a]Gen. 25:23; Is. 45:14; 49:7, 23; 60:12, 14 [b]Gen. 9:26, 27; 27:37 [c]Gen. 37:7, 10 [d]Gen. 12:3; Num. 24:9
31 [1]Lit., *your soul* [a]Gen. 27:19 [b]Gen. 27:4
32 [a]Gen. 27:18 [b]Gen. 25:33, 34
33 [1]Lit., *trembled with a very great trembling* [a]Gen. 27:35 [b]Gen. 25:23; 28:3, 4; Num. 23:20
34 [a]Heb. 12:17
35 [a]Gen. 27:19
36 [1]Or, *Was he then named Jacob that he has* [a]Gen. 25:26, 32-34
37 [1]Lit., *brothers* [2]Lit., *for* [a]Gen. 27:28, 29
38 [a]Heb. 12:17
39 [1]Or, *of* [2]Lit., *fatness* [a]Heb. 11:20 [b]Gen. 27:28; Deut. 33:13, 28
40 [1]Lit., *tear off* [a]Gen. 25:23; 27:29 [b]2 Kin. 8:20-22
41 [1]Lit., *in his heart* [a]Gen. 32:3-11; 37:4, 8 [b]Gen. 50:2-4, 10
43 [1]Lit., *flee for yourself* [a]Gen. 27:8, 13 [b]Gen. 11:31 [c]Gen. 24:29
44 [1]Lit., *turns away* [a]Gen. 31:41
45 [1]Lit., *turns away from you* [a]Gen. 27:12, 19, 35
46 [1]Lit., *my life* [a]Gen. 26:34, 35; 28:8 [b]Gen. 24:3
1 [a]Gen. 27:33 [b]Gen. 24:3, 4

34 When Esau heard the words of his
father, [a]he cried out with an exceedingly
great and bitter cry, and said to his
father, "Bless me, *even* me also, O my
father!"
35 And he said, "[a]Your brother came
deceitfully, and has taken away your
blessing."
36 Then he said, "[1]Is he not rightly
named [a]Jacob, for he has supplanted me
these two times? He took away my
birthright, and behold, now he has taken
away my blessing." And he said, "Have
you not reserved a blessing for me?"
37 But Isaac answered and said to
Esau, "Behold, I have made him [a]your
master, and all his [1]relatives I have given
to him [2]as servants; and with grain and
new wine I have sustained him. Now as
for you then, what can I do, my son?"
38 And Esau said to his father, "Do
you have only one blessing, my father?
Bless me, *even* me also, O my father." So
Esau lifted his voice and [a]wept.
39 Then [a]Isaac his father answered
and said to him,
"Behold, [1b]away from the [2]fertility
of the earth shall be your dwelling,
And [1]away from the dew of
heaven from above.
40 "And by your sword you shall live,
And your brother [a]you shall
serve;
But it shall come about [b]when
you become restless,
That you shall [1]break his yoke
from your neck."
41 So Esau [a]bore a grudge against
Jacob because of the blessing with which
his father had blessed him; and Esau
said [1]to himself, "[b]The days of mourning
for my father are near; then I will kill
my brother Jacob."
42 Now when the words of her elder
son Esau were reported to Rebekah, she
sent and called her younger son Jacob,
and said to him, "Behold your brother
Esau is consoling himself concerning
you, *by planning* to kill you.
43 "Now therefore, my son, [a]obey my
voice, and arise, [1]flee to [b]Haran, to my
brother [c]Laban!
44 "And stay with him [a]a few days,
until your brother's fury [1]subsides,
45 until your brother's anger [1]against
you subsides, and he forgets [a]what you
did to him. Then I shall send and get
you from there. Why should I be bereaved
of you both in one day?"
46 And Rebekah said to Isaac, "I am
tired of [1]living because of [a]the daughters
of Heth; [b]if Jacob takes a wife from the
daughters of Heth, like these, from the
daughters of the land, what good will my
life be to me?"

Jacob Is Sent Away

28 SO Isaac called Jacob and
[a]blessed him and charged him,
and said to him, "[b]You shall not take a
wife from the daughters of Canaan.

2 "Arise, go to Paddan-aram, to the house of [a]Bethuel your mother's father; and from there take to yourself a wife from the daughters of Laban your mother's brother.

3 "And may [1a]God Almighty [b]bless you and [c]make you fruitful and [d]multiply you, that you may become a [e]company of peoples.

4 "May He also give you the [a]blessing of Abraham, to you and to your [1]descendants with you; that you may [b]possess the land of your [c]sojournings, which God gave to Abraham."

5 Then [a]Isaac sent Jacob away, and he went to Paddan-aram to Laban, son of Bethuel the Aramean, the brother of Rebekah, the mother of Jacob and Esau.

6 Now Esau saw that Isaac had blessed Jacob and sent him away to Paddan-aram, to take to himself a wife from there, *and that* when he blessed him he charged him, saying, "[a]You shall not take a wife from the daughters of Canaan,"

7 and that Jacob had obeyed his father and his mother and had gone to Paddan-aram.

8 So Esau saw that [a]the daughters of Canaan displeased [1]his father Isaac;

9 and Esau went to Ishmael, and [1]married, [a]besides the wives that he had, Mahalath the daughter of Ishmael, Abraham's son, the sister of Nebaioth.

Jacob's Dream

10 Then Jacob departed from [a]Beersheba and went toward [b]Haran.

11 And he [1]came to [2]a [a]certain place and spent the night there, because the sun had set; and he took one of the stones of the place and put it [3]under his head, and lay down in that place.

12 And [a]he had a dream, and behold, a ladder was set on the earth with its top reaching to heaven; and behold, [b]the angels of God were ascending and descending on it.

13 And behold, [a]the LORD stood [1]above it and said, "I am the LORD, [b]the God of your father Abraham and the God of Isaac; the land on which you lie, I will give it [c]to you and to [d]your [2]descendants.

14 "Your [1]descendants shall also be like [a]the dust of the earth, and you shall [2]spread out [b]to the west and to the east and to the north and to the south; and [c]in you and in your [1]descendants shall all the families of the earth be blessed.

15 "And behold, [a]I am with you, and [b]will keep you wherever you go, and [c]will bring you back to this land; for [d]I will not leave you until I have done what I have [1]promised you."

16 Then Jacob [a]awoke from his sleep and said, "[b]Surely the LORD is in this place, and I did not know it."

17 And he was afraid and said, "[a]How awesome is this place! This is none other than the house of God, and this is the gate of heaven."

18 So Jacob rose early in the morning, and took [a]the stone that he had put [1]under his head and set it up as a pillar, and poured oil on its top.

19 And he called the name of that place [1a]Bethel; however, [2]previously the name of the city had been [b]Luz.

20 Then Jacob [a]made a vow, saying, "[b]If God will be with me and will keep me on this journey that I [1]take, and will give me [2c]food to eat and garments to wear,

21 and [a]I return to my father's house in [1]safety, [b]then the LORD will be my God.

22 "And this stone, which I have set up as a pillar, [a]will be God's house; and [b]of all that Thou dost give me I will surely give a tenth to Thee."

Jacob Meets Rachel

29 THEN Jacob [1]went on his journey, and came to the land of [a]the sons of the east.

2 And he looked, and [1]saw [a]a well in the field, and behold, three flocks of sheep were lying there beside it, for from that well they watered the flocks. Now the stone on the mouth of the well was large.

3 When all the flocks were gathered there, they would then roll the stone from the mouth of the well, and water the sheep, and put the stone back in its place on the mouth of the well.

4 And Jacob said to them, "My brothers, where are you from?" And they said, "We are from [a]Haran."

5 And he said to them, "Do you know Laban the [a]son of Nahor?" And they said, "We know *him.*"

6 And he said to them, "Is it well with him?" And they said, "It is well, and behold, [a]Rachel his daughter is coming with the sheep."

7 And he said, "Behold, it is still high day; it is not time for the livestock to be gathered. Water the sheep, and go, pasture them."

8 But they said, "We cannot, until all the flocks are gathered, and they roll the stone from the mouth of the well; then we water the sheep."

9 While he was still speaking with them, Rachel came with her father's sheep, for she was a shepherdess.

10 And it came about, when Jacob saw Rachel the daughter of Laban his mother's brother, and the sheep of Laban his mother's brother, that Jacob went up, and rolled the stone from the mouth of the well, and watered the flock of Laban his mother's brother.

11 Then Jacob [a]kissed Rachel, and lifted his voice and wept.

12 And Jacob told Rachel that he was a [1a]relative of her father and that he was Rebekah's son, and [b]she ran and told her father.

13 So it came about, when [a]Laban heard the news of Jacob his sister's son, that he ran to meet him, and [b]embraced

2 [a]Gen. 25:20
3 [1]Heb., *El Shaddai* [a]Gen. 17:1; 35:11; 48:3 [b]Gen. 22:17 [c]Gen. 17:6, 20 [d]Gen. 17:2; 26:4, 24 [e]Gen. 35:11; 48:4
4 [1]Lit., *seed* [a]Gen. 12:2; 22:17 [b]Gen. 15:7, 8; 17:8 [c]1 Chr. 29:15; Ps. 39:12
5 [a]Gen. 27:43
6 [a]Gen. 28:1
8 [1]Lit., *in the eyes of his* [a]Gen. 24:3; 26:34, 35; 27:46
9 [1]Lit., *took for his wife* [a]Gen. 26:34; 36:2
10 [a]Gen. 26:23 [b]Gen. 12:4, 5; 27:43
11 [1]Lit., *lighted on* [2]Lit., *the place* [3]Lit., *at his head-place* [a]Gen. 28:19
12 [a]Gen. 41:1; Num. 12:6 [b]John 1:51
13 [1]Or, *beside him* [2]Lit., *seed* [a]Gen. 35:1; Amos 7:7 [b]Gen. 26:3, 24 [c]Gen. 13:15, 17; 26:3 [d]Gen. 12:7; 15:18
14 [1]Lit., *seed* [2]Lit., *break through* [a]Gen. 13:16; 22:17 [b]Gen. 13:14, 15 [c]Gen. 12:3; 18:18; 22:18; 26:4
15 [1]Lit., *spoken to* [a]Gen. 26:3, 24; 31:3 [b]Num. 6:24; Ps. 121:5, 7, 8 [c]Gen. 48:21; Deut. 30:3 [d]Num. 23:19; Deut. 7:9; 31:6, 8
16 [a]1 Kin. 3:15; Jer. 31:26 [b]Ex. 3:4-6; Josh. 5:13-15; Ps. 139:7-12
17 [a]Ps. 68:35
18 [1]Lit., *at his head-place* [a]Gen. 28:11; 35:14
19 [1]I.e., the house of God [2]Lit., *at the first* [a]Judg. 1:23 [b]Gen. 35:6; 48:3
20 [1]Lit., *go* [2]Lit., *bread* [a]Gen. 31:13; Judg. 11:30; 2 Sam. 15:8 [b]Gen. 28:15 [c]1 Tim. 6:8
21 [1]Lit., *peace* [a]Judg. 11:31 [b]Deut. 26:17
22 [a]Gen. 35:7 [b]Lev. 27:30; Deut. 14:22

1 [1]Lit., *lifted up his feet* [a]Judg. 6:3, 33
2 [1]Lit., *behold* [a]Gen. 24:10, 11; Ex. 2:15, 16
4 [a]Gen. 28:10
5 [a]Gen. 24:24, 29
6 [a]Ex. 2:16
11 [a]Gen. 33:4
12 [1]Lit., *brother* [a]Gen. 28:5 [b]Gen. 24:28
13 [a]Gen. 24:29-31 [b]Gen. 33:4

him and kissed him, and brought him to his house. Then he related to Laban all these things.

14 And Laban said to him, "Surely you are [a]my bone and my flesh." And he stayed with him a month.

15 Then Laban said to Jacob, "Because you are my [1]relative, should you therefore serve me for nothing? Tell me, what shall [a]your wages be?"

16 Now Laban had two daughters; the name of the older was Leah, and the name of the younger was Rachel.

17 And Leah's eyes were weak, but Rachel was [a]beautiful of form and [1]face.

18 Now Jacob [a]loved Rachel, so he said, "[b]I will serve you seven years for your younger daughter Rachel."

19 And Laban said, "It is better that I give her to you than that I should give her to another man; stay with me."

20 So Jacob served seven years for Rachel and they seemed to him but a few days [a]because of his love for her.

Laban's Treachery

21 Then Jacob said to Laban, "Give *me* my wife, for my [1]time is completed, that I may [a]go in to her."

22 And Laban gathered all the men of the place, and made a feast.

23 Now it came about in the evening that he took his daughter Leah, and brought her to him; and *Jacob* went in to her.

24 Laban also gave his maid Zilpah to his daughter Leah as a maid.

25 So it came about in the morning that, behold, it was Leah! And he said to Laban, "[a]What is this you have done to me? Was it not for Rachel that I served with you? Why then have you [b]deceived me?"

26 But Laban said, "It is not [1]the practice in our place, to [2]marry off the younger before the first-born.

27 "Complete the week of this one, and we will give you the other also for the service which [a]you shall serve with me for another seven years."

28 And Jacob did so and completed her week, and he gave him his daughter Rachel as his wife.

29 Laban also gave his maid Bilhah to his daughter Rachel as her maid.

30 So *Jacob* went in to Rachel also, and indeed [a]he loved Rachel more than Leah, and he served with [1]Laban for [b]another seven years.

31 Now the LORD saw that Leah was [1]unloved, and He opened her womb, but Rachel was barren.

32 And Leah conceived and bore a son and named him [1]Reuben, for she said, "Because the LORD has [2a]seen my affliction; surely now my husband will love me."

33 Then she conceived again and bore a son and said, "[a]Because the LORD has [1]heard that I am [2]unloved, He has therefore given me this *son* also." So she named him Simeon.

34 And she conceived again and bore a son and said, "Now this time my husband will become [1]attached to me, because I have borne him three sons." Therefore he was named [a]Levi.

35 And she conceived again and bore a son and said, "This time I will [1]praise the LORD." Therefore she named him [2a]Judah. Then she stopped bearing.

The Sons of Jacob

30 NOW when Rachel saw that [a]she bore Jacob no children, [1]she became jealous of her sister; and she said to Jacob, "[b]Give me children, or else I die."

2 Then Jacob's anger burned against Rachel, and he said, "Am I in the place of God, who has [a]withheld from you the fruit of the womb?"

3 And she said, "[a]Here is my maid Bilhah, go in to her, that she may [b]bear on my knees, that [1c]through her I too may have children."

4 So [a]she gave him her maid Bilhah as a wife, and Jacob went in to her.

5 And Bilhah conceived and bore Jacob a son.

6 Then Rachel said, "God has [1a]vindicated me, and has indeed heard my voice and has given me a son." Therefore she named him [2]Dan.

7 And Rachel's maid Bilhah conceived again and bore Jacob a second son.

8 So Rachel said, "With [1]mighty wrestlings I have [2]wrestled with my sister, *and* I have indeed prevailed." And she named him Naphtali.

9 When Leah saw that she had stopped bearing, she took her maid Zilpah and gave her to Jacob as a wife.

10 And Leah's maid Zilpah bore Jacob a son.

11 Then Leah said, "[1]How fortunate!" So she named him [2]Gad.

12 And Leah's maid Zilpah bore Jacob a second son.

13 Then Leah said, "[1]Happy am I! For women [a]will call me happy." So she named him [2]Asher.

14 Now in the days of wheat harvest Reuben went and found [a]mandrakes in the field, and brought them to his mother Leah. Then Rachel said to Leah, "Please give me some of your son's mandrakes."

15 But she said to her, "Is it a small matter for you to take my husband? And would you take my son's mandrakes also?" So Rachel said, "Therefore he may lie with you tonight in return for your son's mandrakes."

16 When Jacob came in from the field in the evening, then Leah went out to meet him and said, "You must come in to me, for I have surely hired you with my son's mandrakes." So he lay with her that night.

17 And God gave heed to Leah, and she conceived and bore Jacob a fifth son.

14 [a]Gen. 2:23; Judg. 9:2; 2 Sam. 5:1; 19:12, 13

15 [1]Lit., *brother* [a]Gen. 31:41

17 [1]Lit., *beautiful of appearance* [a]Gen. 12:11, 14; 26:7

18 [a]Gen. 24:67 [b]Hos. 12:12

20 [a]Song 8:7

21 [1]Lit., *days are* [a]Judg. 15:1

25 [a]Gen. 12:18; 20:9; 26:10 [b]1 Sam. 28:12

26 [1]Lit., *done thus in* [2]Lit., *give*

27 [a]Gen. 31:41

30 [1]Lit., *him* [a]Gen. 29:17, 18 [b]Gen. 31:41

31 [1]Lit., *hated*

32 [1]I.e., see, a son [2]Lit., *looked upon* [a]Gen. 16:11; 31:42; Ex. 3:7; 4:31; Deut. 26:7; Ps. 25:18

33 [1]Heb., *shama,* related to Simeon [2]Lit., *hated* [a]Deut. 21:15

34 [1]Heb., *lavah,* related to Levi [a]Gen. 49:5

35 [1]Heb., *Jadah,* related to Judah [2]Heb., *Jehudah* [a]Gen. 49:8; Matt. 1:2

1 [1]Lit., *Rachel* [a]Gen. 29:31 [b]1 Sam. 1:5, 6

2 [a]Gen. 20:18; 29:31

3 [1]Lit., *from her I too may be built* [a]Gen. 16:2 [b]Gen. 50:23; Job 3:12 [c]Gen. 16:2

4 [a]Gen. 16:3, 4

6 [1]Lit., *judged* [2]I.e., He judged [a]Ps. 35:24; 43:1; Lam. 3:59

8 [1]Lit., *wrestlings of God* [2]Heb., *niphtal,* related to Naphtali

11 [1]Lit., *With fortune!* Some versions read *Fortune has come* [2]I.e., Fortune

13 [1]Lit., *With my happiness!* [2]I.e., happy [a]Luke 1:48

14 [a]Song 7:13

18 Then Leah said, "God has given me my [1]wages, because I gave my maid to my husband." So she named him Issachar.

19 And Leah conceived again and bore a sixth son to Jacob.

20 Then Leah said, "God has endowed me with a good gift; now my husband [1]will dwell with me, because I have borne him six sons." So she named him Zebulun.

21 And afterward she bore a daughter and named her Dinah.

22 Then [a]God remembered Rachel, and God gave heed to her and [b]opened her womb.

23 So she conceived and bore a son and said, "God has [a]taken away my reproach."

24 And she named him Joseph, saying, "[a]May the LORD [1]give me another son."

Jacob Prospers

25 Now it came about when Rachel had borne Joseph, that Jacob said to Laban, "[a]Send me away, that I may go to my own place and to my own country.

26 "Give *me* my wives and my children [a]for whom I have served you, and let me depart; for you yourself know my service which I have [1]rendered you."

27 But Laban said to him, "If now [1]it pleases you, *stay with me;* I have divined [a]that the LORD has blessed me on your account."

28 And he [1]continued, "[a]Name me your wages, and I will give it."

29 But he said to him, "[a]You yourself know how I have served you and how your cattle have [1]fared with me.

30 "For you had little before [1]I came, and it has [2]increased to a multitude; and the LORD has blessed you [3]wherever I turned. But now, when shall I provide for my own household also?"

31 So he said, "What shall I give you?" And Jacob said, "You shall not give me anything. If you will do this *one* thing for me, I will again pasture *and* keep your flock:

32 let me pass through your entire flock today, removing from there every [a]speckled and spotted sheep, and every black [1]one among the lambs, and the spotted and speckled among the goats; and *such* shall be my wages.

33 "So my [1]honesty will answer for me later, when you come concerning my [2]wages. Every one that is not speckled and spotted among the goats and black among the lambs, *if found* with me, will be considered stolen."

34 And Laban said, "[1]Good, let it be according to your word."

35 So he removed on that day the striped and spotted male goats and all the speckled and spotted female goats, every one with white in it, and all the black ones among the sheep, and gave them into the [1]care of his sons.

36 And he put *a distance of* three days' journey between himself and Jacob, and Jacob fed the rest of Laban's flocks.

37 Then Jacob [1]took fresh rods of poplar and almond and plane trees, and peeled white stripes in them, exposing the white which *was* [2]in the rods.

38 And he set the rods which he had peeled in front of the flocks in the gutters, *even* in the watering troughs, where the flocks came to drink; and they [1]mated when they came to drink.

39 So the flocks [1]mated by the rods, and the flocks brought forth striped, speckled, and spotted.

40 And Jacob separated the lambs, and [1]made the flocks face toward the striped and all the black in the flock of Laban; and he put his own herds apart, and did not put them with Laban's flock.

41 Moreover, it came about whenever the [1]stronger of the flock [2]were mating, that Jacob would place the rods in the sight of the flock in the gutters, so that they might [3]mate by the rods;

42 but when the flock was feeble, he did not put *them* in; so the feebler were Laban's and the [1]stronger Jacob's.

43 So [a]the man [1]became exceedingly prosperous, and had large flocks and female and male servants and camels and donkeys.

Jacob Leaves Secretly for Canaan

31 NOW [1]Jacob heard the words of Laban's sons, saying, "Jacob has taken away all that was our father's, and from what belonged to our father he has made all this [2]wealth."

2 And Jacob saw the [1]attitude of Laban, and behold, it was not *friendly* toward him as formerly.

3 Then the LORD said to Jacob, "[a]Return to the land of your fathers and to your relatives, and [b]I will be with you."

4 So Jacob sent and called Rachel and Leah to his flock in the field,

5 and said to them, "[a]I see your father's [1]attitude, that it is not *friendly* toward me as formerly, but [b]the God of my father has been with me.

6 "And [a]you know that I have served your father with all my strength.

7 "Yet your father has [a]cheated me and [b]changed my wages ten times; however, [c]God did not allow him to hurt me.

8 "If [a]he spoke thus, 'The speckled shall be your wages,' then all the flock brought forth speckled; and if he spoke thus, 'The striped shall be your wages,' then all the flock brought forth striped.

9 "Thus God has [a]taken away your father's livestock and given *them* to me.

10 "And it came about at the time when the flock were [1]mating that I lifted up my eyes and saw in a dream, and behold, the male goats which were [2]mating *were* striped, speckled, and mottled.

11 "Then [a]the angel of God said to me in the dream, 'Jacob,' and I said, 'Here I am.'

18 [1]Heb., *sachar,* related to Issachar

20 [1]Heb., *zabal,* related to Zebulun. Some translate *will honor*

22 [a]1 Sam. 1:19, 20 [b]Gen. 29:31

23 [a]Is. 4:1; Luke 1:25

24 [1]Lit., *add to me;* Heb., *Joseph* [a]Gen. 35:17

25 [a]Gen. 24:54, 56

26 [1]Lit., *served* [a]Gen. 29:18, 20, 27; Hos. 12:12

27 [1]Lit., *I have found favor in your eyes* [a]Gen. 26:24; 39:3, 5; Is. 61:9

28 [1]Lit., *said* [a]Gen. 29:15; 31:7, 41

29 [1]Lit., *been* [a]Gen. 31:6

30 [1]Lit., *me* [2]Lit., *broken forth* [3]Lit., *at my foot*

32 [1]Lit., *sheep* [a]Gen. 31:8

33 [1]Lit., *righteousness* [2]Lit., *wages which are before you*

34 [1]Lit., *Behold, would that it might be*

35 [1]Lit., *hand*

37 [1]Lit., *took to himself* [2]Lit., *on*

38 [1]Or, *conceived*

39 [1]Or, *conceived*

40 [1]Lit., *set the faces*

41 [1]Lit., *bound ones;* i.e., firm and compact [2]Or, *conceived* [3]Or, *conceive*

42 [1]Lit., *bound ones;* i.e., firm and compact

43 [1]Lit., *broke forth* [a]Gen. 12:16; 13:2; 24:35; 26:13, 14; 30:30

1 [1]Lit., *he* [2]Lit., *glory*

2 [1]Lit., *face*

3 [a]Gen. 32:9 [b]Gen. 28:15

5 [1]Lit., *face* [a]Gen. 31:2 [b]Gen. 21:22; 28:13, 15; 31:29, 42, 53; Is. 41:10; Heb. 13:5

6 [a]Gen. 30:29

7 [a]Gen. 29:25 [b]Gen. 31:41 [c]Gen. 15:1; 31:29

8 [a]Gen. 30:32

9 [a]Gen. 31:1, 16

10 [1]Or, *conceiving* [2]Lit., *leaping upon the flock*

11 [a]Gen. 16:7-11; 22:11, 15; 31:13; 48:16

12 "And he said, 'Lift up, now, your eyes and see *that* all the male goats which are [1]mating are striped, speckled, and mottled; for [a]I have seen all that Laban has been doing to you.

13 'I am [a]the God *of* Bethel, where you [b]anointed a pillar, where you made a vow to Me; now arise, [1]leave this land, and [c]return to the land of your birth.' "

14 And Rachel and Leah answered and said to him, "Do we still have any portion or inheritance in our father's house?

15 "Are we not reckoned by him as foreigners? For [a]he has sold us, and has also [1]entirely consumed [2]our purchase price.

16 "Surely all the wealth which God has taken away from our father belongs to us and our children; now then, do whatever God has said to you."

17 Then Jacob arose and put his children and his wives upon camels;

18 and he drove away all his livestock and all his property which he had gathered, his acquired livestock which he had gathered in Paddan-aram, [a]to go to the land of Canaan to his father Isaac.

19 When Laban had gone to shear his flock, then Rachel stole the [1a]household idols that were her father's.

20 And Jacob [1]deceived Laban the Aramean, by not telling him that he was fleeing.

21 So he fled with all that he had; and he arose and crossed the *Euphrates* River, and set his face toward the hill country of [a]Gilead.

Laban Pursues Jacob

22 When it was told Laban on the third day that Jacob had fled,

23 then he took his [1]kinsmen with him, and pursued him *a distance of* seven days' journey; and he overtook him in the hill country of Gilead.

24 And [a]God came to Laban the Aramean in a [b]dream of the night, and said to him, "[1c]Be careful that you do not speak to Jacob either good or bad."

25 And Laban caught up with Jacob. Now Jacob had pitched his tent in the hill country, and Laban with his [1]kinsmen camped in the hill country of Gilead.

26 Then Laban said to Jacob, "What have you done [1]by deceiving me and carrying away my daughters like captives of the sword?

27 "Why did you flee secretly and [1]deceive me, and did not tell me, so that I might have sent you away with joy and with songs, with [a]timbrel and with [b]lyre;

28 and did not allow me [a]to kiss my sons and my daughters? Now you have done foolishly.

29 "It is in [1]my power to do you harm, but [a]the God of your father spoke to me last night, saying, '[2b]Be careful not to speak either good or bad to Jacob.'

30 "And now you have indeed gone away because you longed greatly for your father's house; *but* why did you steal [a]my gods?"

31 Then Jacob answered and said to Laban, "Because I was afraid, for I said, 'Lest you would take your daughters from me by force.'

32 "[a]The one with whom you find your gods shall not live; in the presence of our [1]kinsmen [2]point out what is yours [3]among my belongings and take *it* for yourself." For Jacob did not know that Rachel had stolen them.

33 So Laban went into Jacob's tent, and into Leah's tent, and into the tent of the two maids, but he did not find *them.* Then he went out of Leah's tent and entered Rachel's tent.

34 Now Rachel had taken the [1]household idols and put them in the camel's saddle, and she sat on them. And Laban felt through all the tent, but did not find *them.*

35 And she said to her father, "Let not my lord be angry that I cannot [a]rise before you, for the manner of women is upon me." So he searched, but did not find the [1b]household idols.

36 Then Jacob became angry and contended with Laban; and Jacob answered and said to Laban, "What is my transgression? What is my sin, that you have hotly pursued me?

37 "Though you have felt through all my goods, what have you found of all your household goods? Set *it* here before my [1]kinsmen and your [1]kinsmen, that they may decide between us two.

38 "These twenty years I *have been* with you; your ewes and your female goats have not miscarried, nor have I eaten the rams of your flocks.

39 "That which was torn *of beasts* I did not bring to you; I bore the loss of it myself. You required it of my hand *whether* stolen by day or stolen by night.

40 "*Thus* I was: by day the [1]heat consumed me, and the frost by night, and my sleep fled from my eyes.

41 "These twenty years I have been in your house; [a]I served you fourteen years for your two daughters, and six years for your flock, and you [b]changed my wages ten times.

42 "If [a]the God of my father, the God of Abraham, and the fear of Isaac, had not been for me, surely now you would have sent me away empty-handed. [b]God has seen my affliction and the toil of my hands, so He [c]rendered judgment last night."

The Covenant of Mizpah

43 Then Laban answered and said to Jacob, "The daughters are my daughters, and the children are my children, and [a]the flocks are my flocks, and all that you see is mine. But what can I do this day to these my daughters or to their children whom they have borne?

44 "So now come, let us [a]make a covenant, [1]you and I, and [b]let it be a witness between [2]you and me."

12 [1]Lit., *leaping upon the flock* [a]Ex. 3:7

13 [1]Lit., *go out from* [a]Gen. 28:13, 19 [b]Gen. 28:18, 20 [c]Gen. 28:15; 32:9

15 [1]I.e., enjoyed the benefit of [2]Lit., *our money* [a]Gen. 29:20, 23, 27

18 [a]Gen. 35:27

19 [1]Heb., *teraphim* [a]Gen. 31:30, 34; 35:2; Judg. 17:5; 1 Sam. 19:13; Hos. 3:4

20 [1]Lit., *stole the heart of*

21 [a]Gen. 37:25

23 [1]Lit., *brothers*

24 [1]Lit., *Take heed to yourself* [a]Gen. 20:3; 31:29 [b]Gen. 20:3, 6; 31:11 [c]Gen. 24:50; 31:7, 29

25 [1]Lit., *brothers*

26 [1]Lit., *and you have stolen my heart*

27 [1]Lit., *steal me* [a]Ex. 15:20 [b]Gen. 4:21

28 [a]Gen. 31:55

29 [1]Lit., *the power of my hand* [2]Lit., *Take heed to yourself* [a]Gen. 31:5, 24, 42, 53 [b]Gen. 31:24

30 [a]Gen. 31:19; Josh. 24:2; Judg. 18:24

32 [1]Lit., *brothers* [2]Lit., *recognize* [3]Lit., *with me* [a]Gen. 44:9

34 [1]Heb., *teraphim*

35 [1]Heb., *teraphim* [a]Lev. 19:32 [b]Gen. 31:19

37 [1]Lit., *brothers*

40 [1]Or, *drought*

41 [a]Gen. 29:27, 30 [b]Gen. 31:7

42 [a]Gen. 31:5, 29, 53 [b]Gen. 29:32; Ex. 3:7 [c]Gen. 31:24, 29

43 [a]Gen. 31:1

44 [1]Lit., *I and you* [2]Lit., *me and you* [a]Gen. 21:27, 32; 26:28 [b]Josh. 24:27

45 Then Jacob took [a]a stone and set it up *as* a pillar.

46 And Jacob said to his [1]kinsmen, "Gather stones." So they took stones and made a heap, and they ate there by the heap.

47 Now Laban [a]called it [1]Jegar-sahadutha, but Jacob called it [2]Galeed.

48 And Laban said, "[a]This heap is a witness between [1]you and me this day." Therefore it was named Galeed;

49 and [1a]Mizpah, for he said, "May the LORD watch between [2]you and me when we are [3]absent one from the other.

50 "If you mistreat my daughters, or if you take wives besides my daughters, *although* no man is with us, see, [a]God is witness between [1]you and me."

51 And Laban said to Jacob, "Behold this heap and behold the pillar which I have set between [1]you and me.

52 "This heap is a witness, and the pillar is a witness, that I will not pass by this heap to you for harm, and you will not pass by this heap and this pillar to me, for harm.

53 "[a]The God of Abraham and the God of Nahor, the God of their father, [b]judge between us." So Jacob swore by [c]the fear of his father Isaac.

54 Then Jacob [a]offered a sacrifice on the mountain, and called his [1]kinsmen to [2]the meal; and they ate [3]the meal and spent the night on the mountain.

55 [1]And early in the morning Laban arose, and [a]kissed his sons and his daughters and blessed them. Then Laban departed and returned to his place.

Jacob's Fear of Esau

32 NOW as Jacob went on his way, [a]the angels of God met him.

2 And Jacob said when he saw them, "This is God's [1]camp." So he named that place [2a]Mahanaim.

3 Then Jacob [a]sent messengers before him to his brother Esau in the land of [b]Seir, the [1]country of [c]Edom.

4 He also commanded them saying, "Thus you shall say to my lord Esau: 'Thus says your servant Jacob, "I have sojourned with Laban, and [a]stayed until now;

5 and [a]I have oxen and donkeys *and* flocks and male and female servants; and I have sent to tell my lord, [b]that I may find favor in your sight." ' "

6 And the messengers returned to Jacob, saying, "We came to your brother Esau, and furthermore [a]he is coming to meet you, and four hundred men are with him."

7 Then Jacob was [a]greatly afraid and distressed; and he divided the people who were with him, and the flocks and the herds and the camels, into two companies;

8 for he said, "If Esau comes to the one company and [1]attacks it, then the company which is left will escape."

9 And Jacob said, "O [a]God of my father Abraham and God of my father Isaac, O LORD, who didst say to me, '[b]Return to your country and to your relatives, and I will [1]prosper you,'

10 [1]I am unworthy [a]of all the lovingkindness and of all the [2]faithfulness which Thou hast shown to Thy servant; for with my staff *only* I crossed this Jordan, and now I have become two companies.

11 "[a]Deliver me, I pray, [b]from the hand of my brother, from the hand of Esau; for I fear him, lest he come and [1]attack me, the [c]mothers with the children.

12 "For Thou didst say, '[a]I will surely [1]prosper you, and [b]make your [2]descendants as the sand of the sea, which cannot be numbered for multitude.' "

13 So he spent the night there. Then he [1]selected from what [2]he had with him a [a]present for his brother Esau:

14 two hundred female goats and twenty male goats, two hundred ewes and twenty rams,

15 thirty milking camels and their colts, forty cows and ten bulls, twenty female donkeys and ten male donkeys.

16 And he delivered *them* into the hand of his servants, every drove by itself, and said to his servants, "Pass on before me, and put a space between droves."

17 And he commanded the [1]one in front, saying, "When my brother Esau meets you and asks you, saying, 'To whom do you belong, and where are you going, and to whom do these *animals* in front of you belong?'

18 then you shall say, '*These* belong to your servant Jacob; it is a present sent to my lord Esau. And behold, he also is behind us.' "

19 Then he commanded also the second and the third, and all those who followed the droves, saying, "After this manner you shall speak to Esau when you find him;

20 and you shall say, 'Behold, your servant Jacob also is behind us.' " For he said, "I will appease him with the present that goes before me. Then afterward I will see his face; perhaps he will accept me."

21 So the present passed on before him, while he himself spent that night in the camp.

22 Now he arose that same night and took his two wives and his two maids and his eleven children, and crossed the ford of the [a]Jabbok.

23 And he took them and sent them across the stream. And he sent across whatever he had.

Jacob Wrestles

24 Then Jacob was left alone, and a man [a]wrestled with him until daybreak.

25 And when he saw that he had not prevailed against him, he touched the socket of his thigh; so the socket of Jacob's thigh was dislocated while he wrestled with him.

---

45 [a]Gen. 28:18; Josh. 24:26, 27
46 [1]Lit., *brothers*
47 [1]I.e., the heap of witness, in Aram. [2]I.e., the heap of witness, in Heb. [a]Josh. 22:34
48 [1]Lit., *me and you* [a]Josh. 24:27
49 [1]Lit., *the Mizpah;* i.e., the watchtower [2]Lit., *me and you* [3]Lit., *hidden* [a]Judg. 11:29; 1 Sam. 7:5, 6
50 [1]Lit., *me and you* [a]Jer. 29:23; 42:5
51 [1]Lit., *me and you*
53 [a]Gen. 28:13 [b]Gen. 16:5 [c]Gen. 31:42
54 [1]Lit., *brothers* [2]Lit., *eat bread* [3]Lit., *bread* [a]Ex. 18:12
55 [1]Ch. 32:1 in Heb. [a]Gen. 31:28, 43
1 [a]2 Kin. 6:16, 17; Ps. 34:7
2 [1]Or, *company* [2]I.e., Two Camps, or, Two Companies [a]Josh. 21:38; 2 Sam. 2:8
3 [1]Lit., *field* [a]Gen. 27:41, 42; 32:7, 11 [b]Gen. 14:6; 33:14 [c]Gen. 25:30; 36:8, 9
4 [a]Gen. 31:41
5 [a]Gen. 30:43 [b]Gen. 33:8
6 [a]Gen. 33:1
7 [a]Gen. 32:11
8 [1]Lit., *smites*
9 [1]Lit., *do good with you* [a]Gen. 28:13; 31:42 [b]Gen. 28:15; 31:3, 13
10 [1]Lit., *I am less than all* [2]Or, *truth* [a]Gen. 24:27
11 [1]Lit., *smite* [a]Ps. 59:1, 2 [b]Gen. 27:41, 42; 33:4 [c]Hos. 10:14
12 [1]Lit., *do good with* [2]Lit., *seed* [a]Gen. 28:14 [b]Gen. 22:17
13 [1]Lit., *took* [2]Lit., *had come to his hand* [a]Gen. 43:11
17 [1]Lit., *first*
22 [a]Deut. 3:16; Josh. 12:2
24 [a]Hos. 12:3, 4

26 Then he said, "Let me go, for the
dawn is breaking." But he said, "[a]I will
not let you go unless you bless me."
27 So he said to him, "What is your
name?" And he said, "Jacob."
28 And [a]he said, "Your name shall no
longer be Jacob, but [1]Israel; for you
have striven with God and with men and
have prevailed."
29 Then [a]Jacob asked him and said,
"Please tell me your name." But he said,
"Why is it that you ask my name?" And
he blessed him there.
30 So Jacob named the place [1]Peniel,
for *he said,* "[a]I have seen God face to
face, yet my [2]life has been preserved."
31 Now the sun rose upon him just as
he crossed over [a]Penuel, and he was
limping on his thigh.
32 Therefore, to this day the sons of
Israel do not eat the sinew of the hip
which is on the socket of the thigh,
because he touched the socket of Jacob's
thigh in the sinew of the hip.

Jacob Meets Esau

33 THEN Jacob lifted his eyes and
looked, and behold, [a]Esau was
coming, and four hundred men with
him. So he divided the children [1]among
Leah and Rachel and the two maids.
2 And he put the maids and their
children [1]in front, and Leah and her
children [2]next, and Rachel and Joseph
[2]last.
3 But he himself passed on ahead of
them and [a]bowed down to the ground
seven times, until he came near to his
brother.
4 Then Esau ran to meet him and
embraced him, and [a]fell on his neck and
kissed him, and they wept.
5 And he lifted his eyes and saw the
women and the children, and said,
"[1]Who are these with you?" So he said,
"[a]The children whom God has graciously given your servant."
6 Then the maids came near [1]with
their children, and they bowed down.
7 And Leah likewise came near with
her children, and they bowed down; and
afterward Joseph came near with Rachel, and they bowed down.
8 And he said, "What do you mean
by [a]all this company which I have met?"
And he said, "[b]To find favor in the sight
of my lord."
9 But Esau said, "[a]I have plenty, my
brother; let what you have be your
own."
10 And Jacob said, "No, please, if
now I have found favor in your sight,
then take my present from my hand, [1]for
I see your face as one sees the face of
God, and you have received me favorably.
11 "Please take my [1a]gift which has
been brought to you, [b]because God has
dealt graciously with me, and because I
have [2]plenty." Thus he urged him and he
took *it.*
12 Then [1]Esau said, "Let us take our
journey and go, and I will go before
you."
13 But he said to him, "My lord
knows that the children are frail and that
the flocks and herds which are nursing
are [1]a care to me. And if they are driven
hard one day, all the flocks will die.
14 "Please let my lord pass on before
his servant; and I will proceed at my
leisure, according to the pace of the
cattle that are before me and according
to the pace of the children, until I come
to my lord at [a]Seir."
15 And Esau said, "Please let me leave
with you some of the people who are
with me." But he said, "[1]What need is
there? [a]Let me find favor in the sight of
my lord."
16 So Esau returned that day on his
way to Seir.
17 And Jacob journeyed to [1a]Succoth;
and built for himself a house, and made
booths for his livestock, therefore the
place is named Succoth.

Jacob Settles in Shechem

18 Now Jacob came safely to the city
of [a]Shechem, which is in the land of
Canaan, when he came from [b]Paddan-
aram, and camped before the city.
19 And [a]he bought the piece of land
where he had pitched his tent from the
hand of the sons of Hamor, Shechem's
father, for one hundred [1]pieces of
money.
20 Then he erected there an altar, and
called it [1]El-Elohe-Israel.

The Treachery of Jacob's Sons

34 NOW [a]Dinah the daughter of
Leah, whom she had borne to
Jacob, went out to [1]visit the daughters of
the land.
2 And when Shechem the son of
Hamor [a]the Hivite, the prince of the
land, saw her, he took her and lay with
her [1]by force.
3 And [1]he was deeply attracted to
Dinah the daughter of Jacob, and he
loved the girl and [2]spoke tenderly to her.
4 So Shechem [a]spoke to his father
Hamor, saying, "Get me this young girl
for a wife."
5 Now Jacob heard that he had defiled Dinah his daughter; but his sons
were with his livestock in the field, so
Jacob kept silent until they came in.
6 Then Hamor the father of Shechem
went out to Jacob to speak with him.
7 Now the sons of Jacob came in
from the field when they heard *it;* and
the men were grieved, and they were
very angry because he had done a [1a]dis-
graceful thing in Israel [2]by lying with
Jacob's daughter, for such a thing ought
not to be done.
8 But Hamor spoke with them, saying, "The soul of my son Shechem longs
for your daughter; please give her to him
[1]in marriage.

26 [a]Hos. 12:4

28 [1]I.e., he who strives with God; or, God strives [a]Gen. 35:10; 1 Kin. 18:31

29 [a]Judg. 13:17, 18

30 [1]I.e., the face of God [2]Lit., *soul* [a]Gen. 16:13; Ex. 24:10, 11; 33:20; Num. 12:8; Judg. 6:22; 13:22

31 [a]Judg. 8:8

1 [1]Or, *to* [a]Gen. 32:6

2 [1]Lit., *first* [2]Lit., *behind*

3 [a]Gen. 42:6; 43:26

4 [a]Gen. 45:14, 15

5 [1]Or, *What relation are these to you?* [a]Gen. 48:9; Ps. 127:3; Is. 8:18

6 [1]Lit., *they and*

8 [a]Gen. 32:13-16 [b]Gen. 32:5

9 [a]Gen. 27:39, 40

10 [1]Lit., *for therefore I have seen your face like seeing God's face*

11 [1]Lit., *blessing* [2]Lit., *all* [a]1 Sam. 25:27 [b]Gen. 30:43

12 [1]Lit., *he*

13 [1]Lit., *upon me*

14 [a]Gen. 32:3

15 [1]Lit., *Why this?* [a]Ruth 2:13

17 [1]I.e., booths [a]Josh. 13:27; Judg. 8:5, 14; Ps. 60:6

18 [a]Gen. 12:6; Josh. 24:1; Judg. 9:1 [b]Gen. 25:20; 28:2

19 [1]Heb., *qesitah* [a]Josh. 24:32; John 4:5

20 [1]I.e., God, the God of Israel

1 [1]Lit., *see* [a]Gen. 30:21

2 [1]Lit., *and humbled her* [a]Gen. 34:30

3 [1]Lit., *his soul clung* [2]Lit., *spoke to the heart of the girl*

4 [a]Judg. 14:2

7 [1]Lit., *senseless* [2]Lit., *to lie* [a]Deut. 22:20-30; Judg. 20:6; 2 Sam. 13:12

8 [1]Lit., *for a wife*

9"And intermarry with us; give your
daughters to us, and take our daughters
for yourselves.
10"Thus you shall [1]live with us, and
[a]the land shall be *open* before you; [1]live
and [b]trade in it, and [c]acquire property in
it."
11 Shechem also said to her father and
to her brothers, "If I find favor in your
sight, then I will give whatever you say
to me.
12"Ask me ever so much bridal payment and gift, and I will give according
as you say to me; but give me the girl [1]in
marriage."
13 But Jacob's sons answered Shechem and his father Hamor, with deceit,
and spoke to them, because he had
defiled Dinah their sister.
14 And they said to them, "We cannot
do this thing, to give our sister to [a]one
who is uncircumcised, for that would be
a disgrace to us.
15"Only on this *condition* will we
consent to you: if you will become like
us, in that every male of you be circumcised,
16 then we will give our daughters to
you, and we will take your daughters for
ourselves, and we will [1]live with you and
become one people.
17"But if you will not listen to us to be
circumcised, then we will take our
daughter and go."
18 Now their words seemed [1]reason-
able to Hamor and Shechem, Hamor's
son.
19 And the young man did not delay
to do the thing, because he was delighted
with Jacob's daughter. Now he was more
respected than all the household of his
father.
20 So Hamor and his son Shechem
came to the [a]gate of their city, and spoke
to the men of their city, saying,
21"These men are [1]friendly with us;
therefore let them [2]live in the land and
trade in it, for behold, the land is [3]large
enough for them. Let us take their
daughters [4]in marriage, and give our
daughters to them.
22"Only on this *condition* will the men
consent to us to [1]live with us, to become
one people: that every male among us be
circumcised as they are circumcised.
23"Will not their livestock and their
property and all their animals be ours?
Only let us consent to them, and they
will [1]live with us."
24 And [a]all who went out of the gate
of his city listened to Hamor and to his
son Shechem, and every male was circumcised, all who went out of the gate of
his city.
25 Now it came about on the third
day, when they were in pain, that two of
Jacob's sons, [a]Simeon and Levi, Dinah's
brothers, each took his sword and came
upon the city unawares, and killed every
male.
26 And they killed Hamor and his son
Shechem with the edge of the sword, and
took Dinah from Shechem's house, and
went forth.
27 Jacob's sons came upon the slain
and looted the city, because they had
defiled their sister.
28 They took their flocks and their
herds and their donkeys, and that which
was in the city and that which was in the
field;
29 and they captured and looted all
their wealth and all their little ones and
their wives, even all that *was* in the
houses.
30 Then Jacob said to Simeon and
Levi, "You have [a]brought trouble on me,
by [b]making me odious among the inhabitants of the land, among [c]the Canaanites and the Perizzites; and [1d]my
men being few in number, they will
gather together against me and [2]attack
me and I shall be destroyed, I and my
household."
31 But they said, "Should he [1]treat
our sister as a harlot?"

Jacob Moves to Bethel

35 THEN God said to Jacob,
"Arise, go up to [a]Bethel, and [1]live
there; and make an altar there to [b]God,
who appeared to you [c]when you fled
[2]from your brother Esau."
2 So Jacob said to his [a]household
and to all who were with him, "Put away
[b]the foreign gods which are among you,
and [c]purify yourselves, and change your
garments;
3 and let us arise and go up to
Bethel; and I will make [a]an altar there to
God, [b]who answered me in the day of
my distress, and [c]has been with me
[1]wherever I have gone."
4 So they gave to Jacob all the foreign gods which [1]they had, and the rings
which were in their ears; and Jacob hid
them under the [2]oak which was near
Shechem.
5 As they journeyed, there was [1a]a
great terror upon the cities which were
around them, and they did not pursue
the sons of Jacob.
6 So Jacob came to [a]Luz (that is,
Bethel), which is in the land of Canaan,
he and all the people who were with him.
7 And [a]he built an altar there, and
called the place [1]El-bethel, because there
God had revealed Himself to him, when
he fled [2]from his brother.
8 Now [a]Deborah, Rebekah's nurse,
died, and she was buried below Bethel
under the oak; it was named [1]Allon-
bacuth.

Jacob Is Named Israel

9 Then God appeared to Jacob again
when he came from Paddan-aram, and
He [a]blessed him.
10 And [a]God said to him,
"Your name is Jacob;
[1]You shall no longer be called
Jacob,
But Israel shall be your name."
Thus He called [2]him Israel.

10 [1]Lit., *dwell* [a]Gen. 13:9; 20:15 [b]Gen. 42:34 [c]Gen. 47:27
12 [1]Lit., *for a wife*
14 [a]Gen. 17:14
16 [1]Lit., *dwell*
18 [1]Lit., *good*
20 [a]Ruth 4:1; 2 Sam. 15:2
21 [1]Lit., *peaceful* [2]Lit., *dwell* [3]Lit., *wide of hands before them* [4]Lit., *to us for wives*
22 [1]Lit., *dwell*
23 [1]Lit., *dwell*
24 [a]Gen. 23:10
25 [a]Gen. 49:5-7
30 [1]Lit., *I, few in number* [2]Lit., *smite* [a]Josh. 7:25 [b]Ex. 5:21; 1 Sam. 13:4; 2 Sam. 10:6 [c]Gen. 13:7; 34:2 [d]Gen. 46:26, 27; Deut. 4:27; 1 Chr. 16:19; Ps. 105:12
31 [1]Or, *make*
1 [1]Lit., *dwell* [2]Lit., *from the face of* [a]Gen. 28:19 [b]Gen. 28:13 [c]Gen. 27:43
2 [a]Gen. 18:19; Josh. 24:15 [b]Gen. 31:19, 30, 34 [c]Ex. 19:10, 14
3 [1]Lit., *in the way which* [a]Gen. 28:20-22 [b]Ps. 107:6 [c]Gen. 28:15; 31:3, 42
4 [1]Lit., *were in their hand* [2]Or, *terebinth*
5 [1]Or, *a terror of God* [a]Ex. 15:16; 23:27; Deut. 2:25
6 [a]Gen. 28:19; 48:3
7 [1]I.e., the God of Bethel [2]Lit., *from the face of* [a]Gen. 35:3
8 [1]I.e., oak of weeping [a]Gen. 24:59
9 [a]Gen. 32:29
10 [1]Lit., *Your name* [2]Lit., *his name* [a]Gen. 17:5; 32:28

11 God also said to him,
"I am [1a]God Almighty;
[b]Be fruitful and multiply;
A nation and a [c]company of nations shall [2]come from you,
And [d]kings shall [2]come forth from [3]you.
12 "And [a]the land which I gave to Abraham and Isaac,
I will give it to you,
And I will give the land to your [1]descendants after you."
13 Then [a]God went up from him in
the place where He had spoken with
him.
14 And Jacob set up [a]a pillar in the
place where He had spoken with him, a
pillar of stone, and he poured out a
[1]libation on it; he also poured oil on it.
15 So Jacob named the place where
God had spoken with him, [1a]Bethel.
16 Then they journeyed from Bethel;
and when there was still some distance
to go to [a]Ephrath, Rachel began to give
birth and she [1]suffered severe labor.
17 And it came about when she was in
severe labor that the midwife said to her,
"Do not fear, for now [a]you have *another*
son."
18 And it came about as her soul was
departing (for she died), that she named
him [1]Ben-oni; but his father called him
[2]Benjamin.
19 So [a]Rachel died and was buried on
the way to [b]Ephrath (that is, Bethlehem).
20 And Jacob set up a pillar over her
grave; that is the [a]pillar of Rachel's
grave to this day.
21 Then Israel journeyed on and
pitched his tent beyond the [1a]tower of
[2]Eder.
22 And it came about while Israel was
dwelling in that land, that [a]Reuben went
and lay with Bilhah his father's concubine; and Israel heard *of it.*

The Sons of Israel

Now there were twelve sons of Jacob—
23 [a]the sons of Leah: Reuben, Jacob's
first-born, then Simeon and Levi and
Judah and Issachar and Zebulun;
24 [a]the sons of Rachel: Joseph and
Benjamin;
25 and [a]the sons of Bilhah, Rachel's
maid: Dan and Naphtali;
26 and [a]the sons of Zilpah, Leah's
maid: Gad and Asher. These are the
sons of Jacob who were born to him in
Paddan-aram.
27 And Jacob came to his father Isaac
at [a]Mamre of [b]Kiriath-arba (that is,
Hebron), where Abraham and Isaac had
sojourned.
28 Now the days of Isaac were [a]one
hundred and eighty years.
29 And Isaac breathed his last and
died, and was [a]gathered to his people, an
[b]old man [1]of ripe age; and [c]his sons
Esau and Jacob buried him.

Esau Moves

36 NOW these are *the records of* the
generations of [a]Esau (that is,
Edom).
2 Esau [a]took his wives from the
daughters of Canaan: Adah the daughter
of Elon the Hittite, and [b]Oholibamah
the daughter of Anah and the [c]granddaughter of Zibeon the Hivite;
3 also Basemath, Ishmael's daughter,
the sister of Nebaioth.
4 And Adah bore [a]Eliphaz to Esau,
and Basemath bore Reuel,
5 and Oholibamah bore Jeush and
Jalam and Korah. These are the sons of
Esau who were born to him in the land
of Canaan.
6 [a]Then Esau took his wives and his
sons and his daughters and all [1]his
household, and his livestock and all
his cattle and all his goods which he had
acquired in the land of Canaan, and
went to *another* land away from his
brother Jacob.
7 [a]For their property had become too
great for them to [1]live together, and the
[b]land where they [c]sojourned could not
sustain them because of their livestock.
8 So Esau lived in the hill country of
[a]Seir; Esau is [b]Edom.
9 These then are *the records of* the
generations of Esau the father of [1]the
Edomites in the hill country of Seir.

Descendants of Esau

10 These are the names of Esau's
sons: Eliphaz the son of Esau's wife
Adah, Reuel the son of Esau's wife
Basemath.
11 And the sons of Eliphaz were Teman, Omar, [1]Zepho and Gatam and
Kenaz.
12 And Timna was a concubine of
Esau's son Eliphaz and she bore [a]Amalek to Eliphaz. These are the sons of
Esau's wife Adah.
13 And these are the sons of Reuel:
Nahath and Zerah, Shammah and Mizzah. These were the sons of Esau's wife
Basemath.
14 And these were the sons of Esau's
wife Oholibamah, the daughter of Anah
and the [1]granddaughter of Zibeon: [2]she
bore to Esau, Jeush and Jalam and
Korah.
15 These are the chiefs of the sons of
Esau. The sons of Eliphaz, the first-born
of Esau, are chief Teman, chief Omar,
chief Zepho, chief Kenaz,
16 chief Korah, chief Gatam, chief
Amalek. These are the chiefs [1]descended
from Eliphaz in the land of Edom; these
are the sons of Adah.
17 And these are the sons of Reuel,
Esau's son: chief Nahath, chief Zerah,
chief Shammah, chief Mizzah. These are
the chiefs [1]descended from Reuel in the
land of Edom; these are the sons of
Esau's wife Basemath.
18 And these are the sons of Esau's
wife Oholibamah: chief Jeush, chief

11 [1]Heb., *El Shaddai* [2]Or, *come into being* [3]Lit., *your loins* [a]Gen. 17:1; 28:3; Ex. 6:3 [b]Gen. 9:1, 7 [c]Gen. 48:4 [d]Gen. 17:6, 16; 36:31
12 [1]Lit., *seed* [a]Gen. 12:7; 13:15; 26:3, 4; 28:13; Ex. 32:13
13 [a]Gen. 17:22; 18:33
14 [1]Or, *drink offering* [a]Gen. 28:18, 19; 31:45
15 [1]I.e., the house of God [a]Gen. 28:19
16 [1]Lit., *had difficulty in her giving birth* [a]Gen. 35:19; 48:7; Ruth 4:11; Mic. 5:2
17 [a]Gen. 30:24
18 [1]I.e., the son of my sorrow [2]I.e., the son of the right hand
19 [a]Gen. 48:7 [b]Ruth 1:2; 4:11; Mic. 5:2
20 [a]1 Sam. 10:2
21 [1]Heb., *Migdal-eder* [2]Or, *flock* [a]Mic. 4:8
22 [a]Gen. 49:4; 1 Chr. 5:1
23 [a]Gen. 29:31-35; 30:18-20; 46:8; Ex. 1:1-4
24 [a]Gen. 30:22-24; 35:18
25 [a]Gen. 30:5-8
26 [a]Gen. 30:10-13
27 [a]Gen. 13:18; 18:1; 23:19 [b]Josh. 14:15
28 [a]Gen. 25:26
29 [1]Lit., *and satisfied with days* [a]Gen. 25:8; 49:33 [b]Gen. 15:15 [c]Gen. 25:9

1 [a]Gen. 25:30
2 [a]Gen. 28:9 [b]Gen. 36:25 [c]Gen. 36:24
4 [a]1 Chr. 1:35
6 [1]Lit., *the souls of his house* [a]Gen. 12:5
7 [1]Lit., *dwell* [a]Gen. 13:6 [b]Gen. 17:8; Heb. 11:9 [c]1 Chr. 29:15; Ps. 39:12
8 [a]Gen. 32:3 [b]Gen. 36:1, 19
9 [1]Lit., *Edom*
11 [1]In 1 Chr. 1:36, *Zephi*
12 [a]Ex. 17:8-16; Num. 24:20; Deut. 25:17-19; 1 Sam. 15:2, 3
14 [1]Gr., *son* [2]Lit., *and she*
16 [1]Lit., *of Eliphaz*
17 [1]Lit., *of Reuel*

Jalam, chief Korah. These are the chiefs
[1]descended from Esau's wife Oholibamah, the daughter of Anah.
19 These are the sons of Esau (that is,
Edom), and these are their chiefs.
20 These are the sons of Seir [a]the
Horite, the inhabitants of the land:
Lotan and Shobal and Zibeon and
Anah,
21 and Dishon and Ezer and Dishan.
These are the chiefs [1]descended from the
Horites, the sons of Seir in the land of
Edom.
22 And the sons of Lotan were Hori
and [1]Hemam; and Lotan's sister was
Timna.
23 And these are the sons of Shobal:
[1]Alvan and Manahath and Ebal, [2]She-
pho and Onam.
24 And these are the sons of Zibeon:
Aiah and Anah—he is the Anah who
found the hot springs in the wilderness
when he was pasturing the donkeys of
his father Zibeon.
25 And these are the children of
Anah: Dishon, and Oholibamah, the
daughter of Anah.
26 And these are the sons of [1a]Di-
shon: [2]Hemdan and Eshban and Ithran
and Cheran.
27 These are the sons of Ezer: Bilhan
and Zaavan and [1]Akan.
28 These are the sons of Dishan: Uz
and Aran.
29 These are the chiefs [1]descended
from the Horites: chief Lotan, chief
Shobal, chief Zibeon, chief Anah,
30 chief Dishon, chief Ezer, chief
Dishan. These are the chiefs [1]descended
from the Horites, according to their
various chiefs in the land of Seir.
31 Now these are the kings who
reigned in the land of Edom before any
[a]king reigned over the sons of Israel.
32 [1a]Bela the son of Beor reigned in
Edom, and the name of his city was
Dinhabah.
33 Then Bela died, and Jobab the son
of Zerah of Bozrah became king in his
place.
34 Then Jobab died, and Husham of
the land of the Temanites became king
in his place.
35 Then Husham died, and Hadad the
son of Bedad, who [1]defeated Midian in
the field of Moab, became king in his
place; and the name of his city was
Avith.
36 Then Hadad died, and Samlah of
Masrekah became king in his place.
37 Then Samlah died, and Shaul of
Rehoboth on the *Euphrates* River became king in his place.
38 Then Shaul died, and Baal-hanan
the son of Achbor became king in his
place.
39 Then Baal-hanan the son of Achbor died, and [1]Hadar became king in his
place; and the name of his city was
[2]Pau; and his wife's name was Mehetabel, the daughter of Matred, daughter of
Mezahab.

18 [1]Lit., *of Oholibamah, Esau's wife*
20 [a]Gen. 14:6; Deut. 2:12, 22; 1 Chr. 1:38-42
21 [1]Lit., *of the Horites*
22 [1]In 1 Chr. 1:39, *Homam*
23 [1]In 1 Chr. 1:40, *Alian* [2]In 1 Chr. 1:40, *Shephi*
26 [1]Heb., *Dishan* [2]In 1 Chr. 1:41, *Hamran* [a]1 Chr. 1:41
27 [1]In 1 Chr. 1:42, *Jaakan*
29 [1]Lit., *of the Horites*
30 [1]Lit., *of the Horites*
31 [a]Gen. 17:6, 16; 35:11; 1 Chr. 1:43
32 [1]Lit., *And Bela* [a]1 Chr. 1:43
35 [1]Or, *smote*
39 [1]In 1 Chr. 1:50, *Hadad* [2]In 1 Chr. 1:50, *Pai*
40 [1]Lit., *of Esau* [2]In 1 Chr. 1:51, *Aliah*
43 [1]Heb., *Edom*
1 [1]Lit., *of his father's sojournings* [a]Gen. 17:8; 28:4
2 [a]Gen. 41:46 [b]Gen. 35:25, 26 [c]1 Sam. 2:22-24
3 [1]Or, *full-length robe* [a]Gen. 44:20 [b]Gen. 37:23, 32
4 [1]Lit., *in peace* [a]Gen. 27:41; 1 Sam. 17:28
5 [1]Lit., *dreamed* [a]Gen. 28:12; 31:10, 11, 24
6 [1]Lit., *dreamed*
7 [a]Gen. 42:6, 9; 43:26; 44:14
8 [a]Gen. 49:26; Deut. 33:16
9 [1]Lit., *dreamed*
10 [1]Lit., *dreamed* [a]Gen. 27:29
11 [a]Acts 7:9 [b]Dan. 7:28; Luke 2:19, 51
13 [1]Lit., *Behold me.* [a]Gen. 33:18-20

40 Now these are the names of the
chiefs [1]descended from Esau, according
to their families *and* their localities, by
their names: chief Timna, chief [2]Alvah,
chief Jetheth,
41 chief Oholibamah, chief Elah, chief
Pinon,
42 chief Kenaz, chief Teman, chief
Mibzar,
43 chief Magdiel, chief Iram. These
are the chiefs of Edom (that is, Esau, the
father of [1]the Edomites), according to
their habitations in the land of their
possession.

Joseph's Dream

37 NOW Jacob lived in [a]the land
[1]where his father had sojourned,
in the land of Canaan.
2 These are *the records of* the generations of Jacob.
Joseph, when [a]seventeen years of age,
was pasturing the flock with his brothers
while he was *still* a youth, along with
[b]the sons of Bilhah and the sons of
Zilpah, his father's wives. And Joseph
brought back a [c]bad report about them
to their father.
3 Now Israel loved Joseph more than
all his sons, because he was [a]the son of
his old age; and he made him a [1b]vari-
colored tunic.
4 And his brothers saw that their
father loved him more than all his brothers; and *so* they [a]hated him and could
not speak to him [1]on friendly terms.
5 Then Joseph [1a]had a dream, and
when he told it to his brothers, they
hated him even more.
6 And he said to them, "Please listen
to this dream which I have [1]had;
7 for behold, we were binding
sheaves in the field, and lo, my sheaf
rose up and also stood erect; and behold, your sheaves gathered around and
[a]bowed down to my sheaf."
8 Then his brothers said to him,
"[a]Are you actually going to reign over
us? Or are you really going to rule over
us?" So they hated him even more for his
dreams and for his words.
9 Now he [1]had still another dream,
and related it to his brothers, and said,
"Lo, I have [1]had still another dream;
and behold, the sun and the moon and
eleven stars were bowing down to me."
10 And he related *it* to his father and
to his brothers; and his father rebuked
him and said to him, "What is this
dream that you have [1]had? Shall I and
your mother and [a]your brothers actually
come to bow ourselves down before you
to the ground?"
11 And [a]his brothers were jealous of
him, but his father [b]kept the saying *in
mind.*
12 Then his brothers went to pasture
their father's flock in Shechem.
13 And Israel said to Joseph, "Are not
your brothers pasturing *the flock* in
[a]Shechem? Come, and I will send you to
them." And he said to him, "[1]I will go."

14 Then he said to him, “Go now and see about the welfare of your brothers and the welfare of the flock; and bring word back to me.” So he sent him from the valley of [a]Hebron, and he came to Shechem.

15 And a man found him, and behold, he was wandering in the field; and the man asked him, [1]“What are you looking for?”

16 And he said, “I am looking for my brothers; please tell me where they are pasturing *the flock.*”

17 Then the man said, “They have moved from here; for I heard *them* say, ‘Let us go to [a]Dothan.’ ” So Joseph went after his brothers and found them at Dothan.

The Plot against Joseph

18 [1]When they saw him from a distance and before he came close to them, they [a]plotted against him to put him to death.

19 And they said to one another, “[1]Here comes this dreamer!

20 “Now then, come and let us kill him and throw him into one of the pits; and [a]we will say, ‘A wild beast devoured him.’ Then let us see what will become of his dreams!”

21 But [a]Reuben heard *this* and rescued him out of their hands and said, “Let us not [1]take his life.”

22 Reuben further said to them, “Shed no blood. Throw him into this pit that is in the wilderness, but do not lay hands on him”—that he might rescue him out of their hands, to restore him to his father.

23 So it came about, when Joseph [1]reached his brothers, that they stripped Joseph of his [2]tunic, the varicolored tunic that was on him;

24 and they took him and threw him into the pit. Now the pit was empty, without any water in it.

25 Then they sat down to eat [1]a meal. And as they raised their eyes and looked, behold, a caravan of [a]Ishmaelites was coming from Gilead, with their camels bearing [2b]aromatic gum and [3c]balm and [4]myrrh, [5]on their way to bring *them* down to Egypt.

26 And Judah said to his brothers, “What profit is it for us to kill our brother and [a]cover up his blood?

27 “[a]Come and let us sell him to the Ishmaelites and not lay our hands on him; for he is our brother, our *own* flesh.” And his brothers listened *to him.*

28 Then some [a]Midianite traders passed by, so they pulled *him* up and lifted Joseph out of the pit, and [b]sold [1]him to the Ishmaelites for twenty *shekels* of silver. Thus [c]they brought Joseph into Egypt.

29 Now Reuben returned to the pit, and behold, Joseph was not in the pit; so he [a]tore his garments.

30 And he returned to his brothers and said, “[a]The boy is not *there;* as for me, where am I to go?”

31 So [a]they took Joseph’s tunic, and slaughtered a male goat, and dipped the tunic in the blood;

32 and they sent the varicolored tunic and brought it to their father and said, “We found this; please [1]examine *it* to *see* whether it is your son’s tunic or not.”

33 Then he [1]examined it and said, “It is my son’s tunic. [a]A wild beast has devoured him; [b]Joseph has surely been torn to pieces!”

34 So Jacob [a]tore his clothes, and put sackcloth on his loins, and mourned for his son many days.

35 Then all his sons and all his daughters arose to comfort him, but he refused to be comforted. And he said, “Surely I will [a]go down to Sheol in mourning for my son.” So his father wept for him.

36 Meanwhile, the [1]Midianites [a]sold him in Egypt to Potiphar, Pharaoh’s officer, the captain of the bodyguard.

Judah and Tamar

38 AND it came about at that time, that Judah [1]departed from his brothers, and [2]visited a certain [a]Adullamite, whose name was Hirah.

2 And Judah saw there a daughter of a certain Canaanite whose name was [a]Shua; and he took her and went in to her.

3 So she conceived and bore a son and he named him [a]Er.

4 Then she conceived again and bore a son and named him [a]Onan.

5 And she bore still another son and named him [a]Shelah; and it was at Chezib [1]that she bore him.

6 Now Judah took a wife for Er his first-born, and her name *was* Tamar.

7 But [a]Er, Judah’s first-born, was evil in the sight of the LORD, so the LORD took his life.

8 Then Judah said to Onan, “[a]Go in to your brother’s wife, and perform your duty as a brother-in-law to her, and raise up [1]offspring for your brother.”

9 And Onan knew that the [1a]offspring would not be his; so it came about that when he went in to his brother’s wife, he [2]wasted his seed on the ground, in order not to give [1]offspring to his brother.

10 But what he did was displeasing in the sight of the LORD; so He [a]took his life also.

11 Then Judah said to his daughter-in-law Tamar, “[a]Remain a widow in your father’s house until my son Shelah grows up”; for he [1]thought, “[2]*I am afraid* that he too may die like his brothers.” So Tamar went and lived in her father’s house.

12 Now [1]after a considerable time Shua’s daughter, the wife of Judah, died; and when [2]the time of mourning was ended, Judah went up to his sheepshearers at [a]Timnah, he and his friend Hirah the Adullamite.

13 And it was told to Tamar, “[1]Behold, your father-in-law is going up to [a]Timnah to shear his sheep.”

14 [a]Gen. 13:18; 23:2, 19; 35:27; Josh. 14:14, 15; Judg. 1:10
15 [1]Lit., *saying, “What . . .?”*
17 [a]2 Kin. 6:13
18 [1]Or, *And*
[a]Ps. 31:13; 37:12, 32; Mark 14:1; John 11:53; Acts 23:12
19 [1]Lit., *Behold, this master of dreams comes*
20 [a]Gen. 37:32, 33
21 [1]Lit., *smite his soul*
[a]Gen. 42:22
23 [1]Lit., *came to* [2]Or, *full-length robe*
25 [1]Lit., *bread* [2]Or, *ladanum spice* [3]Or, *mastic* [4]Or, *resinous bark* [5]Lit., *going*
[a]Gen. 16:11, 12; 37:28; 39:1 [b]Gen. 43:11 [c]Jer. 8:22; 46:11
26 [a]Gen. 37:20
27 [a]Gen. 42:21
28 [1]Lit., *Joseph*
[a]Gen. 37:25; Judg. 6:1-3; 8:22, 24 [b]Gen. 45:4, 5; Ps. 105:17; Acts 7:9 [c]Gen. 39:1
29 [a]Gen. 37:34; 44:13
30 [a]Gen. 42:13, 36
31 [a]Gen. 37:3, 23
32 [1]Or, *recognize*
33 [1]Or, *recognized*
[a]Gen. 37:20 [b]Gen. 44:28
34 [a]Gen. 37:29
35 [a]Gen. 25:8; 35:29; 42:38; 44:29, 31
36 [1]Lit., *Medanites*
[a]Gen. 39:1

1 [1]Lit., *went down* [2]Lit., *turned aside to*
[a]Josh. 15:35; 1 Sam. 22:1
2 [a]1 Chr. 2:3
3 [a]Gen. 46:12; Num. 26:19
4 [a]Gen. 46:12
5 [1]Lit., *when*
[a]Num. 26:20
7 [a]Gen. 46:12; Num. 26:19; 1 Chr. 2:3
8 [1]Lit., *seed*
[a]Deut. 25:5, 6; Matt. 22:24
9 [1]Lit., *seed* [2]Lit., *spilled on the ground*
[a]Deut. 25:6
10 [a]Gen. 46:12; Num. 26:19
11 [1]Lit., *said* [2]Lit., *Lest he also die*
[a]Ruth 1:12, 13
12 [1]Lit., *the days became many and* [2]Lit., *Judah was comforted, he*
[a]Josh. 15:10, 57
13 [1]Lit., *saying, Behold*
[a]Josh. 15:10, 57; Judg. 14:1

14 So she [1]removed her widow's garments and [a]covered *herself* with a [2]veil, and wrapped herself, and sat in the gateway of [3]Enaim, which is on the road to Timnah; for she saw that Shelah had grown up, and [b]she had not been given to him as a wife.

15 When Judah saw her, he thought she *was* a harlot, for she had covered her face.

16 So he turned aside to her by the road, and said, "[1]Here now, let me come in to you"; for he did not know that she was his daughter-in-law. And she said, "What will you give me, that you may come in to me?"

17 He said, therefore, "I will send you a [1]kid from the flock." She said, moreover, "Will you give a pledge until you send *it?*"

18 And he said, "What pledge shall I give you?" And she said, "[a]Your seal and your cord, and your staff that is in your hand." So he gave *them* to her, and went in to her, and she conceived by him.

19 Then she arose and departed, and [1]removed her [2]veil and put on her widow's garments.

20 When Judah sent the [1]kid by his friend the Adullamite, to receive the pledge from the woman's hand, he did not find her.

21 And he asked the men of her place, saying, "Where is the temple prostitute who was by the road at Enaim?" But they said, "There has been no temple prostitute here."

22 So he returned to Judah, and said, "I did not find her; and furthermore, the men of the place said, 'There has been no temple prostitute here.' "

23 Then Judah said, "Let her [1]keep them, lest we become a laughingstock. [2]After all, I sent this kid, but you did not find her."

24 Now it was about three months later that Judah was informed, "[1]Your daughter-in-law Tamar has played the harlot, and behold, she is also with child by harlotry." Then Judah said, "Bring her out and [a]let her be burned!"

25 It was while she was being brought out that she sent to her father-in-law, saying, "I am with child by the man to whom these things belong." And she said, "[a]Please examine and see, whose signet ring and cords and staff are these?"

26 And Judah recognized *them,* and said, "[a]She is more righteous than I, inasmuch as [b]I did not give her to my son Shelah." And he did not [1]have relations with her again.

27 And it came about at the time she was giving birth, that behold, there were [a]twins in her womb.

28 Moreover, it took place while she was giving birth, one put out a hand, and the midwife took and tied a scarlet *thread* on his hand, saying, "This one came out first."

29 But it came about as he drew back his hand, that behold, his brother came out. Then she said, "What a breach you have made for yourself!" So he was named [1a]Perez.

30 And afterward his brother came out who had the scarlet *thread* on his hand; and he was named [1a]Zerah.

Joseph's Success in Egypt

39 NOW Joseph had been taken down to Egypt; and Potiphar, an Egyptian officer of Pharaoh, the captain of the bodyguard, bought him [1]from the [a]Ishmaelites, who had taken him down there.

2 And [a]the LORD was with Joseph, so he became a [1]successful man. And he was in the house of his master, the Egyptian.

3 Now his master [a]saw that the LORD was with him and *how* the LORD [b]caused all that he did to prosper in his hand.

4 So Joseph [a]found favor in his sight, and [1]became his personal servant; and he made him overseer over his house, and [b]all that he owned he put in his [2]charge.

5 And it came about that from the time he made him overseer in his house, and over all that he owned, the LORD [a]blessed the Egyptian's house on account of Joseph; thus [b]the LORD's blessing was upon all that he owned, in the house and in the field.

6 So he left everything he owned in Joseph's [1]charge; and with him *there* he did not [2]concern himself with anything except the [3]food which he [4]ate. Now Joseph was [a]handsome in form and appearance.

7 And it came about after these events [a]that his master's wife [1]looked with desire at Joseph, and she said, "[b]Lie with me."

8 But [a]he refused and said to his master's wife, "Behold, with me *here,* my master [1]does not concern himself with anything in the house, and he has put all that he owns in my [2]charge.

9 "[1a]There is no one greater in this house than I, and he has withheld nothing from me except you, because you are his wife. How then could I do this great evil, and [b]sin against God?"

10 And it came about as she spoke to Joseph day after day, that he did not listen to her to lie beside her, *or* be with her.

11 Now it happened [1]one day that he went into the house to do his work, and none of the men of the household was there inside.

12 And she caught him by his garment, saying, "Lie with me!" And he left his garment in her hand and fled, and went outside.

13 [1]When she saw that he had left his garment in her hand, and had fled outside,

14 [1]Lit., *removed from herself* [2]Or, *shawl* [3]In Josh. 15:34, *Enam* [a]Gen. 24:65 [b]Gen. 38:11, 26
16 [1]Or, *Come, now*
17 [1]Lit., *kid of goats*
18 [a]Gen. 38:25; 41:42
19 [1]Lit., *removed from herself* [2]Or, *shawl*
20 [1]Lit., *kid of goats by the hand of*
23 [1]Lit., *take for herself* [2]Lit., *Behold*
24 [1]Lit., *saying, Your* [a]Lev. 21:9
25 [a]Gen. 37:32
26 [1]Lit., *know her yet again* [a]1 Sam. 24:17 [b]Gen. 38:14
27 [a]Gen. 25:24-26
29 [1]I.e., a breach [a]Gen. 46:12; Ruth 4:12
30 [1]I.e., a dawning or brightness [a]1 Chr. 2:4
1 [1]Lit., *from the hand of* [a]Gen. 37:25, 28, 36; Ps. 105:17
2 [1]Or, *prosperous* [a]Gen. 39:3, 21, 23; Acts 7:9
3 [a]Gen. 21:22; 26:28 [b]Ps. 1:3
4 [1]Or, *ministered to him* [2]Lit., *hand* [a]Gen. 18:3; 19:19 [b]Gen. 24:2; 39:8, 22
5 [a]Gen. 30:27 [b]Deut. 28:3, 4, 11
6 [1]Lit., *hand* [2]Lit., *know* [3]Lit., *bread* [4]Or, *used to eat* [a]Gen. 29:17; 1 Sam. 16:12
7 [1]Lit., *lifted up her eyes at* [a]Prov. 7:15-20 [b]2 Sam. 13:11
8 [1]Lit., *does not know what is in the house* [2]Lit., *hand* [a]Prov. 6:23, 24
9 [1]Or, *He is not greater* [a]Gen. 41:40 [b]Gen. 20:6; 42:18; 2 Sam. 12:13; Ps. 51:4
11 [1]Lit., *about this day*
13 [1]Lit., *And it came about when*

14 she called to the men of her household, and said to them, "See, he has brought in a [1]Hebrew to us to make sport of us; he came in to me to lie with me, and I [2]screamed.

15 "And it came about when he heard that I raised my voice and [1]screamed, that he left his garment beside me and fled, and went outside."

16 So she [1]left his garment beside her until his master came home.

17 Then she [a]spoke to him [1]with these words, "[2]The Hebrew slave, whom you brought to us, came in to me to make sport of me;

18 and it happened as I raised my voice and [1]screamed, that he left his garment beside me and fled outside."

Joseph Imprisoned

19 Now it came about when his master heard the words of his wife, which she spoke to him, saying, "[1]This is what your slave did to me," that [a]his anger burned.

20 So Joseph's master took him and [a]put him into the jail, the place where the king's prisoners were confined; and he was there in the jail.

21 But [a]the LORD was with Joseph and extended kindness to him, and [b]gave him favor in the sight of the chief jailer.

22 And the chief jailer [a]committed to Joseph's [1]charge all the prisoners who were in the jail; so that whatever was done there, he was [2]responsible *for it.*

23 [a]The chief jailer did not supervise anything under [1]Joseph's charge because [b]the LORD was with him; and whatever he did, [c]the LORD made to prosper.

Joseph Interprets a Dream

40 THEN it came about after these things [a]the cupbearer and the baker for the king of Egypt offended their lord, the king of Egypt.

2 And Pharaoh was [a]furious with his two officials, the chief cupbearer and the chief baker.

3 So he put them in confinement in the house of the [a]captain of the bodyguard, in the jail, the *same* place where Joseph was imprisoned.

4 And the captain of the bodyguard put Joseph in charge of them, and he [1]took care of them; and they were in confinement for [2]some time.

5 Then the cupbearer and the baker for the king of Egypt, who were confined in jail, both had a dream the same night, each man with his *own* dream *and* each dream with its *own* interpretation.

6 [1]When Joseph came to them in the morning and observed them, [2]behold, they were dejected.

7 And he asked Pharaoh's officials who were with him in confinement in his master's house, "[1][a]Why are your faces so sad today?"

8 Then they said to him, "[a]We have [1]had a dream and there is no one to interpret it." Then Joseph said to them, "[b]Do not interpretations belong to God? Tell *it* to me, please."

9 So the chief cupbearer told his dream to Joseph, and said to him, "In my dream, [1]behold, *there was* a vine in front of me;

10 and on the vine *were* three branches. And as it was budding, its blossoms came out, *and* its clusters produced ripe grapes.

11 "Now Pharaoh's cup was in my hand; so I took the grapes and squeezed them into Pharaoh's cup, and I put the cup into Pharaoh's [1]hand."

12 Then Joseph said to him, "This is the [a]interpretation of it: the three branches are three days;

13 within three more days Pharaoh will [1]lift up your head and restore you to your [2]office; and you will put Pharaoh's cup into his hand according to your former custom when you were his cupbearer.

14 "Only [1]keep me in mind when it goes well with you, and please [a]do me a kindness [2]by mentioning me to Pharaoh, and get me out of this house.

15 "For [a]I was in fact kidnapped from the land of the Hebrews, and even here I have done nothing that they should have put me into the [1]dungeon."

16 When the chief baker saw that he had interpreted favorably, he said to Joseph, "I also *saw* in my dream, and behold, *there were* three baskets of white bread on my head;

17 and in the top basket *there were* some of all [1]sorts of baked food for Pharaoh, and the birds were eating them out of the basket on my head."

18 Then Joseph answered and said, "This is its interpretation: the three baskets are three days;

19 within three more days Pharaoh will lift up your head from you and will hang you on a tree; and the birds will eat your flesh off you."

20 Thus it came about on the third day, *which was* [a]Pharaoh's birthday, that he made a feast for all his servants; [b]and he lifted up the head of the chief cupbearer and the head of the chief baker among his servants.

21 And he restored the chief cupbearer to his [1]office, and [a]he put the cup into Pharaoh's [2]hand;

22 but [a]he hanged the chief baker, just as Joseph had interpreted to them.

23 Yet the chief cupbearer did not remember Joseph, but [a]forgot him.

Pharaoh's Dream

41 NOW it happened at the end of two full years that Pharaoh had a dream, and behold, he was standing by the Nile.

2 And lo, from the Nile there came up seven cows, sleek and [1]fat; and they grazed in the [a]marsh grass.

3 Then behold, seven other cows came up after them from the Nile, ugly and [1]gaunt, and they stood by the *other* cows on the bank of the Nile.

14 [1]Lit., *Hebrew man* [2]Lit., *called with a great voice.*
15 [1]Lit., *called out*
16 [1]Lit., *let . . . lie beside*
17 [1]Lit., *according to* [2]Lit., *saying, "The* [a]Ex. 23:1; Prov. 26:28
18 [1]Lit., *called out*
19 [1]Lit., *According to these things your slave* [a]Prov. 6:34
20 [a]Gen. 40:3; Ps. 105:18
21 [a]Gen. 39:2; Ps. 105:19; Acts 7:9 [b]Ex. 3:21; 11:3; 12:36
22 [1]Lit., *hand* [2]Lit., *the doer* [a]Gen. 39:4; 40:3, 4
23 [1]Lit., *his hand* [a]Gen. 39:3, 8 [b]Gen. 39:2, 3 [c]Gen. 39:3

1 [a]Gen. 40:11, 13; Neh. 1:11
2 [a]Prov. 16:14
3 [a]Gen. 39:1, 20
4 [1]Lit., *ministered to* [2]Lit., *days*
6 [1]Or, *And* [2]Lit., *and behold*
7 [1]Lit., *saying, Why* [a]Neh. 2:2
8 [1]Lit., *dreamed* [a]Gen. 41:15 [b]Gen. 41:16; Dan. 2:27, 28
9 [1]Lit., *and behold*
11 [1]Lit., *palm*
12 [a]Dan. 2:36; 4:18, 19
13 [1]Or possibly, *forgive you* [2]Lit., *place*
14 [1]Lit., *remember me with yourself* [2]Lit., *and mention* [a]Josh. 2:12; 1 Sam. 20:14; 1 Kin. 2:7
15 [1]Or, *pit* [a]Gen. 37:26-28
17 [1]Lit., *food for Pharaoh made by a baker*
20 [a]Matt. 14:6 [b]2 Kin. 25:27; Jer. 52:31
21 [1]Lit., *wine-pouring* [2]Lit., *palm* [a]Gen. 40:13
22 [a]Gen. 40:19; Esth. 7:10
23 [a]Job 19:14; Ps. 31:12; Eccl. 9:15

2 [1]Lit., *fat of flesh* [a]Job 8:11; Is. 19:6, 7
3 [1]Lit., *lean of flesh*

4 And the ugly and [1]gaunt cows ate
up the seven sleek and fat cows. Then
Pharaoh awoke.
5 And he fell asleep and dreamed a
second time; and behold, seven ears of
grain came up on a single stalk, plump
and good.
6 Then behold, seven ears, thin and
scorched by the east wind, sprouted up
after them.
7 And the thin ears swallowed up the
seven plump and full ears. Then Pharaoh
awoke, and behold, *it was* a dream.
8 Now it came about in the morning
that [a]his spirit was troubled, so he sent
and called for all the [1b]magicians of
Egypt, and all its [c]wise men. And Pharaoh told them his [2]dreams, but [d]there
was no one who could interpret them to
Pharaoh.
9 Then the chief cupbearer spoke to
Pharaoh, saying, "I would make mention
today of [a]my *own* [1]offenses.
10 "Pharaoh was [a]furious with his
servants, and [b]he put me in confinement
in the house of the captain of the bodyguard, *both* me and the chief baker.
11 "And [a]we had a dream [1]on the same
night, [2]he and I; each of us dreamed
according to the interpretation of his
own dream.
12 "Now a Hebrew youth *was* with us
there, a [a]servant of the captain of the
bodyguard, and we related *them* to him,
and [b]he interpreted our dreams for us.
To each one he interpreted according to
his *own* dream.
13 "And it came about that just [a]as he
interpreted for us, so it happened; he
restored me in my [1]office, but he hanged
him."

Joseph Interprets

14 Then Pharaoh sent and [a]called for
Joseph, and they [b]hurriedly brought him
out of the dungeon; and when he had
shaved himself and changed his clothes,
he came to Pharaoh.
15 And Pharaoh said to Joseph, "I
have had a dream, [a]but no one can
interpret it; and [b]I have heard [1]it said
about you, that [2]when you hear a dream
you can interpret it."
16 Joseph then answered Pharaoh,
saying, "[1a]It is not in me; [b]God will
[2]give Pharaoh a favorable answer."
17 So Pharaoh spoke to Joseph, "In
my dream, behold, I was standing on the
bank of the Nile;
18 and behold, seven cows, [1]fat and
sleek came up out of the Nile; and they
grazed in the marsh grass.
19 "And lo, seven other cows came up
after them, poor and very ugly and
[1]gaunt, such as I had never seen for
[2]ugliness in all the land of Egypt;
20 and the lean and [1]ugly cows ate up
the first seven fat cows.
21 "Yet when they had [1]devoured
them, it could not be [2]detected that they
had [1]devoured them; [3]for they were just
as ugly as [4]before. Then I awoke.

4 [1]Lit., *lean of flesh*

8 [1]Or, *soothsayer priests* [2]Lit., *dream* [a]Dan. 2:1, 3 [b]Ex. 7:11, 22; Dan. 1:20; 2:2 [c]Matt. 2:1 [d]Dan. 2:27; 4:7

9 [1]Or, *sins* [a]Gen. 40:14, 23

10 [a]Gen. 40:2, 3 [b]Gen. 39:20

11 [1]Lit., *one night* [2]Lit., *I and he* [a]Gen. 40:5

12 [a]Gen. 37:36 [b]Gen. 40:12

13 [1]Lit., *place* [a]Gen. 40:21, 22

14 [a]Ps. 105:20 [b]Dan. 2:25

15 [1]Lit., *about you, saying* [2]Lit., *you hear a dream to interpret it* [a]Gen. 41:8 [b]Dan. 5:16

16 [1]Lit., *Apart from me* [2]Lit., *answer the peace of Pharaoh* [a]Dan. 2:30; Zech. 4:6; Acts 3:12; 2 Cor. 3:5 [b]Gen. 40:8; 41:25, 28, 32; Deut. 29:29; Dan. 2:22, 28, 47

18 [1]Lit., *fat of flesh*

19 [1]Lit., *lean of flesh* [2]Lit., *badness*

20 [1]Lit., *bad*

21 [1]Lit., *entered their inward parts* [2]Or, *known* [3]Lit., *and* [4]Lit., *in the beginning*

24 [1]Or, *soothsayer priests* [a]Is. 8:19; Dan. 4:7

25 [1]Lit., *dream is* [a]Gen. 41:28, 32; Dan. 2:28, 29, 45

26 [1]Lit., *dream is*

27 [a]2 Kin. 8:1

28 [1]Lit., *That is the thing which I spoke* [a]Gen. 41:25, 32

29 [a]Gen. 41:47

30 [1]Lit., *arise* [2]Lit., *destroy* [a]Gen. 41:54, 56; 47:13; Ps. 105:16

32 [a]Gen. 41:25, 28

33 [a]Gen. 41:39

34 [1]Lit., *over*

35 [a]Gen. 41:48

37 [1]Lit., *word* [2]Lit., *in the sight of*

38 [a]Job 32:8; Dan. 4:8, 9, 18; 5:11, 14

39 [a]Gen. 41:33

40 [1]Lit., *mouth* [2]Lit., *kiss* [a]Ps. 105:21; Acts 7:10

22 "I saw also in my dream, and behold, seven ears, full and good, came up
on a single stalk;
23 and lo, seven ears, withered, thin,
and scorched by the east wind, sprouted
up after them;
24 and the thin ears swallowed the
seven good ears. Then [a]I told it to the
[1]magicians, but there was no one who
could explain it to me."
25 Now Joseph said to Pharaoh, "Pharaoh's [1]dreams are one *and the same;*
[a]God has told to Pharaoh what He is
about to do.
26 "The seven good cows are seven
years; and the seven good ears are seven
years; the [1]dreams are one *and the same.*
27 "And the seven lean and ugly cows
that came up after them are seven years,
and the seven thin ears scorched by the
east wind [a]shall be seven years of famine.
28 "[1]It is as I have spoken to Pharaoh:
[a]God has shown to Pharaoh what He is
about to do.
29 "Behold, [a]seven years of great abundance are coming in all the land of
Egypt;
30 and after them [a]seven years of
famine will [1]come, and all the abundance will be forgotten in the land of
Egypt; and the famine will [2]ravage the
land.
31 "So the abundance will be unknown
in the land because of that subsequent
famine; for it *will be* very severe.
32 "Now as for the repeating of the
dream to Pharaoh twice, *it means* that
[a]the matter is determined by God, and
God will quickly bring it about.
33 "And now let Pharaoh look for a
man [a]discerning and wise, and set him
over the land of Egypt.
34 "Let Pharaoh take action to appoint
overseers [1]in charge of the land, and let
him exact a fifth *of the produce* of the
land of Egypt in the seven years of
abundance.
35 "Then let them [a]gather all the food
of these good years that are coming, and
store up the grain for food in the cities
under Pharaoh's authority, and let them
guard *it.*
36 "And let the food become as a
reserve for the land for the seven years
of famine which will occur in the land of
Egypt, so that the land may not perish
during the famine."
37 Now the [1]proposal seemed good
[2]to Pharaoh and [2]to all his servants.

Joseph Is Made a Ruler of Egypt

38 Then Pharaoh said to his servants,
"Can we find a man like this, [a]in whom
is a divine spirit?"
39 So Pharaoh said to Joseph, "Since
God has informed you of all this, there is
no one so [a]discerning and wise as you
are.
40 "[a]You shall be over my house, and
according to your [1]command all my
people shall [2]do homage; only in the
throne I will be greater than you."

41 And Pharaoh said to Joseph, "See I
have set you [a]over all the land of Egypt."
42 Then Pharaoh [a]took off his signet
ring from his hand, and put it on Joseph's hand, and clothed him in garments of fine linen, and [b]put the gold
necklace around his neck.
43 And he had him ride in [1]his second
chariot; and they proclaimed before
him, "[2]Bow the knee!" And he set him
over all the land of Egypt.
44 Moreover, Pharaoh said to Joseph,
"*Though* I am Pharaoh, yet [a]without
[1]your permission no one shall raise his
hand or foot in all the land of Egypt."
45 Then Pharaoh named Joseph
[1]Zaphenath-paneah; and he gave him
Asenath, the daughter of Potiphera
priest of [2a]On, as his wife. And Joseph
went forth over the land of Egypt.
46 Now Joseph was [a]thirty years old
when he [1]stood before Pharaoh, king of
Egypt. And Joseph went out from the
presence of Pharaoh, and went through
all the land of Egypt.
47 And during the seven years of
plenty the land brought forth [1]abun-
dantly.
48 So he gathered all the food of *these*
seven years which occurred in the land
of Egypt, and placed the food in the
cities; he placed in every city the food
from its own surrounding fields.
49 Thus Joseph stored up grain [1]in
great abundance like the sand of the sea,
until he stopped [2]measuring *it*, for it was
[3]beyond measure.

The Sons of Joseph

50 Now before the year of famine
came, [a]two sons were born to Joseph,
whom Asenath, the daughter of Potiphera priest of [1]On, bore to him.
51 And Joseph named the first-born
[1]Manasseh, "For," *he said,* "God has
made me forget all my trouble and all
my father's household."
52 And he named the second
[1]Ephraim, "For," *he said,* "[a]God has
made me fruitful in the land of my
affliction."
53 When the seven years of plenty
which had been in the land of Egypt
came to an end,
54 and [a]the seven years of famine
began to come, just as Joseph had said,
then there was famine in all the lands;
but in all the land of Egypt there was
bread.
55 So when all the land of Egypt was
famished, the people cried out to Pharaoh for bread; and Pharaoh said to all
the Egyptians, "Go to Joseph; [a]whatever
he says to you, you shall do."
56 When the famine was *spread* over
all the face of the earth, then Joseph
opened all [1]the storehouses, and sold to
the Egyptians; and the famine was severe in the land of Egypt.
57 And *the people of* all the earth came
to Egypt to buy grain from Joseph,
because [a]the famine was severe in all the
earth.

41 [a]Gen. 42:6; Ps. 105:21; Dan. 6:3; Acts 7:10
42 [a]Esth. 3:10; 8:2 [b]Dan. 5:7, 16, 29
43 [1]Lit., *the second . . . which was his* [2]Heb., *Abreck: Attention* or *Make way*
44 [1]Lit., *you no one* [a]Ps. 105:22
45 [1]Probably Egyptian for "God speaks; he lives" [2]Or, *Heliopolis* [a]Jer. 43:13; Ezek. 30:17
46 [1]Or, *entered the service of* [a]Gen. 37:2
47 [1]Lit., *by handfuls*
49 [1]Lit., *very much* [2]Lit., *numbering* [3]Or, *without number*
50 [1]Or, *Heliopolis* [a]Gen. 48:5
51 [1]I.e., making to forget
52 [1]I.e., fruitfulness [a]Gen. 17:6; 28:3; 49:22
54 [a]Gen. 41:30; Ps. 105:16; Acts 7:11
55 [a]John 2:5
56 [1]Lit., *that which was in them*
57 [a]Gen. 12:10

1 [a]Acts 7:12
2 [1]Lit., *from there* [a]Acts 7:12 [b]Gen. 43:8; Ps. 33:18, 19
4 [1]Lit., *Lest harm* [a]Gen. 35:24 [b]Gen. 42:38
5 [a]Gen. 12:10; 26:1; 41:57; Acts 7:11
6 [a]Gen. 41:41, 55 [b]Gen. 37:7-10; 41:43; Is. 60:14
7 [a]Gen. 42:30
8 [a]Gen. 37:2; 41:46
9 [1]Lit., *had dreamed* [2]Lit., *nakedness of the land* [a]Gen. 37:6-9
10 [a]Gen. 37:8
11 [a]Gen. 42:16, 19, 31, 34
12 [1]Lit., *nakedness of the land*
13 [a]Gen. 43:7 [b]Gen. 37:30; 42:32; 44:20
14 [1]Lit., *to you, saying*
15 [a]1 Sam. 17:55
16 [a]Gen. 42:11
17 [a]Gen. 40:4, 7
18 [a]Gen. 39:9; Lev. 25:43; Neh. 5:15
19 [1]Lit., *the house of your prison*

Joseph's Brothers Sent to Egypt

42 NOW [a]Jacob saw that there was
grain in Egypt, and Jacob said to
his sons, "Why are you staring at one
another?"
2 And he said, "Behold, [a]I have
heard that there is grain in Egypt; go
down there and buy *some* for us [1]from
that place, [b]so that we may live and not
die."
3 Then ten brothers of Joseph went
down to buy grain from Egypt.
4 But Jacob did not send Joseph's
brother [a]Benjamin with his brothers, for
he said, "[1b]I am afraid that harm may
befall him."
5 So the sons of Israel came to buy
grain among those who were coming,
[a]for the famine was in the land of Canaan *also.*
6 Now [a]Joseph was the ruler over the
land; he was the one who sold to all the
people of the land. And Joseph's brothers came and [b]bowed down to him with
their faces to the ground.
7 When Joseph saw his brothers he
recognized them, but he disguised himself to them and [a]spoke to them harshly.
And he said to them, "Where have you
come from?" And they said, "From the
land of Canaan, to buy food."
8 But Joseph had recognized his
brothers, although [a]they did not recognize him.
9 And Joseph [a]remembered the
dreams which he [1]had about them, and
said to them, "You are spies; you have
come to look at the [2]undefended parts of
our land."
10 Then they said to him, "No, [a]my
lord, but your servants have come to buy
food.
11 "We are all sons of one man; we are
[a]honest men, your servants are not
spies."
12 Yet he said to them, "No, but you
have come to look at the [1]undefended
parts of our land!"
13 But they said, "Your servants are
twelve brothers *in all,* the sons of one
man in the land of Canaan; and behold,
the youngest is with [a]our father today,
and [b]one is no more."
14 And Joseph said to them, "It is as I
said [1]to you, you are spies;
15 by this you will be tested: [a]by the
life of Pharaoh, you shall not go from
this place unless your youngest brother
comes here!
16 "Send one of you that he may get
your brother, while you remain confined,
that your words may be tested, whether
there is [a]truth in you. But if not, by the
life of Pharaoh, surely you are spies."
17 So he put them all together in
[a]prison for three days.
18 Now Joseph said to them on the
third day, "Do this and live, for [a]I fear
God:
19 if you are honest men, let one of
your brothers be confined in [1]your
prison; but as for *the rest of* you, go,

carry grain for the famine of your households,

20 and [a]bring your youngest brother to me, so your words may be verified, and you will not die." And they did so.

21 Then they said to one another, "[a]Truly we are guilty concerning our brother, because we saw the distress of his soul when he pleaded with us, yet we would not listen; therefore this distress has come upon us."

22 And Reuben answered them, saying, "[a]Did I not tell [1]you, 'Do not sin against the boy'; and you would not listen? [2b]Now comes the reckoning for his blood."

23 They did not know, however, that Joseph understood, for there was an interpreter between them.

24 And he turned away from them and [a]wept. But when he returned to them and spoke to them, he [b]took Simeon from them and bound him before their eyes.

25 [a]Then Joseph gave orders to fill their bags with grain and to restore every man's money in his sack, and to give them provisions for the journey. And thus it was done for them.

26 So they loaded their donkeys with their grain, and departed from there.

27 And as one *of them* opened his sack to give his donkey fodder at the lodging place, he saw his [a]money; and behold, it was in the mouth of his sack.

28 Then he said to his brothers, "My money has been returned, and behold, it is even in my sack." And their hearts [1]sank, and they *turned* [2]trembling to one another, saying, "[a]What is this that God has done to us?"

Simeon Is Held Hostage

29 When they came to their father Jacob in the land of Canaan, they told him all that had happened to them, saying,

30 "The man, the lord of the land, [a]spoke harshly with us, and took us for spies of the country.

31 "But we said to him, 'We are [a]honest men; we are not spies.

32 'We are twelve brothers, sons of our father; one is no more, and the youngest is with our father today in the land of Canaan.'

33 "And the man, the lord of the land, said to us, '[a]By this I shall know that you are honest men: leave one of your brothers with me and take *grain for* the famine of your households, and go.

34 'But bring your youngest brother to me that I may know that you are not spies, but [1]honest men. I will give your brother to you, and you may [a]trade in the land.'"

35 Now it came about as they were emptying their sacks, that behold, [a]every man's bundle of money *was* in his sack;

20 [a]Gen. 42:34; 43:5; 44:23

21 [a]Gen. 37:26-28; 45:3; Hos. 5:15

22 [1]Lit., *you saying* [2]Lit., *And behold, his blood also is required* [a]Gen. 37:21, 22 [b]Gen. 9:5, 6; 1 Kin. 2:32; 2 Chr. 24:22; Ps. 9:12

24 [a]Gen. 43:30; 45:14, 15 [b]Gen. 43:14, 23

25 [a]Gen. 44:1; Rom. 12:17, 20, 21; 1 Pet. 3:9

27 [a]Gen. 43:21, 22

28 [1]Lit., *went out* [2]Lit., *trembled* [a]Gen. 43:23

30 [a]Gen. 42:7

31 [a]Gen. 42:11

33 [a]Gen. 42:19, 20

34 [1]Lit., *you are honest* [a]Gen. 34:10

35 [a]Gen. 43:12, 15, 21

36 [a]Gen. 43:14

37 [1]Lit., *hand*

38 [1]Lit., *he* [2]Lit., *on which you are going* [a]Gen. 37:33, 34; 42:13; 44:27, 28 [b]Gen. 42:4 [c]Gen. 37:35; 44:29, 31

1 [a]Gen. 12:10; 26:1; 41:56, 57

3 [1]Lit., *us, saying* [a]Gen. 43:5; 44:23

6 [1]Lit., *to tell*

7 [1]Lit., *told him according to these words* [a]Gen. 42:13; 43:27

8 [a]Gen. 42:2

9 [1]Lit., *from my hand you may require him* [2]Lit., *I shall have sinned before you all the days* [a]Gen. 42:37; 44:32; Philem. 18, 19

11 [1]Or, *vessels* [2]Or, *mastic* [3]Or, *ladanum spice* [4]Or, *resinous bark* [a]Gen. 32:20; 43:25, 26 [b]Gen. 37:25; Jer. 8:22; Ezek. 27:17

12 [a]Gen. 42:25, 35; 43:21, 22

and when they and their father saw their bundles of money, they were dismayed.

36 And their father Jacob said to them, "You have [a]bereaved me of my children: Joseph is no more, and Simeon is no more, and you would take Benjamin; all these things are against me."

37 Then Reuben spoke to his father, saying, "You may put my two sons to death if I do not bring him *back* to you; put him in my [1]care, and I will return him to you."

38 But [1]Jacob said, "My son shall not go down with you; for his [a]brother is dead, and he alone is left. [b]If harm should befall him on the journey [2]you are taking, then you will [c]bring my gray hair down to Sheol in sorrow."

The Return to Egypt

43 [a]NOW the famine was severe in the land.

2 So it came about when they had finished eating the grain which they had brought from Egypt, that their father said to them, "Go back, buy us a little food."

3 Judah spoke to him, however, saying, "[a]The man solemnly warned [1]us, 'You shall not see my face unless your brother is with you.'

4 "If you send our brother with us, we will go down and buy you food.

5 "But if you do not send *him,* we will not go down; for the man said to us, 'You shall not see my face unless your brother is with you.'"

6 Then Israel said, "Why did you treat me so badly [1]by telling the man whether you still had *another* brother?"

7 But they said, "The man questioned particularly about us and our relatives, saying, '[a]Is your father still alive? Have you *another* brother?' So we [1]answered his questions. Could we possibly know that he would say, 'Bring your brother down'?"

8 And Judah said to his father Israel, "Send the lad with me, and we will arise and go, [a]that we may live and not die, we as well as you and our little ones.

9 "[a]I myself will be surety for him; [1]you may hold me responsible for him. If I do not bring him *back* to you and set him before you, then [2]let me bear the blame before you forever.

10 "For if we had not delayed, surely by now we could have returned twice."

11 Then their father Israel said to them, "If *it must be* so, then do this: take some of the best products of the land in your [1]bags, and carry down to the man [a]as a present, a little [2b]balm and a little honey, [3]aromatic gum and [4]myrrh, pistachio nuts and almonds.

12 "And take double *the* money in your hand, and take back in your hand [a]the money that was returned in the mouth of your sacks; perhaps it was a mistake.

13 "Take your brother also, and arise, return to the man;

14 and may [1a]God Almighty [b]grant
you compassion in the sight of the man,
that he may release to you [c]your other
brother and Benjamin. And as for me,
[d]if I am bereaved of my children, I am
bereaved."
15 So the men took [a]this present, and
they took double *the* money in their
hand, and Benjamin; then they arose
and went down to Egypt and stood
before Joseph.

Joseph Sees Benjamin

16 When Joseph saw Benjamin with
them, he said to his [a]house steward,
"Bring the men into the house, and slay
an animal and make ready; for the men
are to dine with me at noon."
17 So the man did as Joseph said, and
[1]brought the men to Joseph's house.
18 Now the men were afraid, because
they were brought to Joseph's house;
and they said, "*It is* because of the
money that was returned in our sacks
the first time that we are being brought
in, that he may [1]seek occasion against us
and fall upon us, and take us for slaves
with our donkeys."
19 So they came near to Joseph's
house steward, and spoke to him at the
entrance of the house,
20 and said, "Oh, my lord, we indeed
came down the first time to buy food,
21 and it came about when we came
to the lodging place, that we opened our
sacks, and behold, [a]each man's money
was in the mouth of his sack, our money
in [1]full. So [b]we have brought it back in
our hand.
22 "We have also brought down other
money in our hand to buy food; we do
not know who put our money in our
sacks."
23 And he said, "[1]Be at ease, do not
be afraid. [a]Your God and the God of
your father has given you treasure in
your sacks; [2]I had your money." Then
[b]he brought Simeon out to them.
24 Then the man brought the men
into Joseph's house and [a]gave them
water, and they [b]washed their feet; and
he gave their donkeys fodder.
25 So they prepared [a]the present [1]for
Joseph's coming at noon; for they had
heard that they were to eat [2]a meal there.
26 When Joseph came home, they
brought into the house to him the present which was in their hand and [a]bowed
to the ground before him.
27 Then he asked them about their
welfare, and said, "[a]Is your old father
well, of whom you spoke? Is he still
alive?"
28 And they said, "Your servant our
father is well; he is still alive." [a]And they
bowed down [1]in homage.
29 As he lifted his eyes and saw his
brother Benjamin, his mother's son, he
said, "Is this [a]your youngest brother, of
whom you spoke to me?" And he said,
"[b]May God be gracious to you, my son."
30 And Joseph hurried *out* for [1a]he
was deeply stirred over his brother, and
he sought *a place* to weep; and he entered his chamber and [b]wept there.
31 Then he washed his face, and came
out; and he [a]controlled himself and said,
"[1]Serve the meal."
32 So they served him by himself, and
them by themselves, and the Egyptians,
who ate with him, by themselves; because the Egyptians could not eat bread
with the Hebrews, for that is [1a]loath-
some to the Egyptians.
33 Now they [1]were seated before him,
[a]the first-born according to his birthright
and the youngest according to his youth,
and the men looked at one another in
astonishment.
34 And he took portions to them from
[1]his own table; [a]but Benjamin's portion
was five times as much as any of theirs.
So they feasted and drank freely with
him.

The Brothers Are Brought Back

44 [a]THEN he commanded his house
steward, saying, "Fill the men's
sacks with food, as much as they can
carry, and put each man's money in the
mouth of his sack.
2 "And put my cup, the silver cup, in
the mouth of the sack of the youngest,
and his money for the grain." And he
did [1]as Joseph had told *him*.
3 [1]As soon as it was light, the men
were sent away, they with their donkeys.
4 They had *just* gone out of [a]the city,
and were not far off, when Joseph said to
his house steward, "Up, follow the men;
and when you overtake them, say to
them, 'Why have you repaid evil for
good?
5 'Is not this the one from which my
lord drinks, and which he indeed uses
for [a]divination? You have done wrong in
doing this.' "
6 So he overtook them and spoke
these words to them.
7 And they said to him, "Why does
my lord speak such words as these? Far
be it from your servants to do such a
thing.
8 "Behold, [a]the money which we
found in the mouth of our sacks we have
brought back to you from the land of
Canaan. How then could we steal silver
or gold from your lord's house?
9 "[a]With whomever of your servants it
is found, let him die, and we also will be
my lord's [b]slaves."
10 So he said, "Now let it also be
according to your words; he with whom
it is found shall be my slave, and *the rest
of* you shall be innocent."
11 Then they hurried, each man lowered his sack to the ground, and each
man opened his sack.
12 And he searched, beginning with
the oldest and ending with the youngest,
and [a]the cup was found in Benjamin's
sack.

14 [1]Heb., *El Shaddai* [a]Gen. 17:1; 28:3; 35:11 [b]Ps. 106:46 [c]Gen. 42:24 [d]Gen. 42:36

15 [a]Gen. 43:11

16 [a]Gen. 44:1

17 [1]Lit., *the man brought*

18 [1]Lit., *roll himself upon us*

21 [1]Lit., *its weight* [a]Gen. 42:27, 35 [b]Gen. 43:12, 15

23 [1]Lit., *Peace be to you* [2]Lit., *your money had come to me* [a]Gen. 42:28 [b]Gen. 42:24

24 [a]Gen. 18:4; 19:2; 24:32 [b]Luke 7:44; John 13:5; 1 Tim. 5:10

25 [1]Lit., *until* [2]Lit., *bread* [a]Gen. 43:11, 15

26 [a]Gen. 37:7, 10

27 [a]Gen. 43:7; 45:3

28 [1]Lit., *and prostrated themselves* [a]Gen. 37:7, 10

29 [a]Gen. 42:13 [b]Num. 6:25; Ps. 67:1

30 [1]Lit., *his compassion grew warm* [a]1 Kin. 3:26 [b]Gen. 42:24; 45:2, 14, 15; 46:29

31 [1]Lit., *Set on bread.* [a]Gen. 45:1

32 [1]Lit., *an abomination* [a]Gen. 46:34; Ex. 8:26

33 [1]Lit., *sat* [a]Gen. 42:7

34 [1]Lit., *his face* [a]Gen. 35:24; 45:22

1 [a]Gen. 42:25

2 [1]Or, *according to the word*

3 [1]Lit., *The morning was light*

4 [a]Gen. 44:13

5 [a]Gen. 30:27; 44:15; Lev. 19:26; Deut. 18:10-14

8 [a]Gen. 43:21

9 [a]Gen. 31:32 [b]Gen. 44:16

12 [a]Gen. 44:2

13 Then they [a]tore their clothes, and when each man loaded his donkey, they returned to [b]the city.

14 When Judah and his brothers came to Joseph's house, he was still there, and [a]they fell to the ground before him.

15 And Joseph said to them, "What is this deed that you have done? Do you not know that such a man as I can indeed practice [a]divination?"

16 So Judah said, "What can we say to my lord? What can we speak? And how can we justify ourselves? God has found out the iniquity of your servants; behold, we are my lord's [a]slaves, both we and the one in whose [1]possession the cup has been found."

17 But he said, "Far be it from me to do this. The man in whose [1]possession the cup has been found, he shall be my slave; but as for you, go up in peace to your father."

18 Then Judah approached him, and said, "Oh my lord, may your servant please speak a word in my lord's ears, and [1a]do not be angry with your servant; for [b]you are equal to Pharaoh.

19 "[a]My lord asked his servants, saying, 'Have you a father or a brother?'

20 "And we said to my lord, 'We have an old father and [a]a little child of *his* old age. Now [b]his brother is dead, so he alone is left of his mother, and his father loves him.'

21 "Then you said to your servants, '[a]Bring him down to me, that I may set my eyes on him.'

22 "But we said to my lord, 'The lad cannot leave his father, for if he should leave his father, [1]his father would die.'

23 "You said to your servants, however, '[a]Unless your youngest brother comes down with you, you shall not see my face again.'

24 "Thus it came about when we went up to your servant my father, we told him the words of my lord.

25 "And [a]our father said, 'Go back, buy us a little food.'

26 "But we said, 'We cannot go down. If our youngest brother is with us, then we will go down; for we cannot see the man's face unless our youngest brother is with us.'

27 "And your servant my father said to us, 'You know that [a]my wife bore me two sons;

28 and the one went out from me, and [a]I said, "Surely he is torn in pieces," and I have not seen him since.

29 'And if you take this one also from [1]me, and harm befalls him, you will [a]bring my gray hair down to Sheol in [2]sorrow.'

30 "Now, therefore, when I come to your servant my father, and the lad is not with us, since [1a]his life is bound up in the lad's life,

31 it will come about when he sees that the lad is not *with us*, that he will die. Thus your servants will [a]bring the gray hair of your servant our father down to Sheol in sorrow.

32 "For your servant [a]became surety for the lad to my father, saying, 'If I do not bring him *back* to you, then [1]let me bear the blame before my father forever.'

33 "Now, therefore, please let your servant remain instead of the lad a slave to my lord, and let the lad go up with his brothers.

34 "For how shall I go up to my father if the lad is not with me, lest I see the evil that would [1]overtake my father?"

Joseph Deals Kindly with His Brothers

45 THEN Joseph could not control himself before all those who stood by him, and he cried, "Have everyone go out from me." So there [1]was no man with him [a]when Joseph made himself known to his brothers.

2 And [a]he [1]wept so loudly that the Egyptians heard *it*, and the household of Pharaoh heard *of it*.

3 Then Joseph said to his brothers, "[a]I am Joseph! [b]Is my father still alive?" But his brothers could not answer him, for [c]they were dismayed at his presence.

4 Then Joseph said to his brothers, "Please come [1]closer to me." And they came [1]closer. And he said, "I am your brother Joseph, whom you [a]sold into Egypt.

5 "And now do not be grieved or angry [1]with yourselves, because [a]you sold me here; for [b]God sent me before you to preserve life.

6 "For the famine *has been* in the land [a]these two years, and there are still five years in which there will be neither plowing nor harvesting.

7 "And [a]God sent me before you to preserve for you a remnant in the earth, and to keep you alive by a great [1]deliverance.

8 "Now, therefore, it was not you who sent me here, but God; and He has made me a [a]father to Pharaoh and lord of all his household and ruler over all the land of Egypt.

9 "Hurry and go up to my father, and [a]say to him, 'Thus says your son Joseph, "God has made me lord of all Egypt; come down to me, do not delay.

10 "And you shall [1]live in the land of [a]Goshen, and you shall be near me, you and your children and your children's children and your flocks and your herds and all that you have.

11 "There I will also [a]provide for you, for there are still five years of famine *to come*, lest you and your household and all that you have be impoverished." '

12 "And behold, your eyes see, and the eyes of my brother Benjamin *see*, that it is my mouth which is speaking to you.

13 "Now you must tell my father of all my splendor in Egypt, and all that you have seen; and you must hurry and [a]bring my father down here."

14 Then he fell on his brother Benjamin's neck and [a]wept; and Benjamin wept on his neck.

13 [a]Gen. 37:29, 34; Num. 14:6; 2 Sam. 1:11 [b]Gen. 44:4
14 [a]Gen. 37:7, 10
15 [a]Gen. 44:5
16 [1]Lit., *hand* [a]Gen. 44:9
17 [1]Lit., *hand*
18 [1]Lit., *let not your anger burn against* [a]Gen. 18:30, 32; Ex. 32:22 [b]Gen. 37:7, 8; 41:40-44
19 [a]Gen. 43:7
20 [a]Gen. 37:3; 43:8; 44:30 [b]Gen. 37:33; 42:13, 38
21 [a]Gen. 42:15, 20
22 [1]Lit., *he would*
23 [a]Gen. 43:3, 5
25 [a]Gen. 43:2
27 [a]Gen. 46:19
28 [a]Gen. 37:31-35
29 [1]Lit., *my face* [2]Lit., *evil* [a]Gen. 42:38; 44:31
30 [1]Lit., *his soul is bound with his soul* [a]1 Sam. 18:1
31 [a]Gen. 44:29
32 [1]Lit., *and I shall have sinned for all the days before my father* [a]Gen. 43:9
34 [1]Lit., *find*
1 [1]Lit., *stood* [a]Acts 7:13
2 [1]Lit., *gave forth his voice in weeping* [a]Gen. 45:14, 15; 46:29
3 [a]Acts 7:13 [b]Gen. 43:27 [c]Gen. 37:20-28; 42:21, 22
4 [1]Lit., *near* [a]Gen. 37:28
5 [1]Lit., *in your eyes* [a]Gen. 37:28 [b]Gen. 45:7, 8; 50:20; Ps. 105:17
6 [a]Gen. 37:2; 41:46, 53
7 [1]Lit., *escaped company* [a]Gen. 45:5
8 [a]Judg. 17:10
9 [a]Acts 7:14
10 [1]Lit., *dwell* [a]Gen. 46:28, 34; 47:1
11 [a]Gen. 47:12
13 [a]Acts 7:14
14 [a]Gen. 45:2

15 And he kissed all his brothers and
wept on them, and afterward his brothers talked with him.
16 Now when [a]the [1]news was heard in
Pharaoh's house [2]that Joseph's brothers
had come, it [3]pleased Pharaoh and his
servants.
17 Then Pharaoh said to Joseph, "Say
to your brothers, 'Do this: load your
beasts and [1]go to the land of Canaan,
18 and take your father and your
households and come to me, and [a]I will
give you the [1]best of the land of Egypt
and you shall eat the fat of the land.'
19 "Now you are ordered, 'Do this:
[1]take [a]wagons from the land of Egypt
for your little ones and for your wives,
and bring your father and come.
20 'And do not [1]concern yourselves
with your goods, for the [2]best of all the
land of Egypt is yours.' "
21 Then the sons of Israel did so; and
Joseph gave them [a]wagons according to
the [1]command of Pharaoh, and gave
them provisions for the journey.
22 To [1]each of them he gave [a]changes
of garments, but to Benjamin he gave
three hundred *pieces of* silver and [b]five
changes of garments.
23 And to his father he sent [1]as follows: ten donkeys loaded with the [2]best
things of Egypt, and ten female donkeys
loaded with grain and bread and sustenance for his father [3]on the journey.
24 So he sent his brothers away, and
[1]as they departed, he said to them, "Do
not [2]quarrel on the journey."
25 Then they went up from Egypt,
and came to the land of Canaan to their
father Jacob.
26 And they told him, saying, "Joseph
is still alive, and indeed he is ruler over
all the land of Egypt." But [1]he was
stunned, for [a]he did not believe them.
27 When they told him all the words
of Joseph that he had spoken to them,
and when he saw the [a]wagons that
Joseph had sent to carry him, the spirit
of their father Jacob revived.
28 Then Israel said, "It is enough; my
son Joseph is still alive. I will go and see
him before I die."

Jacob Moves to Egypt

46 SO Israel set out with all that he
had, and came to [a]Beersheba,
and offered sacrifices to the [b]God of his
father Isaac.
2 And [a]God spoke to Israel [1]in visions of the night and said, "[b]Jacob,
Jacob." And he said, "Here I am."
3 And He said, "[a]I am God, the God
of your father; do not be afraid to go
down to Egypt, for I will [b]make you a
great nation there.
4 "[a]I will go down with you to Egypt,
and [b]I will also surely bring you up
again; and [c]Joseph will [1]close your
eyes."
5 Then Jacob arose from Beersheba;
and the sons of Israel carried their father
Jacob and their little ones and their
wives, in the [a]wagons which Pharaoh
had sent to carry him.
6 And they took their livestock and
their property, which they had acquired
in the land of Canaan, and [a]came to
Egypt, Jacob and all his [1]descendants
with him:
7 his sons and his grandsons with
him, his daughters and his granddaugh-
ters, and all his [1]descendants he brought
with him to Egypt.

Those Who Came to Egypt

8 Now these are the [a]names of the
sons of Israel, Jacob and his sons, who
went to Egypt: Reuben, Jacob's first-
born.
9 And the sons of Reuben: Hanoch
and Pallu and Hezron and Carmi.
10 And the [a]sons of Simeon: [1]Jemuel
and Jamin and Ohad and [2]Jachin and
[3]Zohar and Shaul the son of a Canaanite
woman.
11 And the sons of Levi: [1]Gershon,
Kohath, and Merari.
12 And the sons of Judah: Er and
Onan and Shelah and Perez and Zerah
(but Er and Onan died in the land of
Canaan). And the [a]sons of Perez were
Hezron and Hamul.
13 And the sons of Issachar: Tola and
[1]Puvvah and [2]Iob and Shimron.
14 And the sons of Zebulun: Sered
and Elon and Jahleel.
15 These are the sons of Leah, whom
she bore to Jacob in Paddan-aram, with
his daughter Dinah; [1]all his sons and his
daughters *numbered* thirty-three.
16 And the [a]sons of Gad: [1]Ziphion
and Haggi, Shuni and [2]Ezbon, Eri and
[3]Arodi and Areli.
17 And the [a]sons of Asher: Imnah and
Ishvah and Ishvi and Beriah and their
sister Serah. And the [b]sons of Beriah:
Heber and Malchiel.
18 These are the sons of Zilpah, whom
Laban gave to his daughter Leah; and
she bore to Jacob these sixteen persons.
19 The sons of Jacob's wife Rachel:
Joseph and Benjamin.
20 [a]Now to Joseph in the land of
Egypt were born Manasseh and
Ephraim, whom Asenath, the daughter
of Potiphera, priest of On, bore to him.
21 And the [a]sons of Benjamin: Bela
and Becher and Ashbel, Gera and Naaman, [1]Ehi and Rosh, [2]Muppim and
[3]Huppim and Ard.
22 These are the sons of Rachel, who
were born to Jacob; *there were* fourteen
persons in all.
23 And the sons of Dan: [1]Hushim.
24 And the sons of Naphtali: [1]Jahzeel
and Guni and Jezer and [2]Shillem.
25 These are the [a]sons of Bilhah,
whom [b]Laban gave to his daughter
Rachel, and she bore these to Jacob;
there were seven persons in all.
26 [a]All the persons belonging to Jacob, who came to Egypt, [1]his direct

16 [1]Lit., *voice* [2]Lit., *saying, "Joseph's brothers have come."* [3]Lit., *was good in the eyes of* [a]Acts 7:13
17 [1]Lit., *come, go*
18 [1]Lit., *good* [a]Gen. 27:28
19 [1]Lit., *take for yourselves* [a]Gen. 45:21, 27; 46:5; Num. 7:3-8
20 [1]Lit., *let your eye look with regret upon your vessels* [2]Lit., *good*
21 [1]Lit., *mouth* [a]Gen. 45:19
22 [1]Lit., *all of them he gave each man* [a]2 Kin. 5:5 [b]Gen. 43:34
23 [1]Lit., *like this* [2]Lit., *good* [3]Lit., *for*
24 [1]Lit., *they departed; and he said* [2]Lit., *be agitated*
26 [1]Lit., *his heart grew numb* [a]Gen. 37:31-35
27 [a]Gen. 45:19

1 [a]Gen. 21:31; 28:10 [b]Gen. 26:24; 28:13; 31:42
2 [1]Lit., *in the visions* [a]Gen. 15:1; Num. 12:6; Job 33:14, 15 [b]Gen. 22:11; 31:11
3 [a]Gen. 17:1; 28:13 [b]Gen. 12:2; Ex. 1:9; Deut. 26:5
4 [1]Lit., *put his hand on* [a]Gen. 28:15; 48:21 [b]Gen. 50:24; Ex. 3:8 [c]Gen. 50:1
5 [a]Gen. 45:21
6 [1]Lit., *seed* [a]Deut. 26:5; Josh. 24:4; Ps. 105:23; Is. 52:4; Acts 7:15
7 [1]Lit., *seed*
8 [a]Ex. 1:1-4; Num. 26:4, 5; 1 Chr. 2:1ff.
10 [1]In Num. 26:12 and 1 Chr. 4:24, *Nemuel* [2]In 1 Chr. 4:24, *Jarib* [3]In Num. 26:13 and 1 Chr. 4:24, *Zerah* [a]Ex. 6:15
11 [1]In 1 Chr. 6:16, *Gershom*
12 [a]1 Chr. 2:5
13 [1]In Num. 26:23, *Puvah;* in 1 Chr. 7:1, *Puah* [2]In Num. 26:24 and 1 Chr. 7:1, *Jashub*
15 [1]Lit., *all the souls of*
16 [1]In Num. 26:15, *Zephon* [2]In Num. 26:16, *Ozni* [3]In Num. 26:17, *Arod* [a]Num. 26:15-18
17 [a]1 Chr. 7:30 [b]1 Chr. 7:31
20 [a]Gen. 41:50-52
21 [1]In Num. 26:38, *Ahiram* [2]In Num. 26:39, *Shephupham;* in 1 Chr. 7:12, *Shuppim* [3]In Num. 26:39, *Hupham* [a]1 Chr. 7:6
23 [1]In Num. 26:42, *Shuham*
24 [1]In 1 Chr. 7:13, *Jahziel* [2]In 1 Chr. 7:13, *Shallum*

25 [a]Gen. 30:5, 7 [b]Gen. 29:29
26 [1]Lit., *who came out of his loins* [a]Ex. 1:5

descendants, not including the wives of Jacob's sons, *were* sixty-six persons in all,

27 and the sons of Joseph, who were born to him in Egypt were [1]two; [a]all the persons of the house of Jacob, who came to Egypt, *were* seventy.

28 Now he sent Judah before him to Joseph, to point out *the way* before him to [a]Goshen; and they came into the land of Goshen.

29 And Joseph [1]prepared his chariot and went up to Goshen to meet his father Israel; as soon as he appeared [2]before him, he fell on his neck and [a]wept on his neck a long time.

30 Then Israel said to Joseph, "Now let me die, since I have seen your face, that you are still alive."

31 And Joseph said to his brothers and to his father's household, "[a]I will go up and tell Pharaoh, and will say to him, 'My brothers and my father's household, who *were* in the land of Canaan, have come to me;

32 and the men are shepherds, for they have been [1]keepers of livestock; and they have brought their flocks and their herds and all that they have.'

33 "And it shall come about when Pharaoh calls you and says, '[a]What is your occupation?'

34 that you shall say, 'Your servants have been [1a]keepers of livestock from our youth even until now, both we and our fathers,' that you may [2]live in the land of [b]Goshen; for every shepherd is [3c]loathsome to the Egyptians."

Jacob's Family Settles in Goshen

47 THEN [a]Joseph went in and told Pharaoh, and said, "My father and my brothers and their flocks and their herds and all that they have, have come out of the land of Canaan; and behold, they are in the land of [b]Goshen."

2 And he took five men from among his brothers, and [a]presented them to Pharaoh.

3 Then Pharaoh said to his brothers, "[a]What is your occupation?" So they said to Pharaoh, "Your servants are [b]shepherds, both we and our fathers."

4 And they said to Pharaoh, "[a]We have come to sojourn in the land, for there is no pasture for your servants' flocks, for [b]the famine is severe in the land of Canaan. Now, therefore, please let your servants [1c]live in the land of Goshen."

5 Then Pharaoh said to [1]Joseph, "Your father and your brothers have come to you.

6 "The land of Egypt is [1]at your disposal; [2]settle your father and your brothers in [a]the best of the land, let them [3]live in the land of Goshen; and if you know any [b]capable men among them, then [4]put them in charge of my livestock."

7 Then Joseph brought his father Jacob and [1]presented him to Pharaoh; and Jacob [a]blessed Pharaoh.

8 And Pharaoh said to Jacob, "How many [1]years have you lived?"

9 So Jacob said to Pharaoh, "The [1a]years of my sojourning are one hundred and [2]thirty; few and [3]unpleasant have been the [1]years of my life, nor have they [4]attained [b]the [1]years [5]that my fathers lived during the days of their sojourning."

10 And Jacob [a]blessed Pharaoh, and went out from [1]his presence.

11 So Joseph [1]settled his father and his brothers, and gave them a possession in the land of Egypt, in [a]the best of the land, in the land of [b]Rameses, as Pharaoh had ordered.

12 And Joseph [a]provided his father and his brothers and all his father's household with [1]food, according to their little ones.

13 Now there was no [1]food in all the land, because the famine was very severe, so that [a]the land of Egypt and the land of Canaan languished because of the famine.

14 And [a]Joseph gathered all the money that was found in the land of Egypt and in the land of Canaan for the grain which they bought, and Joseph brought the money into Pharaoh's house.

15 And when the money was all spent in the land of Egypt and in the land of Canaan, all the Egyptians came to Joseph [1]and said, "Give us [2]food, for [a]why should we die in your presence? For *our* money [3]is gone."

16 Then Joseph said, "Give up your livestock, and I will give you *food* for your livestock, since *your* money [1]is gone."

17 So they brought their livestock to Joseph, and Joseph gave them [1]food in exchange for the horses and the [2]flocks and the herds and the donkeys; and he [3]fed them with [1]food in exchange for all their livestock [4]that year.

18 And when that year was ended, they came to him the [1]next year and said to him, "We will not hide from my lord that our money is all spent, and the [2]cattle are my lord's. There is nothing left [3]for my lord except our bodies and our lands.

19 "Why should we die before your eyes, both we and our land? Buy us and our land for [1]food, and we and our land will be slaves to Pharaoh. So give us seed, that we may live and not die, and that the land may not be desolate."

Result of the Famine

20 So Joseph bought all the land of Egypt for Pharaoh, for [1]every Egyptian sold his field, because the famine was severe upon them. Thus the land became Pharaoh's.

21 And as for the people, he removed them to the cities from one end of Egypt's border to the other.

27 [1]Lit., *two souls* [a]Ex. 1:5; Deut. 10:22; Acts 7:14
28 [a]Gen. 45:10
29 [1]Lit., *tied, harnessed* [2]Lit., *to* [a]Gen. 45:14, 15
31 [a]Gen. 47:1
32 [1]Lit., *men*
33 [a]Gen. 47:2, 3
34 [1]Lit., *men* [2]Lit., *dwell* [3]Lit., *an abomination* [a]Gen. 13:7, 8; 26:20; 37:2 [b]Gen. 45:10, 18; 47:6, 11 [c]Gen. 43:32; Ex. 8:26

1 [a]Gen. 46:31 [b]Gen. 45:10; 46:28
2 [a]Acts 7:13
3 [a]Gen. 46:33 [b]Gen. 46:34
4 [1]Lit., *dwell* [a]Gen. 15:13; Deut. 26:5; Ps. 105:23 [b]Gen. 43:1; Acts 7:11 [c]Gen. 46:34
5 [1]Lit., *Joseph, saying*
6 [1]Lit., *before you* [2]Lit., *cause them to dwell* [3]Lit., *dwell* [4]Lit., *appoint them rulers* [a]Gen. 45:10, 18; 47:11 [b]Ex. 18:21, 25; 1 Kin. 11:28; Prov. 22:29
7 [1]Lit., *set him before* [a]Gen. 47:10; 2 Sam. 14:22; 1 Kin. 8:66
8 [1]Lit., *are the days of the years of your life*
9 [1]Lit., *days of the years* [2]Lit., *thirty years* [3]Lit., *evil* [4]Lit., *reached* [5]Lit., *of the life of my fathers* [a]Heb. 11:9, 13 [b]Gen. 25:7; 35:28
10 [1]Lit., *Pharaoh's* [a]Gen. 47:7
11 [1]Lit., *caused to dwell* [a]Gen. 47:6, 27 [b]Ex. 1:11; 12:37
12 [1]Or, *bread* [a]Gen. 45:11
13 [1]Or, *bread* [a]Gen. 41:30; Acts 7:11
14 [a]Gen. 41:56
15 [1]Lit., *saying* [2]Or, *bread* [3]Lit., *ceases* [a]Gen. 47:19
16 [1]Lit., *ceases*
17 [1]Or, *bread* [2]Lit., *livestock of the flocks and livestock of the herds* [3]Lit., *led them as a shepherd* [4]Lit., *in that year*
18 [1]Lit., *second* [2]Lit., *livestock of the cattle* [3]Lit., *in the presence of*
19 [1]Or, *bread*
20 [1]Lit., *Egypt, every man*

22 Only the land of the priests he did not buy, for the priests had an allotment from Pharaoh, and they [1]lived off the allotment which Pharaoh gave them. Therefore, they did not sell their land.

23 Then Joseph said to the people, "Behold, I have today bought you and your land for Pharaoh; now, *here* is seed for you, and you may sow the land.

24 "And [1]at the harvest you shall give a [a]fifth to Pharaoh, and [2]four-fifths shall be your own for seed of the field and for your food and for those of your households and as food for your little ones."

25 So they said, "You have saved our lives! Let us find favor in the sight of my lord, and we will be Pharaoh's slaves."

26 And Joseph made it a statute concerning the land of Egypt *valid* to this day, that Pharaoh should have the fifth; [a]only the land of the priests [1]did not become Pharaoh's.

27 Now Israel [1]lived in the land of Egypt, in [2]Goshen, and they [a]acquired property in it and [b]were fruitful and became very numerous.

28 And Jacob lived in the land of Egypt [a]seventeen years; so the [1]length of Jacob's life was one hundred and forty-seven years.

29 When [1a]the time for Israel to die drew near, he called his son Joseph and said to him, "Please, if I have found favor in your sight, [b]place now your hand under my thigh and [c]deal with me in kindness and [2]faithfulness. Please do not bury me in Egypt,

30 but when I [a]lie down with my fathers, you shall carry me out of Egypt and bury me in [b]their burial place." And he said, "I will do as you have said."

31 And he said, "[a]Swear to me." So he swore to him. Then [b]Israel bowed *in worship* at the head of the bed.

Israel's Last Days

48 NOW it came about after these things that [1]Joseph was told, "Behold, your father is sick." So he took his two sons [a]Manasseh and Ephraim with him.

2 When [1]it was told to Jacob, "Behold, your son Joseph has come to you," Israel [2]collected his strength and sat [3]up in the bed.

3 Then Jacob said to Joseph, "[1a]God Almighty appeared to me at [b]Luz in the land of Canaan and blessed me,

4 and He said to me, 'Behold, I will make you fruitful and numerous, and I will make you a company of peoples, and will give this land to your [1]descendants after you for [a]an everlasting possession.'

5 "And now your two sons, who were born to you in the land of Egypt before I came to you in Egypt, are mine; [a]Ephraim and Manasseh shall be mine, as [b]Reuben and Simeon are.

6 "But your offspring that [1]have been born after them shall be yours; they shall be called by the [2]names of their brothers in their inheritance.

7 "Now as for me, when I came from [a]Paddan, [b]Rachel died, [1]to my sorrow, in the land of Canaan on the journey, when there was still some distance to go to Ephrath; and I buried her there on the way to Ephrath (that is, Bethlehem)."

8 When Israel [a]saw Joseph's sons, he said, "Who are these?"

9 And Joseph said to his father, "[a]They are my sons, whom God has given me here." So he said, "Bring them to me, please, that [b]I may bless them."

10 Now [a]the eyes of Israel were *so* dim from age *that* he could not see. Then [1]Joseph brought them close to him, and he [b]kissed them and embraced them.

11 And Israel said to Joseph, "I never [1]expected to see your face, and behold, God has let me see your [2]children as well."

12 Then Joseph [1]took them from his knees, and [a]bowed with his face to the ground.

13 And Joseph took them both, Ephraim with his right hand toward Israel's left, and Manasseh with his left hand toward Israel's right, and brought them close to him.

14 But Israel stretched out his right hand and laid it on the head of Ephraim, who was the younger, and his left hand on Manasseh's head, [1]crossing his hands, [2]although [a]Manasseh was the first-born.

15 And he blessed Joseph, and said,

"[a]The God before whom my fathers Abraham and Isaac walked,
[b]The God who has been my shepherd [1]all my life to this day,
16 [a]The angel who has redeemed me from all evil,
[b]Bless the lads;
And may my name [1]live on in them,
And the [2]names of my fathers Abraham and Isaac;
And [c]may they grow into a multitude in the midst of the earth."

17 When Joseph saw that his father [a]laid his right hand on Ephraim's head, it displeased him; and he grasped his father's hand to remove it from Ephraim's head to Manasseh's head.

18 And Joseph said to his father, "Not so, my father, for this one is the first-born. Place your right hand on his head."

19 But his father refused and said, "I know, my son, I know; he also shall become a people and he also shall be great. However, his younger brother shall be greater than he, and [a]his [1]descendants shall become a [2]multitude of nations."

20 And [a]he blessed them that day, saying,

"By you Israel shall pronounce blessing, saying,
'May God make you like Ephraim and Manasseh!'"

Thus he put Ephraim before Manasseh.

---

22 [1]Lit., *ate their allotment*
24 [1]Lit., *it shall come about . . . that you shall* [2]Lit., *four parts* [a]Gen. 41:34
26 [1]Lit., *alone did* [a]Gen. 47:22
27 [1]Lit., *dwelt* [2]Lit., *in the land of Goshen* [a]Gen. 47:11 [b]Gen. 17:6; 26:4; 35:11; Ex. 1:7; Deut. 26:5; Acts 7:17
28 [1]Lit., *days of Jacob, the years of his life* [a]Gen. 47:9
29 [1]Lit., *the days of Israel to die drew near* [2]Lit., *truth* [a]Deut. 31:14; 1 Kin. 2:1 [b]Gen. 24:2 [c]Gen. 24:49
30 [a]Gen. 15:15; Deut. 31:16 [b]Gen. 23:17-20; 25:9, 10; 35:29; 49:29-32; 50:5, 13; Acts 7:15, 16
31 [a]Gen. 21:23, 24; 24:3; 31:53; 50:25 [b]1 Kin. 1:47

1 [1]Lit., *one said to Joseph* [a]Gen. 41:51, 52; Josh. 14:4
2 [1]Lit., *one told Jacob and said* [2]Lit., *strengthened himself* [3]Lit., *upon the bed*
3 [1]Heb., *El Shaddai* [a]Gen. 28:13f.; 35:9-12 [b]Gen. 28:19; 35:6
4 [1]Lit., *seed* [a]Gen. 17:8
5 [a]Gen. 41:50-52; 48:1; 46:20; Josh. 14:4 [b]1 Chr. 5:1, 2
6 [1]Lit., *you have begotten* [2]Lit., *name*
7 [1]Lit., *upon me* [a]Gen. 33:18 [b]Gen. 35:19, 20
8 [a]Gen. 48:10
9 [a]Gen. 33:5 [b]Gen. 27:4
10 [1]Lit., *he* [a]Gen. 27:1 [b]Gen. 27:27
11 [1]Lit., *meditated, judged* [2]Lit., *seed*
12 [1]Lit., *made them come out* [a]Gen. 42:6
14 [1]Or, *consciously directing* [2]Lit., *when* [a]Gen. 41:51, 52
15 [1]Lit., *from the continuance of me* [a]Gen. 17:1 [b]Gen. 49:24
16 [1]Lit., *be called* [2]Lit., *name* [a]Gen. 22:11, 15-18; 28:13-15; 31:11 [b]Heb. 11:21 [c]Gen. 28:14; 46:3
17 [a]Gen. 48:14
19 [1]Lit., *seed* [2]Lit., *fulness* [a]Gen. 28:14; 46:3
20 [a]Heb. 11:21

21 Then Israel said to Joseph, "Behold, I am about to die, but [a]God will be
with you, and [b]bring you back to the
land of your fathers.
22 "And I give you one [1]portion more
than your brothers, [a]which I took from
the hand of the Amorite with my sword
and my bow."

Israel's Prophecy concerning His Sons

49 THEN Jacob summoned his sons
and said, "Assemble yourselves
that I may tell you what shall befall you
[a]in the [1]days to come.
2 "Gather together and hear, O sons
of Jacob;
And [a]listen to Israel your father.

3 "Reuben, you are my first-born;
My might and [a]the beginning of
my strength,
[1]Preeminent in dignity and [1]pre-
eminent in power.
4 "[1]Uncontrolled as water, you shall
not have preeminence,
[a]Because you went up to your
father's bed;
Then you defiled *it*—he went up
to my couch.

5 "[a]Simeon and Levi are brothers;
Their swords are implements of
violence.
6 "[a]Let my soul not enter into their
council;
Let not my glory be united with
their assembly;
Because in their anger they slew
[1]men,
And in their self-will they lamed
[2]oxen.
7 "Cursed be their anger, for it is
fierce;
And their wrath, for it is cruel.
[a]I will [1]disperse them in Jacob,
And scatter them in Israel.

8 "Judah, your brothers shall praise
you;
Your hand shall be on the neck of
your enemies;
[a]Your father's sons shall bow
down to you.
9 "Judah is a [a]lion's whelp;
From the prey, my son, you have
gone up.
[b]He [1]couches, he lies down as a
lion,
And as a [2]lion, who [3]dares rouse
him up?
10 "[a]The scepter shall not depart from
Judah,
Nor the ruler's staff from between
his feet,
[1]Until Shiloh comes,
And [b]to him *shall be* the obedience of the peoples.
11 "[1][a]He ties *his* foal to the vine,
And his donkey's colt to the
choice vine;
[b]He washes his garments in wine,
And his robes in the blood of
grapes.

12 "His eyes are [1]dull from wine,
And his teeth [2]white from milk.

13 "[a]Zebulun shall dwell at the sea-
shore;
And he *shall be* [1]a haven for ships,
And his flank *shall be* toward
Sidon.

14 "Issachar is [1]a strong donkey,
[a]Lying down between the [2]sheep-
folds.
15 "When he saw that a resting place
was good
And that the land was pleasant,
He bowed his shoulder to bear
burdens,
And became a slave at forced
labor.

16 "[a]Dan shall [b]judge his people,
As one of the tribes of Israel.
17 "Dan shall be a serpent in the way,
A horned snake in the path,
That bites the horse's heels,
So that his rider falls backward.
18 "[a]For Thy salvation I wait, O
LORD.

19 "[a]As for Gad, [1]raiders shall raid
him,
But he shall raid *at* their [2]heels.

20 "[1][a]As for [b]Asher, his [2]food shall be
[3]rich,
And he shall yield royal dainties.

21 "[a]Naphtali is a doe let loose,
He gives beautiful words.

22 "[a]Joseph is a fruitful [1]bough,
A fruitful [1]bough by a spring;
Its [2]branches run over a wall.
23 "The archers bitterly attacked him,
And shot *at him* and harassed
him;
24 But his [a]bow remained [1]firm,
And [2][b]his arms were agile,
From the hands of the [c]Mighty
One of Jacob
(From there is [d]the Shepherd, [e]the
Stone of Israel),
25 From [a]the God of your father
who helps you,
And [1][b]by the [2]Almighty who
blesses you
With [c]blessings of heaven above,
Blessings of the deep that lies
beneath,
Blessings of the breasts and of the
womb.
26 "The blessings of your father
Have surpassed the blessings of
my ancestors
Up to the [1]utmost bound of [a]the
everlasting hills;
May they be on the head of
Joseph,
And on the crown of the head of
the one distinguished among his
brothers.

27 "Benjamin is a [1]ravenous wolf;
In the morning he devours the
prey,

21 [a]Gen. 26:3 [b]Gen. 28:15; 46:4; 50:24
22 [1]Or, *ridge;* lit., *shoulder;* Heb., *Shechem* [a]Josh. 24:32; John 4:5

1 [1]Lit., *end of the days* [a]Num. 24:14
2 [a]Ps. 34:11
3 [1]Lit., *preeminence* [a]Deut. 21:17; Ps. 78:51; 105:36
4 [1]Or, *Boiling over;* lit., *recklessness* [a]Gen. 35:22; Deut. 27:20; 1 Chr. 5:1
5 [a]Gen. 34:25-30
6 [1]Lit., *a man* [2]Lit., *an ox* [a]Ps. 64:2
7 [1]Lit., *divide* [a]Josh. 19:1, 9; 21:1-42
8 [a]Gen. 27:29; 1 Chr. 5:2
9 [1]Lit., *bows down* [2]Or, *lioness* [3]Lit., *shall* [a]Ezek. 19:5-7; Mic. 5:8 [b]Num. 24:9
10 [1]Or, *Until he comes to Shiloh;* or, *Until he comes to whom it belongs* [a]Num. 24:17; Ps. 60:7; 108:8 [b]Ps. 2:6-9; 72:8-11; Is. 42:1, 4; 49:6
11 [1]Lit., *Binding of* [a]Deut. 8:7, 8; 2 Kin. 18:32 [b]Is. 63:2
12 [1]Or, *darker than* [2]Or, *whiter than*
13 [1]Lit., *for a shore of ships* [a]Deut. 33:18, 19
14 [1]Lit., *a donkey of bone* [2]Or, *saddlebags* [a]Judg. 5:16; Ps. 68:13
16 [a]Deut. 33:22; Judg. 18:26, 27 [b]Gen. 30:6
18 [a]Ex. 15:2; Ps. 25:5; 40:1-3; 119:166, 174; Is. 25:9; Mic. 7:7
19 [1]Lit., *a raiding band* [2]Lit., *heel* [a]Deut. 33:20
20 [1]Lit., *From* [2]Or, *bread* [3]Lit., *fat* [a]Deut. 33:24, 25 [b]Gen. 30:13
21 [a]Deut. 33:23
22 [1]Lit., *son* [2]Lit., *daughters* [a]Deut. 33:13-17
24 [1]I.e., in an unyielding position [2]Lit., *the arms of his hands* [a]Job 29:20 [b]Ps. 18:34; 73:23; Is. 41:10 [c]Ps. 132:2, 5; Is. 1:24; 49:26 [d]Ps. 23:1; 80:1 [e]Ps. 118:22; Is. 28:16; 1 Pet. 2:6-8
25 [1]Or, *with* [2]Heb., *Shaddai* [a]Gen. 28:13; 32:9 [b]Gen. 28:3; 48:3 [c]Gen. 27:28
26 [1]Lit., *limit;* or, *desire* [a]Deut. 33:15, 16
27 [1]Lit., *a wolf that tears*

And in the evening he divides the spoil."

28 All these are the twelve tribes of Israel, and this is what their father said to them [1]when he blessed them. He blessed them, every one [2]with the blessing appropriate to him.

29 Then he charged them and said to them, "I am about to be [a]gathered to my people; [b]bury me with my fathers in the cave that is in [c]the field of Ephron the Hittite,

30 in the [a]cave that is in the field of Machpelah, which is before Mamre, in the land of Canaan, which Abraham bought along with the field from Ephron the Hittite for a [1]burial site.

31 "There they buried [a]Abraham and his wife [b]Sarah, there they buried [c]Isaac and his wife Rebekah, and there I buried Leah—

32 the field and the cave that is in it, purchased from the sons of Heth."

33 When Jacob finished charging his sons, he drew his feet into the bed and [a]breathed his last, and was [b]gathered to his people.

The Death of Israel

50 THEN Joseph fell on his father's face, and wept over him and kissed him.

2 And Joseph commanded his servants the physicians to embalm his father. So the physicians [a]embalmed Israel.

3 Now forty days were [1]required for [2]it, for [3]such is the period required for embalming. And the Egyptians [a]wept for him seventy days.

4 And when the days of [1]mourning for him were past, Joseph spoke to the household of Pharaoh, saying, "If now I have found favor in your sight, please speak [2]to Pharaoh, saying,

5 '[a]My father made me swear, saying, "Behold, I am about to die; in my grave [b]which I dug for myself in the land of Canaan, there you shall bury me." Now therefore, please let me go up and bury my father; then I will return.' "

6 And Pharaoh said, "Go up and bury your father, as he made you swear."

7 So Joseph went up to bury his father, and with him went up all the servants of Pharaoh, the elders of his household and all the elders of the land of Egypt,

8 and all the household of Joseph and his brothers and his father's household; they left only their little ones and their flocks and their herds in the land of Goshen.

9 There also went up with him both chariots and horsemen; and it was a very great company.

10 When they came to the [1]threshing floor of Atad, which is beyond the Jordan, they [a]lamented there with a very great and [2]sorrowful lamentation; and he [3]observed seven days mourning for his father.

11 Now when the inhabitants of the land, the Canaanites, saw the mourning at [1]the threshing floor of Atad, they said, "This is a [2]grievous [3]mourning for the Egyptians." Therefore it was named [4]Abel-mizraim, which is beyond the Jordan.

Burial at Machpelah

12 And thus his sons did for him as he had charged them;

13 for his sons carried him to the land of Canaan, and buried him in [a]the cave of the field of Machpelah before Mamre, which Abraham had bought along with the field for a [1]burial site from Ephron the Hittite.

14 And after he had buried his father, Joseph returned to Egypt, he and his brothers, and all who had gone up with him to bury his father.

15 When Joseph's brothers saw that their father was dead, they said, "[a]What if Joseph should bear a grudge against us and pay us back in full for all the wrong which we did to him!"

16 So they [1]sent *a message* to Joseph, saying, "Your father charged before he died, saying,

17 'Thus you shall say to Joseph, "Please forgive, I beg you, the transgression of your brothers and their sin, for they did you wrong." ' And now, please forgive the transgression of the servants of the God of your father." And Joseph wept when they spoke to him.

18 Then his brothers also came and [a]fell down before him and said, "Behold, we are your servants."

19 But Joseph said to them, "Do not be afraid, for am I in God's place?

20 "And as for you, [a]you meant evil against me, *but* God meant it for good in order to bring about [1]this present result, to preserve many people alive.

21 "So therefore, do not be afraid; [a]I will provide for you and your little ones." So he comforted them and spoke [1]kindly to them.

Death of Joseph

22 Now Joseph stayed in Egypt, he and his father's household, and Joseph lived one hundred and ten years.

23 And Joseph saw the third generation of Ephraim's sons; also the sons of Machir, the son of Manasseh, were [a]born on Joseph's knees.

24 And Joseph said to his brothers, "[a]I am about to die, but God will surely [1]take care of you, and bring you up from this land to the land which He [2]promised on oath to [b]Abraham, to [c]Isaac and to [d]Jacob."

25 Then Joseph made the sons of Israel swear, saying, "God will surely [1]take care of you, and [a]you shall carry my bones up from here."

26 So Joseph died at the age of one hundred and ten years; and [1]he was [a]embalmed and placed in a coffin in Egypt.

---

28 [1]Lit., *and* [2]Lit., *according to his blessing*

29 [a]Gen. 25:8 [b]Gen. 47:30 [c]Gen. 23:16-20; 50:13

30 [1]Lit., *possession of a burial place* [a]Gen. 23:3-20

31 [a]Gen. 25:9 [b]Gen. 23:19 [c]Gen. 35:29

33 [a]Gen. 25:8; Acts 7:15 [b]Gen. 49:29

2 [a]Gen. 50:26; 2 Chr. 16:14; Matt. 26:12; Mark 16:1; John 19:39, 40

3 [1]Lit., *fulfilled* [2]Or, *him* [3]Lit., *so are fulfilled the days of embalming* [a]Gen. 50:10; Num. 20:29; Deut. 34:8

4 [1]Lit., *weeping* [2]Lit., *In the ears of*

5 [a]Gen. 47:29-31 [b]2 Chr. 16:14; Is. 22:16; Matt. 27:60

10 [1]Heb., *Goren ha-Atad* [2]Lit., *heavy* [3]Lit., *made a mourning for seven days* [a]Acts 8:2

11 [1]Heb., *Goren ha-Atad* [2]Lit., *heavy* [3]Heb., *ebel* [4]I.e., the meadow (or mourning) of Egypt

13 [1]Lit., *possession of a burial place* [a]Gen. 23:16-20; Acts 7:16

15 [a]Gen. 37:28; 42:21, 22

16 [1]Lit., *commanded*

18 [a]Gen. 37:8-10; 41:43

20 [1]Lit., *as it is this day* [a]Gen. 37:26, 27; 45:5, 7

21 [1]Lit., *to their heart* [a]Gen. 45:11; 47:12

23 [a]Gen. 30:3

24 [1]Or, *visit* [2]Lit., *swore* [a]Gen. 48:21; Ex. 3:16, 17; Heb. 11:22 [b]Gen. 13:15, 17; 15:7, 8, 18 [c]Gen. 26:3 [d]Gen. 28:13; 35:12

25 [1]Or, *visit* [a]Gen. 47:29, 30; Ex. 13:19; Josh. 24:32; Heb. 11:22

26 [1]Lit., *they embalmed him* [a]Gen. 50:2

EXODUS

Israel Multiplies in Egypt

1 NOW these are the [a]names of the
sons of Israel who came to Egypt
with Jacob; they came each one [1]with
his household:
2 Reuben, Simeon, Levi and Judah;
3 Issachar, Zebulun and Benjamin;
4 Dan and Naphtali, Gad and Asher.
5 And all the [1]persons who came
from the loins of Jacob were [a]seventy [2]in
number, but Joseph was *already* in
Egypt.
6 And [a]Joseph died, and all his
brothers and all that generation.
7 But the sons of Israel [a]were fruitful
and [1]increased greatly, and multiplied,
and became exceedingly [2]mighty, so that
the land was filled with them.
8 Now a new [a]king arose over Egypt,
who did not know Joseph.
9 And [a]he said to his people, "Behold, the people of the sons of Israel are
[1]more and mightier than we.
10 "Come, let us [a]deal wisely with
them, lest they multiply and [1]in the
event of war, they also join themselves to
those who hate us, and fight against us,
and [2]depart from the land."
11 So they appointed [a]taskmasters
over them to afflict them with [1b]hard
labor. And they built for Pharaoh [c]stor-
age cities, Pithom and [d]Raamses.
12 But the more they afflicted them,
[a]the more they multiplied and the more
they [1]spread out, so that they were in
dread of the sons of Israel.
13 And the Egyptians compelled the
sons of Israel [a]to labor rigorously;
14 and they made [a]their lives bitter
with hard labor in mortar and bricks and
at all *kinds* of labor in the field, all their
labors which they rigorously [1]imposed
on them.
15 Then the king of Egypt spoke to
the Hebrew midwives, one of whom
[1]was named Shiphrah, and the other
[1]was named Puah;
16 and he said, "When you are helping the Hebrew women to give birth and
see *them* upon the birthstool, [a]if it is a
son, then you shall put him to death; but
if it is a daughter, then she shall live."
17 But the midwives [1a]feared God,
and [b]did not do as the king of Egypt had
[2]commanded them, but let the boys live.
18 So the king of Egypt called for the
midwives, and said to them, "Why have
you done this thing, and let the boys
live?"
19 And the midwives said to Pharaoh,
"Because the Hebrew women are not as
the Egyptian women; for they are vigorous, and they give birth before the
midwife [1]can get to them."
20 So [a]God was good to the midwives,
and [b]the people multiplied, and became
very [1]mighty.
21 And it came about because the
midwives [1a]feared God, that He [2]estab-
lished [3]households for them.
22 Then Pharaoh commanded all his
people, saying, "[a]Every son who is born
[1]you are to cast into [b]the Nile, and every
daughter you are to keep alive."

The Birth of Moses

2 NOW a man from [a]the house of
Levi went and [1]married a daughter
of Levi.
2 And the woman conceived and
bore a son; and when she saw [1]that he
was [2a]beautiful, she hid him for three
months.
3 But when she could hide him no
longer, she got him a [1a]wicker [2]basket
and covered it over with tar and pitch.
Then she put the child into it, and set *it*
among the [b]reeds by the bank of the
Nile.
4 And [a]his sister stood at a distance
to [1]find out what would [2]happen to him.
5 Then the daughter of Pharaoh
came down [a]to bathe at the Nile, with
her maidens walking alongside the Nile;
and she saw the [1]basket among the reeds
and sent her maid, and she brought it *to
her.*
6 When she opened *it,* she [1]saw the
child, and behold, *the* [2]boy was crying.
And she had pity on him and said, "This
is one of the Hebrews' children."
7 Then his sister said to Pharaoh's
daughter, "Shall I go and call [1]a nurse
for you from the Hebrew women, that
she may nurse the child for you?"
8 And Pharaoh's daughter said to
her, "Go *ahead.*" So the girl went and
called the child's mother.
9 Then Pharaoh's daughter said to
her, "Take this child away and nurse
him for me and I shall give *you* your
wages." So the woman took the child
and nursed him.
10 And the child grew, and she
brought him to Pharaoh's daughter, and
[a]he became her son. And she named him
[1]Moses, and said, "Because I [2]drew him
out of the water."
11 Now it came about in those days,
[a]when Moses had grown up, that he
went out to his brethren and looked on
their [1b]hard labors; and [c]he saw an
Egyptian beating a Hebrew, one of his
brethren.
12 So he [1]looked this way and that,
and when he saw there was no one
around, he [a]struck down the Egyptian
and hid him in the sand.
13 And he went out [a]the next day, and
behold, two Hebrews were [1]fighting with
each other; and he said to the [2]offender,
"Why are you striking your companion?"
14 But he said, "[a]Who made you a
[1]prince or a judge over us? Are you
[2]intending to kill me, as you killed the
Egyptian?" Then Moses was afraid, and
said, "Surely the matter has become
known."

1 [1]Lit., *and*
[a]Gen. 46:8-27
5 [1]Lit., *souls* [2]Lit., *as to souls*
[a]Gen. 46:26, 27; Deut. 10:22
6 [a]Gen. 50:26
7 [1]Lit., *swarmed* [2]Or, *numerous*
[a]Gen. 12:2; 28:3; 35:11; 46:3; 47:27; 48:4; Deut. 26:5; Ps. 105:24; Acts 7:17
8 [a]Acts 7:18, 19
9 [1]Or, *too many and too mighty for us*
[a]Ps. 105:24, 25
10 [1]Lit., *it came about when war befalls that* [2]Lit., *go up from*
[a]Acts 7:19
11 [1]Lit., *their burdens*
[a]Gen. 15:13; Ex. 3:7; 5:6 [b]Ex. 1:14; 2:11; 5:4-9; 6:6f. [c]1 Kin. 9:19; 2 Chr. 8:4 [d]Gen. 47:11
12 [1]Lit., *broke forth*
[a]Ex. 1:7
13 [a]Gen. 15:13; Deut. 4:20
14 [1]Lit., *worked through them*
[a]Ex. 2:23; 6:9; Num. 20:15; Acts 7:19
15 [1]Lit., *the name was*
16 [a]Acts 7:19
17 [1]Or, *revered* [2]Lit., *spoken to*
[a]Ex. 1:21; Prov. 16:6 [b]Acts 4:18-20; 5:29
19 [1]Lit., *comes to*
20 [1]Or, *numerous*
[a]Prov. 11:18; Eccl. 8:12; Heb. 6:10 [b]Ex. 1:12; Is. 3:10
21 [1]Or, *revered* [2]Lit., *made* [3]Or, *families*
[a]Ex. 1:17
[b]1 Sam. 2:35; 2 Sam. 7:11, 27; 1 Kin. 2:24; 11:38
22 [1]Some versions insert *to the Hebrews*
[a]Acts 7:19 [b]Gen. 41:1

1 [1]Lit., *took*
[a]Ex. 6:16, 18, 20
2 [1]Lit., *him that* [2]Lit., *good*
[a]Acts 7:20; Heb. 11:23
3 [1]I.e., papyrus reeds [2]Or, *chest*
[a]Is. 18:2 [b]Is. 19:6
4 [1]Lit., *know* [2]Lit., *be done*
[a]Ex. 15:20; Num. 26:59
5 [1]Or, *chest*
[a]Ex. 7:15; 8:20
6 [1]Heb., *saw it, the child* [2]Or, *lad*
7 [1]Lit., *a woman giving suck*
10 [1]Heb., *Mosheh,* from *mashah* [2]Heb., *mashah*
[a]Acts 7:21
11 [1]Lit., *burdens*
[a]Acts 7:23; Heb. 11:24-26 [b]Ex. 1:11; 5:4, 5; 6:6, 7 [c]Acts 7:24
12 [1]Lit., *turned*
[a]Acts 7:24, 25
13 [1]Or, *quarreling* [2]Or, *the guilty one*
[a]Acts 7:26-28
14 [1]Lit., *man, a prince* [2]Lit., *saying in your heart* [a]Gen. 19:9; Acts 7:27, 28

Moses Escapes to Midian

15 When Pharaoh heard of this matter, he tried to kill Moses. But [a]Moses fled from the presence of Pharaoh and [1]settled in the land of Midian; and he sat down [b]by a well.

16 Now [a]the priest of Midian had seven daughters; and [b]they came to draw water, and filled the troughs to water their father's flock.

17 Then the shepherds came and drove them away, but [a]Moses stood up and helped them, and watered their flock.

18 When they came to [a]Reuel their father, he said, "Why have you come *back* so soon today?"

19 So they said, "An Egyptian delivered us from the hand of the shepherds; and what is more, he even drew the water for us and watered the flock."

20 And he said to his daughters, "Where is he then? Why is it that you have left the man behind? Invite him [1]to have something to eat."

21 [a]And Moses was willing to dwell with the man, and he gave his daughter [b]Zipporah to Moses.

22 Then she gave birth to [a]a son, and he named him [1]Gershom, for he said, "I have been [b]a [2]sojourner in a foreign land."

23 Now it came about in *the course of* those many days that the king of Egypt died. And the sons of Israel [a]sighed because of the bondage, and they cried out; and [b]their cry for help because of *their* bondage rose up to God.

24 So [a]God heard their groaning; and God remembered [b]His covenant with Abraham, Isaac, and Jacob.

25 And [a]God saw the sons of Israel, and God [1]took notice *of them.*

The Burning Bush

3 NOW Moses was pasturing the flock of [a]Jethro his father-in-law, the priest of Midian; and he led the flock to the [1]west side of the wilderness, and came to [b]Horeb, the [c]mountain of God.

2 And [a]the angel of the LORD appeared to him in a blazing fire from the midst of [1]a [b]bush; and he looked, and behold, the bush was burning with fire, yet the bush was not consumed.

3 So Moses said, "[1a]I must turn aside now, and see this [2]marvelous sight, why the bush is not burned up."

4 When the LORD saw that he turned aside to look, [a]God called to him from the midst of the bush, and said, "Moses, Moses!" And he said, "Here I am."

5 Then He said, "Do not come near here; [a]remove your sandals from your feet, for the place on which you are standing is holy ground."

6 He said also, "[a]I am the God of your father, the God of Abraham, the God of Isaac, and the God of Jacob." [b]Then Moses hid his face, for he was [c]afraid to look at God.

7 And the LORD said, "I have surely [a]seen the affliction of My people who are in Egypt, and have given heed to their cry because of their taskmasters, for I am aware of their sufferings.

8 "So I have come down [a]to deliver them from the [1]power of the Egyptians, and to bring them up from that land to a [b]good and spacious land, to a land flowing with milk and honey, to the place of [c]the Canaanite and the Hittite and the Amorite and the Perizzite and the Hivite and the Jebusite.

9 "And now, behold, [a]the cry of the sons of Israel has come to Me; furthermore, I have seen the oppression with which the Egyptians are oppressing them.

The Mission of Moses

10 "Therefore, come now, and I will send you to Pharaoh, [a]so that you may bring My people, the sons of Israel, out of Egypt."

11 But Moses said to God, "[a]Who am I, that I should go to Pharaoh, and that I should bring the sons of Israel out of Egypt?"

12 And He said, "Certainly [a]I will be with you, and this shall be the sign to you that it is I who have sent you: [b]when you have brought the people out of Egypt, [c]you shall [1]worship God at this mountain."

13 Then Moses said to God, "Behold, I am going to the sons of Israel, and I shall say to them, 'The God of your fathers has sent me to you.' Now they may say to me, 'What is His name?' What shall I say to them?"

14 And God said to Moses, "[1a]I AM WHO [1]I AM"; and He said, "Thus you shall say to the sons of Israel, '[1]I AM has sent me to you.' "

15 And God, furthermore, said to Moses, "Thus you shall say to the sons of Israel, '[a]The LORD, the God of your fathers, the God of Abraham, the God of Isaac, and the God of Jacob, has sent me to you.' This is My name forever, and this is My [b]memorial-name [1]to all generations.

16 "Go and [a]gather the elders of Israel together, and say to them, '[b]The LORD, the God of your fathers, the God of Abraham, Isaac and Jacob, has appeared to me, saying, "[1c]I am indeed concerned about you and what has been done to you in Egypt.

17 "So [a]I said, I will bring you up out of the affliction of Egypt to the land of [b]the Canaanite and the Hittite and the Amorite and the Perizzite and the Hivite and the Jebusite, to a land [c]flowing with milk and honey." '

2:15 [1]Lit., *dwelt* [a]Acts 7:29; Heb. 11:27 [b]Gen. 24:11; 29:2
16 [a]Ex. 3:1; 18:12 [b]Gen. 24:11, 13, 19; 29:9, 10; 1 Sam. 9:11
17 [a]Gen. 29:3, 10
18 [a]Ex. 3:1; Num. 10:29
20 [1]Lit., *that he may eat bread*
21 [a]Acts 7:29 [b]Ex. 4:25; 18:2
22 [1]Heb., *ger sham, a stranger there* [2]Heb., *ger* [a]Ex. 4:20; 18:3, 4 [b]Gen. 23:4; Lev. 25:23; Acts 7:29; Heb. 11:13, 14
23 [a]Ex. 6:5, 9 [b]Ex. 3:7, 9; Deut. 26:7; James 5:4
24 [a]Ex. 6:5; Acts 7:34 [b]Gen. 15:13f.; 22:16-18; 26:2-5; 28:13-15; Ps. 105:8, 42
25 [1]Lit., *knew* them [a]Ex. 3:7; 4:31; Acts 7:34

3:1 [1]Or, *rear part* [a]Ex. 2:18; 4:18; 18:12; Num. 10:29 [b]Ex. 3:12; 17:6; 33:6; 1 Kin. 19:8 [c]Ex. 4:27; 18:5; 24:13
2 [1]Lit., *the* [a]Gen. 16:7-11; 21:17; 22:11, 15; Ex. 3:4-11, 16; Judg. 13:13-21; Acts 7:30 [b]Deut. 33:16; Mark 12:26; Luke 20:37; Acts 7:30
3 [1]Lit., *Let me turn* [2]Lit., *great* [a]Acts 7:31
4 [a]Ex. 4:5
5 [a]Josh. 5:15; Acts 7:33
6 [a]Gen. 28:13; Ex. 3:16; 4:5; Matt. 22:32; Mark 12:26; Luke 20:37 [b]Acts 7:32 [c]Judg. 13:22; Rev. 1:17
7 [a]Ex. 2:25; Neh. 9:9; Ps. 106:44; Is. 63:9; Acts 7:34
8 [1]Lit., *hand* [a]Gen. 15:13-16; 46:4; 50:24, 25; Ex. 6:6-8; 12:51 [b]Ex. 3:17; 13:5; Num. 13:27; Deut. 1:25; 8:7-9; Jer. 11:5; Ezek. 20:6 [c]Gen. 15:19-21; Josh. 24:11
9 [a]Ex. 2:23
10 [a]Gen. 15:13, 14; Ex. 12:40, 41; Mic. 6:4; Acts 7:6, 7
11 [a]Ex. 4:10; 6:12; 1 Sam. 18:18
12 [1]Or, *serve* [a]Gen. 31:3; Ex. 4:12, 15; 33:14-16; Deut. 31:23; Josh. 1:5; Is. 43:2 [b]Ex. 19:1 [c]Ex. 19:2, 3; Acts 7:7
14 [1]Related to the name of God, *YHWH*, rendered *LORD*, which is derived from the verb *HAYAH, to be* [a]Ex. 6:3; John 8:24, 28, 58; Heb. 13:8; Rev. 1:8; 4:8
15 [1]Lit., *to generation of generation* [a]Ex. 3:6, 13 [b]Ps. 30:4; 97:12; 102:12; 135:13; Hos. 12:5
16 [1]Lit., *Visiting I have visited* [a]Ex. 4:29 [b]Gen. 28:13; 48:15; Ex. 3:2, 6; 4:5 [c]Ex. 4:31; Ps. 33:18f.
17 [a]Gen. 15:13-21; 46:4; 50:24, 25 [b]Josh. 24:11 [c]Ex. 3:8

18 "And [a]they will [1]pay heed to what you say; and [b]you with the elders of Israel will come to the king of Egypt, and you will say to him, 'The LORD, the God of the Hebrews, has met with us. So now, please, let us go a [c]three days' journey into the wilderness, that we may sacrifice to the LORD our God.'

19 "But I know that the king of Egypt [a]will not permit you to go, [b]except [1]under compulsion.

20 "So I will stretch out [a]My hand, and strike Egypt with all My [b]miracles which I shall do in the midst of it; and [c]after that he will let you go.

21 "And I will grant this people [a]favor in the sight of the Egyptians; and it shall be that when you go, you will not go empty-handed.

22 "But every woman [a]shall ask of her neighbor and the woman who lives in her house, articles of silver and articles of gold, and clothing; and you will put them on your sons and daughters. Thus you will [b]plunder the Egyptians."

Moses Given Powers

4 THEN Moses answered and said, "What if they will not believe me, or [a]listen [1]to what I say? For they may say, '[b]The LORD has not appeared to you.' "

2 And the LORD said to him, "What is that in your hand?" And he said, "[a]A staff."

3 Then He said, "Throw it on the ground." So he threw it on the ground, and [a]it became a serpent; and Moses fled from it.

4 But the LORD said to Moses, "Stretch out your hand and grasp *it* by its tail"—so he stretched out his hand and caught it, and it became a staff in his [1]hand—

5 "that [a]they may believe that [b]the LORD, the God of their fathers, the God of Abraham, the God of Isaac, and the God of Jacob, has appeared to you."

6 And the LORD furthermore said to him, "Now put your hand into your bosom." So he put his hand into his bosom, and when he took it out, behold, his hand was [a]leprous like snow.

7 Then He said, "Put your hand into your bosom again." So he put his hand into his bosom again; and when he took it out of his bosom, behold, [a]it was restored like *the rest of* his flesh.

8 "And it shall come about that if they will not believe you or [1]heed the [2]witness of the first sign, they may believe the [2]witness of the last sign.

9 "But it shall be that if they will not believe even these two signs or heed what you say, then you shall take some water from the Nile and pour it on the dry ground; and the water which you take from the Nile [a]will become blood on the dry ground."

10 Then Moses said to the LORD, "Please, Lord, [a]I have never been [1]eloquent, neither [2]recently nor in time past, nor since Thou hast spoken to Thy servant; for I am [3]slow of speech and [3]slow of tongue."

11 And the LORD said to him, "Who has made man's mouth? Or [a]who makes *him* dumb or deaf, or seeing or blind? Is it not I, the LORD?

12 "Now then go, and [a]I, even I, will be with your mouth, and [b]teach you what you are to say."

13 But he said, "Please, Lord, now [1]send *the message* by whomever Thou wilt."

Aaron to Be Moses' Mouthpiece

14 Then the anger of the LORD burned against Moses, and He said, "Is there not your brother Aaron the Levite? I know that [1]he speaks fluently. And moreover, behold, [a]he is coming out to meet you; when he sees you, he will be glad in his heart.

15 "And you are to speak to him and [a]put the words in his mouth; and I, even I, will be with your mouth and his mouth, and I will teach you what you are to do.

16 "Moreover, [a]he shall speak for you to the people; and it shall come about that he shall be as a mouth for you, and you shall be as God to him.

17 "And you shall take in your hand [a]this staff, [b]with which you shall perform the signs."

18 Then Moses departed and returned to [1]Jethro [a]his father-in-law, and said to him, "Please, let me go, that I may return to my brethren who are in Egypt, and see if they are still alive." And Jethro said to Moses, "Go in peace."

19 Now the LORD said to Moses in Midian, "Go [1]back to Egypt, for [a]all the men who were seeking your life are dead."

20 So Moses took his wife and his [a]sons and mounted them on a donkey, and he returned to the land of Egypt. Moses also took the [b]staff of God in his hand.

21 And the LORD said to Moses, "When you go [1]back to Egypt see that you perform before Pharaoh all [a]the wonders which I have put in your [2]power; but [b]I will harden his heart so that he will not let the people go.

22 "Then you shall say to Pharaoh, 'Thus says the LORD, "[a]Israel is My son, My first-born.

23 "So I said to you, '[a]Let My son go, that he may serve Me'; but you have refused to let him go. Behold, [b]I will kill your son, your first-born." ' "

24 Now it came about at the lodging place on the way that the LORD met him and [a]sought to put him to death.

25 Then Zipporah took [a]a flint and cut off her son's foreskin and [1]threw *it* at Moses' feet, and she said, "You are indeed a bridegroom of blood to me."

18 [1]Lit., *hear your voice* [a]Ex. 4:31 [b]Ex. 5:1 [c]Ex. 5:3; 8:27
19 [1]Lit., *by a strong hand* [a]Ex. 5:2 [b]Ex. 6:1
20 [a]Ex. 6:1; 7:4, 5; 9:15; 13:3, 9, 14 [b]Ex. 7:3; 15:11; Deut. 6:22; Neh. 9:10; Ps. 105:27; 135:9; Jer. 32:20; Acts 7:36 [c]Ex. 11:1; 12:31-33
21 [a]Ex. 11:3; 12:36; 1 Kin. 8:50; Ps. 105:37f.; 106:46; Prov. 16:7
22 [a]Gen. 15:14; Ex. 11:2; 12:35 [b]Ezek. 39:10

1 [1]Lit., *to my voice* [a]Ex. 3:18; 6:30 [b]Ex. 3:15, 16
2 [a]Ex. 4:17, 20
3 [a]Ex. 7:10-12
4 [1]Lit., *palm*
5 [a]Ex. 4:31; 19:9 [b]Gen. 28:13; 48:15; Ex. 3:6, 15
6 [a]Num. 12:10; 2 Kin. 5:27
7 [a]Num. 12:13-15; Deut. 32:39; 2 Kin. 5:14; Matt. 8:3; Luke 17:12-14
8 [1]Lit., *listen to* [2]Lit., *voice*
9 [a]Ex. 7:19, 20
10 [1]Lit., *a man of words* [2]Lit., *yesterday* [3]Lit., *heavy* [a]Ex. 3:11; 4:1; 6:12; Jer. 1:6
11 [a]Ps. 94:9; 146:8; Matt. 11:5; Luke 1:20, 64
12 [a]Ex. 4:15, 16; Deut. 18:18; Is. 50:4; Jer. 1:9 [b]Matt. 10:19, 20; Mark 13:11; Luke 12:11, 12; 21:14, 15
13 [1]Lit., *send by the hand which Thou sendest*
14 [1]Lit., *speaking he speaks* [a]Ex. 4:27
15 [a]Ex. 4:12, 30; 7:1f.; Num. 23:5, 12, 16; Deut. 18:18; Is. 51:16; 59:21; Jer. 1:9
16 [a]Ex. 7:1, 2
17 [a]Ex. 4:2, 20; 17:9 [b]Ex. 7:9-20; 14:16
18 [1]Heb., *Jether* [a]Ex. 2:21; 3:1
19 [1]Lit., *return* [a]Ex. 2:15, 23
20 [a]Ex. 18:3, 4; Acts 7:29 [b]Ex. 4:17; 17:9; Num. 20:8, 9, 11
21 [1]Lit., *to return* [2]Lit., *hand* [a]Ex. 3:20; 11:9, 10 [b]Ex. 7:3, 13; 9:12, 35; 10:1, 20, 27; 14:4, 8; Deut. 2:30; Josh. 11:20; 1 Sam. 6:6; Is. 63:17; John 12:40; Rom. 9:18
22 [a]Is. 63:16; 64:8; Jer. 31:9; Hos. 11:1; Rom. 9:4
23 [a]Ex. 5:1; 6:11; 7:16 [b]Ex. 11:5; 12:29; Ps. 105:36; 135:8; 136:10
24 [a]Num. 22:22

25 [1]Lit., *made it touch at his feet* [a]Gen. 17:14; Josh. 5:2, 3

26 So He let him alone. At that time she said, "*You are* a bridegroom of blood"—[1]because of the circumcision.

27 [a]Now the LORD said to Aaron, "Go to meet Moses in the wilderness." So he went and met him at the [b]mountain of God, and he kissed him.

28 And [a]Moses told Aaron all the words of the LORD with which He had sent him, and [b]all the signs that He had commanded him *to do.*

29 Then Moses and Aaron went and [a]assembled all the elders of the sons of Israel;

30 and [a]Aaron spoke all the words which the LORD had spoken to Moses. He then performed the [b]signs in the sight of the people.

31 So [a]the people believed; and when they heard that the LORD [1b]was concerned about the sons of Israel and that He had seen their affliction, then [c]they bowed low and worshiped.

Israel's Labor Increased

5 AND afterward Moses and Aaron came and said to Pharaoh, "[a]Thus says the LORD, the God of Israel, '[b]Let My people go that they may celebrate a feast to Me in the wilderness.' "

2 But Pharaoh said, "[a]Who is the LORD that I should obey His voice to let Israel go? I do not know the LORD, and besides, [b]I will not let Israel go."

3 Then they said, "[a]The God of the Hebrews has met with us. Please, let us go a three days' journey into the wilderness that we may sacrifice to the LORD our God, lest He fall upon us with pestilence or with the sword."

4 But the king of Egypt said to them, "Moses and Aaron, why do you [1]draw the people away from their [2]work? Get *back* to your [3a]labors!"

5 Again Pharaoh said, "Look, [a]the people of the land are now many, and you would have them cease from their labors!"

6 So the same day Pharaoh commanded [a]the taskmasters over the people and their [b]foremen, saying,

7 "You are no longer to give the people straw to make brick as previously; let them go and gather straw for themselves.

8 "But the quota of bricks which they were making previously, you shall impose on them; you are not to reduce any of it. Because they are [a]lazy, therefore they cry out, '[1]Let us go and sacrifice to our God.'

9 "Let the labor be heavier on the men, and let them work at it that they may pay no attention to false words."

10 So [a]the taskmasters of the people and their foremen went out and spoke to the people, saying, "Thus says Pharaoh, 'I am not going to give you *any* straw.

11 'You go *and* get straw for yourselves wherever you can find *it;* but none of your labor will be reduced.' "

12 So the people scattered through all the land of Egypt to gather stubble for straw.

13 And the taskmasters pressed them, saying, "Complete your [1]work quota, [2]*your* daily amount, just as when [3]you had straw."

14 Moreover, [a]the foremen of the sons of Israel, whom Pharaoh's taskmasters had set over them, [b]were beaten [1]and were asked, "Why have you not completed your required amount either yesterday or today in making brick as previously?"

15 Then the foremen of the sons of Israel came and cried out to Pharaoh, saying, "Why do you deal this way with your servants?

16 "There is no straw given to your servants, yet they keep saying to us, 'Make bricks!' And behold, your servants are being beaten; but it is the fault of your *own* people."

17 But he said, "You are [a]lazy, *very* lazy; therefore you say, 'Let us go *and* sacrifice to the LORD.'

18 "So go now *and* work; for you shall be given no straw, yet you must deliver the quota of bricks."

19 And the foremen of the sons of Israel saw that they were in trouble [1]because they were told, "You must not reduce [2]*your* daily amount of bricks."

20 When they left Pharaoh's presence, they met Moses and Aaron as they were [1]waiting for them.

21 And [a]they said to them, "[b]May the LORD look upon you and judge *you,* for you have [c]made [1]us odious in Pharaoh's sight and in the sight of his servants, to put a sword in their hand to kill us."

22 Then Moses returned to the LORD and said, "[a]O Lord, why hast Thou brought harm to this people? Why didst Thou ever send me?

23 "Ever since I came to Pharaoh to speak in Thy name, he has done harm to this people; [a]and Thou hast not delivered Thy people at all."

God Promises Action

6 THEN the LORD said to Moses, "Now you shall see what I will do to Pharaoh; for [1a]under compulsion he shall let them go, and [1]under compulsion he shall drive them out of his land."

2 God spoke further to Moses and said to him, "I am [a]the LORD;

3 and I appeared to Abraham, Isaac, and Jacob, as [1a]God Almighty, but *by* [b]My name, [2]LORD, I did not make Myself known to them.

4 "And I also established [a]My covenant with them, to give them the land of Canaan, the [1]land in which they sojourned.

5 "And furthermore I have [a]heard the groaning of the sons of Israel, because the Egyptians are holding them in bondage; and I have remembered My covenant.

4:26 [1]Lit., *with reference to*
27 [a]Ex. 4:14 [b]Ex. 3:1; 18:5; 24:13
28 [a]Ex. 4:15f. [b]Ex. 4:8f.
29 [a]Ex. 3:16
30 [a]Ex. 4:15, 16 [b]Ex. 4:1-9
31 [1]Lit., *had visited* [a]Ex. 3:18; 4:8f.; 19:9 [b]Gen. 50:24; Ex. 3:16 [c]Gen. 24:26; Ex. 12:27; 1 Chr. 29:20

5:1 [a]Ex. 3:18 [b]Ex. 4:23; 6:11; 7:16
2 [a]2 Kin. 18:35; 2 Chr. 32:14; Job 21:15 [b]Ex. 3:19
3 [a]Ex. 3:18
4 [1]Lit., *loose* [2]Lit., *works* [3]Lit., *burdens* [a]Ex. 1:11; 2:11; 6:5-7
5 [a]Ex. 1:7, 9
6 [a]Ex. 1:11; 3:7; 5:10, 13, 14 [b]Ex. 5:10, 14, 15, 19
8 [1]Lit., *saying, 'Let* [a]Ex. 5:17
10 [a]Ex. 1:11; 3:7; 5:6
13 [1]Lit., *works* [2]Lit., *the matter of a day in its day* [3]Lit., *there was*
14 [1]Lit., *saying* [a]Ex. 5:6 [b]Is. 10:24
17 [a]Ex. 5:8
19 [1]Lit., *saying* [2]Lit., *from your bricks the matter of a day in its day*
20 [1]Lit., *standing to meet*
21 [1]Lit., *our savor to stink* [a]Ex. 14:11; 15:24; 16:2 [b]Gen. 16:5; 31:53 [c]Gen. 34:30; 1 Sam. 13:4; 27:12; 2 Sam. 10:6; 1 Chr. 19:6
22 [a]Num. 11:11; Jer. 4:10
23 [a]Ex. 3:8

6:1 [1]Lit., *by a strong hand* [a]Ex. 3:19, 20; 7:4, 5; 11:1; 12:31, 33, 39; 13:3
2 [a]Ex. 3:14, 15
3 [1]Heb., *El Shaddai* [2]Heb., *YHWH,* usually rendered *LORD* [a]Gen. 17:1; 35:11; 48:3 [b]Ps. 68:4; 83:18; Is. 52:6; Jer. 16:21; Ezek. 37:6, 13
4 [1]Lit., *land of their sojournings in which . . .* [a]Gen. 12:7; 15:18; 17:4, 7; 26:3, 4; 28:4, 13
5 [a]Ex. 2:24

6 "Say, therefore, to the sons of Israel,
'[a]I am the LORD, and [b]I will bring you
out from under the burdens of the Egyptians, and I will deliver you from their
bondage. I will also [c]redeem you with
[d]an outstretched arm and with great
judgments.
7 'Then I will take you [1a]for My
people, and [b]I will be [2]your God; and
[c]you shall know that I am the LORD your
God, who brought you out from under
the burdens of the Egyptians.
8 'And I will bring you to the land
which [a]I [1]swore to give to Abraham,
Isaac, and Jacob, and [b]I will give it to
you *for* a possession; [c]I am the LORD.' "
9 So Moses spoke thus to the sons of
Israel, but they did not listen to Moses
on [a]account of *their* [1]despondency and
cruel bondage.
10 Now the LORD spoke to Moses,
saying,
11 "[a]Go, [1]tell Pharaoh king of Egypt
[2]to let the sons of Israel go out of his
land."
12 But Moses spoke before the LORD,
saying, "Behold, the sons of Israel have
not listened to me; [a]how then will Pharaoh listen to me, for I am [1b]unskilled in
speech?"
13 Then the LORD spoke to Moses
and to Aaron, and gave them a charge to
the sons of Israel and to Pharaoh king of
Egypt, to bring the sons of Israel out of
the land of Egypt.

The Heads of Israel

14 These are the heads of their fathers'
households. [a]The sons of Reuben, Israel's first-born: Hanoch and Pallu,
Hezron and Carmi; these are the families of Reuben.
15 And the [a]sons of Simeon: Jemuel
and Jamin and Ohad and Jachin and
Zohar and Shaul the son of a Canaanite
woman; these are the families of Simeon.
16 And these are the names of [a]the
sons of Levi according to their generations: Gershon and Kohath and Merari;
and the [1]length of Levi's life was one
hundred and thirty-seven years.
17 [a]The sons of Gershon: [1]Libni and
Shimei, according to their families.
18 And [a]the sons of Kohath: Amram
and Izhar and Hebron and Uzziel; and
the [1]length of Kohath's life was one
hundred and thirty-three years.
19 And [a]the sons of Merari: Mahli
and Mushi. These are the families of the
Levites according to their generations.
20 And [a]Amram [1]married his father's
sister Jochebed, and she bore him Aaron
and Moses; and the [2]length of Amram's
life was one hundred and thirty-seven
years.
21 And [a]the sons of Izhar: Korah and
Nepheg and Zichri.
22 [a]And the sons of Uzziel: Mishael
and [1]Elzaphan and Sithri.
23 And Aaron [1]married Elisheba, the
daughter of [a]Amminadab, the sister of
[b]Nahshon, and she bore him [c]Nadab
and Abihu, Eleazar and Ithamar.
24 And the [a]sons of Korah: Assir and
Elkanah and [1]Abiasaph; these are the
families of the Korahites.
25 And Aaron's son [a]Eleazar [1]married
one of the daughters of Putiel, and she
bore him [b]Phinehas. These are the heads
of the fathers' *households* of the Levites
according to their families.
26 It was *the same* Aaron and Moses
to whom the LORD said, "[a]Bring out the
sons of Israel from the land of Egypt
according to their [b]hosts."
27 They were the ones [a]who spoke to
Pharaoh king of Egypt [1]about bringing
out the sons of Israel from Egypt; it was
the same Moses and Aaron.
28 Now it came about on the day
when the LORD spoke to Moses in the
land of Egypt,
29 that the LORD spoke to Moses,
saying, "[a]I am the LORD; [b]speak to
Pharaoh king of Egypt all that I speak to
you."
30 But Moses said before the LORD,
"Behold, I am [1a]unskilled in speech;
how then will Pharaoh listen to me?"

"I Will Stretch Out My Hand"

7 THEN the LORD said to Moses,
"[a]See, I make you *as* God to Pharaoh, and your brother Aaron shall be
your prophet.
2 "You shall speak all that I command
you, and your brother [a]Aaron shall
speak to Pharaoh that he let the sons of
Israel go out of his land.
3 "But [a]I will harden Pharaoh's heart
that I may [b]multiply My signs and My
wonders in the land of Egypt.
4 "When [a]Pharaoh will not listen to
you, then I will lay My hand on Egypt,
and [b]bring out My hosts, My people the
sons of Israel, from the land of Egypt by
[c]great judgments.
5 "And [a]the Egyptians shall know that
I am the LORD, when I [b]stretch out My
hand on Egypt and bring out the sons of
Israel from their midst."
6 So Moses and Aaron did *it;* [a]as the
LORD commanded them, thus they did.
7 And Moses was [a]eighty years old
and Aaron [1]eighty-three, when they
spoke to Pharaoh.

Aaron's Rod Becomes a Serpent

8 Now the LORD spoke to Moses and
Aaron, saying,
9 "When Pharaoh speaks to you, saying, '[1a]Work a miracle,' then you shall
say to Aaron, '[b]Take your staff and
throw *it* down before Pharaoh, *that* it
may become a serpent.' "

6 [a]Ex. 13:3, 14; 20:2; Deut. 6:12 [b]Ex. 3:17; 7:4; 12:51; 16:6; 18:1; Deut. 26:8; Ps. 136:11 [c]Ex. 15:13; Deut. 7:8; 1 Chr. 17:21; Neh. 1:10 [d]Deut. 4:34; 5:15; 26:8; Ps. 136:11f.
7 [1]Lit., *to Me for a people* [2]Lit., *to you for a God* [a]Ex. 19:5; Deut. 4:20; 7:6; 2 Sam. 7:24 [b]Gen. 17:7f.; Ex. 29:45f.; Lev. 11:45; 26:12, 13, 45; Deut. 29:13 [c]Ex. 16:12; Is. 41:20; 49:23, 26; 60:16
8 [1]Lit., *lifted up My hand* [a]Gen. 15:18; 26:3; Num. 14:30; Neh. 9:15; Ezek. 20:5, 6 [b]Josh. 24:13; Ps. 136:21, 22 [c]Ex. 6:6
9 [1]Lit., *shortness of spirit* [a]Ex. 2:23
11 [1]Lit., *speak to* [2]Lit., *that he let* [a]Ex. 4:22, 23
12 [1]Lit., *uncircumcised of lips* [a]Ex. 4:1, 10; 6:30 [b]Jer. 1:6
14 [a]Gen. 46:9; Num. 26:5-11; 1 Chr. 5:3
15 [a]Gen. 46:10; 1 Chr. 4:24
16 [1]Lit., *years* [a]Gen. 46:11; Num. 3:17; 26:57f.; 1 Chr. 6:1, 16-19
17 [1]In 1 Chr. 23:7, *Ladan* [a]Num. 3:18-20; 1 Chr. 6:17-19
18 [1]Lit., *years* [a]Num. 3:19; 1 Chr. 6:2, 18
19 [a]Num. 3:20; 1 Chr. 6:19; 23:21
20 [1]Lit., *took to him to wife* [2]Lit., *years* [a]Ex. 2:1, 2; Num. 26:59
21 [a]Num. 16:1; 1 Chr. 6:37, 38
22 [1]In Num. 3:30, *Elizaphan* [a]Lev. 10:4; Num. 3:30
23 [1]Lit., *took to him to wife* [a]Ruth 4:19, 20; 1 Chr. 2:10 [b]Num. 1:7; 2:3 [c]Lev. 10:1; Num. 3:2; 26:60; 1 Chr. 6:3; 24:1
24 [1]In 1 Chr. 6:23 and 9:19, *Ebiasaph* [a]Num. 26:11; 1 Chr. 6:22, 23, 37
25 [1]Lit., *took to him to wife* [a]Josh. 24:33 [b]Num. 25:7-13; Josh. 24:33; Ps. 106:30
26 [a]Ex. 3:10; 6:13 [b]Ex. 7:4; 12:17, 51
27 [1]Lit., *to bring out* [a]Ex. 5:1
29 [a]Ex. 6:2, 6, 8 [b]Ex. 6:11; 7:2
30 [1]Lit., *uncircumcised of lips* [a]Ex. 4:10; 6:12; Jer. 1:6

1 [a]Ex. 4:16
2 [a]Ex. 4:15
3 [a]Ex. 4:21 [b]Ex. 11:9; Acts 7:36
4 [a]Ex. 3:19, 20; 7:13, 16, 22; 8:15, 19; 9:12; 11:9 [b]Ex. 12:51; 13:3, 9 [c]Ex. 6:6
5 [a]Ex. 7:17; 8:19, 22; 10:7; 14:4, 18, 25 [b]Ex. 3:20
6 [a]Gen. 6:22; 7:5; Ex. 7:2
7 [1]Lit., *83 years old* [a]Deut. 29:5; 31:2; 34:7; Acts 7:23, 30
9 [1]Lit., *Show a wonder for yourselves* [a]Is. 7:11; John 2:18; 6:30 [b]Ex. 4:2, 17

10 So Moses and Aaron came to Pharaoh, and thus they did just as the LORD had commanded; and Aaron threw his staff down before Pharaoh and [1]his servants, and it [a]became a serpent.

11 Then Pharaoh also [a]called for *the* wise men and *the* sorcerers, and they also, the [1b]magicians of Egypt, did [2]the same with [c]their secret arts.

12 For each one threw down his staff and they turned into serpents. But Aaron's staff swallowed up their staffs.

13 Yet [a]Pharaoh's heart was [1]hardened, and he did not listen to them, as the LORD had said.

Water Is Turned to Blood

14 Then the LORD said to Moses, "Pharaoh's heart is [1]stubborn; he refuses to let the people go.

15 "Go to Pharaoh in the morning [1]as [a]he is going out to the water, and station yourself to meet him on the bank of the Nile; and you shall take in your hand [b]the staff that was turned into a serpent.

16 "[a]And you will say to him, 'The LORD, the God of the Hebrews, sent me to you, saying, "[b]Let My people go, that they may serve Me in the wilderness. But behold, you have not listened until now."

17 'Thus says the LORD, "[a]By this you shall know that I am the LORD: behold, I will strike [1]the water that is in the Nile with the staff that is in my hand, and [b]it shall be turned to blood.

18 "And [a]the fish that are in the Nile will die, and the Nile will [1]become foul; and the Egyptians will [2b]find difficulty in drinking water from the Nile." ' "

19 Then the LORD said to Moses, "Say to Aaron, 'Take your staff and [a]stretch out your hand over the waters of Egypt, over their rivers, over their [1]streams, and over their pools, and over all their reservoirs of water, that they may become blood; and there shall be blood throughout all the land of Egypt, both in *vessels of* wood and in *vessels of* stone.' "

20 So Moses and Aaron did even as the LORD had commanded. And he lifted up [1a]the staff and struck the water that *was* in the Nile, in the sight of Pharaoh and in the sight of his servants, and [b]all the water that *was* in the Nile was turned to blood.

21 And the fish that *were* in the Nile died, and the Nile [1]became foul, so that the Egyptians could not drink water from the Nile. And the blood was through all the land of Egypt.

22 [a]But the [1]magicians of Egypt did [2]the same with their secret arts; and Pharaoh's heart was [3]hardened, and he did not listen to them, as the LORD had said.

23 Then Pharaoh turned and went into his house [1]with no concern even for this.

24 So all the Egyptians dug around the Nile for water to drink, for they could not drink of the water of the Nile.

25 And seven days [1]passed after the LORD had struck the Nile.

Frogs over the Land

8 [1]THEN the LORD said to Moses, "Go to Pharaoh and say to him, 'Thus says the LORD, "[a]Let My people go, that they may serve Me.

2 "But if you refuse to let *them* go, behold, I will smite your whole territory with frogs.

3 "And the Nile will [a]swarm with frogs, which will come up and go into your house and into your bedroom and on your bed, and into the houses of your servants and on your people, and into your ovens and into your kneading bowls.

4 "So the frogs will come up on you and your people and all your servants." ' "

5 [1]Then the LORD said to Moses, "Say to Aaron, '[a]Stretch out your hand with your staff over the rivers, over the [2]streams and over the pools, and make frogs come up on the land of Egypt.' "

6 So Aaron stretched out his hand over the waters of Egypt, and the [1a]frogs came up and covered the land of Egypt.

7 [a]And the [1]magicians did [2]the same with their secret arts, [3]making frogs come up on the land of Egypt.

8 Then Pharaoh [a]called for Moses and Aaron and said, "[b]Entreat the LORD that He remove the frogs from me and from my people; and [c]I will let the people go, that they may sacrifice to the LORD."

9 And Moses said to Pharaoh, "[1]The honor is yours to tell me: when shall I entreat for you and your servants and your people, that the frogs be [2]destroyed from you and your houses, *that* they may be left only in the Nile?"

10 Then he said, "Tomorrow." So he said, "*May it be* according to your word, that you may know that there is [a]no one like the LORD our God.

11 "And the [a]frogs will depart from you and your houses and your servants and your people; they will be left only in the Nile."

12 Then Moses and Aaron went out from Pharaoh, and [a]Moses cried to the LORD concerning the frogs which He had [1]inflicted upon Pharaoh.

13 And the LORD did according to the word of Moses, and the frogs died out of the houses, the courts, and the fields.

14 So they piled them in heaps, and the land [1]became foul.

15 But when Pharaoh saw that there was relief, he [1]hardened his heart and [a]did not listen to them, as the LORD had said.

10 [1]Lit., *before his* [a]Ex. 4:3; 7:9
11 [1]Or, *soothsayer priests* [2]Lit., *thus* [a]Dan. 2:2; 4:6; 5:7 [b]Gen. 41:8; Ex. 7:22; Dan. 2:2; 2 Tim. 3:8 [c]Ex. 7:22; 8:7, 18; 2 Tim. 3:9; Rev. 13:13, 14
13 [1]Lit., *strong* [a]Ex. 4:21; 7:3, 22; 8:15, 19, 32; 9:7, 12, 34, 35; 10:1, 20, 27
14 [1]Or, *hard;* lit., *heavy*
15 [1]Lit., *behold* [a]Ex. 2:5; 8:20 [b]Ex. 4:2, 3; 7:10
16 [a]Ex. 3:13, 18; 4:22; 5:1 [b]Ex. 4:23; 5:1, 3
17 [1]Lit., *upon the waters* [a]Ex. 5:2; 7:5; 10:2; Ps. 9:16; Ezek. 25:17 [b]Ex. 4:9; 7:20; Rev. 11:6; 16:4, 6
18 [1]I.e., have a bad smell [2]Or, *be weary of* [a]Ex. 7:21 [b]Ex. 7:24
19 [1]Or, *canals* [a]Ex. 8:5, 6, 16; 9:22; 10:12, 21; 14:21, 26
20 [1]Lit., *with the staff* [a]Ex. 17:5 [b]Ps. 78:44; 105:29
21 [1]I.e., had a bad smell
22 [1]Or, *soothsayer priests* [2]Lit., *thus* [3]Lit., *strong* [a]Ex. 7:11; 8:7
23 [1]Lit., *and he did not set his heart even to this*
25 [1]Lit., *were fulfilled*

1 [1]Ch. 7:26 in Heb. [a]Ex. 3:18; 4:23; 5:1, 3
3 [a]Ps. 105:30
5 [1]Ch. 8:1 in Heb. [2]Or, *canals* [a]Ex. 7:19
6 [1]Lit., *frog* [a]Ps. 78:45; 105:30
7 [1]Or, *soothsayer priests* [2]Lit., *thus* [3]Lit., *and made* [a]Ex. 7:11, 22
8 [a]Ex. 8:25; 9:27; 10:16 [b]Ex. 8:28; 9:28; 10:17; Num. 21:7; 1 Kin. 13:6 [c]Ex. 8:15, 29, 32
9 [1]Lit., *Glory over me* [2]Lit., *cut off*
10 [a]Ex. 9:14; Deut. 4:35, 39; 33:26; 2 Sam. 7:22; 1 Chr. 17:20; Ps. 86:8; Is. 46:9; Jer. 10:6, 7
11 [a]Ex. 8:13
12 [1]Lit., *placed* [a]Ex. 8:30; 9:33; 10:18
14 [1]I.e., had a bad smell
15 [1]Lit., *made heavy* [a]Ex. 7:4

The Plague of Insects

16 Then the LORD said to Moses, "Say to Aaron, 'Stretch out your staff and strike the dust of the earth, that it may become [1]gnats through all the land of Egypt.' "

17 And they did so; and Aaron stretched out his hand with his staff, and struck the dust of the earth, and there were [1]gnats on man and beast. All the dust of the earth became [1a]gnats through all the land of Egypt.

18 And the [1]magicians tried with their secret arts to bring forth [2]gnats, but [a]they could not; so there were [2]gnats on man and beast.

19 Then the [1]magicians said to Pharaoh, "[a]This is the finger of God." But Pharaoh's heart was [2]hardened, and he did not listen to them, as the LORD had said.

20 Now the LORD said to Moses, "[a]Rise early in the morning and present yourself before Pharaoh, [1]as [b]he comes out to the water, and say to him, 'Thus says the LORD, "[c]Let My people go, that they may serve Me.

21 "For if you will not let My people go, behold, I will send swarms of insects on you and on your servants and on your people and into your houses; and the houses of the Egyptians shall be full of swarms of insects, and also the ground on which they *dwell.*

22 "[a]But on that day I will set apart the land of Goshen, where My people are [1]living, so that no swarms of insects will be there, in order that you may know that [2b]I, the LORD, am in the midst of the land.

23 "And I will [1]put a division between My people and your people. Tomorrow this sign shall occur." ' "

24 Then the LORD did so. And there came [1]great swarms of insects into the house of Pharaoh and the houses of his servants and the land was [a]laid waste because of the swarms of insects in all the land of Egypt.

25 And Pharaoh [a]called for Moses and Aaron and said, "[b]Go, sacrifice to your God within the land."

26 But Moses said, "It is not right to do so, for we shall sacrifice to the LORD our God [1]what is [a]an abomination to the Egyptians. If we sacrifice [1]what is an abomination to the Egyptians before their eyes, will they not then stone us?

27 "We must go a [a]three days' journey into the wilderness and sacrifice to the LORD our God as He [1]commands us."

28 And Pharaoh said, "[a]I will let you go, that you may sacrifice to the LORD your God in the wilderness; only you shall not go very far away. [b]Make supplication for me."

29 Then Moses said, "Behold, I am going out from you, and I shall make supplication to the LORD that the swarms of insects may depart from Pharaoh, from his servants, and from his people tomorrow; only do not let Pharaoh [a]deal deceitfully again in not letting the people go to sacrifice to the LORD."

30 So [a]Moses went out from Pharaoh and made supplication to the LORD.

31 And the LORD did [1]as Moses asked, and removed the swarms of insects from Pharaoh, from his servants and from his people; not one remained.

32 But Pharaoh [1]hardened his heart this time also, and [a]he did not let the people go.

Egyptian Cattle Die

9 THEN the LORD said to Moses, "Go to Pharaoh and speak to him, 'Thus says the LORD, the God of the Hebrews, "[a]Let My people go, that they may serve Me.

2 "For [a]if you refuse to let *them* go, and [1]continue to hold them,

3 behold, [a]the hand of the LORD [1]will come *with* a very severe pestilence on your livestock which are in the field, on the horses, on the donkeys, on the camels, on the herds, and on the flocks.

4 "[a]But the LORD will make a distinction between the livestock of Israel and the livestock of Egypt, so that [b]nothing will die of all that belongs to the sons of Israel." ' "

5 And the LORD set a definite time, saying, "Tomorrow the LORD will do this thing in the land."

6 So the LORD did this thing on the morrow, and [a]all the livestock of Egypt died; [b]but of the livestock of the sons of Israel, not one died.

7 And Pharaoh sent, and behold, there was not even one of the livestock of Israel dead. But [a]the heart of Pharaoh was [1]hardened, and he did not let the people go.

The Plague of Boils

8 Then the LORD said to Moses and Aaron, "Take for yourselves handfuls of soot from a kiln, and let Moses throw it toward the sky in the sight of Pharaoh.

9 "And it will become fine dust over all the land of Egypt, and will become [a]boils breaking out with sores on man and beast through all the land of Egypt."

10 So they took soot from a kiln, and stood before Pharaoh; and Moses threw it toward the sky, and it became boils breaking out with sores on man and beast.

11 [a]And the [1]magicians could not stand before Moses because of the boils, for the boils were on the magicians [2]as well as on all the Egyptians.

12 And [a]the LORD [1]hardened Pharaoh's heart, and he did not listen to them, just as the LORD had spoken to Moses.

13 Then the LORD said to Moses, "[a]Rise up early in the morning and stand before Pharaoh and say to him, 'Thus says the LORD, the God of the Hebrews, "[b]Let My people go, that they may serve Me.

---

16 [1]Or, *lice*

17 [1]Or, *lice* [a]Ps. 105:31

18 [1]Or, *soothsayer priests* [2]Or, *lice* [a]Ex. 7:11, 12; 8:7; 9:11

19 [1]Or, *soothsayer priests* [2]Lit., *strong* [a]Ex. 7:5; 10:7; Ps. 8:3; Luke 11:20

20 [1]Lit., *behold* [a]Ex. 7:15; 9:13 [b]Ex. 2:5; 7:15 [c]Ex. 3:18; 4:23; 5:1, 3; 8:1

22 [1]Lit., *standing* [2]Or, *I am the LORD in the midst of the earth* [a]Ex. 9:4, 6, 24; 10:23; 11:7 [b]Ex. 9:29; 19:5; 20:11

23 [1]Lit., *set a ransom*

24 [1]Lit., *heavy* [a]Ps. 78:45; 105:31

25 [a]Ex. 8:8; 9:27; 10:16 [b]Ex. 9:28; 10:8, 24; 12:31

26 [1]Lit., *the abomination of Egypt* [a]Gen. 43:32; 46:34; Deut. 7:25f.

27 [1]Lit., *says to us* [a]Ex. 3:18; 5:3

28 [a]Ex. 8:8, 15, 29, 32 [b]Ex. 8:8; 9:28; 1 Kin. 13:6

29 [a]Ex. 8:8, 15

30 [a]Ex. 8:12

31 [1]Lit., *according to the word of Moses*

32 [1]Lit., *made heavy* [a]Ex. 4:21; 8:8, 15

1 [a]Ex. 4:23; 8:1

2 [1]Lit., *still hold* [a]Ex. 8:2

3 [1]Lit., *will be* [a]Ex. 7:4; 1 Sam. 5:6; Ps. 39:10; Acts 13:11

4 [a]Ex. 8:22 [b]Ex. 9:6

6 [a]Ex. 9:19, 20, 25; Ps. 78:48 [b]Ex. 9:4

7 [1]Lit., *heavy* [a]Ex. 7:14; 8:32

9 [a]Deut. 28:27; Rev. 16:2

11 [1]Or, *soothsayer priests* [2]Lit., *and on all* [a]Ex. 8:18

12 [1]Lit., *made strong* [a]Ex. 4:21; 10:1, 20; 14:8; Josh. 11:20; John 12:40

13 [a]Ex. 8:20 [b]Ex. 4:23

14 "For this time I will send all My plagues [1]on you and your servants and your people, so that [a]you may know that there is no one like Me in all the earth.

15 "For *if by* now I had put forth My hand and struck you and your people with pestilence, you would then have been cut off from the earth.

16 "But, indeed, [a]for this cause I have allowed you to [1]remain, in order to show you My power, and in order to proclaim My name through all the earth.

17 "Still you exalt yourself against My people [1]by not letting them go.

The Plague of Hail

18 "Behold, about this time tomorrow, [a]I will [1]send a very heavy hail, such as has not been *seen* in Egypt from the day it was founded [2]until now.

19 "Now therefore send, bring [a]your livestock and whatever you have in the field to safety. [b]Every man and beast that is found in the field and is not brought home, when the hail comes down on them, will die." ' "

20 [a]The one among the servants of Pharaoh who [1]feared the word of the LORD made his servants and his livestock flee into the houses;

21 but he who [1]paid no regard to the word of the LORD [2]left his servants and his livestock in the field.

22 Now the LORD said to Moses, "Stretch out your hand toward the sky, that [1a]hail may fall on all the land of Egypt, on man and on beast and on every plant of the field, throughout the land of Egypt."

23 And Moses stretched out his staff toward the sky, and the LORD [1]sent [2]thunder and [a]hail, and fire ran down to the earth. And the LORD rained hail on the land of Egypt.

24 So there was hail, and fire [1]flashing continually in the midst of the hail, very severe, such as had not been in all the land of Egypt since it became a nation.

25 And [a]the hail struck all that was in the field through all the land of Egypt, both man and beast; the hail also struck every plant of the field and shattered every tree of the field.

26 [a]Only in the land of Goshen, where the sons of Israel *were,* there was no hail.

27 Then Pharaoh [1a]sent for Moses and Aaron, and said to them, "[b]I have sinned this time; the LORD is the righteous one, and I and my people are the wicked ones.

28 "[a]Make supplication to the LORD, for there has been enough of God's [1]thunder and hail; and [b]I will let you go, and you shall stay no longer."

29 And Moses said to him, "As soon as I go out of the city, I will [a]spread out my [1]hands to the LORD; the [2]thunder will cease, and there will be hail no longer, that you may know that [b]the earth is the LORD'S.

30 "[a]But as for you and your servants, I know that [b]you do not yet [1]fear [2]the LORD God."

31 (Now the flax and the [a]barley were [1]ruined, for the barley was in the ear and the flax was in bud.

32 But the wheat and the spelt were not [1]ruined, for they *ripen* late.)

33 [a]So Moses went out of the city from Pharaoh, and spread out his [1]hands to the LORD; and the [2]thunder and the hail ceased, and rain [3]no longer poured on the earth.

34 But when Pharaoh saw that the rain and the hail and the [1]thunder had ceased, he sinned again and [2]hardened his heart, he and his servants.

35 And Pharaoh's heart was [1]hardened, and he did not let the sons of Israel go, just as the [a]LORD had spoken through Moses.

The Plague of Locusts

10 THEN the LORD said to Moses, "Go to Pharaoh, for [a]I have [1]hardened his heart and the heart of his servants, that I may [2]perform these signs of Mine [3]among them,

2 and [a]that you may tell in the [1]hearing of your son, and of your grandson, how I made a mockery of the Egyptians, and how I [2]performed My signs among them; [b]that you may know that I am the LORD."

3 And Moses and Aaron went to Pharaoh and said to him, "Thus says the LORD, the God of the Hebrews, 'How long will you refuse to [a]humble yourself before Me? [b]Let My people go, that they may serve Me.

4 'For if you refuse to let My people go, behold, tomorrow I will bring locusts into your territory.

5 'And they shall cover the surface of the land, so that no one shall be able to see the land. [a]They shall also eat the rest of what has escaped—what is left to you from the hail—and they shall eat every tree which sprouts for you out of the field.

6 'Then [a]your houses shall be filled, and the houses of all your servants and the houses of all the Egyptians, *something* which neither your fathers nor your grandfathers have seen, from the day that they [1]came upon the earth until this day.' " And he turned and went out from Pharaoh.

7 And [a]Pharaoh's servants said to him, "How long will this man be [b]a snare to us? Let the men go, that they may serve the LORD their God. Do you not [1]realize that Egypt is destroyed?"

8 So Moses and Aaron [a]were brought back to Pharaoh, and he said to them, "[b]Go, serve the LORD your God! [1]Who are the ones that are going?"

9 And Moses said, "[a]We shall go with our young and our old; with our sons and our daughters, [b]with our flocks and our herds we will go, for we [1]must hold a feast to the LORD."

14 [1]Lit., *to your heart* [a]Ex. 8:10; Deut. 3:24; 2 Sam. 7:22; 1 Chr. 17:20; Ps. 86:8; Is. 45:5-8; 46:9; Jer. 10:6, 7
16 [1]Lit., *stand* [a]Prov. 16:4; Rom. 9:17
17 [1]Lit., *so as not to let*
18 [1]Lit., *cause to rain* [2]Lit., *and until now* [a]Ex. 9:23, 24
19 [a]Ex. 9:6 [b]Ex. 9:25
20 [1]Or, *revered* [a]Prov. 13:13
21 [1]Lit., *did not set his heart to* [2]Lit., *then left*
22 [1]Lit., *there may be hail* [a]Rev. 16:21
23 [1]Lit., *gave* [2]Lit., *sounds* [a]Gen. 19:24; Josh. 10:11; Ps. 18:13; 78:47; 105:32; Is. 30:30; Ezek. 38:22; Rev. 8:7
24 [1]Lit., *taking hold of itself*
25 [a]Ex. 9:19; Ps. 78:47, 48; 105:32, 33
26 [a]Ex. 8:22; 9:4, 6; 11:7
27 [1]Lit., *sent and called* [a]Ex. 8:8 [b]Ex. 10:16, 17; 2 Chr. 12:6; Ps. 129:4; 145:17; Lam. 1:18
28 [1]Lit., *sounds* [a]Ex. 8:8, 28; 10:17 [b]Ex. 8:25; 10:8, 24
29 [1]Lit., *palms* [2]Lit., *sounds* [a]1 Kin. 8:22, 38; Ps. 143:6; Is. 1:15 [b]Ex. 8:22; 19:5; 20:11; Ps. 24:1; 1 Cor. 10:26
30 [1]Or, *reverence* [2]Lit., *before the* LORD [a]Ex. 8:29 [b]Is. 26:10
31 [1]Lit., *smitten* [a]Ruth 1:22; 2:23
32 [1]Lit., *smitten*
33 [1]Lit., *palms* [2]Lit., *sounds* [3]Lit., *was not poured* [a]Ex. 8:12; 9:29
34 [1]Lit., *sounds* [2]Lit., *made heavy*
35 [1]Lit., *strong* [a]Ex. 4:21

1 [1]Lit., *made heavy* [2]Lit., *put* [3]Lit., *in his midst* [a]Ex. 4:21; 7:13; Josh. 11:20; John 12:40; Rom. 9:18
2 [1]Lit., *ears* [2]Lit., *put* [a]Ex. 12:26, 27; 13:8, 14, 15; Deut. 4:9; Ps. 44:1; 78:5; Joel 1:3 [b]Ex. 7:5, 17
3 [a]1 Kin. 21:29; 2 Chr. 34:27; James 4:10; 1 Pet. 5:6 [b]Ex. 4:23
5 [a]Joel 1:4; 2:25
6 [1]Lit., *were* [a]Ex. 8:3, 21
7 [1]Lit., *know* [a]Ex. 7:5; 8:19; 12:33 [b]Ex. 23:33; Josh. 23:13; 1 Sam. 18:21; Eccl. 7:26
8 [1]Lit., *Who and who are* [a]Ex. 8:8 [b]Ex. 8:25
9 [1]Lit., *have a feast* [a]Ex. 12:37, 38 [b]Ex. 10:26

10 Then he said to them, "Thus may
the LORD be with you, [1]if ever I let you
and your little ones go! Take heed, for
evil is [2]in your mind.
11 "Not so! Go now, the men *among*
you, and serve the LORD, for [1]that is
what you desire." So [a]they were driven
out from Pharaoh's presence.
12 Then the LORD said to Moses,
"[a]Stretch out your hand over the land of
Egypt for the locusts, that they may
come up on the land of Egypt, and [b]eat
every plant of the land, *even* all that the
hail has left."
13 So Moses stretched out his staff
over the land of Egypt, and the LORD
directed an east wind on the land all that
day and all that night; and when it was
morning, the east wind [1]brought the
[a]locusts.
14 And [a]the locusts came up over all
the land of Egypt and settled in all the
territory of Egypt; *they were* very [1]nu-
merous. There had never been so *many*
[2]locusts, nor would there be so *many*
[3]again.
15 For they covered the surface of the
whole land, so that the land was darkened; and they [a]ate every plant of the
land and all the fruit of the trees that the
hail had left. Thus nothing green was left
on tree or plant of the field through all
the land of Egypt.
16 Then Pharaoh hurriedly [a]called for
Moses and Aaron, and he said, "[b]I have
sinned against the LORD your God and
against you.
17 "Now therefore, please forgive my
sin only this once, and [a]make supplication to the LORD your God, that He
would only remove this death from me."
18 And [a]he went out from Pharaoh
and made supplication to the LORD.
19 So the LORD shifted *the wind* to a
very strong west wind which took up the
locusts and drove them into the [1]Red
Sea; not one locust was left in all the
territory of Egypt.
20 But [a]the LORD [1]hardened Pharaoh's heart, and he did not let the sons
of Israel go.

Darkness over the Land

21 Then the LORD said to Moses,
"[a]Stretch out your hand toward the sky,
that there may be darkness over the land
of Egypt, even a darkness [b]which may be
felt."
22 So Moses stretched out his hand
toward the sky, and there was [a]thick
darkness in all the land of Egypt for
three days.
23 They did not see one another, nor
did anyone rise from his place for three
days, [a]but all the sons of Israel had light
in their dwellings.
24 Then Pharaoh [a]called to Moses,
and said, "Go, serve the LORD; only let
your flocks and your herds be detained.
Even [b]your little ones may go with you."

10 [1]Lit., *when I* [2]Lit., *before your face*
11 [1]Lit., *you desire it* [a]Ex. 10:28
12 [a]Ex. 7:19 [b]Ex. 10:5, 15
13 [1]Lit., *carried* [a]Ps. 78:46; 105:34
14 [1]Lit., *heavy* [2]Lit., *locusts like them before them* [3]Lit., *after them* [a]Deut. 28:38; Ps. 78:46; 105:34; Joel 1:4, 7; 2:1-11; Rev. 9:3
15 [a]Ex. 10:5; Ps. 105:34f.
16 [a]Ex. 8:8 [b]Ex. 9:27
17 [a]Ex. 8:8, 28; 9:28; 1 Kin. 13:6
18 [a]Ex. 8:30
19 [1]Lit., *Sea of Reeds*
20 [1]Lit., *made strong* [a]Ex. 4:21; 11:10
21 [a]Ex. 9:22 [b]Deut. 28:29
22 [a]Ps. 105:28; Rev. 16:10
23 [a]Ex. 8:22
24 [a]Ex. 8:8, 25 [b]Ex. 10:10
25 [1]Lit., *give into our hand* [2]Lit., *make*
26 [a]Ex. 10:9
27 [1]Lit., *made strong* [a]Ex. 4:21; 10:20; 14:4, 8
28 [1]Lit., *Take heed to yourself* [a]Ex. 10:11
29 [a]Ex. 11:8; Heb. 11:27
1 [a]Ex. 12:31, 33, 39
2 [1]Lit., *ears* [a]Ex. 3:22; 12:35, 36
3 [1]Lit., *very great* [a]Ex. 3:21; 12:36; Ps. 106:46 [b]Deut. 34:10-12
4 [a]Ex. 12:29
5 [a]Ex. 12:12, 29; Ps. 78:51; 105:36; 135:8; 136:10
6 [a]Ex. 12:30
7 [1]Lit., *sharpen his tongue* [2]Lit., *know* [a]Ex. 8:22; Josh. 10:21
8 [1]Lit., *to* [2]Lit., *are at your feet* [a]Ex. 12:31-33 [b]Heb. 11:27
9 [a]Ex. 7:4 [b]Ex. 7:3
10 [1]Lit., *made strong* [a]Ex. 4:21 [b]Ex. 7:3; 9:12; 10:20, 27; Josh. 11:20; Is. 63:17; John 12:40

25 But Moses said, "You must also
[1]let us have sacrifices and burnt offerings, that we may [2]sacrifice *them* to the
LORD our God.
26 "[a]Therefore, our livestock, too, will
go with us; not a hoof will be left
behind, for we shall take some of them
to serve the LORD our God. And until
we arrive there, we ourselves do not
know with what we shall serve the
LORD."
27 But [a]the LORD [1]hardened Pharaoh's heart, and he was not willing to
let them go.
28 Then Pharaoh said to him, "[a]Get
away from me! [1]Beware, do not see my
face again, for in the day you see my face
you shall die!"
29 And Moses said, "You are right; [a]I
shall never see your face again!"

The Last Plague

11 NOW the LORD said to Moses,
"One more plague I will bring on
Pharaoh and on Egypt; [a]after that he
will let you go from here. When he lets
you go, he will surely drive you out from
here completely.
2 "Speak now in the [1]hearing of the
people that [a]each man ask from his
neighbor and each woman from her
neighbor for articles of silver and articles
of gold."
3 [a]And the LORD gave the people
favor in the sight of the Egyptians.
[b]Furthermore, the man Moses *himself*
was [1]greatly esteemed in the land of
Egypt, *both* in the sight of Pharaoh's
servants and in the sight of the people.
4 And Moses said, "Thus says the
LORD, 'About [a]midnight I am going out
into the midst of Egypt,
5 and [a]all the first-born in the land of
Egypt shall die, from the first-born of
the Pharaoh who sits on his throne, even
to the first-born of the slave girl who is
behind the millstones; all the first-born
of the cattle as well.
6 'Moreover, there shall be [a]a great
cry in all the land of Egypt, such as there
has not been *before* and such as shall
never be again.
7 '[a]But against any of the sons of
Israel a dog shall not *even* [1]bark,
whether against man or beast, that you
may [2]understand how the LORD makes a
distinction between Egypt and Israel.'
8 "And [a]all these your servants will
come down to me and bow themselves
[1]before me, saying, 'Go out, you and all
the people who [2]follow you,' and after
that I will go out." [b]And he went out
from Pharaoh in hot anger.
9 Then the LORD said to Moses,
"[a]Pharaoh will not listen to you, so [b]that
My wonders will be multiplied in the
land of Egypt."
10 And [a]Moses and Aaron performed
all these wonders before Pharaoh; yet
[b]the LORD [1]hardened Pharaoh's heart,
and he did not let the sons of Israel go
out of his land.

The Passover Lamb

12 NOW the LORD said to Moses
and Aaron in the land of [1]Egypt,
2 "[a]This month shall be the beginning
of months for you; it is to be the first
month of the year to you.
3 "Speak to all the congregation of
Israel, saying, 'On the tenth of this
month they are each one to take a [1]lamb
for themselves, according to their fathers' households, a [1]lamb for [2]each
household.
4 'Now if the household is too small
for a [1]lamb, then he and his neighbor
nearest to his house are to take one
according to the [2]number of persons *in
them;* according to [3]what each man
should eat, you are to [4]divide the lamb.
5 'Your [1]lamb shall be [a]an unblemished male a year old; you may take it
from the sheep or from the goats.
6 'And [1]you shall keep it until the
[a]fourteenth day of the same month, then
the whole assembly of the congregation
of Israel is to kill it [2][b]at twilight.
7 '[a]Moreover, they shall take some of
the blood and put it on the two doorposts and on the lintel [1]of the houses in
which they eat it.
8 'And they shall eat the flesh [a]that
same night, [b]roasted with fire, and they
shall eat it with [c]unleavened bread [1][d]and
bitter herbs.
9 'Do not eat any of it raw or boiled
at all with water, but rather [a]roasted
with fire, *both* its head and its legs along
with [b]its entrails.
10 '[a]And you shall not leave any of it
over until morning, but whatever is left
of it until morning, you shall burn with
fire.
11 'Now you shall eat it in this manner: *with* your loins girded, your sandals
on your feet, and your staff in your
hand; and you shall eat it in haste—it is
[a]the LORD's Passover.
12 'For [a]I will go through the land of
Egypt on that night, and will strike
down all the first-born in the land of
Egypt, both man and beast; and [b]against
all the gods of Egypt I will execute
judgments—[c]I am the LORD.
13 'And [a]the blood shall be a sign for
you on the houses where you [1]live; and
when I see the blood I will pass over
you, and no plague will befall you [2]to
destroy *you* when I strike the land of
Egypt.

Feast of Unleavened Bread

14 'Now [a]this day will be [b]a memorial
to you, and you shall celebrate it *as* a
feast to the LORD; throughout your
generations you are to celebrate it *as* [1][c]a
permanent ordinance.
15 '[a]Seven days you shall eat unleavened bread, but on the first day you shall
[1]remove leaven from your houses; for
whoever eats anything leavened from the
first day until the seventh day, [b]that
[2]person shall be cut off from Israel.
16 'And [a]on the first day you shall
have a holy assembly, and *another* holy
assembly on the seventh day; no work at
all shall be done on them, except what
must be eaten [1]by every person, that
alone may be [2]prepared by you.
17 'You shall also observe [a]the *Feast of*
Unleavened Bread, for on this [b]very day
I brought your hosts out of the land of
Egypt; therefore you shall observe this
day throughout your generations as [c]a
[1]permanent ordinance.
18 '[a]In the first *month,* on the fourteenth day of the month at evening, you
shall eat unleavened bread, until the
twenty-first day of the month at evening.
19 '[a]Seven days there shall be no
leaven found in your houses; for whoever eats what is leavened, that [1][b]person
shall be cut off from the congregation of
Israel, whether *he is* an alien or a native
of the land.
20 'You shall not eat anything leavened; in all your dwellings you shall eat
unleavened bread.' "
21 Then [a]Moses called for all the
elders of Israel, and said to them, "[1]Go
and [b]take for yourselves [2]lambs according to your families, and slay [c]the Passover *lamb.*
22 "[a]And you shall take a bunch of
hyssop and dip it in the blood which is
in the basin, and [1]apply some of the
blood that is in the basin to the lintel
and the two doorposts; and none of you
shall go outside the door of his house
until morning.

A Memorial of Redemption

23 "For [a]the LORD will pass through to
smite the Egyptians; and when He sees
the blood on the lintel and on the two
doorposts, the LORD will pass over the
door and will [b]not allow the [c]destroyer
to come in to your houses to smite *you.*
24 "And [a]you shall observe this event
as an ordinance for you and your children forever.
25 "And it will come about when you
enter the land which the LORD will give
you, as He has [1]promised, that you shall
observe this [2]rite.
26 "[a]And it will come about when your
children will say to you, '[1]What does this
rite mean to you?'
27 that you shall say, 'It is a Passover
sacrifice to [a]the LORD [1]who passed over
the houses of the sons of Israel in Egypt
when He smote the Egyptians, but
[2]spared our homes.' " [b]And the people
bowed low and worshiped.
28 Then the sons of Israel went and
did *so;* just as the LORD had commanded
Moses and Aaron, so they did.
29 Now it came about at [a]midnight
that [b]the LORD struck all [c]the first-born
in the land of Egypt, from the first-born
of Pharaoh who sat on his throne to the
first-born of the captive who was in the
dungeon, and all the first-born of [d]cattle.
30 And Pharaoh arose in the night, he

1 [1]Lit., *Egypt, saying*
2 [a]Ex. 13:4; 23:15; 34:18; Deut. 16:1
3 [1]Or, *kid* [2]Lit., *the*
4 [1]Or, *kid* [2]Or, *amount* [3]Lit., *each man's eating* [4]Lit., *compute for*
5 [1]Or, *kid* [a]Lev. 22:18-21; 23:12; Heb. 9:14; 1 Pet. 1:19
6 [1]Lit., *it shall be to you for a guarding* [2]Lit., *between the two evenings* [a]Ex. 12:14, 17; Lev. 23:5; Num. 9:1-3, 11; 28:16 [b]Ex. 16:12; Deut. 16:4, 6
7 [1]Lit., *upon* [a]Ex. 12:22
8 [1]Lit., *in addition to* [a]Ex. 34:25; Num. 9:12 [b]Deut. 16:7 [c]Deut. 16:3, 4; 1 Cor. 5:8 [d]Num. 9:11
9 [a]Ex. 12:8 [b]Ex. 29:13, 17, 22
10 [a]Ex. 16:19; 23:18; 34:25
11 [a]Ex. 12:13, 21, 27, 43
12 [a]Ex. 11:4, 5 [b]Num. 33:4; Ps. 82:1 [c]Ex. 6:2
13 [1]Lit., *are* [2]Lit., *for destruction* [a]Heb. 11:28
14 [1]Or, *an eternal* [a]Ex. 12:6; Lev. 23:4, 5; 2 Kin. 23:21 [b]Ex. 13:9 [c]Ex. 12:17, 24; 13:10
15 [1]Lit., *cause to cease* [2]Lit., *soul* [a]Ex. 13:6, 7; 23:15; 34:18; Lev. 23:6; Num. 28:17; Deut. 16:3, 8 [b]Gen. 17:14; Ex. 12:19; Num. 9:13
16 [1]Lit., *pertaining to* [2]Lit., *done* [a]Lev. 23:7, 8; Num. 28:18, 25
17 [1]Or, *eternal* [a]Deut. 16:3-8 [b]Ex. 12:41 [c]Ex. 12:14; 13:3, 10
18 [a]Ex. 12:2; Lev. 23:5-8; Num. 28:16-25
19 [1]Lit., *soul* [a]Ex. 12:15; 23:15; 34:18 [b]Num. 9:13
21 [1]Lit., *Draw out* [2]Lit., *sheep* [a]Num. 9:4; Heb. 11:28 [b]Ex. 12:3 [c]Ex. 12:11
22 [1]Lit., *cause to touch* [a]Ex. 12:7
23 [a]Ex. 11:4; 12:12, 13 [b]Rev. 7:3; 9:4 [c]1 Cor. 10:10; Heb. 11:28
24 [a]Ex. 12:14, 17; 13:5, 10
25 [1]Lit., *spoken* [2]Lit., *service*
26 [1]Lit., *What is this service to you?* [a]Ex. 10:2; 13:8, 14, 15; Deut. 32:7; Josh. 4:6; Ps. 78:6
27 [1]Lit., *because He* [2]Lit., *delivered* [a]Ex. 12:11 [b]Ex. 4:31

29 [a]Ex. 11:4, 5 [b]Num. 8:17; 33:4; Ps. 135:8; 136:10 [c]Ex. 4:23; Ps. 78:51; 105:36 [d]Ex. 9:6

THE JEWISH CALENDAR

Exodus 12:2. The Jewish calendar is a lunar calendar of twenty-eight days, resulting in a shorter year than that in the West. When the calendar became a month out of gear, an additional month called *Adar* was inserted. Months always began with the new moon. Easter always follows Passover, which is at full moon in *Abib*. The Easter festival varies with the moon and a change is made from later April to late March when the additional Jewish month is inserted.

THE PROHIBITION AGAINST LIKENESSES

Exodus 20:4. The commandment against idols *("graven images," KJV)* and likenesses (forms) seems to have been made against the possible incursions of Canaanite religion. This has a spiritual importance, namely that no material representation can be made of a spiritual God, which is covered by the prohibition against idols. The warning against forms *("likeness," KJV)*, however, is something different. The likeness was a mask worn over the face and used in Canaanite religious ritual. Examples of likenesses have been discovered at Hazor.

WHEN DOES SABBATH BEGIN?

Exodus 20:8. Jewish days began not at midnight but at six o'clock in the evening. Monday afternoon, for example, was followed by Tuesday evening. (This is why in Genesis 1 the days of creation are described as an evening and a morning, and why it was necessary for the high priest to be kept awake through the hours of darkness on the Day of Atonement.) The service at the synagogue that welcomed the Sabbath was therefore followed by a night's sleep before teaching was continued the following morning. At six o'clock on the Saturday evening, the Sabbath was over and people were free to go about their normal tasks.

LIVING WATER

John 7. It was on the last day of the festival of Tabernacles (v. 2) that Jesus proclaimed as he stood in the Temple (vv. 14, 37) that if anyone thirsted he could go to him and drink and receive complete inner satisfaction (vv. 37-38). Jesus was obviously saying in a dramatic way that it was not the Jewish faith (symbolized by the pouring out of the water from the pool of Siloam) that would satisfy the world, but rather Jesus through the gift of the Holy Spirit. It was also on the last day that Jesus said he was the light of the world (John 8:12). Jesus is therefore clearly taking up the symbolism of the candelabra from the festival.

THE LAST SUPPER

John 13:1-2. The normal translation of these verses is, *"It was just*

before the Passover Feast. Jesus knew that the time had come for him to leave this world and go to the Father. Having loved his own who were in the world, he now showed them the full extent of his love. The evening meal was being served..." This gives a picture of Jesus holding a special celebration with his disciples with a simulated Passover in contrast to the accounts in other gospels (e.g., Mark 14:12), which say it was actually the day the Passover lamb was killed that the last Supper was held.

Critical scholars therefore teach that John deliberately manipulated the date so that he could represent Jesus as being crucified and hung on the cross at the same time as the Passover lambs were hung. This very nice representation from the critical point of view is based on what appears to be a contradiction. In fact, a contradiction does not necessarily arise. John 13:1 may be regarded as a separate statement in itself–that before Passover began, Jesus knew he was going to die and committed himself to his disciples to see the whole drama through. Then his commitment was fulfilled during the Passover meal.

HONEY

Although the Egyptians kept colonies of bees in hives, this was not developed by the Jews until Roman times. One reason may be that the land was full of honey from wild bees (Exodus 3:8; 13:5), although honey may also refer to grape syrup. Swarms of bees might settle in a hollow tree (1 Samuel 14:25-27), a hole in the rock (Psalm 81:16; Deuteronomy 32:13), or even in an animal carcass (Judges 14:8-9). John the Baptist was able to find honey in the desert (Matthew 3:4).

Honey was used as a natural sweetener in the absence of sugar. God's words are therefore sweet like honey (Psalm 19:10), pleasant words are like it (Proverbs 16:24), and so is wisdom to the soul (Proverbs 24:13-14). It was used for food as well as for sweetening. Jesus was given some of the honeycomb that was part of the meal shortly after his resurrection (Luke 24:41-43).

JOSEPH *- dreamer*

The fact that Joseph was known as a dreamer might sound rather useless. But more important than the fact Joseph had dreams is how Joseph handled them. God made Joseph's dreams a reality because he surrendered to God's plan for his life. When God began to move mightily in Joseph's life, he was still a teenager!

When Joseph began relating his dream of being a ruler, his brothers became fed up and decided to get rid of him. We know from the bible Joseph was the favorite son and was pampered by his father. Joseph did not have to work as hard as his brothers did. But his circumstances changed drastically when his brothers sold him.

God used the circumstances of Joseph's life to mold him into a man who would be the kind of ruler He needed. Joseph went from being the favorite in his father's house to a menial laborer in Potiphar's house. Joseph was forced through his slavery to learn to be a servant.

Joseph also became skilled in self-control while a slave. Though Potiphar's wife tempted Joseph, he resisted her. Many of the early Jewish rulers had fallen into sexual immorality. They became unusable in God's service. God desired to use Joseph greatly, but he needed to be able to control himself.

Joseph had quite a waiting period before his dream of ruling came true. He even served time in prison for something he did not do. Though it must have been hard to spend his youth as he did, Joseph had faith in God and did not become bitter. He was patient and lived to see his dream become a reality.

QUESTIONS

1. **Joseph was proud of his position as a favorite son. Are there things in your life of which you're overly proud? If so, how can you change your attitude to a more humble one?**

2. **Joseph had to wait thirteen years to see his dream fulfilled, but he trusted God. In today's society, great importance is placed on not waiting for anything! Why should you wait for God's timing to see your own dreams come true?**

3. **Through Joseph's suffering was not pleasant, it produced good fruit in his life. When has God used difficulties to produce growth in your life?**

4. **Today's liberal society places little value on self-control and sexual purity. Why do you think God considers it so important?**

and all his servants and all the Egyptians; and there was [a]a great cry in Egypt, for there was no home where there was not someone dead.

31 Then [a]he called for Moses and Aaron at night and said, "Rise up, [b]get out from among my people, both you and the sons of Israel; and go, [1]worship the LORD, as you have said.

32 "Take [a]both your flocks and your herds, as you have said, and go, and bless me also."

Exodus of Israel

33 And [a]the Egyptians urged the people, to send them out of the land in haste, for they said, "We shall all be dead."

34 So the people took [a]their dough before it was leavened, *with* their kneading bowls bound up in the clothes on their shoulders.

35 [a]Now the sons of Israel had done according to the word of Moses, for they had requested from the Egyptians articles of silver and articles of gold, and clothing;

36 and the LORD had given the people favor in the sight of the Egyptians, so that they let them have their request. Thus they [a]plundered the Egyptians.

37 Now the [a]sons of Israel journeyed from [b]Rameses to Succoth, about [c]six hundred thousand men on foot, aside from children.

38 And a [a]mixed multitude also went up with them, [1]along with flocks and herds, a [b]very large number of livestock.

39 And they baked the dough which they had brought out of Egypt into cakes of unleavened bread. For it had not become leavened, since they were [a]driven out of Egypt and could not delay, nor had they [1]prepared any provisions for themselves.

40 Now the time [1]that the sons of Israel lived in Egypt was [a]four hundred and thirty years.

41 And it came about at the end of four hundred and thirty years, [1]to [a]the very day, that [b]all the hosts of the LORD went out from the land of Egypt.

Ordinance of the Passover

42 [a]It is a night [1]to be observed for the LORD for having brought them out from the land of Egypt; this night is for the LORD, [1]to be observed [2]by all the sons of Israel throughout their generations.

43 And the LORD said to Moses and Aaron, "This is the ordinance of [a]the Passover: no [1b]foreigner is to eat of it;

44 but every man's [a]slave purchased with money, after you have circumcised him, then he may eat of it.

45 "[a]A sojourner or a hired servant shall not eat of it.

46 "It is to be eaten in a single house; you are not to bring forth any of the flesh outside of the house, [a]nor are you to break any bone of it.

47 "[a]All the congregation of Israel are to [1]celebrate this.

48 "But [a]if a [1]stranger sojourns with you, and [2]celebrates the Passover to the LORD, let all his males be circumcised, and then let him come near to [3]celebrate it; and he shall be like a native of the land. But no uncircumcised person may eat of it.

49 "[1a]The same law shall [2]apply to the native as to the [3]stranger who sojourns among you."

50 Then all the sons of Israel did *so;* they did just as the LORD had commanded Moses and Aaron.

51 And it came about on that same day that [a]the LORD brought the sons of Israel out of the land of Egypt [1b]by their hosts.

Consecration of the First-born

13 THEN the LORD spoke to Moses, saying,

2 "[a]Sanctify to Me every first-born, the first [1]offspring of every womb among the sons of Israel, both of man and beast; it belongs to Me."

3 And Moses said to the people, "[a]Remember this day in which you went out from Egypt, from the house of [1]slavery; for [b]by [2]a powerful hand the LORD brought you out from this place. [c]And nothing leavened shall be eaten.

4 "On this day in the [a]month of Abib, you are about to go forth.

5 "And it shall be when the LORD [a]brings you to the land of the Canaanite, the Hittite, the Amorite, the Hivite and the Jebusite, which [b]He swore to your fathers to give you, a land flowing with milk and honey, [c]that you shall [1]observe this rite in this month.

6 "For [a]seven days you shall eat unleavened bread, and on the seventh day there shall be a feast to the LORD.

7 "Unleavened bread shall be eaten throughout the seven days; and [a]nothing leavened shall be seen [1]among you, nor shall any leaven be seen [1]among you in all your borders.

8 "[a]And you shall tell your son on that day, saying, 'It is because of what the LORD did for me when I came out of Egypt.'

9 "And [a]it shall [1]serve as a sign to you on your hand, and as a reminder [2]on your forehead, that the law of the LORD may be in your mouth; for with [b]a powerful hand the LORD brought you out of Egypt.

10 "Therefore, you shall [a]keep this ordinance at its appointed time from [1]year to year.

11 "Now it shall come about when [a]the LORD brings you to the land of the Canaanite, as [b]He swore to you and to your fathers, and gives it to you,

12 that [a]you shall [1]devote to the LORD the first [2]offspring of every womb, and [3]the first offspring of every beast that you own; the males belong to the LORD.

30 [a]Ex. 11:6
31 [1]Or, *serve* [a]Ex. 8:8 [b]Ex. 8:25
32 [a]Ex. 10:9, 26
33 [a]Ex. 10:7; 11:1; 12:39; Ps. 105:38
34 [a]Ex. 12:39
35 [a]Ex. 3:21, 22; 11:2, 3; Ps. 105:37
36 [a]Ex. 3:22
37 [a]Num. 33:3, 5 [b]Gen. 47:11 [c]Ex. 38:26; Num. 1:46; 2:32; 11:21; 26:51
38 [1]Lit., *and* [a]Num. 11:4 [b]Ex. 17:3; Num. 20:19; 32:1; Deut. 3:19
39 [1]Lit., *made* [a]Ex. 6:1; 11:1; 12:31-33
40 [1]Or, *of the sons of Israel who dwelt* [a]Gen. 15:13, 16; Acts 7:6; Gal. 3:17
41 [1]Lit., *that it happened on this very day* [a]Ex. 12:17 [b]Ex. 3:8, 10; 6:6
42 [1]Or, *of vigil* [2]Lit., *to the sons* [a]Ex. 13:10; 34:18; Deut. 16:1
43 [1]Lit., *son of a stranger* [a]Ex. 12:11; Num. 9:14 [b]Ex. 12:48
44 [a]Gen. 17:12, 13; Lev. 22:11
45 [a]Lev. 22:10
46 [a]Num. 9:12; Ps. 34:20; John 19:33, 36
47 [1]Lit., *do* [a]Ex. 12:6; Num. 9:13, 14
48 [1]Lit., *sojourner* [2]Lit., *does* [3]Lit., *do* [a]Num. 9:14
49 [1]Lit., *One law* [2]Lit., *be* [3]Lit., *sojourner* [a]Lev. 24:22; Num. 15:15, 16, 29
51 [1]Lit., *according to* [a]Ex. 12:41 [b]Ex. 6:26

2 [1]Lit., *opening* [a]Ex. 13:12, 13, 15; 22:29; Lev. 27:26; Num. 3:13; 8:16f.; 18:15; Deut. 15:19; Luke 2:23
3 [1]Lit., *slaves* [2]Lit., *strength of hand* [a]Ex. 12:42; Deut. 16:3 [b]Ex. 3:20; 6:1 [c]Ex. 12:19
4 [a]Ex. 12:2; 23:15; 34:18; Deut. 16:1
5 [1]Lit., *serve this service* [a]Ex. 3:8, 17; Josh. 24:11 [b]Ex. 6:8 [c]Ex. 12:25
6 [a]Ex. 12:15-20
7 [1]Lit., *to* [a]Ex. 12:19
8 [a]Ex. 10:2; 12:26f.; 13:14; Ps. 44:1
9 [1]Lit., *be for* [2]Lit., *between your eyes* [a]Ex. 12:14; 13:16; Num. 15:39; Deut. 6:8; 11:18 [b]Ex. 13:3
10 [1]Lit., *days to days* [a]Ex. 12:24, 25; 13:5
11 [a]Ex. 13:5 [b]Gen. 15:18; 17:8; 28:15; Ps. 105:42-45

12 [1]Lit., *cause to pass over* [2]Lit., *opening* [3]Lit., *every issue the offspring of a beast* [a]Ex. 13:1, 2; 22:29; 34:19; Lev. 27:26; Num. 18:15; Ezek. 44:30; Luke 2:23

13 "But [a]every first [1]offspring of a donkey you shall redeem with a lamb, but if you do not redeem *it,* then you shall break its neck; and [b]every first-born of man among your sons you shall redeem.

14 "[a]And it shall be when your son asks you in time to come, saying, 'What is this?' then you shall say to him, '[b]With a [1]powerful hand the LORD brought us out of Egypt, from the house of [2]slavery.

15 'And it came about, when Pharaoh was stubborn about letting us go, that the [a]LORD killed every first-born in the land of Egypt, both the first-born of man and the first-born of beast. Therefore, I sacrifice to the LORD the males, the first [1]offspring of every womb, but every first-born of my sons I redeem.'

16 "So [a]it shall [1]serve as a sign on your hand, and as [2]phylacteries [3]on your forehead, for with a [4]powerful hand the LORD brought us out of Egypt."

God Leads the People

17 Now it came about when Pharaoh had let the people go, that God did not lead them by the way of the land of the Philistines, even though it was near; for God said, "[a]Lest the people change their minds when they see war, and they return to Egypt."

18 Hence God led the people around by the way of the wilderness to the [1]Red Sea; and the sons of Israel went up [a]in martial array from the land of Egypt.

19 And Moses took [a]the bones of Joseph with him, for he had made the sons of Israel solemnly swear, saying, "God shall surely [1]take care of you; and you shall carry my bones from here with you."

20 Then they set out from [a]Succoth and camped in Etham on the edge of the wilderness.

21 And [a]the LORD was going before them in a pillar of cloud by day to lead them on the way, and in a pillar of fire by night to give them light, that they might [1]travel by day and by night.

22 [1]He [a]did not take away the pillar of cloud by day, nor the pillar of fire by night, from before the people.

Pharaoh in Pursuit

14 NOW the LORD spoke to Moses, saying,

2 "Tell the sons of Israel to turn back and camp before [a]Pi-hahiroth, between [b]Migdol and the sea; you shall camp in front of Baal-zephon, opposite it, by the sea.

3 "For Pharaoh will say of the sons of Israel, 'They are wandering aimlessly in the land; the wilderness has shut them in.'

4 "Thus [a]I will [1]harden Pharaoh's heart, and [b]he will chase after them; and I will be honored through Pharaoh and all his army, and [c]the Egyptians will know that I am the LORD." And they did so.

5 When the king of Egypt was told that the people had fled, [1]Pharaoh and his servants had a change of heart toward the people, and they said, "What is this we have done, that we have let Israel go from serving us?"

6 So he made his chariot ready and took his people with him;

7 and he took six hundred select chariots, and all the *other* chariots of Egypt with officers over all of them.

8 And [a]the LORD [1]hardened the heart of Pharaoh, king of Egypt, and he chased after the sons of Israel as the sons of Israel were going out [2b]boldly.

9 Then [a]the Egyptians chased after them *with* all the horses *and* chariots of Pharaoh, his horsemen and his army, and they overtook them camping by the sea, [b]beside Pi-hahiroth, in front of Baal-zephon.

10 And as Pharaoh drew near, the sons of Israel [1]looked, and behold, the Egyptians were marching after them, and they became very frightened; [a]so the sons of Israel cried out to the LORD.

11 Then [a]they said to Moses, "Is it because there were no graves in Egypt that you have taken us away to die in the wilderness? Why have you dealt with us in this way, [1]bringing us out of Egypt?

12 "[a]Is this not the word that we spoke to you in Egypt, saying, '[1]Leave us alone that we may serve the Egyptians'? For it would have been better for us to serve the Egyptians than to die in the wilderness."

The Sea Is Divided

13 But Moses said to the people, "[a]Do not fear! [1]Stand by and see [b]the salvation of the LORD which He will accomplish for you today; for the Egyptians whom you have seen today, you will never see them again forever.

14 "[a]The LORD will fight for you while [b]you keep silent."

15 Then the LORD said to Moses, "Why are you crying out to Me? Tell the sons of Israel to go forward.

16 "And as for you, lift up [a]your staff and stretch out your hand over the sea and divide it, and the sons of Israel shall [1]go through the midst of the sea on dry land.

17 "And as for Me, behold, [a]I will [1]harden the hearts of the Egyptians so that they will go in after them; and I will be honored through Pharaoh and all his army, through his chariots and his horsemen.

18 "[a]Then the Egyptians will know that I am the LORD, when I am honored through Pharaoh, through his chariots and his horsemen."

19 And [a]the angel of God, who had been going before the camp of Israel, moved and went behind them; and the pillar of cloud moved from before them and stood behind them.

20 So it came between the camp of Egypt and the camp of Israel; and there

---

13 [1]Lit., *opening* [a]Ex. 34:20; Num. 18:15 [b]Num. 3:46
14 [1]Lit., *strength of hand* [2]Lit., *slaves* [a]Ex. 10:2; 12:26, 27; 13:8; Deut. 6:20; Josh. 4:6, 21 [b]Ex. 13:3, 9
15 [1]Lit., *opening* [a]Ex. 12:29
16 [1]Lit., *be for* [2]Or, *frontlet-bands* [3]Lit., *between your eyes* [4]Lit., *strength of hand* [a]Ex. 13:9; Deut. 6:8
17 [a]Ex. 14:11, 12; Num. 14:1-4; Deut. 17:16
18 [1]Lit., *Sea of Reeds* [a]Josh. 1:14; 4:12, 13
19 [1]Lit., *visit* [a]Gen. 50:24, 25; Josh. 24:32; Acts 7:15, 16
20 [a]Ex. 12:37; Num. 33:6
21 [1]Lit., *go* [a]Ex. 14:19, 24; 33:9, 10; Num. 9:15; 14:14; Deut. 1:33; Neh. 9:12; Ps. 78:14; 99:7; 105:39; Is. 4:5; 1 Cor. 10:1
22 [1]Or, *The pillar of cloud by day and the pillar of fire by night did not depart* [a]Neh. 9:19

2 [a]Num. 33:7 [b]Jer. 44:1
4 [1]Lit., *make strong* [a]Ex. 4:21; 7:3; 14:17 [b]Ex. 14:23 [c]Ex. 7:5; 14:25
5 [1]Lit., *the heart of Pharaoh . . . was changed*
8 [1]Lit., *made strong* [2]Lit., *with a high hand* [a]Ex. 14:4 [b]Num. 33:3; Acts 13:17
9 [a]Ex. 15:9; Josh. 24:6 [b]Ex. 14:2
10 [1]Lit., *lifted up their eyes* [a]Josh. 24:7; Neh. 9:9; Ps. 34:17; 107:6
11 [1]Lit., *so as to bring* [a]Ex. 5:21; 15:24; 16:2; Ps. 106:7, 8
12 [1]Lit., *Cease from us* [a]Ex. 6:9
13 [1]Or, *Take your stand* [a]Gen. 15:1; 46:3; Ex. 20:20; 2 Chr. 20:15, 17; Is. 41:10, 13, 14 [b]Ex. 14:30; 15:2
14 [a]Ex. 14:25; 15:3; Deut. 1:30; 3:22; Josh. 23:3; 2 Chr. 20:29; Neh. 4:20 [b]Is. 30:15
16 [1]Lit., *enter the* [a]Ex. 4:17, 20; 7:19; 14:21, 26; 17:5, 6, 9; Num. 20:8, 9, 11; Is. 10:26
17 [1]Lit., *make strong* [a]Ex. 14:4, 8
18 [a]Ex. 14:25
19 [a]Ex. 13:21, 22

was the cloud [1]along with the darkness,
yet it gave light at night. Thus the one
did not come near the other all night.
21 [a]Then Moses stretched out his
hand over the sea; and the LORD [1]swept
the sea *back* by a strong east wind all
night, and turned the sea into [b]dry land,
so [c]the waters were divided.
22 [a]And the sons of Israel [1]went
through the midst of the sea on the dry
land, and [b]the waters *were like* a wall to
them on their right hand and on their
left.
23 Then [a]the Egyptians took up the
pursuit, and all Pharaoh's horses, his
chariots and his horsemen went in after
them into the midst of the sea.
24 And it came about at the morning
watch, that [a]the LORD looked down on
the [1]army of the Egyptians [2]through the
pillar of fire and cloud and brought the
[1]army of the Egyptians into confusion.
25 And He [1]caused their chariot
wheels to swerve, and He made them
drive with difficulty; so the Egyptians
said, "Let [2]us flee from Israel, [a]for the
LORD is fighting for them against the
Egyptians."
26 Then the LORD said to Moses,
"[a]Stretch out your hand over the sea so
that the waters may come back over the
Egyptians, over their chariots and their
horsemen."
27 So Moses stretched out his hand
over the sea, and [a]the sea returned to its
normal state at daybreak, while the
Egyptians were fleeing [1]right into it;
then the LORD [2b]overthrew the Egyptians in the midst of the sea.
28 And the waters returned and covered the chariots and the horsemen,
[1]even Pharaoh's entire army that had
gone into the sea after them; [a]not even
one of them remained.
29 But the sons of Israel walked on
[a]dry land through the midst of the sea,
and the waters *were like* a wall to them
on their right hand and on their left.
30 [a]Thus the LORD saved Israel that
day from the hand of the Egyptians, and
Israel [b]saw the Egyptians dead on the
seashore.
31 And when Israel saw the great
[1]power which the LORD had [2]used
against the Egyptians, the people [3]feared
the LORD, and [a]they believed in the
LORD and in His servant Moses.

The Song of Moses and Israel

15 [a]THEN Moses and the sons of
Israel sang this song to the LORD,
[1]and said,
"[2b]I will sing to the LORD, for He
[3]is highly exalted;
[c]The horse and its rider He has
hurled into the sea.
2 "[1a]The LORD is my strength and
song,
And He has become my salvation;
[b]This is my God, and I will praise
Him;
[c]My father's God, and I will [d]ex-
tol Him.
3 "[a]The LORD is a warrior;
[1b]The LORD is His name.
4 "[a]Pharaoh's chariots and his army
He has cast into the sea;
And the choicest of his officers are
[1]drowned in the [2]Red Sea.
5 "The deeps cover them;
[a]They went down into the depths
like a stone.
6 "[a]Thy right hand, O LORD, is majestic in power,
[b]Thy right hand, O LORD, shatters
the enemy.
7 "And in the greatness of Thine
[1]excellence Thou [a]dost overthrow those who rise up against
Thee;
[b]Thou dost send forth Thy burning anger, *and* it [c]consumes
them as chaff.
8 "[a]And at the blast of Thy nostrils
the waters were piled up,
[b]The flowing waters stood up like
a heap;
The deeps were congealed in the
heart of the sea.
9 "[a]The enemy said, 'I will pursue, I
will overtake, I will [b]divide the
spoil;
My [1]desire shall be [2]gratified
against them;
I will draw out my sword, my
hand shall [3]destroy them.'
10 "[a]Thou didst blow with Thy wind,
the sea covered them;
[b]They sank like lead in the
[1]mighty waters.
11 "[a]Who is like Thee among the
gods, O LORD?
Who is like Thee, [b]majestic in
holiness,
[c]Awesome in praises, [d]working
wonders?
12 "[a]Thou didst stretch out Thy right
hand,
The earth swallowed them.
13 "In Thy lovingkindness Thou hast
[a]led the people whom Thou hast
[b]redeemed;
In Thy strength Thou hast guided
them [c]to Thy holy habitation.
14 "[a]The peoples have heard, they
tremble;
Anguish has gripped the inhabitants of Philistia.
15 "Then the [a]chiefs of Edom were
dismayed;
[b]The leaders of Moab, trembling
grips them;
[c]All the inhabitants of Canaan
have melted away.

20 [1]Lit., *and the darkness*
21 [1]Lit., *caused to go* [a]Ex. 7:19; 14:16 [b]Ps. 66:6; 106:9; 136:13, 14 [c]Ex. 15:8; Josh. 3:16; 4:23; Neh. 9:11; Ps. 74:13; 78:13; 114:3, 5; Is. 63:12, 13
22 [1]Lit., *entered the* [a]Ex. 15:19; Josh. 3:17; 4:22; Neh. 9:11; Ps. 66:6; 78:13; Heb. 11:29 [b]Ex. 14:29; 15:8
23 [a]Ex. 14:4, 17
24 [1]Lit., *camp* [2]Or, *in* [a]Ex. 13:21
25 [1]Or, *removed* [2]Lit., *me* [a]Ex. 14:4, 14, 18
26 [a]Ex. 14:16
27 [1]Lit., *to meet it* [2]Lit., *shook off* [a]Josh. 4:18 [b]Ex. 15:1, 7; Deut. 11:4; Neh. 9:11; Ps. 78:53; Heb. 11:29
28 [1]Lit., *in respect to* [a]Ps. 78:53; 106:11
29 [a]Ex. 14:22; Ps. 66:6; Is. 11:15
30 [a]Ex. 14:13; Ps. 106:8, 10; Is. 63:8, 11 [b]Ps. 58:10; 59:10
31 [1]Lit., *hand* [2]Lit., *done* [3]Or, *revered* [a]Ex. 4:31; 19:9; Ps. 106:12; John 2:11; 11:45

1 [1]Lit., *and said, saying* [2]Or, *Let me sing* [3]Or, *triumphed gloriously* [a]Ps. 106:12; Rev. 15:3 [b]Is. 12:5; 42:10-12 [c]Jer. 51:21
2 [1]Heb., *YAH* [a]Ps. 18:1, 2; Is. 12:2; Hab. 3:18f. [b]Ps. 48:14 [c]Ex. 3:6, 15, 16 [d]2 Sam. 22:47; Ps. 99:5; Is. 25:1
3 [1]Heb., *YHWH*, usually rendered *LORD* [a]Ex. 14:14; Rev. 19:11 [b]Ex. 3:15; 6:2, 3, 7, 8; Ps. 24:8; 83:18
4 [1]Lit., *sunk* [2]Lit., *Sea of Reeds* [a]Ex. 14:6, 7, 17, 28
5 [a]Ex. 15:10; Neh. 9:11
6 [a]Ex. 3:20; 6:1 [b]Ps. 118:15, 16
7 [1]Or, *exaltation* [a]Ex. 14:27 [b]Ps. 78:49, 50 [c]Deut. 4:24; Is. 5:24; Heb. 12:29
8 [a]Ex. 14:22, 29; Job 4:9 [b]Ps. 78:13
9 [1]Lit., *soul* [2]Lit., *be filled with them* [3]Or, *dispossess, bring to ruin* [a]Ex. 14:5, 8, 9 [b]Judg. 5:30; Is. 53:12; Luke 11:22
10 [1]Or, *majestic* [a]Ex. 14:27, 28 [b]Ex. 15:5
11 [a]Ex. 8:10; 9:14; Deut. 3:24; 2 Sam. 7:22; 1 Kin. 8:23; Ps. 71:19; 86:8; Mic. 7:18 [b]Is. 6:3; Rev. 4:8 [c]Ps. 22:23 [d]Ps. 72:18; 136:4
12 [a]Ex. 15:6
13 [a]Neh. 9:12; Ps. 77:20 [b]Ex. 15:16; Ps. 77:15 [c]Ex. 15:17; Ps. 78:54
14 [a]Deut. 2:25; Hab. 3:7
15 [a]Gen. 36:15, 40 [b]Num. 22:3, 4 [c]Josh. 2:9, 11, 24; 5:1

16 “[a]Terror and dread fall upon them;
[b]By the greatness of Thine arm they are motionless as stone;
Until Thy people pass over, O LORD,
Until the people pass over whom Thou [c]hast purchased.
17 “[a]Thou wilt bring them and [b]plant them in [c]the mountain of Thine inheritance,
[d]The place, O LORD, which Thou hast made for Thy dwelling,
[e]The sanctuary, O Lord, which Thy hands have established.
18 “[a]The LORD shall reign forever and ever.”

19 [a]For the horses of Pharaoh with his chariots and his horsemen went into the sea, and the LORD brought back the waters of the sea on them; but the sons of Israel walked on [b]dry land through the midst of the sea.

20 And [a]Miriam the prophetess, Aaron’s sister, took the [b]timbrel in her hand, and all the women went out after her with timbrels and with [1c]dancing.

21 And Miriam answered them,
“[a]Sing to the LORD, for He [1]is highly exalted;
The horse and his rider He has hurled into the sea.”

The LORD Provides Water

22 [a]Then Moses [1]led Israel from the [2]Red Sea, and they went out into [b]the wilderness of [c]Shur; and they went three days in the wilderness and found no water.

23 And when they came to [a]Marah, they could not drink the waters [1]of Marah, for they were [2]bitter; therefore it was named [3]Marah.

24 So the people [a]grumbled at Moses, saying, “What shall we drink?”

25 Then he [a]cried out to the LORD, and the LORD showed him [b]a tree; and he threw *it* into the waters, and the waters became sweet. There He [c]made for them a statute and regulation, and there He [d]tested them.

26 And He said, “[a]If you will give earnest heed to the voice of the LORD your God, and do what is right in His sight, and give ear [b]to His commandments, and keep all His statutes, [c]I will put none of the diseases on you which I have put on the Egyptians; for I, [d]the LORD, am your healer.”

27 Then they came to [a]Elim where there *were* twelve springs of water and seventy date palms, and they camped there beside the waters.

The LORD Provides Manna

16 THEN they set out from Elim, and all the congregation of the sons of Israel came to the wilderness of [a]Sin, which is between Elim and Sinai, on [b]the fifteenth day of the second month after their departure from the land of Egypt.

2 And the whole congregation of the sons of Israel [a]grumbled against Moses and Aaron in the wilderness.

3 And the sons of Israel said to them, “[a]Would that we had died by the LORD’s hand in the land of Egypt, [b]when we sat by the pots of [1]meat, when we ate bread to the full; for you have brought us out into this wilderness to kill this whole assembly with hunger.”

4 Then the LORD said to Moses, “Behold, [a]I will rain bread from heaven for you; and the people shall go out and gather a day’s portion every day, that I may [b]test them, whether or not they will walk in My [1]instruction.

5 “And it will come about [a]on the sixth day, when they prepare what they bring in, it will be twice as much as they gather daily.”

6 So Moses and Aaron said to all the sons of Israel, “At evening [1a]you will know that the LORD has brought you out of the land of Egypt;

7 and in the morning [1]you will see [a]the glory of the LORD, for [b]He hears your grumblings against the LORD; and [c]what are we, that you grumble against us?”

The LORD Provides Meat

8 And Moses said, “*This will happen* when the LORD gives you [1]meat to eat in the evening, and bread to the full in the morning; for the LORD hears your grumblings which you grumble against Him. And what are we? Your grumblings are [a]not against us but against the LORD.”

9 Then Moses said to Aaron, “Say to all the congregation of the sons of Israel, ‘[a]Come near before the LORD, for He has heard your grumblings.’ ”

10 And it came about as Aaron spoke to the whole congregation of the sons of Israel, that they [1]looked toward the wilderness, and behold, [a]the glory of the LORD appeared in the cloud.

11 And the LORD spoke to Moses, saying,

12 “[a]I have heard the grumblings of the sons of Israel; speak to them, saying, ‘[1]At twilight you shall eat [2]meat, and in the morning you shall be filled with bread; and [b]you shall know that I am the LORD your God.’ ”

13 So it came about at evening that [a]the quails came up and covered the camp, and in the morning [b]there was a layer of dew around the camp.

14 [a]When the layer of dew [1]evaporated, behold, on the [2]surface of the wilderness [b]there was a fine flake-like thing, fine as the frost on the ground.

15 When the sons of Israel saw *it*, they said to one another, “[1]What is it?” For they did not know what it was. And Moses said to them, “[a]It is the bread which the LORD has given you to eat.

16 [a]Ex. 23:27; Deut. 2:25; Josh. 2:9 [b]Ex. 15:5, 6 [c]Ex. 15:13; Ps. 74:2; Is. 43:1; Jer. 31:11; Titus 2:14; 2 Pet. 2:1
17 [a]Ex. 23:20; 32:34 [b]Ps. 44:2; 80:8, 15 [c]Ps. 2:6; 78:54, 68 [d]Ps. 68:16; 76:2; 132:13, 14 [e]Ps. 78:69
18 [a]Ps. 10:16; 29:10; Is. 57:15
19 [a]Ex. 14:23, 28 [b]Ex. 14:22, 29
20 [1]Lit., *dances* [a]Ex. 2:4; Num. 26:59; 1 Chr. 6:3; Mic. 6:4 [b]Judg. 11:34; 1 Sam. 18:6; 1 Chr. 15:16; Ps. 68:25; 81:2; 149:3; Jer. 31:4 [c]Judg. 11:34; 21:21; 1 Sam. 18:6; Ps. 30:11; 150:4
21 [1]Or, *has triumphed gloriously* [a]Ex. 15:1
22 [1]Lit., *caused Israel to journey* [2]Lit., *Sea of Reeds* [a]Ps. 77:20; 78:52, 53 [b]Num. 33:8 [c]Gen. 16:7; 20:1; 25:18
23 [1]Lit., *from* [2]Heb., *Marim* [3]I.e., bitterness [a]Num. 33:8; Ruth 1:20
24 [a]Ex. 14:11; 16:2; Ps. 106:13
25 [a]Ex. 14:10 [b]Ezek. 47:7, 8 [c]Josh. 24:25 [d]Ex. 16:4; Deut. 8:2, 16; Judg. 2:22; 3:1, 4; Ps. 66:10
26 [a]Ex. 19:5, 6; Deut. 7:12 [b]Ex. 20:2-17 [c]Deut. 7:15; 28:58, 60 [d]Ex. 23:25; Deut. 32:39; Ps. 41:3, 4; 103:3; 147:3
27 [a]Num. 33:9

1 [a]Num. 33:10, 11; Ezek. 30:15 [b]Ex. 12:6, 51; 19:1
2 [a]Ex. 14:11; 15:24; Ps. 106:25; 1 Cor. 10:10
3 [1]Or, *flesh* [a]Ex. 17:3; Num. 14:2, 3; 20:3; Lam. 4:9 [b]Num. 11:4, 5
4 [1]Or, *law* [a]Neh. 9:15; Ps. 78:23-25; 105:40; John 6:31; 1 Cor. 10:3 [b]Ex. 15:25; Deut. 8:2, 16
5 [a]Ex. 16:22
6 [1]Lit., *and you* [a]Ex. 6:7
7 [1]Lit., *and you* [a]Ex. 16:10, 12; Is. 35:2; 40:5; John 11:4, 40 [b]Num. 14:27; 17:5 [c]Num. 16:11
8 [1]Or, *flesh* [a]1 Sam. 8:7; Luke 10:16; Rom. 13:2; 1 Thess. 4:8
9 [a]Num. 16:16
10 [1]Lit., *turned* [a]Ex. 13:21; 16:7; Num. 16:19; 1 Kin. 8:10f.

12 [1]Lit., *Between the two evenings* [2]Or, *flesh* [a]Ex. 16:8; Num. 14:27 [b]Ex. 6:7; 16:7; 1 Kin. 20:28; Joel 3:17
13 [a]Num. 11:31; Ps. 78:27-29; 105:40 [b]Num. 11:9
14 [1]Lit., *had gone up* [2]Lit., *face of* [a]Num. 11:7-9 [b]Ex. 16:31; Neh. 9:15; Ps. 78:24; 105:40
15 [1]Heb., *Man hu*, cf. v. 31 [a]Ex. 16:4; Neh. 9:15; Ps. 78:24; John 6:31; 1 Cor. 10:3

16 "This is [1]what the LORD has commanded, 'Gather of it every man [2]as much as he should eat; you shall take [3][a]an omer apiece according to the number of persons each of you has in his tent.' "

17 And the sons of Israel did so, and *some* gathered much and *some* little.

18 When they measured it with an omer, [a]he who had gathered much had no excess, and he who had gathered little had no lack; every man gathered [1]as much as he should eat.

19 And Moses said to them, "[a]Let no man leave any of it until morning."

20 But they did not listen to Moses, and some left part of it until morning, and it bred worms and became foul; and Moses was angry with them.

21 And they gathered it morning by morning, every man [1]as much as he should eat; but when the sun grew hot, it would melt.

The Sabbath Observed

22 [a]Now it came about on the sixth day they gathered twice as much bread, two omers for each one. When all the [b]leaders of the congregation came and told Moses,

23 then he said to them, "This is what the LORD [1]meant: [a]Tomorrow is a sabbath observance, a holy sabbath to the LORD. Bake what you will bake and boil what you will boil, and [b]all that is left over [2]put aside to be kept until morning."

24 So they [1]put it aside until morning, as Moses had ordered, and [a]it did not become foul, nor was there any worm in it.

25 And Moses said, "Eat it today, for today is a sabbath to the LORD; today you will not find it in the field.

26 "[a]Six days you shall gather it, but on the seventh day, *the* sabbath, there will be [1]none."

27 And it came about on the seventh day that some of the people went out to gather, but they found none.

28 Then the LORD said to Moses, "[a]How long do you refuse to keep My commandments and My [1]instructions?

29 "See, [1]the LORD has given you the sabbath; therefore He gives you bread for two days on the sixth day. Remain every man in his place; let no man go out of his place on the seventh day."

30 So the people rested on the seventh day.

31 And the house of [a]Israel named it [1]manna, and it was like [b]coriander seed, white; and its taste was like wafers with honey.

32 Then Moses said, "This is [1]what the LORD has commanded, 'Let an omerful of it be kept throughout your generations, that they may see the bread that I fed you in the wilderness, when I brought you out of the land of Egypt.' "

33 And Moses said to Aaron, "[a]Take a jar and put an omerful of manna in it, and place it before the LORD, to be kept throughout your generations."

34 As the LORD commanded Moses, so Aaron placed it before [a]the Testimony, to be kept.

35 [a]And the sons of Israel ate the manna forty years, until they came to an inhabited land; they ate the manna until they came to the border of the land of Canaan.

36 (Now [a]an omer is a tenth of an [1]ephah.)

Water in the Rock

17 THEN all the congregation of the sons of Israel journeyed by [1]stages from the wilderness of [a]Sin, according to the [2]command of the LORD, and camped at [b]Rephidim, and there was no water for the people to drink.

2 Therefore the people [a]quarreled with Moses and said, "Give us water that we may drink." And Moses said to them, "[b]Why do you quarrel with me? [c]Why do you test the LORD?"

3 But the people thirsted there for water; and [1]they [a]grumbled against Moses and said, "Why, now, have you brought us up from Egypt, to kill [2]us and [3]our children and [3b]our livestock with thirst?"

4 So Moses cried out to the LORD, saying, "What shall I do to this people? A [a]little more and they will stone me."

5 Then the LORD said to Moses, "Pass before the people and take with you some of [a]the elders of Israel; and take in your hand your staff with which [b]you struck the Nile, and go.

6 "Behold, I will stand before you there on the rock at [a]Horeb; and [b]you shall strike the rock, and water will come out of it, that the people may drink." And Moses did so in the sight of the elders of Israel.

7 And he named the place [1a]Massah and [2b]Meribah because of the quarrel of the sons of Israel, and because they [c]tested the LORD, saying, "Is the LORD among us, or not?"

Amalek Fought

8 Then [a]Amalek came and fought against Israel at [b]Rephidim.

9 So Moses said to [a]Joshua, "Choose men for us, and go out, fight against Amalek. Tomorrow I will station myself on the top of the hill with [b]the staff of God in my hand."

10 And Joshua did as Moses [1]told him, [2]and fought against Amalek; and Moses, Aaron, and [a]Hur went up to the top of the hill.

11 So it came about when Moses held his hand up, that Israel prevailed, and when he let his hand [1]down, Amalek prevailed.

12 But Moses' hands were heavy. Then they took a stone and put it under him, and he sat on it; and Aaron and Hur [a]supported his hands, one on one side and one on the other. Thus his hands were steady until the sun set.

---

16 [1]Lit., *the thing which* [2]Lit., *according to his eating* [3]Lit., *an omer for a head* [a]Ex. 16:32, 36
18 [1]Lit., *according to his eating* [a]2 Cor. 8:15
19 [a]Ex. 12:10; 16:23; 23:18
21 [1]Lit., *according to his eating*
22 [a]Ex. 16:5 [b]Ex. 34:31
23 [1]Lit., *spoke* [2]Lit., *lay up for you* [a]Gen. 2:3; Ex. 20:8-11; 23:12; 31:15; 35:2; Lev. 23:3; Neh. 9:13, 14 [b]Ex. 16:19
24 [1]Lit., *laid it up* [a]Ex. 16:20
26 [1]Lit., *none on it* [a]Ex. 20:9, 10
28 [1]Or, *laws* [a]2 Kin. 17:14; Ps. 78:10; 106:13
29 [1]Lit., *for the LORD*
31 [1]Heb., *man*, cf. v. 15 [a]Num. 11:7-9; Deut. 8:3, 16 [b]Ex. 16:14
32 [1]Lit., *the thing which*
33 [a]Heb. 9:4; Rev. 2:17
34 [a]Ex. 25:16, 21; 27:21; 40:20; Num. 17:10
35 [a]Deut. 8:2f.; Josh. 5:12; Neh. 9:20, 21
36 [1]I.e., Approx. one bu. [a]Ex. 16:16

1 [1]Lit., *their journeyings* [2]Lit., *mouth* [a]Ex. 16:1; Num. 33:12 [b]Ex. 19:2; Num. 33:14
2 [a]Ex. 14:11; Num. 20:2, 3, 13 [b]Ex. 16:8 [c]Deut. 6:16; Ps. 78:18, 41; Matt. 4:7; 1 Cor. 10:9
3 [1]Lit., *the people* [2]Lit., *me* [3]Lit., *my* [a]Ex. 16:2, 3 [b]Ex. 12:38
4 [a]Num. 14:10; 1 Sam. 30:6
5 [a]Ex. 3:16, 18 [b]Ex. 7:20
6 [a]Ex. 3:1 [b]Num. 20:10, 11; Deut. 8:15; Neh. 9:15; Ps. 78:15; 105:41; 114:8; 1 Cor. 10:4
7 [1]I.e., test [2]I.e., quarrel [a]Deut. 6:16; 9:22; Ps. 95:8 [b]Num. 20:13, 24; 27:14; Ps. 81:7 [c]Num. 14:22; Deut. 33:8
8 [a]Gen. 36:12; Num. 24:20; Deut. 25:17-19; 1 Sam. 15:2 [b]Ex. 17:1
9 [a]Ex. 24:13 [b]Ex. 4:20
10 [1]Lit., *said to* [2]Lit., *to fight* [a]Ex. 24:14; 31:2
11 [1]Lit., *rest*
12 [a]Is. 35:3

13 So Joshua [1]overwhelmed Amalek and his people with the edge of the sword.

14 Then the LORD said to Moses, "[a]Write this in [1]a book as a memorial, and [2]recite it to Joshua, [3]that [b]I will utterly blot out the memory of Amalek from under heaven."

15 And Moses built an [a]altar, and named it [b]The LORD is My Banner;

16 and he said, "[1a]The LORD has sworn; the LORD will have war against Amalek from generation to generation."

Jethro, Moses' Father-in-law

18 NOW [a]Jethro, the priest of Midian, Moses' father-in-law, heard of all that God had done for Moses and for Israel His people, how the LORD had brought Israel out of Egypt.

2 And Jethro, Moses' father-in-law, took Moses' wife [a]Zipporah, after he had sent her away,

3 and her [a]two sons, of whom [1]one was named Gershom, for he said, "I have been [b]a [2]sojourner in a foreign land."

4 And [1]the other was named [2a]Eliezer, for *he said,* "[b]The God of my father was my help, and delivered me from the sword of Pharaoh."

5 Then Jethro, Moses' father-in-law, came with his sons and his wife to Moses [1]in the wilderness where he was camped, at [a]the mount of God.

6 And he [1]sent word to Moses, "I, your father-in-law Jethro, am coming to you with your wife and her two sons with her."

7 Then Moses went out to meet his father-in-law, and [a]he bowed down and [b]kissed him; and they [c]asked each other of their welfare, and went into the tent.

8 And Moses told his father-in-law all that the LORD had done to Pharaoh and to the Egyptians [a]for Israel's sake, all the [b]hardship that had befallen them on the journey, and *how* [c]the LORD had delivered them.

9 And Jethro rejoiced over all [a]the goodness which the LORD had done to Israel, [1]in delivering [2]them from the hand of the Egyptians.

10 So Jethro said, "[a]Blessed be the LORD who delivered you from the hand of the Egyptians and from the hand of Pharaoh, *and* who delivered the people from under the hand of the Egyptians.

11 "Now I know that [a]the LORD is greater than all the gods; [1]indeed, [b]it was proven when they dealt proudly against [2]the people."

12 [a]Then Jethro, Moses' father-in-law, took a burnt offering and sacrifices for God, and Aaron came with all the elders of Israel to eat [1]a meal with Moses' father-in-law before God.

13 And it came about the next day that Moses sat to judge the people, and the people stood about Moses from the morning until the evening.

14 Now when Moses' father-in-law saw all that he was doing for the people, he said, "What is this thing that you are doing for the people? Why do you alone sit *as judge* and all the people stand about you from morning until evening?"

15 And Moses said to his father-in-law, "Because the people come to me [a]to inquire of God.

16 "When they have a [1a]dispute, it comes to me, and I judge between a man and his neighbor, and make known the statutes of God and His laws."

Jethro Counsels Moses

17 And Moses' father-in-law said to him, "The thing that you are doing is not good.

18 "[a]You will surely wear out, both yourself and [1]these people who are with you, for the [2]task is too heavy for you; [b]you cannot do it alone.

19 "Now listen to [1]me: I shall give you counsel, and God be with you. [2]You be the people's representative before God, and you [a]bring the [3]disputes to God,

20 [a]then teach them the statutes and the laws, and make known to them [b]the way in which they are to walk, and the work they are to do.

21 "Furthermore, you shall [1]select out of all the people [a]able men [b]who fear God, men of truth, those who [c]hate dishonest gain; and you shall place *these* over them, *as* leaders of thousands, [2]of hundreds, [2]of fifties and [2]of tens.

22 "And let them judge the people at all times; and let it be [a]that every major [1]dispute they will bring to you, but every minor [1]dispute they themselves will judge. So it will be easier for you, and [b]they will bear *the burden* with you.

23 "If you do this thing and God *so* commands you, then you will be able to [1]endure, and all [2]these people also will go to [3]their place in peace."

24 So Moses listened [1]to his father-in-law, and did all that he had said.

25 And Moses chose [a]able men out of all Israel, and made them heads over the people, leaders of thousands, [1]of hundreds, [1]of fifties and [1]of tens.

26 And they judged the people at all times; [a]the difficult [1]dispute they would bring to Moses, but every minor [1]dispute they themselves would judge.

27 Then Moses [1a]bade his father-in-law farewell, and he went his way into his own land.

Moses on Sinai

19 [a]IN the third month after the sons of Israel had gone out of the land of Egypt, [1]on that very day they came into the wilderness of [b]Sinai.

2 When they set out from [a]Rephidim, they came to the wilderness of Sinai, and camped in the wilderness; and there Israel camped in front of [b]the mountain.

---

13 [1]Lit., *weakened*
14 [1]Lit., *the book* [2]Lit., *place it in the ears of* [3]Or, *for* [a]Ex. 24:4; 34:27; Num. 33:2 [b]Deut. 25:19; 1 Sam. 15:3
15 [a]Ex. 24:4 [b]Gen. 22:14; Judg. 6:24
16 [1]Or, *Because a hand is against the throne of the LORD;* lit., *Because a hand upon the throne of YAH* [a]Gen. 22:16

1 [a]Ex. 2:16, 18; 3:1
2 [a]Ex. 2:21; 4:25
3 [1]Lit., *the name of the one was* [2]Heb., *ger* [a]Ex. 2:22; 4:20; Acts 7:29 [b]Ex. 2:22
4 [1]Lit., *the name of the other was* [2]Heb., *El-ezer;* i.e., my God is help [a]1 Chr. 23:15, 17 [b]Gen. 49:25
5 [1]Lit., *unto* [a]Ex. 3:1, 12; 4:27; 24:13
6 [1]Lit., *said*
7 [a]Gen. 43:26, 28 [b]Gen. 29:13; Ex. 4:27 [c]Gen. 43:27; 2 Sam. 11:7
8 [a]Ex. 4:23; 7:4, 5 [b]Num. 20:14; Neh. 9:32 [c]Ex. 15:6, 16
9 [1]Lit., *in that He had delivered* [2]Lit., *him* [a]Is. 63:7-14
10 [a]Gen. 14:20; 2 Sam. 18:28; 1 Kin. 8:56; Ps. 68:19, 20
11 [1]Lit., *indeed, in the thing in which they* [2]Lit., *them* [a]Ex. 12:12; 15:11; 2 Chr. 2:5; Ps. 95:3; 97:9; 135:5 [b]Luke 1:51
12 [1]Lit., *bread* [a]Gen. 31:54; Ex. 24:5
15 [a]Num. 9:6, 8; 27:5; Deut. 17:8-13
16 [1]Lit., *matter* [a]Ex. 24:14
18 [1]Lit., *this* [2]Lit., *matter* [a]Num. 11:14, 17; Deut. 1:12 [b]Deut. 1:9
19 [1]Lit., *my voice* [2]Lit., *You be for the people in front of God* [3]Lit., *matters* [a]Num. 27:5
20 [a]Deut. 1:18; 4:1, 5; 5:1 [b]Ps. 143:8
21 [1]Lit., *see* [2]Lit., *leaders of* [a]Ex. 18:25; Deut. 1:13, 15; 2 Chr. 19:5-10; Ps. 15:1-5; Acts 6:3 [b]Gen. 42:18; 2 Sam. 23:3 [c]Deut. 16:19
22 [1]Lit., *matter* [a]Deut. 1:17, 18 [b]Num. 11:17
23 [1]Lit., *stand* [2]Lit., *this* [3]Lit., *his*
24 [1]Lit., *to the voice of*
25 [1]Lit., *leaders of* [a]Ex. 18:21; Deut. 1:15
26 [1]Lit., *matter* [a]Ex. 18:22
27 [1]Lit., *sent off his father-in-law* [a]Num. 10:29, 30

1 [1]Lit., *on this day* [a]Ex. 12:6, 51; 16:1 [b]Deut. 1:6; 4:10, 15; 5:2
2 [a]Ex. 17:1; Num. 33:15 [b]Ex. 3:1, 12; 18:5

3 And Moses went up to God, and [a]the LORD called to him from the mountain, saying, "Thus you shall say to the house of Jacob and tell the sons of Israel:

4 '[a]You yourselves have seen what I did to the Egyptians, and *how* I bore you on [b]eagles' wings, and brought you to Myself.

5 'Now then, [a]if you will indeed obey My voice and [b]keep My covenant, then you shall be [c]My [1]own possession among all the peoples, for [d]all the earth is Mine;

6 and you shall be to Me [a]a kingdom of priests and [b]a holy nation.' These are the words that you shall speak to the sons of Israel."

7 [a]So Moses came and called the elders of the people, and set before them all these words which the LORD had commanded him.

8 [a]And all the people answered together and said, "All that the LORD has spoken we will do!" And Moses brought back the words of the people to the LORD.

9 And the LORD said to Moses, "Behold, I shall come to you in [a]a thick cloud, in order that the [b]people may hear when I speak with you, and may also believe in you forever." Then Moses told the words of the people to the LORD.

10 The LORD also said to Moses, "Go to the people and [a]consecrate them today and tomorrow, and let them [b]wash their garments;

11 and let them be ready for the third day, for on [a]the third day the LORD will come down on Mount Sinai in the sight of all the people.

12 "And you shall set bounds for the people all around, saying, '[1]Beware that you do not go up on the mountain or touch the border of it; [a]whoever touches the mountain shall surely be put to death.

13 'No hand shall touch him, but [a]he shall surely be stoned or [1]shot through; whether beast or man, he shall not live.' When the ram's horn sounds a long blast, they shall come up to [b]the mountain."

14 So Moses went down from the mountain to the people and consecrated the people, and they washed their garments.

15 And he said to the people, "Be ready for the third day; do not go near a woman."

16 [a]So it came about on the third day, when it was morning, that there were [1]thunder and lightning flashes and a thick cloud upon the mountain and a very loud trumpet sound, so that all the people who *were* in the camp trembled.

17 And Moses brought the people out of the camp to meet God, and they stood at the [1]foot of the mountain.

The LORD Visits Sinai

18 [a]Now Mount Sinai *was* all in smoke because the LORD descended upon it [b]in fire; and its smoke ascended like [c]the smoke of a furnace, and [d]the whole mountain [1]quaked violently.

19 When the sound of the trumpet grew louder and louder, Moses spoke and [a]God answered him with [1]thunder.

20 [a]And the LORD came down on Mount Sinai, to the top of the mountain; and the LORD called Moses to the top of the mountain, and Moses went up.

21 Then the LORD spoke to Moses, "Go down, [1]warn the people, lest [a]they break through to the LORD to gaze, and many of them [2]perish.

22 "And also let the [a]priests who come near to the LORD consecrate themselves, lest the LORD break out against them."

23 And Moses said to the LORD, "The people cannot come up to Mount Sinai, for Thou didst [1]warn us, saying, '[a]Set bounds about the mountain and consecrate it.' "

24 Then the LORD said to him, "[1]Go down and come up *again,* [a]you and Aaron with you; but do not let the [b]priests and the people break through to come up to the LORD, lest He break forth upon them."

25 So Moses went down to the people and told them.

The Ten Commandments

20 THEN God spoke all these words, saying,

2 "[a]I am the LORD your God, [b]who brought you out of the land of Egypt, out of the house of [1]slavery.

3 "[a]You shall have no other [b]gods [1]before Me.

4 "[a]You shall not make for yourself [1]an idol, or any likeness of what is in heaven above or on the earth beneath or in the water under the earth.

5 "[a]You shall not worship them or serve them; for I, the LORD your God, am a [b]jealous God, [c]visiting the iniquity of the fathers on the children, on the third and the fourth generations of those who hate Me,

6 but showing lovingkindness to [a]thousands, to those who love Me and keep My commandments.

7 "[a]You shall not take the name of the LORD your God in vain, for the LORD will not [1]leave him unpunished who takes His name in vain.

8 "Remember [a]the sabbath day, to keep it holy.

9 "[a]Six days you shall labor and do all your work,

10 but the seventh day is a sabbath of the LORD your God; *in it* [a]you shall not do any work, you or your son or your daughter, your male or your female servant or your cattle or your sojourner who [1]stays with you.

3 [a]Ex. 3:4
4 [a]Deut. 29:2 [b]Deut. 32:11; Rev. 12:14
5 [1]Or, *special treasure* [a]Ex. 15:26; Deut. 5:2f. [b]Ps. 78:10 [c]Deut. 4:20; 7:6; 14:2; 26:18; Ps. 135:4; Titus 2:14; 1 Pet. 2:9 [d]Ex. 9:29; Deut. 10:14; Job 41:11; Ps. 50:12; 1 Cor. 10:26
6 [a]1 Pet. 2:5, 9; Rev. 1:6; 5:10 [b]Deut. 7:6; 14:21; 26:19; Is. 62:12
7 [a]Ex. 4:29, 30
8 [a]Ex. 4:31; 24:3, 7; Deut. 5:27; 26:17
9 [a]Ex. 19:16; 24:15, 16; Deut. 4:11; Ps. 99:7 [b]Deut. 4:12, 36
10 [a]Lev. 11:44, 45 [b]Gen. 35:2; Lev. 15:5; Num. 8:7, 21; 19:19; Rev. 22:14
11 [a]Ex. 19:16
12 [1]Lit., *Take heed to yourselves* [a]Heb. 12:20
13 [1]I.e., with arrows [a]Heb. 12:20 [b]Ex. 19:17
16 [1]Lit., *sounds* [a]Heb. 12:18, 19, 21
17 [1]Lit., *lower part*
18 [1]Or, *trembled* [a]Deut. 4:11; Ps. 104:32; 144:5 [b]Ex. 3:2; 24:17; Deut. 5:4; 2 Chr. 7:1-3; Heb. 12:18 [c]Gen. 15:17; 19:28 [d]Judg. 5:5; Ps. 68:7, 8; Jer. 4:24
19 [1]Or, *a voice;* lit., *a sound* [a]Ps. 81:7
20 [a]Neh. 9:13
21 [1]Lit., *testify to* [2]Lit., *fall* [a]Ex. 3:5; 1 Sam. 6:19
22 [a]Ex. 19:24; 24:5; Lev. 10:3; 21:6-8
23 [1]Lit., *testify to* [a]Ex. 19:12
24 [1]Lit., *Go, descend* [a]Ex. 24:1, 9, 12 [b]Ex. 19:22

2 [1]Lit., *slaves* [a]Lev. 26:1; Deut. 5:6; Ps. 81:10 [b]Ex. 13:3; 15:13, 16; Deut. 7:8
3 [1]Or, *besides Me* [a]Deut. 6:14; 2 Kin. 17:35; Jer. 25:6; 35:15 [b]Ex. 15:11; 20:23
4 [1]Or, *a graven image* [a]Lev. 19:4; 26:1; Deut. 4:15-19; 27:15
5 [a]Ex. 23:24; Josh. 23:7; 2 Kin. 17:35 [b]Ex. 34:14; Deut. 4:24; Josh. 24:19; Nah. 1:2 [c]Ex. 34:6, 7; Num. 14:18, 33; Deut. 5:9, 10; 1 Kin. 21:29; Jer. 32:18
6 [a]Deut. 7:9
7 [1]Or, *hold him guiltless* [a]Lev. 19:12; Deut. 6:13; 10:20
8 [a]Ex. 23:12; 31:13-16; Lev. 26:2; Deut. 5:12
9 [a]Ex. 34:21; 35:2, 3; Lev. 23:3; Deut. 5:13; Luke 13:14
10 [1]Lit., *is in your gates* [a]Neh. 13:16-19

11 "[a]For in six days the LORD made the
heavens and the earth, the sea and all
that is in them, and rested on the seventh day; therefore the LORD blessed the
sabbath day and made it holy.
12 "[a]Honor your father and your
mother, that your [b]days may be prolonged in the land which the LORD your
God gives you.
13 "[a]You shall not murder.
14 "[a]You shall not commit adultery.
15 "[a]You shall not steal.
16 "[a]You shall not bear false witness
against your [b]neighbor.
17 "[a]You shall not covet your neighbor's house; [b]you shall not covet your
neighbor's wife or his male servant or his
female servant or his ox or his donkey or
anything that belongs to your neighbor."
18 [a]And all the people perceived the
[1]thunder and the lightning flashes and
the sound of the trumpet and the mountain smoking; and when the people saw
it, they trembled and stood at a distance.
19 [a]Then they said to Moses, "Speak
[1]to us yourself and we will listen; but let
not God speak [1]to us, lest we die."
20 And Moses said to the people,
"[a]Do not be afraid; for God has come in
order [b]to test you, and in order that [c]the
fear of Him may [1]remain with you, so
that you may not sin."
21 So the people stood at a distance,
while Moses approached [a]the thick
cloud where God *was.*
22 Then the LORD said to Moses,
"Thus you shall say to the sons of Israel,
'You yourselves have seen that [a]I have
spoken [1]to you from heaven.
23 '[a]You shall not make *other gods*
besides Me; [b]gods of silver or gods of
gold, you shall not make for yourselves.
24 'You shall make [a]an altar of earth
for Me, and you shall sacrifice on it your
[b]burnt offerings and your [c]peace offerings, [d]your sheep and your oxen; in
every place [e]where I cause My name to
be remembered, I will come to you and
bless you.
25 'And if you make an altar of stone
for Me, [a]you shall not build it of cut
stones, for if you wield your tool on it,
you will profane it.
26 'And you shall not go up by steps to
My altar, that [a]your nakedness may not
be exposed on it.'

Ordinances for the People

21 "NOW these are the [a]ordinances
which you are to set before them.
2 "If you buy [a]a Hebrew slave, he
shall serve for six years; but on the
seventh he shall go out as a free man
without payment.
3 "If he comes [1]alone, he shall go out
[1]alone; if he is the husband of a wife,
then his wife shall go out with him.
4 "If his master gives him a wife, and
she bears him sons or daughters, the wife
and her children shall belong to her
master, and he shall go out [1]alone.
5 "But [a]if the slave plainly says, 'I love
my master, my wife and my children; I
will not go out as a free man,'
6 then his master shall bring him to
[1]God, then he shall bring him to the
door or the doorpost. And his master
shall pierce his ear with an awl; and he
shall serve him permanently.
7 "[a]And if a man sells his daughter as
a female slave, she is not to [1]go free [b]as
the male slaves [1]do.
8 "If she is [1]displeasing in the eyes of
her master [2]who designated her for
himself, then he shall let her be redeemed. He does not have authority to
sell her to a foreign people because of his
[3]unfairness to her.
9 "And if he designates her for his
son, he shall deal with her according to
the custom of daughters.
10 "If he takes to himself another
woman, he may not reduce her [1]food,
her clothing, or [a]her conjugal rights.
11 "And if he will not do these three
things for her, then she shall go out for
nothing, without *payment of* money.

Personal Injuries

12 "[a]He who strikes a man so that he
dies shall surely be put to death.
13 "[a]But [1]if he did not lie in wait *for*
him, but [b]God let *him* fall into his hand,
then I will appoint you a place to which
he may flee.
14 "[a]If, however, a man acts presumptuously toward his neighbor, so as to kill
him craftily, you are to take him *even*
from My altar, that he may die.
15 "And he who strikes his father or his
mother shall surely be put to death.
16 "[a]And he who [1]kidnaps a man,
whether he sells him or he is found in his
[2]possession, shall surely be put to death.
17 "[a]And he who curses his father or
his mother shall surely be put to death.
18 "And if men have a quarrel and one
strikes the other with a stone or with *his*
fist, and he does not die but [1]remains in
bed;
19 if he gets up and walks around
outside on his staff, then he who struck
him shall go unpunished; he shall only
pay for his [1]loss of time, and [2]shall take
care of him until he is completely healed.
20 "And if a man strikes his male or
female slave with a rod and he dies [1]at
his hand, he shall [2]be punished.
21 "If, however, he [1]survives a day or
two, no vengeance shall be taken; [a]for he
is his [2]property.
22 "And *if* men struggle with each
other and strike a woman with child so
that [1]she has a miscarriage, yet there is
no *further* injury, he shall surely be fined
as the woman's husband [2]may demand
of him; and he shall [a]pay [3]as the judges
decide.

11 [a]Gen. 2:2, 3; Ex. 31:17
12 [a]Lev. 19:3; Deut. 27:16; Matt. 15:4; 19:19; Mark 7:10; 10:19; Luke 18:20; Eph. 6:2 [b]Deut. 5:16, 33; 6:2; 11:8, 9; Jer. 35:7
13 [a]Gen. 9:6; Ex. 21:12; Lev. 24:17; Matt. 5:21; 19:18; Mark 10:19; Luke 18:20; Rom. 13:9; James 2:11
14 [a]Lev. 20:10; Deut. 5:18; Matt. 5:27; 19:18; Rom. 13:9
15 [a]Ex. 21:16; Lev. 19:11, 13; Matt. 19:18; Rom. 13:9
16 [a]Ex. 23:1, 7; Deut. 5:20; Matt. 19:18 [b]Lev. 19:18
17 [a]Deut. 5:21; Rom. 7:7; 13:9; Eph. 5:3, 5 [b]Prov. 6:29; Matt. 5:28
18 [1]Lit., *sounds* [a]Ex. 19:16, 18; Heb. 12:18, 19
19 [1]Lit., *with* [a]Deut. 5:5, 23-27; Gal. 3:19; Heb. 12:19
20 [1]Lit., *be before* [a]Ex. 14:13; Is. 41:10, 13 [b]Ex. 15:25; Deut. 13:3 [c]Deut. 4:10; 6:24; Prov. 3:7; 16:6; Is. 8:13
21 [a]Ex. 19:16; Deut. 5:22
22 [1]Lit., *with* [a]Deut. 4:36; 5:24, 26; Neh. 9:13
23 [a]Ex. 20:3 [b]Ex. 32:1, 2, 4; Deut. 29:17
24 [a]Ex. 20:25; 27:1-8 [b]Ex. 10:25; 18:12 [c]Ex. 24:5; Lev. 1:2 [d]Deut. 12:5; 16:6, 11; 26:2; 2 Chr. 6:6 [e]Deut. 12:5; 26:2
25 [a]Deut. 27:5, 6; Josh. 8:31
26 [a]Ex. 28:42, 43

1 [a]Ex. 24:3, 4; Deut. 4:14; 6:1
2 [a]Lev. 25:39-43; Deut. 15:12-18; Jer. 34:14
3 [1]Lit., *by himself*
4 [1]Lit., *by himself*
5 [a]Deut. 15:16, 17
6 [1]Or, *the judges who acted in God's name*
7 [1]Lit., *go out* [a]Neh. 5:5 [b]Ex. 21:2, 3
8 [1]Lit., *bad* [2]Another reading is *so that he did not designate her* [3]Lit., *dealing treacherously*
10 [1]Lit., *flesh* [a]1 Cor. 7:3, 5
12 [a]Gen. 9:6; Lev. 24:17; Num. 35:30; Matt. 26:52
13 [1]Lit., *he who* [a]Num. 35:10-34; Deut. 19:1-13; Josh. 20:1-9 [b]1 Sam. 24:4, 10, 18
14 [a]Deut. 19:11, 12; 1 Kin. 2:28-34
16 [1]Lit., *steals* [2]Lit., *hand* [a]Deut. 24:7

17 [a]Lev. 20:9; Prov. 20:20; Matt. 15:4; Mark 7:10
18 [1]Lit., *lies*
19 [1]Lit., *his sitting* [2]Lit., *healing, he shall cause to be healed*
20 [1]Lit., *under* [2]Lit., *suffer vengeance*
21 [1]Lit., *stands* [2]Lit., *money* [a]Lev. 25:44-46
22 [1]Or, *an untimely birth occurs;* lit., *her children come out* [2]Lit., *lays on him* [3]Lit., *by arbitration* [a]Ex. 21:30; Deut. 22:18, 19

23“But if there is *any further* injury,
[a]then you shall appoint *as a penalty* life
for life,
24 [a]eye for eye, tooth for tooth, hand
for hand, foot for foot,
25 burn for burn, wound for wound,
[1]bruise for bruise.
26“And if a man strikes the eye of his
male or female slave, and destroys it, he
shall let him go free on account of his
eye.
27“And if he [1]knocks out a tooth of his
male or female slave, he shall let him go
free on account of his tooth.
28“And if an ox gores a man or a
woman [1]to death, [a]the ox shall surely be
stoned and its flesh shall not be eaten;
but the owner of the ox shall go unpunished.
29“If, however, an ox was previously
in the habit of goring, and its owner has
been warned, yet he does not confine it,
and it kills a man or a woman, the ox
shall be stoned and its owner also shall
be put to death.
30“If a ransom is [1]demanded of him,
then he shall give for the redemption of
his life whatever is [1]demanded of him.
31“Whether it gores a son or [1]a daughter, it shall be done to him according to
[2]the same rule.
32“If the ox gores a male or female
slave, [1]the owner shall give his *or her*
master [a]thirty shekels of silver, and the
ox shall be stoned.
33“And if a man opens a pit, or [1]digs a
pit and does not cover it over, and an ox
or a donkey falls into it,
34 the owner of the pit shall make
restitution; he shall [1]give money to its
owner, and the dead *animal* shall become his.
35“And if one man's ox hurts anoth-
er's so that it dies, then they shall sell the
live ox and divide its price equally; and
also they shall divide the dead *ox*.
36“Or *if* it is known that the ox was
previously in the habit of goring, yet its
owner has not confined it, he shall surely
pay ox for ox, and the dead *animal* shall
become his.

Property Rights

22 “[1]IF a man steals an ox or a
sheep, and slaughters it or sells it,
he shall pay five oxen for the ox and
[a]four sheep for the sheep.
2“[1]If the [a]thief is [2]caught while
breaking in, and is struck so that he dies,
there will be no bloodguiltiness on his
account.
3“*But* if the sun has risen on him,
there will be bloodguiltiness on his
account. He shall surely make restitution; if he owns nothing, then he shall be
[a]sold for his theft.
4“If what he stole is actually found
alive in his [1]possession, whether an ox or
a donkey or a sheep, [a]he shall pay
double.
5“If a man lets a field or vineyard be
grazed *bare* and lets his animal loose so
that it grazes in another man's field, he
shall make restitution from the best of
his own field and the best of his own
vineyard.
6“If a fire breaks out and spreads to
thorn bushes, so that stacked grain or
the standing grain or the field *itself* is
consumed, he who started the fire shall
surely make restitution.
7“[a]If a man gives his neighbor money
or goods to keep *for him,* and it is stolen
from the man's house, if the thief is
[1]caught, he shall pay double.
8“If the thief is not [1]caught, then the
owner of the house shall [2]appear before
[3a]the judges, *to* determine whether he
[4]laid his hands on his neighbor's property.
9“For every [1]breach of trust, *whether
it is* for ox, for donkey, for sheep, for
clothing, *or* for any lost thing about
which one says, 'This is it,' the [2]case of
both parties shall come before [3a]the
judges; he whom [3]the judges condemn
shall pay double to his neighbor.
10“If a man gives his neighbor a
donkey, an ox, a sheep, or any animal to
keep *for him,* and it dies or is hurt or is
driven away while no one is looking,
11 an [a]oath before the LORD shall be
made by the two of them, [1]that he has
not [2]laid hands on his neighbor's property; and its owner shall accept *it,* and he
shall not make restitution.
12“But if it is actually stolen from him,
he shall make restitution to its owner.
13“If it is all torn to pieces, let him
bring it as evidence; he shall not make
restitution for what has been torn to
pieces.
14“And if a man [1]borrows *anything*
from his neighbor, and it is injured or
dies while its owner is not with it, he
shall make full restitution.
15“If its owner is with it, he shall not
make restitution; if it is hired, it came
for its hire.

Sundry Laws

16“[a]And if a man seduces a virgin who
is not engaged, and lies with her, he
must pay a dowry for her *to be* his wife.
17“If her father absolutely refuses to
give her to him, he shall [1]pay money
equal to the [a]dowry for virgins.
18“You shall not allow a [a]sorceress to
live.
19“[a]Whoever lies with an animal shall
surely be put to death.
20“[a]He who sacrifices to [1]any god,
other than to the LORD alone, shall be
[2]utterly destroyed.
21“And [a]you shall not wrong a stranger or oppress him, for you were strangers in the land of Egypt.
22“[a]You shall not afflict any widow or
orphan.
23“If you afflict him at all, *and* [a]if he
does cry out to Me, [b]I will surely hear
his cry;
24 and My anger will be kindled, and
I will kill you with the sword; [a]and your

23 [a]Lev. 24:19; Deut. 19:21
24 [a]Lev. 24:20; Deut. 19:21; Matt. 5:38
25 [1]Lit., *welt*
27 [1]Lit., *causes to fall*
28 [1]Lit., *so that he dies* [a]Gen. 9:5; Ex. 21:32
30 [1]Lit., *laid on him*
31 [1]Lit., *gores a daughter* [2]Lit., *this judgment*
32 [1]Lit., *he* [a]Zech. 11:12; Matt. 26:15; 27:3, 9
33 [1]Lit., *if a man digs*
34 [1]Lit., *give back*

1 [1]Ch. 21:37 in Heb. [a]2 Sam. 12:6; Luke 19:8
2 [1]Ch. 22:1 in Heb. [2]Lit., *found* [a]Matt. 6:19; 24:43; 1 Pet. 4:15
3 [a]Matt. 18:25
4 [1]Lit., *hand* [a]Ex. 22:7
7 [1]Lit., *found* [a]Lev. 6:1-7
8 [1]Lit., *found* [2]Lit., *approach to* [3]Or, *God* [4]Lit., *stretched his hand* [a]Ex. 22:9; Deut. 17:8, 9; 19:17
9 [1]Or, *matter of transgression* [2]Lit., *matter* [3]Or, *God* [a]Ex. 22:8, 28; Deut. 25:1
11 [1]Lit., *whether* [2]Lit., *stretched his hand* [a]Heb. 6:16
14 [1]Lit., *asks*
16 [a]Deut. 22:28, 29
17 [1]Lit., *weigh out silver* [a]Gen. 34:12; 1 Sam. 18:25
18 [a]Lev. 19:31; 20:6, 27; Deut. 18:10, 11; 1 Sam. 28:3; Jer. 27:9, 10
19 [a]Lev. 18:23; 20:15, 16; Deut. 27:21
20 [1]Lit., *the gods* [2]Lit., *put under the ban* [a]Ex. 32:8; 34:15; Lev. 17:7; Num. 25:2; Deut. 17:2, 3, 5; 1 Kin. 18:40; 2 Kin. 10:25
21 [a]Ex. 23:9; Lev. 19:33, 34; 25:35; Deut. 1:16; 10:19; 27:19; Zech. 7:10
22 [a]Deut. 24:17, 18; Prov. 23:10, 11; Jer. 7:6, 7
23 [a]Deut. 15:9; Job 35:9; Luke 18:7 [b]Deut. 10:18; Job 34:28; Ps. 10:14, 17, 18; 18:6; 68:5; James 5:4
24 [a]Ps. 109:2, 9

wives shall become widows and your
children fatherless.
25 “[a]If you lend money to My people,
to the poor [1]among you, you are not to
[2]act as a creditor to him; you shall not
[3]charge him [b]interest.
26 “If you ever take your neighbor’s
cloak [a]as a pledge, you are to return it to
him before the sun sets,
27 for that is his only covering; it is
his cloak for his [1]body. What else shall
he sleep in? And it shall come about that
[a]when he cries out to Me, I will hear *him,*
for [b]I am gracious.
28 “You shall not [1a]curse God, [b]nor
curse a ruler of your people.
29 “[a]You shall not delay *the offering*
from [1]your harvest and your vintage.
[b]The first-born of your sons you shall
give to Me.
30 “[a]You shall do the same with your
oxen *and* with your sheep. It shall be
with its mother seven days; [b]on the
eighth day you shall give it to Me.
31 “[a]And you shall be holy men to
Me, therefore [b]you shall not eat *any* flesh
torn to pieces in the field; you shall
throw it to the dogs.

Sundry Laws

23 “[a]YOU shall not bear a false
report; do not join your hand
with a wicked man to be a [b]malicious
witness.
2 “You shall not follow [1]a multitude
in doing evil, nor shall you [2]testify in a
dispute so as to turn aside after [1]a
multitude in order to [a]pervert *justice;*
3 [a]nor shall you [1]be partial to a poor
man in his dispute.
4 “[a]If you meet your enemy’s ox or his
donkey wandering away, you shall surely
return it to him.
5 “[a]If you see the donkey of one who
hates you lying *helpless* under its load,
you shall refrain from leaving it to him,
you shall surely release *it* with him.
6 “[a]You shall not pervert the justice
due to your needy *brother* in his dispute.
7 “[a]Keep far from a false charge, and
[b]do not kill the innocent or the righteous, for [c]I will not acquit the guilty.
8 “[a]And you shall not take a bribe, for
a bribe blinds the clear-sighted and
[1]subverts the cause of the just.
9 “[a]And you shall not oppress a
[1]stranger, since you yourselves know the
[2]feelings of a [1]stranger, for you *also* were
[1]strangers in the land of Egypt.

The Sabbath and Land

10 “[a]And you shall sow your land for
six years and gather in its yield,
11 but *on* the seventh year you shall
let it [1]rest and lie fallow, so that the
needy of your people may eat; and
whatever they leave the beast of the field
may eat. You are to do the same with
your vineyard *and* your olive grove.
12 “[a]Six days you are to do your work,
but on the seventh day you shall cease
from labor in order that your ox and
your donkey may rest, and the son of
your female slave, as well as [1]your
stranger, may refresh themselves.
13 “Now [a]concerning everything which
I have said to you, be on your guard;
and [b]do not mention the name of other
gods, nor let *them* be heard [1]from your
mouth.

Three National Feasts

14 “[a]Three times a year you shall celebrate a feast to Me.
15 “You shall observe [a]the Feast of
Unleavened Bread; for seven days you
are to eat unleavened bread, as I commanded you, at the appointed time in
the [b]month Abib, for in it you came out
of Egypt. And [1c]none shall appear before Me empty-handed.
16 “Also *you shall observe* [a]the Feast of
the Harvest *of* the first fruits of your
labors *from* what you sow in the field;
also the Feast of the Ingathering at the
end of the year [b]when you gather in *the*
fruit of your labors from the field.
17 “[a]Three times a year all your males
shall appear before the Lord [1]GOD.
18 “[a]You shall not offer the blood of
My sacrifice with leavened bread; [b]nor is
the fat of My [1]feast to remain overnight
until morning.
19 “You shall bring [a]the choice first
fruits of your soil into the house of the
LORD your God. [b]You are not to boil a
kid in the milk of its mother.

Conquest of the Land

20 “Behold, I am going to send [a]an
angel before you to guard you along the
way, and [b]to bring you into the place
which I have prepared.
21 “Be on your guard before him and
obey his voice; [a]do not be rebellious
toward him, for he will not pardon your
transgression, since [b]My name is in him.
22 “But if you will truly obey his voice
and do all that I say, then [a]I will be an
enemy to your enemies and an adversary
to your adversaries.
23 “[a]For My angel will go before you
and bring you in to *the land of* the
Amorites, the Hittites, the Perizzites, the
Canaanites, the Hivites and the Jebusites; and I will completely destroy
them.
24 “[a]You shall not worship their gods,
nor serve them, nor do according to their
deeds; [b]but you shall utterly overthrow
them, and break their [c]*sacred* pillars in
pieces.
25 “[a]But you shall serve the LORD your
God, [1]and He will bless your bread and
your water; and [b]I will remove sickness
from your midst.

25 [1]Lit., *with* [2]Lit., *be* [3]Lit., *lay upon* [a]Lev. 25:35-37; Deut. 15:7-11 [b]Deut. 23:19, 20; Neh. 5:7; Ps. 15:5; Ezek. 18:8
26 [a]Deut. 24:6, 10-13; Job 24:3; Prov. 20:16; Amos 2:8
27 [1]Lit., *skin* [a]Ex. 22:23 [b]Ex. 34:6
28 [1]Or, *revile* [a]Lev. 24:15, 16 [b]Eccl. 10:20; Acts 23:5
29 [1]Lit., *your fulness and your tears* [a]Ex. 23:16, 19; Deut. 26:2-11; Prov. 3:9 [b]Ex. 13:2, 12
30 [a]Deut. 15:19; Lev. 22:27 [b]Gen. 17:12; Lev. 12:3
31 [a]Ex. 19:6; Lev. 11:44; 19:2 [b]Lev. 7:24; 17:15; Ezek. 4:14

1 [a]Ex. 20:16; Lev. 19:11f.; Deut. 5:20; Ps. 101:5; Prov. 10:18 [b]Deut. 19:16-21; Ps. 35:11; Prov. 19:5; Acts 6:11
2 [1]Lit., *many men* [2]Or, *answer* [a]Deut. 16:19; 24:17
3 [1]Lit., *honor* [a]Ex. 23:6; Lev. 19:15; Deut. 1:17; 16:19
4 [a]Deut. 22:1-4
5 [a]Deut. 22:4
6 [a]Ex. 23:2, 3; Lev. 19:15
7 [a]Ex. 20:16; Ps. 119:29; Eph. 4:25 [b]Ex. 20:13; Deut. 27:25 [c]Ex. 34:7; Deut. 25:1; Rom. 1:18
8 [1]Or, *distorts the words* [a]Deut. 10:17; 16:19; Prov. 15:27; 17:8, 23; Is. 5:22, 23
9 [1]Or, *sojourner(s)* [2]Lit., *soul* [a]Ex. 22:21; Lev. 19:33f.; Deut. 24:17f.; 27:19
10 [a]Lev. 25:1-7
11 [1]Lit., *drop*
12 [1]Lit., *the sojourner* [a]Ex. 20:8-11; 31:15; 34:21; 35:2, 3; Lev. 23:3; Deut. 5:13f.
13 [1]Lit., *on* [a]Deut. 4:9, 23; 1 Tim. 4:16 [b]Josh. 23:7; Ps. 16:4; Hos. 2:17
14 [a]Ex. 23:17; 34:22-24; Deut. 16:16
15 [1]Lit., *they . . . not* [a]Ex. 12:14-20; Lev. 23:6-8; Num. 28:16-25 [b]Ex. 12:2; 13:4 [c]Ex. 22:29; 34:20
16 [a]Ex. 34:22; Lev. 23:10; Num. 28:26 [b]Lev. 23:39
17 [1]Heb., *YHWH,* usually rendered *LORD* [a]Ex. 23:14; 34:23; Deut. 16:16
18 [1]Or, *festival* [a]Ex. 34:25; Lev. 2:11 [b]Ex. 12:10; Lev. 7:15; Deut. 16:4

19 [a]Ex. 22:29; 34:26; Deut. 26:2, 10; Neh. 10:35; Prov. 3:9 [b]Deut. 14:21
20 [a]Ex. 3:2; 14:19; 23:23; 32:34; 33:2 [b]Ex. 15:16, 17
21 [a]Deut. 9:7; Ps. 78:40, 56 [b]Ex. 3:14; 6:3; 34:5-7
22 [a]Gen. 12:3; Num. 24:9; Deut. 30:7
23 [a]Ex. 23:20; Josh. 24:8, 11
24 [a]Ex. 20:5; 23:13, 33; Deut. 12:30f. [b]Num. 33:52; Deut. 7:5; 12:3; 2 Kin. 18:4 [c]Ex. 34:13; Lev. 26:1; 2 Kin. 3:2
25 [1]Or, *that He may bless* [a]Lev. 26:3-13; Deut. 6:13; 10:12; 28:1-14; Josh. 22:5; 1 Sam. 12:20; Matt. 4:10 [b]Ex. 15:26; Deut. 7:15

26 "There shall be no one miscarrying or [a]barren in your land; [b]I will fulfill the number of your days.

27 "I will [a]send My terror ahead of you, and [b]throw into confusion all the people among whom you come, and I will [c]make all your enemies turn *their* backs to you.

28 "And I will send [a]hornets ahead of you, that they may [b]drive out the Hivites, the Canaanites, and the Hittites before you.

29 "[a]I will not drive them out before you in a single year, that the land may not become desolate, and the beasts of the field become too numerous for you.

30 "I will drive them out before you [a]little by little, until you become fruitful and take possession of the land.

31 "[a]And I will fix your boundary from the [1]Red Sea to the sea of the Philistines, and from the wilderness to the River *Euphrates;* [b]for I will deliver the inhabitants of the land into your hand, and you will [c]drive them out before you.

32 "[a]You shall [1]make no covenant with them [b]or with their gods.

33 "[a]They shall not live in your land, lest they make you sin against Me; for *if* you serve their gods, [b]it will surely be a snare to you."

People Affirm Their Covenant with God

24 THEN He said to Moses, "[a]Come up to the LORD, you and Aaron, [b]Nadab and Abihu and [c]seventy of the elders of Israel, and you shall worship at a distance.

2 "Moses alone, however, shall come near to the LORD, but they shall not come near, nor shall the people come up with him."

3 Then Moses came and recounted to the people all the words of the LORD and all the [1]ordinances; and all the people answered with one voice, and said, "[a]All the words which the LORD has spoken we will do!"

4 And [a]Moses wrote down all the words of the LORD. Then he arose early in the morning, and built an [b]altar [1]at the foot of the mountain with twelve pillars for the twelve tribes of Israel.

5 And he sent young men of the sons of Israel, [a]and they offered burnt offerings and sacrificed young bulls as peace offerings to the LORD.

6 And [a]Moses took half of the blood and put *it* in basins, and the *other* half of the blood he sprinkled on the altar.

7 Then he took [a]the book of the covenant and read *it* in the hearing of the people; and they said, "[b]All that the LORD has spoken we will do, and we will be obedient!"

8 So [a]Moses took the blood and sprinkled *it* on the people, and said, "Behold [b]the blood of the covenant, which the LORD has [1]made with you [2]in accordance with all these words."

9 Then Moses went up [1]with Aaron, [a]Nadab and Abihu, and seventy of the elders of Israel,

10 and [a]they saw the God of Israel; and under His feet [1b]there appeared to be a pavement of sapphire, [2]as clear as the sky itself.

11 Yet He did not stretch out His hand against the nobles of the sons of Israel; and [a]they beheld God, and they ate and drank.

12 Now the LORD said to Moses, "Come up to Me on the mountain and [1]remain there, and [a]I will give you the stone tablets [2]with the law and the commandment which I have written for their instruction."

13 So Moses arose [1]with [a]Joshua his [2]servant, and Moses went up to [b]the mountain of God.

14 But to the elders he said, "[a]Wait here for us until we return to you. And behold, [b]Aaron and Hur are with you; whoever [1]has a legal matter, let him approach them."

15 Then Moses went up to the mountain, and [a]the cloud covered the mountain.

16 And [a]the glory of the LORD [1]rested on Mount Sinai, and the cloud covered it for six days; and on the seventh day He [b]called to Moses from the midst of the cloud.

17 [a]And to the eyes of the sons of Israel the appearance of the glory of the LORD was like a [b]consuming fire on the mountain top.

18 And Moses entered the midst of the cloud [1]as he went up to the mountain; and Moses was on the mountain [a]forty days and forty nights.

Offerings for the Sanctuary

25 THEN the LORD spoke to Moses, saying,

2 "[a]Tell the sons of Israel to [1]raise a [2]contribution for Me; [b]from every man whose heart moves him you shall [1]raise My [2]contribution.

3 "And this is the [1]contribution which you are to [2]raise from them: gold, silver and bronze,

4 [1a]blue, purple and scarlet *material,* fine linen, goat *hair,*

5 rams' skins dyed red, porpoise skins, acacia wood,

6 [a]oil for lighting, [b]spices for the anointing oil and for the fragrant incense,

7 onyx stones and setting stones, for the [a]ephod and for the [1b]breastpiece.

8 "And let them [a]construct a sanctuary for Me, [b]that I may dwell among them.

9 "[a]According to all that I am going to show you, *as* the pattern of the tabernacle and the pattern of all its furniture, just so you shall construct *it.*

26 [a]Deut. 7:14 [b]Deut. 4:40; Job 5:26
27 [a]Gen. 35:5; Ex. 15:16; Deut. 2:25; Josh. 2:9 [b]Deut. 7:23 [c]Ps. 18:40; 21:12
28 [a]Deut. 7:20; Josh. 24:12 [b]Ex. 33:2; 34:11
29 [a]Deut. 7:22
30 [a]Deut. 7:22
31 [1]Lit., *Sea of Reeds* [a]Gen. 15:18; Deut. 1:7, 8; 11:24 [b]Deut. 2:36; Josh. 21:44 [c]Josh. 24:12, 18
32 [1]Lit., *cut* [a]Ex. 34:12; Deut. 7:2 [b]Ex. 23:13, 24
33 [a]Deut. 7:1-5, 16 [b]Ex. 34:12; Deut. 12:30; Josh. 23:13; Judg. 2:3; Ps. 106:36

1 [a]Ex. 19:24 [b]Ex. 6:23; 28:1; Lev. 10:1, 2 [c]Num. 11:16
3 [1]Or, *judgments* [a]Ex. 19:8; 24:7; Deut. 5:27
4 [1]Lit., *under* [a]Ex. 17:14; 34:27; Deut. 31:9 [b]Ex. 17:15
5 [a]Ex. 18:12
6 [a]Heb. 9:18
7 [a]Ex. 24:4; Heb. 9:19 [b]Ex. 24:3
8 [1]Lit., *cut* [2]Lit., *on all* [a]Heb. 9:19, 20 [b]Zech. 9:11; Matt. 26:28; Mark 14:24; Luke 22:20; 1 Cor. 11:25; Heb. 13:20
9 [1]Lit., *and* [a]Ex. 24:1
10 [1]Lit., *like a pavement* [2]Lit., *and as* [a]Ex. 24:11; Num. 12:8; Is. 6:5; John 1:18; 6:46 [b]Ezek. 1:26; 10:1; Rev. 4:3
11 [a]Gen. 16:13; 32:30; Ex. 24:10
12 [1]Lit., *be* [2]Lit., *and* [a]Ex. 31:18; 32:15; Deut. 5:22
13 [1]Lit., *and* [2]Or, *minister* [a]Ex. 17:9-14; 33:11 [b]Ex. 3:1
14 [1]Lit., *is a master of matters* [a]Gen. 22:5 [b]Ex. 17:10, 12
15 [a]Ex. 19:9
16 [1]Lit., *dwelt* [a]Ex. 16:10; Num. 14:10 [b]Ps. 99:7
17 [a]Ex. 3:2; Ezek. 1:28 [b]Deut. 4:24; 9:3; Heb. 12:29
18 [1]Lit., *and* [a]Ex. 34:28; Deut. 9:9; 10:10

2 [1]Lit., *take* [2]Or, *heave offering* [a]Ex. 35:4-9 [b]Ex. 35:21; 1 Chr. 29:3, 5, 9; Ezra 2:68; 2 Cor. 8:11, 12; 9:7
3 [1]Or, *heave offering* [2]Lit., *take*
4 [1]Or, *violet* [a]Ex. 28:5, 6, 8
6 [a]Ex. 27:20 [b]Ex. 30:23f.
7 [1]Or, *pouch* [a]Ex. 28:4, 6-14 [b]Ex. 28:4, 15-30
8 [a]Ex. 36:1-5 [b]Ex. 29:45, 46; Num. 5:3; Deut. 12:11; 1 Kin. 6:13; 2 Cor. 6:16; Rev. 21:3
9 [a]Ex. 25:40; 26:30; Acts 7:44; Heb. 8:2, 5

Ark of the Covenant

10“[a]And they shall construct an ark of
acacia wood two and a half [1]cubits
[2]long, and one and a half cubits [3]wide,
and one and a half cubits [4]high.
11“And you shall [a]overlay it with pure
gold, inside and out you shall overlay it,
and you shall make a gold molding
[1]around it.
12“And you shall cast four gold rings
for it, and [1]fasten them on its four feet,
and two rings shall be on one side of it
and two rings on the other side of it.
13“And you shall make poles of acacia
wood and overlay them with gold.
14“And you shall put the poles into
the rings on the sides of the ark, to carry
the ark with them.
15“The [a]poles shall [1]remain in the
rings of the ark; they shall not be removed from it.
16“And you shall [a]put into the ark the
testimony which I shall give you.
17“And you shall [a]make a [1]mercy seat
of pure gold, two and a half [2]cubits
[3]long and one and a half cubits [4]wide.
18“And you shall make two cherubim
of gold, make them of hammered work
[1]at the two ends of the mercy seat.
19“And make one cherub [1]at one end
and one cherub [1]at the other end; you
shall make the cherubim *of one piece*
with the mercy seat at its two ends.
20“And [a]the cherubim shall have *their*
wings spread upward, covering the
mercy seat with their wings and [1]facing
one another; the faces of the cherubim
are to be *turned* toward the mercy seat.
21“And [a]you shall put the mercy seat
[1]on top of the ark, and [b]in the ark you
shall put the testimony which I shall give
to you.
22“And [a]there I will meet with you;
and from above the mercy seat, from
[b]between the two cherubim which are
upon the ark of the testimony, I will
speak to you about all that I will give
you in commandment for the sons of
Israel.

The Table of Showbread

23“[a]And you shall make a table of
acacia wood, two cubits [1]long and one
cubit [2]wide and one and a half cubits
[3]high.
24“And you shall overlay it with pure
gold and make a gold [a]border around it.
25“And you shall make for it a rim of
a handbreadth around *it;* and you
shall make a gold border for the rim
around it.
26“And you shall make four gold rings
for it and put rings on the four corners
which are on its four feet.
27“The rings shall be close to the rim
as holders for the poles to carry the
table.
28“And you shall make the poles of
acacia wood and overlay them with gold,
so that with them the table may be
carried.
29“And you shall make its [1a]dishes
and its pans and its jars and its [2]bowls,
with which to pour libations; you shall
make them of pure gold.
30“And you shall set [a]the bread of the
[1]Presence on the table before Me [2]at all
times.

The Golden Lampstand

31“[a]Then you shall make a lampstand
of pure gold. The lampstand *and* its base
and its shaft are to be made of hammered work; its cups, its [1]bulbs and its
flowers shall be *of one piece* with it.
32“And [a]six branches shall go out
from its sides; three branches of the
lampstand from its one side, and three
branches of the lampstand from its
[1]other side.
33“[a]Three cups *shall be* shaped like
almond *blossoms* in the one branch, a
[1]bulb and a flower, and three cups
shaped like almond *blossoms* in the
[2]other branch, a [1]bulb and a flower—so
for six branches going out from the
lampstand;
34 and [a]in the lampstand four cups
shaped like almond *blossoms,* its [1]bulbs
and its flowers.
35“[a]And a [1]bulb shall be under the
first pair of branches *coming* out of it,
and a [1]bulb under the *second* pair of
branches *coming* out of it, and a [1]bulb
under the *third* pair of branches *coming*
out of it, for the six branches coming out
of the lampstand.
36“[a]Their [1]bulbs and their branches
shall be of one piece with it; all of it shall
be one piece of hammered work of pure
gold.
37“Then you shall make its lamps
seven *in number;* and [a]they shall [1]mount
its lamps so as to shed light on the space
in front of it.
38“And its snuffers and [1]their trays
shall be of pure gold.
39“It shall be made from a talent of
pure gold, with all these utensils.
40“And [a]see that you make *them* [b]after
the pattern for them, which was shown
to you on the mountain.

Curtains of Linen

26 “[a]MOREOVER you shall make
the tabernacle with ten curtains
of fine twisted linen and [1]blue and
purple and scarlet *material;* you shall
make them with cherubim, the work of a
skillful workman.
2“The length of each curtain shall be
twenty-eight [1]cubits, and the width of
each curtain four [1]cubits; all the curtains
shall have [2]the same measurements.
3“Five curtains shall be [1]joined to
one another; and *the other* five curtains
shall be [1]joined to one another.
4“And you shall make loops of [1]blue
on the edge of the [2]outermost curtain in
the *first* set; and likewise you shall make
them on the edge of the curtain that is
outermost in the second [3]set.

10 [1]I.e., One cubit equals approx. 18 in. [2]Lit., *its length* [3]Lit., *its width* [4]Lit., *its height* [a]Ex. 37:1-9; Deut. 10:3; Heb. 9:4
11 [1]Lit., *on it round about* [a]Heb. 9:4
12 [1]Or, *put*
15 [1]Lit., *be* [a]1 Kin. 8:8
16 [a]Ex. 40:20; Deut. 10:2; 31:26; 1 Kin. 8:9; Heb. 9:4
17 [1]Lit., *propitiatory,* and so through v. 22 [2]I.e., One cubit equals approx. 18 in. [3]Lit., *its length* [4]Lit., *its width* [a]Ex. 37:6
18 [1]Lit., *from*
19 [1]Lit., *from*
20 [1]Lit., *their faces to* [a]1 Kin. 8:7; 1 Chr. 28:18; Heb. 9:5
21 [1]Lit., *above, upon* [a]Ex. 26:34; 40:20 [b]Ex. 25:16
22 [a]Ex. 29:42, 43; 30:6, 36; Lev. 16:2; Num. 17:4 [b]Num. 7:89; 1 Sam. 4:4; 2 Sam. 6:2; 2 Kin. 19:15; Ps. 80:1; Is. 37:16
23 [1]Lit., *its length* [2]Lit., *its width* [3]Lit., *its height* [a]Ex. 37:10-16
24 [a]Ex. 25:11
29 [1]Or, *platters* [2]Lit., *libation bowls* [a]Ex. 37:16; Num. 4:7
30 [1]Lit., *Face* [2]Or, *continually* [a]Ex. 39:36; 40:23; Lev. 24:5-9
31 [1]Or, *calyx* [a]Ex. 37:17-24; 1 Kin. 7:49; Zech. 4:2
32 [1]Lit., *second* [a]Ex. 37:18
33 [1]Or, *calyx* [2]Lit., *one branch* [a]Ex. 37:19
34 [1]Or, *calyxes* [a]Ex. 37:20
35 [1]Or, *calyx* [a]Ex. 37:21
36 [1]Or, *calyxes* [a]Ex. 37:22
37 [1]Lit., *raise up* [a]Num. 8:2
38 [1]Lit., *its snuff dishes*
40 [a]Heb. 8:5 [b]Ex. 25:9; 26:30; Num. 8:4; Acts 7:44

1 [1]Or, *violet* [a]Ex. 36:8-19
2 [1]I.e., One cubit equals approx. 18 in. [2]Lit., *one measure*
3 [1]Or, *coupled*
4 [1]Or, *violet* [2]Lit., *one curtain from the end in the coupling* [3]Lit., *coupling*

5"You shall make fifty loops in the one curtain, and you shall make fifty loops on the [1]edge of the curtain that is in the second [2]set; the loops shall be opposite each other.

6"And you shall make fifty clasps of gold, and [1]join the curtains to one another with the clasps, that the [2]tabernacle may be a unit.

Curtains of Goats' Hair

7"Then [a]you shall make curtains of goats' *hair* for a tent over the tabernacle; you shall make eleven curtains in all.

8"The length of each curtain *shall be* thirty [1]cubits, and the width of each curtain four cubits; the eleven curtains shall have [2]the same measurements.

9"And you shall [1]join five curtains by themselves, and the *other* six curtains by themselves, and you shall double over the sixth curtain [2]at the front of the tent.

10"And you shall make fifty loops on the edge of the [1]curtain that is outermost in the *first* [2]set, and fifty loops on the edge of the curtain *that is outermost in* the second [2]set.

11"And you shall make fifty clasps of [1]bronze, and you shall put the clasps into the loops and [2]join the tent together, that it may be [3]a unit.

12"And the [1]overlapping part that is left over in the curtains of the tent, the half curtain that is left over, shall lap over the back of the tabernacle.

13"And the cubit on one side and the cubit on the other, of what is left over in the length of the curtains of the tent, shall lap over the sides of the tabernacle on one side and on the other, to cover it.

14"And [a]you shall make a covering for the tent of rams' skins [1]dyed red, and a covering of porpoise skins above.

Boards and Sockets

15"Then you shall make [a]the boards for the tabernacle of acacia wood, standing upright.

16"Ten cubits *shall be* the length of [1]each board, and one and a half cubits the width of each board.

17"There *shall be* two tenons for each board, [1]fitted to one another; thus you shall do for all the boards of the tabernacle.

18"And you shall make the boards for the tabernacle: twenty boards [1]for the south side.

19"And you shall make forty [1a]sockets of silver under the twenty boards, two [1]sockets under one board for its two tenons and two [1]sockets under another board for its two tenons;

20 and for the second side of the tabernacle, on the north side, twenty boards,

21 and their forty [1]sockets of silver; two [1]sockets under one board and two [1]sockets under another board.

22"And for the [1]rear of the tabernacle, to the west, you shall make six boards.

23"And you shall make two boards for the corners of the tabernacle at the [1]rear.

24"And they shall be double beneath, and together they shall be complete [1]to its top [2]to the first ring; thus it shall be with both of them: they shall form the two corners.

25"And there shall be eight boards with their [1]sockets of silver, sixteen [1]sockets; two [1]sockets under one board and two [1]sockets under another board.

26"Then you shall make [a]bars of acacia wood, five for the boards of one side of the tabernacle,

27 and five bars for the boards of the [1]other side of the tabernacle, and five bars for the boards of the side of the tabernacle for the [2]rear *side* to the west.

28"And the middle bar in the [1]center of the boards shall pass through from end to end.

29"And you shall overlay the boards with gold and make their rings of gold *as* holders for the bars; and you shall overlay the bars with gold.

30"Then you shall erect the tabernacle [a]according to its plan which you have been shown in the mountain.

The Veil and Screen

31"And you shall make [a]a veil of [1]blue and purple and scarlet *material* and fine twisted linen; it shall be made with cherubim, the work of a skillful workman.

32"And you shall [1]hang it on four pillars of acacia overlaid with gold, their hooks *also being of* gold, on four [2]sockets of silver.

33"And you shall [1]hang up the veil under the clasps, and shall bring in [a]the ark of the testimony there within the veil; and the veil shall [2]serve for you as a partition [b]between the holy place and the holy of holies.

34"And [a]you shall put the mercy seat on the ark of the testimony in the holy of holies.

35"And [a]you shall set the table outside the veil, and the [b]lampstand opposite the table on the side of the tabernacle toward the south; and you shall put the table on the north side.

36"And [a]you shall make a screen for the doorway of the tent of [1]blue and purple and scarlet *material* and fine twisted linen, the work of a [2]weaver.

37"And [a]you shall make five pillars of acacia for the screen, and overlay them with gold, their hooks *also being of* gold; and you shall cast five [1]sockets of [2]bronze for them.

The Bronze Altar

27 "AND you shall make [a]the altar of acacia wood, five [1]cubits long and five cubits wide; the altar shall be square, and its height shall be three cubits.

2"And you shall make [a]its horns on its four corners; its horns shall be of one piece with it, and you shall overlay it with [1]bronze.

5 [1]Lit., *end* [2]Lit., *coupling*

6 [1]Or, *couple* [2]Or, *dwelling place,* and so throughout the ch.

7 [a]Ex. 36:14

8 [1]I.e., One cubit equals approx. 18 in. [2]Lit., *one measure*

9 [1]Or, *couple* [2]Lit., *toward the front of the face of the tent*

10 [1]Lit., *one curtain* [2]Lit., *coupling*

11 [1]Or, *copper* [2]Or, *couple* [3]Lit., *one*

12 [1]Lit., *excess*

14 [1]Or, *tanned* [a]Ex. 36:19

15 [a]Ex. 36:20-34

16 [1]Lit., *the*

17 [1]Lit., *bound*

18 [1]Lit., *toward the side of the Negev to the south*

19 [1]Or, *bases* [a]Ex. 38:27

21 [1]Or, *bases*

22 [1]Lit., *extreme parts*

23 [1]Lit., *extreme parts*

24 [1]Or, *at its head* [2]Or, *with reference to*

25 [1]Or, *bases*

26 [a]Ex. 36:31

27 [1]Lit., *second* [2]Lit., *extreme parts*

28 [1]Lit., *midst*

30 [a]Ex. 25:9, 40; Acts 7:44; Heb. 8:5

31 [1]Or, *violet* [a]Ex. 36:35, 36; 2 Chr. 3:14; Matt. 27:51; Heb. 9:3

32 [1]Lit., *put* [2]Or, *bases*

33 [1]Lit., *put* [2]Lit., *separate for you between* [a]Ex. 25:16; 40:21 [b]Heb. 9:2f.

34 [a]Ex. 25:21; 40:20; Lev. 16:2

35 [a]Ex. 40:22 [b]Ex. 40:24

36 [1]Or, *violet* [2]Lit., *variegator;* i.e., a weaver in colors [a]Ex. 36:37

37 [1]Or, *bases* [2]Or, *copper* [a]Ex. 36:38

1 [1]I.e., One cubit equals approx. 18 in. [a]Ex. 38:1-7

2 [1]Or, *copper,* and so for *bronze* throughout the ch. [a]Ps. 118:27

3 "And you shall make its pails for removing its ashes, and its shovels and its basins and its forks and its firepans; you shall make all its utensils of bronze.

4 "And you shall make for it a grating of network of bronze, and on the net you shall make four bronze rings [1]at its four corners.

5 "And you shall put it beneath, under the ledge of the altar, that the net may reach halfway up the altar.

6 "And you shall make poles for the altar, poles of acacia wood, and overlay them with bronze.

7 "And its poles shall be inserted into the rings, so that the poles shall be on the two sides of the altar [a]when it is carried.

8 "You shall make it hollow with planks; [a]as it was shown to you in the mountain, so they shall make *it.*

Court of the Tabernacle

9 "And you shall make [a]the court of the [1]tabernacle. [2]On the south side *there shall be* hangings for the court of fine twisted linen one hundred cubits long for one side;

10 and its pillars *shall be* twenty, with their twenty [1]sockets of bronze; the hooks of the pillars and their [2]bands *shall be* of silver.

11 "And likewise for the north side in length *there shall be* hangings one hundred *cubits* long, and its twenty pillars with their twenty [1]sockets of bronze; the hooks of the pillars and their bands *shall be* of silver.

12 "And *for* the width of the court on the west side *shall be* hangings of fifty cubits *with* their ten pillars and their ten [1]sockets.

13 "And the width of the court on the [1]east side *shall be* fifty cubits.

14 "The hangings for the *one* [1]side *of the gate shall be* fifteen cubits *with* their three pillars and their three [2]sockets.

15 "And for the [1]other [2]side *shall be* hangings of fifteen cubits *with* their three pillars and their three [3]sockets.

16 "And for the gate of the court there *shall be* a screen of twenty cubits, of [1]blue and purple and scarlet *material* and fine twisted linen, the work of a [2]weaver, *with* their four pillars and their four [3]sockets.

17 "All the pillars around the court shall be furnished with silver bands *with* their hooks of silver and their [1]sockets of bronze.

18 "The length of the court *shall be* one hundred cubits, and the width fifty throughout, and the height five cubits of fine twisted linen, and their [1]sockets of bronze.

19 "All the utensils of the tabernacle *used* in all its service, and all its pegs, and all the pegs of the court, *shall be* of bronze.

20 "And you shall charge the sons of Israel, that they bring you [a]clear oil of beaten olives for the [1]light, to make a lamp [2]burn continually.

21 "In the [a]tent of meeting, outside [b]the veil which is before the testimony, [c]Aaron and his sons shall keep it in order from evening to morning before the LORD; *it shall be* a perpetual [d]statute throughout their generations [1]for the sons of Israel.

Garments of the Priests

28 "THEN [a]bring near to yourself Aaron your brother, and his sons with him, from among the sons of Israel, to minister as priest to Me—Aaron, [b]Nadab and Abihu, Eleazar and Ithamar, Aaron's sons.

2 "And you shall make [a]holy garments for Aaron your brother, for glory and for beauty.

3 "And you shall speak to all the [1a]skillful persons [b]whom I have endowed with [2]the spirit of wisdom, that they make Aaron's garments to consecrate him, that he may minister as priest to Me.

4 "And these are the garments which they shall make: a [1a]breastpiece and an ephod and a robe and a tunic of checkered work, a turban and a sash, and they shall make holy garments for Aaron your brother and his sons, that he may minister as priest to Me.

5 "And they shall take [a]the gold and the [1]blue and the purple and the scarlet *material* and the fine linen.

6 "They shall also make [a]the ephod of gold, of [1]blue and purple *and* scarlet *material* and fine twisted linen, the work of the skillful workman.

7 "It shall have two shoulder pieces joined to its two ends, that it may be joined.

8 "And the skillfully woven band, which is on it, shall be like its workmanship, [1]of the same material: of gold, of [2]blue and purple and scarlet *material* and fine twisted linen.

9 "And you shall take two onyx stones and engrave on them the names of the sons of Israel,

10 six of their names on the one stone, and the names of the remaining six on the [1]other stone, according to their birth.

11 "[1]As a jeweler engraves a signet, you shall engrave the two stones according to the names of the sons of Israel; you shall [2]set them in filigree *settings* of gold.

12 "And you shall put the two stones on the shoulder pieces of the ephod, *as* stones of memorial for the sons of Israel, and Aaron shall [a]bear their names before the LORD on his two shoulders [b]for a memorial.

13 "[a]And you shall make filigree *settings* of gold,

14 and two chains of pure gold; you shall make them of twisted cordage work, and you shall put the corded chains on the filigree *settings.*

15 "And [a]you shall make a [1]breastpiece of judgment, the work of a skillful workman; like the work of the ephod you shall make it: of gold, of [2]blue and

---

4 [1]Lit., *on*

7 [a]Num. 4:15

8 [a]Ex. 25:40; 26:30; Acts 7:44; Heb. 8:5

9 [1]Or, *dwelling place* [2]Lit., *For the side of the Negev to the south* [a]Ex. 38:9-20

10 [1]Or, *bases* [2]Or, *fillets, rings*

11 [1]Or, *bases*

12 [1]Or, *bases*

13 [1]Lit., *east side eastward*

14 [1]Lit., *shoulder* [2]Or, *bases*

15 [1]Lit., *second* [2]Lit., *shoulder* [3]Or, *bases*

16 [1]Or, *violet* [2]Lit., *variegator;* i.e., a weaver in colors [3]Or, *bases*

17 [1]Or, *bases*

18 [1]Or, *bases*

20 [1]Or, *luminary* [2]Lit., *ascend* [a]Ex. 35:8, 28; Lev. 24:1-4

21 [1]Lit., *from* [a]Ex. 25:22; 29:42; 30:36 [b]Ex. 26:31, 33 [c]Ex. 30:8; 1 Sam. 3:3; 2 Chr. 13:11 [d]Ex. 28:43; 29:9; Lev. 3:17; 16:34; Num. 18:23; 19:21; 1 Sam. 30:25

1 [a]Num. 18:7; Ps. 99:6; Heb. 5:1, 4 [b]Ex. 24:1, 9

2 [a]Ex. 29:5, 29; 31:10; 39:1-31; Lev. 8:7-9, 30

3 [1]Lit., *wise of heart* [2]I.e., artistic skill [a]Ex. 31:6; 35:25, 31-35; 36:1 [b]Ex. 31:3; Is. 11:2; 1 Cor. 12:7-11; Eph. 1:17

4 [1]Or, *pouch* [a]Ex. 28:15-43

5 [1]Or, *violet* [a]Ex. 25:3

6 [1]Or, *violet* [a]Ex. 39:2-7; Lev. 8:7

8 [1]Lit., *from it* [2]Or, *violet*

10 [1]Lit., *second*

11 [1]Lit., *A work of a lapidary, engravings of a seal* [2]Lit., *make them to be surrounded*

12 [a]Ex. 28:29; 39:6f. [b]Ex. 39:7; Lev. 24:7; Num. 31:54; Josh. 4:7; 1 Cor. 11:24f.

13 [a]Ex. 39:16-18

15 [1]Or, *pouch* [2]Or, *violet* [a]Ex. 39:8-21

purple and scarlet *material* and fine twisted linen you shall make it.

16 "It shall be square *and* folded double, a span [1]in length and a span [1]in width.

17 "And you shall [1]mount on it four rows of stones; the first row *shall be* a row of ruby, topaz and emerald;

18 and the second row a turquoise, a sapphire and a diamond;

19 and the third row a jacinth, an agate and an amethyst;

20 and the fourth row a beryl and an onyx and a jasper; they shall be [1]set in gold filigree.

21 "And the stones shall be according to the names of the sons of Israel: twelve, according to their names; they shall be *like* the engravings of a seal, each [a]according to his name for the twelve tribes.

22 "And you shall make on the [1]breastpiece chains of twisted cordage work in pure gold.

23 "And you shall make on the breastpiece two rings of gold, and shall put the two rings on the two ends of the breastpiece.

24 "And you shall put the two cords of gold on the two rings at the ends of the breastpiece.

25 "And you shall put the *other* two ends of the two cords on the two filigree *settings,* and put them on the shoulder pieces of the ephod, at the front of it.

26 "And you shall make two rings of gold and shall place them on the two ends of the breastpiece, on the edge of it, which is toward the inner side of the ephod.

27 "And you shall make two rings of gold and put them on the bottom of the two shoulder pieces of the ephod, on the front of it close to the place where it is joined, above the skillfully woven band of the ephod.

28 "And they shall bind the breastpiece by its rings to the rings of the ephod with a [1]blue cord, that it may be on the skillfully woven band of the ephod, and that the breastpiece may not come loose from the ephod.

29 "And Aaron shall carry the names of the sons of Israel in the breastpiece of judgment over his heart when he enters the holy place, for a memorial before the LORD continually.

30 "And [a]you shall put in the breastpiece of judgment the [1b]Urim and the Thummim, and they shall be over Aaron's heart when he goes in before the LORD; and Aaron shall carry the judgment of the sons of Israel over his heart before the LORD continually.

31 "[a]And you shall make the robe of the ephod all of [1]blue.

32 "And there shall be an opening [1]at its top in the middle of it; around its opening there shall be a binding of woven work, as *it were* the opening of a coat of mail, that it may not be torn.

33 "And you shall make on its hem pomegranates of blue and purple and scarlet *material,* all around on its hem, and bells of gold between them all around:

34 a golden bell and a pomegranate, a golden bell and a pomegranate, all around on the hem of the robe.

35 "And it shall be on Aaron [1]when he ministers; and [2]its tinkling may be heard when he enters and [3]leaves the holy place before the LORD, that he may not die.

36 "You shall also make [a]a plate of pure gold and shall engrave on it, like the engravings of a seal, '[b]Holy to the LORD.'

37 "And you shall [1]fasten it on a [2]blue cord, and it shall be on the turban; it shall be at the front of the turban.

38 "And it shall be on Aaron's forehead, and Aaron shall [1a]take away the iniquity of the holy things which the sons of Israel consecrate, with regard to all their holy gifts; and it shall always be on his forehead, that [b]they may be accepted before the LORD.

39 "And you shall weave [a]the tunic of checkered work of fine linen, and shall make a turban of fine linen, and you shall make a sash, the work of a [1]weaver.

40 "And for Aaron's sons you shall make [a]tunics; you shall also make sashes for them, and you shall make [1b]caps for them, for glory and for beauty.

41 "And you shall put them on Aaron your brother and on his sons with him; and you shall [a]anoint them and [1]ordain them and consecrate them, that they may serve Me as priests.

42 "And you shall make for them [a]linen breeches to cover *their* bare flesh; they shall [1]reach from the loins even to the thighs.

43 "And they shall be on Aaron and on his sons when they enter the tent of meeting, or [a]when they approach the altar to minister in the holy place, so that they do not incur [1]guilt and die. [b]It *shall be* a statute forever to him and to his [2]descendants after him.

Consecration of the Priests

29 "[a]NOW this is [1]what you shall do to them to consecrate them to minister as priests to Me: take one young bull and two rams without blemish,

2 and [a]unleavened bread and unleavened cakes mixed with oil, and unleavened wafers [1]spread with oil; you shall make them of fine wheat flour.

3 "And you shall put them in one basket, and present them in the basket along with the bull and the two rams.

4 "Then [a]you shall bring Aaron and his sons to the doorway of the tent of meeting, and wash them with water.

5 "And you shall take the garments, and put on Aaron the [a]tunic and [b]the robe of the ephod and [c]the ephod and [d]the [1]breastpiece, and gird him with the skillfully [e]woven band of the ephod;

16 [1]Lit., *its*

17 [1]Lit., *fill in a setting of stones, four rows of stones*

20 [1]Lit., *interwoven with gold in their settings*

21 [a]Rev. 7:4-8; 21:12

22 [1]Or, *pouch,* and so through v. 30

28 [1]Or, *violet*

30 [1]I.e., lights and perfections [a]Lev. 8:8 [b]Num. 27:21; Deut. 33:8; Ezra 2:63; Neh. 7:65

31 [1]Or, *violet* [a]Ex. 39:22-26

32 [1]Or, *for his head*

35 [1]Lit., *for ministering* [2]Lit., *its sound* [3]Lit., *comes out* from

36 [a]Ex. 39:30, 31; Lev. 8:9 [b]Zech. 14:20

37 [1]Lit., *place* [2]Or, *violet*

38 [1]Or, *bear* [a]Lev. 10:17; 22:16; Num. 18:1 [b]Lev. 1:4; 22:27; 23:11; Is. 56:7

39 [1]Lit., *variegator;* i.e., a weaver in colors [a]Ex. 39:27-29

40 [1]Lit., *headgear* [a]Ex. 28:4; 39:27, 41 [b]Ex. 29:9; 39:28; Lev. 8:13; Ezek. 44:18

41 [1]Lit., *fill their hand* [a]Ex. 29:7, 9; 30:30; 40:15; Lev. 8:1-36; 10:7

42 [1]Lit., *be* [a]Ex. 39:28; Lev. 6:10; 16:4; Ezek. 44:18

43 [1]Or, *iniquity* [2]Lit., *seed* [a]Ex. 20:26 [b]Ex. 27:21

1 [1]Lit., *the thing which* [a]Lev. 8:1-34

2 [1]Or, *anointed* [a]Lev. 2:4; 6:19-23

4 [a]Ex. 40:12; Lev. 8:6

5 [1]Or, *pouch* [a]Ex. 28:39; Lev. 8:7 [b]Ex. 28:31 [c]Ex. 28:6 [d]Ex. 28:15 [e]Ex. 28:8

6 and you shall set the [a]turban on his head, and put [b]the holy crown on the turban.

7 "Then you shall take [a]the anointing oil, and pour it on his head and anoint him.

8 "And you shall bring his sons and put [a]tunics on them.

9 "And you shall gird them with [a]sashes, Aaron and his sons, and bind [1]caps on them, and they shall have [b]the priesthood by a perpetual statute. So you shall [2c]ordain Aaron and his sons.

The Sacrifices

10 "Then you shall bring the bull before the tent of meeting, and Aaron and his sons shall [a]lay their hands on the head of the bull.

11 "And you shall slaughter the bull before the LORD at the doorway of the tent of meeting.

12 "And you shall [a]take some of the blood of the bull and put *it* on [b]the horns of the altar with your finger; and you shall pour out all the blood at the base of the altar.

13 "And you shall [a]take all the fat that covers the entrails and the [1]lobe of the liver, and the two kidneys and the fat that is on them, and offer them up in smoke on the altar.

14 "But [a]the flesh of the bull and its hide and its refuse, you shall burn with fire outside the camp; it is a sin offering.

15 "[a]You shall also take the one ram, and Aaron and his sons shall lay their hands on the head of the ram;

16 and you shall slaughter the ram and shall take its blood and sprinkle it around on the altar.

17 "Then you shall cut the ram into its pieces, and wash its entrails and its legs, and put *them* [1]with its pieces and [2]its head.

18 "And you shall offer up in smoke the whole ram on the altar; it is a burnt offering to the LORD: [a]it is a soothing aroma, an offering by fire to the LORD.

19 "Then [a]you shall take the [1]other ram, and Aaron and his sons shall lay their hands on the head of the ram.

20 "And you shall slaughter the ram, and take some of its blood and put *it* on the lobe of Aaron's right ear and on the lobes of his sons' right ears and on the thumbs of their right hands and on the big toes of their right feet, and sprinkle the *rest of the* blood around on the altar.

21 "Then you shall take some of the blood that is on the altar and some of the [a]anointing oil, and sprinkle *it* on Aaron and on his garments, and on his sons and on his sons' garments with him; so he and his garments shall be consecrated, as well as his sons and his sons' garments with him.

22 "You shall also take the fat from the ram and the fat tail, and the fat that covers the entrails and the [1]lobe of the liver, and the two kidneys and the fat that is on them and the right thigh (for it is a ram of [2]ordination),

23 and one cake of bread and [a]one cake of bread *mixed with* oil and one wafer from the basket of unleavened bread which is *set* before the LORD;

24 and you shall put [1]all these [2]in the [3]hands of Aaron and [2]in the [3]hands of his sons, and shall wave them as a wave offering before the LORD.

25 "And [a]you shall take them from their hands, and offer them up in smoke on the altar on the burnt offering for a soothing aroma before the LORD; it is an offering by fire to the LORD.

26 "Then you shall take [a]the breast of Aaron's ram of [1]ordination, and wave it as a wave offering before the LORD; and it shall be your portion.

27 "And you shall consecrate the breast of the wave offering and the thigh of the heave offering which was waved and which was [1]offered from the ram of [2]ordination, from the one which was for Aaron and from the one which was for his sons.

28 "And it shall be for Aaron and his sons as *their* portion forever from the sons of Israel, for it is a heave offering; and it shall be a heave offering from the sons of Israel from the sacrifices of their peace offerings, *even* their heave offering to the LORD.

29 "And [a]the holy garments of Aaron shall be for his sons after him, [1]that in them they may be anointed and ordained.

30 "For seven days the one of his sons who is priest in his stead shall put them on when he enters the tent of meeting to minister in the holy place.

Food of the Priests

31 "And you shall take the ram of [1]ordination and [a]boil its flesh in a holy place.

32 "And Aaron and his sons shall eat the flesh of the ram, and the bread that is in the basket, at the doorway of the tent of meeting.

33 "Thus [a]they shall eat [1]those things by which atonement was made [2]at their ordination *and* consecration; but a [3b]layman shall not eat *them,* because they are holy.

34 "And [a]if any of the flesh of [1]ordination or any of the bread remains until morning, then you shall burn the remainder with fire; it shall not be eaten, because it is holy.

35 "And thus you shall do to Aaron and to his sons, according to all that I have commanded you; you shall [1]ordain them through [a]seven days.

36 "And [a]each day you shall offer a bull as a sin offering for atonement, and you shall [1]purify the altar when you make atonement [2]for it; and [b]you shall anoint it to consecrate it.

37 "For seven days you shall make atonement [1]for the altar and consecrate it; then [a]the altar shall be most holy, *and* whatever touches the altar shall be holy.

6 [a]Ex. 28:4, 39 [b]Ex. 28:36, 37; Lev. 8:9

7 [a]Ex. 30:25; Lev. 8:12; 21:10; Num. 35:25; Ps. 133:2

8 [a]Ex. 28:39, 40; Lev. 8:13

9 [1]Lit., *headgear* [2]Lit., *fill the hand of* [a]Ex. 28:40 [b]Ex. 40:15; Num. 3:10; 18:7; 25:13; Deut. 18:5 [c]Ex. 28:41; Lev. 8:1-36

10 [a]Lev. 1:4; 8:14

12 [a]Lev. 8:15 [b]Ex. 27:2; 30:2

13 [1]Or, *appendage on* [a]Lev. 3:3, 4

14 [a]Lev. 4:11, 12, 21; Heb. 13:11

15 [a]Lev. 8:18

17 [1]Lit., *on* [2]Lit., *on its*

18 [a]Gen. 8:21; Ex. 29:25

19 [1]Lit., *second* [a]Lev. 8:22f.

21 [a]Ex. 30:25, 31; Lev. 8:30

22 [1]Or, *appendage on* [2]Lit., *filling*

23 [a]Lev. 8:26

24 [1]Lit., *the whole* [2]Lit., *on* [3]Lit., *palms*

25 [a]Lev. 8:28

26 [1]Lit., *filling* [a]Lev. 7:31, 34; 8:29

27 [1]Lit., *heaved;* or, *lifted up* [2]Lit., *filling*

29 [1]Lit., *for anointing in them and filling their hand in them* [a]Num. 20:26, 28

31 [1]Lit., *filling* [a]Lev. 8:31

33 [1]Lit., *them* [2]Lit., *to fill their hand to sanctify them* [3]Lit., *stranger* [a]Lev. 10:14 [b]Lev. 22:10, 13

34 [1]Lit., *filling* [a]Ex. 12:10; 23:18; 34:25; Lev. 8:32

35 [1]Lit., *fill their hand* [a]Lev. 8:33

36 [1]Or, *offer a sin offering on the altar* [2]Lit., *upon* [a]Heb. 10:11 [b]Ex. 40:10

37 [1]Lit., *upon* [a]Ex. 30:28f.

38 "Now [a]this is what you shall offer on the altar: two one year old lambs each day, continuously.

39 "The [a]one lamb you shall offer in the morning, and the [1]other lamb you shall offer at [2]twilight;

40 and there *shall be* one-tenth *of an ephah* of fine flour mixed with one-fourth of a hin of beaten oil, and one-fourth of a hin of wine for a libation with one lamb.

41 "And the [1]other lamb you shall offer at [2]twilight, and shall offer with it [3]the same grain offering as the morning and [4]the same libation, for a soothing aroma, an offering by fire to the LORD.

42 "It shall be a continual burnt offering throughout your generations at the doorway of the tent of meeting before the LORD, [a]where I will meet with you, to speak to you there.

43 "And I will meet there with the sons of Israel, and it shall be consecrated by My glory.

44 "And I will consecrate the tent of meeting and the altar; I will also consecrate Aaron and his sons to minister as priests to Me.

45 "And [a]I will dwell among the sons of Israel and will be their God.

46 "And they shall know that [a]I am the LORD their God who brought them out of the land of Egypt, that I might dwell among them; I am the LORD their God.

The Altar of Incense

30 "MOREOVER, you shall make [a]an altar as a place for burning incense; you shall make it of acacia wood.

2 "Its length *shall be* a [1]cubit, and its width a cubit, it shall be square, and its height *shall be* two cubits; its horns *shall be* [2]of one piece with it.

3 "And you shall overlay it with pure gold, its top and its [1]sides all around, and its horns; and you shall make a gold molding all around for it.

4 "And you shall make two gold rings for it under its molding; you shall make *them* on its two side walls—on [1]opposite sides—and [2]they shall be holders for poles with which to carry it.

5 "And you shall make the poles of acacia wood and overlay them with gold.

6 "And you shall put [1]this altar in front of the veil that is [2]near the ark of the testimony, in front of the [3a]mercy seat that is over *the ark of* the testimony, where I will meet with you.

7 "And Aaron shall burn fragrant incense on it; he shall burn it every morning when he trims the lamps.

8 "And when Aaron [1]trims the lamps at [2]twilight, he shall burn incense. *There shall be* perpetual incense before the LORD throughout your generations.

9 "You shall not offer any strange incense on [1]this altar, or burnt offering or meal offering; and you shall not pour out a libation on it.

10 "And Aaron shall [a]make atonement on its horns once a year; he shall make atonement on it with the blood of the sin offering of atonement once a year throughout your generations. It is most holy to the LORD."

11 The LORD also spoke to Moses, saying,

12 "When you take [a]a [1]census of the sons of Israel [2]to number them, then each one of them shall give [b]a ransom for [3]himself to the LORD, when you [4]number them, that there may be no plague among them when you [4]number them.

13 "This is what everyone who [1]is numbered shall give: half a shekel according to the shekel of the sanctuary ([a]the shekel is twenty gerahs), half a shekel as a [2]contribution to the LORD.

14 "Everyone who [1]is numbered, from twenty years old and over, shall give the [2]contribution to the LORD.

15 "The rich shall not pay more, and the poor shall not pay less than the half shekel, when you give the [1]contribution to the LORD to make atonement for [2]yourselves.

16 "And you shall take the atonement money from the sons of Israel, and shall give it for the service of the tent of meeting, that it may be a memorial for the sons of Israel before the LORD, to make atonement for [1]yourselves."

17 And the LORD spoke to Moses, saying,

18 "You shall also make [a]a laver of [1]bronze, with its base of bronze, for washing; and you shall [b]put it between the tent of meeting and the altar, and you shall put water in it.

19 "And Aaron and his sons shall [a]wash their hands and their feet from it;

20 when they enter the tent of meeting, they shall wash with water, that they may not die; or when they approach the altar to minister, by offering up in smoke a fire *sacrifice* to the LORD.

21 "So they shall wash their hands and their feet, that they may not die; and [a]it shall be a perpetual statute for them, for [1]Aaron and his [2]descendants throughout their generations."

The Anointing Oil

22 Moreover, the LORD spoke to Moses, saying,

23 "Take also for yourself the finest of spices: of flowing myrrh five hundred *shekels,* and of fragrant cinnamon half as much, two hundred and fifty, and of fragrant cane two hundred and fifty,

24 and of cassia five hundred, according to the shekel of the sanctuary, and of olive oil a hin.

25 "And you shall make [1]of these a holy anointing oil, a perfume mixture, the work of a perfumer; it shall be [a]a holy anointing oil.

26 "And with it [a]you shall anoint the tent of meeting and the ark of the testimony,

38 [a]Num. 28:3-31; 29:6-38

39 [1]Lit., *second* [2]Lit., *between the two evenings* [a]Ezek. 46:13-15

41 [1]Lit., *second* [2]Lit., *between the two evenings* [3]Lit., *according to the grain offering of the morning* [4]Lit., *according to its*

42 [a]Ex. 25:22; Num. 17:4

45 [a]Ex. 25:8; Lev. 26:12; Num. 5:3; Deut. 12:11; Zech. 2:10; 2 Cor. 6:16; Rev. 21:3

46 [a]Ex. 20:2

1 [a]Ex. 37:25-29

2 [1]I.e., One cubit equals approx. 18 in. [2]Lit., *from itself*

3 [1]Lit., *walls*

4 [1]Lit., *its two* [2]Lit., *it*

6 [1]Lit., *it* [2]Lit., *upon* or *over* [3]Lit., *propitiatory* [a]Ex. 25:21f.

8 [1]Lit., *causes to ascend* [2]Lit., *between the two evenings*

9 [1]Lit., *it*

10 [a]Lev. 16:18

12 [1]Lit., *sum* [2]Lit., *for their being mustered* [3]Lit., *his soul* [4]Lit., *muster* [a]Ex. 38:25, 26; Num. 1:2; 26:2 [b]Num. 31:50

13 [1]Lit., *passes over to those who are mustered* [2]Lit., *heave offering* [a]Lev. 27:25; Num. 3:47; Ezek. 45:12

14 [1]V. 13, note 1 [2]Lit., *heave offering of the LORD*

15 [1]Lit., *heave offering of the LORD* [2]Lit., *your souls*

16 [1]Lit., *your souls*

18 [1]Or, *copper* [a]Ex. 38:8 [b]Ex. 40:30

19 [a]Ex. 40:31f.; Is. 52:11

21 [1]Lit., *him* [2]Lit., *seed* [a]Ex. 28:43

25 [1]Lit., *it* [a]Ex. 37:29; 40:9; Lev. 8:10

26 [a]Ex. 40:9; Lev. 8:10; Num. 7:1

27 and the table and all its utensils,
and the lampstand and its utensils, and
the altar of incense,
28 and the altar of burnt offering and
all its utensils, and the laver and its
stand.
29 "You shall also consecrate them,
that they may be most holy; whatever
touches them shall be holy.
30 "[a]And you shall anoint Aaron and
his sons, and consecrate them, that they
may minister as priests to Me.
31 "And you shall speak to the sons of
Israel, saying, 'This shall be a holy
anointing oil to Me throughout your
generations.
32 'It shall not be poured on [1]anyone's
body, nor shall you make *any* like it, in
[2]the same proportions; [a]it is holy, *and* it
shall be holy to you.
33 '[a]Whoever shall mix *any* like it, or
whoever puts any of it on a [1]layman,
[2b]shall be cut off from his people.' "

The Incense

34 Then the LORD said to Moses,
"Take for yourself spices, stacte and
onycha and galbanum, spices with pure
frankincense; there shall be an equal
part of each.
35 "And with it you shall make incense,
a perfume, the work of a perfumer,
salted, pure, *and* holy.
36 "And you shall beat some of it very
fine, and put part of it before the testimony in the tent of meeting, [a]where I
shall meet with you; it shall be most holy
to you.
37 "And the incense which you shall
make, [a]you shall not make in [1]the same
proportions for yourselves; it shall be
holy to you for the LORD.
38 "[a]Whoever shall make *any* like it, to
[1]use as perfume, [2]shall be cut off from
his people."

The Skilled Craftsmen

31 [a]NOW the LORD spoke to Moses,
saying,
2 "See, I have called by name Bezalel,
the [a]son of Uri, the son of Hur, of the
tribe of Judah.
3 "And I have [a]filled him with the
Spirit of God in wisdom, in understanding, in knowledge, and in all *kinds of*
[1]craftsmanship,
4 to [1]make artistic designs for work
in gold, in silver, and in [2]bronze,
5 and in the cutting of stones [1]for
settings, and in the carving of wood, that
he may work in all *kinds of* [2]craftsman-
ship.
6 "And behold, I Myself have [1]ap-
pointed with him [a]Oholiab, the son of
Ahisamach, of the tribe of Dan; and in
the hearts of all who are [2]skillful I have
put [3]skill, that they may make all that I
have commanded you:
7 [a]the tent of meeting, and [b]the ark

30 [a]Ex. 29:7; Lev. 8:12
32 [1]Lit., *the flesh of man* [2]Lit., *its proportion* [a]Ex. 30:25, 37
33 [1]Lit., *stranger* [2]Lit., *even he shall* [a]Ex. 30:38 [b]Gen. 17:14; Ex. 12:15; Lev. 7:20f.
36 [a]Ex. 29:42
37 [1]Lit., *its proportion* [a]Ex. 30:32
38 [1]Lit., *smell of it* [2]Lit., *even he shall* [a]Ex. 30:33

1 [a]Ex. 35:30-36:1
2 [a]1 Chr. 2:20
3 [1]Or, *workmanship* [a]Ex. 35:31; 1 Kin. 7:14; 1 Cor. 12:4-8
4 [1]Lit., *devise devices* [2]Or, *copper*
5 [1]Lit., *to fill in (for a setting)* [2]Or, *workmanship*
6 [1]Lit., *given* [2]Lit., *wise of heart* [3]Lit., *wisdom* [a]Ex. 35:34
7 [1]Lit., *propitiatory* [a]Ex. 36:8-38 [b]Ex. 37:1-5 [c]Ex. 37:6-9
8 [1]Or, *vessels* [a]Ex. 37:10-16 [b]Ex. 37:17-24; Lev. 24:4 [c]Ex. 37:25-29
9 [1]Or, *vessels* [a]Ex. 38:1-7 [b]Ex. 38:8
10 [1]Or, *service garments* [2]Lit., *minister as priests* [a]Ex. 39:1
11 [a]Ex. 30:23-32 [b]Ex. 30:34-38
13 [a]Ex. 20:8 [b]Ex. 31:17; Ezek. 20:12, 20
14 [a]Ex. 31:15; 35:2; Num. 15:32, 35; John 7:23
15 [a]Ex. 20:9-11; 23:12; 34:21; 35:2; Lev. 23:3; Deut. 5:12-14 [b]Gen. 2:2f.; Ex. 16:23; 20:8; 35:2, 3 [c]Ex. 31:14
16 [1]Lit., *do*
17 [a]Ex. 31:13; Ezek. 20:12 [b]Gen. 1:31; 2:2, 3; Ex. 20:11
18 [a]Ex. 24:12; 34:29; Deut. 4:13; 5:22; 9:10f. [b]Ex. 32:15, 16; 34:1, 28; Deut. 9:10

1 [1]Or, *gods* [a]Ex. 24:18; Deut. 9:11, 12 [b]Acts 7:40 [c]Ex. 14:11
2 [a]Ex. 35:22
4 [1]Or, *These are your gods* [a]Deut. 9:16; Neh. 9:18; Ps. 106:19; Acts 7:41

of testimony, and [c]the [1]mercy seat upon
it, and all the furniture of the tent,
8 [a]the table also and its [1]utensils, and
the [b]pure *gold* lampstand with all its
[1]utensils, and [c]the altar of incense,
9 [a]the altar of burnt offering also
with all its [1]utensils, and [b]the laver and
its stand,
10 the [1a]woven garments as well, and
the holy garments for Aaron the priest,
and the garments of his sons, *with which*
to [2]carry on their priesthood;
11 [a]the anointing oil also, and the
[b]fragrant incense for the holy place, they
are to make *them* according to all that I
have commanded you."

The Sign of the Sabbath

12 And the LORD spoke to Moses,
saying,
13 "But as for you, speak to the sons of
Israel, saying, '[a]You shall surely observe
My sabbaths; for *this* is [b]a sign between
Me and you throughout your generations, that you may know that I am the
LORD who sanctifies you.
14 'Therefore you are to observe the
sabbath, for it is holy to you. [a]Everyone
who profanes it shall surely be put to
death; for whoever does any work on it,
that person shall be cut off from among
his people.
15 '[a]For six days work may be done,
but on the seventh day there is a [b]sab-
bath of complete rest, holy to the LORD;
[c]whoever does any work on the sabbath
day shall surely be put to death.
16 'So the sons of Israel shall observe
the sabbath, to [1]celebrate the sabbath
throughout their generations as a perpetual covenant.'
17 "[a]It is a sign between Me and the
sons of Israel forever; [b]for in six days
the LORD made heaven and earth, but on
the seventh day He ceased *from labor,*
and was refreshed."
18 And when He had finished speaking with him upon Mount Sinai, He gave
Moses [a]the two tablets of the testimony,
tablets of stone, [b]written by the finger of
God.

The Golden Calf

32 NOW when the people saw that
Moses [a]delayed to come down
from the mountain, the people assembled about Aaron, and said to him,
"Come, [b]make us [1]a god who will go
before us; as for [c]this Moses, the man
who brought us up from the land of
Egypt, we do not know what has become
of him."
2 And Aaron said to them, "[a]Tear off
the gold rings which are in the ears of
your wives, your sons, and your daughters, and bring *them* to me."
3 Then all the people tore off the
gold rings which were in their ears, and
brought *them* to Aaron.
4 And he took *this* from their hand,
and fashioned it with a graving tool, and
made it into a [a]molten calf; and they
said, "[1]This is your god, O Israel, who
brought you up from the land of Egypt."

5 Now when Aaron saw *this,* he built
an altar before it; and Aaron made a
proclamation and said, "Tomorrow *shall*
be a feast to the LORD."
6 So the next day they rose early and
[a]offered burnt offerings, and brought
peace offerings; and [b]the people sat
down to eat and to drink, and rose up
[c]to play.
7 Then the LORD spoke to Moses,
"Go [1]down at once, for your people,
whom [a]you brought up from the land of
Egypt, have [b]corrupted *themselves.*
8 "They have quickly turned aside
from the way which I commanded them.
[a]They have made for themselves a molten calf, and have worshiped it, and
[b]have sacrificed to it, and said, '[1c]This is
your god, O Israel, who brought you up
from the land of Egypt!' "
9 [a]And the LORD said to Moses, "I
have seen this people, and behold, they
are [1b]an obstinate people.
10 "Now then [a]let Me alone, that My
anger may burn against them, and that I
may destroy them; and [b]I will make of
you a great nation."

Moses' Entreaty

11 Then [a]Moses entreated the LORD
his God, and said, "O LORD, why doth
Thine anger burn against Thy people
whom Thou hast brought out from the
land of Egypt with great power and with
a mighty hand?
12 "Why should [a]the Egyptians speak,
saying, 'With evil *intent* He brought
them out to kill them in the mountains
and to destroy them from the face of the
earth'? Turn from Thy burning anger
and change Thy mind about *doing* harm
to Thy people.
13 "Remember Abraham, Isaac, and
Israel, Thy servants to whom Thou didst
[a]swear by Thyself, and didst say to them,
'I will [b]multiply your [1]descendants as
the stars of the heavens, and [c]all this
land of which I have spoken I will give
to your [1]descendants, and they shall
inherit *it* forever.' "
14 [a]So the LORD changed His mind
about the harm which He said He would
do to His people.
15 [a]Then Moses turned and went
down from the mountain with the two
tablets of the testimony in his hand,
[b]tablets which were written on both
[1]sides; they were written on one *side* and
the other.
16 And the tablets were God's work,
and the writing was God's writing engraved on the tablets.
17 Now when Joshua heard the sound
of the people [1]as they shouted, he said to
Moses, "There is a sound of war in the
camp."
18 But he said,

"It is not the sound of the cry of
triumph,
Nor is it the sound of the cry of
defeat;
But the sound of singing I hear."

Moses' Anger

19 And it came about, as soon as
[1]Moses came near the camp, that [a]he
saw the calf and *the* dancing; and Moses'
anger burned, and [b]he threw the tablets
from his hands and shattered them [2]at
the foot of the mountain.
20 [a]And he took the calf which they
had made and burned *it* with fire, and
ground it to powder, and scattered it
over the surface of the water, and made
the sons of Israel drink *it.*
21 Then Moses said to Aaron, "What
did this people do to you, that you have
brought *such* great sin upon them?"
22 And Aaron said, "Do not let the
anger of my lord burn; you know the
people yourself, [a]that they are [1]prone to
evil.
23 "For [a]they said to me, 'Make [1]a god
for us who will go before us; for this
Moses, the man who brought us up from
the land of Egypt, we do not know what
has become of him.'
24 "And I said to them, 'Whoever has
any gold, let them tear it off.' So they
gave *it* to me, and [a]I threw it into the
fire, and out came this calf."
25 Now when Moses saw that the
people were [1]out of control—for Aaron
had [a]let them [2]get out of control to be a
derision among [3]their enemies—
26 then Moses stood in the gate of the
camp, and said, "Whoever is for the
LORD, *come* to me!" And all the sons of
Levi gathered together to him.
27 And he said to them, "Thus says
the LORD, the God of Israel, 'Every man
of you put his sword upon his thigh, and
go back and forth from gate to gate in
the camp, and kill every man his brother,
and every man his friend, and every man
his [1]neighbor.' "
28 So [a]the sons of Levi did [1]as Moses
instructed, and about three thousand
men of the people fell that day.
29 Then Moses said, "[1]Dedicate yourselves today to the LORD—for every man
has been against his son and against his
brother—in order that He may bestow a
blessing upon you today."
30 And it came about on the next day
that Moses said to the people, "[a]You
yourselves have [1]committed a great sin;
and now I am going up to the LORD,
perhaps I can [b]make atonement for your
sin."
31 Then Moses returned to the LORD,
and said, "Alas, this people has [1]com-
mitted a great sin, and they have made
[2]a [a]god of gold for themselves.
32 "But now, if Thou wilt, forgive their
sin—and if not, please blot me out from
Thy [a]book which Thou hast written!"
33 And the LORD said to Moses,
"Whoever has sinned against Me, [a]I will
blot him out of My book.
34 "But go now, lead the people [a]where
I told you. Behold, [b]My angel shall go
before you; nevertheless [c]in the day
when I [1]punish, [d]I will [2]punish them for
their sin."

6 [a]Acts 7:41 [b]1 Cor. 10:7 [c]Ex. 32:17-19; Num. 25:2
7 [1]Lit., *go down* [a]Ex. 32:4, 11; Deut. 9:12 [b]Gen. 6:11f.
8 [1]Or, *These are your gods* [a]Ex. 20:3, 4, 23 [b]Ex. 22:20; 34:15; Deut. 32:17 [c]1 Kin. 12:28
9 [1]Or, *a stiff-necked* [a]Num. 14:11-20 [b]Ex. 33:3, 5; 34:9; Is. 48:4; Acts 7:51
10 [a]Deut. 9:14 [b]Num. 14:12
11 [a]Deut. 9:18, 26
12 [a]Num. 14:13-19; Deut. 9:28; Josh. 7:9
13 [1]Lit., *seed* [a]Gen. 22:16-18; Heb. 6:13 [b]Gen. 15:5; 26:4 [c]Gen. 12:7; 13:15; 15:18; 17:8; 35:12; Ex. 13:5, 11; 33:1
14 [a]Ps. 106:45
15 [1]Lit., *their sides* [a]Deut. 9:15 [b]Ex. 31:18
17 [1]Lit., *in its shouting*
19 [1]Lit., *he* [2]Lit., *beneath* [a]Ex. 32:6; Deut. 9:16 [b]Deut. 9:17
20 [a]Deut. 9:21
22 [1]Lit., *in evil* [a]Deut. 9:24
23 [1]Or, *gods* [a]Ex. 32:1-4
24 [a]Ex. 32:4
25 [1]Lit., *let loose* [2]Lit., *go loose* [3]Lit., *those who rise against them* [a]1 Kin. 12:28-30; 14:16
27 [1]Or, *kin*
28 [1]Lit., *according to Moses' word* [a]Num. 25:7-13; Deut. 33:9
29 [1]Lit., *Fill your hand*
30 [1]Lit., *sinned* [a]1 Sam. 12:20, 23 [b]Num. 25:13
31 [1]Lit., *sinned* [2]Or, *gods* [a]Ex. 20:23
32 [a]Ps. 69:28; Is. 4:3; Dan. 12:1; Mal. 3:16, 17; Phil. 4:3; Rev. 3:5; 21:27
33 [a]Ex. 17:14; Deut. 29:20; Ps. 9:5; Rev. 3:5
34 [1]Lit., *visit* [2]Lit., *visit their sin upon them* [a]Ex. 3:17 [b]Ex. 23:20 [c]Deut. 32:35; Rom. 2:5, 6 [d]Ps. 99:8

35 [a]Then the LORD smote the people,
because of [b]what they did with the calf
which Aaron had made.

The Journey Resumed

33 THEN the LORD spoke to Moses,
"Depart, go up from here, you
and the people whom you have brought
up from the land of Egypt, to the land of
which [a]I swore to Abraham, [b]Isaac, and
[c]Jacob, saying, '[d]To your [1]descendants I
will give it.'
2 "And I will send [a]an angel before
you and [b]I will drive out the Canaanite,
the Amorite, the Hittite, the Perizzite,
the Hivite and the Jebusite.
3 "*Go up* to a land [a]flowing with milk
and honey; for I will not go up in your
midst, because you are [1][b]an obstinate
people, lest [c]I destroy you on the way."
4 When the people heard this [1]sad
word, [a]they went into mourning, and
none of them put on his ornaments.
5 For the LORD had said to Moses,
"Say to the sons of Israel, 'You are [1][a]an
obstinate people; should I go up in your
midst for one moment, I would destroy
you. Now therefore, put off your ornaments from you, that I may know what I
will do with you.' "
6 So the sons of Israel stripped themselves of their ornaments from Mount
Horeb *onward.*
7 Now Moses used to take [a]the tent
and pitch it outside the camp, a good
distance from the camp, and he called it
the tent of meeting. And it came about,
that [b]everyone who sought the LORD
would go out to the tent of meeting
which was outside the camp.
8 And it came about, whenever Moses went out to the tent, that all the
people would arise and stand, each at
the entrance of his tent, and gaze after
Moses until he entered the tent.
9 And it came about, whenever Mo-
ses entered the tent, [a]the pillar of cloud
would descend and stand at the entrance
of the tent; [b]and [1]the LORD would speak
with Moses.
10 When all the people saw the pillar
of cloud standing at the entrance of the
tent, all the people would arise and
worship, each at the entrance of his tent.
11 Thus [a]the LORD used to speak to
Moses face to face, just as a man speaks
to his friend. When [1]Moses returned to
the camp, [b]his servant Joshua, the son of
Nun, a young man, would not depart
from the tent.

Moses Intercedes

12 Then Moses said to the LORD,
"See, Thou dost say to me, '[a]Bring up
this people!' But Thou Thyself hast not
let me know [b]whom Thou wilt send with
me. [c]Moreover, Thou hast said, 'I have
known you by name, and you have also
found favor in My sight.'
13 "Now therefore, I pray Thee, if I
have found favor in Thy sight, [a]let me
know Thy ways, that I may know Thee,
so that I may find favor in Thy sight.
[b]Consider too, that this nation is Thy
people."
14 And He said, "[a]My presence shall
go *with you,* and [b]I will give you rest."
15 Then he said to Him, "[a]If Thy
presence does not go *with us,* do not lead
us up from here.
16 "For how then can it be known that
I have found favor in Thy sight, I and
Thy people? Is it not by Thy going with
us, so that [a]we, I and Thy people, may
be distinguished from all the *other* people who are upon the face of the [1]earth?"
17 And the LORD said to Moses, "I
will also do this thing of which you have
spoken; [a]for you have found favor in My
sight, and I have known you by name."
18 [a]Then [1]Moses said, "I pray Thee,
show me Thy glory!"
19 And He said, "[a]I Myself will make
all My goodness pass before you, and
will proclaim the name of the LORD
before you; and [b]I will be gracious to
whom I will be gracious, and will show
compassion on whom I will show compassion."
20 But He said, "You cannot see My
face, [a]for no man can see Me and live!"
21 Then the LORD said, "Behold, there
is a place [1]by Me, and [a]you shall stand
there on the rock;
22 and it will come about, while My
glory is passing by, that I will put you in
the cleft of the rock and [a]cover you with
My hand until I have passed by.
23 "Then I will take My hand away and
you shall see My back, but [a]My face
shall not be seen."

The Two Tablets Replaced

34 NOW the LORD said to Moses,
"Cut out for yourself [a]two stone
tablets like the former ones, and [b]I will
write on the tablets the words that were
on the former tablets which you shattered.
2 "So be ready by morning, and come
up in the morning to [a]Mount Sinai, and
[1]present yourself there to Me on the top
of the mountain.
3 "And [a]no man is to come up with
you, nor let any man be seen [1]anywhere
on the mountain; even the flocks and the
herds may not graze in front of that
mountain."
4 So he cut out [a]two stone tablets
like the former ones, and Moses rose up
early in the morning and went up to
Mount Sinai, as the LORD had commanded him, and he took two stone
tablets in his hand.
5 And [a]the LORD descended in the
cloud and stood there with him as [1]he
called upon the name of the LORD.
6 Then the LORD passed by in front
of him and proclaimed, "The LORD, the
LORD God, [a]compassionate and gracious, slow to anger, and abounding in
lovingkindness and [1]truth;

35 [a]Ex. 32:28 [b]Ex. 32:4, 24

1 [1]Lit., *seed* [a]Ex. 32:13 [b]Gen. 26:1-3 [c]Gen. 28:10 [d]Gen. 12:7

2 [a]Ex. 32:34 [b]Ex. 23:27-31; Josh. 24:11

3 [1]Lit., *a stiff-necked* [a]Ex. 3:8, 17 [b]Ex. 32:9; 33:5 [c]Ex. 32:10

4 [1]Lit., *evil* [a]Num. 14:1, 39

5 [1]Lit., *a stiff-necked* [a]Ex. 33:3

7 [a]Ex. 18:7, 12-16 [b]Ex. 29:42f.

9 [1]Lit., *He* [a]Ex. 13:21 [b]Ps. 99:7

11 [1]Lit., *he* [a]Num. 12:8; Deut. 34:10 [b]Ex. 24:13

12 [a]Ex. 3:10; 32:34 [b]Ex. 33:2 [c]Ex. 33:17

13 [a]Ps. 25:4; 27:11; 51:13; 86:11; 119:33 [b]Ex. 3:7, 10; 5:1; 32:12, 14; Deut. 9:26, 29

14 [a]Deut. 4:37; Is. 63:9 [b]Deut. 12:10; 25:19; Josh. 21:44; 22:4

15 [a]Ps. 80:3, 7, 19

16 [1]Lit., *ground* [a]Lev. 20:24, 26

17 [a]Ex. 33:12

18 [1]Lit., *he* [a]Ex. 33:20-23

19 [a]Ex. 34:6, 7 [b]Rom. 9:15

20 [a]Is. 6:5; 1 Tim. 6:16

21 [1]Lit., *with* [a]Ps. 18:2, 46; 27:5; 61:2; 62:7

22 [a]Ps. 91:1, 4; Is. 49:2; 51:16

23 [a]Ex. 33:20; John 1:18

1 [a]Ex. 24:12; 31:18; 32:16, 19 [b]Deut. 10:2, 4

2 [1]Or, *place yourself before* [a]Ex. 19:11, 18, 20

3 [1]Lit., *on all* [a]Ex. 19:12, 13

4 [a]Ex. 34:1

5 [1]Or, *he called out with the name of the LORD* [a]Ex. 19:9; 33:9

6 [1]Or, *faithfulness* [a]Num. 14:18; Deut. 4:31; Neh. 9:17; Ps. 86:15; 103:8; 108:4; 145:8; Joel 2:13; Rom. 2:4

7 who [a]keeps lovingkindness for thousands, who forgives iniquity, transgression and sin; yet He [b]will by no means leave *the guilty* unpunished, [c]visiting the iniquity of fathers on the children and on the grandchildren to the third and fourth generations."

8 And Moses made haste [1][a]to bow low toward the earth and worship.

9 And he said, "[a]If now I have found favor in Thy sight, O Lord, I pray, let the Lord go along in our midst, even though [1][b]the people are so obstinate; and do Thou [c]pardon our iniquity and our sin, and [d]take us as Thine own [2]possession."

The Covenant Renewed

10 Then [1]God said, "Behold, [a]I am going to make a covenant. Before all your people [b]I will perform miracles which have not been [2]produced in all the earth, nor among any of the nations; and all the people [3]among whom you live will see the working of the LORD, for it is a fearful thing that I am going to perform with you.

11 "[1]Be sure to observe what I am commanding you this day: behold, [a]I am going to drive out the Amorite before you, and the Canaanite, the Hittite, the Perizzite, the Hivite and the Jebusite.

12 "[a]Watch yourself that you make no covenant with the inhabitants of the land into which you are going, lest it become a snare in your midst.

13 "[a]But *rather,* you are to tear down their altars and smash their *sacred* pillars and cut down their [1][b]Asherim

14 —for [a]you shall not worship any other god, for the LORD, whose name is Jealous, is a jealous God—

15 lest you make a covenant with the inhabitants of the land and they play the harlot with their gods, and [a]sacrifice to their gods, and someone [b]invite you [1]to eat of his sacrifice;

16 and [a]you take some of his daughters for your sons, and his daughters play the harlot with their gods, and cause your sons *also* to play the harlot with their gods.

17 "[a]You shall make for yourself no molten gods.

18 "You shall observe [a]the Feast of Unleavened Bread. For [b]seven days you are to eat unleavened bread, [1]as I commanded you, at the appointed time in the [c]month of Abib, for in the month of Abib you came out of Egypt.

19 "[a]The first offspring from every womb belongs to Me, and all your male livestock, the first offspring from [1]cattle and sheep.

20 "[a]And you shall redeem with a lamb the [1]first offspring from a donkey; and if you do not redeem *it,* then you shall break its neck. You shall redeem [b]all the first-born of your sons. And [2][c]none shall appear before Me empty-handed.

21 "You shall work [a]six days, but on the seventh day you shall rest; *even* during plowing time and harvest you shall rest.

22 "And you shall celebrate [a]the Feast of Weeks, *that is,* the first fruits of the wheat harvest, and the Feast of Ingathering at the turn of the year.

23 "[a]Three times a year all your males are to appear before the Lord [1]GOD, the God of Israel.

24 "For I will [1][a]drive out nations before you and enlarge your borders, and no man shall covet your land when you go up three times a year to appear before the LORD your God.

25 "[a]You shall not [1]offer the blood of My sacrifice with leavened bread, [b]nor is the sacrifice of the Feast of the Passover to [2]be left over until morning.

26 "You shall bring [a]the very first of the first fruits of your soil into the house of the LORD your God. You shall not boil a kid in its mother's milk."

27 Then the LORD said to Moses, "[a]Write [1]down these words, for in accordance with these words I have made [b]a covenant with you and with Israel."

28 So he was there with the LORD [a]forty days and forty nights; he did not eat bread or drink water. And [b]he wrote on the tablets the words of the covenant, [c]the Ten [1]Commandments.

Moses' Face Shines

29 And it came about when Moses was coming down from Mount Sinai (and the [a]two tablets of the testimony *were* in Moses' hand as he was coming down from the mountain), that Moses did not know that [b]the skin of his face shone because of his speaking with Him.

30 So when Aaron and all the sons of Israel saw Moses, behold, the skin of his face shone, and [a]they were afraid to come near him.

31 Then Moses called to them, and Aaron and all the rulers in the congregation returned to him; and Moses spoke to them.

32 And afterward all the sons of Israel came near, and he commanded them *to do* everything that the LORD had spoken [1]to him on Mount Sinai.

33 When Moses had finished speaking with them, [a]he put a veil over his face.

34 But whenever Moses went in before the LORD to speak with Him, [a]he would take off the veil until he came out; and whenever he came out and spoke to the sons of Israel what he had been commanded,

35 [a]the sons of Israel would see the face of Moses, that the skin of Moses' face shone. So Moses would replace the veil over his face until he went in to speak with Him.

The Sabbath Emphasized

35 THEN Moses assembled all the congregation of the sons of Israel, and said to them, "[a]These are the things that the LORD has commanded *you* to [1]do.

7 [a]Ex. 20:5, 6; Deut. 5:10; 7:9; Ps. 103:3; 130:3, 4; 1 John 1:9 [b]Ex. 23:7; Deut. 7:10; Job 10:14; Nah. 1:3 [c]Deut. 5:9
8 [1]Lit., *and bowed . . . worshiped* [a]Ex. 4:31
9 [1]Lit., *it is a people stiff-necked* [2]Or, *inheritance* [a]Ex. 33:13 [b]Ex. 32:9 [c]Ex. 34:7 [d]Deut. 4:20; 9:26, 29; 32:9; Ps. 33:12
10 [1]Lit., *He* [2]Lit., *created* [3]Lit., *in whose midst you are* [a]Ex. 34:27, 28; Deut. 5:2 [b]Deut. 4:32; Ps. 72:18; 136:4
11 [1]Lit., *Observe for yourself* [a]Ex. 33:2
12 [a]Ex. 23:32, 33
13 [1]I.e., wooden symbols of a female deity [a]Ex. 23:24; Deut. 12:3 [b]Deut. 16:21; Judg. 6:25, 26; 2 Kin. 18:4; 2 Chr. 34:3f.
14 [a]Ex. 20:3, 5; Deut. 4:24
15 [1]Lit., *and you eat* [a]Ex. 22:20; 32:8 [b]Num. 25:1, 2; Deut. 32:37, 38
16 [a]Deut. 7:3; Josh. 23:12, 13; 1 Kin. 11:1-4
17 [a]Ex. 20:4, 23; Lev. 19:4; Deut. 5:8
18 [1]Or, *which* [a]Ex. 12:17; Lev. 23:6; Num. 28:16f. [b]Ex. 12:15, 16 [c]Ex. 12:2; 13:4
19 [1]Or, *oxen* [a]Ex. 13:2; 22:29f.
20 [1]Lit., *first opening of* [2]Lit., *they shall not* [a]Ex. 13:13 [b]Ex. 13:15; Num. 3:45 [c]Ex. 22:29; 23:15; Deut. 16:16
21 [a]Ex. 20:9f.; 23:12; 31:15; 35:2; Lev. 23:3; Deut. 5:13f.
22 [a]Ex. 23:16; Num. 28:26
23 [1]Heb., *YHWH,* usually rendered *LORD* [a]Ex. 23:14-17
24 [1]Or, *dispossess* [a]Ex. 33:2; Ps. 78:55
25 [1]Lit., *slaughter* [2]Lit., *remain overnight* [a]Ex. 23:18 [b]Ex. 12:10
26 [a]Ex. 23:19; Deut. 26:2
27 [1]Lit., *for yourself* [a]Ex. 17:14; 24:4 [b]Ex. 34:10
28 [1]Lit., *Words* [a]Ex. 24:18 [b]Ex. 31:18; 34:1 [c]Deut. 4:13; 10:4
29 [a]Ex. 32:15 [b]Matt. 17:2; 2 Cor. 3:7
30 [a]2 Cor. 3:7
32 [1]Lit., *with*
33 [a]2 Cor. 3:13
34 [a]2 Cor. 3:16
35 [a]2 Cor. 3:13

1 [1]Lit., *do them.* [a]Ex. 34:32

2“[a]For six days work may be done,
but on the seventh day you shall have a
holy *day,* [b]a sabbath of complete rest to
the LORD; [c]whoever does any work on it
shall be put to death.
3“[a]You shall not kindle a fire in any
of your dwellings on the sabbath day.”
4 And Moses spoke to all the congregation of the sons of Israel, saying, “This
is the thing which the LORD has commanded, saying,
5 ‘[a]Take from among you a [1]contri-
bution to the LORD; whoever is of a
willing heart, let him bring it as the
LORD’s [1]contribution: gold, silver, and
[2]bronze,
6 and [1]blue, purple and scarlet *material,* fine linen, goats’ *hair,*
7 and rams’ skins [1]dyed red, and
porpoise skins, and acacia wood,
8 and oil for lighting, and spices for
the anointing oil, and for the fragrant
incense,
9 and onyx stones and setting stones,
for the ephod and for the [1]breastpiece.

Tabernacle Workmen

10 ‘And [a]let every skillful man among
you come, and make all that the LORD
has commanded:
11 the [1a]tabernacle, its tent and its
covering, its hooks and its boards, its
bars, its pillars, and its [2]sockets;
12 the [a]ark and its poles, the [1]mercy
seat, and the curtain of the screen;
13 the [a]table and its poles, and all its
[1]utensils, and the bread of the [2]Presence;
14 the [a]lampstand also for the light
and its utensils and its lamps and the oil
for the light;
15 and the [a]altar of incense and its
poles, and the [b]anointing oil and the
[c]fragrant incense, and the screen for the
doorway at the [1]entrance of the tabernacle;
16 [a]the altar of burnt offering with its
[1]bronze grating, its poles, and all its
[2]utensils, the [3]basin and its stand;
17 [a]the hangings of the court, its
pillars and its [1]sockets, and the screen
for the gate of the court;
18 the pegs of the tabernacle and the
pegs of the court and their cords;
19 the [1a]woven garments, for ministering in the holy place, the holy garments
for Aaron the priest, and the garments of
his sons, to minister as priests.’ ”

Gifts Received

20 Then all the congregation of the
sons of Israel departed from Moses’
presence.
21 And [a]everyone whose heart [1]stirred
him and everyone whose spirit [2]moved
him came *and* brought the LORD’s [3]con-
tribution for the work of the tent of
meeting and for all its service and for the
holy garments.
22 Then all [1]whose hearts moved
them, both men and women, came *and*
brought brooches and [2]earrings and
signet rings and bracelets, all articles of
gold; so *did* every man who [3]presented
an offering of gold to the LORD.
23 And every man, [1]who had in his
possession [2]blue and purple and scarlet
material and fine linen and goats’ *hair*
and rams’ skins [3]dyed red and porpoise
skins, brought them.
24 Everyone who could make a [1]con-
tribution of silver and [2]bronze brought
the LORD’s [1]contribution; and every
man, [3]who had in his possession acacia
wood for any work of the service,
brought it.
25 And all the [1]skilled women spun
with their hands, and brought what they
had spun, *in* [2]blue and purple *and* scarlet
material and *in* fine linen.
26 And all the women whose heart
[1]stirred with a skill spun the goats’ *hair.*
27 And the rulers brought the onyx
stones and the stones for setting for the
ephod and for the [1]breastpiece;
28 and [a]the spice and the oil for the
light and for the anointing oil and for
the fragrant incense.
29 The [1]Israelites, all the men and
women, whose heart [2]moved them to
bring *material* for all the work, which the
LORD had commanded through Moses
to be done, brought a [a]freewill offering
to the LORD.
30 [a]Then Moses said to the sons of
Israel, “See, the LORD has called by
name Bezalel the son of Uri, the son of
Hur, of the tribe of Judah.
31“And He has filled him with the
Spirit of God, in wisdom, in understanding and in knowledge and in all [1]crafts-
manship;
32 [1]to make designs for working in
gold and in silver and in [2]bronze,
33 and in the cutting of stones for
settings, and in the carving of wood, so
as to perform in every inventive work.
34“He also has put in his heart to
teach, both he and [a]Oholiab, the son of
Ahisamach, of the tribe of Dan.
35“[a]He has filled them with [1]skill to
perform every work of an engraver and
of a designer and of an embroiderer, in
[2]blue and in purple *and* in scarlet *material,* and in fine linen, and of a weaver, as
performers of every work and makers of
designs.

The Tabernacle Underwritten

36 “NOW Bezalel and Oholiab, and
every [1]skillful person in whom
the LORD has put [2]skill and understanding to know how to perform all the work
[3]in the construction of the sanctuary,
shall perform in accordance with all that
the LORD has commanded.”
2 Then Moses called Bezalel and
Oholiab and every [1]skillful person in
[2]whom the LORD had put [3]skill, [a]every-
one whose heart stirred him, to come to
the work to perform it.
3 And they received from Moses all
the [1]contributions which the sons of
Israel had brought [2]to perform the work
[3]in the construction of the sanctuary.

2 [a]Ex. 20:9, 10; 23:12; 31:15; 34:21; Lev. 23:3; Deut. 5:13f. [b]Ex. 16:23 [c]Num. 15:32-36
3 [a]Ex. 12:16; 16:23
5 [1]Or, *heave offering* [2]Or, *copper* [a]Ex. 25:1-9
6 [1]Or, *violet*
7 [1]Or, *tanned*
9 [1]Or, *pouch*
10 [a]Ex. 31:6
11 [1]Lit., *dwelling place* [2]Or, *bases* [a]Ex. 26:1-30
12 [1]Lit., *propitiatory* [a]Ex. 25:10-22
13 [1]Or, *vessels* [2]Lit., *Face* [a]Ex. 25:23-30
14 [a]Ex. 25:31ff.
15 [1]Or, *doorway* [a]Ex. 30:1-6 [b]Ex. 30:25 [c]Ex. 30:34-38
16 [1]Or, *copper* [2]Or, *vessels* [3]Or, *laver* [a]Ex. 27:1-8
17 [1]Or, *bases* [a]Ex. 27:9-18
19 [1]Or, *service garments* [a]Ex. 31:10; 39:1
21 [1]Lit., *lifted up* [2]Or, *made him willing* [3]Or, *heave offering* [a]Ex. 25:2; 35:5, 22, 26, 29; 36:2
22 [1]Or, *who were willing-hearted* [2]Or, *nose rings* [3]Lit., *waved a wave offering*
23 [1]Lit., *with whom was found* [2]Or, *violet* [3]Or, *tanned*
24 [1]Or, *heave offering* [2]Or, *copper* [3]Lit., *with whom was found*
25 [1]Lit., *women wise of heart* [2]Or, *violet*
26 [1]Lit., *lifted them up in wisdom*
27 [1]Or, *pouch*
28 [a]Ex. 30:23ff.
29 [1]Lit., *sons of Israel* [2]Lit., *made them willing* [a]Ex. 35:21; 1 Chr. 29:9
30 [a]Ex. 31:1-6
31 [1]Or, *work*
32 [1]Lit., *devise devices* [2]Or, *copper*
34 [a]Ex. 31:6
35 [1]Lit., *wisdom of heart* [2]Or, *violet* [a]Ex. 31:3, 6; 35:31; 1 Kin. 7:14

1 [1]Lit., *man wise of heart* [2]Lit., *wisdom* [3]Or, *connected with the service of;* lit., *of the service of*
2 [1]Lit., *man wise of heart* [2]Lit., *whose heart* [3]Lit., *wisdom* [a]Ex. 35:21, 26
3 [1]Lit., *lifted offering* [2]Lit., *to perform it for the work* [3]Lit., *of the service of*

And they still *continued* bringing to him
freewill offerings every morning.
4 And all the [1]skillful men who were
performing all the work of the sanctuary
came, each from [2]the work which [3]he
was performing,
5 and they said to [1]Moses, "[a]The
people are bringing much more than
enough for the [2]construction work which
the LORD commanded *us* to [3]perform."
6 So Moses issued a command, and a
[1]proclamation was circulated throughout the camp, saying, "Let neither man
nor woman any longer perform work for
the [2]contributions of the sanctuary."
Thus the people were restrained from
bringing *any more.*
7 [a]For the [1]material they had was
sufficient and more than enough for all
the work, to perform it.

Construction Proceeds

8 [a]And all the [1]skillful men among
those who were performing the work
made the [2]tabernacle with ten curtains;
of fine twisted linen and [3]blue and
purple and scarlet *material,* with cherubim, the work of a skillful workman,
[4]Bezalel made them.
9 The length of each curtain was
twenty-eight [1]cubits, and the width of
each curtain four [1]cubits; all the curtains
had [2]the same measurements.
10 And he [1]joined five curtains to one
another, and *the other* five curtains he
[1]joined to one another.
11 And he made loops of [1]blue on the
edge of the [2]outermost curtain in the
first [3]set; he did likewise on the edge of
the curtain that was [2]outermost in the
second [3]set.
12 He made [a]fifty loops in the one
curtain and he made fifty loops on the
[1]edge of the curtain that was in the
second [2]set; the loops were opposite
each other.
13 And he made [a]fifty clasps of gold,
and [1]joined the curtains to one another
with the clasps, so the tabernacle was [2]a
unit.
14 Then [a]he made curtains of goats'
hair for a tent over the tabernacle; he
made eleven curtains [1]in all.
15 The length of each curtain was
thirty cubits, and four cubits the width
of each curtain; the eleven curtains had
[1]the same measurements.
16 And he [1]joined five curtains by
themselves, and *the other* six curtains by
themselves.
17 Moreover, he made fifty loops on
the edge of the curtain that was outermost in the *first* [1]set, and he made fifty
loops on the edge of the curtain *that was*
outermost in the second [1]set.
18 And he made fifty clasps of
[1]bronze to [2]join the tent together, that it
might be [3]a unit.
19 And he made a covering for the
tent of rams' skins [1]dyed red, and a
covering of porpoise skins above.
20 [a]Then he made the boards for the
tabernacle of acacia wood, standing
upright.
21 Ten cubits was the length of [1]each
board, and one and a half cubits the
width of each board.
22 There were two tenons for each
board, [1]fitted to one another; thus he did
for all the boards of the tabernacle.
23 And he made the boards for the
tabernacle: twenty boards [1]for the south
side;
24 and he made forty [1]sockets of silver
under the twenty boards; two [1]sockets
under one board for its two tenons and
two [1]sockets under another board for its
two tenons.
25 Then for the second side of the
tabernacle, on the north side, he made
twenty boards,
26 and their forty [1]sockets of silver;
two [1]sockets under one board and two
[1]sockets under another board.
27 And for the [1]rear of the tabernacle,
to the west, he made six boards.
28 And he made two boards for the
corners of the [1]tabernacle at the [2]rear.
29 And they were double beneath, and
together they were complete to its [1]top
[2]to the first ring; thus he did with both
of them for the two corners.
30 And there were eight boards with
their [1]sockets of silver, sixteen [1]sockets,
[2]two under every board.
31 Then he made [a]bars of acacia
wood, five for the boards of one side of
the tabernacle,
32 and five bars for the boards of the
[1]other side of the tabernacle, and five
bars for the boards of the tabernacle for
the [2]rear *side* to the west.
33 And he made the middle bar to
pass through in the [1]center of the boards
from end to end.
34 And he overlaid the boards with
gold and made their rings of gold *as*
holders for the bars, and overlaid the
bars with gold.
35 [a]Moreover, he made the veil of
[1]blue and purple and scarlet *material,*
and fine twisted linen; he made it with
cherubim, the work of a skillful workman.
36 And he made four pillars of acacia
for it, and overlaid them with gold, with
their hooks of gold; and he cast four
[1]sockets of silver for them.
37 And he made a [a]screen for the
doorway of the tent, of [1]blue and purple
and scarlet *material,* and fine twisted
linen, the work of a [2]weaver;
38 and *he made* its [a]five pillars with
their hooks, and he overlaid their tops
and their [1]bands with gold; but their five
[2]sockets were of [3]bronze.

Construction Continues

37 [a]NOW Bezalel made the ark of
acacia wood; its length was two
and a half [1]cubits, and its width one and
a half cubits, and its height one and a
half cubits;

---

4 [1]Lit., *wise* [2]Lit., *his* [3]Lit., *they were*
5 [1]Lit., *Moses, saying,* [2]Lit., *service for the work* [3]Lit., *perform it* [a]2 Chr. 24:14; 31:6-10
6 [1]Lit., *voice* [2]Lit., *heave offering*
7 [1]Lit., *work* [a]1 Kin. 8:64
8 [1]Lit., *wise of heart* [2]Lit., *dwelling place* [3]Or, *violet* [4]Lit., *he* [a]Ex. 26:1-14
9 [1]I.e., One cubit equals approx. 18 in. [2]Lit., *one measure*
10 [1]Or, *coupled*
11 [1]Or, *violet* [2]Lit., *one curtain from the end in the coupling* [3]Lit., *coupling*
12 [1]Lit., *end* [2]Lit., *coupling* [a]Ex. 26:5
13 [1]Or, *coupled* [2]Lit., *one* [a]Ex. 26:6
14 [1]Lit., *in number* [a]Ex. 26:7-14
15 [1]Lit., *one measure*
16 [1]Or, *coupled*
17 [1]Lit., *coupling*
18 [1]Or, *copper* [2]Or, *couple* [3]Lit., *one*
19 [1]Or, *tanned*
20 [a]Ex. 26:15-29
21 [1]Lit., *the*
22 [1]Lit., *bound*
23 [1]Lit., *to the side of the Negev, to the south*
24 [1]Or, *bases*
26 [1]Or, *bases*
27 [1]Lit., *extreme parts*
28 [1]Lit., *dwelling place* [2]Lit., *extreme parts*
29 [1]Or, *head* [2]Or, *with reference to*
30 [1]Or, *bases* [2]Lit., *two sockets*
31 [a]Ex. 26:26-29
32 [1]Or, *second* [2]Lit., *extreme parts*
33 [1]Lit., *midst*
35 [1]Or, *violet* [a]Ex. 26:31-37
36 [1]Or, *bases*
37 [1]Or, *violet* [2]Lit., *variegator;* i.e., a weaver in colors [a]Ex. 26:36
38 [1]Or, *fillets, rings* [2]Or, *bases* [3]Or, *copper* [a]Ex. 26:37

1 [1]I.e., One cubit equals approx. 18 in. [a]Ex. 25:10-20

2 and he overlaid it with pure gold
inside and out, and made a gold molding
for it all around.
3 And he cast four rings of gold for it
on its four feet; even two rings on one
side of it, and two rings on the [1]other
side of it.
4 And he made poles of acacia wood
and overlaid them with gold.
5 And he put the poles into the rings
on the sides of the ark, to carry [1]it.
6 And he made a [1]mercy seat of pure
gold, two and a half cubits [2]long, and
one and a half cubits [3]wide.
7 And he made two cherubim of
gold; he made them of hammered work,
[1]at the two ends of the mercy seat;
8 one cherub [1]at the one end, and
one cherub [1]at the other end; he made
the cherubim *of one piece* with the mercy
seat [1]at the two ends.
9 And the cherubim had *their* wings
spread upward, covering the [1]mercy seat
with their wings, with their faces toward
each other; the faces of the cherubim
were toward the mercy seat.
10 [a]Then he made the table of acacia
wood, two [1]cubits [2]long and a cubit
[3]wide and one and a half cubits [4]high.
11 And he overlaid it with pure gold,
and made a gold molding for it all
around.
12 And he made a rim for it of a
handbreadth all around, and made a
gold molding for its rim all around.
13 And he cast four gold rings for it
and put the rings on the four corners
that were on its four feet.
14 Close by the rim were the rings, the
holders for the poles to carry the table.
15 And he made the poles of acacia
wood and overlaid them with gold, to
carry the table.
16 And he made the utensils which
were on the table, its [1]dishes and its pans
and its [2]bowls and its jars, with which to
pour out libations, of pure gold.
17 [a]Then he made the lampstand of
pure gold. He made the lampstand of
hammered work, its base and its shaft;
its cups, its [1]bulbs and its flowers were *of
one piece* with it.
18 And there were six branches going
out of its sides; three branches of the
lampstand from the one side of it, and
three branches of the lampstand from
the [1]other side of it;
19 three cups shaped like almond
blossoms, a [1]bulb and a flower in one
branch, and three cups shaped like
almond *blossoms,* a [1]bulb and a flower in
the other branch—so for the six
branches going out of the lampstand.
20 And in the lampstand *there were*
four cups shaped like almond *blossoms,*
its [1]bulbs and its flowers;
21 and a [1]bulb was under the *first* pair
of branches *coming* out of it, and a [1]bulb
under the *second* pair of branches *coming*
out of it, and a [1]bulb under the *third* pair
of branches *coming* out of it, for the six
branches coming out of the lampstand.
22 Their [1]bulbs and their branches
were *of one piece* with it; the whole of it
was a single hammered work of pure
gold.
23 And he made its seven lamps with
its snuffers and its [1]trays of pure gold.
24 He made it and all its utensils from
a talent of pure gold.
25 [a]Then he made the altar of incense
of acacia wood: a cubit [1]long and a cubit
[2]wide, square, and two cubits [3]high; its
horns were *of one piece* with it.
26 And he overlaid it with pure gold,
its top and its [1]sides all around, and its
horns; and he made a gold molding for it
all around.
27 And he made two golden rings for
it under its molding, on its two sides—
on opposite sides—as holders for poles
with which to carry it.
28 And he made the poles of acacia
wood and overlaid them with gold.
29 [a]And he made the holy anointing
oil and the pure, fragrant incense of
spices, the work of a perfumer.

The Tabernacle Completed

38 [a]THEN he made the altar of burnt
offering of acacia wood, five [1]cu-
bits [2]long, and five cubits [3]wide, square,
and three cubits [4]high.
2 And he made its horns on its four
corners, its horns [1]being *of one piece*
with it, and he overlaid it with [2]bronze.
3 And he made all the utensils of the
altar, the pails and the shovels and the
basins, the flesh hooks and the firepans;
he made all its utensils of bronze.
4 And he made for the altar a grating
of bronze network beneath, under its
ledge, reaching halfway up.
5 And he cast four rings on the four
ends of the bronze grating *as* holders for
the poles.
6 And he made the poles of acacia
wood and overlaid them with bronze.
7 And he inserted the poles into the
rings on the sides of the altar, with which
to carry it. He made it hollow with
planks.
8 [a]Moreover, he made the laver of
bronze with its base of bronze, [1]from the
mirrors of the serving women who
served at the doorway of the tent of
meeting.
9 [a]Then he made the court: [1]for the
south side the hangings of the court were
of fine twisted linen, one hundred cubits;
10 their twenty pillars, and their
twenty [1]sockets, *made* of bronze; the
hooks of the pillars and their [2]bands
were of silver.
11 And for the north side *there were*
one hundred cubits; their twenty pillars
and their twenty [1]sockets *were* of bronze,
the hooks of the pillars and their [2]bands
were of silver.
12 And for the west side *there were*
hangings of fifty cubits *with* their ten
pillars and their ten [1]sockets; the hooks
of the pillars and their [2]bands *were* of
silver.

3 [1]Lit., *second*
5 [1]Lit., *the ark*
6 [1]Lit., *propitiatory* [2]Lit., *its length* [3]Lit., *its width*
7 [1]Lit., *from*
8 [1]Lit., *from*
9 [1]Lit., *propitiatory*
10 [1]I.e., One cubit equals approx. 18 in. [2]Lit., *its length* [3]Lit., *its width* [4]Lit., *its height* [a]Ex. 25:23-29
16 [1]Or, *platters* [2]Lit., *libation bowls*
17 [1]Or, *calyxes* [a]Ex. 25:31-39
18 [1]Lit., *second*
19 [1]Or, *calyx*
20 [1]Or, *calyxes*
21 [1]Or, *calyx*
22 [1]Or, *calyxes*
23 [1]Lit., *snuff dishes*
25 [1]Lit., *its length* [2]Lit., *its width* [3]Lit., *its height* [a]Ex. 30:1-5
26 [1]Lit., *walls*
29 [a]Ex. 30:23-25, 34, 35

1 [1]I.e., One cubit equals approx. 18 in. [2]Lit., *its length* [3]Lit., *its width* [4]Lit., *its height* [a]Ex. 27:1-8
2 [1]Lit., *were* [2]Or, *copper,* and so for *bronze* throughout the ch.
8 [1]Lit., *with* [a]Ex. 30:18
9 [1]Lit., *to the side of the Negev, to the south* [a]Ex. 27:9-19
10 [1]Or, *bases* [2]Or, *fillets, rings*
11 [1]Or, *bases* [2]Or, *fillets, rings*
12 [1]Or, *bases* [2]Or, *fillets, rings*

13 And for the [1]east side fifty cubits.
14 The hangings for the *one* [1]side *of*
the gate were fifteen cubits, *with* their
three pillars and their three [2]sockets,
15 and so for the [1]other [2]side. [3]On
both sides of the gate of the court *were*
hangings of fifteen cubits, *with* their
three pillars and their three [4]sockets.
16 All the hangings of the court all
around *were* of fine twisted linen.
17 And the [1]sockets for the pillars
were of [2]bronze, the hooks of the pillars
and their [3]bands, of silver; and the
overlaying of their tops, of silver, and all
the pillars of the court were furnished
with silver [3]bands.
18 And the screen of the gate of the
court was the work of the [1]weaver, of
[2]blue and purple and scarlet *material,*
and fine twisted linen. And the length
was twenty cubits and the [3]height was
five cubits, corresponding to the hangings of the court.
19 And their four pillars and their
four [1]sockets *were* of bronze; their hooks
were of silver, and the overlaying of their
tops and their [2]bands *were* of silver.
20 And all the pegs of the [1]tabernacle
and of the court all around *were* of
bronze.

The Cost of the Tabernacle

21 [1]This is the number of *the things for*
the [2]tabernacle, the [2]tabernacle of the
testimony, as they were [3]numbered according to the [4]command of Moses, for
the service of the Levites, by the hand of
Ithamar, the son of Aaron the priest.
22 Now [a]Bezalel, the son of Uri the
son of Hur, of the tribe of Judah, made
all that the LORD had commanded Moses.
23 And with him was [a]Oholiab, the
son of Ahisamach, of the tribe of Dan,
an engraver and a skillful workman and
a [1]weaver in [2]blue and in purple and in
scarlet *material,* and fine linen.
24 All the gold that was used for the
work, in all the work of the sanctuary,
even the gold of the wave offering, was
29 talents and 730 shekels, according to
[a]the shekel of the sanctuary.
25 [a]And the silver of those of the
congregation who were [1]numbered was
100 talents and 1,775 shekels, according
to the shekel of the sanctuary;
26 [a]a beka a head (*that is,* half a shekel
according to the shekel of the sanctuary), for each one who passed over to
those who were [1]numbered, from twenty
years old and upward, for [b]603,550 men.
27 And the hundred talents of silver
were for casting the [1]sockets of the
sanctuary and the [1]sockets of the veil;
one hundred [1]sockets for the hundred
talents, a talent for a [1]socket.
28 And of the 1,775 *shekels,* he made
hooks for the pillars and overlaid their
tops and made [1]bands for them.
29 And the bronze of the wave offering was 70 talents, and 2,400 shekels.
30 And with it he made the [1]sockets to
the doorway of the tent of meeting, and
the bronze altar and its bronze grating,
and all the utensils of the altar,
31 and the [1]sockets of the court all
around and the [1]sockets of the gate of
the court, and all the pegs of the [2]taber-
nacle and all the pegs of the court all
around.

The Priestly Garments

39 MOREOVER, from the [1a]blue
and purple and scarlet *material,*
they made finely [b]woven garments for
ministering in the holy place, [2]as well as
the holy garments which were for Aaron,
just as the LORD had commanded Moses.
2 [a]And he made the ephod of gold,
and of [1]blue and purple and scarlet
material, and fine twisted linen.
3 Then they hammered out gold
sheets and cut *them* into threads [1]to be
woven in *with* the [2]blue and the purple
and the scarlet *material,* and the fine
linen, the work of a skillful workman.
4 They made attaching shoulder
pieces for [1]the ephod; it was attached at
its two *upper* ends.
5 And the skillfully woven band
which was on it was like its workmanship, [1]of the same material: of gold *and*
of [2]blue and purple and scarlet *material,*
and fine twisted linen, just as the LORD
had commanded Moses.
6 And [a]they made the onyx stones,
set in gold filigree *settings;* they were
engraved *like* the engravings of a signet,
according to the names of the sons of
Israel.
7 And [a]he placed them on the shoulder pieces of the ephod, *as* memorial
stones for the sons of Israel, just as the
LORD had commanded Moses.
8 [a]And he made the breastpiece, the
work of a skillful workman, like the
workmanship of the ephod: of gold *and*
of [1]blue and purple and scarlet *material*
and fine twisted linen.
9 It was square; they made the
breastpiece folded double, a span [1]long
and a span [2]wide when folded double.
10 And they [1]mounted four rows of
stones on it. The first row *was* a row of
ruby, topaz, and emerald;
11 and the second row, a turquoise, a
sapphire and a diamond;
12 and the third row, a jacinth, an
agate, and an amethyst;
13 and the fourth row, a beryl, an
onyx, and a jasper. They were set in gold
filigree *settings* when they were
[1]mounted.
14 And the stones were corresponding
to the names of the sons of Israel; they
were twelve, corresponding to their
names, *engraved with* the engravings of a
signet, each with its name for the twelve
tribes.
15 And they made on the breastpiece
chains like cords, of twisted cordage
work in pure gold.

13 [1]Lit., *east side, eastward*
14 [1]Lit., *shoulder* [2]Or, *bases*
15 [1]Lit., *second* [2]Lit., *shoulder* [3]Lit., *On this side and on that side* [4]Or, *bases*
17 [1]Or, *bases* [2]Or, *copper* [3]Or, *fillets, rings*
18 [1]Lit., *variegator;* i.e., a weaver in colors [2]Or, *violet* [3]Lit., *height in width*
19 [1]Or, *bases* [2]Or, *fillets, rings*
20 [1]Lit., *dwelling place*
21 [1]Lit., *These are the appointed things of the tabernacle* [2]Lit., *dwelling place* [3]Lit., *appointed* [4]Lit., *mouth*
22 [a]Ex. 31:2
23 [1]Lit., *variegator;* i.e., a weaver in colors [2]Or, *violet* [a]Ex. 31:6
24 [a]Ex. 30:13; Lev. 27:25; Num. 3:47; 18:16
25 [1]Lit., *mustered* [a]Ex. 30:11-16
26 [1]Lit., *mustered* [a]Ex. 30:13, 15 [b]Ex. 12:37; Num. 1:46; 26:51
27 [1]Or, *bases*
28 [1]Or, *fillets, rings*
30 [1]Or, *bases*
31 [1]Or, *bases* [2]Lit., *dwelling place*

1 [1]Or, *violet* [2]Lit., *and they made* [a]Ex. 35:23 [b]Ex. 31:10; 35:19
2 [1]Or, *violet* [a]Ex. 28:6-12
3 [1]Lit., *to work* [2]Or, *violet*
4 [1]Lit., *it*
5 [1]Lit., *from it* [2]Or, *violet*
6 [a]Ex. 28:9-11
7 [a]Ex. 28:12
8 [1]Or, *violet* [a]Ex. 28:15-28
9 [1]Lit., *its length* [2]Lit., *its width*
10 [1]Lit., *filled*
13 [1]Lit., *filled*

16 And they made two gold filigree *settings* and two gold rings, and put the two rings on the two ends of the breastpiece.

17 Then they put the two gold cords in the two rings at the ends of the breastpiece.

18 And they put the *other* two ends of the two cords on the two filigree *settings,* and put them on the shoulder pieces of the ephod at the front of it.

19 And they made two gold rings and placed *them* on the two ends of the breastpiece, on its inner edge which was next to the ephod.

20 Furthermore, they made two gold rings and placed them on the bottom of the two shoulder pieces of the ephod, on the front of it, close to the place where it joined, above the woven band of the ephod.

21 And they bound the breastpiece by its rings to the rings of the ephod with a [1]blue cord, that it might be on the woven band of the ephod, and that the breastpiece might not come loose from the ephod, just as the LORD had commanded Moses.

22 [a]Then he made the robe of the ephod of woven work, all of [1]blue;

23 [a]and the opening of the robe was *at the top* in the center, as the opening of a coat of mail, with a binding all around its opening, that it might not be torn.

24 And they made pomegranates of [1]blue and purple and scarlet *material and* twisted *linen* on the hem of the robe.

25 They also made bells of pure gold, and put the bells between the pomegranates all around on the hem of the [1]robe,

26 [1]alternating a bell and a pomegranate all around on the hem of the robe, for the service, just as the LORD had commanded Moses.

27 [a]And they made the tunics of finely woven linen for Aaron and his sons,

28 and the turban of fine linen, and the decorated [1]caps of fine linen, and the linen breeches of fine twisted linen,

29 and the sash of fine twisted linen, and [1]blue and purple and scarlet *material,* the work of the [2]weaver, just as the LORD had commanded Moses.

30 [a]And they made the plate of the holy crown of pure gold, and [1]inscribed it like the engravings of a signet, "Holy to the LORD."

31 And they [1]fastened a [2]blue cord to it, to [1]fasten it on the turban above, just as the LORD had commanded Moses.

32 Thus all the work of the [1]tabernacle of the tent of meeting was completed; and the sons of Israel did according to all that the LORD had commanded Moses; so they did.

33 And they brought the tabernacle to Moses, the tent and all its [1]furnishings: its clasps, its boards, its bars, and its pillars and its [2]sockets;

34 and the covering of rams' skins [1]dyed red, and the covering of porpoise skins, and the screening veil;

35 the ark of the testimony and its poles and the [1]mercy seat;

36 the table, all its utensils, and the bread of the [1]Presence;

37 the pure *gold* lampstand, [1]with its arrangement of lamps and all its utensils, and the oil for the light;

38 and the gold altar, and the anointing oil and the fragrant incense, and the veil for the doorway of the tent;

39 the [1]bronze altar and its [1]bronze grating, its poles and all its utensils, the laver and its stand;

40 the hangings for the court, its pillars and its [1]sockets, and the screen for the gate of the court, its cords and its pegs and all the [2]equipment for the service of the tabernacle, for the tent of meeting;

41 the woven garments for ministering in the holy place and the holy garments for Aaron the priest and the garments of his sons, to minister as priests.

42 So the sons of Israel did all the work according to all that the LORD had commanded Moses.

43 And Moses [1]examined all the work and behold, they had done it; just as the LORD had commanded, this they had done. So Moses [a]blessed them.

The Tabernacle Erected

40 THEN the LORD spoke to Moses, saying,

2 "[a]On the first day of the first month you shall set up the [1]tabernacle of the tent of meeting.

3 "And [a]you shall place the ark of the testimony there, and you shall screen the ark with the veil.

4 "And you shall [a]bring in the table and [1b]arrange what belongs on it; and you shall [c]bring in the lampstand and [2]mount its lamps.

5 "Moreover, you shall [a]set the gold altar of incense before the ark of the testimony, and set up the veil for the doorway to the tabernacle.

6 "And you shall set the altar of burnt offering in front of the doorway of the tabernacle of the tent of meeting.

7 "And you shall [a]set the laver between the tent of meeting and the altar, and put water [1]in it.

8 "And you shall set up the court all around and [1]hang up the veil for the gateway of the court.

9 "Then you shall take the anointing oil and [a]anoint the tabernacle and all that is in it, and shall consecrate it and all its [1]furnishings; and it shall be holy.

10 "And you shall anoint the altar of burnt offering and all its utensils, and consecrate the altar; and [a]the altar shall be most holy.

11 "And you shall anoint the laver and its stand, and consecrate it.

12 "Then you shall [a]bring Aaron and his sons to the doorway of the tent of meeting and wash them with water.

13 "And [a]you shall put the holy garments on Aaron and anoint him and

---

21 [1]Or, *violet*

22 [1]Or, *violet* [a]Ex. 28:31, 34

23 [a]Ex. 28:32

24 [1]Or, *violet*

25 [1]Lit., *robe, between the pomegranates*

26 [1]Lit., *a bell and a pomegranate, a bell . . .*

27 [a]Ex. 28:39, 40, 42

28 [1]Lit., *headgear*

29 [1]Or, *violet* [2]Lit., *variegator;* i.e., a weaver in colors

30 [1]Lit., *wrote on it a writing* [a]Ex. 28:36, 37

31 [1]Lit., *put* [2]Or, *violet*

32 [1]Lit., *dwelling place*

33 [1]Or, *utensils* [2]Or, *bases*

34 [1]Or, *tanned*

35 [1]Lit., *propitiatory*

36 [1]Lit., *Face*

37 [1]Lit., *its lamps, the lamps set in order*

39 [1]Or, *copper*

40 [1]Or, *bases* [2]Or, *utensils*

43 [1]Lit., *saw* [a]Lev. 9:22, 23; Num. 6:23-26

2 [1]Lit., *dwelling place* [a]Ex. 19:1; 40:17; Num. 1:1

3 [a]Ex. 26:33; 40:21; Num. 4:5

4 [1]Lit., *arrange its arrangement* [2]Or, *light* [a]Ex. 26:35; 40:22 [b]Ex. 25:30; 40:23 [c]Ex. 40:24f.

5 [a]Ex. 40:26

7 [1]Lit., *there* [a]Ex. 30:18; 40:30

8 [1]Lit., *put the screen*

9 [1]Or, *utensils* [a]Ex. 30:26; Lev. 8:10

10 [a]Ex. 29:37

12 [a]Lev. 8:1-6

13 [a]Ex. 28:41; Lev. 8:13

consecrate him, that he may minister as a priest to Me.

14 "And you shall bring his sons and put tunics on them;

15 and you shall anoint them even as you have anointed their father, that they may minister as priests to Me; and their anointing shall [1]qualify them for a [a]perpetual priesthood throughout their generations."

16 Thus Moses did; according to all that the LORD had commanded him, so he did.

17 Now it came about [a]in the first month [1]of the second year, on the first day of the month, that the [2]tabernacle was erected.

18 And Moses erected the tabernacle and [1]laid its [2]sockets, and set up its boards, and [1]inserted its bars and erected its pillars.

19 And he spread the tent over the tabernacle and put the covering of the tent [1]on top of it, just as the LORD had commanded Moses.

20 Then he took [a]the testimony and put *it* into the ark, and [1]attached the poles to the ark, and put the [2]mercy seat [3]on top of the ark.

21 And he brought the ark into the tabernacle, and [a]set up a veil for the screen, and screened off the ark of the testimony, just as the LORD had commanded Moses.

22 Then he [a]put the table in the tent of meeting, on the north side of the tabernacle, outside the veil.

23 And he set the arrangement of [a]bread in order on it before the LORD, just as the LORD had commanded Moses.

24 Then he placed the lampstand in the tent of meeting, opposite the table, on the south side of the tabernacle.

25 And he [a]lighted the lamps before the LORD, just as the LORD had commanded Moses.

26 Then he [a]placed the gold altar in the tent of meeting in front of the veil;

27 and he [a]burned fragrant incense on it, just as the LORD had commanded Moses.

28 Then he set up the [1]veil for the doorway of the tabernacle.

29 And he [a]set the altar of burnt offering *before* the doorway of the tabernacle of the tent of meeting, and [b]offered on it the burnt offering and the meal offering, just as the LORD had commanded Moses.

30 And he placed the laver between the tent of meeting and the altar, and put water in it for washing.

31 [a]And from it Moses and Aaron and his sons washed their hands and their feet.

32 When they entered the tent of meeting, and when they approached the altar, they washed, just as the LORD had commanded Moses.

33 And he [a]erected the court all around the [1]tabernacle and the altar, and [2]hung up the veil for the gateway of the court. Thus Moses finished the work.

The Glory of the LORD

34 [a]Then the cloud covered the tent of meeting, and the [b]glory of the LORD filled the tabernacle.

35 And Moses [a]was not able to enter the tent of meeting because the cloud had settled on it, and the glory of the LORD filled the tabernacle.

36 And throughout all their journeys [a]whenever the cloud was taken up from over the tabernacle, the sons of Israel would set out;

37 but [a]if the cloud was not taken up, then they did not set out until the day when it was taken up.

38 For throughout all their journeys, [a]the cloud of the LORD was on the tabernacle by day, and there was fire in it by night, in the sight of all the house of Israel.

15 [1]Lit., *be for them* [a]Ex. 29:9; Num. 25:13

17 [1]Lit., *in* [2]Lit., *dwelling place* [a]Ex. 40:2

18 [1]Lit., *put* [2]Or, *bases*

19 [1]Lit., *over it above*

20 [1]Lit., *set* [2]Lit., *propitiatory* [3]Lit., *over the ark above* [a]Ex. 25:16; Deut. 10:5; 1 Kin. 8:9; 2 Chr. 5:10; Heb. 9:4

21 [a]Ex. 26:33

22 [a]Ex. 26:35

23 [a]Ex. 25:30; Lev. 24:5, 6

25 [a]Ex. 25:37; 40:4

26 [a]Ex. 30:6; 40:5

27 [a]Ex. 30:7

28 [1]Or, *screen*

29 [a]Ex. 40:6 [b]Ex. 29:38-42

31 [a]Ex. 30:19, 20

33 [1]Or, *dwelling place* [2]Lit., *put the screen* [a]Ex. 27:9-18; 40:8

34 [a]Num. 9:15-23 [b]1 Kin. 8:11; Ezek. 43:4f.; Rev. 15:8

35 [a]1 Kin. 8:11; 2 Chr. 5:13, 14

36 [a]Num. 9:17; Neh. 9:19

37 [a]Num. 9:19-22

38 [a]Ex. 13:21; Num. 9:12, 15; Ps. 78:14; Is. 4:5

LEVITICUS

The Law of Burnt Offerings

1 THEN [a]the LORD called to Moses
and spoke to him from the tent of
meeting, saying,
2 "Speak to the sons of Israel and say
to them, 'When any man of you brings
an [1a]offering to the LORD, you shall
bring your [1]offering of animals from
[b]the herd or the flock.
3 'If his offering is a [a]burnt offering
from the herd, he shall offer it, a male
[b]without defect; he shall offer it [c]at the
doorway of the tent of meeting, that he
may be accepted before the LORD.
4 '[a]And he shall lay his hand on the
head of the burnt offering, that it may be
accepted for him to make [b]atonement on
his behalf.
5 'And [a]he shall slay the [1]young bull
before the LORD; and Aaron's sons, the
priests, shall offer up [b]the blood and
[c]sprinkle the blood around on the altar
that is at the doorway of the tent of
meeting.
6 '[a]He shall then skin the burnt offering and cut it into its pieces.
7 '[a]And the sons of Aaron the priest
shall put fire on the altar and arrange
wood on the fire.
8 'Then Aaron's sons, the priests,
shall arrange the pieces, the head, and
the [a]suet over the wood which is on the
fire that is on the altar.
9 'Its [a]entrails, however, and its legs
he shall wash with water. And [b]the priest
shall offer up in smoke all of it on the
altar for a burnt offering, an offering by
fire of [c]a soothing aroma to the LORD.
10 'But if his offering is from the flock,
of the sheep or of the goats, for a burnt
offering, he shall offer it a [a]male without
defect.
11 'And [a]he shall slay it on the side of
the altar northward before the LORD,
and Aaron's sons, the priests, shall
sprinkle its blood around on the altar.
12 'He shall then cut it into its pieces
with its head and its [a]suet, and the priest
shall arrange them on the wood which is
on the fire that is on the altar.
13 'The entrails, however, and the legs
he shall wash with water. And [a]the priest
shall offer all of it, and offer it up in
smoke on the altar; it is a burnt offering,
an offering by fire of a soothing aroma to
the LORD.
14 'But if his offering to the LORD is a
burnt offering of birds, then he shall
bring his offering from the [a]turtledoves
or from young pigeons.
15 'And the priest shall bring it to the
altar and wring off its head, and offer it
up in smoke on the altar; and its blood is
to be drained out [a]on the side of the
altar.
16 'He shall also take away its crop
with its feathers, and cast it beside the
altar eastward, to the place of the
[1a]ashes.
17 'Then he shall tear it by its wings,
but [a]shall not sever *it*. And the priest
shall offer it up in smoke on the altar on
the wood which is on the fire; [b]it is a
burnt offering, an offering by fire of a
soothing aroma to the LORD.

The Law of Grain Offerings

2 'NOW when anyone presents a
[a]grain offering as an offering to the
LORD, his offering shall be of fine flour,
and he shall pour oil on it and put
frankincense on it.
2 'He shall then bring it to Aaron's
sons, the priests; and shall take from it
[a]his handful of its fine flour and of its oil
with all of its frankincense. And the
priest shall offer *it* up in smoke *as* its
[b]memorial portion on the altar, an offering by fire of a soothing aroma to the
LORD.
3 'And [a]the remainder of the grain
offering belongs to [b]Aaron and his sons:
a thing most holy, of the offerings to the
LORD by fire.
4 'Now when you bring an offering of
a grain offering baked in an oven, *it shall
be* [a]unleavened cakes of fine flour mixed
with oil, or unleavened wafers [1]spread
with oil.
5 'And if your offering is a grain
offering *made* [a]on the griddle, *it shall be*
of fine flour, unleavened, mixed with oil;
6 you shall break it into bits, and
pour oil on it; it is a grain offering.
7 'Now if your offering is a grain
offering *made* [a]in a [1]pan, it shall be
made of fine flour with oil.
8 'When you bring in the grain offering which is made of these things to the
LORD, it shall be presented to the priest
and he shall bring it to the altar.
9 'The priest then shall take up from
the grain offering [a]its memorial portion,
and shall offer *it* up in smoke on the
altar *as* an offering by fire of a soothing
aroma to the LORD.
10 'And [a]the remainder of the grain
offering belongs to Aaron and his sons:
a thing most holy, of the offerings to the
LORD by fire.
11 '[a]No grain offering, which you bring
to the LORD, shall be made with leaven,
for you shall not offer [1]up in smoke any
leaven or any honey as an [b]offering by
fire to the LORD.
12 '[a]As an offering of first fruits, you
shall bring them to the LORD, but they
shall not ascend for a soothing aroma on
the altar.
13 'Every grain offering of yours,
moreover, you shall season with salt, so
that [a]the salt of the covenant of your
God shall not be lacking from your grain
offering; with all your offerings you shall
offer salt.
14 'Also if you bring a grain offering of
early ripened things to the LORD, you
shall bring [a]fresh heads of grain roasted
in the fire, grits of new growth, for the
grain offering of your early ripened
things.
15 'You shall then put oil on it and lay
incense on it; it is a grain offering.

1 [a]Ex. 19:3; 25:22; Num. 7:89
2 [1]Heb., *qorban* [a]Mark 7:11 [b]Lev. 22:18f.
3 [a]Lev. 6:8-13 [b]Ex. 12:5; Lev. 22:20-24; Deut. 15:21; 17:1 [c]Lev. 17:8, 9; Deut. 12:5, 6, 11
4 [a]Ex. 29:10, 15, 19; Lev. 3:2, 8 [b]Ex. 29:33; Lev. 4:20, 26, 31; 2 Chr. 29:23, 24
5 [1]Or, *one of the herd;* lit., *son of the herd* [a]Ex. 29:11, 16, 20 [b]Lev. 17:11 [c]Lev. 1:11; 3:2, 8, 13; Heb. 12:24; 1 Pet. 1:2
6 [a]Lev. 7:8
7 [a]Lev. 6:8-13
8 [a]Lev. 1:12; 3:3, 4; 8:20
9 [a]Ex. 12:9 [b]Num. 15:8-10; 28:11-14 [c]Gen. 8:21; Ex. 29:18, 25; Lev. 1:13; Num. 15:3; Eph. 5:2
10 [a]Ex. 12:5; Lev. 1:3; Ezek. 43:22; 1 Pet. 1:19
11 [a]Ex. 24:6; Lev. 1:5; 8:19; 9:12
12 [a]Lev. 3:3, 4
13 [a]Num. 15:4-7; 28:11-14
14 [a]Gen. 15:9; Lev. 5:7, 11; 12:8; Luke 2:24
15 [a]Lev. 5:9
16 [1]Or, *fat ashes* [a]Lev. 6:10
17 [a]Gen. 15:10; Lev. 5:8 [b]Lev. 9:13

1 [a]Lev. 6:14-18; Num. 15:4
2 [a]Lev. 5:12; 6:15 [b]Lev. 2:9, 16; 5:12; 24:7; Acts 10:4
3 [a]Lev. 2:10; 6:16 [b]Lev. 10:12, 13
4 [1]Lit., *anointed* [a]Ex. 29:2
5 [a]Lev. 6:21; 7:9
7 [1]Lit., *lidded cooking pan* [a]Lev. 7:9
9 [a]Lev. 2:2, 16; 5:12
10 [a]Lev. 2:3; 6:16
11 [1]Lit., *up from it* [a]Ex. 23:18; 34:25; Lev. 6:16, 17 [b]Ex. 29:25; Lev. 1:13
12 [a]Ex. 34:22; Lev. 7:13; 23:10, 17, 18
13 [a]Num. 18:19; 2 Chr. 13:5; Ezek. 43:24
14 [a]Lev. 23:14

16 'And the priest shall offer up in smoke [a]its memorial portion, part of its grits and its oil with all its incense as an offering by fire to the LORD.

The Law of Peace Offerings

3 'NOW if his offering is a [a]sacrifice of peace offerings, if he is going to offer out of the herd, whether male or female, he shall offer it [b]without defect before the LORD.

2 '[a]And he shall lay his hand on the head of his offering and [b]slay it at the doorway of the tent of meeting, and Aaron's sons, the priests, shall sprinkle the blood around on the altar.

3 'And from the sacrifice of the peace offerings, he shall present an offering by fire to the LORD, the fat that covers the entrails and all the fat that is on the entrails,

4 and the two kidneys with the fat that is on them, which is on the loins, and the [1]lobe of the liver, which he shall remove with the kidneys.

5 'Then [a]Aaron's sons shall offer *it* up in smoke on the altar [b]on the burnt offering, which is on the wood that is on the fire; [c]it is an offering by fire of a soothing aroma to the LORD.

6 'But if his offering for a sacrifice of peace offerings to the LORD is from the flock, he shall offer it, male or female, [a]without defect.

7 'If he is going to offer [a]a lamb for his offering, then he shall offer it [b]before the LORD,

8 and [a]he shall lay his hand on the head of his offering, and [b]slay it before the tent of meeting; and Aaron's sons shall [c]sprinkle its blood around on the altar.

9 'And from the [a]sacrifice of peace offerings he shall bring as an offering by fire to the LORD, its fat, [1]the entire fat tail which he shall remove close to the backbone, and the fat that covers the entrails and all the fat that is on the entrails,

10 and the two kidneys with the fat that is on them, which is on the loins, and the [1]lobe of the liver, which he shall remove [a]with the kidneys.

11 'Then the priest shall offer *it* up in smoke [a]on the altar, *as* [b]food, an offering by fire to the LORD.

12 'Moreover, if his offering is [a]a goat, then he shall offer it before the LORD,

13 and he shall lay his hand on its head and slay it before the tent of meeting; and the sons of Aaron shall sprinkle its blood around on the altar.

14 'And from it he shall present his offering as an offering by fire to the LORD, the fat that covers the entrails and all the fat that is on the entrails,

15 and the two kidneys with the fat that is on them, which is on the loins, and the [1]lobe of the liver, which he shall remove [a]with the kidneys.

16 'And the priest shall offer them up in smoke on the altar *as* food, an offering by fire for a soothing aroma; [a]all fat is the LORD's.

17 'It is a [a]perpetual statute throughout your generations in all your dwellings: you shall not eat any fat [b]or any blood.' "

The Law of Sin Offerings

4 THEN the LORD spoke to Moses, saying,

2 "Speak to the sons of Israel, saying, 'If a person sins [a]unintentionally in any of the [1]things which the LORD has [b]commanded not to be done, and commits any of them,

3 [a]if the anointed priest sins so as to bring guilt on the people, then let him offer to the LORD a [1]bull without defect as a sin offering for the sin he has [2]committed.

4 'And he shall bring the bull to the doorway of the tent of meeting before the LORD, and [a]he shall lay his hand on the head of the bull, and slay the bull before the LORD.

5 'Then the [a]anointed priest is to take some of the blood of the bull and bring it to the tent of meeting,

6 and the priest shall dip his finger in the blood, and sprinkle some of the blood seven times before the LORD, in front of [a]the veil of the sanctuary.

7 'The priest shall also put some of the blood on the horns of [a]the altar of fragrant incense which is before the LORD in the tent of meeting; and all the blood of the bull he shall pour out at the base of the altar of burnt offering which is at the doorway of the tent of meeting.

8 '[a]And he shall remove from it all the fat of the bull of the sin offering: the fat that covers the entrails, and all the fat which is on the entrails,

9 and the two kidneys with the fat that is on them, which is on the loins, and the [1]lobe of the liver, which he shall remove [a]with the kidneys

10 (just as it is removed from the ox of the sacrifice of peace offerings), and the priest is to offer them up in smoke on the altar of burnt offering.

11 'But [a]the hide of the bull and all its flesh with its head and its legs and its entrails and its refuse,

12 [1]that is, all *the rest of* the bull, he is to bring out to [a]a clean place outside the camp where the [2]ashes are poured out, and burn it on wood with fire; where the [2]ashes are poured out it shall be burned.

13 '[a]Now if the whole congregation of Israel commits error, and the matter [1]escapes the notice of the assembly, and they commit any of the [2]things which the LORD has commanded not to be done, and they become guilty;

14 [a]when the sin [1]which they have [2]committed becomes known, then the assembly shall offer [b]a [3]bull of the herd for a sin offering, and bring it before the tent of meeting.

16 [a]Lev. 2:2

1 [a]Lev. 7:11-34; 17:5 [b]Lev. 1:3; 22:20-24

2 [a]Lev. 1:4 [b]Ex. 29:11, 16, 20

4 [1]Or, *appendage on*

5 [a]Lev. 7:28-34 [b]Ex. 29:38-42; Num. 28:3-10 [c]Num. 15:8-10; 28:12-14

6 [a]Lev. 3:1; 22:20-24

7 [a]Num. 15:4, 5; 28:4-8 [b]Lev. 17:8, 9; 1 Kin. 8:62

8 [a]Lev. 1:4 [b]Lev. 3:2 [c]Lev. 1:5

9 [1]Lit., *the fat tail, entire* [a]Lev. 17:5; Num. 7:88; 1 Sam. 10:8; 2 Sam. 6:17; 1 Kin. 3:15; 8:63, 64; 1 Chr. 16:1

10 [1]Or, *appendage on* [a]Lev. 3:4, 15

11 [a]Lev. 3:5 [b]Lev. 3:16; 21:6, 8, 17, 22

12 [a]Num. 15:6-11

15 [1]Or, *appendage on* [a]Lev. 3:4; 7:4

16 [a]Lev. 7:23-25

17 [a]Lev. 6:18, 22; 7:34, 36; 10:9, 15; 16:29; 17:7; 23:14, 21; 24:3 [b]Lev. 7:26; 17:10-16

2 [1]Lit., *commands of the LORD which are not to be done* [a]Lev. 4:22, 27; 5:15-18; 22:14 [b]Lev. 4:13

3 [1]Or, *bull of the herd* [2]Lit., *sinned* [a]Lev. 4:14, 23, 28

4 [a]Lev. 1:4; 4:15; Num. 8:12

5 [a]Lev. 4:3, 17

6 [a]Ex. 40:21, 26

7 [a]Lev. 4:18, 25, 30, 34; 8:15; 9:9; 16:18

8 [a]Lev. 3:3, 4

9 [1]Or, *appendage on* [a]Lev. 3:4

11 [a]Lev. 9:11; Num. 19:5

12 [1]Lit., *and* [2]Or, *fat ashes are* [a]Lev. 4:21; 6:10, 11; 16:27

13 [1]Lit., *is hidden from the eyes of* [2]Lit., *commands of the LORD which are not to be done* [a]Num. 15:24-26

14 [1]Lit., *concerning which* [2]Lit., *sinned* [3]Lit., *son of the herd* [a]Lev. 4:3 [b]Lev. 4:3, 23, 28

15 'Then [a]the elders of the congregation shall lay their hands on the head of the bull before the LORD, and the bull shall be slain [b]before the LORD.

16 'Then the anointed priest is to bring some of the blood of the bull to the tent of meeting;

17 and [a]the priest shall dip his finger in the blood, and sprinkle *it* seven times before the LORD, in front of the veil.

18 'And he shall put some of the blood on the horns of [a]the altar which is before the LORD [1]in the tent of meeting; and all the blood he shall pour out at the base of the altar of burnt offering which is at the doorway of the tent of meeting.

19 '[a]And he shall remove all its fat from it and offer it up in smoke on the altar.

20 'He shall also do with the bull just as he did with [a]the bull of the sin offering; thus he shall do with it. So [b]the priest shall make atonement for them, and they shall be forgiven.

21 'Then he is to bring out the bull to *a place* outside the camp, and burn it as he burned the first bull; it is [a]the sin offering for the assembly.

22 'When [a]a leader [b]sins and unintentionally does any one of all the [1]things which the LORD God has commanded not to be done, and he becomes guilty,

23 [1a]if his sin [2]which he has committed is made known to him, he shall bring for his offering a [3b]goat, [c]a male without defect.

24 'And he shall lay his hand on the head of the male goat, and slay it in the place where [1]they slay the burnt offering before the LORD; it is a sin offering.

25 'Then the priest is to take some of the blood of the sin offering with his finger, and put it on [a]the horns of the altar of burnt offering; and *the rest of* its blood he shall pour out at the base of the altar of burnt offering.

26 '[a]And all its fat he shall offer up in smoke on the altar as *in the case of* the fat of the sacrifice of peace offerings. Thus [b]the priest shall make atonement for him in regard to his sin, and he shall be forgiven.

27 'Now if [1]anyone of [2]the common people sins [a]unintentionally in doing any of the [3]things which the LORD has commanded not to be done, and becomes guilty,

28 [1a]if his sin, which he has [2]committed is made known to him, then he shall bring for his offering a [3b]goat, a [c]female without defect, for his sin which he has [2]committed.

29 'And [a]he shall lay his hand on the head of the sin offering, and [b]slay the sin offering at the place of the burnt offering.

30 'And the priest shall take some of its blood with his finger and put it on the horns of [a]the altar of burnt offering; and [b]all *the rest of* its blood he shall pour out at the base of the altar.

31 '[a]Then he shall remove all its fat, just as the fat was removed from the sacrifice of peace offerings; and the priest shall offer it up in smoke on the altar for [b]a soothing aroma to the LORD. Thus the priest shall make atonement for him, [1]and he shall be forgiven.

15 [a]Lev. 8:14, 18, 22; Num. 8:10, 12 [b]Lev. 1:3
17 [a]Lev. 4:6
18 [1]Lit., *which is in* [a]Lev. 4:7, 25, 30, 34
19 [a]Lev. 4:8
20 [a]Lev. 4:8, 21 [b]Num. 15:25, 28
21 [a]Lev. 4:13f.; 16:15-17; Num. 15:24-26
22 [1]Lit., *commands of the LORD which are not to be done* [a]Num. 31:13; 32:2 [b]Lev. 4:2, 27
23 [1]Lit., *or* [2]Lit., *in which he has sinned* [3]Lit., *buck of the goats* [a]Lev. 4:3 [b]Lev. 4:3, 14, 28 [c]Lev. 4:28
24 [1]Lit., *one slays*
25 [a]Lev. 4:7, 18, 30, 34
26 [a]Lev. 4:19 [b]Lev. 4:20, 31; 5:10, 13, 16, 18; 6:7
27 [1]Lit., *one soul* [2]Lit., *the people of the land* [3]Lit., *commands of the LORD which are not to be done* [a]Lev. 4:2; Num. 15:27
28 [1]Lit., *or* [2]Lit., *sinned* [3]Or, *female goat* [a]Lev. 4:3 [b]Lev. 4:3, 14, 23, 32 [c]Lev. 4:23
29 [a]Lev. 1:4; 4:4, 24 [b]Lev. 1:5, 11
30 [a]Lev. 4:7, 18, 25, 34 [b]Lev. 4:7
31 [1]Or, *so that he may be* [a]Lev. 4:8 [b]Gen. 8:21; Ex. 29:18; Lev. 1:9, 13; 2:2, 9, 12
32 [a]Lev. 4:28
33 [1]Lit., *one slays* [a]Lev. 1:4, 5 [b]Lev. 4:29
34 [a]Lev. 4:7, 18, 25, 30 [b]Lev. 4:7
35 [1]Lit., *sinned* [a]Lev. 4:26, 31 [b]Lev. 4:20

1 [1]Lit., *voice of an oath* [2]Or, *iniquity* [a]Prov. 29:24; Jer. 23:10
2 [a]Lev. 11:8, 11, 24-40; Num. 19:11-16; Deut. 14:8
4 [a]Num. 30:6, 8; Ps. 106:33
5 [a]Lev. 16:21; 26:40; Num. 5:7; Prov. 28:13
6 [1]Lit., *sinned* [2]Lit., *female goat* [a]Lev. 4:28, 32
7 [1]Lit., *his hand does not reach enough for* [a]Lev. 12:6, 8; 14:22, 30, 31
8 [a]Lev. 1:17

32 'But if he brings [a]a lamb as his offering for a sin offering, he shall bring it, a female without defect.

33 'And [a]he shall lay his hand on the head of the sin offering, and slay it for a sin offering [b]in the place where [1]they slay the burnt offering.

34 'And the priest is to take some of the blood of the sin offering with his finger and put it on the horns of [a]the altar of burnt offering; and [b]all *the rest of* its blood he shall pour out at the base of the altar.

35 'Then he shall remove [a]all its fat, just as the fat of the lamb is removed from the sacrifice of the peace offerings, and the priest shall offer them up in smoke on the altar, on the offerings by fire to the LORD. Thus [b]the priest shall make atonement for him in regard to his sin which he has [1]committed, and he shall be forgiven.

The Law of Guilt Offerings

5 'NOW if a person sins, after he hears a [1]public [a]adjuration *to testify*, when he is a witness, whether he has seen or *otherwise* known, if he does not tell *it*, then he will bear his [2]guilt.

2 'Or if a person touches [a]any unclean thing, whether a carcass of an unclean beast, or the carcass of unclean cattle, or a carcass of unclean swarming things, though it is hidden from him, and he is unclean, then he will be guilty.

3 'Or if he touches human uncleanness, of whatever *sort* his uncleanness *may* be with which he becomes unclean, and it is hidden from him, and then he comes to know *it*, he will be guilty.

4 'Or if a person [a]swears thoughtlessly with his lips to do evil or to do good, in whatever matter a man may speak thoughtlessly with an oath, and it is hidden from him, and then he comes to know *it*, he will be guilty in one of these.

5 'So it shall be when he becomes guilty in one of these, that he shall [a]confess that in which he has sinned.

6 'He shall also bring his guilt offering to the LORD for his sin which he has [1]committed, [a]a female from the flock, a lamb or a [2]goat as a sin offering. So the priest shall make atonement on his behalf for his sin.

7 'But if [1]he cannot afford a lamb, then he shall bring to the LORD his guilt offering for that in which he has sinned, two turtledoves or two young pigeons, [a]one for a sin offering and the other for a burnt offering.

8 'And he shall bring them to the priest, who shall offer first that which is for the sin offering and shall nip its head at the front of its neck, but he [a]shall not sever *it*.

9 'He shall also sprinkle some of the blood of the sin offering [a]on the side of the altar, while the rest of the blood shall be drained out [b]at the base of the altar: it is a sin offering.

10 'The second he shall then prepare as a burnt offering [a]according to the ordinance. [b]So the priest shall make atonement on his behalf for his sin which he has [1]committed, and it shall be forgiven him.

11 'But [a]if his [1]means are insufficient for two turtledoves or two young pigeons, then for his offering for that which he has sinned, he shall bring the tenth of an [2]ephah of fine flour for a sin offering; [b]he shall not put oil on it or place incense on it, for it is a sin offering.

12 'And he shall bring it to the priest, and the priest shall take his handful of it as its memorial portion and offer *it* up in smoke on the altar, [1]with the offerings of the LORD by fire: it is a sin offering.

13 'So the priest shall make atonement for him concerning his sin which he has [1]committed from [a]one of these, and it shall be forgiven him; then [b]*the rest* shall become the priest's, like the grain offering.' "

14 Then the LORD spoke to Moses, saying,

15 "[a]If a person acts unfaithfully and sins [b]unintentionally against the LORD's holy things, then he shall bring his [c]guilt offering to the LORD: [d]a ram without defect from the flock, according to your valuation in silver by shekels, in *terms of* the [e]shekel of the sanctuary, for a guilt offering.

16 "[a]And he shall make restitution for that which he has sinned against the holy thing, and shall add to it a fifth part of it, and give it to the priest. [b]The priest shall then make atonement for him with the ram of the guilt offering, and it shall be forgiven him.

17 "Now if a person sins and does any of the things [1]which the LORD has commanded not to be done, [a]though he was unaware, still he is guilty, and shall bear his punishment.

18 "He is then to bring to the priest [a]a ram without defect from the flock, according to your valuation, for a guilt offering. So the priest shall make atonement for him concerning his error in which he sinned [b]unintentionally and did not know *it*, and it shall be forgiven him.

19 "It is a guilt offering; he was certainly guilty before the LORD."

Guilt Offering

6 [1]THEN the LORD spoke to Moses, saying,

2 "[a]When a person sins and acts unfaithfully against the LORD, and deceives his companion in regard to a deposit or a security entrusted *to him*, or through robbery, or *if* he has extorted from his companion,

9 [a]Lev. 1:15 [b]Lev. 4:7, 18
10 [1]Lit., *sinned* [a]Lev. 1:14-17 [b]Lev. 4:20, 26; 5:13, 16
11 [1]Lit., *hand does not reach* [2]I.e., Approx. one bu. [a]Lev. 14:21-32; 27:8 [b]Lev. 2:1, 2
12 [1]Lit., *upon*
13 [1]Lit., *sinned* [a]Lev. 5:4, 5 [b]Lev. 2:3
15 [a]Num. 5:5-8 [b]Lev. 4:2; 22:14 [c]Lev. 7:1-10 [d]Lev. 6:6 [e]Ex. 30:13
16 [a]Lev. 6:5; 22:14; Num. 5:7, 8 [b]Lev. 7:2-7
17 [1]Lit., *the commands of the LORD which are* [a]Lev. 4:2; 5:19
18 [a]Lev. 5:15 [b]Lev. 5:17
1 [1]Ch. 5:20 in Heb.
2 [a]Ex. 22:7-15
3 [a]Ex. 23:4; Deut. 22:1-4
4 [1]Or, *deposited with* [a]Lev. 24:18, 21
5 [1]Lit., *in its sum* [a]Lev. 5:16 [b]Num. 5:8
6 [a]Lev. 5:15
7 [a]Lev. 7:2-5
8 [1]Ch. 6:1 in Heb.
9 [a]Ex. 29:38-42; Num. 28:3-10 [b]Lev. 6:12, 13
10 [1]Or, *fat ashes* [2]Lit., *consumes* [a]Ex. 28:39, 42; 39:27, 28
11 [1]Or, *fat ashes*
12 [a]Lev. 3:5
15 [1]Lit., *and some of* [a]Lev. 2:2, 9
16 [a]Lev. 2:3; 10:12-14; Ezek. 44:29
17 [a]Lev. 2:11 [b]Ex. 40:10; Lev. 6:25, 26, 29, 30; Num. 18:9 [c]Lev. 7:7; 10:16-18

3 or [a]has found what was lost and lied about it and sworn falsely, so that he sins in regard to any one of the things a man may do;

4 then it shall be, when he sins and becomes guilty, that he shall [a]restore what he took by robbery, or what he got by extortion, or the deposit which was [1]entrusted to him, or the lost thing which he found,

5 or anything about which he swore falsely; [a]he shall make restitution for it [1]in full, and add to it one-fifth more. [b]He shall give it to the one to whom it belongs on the day *he presents* his guilt offering.

6 "Then he shall bring to the priest his guilt offering to the LORD, [a]a ram without defect from the flock, according to your valuation, for a guilt offering,

7 and [a]the priest shall make atonement for him before the LORD; and he shall be forgiven for any one of the things which he may have done to incur guilt."

The Priest's Part in the Offerings

8 [1]Then the LORD spoke to Moses, saying,

9 "Command Aaron and his sons, saying, 'This is [a]the law for the burnt offering: the burnt offering itself *shall remain* on the hearth on the altar all night until the morning, and [b]the fire on the altar is to be kept burning on it.

10 'And the priest is to put on [a]his linen robe, and he shall put on undergarments next to his flesh; and he shall take up the [1]ashes *to* which the fire [2]reduces the burnt offering on the altar, and place them beside the altar.

11 'Then he shall take off his garments and put on other garments, and carry the [1]ashes outside the camp to a clean place.

12 'And the fire on the altar shall be kept burning on it. It shall not go out, but the priest shall burn wood on it every morning; and he shall lay out the burnt offering on it, and offer up in smoke the fat portions of the peace offerings [a]on it.

13 'Fire shall be kept burning continually on the altar; it is not to go out.

14 'Now this is the law of the grain offering: the sons of Aaron shall present it before the LORD in front of the altar.

15 '[a]Then one *of them* shall lift up from it a handful of the fine flour of the grain offering, [1]with its oil and all the incense that is on the grain offering, and he shall offer *it* up in smoke on the altar, a soothing aroma, as its memorial offering to the LORD.

16 '[a]And what is left of it Aaron and his sons are to eat. It shall be eaten as unleavened cakes in a holy place; they are to eat it in the court of the tent of meeting.

17 '[a]It shall not be baked with leaven. I have given it as their share from My offerings by fire; [b]it is most holy, like the sin offering and [c]the guilt offering.

18 ‘[a]Every male among the sons of Aaron may eat it; it is a permanent ordinance throughout your generations, from the offerings by fire to the LORD. [b]Whoever touches them shall become consecrated.’ ”

19 Then the LORD spoke to Moses, saying,

20 “This is the offering which Aaron and his sons are to present to the LORD on the day when he is anointed; the tenth of an [a]ephah of fine flour as [b]a [1]regular grain offering, half of it in the morning and half of it in the evening.

21 “It shall be prepared with oil on a [a]griddle. When it is *well* stirred, you shall bring it. You shall present the grain offering in baked pieces as a soothing aroma to the LORD.

22 “And the anointed priest who will be in his place [1]among his sons shall [2]offer it. By a permanent ordinance it shall be entirely offered up in smoke to the LORD.

23 “So every grain offering of the priest shall be burned entirely. It shall not be eaten.”

24 Then the LORD spoke to Moses, saying,

25 “Speak to Aaron and to his sons, saying, ‘This is the law of the sin offering: [a]in the place where the burnt offering is slain the sin offering shall be slain before the LORD; it is most holy.

26 ‘[a]The priest who offers it for sin shall eat it. It shall be eaten in a holy place, in the court of the tent of meeting.

27 ‘[a]Anyone who touches its flesh shall become consecrated; and when any of its blood [1]splashes on a garment, in a holy place you shall wash what was splashed on.

28 ‘Also [a]the earthenware vessel in which it was boiled shall be broken; and if it was boiled in a bronze vessel, then it shall be scoured and rinsed in water.

29 ‘[a]Every male among the priests may eat of it; [b]it is most holy.

30 ‘But no sin offering [a]of which any of the blood is brought into the tent of meeting to make atonement [b]in the holy place shall be eaten; [c]it shall be burned with fire.

The Priest's Part in the Offerings

7 ‘NOW this is the law of the [a]guilt offering; it is most holy.

2 ‘In [a]the place where they slay the burnt offering they are to slay the guilt offering, and he shall sprinkle its blood around on the altar.

3 ‘Then he shall offer from it all its fat: the [a]fat tail and the fat that covers the entrails,

4 and the two kidneys with the fat that is on them, which is on the loins, and the lobe on the liver he shall remove [a]with the kidneys.

5 ‘And the priest shall offer them up in smoke on the altar as an offering by fire to the LORD; it is a guilt offering.

6 ‘[a]Every male among the priests may eat of it. It shall be eaten in a holy place; it is most holy.

7 ‘The guilt offering is like the [a]sin offering, there is one law for them; the [b]priest who makes atonement with it [1]shall have it.

8 ‘Also the priest who presents any man's burnt offering, [1]that priest shall have for himself the skin of the burnt offering which he has presented.

9 ‘Likewise, every grain offering that is baked in the oven, and everything prepared in a [1]pan or on a [a]griddle, [2]shall belong to the priest who presents it.

10 ‘And every grain offering mixed with oil, or dry, shall [1]belong to all the sons of Aaron, [2]to all alike.

11 ‘Now this is the law of the [a]sacrifice of peace offerings which shall be presented to the LORD.

12 ‘If he offers it by way of [a]thanksgiving, then along with the sacrifice of thanksgiving he shall offer [b]unleavened cakes mixed with oil, and unleavened wafers [1]spread with oil, and cakes *of well* stirred fine flour mixed with oil.

13 ‘With the sacrifice of his peace offerings for thanksgiving, he shall present his offering with cakes of [a]leavened bread.

14 ‘And of [1]this he shall present one of every offering as a [2]contribution to the LORD; [a]it shall [3]belong to the priest who sprinkles the blood of the peace offerings.

15 ‘[a]Now *as for* the flesh of the sacrifice of his thanksgiving peace offerings, it shall be eaten on the day of his offering; he shall not leave any of it over until morning.

16 ‘But if the sacrifice of his offering is a [a]votive or a freewill offering, it shall be eaten on the day that he offers his sacrifice; and on the [1]next day what is left of it may be eaten;

17 [a]but what is left over from the flesh of the sacrifice on the third day shall be burned with fire.

18 ‘So if any of the flesh of the sacrifice of his peace offerings should *ever* be eaten on the third day, he who offers it shall not be accepted, *and* it shall not be reckoned to his *benefit.* It shall be an [a]offensive thing, and the person who eats of it shall bear his *own* iniquity.

19 ‘Also the flesh that touches anything unclean shall not be eaten; it shall be burned with fire. [1]As for *other* flesh, anyone who is clean may eat *such* flesh.

20 ‘[a]But the person who eats the flesh of the sacrifice of peace offerings which belong to the LORD, [1]in his uncleanness, that person [b]shall be cut off from his people.

21 ‘[a]And when anyone touches anything unclean, whether human uncleanness, or an unclean animal, or any unclean [1]detestable thing, and eats of the flesh of the sacrifice of peace offerings which belong to the LORD, that

---

6:18 [a]Lev. 6:29; 7:6; Num. 18:10; 1 Cor. 9:13 [b]Lev. 6:27
6:20 [1]Lit., *grain offering continually* [a]Lev. 5:11 [b]Num. 4:16
6:21 [a]Lev. 2:5
6:22 [1]Lit., *from among* [2]Lit., *do*
6:25 [a]Lev. 1:11
6:26 [a]Lev. 6:29
6:27 [1]Lit., *one sprinkles* [a]Lev. 7:19
6:28 [a]Lev. 11:33; 15:12
6:29 [a]Lev. 6:18 [b]Lev. 6:17, 25
6:30 [a]Lev. 4:1-21 [b]Lev. 4:7, 18 [c]Lev. 4:11, 12, 21
7:1 [a]Lev. 5:14-6:7
7:2 [a]Lev. 1:11
7:3 [a]Lev. 3:9
7:4 [a]Lev. 3:4
7:6 [a]Lev. 6:18, 29; Num. 18:9
7:7 [1]Lit., *it shall be for him* [a]Lev. 6:25, 26, 30 [b]1 Cor. 9:13; 10:18
7:8 [1]Lit., *for the priest, it shall be for him*
7:9 [1]Lit., *lidded cooking pan* [2]Lit., *for the priest, it shall be for him* [a]Lev. 2:5
7:10 [1]Lit., *be* [2]Lit., *a man as his brother*
7:11 [a]Lev. 3:1
7:12 [1]Or, *anointed* [a]Lev. 7:15 [b]Lev. 2:4; Num. 6:15
7:13 [a]Lev. 2:12; 23:17, 18; Amos 4:5
7:14 [1]Lit., *it* [2]Or, *heave offering* [3]Lit., *be for* [a]Num. 18:8, 11, 19
7:15 [a]Lev. 22:29, 30
7:16 [1]Lit., *morrow and what* [a]Lev. 19:5-8
7:17 [a]Ex. 12:10
7:18 [a]Lev. 19:7; Prov. 15:8
7:19 [1]Lit., *And the flesh*
7:20 [1]Lit., *and his uncleanness is on him* [a]Lev. 22:3-7; Num. 19:13 [b]Lev. 7:25
7:21 [1]Some mss. read *swarming thing* [a]Lev. 5:2, 3

person shall be cut off from his people.' "
22 Then the LORD spoke to Moses,
saying,
23 "Speak to the sons of Israel, saying,
'You shall not eat [a]any fat *from* an ox, a
sheep, or a goat.
24 'Also the fat of *an animal* which
dies, and the fat of an animal [a]torn *by*
beasts, may be put to any other use, but
you must certainly not eat it.
25 'For whoever eats the fat of the
animal from which [1]an offering by fire is
offered to the LORD, even the person
who eats shall be cut off from his people.
26 '[a]And you are not to eat any blood,
either of bird or animal, in any of your
dwellings.
27 'Any person who eats any blood,
even that person shall be cut off from his
people.' "
28 Then the LORD spoke to Moses,
saying,
29 "Speak to the sons of Israel, saying,
'He who offers [a]the sacrifice of his peace
offerings to the LORD shall bring his
offering to the LORD from the sacrifice of
his peace offerings.
30 'His own hands are to bring offerings by fire to the LORD. He shall bring
the fat with the breast, that the [a]breast
may be [1]presented as a wave offering
before the LORD.
31 'And the priest shall offer up the fat
in smoke on the altar; but [a]the breast
shall belong to Aaron and his sons.
32 'And you shall give [a]the right thigh
to the priest as a [1]contribution from the
sacrifices of your peace offerings.
33 'The one among the sons of Aaron
who offers the blood of the peace offerings and the fat, the right thigh shall be
his as *his* portion.
34 'For I have taken [a]the breast of the
wave offering and the thigh of the [1]con-
tribution from the sons of Israel from
the sacrifices of their peace offerings,
and have given them to Aaron the priest
and to his sons as *their* due forever from
the sons of Israel.
35 'This is [1]that which is consecrated
to Aaron and [1]that [a]which is consecrated
to his sons from the offerings by fire to
the LORD, in that day when he presented
them to serve as priests to the LORD.
36 '[1]These the LORD had commanded
to be given them from the sons of Israel
in the day that He [a]anointed them. It is
their due forever throughout their generations.' "
37 This is the law of the burnt offering, the grain offering and the sin offering and the guilt offering and [a]the ordination offering and the sacrifice of peace
offerings,
38 [a]which the LORD commanded Moses at Mount Sinai in the day that He
commanded the sons of Israel to [1]pre-
sent their offerings to the LORD in the
wilderness of Sinai.

The Consecration of Aaron and His Sons

8 THEN the LORD spoke to Moses,
saying,
2 "[a]Take Aaron and his sons with
him, and the [b]garments and [c]the anointing oil and the bull of the sin offering,
and the two rams and the basket of
unleavened bread;
3 and assemble all the congregation
at the doorway of the tent of meeting."
4 So Moses did just as the LORD
commanded him. When the congregation was assembled at the doorway of
the tent of meeting,
5 Moses said to the congregation,
"This is the thing which the LORD has
commanded to do."
6 Then [a]Moses had Aaron and his
sons come near, and [b]washed them with
water.
7 And he [a]put the tunic on him and
girded him with the sash, and clothed
him with the robe, and put the ephod on
him; and he girded him with the artistic
band of the ephod, [1]with which he tied *it*
to him.
8 He then placed the [1]breastpiece on
him, and in the [1]breastpiece he put [2a]the
Urim and the Thummim.
9 He also placed the turban on his
head, and on the turban, at its front, he
placed [a]the golden plate, the holy crown,
just as the LORD had commanded Moses.
10 Moses then took [a]the anointing oil
and anointed the [1]tabernacle and all that
was in it, and consecrated them.
11 And he sprinkled some of it on the
altar seven times and anointed the altar
and all its utensils, and the basin and its
stand, to [a]consecrate them.
12 Then he poured some of the
[a]anointing oil on Aaron's head and
anointed him, to consecrate him.
13 [a]Next Moses had Aaron's sons
come near and clothed them with tunics,
and girded them with sashes, and bound
[1]caps on them, just as the LORD had
commanded Moses.
14 Then he brought [a]the bull of the sin
offering, and Aaron and his sons laid
their hands on the head of the bull of the
sin offering.
15 Next [1]Moses slaughtered *it* and
took the blood and with his finger [a]put
some of it around on the horns of the
altar, and purified the altar. Then he
poured out *the rest of* the blood at the
base of the altar and consecrated it, to
make atonement for it.
16 He also [a]took all the fat that was
on the entrails and the [1]lobe of the liver,
and the two kidneys and their fat; and
Moses offered it up in smoke on the
altar.
17 [a]But the bull and its hide and its
flesh and its refuse, he burned in the fire
outside the camp, just as the LORD had
commanded Moses.
18 Then he presented [a]the ram of the
burnt offering, and Aaron and his sons
laid their hands on the head of the ram.

23 [a]Lev. 3:17
24 [a]Ex. 22:31; Lev. 17:15; 22:8
25 [1]Lit., *he offers an offering by fire*
26 [a]Gen. 9:4; Lev. 17:10-16; 19:26; Deut. 12:23; 1 Sam. 14:33; Acts 15:20
29 [a]Lev. 3:1
30 [1]Lit., *waved* [a]Ex. 29:26, 27; Lev. 8:29; Num. 6:20
31 [a]Num. 18:11; Deut. 18:3
32 [1]Or, *heave offering* [a]Ex. 29:27; Lev. 7:34; 9:21; Num. 6:20
34 [1]Or, *heave offering* [a]Ex. 29:27; Lev. 10:14, 15; Num. 18:18
35 [1]Lit., *the anointed portion of* [a]Num. 18:8
36 [1]Lit., *which* [a]Ex. 40:13-15; Lev. 8:12, 30
37 [a]Ex. 29:22-34; Lev. 8:22, 23
38 [1]Or, *offer* [a]Lev. 1:1; 26:46; 27:34; Deut. 4:5
2 [a]Ex. 28:1 [b]Lev. 6:10 [c]Ex. 30:25
6 [a]Ex. 29:4-6 [b]Ex. 30:19, 20; Ps. 26:6; 1 Cor. 6:11; Eph. 5:26
7 [1]Lit., *and with it* [a]Ex. 28:4
8 [1]Lit., *pouch* [2]I.e., the lights and perfections [a]Ex. 28:30; Num. 27:21; Deut. 33:8; 1 Sam. 28:6; Ezra 2:63; Neh. 7:65
9 [a]Ex. 28:36
10 [1]Or, *dwelling place* [a]Ex. 30:26-29; Lev. 8:2
11 [a]Ex. 29:36, 37; 30:29
12 [a]Ex. 29:7; 30:30; Lev. 21:10, 12; Ps. 133:2
13 [1]Lit., *headgear* [a]Ex. 29:8, 9
14 [a]Ex. 29:10; Lev. 4:4; Ps. 66:15; Ezek. 43:19
15 [1]Lit., *he slaughtered it and Moses took* [a]Ex. 29:12; Lev. 4:7; Ezek. 43:20
16 [1]Or, *appendage on* [a]Ex. 29:13
17 [a]Ex. 29:14; Lev. 4:11, 12
18 [a]Ex. 29:15; Lev. 8:2

19 And [1]Moses slaughtered *it* and
sprinkled the blood around on the altar.
20 When he had cut the ram into its
pieces, Moses [a]offered up the head and
the pieces and the suet in smoke.
21 After he had washed the entrails
and the legs with water, Moses [a]offered
up the whole ram in smoke on the altar.
It was a burnt offering for a soothing
aroma; it was an offering by fire to the
LORD, just as the LORD had commanded
Moses.
22 Then he presented the second ram,
[a]the ram of [1]ordination; and Aaron and
his sons laid their hands on the head of
the ram.
23 And [1]Moses slaughtered *it* and
took some of its blood and [a]put it on the
lobe of Aaron's right ear, and on the
thumb of his right hand, and on the big
toe of his right foot.
24 He also had Aaron's sons come
near; and Moses put some of the blood
on the lobe of their right ear, and on the
thumb of their right hand, and on the
big toe of their right foot. Moses then
[a]sprinkled *the rest of* the blood around
on the altar.
25 And he took the fat, and the fat
tail, and all the fat that was on the
entrails, and the [1]lobe of the liver and
the two kidneys and their fat and the
right thigh.
26 And [a]from the basket of unleavened bread that was before the LORD, he
took one unleavened cake and one cake
of bread *mixed with* oil and one wafer,
and placed *them* on the portions of fat
and on the right thigh.
27 He then [a]put all *these* on the hands
of Aaron and on the hands of his sons,
and presented them as a wave offering
before the LORD.
28 Then Moses [a]took them from their
hands and offered them up in smoke on
the altar with the burnt offering. They
were an ordination offering for [b]a soothing aroma; it was an offering by fire to
the LORD.
29 Moses also took [a]the breast and
presented it for a wave offering before
the LORD; it was [b]Moses' portion of the
ram of ordination, just as the LORD had
commanded Moses.
30 So Moses [a]took some of the anointing oil and some of the blood which was
on the altar, and sprinkled it on Aaron,
on his garments, on his sons, and on the
garments of his sons with him; and he
consecrated Aaron, his garments, and
his sons, and the garments of his sons
with him.
31 Then Moses said to Aaron and to
his sons, "[a]Boil the flesh at the doorway
of the tent of meeting, and eat it there
together with the bread which is in the
basket of the ordination offering, just as
I commanded, [b]saying, 'Aaron and his
sons shall eat it.'
32 "And [a]the remainder of the flesh
and of the bread you shall burn in the
fire.
33 "[a]And you shall not go outside the
doorway of the tent of meeting for seven
days, until the day that the period of
your ordination is fulfilled; for he will
[1]ordain you through seven days.
34 "The LORD has commanded to do as
has been done this day, to make atonement on your behalf.
35 "At the doorway of the tent of
meeting, moreover, you shall remain day
and night for seven days, and [a]keep the
charge of the LORD, that you may not
die, for so I have been commanded."
36 Thus Aaron and his sons did all the
things which the LORD had commanded
through Moses.

Aaron Offers Sacrifices

9 NOW it came about [a]on the eighth
day that Moses called Aaron and his
sons and the elders of Israel;
2 and he said to Aaron, "[a]Take for
yourself a calf, a bull, for a sin offering
and a ram for a burnt offering, *both*
without defect, and offer *them* before the
LORD.
3 "Then to the sons of Israel you shall
speak, saying, 'Take a male goat for a sin
offering, and a calf and a lamb, both one
year old, without defect, for a burnt
offering,
4 and an ox and a ram for peace
offerings, to sacrifice before the LORD,
and a grain offering mixed with oil; for
today [a]the LORD shall appear to you.' "
5 So they took what Moses had commanded to the front of the tent of
meeting, and the whole congregation
came near and stood before the LORD.
6 And Moses said, "This is the thing
which the LORD has commanded you to
do, that [a]the glory of the LORD may
appear to you."
7 Moses then said to Aaron, "Come
near to the altar and [1a]offer your sin
offering and your burnt offering, that
you may make atonement for yourself
and for the people; then make the offering [2]for the people, that you may make
atonement for them, just as the LORD
has commanded."
8 [a]So Aaron came near to the altar
and slaughtered the calf of the sin offering which was for himself.
9 [a]And Aaron's sons presented the
blood to him; and he dipped his finger in
the blood, and [b]put *some* on the horns of
the altar, and poured out *the rest of* the
blood at the base of the altar.
10 The fat and the kidneys and the
[1]lobe of the liver of the sin offering, he
then offered up in smoke on the altar
just as the LORD had commanded Moses.
11 [a]The flesh and the skin, however,
he burned with fire outside the camp.
12 Then he slaughtered the burnt
offering; and Aaron's sons handed the
blood to him and he sprinkled it around
on the altar.

19 [1]Lit., *he slaughtered it and Moses sprinkled*
20 [a]Lev. 1:8
21 [a]Ex. 29:18
22 [1]Lit., *filling*, and so throughout the ch. [a]Ex. 29:31; Lev. 8:2
23 [1]Lit., *he slaughtered it and Moses took* [a]Ex. 29:20, 21
24 [a]Heb. 9:18-22
25 [1]Or, *appendage on*
26 [a]Ex. 29:23
27 [a]Ex. 29:24
28 [a]Ex. 29:25 [b]Gen. 8:21
29 [a]Lev. 7:31-34 [b]Ex. 29:26; Ps. 99:6
30 [a]Ex. 29:21
31 [a]Ex. 29:31 [b]Ex. 29:32
32 [a]Ex. 29:34
33 [1]Lit., *fill your hands* [a]Ex. 29:35
35 [a]Num. 3:7; 9:19; Deut. 11:1; 1 Kin. 2:3; Ezek. 48:11
1 [a]Ezek. 43:27
2 [a]Ezek. 29:1; Lev. 4:3
4 [a]Ex. 29:43
6 [a]Ex. 24:16; Lev. 9:23
7 [1]Lit., *make* [2]Lit., *of* [a]Heb. 5:3; 7:27
8 [a]Lev. 4:1-12
9 [a]Lev. 9:12, 18 [b]Lev. 4:7
10 [1]Or, *appendage on*
11 [a]Lev. 4:11, 12; 8:17

13 And they handed the burnt offering to him in [1]pieces with the head, and he offered *them* up in smoke on the altar.

14 He also washed the entrails and the legs, and offered *them* up in smoke with the burnt offering on the altar.

15 Then he presented the people's offering, and took the [a]goat of the sin offering which was for the people, and slaughtered it and offered it for sin, like the first.

16 He also presented the burnt offering, and [1]offered it according to [a]the ordinance.

17 Next he presented [a]the grain offering, and filled his [1]hand with some of it and offered *it* up in smoke on the altar, [b]besides the burnt offering of the morning.

18 Then [a]he slaughtered the ox and the ram, the sacrifice of peace offerings which was for the people; and Aaron's sons handed the blood to him and he sprinkled it around on the altar.

19 As for the portions of fat from the ox and from the ram, the fat tail, and the *fat* [a]covering, and the kidneys and the [1]lobe of the liver,

20 they now placed the portions of fat on the breasts; and he offered [1]them up in smoke on the altar.

21 But [a]the breasts and the right thigh Aaron [1]presented as a wave offering before the LORD, just as Moses had commanded.

22 Then Aaron lifted up his hands toward the people and [a]blessed them, and he stepped down after making the sin offering and the burnt offering and the peace offerings.

23 And Moses and Aaron went into the tent of meeting. When they came out and blessed the people, [a]the glory of the LORD appeared to all the people.

24 [a]Then fire came out from before the LORD and consumed the burnt offering and the portions of fat on the altar; and when all the people saw *it*, they shouted and fell on their faces.

The Sin of Nadab and Abihu

10 NOW [a]Nadab and Abihu, the sons of Aaron, took their respective [b]firepans, and after putting fire in them, placed incense on it and offered strange fire before the LORD, which He had not commanded them.

2 [a]And fire came out from the presence of the LORD and consumed them, and they died before the LORD.

3 Then Moses said to Aaron, "It is what the LORD spoke, saying,

'By those who [a]come near Me I
[1][b]will be treated as holy,
And before all the people I will [c]be
honored.' "

So Aaron, therefore, kept silent.

4 Moses called also to [a]Mishael and Elzaphan, the sons of Aaron's uncle Uzziel, and said to them, "Come forward, carry your [1]relatives away from the front of the sanctuary to the outside of the camp."

5 So they came forward and carried them still in their [a]tunics to the outside of the camp, as Moses had said.

6 Then Moses said to Aaron and to his sons Eleazar and Ithamar, "[a]Do not [1]uncover your heads nor tear your clothes, so that you may not die, and that He may not [b]become wrathful against all the congregation. But your [2]kinsmen, the whole house of Israel, shall bewail the burning which the LORD has [3]brought about.

7 "You shall not even go out from the doorway of the tent of meeting, lest you die; for [a]the LORD's anointing oil is upon you." So they did according to the word of Moses.

8 The LORD then spoke to Aaron, saying,

9 "[a]Do not drink wine or strong drink, neither you nor your sons with you, when you come into the tent of meeting, so that you may not die—it is a perpetual statute throughout your generations—

10 and [a]so as to make a distinction between the holy and the profane, and between the unclean and the clean,

11 and [a]so as to teach the sons of Israel all the statutes which the LORD has spoken to them through Moses."

12 Then Moses spoke to Aaron, and to his surviving sons, [a]Eleazar and Ithamar, "[b]Take the grain offering that is left over from the LORD's offerings by fire and eat it unleavened beside the altar, for it is most holy.

13 "You shall eat it, moreover, in a holy place, because it is your due and your sons' due out of the LORD's offerings by fire; for thus I have been commanded.

14 "[a]The breast of the wave offering, however, and the thigh of the offering you may eat in a clean place, you and your sons and your daughters with you; for they have been given as your due and your sons' due out of the sacrifices of the peace offerings of the sons of Israel.

15 "[a]The thigh offered by lifting up and the breast offered by waving, they shall bring along with the offerings by fire of the portions of fat, to present as a wave offering before the LORD; so it shall be a thing perpetually due you and your sons with you, just as the LORD has commanded."

16 But Moses searched carefully for the [a]goat of the sin offering, and behold, it had been burned up! So he was angry with Aaron's surviving sons Eleazar and Ithamar, saying,

17 "Why [a]did you not eat the sin offering at the holy place? For it is most holy, and [1]He gave it to you to bear away [b]the guilt of the congregation, to make atonement for them before the LORD.

18 "Behold, [a]since its blood had not been brought inside, into the sanctuary, you should certainly have [b]eaten it in the sanctuary, just as I commanded."

13 [1]Lit., *its pieces*
15 [a]Lev. 4:27-31
16 [1]Lit., *made* [a]Lev. 1:1-13
17 [1]Lit., *palm* [a]Lev. 2:1-3 [b]Lev. 3:5
18 [a]Lev. 3:1-11
19 [1]Or, *appendage on* [a]Lev. 3:9
20 [1]Lit., *the portions of fat*
21 [1]Lit., *waved* [a]Ex. 29:26, 27; Lev. 7:30-34
22 [a]Num. 6:22-26; Deut. 21:5; Luke 24:50
23 [a]Lev. 9:6; Num. 16:19
24 [a]1 Kin. 18:38, 39; 2 Chr. 7:1

1 [a]Ex. 24:1, 9; Num. 3:2; 26:61 [b]Lev. 16:12
2 [a]Num. 3:4; 16:35; 26:61
3 [1]Or, *will show Myself holy* [a]Ex. 19:22; Lev. 21:6 [b]Ex. 30:30; Ezek. 38:16 [c]Ex. 14:4, 17; Is. 49:3; Ezek. 28:22
4 [1]Lit., *brothers* [a]Ex. 6:22
5 [a]Ex. 29:5; Lev. 8:13
6 [1]Lit., *unbind* [2]Lit., *brothers* [3]Lit., *burned* [a]Lev. 21:1-5, 10-12 [b]Num. 1:53; 16:22, 46; 18:5; Josh. 7:1; 22:18, 20; 2 Sam. 24:1
7 [a]Ex. 28:41; Lev. 21:12
9 [a]Prov. 20:1; 31:5; Is. 28:7; Ezek. 44:21; Hos. 4:11; Luke 1:15; Eph. 5:18; 1 Tim. 3:3; Titus 1:7
10 [a]Lev. 11:47; 20:25; Ezek. 22:26
11 [a]Deut. 17:10, 11; 33:10
12 [a]Ex. 6:23; Num. 3:2 [b]Lev. 6:14-18
14 [a]Lev. 7:30-34; Num. 18:11
15 [a]Lev. 7:34
16 [a]Lev. 9:3, 15
17 [1]Or, *was given* [a]Lev. 6:24-30 [b]Ex. 28:38; Lev. 22:16; Num. 18:1
18 [a]Lev. 6:30 [b]Lev. 6:26

19 But Aaron spoke to Moses, "Behold, this very day they [a]presented their
sin offering and their burnt offering
before the LORD. When things like these
happened to me, if I had eaten a sin
offering today, would it have been good
in the sight of the LORD?"
20 And when Moses heard *that*, it
seemed good in his sight.

Laws about Animals for Food

11 THE LORD spoke again to Moses
and to Aaron, saying to them,
2 "Speak to the sons of Israel, saying,
'[a]These are the creatures which you may
eat from all the animals that are on the
earth.
3 'Whatever divides a hoof, thus making split hoofs, *and* chews the cud,
among the animals, that you may eat.
4 'Nevertheless, [a]you are not to eat of
these, among those which chew the cud,
or among those which divide the hoof:
the camel, for though it chews cud, it
does not divide the hoof, it is unclean to
you.
5 'Likewise, the rock badger, for
though it chews cud, it does not divide
the hoof, it is unclean to you;
6 the [1]rabbit also, for though it
chews cud, it does not divide the hoof, it
is unclean to you;
7 and the pig, for though it divides
the hoof, thus making a split hoof, it
does not chew cud, it is unclean to you.
8 'You shall not eat of their flesh nor
touch their carcasses; they are unclean
to you.
9 '[a]These you may eat, whatever is in
the water: all that have fins and scales,
those in the water, in the seas or in the
rivers, you may eat.
10 '[a]But whatever is in the seas and in
the rivers, that do not have fins and
scales among all the teeming life of the
water, and among all the living creatures
that are in the water, they are detestable
things to you,
11 and they shall be [1]abhorrent to
you; you may not eat of their flesh, and
their carcasses you shall detest.
12 'Whatever in the water does not
have fins and scales is [1]abhorrent to you.

Avoid the Unclean

13 'These, moreover, [a]you shall detest
among the birds; they are [1]abhorrent,
not to be eaten: the [2]eagle and the
vulture and the [3]buzzard,
14 and the kite and the falcon in its
kind,
15 every raven in its kind,
16 and the ostrich and the owl and the
sea gull and the hawk in its kind,
17 and the little owl and the cormorant and the [1]great owl,
18 and the white owl and the [1]pelican
and the carrion vulture,
19 and the stork, the heron in its
kinds, and the hoopoe, and the bat.
20 'All the [1]winged insects that walk
on *all* fours are detestable to you.
21 'Yet these you may eat among all
the [1]winged insects which walk on *all*
fours: those which have above their feet
jointed legs with which to jump on the
earth.
22 'These of them you may eat: the
locust in its kinds, and the devastating
locust in its kinds, and the cricket in its
kinds, and the grasshopper in its kinds.
23 'But all other [1]winged insects which
are four-footed are detestable to you.
24 'By these, moreover, you will be
made unclean: whoever touches their
carcasses becomes unclean until evening,
25 and [a]whoever picks up any of their
carcasses shall wash his clothes and be
unclean until evening.
26 'Concerning all the animals which
divide the hoof, but do not make a split
hoof, or which do not chew cud, they are
unclean to you: whoever touches them
becomes unclean.
27 'Also whatever walks on its paws,
among all the creatures that walk on *all*
fours, are unclean to you; whoever
touches their carcasses becomes unclean
until evening,
28 and the one who picks up their
carcasses shall wash his clothes and be
unclean until evening; they are unclean
to you.
29 'Now these are to you the unclean
among the swarming things which
swarm on the earth: the mole, and the
mouse, and the [1]great lizard in its kinds,
30 and the gecko, and the [1]crocodile,
and the lizard, and the [2]sand reptile, and
the chameleon.
31 'These are to you the unclean
among all the swarming things; whoever
touches them when they are dead becomes unclean until evening.
32 'Also anything on which one of
them may fall when they are dead,
becomes unclean, including any wooden
article, or clothing, or a skin, or a sack—
any article [1]of which use is made—[a]it
shall be put in the water and be unclean
until evening, then it becomes clean.
33 'As for any [a]earthenware vessel into
which one of them may fall, whatever is
in it becomes unclean and you shall
break [1]the vessel.
34 'Any of the [1]food which may be
eaten, on which water comes, shall become unclean; and any [1]liquid which
may be drunk in every vessel shall
become unclean.
35 'Everything, moreover, on which
part of their carcass may fall becomes
unclean; an oven or a [1]stove shall be
smashed; they are unclean and shall
continue as unclean to you.
36 'Nevertheless a spring or a cistern
[1]collecting water shall be clean, though
the one who touches their carcass shall
be unclean.
37 'And if a part of their carcass falls
on any seed for sowing which is to be
sown, it is clean.

19 [a]Lev. 9:8, 12
2 [a]Deut. 14:3-21
4 [a]Acts 10:14
6 [1]Or, *hare*
9 [a]Deut. 14:9
10 [a]Deut. 14:10
11 [1]Lit., *detestable things*
12 [1]Lit., *detestable things*
13 [1]Lit., *a detestable thing* [2]Or, *vulture* [3]Or, *black vulture* [a]Deut. 14:12-19
17 [1]Specifically, *great horned owl*
18 [1]Or, *owl* or *jackdaw*
20 [1]Lit., *swarming things with wings*
21 [1]V. 20, note 1
23 [1]V. 20, note 1
25 [a]Lev. 11:40
29 [1]Or, *thorn-tailed lizard*
30 [1]Or, *lizard* [2]Species as yet undefined
32 [1]Lit., *with which work is done* [a]Lev. 15:12
33 [1]Lit., *it* [a]Lev. 6:28; 15:12
34 [1]I.e., if touched by a carcass; cf. vv. 29-32
35 [1]Lit., *hearth for supporting (two) pots*
36 [1]Lit., *of a gathering of*

38 ‘Though if water is put on the seed, and a part of their carcass falls on it, it is unclean to you.

39 ‘Also if one of the animals dies which you have for food, the one who touches its carcass becomes unclean until evening.

40 ‘[a]He too, who eats some of its carcass shall wash his clothes and be unclean until evening; and the one who picks up its carcass shall wash his clothes and be unclean until evening.

41 ‘[a]Now every swarming thing that swarms on the earth is detestable, not to be eaten.

42 ‘Whatever crawls on its belly, and whatever walks on *all* fours, whatever has many feet, in respect to every swarming thing that swarms on the earth, you shall not eat them, for they are detestable.

43 ‘[a]Do not render [1]yourselves detestable through any of the swarming things that swarm; and you shall not make yourselves unclean with them so that you become unclean.

44 ‘For [a]I am the LORD your God. Consecrate yourselves therefore, and [b]be holy; for I am holy. And you shall not make yourselves unclean with any of the swarming things that swarm on the earth.

45 ‘[a]For I am the LORD, who brought you up from the land of Egypt, to be your God; thus [b]you shall be holy for I am holy.’ ”

46 This is the law regarding the animal, and the bird, and every living thing that moves in the waters, and everything that swarms on the earth,

47 [a]to make a distinction between the unclean and the clean, and between the edible creature and the creature which is not to be eaten.

Laws of Motherhood

12 THEN the LORD spoke to Moses, saying,

2“Speak to the sons of Israel, saying, ‘When a woman [1]gives birth and bears a male *child*, then she shall be unclean for seven days, [a]as in the days of [2]her menstruation she shall be unclean.

3 ‘And on [a]the eighth day the flesh of his foreskin shall be circumcised.

4 ‘Then she shall remain in the blood of *her* purification for thirty-three days; she shall not touch any consecrated thing, nor enter the sanctuary, until the days of her purification are completed.

5 ‘But if she bears a female *child*, then she shall be unclean for two weeks, as in her [1]menstruation; and she shall remain in the blood of *her* purification for sixty-six days.

6 ‘And [a]when the days of her purification are completed, for a son or for a daughter, she shall bring to the priest at the doorway of the tent of meeting, a one year old lamb for a burnt offering, and a young pigeon or a turtledove [b]for a sin offering.

40 [a]Lev. 17:15; 22:8; Deut. 14:21; Ezek. 44:31

41 [a]Lev. 11:29

43 [1]Lit., *your souls* [a]Lev. 20:25

44 [a]Ex. 6:7; 16:12; 23:25; Is. 43:3; 51:15 [b]Lev. 19:2; 1 Pet. 1:16

45 [a]Ex. 6:7; 20:2; Lev. 22:33; 25:38; 26:45 [b]Lev. 19:2; 1 Pet. 1:16

47 [a]Lev. 10:10; Ezek. 22:26; 44:23

2 [1]Lit., *produces seed* [2]Lit., *the impurity of her sickness* [a]Lev. 15:19; 18:19

3 [a]Gen. 17:12; Luke 1:59; 2:21

5 [1]Lit., *impurity*

6 [a]Luke 2:22 [b]Lev. 5:7

7 [1]Lit., *fountain*

8 [1]Lit., *her hand does not find a sufficiency of a lamb* [a]Luke 2:22-24 [b]Lev. 5:7 [c]Lev. 4:26

2 [1]Lit., *flesh* [2]Lit., *a mark, stroke,* and so throughout the ch. [a]Deut. 24:8

3 [1]Lit., *flesh*

4 [1]Lit., *flesh* [2]Lit., *the appearance of it is not deeper* [3]Lit., *shut up*

5 [1]Lit., *has stood* [2]Lit., *shut up*

6 [a]Lev. 11:25; 14:8

10 [a]Num. 12:10; 2 Kin. 5:27; 2 Chr. 26:19, 20

11 [1]Lit., *an old* [2]Lit., *flesh* [3]Lit., *shut up*

12 [1]Lit., *with regard to the whole sight of the priest's eyes*

7 ‘Then he shall offer it before the LORD and make atonement for her; and she shall be cleansed from the [1]flow of her blood. This is the law for her who bears *a child, whether* a male or a female.

8 ‘But if [1]she cannot afford a lamb, then she shall take [a]two turtledoves or two young pigeons, [b]the one for a burnt offering and the other for a sin offering; and the [c]priest shall make atonement for her, and she shall be clean.’ ”

The Test for Leprosy

13 THEN the LORD spoke to Moses and to Aaron, saying,

2“When a man has on the skin of his [1]body a swelling or a scab or a bright spot, and it becomes [2]an infection of leprosy on the skin of his [1]body, [a]then he shall be brought to Aaron the priest, or to one of his sons the priests.

3“And the priest shall look at the mark on the skin of the [1]body, and if the hair in the infection has turned white and the infection appears to be deeper than the skin of his [1]body, it is an infection of leprosy; when the priest has looked at him, he shall pronounce him unclean.

4“But if the bright spot is white on the skin of his [1]body, and [2]it does not appear to be deeper than the skin, and the hair on it has not turned white, then the priest shall [3]isolate *him who has* the infection for seven days.

5“And the priest shall look at him on the seventh day, and if in his eyes the infection [1]has not changed, *and* the infection has not spread on the skin, then the priest shall [2]isolate him for seven more days.

6“And the priest shall look at him again on the seventh day; and if the infection has faded, and the mark has not spread on the skin, then the priest shall pronounce him clean; it is *only* a scab. And he shall [a]wash his clothes and be clean.

7“But if the scab spreads farther on the skin, after he has shown himself to the priest for his cleansing, he shall appear again to the priest.

8“And the priest shall look, and if the scab has spread on the skin, then the priest shall pronounce him unclean; it is leprosy.

9“When the infection of leprosy is on a man, then he shall be brought to the priest.

10“The priest shall then look, and if there is a [a]white swelling in the skin, and it has turned the hair white, and there is quick raw flesh in the swelling,

11 it is [1]a chronic leprosy on the skin of his [2]body, and the priest shall pronounce him unclean; he shall not [3]isolate him, for he is unclean.

12“And if the leprosy breaks out farther on the skin, and the leprosy covers all the skin of *him who has* the infection from his head even to his feet, [1]as far as the priest can see,

13 then the priest shall look, and
behold, *if* the leprosy has covered all his
[1]body, he shall pronounce clean *him who*
has the infection; it has all turned white
and he is clean.
14 "But whenever raw flesh appears on
him, he shall be unclean.
15 "And the priest shall look at the raw
flesh, and he shall pronounce him unclean; the raw flesh is unclean, it is
leprosy.
16 "Or if the raw flesh turns again and
is changed to white, then he shall [a]come
to the priest,
17 and the priest shall look at him,
and behold, *if* the infection has turned to
white, then the priest shall pronounce
clean *him who has* the infection; he is
clean.
18 "And when the [1]body has a boil on
its skin, and it is healed,
19 and in the place of the boil there is
a white swelling or a reddish-white,
bright spot, then it shall be shown to the
priest;
20 and the priest shall look, and behold, *if* [1]it appears to be lower than the
skin, and the hair on it has turned white,
then the priest shall pronounce him
unclean; it is the infection of leprosy, it
has broken out in the boil.
21 "But if the priest looks at it, and
behold, there are no white hairs in it and
it is not lower than the skin and is faded,
then the priest shall [1]isolate him for
seven days;
22 and if it spreads farther on the
skin, then the priest shall pronounce him
unclean; it is an infection.
23 "But if the bright spot remains in its
place, and does not spread, it is *only* the
scar of the boil; and the priest shall
pronounce him clean.
24 "Or if the [1]body sustains in its skin a
burn by fire, and the raw *flesh* of the
burn becomes a bright spot, reddish-
white, or white,
25 then the priest shall look at it. And
if the hair in the bright spot has [a]turned
white, and it appears to be deeper than
the skin, it is leprosy; it has broken out
in the burn. Therefore, the priest shall
pronounce him unclean; it is an infection of leprosy.
26 "But if the priest looks at it, and
indeed, there is no white hair in the
bright spot, and it is no [1]deeper than the
skin, but is dim, then the priest shall
[2]isolate him for seven days;
27 and the priest shall look at him on
the seventh day. If it spreads farther in
the skin, then the priest shall pronounce
him unclean; it is an infection of leprosy.
28 "But if the bright spot remains in its
place, and has not spread in the skin, but
is dim, it is the swelling from the burn;
and the priest shall pronounce him
clean, for it is *only* the scar of the burn.
29 "Now if a man or woman has an
infection on the head or on the beard,
30 then the priest shall look at the
infection, and if it appears to be deeper
than the skin, and there is thin yellowish
hair in it, then the priest shall pronounce
him unclean; it is a scale, it is leprosy of
the head or of the beard.
31 "But if the priest looks at the infection of the scale, and indeed, it appears
to be no deeper than the skin, and there
is no black hair in it, then the priest shall
[1]isolate *the person* with the scaly infection for seven days.
32 "And on the seventh day the priest
shall look at the infection, and if the
scale has not spread, and no yellowish
hair has [1]grown in it, and the appearance of the scale is no deeper than the
skin,
33 then he shall shave himself, but he
shall not shave the scale; and the priest
shall [1]isolate *the person* with the scale
seven more days.
34 "Then on the seventh day the priest
shall look at the scale, and if the scale
has not spread in the skin, and it appears
to be no deeper than the skin, the priest
shall pronounce him clean; and he shall
wash his clothes and be clean.
35 "But if the scale spreads farther in
the skin after his cleansing,
36 then the priest shall look at him,
and if the scale has spread in the skin,
the priest need not seek for the yellowish
hair; he is unclean.
37 "If in his sight the scale has remained, however, and black hair has
grown in it, the scale has healed, he is
clean; and the priest shall pronounce
him clean.
38 "And when a man or a woman has
bright spots on the skin of the [1]body,
even white bright spots,
39 then the priest shall look, and if the
bright spots on the skin of their [1]bodies
are a faint white, it is [2]eczema that has
broken out on the skin; he is clean.
40 "Now if a [1]man loses the hair of his
head, he is [a]bald; he is clean.
41 "And if his head becomes bald at
the [1]front and sides, he is bald on the
forehead; he is clean.
42 "But if on the bald head or the bald
forehead, there occurs a reddish-white
infection, it is leprosy breaking out on
his bald head or on his bald forehead.
43 "Then [a]the priest shall look at him;
and if the swelling of the infection is
reddish-white on his bald head or on his
bald forehead, like the appearance of
leprosy in the skin of the [1]body,
44 he is a leprous man, he is unclean.
The priest shall surely pronounce him
unclean; his infection is on his head.
45 "As for the leper who has the infection, his clothes shall be torn, and [a]the
hair of his head shall be [1]uncovered, and
he shall [b]cover his mustache and cry,
'[c]Unclean! Unclean!'
46 "He shall remain unclean all the
days during which he has the infection;
he is unclean. He shall live alone; his
dwelling shall be [a]outside the camp.
47 "When a garment has a [1]mark of
leprosy in it, whether it is a wool garment or a linen garment,

13 [1]Lit., *flesh*

16 [a]Luke 5:12-14

18 [1]Lit., *flesh*

20 [1]Lit., *the appearance of it is lower*

21 [1]Lit., *shut up*

24 [1]Lit., *flesh*

25 [a]Ex. 4:6; Num. 12:10; 2 Kin. 5:27

26 [1]Lit., *lower* [2]Lit., *shut up*

31 [1]Lit., *shut up*

32 [1]Lit., *been*

33 [1]Lit., *shut up*

38 [1]Lit., *flesh*

39 [1]Lit., *flesh* [2]Lit., *tetter*

40 [1]Lit., *man's head becomes bald* [a]2 Kin. 2:23; Is. 15:2; Amos 8:10

41 [1]Lit., *border of his face*

43 [1]Lit., *flesh* [a]Lev. 10:10; Ezek. 22:26

45 [1]Or, *disheveled* [a]Lev. 10:6 [b]Ezek. 24:17, 22; Mic. 3:7 [c]Lam. 4:15

46 [a]Num. 5:1-4; 12:14

47 [1]Lit., *infection*, and so throughout the ch.

48 whether in [1]warp or woof, of linen or of wool, whether in leather or in any article made of leather,

49 if the mark is greenish or reddish in the garment or in the leather, or in the [1]warp or in the woof, or in any article of leather, it is a leprous mark and shall be shown to the priest.

50 "Then [a]the priest shall look at the mark, and shall [1]quarantine the article with the mark for seven days.

51 "He shall then look at the mark on the seventh day; if the mark has spread in the garment, whether in the warp or in the woof, or in the leather, whatever the purpose for which the leather is used, the mark is a [1]leprous malignancy, it is unclean.

52 "So he shall burn the garment, whether the warp or the woof, in wool or in linen, or any article of leather in which the mark occurs, for it is a [1]leprous malignancy; it shall be burned in the fire.

53 "But if the priest shall look, and indeed, the mark has not spread in the garment, either in the warp or in the woof, or in any article of leather,

54 then the priest shall order them to wash the thing in which the mark occurs, and he shall [1]quarantine it for seven more days.

55 "After the article with the mark has been washed, the priest shall again look, and if the mark has not changed its appearance, even though the mark has not spread, it is unclean; you shall burn it in the fire, whether an eating away has produced bareness on the top or on the front of it.

56 "Then if the priest shall look, and if the mark has faded after it has been washed, then he shall tear it out of the garment or out of the leather, whether from the warp or from the woof;

57 and if it appears again in the garment, whether in the warp or in the woof, or in any article of leather, it is an outbreak; the article with the mark shall be burned in the fire.

58 "And the garment, whether the warp or the woof, or any article of leather from which the mark has departed when you washed it, it shall then be washed a second time and shall be clean."

59 This is the law for the mark of leprosy in a garment of wool or linen, whether in the warp or in the woof, or in any article of leather, for pronouncing it clean or unclean.

Law of Cleansing a Leper

14 THEN the LORD spoke to Moses, saying,

2 "This shall be the law of the leper in the day of his cleansing. [a]Now he shall be brought to the priest,

3 and the priest shall go [a]out to the outside of the camp. Thus the priest shall look, and if the [1]infection of leprosy has been healed in the leper,

4 then the priest shall give orders to take two live clean birds and [a]cedar wood and a [1]scarlet string and hyssop for the one who is to be cleansed.

5 "The priest shall also give orders to slay the one bird in an earthenware vessel over [1]running water.

6 "*As for* the live bird, he shall take it, together with [a]the cedar wood and the [1]scarlet string and the [b]hyssop, and shall dip them and the live bird in the blood of the bird that was slain over the [2]running water.

7 "[a]He shall then sprinkle seven times the one who is to be cleansed from the leprosy, and shall pronounce him clean, and shall let the live bird go free over the open field.

8 "[a]The one to be cleansed shall then wash his clothes and shave off all his hair, and bathe in water and [b]be clean. Now afterward, he may enter the camp, but he [c]shall stay outside his tent for seven days.

9 "And it will be on the seventh day that he shall shave off all his hair: he shall shave his head and his beard and his eyebrows, even all his hair. He shall then wash his clothes and bathe his [1]body in water and [a]be clean.

10 "Now on the eighth day he is to take two male lambs without defect, and a yearling ewe lamb without defect, and three-tenths *of an* [1]*ephah* of fine flour mixed with oil for a grain offering, and one [2a]log of oil;

11 and the priest who pronounces him clean shall present the man to be cleansed and the [1]aforesaid before the LORD at the doorway of the tent of meeting.

12 "Then the priest shall take the one male lamb and bring it for a [a]guilt offering, with the [1b]log of oil, and present them as a [c]wave offering before the LORD.

13 "Next he shall slaughter the male lamb in [a]the place where they slaughter the sin offering and the burnt offering, at the place of the sanctuary—for the guilt offering, [b]like the sin offering, belongs to the priest; it is most holy.

14 "The priest shall then take some of the blood of the [a]guilt offering, and the priest shall put *it* on [b]the lobe of the right ear of the one to be cleansed, and on the thumb of his right hand, and on the big toe of his right foot.

15 "The priest shall also take some of the [1a]log of oil, and pour *it* into his left palm;

16 the priest shall then dip his right-hand finger into the oil that is in his left palm, and with his finger sprinkle some of the oil seven times before the LORD.

17 "And of the remaining oil which is in his palm, the priest shall put some on the right ear lobe of the one to be cleansed, and on the thumb of his right hand, and on the big toe of his right foot, on the blood of the guilt offering;

48 [1]Or, *weaving or texture*

49 [1]Or, *weaving or texture*

50 [1]Lit., *shut up* [a]Ezek. 44:23

51 [1]Lit., *malignant leprosy*

52 [1]Lit., *malignant leprosy*

54 [1]Lit., *shut up*

2 [a]Matt. 8:4; Mark 1:44; Luke 5:14; 17:14

3 [1]Lit., *mark, stroke,* and so throughout the ch. [a]Lev. 13:46

4 [1]Lit., *scarlet color and* [a]Lev. 14:6, 49, 51, 52; Num. 19:6

5 [1]Lit., *living*

6 [1]Lit., *scarlet color and* [2]Lit., *living* [a]Lev. 14:4 [b]Ps. 51:7

7 [a]Ezek. 36:25

8 [a]Lev. 11:25; 13:6; Num. 8:7 [b]Lev. 14:9, 20 [c]Num. 5:2, 3; 12:14, 15; 2 Chr. 26:21

9 [1]Lit., *flesh* [a]Lev. 14:8, 20

10 [1]I.e., Approx. one bu. [2]I.e., Approx. one pt. [a]Lev. 14:12, 15, 21, 24

11 [1]Lit., *them*

12 [1]I.e., Approx. one pt. [a]Lev. 5:6, 18; 6:6; 14:19 [b]Lev. 14:10 [c]Ex. 29:22-24, 26

13 [a]Ex. 29:11; Lev. 1:11; 4:24 [b]Lev. 6:24-30; 7:7

14 [a]Lev. 14:19 [b]Ex. 29:20; Lev. 8:23, 24

15 [1]I.e., Approx. one pt. [a]Lev. 14:10

18 while the rest of the oil that is in the priest's palm, he shall put on the head of the one to be cleansed. So the priest shall make [a]atonement on his behalf before the LORD.

19"The priest shall next offer the [a]sin offering and make atonement for the one to be cleansed from his uncleanness. Then afterward, he shall slaughter the burnt offering.

20"And the priest shall offer up the burnt offering and the grain offering on the altar. Thus the priest shall make atonement for him, and [a]he shall be clean.

21"[a]But if he is poor, and his [1]means are insufficient, then he is to take one male lamb for a [b]guilt offering as a wave offering to make atonement for him, and one-tenth *of an* [2]*ephah* of fine flour mixed with oil for a grain offering, and a [3][c]log of oil,

22 and two turtledoves or two young pigeons which [1]are within his means, [a]the one shall be a [b]sin offering and the other a burnt offering.

23"[a]Then the eighth day he shall bring them for his cleansing to the priest, at the doorway of the tent of meeting, before the LORD.

24"And the priest shall take the lamb of the guilt offering, and [a]the [1]log of oil, and the priest shall offer them for a wave offering before the LORD.

25"Next he shall slaughter the lamb of the guilt offering; and the priest is to take some of the blood of the guilt offering and put *it* on [a]the lobe of the right ear of the one to be cleansed and on the thumb of his right hand, and on the big toe of his right foot.

26"The priest shall also pour some of the oil into his left palm;

27 and with his right-hand finger the priest shall sprinkle some of the oil that is in his left palm seven times before the LORD.

28"The priest shall then put some of the oil that is in his palm on the lobe of the right ear of the one to be cleansed, and on the thumb of his right hand, and on the big toe of his right foot, on the place of the blood of the guilt offering.

29"Moreover, the rest of the oil that is in the priest's palm he shall put on the head of the one to be cleansed, to make atonement on his behalf before the LORD.

30"He shall then offer one of the turtledoves or young pigeons, [1]which are within his means.

31"*He shall offer* what [1]he can afford, [a]the one for a sin offering, and the other for a burnt offering, together with the grain offering. So the priest shall make atonement before the LORD on behalf of the one to be cleansed.

32"This is the law *for him* in whom there is an infection of leprosy, whose [1]means are limited for his cleansing."

Cleansing a Leprous House

33 The LORD further spoke to Moses and to Aaron, saying,

34"[a]When you enter the land of Canaan, which I give you for a possession, and I put a mark of leprosy on a house in the land of your possession,

35 then the one who owns the house shall come and tell the priest, saying, '*Something* like [a]a mark *of leprosy* has become visible to me in the house.'

36"The priest shall then order that they empty the house before the priest goes in to look at the mark, so that everything in the house need not become unclean; and afterward the priest shall go in to look at the house.

37"So he shall look at the mark, and if the mark on the walls of the house has greenish or reddish depressions, and appears deeper than the [1]surface;

38 then the priest shall come out of the house, to the [1]doorway, and [2]quarantine the house for seven days.

39"And the priest shall return on the seventh day and [1]make an inspection. If the mark has indeed spread in the walls of the house,

40 then the priest shall order them to tear out the stones with the mark in them and throw them away [1]at an unclean place outside the city.

41"And he shall have the house scraped all around [1]inside, and they shall dump the plaster that they scrape off at an unclean place outside the city.

42"Then they shall take other stones and replace *those* stones; and he shall take other plaster and replaster the house.

43"If, however, the mark breaks out again in the house, after he has torn out the stones and scraped the house, and after it has been replastered,

44 then the priest shall come in and [1]make an inspection. If he sees that the mark has indeed spread in the house, it is [a]a malignant mark in the house; it is unclean.

45"He shall therefore tear down the house, its stones, and its timbers, and all the plaster of the house, and he shall take *them* outside the city to an [a]unclean place.

46"Moreover, whoever goes into the house during the time that he has [1]quarantined it, becomes [a]unclean until evening.

47"Likewise, whoever lies down in the house shall wash his clothes, and whoever eats in the house shall wash his clothes.

48"If, on the other hand, the priest comes in and [1]makes an inspection, and the mark has not indeed spread in the house after the house has been replastered, then the priest shall pronounce the house clean because the mark has [2]not reappeared.

49"To cleanse the house then, he shall take [a]two birds and cedar wood and a [1]scarlet string and hyssop,

18 [a]Lev. 4:26; Num. 15:28; Heb. 2:17

19 [a]Lev. 14:12

20 [a]Lev. 14:8, 9

21 [1]Lit., *hand is not reaching* [2]I.e., Approx. one bu. [3]I.e., Approx. one pt. [a]Lev. 5:11; 12:8; 27:8 [b]Lev. 14:22 [c]Lev. 14:10

22 [1]Lit., *his hand reaches* [a]Lev. 5:7 [b]Lev. 14:21, 24, 25

23 [a]Lev. 14:10, 11

24 [1]I.e., Approx. one pt. [a]Lev. 14:10

25 [a]Lev. 14:14

30 [1]Lit., *from those which his hand can reach*

31 [1]Lit., *his hand can reach* [a]Lev. 5:7

32 [1]Lit., *hand does not reach*

34 [a]Gen. 17:8; Num. 32:22; Deut. 7:1; 32:49

35 [a]Ps. 91:10

37 [1]Lit., *wall*

38 [1]Lit., *doorway of the house* [2]Lit., *shut up*

39 [1]Lit., *look*

40 [1]Lit., *to*

41 [1]Lit., *from the house around*

44 [1]Lit., *look* [a]Lev. 13:51

45 [a]Lev. 14:41

46 [1]Lit., *shut up* [a]Num. 19:7, 10, 21, 22

48 [1]Lit., *looks* [2]Lit., *healed*

49 [1]Lit., *scarlet color* [a]Lev. 14:4

50 and he shall slaughter the one bird in an earthenware vessel over [1]running water.

51 "Then he shall take the cedar wood and the [a]hyssop and the [1]scarlet string, with the live bird, and dip them in the blood of the slain bird, as well as in the [2]running water, and sprinkle the house seven times.

52 "He shall thus cleanse the house with the blood of the bird and with the [1]running water, along with the live bird and with the cedar wood and with the hyssop and with the [2]scarlet string.

53 "However, he shall let the live bird go free outside the city into the open field. So he shall make atonement for the house, and it shall be clean."

54 This is the law for any mark of leprosy—even for a [a]scale,

55 and for the [a]leprous garment or house,

56 and [a]for a swelling, and for a scab, and for a bright spot—

57 to teach [1]when they are unclean, and [2]when they are clean. This is the law of leprosy.

Cleansing Unhealthiness

15 THE LORD also spoke to Moses and to Aaron, saying,

2 "Speak to the sons of Israel, and say to them, '[a]When any man has a discharge from his [1]body, [2]his discharge is unclean.

3 'This, moreover, shall be his uncleanness in his discharge: it is his uncleanness whether his body allows its discharge to flow, or whether his body obstructs its discharge.

4 'Every bed on which the person with the discharge lies becomes unclean, and everything on which he sits becomes unclean.

5 'Anyone, moreover, who touches his bed shall wash his clothes and bathe in water and be unclean until evening;

6 and whoever sits on the thing on which the man with the discharge has been sitting, shall wash his clothes and bathe in water and be unclean until evening.

7 'Also whoever touches the [1]person with the discharge shall wash his clothes and bathe in water and be unclean until evening.

8 'Or if the man with the discharge spits on one who is clean, he too shall wash his clothes and bathe in water and be unclean until evening.

9 'And every saddle on which the person with the discharge rides becomes unclean.

10 'Whoever then touches any of the things which were under him shall be unclean until evening, and he who carries them shall wash his clothes and bathe in water and be unclean until evening.

11 'Likewise, whomever the one with the discharge touches without having rinsed his hands in water shall wash his clothes and bathe in water and be unclean until evening.

12 'However, an [a]earthenware vessel which the person with the discharge touches shall be broken, and every wooden vessel shall be rinsed in water.

13 'Now when the man with the discharge becomes cleansed from his discharge, then he [a]shall count off for himself seven days for his cleansing; he shall then wash his clothes and bathe his body in [1]running water and shall become clean.

14 'Then on the eighth day he shall take for himself [a]two turtledoves or two young pigeons, and come before the LORD to the doorway of the tent of meeting, and give them to the priest;

15 and the priest shall offer them, [a]one for a sin offering, and the other for a burnt offering. So [b]the priest shall make atonement on his behalf before the LORD because of his discharge.

16 '[a]Now if a [1]man has a seminal emission, he shall bathe all his body in water and be unclean until evening.

17 'As for any garment or any leather on which there is seminal emission, it shall be washed with water and be unclean until evening.

18 'If a man lies with a woman *so that* there is a seminal emission, they shall both bathe in water and be [a]unclean until evening.

19 '[a]When a woman has a discharge, *if* her discharge in her body is blood, she shall continue in her menstrual impurity for seven days; and whoever touches her shall be unclean until evening.

20 'Everything also on which she lies during her menstrual impurity shall be unclean, and everything on which she sits shall be unclean.

21 'And anyone who touches her bed shall wash his clothes and bathe in water and be unclean until evening.

22 'And whoever touches any thing on which she sits shall wash his clothes and bathe in water and be unclean until evening.

23 'Whether it be on the bed or on the thing on which she is sitting, when he touches it, he shall be unclean until evening.

24 '[a]And if a man actually lies with her, so that her menstrual impurity is on him, he shall be unclean seven days, and every bed on which he lies shall be unclean.

25 '[a]Now if a woman has a discharge of her blood many days, not at the period of her menstrual impurity, or if she has a discharge beyond [1]that period, all the days of her impure discharge she shall continue as though [2]in her menstrual impurity; she is unclean.

26 'Any bed on which she lies all the days of her discharge shall be to her like [1]her bed at menstruation; and every thing on which she sits shall be unclean, like [2]her uncleanness at that time.

50 [1]Lit., *living*

51 [1]Lit., *scarlet color* [2]Lit., *living* [a]1 Kin. 4:33; Ps. 51:7

52 [1]Lit., *living* [2]Lit., *scarlet color*

54 [a]Lev. 13:30

55 [a]Lev. 13:47-52

56 [a]Lev. 13:2

57 [1]Lit., *in the day of uncleanness* [2]Lit., *in the day of cleanness*

2 [1]Lit., *flesh*, and so throughout the ch. [2]Or, *by his discharge, he is unclean* [a]Lev. 22:4; Num. 5:2; 2 Sam. 3:29

7 [1]Lit., *flesh*

12 [a]Lev. 6:28; 11:33

13 [1]Lit., *living* [a]Lev. 8:33; 14:8

14 [a]Lev. 14:22, 23

15 [a]Lev. 5:7; 14:31 [b]Lev. 14:19, 31

16 [1]Lit., *man's . . . goes out from him* [a]Lev. 22:4; Deut. 23:10, 11

18 [a]1 Sam. 21:4

19 [a]Lev. 12:2

24 [a]Lev. 18:19; 20:18

25 [1]Lit., *her menstrual impurity* [2]Lit., *in the days of* [a]Matt. 9:20; Mark 5:25; Luke 8:43

26 [1]Lit., *the bed of her menstrual impurity* [2]Lit., *the uncleanness of her menstrual impurity*

27 'Likewise, whoever touches them shall be unclean and shall wash his clothes and bathe in water and be unclean until evening.

28 'When she becomes clean from her discharge, she shall count off for herself seven days; and afterward she shall be clean.

29 'Then on the eighth day she shall take for herself two turtledoves or two young pigeons, and bring them in to the priest, to the doorway of the tent of meeting.

30 'And the priest shall offer the [a]one for a sin offering and the other for a burnt offering. So the priest shall make atonement on her behalf before the LORD because of her impure discharge.'

31 "Thus you shall keep the sons of Israel separated from their uncleanness, lest they die in their uncleanness by their [a]defiling My [1]tabernacle that is among them."

32 This is the law for the one with a discharge, and for the man [1]who has a seminal emission so that he is unclean by it,

33 and for the woman who is ill because of menstrual impurity, and for the one who has a discharge, whether a male or a female, or a man who lies with an unclean woman.

Law of Atonement

16 NOW the LORD spoke to Moses after [a]the death of the two sons of Aaron, when they had approached the presence of the LORD and died.

2 And the LORD said to Moses, "Tell your brother Aaron that he shall not enter [a]at any time into the holy place inside the veil, before the [1]mercy seat which is on the ark, lest he die; for [b]I will appear in the cloud over the [1]mercy seat.

3 "Aaron shall enter the holy place with this: with a [1]bull for a [a]sin offering and a ram for a burnt offering.

4 "He shall put on the [a]holy linen tunic, and the linen undergarments shall be next to his [1]body, and he shall be girded with the linen sash, and attired with the linen turban (these are holy garments). Then he shall [b]bathe his [1]body in water and put them on.

5 "And he shall take from the congregation of the sons of Israel [a]two male goats for a sin offering and one ram for a burnt offering.

6 "Then [a]Aaron shall offer the bull for the sin offering which is for himself, that he may make atonement for himself and for his household.

7 "And he shall take the two goats and present them before the LORD at the doorway of the tent of meeting.

8 "And Aaron shall cast lots for the two goats, one lot for the LORD and the other lot for the [1]scapegoat.

9 "Then Aaron shall offer the goat on which the lot for the LORD fell, and make it a sin offering.

10 "But the goat on which the lot for the [1]scapegoat fell, shall be presented alive before the LORD, to make [a]atonement upon it, to send it into the wilderness as the [1]scapegoat.

11 "Then Aaron shall offer the bull of the sin offering [a]which is for himself, and make atonement for himself and [b]for his household, and he shall slaughter the bull of the sin offering which is for himself.

12 "And he shall take a [a]firepan full of coals of fire from upon the altar before the LORD, and [1]two handfuls of finely ground [b]sweet incense, and bring *it* inside the veil.

13 "And he shall put the incense on the fire before the LORD, that the cloud of incense may cover the [1a]mercy seat that is on *the ark of* the testimony, [b]lest he die.

14 "Moreover, [a]he shall take some of the blood of the bull and sprinkle *it* [b]with his finger on the [1]mercy seat on the east *side*; also in front of the [1]mercy seat he shall sprinkle some of the blood with his finger seven times.

15 "Then he shall slaughter the goat of the sin offering [a]which is for the people, and bring its blood inside the veil, and do with its blood as he did with the blood of the bull, and sprinkle it on the [1]mercy seat and in front of the [1]mercy seat.

16 "And [a]he shall make atonement for the holy place, because of the impurities of the sons of Israel, and because of their transgressions, in regard to all their sins; and thus he shall do for the tent of meeting which abides with them in the midst of their impurities.

17 "When he goes in to make atonement in the holy place, no one shall be in the tent of meeting until he comes out, that he may make atonement for himself and for his household and for all the assembly of Israel.

18 "Then he shall go out to the altar that is before the LORD and make atonement for it, and shall take some of the blood of the bull and of the blood of the goat, and [a]put it on the horns of the altar on all sides.

19 "And [a]with his finger he shall sprinkle some of the blood on it seven times, and cleanse it, and from the impurities of the sons of Israel consecrate it.

20 "When he finishes atoning for the holy place, and the tent of meeting and the altar, he shall offer the live goat.

21 "Then Aaron shall lay both of his hands on the head of the live goat, and [a]confess over it all the iniquities of the sons of Israel, and all their transgressions [1]in regard to all their sins; and he shall lay them on the head of the goat and send *it* away into the wilderness by the hand of a man who *stands* in readiness.

22 "And the goat shall bear on itself all their iniquities to a solitary land; and he shall release the goat in the wilderness.

30 [a]Lev. 5:7

31 [1]Or, *dwelling place* [a]Lev. 20:3; Num. 19:13, 20; Ezek. 5:11; 36:17

32 [1]Lit., *whose seminal emission goes out from him*

1 [a]Lev. 10:1, 2

2 [1]Lit., *propitiatory* [a]Ex. 30:10; Heb. 6:19; 9:7, 25 [b]Ex. 25:21, 22; 40:34; 1 Kin. 8:10-12

3 [1]Or, *bull of the herd* [a]Lev. 4:1-12; 16:6; Heb. 9:7

4 [1]Lit., *flesh* [a]Ex. 28:39, 42 [b]Ex. 30:20; Lev. 16:24; Heb. 10:22

5 [a]Lev. 4:13-21; 2 Chr. 29:21; Ezek. 45:22

6 [a]Heb. 5:3

8 [1]Lit., *goat of removal,* or else a name: *Azazel*

10 [1]Lit., *goat of removal,* or else a name: *Azazel* [a]Is. 53:4-10; Rom. 3:25; 1 John 2:2

11 [a]Heb. 7:27; 9:7 [b]Lev. 16:33

12 [1]Lit., *the filling of the hollow of his hands* [a]Lev. 10:1; Num. 16:18 [b]Ex. 30:34-38

13 [1]Lit., *propitiatory* [a]Ex. 25:21 [b]Ex. 28:43; Lev. 22:9; Num. 4:15, 20

14 [1]Lit., *propitiatory* [a]Heb. 9:25 [b]Lev. 4:6, 17

15 [1]Lit., *propitiatory* [a]Heb. 7:27; 9:7, 12

16 [a]Ex. 29:36, 37; 30:10; Heb. 2:17

18 [a]Lev. 4:25; Ezek. 43:20, 22

19 [a]Lev. 16:14; Ezek. 43:20

21 [1]Lit., *in addition to* [a]Lev. 5:5

23"Then Aaron shall come into the
tent of meeting, and take off [a]the linen
garments which he put on when he went
into the holy place, and shall leave them
there.
24"And [a]he shall bathe his [1]body with
water in a holy place and put on [b]his
clothes, and come forth and offer his
burnt offering and the burnt offering of
the people, and make atonement for
himself and for the people.
25"Then he shall offer up in smoke the
fat of the sin offering on the altar.
26"And the one who released the goat
as the [1]scapegoat [a]shall wash his clothes
and bathe his [2]body with water; then
afterward he shall come into the camp.
27"But the bull of the sin offering and
the goat of the sin offering, [a]whose blood
was brought in to make atonement in
the holy place, shall be taken outside the
camp, and they shall burn their hides,
their flesh, and their refuse in the fire.
28"Then the [a]one who burns them
shall wash his clothes and bathe his
body with water, then afterward he shall
come into the camp.

An Annual Atonement

29"And *this* shall be a permanent
statute for you: [a]in the seventh month,
on the tenth day of the month, you shall
humble your souls, and not [b]do any
work, whether the native, or the alien
who sojourns among you;
30 for it is on this day that [1]atonement
shall be made for you to [a]cleanse you;
you shall be clean from all your sins
before the LORD.
31"It is to be a sabbath of solemn rest
for you, that you may [a]humble your
souls; it is a permanent statute.
32"So the priest who is anointed and
[1]ordained to serve as priest in his father's place shall make atonement: he
shall thus put on [a]the linen garments, the
holy garments,
33 and make atonement for the holy
sanctuary; and he shall make atonement
for the tent of meeting and for the altar.
He shall also make atonement for [a]the
priests and for all the people of the
assembly.
34"Now you shall have this as a [a]per-
manent statute, to [b]make atonement for
the sons of Israel for all their sins once
every year." And just as the LORD had
commanded Moses, *so* he did.

Blood for Atonement

17 THEN the LORD spoke to Moses,
saying,
2"Speak to Aaron and to his sons,
and to all the sons of Israel, and say to
them, 'This is what the LORD has commanded, saying,
3"Any man from the house of Israel
who slaughters an ox, or a lamb, or a
goat in the camp, or who slaughters it
outside the camp,
4 and [a]has not brought it to the
doorway of the tent of meeting to present *it* as an offering to the LORD before
the [1]tabernacle of the LORD, bloodguiltiness is to be reckoned to that man. He
has shed blood and that man shall be cut
off from among his people.
5"[1]The reason is so that the sons of
Israel may bring their sacrifices which
they were sacrificing in the open field,
that they may bring them in to the
LORD, at the doorway of the tent of
meeting to the priest, and sacrifice them
as sacrifices of peace offerings to the
LORD.
6"And the priest shall sprinkle the
blood on the altar of the LORD at the
doorway of the tent of meeting, and
[a]offer up the fat in smoke as a soothing
aroma to the LORD.
7"And [a]they shall no longer sacrifice
their sacrifices to the [1]goat demons with
which they play the harlot. This shall be
a permanent statute to them throughout
their generations."'
8"Then you shall say to them, 'Any
man from the house of Israel, or from
the aliens who sojourn among them, who
offers a burnt offering or sacrifice,
9 and [a]does not bring it to the doorway of the tent of meeting to [1]offer it to
the LORD, that man also shall be cut off
from his people.
10 '[a]And any man from the house of
Israel, or from the aliens who sojourn
among them, who eats any blood, [b]I will
set My face against that person who eats
blood, and will cut him off from among
his people.
11 'For [a]the [1]life of the flesh is in the
blood, and I have given it to you on the
altar to make atonement for your souls;
for [b]it is the blood by reason of the [1]life
that makes atonement.'
12"Therefore I said to the sons of
Israel, 'No person among you may eat
blood, nor may any alien who sojourns
among you eat blood.'
13"So when any man from the sons of
Israel, or from the aliens who sojourn
among them, [1]in hunting catches a beast
or a bird which may be eaten, [a]he shall
pour out its blood and cover it with
earth.
14"[a]For *as for the* [1]life of all flesh, its
blood is *identified* with its [1]life. Therefore I said to the sons of Israel, 'You are
not to eat the blood of any flesh, for the
[1]life of all flesh is its blood; whoever eats
it shall be cut off.'
15"[a]And when any person eats *an
animal* which dies, or is torn *by beasts*,
whether he is a native or an alien, he
shall wash his clothes and bathe in
water, and remain unclean until evening;
then he will become clean.
16"But if he does not wash *them* or
bathe his body, then [a]he shall bear his
[1]guilt."

Laws on Immoral Relations

18 THEN the LORD spoke to Moses,
saying,
2"Speak to the sons of Israel and say
to them, '[a]I am the LORD your God.

23 [a]Lev. 16:4; Ezek. 42:14; 44:19

24 [1]Lit., *flesh* [a]Lev. 16:4 [b]Ex. 28:40, 41

26 [1]Lit., *goat of removal,* or else a name: *Azazel* [2]Lit., *flesh* [a]Lev. 11:25, 40

27 [a]Lev. 6:30; Heb. 13:11

28 [a]Num. 19:8

29 [a]Lev. 23:27; Num. 29:7 [b]Ex. 31:14, 15

30 [1]Lit., *he shall make atonement* [a]Ps. 51:2; Jer. 33:8; Eph. 5:26

31 [a]Lev. 23:32; Ezra 8:21; Is. 58:3, 5; Dan. 10:12

32 [1]Lit., *whose hand is filled* [a]Lev. 16:4

33 [a]Lev. 16:11

34 [a]Lev. 23:31 [b]Heb. 9:7

4 [1]Lit., *dwelling place* [a]Deut. 12:5-21

5 [1]Lit., *In order that*

6 [a]Num. 18:17

7 [1]Or, *goat-idols* [a]Ex. 22:20; 32:8; 34:15; Deut. 32:17; 2 Chr. 11:15; Ps. 106:37f.; 1 Cor. 10:20

9 [1]Lit., *do* [a]Ex. 20:24; Lev. 17:4

10 [a]Gen. 9:4; Lev. 3:17; 7:26, 27; Deut. 12:16, 23-25; 1 Sam. 14:33 [b]Lev. 20:3, 6; Jer. 44:11

11 [1]Lit., *soul* [a]Gen. 9:4; Lev. 17:14 [b]Heb. 9:22

13 [1]Lit., *who in hunting* [a]Deut. 12:16

14 [1]Lit., *soul* [a]Gen. 9:4; Lev. 17:11

15 [a]Ex. 22:31; Lev. 7:24; 22:8; Deut. 14:21

16 [1]Or, *iniquity* [a]Num. 19:20

2 [a]Ex. 6:7; Lev. 11:44; Ezek. 20:5

3 'You shall not do [1]what is [a]done in
the land of Egypt where you lived, nor
are you to do [1]what is [b]done in the land
of Canaan where I am bringing you; you
shall not walk in their statutes.
4 'You are to perform My judgments
and keep My statutes, [1]to live in accord
with them; [a]I am the LORD your God.
5 'So you shall keep My statutes and
My judgments, [a]by which a man may
live if he does them; I am the LORD.
6 'None of you shall approach any
blood relative [1]of his to uncover nakedness; I am the LORD.
7 '[a]You shall not uncover the nakedness of your father, that is, the nakedness of your mother. She is your mother;
you are not to uncover her nakedness.
8 '[a]You shall not uncover the nakedness of your father's wife; it is your
father's nakedness.
9 '[a]The nakedness of your sister,
either your father's daughter or your
mother's daughter, whether born at
home or born outside, their nakedness
you shall not uncover.
10 'The nakedness of your son's
daughter or your daughter's daughter,
their nakedness you shall not uncover;
for [1]their nakedness is yours.
11 'The nakedness of your father's
wife's daughter, [1]born to your father, she
is your sister, you shall not uncover her
nakedness.
12 '[a]You shall not uncover the nakedness of your father's sister; she is your
father's blood relative.
13 'You shall not uncover the nakedness of your mother's sister, for she is
your mother's blood relative.
14 '[a]You shall not uncover the nakedness of your father's brother; you shall
not approach his wife, she is your aunt.
15 '[a]You shall not uncover the nakedness of your daughter-in-law; she is your
son's wife, you shall not uncover her
nakedness.
16 '[a]You shall not uncover the nakedness of your brother's wife; it is your
brother's nakedness.
17 '[a]You shall not uncover the nakedness of a woman and of her daughter,
nor shall you take her son's daughter or
her daughter's daughter, to uncover her
nakedness; they are blood relatives. It is
[1]lewdness.
18 'And you shall not [1]marry a woman
in addition to [2]her sister [3]as a rival while
she is alive, to uncover her nakedness.
19 '[a]Also you shall not approach a
woman to uncover her nakedness during
her [b]menstrual impurity.
20 '[a]And you shall not have intercourse with your neighbor's wife, to be
defiled with her.
21 'Neither shall you give any of your
offspring [a]to [1]offer them to Molech, nor
shall you [b]profane the name of your
God; I am the LORD.
22 '[a]You shall not lie with a male as
[1]one lies with a female; it is an abomination.
23 '[a]Also you shall not have intercourse with any animal to be defiled
with it, nor shall any woman stand
before an animal to [1]mate with it; it is a
perversion.
24 'Do not defile yourselves by any of
these things; for by all these [a]the nations
which I am casting out before you have
become defiled.
25 'For the land has become defiled,
[a]therefore I have visited its [1]punishment
upon it, so the land [b]has spewed out its
inhabitants.
26 'But as for you, you are to keep My
statutes and My judgments, and shall
not do any of these abominations, *neither* the native, nor the alien who sojourns among you
27 (for the men of the land who have
been before you have done all these
abominations, and the land has become
defiled);
28 so that the land may not spew you
out, should you defile it, as it has spewed
out the nation which has been before
you.
29 'For whoever does any of these
abominations, [1]those persons who do *so*
shall be cut off from among their people.
30 'Thus you are to keep [a]My charge,
that you do not practice any of the
abominable customs which have been
practiced before you, so as not to defile
yourselves with them; [b]I am the LORD
your God.' "

Idolatry Forbidden

19 THEN the LORD spoke to Moses,
saying,
2 "Speak to all the congregation of the
sons of Israel and say to them, '[a]You
shall be holy, for I the LORD your God
am holy.
3 'Every one of you [a]shall reverence
his mother and his father, and you shall
keep [b]My sabbaths; [c]I am the LORD
your God.
4 'Do not turn to [a]idols or make for
yourselves molten [b]gods; I am the LORD
your God.
5 'Now when you offer a sacrifice of
peace offerings to the LORD, you shall
offer it so that you may be accepted.
6 'It shall be eaten the same day you
offer *it*, and the next day; but what
remains until the third day shall be
burned with fire.
7 'So if it is eaten at all on the third
day, it is an offense; it will not be
accepted.
8 'And everyone who eats it will bear
his iniquity, for he has profaned the holy
thing of the LORD; and that person shall
be cut off from his people.

Sundry Laws

9 '[a]Now when you reap the harvest of
your land, you shall not reap to the very
corners of your field, neither shall you
gather the gleanings of your harvest.
10 'Nor shall you glean your vineyard,
nor shall you gather the fallen fruit of

18:3 [1]Lit., *according to the deed of* [a]Ezek. 20:7, 8 [b]Lev. 18:24-30; 20:23
4 [1]Lit., *to walk in them* [a]Lev. 18:2
5 [a]Neh. 9:29; Ezek. 18:9; 20:11; Luke 10:28; Rom. 10:5; Gal. 3:12
6 [1]Lit., *of his flesh*
7 [a]Lev. 20:11; Deut. 27:20; Ezek. 22:10
8 [a]Lev. 20:11; Deut. 22:30; 27:20; 1 Cor. 5:1
9 [a]Lev. 18:11; 20:17; Deut. 27:22
10 [1]Lit., *they are your nakedness*
11 [1]Lit., *begotten of*
12 [a]Lev. 20:19
14 [a]Lev. 20:20
15 [a]Lev. 20:12
16 [a]Lev. 20:21
17 [1]Or, *wickedness* [a]Lev. 20:14
18 [1]Lit., *take a wife* [2]Or, *another* [3]Lit., *to be*
19 [a]Lev. 15:24; 20:18 [b]Lev. 12:2
20 [a]Lev. 20:10; Prov. 6:29; Matt. 5:27, 28; 1 Cor. 6:9; Heb. 13:4
21 [1]Lit., *cause to pass over* [a]Lev. 20:2-5; Deut. 12:31 [b]Lev. 19:12; 20:3; 21:6; Ezek. 36:20; Mal. 1:12
22 [1]Lit., *those who lie* [a]Lev. 20:13; Deut. 23:18 mg.; Rom. 1:27
23 [1]Or, *lie* [a]Ex. 22:19; Lev. 20:15, 16; Deut. 27:21
24 [a]Lev. 18:3; Deut. 18:12
25 [1]Lit., *iniquity* [a]Lev. 20:23; Deut. 9:5; 18:12 [b]Lev. 18:28; 20:22
29 [1]Or, *and the*
30 [a]Lev. 22:9; Deut. 11:1 [b]Lev. 18:2

19:2 [a]Ex. 19:6; Lev. 11:44; 20:7, 26; Eph. 1:4; 1 Pet. 1:16
3 [a]Ex. 20:12; 31:13; Deut. 5:16 [b]Ex. 20:8 [c]Lev. 11:44
4 [a]Lev. 26:1; Ps. 96:5; 115:4-7 [b]Ex. 20:23; 34:17
9 [a]Lev. 23:22; Deut. 24:20-22

your vineyard; you shall leave them for
the needy and for the stranger. I am the
LORD your God.
11 '[a]You shall not steal, nor deal
falsely, [b]nor lie to one another.
12 '[a]And you shall not swear falsely by
My name, so as to [b]profane the name of
your God; I am the LORD.
13 '[a]You shall not oppress your neighbor, nor rob *him.* [b]The wages of a hired
man are not to remain with you all night
until morning.
14 'You shall not curse a deaf man, nor
[a]place a stumbling block before the
blind, but you shall revere your God; I
am the LORD.
15 '[a]You shall do no injustice in judgment; you shall not be partial to the
poor nor defer to the great, but you are
to judge your neighbor fairly.
16 'You shall not go about as [a]a slanderer among your people, and you are
not to [1]act against the [2b]life of your
neighbor; I am the LORD.
17 'You [a]shall not hate your [1]fellow
countryman in your heart; you [b]may
surely reprove your neighbor, but shall
not incur sin because of him.
18 '[a]You shall not take vengeance,
[b]nor bear any grudge against the sons of
your people, but [c]you shall love your
neighbor as yourself; I am the LORD.
19 'You are to keep My statutes. You
shall not breed together two kinds of
your cattle; [a]you shall not sow your field
with two kinds of seed, nor wear a
garment upon you of two kinds of material mixed together.
20 '[a]Now if a man lies carnally with a
woman who is a slave acquired for
another man, but who has in no way
been redeemed, nor given her freedom,
there shall be punishment; they shall
not, *however,* be put to death, because
she was not free.
21 'And he shall bring his guilt offering
to the LORD to the doorway of the tent
of meeting, [a]a ram for a guilt offering.
22 'The priest shall also make atonement for him with the ram of the guilt
offering before the LORD for his sin
which he has committed, and the sin
which he has committed shall be forgiven him.
23 'And when you enter the land and
plant all kinds of trees for food, then you
shall count their fruit as [1]forbidden.
Three years it shall be [1]forbidden to
you; *it* shall not be eaten.
24 'But in the fourth year all its fruit
shall be holy, an offering of praise to the
LORD.
25 'And in the fifth year you are to eat
of its fruit, that its yield may increase for
you; I am the LORD your God.
26 'You shall not eat *anything* [a]with
the blood, nor practice [b]divination or
soothsaying.
27 '[a]You shall not round off the side-
growth of your heads, nor harm the
edges of your beard.
28 'You shall not make any cuts in
your [1]body for the [2]dead, nor make any
tattoo marks on yourselves: I am the
LORD.
29 '[a]Do not [1]profane your daughter by
making her a harlot, so that the land
may not fall to harlotry, and the land
become full of lewdness.
30 'You shall [a]keep My sabbaths and
[b]revere My sanctuary; I am the LORD.
31 'Do not turn to [1a]mediums or spiritists; do not seek them out to be defiled
by them. I am the LORD your God.
32 '[a]You shall rise up before the gray-
headed, and honor the [1]aged, and you
shall revere your God; I am the LORD.
33 '[a]When a stranger resides with you
in your land, you shall not do him
wrong.
34 'The stranger who resides with you
shall be to you as the native among you,
and [a]you shall love him as yourself; for
you were aliens in the land of Egypt: I
am the LORD your God.
35 '[a]You shall do no wrong in judgment, in measurement of weight, or
capacity.
36 'You shall have [a]just balances, just
weights, a just [1]ephah, and a just [2]hin: I
am the LORD your God, who brought
you out from the land of Egypt.
37 'You shall thus observe all My
statutes, and all My ordinances, and do
them: I am the LORD.' "

On Human Sacrifice and Immoralities

20 THEN the LORD spoke to Moses,
saying,
2 "You shall also say to the sons of
Israel, 'Any man from the sons of Israel
or from the aliens sojourning in Israel,
[a]who gives any of his [1]offspring to
Molech, shall surely be put to death;
[b]the people of the land shall stone him
with stones.
3 'I will also set My face against that
man and will cut him off from among his
people, because he has given some of his
[1]offspring to Molech, [a]so as to defile My
sanctuary and [b]to profane My holy
name.
4 'If the people of the land, however,
[1]should ever disregard that man when he
gives any of his [2]offspring to Molech, so
as not to put him to death,
5 then I Myself will set My face
against that man and against his family;
and I will cut off from among their
people both him and all those who play
the harlot after him, by playing the
harlot after Molech.
6 'As for the person who turns to
[1a]mediums and to spiritists, to play the
harlot after them, I will also set My face
against that person and will cut him off
from among his people.
7 'You shall consecrate yourselves
therefore and [a]be holy, for I am the
LORD your God.
8 'And [a]you shall keep My statutes
and practice them; I am the LORD who
sanctifies you.

11 [a]Ex. 20:15, 16 [b]Jer. 9:3-5; Eph. 4:25
12 [a]Ex. 20:7; Deut. 5:11; Matt. 5:33 [b]Lev. 18:21
13 [a]Ex. 22:7-15, 21-27 [b]Deut. 24:15; James 5:4
14 [a]Deut. 27:18
15 [a]Ex. 23:3, 6; Deut. 1:17; 10:17; 16:19
16 [1]Lit., *stand* [2]Lit., *blood* [a]Ps. 15:3; Jer. 6:28; 9:4; Ezek. 22:9 [b]Ex. 23:7; Deut. 27:25
17 [1]Lit., *brother* [a]1 John 2:9, 11; 3:15 [b]Matt. 18:15; Luke 17:3
18 [a]Deut. 32:35; Rom. 12:19; Heb. 10:30 [b]Ps. 103:9 [c]Matt. 19:19; Mark 12:31; Luke 10:27; Rom. 13:9; Gal. 5:14; James 2:8
19 [a]Deut. 22:9, 11
20 [a]Deut. 22:23-27
21 [a]Lev. 6:1-7
23 [1]Lit., *uncircumcised*
26 [a]Gen. 9:4; Lev. 7:26f.; 17:10; Deut. 12:16, 23 [b]Deut. 18:10; 2 Kin. 17:17
27 [a]Lev. 21:5; Deut. 14:1
28 [1]Lit., *flesh* [2]Lit., *soul*
29 [1]Or, *degrade* [a]Lev. 21:9; Deut. 22:21; 23:17, 18
30 [a]Lev. 19:3 [b]Lev. 26:2
31 [1]Or, *ghosts or spirits* [a]Lev. 20:6, 27; Deut. 18:11; 1 Sam. 28:3; Is. 8:19
32 [1]Lit., *face of the aged* [a]Prov. 23:22; Lam. 5:12; 1 Tim. 5:1
33 [a]Ex. 22:21; Deut. 24:17, 18
34 [a]Lev. 19:18
35 [a]Deut. 25:13-16; Ezek. 45:10
36 [1]I.e., Approx. one bu. [2]I.e., Approx. one gal. [a]Deut. 25:13-15; Prov. 20:10

2 [1]Lit., *seed* [a]Lev. 18:21 [b]Lev. 20:27; 24:14-23; Num. 15:35, 36; Deut. 21:21
3 [1]Lit., *seed* [a]Lev. 15:31 [b]Lev. 18:21
4 [1]Lit., *hiding they hide their eyes from* [2]Lit., *seed*
6 [1]Or, *ghosts and spirits* [a]Lev. 19:31
7 [a]Eph. 1:4; 1 Pet. 1:16
8 [a]Ex. 31:13

9 '[a]If *there is* anyone who curses his father or his mother, he shall surely be put to death; he has cursed his father or his mother, his bloodguiltiness is upon him.

10 '[a]If *there is* a man who commits adultery with another man's wife, one who commits adultery with his friend's wife, the adulterer and the adulteress shall surely be put to death.

11 '[a]If *there is* a man who lies with his father's wife, he has uncovered his father's nakedness; both of them shall surely be put to death, their bloodguiltiness is upon them.

12 '[a]If *there is* a man who lies with his daughter-in-law, both of them shall surely be put to death; they have committed [1]incest, their bloodguiltiness is upon them.

13 '[a]If *there is* a man who lies with a male as those who lie with a woman, both of them have committed a detestable act; they shall surely be put to death. Their bloodguiltiness is upon them.

14 '[a]If *there is* a man who [1]marries a woman and her mother, it is immorality; both he and they shall be burned with fire, that there may be no immorality in your midst.

15 '[a]If *there is* a man who lies with an animal, he shall surely be put to death; you shall also kill the animal.

16 'If *there is* a woman who approaches any animal to [1]mate with it, you shall kill the woman and the animal; they shall surely be put to death. Their bloodguiltiness is upon them.

17 '[a]If *there is* a man who takes his sister, his father's daughter or his mother's daughter, so that he sees her nakedness and she sees his nakedness, it is a disgrace; and they shall be cut off in the sight of the sons of their people. He has uncovered his sister's nakedness; he bears his guilt.

18 '[a]If *there is* a man who lies with a [1]menstruous woman and uncovers her nakedness, he has laid bare her flow, and she has [2]exposed the flow of her blood; thus both of them shall be cut off from among their people.

19 '[a]You shall also not uncover the nakedness of your mother's sister or of your father's sister, for such a one has made naked his [1]blood relative; they shall bear their guilt.

20 '[a]If *there is* a man who lies with his uncle's wife he has uncovered his uncle's nakedness; they shall bear their sin. They shall die childless.

21 '[a]If *there is* a man who takes his brother's wife, it is [1]abhorrent; he has uncovered his brother's nakedness. They shall be childless.

22 'You are therefore to keep all My statutes and all My ordinances and do them, so that the land to which I am bringing you to [1]live will not [a]spew you out.

23 'Moreover, you shall not [1]follow [a]the customs of the nation which I shall drive out before you, for they did all these things, and [b]therefore I have abhorred them.

24 'Hence I have said to you, "[a]You are to possess their land, and I Myself will give it to you to possess it, a land flowing with milk and honey." I am the LORD your God, who has [b]separated you from the peoples.

25 '[a]You are therefore to make a distinction between the clean animal and the unclean, and between the unclean bird and the clean; and you shall not make [1]yourselves detestable by animal or by bird or by anything [2]that creeps on the ground, which I have separated for you as unclean.

26 'Thus you are to be holy to Me, for I the LORD am holy; and I [a]have set you apart from the peoples to be Mine.

27 'Now a man or a woman [a]who is a medium or a [1]spiritist shall surely be put to death. They shall be stoned with stones, their bloodguiltiness is upon them.' "

Regulations concerning Priests

21 THEN the LORD said to Moses, "Speak to the priests, the sons of Aaron, and say to them, '[a]No one shall defile himself for a *dead* person among his people,

2 [a]except for his relatives who are nearest to him, his mother and his father and his son and his daughter and his brother,

3 also for his virgin sister, who is near to him [1]because she has had no husband; for her he may defile himself.

4 'He shall not defile himself as a [1]relative by marriage among his people, and so profane himself.

5 '[a]They shall not make any baldness on their heads, [b]nor shave off the edges of their beards, [c]nor make any cuts in their flesh.

6 'They shall be holy to their God and [a]not profane the name of their God, for they present the offerings by fire [1]to the LORD, [b]the bread of their God; so they shall be holy.

7 '[a]They shall not take a woman who is profaned by harlotry, nor shall they take a woman divorced from her husband; for he is holy to his God.

8 'You shall consecrate him, therefore, for he offers [a]the bread of your God; he shall be holy to you; for I the LORD, who sanctifies you, am holy.

9 '[a]Also the daughter of any priest, if she profanes herself by harlotry, she profanes her father; she shall be burned with fire.

10 'And the priest who is the highest among his brothers, on whose head the anointing oil has been poured, and [1]who has been consecrated to wear the garments, [a]shall not [2]uncover his head, nor tear his clothes;

---

9 [a]Ex. 21:17; Deut. 27:16

10 [a]Ex. 20:14; Lev. 18:20; Deut. 5:18

11 [a]Lev. 18:7, 8; Deut. 27:20

12 [1]Lit., *confusion;* i.e., a violation of divine order [a]Lev. 18:15

13 [a]Lev. 18:22

14 [1]Lit., *takes* [a]Lev. 18:17; Deut. 27:23

15 [a]Lev. 18:23; Deut. 27:21

16 [1]Lit., *lie*

17 [a]Lev. 18:9; Deut. 27:22

18 [1]Lit., *sick* [2]Or, *uncovered* [a]Lev. 15:24; 18:19

19 [1]Lit., *flesh* [a]Lev. 18:12, 13

20 [a]Lev. 18:14

21 [1]Or, *an impure deed* [a]Lev. 18:16

22 [1]Lit., *dwell in it* [a]Lev. 18:28

23 [1]Lit., *walk in the statutes* [a]Lev. 18:3 [b]Lev. 18:25

24 [a]Ex. 13:5; 33:1-3 [b]Ex. 33:16; Lev. 20:26

25 [1]Lit., *your souls* [2]Lit., *with which the ground creeps* [a]Lev. 10:10; 11:1-47; Deut. 14:3-21

26 [a]Lev. 20:24

27 [1]Lit., *spiritist among them* [a]Lev. 19:31

1 [a]Lev. 19:28; Ezek. 44:25

2 [a]Lev. 21:11

3 [1]Or, *whom no man has had*

4 [1]Lit., *husband among*

5 [a]Deut. 14:1; Ezek. 44:20 [b]Lev. 19:27 [c]Deut. 14:1

6 [1]Lit., *of* [a]Lev. 18:21 [b]Lev. 3:11

7 [a]Lev. 21:13, 14

8 [a]Lev. 21:6

9 [a]Gen. 38:24; Lev. 19:29

10 [1]Lit., *whose hand has been filled* [2]Lit., *unbind* [a]Lev. 10:6

11 [a]nor shall he approach any dead person, nor defile himself *even* for his father or his mother;

12 [a]nor shall he go out of the sanctuary, nor profane the sanctuary of his God; for [b]the consecration of the anointing oil of his God is on him: I am the LORD.

13 'And he shall take a wife in her virginity.

14 '[a]A widow, or a divorced woman, or one who is profaned by harlotry, these he may not take; but rather he is to [1]marry a virgin of his own people;

15 that he may not profane his [1]offspring among his people: for I am the LORD who sanctifies him.' "

16 Then the LORD spoke to Moses, saying,

17 "Speak to Aaron, saying, 'No man of your [1]offspring throughout their generations who has a defect shall approach to offer the [a]bread of his God.

18 '[a]For no one who has a defect shall approach: a blind man, or a lame man, or he who has a [1a]disfigured *face*, or any deformed *limb*,

19 or a man who has a broken foot or broken hand,

20 or a hunchback or a dwarf, or *one who has* a [1]defect in his eye or eczema or scabs or [a]crushed testicles.

21 'No man among the [1]descendants of Aaron the priest, who has a defect, is to come near to offer the LORD's offerings by fire; *since* he has a defect, he shall not come near to offer [a]the bread of his God.

22 'He may eat [a]the bread of his God, *both* of the most holy and of the holy,

23 only he shall not go in to the veil or come near the altar because he has a defect, that he may not profane My sanctuaries. For I am the LORD who sanctifies them.' "

24 So Moses spoke to Aaron and to his sons and to all the sons of Israel.

Sundry Rules for Priests

22 THEN the LORD spoke to Moses, saying,

2 "Tell Aaron and his sons to be careful with the holy *gifts* of the sons of Israel, which they dedicate to Me, so as not to profane My holy name; I am the LORD.

3 "Say to them, '[a]If any man among all your [1]descendants throughout your generations approaches the holy *gifts* which the sons of Israel dedicate to the LORD, while he has an uncleanness, that person shall be cut off from before Me. I am the LORD.

4 '[a]No man, of the [1]descendants of Aaron, who is a leper or who has a discharge, may eat of the holy *gifts* until he is clean. [b]And if one touches anything made unclean by a corpse or if [c]a man has a seminal emission,

5 or [a]if a man touches any teeming things, by which he is made unclean, or any man by whom he is made unclean, whatever his uncleanness;

6 a [1]person who touches any such shall be unclean until evening, and shall not eat of the holy *gifts*, unless he has bathed his [2]body in water.

7 'But when the sun sets, he shall be clean, and afterward he shall eat of the holy *gifts*, for [a]it is his [1]food.

8 'He shall not eat [a]*an animal* which dies or is torn *by beasts*, becoming unclean by it; I am the LORD.

9 'They shall therefore keep [a]My charge, so that [b]they may not bear sin because of it, and die thereby because they profane it; I am the LORD who sanctifies them.

10 '[a]No [1]layman, however, is to eat the holy *gift*; a sojourner with the priest or a hired man shall not eat of the holy *gift*.

11 '[a]But if a priest buys a [1]slave as *his* property with his money, [2]that one may eat of it, and those who are born in his house may eat of his [3]food.

12 'And if a priest's daughter is married to a [1]layman, she shall not eat of the [2]offering of the *gifts*.

13 'But if a priest's daughter becomes a widow or divorced, and has no child and returns to her father's house as in her youth, she shall eat of her father's [1]food; [a]but no [2]layman shall eat of it.

14 '[a]But if a man eats a holy *gift* unintentionally, then he shall add to it a fifth of it and shall give the holy *gift* to the priest.

15 'And [a]they shall not profane the holy *gifts* of the sons of Israel which they offer to the LORD,

16 and *so* cause them [a]to bear [1]punishment for guilt by eating their holy *gifts*; for I am the LORD who sanctifies them.' "

Flawless Animals for Sacrifice

17 Then the LORD spoke to Moses, saying,

18 "Speak to Aaron and to his sons and to all the sons of Israel, and say to them, '[a]Any man of the house of Israel or of the aliens in Israel who presents his offering, whether it is any of their [1]votive or any of their freewill offerings, which they present to the LORD for a burnt offering—

19 [a]for you to be accepted—*it must be* a male without defect from the cattle, the sheep, or the goats.

20 '[a]Whatever has a defect, you shall not offer, for it will not be accepted for you.

21 'And when a man offers a sacrifice of peace offerings to the LORD [a]to [1]fulfill a special vow, or for a freewill offering, of the herd or of the flock, it must be perfect to be accepted; there shall be no defect in it.

22 'Those *that are* blind or fractured or maimed or having a running sore or eczema or scabs, you shall not offer to the LORD, nor make of them an offering by fire on the altar to the LORD.

23 'In respect to an ox or a lamb which has an [1]overgrown or stunted *member*,

11 [a]Lev. 19:28; Num. 19:14
12 [a]Lev. 10:7 [b]Ex. 29:6, 7
14 [1]Lit., *take as wife* [a]Lev. 21:7; Ezek. 44:22
15 [1]Lit., *seed*
17 [1]Lit., *seed* [a]Lev. 21:6
18 [1]Lit., *slit* [a]Lev. 22:19-25
20 [1]Lit., *obscurity* [a]Deut. 23:1; Is. 56:3-5
21 [1]Lit., *seed* [a]Lev. 21:6
22 [a]1 Cor. 9:13
3 [1]Lit., *seed* [a]Lev. 7:20, 21; Num. 19:13
4 [1]Lit., *seed* [a]Lev. 14:1-32 [b]Lev. 11:24-28, 39, 40 [c]Lev. 15:16, 17
5 [a]Lev. 11:23-28
6 [1]Lit., *soul* [2]Lit., *flesh*
7 [1]Lit., *bread* [a]Num. 18:11
8 [a]Lev. 7:24; 11:39, 40; 17:15
9 [a]Lev. 18:30 [b]Ex. 28:43; Lev. 22:16; Num. 18:22
10 [1]Lit., *stranger* [a]Ex. 29:33; Lev. 22:13; Num. 3:10
11 [1]Lit., *soul* [2]Lit., *he may* [3]Lit., *bread* [a]Gen. 17:13; Ex. 12:44
12 [1]Lit., *stranger* [2]Lit., *heave offering*
13 [1]Lit., *bread* [2]Lit., *stranger* [a]Lev. 22:10
14 [a]Lev. 5:15, 16
15 [a]Num. 18:32
16 [1]Or, *iniquity requiring a guilt offering* [a]Lev. 10:17; 22:9
18 [1]Lit., *vows* [a]Num. 15:14
19 [a]Lev. 21:18-21; Deut. 15:21
20 [a]Deut. 15:21; 17:1; Mal. 1:8, 14; Heb. 9:14; 1 Pet. 1:19
21 [1]Or, *make a special votive offering* [a]Num. 15:3, 8
23 [1]Or, *a deformed*

you may present it for a freewill offering,
but for a vow it shall not be accepted.
24 'Also [a]anything *with its testicles*
bruised or crushed or torn or cut, you
shall not offer to the LORD, or [1]sacrifice
in your land,
25 nor shall you accept any such from
the hand of a foreigner for offering [a]as
the [1]food of your God; for their corruption is in them, they have a defect, they
shall not be accepted for you.' "
26 Then the LORD spoke to Moses,
saying,
27 "When an ox or a sheep or a goat is
born, it shall [1]remain [a]seven days [2]with
its mother, and from the eighth day on it
shall be accepted as a sacrifice of an
offering by fire to the LORD.
28 "[a]But, *whether* it is an ox or a sheep,
you shall not kill *both* it and its young in
one day.
29 "And when you sacrifice [a]a sacrifice
of thanksgiving to the LORD, you shall
sacrifice it so that you may be accepted.
30 "It shall be eaten on the same day,
you shall leave none of it until morning:
I am the LORD.
31 "[a]So you shall keep My commandments, and do them: I am the LORD.
32 "And you shall not profane My holy
name, but I will be sanctified among the
sons of Israel: I am the LORD who
sanctifies you,
33 [a]who brought you out from the
land of Egypt, to be your God: I am the
LORD."

Laws of Religious Festivals

23 THE LORD spoke again to Moses, saying,
2 "Speak to the sons of Israel, and say
to them, '[a]The LORD's appointed times
which you shall [b]proclaim as holy convocations—My appointed times are
these:
3 '[a]For six days work may be done;
but on the seventh day there is a sabbath
of complete rest, a holy convocation.
You shall not do any work; it is a
sabbath to the LORD in all your dwellings.
4 'These are the [a]appointed times of
the LORD, holy convocations which you
shall proclaim at the times appointed for
them.
5 '[a]In the first month, on the fourteenth day of the month [1]at twilight is
the LORD's Passover.
6 'Then on the fifteenth day of the
same month there is the [a]Feast of Unleavened Bread to the LORD; for seven
days you shall eat unleavened bread.
7 'On the first day you shall have a
holy convocation; you shall [a]not do any
laborious work.
8 'But for seven days you shall present an offering by fire to the LORD. On
the seventh day is a holy convocation;
you shall not do any laborious work.' "
9 Then the LORD spoke to Moses,
saying,
10 "Speak to the sons of Israel, and say
to them, 'When you enter the land which
I am going to give to you and [a]reap its
harvest, then you shall bring in the sheaf
of the first fruits of your harvest to the
priest.
11 'And he shall wave the sheaf before
the LORD for you to be accepted; on the
day after the sabbath the priest shall
wave it.
12 'Now on the day when you wave the
sheaf, you shall offer a male lamb one
year old without defect for a burnt
offering to the LORD.
13 'Its [a]grain offering shall then be
two-tenths *of an ephah* of fine flour
mixed with oil, an offering by fire to the
LORD *for* a soothing aroma, with its
libation, a fourth of a [1]hin of wine.
14 'Until this same day, until you have
brought in the offering of your God,
[a]you shall eat neither bread nor roasted
grain nor new growth. It is to be a
perpetual statute throughout your generations in all your dwelling places.
15 '[a]You shall also count for yourselves from the day after the sabbath,
from the day when you brought in the
sheaf of the wave offering; there shall be
seven complete sabbaths.
16 'You shall count fifty days to the
day after the seventh sabbath; then you
shall present a [a]new grain offering to the
LORD.
17 'You shall bring in from your dwelling places two *loaves* of bread for a wave
offering, made of two-tenths *of an*
[1]*ephah*; they shall be of a fine flour,
baked [a]with leaven as first fruits to the
LORD.
18 'Along with the bread, you shall
present seven one year old male lambs
without defect, and a bull of the herd,
and two rams; they are to be a burnt
offering to the LORD, with their grain
offering and their libations, an offering
by fire of a soothing aroma to the LORD.
19 'You shall also offer [a]one male goat
for a sin offering and two male lambs
one year old for a sacrifice of peace
offerings.
20 'The priest shall then wave them
with the bread of the first fruits for a
wave offering with two lambs before the
LORD; they are to be holy to the LORD
for the priest.
21 'On this same day you shall [a]make a
proclamation as well; you are to have a
holy convocation. You shall do no laborious [b]work. It is to be a perpetual
statute in all your dwelling places
throughout your generations.
22 '[a]When you reap the harvest of your
land, moreover, you shall not reap to the
very corners of your field, nor gather the
gleaning of your harvest; you are to
leave them for the needy and the alien. I
am the LORD your God.' "
23 Again the LORD spoke to Moses,
saying,

24 [1]Lit., *do* [a]Lev. 21:20
25 [1]Lit., *bread* [a]Lev. 21:22
27 [1]Lit., *be* [2]Lit., *under* [a]Ex. 22:30
28 [a]Deut. 22:6, 7
29 [a]Lev. 7:12
31 [a]Lev. 19:37; Num. 15:40; Deut. 4:40
33 [a]Lev. 11:45
2 [a]Lev. 23:4, 37, 44; Num. 29:39 [b]Lev. 23:21
3 [a]Ex. 20:9, 10; 23:12; 31:13-17; 35:2, 3; Lev. 19:3; Deut. 5:13, 14
4 [a]Ex. 23:14; Lev. 23:2
5 [1]Lit., *between the two evenings* [a]Ex. 12:18, 19; Num. 28:16-25; Deut. 16:1; Josh. 5:10
6 [a]Ex. 12:14-20; 23:15; 34:18; Deut. 16:3-8
7 [a]Lev. 23:8, 21, 25, 35, 36
10 [a]Ex. 23:19; 34:26
13 [1]I.e., Approx. one gal. [a]Lev. 6:20
14 [a]Ex. 34:26; Num. 15:20, 21
15 [a]Num. 28:26-31; Deut. 16:9-12
16 [a]Num. 28:26
17 [1]I.e., Approx. one bu. [a]Lev. 2:12; 7:13
19 [a]Lev. 4:23; Num. 28:30
21 [a]Lev. 23:2, 4 [b]Lev. 23:7
22 [a]Lev. 19:9, 10; Deut. 24:19; Ruth 2:15f.

24 "Speak to the sons of Israel, saying,
'[a]In the seventh month on the first of the
month, you shall have a [1]rest, a [b]re-
minder by blowing *of trumpets*, a holy
convocation.
25 'You shall [a]not do any laborious
work, but you shall present an offering
by fire to the LORD.' "

The Day of Atonement

26 And the LORD spoke to Moses,
saying,
27 "On exactly [a]the tenth day of this
seventh month is [b]the day of atonement;
it shall be a holy convocation for you,
and you shall humble your souls and
present an offering by fire to the LORD.
28 "Neither shall you do any work on
this same day, for it is a [a]day of atonement, [b]to make atonement on your
behalf before the LORD your God.
29 "If there is any [1]person who will not
humble himself on this same day, [a]he
shall be cut off from his people.
30 "As for any person who does any
work on this same day, that person I will
destroy from among his people.
31 "You shall do no work at all. It is to
be a perpetual statute throughout your
generations in all your dwelling places.
32 "It is to be a sabbath of complete
rest to you, and you shall humble your
souls; on the ninth of the month at
evening, from evening until evening you
shall keep your sabbath."
33 Again the LORD spoke to Moses,
saying,
34 "Speak to the sons of Israel, saying,
'On [a]the fifteenth of this seventh month
is the [b]Feast of Booths for seven days to
the LORD.
35 'On the first day is a holy convocation; you shall do [a]no laborious work of
any kind.
36 '[a]For seven days you shall present
an offering by fire to the LORD. On [b]the
eighth day you shall have a holy convocation and present an offering by fire to
the LORD; it is an assembly. You shall
do no laborious work.
37 'These are [a]the appointed times of
the LORD which you shall proclaim as
holy convocations, to present offerings
by fire to the LORD—burnt offerings and
grain offerings, sacrifices and libations,
[b]*each* day's matter on its own day—
38 besides *those of* the sabbaths of the
LORD, and besides your gifts, and besides all your [1]votive and freewill offerings, which you give to the LORD.
39 'On exactly the fifteenth day of the
seventh month, [a]when you have gathered
in the crops of the land, you shall
celebrate the feast of the LORD for seven
days, with a [1]rest on the first day and a
[1]rest on the eighth day.
40 'Now on the first day you shall take
for yourselves the [1]foliage of beautiful
trees, palm branches and boughs of leafy
trees and willows of the brook; and you
shall rejoice before the LORD your God
for seven days.
41 'You shall thus celebrate it *as* a
feast to the LORD for seven days in the
year. It *shall be* a perpetual statute
throughout your generations; you shall
celebrate it in the seventh month.
42 'You shall [1]live [a]in booths for seven
days; all the native-born in Israel shall
[1]live in booths,
43 so that [a]your generations may
know that I had the sons of Israel live in
booths when I brought them out from
the land of Egypt. I am the LORD your
God.' "
44 So Moses declared to the sons of
Israel [a]the appointed times of the LORD.

The Lamp and the Bread of the Sanctuary

24 THEN the LORD spoke to Moses,
saying,
2 "Command the sons of Israel that
they bring to you [a]clear oil from beaten
olives for the [1]light, to make a lamp
[2]burn continually.
3 "Outside the veil of testimony in the
tent of meeting, Aaron shall keep it in
order from evening to morning before
the LORD continually; *it shall be* a perpetual statute throughout your generations.
4 "He shall keep the lamps in order on
the [a]pure *gold* lampstand before the
LORD continually.
5 "[a]Then you shall take fine flour and
bake twelve cakes with it; two-tenths *of
an ephah* shall be *in* each cake.
6 "And you shall set them *in* two
rows, six *to* a row, on the [a]pure *gold* table
before the LORD.
7 "And you shall put pure frankincense on each row, that it may be [a]a
memorial portion for the bread, *even* an
offering by fire to the LORD.
8 "[a]Every sabbath day he shall set it in
order before the LORD [b]continually; it is
an everlasting covenant [1]for the sons of
Israel.
9 "[a]And it shall be for Aaron and his
sons, and they shall eat it in a holy
place; for it is most holy to him from the
LORD's offerings by fire, *his* portion
forever."
10 Now the son of an Israelite woman,
whose father was an Egyptian, went out
among the sons of Israel; and the Israelite woman's son and a man of Israel
struggled with each other in the camp.
11 And the son of the Israelite woman
blasphemed the [a]Name and cursed. So
they brought him to Moses. (Now his
mother's name was Shelomith, the
daughter of Dibri, of the tribe of Dan.)
12 And they put him in [1]custody [2]so
that [a]the command of the LORD might
be made clear to them.
13 Then the LORD spoke to Moses,
saying,
14 "Bring the one who has cursed
outside the camp, and let all who heard
him [a]lay their hands on his head; then
[b]let all the congregation stone him.

24 [1]Lit., *sabbath rest* [a]Num. 29:1 [b]Num. 10:9, 10
25 [a]Lev. 23:21
27 [a]Lev. 16:29; 25:9; Num. 29:7 [b]Ex. 30:10; Lev. 16:30; 23:28; Num. 29:7-11
28 [a]Lev. 23:27 [b]Lev. 16:34
29 [1]Lit., *soul* [a]Gen. 17:14; Lev. 13:46; Num. 5:2
34 [a]Num. 29:12 [b]Lev. 23:42, 43; Deut. 16:13, 16; Ezra 3:4; Neh. 8:14; Zech. 14:16; John 7:2
35 [a]Lev. 23:25
36 [a]Num. 29:12-34 [b]Num. 29:35-38
37 [a]Lev. 23:2 [b]Num. 28:1-29:38
38 [1]Lit., *vows, and besides all your*
39 [1]Lit., *sabbath rest* [a]Ex. 23:16
40 [1]Lit., *products, fruit*
42 [1]Lit., *dwell* [a]Lev. 23:34
43 [a]Deut. 31:13; Ps. 78:5f.
44 [a]Lev. 23:37
2 [1]Or, *luminary* [2]Lit., *ascend* [a]Ex. 27:20, 21
4 [a]Ex. 25:31; 31:8; 37:17
5 [a]Ex. 25:30; 39:36; 40:23
6 [a]Ex. 25:24; 1 Kin. 7:48
7 [a]Lev. 2:2, 9, 16
8 [1]Lit., *from* [a]Matt. 12:5 [b]Ex. 25:30; Num. 4:7; 2 Chr. 2:4
9 [a]Matt. 12:4; Mark 2:26; Luke 6:4
11 [a]Ex. 3:15; 22:28; Job 2:5, 9; Is. 8:21
12 [1]Or, *prison* [2]Lit., *to declare distinctly to them according to the mouth of the LORD* [a]Ex. 18:15; Num. 15:34
14 [a]Deut. 13:9; 17:7 [b]Lev. 20:2, 27; Deut. 21:21

15"And you shall speak to the sons of
Israel, saying, '[a]If anyone curses his
God, then he shall bear his sin.
16 'Moreover, the one who [a]blas-
phemes the name of the LORD shall
surely be put to death; all the congregation shall certainly stone him. The alien
as well as the native, when he blasphemes the Name, shall be put to death.

"An Eye for an Eye"

17 '[a]And if a man [1]takes the life of any
human being, he shall surely be put to
death.
18 'And [a]the one who [1]takes the life of
an animal shall make it good, life for life.
19 'And if a man [1]injures his neighbor,
just as he has done, so it shall be done to
him:
20 [a]fracture for fracture, [b]eye for eye,
tooth for tooth; just as he has [1]injured a
man, so it shall be [2]inflicted on him.
21 'Thus the one who [1]kills an animal
shall make it good, but [a]the one who
[1]kills a man shall be put to death.
22 'There shall be [a]one [1]standard for
you; it shall be for the stranger as well as
the native, for I am the LORD your
God.' "
23 Then Moses spoke to the sons of
Israel, and they brought the one who
had cursed outside the camp and stoned
him with stones. Thus the sons of Israel
did, just as the LORD had commanded
Moses.

The Sabbatic Year and Year of Jubilee

25 THE LORD then spoke to Moses
[1]at Mount Sinai, saying,
2"Speak to the sons of Israel, and say
to them, 'When you come into the land
which I shall give you, then the land
shall have a sabbath to the LORD.
3 '[a]Six years you shall sow your field,
and six years you shall prune your
vineyard and gather in its crop,
4 but during [a]the seventh year the
land shall have a sabbath rest, a sabbath
to the LORD; you shall not sow your
field nor prune your vineyard.
5 'Your harvest's [1]aftergrowth you
shall not reap, and your grapes of un-
trimmed vines you shall not gather; the
land shall have a sabbatical year.
6 '[a]And all of you shall have the
sabbath *products* of the land for food;
yourself, and your male and female
slaves, and your hired man and your
foreign resident, those who live as aliens
with you.
7 'Even your cattle and the animals
that are in your land shall have all its
crops to eat.
8 'You are also to count off seven
sabbaths of years for yourself, seven
times seven years, so that you have the
time of the seven sabbaths of years,
namely, forty-nine years.
9 'You shall then sound a ram's horn
abroad on [a]the tenth day of the seventh
month; on the day of atonement you
shall sound a horn all through your land.
10 'You shall thus consecrate the fiftieth year and [a]proclaim [1]a release
through the land to all its inhabitants. It
shall be a jubilee for you, [2]and [b]each of
you shall return to his own property,
[2]and each of you shall return to his
family.
11 'You shall have the fiftieth year as a
jubilee; you shall not sow, nor reap its
aftergrowth, nor gather in *from* its un-
trimmed vines.
12 'For it is a jubilee; it shall be holy to
you. You shall eat its crops out of the
field.
13 '[a]On this year of jubilee each of you
shall return to his own property.
14 'If you make a sale, moreover, to
your friend, or buy from your friend's
hand, [a]you shall not wrong one another.
15 'Corresponding to the number of
years after the jubilee, you shall buy
from your [1]friend; he is to sell to you
according to the number of years of
crops.
16 '[a]In proportion to the [1]extent of the
years you shall increase its price, and in
proportion to the fewness of the years,
you shall diminish its price; for *it is* a
number of crops he is selling to you.
17 'So [a]you shall not wrong one another, but you shall [1]fear your God; for I
am the LORD your God.
18 'You shall thus observe My statutes,
and keep My judgments, so as to carry
them out, that [a]you may live securely on
the land.
19 'Then the land will yield its produce, so that you can eat your fill and
live securely on it.
20 'But if you say, "[a]What are we
going to eat on the seventh year [1]if we
do not sow or gather in our crops?"
21 then [a]I will so order My blessing
for you in the sixth year that it will bring
forth the crop for three years.
22 'When you are sowing the eighth
year, you can still eat [a]old things from
the crop, eating *the old* until the ninth
year when its crop comes in.

The Law of Redemption

23 'The land, moreover, shall not be
sold permanently, for [a]the land is Mine;
for [b]you are *but* aliens and sojourners
with Me.
24 'Thus for every [1]piece of your property, you are to provide for the redemption of the land.
25 '[a]If a [1]fellow countryman of yours
becomes so poor he has to sell part of his
property, then his nearest kinsman is to
come and buy back what his [1]relative
has sold.
26 'Or in case a man has no kinsman,
but so [1]recovers his means as to find
sufficient for its redemption,
27 [a]then he shall calculate the years
since its sale and refund the balance to
the man to whom he sold it, and so
return to his property.

15 [a]Ex. 22:28
16 [a]1 Kin. 21:10; Matt. 12:31; Mark 3:28f.
17 [1]Lit., *smites* [a]Gen. 9:6; Ex. 21:12; Num. 35:30, 31; Deut. 27:24
18 [1]Lit., *smites* [a]Lev. 24:21
19 [1]Lit., *gives a blemish*
20 [1]Lit., *given a blemish* [2]Lit., *given* [a]Ex. 21:23; Deut. 19:21 [b]Matt. 5:38
21 [1]Lit., *smites* [a]Lev. 24:17
22 [1]Lit., *judgment* [a]Ex. 12:49; Num. 9:14; 15:15, 16, 29
1 [1]Or, *on*
3 [a]Ex. 23:10, 11
4 [a]Lev. 25:20
5 [1]Lit., *growth from spilled kernels*
6 [a]Lev. 25:20, 21
9 [a]Lev. 23:27
10 [1]Or, *liberty* [2]Or, *when* [a]Jer. 34:8, 15, 17 [b]Lev. 25:13, 28, 54
13 [a]Lev. 25:10; 27:24
14 [a]Lev. 25:17
15 [1]Lit., *friend's hands*
16 [1]Lit., *multitude* [a]Lev. 25:27, 51, 52
17 [1]Or, *reverence* [a]Lev. 25:14; Prov. 14:31; 22:22; Jer. 7:5, 6; 1 Thess. 4:6
18 [a]Lev. 26:5; Deut. 12:10; Jer. 23:6
20 [1]Or, *behold* [a]Lev. 25:4
21 [a]Deut. 28:8
22 [a]Lev. 26:10
23 [a]Ex. 19:5 [b]Gen. 23:4; 1 Chr. 29:15; Ps. 39:12; Heb. 11:13; 1 Pet. 2:11
24 [1]Lit., *land*
25 [1]Lit., *brother* [a]Ruth 2:20; 4:4, 6
26 [1]Lit., *his hand reaches*
27 [a]Lev. 25:16

28 'But if [1]he has not found sufficient means to get it back for himself, then what he has sold shall remain in the hands of its purchaser until the year of jubilee; but at the jubilee it shall [2]revert, that [a]he may return to his property.

29 'Likewise, if a man sells a dwelling house in a walled city, then his redemption right remains valid until a full year from its sale; his right of redemption lasts a full year.

30 'But if it is not bought back for him within the space of a full year, then the house that is in the walled city passes permanently to its purchaser throughout his generations; it does not [1]revert in the jubilee.

31 'The houses of the villages, however, which have no surrounding wall shall be considered [1]as open fields; they have redemption rights and [2]revert in the jubilee.

32 'As for [a]cities of the Levites, the Levites have a permanent right of redemption for the houses of the cities which are their possession.

33 'What, therefore, [1]belongs to the Levites may be redeemed and a house sale [2]in the city of this possession [3]reverts in the jubilee, for the houses of the cities of the Levites are their possession among the sons of Israel.

34 '[a]But pasture fields of their cities shall not be sold, for that is their perpetual possession.

Of Poor Countrymen

35 '[a]Now in case a [1]countryman of yours becomes poor and his [2]means with regard to you falter, then you are to sustain him, like a stranger or a sojourner, that he may live with you.

36 '[a]Do not take [1]usurious interest from him, but revere your God, that your [2]countryman may live with you.

37 'You shall not give him your silver at interest, nor your food for gain.

38 '[a]I am the LORD your God, who brought you out of the land of Egypt to give you the land of Canaan *and* [b]to be your God.

39 '[a]And if a [1]countryman of yours becomes so poor with regard to you that he sells himself to you, you shall not subject him to a slave's service.

40 'He shall be with you as a hired man, as [a]if he were a sojourner; he shall serve with you until the year of jubilee.

41 'He shall then go out from you, he and his sons with him, and shall go back to his family, that he may return to the property of his forefathers.

42 'For they are My servants whom I brought out from the land of Egypt; they are not to be sold *in* a slave sale.

43 '[a]You shall not rule over him with severity, but are to revere your God.

44 'As for your male and female slaves whom you may have—you may acquire male and female slaves from the pagan nations that are around you.

45 'Then, too, *it is* out of the sons of the sojourners who live as aliens among you that you may gain acquisition, and out of their families who are with you, whom they will have [1]produced in your land; they also may become your possession.

46 'You may even bequeath them to your sons after you, to receive as a possession; you can use them as permanent slaves. [a]But in respect to your [1]countrymen, the sons of Israel, you shall not rule with severity over one another.

Of Redeeming a Poor Man

47 'Now if the [1]means of a stranger or of a sojourner with you becomes sufficient, and a [2]countryman of yours becomes so poor with regard to him as to sell himself to a stranger who is sojourning with you, or to the descendants of a stranger's family,

48 then he shall have redemption right after he has been sold. One of his brothers may redeem him,

49 or his uncle, or his uncle's son, may redeem him, or one of his blood relatives from his family may redeem him; or [1a]if he prospers, he may redeem himself.

50 'He then with his purchaser shall calculate from the year when he sold himself to him up to the year of jubilee; and the price of his sale shall correspond to the number of years. *It is* like the days of a hired man *that* he shall be with him.

51 'If there are still many years, [a]he shall refund part of his purchase price in proportion to them for his own redemption;

52 and if few years remain until the year of jubilee, he shall so calculate with him. In proportion to his years he is to refund *the amount for* his redemption.

53 'Like a man hired year by year he shall be with him; [a]he shall not rule over him with severity in your sight.

54 'Even if he is not redeemed by [1]these *means*, [a]he shall still go out in the year of jubilee, he and his sons with him.

55 'For the sons of Israel are My servants; they are My servants whom I brought out from the land of Egypt. I am the LORD your God.

Blessings of Obedience

26 'YOU shall not make for yourselves [1a]idols, nor shall you set up for yourselves [b]an image or [c]a *sacred* pillar, nor shall you place a [d]figured stone in your land to bow down [2]to it; for I am the LORD your God.

2 '[a]You shall keep My sabbaths and reverence My sanctuary; I am the LORD.

3 '[a]If you walk in My statutes and keep My commandments so as to carry them out,

4 then [a]I shall give you rains in their season, so that the land will yield its produce and the trees of the field will bear their fruit.

---

28 [1]Lit., *his hand has not found sufficient to* [2]Lit., *go out* [a]Lev. 25:10, 13

30 [1]Lit., *go out*

31 [1]Lit., *according to* [2]Lit., *go out*

32 [a]Num. 35:1-8; Josh. 21:2

33 [1]Lit., *is from* [2]Lit., *and* [3]Lit., *goes out*

34 [a]Num. 35:2-5

35 [1]Lit., *brother* [2]Lit., *hand* [a]Deut. 15:7-11; 24:14, 15

36 [1]Lit., *interest and usury* [2]Lit., *brother* [a]Ex. 22:25; Deut. 23:19, 20

38 [a]Lev. 11:45 [b]Gen. 17:7

39 [1]Lit., *brother* [a]Ex. 21:2-6; Deut. 15:12-18; 1 Kin. 9:22

40 [a]Ex. 21:2

43 [a]Ex. 1:13, 14; Lev. 25:46, 53; Ezek. 34:4; Col. 4:1

45 [1]Lit., *begotten*

46 [1]Lit., *brothers* [a]Lev. 25:43

47 [1]Lit., *hand . . . reaches* [2]Lit., *brother*

49 [1]Lit., *if his hand has reached and* [a]Lev. 25:26, 27

51 [a]Lev. 25:16

53 [a]Lev. 25:43

54 [1]Or, *these years* [a]Lev. 25:10, 13, 28

1 [1]Or, *graven images* [2]Lit., *over* [a]Lev. 19:4; Deut. 5:8 [b]Ex. 20:4; Deut. 16:21f. [c]Ex. 23:24 [d]Num. 33:52

2 [a]Lev. 19:30

3 [a]Deut. 7:12-26; 11:13; 28:1-14

4 [a]Deut. 11:14

5 '[a]Indeed, your threshing will last for
you until grape gathering, and grape
gathering will last until sowing time.
You will thus eat your [1]food to the full
and [b]live securely in your land.
6 '[a]I shall also grant peace in the
land, so that [b]you may lie down with no
one making *you* tremble. [c]I shall also
eliminate harmful beasts from the land,
and [d]no sword will pass through your
land.
7 'But you will chase your enemies,
and they will fall before you by the
sword;
8 [a]five of you will chase a hundred,
and a hundred of you will chase ten
thousand, and your enemies will fall
before you by the sword.
9 'So I will turn toward you and
[a]make you fruitful and multiply you,
and I will [b]confirm My covenant with
you.
10 '[a]And you will eat the old supply
and clear out the old because of the new.
11 '[a]Moreover, I will make My [1]dwell-
ing among you, and My soul will not
[2]reject you.
12 '[a]I will also walk among you and be
your God, and you shall be My people.
13 '[a]I am the LORD your God, who
brought you out of the land of Egypt so
that *you* should not be their slaves, and
[b]I broke the bars of your yoke and made
you walk erect.

Penalties of Disobedience

14 '[a]But if you do not obey Me and do
not carry out all these commandments,
15 if, instead, you [a]reject My statutes,
and if your soul abhors My ordinances
so as not to carry out all My commandments, *and* so [b]break My covenant,
16 I, in turn, will do this to you: I will
appoint over you a [a]sudden terror, consumption and fever that shall waste
away the eyes and cause the [b]soul to
pine away; also, [c]you shall sow your
seed uselessly, for your enemies shall eat
it up.
17 'And I will set My face against you
so that you shall be struck down before
your enemies; and [a]those who hate you
shall rule over you, and [b]you shall flee
when no one is pursuing you.
18 'If also after these things, you do
not obey Me, then I will punish you
[a]seven times more for your sins.
19 'And I will also [a]break down your
pride of power; I will also make your sky
like iron and your earth like bronze.
20 'And [a]your strength shall be spent
uselessly, for your land shall not yield its
produce and the trees of the land shall
not yield their fruit.
21 'If then, you [1a]act with hostility
against Me and are unwilling to obey
Me, I will increase the plague on you
[b]seven times according to your sins.
22 'And [a]I will let loose among you the
beasts of the field, which shall bereave
you of your children and destroy your
cattle and reduce your number so that
[b]your roads lie deserted.
23 '[a]And if by these things you are not
turned to Me, but act with hostility
against Me,
24 then I will [a]act with hostility
against you; and I, even I, will strike you
[b]seven times for your sins.
25 'I will also bring upon you a sword
which will execute [a]vengeance for the
covenant; and when you gather together
into your cities, I will send [b]pestilence
among you, so that you shall be delivered into enemy hands.
26 '[a]When I break your staff of bread,
ten women will bake your bread in one
oven, and they will bring back your
bread [1]in rationed amounts, so that you
will [b]eat and not be satisfied.
27 'Yet if in spite of this, you do not
obey Me, but act with hostility against
Me,
28 then [a]I will act with wrathful hostility against you; and I, even I, will
punish you seven times for your sins.
29 'Further, [a]you shall eat the flesh of
your sons and the flesh of your daughters you shall eat.
30 'I then [a]will destroy your high
places, and cut down your [b]incense
altars, and heap your [1]remains on the
[1]remains of your idols; for My soul shall
abhor you.
31 'I will [1]lay [a]waste your cities as well,
and will make your [b]sanctuaries desolate; and I will not [c]smell your soothing
aromas.
32 'And I will make [a]the land desolate
[b]so that your enemies who settle in it
shall be appalled over it.
33 'You, however, I [a]will scatter
among the nations and will draw out a
sword after you, as your land becomes
desolate and your cities become waste.
34 '[a]Then the land will [1]enjoy its sabbaths all the days of the desolation,
while you are in your enemies' land;
then the land will rest and [1]enjoy its
sabbaths.
35 'All the days of *its* desolation it will
observe the rest which it did not observe
on your sabbaths, while you were living
on it.
36 'As for those of you who may be
left, I will also bring [a]weakness into their
hearts in the lands of their enemies. And
the sound of a driven leaf will chase
them and even when no one is pursuing,
they will flee [1]as though from the sword,
and they will fall.
37 '[a]They will therefore stumble over
each other as if *running* from the sword,
although no one is pursuing; and you
will have *no strength* [1]to stand up before
your enemies.
38 'But [a]you will perish among the
nations, and your enemies' land will
consume you.
39 '[a]So those of you who may be left
will rot away because of their iniquity in
the lands of your enemies; and also
because of the iniquities of their forefathers they will rot away with them.

5 [1]Lit., *bread* [a]Deut. 11:15; Joel 2:19, 26; Amos 9:13 [b]Lev. 25:18, 19; Ezek. 34:25
6 [a]Ps. 29:11; 85:8; 147:14 [b]Zeph. 3:13 [c]Lev. 26:22 [d]Lev. 26:25
8 [a]Deut. 32:30
9 [a]Gen. 17:6; 22:17; 48:4 [b]Gen. 17:7
10 [a]Lev. 25:22
11 [1]Or, *tabernacle* [2]Lit., *abhor* [a]Ex. 25:8; 29:45, 46; Ezek. 37:26
12 [a]Gen. 3:8; Deut. 23:14; 2 Cor. 6:16
13 [a]Ex. 20:2 [b]Ezek. 34:27
14 [a]Deut. 28:15-68; Josh. 23:15
15 [a]Lev. 26:11; 2 Kin. 17:15 [b]Lev. 26:9
16 [a]Deut. 28:22; Ps. 78:33 [b]1 Sam. 2:33; Ezek. 24:23; 33:10 [c]Judg. 6:3-6; Job 31:8
17 [a]Ps. 106:41 [b]Lev. 26:36, 37; Ps. 53:5; Prov. 28:1
18 [a]Lev. 26:21, 24, 28
19 [a]Is. 28:1-3; Ezek. 24:21
20 [a]Ps. 127:1; Is. 17:10, 11; 49:4; Jer. 12:13
21 [1]Lit., *walk,* and so throughout the ch. [a]Lev. 26:23, 27, 40 [b]Lev. 26:18
22 [a]2 Kin. 17:25 [b]Judg. 5:6
23 [a]Lev. 26:21; Jer. 5:3
24 [a]Lev. 26:28, 41 [b]Lev. 26:21
25 [a]Jer. 50:28; 51:11 [b]Num. 14:12
26 [1]Lit., *by weight* [a]Is. 3:1; Ezek. 4:16, 17; 5:16 [b]Mic. 6:14
28 [a]Lev. 26:24, 41; Is. 59:18
29 [a]2 Kin. 6:29
30 [1]Lit., *corpses* [a]2 Kin. 23:20; Ezek. 6:3, 6; Amos 7:9 [b]2 Chr. 34:4, 7; Is. 27:9
31 [1]Lit., *give desolation to* [a]Neh. 2:3; Jer. 44:2, 6, 22 [b]Is. 63:18; Lam. 2:7 [c]Amos 5:21
32 [a]Jer. 9:11; 12:11; 25:11; 33:10 [b]Jer. 18:16; 19:8
33 [a]Deut. 4:27; 28:64; Ps. 44:11; 106:27; Jer. 31:10; Ezek. 12:15; 20:23; Zech. 7:14
34 [1]Lit., *satisfy* [a]Lev. 26:43; 2 Chr. 36:21
36 [1]Lit., *the flight of the sword* [a]Is. 30:17; Lam. 1:3, 6; 4:19; Ezek. 21:7
37 [1]Lit., *you will stand* [a]Jer. 6:21; Nah. 3:3
38 [a]Deut. 4:26
39 [a]Ezek. 4:17; 33:10

40 '[a]If they confess their iniquity and
the iniquity of their forefathers, in their
unfaithfulness which they committed
against Me, and also in their acting with
hostility against Me—
41 I also was acting with hostility
against them, to bring them into the land
of their enemies—[a]or if their uncircumcised heart becomes humbled so that
[b]they then make amends for their iniquity,
42 then I will remember [a]My covenant
with Jacob, and I will remember also
[b]My covenant with Isaac, and [c]My covenant with Abraham as well, and I will
remember the land.
43 '[a]For the land shall be abandoned
by them, and shall make up for its
sabbaths while it is made desolate without them. They, meanwhile, shall be
making amends for their iniquity, [1]be-
cause they rejected My ordinances and
their [b]soul abhorred My statutes.
44 'Yet in spite of this, when they are
in the land of their enemies, I will not
reject them, nor will I so [a]abhor them as
[b]to destroy them, [c]breaking My covenant with them; for I am the LORD
their God.
45 'But I will remember for them the
[a]covenant with their ancestors, whom I
brought out of the land of Egypt in the
sight of the nations, that [b]I might be
their God. I am the LORD.' "
46 [a]These are the statutes and ordinances and laws which the LORD established between Himself and the sons of
Israel [1]through Moses at Mount Sinai.

Rules concerning Valuations

27 AGAIN, the LORD spoke to Moses, saying,
2 "Speak to the sons of Israel, and say
to them, '[a]When a man makes a difficult
vow, he *shall be valued* according to your
valuation of persons belonging to the
LORD.
3 'If your valuation is of the male
from twenty years even to sixty years
old, then your valuation shall be fifty
shekels of silver, after [a]the shekel of the
sanctuary.
4 'Or if it is a female, then your
valuation shall be thirty shekels.
5 'And if it be from five years even to
twenty years old then your valuation for
the male shall be twenty shekels, and for
the female ten shekels.
6 'But if *they are* from a month even
up to five years old, then your valuation
shall be [a]five shekels of silver for the
male, and for the female your valuation
shall be three shekels of silver.
7 'And if *they are* from sixty years old
and upward, if it is a male, then your
valuation shall be fifteen shekels, and for
the female ten shekels.
8 'But if he is poorer than your valuation, then he shall be placed before the
priest, and the priest shall value him;
[a]according to [1]the means of the one who
vowed, the priest shall value him.
9 'Now if it is an animal of the kind
which [1]men can present as an offering to
the LORD, any such that one gives to the
LORD shall be holy.
10 '[a]He shall not replace it or exchange
it, a good for a bad, or a bad for a good;
or if he does exchange animal for animal, then both it and its substitute shall
become holy.
11 'If, however, it is any unclean animal of the kind which [1]men do not
present as an offering to the LORD, then
he shall place the animal before the
priest.
12 'And the priest shall value it [1]as
either good or bad; as you, the priest,
value it, so it shall be.
13 'But if he should ever *wish to* redeem it, then he shall add one-fifth of it
to your valuation.
14 'Now if a man consecrates his house
as holy to the LORD, then the priest shall
value it [1]as either good or bad; as the
priest values it, so it shall stand.
15 'Yet if the one who consecrates it
should *wish to* redeem his house, then he
shall add one-fifth of your valuation
price to it, so that it may be his.
16 'Again, if a man consecrates to the
LORD part of the fields of his own
property, then your valuation shall be
[1]proportionate to the seed needed for it:
a homer of barley seed at fifty shekels of
silver.
17 'If he consecrates his field as of the
year of jubilee, according to your valuation it shall stand.
18 'If he consecrates his field after the
jubilee, however, then the priest shall
calculate the price for [1]him [2]proportion-
ate to the years that are left until the
year of jubilee; and it shall be deducted
from your valuation.
19 'And if the one who consecrates it
should ever wish to redeem the field,
then he shall add one-fifth of your
valuation price to it, so that it may pass
to him.
20 'Yet if he will not redeem the field,
[1]but has sold the field to another man, it
may no longer be redeemed;
21 and when it [1]reverts in the jubilee,
the field shall be holy to the LORD, like a
field [2]set apart; [a]it shall be for the priest
as his [3]property.
22 'Or if he consecrates to the LORD a
field which he has bought, which is not a
part of the field of his own [1]property,
23 then the priest shall calculate for
[1]him the amount of your valuation up to
the year of jubilee; and he shall on that
day give your valuation as holy to the
LORD.
24 'In the year of jubilee the field shall
return to the one from whom he bought
it, to whom the possession of the land
belongs.
25 'Every valuation of yours, moreover, shall be after [a]the shekel of the
sanctuary. The shekel shall be twenty
gerahs.

40 [a]Jer. 3:12-15; 14:20; Hos. 5:15
41 [a]Jer. 4:4; 9:25, 26; Ezek. 44:7, 9; Acts 7:51 [b]Ezek. 20:43
42 [a]Gen. 28:13-15; 35:11, 12 [b]Gen. 26:2-5 [c]Gen. 22:15-18
43 [1]Lit., *because and by the cause* [a]Lev. 26:34 [b]Lev. 26:11
44 [a]Lev. 26:11 [b]Deut. 4:31; Jer. 30:11 [c]Jer. 33:20-26
45 [a]Ex. 6:6-8 [b]Gen. 17:7
46 [1]Lit., *by the hand of* [a]Lev. 7:38; 27:34; Deut. 4:5; 29:1
2 [a]Num. 6:2; Deut. 23:21-23
3 [a]Ex. 30:13; Lev. 27:25; Num. 3:47; 18:16
6 [a]Num. 18:16
8 [1]Lit., *what the hand reaches* [a]Lev. 5:11; 14:21-24
9 [1]Lit., *they*
10 [a]Lev. 27:33
11 [1]Lit., *they*
12 [1]Lit., *between*
14 [1]Lit., *between good*
16 [1]Lit., *according to its seed*
18 [1]Or, *it* [2]Lit., *according to the years*
20 [1]Or, *if he*
21 [1]Lit., *goes out* [2]Or, *devoted, banned* [3]Lit., *possession* [a]Num. 18:14; Ezek. 44:29
22 [1]Lit., *possession*
23 [1]Or, *it*
25 [a]Ex. 30:13; Lev. 27:3; Num. 3:47; 18:16

26 '[a]However, a first-born among animals, which as a first-born belongs to the LORD, no man may consecrate it; whether ox or sheep, it is the LORD's.

27 'But if *it is* among the unclean animals, then he shall [1]redeem it according to your valuation, and add to it one-fifth of it; and if it is not redeemed, then it shall be sold according to your valuation.

28 'Nevertheless, [a]anything which a man [1]sets apart to the LORD out of all that he has, of man or animal or of the fields of his own property, shall not be sold or redeemed. Anything [2]devoted to destruction is most holy to the LORD.

29 'No [1]one who may have been [2]set apart among men shall be ransomed; he shall surely be put to death.

26 [a]Ex. 13:2

27 [1]Or, *ransom*

28 [1]Lit., *anything devoted;* or, *banned* [2]Or, *puts under the ban* [a]Num. 18:14; Josh. 6:17-19

29 [1]Lit., *one devoted;* or, *banned* [2]Or, *put under the ban*

30 [a]Gen. 28:22; 2 Chr. 31:5; Neh. 13:12

32 [a]Jer. 33:13; Ezek. 20:37

33 [a]Lev. 27:10

34 [a]Lev. 26:46; Deut. 4:5

30 'Thus [a]all the tithe of the land, of the seed of the land or of the fruit of the tree, is the LORD's; it is holy to the LORD.

31 'If, therefore, a man wishes to redeem part of his tithe, he shall add to it one-fifth of it.

32 'And for every tenth part of herd or flock, whatever [a]passes under the rod, the tenth one shall be holy to the LORD.

33 '[a]He is not to be concerned whether *it is* good or bad, nor shall he exchange it; or if he does exchange it, then both it and its substitute shall become holy. It shall not be redeemed.' "

34 [a]These are the commandments which the LORD commanded Moses for the sons of Israel at Mount Sinai.

NUMBERS

The Census of Israel's Warriors

1 THEN the LORD spoke to Moses in the wilderness of Sinai, in the tent of meeting, on [a]the first of the second month, in the second year after they had come out of the land of Egypt, saying,

2 "[a]Take a [1]census of all the congregation of the sons of Israel, by their families, by their fathers' households, according to the number of names, every male, head by head

3 from [a]twenty years old and upward, whoever *is able to* go out to war in Israel, you and Aaron shall [1]number them by their armies.

4 "With you, moreover, there shall be a man of each tribe, [a]each one head of his father's household.

5 "These then are the names of the men who shall stand with you: [a]of Reuben, Elizur the son of Shedeur;

6 of Simeon, Shelumiel the son of Zurishaddai;

7 of Judah, [a]Nahshon the son of Amminadab;

8 of Issachar, Nethanel the son of Zuar;

9 of Zebulun, Eliab the son of Helon;

10 of the sons of Joseph: of Ephraim, Elishama the son of Ammihud; of Manasseh, Gamaliel the son of Pedahzur;

11 of Benjamin, Abidan the son of Gideoni;

12 of Dan, Ahiezer the son of Ammishaddai;

13 of Asher, Pagiel the son of Ochran;

14 of Gad, Eliasaph the son of [a]Deuel;

15 of Naphtali, Ahira the son of Enan.

16 "These are they who were [a]called of the congregation, the leaders of their fathers' tribes; they were the [b]heads of [1]divisions of Israel."

17 So Moses and Aaron took these men who had been designated by name,

1 [a]Ex. 40:2, 17

2 [1]Lit., *sum* [a]Ex. 12:37; 38:25, 26; Num. 26:2

3 [1]Lit., *muster,* and so throughout the ch. [a]Ex. 30:14; 38:26

4 [a]Ex. 18:21, 25; Num. 1:16; Deut. 1:15

5 [a]Gen. 29:32; Ex. 1:2; Deut. 33:6; Rev. 7:5

7 [a]Ruth 4:20; 1 Chr. 2:10; Luke 3:32

14 [a]Num. 2:14

16 [1]Lit., *thousands;* or, *clans* [a]Ex. 18:21; Num. 7:2; 16:2; 26:9 [b]Ex. 18:25

18 [a]Num. 1:1 [b]Ezra 2:59; Heb. 7:3

19 [a]2 Sam. 24:1

20 [a]Num. 26:5-7

22 [a]Num. 26:12-14 [b]Ps. 144:1

24 [a]Gen. 30:11; Num. 26:15-18; Josh. 4:12; Jer. 49:1

26 [a]Gen. 29:35; Num. 26:19-22; 2 Sam. 24:9; Ps. 78:68; Matt. 1:2

28 [a]Num. 26:23-25

18 and they assembled all the congregation together on the [a]first of the second month. Then they registered by [b]ancestry in their families, by their fathers' households, according to the number of names, from twenty years old and upward, head by head,

19 just as [a]the LORD had commanded Moses. So he numbered them in the wilderness of Sinai.

20 [a]Now the sons of Reuben, Israel's first-born, their genealogical registration by their families, by their fathers' households, according to the number of names, head by head, every male from twenty years old and upward, whoever *was able to* go out to war,

21 their numbered men, of the tribe of Reuben, *were* 46,500.

22 [a]Of the sons of Simeon, their genealogical registration by their families, by their fathers' households, their numbered men, according to the number of names, head by head, every male from twenty years old and upward, [b]whoever *was able to* go out to war,

23 their numbered men, of the tribe of Simeon, *were* 59,300.

24 [a]Of the sons of Gad, their genealogical registration by their families, by their fathers' households, according to the number of names, from twenty years old and upward, whoever *was able to* go out to war,

25 their numbered men, of the tribe of Gad, *were* 45,650.

26 [a]Of the sons of Judah, their genealogical registration by their families, by their fathers' households, according to the number of names, from twenty years old and upward, whoever *was able to* go out to war,

27 their numbered men, of the tribe of Judah, *were* 74,600.

28 [a]Of the sons of Issachar, their genealogical registration by their families, by their fathers' households, ac-

cording to the number of names, from twenty years old and upward, whoever *was able to* go out to war,
29 their numbered men, of the tribe of Issachar, *were* 54,400.
30 [a]Of the sons of Zebulun, their genealogical registration by their families, by their fathers' households, according to the number of names, from twenty years old and upward, whoever *was able to* go out to war,
31 their numbered men, of the tribe of Zebulun, *were* 57,400.
32 [a]Of the sons of Joseph, *namely,* of the sons of Ephraim, their genealogical registration by their families, by their fathers' households, according to the number of names, from twenty years old and upward, whoever *was able to* go out to war,
33 their numbered men, of the tribe of Ephraim, *were* 40,500.
34 [a]Of the sons of Manasseh, their genealogical registration by their families, by their fathers' households, according to the number of names, from twenty years old and upward, whoever *was able to* go out to war,
35 their numbered men, of the tribe of Manasseh, *were* 32,200.
36 [a]Of the sons of Benjamin, their genealogical registration by their families, by their fathers' households, according to the number of names, from twenty years old and upward, whoever *was able to* go out to war,
37 their numbered men, of the tribe of Benjamin, *were* 35,400.
38 [a]Of the sons of Dan, their genealogical registration by their families, by their fathers' households, according to the number of names, from twenty years old and upward, whoever *was able to* go out to war,
39 their numbered men, of the tribe of Dan, *were* 62,700.
40 [a]Of the sons of Asher, their genealogical registration by their families, by their fathers' households, according to the number of names, from twenty years old and upward, whoever *was able to* go out to war,
41 their numbered men, of the tribe of Asher, *were* 41,500.
42 [a]Of the sons of Naphtali, their genealogical registration by their families, by their fathers' households, according to the number of names, from twenty years old and upward, whoever *was able to* go out to war,
43 their numbered men, of the tribe of Naphtali, *were* 53,400.
44 These are the ones who were numbered, whom Moses and Aaron numbered, with the leaders of Israel, twelve men, each of whom was of his father's household.
45 So all the numbered men of the sons of Israel by their fathers' households, from twenty years old and upward, whoever *was able to* go out to war in Israel,
46 even all the numbered men were [a]603,550.

Levites Exempted

47 [a]The Levites, however, were not numbered among them by their fathers' tribe.
48 For the LORD had spoken to Moses, saying,
49 "Only the tribe of Levi [a]you shall not number, nor shall you take their [1]census among the sons of Israel.
50 "But you shall [a]appoint the Levites over the [1]tabernacle of the testimony, and over all its furnishings and over all that belongs to it. They shall carry the tabernacle and all its furnishings, and they shall take care of it; they shall also camp around the [1]tabernacle.
51 "[a]So when the tabernacle is to set out, the Levites shall take it down; and when the tabernacle encamps, the Levites shall set it up. But [b]the [1]layman who comes near shall be put to death.
52 "[a]And the sons of Israel shall camp, each man by his own camp, and each man by his own standard, according to their armies.
53 "[a]But the Levites shall camp around the tabernacle of the testimony, that there may be [b]no wrath on the congregation of the sons of Israel. [c]So the Levites shall keep charge of the tabernacle of the testimony."
54 Thus the sons of Israel did; according to all which the LORD had commanded Moses, so they did.

Arrangement of the Camps

2 NOW the LORD spoke to Moses and to Aaron, saying,
2 "[a]The sons of Israel shall camp, each by his own standard, with the [1]banners of their fathers' households; they shall camp around the tent of meeting [2]at a distance.
3 "Now those who camp on the east side toward the sunrise *shall be* of the standard of the camp of Judah, by their armies, and the leader of the sons of Judah: [a]Nahshon the son of Amminadab,
4 and his army, even their [1]numbered men, 74,600.
5 "And those who camp next to him *shall be* the tribe of Issachar, and the leader of the sons of Issachar: [a]Nethanel the son of Zuar,
6 and his army, even their numbered men, 54,400.
7 "Then *comes* the tribe of Zebulun, and the leader of the sons of Zebulun: [a]Eliab the son of Helon,
8 and his army, even his numbered men, 57,400.
9 "The total of the numbered men of the camp of Judah: 186,400, by their armies. [a]They shall set out first.
10 "On the south side *shall be* the standard of the camp of Reuben by their armies, and the leader of the sons of Reuben: [a]Elizur the son of Shedeur,

30 [a]Num. 26:26, 27
32 [a]Num. 26:35-37; Deut. 33:13-17; Jer. 7:15; Obad. 19
34 [a]Num. 26:28-34
36 [a]Gen. 49:27; Num. 26:38-41; 2 Chr. 17:17; Rev. 7:8
38 [a]Gen. 30:6; 46:23; Num. 2:25; 26:42, 43
40 [a]Num. 26:44-47
42 [a]Num. 26:48-50
46 [a]Ex. 12:37; 38:26; Num. 2:32; 26:51
47 [a]Num. 2:33; 3:14-39; 4:49; 26:57-64
49 [1]Lit., *sum* [a]Num. 26:62
50 [1]Lit., *dwelling place,* and so throughout the ch. [a]Ex. 38:21; Num. 3:6-8, 25-37; 4:15, 25-27, 31, 32
51 [1]Lit., *stranger* [a]Num. 4:1-33 [b]Num. 3:10, 38; 4:15, 19, 20
52 [a]Num. 2:2, 34
53 [a]Num. 3:23, 29, 35, 38 [b]Lev. 10:6; Num. 16:46; 18:5 [c]Num. 8:24; 18:2-4; 1 Chr. 23:32
2 [1]Lit., *signs* [2]Or, *facing it* [a]Num. 1:52; 24:2
3 [a]Num. 1:7; 10:14; Ruth 4:20; 1 Chr. 2:10; Luke 3:32, 33
4 [1]Lit., *mustered,* and so throughout the ch.
5 [a]Num. 1:8; 7:18, 23
7 [a]Num. 1:9
9 [a]Num. 10:14
10 [a]Num. 1:5

11 and his army, even their numbered
men, 46,500.
12"And those who camp next to him
shall be the tribe of Simeon, and the
leader of the sons of Simeon: [a]Shelumiel
the son of Zurishaddai,
13 and his army, even their numbered
men, 59,300.
14"Then *comes* the tribe of Gad, and
the leader of the sons of Gad: [a]Eliasaph
the son of [1]Deuel,
15 and his army, even their numbered
men, 45,650.
16"The total of the numbered men of
the camp of Reuben: 151,450 by their
armies. And [a]they shall set out second.
17"[a]Then the tent of meeting shall set
out *with* the camp of the Levites in the
midst of the camps; just as they camp, so
they shall set out, every man in his place,
by their standards.
18"On the west side *shall be* the standard of the camp of [a]Ephraim by their
armies, and the leader of the sons of
Ephraim *shall be* [b]Elishama the son of
Ammihud,
19 and his army, even their numbered
men, 40,500.
20"And next to him *shall be* the tribe
of Manasseh, and the leader of the sons
of Manasseh: [a]Gamaliel the son of Pedahzur,
21 and his army, even their numbered
men, 32,200.
22"Then *comes* the tribe of [a]Benjamin,
and the leader of the sons of Benjamin:
[b]Abidan the son of Gideoni,
23 and his army, even their numbered
men, 35,400.
24"The total of the numbered men of
the camp of Ephraim: 108,100, by their
armies. And [a]they shall set out third.
25"On the north side *shall be* the
standard of the camp of Dan by their
armies, and the leader of the sons of
Dan: [a]Ahiezer the son of Ammishaddai,
26 and his army, even their numbered
men, 62,700.
27"And those who camp next to him
shall be the tribe of Asher, and the leader
of the sons of Asher: [a]Pagiel the son of
Ochran,
28 and his army, even their numbered
men, 41,500.
29"Then *comes* the tribe of [a]Naphtali,
and the leader of the sons of Naphtali:
[b]Ahira the son of Enan,
30 and his army, even their numbered
men, 53,400.
31"The total of the numbered men of
the camp of Dan, *was* 157,600. [a]They
shall set out last by their standards."
32 These are the numbered men of the
sons of Israel by their fathers' households; the total of the numbered men of
the camps by their armies, [a]603,550.
33 [a]The Levites, however, were not
numbered among the sons of Israel, just
as the LORD had commanded Moses.
34 Thus the sons of Israel did; according to all that the LORD commanded

12 [a]Num. 1:6

14 [1]Many mss. read *Reuel*
[a]Num. 1:14; 7:42

16 [a]Num. 10:18

17 [a]Num. 1:53

18 [a]Gen. 48:14-20; Jer. 31:9, 18-20
[b]Num. 1:10

20 [a]Num. 1:10

22 [a]Ps. 68:27
[b]Num. 1:11

24 [a]Num. 10:22

25 [a]Num. 1:12

27 [a]Num. 1:13

29 [a]Gen. 30:8
[b]Num. 1:15

31 [a]Num. 10:25

32 [a]Ex. 38:26; Num. 1:46

33 [a]Num. 1:47; 26:57-62

1 [a]Ex. 6:20-27

2 [a]Ex. 6:23; Num. 26:60

3 [1]Lit., *filled their hand*
[a]Ex. 28:41

4 [1]Lit., *before the face*
[a]Lev. 10:1, 2; Num. 26:61

6 [a]Num. 8:6-22; 18:1-7; Deut. 10:8

7 [1]Lit., *him and the duties of the whole congregation*
[a]Num. 1:50

9 [a]Num. 18:6

10 [1]Lit., *stranger*
[a]Ex. 29:9 [b]Num. 1:51

12 [a]Num. 3:45; 8:14 [b]Ex. 13:2

13 [a]Ex. 13:2; Lev. 27:26; Neh. 10:36

14 [a]Ex. 19:1

15 [1]Lit., *muster*, and so throughout the ch.
[a]Num. 1:47

16 [1]Lit., *mouth*

17 [a]Ex. 6:16-22

18 [a]Ex. 6:17

Moses, so they camped by their standards, and so they set out, every one by
his family, according to his father's
household.

Levites to Be Priesthood

3 [a]NOW these are *the records of* the
generations of Aaron and Moses at
the time when the LORD spoke with
Moses on Mount Sinai.
2 [a]These then are the names of the
sons of Aaron: Nadab the first-born,
and Abihu, Eleazar and Ithamar.
3 These are the names of the sons of
Aaron, the [a]anointed priests, whom he
[1]ordained to serve as priests.
4 [a]But Nadab and Abihu died before
the LORD when they offered strange fire
before the LORD in the wilderness of
Sinai; and they had no children. So
Eleazar and Ithamar served as priests [1]in
the lifetime of their father Aaron.
5 Then the LORD spoke to Moses,
saying,
6"[a]Bring the tribe of Levi near and
set them before Aaron the priest, that
they may serve him.
7"And they shall perform the duties
for [1]him and for the whole congregation
before the tent of meeting, to do the
[a]service of the tabernacle.
8"They shall also keep all the furnishings of the tent of meeting, along with
the duties of the sons of Israel, to do the
service of the tabernacle.
9"You shall thus [a]give the Levites to
Aaron and to his sons; they are wholly
given to him from among the sons of
Israel.
10"So you shall appoint Aaron and his
sons that [a]they may keep their priesthood, but [b]the [1]layman who comes near
shall be put to death."
11 Again the LORD spoke to Moses,
saying,
12"Now, behold, I [a]have taken the
Levites from among the sons of Israel
instead of every [b]first-born, the first
issue of the womb among the sons of
Israel. So the Levites shall be Mine.
13"For [a]all the first-born are Mine; on
the day that I struck down all the first-
born in the land of Egypt, I sanctified to
Myself all the first-born in Israel, from
man to beast. They shall be Mine; I am
the LORD."
14 Then the LORD spoke to Moses [a]in
the wilderness of Sinai, saying,
15"[1a]Number the sons of Levi by their
fathers' households, by their families;
every male from a month old and upward you shall number."
16 So Moses numbered them according to the [1]word of the LORD, just as he
had been commanded.
17 [a]These then are the sons of Levi by
their names: Gershon and Kohath and
Merari.
18 And these are the names of the
[a]sons of Gershon by their families: Libni
and Shimei;

19 and the sons of Kohath by their families: Amram and Izhar, Hebron and Uzziel;

20 and the sons of Merari by their families: Mahli and Mushi. These are the families of the Levites according to their fathers' households.

21 Of Gershon *was* the family of the Libnites and the family of the Shimeites; these *were* the families of the Gershonites.

22 Their numbered men, in the numbering of every male from a month old and upward, *even* their numbered men *were* 7,500.

23 The families of the Gershonites were to camp behind the [1]tabernacle westward,

24 and the leader of the fathers' households of the Gershonites *was* Eliasaph the son of Lael.

Duties of the Priests

25 Now [a]the duties of the sons of Gershon in the tent of meeting *involved* the tabernacle and [b]the tent, its covering, and [c]the screen for the doorway of the tent of meeting,

26 and [a]the hangings of the court, and [b]the screen for the doorway of the court, which is around the tabernacle and the altar, and its cords, according to all the service [1]concerning them.

27 And of Kohath *was* the family of the Amramites and the family of the Izharites and the family of the Hebronites and the family of the Uzzielites; these were the families of the Kohathites.

28 In the numbering of every male from a month old and upward, *there were* 8,600, performing the duties of the sanctuary.

29 The families of the sons of Kohath were to camp on the southward side of the tabernacle,

30 and the leader of the fathers' households of the Kohathite families was [1]Elizaphan the son of Uzziel.

31 Now [a]their duties *involved* [b]the ark, [c]the table, [d]the lampstand, [e]the altars, and the utensils of the sanctuary with which they minister, and the screen, and all the service [1]concerning them;

32 and Eleazar the son of Aaron the priest *was* the chief of the leaders of Levi, *and had* the oversight of those who perform the duties of the sanctuary.

33 Of Merari *was* the family of the Mahlites and the family of the Mushites; these *were* the families of Merari.

34 Their numbered men in the numbering of every male from a month old and upward, *were* 6,200.

35 And the leader of the fathers' households of the families of Merari *was* Zuriel the son of Abihail. They *were* to [a]camp on the northward side of the tabernacle.

36 Now the appointed duties of the sons of Merari *involved* the frames of the tabernacle, its bars, its pillars, its sockets, all its equipment, and the service concerning them,

37 and the pillars around the court with their sockets and their pegs and their cords.

38 Now those who were to [a]camp before the tabernacle eastward, before the tent of meeting toward the sunrise, are Moses and Aaron and his sons, performing the duties of the sanctuary for the obligation of the sons of Israel; but [b]the [1]layman coming near was to be put to death.

39 All the numbered men of the Levites, whom Moses and Aaron numbered at the [1]command of the LORD by their families, every male from a month old and upward, *were* [a]22,000.

First-born Redeemed

40 Then the LORD said to Moses, "[a]Number every first-born male of the sons of Israel from a month old and upward, and [1]make a list of their names.

41 "And you [a]shall take the Levites for Me, I am the LORD, instead of all the first-born among the sons of Israel, and the cattle of the Levites instead of all the first-born among the cattle of the sons of Israel."

42 So Moses numbered all the first-born among the sons of Israel, just as the LORD had commanded him;

43 and all the first-born males by the number of names from a month old and upward, for their numbered men were [a]22,273.

44 Then the LORD spoke to Moses, saying,

45 "[a]Take the Levites instead of all the first-born among the sons of Israel and the cattle of the Levites. And the Levites shall be Mine; I am the LORD.

46 "[a]And for the ransom of the 273 of the first-born of the sons of Israel who are in excess beyond the Levites,

47 you shall take [a]five shekels apiece, per head; you shall take *them* in [b]terms of the shekel of the sanctuary ([c]the shekel is twenty [1]gerahs),

48 and give the money, the ransom of those who are in excess among them, to Aaron and to his sons."

49 So Moses took the ransom money from those who were in excess, beyond those ransomed by the Levites;

50 from the first-born of the sons of Israel he took the money in terms of the shekel of the sanctuary, 1,365.

51 Then Moses gave the ransom money to Aaron and to his sons, at the [1]command of the LORD, just as the LORD had commanded Moses.

Duties of the Kohathites

4 THEN the LORD spoke to Moses and to Aaron, saying,

2 "Take [1]a census of the [2]descendants of Kohath from among the sons of Levi, by their families, by their fathers' households,

3 from [a]thirty years and upward, even to fifty years old, all who enter the

23 [1]Lit., *dwelling place,* and so throughout the ch.

25 [a]Num. 4:24-26 [b]Ex. 26:1, 7, 14 [c]Ex. 26:36

26 [1]Lit., *of it* [a]Ex. 27:9, 12, 14, 15 [b]Ex. 27:16

30 [1]In Ex. 6:22, *Elzaphan*

31 [1]Lit., *of it* [a]Num. 4:15 [b]Ex. 25:10-22 [c]Ex. 25:23-28 [d]Ex. 25:31-40 [e]Ex. 27:1, 2; 30:1-5

35 [a]Num. 1:53; 2:25

38 [1]Lit., *stranger* [a]Num. 1:53; 2:3 [b]Num. 1:51

39 [1]Lit., *word* [a]Num. 3:43; 4:48; 26:62

40 [1]Lit., *take the number* [a]Num. 3:15

41 [a]Num. 3:12, 45

43 [a]Num. 3:39

45 [a]Num. 3:12

46 [a]Ex. 13:13, 15; Num. 18:15, 16

47 [1]I.e., A gerah equals approx. one-fortieth oz. [a]Lev. 27:6; Num. 18:16 [b]Ex. 30:13 [c]Lev. 27:25; Ezek. 45:12

51 [1]Lit., *mouth*

2 [1]Lit., *the sum* [2]Lit., *sons*

3 [a]Num. 4:23, 30, 35; 8:24; 1 Chr. 23:3, 24, 27; Ezra 3:8

service to do the work in the tent of
meeting.
4"This is the work of the [1]descend-
ants of Kohath in the tent of meeting,
concerning the most holy things.
5"When the camp sets out, Aaron
and his sons shall go in and they shall
take down [a]the veil of the screen and
cover the [b]ark of the testimony with it;
6 and they shall lay a [a]covering of
porpoise skin on it, and shall spread over
it a cloth of pure [1]blue, and shall insert
its poles.
7"Over the table of the bread of the
Presence they shall also spread a cloth of
[1]blue and put on it the dishes and the
pans and the sacrificial bowls and the
jars for the libation, and [a]the continual
bread shall be on it.
8"And they shall spread over them a
cloth of scarlet *material,* and cover the
same with a covering of porpoise skin,
and they shall insert its poles.
9"Then they shall take a [1]blue cloth
and cover the [a]lampstand for the light,
[b]along with its lamps and its snuffers,
and its [2]trays and all its oil vessels, by
which they serve it;
10 and they shall put it and all its
utensils in a covering of porpoise skin,
and shall put it on the carrying bars.
11"And over the golden altar they
shall spread a [1]blue cloth and cover it
with a covering of porpoise skin, and
shall insert its poles;
12 and they shall take all the utensils
of service, with which they serve in the
sanctuary, and put them in a [1]blue cloth
and cover them with a covering of porpoise skin, and put them on the carrying
bars.
13"Then they shall take away the
[1]ashes from the [a]altar, and spread a
purple cloth over it.
14"They shall also put on it all its
utensils by which they serve in connection with it: the firepans, the forks and
shovels and the basins, all the utensils of
the altar; and they shall spread a cover
of porpoise skin over it and insert its
poles.
15"And when Aaron and his sons have
finished covering the holy *objects* and all
the furnishings of the sanctuary, when
the camp is to set out, after that the sons
of Kohath shall come to carry *them,* so
that they may not touch the holy *objects*
[a]and die. These are the [1]things in the
tent of meeting which the sons of Kohath are to carry.
16"And the responsibility of Eleazar
the son of Aaron the priest is [a]the oil for
the light and the [b]fragrant incense and
[c]the continual grain offering and [d]the
anointing oil—the responsibility of all
the [1]tabernacle and of all that is in it,
with the sanctuary and its furnishings."
17 Then the LORD spoke to Moses
and to Aaron, saying,
18"Do not let the tribe of the families
of the Kohathites be cut off from among
the Levites.
19"But do this to them that they may
live and [a]not die when they approach the
most holy *objects:* Aaron and his sons
shall go in and assign each of them to his
work and to his load;
20 but [a]they shall not go in to see the
holy *objects* even for a moment, lest they
die."

Duties of the Gershonites

21 Then the LORD spoke to Moses,
saying,
22"Take [1]a census of the sons of
Gershon [2]also, by their fathers' households, by their families;
23 from [a]thirty years and upward to
fifty years old, you shall [1]number them;
all who enter to perform the service to
do the work in the tent of meeting.
24"This is the service of the families of
the Gershonites, in serving and in carrying:
25 they shall carry [a]the curtains of the
tabernacle and the tent of meeting *with*
its covering and [b]the covering of porpoise skin that is on top of it, and the
screen for the doorway of the tent of
meeting,
26 and [a]the hangings of the court, and
the screen for the doorway of the gate of
the court which is around the tabernacle
and the altar, and their cords and all the
equipment for their service; and all that
is to be done, [1]they shall perform.
27"All the service of the sons of the
Gershonites, in all their loads and in all
their work, shall be *performed* at the
[1]command of Aaron and his sons; and
you shall assign to them as a duty all
their loads.
28"This is the service of the families of
the sons of the Gershonites in the tent of
meeting, and their duties *shall be* [1]under
the direction of Ithamar the son of
Aaron the priest.

Duties of the Merarites

29"*As for* the sons of Merari, you shall
number them by their families, by their
fathers' households;
30 from [a]thirty years and upward even
to fifty years old, you shall number
them, everyone who enters the service to
do the work of the tent of meeting.
31"Now this is the duty of their loads,
for all their service in the tent of meeting: the boards of the tabernacle and its
bars and its pillars and its [1]sockets,
32 and the pillars around the court
and their [1]sockets and their pegs and
their cords, with all their equipment and
with all their service; and you shall
assign *each man* by name the items [2]he is
to carry.
33"This is the service of the families of
the sons of Merari, according to all their
service in the tent of meeting, [1]under the
direction of Ithamar the son of Aaron
the priest."
34 So Moses and Aaron and the leaders of the congregation numbered the
sons of the Kohathites by their families,
and by their fathers' households,

4 [1]Lit., *sons*

5 [a]Ex. 40:5; Lev. 16:2; 2 Chr. 3:14; Matt. 27:51; Heb. 9:3 [b]Ex. 25:10-16

6 [1]Or, *violet* [a]Num. 4:25

7 [1]Or, *violet* [a]Ex. 25:30; Lev. 24:5-9

9 [1]Or, *violet* [2]Lit., *snuff dishes* [a]Ex. 25:31 [b]Ex. 25:37, 38

11 [1]Or, *violet*

12 [1]Or, *violet*

13 [1]Or, *fat ashes;* i.e., soaked with fat [a]Ex. 27:1-8

15 [1]Lit., *burden . . . of the sons* [a]Num. 1:51; 4:19, 20; 2 Sam. 6:6, 7

16 [1]Lit., *dwelling place,* and so throughout the ch. [a]Lev. 24:1-3 [b]Ex. 30:34-38 [c]Lev. 6:20 [d]Ex. 30:22-33

19 [a]Num. 4:15

20 [a]Ex. 19:21; 1 Sam. 6:19

22 [1]Lit., *the sum* [2]Lit., *also them*

23 [1]Lit., *muster,* and so throughout the ch. [a]Num. 4:3; 1 Chr. 23:3, 24, 27

25 [a]Ex. 40:19 [b]Ex. 26:14; Num. 4:6

26 [1]Lit., *so they shall serve* [a]Ex. 38:9

27 [1]Lit., *mouth*

28 [1]Lit., *in the hand*

30 [a]Num. 4:3; 8:24-26

31 [1]Or, *bases*

32 [1]Or, *bases* [2]Lit., *of the duty of their loads.*

33 [1]Lit., *in the hand*

35 from [a]thirty years and upward even to fifty years old, everyone who entered the service for work in the tent of meeting.

36 And their numbered men by their families were 2,750.

37 These are the numbered men of the Kohathite families, everyone who was serving in the tent of meeting, whom Moses and Aaron numbered according to the [1]commandment of the LORD [2]through Moses.

38 And the numbered men of the sons of Gershon by their families, and by their fathers' households,

39 from thirty years and upward even to fifty years old, everyone who entered the service for work in the tent of meeting.

40 And their numbered men by their families, by their fathers' households, were 2,630.

41 These are the numbered men of the families of the sons of Gershon, everyone who was serving in the tent of meeting, whom Moses and Aaron numbered according to the [1]commandment of the LORD.

42 And the numbered men of the families of the sons of Merari by their families, by their fathers' households,

43 from [a]thirty years and upward even to fifty years old, everyone who entered the service for work in the tent of meeting.

44 And their numbered men by their families were 3,200.

45 These are the numbered men of the families of the sons of Merari, whom Moses and Aaron numbered according to the [1]commandment of the LORD [2]through Moses.

46 All the numbered men of the Levites, whom Moses and Aaron and the leaders of Israel numbered, by their families and by their fathers' households,

47 from thirty years and upward even to fifty years old, everyone who could enter to do the work of service and the work of carrying in the tent of meeting.

48 And their numbered men were [a]8,580.

49 According to the [1]commandment of the LORD [2]through Moses, they [a]were numbered, everyone by his serving or carrying; thus these were his numbered men, just as the LORD had commanded Moses.

On Defilement

5 THEN the LORD spoke to Moses, saying,

2 "Command the sons of Israel that they [a]send away from the camp every leper and everyone having a [b]discharge and everyone who is [c]unclean because of a *dead* person.

3 "You shall send away both male and female; you shall send them outside the camp so that they will not defile their camp where I dwell [a]in their midst."

4 And the sons of Israel did so and sent them outside the camp; just as the LORD had spoken to Moses, thus the sons of Israel did.

5 Then the LORD spoke to Moses, saying,

6 "Speak to the sons of Israel, '[a]When a man or woman commits any of the sins of mankind, acting unfaithfully against the LORD, and that person is guilty,

7 then [1]he shall [a]confess [2]his sins which [3]he has committed, and he [b]shall make restitution in full for his wrong, and add to it one-fifth of it, and give *it* to him whom he has wronged.

8 'But if the man has no [1]relative to whom restitution may be made for the wrong, the restitution which is made for the wrong *must go* to the LORD for the priest, besides the ram of atonement, by which atonement is made for him.

9 '[a]Also every [1]contribution pertaining to all the holy *gifts* of the sons of Israel, which they offer to the priest, shall be his.

10 'So every man's holy *gifts* shall be his; whatever any man gives to the priest, it [a]becomes his.' "

The Adultery Test

11 Then the LORD spoke to Moses, saying,

12 "Speak to the sons of Israel, and say to them, 'If any man's wife [a]goes astray and is unfaithful to him,

13 and a man has [a]intercourse with her and it is hidden from the eyes of her husband and she is [1]undetected, although she has defiled herself, and there is no witness against her and she has not been caught in the act,

14 [1]if a spirit of [a]jealousy comes over him and he is jealous of his wife when she has defiled herself, or if a spirit of jealousy comes over him and he is jealous of his wife when she has not defiled herself,

15 the man shall then bring his wife to the priest, and shall bring *as* [1]an offering for her one-tenth of an [2]ephah of barley meal; he shall not pour oil on it, nor put frankincense on it, for it is a grain offering of jealousy, a grain offering of memorial, [a]a reminder of iniquity.

16 'Then the priest shall bring her near and have her stand before the LORD,

17 and the priest shall take holy water in an earthenware vessel; and [1]he shall take some of the dust that is on the floor of the tabernacle and put *it* into the water.

18 'The priest shall then have the woman stand before the LORD and let *the hair of* the woman's head go loose, and place the grain offering of memorial [1]in her hands, which is the grain offering of jealousy, and in the hand of the priest is to be the water of bitterness that brings a curse.

19 'And the priest shall have her take an oath and shall say to the woman, "If no man has lain with you and if you

35 [a]1 Chr. 23:24
37 [1]Lit., *mouth* [2]Lit., *by the hand of*
41 [1]Lit., *mouth*
43 [a]Num. 8:24-26
45 [1]Lit., *mouth* [2]Lit., *by the hand of*
48 [a]Num. 3:39
49 [1]Lit., *mouth* [2]Lit., *by the hand of* [a]Num. 1:47
2 [a]Lev. 13:8, 46; Num. 12:10, 14, 15 [b]Lev. 15:2 [c]Lev. 21:1; Num. 9:6-10; 19:11
3 [a]Lev. 26:12; Num. 35:34
6 [a]Lev. 5:14-6:7
7 [1]Lit., *they* [2]Lit., *their* [3]Lit., *they have* [a]Lev. 5:5; 26:40, 41; Josh. 7:19 [b]Lev. 6:4, 5
8 [1]Lit., *redeemer*
9 [1]Lit., *heave offering* [a]Lev. 7:32, 34; 10:14, 15
10 [a]Lev. 10:13
12 [a]Num. 5:19-21, 29
13 [1]Lit., *concealed* [a]Lev. 18:20; 20:10
14 [1]Lit., *and* [a]Prov. 6:34; Song 8:6
15 [1]Lit., *her* [2]I.e., Approx. one bu. [a]1 Kin. 17:18; Ezek. 29:16
17 [1]Lit., *the priest*
18 [1]Lit., *on her palms*

have not [a]gone astray into uncleanness,
being under *the authority of* your husband, be [1]immune to this water of bitterness that brings a curse;
20 if you, however, have [a]gone astray,
being under *the authority of* your husband, and if you have defiled yourself
and a man other than your husband has
had intercourse with you"
21 (then the priest shall have the
woman [a]swear with the oath of the
curse, and the priest shall say to
the woman), "the LORD make you a
curse and an oath among your people by
the LORD's making your thigh [1]waste
away and your abdomen swell;
22 and this water that brings a curse
shall go into your [1]stomach, and make
your abdomen swell and your thigh
[2]waste away." And the woman [a]shall
say, "Amen. Amen."
23 'The priest shall then write these
curses on a scroll, and he shall [1]wash
them off into the water of bitterness.
24 'Then he shall make the woman
drink the water of bitterness that brings
a curse, so that the water which brings a
curse will go into her [1]and *cause* bitterness.
25 'And the priest shall take the grain
offering of jealousy from the woman's
hand, and he shall wave the grain offering before the LORD and bring it to the
altar;
26 and [a]the priest shall take a handful
of the grain offering as its memorial
offering and offer *it* up in smoke on the
altar, and afterward he shall make the
woman drink the water.
27 'When he has made her drink the
water, then it shall come about, if she
has defiled herself and has been unfaithful to her husband, that the water which
brings a curse shall go into her [1]and
cause bitterness, and her abdomen will
swell and her thigh will [2]waste away, and
the woman will become [a]a curse among
her people.
28 'But if the woman has not defiled
herself and is clean, she will then be free
and conceive [1]children.
29 'This is the law of jealousy: when a
wife, *being* under *the authority of* her
husband, [a]goes astray and defiles herself,
30 or when a spirit of jealousy comes
over a man and he is jealous of his wife,
he shall then make the woman stand
before the LORD, and the priest shall
apply all this law to her.
31 'Moreover, the man shall be free
from [1]guilt, but that woman shall [a]bear
her [1]guilt.'"

Law of the Nazirites

6 AGAIN the LORD spoke to Moses,
saying,
2 "Speak to the sons of Israel, and say
to them, 'When a man or woman makes
a [1]special vow, the vow of [a]a [2]Nazirite,
to [3]dedicate himself to the LORD,
3 he shall [a]abstain from wine and
strong drink; he shall drink no vinegar,
whether made from wine or strong
drink, neither shall he drink any grape
juice, nor eat fresh or dried grapes.
4 'All the days of his [1]separation he
shall not eat anything that is produced
by the grape vine, from *the* seeds even to
the skin.
5 'All the days of his vow of separation [a]no razor shall pass over his head.
He shall be holy until the days are
fulfilled for which he separated himself
to the LORD; he shall let the locks of hair
on his head grow long.
6 '[a]All the days of his separation to
the LORD he shall not go near to a dead
person.
7 'He [a]shall not make himself unclean
for his father or for his mother, for his
brother or for his sister, when they die,
because his separation to God is on his
head.
8 'All the days of his separation he is
holy to the LORD.
9 'But if a man dies very suddenly
beside him and he defiles his dedicated
head *of hair,* then [a]he shall shave his
head on the day when he becomes clean;
[b]he shall shave it on the seventh day.
10 'Then on the eighth day he shall
bring [a]two turtledoves or two young
pigeons to the priest, to the doorway of
the tent of meeting.
11 'And the priest shall offer [a]one for a
sin offering and *the* other for a burnt
offering, and make atonement for him
[1]concerning his sin because of the *dead*
person. And that same day he shall
consecrate his head,
12 and shall dedicate to the LORD his
days [1]as a [2]Nazirite, and shall bring a
male lamb a year old for a guilt offering;
but the former days shall be void because his separation was defiled.
13 'Now this is the law of the Nazirite
[a]when the days of his separation are
fulfilled, he shall bring [1]the offering to
the doorway of the tent of meeting.
14 'And he shall present his offering to
the LORD: one male lamb a year old
without defect for a burnt offering and
one [a]ewe-lamb a year old without defect
for a sin offering and one ram without
defect for a peace offering,
15 and a basket of [a]unleavened cakes
of fine flour mixed with oil and unleavened wafers spread with oil, along with
[b]their grain offering and their libations.
16 'Then the priest shall present *them*
before the LORD and shall offer his sin
offering and his burnt offering.
17 'He shall also offer the ram for a
sacrifice of peace offerings to the LORD,
together with the basket of unleavened
cakes; the priest shall likewise offer its
grain offering and its libation.
18 '[a]The Nazirite shall then shave his
dedicated head *of hair* at the doorway of
the tent of meeting, and take the dedicated hair of his head and put *it* on the
fire which is under the sacrifice of peace
offerings.

19 [1]Lit., *free from* [a]Num. 5:12
20 [a]Num. 5:12
21 [1]Lit., *fall* [a]Josh. 6:26; 1 Sam. 14:24; Neh. 10:29
22 [1]Or, *inward parts* [2]Lit., *fall* [a]Deut. 27:15
23 [1]Lit., *wipe*
24 [1]Lit., *to*
26 [a]Lev. 2:2, 9
27 [1]Lit., *to* [2]Lit., *fall* [a]Jer. 29:18; 42:18; 44:12
28 [1]Lit., *seed*
29 [a]Num. 5:12
31 [1]Or, *iniquity* [a]Lev. 20:17
2 [1]Or, *difficult* [2]I.e., one separated [3]Or, *live as a Nazirite* [a]Judg. 13:5; 16:17; Amos 2:11, 12
3 [a]Luke 1:15
4 [1]Or, *living as a Nazirite,* and so through v. 21
5 [a]1 Sam. 1:11
6 [a]Lev. 21:1-3; Num. 19:11-22
7 [a]Num. 9:6
9 [a]Lev. 14:8, 9 [b]Num. 6:18
10 [a]Lev. 5:7; 14:22
11 [1]Lit., *because of that which he sinned* [a]Lev. 5:7
12 [1]Or, *of dedication* [2]I.e., one separated
13 [1]Lit., *it* [a]Acts 21:26
14 [a]Lev. 14:10; Num. 15:27
15 [a]Ex. 29:2; Lev. 2:4 [b]Num. 15:1-7
18 [a]Num. 6:9; Acts 21:23, 24

19 '[a]And the priest shall take the ram's shoulder *when it has been* boiled, and one unleavened cake out of the basket, and one unleavened wafer, and shall put *them* on the [1]hands of the Nazirite after he has shaved his [2]dedicated *hair.*
20 'Then the priest shall wave them for a wave offering before the LORD. It is holy for the priest, together with the breast offered by waving and the thigh offered by lifting up; and [a]afterward the Nazirite may drink wine.'
21 "This is the law of the Nazirite who vows his offering to the LORD according to his separation, in addition to what *else* [1]he can afford; according to his vow which he takes, so he shall do according to the law of his separation."

Aaron's Benediction

22 Then the LORD spoke to Moses, saying,
23 "Speak to Aaron and to his sons, saying, 'Thus [a]you shall bless the sons of Israel. You shall say to them:
24 The LORD [a]bless you, and [b]keep you;
25 The LORD [a]make His face shine on you,
And [b]be gracious to you;
26 The LORD [a]lift up His countenance on you,
And [b]give you peace.'
27 "So they shall [1a]invoke My name on the sons of Israel, and I then will bless them."

Offerings of the Leaders

7 NOW it came about on [a]the day that Moses had finished setting up the tabernacle, he [b]anointed it and consecrated it with all its furnishings and the altar and all its utensils; he anointed them and consecrated them also.
2 Then [a]the leaders of Israel, the heads of their fathers' households, [b]made an offering (they were the leaders of the tribes; they were the ones who [1]were over the [2]numbered men).
3 When they brought their offering before the LORD, six [a]covered carts and twelve oxen, a cart for *every* two of the leaders and an ox for each one, then they presented them before the tabernacle.
4 Then the LORD spoke to Moses, saying,
5 "Accept *these things* from them, that they may be [1]used in the service of the tent of meeting, and you shall give them to the Levites, *to* each man according to his service."
6 So Moses took the carts and the oxen, and gave them to the Levites.
7 Two carts and four oxen he gave to the sons of Gershon, according to [a]their service,
8 and four carts and eight oxen he gave to the sons of Merari, according to [a]their service, under the [1]direction of Ithamar the son of Aaron the priest.
9 But he did not give *any* to the sons of Kohath because theirs *was* [a]the service of the holy *objects, which* they carried on the shoulder.
10 And the leaders offered the dedication *offering* [1]for the altar [2]when [a]it was anointed, so the leaders offered their offering before the altar.
11 Then the LORD said to Moses, "Let them present their offering, one leader each day, for the dedication of the altar."
12 Now the one who presented his offering on the first day *was* Nahshon the son of Amminadab, of the tribe of Judah;
13 and his offering *was* one silver [1a]dish whose weight *was* one hundred and thirty *shekels,* one silver bowl of seventy shekels, [b]according to [2]the shekel of the sanctuary, both of them full of fine flour mixed with oil for a grain offering;
14 one gold pan of ten *shekels,* full of incense;
15 one [1]bull, one ram, one male lamb one year old, for a burnt offering;
16 [a]one male goat for a sin offering;
17 and for the sacrifice of peace offerings, two oxen, five rams, five male goats, five male lambs one year old. This *was* the offering of [a]Nahshon the son of Amminadab.
18 On the second day Nethanel the son of Zuar, leader of Issachar, presented *an offering;*
19 he presented as his offering one silver dish whose weight *was* one hundred and thirty *shekels,* one silver bowl of seventy shekels, according to the shekel of the sanctuary, both of them full of fine flour mixed with oil for a grain offering;
20 one gold pan of ten *shekels,* full of incense;
21 one bull, one ram, one male lamb one year old, for a burnt offering;
22 one male goat for a sin offering;
23 and for the sacrifice of [a]peace offerings, two oxen, five rams, five male goats, five male lambs one year old. This *was* the offering of Nethanel the son of Zuar.
24 On the third day *it was* Eliab the son of Helon, leader of the sons of Zebulun;
25 his offering *was* one silver dish whose weight *was* one hundred and thirty *shekels,* one silver bowl of seventy shekels, according to the shekel of the sanctuary, both of them full of fine flour mixed with oil for a grain offering;
26 one gold pan of ten *shekels,* full of incense;
27 one young bull, one ram, one [a]male lamb one year old, for a burnt offering;
28 one male goat for a sin offering;
29 and for the sacrifice of peace offerings, two oxen, five rams, five male goats, five male lambs one year old. This *was* the offering of Eliab the son of Helon.

19 [1]Lit., *palms* [2]Or, *separated* [a]Lev. 7:28-34
20 [a]Eccl. 9:7
21 [1]Lit., *his hand can reach*
23 [a]1 Chr. 23:13
24 [a]Deut. 28:3-6; Ps. 28:9 [b]1 Sam. 2:9; Ps. 17:8
25 [a]Ps. 80:3, 7, 19 [b]Ps. 86:16
26 [a]Ps. 4:6; 44:3 [b]Ps. 29:11; 37:37
27 [1]Lit., *put* [a]2 Sam. 7:23; 2 Chr. 7:14
1 [a]Ex. 40:17 [b]Ex. 40:9-11; Num. 7:10, 84, 88
2 [1]Lit., *stood* [2]Lit., *mustered* [a]Num. 1:5-16 [b]2 Chr. 35:8
3 [a]Is. 66:20
5 [1]Lit., *for serving*
7 [a]Num. 4:24-26
8 [1]Lit., *hand* [a]Num. 4:31, 32
9 [a]Num. 4:5-15
10 [1]Lit., *of* [2]Lit., *in the day that* [a]Num. 7:1; 2 Chr. 7:9
13 [1]Or, *platter,* and so through v. 85 [2]I.e., Approx. one-half oz., and so through v. 86 [a]Ex. 25:29; 37:16 [b]Num. 3:47
15 [1]Or, *bull of the herd,* and so through v. 81
16 [a]Lev. 4:23
17 [a]Luke 3:32, 33
23 [a]Lev. 7:11-13
27 [a]Is. 53:7; John 1:29; 1 Pet. 1:19

30 On the fourth day *it was* Elizur the son of Shedeur, leader of the sons of Reuben;

31 his offering *was* one silver dish whose weight *was* one hundred and thirty *shekels,* one silver bowl of seventy shekels, according to the shekel of the sanctuary, both of them full of fine flour mixed with oil for a grain offering;

32 one gold pan of ten *shekels,* full of incense;

33 one bull, one ram, one [a]male lamb one year old, for a burnt offering;

34 one male goat for a sin offering;

35 and for the sacrifice of peace offerings, two oxen, five rams, five male goats, five male lambs one year old. This *was* the offering of Elizur the son of Shedeur.

36 On the fifth day *it was* Shelumiel the son of Zurishaddai, leader of the children of Simeon;

37 his offering *was* one silver dish whose weight *was* one hundred and thirty *shekels,* one silver bowl of seventy shekels, according to the shekel of the sanctuary, both of them full of fine flour mixed with oil for a grain offering;

38 one gold pan of ten *shekels,* full of incense;

39 one bull, one ram, one male lamb one year old, for a burnt offering;

40 one male goat for a sin offering;

41 and for the sacrifice of peace offerings, two oxen, five rams, five male goats, five male lambs one year old. This *was* the offering of Shelumiel the son of Zurishaddai.

42 On the sixth day *it was* [a]Eliasaph the son of Deuel, leader of the sons of Gad;

43 his offering *was* one silver dish whose weight *was* one hundred and thirty *shekels,* one silver bowl of seventy shekels, according to the shekel of the sanctuary, both of them full of [a]fine flour mixed with oil for a grain offering;

44 one gold pan of ten *shekels,* full of incense;

45 [a]one bull, one ram, one male lamb one year old, for a burnt offering;

46 one male goat for a sin offering;

47 and for the sacrifice of peace offerings, two oxen, five rams, five male goats, five male lambs one year old. This *was* the offering of Eliasaph the son of Deuel.

48 On the seventh day *it was* [a]Elishama the son of Ammihud, leader of the sons of Ephraim;

49 his offering *was* one silver dish whose weight *was* one hundred and thirty *shekels,* one silver bowl of seventy shekels, according to the shekel of the sanctuary, both of them full of fine flour mixed with oil for a grain offering;

50 one gold pan of ten *shekels,* full of [a]incense;

51 [a]one bull, one ram, one male lamb one year old, for a burnt offering;

52 one male goat for a sin offering;

53 and for the sacrifice of peace offerings, two oxen, five rams, five male goats, five male lambs one year old. This *was* the offering of Elishama the son of Ammihud.

54 On the eighth day *it was* [a]Gamaliel the son of Pedahzur, leader of the sons of Manasseh;

55 his offering *was* one silver dish whose weight *was* one hundred and thirty *shekels,* one silver bowl of seventy shekels, according to the shekel of the sanctuary, both of them full of fine flour mixed with oil for a grain offering;

56 one gold pan of ten *shekels,* full of [a]incense;

57 one bull, one ram, one [a]male lamb one year old, for a burnt offering;

58 one male goat for a sin offering;

59 and for the [a]sacrifice of peace offerings, two oxen, five rams, five male goats, five male lambs one year old. This *was* the offering of Gamaliel the son of Pedahzur.

60 On the ninth day *it was* [a]Abidan the son of Gideoni, leader of the sons of Benjamin;

61 his offering *was* one silver dish whose weight *was* one hundred and thirty *shekels,* one silver bowl of seventy shekels, according to the shekel of the sanctuary, both of them full of fine flour mixed with oil for a grain offering;

62 one gold pan of ten *shekels,* full of [a]incense;

63 one bull, one ram, one male lamb one year old, for a burnt offering;

64 one male goat for a [a]sin offering;

65 and for the sacrifice of [a]peace offerings, two oxen, five rams, five male goats, five male lambs one year old. This *was* the offering of Abidan the son of Gideoni.

66 On the tenth day *it was* [a]Ahiezer the son of Ammishaddai, leader of the sons of Dan;

67 his offering *was* one silver dish whose weight *was* one hundred and thirty *shekels,* one silver bowl of seventy shekels, according to the [a]shekel of the sanctuary, both of them full of fine flour mixed with oil for a grain offering;

68 one gold pan of ten *shekels,* full of [a]incense;

69 one bull, one ram, one male lamb one year old, for a burnt offering;

70 one male goat for a sin offering;

71 and for the sacrifice of peace offerings, two oxen, five rams, five male goats, five male lambs one year old. This *was* the offering of Ahiezer the son of Ammishaddai.

72 On the eleventh day *it was* [a]Pagiel the son of Ochran, leader of the sons of Asher;

73 his offering *was* one silver dish whose weight *was* one hundred and thirty *shekels,* one silver bowl of seventy shekels, according to the shekel of the sanctuary, both of them full of fine flour mixed with oil for a grain offering;

33 [a]Heb. 9:28
42 [a]Num. 1:14; 10:20
43 [a]Lev. 2:5; 14:10
45 [a]Ps. 50:8-14; Is. 1:11
48 [a]Num. 1:10; 2:18; 1 Chr. 7:26
50 [a]Deut. 33:10; Ezek. 8:11; Luke 1:10
51 [a]Mic. 6:6-8
54 [a]Num. 2:20
56 [a]Ex. 30:7
57 [a]Ex. 12:5; Acts 8:32; Rev. 5:6
59 [a]Lev. 3:1-17
60 [a]Num. 1:11; 2:22
62 [a]Rev. 5:8; 8:3, 4
64 [a]2 Cor. 5:21
65 [a]Col. 1:20
66 [a]Num. 1:12; 2:25
67 [a]Ex. 30:13; Lev. 27:25
68 [a]Ps. 141:2
72 [a]Num. 1:13; 2:27

74 one gold pan of ten *shekels,* full of [a]incense;
75 one bull, one ram, one male lamb one year old, for a burnt offering;
76 one male goat for a sin offering;
77 and for the sacrifice of peace offerings, two oxen, five rams, five male goats, five male lambs one year old. This *was* the offering of Pagiel the son of Ochran.
78 On the twelfth day *it was* [a]Ahira the son of Enan, leader of the sons of Naphtali;
79 his offering *was* one [a]silver dish whose weight *was* one hundred and thirty *shekels,* one silver bowl of seventy shekels, according to the shekel of the sanctuary, both of them full of fine flour mixed with oil for a grain offering;
80 one gold pan of ten *shekels,* full of incense;
81 one bull, one ram, one male lamb one year old, for a burnt offering;
82 one male goat for a sin offering;
83 and for the sacrifice of peace offerings, two oxen, five rams, five male goats, five male lambs one year old. This *was* the offering of Ahira the son of Enan.
84 This *was* [a]the dedication *offering* [1]for the altar from the leaders of Israel [2]when [b]it was anointed: twelve silver dishes, twelve silver bowls, twelve gold pans,
85 each silver dish *weighing* one hundred and thirty *shekels* and each bowl seventy; all the silver of the utensils *was* 2,400 *shekels,* according to the shekel of the sanctuary;
86 the twelve gold pans, full of incense, *weighing* ten *shekels* apiece, according to the [a]shekel of the sanctuary, all the gold of the pans 120 *shekels;*
87 all the oxen for the burnt offering twelve bulls, *all* the rams twelve, the male lambs one year old with their grain offering twelve, and the male goats for a sin offering twelve;
88 and all the oxen for the sacrifice of peace offerings 24 bulls, *all* the rams 60, the male goats 60, the male lambs one year old 60. [a]This *was* the dedication *offering* for the altar after it was anointed.
89 Now when [a]Moses went into the tent of meeting to speak with Him, he heard the voice speaking to him from above [b]the [1]mercy seat that was on the ark of the testimony, from [c]between the two cherubim, so He spoke to him.

The Seven Lamps

8 THEN the LORD spoke to Moses, saying,
2 "Speak to Aaron and say to him, 'When you [1]mount the lamps, the seven lamps will [a]give light in the front of the lampstand.' "
3 Aaron therefore did so; he [1]mounted its lamps at the front of the lampstand, just as the LORD had commanded Moses.
4 [a]Now this was the workmanship of the lampstand, hammered work of gold; from its base to its flowers, it was hammered work; [b]according to the pattern which the LORD had showed Moses, so he made the lampstand.

Cleansing the Levites

5 Again the LORD spoke to Moses, saying,
6 "Take the Levites from among the sons of Israel and [a]cleanse them.
7 "And thus you shall do to them, for their [1]cleansing: *sprinkle* [2]purifying [a]water on them, and let them [3][b]use a razor over their whole [4]body, and [c]wash their clothes, and they shall be clean.
8 "Then let them take a [1]bull with [a]its grain offering, fine flour mixed with oil; and a second [1]bull you shall take for a sin offering.
9 "So [a]you shall present the Levites before the tent of meeting. [b]You shall also assemble the whole congregation of the sons of Israel,
10 and present the Levites before the LORD; and the sons of Israel [a]shall lay their hands on the Levites.
11 "Aaron then shall [1]present the Levites before the LORD as a [a]wave offering from the sons of Israel, that they may [2]qualify to perform the service of the LORD.
12 "Now [a]the Levites shall lay their hands on the heads of the bulls; then offer the one for a sin offering and the other for a burnt offering to the LORD, to make atonement for the Levites.
13 "And you shall have the Levites stand before Aaron and before his sons so as to present them as a wave offering to the LORD.
14 "Thus you shall separate the Levites from among the sons of Israel, and [a]the Levites shall be Mine.
15 "Then after that the Levites may go in to serve the tent of meeting. But you shall cleanse them and [a]present them as a wave offering;
16 for they are [a]wholly given to Me from among the sons of Israel. I have taken them for Myself [b]instead of every first issue of the womb, the first-born of all the sons of Israel.
17 "For [a]every first-born among the sons of Israel is Mine, among the men and among the animals; on the day that I struck down all the first-born in the land of Egypt I sanctified them for Myself.
18 "But I have taken the Levites instead of every first-born among the sons of Israel.
19 "And [a]I have given the Levites as [1]a gift to Aaron and to his sons from among the sons of Israel, to perform the service of the sons of Israel at the tent of meeting, and to make atonement on behalf of the sons of Israel, that there may be no [b]plague among the sons of Israel by [2]their coming near to the sanctuary."

74 [a]Mal. 1:11
78 [a]Num. 1:15; 2:29
79 [a]Ezra 1:9, 10; Dan. 5:2
84 [1]Lit., *of* [2]Lit., *in the day that* [a]Num. 7:10 [b]Num. 7:1
86 [a]Ex. 30:13
88 [a]Num. 7:1, 10
89 [1]Lit., *propitiatory* [a]Ex. 40:34, 35 [b]Ex. 25:21, 22 [c]Ps. 80:1; 99:1
2 [1]Lit., *raise up* [a]Ex. 25:37; Lev. 24:2, 4
3 [1]Lit., *raised up*
4 [a]Ex. 25:31-40 [b]Ex. 25:9, 31-40; 26:30; 37:17-24
6 [a]Is. 52:11
7 [1]Lit., *this their cleansing* [2]Lit., *water of sin* [3]Lit., *cause to pass* [4]Lit., *flesh* [a]Num. 19:9, 13, 20 [b]Lev. 14:8, 9 [c]Num. 8:21
8 [1]Or, *bull of the herd* [a]Lev. 2:1; Num. 15:8-10
9 [a]Ex. 29:4; 40:12 [b]Lev. 8:3
10 [a]Lev. 1:4
11 [1]Lit., *wave,* and so throughout the ch. [2]Lit., *be able* [a]Lev. 7:30, 34
12 [a]Ex. 29:10
14 [a]Num. 3:12; 16:9
15 [a]Ex. 29:24
16 [a]Num. 3:9 [b]Ex. 13:2; Num. 3:12, 45
17 [a]Ex. 13:2, 12, 13, 15; Luke 2:23
19 [1]Lit., *given ones* [2]Lit., *the sons of Israel's* [a]Num. 3:9 [b]Num. 1:53; 16:46

20 Thus did Moses and Aaron and all
the congregation of the sons of Israel to
the Levites; according to all that the
LORD had commanded Moses concerning the Levites, so the sons of Israel did
to them.
21 [a]The Levites, too, purified themselves from sin and washed their clothes;
and Aaron presented them as a wave
offering before the LORD. Aaron also
made atonement for them to cleanse
them.
22 Then after that the Levites went in
to perform their service in the tent of
meeting before Aaron and before his
sons; just as the LORD had commanded
Moses concerning the Levites, so they
did to them.

Retirement

23 Now the LORD spoke to Moses,
saying,
24 "This is what *applies* to the Levites:
from [a]twenty-five years old and upward
[1]they shall enter to perform service in
the work of the tent of meeting.
25 "But at the age of fifty years they
shall [1]retire from service in the work and
not work any more.
26 "They may, however, [1]assist their
brothers in the tent of meeting, [a]to keep
an obligation; but they *themselves* shall
do no work. Thus you shall deal with the
Levites concerning their obligations."

The Passover

9 THUS the LORD spoke to Moses in
the wilderness of Sinai, in [a]the first
month of the second year after they had
come out of the land of Egypt, saying,
2 "Now, let the sons of Israel observe
the Passover at [a]its appointed time.
3 "On the fourteenth day of this
month, [1]at twilight, you shall observe it
at its appointed time; you shall observe
it according to all its statutes and according to all its ordinances."
4 So Moses [1]told the sons of Israel to
observe the Passover.
5 And [a]they observed the Passover in
the first *month,* on the fourteenth day of
the month, at twilight, in the wilderness
of Sinai; [b]according to all that the LORD
had commanded Moses, so the sons of
Israel did.
6 But there were *some* men who were
[a]unclean because of *the* [1]dead person, so
that they could not observe Passover on
that day; so [b]they came before Moses
and Aaron on that day.
7 And those men said to him,
"*Though* we are unclean because of *the*
[1]dead person, why are we restrained
from presenting the offering of the LORD
at its appointed time among the sons of
Israel?"
8 Moses therefore said to them,
"[1a]Wait, and I will listen to what the
LORD will command concerning you."
9 Then the LORD spoke to Moses,
saying,
10 "Speak to the sons of Israel, saying,
'If any one of you or of your generations
becomes unclean because of a *dead*
[1]person, or is on a distant journey, he
may, however, observe the Passover to
the LORD.
11 'In the second month on the [a]four-
teenth day at twilight, they shall observe
it; they [b]shall eat it with unleavened
bread and bitter herbs.
12 'They [a]shall leave none of it until
morning, [b]nor break a bone of it; according to all the statute of the Passover
they shall observe it.
13 '[a]But the man who is clean and is
not on a journey, and yet [1]neglects to
observe the Passover, that [2]person shall
then be cut off from his people, for he
did not present the offering of the LORD
at its appointed time. That man [b]shall
bear his sin.
14 '[a]And if an alien sojourns among
you and [1]observes the Passover to the
LORD, according to the statute of the
Passover and according to its ordinance,
so he shall do; you shall have [b]one
statute, both for the alien and for the
native of the land.' "

The Cloud on the Tabernacle

15 Now on [a]the day that the tabernacle was erected [b]the cloud covered the
tabernacle, the [c]tent of the testimony,
and [d]in the evening it was like the
appearance of fire over the tabernacle,
until morning.
16 So it was continuously; [a]the cloud
would cover it *by day,* and the appearance of fire by night.
17 [a]And whenever the cloud was lifted
from over the tent, afterward the sons of
Israel would then set out; and in the
place where the cloud settled down,
there the sons of Israel would camp.
18 At the [1]command of the LORD the
sons of Israel would set out, and at the
[1]command of the LORD they would
camp; [a]as long as the cloud settled over
the tabernacle, they remained camped.
19 Even when the cloud lingered over
the tabernacle for many days, [1]the sons
of Israel would keep the LORD's charge
and not set out.
20 If [1]sometimes the cloud remained a
few days over the tabernacle, [a]according
to the [2]command of the LORD they
remained camped. Then according to the
[2]command of the LORD they set out.
21 If [1]sometimes the cloud [2]remained
from evening until morning, when the
cloud was lifted in the morning, they
would move out; or *if it remained* in the
daytime and at night, whenever the
cloud was lifted, they would set out.
22 Whether it was two days or a
month or a year that the cloud lingered
over the tabernacle, staying above it, the
sons of Israel remained camped and did
not set out; but [a]when it was lifted, they
did set out.
23 [a]At the [1]command of the LORD
they camped, and at the [1]command of
the LORD they set out; they kept the
LORD's charge, according to the [1]com-
mand of the LORD through Moses.

21 [a]Num. 8:7
24 [1]Lit., *he* [a]Num. 4:3; 1 Chr. 23:3, 24, 27
25 [1]Lit., *return*
26 [1]Lit., *serve* [a]Num. 1:53
1 [a]Ex. 40:2, 17; Num. 1:1
2 [a]Ex. 12:6; Lev. 23:5; Deut. 16:1, 2
3 [1]Lit., *between the two evenings,* and so throughout the ch.
4 [1]Lit., *spoke to*
5 [a]Josh. 5:10 [b]Ex. 12:1-13
6 [1]Lit., *soul of man* [a]Num. 5:2; 19:11-22 [b]Ex. 18:15; Num. 27:2
7 [1]Lit., *soul of man*
8 [1]Lit., *Stand* [a]Ex. 18:15; Ps. 85:8
10 [1]Lit., *soul*
11 [a]2 Chr. 30:2, 15 [b]Ex. 12:8
12 [a]Ex. 12:10 [b]Ex. 12:46; John 19:36
13 [1]Or, *ceases* [2]Lit., *soul* [a]Gen. 17:14; Ex. 12:15, 47 [b]Num. 5:31
14 [1]Or, *would observe* [a]Ex. 12:48 [b]Ex. 12:49; Lev. 24:22; Num. 15:15, 16, 29
15 [a]Ex. 40:2, 17 [b]Ex. 40:34 [c]Num. 17:7 [d]Ex. 13:21, 22
16 [a]Ex. 40:34; Neh. 9:12
17 [a]Ex. 40:36-38; Num. 10:11, 12
18 [1]Lit., *mouth* [a]1 Cor. 10:1
19 [1]Lit., *and the*
20 [1]Lit., *it was that* [2]Lit., *mouth* [a]Ps. 48:14; Prov. 3:5, 6
21 [1]Lit., *it was that* [2]Lit., *was*
22 [a]Ex. 40:36, 37
23 [1]Lit., *mouth* [a]Ps. 73:24; 107:7; Is. 63:14

The Silver Trumpets

10 THE LORD spoke further to Moses, saying,
2 "Make yourself two trumpets of
silver, of hammered work you shall make
them; and you shall use them for [a]sum-
moning the congregation and for having
the camps set out.
3 "And [a]when both are blown, all the
congregation shall gather themselves to
you at the doorway of the tent of meeting.
4 "Yet if *only* one is blown, then the
[a]leaders, the heads of the [1]divisions of
Israel, shall assemble before you.
5 "But when you blow an alarm, the
camps that are pitched [a]on the east side
shall set out.
6 "And when you blow an alarm the
second time, the camps that are pitched
on [a]the south side shall set out; an alarm
is to be blown for them to set out.
7 "When convening the assembly,
however, you shall blow without [a]sound-
ing an alarm.
8 "[a]The priestly sons of Aaron, moreover, shall blow the trumpets; and [1]this
shall be for you a perpetual statute
throughout your generations.
9 "And when you go to war in your
land against the adversary who [a]attacks
you, then you shall sound an alarm with
the trumpets, that you may be [b]remem-
bered before the LORD your God, and be
saved from your enemies.
10 "Also in the day of your gladness
and in your appointed [1]feasts, and on
the first *days* of your months, [a]you shall
blow the trumpets over your burnt offerings, and over the sacrifices of your
peace offerings; and they shall be as a
reminder of you before your God. I am
the LORD your God."

The Tribes Leave Sinai

11 Now it came about in [a]the second
year, in the second month, on the twentieth of the month, that the cloud was
lifted from over the [1]tabernacle of the
testimony;
12 and the sons of Israel set out on
[a]their journeys from the wilderness of
Sinai. Then the cloud settled down in the
[b]wilderness of Paran.
13 [a]So they moved out for the first
time according to the [1]commandment of
the LORD through Moses.
14 And the standard of the camp of
the sons of Judah, according to their
armies, [a]set out first, with Nahshon the
son of Amminadab, over its army,
15 and Nethanel the son of Zuar, over
the tribal army of the sons of Issachar;
16 and Eliab the son of Helon over the
tribal army of the sons of Zebulun.
17 [a]Then the tabernacle was taken
down; and the sons of Gershon and the
sons of Merari, who were carrying the
tabernacle, set out.
18 Next [a]the standard of the camp of
Reuben, according to their armies, set
out with Elizur the son of Shedeur, over
its army,
19 and Shelumiel the son of Zurishaddai over the tribal army of the sons of
Simeon,
20 and Eliasaph the son of Deuel was
over the tribal army of the sons of Gad.
21 [a]Then the Kohathites set out, carrying the holy *objects;* and [b]the tabernacle was set up before their arrival.
22 [a]Next the standard of the camp of
the sons of Ephraim, according to their
armies, was set out, with Elishama the
son of Ammihud over its army,
23 and Gamaliel the son of Pedahzur
over the tribal army of the sons of
Manasseh;
24 and Abidan the son of Gideoni
over the tribal army of the sons of
Benjamin.
25 [a]Then the standard of the camp of
the sons of Dan, according to their
armies, *which formed* the [b]rear guard for
all the camps, set out, with Ahiezer the
son of Ammishaddai over its army,
26 and Pagiel the son of Ochran over
the tribal army of the sons of Asher;
27 and Ahira the son of Enan over the
tribal army of the sons of Naphtali.
28 [1]This was the order of march of the
sons of Israel by their armies as they set
out.
29 Then Moses said to [a]Hobab the
son of [b]Reuel the Midianite, Moses'
father-in-law, "We are setting out to the
place of which the LORD said, '[c]I will
give it to you'; [d]come with us and we
will do you good, for the LORD [e]has
[1]promised good concerning Israel."
30 But he said to him, "[a]I will not
come, but rather will go to my *own* land
and relatives."
31 Then he said, "Please do not leave
us, inasmuch as you know where we
should camp in the wilderness, and you
[a]will be as eyes for us.
32 "So it will be, if you go with us, it
will come about that [1a]whatever good
the LORD [2]does for us, [b]we will [3]do for
you."
33 [a]Thus they set out from the mount
of the LORD three days' journey, with
[b]the ark of the covenant of the LORD
journeying in front of them for the
[1]three days, to seek out [c]a resting place
for them.
34 [a]And the cloud of the LORD was
over them by day, when they set out
from the camp.
35 Then it came about when the ark
set out that Moses said,
"[a]Rise up, O LORD!
And let Thine enemies be scattered,
And let those [b]who hate Thee flee
[1]before Thee."
36 And when it came to rest, he said,
"[a]Return Thou, O LORD,
To the myriad [b]thousands of Israel."

2 [a]Is. 1:13
3 [a]Jer. 4:5; Joel 2:15
4 [1]Lit., *thousands;* or, *clans* [a]Ex. 18:21; Num. 1:16; 7:2
5 [a]Num. 10:14
6 [a]Num. 10:18
7 [a]Joel 2:1
8 [1]Lit., *it* [a]Num. 31:6; Josh. 6:4; 2 Chr. 13:12
9 [a]Judg. 2:18; 1 Sam. 10:18; Ps. 106:42 [b]Gen. 8:1; Ps. 106:4
10 [1]Or, *times* [a]Ps. 81:3-5
11 [1]Lit., *dwelling place,* and so throughout the ch. [a]Ex. 40:17
12 [a]Ex. 40:36 [b]Gen. 21:21; Num. 12:16
13 [1]Lit., *mouth* [a]Deut. 1:6
14 [a]Num. 2:3-9
17 [a]Num. 4:21-32
18 [a]Num. 2:10-16
21 [a]Num. 4:4-20 [b]Num. 10:17
22 [a]Num. 2:18-24
25 [a]Num. 2:25-31 [b]Josh. 6:9, 13
28 [1]Lit., *These are the settings out of the sons*
29 [1]Lit., *spoken* [a]Judg. 4:11 [b]Ex. 2:18; 3:1; 18:12 [c]Gen. 12:7; Ex. 6:4-8 [d]Ps. 95:1-7; 100:1-5 [e]Deut. 4:40; 30:5
30 [a]Judg. 1:16; Matt. 21:28, 29
31 [a]Job 29:15
32 [1]Lit., *that good which* [2]Lit., *does good* [3]Lit., *do good* [a]Ps. 22:27-31; 67:5-7 [b]Lev. 19:34; Deut. 10:18
33 [1]Lit., *three days' journey* [a]Num. 10:12 [b]Deut. 1:33 [c]Is. 11:10
34 [a]Num. 9:15-23
35 [1]Or, *from Thy presence* [a]Ps. 68:1, 2; Is. 17:12-14 [b]Deut. 7:10; 32:41
36 [a]Is. 63:17 [b]Deut. 1:10

The People Complain

11 NOW the people became like [a]those who complain of adversity [b]in the hearing of the LORD; and when the LORD heard *it,* His anger was kindled, and the fire of the LORD burned among them and consumed *some* of the outskirts of the camp.

2 [a]The people therefore cried out to Moses, and Moses prayed to the LORD, and the fire [1]died out.

3 So the name of that place was called [1a]Taberah, because the fire of the LORD burned among them.

4 And the [a]rabble who were among them [1]had greedy desires; and also the sons of Israel wept again and said, "[b]Who will give us [2]meat to eat?

5 "[a]We remember the fish which we used to eat free in Egypt, the cucumbers and the melons and the leeks and the onions and the garlic,

6 but now [a]our [1]appetite is gone. There is nothing at all [2]to look at except this manna."

7 [a]Now the manna was like coriander seed, and its appearance like that of [b]bdellium.

8 The people would go about and gather *it* and grind *it* [1]between two millstones or beat *it* in the mortar, and boil *it* in the pot and make cakes with it; and its taste was as the taste of [2]cakes baked with oil.

9 [a]And when the dew fell on the camp at night, the manna would fall [1]with it.

The Complaint of Moses

10 Now Moses heard the people weeping throughout their families, each man at the doorway of his tent; and the anger of the LORD was kindled greatly, and [1]Moses was displeased.

11 [a]So Moses said to the LORD, "Why hast Thou [1]been so hard on Thy servant? And why have I not found favor in Thy sight, that Thou hast laid the burden of all this people on me?

12 "Was it I who conceived all this people? Was it I who brought them forth, that Thou shouldest say to me, 'Carry them in your bosom as a [1a]nurse carries a nursing infant, to the land which [b]Thou didst swear to their fathers'?

13 "Where am I to get meat to give to [a]all this people? For they weep before me, saying, 'Give us meat that we may eat!'

14 "[a]I alone am not able to carry all this people, because it is too [1]burdensome for me.

15 "[a]So if Thou art going to deal thus with me, please kill me at once, if I have found favor in Thy sight, and do not let me see my wretchedness."

Seventy Elders to Assist

16 The LORD therefore said to Moses, "Gather for Me [a]seventy men from the elders of Israel, [b]whom you know to be the elders of the people and their officers and bring them to the tent of meeting, and let them take their stand there with you.

17 "[a]Then I will come down and speak with you there, and I will take of [b]the Spirit who is upon you, and will put *Him* upon them; and they shall bear the burden of the people with you, so that you shall not bear *it* all alone.

18 "And say to the people, '[a]Consecrate yourselves for tomorrow, and you shall eat meat; for you have wept [b]in the ears of the LORD, saying, "Oh that someone would give us meat to eat! For we were well-off in Egypt." Therefore the LORD will give you meat and you shall eat.

19 'You shall eat, not one day, nor two days, nor five days, nor ten days, nor twenty days,

20 [1]but a whole month, until it comes out of your nostrils and becomes loathsome to you; because [a]you have rejected the LORD who is among you and have wept before Him, saying, "Why did we ever leave Egypt?" ' "

21 But Moses said, "The people, among whom I am, are 600,000 on foot; yet Thou hast said, 'I will give them meat in order that they may eat for a whole month.'

22 "Should flocks and herds be slaughtered for them, to be sufficient for them? Or should all the fish of the sea be gathered together for them, to be sufficient for them?"

23 And the LORD said to Moses, "Is [a]the LORD's [1]power limited? Now you shall see whether [b]My word will [2]come true for you or not."

24 So Moses went out and [a]told the people the words of the LORD. Also, he gathered seventy men of the elders of the people, and stationed them around the tent.

25 [a]Then the LORD came down in the cloud and spoke to him; and He took of the Spirit who was upon him and placed *Him* upon the seventy elders. And it came about that when the Spirit rested upon them, they prophesied. But they did not do *it* again.

26 But two men had remained in the camp; the name of one was Eldad and the name of the [1]other Medad. And [a]the Spirit rested upon them (now they were among those who had been registered, but had not gone out to the tent), and they prophesied in the camp.

27 So a young man ran and told Moses and said, "Eldad and Medad are prophesying in the camp."

28 Then [a]Joshua the son of Nun, the attendant of Moses from his youth, answered and said, "[b]Moses, my lord, restrain them."

29 But Moses said to him, "Are you jealous for my sake? [a]Would that all the LORD's people were prophets, that the LORD would put His Spirit upon them!"

30 Then Moses [1]returned to the camp, *both* he and the elders of Israel.

1 [a]Num. 14:2; 16:11; 17:5 [b]Num. 11:18; 14:28

2 [1]Lit., *sank down* [a]Num. 12:11, 13; 21:7

3 [1]I.e., burning [a]Deut. 9:22

4 [1]Lit., *desired a desire* [2]Lit., *flesh,* and so throughout the ch. [a]Ex. 12:38; 1 Cor. 10:6 [b]Ps. 78:20

5 [a]Ex. 16:3

6 [1]Lit., *soul is dried up* [2]Lit., *for our eyes* [a]Num. 21:5

7 [a]Ex. 16:31 [b]Gen. 2:12

8 [1]Lit., *with* [2]Lit., *juice of oil*

9 [1]Lit., *on* [a]Ex. 16:13, 14

10 [1]Lit., it was *evil in Moses' sight*

11 [1]Lit., *dealt ill with* [a]Ex. 5:22; Deut. 1:12

12 [1]Or, *foster-father* [a]2 Kin. 10:1, 5; Is. 49:23 [b]Gen. 24:7; Ex. 13:5, 11; 33:1

13 [a]Num. 11:21, 22; John 6:5-9

14 [1]Lit., *heavy* [a]Ex. 18:18; Deut. 1:12

15 [a]Ex. 32:32

16 [a]Ex. 24:1, 9 [b]Ex. 18:25

17 [a]Num. 11:25 [b]1 Sam. 10:6; Joel 2:28

18 [a]Ex. 19:10, 22 [b]Num. 11:1

20 [1]Lit., *until* [a]Josh. 24:27; 1 Sam. 10:19

23 [1]Lit., *hand short* [2]Lit., *befall you* [a]Is. 50:2; 59:1 [b]Ezek. 12:25; 24:14

24 [a]Num. 11:16

25 [a]Num. 11:17; 12:5

26 [1]Lit., *second* [a]Num. 24:2; 1 Sam. 10:6; 2 Chr. 15:1; Neh. 9:30

28 [a]Ex. 33:11; Josh. 1:1 [b]Mark 9:38-40

29 [a]1 Cor. 14:5

30 [1]Lit., *removed himself*

The Quail and the Plague

31 [a]Now there went forth a wind from
the LORD, and it brought quail from the
sea, and let *them* fall beside the camp,
about a day's journey on this side and a
day's journey on the other side, all
around the camp, and [1]about two [2]cu-
bits *deep* on the surface of the ground.
32 And the people [1]spent all day and
all night and all the next day, and
gathered the quail (he who gathered least
gathered ten [2a]homers) and they spread
them out for themselves all around the
camp.
33 [a]While the meat was still between
their teeth, before it was chewed, the
anger of the LORD was kindled against
the people, and the LORD struck the
people with a very severe plague.
34 So the name of that place was
called [1a]Kibroth-hattaavah, because
there they buried the people who had
been greedy.
35 From Kibroth-hattaavah [a]the people set out for Hazeroth, and they [1]re-
mained at Hazeroth.

The Murmuring of Miriam and Aaron

12 THEN Miriam and Aaron spoke
against Moses because of the
Cushite woman whom he had married
(for he had married a [a]Cushite woman);
2 [a]and they said, "Has the LORD
indeed spoken only through Moses? Has
He not spoken through us as well?" And
the LORD heard it.
3 (Now the man Moses was [a]very
humble, more than any man who was on
the face of the earth.)
4 And suddenly the LORD said to
Moses and Aaron and to Miriam, "You
three come out to the tent of meeting."
So the three of them came out.
5 [a]Then the LORD came down in a
pillar of cloud and stood at the doorway
of the tent, and He called [1]Aaron and
Miriam. When they had both come
forward,
6 He said,
"Hear now My words:
If there is a prophet among you,
I, the LORD, shall make Myself
known to him in a [a]vision.
I shall speak with him in a
[b]dream.
7 "Not so, with [a]My servant Moses,
[b]He is faithful in all My household;
8 [a]With him I speak mouth to
mouth,
Even openly, and not in dark
sayings,
And he beholds [b]the form of the
LORD.
Why then were you not afraid
To speak against My servant,
against Moses?"
9 So the anger of the LORD burned
against them and [a]He departed.
10 But when the cloud had withdrawn
from over the tent, behold, [a]Miriam *was*
leprous, as [b]*white as* snow. As Aaron
turned toward Miriam, behold, she *was*
leprous.
11 Then Aaron said to Moses, "Oh,
my lord, I beg you, [a]do not account *this*
sin to us, in which we have acted foolishly and in which we have sinned.
12 "Oh, do not let her be like one dead,
whose flesh is half eaten away when he
comes from his mother's womb!"
13 And Moses cried out to the LORD,
saying, "O God, [a]heal her, I pray!"
14 But the LORD said to Moses, "If
her father had but [a]spit in her face,
would she not bear her shame for seven
days? Let her be shut up for seven days
[b]outside the camp, and afterward she
may be received again."
15 So [a]Miriam was shut up outside the
camp for seven days, and the people did
not move on until Miriam was received
again.
16 Afterward, however, the people
moved out from Hazeroth and camped
in the wilderness of Paran.

Spies View the Land

13 THEN [a]the LORD spoke to Moses saying,
2 "[a]Send out for yourself men so that
they may spy out the land of Canaan,
which I am going to give to the sons of
Israel; you shall send a man from each
of their fathers' tribes, every one a leader
among them."
3 So Moses sent them from the wilderness of Paran at the [1]command of the
LORD, all of them men who were heads
of the sons of Israel.
4 These then *were* their names: from
the tribe of Reuben, Shammua the son
of Zaccur;
5 from the tribe of Simeon, Shaphat
the son of Hori;
6 from the tribe of Judah, [a]Caleb the
son of Jephunneh;
7 from the tribe of Issachar, Igal the
son of Joseph;
8 from the tribe of Ephraim, [a]Hoshea
the son of Nun;
9 from the tribe of Benjamin, Palti
the son of Raphu;
10 from the tribe of Zebulun, Gaddiel
the son of Sodi;
11 from the tribe of Joseph, from the
tribe of Manasseh, Gaddi the son of
Susi;
12 from the tribe of Dan, Ammiel the
son of Gemalli;
13 from the tribe of Asher, Sethur the
son of Michael;
14 from the tribe of Naphtali, Nahbi
the son of Vophsi;
15 from the tribe of Gad, Geuel the
son of Machi.
16 These are the names of the men
whom Moses sent to spy out the land;
but Moses called [a]Hoshea the son of
Nun, Joshua.
17 When Moses sent them to spy out
the land of Canaan, he said to them,
"Go up [1]there into [a]the [2]Negev; then go
up into the hill country.

31 [1]Or, from *about two cubits above* [2]I.e., One cubit equals approx. 18 in. [a]Ex. 16:13; Ps. 78:26-28; 105:40
32 [1]Lit., *rose* [2]I.e., One homer equals approx. 11 bu. [a]Ezek. 45:11
33 [a]Ps. 78:29-31; 106:15
34 [1]I.e., the graves of greediness [a]Deut. 9:22
35 [1]Lit., *were* [a]Num. 33:17
1 [a]Ex. 2:21
2 [a]Num. 16:3
3 [a]Matt. 11:29
5 [1]Or, *"Aaron and Miriam!"* [a]Ex. 19:9; 34:5
6 [a]Gen. 46:2; 1 Sam. 3:15 [b]Gen. 31:11; 1 Kin. 3:5, 15
7 [a]Josh. 1:1 [b]Heb. 3:2, 5
8 [a]Deut. 34:10; Hos. 12:13 [b]Ex. 20:4; 24:10, 11; Deut. 5:8; Ps. 17:15
9 [a]Gen. 17:22; 18:33
10 [a]Deut. 24:9 [b]Ex. 4:6; 2 Kin. 5:27
11 [a]2 Sam. 19:19; 24:10
13 [a]Ps. 30:2; 41:4; Is. 30:26; Jer. 17:14
14 [a]Deut. 25:9; Job 17:6; 30:10; Is. 50:6 [b]Num. 5:1-4
15 [a]Deut. 24:9
1 [a]Deut. 1:22, 23
2 [a]Deut. 1:22; 9:23
3 [1]Lit., *mouth*
6 [a]Num. 14:6, 30; Josh. 14:6
8 [a]Num. 13:16; Deut. 32:44
16 [a]Num. 13:8; Deut. 32:44
17 [1]Lit., *here* [2]I.e., South country, and so throughout the ch. [a]Gen. 12:9; 13:1, 3

18 "And see what the land is like, and whether the people who live in it are strong *or* weak, whether they are few or many.

19 "And how is the land in which they live, is it good or bad? And how are the cities in which they live, are *they* [1]like *open* camps or with fortifications?

20 "And [a]how is the land, is it fat or lean? Are there trees in it or not? [1]Make an [b]effort then to get some of the fruit of the land." Now the time was the time of the first ripe grapes.

21 So they went up and spied out the land from [a]the wilderness of Zin as far as Rehob, [1b]at Lebo-hamath.

22 When they had gone up into [a]the Negev, [1]they came to Hebron where [b]Ahiman, Sheshai and Talmai, the [2]descendants of [c]Anak were. (Now Hebron was built seven years before [d]Zoan in Egypt.)

23 Then they came to the [1]valley of [2a]Eshcol and from there cut down a branch with a single cluster of grapes; and they carried it on a pole between two *men,* with some of the pomegranates and the figs.

24 That place was called the valley of [1]Eshcol, because of the cluster which the sons of Israel cut down from there.

The Spies' Reports

25 When they returned from spying out the land, at the end of forty days,

26 they proceeded to come to Moses and Aaron and to all the congregation of the sons of Israel [1]in the wilderness of Paran, at [a]Kadesh; and they brought back word to them and to all the congregation and showed them the fruit of the land.

27 Thus they told him, and said, "We went in to the land where you sent us; and [a]it certainly does flow with milk and honey, and [b]this is its fruit.

28 "Nevertheless, [a]the people who live in the land are strong, and the cities are fortified *and* very large; and moreover, we saw [b]the [1]descendants of Anak there.

29 "Amalek is living in the land of [a]the Negev and the Hittites and the Jebusites and [b]the Amorites are living in the hill country, and [c]the Canaanites are living by the sea and by the side of the Jordan."

30 Then Caleb quieted the people [1]before Moses, and said, "We should by all means go up and take possession of it, for we shall surely overcome it."

31 But the men who had gone up with him said, "[a]We are not able to go up against the people, for they are too strong for us."

32 So they gave out to the sons of Israel [a]a bad report of the land which they had spied out, saying, "The land through which we have gone, in spying it out, is [b]a land that devours its [1]inhabitants; and [c]all the people whom we saw in it are men of *great* size.

19 [1]Lit., *in*

20 [1]Lit., *Use your strength* [a]Deut. 1:24, 25 [b]Deut. 31:6, 23

21 [1]Or, *to the entrance of Hamath* [a]Num. 20:1; 27:14; 33:36 [b]Josh. 13:5

22 [1]Lit., Most mss. read *one came* [2]Lit., *children* [a]Num. 13:17 [b]Josh. 15:14 [c]Num. 13:28, 33 [d]Ps. 78:12, 43

23 [1]Or, *wadi* [2]I.e., cluster [a]Gen. 14:13; Num. 13:24; 32:9; Deut. 1:24

24 [1]I.e., cluster

26 [1]Lit., *to* [a]Num. 20:1, 14; 32:8

27 [a]Ex. 3:8, 17; 13:5 [b]Deut. 1:25

28 [1]Lit., *born ones* [a]Deut. 1:28; 9:1, 2 [b]Num. 13:33

29 [a]Num. 13:17; 14:25, 45 [b]Josh. 10:6 [c]Num. 14:43, 45

30 [1]Lit., *toward*

31 [a]Deut. 1:28; 9:1-3

32 [1]Or, *settlers* [a]Num. 14:36, 37; Ps. 106:24 [b]Ezek. 36:13, 14 [c]Amos 2:9

33 [a]Gen. 6:4 [b]Deut. 1:28; 9:2; Josh. 11:21

1 [1]Lit., *lifted and gave their voice* [2]Lit., *in that*

2 [a]Num. 11:1 [b]Num. 11:5; 16:13; 20:3, 4; 21:5

3 [a]Ex. 5:21; 16:3 [b]Num. 14:31; Deut. 1:39

4 [a]Neh. 9:17

5 [a]Num. 16:4

7 [a]Num. 13:27; Deut. 1:25

8 [a]Deut. 10:15 [b]Ex. 3:8; Num. 13:27

9 [1]Lit., *food* [2]Lit., *shadow* [a]Deut. 1:26; 9:23, 24 [b]Deut. 1:21, 29

10 [a]Ex. 17:4 [b]Ex. 16:10; Lev. 9:23

11 [a]Ex. 32:9-13 [b]Ps. 106:24

12 [1]Lit., *the pestilence* [a]Lev. 26:25; Deut. 28:21 [b]Ex. 32:10

13 [a]Ex. 32:11-14; Ps. 106:23

14 [a]Ex. 13:21; Deut. 5:4

33 "There also we saw the [a]Nephilim (the sons of Anak are part of the Nephilim); and [b]we became like grasshoppers in our own sight, and so we were in their sight."

The People Rebel

14 THEN all the congregation [1]lifted up their voices and cried, and the people wept [2]that night.

2 And all the sons of Israel [a]grumbled against Moses and Aaron; and the whole congregation said to them, "[b]Would that we had died in the land of Egypt! Or would that we had died in this wilderness!

3 "And why is the LORD bringing us into this land, [a]to fall by the sword? [b]Our wives and our little ones will become plunder; would it not be better for us to return to Egypt?"

4 So they said to one another, "[a]Let us appoint a leader and return to Egypt."

5 [a]Then Moses and Aaron fell on their faces in the presence of all the assembly of the congregation of the sons of Israel.

6 And Joshua the son of Nun and Caleb the son of Jephunneh, of those who had spied out the land, tore their clothes;

7 and they spoke to all the congregation of the sons of Israel, saying, "[a]The land which we passed through to spy out is an exceedingly good land.

8 "[a]If the LORD is pleased with us, then He will bring us into this land, and give it to us—[b]a land which flows with milk and honey.

9 "Only [a]do not rebel against the LORD; and do not [b]fear the people of the land, for they shall be our [1]prey. Their [2]protection has been removed from them, and the LORD is with us; do not fear them."

10 [a]But all the congregation said to stone them with stones. Then [b]the glory of the LORD appeared in the tent of meeting to all the sons of Israel.

Moses Pleads for the People

11 [a]And the LORD said to Moses, "How long will this people spurn Me? And how long will [b]they not believe in Me, despite all the signs which I have performed in their midst?

12 "I will smite them with [1a]pestilence and dispossess them, and I [b]will make you into a nation greater and mightier than they."

13 [a]But Moses said to the LORD, "Then the Egyptians will hear of it, for by Thy strength Thou didst bring up this people from their midst,

14 and they will tell *it* to the inhabitants of this land. They have heard that Thou, O LORD, art in the midst of this people, for [a]Thou, O LORD, art seen eye to eye, while Thy cloud stands over them; and Thou dost go before them in a pillar of cloud by day and in a pillar of fire by night.

15“Now if Thou dost slay this people
as one man, [a]then the nations who have
heard of Thy fame will [1]say,
16 ‘Because the LORD [a]could not bring
this people into the land which He
promised them by oath, therefore He
slaughtered them in the wilderness.’
17“But now, I pray, let the power of
the Lord be great, just as Thou hast
[1]declared,
18 ‘[a]The LORD is slow to anger and
abundant in lovingkindness, forgiving
iniquity and transgression; but [b]He will
by no means clear *the guilty,* [c]visiting the
iniquity of the fathers on the children [1]to
the third and the fourth *generations.*’
19“[a]Pardon, I pray, the iniquity of this
people according to the greatness of Thy
lovingkindness, just as Thou also hast
forgiven this people, from Egypt even
until now.”

The LORD Pardons and Rebukes

20 So the LORD said, “[a]I have pardoned *them* according to your word;
21 but indeed, [a]as I live, [1b]all the earth
will be filled with the glory of the LORD.
22“Surely [a]all the men who have seen
My glory and My signs, which I performed in Egypt and in the wilderness,
yet [b]have put Me to the test these ten
times and have not listened to My voice,
23 [a]shall by no means see the land
which I swore to their fathers, nor shall
any of those who spurned Me see it.
24“But My servant Caleb, [a]because he
has had a different spirit and has followed Me fully, [1b]I will bring into the
land [2]which he entered, and his [3]de-
scendants shall take possession of it.
25“[a]Now the Amalekites and the Canaanites live in the valleys; turn tomorrow and set out to the wilderness by the
way of the [1]Red Sea.”
26 And the LORD spoke to Moses and
Aaron, saying,
27“How long *shall I bear* with this evil
congregation who are [a]grumbling
against Me? I have heard the complaints
of the sons of Israel, which they are
[1]making against Me.
28“Say to them, ‘[a]As I live,’ says the
LORD, ‘just as [b]you have spoken in My
hearing, so I will surely do to you;
29 [a]your corpses shall fall in this
wilderness, even all [b]your [1]numbered
men, according to your complete number from twenty years old and upward,
who have grumbled against Me.
30 ‘Surely you shall not come into the
land in which I [1]swore to settle you,
[a]except Caleb the son of Jephunneh and
Joshua the son of Nun.
31 ‘[a]Your children, however, whom
you said would become a prey—I will
bring them in, and they shall know the
land which you have rejected.
32 ‘[a]But as for you, your corpses shall
fall in this wilderness.
33 ‘And your sons shall be shepherds
for [a]forty years in the wilderness, and
they shall [1]suffer *for* your [2]unfaithful-
ness, until your corpses [3]lie in the wilderness.
34 ‘According to the [a]number of days
which you spied out the land, forty days,
for every day you shall bear your [1]guilt a
year, *even* forty years, and you shall
know My opposition.
35 ‘[a]I, the LORD, have spoken, surely
this I will do to all this evil congregation
who are gathered together against Me.
In this wilderness they shall be destroyed, and there they shall die.’ ”
36 [a]As for the men whom Moses sent
to spy out the land and who returned
and made all the congregation grumble
against him by bringing out a bad report
concerning the land,
37 even [a]those men who brought out
the very bad report of the land died by a
[b]plague before the LORD.
38 But Joshua the son of Nun and
Caleb the son of Jephunneh remained
alive out of those men who went to spy
out the land.

Israel Repulsed

39 And when Moses spoke [a]these
words to all the sons of Israel, [b]the
people mourned greatly.
40 In the morning, however, they rose
up early and went up to the [1]ridge of the
hill country, saying, “[a]Here we are; [2]we
have indeed sinned, but we will go up to
the place which the LORD has promised.”
41 But Moses said, “[a]Why then are
you transgressing the [1]commandment of
the LORD, when it will not succeed?
42“[a]Do not go up, lest you be struck
down before your enemies, for the LORD
is not among you.
43“For the Amalekites and the Canaanites will be there in front of you,
and you will fall by the sword, inasmuch
as you have turned back from following
the LORD. And the LORD will not be
with you.”
44 But they went up heedlessly to the
[1]ridge of the hill country; neither [a]the
ark of the covenant of the LORD nor
Moses left the camp.
45 Then the Amalekites and the Canaanites who lived in that hill country
came down, and struck them and beat
them down as far as [a]Hormah.

Laws for Canaan

15 NOW the LORD spoke to Moses,
saying,
2“[a]Speak to the sons of Israel, and
say to them, ‘When you enter the land
[1]where you are to live, which I am giving
you,
3 then make [a]an offering by fire to
the LORD, a burnt offering or a sacrifice
to [1b]fulfill a special vow, or as a freewill
offering or in your [c]appointed times, to
make a [d]soothing aroma to the LORD,
from the herd or from the flock.

15 [1]Lit., *speak, saying* [a]Ex. 32:12
16 [a]Josh. 7:7
17 [1]Lit., *spoken, saying*
18 [1]Lit., *on* [a]Ex. 20:6; 34:6, 7; Deut. 5:10; 7:9; Ps. 103:8; 145:8; Jon. 4:2 [b]Ex. 20:5; Deut. 5:9; 7:10 [c]Ex. 34:7
19 [a]Ex. 32:32; 34:9
20 [a]Mic. 7:18-20
21 [1]Lit., *and all* [a]Num. 14:28; Deut. 32:40; Is. 49:18 [b]Is. 6:3; Hab. 2:14
22 [a]1 Cor. 10:5 [b]Ex. 5:21; 14:11; 15:24; 16:2; 17:2, 3; 32:1; Num. 11:1, 4; 12:1; 14:2
23 [a]Num. 26:65; 32:11; Heb. 3:18
24 [1]Lit., *him I* [2]Lit., *where* [3]Lit., *seed* [a]Num. 14:6-9 [b]Num. 26:65; 32:12; Deut. 1:36; Josh. 14:6-15
25 [1]Lit., *Sea of Reeds* [a]Num. 13:29
27 [1]Lit., *complaining* [a]Num. 11:1
28 [a]Num. 14:21 [b]Num. 14:2; Deut. 2:14, 15; Heb. 3:17
29 [1]Lit., *mustered* [a]Heb. 3:17 [b]Num. 1:45, 46
30 [1]Lit., *raised My hand* [a]Num. 14:24
31 [a]Num. 14:3
32 [a]Num. 26:64, 65; 32:13; 1 Cor. 10:5
33 [1]Lit., *bear* [2]Lit., *fornications* [3]Lit., *are finished* [a]Deut. 2:7; 8:2, 4; 29:5
34 [1]Or, *iniquities* [a]Num. 13:25
35 [a]Num. 23:19
36 [a]Num. 13:4-16, 32
37 [a]1 Cor. 10:10; Heb. 3:17, 18 [b]Num. 16:49
39 [a]Num. 14:28-35 [b]Ex. 33:4
40 [1]Or, *top of the mountain* [2]Or, *and we will go up . . . for we have sinned* [a]Deut. 1:41-44
41 [1]Lit., *mouth* [a]2 Chr. 24:20
42 [a]Deut. 1:42
44 [1]Or, *top of the mountain* [a]Num. 31:6
45 [a]Num. 21:3

2 [1]Lit., *of your dwellings* [a]Lev. 23:10
3 [1]Or, *make a special votive offering* [a]Lev. 1:2, 3 [b]Lev. 22:21 [c]Lev. 23:1-44 [d]Gen. 8:21; 2 Cor. 2:15, 16; Phil. 4:18

4 '[a]And the one who presents his
offering shall present to the LORD a
grain offering of one-tenth *of an ephah* of
fine flour mixed with one-fourth of a
[1]hin of oil,
5 and you shall prepare wine for the
libation, one-fourth of a hin, with the
burnt offering or for the sacrifice, for
[a]each lamb.
6 'Or for a ram you shall prepare as a
grain offering two-tenths *of an ephah* of
fine flour mixed with one-third of a hin
of oil;
7 and for the libation you shall offer
one-third of a hin of wine as a soothing
aroma to the LORD.
8 'And when you prepare [a]a bull as a
burnt offering or a sacrifice, to [1]fulfill a
special vow, or for peace offerings to the
LORD,
9 then you shall offer with the bull a
grain offering of three-tenths *of an ephah*
of fine flour mixed with one-half a hin of
oil;
10 and you shall offer as the libation
one-half a hin of wine as an offering by
fire, as a soothing aroma to the LORD.
11 'Thus it shall be done for each ox,
or for each ram, or for each of the male
lambs, or of the goats.
12 'According to the number that you
prepare, so you shall do for everyone
according to their number.
13 'All who are native shall do these
things in this manner, in presenting an
offering by fire, as a soothing aroma to
the LORD.

Law of the Sojourner

14 'And if an alien sojourns with you,
or one who may be among you throughout your generations, and he *wishes to*
make an offering by fire, as a soothing
aroma to the LORD, just as you do, so he
shall do.
15 '*As for* the assembly, there shall be
[a]one statute for you and for the alien
who sojourns *with you,* a perpetual statute throughout your generations; as you
are, so shall the alien be before the
LORD.
16 'There is to be [a]one law and one
ordinance for you and for the alien who
sojourns with you.' "
17 Then the LORD spoke to Moses,
saying,
18 "Speak to the sons of Israel, and say
to them, 'When you enter the land where
I bring you,
19 then it shall be, that when you eat
of the [1a]food of the land, you shall lift up
[2]an offering to the LORD.
20 '[a]Of the first of your [1]dough you
shall lift up a cake as an [2]offering; as
[b]the [2]offering of the threshing floor, so
you shall lift it up.
21 'From the first of your [1]dough you
shall give to the LORD an [2]offering
throughout your generations.
22 'But when you [a]unwittingly fail and
do not observe all these commandments,
which the LORD has spoken to Moses,
23 *even* all that the LORD has commanded you [1]through Moses, from the
day when the LORD gave commandment
and onward throughout your generations,
24 then it shall be, if it is done [a]unin-
tentionally, [1]without the knowledge of
the congregation, that all the congregation shall offer one bull for a burnt
offering, as a soothing aroma to the
LORD, [b]with its grain offering, and its
libation, according to the ordinance, and
one male goat for a sin offering.
25 'Then [a]the priest shall make atonement for all the congregation of the sons
of Israel, and they shall be forgiven; for
it was an error, and they have brought
their offering, an offering by fire to the
LORD, and their sin offering before the
LORD, for their error.
26 'So all the congregation of the sons
of Israel will be forgiven, with the alien
who sojourns among them, for *it happened* to all the people through [a]error.
27 'Also if one person sins [a]uninten-
tionally, then he shall offer a one year
old female goat for a sin offering.
28 'And [a]the priest shall make atonement before the LORD for the person
who goes astray when he sins unintentionally, making atonement for him
[1]that he may be forgiven.
29 'You shall have one law for him
who does *anything* unintentionally, for
him who is native among the sons of
Israel and for the alien who sojourns
among them.
30 'But the person who does *anything*
[a]defiantly, whether he is native or an
alien, that one is blaspheming the LORD;
and that person shall be cut off from
among his people.
31 'Because he has [a]despised the word
of the LORD and has broken His commandment, that person shall be completely cut off; [b]his [1]guilt *shall be* on
him.' "

Sabbath-breaking Punished

32 Now while the sons of Israel were
in the wilderness, they found a man
[a]gathering wood on the sabbath day.
33 And those who found him gathering wood brought him to Moses and
Aaron, and to all the congregation;
34 and they put him in [1]custody [a]be-
cause it had not been [2]declared what
should be done to him.
35 Then the LORD said to Moses,
"The man shall surely be put to death;
[a]all the congregation shall stone him
with stones outside the camp."
36 So all the congregation brought
him outside the camp, and stoned him
[1]to death with stones, just as the LORD
had commanded Moses.
37 The LORD also spoke to Moses,
saying,
38 "Speak to the sons of Israel, and tell
them that they shall make for themselves
[a]tassels on the corners of their garments
throughout their generations, and that

4 [1]I.e., Approx. one gal., and so through v. 10 [a]Num. 28:1-29:40
5 [a]Lev. 1:10; 3:6; Num. 15:11
8 [1]Or, *make a special votive offering* [a]Lev. 1:3; 3:1
15 [a]Num. 9:14; 15:29
16 [a]Lev. 24:22
19 [1]Lit., *bread* [2]Or, *a heave offering* [a]Josh. 5:11, 12
20 [1]Or, *coarse meal* [2]Or, *heave offering* [a]Ex. 34:26; Lev. 23:14 [b]Deut. 14:22, 23; 16:13
21 [1]Or, *coarse meal* [2]Or, *offering lifted up*
22 [a]Lev. 4:2
23 [1]Lit., *by the hand of*
24 [1]Lit., *from the eyes of the congregation* [a]Lev. 4:2, 22, 27; 5:15, 18 [b]Num. 15:8-10
25 [a]Lev. 4:20; Heb. 2:17
26 [a]Num. 15:24
27 [a]Lev. 4:27-31; Luke 12:48
28 [1]Or, *and he shall* [a]Lev. 4:35
30 [a]Num. 14:40-44; Deut. 1:43; 17:12, 13
31 [1]Or, *iniquity* [a]2 Sam. 12:9; Prov. 13:13 [b]Ezek. 18:20
32 [a]Ex. 31:14, 15; 35:2, 3
34 [1]Or, *prison* [2]Lit., *declared distinctly* [a]Num. 9:8
35 [a]Lev. 20:2, 27; 24:14-23; Deut. 21:21
36 [1]Lit., *with stones and he died*
38 [a]Deut. 22:12; Matt. 23:5

they shall put on the tassel of each corner a cord of blue.

39 "And it shall be a tassel for you [1]to look at and [a]remember all the commandments of the LORD, so as to do them and not [2]follow after your own heart and your own eyes, after which you played the harlot,

40 in order that you may remember to do all My commandments, and [a]be holy to your God.

41 "I am the LORD your God who brought you out from the land of Egypt to be your God; I am the LORD your God."

Korah's Rebellion

16 NOW [a]Korah the son of Izhar, the son of Kohath, the son of Levi, with [b]Dathan and Abiram, the sons of Eliab, and On the son of Peleth, sons of Reuben, took *action,*

2 and they rose up before Moses, [1]together with some of the sons of Israel, two hundred and fifty leaders of the congregation, [2a]chosen in the assembly, men of renown.

3 And they assembled together [a]against Moses and Aaron, and said to them, "[1b]You have gone far enough, for all the congregation are holy, every one of them, and [c]the LORD is in their midst; so why do you exalt yourselves above the assembly of the LORD?"

4 When Moses heard *this,* [a]he fell on his face;

5 and he spoke to Korah and all his company, saying, "Tomorrow morning the LORD will show who is His, and [a]who is holy, and will bring *him* near to Himself; even [b]the one whom He will choose, He will bring near to Himself.

6 "Do this: take censers for yourselves, Korah and all [1]your company,

7 and put fire in them, and lay incense upon them in the presence of the LORD tomorrow; and the man whom the LORD chooses *shall be* the one who is holy. [1a]You have gone far enough, you sons of Levi!"

8 Then Moses said to Korah, "Hear now, you sons of Levi,

9 [a]is it [1]not enough for you that the God of Israel has separated you from the *rest of* the congregation of Israel, [b]to bring you near to Himself, to do the service of the tabernacle of the LORD, and to stand before the congregation to minister to them;

10 and that He has brought you near, *Korah,* and all your brothers, sons of Levi, with you? And are you [a]seeking for the priesthood also?

11 "Therefore you and all your company are gathered together [a]against the LORD; but as for Aaron, [1]who is he that [b]you grumble against him?"

12 Then Moses sent [1]a summons to Dathan and Abiram, the sons of Eliab; but they said, "We will not come up.

13 "Is it [1]not enough that you have brought us up out of a [a]land flowing with milk and honey [b]to have us die in the wilderness, but you would also lord it over us?

14 "Indeed, you have not brought us [a]into a land flowing with milk and honey, nor have you given us an inheritance of [b]fields and vineyards. Would you [1c]put out the eyes of [2]these men? We will not come up!"

15 Then Moses became very angry and said to the LORD, "[a]Do not regard their offering! [b]I have not taken a single donkey from them, nor have I done harm to any of them."

16 And Moses said to Korah, "You and all your company be present before the LORD tomorrow, both you and they along with Aaron.

17 "And each of you take his firepan and put incense on [1]it, and each of you bring his censer before the LORD, two hundred and fifty firepans; also you and Aaron *shall* each *bring* his firepan."

18 So they each took his *own* censer and put fire on [1]it, and laid incense on [1]it; and they stood at the doorway of the tent of meeting, with Moses and Aaron.

19 Thus Korah assembled all the congregation against them at the doorway of the tent of meeting. And [a]the glory of the LORD appeared to all the congregation.

20 Then the LORD spoke to Moses and Aaron, saying,

21 "[a]Separate yourselves from among this congregation, [b]that I may consume them instantly."

22 But they fell on their faces, and said, "O God, [a]Thou God of the spirits of all flesh, [b]when one man sins, wilt Thou be angry with the entire congregation?"

23 Then the LORD spoke to Moses, saying,

24 "Speak to the congregation, saying, '[a]Get back from around the dwellings of Korah, Dathan and Abiram.' "

25 Then Moses arose and went to Dathan and Abiram, with the elders of Israel following him,

26 and he spoke to the congregation, saying, "[a]Depart now from the tents of these wicked men, and touch nothing that belongs to them, [b]lest you be swept away in all their sin."

27 So they got back from around the dwellings of Korah, Dathan and Abiram; and Dathan and Abiram came out *and* stood at the doorway of their tents, along with their wives and [a]their sons and their little ones.

28 And Moses said, "By this you shall know that [a]the LORD has sent me to do all these deeds; for this is not [1]my doing.

29 "If these men die [1]the death of all men, or [2]if they suffer the [a]fate of all men, *then* the LORD has not sent me.

30 "But [a]if the LORD [1]brings about an entirely new thing and the ground opens its mouth and swallows them up with all that is theirs, and they [b]descend alive into [2]Sheol, then you will understand that these men have spurned the LORD."

39 [1]Lit., *and you shall look at it* [2]Lit., *seek* [a]Deut. 4:23; 6:12; 8:11, 14, 19
40 [a]Lev. 11:44, 45
1 [a]Ex. 6:21; Jude 11 [b]Num. 26:9; Deut. 11:6
2 [1]Lit., *and men from* [2]Lit., *called ones of* [a]Num. 1:16; 26:9
3 [1]Lit., *It is much for you* [a]Num. 12:2; Ps. 106:16 [b]Num. 16:7 [c]Num. 5:3
4 [a]Num. 14:5
5 [a]Lev. 10:3; Ps. 65:4 [b]Num. 17:5, 8
6 [1]Lit., *his*
7 [1]Lit., *It is much for you* [a]Num. 16:3
9 [1]Or, *too little for you* [a]Is. 7:13 [b]Num. 3:6, 9; Deut. 10:8
10 [a]Num. 3:10; 18:1-7
11 [1]Lit., *what* [a]Ex. 16:7 [b]1 Cor. 10:10
12 [1]Lit., *to call*
13 [1]Lit., *a little thing* [a]Ex. 16:3; Num. 11:4-6 [b]Num. 14:2, 3
14 [1]Lit., *bore out* [2]Lit., *those* [a]Num. 13:27; 14:8 [b]Ex. 22:5; 23:10, 11; Num. 20:5 [c]Judg. 16:21; 1 Sam. 11:2
15 [a]Gen. 4:4, 5 [b]1 Sam. 12:3
17 [1]Lit., *them*
18 [1]Lit., *them*
19 [a]Num. 14:10; 16:42; 20:6
21 [a]Num. 16:45 [b]Ex. 32:10, 12
22 [a]Num. 27:16 [b]Gen. 18:23-32; Lev. 4:3
24 [a]Num. 16:45
26 [a]Is. 52:11 [b]Gen. 19:15, 17
27 [a]Num. 26:11
28 [1]Lit., *from my heart* [a]Ex. 3:12-15; 4:12, 15
29 [1]Lit., *like the death* [2]Lit., *the visitation of all men be visited upon them* [a]Eccl. 3:19
30 [1]Lit., *creates a new creation* [2]I.e., the nether world [a]Job 31:2, 3 [b]Ps. 55:15

31 Then it came about as he finished
speaking all these words, that the ground
that was under them split open;
32 and [a]the earth opened its mouth
and swallowed them up, and their households, and [b]all the men who belonged to
Korah, with *their* possessions.
33 So they and all that belonged to
them went down alive to [1]Sheol; and the
earth closed over them, and they perished from the midst of the assembly.
34 And all Israel who *were* around
them fled at their [1]outcry, for they said,
"[2]The earth may swallow us up!"
35 [a]Fire also came forth from the
LORD and consumed the [b]two hundred
and fifty men who were offering the
incense.
36 [1]Then the LORD spoke to Moses,
saying,
37 "Say to Eleazar, the son of Aaron
the priest, that he shall take up the
censers out of the midst of the [1]blaze, for
they are holy; and you scatter the [2]burn-
ing coals abroad.
38 "As for the censers of these [1]men
who have sinned at the cost of their lives,
let them be made into hammered sheets
for a plating of the altar, since they did
present them before the LORD and they
are holy; and [a]they shall be for a sign to
the sons of Israel."
39 So Eleazar the priest took the
bronze censers which the men who were
burned had offered; and they hammered
them out as a plating for the altar,
40 as a [1]reminder to the sons of Israel
that [a]no [2]layman who is not of the
[3]descendants of Aaron should come near
[b]to burn incense before the LORD; that
he might not become like Korah and his
company—just as the LORD had spoken
to him [4]through Moses.

Murmuring and Plague

41 But on the next day all the congregation of the sons of Israel [a]grumbled
against Moses and Aaron, saying, "You
are the ones who have caused the death
of the LORD's people."
42 It came about, however, when the
congregation had assembled against
Moses and Aaron, that they turned
toward the tent of meeting, and behold,
the cloud covered it and [a]the glory of the
LORD appeared.
43 Then Moses and Aaron came to
the front of the tent of meeting,
44 and the LORD spoke to Moses,
saying,
45 "[1a]Get away from among this congregation, that I may consume them
instantly." Then they fell on their faces.
46 And Moses said to Aaron, "Take
your censer and put in it fire from the
altar, and lay incense *on it;* then bring it
quickly to the congregation and [a]make
atonement for them, for [b]wrath has gone
forth from the LORD, the plague has
begun!"
47 Then Aaron took *it* as Moses had
spoken, and ran into the midst of the
assembly, for behold, the plague had

32 [a]Num. 26:10; Deut. 11:6; Ps. 106:17 [b]Num. 26:11

33 [1]I.e., the nether world

34 [1]Or, *voice* [2]Lit., *Lest the earth*

35 [a]Num. 11:1-3; 26:10 [b]Num. 16:2

36 [1]Ch. 17:1 in Heb.

37 [1]Or, *place of burning* [2]Lit., *the fire*

38 [1]Lit., *sinners against their lives* [a]Ezek. 14:8; 2 Pet. 2:6

40 [1]Or, *memorial* [2]Lit., *stranger* [3]Lit., *seed* [4]Lit., *by the hand of* [a]Num. 1:51 [b]Ex. 30:7-10

41 [a]Num. 16:3

42 [a]Num. 16:19

45 [1]Or, *Arise* [a]Num. 16:21, 24

46 [a]Num. 25:13; Is. 6:6, 7 [b]Num. 18:5; Deut. 9:22

47 [a]Num. 25:6-8, 13

49 [a]Num. 25:9 [b]Num. 16:32, 35

1 [1]Ch. 17:16 in Heb.

4 [a]Ex. 25:16, 21, 22; Num. 17:7

5 [a]Num. 16:5

7 [a]Num. 1:50, 53; 9:15

8 [a]Ezek. 17:24; Heb. 9:4

10 [1]Lit., *for preserving* [2]Lit., *sons of rebellion* [a]Num. 17:4 [b]Deut. 9:7, 24

12 [a]Is. 6:5

13 [a]Num. 1:51

1 [1]Lit., *of the sanctuary* [2]Lit., *of your priesthood* [a]Ex. 28:38; Lev. 10:17; 22:16

begun among the people. [a]So he put *on*
the incense and made atonement for the
people.
48 And he took his stand between the
dead and the living, so that the plague
was checked.
49 [a]But those who died by the plague
were 14,700, besides those who [b]died on
account of Korah.
50 Then Aaron returned to Moses at
the doorway of the tent of meeting, for
the plague had been checked.

Aaron's Rod Buds

17 [1]THEN the LORD spoke to Moses,
saying,
2 "Speak to the sons of Israel, and get
from them a rod for each father's household: twelve rods, from all their leaders
according to their fathers' households.
You shall write each name on his rod,
3 and write Aaron's name on the rod
of Levi; for there is one rod for the head
of each of their fathers' households.
4 "You shall then deposit them in the
tent of meeting in front of [a]the testimony, where I meet with you.
5 "And it will come about that the rod
of [a]the man whom I choose will sprout.
Thus I shall lessen from upon Myself the
grumblings of the sons of Israel, who are
grumbling against you."
6 Moses therefore spoke to the sons
of Israel, and all their leaders gave him a
rod apiece, for each leader according to
their fathers' households, twelve rods,
with the rod of Aaron among their rods.
7 So Moses deposited the rods before
the LORD in [a]the tent of the testimony.
8 Now it came about on the next day
that Moses went into the tent of the
testimony; and behold, [a]the rod of
Aaron for the house of Levi had
sprouted and put forth buds and produced blossoms, and it bore ripe almonds.
9 Moses then brought out all the
rods from the presence of the LORD to
all the sons of Israel; and they looked,
and each man took his rod.
10 But the LORD said to Moses, "Put
back the rod of Aaron [a]before the testimony [1]to be kept as a sign against the
[2b]rebels, that you may put an end to
their grumblings against Me, so that
they should not die."
11 Thus Moses did; just as the LORD
had commanded him, so he did.
12 Then the sons of Israel spoke to
Moses, saying, "[a]Behold, we perish, we
are dying, we are all dying!
13 "[a]Everyone who comes near, who
comes near to the tabernacle of the
LORD, must die. Are we to perish completely?"

Duties of Levites

18 SO the LORD said to Aaron,
"You and your sons and your
father's household with you shall [a]bear
the guilt [1]in connection with the sanctuary; and you and your sons with you
shall bear the guilt [2]in connection with
your priesthood.

2"But bring with you also your brothers, the tribe of Levi, the tribe of your father, that they may be [a]joined with you and serve you, while you and your sons with you are before the tent of the testimony.

3"And they shall thus attend to your obligation and the obligation of all the tent, but [a]they shall not come near to the furnishings of the sanctuary and [b]the altar, lest both they and you die.

4"And they shall be joined with you and attend to the obligations of the tent of meeting, for all the service of the tent; but an [1]outsider may not come near you.

5"So you shall attend to the [a]obligations of the sanctuary and the obligations of the altar, [b]that there may no longer be wrath on the sons of Israel.

6"And behold, I Myself [a]have taken your [1]fellow Levites from among the sons of Israel; they are [b]a gift to you, [2]dedicated to the LORD, to perform the service for the tent of meeting.

7"But you and your sons with you shall [a]attend to your priesthood for everything concerning the altar and inside the veil, and you are to perform service. I am giving you the priesthood as [b]a [1]bestowed service, but [c]the [2]outsider who comes near shall be put to death."

The Priests' Portion

8 Then the LORD spoke to Aaron, "Now behold, I Myself have given you charge of My [1a]offerings, even all the holy gifts of the sons of Israel, I have given them to you as a portion, and to your sons as a perpetual allotment.

9"This shall be yours from the most holy *gifts, reserved* from the fire; every offering of theirs, even [a]every grain offering and every [b]sin offering and every guilt offering, which they shall render to Me, shall be most holy for you and for your sons.

10"As the most holy *gifts* you shall eat it; every male shall eat it. It shall be holy to you.

11"This also is yours, [a]the offering of their gift, even all the wave offerings of the sons of Israel; I have [b]given them to you and to your sons and daughters with you, as a perpetual allotment. Everyone of your household who is clean may eat it.

12"[a]All the [1]best of the fresh oil and all the [1]best of the fresh wine and of the grain, the first fruits of those which they give to the LORD, I give them to you.

13"[a]The first ripe fruits of all that is in their land, which they bring to the LORD, shall be yours; everyone of your household who is clean may eat it.

14"[a]Every devoted thing in Israel shall be yours.

15"[1a]Every first issue of the womb of all flesh, whether man or animal, which they offer to the LORD, shall be yours; nevertheless the first-born of man you shall surely redeem, and the first-born of unclean animals you shall redeem.

16"And as to their redemption price, from a month old you shall redeem them, by your valuation, five [1]shekels in silver, according to the [1]shekel of the sanctuary, which is twenty gerahs.

17"But [a]the first-born of an ox or the first-born of a sheep or the first-born of a goat, you shall not redeem; they are holy. [b]You shall sprinkle their blood on the altar and shall offer up their fat in smoke *as* an offering by fire, for a soothing aroma to the LORD.

18"And their [1]meat shall be yours; it shall be yours like the [a]breast of a wave offering and like the right thigh.

19"[a]All the offerings of the holy *gifts,* which the sons of Israel offer to the LORD, I have given to you and your sons and your daughters with you, as a perpetual allotment. It is [b]an everlasting covenant of salt before the LORD to you and your [1]descendants with you."

20 Then the LORD said to Aaron, "[a]You shall have no inheritance in their land, nor own any portion among them; [b]I am your portion and your inheritance among the sons of Israel.

21"And to the sons of Levi, behold, I have given all the [a]tithe in Israel for an inheritance, in return for their service which they perform, the service of the tent of meeting.

22"And [a]the sons of Israel shall not come near the tent of meeting again, lest they bear sin and die.

23"Only the Levites shall perform the service of the tent of meeting, and they shall [a]bear their iniquity; it shall be a perpetual statute throughout your generations, and among the sons of Israel [b]they shall have no inheritance.

24"For the tithe of the sons of Israel, which they offer as an offering to the LORD, I have given to the Levites for an inheritance; therefore I have said concerning them, '[a]They shall have no inheritance among the sons of Israel.' "

25 Then the LORD spoke to Moses, saying,

26"Moreover, you shall speak to the Levites and say to them, 'When you take from the sons of Israel [a]the tithe which I have given you from them for your inheritance, then you shall present an offering from it to the LORD, a [b]tithe of the tithe.

27 'And your offering shall be reckoned to you as the grain from the threshing floor or the full produce from the wine vat.

28 'So you shall also present an offering to the LORD from your tithes, which you receive from the sons of Israel; and from it you shall give the LORD's offering to Aaron the priest.

29 'Out of all your gifts you shall present every offering due to the LORD, from all the [1]best of them, [2]the sacred part from them.'

30"And you shall say to them, 'When you have [1]offered from it the best of it, then *the rest* shall be reckoned to the

2 [a]Num. 3:5-10
3 [a]Num. 4:15-20 [b]Num. 1:51; 18:7
4 [1]Lit., *a stranger*
5 [a]Ex. 27:21; Lev. 24:3 [b]Num. 16:46
6 [1]Lit., *brethren the* [2]Lit., *given* [a]Num. 3:12, 45 [b]Num. 3:9
7 [1]Lit., *service of gift* [2]Lit., *stranger* [a]Ex. 29:9 [b]Num. 18:20; Deut. 18:2; Matt. 10:8; 1 Pet. 5:2, 3 [c]Num. 1:51
8 [1]Lit., *heave offerings,* and so throughout the ch. [a]Lev. 6:16, 18; 7:28-34
9 [a]Lev. 2:1-16 [b]Lev. 6:30
11 [a]Num. 18:1; Deut. 18:3 [b]Lev. 22:1-16
12 [1]Lit., *fat* [a]Deut. 18:4; 32:14; Ps. 81:16; 147:14
13 [a]Ex. 22:29; 23:19; 34:26
14 [a]Lev. 27:1-33
15 [1]Lit., *Everything that opens* [a]Ex. 13:13, 15; Num. 3:46
16 [1]I.e., A shekel equals approx. one-half oz.
17 [a]Deut. 15:19 [b]Lev. 3:2
18 [1]Lit., *flesh* [a]Lev. 7:31
19 [1]Lit., *seed* [a]Num. 18:11 [b]2 Chr. 13:5
20 [a]Deut. 10:9; 12:12; 14:27, 29 [b]Deut. 18:2; Josh. 13:33; Ezek. 44:28
21 [a]Lev. 27:30-33; Deut. 14:22-29
22 [a]Num. 1:51
23 [a]Num. 18:1 [b]Num. 18:20
24 [a]Deut. 10:9
26 [a]Num. 18:21 [b]Neh. 10:38
29 [1]Lit., *fat* [2]Lit., *its*
30 [1]Lit., *lifted*

Levites as the product of the threshing
floor, and as the product of the wine vat.
31 'And you may eat it anywhere, you
and your households, for it is your
compensation in return for your service
in the tent of meeting.
32 'And you shall bear no sin by reason of it, when you have [1]offered the
[2]best of it. But you shall not [a]profane the
sacred gifts of the sons of Israel, lest you
die.' "

Ordinance of the Red Heifer

19 THEN the LORD spoke to Moses
and Aaron, saying,
2 "This is the statute of the law which
the LORD has commanded, saying,
'Speak to the sons of Israel that they
bring you an [a]unblemished red heifer in
which is no defect, *and* [b]on which a yoke
has never [1]been placed.
3 'And you shall give it to [a]Eleazar
the priest, and it shall [b]be brought
outside the camp and be slaughtered in
his presence.
4 'Next Eleazar the priest shall take
some of its blood with his finger, and
[a]sprinkle some of its blood toward the
front of the tent of meeting seven times.
5 'Then the heifer shall be burned in
his sight; [a]its hide and its flesh and its
blood, with its refuse, shall be burned.
6 'And the priest shall take [a]cedar
wood and hyssop and scarlet *material,*
and cast it into the midst of the [1]burning
heifer.
7 'The priest [a]shall then wash his
clothes and bathe his [1]body in water,
and afterward come into the camp, but
the priest shall be unclean until evening.
8 'The one who burns it shall also
wash his clothes in water and bathe his
[1]body in water, and shall be unclean
until evening.
9 'Now a man who is clean shall
gather up the ashes of the heifer and
deposit them outside the camp in a clean
place, and [1]the congregation of the sons
of Israel shall keep it as [a]water to remove impurity; it is [2]purification from
sin.
10 'And the one who gathers the ashes
of the heifer [a]shall wash his clothes and
be unclean until evening; and it shall be
a perpetual statute to the sons of Israel
and to the alien who sojourns among
them.
11 '[a]The one who touches the corpse of
any [1]person shall be unclean for seven
days.
12 'That one shall [a]purify himself from
uncleanness with [1]the water on the third
day and on the seventh day, *and then* he
shall be clean; but if he does not purify
himself on the third day and on the
seventh day, he shall not be clean.
13 '[a]Anyone who touches a corpse, the
[1]body of a man who has died, and does
not purify himself, [b]defiles the [2]taberna-
cle of the LORD; and that person shall be
cut off from Israel. Because the water for
impurity was not [3c]sprinkled on him, he
shall be unclean; his uncleanness is still
on him.
14 'This is the law when a man dies in
a tent: everyone who comes into the tent
and everyone who is in the tent shall be
unclean for seven days.
15 'And every open vessel, which has
no covering [1]tied down on it, shall be
unclean.
16 '[a]Also, anyone who in the open field
touches one who has been slain with a
sword or who has died *naturally,* or a
human bone or a grave, shall be unclean
for seven days.
17 'Then for the unclean *person* they
shall take some of the [1]ashes of the
[2]burnt [3a]purification from sin and [4]flow-
ing water shall be [5]added to them in a
vessel.
18 'And a clean person shall take
hyssop and dip *it* in the water, and
sprinkle *it* on the tent and on all the
furnishings and on the persons who were
there, and on the one who touched the
bone or the one slain or the one dying
naturally or the grave.
19 'Then the clean *person* [a]shall sprinkle on the unclean on the third day and
on the seventh day; and on the seventh
day he shall purify him from uncleanness, and he shall wash his clothes and
bathe *himself* in water and shall be clean
by evening.
20 'But the man who is unclean and
does not purify himself from uncleanness, that person shall be cut off from
the midst of the assembly, because he
has [a]defiled the sanctuary of the LORD;
the water for impurity has not been
sprinkled on him, he is unclean.
21 'So it shall be a perpetual statute for
them. And he [a]who sprinkles the water
for impurity shall wash his clothes, and
he who touches the water for impurity
shall be unclean until evening.
22 '[a]Furthermore, anything that the
unclean *person* touches shall be unclean;
and the person who touches *it* shall be
unclean until evening.' "

Death of Miriam

20 THEN the sons of Israel, the
whole congregation, came to the
[a]wilderness of Zin in the first month;
and the people stayed at Kadesh. Now
Miriam died there and was buried there.
2 [a]And there was no water for the
congregation; [b]and they assembled
themselves against Moses and Aaron.
3 [a]The people thus contended with
Moses and spoke, saying, "[b]If only we
had perished [c]when our brothers perished before the LORD!
4 "[a]Why then have you brought the
LORD'S assembly into this wilderness,
for us and our beasts to die [1]here?
5 "And why have you made us come
up from Egypt, to bring us in to this
wretched place? [a]It is not a place of
[1]grain or figs or vines or pomegranates,
nor is there water to drink."
6 Then Moses and Aaron came in
from the presence of the assembly to the

---

32 [1]Lit., *lifted* [2]Lit., *fat* [a]Lev. 22:15, 16

2 [1]Lit., *come up* [a]Lev. 22:20-25 [b]Deut. 21:3

3 [a]Num. 3:4 [b]Lev. 4:11, 12, 21; Num. 19:9

4 [a]Lev. 4:6, 17; 16:14

5 [a]Ex. 29:14; Lev. 4:11, 12

6 [1]Lit., *burning of the heifer* [a]Lev. 14:4

7 [1]Lit., *flesh* [a]Lev. 16:26, 28; 22:6

8 [1]Lit., *flesh*

9 [1]Lit., *it shall be to the congregation . . . Israel, for a guarding as water of impurity* [2]Or, *a sin offering* [a]Num. 8:7; 31:23

10 [a]Num. 19:7

11 [1]Lit., *soul of man* [a]Lev. 21:1, 11; Num. 5:2; 6:6; Acts 21:26, 27

12 [1]Lit., *it* [a]Num. 19:19; 31:19

13 [1]Lit., *soul* [2]Lit., *dwelling place* [3]Or, *thrown* [a]Lev. 7:21; 22:3-7 [b]Lev. 15:31; 20:3; Num. 19:20 [c]Num. 19:19

15 [1]Lit., *cord*

16 [a]Num. 31:19

17 [1]Lit., *dust* [2]Lit., *burning of the* [3]Or, *sin offering* [4]Lit., *living* [5]Lit., *put* [a]Num. 19:9

19 [a]Ezek. 36:25; Heb. 10:22

20 [a]Num. 19:13

21 [a]Num. 19:7

22 [a]Lev. 5:2, 3; 7:21; 22:5, 6

1 [a]Num. 13:21; 27:14; 33:36

2 [a]Ex. 17:1 [b]Num. 16:19, 42

3 [a]Ex. 17:2 [b]Num. 14:2, 3 [c]Num. 16:31-35

4 [1]Lit., *there* [a]Ex. 17:3

5 [1]Lit., *seed* [a]Num. 16:14

doorway of the tent of meeting, and [a]fell
on their faces. Then the glory of the
LORD appeared to them;
7 and the LORD spoke to Moses,
saying,

The Water of Meribah

8 "Take [a]the rod; and you and your
brother Aaron assemble the congregation and speak to the rock before their
eyes, that it may yield its water. You
shall thus bring forth water for them out
of the rock and let the congregation and
their beasts drink."
9 So Moses took the rod [a]from before the LORD, just as He had commanded him;
10 and Moses and Aaron gathered the
assembly before the rock. And he said to
them, "[a]Listen now, you rebels; shall we
bring forth water for you out of this
rock?"
11 Then Moses lifted up his hand and
struck the rock twice with his rod; and
[a]water came forth abundantly, and the
congregation and their beasts drank.
12 But the LORD said to Moses and
Aaron, "[a]Because you have not believed
Me, to treat Me as holy in the sight of
the sons of Israel, therefore you shall not
bring this assembly into the land which I
have given them."
13 Those *were* the waters of [1a]Meri-
bah, [2]because the sons of Israel contended with the LORD, and He proved
Himself holy among them.
14 From Kadesh Moses then sent
messengers to [a]the king of Edom: "Thus
your brother Israel has said, 'You [b]know
all the hardship that has befallen us;
15 that our fathers went down to
Egypt, and we stayed in Egypt a long
time, and the Egyptians treated us and
our fathers badly.
16 'But [a]when we cried out to the
LORD, He heard our voice and sent [b]an
angel and brought us out from Egypt;
now behold, we are at Kadesh, a town
on the edge of your territory.
17 'Please [a]let us pass through your
land. We shall not pass through field or
through vineyard; we shall not even
drink water from a well. We shall go
along the king's highway, not turning to
the right or left, until we pass through
your territory.' "
18 [a]Edom, however, said to him, "You
shall not pass through [1]us, lest I come
out with the sword against you."
19 Again, the sons of Israel said to
him, "We shall go up by the highway,
and if I and [a]my livestock do drink any
of your water, [b]then I will [1]pay its price.
Let me only pass through on my feet,
[2]nothing *else.*"
20 But he said, "[a]You shall not pass
through." And Edom came out against
him with a heavy [1]force, and with a
strong hand.
21 [a]Thus Edom refused to allow Israel
to pass through his territory; [b]so Israel
turned away from him.

22 Now when they set out from [a]Ka-
desh, the sons of Israel, the whole congregation, came to Mount Hor.

Death of Aaron

23 Then the LORD spoke to Moses
and Aaron at [a]Mount Hor by the border
of the land of Edom, saying,
24 "Aaron shall be [a]gathered to his
people; for he shall not enter the land
which I have given to the sons of Israel,
because [b]you rebelled against My [1]com-
mand at the waters of Meribah.
25 "Take Aaron and his son [a]Eleazar,
and bring them up to Mount Hor;
26 and strip Aaron of his garments
and put them on his son Eleazar. So
Aaron will be [a]gathered *to his people,*
and will die there."
27 So Moses did just as the LORD had
commanded, and they went up to Mount
Hor in the sight of all the congregation.
28 And after Moses had stripped
Aaron of his garments and [a]put them on
his son Eleazar, [b]Aaron died there on
the mountain top. Then Moses and
Eleazar came down from the mountain.
29 And when all the congregation saw
that Aaron had died, all the house of
Israel wept for Aaron thirty [a]days.

Arad Conquered

21 WHEN the Canaanite, the king
of [a]Arad, who lived in the
[1]Negev, heard that Israel was coming by
the way of [2]Atharim, then he fought
against Israel, and took some of them
captive.
2 So [a]Israel made a vow to the LORD,
and said, "If Thou wilt indeed deliver
this people into my hand, then I will
[1]utterly destroy their cities."
3 And the LORD heard the voice of
Israel, and delivered up the Canaanites;
then they [1]utterly destroyed them and
their cities. Thus the name of the place
was called [2a]Hormah.
4 Then they set out from Mount Hor
by the way of the [1]Red Sea, to [a]go
around the land of Edom; and the [2]peo-
ple became impatient because of the
journey.
5 And the people spoke against God
and Moses, "[a]Why have you brought us
up out of Egypt to die in the wilderness?
For there is no [1]food and no water, and
[2b]we loathe this miserable food."

The Bronze Serpent

6 [a]And the LORD sent fiery serpents
among the people and [b]they bit the
people, so that [c]many people of Israel
died.
7 [a]So the people came to Moses and
said, "We have sinned, because we have
spoken against the LORD and you; [b]in-
tercede with the LORD, that He may
remove the serpents from us." And
Moses interceded for the people.
8 Then the LORD said to Moses,
"[1]Make a [a]fiery *serpent,* and set it on a
standard; and it shall come about, that

6 [a]Num. 14:5
8 [a]Ex. 4:17, 20; 17:5, 6
9 [a]Num. 17:10
10 [a]Ps. 106:33
11 [a]Ps. 78:16; Is. 48:21; 1 Cor. 10:4
12 [a]Num. 20:24; 27:14; Deut. 1:37; 3:26, 27
13 [1]I.e., contention [2]Or, *where* [a]Ex. 17:7; Ps. 95:8
14 [a]Gen. 36:31-39; Deut. 2:4 [b]Josh. 2:9, 10; 9:9, 10, 24
16 [a]Ex. 2:23; 3:7 [b]Ex. 14:19
17 [a]Num. 21:22
18 [1]Lit., *me* [a]Num. 24:18
19 [1]Lit., *give* [2]Or, *no great thing* [a]Ex. 12:38 [b]Deut. 2:6, 28
20 [1]Lit., *people* [a]Judg. 11:17
21 [a]Judg. 11:17 [b]Deut. 2:8
22 [a]Num. 20:1, 14
23 [a]Num. 33:37
24 [1]Lit., *mouth* [a]Gen. 25:8 [b]Num. 20:5, 10
25 [a]Num. 3:4
26 [a]Num. 20:24
28 [a]Ex. 29:29 [b]Num. 33:38; Deut. 10:6; 32:50
29 [a]Gen. 1:5; 50:3, 10; Deut. 34:8

1 [1]I.e., South country [2]Or, *the spies* [a]Num. 33:40; Josh. 12:14; Judg. 1:16
2 [1]Lit., *devote to destruction* [a]Gen. 28:20; Judg. 11:30
3 [1]Lit., *devoted to destruction* [2]I.e., a devoted thing; or, Destruction [a]Num. 14:45
4 [1]Lit., *Sea of Reeds* [2]Lit., *soul of the people was short* [a]Deut. 2:8
5 [1]Lit., *bread* [2]Lit., *our soul loathes* [a]Num. 14:2, 3 [b]Num. 11:6
6 [a]Deut. 8:15 [b]Jer. 8:17 [c]1 Cor. 10:9
7 [a]Num. 11:2; Ps. 78:34; Is. 26:16; Hos. 5:15 [b]Ex. 8:8; 1 Sam. 12:19; Acts 8:24
8 [1]Lit., *Make for yourself* [a]Is. 14:29; 30:6; John 3:14

everyone who is bitten, when he looks at
it, he shall live."
9 And Moses made a [a]bronze serpent
and set it on the standard; and it came
about, that if a serpent bit any man,
when he looked to the bronze serpent, he
lived.
10 [a]Now the sons of Israel moved out
and camped in Oboth.
11 And they journeyed from Oboth,
and camped at Iyeabarim, in the wilderness which is opposite Moab, to the
[1]east.
12 [a]From there they set out and
camped in [1]Wadi Zered.
13 From there they journeyed and
camped on the other side of the Arnon,
which is in the wilderness that comes out
of the border of the Amorites, [a]for the
Arnon is the border of Moab, between
Moab and the Amorites.
14 Therefore it is said in the Book of
the Wars of the LORD,
"Waheb in Suphah,
And the wadis of the Arnon,
15 And the slope of the wadis
That extends to the site of [a]Ar,
And leans to the border of
Moab."
16 [a]And from there *they continued* to
[1]Beer, that is the well where the LORD
said to Moses, "Assemble the people,
that I may give them water."
17 [a]Then Israel sang this song:
"Spring up, O well! Sing to it!
18 "The well, which the leaders sank,
Which the nobles of the people
dug,
With the scepter *and* with their
staffs."
And from the wilderness *they continued*
to Mattanah,
19 and from Mattanah to Nahaliel,
and from Nahaliel to Bamoth,
20 and from Bamoth to the valley that
is in the land of Moab, at the top of
Pisgah which overlooks the [1]wasteland.

Two Victories

21 [a]Then Israel sent messengers to
Sihon, king of the Amorites, saying,
22 "[a]Let me pass through your land.
We will not turn off into field or vineyard; we will not drink water from wells.
We will go by the king's highway until
we have passed through your border."
23 [a]But Sihon would not permit Israel
to pass through his border. So Sihon
gathered all his people and went out
against Israel in the wilderness, and
came to [b]Jahaz and fought against Israel.
24 Then [a]Israel [1]struck him with the
edge of the sword, and took possession
of his land from the Arnon to the Jabbok, as far as the sons of Ammon; for
the [b]border of the sons of Ammon *was*
[2]Jazer.
25 And Israel took all these cities and
[a]Israel lived in all the cities of the
Amorites, in Heshbon, and in all her
[1]villages.

9 [a]2 Kin. 18:4; John 3:14, 15
10 [a]Num. 33:43, 44
11 [1]Lit., *sunrise*
12 [1]I.e., a dry ravine except during rainy season [a]Num. 33:45
13 [a]Num. 22:36; Judg. 11:18
15 [a]Num. 21:28; Deut. 2:9, 18, 29
16 [1]I.e., a well [a]Num. 33:46-49
17 [a]Ex. 15:1; Ps. 105:2
20 [1]Or, *Jeshimon*
21 [a]Deut. 2:26-37; Judg. 11:19
22 [a]Num. 20:16, 17
23 [a]Num. 20:21 [b]Deut. 2:32
24 [1]Lit., *smote,* so with Gr. and Lat. [2]M.T. reads *strong* [a]Amos 2:9 [b]Deut. 2:37
25 [1]Lit., *daughters* [a]Amos 2:10
28 [1]Lit., *lords of the* [2]Or, *Bamoth* [a]Jer. 48:45 [b]Num. 21:15 [c]Num. 22:41; Is. 15:2; 16:12
29 [a]Jer. 48:46 [b]Judg. 11:24; 1 Kin. 11:33; 2 Kin. 23:13 [c]Is. 15:5 [d]Is. 16:2
30 [a]Num. 32:3, 34; Jer. 48:18, 22
32 [a]Num. 32:1, 3, 35; Jer. 48:32
33 [1]Lit., *he and* [a]Deut. 3:1-7 [b]Josh. 13:12
34 [a]Deut. 3:2
35 [1]Lit., *smote* [a]Deut. 3:3, 4
1 [a]Num. 33:48, 49
2 [a]Judg. 11:25
3 [a]Ex. 15:15
4 [1]Lit., *assembly* [a]Num. 25:15-18; 31:1-3
5 [1]I.e., Euphrates [a]Josh. 24:9; 2 Pet. 2:15f.; Jude 11 [b]Deut. 23:4

26 For Heshbon was the city of Sihon,
king of the Amorites, who had fought
against the former king of Moab and
had taken all his land out of his hand, as
far as the Arnon.
27 Therefore those who use proverbs
say,
"Come to Heshbon! Let it be built!
So let the city of Sihon be established.
28 "[a]For a fire went forth from Heshbon,
A flame from the town of Sihon;
It devoured [b]Ar of Moab,
The [1c]dominant [2]heights of the
Arnon.
29 "[a]Woe to you, O Moab!
You are ruined, O people of [b]Che-
mosh!
[c]He has given his sons as fugitives,
[d]And his daughters into captivity,
To an Amorite king, Sihon.
30 "But we have cast them down,
Heshbon is ruined as far as [a]Di-
bon,
Then we have laid waste even to
Nophah,
Which *reaches* to Medeba."
31 Thus Israel lived in the land of the
Amorites.
32 And Moses sent to spy out [a]Jazer,
and they captured its villages and dispossessed the Amorites who *were* there.
33 [a]Then they turned and went up by
the way of Bashan, and Og the king of
Bashan went out [1]with all his people, for
battle at [b]Edrei.
34 But the LORD said to Moses, "[a]Do
not fear him, for I have given him into
your hand, and all his people and his
land; and you shall do to him as you did
to Sihon, king of the Amorites, who
lived at Heshbon."
35 So [a]they [1]killed him and his sons
and all his people, until there was no
remnant left him; and they possessed his
land.

Balak Sends for Balaam

22 [a]THEN the sons of Israel journeyed, and camped in the plains
of Moab beyond the Jordan *opposite*
Jericho.
2 Now [a]Balak the son of Zippor saw
all that Israel had done to the Amorites.
3 [a]So Moab was in great fear because
of the people, for they were numerous;
and Moab was in dread of the sons of
Israel.
4 And Moab said to the elders of
[a]Midian, "Now this [1]horde will lick up
all that is around us, as the ox licks up
the grass of the field." And Balak the son
of Zippor was king of Moab at that time.
5 So he sent messengers to [a]Balaam
the son of Beor, at [b]Pethor, which is near
the [1]River, *in* the land of the sons of his
people, to call him, saying, "Behold, a
people came out of Egypt; behold, they

cover the surface of the land, and they
are living opposite me.
6 "[a]Now, therefore, please come,
[b]curse this people for me since they are
too [1]mighty for me; perhaps I may be
able to [2]defeat them and drive them out
of the land. For I know that he whom
you bless is blessed, and he whom you
curse is cursed."
7 So the elders of Moab and the
elders of Midian departed with the *fees*
for [a]divination in their hand; and they
came to Balaam and [1]repeated Balak's
words to him.
8 And he said to them, "Spend the
night here, and I will bring word back to
you as the LORD may speak to me." And
the leaders of Moab stayed with Balaam.
9 Then [a]God came to Balaam and
said, "Who are these men with you?"
10 And Balaam said to God, "Balak
the son of Zippor, king of Moab, has
sent *word* to me,
11 'Behold, there is a people who came
out of Egypt and they cover the surface
of the land; now come, curse them for
me; perhaps I may be able to fight
against them, and drive them out.' "
12 And God said to Balaam, "Do not
go with them; [a]you shall not curse the
people; for they [b]are blessed."
13 So Balaam arose in the morning
and said to Balak's leaders, "Go back to
your land, for the LORD has refused to
let me go with you."
14 And the leaders of Moab arose and
went to Balak, and said, "Balaam refused to come with us."
15 Then Balak again sent leaders,
more numerous and more distinguished
than [1]the former.
16 And they came to Balaam and said
to him, "Thus says Balak the son of
Zippor, 'Let nothing, I beg you, hinder
you from coming to me;
17 for I will indeed honor you richly,
and I will do whatever you say to me.
[a]Please come then, curse this people for
me.' "
18 And Balaam answered and said to
the servants of Balak, "[a]Though Balak
were to give me his house full of silver
and gold, I could not do anything, either
small or great, contrary to the [1]com-
mand of the LORD my God.
19 "And now please, you also stay here
tonight, and I will find out what else the
LORD will speak to me."
20 And God came to Balaam at night
and said to him, "If the men have come
to call you, rise up *and* go with them; but
[a]only the word which I speak to you
shall you do."
21 [a]So Balaam arose in the morning,
and saddled his donkey, and went with
the leaders of Moab.

The Angel and Balaam

22 But God was angry because he was
going, [a]and the angel of the LORD took
his stand in the way as an adversary
against him. Now he was riding on his
donkey and his two servants were with
him.
23 When the donkey saw the angel of
the LORD standing in the way with his
drawn sword in his hand, the donkey
turned off from the way and went into
the field; but Balaam struck the donkey
to turn her back into the way.
24 Then the angel of the LORD stood
in a narrow path of the vineyards, *with* a
wall on this side and a wall on that side.
25 When the donkey saw the angel of
the LORD, she pressed herself to the wall
and pressed Balaam's foot against the
wall, so he struck her again.
26 And the angel of the LORD went
further, and stood in a narrow place
where there was no way to turn to the
right hand or the left.
27 When the donkey saw the angel of
the LORD, she lay down under Balaam;
so [a]Balaam was angry and struck the
donkey with his stick.
28 And [a]the LORD opened the mouth
of the donkey, and she said to Balaam,
"What have I done to you, that you have
struck me these three times?"
29 Then Balaam said to the donkey,
"Because you have made a mockery of
me! If there had been a sword in my
hand, [a]I would have killed you by now."
30 And the donkey said to Balaam,
"Am I not your donkey on which you
have ridden all your life to this day?
Have I ever been accustomed to do so to
you?" And he said, "No."
31 Then the LORD opened the eyes of
Balaam, and he saw [a]the angel of the
LORD standing in the way with his
drawn sword in his hand; and he bowed
[1]all the way to the ground.
32 And the angel of the LORD said to
him, "Why have you struck your donkey
these three times? Behold, I have come
out as an adversary, because your way
was [1a]contrary to me.
33 "But the donkey saw me and turned
aside from me these three times. If she
had not turned aside from me, I would
surely have killed you just now, and let
her live."
34 And Balaam said to the angel of
the LORD, "[a]I have sinned, for I did not
know that you were standing in the way
against me. Now then, if it is displeasing
to you, I will turn back."
35 But the angel of the LORD said to
Balaam, "Go with the men, but [a]you
shall speak only the word which I shall
[1]tell you." So Balaam went along with
the leaders of Balak.
36 When Balak heard that Balaam
was coming, he went out to meet him at
the city of Moab, which is on the Arnon
border, [1]at the extreme end of the border.
37 Then Balak said to Balaam, "Did I
not urgently send to you to call you?
Why did you not come to me? Am I
really unable to honor you?"

6 [1]Or, *numerous* [2]Lit., *smite* [a]Num. 22:17; 23:7, 8 [b]Num. 22:12; 24:9
7 [1]Lit., *spoke* [a]Num. 23:23; 24:1; Josh. 13:22
9 [a]Gen. 20:3
12 [a]Num. 23:8; 24:9 [b]Gen. 12:2; 22:17
15 [1]Lit., *these*
17 [a]Num. 22:6
18 [1]Lit., *mouth* [a]Num. 22:38; 24:13; 1 Kin. 22:14; 2 Chr. 18:13
20 [a]Num. 22:35; 23:5, 12, 16, 26; 24:13
21 [a]2 Pet. 2:15
22 [a]Ex. 23:20
27 [a]James 1:19
28 [a]2 Pet. 2:16
29 [a]Prov. 12:10; Matt. 15:19
31 [1]Lit., *and prostrated himself to his face* [a]Josh. 5:13-15
32 [1]Lit., *reckless* [a]2 Pet. 2:15
34 [a]Num. 14:40
35 [1]Or, *speak to* [a]Num. 22:20
36 [1]Lit., *which is at*

38 So Balaam said to Balak, "Behold,
I have come now to you! [a]Am I able to
speak anything at all? The word that
God puts in my mouth, that I shall
speak."
39 And Balaam went with Balak, and
they came to Kiriath-huzoth.
40 And Balak sacrificed oxen and
sheep, and sent *some* to Balaam and the
leaders who were with him.
41 Then it came about in the morning
that Balak took Balaam, and brought
him up to [1a]the high places of Baal; and
he saw from there [2]a [b]portion of the
people.

The Prophecies of Balaam

23 THEN Balaam said to Balak,
"Build seven altars for me here,
and prepare seven bulls and seven rams
for me here."
2 And Balak did just as Balaam had
spoken, and Balak and Balaam offered
up a bull and a ram on each altar.
3 Then Balaam said to Balak, "Stand
beside your burnt offering, and I will go;
perhaps the LORD will come to meet me,
and whatever He shows me I will tell
you." So he went to a bare hill.
4 Now God met Balaam, and he said
to Him, "I have set up the seven altars,
and I have offered up a bull and a ram
on each altar."
5 Then the LORD [a]put a word in
Balaam's mouth and said, "Return to
Balak, and you shall speak thus."
6 So he returned to him, and behold,
he was standing beside his burnt offering, he and all the leaders of Moab.
7 And he took up his [1]discourse and
said,

"From [a]Aram Balak has brought
me,
Moab's king from the mountains
of the East,
'[b]Come curse Jacob for me,
And come, denounce Israel!'
8 "[a]How shall I curse, whom God
has not cursed?
And how can I denounce, whom
the LORD has not denounced?
9 "As I see him from the top of the
rocks,
And I look at him from the hills;
[a]Behold, a people *who* dwells
apart,
And shall not be reckoned among
the nations.
10 "[a]Who can count the dust of Jacob,
Or number the fourth part of
Israel?
[b]Let [1]me die the death of the
upright,
[c]And let my end be like his!"

11 Then Balak said to Balaam, "What
have you done to me? [a]I took you to
curse my enemies, but behold, you have
actually blessed them!"
12 And he answered and said, "Must I
not be careful to speak [a]what the LORD
puts in my mouth?"

38 [a]Num. 22:18

41 [1]Or, *Bamoth-baal* [2]Lit., *the end of the camp* [a]Num. 21:28 [b]Num. 23:13

5 [a]Num. 22:20; Deut. 18:18; Jer. 1:9

7 [1]Lit., *parable* [a]Num. 22:5; Deut. 23:4 [b]Num. 22:6

8 [a]Num. 22:12

9 [a]Deut. 32:8; 33:28

10 [1]Lit., *my soul* [a]Gen. 13:16; 28:14 [b]Is. 57:1 [c]Ps. 37:37

11 [a]Neh. 13:2

12 [a]Num. 22:20

16 [a]Num. 22:20

18 [1]Lit., *parable*

19 [a]1 Sam. 15:29 [b]Is. 40:8; 55:11

20 [a]Gen. 12:2; 22:17; Num. 22:12 [b]Is. 43:13

21 [1]Or, *iniquity* [a]Num. 14:18, 19, 34; Ps. 32:2, 5 [b]Deut. 9:24; 32:5; Jer. 50:20 [c]Ex. 3:12; Deut. 31:23 [d]Deut. 33:5; Ps. 89:15-18

22 [a]Num. 24:8 [b]Deut. 33:17

23 [a]Num. 22:7; 24:1; Josh. 13:22

24 [a]Gen. 49:9; Nah. 2:11, 12

26 [1]Lit., *saying, Whatever* [a]Num. 22:18

27 [1]Lit., *right in the sight of God*

13 Then Balak said to him, "Please
come with me to another place from
where you may see them, although you
will only see the extreme end of them,
and will not see all of them; and curse
them for me from there."
14 So he took him to the field of
Zophim, to the top of Pisgah, and built
seven altars and offered a bull and a ram
on *each* altar.
15 And he said to Balak, "Stand here
beside your burnt offering, while I myself meet *the LORD* yonder."
16 Then the LORD met Balaam and
[a]put a word in his mouth and said,
"Return to Balak, and thus you shall
speak."
17 And he came to him, and behold,
he was standing beside his burnt offering, and the leaders of Moab with him.
And Balak said to him, "What has the
LORD spoken?"
18 Then he took up his [1]discourse and
said,

"Arise, O Balak, and hear;
Give ear to me, O son of Zippor!
19 "[a]God is not a man, that He
should lie,
Nor a son of man, that He should
repent;
[b]Has He said, and will He not do
it?
Or has He spoken, and will He
not make it good?
20 "Behold, I have received *a command* to bless;
[a]When He has blessed, then [b]I
cannot revoke it.
21 "[a]He has not observed [1]misfortune
in Jacob;
[b]Nor has He seen trouble in Israel;
[c]The LORD his God is with him,
[d]And the shout of a king is among
them.
22 "[a]God brings them out of Egypt,
He is for them like the [b]horns of
the wild ox.
23 "[a]For there is no omen against
Jacob,
Nor is there any divination
against Israel;
At the proper time it shall be said
to Jacob
And to Israel, what God has
done.
24 "[a]Behold, a people rises like a
lioness,
And as a lion it lifts itself;
It shall not lie down until it devours the prey,
And drinks the blood of the
slain."

25 Then Balak said to Balaam, "Do
not curse them at all nor bless them at
all!"
26 But Balaam answered and said to
Balak, "Did I not tell you, '[1a]Whatever
the LORD speaks, that I must do'?"
27 Then Balak said to Balaam, "Please
come, I will take you to another place;
perhaps it will be [1]agreeable with God
that you curse them for me from there."

28 So Balak took Balaam to the top of
Peor which overlooks the [1]wasteland.
29 And Balaam said to Balak, "Build
seven altars for me here and prepare
seven bulls and seven rams for me here."
30 And Balak did just as Balaam had
said, and offered up a bull and a ram on
each altar.

The Prophecy from Peor

24 WHEN Balaam saw that it
[1]pleased the LORD to bless Israel,
he did not go as at other times to [2]seek
[a]omens but he set his face toward the
[b]wilderness.
2 And Balaam lifted up his eyes and
saw Israel [1]camping tribe by tribe; and
[a]the Spirit of God came upon him.
3 And he took up his [1]discourse and
said,

"[a]The oracle of Balaam the son of
Beor,
And the oracle of the man whose
eye is opened;
4 The oracle of him who [a]hears the
[1]words of God,
Who sees the [b]vision of [2]the Almighty,
Falling down, yet having his eyes
uncovered,
5 How fair are your tents, O Jacob,
Your dwellings, O Israel!
6 "Like [1]valleys that stretch out,
Like gardens beside the river,
Like [a]aloes planted by the LORD,
Like [b]cedars beside the waters.
7 "Water shall flow from his buckets,
And his seed *shall be* by many
waters,
And his king shall be higher than
[a]Agag,
[b]And his kingdom shall be exalted.
8 "[a]God brings him out of Egypt,
He is for him like the horns of the
wild ox.
[b]He shall devour the nations *who
are* his adversaries,
And shall crush their bones in
pieces,
And shatter *them* with his [c]arrows.
9 "[a]He [1]couches, he lies down as a
lion,
And as a [2]lion, who [3]dares rouse
him?
[b]Blessed is everyone who blesses
you,
And cursed is everyone who
curses you."

10 Then Balak's anger burned against
Balaam, and he struck his [1]hands together;
and Balak said to Balaam, "I
called you to curse my enemies, but
behold, you have persisted in blessing
them these three times!
11 "Therefore, [1]flee to your place now.
I said I would honor you greatly, but
behold, the LORD has held you back
from honor."
12 And Balaam said to Balak, "[a]Did I
not tell your messengers whom you had
sent to me, saying,
13 'Though Balak were to give me his
house full of silver and gold, I could not
do anything contrary to the [1]command
of the LORD, either good or bad, [a]of my
own [2]accord. [b]What the LORD speaks,
that I will speak'?
14 "And now behold, [a]I am going to
my people; come, *and* I will advise you
what this people will do to your people
in the [1]days to come."
15 And he took up his discourse and
said,

"[a]The oracle of Balaam the son of
Beor,
And the oracle of the man whose
eye is opened,
16 The oracle of him who hears the
[1]words of God,
And knows the knowledge of the
[2]Most High,
Who sees the vision of [3]the Almighty,
Falling down, yet having his eyes
uncovered.
17 "I see him, but not now;
I behold him, but not near;
A star shall come forth from Jacob,
[a]And a scepter shall rise from
Israel,
[b]And shall crush through the
[1]forehead of Moab,
And [2]tear down all the sons of
[3]Sheth.
18 "[a]And Edom shall be a possession,
[b]Seir, its enemies, also shall be a
possession,
While Israel performs valiantly.
19 "One from Jacob shall have dominion,
And shall destroy the remnant
from the city."

20 And he looked at Amalek and took
up his discourse and said,

"Amalek was the first of the nations,
[a]But his end *shall be* [1]destruction."

21 And he looked at the [a]Kenite, and
took up his discourse and said,

"Your dwelling place is enduring,
And your nest is set in the cliff.
22 "Nevertheless Kain shall be consumed;
How long shall [a]Asshur [1]keep you
captive?"

23 And he took up his discourse and
said,

"Alas, who can live except God has
ordained it?
24 "But ships *shall come* from the
coast of [a]Kittim,
And they shall afflict Asshur and
shall afflict [b]Eber;
[c]So they also *shall come* to destruction."

25 Then Balaam arose and departed
and returned to [a]his place, and Balak
also went his way.

---

28 [1]Or, *Jeshimon*

1 [1]Lit., *was good in the eyes of* [2]Lit., *encounter* [a]Num. 22:7; 23:23 [b]Num. 23:28

2 [1]Lit., *dwelling* [a]Num. 11:26; 1 Sam. 19:20; Rev. 1:10

3 [1]Lit., *parable,* and so throughout the ch. [a]Num. 24:15, 16

4 [1]Lit., *sayings* [2]Heb., *Shaddai* [a]Num. 22:20 [b]Gen. 15:1; Num. 12:6

6 [1]Or possibly, *palm trees* [a]Ps. 45:8 [b]Ps. 1:3

7 [a]Num. 24:20; 1 Sam. 15:8 [b]Ps. 145:11-13

8 [a]Num. 23:22 [b]Num. 23:24; Ps. 2:9 [c]Ps. 45:5

9 [1]Lit., *bows down* [2]Or, *lioness* [3]Lit., *shall* [a]Gen. 49:9; Num. 23:24 [b]Gen. 12:3; 27:29

10 [1]Lit., *palms*

11 [1]Lit., *flee for yourself*

12 [a]Num. 22:18

13 [1]Lit., *mouth* [2]Lit., *heart* [a]Num. 16:28 [b]Num. 22:20

14 [1]Lit., *end of the days* [a]Num. 31:8, 16; Josh. 13:22

15 [a]Num. 24:3, 4

16 [1]Lit., *sayings* [2]Heb., *Elyon* [3]Heb., *Shaddai*

17 [1]Lit., *corners* [2]Another reading is *the crown of the head of* [3]I.e., tumult [a]Gen. 49:10 [b]Num. 21:29; Is. 15:1-16:14

18 [a]Gen. 27:29; Amos 9:11, 12 [b]Gen. 32:3

20 [1]Lit., *to destroying* [a]Num. 24:24

21 [a]Gen. 15:19

22 [1]Lit., *take* [a]Gen. 10:21, 22

24 [a]Gen. 10:4; Ezek. 27:6 [b]Gen. 10:21 [c]Num. 24:20

25 [a]Num. 24:14

The Sin of Peor

25 WHILE Israel remained at [a]Shittim, the people began [b]to play the harlot with the daughters of Moab.

2 For [a]they invited the people to the sacrifices of their gods, and the people ate and bowed down to their gods.

3 So [a]Israel joined themselves to [1]Baal of Peor, and the LORD was angry against Israel.

4 And the LORD said to Moses, "Take all the leaders of the people and execute them [1]in broad daylight before the LORD, [a]so that the fierce anger of the LORD may turn away from Israel."

5 So Moses said to the judges of Israel, "Each of you [a]slay his men who have joined themselves to [1]Baal of Peor."

6 Then behold, one of the sons of Israel came and brought to his [1]relatives a [a]Midianite woman, in the sight of Moses and in the sight of all the congregation of the sons of Israel, [b]while they were weeping at the doorway of the tent of meeting.

7 [a]When Phinehas the son of Eleazar, the son of Aaron the priest, saw it, he arose from the midst of the congregation, and took a spear in his hand;

8 and he went after the man of Israel into the [1]tent, and pierced both of them through, the man of Israel and the woman, through the [2]body. [a]So the plague on the sons of Israel was checked.

9 [a]And those who died by the plague were 24,000.

The Zeal of Phinehas

10 Then the LORD spoke to Moses, saying,

11 "[a]Phinehas the son of Eleazar, the son of Aaron the priest, has turned away My wrath from the sons of Israel, in that he was jealous with My jealousy among them, so that I did not destroy the sons of Israel [b]in My jealousy.

12 "Therefore say, '[a]Behold, I give him My [b]covenant of peace;

13 and it shall be for him and his [1]descendants after him, a covenant of a [a]perpetual priesthood, because he was jealous for his God, and [b]made atonement for the sons of Israel.' "

14 Now the name of the [1]slain man of Israel who was [1]slain with the Midianite woman, was Zimri the son of Salu, a leader of a father's household among the Simeonites.

15 And the name of the Midianite woman who was [1]slain was [a]Cozbi the daughter of [b]Zur, [2]who was head of the people of a father's household in Midian.

16 Then the LORD spoke to Moses, saying,

17 "[a]Be hostile to the Midianites and strike them;

18 for they have been hostile to you with their tricks, with which they have deceived you in the affair of Peor, and in the affair of Cozbi, the daughter of the leader of Midian, their sister who was slain on the day of the plague because of Peor."

Census of a New Generation

26 THEN it came about after the [a]plague, [2]that the LORD spoke to Moses and to Eleazar the son of Aaron the priest, saying,

2 "[a]Take a [1]census of all the congregation of the sons of Israel from twenty years old and upward, by their fathers' households, whoever is able to go out to war in Israel."

3 So Moses and Eleazar the priest spoke with them [a]in the plains of Moab by the Jordan at Jericho, saying,

4 "*Take a census of the people* from twenty years old and upward, as the LORD has commanded Moses."

Now the sons of Israel who came out of the land of Egypt *were:*

5 Reuben, Israel's first-born, the sons of Reuben: *of* Hanoch, the family of the Hanochites; of Pallu, the family of the Palluites;

6 of Hezron, the family of the Hezronites; of Carmi, the family of the Carmites.

7 These are the families of the Reubenites, and those who were numbered of them were [a]43,730.

8 And the son of Pallu: Eliab.

9 And the sons of Eliab: Nemuel and Dathan and Abiram. These are the Dathan and Abiram who were [a]called by the congregation, who contended against Moses and against Aaron in the company of Korah, when they contended against the LORD,

10 and [a]the earth opened its mouth and swallowed them up along with Korah, when that company died, [b]when the fire devoured 250 men, so that they became a [1]warning.

11 [a]The sons of Korah, however, did not die.

12 The sons of Simeon according to their families: of [1]Nemuel, the family of the Nemuelites; of Jamin, the family of the Jaminites; of [2]Jachin, the family of the Jachinites;

13 of [1]Zerah, the family of the Zerahites; of Shaul, the family of the Shaulites.

14 These are the families of the Simeonites, [a]22,200.

15 The sons of Gad according to their families: of [1]Zephon, the family of the Zephonites; of Haggi, the family of the Haggites; of Shuni, the family of the Shunites;

16 of [1]Ozni, the family of the Oznites; of Eri, the family of the Erites;

17 of [1]Arod, the family of the Arodites; of Areli, the family of the Arelites.

18 These are the families of the sons of Gad according to those who were numbered of them, [a]40,500.

19 The [a]sons of Judah *were* Er and Onan, but Er and Onan died in the land of Canaan.

1 [a]Num. 33:49; Josh. 2:1 [b]Num. 31:16; 1 Cor. 10:8; Rev. 2:14
2 [a]Ex. 34:15; Deut. 32:38
3 [1]Or, *Baal-peor* [a]Ps. 106:28, 29; Hos. 9:10
4 [1]Lit., *in front of the sun* [a]Deut. 13:17
5 [1]Or, *Baal-peor* [a]Ex. 32:27
6 [1]Lit., *brothers* [a]Num. 22:4 [b]Joel 2:17
7 [a]Ps. 106:30
8 [1]Or, *inner rooms* [2]Or, *belly* [a]Num. 16:46-48
9 [a]Num. 14:37; 16:48-50; 31:16
11 [a]Ps. 106:30 [b]Ex. 20:5
12 [a]Ps. 106:30, 31 [b]Is. 54:10; Ezek. 34:25; 37:26
13 [1]Lit., *seed* [a]Ex. 29:9 [b]Num. 16:46
14 [1]Lit., *smitten*
15 [1]Lit., *smitten* [2]Lit., *he* [a]Num. 25:18 [b]Num. 31:8
17 [a]Num. 25:1; 22:4; 31:1-3

1 [1]Ch. 25:19 in Heb. [2]Ch. 26:1 in Heb. [a]Num. 25:9
2 [1]Lit., *sum* [a]Ex. 30:11-16; 38:25, 26; Num. 1:2
3 [a]Num. 22:1; 33:48; 35:1
7 [a]Num. 1:21
9 [a]Num. 1:16; 16:2
10 [1]Lit., *sign* [a]Num. 16:32 [b]Num. 16:35, 38
11 [a]Num. 16:27, 33; Deut. 24:16
12 [1]In Gen. 46:10 and Ex. 6:15, *Jemuel* [2]In 1 Chr. 4:24, *Jarib*
13 [1]In Gen. 46:10, *Zohar*
14 [a]Num. 1:23
15 [1]In Gen. 46:16, *Ziphion*
16 [1]In Gen. 46:16, *Ezbon*
17 [1]In Gen. 46:16, *Arodi*
18 [a]Num. 1:25
19 [a]Gen. 38:2; 46:12

20 And the [a]sons of Judah according to their families were: of Shelah, the family of the Shelanites; of Perez, the family of the Perezites; of Zerah, the family of the Zerahites.

21 And the sons of Perez were: of Hezron, the family of the Hezronites; of Hamul, the family of the Hamulites.

22 These are the families of Judah according to those who were numbered of them, [a]76,500.

23 The [a]sons of Issachar according to their families: *of* Tola, the family of the Tolaites; of [1]Puvah, the family of the Punites;

24 of [1]Jashub, the family of the Jashubites; of Shimron, the family of the Shimronites.

25 These are the families of Issachar according to those who were numbered of them, [a]64,300.

26 The [a]sons of Zebulun according to their families: of Sered, the family of the Seredites; of Elon, the family of the Elonites; of Jahleel, the family of the Jahleelites.

27 These are the families of the Zebulunites according to those who were numbered of them, [a]60,500.

28 The [a]sons of Joseph according to their families: Manasseh and Ephraim.

29 The sons of Manasseh: of Machir, the family of the Machirites; and [a]Machir [1]became the father of Gilead: of Gilead, the family of the Gileadites.

30 These are the sons of Gilead: *of* [1]Iezer, the family of the [a]Iezerites; of Helek, the family of the Helekites;

31 and *of* Asriel, the family of the Asrielites; and *of* Shechem, the family of the Shechemites;

32 and *of* Shemida, the family of the Shemidaites; and *of* Hepher, the family of the Hepherites.

33 Now Zelophehad the son of Hepher had no sons, but only daughters; and [a]the names of the daughters of Zelophehad were Mahlah, Noah, Hoglah, Milcah and Tirzah.

34 These are the families of Manasseh; and those who were numbered of them were [a]52,700.

35 These are the sons of Ephraim according to their families: of Shuthelah, the family of the Shuthelahites; of [1]Becher, the family of the Becherites; of Tahan, the family of the Tahanites.

36 And these are the sons of Shuthelah: of Eran, the family of the Eranites.

37 These are the families of the sons of Ephraim according to those who were numbered of them, [a]32,500. These are the sons of Joseph according to their families.

38 The sons of Benjamin according to their families: of Bela, the family of the Belaites; of Ashbel, the family of the Ashbelites; of [1]Ahiram, the family of the Ahiramites;

39 of [1]Shephupham, the family of the Shuphamites; of [2]Hupham, the family of the Huphamites.

40 And the sons of Bela were [1]Ard and Naaman: *of Ard,* the family of the Ardites; of Naaman, the family of the Naamites.

41 These are the sons of Benjamin according to their families; and those who were numbered of them were [a]45,600.

42 These are the sons of Dan according to their families: of [1]Shuham, the family of the Shuhamites. These are the families of Dan according to their families.

43 All the families of the Shuhamites, according to those who were numbered of them, were [a]64,400.

44 The [a]sons of Asher according to their families: of Imnah, the family of the Imnites; of Ishvi, the family of the Ishvites; of Beriah, the family of the Beriites.

45 Of the sons of Beriah: of Heber, the family of the Heberites; of Malchiel, the family of the Malchielites.

46 And the name of the daughter of Asher *was* Serah.

47 These are the families of the sons of Asher according to those who were numbered of them, [a]53,400.

48 The [a]sons of Naphtali according to their families: of Jahzeel, the family of the Jahzeelites; of Guni, the family of the Gunites;

49 of Jezer, the family of the Jezerites; of [a]Shillem, the family of the Shillemites.

50 These are the families of Naphtali according to their families; and those who were numbered of them were [a]45,400.

51 These are those who were numbered of the sons of Israel, [a]601,730.

52 Then the LORD spoke to Moses, saying,

53 "[1]Among these the land shall be divided for an inheritance according to the number of names.

54 "[a]To the larger *group* you shall increase their inheritance, and to the smaller *group* you shall diminish their inheritance; each shall be given their inheritance according to those who were numbered of them.

55 "But the land shall be [a]divided by lot. They shall [1]receive their inheritance according to the names of the tribes of their fathers.

56 "According to the selection by lot, their inheritance shall be divided between the larger and the smaller *groups.*"

57 And [a]these are those who were numbered of the Levites according to their families: of Gershon, the family of the Gershonites; of Kohath, the family of the Kohathites; of Merari, the family of the Merarites.

58 These are the families of Levi: the family of the Libnites, the family of the Hebronites, the family of the Mahlites, the family of the Mushites, the family of the Korahites. [a]And Kohath [1]became the father of Amram.

20 [a]Gen. 49:8; 1 Chr. 2:3; Rev. 7:5
22 [a]Num. 1:27
23 [1]In Gen. 46:13, *Puvvah;* in 1 Chr. 7:1, *Puah* [a]Gen. 46:13; 1 Chr. 7:1
24 [1]In Gen. 46:13, *Iob*
25 [a]Num. 1:29
26 [a]Gen. 46:14
27 [a]Num. 1:31
28 [a]Gen. 46:20; Deut. 33:16f.
29 [1]Lit., *begot* [a]Josh. 17:1; 1 Chr. 7:14f.
30 [1]In Josh. 17:2, *Abiezer* [a]Judg. 6:11, 24, 34
33 [a]Num. 27:1
34 [a]Num. 1:35
35 [1]In 1 Chr. 7:20, *Bered*
37 [a]Num. 1:33
38 [1]In Gen. 46:21, *Ehi;* in 1 Chr. 8:1, *Aharah*
39 [1]In Gen. 46:21, *Muppim;* in 1 Chr. 7:12, *Shuppim* [2]In Gen. 46:21, *Muppim* and *Huppim*
40 [1]In 1 Chr. 8:3, *Addar*
41 [a]Num. 1:37
42 [1]In Gen. 46:23, *Hushim*
43 [a]Num. 1:39
44 [a]Gen. 46:17; 1 Chr. 7:30
47 [a]Num. 1:41
48 [a]Gen. 46:24; 1 Chr. 7:13
49 [a]1 Chr. 7:13
50 [a]Num. 1:43
51 [a]Ex. 12:37; 38:26; Num. 1:46; 11:21
53 [1]Lit., *To*
54 [a]Num. 33:54
55 [1]Lit., *inherit according to* [a]Num. 33:54; 34:13
57 [a]Gen. 46:11; Ex. 6:16; 1 Chr. 6:1, 16
58 [1]Lit., *begot* [a]Ex. 6:20

59 And the name of Amram's wife [a]was Jochebed, the daughter of Levi, who was born to Levi in Egypt; and she bore to Amram: Aaron and Moses and their sister Miriam.

60 [a]And to Aaron were born Nadab and Abihu, Eleazar and Ithamar.

61 [a]But Nadab and Abihu died when they offered strange fire before the LORD.

62 And those who were numbered of them were [a]23,000, every male from a month old and upward, for [b]they were not numbered among the sons of Israel [c]since no inheritance was given to them among the sons of Israel.

63 These are those who were numbered by Moses and Eleazar the priest, who numbered the sons of Israel in the plains of Moab by the Jordan at Jericho.

64 [a]But among these there was not a man of those who were numbered by Moses and Aaron the priest, who numbered the sons of Israel in the wilderness of Sinai.

65 For the LORD had said [1]of them, "[a]They shall surely die in the wilderness." And not a man was left of them, [b]except Caleb the son of Jephunneh, and Joshua the son of Nun.

A Law of Inheritance

27 THEN [a]the daughters of Zelophehad, the son of Hepher, the son of Gilead, the son of Machir, the son of Manasseh, of the families of Manasseh the son of Joseph, came near; and these are [b]the names of his daughters: Mahlah, Noah and Hoglah and Milcah and Tirzah.

2 And they stood before Moses and before Eleazar the priest and before the leaders and all the congregation, at the doorway of the tent of meeting, saying,

3 "Our father [a]died in the wilderness, yet he was not among the company of those who gathered themselves together against the LORD in the company of Korah; but he died in his own sin, and [b]he had no sons.

4 "Why should the name of our father be withdrawn from among his family because he had no son? Give us a possession among our father's brothers."

5 [a]And Moses brought their case before the LORD.

6 Then the LORD spoke to Moses, saying,

7 "[a]The daughters of Zelophehad are right in *their* statements. You shall surely give them a hereditary possession among their father's brothers, and you shall transfer the inheritance of their father to them.

8 "Further, you shall speak to the sons of Israel, saying, 'If a man dies and has no son, then you shall transfer his inheritance to his daughter.

9 'And if he has no daughter, then you shall give his inheritance to his brothers.

10 'And if he has no brothers, then you shall give his inheritance to his father's brothers.

11 'And if his father has no brothers, then you shall give his inheritance to his nearest relative in his own family, and he shall possess it; and it shall be a [a]statutory ordinance to the sons of Israel, just as the LORD commanded Moses.' "

12 [a]Then the LORD said to Moses, "Go up to this [b]mountain of Abarim, and see the land which I have given to the sons of Israel.

13 "And when you have seen it, you too [a]shall be gathered to your people, [b]as Aaron your brother [1]was;

14 for in the wilderness of Zin, during the strife of the congregation, [a]you rebelled against My [1]command [2]to treat Me as holy before their eyes at the water." (These are the waters of Meribah of Kadesh in the wilderness of Zin.)

Joshua to Succeed Moses

15 Then Moses spoke to the LORD, saying,

16 "[a]May the LORD, the God of the spirits of all flesh, appoint a man over the congregation,

17 who [a]will go out [1]and come in before them, and who will lead them out and [2]bring them in, that the congregation of the LORD may not be [b]like sheep which have no shepherd."

18 So the LORD said to Moses, "[1]Take Joshua the son of Nun, a man [a]in whom is the Spirit, and [b]lay your hand on him;

19 and have him stand before Eleazar the priest and before all the congregation; and [a]commission him in their sight.

20 "And you shall put some of your [1]authority on him, in order that all the congregation of the sons of Israel may obey *him.*

21 "Moreover, he shall stand before Eleazar the priest, who shall inquire for him [a]by the judgment of the Urim before the LORD. At his [1]command they shall go out and at his [1]command they shall come in, *both* he and the sons of Israel with him, even all the congregation."

22 And Moses did just as the LORD commanded him; and he took Joshua and set him before Eleazar the priest, and before all the congregation.

23 Then he laid his hands on him and [a]commissioned him, just as the LORD had spoken [1]through Moses.

Laws for Offerings

28 THEN the LORD spoke to Moses, saying,

2 "Command the sons of Israel and say to them, 'You shall [1]be careful to present My offering, My [a]food for My offerings by fire, of a soothing aroma to Me, at their appointed time.'

3 "[a]And you shall say to them, 'This is the offering by fire which you shall offer to the LORD; two male lambs one year old without defect *as* a continual burnt offering every day.

59 [a]Ex. 2:1, 2; 6:20
60 [a]Num. 3:2
61 [a]Lev. 10:1, 2; Num. 3:4
62 [a]Num. 3:39 [b]Num. 1:47 [c]Num. 18:23, 24
64 [a]Num. 14:29-35; Deut. 2:14-16; Heb. 3:17
65 [1]Or, *to* [a]Num. 14:26-35; Ps. 90:3-10; 1 Cor. 10:5 [b]Deut. 1:36; Josh. 14:6-10
1 [a]Num. 26:33; 36:1 [b]Num. 26:33
3 [a]Num. 26:64, 65 [b]Num. 26:33
5 [a]Num. 9:8; 27:21
7 [a]Num. 36:2; Josh. 17:4
11 [a]Num. 35:29
12 [a]Deut. 3:23-27; 32:48-52 [b]Num. 33:47, 48
13 [1]Lit., *was gathered* [a]Num. 31:2 [b]Num. 20:24, 28; Deut. 10:6
14 [1]Lit., *mouth* [2]Lit., *for My sanctity* [a]Num. 20:12; Deut. 32:51; Ps. 106:32
16 [a]Num. 16:22
17 [1]Lit., *before them and who will* [2]Lit., *who will bring* [a]Deut. 31:2; 2 Chr. 1:10 [b]1 Kin. 22:17; Ezek. 34:5; Matt. 9:36; Mark 6:34
18 [1]Lit., *Take for yourself* [a]Num. 11:25-29; Deut. 34:9 [b]Num. 27:23
19 [a]Deut. 3:28; 31:3, 7, 8, 23
20 [1]Lit., *majesty*
21 [1]Lit., *mouth* [a]Ex. 28:30; 1 Sam. 28:6
23 [1]Lit., *by the hand of* [a]Deut. 31:23
2 [1]Lit., *watch* [a]Lev. 3:11
3 [a]Ex. 29:38-42

4 'You shall offer the one lamb in the
morning, and the other lamb you shall
offer [1]at twilight;
5 also [a]a tenth of an ephah of fine
flour for a [b]grain offering, mixed with a
fourth of a hin of beaten oil.
6 'It is a continual burnt offering
which was ordained in Mount Sinai as a
soothing aroma, an offering by fire to the
LORD.
7 'Then the libation with it *shall be* a
fourth of a hin for each lamb, [a]in the
holy place you shall pour out a libation
of strong drink to the LORD.
8 'And the other lamb you shall offer
[1]at twilight; as the grain offering of the
morning and as its libation, you shall
offer it, an offering by fire, a soothing
aroma to the LORD.
9 'Then on the sabbath day two male
lambs one year old without defect, and
two-tenths *of an* [1]*ephah* of fine flour
mixed with oil as a grain offering, and its
libation:
10 '*This is* the burnt offering of every
sabbath in addition to the [a]continual
burnt offering and its libation.
11 'Then [a]at the beginning of each of
your months you shall present a burnt
offering to the LORD; two [1]bulls and one
ram, seven male lambs one year old
without defect,
12 [a]and three-tenths *of an* [1]*ephah* of
fine flour for a grain offering, mixed with
oil, for each bull; and two-tenths of fine
flour for a grain offering, mixed with oil,
for the one ram;
13 and a tenth *of an* [1]*ephah* of fine
flour mixed with oil for a grain offering
for each lamb, for a burnt offering of a
soothing aroma, an offering by fire to the
LORD.
14 'And their libations shall be half a
hin of wine for a bull and a third of a hin
for the ram and a fourth of a hin for a
lamb; this is the burnt offering of each
month throughout the months of the
year.
15 'And one male goat for a sin offering to the LORD; it shall be offered with
its libation in addition to the [a]continual
burnt offering.
16 '[a]Then on the fourteenth day of the
first month shall be the LORD's Passover.
17 'And [a]on the fifteenth day of this
month *shall be* a [b]feast, unleavened
bread *shall be* eaten for seven days.
18 'On the [a]first day *shall be* a holy
convocation; you shall do no laborious
work.
19 'And you shall present an offering
by fire, a burnt offering to the LORD:
two [1]bulls and one ram and seven male
lambs one year old, [a]having them without defect.
20 'And for their grain offering, you
shall offer fine flour mixed with oil:
three-tenths *of an* [1]*ephah* for a bull and
two-tenths for the ram.
21 'A tenth *of an* [1]*ephah* you shall offer
for [2]each of the seven lambs,
22 and one male goat for a [a]sin offering, to make atonement for you.
23 'You shall present these besides [a]the
burnt offering of the morning, which is
for a continual burnt offering.
24 'After this manner you shall present
daily, for seven days, [a]the food of the
offering by fire, of a soothing aroma to
the LORD; it shall be presented with its
libation in addition to the [b]continual
burnt offering.
25 'And on the seventh day you shall
have a holy convocation; [a]you shall do
no laborious work.
26 'Also on [a]the day of the first fruits,
when you present a new grain offering to
the LORD in your *Feast of* Weeks, you
shall have a holy convocation; [b]you shall
do no laborious work.
27 'And you shall offer a burnt offering
for a soothing aroma to the LORD, two
young bulls, one ram, seven male lambs
one year old,
28 and their grain offering, fine flour
mixed with oil, three-tenths *of an* [1]*ephah*
for each bull, two-tenths for the one
ram,
29 a tenth for [1]each of the seven
lambs,
30 one male goat to make atonement
for you.
31 '[a]Besides the continual burnt offering and its grain offering, you shall
present *them* with their libations. They
shall be [1]without defect.

Offerings of the Seventh Month

29 '[a]NOW in the seventh month, on
the first day of the month, you
shall also have a holy convocation; [b]you
shall do no laborious work. It will be to
you a day for blowing trumpets.
2 'And you shall offer a burnt offering
as a soothing aroma to the LORD: one
[1]bull, one ram, *and* seven male lambs
one year old without defect;
3 also their grain offering, fine flour
mixed with oil, three-tenths *of an* [1]*ephah*
for the bull, two-tenths for the ram,
4 and one-tenth for [1]each of the
seven lambs.
5 'And *offer* one male goat for a sin
offering, to make atonement for you,
6 [a]besides the burnt offering of the
new moon, and its grain offering, and
the [b]continual burnt offering and its
grain offering, and their libations, according to their ordinance, for a soothing aroma, an offering by fire to the
LORD.
7 'Then on [a]the tenth day of this
seventh month you shall have a holy
convocation, and you shall humble yourselves; you shall not do any work.
8 'And you shall present a burnt
offering to the LORD *as* a soothing
aroma: one bull, one ram, seven male
lambs one year old, [a]having them without defect;
9 and their grain offering, fine flour
mixed with oil, three-tenths *of an* [1]*ephah*
for the bull, two-tenths for the one ram,
10 a tenth for each of the seven lambs;

4 [1]Lit., *between the two evenings*
5 [a]Ex. 16:36; Num. 15:4 [b]Lev. 2:1
7 [a]Ex. 29:42
8 [1]Lit., *between the two evenings*
9 [1]I.e., Approx. one bu.
10 [a]Num. 28:3
11 [1]Lit., *bulls of the herd* [a]Num. 10:10; Ezek. 46:6, 7
12 [1]I.e., Approx. one bu. [a]Num. 15:4-12
13 [1]I.e., Approx. one bu.
15 [a]Num. 28:3
16 [a]Ex. 12:1-20; Lev. 23:5-8; Deut. 16:1-8
17 [a]Lev. 23:6 [b]Ex. 23:15; 34:18; Deut. 16:3-8
18 [a]Lev. 23:7
19 [1]Or, *bulls of the herd* [a]Deut. 15:21
20 [1]I.e., Approx. one bu.
21 [1]I.e., Approx. one bu. [2]Lit., *each lamb*
22 [a]Lev. 16:18; Rom. 8:3; Gal. 4:4f.
23 [a]Num. 28:3
24 [a]Lev. 3:11 [b]Num. 28:3
25 [a]Num. 28:18
26 [a]Ex. 23:16; 34:22; Lev. 23:15-21; Deut. 16:9-12 [b]Num. 28:18
28 [1]I.e., Approx. one bu.
29 [1]Lit., *each lamb*
31 [1]Lit., *without defect to you* [a]Num. 28:3

1 [a]Ex. 23:16; 34:22; Lev. 23:23-25 [b]Num. 28:26
2 [1]Or, *bull of a herd*, and so throughout the ch.
3 [1]I.e., Approx. one bu.
4 [1]Lit., *each lamb*, and so throughout the ch.
6 [a]Num. 28:27 [b]Num. 28:3
7 [a]Lev. 16:29-34; 23:26-32
8 [a]Lev. 22:20; Deut. 15:21; 17:1
9 [1]I.e., Approx. one bu.

11 one male goat for a sin offering, besides [a]the sin offering of atonement and [b]the continual burnt offering and its grain offering, and their libations.

12 'Then on [a]the fifteenth day of the seventh month you shall have a holy convocation; you [b]shall do no laborious work, and you shall observe a feast to the LORD for seven days.

13 'And you shall present a burnt offering, an offering by fire as a soothing aroma to the LORD: thirteen bulls, two rams, fourteen male lambs one year old, which are without defect,

14 and their grain offering, fine flour mixed with oil, three-tenths *of an* [1]*ephah* for [2]each of the thirteen bulls, two-tenths for [3]each of the two rams,

15 and a tenth for each of the fourteen lambs;

16 and one male goat for a sin offering, [a]besides the continual burnt offering, its grain offering and its libation.

17 'Then on [a]the second day: twelve bulls, two rams, fourteen male lambs one year old without defect;

18 and their grain offering and their libations for the bulls, for the rams and for the lambs, by their number [a]according to the ordinance;

19 and one male goat for a sin offering, [a]besides the continual burnt offering and its grain offering, and their libations.

20 'Then on the third day: eleven bulls, two rams, fourteen male lambs one year old without defect;

21 and their grain offering and their libations for the bulls, for the rams and for the lambs, by their number according to the ordinance;

22 and one male goat for a sin offering, besides the continual burnt offering and its grain offering and its libation.

23 'Then on the fourth day: ten bulls, two rams, fourteen male lambs one year old without defect;

24 their grain offering and their libations for the bulls, for the rams and for the lambs, by their number according to the ordinance;

25 and one male goat for a sin offering, besides the continual burnt offering, its grain offering and its libation.

26 'Then on the fifth day: nine bulls, two rams, fourteen male lambs one year old [a]without defect;

27 and their grain offering and their libations for the bulls, for the rams and for the lambs, by their number according to the ordinance;

28 and one male goat for a sin offering, besides the continual burnt offering and its grain offering and its libation.

29 'Then on the sixth day: eight bulls, two rams, fourteen male lambs one year old without defect;

30 and their grain offering and their libations for the bulls, for the rams and for the lambs, by their number according to the ordinance;

31 and one male goat for a sin offering, besides the continual burnt offering, its grain offering and its libations.

11 [a]Lev. 16:3, 5 [b]Num. 28:3
12 [a]Lev. 23:33-35; Deut. 16:13-15 [b]Num. 29:1
14 [1]I.e., Approx. one bu. [2]Lit., *each bull* [3]Lit., *each ram*
16 [a]Num. 28:3
17 [a]Lev. 23:36
18 [a]Lev. 2:1-16
19 [a]Num. 28:8
26 [a]Heb. 7:26
35 [a]Lev. 23:36
39 [1]Lit., *vows* [a]Lev. 23:2
40 [1]Ch. 30:1 in Heb.
1 [a]Num. 1:4, 16; 7:2
2 [a]Deut. 23:21-23; Matt. 5:33
4 [1]Lit., *is silent to her,* and so throughout the ch.
6 [1]Lit., *be to a husband* [2]Lit., *her vows are on her*

32 'Then on the seventh day: seven bulls, two rams, fourteen male lambs one year old without defect;

33 and their grain offering and their libations for the bulls, for the rams and for the lambs, by their number according to the ordinance;

34 and one male goat for a sin offering, besides the continual burnt offering, its grain offering and its libation.

35 '[a]On the eighth day you shall have a solemn assembly; you shall do no laborious work.

36 'But you shall present a burnt offering, an offering by fire, as a soothing aroma to the LORD: one bull, one ram, seven male lambs one year old without defect;

37 their grain offering and their libations for the bull, for the ram and for the lambs, by their number according to the ordinance;

38 and one male goat for a sin offering, besides the continual burnt offering and its grain offering and its libation.

39 'You shall present these to the LORD at your [a]appointed times, besides your [1]votive offerings and your freewill offerings, for your burnt offerings and for your grain offerings and for your libations and for your peace offerings.' "

40 [1]And Moses spoke to the sons of Israel in accordance with all that the LORD had commanded Moses.

The Law of Vows

30 THEN Moses spoke to [a]the heads of the tribes of the sons of Israel, saying, "This is the word which the LORD has commanded.

2 "[a]If a man makes a vow to the LORD, or takes an oath to bind himself with a binding obligation, he shall not violate his word; he shall do according to all that proceeds out of his mouth.

3 "Also if a woman makes a vow to the LORD, and binds herself by an obligation in her father's house in her youth,

4 and her father hears her vow and her obligation by which she has bound herself, and her father [1]says nothing to her, then all her vows shall stand, and every obligation by which she has bound herself shall stand.

5 "But if her father should forbid her on the day he hears *of it,* none of her vows or her obligations by which she has bound herself shall stand; and the LORD will forgive her because her father had forbidden her.

6 "However, if she should [1]marry while [2]under her vows or the rash statement of her lips by which she has bound herself,

7 and her husband hears of it and says nothing to her on the day he hears *it,* then her vows shall stand and her obligations by which she has bound herself shall stand.

8 "But if on the day her husband hears *of it,* he forbids her, then he shall

annul her vow which [1]she is under and
the rash statement of her lips by which
she has bound herself; and the LORD
will forgive her.
9"But the vow of a widow or of a
divorced woman, everything by which
she has bound herself, shall stand
against her.
10"However, if she vowed in her husband's house, or bound herself by an
obligation with an oath,
11 and her husband heard *it,* but said
nothing to her *and* did not forbid her,
then all her vows shall stand, and every
obligation by which she bound herself
shall stand.
12"But if her husband indeed annuls
them on the day he hears *them,* then
whatever proceeds out of her lips concerning her vows or concerning the
obligation of herself, shall not stand; her
husband has annulled them, and the
LORD will forgive her.
13"Every vow and every binding oath
to humble herself, her husband may
confirm it or her husband may annul it.
14"But if her husband indeed says
nothing to her from day to day, then he
confirms all her vows or all her obligations which are on her; he has confirmed
them, because he said nothing to her on
the day he heard them.
15"But if he indeed annuls them after
he has heard them, then he shall bear her
guilt."
16 These are the statutes which the
LORD commanded Moses, *as* between a
man and his wife, *and as* between a
father and his daughter, *while she is* in
her youth in her father's house.

The Slaughter of Midian

31 THEN the LORD spoke to Moses,
saying,
2"[a]Take full vengeance for the sons of
Israel on the Midianites; afterward you
will be [b]gathered to your people."
3 And Moses spoke to the people,
saying, "Arm men from among you for
the war, that they may [1]go against
Midian, to execute [a]the LORD'S vengeance on Midian.
4"A thousand from each tribe of all
the tribes of Israel you shall send to the
war."
5 So there were [1]furnished from the
thousands of Israel, a thousand from
each tribe, twelve thousand armed for
war.
6 And Moses sent them, a thousand
from each tribe, to the war, and Phinehas the son of Eleazar the priest, to the
war with them, [a]and the holy vessels and
[b]the trumpets for the alarm in his hand.
7 So they made war against Midian,
just as the LORD had commanded Moses, and [a]they killed every male.
8 And they killed the kings of Mid-
ian along with the *rest of* their slain: [a]Evi
and Rekem and [b]Zur and Hur and
Reba, the five kings of Midian; they also
killed [c]Balaam the son of Beor with the
sword.
9 And the sons of Israel captured the
women of Midian and their little ones;
and all their cattle and all their flocks
and all their goods, they plundered.
10 Then they burned all their cities
where they lived and all their camps with
fire.
11 And [a]they took all the spoil and all
the prey, both of man and of beast.
12 And they brought the captives and
the prey and the spoil to Moses, and to
Eleazar the priest and to the congregation of the sons of Israel, to the camp at
the plains of Moab, which are by the
Jordan opposite Jericho.
13 And Moses and Eleazar the priest
and all the leaders of the congregation
went out to meet them outside the camp.
14 And Moses was angry with the
officers of the army, the captains of
thousands and the captains of hundreds,
who had come from service in the war.
15 And Moses said to them, "Have
you [1]spared [a]all the women?
16"[a]Behold, these [1]caused the sons of
Israel, through the [2]counsel of [b]Balaam,
to [3]trespass against the LORD in the
matter of Peor, so the plague was among
the congregation of the LORD.
17"[a]Now therefore, kill every male
among the little ones, and kill every
woman who has known man [1]intimately.
18"But all the [1]girls who have not
known man [2]intimately, [3]spare for yourselves.
19"[a]And you, camp outside the camp
seven days; whoever has killed any
person, and whoever has touched any
slain, purify yourselves, you and your
captives, on the third day and on the
seventh day.
20"And you shall purify for yourselves
every garment and every article of
[1]leather and all the work of goats' *hair,*
and all articles of wood."
21 Then Eleazar the priest said to the
men of war who had gone to battle,
"This is the statute of the law which the
LORD has commanded Moses:
22 only the gold and the silver, the
bronze, the iron, the tin and the lead,
23 everything that can stand the fire,
you shall pass through the fire, and it
shall be clean, but it shall be purified
with [a]water for impurity. But whatever
cannot stand the fire you shall pass
through the water.
24"And you shall wash your clothes on
the seventh day and be clean, and afterward you may enter the camp."

Division of the Booty

25 Then the LORD spoke to Moses,
saying,
26"You and Eleazar the priest and the
heads of the fathers' *households* of the
congregation, take a count of the booty
[1]that was captured, both of man and of
animal;
27 and [a]divide the booty between the
warriors who went out to battle and all
the congregation.

8 [1]Lit., *is on her*
2 [a]Num. 25:1, 16, 17 [b]Num. 20:24, 26; 27:13
3 [1]Lit., *be* [a]Lev. 26:25
5 [1]Lit., *delivered*
6 [a]Num. 14:44 [b]Num. 10:8, 9
7 [a]Deut. 20:13; Judg. 21:11; 1 Kin. 11:15, 16
8 [a]Josh. 13:21 [b]Num. 25:15 [c]Num. 31:16; Josh. 13:22
11 [a]Deut. 20:14
15 [1]Lit., *let . . . live* [a]Deut. 20:14
16 [1]Lit., *were to* [2]Lit., *word* [3]Possibly, *defect from the Lord* [a]Num. 25:1-9 [b]Num. 31:8
17 [1]Lit., *by lying with a man* [a]Deut. 7:2; 20:16-18
18 [1]Lit., *female children* [2]Lit., *by lying with a man* [3]Lit., *keep alive*
19 [a]Num. 19:11-22
20 [1]Or, *skin*
23 [a]Num. 19:9, 17
26 [1]Lit., *of captives*
27 [a]Josh. 22:8

28"[a]And levy a tax for the LORD from
the men of war who went out to battle,
one [1]in five hundred of the persons and
of the cattle and of the donkeys and of
the sheep;
29 take it from their half and give it to
Eleazar the priest, as an [1]offering to the
LORD.
30"And from the sons of Israel's half,
you shall take one drawn out of every
fifty of the persons, of the cattle, of the
donkeys and of the sheep, from all the
animals, and give them to the Levites
who [a]keep charge of the tabernacle of
the LORD."
31 And Moses and Eleazar the priest
did just as the LORD had commanded
Moses.
32 Now the booty that remained from
the spoil which the [1]men of war had
plundered was 675,000 sheep,
33 and 72,000 cattle,
34 and 61,000 donkeys,
35 and of human beings, of the
women who had not known man [1]inti-
mately, all the persons were 32,000.
36 And the half, the portion of those
who went out to war, was *as follows:* the
number of sheep was 337,500,
37 and the LORD's levy of the sheep
was 675,
38 and the cattle were 36,000, from
which the LORD's levy was 72.
39 And the donkeys were 30,500, from
which the LORD's levy was 61.
40 And the human beings were
16,000, from whom the LORD's levy was
32 persons.
41 And Moses gave the levy *which was*
the LORD's offering to Eleazar the priest,
just [a]as the LORD had commanded Moses.
42 As for the sons of Israel's half,
which Moses [1]separated from the men
who had gone to war—
43 now the congregation's half was
337,500 sheep,
44 and 36,000 cattle,
45 and 30,500 donkeys,
46 and the human beings were
16,000—
47 and from the sons of Israel's half,
Moses took one drawn out of every fifty,
both of man and of animals, and gave
them to the Levites, who kept charge of
the tabernacle of the LORD, just as the
LORD had commanded Moses.
48 Then the officers who were over the
thousands of the army, the captains of
thousands and the captains of hundreds,
approached Moses;
49 and they said to Moses, "Your
servants have taken a census of men of
war who are in our charge, and no man
of us is missing.
50"So we have brought as an offering
to the LORD what each man found,
articles of gold, armlets and bracelets,
signet rings, earrings and necklaces, [a]to
make atonement for ourselves before the
LORD."
51 And Moses and Eleazar the priest
took the gold from them, all kinds of
wrought articles.
52 And all the gold of the offering
which they offered up to the LORD, from
the captains of thousands and the captains of hundreds, was 16,750 shekels.
53 [a]The men of war had taken booty,
every man for himself.
54 So Moses and Eleazar the priest
took the gold from the captains of
thousands and of hundreds, and brought
it to the tent of meeting as [a]a memorial
for the sons of Israel before the LORD.

Reuben and Gad Settle in Gilead

32 NOW the sons of Reuben and
the sons of Gad had an [a]exceed-
ingly large number of livestock. So when
they saw the land of [b]Jazer and the land
of Gilead, that [1]it was indeed a place
suitable for livestock,
2 the sons of Gad and the sons of
Reuben came and spoke to Moses and to
Eleazar the priest and to the leaders of
the congregation, saying,
3"[a]Ataroth, Dibon, Jazer, Nimrah,
Heshbon, Elealeh, Sebam, Nebo and
Beon,
4 the land [a]which the LORD [1]con-
quered before the congregation of Israel,
is a land for livestock; and your servants
have livestock."
5 And they said, "If we have found
favor in your sight, let this land be given
to your servants as a possession; do not
take us across the Jordan."
6 But Moses said to the sons of Gad
and to the sons of Reuben, "Shall your
brothers go to war while you yourselves
sit here?
7"[a]Now why are you [1]discouraging
the sons of Israel from crossing over into
the land which the LORD has given
them?
8"[1]This is what your fathers did when
I sent them from [a]Kadesh-barnea to see
the land.
9"For when they went up to [a]the
[1]valley of Eshcol and saw the land, they
[2]discouraged the sons of Israel so that
they did not go into the land which the
LORD had given them.
10"So [a]the LORD's anger burned in
that day, and He swore, saying,
11 '[a]None of the men who came up
from Egypt, from twenty years old and
upward, shall see the land which I swore
to Abraham, to Isaac and to Jacob; for
they did not follow Me fully,
12 except Caleb the son of Jephunneh
the Kenizzite and Joshua the son of
Nun, [a]for they have followed the LORD
fully.'
13"[a]So the LORD's anger burned
against Israel, and He made them wander in the wilderness forty years, until
the entire generation of those who had
done evil in the sight of the LORD was
destroyed.
14"Now behold, you have risen up in
your fathers' place, a brood of sinful

28 [1]Lit., *soul from* [a]Num. 18:21-30
29 [1]Lit., *heave offering,* and so throughout the ch.
30 [a]Num. 3:7, 8, 25, 26, 31, 36, 37; 18:3, 4
32 [1]Lit., *people*
35 [1]Lit., *by lying with a man*
41 [a]Num. 5:9, 10; 18:19
42 [1]Or, *divided*
50 [a]Ex. 30:12-16
53 [a]Num. 31:32; Deut. 20:14
54 [a]Ex. 30:16
1 [1]Lit., *behold, the place, a place for* [a]Ex. 12:38 [b]Num. 21:32
3 [a]Num. 32:34-38
4 [1]Lit., *smote* [a]Num. 21:34
7 [1]Lit., *restraining the hearts of* [a]Num. 13:27-14:4
8 [1]Lit., *Thus your fathers* [a]Num. 13:3, 26; Deut. 1:19-25
9 [1]Or, *wadi* [2]Lit., *restrained the hearts of* [a]Num. 13:24; Deut. 1:24
10 [a]Num. 14:11f.; Deut. 1:34
11 [a]Num. 14:28-30
12 [a]Deut. 1:36; Josh. 14:8f.
13 [a]Num. 14:33-35

men, to add still more to the burning
[a]anger of the LORD against Israel.
15"For if you [a]turn away from following Him, He will once more abandon
them in the wilderness; and you will
destroy all these people."
16 Then they came near to him and
said, "We will build here sheepfolds for
our livestock and cities for our little
ones;
17 [a]but we ourselves will be armed
ready *to go* before the sons of Israel,
until we have brought them to their
place, while our little ones live in the
fortified cities because of the inhabitants
of the land.
18"[a]We will not return to our homes
until every one of the sons of Israel has
possessed his inheritance.
19"For we will not have an inheritance
with them on the other side of the
Jordan and beyond, because our inheritance has fallen to us [a]on this side of the
Jordan toward the east."
20 [a]So Moses said to them, "If you
will do [1]this, if you will arm yourselves
before the LORD for the war,
21 and all of you armed men cross
over the Jordan before the LORD until
He has driven His enemies out from
before Him,
22 [a]and the land is subdued before the
LORD, then afterward you shall return
and be free of obligation toward the
LORD and toward Israel, and this land
shall be yours for a possession before the
LORD.
23"But if you will not do so, behold,
you have sinned against the LORD, and
be sure [a]your sin will find you out.
24"Build yourselves cities for your
little ones, and sheepfolds for your
sheep; and [a]do [1]what you have promised."
25 And the sons of Gad and the sons
of Reuben spoke to Moses, saying,
"Your servants will do just as my lord
commands.
26"[a]Our little ones, our wives, our
livestock and all our cattle shall [1]remain
there in the cities of Gilead;
27 while your servants, everyone who
is armed for war, will [a]cross over in the
presence of the LORD to battle, just as
my lord says."
28 So Moses gave command concerning them to Eleazar the priest, and to
Joshua the son of Nun, and to the heads
of the fathers' *households* of the tribes of
the sons of Israel.
29 And Moses said to them, "If the
sons of Gad and the sons of Reuben,
everyone who is armed for battle, will
cross with you over the Jordan in the
presence of the LORD, and the land will
be subdued before you, then you shall
give them the land of Gilead for a
possession;
30 but if they will not cross over with
you armed, they shall have possessions
among you in the land of Canaan."
31 And the sons of Gad and the sons
of Reuben answered, saying, "As the
LORD has said to your servants, so we
will do.
32"We ourselves will cross over armed
in the presence of the LORD into the land
of Canaan, and the possession of our
inheritance *shall remain* with us across
the Jordan."
33 [a]So Moses gave to them, to the
sons of Gad and to the sons of Reuben
and to the half-tribe of Joseph's son
Manasseh, the kingdom of Sihon, king
of the Amorites and the kingdom of Og,
the king of Bashan, the land with its
cities with *their* [1]territories, the cities of
the surrounding land.
34 And the sons of Gad built Dibon
and Ataroth and [a]Aroer,
35 and Atroth-shophan and Jazer and
Jogbehah,
36 and [a]Beth-nimrah and Beth-haran
as fortified cities, and sheepfolds for
sheep.
37 And the sons of Reuben built
Heshbon and Elealeh and Kiriathaim,
38 and [a]Nebo and Baal-meon—*their*
names being changed—and Sibmah, and
they gave *other* names to the cities which
they built.
39 And the sons of [a]Machir the son of
Manasseh went to Gilead and took it,
and dispossessed the Amorites who were
in it.
40 So Moses gave [a]Gilead to Machir
the son of Manasseh, and he lived in it.
41 And Jair the son of Manasseh went
and took its [1]towns, and called them
[2a]Havvoth-jair.
42 And Nobah went and took Kenath
and its villages, and called it Nobah
after [a]his own name.

Review of the Journey from Egypt to Jordan

33 THESE are the journeys of the
sons of Israel, by which they
came out from the land of Egypt by their
armies, under [a]the [1]leadership of Moses
and Aaron.
2 And Moses recorded their starting
places according to their journeys by the
[1]command of the LORD, and these are
their journeys according to their starting
places.
3 [a]And they journeyed from Rameses in the first month, on the fifteenth
day of the first month; on the [1]next day
after the Passover the sons of Israel
[b]started out [2]boldly in the sight of all the
Egyptians,
4 while the Egyptians were burying
all their first-born whom the LORD had
struck down among them. The LORD
had also executed judgments [a]on their
gods.
5 Then [a]the sons of Israel journeyed
from Rameses, and camped in Succoth.
6 [a]And they journeyed from Succoth,
and camped in Etham, which is on the
edge of the wilderness.
7 [a]And they journeyed from Etham,
and turned back to Pi-hahiroth, which

14 [a]Deut. 1:34f.
15 [a]Deut. 30:17, 18; 2 Chr. 7:19, 20
17 [a]Josh. 4:12, 13
18 [a]Josh. 22:1-4
19 [a]Josh. 12:1; 13:8
20 [1]Lit., *this thing* [a]Deut. 3:18
22 [a]Deut. 3:20
23 [a]Gen. 4:7; 44:16; Is. 59:12
24 [1]Lit., *that which has come out of your mouth* [a]Num. 30:2
26 [1]Lit., *be* [a]Josh. 1:14
27 [a]Josh. 4:12
33 [1]Lit., *borders* [a]Deut. 3:8-17; Josh. 12:1-6
34 [a]Deut. 2:36
36 [a]Num. 32:3
38 [a]Is. 46:1
39 [a]Gen. 50:23
40 [a]Deut. 3:12, 13, 15; Josh. 17:1
41 [1]Lit., *tent villages* [2]I.e., the towns of Jair [a]Deut. 3:14; Judg. 10:4
42 [a]2 Sam. 18:18; Ps. 49:11
1 [1]Lit., *hand* [a]Ps. 77:20; 105:26; Mic. 6:4
2 [1]Lit., *mouth*
3 [1]Lit., *morrow* [2]Lit., *with a high hand* [a]Ex. 12:37 [b]Ex. 14:8
4 [a]Ex. 12:12
5 [a]Ex. 12:37
6 [a]Ex. 13:20
7 [a]Ex. 14:1, 2

faces Baal-zephon; and they camped
before Migdol.
8 [a]And they journeyed [1]from before
Hahiroth, and passed through the midst
of the sea into the wilderness; and [b]they
went three days' journey in the wilderness of Etham, and camped at Marah.
9 [a]And they journeyed from Marah,
and came to Elim; and in Elim there
were twelve springs of water and seventy
palm trees; and they camped there.
10 And they journeyed from Elim,
and camped by the [1]Red Sea.
11 And they journeyed from the [1]Red
Sea, and camped in [a]the wilderness of
Sin.
12 And they journeyed from the wilderness of Sin, and camped at Dophkah.
13 And they journeyed from Dophkah, and camped at Alush.
14 And they journeyed from Alush,
and camped [a]at Rephidim; now it was
there that the people had no water to
drink.
15 And they journeyed from Rephidim, and camped in [a]the wilderness of
Sinai.
16 And they journeyed from the wilderness of Sinai, and camped at [a]Kib-
roth-hattaavah.
17 And they journeyed from Kibroth-
hattaavah, and camped at [a]Hazeroth.
18 And they journeyed from Hazeroth, and camped at Rithmah.
19 And they journeyed from Rithmah,
and camped at Rimmon-perez.
20 And they journeyed from Rimmon-
perez, and camped at [a]Libnah.
21 And they journeyed from Libnah,
and camped at Rissah.
22 And they journeyed from Rissah,
and camped in Kehelathah.
23 And they journeyed from Kehelathah, and camped at Mount Shepher.
24 And they journeyed from Mount
Shepher, and camped at Haradah.
25 And they journeyed from Haradah,
and camped at Makheloth.
26 And they journeyed from Makheloth, and camped at Tahath.
27 And they journeyed from Tahath,
and camped at Terah.
28 And they journeyed from Terah,
and camped at Mithkah.
29 And they journeyed from Mithkah,
and camped at Hashmonah.
30 And they journeyed from Hashmonah, and camped at [a]Moseroth.
31 And they journeyed from Mo-
seroth, and camped at Bene-jaakan.
32 And they journeyed from [a]Bene-
jaakan, and camped at Hor-haggidgad.
33 And they journeyed from Hor-
haggidgad, and camped at [a]Jotbathah.
34 And they journeyed from Jotbathah, and camped at Abronah.
35 And they journeyed from Abronah,
and camped at [a]Ezion-geber.
36 And they journeyed from Ezion-
geber, and camped in the wilderness of
[a]Zin, that is, Kadesh.
37 And they journeyed from Kadesh,
and camped at [a]Mount Hor, [b]at the edge
of the land of Edom.
38 [a]Then Aaron the priest went up to
Mount Hor at the [1]command of the
LORD, and died there, in the fortieth
year after the sons of Israel had come
from the land of Egypt on the first *day* in
the fifth month.
39 And Aaron was one hundred
twenty-three years old when he died on
Mount Hor.
40 Now the Canaanite, the king of
[a]Arad [1]who lived in the [2]Negev in the
land of Canaan, heard of the coming of
the sons of Israel.
41 Then they journeyed from Mount
Hor, and camped at Zalmonah.
42 And they journeyed from Zalmonah, and camped at Punon.
43 And they journeyed from Punon,
and camped at [a]Oboth.
44 And they journeyed from Oboth,
and camped at Iye-abarim, at the border
of Moab.
45 And they journeyed from Iyim, and
camped at Dibon-gad.
46 And they journeyed from Dibon-
gad, and camped at Almon-diblathaim.
47 And they journeyed from Almon-
diblathaim, and camped in the mountains of [a]Abarim, before Nebo.
48 And they journeyed from the
mountains of Abarim, and [a]camped in
the plains of Moab by the Jordan *opposite* Jericho.
49 And they camped by the Jordan,
from Beth-jeshimoth as far as [a]Abel-
shittim in the plains of Moab.

Law of Possessing the Land

50 Then the LORD spoke to Moses in
the plains of Moab by the Jordan *opposite* Jericho, saying,
51 "Speak to the sons of Israel and say
to them, '[a]When you cross over the
Jordan into the land of Canaan,
52 then you shall drive out all the
inhabitants of the land from before you,
and [a]destroy all their figured stones, and
destroy all their molten images and
demolish all their high places;
53 [a]and you shall take possession of
the land and live in it, for I have given
the land to you to possess it.
54 '[a]And you shall inherit the land by
lot according to your families; to the
larger you shall give more inheritance,
and to the smaller you shall give less
inheritance. Wherever the lot falls to
anyone, that shall be his. You shall
inherit according to the tribes of your
fathers.
55 'But if you do not drive out the
inhabitants of the land from before you,
then it shall come about that those
whom you let remain of them *will become* [a]as pricks in your eyes and as
thorns in your sides, and they shall
trouble you in the land in which you live.
56 'And it shall come about that as I
plan to do to them, so I will do to you.'"

8 [1]Many mss. read *from Pi-hahiroth* [a]Ex. 14:22 [b]Ex. 15:22, 23
9 [a]Ex. 15:27
10 [1]Lit., *Sea of Reeds*
11 [1]Lit., *Sea of Reeds* [a]Ex. 16:1
14 [a]Ex. 17:1
15 [a]Ex. 19:1
16 [a]Num. 11:34
17 [a]Num. 11:35
20 [a]Deut. 1:1
30 [a]Deut. 10:6
32 [a]Gen. 36:27; Deut. 10:6; 1 Chr. 1:42
33 [a]Deut. 10:7
35 [a]Deut. 2:8
36 [a]Num. 20:1
37 [a]Num. 20:22 [b]Num. 20:16
38 [1]Lit., *mouth* [a]Num. 20:28; Deut. 10:6
40 [1]Lit., *and he* [2]I.e., South country [a]Num. 21:1
43 [a]Num. 21:10, 11
47 [a]Num. 27:12
48 [a]Num. 22:1
49 [a]Num. 25:1
51 [a]Josh. 3:17
52 [a]Ex. 23:24; Lev. 26:1; Deut. 7:5; 12:3, 30; Ps. 106:34-36
53 [a]Deut. 11:31; 17:14; Josh. 21:43
54 [a]Num. 26:53-56
55 [a]Josh. 23:13

Instruction for Apportioning Canaan

34 THEN the LORD spoke to Moses, saying,

2"Command the sons of Israel and say to them, 'When you enter [a]the land of Canaan, this is the land that shall fall to you as an inheritance, *even the* land of Canaan according to its borders.

3 '[a]Your southern [1]sector shall [2]extend from the wilderness of Zin along the side of Edom, and your southern border shall [2]extend from the end of the Salt Sea [b]eastward.

4 'Then your border shall turn *direction* from the south to the ascent of Akrabbim, and [1]continue to Zin, and its [2]termination shall be to the south of [a]Kadesh-barnea; and it shall [3]reach Hazaraddar, and [1]continue to Azmon.

5 'And the border shall turn *direction* from Azmon to the brook of Egypt, and its termination shall be at [a]the sea.

6 'As for the western border, you shall have the Great Sea, that is, *its* [1]coastline; this shall be your west border.

7 '[a]And this shall be your north border: you shall draw your *border* line from the Great Sea to Mount Hor.

8 'You shall draw a line from Mount Hor to [a]the [1]Lebo-hamath, and the termination of the border shall be at Zedad;

9 and the border shall proceed to Ziphron, and its termination shall be at Hazar-enan. This shall be your north border.

10 'For your eastern border you shall also draw a line from Hazar-enan to Shepham,

11 and the border shall go down from Shepham to [a]Riblah on the east side of Ain; and the border shall go down and reach to the [1]slope on the east side of the Sea of [b]Chinnereth.

12 'And the border shall go down to the Jordan and its termination shall be at the Salt Sea. This shall be your land according to its borders all around.' "

13 So Moses commanded the sons of Israel, saying, "[a]This is the land that you are to apportion by lot among you as a possession, which the LORD has commanded to give to the nine and a half tribes.

14"[a]For the tribe of the sons of Reuben have received *theirs* according to their fathers' households, and the tribe of the sons of Gad according to their fathers' households, and the half-tribe of Manasseh have received their possession.

15"The two and a half tribes have received their possession across the Jordan opposite Jericho, eastward toward the sunrising."

16 Then the LORD spoke to Moses, saying,

17"[a]These are the names of the men who shall apportion the land to you for inheritance: Eleazar the priest and Joshua the son of Nun.

18"And you shall take one leader of every tribe to apportion the land for inheritance.

19"And these are the names of the men: of the tribe of [a]Judah, [b]Caleb the son of Jephunneh.

20"And of the tribe of the sons of [a]Simeon, Samuel the son of Ammihud.

21"Of the tribe of [a]Benjamin, Elidad the son of Chislon.

22"And of the tribe of the sons of Dan a leader, Bukki the son of Jogli.

23"Of the sons of Joseph: of the tribe of the sons of Manasseh a leader, Hanniel the son of Ephod.

24"And of the tribe of the sons of Ephraim a leader, Kemuel the son of Shiphtan.

25"And of the tribe of the sons of Zebulun a leader, Elizaphan the son of Parnach.

26"And of the tribe of the sons of Issachar a leader, Paltiel the son of Azzan.

27"And of the tribe of the sons of Asher a leader, Ahihud the son of Shelomi.

28"And of the tribe of the sons of Naphtali a leader, Pedahel the son of Ammihud."

29 These are those whom the LORD commanded to apportion the inheritance to the sons of Israel in the land of Canaan.

Cities for the Levites

35 [a]NOW the LORD spoke to Moses in the plains of Moab by the Jordan opposite Jericho, saying,

2"Command the sons of Israel that they give to the Levites from the inheritance of their possession, cities to live in; and you shall give to the Levites pasture lands around the cities.

3"And the cities shall be theirs to live in; and their pasture lands shall be for their cattle and for their herds and for all their beasts.

4"And the pasture lands of the cities which you shall give to the Levites *shall extend* from the wall of the city [1]outward a thousand cubits around.

5"You shall also measure outside the city on the east side two thousand cubits, and on the south side two thousand cubits, and on the west side two thousand cubits, and on the north side two thousand cubits, with the city in the center. This shall become theirs as pasture lands for the cities.

Cities of Refuge

6"And the cities which you shall give to the Levites *shall be* the [a]six cities of refuge, which you shall give for the manslayer to flee to; and in addition to them you shall give forty-two cities.

7"All the cities which you shall give to the Levites *shall be* [a]forty-eight cities, [1]together with their pasture lands.

8"[a]As for the cities which you shall give from the possession of the sons of

2 [a]Gen. 17:8; Ps. 78:54, 55; 105:11

3 [1]Lit., *side* [2]Lit., *be* [a]Josh. 15:1-3 [b]Josh. 15:5

4 [1]Lit., *pass along* [2]Lit., *goings out*, and so throughout the ch. [3]Lit., *go forth to* [a]Num. 32:8

5 [a]Josh. 15:4

6 [1]Lit., *border*

7 [a]Ezek. 47:15-17

8 [1]Or, *entrance of Hamath* [a]Josh. 13:5

11 [1]Lit., *shoulder* [a]2 Kin. 23:33 [b]Deut. 3:17; Josh. 13:27

13 [a]Gen. 15:18; Num. 26:52-56; Deut. 11:24; Josh. 14:1-5

14 [a]Num. 32:33

17 [a]Josh. 14:1, 2

19 [a]Gen. 29:35; Deut. 33:7; Ps. 60:7 [b]Num. 13:6, 30; 26:65; Deut. 1:36

20 [a]Gen. 29:33; 49:5; Ezek. 48:24

21 [a]Gen. 49:27; Deut. 33:12; Ps. 68:27

1 [a]Lev. 25:32-34

4 [1]Lit., *and outward*

6 [a]Josh. 20:7-9

7 [1]Lit., *them* [a]Josh. 21:41

8 [a]Lev. 25:32-34; Num. 26:54; 33:54; Josh. 21:1-42

Israel, you shall take more from the larger and you shall take less from the smaller; each shall give some of his cities to the Levites in proportion to his possession which he inherits."

9 Then the LORD spoke to Moses, saying,

10 "[a]Speak to the sons of Israel and say to them, 'When you cross the Jordan into the land of Canaan,

11 [a]then you shall select for yourselves cities to be your [b]cities of refuge, that the manslayer who has [1]killed any person [c]unintentionally may flee there.

12 'And [a]the cities shall be to you as a refuge from the avenger, so that the manslayer may not die until he stands before the congregation for [1]trial.

13 'And the cities which you are to give shall be your six cities of refuge.

14 'You [a]shall give three cities across the Jordan and three cities [1]in the land of Canaan; they are to be cities of refuge.

15 'These six cities shall be for refuge for the sons of Israel, and for the alien and for the sojourner among them; that anyone who [1]kills a person [a]unintentionally may flee there.

16 '[a]But if he struck him down with an iron object, so that he died, he is a murderer; the murderer shall surely be put to death.

17 'And if he struck him down with a stone in the hand, by which he may die, and *as a result* he died, he is a murderer; the murderer [a]shall surely be put to death.

18 'Or if he struck him with a wooden object in the hand, by which he may die, and *as a result* he died, he is a murderer; the murderer shall surely be put to death.

19 'The blood avenger himself shall put the murderer to death; he shall put him to death when he meets him.

20 'And [a]if he pushed him of hatred, or threw something at him [b]lying in wait and *as a result* he died,

21 or if he struck him down with his hand in enmity, and *as a result* he died, the one who struck him shall surely be put to death, he is a murderer; the blood avenger shall put the murderer to death when he meets him.

22 '[a]But if he pushed him suddenly without enmity, or threw something at him without lying in wait,

23 or with any [1]deadly object of stone, and without seeing it dropped on him so that he died, while he was not his enemy nor seeking his injury,

24 then [a]the congregation shall judge between the slayer and the blood avenger according to these ordinances.

25 'And the congregation shall deliver the manslayer from the hand of the blood avenger, and the congregation shall restore him to his city of refuge to which he fled; and he shall live in it until the death of the high priest who was anointed with the holy oil.

26 'But if the manslayer shall at any time go beyond the border of his city of refuge to which he may flee,

27 and the blood avenger finds him outside the border of his city of refuge, and the blood avenger kills the manslayer, he shall not be guilty of blood

28 because he should have remained in his city of refuge until the death of the high priest. But after the death of the high priest the manslayer shall return to the land of his possession.

29 'And these things shall be for a [a]statutory ordinance to you throughout your generations in all your dwellings.

30 '[a]If anyone kills a person, the murderer shall be put to death at the [1]evidence of witnesses, but [b]no person shall be put to death on the testimony of one witness.

31 'Moreover, you shall not take ransom for the life of a murderer who is guilty of death, but he shall surely be put to death.

32 'And you shall not take ransom for him who has fled to his city of refuge, that he may return to live in the land [1]before the death of the priest.

33 '[a]So you shall not pollute the land in which you are; for blood pollutes the land and no expiation can be made for the land for the blood that is shed on it, except [b]by the blood of him who shed it.

34 'And you shall not [a]defile the land in which you live, in the midst of which [b]I dwell; for I the LORD am dwelling in the midst of the sons of Israel.' "

Inheritance by Marriage

36 [a]AND the heads of the fathers' *households* of the family of the sons of Gilead, the son of Machir, the son of Manasseh, of the families of the sons of Joseph, came near and spoke before Moses and before the leaders, the heads of the fathers' *households* of the sons of Israel,

2 and they said, "The LORD commanded my lord to give the land by lot to the sons of Israel as an inheritance, and my lord [a]was commanded by the LORD to give the inheritance of Zelophehad our brother to his daughters.

3 "But if they [1]marry one of the sons of the *other* tribes of the sons of Israel, their inheritance will be withdrawn from the inheritance of our fathers and will be added to the inheritance of the tribe to which they belong; thus it will be withdrawn from our allotted inheritance.

4 "And when the [a]jubilee of the sons of Israel [1]comes, then their inheritance will be added to the inheritance of the tribe to which they belong; so their inheritance will be withdrawn from the inheritance of the tribe of our fathers."

5 Then Moses commanded the sons of Israel according to the [1]word of the LORD, saying, "The tribe of the sons of Joseph are right in *their* statements.

---

10 [a]Josh. 20:1-9

11 [1]Lit., *smote* [a]Deut. 19:1-13 [b]Josh. 20:2f. [c]Ex. 21:13; Lev. 4:2f., 22f.; Num. 35:22-25

12 [1]Lit., *judgment* [a]Deut. 19:4-6; Josh. 20:2, 3

14 [1]Lit., *you shall give in* [a]Deut. 4:41

15 [1]Lit., *smites* [a]Num. 35:11

16 [a]Ex. 21:12, 14; Lev. 24:17

17 [a]Num. 35:31

20 [a]Gen. 4:8; 2 Sam. 3:27; 20:10 [b]Ex. 21:14; Deut. 19:11

22 [a]Num. 35:11

23 [1]Lit., *by which he may die*

24 [a]Josh. 20:6

29 [a]Num. 27:11

30 [1]Lit., *mouth* [a]Num. 35:16 [b]Deut. 17:6; 19:15; Matt. 18:16; John 7:51; 8:17, 18

32 [1]Or, *until*

33 [a]Deut. 21:7, 8; Ps. 106:38 [b]Gen. 9:6

34 [a]Lev. 18:24, 25 [b]Num. 5:3

1 [a]Num. 27:1

2 [a]Num. 27:5-7

3 [1]Lit., *become wives to,* in this ch.

4 [1]Lit., *shall be* [a]Lev. 25:10

5 [1]Lit., *mouth*

6"[a]This is [1]what the LORD has commanded concerning the daughters of
Zelophehad, saying, 'Let them marry
[2]whom they wish; only they must marry
within the family of the tribe of their
father.'
7"Thus [a]no inheritance of the sons of
Israel shall [1]be transferred from tribe to
tribe, for the sons of Israel shall each
[2]hold to the inheritance of the tribe of
his fathers.
8"[a]And every daughter who comes
into possession of an inheritance of any
tribe of the sons of Israel, shall be wife
to one of the family of the tribe of her
father, so that the sons of Israel each
may possess the inheritance of his fathers.
9"Thus no inheritance shall [1]be transferred from one tribe to another tribe,
for the tribes of the sons of Israel shall
each [2]hold to his own inheritance."
10 Just as the LORD had commanded
Moses, so the daughters of Zelophehad
did:
11 [a]Mahlah, Tirzah, Hoglah, Milcah
and Noah, the daughters of Zelophehad
married their uncles' sons.
12 They married *those* from the families of the sons of Manasseh the son of
Joseph, and their inheritance [1]remained
with the tribe of the family of their
father.
13 [a]These are the commandments and
the ordinances which the LORD commanded to the sons of Israel through
Moses in the plains of Moab by the
Jordan *opposite* Jericho.

6 [1]Lit., *the thing which* [2]Lit., *to the good one in their eyes* [a]Num. 27:7
7 [1]Lit., *turn about* [2]Lit., *cleave* [a]1 Kin. 21:3
8 [a]1 Chr. 23:22
9 [1]Lit., *turn about* [2]Lit., *cleave*
11 [a]Num. 26:33
12 [1]Lit., *was*
13 [a]Lev. 26:46; 27:34; Num. 22:1

DEUTERONOMY

Israel's History after the Exodus

1 THESE are the words which Moses
spoke to all Israel [a]across the Jordan
in the wilderness, in the [b]Arabah opposite [1]Suph, between Paran and Tophel
and Laban and Hazeroth and Dizahab.
2 It is eleven days' *journey* from
[a]Horeb by the way of Mount [b]Seir to
[c]Kadesh-barnea.
3 And it came about in the [a]fortieth
year, on the first day of the eleventh
month, that Moses spoke to the children
of Israel, [b]according to all that the LORD
had commanded him *to give* to them,
4 after he had [1a]defeated Sihon the
king of the Amorites, who lived in
Heshbon, and [b]Og the king of Bashan,
who lived in [c]Ashtaroth [2]and Edrei.
5 Across the Jordan in the land of
Moab, Moses undertook to expound this
law, saying,
6"The LORD our God [a]spoke to us at
Horeb, saying, 'You have [1]stayed long
enough at this mountain.
7 'Turn and set your journey, and go
to [a]the hill country of the Amorites, and
to all their neighbors in the Arabah, in
the hill country and in the lowland and
in [b]the [1]Negev and by the seacoast, the
land of the Canaanites, and Lebanon, as
far as the great river, the river Euphrates.
8 'See, I have placed the land before
you; go in and possess the land which
the LORD [a]swore to give to your fathers,
to Abraham, to Isaac, and to Jacob, to
them and their [1]descendants after them.'
9"And I spoke to you at that time,
saying, '[a]I am not able to bear *the burden*
of you alone.
10 'The LORD your God has [a]multi-
plied you, and behold, you are this day
as the stars of heaven for multitude.
11 'May the LORD, the God of your
fathers, increase you a thousand-fold
more than you are, and bless you, [a]just
as He has [1]promised you!
12 'How can I alone bear the load and
burden of you and your strife?
13 '[1a]Choose wise and discerning and
experienced men from your tribes, and I
will appoint them as your heads.'
14"And you answered me and said,
'The thing which you have said to do is
good.'
15"So I took the heads of your tribes,
wise and experienced men, and [1]ap-
pointed them heads over you, leaders of
thousands, and [2]of hundreds, [2]of fifties
and [2]of tens, and officers for your tribes.
16"Then I charged your judges at that
time, saying, 'Hear *the cases* between
your [1]fellow countrymen, and [a]judge
righteously between a man and his [2]fel-
low countryman, or the alien who is with
him.
17 '[a]You shall not show partiality in
judgment; you shall hear the small and
the great alike. You shall [b]not fear [1]man,
for the judgment is God's. And [c]the case
that is too hard for you, you shall bring
to me, and I will hear it.'
18"[a]And I commanded you at that
time all the things that you should do.
19"Then we set out from [a]Horeb, and
went through all that [b]great and terrible
wilderness which you saw, on the way to
the [c]hill country of the Amorites, just as
the LORD our God had commanded us;
and we came to [d]Kadesh-barnea.
20"And I said to you, 'You have come
to the hill country of the Amorites which
the LORD our God is about to give us.
21 'See, the LORD your God has placed
the land before you; go up, take possession, as the LORD, the God of your
fathers, has spoken to you. [a]Do not fear
or be dismayed.'
22"[a]Then all of you approached me
and said, 'Let us send men before us,
that they may search out the land for us,
and bring back to us word of the way by

1 [1]Perhaps Red Sea [a]Deut. 4:46 [b]Deut. 2:8
2 [a]Ex. 3:1; 17:6 [b]Gen. 32:3 [c]Num. 13:26; 32:8; Deut. 9:23
3 [a]Num. 33:38 [b]Deut. 4:1, 2
4 [1]Lit., *smitten* [2]So with ancient versions; M.T. omits *and* [a]Num. 21:21-26; Deut. 2:26-35; Josh. 13:10; Neh. 9:22 [b]Num. 21:33-35; Josh. 13:12 [c]Josh. 12:4
6 [1]Lit., *dwelt* [a]Num. 10:11-13
7 [1]I.e., South country [a]Gen. 15:18; Deut. 11:24; Josh. 10:40 [b]Gen. 12:9
8 [1]Lit., *seed* [a]Gen. 12:7; 26:3; 28:13; Ex. 33:1; Num. 14:23; 32:11; Heb. 6:13, 14
9 [a]Ex. 18:18, 24; Num. 11:14
10 [a]Gen. 15:5; 22:17; Ex. 32:13; Deut. 7:7; 10:22; 26:5; 28:62
11 [1]Lit., *spoken to* [a]Deut. 1:8, 10
13 [1]Lit., *Give for yourselves* [a]Ex. 18:21
15 [1]Lit., *gave* [2]Lit., *leaders of*
16 [1]Lit., *brothers* [2]Lit., *brother* [a]Deut. 16:18; John 7:24
17 [1]Lit., *because of man* [a]Deut. 10:17; 16:19; 24:17; 2 Chr. 19:5, 6; Prov. 24:23-26; Acts 10:34; James 2:1, 9 [b]Prov. 29:25 [c]Ex. 18:22, 26
18 [a]Ex. 18:20
19 [a]Deut. 1:2 [b]Deut. 2:7; 8:15; 32:10; Jer. 2:6 [c]Deut. 1:7 [d]Deut. 1:2
21 [a]Josh. 1:6, 9
22 [a]Num. 13:1-3

which we should go up, and the cities
which we shall enter.'
23"And the thing pleased me and I
took twelve of your men, one man for
each tribe.
24"And [a]they turned and went up into
the hill country, and came to the valley
of Eshcol, and spied it out.
25"Then they took *some* of the fruit of
the land in their hands and brought it
down to us; and they brought us back a
report and said, 'It is a good land which
the LORD our God is about to give us.'
26"[a]Yet you were not willing to go up,
but [b]rebelled against the [1]command of
the LORD your God;
27 and [a]you grumbled in your tents
and said, 'Because the LORD hates us,
He has brought us out of the land of
Egypt to deliver us into the hand of the
Amorites to destroy us.
28 'Where can we go up? Our brethren
have made our hearts melt, saying, "The
people are bigger and taller than we; the
cities are large and fortified to heaven.
And besides, we saw [a]the sons of the
Anakim there." '
29"Then I said to you, 'Do not be
shocked, nor fear them.
30 'The LORD your God who goes
before you will [a]Himself fight on your
behalf, [1]just as He did for you in Egypt
before your eyes,
31 and in the wilderness where you
saw how [a]the LORD your God carried
you, just as a man carries his son, in all
the way which you have walked, until
you came to this place.'
32"But [1a]for all this, you did not trust
the LORD your God,
33 [a]who goes before you on *your* way,
[b]to seek out a place for you to encamp,
in fire by night and cloud by day, to
show you the way in which you should
go.
34"Then the LORD heard the sound of
your words, and He was angry and [a]took
an oath, saying,
35 '[a]Not one of these men, this evil
generation, shall see the good land which
I swore to give your fathers,
36 except Caleb the son of Jephunneh; he shall see it, and [a]to him and to
his sons I will give the land on which he
has set foot, because he has followed the
LORD fully.'
37"[a]The LORD was angry with me also
on your account, saying, '[b]Not even you
shall enter there.
38 'Joshua the son of Nun, who stands
before you, [a]he shall enter there; encourage him, for [b]he shall cause Israel to
inherit it.
39 'Moreover, [a]your little ones who
you said would become a prey, and your
sons, who this day have [b]no knowledge
of good or evil, shall enter there, and I
will give it to them, and they shall
possess it.
40 'But as for you, [a]turn around and
set out for the wilderness by the way to
the [1]Red Sea.'

41"[a]Then you answered and said to
me, 'We have sinned against the LORD;
we will indeed go up and fight, just as
the LORD our God commanded us.' And
every man of you girded on his weapons
of war, and regarded it as easy to go up
into the hill country.
42"[a]And the LORD said to me, 'Say to
them, "Do not go up, nor fight, for I am
not among you; lest you be [1]defeated
before your enemies." '
43"So I spoke to you, but you would
not listen. Instead [a]you rebelled against
the [1]command of the LORD, and acted
presumptuously and went up into the
hill country.
44"[a]And the Amorites who [1]lived in
that hill country came out against you,
and chased you [b]as bees do, and crushed
you from Seir to Hormah.
45"Then you returned and wept before
the LORD; but the [a]LORD did not listen
to your voice, nor give ear to you.
46"So you remained in [a]Kadesh many
days, [1]the days that you spent *there*.

Wanderings in the Wilderness

2 "[a]THEN we turned and set out for
the wilderness by the way to the
[1]Red Sea, as the LORD spoke to me, and
circled [b]Mount Seir for many days.
2"And the LORD spoke to me, saying,
3 'You have circled this mountain
long enough. *Now* turn north,
4 [a]and command the people, saying,
"You will pass through the [b]territory of
your brothers the sons of Esau who live
in Seir; and [c]they will be afraid of you.
So be very careful;
5 do not [1]provoke them, for I will
not give you any of their land, even *as
little as* a [2]footstep [a]because I have given
Mount Seir to Esau as a possession.
6"You shall buy food from them with
money so that you may eat, and you
shall also purchase water from them
with money so that you may drink.
7"For the LORD your God has
blessed you in all [1]that you have done;
He has known your [2]wanderings
through this [a]great wilderness. These
[b]forty years the LORD your God has
been with you; you have not lacked a
thing." '
8"So we passed beyond our brothers
the sons of Esau, who live in Seir, away
from the [a]Arabah road, away from Elath
and [b]from Ezion-geber. And we turned
and passed through by the way of the
wilderness of Moab.
9"Then the LORD said to me, 'Do not
harass Moab, nor provoke them to war,
for I will not give you any of [1]their land
as a possession, because I have given [a]Ar
to [b]the sons of Lot as a possession.
10 (The [a]Emim lived there formerly, a
people as great, numerous, and tall as
the Anakim.
11 Like the Anakim, they are also
regarded as [a]Rephaim, but the Moabites
call them Emim.

24 [a]Num. 13:21-25
26 [1]Lit., *mouth* [a]Num. 14:1-4 [b]Deut. 9:23
27 [a]Deut. 9:28; Ps. 106:25
28 [a]Num. 13:28, 33; Deut. 9:2
30 [1]Lit., *according to all that* [a]Ex. 14:14; Deut. 3:22; 20:4; Neh. 4:20
31 [a]Deut. 32:10-12; Is. 46:3, 4; 63:9; Hos. 11:3; Acts 13:18
32 [1]Lit., *in this matter* [a]Num. 14:11; Ps. 106:24; Heb. 3:19; 4:2; Jude 5
33 [a]Ex. 13:21; Num. 9:15-23; Neh. 9:12; Ps. 78:14 [b]Num. 10:33
34 [a]Num. 14:28-30; Heb. 3:18
35 [a]Ps. 95:11; 106:26; Ezek. 20:15; 1 Cor. 10:5; Heb. 3:14-19
36 [a]Num. 14:24; Josh. 14:9
37 [a]Num. 20:12; Deut. 3:26; 4:21 [b]Num. 27:13, 18
38 [a]Num. 14:30 [b]Num. 34:17; Deut. 3:28; 31:7; Josh. 11:23
39 [a]Num. 14:3, 31 [b]Is. 7:15, 16
40 [1]Lit., *Sea of Reeds* [a]Num. 14:25
41 [a]Num. 14:40
42 [1]Lit., *smitten* [a]Num. 14:41-43
43 [1]Lit., *mouth* [a]Num. 14:40
44 [1]Lit., *dwelt* [a]Num. 14:45 [b]Ps. 118:12
45 [a]Job 27:8, 9; Ps. 66:18; John 9:31
46 [1]Lit., *as the days* [a]Num. 20:1, 22; Deut. 2:7, 14; Judg. 11:17

1 [1]Lit., *Sea of Reeds* [a]Num. 21:4 [b]Deut. 1:2
4 [a]Num. 20:14-21 [b]Gen. 36:8 [c]Ex. 15:15, 16
5 [1]Or, *engage in strife with* [2]Lit., *treading of a sole of a foot* [a]Gen. 36:8; Josh. 24:4
7 [1]Lit., *the work of your hand* [2]Lit., *goings* [a]Deut. 1:19 [b]Num. 14:33, 34; 32:13; Deut. 2:14
8 [a]Deut. 1:1 [b]Num. 33:35; 1 Kin. 9:26
9 [1]Lit., *his* [a]Num. 21:15, 28; Deut. 2:18, 29 [b]Gen. 19:36, 37
10 [a]Gen. 14:5
11 [a]Gen. 14:5; Deut. 2:20

12 [a]The Horites formerly lived in Seir, but the sons of Esau dispossessed them and destroyed them from before them and settled in their place, [b]just as Israel did to the land of [1]their possession which the LORD gave to them.)

13 'Now arise and cross over the [1]brook Zered yourselves.' So we crossed over the [1]brook Zered.

14 "Now the [1]time that it took for us to come from Kadesh-barnea, until we crossed over the [2]brook Zered, was [a]thirty-eight years; until [b]all the generation of the men of war perished from within the camp, as [c]the LORD had sworn to them.

15 "[a]Moreover the hand of the LORD was against them, to destroy them from within the camp, until they all perished.

16 "So it came about when [a]all the men of war had finally perished from among the people,

17 that the LORD spoke to me, saying,

18 'You shall cross over [a]Ar, the border of Moab, today.

19 'And when you come opposite the [a]sons of Ammon, do not harass them nor provoke them, for I will not give you any of the land of the sons of Ammon as a possession, because I have given it to [b]the sons of Lot as a possession.'

20 (It is also regarded as the land of the [a]Rephaim, *for* Rephaim formerly lived in it, but the Ammonites call them Zamzummin,

21 a people as great, numerous, and tall as the Anakim, but the LORD destroyed them before them. And they dispossessed them and settled in their place,

22 just as He did for the sons of Esau, who [a]live in Seir, when He destroyed [b]the Horites from before them; and they dispossessed them, and settled in their place even to this day.

23 And the [a]Avvim, who lived in villages as far as Gaza, the [1b]Caphtorim who came from [2c]Caphtor, destroyed them and lived in their place.)

24 'Arise, set out, and pass through the [1a]valley of Arnon. Look! I have given Sihon the Amorite, king of Heshbon, and his land into your hand; begin to take possession and contend with him in battle.

25 'This day I will begin to put [a]the dread and fear of you [1]upon the peoples [2]everywhere under the heavens, who, when they hear the report of you, [b]shall tremble and be in anguish because of you.'

26 "[a]So I sent messengers from the wilderness of Kedemoth to Sihon king of Heshbon with words of peace, saying,

27 'Let me pass through your land, I will [1]travel only on the highway; I will not turn aside to the right or to the left.

28 'You will sell me food for money so that I may eat, and give me water for money so that I may drink, [a]only let me pass through on [1]foot,

29 just as the sons of Esau who live in Seir and the Moabites who live in [a]Ar did for me, until I cross over the Jordan into the land which the LORD our God is giving to us.'

30 "But [a]Sihon king of Heshbon was not willing for us to pass [1]through his land; for the [b]LORD your God hardened his spirit and made his heart obstinate, in order to deliver him into your hand, as *he is* today.

31 "And the LORD said to me, 'See, I have begun to deliver Sihon and his land [1]over to you. Begin to [2]occupy, that you may possess his land.'

32 "Then Sihon [1]with all his people came out to meet us in battle at Jahaz.

33 "And [a]the LORD our God delivered him [1]over to us; and we [2b]defeated him with his sons and all his people.

34 "So we captured all his cities at that time, and [1a]utterly destroyed [2]the men, women and children of every city. We left no survivor.

35 "We took [a]only the animals as our booty and the spoil of the cities which we had captured.

36 "From [a]Aroer which is on the edge of the [1]valley of Arnon and *from* the city which is in the [1]valley, even to Gilead, there was no city that was too high for us; the LORD our God delivered all [2]over to us.

37 "[a]Only you did not go near to the land of the sons of Ammon, all along the [1]river [b]Jabbok and the cities of the hill country, and wherever the LORD our God had commanded us.

Conquests Recounted

3 "[a]THEN we turned and went up the road to Bashan, and Og, king of Bashan, [1]with all his people came out to meet us in battle at Edrei.

2 "But the LORD said to me, 'Do not fear him, for I have delivered him and all his people and his land into your hand; and you shall do to him just as you did to Sihon king of the Amorites, who lived at Heshbon.'

3 "So the LORD our God delivered Og also, king of Bashan, with all his people into our hand, and we smote [1]them until no survivor was [2]left.

4 "And we captured all his cities at that time; there was not a city which we did not take from them: sixty cities, all the region of [a]Argob, the kingdom of Og in Bashan.

5 "All these were cities fortified with high walls, gates and bars, besides a great many [1]unwalled towns.

6 "And we [1]utterly destroyed them, as we did to [a]Sihon king of Heshbon, [2b]utterly destroying [3]the men, women and children of every city.

7 "[a]But all the animals and the spoil of the cities we took as our booty.

8 "[a]Thus we took the land at that time from the hand of the two kings of the Amorites who were beyond the Jordan, from the [1]valley of Arnon to Mount Hermon

9 (Sidonians [a]call Hermon [b]Sirion, and the Amorites call it [c]Senir):

---

12 [1]Lit., *his* [a]Gen. 36:20; Deut. 2:22 [b]Num. 21:25, 35
13 [1]Or, *wadi*
14 [1]Lit., *days in which we went* [2]Or, *wadi* [a]Deut. 2:7 [b]Num. 14:29-35; 26:64, 65; Ps. 106:26; 1 Cor. 10:5 [c]Deut. 1:34, 35
15 [a]Jude 5
16 [a]Deut. 2:14
18 [a]Deut. 2:9
19 [a]Gen. 19:38 [b]Deut. 2:9
20 [a]Deut. 2:11
22 [a]Gen. 36:8; Deut. 2:5 [b]Deut. 2:12
23 [1]I.e., Philistines [2]I.e., Crete [a]Josh. 13:3 [b]Gen. 10:14; 1 Chr. 1:12 [c]Jer. 47:4; Amos 9:7
24 [1]Or, *wadi* [a]Num. 21:13, 14; Judg. 11:18
25 [1]Lit., *in front of* [2]Lit., *under all the heavens* [a]Ex. 23:27; Deut. 11:25; Josh. 2:9 [b]Ex. 15:14-16
26 [a]Num. 21:21-32; Deut. 1:4; Judg. 11:19-21
27 [1]Lit., *go by the way*
28 [1]Lit., *my feet* [a]Num. 20:19
29 [a]Deut. 2:9
30 [1]Lit., *by him* [a]Num. 21:23 [b]Ex. 4:21; Josh. 11:20
31 [1]Lit., *before you* [2]Lit., *possess*
32 [1]Lit., *he and*
33 [1]Lit., *before us* [2]Lit., *smote* [a]Ex. 23:31; Deut. 7:2 [b]Deut. 29:7
34 [1]Or, *put under the ban* [2]Lit., *every city of man . . .* [a]Deut. 3:6; 7:2
35 [a]Deut. 3:7
36 [1]Or, *wadi* [2]Lit., *before us* [a]Deut. 3:12; 4:48; Josh. 12:2; 13:9
37 [1]Or, *wadi* [a]Deut. 2:19 [b]Gen. 32:22; Num. 21:24; Deut. 3:16

1 [1]Lit., *he and* [a]Num. 21:33-35
3 [1]Lit., *him* [2]Lit., *left to him*
4 [a]Deut. 3:13, 14; 1 Kin. 4:13
5 [1]Or, *rural*
6 [1]Or, *put them under the ban* [2]Or, *putting under the ban* [3]Lit., *every city of men . . .* [a]Deut. 1:4 [b]Deut. 2:34
7 [a]Deut. 2:35
8 [1]Or, *wadi* [a]Num. 32:33; Josh. 12:1-7; 13:8-12
9 [a]Deut. 4:48; Josh. 11:17; Ps. 42:6; 133:3 [b]Ps. 29:6 [c]1 Chr. 5:23

10 all the cities of the tableland and
all Gilead and [a]all Bashan, as far as
Salecah and Edrei, cities of the kingdom
of Og in Bashan.
11 (For only Og king of Bashan was
left of the remnant of the [a]Rephaim.
Behold, his [1]bedstead was an iron [1]bed-
stead; it is in [b]Rabbah of the sons of
Ammon. Its length was nine cubits and
its width four cubits [2]by ordinary cubit.)
12“So we took possession of this land
at that time. From [a]Aroer, which is by
the [1]valley of Arnon, and half the hill
country of [b]Gilead and its cities, I gave
to the Reubenites and to the Gadites.
13“And the rest of Gilead, and all
Bashan, the kingdom of Og, I gave to the
half-tribe of Manasseh, all the region of
Argob (concerning all Bashan, it is
called the land of Rephaim.
14 [a]Jair the son of Manasseh took all
the region of Argob as far as the border
of the Geshurites and the Maacathites,
and called [1]it, *that is*, Bashan, after his
own name, [2]Havvoth-jair, *as it is* to this
day.)
15“[a]And to Machir I gave Gilead.
16“And to the Reubenites and to the
Gadites, I gave from Gilead even as far
as the [1]valley of Arnon, the middle of
the [1]valley [2]as a border and as far as the
[1]river [a]Jabbok, the border of the sons of
Ammon;
17 the Arabah also, with the Jordan
[1]as *a* border, from [2][a]Chinnereth [b]even as
far as the sea of the Arabah, [c]the Salt
Sea, [3]at the foot of the slopes of Pisgah
on the east.
18“Then I commanded you at that
time, saying, ‘[a]The LORD your God has
given you this land to possess it; [b]all you
valiant men shall cross over armed
before your brothers, the sons of Israel.
19 ‘[a]But your wives and your little
ones and your livestock (I know that you
have [b]much livestock), shall remain in
your cities which I have given you,
20 [a]until the LORD gives rest to your
fellow countrymen as to you, and they
also possess the land which the LORD
your God will give them beyond the
Jordan. [b]Then you may return every
man to his possession, which I have
given you.’
21“And I commanded Joshua at that
time, saying, ‘Your eyes have seen all
that the LORD your God has done to
these two kings; so the LORD shall do to
all the kingdoms into which you are
about to cross.
22 ‘Do not fear them, for the LORD
your God [a]is the one fighting for you.’
23“I also pleaded with the LORD at
that time, saying,
24 ‘O Lord [1]GOD, Thou hast begun to
show Thy servant [a]Thy greatness and
Thy strong hand; for what [b]god is there
in heaven or on earth who can do such
works and mighty acts as Thine?
25 ‘Let me, I pray, cross over and see
the [a]fair land that is beyond the Jordan,
[1]that good hill country and Lebanon.’
26“But [a]the LORD was angry with me
on your account, and would not listen to
me; and the LORD said to me, ‘[1]Enough!
Speak to Me no more of this matter.
27 ‘Go up to the top of [a]Pisgah and lift
up your eyes to the west and north and
south and east, and see *it* with your eyes,
[b]for you shall not cross over this Jordan.
28 ‘[a]But charge Joshua and encourage
him and strengthen him; [b]for he shall go
across [1]at the head of this people, and he
shall give them as an inheritance the
land which you will see.’
29“So we remained in the valley opposite [a]Beth-peor.

Israel Urged to Obey God’s Law

4 “AND now, O Israel, listen to the
statutes and the judgments which [a]I
am teaching you to perform, in order
that [b]you may live and go in and take
possession of the land which the LORD,
the God of your fathers, is giving you.
2“[a]You shall not add to the word
which [b]I am commanding you, nor take
away from it, that you may keep the
commandments of the LORD your God
which I command you.
3“[a]Your eyes have seen what the
LORD has done in the case of Baal-peor,
for all the men who followed Baal-peor,
the LORD your God has destroyed [1]them
from among you.
4“But you who held fast to the LORD
your God are alive today, every one of
you.
5“See, I have taught you statutes and
judgments [a]just as the LORD my God
commanded me, that you should do thus
in the land where you are entering to
possess it.
6“So keep and do *them*, [a]for that is
your wisdom and your understanding in
the sight of the peoples who will hear all
these statutes and say, ‘Surely this great
nation is a wise and understanding
people.’
7“For [a]what great nation is there that
has a god [b]so near to it as is the LORD
our God [c]whenever we call on Him?
8“Or what great nation is there that
has [a]statutes and judgments as righteous
as this whole law which I am setting
before you today?
9“Only [a]give heed to yourself and
keep your soul diligently, lest you forget
the things which your eyes have seen,
and lest they depart from your heart [b]all
the days of your life; but [c]make them
known to your sons and your grandsons.
10“*Remember* the day you stood before the LORD your God at Horeb, when
the LORD said to me, ‘Assemble the
people to Me, that I may let them hear
My words [a]so they may learn to [1]fear
Me all the days they live on the earth,
and that they may [b]teach their children.’
11“And you came near and stood at
the foot of the mountain, [a]and the
mountain burned with fire to the *very*
heart of the heavens: darkness, cloud
and thick gloom.

10 [a]Josh. 13:11
11 [1]Or, *couch* [2]Lit., *by a man’s forearm* [a]Gen. 14:5; Deut. 2:11, 20 [b]2 Sam. 11:1; 12:26; Jer. 49:2
12 [1]Or, *wadi* [a]Deut. 2:36 [b]Num. 32:32-38; Josh. 13:8-13
14 [1]Lit., *them* [2]I.e., the towns of Jair [a]Num. 32:41; 1 Chr. 2:22
15 [a]Num. 32:39, 40
16 [1]Or, *wadi* [2]Lit., *and* [a]Num. 21:24; Deut. 2:37
17 [1]Lit., *and* [2]I.e., the Sea of Galilee [3]Lit., *under* [a]Num. 34:11; Josh. 13:27 [b]Josh. 12:3 [c]Gen. 14:3; Josh. 3:16
18 [a]Josh. 1:13 [b]Num. 32:20; Josh. 4:12, 13
19 [a]Josh. 1:14 [b]Ex. 12:38
20 [a]Josh. 1:15 [b]Josh. 22:4
22 [a]Ex. 14:14; Deut. 1:30; 20:4; Neh. 4:20
24 [1]Heb., *YHWH*, usually rendered *LORD* [a]Deut. 11:2 [b]Ex. 8:10; 15:11; 2 Sam. 7:22; Ps. 71:19; 86:8
25 [1]Lit., *this* [a]Deut. 4:22
26 [1]Lit., *Enough for you* [a]Deut. 1:37
27 [a]Num. 23:14; 27:12 [b]Deut. 1:37
28 [1]Lit., *before this people* [a]Num. 27:18; Deut. 31:3, 7, 8, 23 [b]Deut. 1:38
29 [a]Num. 25:1-3; Deut. 4:46; 34:6

1 [a]Deut. 1:3 [b]Lev. 18:5; Deut. 5:33; 8:1; 16:20; 30:16, 19; Ezek. 20:11; Rom. 10:5
2 [a]Deut. 12:32; Prov. 30:6; Rev. 22:18 [b]Deut. 4:5, 14, 40
3 [1]Lit., *him* [a]Num. 25:1-9
5 [a]Lev. 26:46; 27:34
6 [a]Deut. 30:19, 20; 32:46, 47; Job 28:28; Ps. 19:7; 111:10; Prov. 1:7; 2 Tim. 3:15
7 [a]Deut. 4:32-34; 2 Sam. 7:23 [b]Ps. 34:17, 18; 145:18; 148:14; Is. 55:6 [c]Ps. 34:18; 85:9
8 [a]Ps. 89:14; 97:2; 119:144, 160, 172
9 [a]Deut. 4:23; 6:12; 8:11, 14, 19; Prov. 4:23; 23:19 [b]Deut. 6:2; 12:1; 16:3 [c]Gen. 18:19; Deut. 4:10; 6:7, 20-25; 11:19; 32:46; Ps. 78:5, 6; Prov. 22:6; Eph. 6:4
10 [1]Or, *reverence* [a]Deut. 14:23; 17:19; 31:12, 13 [b]Deut. 4:9
11 [a]Ex. 19:18; Heb. 12:18, 19

12"Then the LORD spoke to you from the midst of the fire; you heard the sound of words, but you saw no form—only a voice.

13"So He declared to you His covenant which He commanded you to perform, *that is,* [a]the ten [1]commandments; and [b]He wrote them on two tablets of stone.

14"And the LORD commanded me at that time to teach you statutes and judgments, that you might perform them in the land where you are going over to possess it.

15"So [a]watch yourselves carefully, since you did not see any [b]form on the day the LORD spoke to you at Horeb from the midst of the fire,

16 lest you [a]act corruptly and [b]make a graven image for yourselves in the form of any figure, the likeness of male or female,

17 the likeness of any animal that is on the earth, the likeness of [a]any winged bird that flies in the sky,

18 the likeness of anything that creeps on the ground, the likeness of any fish that is in the water below the earth.

19"And *beware,* lest you lift up your eyes to heaven and see the sun and the moon and the stars, [a]all the host of heaven, [b]and be drawn away and worship them and serve them, those which the LORD your God has allotted to all the peoples under the whole heaven.

20"But the LORD has taken you and brought you out of [a]the iron furnace, from Egypt, to [b]be a people for His own possession, as today.

21"[a]Now the LORD was angry with me on your account, and swore that I should not cross the Jordan, and that I should not enter the good land which the LORD your God is giving you as an inheritance.

22"For [a]I shall die in this land, I shall not cross the Jordan, but you shall cross and take possession of this [b]good land.

23"So watch yourselves, [a]lest you forget the covenant of the LORD your God, which He made with you, and [b]make for yourselves a graven image in the form of anything *against* which the LORD your God has commanded you.

24"For the LORD your God is a [a]consuming fire, a [b]jealous God.

25"When you [1]become the father of children and children's children and have remained long in the land, and [a]act corruptly, and [b]make an [2]idol in the form of anything, and [c]do that which is evil in the sight of the LORD your God *so as* to provoke Him to anger,

26 I [a]call heaven and earth to witness against you today, that you shall [b]surely perish quickly from the land where you are going over the Jordan to possess it. You shall not [1]live long on it, but shall be utterly destroyed.

27"And the LORD will [a]scatter you among the peoples, and you shall be left few in number among the nations, where the LORD shall drive you.

28"And [a]there you will serve gods, the work of man's hands, [b]wood and stone, [c]which neither see nor hear nor eat nor smell.

29"[a]But from there you will seek the LORD your God, and you will find *Him* if you search for Him [b]with all your heart and all your soul.

30"When you [a]are in distress and all these things have come upon you, [b]in the latter days, [c]you will return to the LORD your God and listen to His voice.

31"For the LORD your God is a [a]compassionate God; [b]He will not fail you nor [c]destroy you nor [d]forget the covenant with your fathers which He swore to them.

32"Indeed, [a]ask now concerning the former days which were before you, since the [b]day that God created [1]man on the earth, and *inquire* [c]from one end of the heavens to the other. [d]Has *anything* been done like this great thing, or has *anything* been heard like it?

33"[a]Has *any* people heard the voice of God speaking from the midst of the fire, as you have heard *it,* and survived?

34"[a]Or has a god tried to go to take for himself a nation from within *another* nation [b]by trials, by signs and wonders and by war and [c]by a mighty hand and by an outstretched arm and by great terrors, [1]as the LORD your God did for you in Egypt before your eyes?

35"To you it was shown that you might know that the LORD, He is God; [a]there is no other besides Him.

36"[a]Out of the heavens He let you hear His voice [b]to discipline you; and on earth He let you see His great fire, and you heard His words from the midst of the fire.

37"[1a]Because He loved your fathers, therefore He chose [2]their descendants after them. And He [3b]personally brought you from Egypt by His great power,

38 driving out from before you nations greater and mightier than you, to bring you in *and* [a]to give you their land for an inheritance, as it is today.

39"Know therefore today, and take it to your heart, that [a]the LORD, He is God in heaven above and on the earth below; there is no other.

40"[a]So you shall keep His statutes and His commandments which I am [1]giving you today, that [b]it may go well with you and with your children after you, and [c]that you may [2]live long on the land which the LORD your God is giving you for all time."

41 [a]Then Moses set apart three cities across the Jordan to the [1]east,

42 that a manslayer might flee there, who unintentionally slew his neighbor without having enmity toward him in time past; and by fleeing to one of these cities he might live:

13 [1]Lit., *words* [a]Ex. 34:28; Deut. 10:4 [b]Ex. 31:18; 34:1, 28
15 [a]Josh. 23:11 [b]Is. 40:18
16 [a]Deut. 4:25; 9:12; 31:29 [b]Ex. 20:4; Lev. 26:1; Deut. 5:8, 9; 27:15; Rom. 1:23
17 [a]Rom. 1:23
19 [a]Gen. 2:1; Deut. 17:3; 2 Kin. 17:16; 21:3 [b]Deut. 13:5, 10; Job 31:26-28
20 [a]1 Kin. 8:51; Jer. 11:4 [b]Ex. 19:5; Deut. 7:6; 14:2; 26:18; Titus 2:14; 1 Pet. 2:9
21 [a]Num. 20:12; Deut. 1:37
22 [a]Num. 27:13, 14 [b]Deut. 3:25
23 [a]Deut. 4:9 [b]Deut. 4:16
24 [a]Ex. 24:17; Deut. 9:3; Is. 30:27; 33:14; Heb. 12:29 [b]Deut. 5:9; 6:15
25 [1]Lit., *beget* [2]Or, *a graven image* [a]Deut. 4:16 [b]Deut. 4:23 [c]2 Kin. 17:17
26 [1]Lit., *prolong your days* [a]Deut. 30:19; 31:28; 32:1; Is. 1:2; Mic. 6:2 [b]Deut. 7:4; 8:19, 20
27 [a]Lev. 26:33; Deut. 28:64; 29:28; Neh. 1:8
28 [a]Deut. 28:36, 64; Jer. 16:13 [b]Deut. 29:17 [c]Ps. 115:4-8; 135:15-18; Is. 44:12-20
29 [a]Deut. 30:1-3, 10; 2 Chr. 15:4; Is. 55:6; Jer. 29:13 [b]Deut. 6:5; 10:12
30 [a]Ps. 18:6; 59:16; 107:6, 13 [b]Deut. 31:29; Jer. 23:20; Hos. 3:5; Heb. 1:2 [c]Jer. 4:1, 2
31 [a]Ex. 34:6; 2 Chr. 30:9; Neh. 9:31; Ps. 103:8; 111:4; 116:5; Jon. 4:2 [b]Deut. 31:6, 8; Josh. 1:5; 1 Chr. 28:20; Heb. 13:5 [c]Jer. 30:11 [d]Lev. 26:45
32 [1]Or, *Adam* [a]Deut. 32:7; Job 8:8 [b]Gen. 1:27; Is. 45:12 [c]Deut. 28:64; Matt. 24:31 [d]Deut. 4:7; 2 Sam. 7:23
33 [a]Ex. 20:22; Deut. 5:24, 26
34 [1]Lit., *according to all that* [a]Ex. 14:30; Deut. 33:29 [b]Deut. 7:19 [c]Deut. 5:15; 6:21; Ps. 136:12
35 [a]Ex. 8:10; 9:14; Deut. 4:39; 32:12, 39; 1 Sam. 2:2; Is. 43:10-12; 44:6-8; 45:5-7; Mark 12:32
36 [a]Ex. 19:9, 19; 20:18, 22; Deut. 4:33; Neh. 9:13; Heb. 12:25 [b]Deut. 8:5
37 [1]Lit., *And instead, because* [2]Lit., *his seed* [3]Lit., *with His presence* [a]Deut. 7:7, 8; 10:15; 33:3 [b]Ex. 33:14; Is. 63:9
38 [a]Num. 32:4; 34:14, 15
39 [a]Deut. 4:35; Josh. 2:11
40 [1]Lit., *commanding* [2]Lit., *prolong your days* [a]Lev. 22:31; Deut. 4:2; Ps. 105:45 [b]Deut. 4:1; 5:16, 29, 33; 6:3, 18; 12:25, 28; 22:7 [c]Ex. 23:26; Deut. 32:47
41 [1]Lit., *sunrise* [a]Num. 35:6; Deut. 19:2-13; Josh. 20:7-9

43 [a]Bezer in the wilderness on the plateau for the Reubenites, and Ramoth in Gilead for the Gadites, and Golan in Bashan for the Manassites.

44 Now this is the law which Moses set before the sons of Israel;

45 these are the testimonies and the statutes and the ordinances which Moses spoke to the sons of Israel, when they came out from Egypt,

46 across the Jordan, in the valley [a]opposite Beth-peor, in the land of [b]Sihon king of the Amorites who lived at Heshbon, whom Moses and the sons of Israel [1]defeated when they came out from Egypt.

47 And they took possession of his land and the land of [a]Og king of Bashan, the two kings of the Amorites, *who were* across the Jordan to the [1]east,

48 from [a]Aroer, which is on the edge of the [1]valley of Arnon, even as far as [b]Mount Sion (that is, Hermon),

49 with all the Arabah across the Jordan to the east, even as far as the sea of the Arabah, [1]at the foot of the slopes of Pisgah.

The Ten Commandments Repeated

5 THEN Moses summoned all Israel, and said to them, "Hear, O Israel, the statutes and the ordinances which I am speaking today in your [1]hearing, that you may learn them and observe [2]them carefully.

2"The LORD our God made [a]a covenant with us at Horeb.

3"[a]The LORD did not make this covenant with our fathers, but with us, *with* all those of [1]us alive here today.

4"The LORD spoke to you [a]face to face at the mountain [b]from the midst of the fire,

5 *while* [a]I was standing between the LORD and you at that time, to declare to you the word of the LORD; [b]for you were afraid because of the fire and did not go up the mountain. [1]He said,

6 '[a]I am the LORD your God, who brought you out of the land of Egypt, out of the house of [1]slavery.

7 '[a]You shall have no other gods [1]before Me.

8 '[a]You shall not make for yourself [1]an idol, *or* any likeness *of* what is in heaven above [2]or on the earth beneath [2]or in the water under the earth.

9 'You shall not worship them or serve them; for I, the LORD your God, am a jealous God, [a]visiting the iniquity of the fathers on the children, and on the third and the fourth *generations* of those who hate Me,

10 but [a]showing lovingkindness to thousands, to those who love Me and keep My commandments.

11 '[a]You shall not take the name of the LORD your God in vain, for the LORD will not [1]leave him unpunished who takes His name in vain.

12 '[a]Observe the sabbath day to keep it holy, as the LORD your God commanded you.

13 'Six days you shall labor and do all your work,

14 but [a]the seventh day is a sabbath of the LORD your God; *in it* you shall not do any work, you or your son or your daughter or your male servant or your female servant or your ox or your donkey or any of your cattle or your sojourner who [1]stays with you, so that your male servant and your female servant may rest as well as you.

15 '[a]And you shall remember that you were a slave in the land of Egypt, and the LORD your God brought you out of there by a mighty hand and by an outstretched arm; therefore the LORD your God commanded you to observe the sabbath day.

16 '[a]Honor your father and your mother, as the LORD your God has commanded you, [b]that your days may be prolonged, and that it may go well with you on the land which the LORD your God gives you.

17 '[a]You shall not murder.

18 '[a]You shall not commit adultery.

19 '[a]You shall not steal.

20 '[a]You shall not bear false witness against your neighbor.

21 '[a]You shall not covet your neighbor's wife, and you shall not desire your neighbor's house, his field or his male servant or his female servant, his ox or his donkey or anything that belongs to your neighbor.'

Moses Interceded

22"These words the LORD spoke to all your assembly at the mountain from the midst of the fire, *of* the cloud and *of* the thick gloom, with a great voice, and He added no more. And [a]He wrote them on two tablets of stone and gave them to me.

23"And it came about, when you heard the voice from the midst of the darkness, while the mountain was burning with fire, that you came near to me, all the heads of your tribes and your elders.

24"And you said, 'Behold, the LORD our God has shown us His glory and His greatness, and we have heard His voice from the midst of the fire; we have seen today that God speaks with man, yet he lives.

25 '[a]Now then why should we die? For this great fire will consume us; if we hear the voice of the LORD our God any longer, then we shall die.

26 'For [a]who is there of all flesh, who has heard the voice of the living God speaking from the midst of the fire, as we *have*, and lived?

27 '[1]Go near and hear all that the LORD our God says; then speak to us all that the LORD our God will speak to you, and we will hear and do *it*.'

28"And the LORD heard the voice of your words when you spoke to me, [a]and the LORD said to me, 'I have heard the voice of the words of this people which

43 [a]Josh. 20:8
46 [1]Lit., *smote* [a]Deut. 3:29 [b]Num. 21:21-25
47 [1]Lit., *sunrise* [a]Deut. 1:4; 3:3, 4
48 [1]Or, *wadi* [a]Deut. 2:36; 3:12 [b]Deut. 3:9; Ps. 133:3
49 [1]Lit., *under*
1 [1]Lit., *ears* [2]Lit., *to do them*
2 [a]Ex. 19:5; Mal. 4:4
3 [1]Lit., *us ourselves* [a]Jer. 31:32; Heb. 8:9
4 [a]Num. 14:14; Deut. 34:10 [b]Deut. 4:33
5 [1]Lit., *saying* [a]Gal. 3:19 [b]Ex. 19:16, 21-24; 20:18; Heb. 12:18-21
6 [1]Lit., *slaves* [a]Ex. 20:2-17; Lev. 26:1; Deut. 6:4; Ps. 81:10
7 [1]Or, *besides* [a]Ex. 20:3
8 [1]Or, *a graven image* [2]Lit., *or what is* [a]Ex. 20:4-6; Lev. 26:1; Deut. 4:15-18; 27:15; Ps. 97:7
9 [a]Ex. 34:7; Num. 14:18; Deut. 7:10
10 [a]Num. 14:18; Deut. 7:9; Jer. 32:18
11 [1]Or, *hold him guiltless* [a]Ex. 20:7; Lev. 19:12; Deut. 6:13; 10:20; Matt. 5:33
12 [a]Ex. 16:23-30; 20:8-11; 31:13f.; Mark 2:27f.
14 [1]Lit., *is in your gates* [a]Gen. 2:2; Heb. 4:4
15 [a]Ex. 20:11
16 [a]Ex. 20:12; Lev. 19:3; Deut. 27:16; Matt. 15:4; 19:19; Mark 7:10; 10:19; Luke 18:20; Eph. 6:2, 3; Col. 3:20 [b]Deut. 4:40
17 [a]Gen. 9:6; Ex. 20:13; Lev. 24:17; Matt. 5:21f.; 19:18; Mark 10:19; Rom. 13:9; James 2:11
18 [a]Ex. 20:14; Lev. 20:10; Matt. 5:27f.; 19:18; Mark 10:19; Luke 18:20; Rom. 13:9; James 2:11
19 [a]Ex. 20:15; Lev. 19:11
20 [a]Ex. 20:16; 23:1; Matt. 19:18
21 [a]Ex. 20:17; Rom. 7:7; 13:9
22 [a]Ex. 24:12; 31:18; Deut. 4:13
25 [a]Ex. 20:18, 19; Deut. 18:16
26 [a]Deut. 4:33
27 [1]Lit., *Go yourself*
28 [a]Deut. 18:17

GREAT MILITARY LOSSES

Amos 5:3. Although there was a regular army in Amos' time, recruiting officers still went about in times of national emergency and conscripted ninety percent of the able-bodied men. The point about this passage is that the armies are to be so totally destroyed that there will be none who return.

NUMBERS

There are problems of understanding numbers in connection with groups of people in the Bible. Judges 20:17 says that 400,000 men marched against Benjamin, but Judges 5:8 says that 40,000 was the greatest number that could be raised from all the tribes put together. The lower number fits with the number who went into battle at Jericho (Joshua 4:13). When David took his military census (2 Samuel 24:1-9), 800,000 men were available in Israel and 500,000 in Judah, but many years later there were only 60,000 heads of families prosperous enough to pay tax (2 Kings 15:19-20), which would give a total population of about 800,000.

The disparity in the numbers may be due to the fact that we still do not understand the system of numbering. It sometimes happens that a particular word can represent a number or can have an entirely different meaning. A *"score"* means *"twenty,"* but it also means a *"tally."* (If a newspaper reporter records that Liverpool made a score against Everton in a British football [soccer] match, it does not mean that they put the ball twenty times into the Everton net, although someone reading the account many years later might *mis*understand it that way.) It may be that *"fifties," "hundreds,"* and *"thousands"* refer to units within an organization and not to actual numbers. We will have to wait for full understanding.

REMOVING THE SHOES

Exodus 3:5. When one entered a house it was the usual practice to take off one's shoes, because otherwise the dirt from the unpaved streets and pathways would defile the house. If the floors were carpeted, the carpets would be ruined. Removal of shoes was therefore a mark of consideration and respect, and since God can be given no less respect, the removal of shoes is mark of respect toward God. This practice continues in Muslim places of worship in contemporary society.

ENTERING WOMEN'S QUARTERS

Judges 4:17-22. The story is normally told as an example of Jael's treachery, for when an enemy was at rest in a tent, he was supposed to be completely safe. But there may be more to the story than meets the eye and we are probably not given all the details. A guest in a tent slept in the porch and was never allowed inside, which were the women's quarters. Invasion of the women's quarters was punishable by death.

THE LEVITE AND HIS CONCUBINE

Judges 19-21. This is one of two appendixes to the book of Judges that illustrate the spiritual chaos into which the people had fallen. The book is set in a period when the twelve tribes of Israel were united in their allegiance to Yahweh–a relationship called an *amphictyony*. When the Levite was returning home with his concubine, they went to Gibeah–within the tribal territory of Benjamin–to look for a place to stay for the night, but the house was raided and the woman taken away and murdered by a repetitive rape. The division of the woman's body was the call to the twelve tribes to assemble at the central sanctuary. It became clear to the assembly that the attitude of the men of Gibeah was not just lust, but was part of an attitude that lay claim to independence on the part of the whole tribe. Benjamin wanted to be out of the amphictyony. It was because the tribes believed that the protection of God depended on their loyalty to one another that they took such drastic action against the show of independence.

THE DRINK OF WATER

Mark 9:41. One of the first things done for a guest was to give him a drink of cool water. It was a pledge of friendship (Abraham's servant Eleizer looked for a welcome by waiting for a drink of water, Genesis 24:17-18). When Jesus said *"Whoever gives you a cup of water to drink because of your name as followers of Christ"* he was saying that if we pledge a person our friendship for Christ's sake we shall not lose our reward.

THE BROKEN TILE

Revelation 2:17. Christ tells the angel of the church at Pergamum that *"To him that overcomes...I will give...a white stone, and a new name written on the stone which no one knows but him who receives it."* This statement may be an allusion to a common practice between friends. A tile was taken and broken in half. One friend wrote his name on one of the halves, and the other friend wrote his name on the other. The two halves were then exchanged. Often the pieces were handed down from father to son. To be able to produce the counterpart of a piece of tile held by another person, even years later, was to guarantee friendship and hospitality.

GIDEON *- bravery*

Gideon was a young man when God chose him to lead as incredibly small army to defeat the Midianites. Truly Gideon was a brave man.

Gideon's family background was not particularly outstanding. Though he was young and poor, Gideon had not proven his courage. God's angel addressed him as a *"valiant warrior"* (Judges 6:12). Gideon worshipped God, even when his own father had built an altar to Baal.

When God called Gideon to deliver Israel, he was not afraid. His greatest concern was to be sure God was with him. Though he was a brave man, Gideon knew the true delivering power would come from God. Once he had assurance of God's presence, he moved out boldly.

Gideon did not dispute God's directions to cut down the size of the large army of Israel that gathered. God explained his reason, saying in Judges 7:2 *"... lest Israel become boastful, saying 'My own power has delivered me.'"* Even when God had Gideon cut the army down to three hundred men, Gideon was obedient and courageous.

God strengthened and built up Gideon's courage along the way to the battle. God did not give Gideon a call and then abandon him. He continued with him constantly, advising and guiding Gideon. Gideon was brave because he knew God was with him and would deliver Israel.

He believed in God's delivering power so strongly that he went out to fight his greatest battle with trumpets, pitchers and torches — not swords! Gideon learned an important truth at a young age: with God anything is possible.

QUESTIONS

1. Gideon's obscurity and lack of wealth were unimportant to God when He chose him. Are there circumstances in your life that make you feel unworthy to be used by God? How can you overcome feelings of unworthiness?

2. Gideon's only questions to God were directed at receiving assurance God was with him. How can you know God is with you?

3. God's directions to Gideon seemed unwise against the strength of the Midianite army, yet Gideon won. When has God brought you victory against seemingly insurmountable odds?

4. Gideon followed God's very specific instructions exactly. How important do you think it is to be obedient to the extent Gideon was?

they have spoken to you. They have
done well in all that they have spoken.
29 '[a]Oh that they had such a heart in
them, that they would fear Me, and
[b]keep all My commandments always,
that [c]it may be well with them and with
their sons forever!
30 'Go, say to them, "Return to your
tents."
31 '[a]But as for you, stand here by Me,
that I may speak to you all the commandments and the statutes and the
judgments which you shall teach them,
that they may observe *them* in the land
which I give them to possess.'
32 "So you shall observe to do just as
the LORD your God has commanded
you; [a]you shall not turn aside to the
right or to the left.
33 "[a]You shall walk in all the way
which the LORD your God has commanded you, [b]that you may live, and
that it may be well with you, and that
you may prolong *your* days in the land
which you shall possess.

Obey God and Prosper

6 "NOW this is the commandment,
the statutes and the judgments
which the LORD your God has commanded *me* to teach you, that you might
do *them* in the land where you are going
over to possess it,
2 so that you and your son and your
grandson might [a]fear the LORD your
God, to keep all His statutes and His
commandments, which I command you,
[b]all the days of your life, and that your
days may be prolonged.
3 "O Israel, you should listen and [1]be
careful to do *it*, that [a]it may be well with
you and that you may multiply greatly,
just as the LORD, the God of your
fathers, has promised you, *in* [b]a land
flowing with milk and honey.
4 "[a]Hear, O Israel! The LORD is our
God, the [b]LORD is one!
5 "And [a]you shall love the LORD your
God [b]with all your heart and with all
your soul and with all your might.
6 "And [a]these words, which I am
commanding you today, shall be on your
heart;
7 and [a]you shall teach them diligently to your sons and shall talk of
them when you sit in your house and
when you walk by the way and when you
lie down and when you rise up.
8 "[a]And you shall bind them as a sign
on your hand and they shall be as
[1]frontals [2]on your forehead.
9 "[a]And you shall write them on the
doorposts of your house and on your
gates.
10 "Then it shall come about when the
LORD your God brings you into the land
which He swore to your fathers, Abraham, Isaac and Jacob, to give you, [a]great
and splendid cities which you did not
build,
11 and houses full of all good things
which you did not fill, and hewn cisterns
which you did not dig, vineyards and
olive trees which you did not plant, and
[a]you shall eat and be satisfied,
12 then watch yourself, lest [a]you forget the LORD who brought you from the
land of Egypt, out of the house of
[1]slavery.
13 "[a]You shall [1]fear *only* the LORD
your God; and you shall [2]worship Him,
and [b]swear by His name.
14 "[a]You shall not follow other gods,
any of the gods of the peoples who
surround you,
15 for the LORD your God in the
midst of you is a [a]jealous God; otherwise the anger of the LORD your God
will be kindled against you, and He will
[1]wipe you off the face of the earth.
16 "[a]You shall not put the LORD your
God to the test, [b]as you tested *Him* at
Massah.
17 "[a]You should diligently keep the
commandments of the LORD your God,
and His testimonies and His statutes
which He has commanded you.
18 "And you shall do what is right and
good in the sight of the LORD, that [a]it
may be well with you and that you may
go in and possess the good land which
the LORD swore to *give* your fathers,
19 by driving out all your enemies
from before you, as the LORD has spoken.
20 "[a]When your son asks you in time to
come, saying, 'What *do* the testimonies
and the statutes and the judgments *mean*
which the LORD our God commanded
you?'
21 then you shall say to your son, 'We
were slaves to Pharaoh in Egypt; and the
LORD brought us from Egypt with a
mighty hand.
22 'Moreover, the LORD showed great
and distressing signs and wonders before
our eyes against Egypt, Pharaoh and all
his household;
23 and He brought us out from there
in order to bring us in, to give us the
land which He had sworn to our fathers.'
24 "So the LORD commanded us to
observe all these statutes, [a]to fear the
LORD our God for our good always and
[b]for our survival, as *it is* today.
25 "And [a]it will be righteousness for us
if we [1]are careful to observe all this
commandment before the LORD our
God, just as He commanded us.

Warnings

7 "[a]WHEN the LORD your God shall
bring you into the land where you
are entering to possess it, and shall clear
away many nations before you, the
Hittites and the Girgashites and the
Amorites and the Canaanites and the
Perizzites and the Hivites and the Jebusites, [b]seven nations greater and stronger
than you,
2 and when the LORD your God shall
deliver them before you, and you shall

29 [a]Ps. 81:13; Is. 48:18 [b]Deut. 11:1 [c]Deut. 5:16, 33
31 [a]Ex. 24:12
32 [a]Deut. 17:20; 28:14; Josh. 1:7; 23:6; Prov. 4:27
33 [a]Deut. 10:12; Jer. 7:23; Luke 1:6 [b]Deut. 4:1, 40; 12:25, 28; 22:7; Eph. 6:3
2 [a]Ex. 20:20; Deut. 10:12; Ps. 111:10; 128:1; Eccl. 12:13 [b]Deut. 4:9
3 [1]Lit., *keep* [a]Deut. 5:33 [b]Ex. 3:8, 17
4 [a]Matt. 22:37; Mark 12:29, 30; Luke 10:27 [b]Deut. 4:35, 39; John 10:30; 1 Cor. 8:4; Eph. 4:6
5 [a]Matt. 22:37; Mark 12:30; Luke 10:27 [b]Deut. 4:29; 10:12
6 [a]Deut. 11:18
7 [a]Deut. 4:9; 11:19; Eph. 6:4
8 [1]Or, *frontlet bands* [2]Lit., *between your eyes* [a]Ex. 12:14; 13:9, 16; Deut. 11:18; Prov. 3:3; 6:21; 7:3
9 [a]Deut. 11:20
10 [a]Deut. 9:1; 19:1; Josh. 24:13; Ps. 105:44
11 [a]Deut. 8:10; 11:15; 14:29
12 [1]Lit., *slaves* [a]Deut. 4:9
13 [1]Or, *reverence* [2]Or, *serve* [a]Deut. 13:4; Matt. 4:10; Luke 4:8 [b]Deut. 5:11; 10:20; Ps. 63:11; Matt. 5:33
14 [a]Jer. 25:6
15 [1]Lit., *destroy* [a]Deut. 4:24; 5:9
16 [a]Matt. 4:7; Luke 4:12 [b]Ex. 17:7
17 [a]Deut. 11:22; Ps. 119:4
18 [a]Deut. 4:40
20 [a]Ex. 13:8, 14
24 [a]Deut. 10:12; Jer. 32:39 [b]Ps. 41:2; Luke 10:28
25 [1]Lit., *keep* [a]Deut. 24:13; Rom. 10:3
1 [a]Deut. 20:16-18 [b]Acts 13:19

[1]defeat them, [a]then you shall [2]utterly
destroy them. [b]You shall make no covenant with them [c]and show no favor to
them.
3"Furthermore, [a]you shall not intermarry with them; you shall not give your
[1]daughters to [2]their sons, nor shall you
take [3]their daughters for your [4]sons.
4"For [1]they will turn your [2]sons away
from [3]following Me to serve other gods;
then the anger of the LORD will be
kindled against you, and [a]He will
quickly destroy you.
5"But thus you shall do to them: [a]you
shall tear down their altars, and smash
their *sacred* pillars, and hew down their
[1]Asherim, and burn their graven images
with fire.
6"For you are [a]a holy people to the
LORD your God; the LORD your God
has chosen you to be [b]a people for His
[1]own possession out of all the peoples
who are on the face of the [2]earth.
7"[a]The LORD did not set His love on
you nor choose you because you were
more in number than any of the peoples,
for you were the fewest of all peoples,
8 but because the LORD loved you
and kept the [a]oath which He swore to
your forefathers, [b]the LORD brought you
out by a mighty hand, and redeemed you
from the house of [1]slavery, from the
hand of Pharaoh king of Egypt.
9"Know therefore that the LORD
your God, [a]He is God, [b]the faithful
God, [c]who keeps [1]His covenant and [1]His
lovingkindness to a thousandth generation with those who [d]love Him and keep
His commandments;
10 but [a]repays those who hate Him to
[1]their faces, to destroy [2]them; He will
not delay [3]with him who hates Him, He
will repay him to his face.
11"Therefore, you shall keep the commandment and the statutes and the
judgments which I am commanding you
today, to do them.

Promises of God

12"[a]Then it shall come about, because
you listen to these judgments and keep
and do them, that the LORD your God
will keep with you [1]His covenant and
[1]His lovingkindness which He swore to
your forefathers.
13"And He will [a]love you and bless
you and [b]multiply you; He will also
bless the fruit of your womb and the
fruit of your ground, your grain and
your new wine and your oil, the increase
of your herd and the young of your
flock, [1]in the land which He swore to
your forefathers to give you.
14"You shall be blessed above all
peoples; there shall be no male or female
[a]barren among you or among your cattle.
15"And [a]the LORD will remove from
you all sickness; and He will not put on
you any of the harmful diseases of Egypt
which you have known, but He will lay
them on all who hate you.
16"And you shall consume all the
peoples whom the LORD your God will
deliver to you; [a]your eye shall not pity
them, neither shall you serve their gods,
for that *would be* [b]a snare to you.
17"If you should say in your heart,
'These nations are greater than I; how
can I [a]dispossess them?'
18 you shall not be afraid of them;
you shall well [a]remember what the LORD
your God did to Pharaoh and to all
Egypt:
19 [a]the great trials which your eyes
saw and the signs and the wonders and
the mighty hand and the outstretched
arm by which the LORD your God
brought you out. So shall the LORD your
God do to all the peoples of whom you
are afraid.
20"Moreover, the LORD your God will
send [a]the hornet against them, until
those who are left and hide themselves
from you perish.
21"You shall not dread [1]them, for [a]the
LORD your God is in your midst, [b]a
great and awesome God.
22"[a]And the LORD your God will clear
away these nations before you little by
little; you will not be able to put an end
to them quickly, lest the [1]wild beasts
grow too numerous for you.
23"[a]But the LORD your God shall
deliver them before you, and will [1]throw
them into great confusion until they are
destroyed.
24"[a]And He will deliver their kings
into your hand so that you shall make
their name perish from under heaven;
[b]no man will be able to stand before you
until you have destroyed them.
25"The graven images of their gods
you are to [a]burn with fire; you shall [b]not
covet the silver or the gold that is on
them, nor take it for yourselves, lest you
be [c]snared by it, for it is an [d]abomina-
tion to the LORD your God.
26"And you shall not bring an abomination into your house, and like it come
under the [a]ban; you shall utterly detest
it and you shall utterly abhor it, for it is
something banned.

God's Gracious Dealings

8 "ALL the commandments that I am
commanding you today you shall be
careful to do, that you [a]may live and
multiply, and go in and possess the land
which the LORD swore *to give* to your
forefathers.
2"[a]And you shall remember all the
way which the LORD your God has [b]led
you in the wilderness these forty years,
that He might humble you, [c]testing you,
to know what was in your heart, whether
you would keep His commandments or
not.
3"And He humbled you and let you
be hungry, and fed you with manna
which you did not know, nor did your
fathers know, that He might make you
[1]understand that [a]man does not live by

2 [1]Lit., *smite* [2]Lit., *surely devote to the ban*
[a]Num. 31:17; Josh. 11:11 [b]Ex. 23:32
[c]Deut. 7:16; 13:8
3 [1]Lit., *daughter* [2]Lit., *his son* [3]Lit., *his daughter* [4]Lit., *son*
[a]Ex. 34:15, 16; Josh. 23:12; Ezra 9:2
4 [1]Lit., *he* [2]Lit., *son* [3]Lit., *after*
[a]Deut. 4:26
5 [1]I.e., wooden symbols of a female deity
[a]Ex. 23:24; 34:13; Deut. 12:3
6 [1]Or, *special treasure* [2]Lit., *ground*
[a]Ex. 19:6; Deut. 14:2, 21; Ps. 50:5; Jer. 2:3 [b]Ex. 19:5; Deut. 4:20; 14:2; 26:18; Ps. 135:4; Titus 2:14; 1 Pet. 2:9
7 [a]Deut. 4:37
8 [1]Lit., *slaves*
[a]Ex. 32:13 [b]Ex. 13:3
9 [1]Lit., *the*
[a]Deut. 4:35, 39 [b]Is. 49:7; 1 Cor. 1:9; 1 Thess. 5:24; 2 Tim. 2:13 [c]Ex. 20:6; Dan. 9:4 [d]Deut. 5:10
10 [1]Lit., *his face* [2]Lit., *him* [3]Lit., *to*
[a]Is. 59:18; Nah. 1:2
12 [1]Lit., *the*
[a]Lev. 26:3-13; Deut. 28:1-14
13 [1]Lit., *on the ground*
[a]Ps. 146:8; Prov. 15:9; John 14:21 [b]Lev. 26:9; Deut. 13:17; 30:5
14 [a]Ex. 23:26
15 [a]Ex. 15:26
16 [a]Deut. 7:2 [b]Ex. 23:33; Judg. 8:27; Ps. 106:36
17 [a]Num. 33:53
18 [a]Ps. 105:5
19 [a]Deut. 4:34
20 [a]Ex. 23:28; Josh. 24:12
21 [1]Lit., *from before them*
[a]Ex. 29:45; Josh. 3:10 [b]Deut. 10:17; Neh. 1:5; 9:32
22 [1]Lit., *beasts of the field*
[a]Ex. 23:29, 30
23 [1]Lit., *confuse them with*
[a]Ex. 23:27; Josh. 10:10
24 [a]Josh. 6:2; 10:23-25 [b]Deut. 11:25; Josh. 1:5; 10:8; 23:9
25 [a]Ex. 32:20; Deut. 12:3; 1 Chr. 14:12 [b]Ex. 20:17 [c]Deut. 7:16; Judg. 8:27 [d]Deut. 17:1
26 [a]Lev. 27:28f.

1 [a]Deut. 4:1
2 [a]Deut. 8:16 [b]Ps. 136:16; Amos 2:10 [c]Ex. 15:25; 20:20; 2 Chr. 32:31
3 [1]Lit., *know*
[a]Matt. 4:4; Luke 4:4

bread alone, but man lives by everything that proceeds out of the mouth of the LORD.

4 "[a]Your clothing did not wear out on you, nor did your foot swell these forty years.

5 "[a]Thus you are to know in your heart that the LORD your God was disciplining you just as a man disciplines his son.

6 "Therefore, you shall keep the commandments of the LORD your God, to walk in His ways and to [1]fear Him.

7 "For [a]the LORD your God is bringing you into a good land, a land of brooks of water, of fountains and springs, flowing forth in valleys and hills;

8 a land of wheat and barley, of vines and fig trees and pomegranates, a land of olive oil and honey;

9 a land where you shall eat food without scarcity, in which you shall not lack anything; a land whose stones are iron, and out of whose hills you can dig copper.

10 "When [a]you have eaten and are satisfied, you shall bless the LORD your God for the good land which He has given you.

11 "[1]Beware lest you [a]forget the LORD your God by not keeping His commandments and His ordinances and His statutes which I am commanding you today;

12 lest, [a]when you have eaten and are satisfied, and have built good houses and lived *in them,*

13 and when your herds and your flocks multiply, and your silver and gold multiply, and all that you have multiplies,

14 then your heart becomes [1]proud, and you [a]forget the LORD your God who brought you out from the land of Egypt, out of the house of [2]slavery.

15 "He led you through [a]the great and terrible wilderness, *with its* [b]fiery serpents and scorpions and thirsty ground where there was no water; He [c]brought water for you out of the rock of flint.

16 "In the wilderness He fed you manna [a]which your fathers did not know, that He might humble you and that He might [b]test you, to do good for you [1]in the end.

17 "Otherwise, [a]you may say in your heart, 'My power and the strength of my hand made me this wealth.'

18 "But you shall remember the LORD your God, for [a]it is He who is giving you power to make wealth, that He may confirm His covenant which He swore to your fathers, as *it is* this day.

19 "And it shall come about if you ever forget the LORD your God, and go after other gods and serve them and worship them, [a]I testify against you today that you shall surely perish.

20 "Like the nations that the LORD makes to perish before you, so [a]you shall perish; because you would not listen to the voice of the LORD your God.

Israel Provoked God

9 "HEAR, O Israel! You are crossing over the Jordan today to go in to dispossess [a]nations greater and mightier than you, great cities [1b]fortified to heaven,

2 a people great and tall, the sons of the Anakim, whom you know and of whom you have heard *it said,* '[a]Who can stand before the sons of Anak?'

3 "Know therefore today that [a]it is the LORD your God who is crossing over before you as [b]a consuming fire. He will destroy them and He will subdue them before you, so that [c]you may drive them out and destroy them quickly, just as the LORD has spoken to you.

4 "[a]Do not say in your heart when the LORD your God has driven them out before [1]you, 'Because of my righteousness the LORD has brought me in to possess this land,' but *it is* [b]because of the wickedness of these nations *that* the LORD is dispossessing them before you.

5 "It is [a]not for your righteousness or for the uprightness of your heart that you are going to possess their land, but *it is* because of the wickedness of these nations *that* the LORD your God is driving them out before you, in order to confirm [b]the [1]oath which the LORD swore to your fathers, to Abraham, Isaac and Jacob.

6 "Know, then, *it is* not because of your righteousness *that* the LORD your God is giving you this good land to possess, for you are [a]a [1]stubborn people.

7 "Remember, do not forget how you provoked the LORD your God to wrath in the wilderness; [a]from the day that you left the land of Egypt until you arrived at this place, you have been rebellious against the LORD.

8 "Even [a]at Horeb you provoked the LORD to wrath, and the LORD was so angry with you that He would have destroyed you.

9 "When I went up to the mountain to receive the tablets of stone, the tablets of the covenant which the LORD had made with you, then I remained on the mountain forty days and nights; [a]I neither ate bread nor drank water.

10 "And the LORD gave me the two tablets of stone [a]written by the finger of God; and on them *were* all the words which the LORD had spoken with you at the mountain from the midst of the fire on the day of the assembly.

11 "And it came about [a]at the end of forty days and nights that the LORD gave me the two tablets of stone, the tablets of the covenant.

12 "[a]Then the LORD said to me, 'Arise, go down from here quickly, for your people whom you brought out of Egypt have acted corruptly. They have [b]quickly turned aside from the way which I commanded them; they have made a molten image for themselves.'

---

4 [a]Deut. 29:5; Neh. 9:21
5 [a]Deut. 4:36; 2 Sam. 7:14; Prov. 3:12; Heb. 12:6; Rev. 3:19
6 [1]Or, *reverence*
7 [a]Deut. 11:9-12; Jer. 2:7
10 [a]Deut. 6:11
11 [1]Lit., *Take heed to yourself* [a]Deut. 4:9
12 [a]Prov. 30:9; Hos. 13:6
14 [1]Lit., *lifted up* [2]Lit., *slaves* [a]Deut. 8:11; Ps. 106:21
15 [a]Deut. 1:19; Jer. 2:6 [b]Num. 21:6 [c]Ex. 17:6; Num. 20:11; Deut. 32:13; Ps. 78:15; 114:8
16 [1]Lit., *at your end* [a]Ex. 16:15 [b]Deut. 8:2
17 [a]Deut. 9:4
18 [a]Prov. 10:22; Hos. 2:8
19 [a]Deut. 4:26; 30:18
20 [a]Ezek. 5:5-17

1 [1]Lit., *and fortified* [a]Deut. 4:38; 7:1; 11:23 [b]Deut. 1:28
2 [a]Num. 13:22, 28, 33; Josh. 11:21, 22
3 [a]Deut. 31:3; Josh. 3:11 [b]Deut. 4:24; Heb. 12:29 [c]Ex. 23:31; Deut. 7:24
4 [1]Lit., *you saying* [a]Deut. 8:17; 9:7, 24; 31:27 [b]Lev. 18:3, 24-30; Deut. 12:31; 18:9-14
5 [1]Lit., *word* [a]Titus 3:5 [b]Gen. 12:7; 13:15; 15:7; 17:8; 26:4; 28:13
6 [1]Or, *stiff-necked* [a]Deut. 9:13; 10:16; 31:27
7 [a]Ex. 14:10f.; Num. 14:22
8 [a]Ex. 32:7-10; Ps. 106:19
9 [a]Ex. 24:18; 34:28; Deut. 8:3; 9:18
10 [a]Deut. 4:13
11 [a]Deut. 9:9
12 [a]Ex. 32:7, 8 [b]Judg. 2:17

13“The [a]LORD spoke further to me,
saying, ‘I have seen this people, and
indeed, it is a [1][b]stubborn people.
14 ‘[a]Let Me alone, that I may destroy
them and [b]blot out their name from
under heaven; and I will make of you a
nation mightier and greater than they.’
15“[a]So I turned and came down from
the mountain while the mountain was
burning with fire, and the two tablets of
the covenant were in my two hands.
16“And I saw that you had indeed
sinned against the LORD your God. You
had made for yourselves a molten calf;
you had turned aside quickly from the
way which the LORD had commanded
you.
17“And I took hold of the two tablets
and threw them from my hands, and
smashed them before your eyes.
18“[a]And I fell down before the LORD,
[b]as at the first, forty days and nights; [c]I
neither ate bread nor drank water, [d]be-
cause of all your sin which you had
committed in doing what was evil in the
sight of the LORD to provoke Him to
anger.
19“For [a]I was afraid of the anger and
hot displeasure with which the LORD
was wrathful against you in order to
destroy you, [b]but the LORD listened to
me that time also.
20“And the LORD was angry enough
with Aaron to destroy him; so I also
prayed for Aaron at the same time.
21“[a]And I took your [1]sinful *thing*, the
calf which you had made, and burned it
with fire and crushed it, grinding it very
small until it was as fine as dust; and I
threw its dust into the brook that came
down from the mountain.
22“Again at [a]Taberah and at [b]Massah
and at [c]Kibroth-hattaavah you provoked
the LORD to wrath.
23“And when the LORD sent you from
[a]Kadesh-barnea, saying, ‘[b]Go up and
possess the land which I have given you,’
then you rebelled against the [1]command
of the LORD your God; [c]you neither
believed Him nor listened to His voice.
24“[a]You have been rebellious against
the LORD from the day I knew you.
25“[a]So I fell down before the LORD the
forty days and nights, which I [1]did
because the LORD had said He would
destroy you.
26“[a]And I prayed to the LORD, and
said, ‘O Lord GOD, do not destroy Thy
people, even Thine inheritance, whom
Thou hast redeemed through Thy greatness, whom Thou hast brought out of
Egypt with a mighty hand.
27 ‘Remember Thy servants, Abraham, Isaac, and Jacob; do not look at
the stubbornness of this people or at
their wickedness or their sin.
28 ‘Otherwise the land from which
Thou didst bring us may say, “[a]Because
the LORD was not able to bring them
into the land which He had [1]promised
them and because He hated them He has
brought them out to slay them in the
wilderness.”

13 [1]Or, *stiff-necked* [a]Ex. 32:9 [b]Deut. 10:16; 31:27; 2 Kin. 17:14
14 [a]Ex. 32:10 [b]Ps. 9:5; 109:13
15 [a]Ex. 32:15-19
18 [a]Ex. 34:28 [b]Deut. 10:10 [c]Deut. 9:9 [d]Ex. 34:9
19 [a]Ex. 32:10f.; Heb. 12:21 [b]Ex. 34:10; Deut. 10:10
21 [1]Lit., *sin* [a]Ex. 32:20
22 [a]Num. 11:3 [b]Ex. 17:7 [c]Num. 11:34
23 [1]Lit., *mouth* [a]Deut. 1:2 [b]Deut. 1:21 [c]Deut. 1:26; Ps. 106:24
24 [a]Deut. 9:7; 31:27
25 [1]Lit., *fell down* [a]Deut. 9:18
26 [a]Ex. 32:11-13; 1 Sam. 7:9; Jer. 15:1
28 [1]Lit., *spoken to* [a]Ex. 32:12; Num. 14:16
29 [a]Deut. 4:20; 1 Kin. 8:51; Neh. 1:10; Ps. 106:40 [b]Deut. 4:34
1 [a]Ex. 34:1 [b]Ex. 25:10
2 [a]Deut. 4:13 [b]Ex. 25:16
3 [a]Ex. 25:5; 37:1-9 [b]Ex. 34:4
4 [1]Lit., *Words* [a]Ex. 34:28; Deut. 4:13 [b]Ex. 20:1 [c]Deut. 9:10; 18:16
5 [a]Ex. 34:29 [b]Ex. 40:20 [c]1 Kin. 8:9
6 [1]Or, *the wells of the sons of Jaakan* [a]Num. 33:30, 31 [b]Num. 20:25-28; 33:38
7 [a]Num. 33:33, 34
8 [a]Num. 3:6; 18:1-7; Deut. 31:9 [b]Deut. 17:12; 18:5; 21:5
9 [a]Num. 18:20, 24; Deut. 18:1, 2; Ezek. 44:28
10 [a]Ex. 34:28; Deut. 9:18
12 [1]Or, *reverence* [a]Mic. 6:8 [b]Deut. 6:5; Matt. 22:37; 1 Tim. 1:5 [c]Deut. 4:29
14 [1]Lit., *heaven of heavens* [a]1 Kin. 8:27; Neh. 9:6; Ps. 68:33; 115:16 [b]Ps. 24:1
15 [1]Lit., *seed* [a]Deut. 4:37

29 ‘Yet they are Thy people, even
[a]Thine inheritance, whom Thou hast
brought out by Thy [b]great power and
Thine outstretched arm.’

The Tablets Rewritten

10 “AT that time the LORD said to
me, ‘[a]Cut out for yourself two
tablets of stone like the former ones, and
come up to Me on the mountain, and
[b]make an ark of wood for yourself.
2 ‘And [a]I will write on the tablets the
words that were on the former tablets
which you shattered, and [b]you shall put
them in the ark.’
3“So [a]I made an ark of acacia wood
and [b]cut out two tablets of stone like the
former ones, and went up on the mountain with the two tablets in my hand.
4“And He wrote on the tablets, like
the former writing, [a]the Ten [1]Command-
ments [b]which the LORD had spoken to
you on the mountain from the midst of
the fire [c]on the day of the assembly; and
the LORD gave them to me.
5“Then I turned and [a]came down
from the mountain, and [b]put the tablets
in the ark which I had made; [c]and there
they are, as the LORD commanded me.”
6 (Now the sons of Israel set out
from [1]Beeroth [a]Bene-jaakan to Moserah.
[b]There Aaron died and there he was
buried and Eleazar his son ministered as
priest in his place.
7 [a]From there they set out to Gudgodah; and from Gudgodah to Jotbathah,
a land of brooks of water.
8 [a]At that time the LORD set apart
the tribe of Levi to carry the ark of the
covenant of the LORD, to stand before
the LORD [b]to serve Him and to bless in
His name until this day.
9 [a]Therefore, Levi does not have a
portion or inheritance with his brothers;
the LORD is his inheritance, just as the
LORD your God spoke to him.)
10“[a]I, moreover, stayed on the mountain forty days and forty nights like the
first time, and the LORD listened to me
that time also; the LORD was not willing
to destroy you.
11“Then the LORD said to me, ‘Arise,
proceed on your journey ahead of the
people, that they may go in and possess
the land which I swore to their fathers to
give them.’
12“[a]And now, Israel, what does the
LORD your God require from you, but to
[1]fear the LORD your God, to walk in all
His ways and [b]love Him, and to serve
the LORD your God with [c]all your heart
and with all your soul,
13 *and* to keep the LORD's commandments and His statutes which I am
commanding you today for your good?
14“Behold, [a]to the LORD your God
belong heaven and the [1]highest heavens,
[b]the earth and all that is in it.
15“[a]Yet on your fathers did the LORD
set His affection to love them, and He
chose their [1]descendants after them, *even*
you above all peoples, as *it is* this day.

16 “[a]Circumcise then [1]your heart, and [b]stiffen your neck no more.

17 “[a]For the LORD your God is the God of gods and the [b]Lord of lords, the great, the mighty, and the awesome God [c]who does not show partiality, nor [d]take a bribe.

18 “He executes justice for [a]the orphan and the widow, and shows His love for the alien by giving him food and clothing.

19 “[a]So show your love for the alien, for you were aliens in the land of Egypt.

20 “You shall fear the LORD your God; you shall serve Him and [a]cling to Him, and [b]you shall swear by His name.

21 “He is [a]your praise and He is your God, who has done these great and awesome things for you which your eyes have seen.

22 “[a]Your fathers went down to Egypt seventy persons *in all,* [b]and now the LORD your God has made you as numerous as the stars of heaven.

Rewards of Obedience

11 “YOU shall therefore [a]love the LORD your God, and always [b]keep His charge, His statutes, His ordinances, and His commandments.

2 “And know this day [a]that I *am* not *speaking* with your sons who have not known and who have not seen the [1]discipline of the LORD your God—His greatness, His mighty hand, and His outstretched arm,

3 and [a]His signs and His works which He did in the midst of Egypt to Pharaoh the king of Egypt and to all his land;

4 and what He did to Egypt's army, to its horses and its chariots, [a]when He made the water of the [1]Red Sea to [2]engulf them while they were pursuing you, and the LORD [3]completely destroyed them;

5 and what He did to you in the wilderness until you came to this place;

6 and [a]what He did to Dathan and Abiram, the sons of Eliab, the son of Reuben, when the earth opened its mouth and swallowed them, their households, their tents, and [b]every living thing that [1]followed them, among all Israel—

7 but your own eyes have seen all the great work of the LORD which He did.

8 “You shall therefore keep every commandment which I am commanding you today, [a]so that you may be strong and go in and possess the land into which you are about to cross to possess it;

9 [a]so that you may prolong *your* days on the land which the LORD swore to your fathers to give to them and to their [1]descendants, [b]a land flowing with milk and honey.

10 “For the land, into which you are entering to possess it, is not like the land of Egypt from which you came, where you used to sow your seed and water it with your [1]foot like a vegetable garden.

16 [1]Lit., *the foreskin of your heart* [a]Lev. 26:41; Jer. 4:4 [b]Deut. 9:6
17 [a]Josh. 22:22; Ps. 136:2; Dan. 2:47; 1 Tim. 6:15; Rev. 19:16 [b]Rev. 17:14 [c]Deut. 1:17; Acts 10:34; Rom. 2:11; Gal. 2:6; Eph. 6:9 [d]Deut. 16:19
18 [a]Ex. 22:22-24; Ps. 68:5; 146:9
19 [a]Lev. 19:34; Ezek. 47:22, 23
20 [a]Deut. 11:22; 13:4 [b]Deut. 5:11; 6:13; Ps. 63:11
21 [a]Ps. 109:1; 148:14; Jer. 17:14
22 [a]Gen. 46:27 [b]Gen. 15:5; 22:17; Deut. 1:10

1 [a]Deut. 6:5; 10:12 [b]Lev. 18:30; 22:9
2 [1]Or, *instruction* [a]Deut. 4:34
3 [a]Ex. 7:8-21
4 [1]Lit., *Sea of Reeds* [2]Lit., *flow over their faces* [3]Lit., *to this day* [a]Ex. 14:28; Deut. 1:40; 2:1
6 [1]Lit., *was at their feet* [a]Num. 16:1-35; Ps. 106:16-18 [b]Num. 26:10, 11
8 [a]Deut. 31:6, 7, 23; Josh. 1:6, 7
9 [1]Lit., *seed* [a]Deut. 4:40; 5:16, 33; 6:2; Prov. 10:27 [b]Ex. 3:8
10 [1]I.e., probably a treadmill
11 [a]Deut. 8:7
12 [1]Lit., *beginning of the year* [a]1 Kin. 9:3
13 [a]Lev. 26:3; Deut. 7:12 [b]Deut. 11:1 [c]Deut. 4:29
14 [1]So some ancient versions; M.T. reads *I* [2]I.e., autumn [3]I.e., spring [a]Lev. 26:4; Deut. 28:12 [b]Joel 2:23; James 5:7
15 [1]So some ancient versions; M.T. reads *I* [a]Ps. 104:14 [b]Deut. 6:11
16 [1]Lit., *Watch yourselves* [a]Job 31:27
17 [a]Deut. 6:15; 9:19 [b]1 Kin. 8:35; 2 Chr. 6:26; 7:13 [c]Deut. 28:24 [d]Deut. 4:26
18 [1]Lit., *put* [2]Lit., *frontlet bands* [3]Lit., *between your eyes* [a]Ex. 13:9, 16; Deut. 6:8
19 [a]Deut. 4:9, 10; 6:7; Prov. 22:6
20 [a]Deut. 6:9
21 [1]Lit., *the days of the heavens* [a]Prov. 3:2; 4:10; 9:11 [b]Ps. 72:5
22 [a]Deut. 6:17 [b]Deut. 11:1 [c]Deut. 10:20
23 [a]Deut. 4:38 [b]Deut. 9:1

11 “But [a]the land into which you are about to cross to possess it, a land of hills and valleys, drinks water from the rain of heaven,

12 a land for which the LORD your God cares; [a]the eyes of the LORD your God are always on it, from the [1]beginning even to the end of the year.

13 “And it shall come about, [a]if you listen obediently to my commandments which I am commanding you today, [b]to love the LORD your God and to serve Him [c]with all your heart and all your soul,

14 that [1a]He will give the rain for your land in its season, the [2b]early and [3]late rain, that you may gather in your grain and your new wine and your oil.

15 “And [1a]He will give grass in your fields for your cattle, and [b]you shall eat and be satisfied.

16 “[1a]Beware, lest your hearts be deceived and you turn away and serve other gods and worship them.

17 “Or [a]the anger of the LORD will be kindled against you, and He will [b]shut up the heavens [c]so that there will be no rain and the ground will not yield its fruit; and [d]you will perish quickly from the good land which the LORD is giving you.

18 “[a]You shall therefore [1]impress these words of mine on your heart and on your soul; and you shall bind them as a sign on your hand, and they shall be as [2]frontals [3]on your forehead.

19 “[a]And you shall teach them to your sons, talking of them when you sit in your house and when you walk along the road and when you lie down and when you rise up.

20 “[a]And you shall write them on the doorposts of your house and on your gates,

21 so that [a]your days and the days of your sons may be multiplied on the land which the LORD swore to your fathers to give them, as [1b]long as the heavens *remain* above the earth.

22 “For if you are [a]careful to keep all this commandment which I am commanding you, to do it, [b]to love the LORD your God, to walk in all His ways and [c]hold fast to Him;

23 then the LORD will [a]drive out all these nations from before you, and you will [b]dispossess nations greater and mightier than you.

24 “[a]Every place on which the sole of your foot shall tread shall be yours; [b]your border shall be from the wilderness to Lebanon, *and* from the river, the river Euphrates, as far as [1]the western sea.

25 “[a]There shall no man be able to stand before you; the LORD your God shall lay the dread of you and the fear of you on all the land on which you set foot, as He has spoken to you.

24 [1]I.e., the Mediterranean [a]Josh. 1:3; 14:9 [b]Gen. 15:18; Ex. 23:31; Deut. 1:7, 8
25 [a]Ex. 23:27; Deut. 7:24

26"[a]See, I am setting before you today a blessing and a curse:

27 the [a]blessing, if you listen to the commandments of the LORD your God, which I am commanding you today;

28 and the [a]curse, if you do not listen to the commandments of the LORD your God, but turn aside from the way which I am commanding you today, [1]by following other gods which you have not known.

29"And it shall come about, when the LORD your God brings you into the land where you are entering to possess it, [a]that you shall place the blessing on Mount Gerizim and the curse on Mount Ebal.

30"Are they not across the Jordan, west of the way toward the sunset, in the land of the Canaanites who live in the Arabah, opposite [a]Gilgal, beside [b]the [1]oaks of Moreh?

31"For you are about to cross the Jordan to go in to possess the land which the LORD your God is giving you, and [a]you shall possess it and live in it,

32 and you shall be careful to do all the statutes and the judgments which I am setting before you today.

Laws of the Sanctuary

12 "THESE are the statutes and the judgments which you shall carefully observe in the land which the LORD, the God of your fathers, has given you to possess [1a]as long as you live on the [2]earth.

2"You shall utterly destroy all the places where the nations whom you shall dispossess serve their gods, on the [a]high mountains and on the hills and under every green tree.

3"And [a]you shall tear down their altars and smash their *sacred* pillars and burn their [1]Asherim with fire, and you shall cut down the engraved images of their gods, and you shall [b]obliterate their name from that place.

4"You shall not act like this toward the LORD your God.

5"[a]But you shall seek *the LORD* at the place which the LORD your God shall choose from all your tribes, to establish His name there for His dwelling, and there you shall come.

6"And there you shall bring your burnt offerings, your sacrifices, [a]your tithes, the [1]contribution of your hand, your votive offerings, your freewill offerings, and the first-born of your herd and of your flock.

7"There also you and your households shall eat before the LORD your God, and [a]rejoice in all [1]your undertakings in which the LORD your God has blessed you.

8"You shall not do at all what we are doing here today, every man *doing* whatever is right in his own eyes;

9 for you have not as yet come to [a]the resting place and the [b]inheritance which the LORD your God is giving you.

10"When you cross the Jordan and live in the land which the LORD your God is giving you to inherit, and [a]He gives you rest from all your enemies around *you* so that you live in security,

11 [a]then it shall come about that the place in which the LORD your God shall choose for His name to dwell, there you shall bring all that I command you: your burnt offerings and your sacrifices, your tithes and the [1]contribution of your hand, and all your choice votive offerings which you will vow to the LORD.

12"And you shall [a]rejoice before the LORD your God, you and your sons and daughters, your male and female servants, and the [b]Levite who is within your gates, since [c]he has no portion or inheritance with you.

13"[a]Be careful that you do not offer your burnt offerings in every *cultic* place you see,

14 but in the place which the LORD chooses in one of your tribes, there you shall offer your burnt offerings, and there you shall do all that I command you.

15"[a]However, you may slaughter and eat meat within any of your gates, [1]whatever you desire, according to the blessing of the LORD your God which He has given you; the unclean and the clean may eat of it, as of [b]the gazelle and the deer.

16"[a]Only you shall not eat the blood; [b]you are to pour it out on the ground like water.

17"[a]You are not allowed to eat within your gates the tithe of your grain, or new wine, or oil, or the first-born of your herd or flock, or any of your votive offerings which you vow, or your freewill offerings, or the [1]contribution of your hand.

18"But [a]you shall eat them before the LORD your God in [b]the place which the LORD your God will choose, you and your son and daughter, and your male and female servants, and the [c]Levite who is within your gates; and you shall [d]rejoice before the LORD your God in all [1]your undertakings.

19"[a]Be careful that you do not forsake the Levite [1]as long as you live in your land.

20"When the LORD your God extends your border [a]as He has promised you, and you say, 'I will eat meat,' because [1]you desire to eat meat, *then* you may eat meat, [2]whatever you desire.

21"If the place which the LORD your God chooses to put His name is too far from you, then you may slaughter of your herd and flock which the LORD has given you, as I have commanded you; and you may eat within your gates [1]whatever you desire.

22"Just as a gazelle or a deer is eaten, so you shall eat it; the unclean and the clean alike may eat of it.

23"Only be sure [a]not to eat the blood, for the blood is the [1]life, and you shall not eat the [1]life with the flesh.

26 [a]Deut. 30:1, 19
27 [a]Deut. 28:1-14
28 [1]Lit., *to follow* [a]Deut. 28:15-68
29 [a]Deut. 27:12; Josh. 8:33
30 [1]Lit., *terebinths* [a]Josh. 4:19 [b]Gen. 12:6
31 [a]Deut. 17:14; Josh. 21:43

1 [1]Lit., *all the days* [2]Lit., *ground* [a]Deut. 4:9, 10; 1 Kin. 8:40
2 [a]2 Kin. 16:4; 17:10, 11
3 [1]I.e., wooden symbols of a female deity [a]Num. 33:52; Deut. 7:5; Judg. 2:2 [b]Ex. 23:13; Ps. 16:4; Zech. 13:2
5 [a]Ex. 20:24; Deut. 12:11, 13; 2 Chr. 7:12; Ps. 78:68
6 [1]Or, *heave offering* [a]Deut. 14:22
7 [1]Lit., *the putting forth of your hand* [a]Lev. 23:40; Deut. 12:12, 18; 14:26; 28:47; Eccl. 3:12, 13; 5:18-20
9 [a]Deut. 3:20; 25:19; Ps. 95:11 [b]Deut. 4:21
10 [a]Josh. 11:23
11 [1]Or, *heave offering* [a]Deut. 12:5; 15:20; 16:2; 17:8; 18:6
12 [a]Deut. 12:7 [b]Deut. 12:18, 19; 26:11-13 [c]Deut. 10:9; 14:29
13 [a]Deut. 12:5, 11
15 [1]Lit., *in every desire of your soul* [a]Deut. 12:20-23 [b]Deut. 12:22; 14:5; 15:22
16 [a]Gen. 9:4; Lev. 7:26; 17:10-12; 1 Sam. 14:33f.; Acts 15:20, 29 [b]Deut. 15:23
17 [1]Lit., *heave offering* [a]Deut. 12:26
18 [1]Lit., *the putting forth of your hand* [a]Deut. 14:23 [b]Deut. 12:5 [c]Deut. 12:12 [d]Deut. 12:7; Eccl. 3:12f.; 5:18-20
19 [1]Lit., *all your days upon your land* [a]Deut. 14:27
20 [1]Lit., *your soul desires* [2]Lit., *in every desire of your soul* [a]Gen. 15:18; Deut. 11:24; 19:8
21 [1]Lit., *in every desire of your soul*
23 [1]Lit., *soul* [a]Gen. 9:4; Lev. 17:10-14; Deut. 12:16

24 "You shall not eat it; you shall pour it out on the ground like water.

25 "You shall not eat it, in order that [a]it may be well with you and your sons after you, for [b]you will be doing what is right in the sight of the LORD.

26 "[a]Only your holy things which you may have and your votive offerings, you shall take and go to the place which the LORD chooses.

27 "And [a]you shall offer your burnt offerings, the flesh and the blood, on the altar of the LORD your God; and the blood of your sacrifices shall be poured out on the altar of the LORD your God, and [b]you shall eat the flesh.

28 "Be careful to listen to all these words which I command you, in order that [a]it may be well with you and your sons after you forever, for you will be doing what is good and right in the sight of the LORD your God.

29 "When [a]the LORD your God cuts off before you the nations which you are going in to dispossess, and you dispossess them and dwell in their land,

30 beware that you are not ensnared [1]to follow them, after they are destroyed before you, and that you do not inquire after their gods, saying, 'How do these nations serve their gods, that I also may do likewise?'

31 "[a]You shall not behave thus toward the LORD your God, for every abominable act which the LORD hates they have done for their gods; for [b]they even burn their sons and daughters in the fire to their gods.

32 "[1a]Whatever I command you, you shall be careful to do; [b]you shall not add to nor take away from it.

Shun Idolatry

13 "[1a]IF a prophet or a dreamer of dreams arises among you and gives you a sign or a wonder,

2 and the sign or the wonder comes true, concerning which he spoke to you, saying, '[a]Let us go after other gods (whom you have not known) and let us serve them,'

3 you shall not listen to the words of that prophet or that dreamer of dreams; for the LORD your God is [a]testing you to find out if [b]you love the LORD your God with all your heart and with all your soul.

4 "[a]You shall follow the LORD your God and fear Him; and you shall keep His commandments, listen to His voice, serve Him, and [b]cling to Him.

5 "But that prophet or that dreamer of dreams shall be [a]put to death, because he has [1]counseled [2]rebellion against the LORD your God who brought you from the land of Egypt and redeemed you from the house of [3]slavery, [b]to seduce you from the way in which the LORD your God commanded you to walk. [c]So you shall purge the evil from among you.

6 "[a]If your brother, your mother's son, or your son or daughter, or the wife [1]you cherish, or your friend who is as your own soul, entice you secretly, saying, '[b]Let us go and serve other gods' (whom neither you nor your fathers have known,

7 of the gods of the peoples who are around you, near you or far from you, from one end of the earth to the other end),

8 [a]you shall not yield to him or listen to him; [b]and your eye shall not pity him, nor shall you spare or conceal him.

9 "[a]But you shall surely kill him; [b]your hand shall be first against him to put him to death, and afterwards the hand of all the people.

10 "So you shall stone him [1]to death because he has sought [a]to seduce you from the LORD your God who brought you out from the land of Egypt, out of the house of [2]slavery.

11 "Then [a]all Israel will hear and be afraid, and will never again do such a wicked thing among you.

12 "If you hear in one of your cities, which the LORD your God is giving you to live in, *anyone* saying *that*

13 some worthless men have gone out from among you and have seduced the inhabitants of their city, saying, '[a]Let us go and serve other gods' (whom you have not known),

14 then you shall investigate and search out and inquire thoroughly. And if it is true *and* the matter established that this abomination has been done among you,

15 [a]you shall surely strike the inhabitants of that city with the edge of the sword, [1]utterly destroying it and all that is in it and its cattle with the edge of the sword.

16 "[a]Then you shall gather all its booty into the middle of its open square and burn the city and all its booty with fire as a whole burnt offering to the LORD your God; and it shall be a [1b]ruin forever. It shall never be rebuilt.

17 "And nothing from that which is put under the ban shall cling to your hand, in order that the LORD may turn from [a]His burning anger and [b]show mercy to you, and have compassion on you and [c]make you increase, just [d]as He has sworn to your fathers,

18 [1]if you will listen to the voice of the LORD your God, [2]keeping all His commandments which I am commanding you today, [3]and doing what is right in the sight of the LORD your God.

Clean and Unclean Animals

14 "YOU are [a]the sons of the LORD your God; [b]you shall not cut yourselves nor [1]shave your forehead for the sake of the dead.

2 "For you are [a]a holy people to the LORD your God; and the LORD has chosen you to be a [b]people for His [1]own possession out of all the peoples who are on the face of the earth.

25 aDeut. 4:40; Is. 3:10 bEx. 15:26; 1 Kin. 11:38
26 aNum. 5:9f.; 18:19; Deut. 12:17
27 aLev. 1:9, 13 bLev. 3:1-17
28 aDeut. 4:40; Eccl. 8:12
29 aJosh. 23:4
30 1Lit., *after them*
31 aDeut. 9:5 bLev. 18:21; Deut. 18:10; Ps. 106:37; Jer. 32:35
32 1Lit., *Everything that* aDeut. 4:2; Josh. 1:7 bProv. 30:6; Rev. 22:18

1 1Ch. 13:2 in Heb. aMatt. 24:24; Mark 13:22; 2 Thess. 2:9
2 aDeut. 13:6, 13
3 aEx. 20:20; Deut. 8:2, 16; 1 Cor. 11:19 bDeut. 6:5
4 a2 Kin. 23:3; 2 Chr. 34:31; 2 John 6 bDeut. 10:20
5 1Lit., *spoken* 2Lit., *turning aside* 3Lit., *slaves* aDeut. 13:9, 15; 17:5; 1 Kin. 18:40 bDeut. 4:19; 13:10 c1 Cor. 5:13
6 1Lit., *of your bosom* aDeut. 17:2-7; 29:18 bDeut. 13:2
8 aProv. 1:10 bDeut. 7:2
9 aDeut. 13:5 bLev. 24:14; Deut. 17:7
10 1Lit., *with stones so that he dies* 2Lit., *slaves* aDeut. 13:5
11 aDeut. 19:20
13 aDeut. 13:2
15 1Or, *putting it under the ban* aDeut. 13:5
16 1Lit., *mound* aDeut. 7:25, 26 bJosh. 8:28; Is. 17:1; 25:2; Jer. 49:2
17 aEx. 32:12; Num. 25:4 bDeut. 30:3 cDeut. 7:13 dGen. 22:17; 26:4, 24; 28:14
18 1Or, *for* 2Lit., *to keep* 3Lit., *to do*

1 1Lit., *make a baldness between your eyes* aRom. 8:16; 9:8, 26; Gal. 3:26; 1 John 3:1 bLev. 19:28; 21:5; Jer. 16:6; 41:5
2 1Or, *special treasure* aLev. 20:26; Deut. 7:6; Rom. 12:1 bEx. 19:5; Deut. 4:20; 26:18; Titus 2:14; 1 Pet. 2:9

3"[a]You shall not eat any detestable
thing.
4"[a]These are the animals which you
may eat: the ox, the sheep, the goat,
5 [1]the deer, the gazelle, the roebuck,
the wild goat, the ibex, the antelope and
the mountain sheep.
6"And any animal that divides the
hoof and has the hoof split in [1]two *and*
[2]chews the cud, among the animals, that
you may eat.
7"Nevertheless, you are not to eat of
these among those which [1]chew the cud,
or among those that divide the hoof in
[2]two: the camel and the [3]rabbit and the
rock-badger, for though they [1]chew the
cud, they do not divide the hoof; they
are unclean for you.
8"And the pig, because it divides the
hoof but *does* not *chew* the cud, it is
unclean for you. You shall not eat any of
their flesh nor touch their carcasses.
9"These you may eat of all that are in
water: anything that has fins and scales
you may eat,
10 but anything that does not have
fins and scales you shall not eat; it is
unclean for you.
11"You may eat any clean bird.
12"But [a]these are the ones which you
shall not eat: the [1]eagle and the vulture
and the [2]buzzard,
13 and the red kite, the falcon, and the
kite in their kinds,
14 and every raven in its kind,
15 and the ostrich, the owl, the sea
gull, and the hawk in their kinds,
16 the little owl, the [1]great owl, the
white owl,
17 the pelican, the carrion vulture, the
cormorant,
18 the stork, and the heron in their
kinds, and the hoopoe and the bat.
19"And all the [1]teeming life with
wings are unclean to you; they shall not
be eaten.
20"You may eat any clean bird.
21"[a]You shall not eat anything which
dies *of itself.* You may give it to the alien
who is in your [1]town, so that he may eat
it, or you may sell it to a foreigner, for
you are [b]a holy people to the LORD your
God. [c]You shall not boil a kid in its
mother's milk.
22"You [a]shall surely tithe all the
produce from [1]what you sow, which
comes out of the field every year.
23"And you shall eat in the presence
of the LORD your God, [a]at the place
where He chooses to establish His name,
the tithe of your grain, your new wine,
your oil, and the first-born of your herd
and your flock, in order that you may
[b]learn to fear the LORD your God always.
24"And if the [1]distance is so great for
you that you are not able to [2]bring *the
tithe,* since the place where the LORD
your God chooses [a]to set His name is
too far away from you when the LORD
your God blesses you,
25 then you shall [1]exchange *it* for
money, and bind the money in your
hand and go to the place which the
LORD your God chooses.
26"And you may spend the money for
whatever your [1]heart desires, for oxen,
or sheep, or wine, or strong drink, or
whatever your [1]heart [2]desires; and [a]there
you shall eat in the presence of the LORD
your God and rejoice, you and your
household.
27"Also you shall not neglect [a]the
Levite who is in your [1]town, [b]for he has
no portion or inheritance among you.
28"[a]At the end of every third year you
shall bring out all the tithe of your
produce in that year, and shall deposit *it*
in your [1]town.
29"And the Levite, [a]because he has no
portion or inheritance among you, and
[b]the alien, the [1]orphan and the widow
who are in your [2]town, shall come and
[c]eat and be satisfied, in order that [d]the
LORD your God may bless you in all the
work of your hand which you do.

The Sabbatic Year

15 "[a]AT the end of *every* seven years
you shall [1]grant a remission *of
debts.*
2"And this is the manner of remission: every creditor shall release what he
has loaned to his neighbor; he shall not
exact it of his neighbor and his brother,
because the LORD's remission has been
proclaimed.
3"[a]From a foreigner you may exact *it,*
but your hand shall release whatever of
yours is with your brother.
4"However, there shall be no poor
among you, since [a]the LORD will surely
bless you in the land which the LORD
your God is giving you as an inheritance
to possess,
5 if only you listen obediently to the
voice of the LORD your God, to observe
carefully all this commandment which I
am commanding you today.
6"[a]For the LORD your God shall
bless you as He has promised you, and
you will lend to many nations, but you
will not borrow; and you will rule over
many nations, but they will not rule over
you.
7"If there is [a]a poor man with you,
one of your brothers, in any of your
[1]towns in your land which the LORD
your God is giving you, [b]you shall not
harden your heart, nor close your hand
from your poor brother;
8 but [a]you shall freely open your
hand to him, and shall generously lend
him sufficient for his need *in* whatever he
lacks.
9"Beware, lest there is a base
[1]thought in your heart, saying, '[a]The
seventh year, the year of remission, is
near,' and [b]your eye is hostile toward
your poor brother, and you give him
nothing; then he [c]may cry to the LORD
against you, and it will be a sin in you.

3 [a]Ezek. 4:14
4 [a]Lev. 11:2-45; Acts 10:14
5 [1]Exact identification of these animals is uncertain
6 [1]Lit., *two hoofs* [2]Lit., *brings up*
7 [1]Lit., *brings up* [2]Lit., *a cleaving* [3]Or, *hare*
12 [1]Or, *vulture* [2]Or, *black vulture* [a]Lev. 11:13
16 [1]Or, *great horned owl*
19 [1]I.e., flying insects
21 [1]Lit., *gates* [a]Lev. 17:15; 22:8; Ezek. 4:14; 44:31 [b]Deut. 14:2 [c]Ex. 23:19; 34:26
22 [1]Lit., *your seed* [a]Lev. 27:30; Deut. 12:6, 17; Neh. 10:37
23 [a]Deut. 12:5 [b]Deut. 4:10; Ps. 2:11; 111:10; 147:11; Is. 8:13; Jer. 32:38-40
24 [1]Lit., *way* [2]Lit., *carry it* [a]Deut. 12:5, 21
25 [1]Lit., *give in money*
26 [1]Lit., *soul* [2]Lit., *asks of you* [a]Deut. 12:7
27 [1]Lit., *gates* [a]Deut. 12:12 [b]Num. 18:20; Deut. 10:9; 18:12
28 [1]Lit., *gates* [a]Deut. 26:12
29 [1]Or, *fatherless* [2]Lit., *gates* [a]Deut. 10:9 [b]Deut. 16:11, 14; 24:19-21; 26:12; Ps. 94:6; Is. 1:17 [c]Deut. 6:11 [d]Deut. 15:10; Mal. 3:10
1 [1]Lit., *make a release* [a]Deut. 31:10
3 [a]Deut. 23:20
4 [a]Deut. 28:8
6 [a]Deut. 28:12, 13
7 [1]Lit., *gates* [a]Lev. 25:35; Deut. 15:11 [b]1 John 3:17
8 [a]Matt. 5:42; Luke 6:34; Gal. 2:10
9 [1]Lit., *word* [a]Deut. 15:1 [b]Matt. 20:15 [c]Ex. 22:23; Deut. 24:15; Job 34:28; Ps. 12:5; James 5:4

10"You shall generously give to him,
and your heart shall not be grieved when
you give to him, because [a]for this thing
the LORD your God will bless you in all
your work and in all [1]your undertakings.
11"[a]For the poor will never cease *to be*
[1]in the land; therefore I command you,
saying, 'You shall freely open your hand
to your brother, to your needy and poor
in your land.'
12"[a]If your [1]kinsman, a Hebrew man
or woman, is sold to you, then he shall
serve you six years, but in the seventh
year you shall set him [2]free.
13"And when you set him [1]free, you
shall not send him away empty-handed.
14"You shall furnish him liberally
from your flock and from your threshing
floor and from your wine vat; you shall
give to him as the LORD your God has
blessed you.
15"And you shall remember that you
were a slave in the land of Egypt, and
the LORD your God redeemed you;
therefore I command you [1]this today.
16"And it shall come about [a]if he says
to you, 'I will not go out from you,'
because he loves you and your household, since he fares well with you;
17 then you shall take an awl and
pierce it through his ear into the door,
and he shall be your servant forever.
And also you shall do likewise to your
maidservant.
18"It shall not seem hard to you when
you set him [1]free, for he has given you
six years *with* [2]double the service of a
hired man; so the LORD your God will
bless you in whatever you do.
19"[a]You shall consecrate to the LORD
your God all the first-born males that
are born of your herd and of your flock;
you shall not work with the first-born of
your herd, nor shear the first-born of
your flock.
20"[a]You and your household shall eat
it every year before the LORD your God
in the place which the LORD chooses.
21"[a]But if it has any [1]defect, *such as*
lameness or blindness, *or* any serious
[1]defect, you shall not sacrifice it to the
LORD your God.
22"You shall eat it within your gates;
[a]the unclean and the clean alike *may eat*
it, as [a]a gazelle or a deer.
23"Only [a]you shall not eat its blood;
you are to pour it out on the ground like
water.

The Feasts of Passover, of Weeks, and of Booths

16 "OBSERVE [a]the month of Abib
and [1b]celebrate the Passover to
the LORD your God, for in the month of
Abib the LORD your God brought you
out of Egypt by night.
2"And you shall sacrifice the Passover to the LORD your God from the
flock and the herd, in the place where
the LORD chooses to establish His name.
3"[a]You shall not eat leavened bread
with it; seven days you shall eat with it
unleavened bread, the bread of affliction
(for you came out of the land of Egypt in
haste), in order that you may remember
[b]all the days of your life the day when
you came out of the land of Egypt.
4"For seven days no leaven shall be
seen with you in all your territory, and
[a]none of the flesh which you sacrifice on
the evening of the first day shall remain
overnight until morning.
5"You are not allowed to sacrifice the
Passover in any of your [1]towns which
the LORD your God is giving you;
6 but [a]at the place where the LORD
your God chooses to establish His name,
you shall sacrifice the Passover in the
evening at sunset, at the time that you
came out of Egypt.
7"And you shall [a]cook and eat *it* in
the place which the LORD your God
chooses. And in the morning you are to
return to your tents.
8"Six days you shall eat unleavened
bread, and [a]on the seventh day there
shall be [b]a solemn assembly to the LORD
your God; you shall do no work *on it.*
9"[a]You shall count seven weeks for
yourself; you shall begin to count seven
weeks from the time you begin to put the
sickle to the standing grain.
10"Then you shall [1]celebrate the Feast
of Weeks to the LORD your God with a
tribute of a freewill offering of your
hand, which you shall give just as the
LORD your God blesses you;
11 and you shall [a]rejoice before the
LORD your God, you and your son and
your daughter and your male and female
servants and [b]the Levite who is in your
[1]town, and [c]the stranger and the [2]orphan
and the widow who are in your midst, in
the place where the LORD your God
chooses to establish His name.
12"And [a]you shall remember that you
were a slave in Egypt, and you shall be
careful to observe these statutes.
13"[a]You shall [1]celebrate the Feast of
Booths seven days after you have gathered in from your threshing floor and
your wine vat;
14 and you shall [a]rejoice in your feast,
you and your son and your daughter and
your male and female servants and the
Levite and the stranger and the [1]orphan
and the widow who are in your [2]towns.
15"Seven days you shall celebrate a
feast to the LORD your God in the place
which the LORD chooses, because the
LORD your God will bless you in all your
produce and in all the work of your
hands, so that you shall be altogether
joyful.
16"[a]Three times in a year all your
males shall appear before the LORD your
God in the place which He chooses, at
the Feast of Unleavened Bread and at
the Feast of Weeks and at the Feast of
Booths, and [b]they shall not appear
before the LORD empty-handed.
17"Every man [1]shall give as he is able,
according to the blessing of the LORD
your God which He has given you.

10 [1]Lit., *the putting forth of your hand* [a]Deut. 14:29; Ps. 41:1; Prov. 22:9

11 [1]Lit., *in the midst of* [a]Matt. 26:11; Mark 14:7; John 12:8

12 [1]Lit., *brother* [2]Lit., *free from you* [a]Ex. 21:2-6; Lev. 25:39-43; Jer. 34:14

13 [1]Lit., *free from you*

15 [1]Lit., *this thing*

16 [a]Ex. 21:5, 6

18 [1]Lit., *free from you* [2]Lit., *double the amount*

19 [a]Ex. 13:2, 12

20 [a]Lev. 7:15-18; Deut. 12:5; 14:23

21 [1]Lit., *blemish* [a]Lev. 22:19-25; Deut. 17:1

22 [a]Deut. 12:15, 16, 22

23 [a]Gen. 9:4; Lev. 7:26; 17:10; 19:26; Deut. 12:16, 23

1 [1]Lit., *perform* [a]Ex. 12:2 [b]Num. 28:16

3 [a]Ex. 12:8, 15, 19, 39; 13:3; 34:18 [b]Deut. 4:9

4 [a]Ex. 12:8, 10; 34:25

5 [1]Lit., *gates*

6 [a]Deut. 12:5

7 [a]Ex. 12:8; 2 Chr. 35:13

8 [a]Num. 28:25 [b]Ex. 12:16; 13:6; Lev. 23:8, 36

9 [a]Ex. 23:16; 34:22; Lev. 23:15; Num. 28:26

10 [1]Lit., *perform*

11 [1]Lit., *gates* [2]Or, *fatherless* [a]Deut. 12:7 [b]Deut. 12:12 [c]Deut. 14:29

12 [a]Deut. 15:15

13 [1]Lit., *perform* [a]Lev. 23:34-43

14 [1]Or, *fatherless* [2]Lit., *gates* [a]Deut. 16:11

16 [a]Ex. 23:14-17; 34:23, 24 [b]Ex. 34:20

17 [1]Lit., *according to the gift of his hand*

18 "You shall appoint for yourself judges and officers in all your [1]towns which the LORD your God is giving you, according to your tribes, and they shall judge the people with righteous judgment.

19 "[a]You shall not distort justice; [b]you shall not [1]be partial, and [c]you shall not take a bribe, for a bribe blinds the eyes of the wise and perverts the words of the righteous.

20 "Justice, *and only* justice, you shall pursue, that [a]you may live and possess the land which the LORD your God is giving you.

21 "[a]You shall not plant for yourself an [1]Asherah of any kind of tree beside the altar of the LORD your God, which you shall make for yourself.

22 "[a]Neither shall you set up for yourself a *sacred* pillar which the LORD your God hates.

Administration of Justice

17 "[a]YOU shall not sacrifice to the LORD your God an ox or a sheep which has a blemish or any [1]defect, for that is a detestable thing to the LORD your God.

2 "[a]If there is found in your midst, in any of your [1]towns, which the LORD your God is giving you, a man or a woman who does what is evil in the sight of the LORD your God, by transgressing His covenant,

3 and has gone and [a]served other gods and worshiped them, [b]or the sun or the moon or any of the heavenly host, [c]which I have not commanded,

4 and if it is told you and you have heard of it, then you shall inquire thoroughly. And behold, if it is true and the thing certain that this detestable thing has been done in Israel,

5 then you shall bring out that man or that woman who has done this evil deed, to your gates, *that is,* the man or the woman, and [a]you shall stone them to [1]death.

6 "[a]On the [1]evidence of two witnesses or three witnesses, he who is to die shall be put to death; he shall not be put to death on the [1]evidence of one witness.

7 "[a]The hand of the witnesses shall be first against him to put him to death, and afterward the hand of all the people. [b]So you shall purge the evil from your midst.

8 "[a]If any case is too difficult for you to decide, between [1]one kind of homicide or another, between [2]one kind of lawsuit or another, and between [3]one kind of assault or another, being cases of dispute in your [4]courts, then you shall arise and go up to [b]the place which the LORD your God chooses.

9 "So you shall come to [a]the Levitical priest or the judge who is *in office* in those days, and you shall inquire *of them,* and they will declare to you the verdict in the case.

10 "And you shall do according to the [1]terms of the verdict which they declare to you from that place which the LORD chooses; and you shall be careful to observe according to all that they teach you.

11 "[a]According to the [1]terms of the law which they teach you, and according to the verdict which they tell you, you shall do; you shall not turn aside from the word which they declare to you, to the right or the left.

12 "And the man who acts [a]presumptuously by not listening to the priest who stands there to serve the LORD your God, nor to the judge, that man shall die; thus you shall purge the evil from Israel.

13 "Then all the people will hear and be afraid, and will not act [a]presumptuously again.

14 "When you enter the land which the LORD your God gives you, and you [a]possess it and live in it, and you say, '[b]I will set a king over me like all the nations who are around me,'

15 you shall surely set a king over you whom the LORD your God chooses, *one* [a]from among your [1]countrymen you shall set as king over yourselves; you may not put a foreigner over yourselves who is not your [1]countryman.

16 "[a]Moreover, he shall not multiply horses for himself, nor shall he [b]cause the people to return to Egypt to multiply horses, since [c]the LORD has said to you, 'You shall never again return that way.'

17 "[a]Neither shall he multiply wives for himself, [1]lest his heart turn away; nor shall he greatly increase silver and gold for himself.

18 "Now it shall come about when he sits on the throne of his kingdom, he shall write for himself a copy of this law on a scroll [1][a]in the presence of the Levitical priests.

19 "And it shall be with him, and he shall read it [a]all the days of his life, that he may learn to fear the LORD his God, [1]by carefully observing all the words of this law and these statutes,

20 that his heart may not be lifted up above his [1]countrymen [a]and that he may not turn aside from the commandment, to the right or the left; in order that he and his sons may continue long in his kingdom in the midst of Israel.

Portion of the Levites

18 "[a]THE Levitical priests, the whole tribe of Levi, shall have no portion or inheritance with Israel; they shall eat the LORD's offerings by fire and His [1]portion.

2 "[a]And they shall have no inheritance among their [1]countrymen; the LORD is their inheritance, as He [2]promised them.

3 "[a]Now this shall be the priests' due from the people, from those who offer a sacrifice, either an ox or a sheep, of which they shall give to the priest the shoulder and the two cheeks and the stomach.

---

18 [1]Lit., *gates*
19 [1]Lit., *regard persons* [a]Ex. 23:2; Lev. 19:15; Deut. 1:17; 10:17 [b]Prov. 24:23 [c]Ex. 23:8; Prov. 17:23; Eccl. 7:7
20 [a]Deut. 4:1
21 [1]I.e., wooden symbol of a female deity [a]Deut. 7:5; 2 Kin. 17:16; 21:3; 2 Chr. 33:3
22 [a]Lev. 26:1

1 [1]Lit., *evil thing* [a]Deut. 15:21
2 [1]Lit., *gates* [a]Deut. 13:6-11
3 [a]Ex. 22:20 [b]Job 31:26-28 [c]Jer. 7:22
5 [1]Lit., *death with stones* [a]Lev. 24:14; Josh. 7:25
6 [1]Lit., *mouth* [a]Num. 35:30; Deut. 19:15; Matt. 18:16; John 8:17; 2 Cor. 13:1; 1 Tim. 5:19; Heb. 10:28
7 [a]Lev. 24:14; Deut. 13:9 [b]1 Cor. 5:13
8 [1]Lit., *blood to blood* [2]Lit., *judgment to judgment* [3]Lit., *stroke to stroke* [4]Lit., *gates* [a]2 Chr. 19:10; Hag. 2:11 [b]Deut. 12:5; Ps. 122:5
9 [a]Deut. 19:17
10 [1]Lit., *mouth*
11 [1]Lit., *mouth* [a]Deut. 25:1
12 [a]Num. 15:30; Deut. 1:43; 17:13; 18:20; Hos. 4:4
13 [a]Deut. 17:12
14 [a]Deut. 11:31; Josh. 21:43 [b]1 Sam. 8:5, 19, 20; 10:19
15 [1]Lit., *brother(s)* [a]Jer. 30:21
16 [a]1 Kin. 4:26; 10:26-29; Ps. 20:7 [b]Is. 31:1; Ezek. 17:15 [c]Ex. 13:17, 18; Hos. 11:5
17 [1]Lit., *nor* [a]2 Sam. 5:13; 12:11; 1 Kin. 11:3, 4
18 [1]Lit., *from before* [a]Deut. 31:24-26
19 [1]Lit., *to keep to do them* [a]Deut. 4:9, 10; Josh. 1:8
20 [1]Lit., *brothers* [a]Deut. 5:32; 1 Kin. 15:5

1 [1]Or, *inheritance* [a]Deut. 10:9; 1 Cor. 9:13
2 [1]Lit., *brothers* [2]Lit., *spoke to* [a]Num. 18:20
3 [a]Lev. 7:32-34; Num. 18:11, 12

4"You shall give him the [a]first fruits of your grain, your new wine, and your oil, and the first shearing of your sheep.

5"[a]For the LORD your God has chosen him and his sons from all your tribes, to [b]stand [1]and serve in the name of the LORD forever.

6"Now if a Levite comes from any of your [1]towns throughout Israel where he [a]resides, and comes [2]whenever he desires to the place which the LORD chooses,

7 then he shall serve in the name of the LORD his God, like all his fellow Levites who stand there before the LORD.

8"[a]They shall eat [1]equal portions, except *what they receive* from the sale of their fathers' *estates.*

Spiritism Forbidden

9"When you enter the land which the LORD your God gives you, you shall not learn to [1a]imitate the detestable things of those nations.

10"There shall not be found among you anyone [a]who makes his son or his daughter pass through the fire, one who uses divination, one [b]who practices witchcraft, or one who interprets omens, or a sorcerer,

11 or one who casts a spell, [a]or a medium, or a spiritist, or one who calls up the dead.

12"For whoever does these things is detestable to the LORD; and [a]because of these detestable things the LORD your God will drive them out before you.

13"[a]You shall be [1]blameless before the LORD your God.

14"For those nations, which you shall dispossess, listen to those who [a]practice witchcraft and to diviners, but as for you, the LORD your God has not allowed you *to do* so.

15"[a]The LORD your God will raise up for you a prophet like me from among you, from your [1]countrymen, you shall listen to him.

16"This is [a]according to all that you asked of the LORD your God in Horeb on the day of the assembly, saying, 'Let me not hear again the voice of the LORD my God, let me not see this great fire anymore, lest I die.'

17"[a]And the LORD said to me, 'They have [1]spoken well.

18 'I will raise up a prophet from among their [1]countrymen like you, and [a]I will put My words in his mouth, and [b]he shall speak to them all that I command him.

19 '[a]And it shall come about that whoever will not listen to My words which he shall speak in My name, I Myself will require *it* of him.

20 'But the prophet who shall speak a word [a]presumptuously in My name which I have not commanded him to speak, or [b]which he shall speak in the name of other gods, [1]that prophet shall die.'

21"And [1]you may say in your heart, 'How shall we know the word which the LORD has not spoken?'

22"[a]When a prophet speaks in the name of the LORD, if the thing does not come about or come true, that is the thing which the LORD has not spoken. The prophet has spoken it [b]presumptuously; you shall not be afraid of him.

Cities of Refuge

19 "[a]WHEN the LORD your God cuts off the nations, whose land the LORD your God gives you, and you dispossess them and settle in their cities and in their houses,

2 [a]you shall set aside three cities for yourself in the midst of your land, which the LORD your God gives you to [1]possess.

3"You shall prepare the [1]roads for yourself, and divide into three parts the territory of your land, which the LORD your God will give you as a possession, [2]so that any manslayer may flee there.

4"[a]Now this is the case of the manslayer who may flee there and live: when he [1]kills his friend [2]unintentionally, [3]not hating him previously—

5 as when *a man* goes into the forest with his friend to cut wood, and his hand [1]swings the axe to cut down the tree, and the iron *head* slips off the [2]handle and [3]strikes his friend so that he dies—he may flee to one of these cities and live;

6 lest the avenger of blood pursue the manslayer [1]in the heat of his anger, and overtake him, because the way is long, and [2]take his life, though he was not deserving of death, since he had not hated him previously.

7"Therefore, I command you, saying, 'You shall set aside three cities for yourself.'

8"And if the LORD your God [a]enlarges your territory, just as He has sworn to your fathers, and gives you all the land which He [1]promised to give your fathers—

9 if you [1]carefully observe all this commandment, which I command you today, [a]to love the LORD your God, and to walk in His ways always—[b]then you shall add three more cities for yourself, besides these three.

10"So innocent blood will not be shed in the midst of your land which the LORD your God gives you as an inheritance, and [a]bloodguiltiness be on you.

11"But [a]if there is a man who hates his neighbor and lies in wait for him and rises up against him and strikes [1]him so that he dies, and he flees to one of these cities,

12 then the elders of his city shall send and take him from there and deliver him into the hand of the avenger of blood, that he may die.

13"[1a]You shall not pity him, but [b]you shall purge the blood of the innocent from Israel, that it may go well with you.

4 [a]Num. 18:12
5 [1]Lit., *to* [a]Ex. 29:9 [b]Deut. 10:8
6 [1]Lit., *gates* [2]Lit., *with all the desire of his soul* [a]Num. 35:2, 3
8 [1]Lit., *portion like portion* [a]Lev. 27:30-33; Num. 18:21-24; 2 Chr. 31:4; Neh. 12:44
9 [1]Lit., *do according to* [a]Deut. 9:5
10 [a]Deut. 12:31 [b]Ex. 22:18; Lev. 19:26, 31; 20:6; Jer. 27:9, 10; Mal. 3:5
11 [a]Lev. 19:31
12 [a]Lev. 18:24
13 [1]Lit., *complete, perfect;* or, *having integrity* [a]Gen. 6:9; 17:1; Matt. 5:48
14 [a]2 Kin. 21:6
15 [1]Lit., *brothers* [a]Matt. 21:11; Luke 2:25-34; 7:16; 24:19; John 1:21, 25; 4:19; Acts 3:22; 7:37
16 [a]Ex. 20:18, 19; Deut. 5:23-27
17 [1]Lit., *done well what they have spoken* [a]Deut. 5:28
18 [1]Lit., *brothers* [a]Is. 51:16; John 17:8 [b]John 4:25; 8:28; 12:49, 50
19 [a]Acts 3:23; Heb. 12:25
20 [1]Lit., *and that* [a]Deut. 13:5; 17:12 [b]Deut. 13:1, 2; Jer. 14:14; Zech. 13:3
21 [1]Lit., *if you say*
22 [a]Jer. 28:9 [b]Deut. 18:20

1 [a]Deut. 6:10, 11
2 [1]Lit., *possess it* [a]Deut. 4:41; Josh. 20:2
3 [1]Lit., *road* [2]Lit., *and it shall be for every manslayer to flee there*
4 [1]Lit., *smites* [2]Lit., *without knowledge* [3]Lit., *and he was not hating him previously* [a]Num. 35:9-34
5 [1]Lit., *is thrust with* [2]Lit., *wood* [3]Lit., *finds*
6 [1]Lit., *while his heart is hot* [2]Lit., *smite him in the soul*
8 [1]Lit., *spoke* [a]Gen. 15:18
9 [1]Lit., *keep . . . to do it* [a]Deut. 6:5 [b]Josh. 20:7
10 [a]Num. 35:33; Deut. 21:1-9
11 [1]Lit., *him in the soul* [a]Ex. 21:12; Num. 35:16; 1 John 3:15
13 [1]Lit., *Your eye* [a]Deut. 7:2 [b]1 Kin. 2:31

Laws of Landmark and Testimony

14 "[a]You shall not move your neighbor's boundary mark, which the ancestors have set, in your inheritance which
you shall inherit in the land that the
LORD your God gives you to [1]possess.
15 "[a]A single witness shall not rise up
against a man on account of any iniquity
or any sin [1]which he has committed; on
the [2]evidence of two or three witnesses a
matter shall be confirmed.
16 "[a]If a malicious witness rises up
against a man to [1]accuse him of [2]wrong-
doing,
17 then both the men who have the
dispute shall stand [a]before the LORD,
before the priests and the judges who
will be *in office* in those days.
18 "And the judges [a]shall investigate
thoroughly; and if the witness is a false
witness *and* he has [1]accused his brother
falsely,
19 then [a]you shall do to him just as he
had intended to do to his brother. Thus
you shall purge the evil from among you.
20 "And [a]the rest will hear and be
afraid, and will never again do such an
evil thing among you.
21 "Thus [1a]you shall not show pity:
[b]life for life, [c]eye for eye, tooth for tooth,
hand for hand, foot for foot.

Laws of Warfare

20 "WHEN you go out to battle
against your enemies and see
[a]horses and chariots *and* people more
numerous than you, [b]do not be afraid of
them; for the LORD your God, who
brought you up from the land of Egypt,
is with you.
2 "Now it shall come about that when
you are approaching the battle, the
priest shall come near and speak to the
people.
3 "And he shall say to them, 'Hear, O
Israel, you are approaching the battle
against your enemies today. Do not be
fainthearted. [a]Do not be afraid, or panic,
or tremble before them,
4 for the LORD your God [a]is the one
who goes with you, to fight for you
against your enemies, to save you.'
5 "The officers also shall speak to the
people, saying, 'Who is the man that has
built a new house and has not [a]dedicated
it? Let him depart and return to his
house, lest he die in the battle and
another man dedicate it.
6 'And who is the man that has
planted a vineyard and has not [1]begun
to use its fruit? Let him depart and
return to his house, lest he die in the
battle and another man [1]begin to use its
fruit.
7 '[a]And who is the man that is engaged to a woman and has not [1]married
her? Let him depart and return to his
house, lest he die in the battle and
another man [2]marry her.'
8 "Then the officers shall speak further to the people, and they shall say,
'[a]Who is the man that is afraid and
fainthearted? Let him depart and return
to his house, so that [1]he might not make
his brothers' hearts melt like his heart.'
9 "And it shall come about that when
the officers have finished speaking to the
people, they shall appoint commanders
of armies at the head of the people.
10 "When you approach a city to fight
against it, you shall [1]offer it terms of
peace.
11 "And it shall come about, if it
[1]agrees to make peace with you and
opens to you, then it shall be that all the
people who are found in it shall become
your [a]forced labor and shall serve you.
12 "However, if it does not make peace
with you, but makes war against you,
then you shall besiege it.
13 "When the LORD your God gives it
into your hand, [a]you shall strike all the
[1]men in it with the edge of the sword.
14 "Only the women and the children
and [a]the animals and all that is in the
city, all its spoil, you shall take as booty
for yourself; and you shall [1]use the spoil
of your enemies which the LORD your
God has given you.
15 "Thus you shall do to all the cities
that are very far from you, which are not
of the cities of these nations [1]nearby.
16 "[a]Only in the cities of these peoples
that the LORD your God is giving you as
an inheritance, you shall not leave alive
anything that breathes.
17 "But you shall [1]utterly destroy them,
the Hittite and the Amorite, the Canaanite and the Perizzite, the Hivite and the
Jebusite, as the LORD your God has
commanded you,
18 in order that they may not teach
you to do [a]according to all their detestable things which they have done for
their gods, so that you would [b]sin
against the LORD your God.
19 "When you besiege a city a long
time, to make war against it in order to
capture it, you shall not destroy its trees
by swinging an axe against them; for
you may eat from them, and you shall
not cut them down. [1]For is the tree of
the field a man, that it should [2]be besieged by you?
20 "Only the trees which you know [1]are
not fruit trees you shall destroy and cut
down, that you may construct siegeworks against the city that is making war
with you until it falls.

Expiation of a Crime

21 "IF a slain person is found lying
in the open country in the land
which the LORD your God gives you to
[1]possess, *and* it is not known who has
struck him,
2 then your elders and your judges
shall go out and measure *the distance* to
the cities which are around the slain one.
3 "And it shall be that the city which
is nearest to the slain man, that is, the
elders of that city, shall take a heifer of
the herd, which has not been worked
and which has not pulled in a yoke;

14 [1]Lit., *possess it* [a]Deut. 27:17; Job 24:2; Prov. 22:28; Hos. 5:10

15 [1]Lit., *in any sin, which he sins* [2]Lit., *mouth of two witnesses, or by the mouth of three* [a]Num. 35:30; Deut. 17:6; Matt. 18:16; John 8:17; 2 Cor. 13:1; 1 Tim. 5:19; Heb. 10:28

16 [1]Lit., *testify against* [2]Lit., *turning aside* [a]Ex. 23:1; Ps. 27:12

17 [a]Deut. 17:9

18 [1]Lit., *testified against* [a]Deut. 25:1

19 [a]Prov. 19:5

20 [a]Deut. 17:13; 21:21

21 [1]Lit., *your eye* [a]Deut. 19:13 [b]Ex. 21:23; Lev. 24:20 [c]Matt. 5:38

1 [a]Deut. 3:22; 7:18; 31:6, 8; Ps. 20:7; Is. 31:1 [b]2 Chr. 32:7, 8; Ps. 23:4; Is. 41:10

3 [a]Deut. 20:1; Josh. 23:10

4 [a]Deut. 1:30; 3:22; Josh. 23:10

5 [a]Neh. 12:27

6 [1]Lit., *treat(ed) it as common*

7 [1]Lit., *taken* [2]Lit., *take* [a]Deut. 24:5

8 [1]So with Gr. and other ancient versions [a]Judg. 7:3

10 [1]Lit., *call to it for peace*

11 [1]Lit., *answers peace* [a]1 Kin. 9:21

13 [1]Lit., *males* [a]Num. 31:7

14 [1]Lit., *eat* [a]Josh. 8:2

15 [1]Lit., *here*

16 [a]Ex. 23:31-33; Num. 21:2, 3; Deut. 7:1-5; Josh. 11:14

17 [1]Or, *put them under the ban*

18 [a]Ex. 34:12-16; Deut. 7:4; 9:5; 12:30, 31 [b]Ex. 23:33; 2 Kin. 21:3-15; Ps. 106:34-41

19 [1]Read as interrogative with ancient versions [2]Lit., *come before you in the siege*

20 [1]Lit., *they are not trees for food*

1 [1]Lit., *possess it*

4 and the elders of that city shall bring the heifer down to a valley with running water, which has not been plowed or sown, and shall break the heifer's neck there in the valley.

5 "Then [a]the priests, the sons of Levi, shall come near, for the LORD your God has chosen them to serve Him and to bless in the name of the LORD; and every dispute and every [1]assault [2]shall be settled by them.

6 "And all the elders of that city [1]which is nearest to the slain man shall [a]wash their hands over the heifer whose neck was broken in the valley;

7 and they shall answer and say, 'Our hands have not shed this blood, nor did our eyes see *it.*

8 '[1]Forgive Thy people Israel whom Thou hast redeemed, O LORD, and do not place the guilt of [a]innocent blood in the midst of Thy people Israel.' And the bloodguiltiness shall be [2]forgiven them.

9 "[a]So you shall remove the guilt of innocent blood from your midst, when you do what is right in the eyes of the LORD.

Domestic Relations

10 "When you go out to battle against your enemies, and [a]the LORD your God delivers them into your hands, and you take them away captive,

11 and see among the captives a beautiful woman, and have a desire for her and would take her as a wife for yourself,

12 then you shall bring her home to your house, and she shall [a]shave her head and [1]trim her nails.

13 "She shall also [1]remove the clothes of her captivity and shall remain in your house, and [a]mourn her father and mother a full month; and after that you may go in to her and be her husband and she shall be your wife.

14 "And it shall be, if you are not pleased with her, then you shall let her go [1]wherever she wishes; but you shall certainly not sell her for money, you shall not [2]mistreat her, because you have [a]humbled her.

15 "If a man has two wives, the one loved and [a]the other [1]unloved, and *both* the loved and the [1]unloved have borne him sons, if the first-born son belongs to the [1]unloved,

16 then it shall be in the day he [1]wills what he has to his sons, he cannot make the son of the loved the first-born before the son of the [2]unloved, who is the first-born.

17 "But he shall acknowledge the first-born, the son of the [1]unloved, by giving him a double portion of all that [2]he has, for he is the [a]beginning of his strength; [b]to him belongs the right of the first-born.

18 "If any man has a stubborn and rebellious son who will [a]not obey his father or his mother, and when they chastise him, he will not even listen to them,

19 then his father and mother shall seize him, and bring him out to the elders of his city [1]at the gateway of his home town.

20 "And they shall say to the elders of his city, 'This son of ours is stubborn and rebellious, he will not obey us, he is a glutton and a drunkard.'

21 "[a]Then all the men of his city shall stone him to death; so [b]you shall remove the evil from your midst, and [c]all Israel shall hear *of it* and fear.

22 "And if a man has committed a sin [a]worthy of death, and he is put to death, and you hang him on a tree,

23 [a]his corpse shall not hang all night on the tree, but you shall surely bury him on the same day (for [b]he who is hanged is [1]accursed of God), so that you [c]do not defile your land which the LORD your God gives you as an inheritance.

Sundry Laws

22 "[a]YOU shall not see your [1]countryman's ox or his sheep straying away, and [2]pay no attention to them; you shall certainly bring them back to your countryman.

2 "And if your countryman is not near you, or if you do not know him, then you shall bring it home to your house, and it shall remain with you until your countryman looks for it; then you shall restore it to him.

3 "And thus you shall do with his donkey, and you shall do the same with his garment, and you shall do likewise with anything lost by your countryman, which he has lost and you have found. You are not allowed to [1]neglect *them.*

4 "You shall not see your countryman's donkey or his ox fallen down on the way, and [1]pay no attention to them; you shall certainly help him to raise *them* up.

5 "A woman shall not wear man's clothing, nor shall a man put on a woman's clothing; for whoever does these things is an abomination to the LORD your God.

6 "If you happen to come upon a bird's nest along the way, in any tree or on the ground, with young ones or eggs, and the mother sitting on the young or on the eggs, [a]you shall not take the mother with the young;

7 you shall certainly let the mother go, but the young you may take for yourself, [a]in order that it may be well with you, and that you may prolong your days.

8 "When you build a new house, you shall make a parapet for your roof, that you may not bring bloodguilt on your house if anyone falls from it.

9 "[a]You shall not sow your vineyard with two kinds of seed, lest [1]all the produce of the seed which you have sown, and the increase of the vineyard become defiled.

5 [1]Lit., *stroke* [2]Lit., *shall be according to their mouth* [a]Deut. 17:9-11; 19:17; 1 Chr. 23:13

6 [1]Lit., *who are* [a]Matt. 27:24

8 [1]Lit., *Cover over, atone for* [2]Lit., *covered over, atoned for* [a]Num. 35:33, 34; Jon. 1:14

9 [a]Deut. 19:13

10 [a]Josh. 21:44

12 [1]Lit., *do* [a]Lev. 14:8, 9; Num. 6:9

13 [1]Lit., *remove from her* [a]Ps. 45:10

14 [1]Lit., *according to her soul* [2]Or, *enslave* [a]Gen. 34:2

15 [1]Lit., *hated* [a]Gen. 29:33

16 [1]Lit., *makes to inherit* [2]Lit., *hated*

17 [1]Lit., *hated* [2]Lit., *is found with him* [a]Gen. 49:3 [b]Gen. 25:31

18 [a]Ex. 20:12; Lev. 19:3; Prov. 1:8; Eph. 6:1-3

19 [1]Lit., *and to the gate of his place*

21 [a]Lev. 20:2, 27; 24:14-23; Num. 15:25, 36 [b]Deut. 19:19 [c]Deut. 13:11

22 [a]Deut. 22:26; Matt. 26:66; Mark 14:64; Acts 23:29

23 [1]Lit., *the curse of God* [a]Josh. 8:29; 10:26, 27; John 19:31 [b]Gal. 3:13 [c]Lev. 18:25; Num. 35:34

1 [1]Lit., *brother,* and so through v. 4 [2]Lit., *hide yourself from them* [a]Ex. 23:4, 5; Prov. 27:10; Zech. 7:9

3 [1]Lit., *hide yourself*

4 [1]Lit., *hide yourself from them*

6 [a]Lev. 22:28

7 [a]Deut. 4:40

9 [1]Lit., *the fulness* [a]Lev. 19:19

10“[a]You shall not plow with an ox and a donkey together.

11“[a]You shall not wear a material mixed of wool and linen together.

12“[a]You shall make yourself tassels on the four corners of your garment with which you cover yourself.

Laws on Morality

13“[a]If any man takes a wife and goes in to her and *then* [1]turns against her,

14 and charges her with shameful deeds and [1]publicly defames her, and says, ‘I took this woman, *but* when I came near her, I did not find her a virgin,’

15 then the girl’s father and her mother shall take and bring out the *evidence* of the girl’s virginity to the elders of the city at the gate.

16“And the girl’s father shall say to the elders, ‘I gave my daughter to this man for a wife, but he [1]turned against her;

17 and behold, he has charged her with shameful deeds, saying, “I did not find your daughter a virgin.” But [1]this is the *evidence* of my daughter’s virginity.’ And they shall spread the garment before the elders of the city.

18“So [a]the elders of that city shall take the man and chastise him,

19 and they shall fine him a hundred *shekels* of silver and give it to the girl’s father, because he [1]publicly defamed a virgin of Israel. And she shall remain his wife; he cannot [2]divorce her all his days.

20“But if this [1a]charge is true, that the girl was not found a virgin,

21 then they shall bring out the girl to the doorway of her father’s house, and the men of her city shall stone her [1]to death because she has [a]committed an act of folly in Israel, by playing the harlot in her father’s house; thus [b]you shall purge the evil from among you.

22“[a]If a man is found lying with a married woman, then both of them shall die, the man who lay with the woman, and the woman; thus you shall purge the evil from Israel.

23“[a]If there is a girl who is a virgin engaged to a man, and *another* man finds her in the city and lies with her,

24 then you shall bring them both out to the gate of that city and you shall stone them [1]to death; the girl, because she did not cry out in the city, and the man, because he has violated his neighbor’s wife. Thus you shall purge the evil from among you.

25“But if in the field the man finds the girl who is engaged, and the man forces her and lies with her, then only the man who lies with her shall die.

26“But you shall do nothing to the girl; there is no sin in the girl worthy of death, for just as a man rises against his neighbor and murders him, so is this case.

27“When he found her in the field, the engaged girl cried out, but there was no one to save her.

28“[a]If a man finds a girl who is a virgin, who is not engaged, and seizes her and lies with her and they are discovered,

29 then the man who lay with her shall give to the girl’s father fifty *shekels* of silver, and she shall become his wife because he has violated her; he cannot divorce her all his days.

30“[1a]A man shall not take his father’s wife so that he shall not uncover his father’s skirt.

Persons Excluded from the Assembly

23 “[a]NO one who is [1]emasculated, or has his male organ cut off, shall enter the assembly of the LORD.

2“No one of illegitimate birth shall enter the assembly of the LORD; none of his *descendants,* even to the tenth generation, shall enter the assembly of the LORD.

3“[a]No Ammonite or Moabite shall enter the assembly of the LORD; none of their *descendants,* even to the tenth generation, shall ever enter the assembly of the LORD,

4 [a]because they did not meet you with [1]food and water on the way when you came out of Egypt, and because they hired against you [b]Balaam the son of Beor from Pethor of [2]Mesopotamia, to curse you.

5“Nevertheless, the LORD your God was not willing to listen to Balaam, but the LORD your God [a]turned the curse into a blessing for you because the LORD your God [b]loves you.

6“[a]You shall never seek their peace or their prosperity all your days.

7“You shall not detest an Edomite, for [a]he is your brother; you shall not detest an Egyptian, [b]because you were an alien in his land.

8“The sons of the third generation who are born to them may enter the assembly of the LORD.

9“When you go out as [1]an army against your enemies, then you shall keep yourself from every evil thing.

10“[a]If there is among you any man who is unclean because of a nocturnal emission, then he must go outside the camp; he may not [1]reenter the camp.

11“But it shall be when evening approaches, he shall bathe himself with water, and at sundown he may [1]reenter the camp.

12“You shall also have a place outside the camp and go out there,

13 and you shall have a [1]spade among your tools, and it shall be when you sit down outside, you shall dig with it and shall turn [2]to cover up your excrement.

14“Since [a]the LORD your God walks in the midst of your camp to deliver you and to [1]defeat your enemies before you, therefore your camp must be [b]holy; and He must not see [2]anything indecent among you [3]lest He turn away from you.

15“[a]You shall not hand over to his master a slave who has [1]escaped from his master to you.

---

10 [a]2 Cor. 6:14-16
11 [a]Lev. 19:19
12 [a]Num. 15:37-41; Matt. 23:5
13 [1]Lit., *hates her* [a]Gen. 29:21; Deut. 24:1; Judg. 15:1
14 [1]Lit., *causes an evil name to go out against her*
16 [1]Lit., *hated her*
17 [1]Lit., *these are*
18 [a]Ex. 18:21; Deut. 1:9-18
19 [1]Lit., *caused an evil name to go out against a virgin* [2]Lit., *send her away*
20 [1]Lit., *matter* [a]Deut. 17:4
21 [1]Lit., *with stones so that she dies* [a]Gen. 34:7; Lev. 19:29; 21:9; Deut. 23:17, 18; Judg. 20:5-10; 2 Sam. 13:12, 13 [b]Deut. 13:5; 17:7; 19:19
22 [a]Lev. 20:10; Ezek. 16:38; Matt. 5:27, 28; John 8:5; 1 Cor. 6:9; Heb. 13:4
23 [a]Lev. 19:20-22; Matt. 1:18, 19
24 [1]Lit., *with stones so that they die*
28 [a]Ex. 22:16
30 [1]Ch. 23:1 in Heb. [a]Lev. 18:8; 20:11; Deut. 27:20; 1 Cor. 5:1

1 [1]Lit., *wounded by crushing* of testicles [a]Lev. 21:20; 22:24
3 [a]Neh. 13:1, 2
4 [1]Lit., *bread* [2]Heb., *Aram-naharaim* [a]Neh. 13:2 [b]Num. 22:5; 23:7; Josh. 24:9; 2 Pet. 2:15; Jude 11
5 [a]Prov. 26:2 [b]Deut. 4:37
6 [a]Ezra 9:12
7 [a]Gen. 25:24-26; Obad. 10, 12 [b]Ex. 22:21; 23:9; Lev. 19:34; Deut. 10:19
9 [1]Or, *a camp*
10 [1]Lit., *come to the midst of* [a]Lev. 15:16
11 [1]Lit., *come to the midst of*
13 [1]Lit., *peg* [2]Lit., *and*
14 [1]Lit., *give* [2]Lit., *nakedness of anything* [3]Lit., *and* [a]Lev. 26:12 [b]Ex. 3:5
15 [1]Lit., *delivered himself* [a]1 Sam. 30:15

16"He shall live with you in your midst, in the place which he shall choose in one of your [1]towns where it pleases him; [a]you shall not mistreat him.

17"[a]None of the daughters of Israel shall be a cult prostitute, [b]nor shall any of the sons of Israel be a cult prostitute.

18"You shall not bring the hire of a harlot or the wages of a [1][a]dog into the house of the LORD your God for any votive offering, for both of these are an abomination to the LORD your God.

19"[a]You shall not charge interest to your [1]countrymen: interest on money, food, *or* anything that may be loaned at interest.

20"[a]You may charge interest to a foreigner, but to your [1]countryman you shall not charge interest, so that [b]the LORD your God may bless you in all [2]that you undertake in the land which you are about to enter to [3]possess.

21"[a]When you make a vow to the LORD your God, you shall not delay to pay it, for it would be sin in you, [1]and the LORD your God will surely require it of you.

22"However, if you refrain from vowing, it would not be sin in you.

23"You shall be careful to perform what goes out from your lips, just as you have voluntarily vowed to the LORD your God, what you have [1]promised.

24"When you enter your neighbor's vineyard, then you may eat grapes [1]until you are fully satisfied, but you shall not put any in your [2]basket.

25"[a]When you enter your neighbor's standing grain, then you may pluck the heads with your hand, but you shall not wield a sickle in your neighbor's standing grain.

Law of Divorce

24 "WHEN a man takes a wife and marries her, and it happens [1]that she finds no favor in his eyes because he has found some [a]indecency in her, and [b]he writes her a certificate of divorce and puts *it* in her hand and sends her out from his house,

2 and she leaves his house and goes and becomes another man's *wife,*

3 and if the latter husband [1]turns against her and writes her a certificate of divorce and puts *it* in her hand and sends her out of his house, or if the latter husband dies who took her to be his wife,

4 *then* her [a]former husband who sent her away is not allowed to take her again to be his wife, since she has been defiled; for that is an abomination before the LORD, and you shall not bring sin on the land which the LORD your God gives you as an inheritance.

5"[a]When a man takes a new wife, he shall not go out with the army, nor be charged with any duty; he shall be free at home one year and shall [b]give happiness to his wife whom he has taken.

Sundry Laws

6"No one shall take a handmill or an upper millstone in pledge, for he would be taking a life in pledge.

7"[a]If a man is [1]caught kidnapping any of his [2]countrymen of the sons of Israel, and he deals with him violently, or sells him, then that thief shall die; so you shall purge the evil from among you.

8"[a]Be careful against [1]an infection of leprosy, that you diligently observe and do according to all that the Levitical priests shall teach you; as I have commanded them, so you shall be careful to do.

9"Remember what the LORD your God did [a]to Miriam on the way as you came out of Egypt.

10"[a]When you make your neighbor a loan of any sort, you shall not enter his house to take his pledge.

11"You shall remain outside, and the man to whom you make the loan shall bring the pledge out to you.

12"And if he is a poor man, you shall not sleep with his pledge.

13"[a]When the sun goes down you shall surely return the pledge to him, that he may sleep in his cloak and bless you; and [b]it will be righteousness for you before the LORD your God.

14"[a]You shall not oppress a hired servant *who is* poor and needy, whether *he is* one of your [1]countrymen or one of your aliens who is in your land in your [2]towns.

15"[a]You shall give him his wages on his day [1]before the sun sets, for he is poor and sets his [2]heart on it; so that [b]he may not cry against you to the LORD and it become sin in you.

16"[a]Fathers shall not be put to death [1]for *their* sons, nor shall sons be put to death [1]for *their* fathers; everyone shall be put to death for his own sin.

17"[a]You shall not pervert the justice [1]due an alien *or* [2]an orphan, nor [b]take a widow's garment in pledge.

18"But you shall remember that you were a slave in Egypt, and that the LORD your God redeemed you from there; therefore I am commanding you to do this thing.

19"[a]When you reap your harvest in your field and have forgotten a sheaf in the field, you shall not go back to get it; it shall be [b]for the alien, for the [1]orphan, and for the widow, in order that the LORD your God [c]may bless you in all the work of your hands.

20"[a]When you beat your olive tree, you shall not go over the boughs [1]again; it shall be [b]for the alien, for the [2]orphan, and for the widow.

21"When you gather the grapes of your vineyard, you shall not [1]go over it again; it shall be for the alien, for the [2]orphan, and for the widow.

22"And you shall remember that you were a slave in the land of Egypt; therefore I am commanding you to do this thing.

---

16 [1]Lit., *gates* [a]Ex. 22:21; Prov. 22:22
17 [a]Lev. 19:29; Deut. 22:21 [b]Gen. 19:5; 2 Kin. 23:7
18 [1]I.e., male prostitute, sodomite [a]Lev. 18:22; 20:13
19 [1]Lit., *brothers* [a]Ex. 22:25; Lev. 25:35-37; Neh. 5:2-7; Ps. 15:5
20 [1]Lit., *brother* [2]Lit., *the putting forth of your hand* [3]Lit., *possess it* [a]Deut. 28:12 [b]Deut. 15:10
21 [1]Lit., *for* [a]Num. 30:1, 2; Job 22:27; Ps. 61:8; Eccl. 5:4, 5; Matt. 5:33
23 [1]Lit., *spoken with your mouth*
24 [1]Lit., *according to your satisfaction of your soul* [2]Or, *vessel*
25 [a]Matt. 12:1; Mark 2:23; Luke 6:1

1 [1]Lit., *if* [a]Num. 5:12, 28; Deut. 22:13-21 [b]Matt. 5:31; 19:7-9; Mark 10:4, 5
3 [1]Lit., *hates her*
4 [a]Jer. 3:1
5 [a]Deut. 20:7 [b]Prov. 5:18
7 [1]Lit., *found stealing* [2]Lit., *brothers* [a]Ex. 21:16
8 [1]Lit., *a mark* or *stroke* [a]Lev. 13:1-14, 57
9 [a]Num. 12:10
10 [a]Ex. 22:26, 27
13 [a]Ex. 22:26 [b]Deut. 6:25; Ps. 106:31; Dan. 4:27
14 [1]Lit., *brothers* [2]Lit., *gates* [a]Lev. 19:13; 25:35-43; Deut. 15:7-18; Prov. 14:31; Amos 4:1; 1 Tim. 5:18
15 [1]Lit., *that the sun shall not go down on it* [2]Lit., *soul* [a]Lev. 19:13; Jer. 22:13; James 5:4 [b]Ex. 22:23; Deut. 15:9; Job 35:9; James 5:4
16 [1]Or, *with* [a]2 Kin. 14:6; 2 Chr. 25:4; Jer. 31:29, 30; Ezek. 18:20
17 [1]Lit., *of* [2]Or, *the fatherless* [a]Ex. 23:9; Lev. 19:33; Deut. 1:17; 10:17; 16:19; 27:19 [b]Ex. 22:22
19 [1]Or, *fatherless* [a]Lev. 19:9, 10; 23:22 [b]Deut. 14:29 [c]Prov. 19:17
20 [1]Lit., *after yourself* [2]Or, *fatherless* [a]Lev. 19:10 [b]Deut. 24:19
21 [1]Lit., *glean it after yourself* [2]Or, *fatherless*

Sundry Laws

25 "[a]IF there is a dispute between men and they go to [1]court, and [2]the judges decide their case, [b]and they justify the righteous and condemn the wicked,

2 then it shall be if the wicked man [1a]deserves to be beaten, the judge shall then make him lie down and be beaten in his presence with the number of stripes according to his [2]guilt.

3 "[a]He may beat him forty times *but* no more, lest he beat him with many more stripes than these, and your brother be [b]degraded in your eyes.

4 "[a]You shall not muzzle the ox while he is threshing.

5 "When brothers live together and one of them dies and has no son, the wife of the deceased shall not be *married* outside *the family* to a strange man. [a]Her husband's brother shall go in to her and take her to himself as wife and perform the duty of a husband's brother to her.

6 "And it shall be that the first-born whom she bears shall [1]assume the name of his dead brother, that [a]his name may not be blotted out from Israel.

7 "[a]But if the man does not desire to take his brother's wife, then his brother's wife shall go up to the gate to the elders and say, 'My husband's brother refuses to establish a name for his brother in Israel; he is not willing to perform the duty of a husband's brother to me.'

8 "Then the elders of his city shall summon him and speak to him. And *if* he persists and says, 'I do not desire to take her,'

9 [a]then his brother's wife shall come to him in the sight of the elders, and pull his sandal off his foot and [b]spit in his face; and she shall [1]declare, 'Thus it is done to the man who does not build up his brother's house.'

10 "And in Israel his name shall be called, 'The house of him whose sandal is removed.'

11 "If *two* men, a man and his [1]countryman, are struggling together, and the wife of one comes near to deliver her husband from the hand of the one who is striking him, and puts out her hand and seizes his genitals,

12 then you shall cut off her [1]hand; [2a]you shall not show pity.

13 "[a]You shall not have in your bag [1]differing weights, a large and a small.

14 "You shall not have in your house [1]differing measures, a large and a small.

15 "You shall have a full and just weight; you shall have a full and just [1]measure, [a]that your days may be prolonged in the [2]land which the LORD your God gives you.

16 "For [a]everyone who does these things, everyone who acts unjustly is an abomination to the LORD your God.

17 "[a]Remember what Amalek did to you along the way when you came out from Egypt,

18 how he met you along the way and attacked among you all the stragglers at your rear when you were faint and weary; and he [a]did not [1]fear God.

19 "Therefore it shall come about when the LORD your God has given you [a]rest from all your surrounding enemies, in the land which the LORD your God gives you as an inheritance to [1]possess, you shall blot out the memory of Amalek from under heaven; you must not forget.

Offering First Fruits

26 "THEN it shall be, when you enter the land which the LORD your God gives you as an inheritance, and you possess it and live in it,

2 that you shall take some of [a]the first of all the produce of the ground which you shall bring in from your land that the LORD your God gives you, and you shall put *it* in a basket and [b]go to the place where the LORD your God chooses to establish His name.

3 "And you shall go to the priest who is in office at that time, and say to him, 'I declare this day to the LORD [1]my God that I have entered the land which the LORD swore to our fathers to give us.'

4 "Then the priest shall take the basket from your hand and set it down before the altar of the LORD your God.

5 "And you shall answer and say before the LORD your God, '[a]My father was a [1]wandering Aramean, and he went down to Egypt and [2]sojourned there, [b]few in number; but there he became a [c]great, mighty and populous nation.

6 'And the [a]Egyptians treated us harshly and afflicted us, and imposed hard labor on us.

7 'Then [a]we cried to the LORD, the God of our fathers, and the LORD heard our voice and saw our affliction and our toil and our oppression;

8 [a]and the LORD brought us out of Egypt with a mighty hand and an outstretched arm and with great terror and with signs and wonders;

9 and He has brought us to this place, and has given us this land, [a]a land flowing with milk and honey.

10 'And now behold, I have brought the first of the produce of the ground [a]which Thou, O LORD hast given me.' And you shall set it down before the LORD your God, and worship before the LORD your God;

11 and you and [a]the Levite and the alien who is among you shall [b]rejoice in all the good which the LORD your God has given you and your household.

12 "[a]When you have finished [1]paying all the tithe of your increase in the third year, the year of tithing, then you shall give it to the Levite, to the stranger, to the [2]orphan and to the widow, that they may eat in your [3]towns, and be satisfied.

13 "And you shall say before the LORD your God, 'I have removed the sacred *portion* from *my* house, and also have

1 [1]Lit., *the judgment* [2]Lit., *they judge them* [a]Deut. 17:8-13; 19:17 [b]Deut. 1:16, 17

2 [1]Lit., *is a son of beating* [2]Or, *wickedness* [a]Prov. 19:29; Luke 12:48

3 [a]2 Cor. 11:24 [b]Job 18:3

4 [a]Prov. 12:10; 1 Cor. 9:9; 1 Tim. 5:18

5 [a]Matt. 22:24; Mark 12:19; Luke 20:28

6 [1]Lit., *stand on* [a]Ruth 4:5, 10

7 [a]Ruth 4:5, 6

9 [1]Lit., *answer and say* [a]Ruth 4:7, 8 [b]Num. 12:14

11 [1]Lit., *brother*

12 [1]Lit., *palm* [2]Lit., *your eye* [a]Deut. 7:2; 19:13

13 [1]Lit., *a stone and a stone* [a]Lev. 19:35-37; Prov. 11:1; 20:23; Ezek. 45:10; Mic. 6:11

14 [1]Lit., *an ephah and an ephah*

15 [1]Lit., *ephah* [2]Lit., *ground* [a]Ex. 20:12

16 [a]Prov. 11:1

17 [a]Ex. 17:8-16

18 [1]Or, *reverence* [a]Ps. 36:1; Rom. 3:18

19 [1]Lit., *possess it* [a]Deut. 12:9

2 [a]Ex. 22:29; 23:16, 19; Num. 18:13; Prov. 3:9 [b]Deut. 12:5

3 [1]So with Gr.; Heb., *your*

5 [1]Or, *perishing* [2]Or, *lived as an alien* [a]Gen. 43:1-14 [b]Gen. 46:27 [c]Deut. 1:10; 10:22

6 [a]Ex. 1:8-11

7 [a]Ex. 2:23-25; 3:9

8 [a]Deut. 4:34; 34:11, 12

9 [a]Ex. 3:8, 17

10 [a]Deut. 8:18; Prov. 10:22

11 [a]Deut. 12:12 [b]Deut. 12:7; 16:11; Eccl. 3:12, 13; 5:18-20

12 [1]Lit., *tithing* [2]Or, *fatherless* [3]Lit., *gates* [a]Lev. 27:30; Num. 18:24; Deut. 14:28, 29; Heb. 7:5, 9, 10

given it to the Levite and the alien, the [1]orphan and the widow, according to all Thy commandments which Thou hast commanded me; [a]I have not transgressed or forgotten any of Thy commandments.

14 'I have not eaten of it [1]while mourning, nor have I removed any of it while I was unclean, nor offered any of it to the dead. I have listened to the voice of the LORD my God; I have done according to all that Thou hast commanded me.

15 '[a]Look down from Thy holy habitation, from heaven, and bless Thy people Israel, and the ground which Thou hast given us, [b]a land flowing with milk and honey, as Thou didst swear to our fathers.'

16 "This day the LORD your God commands you to do these statutes and ordinances. You shall therefore be careful to do them [a]with all your heart and with all your soul.

17 "[a]You have today declared the LORD to be your God, and [1]that you would walk in His ways and keep His statutes, His commandments and His ordinances, and listen to His voice.

18 "And the LORD has today declared you to be [a]His people, a treasured possession, as He promised you, and [1]that you should keep all His commandments;

19 and [1]that He shall [a]set you high above all nations which He has made, for praise, fame, and honor; and that you shall be [b]a consecrated people to the LORD your God, as He has spoken."

The Curses of Mount Ebal

27 THEN Moses and the elders of Israel charged the people, saying, "Keep all the commandments which I command you today.

2 "[a]So it shall be on the day when you shall cross the Jordan to the land which the LORD your God gives you, that you shall set up for yourself large stones, and coat them with lime

3 and write on them all the words of this law, when you cross over, in order that you may enter the land which the LORD your God gives you, [a]a land flowing with milk and honey, as the LORD, the God of your fathers, [1]promised you.

4 "So it shall be when you cross the Jordan, you shall set up [a]on Mount Ebal, these stones, [1]as I am commanding you today, and you shall coat them with lime.

5 "Moreover, you shall build there an altar to the LORD your God, an altar of stones; you [a]shall not [1]wield an iron *tool* on them.

6 "You shall build the altar of the LORD your God of [1]uncut stones; and you shall offer on it burnt offerings to the LORD your God;

7 and you shall sacrifice peace offerings and eat there, and you shall [a]rejoice before the LORD your God.

8 "And you shall write on the [1]stones all the words of this law very distinctly."

9 Then Moses and the Levitical priests spoke to all Israel, saying, "Be silent and listen, O Israel! This day you have become a people for the LORD your God.

10 "You shall therefore [1]obey the LORD your God, and do His commandments and His statutes which I command you today."

11 Moses also charged the people on that day, saying,

12 "When you cross the Jordan, these shall stand on [a]Mount Gerizim to bless the people: [b]Simeon, Levi, Judah, Issachar, Joseph, and Benjamin.

13 "And for the curse, these shall stand on Mount Ebal: Reuben, Gad, Asher, Zebulun, Dan, and Naphtali.

14 "The Levites shall then answer and say to all the men of Israel with a loud voice,

15 'Cursed is the man who makes [1a]an idol or a molten image, an abomination to the LORD, the work of the hands of the craftsman, and sets *it* up in secret.' And [b]all the people shall answer and say, 'Amen.'

16 '[a]Cursed is he who dishonors his father or mother.' And all the people shall say, 'Amen.'

17 '[a]Cursed is he who moves his neighbor's boundary mark.' And all the people shall say, 'Amen.'

18 '[a]Cursed is he who misleads a blind *person* on the road.' And all the people shall say, 'Amen.'

19 '[a]Cursed is he who distorts the justice due an alien, [1]orphan, and widow.' And all the people shall say, 'Amen.'

20 '[a]Cursed is he who lies with his father's wife, because he has uncovered his father's skirt.' And all the people shall say, 'Amen.'

21 '[a]Cursed is he who lies with any animal.' And all the people shall say, 'Amen.'

22 '[a]Cursed is he who lies with his sister, the daughter of his father or of his mother.' And all the people shall say, 'Amen.'

23 '[a]Cursed is he who lies with his mother-in-law.' And all the people shall say, 'Amen.'

24 '[a]Cursed is he who strikes his neighbor in secret.' And all the people shall say, 'Amen.'

25 '[a]Cursed is he who accepts a bribe to strike down an innocent person.' And all the people shall say, 'Amen.'

26 '[a]Cursed is he who does not confirm the words of this law by doing them.' And all the people shall say, 'Amen.'

Blessings at Gerizim

28 "[a]NOW it shall be, if you will diligently [1]obey the LORD your God, being careful to do all His commandments which I command you today, the LORD your God [b]will set you high above all the nations of the earth.

13 [1]Or, *fatherless* [a]Ps. 119:141, 153, 176

14 [1]Lit., *while in my*

15 [a]Ps. 80:14; Is. 63:15; Zech. 2:13 [b]Deut. 26:9

16 [a]Deut. 4:29

17 [1]Lit., *to walk in* [a]Ps. 48:14

18 [1]Lit., *to keep all* [a]Ex. 6:7; 19:5; Deut. 4:20; 7:6; 14:2; 28:9; 29:13; Titus 2:14; 1 Pet. 2:9

19 [1]Lit., *to set you* [a]Deut. 4:7, 8; 28:1, 13 [b]Ex. 19:6; Deut. 7:6; Is. 62:12; Jer. 2:3; 1 Pet. 2:9

2 [a]Josh. 8:30-32

3 [1]Lit., *spoke to* [a]Deut. 26:9

4 [1]Lit., *which* [a]Deut. 11:29; Josh. 8:30

5 [1]Lit., *lift up* [a]Ex. 20:25; Josh. 8:31

6 [1]Lit., *whole*

7 [a]Deut. 26:11

8 [1]I.e., stones coated with lime, cf. v. 4

10 [1]Lit., *listen to the voice of*

12 [a]Deut. 11:29 [b]Josh. 8:33-35

15 [1]Or, *a graven image* [a]Ex. 20:4, 23; 34:17; Lev. 19:4; 26:1; Deut. 4:16, 23; 5:8; Is. 44:9 [b]1 Cor. 14:16

16 [a]Ex. 20:12; 21:17; Lev. 19:3; 20:9; Deut. 5:16; Ezek. 22:7

17 [a]Deut. 19:14; Prov. 22:28

18 [a]Lev. 19:14

19 [1]Or, *fatherless* [a]Ex. 22:21; 23:9; Lev. 19:33; Deut. 10:18; 24:17

20 [a]Lev. 18:8; 20:11; Deut. 22:30; 1 Cor. 5:1

21 [a]Ex. 22:19; Lev. 18:23; 20:15

22 [a]Lev. 18:9; 20:17

23 [a]Lev. 20:14

24 [a]Ex. 21:12; Lev. 24:17; Num. 35:30, 31

25 [a]Ex. 23:7; Deut. 10:17; Ps. 15:5; Ezek. 22:12

26 [a]Ps. 119:21; Jer. 11:3; Gal. 3:10

1 [1]Lit., *listen to the voice of* [a]Ex. 15:26; 23:22-27; Lev. 26:3-13; Deut. 7:12-26; 11:13 [b]Deut. 28:13; 26:19; 1 Chr. 14:2

2"And all these blessings shall come
upon you and [a]overtake you, if you will
[1]obey the LORD your God.
3"Blessed *shall* you *be* in the city, and
blessed *shall* you *be* [a]in the [1]country.
4"Blessed *shall be* the [1]offspring of
your [2]body and the [1]produce of your
ground and the [1]offspring of your beasts,
the increase of your herd and the young
of your flock.
5"Blessed *shall be* your basket and
your kneading bowl.
6"Blessed *shall* you *be* [a]when you
come in, and blessed *shall* you *be* when
you go out.
7"The LORD will cause your enemies
who rise up against you to be [1]defeated
before you; they shall come out against
you one way and shall flee before you
seven ways.
8"The LORD will command the blessing upon you in your barns and in [a]all
that you put your hand to, and He will
bless you in the land which the LORD
your God gives you.
9"[a]The LORD will establish you as a
holy people to Himself, as He swore to
you, if you will keep the commandments
of the LORD your God, and walk in His
ways.
10"So all the peoples of the earth shall
see that [1a]you are called by the name of
the LORD; and they shall be afraid of
you.
11"[a]And the LORD will make you
abound in prosperity, in the [1]offspring
of your [2]body and in the [1]offspring of
your beast and in the [1]produce of your
ground, in the land which the LORD
swore to your fathers to give you.
12"The LORD will open for you His
good storehouse, the heavens, to give
rain to your land in its season and to
bless all the work of your hand; and
[a]you shall lend to many nations, but you
shall not borrow.
13"[a]And the LORD shall make you the
head and not the tail, and you only shall
be above, and you shall not be underneath, if you will listen to the commandments of the LORD your God, which I
charge you today, to [1]observe *them*
carefully,
14 and [a]do not turn aside from any of
the words which I command you today,
to the right or to the left, to go after
other gods to serve them.

Consequences of Disobedience

15"[a]But it shall come about, if you will
not [1]obey the LORD your God, to observe to do all His commandments and
His statutes with which I charge you
today, that all these curses shall come
upon you and overtake you.
16"[a]Cursed *shall* you *be* in the city,
and cursed *shall* you *be* in the [1]country.
17"[a]Cursed *shall be* your basket and
your kneading bowl.
18"[a]Cursed *shall be* the [1]offspring of
your [2]body and the [1]produce of your
ground, the increase of your herd and
the young of your flock.
19"[a]Cursed *shall* you *be* when you
come in, and cursed *shall* you *be* when
you go out.
20"[a]The LORD will send upon you
curses, confusion, and [b]rebuke, in all
[1]you undertake to do, until you are
destroyed and until [c]you perish quickly,
on account of the evil of your deeds,
because you have forsaken Me.
21"[a]The LORD will make the pestilence
cling to you until He has consumed you
from the land, where you are entering to
possess it.
22"[a]The LORD will smite you with
consumption and with fever and with
inflammation and with fiery heat and
with [1]the sword and [b]with blight and
with mildew, and they shall pursue you
until [c]you perish.
23"And [1]the heaven which is over your
head shall be bronze, and the earth
which is under you, iron.
24"[a]The LORD will make the rain of
your land powder and dust; from heaven
it shall come down on you until you are
destroyed.
25"[a]The LORD will cause you to be
[1]defeated before your enemies; you shall
go out one way against them, but you
shall flee seven ways before them, and
you shall [b]be *an example of* terror to all
the kingdoms of the earth.
26"[a]And your carcasses shall be food
to all birds of the sky and to the beasts
of the earth, and there shall be no one to
frighten *them* away.
27"[a]The LORD will smite you with the
boils of Egypt and with [b]tumors and
with the scab and with the itch, from
which you cannot be healed.
28"The LORD will smite you with
madness and with blindness and with
bewilderment of heart;
29 and you shall [1a]grope at noon, as
the blind man gropes in darkness, and
you shall not prosper in your ways; but
you shall only be oppressed and robbed
continually, with none to save you.
30"[a]You shall betroth a wife, but
another man shall violate her; [b]you shall
build a house, but you shall not live in it;
you shall plant a vineyard, but you shall
not [1]use its fruit.
31"Your ox shall be slaughtered before
your eyes, but you shall not eat of it;
your donkey shall be torn away from
you, and shall not be restored to you;
your sheep shall be given to your enemies, and you shall have none to save
you.
32"[a]Your sons and your daughters
shall be given to another people, while
your eyes shall look on and yearn for
them continually; but there shall be
nothing [1]you can do.
33"[a]A people whom you do not know
shall eat up the produce of your ground
and all your labors, and you shall never
be anything but oppressed and crushed
continually.
34"And you shall be driven mad by
the sight of [1]what you see.

2 [1]Lit., *listen to the voice of* [a]Zech. 1:6
3 [1]Or, *field* [a]Gen. 39:5
4 [1]Lit., *fruit* [2]Lit., *womb*
6 [a]Ps. 121:8
7 [1]Lit., *smitten*
8 [a]Deut. 15:10
9 [a]Ex. 19:5
10 [1]Lit., *the name of the LORD is called upon you* [a]2 Chr. 7:14
11 [1]Lit., *fruit* [2]Or, *womb* [a]Deut. 28:4; Prov. 10:22
12 [a]Deut. 23:20
13 [1]Lit., *keep and do* [a]Deut. 28:1, 44
14 [a]Deut. 5:32; Josh. 1:7
15 [1]Lit., *listen to the voice of* [a]Lev. 26:14-43; Josh. 23:15; Dan. 9:11
16 [1]Or, *field* [a]Deut. 28:3
17 [a]Deut. 28:5
18 [1]Lit., *fruit* [2]Or, *womb* [a]Deut. 28:4
19 [a]Deut. 28:6
20 [1]Lit., *the putting forth of your hand which you do* [a]Deut. 28:8; Mal. 2:2 [b]Ps. 80:16; Is. 51:20; 66:15 [c]Deut. 4:26
21 [a]Lev. 26:25; Num. 14:12; Jer. 24:10; Amos 4:10
22 [1]Another reading is *drought* [a]Lev. 26:16 [b]Amos 4:9 [c]Deut. 4:26
23 [1]Lit., *your*
24 [a]Deut. 11:17; 28:12
25 [1]Lit., *smitten* [a]Deut. 28:7; Is. 30:17 [b]2 Chr. 29:8; Jer. 15:4; 24:9; Ezek. 23:46
26 [a]Jer. 7:33; 16:4; 19:7; 34:20
27 [a]Ex. 9:9; Deut. 7:15; 28:60, 61 [b]1 Sam. 5:6
29 [1]Lit., *be groping* [a]Ex. 10:21
30 [1]Lit., *begin it* [a]Job 31:10; Jer. 8:10 [b]Amos 5:11
32 [1]Lit., *in the power of your hand* [a]Deut. 28:41
33 [a]Jer. 5:15, 17
34 [1]Lit., *your eyes which you*

35 "[a]The LORD will strike you on the knees and legs with sore boils, from which you cannot be healed, from the sole of your foot to the crown of your head.

36 "[a]The LORD will bring you and your king, whom you shall set over you, to a nation which neither you nor your fathers have known, and there you shall serve other gods, [b]wood and stone.

37 "And [a]you shall become a horror, a proverb, and a taunt among all the people where the LORD will drive you.

38 "[a]You shall bring out much seed to the field but you shall gather in little, for [b]the locust shall consume it.

39 "[a]You shall plant and cultivate vineyards, but you shall neither drink of the wine nor gather *the grapes,* for the worm shall devour them.

40 "[a]You shall have olive trees throughout your territory but you shall not anoint yourself with the oil, for your olives shall drop off.

41 "[a]You shall [1]have sons and daughters but they shall not be yours, for they shall go into captivity.

42 "[a]The cricket shall possess all your trees and the produce of your ground.

43 "[a]The alien who is among you shall rise above you higher and higher, but you shall go down lower and lower.

44 "[a]He shall lend to you, but you shall not lend to him; [b]he shall be the head, and you shall be the tail.

45 "So all these curses shall come on you and pursue you and overtake you [a]until you are destroyed, because you would not [1]obey the LORD your God by keeping His commandments and His statutes which He commanded you.

46 "And they shall become [a]a sign and a wonder on you and your [1]descendants forever.

47 "[a]Because you did not serve the LORD your God with joy and a glad heart, for the abundance of all things;

48 therefore you shall serve your enemies whom the LORD shall send against you, [a]in hunger, in thirst, in nakedness, and in the lack of all things; and He [b]will put an iron yoke on your neck until He has destroyed you.

49 "[a]The LORD will bring a nation against you from afar, from the end of the earth, [b]as the eagle swoops down, a nation whose language you shall not understand,

50 a nation of fierce countenance who shall [a]have no respect for the old, nor show favor to the young.

51 "Moreover, it shall eat the [1]offspring of your herd and the produce of your ground until you are destroyed, who also leaves you no grain, new wine, or oil, nor the increase of your herd or the young of your flock until they have caused you to perish.

52 "[a]And it shall besiege you in all your [1]towns until your high and fortified walls in which you trusted come down throughout your land, and it shall besiege you in all your [1]towns throughout your land which the LORD your God has given you.

53 "[a]Then you shall eat the [1]offspring of your own body, the flesh of your sons and of your daughters whom the LORD your God has given you, during the siege and the distress by which your enemy shall [2]oppress you.

54 "The man who is [1]refined and very delicate among you [2]shall be hostile toward his brother and toward the wife [3]he cherishes and toward the rest of his children who remain,

55 so that he will not give *even* one of them any of the flesh of his children which he shall eat, since he has nothing *else* left, during the siege and the distress by which your enemy shall [1]oppress you in all your [2]towns.

56 "[a]The [1]refined and delicate woman among you, who would not venture to set the sole of her foot on the ground for delicateness and [2]refinement, [3]shall be hostile toward the husband [4]she cherishes and toward her son and daughter,

57 and toward her afterbirth which issues from between her [1]legs and toward her children whom she bears; for [a]she shall eat them secretly for lack of anything *else,* during the siege and the distress by which your enemy shall [2]oppress you in your [3]towns.

58 "If you are not careful to observe all the words of this law which are written in this book, to [1a]fear this honored and awesome [b]name, [2]the LORD your God,

59 then the LORD will bring extraordinary plagues on you and [1]your descendants, even [2]severe and lasting plagues, and miserable and chronic sicknesses.

60 "[a]And He will bring back on you all the diseases of Egypt of which you were afraid, and they shall cling to you.

61 "Also every sickness and every plague which, not written in the book of this law, the LORD will bring on you [a]until you are destroyed.

62 "Then you shall be left few in number, [a]whereas you were as the stars of heaven for multitude, because you did not [1]obey the LORD your God.

63 "And it shall come about that as the LORD [a]delighted over you to prosper you, and multiply you, so the LORD will [b]delight over you to make you perish and destroy you; and you shall be [c]torn from the land where you are entering to possess it.

64 "Moreover, the LORD will [a]scatter you among all peoples, from one end of the earth to the other end of the earth; and there you shall [b]serve other gods, wood and stone, which you or your fathers have not known.

65 "And [a]among those nations you shall find no rest, and there shall be no resting place for the sole of your foot; but there [b]the LORD will give you a trembling heart, failing of eyes, and despair of soul.

35 [a]Deut. 28:27
36 [a]2 Kin. 17:4, 6; 24:12, 14; 25:7, 11; 2 Chr. 36:1-21; Jer. 39:1-9 [b]Deut. 4:28; Jer. 16:13
37 [a]1 Kin. 9:7, 8; Jer. 19:8; 24:9; 25:9; 29:18
38 [a]Is. 5:10; Mic. 6:15; Hag. 1:6 [b]Ex. 10:4; Joel 1:4
39 [a]Is. 5:10; 17:10, 11
40 [a]Jer. 11:16; Mic. 6:15
41 [1]Lit., *beget* [a]Deut. 28:32
42 [a]Deut. 28:38
43 [a]Deut. 28:13
44 [a]Deut. 28:12 [b]Deut. 28:13
45 [1]Lit., *listen to the voice of* [a]Deut. 4:25, 26
46 [1]Lit., *seed* [a]Num. 26:10; Is. 8:18; Ezek. 5:15; 14:8
47 [a]Deut. 12:7; Neh. 9:35-37
48 [a]Lam. 4:4-6 [b]Jer. 28:13, 14
49 [a]Is. 5:26-30; 7:18-20; Jer. 5:15; 6:22, 23 [b]Jer. 48:40; 49:22; Lam. 4:19; Hos. 8:1
50 [a]Is. 47:6
51 [1]Lit., *fruit*
52 [1]Lit., *gates* [a]Jer. 10:17, 18; Zeph. 1:15, 16
53 [1]Lit., *fruit* [2]Or, *distress* [a]Lev. 26:29; 2 Kin. 6:28, 29; Jer. 19:9; Lam. 2:20; 4:10
54 [1]Lit., *tender* [2]Lit., *his eye shall be evil toward* [3]Lit., *of his bosom*
55 [1]Or, *distress* [2]Lit., *gates*
56 [1]Lit., *tender* [2]Lit., *tenderness* [3]Lit., *her eye shall be evil toward* [4]Lit., *of her bosom* [a]Lam. 4:10
57 [1]Lit., *feet* [2]Or, *distress* [3]Lit., *gates* [a]2 Kin. 6:28, 29; Lam. 4:10
58 [1]Or, *reverence* [2]Heb., *YHWH* [a]Ps. 99:3; Mal. 1:14 [b]Is. 42:8
59 [1]Lit., *plague on your seed* [2]Lit., *great*
60 [a]Deut. 28:27
61 [a]Deut. 4:25, 26
62 [1]Lit., *listen to the voice of* [a]Deut. 1:10; Neh. 9:23
63 [a]Jer. 32:41 [b]Prov. 1:26 [c]Jer. 12:14; 45:4
64 [a]Lev. 26:33; Deut. 4:27; Neh. 1:8 [b]Deut. 4:28; 29:26; 32:17
65 [a]Lam. 1:3 [b]Lev. 26:36

66"So your life shall [1]hang in doubt
before you; and you shall be in dread
night and day, and shall have no assurance of your life.
67"[a]In the morning you shall say,
'Would that it were evening!' And at
evening you shall say, 'Would that it
were morning!' because of the dread of
your heart which you dread, and for the
sight of your eyes which you shall see.
68"And the LORD will bring you back
to Egypt in ships, by the way about
which I spoke to you, 'You will never see
it again!' And there you shall offer
yourselves for sale to your enemies as
male and female slaves, but there will be
no buyer."

The Covenant in Moab

29 [1a]THESE are the words of the
covenant which the LORD commanded Moses to make with the sons of
Israel in the land of Moab, besides the
[b]covenant which He had made with
them at Horeb.
2 [1]And Moses summoned all Israel
and said to them, "You have seen all
that the LORD did before your eyes in
the land of Egypt to Pharaoh and all his
servants and all his land;
3 [a]the great trials which your eyes
have seen, those great signs and wonders.
4"Yet to this day [a]the LORD has not
given you a heart to know, nor eyes to
see, nor ears to hear.
5"And I have led you forty years in
the wilderness; [a]your clothes have not
worn out on you, and your sandal has
not worn out on your foot.
6"[a]You have not eaten bread, nor
have you drunk wine or strong drink, in
order that you might know that I am the
LORD your God.
7"[a]When you [1]reached this place,
Sihon the king of Heshbon and Og the
king of Bashan came out to meet us for
battle, but we [2]defeated them;
8 and we took their land and [a]gave it
as an inheritance to the Reubenites, the
Gadites, and the half-tribe of the Manassites.
9"[a]So keep the words of this covenant
to do them, [b]that you may prosper in all
that you do.
10"You stand today, all of you, before
the LORD your God: your chiefs, your
tribes, your elders and your officers, *even*
all the men of Israel,
11 your little ones, your wives, and the
alien who is within your camps, from
[a]the one who chops your wood to the
one who draws your water,
12 that you may enter into the covenant with the LORD your God, and into
His oath which the LORD your God is
making with you today,
13 in order that He may establish you
today as His people and that [a]He may be
your God, just as He spoke to you and
as He swore to your fathers, to Abraham, Isaac, and Jacob.
14"Now not with you alone am I
[a]making this covenant and this oath,
15 [a]but both with those who stand
here with us today in the presence of the
LORD our God and with those who are
not with us here today
16 (for you know how we lived in the
land of Egypt, and how we came
through the midst of the nations through
which you passed.
17"Moreover, you have seen their
abominations and their idols *of* [a]wood,
stone, silver, and gold, which *they had*
with them);
18 [a]lest there shall be among you a
man or woman, or family or tribe, whose
heart turns away today from the LORD
our God, to go and serve the gods of
those nations; lest there shall be among
you [b]a root bearing poisonous fruit and
wormwood.
19"And it shall be when he hears the
words of this curse, that he will [1]boast,
saying, 'I have peace though I walk in
the stubbornness of my heart in order
[2]to destroy the watered *land* with the
dry.'
20"The LORD shall never be willing to
forgive him, but rather the anger of the
LORD and [a]His jealousy will [1b]burn
against that man, and every curse which
is written in this book will [2]rest on him,
and the LORD will [c]blot out his name
from under heaven.
21"Then the LORD will single him out
for [1]adversity from all the tribes of
Israel, according to all the curses of the
covenant [a]which are written in this book
of the law.
22"Now the generation to come, your
sons who rise up after you and [a]the
foreigner who comes from a distant
land, when they see the plagues of the
land and the diseases with which the
LORD has [1]afflicted it, will say,
23 'All its land is [a]brimstone and salt,
[b]a burning waste, [1]unsown and unpro-
ductive, and no grass grows in it, like the
overthrow of [c]Sodom and Gomorrah,
Admah and Zeboiim, which the LORD
overthrew in His anger and in His
wrath.'
24"And all the nations shall say,
'[a]Why has the LORD done thus to this
land? Why this great [1]outburst of anger?'
25"Then *men* shall say, '[a]Because they
forsook the covenant of the LORD, the
God of their fathers, which He made
with them when He brought them out of
the land of Egypt.
26 'And they went and served other
gods and worshiped them, gods whom
they have not known and whom He had
not [1]allotted to them.
27 'Therefore, the anger of the LORD
burned against that land, [a]to bring upon
it every curse which is written in this
book;
28 and [a]the LORD uprooted them from
their land in anger and in fury and in
great wrath, and cast them into another
land, as *it is* this day.'

66 [1]Lit., *be hung for you in front*
67 [a]Job 7:4
1 [1]Ch. 28:69 in Heb. [a]Lev. 26:46; 27:34 [b]Deut. 5:2, 3
2 [1]Ch. 29:1 in Heb.
3 [a]Deut. 4:34; 7:19
4 [a]Is. 6:9, 10; Ezek. 12:2; Matt. 13:14; Acts 28:26, 27; Rom. 11:8
5 [a]Deut. 8:4
6 [a]Deut. 8:3
7 [1]Lit., *came to* [2]Lit., *smote* [a]Num. 21:21-24, 33, 35; Deut. 2:26-3:17
8 [a]Num. 32:32, 33; Deut. 3:12, 13
9 [a]Deut. 4:6; 1 Kin. 2:3 [b]Josh. 1:7
11 [a]Josh. 9:21, 23, 27
13 [a]Gen. 17:7; Ex. 6:7
14 [a]Jer. 31:31; Heb. 8:7, 8
15 [a]Acts 2:39
17 [a]Ex. 20:23; Deut. 4:28; 28:36
18 [a]Deut. 13:6 [b]Deut. 32:32; Heb. 12:15
19 [1]Lit., *bless himself in his heart* [2]I.e., to destroy everything
20 [1]Lit., *smoke* [2]Lit., *lie down* [a]Ps. 79:5; Ezek. 23:25 [b]Ps. 74:1; 80:4 [c]Ex. 32:33; Deut. 9:14; 2 Kin. 14:27
21 [1]Lit., *evil* [a]Deut. 30:10
22 [1]Lit., *made it sick* [a]Jer. 19:8; 49:17; 50:13
23 [1]Lit., *it is not sown and does not cause to sprout* [a]Gen. 19:24; Is. 34:9; Jer. 17:6; Zeph. 2:9 [b]Is. 1:7; 64:11 [c]Jude 7
24 [1]Lit., *heat* [a]1 Kin. 9:8; Jer. 22:8
25 [a]2 Kin. 17:9-23; 2 Chr. 36:13-21
26 [1]Lit., *portioned*
27 [a]Dan. 9:11
28 [a]2 Chr. 7:20; Ps. 52:5; Prov. 2:22; Ezek. 19:12, 13

29“[a]The secret things belong to the
LORD our God, but [b]the things revealed
belong to us and to our sons forever,
that we may observe all the words of this
law.

Restoration Promised

30 “SO it shall be when all of these
things have come upon you, [a]the
blessing and the curse which I have set
before you, and you [1]call *them* to mind
[b]in all nations where the LORD your God
has banished you,
2 and you [a]return to the LORD your
God and [1]obey Him [b]with all your heart
and soul according to all that I command you today, you and your sons,
3 then the LORD your God will [a]re-
store [1]you from captivity, and have
compassion on you, and [b]will gather you
again from all the peoples where the
LORD your God has [c]scattered you.
4“If your outcasts are at the ends of
the [1]earth, [a]from there the LORD your
God will gather you, and from there He
will [2]bring you back.
5“And [a]the LORD your God will
bring you into the land which your
fathers possessed, and you shall possess
it; and He will prosper you and [b]multi-
ply you more than your fathers.
6“Moreover [a]the LORD your God will
circumcise your heart and the heart of
your [1]descendants, [b]to love the LORD
your God with all your heart and with
all your soul, in order that you may live.
7“[a]And the LORD your God will
[1]inflict all these curses on your enemies
and on those who hate you, who persecuted you.
8“And you shall again [1]obey the
LORD, and observe all His commandments which I command you today.
9“[a]Then the LORD your God will
[1]prosper you abundantly in all the work
of your hand, in the [2]offspring of your
[3]body and in the [2]offspring of your
cattle and in the [2]produce of
your ground, for [b]the LORD will again
rejoice over you for good, just as He
rejoiced over your fathers;
10 [1]if you [2]obey the LORD your God
to keep His commandments and His
statutes which [a]are written in this book
of the law, [1]if you turn to the LORD your
God [b]with all your heart and soul.
11“For this commandment which I
command you today is not too difficult
for you, nor is it [1]out of reach.
12“It is not in heaven, [1]that you
should say, ‘[a]Who will go up to heaven
for us to get it for us and make us hear
it, that we may observe it?’
13“Nor is it beyond the sea, [1]that you
should say, ‘Who will cross the sea for us
to get it for us and make us hear it, that
we may observe it?’
14“But the word is very near you, in
your mouth and in your heart, that you
may observe it.

Choose Life

15“See, [a]I have set before you today
life and [1]prosperity, and death and
[2]adversity;
16 in that I command you today [a]to
love the LORD your God, to walk in His
ways and to keep His commandments
and His statutes and His judgments, that
you [b]may live and multiply, and that the
LORD your God may bless you in the
land where you are entering to possess it.
17“But if your heart turns away and
you will not obey, but are drawn away
and worship other gods and serve them,
18 I declare to you today that [a]you
shall surely perish. You shall not prolong *your* days in the land where you
are crossing the Jordan to enter [1]and
possess it.
19“[a]I call heaven and earth to witness
against you today, that I have set before
you life and death, [b]the blessing and the
curse. So choose life in order that you
may live, you and your [1]descendants,
20 [a]by loving the LORD your God, by
obeying His voice, and [b]by holding fast
to Him; [c]for [1]this is your life and the
length of your days, [2]that you may live
in [d]the land which the LORD swore to
your fathers, to Abraham, Isaac, and
Jacob, to give them.”

Moses’ Last Counsel

31 SO Moses went and spoke these
words to all Israel.
2 And he said to them, “I am [a]a
hundred and twenty years old today; [b]I
am no longer able to come and go, and
the LORD has said to me, ‘[c]You shall not
cross this Jordan.’
3“[a]It is the LORD your God who will
cross ahead of you; He will destroy these
nations before you, and you shall dispossess them. [b]Joshua is the one who will
cross ahead of you, just as the LORD has
spoken.
4“And the LORD will do to them just
as He did to Sihon and Og, the kings of
the Amorites, and to their land, when He
destroyed them.
5“And [a]the LORD will deliver them
up before you, and you shall do to them
according to all the commandments
which I have commanded you.
6“[a]Be strong and courageous, [b]do not
be afraid or tremble at them, for [c]the
LORD your God is the one who goes with
you. [d]He will not fail you or forsake
you.”
7 Then Moses called to Joshua and
said to him in the sight of all Israel, “[a]Be
strong and courageous, for you shall go
with this people into the land which the
LORD has sworn to their fathers to give
them, and you shall give it to them as an
inheritance.
8“And [a]the LORD is the one who goes
ahead of you; He will be with you. [b]He
will not fail you or forsake you. Do not
fear, or be dismayed.”

29 [a]Acts 1:7 [b]John 5:39; Acts 17:11; 2 Tim. 3:16

1 [1]Lit., *cause them to return to your heart* [a]Deut. 11:26; 30:15, 19 [b]Lev. 26:40-45; Deut. 28:64; 29:28; 1 Kin. 8:47

2 [1]Lit., *listen to His voice* [a]Deut. 4:29, 30; Neh. 1:9 [b]Deut. 4:29

3 [1]Lit., *your captivity* [a]Gen. 28:15; 48:21; Ps. 126:1, 4; Jer. 29:14 [b]Ps. 147:2; Jer. 32:37; Ezek. 34:13 [c]Deut. 4:27

4 [1]Lit., *sky* [2]Lit., *take you* [a]Neh. 1:9; Is. 43:6; 48:20; 62:11

5 [a]Jer. 29:14; 30:3 [b]Deut. 7:13; 13:17

6 [1]Lit., *seed* [a]Deut. 10:16 [b]Deut. 6:5

7 [1]Lit., *put* [a]Deut. 7:15

8 [1]Lit., *listen to the voice of*

9 [1]Lit., *make you have excess for good* [2]Lit., *fruit* [3]Lit., *womb* [a]Jer. 31:27, 28 [b]Jer. 32:41

10 [1]Or, *for you will* [2]Lit., *listen to the voice of* [a]Deut. 29:21 [b]Deut. 4:29

11 [1]Lit., *far off*

12 [1]Lit., *to say* [a]Rom. 10:6-8

13 [1]Lit., *to say*

15 [1]Lit., *good* [2]Lit., *evil* [a]Deut. 11:26

16 [a]Deut. 6:5 [b]Deut. 4:1; 30:19

18 [1]Lit., *to* [a]Deut. 4:26; 8:19

19 [1]Lit., *seed* [a]Deut. 4:26 [b]Deut. 30:1

20 [1]Lit., *that* [2]Lit., *to dwell* [a]Deut. 6:5 [b]Deut. 10:20 [c]Deut. 4:1; 32:47; Acts 17:25, 28 [d]Gen. 12:7; 17:1-8

2 [a]Deut. 34:7 [b]Num. 27:17; 1 Kin. 3:7 [c]Deut. 1:37; 3:27

3 [a]Deut. 9:3 [b]Num. 27:18

5 [a]Deut. 7:2

6 [a]Josh. 10:25; 1 Chr. 22:13 [b]Deut. 1:29; 7:18; 20:1 [c]Deut. 20:4 [d]Josh. 1:5; Heb. 13:5

7 [a]Deut. 1:38; 3:28

8 [a]Ex. 13:21; 33:14 [b]Deut. 31:6; Josh. 1:5; Heb. 13:5

9 So Moses wrote this law and gave it to the priests, the sons of Levi [a]who carried the ark of the covenant of the LORD, and to all the elders of Israel.

10 Then Moses commanded them, saying, "At the end of *every* seven years, at the time of [a]the year of remission of debts, at the [b]Feast of Booths,

11 when all Israel comes [a]to appear before the LORD your God at [b]the place which He will choose, [c]you shall read this law in front of all Israel in their hearing.

12 "Assemble the people, the men and the women and children and [1]the alien who is in your [2]town, in order that they may hear and [a]learn and fear the LORD your God, and be careful to observe all the words of this law.

13 "And their children, who have not known, will hear and learn to fear the LORD your God, as long as you live on the land [1]which you are about to cross the Jordan to [2]possess."

Israel Will Fall Away

14 Then the LORD said to Moses, "Behold, [1a]the time for you to die is near; call Joshua, and present yourselves at the tent of meeting, that I may commission him." [b]So Moses and Joshua went and presented themselves at the tent of meeting.

15 [a]And the LORD appeared in the tent in a pillar of cloud, and the pillar of cloud stood at the doorway of the tent.

16 And the LORD said to Moses, "Behold, [a]you are about to lie down with your fathers; and [b]this people will arise and play the harlot with the strange gods of the land, into the midst of which they are going, and [c]will forsake Me and break My covenant which I have made with them.

17 "[a]Then My anger will be kindled against them in that day, and [b]I will forsake them and [c]hide My face from them, and they shall be consumed, and many evils and troubles shall come upon them; so that they will say in that day, '[d]Is it not because our God is not among us that these evils have come upon us?'

18 "But I will surely hide My face in that day because of all the evil which they will do, for they will turn to other gods.

19 "Now therefore, [a]write this song for yourselves, and teach it to the sons of Israel; put it [1]on their lips, in order that this song may be a witness for Me against the sons of Israel.

20 "[a]For when I bring them into the land flowing with milk and honey, which I swore to their fathers, and they have eaten and are satisfied and [b]become [1]prosperous, then they will turn to other gods and serve them, and spurn Me and break My covenant.

21 "Then it shall come about, [a]when many evils and troubles have come upon them, that this song will testify before them as a witness (for it shall not be forgotten from the [1]lips of their descendants); for [b]I know their intent which they are [2]developing today, before I have brought them into the land which I swore."

22 [a]So Moses wrote this song the same day, and taught it to the sons of Israel.

Joshua Is Commissioned

23 [a]Then He commissioned Joshua the son of Nun, and said, "[b]Be strong and courageous, for you shall bring the sons of Israel into the land which I swore to them, and [c]I will be with you."

24 And it came about, when Moses finished writing the words of this law in a book until they were complete,

25 that Moses commanded the Levites [a]who carried the ark of the covenant of the LORD, saying,

26 "Take this book of the law and place it beside the ark of the covenant of the LORD your God, that it may [1]remain there as a witness against you.

27 "For I know [a]your rebellion and [b]your [1]stubbornness; behold, while I am still alive with you today, you have been rebellious against the LORD; how much more, then, after my death?

28 "Assemble to me all the elders of your tribes and your officers, that I may speak these words in their hearing and [a]call the heavens and the earth to witness against them.

29 "For I know that after my death you will [a]act corruptly and turn from the way which I have commanded you; and evil will befall you in the latter days, for you will do that which is evil in the sight of the LORD, provoking Him to anger with the work of your hands."

30 Then Moses spoke in the hearing of all the assembly of Israel the words of this song, until they were complete:

The Song of Moses

32 "[a]GIVE ear, O heavens, and let me speak;
And let the earth hear the words of my mouth.
2 "[a]Let my teaching drop as the rain,
My speech distill as the dew,
[b]As the droplets on the fresh grass
And as the showers on the herb.
3 "[a]For I proclaim the name of the LORD;
[b]Ascribe greatness to our God!
4 "[a]The Rock! His work is perfect,
[b]For all His ways are [1]just;
[c]A God of faithfulness and without injustice,
Righteous and upright is He.
5 "[1a]They have acted corruptly toward Him,
They are not His children, because of their defect;
[b]*But are* a perverse and crooked generation.
6 "Do you thus [a]repay the LORD,
[b]O foolish and unwise people?
[c]Is not He your Father who has bought you?
[d]He has made you and established you.

9 [a]Num. 4:5, 6, 15; Deut. 10:8; 31:25, 26; Josh. 3:3
10 [a]Deut. 15:1, 2 [b]Lev. 23:34; Deut. 16:13
11 [a]Deut. 16:16 [b]Deut. 12:5 [c]Josh. 8:34; 2 Kin. 23:2
12 [1]Lit., *your alien* [2]Lit., *gates* [a]Deut. 4:10
13 [1]Lit., *where* [2]Lit., *possess it*
14 [1]Lit., *your days to die are* [a]Num. 27:12, 13; Deut. 4:22; 32:50 [b]Ex. 33:9-11
15 [a]Ex. 33:9
16 [a]Gen. 15:15 [b]Ex. 34:15; Deut. 4:25-28; Judg. 2:11, 12, 17 [c]Judg. 10:6; 1 Kin. 18:18; 19:10; Jer. 2:13
17 [a]Judg. 2:14; 6:13 [b]2 Chr. 15:2; 24:20 [c]Ps. 104:29; Is. 8:17 [d]Num. 14:42
19 [1]Lit., *in their mouths* [a]Deut. 31:22
20 [1]Lit., *fat* [a]Deut. 6:10-12; 8:10, 19; 11:16, 17 [b]Deut. 32:15-17
21 [1]Lit., *mouth of its seed* [2]Lit., *making* [a]Lev. 26:41; Deut. 4:30 [b]1 Chr. 28:9; John 2:24, 25
22 [a]Deut. 31:19
23 [a]Num. 27:23; Deut. 31:7 [b]Josh. 1:6 [c]Ex. 3:12
25 [a]Deut. 31:9
26 [1]Lit., *be*
27 [1]Lit., *stiff neck* [a]Deut. 9:7, 24 [b]Ex. 32:9; Deut. 9:6, 13
28 [a]Deut. 4:26; 30:19; 32:1
29 [a]Judg. 2:19
1 [a]Deut. 4:26; Ps. 50:4; Is. 1:2; Jer. 6:19
2 [a]Is. 55:10, 11 [b]Ps. 72:6
3 [a]Ex. 33:19; 34:5, 6 [b]Deut. 3:24; 5:24
4 [1]Or, *judgment* [a]Deut. 32:15, 18, 30; 2 Sam. 22:31 [b]Gen. 18:25; Dan. 4:37 [c]Deut. 7:9
5 [1]Lit., *It has* [a]Deut. 4:25; 31:29 [b]Matt. 17:17
6 [a]Ps. 116:12 [b]Deut. 32:28 [c]Deut. 1:31; Ps. 74:2; Is. 63:16 [d]Deut. 32:15

7 "Remember the days of old,
Consider the years of all generations.
[a]Ask your father, and he will inform you,
Your elders, and they will tell you.
8 "[a]When the Most High gave the nations their inheritance,
When He separated the sons of [1]man,
He set the boundaries of the peoples
[b]According to the number of the sons of Israel.
9 "[a]For the LORD's portion is His people;
Jacob is the allotment of His inheritance.
10 "[a]He found him in a desert land,
And in the howling waste of a wilderness;
He encircled him, He cared for him,
He guarded him as [b]the pupil of His eye.
11 "[a]Like an eagle that stirs up its nest,
That hovers over its young,
[b]He spread His wings and caught them,
He carried them on His pinions.
12 "[a]The LORD alone guided him,
[b]And there was no foreign god with him.
13 "[a]He made him ride on the high places of the earth,
And he ate the produce of the field;
[b]And He made him suck honey from the rock,
And [c]oil from the flinty rock,
14 Curds of cows, and milk of the flock,
With fat of lambs,
And rams, the breed of Bashan, and goats,
[a]With the finest of the wheat—
And of the [b]blood of grapes you drank wine.

15 "[a]But [1]Jeshurun grew fat and kicked—
You are grown fat, thick, and sleek—
[b]Then he forsook God [c]who made him,
And scorned [d]the Rock of his salvation.
16 "[a]They made Him jealous with strange *gods;*
[b]With abominations they provoked Him to anger.
17 "[a]They sacrificed to demons who were not God,
[b]To gods whom they have not known,
[c]New *gods* who came lately,
Whom your fathers did not dread.
18 "You neglected [a]the Rock who begot you,
[b]And forgot the God who gave you birth.

19 "[a]And the LORD saw *this,* and spurned *them*
[b]Because of the provocation of His sons and daughters.
20 "Then He said, 'I will hide My face from them,
[a]I will see what their end *shall be;*
[b]For they are a perverse generation,
[c]Sons in whom is no faithfulness.
21 '[a]They have made Me jealous with *what* is not God;
They have provoked Me to anger with their [1b]idols.
[c]So I will make them jealous with *those who* are not a people;
I will provoke them to anger with a foolish nation,
22 [a]For a fire is kindled in My anger,
And burns to the lowest part of [1]Sheol,
[b]And consumes the earth with its yield,
And sets on fire the foundations of the mountains.

23 '[a]I will heap misfortunes on them;
[b]I will use My arrows on them.
24 '[a]*They shall be* wasted by famine, and consumed by [1]plague
[b]And bitter destruction;
[c]And the teeth of beasts I will send upon them,
[d]With the venom of crawling things of the dust.
25 '[a]Outside the sword shall bereave,
And inside terror—
[b]Both young man and virgin,
The nursling with the man of gray hair.
26 'I would have said, "[a]I will cut them to pieces,
[b]I will remove the memory of them from men,"
27 Had I not feared the provocation by the enemy,
Lest their adversaries should misjudge,
Lest they should say, "[a]Our hand is [1]triumphant,
And the LORD has not done all this." '

28 "[a]For they are a nation [1]lacking in counsel,
And there is no understanding in them.
29 "[a]Would that they were wise, that they understood this,
[b]That they would discern their [1]future!
30 "[a]How could one chase a thousand,
And two put ten thousand to flight,
Unless their [b]Rock had sold them,
And the LORD had given them up?
31 "Indeed their rock is not like our Rock,
[a]Even our enemies [1]themselves judge this.
32 "For their vine is from the vine of Sodom,
And from the fields of Gomorrah;

7 [a]Ex. 12:26; Ps. 78:5-8
8 [1]Or, *Adam* [a]Acts 17:26 [b]Num. 23:9; Deut. 33:28
9 [a]1 Sam. 10:1; 1 Kin. 8:51, 53; Jer. 10:16
10 [a]Deut. 1:19 [b]Ps. 17:8; Prov. 7:2; Zech. 2:8
11 [a]Ex. 19:4; Deut. 33:12 [b]Ps. 18:10-18
12 [a]Deut. 4:35, 39 [b]Deut. 32:39; Is. 43:12
13 [a]Is. 58:14 [b]Deut. 8:8; Ps. 81:16 [c]Job 29:6
14 [a]Ps. 81:16; 147:14 [b]Gen. 49:11
15 [1]I.e., Israel [a]Deut. 31:20 [b]Judg. 10:6 [c]Deut. 32:6 [d]Deut. 32:4; Ps. 89:26
16 [a]Ps. 78:58 [b]Ps. 106:29
17 [a]Lev. 17:7; 1 Cor. 10:20 [b]Deut. 28:64 [c]Judg. 5:8
18 [a]Deut. 32:4 [b]Ps. 106:21
19 [a]Lev. 26:30; Ps. 106:40 [b]Jer. 44:21-23
20 [a]Deut. 31:29 [b]Deut. 32:5 [c]Deut. 9:23
21 [1]Lit., *vanities* [a]Deut. 32:16; 1 Cor. 10:22 [b]Deut. 32:17; 1 Kin. 16:13, 26 [c]Rom. 10:19
22 [1]I.e., the nether world [a]Num. 16:33-35; Ps. 18:7, 8; Lam. 4:11 [b]Lev. 26:20
23 [a]Deut. 29:21 [b]Ps. 18:14; 45:5
24 [1]Lit., *burning heat* [a]Deut. 28:22, 48 [b]Ps. 91:6 [c]Lev. 26:22 [d]Amos 5:18, 19
25 [a]Lam. 1:20; Ezek. 7:15 [b]2 Chr. 36:17; Lam. 2:21
26 [a]Deut. 4:27; 28:64 [b]Deut. 9:14
27 [1]Lit., *high* [a]Num. 15:30
28 [1]Lit., *perishing* [a]Deut. 32:6
29 [1]Or, *latter end* [a]Deut. 5:29 [b]Deut. 31:29
30 [a]Lev. 26:7, 8 [b]Deut. 32:4; Ps. 44:12
31 [1]Lit., *are judges* [a]Ex. 14:25

Their grapes are grapes of [a]poison,
Their clusters, bitter.
33 "Their wine is the venom of [1]ser-
pents,
And the [2]deadly poison of cobras.

34 '[a]Is it not laid up in store with Me,
Sealed up in My treasuries?
35 '[a]Vengeance is Mine, and retribution,
[b]In due time their foot will slip;
[c]For the day of their calamity is
near,
And the impending things are hastening upon them.'
36 "[a]For the LORD will vindicate His
people,
[b]And will have compassion on His
servants;
When He sees that *their* [1]strength is
gone,
And there is none *remaining,* bond
or free.
37 "And He will say, '[a]Where are their
gods,
The rock in which they sought
refuge?
38 '[a]Who ate the fat of their sacrifices,
And drank the wine of their libation?
[b]Let them rise up and help you,
Let them be your hiding place!
39 '[a]See now that I, I am He,
[b]And there is no god besides Me;
[c]It is I who put to death and give
life.
[d]I have wounded, and it is I who
heal;
[e]And there is no one who can
deliver from My hand.
40 'Indeed, [a]I lift up My hand to
heaven,
And say, as I live forever,
41 [a]If I sharpen My [1]flashing sword,
And My hand takes hold on justice,
[b]I will render vengeance on My
adversaries,
And I will repay those who hate
Me.
42 '[a]I will make My arrows drunk with
blood,
[b]And My sword shall devour flesh,
With the blood of the slain and the
captives,
From the long-haired [1]leaders of
the enemy.'
43 "[a]Rejoice, O nations, *with* His people;
[b]For He will avenge the blood of
His servants,
[c]And will render vengeance on His
adversaries,
[d]And will atone for His land *and*
His people."
44 Then Moses came and spoke all the
words of this song in the hearing of the
people, he, with [1][a]Joshua the son of
Nun.
45 When Moses had finished speaking
all these words to all Israel,
46 he said to them, "[a]Take to your
heart all the words with which I am

32 [a]Deut. 29:18
33 [1]Lit., *dragons* [2]Lit., *cruel*
34 [a]Job 14:17; Jer. 44:21
35 [a]Ps. 94:1; Rom. 12:19; Heb. 10:30 [b]Jer. 23:12 [c]Ezek. 7:5-10
36 [1]Lit., *hand* [a]Ps. 135:14; Heb. 10:30 [b]Lev. 26:43-45; Deut. 30:1-3
37 [a]Judg. 10:14; Jer. 2:28
38 [a]Num. 25:1, 2 [b]Jer. 11:12
39 [a]Is. 41:4; 43:10 [b]Deut. 32:12; Is. 45:5 [c]1 Sam. 2:6; Ps. 68:20 [d]Ps. 51:8 [e]Ps. 50:22
40 [a]Ezek. 20:5, 6; 21:4, 5
41 [1]Or, *lightning* [a]Is. 34:6-8 [b]Jer. 50:28-32
42 [1]Lit., *head* [a]Deut. 32:23 [b]Jer. 12:12; 46:10, 14
43 [a]Rom. 15:10 [b]2 Kin. 9:7; Rev. 6:10; 19:2 [c]Is. 1:24, 25 [d]Ps. 65:3; 79:9; 85:1
44 [1]Lit., *Hoshea* [a]Num. 13:8, 16
46 [1]Lit., *to do* [a]Ezek. 40:4; 44:5 [b]Deut. 4:9
47 [1]Lit., *where* [2]Lit., *possess it* [a]Deut. 8:3; 30:20 [b]Deut. 4:40; 33:25
48 [a]Num. 27:12
49 [1]Lit., *which is opposite* [a]Num. 27:12-14; Deut. 3:27
50 [a]Gen. 25:8
51 [a]Num. 20:12 [b]Num. 27:14
52 [a]Deut. 34:1-3 [b]Deut. 1:37; 3:27

1 [a]Josh. 14:6
2 [1]Lit., *rose to* [2]Lit., *myriads of holiness* [3]Or, *a fiery law* [a]Ex. 19:18, 20; Ps. 68:8, 17 [b]Judg. 5:4 [c]Num. 10:12; Hab. 3:3 [d]Dan. 7:10; Acts 7:53 [e]Ex. 23:20-22
3 [1]Lit., *peoples* [2]Lit., *His* [3]Or, *lie down at Thy feet* [a]Deut. 4:37; Mal. 1:2 [b]Deut. 7:6; 14:2 [c]Deut. 6:1-9; Luke 10:39
4 [a]Deut. 4:2; John 7:19 [b]Ps. 119:111
5 [a]Num. 23:21
6 [a]Gen. 49:3, 4
7 [1]Lit., *him* [a]Gen. 49:8-12

warning you today, which you shall
command [b]your sons to observe [1]care-
fully, *even* all the words of this law.
47 "For it is not an idle word for you;
indeed [a]it is your life. And [b]by this word
you shall prolong your days in the land,
[1]which you are about to cross the Jordan
to [2]possess."
48 And [a]the LORD spoke to Moses
that very same day, saying,
49 "[a]Go up to this mountain of the
Abarim, Mount Nebo, which is in the
land of Moab [1]opposite Jericho, and
look at the land of Canaan, which I am
giving to the sons of Israel for a possession.
50 "Then die on the mountain where
you ascend, and be [a]gathered to your
people, as Aaron your brother died on
Mount Hor and was gathered to his
people,
51 [a]because you broke faith with Me
in the midst of the sons of Israel at the
waters of Meribah-kadesh, in the [b]wil-
derness of Zin, because you did not treat
Me as holy in the midst of the sons of
Israel.
52 "[a]For you shall see the land at a
distance, but [b]you shall not go there,
into the land which I am giving the sons
of Israel."

The Blessing of Moses

33 NOW this is the blessing with
which Moses [a]the man of God
blessed the sons of Israel before his
death.
2 And he said,
"[a]The LORD came from Sinai,
[b]And [1]dawned on them from Seir;
[c]He shone forth from Mount Paran,
And He came from [d]the [2]midst of
ten thousand holy ones;
[e]At His right hand there was
[3]flashing lightning for them.
3 "[a]Indeed, He loves [1]the people;
[b]All [2]Thy holy ones are in Thy
hand,
[c]And they [3]followed in Thy steps;
Everyone receives of Thy words.
4 "[a]Moses charged us with a law,
[b]A possession for the assembly of
Jacob.
5 "[a]And He was king in Jeshurun,
When the heads of the people
were gathered,
The tribes of Israel together.

6 "[a]May Reuben live and not die,
Nor his men be few."

7 [a]And this regarding Judah; so he
said,
"Hear, O LORD, the voice of Judah,
And bring him to his people.
With his hands he contended for
[1]them;
And mayest Thou be a help
against his adversaries."

8 And of Levi he said,
"*Let* Thy [a]Thummim and Thy Urim *belong* to [1]Thy [b]godly man,
[c]Whom Thou didst prove at Massah,
With whom Thou didst contend at the waters of Meribah;
9 [a]Who said of his father and his mother,
'I did not consider them';
And he did not acknowledge his brothers,
Nor did he regard his own sons,
For [b]they observed Thy word,
And kept Thy covenant.
10 "[a]They shall teach Thine ordinances to Jacob,
And Thy law to Israel.
[b]They shall put incense [1]before Thee,
And [c]whole burnt offerings on Thine altar.
11 "O LORD, bless his substance,
And accept the work of his hands;
Shatter the loins of those who rise up against him,
And those who hate him, so that they may not rise *again*."

12 Of Benjamin he said,
"[a]May the beloved of the LORD dwell in security by Him,
[b]Who shields him all the day,
[c]And he dwells between His shoulders."

13 And of Joseph he said,
"[a]Blessed of the LORD *be* his land,
With the choice things of heaven, with the dew,
And from the deep lying beneath,
14 And with the choice yield of the sun,
And with the choice produce of the months.
15 "And with the [1]best things of [a]the ancient mountains,
And with the choice things of the everlasting hills,
16 And with the choice things of the earth and its fulness,
And the favor [a]of Him who dwelt in the bush.
Let it come to the head of Joseph,
And to the crown of the head of the one distinguished among his brothers.
17 "As the first-born of his ox, majesty is his,
And his horns are the horns of [a]the wild ox;
With them he shall [b]push the peoples,
All [1]at once, *to* the ends of the earth.
And those are the ten thousands of Ephraim,
And those are the thousands of Manasseh."

18 [a]And of Zebulun he said,
"Rejoice, Zebulun, in your going forth,
And, Issachar, in your tents.
19 "[a]They shall call peoples *to* the mountain;
There they shall offer [b]righteous sacrifices;
For they shall [1]draw out [c]the abundance of the seas,
And the hidden treasures of the sand."

20 [a]And of Gad he said,
"Blessed is the one who enlarges Gad;
He lies down [b]as a [1]lion,
And tears the arm, also the crown of the head.
21 "[a]Then he [1]provided the first *part* for himself,
[b]For there the ruler's portion was [2]reserved;
[c]And he came *with* the leaders of the people;
[d]He executed the justice of the LORD,
And His ordinances with Israel."

22 [a]And of Dan he said,
"Dan is [b]a lion's whelp,
That leaps forth from Bashan."

23 And of Naphtali he said,
"[a]O Naphtali, satisfied with favor,
And full of the blessing of the LORD,
Take possession of the sea and the south."

24 [a]And of Asher he said,
"More blessed than sons is Asher;
May he be favored by his brothers,
[b]And may he dip his foot in oil.
25 "[a]Your locks shall be iron and bronze,
[b]And according to your days, so shall your leisurely walk be.

26 "[a]There is none like the God of [1]Jeshurun,
[b]Who rides the heavens [2]to your help,
And through the skies in His majesty.
27 "[a]The eternal God is a [1]dwelling place,
[b]And underneath are the everlasting arms;
[c]And He drove out the enemy from before you,
[d]And said, 'Destroy!'
28 "[a]So Israel dwells in security,
[b]The fountain of Jacob secluded,
[c]In a land of grain and new wine;
[d]His heavens also drop down dew.
29 "[a]Blessed are you, O Israel;
[b]Who is like you, a people saved by the LORD,
[c]Who is the shield of your help,
[d]And the sword of your majesty!
[e]So your enemies shall cringe before you,
[f]And you shall tread upon their high places."

8 [1]Lit., *him* [a]Ex. 28:30; Lev. 8:8 [b]Ps. 106:16 [c]Ex. 17:7; Num. 20:13, 24; Deut. 6:16
9 [a]Ex. 32:27-29 [b]Mal. 2:5
10 [1]Lit., *in Thy nostrils* [a]Lev. 10:11; Deut. 31:9-13 [b]Lev. 16:12, 13 [c]Ps. 51:19
12 [a]Deut. 4:37f.; 12:10 [b]Deut. 32:11 [c]Ex. 28:12
13 [a]Gen. 27:27, 28; 49:22-26
15 [1]Or, *chief* [a]Hab. 3:6
16 [a]Ex. 2:2-6; 3:2, 4
17 [1]Or, *together* [a]Num. 23:22 [b]1 Kin. 22:11; Ps. 44:5
18 [a]Gen. 49:13-15
19 [1]Lit., *suck* [a]Ex. 15:17; Ps. 2:6; Is. 2:3 [b]Ps. 4:5; 51:19 [c]Is. 60:5
20 [1]Or, *lioness* [a]Gen. 49:19 [b]Gen. 49:9
21 [1]Lit., *saw* [2]Or, *covered up* [a]Num. 32:1-5 [b]Num. 34:14 [c]Josh. 4:12 [d]Josh. 22:1-3
22 [a]Gen. 49:16 [b]Ezek. 19:2, 3
23 [a]Gen. 49:21
24 [a]Gen. 49:20 [b]Job 29:6
25 [a]Ps. 147:13 [b]Deut. 4:40; 32:47
26 [1]I.e., Israel [2]Lit., *in* [a]Ex. 15:11; Deut. 4:35; Ps. 86:8; Jer. 10:6 [b]Deut. 10:14; Ps. 68:33, 34; 104:3; Hab. 3:8
27 [1]Or, *refuge* [a]Ps. 90:1, 2 [b]Gen. 49:24 [c]Ex. 34:11; Josh. 24:18 [d]Deut. 7:2
28 [a]Deut. 33:12; Jer. 23:6 [b]Num. 23:9; Deut. 32:8 [c]Gen. 27:28, 37 [d]Deut. 33:13
29 [a]Ps. 1:1; 32:1, 2 [b]Deut. 4:32; 2 Sam. 7:23 [c]Gen. 15:1; Ps. 33:20; 115:9-11 [d]Ps. 68:34 [e]Ps. 66:3 [f]Num. 33:52

The Death of Moses

34 [a]NOW Moses went up from the plains of Moab to Mount Nebo, to the top of Pisgah, which is opposite Jericho. And the LORD [b]showed him all the land, Gilead as far as Dan,

2 and all Naphtali and the land of Ephraim and Manasseh, and all the land of Judah as far as the [1a]western sea,

3 and the [1]Negev and the plain in the valley of Jericho, [a]the city of palm trees, as far as Zoar.

4 Then the LORD said to him, "This is the land which [a]I swore to Abraham, Isaac, and Jacob, saying, 'I will give it to your [1]descendants'; I have let you see *it* with your eyes, but you shall not go over there."

5 So Moses [a]the servant of the LORD [b]died there in the land of Moab, according to the [1]word of the LORD.

6 And He buried him in the valley in the land of Moab, [a]opposite Beth-peor; but [b]no man knows his burial place to this day.

7 Although Moses was [a]one hundred and twenty years old when he died, [b]his eye was not dim, nor his vigor abated.

8 So the sons of Israel wept for Moses in the plains of Moab thirty days; then the days of weeping *and* mourning for Moses came to an end.

9 Now Joshua the son of Nun was [a]filled with the spirit of wisdom, for Moses had laid his hands on him; and the sons of Israel listened to him and did as the LORD had commanded Moses.

10 Since then [a]no prophet has risen in Israel like Moses, whom [b]the LORD knew face to face,

11 for all the signs and wonders which the LORD sent him to perform in the land of Egypt against Pharaoh, all his servants, and all his land,

12 and for all the mighty [1]power and for all the great terror which Moses performed in the sight of all Israel.

1 [a]Deut. 32:49 [b]Deut. 32:52
2 [1]I.e., Mediterranean Sea [a]Deut. 11:24
3 [1]I.e., South country [a]Judg. 1:16; 3:13; 2 Chr. 28:15
4 [1]Lit., *seed* [a]Gen. 12:7; 26:3; 28:13
5 [1]Lit., *mouth* [a]Num. 12:7; Josh. 1:1, 2 [b]Deut. 32:50
6 [a]Deut. 3:29; 4:46 [b]Jude 9
7 [a]Deut. 31:2 [b]Gen. 27:1; 48:10
9 [a]Num. 27:18, 23; Is. 11:2
10 [a]Deut. 18:15, 18 [b]Ex. 33:11; Num. 12:8; Deut. 5:4
12 [1]Lit., *hand*

THE BOOK OF JOSHUA

God's Charge to Joshua

1 NOW it came about after the death of Moses the servant of the LORD that the LORD spoke to Joshua the son of Nun, Moses' [1]servant, saying,

2 "Moses [a]My servant is dead; now therefore arise, [b]cross this Jordan, you and all this people, to the land which I am giving to them, to the sons of Israel.

3 "[a]Every place on which the sole of your foot treads, I have given it to you, just as I spoke to Moses.

4 "[a]From the wilderness and this Lebanon, even as far as the great river, the river Euphrates, all the land of the Hittites, and as far as the Great Sea toward the setting of the sun, will be your territory.

5 "[a]No man will *be able to* stand before you all the days of your life. Just as I have been with Moses, I will be with you; [b]I will not fail you or forsake you.

6 "[a]Be strong and courageous, for you shall give this people possession of the land which I swore to their fathers to give them.

7 "Only be strong and very courageous; [1a]be careful to do according to all the law which Moses My servant commanded you; do not turn from it to the right or to the left, so that you may [2]have success wherever you go.

8 "[a]This book of the law shall not depart from your mouth, but you shall meditate on it day and night, so that you may [1]be careful to do according to all that is written in it; [b]for then you will make your way prosperous, and then you will [2]have success.

9 "Have I not commanded you? [a]Be strong and courageous! [b]Do not tremble or be dismayed, for the LORD your God is with you wherever you go."

Joshua Assumes Command

10 Then Joshua commanded the officers of the people, saying,

11 "Pass through the midst of the camp and command the people, saying, 'Prepare provisions for yourselves, for within [a]three days you are to cross this Jordan, to go in to possess the land which the LORD your God is giving you, to possess it.' "

12 [a]And to the Reubenites and to the Gadites and to the half-tribe of Manasseh, Joshua [1]said,

13 "Remember the word which Moses the servant of the LORD commanded you, saying, '[a]The LORD your God gives you rest, and will give you this land.'

14 "Your wives, your little ones, and your cattle shall remain in the land which Moses gave you beyond the Jordan, but you shall cross before your brothers in battle array, all your valiant warriors, and shall help them,

15 until the LORD gives your brothers rest, as *He gives* you, and they also possess the land which the LORD your God is giving them. [a]Then you shall return to [1]your own land, and possess [2]that which Moses [b]the servant of the LORD gave you beyond the Jordan toward the sunrise."

16 And they answered Joshua, saying, "All that you have commanded us we will do, and wherever you send us we will go.

17 "Just as we obeyed Moses in all things, so we will obey you; only [a]may

1 [1]Or, *minister*
2 [a]Num. 12:7; Deut. 34:5 [b]Josh. 1:11
3 [a]Deut. 11:24
4 [a]Gen. 15:18; Num. 34:3
5 [a]Deut. 7:24 [b]Deut. 31:6, 7; Heb. 13:5
6 [a]Deut. 31:6, 7, 23
7 [1]Lit., *observe* [2]Or, *act wisely* [a]Deut. 5:32
8 [1]Lit., *observe* [2]Or, *act wisely* [a]Deut. 31:24; Josh. 8:34 [b]Deut. 29:9; Ps. 1:1-3
9 [a]Josh. 1:7 [b]Deut. 31:8
11 [a]Josh. 3:2
12 [1]Lit., *said, saying* [a]Num. 32:20-22
13 [a]Deut. 3:18-20
15 [1]Lit., *the land of your possession* [2]Lit., *it* [a]Josh. 22:4 [b]Josh. 1:1
17 [a]Josh. 1:5, 9

the LORD your God be with you, as He was with Moses.

18 "Anyone who rebels against your [1]command and does not obey your words in all that you command him, shall be put to death; only be strong and courageous."

Rahab Shelters Spies

2 THEN Joshua the son of Nun sent two men as spies secretly from [a]Shittim, saying, "Go, view the land, especially Jericho." So they went and came into the house of [b]a harlot whose name was Rahab, and [1]lodged there.

2 And it was told the king of Jericho, saying, "Behold, men from the sons of Israel have come here tonight to search out the land."

3 And the king of Jericho sent *word* to Rahab, saying, "Bring out the men who have come to you, who have entered your house, for they have come to search out all the land."

4 But the [a]woman had taken the two men and hidden them, and she said, "Yes, the men came to me, but I did not know where they were from.

5 "And it came about when *it was time* to shut the gate, at dark, that the men went out; I do not know where the men went. Pursue them quickly, for you will overtake them."

6 But [a]she had brought them up to the roof and hidden them in the stalks of flax which she had laid in order on the roof.

7 So the men pursued them on the road to the Jordan to the fords; and as soon as those who were pursuing them had gone out, they shut the gate.

8 Now before they lay down, [1]she came up to them on the roof,

9 and said to the men, "[a]I know that the LORD has given you the land, and that the [b]terror of you has fallen on us, and that all the inhabitants of the land have [1]melted away before you.

10 "[a]For we have heard how the LORD dried up the water of the [1]Red Sea before you when you came out of Egypt, and [b]what you did to the two kings of the Amorites who were beyond the Jordan, to Sihon and Og, whom you [2]utterly destroyed.

11 "And when we heard *it,* [a]our hearts melted and no [1]courage remained in any man any longer because of you; for the [b]LORD your God, He is God in heaven above and on earth beneath.

12 "Now therefore, please swear to me by the LORD, since I have dealt kindly with you, that you also will deal kindly with my father's household, and give me a [a]pledge of [1]truth,

13 and [1]spare my father and my mother and my brothers and my sisters, with all who belong to them, and deliver our [2]lives from death."

14 So the men said to her, "Our [1]life [2]for yours if you do not tell this business of ours; and it shall come about when the LORD gives us the land that we will [a]deal kindly and [3]faithfully with you."

The Promise to Rahab

15 Then she let them down by a rope through the window, for her house was on the city wall, so that she was living on the wall.

16 And she said to them, "[a]Go to the hill country, lest the pursuers happen upon you, and hide yourselves there for three days, until the pursuers return. Then afterward you may go on your way."

17 And the men said to her, "[a]We *shall be* free from this oath [1]to you which you have made us swear,

18 [1]unless, when we come into the land, you tie this cord of scarlet thread in the window through which you let us down, and [a]gather to yourself into the house your father and your mother and your brothers and all your father's household.

19 "And it shall come about that anyone who goes out of the doors of your house into the street, his blood *shall be* on his own head, and we *shall be* free; but anyone who is with you in the house, [a]his blood *shall be* on our head, if a hand is *laid* on him.

20 "But if you tell this business of ours, then we shall be free from the oath which you have made us swear."

21 And she said, "According to your words, so be it." So she sent them away, and they departed; and she tied the scarlet cord in the window.

22 And they departed and came to the hill country, and remained there for three days until the pursuers returned. Now the pursuers had sought *them* [1]all along the road, but had not found *them.*

23 Then the two men returned and came down from the hill country and crossed over and came to Joshua the son of Nun, and they related to him all that had happened to them.

24 And they said to Joshua, "Surely the LORD has given all the land into our hands, and [a]all the inhabitants of the land, moreover, have [1]melted away before us."

Israel Crosses the Jordan

3 THEN Joshua rose early in the morning; and he and all the sons of Israel set out from [a]Shittim and came to the Jordan, and they lodged there before they crossed.

2 And it came about [a]at the end of three days that the officers went through the midst of the camp;

3 and they commanded the people, saying, "When you see the [a]ark of the covenant of the LORD your God with the Levitical priests carrying it, then you shall set out from your place and go after it.

4 "However, there shall be between you and it a distance of about 2,000 [1]cubits by measure. Do not come near it, that you may know the way by which

18 [1]Lit., *mouth*

1 [1]Lit., *lay down* [a]Num. 25:1; Josh. 3:1 [b]Heb. 11:31; James 2:25

4 [a]2 Sam. 17:19

6 [a]James 2:25

8 [1]Lit., *then she*

9 [1]Or, *become demoralized* [a]Num. 20:24; Josh. 9:24 [b]Ex. 23:27; Deut. 2:25; Josh. 9:9, 10

10 [1]Lit., *Sea of Reeds* [2]Or, *put under the ban* [a]Ex. 14:21; Num. 23:22; 24:8 [b]Num. 21:21-35

11 [1]Lit., *spirit arose* [a]Josh. 5:1; 7:5; Ps. 22:14; Is. 13:7; 19:1 [b]Deut. 4:39

12 [1]Or, *faithfulness* [a]Josh. 2:18, 19

13 [1]Lit., *let live* [2]Lit., *souls*

14 [1]Lit., *soul* [2]Lit., *instead of you to die* [3]Or, *truly* [a]Gen. 24:49

16 [a]James 2:25

17 [1]Lit., *of yours* [a]Gen. 24:8

18 [1]Lit., *behold* [a]Josh. 2:12

19 [a]Matt. 27:25

22 [1]Lit., *through all the road*

24 [1]Or, *become demoralized* [a]Josh. 2:9

1 [a]Josh. 2:1

2 [a]Josh. 1:11

3 [a]Deut. 31:9

4 [1]I.e., One cubit equals approx. 18 in.

you shall go, for you have not passed this way before."

5 Then Joshua said to the people, "[a]Consecrate yourselves, for tomorrow the LORD will do wonders among you."

6 And Joshua spoke to the priests, saying, "Take up the ark of the covenant and cross over ahead of the people." So they took up the ark of the covenant and went ahead of the people.

7 Now the LORD said to Joshua, "This day I will begin to [a]exalt you in the sight of all Israel, that they may know that just as I have been with Moses, I will be with you.

8 "You shall, moreover, command the priests who are carrying the ark of the covenant, saying, 'When you come to the edge of the waters of the Jordan, you shall stand *still* in the Jordan.' "

9 Then Joshua said to the sons of Israel, "Come here, and hear the words of the LORD your God."

10 And Joshua said, "By this you shall know that [a]the living God is among you, and that He will assuredly [b]dispossess from before you the Canaanite, the Hittite, the Hivite, the Perizzite, the Girgashite, the Amorite, and the Jebusite.

11 "Behold, the ark of the covenant of [a]the Lord of all the earth is crossing over ahead of you into the Jordan.

12 "Now then, [a]take for yourselves twelve men from the tribes of Israel, one man for each tribe.

13 "And it shall come about when the soles of the feet of the priests who carry the ark of the LORD, the Lord of all the earth, shall rest in the waters of the Jordan, the waters of the Jordan shall be cut off, *and* the waters which are [1]flowing down from above [2]shall [a]stand in one heap."

14 So it came about when the people set out from their tents to cross the Jordan with the priests carrying [a]the ark of the covenant before the people,

15 and when those who carried the ark came into the Jordan, and the feet of the priests carrying the ark were dipped in the edge of the water (for the [a]Jordan overflows all its banks all the days of harvest),

16 [a]that the waters which were [1]flowing down from above stood *and* rose up in [b]one heap, a great distance away at Adam, the city that is beside Zarethan; and those which were [1]flowing down toward the sea of the [c]Arabah, the Salt Sea, were completely cut off. So the people crossed opposite Jericho.

17 And the priests who carried the ark of the covenant of the LORD stood firm [a]on dry ground in the middle of the Jordan while all Israel crossed on dry ground, until all the nation had finished crossing the Jordan.

Memorial Stones from Jordan

4 NOW it came about when all the nation had finished crossing the [a]Jordan, that the LORD spoke to Joshua, saying,

2 "[a]Take for yourselves twelve men from the people, one man from each tribe,

3 and command them, saying, 'Take up for yourselves twelve stones from here out of the middle of the Jordan, from the place where the priests' feet are standing firm, and carry them over with you, and lay them down in [a]the lodging place where you will lodge tonight.' "

4 So Joshua called the twelve men whom he had appointed from the sons of Israel, one man from each tribe;

5 and Joshua said to them, "[1]Cross again to the ark of the LORD your God into the middle of the Jordan, and each of you take up a stone on his shoulder, according to the number of the tribes of the sons of Israel.

6 "[1]Let this be a sign among you, so that [a]when your children ask [2]later, saying, 'What do these stones mean to you?'

7 then you shall say to them, 'Because the [a]waters of the Jordan were cut off before the ark of the covenant of the LORD; when it crossed the Jordan, the waters of the Jordan were cut off.' So these stones shall become a [b]memorial to the sons of Israel forever."

8 And thus the sons of Israel did, as Joshua commanded, and took up twelve stones from the middle of the Jordan, just as the LORD spoke to Joshua, according to the number of the tribes of the sons of Israel; and they carried them over with them to [a]the lodging place, and put them down there.

9 Then Joshua set up twelve [a]stones in the middle of the Jordan at the place where the feet of the priests who carried the ark of the covenant were standing, and they are there to this day.

10 For the priests who carried the ark were standing in the middle of the Jordan until everything was completed that the LORD had commanded Joshua to speak to the people, according to all that Moses had commanded Joshua. And the people hurried and crossed;

11 and it came about when all the people had finished crossing, that the ark of the LORD and the priests crossed before the people.

12 [a]And the sons of Reuben and the sons of Gad and the half-tribe of Manasseh crossed over in battle array before the sons of Israel, just as Moses had spoken to them;

13 about 40,000, equipped for war, crossed for battle before the LORD to the desert plains of Jericho.

14 [a]On that day the LORD exalted Joshua in the sight of all Israel; so that they [1]revered him, just as they had [1]revered Moses all the days of his life.

15 Now the LORD said to [1]Joshua,

16 "Command the priests who carry [a]the ark of the testimony that they come up from the Jordan."

5 [a]Ex. 19:10, 11; Josh. 7:13
7 [a]Josh. 4:14
10 [a]Deut. 5:26; 1 Thess. 1:9 [b]Ex. 33:2; Deut. 7:1
11 [a]Job 41:11; Ps. 24:1; Zech. 6:5
12 [a]Josh. 4:2
13 [1]Lit., *going* [2]Lit., *and they shall* [a]Ex. 15:8
14 [a]Ps. 132:8; Acts 7:44f.
15 [a]1 Chr. 12:15; Jer. 12:5; 49:19
16 [1]Lit., *going* [a]Ps. 66:6; 74:15; 114:3, 5 [b]Josh. 3:13 [c]Deut. 1:1
17 [a]Ex. 14:21, 22, 29

1 [a]Deut. 27:2; Josh. 3:17
2 [a]Josh. 3:12
3 [a]Josh. 4:20
5 [1]Lit., *Cross before the ark*
6 [1]Lit., *That this may be* [2]Lit., *tomorrow* [a]Ex. 12:26; 13:14; Josh. 4:21
7 [a]Josh. 3:13 [b]Ex. 12:14; Num. 16:40
8 [a]Josh. 4:20
9 [a]Gen. 28:18; Josh. 24:26f.; 1 Sam. 7:12
12 [a]Num. 32:17
14 [1]Or, *feared* [a]Josh. 3:7
15 [1]Lit., *Joshua, saying*
16 [a]Ex. 25:16

17 So Joshua commanded the priests,
saying, "Come up from the Jordan."
18 And it came about when the priests
who carried the ark of the covenant of
the LORD had come up from the middle
of the Jordan, and the soles of the
priests' feet were [1]lifted up to the dry
ground, that the waters of the Jordan
returned to their place, and went over all
its banks as before.
19 Now the people came up from the
Jordan on the [a]tenth of the first month
and camped at Gilgal on the eastern
edge of Jericho.
20 [a]And [1]those twelve stones which
they had taken from the Jordan, Joshua
set up [b]at Gilgal.
21 And he said to the sons of [1]Israel,
"When your children ask their fathers in
time to come, saying, 'What are these
stones?'
22 then you shall inform your children, saying, 'Israel crossed this Jordan
on [a]dry ground.'
23 "For the LORD your God dried up
the waters of the Jordan before you until
you had crossed, just as the LORD your
God had done to the [1]Red Sea, [a]which
He dried up before us until we had
crossed;
24 that [a]all the peoples of the earth
may know that the [b]hand of the LORD is
mighty, so that you may [1c]fear the LORD
your God [2]forever."

Israel Is Circumcised

5 NOW it came about when all the
kings of the Amorites who *were*
beyond the Jordan to the west, and all
the kings of the [a]Canaanites who *were* by
the sea, [b]heard how the LORD had dried
up the waters of the Jordan before the
sons of Israel until [1]they had crossed,
that their hearts melted, and there was
no spirit in them any longer, because of
the sons of Israel.
2 At that time the LORD said to
Joshua, "Make for yourself [a]flint knives
and circumcise again the sons of Israel
the second time."
3 So Joshua made himself flint knives
and circumcised the sons of Israel at
[1]Gibeath-haaraloth.
4 And this is the reason why Joshua
circumcised them: [a]all the people who
came out of Egypt who were males, all
the men of war, died in the wilderness
along the way, after they came out of
Egypt.
5 For all the people who came out
were circumcised, but all the people who
were born in the wilderness along the
way as they came out of Egypt had not
been circumcised.
6 For the sons of Israel walked [a]forty
years in the wilderness, until all the
nation, *that is,* the men of war who came
out of Egypt, [1]perished because they did
not listen to the voice of the LORD, [b]to
whom the LORD had sworn that He
would not let them see the land which
the LORD had sworn to their fathers to

18 [1]Lit., *drawn out*

19 [a]Deut. 1:3

20 [1]Lit., *these* [a]Josh. 4:8 [b]Josh. 4:3, 8

21 [1]Lit., *Israel, saying,*

22 [a]Josh. 3:17

23 [1]Lit., *Sea of Reeds* [a]Ex. 14:21

24 [1]Or, *reverence* [2]Lit., *all the days* [a]1 Kin. 8:42; 2 Kin. 19:19; Ps. 106:8 [b]Ex. 15:16; 1 Chr. 29:12; Ps. 89:13 [c]Ex. 14:31; Ps. 76:7f.; Jer. 10:7

1 [1]Other mss. read *we* [a]Num. 13:29 [b]Josh. 2:10, 11

2 [a]Ex. 4:25

3 [1]I.e., the hill of the foreskins

4 [a]Deut. 2:14

6 [1]Lit., *were finished* [a]Deut. 2:7, 14 [b]Num. 14:29-35; 26:63-65

7 [1]Lit., *circumcised them*

8 [1]Lit., *revived*

9 [1]I.e., rolling [a]Zeph. 2:8

10 [a]Ex. 12:18 [b]Josh. 4:19

11 [1]Lit., *morrow* [2]Lit., *this*

12 [1]Lit., *morrow* [a]Ex. 16:35

13 [a]Gen. 18:1, 2; 32:24, 30; Num. 22:31

14 [a]Gen. 17:3

15 [a]Ex. 3:5

2 [a]Deut. 7:24

4 [a]Lev. 25:9

5 [1]Lit., *in its place* [2]Lit., *before himself*

give us, a land flowing with milk and
honey.
7 And their children whom He raised
up in their place, Joshua [1]circumcised;
for they were uncircumcised, because
they had not circumcised them along the
way.
8 Now it came about when they had
finished circumcising all the nation, that
they remained in their places in the
camp until they were [1]healed.
9 Then the LORD said to Joshua,
"Today I have rolled away [a]the reproach
of Egypt from you." So the name of that
place is called [1]Gilgal to this day.
10 While the sons of Israel camped at
Gilgal, [a]they observed the Passover on
the evening of the [b]fourteenth day of the
month on the desert plains of Jericho.
11 And on the [1]day after the Passover,
on [2]that very day, they ate some of the
produce of the land, unleavened cakes
and parched *grain.*
12 And [a]the manna ceased on the
[1]day after they had eaten some of the
produce of the land, so that the sons of
Israel no longer had manna, but they ate
some of the yield of the land of Canaan
during that year.
13 Now it came about when Joshua
was by Jericho, that he lifted up his eyes
and looked, and behold, [a]a man was
standing opposite him with his sword
drawn in his hand, and Joshua went to
him and said to him, "Are you for us or
for our adversaries?"
14 And he said, "No, rather I indeed
come now *as* captain of the host of the
LORD." And Joshua [a]fell on his face to
the earth, and bowed down, and said to
him, "What has my lord to say to his
servant?"
15 And the captain of the LORD's host
said to Joshua, "[a]Remove your sandals
from your feet, for the place where you
are standing is holy." And Joshua did so.

The Conquest of Jericho

6 NOW Jericho was tightly shut because of the sons of Israel; no one
went out and no one came in.
2 And the LORD said to Joshua, "See,
I have given Jericho into your hand, with
[a]its king *and* the valiant warriors.
3 "And you shall march around the
city, all the men of war circling the city
once. You shall do so for six days.
4 "Also seven priests shall carry seven
[a]trumpets of rams' horns before the ark;
then on the seventh day you shall march
around the city seven times, and the
priests shall blow the trumpets.
5 "And it shall be that when they
make a long blast with the ram's horn,
and when you hear the sound of the
trumpet, all the people shall shout with a
great shout; and the wall of the city will
fall down [1]flat, and the people will go up
every man straight [2]ahead."
6 So Joshua the son of Nun called
the priests and said to them, "Take up
the ark of the covenant, and let seven

priests carry seven trumpets of rams'
horns before the ark of the LORD."
7 Then [1]he said to the people, "Go
forward, and march around the city, and
let the armed men go on before the ark
of the LORD."
8 And it was *so,* that when Joshua
had spoken to the people, the seven
priests carrying the seven trumpets of
rams' horns before the LORD went forward and blew the trumpets; and the ark
of the covenant of the LORD followed
them.
9 And the armed men went before
the priests who blew the trumpets, and
[a]the rear guard came after the ark, while
they continued to blow the trumpets.
10 But Joshua commanded the people,
saying, "You shall not shout nor let your
voice be heard, nor let a word proceed
out of your mouth, until the day I tell
you, 'Shout!' Then you shall shout!"
11 So he had the ark of the LORD
[1]taken around the city, circling *it* once;
then they came into the camp and spent
the night in the camp.
12 Now Joshua rose early in the
morning, and the priests took up the ark
of the LORD.
13 And [a]the seven priests carrying the
seven trumpets of rams' horns before the
ark of the LORD went on continually,
and blew the trumpets; and the armed
men went before them, and [b]the rear
guard came after the ark of the LORD,
while they continued to blow the trumpets.
14 Thus the second day they marched
around the city once and returned to the
camp; they did so for six days.
15 Then it came about on the seventh
day that they rose early at the dawning
of the day and marched around the city
in the same manner seven times; only on
that day they marched around the city
seven times.
16 And it came about at the seventh
time, when the priests blew the trumpets,
Joshua said to the people, "[a]Shout! For
the LORD has given you the city.
17 "And the city shall be [a]under the
ban, it and all that is in it belongs to the
LORD; only Rahab the harlot [1]and all
who are with her in the house shall live,
because she hid the messengers whom
we sent.
18 "But as for you, only keep yourselves from the things under the ban, lest
you [1]covet *them* and [a]take some of the
things under the ban, so you would
make the camp of Israel accursed and
bring trouble on it.
19 "[a]But all the silver and gold and
articles of bronze and iron are holy to
the LORD; they shall go into the treasury
of the LORD."
20 So the people shouted, and [1]*priests*
blew the trumpets; and it came about,
when the people heard the sound of the
trumpet, that the people shouted with a
great shout and the [a]wall fell down [2]flat,
so that the people went up into the city,
every man straight [3]ahead, and they
took the city.
21 [a]And they [1]utterly destroyed everything in the city, both man and woman,
young and old, and ox and sheep and
donkey, with the edge of the sword.
22 And Joshua said to the two men
who had spied out the land, "[a]Go into
the harlot's house and bring the woman
and all she has out of there, as you have
sworn to her."
23 So the young men who were spies
went in and [a]brought out Rahab and her
father and her mother and her brothers
and all she had; they also brought out all
her relatives, and placed them outside
the camp of Israel.
24 [a]And they burned the city with fire,
and all that was in it. Only the silver and
gold and articles of bronze and iron,
they put into the treasury of the [1]house
of the LORD.
25 However, [a]Rahab the harlot and
her father's household and all she had,
Joshua [1]spared; and she has lived in the
midst of Israel to this day, for [b]she hid
the messengers whom Joshua sent to spy
out Jericho.
26 Then Joshua made them take an
oath at that time, saying, "[a]Cursed
before the LORD is the man who rises up
and builds this city Jericho; with *the loss*
of his first-born he shall lay its foundation, and with *the loss of* his youngest
son he shall set up its gates."
27 So [a]the LORD was with Joshua, and
his [b]fame was in all the land.

Israel Is Defeated at Ai

7 [a]BUT the sons of Israel acted unfaithfully in regard to the things
under the ban, for Achan, the son of
Carmi, the son of Zabdi, the son of
Zerah, from the tribe of Judah, took
some of the things under the ban, therefore the anger of the LORD burned
against the sons of Israel.
2 Now Joshua sent men from Jericho
to Ai, which is near [a]Beth-aven, east of
Bethel, and said to them, "[1]Go up and
spy out the land." So the men went up
and spied out Ai.
3 And they returned to Joshua and
said to him, "Do not let all the people go
up; *only* about two or three thousand
men need go up [1]to Ai; do not make all
the people toil up there, for they are
few."
4 So about three thousand men from
the people went up there, but [a]they fled
[1]from the men of Ai.
5 And the men of Ai struck down
about thirty-six of their men, and pursued them [1]from the gate as far as
Shebarim, and struck them down on the
descent, so the [a]hearts of the people
melted and became as water.
6 Then Joshua [a]tore his clothes and
fell to the earth on his face before the
ark of the LORD until the evening, *both*
he and the elders of Israel; and [b]they put
dust on their heads.

7 [1]Or, *they*
9 [a]Josh. 6:13; Is. 52:12
11 [1]Lit., *to go around*
13 [a]Josh. 6:4 [b]Josh. 6:9
16 [a]2 Chr. 13:14f.
17 [1]Lit., *she and all* [a]Lev. 27:28; Deut. 20:17
18 [1]Lit., *devote* [a]Josh. 7:1
19 [a]Num. 31:11, 12, 21-23
20 [1]Or, *they* [2]Lit., *in its place* [3]Lit., *before himself* [a]Heb. 11:30
21 [1]Or, *put under the ban* [a]Deut. 20:16
22 [a]Josh. 2:12-19
23 [a]Heb. 11:31
24 [1]I.e., tabernacle [a]Deut. 20:16-18
25 [1]Lit., *let live* [a]Heb. 11:31 [b]Josh. 2:6
26 [a]1 Kin. 16:34
27 [a]Gen. 39:2; Judg. 1:19 [b]Josh. 9:1, 3
1 [a]Josh. 6:17-19
2 [1]Lit., *saying, Go* [a]Josh. 18:12; 1 Sam. 13:5; 14:23
3 [1]Lit., *and smite*
4 [1]Lit., *before* [a]Lev. 26:17; Deut. 28:25
5 [1]Or, *before* [a]Lev. 26:36; Josh. 2:11; Ezek. 21:7; Nah. 2:10
6 [a]Job 2:12 [b]Job 42:6; Lam. 2:10; Rev. 18:19

7 And Joshua said, "Alas, O Lord [1]GOD, why didst Thou ever bring this people over the Jordan, *only* to deliver us into the hand of the Amorites, to destroy us? If only we had been willing [2]to dwell beyond the Jordan!

8 "O Lord, what can I say since Israel has turned *their* [1]back before their enemies?

9 "[a]For the Canaanites and all the inhabitants of the land will hear of it, and they will surround us and cut off our name from the earth. And what wilt Thou do for Thy great name?"

10 So the LORD said to Joshua, "Rise up! Why is it that you have fallen on your face?

11 "Israel has sinned, and [a]they have also transgressed My covenant which I commanded them. And they have even taken some of the things under the ban and have both stolen and deceived. Moreover, they have also put *them* among their own things.

12 "Therefore the [a]sons of Israel cannot stand before their enemies; they turn *their* [1]backs before their enemies, for they have become accursed. I will not be with you anymore unless you destroy the things under the ban from your midst.

13 "Rise up! [a]Consecrate the people and say, 'Consecrate yourselves for tomorrow, for thus the LORD, the God of Israel, has said, "[b]There are things under the ban in your midst, O Israel. You cannot stand before your enemies until you have removed the things under the ban from your midst."

14 'In the morning then you shall come near by your tribes. And it shall be that the tribe which [a]the LORD takes *by lot* shall come near by families, and the family which the LORD takes shall come near by households, and the household which the LORD takes shall come near man by man.

15 'And [a]it shall be that the one who is taken with the things under the ban shall be burned with fire, he and all that belongs to him, because he has transgressed the covenant of the LORD, and because he [b]has committed a disgraceful thing in Israel.' "

The Sin of Achan

16 So Joshua arose early in the morning and brought Israel near by [1]tribes, and the tribe of Judah was taken.

17 And he brought the family of Judah near, and he took the family of the Zerahites; and he brought the family of the Zerahites near man by man, and Zabdi was taken.

18 And he brought his household near man by man; and [a]Achan, son of Carmi, son of Zabdi, son of Zerah, from the tribe of Judah, was taken.

19 Then Joshua said to Achan, "My son, I implore you, [a]give glory to the LORD, the God of Israel, and give praise to Him; and tell me now what you have done. Do not hide it from me."

20 So Achan answered Joshua and said, "Truly, I have sinned against the LORD, the God of Israel, and [1]this is what I did:

21 when I saw among the spoil a beautiful mantle from Shinar and two hundred shekels of silver and a bar of gold fifty shekels in weight, then I [a]coveted them and took them; and behold, they are concealed in the earth inside my tent with the silver underneath it."

22 So Joshua sent messengers, and they ran to the tent; and behold, it was concealed in his tent with the silver underneath it.

23 And they took them from inside the tent and brought them to Joshua and to all the sons of Israel, and they poured them out before the LORD.

24 Then Joshua and all Israel with him, took Achan the son of Zerah, the silver, the mantle, the bar of gold, his sons, his daughters, his [1]oxen, his donkeys, his sheep, his tent and all that belonged to him; and they brought them up to [a]the valley of [2]Achor.

25 And Joshua said, "Why have you [a]troubled us? The LORD will trouble you this day." And all Israel stoned [1]them with stones; and they burned them with fire [2]after they had stoned them with stones.

26 And they raised over him a great heap of stones that stands to this day, and the LORD turned from the fierceness of His anger. Therefore the name of that place has been called [a]the valley of [1]Achor to this day.

The Conquest of Ai

8 NOW the LORD said to Joshua, "[a]Do not fear or be dismayed. Take all the people of war with you and arise, go up to Ai; see, [b]I have given into your hand the king of Ai, his people, his city, and his land.

2 "And you shall do to Ai and its king just as you did to Jericho and its king; you shall [a]take only its spoil and its cattle as plunder for yourselves. [1]Set an ambush for the city behind it."

3 So Joshua rose with all the people of war to go up to Ai; and Joshua chose 30,000 men, valiant warriors, and sent them out at night.

4 And he commanded them, saying, "See, you are [a]going to ambush the city from behind [1]it. Do not go very far from the city, but all of you be ready.

5 "Then I and all the people who are with me will approach the city. And it will come about when they come out to meet us as at the first, that [a]we will flee before them.

6 "And they will come out after us until we have drawn them away from the city, for they will say, '*They* are fleeing before us as at the first.' So we will flee before them.

7 "And you shall rise from *your* ambush and take possession of the city, for the LORD your God will deliver it into your hand.

7 [1]Heb., *YHWH*, usually rendered *LORD* [2]Lit., *and had dwelt*

8 [1]Lit., *neck*

9 [a]Ex. 32:12; Deut. 9:28

11 [a]Josh. 6:18, 19

12 [1]Lit., *necks* [a]Num. 14:39, 45; Judg. 2:14

13 [a]Josh. 3:5 [b]Josh. 6:18

14 [a]Prov. 16:33

15 [a]1 Sam. 14:38f. [b]Gen. 34:7; Judg. 20:6

16 [1]Lit., *its tribes*

18 [a]Num. 32:23; Acts 5:1-10

19 [a]1 Sam. 6:5; 2 Chr. 30:22; Jer. 13:16; John 9:24

20 [1]Lit., *thus and thus I did*

21 [a]Eph. 5:5; 1 Tim. 6:10

24 [1]Or, *cattle* [2]I.e., trouble [a]Josh. 15:7

25 [1]Lit., *him* [2]Lit., *and they stoned* [a]Josh. 6:18

26 [1]I.e., trouble [a]Is. 65:10; Hos. 2:15

1 [a]Josh. 1:9; 10:8 [b]Josh. 6:2

2 [1]Lit., *Set for yourself* [a]Deut. 20:14; Josh. 8:27

4 [1]Lit., *the city* [a]Judg. 20:29

5 [a]Judg. 20:32

8 "Then it will be when you have seized the city, that you shall set the city on fire. You shall do *it* [a]according to the word of the LORD. See, I have commanded you."

9 So Joshua sent them away, and they went to the place of ambush and remained between Bethel and Ai, on the west side of Ai; but Joshua spent that night among the people.

10 Now Joshua [a]rose early in the morning and mustered the people, and he went up with the elders of Israel before the people to Ai.

11 Then all the people of war who *were* with him went up and drew near and arrived in front of the city, and camped on the north side of Ai. Now *there was* a valley between him and Ai.

12 And he took about 5,000 men and set them in ambush between [a]Bethel and Ai, on the west side of the [1]city.

13 So they stationed the people, all the army that was on the north side of the city, and its rear guard on the west side of the city, and Joshua spent that night in the midst of the valley.

14 And it came about when the king of Ai saw *it,* that the men of the city hurried and rose up early and went out to meet Israel in battle, he and all his people at the appointed place before the desert plain. But he did not know that *there was* an ambush against him behind the city.

15 And Joshua and all Israel pretended to be beaten before them, and fled [a]by the way of the wilderness.

16 And all the people who were in the city were called together to pursue them, and they pursued Joshua, and [a]were drawn away from the city.

17 So not a man was left in Ai or Bethel who had not gone out after Israel, and they left the city [1]unguarded and pursued Israel.

18 Then the LORD said to Joshua, "[a]Stretch out the javelin that is in your hand toward Ai, for I will give it into your hand." So Joshua stretched out the javelin that was in his hand toward the city.

19 And the *men in* ambush rose quickly from their place, and when he had stretched out his hand, they ran and entered the city and captured it; and they quickly set the city on fire.

20 When the men of Ai turned [1]back and looked, behold, the smoke of the city ascended to the sky, and they had no place to flee this way or that, for the people who had been fleeing to the wilderness turned against the pursuers.

21 When Joshua and all Israel saw that the *men in* ambush had captured the city and that the smoke of the city ascended, they turned back and [1]slew the men of Ai.

22 And [1]the others came out from the city to encounter them, so that they were *trapped* in the midst of Israel, [2]some on this side and some on that side; and they [3]slew them until [a]no one was left [4]of those who survived or escaped.

23 But they took alive the king of Ai and brought him to Joshua.

24 Now it came about when Israel had finished killing all the inhabitants of Ai in the field in the wilderness where they pursued them, and all of them were fallen by the edge of the sword until they were destroyed, then all Israel returned to Ai and struck it with the edge of the sword.

25 [a]And all who fell that day, both men and women, were 12,000—all the [1]people of Ai.

26 For Joshua [a]did not withdraw his hand with which he stretched out the javelin until he had [1]utterly destroyed all the inhabitants of Ai.

27 [a]Israel took only the cattle and the spoil of that city as plunder for themselves, according to the word of the LORD which He had commanded Joshua.

28 So Joshua burned Ai and made it [a]a heap forever, a desolation until this day.

29 [a]And he hanged the king of Ai on a tree until evening; and at sunset Joshua gave command and they took his body down from the tree, and threw it at the entrance of the city gate, and raised over it a great heap of stones *that stands* to this day.

30 Then Joshua built an altar to the LORD, the God of Israel, in [a]Mount Ebal,

31 just as Moses the servant of the LORD had commanded the sons of Israel, as it is written in the book of the law of Moses, [a]an altar of uncut stones, on which no man had wielded an iron *tool;* and they offered burnt offerings on it to the LORD, and sacrificed peace offerings.

32 And he [a]wrote there on the stones a copy of the law of Moses, which [1]he had written, in the presence of the sons of Israel.

33 [a]And all Israel with their elders and officers and their judges were standing on both sides of the ark before the Levitical priests who carried the ark of the covenant of the LORD, the stranger as well as the native. Half of them *stood* in front of [b]Mount Gerizim and half of them in front of Mount Ebal, just as Moses the servant of the LORD had given command at first to bless the people of Israel.

34 Then afterward he read all the words of the law, the blessing and the curse, according to all that is written in [a]the book of the law.

35 There was not a word of all that Moses had commanded which Joshua did not read before all the assembly of Israel [a]with the women and the little ones and the strangers who were [1]living among them.

8 [a]Deut. 20:16-18; Josh. 8:2
10 [a]Gen. 22:3
12 [1]I.e., Ai [a]Gen. 12:8; 28:19; Judg. 1:22
15 [a]Josh. 15:61; 16:1; 18:12
16 [a]Judg. 20:31
17 [1]Lit., *open*
18 [a]Ex. 14:16; 17:9-13; Josh. 8:26
20 [1]Lit., *behind them*
21 [1]Lit., *smote*
22 [1]Lit., *these came* [2]Lit., *these . . . those* [3]Lit., *smote* [4]Lit., *for it* [a]Josh. 8:8
25 [1]Lit., *men* [a]Deut. 20:16-18
26 [1]Or, *put under the ban* [a]Ex. 17:11, 12
27 [a]Josh. 8:2
28 [a]Deut. 13:16
29 [a]Deut. 21:22, 23
30 [a]Deut. 27:2-8
31 [a]Ex. 20:25
32 [1]I.e., Moses [a]Deut. 27:2, 3, 8
33 [a]Deut. 27:11-14 [b]Deut. 11:29
34 [a]Josh. 1:8
35 [1]Lit., *walking* [a]Ex. 12:38; Deut. 31:12; Zech. 8:23

Guile of the Gibeonites

9 NOW it came about when [a]all the kings who were beyond the Jordan, in the hill country and in the lowland and on all the [b]coast of the Great Sea toward Lebanon, [c]the Hittite and the Amorite, the Canaanite, the Perizzite, the Hivite and the Jebusite, heard of it,

2 that they gathered themselves together with [1][a]one accord to fight with Joshua and with Israel.

3 When the inhabitants of [a]Gibeon heard what Joshua had done to Jericho and to Ai,

4 they also acted craftily and [1]set out as envoys, and took worn-out sacks on their donkeys, and wineskins, worn-out and torn and [2]mended,

5 and worn-out and patched sandals on their feet, and worn-out clothes on themselves; and all the bread of their provision was dry *and* had become crumbled.

6 And they went to Joshua to the [a]camp at Gilgal, and said to him and to the men of Israel, "We have come from a far country; now therefore, make a covenant with us."

7 And the men of Israel said to the [a]Hivites, "Perhaps you are living [1]within our land; [b]how then shall we make a covenant with you?"

8 But they said to Joshua, "[a]We are your servants." Then Joshua said to them, "Who are you, and where do you come from?"

9 And they said to him, "Your servants have come from [a]a very far country because of the [1]fame of the LORD your God; for [b]we have heard the report of Him and all that He did in Egypt,

10 and all that He did to the two kings of the Amorites who were beyond the Jordan, to Sihon king of Heshbon and to Og king of Bashan who was at Ashtaroth.

11 "So our elders and all the inhabitants of our country spoke to us, saying, 'Take provisions in your hand for the journey, and go to meet them and say to them, "[a]We are your servants; now then, make a covenant with us." '

12 "This our bread *was* warm *when* we took it for our provisions out of our houses on the day that we left to come to you; but now behold, it is dry and has become crumbled.

13 "And these wineskins which we filled were new, and behold, they are torn; and these our clothes and our sandals are worn out because of the very long journey."

14 So the men *of Israel* took some of their provisions, and [a]did not ask for the [1]counsel of the LORD.

15 [a]And Joshua made peace with them and made a covenant with them, to let them live; and the leaders of the congregation swore *an oath* to them.

16 And it came about at the end of three days after they had made a covenant with them, that they heard that they were neighbors and that they were living [1]within their land.

17 Then the sons of Israel set out and came to their cities on the third day. Now their cities *were* [a]Gibeon and Chephirah and Beeroth and Kiriath-jearim.

18 And the sons of Israel did not strike them because the leaders of the congregation had sworn to them by the LORD the God of Israel. And the whole congregation grumbled against the leaders.

19 But all the leaders said to the whole congregation, "We have sworn to them by the LORD, the God of Israel, and now we cannot touch them.

20 "This we will do to them, even let them live, lest wrath be upon us for the oath which we swore to them."

21 And the leaders said to them, "Let them live." So they became [a]hewers of wood and drawers of water for the whole congregation, just as the leaders had spoken to them.

22 Then Joshua called for them and spoke to them, saying, "Why have you deceived us, saying, 'We are very far from you,' [a]when you are living [1]within our land?

23 "Now therefore, you are [a]cursed, and [1]you shall never cease being slaves, both hewers of wood and drawers of water for the house of my God."

24 So they answered Joshua and said, "[a]Because it was certainly told your servants that the LORD your God had commanded His servant Moses to give you all the land, and to destroy all the inhabitants of the land before you; therefore we feared greatly for our lives because of you, and have done this thing.

25 "And now behold, [a]we are in your hands; do as it seems good and right in your sight to do to us."

26 Thus he did to them, and delivered them from the hands of the sons of Israel, and they did not kill them.

27 But Joshua made them that day hewers of wood and drawers of water for the congregation and for the altar of the LORD, to this day, [a]in the place which He would choose.

Five Kings Attack Gibeon

10 NOW it came about when Adoni-zedek king of Jerusalem heard that Joshua had captured Ai, and had [1]utterly destroyed it (just [a]as he had done to Jericho and its king, so he had done to Ai and its king), and that the inhabitants of Gibeon had [b]made peace with Israel and were [2]within their land,

2 that [1]he [a]feared greatly, because Gibeon *was* a great city, like one of the royal cities, and because it was greater than Ai, and all its men *were* mighty.

3 Therefore Adoni-zedek king of Jerusalem sent *word* [a]to Hoham king of Hebron and to Piram king of Jarmuth and to Japhia king of Lachish and to Debir king of Eglon, saying,

---

Chapter 9:
1 [a]Num. 13:29; Josh. 3:10 [b]Num. 34:6 [c]Ex. 3:17; 23:23
2 [1]Lit., *one mouth* [a]Ps. 83:3, 5
3 [a]Josh. 9:17, 22; 10:2; 21:17
4 [1]Lit., *went and traveled as envoys* [2]Lit., *tied up*
6 [a]Josh. 5:10
7 [1]Lit., *among us* [a]Josh. 9:1; 11:19 [b]Ex. 23:32; Deut. 7:2
8 [a]Deut. 20:11; 2 Kin. 10:5
9 [1]Or, *name* [a]Josh. 9:16, 17 [b]Josh. 2:9; 9:24
11 [a]Josh. 9:8
14 [1]Lit., *mouth* [a]Num. 27:21
15 [a]Ex. 23:32
16 [1]Lit., *among them*
17 [a]Josh. 18:25
21 [a]Deut. 29:11
22 [1]Lit., *among us* [a]Josh. 9:16
23 [1]Lit., *a servant shall not be cut off from you* [a]Gen. 9:25
24 [a]Josh. 9:9
25 [a]Gen. 16:6
27 [a]Deut. 12:5

Chapter 10:
1 [1]Or, *put under the ban* [2]Lit., *among them* [a]Josh. 8:21f. [b]Josh. 9:15
2 [1]Lit., *they* [a]Ex. 15:14-16
3 [a]Josh. 10:23

4 "Come up to me and help me, and
let us [1]attack Gibeon, for it has [a]made
peace with Joshua and with the sons of
Israel."
5 So the five kings of [a]the Amorites,
the king of Jerusalem, the king of Hebron, the king of Jarmuth, the king of
Lachish, *and* the king of Eglon, gathered
together and went up, they with all their
armies, and camped by Gibeon and
fought against it.
6 Then the men of Gibeon sent *word*
to Joshua to the camp at Gilgal, saying,
"Do not [1]abandon your servants; come
up to us quickly and save us and help us,
for all the kings of the Amorites that live
in the hill country have assembled
against us."
7 So Joshua went up from Gilgal, he
and [a]all the people of war with him and
all the valiant warriors.
8 And the LORD said to Joshua,
"[a]Do not fear them, for I have given
them into your hands; not [1]one of them
shall stand before you."
9 So Joshua came upon them suddenly [1]by marching all night from Gilgal.
10 [a]And the LORD confounded them
before Israel, and He [1]slew them with a
great slaughter at Gibeon, and pursued
them by the way of the ascent of Beth-
horon, and struck them as far as Azekah
and Makkedah.
11 And it came about as they fled
from before Israel, *while* they were at the
descent of Beth-horon, that [a]the LORD
threw large stones from heaven on them
as far as Azekah, and they died; *there
were* more who died [1]from the hailstones
than those whom the sons of Israel killed
with the sword.
12 Then Joshua spoke to the LORD in
the day when the LORD delivered up the
Amorites before the sons of Israel, and
he said in the sight of Israel,
"O [a]sun, stand still at Gibeon,
And O moon in the valley of
Aijalon."
13 [a]So the sun stood still, and the
moon stopped,
Until the nation avenged themselves of their enemies.
Is it not written in [b]the book of Jashar?
And [c]the sun stopped in the middle of
the sky, and did not hasten to go *down*
for about a whole day.
14 And there was no day like that
before it or after it, when the LORD
listened to the voice of a man; for [a]the
LORD fought for Israel.
15 Then Joshua and all Israel with
him returned to the camp to Gilgal.

Victory at Makkedah

16 Now these [a]five kings had fled and
hidden themselves in the cave at Makkedah.
17 And it was told Joshua, saying,
"The five kings have been found hidden
in the cave at Makkedah."
18 And Joshua said, "Roll large stones
against the mouth of the cave, and
assign men by it to guard them,
19 but do not stay *there* yourselves;
pursue your enemies and [1]attack them in
the rear. Do not allow them to enter
their cities, for the LORD your God has
delivered them into your hand."
20 And it came about when Joshua
and the sons of Israel had finished
[1]slaying them with a very great slaughter, [a]until they were destroyed, and the
survivors *who* remained of them [2]had
entered the fortified cities,
21 that all the people returned to the
camp to Joshua at Makkedah in peace.
No one [1]uttered a word against any of
the sons of Israel.
22 Then Joshua said, "Open the
mouth of the cave and bring these five
kings out to me from the cave."
23 And they did so, and [a]brought
these five kings out to him from the
cave: the king of Jerusalem, the king of
Hebron, the king of Jarmuth, the king of
Lachish, *and* the king of Eglon.
24 And it came about when they
brought these kings out to Joshua, that
Joshua called for all the men of Israel,
and said to the chiefs of the men of war
who had gone with him, "Come near,
[a]put your feet on the necks of these
kings." So they came near and put their
feet on their necks.
25 Joshua then said to them, "[a]Do not
fear or be dismayed! Be strong and
courageous, for thus the LORD will do to
all your enemies with whom you fight."
26 So afterward Joshua struck them
and put them to death, and he [a]hanged
them on five trees; and they hung on the
trees until evening.
27 And it came about at [1]sunset that
Joshua commanded, and [a]they took
them down from the trees and threw
them into the cave where they had
hidden themselves, and put large stones
over the mouth of the cave, to this very
day.
28 Now Joshua captured Makkedah
on that day, and struck it and its king
with the edge of the sword; [a]he [1]utterly
destroyed [2]it and every [3]person who was
in it. He left no survivor. Thus he did to
the king of Makkedah [b]just as he had
done to the king of Jericho.

Joshua's Conquest of Southern Palestine

29 Then Joshua and all Israel with
him passed on from Makkedah to [a]Lib-
nah, and fought against Libnah.
30 And the LORD gave it also with its
king into the hands of Israel, and he
struck it and every person who *was* in it
with the edge of the sword. He left no
survivor in it. Thus he did to its king just
as he had done to the king of Jericho.
31 And Joshua and all Israel with him
passed on from Libnah to Lachish, and
they camped by it and fought against it.
32 And the LORD gave Lachish into
the hands of Israel; and he captured it
on the second day, and struck it and

4 [1]Lit., *smite* [a]Josh. 9:15
5 [a]Num. 13:29
6 [1]Lit., *slacken your hands from*
7 [a]Josh. 8:1
8 [1]Lit., *a man* [a]Josh. 1:5, 9
9 [1]Lit., *he went up*
10 [1]Lit., *struck* [a]Deut. 7:23
11 [1]Lit., *with* [a]Ps. 18:12f.; Is. 28:2
12 [a]Hab. 3:11
13 [a]Hab. 3:11 [b]2 Sam. 1:18 [c]Is. 38:8
14 [a]Ex. 14:14; Deut. 1:30; Josh. 10:42
16 [a]Josh. 10:5
19 [1]Lit., *smite their tail*
20 [1]Lit., *striking* [2]Lit., *and had* [a]Deut. 20:16
21 [1]Lit., *sharpened his tongue*
23 [a]Deut. 7:24
24 [a]Mal. 4:3
25 [a]Josh. 10:8
26 [a]Josh. 8:29
27 [1]Lit., *the time of the going of the sun* [a]Deut. 21:22, 23
28 [1]Or, *put under the ban* [2]Some mss. read *them* [3]Lit., *soul,* and so throughout the ch. [a]Deut. 20:16 [b]Josh. 6:21
29 [a]Josh. 15:42; 21:13

every person who *was* in it with the edge
of the sword, according to all that he had
done to Libnah.
33 Then Horam king of [a]Gezer came
up to help Lachish, and Joshua [1]de-
feated him and his people until he had
left him no survivor.
34 And Joshua and all Israel with him
passed on from Lachish to Eglon, and
they camped by it and fought against it.
35 And they captured it on that day
and struck it with the edge of the sword;
and he [1]utterly destroyed that day every
person who *was* in it, according to all
that he had done to Lachish.
36 Then Joshua and all Israel with
him went up from Eglon to [a]Hebron,
and they fought against it.
37 And they captured it and struck it
and its king and all its cities and all the
persons who *were* in it with the edge of
the sword. He left no survivor, according
to all that he had done to Eglon. And he
[1]utterly destroyed it and every person
who *was* in it.
38 Then Joshua and all Israel with
him returned to [a]Debir, and they fought
against it.
39 And he captured it and its king and
all its cities, and they struck them with
the edge of the sword, and [1]utterly
destroyed every person *who was* in it. He
left no survivor. Just as he had done to
Hebron, so he did to Debir and its king,
as he had also done to Libnah and its
king.
40 Thus Joshua struck all the land,
[a]the hill country and the [1]Negev and the
lowland and the slopes and [b]all their
kings. He left no survivor, but [c]he [2]ut-
terly destroyed all who breathed, just as
the LORD, the God of Israel, had commanded.
41 And Joshua struck them from Kadesh-barnea even as far as Gaza, and all
the country of [a]Goshen even as far as
Gibeon.
42 And Joshua captured all these
kings and their lands at one time, because [a]the LORD, the God of Israel,
fought for Israel.
43 So Joshua and all Israel with him
returned to the camp at Gilgal.

Northern Palestine Taken

11 THEN it came about, when Jabin
king of [a]Hazor heard *of it,* that he
sent to Jobab king of Madon and to the
king of Shimron and to the king of
Achshaph,
2 and to the kings who were of the
north in the hill country, and in the
[a]Arabah—south of [1]Chinneroth and in
the lowland and on the [2]heights of Dor
on the west—
3 to the Canaanite on the east and on
the west, and the Amorite and the Hittite and the Perizzite and the Jebusite in
the hill country, and [a]the Hivite [1]at the
foot of [b]Hermon in the land of [c]Mizpeh.
4 And they came out, they and all
their armies with them, [a]*as* many people
as the sand that is on the seashore, with
very many horses and chariots.
5 So all of these kings having agreed
to meet, came and encamped together at
the waters of Merom, to fight against
Israel.
6 Then the LORD said to Joshua,
"[a]Do not be afraid because of them, for
tomorrow at this time I will deliver all of
them slain before Israel; you shall [b]ham-
string their horses and burn their chariots with fire."
7 So Joshua and all the people of war
with him came upon them suddenly by
the waters of Merom, and attacked
them.
8 And the LORD delivered them into
the hand of Israel, so that they [1]defeated
them, and pursued them as far as Great
Sidon and [a]Misrephoth-maim and the
valley of [b]Mizpeh to the east; and they
struck them until no survivor was left to
them.
9 And Joshua did to them as the
LORD had told him; he [a]hamstrung their
horses, and burned their chariots with
fire.
10 Then Joshua turned back at that
time, and captured [a]Hazor and struck its
king with the sword; for Hazor formerly
was the head of all these kingdoms.
11 [a]And they struck every person who
was in it with the edge of the sword,
[1]utterly destroying *them;* there was no
one left who breathed. And he burned
Hazor with fire.
12 And Joshua captured all the cities
of these kings, and all their kings, and he
struck them with the edge of the sword,
and utterly destroyed them; just [a]as
Moses the servant of the LORD had
commanded.
13 However, Israel did not burn any
cities that stood on their mounds, except
Hazor alone, *which* Joshua burned.
14 [a]And all the spoil of these cities
and the cattle, the sons of Israel took as
their plunder; but they struck every man
with the edge of the sword, until they
had destroyed them. They left no one
who breathed.
15 Just as the LORD had commanded
Moses his servant, so Moses commanded Joshua, and so Joshua did; he
left nothing undone of all that the LORD
had commanded Moses.
16 Thus Joshua took all that land:
[a]the hill country and all the [1]Negev, all
that land of Goshen, the lowland, [b]the
Arabah, the hill country of Israel and its
lowland
17 from [a]Mount Halak, that rises
toward Seir, even as far as Baal-gad in
the valley of Lebanon [1]at the foot of
Mount Hermon. And he captured [b]all
their kings and struck them down and
put them to death.
18 Joshua waged war a long time with
all these kings.
19 There was not a city which made
peace with the sons of Israel except [a]the
Hivites living in Gibeon; they took them
all in battle.

33 [1]Lit., *smote* [a]Josh. 16:3, 10; Judg. 1:29; 1 Kin. 9:16f.

35 [1]Or, *put under the ban*

36 [a]Num. 13:22; Judg. 1:10, 20; 2 Sam. 5:1, 3, 5, 13; 2 Chr. 11:10

37 [1]Or, *put it under the ban*

38 [a]Josh. 15:15; Judg. 1:11; 1 Chr. 6:58

39 [1]Or, *put it under the ban*

40 [1]I.e., South country [2]Or, *put it under the ban* [a]Deut. 1:7 [b]Deut. 7:24 [c]Deut. 20:16

41 [a]Josh. 11:16; 15:51

42 [a]Josh. 10:14

1 [a]Josh. 11:10

2 [1]I.e., Sea of Galilee [2]Or, *Naphoth-dor* [a]Josh. 12:3; 13:27

3 [1]Lit., *under* [a]Deut. 7:1; Judg. 3:3, 5; 1 Kin. 9:20 [b]Josh. 11:17; 13:5, 11 [c]Josh. 15:38; 18:26

4 [a]Judg. 7:12

6 [a]Josh. 10:8 [b]2 Sam. 8:4

8 [1]Lit., *smote* [a]Josh. 13:6 [b]Josh. 11:3

9 [a]Josh. 11:6

10 [a]Josh. 11:1

11 [1]Or, *putting them under the ban,* and so throughout the ch. [a]Deut. 20:16

12 [a]Num. 33:50-52; Deut. 7:2; 20:16f.

14 [a]Num. 31:11, 12

16 [1]I.e., South country [a]Josh. 10:40, 41 [b]Josh. 11:2

17 [1]Lit., *under* [a]Josh. 12:7 [b]Deut. 7:24

19 [a]Josh. 9:3, 7

20 [a]For it was of the LORD to [1]harden their hearts, to meet Israel in battle in order that he might [b]utterly destroy them, that they might [2]receive no mercy, but that he might destroy them, just as the LORD had commanded Moses.

21 Then Joshua came at that time and cut off [a]the Anakim from the hill country, from Hebron, from Debir, from Anab and from all the hill country of Judah and from all the hill country of Israel. Joshua utterly destroyed them with their cities.

22 There were no Anakim left in the land of the sons of Israel; only in Gaza, in [a]Gath, and in [b]Ashdod some remained.

23 So Joshua took the whole land, according to all that the LORD had spoken to Moses, and [a]Joshua gave it for an inheritance to Israel according to their divisions by their tribes. [b]Thus the land had rest from war.

Kings Defeated by Israel

12 NOW these are the [a]kings of the land whom the sons of Israel [1]defeated, and whose land they possessed beyond the Jordan toward the sunrise, from the valley of the Arnon as far as Mount Hermon, and all the Arabah to the east:

2 Sihon king of the Amorites, who lived in Heshbon, *and* ruled [a]from Aroer, which is on the edge of the valley of the Arnon, both the middle of the valley and half of Gilead, even as far as the brook Jabbok, the border of the sons of Ammon;

3 and the [a]Arabah as far as the Sea of [1]Chinneroth toward the east, and as far as the sea of the Arabah, *even* the Salt Sea, eastward [2]toward [b]Beth-jeshimoth, and on the south, [3]at the foot of the slopes of Pisgah;

4 and the territory of Og king of Bashan, one of [a]the remnant of Rephaim, who lived at [b]Ashtaroth and at Edrei,

5 and ruled over Mount Hermon and [a]Salecah and all Bashan, as far as [b]the border of the Geshurites and the Maacathites, and half of Gilead, *as far as* the border of Sihon king of Heshbon.

6 Moses the servant of the LORD and the sons of Israel [1]defeated them; and [a]Moses the servant of the LORD gave it to the Reubenites and the Gadites, and the half-tribe of Manasseh as a possession.

7 Now these are the kings of the land whom Joshua and the sons of Israel [1]defeated beyond the Jordan toward the west, from Baal-gad in the valley of Lebanon even as far as [a]Mount Halak, which rises toward Seir; and Joshua gave it to the tribes of Israel as a possession according to their divisions,

8 in [a]the hill country, in the lowland, in the Arabah, on the slopes, and in the wilderness, and in the [1]Negev; the Hittite, the Amorite and the Canaanite, the Perizzite, the Hivite and the Jebusite:

9 the [a]king of Jericho, one; the [b]king of Ai, which is beside Bethel, one;

10 the [a]king of Jerusalem, one; the king of Hebron, one;

11 the king of Jarmuth, one; the king of Lachish, one;

12 the king of Eglon, one; the king of Gezer, one;

13 the king of Debir, one; the king of Geder, one;

14 the king of Hormah, one; the king of [a]Arad, one;

15 the king of Libnah, one; the king of Adullam, one;

16 the king of Makkedah, one; the king of Bethel, one;

17 the king of Tappuah, one; the [a]king of Hepher, one;

18 the king of [a]Aphek, one; the king of Lasharon, one;

19 the king of Madon, one; the king of Hazor, one;

20 the king of Shimron-meron, one; the king of Achshaph, one;

21 the king of Taanach, one; the king of Megiddo, one;

22 the king of [a]Kedesh, one; the king of Jokneam in Carmel, one;

23 the king of Dor in the [1]heights of Dor, one; the king of [a]Goiim in Gilgal, one;

24 the king of Tirzah, one: [a]in all, thirty-one kings.

Canaan Divided among the Tribes

13 NOW [a]Joshua was old *and* advanced in years when the LORD said to him, "You are old *and* advanced in years, and very much of the land remains to be possessed.

2 "This is the land that remains: all the regions *of* the Philistines and all *those of* the [a]Geshurites;

3 from the Shihor which is [1]east of Egypt, even as far as the border of Ekron to the north (it is counted as Canaanite); the [a]five lords of the Philistines: the Gazite, the Ashdodite, the Ashkelonite, the Gittite, the Ekronite; and the Avvite

4 [1]to the south, all the land of the Canaanite, and Mearah that belongs to the Sidonians, as far as [a]Aphek, to the border of the [b]Amorite;

5 and the land of the [a]Gebalite, and all of Lebanon, toward the [1]east, [b]from Baal-gad below Mount Hermon as far as [2]Lebo-hamath.

6 "All the inhabitants of the hill country from Lebanon as far as [a]Misrephoth-maim, all the Sidonians, I will [1]drive them out from before the sons of Israel; [b]only allot it to Israel for an inheritance as I have commanded you.

7 "Now therefore, apportion this land for an inheritance to the nine tribes, and the half-tribe of Manasseh."

8 With [1]the other half-tribe, the Reubenites and the Gadites received their inheritance which Moses gave them [a]beyond the Jordan to the east, just as Moses the servant of the LORD gave to them;

---

20 [1]Lit., *make strong* [2]Lit., *have* [a]Ex. 14:17 [b]Deut. 7:16
21 [a]Num. 13:33; Deut. 9:2
22 [a]1 Sam. 17:4; 1 Kin. 2:39; 1 Chr. 8:13 [b]Josh. 15:46f.; 1 Sam. 5:1; Is. 20:1
23 [a]Deut. 1:38 [b]Deut. 12:9, 10; 25:19; Heb. 4:8
1 [1]Lit., *smote* [a]Num. 32:33; Deut. 3:8-17
2 [a]Deut. 2:36
3 [1]I.e., Galilee [2]Lit., *the way of* [3]Lit., *under* [a]Josh. 11:2 [b]Josh. 13:20
4 [a]Deut. 3:11 [b]Deut. 1:4
5 [a]Deut. 3:10; Josh. 13:11; 1 Chr. 5:11 [b]Deut. 3:14; 1 Sam. 27:8
6 [1]Lit., *smote* [a]Num. 32:33; Deut. 3:12
7 [1]Lit., *smote* [a]Josh. 11:17
8 [1]I.e., South country [a]Josh. 11:16
9 [a]Josh. 6:2 [b]Josh. 8:29
10 [a]Josh. 10:23
14 [a]Num. 21:1
17 [a]1 Kin. 4:10
18 [a]Josh. 13:4; 2 Kin. 13:17
22 [a]Josh. 19:37; 20:7; 21:32
23 [1]Or, *Naphath-dor* [a]Gen. 14:1
24 [a]Deut. 7:24
1 [a]Josh. 14:10
2 [a]Josh. 13:11; 1 Sam. 27:8
3 [1]Lit., *on the face of* [a]1 Sam. 6:4, 16
4 [1]Or, *from the Teman* [a]Josh. 12:18; 19:30; 1 Sam. 4:1; 1 Kin. 20:26, 30 [b]Ezek. 16:3; Amos 2:10
5 [1]Lit., *sunrise* [2]Or, *the entrance of Hamath* [a]1 Kin. 5:18 [b]Josh. 12:7
6 [1]Or, *dispossess* [a]Josh. 11:8 [b]Num. 33:54
8 [1]Lit., *it, the* [a]Josh. 12:1-6

9 from Aroer, which is on the edge of
the valley of the Arnon, with the city
which is in the middle of the valley, and
all the plain of Medeba, as far as Dibon;
10 and all the cities of Sihon king of
the Amorites, who reigned in Heshbon,
as far as the border of the sons of
Ammon;
11 and [a]Gilead, and the [1]territory of
the Geshurites and Maacathites, and all
Mount Hermon, and all Bashan as far as
Salecah;
12 all the kingdom of [a]Og in Bashan,
who reigned in Ashtaroth and in Edrei
(he alone was left of the remnant of the
Rephaim); for Moses [b]struck them and
dispossessed them.
13 But the sons of Israel did not
dispossess the Geshurites or the Maacathites; for Geshur and Maacath live
among Israel until this day.
14 [a]Only to the tribe of Levi he did
not give an inheritance; the offerings by
fire to the LORD, the God of Israel, are
[1]their inheritance, as He spoke to him.
15 So Moses gave *an inheritance* to the
tribe of the sons of Reuben according to
their families.
16 And their [1]territory was [a]from
Aroer, which is on the edge of the valley
of the Arnon, with the city which is in
the middle of the valley and all the plain
by Medeba;
17 Heshbon, and all its cities which
are on the plain: Dibon and Bamoth-
baal and Beth-baal-meon,
18 and [a]Jahaz and Kedemoth and
Mephaath,
19 and [a]Kiriathaim and Sibmah and
Zereth-shahar on the hill of the valley,
20 and Beth-peor and the slopes of
Pisgah and Beth-jeshimoth,
21 even all the cities of the plain and
all the kingdom of Sihon king of the
Amorites who reigned in Heshbon,
whom Moses struck with the chiefs of
Midian, [a]Evi and Rekem and Zur and
Hur and Reba, the princes of Sihon, who
lived in the land.
22 The sons of Israel also killed [a]Ba-
laam the son of Beor, the diviner, with
the sword among *the rest of* their slain.
23 And the border of the sons of
Reuben was the [1]Jordan. This was the
inheritance of the sons of Reuben according to their families, the cities and
their villages.
24 Moses also gave *an inheritance* to
the tribe of Gad, to the sons of Gad,
according to their families.
25 And their territory was [a]Jazer, and
all the cities of Gilead, and half the land
of the sons of Ammon, as far as Aroer
which is before Rabbah;
26 and from Heshbon as far as Ra-
math-mizpeh and Betonim, and from
Mahanaim as far as the border of [1]De-
bir;
27 and in the valley, Beth-haram and
Beth-nimrah and Succoth and Zaphon,
the rest of the kingdom of Sihon king of
Heshbon, with the Jordan [1]as a border,
as far as the *lower* end of the Sea of
[2a]Chinnereth beyond the Jordan to the
east.
28 This is the inheritance of the sons
of Gad according to their families, the
cities and their villages.
29 Moses also gave *an inheritance* to
the half-tribe of Manasseh; and it was
for the half-tribe of the sons of Manasseh according to their families.
30 And their territory was from Mahanaim, all Bashan, all the kingdom of
Og king of Bashan, and all [a]the [1]towns
of Jair, which are in Bashan, sixty cities;
31 also half of Gilead, with [a]Ashta-
roth and Edrei, the cities of the kingdom
of Og in Bashan, *were* for the sons of
Machir the son of Manasseh, for half of
the sons of Machir according to their
families.
32 These are *the territories* which Moses apportioned for an inheritance in the
plains of Moab, beyond the Jordan at
Jericho to the east.
33 But [a]to the tribe of Levi, Moses did
not give an inheritance; the LORD, the
God of Israel, is their inheritance, as He
had [1]promised to them.

Caleb's Request

14 NOW these are *the territories*
which the sons of Israel inherited
in the land of Canaan, which [a]Eleazar
the priest, and Joshua the son of Nun,
and the heads of the [1]households of the
tribes of the sons of Israel apportioned
to them for an inheritance,
2 by the [a]lot of their inheritance, as
the LORD commanded [1]through Moses,
for the nine tribes and the half-tribe.
3 For [a]Moses had given the inheritance of the two tribes and the half-tribe
beyond the Jordan; but [b]he did not give
an inheritance to the Levites among
them.
4 For the sons of Joseph were two
tribes, [a]Manasseh and Ephraim, and
they did not give a portion to the Levites
in the land, except cities to live in, with
their pasture lands for their livestock
and for their property.
5 Thus the sons of Israel did just [a]as
the LORD had commanded Moses, and
they divided the land.
6 Then the sons of Judah drew near
to Joshua in Gilgal, and [a]Caleb the son
of Jephunneh the Kenizzite said to him,
"You know the word which the LORD
spoke to Moses the man of God concerning [1]you and me in Kadesh-barnea.
7 "I was forty years old when [a]Moses
the servant of the LORD sent me from
Kadesh-barnea to spy out the land, and
I brought word back to him as *it was* in
my heart.
8 "Nevertheless my brethren who
went up with me made the heart of the
people [1]melt with fear; but [a]I followed
the LORD my God fully.
9 "So Moses swore on that day, saying, 'Surely [a]the land on which your foot
has trodden shall be an inheritance to

13:11 [1]Or, *border* [a]Gen. 37:25; Num. 32:29; Josh. 13:25; 17:5f.
12 [a]Deut. 3:11 [b]Num. 21:24
14 [1]Lit., *his* [a]Deut. 18:1, 2
16 [1]Or, *border* [a]Josh. 13:9
18 [a]Num. 21:23; Judg. 11:20; Is. 15:4; Jer. 48:34
19 [a]Num. 32:37; Jer. 48:1, 23; Ezek. 25:9
21 [a]Num. 31:8
22 [a]Num. 31:8
23 [1]Lit., *Jordan and border*
25 [a]Num. 21:32; Josh. 21:39; 2 Sam. 24:5; 1 Chr. 6:81; 26:31; Is. 16:8f.; Jer. 48:32
26 [1]Or, *Lidebir*
27 [1]Lit., *and border* [2]I.e., Galilee [a]Num. 34:11; Deut. 3:17
30 [1]Lit., *tent villages* [a]Num. 32:41
31 [a]Josh. 9:10; 12:4; 13:12; Judg. 10:6; 1 Sam. 7:3f.; 12:10; 1 Chr. 6:71
33 [1]Lit., *spoken to* [a]Deut. 18:1f.; Josh. 13:14
14:1 [1]Lit., *fathers'* [a]Num. 34:16-29
2 [1]Lit., *by the hand of* [a]Num. 26:55; 33:54; 34:13
3 [a]Num. 32:33 [b]Josh. 13:14
4 [a]Gen. 41:51f.; 46:20; 48:1, 5; Num. 26:28; 2 Chr. 30:1
5 [a]Num. 35:1f.; Josh. 21:2
6 [1]Lit., *me and concerning you* [a]Num. 13:6, 30; 14:6, 24, 30
7 [a]Num. 13:1-31
8 [1]Lit., *become demoralized* [a]Num. 14:24; Deut. 1:36
9 [a]Deut. 1:36

you and to your children forever, because you have followed the LORD my God fully.'

10 "And now behold, the LORD has let me live, just as He spoke, these forty-five years, from the time that the LORD spoke this word to Moses, when Israel walked in the wilderness; and now behold, I am eighty-five years old today.

11 "[a]I am still as strong today as I was in the day Moses sent me; as my strength was then, so my strength is now, for war and for [b]going out and coming in.

12 "Now then, give me this hill country about which the LORD spoke on that day, for you heard on that day that [a]Anakim *were* there, with great fortified cities; perhaps the LORD will be with me, and I shall [1]drive them out as the LORD has spoken."

13 So Joshua [a]blessed him, and [b]gave Hebron to Caleb the son of Jephunneh for an inheritance.

14 Therefore, Hebron became the inheritance of Caleb the son of Jephunneh the Kenizzite until this day, because he followed the LORD God of Israel fully.

15 Now the name of Hebron was formerly [1]Kiriath-arba; *for Arba* was the greatest man among the Anakim. [a]Then the land had rest from war.

Territory of Judah

15 NOW [a]the lot for the tribe of the sons of Judah according to their families [1]reached the [b]border of Edom, southward to the [c]wilderness of Zin at the extreme south.

2 And their south border was from the lower end of the Salt Sea, from the bay that turns to the south.

3 Then it proceeded southward to the ascent of Akrabbim and continued to Zin, then went up by the south of Kadesh-barnea and continued to Hezron, and went up to Addar and turned about to Karka.

4 And it [a]continued to Azmon and proceeded to the [1b]brook of Egypt; and the [2]border ended at the sea. This shall be your south border.

5 And the [a]east border *was* the Salt Sea, as far as the [1]mouth of the Jordan. And the [b]border of the north side was from the bay of the sea at the [1]mouth of the Jordan.

6 Then the border went up to Beth-hoglah, and continued on the north of Beth-arabah, and the border went up to the stone of Bohan the son of Reuben.

7 And the border went up to Debir from [a]the valley of Achor, and turned northward toward Gilgal which is opposite the ascent of Adummim, which is on the south of the valley; and the border continued to the waters of En-shemesh, and [1]it ended at En-rogel.

8 Then the border went up the valley of Ben-hinnom to the slope of the [a]Jebusite on the south (that is, Jerusalem); and the border went up to the top of the mountain which is before the valley of Hinnom to the west, which is at the end of the valley of Rephaim toward the north.

9 And from the top of the mountain the border curved to the spring of the waters of Nephtoah and proceeded to the cities of Mount Ephron, then the border curved to [a]Baalah (that is, [b]Kiriath-jearim).

10 And the border turned about from Baalah westward to Mount Seir, and continued to the slope of Mount Jearim on the north (that is, Chesalon), and went down to Beth-shemesh and continued through [a]Timnah.

11 And the border proceeded to the side of Ekron northward. Then the border curved to Shikkeron and continued to Mount Baalah and proceeded to Jabneel, and the [1]border ended at the sea.

12 And the west border *was* [a]at the Great Sea, even *its* [1]coastline. This is the border around the sons of Judah according to their families.

13 Now [a]he gave to Caleb the son of Jephunneh a portion [b]among the sons of Judah, according to the [1]command of the LORD to Joshua, *namely,* [2]Kiriath-arba, *Arba being* the father of Anak (that is, Hebron).

14 And [a]Caleb [1]drove out from there the three [b]sons of Anak: Sheshai and Ahiman and Talmai, the children of Anak.

15 Then [a]he went up from there against the inhabitants of Debir; now the name of Debir formerly was Kiriath-sepher.

16 And Caleb said, "The one who [1]attacks Kiriath-sepher and captures it, [2]I will give him Achsah my daughter as a wife."

17 And [a]Othniel the son of Kenaz, the brother of Caleb, captured it; so he gave him Achsah his daughter as a wife.

18 [a]And it came about that when she came *to him,* she persuaded him to ask her father for a field. So she alighted from the donkey, and Caleb said to her, "What do you want?"

19 Then she said, "Give me a blessing; since you have given me the land of the [1]Negev, give me also springs of water." So he gave her the upper springs and the lower springs.

20 This is the inheritance of the tribe of the sons of Judah according to their families.

21 Now the cities at the extremity of the tribe of the sons of Judah toward the border of Edom in the south were Kabzeel and [a]Eder and Jagur,

22 and Kinah and Dimonah and Adadah,

23 and Kedesh and Hazor and Ithnan,

24 Ziph and Telem and Bealoth,

25 and Hazor-hadattah and Kerioth-hezron (that is, Hazor),

26 Amam and Shema and Moladah,

27 and Hazar-gaddah and Heshmon and Beth-pelet,

11 [a]Deut. 34:7 [b]Deut. 31:2
12 [1]Or, *dispossess* [a]Num. 13:33
13 [a]Josh. 22:6 [b]Judg. 1:20; 1 Chr. 6:55f.
15 [1]I.e., the city of Arba [a]Josh. 11:23
1 [1]Lit., *was to* [a]Num. 34:3, 4 [b]Num. 20:16 [c]Deut. 32:51
4 [1]Or, *wadi* [2]Lit., *goings out of the border were* [a]Num. 34:5 [b]Gen. 15:18; 1 Kin. 8:65
5 [1]Lit., *end* [a]Num. 34:3, 10-12 [b]Josh. 18:15-19
7 [1]Lit., *the goings out of it were* [a]Josh. 7:24
8 [a]Josh. 15:63
9 [a]1 Chr. 13:6 [b]Judg. 18:12
10 [a]Gen. 38:13; Judg. 14:1
11 [1]Lit., *goings out . . . were*
12 [1]Lit., *border* [a]Num. 34:6
13 [1]Lit., *mouth* [2]I.e., the city of Arba [a]Josh. 14:13-15 [b]Num. 13:6
14 [1]Or, *dispossessed* [a]Josh. 11:21, 22 [b]Num. 13:33; Deut. 9:2
15 [a]Josh. 10:38
16 [1]Lit., *smites* [2]Lit., *and I*
17 [a]Judg. 1:13; 3:9
18 [a]Judg. 1:14
19 [1]I.e., South country
21 [a]Gen. 35:21

28 and Hazar-shual and [a]Beersheba
and Biziothiah,
29 Baalah and Iim and Ezem,
30 and Eltolad and Chesil and Hormah,
31 and [a]Ziklag and Madmannah and
Sansannah,
32 and Lebaoth and Shilhim and Ain
and Rimmon; in all, twenty-nine cities
with their villages.
33 In the lowland: [a]Eshtaol and Zorah
and Ashnah,
34 and Zanoah and En-gannim, Tappuah and Enam,
35 Jarmuth and [a]Adullam, Socoh and
Azekah,
36 and Shaaraim and Adithaim and
Gederah and Gederothaim; fourteen
cities with their villages.
37 Zenan and Hadashah and Migdal-
gad,
38 and Dilean and Mizpeh and Jok-
theel,
39 [a]Lachish and Bozkath and Eglon,
40 and Cabbon and Lahmas and Chit-
lish,
41 and Gederoth, Beth-dagon and
Naamah and Makkedah; sixteen cities
with their villages.
42 Libnah and Ether and Ashan,
43 and Iphtah and Ashnah and Nezib,
44 and Keilah and Achzib and Mareshah; nine cities with their villages.
45 Ekron, with its towns and its villages;
46 from Ekron even to the sea, all that
were by the [1]side of Ashdod, with their
villages.
47 Ashdod, its towns and its villages;
Gaza, its towns and its villages; as far as
[a]the [1]brook of Egypt and the Great Sea,
even *its* [2]coastline.
48 And in the hill country: Shamir
and Jattir and Socoh,
49 and Dannah and Kiriath-sannah
(that is, Debir),
50 and Anab and Eshtemoh and
Anim,
51 and Goshen and Holon and Giloh;
eleven cities with their villages.
52 Arab and Dumah and Eshan,
53 and Janum and Beth-tappuah and
Aphekah,
54 and Humtah and Kiriath-arba
(that is, Hebron), and Zior; nine cities
with their villages.
55 Maon, Carmel and Ziph and Jut-
tah,
56 and Jezreel and Jokdeam and Zanoah,
57 Kain, Gibeah and Timnah; ten
cities with their villages.
58 Halhul, Beth-zur and Gedor,
59 and Maarath and Beth-anoth and
Eltekon; six cities with their villages.
60 Kiriath-baal (that is, Kiriath-jearim), and Rabbah; two cities with their
villages.
61 In the wilderness: Beth-arabah,
Middin and Secacah,
62 and Nibshan and the City of Salt
and Engedi; six cities with their villages.

63 Now as for the [a]Jebusites, the
inhabitants of Jerusalem, the sons of
Judah could not [1]drive them out; so the
Jebusites live with the sons of Judah at
Jerusalem until this day.

Territory of Ephraim

16 THEN the lot for the sons of
Joseph went from the Jordan at
Jericho to the waters of Jericho on the
east into [a]the wilderness, going up from
Jericho through the hill country to
Bethel.
2 And it went from Bethel to Luz,
and [a]continued to the border of the
Archites at Ataroth.
3 And it went down westward to the
territory of the Japhletites, as far as the
territory of lower [a]Beth-horon even to
[b]Gezer, and [1]it ended at the sea.
4 And the [a]sons of Joseph, Manasseh
and Ephraim, received their inheritance.
5 Now *this* was the territory of the
sons of Ephraim according to their
families: the border of their inheritance
eastward was [a]Ataroth-addar, as far as
upper Beth-horon.
6 Then the border went westward at
[a]Michmethath on the north, and the
border turned about eastward to Taa-
nath-shiloh, and continued *beyond* it to
the east of Janoah.
7 And it went down from Janoah to
Ataroth and to [a]Naarah, then reached
Jericho and came out at the Jordan.
8 From [a]Tappuah the border continued westward to the [1]brook of Kanah,
and [2]it ended at the sea. This is the
inheritance of the tribe of the sons of
Ephraim according to their families,
9 *together* with the cities which were
set apart for the sons of Ephraim in the
midst of the inheritance of the sons of
Manasseh, all the cities with their villages.
10 [a]But they did not [1]drive out the
Canaanites who lived in Gezer, so [b]the
Canaanites live in the midst of Ephraim
to this day, and they became forced
laborers.

Territory of Manasseh

17 NOW *this* was the lot for the
tribe of [a]Manasseh, for he was
the first-born of Joseph. To Machir the
first-born of Manasseh, the father of
Gilead, [1]was allotted Gilead and Bashan, because he was a man of war.
2 So *the lot* was *made* for the rest of
the sons of Manasseh according to their
families: for the sons of Abiezer and for
the sons of Helek and for the sons of
Asriel and for the sons of Shechem and
for the sons of Hepher and for the sons
of Shemida; these *were* the male *descendants* of Manasseh the son of Joseph
according to their families.
3 However, [a]Zelophehad, the son of
Hepher, the son of Gilead, the son of
Machir, the son of Manasseh, had no
sons, only daughters; and these are the
names of his daughters: Mahlah and
Noah, Hoglah, Milcah and Tirzah.

28 [a]Gen. 21:31
31 [a]1 Sam. 27:6; 30:1
33 [a]Judg. 13:25; 16:31
35 [a]1 Sam. 22:1
39 [a]Josh. 10:3; 2 Kin. 14:19
46 [1]Lit., *hand*
47 [1]Or, *wadi* [2]Lit., *border* [a]Josh. 15:4
63 [1]Or, *dispossess them* [a]Judg. 1:21; 2 Sam. 5:6; 1 Chr. 11:4
1 [a]Josh. 8:15; 18:12
2 [a]Josh. 18:13
3 [1]Lit., *the goings out of it were* [a]Josh. 18:13; 1 Kin. 9:17 [b]Josh. 10:33
4 [a]Josh. 17:14
5 [a]Josh. 18:13
6 [a]Josh. 17:7
7 [a]1 Chr. 7:28
8 [1]Or, *wadi* [2]Lit., *the goings out of it were* [a]Josh. 17:8
10 [1]Or, *dispossess* [a]Judg. 1:29; 1 Kin. 9:16 [b]Josh. 17:12, 13
1 [1]Lit., *and there was to him* [a]Gen. 41:51; 46:20; 48:17f.
3 [a]Num. 26:33; 27:1-7

4 And they came near before Eleazar
the priest and before Joshua the son of
Nun and before the leaders, saying,
"The LORD commanded Moses to give
us an inheritance among our brothers."
So [a]according to the [1]command of the
LORD he gave them an inheritance
among their father's brothers.
5 Thus there fell ten portions to
Manasseh, besides the land of Gilead
and Bashan, which is beyond the Jordan,
6 because the daughters of Manasseh
received an inheritance among his sons.
And the [a]land of Gilead belonged to the
rest of the sons of Manasseh.
7 And the border of Manasseh [1]ran
from Asher to Michmethath which was
east of Shechem; then the border went
[2]southward to the inhabitants of En-
tappuah.
8 The land of Tappuah belonged to
Manasseh, but [a]Tappuah on the border
of Manasseh *belonged* to the sons of
Ephraim.
9 And the [a]border went down to the
[1]brook of Kanah, southward of the
[1]brook (these cities *belonged* to Ephraim
among the cities of Manasseh), and the
border of Manasseh *was* on the north
side of the [1]brook, and [2]it ended at the
sea.
10 The south side *belonged* to Ephraim
and the north side to Manasseh, and the
sea was [1]their border; and they reached
to Asher on the north and to Issachar on
the east.
11 And in Issachar and in Asher,
[a]Manasseh had Beth-shean and its towns
and Ibleam and its towns, and the inhabitants of Dor and its towns, and the
inhabitants of En-dor and its towns, and
the inhabitants of Taanach and its
towns, and the inhabitants of Megiddo
and its towns, the third is [b]Napheth.
12 [a]But the sons of Manasseh could
not take possession of these cities, because the Canaanites persisted in living
in that land.
13 And it came about when the sons
of Israel became strong, [a]they put the
Canaanites to forced labor, but they did
not [1]drive them out completely.
14 Then the [a]sons of Joseph spoke to
Joshua, saying, "Why have you given me
only one lot and one portion for an
inheritance, since I am a numerous
people whom the LORD has thus far
blessed?"
15 And Joshua said to them, "If you
are a numerous people, go [1]up to the
forest and [2]clear a place for yourself
there in the land of the Perizzites and of
the Rephaim, since the hill country of
Ephraim is too narrow for you."
16 And the sons of Joseph said, "The
hill country is not enough for us, and all
the Canaanites who live in the valley
land have [a]chariots of iron, both those
who are in Beth-shean and its towns,
and those who are in the valley of
Jezreel."
17 And Joshua spoke to the house of
Joseph, to Ephraim and Manasseh, saying, "You are a numerous people and
have great power; you shall not have one
lot *only,*
18 but the hill country shall be yours.
For though it is a forest, you shall [1]clear
it, and to its [2]farthest borders it shall be
yours; for you shall [3]drive out the Canaanites, even though they have [a]chari-
ots of iron *and* though they are strong."

Rest of the Land Divided

18 THEN the whole congregation of
the sons of Israel assembled
themselves at [a]Shiloh, and set up the
tent of meeting there; and the land was
subdued before them.
2 And there remained among the
sons of Israel seven tribes who had not
divided their inheritance.
3 So Joshua said to the sons of Israel,
"[a]How long will you put off entering to
take possession of the land which the
LORD, the God of your fathers, has given
you?
4 "Provide for yourselves three men
from [1]each tribe that I may send them,
and that they may arise and walk
through the land and write a description
of it according to their inheritance; then
they shall [2]return to me.
5 "And they shall divide it into seven
portions; [a]Judah shall stay in its territory on the south, and the house of
Joseph shall stay in their territory on the
north.
6 "And you shall describe the land in
seven divisions, and bring *the description*
here to me. [a]And I will cast lots for you
here before the LORD our God.
7 "For [a]the Levites have no portion
among you, because the priesthood of
the LORD is [1]their inheritance. Gad and
Reuben and the half-tribe of Manasseh
also have received their inheritance
eastward beyond the Jordan, which
Moses the servant of the LORD gave
them."
8 Then the men arose and went, and
Joshua commanded those who went to
describe the land, saying, "Go and walk
through the land and describe it, and
return to me; then I will cast lots for you
here before the LORD in [a]Shiloh."
9 So the men went and passed
through the land, and described it by
cities in seven divisions in a book; and
they came to Joshua to the camp at
Shiloh.
10 And [a]Joshua cast lots for them in
Shiloh before the LORD, and there
Joshua divided the land to the sons of
Israel according to their divisions.

The Territory of Benjamin

11 Now the lot of the tribe of the sons
of Benjamin came up according to their
families, and the territory of their lot
[1]lay between the sons of Judah and the
sons of Joseph.

4 [1]Lit., *mouth* [a]Num. 27:5-7
6 [a]Josh. 13:30, 31
7 [1]Lit., *was* [2]Lit., *to the right hand*
8 [a]Josh. 16:8
9 [1]Or, *wadi* [2]Lit., *goings out of it were* [a]Josh. 16:8f.
10 [1]Lit., *its*
11 [a]1 Chr. 7:29 [b]Josh. 11:2; 12:23
12 [a]Judg. 1:27
13 [1]Or, *dispossess* [a]Josh. 16:10
14 [a]Num. 13:7
15 [1]Lit., *up for yourself* [2]Lit., *cut down*
16 [a]Josh. 17:18; Judg. 1:19; 4:3, 13
18 [1]Lit., *cut it down* [2]Lit., *goings out* [3]Or, *dispossess* [a]Josh. 17:16
1 [a]Judg. 21:19; Jer. 7:12; 26:6, 9
3 [a]Judg. 18:9
4 [1]Lit., *the* [2]Lit., *come*
5 [a]Josh. 15:1
6 [a]Josh. 14:2
7 [1]Lit., *his* [a]Num. 18:7, 20; Josh. 13:33
8 [a]Josh. 18:1
10 [a]Num. 34:16-29; Josh. 19:51
11 [1]Lit., *went out*

12 And [a]their border on the north side was from the Jordan, then the border went up to the side of Jericho on the north, and went up through the hill country westward; and [1]it ended at the wilderness of Beth-aven.

13 And from there the border continued to [a]Luz, to the side of Luz (that is, Bethel) southward; and the border went down to Ataroth-addar, near the hill which *lies* on the south of [b]lower Beth-horon.

14 And the border extended *from there,* and turned round on the west side southward, from the hill which *lies* before Beth-horon southward; and [1]it ended at Kiriath-baal (that is, Kiriath-jearim), a city of the sons of Judah. This *was* the west side.

15 Then the [a]south side *was* from the edge of Kiriath-jearim, and the border went westward and went to the fountain of the waters of Nephtoah.

16 And the border went down to the edge of the hill which is in the [a]valley of Ben-hinnom, which is in the valley of Rephaim northward; and it went down to the valley of Hinnom, to the slope of the Jebusite southward, and went down to En-rogel.

17 And it extended northward and went to En-shemesh and went to Geliloth, which is opposite the ascent of Adummim, and it went down to the [a]stone of Bohan the son of Reuben.

18 And it continued to the side in front of the Arabah northward, and went down to the Arabah.

19 And the border continued to the side of Beth-hoglah northward; and the [1]border ended at the north bay of the Salt Sea, at the south end of the Jordan. This *was* the south border.

20 Moreover, the Jordan was its border on the east side. This *was* the inheritance of the sons of Benjamin, according to their families *and* according to its borders all around.

21 Now the cities of the tribe of the sons of Benjamin according to their families were Jericho and Beth-hoglah and Emek-keziz,

22 and Beth-arabah and Zemaraim and Bethel,

23 and Avvim and Parah and Ophrah,

24 and Chephar-ammoni and Ophni and [a]Geba; twelve cities with their villages.

25 Gibeon and Ramah and Beeroth,

26 and Mizpeh and Chephirah and Mozah,

27 and Rekem and Irpeel and Taralah,

28 and [a]Zelah, Haeleph and the Jebusite (that is, Jerusalem), Gibeah, Kiriath; fourteen cities with their villages. This is the inheritance of the [b]sons of Benjamin according to their families.

Territory of Simeon

19 THEN the second lot [1]fell to Simeon, to the tribe of the sons of Simeon according to their families, and their inheritance was in the midst of the inheritance of the sons of Judah.

2 So they had as their inheritance Beersheba or [1]Sheba and Moladah,

3 and Hazar-shual and Balah and Ezem,

4 and Eltolad and Bethul and Hormah,

5 and Ziklag and Beth-marcaboth and Hazar-susah,

6 and Beth-lebaoth and Sharuhen, thirteen cities with their villages;

7 Ain, Rimmon and Ether and Ashan, four cities with their villages;

8 and all the villages which *were* around these cities as far as Baalath-beer, Ramah of the [1]Negev. This *was* the inheritance of the tribe of the sons of Simeon according to their families.

9 The inheritance of the sons of Simeon *was taken* from the portion of the sons of Judah, for the share of the sons of Judah was too large for them; so the sons of Simeon received *an* inheritance in the midst of [1]Judah's inheritance.

Territory of Zebulun

10 Now the third lot came up for the sons of Zebulun according to their families. And the territory of their inheritance was as far as Sarid.

11 Then their border went up to the west and to Maralah, it then [1]touched Dabbesheth, and reached to the [2]brook that is before Jokneam.

12 Then it turned from Sarid to the east toward the sunrise as far as the border of Chisloth-tabor, and it proceeded to Daberath and [1]up to Japhia.

13 And from there it continued eastward toward the sunrise to Gath-hepher, to Eth-kazin, and it proceeded to Rimmon [1]which stretches to Neah.

14 And the border circled around it on the north to Hannathon, and [1]it ended at the valley of Iphtahel.

15 *Included* also *were* Kattah and Nahalal and Shimron and Idalah and Bethlehem; twelve cities with their villages.

16 This *was* the inheritance of the sons of Zebulun according to their families, these cities with their villages.

Territory of Issachar

17 The fourth lot [1]fell to Issachar, to the sons of Issachar according to their families.

18 And their territory was to Jezreel and *included* Chesulloth and [a]Shunem,

19 and Hapharaim and Shion and Anaharath,

20 and Rabbith and Kishion and Ebez,

21 and Remeth and En-gannim and En-haddah and Beth-pazzez.

22 And the border reached to [a]Tabor and Shahazumah and Beth-shemesh, and [1]their border ended at the Jordan; sixteen cities with their villages.

23 This *was* the inheritance of the tribe of the sons of Issachar according to

---

12 [1]Lit., *the goings out of it were* [a]Josh. 16:1

13 [a]Gen. 28:19; Judg. 1:23 [b]Josh. 16:3

14 [1]Lit., *the goings out of it were*

15 [a]Josh. 15:5-9

16 [a]2 Kin. 23:10

17 [a]Josh. 15:6

19 [1]Lit., *goings out of the border were*

24 [a]Ezra 2:26; Is. 10:29

28 [a]2 Sam. 21:14 [b]Num. 26:38

1 [1]Lit., *came out*

2 [1]In Josh. 15:26, *Shema*

8 [1]I.e., South country

9 [1]Lit., *their*

11 [1]Or, *reached to* [2]Or, *wadi*

12 [1]Lit., *went up*

13 [1]Or, *and is marked off*

14 [1]Lit., *the goings out of it were*

17 [1]Lit., *came out*

18 [a]1 Sam. 28:4; 2 Kin. 4:8

22 [1]Lit., *the goings out of their border were* [a]Judg. 4:6; Ps. 89:12

their families, the cities with their villages.

Territory of Asher

24 Now the fifth lot [1]fell to the tribe of
the sons of Asher according to their
families.
25 And their territory was Helkath
and Hali and Beten and Achshaph,
26 and Allammelech and Amad and
Mishal; and it reached to Carmel on the
west and to Shihor-libnath.
27 And it turned toward the [1]east to
Beth-dagon, and reached to Zebulun,
and to the valley of Iphtahel northward
to Beth-emek and Neiel; then it proceeded on [2]north to [a]Cabul,
28 and Ebron and Rehob and Hammon and Kanah, as far as Great [a]Sidon.
29 And the border turned to Ramah,
and to the fortified city of Tyre; then the
border turned to Hosah, and [1]it ended at
the sea by the region of [a]Achzib.
30 *Included* also *were* Ummah, and
Aphek and Rehob; twenty-two cities
with their villages.
31 This *was* the inheritance of the
tribe of the sons of Asher according to
their families, these cities with their
villages.

Territory of Naphtali

32 The sixth lot [1]fell to the sons of
Naphtali; to the sons of Naphtali according to their families.
33 And their border was from Heleph,
from the oak in Zaanannim and Adami-
nekeb and Jabneel, as far as Lakkum;
and [1]it ended at the Jordan.
34 Then the border turned westward
to Aznoth-tabor, and proceeded from
there to Hukkok; and it reached to
Zebulun on the south and [1]touched
Asher on the west, and to Judah at the
Jordan toward the [2]east.
35 And the fortified cities *were* Zid-
dim, Zer and [a]Hammath, Rakkath and
[b]Chinnereth,
36 and Adamah and Ramah and Hazor,
37 and Kedesh and Edrei and En-
hazor,
38 and Yiron and Migdal-el, Horem
and Beth-anath and Beth-shemesh; nineteen cities with their villages.
39 This *was* the inheritance of the
tribe of the sons of Naphtali according
to their families, the cities with their
villages.

Territory of Dan

40 The seventh lot [1]fell to the tribe of
the sons of Dan according to their
families.
41 And the territory of their inheritance was Zorah and Eshtaol and Ir-
shemesh,
42 and Shaalabbin and Aijalon and
Ithlah,
43 and Elon and Timnah and Ekron,
44 and Eltekeh and Gibbethon and
Baalath,
45 and Jehud and Bene-berak and
Gath-rimmon,
46 and Me-jarkon and Rakkon, with
the territory over against [1]Joppa.
47 And the territory of the [a]sons of
Dan proceeded [1]beyond them; for the
sons of Dan went up and fought with
Leshem and captured it. Then they
struck it with the edge of the sword and
possessed it and [2]settled in it; and they
called [3b]Leshem Dan after the name of
Dan their father.
48 This *was* the inheritance of the
tribe of the sons of Dan according to
their families, these cities with their
villages.
49 When they finished apportioning
the land for inheritance by its borders,
the sons of Israel gave an inheritance in
their midst to Joshua the son of Nun.
50 In accordance with the [1]command
of the LORD they gave him the city for
which he asked, [a]Timnath-serah in the
hill country of Ephraim. So he built the
city and [2]settled in it.
51 [a]These are the inheritances which
Eleazar the priest and Joshua the son of
Nun and the heads of the [1]households of
the tribes of the sons of Israel distributed by lot in Shiloh before the LORD, at
the doorway of the tent of meeting. So
they finished dividing the land.

Six Cities of Refuge

20 THEN the LORD spoke to
Joshua, saying,
2 "Speak to the sons of Israel, saying,
'[1]Designate [a]the cities of refuge, of
which I spoke to you [2]through Moses,
3 that the manslayer who [1]kills any
person unintentionally, without pre-
meditation, may flee there, and they
shall become your refuge from the
avenger of blood.
4 'And he shall flee to one of these
cities, and shall stand at the entrance of
the [a]gate of the city and state his case in
the hearing of the elders of that city; and
they shall [1]take him into the city to them
and give him a place, so that he may
dwell among them.
5 'Now [a]if the avenger of blood pursues him, then they shall not deliver the
manslayer into his hand, because he
struck his neighbor without premedita-
tion and did not hate him beforehand.
6 'And he shall dwell in that city
[a]until he stands before the congregation
for judgment, until the death of the one
who is high priest in those days. Then
the manslayer shall [1]return to his own
city and to his own house, to the city
from which he fled.' "
7 So they [1]set apart [a]Kedesh in
[2]Galilee in the hill country of Naphtali
and Shechem in the hill country of
Ephraim, and Kiriath-arba (that is,
Hebron) in [b]the hill country of Judah.
8 And beyond the Jordan east of
Jericho, they [1]designated Bezer in the
wilderness on the plain from the tribe of
Reuben, and Ramoth in Gilead from the

24 [1]Lit., *came out*

27 [1]Lit., *sunrise* [2]Lit., *from the left hand* [a]1 Kin. 9:13

28 [a]Gen. 10:19; Judg. 1:31; Acts 27:3

29 [1]Lit., *the goings out of it were* [a]Judg. 1:31

32 [1]Lit., *came out*

33 [1]Lit., *the goings out of it were*

34 [1]Or, *reached to* [2]Lit., *sunrise*

35 [a]Gen. 10:18; 1 Kin. 8:65 [b]Deut. 3:17

40 [1]Lit., *came out*

46 [1]Heb., *Japho*

47 [1]Lit., *from* [2]Lit., *dwelt* [3]I.e., Laish [a]Judg. 18:1 [b]Judg. 18:29

50 [1]Lit., *mouth* [2]Lit., *dwelt* [a]Num. 13:8; Josh. 24:30

51 [1]Lit., *fathers* [a]Josh. 18:10

2 [1]Lit., *Set for yourselves* [2]Lit., *by the hand of* [a]Num. 35:6-34; Deut. 4:41-43; 19:2ff.

3 [1]Lit., *smites*

4 [1]Lit., *gather* [a]Ruth 4:1; Job 5:4; Jer. 38:7

5 [a]Num. 35:12

6 [1]Lit., *return and come* [a]Num. 35:12

7 [1]Lit., *sanctified* [2]Heb., *Galil* [a]Josh. 21:32; 1 Chr. 6:76 [b]Josh. 21:11; Luke 1:39

8 [1]Lit., *set*

tribe of Gad, and Golan in Bashan from
the tribe of Manasseh.
9 [a]These were the appointed cities
for all the sons of Israel and for the
stranger who sojourns among them, that
whoever [1]kills any person unintentionally may flee there, and not die by the
hand of the avenger of blood until he
stands before the congregation.

Forty-eight Cities of the Levites

21 THEN the heads of [1]households
of [a]the Levites approached Eleazar the priest and Joshua the son of Nun
and the heads of [1]households of the
tribes of the sons of Israel.
2 And they spoke to them at Shiloh
in the land of Canaan, saying, "[a]The
LORD commanded [1]through Moses to
give us cities to live in, with their pasture
lands for our cattle."
3 So the sons of Israel gave the
Levites from their inheritance these
cities with their pasture lands, according
to the [1]command of the LORD.
4 Then the lot came out for the
families of the Kohathites. And the sons
of Aaron the priest, who were of the
Levites, [1]received thirteen cities by lot
from the tribe of Judah and from the
tribe of the Simeonites and from the
tribe of Benjamin.
5 And the rest of the sons of Kohath
[1]received ten cities by lot from the
families of the tribe of Ephraim and
from the tribe of Dan and from the half-
tribe of Manasseh.
6 And the sons of Gershon [1]received
thirteen cities by lot from the families of
the tribe of Issachar and from the tribe
of Asher and from the tribe of Naphtali
and from the half-tribe of Manasseh in
Bashan.
7 The sons of Merari according to
their families [1]received twelve cities from
the tribe of Reuben and from the tribe of
Gad and from the tribe of Zebulun.
8 Now the [a]sons of Israel gave by lot
to the Levites these cities with their
pasture lands, as the LORD had commanded [1]through Moses.
9 And they gave these cities which
are *here* mentioned by name from the
tribe of the sons of Judah and from the
tribe of the sons of Simeon;
10 and they were for the sons of
Aaron, one of the families of the Kohathites, of the sons of Levi, for the lot
was theirs first.
11 Thus [a]they gave them Kiriath-arba,
Arba being the [b]father of Anak (that is,
Hebron), in the hill country of Judah,
with its surrounding pasture lands.
12 But the fields of the city and its
villages, they gave to Caleb the son of
Jephunneh as his possession.
13 So [a]to the sons of Aaron the priest
they gave [b]Hebron, the city of refuge for
the manslayer, with its pasture lands,
and [c]Libnah with its pasture lands,
14 and [a]Jattir with its pasture lands
and [b]Eshtemoa with its pasture lands,
15 and [1]Holon with its pasture lands
and [a]Debir with its pasture lands,
16 and [1]Ain with its pasture lands and
[a]Juttah with its pasture lands *and* [b]Beth-
shemesh with its pasture lands; nine
cities from these two tribes.
17 And from the tribe of Benjamin,
[a]Gibeon with its pasture lands, [b]Geba
with its pasture lands,
18 Anathoth with its pasture lands
and [1]Almon with its pasture lands; four
cities.
19 All the cities of the sons of Aaron,
the priests, were thirteen cities with their
pasture lands.
20 Then the cities from the tribe of
Ephraim were allotted to the [a]families of
the sons of Kohath, the Levites, *even to*
the rest of the sons of Kohath.
21 And they gave them [a]Shechem, the
city of refuge for the manslayer, with its
pasture lands, in the hill country of
Ephraim, and Gezer with its pasture
lands,
22 and Kibzaim with its pasture lands
and Beth-horon with its pasture lands;
four cities.
23 And from the tribe of Dan, Elteke
with its pasture lands, Gibbethon with
its pasture lands,
24 Aijalon with its pasture lands,
Gath-rimmon with its pasture lands;
four cities.
25 And from the half-tribe of Manasseh, *they allotted* Taanach with its pasture lands and Gath-rimmon with its
pasture lands; two cities.
26 All the cities with their pasture
lands for the families of the rest of the
sons of Kohath were ten.
27 And [a]to the sons of Gershon, one
of the families of the Levites, from the
half-tribe of Manasseh, *they gave* Golan
in Bashan, the city of refuge for the
manslayer, with its pasture lands, and
Be-eshterah with its pasture lands; two
cities.
28 And from the tribe of Issachar, *they
gave* Kishion with its pasture lands,
Daberath with its pasture lands,
29 Jarmuth with its pasture lands, En-
gannim with its pasture lands; four
cities.
30 And from the tribe of Asher, *they
gave* Mishal with its pasture lands, Abdon with its pasture lands,
31 Helkath with its pasture lands and
Rehob with its pasture lands; four cities.
32 And from the tribe of Naphtali,
they gave [a]Kedesh in Galilee, the city of
refuge for the manslayer, with its pasture
lands and Hammoth-dor with its pasture
lands and Kartan with its pasture lands;
three cities.
33 All the cities of the Gershonites
according to their families were thirteen
cities with their pasture lands.
34 And to the families of [a]the sons of
Merari, the rest of the Levites, *they gave*
from the tribe of Zebulun, Jokneam with
its pasture lands and Kartah with its
pasture lands.

9 [1]Lit., *smites* [a]Num. 35:13ff.
1 [1]Lit., *fathers* [a]Num. 35:1-8
2 [1]Lit., *by the hand of* [a]Num. 35:2
3 [1]Lit., *mouth*
4 [1]Lit., *had*
5 [1]Lit., *had*
6 [1]Lit., *had*
7 [1]Lit., *had*
8 [1]Lit., *by the hand of* [a]Gen. 49:5ff.
11 [a]1 Chr. 6:55 [b]Josh. 14:15; 15:13
13 [a]1 Chr. 6:57 [b]Josh. 15:54 [c]Josh. 15:42
14 [a]Josh. 15:48 [b]Josh. 15:50
15 [1]In 1 Chr. 6:58, *Hilen* [a]Josh. 15:49
16 [1]In 1 Chr. 6:59, *Ashan* [a]Josh. 15:55 [b]Josh. 15:10
17 [a]Josh. 18:25 [b]Josh. 18:24
18 [1]In 1 Chr. 6:60, *Allemeth*
20 [a]1 Chr. 6:66
21 [a]Josh. 20:7
27 [a]1 Chr. 6:71
32 [a]Josh. 20:7
34 [a]1 Chr. 6:77

35 Dimnah with its pasture lands,
Nahalal with its pasture lands; four
cities.
36 And from the tribe of Reuben, *they*
gave [a]Bezer with its pasture lands and
Jahaz with its pasture lands,
37 Kedemoth with its pasture lands
and Mephaath with its pasture lands;
four cities.
38 And from the tribe of Gad, *they*
gave [a]Ramoth in Gilead, the city of
refuge for the manslayer, with its pasture
lands and [b]Mahanaim with its pasture
lands,
39 Heshbon with its pasture lands,
Jazer with its pasture lands; four cities in
all.
40 All *these were* the cities of the sons
of Merari according to their families, the
rest of the families of the Levites; and
their lot was twelve cities.
41 [a]All the cities of the Levites in the
midst of the possession of the sons of
Israel were forty-eight cities with their
pasture lands.
42 These cities each had its surrounding pasture lands; thus *it was* with all
these cities.
43 [a]So the LORD gave Israel all the
land which He had sworn to give to their
fathers, and [b]they possessed it and lived
in it.
44 And the LORD [a]gave them rest on
every side, according to all that He had
sworn to their fathers, and [b]no one of all
their enemies stood before them; [c]the
LORD gave all their enemies into their
hand.
45 [a]Not [1]one of the good promises
which the LORD had [2]made to the house
of Israel failed; all came to pass.

Tribes beyond Jordan Return

22 [a]THEN Joshua summoned the
Reubenites and the Gadites and
the half-tribe of Manasseh,
2 and said to them, "You have kept
all that Moses the servant of the LORD
commanded you, [a]and have listened to
my voice in all that I commanded you.
3 "You have not forsaken your brothers these many days to this day, but have
kept the charge of the commandment of
the LORD your God.
4 "And now [a]the LORD your God has
given rest to your brothers, as He spoke
to them; therefore turn now and go to
your tents, to the land of your possession, which Moses the servant of the
LORD gave you beyond the Jordan.
5 "Only be very careful to observe the
commandment and the law which Moses
the servant of the LORD commanded
you, to [a]love the LORD your God and
walk in all His ways and keep His
commandments and hold fast to Him
and serve Him [b]with all your heart and
with all your soul."
6 So Joshua [a]blessed them and sent
them away, and they went to their tents.
7 Now [a]to the one half-tribe of Manasseh Moses had given *a possession* in
Bashan, but [b]to the other half Joshua
gave *a possession* among their brothers
westward beyond the Jordan. So when
Joshua sent them away to their tents, he
blessed them,
8 and said to [1]them, "Return to your
tents with great riches and with very
much livestock, with silver, gold, bronze,
iron, and with very many clothes; [a]di-
vide the spoil of your enemies with your
brothers."
9 And the sons of Reuben and the
sons of Gad and the half-tribe of Manasseh returned *home* and departed from
the sons of Israel at Shiloh which is in
the land of Canaan, to go to the [a]land of
Gilead, to the land of their possession
which they had possessed, according to
the [1]command of the LORD [2]through
Moses.

The Offensive Altar

10 And when they came to the region
of the Jordan which is in the land of
Canaan, the sons of Reuben and the
sons of Gad and the half-tribe of Manasseh built an altar there by the Jordan, a
large altar in appearance.
11 And the sons of Israel heard *it*
[1]said, "Behold, the sons of Reuben and
the sons of Gad and the half-tribe of
Manasseh have [a]built an altar at the
[2]frontier of the land of Canaan, in the
region of the Jordan, on the side *belong-*
ing to the sons of Israel."
12 And when the sons of Israel heard
of it, the whole congregation of the sons
of Israel gathered themselves at [a]Shiloh,
to go up against them in war.
13 Then the sons of Israel sent to the
sons of Reuben and to the sons of Gad
and to the half-tribe of Manasseh, into
the land of Gilead, [a]Phinehas the son of
Eleazar the priest,
14 and with him ten chiefs, one chief
for each father's household from each of
the tribes of Israel; and [a]each one of
them *was* the head of his father's household among the [1]thousands of Israel.
15 And they came to the sons of
Reuben and to the sons of Gad and to
the half-tribe of Manasseh, to the land of
Gilead, and they spoke with them saying,
16 "Thus says the whole congregation
of the LORD, 'What is this unfaithful act
which you have committed against the
God of Israel, turning away from following the LORD this day, by [a]building
yourselves an altar, to rebel against the
LORD this day?
17 'Is not [a]the iniquity of Peor [1]enough
for us, from which we have not cleansed
ourselves to this day, although a plague
came on the congregation of the LORD,
18 that you must turn away this day
from following the LORD? And it will
come about if you rebel against the
LORD today, that [a]He will be angry with
the whole congregation of Israel tomorrow.

36 [a]Deut. 4:43; Josh. 20:8
38 [a]Deut. 4:43; 1 Kin. 4:13 [b]Gen. 32:2; 2 Sam. 2:8
41 [a]Num. 35:7
43 [a]Deut. 34:4 [b]Num. 33:53; Deut. 11:31; 17:14
44 [a]Josh. 1:13; 23:1 [b]Deut. 7:24 [c]Ex. 23:31
45 [1]Lit., *a word from every good word* [2]Lit., *spoken* [a]Josh. 23:14; 1 Kin. 8:56
1 [a]Num. 32:20-22
2 [a]Josh. 1:12-18
4 [a]Num. 32:18; Deut. 3:20
5 [a]Deut. 5:10 [b]Deut. 4:29
6 [a]Gen. 47:7; Josh. 14:13; 2 Sam. 6:18; Luke 24:50
7 [a]Num. 32:33 [b]Josh. 17:1-13
8 [1]Lit., *them, saying, "Return* [a]Num. 31:27; 1 Sam. 30:16
9 [1]Lit., *mouth* [2]Lit., *by the hand of* [a]Num. 32:1, 26, 29
11 [1]Lit., *saying* [2]Lit., *front* [a]Deut. 12:5; Josh. 22:19
12 [a]Josh. 18:1
13 [a]Num. 25:7, 11; 31:6
14 [1]Or, *families* [a]Num. 1:4
16 [a]Josh. 22:11
17 [1]Lit., *little for us* [a]Num. 25:1-9
18 [a]Num. 16:22

19 'If, however, the land of your possession is unclean, then [1]cross into the
land of the possession of the LORD,
where the LORD's tabernacle [2]stands,
and take possession among us. Only do
not rebel against the LORD, or rebel
against us by [a]building an altar for
yourselves, besides the altar of the LORD
our God.
20 'Did not [a]Achan the son of Zerah
act unfaithfully in the things under the
ban, and wrath fall on all the congregation of Israel? And that man did not
perish alone in his iniquity.' "
21 Then the sons of Reuben and the
sons of Gad and the half-tribe of Manasseh answered, and spoke to the heads of
the [1]families of Israel.
22 "The [a]Mighty One, God, the LORD,
the Mighty One, God, the LORD! [b]He
knows, and may Israel itself know. If *it*
was in rebellion, or if in an unfaithful act
against the LORD do not Thou save us
this day!
23 "If we have built us an altar to turn
away from following the LORD, or if to
[a]offer a burnt offering or grain offering
on it, or if to offer sacrifices of peace
offerings on it, may the LORD Himself
require it.
24 "But truly we have done this out of
concern, [1]for a reason, saying, 'In time
to come your sons may say to our [2]sons,
"What have you to do with the LORD,
the God of Israel?
25 "For the LORD has made the Jordan
a border between us and you, *you* sons of
Reuben and sons of Gad; you have no
portion in the LORD." So your sons may
make our sons stop fearing the LORD.'
26 "Therefore we said, 'Let us [1]build an
altar, not for burnt offering or for sacrifice;
27 rather it shall be [a]a witness between us and you and between our
generations after us, that we are to
[b]perform the service of the LORD before
Him with our burnt offerings, and with
our sacrifices and with our peace offerings, that your sons may not say to our
sons in time to come, "You have no
portion in the LORD." '
28 "Therefore we said, 'It shall also
come about if they say *this* to us or to
our generations in time to come, then we
shall say, "See the copy of the altar of
the LORD which our fathers made, not
for burnt offering or for sacrifice; rather
it is a witness between us and you." '
29 "Far be it from us that we should
rebel against the LORD and turn away
from following the LORD this day, by
[a]building an altar for burnt offering, for
grain offering or for sacrifice, besides the
altar of the LORD our God which is
before His [1]tabernacle."
30 So when Phinehas the priest and
the leaders of the congregation, even the
heads of the [1]families of Israel who *were*
with him, heard the words which the
sons of Reuben and the sons of Gad and
the sons of Manasseh spoke, it pleased
them.
31 And Phinehas the son of Eleazar
the priest said to the sons of Reuben and
to the sons of Gad and to the sons of
Manasseh, "Today we know that the
[a]LORD is in our midst, because you have
not committed this unfaithful act against
the LORD; now you have delivered the
sons of Israel from the hand of the
LORD."
32 Then Phinehas the son of Eleazar
the priest and the leaders returned from
the sons of Reuben and from the sons of
Gad, from the land of Gilead, to the
land of Canaan, to the sons of Israel,
and brought back word to them.
33 And the word pleased the sons of
Israel, and the sons of Israel [a]blessed
God; and they did not speak of going up
against them in war, to destroy the land
in which the sons of Reuben and the
sons of Gad were living.
34 And the sons of Reuben and the
sons of Gad [a]called the altar *Witness;*
"For," *they said,* "it is a witness between
us that the LORD is God."

Joshua's Farewell Address

23 NOW it came about after many
days, when the LORD had given
[a]rest to Israel from all their enemies [1]on
every side, and Joshua was old, advanced in years,
2 that [a]Joshua called for all Israel,
for their elders and their heads and their
judges and their officers, and said to
them, "I am old, advanced in years.
3 "And you have seen all that the
LORD your God has done to all these
nations because of you, for [a]the LORD
your God is He who has been fighting
for you.
4 "See, [a]I have apportioned to you
these nations which remain as an inheritance for your tribes, with all the nations
which I have cut off, from the Jordan
even to the Great Sea toward the setting
of the sun.
5 "And the LORD your God, He shall
thrust them out from before you and
[1a]drive them from before you; and [b]you
shall possess their land, just as the LORD
your God [2]promised you.
6 "[a]Be very firm, then, to keep and do
all that is written in the book of the law
of Moses, so that you may not turn aside
from it to the right hand or to the left,
7 in order that you may not [1]asso-
ciate with these nations, these which
remain among you, or [a]mention the
name of their gods, or [b]make *anyone*
swear *by them,* or [c]serve them, or bow
down to them.
8 "But you are to cling to the LORD
your God, as you have done to this day.
9 "[a]For the LORD has [1]driven out
great and strong nations from before
you; and as for you, [b]no man has stood
before you to this day.
10 "[a]One of your men puts to flight a
thousand, for the LORD your God is [b]He
who fights for you, just as He [1]promised
you.

19 [1]Lit., *cross for yourselves* [2]Lit., *abides* [a]Josh. 22:11
20 [a]Josh. 7:1-26
21 [1]Lit., *thousands*
22 [a]Deut. 10:17 [b]1 Kin. 8:39; Job 10:7; Ps. 44:21
23 [a]Deut. 12:11
24 [1]Lit., *from* [2]Lit., *sons, saying*
26 [1]Lit., *prepare to build for ourselves*
27 [a]Gen. 31:48; Josh. 24:27 [b]Deut. 12:6, 11, 26f.
29 [1]Lit., *dwelling place* [a]Deut. 12:13f.
30 [1]Lit., *thousands*
31 [a]Ex. 25:8; Lev. 26:11f.; 2 Chr. 15:2
33 [a]1 Chr. 29:20; Dan. 2:19; Luke 2:28
34 [a]Gen. 31:47-49
1 [1]Lit., *from round about* [a]Josh. 21:44
2 [a]Josh. 24:1
3 [a]Deut. 1:30
4 [a]Ex. 23:30
5 [1]Or, *dispossess* [2]Lit., *spoke to* [a]Ex. 23:20 [b]Num. 33:53
6 [a]Deut. 5:32; Josh. 1:7
7 [1]Lit., *go among* [a]Ex. 23:13; Ps. 16:4 [b]Deut. 6:13; 10:20 [c]Ex. 20:5
9 [1]Or, *dispossessed* [a]Ex. 23:23, 30 [b]Deut. 7:24
10 [1]Lit., *spoke to* [a]Lev. 26:8; Deut. 28:7; 32:20 [b]Deut. 3:22; Josh. 23:3

11"So take diligent heed to yourselves
to love the LORD your God.
12"For if you ever go back and [a]cling
to the rest of these nations, these which
remain among you, and [b]intermarry
with them, so that you [1]associate with
them and they with you,
13 know with certainty that the LORD
your God will not continue to [1]drive
these nations out from before you; but
they shall be a [a]snare and a trap to you,
and a whip on your sides and thorns in
your eyes, until you perish from off this
good land which the LORD your God has
given you.
14"Now behold, today [a]I am going the
way of all the earth, and you know in all
your hearts and in all your souls that
[b]not one word of all the good words
which the LORD your God spoke concerning you has failed; all have [1]been
fulfilled for you, not [2]one of them has
failed.
15"And it shall come about that just as
all the good words which the LORD your
God spoke to you have come upon you,
so [a]the LORD will bring upon you all the
threats, until He has destroyed you from
off this good land which the LORD your
God has given you.
16"[a]When you transgress the covenant
of the LORD your God, which He commanded you, and go and serve other
gods, and bow down to them, then the
anger of the LORD will burn against you,
and you shall perish quickly from off the
good land which He has given you."

Joshua Reviews Israel's History

24 THEN [a]Joshua gathered all the
tribes of Israel to Shechem, and
called for the elders of Israel and for
their heads and their judges and their
officers; and they presented themselves
before God.
2 And Joshua said to all the people,
"Thus says the LORD, the God of Israel,
'From ancient times your fathers lived
beyond the [1]River, *namely,* [a]Terah, the
father of Abraham and the father of
Nahor, and they served other gods.
3 'Then [a]I took your father Abraham
from beyond the [1]River, and led him
through all the land of Canaan, and
[b]multiplied his [2]descendants and gave
him [c]Isaac.
4 'And to Isaac I gave [a]Jacob and
Esau, and [b]to Esau I gave Mount Seir, to
possess it; but [c]Jacob and his sons went
down to Egypt.
5 'Then [a]I sent Moses and Aaron, and
I plagued Egypt [1]by what I did in its
midst; and afterward I brought you out.
6 'And I brought your fathers out of
Egypt, and [a]you came to the sea; and
Egypt pursued your fathers with chariots
and horsemen to the [1]Red Sea.
7 'But when they cried out to the
LORD, He put darkness between you and
the Egyptians, and brought the sea upon
them and covered them; and your own
eyes saw what I did in Egypt. And [a]you
lived in the wilderness for a long time.
8 'Then [a]I brought you into the land
of the Amorites who lived beyond the
Jordan, and they fought with you; and I
gave them into your hand, and you took
possession of their land when I destroyed them before you.
9 'Then [a]Balak the son of Zippor,
king of Moab, arose and fought against
Israel, and he sent and summoned Balaam the son of Beor to curse you.
10 'But I [a]was not willing to listen to
Balaam. So he had to bless you, and I
delivered you from his hand.
11 'And [a]you crossed the Jordan and
came to Jericho; and the citizens of
Jericho fought against you, *and* [b]the
Amorite and the Perizzite and the Canaanite and the Hittite and the Girgashite, the Hivite and the Jebusite. Thus
[c]I gave them into your hand.
12 'Then I [a]sent the hornet before you
and it [1]drove out the two kings of the
Amorites from before you, *but* [b]not by
your sword or your bow.
13 'And [a]I gave you a land on which
you had not labored, and cities which
you had not built, and you have lived in
them; you are eating of vineyards and
olive groves which you did not plant.'

"We Will Serve the LORD"

14"Now, therefore, [1][a]fear the LORD
and serve Him in sincerity and [2]truth;
and put away the gods which your
fathers served beyond the [3]River and in
Egypt, and serve the LORD.
15"And if it is disagreeable in your
sight to serve the LORD, choose for
yourselves today whom you will serve:
whether the gods which your fathers
served which were beyond the River, or
[a]the gods of the Amorites in whose land
you are living; but as for me and my
house, we will serve the LORD."
16 And the people answered and said,
"Far be it from us that we should forsake the LORD to serve other gods;
17 for the LORD our God is He who
brought us and our fathers up out of the
land of Egypt, from the house of [1]bond-
age, and who did these great signs in our
sight and preserved us through all the
way in which we went and among all the
peoples through whose midst we passed.
18"And the LORD drove out from
before us all the peoples, even the Amorites who lived in the land. We also will
serve the LORD, for He is our God."
19 Then Joshua said to the people,
"You will not be able to serve the LORD,
[a]for He is a holy God. He is [b]a jealous
God; [c]He will not forgive your transgression or your sins.
20"[a]If you forsake the LORD and serve
foreign gods, then He will turn and do
you harm and consume you after He has
done good to you."
21 And the people said to Joshua,
"No, but we will serve the LORD."
22 And Joshua said to the people,
"You are witnesses against yourselves
that [a]you have chosen for yourselves the

12 [1]Lit., *go among* [a]Ex. 34:15, 16; Ps. 106:34, 35 [b]Deut. 7:3, 4; Ezra 9:2; Neh. 13:25
13 [1]Or, *dispossess* [a]Ex. 23:33; 34:12; Deut. 7:16
14 [1]Lit., *come* [2]Lit., *one word* [a]1 Kin. 2:2 [b]Josh. 21:45
15 [a]Lev. 26:14-33; Deut. 28:15
16 [a]Deut. 4:25, 26
1 [a]Josh. 23:2
2 [1]I.e., Euphrates [a]Gen. 11:27-32
3 [1]I.e., Euphrates [2]Lit., *seed* [a]Gen. 12:1; 24:7 [b]Gen. 15:5 [c]Gen. 21:3
4 [a]Gen. 25:25, 26 [b]Gen. 36:8; Deut. 2:5 [c]Gen. 46:6, 7
5 [1]Lit., *according to* [a]Ex. 4:14-17
6 [1]Lit., *Sea of Reeds* [a]Ex. 14:2-31
7 [a]Deut. 1:46; 2:14
8 [a]Num. 21:21-32
9 [a]Num. 22:2-6
10 [a]Deut. 23:5
11 [a]Josh. 3:14-17 [b]Ex. 23:23, 28; Deut. 7:1 [c]Ex. 23:31
12 [1]Lit., *drove them out* [a]Ex. 23:28; Deut. 7:20 [b]Ps. 44:3
13 [a]Deut. 6:10, 11
14 [1]Or, *reverence* [2]Or, *faithfulness* [3]I.e., Euphrates [a]Deut. 10:12; 18:13; 1 Sam. 12:24
15 [a]Judg. 6:10
17 [1]Lit., *bondmen*
19 [a]Lev. 19:2; 20:7, 26 [b]Ex. 20:5; 34:14 [c]Ex. 23:21
20 [a]Deut. 4:25, 26
22 [a]Ps. 119:173

LORD, to serve Him." And they said,
"We are witnesses."
23 "Now therefore, put away the foreign gods which are in your midst, and
[a]incline your hearts to the LORD, the
God of Israel."
24 [a]And the people said to Joshua,
"We will serve the LORD our God and
we will [1]obey His voice."
25 [a]So Joshua made a covenant with
the people that day, and made for them
a statute and an ordinance in Shechem.
26 And Joshua [a]wrote these words in
the book of the law of God; and he took
a large stone and set it up there under
the oak that was by the sanctuary of the
LORD.
27 And Joshua said to all the people,
"Behold, [a]this stone shall be for a witness against us, for it has heard all the
words of the LORD which He spoke [1]to
us; thus it shall be for a witness against
you, lest you deny your God."
28 Then Joshua dismissed the people,
each to his inheritance.

23 [a]1 Kin. 8:57, 58; Ps. 119:36; 141:4
24 [1]Lit., *listen to* [a]Ex. 19:8; 24:3, 7; Deut. 5:27
25 [a]Ex. 24:8
26 [a]Deut. 31:24
27 [1]Lit., *with* [a]Josh. 22:27, 34
30 [a]Josh. 19:50
31 [1]Lit., *prolonged days after* [a]Judg. 2:6f.
32 [1]Heb., *qesitah* [a]Gen. 50:24, 25; Ex. 13:19 [b]Gen. 33:19; John 4:5; Acts 7:15f.
33 [1]Or, *on the hill* [a]Josh. 22:13

Joshua's Death and Burial

29 And it came about after these
things that Joshua the son of Nun, the
servant of the LORD, died, being one
hundred and ten years old.
30 And they buried him in the territory of his inheritance in [a]Timnath-
serah, which is in the hill country of
Ephraim, on the north of Mount Gaash.
31 And [a]Israel served the LORD all the
days of Joshua and all the days of the
elders who [1]survived Joshua, and had
known all the deeds of the LORD which
He had done for Israel.
32 Now [a]they buried the bones of
Joseph, which the sons of Israel brought
up from Egypt, at Shechem, in the piece
of ground [b]which Jacob had bought
from the sons of Hamor the father of
Shechem for one hundred [1]pieces of
money; and they became the inheritance
of Joseph's sons.
33 And Eleazar the son of Aaron died;
and they buried him [1]at Gibeah of
[a]Phinehas his son, which was given him
in the hill country of Ephraim.

THE BOOK OF JUDGES

Jerusalem Is Captured

1 NOW it came about after the death
of Joshua that the sons of Israel
[a]inquired of the LORD, saying, "Who
shall go up first for us [b]against the
Canaanites, to fight against them?"
2 And the LORD said, "[a]Judah shall
go up; behold, I have given the land into
his hand."
3 Then Judah said to Simeon his
brother, "Come up with me into [1]the
territory allotted me, that we may fight
against the Canaanites; and [2]I in turn
will go with you into [3]the territory
allotted you." So Simeon went with him.
4 And Judah went up, and [a]the LORD
gave the Canaanites and the Perizzites
into their hands; and they [1]defeated ten
thousand men at Bezek.
5 And they found Adoni-bezek in
Bezek and fought against him and they
[1]defeated the Canaanites and the Perizzites.
6 But Adoni-bezek fled; and they
pursued him and caught him and cut off
his [1]thumbs and big toes.
7 And Adoni-bezek said, "Seventy
kings with their thumbs and their big
toes cut off used to gather up *scraps*
under my table; [a]as I have done, so God
has repaid me." So they brought him to
Jerusalem and he died there.
8 Then the sons of Judah fought
against [a]Jerusalem and captured it and
struck it with the edge of the sword and
set the city on fire.
9 And afterward the sons of Judah
went down to fight against the Canaan-

1 [a]Num. 27:21 [b]Judg. 1:27; 2:21-23; 3:1-6
2 [a]Gen. 49:8
3 [1]Lit., *my lot* [2]Lit., *I, even I* [3]Lit., *your lot*
4 [1]Lit., *smote them* [a]Ps. 44:2; 78:55
5 [1]Lit., *smote*
6 [1]Lit., *thumbs of his hands and his feet*
7 [a]Lev. 24:19
8 [a]Josh. 15:63; Judg. 1:21
9 [1]I.e., South country
10 [a]Josh. 15:13-19
11 [a]Josh. 15:15
13 [a]Judg. 3:9
14 [1]Lit., *the* [2]Lit., *for yourself* [a]Josh. 15:18
15 [1]I.e., South country
16 [1]Lit., *sons* [a]Num. 10:29-32; Judg. 4:11 [b]Deut. 34:3; Judg. 3:13 [c]Num. 21:1

ites living in the hill country and in the
[1]Negev and in the lowland.
10 [a]So Judah went against the Canaanites who lived in Hebron (now the
name of Hebron formerly *was* Kiriath-
arba); and they struck Sheshai and
Ahiman and Talmai.

Capture of Other Cities

11 Then [a]from there he went against
the inhabitants of Debir (now the name
of Debir formerly *was* Kiriath-sepher).
12 And Caleb said, "The one who
attacks Kiriath-sepher and captures it, I
will even give him my daughter Achsah
for a wife."
13 And [a]Othniel the son of Kenaz,
Caleb's younger brother, captured it; so
he gave him his daughter Achsah for a
wife.
14 Then [a]it came about when she
came *to him,* that she persuaded him to
ask her father for a field. Then she
alighted from [1]her donkey, and Caleb
said to her, "What [2]do you want?"
15 And she said to him, "Give me a
blessing, since you have given me the
land of the [1]Negev, give me also springs
of water." So Caleb gave her the upper
springs and the lower springs.
16 And the [1]descendants of [a]the Kenite, Moses' father-in-law, went up from
the [b]city of palms with the sons of
Judah, to the wilderness of Judah which
is in the south of [c]Arad; and they went
and lived with the people.
17 Then Judah went with Simeon his
brother, and they struck the Canaanites
living in Zephath, and utterly destroyed

it. So the name of the city was called
[a]Hormah.
18 And Judah took [a]Gaza with its
territory and Ashkelon with its territory
and Ekron with its territory.
19 Now the LORD was with Judah,
and they took possession of the hill
country; but they could not [1]drive out
the inhabitants of the valley because
they had [a]iron chariots.
20 Then they gave Hebron to Caleb,
[a]as Moses had [1]promised; and he drove
out from there [b]the three sons of Anak.
21 [a]But the sons of Benjamin did not
drive out the [b]Jebusites who lived in
Jerusalem; so the Jebusites have lived
with the sons of Benjamin in Jerusalem
to this day.
22 Likewise the house of Joseph went
up against Bethel, and the LORD was
with them.
23 And the house of Joseph spied out
Bethel ([a]now the name of the city was
formerly Luz).
24 And the spies saw a man coming
out of the city, and they said to him,
"Please show us the entrance to the city
and [a]we will treat you kindly."
25 So he showed them the entrance to
the city, and they struck the city with the
edge of the sword, [a]but they let the man
and all his family go free.
26 And the man went into the land of
the Hittites and built a city and named it
Luz [1]which is its name to this day.

Places Not Conquered

27 [a]But Manasseh did not take possession of Beth-shean and its villages, or
Taanach and its villages, or the inhabitants of Dor and its villages, or the
inhabitants of Ibleam and its villages, or
the inhabitants of Megiddo and its
villages; so [b]the Canaanites persisted in
living in that land.
28 And it came about when Israel
became strong, that they put the Canaanites to forced labor, but they did
not drive them out completely.
29 [a]Neither did Ephraim drive out the
Canaanites who were living in Gezer; so
the Canaanites lived in Gezer among
them.
30 Zebulun did not drive out the
inhabitants of Kitron, or the inhabitants
of Nahalol; so the Canaanites lived
among them and became subject to
forced labor.
31 Asher did not drive out the inhabitants of Acco, or the inhabitants of
Sidon, or of Ahlab, or of Achzib, or of
Helbah, or of Aphik, or of Rehob.
32 So the Asherites lived among the
Canaanites, the inhabitants of the land;
for they did not drive them out.
33 Naphtali did not drive out the
inhabitants of Beth-shemesh, or the
inhabitants of Beth-anath, but lived
among the Canaanites, the inhabitants
of the land; and the inhabitants of Beth-
shemesh and Beth-anath became forced
labor for them.
34 Then the Amorites [1]forced the sons
of Dan into the hill country, for they did
not allow them to come down to the
valley;
35 yet the Amorites persisted in [1]liv-
ing in Mount Heres, in Aijalon and in
Shaalbim; but when the [2]power of the
house of Joseph [3]grew strong, they became forced labor.
36 And the border of the Amorites ran
from the [a]ascent of Akrabbim, from Sela
and upward.

Israel Rebuked

2 NOW [a]the angel of the LORD came
up from Gilgal to [b]Bochim. And he
said, "[c]I brought you up out of Egypt
and led you into the land which I have
sworn to your fathers; and I said, '[d]I will
never break My covenant with you,
2 and as for you, [a]you shall make no
covenant with the inhabitants of this
land; [b]you shall tear down their altars.'
But you have not [1]obeyed Me; what is
this you have done?
3 "Therefore I also said, '[a]I will not
drive them out before you; but they shall
[1]become [b]*as thorns* in your sides, and
their gods shall be a snare to you.' "
4 And it came about when the angel
of the LORD spoke these words to all the
sons of Israel, that the people lifted up
their voices and wept.
5 So they named that place [1]Bochim;
and there they sacrificed to the LORD.

Joshua Dies

6 [a]When Joshua had dismissed the
people, the sons of Israel went each to
his inheritance to possess the land.
7 And the people served the LORD all
the days of Joshua, and all the days of
the elders who [1]survived Joshua, who
had seen all the great work of the LORD
which He had done for Israel.
8 Then Joshua the son of Nun, the
servant of the LORD, died at the age of
one hundred and ten.
9 And they buried him in the territory of [a]his inheritance in Timnath-
heres, in the hill country of Ephraim,
north of Mount Gaash.
10 And all that generation also were
gathered to their fathers; and there arose
another generation after them who [a]did
not know the LORD, nor yet the work
which He had done for Israel.

Israel Serves Baals

11 Then the sons of Israel did [a]evil in
the sight of the LORD, and [1]served the
[b]Baals,
12 and [a]they forsook the LORD, the
God of their fathers, who had brought
them out of the land of Egypt, and
followed other gods from *among* the
gods of the peoples who were around
them, and bowed themselves down to
them; thus they provoked the LORD to
anger.
13 So they forsook the LORD and
[a]served Baal and the Ashtaroth.

---

17 [a]Num. 21:3
18 [a]Josh. 11:22
19 [1]Or, *dispossess* [a]Josh. 17:16; Judg. 4:3, 13
20 [1]Lit., *spoken* [a]Josh. 14:9 [b]Josh. 15:14; Judg. 1:10
21 [a]Josh. 15:63; Judg. 1:8 [b]1 Chr. 11:4
23 [a]Gen. 28:19
24 [a]Josh. 2:12
25 [a]Josh. 6:25
26 [1]Lit., *it*
27 [a]Josh. 17:12 [b]Judg. 1:1
29 [a]Josh. 16:10
34 [1]Lit., *pressed*
35 [1]Lit., *dwelling* [2]Lit., *hand* [3]Lit., *was heavy*
36 [a]Josh. 15:3
1 [a]Judg. 6:11; 13:2-21 [b]Judg. 2:5 [c]Ex. 20:2 [d]Gen. 17:7, 8; Lev. 26:42, 44; Deut. 7:9
2 [1]Lit., *listened to My voice* [a]Ex. 23:32; Deut. 7:2-5 [b]Ex. 34:12, 13
3 [1]Some ancient mss. read *be adversaries, and* [a]Josh. 23:13 [b]Num. 33:55
5 [1]I.e., weepers
6 [a]Josh. 24:28-31
7 [1]Lit., *prolonged days after*
9 [a]Josh. 19:49f.
10 [a]Ex. 5:2; 1 Sam. 2:12
11 [1]Or, *worshiped* [a]Judg. 3:7, 12; 4:1; 6:1 [b]Judg. 6:25; 8:33; 10:6
12 [a]Deut. 31:16
13 [a]Judg. 10:6

14 [a]And the anger of the LORD burned
against Israel, and He gave them into the
hands of plunderers who plundered
them; and [b]He sold them into the hands
of their enemies around *them,* so that
they could no longer stand before their
enemies.
15 Wherever they went, the hand of
the LORD was against them for evil, as
the LORD had spoken and [a]as the LORD
had sworn to them, so that they were
severely distressed.
16 [a]Then the LORD raised up judges
[1]who delivered them from the hands of
those who plundered them.
17 And yet they did not listen to their
judges, for they played the harlot after
other gods and bowed themselves down
to them. They turned aside quickly from
the way [a]in which their fathers had
walked in obeying the commandments
of the LORD; they did not do as *their
fathers.*
18 And when the LORD raised up
judges for them, [a]the LORD was with the
judge and delivered them from the hand
of their enemies all the days of the
judge; for the LORD was [b]moved to pity
by their groaning because of those who
oppressed and afflicted them.
19 But it came about when the judge
died, that they would turn back and act
more corruptly than their fathers, in
following other gods to serve them and
bow down to them; they did not abandon their practices or their stubborn
ways.
20 [a]So the anger of the LORD burned
against Israel, and He said, "Because
this nation has transgressed My covenant which I commanded their fathers,
and has not listened to My voice,
21 [a]I also will no longer drive out
before them any of the nations which
Joshua left when he died,
22 in order to [a]test Israel by them,
whether they will keep the way of the
LORD to walk in it as their fathers [1]did,
or not."
23 So the LORD allowed those nations
to remain, not driving them out quickly;
and He did not give them into the hand
of Joshua.

Idolatry Leads to Servitude

3 [a]NOW these are the nations which
the LORD left, to test Israel by them
(*that is,* all who had not [1]experienced
any of the wars of Canaan;
2 only in order that the generations
of the sons of Israel might [1]be taught
war, [2]those who had not [3]experienced it
formerly).
3 *These nations are:* the five lords of
the Philistines and all the Canaanites
and the Sidonians and [a]the Hivites who
lived in Mount Lebanon, from Mount
Baal-hermon as far as [1]Lebo-hamath.
4 And they were for [1a]testing Israel,
to find out if they would [2]obey the
commandments of the LORD, which He
had commanded their fathers [3]through
Moses.

14 [a]Deut. 31:17; Ps. 106:40-42 [b]Deut. 28:25; 32:30
15 [a]Lev. 26:14-39; Deut. 28:15-68
16 [1]Lit., *and they* [a]Ps. 106:43-45
17 [a]Judg. 2:7
18 [a]Josh. 1:5 [b]Deut. 32:36; Ps. 106:44
20 [a]Judg. 2:14
21 [a]Josh. 23:4, 5, 13
22 [1]Lit., *kept* [a]Deut. 8:2; 13:3
1 [1]Lit., *known* [a]Judg. 1:1; 2:21, 22
2 [1]Lit., *know, to teach them* [2]Lit., *only* [3]Lit., *known*
3 [1]Or, *the entrance of Hamath* [a]Josh. 9:7; 11:19
4 [1]Lit., *testing by them* [2]Lit., *hear* [3]Lit., *by the hand of* [a]Deut. 8:2
5 [a]Ps. 106:35
6 [a]Ex. 34:15, 16; Deut. 7:3, 4; Josh. 23:12
7 [1]I.e., wooden symbol of a female deity [a]Judg. 2:11 [b]Deut. 4:9 [c]Judg. 2:13
8 [1]Heb., *Aram-naharaim*
9 [a]Judg. 1:13
10 [1]Heb., *Aram* [2]Lit., *his hand was strong* [a]Num. 11:25-29; 24:2
12 [a]Judg. 2:11 [b]Judg. 2:14
13 [1]Lit., *smote* [a]Deut. 34:3; Judg. 1:16
15 [1]Lit., *his hand* [a]Ps. 78:34

5 And [a]the sons of Israel lived
among the Canaanites, the Hittites, the
Amorites, the Perizzites, the Hivites, and
the Jebusites;
6 and [a]they took their daughters for
themselves as wives, and gave their own
daughters to their sons, and served their
gods.
7 And the sons of Israel did [a]what
was evil in the sight of the LORD, and
[b]forgot the LORD their God, and [c]served
the Baals and the [1]Asheroth.
8 Then the anger of the LORD was
kindled against Israel, so that He sold
them into the hands of Cushan-rishathaim king of [1]Mesopotamia; and the
sons of Israel served Cushan-rishathaim
eight years.

The First Judge Delivers Israel

9 And when the sons of Israel cried
to the LORD, the LORD raised up a
deliverer for the sons of Israel to deliver
them, [a]Othniel the son of Kenaz, Caleb's
younger brother.
10 And [a]the Spirit of the LORD came
upon him, and he judged Israel. When
he went out to war, the LORD gave
Cushan-rishathaim king of [1]Mesopota-
mia into his hand, so that [2]he prevailed
over Cushan-rishathaim.
11 Then the land had rest forty years.
And Othniel the son of Kenaz died.
12 Now the sons of Israel again [a]did
evil in the sight of the LORD. So [b]the
LORD strengthened Eglon the king of
Moab against Israel, because they had
done evil in the sight of the LORD.
13 And he gathered to himself the
sons of Ammon and Amalek; and he
went and [1]defeated Israel, and they
possessed [a]the city of the palm trees.
14 And the sons of Israel served Eglon
the king of Moab eighteen years.

Ehud Delivers from Moab

15 But when the sons of Israel [a]cried
to the LORD, the LORD raised up a
deliverer for them, Ehud the son of
Gera, the Benjamite, a left-handed man.
And the sons of Israel sent tribute by
[1]him to Eglon the king of Moab.
16 And Ehud made himself a sword
which had two edges, a cubit in length;
and he bound it on his right thigh under
his cloak.
17 And he presented the tribute to
Eglon king of Moab. Now Eglon was a
very fat man.
18 And it came about when he had
finished presenting the tribute, that he
sent away the people who had carried
the tribute.
19 But he himself turned back from
the idols which were at Gilgal, and said,
"I have a secret message for you, O
king." And he said, "Keep silence." And
all who attended him left him.
20 And Ehud came to him while he
was sitting alone in his cool roof chamber. And Ehud said, "I have a message
from God for you." And he arose from
his seat.

21 And Ehud stretched out his left hand, took the sword from his right thigh and thrust it into his belly.

22 The handle also went in after the blade, and the fat closed over the blade, for he did not draw the sword out of his belly; and the refuse came out.

23 Then Ehud went out into the vestibule and shut the doors of the roof chamber behind him, and locked *them*.

24 When he had gone out, his servants came and looked, and behold, the doors of the roof chamber were locked; and they said, "[a]He is only [1]relieving himself in the cool room."

25 And they waited until they [1]became anxious; but behold, he did not open the doors of the roof chamber. Therefore they took the key and opened them, and behold, their master had fallen to the [2]floor dead.

26 Now Ehud escaped while they were delaying, and he passed by the idols and escaped to Seirah.

27 And it came about when he had arrived, that [a]he blew the trumpet in the hill country of Ephraim; and the sons of Israel went down with him from the hill country, and he *was* in front of them.

28 And he said to them, "Pursue *them*, for the LORD has given your enemies the Moabites into your hands." So they went down after him and seized [a]the fords of the Jordan opposite Moab, and did not allow anyone to cross.

29 And they struck down at that time about ten thousand Moabites, all robust and valiant men; and no one escaped.

30 So Moab was subdued that day under the hand of Israel. And the land was undisturbed for eighty years.

Shamgar Delivers from Philistines

31 And after him came [a]Shamgar the son of Anath, who struck down six hundred Philistines with an oxgoad; and he also saved Israel.

Deborah and Barak Deliver from Canaanites

4 THEN [a]the sons of Israel again did evil in the sight of the LORD, after Ehud died.

2 And the LORD sold them into the hand of [a]Jabin king of Canaan, who reigned in Hazor; and the commander of his army was Sisera, who lived in [b]Harosheth-hagoyim.

3 And the sons of Israel cried to the LORD; for he had nine hundred [a]iron chariots, and he oppressed the sons of Israel severely for twenty years.

4 Now Deborah, a [1]prophetess, the wife of Lappidoth, was judging Israel at that time.

5 And she used to [1]sit under the [a]palm tree of Deborah between Ramah and Bethel in the hill country of Ephraim; and the sons of Israel came up to her for judgment.

6 Now she sent and summoned [a]Barak the son of Abinoam from Kedesh-naphtali, and said to him, "[1]Behold, the LORD, the God of Israel, has commanded, 'Go and march to Mount Tabor, and take with you ten thousand men from the sons of Naphtali and from the sons of Zebulun.

7 'And I will draw out to you Sisera, the commander of Jabin's army, with his chariots and his [1]many *troops* to the river Kishon; and [a]I will give him into your hand.' "

8 Then Barak said to her, "If you will go with me, then I will go; but if you will not go with me, I will not go."

9 And she said, "I will surely go with you; nevertheless, the honor shall not be yours on the journey that you are about to take, [a]for the LORD will sell Sisera into the hands of a woman." Then Deborah arose and went with Barak to Kedesh.

10 And Barak called [a]Zebulun and Naphtali together to Kedesh, and ten thousand men went up [1b]with him; Deborah also went up with him.

11 Now Heber [a]the Kenite had separated himself from the Kenites, from the sons of Hobab the father-in-law of Moses, and had pitched his tent as far away as the [1]oak in [b]Zaanannim, which is near Kedesh.

12 Then they told Sisera that Barak the son of Abinoam had gone up to Mount Tabor.

13 And Sisera called together all his chariots, [a]nine hundred iron chariots, and all the people who *were* with him, from [b]Harosheth-hagoyim to the river Kishon.

14 And Deborah said to Barak, "Arise! For this is the day in which the LORD has given Sisera into your hands; [1]behold, [a]the LORD has gone out before you." So Barak went down from Mount Tabor with ten thousand men following him.

15 [a]And the LORD [1]routed Sisera and all *his* chariots and all *his* army, with the edge of the sword before Barak; and Sisera alighted from *his* chariot and fled away on foot.

16 But Barak pursued the chariots and the army as far as Harosheth-hagoyim, and all the army of Sisera fell by the edge of the sword; [a]not even one was left.

17 Now Sisera fled away on foot to the tent of Jael the wife of Heber the Kenite, for *there was* peace between Jabin the king of Hazor and the house of Heber the Kenite.

18 And Jael went out to meet Sisera, and said to him, "Turn aside, my master, turn aside to me! Do not be afraid." And he turned aside to her into the tent, and she covered him with a [1]rug.

19 [a]And he said to her, "Please give me a little water to drink, for I am thirsty." So she opened a [1]bottle of milk and gave him a drink; then she covered him.

20 And he said to her, "Stand in the doorway of the tent, and it shall be if anyone comes and inquires of you, and

24 [1]Lit., *covering his feet* [a]1 Sam. 24:3
25 [1]Lit., *were ashamed* [2]Lit., *earth*
27 [a]Judg. 6:34; 1 Sam. 13:3
28 [a]Judg. 7:24; 12:5
31 [a]Judg. 5:6
1 [a]Judg. 2:19
2 [a]Josh. 11:1, 10 [b]Judg. 4:13, 16
3 [a]Judg. 1:19
4 [1]Lit., *woman prophetess*
5 [1]Or, *live* [a]Gen. 35:8
6 [1]Or, *Has not . . . commanded . . . ?* [a]Heb. 11:32
7 [1]Lit., *multitude* [a]Ps. 83:9
9 [a]Judg. 4:21
10 [1]Lit., *at his feet* [a]Judg. 5:18 [b]Judg. 4:14; 5:15
11 [1]Or, *terebinth* [a]Judg. 1:16 [b]Josh. 19:33
13 [a]Judg. 4:3 [b]Judg. 4:2
14 [1]Or, *has not the LORD gone . . . ?* [a]Deut. 9:3; 2 Sam. 5:24; Ps. 68:7
15 [1]Lit., *confused* [a]Deut. 7:23; Josh. 10:10
16 [a]Ex. 14:28; Ps. 83:9
18 [1]Or, *blanket*
19 [1]I.e., skin container [a]Judg. 5:24-27

says, 'Is there anyone here?' that you
shall say, 'No.' "
21 But Jael, Heber's wife, [a]took a tent
peg and [1]seized a hammer in her hand,
and went secretly to him and drove the
peg into his temple, and it went through
into the ground; for he was sound asleep
and exhausted. So he died.
22 And behold, as Barak pursued
Sisera, Jael came out to meet him and
said to him, "Come, and I will show you
the man whom you are seeking." And he
entered [1]with her, and behold Sisera was
lying dead with the tent peg in his
temple.
23 So [a]God subdued on that day
Jabin the king of Canaan before the sons
of Israel.
24 And the hand of the sons of Israel
pressed heavier and heavier upon Jabin
the king of Canaan, until they had
[1]destroyed Jabin the king of Canaan.

The Song of Deborah and Barak

5 [a]THEN Deborah and Barak the son
of Abinoam sang on that day, saying,

2 "[a]That [1]the leaders led in Israel,
That [b]the people volunteered,
Bless the LORD!
3 "Hear, O kings; give ear, O rulers!
[a]I—to the LORD, I will sing,
I will sing praise to the LORD, the God of Israel.
4 "[a]LORD, when Thou didst go out from Seir,
When Thou didst march from the field of Edom,
[b]The earth quaked, the heavens also dripped,
Even the clouds dripped water.
5 "[a]The mountains [1]quaked at the presence of the LORD,
[b]This Sinai, at the presence of the LORD, the God of Israel.

6 "In the days of [a]Shamgar the son of Anath,
In the days of [b]Jael, the highways [1]were deserted,
And travelers [2]went by [3]roundabout ways.
7 "The peasantry ceased, they ceased in Israel,
Until I, Deborah, arose,
Until I arose, a mother in Israel.
8 "[a]New gods were chosen;
Then war *was* in the gates.
Not a shield or a spear was seen
Among forty thousand in Israel.
9 "My heart *goes out* to [a]the commanders of Israel,
The volunteers among the people;
Bless the LORD!
10 "[a]You who ride on [1]white donkeys,
You who sit on *rich* carpets,
And you who travel on the road—[2]sing!
11 "At the sound of those who divide *flocks* among [a]the watering places,
There they shall recount [b]the righteous deeds of the LORD,
The righteous deeds for His [1]peasantry in Israel.
Then the people of the LORD went down [c]to the gates.

12 "[a]Awake, awake, Deborah;
Awake, awake, [1]sing a song!
Arise, Barak, and [b]take away your captives, O son of Abinoam.
13 "Then survivors came down to the nobles;
The people of the LORD came down to me as warriors.
14 "From Ephraim those whose root is [a]in Amalek *came down,*
Following you, Benjamin, with your peoples;
From Machir commanders came down,
And from Zebulun those who wield the staff of [1]office.
15 "And the [1]princes of Issachar *were* with Deborah;
As *was* Issachar, so *was* Barak;
Into the valley they rushed [a]at his [2]heels;
Among the divisions of Reuben
There were great resolves of heart.
16 "Why did you sit among [a]the [1]sheepfolds,
To hear the piping for the flocks?
Among the divisions of Reuben
There were great searchings of heart.
17 "[a]Gilead [1]remained across the Jordan;
And why did Dan stay in ships?
Asher sat at the seashore,
And [1]remained by its landings.
18 "[a]Zebulun *was* a people who despised their lives *even* to death,
And Naphtali also, on the high places of the field.

19 "[a]The kings came *and* fought;
Then fought the kings of Canaan
[b]At Taanach near the waters of Megiddo;
[c]They took no plunder in silver.
20 "[a]The stars fought from heaven,
From their courses they fought against Sisera.
21 "The torrent of Kishon swept them away,
The ancient torrent, the torrent Kishon.
[a]O my soul, march on with strength.
22 "[a]Then the horses' hoofs beat
From the dashing, the dashing of his [1]valiant steeds.
23 'Curse Meroz,' said the angel of the LORD,
'Utterly curse its inhabitants;
[a]Because they did not come to the help of the LORD,
To the help of the LORD against the warriors.'

4:21 [1]Lit., *placed* [a]Judg. 5:26
4:22 [1]Lit., *to*
4:23 [a]Neh. 9:24; Ps. 18:47
4:24 [1]Lit., *cut off*
5:1 [a]Ex. 15:1
5:2 [1]Or, *locks hung loose in* [a]Judg. 5:9 [b]Ps. 110:3
5:3 [a]Ps. 27:6
5:4 [a]Deut. 33:2; Ps. 68:7 [b]Ps. 68:8, 9
5:5 [1]Lit., *flowed* [a]Ex. 19:18 [b]Ps. 68:8
5:6 [1]Lit., *had ceased* [2]Lit., *walked* [3]Lit., *twisted* [a]Judg. 3:31 [b]Judg. 4:17
5:8 [a]Deut. 32:17
5:9 [a]Judg. 5:2
5:10 [1]Or, *tawny* [2]Or, *declare it* [a]Judg. 10:4; 12:14
5:11 [1]Or, *rural dwellers* [a]Gen. 24:11; 29:2, 3 [b]1 Sam. 12:7; Mic. 6:5 [c]Judg. 5:8
5:12 [1]Or, *utter* [a]Ps. 57:8 [b]Ps. 68:18; Eph. 4:8
5:14 [1]Lit., *the scribe* [a]Judg. 12:15
5:15 [1]So with ancient versions; Heb., *My princes* [2]Lit., *feet* [a]Judg. 4:10
5:16 [1]Or, *saddlebags* [a]Num. 32:1, 2, 24, 36
5:17 [1]Or, *dwelt* [a]Josh. 22:9
5:18 [a]Judg. 4:6, 10
5:19 [a]Josh. 11:1-5; Judg. 4:13 [b]Judg. 1:27 [c]Judg. 5:30
5:20 [a]Josh. 10:12-14
5:21 [a]Ex. 15:2; Ps. 44:5
5:22 [1]Lit., *mighty ones* [a]Job 39:19-25
5:23 [a]Judg. 5:13

24 "[a]Most blessed of women is Jael,
The wife of Heber the Kenite;
Most blessed is she of women in the tent.
25 "He asked for water *and* she gave him milk;
In a magnificent bowl she brought him curds.
26 "She reached out her hand for the tent peg,
And her right hand for the workmen's hammer.
Then she struck Sisera, she smashed his head;
And she shattered and pierced his temple.
27 "Between her feet he bowed, he fell, he lay;
Between her feet he bowed, he fell;
Where he bowed, there he fell [1]dead.
28 "Out of the window she looked and lamented,
The mother of Sisera through the [1]lattice,
'Why does his chariot delay in coming?
Why do the [2]hoofbeats of his chariots tarry?'
29 "Her wise princesses would answer her,
Indeed she repeats her words to herself,
30 '[a]Are they not finding, are they not dividing the spoil?
A maiden, two maidens for every warrior;
To Sisera a spoil of dyed work,
A spoil of dyed work embroidered,
Dyed work of double embroidery on the [1]neck of the spoiler?'
31 "[a]Thus let all Thine enemies perish, O LORD;
[b]But let those who love Him be like the rising of the sun in its might."
And the land was undisturbed for forty years.

Israel Oppressed by Midian

6 THEN the sons of Israel [a]did what
was evil in the sight of the LORD;
and the LORD gave them into the hands
of [b]Midian seven years.
2 And the [1]power of Midian prevailed against Israel. Because of Midian
the sons of Israel made for themselves
[a]the dens which were in the mountains
and the caves and the strongholds.
3 For it was when Israel had sown,
that the Midianites would come up with
the Amalekites and the sons of the east
and [1]go against them.
4 So they would camp against them
and [a]destroy the produce of the earth [1]as
far as Gaza, and [b]leave no sustenance in
Israel as well as no sheep, ox, or donkey.
5 For they would come up with their
livestock and their tents, they would
come in [a]like locusts for number,
both they and their camels were innumerable; and they came into the land to
devastate it.
6 So Israel was brought [a]very low
because of Midian, and the sons of Israel
cried to the LORD.
7 Now it came about when the sons
of Israel cried to the LORD on account of
Midian,
8 that the LORD sent a prophet to the
sons of Israel, and [a]he said to them,
"Thus says the LORD, the God of Israel,
'It was I who brought you up from
Egypt; and brought you out from the
house of [1]slavery.
9 'And I delivered you from the
hands of the Egyptians and from the
hands of all your oppressors, and dispossessed them before you and gave you
their land,
10 and I said to you, "I am the LORD
your God; you [a]shall not fear the gods of
the Amorites in whose land you live. But
you have not [1]obeyed Me."' "

Gideon Is Visited

11 Then [a]the angel of the LORD came
and sat under the [1]oak that was in
Ophrah, which belonged to Joash the
[b]Abiezrite as his son [c]Gideon was beating out wheat in the wine press in order
to save *it* from the Midianites.
12 And the angel of the LORD appeared to him and said to him, "The
LORD is with you, O valiant warrior."
13 Then Gideon said to him, "O my
lord, if the LORD is with us, why then
has all this happened to us? And where
are all His miracles which our fathers
told us about, saying, 'Did not the LORD
bring us up from Egypt?' But [a]now the
LORD has abandoned us and given us
into the hand of Midian."
14 And the LORD [1]looked at him and
said, "[a]Go in this your strength and
deliver Israel from the hand of Midian.
Have I not sent you?"
15 [a]And he said to Him, "O Lord,
[1]how shall I deliver Israel? Behold, my
family is the least in [b]Manasseh, and I
am the youngest in my father's house."
16 [a]But the LORD said to him, "Surely
I will be with you, and you shall [1]defeat
Midian as one man."
17 So [1]Gideon said to Him, "If now I
have found favor in Thy sight, then show
me [a]a sign that it is Thou who speakest
with me.
18 "Please do not depart from here,
until I come *back* to Thee, and bring out
my offering and lay it before Thee." And
He said, "I will remain until you return."
19 Then Gideon went in and [a]pre-
pared a kid and unleavened bread from
an [1]ephah of flour; he put the meat in a
basket [2]and the broth in a pot, and
brought *them* out to him under the [3]oak,
and presented *them*.
20 And the angel of God said to him,
"Take the meat and the unleavened
bread and lay them on this rock, and
pour out the broth." And he did so.

24 [a]Judg. 4:19-21
27 [1]Lit., *devastated*
28 [1]Or, *window* [2]Lit., *steps*
30 [1]Lit., *necks of the spoil* [a]Ex. 15:9
31 [a]Ps. 68:2; 92:9 [b]Ps. 19:4-6; 89:36, 37
1 [a]Judg. 2:11 [b]Num. 22:4; 25:15-18; 31:1-3
2 [1]Lit., *hand* [a]1 Sam. 13:6; Heb. 11:38
3 [1]Lit., *go up*
4 [1]Lit., *until your coming to* [a]Lev. 26:16 [b]Deut. 28:31
5 [a]Judg. 7:12; 8:10
6 [a]Deut. 28:43
8 [1]Lit., *slaves* [a]Judg. 2:1, 2
10 [1]Lit., *listened to My voice* [a]2 Kin. 17:35; Jer. 10:2
11 [1]Or, *terebinth* [a]Judg. 2:1; 6:14; 13:3 [b]Josh. 17:2; Judg. 6:15 [c]Heb. 11:32
13 [a]Judg. 6:1; Ps. 44:9
14 [1]Or, *turned toward* [a]Heb. 11:32-34
15 [1]Lit., *with what* [a]Ex. 3:11 [b]Judg. 6:11
16 [1]Lit., *smite* [a]Ex. 3:12; Josh. 1:5
17 [1]Lit., *he* [a]Judg. 6:37; Is. 38:7, 8
19 [1]I.e., Approx. one bu. [2]Lit., *and he put* [3]Or, *terebinth* [a]Gen. 18:6-8

21 Then the angel of the LORD put out
the end of the staff that was in his hand
and touched the meat and the unleavened bread; and [a]fire sprang up from the
rock and consumed the meat and the
unleavened bread. Then the angel of
the LORD [1]vanished from his sight.
22 [a]When Gideon saw that he was the
angel of the LORD, [1]he said, "Alas, O
Lord [2]GOD! For now I have seen the
angel of the LORD face to face."
23 And the LORD said to him, "Peace
to you, do not fear; you shall not die."
24 Then Gideon built an altar there to
the LORD and named it [1]The LORD is
Peace. To this day it is still [a]in Ophrah
of the Abiezrites.
25 Now the same night it came about
that the LORD said to him, "Take your
father's bull [1]and a second bull seven
years old, and pull down the altar of
Baal which belongs to your father, and
cut down the [2a]Asherah that is beside it;
26 and build an altar to the LORD
your God on the top of this stronghold
in an orderly manner, and take a second
bull and offer a burnt offering with the
wood of the Asherah which you shall cut
down."
27 Then Gideon took ten men of his
servants and did as the LORD had spoken to him; and it came about, because
he was too afraid of his father's household and the men of the city to do it by
day, that he did it by night.

The Altar of Baal Destroyed

28 When the men of the city arose
early in the morning, behold, the altar of
Baal was torn down, and the Asherah
which was beside it was cut down, and
the second bull was offered on the altar
which had been built.
29 And they said to one another,
"Who did this thing?" And when they
searched about and inquired, they said,
"Gideon the son of Joash did this
thing."
30 Then the men of the city said to
Joash, "Bring out your son, that he may
die, for he has torn down the altar of
Baal, and indeed, he has cut down the
Asherah which was beside it."
31 But Joash said to all who stood
against him, "Will you contend for Baal,
or will you deliver him? Whoever will
[1]plead for him shall be put to death by
morning. If he is a god, let him contend
for himself, because someone has torn
down his altar."
32 Therefore on that day he named
him [a]Jerubbaal, that is to say, "Let Baal
contend against him," because he had
torn down his altar.
33 Then all the Midianites and the
Amalekites and the sons of the east
assembled themselves; and they crossed
over and camped in [a]the valley of Jezreel.
34 So [a]the Spirit of the LORD [1]came
upon Gideon; and he [b]blew a trumpet,
and the Abiezrites were called together
to follow him.
35 And he sent messengers throughout Manasseh, and they also were called
together to follow him; and he sent
messengers to Asher, [a]Zebulun, and
Naphtali, and [b]they came up to meet
them.

Sign of the Fleece

36 Then Gideon said to God, "[a]If
Thou wilt deliver Israel [1]through me, as
Thou hast spoken,
37 behold, I will put a fleece of wool
on the threshing floor. If there is dew on
the fleece only, and it is dry on all the
ground, then I will know that Thou wilt
deliver Israel [1]through me, as Thou hast
spoken."
38 And it was so. When he arose early
the next morning and squeezed the
fleece, he drained the dew from the
fleece, a bowl full of water.
39 Then Gideon said to God, "[a]Do
not let Thine anger burn against me that
I may speak once more; please let me
make a test once more with the fleece, let
it now be dry only on the fleece, and let
there be dew on all the ground."
40 And God did so that night; for it
was dry only on the fleece, and dew was
on all the ground.

Gideon's 300 Chosen Men

7 THEN [a]Jerubbaal (that is, Gideon)
and all the people who were with
him, rose early and camped beside [1]the
spring of Harod; and the camp of Midian was on the north side of [2]them by
the hill of [b]Moreh in the valley.
2 And the LORD said to Gideon,
"The people who are with you are too
many for Me to give Midian into their
hands, [a]lest Israel [1]become boastful,
saying, 'My own [2]power has delivered
me.'
3 "Now therefore [1]come, proclaim in
the hearing of the people, saying, '[a]Who-
ever is afraid and trembling, let him
return and depart from Mount Gilead.' "
So 22,000 people returned, but 10,000
remained.
4 [a]Then the LORD said to Gideon,
"The people are still too many; bring
them down to the water and I will test
them for you there. Therefore it shall be
that he of whom I say to you, 'This one
shall go with you,' he shall go with you;
but everyone of whom I say to you, 'This
one shall not go with you,' he shall not
go."
5 So he brought the people down to
the water. And the LORD said to Gideon,
"You shall separate everyone who laps
the water with his tongue, as a dog laps,
as well as everyone who kneels to drink."
6 Now the number of those who
lapped, putting their hand to their
mouth, was 300 men; but all the rest of
the people kneeled to drink water.
7 And the LORD said to Gideon, "I
will deliver you [a]with the 300 men who
lapped and will give the Midianites into
your hands; so let all the *other* people go,
each man to his [1]home."

21 [1]Or, *departed* [a]Lev. 9:24

22 [1]Lit., *Gideon* [2]Heb., *YHWH*, usually rendered *LORD* [a]Gen. 32:30; Ex. 33:20; Judg. 13:21, 22

24 [1]Heb., *Yahweh-shalom* [a]Judg. 8:32

25 [1]Or, *even* [2]I.e., wooden symbol of a female deity, also vv. 26, 28, 30 [a]Ex. 34:13

31 [1]Or, *contend*

32 [a]Judg. 7:1

33 [a]Josh. 17:16

34 [1]Lit., *clothed* [a]Judg. 3:10 [b]Judg. 3:27

35 [a]Judg. 4:6, 10; 5:18 [b]Judg. 7:3

36 [1]Lit., *by my hand* [a]Judg. 6:14, 16, 17

37 [1]Lit., *by my hand*

39 [a]Gen. 18:32

1 [1]Or, *En-Harod* [2]Lit., *him* [a]Judg. 6:32 [b]Gen. 12:6; Deut. 11:30

2 [1]Lit., *glorify itself against me* [2]Lit., *hand* [a]Deut. 8:17, 18

3 [1]Or, *please* [a]Deut. 20:8

4 [a]1 Sam. 14:6

7 [1]Lit., *place* [a]1 Sam. 14:6

8 So [1]the 300 men took the people's
provisions and their trumpets into their
hands. And [2]Gideon sent all the *other*
men of Israel, each to his tent, but
retained the 300 men; and the camp of
Midian was below him in the valley.
9 Now the same night it came about
that the LORD said to him, "Arise, go
down against the camp, [a]for I have given
it into your hands.
10 "But if you are afraid to go down, go
with Purah your servant down to the
camp,
11 and you will hear what they say;
and [a]afterward your hands will be
strengthened that you may go down
against the camp." So he went with
Purah his servant down to the [1]outposts
of the army that was in the camp.
12 Now the Midianites and the Amalekites and all the sons of the east were
lying in the valley [a]as numerous as
locusts; and their camels were without
number, [b]as numerous as the sand on
the seashore.
13 When Gideon came, behold, a man
was relating a dream to his friend. And
he said, "Behold, I [1]had a dream; [2]a loaf
of barley bread was tumbling into the
camp of Midian, and it came to the tent
and struck it so that it fell, and turned it
[3]upside down so that the tent lay flat."
14 And his friend answered and said,
"This is nothing less than the sword of
Gideon the son of Joash, a man of
Israel; God has given Midian and all the
camp [a]into his hand."
15 And it came about when Gideon
heard the account of the dream and its
interpretation, that he bowed in worship.
He returned to the camp of Israel and
said, "Arise, for the LORD has given the
camp of Midian into your hands."
16 And he divided the 300 men into
three [1]companies, and he put trumpets
and empty pitchers into the hands of all
of them, with torches inside the pitchers.
17 And he said to them, "Look at me,
and do likewise. And behold, when I
come to the outskirts of the camp, [1]do as
I do.
18 "When I and all who are with me
blow the trumpet, then you also blow the
trumpets all around the camp, and say,
'For the LORD and for Gideon.' "

Confusion of the Enemy

19 So Gideon and the hundred men
who were with him came to the outskirts
of the camp at the beginning of the
middle watch, when they had just posted
the watch; and they blew the trumpets
and smashed the pitchers that were in
their hands.
20 When the three [1]companies blew
the trumpets and broke the pitchers,
they held the torches in their left hands
and the trumpets in their right hands for
blowing, and cried, "A sword for the
LORD and for Gideon!"
21 And each stood in his place around
the camp; and [a]all the [1]army ran, crying
out as they fled.
22 And when they blew 300 trumpets,
the [a]LORD set the sword of one against
another even throughout the whole
[1]army; and the [1]army fled as far as Beth-
shittah toward Zererah, as far as the
edge of [b]Abel-meholah, by Tabbath.
23 And the men of Israel were summoned from [a]Naphtali and Asher and
all Manasseh, and they pursued Midian.
24 And Gideon sent messengers
throughout all the hill country of
Ephraim, saying, "Come down [1]against
Midian and [a]take the waters before
them, as far as Beth-barah and the
Jordan." So all the men of Ephraim were
summoned, and they took the waters as
far as Beth-barah and the Jordan.
25 And they captured the two leaders
of Midian, [a]Oreb and Zeeb, and they
killed Oreb at the rock of Oreb, and they
killed Zeeb at the wine press of Zeeb,
while they pursued Midian; and they
brought the heads of Oreb and Zeeb to
Gideon [b]from across the Jordan.

Zeba and Zalmunna Routed

8 THEN the men of Ephraim said to
him, "[a]What is this thing you have
done to us, not calling us when you went
to fight against Midian?" And they
contended with him vigorously.
2 But he said to them, "What have I
done now in comparison with you? Is
not the gleaning *of the grapes* of
Ephraim better than the vintage of
Abiezer?
3 "God has given the leaders of Midian, Oreb and Zeeb into your hands; and
what was I able to do in comparison
with you?" Then their [1]anger toward
him subsided when he said [2]that.
4 Then Gideon and the 300 men who
were with him came [a]to the Jordan *and*
crossed over, weary yet pursuing.
5 And he said to the men of [a]Suc-
coth, "Please give loaves of bread to the
people who are following me, for they
are weary, and I am pursuing Zebah and
Zalmunna, the kings of Midian."
6 And the leaders of Succoth said,
"[1a]Are the hands of Zebah and Zalmunna already in your hands, that we
should give bread to your army?"
7 And Gideon said, "[1]All right,
[a]when the LORD has given Zebah and
Zalmunna into my hand, then I will
[2]thrash your [3]bodies with the thorns of
the wilderness and with briers."
8 And he went up from there to
[1a]Penuel, and spoke similarly to them;
and the men of Penuel answered him
just as the men of Succoth had answered.
9 So he spoke also to the men of
Penuel, saying, "When I return safely, [a]I
will tear down this tower."
10 Now Zebah and Zalmunna were in
Karkor, and their [1]armies with them,
about 15,000 men, all who were left of
the entire [2]army of the sons of the east;
[a]for the fallen were 120,000 [3]swordsmen.

8 [1]Lit., *they* [2]Lit., *he*
9 [a]Josh. 2:24; 10:8; 11:6
11 [1]Lit., *extremity of the battle array* [a]Judg. 7:15; 1 Sam. 14:9, 10
12 [a]Judg. 6:5; 8:10 [b]Josh. 11:4
13 [1]Lit., *dreamed* [2]Lit., *and behold, a loaf* [3]Lit., *upwards*
14 [a]Josh. 2:9
16 [1]Lit., *heads*
17 [1]Lit., *it shall come about that just as I do, so you shall do.*
20 [1]Lit., *heads*
21 [1]Or, *camp* [a]2 Kin. 7:7
22 [1]Or, *camp* [a]1 Sam. 14:20 [b]1 Kin. 4:12; 19:16
23 [a]Judg. 6:35
24 [1]Lit., *to meet* [a]Judg. 3:28
25 [a]Ps. 83:11; Is. 10:26 [b]Judg. 8:4
1 [a]Judg. 12:1
3 [1]Lit., *spirit* [2]Lit., *this thing*
4 [a]Judg. 7:25
5 [a]Gen. 33:17
6 [1]Lit., *Is the palm* [a]Judg. 8:15
7 [1]Lit., *For thus* [2]Or, *trample* [3]Lit., *flesh* [a]Judg. 7:15
8 [1]In Gen. 32:30, *Peniel* [a]Gen. 32:31
9 [a]Judg. 8:17
10 [1]Or, *camps* [2]Or, *camp* [3]Lit., *men who drew sword* [a]Judg. 6:5; 7:12; Is. 9:4

11 And Gideon went up by the way of
those who lived in tents on the east of
Nobah and Jogbehah, and [1]attacked the
camp, when the camp was [2]unsuspect-
ing.
12 When Zebah and Zalmunna fled,
he pursued them and captured the two
kings of Midian, Zebah and Zalmunna,
and routed the whole [1]army.
13 Then Gideon the son of Joash
returned from the battle [1]by the ascent
of Heres.
14 And he captured a youth [1]from
Succoth and questioned him. Then *the
youth* wrote down for him the princes of
Succoth and its elders, seventy-seven
men.
15 And he came to the men of Succoth
and said, "Behold Zebah and Zalmunna,
concerning whom you taunted me, saying, '[1][a]Are the hands of Zebah and
Zalmunna already in your hand, that we
should give bread to your men who are
weary?' "
16 And he took the elders of the city,
and thorns of the wilderness and briers,
and he [1]disciplined the men of Succoth
with them.
17 [a]And he tore down the tower of
Penuel and killed the men of the city.
18 Then he said to Zebah and Zalmunna, "What kind of men *were* they
whom you killed at Tabor?" And they
said, "They were like you, each one
[1]resembling the son of a king."
19 And he said, "They *were* my brothers, the sons of my mother. *As* the LORD
lives, if only you had let them live, I
would not kill you."
20 So he said to Jether his first-born,
"Rise, kill them." But the youth did not
draw his sword, for he was afraid, because he was still a youth.
21 Then Zebah and Zalmunna said,
"Rise up yourself, and fall on us; for as
the man, so is his strength." [a]So Gideon
arose and killed Zebah and Zalmunna,
and [b]took the crescent ornaments which
were on their camels' necks.
22 Then the men of Israel said to
Gideon, "Rule over us, both you and
your son, also your son's son, for you
have delivered us from the hand of
Midian."
23 But Gideon said to them, "I will
not rule over you, nor shall my son rule
over you; [a]the LORD shall rule over
you."
24 Yet Gideon said to them, "I would
[1]request of you, that each of you give me
[2]an earring from his spoil." (For they
had gold earrings, because they were
[a]Ishmaelites.)
25 And they said, "We will surely give
them." So they spread out a garment,
and every one of them threw an earring
there from his spoil.
26 And the weight of the gold earrings
that he requested was 1,700 *shekels* of
gold, besides the crescent ornaments and
the pendants and the purple robes which
were on the kings of Midian, and besides
the neck bands that *were* on their camels' necks.
27 And Gideon made it into [a]an
ephod, and placed it in his city, Ophrah,
and all Israel played the harlot with it
there, so that it became a snare to
Gideon and his household.

Forty Years of Peace

28 So Midian was subdued before the
sons of Israel, and they did not lift up
their heads anymore. And the land was
undisturbed for forty years in the days
of Gideon.
29 Then [a]Jerubbaal the son of Joash
went and lived in his own house.
30 Now Gideon had [a]seventy sons
who [1]were his direct descendants, for he
had many wives.
31 And his concubine who was in
Shechem also bore him a son, and he
[1]named him Abimelech.
32 And Gideon the son of Joash died
at a ripe old age and was buried in the
tomb of his father Joash, in Ophrah of
the Abiezrites.
33 Then it came about, as soon as
Gideon was dead, [a]that the sons of Israel
again played the harlot with the Baals,
and made [b]Baal-berith their god.
34 Thus the sons of Israel [a]did not
remember the LORD their God, who had
delivered them from the hands of all
their enemies on every side;
35 [a]nor did they show kindness to the
household of Jerubbaal (*that is,* Gideon),
in accord with all the good that he had
done to Israel.

Abimelech's Conspiracy

9 AND [a]Abimelech the son of Jerubbaal went to Shechem to his moth-
er's [1]relatives, and spoke to them and to
the whole clan of the household of his
mother's father, saying,
2 "Speak, now, in the hearing of all
the leaders of Shechem, 'Which is better
for you, that [a]seventy men, all the sons
of Jerubbaal, rule over you, or that one
man rule over you?' Also, remember that
I am [b]your bone and your flesh."
3 And his mother's [1]relatives spoke
all these words on his behalf in the
hearing of all the leaders of Shechem;
and [2]they were inclined to follow Abimelech, for they said, "He is [a]our [3]rela-
tive."
4 And they gave him seventy *pieces*
of silver from the house of [a]Baal-berith
with which Abimelech hired worthless
and reckless fellows, and they followed
him.
5 Then he went to his father's house
at Ophrah, and [a]killed his brothers the
sons of Jerubbaal, [b]seventy men, on one
stone. But Jotham the youngest son of
Jerubbaal was left, for he hid himself.
6 And all the men of Shechem and
all [1]Beth-millo assembled together, and
they went and made Abimelech king, by
the [2]oak of the pillar which was in
Shechem.

11 [1]Lit., *smote* [2]Or, *secure*
12 [1]Or, *camp*
13 [1]Or, *from*
14 [1]Lit., *of the men of*
15 [1]Lit., *Is the palm* [a]Judg. 8:6
16 [1]Lit., *made the men . . . to know*
17 [a]Judg. 8:9
18 [1]Lit., *like the form of the sons*
21 [a]Ps. 83:11 [b]Judg. 8:26
23 [a]1 Sam. 8:7; 10:19; 12:12; Ps. 10:16
24 [1]Lit., *request a request* [2]Or, *a nose ring* [a]Gen. 25:13-16
27 [a]Ex. 28:6-35; Judg. 17:5; 18:14-20
29 [a]Judg. 7:1
30 [1]Lit., *came from his loins* [a]Judg. 9:2, 5
31 [1]Lit., *appointed his name*
33 [a]Judg. 2:11, 12 [b]Judg. 9:4, 27, 46
34 [a]Deut. 4:9; Judg. 3:7
35 [a]Judg. 9:16-18
1 [1]Lit., *brothers* [a]Judg. 8:31, 35
2 [a]Judg. 8:30; 9:5, 18 [b]Gen. 29:14
3 [1]Lit., *brothers* [2]Lit., *their hearts inclined after* [3]Lit., *brother* [a]Gen. 29:15
4 [a]Judg. 8:33
5 [a]2 Kin. 11:1, 2 [b]Judg. 8:30; 9:2, 18
6 [1]Or, *the house of Millo* [2]Or, *terebinth*

7 Now when they told Jotham, he
went and stood on the top of [a]Mount
Gerizim, and lifted his voice and called
out. Thus he said to them, "Listen to me,
O men of Shechem, that God may listen
to you.
8 "Once the trees went forth to anoint
a king over them, and they said to the
olive tree, 'Reign over us!'
9 "But the olive tree said to them,
'Shall I leave my fatness with [1]which
God and men are honored, and go to
wave over the trees?'
10 "Then the trees said to the fig tree,
'You come, reign over us!'
11 "But the fig tree said to them, 'Shall
I leave my sweetness and my good [1]fruit,
and go to wave over the trees?'
12 "Then the trees said to the vine,
'You come, reign over us!'
13 "But the vine said to them, 'Shall I
leave my new wine, which cheers God
and men, and go to wave over the trees?'
14 "Finally all the trees said to the
bramble, 'You come, reign over us!'
15 "And the bramble said to the trees,
'If in [1]truth you are anointing me as king
over you, come and take refuge in my
shade; but if not, may fire come out
from the bramble and consume the
cedars of Lebanon.'
16 "Now therefore, if you have dealt in
[1]truth and integrity in making Abimelech king, and if you have dealt well
with [a]Jerubbaal and his house, and
[2]have dealt with him [3]as he deserved—
17 for my father fought for you and
[1]risked his life and delivered you from
the hand of Midian;
18 but you have risen against my
father's house today and have killed [a]his
sons, seventy men, on one stone, and
have made Abimelech, [b]the son of his
maidservant, king over the men of Shechem, because he is your [1]relative—
19 if then you have dealt in [1]truth and
integrity with Jerubbaal and his house
this day, rejoice in Abimelech, and let
him also rejoice in you.
20 "But if not, let fire come out from
Abimelech and consume the men of
Shechem and [1]Beth-millo; and let fire
come out from the men of Shechem and
from [1]Beth-millo, and consume Abimelech."
21 Then Jotham escaped and fled, and
went to Beer and remained there because of Abimelech his brother.

Shechem and Abimelech Fall

22 Now Abimelech ruled over Israel
three years.
23 [a]Then God sent an evil spirit between Abimelech and the men of Shechem; and the men of Shechem [b]dealt
treacherously with Abimelech,
24 [a]in order that the violence [1]done to
the seventy sons of Jerubbaal might
come, and [b]their blood might be laid on
Abimelech their brother, who killed
them, and on the men of Shechem, who
strengthened his hands to kill his
brothers.
25 And the men of Shechem set [1]men
in ambush against him on the tops of the
mountains, and they robbed all who
might pass by them along the road; and
it was told to Abimelech.
26 Now Gaal the son of Ebed came
with his [1]relatives, and crossed over into
Shechem; and the men of Shechem put
their trust in him.
27 And they went out into the field
and gathered *the grapes of* their vineyards and trod *them,* and held a [1]festi-
val; and they went into the house of
[a]their god, and ate and drank and cursed
Abimelech.
28 Then Gaal the son of Ebed said,
"Who is Abimelech, and who is Shechem, that we should serve him? Is he
not the son of Jerubbaal, and *is* Zebul
not his [1]lieutenant? Serve the men of
[a]Hamor the father of Shechem; but why
should we serve him?
29 "[1][a]Would, therefore, that this people
were under my authority! Then I would
remove Abimelech." And he said to
Abimelech, "Increase your army, and
come out."
30 And when Zebul the ruler of the
city heard the words of Gaal the son of
Ebed, his anger burned.
31 And he sent messengers to Abimelech [1]deceitfully, saying, "Behold, Gaal
the son of Ebed and his [2]relatives have
come to Shechem; and behold, they are
[3]stirring up the city against you.
32 "Now therefore, arise by night, you
and the people who are with you, and lie
in wait in the field.
33 "And it shall come about in the
morning, as soon as the sun is up, that
you shall rise early and rush upon the
city; and behold, when he and the people who are with him come out against
you, you shall [a]do to them [1]whatever
you can."
34 So Abimelech and all the people
who *were* with him arose by night and
lay in wait against Shechem in four
[1]companies.
35 Now Gaal the son of Ebed went
out and stood in the entrance of the city
gate; and Abimelech and the people who
were with him arose from the ambush.
36 And when Gaal saw the people, he
said to Zebul, "[1]Look, people are coming down from the tops of the mountains." But Zebul said to him, "You are
seeing the shadow of the mountains as *if
they were* men."
37 And Gaal spoke again and said,
"Behold, people are coming down from
[a]the [1]highest part of the land, and one
[2]company comes by the way of [3]the
diviners' [4]oak."
38 Then Zebul said to him, "Where is
your [1]boasting now with which you said,
'Who is Abimelech that we should serve
him?' Is this not the people whom you
despised? Go out now and fight with
them!"
39 So Gaal went out before the leaders of Shechem and fought with Abimelech.

7 [a]Deut. 11:29, 30
9 [1]Lit., *which by me*
11 [1]Or, *produce*
15 [1]Or, *sincerity*
16 [1]Or, *sincerity* [2]Lit., *if you have* [3]Lit., *according to the dealing of his hands* [a]Judg. 8:35
17 [1]Lit., *cast his soul in front*
18 [1]Lit., *brother* [a]Judg. 8:30; 9:2, 5 [b]Judg. 8:31
19 [1]Or, *sincerity*
20 [1]Or, *the house of Millo*
23 [a]1 Sam. 16:14; Is. 19:2, 14 [b]Is. 33:1
24 [1]Lit., *of the seventy* [a]Deut. 27:25; Judg. 9:56, 57 [b]Num. 35:33
25 [1]Lit., *liers-in-wait for*
26 [1]Lit., *brothers*
27 [1]Lit., *rejoicing* [a]Judg. 8:33; 9:46
28 [1]Lit., *overseer* [a]Gen. 34:2
29 [1]Lit., *And who will give this people into my hand* [a]2 Sam. 15:4
31 [1]Or, *in Tormah* [2]Lit., *brothers* [3]Lit., *besieging*
33 [1]Lit., *as your hand can find* [a]1 Sam. 10:7
34 [1]Lit., *heads*
36 [1]Lit., *Behold*
37 [1]Or, *center* [2]Lit., *head* [3]Heb., *Elommeonenim* [4]Or, *terebinth* [a]Ezek. 38:12
38 [1]Lit., *mouth*

40 And Abimelech chased him, and he fled before him; and many fell wounded up to the entrance of the gate.

41 Then Abimelech remained at Arumah, but Zebul drove out Gaal and his [1]relatives so that they could not remain in Shechem.

42 Now it came about the next day, that the people went out to the field, and it was told to Abimelech.

43 So he took [1]his people and divided them into three [2]companies, and lay in wait in the field; when he looked and [3]saw the people coming out from the city, he arose against them and [4]slew them.

44 Then Abimelech and the [1]company who was with him dashed forward and stood in the entrance of the city gate; the other two [2]companies then dashed against all who *were* in the field and [3]slew them.

45 And Abimelech fought against the city all that day, and he captured the city and killed the people who *were* in it; then he [a]razed the city and sowed it with salt.

46 When all the leaders of the tower of Shechem heard of *it,* they entered the inner chamber of the [1]temple of [a]El-berith.

47 And it was told Abimelech that all the leaders of the tower of Shechem were gathered together.

48 So Abimelech went up to Mount [a]Zalmon, he and all the people who *were* with him; and Abimelech took [1]an axe in his hand and cut down a branch from the trees, and lifted it and laid *it* on his shoulder. Then he said to the people who *were* with him, "What you have seen me do, hurry *and* do [2]likewise."

49 And all the people also cut down each one his branch and followed Abimelech, and put *them* on the inner chamber and set the inner chamber on fire over those *inside,* so that all the men of the tower of Shechem also died, about a thousand men and women.

50 Then Abimelech went to Thebez, and he camped against Thebez and captured it.

51 But there was a strong tower in the center of the city, and all the men and women with all the leaders of the city fled there and shut themselves in; and they went up on the roof of the tower.

52 So Abimelech came to the tower and fought against it, and approached the entrance of the tower to burn it with fire.

53 But [a]a certain woman threw an upper millstone on Abimelech's head, crushing his skull.

54 Then [a]he called quickly to the young man, his armor bearer, and said to him, "Draw your sword and kill me, lest it be said of me, 'A woman slew him.' " So [1]the young man pierced him through, and he died.

55 And when the men of Israel saw that Abimelech was dead, each departed to his [1]home.

56 Thus [a]God repaid the wickedness of Abimelech, which he had done to his father, in killing his seventy brothers.

57 Also God returned all the wickedness of the men of Shechem on their heads, and the curse of Jotham the son of Jerubbaal came [1]upon them.

Oppression of Philistines and Ammonites

10 NOW after Abimelech died, Tola the son of Puah, the son of Dodo, a man of Issachar, [a]arose to save Israel; and he lived in Shamir in the hill country of Ephraim.

2 And he judged Israel twenty-three years. Then he died and was buried in Shamir.

3 And after him, Jair the Gileadite arose, and judged Israel twenty-two years.

4 And he had thirty sons who rode on thirty donkeys, and they had thirty cities [1]in the land of Gilead [a]that are called [2]Havvoth-jair to this day.

5 And Jair died and was buried in Kamon.

6 Then the sons of Israel again did evil in the sight of the LORD, [a]served the Baals and the Ashtaroth, the gods of Aram, the gods of Sidon, the gods of Moab, [b]the gods of the sons of Ammon, and the gods of the Philistines; thus [c]they forsook the LORD and did not serve Him.

7 And the anger of the LORD burned against Israel, and He [a]sold them into the hands of the Philistines, and into the hands of the sons of Ammon.

8 And they [1]afflicted and crushed the sons of Israel [2]that year; for eighteen years they *afflicted* all the sons of Israel who were beyond the Jordan [3]in Gilead in the land of the Amorites.

9 And the sons of Ammon crossed the Jordan to fight also against Judah, Benjamin, and the house of Ephraim, so that Israel was greatly distressed.

10 Then the [a]sons of Israel cried out to the LORD, saying, "We have sinned against Thee, for indeed, we have forsaken our God and served the Baals."

11 And the LORD said to the sons of Israel, "*Did I* not *deliver you* [a]from the Egyptians, [b]the Amorites, [c]the sons of Ammon, and the Philistines?

12 "Also when the Sidonians, the Amalekites and the Maonites [a]oppressed you, you cried out to Me, and I delivered you from their hands.

13 "Yet [a]you have forsaken Me and served other gods; therefore I will deliver you no more.

14 "[a]Go and cry out to the gods which you have chosen; let them deliver you in the time of your distress."

15 And the sons of Israel said to the LORD, "We have sinned, [a]do to us whatever seems good to Thee; only please deliver us this day."

16 [a]So they put away the foreign gods from among them, and served the LORD; and [1b]He could bear the misery of Israel no longer.

41 [1]Lit., *brothers*
43 [1]Lit., *the* [2]Lit., *heads* [3]Lit., *behold* [4]Lit., *smote*
44 [1]Singular with Gr.; Heb. plural, *heads* [2]Lit., *heads* [3]Lit., *smote*
45 [a]2 Kin. 3:25
46 [1]Lit., *house* [a]Judg. 8:33
48 [1]Lit., *the axes* [2]Lit., *like me* [a]Ps. 68:14
53 [a]2 Sam. 11:21
54 [1]Lit., *his* [a]1 Sam. 31:4
55 [1]Lit., *place*
56 [a]Gen. 9:5, 6; Ps. 94:23
57 [1]Lit., *to*
1 [a]Judg. 2:16
4 [1]Lit., *which are in* [2]I.e., the towns of Jair [a]Num. 32:41
6 [a]Judg. 2:13 [b]Judg. 11:24 [c]Deut. 31:16, 17; 32:15
7 [a]1 Sam. 12:9
8 [1]Lit., *shattered* [2]Lit., *in that* [3]Lit., *which is in*
10 [a]1 Sam. 12:10
11 [a]Judg. 2:12 [b]Num. 21:21-25 [c]Judg. 3:13
12 [a]Ps. 106:42
13 [a]Jer. 2:13
14 [a]Deut. 32:37
15 [a]1 Sam. 3:18
16 [1]Lit., *His soul was short with the misery* [a]Josh. 24:23 [b]Deut. 32:36

17 Then the sons of Ammon were
summoned, and they camped in Gilead.
And the sons of Israel gathered together,
and camped in [a]Mizpah.
18 And the people, the leaders of
Gilead, said to one another, "Who is the
man who will begin to fight against the
sons of Ammon? He shall become head
over all the inhabitants of Gilead."

Jephthah the Ninth Judge

11 NOW [a]Jephthah the Gileadite
was a [1]valiant warrior, but he was
the son of a harlot. And Gilead [2]was the
father of Jephthah.
2 And Gilead's wife bore him sons;
and when his wife's sons grew up, they
drove Jephthah out and said to him,
"You shall not have an inheritance in
our father's house, for you are the son of
another woman."
3 So Jephthah fled from his brothers
and lived in the land of [a]Tob; and
worthless fellows gathered themselves
[1]about Jephthah, and they went out with
him.
4 And it came about after a while
that [a]the sons of Ammon fought against
Israel.
5 And it happened when the sons of
Ammon fought against Israel that the
elders of Gilead went to get Jephthah
from the land of Tob;
6 and they said to Jephthah, "Come
and be our chief that we may fight
against the sons of Ammon."
7 Then Jephthah said to the elders of
Gilead, "[a]Did you not hate me and drive
me from my father's house? So why have
you come to me now when you are in
trouble?"
8 And the elders of Gilead said to
Jephthah, "For this reason we have now
returned to you, that you may go with us
and fight with the sons of Ammon and
[a]become head over all the inhabitants of
Gilead."
9 So Jephthah said to the elders of
Gilead, "If you take me back to fight
against the sons of Ammon and the
LORD gives them up [1]to me, will I
become your head?"
10 And the elders of Gilead said to
Jephthah, "[a]The LORD is [1]witness between us; surely we will do [2]as you have
said."
11 Then Jephthah went with the elders
of Gilead, and the people made him
head and chief over them; and Jephthah
spoke all his words before the LORD at
[a]Mizpah.
12 Now Jephthah sent messengers to
the king of the sons of Ammon, saying,
"What is between you and me, that you
have come to me to fight against my
land?"
13 And the king of the sons of Ammon said to the messengers of Jephthah,
"Because Israel [a]took away my land
when they came up from Egypt, from
the Arnon as far as the [b]Jabbok and the
Jordan; therefore, return them peaceably
now."
14 But Jephthah sent messengers
again to the king of the sons of Ammon,
15 and they said to him, "Thus says
Jephthah, 'Israel did not take away the
land of Moab, nor the land of the sons
of Ammon.
16 'For when they came up from
Egypt, and Israel [a]went through the
wilderness to the [1]Red Sea and [b]came to
Kadesh,
17 then Israel [a]sent messengers to the
king of Edom, saying, "Please let us pass
through your land," but the king of
Edom would not listen. [b]And they also
sent to the king of Moab, but he would
not consent. So Israel remained at Kadesh.
18 'Then they went through the wilderness and [a]around the land of Edom and
the land of Moab, and came to the east
side of the land of Moab, and they
camped beyond the Arnon; but they
[b]did not enter the territory of Moab, for
the Arnon *was* the border of Moab.
19 'And Israel sent [a]messengers to
Sihon king of the Amorites, the king of
Heshbon, and Israel said to him, "Please
let us pass through your land to our
place."
20 'But Sihon did not trust Israel to
pass through his territory; so Sihon
gathered all his people and camped in
Jahaz, and fought with Israel.
21 'And the LORD, the God of Israel,
gave Sihon and all his people into the
hand of Israel, and they [1a]defeated
them; so Israel possessed all the land of
the Amorites, the inhabitants of that
country.
22 '[a]So they possessed all the territory
of the Amorites, from the Arnon as far
as the Jabbok, and from the wilderness
as far as the Jordan.
23 'Since now the LORD, the God of
Israel, drove out the Amorites from
before His people Israel, are you then to
possess it?
24 'Do you not possess what [a]Che-
mosh your god gives you to possess? So
whatever the LORD our God has driven
out before us, we will possess it.
25 'And now are you any better than
[a]Balak the son of Zippor, king of Moab?
Did he ever strive with Israel, or did he
ever fight against them?
26 '[a]While Israel lived in Heshbon and
its villages, and in Aroer and its villages,
and in all the cities that are on the banks
of the Arnon, three hundred years, why
did you not recover them within that
time?
27 'I therefore have not sinned against
you, but you are doing me wrong by
making war against me; [a]may the LORD,
the Judge, judge today between the sons
of Israel and the sons of Ammon.'"
28 But the king of the sons of Ammon
[1]disregarded the message which Jephthah sent him.

17 [a]Judg. 11:29
1 [1]Or, *mighty man of valor* [2]Lit., *begat* [a]Heb. 11:32
3 [1]Lit., *to* [a]2 Sam. 10:6, 8
4 [a]Judg. 10:9, 17
7 [a]Gen. 26:27
8 [a]Judg. 10:18
9 [1]Lit., *before*
10 [1]Lit., *hearer* [2]Lit., *according to your word* [a]Gen. 31:50; Jer. 29:23; 42:5; Mic. 1:2
11 [a]Judg. 10:17; 11:29; 20:1; 1 Sam. 10:17
13 [a]Num. 21:24 [b]Gen. 32:22
16 [1]Lit., *Sea of Reeds* [a]Num. 14:25; Deut. 1:40 [b]Num. 20:1, 4-21
17 [a]Num. 20:14-21 [b]Josh. 24:9
18 [a]Num. 21:4; Deut. 2:8 [b]Deut. 2:9, 18, 19
19 [a]Num. 21:21-32; Deut. 2:26-36
21 [1]Lit., *smote* [a]Num. 21:24; Deut. 2:32-34
22 [a]Deut. 2:36, 37
24 [a]Num. 21:29; 1 Kin. 11:7
25 [a]Num. 22:2; Josh. 24:9; Mic. 6:5
26 [a]Num. 21:25, 26; Deut. 2:36
27 [a]Gen. 16:5; 18:25; 31:53; 1 Sam. 24:12, 15
28 [1]Lit., *did not listen to the words*

Jephthah's Tragic Vow

29 Now [a]the Spirit of the LORD came upon Jephthah, so that he passed through Gilead and Manasseh; then he passed through Mizpah of Gilead, and from Mizpah of Gilead he went on to the sons of Ammon.

30 And Jephthah made a vow to the LORD and said, "If Thou wilt indeed give the sons of Ammon into my hand,

31 then it shall be that whatever comes out of the doors of my house to meet me when I return in peace from the sons of Ammon, it shall be the LORD'S, and I will offer it up as a burnt offering."

32 So Jephthah crossed over to the sons of Ammon to fight against them; and the LORD gave them into his hand.

33 And he struck them with a very great slaughter from Aroer [1]to the entrance of [a]Minnith, twenty cities, and as far as Abel-keramim. So the sons of Ammon were subdued before the sons of Israel.

34 When Jephthah came to his house at [a]Mizpah, behold, his daughter was coming out to meet him [b]with tambourines and with dancing. Now she was his one *and* only child; besides her he had neither son nor daughter.

35 And it came about when he saw her, that he tore his clothes and said, "Alas, my daughter! You have brought me very low, and you are among those who trouble me; for I have [1]given my word to the LORD, and [a]I cannot take *it* back."

36 So she said to him, "My father, you have [1]given your word to the LORD; [a]do to me [2]as you have said, since the LORD has avenged you of your enemies, the sons of Ammon."

37 And she said to her father, "Let this thing be done for me; let me alone two months, that I may [1]go to the mountains and weep because of [a]my virginity, I and my companions."

38 Then he said, "Go." So he sent her away for two months; and she left with her companions, and wept on the mountains because of her virginity.

39 And it came about at the end of two months that she returned to her father, who did to her according to the vow which he had made; and she [1]had no relations with a man. Thus it became a custom in Israel,

40 that the daughters of Israel went yearly to [1]commemorate the daughter of Jephthah the Gileadite four days in the year.

Jephthah and His Successors

12 THEN the men of Ephraim were summoned, and they crossed [1]to Zaphon and [a]said to Jephthah, "Why did you cross over to fight against the sons of Ammon without calling us to go with you? We will burn your house down on you."

2 And Jephthah said to them, "I and my people were at great strife with the sons of Ammon; when I called you, you did not deliver me from their hand.

3 "And when I saw that you would not deliver *me,* I [1a]took my life in my hands and crossed over against the sons of Ammon, and the LORD gave them into my hand. Why then have you come up to me this day, to fight against me?"

4 Then Jephthah gathered all the men of Gilead and fought Ephraim; and the men of Gilead [1]defeated Ephraim, because they said, "You are fugitives of Ephraim, O Gileadites, in the midst of Ephraim *and* in the midst of Manasseh."

5 And the Gileadites [a]captured the fords of the Jordan opposite Ephraim. And it happened when *any of* the fugitives of Ephraim said, "Let me cross over," the men of Gilead would say to him, "Are you an Ephraimite?" If he said, "No,"

6 then they would say to him, "Say now, 'Shibboleth.' " But he said, "Sibboleth," for he could not [1]pronounce it correctly. Then they seized him and slew him at the fords of the Jordan. Thus there fell at that time 42,000 of Ephraim.

7 And Jephthah judged Israel six years. Then Jephthah the Gileadite died and was buried in *one of* the cities of Gilead.

8 Now Ibzan of Bethlehem judged Israel after him.

9 And he had thirty sons, and thirty daughters *whom* he [1]gave in marriage outside *the family,* and he brought in thirty daughters from outside for his sons. And he judged Israel seven years.

10 Then Ibzan died and was buried in Bethlehem.

11 Now Elon the Zebulunite judged Israel after him; and he judged Israel ten years.

12 Then Elon the Zebulunite died and was buried at Aijalon in the land of Zebulun.

13 Now Abdon the son of Hillel the Pirathonite judged Israel after him.

14 And he had forty sons and thirty grandsons who rode on seventy donkeys; and he judged Israel eight years.

15 Then Abdon the son of Hillel the Pirathonite died and was buried at Pirathon in the land of Ephraim, in the hill country of the Amalekites.

Philistines Oppress Again

13 NOW the sons of Israel [a]again did evil in the sight of the LORD, so that the LORD gave them into the hands of the Philistines forty years.

2 And there was a certain man of [a]Zorah, of the family of the Danites, whose name was Manoah; and his wife was barren and had borne no *children.*

3 [a]Then the angel of the LORD appeared to the woman, and said to her, "Behold now, you are barren and have borne no *children,* but you shall conceive and give birth to a son.

4 "Now therefore, be careful [a]not to drink wine or strong drink, nor eat any unclean thing.

29 [a]Judg. 3:10

33 [1]Lit., *even until you are coming to* [a]Ezek. 27:17

34 [a]Judg. 10:17; 11:11 [b]Ex. 15:20; 1 Sam. 18:6; Jer. 31:4

35 [1]Lit., *opened my mouth* [a]Num. 30:2; Eccl. 5:4, 5

36 [1]Lit., *opened your mouth* [2]Lit., *according to what has proceeded from your mouth* [a]Num. 30:2

37 [1]Lit., *go and go down on* [a]Gen. 30:23; Luke 1:25

39 [1]Lit., *knew no man*

40 [1]Lit., *recount;* ancient versions, *lament*

1 [1]Or, *northward* [a]Judg. 8:1

3 [1]Lit., *put my soul in my palm* [a]1 Sam. 19:5; 28:21; Job 13:14

4 [1]Lit., *smote*

5 [a]Judg. 3:28

6 [1]Lit., *speak so*

9 [1]Lit., *sent outside*

1 [a]Judg. 2:11

2 [a]Josh. 19:41

3 [a]Judg. 6:11, 14; 13:6, 8, 10, 11; Luke 1:11-13

4 [a]Num. 6:2, 3; Luke 1:15

5 "[a]For behold, you shall conceive
and give birth to a son, and no razor
shall come upon his head, for the boy
shall be a [b]Nazirite to God from the
womb; and he shall begin to deliver
Israel from the hands of the Philistines."
6 Then the woman came and told her
husband, saying, "[a]A man of God came
to me and his appearance was like the
appearance of the angel of God, very
awesome. And I did not ask him where
he *came* from, nor did he tell me his
name.
7 "But he said to me, 'Behold, you
shall conceive and give birth to a son,
and now you shall not drink wine or
strong drink nor eat any unclean thing,
for the boy shall be a Nazirite to God
from the womb to the day of his
death.'"
8 Then Manoah entreated the LORD
and said, "O Lord, please let [a]the man of
God whom Thou hast sent come to us
again that he may teach us what to do
for the boy who is to be born."
9 And God listened to the voice of
Manoah; and [a]the angel of God came
again to the woman as she was sitting in
the field, but Manoah her husband was
not with her.
10 So the woman ran quickly and told
her [1]husband, "Behold, [a]the man who
[2]came the *other* day has appeared to
me."
11 Then Manoah arose and followed
his wife, and when he came to the man
he said to him, "Are you [a]the man who
spoke to the woman?" And he said, "I
am."
12 And Manoah said, "Now when
your words come *to pass,* what shall be
the boy's mode of life and his vocation?"
13 So [a]the angel of the LORD said to
Manoah, "[b]Let the woman pay attention
[1]to all that I said.
14 "She should not eat anything that
comes from the [a]vine nor drink wine or
strong drink, nor eat any unclean thing;
let her observe all that I commanded."
15 Then Manoah said to [a]the angel of
the LORD, "Please let us detain you so
that we may prepare a kid for you."
16 And the angel of the LORD said to
Manoah, "Though you detain me, [a]I will
not eat your [1]food, but if you prepare a
burnt offering, *then* offer it to the
LORD." For Manoah did not know that
he was the angel of the LORD.
17 And Manoah said to the angel of
the LORD, "[a]What is your name, so that
when your words come *to pass,* we may
honor you?"
18 But the angel of the LORD said to
him, "Why do you ask my name, seeing
it is [1a]wonderful?"
19 So [a]Manoah took the kid with the
grain offering and offered it on the rock
to the LORD, and He performed wonders
while Manoah and his wife looked on.
20 For it came about when the flame
went up from the altar toward heaven,
that the angel of the LORD ascended in
the flame of the altar. When Manoah
and his wife saw *this,* they [a]fell on their
faces to the ground.
21 Now the angel of the LORD appeared no more to Manoah or his wife.
[a]Then Manoah knew that he was the
angel of the LORD.
22 So Manoah said to his wife, "[a]We
shall surely die, for we have seen God."
23 But his wife said to him, "If the
LORD had desired to kill us, He would
not have accepted a burnt offering and a
grain offering from our hands, nor would
He have [a]shown us all these things, nor
would He have let us hear *things* like this
at this time."
24 Then the woman gave birth to a
son and named him Samson; and the
[a]child grew up and the LORD blessed
him.
25 And [a]the Spirit of the LORD began
to stir him in [1b]Mahaneh-dan, between
Zorah and Eshtaol.

Samson's Marriage

14 THEN Samson went down to
Timnah and saw a woman in
Timnah, *one* of the daughters of the
Philistines.
2 So he came [1]back and told his
father and [2]mother, "I saw a woman in
Timnah, *one* of the daughters of the
Philistines; now therefore, get her for me
as a wife."
3 Then his father and his mother said
to him, "Is there no woman among the
daughters of your [1a]relatives, or among
all [2]our people, that you go to [b]take a
wife from the uncircumcised Philistines?" But Samson said to his father,
"Get her for me, for she [3]looks good to
me."
4 However, his father and mother
did not know that [a]it was of the LORD,
for He was seeking an occasion against
the Philistines. Now at that time the
Philistines were ruling over Israel.
5 Then Samson went down to Timnah with his father and mother, and
came as far as the vineyards of Timnah;
and behold, a young lion *came* roaring
toward him.
6 And [a]the Spirit of the LORD [1]came
upon him mightily, so that [b]he tore him
as one tears a kid though he had nothing
in his hand; but he did not tell his father
or mother what he had done.
7 So he went down and talked to the
woman; and she [1]looked good to Samson.
8 When he returned later to take her,
he turned aside to look at the carcass of
the lion; and behold, a swarm of bees
and honey were in the body of the lion.
9 So he scraped [1]the honey into his
[2]hands and went on, eating as he went.
When he came to his father and mother,
he gave *some* to them and they ate *it;* but
he did not tell them that he had scraped
the honey out of the body of the lion.
10 Then his father went down to the
woman; and Samson made a feast there,
for the young men customarily did this.

5 [a]Luke 1:15 [b]Num. 6:2-5
6 [a]Judg. 6:11; 13:8, 10, 11
8 [a]Judg. 13:3, 7
9 [a]Judg. 13:8
10 [1]Lit., *husband, and said to him* [2]Lit., *came to me* [a]Judg. 13:9
11 [a]Judg. 13:8
13 [1]Lit., *from* [a]Judg. 13:11 [b]Judg. 13:4
14 [a]Num. 6:4
15 [a]Judg. 13:3
16 [1]Lit., *bread* [a]Judg. 6:20
17 [a]Gen. 32:29
18 [1]I.e., incomprehensible [a]Is. 9:6
19 [a]Judg. 6:20, 21
20 [a]Lev. 9:24; 1 Chr. 21:16; Ezek. 1:28; Matt. 17:6
21 [a]Judg. 13:16
22 [a]Gen. 32:30; Deut. 5:26; Judg. 6:22
23 [a]Ps. 25:14
24 [a]1 Sam. 3:19; Luke 1:80
25 [1]I.e., the camp of Dan [a]Judg. 3:10 [b]Judg. 18:11, 12

2 [1]Lit., *up* [2]Lit., *mother, saying,*
3 [1]Lit., *brothers* [2]Lit., *my* [3]Lit., *is right in my eyes* [a]Gen. 24:3, 4 [b]Ex. 34:16; Deut. 7:3
4 [a]Josh. 11:20
6 [1]Lit., *rushed upon* [a]Judg. 3:10 [b]1 Sam. 17:34-36
7 [1]Lit., *was right in Samson's eyes*
9 [1]Lit., *it* [2]Lit., *palms*

11 And it came about when they saw
him that they brought thirty companions
to be with him.

Samson's Riddle

12 Then Samson said to them, "Let
me now [a]propound a riddle to you; if
you will indeed tell it to me within the
seven days of the feast, and find it out,
then I will give you thirty linen wraps
and thirty [b]changes of clothes.
13"But if you are unable to tell me,
then you shall give me thirty linen wraps
and thirty changes of clothes." And they
said to him, "Propound your riddle, that
we may hear it."
14 So he said to them,
"Out of the eater came something
to eat,
And out of the strong came something
sweet."
But they could not tell the riddle in three
days.
15 Then it came about on the [1]fourth
day that they said to Samson's wife,
"[a]Entice your husband, that he may tell
us the riddle, [b]lest we burn you and your
father's house with fire. Have you invited
us to impoverish us? Is this not
so?"
16 And Samson's wife wept before
him and said, "[a]You only hate me, and
you do not love me; you have propounded
a riddle to the sons of my
people, and have not told *it* to me." And
he said to her, "Behold, I have not told *it*
to my father or mother; so should I tell
you?"
17 However she wept before him
seven days while their feast lasted. And
it came about on the seventh day that he
told her because she pressed him so
hard. She then told the riddle to the sons
of her people.
18 So the men of the city said to him
on the seventh day before the sun went
down,
"What is sweeter than honey?
And what is stronger than a
lion?"
And he said to them,
"If you had not plowed with my
heifer,
You would not have found out
my riddle."
19 Then [a]the Spirit of the LORD [1]came
upon him mightily, and he went down to
Ashkelon and killed thirty of them and
took their spoil, and gave the changes *of
clothes* to those who told the riddle. And
his anger burned, and he went up to his
father's house.
20 But Samson's wife was [a]*given* to his
companion who had been his [1]friend.

Samson Burns Philistine Crops

15 BUT after a while, in the time of
wheat harvest, it came about that
Samson visited his wife [a]with a young
goat, and said, "I will go in to my wife in
her room." But her father did not let him
enter.
2 And her father said, "I really
thought that you hated her intensely; so
I [a]gave her to your companion. Is not
her younger sister [1]more beautiful than
she? Please let her be yours [2]instead."
3 Samson then said to them, "This
time I shall be blameless in regard to the
Philistines when I do them harm."
4 And Samson went and caught three
hundred foxes, and took torches, and
turned *the foxes* tail to tail, and put one
torch in the middle between two tails.
5 When he had set fire to the torches,
he released [1]the foxes into the standing
grain of the Philistines, thus burning up
both the shocks and the standing grain,
along with the vineyards *and* groves.
6 Then the Philistines said, "Who did
this?" And they said, "Samson, the son-in-law
of the Timnite, because [1]he took
his wife and gave her to his companion."
So the Philistines came up and [a]burned
her and her father with fire.
7 And Samson said to them, "Since
you act like this, I will surely take
revenge on you, but after that I will
quit."
8 And he struck them [1]ruthlessly
with a great slaughter; and he went
down and lived in the cleft of the rock of
Etam.
9 Then the Philistines went up and
camped in Judah, and spread out in
Lehi.
10 And the men of Judah said, "Why
have you come up against us?" And they
said, "We have come up to bind Samson
in order to do to him as he did to us."
11 Then 3,000 men of Judah went
down to the cleft of the rock of Etam
and said to Samson, "Do you not know
[a]that the Philistines are rulers over us?
What then is this that you have done to
us?" And he said to them, "As they did
to me, so I have done to them."
12 And they said to him, "We have
come down to bind you so that we may
give you into the hands of the Philistines."
And Samson said to them,
"Swear to me that you will not [1]kill me."
13 So they said to [1]him, "No, but we
will bind you fast and give you into their
hands; yet surely we will not kill you."
Then they bound him with two new
ropes and brought him up from the rock.
14 When he came to Lehi, the Philistines
shouted as they met him. And [a]the
Spirit of the LORD [1]came upon him
mightily so that the ropes that were on
his arms were as flax that is burned with
fire, and his bonds [2]dropped from his
hands.
15 And he found a fresh jawbone of a
donkey, so he [1]reached out and took it
and [2]killed [a]a thousand men with it.
16 Then Samson said,
"With the jawbone of a donkey,
[1]Heaps upon heaps,
With the jawbone of a donkey
I have [2]killed a thousand men."
17 And it came about when he had
finished speaking, that he threw the

12 [a]Ezek. 17:2 [b]Gen. 45:22; 2 Kin. 5:22

15 [1]So with some ancient versions; Heb., *seventh* [a]Judg. 16:5 [b]Judg. 15:6

16 [a]Judg. 16:15

19 [1]Lit., *rushed upon* [a]Judg. 3:10; 13:25

20 [1]Or, *best man* [a]Judg. 15:2

1 [a]Gen. 38:17

2 [1]Lit., *better* [2]Lit., *instead of her* [a]Judg. 14:20

5 [1]Lit., *them*

6 [1]I.e., the Timnite [a]Judg. 14:15

8 [1]Lit., *leg on thigh*

11 [a]Lev. 26:25; Deut. 28:43f.; Judg. 13:1; 14:4; Ps. 106:40-42

12 [1]Lit., *fall upon me yourselves*

13 [1]Lit., *him, saying*

14 [1]Lit., *rushed upon* [2]Lit., *were melted* [a]Judg. 14:19; 1 Sam. 11:6

15 [1]Lit., *stretched out his hand* [2]Lit., *smote* [a]Lev. 26:8; Josh. 23:10

16 [1]Lit., *Heap, two heaps;* Heb. is same root as donkey [2]Lit., *smitten*

jawbone from his hand; and he named that place [1]Ramath-lehi.

18 Then he became very thirsty, and he [a]called to the LORD and said, "Thou hast given this great deliverance by the hand of Thy servant, and now [1]shall I die of thirst [2]and fall into the hands of the uncircumcised?"

19 But God split the hollow place that is in Lehi so that water came out of it. When he drank, [a]his [1]strength returned and he revived. Therefore, he named it [2]En-hakkore, which is in Lehi to this day.

20 So [a]he judged Israel twenty years in [b]the days of the Philistines.

Samson's Weakness

16 NOW Samson went to [a]Gaza and saw a harlot there, and went in to her.

2 *When it was told* to the Gazites, saying, "Samson has come here," they [a]surrounded *the place* and lay in wait for him all night at the gate of the city. And they kept silent all night, saying, "*Let us wait* until the morning light, then we will kill him."

3 Now Samson lay until midnight, and at midnight he arose and took hold of the doors of the city gate and the two posts and pulled them up along with the bars; then he put them on his shoulders and carried them up to the top of the mountain which is opposite Hebron.

4 After this it came about that he loved a woman in the valley of Sorek, whose name was Delilah.

5 And the [a]lords of the Philistines came up to her, and said to her, "[b]Entice him, and see where his great strength *lies* and [1]how we may overpower him that we may bind him to afflict him. Then we will each give you eleven hundred *pieces* of silver."

6 So Delilah said to Samson, "Please tell me where your great strength is and [1]how you may be bound to afflict you."

7 And Samson said to her, "If they bind me with seven fresh cords that have not been dried, then I shall become weak and be like any *other* man."

8 Then the lords of the Philistines brought up to her seven fresh cords that had not been dried, and she bound him with them.

9 Now she had *men* lying in wait in an inner room. And she said to him, "The Philistines are upon you, Samson!" But he snapped the cords as a string of tow snaps when it [1]touches fire. So his strength was not discovered.

10 Then Delilah said to Samson, "Behold, you have deceived me and told me lies; now please tell me, [1]how you may be bound."

11 And he said to her, "If they bind me tightly with new ropes [1]which have not been used, then I shall become weak and be like any *other* man."

12 So Delilah took new ropes and bound him with them and said to him, "The Philistines are upon you, Samson!" For the *men* were lying in wait in the inner room. But he snapped [1]the ropes from his arms like a thread.

13 Then Delilah said to Samson, "Up to now you have deceived me and told me lies; tell me [1]how you may be bound." And he said to her, "If you weave the seven locks of my [2]hair with the web [3][and fasten it with a pin, then I shall become weak and be like any other man."

14 So while he slept, Delilah took the seven locks of his [1]hair and wove them into the web]. And she fastened *it* with the pin, and said to him, "The Philistines are upon you, Samson!" But he awoke from his sleep and pulled out the pin of the loom and the web.

Delilah Extracts His Secret

15 Then she said to him, "[a]How can you say, 'I love you,' when your heart is not with me? You have deceived me these three times and have not told me where your great strength is."

16 And it came about when she pressed him daily with her words and urged him, that his soul was [1]annoyed to death.

17 So he told her all *that was* in his heart and said to her, "A razor has never come on my head, for I have been a [a]Nazirite to God from my mother's womb. If I am shaved, then my strength will leave me and I shall become weak and be like any *other* man."

18 When Delilah saw that he had told her all *that was* in his heart, she sent and called the lords of the Philistines, saying, "Come up once more, for he has told me all *that is* in his heart." Then the lords of the Philistines came up to her, and brought the money in their hands.

19 And she made him sleep on her knees, and called for a man and had him shave off the seven locks of his [1]hair. Then she began to afflict him, and his strength left him.

20 And she said, "The Philistines are upon you, Samson!" And he awoke from his sleep and said, "I will go out as at other times and shake myself free." But he did not know that [a]the LORD had departed from him.

21 Then the Philistines seized him and gouged out his eyes; and they brought him down to Gaza and bound him with bronze chains, and he was a grinder in the prison.

22 However, the hair of his head began to grow again after it was shaved off.

23 Now the lords of the Philistines assembled to offer a great sacrifice to [a]Dagon their god, and to rejoice, for they said,

"Our god has given Samson our
enemy into our hands."

24 When the people saw him, [a]they praised their god, for they said,

"Our god has given our enemy into
our hands,
Even the destroyer of our country,
Who has slain many of us."

17 [1]I.e., the high place of the jawbone
18 [1]Or, *I shall . . . uncircumcised* [2]Or, *or* [a]Judg. 16:28
19 [1]Lit., *spirit* [2]I.e., the spring of him who called [a]Is. 40:29
20 [a]Judg. 16:31; Heb. 11:32 [b]Judg. 13:1
1 [a]Josh. 15:47
2 [a]1 Sam. 23:26; Ps. 118:10–12
5 [1]Lit., *by what* [a]Josh. 13:3 [b]Judg. 14:15
6 [1]Lit., *by what*
9 [1]Lit., *smells*
10 [1]Lit., *by what*
11 [1]Lit., *with which work has not been done*
12 [1]Lit., *them*
13 [1]Lit., *by what* [2]Lit., *head* [3]The passage in brackets is found in Gr. but not in any Heb. mss.
14 [1]Lit., *head*
15 [a]Judg. 14:16
16 [1]Lit., *impatient to the point of*
17 [a]Num. 6:2, 5; Judg. 13:5
19 [1]Lit., *head*
20 [a]Num. 14:42, 43; Josh. 7:12; 1 Sam. 16:14
23 [a]1 Sam. 5:2
24 [a]1 Sam. 31:9; 1 Chr. 10:9; Ps. 97:7

25 It so happened when [1]they were in
high spirits, that they said, "Call for
Samson, that he may amuse us." So they
called for Samson from the prison, and
he [2]entertained them. And they made
him stand between the pillars.
26 Then Samson said to the boy who
was holding his hand, "Let me feel the
pillars on which the house rests, that I
may lean against them."
27 Now the house was full of men and
women, and all the lords of the Philistines were there. And about 3,000 men
and women were on the roof looking on
while Samson was amusing *them.*

Samson Is Avenged

28 [a]Then Samson called to the LORD
and said, "O Lord [1]GOD, please remember me and please strengthen me just
this time, O God, that I may at once [b]be
avenged of the Philistines for my two
eyes."
29 And Samson grasped the two middle pillars on which the house rested,
and braced himself against them, the one
with his right hand and the other with
his left.
30 And Samson said, "Let me die with
the Philistines!" And he bent with [1]all
his might so that the house fell on the
lords and all the people who were in it.
So the dead whom he killed at his death
were more than those whom he killed in
his life.
31 Then his brothers and all his father's household came down, took him,
brought him up, and buried him between Zorah and Eshtaol in the tomb of
Manoah his father. [a]Thus he had judged
Israel twenty years.

Micah's Idolatry

17 NOW there was a man of the hill
country of Ephraim whose name
was Micah.
2 And he said to his mother, "The
eleven hundred *pieces* of silver which
were taken from you, about which you
uttered a curse [1]in my hearing, behold,
the silver is with me; I took it." And his
mother said, "Blessed be my son by the
LORD."
3 He then returned the eleven hundred *pieces* of silver to his mother, and
his mother said, "I wholly dedicate the
silver from my hand to the LORD for my
son [a]to make a graven image and a
molten image; now therefore, I will
return [1]them to you."
4 So when he returned the silver to
his mother, his mother took two hundred
pieces of silver and gave them to the
silversmith who made [1]them into a
graven image and a molten image, and
[2]they were in the house of Micah.
5 And the man Micah had a [1a]shrine
and he made an [b]ephod and [2c]household
idols and [3]consecrated one of his sons,
[d]that he might become his priest.
6 In those days [a]there was no king in
Israel; [b]every man did what was right in
his own eyes.
7 Now there was a young man from
[a]Bethlehem in Judah, of the family of
Judah, who was a Levite; and he was
[1]staying there.
8 Then the man departed from the
city, from Bethlehem in Judah, to [1]stay
wherever he might find *a place;* and as
he made his journey, he came to the [a]hill
country of Ephraim to the house of
Micah.
9 And Micah said to him, "Where do
you come from?" And he said to him, "I
am a Levite from Bethlehem in Judah,
and I am going to [1]stay wherever I may
find *a place.*"
10 Micah then said to him, "Dwell
with me and be [a]a father and a priest to
me, and I will give you ten *pieces* of
silver a year, a suit of clothes, and your
maintenance." So the Levite went *in.*
11 And the Levite agreed to live with
the man; and the young man became to
him like one of his sons.
12 So Micah [1]consecrated the Levite,
and the young man [a]became his priest
and [2]lived in the house of Micah.
13 Then Micah said, "Now I know
that the LORD will prosper me, seeing I
have a Levite as priest."

Danites Seek Territory

18 [a]IN those days there was no king
of Israel; and [b]in those days the
tribe of the Danites was seeking an
inheritance for themselves to live in, for
until that day [1]an inheritance had not
[2]been allotted to them as a possession
among the tribes of Israel.
2 So the sons of Dan sent from their
family five men out of their whole number, [1]valiant men from [a]Zorah and Eshtaol, to spy out the land and to search it;
and they said to them, "Go, search the
land." And they came to [b]the hill country of Ephraim, to the house of Micah,
and lodged there.
3 When they were near the house of
Micah, they recognized the voice of the
young man, the Levite; and they turned
aside there, and said to him, "Who
brought you here? And what are you
doing in this *place?* And what do you
have here?"
4 And he said to them, "Thus and so
has Micah done to me, and he has hired
me, and [a]I have become his priest."
5 And they said to him, "Inquire of
God, please, that we may know whether
our way on which we are going will be
prosperous."
6 And the priest said to them, "Go in
peace; your way in which you are going
[1]has the LORD's approval."
7 Then the five men departed and
came to [a]Laish and saw the people who
were in it living in security, after the
manner of the Sidonians, quiet and
secure; for there was no [1]ruler humiliating *them* for anything in the land, and
they were far from the Sidonians and
had no dealings with anyone.

25 [1]Lit., *their heart was pleasant* [2]Lit., *made sport before them*

28 [1]Heb., *YHWH,* usually rendered *LORD* [a]Judg. 15:18 [b]Jer. 15:15

30 [1]Lit., *strength*

31 [a]Judg. 15:20

2 [1]Lit., *and also spoke it in my ears*

3 [1]Lit., *it* [a]Ex. 20:4, 23; 34:17

4 [1]Lit., *it* [2]Lit., *it was*

5 [1]Lit., *house of gods* [2]Heb., *teraphim* [3]Lit., *filled the hand of* [a]Judg. 18:24 [b]Judg. 8:27; 18:14 [c]Gen. 31:19 [d]Num. 3:10

6 [a]Judg. 18:1; 19:1 [b]Deut. 12:8; Judg. 21:25

7 [1]Or, *sojourning* [a]Judg. 19:1; Ruth 1:1, 2; Mic. 5:2; Matt. 2:1

8 [1]Or, *sojourn* [a]Josh. 24:33

9 [1]Or, *sojourn*

10 [a]Judg. 18:19

12 [1]Lit., *filled the hand of* [2]Lit., *was* [a]Num. 16:10; 18:1-7

1 [1]Lit., *it* [2]Lit., *fallen* [a]Judg. 17:6; 19:1 [b]Josh. 19:40-48

2 [1]Lit., *men, sons of valor* [a]Judg. 13:25 [b]Judg. 17:1

4 [a]Judg. 17:12

6 [1]Lit., *is before the LORD*

7 [1]Lit., *possessor of restraint* [a]Josh. 19:47; Judg. 18:29

8 When they came back to their
brothers at Zorah and Eshtaol, their
brothers said to them, "What *do* you
report?"
9 And they said, "Arise, and let us go
up against them; for we have seen the
land, and behold, it is very good. And
will you [1]sit still? Do not delay to go, to
enter, to possess the land.
10 "When you enter, you shall come to
a secure people with a spacious land; for
God has given it into your hand, [a]a place
where there is no lack of anything that is
on the earth."
11 Then from the family of the Danites, from Zorah and from Eshtaol, six
hundred men armed with weapons of
war set out.
12 And they went up and camped at
Kiriath-jearim in Judah. Therefore they
called that place [1a]Mahaneh-dan to this
day; behold, it is [2]west of Kiriath-jearim.
13 And they passed from there to the
hill country of Ephraim and came to the
house of Micah.

Danites Take Micah's Idols

14 Then the five men who went to spy
out the country of Laish answered and
said to their kinsmen, "Do you know
that there are in these houses [a]an ephod
and [1]household idols and a graven image
and a molten image? Now therefore,
consider what you should do."
15 And they turned aside there and
came to the house of the young man, the
Levite, to the house of Micah, and asked
him of his welfare.
16 And the six hundred men armed
with their weapons of war, who were of
the sons of Dan, stood by the entrance
of the gate.
17 Now the five men who went to spy
out the land went up *and* entered there,
and took [a]the graven image and the
ephod and [1]household idols and the
molten image, while the priest stood by
the entrance of the gate with the six
hundred men armed with weapons of
war.
18 And when these went into Micah's
house and took the graven image, the
ephod and [1]household idols and the
molten image, the priest said to them,
"What are you doing?"
19 And they said to him, "Be silent,
[a]put your hand over your mouth and
come with us, and be to us [b]a father and
a priest. Is it better for you to be a priest
to the house of one man, or to be priest
to a tribe and a family in Israel?"
20 And the priest's heart was glad,
and he took the ephod and [1]household
idols and the graven image, and went
among the people.
21 Then they turned and departed,
and put the little ones and the livestock
and the valuables in front of them.
22 When they had gone some distance
from the house of Micah, the men who
were in the houses near Micah's house

9 [1]Lit., *be*

10 [a]Deut. 8:9

12 [1]I.e., the camp of Dan [2]Lit., *behind* [a]Judg. 13:25

14 [1]Heb., *teraphim* [a]Judg. 17:5

17 [1]Heb., *teraphim* [a]Gen. 31:19, 30; Is. 41:29; Mic. 5:13

18 [1]Heb., *teraphim*

19 [a]Job 21:5; 29:9; 40:4 [b]Judg. 17:10

20 [1]Heb., *teraphim*

23 [1]Lit., *their faces*

25 [1]Lit., *bitter of soul* [2]Lit., *gather*

27 [a]Josh. 19:47; Judg. 18:7

28 [a]2 Sam. 10:6

29 [a]Josh. 19:47

30 [1]Some ancient versions read *Moses* [a]Judg. 17:3, 5 [b]Ex. 2:22; 18:3 [c]Judg. 17:3, 5

31 [a]Josh. 18:1

1 [1]Or, *sojourning* [a]Judg. 18:1

3 [1]Lit., *to her heart* [2]Lit., *and* [a]Gen. 34:3; 50:21

assembled and overtook the sons of
Dan.
23 And they cried to the sons of Dan,
who turned [1]around and said to Micah,
"What is *the matter* with you, that you
have assembled together?"
24 And he said, "You have taken
away my gods which I made, and the
priest, and have gone away, and what do
I have besides? So how can you say to
me, 'What is *the matter* with you?' "
25 And the sons of Dan said to him,
"Do not let your voice be heard among
us, lest [1]fierce men fall upon you and
you [2]lose your life, with the lives of your
household."
26 So the sons of Dan went on their
way; and when Micah saw that they
were too strong for him, he turned and
went back to his house.
27 Then they took what Micah had
made and the priest who had belonged
to him, and came to [a]Laish, to a people
quiet and secure, and struck them with
the edge of the sword; and they burned
the city with fire.
28 And there was no one to deliver
them, because it was far from Sidon and
they had no dealings with anyone, and it
was in the valley which is near [a]Beth-
rehob. And they rebuilt the city and
lived in it.
29 And [a]they called the name of the
city Dan, after the name of Dan their
father who was born in Israel; however,
the name of the city formerly was Laish.
30 And the sons of Dan set up for
themselves [a]the graven image; and Jonathan, the son of [b]Gershom, the son of
[1]Manasseh, [c]he and his sons were priests
to the tribe of the Danites until the day
of the captivity of the land.
31 So they set up for themselves Micah's graven image which he had made,
all the time that the [a]house of God was
at Shiloh.

A Levite's Concubine Degraded

19 NOW it came about in those
days, when [a]there was no king in
Israel, that there was a certain Levite
[1]staying in the remote part of the hill
country of Ephraim, who took a concubine for himself from Bethlehem in
Judah.
2 But his concubine played the harlot
against him, and she went away from
him to her father's house in Bethlehem
in Judah, and was there for a period of
four months.
3 Then her husband arose and went
after her to [a]speak [1]tenderly to her in
order to bring her back, [2]taking with
him his servant and a pair of donkeys.
So she brought him into her father's
house, and when the girl's father saw
him, he was glad to meet him.
4 And his father-in-law, the girl's
father, detained him; and he remained
with him three days. So they ate and
drank and lodged there.

WEIGHT

Deuteronomy 25. The verb *"to weigh"* is *shaqual* (shekel) in Hebrew, and for this reason the "shekel" became the basic weight. Absalom's hair weighed two hundred of them (2 Samuel 14:26). From the figures given in Exodus 38:25-26, we can work out that a beka was half a shekel, and a talent was three hundred shekels. At a later date another weight was added, called a *mina*, which was probably fifty shekels.

These names were adopted in other countries, but the multiples and the actual weights were different. Added to this was the complication that there seem to have been two sets of weights used by the merchant. A light set was used when purchasing and a heavy set when selling (Deuteronomy 25:13). This gave the trader a legitimate percentage profit and was not wrong in itself. It was *mixed* weights that were the problem, or the deliberate use of *false* weights in order to cheat people (Leviticus 19:35-36; Micah 6:10-11). Weights themselves were often shaped stones, carved into animals and other subjects, and marked with their weight. They were used in scales and balances (Isaiah 40:12). It is estimated that the talent weighed between seventy-five and eighty pounds. It took its name from the large, heavy lid of a container.

COINAGE

In the earliest days of the Bible, trade was done through barter, but it was soon recognized that it was more convenient to exchange something that in its turn could be exchanged for something else. This was done through weighed quantities of metal. Abraham therefore weighed out four hundred shekels of silver in payment for a burial place for his family (Genesis 23:16). The metals used in exchange were mainly gold, silver and copper. At one point metals were made into standard shapes such as discs, bars and rings, but true coinage did not start until the seventh century BC. The king's mark was then put on a piece to guarantee its weight and to purity and therefore its value.

Coins are not mentioned until quite late in the Bible. Only in Nehemiah's time do we read about *"darics of gold"* (Nehemiah 7:71), which were minted by Darius of Persia and took his name. Coins became more plentiful in New Testament times, but there were so many types that money was quite confusing. Three systems of coinage were in operation. The Roman coinage had international currency and was made in coins of copper, bronze, silver and gold. When Jesus told his disciples to take no gold, silver, or copper in their purses (Matthew 10:9), he was probably referring to the coinage.

JEWISH COINAGE

The Romans allowed local coinage to circulate in addition to their own. There was a very limited Jewish coinage. Coinage seems to have

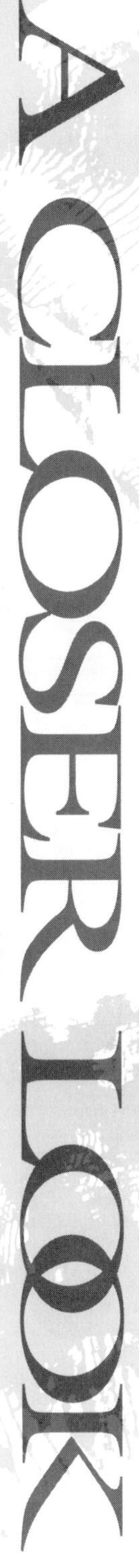

been minted by Nehemiah, probably to pay the temple tax. Nothing else was heard of coinage until one of the descendants of the Maccabees wrested the privilege from the Syrian overlords (1 Maccabees 15:6), In New Testament times the sole Jewish coin was a copper lepton, which means *"thin."* The widow put them in the treasury (Mark 12:42). It was equivalent to about half a quadrans. The first *"real"* Jewish coins were produced at times of revolt, between AD 66 and 70, and between AD 132 and 135.

LINEAR MEASUREMENTS

Linear measurements were developed from the proportions of the human body, the finger, the palm, the span (distance from spread thumb to little fingertip), the cubit (distance from the elbow to the middle fingertip), and the rope or fathom was the distance from the tip of one middle finger to the other middle finger with the arms extended.

The system was not without its problems. Body measurements vary from person to person, and there is evidence that there were differing lengths of cubit, from about 17.7 inches to about 20.5 inches. There was a long or *"royal"* cubit of 7 palms or 28 fingers (all royal measurements were larger than standard); there were also old cubits (2 Chronicles 3:3) and new ones (Ezekiel 40:5). In general, however, the system was easily understood, and approximate measurements could be calculated.

Longer distances were vaguely worked out in terms of several days' journey (e.g., Genesis 30:36). Much later, the Greeks used a measurement called a stadion (plural, stadia), which was just over 200 yards and is mentioned in the book of Maccabees. Distance was not used for calculating area as in our system. An acre was the amount of land that could be ploughed by an ox in a day (Isaiah 5:10). The maximum distance that could be walked on the Sabbath (a Sabbath day's journey, Acts 1:12) was 2,000 paces, a there-and-back distance (each way) of a Roman mile (1,000 paces).

THE MARKET

Acts 16. The market normally opened off the gate and was associated with it (Acts 16:19). It was the area where the villagers brought in their produce to sell and where traders from other parts of the country brought their wares. It was normally open every weekday (see Nehemiah 10:13) for in the absence of refrigeration it was necessary for people to purchase food on a daily basis.

RUTH - *loyalty*

As noted in the Bible, Ruth came from Noab, a people hated by the Israelites. Yet she earned the admiration and respect of the Jews in Bethlehem. Why did she gain this unusual acceptance? It was due to her loyalty.

She was a very young woman when her husband died. It was quite common in Biblical times to be married well before eighteen. Yet she did not spend her days feeling sorry for herself, seeking sympathy or blaming others for her predicament. Instead, we will see in the Scriptures how she honored her marriage and her husband's memory by her love for his mother.

Ruth had chosen her husband's people, his country and his God. She built her life on these things. When the circumstances of her life changed, Ruth's beliefs did not. Her attitude was unwavering in love and loyalty.

Ruth's own words, often used today as wedding vows, speak of her deep love for Naomi. This beautiful passage is a heart-cry of sincerity (Ruth 1:16-17).

Do not urge me to leave you
Or turn back from following you;
For where you go, I will go,
And where you lodge, I will lodge.
Your people shall be my people,
And your God, my God.
Where you die, I will die,
And there I will be buried.

There was little for Ruth to gain by remaining with her mother-in-law. In truth, she would have been more comfortable had she returned to her parents' home. And yet she did not put her own well-being first. She was concerned about Naomi's welfare and committed to the choices she made.

And so they moved to Bethlehem. Ruth supported herself and Naomi by hard physical labor, picking up what was left by the harvesters in the grain fields. Because her love was real, even her attitude toward work was joyful. Ruth appreciated God meeting their needs, and did not complain at how it was done.

God, in turn, blessed Ruth greatly through her marriage to Boaz. Her living conditions greatly improved, and her son, Obed, was King David's grandfather. Naomi moved into the household and help care for Obed. Ruth's depth of commitment blessed her entire family. Ruth's gift of loving loyalty brought her much love in return.

QUESTIONS

1. Ruth lived a life of no regrets, making Godly choices and seeing them through. You face many important decisions, such as education, love and marriage, friendships and service to God. What can you do to make sure you can follow your choices through without regret?

2. Ruth is presented as being sweet, kind, caring and content. She did not spend her time wishing "What if" or "If only". How can you eliminate doubt and live content with your life?

3. If God called you to handle a lowly task, would you be humiliated? If so, how would you regain your joy?

4. Are you able to express real gratitude as God meets your needs. How can you avoid the trap of wishing He had done things differently?

5 Now it came about on the fourth day that they got up early in the morning, and he [1]prepared to go; and the girl's father said to his son-in-law, "[a]Sustain [2]yourself with a piece of bread, and afterward you may go."

6 So both of them sat down and ate and drank together; and the girl's father said to the man, "Please be willing to spend the night, and [a]let your heart be merry."

7 Then the man arose to go, but his father-in-law urged him so that he spent the night there again.

8 And on the fifth day he arose to go early in the morning, and the girl's father said, "Please sustain [1]yourself, and wait until [2]afternoon"; so both of them ate.

9 When the man arose to go along with his concubine and servant, his father-in-law, the girl's father, said to him, "Behold now, the day has drawn [1]to a close; please spend the night. Lo, the day is [2]coming to an end; spend the night here that your heart may be merry. Then tomorrow you may arise early for your journey so that you may go [3]home."

10 But the man was not willing to spend the night, so he arose and departed and came to *a place* opposite [a]Jebus (that is, Jerusalem). And there were with him a pair of saddled donkeys; his concubine also was with him.

11 When they *were* near Jebus, the day was almost gone; and [a]the servant said to his master, "Please come, and let us turn aside into this city of the Jebusites and spend the night in it."

12 However, his master said to him, "We will not turn aside into the city of foreigners who are not of the sons of Israel; but we will go on as far as Gibeah."

13 And he said to his servant, "Come and let us approach one of these places; and we will spend the night in Gibeah or Ramah."

14 So they passed along and went their way, and the sun set on them near Gibeah which belongs to Benjamin.

15 And they turned aside there in order to enter *and* lodge in Gibeah. When [1]they entered, [1]they sat down in the open square of the city, for no one took them into *his* house to spend the night.

16 Then behold, an old man was coming out of the field from his work at evening. Now the man was from [a]the hill country of Ephraim, and he was [1]staying in Gibeah, but the men of the place [b]were Benjamites.

17 And he lifted up his eyes and saw the traveler in the open square of the city; and the old man said, "Where are you going, and where do you come from?"

18 And he said to him, "We are passing from Bethlehem in Judah to the remote part of the hill country of Ephraim, *for* I am from there, and I went to Bethlehem in Judah. But I am *now* going to [1]my house, and no man will take me into his house.

19 "Yet there is both straw and fodder for our donkeys, and also bread and wine for me, [1]your maidservant, and [a]the young man who is with your servants; there is no lack of anything."

20 And the old man said, "[a]Peace to you. Only let me *take care of* all your needs; however, do not spend the night in the open square."

21 [a]So he took him into his house and gave the donkeys fodder, and they washed their feet and ate and drank.

22 While they were [1]making merry, behold, [a]the men of the city, certain [2b]worthless fellows, surrounded the house, pounding the door; and they spoke to the owner of the house, the old man, saying, "Bring out the man who came into your house that we may have [3]relations with him."

23 Then the man, the owner of the house, went out to them and said to them, "No, my fellows, please do not act so wickedly; since this man has come into my house, [a]do not commit this act of folly.

24 "[a]Here is my virgin daughter and his concubine. Please let me bring them out that you may ravish them and do to them [1]whatever you wish. But do not commit such an act of folly against this man."

25 But the men would not listen to him, so the man seized his concubine and brought *her* out to them. And they raped her and abused her all night until morning, then let her go at the approach of dawn.

26 [1]As the day began to dawn, the woman came and fell down at the doorway of the man's house where her master was, until *full* daylight.

27 When her master arose in the morning and opened the doors of the house and went out to go on his way, then behold, his concubine was lying at the doorway of the house, with her hands on the threshold.

28 And he said to her, "Get up and let us go," [a]but there was no answer. Then he placed her on the donkey; and the man arose and went to his [1]home.

29 When he entered his house, he took a knife and laid hold of his concubine and [a]cut her in twelve pieces, limb by limb, and sent her throughout the territory of Israel.

30 And it came about that all who saw *it* said, "Nothing like this has *ever* happened or been seen from the day when the sons of Israel came up from the land of Egypt to this day. Consider it, [a]take counsel and speak up!"

Resolve to Punish the Guilty

20 THEN all the sons of Israel from Dan to Beersheba, including the land of Gilead, came out, and the congregation assembled as one man to the LORD at [a]Mizpah.

5 [1]Lit., *arose* [2]Lit., *your heart* [a]Gen. 18:5; Judg. 19:8

6 [a]Judg. 16:25; 19:9, 22; Ruth 3:7; 1 Kin. 21:7; Esth. 1:10

8 [1]Lit., *your heart* [2]Lit., *the day declines*

9 [1]Lit., *toward evening* [2]Lit., *declining* [3]Lit., *to your tent*

10 [a]1 Chr. 11:4, 5

11 [a]Judg. 19:19

15 [1]So with Gr.; M.T., *he*

16 [1]Or, *sojourning* [a]Judg. 19:1 [b]Judg. 19:14

18 [1]Heb., *the house of the LORD*, cf. v. 29

19 [1]I.e., my concubine [a]Judg. 19:11

20 [a]Gen. 43:23; Judg. 6:23

21 [a]Gen. 24:32, 33

22 [1]Lit., *making their hearts merry* [2]Lit., *sons of Belial* [3]Lit., *intercourse* [a]Gen. 19:4, 5; Ezek. 16:46-48 [b]Deut. 13:13; 1 Sam. 2:12; 1 Kin. 21:10; 2 Cor. 6:15

23 [a]Gen. 34:7; Deut. 22:21; Judg. 20:6; 2 Sam. 13:12

24 [1]Lit., *the good in your eyes* [a]Gen. 19:8

26 [1]Lit., *At the turning of the morning*

28 [1]Lit., *place* [a]Judg. 20:5

29 [a]1 Sam. 11:7

30 [a]Judg. 20:7; Prov. 13:10

1 [a]1 Sam. 7:5

2 And the [1]chiefs of all the people, *even* of all the tribes of Israel, took their stand in the assembly of the people of God, 400,000 foot [2]soldiers [a]who drew the sword.

3 (Now the sons of Benjamin heard that the sons of Israel had gone up to Mizpah.) And the sons of Israel said, "Tell *us,* how did this wickedness take place?"

4 So the Levite, the husband of the woman who was murdered, answered and said, "I came with my concubine to spend the night at Gibeah which belongs to Benjamin.

5 "But the [a]men of Gibeah rose up against me and surrounded the house at night because of me. They intended to kill me; instead, they [b]ravished my concubine so that she died.

6 "And I [a]took hold of my concubine and cut her in pieces and sent her throughout the land of Israel's inheritance; for [b]they have committed a lewd and disgraceful act in Israel.

7 "Behold, all you sons of Israel, [a]give your advice and counsel here."

8 Then all the people arose as one man, saying, "Not one of us will go to his tent, nor will any of us return to his house.

9 "But now this is the thing which we will do to Gibeah; *we will go up* against it by lot.

10 "And we will take 10 men out of 100 throughout the tribes of Israel, and 100 out of 1,000, and 1,000 out of 10,000 to [1]supply food for the people, that when they come to [2]Gibeah of Benjamin, they may [3]punish *them* for all the disgraceful acts that they have committed in Israel."

11 Thus all the men of Israel were gathered against the city, united as one man.

12 Then the tribes of Israel sent men through the entire [1]tribe of Benjamin, saying, "What is this wickedness that has taken place among you?

13 "Now then, deliver up the men, the [1a]worthless fellows in Gibeah, that we may put them to death and [b]remove *this* wickedness from Israel." But the sons of Benjamin would not listen to the voice of their brothers, the sons of Israel.

14 And the sons of Benjamin gathered from the cities to Gibeah, to go out to battle against the sons of Israel.

15 And from the cities on that day the [a]sons of Benjamin were [1]numbered, 26,000 men who draw the sword, besides the inhabitants of Gibeah who were [1]numbered, 700 choice men.

16 Out of all these people 700 [a]choice men were left-handed; each one could sling a stone at a hair and not miss.

17 Then the men of Israel besides Benjamin were [1]numbered, 400,000 men who draw the sword; all these were men of war.

Civil War, Benjamin Defeated

18 Now the sons of Israel arose, went up to Bethel, and [a]inquired of God, and said, "Who shall go up first for us to battle against the sons of Benjamin?" Then the LORD said, "Judah *shall go up* first."

19 So the sons of Israel arose in the morning and camped against Gibeah.

20 And the men of Israel went out to battle against Benjamin, and the men of Israel arrayed for battle against them at Gibeah.

21 Then the sons of Benjamin came out of Gibeah and [1a]felled to the ground on that day 22,000 men of Israel.

22 But the people, the men of Israel, encouraged themselves and arrayed for battle again in the place where they had arrayed themselves the first day.

23 [a]And the sons of Israel went up and wept before the LORD until evening, and [b]inquired of the LORD, saying, "Shall we again draw near for battle against the sons of my brother Benjamin?" And the LORD said, "Go up against him."

24 Then the sons of Israel [1]came against the sons of Benjamin the second day.

25 And Benjamin went out [1]against them from Gibeah the second day and [2]felled to the ground again 18,000 men of the sons of Israel; all these drew the sword.

26 Then [a]all the sons of Israel and all the people went up and came to Bethel and wept; thus they remained there before the LORD and fasted that day until evening. And they offered burnt offerings and peace offerings before the LORD.

27 And the sons of Israel [a]inquired of the LORD (for the ark of the covenant of God *was* there in those days,

28 and Phinehas the son of Eleazar, Aaron's son, stood before it to *minister* in those days), saying, "Shall I yet again go out to battle against the sons of my brother Benjamin, or shall I cease?" And the LORD said, "Go up, [a]for tomorrow I will deliver them into your hand."

29 [a]So Israel set men in ambush around Gibeah.

30 And the sons of Israel went up against the sons of Benjamin on the third day and arrayed themselves against Gibeah, as at other times.

31 [a]And the sons of Benjamin went out [1]against the people and were drawn away from the city, and they began to strike [2]and kill some of the people, as at other times, on the highways, one of which goes up to Bethel and the other to Gibeah, *and* in the field, about thirty men of Israel.

32 And the sons of Benjamin said, "They are struck down before us, as at the first." But the sons of Israel said, "Let us flee that we may draw them away from the city to the highways."

33 Then all the men of Israel arose from their place and arrayed themselves at Baal-tamar; [a]and the men of Israel in ambush broke out of their place, even out of Maareh-geba.

2 [1]Lit., *cornerstones* [2]Lit., *men* [a]Judg. 8:10
5 [a]Judg. 19:22 [b]Judg. 19:25f.
6 [a]Judg. 19:29 [b]Gen. 34:7; Josh. 7:15
7 [a]Judg. 19:30
10 [1]Lit., *take* [2]Heb., *Geba* [3]Lit., *do*
12 [1]Lit., *tribes*
13 [1]Lit., *sons of Belial* [a]2 Cor. 6:15 [b]Deut. 13:5; 17:12; 1 Cor. 5:13
15 [1]Or, *mustered* [a]Num. 1:36, 37; 2:23; 26:41
16 [a]Judg. 3:15; 1 Chr. 12:2
17 [1]Or, *mustered*
18 [a]Num. 27:21; Judg. 20:23, 27
21 [1]Lit., *destroyed* [a]Judg. 20:25
23 [a]Josh. 7:6, 7 [b]Judg. 20:18
24 [1]Lit., *approached*
25 [1]Lit., *to meet* [2]Lit., *destroyed*
26 [a]Judg. 20:23; 21:2
27 [a]Judg. 20:18
28 [a]Judg. 7:9
29 [a]Josh. 8:4
31 [1]Lit., *to meet* [2]Lit., *slain ones* [a]Josh. 8:16
33 [a]Josh. 8:19

34 When ten thousand choice men
from all Israel came against Gibeah, the
battle became [1]fierce; [a]but [2]Benjamin
did not know that [3]disaster was [4]close to
them.
35 And the LORD struck Benjamin
before Israel, so that the sons of Israel
destroyed 25,100 men of Benjamin that
day, all [1]who draw the sword.
36 So the sons of Benjamin saw that
they were [1]defeated. [a]When the men of
Israel gave [2]ground to Benjamin because
they relied on the men in ambush whom
they had set against Gibeah,
37 [a]the men in ambush hurried and
rushed against Gibeah; the men in ambush also deployed and struck all the
city with the edge of the sword.
38 Now the appointed sign between
the men of Israel and the men in ambush
was [a]that they should make a great cloud
of smoke rise from the city.
39 Then the men of Israel turned in
the battle, and Benjamin began to strike
[1]and kill about thirty men of Israel, [a]for
they said, "Surely they are [2]defeated
before us, as in the first battle."
40 But when the cloud began to rise
from the city in a column of smoke,
Benjamin looked [a]behind them; and
behold, the whole city was going up *in
smoke* to heaven.
41 Then the men of Israel turned, and
the men of Benjamin were terrified; for
they saw that [1a]disaster was [2]close to
them.
42 Therefore, they turned their backs
before the men of Israel [a]toward the
direction of the wilderness, but the
battle overtook them while those who
came out of the cities destroyed them in
the midst of them.
43 [a]They surrounded Benjamin, pursued them without rest *and* trod them
down opposite Gibeah toward the [1]east.
44 Thus 18,000 men of Benjamin fell;
all these were valiant warriors.
45 [1]The rest turned and fled toward
the wilderness to the rock of [a]Rimmon,
but they [2]caught 5,000 of them on the
highways and overtook them [3]at Gidom
and [4]killed 2,000 of them.
46 So all of Benjamin who fell that
day were 25,000 men who draw the
sword; all these were valiant warriors.
47 But 600 men turned and fled
toward the wilderness to the rock of
Rimmon, and they remained at the rock
of Rimmon four months.
48 The men of Israel then turned back
against the sons of Benjamin and struck
them with the edge of the sword, both
the entire city with the cattle and all that
they found; they also set on fire all the
cities which they found.

Mourning Lost Tribe

21 NOW the men of Israel [a]had
sworn in Mizpah, saying, "None
of us shall give his daughter to Benjamin
[1]in marriage."
2 [a]So the people came to Bethel and
sat there before God until evening, and
lifted up their voices and wept [1]bitterly.
3 And they said, "Why, O LORD,
God of Israel, has this come about in
Israel, so that one tribe should be *missing* today in Israel?"
4 And it came about the next day
that the people arose early and built [a]an
altar there, and offered burnt offerings
and peace offerings.
5 Then the sons of Israel said, "Who
is there among all the tribes of Israel
who did not come up in the assembly to
the LORD?" For [1]they had taken a great
oath concerning him [a]who did not come
up to the LORD at Mizpah, saying, "He
shall surely be put to death."
6 And the sons of Israel were sorry
for their brother Benjamin and said,
"One tribe is cut off from Israel today.
7 "What shall we do for wives for
those who are left, since we have [a]sworn
by the LORD not to give them any of our
daughters in marriage?"

Provision for Their Survival

8 And they said, "What one is there
of the tribes of Israel who did not come
up to the LORD at Mizpah?" And behold, no one had come to the camp from
Jabesh-gilead to the assembly.
9 For when the people were [1]num-
bered, behold, not one of the inhabitants
of Jabesh-gilead was there.
10 And the congregation sent 12,000
of the valiant warriors there, and commanded them, saying, "Go and [a]strike
the inhabitants of Jabesh-gilead with the
edge of the sword, with the women and
the little ones.
11 "And this is the thing that you shall
do: you [a]shall utterly destroy every man
and every woman who has [1]lain with a
man."
12 And they found among the inhabitants of Jabesh-gilead 400 young virgins
who had not known a man by lying with
[1]him; and they brought them to the
camp at Shiloh, which is in the land of
Canaan.
13 Then the whole congregation sent
word and spoke to the sons of Benjamin
who were [a]at the rock of Rimmon, and
[b]proclaimed peace to them.
14 And Benjamin returned at that
time, and they gave them the women
whom they had kept alive from the
women of Jabesh-gilead; yet they [1]were
not enough for them.
15 And the people were sorry for
Benjamin because the LORD had made a
breach in the tribes of Israel.
16 Then the elders of the congregation
said, "What shall we do for wives for
those who are left, since the women are
destroyed out of Benjamin?"
17 And they said, "*There must be* an
inheritance for the survivors of Benjamin, that a tribe may not be blotted out
from Israel.
18 "But we cannot give them wives of
our daughters." For the sons of Israel
[a]had sworn, saying, "Cursed is he who
gives a wife to Benjamin."

20:34 [1]Lit., *heavy* [2]Lit., *they* [3]Lit., *evil* [4]Lit., *touching* [a]Josh. 8:14; Job 21:13
35 [1]Lit., *these*
36 [1]Lit., *smitten* [2]Lit., *place* [a]Josh. 8:15
37 [a]Josh. 8:19
38 [a]Josh. 8:20
39 [1]Lit., *slain ones* [2]Lit., *smitten* [a]Judg. 20:32
40 [a]Josh. 8:20
41 [1]Lit., *evil* [2]Lit., *touching* [a]Prov. 5:22; 11:5, 6; 29:6
42 [a]Josh. 8:15, 24
43 [1]Lit., *sunrise* [a]Hos. 9:9; 10:9
45 [1]So with Gr.; Heb., *And they* [2]Lit., *gleaned* [3]Lit., *as far as* [4]Lit., *smote* [a]Judg. 21:13
21:1 [1]Lit., *for a wife* [a]Judg. 21:7, 18
2 [1]Lit., *with great weeping* [a]Judg. 20:26
4 [a]Deut. 12:5; 2 Sam. 24:25
5 [1]Lit., *there was a great oath* [a]Judg. 5:23
7 [a]Judg. 21:1
9 [1]Or, *mustered*
10 [a]Num. 31:17; Judg. 5:23; 1 Sam. 11:7
11 [1]Lit., *known lying with* [a]Num. 31:17
12 [1]Lit., *a male*
13 [a]Judg. 20:47 [b]Deut. 20:10
14 [1]Lit., *did not find it so*
18 [a]Judg. 21:1

19 So they said, "Behold, there is a feast of the LORD from year to year in [a]Shiloh, which is on the north side of Bethel, on the east side of the highway that goes up from Bethel to Shechem, and on the south side of Lebonah."

20 And they commanded the sons of Benjamin, saying, "Go and lie in wait in the vineyards,

21 and watch; and behold, if the daughters of Shiloh come out to [1][a]take part in the dances, then you shall come out of the vineyards and each of you shall catch his wife from the daughters of Shiloh, and go to the land of Benjamin.

22 "And it shall come about, when their fathers or their brothers come to complain to us, that we shall say to them, 'Give them to us voluntarily, because we did not take for each man *of Benjamin* [1]a wife in battle, [2][a]nor did you give *them* to them, *else* you would now be guilty.' "

23 And the sons of Benjamin did so, and took wives according to their number from those who danced, whom they carried away. And they went and returned to their inheritance, and [a]rebuilt the cities and lived in them.

24 And the sons of Israel departed from there at that time, every man to his tribe and family, and each one of them went out from there to his inheritance.

25 [a]In those days there was no king in Israel; everyone did what was right in his own eyes.

19 [a]Josh. 18:1; Judg. 18:31; 1 Sam. 1:3
21 [1]Lit., *dance* [a]Ex. 15:20; Judg. 11:34
22 [1]Lit., *his* [2]Lit., *because* [a]Judg. 21:1, 18
23 [a]Judg. 20:48
25 [a]Judg. 17:6; 18:1; 19:1

THE BOOK OF RUTH

Naomi Widowed

1 NOW it came about in the days [a]when the judges [1]governed, that there was [b]a famine in the land. And a certain man [c]of Bethlehem in Judah went to sojourn in the land of Moab [2]with his wife and his two sons.

2 And the name of the man *was* Elimelech, and the name of his wife, Naomi; and the names of his two sons *were* Mahlon and Chilion, Ephrathites of Bethlehem in Judah. Now they [a]entered the land of Moab and remained there.

3 Then Elimelech, Naomi's husband, died; and she was left with her two sons.

4 And they took for themselves Moabite women *as* wives; the name of the one was Orpah and the name of the other Ruth. And they lived there about ten years.

5 Then [1]both Mahlon and Chilion also died; and the woman was bereft of her two children and her husband.

6 Then she arose with her daughters-in-law that she might return from the land of Moab, for she had heard in the land of Moab that the LORD had [a]visited His people in [b]giving them food.

7 So she departed from the place where she was, and her two daughters-in-law with her; and they went on the way to return to the land of Judah.

8 And Naomi said to her two daughters-in-law, "Go, return each of you to her mother's house. [a]May the LORD deal kindly with you as you have dealt with the dead and with me.

9 "May the LORD grant that you may find rest, each in the house of her husband." Then she kissed them, and they lifted up their voices and wept.

10 And they said to her, "*No,* but we will surely return with you to your people."

11 But Naomi said, "Return, my daughters. Why should you go with me? Have I yet sons in my womb, that [a]they may be your husbands?

12 "Return, my daughters! Go, for I am too old to have a husband. If I said I have hope, if I should even have a husband tonight and also bear sons,

13 would you therefore wait until they were grown? Would you therefore refrain from marrying? No, my daughters; for it is [1]harder for me than for you, for [a]the hand of the LORD has gone forth against me."

Ruth's Loyalty

14 And they lifted up their voices and wept again; and Orpah kissed her mother-in-law, but Ruth clung to her.

15 Then she said, "Behold, your sister-in-law has gone back to her people and her [a]gods; return after your sister-in-law."

16 But Ruth said, "Do not urge me to leave you *or* turn back from following you; for where you go, I will go, and where you lodge, I will lodge. Your people *shall be* my people, and your God, my God.

17 "Where you die, I will die, and there I will be buried. Thus may [a]the LORD do to me, and worse, if *anything but* death parts you and me."

18 When [a]she saw that she was determined to go with her, she [1]said no more to her.

19 So they both went until they came to Bethlehem. And it came about when they had come to Bethlehem, that [a]all the city was stirred because of them, and [1]the women said, "Is this Naomi?"

20 And she said to them, "Do not call me [1]Naomi; call me [2]Mara, for [3][a]the Almighty has dealt very bitterly with me.

1 [1]Or, *judged* [2]Lit., *he, and* [a]Judg. 2:16-18 [b]Gen. 12:10; 26:1; 2 Kin. 8:1 [c]Judg. 17:8; Mic. 5:2
2 [a]Judg. 3:30
5 [1]Lit., *both of them*
6 [a]Ex. 4:31; Jer. 29:10; Zeph. 2:7 [b]Ps. 132:15; Matt. 6:11
8 [a]2 Tim. 1:16
11 [a]Gen. 38:11; Deut. 25:5
13 [1]Lit., *more bitter* [a]Judg. 2:15; Job 19:21; Ps. 32:4
15 [a]Josh. 24:15; Judg. 11:24
17 [a]1 Sam. 3:17; 2 Kin. 6:31
18 [1]Lit., *ceased to speak* [a]Acts 21:14
19 [1]Lit., *they* [a]Matt. 21:10
20 [1]I.e., pleasant [2]I.e., bitter [3]Heb., *Shaddai* [a]Ex. 6:3; Job 6:4

21 "I went out full, but [a]the LORD has
brought me back empty. Why do you
call me Naomi, since the LORD has
witnessed against me and [1]the Almighty
has afflicted me?"
22 So Naomi returned, and with her
Ruth the Moabitess, her daughter-in-
law, who returned from the land of
Moab. And they came to Bethlehem at
[a]the beginning of barley harvest.

Ruth Gleans in Boaz' Field

2 NOW Naomi had [1]a kinsman of her
husband, a [2]man of great wealth, of
the family of [a]Elimelech, whose name
was Boaz.
2 And Ruth the Moabitess said to
Naomi, "Please let me go to the field and
[a]glean among the ears of grain after one
in whose sight I may find favor." And
she said to her, "Go, my daughter."
3 So she departed and went and
gleaned in the field after the reapers; and
[1]she happened to come to the portion of
the field belonging to Boaz, who was of
the family of Elimelech.
4 Now behold, Boaz came from
Bethlehem and said to the reapers,
"[a]May the LORD be with you." And they
said to him, "May the LORD bless you."
5 Then Boaz said to his servant who
was [1]in charge of the reapers, "Whose
young woman is this?"
6 And the servant [1]in charge of the
reapers answered and said, "She is the
young Moabite woman who returned
with Naomi from the land of Moab.
7 "And she said, 'Please let me glean
and gather after the reapers among the
sheaves.' Thus she came and has remained from the morning until now; she
has been sitting in the house for a little
while."
8 Then Boaz said to Ruth, "[1]Listen
carefully, my daughter. Do not go to
glean in another field; furthermore, do
not go on from this one, but stay here
with my maids.
9 "Let your eyes be on the field which
they reap, and go after them. Indeed, I
have commanded the servants not to
touch you. When you are thirsty, go to
the [1]water jars and drink from what the
servants draw."
10 Then she [a]fell on her face, bowing
to the ground and said to him, "Why
have I found favor in your sight that you
should take notice of me, since I am a
foreigner?"
11 And Boaz answered and said to
her, "All that you have done for your
mother-in-law after the death of your
husband has been fully reported to me,
and how you left your father and your
mother and the land of your birth, and
came to a people that you did not
previously know.
12 "[a]May the LORD reward your work,
and your wages be full from the LORD,
the God of Israel, [b]under whose wings
you have come to seek refuge."
13 Then she said, "I have found favor
in your sight, my lord, for you have
comforted me and indeed have spoken
[1]kindly to your maidservant, though I
am not like one of your maidservants."
14 And at mealtime Boaz said to her,
"[1]Come here, that you may eat of the
bread and dip your piece of bread in the
vinegar." So she sat beside the reapers;
and he [2]served her roasted grain, and she
ate and was satisfied [a]and had some left.
15 When she rose to glean, Boaz commanded his servants, saying, "Let her
glean even among the sheaves, and do
not insult her.
16 "And also you shall purposely pull
out for her *some grain* from the bundles
and leave *it* that she may glean, and do
not rebuke her."
17 So she gleaned in the field until
evening. Then she beat out what she had
gleaned, and it was about an ephah of
barley.
18 And she took *it* up and went into
the city, and her mother-in-law saw what
she had gleaned. She also took *it* out and
[a]gave [1]Naomi what she had left after
[2]she was satisfied.
19 Her mother-in-law then said to her,
"Where did you glean today and where
did you work? May he who [a]took notice
of you be blessed." So she told her
mother-in-law with whom she had
worked and said, "The name of the man
with whom I worked today is Boaz."
20 And Naomi said to her daughter-
in-law, "[a]May he be blessed of the LORD
who has not withdrawn his kindness to
the living and to the dead." Again
Naomi said to her, "The man is [1]our
relative, he is one of our [2]closest relatives."
21 Then Ruth the Moabitess said,
"[1]Furthermore, he said to me, 'You
should stay close to my servants until
they have finished all my harvest.' "
22 And Naomi said to Ruth her
daughter-in-law, "It is good, my daughter, that you go out with his maids, lest
others fall upon you in another field."
23 So she stayed close by the maids of
Boaz in order to glean until [a]the end of
the barley harvest and the wheat harvest.
And she lived with her mother-in-law.

Boaz Will Redeem Ruth

3 THEN Naomi her mother-in-law
said to her, "My daughter, shall I
not seek [1]security for you, that it may be
well with you?
2 "And now is not Boaz [a]our [1]kins-
man, with whose maids you were? Behold, he winnows barley at the threshing
floor tonight.
3 "Wash yourself therefore, and
anoint yourself and put on your *best*
clothes, and go down to the threshing
floor; *but* do not make yourself known to
the man until he has finished eating and
drinking.
4 "And it shall be when he lies down,
that you shall [1]notice the place where he

21 [1]Heb., *Shaddai* [a]Job 1:21
22 [a]Ex. 9:31; Lev. 23:10, 11
1 [1]Or, *an acquaintance* [2]Or, *mighty, valiant man* [a]Ruth 1:2
2 [a]Lev. 19:9, 10; 23:22; Deut. 24:19; Ruth 2:7
3 [1]Lit., *her chance chanced upon*
4 [a]Judg. 6:12; Ps. 129:8; Luke 1:28; 2 Thess. 3:16
5 [1]Lit., *appointed over*
6 [1]Lit., *who was appointed over*
8 [1]Lit., *Have you not heard*
9 [1]Lit., *vessels*
10 [a]1 Sam. 25:23
12 [a]1 Sam. 24:19 [b]Ruth 1:16; Ps. 17:8; 36:7; 57:1; 61:4; 63:7; 91:4
13 [1]Lit., *to the heart of your*
14 [1]Lit., *Draw near* [2]Lit., *held out to* [a]Ruth 2:18
18 [1]Lit., *her* [2]Lit., *her satiety* [a]Ruth 2:14
19 [a]Ps. 41:1
20 [1]Lit., *near to us* [2]Lit., *redeemers* [a]2 Sam. 2:5
21 [1]Lit., *Also that*
23 [a]Deut. 16:9
1 [1]Lit., *rest*
2 [1]Or, *acquaintance* [a]Deut. 25:5-10
4 [1]Lit., *know*

lies, and you shall go and uncover his
feet and lie down; then he will tell you
what you shall do."
5 And she said to her, "[a]All that you
say I will do."
6 So she went down to the threshing
floor and did according to all that her
mother-in-law had commanded her.
7 When Boaz had eaten and drunk
and [a]his heart was merry, he went to lie
down at the end of the heap of grain;
and she came secretly, and uncovered his
feet and lay down.
8 And it happened in the middle of
the night that the man was startled and
[1]bent forward; and behold, a woman
was lying at his feet.
9 And he said, "Who are you?" And
she answered, "I am Ruth your maid. So
spread your covering over your maid, for
you are a [1]close relative."
10 Then he said, "[a]May you be
blessed of the LORD, my daughter. You
have shown your last kindness to be
better than the first by not going after
young men, whether poor or rich.
11 "And now, my daughter, do not
fear. I will do for you whatever you [1]ask,
for all my people in the [2]city know that
you are [a]a woman of excellence.
12 "And now it is true I am a [1]close
relative; however, there is a [1]relative
closer than I.
13 "Remain this night, and when morning comes, [a]if he will [1]redeem you, good;
let him redeem you. But if he does not
wish to [1]redeem you, then I will redeem
you, [b]as the LORD lives. Lie down until
morning."
14 So she lay at his feet until morning
and rose before one could recognize
another; and he said, "[a]Let it not be
known that the woman came to the
threshing floor."
15 Again he said, "Give me the cloak
that is on you and hold it." So she held
it, and he measured six *measures* of
barley and laid *it* on her. Then [1]she went
into the city.
16 And when she came to her mother-
in-law, she said, "[1]How did it go, my
daughter?" And she told her all that the
man had done for her.
17 And she said, "These six *measures*
of barley he gave to me, for he said, 'Do
not go to your mother-in-law empty-
handed.'"
18 Then she said, "Wait, my daughter,
until you know how the matter [1]turns
out; for the man will not rest until he has
[2]settled it today."

The Marriage of Ruth

4 NOW Boaz went up to the gate and
sat down there, and behold, [a]the
[1]close relative of whom Boaz spoke was
passing by, so he said, "Turn aside,
[2]friend, sit down here." And he turned
aside and sat down.
2 And he took ten men of the [a]elders
of the city and said, "Sit down here." So
they sat down.
3 Then he said to the [1]closest relative, "Naomi, who has come back from
the land of Moab, has to sell the piece of
land [a]which belonged to our brother
Elimelech.
4 "So I thought to [1]inform you, saying, '[a]Buy *it* before those who are sitting
here, and before the elders of my people.
If you will redeem *it,* redeem *it;* but if
[2]not, tell me that I may know; for [b]there
is no one but you to redeem *it,* and I am
after you.'" And he said, "I will redeem
it."
5 Then Boaz said, "On the day you
buy the field from the hand of Naomi,
you must also acquire Ruth the Moabitess, the widow of the deceased, in order
[a]to raise up the name of the deceased on
his inheritance."
6 And [a]the [1]closest relative said, "I
cannot redeem *it* for myself, lest I [2]jeop-
ardize my own inheritance. Redeem *it*
for yourself; you *may have* my right of
redemption, for I cannot redeem *it.*"
7 Now this was [a]*the custom* in former
times in Israel concerning the redemption and the exchange *of land* to confirm
any matter: a man removed his sandal
and gave it to another; and this was the
manner of attestation in Israel.
8 So the [1]closest relative said to
Boaz, "Buy *it* for yourself." And he
removed his sandal.
9 Then Boaz said to the elders and
all the people, "You are witnesses today
that I have bought from the hand of
Naomi all that belonged to Elimelech
and all that belonged to Chilion and
Mahlon.
10 "Moreover, I have acquired Ruth
the Moabitess, the widow of Mahlon, to
be my wife in order to raise up the name
of the deceased on his inheritance, so
[a]that the name of the deceased may not
be cut off from his brothers or from the
[1]court of his *birth* place; you are witnesses today."
11 And all the people who were in the
[1]court, and the elders, said, "*We are*
witnesses. May the LORD make the
woman who is coming into your home
[a]like Rachel and Leah, both of whom
built the house of Israel; and may you
achieve [2]wealth in Ephrathah and [3]be-
come famous in Bethlehem.
12 "Moreover, may your house be like
the house of [a]Perez whom Tamar bore to
Judah, through the [1]offspring which the
LORD shall give you by this young
woman."
13 So Boaz took Ruth, and she became his wife, and he went in to her.
And [a]the LORD [1]enabled her to conceive,
and she gave birth to a son.
14 Then the [a]women said to Naomi,
"Blessed is the LORD who has not left
you without a [1]redeemer today, and may
his name [2]become famous in Israel.
15 "May he also be to you a restorer of
life and a sustainer of your old age; for
your daughter-in-law, who loves you

5 [a]Eph. 6:1; Col. 3:20
7 [a]Judg. 19:6, 9; 2 Sam. 13:28; 1 Kin. 21:7; Esth. 1:10
8 [1]Lit., *twisted himself*
9 [1]Or, *redeemer*
10 [a]Ruth 2:20
11 [1]Lit., *say* [2]Lit., *gate* [a]Prov. 12:4; 31:10
12 [1]Or, *redeemer*
13 [1]Or, *act as close relative to* [a]Deut. 25:5; Matt. 22:24 [b]Judg. 8:19; Jer. 4:2; 12:16
14 [a]Rom. 14:16; 2 Cor. 8:21
15 [1]So with many mss.; M.T., *he*
16 [1]Lit., *Who are you?*
18 [1]Lit., *falls* [2]Lit., *finished the matter*

1 [1]Or, *redeemer* [2]Lit., *a certain one* [a]Ruth 3:12
2 [a]1 Kin. 21:8; Prov. 31:23
3 [1]Lit., *redeemer* [a]Lev. 25:25
4 [1]Lit., *uncover your ear* [2]Lit., *no one will redeem* [a]Jer. 32:7f. [b]Lev. 25:25
5 [a]Gen. 38:8; Deut. 25:5f.; Matt. 22:24
6 [1]Lit., *redeemer* [2]Lit., *ruin* [a]Lev. 25:25
7 [a]Deut. 25:8-10
8 [1]Lit., *redeemer*
10 [1]Lit., *gate* [a]Deut. 25:6
11 [1]Lit., *gate* [2]Or, *power* [3]Lit., *call the name in* [a]Gen. 29:25-30
12 [1]Lit., *seed* [a]Gen. 38:29; 46:12; Ruth 4:18
13 [1]Lit., *gave her conception* [a]Gen. 29:31; 33:5
14 [1]Or, *closest relative* [2]Lit., *be called in* [a]Luke 1:58

[1a]and is better to you than seven sons,
has given birth to him."

The Line of David Began Here

16 Then Naomi took the child [1]and
laid him in her lap, and became his
nurse.
17 And the neighbor women gave him
a name, saying, "A son has been born to
Naomi!" So they named him Obed. He
is the father of Jesse, the father of David.

15 [1]Lit., *who* [a]Ruth 1:16, 17; 2:11, 12
16 [1]I.e., as her own
18 [1]Lit., *begot,* and so through v. 22 [a]Matt. 1:3-6

18 Now these are the generations of
Perez: [a]to Perez [1]was born Hezron,
19 and to Hezron was born Ram, and
to Ram, Amminadab,
20 and to Amminadab was born Nahshon, and to Nahshon, Salmon,
21 and to Salmon was born Boaz, and
to Boaz, Obed,
22 and to Obed was born Jesse, and to
Jesse, David.

THE FIRST BOOK OF SAMUEL

Elkanah and His Wives

1 NOW there was a certain man from
[a]Ramathaim-zophim from the [b]hill
country of Ephraim, and his name was
[c]Elkanah the son of Jeroham, the son of
Elihu, the son of Tohu, the son of Zuph,
an Ephraimite.
2 And he had [a]two wives: the name
of one was [b]Hannah and the name of the
other Peninnah; and Peninnah had children, but Hannah had no children.
3 Now this man would go up from
his city [a]yearly [b]to worship and to
sacrifice to the LORD of hosts in [c]Shiloh.
And the two sons of Eli, Hophni and
Phinehas were priests to the LORD there.
4 And when the day came that Elkanah sacrificed, he [a]would give portions
to Peninnah his wife and to all her sons
and her daughters;
5 but to Hannah he would give a
double portion, for he loved Hannah,
[a]but the LORD had closed her womb.
6 Her rival, however, [a]would provoke
her bitterly to irritate her, because the
LORD had closed her womb.
7 And it happened year after year, as
often as she went up to the house of the
LORD, she would provoke her, so she
wept and would not eat.
8 Then Elkanah her husband said to
her, "Hannah, why do you weep and
why do you not eat and why is your
heart sad? [a]Am I not better to you than
ten sons?"
9 Then Hannah rose after eating and
drinking in Shiloh. Now Eli the priest
was sitting on the seat by the doorpost
of [a]the temple of the LORD.
10 And she, [1]greatly distressed,
prayed to the LORD and wept bitterly.
11 And she [a]made a vow and said, "O
LORD of hosts, if Thou wilt indeed [b]look
on the affliction of Thy maidservant and
remember me, and not forget Thy maidservant, but wilt give Thy maidservant a
[1]son, then I will give him to the LORD all
the days of his life, and [c]a razor shall
never come on his head."
12 Now it came about, as she [1]contin-
ued praying before the LORD, that Eli
was watching her mouth.

1 [a]1 Sam. 1:19 [b]Josh. 17:17, 18; 24:33 [c]1 Chr. 6:22-28, 33-38
2 [a]Deut. 21:15-17 [b]Luke 2:36
3 [a]Ex. 34:23; 1 Sam. 1:21; Luke 2:41 [b]Ex. 23:14; Deut. 12:5-7; 16:16 [c]Josh. 18:1
4 [a]Deut. 12:17, 18
5 [a]Gen. 16:1; 30:1
6 [a]Job 24:21
8 [a]Ruth 4:15
9 [a]1 Sam. 3:3
10 [1]Lit., *bitter of soul*
11 [1]Lit., *seed of men* [a]Num. 30:6-11 [b]Gen. 29:32 [c]Num. 6:5; Judg. 13:5
12 [1]Lit., *multiplied*
13 [a]Gen. 24:42-45
14 [a]Acts 2:4, 13
15 [1]Lit., *severe* [a]Job 30:16; Ps. 42:4; 62:8; Lam. 2:19
16 [1]Lit., *give* [2]Lit., *my provocation*
17 [a]Judg. 18:6; 1 Sam. 25:35; 2 Kin. 5:19; Mark 5:34; Luke 7:50 [b]Ps. 20:3-5
18 [a]Gen. 33:15; Ruth 2:13 [b]Rom. 15:13
19 [1]Lit., *knew* [a]1 Sam. 1:1; 2:11 [b]Gen. 21:1; 30:22
20 [1]Lit., *at the circuit of the days* [a]Gen. 41:51, 52; Ex. 2:10, 22; Matt. 1:21
21 [a]Deut. 12:11; 1 Sam. 1:3
22 [a]Luke 2:22 [b]1 Sam. 1:11, 28
23 [1]Lit., *in your eyes* [a]Num. 30:7, 10, 11 [b]1 Sam. 1:17

13 As for Hannah, [a]she was speaking
in her heart, only her lips were moving,
but her voice was not heard. So Eli
thought she was drunk.
14 Then Eli said to her, "[a]How long
will you make yourself drunk? Put away
your wine from you."
15 But Hannah answered and said,
"No, my lord, I am a woman [1]oppressed
in spirit; I have drunk neither wine nor
strong drink, but I [a]have poured out my
soul before the LORD.
16 "Do not [1]consider your maidservant
as a worthless woman; for I have spoken
until now out of my great concern and
[2]provocation."
17 Then Eli answered and said, "[a]Go
in peace; and may the God of Israel
[b]grant your petition that you have asked
of Him."
18 And she said, "[a]Let your maidservant find favor in your sight." So the
woman went her way and ate, and [b]her
face was no longer *sad.*

Samuel Is Born to Hannah

19 Then they arose early in the morning and worshiped before the LORD, and
returned again to their house in [a]Ramah.
And Elkanah [1]had relations with Hannah his wife, and [b]the LORD remembered her.
20 And it came about [1]in due time,
after Hannah had conceived, that she
gave birth to a son; and she named him
Samuel, *saying,* "[a]Because I have asked
him of the LORD."
21 Then the man Elkanah [a]went up
with all his household to offer to the
LORD the yearly sacrifice and *pay* his
vow.
22 But Hannah did not go up, for she
said to her husband, "*I will not go up*
until the child is weaned; then I will
[a]bring him, that he may appear before
the LORD and [b]stay there forever."
23 And [a]Elkanah her husband said to
her, "Do what seems best [1]to you. Remain until you have weaned him; only
[b]may the LORD confirm His word." So
the woman remained and nursed her son
until she weaned him.

24 Now when she had weaned him,
[a]she took him up with her, with a three-
year-old bull and one ephah of flour and
a jug of wine, and brought him to [b]the
house of the LORD in Shiloh, although
the child was young.
25 Then [a]they slaughtered the bull,
and [b]brought the boy to Eli.
26 And she said, "Oh, my lord! [a]As
your soul lives, my lord, I am the woman
who stood here beside you, praying to
the LORD.
27 "[a]For this boy I prayed, and the
LORD has given me my petition which I
asked of Him.
28 "[a]So I have also [1]dedicated him to
the LORD; as long as he lives he is
[1]dedicated to the LORD." And [b]he worshiped the LORD there.

Hannah's Song of Thanksgiving

2 THEN Hannah [a]prayed and said,
"My heart exults in the LORD;
[b]My [1]horn is exalted in the LORD,
My mouth [2]speaks boldly against my enemies,
Because [c]I rejoice in Thy salvation.
2 "[a]There is no one holy like the LORD,
Indeed, [b]there is no one besides Thee,
[c]Nor is there any rock like our God.
3 "[1]Boast no more so very proudly,
[a]Do not let arrogance come out of your mouth;
[b]For the LORD is a God of knowledge,
[c]And with Him actions are weighed.
4 "[a]The bows of the mighty are shattered,
[b]But the feeble gird on strength.
5 "Those who were full hire themselves out for bread,
But those who were hungry cease *to hunger*.
[a]Even the barren gives birth to seven,
But [b]she who has many children languishes.
6 "[a]The LORD kills and makes alive;
[b]He brings down to [1]Sheol and raises up.
7 "[a]The LORD makes poor and rich;
[b]He brings low, He also exalts.
8 "[a]He raises the poor from the dust,
[b]He lifts the needy from the ash heap
[c]To make them sit with nobles,
And inherit a seat of honor;
[d]For the pillars of the earth are the LORD's,
And He set the world on them.
9 "[a]He keeps the feet of His godly ones,
[b]But the wicked ones are silenced in darkness;
[c]For not by might shall a man prevail.
10 "[a]Those who contend with the LORD will be shattered;
[b]Against them He will thunder in the heavens,
[c]The LORD will judge the ends of the earth;
[d]And He will give strength to His king,
[e]And will exalt the [1]horn of His anointed."
11 Then Elkanah went to his home at
[a]Ramah. [b]But the boy ministered to the
LORD before Eli the priest.

The Sin of Eli's Sons

12 Now the sons of Eli were [1a]worth-
less men; they did not know the LORD
13 [a]and the custom of the priests with
the people. When any man was offering
a sacrifice, the priest's servant would
come while the meat was boiling, with a
three-pronged fork in his hand.
14 Then he would thrust it into the
pan, or kettle, or caldron, or pot; all that
the fork brought up the priest would
take for himself. Thus they did in Shiloh
to all the Israelites who came there.
15 Also, before [a]they burned the fat,
the priest's servant would come and say
to the man who was sacrificing, "Give
the priest meat for roasting, as he will
not take boiled meat from you, only
raw."
16 And if the man said to him, "They
must surely [1]burn the fat [2]first, and then
take as much as [3]you desire," then he
would say, "No, but you shall give *it to*
me now; and if not, I will take it by
force."
17 Thus the sin of the young men was
very great before the LORD, for the men
[a]despised the offering of the LORD.

Samuel before the LORD as a Boy

18 Now [a]Samuel was ministering before the LORD, *as* a boy [1b]wearing a
linen ephod.
19 And his mother would make him a
little [a]robe and bring it to him from year
to year when she would come up with
her husband to offer [b]the yearly sacrifice.
20 Then Eli would [a]bless Elkanah and
his wife and say, "May the LORD give
you [1]children from this woman in place
of [2]the one she [b]dedicated to the LORD."
And they went to their own [3]home.
21 And [a]the LORD visited Hannah;
and she conceived and gave birth to
three sons and two daughters. And [b]the
boy Samuel grew before the LORD.

Eli Rebukes His Sons

22 Now Eli was very old; and he
heard [a]all that his sons were doing to all
Israel, and how they lay with [b]the
women who served at the doorway of the
tent of meeting.
23 And he said to them, "Why do you
do such things, the evil things that I hear
from all these people?

24 [a]Num. 15:9, 10; Deut. 12:5, 6 [b]Josh. 18:1; 1 Sam. 4:3, 4
25 [a]Lev. 1:5 [b]Luke 2:22
26 [a]2 Kin. 2:2, 4, 6; 4:30
27 [a]1 Sam. 1:11-13; Ps. 6:9; 66:19, 20
28 [1]Lit., *lent* [a]1 Sam. 1:11, 22 [b]Gen. 24:26, 52

1 [1]I.e., strength [2]Lit., *is enlarged* [a]1 Sam. 2:1-10; Luke 1:46-55 [b]Deut. 33:17; Job 16:15; Ps. 75:10; 89:17, 24; 92:10; 112:9 [c]Ps. 9:14; 13:5; 35:9; Is. 12:2, 3
2 [a]Ex. 15:11; Lev. 19:2; Ps. 86:8 [b]2 Sam. 22:32 [c]Deut. 32:30, 31
3 [1]Lit., *Talk much* [a]Prov. 8:13 [b]1 Sam. 16:7; 1 Kin. 8:39 [c]Prov. 16:2; 24:12
4 [a]Ps. 37:15; 46:9 [b]Ps. 18:39; Heb. 11:32-34
5 [a]Ruth 4:15; Ps. 113:9 [b]Jer. 15:9
6 [1]I.e., the nether world [a]Deut. 32:39; 2 Kin. 5:7; Rev. 1:18 [b]Is. 26:19
7 [a]Deut. 8:17, 18 [b]Job 5:11; Ps. 75:7; James 4:10
8 [a]Job 42:10-12; Ps. 75:7; 113:7 [b]2 Sam. 7:8; Dan. 2:48; James 2:5 [c]Job 36:7; Ps. 113:8 [d]Job 38:4-6; Ps. 75:3; 104:5
9 [a]Ps. 91:11, 12; 121:3; Prov. 3:26; 1 Pet. 1:5 [b]Matt. 8:12 [c]Ps. 33:16, 17
10 [1]I.e., strength [a]Ex. 15:6; Ps. 2:9 [b]1 Sam. 7:10; 2 Sam. 22:14; Ps. 18:13, 14 [c]Ps. 96:13; 98:9; Matt. 25:31, 32 [d]Ps. 21:1, 7 [e]Ps. 89:24
11 [a]1 Sam. 1:1, 19 [b]1 Sam. 1:28; 2:18; 3:1
12 [1]Lit., *sons of Belial* [a]Jer. 2:8; 9:3, 6; 2 Cor. 6:15
13 [a]Lev. 7:29-34
15 [a]Lev. 3:3-5, 16
16 [1]Lit., *offer up in smoke* [2]Lit., *like the day* [3]Lit., *your soul*
17 [a]Mal. 2:7-9
18 [1]Lit., *girded with* [a]1 Sam. 2:11; 3:1 [b]1 Sam. 2:28; 22:18; 2 Sam. 6:14; 1 Chr. 15:27
19 [a]Ex. 28:31 [b]1 Sam. 1:3, 21
20 [1]Lit., *seed* [2]Lit., *the one asked for which was lent* [3]Lit., *place* [a]Luke 2:34 [b]1 Sam. 1:11, 27, 28
21 [a]Gen. 21:1 [b]Judg. 13:24; 1 Sam. 2:26; 3:19-21; Luke 1:80; 2:40
22 [a]1 Sam. 2:13-17 [b]Ex. 38:8

24 "No, my sons; for the report is not good [a]which I hear [1]the LORD's people circulating.

25 "If one man sins against another, [a]God will mediate for him; but [b]if a man sins against the LORD, who can intercede for him?" But they would not listen to the voice of their father, for the [c]LORD desired to put them to death.

26 Now the boy [a]Samuel [1]was growing in stature and in favor both with the LORD and with men.

27 Then [a]a man of God came to Eli and said to him, "Thus says the LORD, '[b]Did I *not* indeed reveal Myself to the house of your father when they were in Egypt *in bondage* to Pharaoh's house?

28 'And [a]did I *not* choose them from all the tribes of Israel to be My priests, to go up to My altar, to burn incense, to carry an ephod before Me; and did I *not* [b]give to the house of your father all the fire *offerings* of the sons of Israel?

29 'Why do you [a]kick at My sacrifice and at My offering [b]which I have commanded *in My* [c]dwelling, and [d]honor your sons above Me, by making yourselves fat with the [1]choicest of every offering of My people Israel?'

30 "Therefore the LORD God of Israel declares, '[a]I did indeed say that your house and the house of your father should walk before Me forever'; but now the LORD declares, 'Far be it from Me—for [b]those who honor Me I will honor, and those [c]who despise Me will be lightly esteemed.

31 'Behold, [a]the days are coming when I will break your [1]strength and the [1]strength of your father's house so that there will not be an old man in your house.

32 'And you will see [a]the distress of *My* dwelling, in *spite of* all that [1]I do good for Israel; and an [b]old man will not be in your house forever.

33 'Yet I will not cut off every man of yours from My altar [1]that your eyes may fail *from weeping* and your soul grieve, and all the increase of your house will die [2]in the prime of life.

34 'And this will be [a]the sign to you which shall come concerning your two sons, Hophni and Phinehas: [b]on the same day both of them shall die.

35 'But [a]I will raise up for Myself a faithful priest who will do according to what is in My heart and in My soul; and [b]I will build him an enduring house, and he will walk before [c]My anointed always.

36 'And it shall come about that everyone who is left in your house shall come and bow down to him for a [1]piece of silver or a loaf of bread, and say, "Please [2]assign me to one of the priest's offices so that I may eat a piece of bread." ' "

The Prophetic Call to Samuel

3 NOW [a]the boy Samuel was ministering to the LORD before Eli. And [b]word from the LORD was rare in those days, [1]visions were infrequent.

2 And it happened at that time as Eli was lying down in his place (now [a]his eyesight had begun to grow dim *and* he could not see well),

3 and [a]the lamp of God had not yet gone out, and Samuel was lying down in the temple of the LORD where the ark of God *was*,

4 that the LORD called Samuel; and he said, "[a]Here I am."

5 Then he ran to Eli and said, "Here I am, for you called me." But he said, "I did not call, lie down again." So he went and lay down.

6 And the LORD called yet again, "Samuel!" So Samuel arose and went to Eli, and said, "Here I am, for you called me." But he [1]answered, "I did not call, my son, lie down again."

7 [a]Now Samuel did not yet know the LORD, nor had the word of the LORD yet been revealed to him.

8 So the LORD called Samuel again for the third time. And he arose and went to Eli, and said, "Here I am, for you called me." Then Eli discerned that the LORD was calling the boy.

9 And Eli said to Samuel, "Go lie down, and it shall be if He calls you, that you shall say, 'Speak, LORD, for Thy servant is listening.' " So Samuel went and lay down in his place.

10 Then the LORD came and stood and called as at other times, "Samuel! Samuel!" And Samuel said, "Speak, for Thy servant is listening."

11 And the LORD said to Samuel, "Behold, [a]I am about to do a thing in Israel at which both ears of everyone who hears it will tingle.

12 "In that day [a]I will carry out against Eli all that I have spoken concerning his house, from beginning to end.

13 "For [a]I have told him that I am about to judge his house forever for [b]the iniquity which he knew, because [c]his sons brought a curse on themselves and [d]he did not rebuke them.

14 "And therefore I have sworn to the house of Eli that [a]the iniquity of Eli's house shall not be atoned for by sacrifice or offering forever."

15 So Samuel lay down until morning. Then he [a]opened the doors of the house of the LORD. But Samuel was afraid to tell [b]the vision to Eli.

16 Then Eli called Samuel and said, "Samuel, my son." And he said, "Here I am."

17 And he said, "What is the word that He spoke to you? Please do not hide it from me. [a]May God do so to you, and more also, if you hide anything from me of all the words that He spoke to you."

18 So Samuel told him everything and hid nothing from him. And he said, "[a]It is the LORD; let Him do what seems good to Him."

19 Thus [a]Samuel grew and [b]the LORD was with him and [c]let none of his words [1]fail.

24 [1]Or, *making the LORD'S people transgress* [a]1 Kin. 15:26

25 [a]Deut. 1:17 [b]Num. 15:30; 1 Sam. 3:14; Heb. 10:26, 27 [c]Josh. 11:20

26 [1]Lit., *was going on both great and good* [a]1 Sam. 2:21; Luke 2:52

27 [a]Deut. 33:1; Judg. 13:6 [b]Ex. 4:14-16; 12:1, 43

28 [a]Ex. 28:1-4; 30:7, 8; Lev. 8:7, 8 [b]Lev. 7:35, 36

29 [1]Or, *first* [a]1 Sam. 2:13-17 [b]Deut. 12:5-9 [c]Ps. 26:8 [d]Matt. 10:37

30 [a]Ex. 29:9; Num. 25:13 [b]Ps. 50:23 [c]Mal. 2:9

31 [1]Or, *arm* [a]1 Sam. 4:11-18; 22:17-20

32 [1]Lit., *He does* [a]1 Kin. 2:26, 27 [b]Zech. 8:4

33 [1]Lit., *to waste away your eyes and to grieve your soul* [2]Lit., *as men*

34 [a]1 Sam. 10:7-9; 1 Kin. 13:3 [b]1 Sam. 4:11, 17

35 [a]1 Sam. 3:1; 7:9; 9:12, 13 [b]1 Sam. 8:3-5; 25:28; 2 Sam. 7:11, 27; 1 Kin. 11:38 [c]1 Sam. 10:9, 10; 12:3; 16:13

36 [1]Or, *payment* [2]Lit., *attach*

1 [1]Lit., *no vision spread abroad* [a]1 Sam. 2:11, 18 [b]Ps. 74:9; Ezek. 7:26; Amos 8:11, 12

2 [a]Gen. 27:1; 48:10; 1 Sam. 4:15

3 [a]Ex. 25:31-37; Lev. 24:2, 3

4 [a]Is. 6:8

6 [1]Lit., *said*

7 [a]Acts 19:2; 1 Cor. 13:11

11 [a]2 Kin. 21:12; Jer. 19:3

12 [a]1 Sam. 2:27-36

13 [a]1 Sam. 2:29-31 [b]1 Sam. 2:22 [c]1 Sam. 2:12, 17, 22 [d]Deut. 17:12; 21:18

14 [a]Lev. 15:31; Is. 22:14

15 [a]1 Chr. 15:23 [b]1 Sam. 3:10

17 [a]2 Sam. 3:35

18 [a]Ex. 34:5-7; Lev. 10:3; Job 2:10; Is. 39:8

19 [1]Lit., *fall to the ground* [a]1 Sam. 2:21 [b]Gen. 21:22; 28:15; 39:2 [c]1 Sam. 9:6

20 And all Israel [a]from Dan even to Beersheba knew that Samuel was confirmed as a prophet of the LORD.

21 And [a]the LORD appeared again at Shiloh, [b]because the LORD revealed Himself to Samuel at Shiloh by the word of the LORD.

Philistines Take the Ark in Victory

4 THUS the word of Samuel came to all Israel. Now Israel went out to meet the Philistines in battle and camped beside [a]Ebenezer while the Philistines camped in [b]Aphek.

2 And the Philistines drew up in battle array to meet Israel. When the battle spread, Israel was [1]defeated before the Philistines who killed about four thousand men on the battlefield.

3 When the people came into the camp, the elders of Israel said, "[a]Why has the LORD defeated us today before the Philistines? [b]Let us take to ourselves from Shiloh the ark of the covenant of the LORD, that [1]it may come among us and deliver us from the power of our enemies."

4 So the people sent to Shiloh, and from there they carried the ark of the covenant of the LORD of hosts [a]who sits *above* the cherubim; and the two sons of Eli, Hophni and Phinehas, *were* there with the ark of the covenant of God.

5 And it happened as the ark of the covenant of the LORD came into the camp, that [a]all Israel shouted with a great shout, so that the earth resounded.

6 And when the Philistines heard the noise of the shout, they said, "What *does* the noise of this great shout in the camp of the Hebrews *mean?*" Then they understood that the ark of the LORD had come into the camp.

7 And the Philistines were afraid, for they said, "God has come into the camp." And they said, "[a]Woe to us! For nothing like this has happened before.

8 "Woe to us! Who shall deliver us from the hand of these mighty gods? These are the gods who smote the Egyptians with all *kinds of* plagues in the wilderness.

9 "[a]Take courage and be men, O Philistines, lest you become slaves to the Hebrews, [b]as they have been slaves to you; therefore, be men and fight."

10 So the Philistines fought and [a]Israel was [1]defeated, and [b]every man fled to his tent, and the slaughter was very great; for there fell of Israel thirty thousand foot soldiers.

11 And the ark of God was taken; and [a]the two sons of Eli, Hophni and Phinehas, died.

12 Now a man of Benjamin ran from the battle line and came to Shiloh the same day with [a]his clothes torn and [1]dust on his head.

13 When he came, behold, [a]Eli was sitting on *his* seat [1]by the road eagerly watching, because his heart was trembling for the ark of God. So the man came to tell *it* in the city, and all the city cried out.

14 When Eli heard the noise of the outcry, he said, "What *does* the noise of this commotion *mean?*" Then the man came hurriedly and told Eli.

15 Now Eli was ninety-eight years old, and [a]his eyes were set so that he could not see.

16 And the man said to Eli, "I am the one who came from the battle line. Indeed, I escaped from the battle line today." And he said, "[a]How did things go, my son?"

17 Then the one who brought the news answered and said, "Israel has fled before the Philistines and there has also been a great slaughter among the people, and your two sons also, Hophni and Phinehas, are dead, and the ark of God has been taken."

18 And it came about when he mentioned the ark of God that [1][a]Eli fell off the seat backward beside the gate, and his neck was broken and he died, for [2]he was old and heavy. Thus he judged Israel forty years.

19 Now his daughter-in-law, Phinehas' wife, was pregnant and about to give birth; and when she heard the news that the ark of God was taken and that her father-in-law and her husband had died, she kneeled down and gave birth, for her pains came upon her.

20 And about the time of her death the women who stood by her said to her, "[a]Do not be afraid, for you have given birth to a son." But she did not answer or pay attention.

21 And she called the boy [1]Ichabod, saying, "[a]The glory has departed from Israel," because [b]the ark of God was taken and because of her father-in-law and her husband.

22 And she said, "The glory has departed from Israel, for the ark of God was taken."

Capture of the Ark Provokes God

5 NOW the Philistines took the ark of God and [a]brought it from Ebenezer to [b]Ashdod.

2 Then the Philistines took the ark of God and brought it to [a]the house of Dagon, and set it by Dagon.

3 When the Ashdodites arose early the next morning, behold, [a]Dagon had fallen on his face to the ground before the ark of the LORD. So they took Dagon and [b]set him in his place again.

4 But when they arose early the next morning, behold, [a]Dagon had fallen on his face to the ground before the ark of the LORD. And the head of Dagon and both the palms of his hands *were* cut off on the threshold; [1]only the trunk of Dagon was left to him.

5 Therefore neither the priests of Dagon nor all who enter Dagon's house [a]tread on the threshold of Dagon in Ashdod to this day.

20 [a]Judg. 20:1
21 [a]Gen. 12:7 [b]1 Sam. 3:10
1 [a]1 Sam. 7:12 [b]Josh. 12:18; 1 Sam. 29:1
2 [1]Lit., *smitten*
3 [1]Or, *he* [a]Josh. 7:7, 8 [b]Num. 10:35; Josh. 6:6
4 [a]Ex. 25:22; 2 Sam. 6:2; Ps. 80:1
5 [a]Josh. 6:5, 20
7 [a]Ex. 15:14
9 [a]1 Cor. 16:13 [b]Judg. 13:1; 1 Sam. 14:21
10 [1]Lit., *smitten* [a]Deut. 28:15, 25; 1 Sam. 4:2 [b]2 Sam. 18:17; 19:8; 2 Kin. 14:12; 2 Chr. 25:22
11 [a]1 Sam. 2:34; Ps. 78:56-64
12 [1]Lit., *ground* [a]Josh. 7:6; 2 Sam. 1:2; 15:32; Neh. 9:1; Job 2:12
13 [1]Gr. version reads *beside the gate watching the road* [a]1 Sam. 1:9; 4:18
15 [a]1 Sam. 3:2; 1 Kin. 14:4
16 [a]2 Sam. 1:4
18 [1]Lit., *he* [2]Lit., *the man* [a]1 Sam. 4:13
20 [a]Gen. 35:16-19
21 [1]I.e., No glory [a]Ps. 26:8; Jer. 2:11 [b]1 Sam. 4:11
1 [a]1 Sam. 4:1; 7:12 [b]Josh. 13:3
2 [a]Judg. 16:23-30; 1 Chr. 10:8-10
3 [a]Is. 19:1; 46:1, 2 [b]Is. 46:7
4 [1]So with ancient versions; Heb., *only Dagon* [a]Ezek. 6:4, 6; Mic. 1:7
5 [a]Zeph. 1:9

6 Now [a]the hand of the LORD was
heavy on the Ashdodites, and [b]He ravaged them and smote them with [c]tumors,
both Ashdod and its territories.
7 When the men of Ashdod saw that
it was so, they said, "The ark of the God
of Israel must not remain with us, for
His hand is severe on us and on Dagon
our god."
8 So they sent and [a]gathered all the
lords of the Philistines to them and said,
"What shall we do with the ark of the
God of Israel?" And they said, "Let the
ark of the God of Israel be brought
around to Gath." And they brought the
ark of the God of Israel *around.*
9 And it came about that after they
had brought it around, [a]the hand of the
LORD was against the city with very
great confusion; and He smote the men
of the city, both young and old, so that
[b]tumors broke out on them.
10 So they sent the ark of God to
Ekron. And it happened as the ark of
God came to Ekron that the Ekronites
cried out, saying, "They have brought
the ark of the God of Israel around to
[1]us, to kill [1]us and [2]our people."
11 They [a]sent therefore and gathered
all the lords of the Philistines and said,
"Send away the ark of the God of Israel,
and let it return to its own place, that it
may not kill [1]us and [2]our people." For
there was a deadly confusion throughout
the city; [b]the hand of God was very
heavy there.
12 And the men who did not die were
smitten with tumors and [a]the cry of the
city went up to heaven.

The Ark Returned to Israel

6 NOW the ark of the LORD had been
in the [1]country of the Philistines
seven months.
2 And [a]the Philistines called for the
priests and the diviners, saying, "What
shall we do with the ark of the LORD?
Tell us [1]how we shall send it to its
place."
3 And they said, "If you send away
the ark of the God of Israel, [a]do not
send it empty; but you shall surely
[b]return to Him a guilt offering. Then you
shall be healed and it shall be known to
you why His hand is not removed from
you."
4 Then they said, "What shall be the
guilt offering which we shall return to
Him?" And they said, "Five golden
[a]tumors and five golden mice [b]*according
to* the number of the lords of the Philistines, for one plague was on all of [1]you
and on your lords.
5 "So you shall make likenesses of
your tumors and likenesses of your mice
that ravage the land, and [a]you shall give
glory to the God of Israel; perhaps [b]He
will ease His hand from you, [c]your gods,
and your land.
6 "Why then do you harden your
hearts [a]as the Egyptians and Pharaoh
hardened their hearts? When He had
severely dealt with them, [b]did they not

6 [a]Ex. 9:3; 1 Sam. 5:7, 11; Ps. 32:4; 145:20; 147:6; Acts 13:11 [b]1 Sam. 6:5 [c]Deut. 28:27; Ps. 78:66
8 [a]1 Sam. 5:11; 29:6-11
9 [a]Deut. 2:15; 1 Sam. 5:11; 7:13; 12:15 [b]1 Sam. 5:6
10 [1]Lit., *me* [2]Lit., *my*
11 [1]Lit., *me* [2]Lit., *my* [a]1 Sam. 5:8 [b]1 Sam. 5:6, 9
12 [a]Ex. 12:30; Is. 15:3
1 [1]Lit., *field*
2 [1]Or, *with what* [a]Gen. 41:8; Ex. 7:11; Is. 2:6
3 [a]Ex. 23:15; Deut. 16:16 [b]Lev. 5:15, 16
4 [1]Lit., *them* [a]1 Sam. 5:6, 9, 12; 6:17 [b]Josh. 13:3; Judg. 3:3; 1 Sam. 6:17, 18
5 [a]Josh. 7:19; 1 Chr. 16:28, 29; Is. 42:12; Jer. 13:16; John 9:24; Rev. 14:7 [b]1 Sam. 5:6, 11 [c]1 Sam. 5:3, 4, 7
6 [1]Lit., *them* [a]Ex. 7:13; 8:15, 32; 9:34; 14:17 [b]Ex. 12:31
7 [a]2 Sam. 6:3 [b]Num. 19:2; Deut. 21:3, 4
8 [a]1 Sam. 6:4, 5 [b]1 Sam. 6:3
9 [a]Josh. 15:10; 21:16 [b]1 Sam. 6:3
12 [1]Lit., *way* [a]1 Sam. 6:9 [b]Num. 20:19
14 [a]2 Sam. 24:22; 1 Kin. 19:21
15 [a]Josh. 3:3
16 [a]Josh. 13:3; Judg. 3:3
17 [a]1 Sam. 6:4
18 [1]So some mss. and versions; Heb., *Abel* [a]Deut. 3:5 [b]1 Sam. 6:14, 15
19 [a]Ex. 19:21; Num. 4:5, 15, 20; 2 Sam. 6:7
20 [a]Lev. 11:44, 45; 2 Sam. 6:9; Mal. 3:2; Rev. 6:17

allow [1]the people to go, and they departed?
7 "Now therefore take and [a]prepare a
new cart and two milch cows on which
there [b]has never been a yoke; and hitch
the cows to the cart and take their calves
home, away from them.
8 "And take the ark of the LORD and
place it on the cart; and put [a]the articles
of gold which you return to Him as [b]a
guilt offering in a box by its side. Then
send it away that it may go.
9 "And watch, if it goes up by the way
of its own territory to [a]Beth-shemesh,
then He has done us this great evil. But
if not, then [b]we shall know that it was
not His hand that struck us; it happened
to us by chance."
10 Then the men did so, and took two
milch cows and hitched them to the cart,
and shut up their calves at home.
11 And they put the ark of the LORD
on the cart, and the box with the golden
mice and the likenesses of their tumors.
12 And the cows took the straight way
in the [1]direction of [a]Beth-shemesh; they
went along [b]the highway, lowing as they
went, and did not turn aside to the right
or to the left. And the lords of the
Philistines followed them to the border
of Beth-shemesh.
13 Now *the people of* Beth-shemesh
were reaping their wheat harvest in the
valley, and they raised their eyes and
saw the ark and were glad to see *it.*
14 And the cart came into the field of
Joshua the Beth-shemite and stood there
where there *was* a large stone; and they
split the wood of the cart and [a]offered
the cows as a burnt offering to the LORD.
15 And [a]the Levites took down the
ark of the LORD and the box that was
with it, in which were the articles of
gold, and put them on the large stone;
and the men of Beth-shemesh offered
burnt offerings and sacrificed sacrifices
that day to the LORD.
16 And when the [a]five lords of the
Philistines saw it, they returned to Ekron
that day.
17 And [a]these are the golden tumors
which the Philistines returned for a guilt
offering to the LORD: one for Ashdod,
one for Gaza, one for Ashkelon, one for
Gath, one for Ekron;
18 and the golden mice, *according* to
the number of all the cities of the Philistines belonging to the five lords, [a]both of
fortified cities and of country villages.
[b]The large [1]stone on which they set the
ark of the LORD *is a witness* to this day
in the field of Joshua the Beth-shemite.
19 And [a]He struck down some of the
men of Beth-shemesh because they had
looked into the ark of the LORD. He
struck down of all the people, 50,070
men, and the people mourned because
the LORD had struck the people with a
great slaughter.
20 And the men of Beth-shemesh said,
"[a]Who is able to stand before the LORD,
this holy God? And to whom shall He go
up from us?"

21 So they sent messengers to the
inhabitants of [a]Kiriath-jearim, saying,
"The Philistines have brought back the
ark of the LORD; come down and take it
up to you."

Deliverance from the Philistines

7 AND the men of Kiriath-jearim
came and took the ark of the LORD
and [a]brought it into the house of Abinadab on the hill, and consecrated Eleazar
his son to keep the ark of the LORD.
2 And it came about from the day
that the ark remained at Kiriath-jearim
that the time was long, for it was twenty
years; and all the house of Israel lamented after the LORD.
3 Then Samuel spoke to all the house
of Israel, saying, "[a]If you return to the
LORD with all your heart, [b]remove the
foreign gods and the [c]Ashtaroth from
among you and [d]direct your hearts to
the LORD and [e]serve Him alone; and He
will deliver you from the hand of the
Philistines."
4 So the sons of Israel removed the
Baals and the Ashtaroth and served the
LORD alone.
5 Then Samuel said, "Gather all
Israel to [a]Mizpah, and [b]I will pray to the
LORD for you."
6 And they gathered to Mizpah, and
drew water and [a]poured it out before the
LORD, and [b]fasted on that day, and said
there, "[c]We have sinned against the
LORD." And Samuel judged the sons of
Israel at Mizpah.
7 Now when the Philistines heard
that the sons of Israel had gathered to
Mizpah, the lords of the Philistines went
up against Israel. And when the sons of
Israel heard it, [a]they were afraid of the
Philistines.
8 Then the sons of Israel said to
Samuel, "[a]Do not cease to cry to the
LORD our God for us, that He may save
us from the hand of the Philistines."
9 And Samuel took [a]a suckling lamb
and offered it for a whole burnt offering
to the LORD; and Samuel cried to the
LORD for Israel and [b]the LORD answered
him.
10 Now Samuel was offering up the
burnt offering, and the Philistines drew
near to battle against Israel. But [a]the
LORD thundered with a great [1]thunder
on that day against the Philistines and
[b]confused them, so that they were
[2]routed before Israel.
11 And the men of Israel went out of
Mizpah and pursued the Philistines, and
struck them down as far as below Beth-
car.
12 Then Samuel [a]took a stone and set
it between Mizpah and Shen, and named
it [1]Ebenezer, saying, "Thus far the LORD
has helped us."
13 [a]So the Philistines were subdued
and [b]they did not come anymore within
the border of Israel. And the hand of the
LORD was against the Philistines all the
days of Samuel.
14 And the cities which the Philistines
had taken from Israel were restored to
Israel, from Ekron even to Gath; and
Israel delivered their territory from the
hand of the Philistines. So there was
peace between Israel and [a]the Amorites.

Samuel's Ministry

15 Now Samuel [a]judged Israel all the
days of his life.
16 And he used to go annually on
circuit to [a]Bethel and [b]Gilgal and [c]Miz-
pah, and he judged Israel in all these
places.
17 Then his return *was* to [a]Ramah, for
his house *was* there, and there he judged
Israel; and he [b]built there an altar to the
LORD.

Israel Demands a King

8 AND it came about when Samuel
was old that [a]he appointed his sons
judges over Israel.
2 Now the name of his first-born was
Joel, and the name of his second, Abijah; *they* were judging in [a]Beersheba.
3 His sons, however, did not walk in
his ways, but turned aside after dishonest gain and [a]took bribes and perverted
justice.
4 Then all the elders of Israel gathered together and came to Samuel at
[a]Ramah;
5 and they said to him, "Behold, you
have grown old, and your sons do not
walk in your ways. Now [a]appoint a king
for us to judge us like all the nations."
6 But the thing was [1a]displeasing in
the sight of Samuel when they said,
"Give us a king to judge us." And
[b]Samuel prayed to the LORD.
7 And the LORD said to Samuel,
"Listen to the voice of the people in
regard to all that they say to you, for
[a]they have not rejected you, but they
have rejected Me from being king over
them.
8"Like all the deeds which they have
done since the day that I brought them
up from Egypt even to this day—in that
they have forsaken Me and served other
gods—so they are doing to you also.
9"Now then, listen to their voice;
[a]however, you shall solemnly [1]warn
them and tell them of [b]the [2]procedure of
the king who will reign over them."

Warning concerning a King

10 So Samuel spoke all the words of
the LORD to [a]the people who had asked
of him a king.
11 And he said, "[a]This will be the
[1]procedure of the king who will reign
over you: [b]he will take your sons and
place *them* for himself in his chariots and
among his horsemen and [c]they will run
before his chariots.
12"And [a]he will appoint for himself
commanders of thousands and of fifties,
and *some* to [1]do his plowing and to reap
his harvest and to make his weapons of
war and equipment for his chariots.

---

21 [a]Josh. 9:17; 15:9, 60; 1 Chr. 13:5, 6

1 [a]2 Sam. 6:3, 4

3 [a]1 Kin. 8:48; Is. 55:7; Hos. 6:1; Joel 2:12-14 [b]Gen. 35:2; Josh. 24:14, 23; Judg. 10:16 [c]Judg. 2:13; 1 Sam. 31:10 [d]Deut. 13:4; 2 Chr. 19:3 [e]Deut. 6:13; 10:20; 13:4; Josh. 24:14; Matt. 4:10; Luke 4:8

5 [a]Judg. 10:17; 20:1 [b]1 Sam. 8:6; 12:17-19

6 [a]1 Sam. 1:15; Ps. 62:8; Lam. 2:19 [b]Lev. 16:29; Neh. 9:1 [c]Judg. 10:10; 1 Kin. 8:47; Ps. 106:6

7 [a]1 Sam. 13:6; 17:11

8 [a]1 Sam. 12:19-24; Is. 37:4

9 [a]Lev. 22:27 [b]Ps. 99:6; Jer. 15:1

10 [1]Lit., *voice* [2]Lit., *smitten* [a]1 Sam. 2:10; 2 Sam. 22:14, 15; Ps. 29:3, 4 [b]Josh. 10:10; Ps. 18:14

12 [1]I.e., The stone of help [a]Gen. 35:14; Josh. 4:9; 24:26

13 [a]Judg. 13:1-15 [b]1 Sam. 13:5

14 [a]Num. 13:29; Josh. 10:5-10

15 [a]1 Sam. 7:6

16 [a]Gen. 28:19; 35:6 [b]Josh. 5:9, 10 [c]1 Sam. 7:5

17 [a]1 Sam. 1:1, 19; 2:11 [b]Judg. 21:4

1 [a]Deut. 16:18, 19

2 [a]Gen. 22:19; 1 Kin. 19:3; Amos 5:5

3 [a]Ex. 23:6, 8; Deut. 16:19

4 [a]1 Sam. 7:17

5 [a]Deut. 17:14, 15

6 [1]Or, *evil* [a]1 Sam. 12:17 [b]1 Sam. 15:11

7 [a]Ex. 16:8; 1 Sam. 10:19

9 [1]Lit., *testify to* [2]Lit., *custom* [a]Ezek. 3:18 [b]1 Sam. 8:11-18; 10:25

10 [a]1 Sam. 8:4

11 [1]Lit., *custom* [a]Deut. 17:14-20; 1 Sam. 10:25 [b]1 Sam. 14:52 [c]2 Sam. 15:1

12 [1]Lit., *plow his plowing* [a]Num. 31:14; 1 Sam. 22:7

13 "He will also take your daughters for perfumers and cooks and bakers.

14 "And [a]he will take the best of your fields and your vineyards and your olive groves, and give *them* to his servants.

15 "And he will take a tenth of your seed and of your vineyards, and give to his officers and to his servants.

16 "He will also take your male servants and your female servants and your best young men and your donkeys, and [1]use *them* for his work.

17 "He will take a tenth of your flocks, and you yourselves will become his servants.

18 "Then [a]you will cry out in that day because of your king whom you have chosen for yourselves, but [b]the LORD will not answer you in that day."

19 Nevertheless, the people [a]refused to listen to the voice of Samuel, and they said, "No, but there shall be a king over us,

20 [a]that we also may be like all the nations, that our king may judge us and go out before us and fight our battles."

21 Now after Samuel had heard all the words of the people, [a]he repeated them in the LORD's hearing.

22 And the LORD said to Samuel, "[a]Listen to their voice, and [1]appoint them a king." So Samuel said to the men of Israel, "Go every man to his city."

Saul's Search

9 NOW there was a man of Benjamin whose name was [a]Kish the son of Abiel, the son of Zeror, the son of Becorath, the son of Aphiah, the son of a Benjamite, a mighty man of [1]valor.

2 And he had a son whose name was Saul, a [a]choice and handsome *man,* and there was not a more handsome person than he among the sons of Israel; [b]from his shoulders and up he was taller than any of the people.

3 Now the donkeys of Kish, Saul's father, were lost. So Kish said to his son Saul, "Take now with you one of the servants, and arise, go search for the donkeys."

4 And he passed through [a]the hill country of Ephraim and passed through the land of [b]Shalishah, but they did not find *them.* Then they passed through the land of [c]Shaalim, but *they were* not *there.* Then he passed through the land of the Benjamites, but they did not find *them.*

5 When they came to the land of [a]Zuph, Saul said to his servant who was with him, "Come, and let us return, [b]lest my father cease *to be concerned* about the donkeys and become anxious for us."

6 And he said to him, "Behold now, there is [a]a man of God in this city, and the man is held in honor; [b]all that he says surely comes true. Now let us go there, [c]perhaps he can tell us about our journey on which we have set out."

7 Then Saul said to his servant, "But behold, if we go, what shall we bring the man? For the bread is gone from our sack and there is [a]no present to bring to the man of God. What do we have?"

8 And the servant answered Saul again and said, "Behold, I have in my hand a fourth of a shekel of silver; I will give *it* to the man of God and he will [a]tell us our way."

9 (Formerly in Israel, when a man went to inquire of God, he used to say, "Come, and let us go to the seer"; for *he who is called* a prophet now was formerly called [a]a seer.)

10 Then Saul said to his servant, "Well said; come, let us go." So they went to the city where the man of God was.

11 As they went up the slope to the city, [a]they found young women going out to draw water, and said to them, "Is the seer here?"

12 And they answered them and said, "He is; [1]see, *he is* ahead of you. Hurry now, for he has come into the city today, for [a]the people have a sacrifice on [b]the high place today.

13 "As soon as you enter the city you will find him before he goes up to the high place to eat, for the people will not eat until he comes, because [a]he must bless the sacrifice; afterward those who are invited will eat. Now therefore, go up for you will find him at once."

14 So they went up to the city. As they came into the city, behold, Samuel was coming out toward them to go up to the high place.

God's Choice for King

15 Now a day before Saul's coming, [a]the LORD had [1]revealed *this* to Samuel saying,

16 "About this time tomorrow I will send you a man from the land of Benjamin, and [a]you shall anoint him to be prince over My people Israel; and he shall deliver My people from the hand of the Philistines. For [b]I have regarded My people, because their cry has come to Me."

17 When Samuel saw Saul, the LORD [1]said to him, "[a]Behold, the man of whom I spoke to you! This one shall rule over My people."

18 Then Saul approached Samuel in the gate, and said, "Please tell me where the seer's house is."

19 And Samuel answered Saul and said, "I am the seer. Go up before me to the high place, for you shall eat with me today; and in the morning I will let you go, and will tell you all that is on your mind.

20 "And [a]as for your donkeys which were lost three days ago, do not set your mind on them, for they have been found. And [b]for whom is all that is desirable in Israel? Is it not for you and for all your father's household?"

14 [a]1 Kin. 21:7; Ezek. 46:18
16 [1]Lit., *make*
18 [a]Is. 8:21 [b]Prov. 1:25-28; Is. 1:15; Mic. 3:4
19 [a]Is. 66:4; Jer. 44:16
20 [a]1 Sam. 8:5
21 [a]Judg. 11:11
22 [1]Lit., *cause a king to reign for them* [a]1 Sam. 8:7
1 [1]Or, *wealth* or *influence* [a]1 Sam. 14:51; 1 Chr. 8:33; 9:36-39
2 [a]1 Sam. 10:24 [b]1 Sam. 10:23
4 [a]Josh. 24:33 [b]2 Kin. 4:42 [c]Josh. 19:42
5 [a]1 Sam. 1:1 [b]1 Sam. 10:2
6 [a]Deut. 33:1; 1 Kin. 13:1; 2 Kin. 5:8 [b]1 Sam. 3:19 [c]Gen. 24:42
7 [a]1 Kin. 14:3; 2 Kin. 5:15; 8:8, 9; Ezek. 13:19
8 [a]1 Sam. 9:6
9 [a]2 Sam. 24:11; 2 Kin. 17:13; 1 Chr. 9:22; 26:28; 29:29; Is. 30:10; Amos 7:12
11 [a]Gen. 24:11, 15; 29:8, 9; Ex. 2:16
12 [1]Or, *behold* [a]Gen. 31:54; Num. 28:11-15; 1 Kin. 3:2 [b]1 Sam. 7:17; 10:5
13 [a]Luke 9:16; John 6:11
15 [1]Lit., *uncovered the ear* [a]1 Sam. 15:1; Acts 13:21
16 [a]1 Sam. 10:1 [b]Ex. 3:7, 9
17 [1]Lit., *answered* [a]1 Sam. 16:12
20 [a]1 Sam. 9:3 [b]1 Sam. 8:5; 12:13

21 And Saul answered and said, "[a]Am
I not a Benjamite, of [b]the smallest of the
tribes of Israel, and my family the least
of all the families of the [1]tribe of Benjamin? Why then do you speak to me in
this way?"
22 Then Samuel took Saul and his
servant and brought them into the hall,
and gave them a place at the head of
those who were invited, who were about
thirty men.
23 And Samuel said to the cook,
"[1]Bring the portion that I gave you,
concerning which I said to you, 'Set it
[2]aside.' "
24 Then the cook [a]took up the leg
with what was on it and set *it* before
Saul. And *Samuel* said, "Here is what
has been reserved! Set *it* before you *and*
eat, because it has been kept for you
until the appointed time, [1]since I said I
have invited the people." So Saul ate
with Samuel that day.
25 When they came down from the
high place into the city, *Samuel* spoke
with Saul [a]on the roof.[1]
26 And they arose early; and it came
about at daybreak that Samuel called to
Saul on the roof, saying, "Get up, that I
may send you away." So Saul arose, and
both he and Samuel went out into the
street.
27 As they were going down to the
edge of the city, Samuel said to Saul,
"Say to the servant that he might go
ahead of us and pass on, but you remain
standing now, that I may proclaim the
word of God to you."

Saul among Prophets

10 THEN [a]Samuel took the flask of
oil, poured it on his head, [b]kissed
him and said, "Has not [c]the LORD
anointed you a ruler over [d]His inheritance?
2 "When you go from me today, then
you will find two men close to [a]Rachel's
tomb in the territory of Benjamin at
Zelzah; and they will say to you, '[b]The
donkeys which you went to look for have
been found. Now behold, your father
has [1]ceased to be concerned about the
donkeys and is anxious for you, saying,
"What shall I do about my son?" '
3 "Then you will go on further from
there, and you will come as far as the
[1a]oak of Tabor, and there three men
going up [b]to God at Bethel will meet
you, one carrying three kids, another
carrying three loaves of bread, and
another carrying a jug of wine;
4 and they will greet you and give
you two *loaves* of bread, which you will
accept from their hand.
5 "Afterward you will come to [1a]the
hill of God where the Philistine garrison
is; and it shall be as soon as you have
come there to the city, that you will meet
[b]a group of prophets coming down from
the high place with harp, tambourine,
flute, and a lyre before them, and [c]they
will be prophesying.
6 "Then [a]the Spirit of the LORD will
come upon you mightily, and [b]you shall
prophesy with them and be changed into
another man.
7 "And it shall be when these signs
come to you, [a]do for yourself what [1]the
occasion requires; for [b]God is with you.
8 "And [a]you shall go down before me
to Gilgal; and behold, I will come down
to you to offer burnt offerings and [b]sac-
rifice peace offerings. [c]You shall wait
seven days until I come to you and show
you what you should do."
9 Then it happened when he turned
his back to leave Samuel, God [a]changed
[1]his heart; and all those signs came
about on that day.
10 [a]When they came to [1]the hill there,
behold, a group of prophets met him;
and the Spirit of God came upon him
mightily, so that he prophesied among
them.
11 And it came about, when all who
knew him previously saw that he prophesied now with the prophets, that the
people said to one another, "What has
happened to the son of Kish? [a]Is Saul
also among the prophets?"
12 And a man there answered and
said, "Now, who is their father?" Therefore it became a proverb: "[a]Is Saul also
among the prophets?"
13 When he had finished prophesying,
he came to the high place.
14 Now [a]Saul's uncle said to him and
his servant, "Where did you go?" And he
said, "[b]To look for the donkeys. When
we saw that they could not be found, we
went to Samuel."
15 And Saul's uncle said, "Please tell
me what Samuel said to you."
16 So Saul said to his uncle, "[a]He told
us plainly that the donkeys had been
found." But he did not tell him about
the matter of the kingdom which Samuel
had mentioned.

Saul Publicly Chosen King

17 Thereafter Samuel called the [a]peo-
ple together to the LORD at Mizpah;
18 and he said to the sons of Israel,
"[a]Thus says the LORD, the God of Israel,
'I brought Israel up from Egypt, and I
delivered you from the hand of the
Egyptians, and from the [1]power of all
the kingdoms that were oppressing you.'
19 "But you [a]today rejected your God,
who delivers you from all your calamities and your distresses; yet you have
[1]said, 'No, but set a king over us!' Now
therefore, [b]present yourselves before the
LORD by your tribes and by your clans."
20 Thus Samuel brought all the tribes
of Israel near, and the tribe of Benjamin
was taken by lot.
21 Then he brought the tribe of Benjamin near by its families, and the Matrite
family was taken. And Saul the son of
Kish was taken; but when they looked
for him, he could not be found.
22 Therefore [a]they inquired further of
the LORD, "Has the man come here

21 [1]So some ancient versions; Heb., *tribes* [a]1 Sam. 15:17 [b]Judg. 20:46-48
23 [1]Lit., *Give* [2]Lit., *with you*
24 [1]Lit., *saying* [a]Ex. 29:22, 27; Lev. 7:32, 33; Num. 18:18
25 [1]Gr. adds *and they spread a bed for Saul on the roof and he slept.* [a]Deut. 22:8; Luke 5:19; Acts 10:9
1 [a]Ex. 30:23-33; 1 Sam. 16:13; 2 Kin. 9:3, 6 [b]Ps. 2:12 [c]1 Sam. 16:13; 26:9; 2 Sam. 1:14 [d]Deut. 32:9; Ps. 78:71
2 [1]Lit., *abandoned the matter of* [a]Gen. 35:16-20; 48:7 [b]1 Sam. 9:3-5
3 [1]Or, *terebinth* [a]Gen. 35:8 [b]Gen. 28:19; 35:1, 3, 7
5 [1]Or, *Gibeath-haelohim* [a]1 Sam. 13:2, 3 [b]1 Sam. 19:20; 2 Kin. 2:3, 5, 15 [c]2 Kin. 3:15; 1 Chr. 25:1-6; 1 Cor. 14:1
6 [a]Num. 11:25, 29; Judg. 14:6 [b]1 Sam. 10:10; 19:23, 24
7 [1]Lit., *your hand finds* [a]Eccl. 9:10 [b]Josh. 1:5; Judg. 6:12; Heb. 13:5
8 [a]1 Sam. 11:14; 13:8 [b]1 Sam. 11:15 [c]1 Sam. 13:8
9 [1]Lit., *for him another heart* [a]1 Sam. 10:6
10 [1]Or, *Gibeath* [a]1 Sam. 10:5, 6; 19:20
11 [a]1 Sam. 19:24; Amos 7:14, 15; Matt. 13:54-57; John 7:15
12 [a]1 Sam. 19:23, 24
14 [a]1 Sam. 14:50 [b]1 Sam. 9:3-6
16 [a]1 Sam. 9:20
17 [a]Judg. 20:1; 1 Sam. 7:5
18 [1]Lit., *hand* [a]Judg. 6:8, 9
19 [1]So with several mss. and versions; M.T., *said to Him* [a]1 Sam. 8:6, 7; 12:12 [b]Josh. 7:14-18; 24:1; Prov. 16:33
22 [a]1 Sam. 23:2, 4

yet?" So the LORD said, "Behold, he is
hiding himself by the baggage."
23 So they ran and took him from
there, and when he stood among the
people, [a]he was taller than any of the
people from his shoulders upward.
24 And Samuel said to all the people,
"Do you see him [a]whom the LORD has
chosen? Surely there is no one like him
among all the people." So all the people
shouted and said, "[1b]*Long* live the
king!"
25 Then Samuel told the people [a]the
ordinances of the kingdom, and wrote
them in the book and [b]placed *it* before
the LORD. And Samuel sent all the
people away, each one to his house.
26 And Saul also went [a]to his house at
Gibeah; and the valiant *men* whose
hearts God had touched went with him.
27 But certain [1a]worthless men said,
"How can this one deliver us?" And they
despised him and [b]did not bring him any
present. But he kept silent.

Saul Defeats the Ammonites

11 NOW [a]Nahash the Ammonite
came up and [1]besieged [b]Jabesh-
gilead; and all the men of Jabesh said to
Nahash, "Make [c]a covenant with us and
we will serve you."
2 But Nahash the Ammonite said to
them, "I will make *it* with you on this
condition, [a]that I will gouge out the right
eye of every one of you, thus I will make
it [b]a reproach on all Israel."
3 And [a]the elders of Jabesh said to
him, "Let us alone for seven days, that
we may send messengers throughout the
territory of Israel. Then, if there is no
one to deliver us, we will come out to
you."
4 Then the messengers came [a]to Gibeah of Saul and spoke these words in the
hearing of the people, and all the people
[b]lifted up their voices and wept.
5 Now behold, Saul was coming
from the field [a]behind the oxen; and [1]he
said, "What is *the matter* with the people
that they weep?" So they related to him
the words of the men of Jabesh.
6 Then [a]the Spirit of God came upon
Saul mightily when he heard these
words, and [1]he became very angry.
7 And he took a yoke of oxen and
[a]cut them in pieces, and sent *them*
throughout the territory of Israel by the
hand of messengers, saying, "[b]Whoever
does not come out after Saul and after
Samuel, so shall it be done to his oxen."
Then the dread of the LORD fell on the
people, and they came out [c]as one man.
8 And he [1]numbered them in [a]Bezek;
and the [b]sons of Israel were 300,000, and
the men of Judah 30,000.
9 And they said to the messengers
who had come, "Thus you shall say to
the men of Jabesh-gilead, 'Tomorrow, by
the time the sun is hot, you shall have
deliverance.'" So the messengers went
and told the men of Jabesh; and they
were glad.
10 Then the men of Jabesh said, "[a]To-
morrow we will come out to you, and
you may do to us whatever seems good
[1]to you."
11 And it happened the next morning
that Saul put the people [a]in three companies; and they came into the midst of
the camp at the morning watch, and
struck down the Ammonites until the
heat of the day. And it came about that
those who survived were scattered, so
that no two of them were left together.
12 Then the people said to Samuel,
"[a]Who is he that said, 'Shall Saul reign
over us?' [1b]Bring the men, that we may
put them to death."
13 But Saul said, "[a]Not a man shall be
put to death this day, for today [b]the
LORD has accomplished deliverance in
Israel."
14 Then Samuel said to the people,
"Come and let us go to [a]Gilgal and
[b]renew the kingdom there."
15 So all the people went to Gilgal,
and there they made Saul king [a]before
the LORD in Gilgal. There they also
[b]offered sacrifices of peace offerings
before the LORD; and there Saul and all
the men of Israel rejoiced greatly.

Samuel Addresses Israel

12 THEN Samuel said to all Israel,
"Behold, [a]I have listened to your
voice in all that you said to me, and I
[b]have [1]appointed a king over you.
2 "And now, [a]here is the king walking
before you, but [b]I am old and gray, and
behold [c]my sons are with you. And [d]I
have walked before you from my youth
even to this day.
3 "Here I am; bear witness against me
before the LORD and [a]His anointed.
[b]Whose ox have I taken, or whose donkey have I taken, or whom have I defrauded? Whom have I oppressed, or
[c]from whose hand have I taken a bribe
to blind my eyes with it? I will restore *it*
to you."
4 And they said, "You have not
defrauded us, or oppressed us, or taken
anything from any man's hand."
5 And he said to them, "The LORD is
witness against you, and His anointed is
witness this day that [a]you have found
nothing [b]in my hand." And they said,
"*He is* witness."
6 Then Samuel said to the people, "It
is the LORD who [1a]appointed Moses and
Aaron and who brought your fathers up
from the land of Egypt.
7 "So now, take your stand, [a]that I
may plead with you before the LORD
concerning all the righteous acts of the
LORD which He did for you and your
fathers.
8 "[a]When Jacob went into Egypt and
[b]your fathers cried out to the LORD, then
[c]the LORD sent Moses and Aaron [1d]who
brought your fathers out of Egypt and
settled them in this place.

23 [a]1 Sam. 9:2
24 [1]Lit., *May the king live* [a]Deut. 17:15; 2 Sam. 21:6 [b]1 Kin. 1:25, 34, 39
25 [a]Deut. 17:14-20; 1 Sam. 8:11-18 [b]Deut. 31:26
26 [a]1 Sam. 11:4; 15:34
27 [1]Lit., *sons of Belial*, cf. 2 Cor. 6:15 [a]Deut. 13:13; 1 Sam. 25:17 [b]1 Kin. 10:25; 2 Chr. 17:5

1 [1]Lit., *camped against* [a]1 Sam. 12:12 [b]Judg. 21:8; 1 Sam. 31:11 [c]Gen. 26:28; 1 Kin. 20:34; Job 41:4; Ezek. 17:13
2 [a]Num. 16:14 [b]1 Sam. 17:26; Ps. 44:13
3 [a]1 Sam. 8:4
4 [a]1 Sam. 10:26; 15:34 [b]Gen. 27:38; Judg. 2:4; 20:23, 26; 21:2; 1 Sam. 30:4
5 [1]Lit., *Saul* [a]1 Kin. 19:19
6 [1]Lit., *his anger burned exceedingly* [a]Judg. 3:10; 6:34; 11:29; 13:25; 14:6; 1 Sam. 10:10; 16:13
7 [a]Judg. 19:29 [b]Judg. 21:5, 8 [c]Judg. 20:1
8 [1]Lit., *mustered* [a]Judg. 1:5 [b]Judg. 20:2
10 [1]Lit., *in your sight* [a]1 Sam. 11:3
11 [a]Judg. 7:16, 20
12 [1]Lit., *Give* [a]1 Sam. 10:27 [b]Luke 19:27
13 [a]1 Sam. 10:27; 2 Sam. 19:22 [b]Ex. 14:13, 30; 1 Sam. 19:5
14 [a]1 Sam. 7:16; 10:8 [b]1 Sam. 10:25
15 [a]1 Sam. 10:17 [b]1 Sam. 10:8

1 [1]Lit., *made* [a]1 Sam. 8:7, 9, 22 [b]1 Sam. 10:24; 11:14, 15
2 [a]1 Sam. 8:20 [b]1 Sam. 8:1, 5 [c]1 Sam. 8:3, 5 [d]1 Sam. 3:10, 19, 20
3 [a]1 Sam. 10:1; 24:6; 2 Sam. 1:14 [b]Ex. 20:17; Num. 16:15; Acts 20:33 [c]Ex. 23:8; Deut. 16:19
5 [a]Acts 23:9; 24:20 [b]Ex. 22:4
6 [1]Lit., *made* [a]Ex. 6:26; Mic. 6:4
7 [a]Ezek. 20:35; Mic. 6:1-5
8 [1]Lit., *and they brought* [a]Gen. 46:5, 6 [b]Ex. 2:23-25 [c]Ex. 3:10; 4:14-16 [d]1 Sam. 10:18

9 "But [a]they forgot the LORD their God, so [b]He sold them into the hand of Sisera, captain of the army of Hazor, and [c]into the hand of the Philistines and [d]into the hand of the king of Moab, and they fought against them.

10 "And [a]they cried out to the LORD and said, 'We have sinned because we have forsaken the LORD and have served [b]the Baals and the Ashtaroth; but [c]now deliver us from the hands of our enemies, and we will serve Thee.'

11 "Then the LORD sent [a]Jerubbaal and [1b]Bedan and [c]Jephthah and [d]Samuel, and delivered you from the hands of your enemies all around, so that you lived in security.

The King Confirmed

12 "When you saw [a]that Nahash the king of the sons of Ammon came against you, you said to me, '[b]No, but a king shall reign over us,' [c]although the LORD your God *was* your king.

13 "Now therefore, [a]here is the king whom you have chosen, [b]whom you have asked for, and behold, the LORD has set a king over you.

14 "[a]If you will fear the LORD and serve Him, and listen to His voice and not rebel against the [1]command of the LORD, then both you and also the king who reigns over you will follow the LORD your God.

15 "And [a]if you will not listen to the voice of the LORD, but rebel against the [1]command of the LORD, then [b]the hand of the LORD will be against you, [c]*as it was* against your fathers.

16 "Even now, [a]take your stand and see this great thing which the LORD will do before your eyes.

17 "[a]Is it not the wheat harvest today? [b]I will call to the LORD, that He may send [1]thunder and rain. Then you will know and see that [c]your wickedness is great which you have done in the sight of the LORD by asking for yourselves a king."

18 So Samuel called to the LORD, and the LORD sent [1]thunder and rain that day; and [a]all the people greatly feared the LORD and Samuel.

19 Then all the people said to Samuel, "[a]Pray for your servants to the LORD your God, so that we may not die, for we have added to all our sins [b]*this* evil by asking for ourselves a king."

20 And Samuel said to the people, "Do not fear. You have committed all this evil, yet [a]do not turn aside from following the LORD, but serve the LORD with all your heart.

21 "And you must not turn aside, for *then you would go* after [a]futile things which can not profit or deliver, because they are futile.

22 "For [a]the LORD will not abandon His people [b]on account of His great name, because the LORD [c]has been pleased to make you a people for Himself.

9 [a]Deut. 32:18; Judg. 3:7 [b]Judg. 4:2 [c]Judg. 3:31; 10:7; 13:1 [d]Judg. 3:12-30
10 [a]Judg. 10:10 [b]Judg. 2:13; 3:7 [c]Judg. 10:15, 16
11 [1]Gr. and Syr. read *Barak* [a]Judg. 6:31, 32; 7:1 [b]Judg. 4:6; 11:1 [c]Judg. 11:29 [d]1 Sam. 3:20
12 [a]1 Sam. 11:1, 2 [b]1 Sam. 8:6, 19 [c]Judg. 8:23; 1 Sam. 8:7
13 [a]1 Sam. 10:24 [b]1 Sam. 8:5; 12:17, 19; Hos. 13:11
14 [1]Lit., *mouth* [a]Josh. 24:14
15 [1]Lit., *mouth* [a]Lev. 26:14, 15; Josh. 24:20; Is. 1:20 [b]1 Sam. 5:9 [c]1 Sam. 12:9
16 [a]Ex. 14:13, 31
17 [1]Lit., *sounds* [a]Prov. 26:1 [b]1 Sam. 7:9, 10; James 5:16ff. [c]1 Sam. 8:7
18 [1]Lit., *sounds* [a]Ex. 14:31
19 [a]Ex. 9:28; 1 Sam. 12:23; Jer. 15:1; 1 John 5:16 [b]1 Sam. 12:17, 20
20 [a]Deut. 11:16
21 [a]Deut. 11:16; Is. 41:29; Hab. 2:18
22 [a]Deut. 31:6; 1 Kin. 6:13 [b]Ex. 32:12; Num. 14:13; Josh. 7:9; Ps. 106:8; Jer. 14:21 [c]Deut. 7:6-11; 1 Pet. 2:9
23 [a]Rom. 1:9; 1 Cor. 9:16; Col. 1:9; 1 Thess. 3:10; 2 Tim. 1:3 [b]1 Kin. 8:36; Ps. 34:11; Prov. 4:11
24 [1]Or, *reverence* [a]Eccl. 12:13 [b]Deut. 10:21; Is. 5:12
25 [a]Is. 1:20; 3:11 [b]Josh. 24:20 [c]1 Sam. 31:1-5; Hos. 10:3

2 [a]1 Sam. 13:5; 14:31 [b]1 Sam. 10:26
3 [a]1 Sam. 10:5 [b]1 Sam. 13:16; 14:5 [c]Judg. 3:27; 6:34
4 [1]Lit., *saying* [2]Lit., *after* [a]Gen. 34:30; Ex. 5:21; 2 Sam. 10:6
5 [a]Josh. 11:4 [b]Josh. 18:12; 1 Sam. 14:23
6 [a]Judg. 6:2
7 [a]Num. 32:33
8 [a]1 Sam. 10:8
9 [a]Deut. 12:5-14; 2 Sam. 24:25; 1 Kin. 3:4
10 [1]Lit., *bless* [a]1 Sam. 15:13
11 [a]1 Sam. 13:2, 5, 16, 23

23 "Moreover, as for me, [a]far be it from me that I should sin against the LORD by ceasing to pray for you; but [b]I will instruct you in the good and right way.

24 "[a]Only [1]fear the LORD and serve Him in truth with all your heart; for consider [b]what great things He has done for you.

25 "[a]But if you still do wickedly, [b]both you and your king [c]shall be swept away."

War with the Philistines

13 SAUL was *forty* years old when he began to reign, and he reigned *thirty*-two years over Israel.

2 Now Saul chose for himself 3,000 men of Israel, of which 2,000 were with Saul in [a]Michmash and in the hill country of Bethel, while 1,000 were with Jonathan at [b]Gibeah of Benjamin. But he sent away the rest of the people, each to his tent.

3 And Jonathan smote [a]the garrison of the Philistines that was in [b]Geba, and the Philistines heard of *it*. Then Saul [c]blew the trumpet throughout the land, saying, "Let the Hebrews hear."

4 And all Israel heard [1]the news that Saul had smitten the garrison of the Philistines, and also that Israel [a]had become odious to the Philistines. The people were then summoned [2]to Saul at Gilgal.

5 Now the Philistines assembled to fight with Israel, 30,000 chariots and 6,000 horsemen, and [a]people like the sand which is on the seashore in abundance; and they came up and camped in Michmash, east of [b]Beth-aven.

6 When the men of Israel saw that they were in a strait (for the people were hard-pressed), then [a]the people hid themselves in caves, in thickets, in cliffs, in cellars, and in pits.

7 Also *some of* the Hebrews crossed the Jordan into the land of [a]Gad and Gilead. But as for Saul, he *was* still in Gilgal, and all the people followed him trembling.

8 Now [a]he waited seven days, according to the appointed time set by Samuel, but Samuel did not come to Gilgal; and the people were scattering from him.

9 So Saul said, "Bring to me the burnt offering and the peace offerings." And [a]he offered the burnt offering.

10 And it came about as soon as he finished offering the burnt offering, that behold, Samuel came; and [a]Saul went out to meet him *and* to [1]greet him.

Saul Assumes Priestly Office

11 But Samuel said, "What have you done?" And Saul said, "Because I saw that the people were scattering from me, and that you did not come within the appointed days, and that [a]the Philistines were assembling at Michmash,

12 therefore I said, 'Now the Philistines will come down against me at

Gilgal, and I have not asked the favor of
the LORD.' So I forced myself and offered the burnt offering."
13 And Samuel said to Saul, "[a]You
have acted foolishly; [b]you have not kept
the commandment of the LORD your
God, which He commanded you, for
now the LORD would have established
your kingdom [1]over Israel [c]forever.
14"But [a]now your kingdom shall not
endure. [b]The LORD has sought out for
Himself a man after His own heart, and
the LORD has appointed him as ruler
over His people, because you have not
kept what the LORD commanded you."
15 Then Samuel arose and went up
from Gilgal to [a]Gibeah of Benjamin.
And Saul [1]numbered the people who
were present with him, [b]about six hundred men.
16 Now Saul and his son Jonathan
and the people who were present with
them were staying in [a]Geba of Benjamin
while the Philistines camped at Michmash.
17 And [a]the [1]raiders came from the
camp of the Philistines in three [2]compa-
nies: one [3]company turned [4]toward
[b]Ophrah, to the land of Shual,
18 and another [1]company turned
[2]toward [a]Beth-horon, and another [1]com-
pany turned [2]toward the border which
overlooks the valley of [b]Zeboim toward
the wilderness.
19 Now [a]no blacksmith could be
found in all the land of Israel, for the
Philistines said, "Lest the Hebrews make
[1b]swords or spears."
20 So all Israel went down to the
Philistines, each to sharpen his plow-
share, his mattock, his axe, and his hoe.
21 And the charge was [1]two-thirds of
a shekel for the plowshares, the mat-
tocks, the forks, and the axes, and to fix
the hoes.
22 So it came about on the day of
battle that [a]neither sword nor spear was
found in the hands of any of the people
who *were* with Saul and Jonathan, but
they were found with Saul and his son
Jonathan.
23 And [a]the garrison of the Philistines
went out to [b]the pass of Michmash.

Jonathan's Victory

14 NOW the day came that Jonathan, the son of Saul, said to the
young man who was carrying his armor,
"Come and let us cross over to the
Philistines' garrison that is on yonder
side." But he did not tell his father.
2 And Saul was staying in the outskirts of [a]Gibeah under the pomegranate
tree which is in [b]Migron. And the people
who *were* with him *were* [c]about six
hundred men,
3 and Ahijah, the [a]son of Ahitub,
[b]Ichabod's brother, the son of Phinehas,
the son of Eli, the priest of the LORD at
[c]Shiloh, [d]was [1]wearing an ephod. And
the people did not know that Jonathan
had gone.
4 And [a]between the passes by which
Jonathan sought to cross over to the
Philistines' garrison, there was a sharp
crag on the one side, and a sharp crag on
the other side, and the name of the one
was Bozez, and the name of the other
Seneh.
5 The one crag rose on the north
opposite Michmash, and the other on
the south opposite Geba.
6 Then Jonathan said to the young
man who was carrying his armor, "Come
and let us cross over to the garrison of
[a]these uncircumcised; perhaps the LORD
will work for us, for [b]the LORD is not
restrained to save by many or by few."
7 And his armor bearer said to him,
"Do all that is in your heart; turn
yourself, *and* here I am with you according to your [1]desire."
8 Then Jonathan said, "[a]Behold, we
will cross over to the men and reveal
ourselves to them.
9"If they [1]say to us, 'Wait until we
come to you'; then we will stand in our
place and not go up to them.
10"But if they [1]say, 'Come up to us,'
then we will go up, for the LORD has
given them into our hands; and [a]this
shall be the sign to us."
11 And when both of them revealed
themselves to the garrison of the Philistines, the Philistines said, "Behold, [a]He-
brews are coming out of the holes where
they have hidden themselves."
12 So the men of the garrison [1]hailed
Jonathan and his armor bearer and said,
"Come up to us and [a]we will tell you
something." And Jonathan said to his
armor bearer, "Come up after me, for
[b]the LORD has given them into the hands
of Israel."
13 Then Jonathan climbed up on his
hands and feet, with his armor bearer
behind him; and they fell before Jonathan, and his armor bearer put some to
death after him.
14 And that first slaughter which
Jonathan and his armor bearer made
was about twenty men within about half
a furrow in an acre of land.
15 And there was a trembling in the
camp, in the field, and among all the
people. Even the garrison and [a]the raiders trembled, and [b]the earth quaked so
[c]that it became a [1]great trembling.
16 Now Saul's watchmen in Gibeah of
Benjamin looked, and behold, the multitude melted away; and they went here
and *there.*
17 And Saul said to the people who
were with him, "[1]Number now and see
who has gone from us." And when they
had [1]numbered, behold, Jonathan and
his armor bearer were not *there.*
18 Then Saul said to Ahijah, "[a]Bring
the ark of God here." For the ark of God
was at that time with the sons of Israel.
19 And it happened [a]while Saul talked
to the priest, that the commotion in the
camp of the Philistines continued and
increased; so Saul said to the priest,
"Withdraw your hand."

13 [1]Lit., *to* [a]2 Chr. 16:9 [b]1 Sam. 15:11, 22, 28 [c]1 Sam. 1:22

14 [a]1 Sam. 15:28 [b]Acts 7:46; 13:22

15 [1]Lit., *mustered* [a]1 Sam. 13:2 [b]1 Sam. 13:2, 6, 7; 14:2

16 [a]1 Sam. 13:2, 3

17 [1]Lit., *destroyers* [2]Lit., *heads* [3]Lit., *head* [4]Lit., *toward the direction of* [a]1 Sam. 14:15 [b]Josh. 18:23

18 [1]Lit., *head* [2]Lit., *the direction of* [a]Josh. 16:3; 18:13, 14 [b]Neh. 11:34

19 [1]Lit., *sword or spear* [a]Judg. 5:8; 2 Kin. 24:14; Jer. 24:1; 29:2 [b]Judg. 5:8

21 [1]Heb., *pim*

22 [a]Judg. 5:8

23 [a]1 Sam. 14:1; 2 Sam. 23:14 [b]1 Sam. 14:4, 5; Is. 10:28

2 [a]1 Sam. 13:15, 16 [b]Is. 10:28 [c]1 Sam. 13:15

3 [1]Lit., *carrying* [a]1 Sam. 22:9-12, 20 [b]1 Sam. 4:21 [c]1 Sam. 1:3 [d]1 Sam. 2:28

4 [a]1 Sam. 13:23

6 [a]1 Sam. 17:26, 36; Jer. 9:25, 26 [b]Judg. 7:4, 7; 1 Sam. 17:46, 47; Ps. 115:3; 135:6; Zech. 4:6; Matt. 19:26

7 [1]Lit., *heart*

8 [a]Judg. 7:9-14

9 [1]Lit., *say thus*

10 [1]Lit., *say thus* [a]Gen. 24:14; Judg. 6:36

11 [a]1 Sam. 13:6; 14:22

12 [1]Lit., *answered* [a]1 Sam. 17:43, 44 [b]2 Sam. 5:24

15 [1]Lit., *trembling of God* [a]1 Sam. 13:17, 18 [b]1 Sam. 7:10 [c]Gen. 35:5; 2 Kin. 7:6

17 [1]Lit., *muster(ed)*

18 [a]1 Sam. 23:9; 30:7

19 [a]Num. 27:21

20 Then Saul and all the people who *were* with him rallied and came to the battle; and behold, [a]every man's sword was against his fellow, *and there was* very great confusion.

21 Now the Hebrews *who* were with the Philistines previously, who went up with them all around in the camp, even [a]they also *turned* to be with the Israelites who *were* with Saul and Jonathan.

22 When all the [a]men of Israel who had hidden themselves in the hill country of Ephraim heard that the Philistines had fled, even they also pursued them closely in the battle.

23 So [a]the LORD delivered Israel that day, and the battle [1]spread beyond [b]Beth-aven.

Saul's Foolish Order

24 Now the men of Israel were hard-pressed on that day, for Saul had [a]put the people under oath, saying, "Cursed be the man who eats food [1]before evening, and until I have avenged myself on my enemies." So none of the people tasted food.

25 And all *the people of* the land entered the forest, and there was honey on the ground.

26 When the people entered the forest, behold, [a]*there was* a flow of honey; but no man put his hand to his mouth, for the people feared the oath.

27 But Jonathan had not heard when his father put the people under oath; therefore, [a]he put out the end of the staff that *was* in his hand and dipped it in the honeycomb, and put his hand to his mouth, and [b]his eyes brightened.

28 Then one of the people answered and said, "Your father strictly put the people under oath, saying, 'Cursed be the man who eats food today.' " And the people were weary.

29 Then Jonathan said, "[a]My father has troubled the land. See now, how my eyes have brightened because I tasted a little of this honey.

30 "How much more, if only the people had eaten freely today of the spoil of their enemies which they found! For now the slaughter among the Philistines has not been great."

31 And they struck among the Philistines that day from [a]Michmash to [b]Aijalon. And the people were very weary.

32 And [a]the people [1]rushed greedily upon the spoil, and took sheep and oxen and calves, and slew *them* on the ground; and the people ate *them* [b]with the blood.

33 Then they told Saul, saying, "Behold, the people are [a]sinning against the LORD by eating with the blood." And he said, "You have acted treacherously; roll a great stone to me today."

34 And Saul said, "Disperse yourselves among the people and say to them, 'Each one of you bring me his ox or his sheep, and slaughter *it* here and eat; and do not sin against the LORD by eating with the blood.' " So all the people that night brought each one his ox [1]with him, and slaughtered *it* there.

35 And [a]Saul built an altar to the LORD; it was the first altar that he built to the LORD.

36 Then Saul said, "Let us go down after the Philistines by night and take spoil among them until the morning light, and let us not leave a man of them." And they said, "Do whatever seems good [1]to you." So [a]the priest said, "Let us draw near to God here."

37 And Saul [a]inquired of God, "Shall I go down after the Philistines? Wilt Thou give them into the hand of Israel?" But [b]He did not answer him on that day.

38 And Saul said, "[a]Draw near here, all you [1]chiefs of the people, and investigate and see how this sin has happened today.

39 "For [a]as the LORD lives, who delivers Israel, though it is in Jonathan my son, he shall surely die." But not one of all the people answered him.

40 Then he said to all Israel, "You shall be on one side and I and Jonathan my son will be on the other side." And the people said to Saul, "Do what seems good [1]to you."

41 Therefore, Saul said to the LORD, the God of Israel, "[a]Give a perfect *lot.*" And Jonathan and Saul were taken, but the people escaped.

42 And Saul said, "Cast *lots* between me and Jonathan my son." And Jonathan was taken.

43 Then Saul said to Jonathan, "[a]Tell me what you have done." So Jonathan told him and said, "[b]I indeed tasted a little honey with the end of the staff that was in my hand. Here I am, I must die!"

44 And Saul said, "[a]May God do [1]this *to me* and more also, for [b]you shall surely die, Jonathan."

45 But the people said to Saul, "Must Jonathan die, who has [1]brought about this great deliverance in Israel? Far from it! As the LORD lives, [a]there shall not one hair of his head fall to the ground, for [b]he has worked with God this day." So the people [2]rescued Jonathan and he did not die.

46 Then Saul went up from [1]pursuing the Philistines, and the Philistines went to their own place.

Constant Warfare

47 Now when Saul had taken the kingdom over Israel, he fought against all his enemies on every side, against Moab, [a]the sons of Ammon, Edom, [b]the kings of Zobah, and [c]the Philistines; and wherever he turned, he [1]inflicted punishment.

48 And he acted valiantly and [1a]defeated the Amalekites, and delivered Israel from the hands of [2]those who plundered them.

49 Now [a]the sons of Saul were Jonathan and Ishvi and Malchi-shua; and the names of his two daughters *were these:* the name of the first-born [b]Merab and the name of the younger [c]Michal.

---

20 [a]Judg. 7:22; 2 Chr. 20:23
21 [a]1 Sam. 29:4
22 [a]1 Sam. 13:6
23 [1]Lit., *passed over* [a]Ex. 14:30; 1 Sam. 10:19; 14:23; 1 Chr. 11:14; 2 Chr. 32:22; Ps. 44:7 [b]1 Sam. 13:5
24 [1]Lit., *until* [a]Josh. 6:26
26 [a]Matt. 3:4
27 [a]1 Sam. 14:43 [b]1 Sam. 30:12
29 [a]Josh. 7:25; 1 Kin. 18:18
31 [a]1 Sam. 14:5 [b]Josh. 10:12
32 [1]Lit., *did with regard to the spoil* [a]1 Sam. 15:19 [b]Gen. 9:4; Lev. 3:17; 17:10-14; 19:26; Deut. 12:16, 23; Acts 15:20
33 [a]Lev. 7:26, 27; 19:26; Deut. 12:16, 23-25; 15:23
34 [1]Lit., *in his hand*
35 [a]1 Sam. 7:12, 17; 2 Sam. 24:25; James 4:8
36 [1]Lit., *in your eyes* [a]1 Sam. 14:3, 18, 19
37 [a]1 Sam. 10:22 [b]1 Sam. 28:6
38 [1]Lit., *corners* [a]Josh. 7:11, 12; 1 Sam. 10:19, 20
39 [a]1 Sam. 14:24, 44; 2 Sam. 12:5
40 [1]Lit., *in your eyes*
41 [a]Acts 1:24
43 [a]Josh. 7:19 [b]1 Sam. 14:27
44 [1]Lit., *thus* [a]Ruth 1:17; 1 Sam. 25:22 [b]1 Sam. 14:39
45 [1]Lit., *worked* [2]Lit., *ransomed* [a]2 Sam. 14:11; 1 Kin. 1:52; Luke 21:18; Acts 27:34 [b]2 Cor. 6:1
46 [1]Lit., *after*
47 [1]Or, *condemned* [a]1 Sam. 11:1-13 [b]2 Sam. 8:3-10 [c]1 Sam. 14:52
48 [1]Lit., *smote* [2]Lit., *its plunderers* [a]1 Sam. 15:3, 7
49 [a]1 Sam. 31:2; 1 Chr. 8:33; 10:2 [b]1 Sam. 18:17-19 [c]1 Sam. 18:20, 27; 19:12; 2 Sam. 6:20-23

50 And the name of Saul's wife was
Ahinoam the daughter of Ahimaaz. And
[a]the name of the captain of his army was
Abner the son of Ner, Saul's uncle.
51 [a]And Kish *was* the father of Saul,
and Ner the father of Abner *was* the son
of Abiel.
52 Now the war against the Philistines
was severe all the days of Saul; and
when Saul saw any mighty man or any
valiant man, he [1a]attached him to [2]his
staff.

Saul's Disobedience

15 THEN Samuel said to Saul,
"[a]The LORD sent me to anoint
you as king over His people, over Israel;
now therefore, listen to the [1]words of the
LORD.
2 "Thus says the LORD of hosts, 'I will
[1]punish Amalek [a]*for* what he did to
Israel, how he set himself against him on
the way while he was coming up from
Egypt.
3 'Now go and strike Amalek and
[a]utterly destroy all that he has, and do
not spare him; but [b]put to death both
man and woman, child and infant, ox
and sheep, camel and donkey.' "
4 Then Saul summoned the people
and [1]numbered them in [a]Telaim,
200,000 foot soldiers and 10,000 men of
Judah.
5 And Saul came to the city of Amalek, and set an ambush in the valley.
6 And Saul said to [a]the Kenites,
"Go, depart, go down from among the
Amalekites, lest I destroy you with
them; for [b]you showed kindness to all
the sons of Israel when they came up
from Egypt." So the Kenites departed
from among the Amalekites.
7 So [a]Saul [1]defeated the Amalekites,
from [b]Havilah as you go to [c]Shur, which
is [2]east of Egypt.
8 And he captured [a]Agag the king of
the Amalekites alive, and [b]utterly destroyed all the people with the edge of
the sword.
9 But Saul and the people [a]spared
Agag and the best of the sheep, the oxen,
the fatlings, the lambs, and all that was
good, and were not willing to destroy
them utterly; but everything despised
and worthless, that they utterly destroyed.

Samuel Rebukes Saul

10 Then the word of the LORD came
to Samuel, saying,
11 "[a]I regret that I have made Saul
king, for [b]he has turned back from
[1]following Me, and has not carried out
My commands." And Samuel was distressed and [c]cried out to the LORD all
night.
12 And Samuel rose early in the
morning to meet Saul; and it was told
Samuel, saying, "Saul came to [a]Carmel,
and behold, he set up a monument for
himself, then turned and proceeded on
[1]down to [b]Gilgal."
13 And Samuel came to Saul, and
Saul said to him, "[a]Blessed are you of
the LORD! I have carried out the command of the LORD."
14 But Samuel said, "[a]What then is
this [1]bleating of the sheep in my ears,
and the [1]lowing of the oxen which I
hear?"
15 And Saul said, "They have brought
them from the Amalekites, for [a]the
people spared the best of the sheep and
oxen, to sacrifice to the LORD your God;
but the rest we have utterly destroyed."
16 Then Samuel said to Saul, "Wait,
and let me tell you what the LORD said
to me last night." And he said to him,
"Speak!"
17 And Samuel said, "Is it not true,
[a]though you were little in your own eyes,
you were *made* the head of the tribes of
Israel? And the LORD anointed you king
over Israel,
18 and the LORD sent you on a [1]mis-
sion, and said, '[a]Go and utterly destroy
the sinners, the Amalekites, and fight
against them until they are exterminated.'
19 "Why then did you not obey the
voice of the LORD, [a]but rushed upon the
spoil and did what was evil in the sight
of the LORD?"
20 Then Saul said to Samuel, "[a]I did
obey the voice of the LORD, and went on
the [1]mission on which the LORD sent me,
and have brought back Agag the king of
Amalek, and have utterly destroyed the
Amalekites.
21 "But [a]the people took *some* of the
spoil, sheep and oxen, the choicest of the
things devoted to destruction, to sacrifice to the LORD your God at Gilgal."
22 And Samuel said,
"[a]Has the LORD as much delight in
burnt offerings and sacrifices
As in obeying the voice of the
LORD?
Behold, [b]to obey is better than
sacrifice,
And to heed than the fat of rams.
23 "For rebellion is as the sin of
[a]divination,
And insubordination is as [b]iniq-
uity and idolatry.
Because you have rejected the
word of the LORD,
[c]He has also rejected you from
being king."
24 Then Saul said to Samuel, "[a]I have
sinned; [b]I have indeed transgressed the
[1]command of the LORD and your words,
because I feared the people and listened
to their voice.
25 "Now therefore, [a]please pardon my
sin and return with me, that I may
worship the LORD."
26 But Samuel said to Saul, "I will not
return with you; for [a]you have rejected
the word of the LORD, and the LORD has
rejected you from being king over Israel."
27 And as Samuel turned to go, [a]*Saul*
seized the edge of his robe, and it tore.

50 [a]2 Sam. 2:8
51 [a]1 Sam. 9:1, 21
52 [1]Lit., *gathered* [2]Lit., *himself* [a]1 Sam. 8:11
1 [1]Lit., *sound of the words* [a]1 Sam. 9:16; 10:1
2 [1]Or, *visit* [a]Ex. 17:8-16; Num. 24:20; Deut. 25:17-19
3 [a]Num. 24:20; Deut. 20:16-18; Josh. 6:17-21 [b]1 Sam. 22:19
4 [1]Lit., *mustered* [a]Josh. 15:24
6 [a]Num. 24:21; Judg. 1:16; 4:11 [b]Ex. 18:9, 10; Num. 10:29-32
7 [1]Lit., *smote* [2]Lit., *before* [a]1 Sam. 14:48 [b]Gen. 25:18 [c]Gen. 16:7; Ex. 15:22; 1 Sam. 27:8
8 [a]Num. 24:7; 1 Sam. 15:20; Esth. 3:1 [b]1 Sam. 27:8, 9; 30:1; 2 Sam. 8:12
9 [a]1 Sam. 15:3, 15, 19
11 [1]Lit., *after* [a]Gen. 6:6, 7; Ex. 32:14; 1 Sam. 15:35; 2 Sam. 24:16 [b]Josh. 22:16; 1 Sam. 13:13; 1 Kin. 9:6, 7 [c]Ex. 32:11-13; Luke 6:12
12 [1]Lit., *and went down* [a]Josh. 15:55; 1 Sam. 25:2 [b]1 Sam. 13:12, 15
13 [a]Gen. 14:19; Judg. 17:2; Ruth 3:10; 2 Sam. 2:5
14 [1]Lit., *sound* [a]Ex. 32:21-24
15 [a]Gen. 3:12, 13; Ex. 32:22, 23; 1 Sam. 15:9, 21
17 [a]1 Sam. 9:21; 10:22
18 [1]Lit., *way* [a]1 Sam. 15:3
19 [a]1 Sam. 14:32
20 [1]Lit., *way* [a]1 Sam. 15:13
21 [a]Ex. 32:22, 23; 1 Sam. 15:15
22 [a]Ps. 40:6-8; 51:16, 17; Is. 1:11-15; Mic. 6:6-8; Heb. 10:6-9 [b]Jer. 7:22, 23; Hos. 6:6; Matt. 12:7; Mark 12:33
23 [a]Deut. 18:10 [b]Gen. 31:19, 34 [c]1 Sam. 13:14
24 [1]Lit., *mouth* [a]Num. 22:34; 2 Sam. 12:13; Ps. 51:4 [b]Prov. 29:25; Is. 51:12, 13
25 [a]Ex. 10:17
26 [a]1 Sam. 13:14; 16:1
27 [a]1 Kin. 11:30, 31

28 So Samuel said to him, "[a]The
LORD has torn the kingdom of Israel
from you today, and has given it to your
neighbor who is better than you.
29 "And also the [1a]Glory of Israel [b]will
not lie or change His mind; for He is not
a man that He should change His mind."
30 Then he said, "I have sinned; [a]*but*
please honor me now before the elders of
my people and before Israel, and go
back with me, [b]that I may worship the
LORD your God."
31 So Samuel went back following
Saul, and Saul worshiped the LORD.
32 Then Samuel said, "Bring me
Agag, the king of the Amalekites." And
Agag came to him [1]cheerfully. And Agag
said, "Surely the bitterness of death is
past."
33 But Samuel said, "[a]As your sword
has made women childless, so shall your
mother be childless among women."
And Samuel hewed Agag to pieces before the LORD at Gilgal.
34 Then Samuel went to [a]Ramah, but
Saul went up to his house at [b]Gibeah of
Saul.
35 And [a]Samuel did not see Saul
again until the day of his death; for
Samuel [b]grieved over Saul. And the
LORD regretted that He had made Saul
king over Israel.

Samuel Goes to Bethlehem

16 NOW the LORD said to Samuel,
"[a]How long will you grieve over
Saul, since [b]I have rejected him from
being king over Israel? [c]Fill your horn
with oil, and go; I will send you to [d]Jesse
the Bethlehemite, for I have [e]selected a
king for Myself among his sons."
2 But Samuel said, "How can I go?
When Saul hears *of it,* he will kill me."
And the LORD said, "[a]Take a heifer with
you, and say, 'I have come to sacrifice to
the LORD.'
3 "And you shall invite Jesse to the
sacrifice, and [a]I will show you what you
shall do; and [b]you shall anoint for Me
the one whom I [1]designate to you."
4 So Samuel did what the LORD said,
and came to [a]Bethlehem. And the elders
of the city came trembling to meet him
and said, "[b]Do you come in peace?"
5 And he said, "In peace; I have
come to sacrifice to the LORD. [a]Conse-
crate yourselves and come with me to
the sacrifice." He also consecrated Jesse
and his sons, and invited them to the
sacrifice.
6 Then it came about when they
entered, that he looked at [a]Eliab and
thought, "Surely the LORD's anointed is
before Him."
7 But the LORD said to Samuel, "Do
not look at his appearance or at the
height of his stature, because I have
rejected him; for [1]God *sees* not as man
sees, for man looks at the outward
appearance, [a]but the LORD looks at the
heart."

28 [a]1 Sam. 28:17, 18; 1 Kin. 11:31
29 [1]Or, *Eminence* [a]1 Chr. 29:11 [b]Num. 23:19; Ezek. 24:14; Titus 1:2
30 [a]John 5:44; 12:43 [b]Is. 29:13
32 [1]Or, *in bonds*
33 [a]Gen. 9:6; Judg. 1:7; Matt. 7:2
34 [a]1 Sam. 7:17 [b]1 Sam. 11:4
35 [a]1 Sam. 19:24 [b]1 Sam. 16:1
1 [a]1 Sam. 15:35 [b]1 Sam. 13:13, 14; 15:23 [c]1 Sam. 9:16; 10:1; 2 Kin. 9:1 [d]Ruth 4:17-22 [e]Ps. 78:70, 71; Acts 13:22
2 [a]1 Sam. 20:29
3 [1]Lit., *say to you* [a]Ex. 4:15; Acts 9:6 [b]Deut. 17:14, 15; 1 Sam. 9:16
4 [a]Gen. 48:7; Luke 2:4 [b]1 Kin. 2:13; 2 Kin. 9:22; 1 Chr. 12:17, 18
5 [a]Gen. 35:2; Ex. 19:10
6 [a]1 Sam. 17:13
7 [1]So with Gr.; Heb., He does *not see what man sees* [a]1 Sam. 2:3; 1 Kin. 8:39; 1 Chr. 28:9; Luke 16:15
8 [a]1 Sam. 17:13
9 [1]In 2 Sam. 13:3, *Shimeah;* in 1 Chr. 2:13, *Shimea* [a]1 Sam. 17:13
11 [1]Lit., *take* [a]1 Sam. 17:12; 2 Sam. 13:3
12 [a]Gen. 39:6; Ex. 2:2; Acts 7:20 [b]1 Sam. 9:17
13 [a]1 Sam. 10:1 [b]Num. 27:18; 1 Sam. 10:6, 9, 10
14 [a]Judg. 16:20; 1 Sam. 11:6; 18:12; 28:15 [b]Judg. 9:23; 1 Sam. 16:15, 16; 18:10; 19:9; 1 Kin. 22:19-22
16 [a]1 Sam. 18:10; 19:9; 2 Kin. 3:15
18 [a]1 Sam. 17:32-36 [b]1 Sam. 3:19
20 [a]1 Sam. 10:4, 27; Prov. 18:16
21 [1]Lit., *stood before him* [2]Lit., *he* [a]Gen. 41:46; Prov. 22:29
23 [a]1 Sam. 16:14-16

8 Then Jesse called [a]Abinadab, and
made him pass before Samuel. And he
said, "Neither has the LORD chosen this
one."
9 Next Jesse made [1a]Shammah pass
by. And he said, "Neither has the LORD
chosen this one."
10 Thus Jesse made seven of his sons
pass before Samuel. But Samuel said to
Jesse, "The LORD has not chosen these."
11 And Samuel said to Jesse, "Are
these all the children?" And he said,
"[a]There remains yet the youngest, and
behold, he is tending the sheep." Then
Samuel said to Jesse, "Send and [1]bring
him; for we will not sit down until he
comes here."

David Anointed

12 So he sent and brought him in.
Now he was ruddy, with [a]beautiful eyes
and a handsome appearance. And the
LORD said, "[b]Arise, anoint him; for this
is he."
13 Then Samuel took the horn of oil
and [a]anointed him in the midst of his
brothers; and [b]the Spirit of the LORD
came mightily upon David from that day
forward. And Samuel arose and went to
Ramah.
14 [a]Now the Spirit of the LORD departed from Saul, and [b]an evil spirit
from the LORD terrorized him.
15 Saul's servants then said to him,
"Behold now, an evil spirit from God is
terrorizing you.
16 "Let our lord now command your
servants who are before you. Let them
seek a man who is a skillful player on the
harp; and it shall come about when the
evil spirit from God is on you, that [a]he
shall play *the harp* with his hand, and
you will be well."
17 So Saul said to his servants, "Provide for me now a man who can play
well, and bring *him* to me."
18 Then one of the young men answered and said, "Behold, I have seen a
son of Jesse the Bethlehemite who is a
skillful musician, [a]a mighty man of
valor, a warrior, one prudent in speech,
and a handsome man; and [b]the LORD is
with him."
19 So Saul sent messengers to Jesse,
and said, "Send me your son David who
is with the flock."
20 And Jesse [a]took a donkey *loaded
with* bread and a jug of wine and a
young goat, and sent *them* to Saul by
David his son.
21 Then David came to Saul and
[1a]attended him, and [2]Saul loved him
greatly; and he became his armor bearer.
22 And Saul sent to Jesse, saying, "Let
David now stand before me; for he has
found favor in my sight."
23 So it came about whenever [a]the *evil*
spirit from God came to Saul, David
would take the harp and play *it* with his
hand; and Saul would be refreshed and
be well, and the evil spirit would depart
from him.

Goliath's Challenge

17 NOW [a]the Philistines gathered
their armies for battle; and they
were gathered at Socoh which belongs to
Judah, and they camped between [b]Socoh
and [c]Azekah, in [d]Ephes-dammim.
2 And Saul and the men of Israel
were gathered, and camped in [a]the valley
of Elah, and drew up in battle array to
encounter the Philistines.
3 And the Philistines stood on the
mountain on one side while Israel stood
on the mountain on the other side, with
the valley between them.
4 Then a champion came out from
the armies of the Philistines named
[a]Goliath, from [b]Gath, whose height was
six [1]cubits and a span.
5 And *he had* a bronze helmet on his
head, and he was clothed with scale-
armor [1]which weighed five thousand
shekels of bronze.
6 *He* also *had* bronze [1]greaves on his
legs and a [a]bronze javelin *slung* between
his shoulders.
7 And [a]the shaft of his spear was like
a weaver's beam, and the head of his
spear *weighed* six hundred shekels of
iron; [b]his shield-carrier also walked
before him.
8 And he stood and shouted to the
ranks of Israel, and said to them, "Why
do you come out to draw up in battle
array? Am I not the Philistine and you
[a]servants of Saul? Choose a man for
yourselves and let him come down to
me.
9 "[a]If he is able to fight with me and
[1]kill me, then we will become your
servants; but if I prevail against him and
[1]kill him, then you shall become our
servants and serve us."
10 Again the Philistine said, "[a]I defy
the ranks of Israel this day; give me a
man that we may fight together."
11 When Saul and all Israel heard
these words of the Philistine, they were
dismayed and greatly afraid.
12 Now David was [a]the son of [1]the
[b]Ephrathite of Bethlehem in Judah,
whose name was Jesse, and [c]he had eight
sons. And [2]Jesse was old in the days of
Saul, advanced *in years* among men.
13 And the three older sons of Jesse
had [1]gone after Saul to the battle. And
[a]the names of his three sons who went to
the battle were Eliab the first-born, and
the second to him Abinadab, and the
third Shammah.
14 And [a]David was the youngest.
Now the three oldest followed Saul,
15 [a]but David went back and forth
from Saul [b]to tend his father's flock at
Bethlehem.
16 And the Philistine came [1]forward
morning and evening for forty days, and
took his stand.
17 Then Jesse said to David his son,
"[a]Take now for your brothers an ephah
of this roasted grain and these ten
loaves, and run to the camp to your
brothers.
18 "[a]Bring also these ten cuts of cheese
to the commander of *their* thousand,
[b]and look into the welfare of your brothers, and bring back [1]news of them.
19 "For Saul and they and all the men
of Israel are in the valley of Elah, fighting with the Philistines."

David Accepts the Challenge

20 So David arose early in the morning and left the flock with a keeper and
took *the supplies* and went as Jesse had
commanded him. And he came to the
[a]circle of the camp while the army was
going out in battle array shouting the
war cry.
21 And Israel and the Philistines drew
up in battle array, army against army.
22 Then David left his [a]baggage in the
[1]care of the baggage keeper, and ran to
the battle line and entered in order to
greet his brothers.
23 As he was talking with them, behold, the champion, the Philistine from
Gath named Goliath, was coming up
from the army of the Philistines, and he
spoke [a]these same words; and David
heard *them*.
24 When all the men of Israel saw the
man, they fled from him and were
greatly afraid.
25 And the men of Israel said, "Have
you seen this man who is coming up?
Surely he is coming up to defy Israel.
And it will be that the king will enrich
the man who kills him with great riches
and [a]will give him his daughter and
make his father's house [1]free in Israel."
26 Then David spoke to the men who
were standing by him, saying, "What
will be done for the man who kills this
Philistine, and takes away [a]the reproach
from Israel? For who is this [b]uncircum-
cised Philistine, that he should [c]taunt the
armies of [d]the living God?"
27 And the people [1]answered him in
accord with this word, saying, "[a]Thus it
will be done for the man who kills him."
28 Now Eliab his oldest brother heard
when he spoke to the men; and [a]Eliab's
anger burned against David and he said,
"Why have you come down? And with
whom have you left those few sheep in
the wilderness? I know your insolence
and the wickedness of your heart; for
you have come down in order to see the
battle."
29 But David said, "What have I done
now? Was it not just a [1]question?"
30 Then he turned [1]away from him to
another and [a]said the same thing; and
the people answered the same thing as
[2]before.

David Kills Goliath

31 When the words which David
spoke were heard, they told *them* [1]to
Saul, and he sent for him.
32 And David said to Saul, "[a]Let no
man's heart fail on account of him;
[b]your servant will go and fight with this
Philistine."

1 [a]1 Sam. 13:5 [b]Josh. 15:35; 2 Chr. 28:18 [c]Josh. 10:10 [d]1 Chr. 11:13
2 [a]1 Sam. 21:9
4 [1]I.e., One cubit equals approx. 18 in. [a]2 Sam. 21:19 [b]Josh. 11:22
5 [1]Lit., *and the weight of the armor* was
6 [1]Or, *shin guards* [a]1 Sam. 17:45
7 [a]2 Sam. 21:19; 1 Chr. 11:23 [b]1 Sam. 17:41
8 [a]1 Sam. 8:17
9 [1]Lit., *smite* [a]2 Sam. 2:12-16
10 [a]1 Sam. 17:26, 36, 45; 2 Sam. 21:21
12 [1]Lit., *this* [2]Lit., *the man* [a]Ruth 4:22; 1 Sam. 16:18 [b]Gen. 35:19 [c]1 Sam. 16:10, 11; 1 Chr. 2:13-15
13 [1]Lit., *gone; they went* [a]1 Sam. 16:6, 8, 9
14 [a]1 Sam. 16:11
15 [a]1 Sam. 16:21-23 [b]1 Sam. 16:11, 19
16 [1]Lit., *near*
17 [a]1 Sam. 25:18
18 [1]Lit., *their pledge* [a]1 Sam. 16:20 [b]Gen. 37:13, 14
20 [a]1 Sam. 26:5, 7
22 [1]Lit., *hand* [a]Judg. 18:21; Is. 10:28
23 [a]1 Sam. 17:8-10
25 [1]I.e., free from taxes and public service [a]Josh. 15:16
26 [a]1 Sam. 11:2 [b]1 Sam. 14:6; 17:36; Jer. 9:25, 26 [c]1 Sam. 17:10 [d]Deut. 5:26; 2 Kin. 19:4; Jer. 10:10
27 [1]Lit., *said to* [a]1 Sam. 17:25
28 [a]Gen. 37:4, 8-36; Prov. 18:19; Matt. 10:36
29 [1]Lit., *word*
30 [1]Lit., *from beside him* [2]Lit., *the former word* [a]1 Sam. 17:26, 27
31 [1]Lit., *before*
32 [a]Deut. 20:1-4 [b]1 Sam. 16:18

33 Then Saul said to David, "[a]You are not able to go against this Philistine to fight with him; for you are *but* a youth while he has been a warrior from his youth."

34 But David said to Saul, "Your servant was tending his father's sheep. When a lion or a bear came and took a lamb from the flock,

35 I went out after him and [1]attacked him, and [a]rescued *it* from his mouth; and when he rose up against me, I seized *him* by his beard and [1]struck him and killed him.

36 "Your servant has [1]killed both the lion and the bear; and this uncircumcised Philistine will be like one of them, since he has taunted the armies of the living God."

37 And David said, "[a]The LORD who delivered me from the paw of the lion and from the paw of the bear, He will deliver me from the hand of this Philistine." And Saul said to David, "[b]Go, and may the LORD be with you."

38 Then Saul clothed David with his garments and put a bronze helmet on his head, and he clothed him with armor.

39 And David girded his sword over his armor and tried to walk, for he had not tested *them.* So David said to Saul, "I cannot go with these, for I have not tested *them.*" And David took them [1]off.

40 And he took his stick in his hand and chose for himself five smooth stones from the brook, and put them in the shepherd's bag which he had, even in *his* pouch, and [a]his sling was in his hand; and he approached the Philistine.

41 Then the Philistine came on and approached David, with the shield-bearer in front of him.

42 When the Philistine looked and saw David, [a]he disdained him; for he was *but* a youth, and [b]ruddy, with a handsome appearance.

43 And the Philistine said to David, "[a]Am I a dog, that you come to me with sticks?" And [b]the Philistine cursed David by his gods.

44 The Philistine also said to David, "Come to me, and I will give your flesh [a]to the birds of the sky and the beasts of the field."

45 Then David said to the Philistine, "You come to me with a sword, a spear, and a javelin, [a]but I come to you in the name of the LORD of hosts, the God of the armies of Israel, whom you have taunted.

46 "This day the LORD will deliver you up into my hands, and I will strike you down and remove your head from you. And I will give the [a]dead bodies of the army of the Philistines this day to the birds of the sky and the wild beasts of the earth, [b]that all the earth may know that there is a God in Israel,

47 and that all this assembly may know that [a]the LORD does not deliver by sword or by spear; [b]for the battle is the LORD's and He will give you into our hands."

48 Then it happened when the Philistine rose and came and drew near to meet David, that [a]David ran quickly toward the battle line to meet the Philistine.

49 And David put his hand into his bag and took from it a stone and slung *it,* and struck the Philistine on his forehead. And the stone sank into his forehead, so that he fell on his face to the ground.

50 Thus David prevailed over the Philistine with a sling and a stone, and he struck the Philistine and killed him; but there was no sword in David's hand.

51 Then David ran and stood over the Philistine and [a]took his sword and drew it out of its sheath and killed him, and cut off his head with it. [b]When the Philistines saw that their champion was dead, they fled.

52 And the men of Israel and Judah arose and shouted and pursued the Philistines [1]as far as the valley, and to the gates of [a]Ekron. And the slain Philistines [2]lay along the way to [b]Shaaraim, even to Gath and Ekron.

53 And the sons of Israel returned from chasing the Philistines and plundered their camps.

54 Then David took the Philistine's head and brought it to Jerusalem, but he put his weapons in his tent.

55 Now when Saul saw David going out against the Philistine, he said to Abner the commander of the army, "Abner, whose son is [a]this young man?" And Abner said, "By your life, O king, I do not know."

56 And the king said, "You inquire whose son the youth is."

57 So when David returned from killing the Philistine, Abner took him and [a]brought him before Saul with the Philistine's head in his hand.

58 And Saul said to him, "Whose son are you, young man?" And David answered, "[a]*I am* the son of your servant Jesse the Bethlehemite."

Jonathan and David

18 NOW it came about when he had finished speaking to Saul, that [a]the soul of Jonathan was knit to the soul of David, and [b]Jonathan loved him as himself.

2 And Saul took him that day and [a]did not let him return to his father's house.

3 Then [a]Jonathan made a covenant with David because he loved him as himself.

4 And [a]Jonathan stripped himself of the robe that was on him and gave it to David, with his armor, including his sword and his bow and his belt.

5 So David went out wherever Saul sent him, *and* [1]prospered; and Saul set him over the men of war. And it was pleasing in the sight of all the people and also in the sight of Saul's servants.

---

33 [a]Num. 13:31
35 [1]Lit., *smote* [a]Amos 3:12
36 [1]Lit., *smitten*
37 [a]2 Cor. 1:10; 2 Tim. 4:17, 18 [b]1 Sam. 20:13; 1 Chr. 22:11, 16
39 [1]Lit., *off from himself*
40 [a]Judg. 20:16
42 [a]Ps. 123:4; Prov. 16:18 [b]1 Sam. 16:12
43 [a]1 Sam. 24:14; 2 Sam. 3:8; 2 Kin. 8:13 [b]1 Kin. 20:10
44 [a]1 Sam. 17:46
45 [a]2 Sam. 22:35; 2 Chr. 32:8; Ps. 124:8; Heb. 11:32-34
46 [a]Deut. 28:26 [b]Josh. 4:24; 1 Kin. 8:43; 18:36; 2 Kin. 19:19; Is. 37:20
47 [a]1 Sam. 14:6; 2 Chr. 14:11; 20:15; Ps. 44:6; Hos. 1:7; Zech. 4:6 [b]2 Chr. 20:15
48 [a]Ps. 27:3
51 [a]1 Sam. 21:9; 2 Sam. 23:21 [b]Heb. 11:34
52 [1]Lit., *until your coming to* [2]Lit., *fell* [a]Josh. 15:11 [b]Josh. 15:36
55 [a]1 Sam. 16:12, 21, 22
57 [a]1 Sam. 17:54
58 [a]1 Sam. 17:12
1 [a]Gen. 44:30 [b]Deut. 13:6; 1 Sam. 20:17; 2 Sam. 1:26
2 [a]1 Sam. 17:15
3 [a]1 Sam. 20:8-17
4 [a]Gen. 41:42; 1 Sam. 17:38; Esth. 6:8
5 [1]Or, *acted wisely*

6 And it happened as they were
coming, when David returned from killing the Philistine, that [a]the women came
out of all the cities of Israel, singing and
dancing, to meet King Saul, with tambourines, with joy and with [1]musical
instruments.
7 And the women [a]sang as they
[1]played, and said,
"[b]Saul has slain his thousands,
[c]And David his ten thousands."
8 Then Saul became very angry, for
this saying [1]displeased him; and he said,
"They have ascribed to David ten thousands, but to me they have ascribed
thousands. Now [a]what more can he have
but the kingdom?"
9 And Saul looked at David with
suspicion from that day on.

Saul Turns against David

10 Now it came about on the next day
that [a]an evil spirit from God came
mightily upon Saul, and [b]he raved in the
midst of the house, while David was
playing *the harp* with his hand, [1c]as
usual; and [2d]a spear *was* in Saul's hand.
11 And [a]Saul hurled the spear for he
thought, "I will [1]pin David to the wall."
But David [2]escaped from his presence
twice.
12 Now [a]Saul was afraid of David,
[b]for the LORD was with him but [c]had
departed from Saul.
13 Therefore Saul removed him from
[1]his presence, and appointed him as his
commander of a thousand; and [a]he went
out and came in before the people.
14 And David was [1]prospering in all
his ways for [a]the LORD *was* with him.
15 When Saul saw that he was [1]pros-
pering greatly, he dreaded him.
16 But [a]all Israel and Judah loved
David, and he went out and came in
before them.
17 Then Saul said to David, "[a]Here is
my older daughter Merab; I will give her
to you as a wife, only be a valiant man
for me and fight [b]the LORD's battles."
For Saul thought, "My hand shall not be
against him, but [c]let the hand of the
Philistines be against him."
18 But David said to Saul, "[a]Who am
I, and what is my life *or* my father's
family in Israel, that I should be the
king's son-in-law?"
19 So it came about at the time when
Merab, Saul's daughter, should have
been given to David, that she was given
to [a]Adriel [b]the Meholathite for a wife.

David Marries Saul's Daughter

20 Now [a]Michal, Saul's daughter,
loved David. When they told Saul, the
thing was agreeable [1]to him.
21 And Saul thought, "I will give her
to him that she may become a snare to
him, and [a]that the hand of the Philistines
may be against him." Therefore Saul
said to David, "[b]For a second time you
may be my son-in-law today."

6 [1]I.e., triangles; or, three-stringed instruments [a]Ex. 15:20, 21; Judg. 11:34; Ps. 68:25; 149:3
7 [1]Or, *danced* [a]Ex. 15:21; 1 Sam. 21:11; 29:5 [b]1 Sam. 21:11 [c]2 Sam. 18:3
8 [1]Lit., *was evil in his eyes* [a]1 Sam. 15:28
10 [1]Lit., *day by day* [2]Lit., *the* [a]1 Sam. 16:14 [b]1 Sam. 19:23, 24 [c]1 Sam. 16:23 [d]1 Sam. 19:9
11 [1]Lit., *strike David and the wall* [2]Lit., *turned about* [a]1 Sam. 19:10; 20:33
12 [a]1 Sam. 18:15, 29 [b]1 Sam. 16:13, 18 [c]1 Sam. 16:14; 28:15
13 [1]Lit., *with him* [a]Num. 27:17; 1 Sam. 18:16; 2 Sam. 5:2
14 [1]Or, *acting wisely* [a]Gen. 39:2, 3, 23; Josh. 6:27; 1 Sam. 16:18
15 [1]Or, *acting very wisely*
16 [a]1 Sam. 18:5
17 [a]1 Sam. 17:25 [b]Num. 21:14; 1 Sam. 17:36, 47; 25:28 [c]1 Sam. 18:21, 25
18 [a]1 Sam. 9:21; 18:23; 2 Sam. 7:18
19 [a]2 Sam. 21:8 [b]Judg. 7:22; 1 Kin. 19:16
20 [1]Lit., *in his sight* [a]1 Sam. 18:28
21 [a]1 Sam. 18:17 [b]1 Sam. 18:26
23 [1]Lit., *in the ears of* [a]Gen. 29:20; 34:12
24 [1]Lit., *by saying according*
25 [a]Gen. 34:12; Ex. 22:17 [b]1 Sam. 14:24 [c]1 Sam. 18:17
26 [1]Lit., *it was agreeable in the sight of* [2]Lit., *And the days had not expired* [a]1 Sam. 18:21
27 [a]1 Sam. 18:17 [b]2 Sam. 3:14
30 [a]2 Sam. 11:1 [b]1 Sam. 18:5

1 [a]1 Sam. 18:8, 9 [b]1 Sam. 18:1-3
3 [1]Lit., *see* [a]1 Sam. 20:9, 13
4 [1]Lit., *good* [a]1 Sam. 20:32; Prov. 31:8, 9 [b]Gen. 42:22; Prov. 17:13; Jer. 18:20
5 [a]Judg. 9:17; 1 Sam. 17:49, 50; 28:21; Ps. 119:109 [b]1 Sam. 11:13; 1 Chr. 11:14 [c]Deut. 19:10-13; 1 Sam. 20:32; Ps. 94:21; Matt. 27:4

22 Then Saul commanded his servants, "Speak to David secretly, saying,
'Behold, the king delights in you, and all
his servants love you; now therefore,
become the king's son-in-law.' "
23 So Saul's servants spoke these
words [1]to David. But David said, "Is it
trivial in your sight to become the king's
son-in-law, [a]since I am a poor man and
lightly esteemed?"
24 And the servants of Saul reported
to him [1]according to these words *which*
David spoke.
25 Saul then said, "Thus you shall say
to David, 'The king does not desire any
[a]dowry except a hundred foreskins of
the Philistines, [b]to take vengeance on the
king's enemies.' " Now [c]Saul planned to
make David fall by the hand of the
Philistines.
26 When his servants told David these
words, [1]it pleased David to become the
king's son-in-law. [2a]Before the days had
expired
27 David rose up and went, [a]he and
his men, and struck down two hundred
men among the Philistines. Then [b]David
brought their foreskins, and they gave
them in full number to the king, that he
might become the king's son-in-law. So
Saul gave him Michal his daughter for a
wife.
28 When Saul saw and knew that the
LORD was with David, and *that* Michal,
Saul's daughter, loved him,
29 then Saul was even more afraid of
David. Thus Saul was David's enemy
continually.
30 Then the commanders of the Philistines [a]went out *to battle*, and it happened as often as they went out, that
David [b]behaved himself more wisely
than all the servants of Saul. So his name
was highly esteemed.

David Protected from Saul

19 NOW Saul told Jonathan his son
and all his servants [a]to put David
to death. But [b]Jonathan, Saul's son,
greatly delighted in David.
2 So Jonathan told David saying,
"Saul my father is seeking to put you to
death. Now therefore, please be on
guard in the morning, and stay in a
secret place and hide yourself.
3 "And I will go out and stand beside
my father in the field where you are, and
I will speak with my father about you;
[a]if I [1]find out anything, then I shall tell
you."
4 Then Jonathan [a]spoke well of David to Saul his father, and said to him,
"[b]Do not let the king sin against his
servant David, since he has not sinned
against you, and since his deeds *have
been* very [1]beneficial to you.
5 "For [a]he took his life in his hand
and struck the Philistine, and [b]the LORD
brought about a great deliverance for all
Israel; you saw *it* and rejoiced. [c]Why
then will you sin against innocent blood,
by putting David to death without a
cause?"

6 And Saul listened to the voice of
Jonathan, and Saul vowed, "As the
LORD lives, he shall not be put to
death."
7 Then Jonathan called David, and
Jonathan told him all these words. And
Jonathan brought David to Saul, and he
was in his presence as [a]formerly.
8 When there was war again, David
went out and fought with the Philistines,
and [1]defeated them with great slaughter,
so that they fled before him.
9 Now there was [a]an evil spirit from
the LORD on Saul as he was sitting in his
house [b]with his spear in his hand, [c]and
David was playing *the harp* with *his*
hand.
10 [a]And Saul tried to [1]pin David to
the wall with the spear, but he slipped
away out of Saul's presence, so that he
[2]stuck the spear into the wall. And
David fled and escaped that night.
11 Then [a]Saul sent messengers to
David's house to watch him, in order to
put him to death in the morning. But
Michal, David's wife, told him, saying,
"If you do not save your life tonight,
tomorrow you will be put to death."
12 [a]So Michal let David down
through a window, and he went out and
fled and escaped.
13 And Michal took [a]the [1]household
idol and laid *it* on the bed, and put a
quilt of goats' *hair* at its head, and
covered *it* with clothes.
14 When Saul sent messengers to take
David, she said, "[a]He is sick."
15 Then Saul sent messengers to see
David, saying, "Bring him up to me on
[1]his bed, that I may put him to death."
16 When the messengers entered, behold, the [1]household idol *was* on the bed
with the quilt of goats' *hair* at its head.
17 So Saul said to Michal, "Why have
you deceived me like this and let my
enemy go, so that he has escaped?" And
Michal said to Saul, "He said to me, 'Let
me go! [a]Why should I put you to
death?' "
18 Now David fled and escaped and
came [a]to Samuel at Ramah, and told
him all that Saul had done to him. And
he and Samuel went and stayed in
[b]Naioth.
19 And it was told Saul, saying, "Behold, David is at Naioth in Ramah."
20 Then [a]Saul sent messengers to take
David, but when they saw [b]the company
of the prophets prophesying, with Samuel standing *and* presiding over them,
the Spirit of God came upon the messengers of Saul; and [c]they also prophesied.
21 And when it was told Saul, he sent
other messengers, and they also prophesied. So Saul sent messengers again the
third time, and they also prophesied.
22 Then he himself went to Ramah,
and came as far as the large well that is
in Secu; and he asked and said, "Where
are Samuel and David?" And *someone*
said, "Behold, they are at Naioth in
Ramah."
23 And he [1]proceeded there to Naioth
in Ramah; and [a]the Spirit of God came
upon him also, so that he went along
prophesying continually until he came to
Naioth in Ramah.
24 And he also stripped off his
clothes, and he too prophesied before
Samuel and [1]lay down [2a]naked all that
day and all that night. Therefore they
say, "[b]Is Saul also among the prophets?"

David and Jonathan Covenant

20 THEN David fled from Naioth in
Ramah, and came and [a]said [1]to
Jonathan, "What have I done? What is
my iniquity? And what is my sin before
your father, that he is seeking my life?"
2 And he said to him, "Far from it,
you shall not die. Behold, my father does
nothing either great or small [1]without
disclosing it to me. So why should my
father hide this thing from me? It is not
so!"
3 Yet David [a]vowed again, [1]saying,
"Your father knows well that I have
found favor in your sight, and he has
said, 'Do not let Jonathan know this, lest
he be grieved.' But truly [b]as the LORD
lives and as your soul lives, there is
[2]hardly a step between me and death."
4 Then Jonathan said to David,
"Whatever [1]you say, I will do for you."
5 So David said to Jonathan, "Behold, tomorrow is [a]the new moon, and I
ought [b]to sit down to eat with the king.
But let me go, [c]that I may hide myself in
the field until the third evening.
6 "If your father misses me at all, then
say, 'David earnestly asked *leave* of me
to run to [a]Bethlehem his city, because it
is [b]the yearly sacrifice there for the
whole family.'
7 "If he [1]says, 'It is good,' your servant *shall be* safe; but if he is very angry,
[a]know that he has decided on evil.
8 "Therefore deal kindly with your
servant, for [a]you have brought your
servant into a covenant of the LORD with
you. But [b]if there is iniquity in me, put
me to death yourself; for why then
should you bring me to your father?"
9 And Jonathan said, "Far be it from
you! For if I should indeed learn that
evil has been decided by my father to
come upon you, then would I not tell
you about it?"
10 Then David said to Jonathan,
"Who will tell me [1]if your father answers
you harshly?"
11 And Jonathan said to David,
"Come, and let us go out into the field."
So both of them went out to the field.
12 Then Jonathan said to David, "The
LORD, the God of Israel, *be witness*!
When I have sounded out my father
about this time tomorrow, *or* the third
day, behold, if there is good *feeling*
toward David, shall I not then send to
you and [1]make it known to you?
13 "If it please my father *to do* you
harm, [a]may the LORD do so to Jonathan
and more also, if I do not [1]make it
known to you and send you away, that
you may go in safety. And [b]may the

7 [a]1 Sam. 16:21; 18:2, 10, 13
8 [1]Lit., *smote*
9 [a]1 Sam. 16:14; 18:10, 11 [b]1 Sam. 18:10 [c]1 Sam. 16:16
10 [1]Lit., *strike David and the wall* [2]Lit., *struck* [a]1 Sam. 18:11; 20:33; Prov. 1:16
11 [a]Judg. 16:2; Ps. 59:title
12 [a]Josh. 2:15; Acts 9:25; 2 Cor. 11:33
13 [1]Heb., *teraphim* [a]Gen. 31:19; Judg. 18:14, 17
14 [a]Josh. 2:5
15 [1]Lit., *the*
16 [1]Heb., *teraphim*
17 [a]2 Sam. 2:22
18 [a]1 Sam. 7:17 [b]1 Sam. 19:22, 23
20 [a]1 Sam. 19:11, 14; John 7:32 [b]1 Sam. 10:5, 6, 10 [c]Num. 11:25; Joel 2:28
23 [1]Lit., *went* [a]1 Sam. 10:10
24 [1]Lit., *fell* [2]I.e., without outward garments [a]2 Sam. 6:20; Is. 20:2; Mic. 1:8 [b]1 Sam. 10:10-12

1 [1]Lit., *before* [a]1 Sam. 24:9
2 [1]Lit., *and he does not uncover my ear*
3 [1]Lit., *and said* [2]Lit., *about* [a]Deut. 6:13 [b]1 Sam. 25:26; 2 Kin. 2:6
4 [1]Lit., *your soul says*
5 [a]Num. 10:10; 28:11-15; Amos 8:5 [b]1 Sam. 20:24, 27 [c]1 Sam. 19:2
6 [a]1 Sam. 17:58 [b]Deut. 12:5; 1 Sam. 9:12
7 [1]Lit., *says thus* [a]1 Sam. 25:17
8 [a]1 Sam. 18:3; 23:18 [b]2 Sam. 14:32
10 [1]Lit., *or what*
12 [1]Lit., *uncover your ear*
13 [1]Lit., *uncover your ear* [a]Ruth 1:17; 1 Sam. 3:17 [b]Josh. 1:5; 1 Sam. 17:37; 18:12; 1 Chr. 22:11, 16

LORD be with you as He has been with
my father.
14 "And if I am still alive, will you not
show me the lovingkindness of the
LORD, that I may not die?
15 "And [a]you shall not cut off your
lovingkindness from my house forever,
not even when the LORD cuts off every
one of the enemies of David from the
face of the earth."
16 So Jonathan made a *covenant* with
the house of David, *saying*, "[a]May the
LORD require *it* at the hands of David's
enemies."
17 And Jonathan made David vow
again because of his love for him, because [a]he loved him as he loved his own
life.
18 Then Jonathan said to him, "[a]To-
morrow is the new moon, and you will
be missed because your seat will be
empty.
19 "When you have stayed for three
days, you shall go down quickly and
come to the place where you hid yourself
on that eventful day, and you shall
remain by the stone Ezel.
20 "And I will shoot three arrows to the
side, as though I shot at a target.
21 "And behold, I will send the lad,
saying, 'Go, find the arrows.' If I specifically say to the lad, 'Behold, the arrows
are on this side of you, get them,' then
come; for there is safety for you and [1]no
harm, as the LORD lives.
22 "But if I [1]say to the youth, '[a]Behold,
the arrows are beyond you,' go, for the
LORD has sent you away.
23 "[a]As for the [1]agreement of which
you and I have spoken, behold, [b]the
LORD is between you and me forever."
24 So David hid in the field; and when
the new moon came, the king sat down
to eat food.
25 And the king sat on his seat as
usual, the seat by the wall; then Jonathan rose up and Abner sat down by
Saul's side, but [a]David's place was
empty.
26 Nevertheless Saul did not speak
anything that day, for he thought, "It is
an accident, [a]he is not clean, surely *he is*
not clean."
27 And it came about the next day,
the second *day* of the new moon, that
David's place was empty; so Saul said to
Jonathan his son, "Why has the son of
Jesse not come to the meal, either yesterday or today?"
28 Jonathan then answered Saul,
"[a]David earnestly asked leave of me *to*
go to Bethlehem,
29 for he said, 'Please [1]let me go, since
our family has a sacrifice in the city, and
my brother has commanded me to attend. And now, if I have found favor in
your sight, please let me get away that I
may see my brothers.' For this reason he
has not come to the king's table."

Saul Is Angry with Jonathan

30 Then Saul's anger burned against
Jonathan and he said to him, "You son
of a perverse, rebellious woman! Do I
not know that you are choosing the son
of Jesse to your own shame and to the
shame of your mother's nakedness?
31 "For [1]as long as the son of Jesse
lives on the earth, neither you nor your
kingdom will be established. Therefore
now, send and bring him to me, for [a]he
[2]must surely die."
32 But Jonathan answered Saul his
father and said to him, "[a]Why should he
be put to death? What has he done?"
33 Then [a]Saul hurled his spear at him
to strike him down; [b]so Jonathan knew
that his father had decided to put David
to death.
34 Then Jonathan arose from the
table in fierce anger, and did not eat
food on the second day of the new
moon, for he was grieved over David
because his father had dishonored him.
35 Now it came about in the morning
that Jonathan went out into the field for
the appointment with David, and a little
lad *was* with him.
36 And he said to his lad, "[a]Run, find
now the arrows which I am about to
shoot." As the lad was running, he shot
[1]an arrow past him.
37 When the lad reached the place of
the arrow which Jonathan had shot,
Jonathan called after the lad, and said,
"[a]Is not the arrow beyond you?"
38 And Jonathan called after the lad,
"Hurry, be quick, do not stay!" And
Jonathan's lad picked up the arrow and
came to his master.
39 But the lad was not aware of anything; only Jonathan and David knew
about the matter.
40 Then Jonathan gave his weapons to
his lad and said to him, "Go, bring *them*
to the city."
41 When the lad was gone, David rose
from the south side and fell on his face
to the ground, and [a]bowed three times.
And they kissed each other and wept
together, but [b]David more.
42 And Jonathan said to David, "[a]Go
in safety, inasmuch as we have sworn to
each other in the name of the LORD,
saying, '[b]The LORD will be between me
and you, and between my [1]descendants
and your [1]descendants forever.' " [2]Then
he rose and departed, while Jonathan
went into the city.

David Takes Consecrated Bread

21 THEN David came to [a]Nob to
Ahimelech the priest; and
Ahimelech [b]came trembling to meet
David, and said to him, "Why are you
alone and no one with you?"
2 And David said to Ahimelech the
priest, "The king has commissioned me
with a matter, and has said to me, '[a]Let
no one know anything about the matter
on which I am sending you and with
which I have commissioned you; and I
have directed the young men to a certain
place.'

15 [a]2 Sam. 9:1, 3
16 [a]Deut. 23:21; 1 Sam. 25:22
17 [a]1 Sam. 18:1
18 [a]1 Sam. 20:5, 25
21 [1]Lit., *there is nothing*
22 [1]Lit., *say thus* [a]1 Sam. 20:37
23 [1]Lit., *word* [a]1 Sam. 20:14, 15 [b]Gen. 31:49, 53; 1 Sam. 20:42
25 [a]1 Sam. 20:18
26 [a]Lev. 7:20, 21; 15:5; 1 Sam. 16:5
28 [a]1 Sam. 20:6
29 [1]Lit., *send me away*
31 [1]Lit., *all the days which* [2]Lit., *is a son of death* [a]2 Sam. 12:5
32 [a]Gen. 31:36; 1 Sam. 19:5; Prov. 31:9; Matt. 27:23
33 [a]1 Sam. 18:11; 19:10 [b]1 Sam. 20:7
36 [1]Lit., *the* [a]1 Sam. 20:20, 21
37 [a]1 Sam. 20:22
41 [a]Gen. 42:6 [b]1 Sam. 18:3
42 [1]Lit., *seed* [2]Ch. 21:1 in Heb. [a]1 Sam. 20:22 [b]1 Sam. 20:15, 16,
1 [a]1 Sam. 22:19; Neh. 11:32; Is. 10:32 [b]1 Sam. 16:4
2 [a]Ps. 141:3

3"Now therefore, what [1]do you have
on hand? Give [2]me five loaves of bread,
or whatever can be found."
4 And the priest answered David and
said, "There is no ordinary bread [1]on
hand, but there is [a]consecrated bread; if
only the young men have [b]kept themselves from women."
5 And David answered the priest and
said to him, "[a]Surely women have been
kept from us as previously when I set out
and the [b]vessels of the young men were
holy, though it was an ordinary journey;
how much more then today will [1]their
vessels *be holy*?"
6 So [a]the priest gave him consecrated
bread; for there was no bread there but
the [b]bread of the Presence which was
removed from before the LORD, in order
to put hot bread *in its place* when it was
taken away.
7 Now one of the servants of Saul
was there that day, detained before the
LORD; and his name was [a]Doeg the
Edomite, the [b]chief of Saul's shepherds.
8 And David said to Ahimelech,
"Now is there not a spear or a sword [1]on
hand? For I brought neither my sword
nor my weapons [2]with me, because the
king's matter was urgent."
9 Then the priest said, "[a]The sword
of Goliath the Philistine, whom you
[1]killed [b]in the valley of Elah, behold, it is
wrapped in a cloth behind the ephod; if
you would take it for yourself, take *it*.
For there is no other except it here."
And David said, "There is none like it;
give it to me."
10 Then David arose and fled that day
from Saul, and went to [a]Achish king of
Gath.
11 But the [a]servants of Achish said to
him, "Is this not David the king of the
land? [b]Did they not sing of this one as
they danced, saying,

'Saul has slain his thousands,
And David his ten thousands'?"

12 And David [a]took these words [1]to
heart, and greatly feared Achish king of
Gath.
13 So he [a]disguised his sanity before
them, and acted insanely in their hands,
and scribbled on the doors of the gate,
and let his saliva run down into his
beard.
14 Then Achish said to his servants,
"Behold, you see the man behaving as a
madman. Why do you bring him to me?
15"Do I lack madmen, that you have
brought this one to act the madman in
my presence? Shall this one come into
my house?"

The Priests Slain at Nob

22 SO David departed from there
and [a]escaped to [b]the cave of
Adullam; and when his brothers and all
his father's household heard *of it*, they
went down there to him.
2 And everyone who was in distress,
and everyone who [1]was in debt, and
everyone who was [2]discontented, gathered to him; and he became captain over
them. Now there were [a]about four hundred men with him.
3 And David went from there to
Mizpah of Moab; and he said to the king
of Moab, "Please let my father and my
mother come *and stay* with you until I
know what God will do for me."
4 Then he left them with the king of
Moab; and they stayed with him all the
time that David was in the stronghold.
5 And [a]the prophet Gad said to
David, "Do not stay in the stronghold;
depart, and go into the land of Judah."
So David departed and went into the
forest of Hereth.
6 Then Saul heard that David and
the men who were with him had been
discovered. Now [a]Saul was sitting in
Gibeah, under the tamarisk tree on the
height with his spear in his hand, and all
his servants were standing around him.
7 And Saul said to his servants who
stood around him, "Hear now, O Benjamites! Will the son of Jesse also give to
all of you fields and vineyards? [a]Will he
make you all commanders of thousands
and commanders of hundreds?
8"For all of you have conspired
against me so that there is no one who
[1]discloses to me [a]when my son makes *a
covenant* with the son of Jesse, and there
is none of you [b]who is sorry for me or
[1]discloses to me that my son has stirred
up my servant against me to lie in
ambush, as *it is* this day."
9 Then [a]Doeg the Edomite, who was
[1]standing by the servants of Saul, answered and said, "[b]I saw the son of Jesse
coming to Nob, to [c]Ahimelech the son of
Ahitub.
10"And [a]he inquired of the LORD for
him, [b]gave him provisions, and [c]gave
him the sword of Goliath the Philistine."
11 Then the king sent someone to
summon Ahimelech the priest, the son of
Ahitub, and all his father's household,
the priests who were in Nob; and all of
them came to the king.
12 And Saul said, "Listen now, son of
Ahitub." And he [1]answered, "Here I am,
my lord."
13 Saul then said to him, "Why have
you and the son of Jesse conspired
against me, in that you have given him
bread and a sword and have inquired of
God for him, that he should rise up
against me [a]by lying in ambush as *it is*
this day?"
14 [a]Then Ahimelech answered the
king and said, "And who among all your
servants is as faithful as David, even the
king's son-in-law, who [1]is captain over
your guard, and is honored in your
house?
15"Did I *just* begin [a]to inquire of God
for him today? Far be it from me! [b]Do
not let the king impute anything to his
servant *or* to any of the household of my
father, for your servant knows nothing
[1]at all of this whole affair."
16 But the king said, "You shall surely
die, Ahimelech, you and all your father's
household!"

---

3 [1]Lit., *is under your hand?* [2]Lit., *in my hand*

4 [1]Lit., *under my hand* [a]Ex. 25:30; Lev. 24:5-9; Matt. 12:4 [b]Ex. 19:15

5 [1]Lit., *it* be holy *in the vessel* [a]Ex. 19:14, 15 [b]1 Thess. 4:4

6 [a]Matt. 12:3, 4; Luke 6:3, 4 [b]Lev. 24:5-9

7 [a]1 Sam. 14:47; 22:9; Ps. 52: title [b]1 Chr. 27:29, 31

8 [1]Lit., *under your hand* [2]Lit., *in my hand*

9 [1]Lit., *smote* [a]1 Sam. 17:51, 54 [b]1 Sam. 17:2

10 [a]Ps. 34:title

11 [a]Ps. 56:title [b]1 Sam. 18:7; 29:5

12 [1]Lit., *in his* [a]Luke 2:19

13 [a]Ps. 34:title

1 [a]Ps. 57:title [b]Josh. 12:15; 15:35; 2 Sam. 23:13; Ps. 142:title

2 [1]Lit., *had a creditor* [2]Lit., *bitter of soul* [a]1 Sam. 23:13; 25:13

5 [a]2 Sam. 24:11; 1 Chr. 21:9; 29:29; 2 Chr. 29:25

6 [a]Judg. 4:5; 1 Sam. 14:2

7 [a]1 Sam. 8:12; 1 Chr. 12:16-18

8 [1]Lit., *uncovers my ear* [a]1 Sam. 18:3; 20:16 [b]1 Sam. 23:21

9 [1]Or, *set over* [a]Ps. 52:title [b]1 Sam. 21:1 [c]1 Sam. 14:3; 21:1

10 [a]Num. 27:21; 1 Sam. 10:22 [b]1 Sam. 21:6 [c]1 Sam. 21:9

12 [1]Lit., *said*

13 [a]1 Sam. 22:8

14 [1]So with Gr.; Heb., *turns aside to* [a]1 Sam. 19:4, 5; 20:32

15 [1]Lit., *small or great* [a]2 Sam. 5:19, 23 [b]2 Sam. 19:18, 19

17 And [a]the king said to the [1]guards
who were attending him, "Turn around
and put the priests of the LORD to death,
because their hand also is with David
and because they knew that he was
fleeing and did not [2]reveal it to me." But
the [b]servants of the king were not willing
to put forth their hands to [3]attack the
priests of the LORD.
18 Then the king said to Doeg, "You
turn around and [1]attack the priests."
And Doeg the Edomite turned around
and [2]attacked the priests, and [a]he killed
that day eighty-five men [b]who wore the
linen ephod.
19 And [a]he struck Nob the city of the
priests with the edge of the sword, both
men and women, children and infants;
also oxen, donkeys, and sheep, *he struck*
with the edge of the sword.
20 But [a]one son of Ahimelech the son
of Ahitub, named Abiathar, [b]escaped
and fled after David.
21 And Abiathar told David that Saul
had killed the priests of the LORD.
22 Then David said to Abiathar, "I
knew on that day, when [a]Doeg the
Edomite was there, that he would surely
tell Saul. I have brought about *the death*
of every person in your father's household.
23 "Stay with me, do not be afraid, for
[a]he who seeks my life seeks your life; for
you are [1]safe with me."

David Delivers Keilah

23 THEN they told David, saying,
"Behold, the Philistines are fighting against [a]Keilah, and are plundering
the threshing floors."
2 So David [a]inquired of the LORD,
saying, "Shall I go and [1]attack these
Philistines?" And the LORD said to
David, "Go and [1]attack the Philistines,
and deliver Keilah."
3 But David's men said to him, "Behold, we are afraid here in Judah. How
much more then if we go to Keilah
against the ranks of the Philistines?"
4 Then David inquired of the LORD
once more. And the LORD answered him
and said, "Arise, go down to Keilah, for
[a]I will give the Philistines into your
hand."
5 So David and his men went to
Keilah and fought with the Philistines;
and he led away their livestock and
struck them with a great slaughter. Thus
David delivered the inhabitants of Keilah.
6 Now it came about, when Abiathar
the son of Ahimelech [a]fled to David at
Keilah, *that* he came down *with* an
ephod in his hand.
7 When it was told Saul that David
had come to Keilah, Saul said, "God has
[1]delivered him into my hand, for he shut
himself in by entering a city with double
gates and bars."
8 So Saul summoned all the people
for war, to go down to Keilah to besiege
David and his men.
9 Now David knew that Saul was
plotting evil against him; so he said to
[a]Abiathar the priest, "[b]Bring the ephod
here."
10 Then David said, "O LORD God of
Israel, Thy servant has heard for certain
that Saul is seeking to come to Keilah to
destroy the city on my account.
11 "Will the men of Keilah surrender
me into his hand? Will Saul come down
just as Thy servant has heard? O LORD
God of Israel, I pray, tell Thy servant."
And the LORD said, "He will come
down."
12 Then David said, "Will the men of
Keilah surrender me and my men into
the hand of Saul?" And the LORD said,
"[a]They will surrender you."
13 Then David and his men, [a]about
six hundred, arose and departed from
Keilah, and they went [b]wherever they
could go. When it was told Saul that
David had escaped from Keilah, he
[1]gave up the pursuit.
14 And David stayed in the wilderness
in the strongholds, and remained in the
hill country in the wilderness of [a]Ziph.
And Saul sought him every day, but
[b]God did not deliver him into his hand.

Saul Pursues David

15 Now David [1]became aware that
Saul had come out to seek his life while
David was in the wilderness of Ziph at
Horesh.
16 And Jonathan, Saul's son, arose
and went to David at Horesh, and [1a]en-
couraged him in God.
17 Thus he said to him, "[a]Do not be
afraid, because the hand of Saul my
father shall not find you, and you will be
king over Israel and I will be next to
you; and [b]Saul my father knows that
also."
18 So [a]the two of them made a covenant before the LORD; and David
stayed at Horesh while Jonathan went to
his house.
19 Then [a]Ziphites came up to Saul at
Gibeah, saying, "Is David not hiding
with us in the strongholds at Horesh, on
[b]the hill of Hachilah, which is on the
[1]south of [2]Jeshimon?
20 "Now then, O king, come down
according to all the desire of your soul to
[1]do so; and [a]our part *shall be* to surrender him into the king's hand."
21 And Saul said, "May you be
blessed of the LORD; [a]for you have had
compassion on me.
22 "Go now, make more sure, and
investigate and see his place where his
[1]haunt is, *and* who has seen him there;
for I am told that he is very cunning.
23 "So look, and learn about all the
hiding places where he hides himself,
and return to me with certainty, and I
will go with you; and it shall come about
if he is in the land that I will search him
out among all the thousands of Judah."

17 [1]Lit., *runners* [2]Lit., *uncover my ear* [3]Lit., *fall upon* [a]2 Kin. 10:25 [b]Ex. 1:17
18 [1]Lit., *smite* [2]Lit., *smote* [a]1 Sam. 2:31 [b]1 Sam. 2:18
19 [a]1 Sam. 15:3
20 [a]1 Sam. 23:6, 9; 30:7; 1 Kin. 2:26, 27 [b]1 Sam. 23:6
22 [a]1 Sam. 21:7
23 [1]Lit., *a charge* [a]1 Kin. 2:26
1 [a]Josh. 15:44; Neh. 3:17, 18
2 [1]Lit., *smite* [a]1 Sam. 23:4, 6, 9-12; 2 Sam. 5:19, 23
4 [a]Josh. 8:7; Judg. 7:7
6 [a]1 Sam. 22:20
7 [1]Lit., *alienated*
9 [a]1 Sam. 22:20 [b]1 Sam. 23:6; 30:7
12 [a]Judg. 15:10-13; 1 Sam. 23:20
13 [1]Lit., *ceased going out* [a]1 Sam. 22:2; 25:13 [b]2 Sam. 15:20
14 [a]Josh. 15:55; 2 Chr. 11:8 [b]Ps. 32:7
15 [1]Lit., *saw*
16 [1]Lit., *strengthened his hand* [a]1 Sam. 30:6; Neh. 2:18
17 [a]Ps. 27:1, 3; 118:6; Is. 54:17; Heb. 13:6 [b]1 Sam. 20:31; 24:20
18 [a]1 Sam. 18:3; 20:12-17, 42; 2 Sam. 9:1; 21:7
19 [1]Lit., *right side* [2]Or, *the desert* [a]1 Sam. 26:1; Ps. 54:title [b]1 Sam. 26:3
20 [1]Lit., *come down* [a]1 Sam. 23:12
21 [a]1 Sam. 22:8
22 [1]Lit., *foot*

24 Then they arose and went to Ziph before Saul. Now David and his men were in the wilderness of [a]Maon, in the Arabah to the [1]south of [2]Jeshimon.

25 When Saul and his men went to seek *him,* they told David, and he came down to the rock and stayed in the wilderness of Maon. And when Saul heard *it,* he pursued David in the wilderness of Maon.

26 And Saul went on one side of the mountain, and David and his men on the other side of the mountain; and David was hurrying to get away from Saul, for Saul and his men [a]were surrounding David and his men to seize them.

27 But a messenger came to Saul, saying, "Hurry and come, for the Philistines have made a raid on the land."

28 So Saul returned from pursuing David, and went to meet the Philistines; therefore they called that place [1]the Rock of Escape.

29 [1]And David went up from there and stayed in the strongholds of [a]Engedi.

David Spares Saul's Life

24 NOW it came about [a]when Saul returned from pursuing the Philistines, [b]he was told, saying, "Behold, David is in the wilderness of Engedi."

2 Then [a]Saul took three thousand chosen men from all Israel, and went to seek David and his men in front of the Rocks of the Wild Goats.

3 And he came to the sheepfolds on the way, where there *was* a cave; and Saul [a]went in to [1]relieve himself. Now [b]David and his men were sitting in the inner recesses of the cave.

4 And the men of David said to him, "Behold, [a]*this is* the day of which the LORD said to you, 'Behold; [b]I am about to give your enemy into your hand, and you shall do to him as it seems good [1]to you.' " Then David arose and cut off the edge of Saul's robe secretly.

5 And it came about afterward that [a]David's [1]conscience bothered him because he had cut off the edge of Saul's *robe.*

6 So he said to his men, "[a]Far be it from me because of the LORD that I should do this thing to my lord, the LORD's anointed, to stretch out my hand against him, since he is the LORD's anointed."

7 And David [1]persuaded his men with *these* words and did not allow them to rise up against Saul. And Saul arose, [2]left the cave, and went on *his* way.

8 Now afterward David arose and went out of the cave and called after Saul, saying, "My lord the king!" And when Saul looked behind him, [a]David bowed with his face to the ground and prostrated himself.

9 And David said to Saul, "Why do you listen to the words of men, saying, 'Behold, David seeks [1]to harm you'?

10 "[a]Behold, this day your eyes have seen that the LORD had given you today into my hand in the cave, and [b]some said to kill you, but *my eye* had pity on you; and I said, 'I will not stretch out my hand against my lord, for he is the LORD's anointed.'

11 "Now, [a]my father, see! Indeed, see the edge of your robe in my hand! For in that I cut off the edge of your robe and did not kill you, know and perceive that there is no evil or [1]rebellion in my hands, and I have not sinned against you, though you [b]are lying in wait for my life to take it.

12 "[a]May the LORD judge between [1]you and me, and may the LORD avenge me on you; but my hand shall not be against you.

13 "As the proverb of the ancients says, '[a]Out of the wicked comes forth wickedness'; but my hand shall not be against you.

14 "After whom has the king of Israel come out? Whom are you pursuing? [a]A dead dog, [b]a single flea?

15 "[a]The LORD therefore be judge and decide between [1]you and me; and may He see and [b]plead my cause, and [2]deliver me from your hand."

16 Now it came about when David had finished speaking these words to Saul, that Saul said, "[a]Is this your voice, my son David?" Then Saul lifted up his voice and wept.

17 [a]And he said to David, "You are more righteous than I; for [b]you have dealt well with me, while I have dealt wickedly with you.

18 "And you have declared today that you have done good to me, that [a]the LORD delivered me into your hand and *yet* you did not kill me.

19 "For if a man [a]finds his enemy, will he let him go away [1]safely? May the LORD therefore reward you with good in return for what you have done to me this day.

20 "And now, behold, [a]I know that you shall surely be king, and that [b]the kingdom of Israel shall be established in your hand.

21 "So now [a]swear to me by the LORD that you will not cut off my [1]descendants after me, and that you will not destroy my name from my father's household."

22 And David swore to Saul. And Saul went to his home, but David and his men went up to [a]the stronghold.

Samuel's Death

25 [a]THEN Samuel died; and all Israel gathered together and [b]mourned for him, and [c]buried him at his house in Ramah. And David arose and went down to the [d]wilderness of Paran.

---

24 [1]Lit., *right side* [2]Or, *the desert* [a]Josh. 15:55; 1 Sam. 25:2
26 [a]Ps. 17:9
28 [1]Heb., *Sela-hammahlekoth*
29 [1]Ch. 24:1 in Heb. [a]Josh. 15:62; 2 Chr. 20:2
1 [a]1 Sam. 23:28, 29 [b]1 Sam. 23:19
2 [a]1 Sam. 26:2
3 [1]Lit., *cover his feet* [a]Judg. 3:24 [b]Ps. 57:title; 142:title
4 [1]Lit., *in your sight* [a]1 Sam. 23:17; 25:28-30 [b]1 Sam. 26:8, 11
5 [1]Lit., *heart struck* [a]2 Sam. 24:10
6 [a]1 Sam. 26:11
7 [1]Lit., *tore apart* [2]Lit., *from*
8 [a]1 Sam. 25:23, 24; 1 Kin. 1:31
9 [1]Lit., *your hurt*
10 [a]Ps. 7:3, 4 [b]1 Sam. 24:4
11 [1]Lit., *transgression* [a]2 Kin. 5:13 [b]1 Sam. 23:14, 23; 26:20
12 [1]Lit., *me and you* [a]Gen. 16:5; 31:53; Judg. 11:27; 1 Sam. 26:10, 23
13 [a]Matt. 7:16-20
14 [a]2 Sam. 9:8 [b]1 Sam. 26:20
15 [1]Lit., *me and you* [2]Lit., *vindicate* [a]1 Sam. 24:12 [b]Ps. 35:1; 43:1; 119:154; Mic. 7:9
16 [a]1 Sam. 26:17
17 [a]1 Sam. 26:21 [b]Matt. 5:44
18 [a]1 Sam. 26:23
19 [1]Lit., *on a good road* [a]1 Sam. 23:17
20 [a]1 Sam. 23:17 [b]1 Sam. 13:14
21 [1]Lit., *seed* [a]Gen. 21:23; 1 Sam. 20:14-17; 2 Sam. 21:6-8
22 [a]1 Sam. 23:29
1 [a]1 Sam. 28:3 [b]Num. 20:29; Deut. 34:8 [c]2 Kin. 21:18; 2 Chr. 33:20 [d]Gen. 21:21; Num. 10:12; 13:3

Nabal and Abigail

2 Now *there was* a man in [a]Maon
whose business was in [b]Carmel; and the
man was very [1]rich, and he had three
thousand sheep and a thousand goats.
And it came about while [c]he was shearing his sheep in Carmel
3 (now the man's name was Nabal,
and his [a]wife's name was Abigail. And
the woman was [1]intelligent and beautiful
in appearance, but the man was harsh
and evil in *his* dealings, and he was [b]a
Calebite),
4 that David heard in the wilderness
that Nabal was shearing his sheep.
5 So David sent ten young men, and
David said to the young men, "Go up to
Carmel, [1]visit Nabal and greet him in
my name;
6 and thus you shall say, '[1]Have a
long life, [a]peace be to you, and peace be
to your house, and peace be to all that
you have.
7 'And now I have heard [a]that you
have shearers; now your shepherds have
been with us and we have not insulted
them, [b]nor have they missed anything all
the days they were in Carmel.
8 'Ask your young men and they will
tell you. Therefore let *my* young men
find favor in your eyes, for we have come
on [a]a [1]festive day. Please give whatever
you find at hand to your servants and to
your son David.'"
9 When David's young men came,
they spoke to Nabal according to all
these words in David's name; then they
waited.
10 But Nabal answered David's servants, and said, "[a]Who is David? And
who is the son of Jesse? There are many
servants today who are each breaking
away from his master.
11 "Shall I then [a]take my bread and my
water and my meat that I have slaughtered for my shearers, and give it to men
[1]whose origin I do not know?"
12 So David's young men retraced
their way and went back; and they came
and told him according to all these
words.
13 And David said to his men, "Each
of you gird on his sword." So each man
girded on his sword. And David also
girded on his sword, and about [a]four
hundred men went up behind David
while two hundred [b]stayed with the
baggage.
14 But one of the young men told
Abigail, Nabal's wife, saying, "Behold,
David sent messengers from the wilderness to [1a]greet our master, and he
scorned them.
15 "Yet the men were very good to us,
and we were not [a]insulted, nor did we
miss anything [1]as long as we went about
with them, while we were in the fields.
16 "[a]They were a wall to us both by
night and by day, all the time we were
with them tending the sheep.
17 "Now therefore, know and [1]consider
what you should do, for evil is plotted
against our master and against all his
household; and he is such a [2]worthless
man that no one can speak to him."

Abigail Intercedes

18 Then Abigail hurried and [a]took
two hundred *loaves* of bread and two
jugs of wine and five sheep already
prepared and five measures of roasted
grain and a hundred clusters of raisins
and two hundred cakes of figs, and
loaded *them* on donkeys.
19 And she said to her young men,
"[a]Go on before me; behold, I am coming
after you." But she did not tell her
husband Nabal.
20 And it came about as she was
riding on her donkey and coming down
by the hidden part of the mountain, that
behold, David and his men were coming
down toward her; so she met them.
21 Now David had said, "Surely in
vain I have guarded all that this *man* has
in the wilderness, so that nothing was
missed of all that belonged to him; and
he has [a]returned me evil for good.
22 "[a]May God do so to the enemies of
David, and more also, [b]if by morning I
leave *as much as* one [1]male of any who
belong to him."
23 When Abigail saw David, she hurried and dismounted from her donkey,
and fell on her face before David, [a]and
bowed herself to the ground.
24 And she fell at his feet and said,
"On me [1]alone, my lord, be the blame.
And please let your maidservant speak
[2]to you, and listen to the words of your
maidservant.
25 "Please do not let my lord [1]pay
attention to this [2]worthless man, Nabal,
for as his name is, so is he. [3]Nabal is his
name and folly is with him; but I your
maidservant did not see the young men
of my lord whom you sent.
26 "Now therefore, my lord, as the
LORD lives, and as your soul lives, since
the LORD has restrained you from [1]shed-
ding blood, and [a]from [2]avenging yourself by your own hand, now then [b]let
your enemies, and those who seek evil
against my lord, be as Nabal.
27 "And now let [a]this [1]gift which your
maidservant has brought to my lord be
given to the young men who [2]accom-
pany my lord.
28 "Please forgive [a]the transgression of
your maidservant; for [b]the LORD will
certainly make for my lord an enduring
house, because my lord is [c]fighting the
battles of the LORD, and [d]evil shall not
be found in you all your days.
29 "And should anyone rise up to
pursue you and to seek your [1]life, then
the [1]life of my lord shall be bound in the
bundle of the living with the LORD your
God; but the [1]lives of your enemies [a]He
will sling out [2]as from the hollow of a
sling.
30 "And it shall come about when the
LORD shall do for my lord according to

2 [1]Lit., *great* [a]1 Sam. 23:24 [b]Josh. 15:55 [c]Gen. 38:13; 2 Sam. 13:23
3 [1]Lit., *of good understanding* [a]Prov. 31:10 [b]Josh. 15:13; 1 Sam. 30:14
5 [1]Lit., *go into*
6 [1]Lit., *To life* [a]1 Chr. 12:18; Ps. 122:7; Luke 10:5
7 [a]2 Sam. 13:23, 24 [b]1 Sam. 25:15, 21
8 [1]Lit., *good* [a]Neh. 8:10-12; Esth. 9:19, 22
10 [a]Judg. 9:28
11 [1]Lit., *from where they are* [a]Judg. 8:6, 15
13 [a]1 Sam. 23:13 [b]1 Sam. 30:24
14 [1]Lit., *bless* [a]1 Sam. 13:10; 15:13
15 [1]Lit., *all the days* [a]1 Sam. 25:7, 21
16 [a]Ex. 14:22; Job 1:10
17 [1]Lit., *see* [2]Lit., *son of Belial*
18 [a]2 Sam. 16:1; 1 Chr. 12:40
19 [a]Gen. 32:16, 20
21 [a]Ps. 109:5; Prov. 17:13
22 [1]Lit., *who urinates against the wall* [a]1 Sam. 3:17; 20:13 [b]1 Kin. 14:10
23 [a]1 Sam. 20:41
24 [1]Lit., *even me* [2]Lit., *in your ears*
25 [1]Lit., *set his heart to* [2]Lit., *man of Belial* [3]I.e., Fool
26 [1]Lit., *coming in with blood* [2]Lit., *saving* [a]Heb. 10:30 [b]2 Sam. 18:32
27 [1]Lit., *blessing* [2]Lit., *walk at the feet of* [a]Gen. 33:11; 1 Sam. 30:26
28 [a]1 Sam. 25:24 [b]1 Sam. 22:14; 2 Sam. 7:11, 16 [c]1 Sam. 18:17 [d]1 Sam. 24:11; Ps. 7:3
29 [1]Lit., *soul* [2]Lit., *in the midst* [a]Jer. 10:18

all the good that He has spoken concerning you, and [a]shall appoint you ruler over Israel,

31 that this will not [1]cause grief or a troubled heart to my lord, both by having shed blood without cause and by my lord having [2]avenged himself. [a]When the LORD shall deal well with my lord, then remember your maidservant."

32 Then David said to Abigail, "[a]Blessed be the LORD God of Israel, who sent you this day to meet me,

33 and blessed be your discernment, and blessed be you, [a]who have kept me this day from [1]bloodshed, and from [2]avenging myself by my own hand.

34 "Nevertheless, as the LORD God of Israel lives, [a]who has restrained me from harming you, unless you had come quickly to meet me, surely there would not have been left to Nabal until the morning light *as much as* one [1]male."

35 So David received from her hand what she had brought him, and he said to her, "[a]Go up to your house in peace. See, I have listened to [1]you and [2b]granted your request."

36 Then Abigail came to Nabal, and behold, he was holding [a]a feast in his house, like the feast of a king. And Nabal's heart was merry within him, [b]for he was very drunk; so [c]she did not tell him anything [1]at all until the morning light.

37 But it came about in the morning, when the wine had gone out of Nabal, that his wife told him these things, and his heart died within him so that he became *as* a stone.

38 And about ten days later, it happened that [a]the LORD struck Nabal, and he died.

David Marries Abigail

39 When David heard that Nabal was dead, he said, "Blessed be the LORD, who has [a]pleaded the cause of my reproach from the hand of Nabal, and [b]has kept back His servant from evil. The LORD has also returned the evildoing of Nabal on his own head." Then David sent [1c]a proposal to Abigail, to take her as his wife.

40 When the servants of David came to Abigail at Carmel, they spoke to her, saying, "David has sent us to you, to take you as his wife."

41 And she arose [a]and bowed with her face to the ground and said, "Behold, your maidservant is a maid [b]to wash the feet of my lord's servants."

42 Then [a]Abigail quickly arose, and rode on a donkey, with her five maidens who [1]attended her; and she followed the messengers of David, and became his wife.

43 David had also taken Ahinoam of [a]Jezreel, and [b]they both became his wives.

44 Now Saul had given [a]Michal his daughter, David's wife, to Palti the son of Laish, who was from [b]Gallim.

David Again Spares Saul

26 THEN the Ziphites came to Saul at Gibeah, saying, "[a]Is not David hiding on the hill of Hachilah, *which is* before [1]Jeshimon?"

2 So Saul arose and went down to the wilderness of Ziph, having with him [a]three thousand chosen men of Israel, to search for David in the wilderness of Ziph.

3 And Saul camped in the hill of Hachilah, which is before [1]Jeshimon, [a]beside the road, and David was staying in the wilderness. When [b]he saw that Saul came after him into the wilderness,

4 David sent out spies, and he knew that Saul was definitely coming.

5 David then arose and came to the place where Saul had camped. And David saw the place where Saul lay, and [a]Abner the son of Ner, the commander of his army; and Saul was lying in the circle of the camp, and the people were camped around him.

6 Then David answered and said to Ahimelech [a]the Hittite and to [b]Abishai the son of Zeruiah, Joab's brother, saying, "Who [c]will go down with me to Saul in the camp?" And Abishai said, "I will go down with you."

7 So David and Abishai came to the people by night, and behold, Saul lay sleeping inside the circle of the camp, with his spear stuck in the ground at his head; and Abner and the people were lying around him.

8 Then Abishai said to David, "Today God has delivered your enemy into your hand; now therefore, please let me strike him with the spear [1]to the ground with one stroke, and I will not [2]strike him the second time."

9 But David said to Abishai, "Do not destroy him, for [a]who can stretch out his hand against the LORD's anointed and be without guilt?"

10 David also said, "As the LORD lives, [a]surely the LORD will strike him, or [b]his day will come that he dies, or [c]he will go down into battle and perish.

11 "[a]The LORD forbid that I should stretch out my hand against the LORD's anointed; but now please take the spear that is at his head and the jug of water, and let us go."

12 So David took the spear and the jug of water from *beside* Saul's head, and they went away, but no one saw or knew *it,* nor did any awake, for they were all asleep, because [a]a sound sleep from the LORD had fallen on them.

13 Then David crossed over to the other side, and stood on top of the mountain at a distance *with* a large area between them.

14 And David called to the people and to Abner the son of Ner, saying, "Will you not answer, Abner?" Then Abner answered and said, "Who are you who calls to the king?"

15 So David said to Abner, "Are you not a man? And who is like you in

30 [a]1 Sam. 13:14
31 [1]Lit., *become staggering to you or a stumbling of the heart* [2]Lit., *saved* [a]Gen. 40:14; 1 Sam. 25:30
32 [a]Ex. 18:10; 1 Kin. 1:48; Ps. 41:13; 72:18; 106:48; Luke 1:68
33 [1]Lit., *coming in with blood* [2]Lit., *saving* [a]1 Sam. 25:26
34 [1]Lit., *who urinates against the wall* [a]1 Sam. 25:26
35 [1]Lit., *your voice* [2]Lit., *lifted up your face* [a]1 Sam. 20:42; 2 Kin. 5:19 [b]Gen. 19:21
36 [1]Lit., *small or large* [a]2 Sam. 13:28 [b]Prov. 20:1; Is. 5:11; Hos. 4:11 [c]1 Sam. 25:19
38 [a]1 Sam. 26:10; 2 Sam. 6:7; Ps. 104:29
39 [1]Lit., *and spoke* [a]1 Sam. 24:15; Prov. 22:23 [b]1 Sam. 25:26, 34 [c]Song 8:8
41 [a]1 Sam. 25:23 [b]Mark 1:7
42 [1]Lit., *walked at her feet* [a]Gen. 24:61-67
43 [a]Josh. 15:56 [b]1 Sam. 27:3; 30:5
44 [a]1 Sam. 18:27; 2 Sam. 3:14 [b]Is. 10:30

1 [1]Or, *the desert* [a]1 Sam. 23:19; Ps. 54:title
2 [a]1 Sam. 13:2; 24:2
3 [1]Or, *the desert* [a]1 Sam. 24:3 [b]1 Sam. 23:15
5 [a]1 Sam. 14:50, 51; 17:55
6 [a]Gen. 23:3; 26:34; Josh. 3:10; 1 Kin. 10:29; 2 Kin. 7:6 [b]1 Chr. 2:16 [c]Judg. 7:10, 11
8 [1]Lit., *even into* [2]Lit., *repeat with respect to him*
9 [a]1 Sam. 24:6, 7; 2 Sam. 1:14, 16
10 [a]Deut. 32:35; 1 Sam. 25:26, 38; Rom. 12:19; Heb. 10:30 [b]Gen. 47:29; Deut. 31:14; Ps. 37:13 [c]1 Sam. 31:6
11 [a]1 Sam. 24:6, 12; Rom. 12:17, 19; 1 Pet. 3:9
12 [a]Gen. 2:21; 15:12; Is. 29:10

Israel? Why then have you not guarded
your lord the king? For one of the
people came to destroy the king your
lord.
16 "This thing that you have done is
not good. As the LORD lives, *all* of you
[1][a]must surely die, because you did not
guard your lord, the LORD's anointed.
And now, see where the king's spear is,
and the jug of water that was at his
head."
17 Then Saul recognized David's voice
and said, "[a]Is this your voice, my son
David?" And David said, "It is my
voice, my lord the king."
18 He also said, "[a]Why then is my
lord pursuing his servant? For what have
I done? Or what evil is in my hand?
19 "Now therefore, please let my lord
the king listen to the words of his servant. If [a]the LORD has stirred you up
against me, [b]let Him [1]accept an offering;
but [c]if it is [2]men, cursed are they before
the LORD, for [d]they have driven me out
today that I should have no attachment
with the inheritance of the LORD, saying,
'Go, serve other gods.'
20 "Now then, do not let my blood fall
to the ground away from the presence of
the LORD; for the king of Israel has
come out to search for [a]a single flea, just
as one hunts a partridge in the mountains."
21 Then Saul said, "[a]I have sinned.
Return, my son David, for I will not
harm you again because my life was
precious in your sight this day. Behold, I
have played the fool and have committed a serious error."
22 And David answered and said,
"Behold the spear of the king! Now let
one of the young men come over and
take it.
23 "And [a]the LORD will repay each
man *for* his righteousness and his faithfulness; for the LORD delivered you into
my hand today, but [b]I refused to stretch
out my hand against the LORD's
anointed.
24 "Now behold, as your life was
[a]highly valued in my sight this day, so
may my life be highly valued in the sight
of the LORD, and may He [b]deliver me
from all distress."
25 Then Saul said to David, "[a]Blessed
are you, my son David; you will both
accomplish much and surely prevail." So
[b]David went on his way, and Saul returned to his place.

David Flees to the Philistines

27 THEN David said [1]to himself,
"Now I will perish one day by
the hand of Saul. [a]There is nothing
better for me than [2]to escape into the
land of the Philistines. Saul then will
despair of searching for me anymore in
all the territory of Israel, and I will
escape from his hand."
2 So David arose and crossed over,
he and [a]the six hundred men who were
with him, to [b]Achish the son of Maoch,
king of Gath.
3 And David lived with Achish at
Gath, he and his men, [a]each with his
household, *even* David with [b]his two
wives, Ahinoam the Jezreelitess, and
Abigail the Carmelitess, Nabal's [1]widow.
4 Now it was told Saul that David
had fled to Gath, so he no longer
searched for him.
5 Then David said to Achish, "If
now I have found favor in your sight, let
them give me a place in one of the cities
in the country, that I may live there; for
why should your servant live in the royal
city with you?"
6 So Achish gave him Ziklag that
day; therefore [a]Ziklag has belonged to
the kings of Judah to this day.
7 And the number of days that David lived in the country of the Philistines
was [a]a year and four months.
8 Now David and his men went up
and raided [a]the Geshurites and the
Girzites and [b]the Amalekites; for they
were the inhabitants of the land from
ancient times, as you come to [c]Shur even
as far as the land of Egypt.
9 And David [1]attacked the land and
did not leave a man or a woman alive,
and he [a]took away the sheep, the cattle,
the donkeys, the camels, and the clothing. Then he returned and came to
Achish.
10 Now Achish said, "Where have you
[a]made a raid today?" And David said,
"Against the [1]Negev of Judah and
against the [1]Negev of [b]the Jerahmeelites
and against the [1]Negev of [c]the Kenites."
11 And David did not leave a man or
a woman alive, to bring to Gath, saying,
"Lest they should tell about us, saying,
'So has David done and so *has been* his
practice all the time he has lived in the
country of the Philistines.'"
12 So Achish believed David, saying,
"He has surely made himself odious
among his people Israel; therefore he
will become my servant forever."

Saul and the Spirit Medium

28 NOW it came about in those
days that [a]the Philistines gathered their armed camps for war, to fight
against Israel. And Achish said to David, "Know assuredly that you will go
out with me in the camp, you and your
men."
2 And David said to Achish, "Very
well, you shall know what your servant
can do." So Achish said to David, "Very
well, I will make you [1]my bodyguard
[a]for life."
3 Now [a]Samuel was dead, and all
Israel had lamented him and buried him
[b]in Ramah his own city. And Saul had
removed from the land those who [c]were
mediums and spiritists.
4 So the Philistines gathered together
and came and camped [a]in Shunem; and
Saul gathered all Israel together and
they camped in [b]Gilboa.

16 [1]Lit., *are surely sons of death* [a]1 Sam. 20:31
17 [a]1 Sam. 24:16
18 [a]1 Sam. 24:9, 11-14
19 [1]Lit., *smell* [2]Lit., *sons of men* [a]2 Sam. 16:11 [b]Gen. 8:21 [c]1 Sam. 24:9 [d]Josh. 22:25-27
20 [a]1 Sam. 24:14
21 [a]Ex. 9:27; 1 Sam. 15:24, 30; 24:17
23 [a]1 Sam. 24:19; Ps. 7:8; 18:20; 62:12 [b]1 Sam. 24:12
24 [a]1 Sam. 18:30 [b]Ps. 54:7
25 [a]1 Sam. 24:19 [b]1 Sam. 24:22

1 [1]Lit., *in his heart* [2]Lit., *that I should surely escape* [a]1 Sam. 26:19
2 [a]1 Sam. 25:13 [b]1 Sam. 21:10; 1 Kin. 2:39
3 [1]Lit., *wife* [a]1 Sam. 30:3; 2 Sam. 2:3 [b]1 Sam. 25:42, 43
6 [a]Josh. 15:31; 19:5; Neh. 11:28
7 [a]1 Sam. 29:3
8 [a]Josh. 13:2, 13 [b]Ex. 17:8; 1 Sam. 15:7, 8 [c]Ex. 15:22
9 [1]Lit., *smote* [a]1 Sam. 15:3; Job 1:3
10 [1]I.e., South country [a]1 Sam. 23:27 [b]1 Sam. 30:29; 1 Chr. 2:9, 25 [c]Judg. 1:16; 4:11

1 [a]1 Sam. 29:1
2 [1]Lit., *keeper of my head* [a]1 Sam. 1:22, 28
3 [a]1 Sam. 25:1 [b]1 Sam. 7:17 [c]Lev. 19:31; 20:27; Deut. 18:10; 1 Sam. 15:23
4 [a]Josh. 19:18; 1 Sam. 28:4; 1 Kin. 1:3; 2 Kin. 4:8 [b]1 Sam. 31:1

5 When Saul saw the camp of the
Philistines, he was afraid and his heart
trembled greatly.
6 [a]When Saul inquired of the LORD,
[b]the LORD did not answer him, either by
[c]dreams or by [d]Urim or by prophets.
7 Then Saul said to his servants,
"Seek for me a woman who is a medium,
that I may go to her and inquire of her."
And his servants said to him, "Behold,
[a]there is a woman who is a medium at
[b]En-dor."
8 Then Saul [a]disguised himself by
putting on other clothes, and went, he
and two men with him, and they came to
the woman by night; and he said,
"[b]Conjure up for me, please, and [c]bring
up for me whom I shall [1]name to you."
9 But the woman said to him, "Behold, you know [a]what Saul has done,
how he has cut off those who are mediums and spiritists from the land. Why
are you then laying a snare for my life to
bring about my death?"
10 And Saul vowed to her by the
LORD, saying, "As the LORD lives, there
shall no punishment come upon you for
this thing."
11 Then the woman said, "Whom
shall I bring up for you?" And he said,
"Bring up Samuel for me."
12 When the woman saw Samuel, she
cried out with a loud voice; and the
woman spoke to Saul, saying, "Why
have you deceived me? For you are
Saul."
13 And the king said to her, "Do not
be afraid; but what do you see?" And
the woman said to Saul, "I see a [1]divine
being coming up out of the earth."
14 And he said to her, "What is his
form?" And she said, "An old man is
coming up, and [a]he is wrapped with a
robe." And Saul knew that it was Samuel, and [b]he bowed with his face to the
ground and did homage.
15 Then Samuel said to Saul, "Why
have you disturbed me by bringing me
up?" And Saul answered, "I am greatly
distressed; for the Philistines are waging
war against me, and [a]God has departed
from me and [b]answers me no more,
either through prophets or by dreams;
therefore I have called you, that you may
make known to me what I should do."
16 And Samuel said, "Why then do
you ask me, since the LORD has departed
from you and has become your adversary?
17 "And the LORD has done [1]accord-
ingly [a]as He spoke through me; for the
LORD has torn the kingdom out of your
hand and given it to your neighbor, to
David.
18 "As [a]you did not [1]obey the LORD
and did not execute His fierce wrath on
Amalek, so the LORD has done this thing
to you this day.
19 "Moreover the LORD will also give
over Israel along with you into the hands
of the Philistines, therefore tomorrow
[a]you and your sons will be with me.

6 [a]1 Chr. 10:13, 14 [b]1 Sam. 14:37; Prov. 1:24-31 [c]Num. 12:6; Joel 2:28 [d]Ex. 28:30; Num. 27:21

7 [a]Acts 16:16 [b]Josh. 17:11; Ps. 83:10

8 [1]Lit., *say* [a]2 Chr. 18:29; 35:22 [b]1 Chr. 10:13; Is. 8:19 [c]Deut. 18:10, 11

9 [a]1 Sam. 28:3

13 [1]Or, *god*

14 [a]1 Sam. 15:27 [b]1 Sam. 24:8

15 [a]1 Sam. 16:14; 18:12 [b]1 Sam. 28:6

17 [1]Lit., *for himself* [a]1 Sam. 15:28

18 [1]Lit., *listen to the voice of* [a]1 Sam. 15:20, 26; 1 Kin. 20:42

19 [a]1 Sam. 31:2; Job 3:17-19

20 [1]Lit., *bread*

21 [1]Lit., *listened to your voice* [2]Lit., *put* [a]Judg. 12:3; 1 Sam. 19:5; Job 13:14

23 [1]Lit., *their voices* [a]1 Kin. 21:4 [b]2 Kin. 5:13 [c]Esth. 1:6; Ezek. 23:41

24 [a]Gen. 18:7; Luke 15:23, 27, 30 [b]Gen. 18:6

1 [a]1 Sam. 28:1 [b]Josh. 12:18; 19:30; 1 Sam. 4:1; 1 Kin. 20:30 [c]1 Kin. 21:1; 2 Kin. 9:30

2 [a]1 Sam. 28:1, 2

3 [1]Lit., *fell* [a]1 Sam. 27:7 [b]1 Sam. 27:1-6; 1 Chr. 12:19, 20; Dan. 6:5

4 [1]Lit., *those* [a]1 Sam. 27:6 [b]1 Sam. 14:21

5 [a]1 Sam. 18:7; 21:11

6 [a]2 Sam. 3:25; 2 Kin. 19:27; Is. 37:28 [b]1 Sam. 27:8-12; 29:3

Indeed the LORD will give over the army
of Israel into the hands of the Philistines!"
20 Then Saul immediately fell full
length upon the ground and was very
afraid because of the words of Samuel;
also there was no strength in him, for he
had eaten no [1]food all day and all night.
21 And the woman came to Saul and
saw that he was terrified, and said to
him, "Behold, your maidservant has
[1]obeyed you, and [a]I have [2]taken my life
in my hand, and have listened to your
words which you spoke to me.
22 "So now also, please listen to the
voice of your maidservant, and let me set
a piece of bread before you that *you may*
eat and have strength when you go on
your way."
23 But he refused and said, "[a]I will
not eat." [b]However, his servants together with the woman urged him, and
he listened to [1]them. So he arose from
the ground and sat on [c]the bed.
24 And the woman had a [a]fattened
calf in the house, and she quickly slaughtered it; and she [b]took flour, kneaded it,
and baked unleavened bread from it.
25 And she brought *it* before Saul and
his servants, and they ate. Then they
arose and went away that night.

The Philistines Mistrust David

29 NOW [a]the Philistines gathered
together all their armies to
[b]Aphek, while the Israelites were camping by the spring which is in [c]Jezreel.
2 And the lords of the Philistines
were proceeding on by hundreds and by
thousands, and [a]David and his men were
proceeding on in the rear with Achish.
3 Then the commanders of the Philistines said, "What *are* these Hebrews
doing here?" And Achish said to the
commanders of the Philistines, "Is this
not David, the servant of Saul the king
of Israel, [a]who has been with me these
days, or *rather* these years, and [b]I have
found no fault in him from the day he
[1]deserted *to me* to this day?"
4 But the commanders of the Philistines were angry with him, and the
commanders of the Philistines said to
him, "Make the man go back, that he
may return [a]to his place where you have
assigned him, and do not let him go
down to battle with us, [b]lest in the battle
he become an adversary to us. For with
what could this *man* make himself acceptable to his lord? *Would it* not *be* with
the heads of [1]these men?
5 "Is this not David, [a]of whom they
sing in the dances, saying,
'Saul has slain his thousands,
And David his ten thousands'?"
6 Then Achish called David and said
to him, "*As* the LORD lives, you *have
been* upright, and [a]your going out and
your coming in with me in the army are
pleasing in my sight; [b]for I have not
found evil in you from the day of your
coming to me to this day. Nevertheless,

you are not pleasing in the sight of the lords.

7 "Now therefore return, and go in peace, that you may not displease the lords of the Philistines."

8 And David said to Achish, "[a]But what have I done? And what have you found in your servant from the day when I came before you to this day, that I may not go and fight against the enemies of my lord the king?"

9 But Achish answered and said to David, "I know that you are pleasing in my sight, [a]like an angel of God; nevertheless [b]the commanders of the Philistines have said, 'He must not go up with us to the battle.'

10 "Now then arise early in the morning [a]with the servants of your lord who have come with you, and as soon as you have arisen early in the morning and have light, depart."

11 So David arose early, he and his men, to depart in the morning, to return to the land of the Philistines. And the Philistines went up to Jezreel.

David's Victory over the Amalekites

30 THEN it happened when David and his men came to [a]Ziklag on the third day, that [b]the Amalekites had made a raid on the [1]Negev and on [c]Ziklag, and had [2]overthrown Ziklag and burned it with fire;

2 and they took captive the women *and all* who were in it, both small and great, [1a]without killing anyone, and carried *them* off and went their way.

3 And when David and his men came to the city, behold, it was burned with fire, and their wives and their sons and their daughters had been taken captive.

4 Then David and the people who were with him [a]lifted their voices and wept until there was no strength in them to weep.

5 Now [a]David's two wives had been taken captive, Ahinoam the Jezreelitess and Abigail the [1]widow of Nabal the Carmelite.

6 Moreover David was greatly distressed because [a]the people spoke of stoning him, for all the people were [1]embittered, each one because of his sons and his daughters. But [b]David strengthened himself in the LORD his God.

7 Then [a]David said to [b]Abiathar the priest, the son of Ahimelech, "Please bring me the ephod." So Abiathar brought the ephod to David.

8 And [a]David inquired of the LORD, saying, "[b]Shall I pursue this band? Shall I overtake them?" And He said to him, "Pursue, for you shall surely overtake them, [c]and you shall surely rescue *all*."

9 So David went, [a]he and the six hundred men who were with him, and came to the brook Besor, *where* those left behind remained.

10 But David pursued, he and four hundred men, for [a]two hundred who were too exhausted to cross the brook Besor, remained *behind.*

11 Now they found an Egyptian in the field and brought him to David, and gave him bread and he ate, and they provided him water to drink.

12 And they gave him a piece of fig cake and two clusters of raisins, and he ate; [a]then his spirit [1]revived. For he had not eaten bread or drunk water for three days and three nights.

13 And David said to him, "To whom do you belong? And where are you from?" And he said, "I am a young man of Egypt, a servant of an Amalekite; and my master left me behind when I fell sick three days ago.

14 "We made a raid on [a]the [1]Negev of the Cherethites, and on that which belongs to Judah, and on [b]the [1]Negev of Caleb, and [c]we burned Ziklag with fire."

15 Then David said to him, "Will you bring me down to this band?" And he said, "Swear to me by God that you will not kill me or deliver me into the hands of my master, and I will bring you down to this band."

16 And when he had brought him down, behold, they were [1]spread over all the land, [a]eating and drinking and [2]dancing because of [b]all the great spoil that they had taken from the land of the Philistines and from the land of Judah.

17 And David [1]slaughtered them [a]from the twilight [2]until the evening of [3]the next day; and not a man of them escaped, except four hundred young men who rode on [b]camels and fled.

18 So David [a]recovered all that the Amalekites had taken, and [1]rescued his two wives.

19 But nothing of theirs was missing, whether small or great, sons or daughters, spoil or anything that they had taken for themselves; [a]David brought *it* all back.

20 So David had [1]captured all the sheep and the cattle *which the people* drove ahead of [2]the *other* livestock, and they said, "[a]This is David's spoil."

The Spoils Are Divided

21 When [a]David came to the two hundred men who were too exhausted to follow David, who had also been left at the brook Besor, and they went out to meet David and to meet the people who were with him, then David approached the people and greeted them.

22 Then all the wicked and worthless men among those who went with David answered and said, "Because they did not go with [1]us, we will not give them any of the spoil that we have recovered, except to every man his wife and his children, that they may lead *them* away and depart."

23 Then David said, "You must not do so, my brothers, with what the LORD has given us, who has kept us and delivered into our hand the band that came against us.

8 [a]1 Sam. 27:10-12

9 [a]2 Sam. 14:17, 20; 19:27 [b]1 Sam. 29:4

10 [a]1 Chr. 12:19, 22

1 [1]I.e., South country [2]Lit., *smote* [a]1 Sam. 29:4, 11 [b]1 Sam. 15:7; 27:8-10 [c]1 Sam. 27:6, 8

2 [1]Lit., *they did not kill* [a]1 Sam. 27:11

4 [a]Num. 14:1

5 [1]Lit., *wife* [a]1 Sam. 25:42, 43; 2 Sam. 2:2

6 [1]Lit., *bitter in soul* [a]Ex. 17:4; John 8:59 [b]1 Sam. 23:16; Ps. 18:2; 27:14; 31:24; 71:4, 5; Rom. 4:20

7 [a]1 Sam. 23:6, 9 [b]1 Sam. 22:20-23

8 [a]1 Sam. 23:2, 4; Ps. 50:15; 91:15 [b]Ex. 15:9 [c]1 Sam. 30:18

9 [a]1 Sam. 27:2

10 [a]1 Sam. 30:9, 21

12 [1]Lit., *returned to him* [a]Judg. 15:19

14 [1]I.e., South country [a]1 Sam. 30:1, 16; 2 Sam. 8:18; 1 Kin. 1:38, 44; Ezek. 25:16; Zeph. 2:5 [b]Josh. 14:13; 15:13; 21:12 [c]1 Sam. 30:1

16 [1]Lit., *left* [2]Lit., *keeping a pilgrim-feast* [a]Luke 12:19; 17:27f. [b]1 Sam. 30:14

17 [1]Lit., *smote* [2]Lit., *even until* [3]Lit., *their* [a]1 Sam. 11:11 [b]Judg. 7:12; 1 Sam. 15:3

18 [1]Lit., *David rescued* [a]Gen. 14:16

19 [a]1 Sam. 30:8

20 [1]Lit., *taken* [2]Lit., *those livestock* [a]1 Sam. 30:26-31

21 [a]1 Sam. 30:10

22 [1]Lit., *me*

24"And who will listen to you in this
matter? For [a]as his share is who goes
down to the battle, so shall his share be
who stays by the baggage; they shall
share alike."
25 And so it has been from that day
forward, that he made it a statute and an
ordinance for Israel to this day.
26 Now when David came to Ziklag,
he sent *some* of the spoil to the elders of
Judah, to his friends, saying, "Behold, [a]a
[1]gift for you from the spoil of [b]the
enemies of the LORD:
27 to those who were in [a]Bethel, and
to those who were in [b]Ramoth of the
[1]Negev, and to those who were in [c]Jattir,
28 and to those who were in [a]Aroer,
and to those who were in Siphmoth, and
to those who were in [b]Eshtemoa,
29 and to those who were in Racal,
and to those who were in the cities of
[a]the Jerahmeelites, and to those who
were in the cities of [b]the Kenites,
30 and to those who were in [a]Hormah,
and to those who were in [b]Bor-ashan,
and to those who were in Athach,
31 and to those who were in [a]Hebron,
and to all the places where David himself and his men were accustomed to
[b]go."

Saul and His Sons Slain

31 [a]NOW the Philistines were fighting against Israel, and the men of
Israel fled from before the Philistines
and fell slain [b]on Mount Gilboa.
2 And the Philistines overtook Saul
and his sons; and the Philistines [1]killed
[a]Jonathan and Abinadab and Malchi-
shua the sons of Saul.
3 And [a]the battle went heavily
against Saul, and the archers [1]hit him;
and he was badly wounded by the archers.
4 [a]Then Saul said to his armor
bearer, "Draw your sword and pierce me
through with it, lest [b]these uncircumcised come and pierce me through and
make sport of me." But his armor bearer
would not, for he was greatly afraid. [c]So
Saul took his sword and fell on it.
5 And when his armor bearer saw
that Saul was dead, he also fell on his
sword and died with him.
6 Thus Saul died with his three sons,
his armor bearer, and all his men on that
day together.
7 And when the men of Israel who
were on the other side of the valley, with
those who were beyond the Jordan, saw
that the men of Israel had fled and that
Saul and his sons were dead, they abandoned the cities and fled; then the Philistines came and lived in them.
8 And it came about on the [1]next day
when the Philistines came to strip the
slain, that they found Saul and his three
sons fallen on Mount Gilboa.
9 And they cut off his head, and
stripped off his weapons, and sent *them*
[1]throughout the land of the Philistines,
[a]to carry the good news [b]to the house of
their idols and to the people.
10 And they put his weapons in the
[1]temple of [a]Ashtaroth, and [b]they fastened his body to the wall of [c]Beth-shan.
11 Now when [a]the inhabitants of Jabesh-gilead heard [1]what the Philistines
had done to Saul,
12 [a]all the valiant men rose and
walked all night, and took the body of
Saul and the bodies of his sons from the
wall of Beth-shan, and they came to
Jabesh, and [b]burned them there.
13 And they took their bones and
[a]buried them under [b]the tamarisk tree at
Jabesh, and [c]fasted seven days.

24 [a]Num. 31:27; Josh. 22:8
26 [1]Lit., *blessing* [a]1 Sam. 25:27 [b]1 Sam. 18:17; 25:28
27 [1]I.e., South country [a]Gen. 12:8; Josh. 7:2; 8:9; 16:1 [b]Josh. 19:8 [c]Josh. 15:48; 21:14
28 [a]Josh. 13:16; 1 Chr. 11:44 [b]Josh. 15:50
29 [a]1 Sam. 27:10 [b]Judg. 1:16; 1 Sam. 15:6
30 [a]Num. 14:45; 21:3; Josh. 12:14; 15:30; 19:4; Judg. 1:17 [b]Josh. 15:42; 19:7
31 [a]Num. 13:22; Josh. 14:13-15; 21:11-13; 2 Sam. 2:1 [b]1 Sam. 23:22

1 [a]1 Chr. 10:1-12 [b]1 Sam. 28:4
2 [1]Lit., *smote* [a]1 Chr. 8:33f.
3 [1]Lit., *found* [a]2 Sam. 1:6
4 [a]Judg. 9:54; 1 Chr. 10:4 [b]Judg. 14:3; 1 Sam. 14:6; 17:26, 36 [c]2 Sam. 1:6, 10
8 [1]Lit., *morrow*
9 [1]Lit., *into . . . around* [a]2 Sam. 1:20 [b]Judg. 16:23, 24
10 [1]Lit., *house* [a]Judg. 2:13; 1 Sam. 7:3 [b]1 Sam. 31:12; 2 Sam. 21:12 [c]Josh. 17:11
11 [1]Lit., *about him what* [a]1 Sam. 11:1-13
12 [a]2 Sam. 2:4-7 [b]2 Chr. 16:14
13 [a]2 Sam. 21:12-14 [b]1 Sam. 22:6 [c]2 Sam. 1:12

THE SECOND BOOK OF
SAMUEL

David Learns of Saul's Death

1 NOW it came about after [a]the death
of Saul, when David had returned
from [b]the slaughter of the Amalekites,
that David remained two days in Ziklag.
2 And it happened on the third day,
that behold, [a]a man came out of the
camp from Saul, [b]with his clothes torn
and [1]dust on his head. And it came
about when he came to David that [c]he
fell to the ground and prostrated himself.
3 Then David said to him, "From
where do you come?" And he said to
him, "I have escaped from the camp of
Israel."
4 And David said to him, "[a]How did
things go? Please tell me." And he said,
"The people have fled from the battle,
and also many of the people have fallen
and are dead; and Saul and Jonathan his
son are dead also."
5 So David said to the young man
who told him, "How do you know that
Saul and his son Jonathan are dead?"
6 And the young man who told him
said, "By chance I happened to be on
[a]Mount Gilboa, and behold, [b]Saul was
leaning on his spear. And behold, the
chariots and the horsemen pursued him
closely.
7 "And when he looked behind him,
he saw me and called to me. And I said,
'Here I am.'
8 "And he said to me, 'Who are you?'
And I [1]answered him, '[a]I am an Amalekite.'
9 "Then he said to me, 'Please stand
beside me and kill me; for agony has
seized me because my [1]life still lingers in
me.'
10 "So I stood beside him [a]and killed
him, because I knew that he could not
live after he had fallen. And [b]I took the
crown which *was* on his head and the
bracelet which *was* on his arm, and I
have brought them here to my lord."
11 Then [a]David took hold of his
clothes and tore them, and *so* also *did* all
the men who *were* with him.
12 And they mourned and wept and
[a]fasted until evening for Saul and his son
Jonathan and for the people of the LORD
and the house of Israel, because they had
fallen by the sword.
13 And David said to the young man
who told him, "Where are you from?"
And he [1]answered, "[a]I am the son of an
alien, an Amalekite."
14 Then David said to him, "How is it
you were not afraid [a]to stretch out your
hand to destroy the LORD's anointed?"
15 And David called one of the young
men and said, "Go, [1]cut him down." [a]So
he struck him and he died.
16 And David said to him, "[a]Your
blood is on your head, for [b]your mouth
has testified against you, saying, 'I have
killed the LORD's anointed.'"

1 [a]1 Sam. 31:6 [b]1 Sam. 30:1, 17, 26
2 [1]Lit., *ground* [a]2 Sam. 4:10 [b]1 Sam. 4:12 [c]1 Sam. 25:23
4 [a]1 Sam. 4:16
6 [a]1 Sam. 28:4; 31:1-6; 1 Chr. 10:4-10 [b]1 Sam. 31:2-4
8 [1]Lit., *said to* [a]1 Sam. 15:3; 30:1, 13, 17
9 [1]Lit., *whole life is still in me*
10 [a]Judg. 9:54 [b]2 Kin. 11:12
11 [a]Gen. 37:29, 34; Josh. 7:6; 2 Chr. 34:27; Ezra 9:3
12 [a]2 Sam. 3:35
13 [1]Lit., *said* [a]2 Sam. 1:8
14 [a]1 Sam. 24:6; 26:9, 11, 16
15 [1]Lit., *fall upon him* [a]2 Sam. 4:10, 12
16 [a]1 Sam. 26:9; 2 Sam. 3:28, 29; 1 Kin. 2:32 [b]2 Sam. 1:10; Luke 19:22
17 [a]2 Chr. 35:25
18 [a]Josh. 10:13
19 [1]Lit., *The* [a]2 Sam. 1:25, 27
20 [a]1 Sam. 31:8-13; Mic. 1:10 [b]Ex. 15:20, 21; 1 Sam. 18:6 [c]1 Sam. 14:6
21 [a]1 Sam. 31:1 [b]Ezek. 31:15 [c]Is. 21:5
22 [a]Deut. 32:42; Is. 34:6 [b]1 Sam. 18:4
23 [a]Jer. 4:13 [b]Judg. 14:18
25 [a]2 Sam. 1:19, 27
26 [a]1 Sam. 18:1-4
27 [a]2 Sam. 1:19, 25 [b]Is. 13:5
1 [a]1 Sam. 23:2, 4, 9-12 [b]Josh. 14:13; 1 Sam. 30:31
2 [1]Lit., *wife* [a]1 Sam. 25:42, 43

David's Dirge for Saul and Jonathan

17 Then David [a]chanted with this
lament over Saul and Jonathan his son,
18 and he told *them* to teach the sons
of Judah *the song of* the bow; behold, it
is written in [a]the book of Jashar.
19 "[1]Your beauty, O Israel, is slain on
your high places!
[a]How have the mighty fallen!
20 "[a]Tell *it* not in Gath,
Proclaim it not in the streets of
Ashkelon;
Lest [b]the daughters of the Philistines rejoice,
Lest the daughters of [c]the uncircumcised exult.
21 "[a]O mountains of Gilboa,
[b]Let not dew or rain be on you,
nor fields of offerings;
For there the shield of the mighty
was defiled,
The shield of Saul, not [c]anointed
with oil.
22 "[a]From the blood of the slain, from
the fat of the mighty,
[b]The bow of Jonathan did not
turn back,
And the sword of Saul did not
return empty.
23 "Saul and Jonathan, beloved and
pleasant in their life,
And in their death they were not
parted;
[a]They were swifter than eagles,
[b]They were stronger than lions.
24 "O daughters of Israel, weep over
Saul,
Who clothed you luxuriously in
scarlet,
Who put ornaments of gold on
your apparel.
25 "[a]How have the mighty fallen in
the midst of the battle!
Jonathan is slain on your high
places.
26 "I am distressed for you, my
brother Jonathan;
You have been very pleasant to
me.
[a]Your love to me was more wonderful
Than the love of women.
27 "[a]How have the mighty fallen,
And [b]the weapons of war perished!"

David Made King over Judah

2 THEN it came about afterwards
that [a]David inquired of the LORD,
saying, "Shall I go up to one of the cities
of Judah?" And the LORD said to him,
"Go up." So David said, "Where shall I
go up?" And He said, "[b]To Hebron."
2 So David went up there, and [a]his
two wives also, Ahinoam the Jezreelitess
and Abigail the [1]widow of Nabal the
Carmelite.

3 And [a]David brought up his men
who *were* with him, each with his household; and they lived in the cities of
Hebron.
4 Then the men of Judah came and
there [a]anointed David king over the
house of Judah.
And they told David, saying, "It was
[b]the men of Jabesh-gilead who buried
Saul."
5 And David sent messengers to the
men of Jabesh-gilead, and said to them,
"[a]May you be blessed of the LORD
because you have [1]shown this kindness
to Saul your lord, and have buried him.
6 "And now [a]may the LORD [1]show
lovingkindness and truth to you; and I
also will [1]show this goodness to you,
because you have done this thing.
7 "Now therefore, let your hands be
strong, and be [1]valiant; for Saul your
lord is dead, and also the house of Judah
has anointed me king over them."

Ish-bosheth Made King over Israel

8 But [a]Abner the son of Ner, commander of Saul's army, had taken [1]Ish-
bosheth the son of Saul, and brought
him over to [b]Mahanaim.
9 And he made him king over [a]Gil-
ead, over the [b]Ashurites, over [c]Jezreel,
over Ephraim, and over Benjamin, even
over all Israel.
10 Ish-bosheth, Saul's son, was forty
years old when he became king over
Israel, and he was king for two years.
The house of Judah, however, followed
David.
11 And [a]the [1]time that David was
king in Hebron over the house of Judah
was seven years and six months.

Civil War

12 Now Abner the son of Ner, went
out from Mahanaim to [a]Gibeon with the
servants of Ish-bosheth the son of Saul.
13 And [a]Joab the son of Zeruiah and
the servants of David went out and met
[1]them by the pool of Gibeon; and they
sat down, [2]one on the one side of the
pool and [2]the other on the other side of
the pool.
14 Then Abner said to Joab, "Now let
the young men arise and [1][a]hold a contest
before us." And Joab said, "Let them
arise."
15 So they arose and went over by
count, twelve for Benjamin and Ish-
bosheth the son of Saul, and twelve of
the servants of David.
16 And each one of them seized his
[1]opponent by the head, and *thrust* his
sword in his [2]opponent's side; so they
fell down together. Therefore that place
was called [3]Helkath-hazzurim, which is
in Gibeon.
17 And that day the battle was very
severe, and [a]Abner and the men of Israel
were beaten before the servants of David.
18 Now [a]the three sons of Zeruiah
were there, Joab and Abishai and Asahel; and Asahel *was* [b]*as* [1]swift-footed as
one of the gazelles which is in the field.
19 And Asahel pursued Abner and
did not [1]turn to the right or to the left
from following Abner.
20 Then Abner looked behind him
and said, "Is that you, Asahel?" And he
answered, "It is I."
21 So Abner said to him, "[1]Turn to
your right or to your left, and take hold
of one of the young men for yourself,
and take for yourself his spoil." But
Asahel was not willing to turn aside
from following him.
22 And Abner repeated again to Asahel, "Turn [1]aside from following me.
Why should I strike you to the ground?
[a]How then could I lift up my face to
your brother Joab?"
23 However, he refused to turn aside;
therefore Abner struck him in the belly
with the butt end of the spear, so that
the spear came out at his back. And he
fell there and died on the spot. And it
came about that all who came to the
place where [a]Asahel had fallen and died,
stood still.
24 But Joab and Abishai pursued
Abner, and when the sun was going
down, they came to the hill of Ammah,
which is in front of Giah by the way of
the wilderness of Gibeon.
25 And the sons of Benjamin gathered
together behind Abner and became one
band, and they stood on the top of a
certain hill.
26 Then Abner called to Joab and
said, "Shall the sword devour forever?
Do you not know that it will be bitter in
the end? How long will you [1]refrain
from telling the people to turn back
from following their brothers?"
27 And Joab said, "As God lives, if
you had not spoken, surely then the
people would have gone away in the
morning, each from following his
brother."
28 So Joab blew the trumpet; and all
the people halted and pursued Israel no
longer, [a]nor did they continue to fight
anymore.
29 Abner and his men then went
through the Arabah all that night; so
they crossed the Jordan, walked all
morning, and came to [a]Mahanaim.
30 Then Joab returned from following
Abner; when he had gathered all the
people together, [1]nineteen of David's
servants besides Asahel were missing.
31 But the servants of David had
struck down many of Benjamin and
Abner's men, *so that* three hundred and
sixty men died.
32 And they took up Asahel and buried him [a]in his father's tomb which was
in Bethlehem. Then Joab and his men
went all night until the day [1]dawned at
Hebron.

The House of David Strengthened

3 NOW [a]there was a long war between the house of Saul and the
house of David; and David grew steadily

3 [a]1 Sam. 30:9; 1 Chr. 12:1
4 [a]1 Sam. 16:13; 2 Sam. 5:3, 5 [b]1 Sam. 31:11-13
5 [1]Lit., *done* [a]1 Sam. 23:21; Ps. 115:15
6 [1]Lit., *do* [a]Ex. 34:6; 2 Tim. 1:16
7 [1]Lit., *sons of valor*
8 [1]I.e., man of shame; cf. 1 Chr. 8:33, *Eshbaal* [a]1 Sam. 14:50 [b]Gen. 32:2; 2 Sam. 17:24
9 [a]Josh. 22:9 [b]Judg. 1:32 [c]1 Sam. 29:1
11 [1]Lit., *number of days* [a]2 Sam. 5:5
12 [a]Josh. 10:12; 18:25
13 [1]Lit., *them together* [2]Lit., *these* [a]2 Sam. 8:16; 1 Chr. 2:16; 11:6
14 [1]Lit., *make sport* [a]2 Sam. 2:16, 17
16 [1]Lit., *fellow* [2]Lit., *fellow's* [3]I.e., the field of sword-edges
17 [a]2 Sam. 3:1
18 [1]Lit., *light in his feet* [a]1 Chr. 2:16 [b]1 Chr. 12:8; Hab. 3:19
19 [1]Lit., *turn to go to*
21 [1]Lit., *Turn for yourself*
22 [1]Lit., *aside for yourself* [a]2 Sam. 3:27
23 [a]2 Sam. 20:12
26 [1]Lit., *not tell the people*
28 [a]2 Sam. 3:1
29 [a]2 Sam. 2:8
30 [1]Lit., *nineteen men*
32 [1]Lit., *lighted on them* [a]Gen. 47:29, 30; Judg. 8:32
1 [a]1 Kin. 14:30; Ps. 46:9

stronger, but the house of Saul grew weaker continually.

2 [a]Sons were born to David at Hebron: his first-born was Amnon, by [b]Ahinoam the Jezreelitess;

3 and his second, Chileab, by Abigail the [1]widow of Nabal the Carmelite; and the third, Absalom the son of [a]Maacah, the daughter of Talmai, king of [b]Geshur;

4 and the fourth, [a]Adonijah the son of Haggith; and the fifth, Shephatiah the son of Abital;

5 and the sixth, Ithream, by David's wife Eglah. These were born to David at Hebron.

Abner Joins David

6 And it came about while there was war between the house of Saul and the house of David that [a]Abner was making himself strong in the house of Saul.

7 Now Saul had a concubine whose name was [a]Rizpah, the daughter of Aiah; and [1]Ish-bosheth said to Abner, "Why have you gone in to my father's concubine?"

8 Then Abner was very angry over the words of Ish-bosheth and said, "[a]Am I a dog's head that belongs to Judah? Today I show kindness to the house of Saul your father, to his brothers and to his friends, and have not delivered you into the hands of David; and yet today you charge me with a guilt concerning the woman.

9 "[a]May God do so to Abner, and more also, if [b]as the LORD has sworn to David, I do not accomplish this for him,

10 [a]to transfer the kingdom from the house of Saul, and to establish the throne of David over Israel and over Judah, [b]from Dan even to Beersheba."

11 And he could no longer answer Abner a word, because he was afraid of him.

12 Then Abner sent messengers to David in his place, saying, "Whose is the land? Make your covenant with me, and behold, my hand shall be with you to bring all Israel over to you."

13 And he said, "Good! I will make a covenant with you, but I demand one thing of you, [1]namely, [a]you shall not see my face unless you [b]first bring Michal, Saul's daughter, when you come to see [2]me."

14 So David sent messengers to Ish-bosheth, Saul's son, saying, "Give me my wife Michal, to whom I was betrothed [a]for a hundred foreskins of the Philistines."

15 And Ish-bosheth sent and took her from *her* husband, from [1]Paltiel the son of Laish.

16 But her husband went with her, weeping as he went, and followed her as far as [a]Bahurim. Then Abner said to him, "Go, return." So he returned.

17 Now Abner had [1]consultation with [a]the elders of Israel, saying, "In times past you were seeking for David to be king over you.

18 "Now then, do *it*! For the LORD has spoken of David, saying, '[a]By the hand of My servant David [1]I will save My people Israel from the hand of the Philistines and from the hand of all their enemies.' "

19 And Abner also spoke in the hearing of Benjamin; and in addition Abner went to speak in the hearing of David in Hebron all that seemed good to Israel and to [a]the whole house of Benjamin.

20 Then Abner and twenty men with him came to David at Hebron. And David made a feast for Abner and the men who were with him.

21 And Abner said to David, "Let me arise and go, and [a]gather all Israel to my lord the king that they may make a covenant with you, and that [b]you may be king over all that your soul desires." So David sent Abner away, and he went in peace.

22 And behold, [a]the servants of David and Joab came from a raid and brought much spoil with them; but Abner was not with David in Hebron, for he had sent him away, and he had gone in peace.

23 When Joab and all the army that was with him arrived, they told Joab, saying, "Abner the son of Ner came to the king, and he has sent him away, and he has gone in peace."

24 Then Joab came to the king and said, "What have you done? Behold, Abner came to you; why then have you sent him away and he is already gone?

25 "You know Abner the son of Ner, that he came to deceive you and to learn of [a]your going out and coming in, and to find out all that you are doing."

Joab Murders Abner

26 When Joab came out from David, he sent messengers after Abner, and they brought him back from the well of Sirah; but David did not know *it*.

27 So when Abner returned to Hebron, Joab took him aside into the middle of the gate to speak with him privately, and there [a]he struck him in the belly so that he died on account of the blood of Asahel his brother.

28 And afterward when David heard it, he said, "I and my kingdom are innocent before the LORD forever of the blood of Abner the son of Ner.

29 "[a]May it [1]fall on the head of Joab and on all his father's house; and may there not fail from the house of Joab [b]one who has a discharge, or who is a leper, or who takes hold of a distaff, or who falls by the sword, or who lacks bread."

30 So Joab and Abishai his brother killed Abner [a]because he had put their brother Asahel to death in the battle at Gibeon.

David Mourns Abner

31 Then David said to Joab and to all the people who were with him, "[a]Tear your clothes and gird on sackcloth and

2 [a]1 Chr. 3:1-3 [b]1 Sam. 25:42, 43
3 [1]Lit., *wife* [a]1 Sam. 27:8; 1 Chr. 3:2 [b]2 Sam. 14:32; 15:8
4 [a]1 Kin. 1:5
6 [a]2 Sam. 2:8, 9
7 [1]So some ancient mss. and versions; M.T., *he* [a]2 Sam. 21:8-11
8 [a]1 Sam. 24:14; 2 Sam. 9:8
9 [a]1 Kin. 19:2 [b]1 Sam. 15:28
10 [a]1 Sam. 15:28 [b]1 Sam. 3:20
13 [1]Lit., *saying* [2]Lit., *my face* [a]Gen. 43:3 [b]1 Sam. 18:20; 19:11
14 [a]1 Sam. 18:25, 27
15 [1]In 1 Sam. 25:44, *Palti*
16 [a]2 Sam. 16:5; 19:16
17 [1]Lit., *a word* [a]1 Sam. 8:4
18 [1]So many ancient mss. and versions; M.T., *he* [a]1 Sam. 9:16; 15:28
19 [a]1 Sam. 10:20, 21; 1 Chr. 12:29
21 [a]2 Sam. 3:10, 12 [b]1 Kin. 11:37
22 [a]1 Sam. 27:8
25 [a]Deut. 28:6; 1 Sam. 29:6; Is. 37:28
27 [a]2 Sam. 2:23; 20:9, 10; 1 Kin. 2:5
29 [1]Lit., *whirl* [a]Deut. 21:6-9; 1 Kin. 2:31-33 [b]Lev. 13:46
30 [a]2 Sam. 2:23
31 [a]Gen. 37:34; Judg. 11:35

lament before Abner." And King David
walked behind the bier.
32 Thus they buried Abner in Hebron; and the king lifted up his voice
and wept at [a]the grave of Abner, and all
the people wept.
33 And [a]the king chanted a *lament* for
Abner and said,
"Should Abner die as a fool dies?
34 "Your hands were not bound, nor
your feet put in fetters;
As one falls before the [1]wicked,
you have fallen."
And all the people wept again over him.
35 Then all the people came [a]to [1]per-
suade David to eat bread while it was
still day; but David vowed, saying,
"[b]May God do so to me, and more also,
if I taste bread or anything else [c]before
the sun goes down."
36 Now all the people took note *of it,*
and it [1]pleased them, just as everything
the king did [2]pleased all the people.
37 So all the people and all Israel
understood that day that it had not been
the will of the king to put Abner the son
of Ner to death.
38 Then the king said to his servants,
"Do you not know that a prince and a
great man has fallen this day in Israel?
39 "And I am [a]weak today, though
anointed king; and these men [b]the sons
of Zeruiah are too difficult for me. [c]May
the LORD repay the evildoer according
to his evil."

Ish-bosheth Murdered

4 NOW when [1]Ish-bosheth, Saul's
son, heard that [a]Abner had died in
Hebron, [2b]he lost courage, and all Israel
was disturbed.
2 And Saul's son *had* two men who
were commanders of bands: the name of
the one was Baanah and the name of the
other Rechab, sons of Rimmon the
Beerothite, of the sons of Benjamin (for
[a]Beeroth is also considered [b]*part* of
Benjamin,
3 and the Beerothites fled to [a]Git-
taim, and have been aliens there until
this day).
4 Now [a]Jonathan, Saul's son, had a
son crippled in his feet. He was five
years old when the [b]report of Saul and
Jonathan came from Jezreel, and his
nurse took him up and fled. And it
happened that in her hurry to flee, he fell
and became lame. And his name was
[1c]Mephibosheth.
5 So the sons of Rimmon the Beerothite, Rechab and Baanah, departed and
came to the house of [a]Ish-bosheth in the
heat of the day while he was taking his
midday rest.
6 [1]And they came to the middle of
the house as [2]if to get wheat, and [a]they
struck him in the belly; and Rechab and
Baanah his brother escaped.
7 Now when they came into the
house, as he was lying on his bed in his
bedroom, they struck him and killed him
and beheaded him. And they took his
head and [1a]traveled by way of the Arabah all night.
8 Then they brought the head of Ish-
bosheth to David at Hebron, and said to
the king, "Behold, the head of Ish-
bosheth, [a]the son of Saul, your enemy,
who sought your life; thus the LORD has
given my lord the king vengeance this
day on Saul and his [1]descendants."
9 And David answered Rechab and
Baanah his brother, sons of Rimmon the
Beerothite, and said to them, "As the
LORD lives, [a]who has redeemed my life
from all distress,
10 [a]when one told me, saying, 'Behold, Saul is dead,' and [1]thought he was
bringing good news, I seized him and
killed him in Ziklag, which was the
reward I gave him for *his* news.
11 "How much more, when wicked
men have killed a righteous man in his
own house on his bed, shall I not now
[a]require his blood from your hand, and
[1]destroy you from the earth?"
12 Then [a]David commanded the
young men, and they killed them and cut
off their hands and feet, and hung them
up beside the pool in Hebron. But they
took the head of Ish-bosheth [b]and buried it in the grave of Abner in Hebron.

David King over All Israel

5 [a]THEN all the tribes of Israel came
to David at Hebron and [1]said, "Behold, we are [b]your bone and your flesh.
2 "Previously, when Saul was king
over us, [a]you were the one who led Israel
out and in. And the LORD said to you,
'[b]You will shepherd My people Israel,
and you will be [c]a ruler over Israel.' "
3 So all the elders of Israel came to
the king at Hebron, and King David
[a]made a covenant with them before the
LORD at Hebron; then [b]they anointed
David king over Israel.
4 David was [a]thirty years old when
he became king, *and* [b]he reigned forty
years.
5 At Hebron [a]he reigned over Judah
seven years and six months, and in
Jerusalem he reigned thirty-three years
over all Israel and Judah.
6 [a]Now the king and his men went to
[b]Jerusalem against the Jebusites, the
inhabitants of the land, and they said to
[1]David, "You shall not come in here, but
the blind and lame shall turn you away";
[2]thinking, "David cannot enter here."
7 Nevertheless, David captured the
stronghold of Zion, that is [a]the city of
David.
8 And David said on that day,
"Whoever would strike the Jebusites, let
him reach the lame and the blind, who
are hated by David's soul, through the
water tunnel." Therefore they say, "The
blind or the lame shall not come into the
house."
9 So David lived in the stronghold,
and called it [a]the city of David. And
David built all around from the [1b]Millo
and inward.

32 [a]Job 31:28, 29; Prov. 24:17
33 [a]2 Sam. 1:17; 2 Chr. 35:25
34 [1]Lit., *sons of wickedness*
35 [1]Lit., *cause* [a]2 Sam. 12:17 [b]1 Sam. 3:17 [c]2 Sam. 1:12
36 [1]Lit., *was good in their eyes* [2]Lit., *was good in the eyes of all*
39 [a]1 Chr. 29:1; 2 Chr. 13:7 [b]2 Sam. 19:5-7 [c]1 Kin. 2:32-34

1 [1]So some ancient mss.; M.T., *he* [2]Lit., *his hands dropped* [a]2 Sam. 3:27 [b]Ezra 4:4
2 [a]Josh. 9:17 [b]Josh. 18:25
3 [a]Neh. 11:33
4 [1]I.e., Merib-baal [a]2 Sam. 9:3, 6 [b]1 Sam. 31:1-4 [c]1 Chr. 8:34; 9:40
5 [a]2 Sam. 2:8
6 [1]Lit., *And here* [2]Lit., *takers of wheat* [a]2 Sam. 2:23
7 [1]Lit., *went* [a]2 Sam. 2:29
8 [1]Lit., *seed* [a]1 Sam. 24:4; 25:29
9 [a]Gen. 48:16; 1 Kin. 1:29; Ps. 31:7
10 [1]Lit., *he was as a bearer of good news in his own eyes* [a]2 Sam. 1:2, 4, 15
11 [1]Lit., *burn* [a]Gen. 9:5; Ps. 9:12
12 [a]2 Sam. 1:15 [b]2 Sam. 3:32

1 [1]Lit., *said, saying* [a]1 Chr. 11:1-3 [b]2 Sam. 19:13
2 [a]1 Sam. 18:5, 13, 16 [b]Gen. 49:24; 2 Sam. 7:7 [c]1 Sam. 25:30
3 [a]2 Sam. 3:21 [b]1 Sam. 16:13; 2 Sam. 2:4
4 [a]Gen. 41:46; Num. 4:3; Luke 3:23 [b]1 Kin. 2:11; 1 Chr. 26:31
5 [a]2 Sam. 2:11; 1 Chr. 3:4; 29:27
6 [1]Lit., *David, saying* [2]Lit., *saying* [a]1 Chr. 11:4-9 [b]Josh. 15:63; 18:28; Judg. 1:21
7 [a]2 Sam. 6:12, 16; 1 Kin. 2:10; 9:24
9 [1]I.e., citadel [a]2 Sam. 5:7 [b]1 Kin. 9:15, 24

10 And [a]David became greater and
greater, for the LORD God of hosts was
with him.
11 [a]Then Hiram king of Tyre sent
messengers to David with cedar trees
and carpenters and stonemasons; and
[b]they built a house for David.
12 And David realized that the LORD
had established him as king over Israel,
and that He had exalted his kingdom for
the sake of His people Israel.
13 Meanwhile [a]David took more concubines and wives from Jerusalem, after
he came from Hebron; and more sons
and daughters were born to David.
14 Now [a]these are the names of those
who were born to him in Jerusalem:
Shammua, Shobab, Nathan, Solomon,
15 Ibhar, Elishua, Nepheg, Japhia,
16 Elishama, Eliada and Eliphelet.

War with the Philistines

17 When the Philistines heard that
they had anointed David king over
Israel, [a]all the Philistines went up to seek
out David; and when David heard *of it,*
he went down to the [b]stronghold.
18 Now the Philistines came and
spread themselves out in [a]the valley of
Rephaim.
19 Then [a]David inquired of the LORD,
saying, "Shall I go up against the Philistines? Wilt Thou give them into my
hand?" And [b]the LORD said to David,
"Go up, for I will certainly give the
Philistines into your hand."
20 So David came to [a]Baal-perazim,
and [1]defeated them there; and he said,
"The LORD has broken through my
enemies before me like the breakthrough
of waters." Therefore he named that
place [2]Baal-perazim.
21 And they abandoned their idols
there, so [a]David and his men carried
them away.
22 Now [a]the Philistines came up once
again and spread themselves out in the
valley of Rephaim.
23 And when [a]David inquired of the
LORD, He said, "You shall not go *di-*
rectly up; circle around behind them and
come at them in front of the [1]balsam
trees.
24 "And it shall be, when [a]you hear the
sound of marching in the tops of the
[1]balsam trees, then you shall act
promptly, for then [b]the LORD will have
gone out before you to strike the army of
the Philistines."
25 Then David did so, just as the
LORD had commanded him, and struck
down the Philistines from [1a]Geba [2]as far
as [b]Gezer.

Peril in Moving the Ark

6 [a]NOW David again gathered all the
chosen men of Israel, thirty thousand.
2 And David arose and went with all
the people who were with him to
[1a]Baale-judah, to bring up from there
the ark of God which is called by the
[b]Name, the very name of the LORD of
hosts who [c]is [2]enthroned *above* the
cherubim.
3 And they [1]placed the ark of God
on [a]a new cart that they might bring it
from the house of Abinadab which was
on the hill; and Uzzah and Ahio, the
sons of Abinadab, were leading the new
cart.
4 So [a]they brought it with the ark of
God from the house of Abinadab, which
was on the hill; and Ahio was walking
ahead of the ark.
5 Meanwhile, David and all the
house of Israel [a]were celebrating before
the LORD [b]with all kinds of *instruments*
made of [1]fir wood, and with lyres, harps,
tambourines, castanets and cymbals.
6 But when they came to the [a]thresh-
ing floor of Nacon, Uzzah [b]reached out
toward the ark of God and took hold of
it, for the oxen nearly upset *it.*
7 And the anger of the LORD burned
against Uzzah, and [a]God struck him
down there for [1]his irreverence; and he
died there by the ark of God.
8 And David became angry because
[1]of the LORD's outburst against Uzzah,
and that place is called [2]Perez-uzzah to
this day.
9 So [a]David was afraid of the LORD
that day; and he said, "How can the ark
of the LORD come to me?"
10 And David was unwilling to move
the ark of the LORD into the city of
David with him; but David took it aside
to the house of [a]Obed-edom the Gittite.
11 Thus the ark of the LORD remained
in the house of Obed-edom the Gittite
three months, and the LORD [a]blessed
Obed-edom and all his household.

The Ark Is Brought to Jerusalem

12 Now it was told King David, saying, "The LORD has blessed the house of
Obed-edom and all that belongs to him,
on account of the ark of God." [a]And
David went and brought up the ark of
God from the house of Obed-edom into
[b]the city of David with gladness.
13 And so it was, that when the [a]bear-
ers of the ark of the LORD had gone six
paces, he sacrificed an [b]ox and a fatling.
14 And [a]David was dancing before
the LORD with all *his* might, and David
was [1b]wearing a linen ephod.
15 So David and all the house of
Israel were bringing up the ark of the
LORD with shouting and the sound of
the trumpet.
16 Then it happened *as* the ark of the
LORD came into the city of David that
[a]Michal the daughter of Saul looked out
of the window and saw King David
leaping and dancing before the LORD;
and she despised him in her heart.
17 So they brought in the ark of the
LORD and set it [a]in its place inside the
tent which David had pitched for it; and
[b]David offered burnt offerings and peace
offerings before the LORD.
18 And when David had finished offering the burnt offering and the peace

10 [a]2 Sam. 3:1

11 [a]1 Kin. 5:1, 10, 18; 1 Chr. 14:1 [b]Ps. 30:title

13 [a]Deut. 17:17; 1 Chr. 3:9

14 [a]1 Chr. 3:5-8

17 [a]1 Sam. 29:1 [b]2 Sam. 23:14; 1 Chr. 11:16

18 [a]Gen. 14:5; Josh. 15:8; 17:15; 18:16

19 [a]1 Sam. 23:2 [b]2 Sam. 2:1

20 [1]Lit., *David smote* [2]I.e., the master of breakthrough [a]1 Chr. 14:11; Is. 28:21

21 [a]1 Chr. 14:12

22 [a]2 Sam. 5:18

23 [1]Or, *baka-shrubs* [a]2 Sam. 5:19

24 [1]Or, *baka-shrubs* [a]2 Kin. 7:6 [b]Judg. 4:14

25 [1]In 1 Chr. 14:16, *Gibeon* [2]Lit., *until you are coming to* [a]Is. 28:21 [b]Josh. 12:12; 21:21

1 [a]1 Chr. 13:5-14

2 [1]I.e., Kiriath-jearim [2]Lit., *sitting* [a]Josh. 15:9, 10; 1 Sam. 7:1 [b]Lev. 24:16 [c]Ex. 25:22

3 [1]Lit., *caused to ride* [a]Num. 7:4-9; 1 Sam. 6:7

4 [a]1 Sam. 7:1; 1 Chr. 13:7

5 [1]Or, *cypress* [a]1 Sam. 18:6, 7 [b]1 Chr. 13:8

6 [a]1 Chr. 13:9 [b]Num. 4:15, 19, 20

7 [1]Lit., *the* [a]1 Sam. 6:19

8 [1]Lit., *the LORD broke through a breakthrough* [2]I.e., the breakthrough of Uzzah

9 [a]Ps. 119:120; Luke 5:8

10 [a]1 Chr. 26:4-8

11 [a]Gen. 30:27; 39:5

12 [a]1 Chr. 15:25-16:3 [b]1 Kin. 8:1

13 [a]Num. 4:15; Josh. 3:3; 1 Chr. 15:2, 15 [b]1 Kin. 8:5

14 [1]Lit., *girded with* [a]Ex. 15:20, 21; Judg. 11:34 [b]Ex. 19:6; 1 Sam. 2:18, 28

16 [a]2 Sam. 3:14

17 [a]1 Chr. 15:1; 2 Chr. 1:4 [b]1 Kin. 8:62-65

offering, [a]he blessed the people in the
name of the LORD of hosts.
19 Further, he distributed to all the
people, to all the multitude of Israel,
both to men and women, a cake of bread
and one of dates and one of raisins to
each one. Then all the people departed
each to his house.
20 But when David returned to bless
his household, Michal the daughter of
Saul came out to meet David and said,
"How the king of Israel distinguished
himself today! [a]He uncovered himself
today in the eyes of his servants' maids
as one of the [b]foolish ones shamelessly
uncovers himself!"
21 So David said to Michal, "[a]*It was*
before the LORD, who chose me above
your father and above all his house, to
appoint me ruler over the people of the
LORD, over Israel; therefore I will celebrate before the LORD.
22 "And I will be more lightly esteemed
than this and will be humble in my own
eyes, but with the maids of whom you
have spoken, with them I will be distinguished."
23 And Michal the daughter of Saul
had no child to the day of her death.

David Plans to Build a Temple

7 [a]NOW it came about when the king
lived in his house, and the LORD had
given him rest on every side from all his
enemies,
2 that the king said to [a]Nathan the
prophet, "See now, I dwell in [b]a house of
cedar, but the ark of God [c]dwells within
tent curtains."
3 And Nathan said to the king, "[a]Go,
do all that is in your mind, for the LORD
is with you."
4 But it came about in the same night
that the word of the LORD came to
Nathan, saying,
5 "Go and say to My servant David,
'Thus says the LORD, "[a]Are you the one
who should build Me a house to dwell
in?
6 "For [a]I have not dwelt in a house
since the day I brought up the sons of
Israel from Egypt, even to this day; but I
have been moving about [b]in a tent, even
in a [1]tabernacle.
7 "[a]Wherever I have gone with all the
sons of Israel, did I speak a word with
one of the tribes of Israel, [b]which I
commanded to shepherd My people
Israel, saying, 'Why have you not built
Me a house of cedar?' " '

God's Covenant with David

8 "Now therefore, thus you shall say
to My servant David, 'Thus says the
LORD of hosts, "[a]I took you from the
pasture, from following the sheep, [b]that
you should be ruler over My people
Israel.
9 "And [a]I have been with you wherever you have gone and [b]have cut off all
your enemies from before you; and I will
make you a great name, like the names
of the great men who are on the earth.

18 [a]1 Kin. 8:14, 15
20 [a]2 Sam. 6:14, 16; Eccl. 7:17 [b]Judg. 9:4
21 [a]1 Sam. 13:14; 15:28
1 [a]1 Chr. 17:1-27
2 [a]2 Sam. 7:17; 12:1; 1 Kin. 1:22; 1 Chr. 29:29; 2 Chr. 9:29 [b]2 Sam. 5:11 [c]Ex. 26:1
3 [a]1 Kin. 8:17, 18; 1 Chr. 22:7
5 [a]1 Kin. 5:3, 4; 8:19
6 [1]Lit., *dwelling place* [a]Josh. 18:1; 1 Kin. 8:16 [b]Ex. 40:18, 34
7 [a]Lev. 26:11, 12 [b]2 Sam. 5:2
8 [a]1 Sam. 16:11, 12; Ps. 78:70, 71 [b]2 Sam. 6:21
9 [a]1 Sam. 5:10 [b]Ps. 18:37-42
10 [1]Lit., *sons of wickedness* [a]Ex. 15:17; Is. 5:2, 7 [b]Ps. 89:22, 23; Is. 60:18
11 [a]Judg. 2:14-16; 1 Sam. 12:9-11 [b]2 Sam. 7:1 [c]1 Sam. 25:28; 2 Sam. 7:27
12 [1]Lit., *seed* [2]Lit., *your bowels* [a]1 Kin. 2:1 [b]Deut. 31:16; Acts 13:36 [c]1 Kin. 8:20; Ps. 132:11
13 [a]1 Kin. 6:12; 8:19 [b]Is. 9:7; 49:8
14 [a]Ps. 89:26, 27; 2 Cor. 6:18; Heb. 1:5 [b]1 Kin. 11:34; Ps. 89:30-33
15 [a]1 Sam. 15:23; 16:14
16 [1]So with Gr. and some ancient mss.; M.T., *you* [a]2 Sam. 7:13; Ps. 89:36, 37
18 [1]Heb., *YHWH*, usually rendered *LORD*, and so throughout the ch. [a]Ex. 3:11; 1 Sam. 18:18
19 [1]Or, *law* [a]2 Sam. 7:11-16; 1 Chr. 17:17 [b]Is. 55:8, 9
20 [a]1 Sam. 16:7; John 21:17
21 [a]1 Chr. 17:19; Eph. 4:32
22 [a]Deut. 3:24; Ps. 48:1; 86:10 [b]Ex. 15:11; 1 Sam. 2:2 [c]Ex. 10:2; Ps. 44:1
23 [a]Deut. 4:32-38 [b]Deut. 10:21 [c]Deut. 15:15 [d]Deut. 9:26
24 [a]Deut. 32:6 [b]Gen. 17:7, 8; Ex. 6:7

10 "I will also appoint a place for My
people Israel and [a]will plant them, that
they may live in their own place and not
be disturbed again, [b]nor will the [1]wicked
afflict them any more as formerly,
11 even [a]from the day that I commanded judges to be over My people
Israel; and [b]I will give you rest from all
your enemies. The LORD also declares to
you that [c]the LORD will make a house
for you.
12 "[a]When your days are complete and
you [b]lie down with your fathers, [c]I will
raise up your [1]descendant after you, who
will come forth from [2]you, and I will
establish his kingdom.
13 "[a]He shall build a house for My
name, and [b]I will establish the throne of
his kingdom forever.
14 "[a]I will be a father to him and he
will be a son to Me; [b]when he commits
iniquity, I will correct him with the rod
of men and the strokes of the sons of
men,
15 but My lovingkindness shall not
depart from him, [a]as I took *it* away from
Saul, whom I removed from before you.
16 "And [a]your house and your kingdom shall endure before [1]Me forever;
your throne shall be established forever." ' "
17 In accordance with all these words
and all this vision, so Nathan spoke to
David.

David's Prayer

18 Then David the king went in and
sat before the LORD, and he said, "[a]Who
am I, O Lord [1]GOD, and what is my
house, that Thou hast brought me this
far?
19 "And yet this was insignificant in
Thine eyes, O Lord GOD, [a]for Thou hast
spoken also of the house of Thy servant
concerning the distant future. And [b]this
is the [1]custom of man, O Lord GOD.
20 "And again what more can David
say to Thee? For [a]Thou knowest Thy
servant, O Lord GOD!
21 "[a]For the sake of Thy word, and
according to Thine own heart, Thou hast
done all this greatness to let Thy servant
know.
22 "For this reason [a]Thou art great, O
Lord GOD; for [b]there is none like Thee,
and there is no God besides Thee, [c]ac-
cording to all that we have heard with
our ears.
23 "And [a]what one nation on the earth
is like Thy people Israel, whom God
went to redeem for Himself as a people
and to make a name for Himself, and [b]to
do a great thing for Thee and awesome
things for Thy land, before [c]Thy people
whom [d]Thou hast redeemed for Thyself
from Egypt, *from* nations and their
gods?
24 "For [a]Thou hast established for
Thyself Thy people Israel as Thine own
people forever, and [b]Thou, O LORD, hast
become their God.

25“Now therefore, O LORD God, the
word that Thou hast spoken concerning
Thy servant and his house, confirm *it*
forever, and do as Thou hast spoken,
26 [a]that Thy name may be magnified
forever, by saying, ‘The LORD of hosts is
God over Israel’; and may the house of
Thy servant David be established before
Thee.
27“For Thou, O LORD of hosts, the
God of Israel, hast [1]made a revelation to
Thy servant, saying, ‘[a]I will build you a
house’; therefore Thy servant has found
[2]courage to pray this prayer to Thee.
28“And now, O Lord GOD, Thou art
God, and [a]Thy words are truth, and
Thou hast [1]promised this good thing to
Thy servant.
29“Now therefore, may it please Thee
to bless the house of Thy servant, that it
may continue forever before Thee. For
Thou, O Lord GOD, hast spoken; and
[a]with Thy blessing may the house of Thy
servant be blessed forever.”

David’s Triumphs

8 [a]NOW after this it came about that
David [1]defeated the Philistines and
subdued them; and David took [2]control
of the chief city from the hand of the
Philistines.
2 And [a]he [1]defeated [b]Moab, and
measured them with the line, making
them lie down on the ground; and he
measured two lines to put to death and
one full line to keep alive. And [c]the
Moabites became servants to David,
[d]bringing tribute.
3 Then David [1]defeated [a]Hadadezer,
the son of Rehob king of Zobah, as [b]he
went to restore his [2]rule at the [3]River.
4 And David captured from him
1,700 horsemen and 20,000 foot soldiers;
and David [a]hamstrung the chariot
horses, but reserved *enough* of them for
100 chariots.
5 And when [a]the Arameans of Damascus came to help Hadadezer, king of
Zobah, David [1]killed 22,000 Arameans.
6 Then David put garrisons among
the Arameans of Damascus, and [a]the
Arameans became servants to David,
bringing tribute. And [b]the LORD helped
David wherever he went.
7 And David took the shields of gold
which were [1]carried by the servants of
Hadadezer, and brought them to Jerusalem.
8 And from [1]Betah and from [a]Bero-
thai, cities of Hadadezer, King David
took a very large amount of bronze.
9 Now when Toi king of [a]Hamath
heard that David had [1]defeated all the
army of Hadadezer,
10 Toi sent [1]Joram his son to King
David to [2]greet him and bless him,
because he had fought against Hadadezer and [3]defeated him; for Hadadezer
[4]had been at war with Toi. And [5]*Joram*
brought with him articles of silver, of
gold and of bronze.
11 King David also [a]dedicated these
to the LORD, with the silver and gold
that he had dedicated from all the nations which he had subdued:
12 from [1]Aram and [a]Moab and [b]the
sons of Ammon and [c]the Philistines and
[d]Amalek, and from the spoil of Hadadezer, son of Rehob, king of Zobah.
13 So [a]David made a name *for himself*
when he returned from [1]killing 18,000
[2]Arameans in [b]the Valley of Salt.
14 And he put garrisons in Edom. In
all Edom he put garrisons, and [a]all the
Edomites became servants to David.
And [b]the LORD helped David wherever
he went.
15 So David reigned over all Israel;
and David [1]administered justice and
righteousness for all his people.
16 And [a]Joab the son of Zeruiah *was*
over the army, and [b]Jehoshaphat the son
of Ahilud *was* [c]recorder.
17 And [a]Zadok the son of Ahitub and
Ahimelech the son of Abiathar *were*
[b]priests, and Seraiah *was* [c]secretary.
18 And [a]Benaiah the son of Jehoiada
[1]was over the [b]Cherethites and the Pelethites; and David’s sons were [2c]chief
ministers.

David’s Kindness to Mephibosheth

9 THEN David said, “Is there yet
[1]anyone left of the house of Saul,
[a]that I may show him kindness for
Jonathan’s sake?”
2 Now there was a servant of the
house of Saul whose name was Ziba, and
they called him to David; and the king
said to him, “Are you [a]Ziba?” And he
said, “*I am* your servant.”
3 And the king said, “Is there not yet
anyone of the house of Saul to whom I
may show the [a]kindness of God?” And
Ziba said to the king, “[b]There is still a
son of Jonathan who is crippled in both
feet.”
4 So the king said to him, “Where is
he?” And Ziba said to the king, “Behold,
he is [a]in the house of Machir the son of
Ammiel in Lo-debar.”
5 Then King David sent and brought
him from the house of Machir the son of
Ammiel, from Lo-debar.
6 And [a]Mephibosheth, the son of
Jonathan the son of Saul, came to David
and [b]fell on his face and prostrated
himself. And David said, “Mephibosheth.” And he said, “Here is your
servant!”
7 And David said to him, “Do not
fear, for [a]I will surely show kindness to
you for the sake of your father Jonathan,
and [b]will restore to you all the [1]land of
your [2]grandfather Saul; and [c]you shall
[3]eat at my table regularly.”
8 Again he prostrated himself and
said, “What is your servant, that you
should regard [a]a dead dog like me?”

26 [a]Ps. 72:18, 19; Matt. 6:9
27 [1]Lit., *uncovered the ear of* [2]Lit., *his heart*
[a]2 Sam. 7:13
28 [1]Or, *spoken*
[a]Ex. 34:6; John 17:17
29 [a]Num. 6:24-26

1 [1]Lit., *smote* [2]Lit., *the bridle of the mother city*
[a]1 Chr. 18
2 [1]Lit., *smote*
[a]Num. 24:17
[b]1 Sam. 22:3, 4
[c]2 Sam. 8:6; 1 Kin. 4:21
[d]2 Kin. 3:4; 17:3
3 [1]Lit., *smote* [2]Lit., *hand* [3]I.e., Euphrates
[a]1 Sam. 14:47; 2 Sam. 10:16, 19
[b]2 Sam. 10:15-19
4 [a]Josh. 11:6, 9
5 [1]Lit., *smote*
[a]1 Kin. 11:23-25
6 [a]2 Sam. 8:2
[b]2 Sam. 3:18
7 [1]Lit., *on*
8 [1]In 1 Chr. 18:8, *Tibhath*
[a]Ezek. 47:16
9 [1]Lit., *smitten*
[a]1 Kin. 8:65; 2 Chr. 8:4
10 [1]In 1 Chr. 18:10, *Hadoram* [2]Lit., *ask him of his welfare* [3]Lit., *smitten* [4]Lit., *was a man of wars* [5]Lit., *there were in his hand*
11 [a]1 Kin. 7:51
12 [1]Some mss. read *Edom*
[a]2 Sam. 8:2 [b]2 Sam. 10:14 [c]2 Sam. 5:17-25 [d]1 Sam. 27:8; 30:17-20
13 [1]Lit., *smiting* [2]Some mss. read *Edom*
[a]2 Sam. 7:9 [b]2 Kin. 14:7
14 [a]Gen. 27:37-40; Num. 24:17, 18
[b]2 Sam. 8:6
15 [1]Lit., *was doing*
16 [a]1 Chr. 11:6
[b]1 Kin. 4:3 [c]2 Kin. 18:18, 37
17 [a]1 Chr. 6:4-8
[b]1 Chr. 16:39, 40
[c]2 Kin. 18:18
18 [1]Lit., *and the Cherethites* [2]Lit., *priests*
[a]1 Kin. 4:4
[b]1 Sam. 30:14; 2 Sam. 15:18; 20:7, 23; 1 Kin. 1:38, 44
[c]1 Chr. 18:17

1 [1]Lit., *he who is*
[a]1 Sam. 20:14-17, 42
2 [a]2 Sam. 16:1-4; 19:17, 29
3 [a]1 Sam. 20:14
[b]2 Sam. 4:4
4 [a]2 Sam. 17:27-29
6 [a]2 Sam. 16:4; 19:24-30 [b]1 Sam. 25:23
7 [1]Lit., *field* [2]Lit., *father* [3]Lit., *eat bread*
[a]2 Sam. 9:1, 3
[b]2 Sam. 12:8 [c]2 Sam. 19:28; 1 Kin. 2:7; 2 Kin. 25:29

8 [a]2 Sam. 16:9; 24:14

9 Then the king called Saul's servant Ziba, and said to him, "[a]All that belonged to Saul and to all his house I have given to your master's [1]grandson.

10 "And you and your sons and your servants shall cultivate the land for him, and you shall bring in *the produce* so that your master's grandson may have food; nevertheless [a]Mephibosheth your master's grandson [b]shall [1]eat at my table regularly." Now Ziba had fifteen sons and twenty servants.

11 Then Ziba said to the king, "According [a]to all that my lord the king commands his servant so your servant will do." So Mephibosheth ate at [1]David's table as one of the king's sons.

12 And Mephibosheth had a young son whose name was Mica. And all who lived in the house of Ziba were servants to Mephibosheth.

13 So Mephibosheth lived in Jerusalem, for [a]he ate at the king's table regularly. Now [b]he was lame in both feet.

Ammon and Aram Defeated

10 [a]NOW it happened afterwards that [b]the king of the Ammonites died, and Hanun his son became king in his place.

2 Then David said, "I will show kindness to Hanun the son of [a]Nahash, just as his father showed kindness to me." So David sent [1]some of his servants to console him concerning his father. But when David's servants came to the land of the Ammonites,

3 the princes of the Ammonites said to Hanun their lord, "[1]Do you think that David is honoring your father because he has sent consolers to you? [a]Has David not sent his servants to you in order to search the city, to spy it out and overthrow it?"

4 So Hanun took David's servants and [a]shaved off half of their beards, and [b]cut off their garments in the middle as far as their hips, and sent them away.

5 When they told *it* to David, he sent to meet them, for the men were greatly humiliated. And the king said, "[1]Stay at Jericho until your beards grow, and *then* return."

6 Now when the sons of Ammon saw that [a]they had become odious to David, the sons of Ammon sent and [b]hired the Arameans of [c]Beth-rehob and the [d]Arameans of Zobah, 20,000 foot soldiers, and the king of [e]Maacah with 1,000 men, and the men of Tob with 12,000 men.

7 When David heard *of it,* he sent Joab and all the army, the mighty men.

8 And the sons of Ammon came out and drew up in battle array [a]at the entrance of the [1]city, while the Arameans of Zobah and of Rehob and the men of [b]Tob and Maacah *were* by themselves in the field.

9 Now when Joab saw that [1]the battle was set against him in front and in the rear, he selected from all the choice men of Israel, and arrayed *them* against the Arameans.

10 But the remainder of the people he placed in the hand of Abishai his brother, and he arrayed *them* against the sons of Ammon.

11 And he said, "If the Arameans are too strong for me, then you shall help me, but if the sons of Ammon are too strong for you, then I will come to help you.

12 "[a]Be strong, and let us show ourselves courageous for the sake of our people and for the cities of our God; and [b]may the LORD do what is good in His sight."

13 So Joab and the people who were with him drew near to the battle against the Arameans, and [a]they fled before him.

14 When the sons of Ammon saw that the Arameans fled, they *also* fled before Abishai and entered the city. [a]Then Joab returned from *fighting* against the sons of Ammon and came to Jerusalem.

15 When the Arameans saw that they had been [1]defeated by Israel, they gathered themselves together.

16 [a]And Hadadezer sent and brought out the Arameans who were beyond the [1]River, and they came to Helam; and [b]Shobach the commander of the army of Hadadezer [2]led them.

17 Now when it was told David, he gathered all Israel together and crossed the Jordan, and came to Helam. And the Arameans arrayed themselves to meet David and fought against him.

18 But the Arameans fled before Israel, and David killed [a]700 charioteers of the Arameans and 40,000 horsemen and struck down Shobach the commander of their army, and he died there.

19 When all the kings, servants of Hadadezer, saw that they were [1]defeated by Israel, [a]they made peace with Israel and served them. So the Arameans feared to help the sons of Ammon anymore.

Bathsheba, David's Great Sin

11 [a]THEN it happened [1b]in the spring, at the time when kings go out *to battle,* that David sent Joab and his servants with him and all Israel, and they destroyed the sons of Ammon and [c]besieged Rabbah. But David stayed at Jerusalem.

2 Now when evening came David arose from his bed and walked around on [a]the roof of the king's house, and from the roof he saw a woman bathing; and the woman was very beautiful in appearance.

3 So David sent and inquired about the woman. And one said, "Is this not [a]Bathsheba, the daughter of Eliam, the wife of [b]Uriah the Hittite?"

4 And David sent messengers and took her, and when she came to him, [a]he lay with her; [b]and when she had purified herself from her uncleanness, she returned to her house.

---

9 [1]Lit., *son* [a]2 Sam. 16:4; 19:29

10 [1]Lit., *eat bread* [a]2 Sam. 9:7, 11, 13 [b]2 Sam. 19:28; 1 Kin. 2:7

11 [1]Lit., *my* [a]2 Sam. 16:1-4; 19:24-30

13 [a]2 Sam. 9:7, 11 [b]2 Sam. 9:3

1 [a]1 Chr. 19:1-19 [b]1 Sam. 11:1

2 [1]Lit., *by the hand of* [a]1 Sam. 11:1

3 [1]Lit., *In your eyes is David honoring* [a]Gen. 42:9, 16

4 [a]Is. 15:2; Jer. 41:5 [b]Is. 20:4

5 [1]Lit., *Return to*

6 [a]Gen. 34:30; 1 Sam. 27:12 [b]2 Sam. 8:3, 5; 2 Kin. 7:6 [c]Judg. 18:28 [d]2 Sam. 8:3 [e]Deut. 3:14

8 [1]Lit., *gate* [a]1 Chr. 19:9 [b]Judg. 11:3, 5

9 [1]Lit., *the faces of the battle were against*

12 [a]Deut. 31:6; Josh. 1:6; 1 Cor. 16:13 [b]1 Sam. 3:18

13 [a]1 Kin. 20:13-21

14 [a]2 Sam. 11:1

15 [1]Lit., *smitten before*

16 [1]I.e., Euphrates [2]Lit., *before* [a]2 Sam. 8:3-8 [b]1 Chr. 19:16

18 [a]1 Chr. 19:18

19 [1]Lit., *smitten before* [a]2 Sam. 8:6

1 [1]Lit., *at the return of the year* [a]1 Chr. 20:1 [b]2 Sam. 10:14; 1 Kin. 20:22, 26 [c]2 Sam. 12:26-29; Jer. 49:2, 3; Amos 1:14

2 [a]Deut. 22:8; 1 Sam. 9:25; Matt. 24:17; Acts 10:9

3 [a]1 Chr. 3:5 [b]2 Sam. 23:39

4 [a]Ps. 51:title; James 1:14, 15 [b]Lev. 12:2-5; 15:18-28; 18:19

5 And the woman conceived; and she sent and told David, and said, "[a]I am pregnant."

6 Then David sent to Joab, *saying,* "Send me Uriah the Hittite." So Joab sent Uriah to David.

7 When Uriah came to him, [a]David asked concerning the welfare of Joab and [1]the people and the state of the war.

8 Then David said to Uriah, "Go down to your house, and [a]wash your feet." And Uriah went out of the king's house, and a present from the king [1]was sent out after him.

9 But Uriah slept [a]at the door of the king's house with all the servants of his lord, and did not go down to his house.

10 Now when they told David, saying, "Uriah did not go down to his house," David said to Uriah, "Have you not come from a journey? Why did you not go down to your house?"

11 And Uriah said to David, "[a]The ark and Israel and Judah are staying in [1]temporary shelters, and my lord Joab and [b]the servants of my lord are camping in the open field. Shall I then go to my house to eat and to drink and to lie with my wife? By your life and the life of your soul, I will not do this thing."

12 Then David said to Uriah, "[a]Stay here today also, and tomorrow I will let you go." So Uriah remained in Jerusalem that day and the [1]next.

13 Now David called him, and he ate and drank before him, and he [a]made him drunk; and in the evening he went out to lie on his bed [b]with his lord's servants, but he did not go down to his house.

14 Now it came about in the morning that David [a]wrote a letter to Joab, and sent *it* by the hand of Uriah.

15 And [a]he had written in the letter, saying, "[1]Place Uriah in the front line of the [2]fiercest battle and withdraw from him, [b]so that he may be struck down and die."

16 So it was as Joab kept watch on the city, that he put Uriah at the place where he knew there *were* valiant men.

17 And the men of the city went out and fought against Joab, and some of the people among David's servants fell; and [a]Uriah the Hittite also died.

18 Then Joab sent and reported to David all the events of the war.

19 And he charged the messenger, saying, "When you have finished telling all the events of the war to the king,

20 and if it happens that the king's wrath rises and he says to you, 'Why did you go so near to the city to fight? Did you not know that they would shoot from the wall?

21 'Who [a]struck down Abimelech the son of Jerubbesheth? Did not a woman throw an upper millstone on him from the wall so that he died at Thebez? Why did you go so near the wall?'—then you shall say, 'Your servant Uriah the Hittite is dead also.' "

5 [a]Lev. 20:10; Deut. 22:22
7 [1]Lit., *welfare of* [a]Gen. 37:14; 1 Sam. 17:22
8 [1]Lit., *went out* [a]Gen. 43:24; Luke 7:44
9 [a]1 Kin. 14:27, 28
11 [1]Or, *booths* [a]2 Sam. 7:2, 6 [b]2 Sam. 20:6
12 [1]Lit., *morrow* [a]Job 20:12-14
13 [a]Prov. 20:1; 23:29-35 [b]2 Sam. 11:9
14 [a]1 Kin. 21:8-10
15 [1]Lit., *Give* [2]Lit., *strong* [a]Eccl. 8:11; Jer. 17:9 [b]2 Sam. 12:9
17 [a]2 Sam. 11:21
21 [a]Judg. 9:50-54
23 [1]Lit., *were upon*
25 [1]Lit., *be evil in your sight*
26 [a]Gen. 50:10; Deut. 34:8; 1 Sam. 31:13
27 [1]Lit., *gathered* [a]2 Sam. 12:9 [b]Ps. 51:4, 5
1 [1]Lit., *said to him* [a]2 Sam. 7:2, 4, 17 [b]Ps. 51:title
3 [1]Lit., *morsel* [a]2 Sam. 11:3
4 [1]Lit., *spared*
5 [1]Lit., *is a son of death* [a]1 Sam. 26:16
6 [a]Ex. 22:1; Luke 19:8
7 [a]1 Kin. 20:42 [b]1 Sam. 16:13
8 [1]Lit., *bosom* [a]2 Sam. 9:7

22 So the messenger departed and came and reported to David all that Joab had sent him *to tell.*

23 And the messenger said to David, "The men prevailed against us and came out against us in the field, but we [1]pressed them as far as the entrance of the gate.

24 "Moreover, the archers shot at your servants from the wall; so some of the king's servants are dead, and your servant Uriah the Hittite is also dead."

25 Then David said to the messenger, "Thus you shall say to Joab, 'Do not let this thing [1]displease you, for the sword devours one as well as another; make your battle against the city stronger and overthrow it'; and *so* encourage him."

26 Now when the wife of Uriah heard that Uriah her husband was dead, [a]she mourned for her husband.

27 When the *time of* mourning was over, David sent and [1]brought her to his house and [a]she became his wife; then she bore him a son. But [b]the thing that David had done was evil in the sight of the LORD.

Nathan Rebukes David

12 THEN the LORD sent [a]Nathan to David. And [b]he came to him, and [1]said,

"There were two men in one city,
the one rich and the other poor.
2 "The rich man had a great many
flocks and herds.
3 "But the poor man had nothing
except [a]one little ewe lamb
Which he bought and nourished;
And it grew up together with him
and his children.
It would eat of his [1]bread and
drink of his cup and lie in his
bosom,
And was like a daughter to him.
4 "Now a traveler came to the rich
man,
And he [1]was unwilling to take
from his own flock or his own
herd,
To prepare for the wayfarer who
had come to him;
Rather he took the poor man's
ewe lamb and prepared it for the
man who had come to him."

5 Then David's anger burned greatly against the man, and he said to Nathan, "As the LORD lives, surely the man who has done this [1a]deserves to die.

6 "And he must make restitution for the lamb [a]fourfold, because he did this thing and had no compassion."

7 Nathan then said to David, "[a]You are the man! Thus says the LORD God of Israel, '[b]It is I who anointed you king over Israel and it is I who delivered you from the hand of Saul.

8 'I also gave you [a]your master's house and your master's wives into your [1]care, and I gave you the house of Israel and Judah; and if *that had been* too little, I would have added to you many more things like these!

9 'Why [a]have you despised the word
of the LORD by doing evil in His sight?
[b]You have struck down Uriah the Hittite
with the sword, [c]have taken his wife to
be your wife, and have killed him with
the sword of the sons of Ammon.
10 'Now therefore, [a]the sword shall
never depart from your house, because
you have despised Me and have taken
the wife of Uriah the Hittite to be your
wife.'
11 "Thus says the LORD, 'Behold, I will
raise up evil against you from your own
household; [a]I will even take your wives
before your eyes, and give *them* to your
companion, and he shall lie with your
wives in [1]broad daylight.
12 'Indeed [a]you did it secretly, but [b]I
will do this thing before all Israel, and
[1]under the sun.' "
13 Then David said to Nathan, "[a]I
have sinned against the LORD." And
Nathan said to David, "The LORD also
has [1b]taken away your sin; you shall not
die.
14 "However, because by this deed you
have [a]given occasion to the enemies of
the LORD to blaspheme, the child also
that is born to you shall surely die."
15 So Nathan went to his house.

Loss of a Child

Then the LORD struck the child that
Uriah's [1]widow bore to David, so that he
was *very* sick.
16 David therefore inquired of God
for the child; and David [a]fasted and
went and [b]lay all night on the ground.
17 And [a]the elders of his household
stood beside him in order to raise him
up from the ground, but he was unwilling and would not eat food with them.
18 Then it happened on the seventh
day that the child died. And the servants
of David were afraid to tell him that the
child was dead, for they said, "Behold,
while the child was *still* alive, we spoke
to him and he did not listen to our voice.
How then can we tell him that the child
is dead, since he might do *himself*
harm!"
19 But when David saw that his servants were whispering together, David
perceived that the child was dead; so
David said to his servants, "Is the child
dead?" And they said, "He is dead."
20 So David arose from the ground,
[a]washed, anointed *himself*, and changed
his clothes; and he came into the house
of the LORD and [b]worshiped. Then he
came to his own house, and when he
requested, they set food before him and
he ate.
21 Then his servants said to him,
"What is this thing that you have done?
[1]While the child was alive, you fasted
and wept; but when the child died, you
arose and ate food."
22 And he said, "While the child was
still alive, [a]I fasted and wept; for I said,
'[b]Who knows, the LORD may be gracious
to me, that the child may live.'
23 "But now he has died; why should I
fast? Can I bring him back again? [a]I
shall go to him, but [b]he will not return to
me."

Solomon Born

24 Then David comforted his wife
Bathsheba, and went in to her and lay
with her; and she gave birth to a son,
and [1a]he named him Solomon. Now the
LORD loved him
25 and sent *word* through Nathan the
prophet, and he named him [1]Jedidiah
for the LORD's sake.

War Again

26 [a]Now Joab fought against [b]Rabbah
of the sons of Ammon, and captured the
royal city.
27 And Joab sent messengers to David and said, "I have fought against
Rabbah, I have even captured the city of
waters.
28 "Now therefore, gather the rest of
the people together and camp against
the city and capture it, lest I capture the
city myself and it be named after me."
29 So David gathered all the people
and went to Rabbah, fought against it,
and captured it.
30 Then [a]he took the crown of [1]their
king from his head; and its weight *was* a
talent of gold, and *in it* [2]*was* a precious
stone; and it was *placed* on David's
head. And he brought out the spoil of
the city in great amounts.
31 He also brought out the people
who were in it, and [a]set *them* under saws,
sharp iron instruments, and iron axes,
and made them pass through the brick-
kiln. And thus he did to all the cities of
the sons of Ammon. Then David and all
the people returned *to* Jerusalem.

Amnon and Tamar

13 NOW it was after this that [a]Ab-
salom the son of David had a
beautiful sister whose name was [b]Tamar,
and [c]Amnon the son of David loved her.
2 And Amnon was so frustrated because of his sister Tamar that he made
himself ill, for she was a virgin, and it
seemed [1]hard to Amnon to do anything
to her.
3 But Amnon had a friend whose
name was Jonadab, the son of [1a]Shim-
eah, David's brother; and Jonadab was a
very shrewd man.
4 And he said to him, "O son of the
king, why are you so depressed morning
after morning? Will you not tell me?"
Then Amnon said to him, "I am in love
with Tamar, the sister of my brother
Absalom."
5 Jonadab then said to him, "Lie
down on your bed and pretend to be ill;
when your father comes to see you, say
to him, 'Please let my sister Tamar come
and give me *some* food to eat, and let her
prepare the food in my sight, that I may
see *it* and eat from her hand.' "

9 [a]1 Sam. 15:23, 26 [b]2 Sam. 11:14-17 [c]2 Sam. 11:27
10 [a]2 Sam. 13:28; 18:14; 1 Kin. 2:25
11 [1]Lit., *the sight of this sun* [a]Deut. 28:30; 2 Sam. 16:21, 22
12 [1]Lit., *before* [a]2 Sam. 11:4-15 [b]2 Sam. 16:22
13 [1]Lit., *caused your sin to pass away* [a]1 Sam. 15:24, 30; 2 Sam. 24:10; Luke 18:13 [b]Lev. 20:10; 24:17; Prov. 28:13; Mic. 7:18
14 [a]Is. 52:5; Rom. 2:24
15 [1]Lit., *wife*
16 [a]Neh. 1:4 [b]2 Sam. 13:31
17 [a]Gen. 24:2
20 [a]Ruth 3:3; Matt. 6:17 [b]Ps. 95:6-8; 103:1, 8-17; Prov. 3:7
21 [1]Lit., *On account of*
22 [a]Is. 38:1-3 [b]Jon. 3:9
23 [a]Gen. 37:35 [b]Job 7:8-10
24 [1]Some mss. read *she* [a]1 Chr. 22:9; Matt. 1:6
25 [1]I.e., beloved of the LORD
26 [a]1 Chr. 20:1-3 [b]Deut. 3:11
30 [1]Or, *Malcam;* c.f. Zeph. 1:5 [2]Or, *were precious stones* [a]1 Chr. 20:2
31 [a]1 Chr. 20:3; Heb. 11:37
1 [a]2 Sam. 3:2, 3; 1 Chr. 3:2 [b]1 Chr. 3:9 [c]2 Sam. 3:2
2 [1]Lit., *hard in Amnon's eyes*
3 [1]In 1 Sam. 16:9, *Shammah;* in 1 Chr. 2:13, *Shimea* [a]1 Sam. 16:9

6 So Amnon lay down and pretended
to be ill; when the king came to see him,
Amnon said to the king, "Please let my
sister Tamar come and [a]make me a
couple of cakes in my sight, that I may
eat from her hand."
7 Then David sent to the house for
Tamar, saying, "Go now to your brother
Amnon's house, and prepare food for
him."
8 So Tamar went to her brother
Amnon's house, and he was lying down.
And she took dough, kneaded *it,* made
cakes in his sight, and baked the cakes.
9 And she took the pan and [1]dished
them out before him, but he refused to
eat. And Amnon said, "[a]Have everyone
go out from me." So everyone went out
from him.
10 Then Amnon said to Tamar,
"Bring the food into the [1]bedroom, that
I may eat from your hand." So Tamar
took the cakes which she had made and
brought them into the bedroom to her
brother Amnon.
11 When she brought *them* to him to
eat, he [a]took hold of her and said to her,
"Come, lie with me, my sister."
12 But she answered him, "No, my
brother, do not violate me, for [a]such a
thing is not done in Israel; do not do this
[b]disgraceful thing!
13 "As for me, where could I [1]get rid of
my reproach? And as for you, you will
be like one of the [2]fools in Israel. Now
therefore, please speak to the king, for
[a]he will not withhold me from you."
14 However, he would not listen to
[1]her; since he was stronger than she, he
[a]violated her and lay with her.
15 Then Amnon hated her with a very
great hatred; for the hatred with which
he hated her was greater than the love
with which he had loved her. And Amnon said to her, "Get up, go away!"
16 But she said to him, "No, because
this wrong in sending me away is greater
than the other that you have done to
me!" Yet he would not listen to her.
17 Then he called his young man who
attended him and said, "Now throw this
woman out of my *presence,* and lock the
door behind her."
18 Now she had on [a]a [1]long-sleeved
garment; for in this manner the virgin
daughters of the king dressed themselves
in robes. Then his attendant took her out
and locked the door behind her.
19 And [a]Tamar put [1]ashes on her
head, and [b]tore her [2]long-sleeved garment which *was* on her; and [c]she put her
hand on her head and went away, crying
aloud as she went.
20 Then Absalom her brother said to
her, "Has Amnon your brother been
with you? But now keep silent, my sister,
he is your brother; do not take this
matter to heart." So Tamar remained
and was desolate in her brother Absalom's house.
21 Now when King David heard of all
these matters, he was very angry.

22 But Absalom did not speak to
Amnon [a]either good or bad; for [b]Absa-
lom hated Amnon because he had violated his sister Tamar.
23 Now it came about after two full
years that Absalom [a]had sheepshearers
in Baal-hazor, which is near Ephraim,
and Absalom invited all the king's sons.

Absalom Avenges Tamar

24 And Absalom came to the king and
said, "Behold now, your servant has
sheepshearers; please let the king and his
servants go with your servant."
25 But the king said to Absalom, "No,
my son, we should not all go, lest we be
burdensome to you." Although he
[1]urged him, he would not go, but blessed
him.
26 Then [a]Absalom said, "If not,
please let my brother Amnon go with
us." And the king said to him, "Why
should he go with you?"
27 But when Absalom [1]urged him, he
let Amnon and all the king's sons go
with him.
28 And Absalom commanded his servants, saying, "See now, [a]when Amnon's
heart is merry with wine, and when I say
to you, 'Strike Amnon,' then put him to
death. Do not fear; have not I myself
commanded you? Be courageous and be
[1]valiant."
29 And the servants of Absalom did
to Amnon just as Absalom had commanded. Then all the king's sons arose
and each mounted [a]his mule and fled.
30 Now it was while they were on the
way that the report came to David,
saying, "Absalom has struck down all
the king's sons, and not one of them is
left."
31 Then the king arose, [a]tore his
clothes and [b]lay on the ground; and all
his servants were standing by with
clothes torn.
32 And [a]Jonadab, the son of Shimeah,
David's brother, [1]responded, "Do not let
my lord [2]suppose they have put to death
all the young men, the king's sons, for
Amnon alone is dead; because by the
[3]intent of Absalom this has been determined since the day that he violated his
sister Tamar.
33 "Now therefore, do not let my lord
the king [a]take the report to [1]heart,
namely, 'all the king's sons are dead,' for
only Amnon is dead."
34 Now [a]Absalom had fled. And [b]the
young man who was the watchman
raised his eyes and looked, and behold,
many people were coming from the road
behind him by the side of the mountain.
35 And Jonadab said to the king,
"Behold, the king's sons have come;
according to your servant's word, so it
happened."
36 And it came about as soon as he
had finished speaking, that behold, the
king's sons came and lifted their voices
and wept; and also the king and all his
servants wept [1]very bitterly.

6 [a]Gen. 18:6
9 [1]Lit., *poured* [a]Gen. 45:1
10 [1]Or, *inner room*
11 [a]Gen. 39:12
12 [a]Lev. 20:17 [b]Judg. 19:23; 20:6
13 [1]Lit., *cause to go* [2]Or, *disgraceful ones* [a]Gen. 20:12
14 [1]Lit., *her voice* [a]Lev. 18:9; Deut. 22:25; 27:22; 2 Sam. 12:11
18 [1]Lit., *a varicolored tunic* [a]Gen. 37:3, 23
19 [1]Or, *dust* [2]Lit., *varicolored tunic* [a]1 Sam. 4:12; Esth. 4:1 [b]Gen. 37:29; 2 Sam. 1:11 [c]Jer. 2:37
22 [a]Gen. 31:24 [b]Lev. 19:17; 1 John 2:9, 11; 3:10, 12, 15
23 [a]1 Sam. 25:7
25 [1]Lit., *broke through*
26 [a]2 Sam. 3:27; 11:13-15
27 [1]Lit., *broke through*
28 [1]Lit., *sons of valor* [a]Judg. 19:6, 9, 22; 1 Sam. 25:36-38
29 [a]2 Sam. 18:9; 1 Kin. 1:33, 38
31 [a]2 Sam. 1:11 [b]2 Sam. 12:16
32 [1]Lit., *answered and said* [2]Lit., *say* [3]Lit., *mouth* [a]2 Sam. 13:3-5
33 [1]Lit., *his heart* [a]2 Sam. 19:19
34 [a]2 Sam. 13:37, 38 [b]2 Sam. 18:24
36 [1]Lit., *with a very great weeping*

37 Now [a]Absalom fled and went to [b]Talmai the son of Ammihud, the king of [c]Geshur. And *David* mourned for his son every day.

38 [a]So Absalom had fled and gone to Geshur, and was there three years.

39 And *the heart of* King David longed to go out to Absalom; for [a]he was comforted concerning Amnon, since he was dead.

The Woman of Tekoa

14 NOW Joab the son of Zeruiah perceived that [a]the king's heart *was inclined* toward Absalom.

2 So Joab sent to [a]Tekoa and [1]brought a wise woman from there and said to her, "Please pretend to be a mourner, and put on mourning garments now, and do not [b]anoint yourself with oil, but be like a woman who has been mourning for the dead many days;

3 then go to the king and speak to him in this manner." So Joab put [a]the words in her mouth.

4 Now when the woman of Tekoa [1]spoke to the king, she fell on her face to the ground and [a]prostrated herself and said, "[b]Help, O king."

5 And the king said to her, "What is your trouble?" And she [1]answered, "Truly I am a widow, for my husband is dead.

6 "And your maidservant had two sons, but the two of them struggled together in the field, and there was no [1]one to separate them, so one struck the other and killed him.

7 "Now behold, [a]the whole family has risen against your maidservant, and they say, 'Hand over the one who struck his brother, that we may put him to death for the life of his brother whom he killed, [b]and destroy the heir also.' Thus they will extinguish my coal which is left, so as to [1]leave my husband neither name nor remnant on the face of the earth."

8 Then the king said to the woman, "Go to your house, and I will give orders concerning you."

9 And the woman of Tekoa said to the king, "O my lord, the king, [a]the iniquity is on me and my father's house, but [b]the king and his throne are guiltless."

10 So the king said, "Whoever speaks to you, bring him to me, and he will not touch you anymore."

11 Then she said, "Please let the king remember the LORD your God, [a]*so that* the avenger of blood may not continue to destroy, lest they destroy my son." And he said, "[b]As the LORD lives, not one hair of your son shall fall to the ground."

12 Then the woman said, "Please let your maidservant speak a word to my lord the king." And he said, "Speak."

13 And the woman said, "[a]Why then have you planned such a thing against the people of God? For in speaking this word the king is as one who is guilty, *in that* the king does not bring back [b]his banished one.

14 "For [a]we shall surely die and are [b]like water spilled on the ground which cannot be gathered up again. Yet God does not take away life, but plans [1]ways so that [c]the banished one may not be cast out from him.

15 "Now [1]the reason I have come to speak this word to my lord the king is because the people have made me afraid; so your maidservant said, 'Let me now speak to the king, perhaps the king will perform the [2]request of his maidservant.

16 'For the king will hear [1]and deliver his maidservant from the [2]hand of the man who would destroy [3]both me and my son from [a]the inheritance of God.'

17 "Then your maidservant said, 'Please let the word of my lord the king be [1]comforting, for as [a]the angel of God, so is my lord the king to discern good and evil. And may the LORD your God be with you.' "

18 Then the king answered and said to the woman, "Please do not hide anything from me that I am about to ask you." And the woman said, "Let my lord the king please speak."

19 So the king said, "Is the hand of Joab with you in all this?" And the woman answered and said, "As your soul lives, my lord the king, no one can turn to the right or to the left from anything that my lord the king has spoken. Indeed, it was [a]your servant Joab who commanded me, and it was he who put all these words in the mouth of your maidservant;

20 in order to change the appearance of things your servant Joab has done this thing. But my lord is wise, [a]like the wisdom of the angel of God, to know all that is in the earth."

Absalom Is Recalled

21 Then the king said to Joab, "Behold now, [a]I will surely do this thing; go therefore, bring back the young man Absalom."

22 And Joab fell on his face to the ground, prostrated himself and blessed the king; then Joab said, "Today your servant knows that I have found favor in your sight, O my lord, the king, in that the king has performed the [1]request of his servant."

23 So Joab arose and went to [a]Geshur, and brought Absalom to Jerusalem.

24 However the king said, "Let him turn to [a]his own house, and let him not see my face." So Absalom turned to his own house and did not see the king's face.

25 Now in all Israel was no one as handsome as Absalom, so highly praised; [a]from the sole of his foot to the crown of his head there was no defect in him.

26 And when he [a]cut the hair of his head (and it was at the end of every year

37 [a]2 Sam. 13:34 [b]2 Sam. 3:3 [c]2 Sam. 14:23, 32
38 [a]2 Sam. 13:34
39 [a]2 Sam. 12:19-23
1 [a]2 Sam. 13:39
2 [1]Lit., *took* [a]2 Sam. 23:26; 2 Chr. 11:6; Amos 1:1 [b]2 Sam. 12:20
3 [a]2 Sam. 14:19
4 [1]Many mss. and ancient versions read *came* [a]1 Sam. 25:23 [b]2 Kin. 6:26-28
5 [1]Lit., *said*
6 [1]Lit., *deliverer between*
7 [1]Lit., *set* [a]Num. 35:19; Deut. 19:12, 13 [b]Matt. 21:38
9 [a]Gen. 43:9; 1 Sam. 25:24 [b]1 Kin. 2:33
11 [a]Num. 35:19, 21; Deut. 19:4-10 [b]1 Sam. 14:45; 1 Kin. 1:52; Matt. 10:30
13 [a]2 Sam. 12:7; 1 Kin. 20:40-42 [b]2 Sam. 13:37, 38
14 [1]Lit., *devices* [a]Job 30:23; 34:15; Heb. 9:27 [b]Ps. 58:7 [c]Num. 35:15, 25, 28
15 [1]Lit., *that* [2]Lit., *word*
16 [1]Lit., *to* [2]Lit., *palm* [3]Lit., *together* [a]Deut. 32:9; 1 Sam. 26:19
17 [1]Lit., *for rest* [a]1 Sam. 29:9; 2 Sam. 14:20; 19:27
19 [a]2 Sam. 14:3
20 [a]2 Sam. 14:17; 19:27
21 [a]2 Sam. 14:11
22 [1]Lit., *word*
23 [a]Deut. 3:14; 2 Sam. 13:37, 38
24 [a]2 Sam. 13:20
25 [a]Deut. 28:35; Job 2:7; Is. 1:6
26 [a]Ezek. 44:20

that he cut *it,* for it was heavy on him so
he cut it), he weighed the hair of his head
at 200 shekels by the king's weight.
27 And [a]to Absalom there were born
three sons, and one daughter whose
name was [b]Tamar; she was a woman of
beautiful appearance.
28 Now Absalom lived two full years
in Jerusalem, [a]and did not see the king's
face.
29 Then Absalom sent for Joab, to
send him to the king, but he would not
come to him. So he sent again a second
time, but he would not come.
30 Therefore he said to his servants,
"See, [a]Joab's [1]field is next to mine, and
he has barley there; go and set it on
fire." So Absalom's servants set the [1]field
on fire.
31 Then Joab arose, came to Absalom
at his house and said to him, "Why have
your servants set my [1]field on fire?"
32 And Absalom [1]answered Joab,
"Behold, I sent for you, saying, 'Come
here, that I may send you to the king, to
say, "Why have I come from Geshur? It
would be better for me still to be
there." ' Now therefore, let me see the
king's face; [a]and if there is iniquity in
me, let him put me to death."
33 So when Joab came to the king and
told him, he called for Absalom. Thus he
came to the king and prostrated himself
on his face to the ground before the
king, and [a]the king kissed Absalom.

Absalom's Conspiracy

15 NOW it came about after this
that [a]Absalom provided for himself a chariot and horses, and fifty men
as runners before him.
2 And Absalom used to rise early
and [a]stand beside the way to the gate;
and it happened that when any man had
a suit to come to the king for judgment,
Absalom would call to him and say,
"From what city are you?" And he
would say, "Your servant is from one of
the tribes of Israel."
3 Then Absalom would say to him,
"See, [a]your [1]claims are good and right,
but no man listens to you on the part of
the king."
4 Moreover, Absalom would say,
"[a]Oh that one would appoint me judge
in the land, then every man who has any
suit or cause could come to me, and I
would give him justice."
5 And it happened that when a man
came near to prostrate himself before
him, he would put out his hand and take
hold of him and [a]kiss him.
6 And in this manner Absalom dealt
with all Israel who came to the king for
judgment; [a]so Absalom stole away the
hearts of the men of Israel.
7 Now it came about at the end of
[1]forty years that Absalom said to the
king, "Please let me go and pay my vow
which I have vowed to the LORD, in
[a]Hebron.

27 [a]2 Sam. 18:18 [b]2 Sam. 13:1
28 [a]2 Sam. 14:24
30 [1]Lit., *portion* [a]Judg. 15:3-5
31 [1]Lit., *portion*
32 [1]Lit., *said to* [a]1 Sam. 20:8; Prov. 28:13
33 [a]Gen. 33:4; Luke 15:20
1 [a]1 Kin. 1:5
2 [a]Ruth 4:1; 2 Sam. 19:8
3 [1]Lit., *words* [a]Prov. 12:2
4 [a]Judg. 9:29
5 [a]2 Sam. 14:33; 20:9
6 [a]Rom. 16:18
7 [1]Some ancient versions render *four* [a]2 Sam. 3:2, 3
8 [a]2 Sam. 13:37, 38 [b]Gen. 28:20, 21
10 [a]1 Kin. 1:34; 2 Kin. 9:13
11 [1]Lit., *in their integrity* [a]1 Sam. 9:13 [b]1 Sam. 22:15
12 [a]2 Sam. 15:31 [b]Josh. 15:51 [c]Ps. 3:1
13 [1]Lit., *after* [a]Judg. 9:3; 2 Sam. 15:6
14 [a]2 Sam. 12:11; Ps. 3:title
16 [1]Lit., *at his feet* [a]2 Sam. 16:21, 22
17 [1]Lit., *at his feet*
18 [1]Lit., *at his feet* [a]2 Sam. 8:18 [b]1 Sam. 23:13; 25:13; 30:1, 9
19 [a]2 Sam. 18:2
20 [1]Or, *faithfulness* [a]1 Sam. 23:13 [b]2 Sam. 2:6
21 [a]Ruth 1:16, 17; Prov. 17:17
23 [a]1 Kin. 15:13; 2 Chr. 29:16 [b]2 Sam. 15:28; 16:2

8 "For your servant [a]vowed a vow
while I was living at Geshur in Aram,
saying, '[b]If the LORD shall indeed bring
me back to Jerusalem, then I will serve
the LORD.' "
9 And the king said to him, "Go in
peace." So he arose and went to Hebron.
10 But Absalom sent spies throughout
all the tribes of Israel, saying, "As soon
as you hear the sound of the trumpet,
then you shall say, '[a]Absalom is king in
Hebron.' "
11 Then two hundred men went with
Absalom from Jerusalem, [a]who were
invited and [b]went [1]innocently, and they
did not know anything.
12 And Absalom sent for [a]Ahithophel
the Gilonite, David's counselor, from his
city [b]Giloh, while he was offering the
sacrifices. And the conspiracy was
strong, for [c]the people increased continually with Absalom.

David Flees Jerusalem

13 Then a messenger came to David,
saying, "[a]The hearts of the men of Israel
are [1]with Absalom."
14 And David said to all his servants
who were with him at Jerusalem, "[a]Arise
and let us flee, for *otherwise* none of us
shall escape from Absalom. Go in haste,
lest he overtake us quickly and bring
down calamity on us and strike the city
with the edge of the sword."
15 Then the king's servants said to the
king, "Behold, your servants *are ready to
do* whatever my lord the king chooses."
16 So the king went out and all his
household [1]with him. But [a]the king left
ten concubines to keep the house.
17 And the king went out and all the
people [1]with him, and they stopped at
the last house.
18 Now all his servants passed on
beside him, [a]all the Cherethites, all the
Pelethites, and all the Gittites, [b]six
hundred men who had come [1]with him
from Gath, passed on before the king.
19 Then the king said to [a]Ittai the
Gittite, "Why will you also go with us?
Return and remain with the king, for
you are a foreigner and also an exile;
return to your own place.
20 "You came *only* yesterday, and shall
I today make you wander with us, while
[a]I go where I will? Return and take back
your brothers; [b]mercy and [1]truth be
with you."
21 But Ittai answered the king and
said, "As the LORD lives, and as my lord
the king lives, surely [a]wherever my lord
the king may be, whether for death or
for life, there also your servant will be."
22 Therefore David said to Ittai, "Go
and pass over." So Ittai the Gittite
passed over with all his men and all the
little ones who *were* with him.
23 While all the country was weeping
with a loud voice, all the people passed
over. The king also passed over [a]the
brook Kidron, and all the people passed
over toward [b]the way of the wilderness.

24 Now behold, [a]Zadok also *came,* and all the Levites with him [b]carrying the ark of the covenant of God. And they set down the ark of God, and [c]Abiathar came up until all the people had finished passing from the city.

25 And the king said to Zadok, "Return the ark of God to the city. If I find favor in the sight of the LORD, then [a]He will bring me back again, and show me both it and [b]His habitation.

26 "But if He should say thus, '[a]I have no delight in you,' behold, here I am, [b]let Him do to me as seems good [1]to Him."

27 The king said also to Zadok the priest, "Are you *not* [a]a seer? Return to the city in peace and your [b]two sons with you, your son Ahimaaz and Jonathan the son of Abiathar.

28 "See, I am going to wait [a]at the fords of the wilderness until word comes from you to inform me."

29 Therefore Zadok and Abiathar returned the ark of God to Jerusalem and remained there.

30 And David went up the ascent of the *Mount of* Olives, and wept as he went, and [a]his head was covered and he walked [b]barefoot. Then all the people who were with him each covered his head and went up weeping as they went.

31 Now someone told David, saying, "[a]Ahithophel is among the conspirators with Absalom." And David said, "O LORD, I pray, [b]make the counsel of Ahithophel foolishness."

32 It happened as David was coming to the summit, where God was worshiped, that behold, Hushai the [a]Archite met him with his [1]coat torn, and [2]dust on his head.

33 And David said to him, "If you pass over with me, then you will be [a]a burden to me.

34 "But if you return to the city, and [a]say to Absalom, 'I will be your servant, O king; as I have been your father's servant in time past, so I will now be your servant,' then you can thwart the counsel of Ahithophel for me.

35 "And are not Zadok and Abiathar the priests with you there? So it shall be that [a]whatever you hear from the king's house, you shall report to Zadok and Abiathar the priests.

36 "Behold [a]their two sons are with them there, Ahimaaz, Zadok's son and Jonathan, Abiathar's son; and [b]by them you shall send me everything that you hear."

37 So Hushai, [a]David's friend, came into the city, and [b]Absalom came into Jerusalem.

Ziba, a False Servant

16 NOW when David had passed [a]a little beyond the summit, behold, [b]Ziba the servant of Mephibosheth met him [c]with a couple of saddled donkeys, and on them *were* two hundred loaves of bread, a hundred clusters of raisins, a hundred summer fruits, and a jug of wine.

2 And the king said to Ziba, "Why do you have these?" And Ziba said, "[a]The donkeys are for the king's household to ride, and the bread and summer fruit for the young men to eat, and the wine, [b]for whoever is faint in the wilderness to drink."

3 Then the king said, "And where is [a]your master's son?" And [b]Ziba said to the king, "Behold, he is staying in Jerusalem, for he said, 'Today the house of Israel will restore the kingdom of my father to me.' "

4 So the king said to Ziba, "Behold, all that belongs to Mephibosheth is yours." And Ziba said, "I prostrate myself; let me find favor in your sight, O my lord, the king!"

David Is Cursed

5 When King David came to [a]Bahurim, behold, there came out from there a man of the family of the house of Saul [b]whose name was Shimei, the son of Gera; he came out [c]cursing continually as he came.

6 And he threw stones at David and at all the servants of King David; and all the people and all the mighty men were at his right hand and at his left.

7 And thus Shimei said when he cursed, "Get out, get out, [a]you man of bloodshed, and worthless fellow!

8 "[a]The LORD has returned upon you all [b]the bloodshed of the house of Saul, in whose place you have reigned; and the LORD has given the kingdom into the hand of your son Absalom. And behold, you are *taken* in your own evil, for you are a man of bloodshed!"

9 Then [a]Abishai the son of Zeruiah said to the king, "Why should [b]this dead dog [c]curse my lord the king? Let me go over now, and [1]cut off his head."

10 But the king said, "[a]What have I to do with you, O sons of Zeruiah? [b]If he curses, and if the LORD has told him, 'Curse David,' [c]then who shall say, 'Why have you done so?' "

11 Then David said to Abishai and to all his servants, "Behold, [a]my son who came out from [1]me seeks my life; how much more now this Benjamite? Let him alone and let him curse, [b]for the LORD has told him.

12 "Perhaps the LORD will look on my affliction and [1a]return good to me instead of his cursing this day."

13 So David and his men went on the way; and Shimei went along on the hillside parallel with him and as he went he cursed, and cast stones and threw dust at him.

14 And the king and all the people who were with him arrived weary and he refreshed himself there.

Absalom Enters Jerusalem

15 [a]Then Absalom and all the people, the men of Israel, entered Jerusalem, and Ahithophel with him.

---

24 [a]2 Sam. 8:17; 20:25 [b]Num. 4:15; 1 Sam. 4:4, 5 [c]1 Sam. 22:20
25 [a]Ps. 43:3 [b]Ex. 15:13; Jer. 25:30
26 [1]Lit., *in His sight* [a]2 Sam. 11:27; 1 Chr. 21:7 [b]1 Sam. 3:18
27 [a]1 Sam. 9:6-9 [b]2 Sam. 17:17
28 [a]Josh. 5:10; 2 Sam. 17:16
30 [a]Esth. 6:12; Ezek. 24:17, 23 [b]Is. 20:2-4
31 [a]2 Sam. 15:12 [b]2 Sam. 16:23; 17:14, 23
32 [1]Or, *tunic* [2]Lit., *ground* [a]Josh. 16:2
33 [a]2 Sam. 19:35
34 [a]2 Sam. 16:19
35 [a]2 Sam. 17:15, 16
36 [a]2 Sam. 15:27 [b]2 Sam. 17:17
37 [a]2 Sam. 16:16; 1 Chr. 27:33 [b]2 Sam. 16:15
1 [a]2 Sam. 15:32 [b]2 Sam. 9:2-13 [c]1 Sam. 25:18
2 [a]Judg. 10:4 [b]2 Sam. 17:29
3 [a]2 Sam. 9:9, 10 [b]2 Sam. 19:26, 27
5 [a]2 Sam. 3:16; 17:18 [b]2 Sam. 19:16-23; 1 Kin. 2:8, 9, 44 [c]Ex. 22:28; 1 Sam. 17:43
7 [a]2 Sam. 12:9
8 [a]2 Sam. 21:1-9 [b]2 Sam. 1:16; 3:28, 29; 4:11, 12
9 [1]Lit., *take off* [a]1 Sam. 26:8; 2 Sam. 19:21; Luke 9:54 [b]2 Sam. 9:8 [c]Ex. 22:28
10 [a]2 Sam. 3:39; 19:22 [b]John 18:11 [c]Rom. 9:20
11 [1]Lit., *my body* [a]2 Sam. 12:11 [b]Gen. 45:5; 1 Sam. 26:19
12 [1]Lit., *the LORD will return* [a]Deut. 23:5; Rom. 8:28
15 [a]2 Sam. 15:12, 37

16 Now it came about when [a]Hushai the Archite, David's friend, came to Absalom, that [b]Hushai said to Absalom, "[c]*Long* live the king! *Long* live the king!"

17 And Absalom said to Hushai, "Is this your [1]loyalty to your friend? [a]Why did you not go with your friend?"

18 Then Hushai said to Absalom, "No! For whom the LORD, this people, and all the men of Israel have chosen, his will I be, and with him I will remain.

19 "And besides, [a]whom should I serve? *Should I* not *serve* in the presence of his son? As I have served in your father's presence, so I will be in your presence."

20 Then Absalom said to Ahithophel, "Give your advice. What shall we do?"

21 And Ahithophel said to Absalom, "[a]Go in to your father's concubines, whom he has left to keep the house; then all Israel will hear that you have made yourself odious to your father. The hands of all who are with you will also be strengthened."

22 So they pitched a tent for Absalom on the roof, [a]and Absalom went in to his father's concubines [b]in the sight of all Israel.

23 And [a]the advice of Ahithophel, which he [1]gave in those days, *was* as if one inquired of the word of God; [b]so was all the advice of Ahithophel *regarded* by both David and Absalom.

Hushai's Counsel

17 FURTHERMORE, Ahithophel said to Absalom, "Please let me choose 12,000 men that I may arise and pursue David tonight.

2 "And [a]I will come upon him while he is weary and [1]exhausted and will terrify him so that all the people who are with him will flee. Then [b]I will strike down the king alone,

3 and I will bring back all the people to you. [1]The return of everyone depends on the man you seek; *then* all the people shall be at [a]peace."

4 So the [1]plan pleased Absalom and all the elders of Israel.

5 Then Absalom said, "Now call [a]Hushai the Archite also, and let us hear what [1]he has to say."

6 When Hushai had come to Absalom, Absalom said to [1]him, "Ahithophel has spoken [2]thus. Shall we [3]carry out his plan? If not, you speak."

7 So Hushai said to Absalom, "[a]This time the advice that Ahithophel has [1]given is not good."

8 Moreover, Hushai said, "You know your father and his men, that they are mighty men and they are [1]fierce, [a]like a bear robbed of her cubs in the field. And your father is an [2]expert in warfare, and will not spend the night with the people.

9 "Behold, he has now hidden himself in one of the [1]caves or in another place; and it will be [2]when he falls on them at the first attack, that whoever hears *it* will say, 'There has been a slaughter among the people who follow Absalom.'

10 "And even the one who is valiant, whose heart is like the heart of a lion, [a]will completely [1]lose heart; for all Israel knows that your father is a mighty man and those who are with him are valiant men.

11 "But I counsel that all Israel be surely gathered to you, [a]from Dan even to Beersheba, [b]as the sand that is by the sea in abundance, and that [1]you personally go into battle.

12 "So we shall come to him in one of the places where he can be found, and we will [1]fall on him [a]as the dew falls on the ground; and of him and of all the men who are with him, not even one will be left.

13 "And if he withdraws into a city, then all Israel shall bring ropes to that city, and we will [a]drag it into the [1]valley until not even a small stone is found there."

14 Then Absalom and all the men of Israel said, "The counsel of Hushai the Archite is better than the counsel of Ahithophel." For [a]the LORD had ordained to thwart the good counsel of Ahithophel, in order that the LORD might bring calamity on Absalom.

Hushai's Warning Saves David

15 Then [a]Hushai said to Zadok and to Abiathar the priests, "[1]This is what Ahithophel counseled Absalom and the elders of Israel, and [1]this is what I have counseled.

16 "Now therefore, send quickly and tell David, saying, '[a]Do not spend the night at the fords of the wilderness, but by all means cross over, lest the king and all the people who are with him be [1]destroyed.'"

17 [a]Now Jonathan and Ahimaaz were staying at [b]En-rogel, and a maidservant would go and tell them, and they would go and tell King David, for they could not be seen entering the city.

18 But a lad did see them, and told Absalom; so the two of them departed quickly and came to the house of a man [a]in Bahurim, who had a well in his courtyard, and they went down [1]into it.

19 And [a]the woman [1]took a covering and spread it over the well's mouth and scattered grain on it, so that nothing was known.

20 Then Absalom's servants came to the woman at the house and said, "Where are Ahimaaz and Jonathan?" And [a]the woman said to them, "They have crossed the brook of water." And when they searched and could not find *them*, they returned to Jerusalem.

21 And it came about after they had departed that they came up out of the well and went and told King David; and they said to David, "[a]Arise and cross over the water quickly for thus Ahithophel has counseled against you."

---

16 [a]2 Sam. 15:37 [b]2 Sam. 15:34 [c]1 Sam. 10:24; 2 Kin. 11:12

17 [1]Or, *kindness* [a]2 Sam. 19:25

19 [a]2 Sam. 15:34

21 [a]2 Sam. 15:16; 20:3

22 [a]2 Sam. 15:16; 20:3 [b]2 Sam. 12:11, 12

23 [1]Lit., *advised* [a]2 Sam. 17:14, 23 [b]2 Sam. 15:12

2 [1]Lit., *slack of hands* [a]2 Sam. 16:14 [b]1 Kin. 22:31

3 [1]Lit., *Like the return of the whole is the man whom you seek* [a]Jer. 6:14

4 [1]Lit., *word was pleasing in the sight of*

5 [1]Lit., *is in his mouth—even he* [a]2 Sam. 15:32-34

6 [1]Lit., *him, saying* [2]Lit., *according to this word* [3]Lit., *do his word*

7 [1]Lit., *advised* [a]2 Sam. 16:21

8 [1]Lit., *bitter of soul* [2]Lit., *man of war* [a]Hos. 13:8

9 [1]Lit., *pits* [2]Lit., *according to a falling among them*

10 [1]Lit., *melt* [a]Josh. 2:9-11

11 [1]Lit., *your face go* [a]1 Sam. 3:20 [b]Gen. 22:17; 1 Sam. 13:5

12 [1]Lit., *settle down* [a]Ps. 110:3; Mic. 5:7

13 [1]Or, *wadi* [a]Mic. 1:6

14 [a]2 Sam. 15:31, 34; Ps. 9:15, 16

15 [1]Lit., *Thus and thus* [a]2 Sam. 15:35, 36

16 [1]Lit., *swallowed up* [a]2 Sam. 15:28

17 [a]2 Sam. 15:27, 36 [b]Josh. 15:7; 18:16

18 [1]Lit., *there* [a]2 Sam. 3:16; 16:5

19 [1]Lit., *took and spread the covering* [a]Josh. 2:4-6

20 [a]Lev. 19:11; Josh. 2:3-5; 1 Sam. 19:12-17

21 [a]2 Sam. 17:15, 16

22 Then David and all the people who
were with him arose and crossed the
Jordan; and by [1]dawn not even one
remained who had not crossed the Jordan.
23 Now when Ahithophel saw that his
counsel was not [1]followed, he [2]saddled
his donkey and arose and went to his
home, to [a]his city, and [3b]set his house in
order, and [c]strangled himself; thus he
died and was buried in the grave of his
father.
24 Then David came to [a]Mahanaim.
And Absalom crossed the Jordan, he
and all the men of Israel with him.
25 And Absalom set [a]Amasa over the
army in place of Joab. Now Amasa was
the son of a man whose name was [1]Ithra
the Israelite, who went in to Abigail the
daughter of [b]Nahash, sister of Zeruiah,
Joab's mother.
26 And Israel and Absalom camped in
the land of Gilead.
27 Now when David had come to
Mahanaim, Shobi [a]the son of Nahash
from [b]Rabbah of the sons of Ammon,
[c]Machir the son of Ammiel from Lo-
debar, and [d]Barzillai the Gileadite from
Rogelim,
28 brought [a]beds, basins, pottery,
wheat, barley, flour, parched *grain,*
beans, lentils, parched *seeds,*
29 honey, curds, sheep, and cheese of
the herd, for David and for the people
who *were* with him, [a]to eat; for they said,
"The people are hungry and weary and
thirsty in the wilderness."

Absalom Slain

18 THEN David [1]numbered the
people who were with him and
[a]set over them commanders of thousands and commanders of hundreds.
2 And David sent the people out,
[a]one third under the [1]command of Joab,
one third under the [1]command of
Abishai the son of Zeruiah, Joab's
brother, and one third under the [1]com-
mand of [b]Ittai the Gittite. And the king
said to the people, "I myself will surely
go out with you also."
3 But the people said, "[a]You should
not go out; for if we indeed flee, they
will not care about us, even if half of us
die, they will not care about us. But [1]you
are worth ten thousand of us; therefore
now it is better that you *be ready* to help
us from the city."
4 Then the king said to them, "Whatever seems best to you I will do." So [a]the
king stood beside the gate, and all the
people went out by hundreds and thousands.
5 And the king charged Joab and
Abishai and Ittai, saying, "*Deal* gently
for my sake with the young man Absalom." And [a]all the people heard when
the king charged all the commanders
concerning Absalom.
6 Then the people went out into the
field against Israel, and the battle took
place in [a]the forest of Ephraim.
7 And the people of Israel were
[1]defeated there before the servants of
David, and the slaughter there that day
was great, 20,000 men.
8 For the battle there was spread
over the whole countryside, and the
forest devoured more people that day
than the sword devoured.
9 Now Absalom happened to meet
the servants of David. For Absalom was
riding on *his* mule, and the mule went
under the thick branches of a great oak.
And [a]his head caught fast in the oak, so
he was [1]left hanging between heaven and
earth, while the mule that was under him
kept going.
10 When a certain man saw *it,* he told
Joab and said, "Behold, I saw Absalom
hanging in an oak."
11 Then Joab said to the man who
had told him, "Now behold, you saw
him! Why then did you not strike him
there to the ground? And I would have
given you ten *pieces* of silver and a belt."
12 And the man said to Joab, "Even if
I should receive a thousand *pieces of*
silver in my hand, I would not put out
my hand against the king's son; for [a]in
our hearing the king charged you and
Abishai and Ittai, saying, '[1]Protect for
me the young man Absalom!'
13 "Otherwise, if I had dealt treacherously against his life (and [a]there is
nothing hidden from the king), then you
yourself would have stood aloof."
14 Then Joab said, "I will not [1]waste
time here with you." [a]So he took three
spears in his hand and thrust them
through the heart of Absalom while he
was yet alive in the [2]midst of the oak.
15 And ten young men who carried
Joab's armor gathered around and
struck Absalom and killed him.
16 Then [a]Joab blew the trumpet, and
the people returned from pursuing Israel, for Joab restrained the people.
17 And they took Absalom and cast
him into [1]a deep pit in the forest and
[a]erected over him a very great heap of
stones. And [b]all Israel fled, each to his
tent.
18 Now Absalom in his lifetime had
taken and [a]set up for himself a pillar
which is in [b]the King's Valley, for he
said, "[c]I have no son [1]to preserve my
name." So he named the pillar after his
own name, and it is called Absalom's
monument to this day.

David Is Grief-stricken

19 Then [a]Ahimaaz the son of Zadok
said, "Please let me run and bring the
king news [b]that the LORD has [1]freed him
from the hand of his enemies."
20 But Joab said to him, "You are not
the man to carry news this day, but you
shall carry news another day; however,
you shall carry no news today because
the king's son is dead."
21 Then Joab said to the Cushite,
"Go, tell the king what you have seen."
So the Cushite bowed to Joab and ran.

22 [1]Lit., *the light of the morning*
23 [1]Lit., *done* [2]Lit., *bound* [3]Lit., *gave charge to* [a]2 Sam. 15:12 [b]2 Kin. 20:1 [c]Matt. 27:5
24 [a]Gen. 32:2, 10; 2 Sam. 2:8
25 [1]In 1 Chr. 2:17, *Jether the Ishmaelite* [a]2 Sam. 19:13; 20:9-12; 1 Kin. 2:5, 32 [b]1 Chr. 2:16
27 [a]1 Sam. 11:1; 2 Sam. 10:1, 2 [b]2 Sam. 12:26, 29 [c]2 Sam. 9:4 [d]2 Sam. 19:31-39; 1 Kin. 2:7
28 [a]Prov. 11:25; Matt. 5:7
29 [a]2 Sam. 16:2, 14; Prov. 21:26; Eccl. 11:1; Rom. 12:13
1 [1]Lit., *mustered* [a]Ex. 18:25; Num. 31:14; 1 Sam. 22:7
2 [1]Lit., *hand* [a]Judg. 7:16; 1 Sam. 11:11 [b]2 Sam. 15:19-22
3 [1]So with some ancient versions; M.T., *for now there are ten thousand like us* [a]2 Sam. 21:17
4 [a]2 Sam. 18:24
5 [a]2 Sam. 18:12
6 [a]Josh. 17:15, 18; 2 Sam. 17:26
7 [1]Lit., *smitten*
9 [1]Lit., *placed* [a]2 Sam. 14:26
12 [1]So with some mss. and the ancient versions; M.T., *Take care whoever* you are *of* [a]2 Sam. 18:5
13 [a]2 Sam. 14:19, 20
14 [1]Lit., *tarry thus* [2]Lit., *heart* [a]2 Sam. 14:30
16 [a]2 Sam. 2:28; 20:22
17 [1]Lit., *the great* [a]Deut. 21:20, 21; Josh. 7:26; 8:29 [b]2 Sam. 19:8; 20:1, 22
18 [1]Lit., *for the sake of remembering* [a]1 Sam. 15:12 [b]Gen. 14:17 [c]2 Sam. 14:27
19 [1]Lit., *vindicated* [a]2 Sam. 15:36 [b]2 Sam. 18:31

22 Now Ahimaaz the son of Zadok
said once more to Joab, "But whatever
happens, please let me also run after the
Cushite." And Joab said, "Why would
you run, my son, since [a]you will have no
reward for going?"
23"But whatever happens," *he said,* "I
will run." So he said to him, "Run."
Then Ahimaaz ran by way of the plain
and passed up the Cushite.
24 Now [a]David was sitting between
the two gates; and [b]the watchman went
up to the roof of the gate by the wall,
and raised his eyes and looked, and
behold, a man running by himself.
25 And the watchman called and told
the king. And the king said, "If he is by
himself there is good news in his
mouth." And he came nearer and nearer.
26 Then the watchman saw another
man running; and the watchman called
to the gatekeeper and said, "Behold,
another man running by himself." And
the king said, "This one also is bringing
good news."
27 And the watchman said, "I [1]think
the running of the first one [a]is like the
running of Ahimaaz the son of Zadok."
And the king said, "[b]This is a good man
and comes with good news."
28 And Ahimaaz called and said to
the king, "[1]All is well." And [a]he prostrated himself before the king with his
face to the ground. And he said,
"[b]Blessed is the LORD your God, who
has delivered up the men who lifted their
hands against my lord the king."
29 And the king said, "[a]Is it well with
the young man Absalom?" And Ahimaaz answered, "When Joab sent the
king's servant, and your servant, I saw a
great tumult, but [b]I did not know what *it*
was."
30 Then the king said, "Turn aside
and stand here." So he turned aside and
stood still.
31 And behold, the Cushite arrived,
and the Cushite said, "Let my lord the
king receive good news, for [a]the LORD
has [1]freed you this day from the hand of
all those who rose up against you."
32 Then the king said to the Cushite,
"[a]Is it well with the young man Absalom?" And the Cushite answered, "[b]Let
the enemies of my lord the king, and all
who rise up against you for evil, be as
that young man!"
33 [1]And the king was deeply moved
and went up to the chamber over the
gate and wept. And thus he said as he
walked, "[a]O my son Absalom, my son,
my son Absalom! [b]Would I had died
instead of you, O Absalom, my son, my
son!"

Joab Reproves David's Lament

19 THEN it was told Joab, "Behold,
[a]the king is weeping and mourns
for Absalom."
2 And the [1]victory that day was
turned to mourning for all the people,
for the people heard *it* said that day,
"The king is grieved for his son."

22 [a]2 Sam. 18:29

24 [a]2 Sam. 19:8 [b]2 Sam. 13:34; 2 Kin. 9:17

27 [1]Lit., *see* [a]2 Kin. 9:20 [b]1 Kin. 1:42

28 [1]Lit., *Peace.* [a]1 Sam. 25:23; 2 Sam. 14:4 [b]1 Sam. 17:46

29 [a]2 Sam. 20:9; 2 Kin. 4:26 [b]2 Sam. 18:22

31 [1]Lit., *vindicated* [a]Judg. 5:31; 2 Sam. 18:19

32 [a]2 Sam. 18:29 [b]1 Sam. 25:26

33 [1]Ch. 19:1 in Heb. [a]2 Sam. 19:4 [b]Ex. 32:32; Rom. 9:3

1 [a]2 Sam. 18:5, 14

2 [1]Lit., *salvation*

4 [1]Lit., *the king cried* [a]2 Sam. 15:30 [b]2 Sam. 18:33

6 [1]Or, *commanders* [2]Lit., *it would be right in your eyes*

7 [1]Lit., *to the heart* [a]Prov. 14:28

8 [a]2 Sam. 15:2; 18:24 [b]2 Sam. 18:17

9 [1]Lit., *palm* [a]2 Sam. 8:1-14 [b]2 Sam. 5:20; 8:1 [c]2 Sam. 15:14

11 [a]2 Sam. 15:29

12 [a]2 Sam. 5:1

13 [a]2 Sam. 17:25 [b]1 Kin. 19:2 [c]2 Sam. 8:16 [d]2 Sam. 3:27-39; 19:5-7

14 [a]Judg. 20:1

15 [a]Josh. 5:9; 1 Sam. 11:14, 15

16 [a]2 Sam. 16:5-13; 1 Kin. 2:8

3 So the people went by stealth into
the city that day, as people who are
humiliated steal away when they flee in
battle.
4 And the king [a]covered his face and
[1]cried out with a loud voice, "[b]O my son
Absalom, O Absalom, my son, my son!"
5 Then Joab came into the house to
the king and said, "Today you have
covered with shame the faces of all your
servants, who today have saved your life
and the lives of your sons and daughters,
the lives of your wives, and the lives of
your concubines,
6 by loving those who hate you, and
by hating those who love you. For you
have shown today that [1]princes and
servants are nothing to you; for I know
this day that if Absalom were alive and
all of us were dead today, then [2]you
would be pleased.
7"Now therefore arise, go out and
speak [1]kindly to your servants, for I
swear by the LORD, if you do not go out,
surely [a]not a man will pass the night
with you, and this will be worse for you
than all the evil that has come upon you
from your youth until now."

David Restored as King

8 So the king arose and sat in the
gate. When they told all the people,
saying, "Behold, the king is [a]sitting in
the gate," then all the people came
before the king.
Now [b]Israel had fled, each to his tent.
9 And all the people were quarreling
throughout all the tribes of Israel, saying, "[a]The king delivered us from the
[1]hand of our enemies and [b]saved us
from the [1]hand of the Philistines, but
now [c]he has fled out of the land from
Absalom.
10"However, Absalom, whom we
anointed over us, has died in battle.
Now then, why are you silent about
bringing the king back?"
11 Then King David sent to [a]Zadok
and Abiathar the priests, saying, "Speak
to the elders of Judah, saying, 'Why are
you the last to bring the king back to his
house, since the word of all Israel has
come to the king, *even* to his house?
12 'You are my brothers; [a]you are my
bone and my flesh. Why then should you
be the last to bring back the king?'
13"And say to [a]Amasa, 'Are you not
my bone and my flesh? [b]May God do so
to me, and more also, if you will not be
[c]commander of the army before me
continually [d]in place of Joab.' "
14 Thus he turned the hearts of all the
men of Judah [a]as one man, so that they
sent *word* to the king, *saying,* "Return,
you and all your servants."
15 The king then returned and came
as far as the Jordan. And Judah came to
[a]Gilgal in order to go to meet the king,
to bring the king across the Jordan.
16 Then [a]Shimei the son of Gera, the
Benjamite who was from Bahurim, hurried and came down with the men of
Judah to meet King David.

17 And there were a thousand men of
Benjamin with him, with [a]Ziba the servant of the house of Saul, and his fifteen
sons and his twenty servants with him;
and they rushed to the Jordan before the
king.
18 Then they kept crossing the ford to
bring over the king's household, and to
do what was good in his sight. And
Shimei the son of Gera fell down before
the king as he was about to cross the
Jordan.
19 So he said to the king, "[a]Let not
my lord consider me guilty, nor remember what your servant did wrong on the
day when my lord the king came out
from Jerusalem, so that the king should
[1]take *it* to heart.
20 "For your servant knows that I have
sinned; therefore behold, I have come
today, [a]the first of all the house of
Joseph to go down to meet my lord the
king."
21 But Abishai the son of Zeruiah
answered and said, "[a]Should not Shimei
be put to death for this, [b]because he
cursed the LORD's anointed?"
22 David then said, "[a]What have I to
do with you, O sons of Zeruiah, that you
should this day be an adversary to me?
[b]Should any man be put to death in
Israel today? For do I not know that I
am king over Israel today?"
23 And the king said to Shimei, "[a]You
shall not die." Thus the king swore to
him.
24 Then [a]Mephibosheth the [1]son of
Saul came down to meet the king; and
[b]he had neither [2]cared for his feet, nor
[2]trimmed his mustache, nor [c]washed his
clothes, from the day the king departed
until the day he came *home* in peace.
25 And it was when he came from
Jerusalem to meet the king, that the king
said to him, "[a]Why did you not go with
me, Mephibosheth?"
26 So he answered, "O my lord, the
king, my servant deceived me; for your
servant said, 'I will saddle a donkey for
myself that I may ride on it and go with
the king,' [a]because your servant is lame.
27 "Moreover, [a]he has slandered your
servant to my lord the king; but my lord
the king is [b]like the angel of God,
therefore do what is good in your sight.
28 "For [a]all my father's household was
nothing but dead men before my lord
the king; [b]yet you set your servant
among those who ate at your own table.
What right do I have yet that I should
[1]complain anymore to the king?"
29 So the king said to him, "Why do
you still speak of your affairs? I have
[1]decided, 'You and Ziba shall divide the
land.' "
30 And Mephibosheth said to the
king, "Let him even take it all, since my
lord the king has come safely to his own
house."
31 Now [a]Barzillai the Gileadite had
come down from Rogelim; and he went
on to the Jordan with the king to [1]escort
him over the Jordan.
32 Now Barzillai was very old, being
eighty years old; and he had [1a]sustained
the king while he stayed at Mahanaim,
for he was a very great man.
33 And the king said to Barzillai,
"You cross over with me and I will
[1]sustain you in Jerusalem with me."
34 But Barzillai said to the king,
"[a]How long [1]have I yet to live, that I
should go up with the king to Jerusalem?
35 "I am [1]now [a]eighty years old. Can I
distinguish between good and bad? Or
can your servant taste what I eat or what
I drink? Or can I hear anymore [b]the
voice of singing men and women? [c]Why
then should your servant be an added
burden to my lord the king?
36 "Your servant would merely cross
over the Jordan with the king. Why
should the king compensate me *with* this
reward?
37 "Please let your servant return, that
I may die in my own city near the grave
of my father and my mother. However,
here is your servant [a]Chimham, let him
cross over with my lord the king, and do
for him what is good in your sight."
38 And the king answered, "Chimham
shall cross over with me, and I will do
for him what is good in your sight; and
whatever you [1]require of me, I will do
for you."
39 All the people crossed over the
Jordan and the king crossed too. The
king then [a]kissed Barzillai and blessed
him, and he returned to his place.
40 Now the king went on to Gilgal,
and Chimham went on with him; and all
the people of Judah and also [a]half the
people of Israel [1]accompanied the king.
41 And behold, all the men of Israel
came to the king and said to the king,
"[a]Why had our brothers [b]the men of
Judah stolen you away, and brought the
king and his household and all David's
men with him over the Jordan?"
42 Then all the men of Judah answered the men of Israel, "Because [a]the
king is a close relative to [1]us. Why then
[2]are you angry about this matter? Have
we eaten at all at the king's *expense*, or
has [3]anything been taken for us?"
43 But the men of Israel answered the
men of Judah and said, "[1a]We have ten
parts in the king, therefore [1]we also have
more *claim* on David than you. Why
then did you treat us with contempt?
Was it not [1]our advice first to bring back
[1]our king?" Yet the words of the men of
Judah were harsher than the words of
the men of Israel.

Sheba's Revolt

20 NOW [a]a worthless fellow happened to be there whose name
was Sheba, the son of [b]Bichri, a Benjamite; and he blew the trumpet and said,
"[c]We have no portion in David,
Nor do we have inheritance in
[d]the son of Jesse;
[e]Every man to his tents, O Israel!"

17 [a]2 Sam. 16:1-4; 19:26, 27
19 [1]Lit., *set* [a]1 Sam. 22:15; 2 Sam. 16:6-8
20 [a]2 Sam. 16:5
21 [a]2 Sam. 16:7, 8 [b]Ex. 22:28
22 [a]2 Sam. 3:39; 16:9, 10 [b]1 Sam. 11:13
23 [a]1 Kin. 2:8
24 [1]I.e., grandson [2]Lit., *done* [a]2 Sam. 9:6-10 [b]2 Sam. 12:20 [c]Ex. 19:10
25 [a]2 Sam. 16:17
26 [a]2 Sam. 9:3
27 [a]2 Sam. 16:3, 4 [b]2 Sam. 14:17, 20
28 [1]Lit., *cry out* [a]2 Sam. 21:6-9 [b]2 Sam. 9:7, 10, 13
29 [1]Lit., *said*
31 [1]Lit., *send* [a]2 Sam. 17:27-29; 1 Kin. 2:7
32 [1]Or, *provided food for* [a]2 Sam. 17:27-29
33 [1]Or, *provide food for*
34 [1]Lit., *are the days of the years of my life* [a]Gen. 47:8
35 [1]Lit., *today* [a]Ps. 90:10 [b]Eccl. 2:8; Is. 5:11, 12 [c]2 Sam. 15:33
37 [a]2 Sam. 19:40; 1 Kin. 2:7; Jer. 41:17
38 [1]Lit., *choose*
39 [a]Gen. 31:55; Ruth 1:14; 2 Sam. 14:33
40 [1]Lit., *crossed over with* [a]2 Sam. 19:9, 10
41 [a]Judg. 8:1; 12:1 [b]2 Sam. 19:11, 12
42 [1]Lit., *me* [2]Lit., *is it hot to you* [3]Or, *a gift* [a]2 Sam. 19:12
43 [1]Singular in Heb. [a]2 Sam. 5:1; 1 Kin. 11:30, 31
1 [a]2 Sam. 16:7 [b]Gen. 46:21 [c]2 Sam. 19:43; 1 Kin. 12:16 [d]1 Sam. 22:7-9 [e]1 Sam. 13:2; 2 Sam. 18:17; 2 Chr. 10:16

2 So all the men of Israel [1]withdrew from following David, *and* followed Sheba the son of Bichri; but the men of Judah [2]remained steadfast to their king, from the Jordan even to Jerusalem.

3 Then David came to his house at Jerusalem, and [a]the king took the ten women, the concubines whom he had left to keep the house, and placed them under guard and provided them with sustenance, but did not go in to them. So they were shut up until the day of their death, living as widows.

4 Then the king said to [a]Amasa, "Call out the men of Judah for me within three days, and be present here yourself."

5 So Amasa went to call out *the men of* Judah, but he [a]delayed longer than the set time which he had appointed him.

6 And David said to [a]Abishai, "Now Sheba the son of Bichri will do us more harm than Absalom; [b]take your lord's servants and pursue him, lest he find for himself fortified cities and escape from our sight."

7 So Joab's men went out after him, [a]along with the Cherethites and the Pelethites and all the mighty men; and they went out from Jerusalem to pursue Sheba the son of Bichri.

8 When they were at the large stone which is in [a]Gibeon, Amasa came [1]to meet them. Now Joab was [2]dressed in his military attire, and over it was a belt with a sword in its sheath fastened at his waist; and as he went forward, it fell out.

9 And Joab said to Amasa, "Is it well with you, my brother?" And [a]Joab took Amasa by the beard with his right hand to kiss him.

Amasa Murdered

10 But Amasa was not on guard against the sword which was in Joab's hand so [a]he struck him in the belly with it and poured out his inward parts on the ground, and did not *strike* him again; and he died. Then Joab and Abishai his brother pursued Sheba the son of Bichri.

11 Now there stood by him one of Joab's young men, and said, "Whoever favors Joab and whoever is for David, [a]*let him* follow Joab."

12 But Amasa lay wallowing in *his* blood in the middle of the highway. And when the man saw that all the people stood still, he [1]removed Amasa from the highway into the field and threw a garment over him when he saw that everyone who came by him stood still.

Revolt Put Down

13 As soon as he was removed from the highway, all the men passed on after Joab to pursue Sheba the son of Bichri.

14 Now he went through all the tribes of Israel to Abel even to Beth-maacah and all the Berites; and they were gathered together and also went after him.

15 And they came and besieged him in [a]Abel Beth-maacah, and [b]they [1]cast up a mound against the city, and it stood by the rampart; and all the people who were with Joab were wreaking destruction in order to topple the wall.

16 Then [a]a wise woman called from the city, "Hear, hear! Please tell Joab, 'Come here that I may speak with you.' "

17 So he approached her, and the woman said, "Are you Joab?" And he answered, "I am." Then she said to him, "Listen to the words of your maidservant." And he answered, "I am listening."

18 Then she spoke, saying, "Formerly they used to say, 'They will surely ask *advice* at Abel,' and thus they ended *the dispute.*

19 "I am of those who are peaceable *and* faithful in Israel. [a]You are seeking to destroy a city even a mother in Israel. Why would you swallow up [b]the inheritance of the LORD?"

20 And Joab answered and said, "Far be it, far be it from me that I should swallow up or destroy!

21 "Such is not the case. But a man from [a]the hill country of Ephraim, [b]Sheba the son of Bichri by name, has lifted up his hand against King David. Only hand him over, and I will depart from the city." And the woman said to Joab, "Behold, his head will be thrown to you over the wall."

22 Then the woman [a]wisely came to all the people. And they cut off the head of Sheba the son of Bichri and threw it to Joab. So [b]he blew the trumpet, and they were dispersed from the city, each to his tent. Joab also returned to the king at Jerusalem.

23 [a]Now Joab was over the whole army of Israel, and Benaiah the son of Jehoiada was over the Cherethites and the Pelethites;

24 and Adoram was over the forced labor, and [a]Jehoshaphat the son of Ahilud was the recorder;

25 and Sheva was scribe, and Zadok and [a]Abiathar were priests;

26 and Ira the Jairite was also a priest to David.

Gibeonite Revenge

21 NOW there was [a]a famine in the days of David for three years, year after year; and [b]David sought the presence of the LORD. And the LORD said, "It is for Saul and his bloody house, because he put the Gibeonites to death."

2 So the king called the Gibeonites and spoke to them (now the Gibeonites were not of the sons of Israel but of the remnant of the Amorites, and [a]the sons of Israel [1]made a covenant with them, but Saul had sought to [2]kill them in his zeal for the sons of Israel and Judah).

3 Thus David said to the Gibeonites, "What should I do for you? And how can I make atonement that you may bless [a]the inheritance of the LORD?"

2 [1]Lit., *went up* [2]Lit., *clung to*
3 [a]2 Sam. 15:16; 16:21, 22
4 [a]2 Sam. 17:25; 19:13
5 [a]1 Sam. 13:8
6 [a]2 Sam. 21:17 [b]2 Sam. 11:11; 1 Kin. 1:33
7 [a]2 Sam. 8:18; 1 Kin. 1:38
8 [1]Lit., *before* [2]Lit., *girded with military garment as clothing* [a]2 Sam. 2:13; 3:30
9 [a]Matt. 26:49
10 [a]2 Sam. 2:23; 3:27; 1 Kin. 2:5
11 [a]2 Sam. 20:13
12 [1]Lit., *caused to turn*
15 [1]Lit., *poured out* [a]1 Kin. 15:20; 2 Kin. 15:29 [b]2 Kin. 19:32; Ezek. 4:2
16 [a]2 Sam. 14:2
19 [a]Deut. 20:10 [b]1 Sam. 26:19; 2 Sam. 14:16; 21:3
21 [a]Josh. 24:33 [b]2 Sam. 20:2
22 [a]2 Sam. 20:16; Eccl. 9:13-16 [b]2 Sam. 20:1
23 [a]2 Sam. 8:16-18; 1 Kin. 4:3-6
24 [a]1 Kin. 4:3
25 [a]1 Kin. 4:4
1 [a]Gen. 12:10; 26:1; 42:5 [b]Num. 27:21
2 [1]Lit., *had sworn to* [2]Lit., *smite* [a]Josh. 9:3, 15-20
3 [a]1 Sam. 26:19; 2 Sam. 20:19

4 Then the Gibeonites said to him, "[a]We have no *concern* of silver or gold with Saul or his house, nor is it for us to put any man to death in Israel." And he said, "I will do for you whatever you say."

5 So they said to the king, "[a]The man who consumed us, and who planned [1]to exterminate us from remaining within any border of Israel,

6 let seven men from his sons be given to us, and we will [1]hang them [a]before the LORD in Gibeah of Saul, [b]the chosen of the LORD." And the king said, "I will give *them.*"

7 But the king spared [a]Mephibosheth, the son of Jonathan the son of Saul, [b]because of the oath of the LORD which was between them, between David and Saul's son Jonathan.

8 So the king took the two sons of [a]Rizpah the daughter of Aiah, Armoni and Mephibosheth whom she had born to Saul, and the five sons of [1b]Merab the daughter of Saul, whom she had born to Adriel the son of Barzillai the [c]Meholathite.

9 Then he gave them into the hands of the Gibeonites, and they [1]hanged them in the mountain before the LORD, so that the seven of them fell together; and they were put to death in the first days of harvest at [a]the beginning of barley harvest.

10 [a]And Rizpah the daughter of Aiah took sackcloth and spread it for herself on the rock, from the beginning of harvest until [1]it rained on them from the sky; and [b]she [2]allowed neither the birds of the sky to rest on them by day nor the beasts of the field by night.

11 When it was told David what Rizpah the daughter of Aiah, the concubine of Saul, had done,

12 then David went and took [a]the bones of Saul and the bones of Jonathan his son from the men of Jabesh-gilead, who had stolen them from the open square of [b]Beth-shan, [c]where the Philistines had hanged them on the day [d]the Philistines struck down Saul in Gilboa.

13 And he brought up the bones of Saul and the bones of Jonathan his son from there, and they gathered the bones of those who had been [1]hanged.

14 And they buried the bones of Saul and Jonathan his son in the country of Benjamin in [a]Zela, in the grave of Kish his father; thus they did all that the king commanded, and after that [b]God was moved by entreaty for the land.

15 Now when [a]the Philistines were at war again with Israel, David went down and his servants with him; and as they fought against the Philistines, David became weary.

16 Then Ishbi-benob, who was [a]among the descendants of the [1]giant, the weight of whose spear was three hundred *shekels* of bronze in weight, [2]was girded with a new *sword,* and he [3]intended to kill David.

17 But [a]Abishai the son of Zeruiah helped him, and struck the Philistine and killed him. Then the men of David swore to him, saying, "[b]You shall not go out again with us to battle, that you may not extinguish [c]the lamp of Israel."

18 [a]Now it came about after this that there was war again with the Philistines at Gob; then [b]Sibbecai the Hushathite struck down Saph, who was among the descendants of the [1]giant.

19 And there was war with the Philistines again at Gob, and Elhanan the son of Jaare-oregim the Bethlehemite [1]killed [2]Goliath the Gittite, [a]the shaft of whose spear was like a weaver's beam.

20 And there was war at Gath again, where there was a man of *great* stature who had six fingers on each hand and six toes on each foot, twenty-four in number; and he also had been born [a]to the [1]giant.

21 And when he defied Israel, Jonathan the son of Shimei, David's brother, struck him down.

22 [a]These four were born to the [1]giant in Gath, and they fell by the hand of David and by the hand of his servants.

David's Psalm of Deliverance

22 [a]AND David spoke [b]the words of this song to the LORD in the day that the LORD delivered him from the [1]hand of all his enemies and from the [1]hand of Saul.

2 And he said,
"[a]The LORD is my [1]rock and my fortress and my deliverer;
3 [1a]My God, my rock, in whom I take refuge;
My [b]shield and [c]the horn of my salvation, my stronghold and [d]my refuge;
My savior, Thou dost save me from violence.
4 "I call upon the LORD, [a]who is worthy to be praised;
And I am saved from my enemies.
5 "For [a]the waves of death encompassed me;
[b]The torrents of [1]destruction [2]overwhelmed me;
6 [a]The cords of [1]Sheol surrounded me;
The snares of death confronted me.
7 "[a]In my distress I called upon the LORD,
Yes, I [1]cried to my God;
And from His temple He heard my voice,
And my cry for help *came* into His ears.
8 "Then [a]the earth shook and quaked,
[b]The foundations of heaven were trembling
And were shaken, because He was angry.
9 "Smoke went up [1]out of His nostrils,
[a]And fire from His mouth devoured;
[b]Coals were kindled by it.

4 [a]Num. 35:31, 32
5 [1]Lit., *against us that we should be exterminated* [a]2 Sam. 21:1
6 [1]Lit., *expose them* [a]Num. 25:4 [b]1 Sam. 10:24
7 [a]2 Sam. 4:4; 9:10 [b]1 Sam. 18:3; 20:12-17; 23:18; 2 Sam. 9:1-7
8 [1]So Gr. and Heb. mss. [a]2 Sam. 3:7 [b]1 Sam. 18:19 [c]1 Kin. 19:16
9 [1]Lit., *exposed them* [a]Ex. 9:31, 32
10 [1]Lit., *water was poured* [2]Lit., *gave* [a]Deut. 21:23 [b]1 Sam. 17:44, 46
12 [a]1 Sam. 31:11-13 [b]Josh. 17:11 [c]1 Sam. 31:10 [d]1 Sam. 31:3, 4
13 [1]Lit., *exposed*
14 [a]Josh. 18:28 [b]Josh. 7:26; 2 Sam. 24:25
15 [a]2 Sam. 5:17-25
16 [1]Heb., *Raphah* [2]Lit., *and he was* [3]Lit., *said* [a]Num. 13:22, 28; Josh. 15:14; 2 Sam. 21:18-22
17 [a]2 Sam. 20:6-10 [b]2 Sam. 18:3 [c]2 Sam. 22:29 1 Kin. 11:36
18 [1]Heb., *Raphah* [a]1 Chr. 20:4-8 [b]1 Chr. 11:29; 27:11
19 [1]Lit., *smote* [2]In 1 Chr. 20:5, *Lahmi, the brother of Goliath* [a]1 Sam. 17:7
20 [1]Heb., *Raphah* [a]2 Sam. 21:16, 18
22 [1]Heb., *Raphah* [a]1 Chr. 20:8

1 [1]Lit., *palm* [a]Ps. 18:2-50 [b]Ex. 15:1; Deut. 31:30
2 [1]Lit., *crag* [a]1 Sam. 23:25; 24:2; Ps. 31:3; 71:3
3 [1]Lit., *God of my rock* [a]Deut. 32:4, 37; 1 Sam. 2:2 [b]Gen. 15:1; Deut. 33:29 [c]Luke 1:69 [d]Ps. 9:9
4 [a]Ps. 48:1; 96:4
5 [1]Heb., *Belial* [2]Or, *terrified* [a]Ps. 93:4; Jon. 2:3 [b]Ps. 69:14, 15
6 [1]I.e., the nether world [a]Ps. 116:3
7 [1]Or, *called* [a]Ps. 116:4; 120:1
8 [a]Judg. 5:4; Ps. 97:4 [b]Job 26:11
9 [1]Or, *in His wrath* [a]Ps. 97:3; Heb. 12:29 [b]2 Sam. 22:13

10 "He bowed the heavens also, and came down
With [a]thick darkness under His feet.
11 "[a]And He rode on a cherub and flew;
And He [1]appeared on [b]the wings of the wind.
12 "[a]And He made darkness [1]canopies around Him,
A mass of waters, thick clouds of the sky.
13 "From the brightness before Him
[a]Coals of fire were kindled.
14 "[a]The LORD thundered from heaven,
And the Most High uttered His voice.
15 "[a]And He sent out arrows, and scattered them,
Lightning, and [1]routed them.
16 "Then the channels of the sea appeared,
The foundations of the world were [1]laid bare,
By the rebuke of the LORD,
[a]At the blast of the breath of His nostrils.
17 "[a]He sent from on high, He took me;
[b]He drew me out of many waters.
18 "He delivered me from my strong enemy,
From those who hated me, for they were too strong for me.
19 "They confronted me in the day of my calamity,
[a]But the LORD was my support.
20 "[a]He also brought me forth into a broad place;
He rescued me, [b]because He delighted in me.
21 "[a]The LORD has rewarded me according to my righteousness;
[b]According to the cleanness of my hands He has recompensed me.
22 "[a]For I have kept the ways of the LORD,
And have not acted wickedly against my God.
23 "[a]For all His ordinances *were* before me;
And *as for* His statutes, I did not depart from [1]them.
24 "[a]I was also [1]blameless toward Him,
And I kept myself from my iniquity.
25 "[a]Therefore the LORD has recompensed me according to my righteousness,
According to my cleanness before His eyes.
26 "[a]With the [1]kind Thou dost show Thyself [1]kind,
With the [2]blameless Thou dost show Thyself [2]blameless;
27 [a]With the pure Thou dost show Thyself pure,
[b]And with the perverted Thou dost show Thyself [1]astute.
28 "[a]And Thou dost save an afflicted people;
[b]But Thine eyes are on the haughty *whom* Thou dost abase.
29 "[a]For Thou art my lamp, O LORD;
And the LORD illumines my darkness.
30 "[a]For by Thee I can [1]run upon a troop;
By my God I can leap over a wall.
31 "[a]As for God, His way is [1]blameless;
[b]The word of the LORD is tested;
[c]He is a shield to all who take refuge in Him.
32 "[a]For who is God, besides the LORD?
[b]And who is a rock, besides our God?
33 "[a]God is my strong fortress;
And He [1]sets the [2]blameless in [3]His way.
34 "[a]He makes [1]my feet like hinds' *feet*,
[b]And sets me on my high places.
35 "[a]He trains my hands for battle,
[b]So that my arms can bend a bow of bronze.
36 "Thou hast also given me [a]the shield of Thy salvation,
And Thy [1]help makes me great.
37 "[a]Thou dost enlarge my steps under me,
And my [1]feet have not slipped.
38 "I pursued my enemies and [a]destroyed them,
And I did not turn back until they were consumed.
39 "And I have devoured them and shattered them, so that they did not rise;
And [a]they fell under my feet.
40 "For Thou hast girded me with strength for battle;
Thou hast [1]subdued under me [a]those who rose up against me.
41 "Thou hast also [a]made my enemies turn *their* backs to me,
And I [1]destroyed those who hated me.
42 "[a]They looked, but there was none to save;
[b]*Even* to the LORD, but He did not answer them.
43 "[a]Then I pulverized them as the dust of the earth,
[b]I crushed *and* stamped them as the mire of the streets.
44 "[a]Thou hast also delivered me from the contentions of my people;
[b]Thou hast kept me as head of the nations;
[c]A people whom I have not known serve me.
45 "[a]Foreigners pretend obedience to me;
As soon as they hear, they obey me.
46 "Foreigners [1]lose heart,
[a]And [2]come trembling out of their [3]fortresses.

10 [a]Ex. 19:16; 1 Kin. 8:12; Ps. 97:2; Nah. 1:3
11 [1]Many mss. read *sped* [a]2 Sam. 6:2 [b]Ps. 104:3
12 [1]Or, *pavilions* [a]Job 36:29
13 [a]2 Sam. 22:9
14 [a]Job 37:2-5; Ps. 29:3
15 [1]Lit., *confused* [a]Deut. 32:23; Josh. 10:10; 1 Sam. 7:10
16 [1]Or, *uncovered* [a]Ex. 15:8; Nah. 1:4
17 [a]Ps. 144:7 [b]Ex. 2:10
19 [a]Ps. 23:4
20 [a]Ps. 31:8; 118:5 [b]2 Sam. 15:26
21 [a]1 Sam. 26:23; 1 Kin. 8:32 [b]Ps. 24:4
22 [a]Gen. 18:19; Ps. 128:1; Prov. 8:32
23 [1]Lit., *it* [a]Deut. 6:6-9; Ps. 119:30, 102
24 [1]Lit., *complete;* or, *having integrity* [a]Gen. 6:9; 7:1; Eph. 1:4; Col. 1:21, 22
25 [a]2 Sam. 22:21
26 [1]Or, *loyal* [2]Lit., *complete;* or, *having integrity* [a]Matt. 5:7
27 [1]Lit., *twisted* [a]Matt. 5:8; 1 John 3:3 [b]Lev. 26:23, 24; Rom. 1:28
28 [a]Ex. 3:7, 8; Ps. 72:12, 13 [b]Is. 2:11, 12, 17; 5:15
29 [a]2 Sam. 21:17; 1 Kin. 11:36; Ps. 27:1
30 [1]Or, *crush a troop* [a]2 Sam. 5:6-8
31 [1]Lit., *complete;* or, *having integrity* [a]Deut. 32:4; Matt. 5:48 [b]Ps. 12:6; 119:140; Prov. 30:5 [c]2 Sam. 22:3; Ps. 84:9
32 [a]1 Sam. 2:2 [b]2 Sam. 22:2
33 [1]Or, *sets free* [2]Lit., *complete;* or, *having integrity* [3]Another reading is *my* [a]2 Sam. 22:2; Ps. 31:3, 4
34 [1]Another reading is *His* [a]2 Sam. 2:18; Hab. 3:19 [b]Deut. 32:13
35 [a]Ps. 144:1 [b]Job 20:24
36 [1]Lit., *answering* [a]Eph. 6:16, 17
37 [1]Lit., *ankles* [a]2 Sam. 22:20; Prov. 4:12
38 [a]Ex. 15:9
39 [a]Mal. 4:3
40 [1]Lit., *caused to bow down* [a]Ps. 44:5
41 [1]Or, *silenced* [a]Ex. 23:27; Josh. 10:24
42 [a]Is. 17:7, 8 [b]1 Sam. 28:6; Is. 1:15
43 [a]2 Kin. 13:7 [b]Is. 10:6; Mic. 7:10
44 [a]2 Sam. 3:1; 19:9, 14 [b]2 Sam. 8:1-14 [c]Is. 55:5
45 [a]Ps. 66:3; 81:15
46 [1]Lit., *languish* [2]Lit., *gird themselves* [3]Lit., *fastnesses* [a]1 Sam. 14:11; Mic. 7:17

47 "The LORD lives, and blessed be my rock;
And exalted be [1][a]God, the rock of my salvation,
48 [a]The God who executes vengeance for me,
[b]And brings down peoples under me,
49 Who also brings me out from my enemies;
Thou dost even lift me above [a]those who rise up against me;
[b]Thou dost rescue me from the violent man.
50 "[a]Therefore I will give thanks to Thee, O LORD, among the nations,
And I will sing praises to Thy name.
51 "[a]*He* is a tower of [1]deliverance to His king,
And [b]shows lovingkindness to His anointed,
[c]To David and his [2]descendants forever."

David's Last Song

23 NOW these are the last words of David.
David the son of Jesse declares,
[a]And the man who was raised on high declares,
[b]The anointed of the God of Jacob,
And the sweet psalmist of Israel,
2 "[a]The Spirit of the LORD spoke by me,
And His word was on my tongue.
3 "The God of Israel said,
[a]The Rock of Israel spoke to me,
'[b]He who rules over men righteously,
[c]Who rules in the fear of God,
4 [a]Is as the light of the morning *when* the sun rises,
A morning without clouds,
When the tender grass *springs* out of the earth,
Through sunshine after rain.'
5 "Truly is not my house so with God?
For [a]He has made an everlasting covenant with me,
Ordered in all things, and secured;
For all my salvation and all *my* desire,
Will He not indeed make *it* grow?
6 "[a]But the worthless, every one of them will be thrust away like thorns,
Because they cannot be taken in hand;
7 But the man who touches them
Must be [1]armed with iron and the shaft of a spear,
And [a]they will be completely burned with fire in *their* [2]place."

His Mighty Men

8 [a]These are the names of the mighty
men whom David had: Josheb-basshebeth a Tahchemonite, chief of the [1]captains, he was *called* Adino the Eznite, because of eight hundred slain *by him* at one time;
9 and after him was Eleazar the son
of [a]Dodo the [b]Ahohite, one of the three mighty men with David when they [1]defied the Philistines who were gathered there to battle and the men of Israel had [2]withdrawn.
10 [a]He arose and struck the Philistines
until his hand was weary and [1]clung to the sword, and [b]the LORD brought about a great [2]victory that day; and the people returned after him only to strip *the slain.*
11 Now after him was Shammah the
son of Agee a [a]Hararite. And the Philistines were gathered [1]into a troop, where there was a plot of ground full of lentils, and the people fled from the Philistines.
12 But he took his stand in the midst
of the plot, defended it and struck the Philistines; and [a]the LORD brought about a great [1]victory.
13 Then three of the thirty chief men
went down and came to David in the harvest time to the [a]cave of Adullam, while the troop of the Philistines was camping in [b]the valley of Rephaim.
14 And David was then [a]in the strong-
hold, while the garrison of the Philistines was then in Bethlehem.
15 [a]And David had a craving and
said, "Oh that someone would give me water to drink from the well of Bethlehem which is by the gate!"
16 [a]So the three mighty men broke
through the camp of the Philistines, and drew water from the well of Bethlehem which was by the gate, and took *it* and brought *it* to David. Nevertheless he would not drink it, but [b]poured it out to the LORD;
17 and he said, "Be it far from me, O
LORD, that I should do this. [a]*Shall I drink* the blood of the men who went in *jeopardy* of their lives?" Therefore he would not drink it. These things the three mighty men did.
18 And [a]Abishai, the brother of Joab,
the son of Zeruiah, was [b]chief of the [1]thirty. And he swung his spear against three hundred [2]and killed *them,* and had a name as well as the three.
19 He was most honored of the thirty,
therefore he became their commander; however, he did not attain to the three.
20 Then [a]Benaiah the son of Jehoiada,
the son of a valiant man of [b]Kabzeel, who had done mighty deeds, [1]killed the [2]two *sons of* Ariel of Moab. He also went down and killed a lion in the middle of a pit on a snowy day.
21 And he [1]killed an Egyptian, [2]an
impressive man. Now the Egyptian *had* a spear in his hand, but he went down to him with a club and snatched the spear from the Egyptian's hand, and killed him with his own spear.
22 These *things* [a]Benaiah the son of
Jehoiada did, and had a name as well as the three mighty men.

47 [1]Lit., *the God of the rock* [a]2 Sam. 22:3; Ps. 89:26
48 [a]1 Sam. 24:12; 25:39; 2 Sam. 4:8; Ps. 94:1 [b]Ps. 144:2
49 [a]Ps. 44:5 [b]Ps. 140:1, 4, 11
50 [a]Rom. 15:9
51 [1]I.e., victories; lit., *salvation* [2]Lit., *seed* [a]Ps. 144:10 [b]Ps. 89:24 [c]2 Sam. 7:12-16
1 [a]2 Sam. 7:8, 9; Ps. 78:70, 71 [b]1 Sam. 16:12, 13; Ps. 89:20
2 [a]Matt. 22:43; 2 Pet. 1:21
3 [a]2 Sam. 22:2, 3, 32 [b]Ps. 72:1-3; Is. 11:1-5 [c]2 Chr. 19:7, 9
4 [a]Judg. 5:31; Ps. 72:6
5 [a]2 Sam. 7:12-16; Ps. 89:29; Is. 55:3
6 [a]Matt. 13:41
7 [1]Lit., *filled* [2]Lit., *sitting* [a]Matt. 3:10; 13:30; Heb. 6:8
8 [1]Or, *three* [a]1 Chr. 11:11-47
9 [1]Lit., *reproached* [2]Lit., *gone up* [a]1 Chr. 27:4 [b]1 Chr. 8:4
10 [1]Lit., *his hand clung* [2]Lit., *salvation* [a]1 Chr. 11:13 [b]1 Sam. 11:13; 19:5
11 [1]Possibly, at Lehi [a]2 Sam. 23:33
12 [1]Lit., *salvation* [a]2 Sam. 23:10
13 [a]1 Sam. 22:1 [b]2 Sam. 5:18
14 [a]1 Sam. 22:4, 5
15 [a]1 Chr. 11:17
16 [a]1 Chr. 11:18 [b]Gen. 35:14
17 [a]Lev. 17:10
18 [1]So two Heb. mss. and Syriac; M.T., *three* [2]Lit., *slain ones* [a]2 Sam. 10:10, 14; 18:2 [b]1 Chr. 11:20, 21
20 [1]Lit., *smote* [2]Or, *two lion-like heroes* [a]2 Sam. 8:18; 20:23 [b]Josh. 15:21
21 [1]Lit., *smote* [2]Lit., *a man of appearance*
22 [a]2 Sam. 23:20

23 He was honored among the thirty,
but he did not attain to the three. And
David appointed him over his guard.
24 [a]Asahel the brother of Joab was
among the thirty; Elhanan the son of
Dodo of Bethlehem,
25 [a]Shammah the [b]Harodite, Elika the
Harodite,
26 Helez the Paltite, Ira the son of
Ikkesh the [a]Tekoite,
27 Abiezer the [a]Anathothite, Mebunnai the Hushathite,
28 Zalmon the Ahohite, Maharai the
[a]Netophathite,
29 [a]Heleb the son of Baanah the Netophathite, Ittai the son of Ribai of
[b]Gibeah of the sons of Benjamin,
30 Benaiah a [a]Pirathonite, Hiddai of
the brooks of [b]Gaash,
31 Abi-albon the Arbathite, Azmaveth
the [a]Barhumite,
32 Eliahba the [a]Shaalbonite, the sons
of Jashen, Jonathan,
33 [a]Shammah the Hararite, Ahiam the
son of Sharar the Ararite,
34 Eliphelet the son of Ahasbai, the
son of [a]the Maacathite, [b]Eliam the son
of [c]Ahithophel the Gilonite,
35 [a]Hezro the [b]Carmelite, Paarai the
Arbite,
36 Igal the son of Nathan of [a]Zobah,
Bani the Gadite,
37 Zelek the Ammonite, Naharai the
[a]Beerothite, armor bearers of Joab the
son of Zeruiah,
38 Ira the [a]Ithrite, Gareb the Ithrite,
39 [a]Uriah the Hittite; thirty-seven in
all.

The Census Taken

24 [a]NOW [b]again the anger of the
LORD burned against Israel, and
it incited David against them to say,
"[c]Go, number Israel and Judah."
2 And the king said to Joab the
commander of the army who was with
him, "Go about now through all the
tribes of Israel, [a]from Dan to Beersheba,
and [1]register the people, that I may
know the number of the people."
3 But Joab said to the king, "[a]Now
may the LORD your God add to the
people a hundred times as many as they
are, while the eyes of my lord the king
still see; but why does my lord the king
delight in this thing?"
4 Nevertheless, the king's word prevailed against Joab and against the
commanders of the army. So Joab and
the commanders of the army went out
from the presence of the king, to [1]regis-
ter the people of Israel.
5 And they crossed the Jordan and
camped in [a]Aroer, on the right side of
the city that is in the middle of the valley
of Gad, and toward [b]Jazer.
6 Then they came to Gilead and to
[1]the land of Tahtim-hodshi, and they
came to Dan-jaan and around to [a]Sidon,
7 and came to the [a]fortress of Tyre
and to all the cities of the [b]Hivites and
of the Canaanites, and they went out to
the south of Judah, *to* [c]Beersheba.
8 So when they had gone about
through the whole land, they came to
Jerusalem at the end of nine months and
twenty days.
9 And Joab gave [a]the number of the
[1]registration of the people to the king;
and there were in Israel [b]eight hundred
thousand valiant men who drew the
sword, and the men of Judah were five
hundred thousand men.
10 Now [a]David's heart [1]troubled him
after he had numbered the people. So
David said to the LORD, "[b]I have sinned
greatly in what I have done. But now, O
LORD, please [2]take away the iniquity of
Thy servant, for [c]I have acted very
foolishly."
11 When David arose in the morning,
the word of the LORD came to [a]the
prophet Gad, David's [b]seer, saying,
12 "Go and speak to David, 'Thus the
LORD says, "I am offering you three
things; choose for yourself one of them,
which I may do to you." ' "
13 So Gad came to David and told
him, and said to him, "Shall [a]seven years
of famine come to you in your land? Or
will you flee three months before your
foes while they pursue you? Or shall
there be three days' pestilence in your
land? Now consider and see what answer I shall return to Him who sent me."
14 Then David said to Gad, "I am in
great distress. Let us now fall into the
hand of the LORD [a]for His mercies are
great, but do not let me fall into the
hand of man."

Pestilence Sent

15 So [a]the LORD [1]sent a pestilence
upon Israel from the morning until the
appointed time; and seventy thousand
men of the people [b]from Dan to Beersheba died.
16 [a]When the angel stretched out his
hand toward Jerusalem to destroy it,
[b]the LORD relented from the calamity,
and said to the angel who destroyed the
people, "It is enough! Now relax your
hand!" And the angel of the LORD was
by the threshing floor of Araunah the
Jebusite.
17 Then David spoke to the LORD
when he saw the angel who was striking
down the people, and said, "Behold, [a]it
is I who have sinned, and it is I who
have done wrong; but [b]these sheep, what
have they done? Please let Thy hand be
against me and against my father's
house."

David Builds an Altar

18 So Gad came to David that day
and said to him, "[a]Go up, erect an altar
to the LORD on the threshing floor of
[1]Araunah the Jebusite."
19 And David went up according to
the word of Gad, just as the LORD had
commanded.
20 And Araunah looked down and
saw the king and his servants crossing
over toward him; and Araunah went out

24 [a]2 Sam. 2:18; 1 Chr. 27:7
25 [a]1 Chr. 11:27 [b]Judg. 7:1
26 [a]2 Sam. 14:2
27 [a]Josh. 21:18
28 [a]2 Kin. 25:23
29 [a]1 Chr. 11:30 [b]Josh. 18:28
30 [a]Judg. 12:13, 15 [b]Josh. 24:30
31 [a]2 Sam. 3:16
32 [a]Josh. 19:42
33 [a]2 Sam. 23:11
34 [a]2 Sam. 10:6, 8; 20:14 [b]2 Sam. 11:3 [c]2 Sam. 15:12
35 [a]1 Chr. 11:37 [b]Josh. 15:55
36 [a]2 Sam. 8:3
37 [a]2 Sam. 4:2
38 [a]1 Chr. 2:53
39 [a]2 Sam. 11:3, 6

1 [a]1 Chr. 21:1 [b]2 Sam. 21:1, 2 [c]1 Chr. 27:23, 24
2 [1]Lit., *muster* [a]Judg. 20:1; 2 Sam. 3:10
3 [a]Deut. 1:11
4 [1]Lit., *muster*
5 [a]Deut. 2:36; Josh. 13:9, 16 [b]Num. 21:32; 32:35
6 [1]Or, *Kadesh in the land of the Hittite* [a]Josh. 19:28; Judg. 1:31
7 [a]Josh. 19:29 [b]Josh. 11:3; Judg. 3:3 [c]Gen. 21:22-33
9 [1]Lit., *muster* [a]Num. 1:44-46 [b]1 Chr. 21:5
10 [1]Lit., *smote* [2]Lit., *cause to pass away* [a]1 Sam. 24:5 [b]2 Sam. 12:13 [c]1 Sam. 13:13; 2 Chr. 16:9
11 [a]1 Sam. 22:5; 1 Chr. 29:29 [b]1 Sam. 9:9
13 [a]1 Chr. 21:12; Ezek. 14:21
14 [a]Ps. 51:1; 130:4, 7
15 [1]Lit., *gave* [a]1 Chr. 21:14; 27:24 [b]2 Sam. 24:2
16 [a]Ex. 12:23; 2 Kin. 19:35; Acts 12:23 [b]Ex. 32:14; 1 Sam. 15:11
17 [a]2 Sam. 24:10 [b]2 Sam. 7:8; Ps. 74:1
18 [1]In 2 Chr. 3:1, *Ornan* [a]1 Chr. 21:18

and bowed his face to the ground before the king.

21 Then Araunah said, "Why has my lord the king come to his servant?" And David said, "To buy the threshing floor from you, in order to build an altar to the LORD, [a]that the plague may be held back from the people."

22 And Araunah said to David, "Let my lord the king take and offer up what is good in his sight. Look, [a]the oxen for the burnt offering, the threshing sledges and the yokes of the oxen for the wood.

23 "Everything, O king, Araunah gives to the king." And Araunah said to the king, "May the LORD your God [a]accept you."

24 However, the king said to Araunah, "No, but I will surely buy *it* from you for a price, for [a]I will not offer burnt offerings to the LORD my God [1]which cost me nothing." So [b]David bought the threshing floor and the oxen for fifty shekels of silver.

25 And David built there an altar to the LORD, and offered burnt offerings and peace offerings. [a]Thus the LORD was moved by entreaty for the land, and the plague was held back from Israel.

21 [a]Num. 16:44-50
22 [a]1 Sam. 6:14; 1 Kin. 19:21
23 [a]Ezek. 20:40, 41
24 [1]Lit., *gratuitously* [a]Mal. 1:13, 14 [b]1 Chr. 21:24, 25
25 [a]2 Sam. 21:14

THE FIRST BOOK OF THE KINGS

David in Old Age

1 NOW King David was old, advanced in age; and they covered him with clothes, but he could not keep warm.

2 So his servants said to him, "Let them seek a young virgin for my lord the king, and let her [1]attend the king and become his nurse; and let her lie in your bosom, that my lord the king may keep warm."

3 So they searched for a beautiful girl throughout all the territory of Israel, and found Abishag the [a]Shunammite, and brought her to the king.

4 And the girl was very beautiful; and she became the king's nurse and served him, but the king did not [1]cohabit with her.

5 Now [a]Adonijah the son of Haggith exalted himself, saying, "I will be king." So [b]he prepared for himself chariots and horsemen with fifty men to run before him.

6 And his father had never [1]crossed him at any time by asking, "Why have you done so?" And he was also a very handsome man; and [2][a]he was born after Absalom.

7 And [1]he had conferred with [a]Joab the son of Zeruiah and with [b]Abiathar the priest; and following [c]Adonijah they helped him.

8 But [a]Zadok the priest, [b]Benaiah the son of Jehoiada, [c]Nathan the prophet, [d]Shimei, Rei, and [e]the mighty men who belonged to David, were not with Adonijah.

9 And Adonijah sacrificed sheep and oxen and fatlings by the [1]stone of Zoheleth, which is beside [a]En-rogel; and he invited all his brothers, the king's sons, and all the men of Judah, the king's servants.

10 But he did not invite Nathan the prophet, Benaiah, the mighty men, and [a]Solomon his brother.

Nathan and Bathsheba

11 Then Nathan spoke to [a]Bathsheba the mother of Solomon, saying, "Have you not heard that Adonijah the son of Haggith has become king, and David our lord does not know *it?*

12 "So now come, please let me [a]give you counsel and save your life and the life of your son Solomon.

13 "Go [1]at once to King David and say to him, 'Have you not, my lord, O king, sworn to your maidservant, saying, "[a]Surely Solomon your son shall be king after me, and he shall sit on my throne"? Why then has Adonijah become king?'

14 "Behold, while you are still there speaking with the king, I will come in after you and confirm your words."

15 So Bathsheba went in to the king in the bedroom. Now [a]the king was very old, and Abishag the Shunammite was ministering to the king.

16 Then Bathsheba bowed and prostrated herself [1]before the king. And the king said, "What [2]do you wish?"

17 And she said to him, "My lord, you swore to your maidservant by the LORD your God, *saying,* '[a]Surely your son Solomon shall be king after me and he shall sit on my throne.'

18 "And now, behold, Adonijah is king; and now, my lord the king, you do not know *it.*

19 "And [a]he has sacrificed oxen and fatlings and sheep in abundance, and has invited all the sons of the king and Abiathar the priest and Joab the commander of the army; but he has not invited Solomon your servant.

20 "And as for you now, my lord the king, the eyes of all Israel are on you, to tell them who shall sit on the throne of my lord the king after him.

21 "Otherwise it will come about, [a]as soon as my lord the king sleeps with his fathers, that I and my son Solomon will be considered [1]offenders."

2 [1]Lit., *stand before*
3 [a]Josh. 19:18; 1 Sam. 28:4
4 [1]Lit., *know her*
5 [a]2 Sam. 3:4 [b]2 Sam. 15:1
6 [1]Lit., *pained him* [2]Lit., *she gave him birth* [a]2 Sam. 3:3, 4
7 [1]Lit., *his words were* [a]1 Chr. 11:6 [b]1 Sam. 22:20, 23; 2 Sam. 20:25 [c]1 Kin. 2:22
8 [a]2 Sam. 20:25; 1 Chr. 16:39 [b]2 Sam. 8:18 [c]2 Sam. 12:1 [d]1 Kin. 4:18 [e]2 Sam. 23:8-39
9 [1]Or, *Gliding* or *Serpent Stone* [a]Josh. 15:7; 18:16; 2 Sam. 17:17
10 [a]2 Sam. 12:24
11 [a]2 Sam. 12:24
12 [a]Prov. 15:22
13 [1]Lit., *and enter* [a]1 Kin. 1:30; 1 Chr. 22:9-13
15 [a]1 Kin. 1:1
16 [1]Lit., *to* [2]Lit., *to you*
17 [a]1 Kin. 1:13
19 [a]1 Kin. 1:9
21 [1]Lit., *sinners* [a]Deut. 31:16; 2 Sam. 7:12; 1 Kin. 2:10

22 And behold, while she was still speaking with the king, Nathan the prophet came in.

23 And they told the king, saying, "Here is Nathan the prophet." And when he came in before the king, he prostrated himself [1]before the king with his face to the ground.

24 Then Nathan said, "My lord the king, have you said, 'Adonijah shall be king after me, and he shall sit on my throne'?

25 "[a]For he has gone down today and has sacrificed oxen and fatlings and sheep in abundance, and has invited all the king's sons and the commanders of the army and Abiathar the priest, and behold, they are eating and drinking before him; and they say, '[b]*Long* live King Adonijah!'

26 "[a]But me, *even* me your servant, and Zadok the priest and Benaiah the son of Jehoiada and your servant Solomon, he has not invited.

27 "Has this thing been done by my lord the king, and you have not shown to your [1]servants who should sit on the throne of my lord the king after him?"

28 Then King David answered and said, "Call Bathsheba to me." And she came into the king's presence and stood before the king.

29 And the king vowed and said, "[a]As the LORD lives, who has redeemed my life from all distress,

30 surely as [a]I vowed to you by the LORD the God of Israel, saying, 'Your son Solomon shall be king after me, and he shall sit on my throne in my place'; I will indeed do so this day."

31 Then Bathsheba bowed with her face to the ground, and prostrated herself [1]before the king and said, "[a]May my lord King David live forever."

32 Then King David said, "Call to me [a]Zadok the priest, Nathan the prophet, and Benaiah the son of Jehoiada." And they came into the king's presence.

33 And the king said to them, "Take with you [a]the servants of your lord, and have my son Solomon ride on my own mule, and bring him down to [b]Gihon.

34 "And let Zadok the priest and Nathan the prophet [a]anoint him there as king over Israel, and [b]blow the trumpet and say, '[c]*Long* live King Solomon!'

35 "Then you shall come up after him, and he shall come and sit on my throne and be king in my place; for I have appointed him to be ruler over Israel and Judah."

36 And Benaiah the son of Jehoiada answered the king and said, "Amen! Thus may the LORD, the God of my lord the king, say.

37 "[a]As the LORD has been with my lord the king, so may He be with Solomon, and [b]make his throne greater than the throne of my lord King David!"

Solomon Anointed King

38 So [a]Zadok the priest, Nathan the prophet, Benaiah the son of Jehoiada, [b]the Cherethites, and the Pelethites went down and had Solomon ride on King David's mule, and brought him to [c]Gihon.

39 Zadok the priest then [a]took the horn of oil from the tent and [b]anointed Solomon. Then they [c]blew the trumpet, and all the people said, "[d]*Long* live King Solomon!"

40 And all the people went up after him, and the people [1]were playing on flutes and rejoicing with great joy, so that the earth [2]shook at their noise.

41 Now Adonijah and all the guests who were with him heard *it,* as they finished eating. When Joab heard the sound of the trumpet, he said, "Why [1]is the city making such an uproar?"

42 While he was still speaking, behold, [a]Jonathan the son of Abiathar the priest came. Then Adonijah said, "Come in, for [b]you are a valiant man and bring good news."

43 But Jonathan answered and said to Adonijah, "No! Our lord King David has made Solomon king.

44 "The king has also sent with him Zadok the priest, Nathan the prophet, Benaiah the son of Jehoiada, the Cherethites, and the Pelethites; and they have made him ride on the king's mule.

45 "And Zadok the priest and Nathan the prophet have anointed him king in Gihon, and they have come up from there rejoicing, [a]so that the city is in an uproar. This is the noise which you have heard.

46 "Besides, [a]Solomon has even taken his seat on the throne of the kingdom.

47 "And moreover, the king's servants came to bless our lord King David, saying, 'May [a]your God make the name of Solomon better than your name and his throne greater than your throne!' And [b]the king bowed himself on the bed.

48 "The king has also said thus, 'Blessed be the LORD, the God of Israel, who [a]has granted one to sit on my throne today while my own eyes see *it.*' "

49 Then all the guests of Adonijah were terrified; and they arose and each went on his way.

50 And Adonijah was afraid of Solomon, and he arose, went and [a]took hold of the horns of the altar.

51 Now it was told Solomon, saying, "Behold, Adonijah is afraid of King Solomon, for behold, he has taken hold of the horns of the altar, saying, 'Let King Solomon swear to me today that he will not put his servant to death with the sword.' "

52 And Solomon said, "If he will be a worthy man, [a]not one of his hairs will fall to the ground; but if wickedness is found in him, he will die."

53 So King Solomon sent, and they brought him down from the altar. And he came and prostrated himself [1]before King Solomon, and Solomon said to him, "Go to your house."

23 [1]Lit., *to*
25 [a]1 Kin. 1:9 [b]1 Sam. 10:24
26 [a]1 Kin. 1:8, 10
27 [1]Some mss. read *servant*
29 [a]2 Sam. 4:9
30 [a]1 Kin. 1:13, 17
31 [1]Lit., *to* [a]Dan. 2:4; 3:9
32 [a]1 Kin. 1:8
33 [a]2 Sam. 20:6, 7 [b]2 Chr. 32:30; 33:14
34 [a]1 Sam. 10:1; 16:3, 12; 2 Sam. 5:3; 1 Kin. 19:16; 2 Kin. 9:3 [b]2 Sam. 15:10 [c]1 Kin. 1:25
37 [a]Josh. 1:5, 17; 1 Sam. 20:13 [b]1 Kin. 1:47
38 [a]1 Kin. 1:8 [b]2 Sam. 8:18 [c]1 Kin. 1:33
39 [a]Ex. 30:23-32; Ps. 89:20 [b]1 Chr. 29:22 [c]1 Kin. 1:34 [d]1 Sam. 10:24
40 [1]Lit., *fluting* [2]Lit., *was split*
41 [1]Lit., *is the sound of the city an uproar*
42 [a]2 Sam. 15:27, 36; 17:17 [b]2 Sam. 18:27
45 [a]1 Kin. 1:40
46 [a]1 Chr. 29:23
47 [a]1 Kin. 1:37 [b]Gen. 47:31
48 [a]2 Sam. 7:12; 1 Kin. 3:6
50 [a]Ex. 27:2; 30:10; 1 Kin. 2:28
52 [a]1 Sam. 14:45; 2 Sam. 14:11; Acts 27:34
53 [1]Lit., *to*

David's Charge to Solomon

2 AS David's [1a]time to die drew near,
he charged Solomon his son, saying,
2 "[a]I am going the way of all the
earth. [b]Be strong, therefore, and [1]show
yourself a man.
3 "And keep the charge of the LORD
your God, to walk in His ways, to keep
His statutes, His commandments, His
ordinances, and His testimonies, [a]ac-
cording to what is written in the law of
Moses, that [b]you may succeed in all that
you do and wherever you turn,
4 so that [a]the LORD may carry out
His promise which He spoke concerning
me, saying, [b]'If your sons are careful of
their way, [c]to walk before Me in [1]truth
with all their heart and with all their
soul, [2d]you shall not lack a man on the
throne of Israel.'
5 "Now you also know what Joab the
[a]son of Zeruiah did to me, what he did
to the two commanders of the armies of
Israel, to [b]Abner the son of Ner, and to
[c]Amasa the son of Jether, whom he
killed; he also [1]shed the blood of war in
peace. And he put the blood of war on
his belt [2]about his waist, and on his
sandals [3]on his feet.
6 "[a]So act according to your wisdom,
and do not let his gray hair go down to
[1]Sheol in peace.
7 "But [a]show kindness to the sons of
Barzillai the Gileadite, and [b]let them be
among those who eat at your table; [c]for
they [1]assisted me when I fled from
Absalom your brother.
8 "And behold, [a]there is with you
Shimei the son of Gera the Benjamite, of
Bahurim; now it was he who cursed me
with a [1]violent curse on the day I went
to Mahanaim. But when [b]he came down
to me at the Jordan, I swore to him by
the LORD, saying, 'I will not put you to
death with the sword.'
9 "Now therefore, do not let him go
unpunished, [a]for you are a wise man;
and you will know what you ought to do
to him, and you will bring his gray hair
down to [1]Sheol with blood."

Death of David

10 Then [a]David slept with his fathers
and was buried in [b]the city of David.
11 And [a]the days that David reigned
over Israel *were* forty years: [b]seven years
he reigned in Hebron, and thirty-three
years he reigned in Jerusalem.
12 And [a]Solomon sat on the throne of
David his father, and his kingdom was
firmly established.
13 Now Adonijah the son of Haggith
came to Bathsheba the mother of Solomon. And she said, "[a]Do you come
peacefully?" And he said, "Peacefully."
14 Then he said, "I have something *to
say* to you." And she said, "Speak."
15 So he said, "You know that [a]the
kingdom was mine and [b]that all Israel
[1]expected me to be king; [c]however, the
kingdom has turned about and become
my brother's, [d]for it was his from the
LORD.
16 "And now I am making one request
of you; do not [1]refuse me." And she said
to him, "Speak."
17 Then he said, "Please speak to
Solomon the king, for he will not [1]refuse
you, that he may give me [a]Abishag the
Shunammite as a wife."
18 And Bathsheba said, "Very well; I
will speak to the king for you."

Adonijah Executed

19 So Bathsheba went to King Solomon to speak to him for Adonijah. And
the king arose to meet her, bowed before
her, and sat on his throne; then he [a]had
a throne set for the king's mother, and
[b]she sat on his right.
20 Then she said, "I am making one
small request of you; [a]do not [1]refuse
me." And the king said to her, "Ask, my
mother, for I will not [2]refuse you."
21 So she said, "[a]Let Abishag the
Shunammite be given to Adonijah your
brother as a wife."
22 And King Solomon answered and
said to his mother, "And why are you
asking Abishag the Shunammite for
Adonijah? [a]Ask for him also the kingdom—[b]for he is my older brother—even
for him, for [c]Abiathar the priest, and for
Joab the son of Zeruiah!"
23 Then King Solomon swore by the
LORD, saying, "May God do so to me
and more also, if Adonijah has [a]not
spoken this word against his own [1]life.
24 "Now therefore, as the LORD lives,
who has established me and set me on
the throne of David my father, and [a]who
has made me a house as He promised,
surely Adonijah will be put to death
today."
25 So King Solomon [a]sent Benaiah
the son of Jehoiada; and he fell upon
him so that he died.
26 Then to Abiathar the priest the
king said, "[a]Go to Anathoth to your own
field, [b]for you [1]deserve to die; but I will
not put you to death at this time, because [c]you carried the ark of the Lord
[2]GOD before my father David, and because [d]you were afflicted in everything
with which my father was afflicted."
27 So Solomon dismissed Abiathar
from being priest to the LORD, in order
to fulfill [a]the word of the LORD, which
He had spoken concerning the house of
Eli in Shiloh.

Joab Executed

28 Now the news came to Joab, [a]for
Joab had followed Adonijah, [b]although
he had not followed Absalom. And Joab
fled to the tent of the LORD and [c]took
hold of the horns of the altar.
29 And it was told King Solomon that
Joab had fled to the tent of the LORD,
and behold, he is beside the altar. Then
Solomon [a]sent Benaiah the son of Jehoiada, saying, "[b]Go, fall upon him."

1 [1]Lit., *days* [a]Gen. 47:29; Deut. 31:14
2 [1]Lit., *become a man* [a]Josh. 23:14 [b]Deut. 31:7, 23; Josh. 1:6, 7
3 [a]Deut. 17:18-20 [b]1 Chr. 22:12, 13
4 [1]Or, *faithfulness* [2]Lit., *there shall not be cast off to you a man from before Me* [a]2 Sam. 7:25 [b]Ps. 132:12 [c]2 Kin. 20:3 [d]2 Sam. 7:12, 13; 1 Kin. 8:25; 9:5
5 [1]Lit., *made* [2]Lit., *that was about* [3]Lit., *that were on* [a]2 Sam. 2:13, 18 [b]2 Sam. 3:27; 1 Kin. 2:32 [c]2 Sam. 20:10
6 [1]I.e., the nether world [a]1 Kin. 2:9
7 [1]Lit., *came near to* [a]2 Sam. 19:31-38 [b]2 Sam. 9:7, 10 [c]2 Sam. 17:27-29
8 [1]Or, *grievous* [a]2 Sam. 16:5-8 [b]2 Sam. 19:18-23
9 [1]I.e., the nether world [a]1 Kin. 2:6
10 [a]Acts 2:29; 13:36 [b]2 Sam. 5:7; 1 Kin. 3:1
11 [a]2 Sam. 5:4, 5; 1 Chr. 3:4; 29:26, 27 [b]2 Sam. 5:5
12 [a]1 Chr. 29:23; 2 Chr. 1:1
13 [a]1 Sam. 16:4
15 [1]Lit., *set their faces on me* [a]2 Sam. 3:3, 4; 1 Kin. 2:22 [b]1 Kin. 1:5-25 [c]1 Kin. 1:38-50 [d]1 Chr. 22:9, 10; 28:5-7
16 [1]Lit., *turn away my face*
17 [1]Lit., *turn away your face* [a]1 Kin. 1:3, 4
19 [a]1 Kin. 15:13 [b]Ps. 45:9
20 [1]Lit., *turn away my face* [2]Lit., *turn away your face* [a]1 Kin. 2:16
21 [a]1 Kin. 1:3, 4
22 [a]2 Sam. 12:8 [b]1 Kin. 1:6; 2:15; 1 Chr. 3:2, 5 [c]1 Kin. 1:7
23 [1]Lit., *soul* [a]Ruth 1:17
24 [a]2 Sam. 7:11, 13; 1 Chr. 22:10
25 [a]2 Sam. 8:18
26 [1]Lit., *are a man of death* [2]Heb., *YHWH,* usually rendered *LORD* [a]Josh. 21:18; Jer. 1:1 [b]1 Sam. 26:16 [c]1 Sam. 23:6; 2 Sam. 15:24-29 [d]1 Sam. 22:20-23; 23:8, 9
27 [a]1 Sam. 2:27-36
28 [a]1 Kin. 1:7 [b]2 Sam. 17:25; 18:2 [c]1 Kin. 1:50
29 [a]1 Kin. 2:25 [b]Ex. 21:14

30 So Benaiah came to the tent of the
LORD, and said to him, "Thus the king
has said, 'Come out.'" But he said, "No,
for I will die here." And Benaiah
brought the king word again, saying,
"Thus spoke Joab, and thus he answered
me."
31 And the king said to him, "[a]Do as
he has spoken and fall upon him and
bury him, [b]that you may remove from
me and from my father's house the
blood which Joab shed without cause.
32"And [a]the LORD will return his
blood on his own head, [b]because he fell
upon two men more righteous and better
than he and killed them with the sword,
while my father David did not know *it:*
[c]Abner the son of Ner, commander of
the army of Israel, and [d]Amasa the son
of Jether, commander of the army of
Judah.
33"[a]So shall their blood return on the
head of Joab and on the head of his
[1]descendants forever; but to David and
his [1]descendants and his house and his
throne, may there be peace from the
LORD forever."
34 Then [a]Benaiah the son of Jehoiada
went up and fell upon him and put him
to death, and he was buried at his own
house [b]in the wilderness.
35 And [a]the king appointed Benaiah
the son of Jehoiada over the army in his
place, and the king appointed [b]Zadok
the priest [c]in the place of Abiathar.

Shimei Executed

36 Now the king sent and called for
[a]Shimei and said to him, "Build for
yourself a house in Jerusalem and live
there, and do not go out from there to
any place.
37"For it will happen on the day you
go out and [a]cross over the [1]brook Kidron, you will know for certain that you
shall surely die; [b]your blood shall be on
your own head."
38 Shimei then said to the king, "The
word is good. As my lord the king has
said, so your servant will do." So Shimei
lived in Jerusalem many days.
39 But it came about at the end of
three years, that two of the servants
of Shimei ran away [a]to Achish son of
Maacah, king of Gath. And they told
Shimei, saying, "Behold, your servants
are in Gath."
40 Then Shimei arose and saddled his
donkey, and went to Gath to Achish to
look for his servants. And Shimei went
and brought his servants from Gath.
41 And it was told Solomon that
Shimei had gone from Jerusalem to
Gath, and had returned.
42 So the king sent and called for
Shimei and said to him, "Did I not make
you swear by the LORD and solemnly
warn you, saying, 'You will know for
certain that on the day you depart and
go anywhere, you shall surely die'? And
you said to me, 'The word which I have
heard is good.'
43"Why then have you not kept the
oath of the LORD, and the command
which I [1]have laid on you?"
44 The king also said to Shimei,
"[a]You know all the evil which [1]you
acknowledge in your heart, which you
did to my father David; therefore [b]the
LORD shall return your evil on your own
head.
45"But King Solomon shall be blessed,
and [a]the throne of David shall be established before the LORD forever."
46 [a]So the king commanded Benaiah
the son of Jehoiada, and he went out and
fell upon him so that he died. [b]Thus the
kingdom was established in the hands of
Solomon.

Solomon's Rule Consolidated

3 THEN [a]Solomon [1]formed a marriage alliance with Pharaoh king of
Egypt, and took Pharaoh's daughter
[b]and brought her to the city of David,
[c]until he had finished building his own
house and the house of the LORD and
[d]the wall around Jerusalem.
2 [a]The people were still sacrificing on
the high places, because there was no
house built for the name of the LORD
until those days.
3 Now [a]Solomon loved the LORD,
[b]walking in the statutes of his father
David, except he sacrificed and burned
incense on the high places.
4 [a]And the king went to [b]Gibeon to
sacrifice there, [c]for that was the great
high place; Solomon offered a thousand
burnt offerings on that altar.
5 [a]In Gibeon the LORD appeared to
Solomon [b]in a dream at night; and God
said, "[c]Ask what *you wish* me to give
you."

Solomon's Prayer

6 Then Solomon said, "[a]Thou hast
shown great lovingkindness to Thy servant David my father, [b]according as he
walked before Thee in [1]truth and righteousness and uprightness of heart
toward Thee; and [c]Thou hast [2]reserved
for him this great lovingkindness, that
Thou hast given him a son to sit on his
throne, as *it is* this day.
7"And now, O LORD my God, [a]Thou
hast made Thy servant king in place of
my father David, yet [b]I am but a little
child; [c]I do not know how to go out or
come in.
8"And [a]Thy servant is in the midst of
Thy people which Thou hast chosen, [b]a
great people who cannot be numbered or
counted for multitude.
9"So [a]give Thy servant [1]an understanding heart to judge Thy people [b]to
discern between good and evil. For who
is able to judge this [2]great people of
Thine?"

God's Answer

10 And [1]it was pleasing in the sight of
the Lord that Solomon had asked this
thing.

31 [a]Ex. 21:14 [b]Num. 35:33; Deut. 19:13; 21:8, 9
32 [a]Gen. 9:6; Judg. 9:24, 57; Ps. 7:16 [b]2 Chr. 21:13, 14 [c]2 Sam. 3:27 [d]2 Sam. 20:9, 10
33 [1]Lit., *seed* [a]2 Sam. 3:29
34 [a]1 Kin. 2:25 [b]Josh. 15:61; Matt. 3:1
35 [a]1 Kin. 4:4 [b]1 Chr. 6:53; 24:3; 29:22 [c]1 Kin. 2:27
36 [a]2 Sam. 16:5; 1 Kin. 2:8
37 [1]Or, *wadi* [a]2 Sam. 15:23; 2 Kin. 23:6; John 18:1 [b]Josh. 2:19; 2 Sam. 1:16; Ezek. 18:13
39 [a]1 Sam. 27:2
43 [1]Lit., *commanded*
44 [1]Lit., *your heart acknowledges* [a]2 Sam. 16:5-13 [b]1 Sam. 25:39; 2 Kin. 11:1, 12-16; Ps. 7:16
45 [a]2 Sam. 7:13; Prov. 25:5
46 [a]1 Kin. 2:25, 34 [b]1 Kin. 2:12; 2 Chr. 1:1

1 [1]Lit., *made himself a son-in-law of Pharaoh* [a]1 Kin. 7:8; 9:16, 24; 2 Chr. 8:11 [b]1 Kin. 9:24 [c]1 Kin. 7:1; 9:10 [d]1 Kin. 9:15
2 [a]Lev. 17:3-5; Deut. 12:2, 13, 14; 1 Kin. 22:43
3 [a]Deut. 6:5; 10:12, 13; 11:13; 30:16; Ps. 31:23; 145:20; 1 Cor. 8:3 [b]1 Kin. 2:3; 9:4; 11:4, 6, 38
4 [a]2 Chr. 1:3 [b]Josh. 18:21-25 [c]1 Chr. 16:39; 21:29
5 [a]1 Kin. 9:2; 11:9 [b]Num. 12:6; Matt. 1:20; 2:13 [c]John 15:7
6 [1]Or, *faithfulness* [2]Lit., *kept* [a]2 Sam. 7:8-17; 2 Chr. 1:8 [b]1 Kin. 9:4 [c]1 Kin. 1:48
7 [a]1 Chr. 22:9-13 [b]1 Chr. 29:1; Jer. 1:6, 7 [c]Num. 27:17
8 [a]Ex. 19:6; Deut. 7:6 [b]Gen. 15:5; 22:17
9 [1]Lit., *a hearing* [2]Lit., *heavy* [a]2 Chr. 1:10; Ps. 72:1, 2; Prov. 2:3-9; James 1:5 [b]2 Sam. 14:17; Heb. 5:14
10 [1]Lit., *the thing*

11 And God said to him, "Because you have asked this thing and have [a]not asked for yourself [1]long life, nor have asked riches for yourself, nor have you asked for the life of your enemies, but have asked for yourself [2]discernment to understand justice,

12 behold, [a]I have done according to your words. Behold, [b]I have given you a wise and discerning heart, so that there has been no one like you before you, nor shall one like you arise after you.

13 "[a]And I have also given you what you have not asked, both [b]riches and honor, so that there will not be any among the kings like you all your days.

14 "And [a]if you walk in My ways, keeping My statutes and commandments, as your father David walked, then I will [b]prolong your days."

15 Then [a]Solomon awoke, and behold, it was a dream. And he came to Jerusalem and stood before the ark of the covenant of the Lord, and offered burnt offerings and made peace offerings, and [b]made a feast for all his servants.

Solomon Wisely Judges

16 Then two women who were harlots came to the king and stood before him.

17 And the one woman said, "Oh, my lord, [1]this woman and I live in the same house; and I gave birth to a child while she *was* in the house.

18 "And it happened on the third day after I gave birth, that this woman also gave birth to a child, and we were together. There was no stranger with us in the house, only the two of us in the house.

19 "And this woman's son died in the night, because she lay on it.

20 "So she arose in the middle of the night and took my son from beside me while your maidservant slept, and laid him in her bosom, and laid her dead son in my bosom.

21 "And when I rose in the morning to nurse my son, behold, he was dead; but when I looked at him carefully in the morning, behold, he was not my son, whom I had borne."

22 Then the other woman said, "No! For the living one is my son, and the dead one is your son." But [1]the first woman said, "No! For the dead one is your son, and the living one is my son." Thus they spoke before the king.

23 Then the king said, "[1]The one says, 'This is my son who is living, and your son is the dead one'; and [1]the other says, 'No! For your son is the dead one, and my son is the living one.' "

24 And the king said, "Get me a sword." So they brought a sword before the king.

25 And the king said, "Divide the living child in two, and give half to the one and half to the other."

26 Then the woman whose child *was* the living one spoke to the king, for [1][a]she was deeply stirred over her son and said, "Oh, my lord, give her the living child, and by no means kill him." But the other said, "He shall be neither mine nor yours; divide *him!*"

27 Then the king answered and said, "Give [1]the first woman the living child, and by no means kill him. She is his mother."

28 When all Israel heard of the judgment which the king had [1]handed down, they feared the king; for [a]they saw that the wisdom of God was in him to [2]administer justice.

Solomon's Officials

4 NOW King Solomon was king over all Israel.

2 And these were his officials: Azariah the son of Zadok *was* [a]the priest;

3 Elihoreph and Ahijah, the sons of Shisha *were* secretaries; [a]Jehoshaphat the son of Ahilud *was* the recorder;

4 and [a]Benaiah the son of Jehoiada *was* over the army; and Zadok and [b]Abiathar *were* priests;

5 and Azariah the son of Nathan *was* over [a]the deputies; and Zabud the son of Nathan, a priest, *was* the king's friend;

6 and Ahishar was over the household; and Adoniram the son of Abda *was* over the men subject to forced labor.

7 And Solomon had twelve deputies over all Israel, who [1]provided for the king and his household; each man had to [2]provide for a month in the year.

8 And these are their names: Ben-hur, in the [a]hill country of Ephraim;

9 Ben-deker in Makaz and [a]Shaalbim and [b]Beth-shemesh and Elonbeth-hanan;

10 Ben-hesed, in Arubboth ([a]Socoh *was* his and all the land of [b]Hepher);

11 Ben-abinadab, *in* all [1]the [a]height of Dor (Taphath the daughter of Solomon was his wife);

12 Baana the son of Ahilud, *in* [a]Taanach and Megiddo, and all [b]Beth-shean which is beside [c]Zarethan below Jezreel, from Beth-shean to [d]Abel-meholah as far as the other side of [e]Jokmeam;

13 Ben-geber, in [a]Ramoth-gilead ([b]the towns of Jair, the son of Manasseh, which are in Gilead were his: [c]the region of Argob, which is in Bashan, sixty great cities with walls and bronze bars *were* his);

14 Ahinadab the son of Iddo, *in* [a]Mahanaim;

15 [a]Ahimaaz, in Naphtali (he also married Basemath the daughter of Solomon);

16 Baana the son of [a]Hushai, in Asher and [1]Bealoth;

17 Jehoshaphat the son of Paruah, in Issachar;

18 [a]Shimei the son of Ela, in Benjamin;

19 Geber the son of Uri, in the land of Gilead, [a]the country of Sihon king of the Amorites and of Og king of Bashan; and *he was* the only deputy who *was* in the land.

11 [1]Lit., *many days* [2]Lit., *hearing* [a]James 4:3
12 [a]1 John 5:14, 15 [b]1 Kin. 4:29-31; 5:12; 10:23, 24; Eccl. 1:16
13 [a]1 Kin. 4:21-24; 10:23, 27; Matt. 6:33; Eph. 3:20 [b]Prov. 3:16
14 [a]1 Kin. 3:6 [b]Ps. 91:16; Prov. 3:2
15 [a]Gen. 41:7 [b]1 Kin. 8:65
17 [1]Lit., *I and this woman*
22 [1]Lit., *this one was saying*
23 [1]Lit., *this one*
26 [1]Lit., *her compassion grew warm* [a]Gen. 43:30; Is. 49:15; Jer. 31:20; Hos. 11:8
27 [1]Lit., *her the living child*
28 [1]Lit., *judged* [2]Lit., *do* [a]1 Kin. 3:9, 11, 12; Dan. 1:17; Col. 2:2, 3
2 [a]1 Chr. 6:10
3 [a]2 Sam. 8:16
4 [a]1 Kin. 2:35 [b]1 Kin. 2:27
5 [a]1 Kin. 4:7
7 [1]Lit., *nourished* [2]Lit., *nourish*
8 [a]Josh. 24:33
9 [a]Judg. 1:35 [b]Josh. 21:16
10 [a]Josh. 15:35 [b]Josh. 12:17
11 [1]Or, *Naphoth-dor* [a]Josh. 11:1, 2
12 [a]Judg. 5:19 [b]Josh. 17:11 [c]Josh. 3:16 [d]1 Kin. 19:16 [e]1 Chr. 6:68
13 [a]1 Kin. 22:3-15 [b]Num. 32:41 [c]Deut. 3:4
14 [a]Josh. 13:26
15 [a]2 Sam. 15:27
16 [1]Or, *in Aloth* [a]2 Sam. 15:32
18 [a]1 Kin. 1:8
19 [a]Deut. 3:8-10

Solomon's Power, Wealth and Wisdom

20 [a]Judah and Israel *were* as numerous as the sand that is on the [1]seashore in abundance; *they* were eating and drinking and rejoicing.

21 [1a]Now Solomon ruled over all the kingdoms [b]from the [2]River *to* the land of the Philistines and to the border of Egypt; [c]*they* brought tribute and served Solomon all the days of his life.

22 And Solomon's [1]provision for one day was thirty [2]kors of fine flour and sixty [2]kors of meal,

23 ten fat oxen, twenty [1]pasture-fed oxen, a hundred sheep besides deer, gazelles, roebucks, and fattened fowl.

24 For he had dominion over everything [1]west of the [2]River, from Tiphsah even to [a]Gaza, [b]over all the kings [1]west of the [2]River; and [c]he had peace on all sides around about him.

25 [a]So Judah and Israel lived in safety, every man under his vine and his fig tree, [b]from Dan even to Beersheba, all the days of Solomon.

26 [a]And Solomon had [1]40,000 stalls of horses for his chariots, and 12,000 horsemen.

27 And those deputies [1]provided for King Solomon and all who came to King Solomon's table, each in his month; they left nothing lacking.

28 They also brought barley and straw for the horses and [a]swift steeds to the place where it should be, each according to his charge.

29 Now [a]God gave Solomon wisdom and very great discernment and breadth of [1]mind, [b]like the sand that is on the seashore.

30 And Solomon's wisdom surpassed the wisdom of all [a]the sons of the east and [b]all the wisdom of Egypt.

31 For [a]he was wiser than all men, than [b]Ethan the Ezrahite, Heman, [c]Calcol and [1]Darda, the sons of Mahol; and his [2]fame was *known* in all the surrounding nations.

32 [a]He also spoke 3,000 proverbs, and his songs were 1,005.

33 And he spoke of trees, from the cedar that is in Lebanon even to the hyssop that grows on the wall; he spoke also of animals and birds and creeping things and fish.

34 And [1]men [a]came from all peoples to hear the wisdom of Solomon, from all the kings of the earth who had heard of his wisdom.

Alliance with King Hiram

5 [1a]NOW Hiram king of Tyre sent his servants to Solomon, when he heard that they had anointed him king in place of his father, for [b]Hiram had [2]always been a friend of David.

2 Then [a]Solomon sent *word* to Hiram, saying,

3 "You know that [a]David my father was unable to build a house for the name of the LORD his God because of the wars which surrounded him, until the LORD put them under the soles of his feet.

4 "But now [a]the LORD my God has given me rest on every side; there is neither adversary nor [1]misfortune.

5 "And behold, [a]I [1]intend to build a house for the name of the LORD my God, as the LORD spoke to David my father, saying, 'Your son, whom I will set on your throne in your place, he will build the house for My name.'

6 "Now therefore, command that they cut for me [a]cedars from Lebanon, and my servants will be with your servants; and I will give you wages for your servants according to all that you say, for you know that there is no one among us who knows how to cut timber like the Sidonians."

7 And it came about when Hiram heard the words of Solomon, that he rejoiced greatly and said, "Blessed be the LORD today, who has given to David a wise son over this great people."

8 So Hiram sent *word* to Solomon, saying, "I have heard *the message* which you have sent me; I will do [1]what you desire concerning the cedar and cypress timber.

9 "My servants will bring *them* down from Lebanon to the sea; and I will make them into rafts *to go* by sea [a]to the place where you [1]direct me, and I will have them broken up there, and you shall carry *them* away. Then [b]you shall accomplish my desire by giving food to my household."

10 So [1]Hiram [2]gave Solomon [3]as much as he desired of the cedar and cypress timber.

11 [a]Solomon then gave Hiram 20,000 [1]kors of wheat as food for his household, and twenty [1]kors of beaten oil; thus Solomon would give Hiram year by year.

12 And [a]the LORD gave wisdom to Solomon, just as He [1]promised him; and there was peace between Hiram and Solomon, and the two of them made a covenant.

Conscription of Laborers

13 Now [a]King Solomon [1]levied forced laborers from all Israel; and the forced laborers [2]numbered 30,000 men.

14 And he sent them to Lebanon, 10,000 a month in relays; they were in Lebanon a month *and* two months at home. And [a]Adoniram *was* over the forced laborers.

15 Now [a]Solomon had 70,000 [1]transporters, and 80,000 hewers *of stone* in the mountains,

16 [a]besides Solomon's 3,300 chief deputies who *were* over the [1]project *and* who ruled over the people who were doing the work.

17 Then [a]the king commanded, and they quarried great stones, costly stones, to lay the foundation of the house with cut stones.

18 So Solomon's builders and [1]Hiram's builders and [a]the Gebalites [2]cut

---

20 [1]Lit., *sea* [a]Gen. 22:17; 32:12; 1 Kin. 3:8
21 [1]Ch. 5:1 in Heb. [2]I.e., Euphrates [a]2 Chr. 9:26 [b]Gen. 15:18; Josh. 1:4 [c]2 Sam. 8:2, 6
22 [1]Lit., *bread* [2]I.e., 1 kor equals approx. 10 bu.
23 [1]Lit., *oxen of the pasture*
24 [1]Lit., *beyond* [2]I.e., Euphrates [a]Judg. 1:18 [b]Ps. 72:11 [c]1 Chr. 22:9
25 [a]Jer. 23:6; Mic. 4:4; Zech. 3:10 [b]1 Sam. 3:20
26 [1]One ms. reads *4000*, cf. 2 Chr. 9:25 [a]1 Kin. 10:26; 2 Chr. 1:14
27 [1]Or, *nourished*
28 [a]Esth. 8:10, 14; Mic. 1:13
29 [1]Lit., *heart* [a]1 Kin. 3:12 [b]1 Kin. 4:20
30 [a]Gen. 29:1; Judg. 6:33 [b]Is. 19:11; Acts 7:22
31 [1]In 1 Chr. 2:6, *Dara* [2]Lit., *name* [a]1 Kin. 3:12 [b]1 Chr. 15:19; Ps. 89:title [c]1 Chr. 2:6
32 [a]Prov. 1:1; 10:1; 25:1; Eccl. 12:9; Song 1:1
34 [1]Lit., *they* [a]1 Kin. 10:1; 2 Chr. 9:23

1 [1]Ch. 5:15 in Heb. [2]Lit., *all the day* [a]2 Chr. 2:3 [b]2 Sam. 5:11; 1 Chr. 14:1
2 [a]2 Chr. 2:3
3 [a]2 Sam. 7:5; 1 Chr. 28:2, 3
4 [1]Lit., *evil occurrence* [a]1 Kin. 4:24; 1 Chr. 22:9
5 [1]Lit., *say* [a]2 Sam. 7:12, 13; 1 Chr. 17:12; 22:10; 28:6; 2 Chr. 2:4
6 [a]2 Chr. 2:8
8 [1]Lit., *all your pleasure*
9 [1]Lit., *send* [a]2 Chr. 2:16 [b]Ezra 3:7; Ezek. 27:17
10 [1]Heb., *Hirom* [2]Lit., *was giving* [3]Lit., *all his desire*
11 [1]I.e., 1 kor equals approx. 10 bu. [a]2 Chr. 2:10
12 [1]Lit., *spoke to* [a]1 Kin. 3:12
13 [1]Lit., *raised up* [2]Lit., *was* [a]1 Kin. 4:6; 9:15
14 [a]1 Kin. 4:6; 12:18
15 [1]Or, *burden bearers* [a]1 Kin. 9:20-22; 2 Chr. 2:17, 18
16 [1]Lit., *work* [a]1 Kin. 9:23
17 [a]1 Kin. 6:7; 1 Chr. 22:2
18 [1]Heb., *Hirom's* [2]Or, *chiseled* [a]Josh. 13:5; Ezek. 27:9

them, and prepared the timbers and the stones to build the house.

The Building of the Temple

6 [a]NOW it came about in the four hundred and eightieth year after the sons of Israel came out of the land of Egypt, in the fourth year of Solomon's reign over Israel, in the month of Ziv which is the second month, that he [1]began to build the house of the LORD.

2 As for the house which King Solomon built for the LORD, its length *was* sixty [1]cubits and its width twenty *cubits* and its height thirty cubits.

3 And the porch in front of the nave of the house *was* twenty cubits [1]in length, [2]corresponding to the width of the house, *and* its [3]depth along the front of the house *was* ten cubits.

4 Also for the house [a]he made windows with *artistic* frames.

5 And [a]against the wall of the house he built stories encompassing the walls of the house around both the nave and the [b]inner sanctuary; thus he made [c]side chambers all around.

6 The lowest story *was* five cubits wide, and the middle *was* six cubits wide, and the third *was* seven cubits wide; for on the outside he [1]made offsets *in the wall* of the house all around in order that *the beams* should not [2]be inserted in the walls of the house.

7 And [a]the house, while it was being built, was built of stone [1]prepared at the quarry, and there was neither hammer nor axe nor any iron tool heard in the house while it was being built.

8 The doorway for the [1]lowest side chamber *was* on the right side of the house; and they would go up by winding stairs to the middle *story*, and from the middle to the third.

9 So [a]he built the house and finished it; and he covered the house with beams and [1]planks of cedar.

10 He also built the stories against the whole house, each five [1]cubits high; and they [2]were fastened to the house with timbers of cedar.

11 Now the word of the LORD came to Solomon saying,

12 "*Concerning* this house which you are building, [a]if you will walk in My statutes and execute My ordinances and keep all My commandments by walking in them, then I will carry out My word with you which I spoke to David your father.

13 "And [a]I will dwell among the sons of Israel, and [b]will not forsake My people Israel."

14 [a]So Solomon built the house and finished it.

15 Then he [a]built the walls of the house on the inside with boards of cedar; from the floor of the house to the [1]ceiling he overlaid *the walls* on the inside with wood, and he overlaid the floor of the house with boards of cypress.

16 [a]And he built twenty cubits on the rear part of the house with boards of cedar from the floor to the [1]ceiling; he built *them* for it on the inside as an inner sanctuary, *even* as [b]the most holy place.

17 And the house, that is, the nave in front of *the inner sanctuary,* was forty [1]cubits *long.*

18 And there was cedar on the house within, carved *in the shape* of [a]gourds and open flowers; all was cedar, there was no stone seen.

19 Then he prepared an inner sanctuary within the house in order to place there the ark of the covenant of the LORD.

20 And [1]the inner sanctuary *was* twenty cubits in length, twenty cubits in width, and twenty cubits in height, and he overlaid it with pure gold. He also overlaid the altar with cedar.

21 So Solomon overlaid the inside of the house with pure gold. And he drew chains of gold across the front of the inner sanctuary; and he overlaid it with gold.

22 And he overlaid the whole house with gold, until all the house was finished. Also [a]the whole altar which was by the inner sanctuary he overlaid with gold.

23 [a]Also in the inner sanctuary he made two cherubim of olive wood, each ten cubits high.

24 And five cubits *was* the one wing of the cherub and five cubits the other wing of the cherub; from the end of one wing to the end of the other wing *were* ten cubits.

25 And the other cherub *was* ten cubits; both the cherubim were of the same measure and the same form.

26 The height of the one cherub *was* ten cubits, and so *was* the other cherub.

27 And he placed the cherubim in the midst of the inner house, and [a]the wings of the cherubim were spread out, so that the wing of the one was touching the *one* wall, and the wing of the other cherub was touching the other wall. So their wings were touching each other in the center of the house.

28 He also overlaid the cherubim with gold.

29 Then he carved all the walls of the house round about with carved engravings of cherubim, palm trees, and open flowers, inner and outer *sanctuaries.*

30 And he overlaid the floor of the house with gold, inner and outer *sanctuaries.*

31 And for the entrance of the inner sanctuary he made doors of olive wood, the lintel *and* five-sided doorposts.

32 So *he made* two doors of olive wood, and he carved on them carvings of cherubim, palm trees, and open flowers, and overlaid them with gold; and he spread the gold on the cherubim and on the palm trees.

33 So also he made for the entrance of the nave four-sided doorposts of olive wood

1 [1]Lit., *built* [a]2 Chr. 3:1, 2
2 [1]I.e., One cubit equals approx. 18 in.
3 [1]Lit., *in its length* [2]Lit., *on the face of* [3]Lit., *width*
4 [a]Ezek. 40:16; 41:16
5 [a]Ezek. 41:6 [b]1 Kin. 6:16, 19, 20 [c]Ezek. 41:5
6 [1]Lit., *gave* [2]Lit., *take hold*
7 [1]Lit., *finished* [a]Ex. 20:25; Deut. 27:5, 6
8 [1]So with Gr. and versions; M.T., *middle*
9 [1]Lit., *rows* [a]1 Kin. 6:14, 38
10 [1]I.e., One cubit equals approx. 18 in. [2]Lit., *took hold*
12 [a]2 Sam. 7:5-16; 1 Kin. 9:4
13 [a]Ex. 25:8; 29:45; Lev. 26:11 [b]Deut. 31:6; Josh. 1:5; Heb. 13:5
14 [a]1 Kin. 6:9, 38
15 [1]Lit., *walls of ceiling* [a]1 Kin. 7:7
16 [1]Lit., *walls* [a]2 Chr. 3:8 [b]Ex. 26:33, 34; Lev. 16:2; 1 Kin. 8:6; Heb. 9:3
17 [1]I.e., One cubit equals approx. 18 in.
18 [a]1 Kin. 7:24
20 [1]Lit., *before*
22 [a]Ex. 30:1, 3, 6
23 [a]Ex. 37:7-9; 2 Chr. 3:10-12
27 [a]Ex. 25:20; 37:9; 1 Kin. 8:7

34 and [a]two doors of cypress wood;
the two leaves of the one door turned on
pivots, and the two [1]leaves of the other
door turned on pivots.
35 And he carved *on it* cherubim,
palm trees, and open flowers; and he
overlaid *them* with gold evenly applied
on the engraved work.
36 And [a]he built the inner court with
three rows of cut stone and a row of
cedar beams.
37 [a]In the fourth year the foundation
of the house of the LORD was laid, in the
month of Ziv.
38 And in the eleventh year, in the
month of Bul, which is the eighth month,
the house was finished throughout all its
parts and according to all its plans. So
he was seven years in building it.

Solomon's Palace

7 NOW [a]Solomon was building his
own house thirteen years, and he
finished all his house.
2 And [a]he built the house of the
forest of Lebanon; its length was 100
[1]cubits and its width 50 cubits and its
height 30 cubits, on four rows of cedar
pillars with cedar beams on the pillars.
3 And it was paneled with cedar
above the side chambers which were on
the 45 pillars, 15 in each row.
4 And *there were artistic window*
frames in three rows, and window was
opposite window in three ranks.
5 And all the doorways and doorposts *had* squared *artistic* frames, and
window was opposite window in three
ranks.
6 Then he made [a]the hall of pillars;
its length was 50 cubits and its width 30
cubits, and a porch *was* in front of them
and pillars and a [b]threshold in front of
them.
7 And he made the hall of the
[a]throne where he was to judge, the hall
of judgment, and [b]it was paneled with
cedar from floor to floor.
8 And his house where he was to live,
the other court inward from the hall, was
of the same workmanship. [a]He also
made a house like this hall for Pharaoh's
daughter, [b]whom Solomon had married.
9 All these were of costly stones, of
stone cut according to measure, sawed
with saws, inside and outside; even from
the foundation to the coping, and so on
the outside to the great court.
10 And the foundation was of costly
stones, *even* large stones, stones of ten
cubits and stones of eight cubits.
11 And above were costly stones,
stone cut according to measure, and
cedar.
12 So [a]the great court all around *had*
three rows of cut stone and a row of
cedar beams even as the inner court of
the house of the LORD, and [b]the porch
of the house.

Hiram's Work in the Temple

13 Now [a]King Solomon sent and
brought Hiram from Tyre.
14 [a]He was a widow's son from the
tribe of Naphtali, and his father was a
man of Tyre, a worker in bronze; and
[b]he was filled with wisdom and understanding and skill for doing any work in
bronze. So he came to King Solomon
and [c]performed all his work.
15 And he fashioned [a]the two pillars
of bronze; [b]eighteen cubits was the
height of one pillar, and a line of twelve
cubits [1]measured the circumference of
both.
16 He also made two capitals of molten bronze to set on the tops of the
pillars; the height of the one capital was
five [1]cubits and the height of the other
capital was five cubits.
17 *There were* nets of network and
twisted threads of chainwork for the
capitals which were on the top of the
pillars; seven for the one capital and
seven for the other capital.
18 So he made the pillars, and two
rows around on the one network to
cover the capitals which were on the top
of the pomegranates; and so he did for
the other capital.
19 And the capitals which *were* on the
top of the pillars in the porch were of lily
design, four cubits.
20 And *there were* capitals on the two
pillars, even above *and* close to the
[1]rounded projection which was beside
the network; and [a]the pomegranates
numbered two hundred in rows around
[2]both capitals.
21 [a]Thus he set up the pillars at the
[b]porch of the nave; and he set up the
right pillar and named it [1]Jachin, and he
set up the left pillar and named it [2]Boaz.
22 And on the top of the pillars was
lily design. So the work of the pillars was
finished.
23 [a]Now he made the sea of [b]cast
metal ten cubits from brim to brim,
circular in form, and its height was five
cubits, and [1]thirty cubits in circumference.
24 And under its brim [a]gourds went
around encircling it ten to a cubit,
[b]completely surrounding the sea; the
gourds were in two rows, cast [1]with the
rest.
25 [a]It stood on twelve oxen, three
facing north, three facing west, three
facing south, and three facing east; and
the sea *was set* on top of them, and all
their rear parts *turned* inward.
26 And it was a handbreadth thick,
and its brim was made like the brim of a
cup, *as* a lily blossom; it could hold two
thousand baths.
27 Then [a]he made the ten stands of
bronze; the length of each stand was
four cubits and its width four cubits and
its height three cubits.
28 And this was the design of the
stands: they had borders, even borders
between the [1]frames,
29 and on the borders which were
between the [1]frames *were* lions, oxen
and cherubim; and on the [1]frames there
was a pedestal above, and beneath the

34 [1]So with Gr.; M.T., *curtains* [a]Ezek. 41:23-25
36 [a]1 Kin. 7:12; Jer. 36:10
37 [a]1 Kin. 6:1
1 [a]1 Kin. 3:1; 9:10; 2 Chr. 8:1
2 [1]I.e., One cubit equals approx. 18 in. [a]1 Kin. 10:17, 21; 2 Chr. 9:16
6 [a]1 Kin. 7:12 [b]Ezek. 41:25, 26
7 [a]Ps. 122:5; Prov. 20:8 [b]1 Kin. 6:15, 16
8 [a]1 Kin. 9:24; 2 Chr. 8:11 [b]1 Kin. 3:1
12 [a]1 Kin. 6:36 [b]1 Kin. 7:6
13 [a]2 Chr. 2:13, 14; 4:11
14 [a]2 Chr. 2:14 [b]Ex. 28:3; 31:3-5; 35:31; 36:1 [c]2 Chr. 4:11-16
15 [1]Lit., *went around the other pillar* [a]2 Kin. 25:17; 2 Chr. 3:15; 4:12; Jer. 52:21 [b]1 Kin. 7:41
16 [1]I.e., One cubit equals approx. 18 in.
20 [1]Lit., *belly* [2]Lit., *on the other capital* [a]1 Kin. 7:42; 2 Chr. 3:16; 4:13; Jer. 52:23
21 [1]I.e., he shall establish [2]I.e., in it is strength [a]2 Chr. 3:17 [b]1 Kin. 6:3
23 [1]Lit., *a line of 30 cubits went around it* [a]2 Chr. 4:2 [b]2 Kin. 16:17; 25:13
24 [1]Lit., *in its casting* [a]1 Kin. 6:18 [b]2 Chr. 4:3
25 [a]2 Chr. 4:4, 5; Jer. 52:20
27 [a]1 Kin. 7:38; 2 Kin. 25:13; 2 Chr. 4:14
28 [1]Or, *crossbars*
29 [1]Or, *crossbars*

lions and oxen *were* wreaths of hanging
work.
30 Now each stand had four bronze
wheels with bronze axles, and its four
feet had supports; beneath the basin
were cast supports with wreaths at each
side.
31 And its opening inside the crown at
the top *was* a cubit, and its opening *was*
round like the design of a pedestal, a
cubit and a half; and also on its opening
there were engravings, and their borders
were square, not round.
32 And the four wheels *were* underneath the borders, and the axles of the
wheels *were* on the stand. And the height
of a wheel *was* a cubit and a half.
33 And the workmanship of the
wheels *was* like the workmanship of a
chariot wheel. Their axles, their rims,
their spokes, and their hubs *were* all cast.
34 Now *there were* four supports at
the four corners of each stand; its supports *were* part of the stand itself.
35 And on the top of the stand *there*
was a circular form half a [1]cubit high,
and on the top of the stand its [2]stays and
its borders *were* part of it.
36 And he engraved on the plates of
its stays and on its borders, cherubim,
lions and palm trees, according to the
clear space on each, with wreaths *all*
around.
37 [a]He made the ten stands like this:
all of them had one casting, one measure
and one form.
38 [a]And he made ten basins of bronze,
one basin held forty baths; each basin
was four cubits, *and* on each of the ten
stands *was* one basin.
39 Then he set the stands, five on the
right side of the house and five on the
left side of the house; and he set the sea
of cast metal on the right side of the
house eastward toward the south.
40 Now Hiram made the basins and
the shovels and the bowls. So Hiram
finished doing all the work which he
performed for King Solomon *in* the
house of the LORD:
41 the two pillars and the *two* bowls of
the capitals which *were* on the top of the
[a]two pillars, and the two networks to
cover the two bowls of the capitals
which *were* on the top of the pillars;
42 and the [a]four hundred pomegranates for the two networks, two rows of
pomegranates for each network to cover
the two bowls of the capitals which *were*
on the tops of the pillars;
43 and the ten stands with the ten
basins on the stands;
44 and [a]the one sea and the twelve
oxen under the sea;
45 and [a]the pails and the shovels and
the bowls; even all these utensils which
Hiram made for King Solomon *in* the
house of the LORD *were* of polished
bronze.
46 [a]In the plain of the Jordan the king
cast them, in the clay ground between
[b]Succoth and [c]Zarethan.

35 [1]I.e., One cubit equals approx. 18 in. [2]Lit., *hands*
37 [a]2 Chr. 4:14
38 [a]Ex. 30:18; 2 Chr. 4:6
41 [a]1 Kin. 7:17, 18
42 [a]1 Kin. 7:20
44 [a]1 Kin. 7:23, 25
45 [a]Ex. 27:3; 2 Chr. 4:16
46 [a]2 Chr. 4:17 [b]Gen. 33:17; Josh. 13:27 [c]Josh. 3:16
47 [a]1 Chr. 22:3, 14
48 [a]Ex. 30:1-3; 37:10-29; 2 Chr. 4:8 [b]Ex. 25:30
49 [a]Ex. 25:31-38
50 [a]Ex. 27:3; 2 Kin. 25:15
51 [a]2 Chr. 5:1 [b]2 Sam. 8:11; 1 Chr. 18:11; 2 Chr. 5:1
1 [a]2 Chr. 5:2-10 [b]Num. 1:4; 7:2 [c]2 Sam. 6:12-17; 1 Chr. 15:25-29 [d]2 Sam. 5:7
2 [a]Lev. 23:34; 1 Kin. 8:65; 2 Chr. 7:8-10
3 [a]Num. 7:9; Deut. 31:9; Josh. 3:3, 6
4 [a]1 Kin. 3:4; 2 Chr. 1:3
5 [1]Lit., *sheep and oxen . . . numbered for multitude* [a]2 Sam. 6:13; 2 Chr. 1:6
6 [a]1 Kin. 8:3 [b]1 Kin. 6:19 [c]1 Kin. 6:27
8 [a]Ex. 25:13-15; 37:4, 5
9 [a]Ex. 25:16, 21; Deut. 10:2-5; Heb. 9:4 [b]Ex. 24:7, 8; 40:20; Deut. 4:13

47 And Solomon left all the utensils
unweighed, because *they were* too many;
[a]the weight of the bronze could not be
ascertained.
48 And Solomon made all the furniture which *was in* the house of the LORD:
[a]the golden altar and the golden table on
which *was* the [b]bread of the Presence;
49 and the lampstands, five on the
right side and five on the left, in front of
the inner sanctuary, of pure gold; and
[a]the flowers and the lamps and the
tongs, of gold;
50 and the cups and the snuffers and
the bowls and the spoons and the [a]fire-
pans, of pure gold; and the hinges both
for the doors of the inner house, the
most holy place, *and* for the doors of the
house, *that is,* of the nave, of gold.
51 [a]Thus all the work that King Solomon performed *in* the house of the LORD
was finished. And [b]Solomon brought in
the things dedicated by his father David,
the silver and the gold and the utensils,
and he put them in the treasuries of the
house of the LORD.

The Ark Brought into the Temple

8 [a]THEN Solomon assembled the elders of Israel and all [b]the heads of
the tribes, the leaders of the fathers'
households of the sons of Israel, to King
Solomon in Jerusalem, [c]to bring up the
ark of the covenant of the LORD from
[d]the city of David, which is Zion.
2 And all the men of Israel assembled themselves to King Solomon at [a]the
feast, in the month Ethanim, which is
the seventh month.
3 Then all the elders of Israel came,
and [a]the priests took up the ark.
4 And they brought up the ark of the
LORD and [a]the tent of meeting and all
the holy utensils, which were in the tent,
and the priests and the Levites brought
them up.
5 And King Solomon and all the
congregation of Israel, who were assembled to him, [a]were with him before the
ark, sacrificing [1]so many sheep and oxen
they could not be counted or numbered.
6 Then [a]the priests brought the ark
of the covenant of the LORD [b]to its
place, into the inner sanctuary of the
house, to the most holy place, [c]under the
wings of the cherubim.
7 For the cherubim spread *their*
wings over the place of the ark, and the
cherubim made a covering over the ark
and its poles from above.
8 But [a]the poles were so long that the
ends of the poles could be seen from the
holy place before the inner sanctuary,
but they could not be seen outside; they
are there to this day.
9 [a]There was nothing in the ark
except the two tablets of stone which
Moses put there at Horeb, where [b]the
LORD made a covenant with the sons of
Israel, when they came out of the land of
Egypt.

10 And it came about when the priests came from the holy place, that [a]the cloud filled the house of the LORD,
11 so that the priests could not stand to minister because of the cloud, for the glory of the LORD filled the house of the LORD.

Solomon Addresses the People

12 [a]Then Solomon said,
"The LORD has said that [b]He would dwell in the thick cloud.
13 "[a]I have surely built Thee a lofty house,
[b]A place for Thy dwelling forever."
14 Then the king [1]faced about and [a]blessed all the assembly of Israel, while all the assembly of Israel was standing.
15 And he said, "[a]Blessed be the LORD, the God of Israel, [b]who spoke with His mouth to my father David and has fulfilled *it* with His hand, saying,
16 '[a]Since the day that I brought My people Israel from Egypt, I did not choose a city out of all the tribes of Israel *in which* to build a house that [b]My name might be there, but [c]I chose David to be over My people Israel.'
17 "[a]Now it was [1]in the heart of my father David to build a house for the name of the LORD, the God of Israel.
18 "But the LORD said to my father David, 'Because it was [1]in your heart to build a house for My name, you did well that it was [1]in your heart.
19 '[a]Nevertheless you shall not build the house, but your son who [1]shall be born to you, he shall build the house for My name.'
20 "Now the LORD has fulfilled His word which He spoke; for [a]I have risen in place of my father David and sit on the throne of Israel, as the LORD [1]promised, and have built the house for the name of the LORD, the God of Israel.
21 "And there I have set a place for the ark, [a]in which is the covenant of the LORD, which He made with our fathers when He brought them from the land of Egypt."

The Prayer of Dedication

22 Then [a]Solomon stood before the altar of the LORD in the presence of all the assembly of Israel and [b]spread out his hands toward heaven.
23 And he said, "O LORD, the God of Israel, [a]there is no God like Thee in heaven above or on earth beneath, [b]who art keeping covenant and *showing* lovingkindness to Thy servants who walk before Thee with all their heart,
24 who hast kept with Thy servant, my father David, that which Thou hast [1]promised him; indeed, Thou hast spoken with Thy mouth and hast fulfilled it with Thy hand as it is this day.
25 "Now therefore, O LORD, the God of Israel, keep with Thy servant David my father that which Thou hast [1]promised him, saying, '[2][a]You shall not lack a man to sit on the throne of Israel, if only your sons take heed to their way to walk before Me as you have walked.'
26 "Now therefore, O God of Israel, let Thy word, I pray Thee, be confirmed [a]which Thou hast spoken to Thy servant, my father David.
27 "But will God indeed dwell on the earth? Behold, [a]heaven and the [1]highest heaven cannot contain Thee, how much less this house which I have built!
28 "Yet have regard to the [a]prayer of Thy servant and to his supplication, O LORD my God, to listen to the cry and to the prayer which Thy servant prays before Thee today;
29 [a]that Thine eyes may be open toward this house night and day, toward [b]the place of which Thou hast said, 'My name shall be there,' to listen to the prayer which Thy servant shall pray toward this place.
30 "And [a]listen to the supplication of Thy servant and of Thy people Israel, [b]when they pray toward this place; hear Thou in heaven Thy dwelling place; hear and [c]forgive.
31 "[a]If a man sins against his neighbor and is made to take an oath, and he comes *and* takes an oath before Thine altar in this house,
32 then hear Thou in heaven and act and judge Thy servants, [a]condemning the wicked by bringing his way on his own head and justifying the righteous by giving him according to his righteousness.
33 "[a]When Thy people Israel are [1]defeated before an enemy, because they have sinned against Thee, [b]if they turn to Thee again and confess Thy name and pray and make supplication to Thee in this house,
34 then hear Thou in heaven, and forgive the sin of Thy people Israel, and bring them back to the land which Thou didst give to their fathers.
35 "[a]When the heavens are shut up and there is no rain, because they have sinned against Thee, and they pray toward this place and confess Thy name and turn from their sin when Thou dost afflict them,
36 then hear Thou in heaven and forgive the sin of Thy servants and of Thy people Israel, [a]indeed, teach them the good way in which they should walk. And [b]send rain on Thy land, which Thou hast given Thy people for an inheritance.
37 "[a]If there is famine in the land, if there is pestilence, if there is blight *or* mildew, locust *or* grasshopper, if their enemy besieges them in the land of their [1]cities, whatever plague, whatever sickness there is,
38 whatever prayer or supplication is made by any man *or* by all Thy people Israel, [1]each knowing the [2]affliction of his own heart, and spreading his [3]hands toward this house;
39 then hear Thou in heaven Thy dwelling place, and forgive and act and render to each according to all his ways,

10 [a]Ex. 40:34, 35; 2 Chr. 7:1, 2
12 [a]2 Chr. 6:1 [b]Lev. 16:2; Ps. 18:11; 97:2
13 [a]2 Sam. 7:13 [b]Ex. 15:17; Ps. 132:14
14 [1]Lit., *turned his face about* [a]2 Sam. 6:18; 1 Kin. 8:55
15 [a]1 Chr. 29:10, 20; Neh. 9:5; Luke 1:68 [b]2 Sam. 7:12, 13; 1 Chr. 22:10
16 [a]2 Sam. 7:4, 5; 1 Chr. 17:3-10; 2 Chr. 6:5 [b]Deut. 12:5, 11 [c]1 Sam. 16:1; 2 Sam. 7:8
17 [1]Lit., *with* [a]2 Sam. 7:2, 3; 1 Chr. 17:1, 2
18 [1]Lit., *with*
19 [1]Lit., *is to come forth from your loins* [a]2 Sam. 7:5, 12, 13; 1 Kin. 5:3, 5; 1 Chr. 17:11, 12; 22:8-10
20 [1]Lit., *spoke* [a]1 Chr. 28:5, 6
21 [a]Deut. 31:26; 1 Kin. 8:9
22 [a]1 Kin. 8:54; 2 Chr. 6:12 [b]Ex. 9:33; Ezra 9:5
23 [a]1 Sam. 2:2; 2 Sam. 7:22 [b]Deut. 7:9; Neh. 1:5; 9:32; Dan. 9:4
24 [1]Lit., *spoken to*
25 [1]Lit., *spoken to* [2]Lit., *There shall not be cut off to you a man from before Me.* [a]1 Kin. 2:4
26 [a]2 Sam. 7:25
27 [1]Lit., *heaven of heavens* [a]2 Chr. 2:6; Ps. 139:7-16; Is. 66:1; Jer. 23:24; Acts 7:49
28 [a]Phil. 4:6
29 [a]2 Chr. 7:15; Neh. 1:6 [b]Deut. 12:11
30 [a]Neh. 1:6 [b]Dan. 6:10 [c]Ex. 34:6, 7; Ps. 85:2; Dan. 9:9; 1 John 1:9
31 [a]Ex. 22:8-11
32 [a]Deut. 25:1
33 [1]Lit., *smitten* [a]Lev. 26:17, 25; Deut. 28:25, 48 [b]Lev. 26:40-42
35 [a]Lev. 26:19; Deut. 11:16, 17; 2 Sam. 24:10-13
36 [a]1 Sam. 12:23; Ps. 5:8; 25:4, 5; 27:11; 86:11; 119:133; Jer. 6:16 [b]1 Kin. 18:1, 41-45; Jer. 14:22
37 [1]Lit., *gates* [a]Lev. 26:16, 25, 26; Deut. 28:21-23, 38-42
38 [1]Lit., *who shall know each* [2]Lit., *plague* [3]Lit., *palms*

[a]whose heart Thou knowest, for [b]Thou alone dost know the hearts of all the sons of men,

40 that they may [1]fear Thee all the days that they live [2]in the land which Thou hast given to our fathers.

41 "Also concerning the foreigner who is not of Thy people Israel, when he comes from a far country for Thy name's sake

42 (for they will hear of Thy great name [a]and Thy mighty hand, and of Thine outstretched arm); when he comes and prays toward this house,

43 hear Thou in heaven Thy dwelling place, and do according to all for which the foreigner calls to Thee, in order [a]that all the peoples of the earth may know Thy name, to [1]fear Thee, as *do* Thy people Israel, and that they may know that [2]this house which I have built is called by Thy name.

44 "When Thy people go out to battle against [1]their enemy, by whatever way Thou shalt send them, and [a]they pray to the LORD [2]toward the city which Thou hast chosen and the house which I have built for Thy name,

45 then hear in heaven their prayer and their supplication, and maintain their [1]cause.

46 "When they sin against Thee (for [a]there is no man who does not sin) and Thou art angry with them and dost deliver them to an enemy, so that [1]they take them away captive [b]to the land of the enemy, far off or near;

47 [a]if they [1]take thought in the land where they have been taken captive, and repent and make supplication to Thee in the land of those who have taken them captive, saying, '[b]We have sinned and have committed iniquity, we have acted wickedly';

48 [a]if they return to Thee with all their heart and with all their soul in the land of their enemies who have taken them captive, and [b]pray to Thee toward their land which Thou hast given to their fathers, the city which Thou hast chosen, and the house which I have built for Thy name;

49 then hear their prayer and their supplication in heaven Thy dwelling place, and maintain their [1]cause,

50 and forgive Thy people who have sinned against Thee and all their transgressions which they have transgressed against Thee, and [a]make them *objects of* compassion before those who have taken them captive, that they may have compassion on them

51 ([a]for they are Thy people and Thine inheritance which Thou hast brought forth from Egypt, [b]from the midst of the iron furnace),

52 [a]that Thine eyes may be open to the supplication of Thy servant and to the supplication of Thy people Israel, to listen to them whenever they call to Thee.

53 "For Thou hast separated them from all the peoples of the earth as Thine inheritance, [a]as Thou didst speak through Moses Thy servant, when Thou didst bring our fathers forth from Egypt, O Lord [1]GOD."

Solomon's Benediction

54 [a]And it came about that when Solomon had finished praying this entire prayer and supplication to the LORD, [b]he arose from before the altar of the LORD, from kneeling on his knees with his [1]hands spread toward heaven.

55 And he stood and [a]blessed all the assembly of Israel with a loud voice, saying,

56 "Blessed be the LORD, who has given rest to His people Israel, [a]according to all that He [1]promised; [b]not one word has [2]failed of all His good [3]promise, which He [1]promised through Moses His servant.

57 "May the LORD our God be with us, as He was with our fathers; [a]may He not leave us or forsake us,

58 that [a]He may incline our hearts to Himself, to walk in all His ways and to keep His commandments and His statutes and His ordinances, which He commanded our fathers.

59 "And may these words of mine, with which I have made supplication before the LORD, be near to the LORD our God day and night, that He may maintain the [1]cause of His servant and the [1]cause of His people Israel, [2]as each day requires,

60 so [a]that all the peoples of the earth may know that [b]the LORD is God; there is no one else.

61 "[a]Let your heart therefore be [1]wholly devoted to the LORD our God, to walk in His statutes and to keep His commandments, as at this day."

Dedicatory Sacrifices

62 [a]Now the king and all Israel with him [b]offered sacrifice before the LORD.

63 And Solomon offered for the sacrifice of peace offerings, which he offered to the LORD, 22,000 oxen and 120,000 sheep. [a]So the king and all the sons of Israel dedicated the house of the LORD.

64 On the same day the king consecrated the middle of the court that *was* before the house of the LORD, because there he [1]offered the burnt offering and the grain offering and the fat of the peace offerings; for [a]the bronze altar that *was* before the LORD *was* too small to hold the burnt offering and the grain offering and the fat of the peace offerings.

65 So [a]Solomon observed the feast at that time, and all Israel with him, a great assembly [b]from the entrance of Hamath [c]to the brook of Egypt, before the LORD our God, for seven days and seven *more* days, *even* fourteen days.

66 On the eighth day he sent the people away and they blessed the king. Then they went to their tents joyful and glad of heart for all the goodness that the LORD had [1]shown to David His servant and to Israel His people.

39 [a]1 Sam. 2:3; 16:7 [b]1 Chr. 28:9; Ps. 11:4; Jer. 17:10; John 2:24, 25; Acts 1:24
40 [1]Or, *revere* [2]Lit., *on the face of the land*
42 [a]Ex. 13:3; Deut. 3:24
43 [1]Or, *reverence* [2]Lit., *Thy name is called upon this house which I have built* [a]Josh. 4:23, 24; 1 Sam. 17:46; Ps. 67:2
44 [1]Lit., *his* [2]Lit., in *the way of* [a]2 Chr. 14:11
45 [1]Lit., *right* or *justice*
46 [1]Lit., *their captors take them captive* [a]Ps. 130:3, 4; 143:2; Prov. 20:9; Eccl. 7:20; Rom. 3:23; 1 John 1:8-10 [b]Lev. 26:34-39; 2 Kin. 17:6, 18; 25:21
47 [1]Lit., *return to their heart* [a]Lev. 26:40-42; Neh. 9:2 [b]Ezra 9:6, 7; Neh. 1:6; Ps. 106:6; Dan. 9:5
48 [a]Deut. 4:29; 1 Sam. 7:3, 4; Neh. 1:9 [b]Dan. 6:10; Jon. 2:4
49 [1]Lit., *judgment*
50 [a]2 Chr. 30:9; Ps. 106:46; Acts 7:10
51 [a]Ex. 32:11, 12; Deut. 9:26-29 [b]Deut. 4:20; Jer. 11:4
52 [a]1 Kin. 8:29
53 [1]Heb., *YHWH*, usually rendered *LORD* [a]Ex. 19:5, 6; Deut. 9:26-29
54 [1]Lit., *palms* [a]2 Chr. 7:1 [b]2 Chr. 6:13
55 [a]Num. 6:23-26; 2 Sam. 6:18; 1 Kin. 8:14
56 [1]Lit., *spoke* [2]Lit., *fallen* [3]Lit., *word* [a]Deut. 12:10 [b]Josh. 21:45; 23:14, 15
57 [a]Deut. 31:6, 17; Josh. 1:5; 1 Sam. 12:22; Rom. 8:31; Heb. 13:5
58 [a]Ps. 119:36; Jer. 31:33
59 [1]Lit., *judgment* [2]Lit., *the thing of a day in its day*
60 [a]Josh. 4:24; 1 Sam. 17:46; 1 Kin. 8:43; 2 Kin. 19:19 [b]Deut. 4:35; 1 Kin. 18:39; Jer. 10:10-12
61 [1]Lit., *complete with* [a]Deut. 18:13; 1 Kin. 11:4; 2 Kin. 20:3
62 [a]2 Chr. 7:4-10 [b]2 Sam. 6:17-19; Ezra 6:16, 17
63 [a]Ezra 6:15-18; Neh. 12:27
64 [1]Lit., *made* [a]2 Chr. 4:1
65 [a]Lev. 23:34-42; 1 Kin. 8:2 [b]Num. 34:8; Josh. 13:5; Judg. 3:3; 2 Kin. 14:25 [c]Gen. 15:18; Ex. 23:31; Num. 34:5; Josh. 13:3
66 [1]Lit., *done*

God's Promise and Warning

9 [a]NOW it came about when Solomon had finished building the house of the LORD, and [b]the king's house, and [c]all [1]that Solomon desired to do,

2 that [a]the LORD appeared to Solomon a second time, as He had appeared to him at Gibeon.

3 And the LORD said to him, "[a]I have heard your prayer and your supplication, which you have made before Me; I have consecrated this house which you have built [b]by putting My name there forever, and [c]My eyes and My heart will be there perpetually.

4 "And as for you, [a]if you will walk before Me as your father David walked, in integrity of heart and uprightness, doing according to all that I have commanded you *and* will keep My statutes and My ordinances,

5 then [a]I will establish the throne of your kingdom over Israel forever, just as I [1]promised to your father David, saying, '[2]You shall not lack a man on the throne of Israel.'

6 "[a]But if you or your sons shall indeed turn away from following Me, and shall not keep My commandments and My statutes which I have set before you and shall go and serve other gods and worship them,

7 [a]then I will cut off Israel from the land which I have given them, and [b]the house which I have consecrated for My name, I will [1]cast out of My sight. So [c]Israel will become a proverb and a byword among all peoples.

8 "And this house will become [1a]a heap of ruins; everyone who passes by will be astonished and hiss and say, '[b]Why has the LORD done thus to this land and to this house?'

9 "And they will say, '[a]Because they forsook the LORD their God, who brought their fathers out of the land of Egypt, and adopted other gods and worshiped them and served them, therefore the LORD has brought all this adversity on them.' "

Cities Given to Hiram

10 [a]And it came about [b]at the end of twenty years in which Solomon had built the two houses, the house of the LORD and the king's house

11 (Hiram king of Tyre had supplied Solomon with cedar and cypress timber and gold according to all his desire), then King Solomon gave Hiram twenty cities in the land of Galilee.

12 So Hiram came out from Tyre to see the cities which Solomon had given him, and they [1]did not please him.

13 And he said, "What are these cities which you have given me, my brother?" So [1]they were called the land of [2a]Cabul to this day.

14 [a]And Hiram sent to the king 120 talents of gold.

15 Now this is the account of the forced labor which King Solomon [a]levied to build the house of the LORD, his own house, the [1b]Millo, the wall of Jerusalem, [c]Hazor, [d]Megiddo, and [e]Gezer.

16 *For* Pharaoh king of Egypt had gone up and captured Gezer, and burned it with fire, and killed the [a]Canaanites who lived in the city, and had [b]given it *as* a dowry to his daughter, Solomon's wife.

17 So Solomon rebuilt Gezer and the lower [a]Beth-horon

18 and [a]Baalath and Tamar in the wilderness, in the land *of Judah,*

19 and all the storage cities which Solomon had, even [a]the cities for [1]his chariots and the cities for [1b]his horsemen, and [2c]all that it pleased Solomon to build in Jerusalem, in Lebanon, and in all the land [3]under his rule.

20 *As for* all the people who were left of the Amorites, the Hittites, the Perizzites, the Hivites and the Jebusites, who were not of the sons of Israel,

21 [a]their descendants who were left after them in the land [b]whom the sons of Israel were unable to destroy utterly, [c]from them Solomon levied [d]forced laborers, even to this day.

22 But Solomon [a]did not make slaves of the sons of Israel; for they were men of war, his servants, his princes, his captains, his chariot commanders, and his horsemen.

23 These *were* the [1a]chief officers who were over Solomon's work, five hundred and fifty, [b]who ruled over the people doing the work.

24 As soon as [a]Pharaoh's daughter came up from the city of David to her house which *Solomon* had built for her, [b]then he built the Millo.

25 Now [a]three times in a year Solomon offered burnt offerings and peace offerings on the altar which he built to the LORD, burning incense with them *on the altar* which *was* before the LORD. So he finished the house.

26 King Solomon also built a [a]fleet of ships in [b]Ezion-geber, which is near Eloth on the shore of the [1]Red Sea, in the land of Edom.

27 [a]And Hiram sent his servants with the fleet, sailors who knew the sea, along with the servants of Solomon.

28 And they went to [a]Ophir, and took four hundred and twenty talents of gold from there, and brought *it* to King Solomon.

The Queen of Sheba

10 NOW when the [a]queen of [b]Sheba heard about the fame of Solomon concerning the name of the LORD, she came [c]to test him with difficult questions.

2 So she came to Jerusalem with a very large retinue, with camels [a]carrying spices and very much gold and precious stones. When she came to Solomon, she

1 [1]Lit., *Solomon's desire which he was pleased to do* [a]2 Chr. 7:11 [b]1 Kin. 7:1, 2 [c]2 Chr. 8:6
2 [a]1 Kin. 3:5; 11:9; 2 Chr. 1:7
3 [a]2 Kin. 20:5; Ps. 10:17; 34:17 [b]1 Kin. 8:29 [c]Deut. 11:12; 2 Chr. 6:40
4 [a]1 Kin. 3:6, 14; 11:4, 6, 8; 2 Kin. 20:3; Ps. 128:1
5 [1]Lit., *spoke* [2]Lit., *There shall not be cut off to you a man* [a]2 Sam. 7:12, 16; 1 Kin. 2:4; 6:12; 1 Chr. 22:10
6 [a]2 Sam. 7:14-16; 1 Chr. 28:9; Ps. 89:30ff.
7 [1]Lit., *send* [a]Lev. 18:24-29; Deut. 4:26; 2 Kin. 17:23 [b]Jer. 7:4-14 [c]Deut. 28:37; Ps. 44:14; Jer. 24:9
8 [1]Heb., *high* [a]2 Kin. 25:9; 2 Chr. 36:19 [b]Deut. 29:24-26; 2 Chr. 7:21; Jer. 22:8, 9, 28
9 [a]Deut. 29:25-28; Jer. 2:10-13
10 [a]2 Chr. 8:1 [b]1 Kin. 6:37, 38; 7:1; 9:1
12 [1]Lit., *were not right in his sight*
13 [1]Lit., *he called them* [2]I.e., as good as nothing [a]Josh. 19:27
14 [a]1 Kin. 9:11
15 [1]I.e., citadel [a]1 Kin. 5:13 [b]2 Sam. 5:9; 1 Kin. 9:24 [c]Josh. 11:1; 19:36 [d]Josh. 17:11 [e]Judg. 1:29
16 [a]Josh. 16:10 [b]1 Kin. 3:1; 7:8
17 [a]Josh. 10:10; 16:3; 21:22; 2 Chr. 8:5
18 [a]Josh. 19:44
19 [1]Lit., *the* [2]Lit., *the desire of Solomon which he desired to build in Jerusalem* [3]Lit., *of* [a]1 Kin. 10:26; 2 Chr. 1:14 [b]1 Kin. 4:26 [c]1 Kin. 9:1
21 [a]Judg. 1:21-29; 3:1 [b]Josh. 15:63; 17:12, 13 [c]Judg. 1:28, 35 [d]Gen. 9:25, 26; Ezra 2:55, 58
22 [a]Lev. 25:39
23 [1]Or, *officers of the deputies* [a]2 Chr. 8:10 [b]1 Kin. 5:16
24 [a]1 Kin. 3:1; 7:8 [b]2 Sam. 5:9; 1 Kin. 9:15; 11:27; 2 Chr. 32:5
25 [a]Ex. 23:14-17; Deut. 16:16
26 [1]Lit., *Sea of Reeds* [a]1 Kin. 22:48 [b]Num. 33:35; Deut. 2:8; 1 Kin. 22:48
27 [a]1 Kin. 5:6, 9; 10:11
28 [a]1 Chr. 29:4; 2 Chr. 8:18

1 [a]2 Chr. 9:1; Matt. 12:42; Luke 11:31 [b]Gen. 10:7, 28; Ps. 72:10, 15 [c]Judg. 14:12-14; Ps. 49:4

2 [a]1 Kin. 10:10

spoke with him about all that was in her heart.

3 And Solomon [1]answered all her questions; nothing was hidden from the king which he did not [2]explain to her.

4 When the queen of Sheba perceived all the wisdom of Solomon, the house that he had built,

5 the food of his table, the seating of his servants, the attendance of his waiters and their attire, his cupbearers, and [1]his stairway by which he went up to the house of the LORD, there was no more spirit in her.

6 Then she said to the king, "It was a true report which I heard in my own land about your words and your wisdom.

7 "Nevertheless I did not believe the [1]reports, until I came and my eyes had seen it. And behold, the half was not told me. You exceed *in* wisdom and prosperity the report which I heard.

8 "How [a]blessed are your men, how blessed are these your servants who stand before you continually *and* hear your wisdom.

9 "[a]Blessed be the LORD your God who delighted in you to set you on the throne of Israel; [b]because the LORD loved Israel forever, therefore He made you king, [c]to do justice and righteousness."

10 And [a]she gave the king a hundred and twenty talents of gold, and a very great *amount* of spices and precious stones. Never again did such abundance of spices come in as that which the queen of Sheba gave King Solomon.

11 [a]And also the ships of Hiram, which brought gold from Ophir, brought in from Ophir a very great *number of* almug trees and precious stones.

12 And [a]the king made of the almug trees supports for the house of the LORD and for the king's house, also lyres and harps for the singers; such almug trees have not come in *again,* nor have they been seen to this day.

13 And King Solomon gave to the queen of Sheba all her desire which she requested, besides what he gave her according to [1]his royal bounty. Then she turned and went to her own land [2]together with her servants.

Wealth, Splendor and Wisdom

14 [a]Now the weight of gold which came in to Solomon in one year *was* 666 talents of gold,

15 besides *that* from the traders and the [1]wares of the merchants and all the kings of the [a]Arabs and the governors of the country.

16 And [a]King Solomon made 200 large shields of beaten gold, [1]using 600 *shekels of* gold on each large shield.

17 And *he made* [a]300 shields of beaten gold, [1]using three minas of gold on each shield, and [b]the king put them in the house of the forest of Lebanon.

3 [1]Lit., *told her all her words* [2]Lit., *tell her*

5 [1]Or, *his burnt offering which he offered*

7 [1]Lit., *words*

8 [a]Prov. 8:34

9 [a]1 Kin. 5:7 [b]1 Chr. 17:22; 2 Chr. 2:11 [c]2 Sam. 8:15; 23:3; Ps. 72:2

10 [a]1 Kin. 10:2

11 [a]1 Kin. 9:27, 28; Job 22:24

12 [a]2 Chr. 9:11

13 [1]Lit., *the hand of King Solomon* [2]Lit., *she and*

14 [a]2 Chr. 9:13-28

15 [1]Or, *traffic* [a]2 Chr. 9:14

16 [1]Lit., *he brought up* [a]1 Kin. 14:26-28; 2 Chr. 12:9, 10

17 [1]Lit., *he brought up* [a]1 Kin. 14:26 [b]1 Kin. 7:2

18 [a]1 Kin. 10:22; 2 Chr. 9:17; Ps. 45:8

19 [1]Lit., *hands* [2]Lit., *on this side and on this at the place of the seat*

21 [1]Lit., *anything*

22 [a]1 Kin. 9:26-28; 22:48; 2 Chr. 20:36

23 [a]1 Kin. 3:12, 13; 4:30

24 [a]1 Kin. 3:9, 12, 28

25 [a]Ps. 68:29

26 [1]So with ancient versions; Heb., *led* [a]1 Kin. 4:26; 2 Chr. 1:14-17; 9:25 [b]1 Kin. 9:19

27 [1]Heb., *Shephelah* [a]Deut. 17:17; 2 Chr. 1:15

28 [a]Deut. 17:16; 2 Chr. 1:16; 9:28

29 [1]Lit., *came up and went out from* [2]Lit., *in like manner by their hand* [a]2 Kin. 7:6, 7

1 [a]Deut. 17:17; Neh. 13:23-27

2 [1]Lit., *go among* [a]Ex. 23:31-33; 34:12-16; Deut. 7:3

3 [a]2 Sam. 5:13-16

18 Moreover, the king made a great throne of [a]ivory and overlaid it with refined gold.

19 There *were* six steps to the throne and a round top to the throne at its rear, and [1]arms [2]on each side of the seat, and two lions standing beside the [1]arms.

20 And twelve lions were standing there on the six steps on the one side and on the other; nothing like *it* was made for any other kingdom.

21 And all King Solomon's drinking vessels *were* of gold, and all the vessels of the house of the forest of Lebanon *were* of pure gold. None was of silver; it was not considered [1]valuable in the days of Solomon.

22 For [a]the king had at sea the ships of Tarshish with the ships of Hiram; once every three years the ships of Tarshish came bringing gold and silver, ivory and apes and peacocks.

23 [a]So King Solomon became greater than all the kings of the earth in riches and in wisdom.

24 And all the earth was seeking the presence of Solomon, [a]to hear his wisdom which God had put in his heart.

25 And [a]they brought every man his gift, articles of silver and gold, garments, weapons, spices, horses, and mules, so much year by year.

26 [a]Now Solomon gathered chariots and horsemen; and he had 1,400 chariots and 12,000 horsemen, and he [1]stationed them in the [b]chariot cities and with the king in Jerusalem.

27 [a]And the king made silver *as common* as stones in Jerusalem, and he made cedars as plentiful as sycamore trees that are in the [1]lowland.

28 [a]Also Solomon's import of horses was from Egypt and Kue, and the king's merchants procured *them* from Kue for a price.

29 And a chariot [1]was imported from Egypt for 600 *shekels* of silver, and a horse for 150; and [2]by the same means they exported them [a]to all the kings of the Hittites and to the kings of the Arameans.

Solomon Turns from God

11 NOW [a]King Solomon loved many foreign women along with the daughter of Pharaoh: Moabite, Ammonite, Edomite, Sidonian, and Hittite women,

2 from the nations concerning which the LORD had said to the sons of Israel, "[a]You shall not [1]associate with them, neither shall they [1]associate with you, *for* they will surely turn your heart away after their gods." Solomon held fast to these in love.

3 [a]And he had seven hundred wives, princesses, and three hundred concubines, and his wives turned his heart away.

4 For it came about when Solomon was old, his wives turned his heart away

after other gods; and [a]his heart was not [1]wholly devoted to the LORD his God, as the heart of David his father *had been.*

5 For Solomon went after [a]Ashtoreth the goddess of the Sidonians and after [1b]Milcom the detestable idol of the Ammonites.

6 And Solomon did what was evil in the sight of the LORD, and did not follow the LORD fully, as David his father *had done.*

7 Then Solomon built a high place for [a]Chemosh the detestable idol of Moab, on the mountain which is [1]east of Jerusalem, and for [b]Molech the detestable idol of the sons of Ammon.

8 Thus also he did for all his foreign wives, who burned incense and sacrificed to their gods.

9 Now [a]the LORD was angry with Solomon [b]because his heart was turned away from the LORD, the God of Israel, [c]who had appeared to him twice,

10 and [a]had commanded him concerning this thing, that he should not go after other gods; but he did not observe what the LORD had commanded.

11 So the LORD said to Solomon, "Because [1]you have done this, and you have not kept My covenant and My statutes, which I have commanded you, [a]I will surely tear the kingdom from you, and will give it to your servant.

12 "Nevertheless I will not do it in your days for the sake of your father David, *but* I will tear it out of the hand of your son.

13 "However, [a]I will not tear away all the kingdom, *but* [b]I will give one tribe to your son for the sake of My servant David and [c]for the sake of Jerusalem which I have chosen."

God Raises Adversaries

14 Then the LORD raised up an adversary to Solomon, Hadad the Edomite; he was of the [1]royal line in Edom.

15 For it came about, [a]when David was in Edom, and Joab the commander of the army had gone up to bury the slain, and had [b]struck down every male in Edom

16 (for Joab and all Israel stayed there six months, until he had cut off every male in Edom),

17 that Hadad fled [1]to Egypt, he and certain Edomites of his father's servants with him, while Hadad *was* a young boy.

18 And they arose from Midian and came to [a]Paran; and they took men with them from Paran and came to Egypt, to Pharaoh king of Egypt, who gave him a house and assigned him food and gave him land.

19 Now Hadad found great favor [1]before Pharaoh, so that he gave him in marriage the sister of his own wife, the sister of Tahpenes the queen.

20 And the sister of Tahpenes bore his son Genubath, whom Tahpenes weaned in Pharaoh's house; and Genubath was in Pharaoh's house among the sons of Pharaoh.

21 But [a]when Hadad heard in Egypt that David slept with his fathers, and that Joab the commander of the army was dead, Hadad said to Pharaoh, "Send me away, that I may go to my own country."

22 Then Pharaoh said to him, "But what have you lacked with me, that behold, you are seeking to go to your own country?" And he answered, "Nothing; nevertheless you must surely [1]let me go."

23 [a]God also raised up *another* adversary to him, Rezon the son of Eliada, who had fled from his lord [b]Hadadezer king of Zobah.

24 And he gathered men to himself and became leader of a marauding band, [a]after David slew them of *Zobah;* and they went to Damascus and stayed [1]there, and reigned in Damascus.

25 So he was an adversary to Israel all the days of Solomon, along with the evil that Hadad *did;* and he abhorred Israel and reigned over Aram.

26 Then [a]Jeroboam the son of Nebat, an Ephraimite of Zeredah, Solomon's servant, whose mother's name was Zeruah, a widow, [b]also [1]rebelled against the king.

27 Now this was the reason why he [1]rebelled against the king: [a]Solomon built the [2]Millo, *and* closed up the breach of the city of his father David.

28 Now the man Jeroboam was a valiant warrior, and when [a]Solomon saw that the young man was [1]industrious, he appointed him over all the [2]forced labor of the house of Joseph.

29 And it came about at that time, when Jeroboam went out of Jerusalem, that [a]the prophet Ahijah the Shilonite found him on the road. Now [1]Ahijah had clothed himself with a new cloak; and both of them were alone in the field.

30 Then [a]Ahijah took hold of the new cloak which was on him, and tore it into twelve pieces.

31 And he said to Jeroboam, "Take for yourself ten pieces; for thus says the LORD, the God of Israel, 'Behold, [a]I will tear the kingdom out of the hand of Solomon and give you ten tribes

32 ([a]but he will have one tribe, for the sake of My servant David and for the sake of Jerusalem, [b]the city which I have chosen from all the tribes of Israel),

33 because they have forsaken Me, and [a]have worshiped Ashtoreth the goddess of the Sidonians, [b]Chemosh the god of Moab, and Milcom the god of the sons of Ammon; and they have not walked in My ways, doing what is right in My sight and *observing* My statutes and My ordinances, as his father David *did.*

34 'Nevertheless I will not take the whole kingdom out of his hand, but I will make him [1]ruler all the days of his life, for the sake of My servant David whom I chose, who observed My commandments and My statutes;

4 [1]Lit., *complete with* [a]1 Kin. 9:4

5 [1]In Jer. 49:1, 3, *Malcam* [a]Judg. 2:13; 10:6; 1 Sam. 7:3, 4 [b]1 Kin. 11:7

7 [1]Lit., *before* [a]Num. 21:29; Judg. 11:24; 2 Kin. 23:13 [b]Lev. 20:2-5; 2 Kin. 23:10; Acts 7:43

9 [a]Ps. 90:7 [b]1 Kin. 11:2, 4 [c]1 Kin. 3:5; 9:2

10 [a]1 Kin. 6:12; 9:6, 7

11 [1]Lit., *this is with you* [a]1 Sam. 2:30; 1 Kin. 11:29-31; 12:15, 16, 20; 2 Kin. 17:15, 21

13 [a]2 Sam. 7:15; 1 Chr. 17:13; Ps. 89:33 [b]1 Kin. 11:32, 36; 12:20 [c]1 Kin. 8:29

14 [1]Lit., *king's seed*

15 [a]2 Sam. 8:14; 1 Chr. 18:12, 13 [b]Deut. 20:13

17 [1]Lit., *to go into*

18 [a]Num. 10:12; Deut. 1:1

19 [1]Lit., *in the sight of*

21 [a]1 Kin. 2:10

22 [1]Lit., *send me away*

23 [a]1 Kin. 11:14 [b]2 Sam. 8:3; 10:16

24 [1]Lit., *in it* [a]2 Sam. 10:8, 18

26 [1]Lit., *lifted up a hand* [a]1 Kin. 11:11, 28; 12:2, 20; 2 Chr. 13:6 [b]2 Sam. 20:21

27 [1]Lit., *lifted up a hand* [2]I.e., citadel [a]1 Kin. 9:15, 24

28 [1]Lit., *a doer of work* [2]Lit., *burden* [a]Prov. 22:29

29 [1]Lit., *he* [a]1 Kin. 12:15; 14:2; 2 Chr. 9:29

30 [a]1 Sam. 15:27, 28

31 [a]1 Kin. 11:11, 12

32 [a]1 Kin. 11:13; 12:21 [b]1 Kin. 11:13; 14:21

33 [a]1 Sam. 7:3; 1 Kin. 11:5-8 [b]Num. 21:29; Jer. 48:7, 13

34 [1]Or, *prince*

35 but [a]I will take the kingdom from
his son's hand and give it to you, *even*
ten tribes.
36 'But [a]to his son I will give one tribe,
[b]that My servant David may have a
lamp always before Me in Jerusalem,
[c]the city where I have chosen for Myself
to put My name.
37 'And I will take you, and you shall
reign over whatever [1]you desire, and you
shall be king over Israel.
38 'Then it will be, that if you listen to
all that I command you and walk in My
ways, and do what is right in My sight
by observing My statutes and My commandments, as My servant David did,
then [a]I will be with you and [b]build you
an enduring house as I built for David,
and I will give Israel to you.
39 'Thus I will afflict the [1]descendants
of David for this, but not always.' "
40 Solomon sought therefore to put
Jeroboam to death; but Jeroboam arose
and fled to Egypt to [a]Shishak king of
Egypt, and he was in Egypt until the
death of Solomon.

The Death of Solomon

41 [a]Now the rest of the acts of Solomon and whatever he did, and his wisdom, are they not written in the book of
the acts of Solomon?
42 Thus [a]the time that Solomon
reigned in Jerusalem over all Israel was
forty years.
43 And Solomon [a]slept with his fathers and was buried in the city of his
father David, and his son [b]Rehoboam
reigned in his place.

King Rehoboam Acts Foolishly

12 THEN Rehoboam [a]went to Shechem, for all Israel had come to
[b]Shechem to make him king.
2 Now it came about [a]when Jeroboam the son of Nebat heard *of it,* that
[1]he was living in Egypt (for he was yet in
Egypt, where he had fled from the presence of King Solomon).
3 Then they sent and called him, and
Jeroboam and all the assembly of Israel
came and spoke to Rehoboam, saying,
4 "[a]Your father made our yoke hard;
now therefore lighten the hard service of
your father and his heavy yoke which he
put on us, and we will serve you."
5 Then he said to them, "[a]Depart
[1]for three days, then return to me." So
the people departed.
6 And King Rehoboam [a]consulted
with the elders who had [1]served his
father Solomon while he was still alive,
saying, "How do you counsel *me* to
answer this people?"
7 Then they spoke to him, saying,
"[a]If you will be a servant to this people
today, will serve them, [1]grant them their
petition, and speak good words to them,
then they will be your servants forever."
8 But he forsook the counsel of the
elders which they had given him, and
consulted with the young men who grew
up with him [1]and served him.
9 So he said to them, "What counsel
do you give that we may answer this
people who have spoken to me, saying,
'Lighten the yoke which your father put
on us' ?"
10 And the young men who grew up
with him spoke to him, saying, "Thus
you shall say to this people who spoke to
you, saying, 'Your father made our yoke
heavy, now you make it lighter for us!'
But you shall speak to them, 'My little
finger is thicker than my father's loins!
11 'Whereas my father loaded you with
a heavy yoke, I will add to your yoke;
my father disciplined you with whips,
but I will discipline you with scorpions.' "
12 Then Jeroboam and all the people
came to Rehoboam on the third day as
the king had [1]directed, saying, "[a]Return
to me on the third day."
13 And the king answered the people
harshly, for he forsook the advice of the
elders which they had [1]given him,
14 and he spoke to them according to
the advice of the young men, saying,
"[a]My father made your yoke heavy, but
I will add to your yoke; my father
disciplined you with whips, but I will
discipline you with scorpions."
15 So the king did not listen to the
people; [a]for it was a turn *of events* from
the LORD, [b]that He might establish His
word, which the LORD spoke through
Ahijah the Shilonite to Jeroboam the son
of Nebat.

The Kingdom Divided
Jeroboam Rules Israel

16 When all Israel *saw* that the king
did not listen to them, the people answered the king, saying,
"What portion do we have in David?
We have no inheritance in the son
of Jesse;
[a]To your tents, O Israel!
Now look after your own house,
David!"
So Israel departed to their tents.
17 But [a]as for the sons of Israel who
lived in the cities of Judah, Rehoboam
reigned over them.
18 Then King Rehoboam sent
[a]Adoram, who was over the forced labor,
and all Israel stoned him [1]to death. And
King Rehoboam made haste to mount
his chariot to flee to Jerusalem.
19 [a]So Israel has been in rebellion
against the house of David to this day.
20 And it came about when all Israel
heard that Jeroboam had returned, that
they sent and called him to the assembly
and made him king over all Israel.
[a]None but the tribe of Judah followed
the house of David.
21 [a]Now when Rehoboam had come
to Jerusalem, he assembled all the house
of Judah and the tribe of Benjamin,
180,000 chosen men who were warriors,
to fight against the house of Israel to
restore the kingdom to Rehoboam the
son of Solomon.

35 [a]1 Kin. 11:12; 12:16, 17
36 [a]1 Kin. 11:13 [b]1 Kin. 15:4; 2 Kin. 8:19; Ps. 132:17 [c]1 Kin. 11:13
37 [1]Lit., *your soul desires*
38 [a]Deut. 31:8; Josh. 1:5 [b]2 Sam. 7:11, 27
39 [1]Lit., *seed*
40 [a]1 Kin. 14:25; 2 Chr. 12:2-9
41 [a]2 Chr. 9:29
42 [a]2 Chr. 9:30
43 [a]1 Kin. 2:10; 2 Chr. 9:31 [b]1 Kin. 14:21; Matt. 1:7
1 [a]2 Chr. 10:1 [b]Judg. 9:6
2 [1]Lit., *Jeroboam* [a]1 Kin. 11:26, 40
4 [a]1 Sam. 8:11-18; 1 Kin. 4:7, 21-25; 9:15
5 [1]Lit., *yet three* [a]1 Kin. 12:12
6 [1]Lit., *stood before* [a]1 Kin. 4:1-6; Job 12:12; 32:7
7 [1]Lit., *answer them* [a]2 Chr. 10:7; Prov. 15:1
8 [1]Lit., *who stood before*
12 [1]Lit., *spoken* [a]1 Kin. 12:5
13 [1]Lit., *advised*
14 [a]Ex. 1:13, 14; 5:5-9, 16-18
15 [a]Deut. 2:30; Judg. 14:4; 1 Kin. 12:24; 2 Chr. 10:15 [b]1 Kin. 11:11, 31
16 [a]2 Sam. 20:1
17 [a]1 Kin. 11:13, 36
18 [1]Lit., *with stones that he died* [a]2 Sam. 20:24; 1 Kin. 4:6; 5:14
19 [a]2 Kin. 17:21
20 [a]1 Kin. 11:13, 32, 36
21 [a]2 Chr. 11:1

22 But the word of God came to
[a]Shemaiah the man of God, saying,
23 "Speak to Rehoboam the son of
Solomon, king of Judah, and to all the
house of Judah and Benjamin and to the
[a]rest of the people, saying,
24 'Thus says the LORD, "You must
not go up and fight against your [1]relatives the sons of Israel; return every man
to his house, [a]for this thing has come
from Me." ' " So they listened to the
word of the LORD, and returned and
went *their way* according to the word of
the LORD.

Jeroboam's Idolatry

25 Then [a]Jeroboam built Shechem in
the hill country of Ephraim, and lived
[1]there. And he went out from there and
built [b]Penuel.
26 And Jeroboam said in his heart,
"Now the kingdom will return to the
house of David.
27 "[a]If this people go up to offer sacrifices in the house of the LORD at Jerusalem, then the heart of this people will
return to their lord, *even* to Rehoboam
king of Judah; and they will kill me and
return to Rehoboam king of Judah."
28 So the king [1]consulted, and [a]made
two golden [b]calves, and he said to them,
"It is too much for you to go up to
Jerusalem; [c]behold your gods, O Israel,
that brought you up from the land of
Egypt."
29 And he set [a]one in [b]Bethel, and the
other he put in [c]Dan.
30 Now [a]this thing became a sin, for
the people went *to worship* before the
one as far as Dan.
31 And [a]he made houses on high
places, and [b]made priests from among
[1]all the people who were not of the sons
of Levi.
32 And Jeroboam [1]instituted a feast in
the eighth month on the fifteenth day of
the month, [a]like the feast which is in
Judah, and he [2]went up to the altar; thus
he did in Bethel, sacrificing to the calves
which he had made. And he stationed in
Bethel [b]the priests of the high places
which he had made.
33 Then he [1]went up to the altar
which he had made in Bethel on the
fifteenth day in the eighth month, even
in the month which he had [2a]devised [3]in
his own heart; and he [2]instituted a feast
for the sons of Israel, and [1]went up to
the altar [b]to burn [4]incense.

Jeroboam Warned, Stricken

13 NOW behold, there came [a]a man
of God from Judah to Bethel by
the word of the LORD, while Jeroboam
was standing by the altar [b]to burn
incense.
2 And [a]he cried against the altar by
the word of the LORD, and said, "O
altar, altar, thus says the LORD, 'Behold,
a son shall be born to the house of
David, [b]Josiah by name; and on you he
shall sacrifice the priests of the high
places who burn incense on you, and
human bones shall be burned on you.' "
3 Then he gave a [1]sign the same day,
saying, "[a]This is the [1]sign which the
LORD has spoken, 'Behold, the altar
shall be split apart and the [2]ashes which
are on it shall be poured out.' "
4 Now it came about when the king
heard the saying of the man of God,
which he cried against the altar in
Bethel, that Jeroboam stretched out his
hand from the altar, saying, "Seize him."
But his hand which he stretched out
against him dried up, so that he could
not draw it back to himself.
5 The altar also was split apart and
the [1]ashes were poured out from the
altar, according to the [2]sign which the
man of God had given by the word of
the LORD.
6 And the king answered and said to
the man of God, "Please [1a]entreat the
LORD your God, and pray for me, that
my hand may be restored to me." So
[b]the man of God [2]entreated the LORD,
and the king's hand was restored to him,
and it became as it was before.
7 Then the king said to the man of
God, "Come home with me and refresh
yourself, and [a]I will give you a reward."
8 But the man of God said to the
king, "[a]If you were to give me half your
house I would not go with you, nor
would I eat bread or drink water in this
place.
9 "For so [1]it was commanded me by
the word of the LORD, saying, 'You shall
eat no bread, nor drink water, nor return
by the way which you came.' "
10 So he went another way, and did
not return by the way which he came to
Bethel.

The Disobedient Prophet

11 Now [a]an old prophet was living in
Bethel; and his [1]sons came and told him
all the deeds which the man of God had
done that day in Bethel; the words
which he had spoken to the king, these
also they related to their father.
12 And their father said to them,
"[1]Which way did he go?" Now his sons
[2]had seen the way which the man of God
who came from Judah had gone.
13 Then he said to his sons, "Saddle
the donkey for me." So they saddled the
donkey for him and he rode away on it.
14 So he went after the man of God
and found him sitting under [1]an oak;
and he said to him, "Are you the man of
God who came from Judah?" And he
said, "I am."
15 Then he said to him, "Come home
with me and eat bread."
16 And he said, "[a]I cannot return with
you, nor go with you, nor will I eat bread
or drink water with you in this place.
17 "For a command *came* to me [a]by the
word of the LORD, 'You shall eat no
bread, nor drink water there; do not
return by going the way which you
came.' "

22 [a]2 Chr. 11:2; 12:5-7
23 [a]1 Kin. 12:17
24 [1]Lit., *brothers* [a]1 Kin. 12:15
25 [1]Lit., *in it* [a]Gen. 12:6; Judg. 9:45-49 [b]Gen. 32:30, 31; Judg. 8:8, 17
27 [a]Deut. 12:5-7, 14
28 [1]Lit., *took counsel* [a]2 Kin. 10:29; 17:16; Hos. 8:4-7 [b]Hos. 10:5 [c]Ex. 32:4, 8
29 [a]Hos. 10:5 [b]Gen. 28:19 [c]Judg. 18:26-31
30 [a]1 Kin. 13:34; 2 Kin. 17:21
31 [1]Or, *extremities of* [a]1 Kin. 13:32 [b]1 Kin. 13:33; 2 Kin. 17:32; 2 Chr. 11:15; 13:9
32 [1]Lit., *made* [2]Or, *offered upon* [a]Lev. 23:33, 34; Num. 29:12; 1 Kin. 8:2, 5 [b]Amos 7:10-13
33 [1]Or, *offered upon* [2]Lit., *made* [3]Lit., *from* [4]Or, *sacrifices* [a]Num. 15:39 [b]1 Kin. 13:1
1 [a]1 Kin. 12:22; 2 Kin. 23:17 [b]1 Kin. 12:33
2 [a]1 Kin. 13:32 [b]2 Kin. 23:15, 16
3 [1]Lit., *wonder* [2]Lit., *ashes of fat* [a]Ex. 4:1-5; Judg. 6:17; Is. 38:7; John 2:18; 1 Cor. 1:22
5 [1]Lit., *ashes of fat* [2]Lit., *wonder*
6 [1]Lit., *soften the face of* [2]Lit., *softened the face of* [a]Ex. 8:8, 28; 9:28; 10:17; Acts 8:24; James 5:16 [b]Luke 6:27, 28
7 [a]1 Sam. 9:7, 8; 2 Kin. 5:15
8 [a]Num. 22:18; 24:13; 1 Kin. 13:16, 17
9 [1]Lit., *he commanded me*
11 [1]Lit., *son* [a]1 Kin. 13:25; 2 Kin. 23:18
12 [1]Lit., *Where is the way he went* [2]Some ancient versions read *showed him*
14 [1]Or, a *terebinth*
16 [a]1 Kin. 13:8, 9
17 [a]1 Kin. 20:35

18 And he said to him, "[a]I also am a prophet like you, and [b]an angel spoke to me by the word of the LORD, saying, 'Bring him back with you to your house, that he may eat bread and drink water.'" *But* [c]he lied to him.

19 So he went back with him, and ate bread in his house and drank water.

20 Now it came about, as they were sitting down at the table, that the word of the LORD came to the prophet who had brought him back;

21 and he cried to the man of God who came from Judah, saying, "Thus says the LORD, 'Because you have [1]disobeyed the [2]command of the LORD, and have not observed the commandment which the LORD your God commanded you,

22 but have returned and eaten bread and drunk water in the place of which He said to you, "Eat no bread and drink no water"; your body shall not come to the grave of your fathers.'"

23 And it came about after he had eaten bread and after he had drunk, that he saddled the donkey for him, for the prophet whom he had brought back.

24 Now when he had gone, [a]a lion met him on the way and killed him, and his body was thrown on the road, with the donkey standing beside it; the lion also was standing beside the body.

25 And behold, men passed by and saw the body thrown on the road, and the lion standing beside the body; so they came and told *it* in the city where [a]the old prophet lived.

26 Now when the prophet who brought him back from the way heard *it,* he said, "It is the man of God, who [1]disobeyed the [2]command of the LORD; therefore the LORD has given him to the lion, which has torn him and killed him, according to the word of the LORD which He spoke to him."

27 Then he spoke to his sons, saying, "Saddle the donkey for me." And they saddled *it.*

28 And he went and found his body thrown on the road with the donkey and the lion standing beside the body; the lion had not eaten the body nor torn the donkey.

29 So the prophet took up the body of the man of God and laid it on the donkey, and brought it back and he came to the city of the old prophet to mourn and to bury him.

30 And he laid his body in his own grave, and they mourned over him, *saying,* "[a]Alas, my brother!"

31 And it came about after he had buried him, that he spoke to his sons, saying, "When I die, bury me in the grave in which the man of God is buried; [a]lay my bones beside his bones.

32 "[a]For the thing shall surely come to pass which he cried by the word of the LORD against the altar in Bethel and [b]against all the houses of the high places which are in the cities of [c]Samaria."

33 After this event Jeroboam did not return from his evil way, but [a]again he made priests of the high places from among [1]all the people; [b]any who would, he ordained, to be priests of the high places.

34 [a]And [1]this event became sin to the house of Jeroboam, [b]even to blot *it* out and destroy *it* from off the face of the earth.

Ahijah Prophesies against the King

14 AT that time Abijah the son of Jeroboam became sick.

2 And Jeroboam said to his wife, "Arise now, and [a]disguise yourself so that they may not know that you are the wife of Jeroboam, and go to [b]Shiloh; behold, Ahijah the prophet is there, who [c]spoke concerning me *that I would be* king over this people.

3 "[a]And take ten loaves with you, *some* cakes and a jar of honey, and go to him. He will tell you what will happen to the boy."

4 And Jeroboam's wife did so, and arose and went to [a]Shiloh, and came to the house of [b]Ahijah. Now Ahijah could not see, [c]for his eyes were [1]dim because of his age.

5 Now the LORD had said to Ahijah, "Behold, the wife of Jeroboam is coming to [1]inquire of you concerning her son, for he is sick. You shall say thus and thus to her, for it will be when she arrives that [a]she will pretend to be another woman."

6 And it came about when Ahijah heard the sound of her feet coming in the doorway, that he said, "Come in, wife of Jeroboam, why do you pretend to be another woman? For I am sent to you *with* a harsh *message.*

7 "Go, say to Jeroboam, 'Thus says the LORD God of Israel, "[a]Because I exalted you from among the people and made you leader over My people Israel,

8 and [a]tore the kingdom away from the house of David and gave it to you—[b]yet you have not been like My servant David, who kept My commandments and who followed Me with all his heart, [c]to do only that which was right in My sight;

9 you also have done more evil than all who were before you, and [a]have gone and made for yourself other gods and [b]molten images to provoke Me to anger, and have [c]cast Me behind your back—

10 therefore behold, I am bringing calamity on the house of Jeroboam, and [a]will cut off from Jeroboam [1]every male person, [b]both bond and free in Israel, and I [c]will make a clean sweep of the house of Jeroboam, as one sweeps away dung until it is all gone.

11 "[a]Anyone belonging to Jeroboam who dies in the city the dogs will eat. And he who dies in the field the birds of the heavens will eat; for the LORD has spoken *it.*"'

18 [a]Matt. 7:15; 1 John 4:1 [b]Gal. 1:8 [c]Prov. 12:19, 22; 19:5; Jer. 29:31, 32; Ezek. 13:8, 9; 1 Tim. 4:1, 2

21 [1]Lit., *rebelled against* [2]Lit., *mouth*

24 [a]1 Kin. 20:36

25 [a]1 Kin. 13:11

26 [1]Lit., *rebelled against* [2]Lit., *mouth*

30 [a]Jer. 22:18

31 [a]Ruth 1:17; 2 Kin. 23:17, 18

32 [a]1 Kin. 13:2 [b]Lev. 26:30; 1 Kin. 12:31 [c]1 Kin. 16:24; John 4:5; Acts 8:14

33 [1]Or, *extremities of* [a]1 Kin. 12:31, 32 [b]Judg. 17:5

34 [1]Lit., *by this thing he became* [a]1 Kin. 12:30; 2 Kin. 17:21 [b]1 Kin. 14:10; 15:29, 30

2 [a]1 Sam. 28:8; 2 Sam. 14:2; 2 Chr. 18:29 [b]Josh. 18:1 [c]1 Kin. 11:29-31

3 [a]1 Sam. 9:7, 8; 1 Kin. 13:7; 2 Kin. 4:42

4 [1]Lit., *set* [a]1 Kin. 14:2 [b]1 Kin. 11:29 [c]1 Sam. 3:2; 4:15

5 [1]Lit., *seek a word from* [a]2 Sam. 14:2

7 [a]2 Sam. 12:7; 1 Kin. 11:28-31; 16:2

8 [a]1 Kin. 11:31 [b]1 Kin. 11:33, 38 [c]1 Kin. 15:5

9 [a]1 Kin. 12:28; 2 Chr. 11:15 [b]Ex. 34:17 [c]Neh. 9:26; Ps. 50:17; Ezek. 23:35

10 [1]Lit., *him who urinates against the wall* [a]1 Kin. 21:21; 2 Kin. 9:8 [b]Deut. 32:36; 2 Kin. 14:26 [c]1 Kin. 15:29

11 [a]1 Kin. 16:4; 21:24

12"Now you arise, go to your house. [a]When your feet enter the city the child will die.

13"And all Israel shall mourn for him and bury him, for [1]he alone of Jeroboam's *family* shall come to the grave, because in him [a]something good was found toward the LORD God of Israel in the house of Jeroboam.

14"Moreover, [a]the LORD will raise up for Himself a king over Israel who shall cut off the house of Jeroboam this day [1]and from now on.

15"For the LORD will strike Israel, as a reed is shaken in the water; and [a]He will uproot Israel from [b]this good land which He gave to their fathers, and [c]will scatter them beyond the *Euphrates* River, [d]because they have made their [1]Asherim, provoking the LORD to anger.

16"And He will give up Israel [a]on account of the sins of Jeroboam, which he [1]committed and with which he made Israel to sin."

17 Then Jeroboam's wife arose and departed and came to [a]Tirzah. [b]As she was entering the threshold of the house, the child died.

18 [a]And all Israel buried him and mourned for him, according to the word of the LORD which He spoke through His servant Ahijah the prophet.

19 Now the rest of the acts of Jeroboam, [a]how he made war and how he reigned, behold, they are written in the Book of the Chronicles of the Kings of Israel.

20 And the time that Jeroboam reigned *was* twenty-two years; and he slept with his fathers, and Nadab his son reigned in his place.

Rehoboam Misleads Judah

21 [a]Now Rehoboam the son of Solomon reigned in Judah. Rehoboam was forty-one years old when he became king, and he reigned seventeen years in Jerusalem, [b]the city which the LORD had chosen from all the tribes of Israel to put His name there. And his mother's name was Naamah the Ammonitess.

22 [a]And Judah did evil in the sight of the LORD, and they [b]provoked Him to jealousy more than all that their fathers had done, with [1]the sins which they [2]committed.

23 For they also built for themselves [a]high places and *sacred* [b]pillars and [1c]Asherim on every high hill and [d]beneath every luxuriant tree.

24 And there were also [a]male cult prostitutes in the land. They did according to all the abominations of the nations which the LORD dispossessed before the sons of Israel.

25 [a]Now it came about in the fifth year of King Rehoboam, that Shishak the king of Egypt came up against Jerusalem.

26 And he took away the treasures of the house of the LORD and the treasures of the king's house, and [a]he took everything, [1b]even taking all the shields of gold which Solomon had made.

27 So King Rehoboam made shields of bronze in their place, and [a]committed them to the [1]care of the commanders of the [2]guard who guarded the doorway of the king's house.

28 Then it happened as often as the king entered the house of the LORD, that the [1]guards would carry them and would bring them back into the [1]guards' room.

29 [a]Now the rest of the acts of Rehoboam and all that he did, are they not written in the Book of the Chronicles of the Kings of Judah?

30 [a]And there was war between Rehoboam and Jeroboam continually.

31 And Rehoboam slept with his fathers, and was buried with his fathers in the city of David; and [a]his mother's name was Naamah the Ammonitess. And Abijam his son became king in his place.

Abijam Reigns over Judah

15 [a]NOW in the eighteenth year of King Jeroboam, the son of Nebat, Abijam became king over Judah.

2 He reigned three years in Jerusalem; and his mother's name was [1a]Maacah the daughter of [2b]Abishalom.

3 And he walked in all the sins of his father which he had committed before him; and [a]his heart was not [1]wholly devoted to the LORD his God, like the heart of his father David.

4 But for David's sake the LORD his God gave him a [a]lamp in Jerusalem, to raise up his son after him and to establish Jerusalem;

5 [a]because David did what was right in the sight of the LORD, and had not turned aside from anything that He commanded him all the days of his life, [b]except in the case of Uriah the Hittite.

6 [a]And there was war between Rehoboam and Jeroboam all the days of his life.

7 Now [a]the rest of the acts of Abijam and all that he did, are they not written in the Book of the Chronicles of the Kings of Judah? [b]And there was war between Abijam and Jeroboam.

Asa Succeeds Abijam

8 [a]And Abijam slept with his fathers and they buried him in the city of David; and Asa his son became king in his place.

9 So in the twentieth year of Jeroboam the king of Israel, Asa began to reign as king of Judah.

10 And he reigned forty-one years in Jerusalem; and [a]his mother's name was Maacah the daughter of Abishalom.

11 And [a]Asa did what was right in the sight of the LORD, like David his father.

12 [a]He also put away the male cult prostitutes from the land, and [b]removed all the idols which his fathers had made.

12 [a]1 Kin. 14:17
13 [1]Lit., *the one* [a]2 Chr. 19:3
14 [1]Lit., *and what even now?* [a]1 Kin. 15:27-29
15 [1]I.e., wooden symbols of a female deity [a]Deut. 29:28; 2 Kin. 17:6; Ps. 52:5 [b]Josh. 23:15, 16 [c]2 Kin. 15:29 [d]Ex. 34:13, 14; Deut. 12:3, 4
16 [1]Lit., *sinned* [a]1 Kin. 12:30; 13:34; 15:30, 34; 16:2
17 [a]1 Kin. 15:21, 33; 16:6-9, 15, 23; Song 6:4 [b]1 Kin. 14:12
18 [a]1 Kin. 14:13
19 [a]1 Kin. 14:30; 2 Chr. 13:2-20
21 [a]2 Chr. 12:13 [b]1 Kin. 11:32, 36
22 [1]Lit., *their* [2]Lit., *sinned* [a]2 Chr. 12:1, 14 [b]Deut. 32:21; Ps. 78:58; 1 Cor. 10:22
23 [1]I.e., wooden symbols of a female deity [a]Deut. 12:2; Ezek. 16:24 [b]Deut. 16:22 [c]1 Kin. 14:15 [d]2 Kin. 17:10; Is. 57:5; Jer. 2:20
24 [a]Gen. 19:5; Deut. 23:17; 1 Kin. 15:12; 22:46; 2 Kin. 23:7
25 [a]1 Kin. 11:40; 2 Chr. 12:2; 9
26 [1]Lit., *and he took away* [a]1 Kin. 15:18; 2 Chr. 12:9 [b]1 Kin. 10:17; 2 Chr. 9:15, 16
27 [1]Lit., *hand* [2]Lit., *runner* [a]1 Sam. 8:11; 22:17
28 [1]Lit., *runners*
29 [a]2 Chr. 12:15, 16
30 [a]1 Kin. 12:21; 15:6
31 [a]1 Kin. 14:21

1 [a]2 Chr. 13:1
2 [1]In 2 Chr. 13:2, *Micaiah, the daughter of Uriel* [2]In 2 Chr. 11:20, *Absalom* [a]2 Chr. 13:2 [b]2 Chr. 11:21
3 [1]Lit., *complete with* [a]1 Kin. 11:4; Ps. 119:80
4 [a]2 Sam. 21:17; 1 Kin. 11:36; 2 Chr. 21:7
5 [a]1 Kin. 9:4; 14:8; Luke 1:6 [b]2 Sam. 11:3f., 15-17; 12:9, 10
6 [a]1 Kin. 14:30; 2 Chr. 12:15-13:20
7 [a]2 Chr. 13:2, 21, 22 [b]2 Chr. 13:3-20
8 [a]2 Chr. 14:1
10 [a]1 Kin. 15:2
11 [a]2 Chr. 14:2
12 [a]Deut. 23:17; 1 Kin. 14:24; 22:46 [b]1 Kin. 11:7, 8; 14:23; 2 Chr. 14:2-5

13 [a]And [1]he also removed Maacah his
mother from *being* queen mother, because she had made a horrid image [2]as
an Asherah; and Asa cut down her
horrid image and [b]burned *it* at the brook
Kidron.
14 [a]But the high places were not taken
away; nevertheless [b]the heart of Asa was
[1]wholly devoted to the LORD all his
days.
15 And [a]he brought into the house of
the LORD the dedicated things of his
father and his own dedicated things:
silver and gold and utensils.
16 [a]Now there was war between Asa
and Baasha king of Israel all their days.
17 [a]And Baasha king of Israel went up
against Judah and [1b]fortified Ramah [c]in
order to prevent *anyone* from going out
or coming in to Asa king of Judah.
18 Then [a]Asa took all the silver and
the gold which were left in the treasuries
of the house of the LORD and the treasuries of the king's house, and delivered
them into the hand of his servants. And
[b]King Asa sent them to Ben-hadad the
son of Tabrimmon, the son of Hezion,
king of Aram, who lived in [c]Damascus,
saying,
19 "*Let there be* a [a]treaty between [1]you
and me, *as* between my father and your
father. Behold, I have sent you a present
of silver and gold; go, break your treaty
with Baasha king of Israel so that he will
withdraw from me."
20 So Ben-hadad listened to King Asa
and sent the commanders of his armies
against the cities of Israel, and [1]con-
quered [a]Ijon, [b]Dan, [c]Abel-beth-maacah
and all [d]Chinneroth, besides all the land
of Naphtali.
21 And it came about when Baasha
heard *of it* that [a]he ceased [1]fortifying
Ramah, and remained in [b]Tirzah.
22 Then King Asa made a proclamation to all Judah—none was exempt—
and they carried away the stones of
Ramah and its timber with which Baasha had built. And King Asa built with
them [a]Geba of Benjamin and Mizpah.

Jehoshaphat Succeeds Asa

23 [a]Now the rest of all the acts of Asa
and all his might and all that he did and
the cities which he built, are they not
written in the Book of the Chronicles of
the Kings of Judah? But in the time of
his old age he was diseased in his feet.
24 And Asa slept with his fathers and
was buried with his fathers in the city of
David his father; and [a]Jehoshaphat his
son reigned in his place.

Nadab, then Baasha, Rules over Israel

25 Now [a]Nadab the son of Jeroboam
became king over Israel in the second
year of Asa king of Judah, and he
reigned over Israel two years.
26 And he did evil in the sight of the
LORD, and [a]walked in the way of his
father and [b]in his sin which he made
Israel sin.
27 Then [a]Baasha the son of Ahijah of
the house of Issachar conspired against
him, and Baasha struck him down at
[b]Gibbethon, which belonged to the Philistines, while Nadab and all Israel were
laying siege to Gibbethon.
28 So Baasha killed him in the third
year of Asa king of Judah, and reigned
in his place.
29 And it came about, as soon as he
was king, he struck down all the household of Jeroboam. He did not leave to
Jeroboam [1]any persons alive, until he
had destroyed them, [a]according to the
word of the LORD, which He spoke by
His servant Ahijah the Shilonite,
30 *and* because of the sins of Jeroboam which he sinned, and [a]which he
made Israel sin, because of his provocation with which he provoked the LORD
God of Israel to anger.
31 [a]Now the rest of the acts of Nadab
and all that he did, are they not written
in the Book of the Chronicles of the
Kings of Israel?

War with Judah

32 [a]And there was war between Asa
and Baasha king of Israel all their days.
33 In the third year of Asa king of
Judah, Baasha the son of Ahijah became
king over all Israel at Tirzah, *and reigned*
twenty-four years.
34 And he did evil in the sight of the
LORD, and [a]walked in the way of Jeroboam and in his sin which he made
Israel sin.

Prophecy against Baasha

16 NOW the word of the LORD
came to [a]Jehu the son of [b]Hanani
against Baasha, saying,
2 "Inasmuch as I [a]exalted you from
the dust and made you leader over My
people Israel, and [b]you have walked in
the way of Jeroboam and have made My
people Israel sin, provoking Me to anger
with their sins,
3 behold, [a]I will consume [b]Baasha
and his house, and [c]I will make your
house like the house of Jeroboam the son
of Nebat.
4 "[a]Anyone of Baasha who dies in the
city the dogs shall eat, and anyone of his
who dies in the field the birds of the
heavens will eat."
5 [a]Now the rest of the acts of Baasha
and what he did and his might, are they
not written in the Book of the Chronicles
of the Kings of Israel?

The Israelite Kings

6 And Baasha slept with his fathers
and was buried in [a]Tirzah, and Elah his
son became king in his place.
7 Moreover, the word of the LORD
through [a]the prophet Jehu the son of
Hanani also came against Baasha and
his household, both because of all the
evil which he did in the sight of the
LORD, provoking Him to anger with
[b]the work of his hands, in being like the
house of Jeroboam, and because [c]he
struck [1]it.

---

13 [1]Lit., *also Maacah his mother and he removed her* [2]Or, *for Asherah* [a]2 Chr. 15:16-18 [b]Ex. 32:20
14 [1]Lit., *complete with* [a]1 Kin. 22:43; 2 Kin. 12:3 [b]1 Kin. 8:61; 15:3
15 [a]1 Kin. 7:51
16 [a]1 Kin. 15:32
17 [1]Lit., *built* [a]2 Chr. 16:1-6 [b]Josh. 18:25; 1 Kin. 15:21, 22 [c]1 Kin. 12:26-29
18 [a]1 Kin. 14:26; 15:15 [b]2 Kin. 12:17, 18; 2 Chr. 16:2 [c]Gen. 14:15; 1 Kin. 11:23, 24
19 [1]Lit., *me and you* [a]2 Chr. 16:7
20 [1]Lit., *smote* [a]2 Kin. 15:29 [b]Judg. 18:29; 1 Kin. 12:29 [c]2 Sam. 20:15; 2 Kin. 15:29 [d]Josh. 11:2; 12:3
21 [1]Lit., *building* [a]1 Kin. 15:17 [b]1 Kin. 14:17; 16:15-18
22 [a]Josh. 18:24; 21:17
23 [a]2 Chr. 16:11-14
24 [a]1 Kin. 22:41-44; 2 Chr. 17:1; Matt. 1:8
25 [a]1 Kin. 14:20
26 [a]1 Kin. 12:28-33; 13:33, 34 [b]1 Kin. 14:16; 15:30, 34
27 [a]1 Kin. 14:14 [b]Josh. 19:44; 21:23; 1 Kin. 16:15
29 [1]Lit., *any breath* [a]1 Kin. 14:9-16
30 [a]1 Kin. 15:26
31 [a]1 Kin. 14:19
32 [a]1 Kin. 15:16
34 [a]1 Kin. 15:26
1 [a]1 Kin. 16:7; 2 Chr. 19:2; 20:34 [b]2 Chr. 16:7-10
2 [a]1 Sam. 2:8; 1 Kin. 14:7 [b]1 Kin. 15:34
3 [a]1 Kin. 14:10; 21:21 [b]1 Kin. 16:11 [c]1 Kin. 15:29
4 [a]1 Kin. 14:11; 21:24
5 [a]1 Kin. 14:19; 15:31
6 [a]1 Kin. 14:17; 15:21
7 [1]Or, *him* [a]1 Kin. 16:1 [b]Ps. 115:4; Is. 2:8 [c]1 Kin. 14:14; 15:27, 29

8 In the twenty-sixth year of Asa
king of Judah, Elah the son of Baasha
became king over Israel at Tirzah, *and*
reigned two years.
9 And his servant [a]Zimri, commander of half his chariots, conspired
against him. Now he *was* at Tirzah
drinking himself drunk in the house of
Arza, [b]who *was* over the household at
Tirzah.
10 Then Zimri went in and struck him
and put him to death, in the twenty-
seventh year of Asa king of Judah, and
became king in his place.
11 And it came about, when he became king, as soon as he sat on his
throne, that [a]he [1]killed all the household
of Baasha; he did not leave [2]a single
male, neither of his [3]relatives nor of his
friends.
12 Thus Zimri destroyed all the household of Baasha, [a]according to the word
of the LORD, which He spoke against
Baasha through [b]Jehu the prophet,
13 for all the sins of Baasha and the
sins of Elah his son, which they sinned
and which they made Israel sin, [a]provok-
ing the LORD God of Israel to anger with
their [1]idols.
14 [a]Now the rest of the acts of Elah
and all that he did, are they not written
in the Book of the Chronicles of the
Kings of Israel?
15 In the twenty-seventh year of Asa
king of Judah, Zimri reigned seven days
at Tirzah. Now the people were camped
against [a]Gibbethon, which belonged to
the Philistines.
16 And the people who were camped
heard [1]it said, "Zimri has conspired and
has also struck down the king." Therefore all Israel made Omri, the commander of the army, king over Israel
that day in the camp.
17 Then Omri and all Israel with him
went up from Gibbethon, and they
besieged Tirzah.
18 And it came about, when Zimri
saw that the city was taken, that he went
into the citadel of the king's house and
burned the king's house over him with
fire, and [a]died,
19 because of his sins which he sinned,
doing evil in the sight of the LORD,
[a]walking in the way of Jeroboam, and in
his sin which he did, making Israel sin.
20 [a]Now the rest of the acts of Zimri
and his conspiracy which he [1]carried
out, are they not written in the Book of
the Chronicles of the Kings of Israel?
21 Then the people of Israel were
divided into two parts: half of the people
followed Tibni the son of Ginath, to
make him king; the *other* half followed
Omri.
22 But the people who followed Omri
prevailed over the people who followed
Tibni the son of Ginath. And Tibni died
and Omri became king.
23 In the thirty-first year of Asa king
of Judah, Omri became king over Israel,
and reigned twelve years; he reigned six
years at [a]Tirzah.
24 And he bought the hill [1]Samaria
from Shemer for two talents of silver;
and he built on the hill, and named the
city which he built [1a]Samaria, after the
name of Shemer, the owner of the hill.
25 And [a]Omri did evil in the sight of
the LORD, and [b]acted more wickedly
than all who *were* before him.
26 For he [a]walked in all the way of
Jeroboam the son of Nebat and in his
sins which he made Israel sin, provoking
the LORD God of Israel with their [1]idols.
27 Now the rest of the acts of Omri
which he did and his might which he
[1]showed, are they not written in the
Book of the Chronicles of the Kings of
Israel?
28 So Omri slept with his fathers, and
was buried in Samaria; and Ahab his
son became king in his place.
29 Now Ahab the son of Omri became
king over Israel in the thirty-eighth year
of Asa king of Judah, and Ahab the son
of Omri reigned over Israel in Samaria
twenty-two years.
30 And Ahab the son of Omri did evil
in the sight of the LORD [a]more than all
who were before him.
31 And it came about, as though it
had been a trivial thing for him to walk
in the sins of Jeroboam the son of
Nebat, that [a]he married Jezebel the
daughter of Ethbaal king of the [b]Sidoni-
ans, and went to serve Baal and worshiped him.
32 So he erected an altar for Baal in
[a]the house of Baal, which he built in
Samaria.
33 And Ahab also made [a]the [1]Ashe-
rah. Thus [b]Ahab did more to provoke
the LORD God of Israel than all the
kings of Israel who were before him.
34 [a]In his days Hiel the Bethelite built
Jericho; he laid its foundations with the
loss of Abiram his first-born, and set up
its gates with the *loss of* his youngest son
Segub, according to the word of the
LORD, which He spoke by Joshua the
son of Nun.

Elijah Predicts Drought

17 NOW Elijah the Tishbite, who
was of [1a]the settlers of Gilead,
said to Ahab, "[b]As the LORD, the God of
Israel lives, before whom I stand, surely
[c]there shall be neither dew nor rain these
years, except by my word."
2 And the word of the LORD came to
him, saying,
3 "Go away from here and turn eastward, and hide yourself by the brook
Cherith, which is [1]east of the Jordan.
4 "And it shall be that you shall drink
of the brook, and [a]I have commanded
the ravens to provide for you there."
5 So he went and did according to
the word of the LORD, for he went and
lived by the brook Cherith, which is
[1]east of the Jordan.
6 And the ravens brought him bread
and meat in the morning and bread and

9 [a]2 Kin. 9:30-33 [b]Gen. 24:2; 39:4; 1 Kin. 18:3
11 [1]Lit., *smote* [2]Lit., *him who urinates against the wall* [3]Lit., *redeemers* [a]1 Kin. 15:29; 16:3
12 [a]1 Kin. 16:3 [b]2 Chr. 19:2; 20:34
13 [1]Lit., *vanities* [a]Deut. 32:21; 1 Kin. 15:30
14 [a]1 Kin. 16:5
15 [a]1 Kin. 15:27
16 [1]Lit., *saying*
18 [a]1 Sam. 31:4, 5; 2 Sam. 17:23
19 [a]1 Kin. 12:28; 14:16; 15:26
20 [1]Lit., *conspired* [a]1 Kin. 16:5, 14, 27
23 [a]1 Kin. 15:21
24 [1]Heb., *Shomeron* [a]1 Kin. 16:28, 29, 32
25 [a]Mic. 6:16 [b]1 Kin. 14:9; 16:30-33
26 [1]Lit., *vanities* [a]1 Kin. 16:19
27 [1]Lit., *did*
30 [a]1 Kin. 14:9; 16:25
31 [a]Deut. 7:1-5 [b]Judg. 18:7; 1 Kin. 11:1-5; 2 Kin. 10:18; 17:16
32 [a]2 Kin. 10:21, 26, 27
33 [1]I.e., wooden symbol of a female deity [a]2 Kin. 13:6 [b]1 Kin. 14:9; 16:29, 30; 21:25
34 [a]Josh. 6:26
1 [1]Or, *Tishbe in Gilead* [a]Judg. 12:4 [b]1 Kin. 18:10; 22:14; 2 Kin. 3:14; 5:20 [c]1 Kin. 18:1; Luke 4:25; James 5:17
3 [1]Lit., *before*
4 [a]1 Kin. 17:9
5 [1]Lit., *before*

meat in the evening, and he would drink
from the brook.
7 And it happened after a while, that
the brook dried up, because there was no
rain in the land.
8 Then the word of the LORD came
to him, saying,
9 "Arise, go to [a]Zarephath, which
belongs to Sidon, and stay there; behold,
[b]I have commanded a widow there to
provide for you."
10 So he arose and went to Zarephath,
and when he came to the gate of the city,
behold, a widow was there gathering
sticks; and [a]he called to her and said,
"Please get me a little water in a [1]jar,
that I may drink."
11 And as she was going to get *it,* he
called to her and said, "Please bring me
a piece of bread in your hand."
12 But she said, "[a]As the LORD your
God lives, [b]I have no [1]bread, only a
handful of flour in the [2]bowl and a little
oil in the jar; and behold, I am gathering
[3]a few sticks that I may go in and
prepare for me and my son, that we may
eat it and [c]die."
13 Then Elijah said to her, "Do not
fear; go, do as you have said, but make
me a little bread cake from [1]it first, and
bring *it* out to me, and afterward you
may make *one* for yourself and for your
son.
14 "For thus says the LORD God of
Israel, 'The [1]bowl of flour shall not be
exhausted, nor shall the jar of oil [2]be
empty, until the day that the LORD sends
rain on the face of the earth.' "
15 So she went and did according to
the word of Elijah, and she and he and
her household ate for *many* days.
16 The [1]bowl of flour was not exhausted nor did the jar of oil [2]become
empty, according to the word of the
LORD which He spoke through Elijah.

Elijah Raises Widow's Son

17 Now it came about after these
things, that the son of the woman, the
mistress of the house, became sick; and
his sickness was so severe, that there was
no breath left in him.
18 So she said to Elijah, "[a]What do I
have to do with you, O [b]man of God?
[1]You have come to me to bring my
iniquity to remembrance, and to put my
son to death!"
19 And he said to her, "Give me your
son." Then he took him from her bosom
and carried him up to the upper room
where he was living, and laid him on his
own bed.
20 And he called to the LORD and
said, "O LORD my God, hast Thou also
brought calamity to the widow with
whom I am [1]staying, by causing her son
to die?"
21 [a]Then he stretched himself upon
the child three times, and called to the
LORD, and said, "O LORD my God, I
pray Thee, let this child's life return [1]to
him."
22 And the LORD heard the voice of
Elijah, [a]and the life of the child returned
[1]to him and he revived.
23 And Elijah took the child, and
brought him down from the upper room
into the house and gave him to his
mother; and Elijah said, "See, your son
is alive."
24 Then the woman said to Elijah,
"[a]Now I know that you are a man of
God, and that the word of the LORD in
your mouth is truth."

Obadiah Meets Elijah

18 NOW it came about [a]*after* many
days, that the word of the LORD
came to Elijah in the third year, saying,
"Go, show yourself to Ahab, and [b]I will
send rain on the face of the earth."
2 So Elijah went to show himself to
Ahab. Now the famine *was* severe in
Samaria.
3 And Ahab called Obadiah [a]who
was over the household. (Now Obadiah
[1b]feared the LORD greatly;
4 for it came about, [a]when Jezebel
[1]destroyed the prophets of the LORD,
that Obadiah took a hundred prophets
and hid them by fifties in a cave, and
[b]provided them with bread and water.)
5 Then Ahab said to Obadiah, "Go
through the land to all the springs of
water and to all the valleys; perhaps we
will find grass and keep the horses and
mules alive, and not [1]have to kill some
of the cattle."
6 So they divided the land between
them to [1]survey it; Ahab went one way
by himself and Obadiah went another
way by himself.
7 Now as Obadiah was on the way,
behold, Elijah [1]met him, [a]and he recognized him and fell on his face and said,
"Is this you, Elijah my master?"
8 And he said to him, "It is I. Go,
say to your master, 'Behold, Elijah *is
here.*' "
9 And he said, "What [1]sin have I
committed, that you are giving your
servant into the hand of Ahab, to put me
to death?
10 "[a]As the LORD your God lives, there
is no nation or kingdom where my
master has not sent to search for you;
and when they said, 'He is not *here,*' he
made the kingdom or nation swear that
they could not find you.
11 "And now you are saying, 'Go, say
to your master, "Behold, Elijah *is here.*" '
12 "And it will come about when I
leave you [a]that the Spirit of the LORD
will carry you where I do not know; so
when I come and tell Ahab and he
cannot find you, he will kill me, although
I your servant have [1]feared the LORD
from my youth.
13 "[a]Has it not been told to my master
what I did when Jezebel killed the
prophets of the LORD, that I hid [1]a
hundred prophets of the LORD by fifties
in a cave, and provided them with bread
and water?

9 [a]Obad. 20; Luke 4:26 [b]1 Kin. 17:4
10 [1]Or, *vessel* [a]Gen. 24:17; John 4:7
12 [1]Lit., *cake* [2]Lit., *pitcher* [3]Lit., *two* [a]1 Kin. 17:1 [b]2 Kin. 4:2-7 [c]Gen. 21:15, 16
13 [1]Lit., *there*
14 [1]Lit., *pitcher* [2]Lit., *lack*
16 [1]Lit., *pitcher* [2]Lit., *lack*
18 [1]Or, *Have you come . . . death?* [a]2 Sam. 16:10; 2 Kin. 3:13; Luke 4:34; John 2:4 [b]1 Kin. 12:22
20 [1]Lit., *sojourning*
21 [1]Lit., *upon his inward part* [a]2 Kin. 4:34, 35; Acts 20:10
22 [1]Lit., *upon his inward part* [a]Luke 7:14; Heb. 11:35
24 [a]John 2:11; 3:2; 16:30
1 [a]1 Kin. 17:1; Luke 4:25; James 5:17 [b]Deut. 28:12
3 [1]Or, *revered* [a]1 Kin. 16:9 [b]Neh. 7:2; Job 28:28
4 [1]Lit., *cut off* [a]1 Kin. 18:13 [b]Matt. 10:40-42
5 [1]Lit., *cut off*
6 [1]Lit., *pass through*
7 [1]Lit., *to meet* [a]2 Kin. 1:6-8
9 [1]Lit., *have I sinned*
10 [a]1 Kin. 17:1
12 [1]Or, *revered* [a]2 Kin. 2:16; Ezek. 3:12, 14; Acts 8:39
13 [1]Lit., *a hundred men of the prophets* [a]1 Kin. 18:4

14 "And now you are saying, 'Go, say
to your master, "Behold, Elijah *is*
here" '; he will then kill me."
15 And Elijah said, "[a]As the LORD of
hosts lives, before whom I stand, I will
surely show myself to him today."
16 So Obadiah went to meet Ahab,
and told him; and Ahab went to meet
Elijah.
17 And it came about, when Ahab saw
Elijah that [a]Ahab said to him, "Is this
you, you troubler of Israel?"
18 And he said, "I have not troubled
Israel, but you and your father's house
have, because [a]you have forsaken the
commandments of the LORD, and [b]you
have followed the Baals.
19 "Now then send *and* gather to me all
Israel at [a]Mount Carmel, [b]*together* with
450 prophets of Baal and 400 prophets
of [c]the Asherah, who eat at Jezebel's
table."

God or Baal on Mount Carmel

20 So Ahab sent *a message* among all
the sons of Israel, and brought the
prophets together at Mount Carmel.
21 And Elijah came near to all the
people and said, "[a]How long *will* you
[1]hesitate between two opinions? [b]If the
LORD is God, follow Him; but if Baal,
follow him." But the people did not
answer him a word.
22 Then Elijah said to the people, "I
[a]alone am left a prophet of the LORD,
but Baal's prophets are [b]450 men.
23 "Now let them give us two oxen;
and let them choose one ox for themselves and cut it up, and place it on the
wood, but put no fire *under it*; and I will
prepare the other ox, and lay it on the
wood, and I will not put a fire *under it.*
24 "Then you call on the name of your
god, and I will call on the name of the
LORD, and [a]the God who answers by
fire, He is God." And all the people
answered and said, "[1]That is a good
idea."
25 So Elijah said to the prophets of
Baal, "Choose one ox for yourselves and
prepare it first for you are many, and call
on the name of your god, but put no fire
under it."
26 Then they took the ox which [1]was
given them and they prepared it and
called on the name of Baal from morning until noon saying, "O Baal, answer
us." But there was [a]no voice and no one
answered. And they [2]leaped about the
altar which [3]they made.
27 And it came about at noon, that
Elijah mocked them and said, "Call out
with a loud voice, for he is a god; either
he is occupied or gone aside, or is on a
journey, or perhaps he is asleep and
needs to be awakened."
28 So they cried with a loud voice and
[a]cut themselves according to their custom with swords and lances until the
blood gushed out on them.
29 And it came about when midday
was past, that they [1]raved [a]until the time
of the offering of the *evening* sacrifice;
but there was no voice, no one answered,
and no [2]one paid attention.
30 Then Elijah said to all the people,
"Come near to me." So all the people
came near to him. And [a]he repaired the
altar of the LORD which had been torn
down.
31 And Elijah took twelve stones according to the number of the tribes of
the sons of Jacob, to whom the word of
the LORD had come, saying, "[a]Israel
shall be your name."
32 So with the stones he built an altar
in [a]the name of the LORD, and he made
a trench around the altar, large enough
to hold two [1]measures of seed.
33 [a]Then he arranged the wood and
cut the ox in pieces and laid *it* on the
wood. And he said, "Fill four pitchers
with water and pour *it* on the burnt
offering and on the wood."
34 And he said, "Do it a second time,"
and they did it a second time. And he
said, "Do it a third time," and they did it
a third time.
35 And the water flowed around the
altar, and he also filled the trench with
water.
36 Then it came about [a]at the time of
the offering of the *evening* sacrifice, that
Elijah the prophet came near and said,
"[b]O LORD, the God of Abraham, Isaac
and Israel, today let it be known that
[c]Thou art God in Israel, and that I am
Thy servant, and [d]that I have done all
these things at Thy word.

Elijah's Prayer

37 "Answer me, O LORD, answer me,
that this people may know that Thou, O
LORD, art God, and *that* Thou hast
turned their heart back again."
38 Then the [a]fire of the LORD fell, and
consumed the burnt offering and the
wood and the stones and the dust, and
licked up the water that was in the
trench.
39 And when all the people saw it,
they fell on their faces; and they said,
"[a]The LORD, He is God; the LORD, He is
God."
40 Then Elijah said to them, "Seize
the prophets of Baal; do not let one of
them escape." So they seized them; and
Elijah brought them down to [a]the brook
Kishon, [b]and slew them there.
41 Now Elijah said to Ahab, "Go up,
eat and drink; for there is the sound of
the roar of a *heavy* shower."
42 So Ahab went up to eat and drink.
But Elijah went up to the top of [a]Car-
mel; and he [b]crouched down on the
earth, and put his face between his
knees.
43 And he said to his servant, "Go up
now, look toward the sea." So he went
up and looked and said, "There is nothing." And he said, "Go back" seven
times.

15 [a]1 Kin. 17:1
17 [a]Josh. 7:25; 1 Kin. 21:20
18 [a]1 Kin. 9:9; 2 Chr. 15:2 [b]1 Kin. 16:31; 21:25, 26
19 [a]Josh. 19:26; 2 Kin. 2:25 [b]1 Kin. 18:22 [c]1 Kin. 16:33
21 [1]Lit., *limp on the two divided opinions* [a]2 Kin. 17:41; Matt. 6:24 [b]Josh. 24:15
22 [a]1 Kin. 19:10, 14 [b]1 Kin. 18:19
24 [1]Lit., *The matter is good* [a]1 Kin. 18:38
26 [1]Lit., *he gave* [2]Lit., *limped;* i.e., a type of ceremonial dance [3]So some mss. and the ancient versions; M.T., *he* [a]Ps. 115:4, 5; Jer. 10:5
28 [a]Lev. 19:28; Deut. 14:1
29 [1]Lit., *prophesied* [2]Lit., *attentiveness* [a]Ex. 29:39, 41
30 [a]1 Kin. 19:10, 14; 2 Chr. 33:16
31 [a]Gen. 32:28; 35:10; 2 Kin. 17:34
32 [1]Heb., *seahs;* i.e., one seah equals approx. 11 qts. [a]Col. 3:17
33 [a]Gen. 22:9; Lev. 1:7, 8
36 [a]1 Kin. 18:29 [b]Gen. 28:13; Ex. 3:6; 4:5; Matt. 22:32 [c]1 Kin. 8:43 [d]Num. 16:28-32
38 [a]Gen. 15:17; Lev. 9:24; 10:1, 2; Judg. 6:21; 2 Kin. 1:12; 1 Chr. 21:26; 2 Chr. 7:1; Job 1:16
39 [a]1 Kin. 18:21, 24
40 [a]Judg. 4:7; 5:21 [b]Deut. 13:5; 18:20; 2 Kin. 10:24, 25
42 [a]1 Kin. 18:19, 20 [b]James 5:18

44 And it came about at the seventh
time, that he said, "Behold, [a]a cloud as
small as a man's hand is coming up from
the sea." And he said, "Go up, say to
Ahab, '[1]Prepare *your chariot* and go
down, so that the *heavy* shower does not
stop you.' "
45 So it came about in a little while,
that the sky grew black with clouds and
wind, and there was a heavy shower.
And Ahab rode and went to [a]Jezreel.
46 Then [a]the hand of the LORD was
on Elijah, and [b]he girded up his loins
and [1]outran Ahab [2]to Jezreel.

Elijah Flees from Jezebel

19 NOW Ahab told Jezebel all that
Elijah had done, and [1a]how he
had killed all the prophets with the
sword.
2 Then Jezebel sent a messenger to
Elijah, saying, "[a]So may the gods do to
me and even more, if I do not make your
[1]life as the [1]life of one of them by
tomorrow about this time."
3 And he [1]was afraid and arose and
ran for his [2]life and came to [a]Beersheba,
which belongs to Judah, and left his
servant there.
4 But he himself went a day's journey
into the wilderness, and came and sat
down under a [1]juniper tree; and [a]he
requested for himself that he might die,
and said, "It is enough; now, O LORD,
take my [2]life, for I am not better than
my fathers."
5 And he lay down and slept under a
[1]juniper tree; and behold, there was [a]an
angel touching him, and he said to him,
"Arise, eat."
6 Then he looked and behold, there
was at his head a bread cake *baked on*
hot stones, and a jar of water. So he ate
and drank and lay down again.
7 And the angel of the LORD came
again a second time and touched him
and said, "Arise, eat, because the journey is too great for you."
8 So he arose and ate and drank, and
went in the strength of that food [a]forty
days and forty nights to [b]Horeb, the
mountain of God.

Elijah at Horeb

9 Then he came there to a cave, and
lodged there; and behold, [a]the word of
the LORD *came* to him, and He said to
him, "What are you doing here, Elijah?"
10 And he said, "[a]I have been very
zealous for the LORD, the God of hosts;
for the sons of Israel have forsaken Thy
covenant, [b]torn down Thine altars and
killed Thy prophets with the sword. And
[c]I alone am left; and they seek my life, to
take it away."
11 So He said, "[a]Go forth, and stand
on the mountain before the LORD." And
behold, the LORD was passing by! And
[b]a great and strong wind was rending the
mountains and breaking in pieces the
rocks before the LORD; *but* the LORD
was not in the wind. And after the wind
an earthquake, *but* the LORD *was* not in
the earthquake.
12 And after the earthquake a fire, *but*
the LORD *was* not in the fire; and after
the fire [a]a sound of a gentle blowing.
13 And it came about when Elijah
heard *it,* that [a]he wrapped his face in his
mantle, and went out and stood in the
entrance of the cave. And behold, [b]a
voice *came* to him and said, "What are
you doing here, Elijah?"
14 Then he said, "[a]I have been very
zealous for the LORD, the God of hosts;
for the sons of Israel have forsaken Thy
covenant, torn down Thine altars and
killed Thy prophets with the sword. And
I alone am left; and they seek my life, to
take it away."
15 And the LORD said to him, "Go,
return on your way to the wilderness of
Damascus, and when you have arrived,
[a]you shall anoint Hazael king over
Aram;
16 and [a]Jehu the son of Nimshi you
shall anoint king over Israel; and [b]Elisha
the son of Shaphat of Abel-meholah you
shall anoint as prophet in your place.
17 "And it shall come about, the [a]one
who escapes from the sword of Hazael,
Jehu [b]shall put to death, and the one
who escapes from the sword of Jehu,
Elisha shall put to death.
18 "[a]Yet I will leave 7,000 in Israel, all
the knees that have not bowed to Baal
and every mouth that has not [b]kissed
him."
19 So he departed from there and
found Elisha the son of Shaphat, while
he was plowing with twelve pairs *of oxen*
before him, and he with the twelfth. And
Elijah passed over to him and threw [a]his
mantle on him.
20 And he left the oxen and ran after
Elijah and said, "Please [a]let me kiss my
father and my mother, then I will follow
you." And he said to him, "Go back
again, for what have I done to you?"
21 So he returned from following him,
and took the pair of oxen and sacrificed
them and [a]boiled their flesh with the
implements of the oxen, and gave *it* to
the people and they ate. Then he arose
and followed Elijah and ministered to
him.

War with Aram

20 NOW [a]Ben-hadad king of Aram
gathered all his army, [b]and there
were thirty-two kings with him, and
horses and chariots. And he went up and
[c]besieged Samaria, and fought against it.
2 Then he sent messengers to the city
to Ahab king of Israel, and said to him,
"Thus says Ben-hadad,
3 'Your silver and your gold are
mine; your most beautiful wives and
children are also mine.' "
4 And the king of Israel answered
and said, "It is according to your word,
my lord, O king; I am yours, and all that
I have."

44 [1]Lit., *Tie, harness* [a]Luke 12:54
45 [a]Josh. 17:16; Judg. 6:33
46 [1]Lit., *ran before* [2]Lit., *until you are coming to* [a]2 Kin. 3:15; Is. 8:11; Ezek. 3:14 [b]2 Kin. 4:29; Jer. 1:17; 1 Pet. 1:13
1 [1]Lit., *all about how* [a]1 Kin. 18:40
2 [1]Lit., *soul* [a]Ruth 1:17; 1 Kin. 20:10; 2 Kin. 6:31
3 [1]Reading of many mss.; Heb. text may read *saw* [2]Lit., *soul* [a]Gen. 21:31
4 [1]Or, *broom-tree* [2]Lit., *soul* [a]Num. 11:15; Jer. 20:14-18; Jon. 4:3, 8
5 [1]Or, *broom-tree* [a]Gen. 28:12
8 [a]Ex. 24:18; 34:28; Deut. 9:9-11, 18; Matt. 4:2 [b]Ex. 3:1; 4:27
9 [a]Ex. 33:21, 22
10 [a]Ex. 20:5; 34:14 [b]Rom. 11:3, 4 [c]1 Kin. 18:22
11 [a]Ex. 19:20; 24:12, 18 [b]Ezek. 1:4
12 [a]Job 4:16; Zech. 4:6
13 [a]Ex. 3:6 [b]1 Kin. 19:9
14 [a]1 Kin. 19:10
15 [a]2 Kin. 8:8-15
16 [a]2 Kin. 9:1-10 [b]1 Kin. 19:19-21; 2 Kin. 2:9, 15
17 [a]2 Kin. 8:12; 13:3, 22 [b]2 Kin. 9:14-10:25
18 [a]Rom. 11:4 [b]Hos. 13:2
19 [a]1 Sam. 28:14; 2 Kin. 2:8, 13, 14
20 [a]Matt. 8:21, 22; Luke 9:61, 62; Acts 20:37
21 [a]2 Sam. 24:22
1 [a]1 Kin. 15:18, 20; 2 Kin. 6:24 [b]1 Kin. 22:31 [c]1 Kin. 16:24; 2 Kin. 6:24

5 Then the messengers returned and
said, "Thus says [1]Ben-hadad, 'Surely, I
sent to you saying, "You shall give me
your silver and your gold and your wives
and your children,"
6 but about this time tomorrow I will
send my servants to you, and they will
search your house and the houses of
your servants; and it shall come about,
[1]whatever is desirable in your eyes, they
will [2]take in their hand and carry
away.' "
7 Then the king of Israel called all
the elders of the land and said, "Please
observe and [a]see how this man is looking
for trouble; for he sent to me for my
wives and my children and my silver and
my gold, and I did not refuse him."
8 And all the elders and all the
people said to him, "Do not listen or
consent."
9 So he said to the messengers of
Ben-hadad, "Tell my lord the king, 'All
that you sent for to your servant at the
first I will do, but this thing I cannot
do.' " And the messengers departed and
brought him word again.
10 And Ben-hadad sent to him and
said, "May [a]the gods do so to me and
more also, if the dust of Samaria shall
suffice for handfuls for all the people
who [1]follow me."
11 Then the king of Israel answered
and said, "Tell *him,* '[a]Let not him who
girds on *his armor* boast like him who
takes *it* off.' "
12 And it came about when *Ben-
hadad* heard this message, as [a]he was
drinking [1]with the kings in the [2]tempo-
rary shelters, that he said to his servants,
"Station *yourselves.*" So they stationed
themselves against the city.

Ahab Victorious

13 Now behold, a prophet approached
Ahab king of Israel and said, "Thus says
the LORD, 'Have you seen all this great
multitude? Behold, [a]I will deliver them
into your hand today, and [b]you shall
know that I am the LORD.' "
14 And Ahab said, "By whom?" So he
said, "Thus says the LORD, 'By the
young men of the rulers of the provinces.' " Then he said, "Who shall [1]begin
the battle?" And he [2]answered, "You."
15 Then he mustered the young men
of the rulers of the provinces, and there
were 232; and after them he mustered all
the people, *even* all the sons of Israel,
7,000.
16 And they went out at noon, while
[a]Ben-hadad was drinking himself drunk
in the [1]temporary shelters [2]with the
thirty-two kings who helped him.
17 And the young men of the rulers of
the provinces went out first; and Ben-
hadad sent out and they told him, saying, "Men have come out from Samaria."
18 [a]Then he said, "If they have come

5 [1]Lit., *Ben-hadad, saying*
6 [1]Lit., *all the desire of your eyes* [2]Lit., *put*
7 [a]2 Kin. 5:7
10 [1]Lit., *are at my feet* [a]1 Kin. 19:2; 2 Kin. 6:31
11 [a]Prov. 27:1
12 [1]Lit., *he and* [2]Or, *booths* [a]1 Kin. 16:9; Prov. 31:4, 5
13 [a]1 Kin. 20:28 [b]1 Kin. 18:36
14 [1]Lit., *bind* [2]Lit., *said*
16 [1]Or, *booths* [2]Lit., *he and the 32 kings* [a]1 Kin. 16:9; 20:12; Prov. 20:1
18 [a]2 Kin. 14:8-12
20 [1]Lit., *smote*
21 [1]Lit., *smote*
22 [a]1 Kin. 20:13 [b]2 Sam. 11:1; 1 Kin. 20:26
23 [a]1 Kin. 14:23; Jer. 16:19-21; Rom. 1:21-23
25 [1]Lit., *number*
26 [a]1 Kin. 20:22 [b]2 Kin. 13:17
27 [a]Judg. 6:3-5; 1 Sam. 13:5-8
28 [a]1 Kin. 17:18 [b]1 Kin. 20:23 [c]1 Kin. 20:13
29 [1]Lit., *smote*
30 [a]1 Kin. 20:26 [b]1 Kin. 22:25; 2 Chr. 18:24
31 [1]Lit., *soul* [a]1 Kin. 20:23-26 [b]Gen. 37:34; 2 Sam. 3:31

out for peace, take them alive; or if they
have come out for war, take them alive."
19 So these went out from the city, the
young men of the rulers of the provinces,
and the army which followed them.
20 And they [1]killed each his man; and
the Arameans fled, and Israel pursued
them, and Ben-hadad king of Aram
escaped on a horse with horsemen.
21 And the king of Israel went out and
[1]struck the horses and chariots, and
[1]killed the Arameans with a great
slaughter.
22 Then [a]the prophet came near to the
king of Israel, and said to him, "Go,
strengthen yourself and observe and see
what you have to do; for [b]at the turn of
the year the king of Aram will come up
against you."
23 Now the servants of the king of
Aram said to him, "[a]Their gods are gods
of the mountains, therefore they were
stronger than we; but rather let us fight
against them in the plain, *and* surely we
shall be stronger than they.
24 "And do this thing: remove the
kings, each from his place, and put
captains in their place,
25 and [1]muster an army like the army
that you have lost, horse for horse, and
chariot for chariot. Then we will fight
against them in the plain, and surely we
shall be stronger than they." And he
listened to their voice and did so.

Another Aramean War

26 So it came about [a]at the turn of the
year, that Ben-hadad mustered the Arameans and went up to [b]Aphek to fight
against Israel.
27 And the sons of Israel were mustered and were provisioned and went to
meet them; and the sons of Israel
camped before them like two little flocks
of goats, [a]but the Arameans filled the
country.
28 Then [a]a man of God came near
and spoke to the king of Israel and said,
"Thus says the LORD, 'Because the
Arameans have said, "[b]The LORD is a
god of *the* mountains, but He is not a
god of *the* valleys"; therefore [c]I will give
all this great multitude into your hand,
and you shall know that I am the
LORD.' "
29 So they camped one over against
the other seven days. And it came about
that on the seventh day, the battle was
joined, and the sons of Israel [1]killed *of*
the Arameans 100,000 foot soldiers in
one day.
30 But the rest fled to [a]Aphek into the
city, and the wall fell on 27,000 men who
were left. And Ben-hadad fled and came
into the city [b]into an inner chamber.
31 And [a]his servants said to him,
"Behold now, we have heard that the
kings of the house of Israel are merciful
kings, please let us [b]put sackcloth on our
loins and ropes on our heads, and go out
to the king of Israel; perhaps he will save
your [1]life."

32 So [a]they girded sackcloth on their
loins and *put* ropes on their heads, and
came to the king of Israel and said,
"[b]Your servant Ben-hadad says, 'Please
let me live.' " And he said, "Is he still
alive? He is my brother."
33 Now the men [1]took this as an
omen, and quickly [2]catching his word
said, "Your brother Ben-hadad." Then
he said, "Go, bring him." Then Ben-
hadad came out to him, and he [3]took
him up into the chariot.
34 And *Ben-hadad* said to him, "[a]The
cities which my father took from your
father I will restore, and you shall make
streets for yourself in Damascus, as my
father made in Samaria." *Ahab said,*
"And I will let you go with this covenant." So he made a covenant with him
and let him go.
35 Now a certain man of [a]the sons of
the prophets said to [1]another [b]by the
word of the LORD, "Please strike me."
But the man refused to strike him.
36 Then he said to him, "Because you
have not listened to the voice of the
LORD, behold, as soon as you have
departed from me, [a]a lion will [1]kill you."
And as soon as he had departed from
him a lion found him, and [2]killed him.
37 Then he found another man and
said, "Please [1]strike me." And the man
[2]struck him, [3]wounding him.
38 So the prophet departed and
waited for the king by the way, and
[a]disguised himself with a bandage over
his eyes.
39 And as the king passed by, he cried
to the king and said, "Your servant went
out into the midst of the battle; and
behold, a man turned aside and brought
a man to me and said, 'Guard this man;
if for any reason he is missing, [a]then
your life shall be for his life, or else you
shall pay a talent of silver.'
40 "And while your servant was busy
here and there, he was gone." And the
king of Israel said to him, "So shall your
judgment be; you yourself have decided
it."
41 Then he hastily took the bandage
away from his eyes, and the king of
Israel recognized him that he was of the
prophets.
42 And he said to him, "Thus says the
LORD, 'Because you have let go out of
your hand the man whom I had devoted
to destruction, therefore [a]your [1]life shall
go for his [1]life, and your people for his
people.' "
43 So [a]the king of Israel went to his
house sullen and vexed, and came to
Samaria.

Ahab Covets Naboth's Vineyard

21 NOW it came about after these
things, that Naboth the Jezreelite
had a vineyard which *was* in [a]Jezreel
beside the palace of Ahab king of Samaria.
2 And Ahab spoke to Naboth, saying, "[a]Give me your vineyard, that I may
have it for a vegetable garden because it
is close beside my house, and I will give
you a better vineyard than it in its place;
if [1]you like, I will give you the price of
[2]it in money."
3 But Naboth said to Ahab, "The
LORD forbid me [a]that I should give you
the inheritance of my fathers."
4 [a]So Ahab came into his house
sullen and vexed because of the word
which Naboth the Jezreelite had spoken
to him; for he said, "I will not give you
the inheritance of my fathers." And he
lay down on his bed and turned away his
face and ate no [1]food.
5 But Jezebel his wife came to him
and said to him, "How is it that your
spirit is so sullen that you are not eating
[1]food?"
6 So he said to her, "Because I spoke
to Naboth the Jezreelite, and said to
him, 'Give me your vineyard for money;
or else, if it pleases you, I will give you a
vineyard in its place.' But he said, 'I will
not give you my vineyard.' "
7 And Jezebel his wife said to him,
"[a]Do you now [1]reign over Israel? Arise,
eat bread, and let your heart be joyful; I
will give you the vineyard of Naboth the
Jezreelite."
8 [a]So she wrote letters in Ahab's
name and sealed them with his seal, and
sent letters to [b]the elders and to the
nobles who were living with Naboth in
his city.
9 Now she wrote in the letters, saying, "Proclaim a fast, and seat Naboth at
the head of the people;
10 and seat two [a]worthless men before
him, and let them testify against him,
saying, '[b]You cursed God and the king.'
Then take him out and [c]stone him [1]to
death."

Jezebel's Plot

11 So the men of his city, the elders
and the nobles who lived in his city, did
as Jezebel had sent *word* to them, just as
it was written in the letters which she
had sent them.
12 They [a]proclaimed a fast and seated
Naboth at the head of the people.
13 Then the two worthless men came
in and sat before him; and the worthless
men testified against him, even against
Naboth, before the people, saying, "Naboth cursed God and the king." [a]So they
took him outside the city and stoned him
[1]to death with stones.
14 Then they sent *word* to Jezebel,
saying, "Naboth has been stoned, and is
dead."
15 And it came about when Jezebel
heard that Naboth had been stoned and
was dead, that Jezebel said to Ahab,
"Arise, take possession of the vineyard
of Naboth, the Jezreelite, which he
refused to give you for money; for
Naboth is not alive, but dead."

32 [a]1 Kin. 20:31 [b]1 Kin. 20:3-6
33 [1]Lit., *divined* [2]Lit., *caught from him* [3]Lit., *caused him to come up*
34 [a]1 Kin. 15:20
35 [1]Lit., *his neighbor* [a]2 Kin. 2:3-7 [b]1 Kin. 13:17, 18
36 [1]Lit., *smite* [2]Lit., *smote* [a]1 Kin. 13:24
37 [1]Lit., *smite* [2]Lit., *smote* [3]Lit., *striking and wounding*
38 [a]1 Kin. 14:2
39 [a]2 Kin. 10:24
42 [1]Lit., *soul* [a]1 Kin. 20:39
43 [a]1 Kin. 21:4
1 [a]Judg. 6:33; 1 Kin. 18:45, 46
2 [1]Lit., *it is good in your eyes* [2]Lit., *this* [a]1 Sam. 8:14
3 [a]Lev. 25:23; Num. 36:7; Ezek. 46:18
4 [1]Lit., *bread* [a]1 Kin. 20:43
5 [1]Lit., *bread*
7 [1]Lit., *exercise kingship* [a]1 Sam. 8:14
8 [a]Esth. 3:12; 8:8, 10 [b]1 Kin. 20:7
10 [1]Lit., *so that he dies* [a]1 Sam. 2:12; 2 Sam. 20:1 [b]Ex. 22:28; Lev. 24:15, 16; Acts 6:11 [c]Lev. 24:14
12 [a]Is. 58:4
13 [1]Lit., *with stones so that he died* [a]2 Kin. 9:26; 2 Chr. 24:21; Acts 7:58, 59; Heb. 11:37

16 And it came about when Ahab heard that Naboth was dead, that Ahab arose to go down to the vineyard of Naboth the Jezreelite, to take possession of it.

17 Then the word of the LORD came to Elijah the Tishbite, saying,

18 "Arise, go down to meet Ahab king of Israel, [a]who is in Samaria; behold, he is in the vineyard of Naboth where he has gone down to take possession of it.

19 "And you shall speak to him, saying, 'Thus says the LORD, "[a]Have you murdered, and also taken possession?" ' And you shall speak to him, saying, 'Thus says the LORD, "[b]In the place where the dogs licked up the blood of Naboth the dogs shall lick up your blood, even yours." ' "

20 And Ahab said to Elijah, "[a]Have you found me, O my enemy?" And he [1]answered, "I have found *you,* [b]because you have sold yourself to do evil in the sight of the LORD.

21 "Behold, I will bring evil upon you, and [a]will utterly sweep you away, and will cut off from Ahab every male, both bond and free in Israel;

22 and [a]I will make your house [b]like the house of Jeroboam the son of Nebat, and like the house of Baasha the son of Ahijah, because of the provocation with which you have provoked *Me* to anger, and *because* you [c]have made Israel sin.

23 "And of Jezebel also has the LORD spoken, saying, '[a]The dogs shall eat Jezebel in the [1]district of Jezreel.'

24 "[a]The one belonging to Ahab, who dies in the city, the dogs shall eat, and the one who dies in the field the birds of heaven shall eat."

25 [a]Surely there was no one like Ahab who sold himself to do evil in the sight of the LORD, [1]because Jezebel his wife incited him.

26 And [a]he acted very abominably in following idols, [b]according to all that the Amorites had done, whom the LORD cast out before the sons of Israel.

27 And it came about when Ahab heard these words, that [a]he tore his clothes and put [1]on sackcloth and fasted, and he lay in sackcloth and went about [2]despondently.

28 Then the word of the LORD came to Elijah the Tishbite, saying,

29 "Do you see how Ahab has humbled himself before Me? Because he has humbled himself before Me, I will not bring the evil in his days, *but* I will bring the evil upon his house [a]in his son's days."

Ahab's Third Campaign against Aram

22 AND [1]three years passed without war between Aram and Israel.

2 [a]And it came about in the third year, that [b]Jehoshaphat the king of Judah came down to the king of Israel.

18 [a]1 Kin. 16:29

19 [a]2 Sam. 12:9 [b]1 Kin. 22:38; 2 Kin. 9:26

20 [1]Lit., *said* [a]1 Kin. 18:17 [b]1 Kin. 21:25; 2 Kin. 17:17; Rom. 7:14

21 [a]1 Kin. 14:10; 2 Kin. 9:8

22 [a]1 Kin. 15:29 [b]1 Kin. 16:3, 11 [c]1 Kin. 12:30; 13:34; 14:16

23 [1]Lit., *portion;* some mss. read *rampart* [a]2 Kin. 9:10, 30-37

24 [a]1 Kin. 14:11; 16:4

25 [1]Or, *whom Jezebel his wife incited* [a]1 Kin. 16:30-33; 21:20

26 [a]1 Kin. 15:12; 2 Kin. 17:12 [b]Gen. 15:16; Lev. 18:25-30; 2 Kin. 21:11

27 [1]Lit., *sackcloth on his flesh* [2]Or, *softly* [a]Gen. 37:34; 2 Sam. 3:31; 2 Kin. 6:30

29 [a]2 Kin. 9:25-37

1 [1]Lit., *they sat for three years*

2 [a]2 Chr. 18:2 [b]1 Kin. 15:24

3 [1]Lit., *are silent so as not* [a]Deut. 4:43; Josh. 21:38; 1 Kin. 4:13

4 [a]2 Kin. 3:7

5 [1]Lit., *as the day*

6 [a]1 Kin. 18:19

7 [a]2 Kin. 3:11

9 [1]Lit., *Hasten Micaiah*

10 [a]1 Kin. 22:6

11 [a]Zech. 1:18-21 [b]Deut. 33:17

14 [a]1 Kin. 18:10, 15 [b]Num. 22:18; 24:13

15 [1]Lit., *said to* [a]1 Kin. 22:12

3 Now the king of Israel said to his servants, "Do you know that [a]Ramoth-gilead belongs to us, and we [1]are still doing nothing to take it out of the hand of the king of Aram?"

4 And he said to Jehoshaphat, "Will you go with me to battle at Ramoth-gilead?" And Jehoshaphat said to the king of Israel, "[a]I am as you are, my people as your people, my horses as your horses."

5 Moreover, Jehoshaphat said to the king of Israel, "Please inquire [1]first for the word of the LORD."

6 Then [a]the king of Israel gathered the prophets together, about four hundred men, and said to them, "Shall I go against Ramoth-gilead to battle or shall I refrain?" And they said, "Go up, for the Lord will give *it* into the hand of the king."

7 But [a]Jehoshaphat said, "Is there not yet a prophet of the LORD here, that we may inquire of him?"

8 And the king of Israel said to Jehoshaphat, "There is yet one man by whom we may inquire of the LORD, but I hate him, because he does not prophesy good concerning me, but evil. *He is* Micaiah son of Imlah." But Jehoshaphat said, "Let not the king say so."

9 Then the king of Israel called an officer and said, "[1]Bring quickly Micaiah son of Imlah."

10 Now the king of Israel and Jehoshaphat king of Judah were sitting each on his throne, arrayed in *their* robes, at the threshing floor at the entrance of the gate of Samaria; and [a]all the prophets were prophesying before them.

11 Then Zedekiah the son of Chenaanah made [a]horns of iron for himself and said, "Thus says the LORD, '[b]With these you shall gore the Arameans until they are consumed.' "

12 And all the prophets were prophesying thus, saying, "Go up to Ramoth-gilead and prosper, for the LORD will give *it* into the hand of the king."

Micaiah Predicts Defeat

13 Then the messenger who went to summon Micaiah spoke to him saying, "Behold now, the words of the prophets are uniformly favorable to the king. Please let your word be like the word of one of them, and speak favorably."

14 But Micaiah said, "[a]As the LORD lives, what [b]the LORD says to me, that I will speak."

15 When he came to the king, the king said to him, "Micaiah, shall we go to Ramoth-gilead to battle, or shall we refrain?" And he [1]answered him, "[a]Go up and succeed, and the LORD will give *it* into the hand of the king."

16 Then the king said to him, "How many times must I adjure you to speak to me nothing but the truth in the name of the LORD?"

17 So he said,
"I saw all Israel
Scattered on the mountains,
[a]Like sheep which have no shepherd.
And the LORD said, 'These have
no master.
Let each of them return to his
house in peace.' "
18 Then the king of Israel said to
Jehoshaphat, "[a]Did I not tell you that he
would not prophesy good concerning
me, but evil?"
19 And [1]Micaiah said, "Therefore,
hear the word of the LORD. [a]I saw the
LORD sitting on His throne, and [b]all the
host of heaven standing by Him on His
right and on His left.
20 "And the LORD said, 'Who will
entice Ahab to go up and fall at Ramoth-gilead?' And one said this while
another said that.
21 "Then a spirit came forward and
stood before the LORD and said, 'I will
entice him.'
22 "And the LORD said to him, 'How?'
And he said, 'I will go out and [a]be a
deceiving spirit in the mouth of all his
prophets.' Then He said, 'You are to
entice *him* and also prevail. Go and do
so.'
23 "Now therefore, behold, [a]the LORD
has put a deceiving spirit in the mouth of
all these your prophets; and the LORD
has proclaimed disaster against you."
24 Then [a]Zedekiah the son of Chenaanah came near and struck Micaiah on
the cheek and said, "[b]How did the Spirit
of the LORD pass from me to speak to
you?"
25 And Micaiah said, "Behold, you
shall see on that day when you [a]enter an
inner room to hide yourself."
26 Then the king of Israel said, "Take
Micaiah and return him to Amon the
governor of the city and to Joash the
king's son;
27 and say, 'Thus says the king, "[a]Put
this man in prison, and feed him [1]spar-
ingly with bread and water until I return
safely." ' "
28 And Micaiah said, "[a]If you indeed
return safely the LORD has not spoken
by me." And he said, "[b]Listen, all you
people."

Defeat and Death of Ahab

29 So [a]the king of Israel and Jehoshaphat king of Judah went up against
Ramoth-gilead.
30 And the king of Israel said to
Jehoshaphat, "[a]I will disguise myself and
go into the battle, but you put on your
robes." So the king of Israel disguised
himself and went into the battle.
31 Now [a]the king of Aram had commanded the thirty-two captains of his
chariots, saying, "Do not fight with
small or great, but with the king of Israel
alone."
32 So it came about, when the captains of the chariots saw Jehoshaphat,
that they said, "Surely it is the king of
Israel," and they turned aside to fight
against him, and Jehoshaphat cried out.
33 Then it happened, when the captains of the chariots saw that it was not
the king of Israel, that they turned back
from pursuing him.
34 Now a certain man drew his bow at
random and struck the king of Israel [1]in
a joint of the armor. So he said to the
driver of his chariot, "Turn [2]around, and
take me out of the [3]fight; [a]for I am
severely wounded."
35 And the battle [1]raged that day, and
the king was propped up in his chariot in
front of the Arameans, and died at
evening, and the blood from the wound
ran into the bottom of the chariot.
36 [a]Then a cry passed throughout the
army close to sunset, saying, "Every man
to his city and every man to his [1]coun-
try."
37 So the king died and was brought
to Samaria, and they buried the king in
Samaria.
38 And they washed the chariot by the
pool of Samaria, and the dogs licked up
his blood (now the harlots bathed themselves *there*), [a]according to the word of
the LORD which He spoke.
39 Now the rest of the acts of Ahab
and all that he did and [a]the ivory house
which he built and all the cities which he
built, are they not written in the Book of
the Chronicles of the Kings of Israel?
40 So Ahab slept with his fathers, and
Ahaziah his son became king in his
place.

The New Rulers

41 [a]Now Jehoshaphat the son of Asa
became king over Judah in the fourth
year of Ahab king of Israel.
42 Jehoshaphat was thirty-five years
old when he became king, and he
reigned twenty-five years in Jerusalem.
And his mother's name was Azubah the
daughter of Shilhi.
43 [a]And he walked in all the way of
Asa his father; he did not turn aside
from it, doing right in the sight of the
LORD. [b]However, the high places were
not taken away; the people still sacrificed and burnt incense on the high
places.
44 [a]Jehoshaphat also made peace with
the king of Israel.
45 Now the rest of the acts of Jehoshaphat, and his might which he
showed and how he warred, are they not
written [a]in the Book of the Chronicles of
the Kings of Judah?
46 And the remnant of [a]the sodomites
who remained in the days of his father
Asa, he [1]expelled from the land.
47 Now [a]there was no king in Edom;
a deputy was king.
48 Jehoshaphat made [a]ships of Tarshish to go to [b]Ophir for gold, but [c]they
did not go for the ships were broken at
[d]Ezion-geber.

17 [a]Num. 27:17; 1 Kin. 22:34-36; 2 Chr. 18:16; Matt. 9:36; Mark 6:34
18 [a]1 Kin. 22:8
19 [1]Lit., *he* [a]Is. 6:1; Ezek. 1:26-28; Dan. 7:9, 10 [b]Job 1:6; 2:1; Ps. 103:20, 21; Dan. 7:10; Matt. 18:10; Heb. 1:7, 14
22 [a]Judg. 9:23; 1 Sam. 16:14; 18:10; 19:9; Ezek. 14:9; 2 Thess. 2:11
23 [a]Ezek. 14:9
24 [a]1 Kin. 22:11; Matt. 5:39; Acts 23:2, 3 [b]2 Chr. 18:23
25 [a]1 Kin. 20:30
27 [1]Lit., *with bread of affliction and water of affliction* [a]2 Chr. 16:10; 18:25-27
28 [a]Deut. 18:22 [b]Mic. 1:2
29 [a]1 Kin. 22:3, 4
30 [a]2 Chr. 35:22
31 [a]1 Kin. 20:1, 16, 24; 2 Chr. 18:30
34 [1]Lit., *between the scale-armor and the breastplate* [2]Lit., *your hand* [3]Lit., *camp* [a]2 Chr. 35:23
35 [1]Lit., *went up*
36 [1]Lit., *land* [a]2 Kin. 14:12
38 [a]1 Kin. 21:19
39 [a]Amos 3:15
41 [a]2 Chr. 20:31
43 [a]2 Chr. 17:3 [b]1 Kin. 15:14; 2 Kin. 12:3
44 [a]1 Kin. 22:2; 2 Kin. 8:16, 18; 2 Chr. 19:2
45 [a]2 Chr. 20:34
46 [1]Lit., *consumed* [a]Gen. 19:5; Deut. 23:17; 1 Kin. 14:24; 15:12; Jude 7
47 [a]2 Sam. 8:14; 2 Kin. 3:9
48 [a]1 Kin. 10:22; 2 Chr. 20:36 [b]1 Kin. 9:28 [c]2 Chr. 20:37 [d]1 Kin. 9:26

49 Then Ahaziah the son of Ahab said
to Jehoshaphat, "Let my servants go
with your servants in the ships." But
Jehoshaphat was not willing.
50 [a]And Jehoshaphat slept with his
fathers and was buried with his fathers
in the city of his father David, and
Jehoram his son became king in his
place.
51 Ahaziah the son of Ahab [a]became
king over Israel in Samaria in the seventeenth year of Jehoshaphat king of Judah, and he reigned two years over
Israel.
52 And he did evil in the sight of the
LORD and [a]walked in the way of his
father and in the way of his mother and
in the way of Jeroboam the son of
Nebat, who caused Israel to sin.
53 [a]So he served Baal and worshiped
him and provoked the LORD God of
Israel to anger according to all that his
father had done.

50 [a]2 Chr. 21:1
51 [a]1 Kin. 22:40
52 [a]1 Kin. 15:26; 21:25
53 [a]Judg. 2:11; 1 Kin. 16:30-32

THE SECOND BOOK OF THE KINGS

Ahaziah's Messengers Meet Elijah

1 NOW [a]Moab rebelled against Israel
after the death of Ahab.
2 And Ahaziah fell through the lattice in his upper chamber which *was* in
Samaria, and became ill. So he sent
messengers and said to them, "Go,
[a]inquire of Baal-zebub, the god of Ekron, [b]whether I shall recover from this
sickness."
3 But the angel of the LORD said to
[a]Elijah the Tishbite, "Arise, go up to
meet the messengers of the king of
Samaria and say to them, 'Is it because
there is no God in Israel *that* you are
going to inquire of [b]Baal-zebub, the god
of Ekron?'
4 "Now therefore thus says the LORD,
'[1a]You shall not come down from the
bed where you have gone up, but you
shall surely die.' " Then Elijah departed.
5 When the messengers returned to
him he said to them, "[1]Why have you
returned?"
6 And they said to him, "A man
came up to meet us and said to us, 'Go,
return to the king who sent you and say
to him, "Thus says the LORD, 'Is it
because there is no God in Israel *that*
you are sending [a]to inquire of Baal-
zebub, the god of Ekron? Therefore [1]you
shall not come down from the bed where
you have gone up, but shall surely
die.' " ' "
7 And he said to them, "What kind
of man was he who came up to meet you
and spoke these words to you?"
8 And they [1]answered him, "[a]*He was*
a hairy man with a leather girdle [2]bound
about his loins." And he said, "It is
Elijah the Tishbite."
9 Then *the king* [a]sent to him a captain of fifty with his fifty. And he went
up to him, and behold, he was sitting on
the top of the hill. And he said to him,
"O man of God, the king says, 'Come
down.' "
10 And Elijah answered and said to
the captain of fifty, "If I am a man of
God, [a]let fire come down from heaven
and consume you and your fifty." [b]Then
fire came down from heaven and consumed him and his fifty.
11 So he again sent to him another
captain of fifty with his fifty. And he
answered and said to him, "O man of
God, thus says the king, 'Come down
quickly.' "
12 And Elijah answered and said to
them, "If I am a man of God, let fire
come down from heaven and consume
you and your fifty." Then the fire of God
came down from heaven and consumed
him and his fifty.
13 So he [a]again sent the captain of a
third fifty with his fifty. When the third
captain of fifty went up, he came and
bowed down on his knees before Elijah,
and begged him and said to him, "O
man of God, please let my life and the
lives of these fifty servants of yours be
precious in your sight.
14 "Behold fire came down from
heaven, and consumed the first two
captains of fifty with their fifties; but
now let my [1]life be precious in your
sight."
15 And [a]the angel of the LORD said to
Elijah, "Go down with him; [b]do not be
afraid of him." So he arose and went
down with him to the king.
16 Then he said to him, "Thus says
the LORD, 'Because you have sent messengers [a]to inquire of Baal-zebub, the
god of Ekron—is it because there is no
God in Israel to inquire of His word?—
therefore [1]you shall not come down from
the bed where you have gone up, but
shall surely die.' "

Jehoram Reigns over Israel

17 So Ahaziah died according to the
word of the LORD which Elijah had
spoken. And because he had no son,
Jehoram became king in his place [a]in the
second year of Jehoram the son of Jehoshaphat, king of Judah.
18 Now the rest of the acts of Ahaziah
which he did, are they not written in the
Book of the Chronicles of the Kings of
Israel?

Elijah Taken to Heaven

2 AND it came about when the LORD
was about to [a]take up Elijah by a
[1]whirlwind to heaven, that Elijah went
with [b]Elisha from [c]Gilgal.

1 [a]2 Sam. 8:2; 2 Kin. 3:5
2 [a]2 Kin. 1:3, 6, 16; Matt. 10:25; Mark 3:22 [b]2 Kin. 8:7-10
3 [a]1 Kin. 17:1; 21:17 [b]2 Kin. 1:2
4 [1]Lit., *The bed where you went up, you shall not come down from it* [a]2 Kin. 1:6, 16
5 [1]Lit., *What is this that you have returned?*
6 [1]V. 4, note 1 [a]2 Kin. 1:2
8 [1]Lit., *said* [2]Or, *girt* [a]Zech. 13:4; Matt. 3:4; Mark 1:6
9 [a]2 Kin. 6:13, 14
10 [a]1 Kin. 18:36-38; Luke 9:54 [b]Job 1:16
13 [a]Is. 1:5; Jer. 5:3
14 [1]Lit., *soul*
15 [a]2 Kin. 1:3 [b]Is. 51:12; Jer. 1:17; Ezek. 2:6
16 [1]V. 4, note 1 [a]2 Kin. 1:3
17 [a]2 Kin. 3:1; 8:16
1 [1]Or, *windstorm* [a]Gen. 5:24; Heb. 11:5 [b]1 Kin. 19:16-21 [c]Josh. 4:19

2 And Elijah said to Elisha, "[a]Stay
here please, for the LORD has sent me as
far as [b]Bethel." But Elisha said, "[c]As the
LORD lives and as you yourself live, I
will not leave you." So they went down
to Bethel.
3 Then [a]the sons of the prophets who
were at Bethel came out to Elisha and
said to him, "Do you know that the
LORD will take away your master from
over [1]you today?" And he said, "Yes, I
know; be still."
4 And Elijah said to him, "Elisha,
please [a]stay here, for the LORD has sent
me to [b]Jericho." But he said, "[c]As the
LORD lives, and as you yourself live, I
will not leave you." So they came to
Jericho.
5 And [a]the sons of the prophets who
were at Jericho approached Elisha and
said to him, "[b]Do you know that the
LORD will take away your master from
over [1]you today?" And he [2]answered,
"Yes, I know; be still."
6 Then Elijah said to him, "Please
[a]stay here, for the LORD has sent me to
[b]the Jordan." And he said, "As the
LORD lives, and as you yourself live, I
will not leave you." So the two of them
went on.
7 Now [a]fifty men of the sons of the
prophets went and stood opposite *them*
at a distance, while the two of them
stood by the Jordan.
8 And Elijah [a]took his mantle and
folded it together and [b]struck the waters,
and they were divided here and there, so
that the two of them crossed over on dry
ground.
9 Now it came about when they had
crossed over, that Elijah said to Elisha,
"Ask what I shall do for you before I am
taken from you." And Elisha said,
"Please, let a [a]double portion of your
spirit be upon me."
10 And he said, "You have asked a
hard thing. *Nevertheless,* if you [a]see me
when I am taken from you, it shall be so
for you; but if not, it shall not be *so.*"
11 Then it came about as they were
going along and talking, that behold,
there appeared [a]a chariot of fire and
horses of fire which separated the two of
them. And Elijah went up by a [1]whirl-
wind to heaven.
12 And Elisha saw *it* and cried out,
"[a]My father, my father, the [1]chariots of
Israel and its horsemen!" And he saw
him no more. Then [b]he took hold of his
own clothes and tore them in two pieces.
13 He also took up the mantle of
Elijah that fell from him, and returned
and stood by the bank of the Jordan.
14 And he took the mantle of Elijah
that fell from him, and struck the waters
and said, "Where is the LORD, the God
of Elijah?" And when he also had
[a]struck the waters, they were divided
here and there; and Elisha crossed over.

Elisha Succeeds Elijah

15 Now when [a]the sons of the prophets who *were* at Jericho opposite *him* saw
him, they said, "The spirit of Elijah rests
on Elisha." And they came to meet him
and bowed themselves to the ground
before him.
16 And they said to him, "Behold
now, there are with your servants fifty
strong men, please let them go and
search for your master; [1]perhaps [a]the
Spirit of the LORD has taken him up and
cast him on some mountain or into some
valley." And he said, "You shall not
send."
17 But when [a]they urged him until he
was ashamed, he said, "Send." They sent
therefore fifty men; and they searched
three days, but did not find him.
18 And they returned to him while he
was staying at Jericho; and he said to
them, "Did I not say to you, 'Do not
go'?"
19 Then the men of the city said to
Elisha, "Behold now, the situation of
this city is pleasant, as my lord sees; but
the water is bad, and the land [1]is unfruitful."
20 And he said, "Bring me a new jar,
and put salt [1]in it." So they brought *it* to
him.
21 And he went out to the spring of
water, and [a]threw salt [1]in it and said,
"Thus says the LORD, 'I have [2]purified
these waters; there shall not be from
there death or [3]unfruitfulness any
longer.' "
22 So the waters have been [1]purified
to this day, according to the word of
Elisha which he spoke.
23 Then he went up from there to
Bethel; and as he was going up by the
way, young lads came out from the city
and [a]mocked him and said to him, "Go
up, you baldhead; go up, you baldhead!"
24 When he looked behind him and
saw them, he [a]cursed them in the name
of the LORD. Then two female bears
came out of the woods and tore up forty-
two lads of [1]their number.
25 And he went from there to [a]Mount
Carmel, and from there he returned to
Samaria.

Jehoram Meets Moab Rebellion

3 NOW Jehoram the son of Ahab
became king over Israel at Samaria
[a]in the eighteenth year of Jehoshaphat
king of Judah, and reigned twelve years.
2 And he did evil in the sight of the
LORD, though not like his father and his
mother; for [a]he put away the *sacred*
pillar of Baal [b]which his father had
made.
3 Nevertheless, [a]he clung to the sins
of Jeroboam the son of Nebat, [b]which he
made Israel sin; he did not depart from
them.
4 Now Mesha king of Moab was a
sheep breeder, and [a]used to pay the king
of Israel 100,000 lambs and the wool of
100,000 rams.
5 But it came about, [a]when Ahab
died, the king of Moab rebelled against
the king of Israel.

2 [a]Ruth 1:15 [b]1 Kin. 12:28, 29 [c]1 Sam. 1:26; 2 Kin. 2:4, 6
3 [1]Lit., *your head* [a]2 Kin. 4:1, 38; 5:22
4 [a]2 Kin. 2:2 [b]Josh. 6:26 [c]2 Kin. 2:2
5 [1]Lit., *your head* [2]Lit., *said* [a]2 Kin. 2:3 [b]2 Kin. 2:3
6 [a]2 Kin. 2:2 [b]Josh. 3:8, 15-17
7 [a]2 Kin. 2:15, 16
8 [a]1 Kin. 19:13, 19 [b]Ex. 14:21, 22; 2 Kin. 2:14
9 [a]Num. 11:17-25; Deut. 21:17
10 [a]Acts 1:10
11 [1]Or, *windstorm* [a]2 Kin. 6:17
12 [1]Lit., *chariot* [a]2 Kin. 13:14 [b]Gen. 37:34; Job 1:20
14 [a]2 Kin. 2:8
15 [a]2 Kin. 2:7
16 [1]Lit., *lest* [a]1 Kin. 18:12; Acts 8:39
17 [a]2 Kin. 8:11
19 [1]Lit., *causes barrenness*
20 [1]Lit., *there*
21 [1]Lit., *there* [2]Lit., *healed* [3]Lit., *barrenness* [a]Ex. 15:25, 26; 2 Kin. 4:41; 6:6
22 [1]Lit., *healed*
23 [a]2 Chr. 36:16; Ps. 31:17, 18
24 [1]Lit., *them* [a]Neh. 13:25-27
25 [a]1 Kin. 18:19, 20; 2 Kin. 4:25
1 [a]2 Kin. 1:17
2 [a]Ex. 23:24; 2 Kin. 10:18, 26-28 [b]1 Kin. 16:31, 32
3 [a]1 Kin. 12:28-32 [b]1 Kin. 14:9, 16
4 [a]2 Sam. 8:2; Is. 16:1, 2
5 [a]2 Kin. 1:1

6 And King Jehoram went out of Samaria [1]at that time and mustered all Israel.

7 Then he went and sent *word* to Jehoshaphat the king of Judah, saying, "The king of Moab has rebelled against me. Will you go with me to fight against Moab?" And he said, "I will go up; [a]I am as you are, my people as your people, my horses as your horses."

8 And he said, "Which way shall we go up?" And he [1]answered, "The way of the wilderness of Edom."

9 So [a]the king of Israel went with [b]the king of Judah and [c]the king of Edom; and they made a circuit of seven days' journey, and there was no water for the army or for the cattle that followed them.

10 Then the king of Israel said, "Alas! For the LORD has called these three kings to give them into the hand of Moab."

11 But Jehoshaphat said, "[a]Is there not a prophet of the LORD here, that we may inquire of the LORD by him?" And one of the king of Israel's servants answered and said, "[b]Elisha the son of Shaphat is here, [c]who used to pour water on the hands of Elijah."

12 And Jehoshaphat said, "The word of the LORD is with him." So the king of Israel and Jehoshaphat and the king of Edom went down to him.

13 Now Elisha said to the king of Israel, "What do I have to do with you? [a]Go to the prophets of your father and to the prophets of your mother." And the king of Israel said to him, "No, for the LORD has called these three kings *together* to give them into the hand of Moab."

14 And Elisha said, "[a]As the LORD of hosts lives, before whom I stand, were it not that I regard the presence of Jehoshaphat the king of Judah, I would not look at you nor see you.

15 "But now [a]bring me a minstrel." And it came about, when the minstrel played, that [b]the hand of the LORD came upon him.

16 And he said, "Thus says the LORD, 'Make this valley full of trenches.'

17 "For thus says the LORD, 'You shall not see wind nor shall you see rain; yet that valley [a]shall be filled with water, so that you shall drink, both you and your cattle and your beasts.

18 'And this is but a [a]slight thing in the sight of the LORD; He shall also give the Moabites into your hand.

19 '[a]Then you shall strike every fortified city and every choice city, and fell every good tree and stop all springs of water, and mar every good piece of land with stones.' "

20 And it happened in the morning [a]about the time of offering the sacrifice, that behold, water came by the way of Edom, and the country was filled with water.

21 Now all the Moabites heard that the kings had come up to fight against them. And all who were able to [1]put on armor and older were summoned, and stood on the border.

22 And they rose early in the morning, and the sun shone on the water, and the Moabites saw the water opposite *them* as red as blood.

23 Then they said, "This is blood; the kings have surely fought together, and they have slain one another. Now therefore, Moab, to the spoil!"

24 But when they came to the camp of Israel, the Israelites arose and struck the Moabites, so that they fled before them; and they went forward [1]into the land, [2]slaughtering the Moabites.

25 [a]Thus they destroyed the cities; and each one threw a stone on every piece of good land and filled it. So they stopped all the springs of water and felled all the good trees, until in [b]Kir-hareseth *only* they left its stones; however, the slingers went about *it* and struck it.

26 When the king of Moab saw that the battle was too fierce for him, he took with him 700 men who drew swords, to break through to the king of Edom; but they could not.

27 Then he took his oldest son who was to reign in his place, and [a]offered him as a burnt offering on the wall. And there came great wrath against Israel, and they departed from him and returned to their own land.

The Widow's Oil

4 NOW a certain woman of the wives of [a]the sons of the prophets cried out to [1]Elisha, "Your servant my husband is dead, and you know that your servant feared the LORD; and [b]the creditor has come to take my two children to be his slaves."

2 And Elisha said to her, "What shall I do for you? Tell me, what do you have in the house?" And she said, "Your maidservant has nothing in the house except [a]a jar of oil."

3 Then he said, "Go, borrow vessels at large for yourself from all your neighbors, *even* empty vessels; do not get a few.

4 "And you shall go in and shut the door behind you and your sons, and pour out into all these vessels; and you shall set aside what is full."

5 So she went from him and shut the door behind her and her sons; they were bringing *the vessels* to her and she poured.

6 And it came about when [a]the vessels were full, that she said to her son, "Bring me another vessel." And he said to her, "There is not one vessel more." And the oil stopped.

7 Then she came and told [a]the man of God. And he said, "Go, sell the oil and pay your debt, and you *and* your sons can live on the rest."

6 [1]Lit., *in that day*
7 [a]1 Kin. 22:4
8 [1]Lit., *said*
9 [a]2 Kin. 3:1 [b]2 Kin. 3:7 [c]1 Kin. 22:47
11 [a]1 Kin. 22:7 [b]2 Kin. 2:25 [c]1 Kin. 19:21; John 13:4, 5, 13, 14
13 [a]1 Kin. 18:19; 22:6-11, 22-25
14 [a]1 Kin. 17:1; 2 Kin. 5:16
15 [a]1 Sam. 16:23; 1 Chr. 25:1 [b]1 Kin. 18:46; Ezek. 1:3
17 [a]Ps. 107:35
18 [a]Jer. 32:17, 27; Mark 10:27; Luke 1:37
19 [a]2 Kin. 3:25
20 [a]Ex. 29:39, 40
21 [1]Lit., *gird themselves with a belt*
24 [1]Lit., *into it* [2]Lit., *smiting*
25 [a]2 Kin. 3:19 [b]Is. 16:7; Jer. 48:31, 36
27 [a]Amos 2:1; Mic. 6:7
1 [1]Lit., *Elisha, saying* [a]2 Kin. 2:3 [b]Lev. 25:39-41, 48; 1 Sam. 22:2; Neh. 5:2-5
2 [a]1 Kin. 17:12
6 [a]Matt. 14:20
7 [a]1 Kin. 12:22

The Shunammite Woman

8 Now there came a day when Elisha passed over to [a]Shunem, where there was a [1]prominent woman, and she persuaded him to eat [2]food. And so it was, as often as he passed by, he turned in there to eat [2]food.

9 And she said to her husband, "Behold now, I perceive that this is a holy [a]man of God passing by us continually.

10 "Please, let us [a]make a little walled upper chamber and let us set a bed for him there, and a table and a chair and a lampstand; and it shall be, when he comes to us, *that* he can turn in there."

11 [1]One day he came there and turned in to the upper chamber and [2]rested.

12 Then he said to [a]Gehazi his servant, "Call this Shunammite." And when he had called her, she stood before him.

13 And he said to him, "Say now to her, 'Behold, you have been [1]careful for us with all this [2]care; what can I do for you? Would you be spoken for to the king or to the captain of the army?' " And she [3]answered, "I live among my own people."

14 So he said, "What then is to be done for her?" And Gehazi [1]answered, "Truly she has no son and her husband is old."

15 And he said, "Call her." When he had called her, she stood in the doorway.

16 Then he said, "[a]At this season [1]next year you shall embrace a son." And she said, "No, my lord, O man of God, [b]do not lie to your maidservant."

17 And the woman conceived and bore a son at that season [1]the next year, as Elisha had said to her.

The Shunammite's Son

18 When the child was grown, the day came that he went out to his father to the reapers.

19 And he said to his father, "My head, my head." And he said to his servant, "Carry him to his mother."

20 When he had taken him and brought him to his mother, he sat on her [1]lap until noon, and *then* died.

21 And she went up and [a]laid him on the bed of [b]the man of God, and shut *the door* behind him, and went out.

22 Then she called to her husband and said, "Please send me one of the servants and one of the donkeys, that I may run to the man of God and return."

23 And he said, "Why will you go to him today? It is neither [a]new moon nor sabbath." And she said, "*It will be* well."

24 Then she saddled a donkey and said to her servant, "Drive and go forward; do not slow down [1]the pace for me unless I tell you."

25 So she went and came to the man of God to [a]Mount Carmel. And it came about when the man of God saw her at a distance, that he said to Gehazi his servant, "Behold, [1]yonder is the Shunammite.

26 "Please run now to meet her and say to her, 'Is it well with you? Is it well with your husband? Is it well with the child?' " And she [1]answered, "It is well."

27 When she came to the man of God [a]to the hill, she caught hold of his feet. And Gehazi came near to push her away; but the man of God said, "Let her alone, for her soul is [1]troubled within her; and the LORD has hidden it from me and has not told me."

28 Then she said, "Did I ask for a son from my lord? Did I not say, '[a]Do not deceive me'?"

29 Then he said to Gehazi, "[a]Gird up your loins and [b]take my staff in your hand, and go your way; if you meet any man, do not [c]salute him, and if anyone salutes you, do not answer him; and [d]lay my staff on the lad's face."

30 And the mother of the lad said, "[a]As the LORD lives and as you yourself live, I will not leave you." And he arose and followed her.

31 Then Gehazi passed on before them and laid the staff on the lad's face, but there was neither sound nor [1]response. So he returned to meet him and told [2]him, "The lad [a]has not awakened."

32 When Elisha came into the house, behold the lad was dead and laid on his bed.

33 So he entered and [a]shut the door behind them both, and prayed to the LORD.

34 And [a]he went up and lay on the child, and put his mouth on his mouth and his eyes on his eyes and his hands on his hands, and he stretched himself on him; and the flesh of the child became warm.

35 Then he returned and walked in the house once back and forth, and went up and [a]stretched himself on him; and the lad sneezed seven times and the lad opened his eyes.

36 And he called Gehazi and said, "Call this Shunammite." So he called her. And when she came in to him, he said, "Take up your son."

37 Then she went in and fell at his feet and bowed herself to the ground, and [a]she took up her son and went out.

The Poisonous Stew

38 When Elisha returned to [a]Gilgal, *there was* [b]a famine in the land. [1]As [c]the sons of the prophets [d]were sitting before him, he said to his servant, "[e]Put on the large pot and boil stew for the sons of the prophets."

39 Then one went out into the field to gather herbs, and found a wild vine and gathered from it his lap full of wild gourds, and came and sliced them into the pot of stew, for they did not know *what they were.*

40 So they poured *it* out for the men to eat. And it came about as they were eating of the stew, that they cried out and said, "O man of God, there is [a]death in the pot." And they were unable to eat.

---

8 [1]Lit., *great* [2]Lit., *bread* [a]Josh. 19:18

9 [a]2 Kin. 4:7

10 [a]Matt. 10:41, 42; 25:40; Rom. 12:13

11 [1]Lit., *Now a day came that* [2]Lit., *lay there*

12 [a]2 Kin. 4:29-31; 5:20-27; 8:4, 5

13 [1]Lit., *fearful* [2]Lit., *fear* [3]Lit., *said*

14 [1]Lit., *said*

16 [1]Lit., *when the time revives* [a]Gen. 18:14 [b]2 Kin. 4:28

17 [1]Lit., *when the time revived*

20 [1]Lit., *knees*

21 [a]2 Kin. 4:32 [b]2 Kin. 4:7

23 [a]Num. 10:10; 28:11; 1 Chr. 23:31

24 [1]Lit., *riding*

25 [1]Lit., *this Shunammite* [a]2 Kin. 2:25

26 [1]Lit., *said*

27 [1]Lit., *bitter* [a]2 Kin. 4:25

28 [a]2 Kin. 4:16

29 [a]1 Kin. 18:46; 2 Kin. 9:1 [b]Ex. 4:17; 2 Kin. 2:14 [c]Luke 10:4 [d]Ex. 7:19, 20; 14:16

30 [a]2 Kin. 2:2, 4

31 [1]Lit., *attentiveness* [2]Lit., *him, saying* [a]John 11:11

33 [a]2 Kin. 4:4; Matt. 6:6; Luke 8:51

34 [a]1 Kin. 17:21-23

35 [a]1 Kin. 17:21

37 [a]Heb. 11:35

38 [1]Lit., *And* [a]2 Kin. 2:1 [b]2 Kin. 8:1 [c]2 Kin. 2:3 [d]Luke 10:39; Acts 22:3 [e]Ezek. 11:3, 7, 11; 24:3

40 [a]Ex. 10:17

41 But he said, "Now bring meal." [a]And he threw it into the pot, and he said, "Pour *it* out for the people that they may eat." Then there was no harm in the pot.

42 Now a man came from Baal-shalishah, and brought the man of God bread of the first fruits, twenty loaves of barley and fresh ears of grain in his sack. And he said, "[a]Give *them* to the people that they may eat."

43 And his attendant said, "What, [a]shall I set this before a hundred men?" But he said, "Give *them* to the people that they may eat, for thus says the LORD, 'They shall eat and have *some* left over.' "

44 So he set *it* before them, and they ate and [a]had *some* left over, according to the word of the LORD.

Naaman Is Healed

5 NOW [a]Naaman, captain of the army of the king of Aram, was a great man [1]with his master, and highly respected, because by him the LORD had given victory to Aram. The man was also a valiant warrior, *but he was* a leper.

2 Now the Arameans had gone out [a]in bands, and had taken captive a little girl from the land of Israel; and she [1]waited on Naaman's wife.

3 And she said to her mistress, "I wish that my master were [1]with the prophet who is in Samaria! Then he would cure him of his leprosy."

4 And [1]Naaman went in and told his master, saying, "Thus and thus spoke the girl who is from the land of Israel."

5 Then the king of Aram said, "Go [1]now, and I will send a letter to the king of Israel." And he departed and [a]took with him ten talents of silver and six thousand *shekels* of gold and ten [b]changes of clothes.

6 And he brought the letter to the king of Israel, saying, "And now as this letter comes to you, behold, I have sent Naaman my servant to you, that you may cure him of his leprosy."

7 And it came about when the king of Israel read the letter, that [a]he tore his clothes and said, "[b]Am I God, to kill and to make alive, that this man is sending *word* to me to cure a man of his leprosy? But [c]consider now, and see how he is seeking [1]a quarrel against me."

8 And it happened when Elisha [a]the man of God heard that the king of Israel had torn his clothes, that he sent *word* to the king, saying, "Why have you torn your clothes? Now let him come to me, and he shall know that there is a prophet in Israel."

9 So Naaman came with his horses and his chariots, and stood at the doorway of the house of Elisha.

10 And Elisha sent a messenger to him, saying, "[a]Go and wash in the Jordan seven times, and your flesh shall be restored to you and *you shall* be clean."

11 But Naaman was furious and went away and said, "Behold, I [1]thought, 'He will surely come out to me, and stand and call on the name of the LORD his God, and wave his hand over the place, and cure the leper.'

12 "Are not [1]Abanah and Pharpar, the rivers of Damascus, better than all the waters of Israel? Could I not wash in them and be clean?" So he turned and [a]went away in a rage.

13 [a]Then his servants came near and spoke to him and said, "[b]My father, had the prophet told you *to do some* great thing, would you not have done *it*? How much more *then*, when he says to you, 'Wash, and be clean'?"

14 So he went down and dipped *himself* seven times in the Jordan, according to the word of the man of God; and [a]his flesh was restored like the flesh of a little child, and [b]he was clean.

Gehazi's Greed

15 When he returned to the man of God [1]with all his company, and came and stood before him, he said, "Behold now, [a]I know that there is no God in all the earth, but in Israel; so please [b]take a [2]present from your servant now."

16 But he said, "[a]As the LORD lives, before whom I stand, [b]I will take nothing." And he urged him to take *it*, but he refused.

17 And Naaman said, "If not, please let your servant at least be given two mules' load of [a]earth; for your servant will no more offer burnt offering nor will he sacrifice to other gods, but to the LORD.

18 "In this matter may the LORD pardon your servant: when my master goes into the house of Rimmon to worship there, and [a]he leans on my hand and I bow myself in the house of Rimmon, when I bow myself in the house of Rimmon, the LORD pardon your servant in this matter."

19 And he said to him, "[a]Go in peace." So he departed from him some distance.

20 But [a]Gehazi, the servant of Elisha the man of God, [1]thought, "Behold, my master has spared this Naaman the Aramean, [2]by not receiving from his hands what he brought. [b]As the LORD lives, I will run after him and take something from him."

21 So Gehazi pursued Naaman. When Naaman saw one running after him, he came down from the chariot to meet him and said, "Is all well?"

22 And he said, "[a]All is well. My master has sent me, saying, 'Behold, just now two young men of the sons of the prophets have come to me from [b]the hill country of Ephraim. Please give them a talent of silver and [c]two changes of clothes.' "

23 And Naaman said, "[a]Be pleased to take two talents." And he urged him, and bound two talents of silver in two bags with two changes of clothes, and

41 [a]Ex. 15:25; 2 Kin. 2:21
42 [a]Matt. 14:16-21; 15:32-38
43 [a]Luke 9:13; John 6:9
44 [a]Matt. 14:20; 15:37; John 6:13
1 [1]Lit., *before* [a]Luke 4:27
2 [1]Lit., *was before* [a]2 Kin. 6:23; 13:20
3 [1]Lit., *before*
4 [1]Lit., *he*
5 [1]Lit., *enter* [a]1 Sam. 9:7; 2 Kin. 4:42 [b]Judg. 14:12; 2 Kin. 5:22, 23
7 [1]Lit., *an occasion* [a]Gen. 37:29 [b]Gen. 30:2; 1 Sam. 2:6 [c]1 Kin. 20:7; Luke 11:54
8 [a]1 Kin. 12:22
10 [a]John 9:7
11 [1]Lit., *said*
12 [1]Another reading is *Amanah* [a]Prov. 14:17; 16:32; 19:11
13 [a]1 Sam. 28:23 [b]2 Kin. 2:12; 6:21; 8:9
14 [a]2 Kin. 5:10; Job 33:25 [b]Luke 4:27; 5:13
15 [1]Lit., *he and* [2]Lit., *blessing* [a]Josh. 2:11; 1 Sam. 17:46, 47; 2 Kin. 5:8 [b]1 Sam. 25:27
16 [a]2 Kin. 3:14 [b]Gen. 14:22, 23; 2 Kin. 5:20, 26
17 [a]Ex. 20:24
18 [a]2 Kin. 7:2, 17
19 [a]Ex. 4:18; 1 Sam. 1:17; Mark 5:34
20 [1]Lit., *said* [2]Lit., *from* [a]2 Kin. 4:12, 31, 36 [b]Ex. 20:7; 2 Kin. 6:31
22 [a]2 Kin. 4:26 [b]Josh. 24:33 [c]2 Kin. 5:5
23 [a]2 Kin. 6:3

gave them to two of his servants; and they carried *them* before him.

24 When he came to the [1]hill, he took them from their hand and [a]deposited them in the house, and he sent the men away, and they departed.

25 But he went in and stood before his master. And Elisha said to him, "Where have you been, Gehazi?" And he said, "[a]Your servant went nowhere."

26 Then he said to him, "Did not my heart go *with you,* when the man turned from his chariot to meet you? [a]Is it a time to receive money and to receive clothes and olive groves and vineyards and sheep and oxen and male and female servants?

27 "Therefore, the leprosy of Naaman shall cleave to you and to your [1]descendants forever." So he went out from his presence [a]a leper *as white* as snow.

The Axe Head Recovered

6 NOW [a]the sons of the prophets said to Elisha, "Behold now, the place before you where we are living is too limited for us.

2 "Please let us go to the Jordan, and each of us take from there a beam, and let us make a place there for ourselves where we may live." So he said, "Go."

3 Then one said, "Please be willing to go with your servants." And he [1]answered, "I shall go."

4 So he went with them; and when they came to the Jordan, they cut down trees.

5 But as one was felling a beam, [1]the axe head fell into the water; and he cried out and said, "Alas, my master! For it was borrowed."

6 Then the man of God said, "Where did it fall?" And when he showed him the place, [a]he cut off a stick, and threw *it* in there, and made the iron float.

7 And he said, "Take it up for yourself." So he put out his hand and took it.

The Arameans Plot to Capture Elisha

8 Now the king of Aram was warring against Israel; and he [1]counseled with his servants saying, "In such and such a place shall be my camp."

9 And [a]the man of God sent *word* to the king of Israel saying, "Beware that you do not pass this place, for the Arameans are coming down there."

10 And the king of Israel sent to the place about which the man of God had told him; thus he warned him, so that he guarded himself there, [1]more than once or twice.

11 Now the heart of the king of Aram was enraged over this thing; and he called his servants and said to them, "Will you tell me which of us is for the king of Israel?"

12 And one of his servants said, "No, my lord, O king; but Elisha, the prophet who is in Israel, tells the king of Israel the words that you speak in your bedroom."

13 So he said, "Go and see where he is, that I may send and take him." And it was told him, saying, "Behold, he is in [a]Dothan."

14 And he sent horses and chariots and a great army there, and they came by night and surrounded the city.

15 Now when the attendant of the man of God had risen early and gone out, behold, an army with horses and chariots was circling the city. And his servant said to him, "Alas, my master! [1]What shall we do?"

16 So he [1]answered, "[a]Do not fear, for [b]those who are with us are more than those who are with them."

17 Then Elisha prayed and said, "[a]O LORD, I pray, open his eyes that he may see." And the LORD opened the servant's eyes, and he saw; and behold, the mountain was full of [b]horses and chariots of fire all around Elisha.

18 And when they came down to him, Elisha prayed to the LORD and said, "Strike this [1]people with blindness, I pray." So He [a]struck them with blindness according to the word of Elisha.

19 Then Elisha said to them, "This is not the way, nor is this the city; follow me and I will bring you to the man whom you seek." And he brought them to Samaria.

20 And it came about when they had come into Samaria, that Elisha said, "O [a]LORD, open the eyes of these *men,* that they may see." So the LORD opened their eyes, and they saw; and behold, they were in the midst of Samaria.

21 Then the king of Israel when he saw them, said to Elisha, "[a]My father, shall I [1]kill them? Shall I [1]kill them?"

22 And he [1]answered, "You shall not [2]kill *them.* Would you [2a]kill those you have taken captive with your sword and with your bow? [b]Set bread and water before them, that they may eat and drink and go to their master."

23 So he prepared a great feast for them; and when they had eaten and drunk he sent them away, and they went to their master. And [a]the marauding bands of Arameans did not come again into the land of Israel.

The Siege of Samaria—Cannibalism

24 Now it came about after this, that [a]Ben-hadad king of Aram gathered all his army and went up and besieged Samaria.

25 And there was a great [a]famine in Samaria; and behold, they besieged it, until a donkey's head was sold for eighty *shekels* of silver, and a fourth of a [1]kab of dove's dung for five *shekels* of silver.

26 And as the king of Israel was passing by on the wall a woman cried out to him, saying, "Help, my lord, O king!"

27 And he said, "[1]If the LORD does not help you, from where shall I help you? From the threshing floor, or from the wine press?"

24 [1]Lit., *Ophel* [a]Josh. 7:1, 11, 12, 21; 1 Kin. 21:16
25 [a]2 Kin. 5:22
26 [a]2 Kin. 5:16
27 [1]Lit., *seed* [a]Ex. 4:6; Num. 12:10
1 [a]2 Kin. 2:3
3 [1]Lit., *said*
5 [1]Lit., *as for the iron, it fell*
6 [a]Ex. 15:25; 2 Kin. 2:21; 4:41
8 [1]Lit., *took counsel*
9 [a]2 Kin. 4:1, 7; 6:12
10 [1]Lit., *not once or twice*
13 [a]Gen. 37:17
15 [1]Lit., *How*
16 [1]Lit., *said* [a]Ex. 14:13 [b]2 Chr. 32:7, 8; Rom. 8:31
17 [a]2 Kin. 6:20 [b]2 Kin. 2:11; Ps. 68:17; Zech. 6:1-7
18 [1]Lit., *nation* [a]Gen. 19:11
20 [a]2 Kin. 6:17
21 [1]Lit., *smite* [a]2 Kin. 2:12; 5:13; 8:9
22 [1]Lit., *said* [2]Lit., *smite* [a]Deut. 20:11-16; 2 Chr. 28:8-15 [b]Rom. 12:20
23 [a]2 Kin. 5:2; 24:2
24 [a]1 Kin. 20:1
25 [1]I.e., one kab equals approx. 2 qts. [a]Lev. 26:26
27 [1]Lit., *No, let the LORD help you*

28 And the king said to her, "[a]What [1]is the matter with you?" And she [2]answered, "This woman said to me, 'Give your son that we may eat him today, and we will eat my son tomorrow.'

29 "[a]So we boiled my son and ate him; and I said to her on the next day, 'Give your son, that we may eat him'; but she has hidden her son."

30 And it came about when the king heard the words of the woman, that [a]he tore his clothes—now he was passing by on the wall—and the people looked, and behold, he had sackcloth [1]beneath on his [2]body.

31 Then he said, "May [a]God do so to me and more also, if the head of Elisha the son of Shaphat [1]remains on him today."

32 Now Elisha was sitting in his house, and [a]the elders were sitting with him. And *the king* sent a man from his presence; but before the messenger came to him, he said to the elders, "Do you [b]see how this son of a murderer has sent to take away my head? Look, when the messenger comes, shut the door and [1]hold the door shut against him. Is not the sound of his master's feet behind him?"

33 And while he was still talking with them, behold, the messenger came down to him, and he said, "[a]Behold, this evil is from the LORD; why should I wait for the LORD any longer?"

Elisha Promises Food

7 THEN Elisha said, "Listen to the word of the LORD; thus says the LORD, '[a]Tomorrow about this time a [1]measure of fine flour shall be *sold* for a shekel, and two measures of barley for a shekel, in the gate of Samaria.' "

2 And [a]the royal officer on whose hand the king was leaning answered the man of God and said, "Behold, [b]if the LORD should make windows in heaven, could this thing be?" Then he said, "Behold you shall see it with your own eyes, but you shall not eat [1]of it."

Four Lepers Relate Arameans' Flight

3 Now there were four [a]leprous men at the entrance of the gate; and they said to one another, "Why do we sit here until we die?

4 "If we say, 'We will enter the city,' then the famine is in the city and we shall die there; and if we sit here, we die also. Now therefore come, and let us [1]go over to [a]the camp of the Arameans. If they spare us, we shall live; and if they kill us, we shall but die."

5 And they arose at twilight to go to the camp of the Arameans; when they came to the outskirts of the camp of the Arameans, behold, there was no one there.

6 For [a]the Lord had caused the army of the Arameans to hear a sound of chariots and a sound of horses, *even* the sound of a great army, so that they said to one another, "Behold, the king of Israel has hired against us [b]the kings of the Hittites and [c]the kings of the Egyptians, to come upon us."

7 Therefore they [a]arose and fled in the twilight, and left their tents and their horses and their donkeys, even the camp just as it was, and fled for their life.

8 When these lepers came to the outskirts of the camp, they entered one tent and ate and drank, and [a]carried from there silver and gold and clothes, and went and hid *them*; and they returned and entered another tent and carried from there *also,* and went and hid *them*.

9 Then they said to one another, "We are not doing right. This day is a day of good news, but we are keeping silent; if we wait until morning light, punishment will [1]overtake us. Now therefore come, let us go and tell the king's household."

10 So they came and called to the gatekeepers of the city, and they told them, saying, "We came to the camp of the Arameans, and behold, there was no one there, nor the voice of man, only the horses tied and the donkeys tied, and the tents just as they were."

11 And the gatekeepers called, and told *it* within the king's household.

12 Then the king arose in the night and said to his servants, "I will now tell you what the Arameans have done to us. They know that [a]we are hungry; therefore they have gone from the camp [b]to hide themselves in the field, saying, 'When they come out of the city, we shall capture them alive and get into the city.' "

13 And one of his servants answered and said, "Please, let some *men* take five of the horses which remain, which are left [1]in the city. Behold, they *will be in any case* like all the multitude of Israel who are left in it; behold, they *will be in any case* like all the multitude of Israel who have already perished, so let us send and see."

14 They took therefore two chariots with horses, and the king sent after the army of the Arameans, saying, "Go and see."

The Promise Fulfilled

15 And they went after them to the Jordan, and behold, all the way was full of clothes and equipment, which the Arameans had thrown away in their haste. Then the messengers returned and told the king.

16 So the people went out and plundered the camp of the Arameans. Then a [1]measure of fine flour *was sold* for a shekel and two [1]measures of barley for a shekel, [a]according to the word of the LORD.

17 Now the king appointed [a]the royal officer on whose hand he leaned [1]to have charge of the gate; but the people trampled on him at the gate, and he died just as the man of God had said, [b]who spoke when the king came down to him.

6:28 [1]Lit., *to you* [2]Lit., *said* [a]Judg. 18:23
6:29 [a]Lev. 26:27-29; Deut. 28:52, 53, 57; Lam. 4:10
6:30 [1]Lit., *within* [2]Lit., *flesh* [a]1 Kin. 21:27
6:31 [1]Lit., *stands* [a]Ruth 1:17; 1 Kin. 19:2
6:32 [1]Lit., *press him with the door* [a]Ezek. 8:1; 14:1; 20:1 [b]1 Kin. 18:4, 13, 14; 21:10, 13
6:33 [a]Is. 8:21
7:1 [1]Heb., *seah* [a]2 Kin. 7:18
7:2 [1]Lit., *from there* [a]2 Kin. 5:18; 7:17, 19 [b]Gen. 7:11; Mal. 3:10
7:3 [a]Lev. 13:45, 46; Num. 5:2-4; 12:10-14
7:4 [1]Lit., *fall* [a]2 Kin. 6:24
7:6 [a]2 Sam. 5:24 [b]1 Kin. 10:29 [c]2 Chr. 12:2, 3; Is. 31:1; 36:9
7:7 [a]Ps. 48:4-6; Prov. 28:1
7:8 [a]Josh. 7:21
7:9 [1]Lit., *find*
7:12 [a]2 Kin. 6:25-29 [b]Josh. 8:4-12
7:13 [1]Lit., *in it*
7:16 [1]Heb., *seah;* i.e., one seah equals approx. 11 qts. [a]2 Kin. 7:1
7:17 [1]Lit., *over the gate* [a]2 Kin. 7:2 [b]2 Kin. 6:32

18 And it came about just as the man
of God had spoken to the king, saying,
"[a]Two [1]measures of barley for a shekel
and a [1]measure of fine flour for a shekel,
shall be *sold* tomorrow about this time at
the gate of Samaria."
19 Then the royal officer answered the
man of God and said, "Now behold, [a]if
the LORD should make windows in
heaven, could such a thing be?" And he
said, "Behold, you shall see it with your
own eyes, but you shall not eat [1]of it."
20 And so it happened to him, for the
people trampled on him at the gate, and
he died.

Jehoram Restores the Shunammite's Land

8 NOW [a]Elisha spoke to the woman
whose son he had restored to life,
saying, "Arise and go [1]with your household, and sojourn wherever you can
sojourn; for the [b]LORD has called for a
famine, and [c]it shall even come on the
land for seven years."
2 So the woman arose and did according to the word of the man of God,
and she went with her household and
sojourned in the land of the Philistines
seven years.
3 And it came about at the end of
seven years, that the woman returned
from the land of the Philistines; and she
went out to [1]appeal to the king for her
house and for her field.
4 Now the king was talking with
[a]Gehazi, the servant of the man of God,
saying, "Please relate to me all the great
things that Elisha has done."
5 And it came about, as he was
relating to the king [a]how he had restored
to life the one who was dead, that
behold, the woman whose son he had
restored to life, [1]appealed to the king for
her house and for her field. And Gehazi
said, "My lord, O king, this is the
woman and this is her son, whom Elisha
restored to life."
6 When the king asked the woman,
she related *it* to him. So the king appointed for her a certain officer, saying,
"Restore all that was hers and all the
produce of the field from the day that
she left the land even until now."

Elisha Predicts Evil from Hazael

7 Then Elisha came to [a]Damascus.
Now [b]Ben-hadad king of Aram was sick,
and it was told him, saying, "[c]The man
of God has come here."
8 And the king said to [a]Hazael,
"[b]Take a gift in your hand and go to
meet the man of God, and [c]inquire of
the LORD by him, saying, 'Will I recover
from this sickness?' "
9 So Hazael went to meet him and
took a gift in his hand, even every kind
of good thing of Damascus, forty camels' loads; and he came and stood before
him and said, "[a]Your son Ben-hadad
king of Aram has sent me to you, saying,
'Will I recover from this sickness?' "
10 Then Elisha said to him, "[a]Go, say
to him, 'You shall surely recover,' but
the [b]LORD has shown me that he will
certainly die."
11 And he [1]fixed his gaze steadily *on*
him [a]until he was ashamed, and [b]the
man of God wept.
12 And Hazael said, "Why does my
lord weep?" Then he [1]answered, "Because [a]I know the evil that you will do to
the sons of Israel: their strongholds you
will set on fire, and their young men you
will kill with the sword, and their little
ones you [b]will dash in pieces, and their
women with child you will rip up."
13 Then Hazael said, "But what is
your servant, [a]*who is but* a dog, that he
should do this great thing?" And Elisha
[1]answered, "[b]The LORD has shown me
that you will be king over Aram."
14 So he departed from Elisha and
returned to his master, who said to him,
"What did Elisha say to you?" And he
[1]answered, "He told me that [a]you would
surely recover."
15 And it came about on the morrow,
that he took the cover and dipped it in
water and spread it on his face, [a]so that
he died. And Hazael became king in his
place.

Another Jehoram Reigns in Judah

16 Now in the fifth year of [a]Joram the
son of Ahab king of Israel, Jehoshaphat
being then the king of Judah, Jehoram
the son of Jehoshaphat king of Judah
became king.
17 He was [a]thirty-two years old when
he became king, and he reigned eight
years in Jerusalem.
18 And he walked in the way of the
kings of Israel, just as the house of Ahab
had done, for [a]the daughter of Ahab
became his wife; and he did evil in the
sight of the LORD.
19 However, the LORD was not willing
to destroy Judah, for the sake of David
His servant, [a]since He had [1]promised
him to give a [2]lamp to him through his
sons always.
20 In his days [a]Edom revolted from
under the hand of Judah, and made a
king over themselves.
21 Then Joram crossed over to Zair,
and all his chariots with him. And it
came about that he arose by night and
struck the Edomites who had surrounded him and the captains of the
chariots; [a]but *his* [1]army fled to their
tents.
22 [a]So Edom revolted [1]against Judah
to this day. Then [b]Libnah revolted at the
same time.
23 And the rest of the acts of Joram
and all that he did, are they not written
in the Book of the Chronicles of the
Kings of Judah?

Ahaziah Succeeds Jehoram in Judah

24 So Joram slept with his fathers, and
[a]was buried with his fathers in the city of
David; and [b]Ahaziah his son became
king in his place.
25 [a]In the twelfth year of Joram the
son of Ahab king of Israel, Ahaziah the

18 [1]Heb., *seah;* i.e., one seah equals approx. 11 qts. [a]2 Kin. 7:1

19 [1]Lit., *from there* [a]2 Kin. 7:2

1 [1]Lit., *you and your* [a]2 Kin. 4:18, 31-35; [b]Ps. 105:16; Hag. 1:11 [c]Gen. 41:27, 54

3 [1]Lit., *cry out*

4 [a]2 Kin. 4:12; 5:20-27

5 [1]Lit., *cried out* [a]2 Kin. 4:35

7 [a]1 Kin. 11:24 [b]2 Kin. 6:24 [c]2 Kin. 5:20

8 [a]1 Kin. 19:15, 17 [b]1 Kin. 14:3 [c]2 Kin. 1:2

9 [a]2 Kin. 5:13

10 [a]2 Kin. 8:14 [b]2 Kin. 8:15

11 [1]Lit., *made his face stand fast and he set* [a]2 Kin. 2:17 [b]Luke 19:41

12 [1]Lit., *said* [a]2 Kin. 10:32, 33; 12:17; 13:3, 7 [b]2 Kin. 15:16; Nah. 3:10

13 [1]Lit., *said* [a]1 Sam. 17:43; 2 Sam. 9:8 [b]1 Kin. 19:15

14 [1]Lit., *said* [a]2 Kin. 8:10

15 [a]2 Kin. 8:10

16 [a]2 Kin. 1:17; 3:1

17 [a]2 Chr. 21:5-10

18 [a]2 Kin. 8:27

19 [1]Lit., *said* [2]I.e., descendant on the throne [a]2 Sam. 7:12-15; 1 Kin. 11:36

20 [a]1 Kin. 22:47; 2 Kin. 3:9, 26, 27; 8:22

21 [1]Lit., *the people* [a]2 Sam. 18:17; 19:8

22 [1]Lit., *from under the hand of* [a]Gen. 27:40 [b]Josh. 21:13; 2 Kin. 19:8

24 [a]2 Chr. 21:20 [b]2 Chr. 21:1, 7

25 [a]2 Chr. 22:1-6

son of Jehoram king of Judah began to reign.

26 [a]Ahaziah *was* twenty-two years old when he became king, and he reigned one year in Jerusalem. And his mother's name *was* Athaliah the granddaughter of Omri king of Israel.

27 And [a]he walked in the way of the house of Ahab, and did evil in the sight of the LORD, like the house of Ahab *had done,* because he was a son-in-law of the house of Ahab.

28 Then he went with Joram the son of Ahab to war against [a]Hazael king of Aram at [b]Ramoth-gilead, and the Arameans [1]wounded Joram.

29 So [a]King Joram returned to be healed in Jezreel of the wounds which the Arameans had [1]inflicted on him at [b]Ramah, when he fought against Hazael king of Aram. Then [c]Ahaziah the son of Jehoram king of Judah went down to see Joram the son of Ahab in Jezreel because he was sick.

Jehu Reigns over Israel

9 NOW Elisha the prophet called one of [a]the sons of the prophets, and said to him, "[b]Gird up your loins, and [c]take this flask of oil in your hand, and go to [d]Ramoth-gilead.

2 "When you arrive there, [1]search out [a]Jehu the son of Jehoshaphat the son of Nimshi, and go in and [2b]bid him arise from among his brothers, and bring him to an inner room.

3 "Then take the flask of oil and pour it on his head and say, 'Thus says the LORD, "[a]I have anointed you king over Israel."' Then open the door and flee and do not wait."

4 So [a]the young man, the servant of the prophet, went to Ramoth-gilead.

5 When he came, behold, the captains of the army were sitting, and he said, "I have a word for you, O captain." And Jehu said, "[1]For which *one* of us?" And he said, "For you, O captain."

6 And he arose and went into the house, and he poured the oil on his head and said to him, "Thus says the LORD, the God of Israel, '[a]I have anointed you king over the people of the LORD, *even* over Israel.

7 'And you shall strike the house of Ahab your master, [a]that I may avenge [b]the blood of My servants the prophets, and the blood of all the servants of the LORD, [c]at the hand of Jezebel.

8 'For the whole house of Ahab shall perish, and [a]I will cut off from Ahab [b]every male person [c]both bond and free in Israel.

9 'And [a]I will make the house of Ahab like the house of Jeroboam the son of Nebat, and [b]like the house of Baasha the son of Ahijah.

10 'And [a]the dogs shall eat Jezebel in the territory of Jezreel, and none shall bury *her.*'" Then he opened the door and fled.

11 Now Jehu came out to the servants of his master, and one said to him, "[a]Is all well? Why did this [b]mad fellow come to you?" And he said to them, "You know *very well* the man and his talk."

12 And they said, "It is a lie, tell us now." And he said, "Thus and thus he said to me, 'Thus says the LORD, "I have anointed you king over Israel."'"

13 Then [a]they hurried and each man took his garment and placed it under him on the bare steps, and [b]blew the trumpet, saying, "Jehu is king!"

Jehoram (Joram) Is Assassinated

14 So Jehu the son of Jehoshaphat the son of Nimshi conspired against Joram. [a]Now Joram [1]with all Israel was [2]defending Ramoth-gilead against Hazael king of Aram,

15 but [a]King [1]Joram had returned to Jezreel to be healed of the wounds which the Arameans had [2]inflicted on him when he fought with Hazael king of Aram. So Jehu said, "If this is your mind, *then* let no one escape *or* [3]leave the city to go tell *it* in Jezreel."

16 Then Jehu rode in a chariot and went to Jezreel, for Joram was lying there. [a]And Ahaziah king of Judah had come down to see Joram.

17 Now the watchman was standing on the tower in Jezreel and he saw the [1]company of Jehu as he came, and said, "I see a [1]company." And Joram said, "Take a horseman and send him to meet them and let him say, 'Is it peace?'"

18 So a horseman went to meet him and said, "Thus says the king, 'Is it peace?'" And Jehu said, "[a]What have you to do with peace? Turn behind me." And the watchman [1]reported, "The messenger came to them, but he did not return."

19 Then he sent out a second horseman, who came to them and said, "Thus says the king, 'Is it peace?'" And Jehu [1]answered, "What have you to do with peace? Turn behind me."

20 And the watchman [1]reported, "He came even to them, and he did not return; and [a]the driving is like the driving of [b]Jehu the son of Nimshi, for he drives furiously."

21 Then [1]Joram said, "[2]Get ready." And they made his chariot ready. [a]And [1]Joram king of Israel and Ahaziah king of Judah went out, each in his chariot, and they went out to meet Jehu and found him in the [3b]property of Naboth the Jezreelite.

22 And it came about, when [1]Joram saw Jehu, that he said, "Is it peace, Jehu?" And he [2]answered, "What peace, [a]so long as the harlotries of your mother Jezebel and her witchcrafts are so many?"

23 So [1]Joram [2]reined about and fled and said to Ahaziah, "[a]*There is* treachery, O Ahaziah!"

24 And [a]Jehu [1]drew his bow with his full strength and [2]shot [3]Joram between his arms; and the arrow went [4]through his heart, and he sank in his chariot.

---

26 [a]2 Chr. 22:2
27 [a]2 Chr. 22:3
28 [1]Lit., *smote* [a]2 Kin. 8:15 [b]1 Kin. 22:3, 29
29 [1]Lit., *struck* [a]2 Kin. 9:15 [b]2 Kin. 8:28; 2 Chr. 22:5, 6 [c]2 Kin. 9:16

1 [a]2 Kin. 2:3 [b]2 Kin. 4:29 [c]1 Sam. 10:1; 16:1; 1 Kin. 1:39 [d]2 Kin. 8:28, 29
2 [1]Lit., *and look there for* [2]Lit., *cause him to* [a]1 Kin. 19:16, 17; 2 Kin. 9:14, 20 [b]2 Kin. 9:5, 11
3 [a]2 Chr. 22:7
4 [a]2 Kin. 9:1
5 [1]Lit., *To whom of us all?*
6 [a]1 Sam. 2:7, 8; 1 Kin. 19:16; 2 Kin. 9:3; 2 Chr. 22:7
7 [a]Deut. 32:35, 43 [b]1 Kin. 18:4; 21:15, 21, 25 [c]2 Kin. 9:32-37
8 [a]1 Kin. 21:21; 2 Kin. 10:17 [b]1 Sam. 25:22 [c]Deut. 32:36; 2 Kin. 14:26
9 [a]1 Kin. 14:10, 11; 15:29 [b]1 Kin. 16:3-5, 11, 12
10 [a]1 Kin. 21:23; 2 Kin. 9:35, 36
11 [a]2 Kin. 9:17, 19, 22 [b]Jer. 29:26; Hos. 9:7; Mark 3:21
13 [a]Matt. 21:7, 8; Mark 11:7, 8 [b]2 Sam. 15:10; 1 Kin. 1:34, 39
14 [1]Lit., *he and* [2]Lit., *keeping* [a]1 Kin. 22:3; 2 Kin. 8:28
15 [1]Heb., *Jehoram* [2]Lit., *struck* [3]Lit., *go out from* [a]2 Kin. 8:29
16 [a]2 Kin. 8:29
17 [1]Lit., *multitude*
18 [1]Lit., *told, saying* [a]2 Kin. 9:19, 22
19 [1]Lit., *said*
20 [1]Lit., *told, saying* [a]2 Sam. 18:27 [b]1 Kin. 19:17
21 [1]Heb., *Jehoram* [2]Lit., *Yoke the chariot* [3]Lit., *portion* [a]2 Chr. 22:7 [b]1 Kin. 21:1-7, 15-19; 2 Kin. 9:26
22 [1]Heb., *Jehoram* [2]Lit., *said* [a]1 Kin. 16:30-33; 18:19; 2 Chr. 21:13
23 [1]Heb., *Jehoram* [2]Lit., *turned his hands* [a]2 Kin. 11:14
24 [1]Lit., *filled his hand with the bow* [2]Lit., *smote* [3]Heb., *Jehoram* [4]Lit., *out at* [a]1 Kin. 22:34

25 Then *Jehu* said to Bidkar his officer, "Take *him* up and [a]cast him into the
[1]property of the field of Naboth the
Jezreelite, for I remember when [2]you
and I were riding together after Ahab his
father, that the [b]LORD laid this [c]oracle
against him:
26 'Surely [a]I have seen yesterday the
blood of Naboth and the blood of his
sons,' says the LORD, 'and [b]I will repay
you in this [1]property,' says the LORD.
Now then, take and cast him into the
[1]property, according to the word of the
LORD."

Jehu Assassinates Ahaziah

27 [a]When Ahaziah the king of Judah
saw *this,* he fled by the way of the garden
house. And Jehu pursued him and said,
"[1]Shoot him too, in the chariot." *So they*
shot him at the ascent of Gur, which is at
[b]Ibleam. But he fled to Megiddo and
died there.
28 [a]Then his servants carried him in a
chariot to Jerusalem, and buried him in
his grave with his fathers in the city of
David.
29 Now in [a]the eleventh year of Joram, the son of Ahab, Ahaziah became
king over Judah.
30 When Jehu came to Jezreel, Jezebel
heard *of it,* and [a]she painted her eyes
and adorned her head, and looked out
the window.
31 And as Jehu entered the gate, she
said, "[a]Is it [1]well, Zimri, [2]your master's
murderer?"
32 Then he lifted up his face to the
window and said, "Who is on my side?
Who?" And two or three officials looked
down at him.

Jezebel Is Slain

33 And he said, "Throw her down."
So they threw her down, and some of her
blood was sprinkled on the wall and on
the horses, and he trampled her under
foot.
34 When he came in, he ate and
drank; and he said, "See now to [a]this
cursed woman and bury her, for [b]she is a
king's daughter."
35 And they went to bury her, but
they found no more of her than the skull
and the feet and the palms of her hands.
36 Therefore they returned and told
him. And he said, "This is the word of
the LORD, which He spoke by His servant Elijah the Tishbite, saying, '[a]In the
[1]property of Jezreel the dogs shall eat
the flesh of Jezebel;
37 and [a]the corpse of Jezebel shall be
as dung on the face of the field in the
[1]property of Jezreel, so they cannot say,
"This is Jezebel." ' "

Judgment upon Ahab's House

10 NOW Ahab had seventy sons in
[a]Samaria. And Jehu wrote letters
and sent *them* to Samaria, to the rulers
of Jezreel, the elders, and to the guardians of *the children of* Ahab, saying,
2 "And now, [a]when this letter comes
to you, since your master's sons are with
you, [1]as well as the chariots and horses
and a fortified city and the weapons,
3 select the best and [1]fittest of your
master's sons, and set *him* on his father's
throne, and fight for your master's
house."
4 But they feared greatly and said,
"Behold, [a]the two kings did not stand
before him; how then can we stand?"
5 And the one who *was* over the
household, and he who *was* over the city,
the elders, and the guardians of *the*
children, sent *word* to Jehu, saying, "[a]We
are your servants, all that you say to us
we will do, we will not make any man
king; do what is good in your sight."
6 Then he wrote a letter to them a
second time saying, "If you are on my
side, and you will listen to my voice, take
the heads of the men, your master's sons,
and come to me at Jezreel tomorrow
about this time." Now the king's sons,
seventy persons, *were* with the great men
of the city, *who* were rearing them.
7 And it came about when the letter
came to them, that they took the king's
sons, and [a]slaughtered *them,* seventy
persons, and put their heads in baskets,
and sent *them* to him at Jezreel.
8 When the messenger came and told
him, saying, "They have brought the
heads of the king's sons," he said, "Put
them in two heaps at the entrance of the
gate until morning."
9 Now it came about in the morning,
that he went out and stood, and said to
all the people, "You are [1]innocent;
behold, [a]I conspired against my master
and killed him, but [b]who [2]killed all
these?
10 "Know then that [a]there shall fall to
the earth nothing of the word of the
LORD, which the LORD spoke concerning
the house of Ahab, for the LORD has
done [b]what He spoke [1]through His
servant Elijah."
11 So Jehu [1]killed all who remained of
the house of Ahab in [a]Jezreel, and all his
great men and his acquaintances and his
priests, until he left him without a
survivor.
12 Then he arose and departed, and
went to Samaria. On the way while he
was at [1]Beth-eked of the shepherds,
13 [a]Jehu [1]met the [2]relatives of Ahaziah king of Judah and said, "Who are
you?" And they [3]answered, "We are the
[2]relatives of Ahaziah; and we have come
down [4]to greet the sons of the king and
the sons of the queen mother."
14 And he said, "Take them alive." So
they took them alive, and killed them at
the pit of Beth-eked, forty-two men; and
he left none of them.
15 Now when he had departed from
there, he [1]met [a]Jehonadab the son of
[b]Rechab *coming* to meet him; and he
[2]greeted him and said to him, "Is your
heart right, as my heart is with your
heart?" And Jehonadab [3]answered, "It
is." *Jehu said,* "If it is, [c]give *me* your

25 [1]Lit., *portion* [2]Lit., *I and you* [a]1 Kin. 21:1 [b]1 Kin. 21:19, 24-29 [c]Is. 13:1
26 [1]Lit., *portion* [a]1 Kin. 21:13, 19 [b]2 Kin. 9:21, 25
27 [1]Lit., *smite* [a]2 Chr. 22:7, 9 [b]Josh. 17:11; Judg. 1:27
28 [a]2 Kin. 23:30
29 [a]2 Kin. 8:25
30 [a]Jer. 4:30; Ezek. 23:40
31 [1]Lit., *peace* [2]Lit., *his* [a]1 Kin. 16:9-20; 2 Kin. 9:18-22
34 [a]1 Kin. 21:25 [b]1 Kin. 16:31
36 [1]Lit., *portion* [a]1 Kin. 21:23
37 [1]Lit., *portion* [a]Jer. 8:1-3
1 [a]1 Kin. 16:24-29
2 [1]Lit., *and with you the* [a]2 Kin. 5:6
3 [1]Lit., *most upright*
4 [a]2 Kin. 9:24, 27
5 [a]Josh. 9:8, 11; 1 Kin. 20:4, 32; 2 Kin. 18:14
7 [a]Judg. 9:5; 2 Kin. 11:1
9 [1]Lit., *just* [2]Lit., *smote* [a]2 Kin. 9:14-24 [b]2 Kin. 10:6
10 [1]Lit., *by the hand of* [a]2 Kin. 9:7-10 [b]1 Kin. 21:19-29
11 [1]Lit., *smote* [a]Hos. 1:4
12 [1]I.e., house of binding
13 [1]Lit., *found* [2]Lit., *brothers* [3]Lit., *said* [4]Lit., *about the welfare of* [a]2 Kin. 8:24, 29; 2 Chr. 21:17; 22:8
15 [1]Lit., *found* [2]Lit., *blessed* [3]Lit., *said* [a]Jer. 35:6-19 [b]1 Chr. 2:55 [c]Ezra 10:19; Ezek. 17:18

hand." And he gave him his hand, and
he took him up to him into the chariot.
16 And he said, "Come with me and
[a]see my zeal for the LORD." So [1]he made
him ride in his chariot.
17 And when he came to Samaria, [a]he
[1]killed all who remained to Ahab in
Samaria, until he had destroyed him,
[b]according to the word of the LORD,
which He spoke to Elijah.

Jehu Destroys Baal Worshipers

18 Then Jehu gathered all the people
and said to them, "[a]Ahab served Baal a
little; Jehu will serve him much.
19 "And now, [a]summon all the prophets of Baal, all his worshipers and all his
priests; let no one be missing, for I have
a great sacrifice for Baal; whoever is
missing shall not live." But Jehu did it in
[1]cunning, in order that he might destroy
the worshipers of Baal.
20 And Jehu said, "[a]Sanctify a solemn
assembly for Baal." And [b]they proclaimed *it.*
21 Then Jehu sent [1]throughout Israel
and all the worshipers of Baal came, so
that there was not a man left who did
not come. And when they went into [a]the
house of Baal, the house of Baal was
filled from one end to the other.
22 And he said to the one who *was* [1]in
charge of the wardrobe, "Bring out
garments for all the worshipers of Baal."
So he brought out garments for them.
23 And Jehu went into the house of
Baal with Jehonadab the son of Rechab;
and he said to the worshipers of Baal,
"Search and see that there may be here
with you none of the servants of the
LORD, but only the worshipers of Baal."
24 Then they went in to offer sacrifices
and burnt offerings. Now Jehu had
stationed for himself eighty men outside,
and he had said, "[a]The one who permits
any of the men whom I bring into your
hands to escape, [1]shall give up his life in
exchange."
25 Then it came about, as soon as he
had finished offering the burnt offering,
that Jehu said to the [1a]guard and to the
royal officers, "[b]Go in, [2]kill them; let
none come out." And they [3]killed them
with the edge of the sword; and the
[1]guard and the royal officers threw *them*
out, and went to the [4]inner room of the
house of Baal.
26 And they brought out the *sacred*
[a]pillars of the house of Baal, and burned
them.
27 They also broke down the *sacred*
pillar of Baal and broke down the house
of Baal, and [a]made it a latrine to this
day.
28 Thus Jehu eradicated Baal out of
Israel.
29 However, [a]*as for* the sins of Jeroboam the son of Nebat, which he made
Israel sin, from these Jehu did not
depart, *even* the [b]golden calves that *were*
at Bethel and that *were* at Dan.
30 And the LORD said to Jehu, "Because you have done well in executing
what is right in My eyes, *and* have done
to the house of Ahab according to all
that *was* in My heart, [a]your sons of the
fourth generation shall sit on the throne
of Israel."
31 But Jehu [1a]was not careful to walk
in the law of the LORD, the God of
Israel, with all his heart; [b]he did not
depart from the sins of Jeroboam, which
he made Israel sin.
32 In those days the [a]LORD began to
cut off *portions* [1]from Israel; and [b]Haz-
ael [2]defeated them throughout the territory of Israel:
33 from the Jordan eastward, all the
land of Gilead, the Gadites and the
Reubenites and the Manassites, from
[a]Aroer, which is by the valley of the
Arnon, even [b]Gilead and Bashan.

Jehoahaz Succeeds Jehu

34 Now the rest of the acts of Jehu
and all that he did and all his might, are
they not written in the Book of the
Chronicles of the Kings of Israel?
35 And Jehu slept with his fathers,
and they buried him in Samaria. And
Jehoahaz his son became king in his
place.
36 Now the [1]time which Jehu reigned
over Israel in Samaria *was* twenty-eight
years.

[a]Athaliah Queen of Judah

11 WHEN Athaliah the mother of
Ahaziah saw that her son was
dead, she rose and destroyed all the
royal [1]offspring.
2 But Jehosheba, the daughter of
King Joram, sister of Ahaziah, [a]took
Joash the son of Ahaziah and stole him
from among the king's sons who were
being put to death, and placed him and
his nurse in the bedroom. So they hid
him from Athaliah, and he was not put
to death.
3 So he was hidden with her in the
house of the LORD six years, while
Athaliah was reigning over the land.
4 [a]Now in the seventh year Jehoiada
sent and brought the captains of hundreds of [b]the Carites and of the [1]guard,
and brought them to him in the house of
the LORD. Then he made a covenant
with them and put them under oath in
the house of the LORD, and showed them
the king's son.
5 And he commanded them, saying,
"This is the thing that you shall do: [a]one
third of you, who come in on the sabbath and keep watch over the king's
house
6 (one third also *shall be* at the gate
Sur, and one third at the gate behind the
[1]guards), [2]shall keep watch over the
house for defense.
7 "And two parts of you, *even* all who
go out on the sabbath, shall also keep
watch over the house of the LORD for the
king.
8 "Then you shall surround the king,
each with his weapons in his hand; and
whoever comes within the ranks shall be

16 [1]Lit., *they* [a]1 Kin. 19:10
17 [1]Lit., *smote* [a]2 Kin. 9:8 [b]2 Kin. 10:10
18 [a]1 Kin. 16:31,32
19 [1]Lit., *insidiousness* [a]1 Kin. 18:19; 22:6
20 [a]Joel 1:14 [b]Ex. 32:4-6
21 [1]Lit., *in all* [a]1 Kin. 16:32; 2 Kin. 11:18
22 [1]Lit., *over the*
24 [1]Lit., *his soul for his soul* [a]1 Kin. 20:30-42
25 [1]Lit., *runners* [2]Lit., *smite* [3]Lit., *smote* [4]Lit., *city* [a]1 Sam. 22:17 [b]1 Kin. 18:40
26 [a]1 Kin. 14:23; 2 Kin. 3:2
27 [a]Ezra 6:11; Dan. 2:5; 3:29
29 [a]1 Kin. 12:28-30; 13:33, 34 [b]1 Kin. 12:29
30 [a]2 Kin. 15:12
31 [1]Lit., *did not watch* [a]Prov. 4:23 [b]2 Kin. 10:29
32 [1]Lit., *in* [2]Lit., *smote* [a]2 Kin. 13:25; 14:25 [b]1 Kin. 19:17; 2 Kin. 8:12; 13:22
33 [a]Deut. 2:36 [b]Amos 1:3-5
36 [1]Lit., *days*
1 [1]Lit., *seed* [a]2 Chr. 22:10-12
2 [a]2 Kin. 11:21; 12:1
4 [1]Lit., *runners* [a]2 Chr. 23:1-21 [b]2 Sam. 20:23; 2 Kin. 11:19
5 [a]1 Chr. 9:25
6 [1]Lit., *runners* [2]Lit., *and shall*

put to death. And [a]be with the king when he goes out and when he comes in."

9 So the captains of hundreds [a]did according to all that Jehoiada the priest commanded. And each one of them took his men who were to come in on the sabbath, with those who were to go out on the sabbath, and came to Jehoiada the priest.

10 And [a]the priest gave to the captains of hundreds the spears and shields that had been King David's, which *were* in the house of the LORD.

11 And the [1]guards stood each with his weapons in his hand, from the right [2]side of the house to the left [2]side of the house, by the altar and by the house, around the king.

12 Then he brought the king's son out and [a]put the crown on him, and *gave him* [b]the testimony; and they made him king and anointed him, and they clapped their hands and said, "[c]*Long* live the king!"

13 [a]When Athaliah heard the noise of the guard *and of* the people, she came to the people in the house of the LORD.

14 And she looked and behold, the king was standing [a]by the pillar, according to the custom, with the captains and the [1]trumpeters beside the king; and [b]all the people of the land rejoiced and blew trumpets. Then Athaliah [c]tore her clothes and cried, "[d]Treason! Treason!"

15 And Jehoiada the priest commanded the captains of hundreds who were appointed over the army, and said to them, "Bring her out [1]between the ranks, and whoever follows her put to death with the sword." For the priest said, "Let her not be put to death in the house of the LORD."

16 So they [1]seized her, and when she arrived at the horses' entrance of the king's house, she was [a]put to death there.

17 Then [a]Jehoiada made a covenant between the LORD and the king and the people, that they should be the LORD's people, also [b]between the king and the people.

18 And all the people of the land went to [a]the house of Baal, and tore it down; [b]his altars and his images they broke in pieces thoroughly, and [c]killed Mattan the priest of Baal before the altars. And the priest appointed [1]officers over the house of the LORD.

19 And he took the captains of hundreds and the [a]Carites and the [1]guards and all the people of the land; and they brought the king down from the house of the LORD, and came by the way of [b]the gate of the [1]guards to the king's house. And he sat on the throne of the kings.

20 So [a]all the people of the land rejoiced and the city was quiet. For they had put Athaliah to death with the sword at the king's house.

21 [1a]Jehoash was seven years old when he became king.

8 [a]Num. 27:16, 17
9 [a]2 Chr. 23:8
10 [a]2 Sam. 8:7; 1 Chr. 18:7
11 [1]Lit., *runners* [2]Lit., *shoulder*
12 [a]2 Sam. 1:10 [b]Ex. 25:16; 31:18 [c]1 Sam. 10:24
13 [a]2 Chr. 23:12
14 [1]Lit., *trumpets* [a]2 Kin. 23:3; 2 Chr. 34:31 [b]1 Kin. 1:39, 40 [c]Gen. 37:29; 44:13 [d]2 Kin. 9:23
15 [1]Lit., *from within*
16 [1]Lit., *placed hands to her* [a]Gen. 9:6; Lev. 24:17
17 [a]Josh. 24:25; 2 Chr. 15:12-14; 34:31 [b]1 Sam. 10:25; 2 Sam. 5:3
18 [1]Lit., *offices* [a]2 Kin. 10:26, 27 [b]Deut. 12:2, 3 [c]1 Kin. 18:40
19 [1]Lit., *runners* [a]2 Kin. 11:4 [b]2 Kin. 11:6
20 [a]Prov. 11:10
21 [1]Ch. 12:1 in Heb. [a]2 Chr. 24:1-14
1 [a]2 Chr. 24:1
3 [a]2 Kin. 14:4; 15:35
4 [1]Lit., *which it comes into . . . to bring* [a]2 Kin. 22:4 [b]Ex. 30:13-16; 35:5, 22, 29; 1 Chr. 29:3-9
5 [1]Lit., *breaches*, and so through v. 12
6 [a]2 Chr. 24:5
9 [a]Mark 12:41; Luke 21:1
10 [a]2 Sam. 8:17; 2 Kin. 19:2; 22:3, 4, 12
11 [1]Lit., *brought*
12 [1]Lit., *went out* [a]2 Kin. 22:5, 6
13 [a]2 Chr. 24:14 [b]1 Kin. 7:48, 50

Joash (Jehoash) Reigns over Judah

12 IN the seventh year of Jehu, [a]Jehoash became king, and he reigned forty years in Jerusalem; and his mother's name was Zibiah of Beersheba.

2 And Jehoash did right in the sight of the LORD all his days in which Jehoiada the priest instructed him.

3 Only [a]the high places were not taken away; the people still sacrificed and burned incense on the high places.

The Temple to Be Repaired

4 Then Jehoash said to the priests, "All the money of the sacred things [a]which is brought into the house of the LORD, in current money, *both* [b]the money of each man's assessment *and* all the money [1]which any man's heart prompts him to bring into the house of the LORD,

5 let the priests take it for themselves, each from his acquaintance; and they shall repair the [1]damages of the house wherever any damage may be found."

6 But it came about that in the twenty-third year of King Jehoash [a]the priests had not repaired the damages of the house.

7 Then King Jehoash called for Jehoiada the priest, and for the *other* priests and said to them, "Why do you not repair the damages of the house? Now therefore take no *more* money from your acquaintances, but pay it for the damages of the house."

8 So the priests agreed that they should take no *more* money from the people, nor repair the damages of the house.

9 But [a]Jehoiada the priest took a chest and bored a hole in its lid, and put it beside the altar, on the right side as one comes into the house of the LORD; and the priests who guarded the threshold put in it all the money which was brought into the house of the LORD.

10 And when they saw that there was much money in the chest, [a]the king's scribe and the high priest came up and tied *it* in bags and counted the money which was found in the house of the LORD.

11 And they gave the money which was weighed out into the hands of those who did the work, who had the oversight of the house of the LORD; and they [1]paid it out to the carpenters and the builders, who worked on the house of the LORD;

12 and [a]to the masons and the stonecutters, and for buying timber and hewn stone to repair the damages to the house of the LORD, and for all that was [1]laid out for the house to repair it.

13 But [a]there were not made for the house of the LORD [b]silver cups, snuffers, bowls, trumpets, any vessels of gold, or vessels of silver from the money which was brought into the house of the LORD;

14 for they gave that to those who did the work, and with it they repaired the house of the LORD.

MEN'S CLOTHES/WOMEN'S CLOTHES

Deuteronomy 22:5. Because the tunic was so basic, it was identical for men and women, except that the man's tunic was often shorter (knee length) and the woman's was often longer (ankle length) and blue. The prohibition against exchanging clothes had its origin in the sexual stimulation that was part of the Canaanite religion.

JOSEPH'S "COAT OF MANY COLOURS"

Genesis 37:3. Joseph received a tunic of many pieces. The additional pieces were probably long sleeves that were a nuisance and got in the way when work was to be done. (When women had long, wide sleeves, they tied them up behind their necks to that their arms would be free.) This indicated that Joseph was not expected to do heavy work; he was the chosen heir to rule over the family.

THE CLOAK AND THE TUNIC

Matthew 5:40; Luke 6:29. Jesus hadn't got it wrong and he was not contradicting himself. In the first case, Jesus was talking about the law court that could take away a person's tunic but not his cloak. In the second case, a robber would grab the outer garment first; it was valuable.

COVERING WOMEN'S HEADS

1 Corinthians 11:10. Respectable women went out with their heads covered and wore veils. Only prostitutes displayed their faces and showed off their hair in order to attract men. Paul therefore tells the Christians that if a woman in the church will not wear a veil then she should be shorn; but it is best that her head be covered. Even when Christians have liberty in the practice of their faith, they are not to shock propriety.

GOD'S ARMOUR

Ephesians 6:10-11. Paul refers to the clothing worn by a soldier. He combines Isaiah's prophecy of the armour of God (Isaiah 59:16-17) with what he knows of the Roman soldier. Underneath the soldier's armour was a foundation garment to *"hold him in"* so that the armour (leather jacket and skirt, covered with metal plates) could fit on top. Roman soldiers had hob-nailed sandals that gripped the ground well. Paul uses the description to say that the devil will not be able to bring Christians down if they are strictly honest, utterly just in their dealings, and not easily upset. Add to this a salvation that enables them to live according to God's standard, with access to and trust in what God has said, and the Christian is well-protected.

THE PRIESTS' CLOTHING

Exodus 28. Priests wore a linen garment over the top of the tunic, perhaps to keep it clean. It was called an ephod (1 Samuel 2:18-19). The high priest wore special clothes, but they still followed the basic provision. The tunic was blue, the ephod was richly embroidered and carried a jewel-encrusted pouch containing two lots from which the will of God might be ascertained. The cloak was white. He wore a special turban on the head.

THE WOMAN AT THE WELL

John 4:6. The Samaritan woman came at the sixth hour of the day (midday), despite the heat, because she knew there would be no other women at the well. Furthermore, because of the life-style she was following, she did not want to talk to them. She had brought her own leather bucket to the well to get the water out (v.7).

A WOMAN'S JOB

Mark 14:13. Since it was always the woman's job to carry water, a man doing the job would be distinctive enough to be identified quickly. Jesus therefore used this means to help Peter and John locate the room where the Last Supper was to be prepared (see Luke 22:8-12).

TWO BASIC MEALS

Luke 14:12. Jesus literally said, *"When you make a **breakfast** or an **evening meal**, call not your friends."* He was referring to the two basic meals of the day.

JONATHAN - *friendship*

Jonathan is known to most Christians as a great example of friendship. In fact, the covenant relationship between David and Jonathan gives us a rare picture of two young men who loved each other deeply.

Jonathan and David became friends during David's early years at Saul's court. Jonathan was the eldest son of King Saul, a brave and mighty leader in his father's army, next in line to the throne. By the time David came to Saul's court, the Bible says the Lord was no longer with Saul. He was tormented by evil spirits, suspicious and violent. Yet from David's arrival, Jonathan loved him. Jonathan gave David his robe, his armor and his sword, mighty symbols of power and position.

As Saul's reasons declined, he plotted against David and tried many times to kill him. The Bible says Saul knew the Lord was with David, so we know his Godliness must have been outstanding. Surely this quality drew Jonathan.

The story of Jonathan's faithfulness to David, his help and love, is old and well-known. Though he was capable of the greatest love, David is the only friend with whom such a relationship is recorded. Jonathan chose wisely who he would love. There was only one friend with whom he would covenant, risk his life and entrust the well-being of his descendants — David! Because of their strong commitment to each other, David and Jonathan were willing to risk it all.

The Bible tells us Jonathan loved David as he loved his own life (1 Sam. 20:17), truly obeying the commandment to love our neighbor as ourselves (Lev. 19:18). Though David was anointed to succeed Saul as king, Jonathan expressed no jealously or resentment. Though Jonathan's father wrongfully turned against David, Jonathan did not.

When Jonathan was slain with his father by the Philistines, David said *"Your love to me was more wonderful than the love of women"* (2 Sam. 1:26). Though David had many wives, his friendship with Jonathan held a special and unique place in his heart.

QUESTIONS

1. **Though Jonathan loved well, he loved wisely. Can you think of times when you placed your loyalty and trust in someone who betrayed you? How could you have avoided this?**

2. **Jonathan and David made a covenant of their friendship, declaring their feelings openly. How have you demonstrated your love to a special friend?**

3. **Jonathan repeatedly risked his life for David's sake. When have you risked embarrassment, unpopularity or even danger for a friend?**

4. **Though they were of opposing powers in Israel and sometimes separated, David and Jonathan's feelings remained true. How do you and your friends overcome difficulties or disagreements?**

15 Moreover, [a]they did not require an
accounting from the men into whose
hand they gave the money to pay to
those who did the work, for they dealt
faithfully.
16 The [a]money from the guilt offerings and [b]the money from the sin offerings, was not brought into the house of
the LORD; [c]it was for the priests.
17 Then [a]Hazael king of Aram went
up and fought against Gath and captured it, and [b]Hazael set his face to go
up to Jerusalem.
18 And [a]Jehoash king of Judah took
all the sacred things that Jehoshaphat
and Jehoram and Ahaziah, his fathers,
kings of Judah, had dedicated, and [b]his
own sacred things and all the gold that
was found among the treasuries of the
house of the LORD and of the king's
house, and sent *them* to Hazael king of
Aram. Then he went away from Jerusalem.

Joash (Jehoash) Succeeded by Amaziah in Judah

19 Now the rest of the acts of Joash
and all that he did, are they not written
in the Book of the Chronicles of the
Kings of Judah?
20 [a]And his servants arose and made a
conspiracy, and [b]struck down Joash at
[c]the house of Millo *as he was* going down
to Silla.
21 For Jozacar the son of Shimeath,
and Jehozabad the son of [a]Shomer, his
servants, struck *him,* and he died; and
they buried him with his fathers in the
city of David, and [b]Amaziah his son
became king in his place.

Kings of Israel: Jehoahaz and Jehoash

13 IN the twenty-third year of Joash
the son of Ahaziah, king of Judah, Jehoahaz the son of Jehu became
king over Israel at Samaria, *and he
reigned* seventeen years.
2 And he did evil in the sight of the
LORD, and followed the sins of Jeroboam the son of Nebat, [a]with which he
made Israel sin; he did not turn from
them.
3 [a]So the anger of the LORD was
kindled against Israel, and He gave them
continually into the hand of [b]Hazael
king of Aram, and into the hand of
[c]Ben-hadad the son of Hazael.
4 Then [a]Jehoahaz entreated the favor
of the LORD, and the LORD listened to
him; for [b]He saw the oppression of
Israel, how the king of Aram oppressed
them.
5 And the LORD gave Israel a [1a]deliv-
erer, so that they [2]escaped from under
the hand of the Arameans; and the sons
of Israel lived in their tents as formerly.
6 Nevertheless they did not turn
away from the sins of the house of
Jeroboam, [a]with which he made Israel
sin, but walked in [1]them; and [b]the
Asherah also remained standing in Samaria.
7 For he left to Jehoahaz of the
[1]army not more than fifty horsemen and
ten chariots and 10,000 footmen, for the
king of Aram had destroyed them and
[a]made them like the dust at threshing.
8 Now the rest of the acts of Jehoahaz, and all that he did and his might,
are they not written in the Book of the
Chronicles of the Kings of Israel?
9 And Jehoahaz slept with his fathers, and they buried him in Samaria;
and Joash his son became king in his
place.
10 In the thirty-seventh year of Joash
king of Judah, Jehoash the son of Jehoahaz, became king over Israel in Samaria,
and reigned sixteen years.
11 And he did evil in the sight of the
LORD; he did not turn away from all the
sins of Jeroboam the son of Nebat, with
which he made Israel sin, but he walked
in [1]them.
12 [a]Now the rest of the acts of Joash
and all that he did and his might with
which he fought against Amaziah king of
Judah, are they not written in the Book
of the Chronicles of the Kings of Israel?
13 So Joash slept with his fathers, and
Jeroboam sat on his throne; and Joash
was buried in Samaria with the kings of
Israel.

Death of Elisha

14 When Elisha [1]became sick with the
illness of which he was to die, Joash the
king of Israel came down to him and
wept over [2]him and said, "[a]My father,
my father, the chariots of Israel and its
horsemen!"
15 And Elisha said to him, "Take a
bow and arrows." So he [1]took a bow and
arrows.
16 Then he said to the king of Israel,
"Put your hand on the bow." And he put
his hand *on it,* then Elisha laid his hands
on the king's hands.
17 And he said, "Open the window
toward the east," and he opened *it.* Then
Elisha said, "Shoot!" And he shot. And
he said, "The LORD's arrow of victory,
even the arrow of victory over Aram; for
you shall [1]defeat the Arameans at
[a]Aphek until you have [2]destroyed *them.*"
18 Then he said, "Take the arrows,"
and he took them. And he said to the
king of Israel, "Strike the ground," and
he struck *it* three times and [1]stopped.
19 So [a]the man of God was angry with
him and said, "You should have struck
five or six times, then you would have
struck Aram until you would have [1]de-
stroyed *it.* But now you shall strike
Aram [b]*only* three times."
20 And Elisha died, and they buried
him. Now [a]the bands of the Moabites
would invade the land in the spring of
the year.
21 And as they were burying a man,
behold, they saw a marauding band; and
they cast the man into the grave of
Elisha. And when the man [1]touched the
bones of Elisha he [a]revived and stood up
on his feet.

---

15 [a]2 Kin. 22:7; 1 Cor. 4:2; 2 Cor. 8:20

16 [a]Lev. 5:15-18 [b]Lev. 4:24, 29 [c]Lev. 7:7; Num. 18:19

17 [a]1 Kin. 19:17; 2 Kin. 8:12; 10:32, 33 [b]2 Chr. 24:23, 24

18 [a]1 Kin. 14:26; 15:18; 2 Kin. 16:8; 18:15, 16 [b]2 Kin. 12:4

20 [a]2 Chr. 24:25-27 [b]2 Kin. 14:5 [c]Judg. 9:6; 2 Sam. 5:9; 1 Kin. 11:27

21 [a]2 Chr. 24:26 [b]2 Kin. 14:1

2 [a]1 Kin. 12:26-33

3 [a]Judg. 2:14 [b]2 Kin. 12:17 [c]2 Kin. 13:24, 25

4 [a]Num. 21:7-9 [b]Ex. 3:7, 9; 2 Kin. 14:26

5 [1]Or, *savior* [2]Lit., *went out* [a]2 Kin. 13:25; 14:25, 27; Neh. 9:27

6 [1]Lit., *it* [a]2 Kin. 13:2 [b]1 Kin. 16:33

7 [1]Lit., *people* [a]Amos 1:3

11 [1]Lit., *it*

12 [a]2 Kin. 13:14-19; 14:8-15

14 [1]Lit., *was sick with his sickness* [2]Lit., *his face* [a]2 Kin. 2:12

15 [1]Lit., *took to himself*

17 [1]Lit., *smite* [2]Lit., *made an end of* [a]1 Kin. 20:26

18 [1]Lit., *stood*

19 [1]Lit., *made an end of* [a]2 Kin. 5:20 [b]2 Kin. 13:25

20 [a]2 Kin. 3:7; 24:2

21 [1]Lit., *went and touched* [a]Matt. 27:52

22 Now [a]Hazael king of Aram had oppressed Israel all the days of Jehoahaz.

23 But the [a]LORD was gracious to them and [b]had compassion on them and turned to them because of [c]His covenant with Abraham, Isaac, and Jacob, and would not destroy them or cast them from His presence until now.

24 When Hazael king of Aram died, Ben-hadad his son became king in his place.

25 Then [a]Jehoash the son of Jehoahaz took again from the hand of Ben-hadad the son of Hazael the cities which he had taken in war from the hand of Jehoahaz his father. [b]Three times Joash [1]defeated him and recovered the cities of Israel.

Amaziah Reigns over Judah

14 [a]IN the second year of Joash son of Joahaz king of Israel, [b]Amaziah the son of Joash king of Judah became king.

2 He was twenty-five years old when he became king, and he reigned twenty-nine years in Jerusalem. And his mother's name was Jehoaddin of Jerusalem.

3 And he did right in the sight of the LORD, yet not like David his father; he did according to all that Joash his father had done.

4 Only [a]the high places were not taken away; [b]the people still sacrificed and burned incense on the high places.

5 Now it came about, as soon as the kingdom was firmly in his hand, that he [1a]killed his servants who had slain the king his father.

6 But the sons of the [1]slayers he did not put to death, according to what is written in the book of the law of Moses, as the LORD commanded, saying, "[a]The fathers shall not be put to death for the sons, nor the sons be put to death for the fathers; but [b]each shall be put to death for his own sin."

7 He [1]killed *of* Edom in [a]the Valley of Salt 10,000 and took [b]Sela by war, and named it [c]Joktheel to this day.

8 [a]Then Amaziah sent messengers to Jehoash, the son of Jehoahaz son of Jehu, king of Israel, saying, "[b]Come, let us face each other."

9 And Jehoash king of Israel sent to Amaziah king of Judah, saying, "[a]The thorn bush which was in Lebanon sent to the cedar which was in Lebanon, saying, 'Give your daughter to my son in marriage.' But there passed by a wild beast that was in Lebanon, and trampled the thorn bush.

10 "[a]You have indeed [1]defeated Edom, and [b]your heart has [2]become proud. Enjoy your glory and stay at home; for why should you provoke trouble so that you, even you, should fall, and Judah with you?"

11 But Amaziah would not listen. So Jehoash king of Israel went up; and he and Amaziah king of Judah faced each other at [a]Beth-shemesh, which belongs to Judah.

12 And Judah was defeated [1]by Israel, and [a]they fled each to his tent.

13 Then Jehoash king of Israel captured Amaziah king of Judah, the son of Jehoash the son of Ahaziah, at Beth-shemesh, and came to Jerusalem and tore down the wall of Jerusalem from [a]the Gate of Ephraim to [b]the Corner Gate, 400 [1]cubits.

14 And [a]he took all the gold and silver and all the utensils which were found in the house of the LORD, and in the treasuries of the king's house, the hostages also, and returned to Samaria.

Jeroboam II Succeeds Jehoash in Israel

15 [a]Now the rest of the acts of Jehoash which he did, and his might and how he fought with Amaziah king of Judah, are they not written in the Book of the Chronicles of the Kings of Israel?

16 So Jehoash slept with his fathers and was buried in Samaria with the kings of Israel; and Jeroboam his son became king in his place.

Azariah (Uzziah) Succeeds Amaziah in Judah

17 [a]And Amaziah the son of Joash king of Judah lived fifteen years after the death of Jehoash son of Jehoahaz king of Israel.

18 Now the rest of the acts of Amaziah, are they not written in the Book of the Chronicles of the Kings of Judah?

19 And they conspired against him in Jerusalem, and he fled to [a]Lachish; but they sent after him to Lachish and killed him there.

20 Then they brought him on horses and he was buried at Jerusalem with his fathers in the city of David.

21 And all the people of Judah took [1]Azariah, who *was* sixteen years old, and made him king in the place of his father Amaziah.

22 [a]He built Elath and restored it to Judah, after the king slept with his fathers.

23 In the fifteenth year of Amaziah the son of Joash king of Judah, Jeroboam the son of Joash king of Israel became king in Samaria, *and reigned* forty-one years.

24 And he did evil in the sight of the LORD; he did not depart from all the sins of Jeroboam the son of Nebat, which he made Israel sin.

25 [a]He restored the border of Israel from [b]the entrance of Hamath as far as [c]the Sea of the Arabah, according to the word of the LORD, the God of Israel, which He spoke [1]through His servant [d]Jonah the son of Amittai, the prophet, who was of [e]Gath-hepher.

26 For the [a]LORD saw the affliction of Israel, *which was* very bitter; for [b]there was neither bond nor free, nor was there any helper for Israel.

27 And the [a]LORD did not say that He would blot out the name of Israel from under heaven, but He saved them by the hand of Jeroboam the son of Joash.

---

22 [a]2 Kin. 8:12, 13

23 [a]2 Kin. 14:27 [b]1 Kin. 8:28 [c]Gen. 13:16, 17; 17:2-5

25 [1]Lit., *smote* [a]2 Kin. 10:32, 33; 14:25 [b]2 Kin. 13:18, 19

1 [a]2 Chr. 25:1 [b]2 Kin. 13:10

4 [a]2 Kin. 12:3 [b]2 Kin. 16:4

5 [1]Lit., *smote* [a]2 Kin. 12:20

6 [1]Lit., *smiters* [a]Deut. 24:16 [b]Jer. 31:30; Ezek. 18:4, 20

7 [1]Lit., *smote* [a]2 Sam. 8:13; 1 Chr. 18:12; 2 Chr. 25:11 [b]Is. 16:1 [c]Josh. 15:38

8 [a]2 Chr. 25:17-24 [b]2 Sam. 2:14-17

9 [a]Judg. 9:8-15

10 [1]Lit., *smitten* [2]Lit., *lifted you up* [a]2 Kin. 14:7 [b]Deut. 8:14; 2 Chr. 26:16

11 [a]Josh. 19:38

12 [1]Lit., *before* [a]2 Sam. 18:17

13 [1]I.e., One cubit equals approx. 18 in. [a]Neh. 8:16; 12:39 [b]2 Chr. 25:23

14 [a]1 Kin. 14:26; 2 Kin. 12:18

15 [a]2 Kin. 13:12, 13

17 [a]2 Chr. 25:25-28

19 [a]Josh. 10:31; 2 Kin. 18:14, 17

21 [1]In 2 Chr. 26:1, *Uzziah*

22 [a]1 Kin. 9:26; 2 Kin. 16:6; 2 Chr. 8:17

25 [1]Lit., *by* [a]2 Kin. 10:32; 13:25 [b]1 Kin. 8:65 [c]Deut. 3:17 [d]Jon. 1:1; Matt. 12:39, 40 [e]Josh. 19:13

26 [a]2 Kin. 13:4 [b]Deut. 32:36

27 [a]2 Kin. 13:23

Zechariah Reigns over Israel

28 Now the rest of the acts of Jeroboam and all that he did and his might,
how he fought and how he recovered for
Israel, [a]Damascus and [b]Hamath, *which
had belonged* to Judah, are they not
written in the Book of the Chronicles of
the Kings of Israel?
29 And Jeroboam slept with his fathers, even with the kings of Israel, and
Zechariah his son became king in his
place.

Series of Kings: Azariah (Uzziah) over Judah

15 [a]IN the twenty-seventh year of
Jeroboam king of Israel, Azariah
son of Amaziah king of Judah became
king.
2 He was [a]sixteen years old when he
became king, and he reigned fifty-two
years in Jerusalem; and his mother's
name was [1]Jecoliah of Jerusalem.
3 And he did right in the sight of the
LORD, according to all that his father
Amaziah had done.
4 Only [a]the high places were not
taken away; the people still sacrificed
and burned incense on the high places.
5 [a]And the LORD struck the king, so
that he was a leper to the day of his
death. And he [b]lived in a separate house,
[1]while Jotham the king's son was over
the household, judging the people of the
land.
6 Now the rest of the acts of Azariah
and all that he did, are they not written
in the Book of the Chronicles of the
Kings of Judah?
7 And Azariah slept with his fathers,
and they buried him with his fathers in
the city of David, and Jotham his son
became king in his place.

Zechariah over Israel

8 [a]In the thirty-eighth year of Azariah king of Judah, Zechariah the son of
Jeroboam became king over Israel in
Samaria *for* six months.
9 And he did evil in the sight of the
LORD, as his fathers had done; he did
not depart from the sins of Jeroboam the
son of Nebat, which he made Israel sin.
10 Then Shallum the son of Jabesh
conspired against him and [a]struck him
before the people and [1]killed him, and
reigned in his place.
11 Now the rest of the acts of Zechariah, behold they are written in the Book
of the Chronicles of the Kings of Israel.
12 This is [a]the word of the LORD
which He spoke to Jehu, saying, "Your
sons to the fourth generation shall sit on
the throne of Israel." And so it was.
13 Shallum son of Jabesh became king
in the [a]thirty-ninth year of Uzziah king
of Judah, and he reigned one month in
[b]Samaria.
14 Then Menahem son of Gadi went
up from [a]Tirzah and came to Samaria,
and struck Shallum son of Jabesh in
Samaria, and killed him and became
king in his place.
15 Now the rest of the acts of Shallum
and his conspiracy which he made,
behold they are written in the Book of
the Chronicles of the Kings of Israel.
16 Then Menahem struck Tiphsah
and all who were in it and its borders
from Tirzah, because they did not open
to him, therefore he struck *it;* and he
ripped up [a]all its women who were with
child.

Menahem over Israel

17 In the [a]thirty-ninth year of Azariah
king of Judah, Menahem son of Gadi
became king over Israel *and reigned* ten
years in Samaria.
18 And he did evil in the sight of the
LORD; he did not depart all his days
from the sins of Jeroboam the son of
Nebat, which he made Israel sin.
19 [a]Pul, king of Assyria, came against
the land, and Menahem gave Pul a
thousand talents of silver so that his
hand might be with him to [b]strengthen
the kingdom [1]under his rule.
20 Then Menahem exacted the money
from Israel, even from all the mighty
men of wealth, from each man fifty
shekels of silver to pay the king of
Assyria. So the king of Assyria returned
and did not remain there in the land.
21 Now the rest of the acts of Menahem and all that he did, are they not
written in the Book of the Chronicles of
the Kings of Israel?
22 And Menahem slept with his fathers, and Pekahiah his son became king
in his place.

Pekahiah over Israel

23 In [a]the fiftieth year of Azariah king
of Judah, Pekahiah son of Menahem
became king over Israel in Samaria, *and
reigned* two years.
24 And he did evil in the sight of the
LORD; he did not depart from the sins of
Jeroboam son of Nebat, which he made
Israel sin.
25 Then Pekah son of Remaliah, his
officer, conspired against him and struck
him in Samaria, in [a]the castle of the
king's house with Argob and Arieh; and
with him were fifty men of the Gileadites, and he killed him and became king
in his place.
26 Now the rest of the acts of Pekahiah and all that he did, behold they are
written in the Book of the Chronicles of
the Kings of Israel.

Pekah over Israel

27 In [a]the fifty-second year of Azariah
king of Judah, [b]Pekah son of Remaliah
became king over Israel in Samaria, *and
reigned* twenty years.
28 And he did evil in the sight of the
LORD; he did not depart from the sins of
Jeroboam son of Nebat, which he made
Israel sin.

28 [a]1 Kin. 11:24 [b]2 Chr. 8:3
1 [a]2 Kin. 14:17
2 [1]In 2 Chr. 26:3, *Jechiliah* [a]2 Chr. 26:3, 4
4 [a]2 Kin. 12:3
5 [1]Lit., *and* [a]2 Chr. 26:21-23 [b]Lev. 13:46; Num. 12:14
8 [a]2 Kin. 15:1
10 [1]Lit., *smote* [a]Amos 7:9
12 [a]2 Kin. 10:30
13 [a]2 Kin. 15:1, 8 [b]1 Kin. 16:24
14 [a]1 Kin. 14:17
16 [a]2 Kin. 8:12; Hos. 13:16
17 [a]2 Kin. 15:1, 8, 13
19 [1]Lit., *in his hand* [a]1 Chr. 5:25, 26 [b]2 Kin. 14:5
23 [a]2 Kin. 15:1, 8, 13, 17
25 [a]1 Kin. 16:18
27 [a]2 Kin. 15:23 [b]2 Chr. 28:6; Is. 7:1

29 In the days of Pekah king of Israel,
[1a]Tiglath-pileser king of Assyria came
and [2]captured Ijon and Abel-beth-maa-
cah and Janoah and Kedesh and Hazor
and Gilead and Galilee, all the land of
Naphtali; and [b]he carried them captive
to Assyria.
30 And Hoshea the son of Elah made
a conspiracy against Pekah the son of
Remaliah, and struck him and put him
to death and became king in his place, in
the twentieth year of Jotham the son of
Uzziah.
31 Now the rest of the acts of Pekah
and all that he did, behold, they are
written in the Book of the Chronicles of
the Kings of Israel.

Jotham over Judah

32 In the second year of Pekah the son
of Remaliah king of Israel, Jotham the
son of [1]Uzziah king of Judah became
king.
33 [a]He was twenty-five years old when
he became king, and he reigned sixteen
years in Jerusalem; and his mother's
name *was* Jerusha the daughter of Zadok.
34 And [a]he did what was right in the
sight of the LORD; he did according to
all that his father Uzziah had done.
35 Only [a]the high places were not
taken away; the people still sacrificed
and burned incense on the high places.
[b]He built the upper gate of the house of
the LORD.
36 Now the rest of the acts of Jotham
and all that he did, are they not written
in the Book of the Chronicles of the
Kings of Judah?
37 In those days [a]the LORD began to
send Rezin king of Aram and Pekah the
son of Remaliah against Judah.
38 And Jotham slept with his fathers,
and he was buried with his fathers in the
city of David his father; and Ahaz his
son became king in his place.

Ahaz Reigns over Judah

16 IN the seventeenth year of Pekah
the son of Remaliah, [a]Ahaz the
son of Jotham, king of Judah, became
king.
2 [a]Ahaz *was* twenty years old when
he became king, and he reigned sixteen
years in Jerusalem; and he did not do
what was right in the sight of the LORD
his God, as his father David *had done.*
3 But he walked in the way of the
kings of Israel, [a]and even made his son
pass through the fire, [b]according to the
abominations of the nations whom the
LORD had [1]driven out from before
the sons of Israel.
4 And he [a]sacrificed and burned
incense on the high places and on the
hills and under every green tree.
5 Then [a]Rezin king of Aram and
Pekah son of Remaliah, king of Israel,
came up to Jerusalem to *wage* war; and
they besieged Ahaz, [b]but could not
[1]overcome him.
6 At that time Rezin king of Aram
recovered [a]Elath for Aram, and cleared
the Judeans out of [1]Elath entirely; and
the [2]Arameans came to Elath, and have
lived there to this day.

Ahaz Seeks Help of Aram

7 [a]So Ahaz sent messengers to [b]Tig-
lath-pileser king of Assyria, saying, "I
am your servant and your son; come up
and deliver me from the [1]hand of the
king of Aram, and from the [1]hand of the
king of Israel, who are rising up against
me."
8 And [a]Ahaz took the silver and gold
that was found in the house of the LORD
and in the treasuries of the king's house,
and sent a present to the king of Assyria.
9 [a]So the king of Assyria listened to
him; and the king of Assyria went up
against Damascus and [b]captured it, and
carried *the people of* it away into exile to
[c]Kir, and put Rezin to death.

Damascus Falls

10 Now King Ahaz went to Damascus
to meet [a]Tiglath-pileser king of Assyria,
and saw the altar which *was* at Damascus; and King Ahaz sent to [b]Urijah the
priest the [1]pattern of the altar and its
model, according to all its workmanship.
11 So Urijah the priest built an altar;
according to all that King Ahaz had sent
from Damascus, thus Urijah the priest
made *it,* [1]before the coming of King
Ahaz from Damascus.
12 And when the king came from
Damascus, the king saw the altar; then
[a]the king approached the altar and
[1]went up to it,
13 and [1]burned his burnt offering and
his meal offering, and poured his libation and sprinkled the blood of his peace
offerings on the altar.
14 And [a]the bronze altar, which *was*
before the LORD, [1]he brought from the
front of the house, from between [b]*his*
altar and the house of the LORD, and he
put it on the north side of *his* altar.
15 Then King Ahaz [1]commanded Urijah the priest, saying, "Upon the great
altar [2]burn [a]the morning burnt offering
and the evening meal offering and the
king's burnt offering and his meal offering, with the burnt offering of all the
people of the land and their meal offering and their libations; and sprinkle on
it all the blood of the burnt offering and
all the blood of the sacrifice. But [b]the
bronze altar shall be for me to inquire
by."
16 So Urijah the priest did according
to all that King Ahaz commanded.
17 Then King Ahaz [a]cut off the borders of the stands, and removed the laver
from them; he also [b]took down the sea
from the bronze oxen which were under
it, and put it on a pavement of stone.
18 And the covered way for the sabbath which they had built in the house,
and the outer entry of the king, he
removed from the house of the LORD
because of the king of Assyria.

29 [1]In 1 Chr. 5:6, 26, *Tilgath-pilneser* [2]Lit., *took* [a]2 Kin. 15:19 [b]2 Kin. 17:6
32 [1]I.e., Azariah
33 [a]2 Chr. 27:1
34 [a]2 Kin. 15:3, 4; 2 Chr. 26:4, 5
35 [a]2 Kin. 12:3 [b]2 Chr. 23:20; 27:3
37 [a]2 Kin. 16:5; Is. 7:1
1 [a]2 Chr. 28:1
2 [a]2 Chr. 28:1-4
3 [1]Or, *dispossessed* [a]Lev. 18:21; 2 Kin. 17:17; 21:6 [b]Deut. 12:31; 2 Kin. 21:2, 11
4 [a]Deut. 12:2; 2 Kin. 14:4
5 [1]Lit., *fight* [a]2 Kin. 15:37; Is. 7:1 [b]2 Chr. 28:5, 6
6 [1]Heb., *Eloth* [2]So with some ancient versions; Heb., *Edomites* [a]2 Kin. 14:22; 2 Chr. 26:2
7 [1]Lit., *palm* [a]2 Chr. 28:16 [b]2 Kin. 15:29
8 [a]2 Kin. 12:17, 18; 18:15
9 [a]2 Chr. 28:21 [b]Amos 1:3-5 [c]Is. 22:6; Amos 9:7
10 [1]Lit., *likeness* [a]2 Kin. 15:29 [b]Is. 8:2
11 [1]Lit., *until*
12 [1]Or, *offered on it* [a]2 Chr. 26:16, 19
13 [1]Lit., *offered in smoke*
14 [1]Lit., *he also* [a]Ex. 27:1, 2; 40:6, 29; 2 Chr. 4:1 [b]2 Kin. 16:11
15 [1]Lit., *commanded him, Urijah* [2]Lit., *offer in smoke* [a]Ex. 29:39-41 [b]2 Kin. 16:14
17 [a]1 Kin. 7:27, 28, 38 [b]1 Kin. 7:23, 25

Hezekiah Reigns over Judah

19 Now the rest of the acts of Ahaz which he did, are they not written [a]in the Book of the Chronicles of the Kings of Judah?

20 So [a]Ahaz slept with his fathers, and [b]was buried with his fathers in the city of David; and his son Hezekiah reigned in his place.

Hoshea Reigns over Israel

17 IN the twelfth year of Ahaz king of Judah, [a]Hoshea the son of Elah became king over Israel in Samaria, *and reigned* nine years.

2 And he did evil in the sight of the LORD, only not as the kings of Israel who were before him.

3 [a]Shalmaneser king of Assyria came up [b]against him, and Hoshea became his servant and paid him tribute.

4 But the king of Assyria found conspiracy in Hoshea, who had sent messengers to So king of Egypt and had offered no tribute to the king of Assyria, as *he had done* year by year; so the king of Assyria shut him up and bound him in prison.

5 Then the king of Assyria invaded the whole land and went up to [a]Samaria and besieged it three years.

Israel Captive

6 In the ninth year of Hoshea, [a]the king of Assyria captured Samaria and [b]carried Israel away into exile to Assyria, and [c]settled them in Halah and Habor, *on* the river of [d]Gozan, and [e]in the cities of the Medes.

Why Israel Fell

7 Now [a]*this* came about, because the sons of Israel had sinned against the LORD their God, [b]who had brought them up from the land of Egypt from under the hand of Pharaoh, king of Egypt, [c]and they had [1]feared other gods

8 and [a]walked in the [1]customs of the nations whom the LORD had driven out before the sons of Israel, and *in the customs* [b]of the kings of Israel which they had [2]introduced.

9 And the sons of Israel [1]did things secretly which were not right, against the LORD their God. Moreover, they built for themselves high places in all their towns, from [a]watchtower to fortified city.

10 And [a]they set for themselves *sacred* pillars and [1b]Asherim on every high hill and under every green tree,

11 and there they burned incense on all the high places as the nations *did* which the LORD had carried away to exile before them; and they did evil things provoking the LORD.

12 And they served idols, [a]concerning which the LORD had said to them, "You shall not do this thing."

13 Yet the [a]LORD warned Israel and Judah, [b]through all His prophets *and* [c]every seer, saying, "[d]Turn from your evil ways and keep My commandments, My statutes according to all the law which I commanded your fathers, and which I sent to you through My servants the prophets."

14 However, they did not listen, but [a]stiffened their neck [1]like their fathers, who did not believe in the LORD their God.

15 And [a]they rejected His statutes and [b]His covenant which He made with their fathers, and His warnings with which He warned them. And [c]they followed vanity and [d]became vain, and *went* after the nations which surrounded them, concerning which the [e]LORD had commanded them not to do like them.

16 And they forsook all the commandments of the LORD their God and made for themselves molten images, *even* [a]two calves, and [b]made an [1]Asherah and [c]worshiped all the host of heaven and [d]served Baal.

17 Then [a]they made their sons and their daughters pass through the fire, and [b]practiced divination and enchantments, and [c]sold themselves to do evil in the sight of the LORD, provoking Him.

18 So the LORD was very angry with Israel, and [a]removed them from His [1]sight; [b]none was left except the tribe of Judah.

19 Also [a]Judah did not keep the commandments of the LORD their God, but [b]walked in the [1]customs [2]which Israel had [3]introduced.

20 And the LORD rejected all the [1]descendants of Israel and afflicted them and [a]gave them into the hand of plunderers, until He had cast them [2]out of His sight.

21 When [a]He had torn Israel from the house of David, [b]they made Jeroboam the son of Nebat king. Then [c]Jeroboam drove Israel away from following the LORD, and made them [1]commit a great sin.

22 And the sons of Israel walked in all the sins of Jeroboam which he did; they did not depart from them,

23 [a]until the LORD removed Israel from His sight, [b]as He spoke through all His servants the prophets. [c]So Israel was carried away into exile from their own land to Assyria until this day.

Cities of Israel Filled with Strangers

24 [a]And the king of Assyria brought *men* from Babylon and from Cuthah and from [1b]Avva and from [c]Hamath and Sephar-vaim, and settled *them* in the cities of Samaria in place of the sons of Israel. So they possessed Samaria and lived in its cities.

19 [a]2 Chr. 28:26
20 [a]Is. 14:28 [b]2 Chr. 28:27
1 [a]2 Kin. 15:30
3 [a]Hos. 10:14 [b]2 Kin. 18:9-12
5 [a]Hos. 13:16
6 [a]Hos. 13:16 [b]Deut. 28:64; 29:27, 28 [c]2 Kin. 18:11; 1 Chr. 5:26 [d]Is. 37:12 [e]Is. 13:17; 21:2
7 [1]Lit., *revered*, and so throughout the ch. [a]Josh. 23:16 [b]Ex. 14:15-30 [c]Judg. 6:10
8 [1]Lit., *statutes* [2]Lit., *made* [a]Lev. 18:3; Deut. 18:9 [b]2 Kin. 16:3; 17:19
9 [1]Or, *uttered words which* [a]2 Kin. 18:8
10 [1]I.e., wooden symbols of a female deity [a]Ex. 34:12-14 [b]1 Kin. 14:23; Mic. 5:14
12 [a]Ex. 20:4
13 [a]Neh. 9:29, 30 [b]2 Kin. 17:23 [c]1 Sam. 9:9 [d]Jer. 7:3-7; 18:11; Ezek. 18:31
14 [1]Lit., *like the neck of* [a]Ex. 32:9; 33:3; Acts 7:51
15 [a]Jer. 8:9 [b]Ex. 24:6-8; Deut. 29:25 [c]Deut. 32:21 [d]Jer. 2:5; Rom. 1:21-23 [e]Deut. 12:30, 31
16 [1]I.e., a wooden symbol of a female deity [a]1 Kin. 12:28 [b]1 Kin. 14:15, 23 [c]Deut. 4:19; 2 Kin. 21:3 [d]1 Kin. 16:31
17 [a]2 Kin. 16:3 [b]Lev. 19:26; Deut. 18:10-12 [c]1 Kin. 21:20
18 [1]Lit., *face* [a]2 Kin. 17:6 [b]1 Kin. 11:13, 32, 36

19 [1]Lit., *statutes* [2]Lit., *of Israel which they* [3]Lit., *made* [a]1 Kin. 14:22, 23 [b]2 Kin. 16:3
20 [1]Lit., *seed* [2]Lit., *from His face* [a]2 Kin. 15:29
21 [1]Lit., *sin* [a]1 Kin. 11:11, 31 [b]1 Kin. 12:20 [c]1 Kin. 12:28-33
23 [a]2 Kin. 17:6 [b]2 Kin. 17:13 [c]2 Kin. 17:6
24 [1]In 2 Kin. 18:34, *Ivvah* [a]Ezra 4:2, 10 [b]2 Kin. 18:34 [c]1 Kin. 8:65

25 And it came about at the beginning of their living there, that they [a]did not fear the LORD; therefore the LORD sent lions among them which killed some of them.

26 So they spoke to the king of Assyria, saying, "The nations whom you have carried away into exile in the cities of Samaria do not know the custom of the god of the land; so he has sent lions among them, and behold, they kill them because they do not know the custom of the god of the land."

27 Then the king of Assyria commanded, saying, "Take there one of the priests whom you carried away into [1]exile, and let [2]him go and live there; and let him teach them the custom of the god of the land."

28 So one of the priests whom they had carried away into exile from Samaria came and lived at Bethel, and taught them how they should fear the LORD.

29 But every nation still made gods of its own and put them [a]in the houses of the high places which the people of Samaria had made, every nation in their cities in which they lived.

30 And [a]the men of Babylon made Succoth-benoth, the men of Cuth made Nergal, the men of Hamath made Ashima,

31 and the Avvites made Nibhaz and Tartak; and [a]the Sepharvites burned their children in the fire to [b]Adrammelech and Anammelech the gods of [c]Sepharvaim.

32 [a]They also feared the LORD and [1b]appointed from among themselves priests of the high places, who acted for them in the houses of the high places.

33 They feared the LORD and served their own gods according to the custom of the nations from among whom they had been carried away into exile.

34 To this day they do according to the earlier customs: they do not fear the LORD, nor do they [1]follow their statutes or their ordinances or the law, or the commandments which the LORD commanded the sons of Jacob, [a]whom He named Israel;

35 with whom the LORD made a covenant and commanded them, saying, "[a]You shall not fear other gods, nor [b]bow down yourselves to them nor [c]serve them nor sacrifice to them.

36 "But the LORD, [a]who brought you up from the land of Egypt with great power and with [b]an outstretched arm, [c]Him you shall fear, and to Him you shall bow yourselves down, and to Him you shall sacrifice.

37 "And the statutes and the ordinances and the law and the commandment, which He wrote for you, [a]you shall observe to do forever; and you shall not fear other gods.

38 "And the covenant that I have made with you, [a]you shall not forget, nor shall you fear other gods.

39 "But the LORD your God you shall fear; and He will deliver you from the hand of all your enemies."

40 However, they did not listen, but they did according to their earlier custom.

41 [a]So while these nations feared the LORD, they also served their [1]idols; their children likewise and their grandchildren, as their fathers did, so they do to this day.

Hezekiah Reigns over Judah

18 NOW it came about [a]in the third year of Hoshea, the son of Elah king of Israel, that [b]Hezekiah the son of Ahaz king of Judah became king.

2 He was [a]twenty-five years old when he became king, and he reigned twenty-nine years in Jerusalem; and his mother's name was Abi the daughter of Zechariah.

3 [a]And he did right in the sight of the LORD, according to all that his father David had done.

4 [a]He removed the high places and broke down the *sacred* pillars and cut down the [1]Asherah. He also broke in pieces [b]the bronze serpent that Moses had made, for until those days the sons of Israel burned incense to it; and it was called [2]Nehushtan.

5 [a]He trusted in the LORD, the God of Israel; [b]so that after him there was none like him among all the kings of Judah, nor *among those* who were before him.

6 For he [a]clung to the LORD; he did not depart from following Him, but kept His commandments, which the LORD had commanded Moses.

Hezekiah Victorious

7 [a]And the LORD was with him; wherever he went he prospered. And [b]he rebelled against the king of Assyria and did not serve him.

8 [a]He [1]defeated the Philistines as far as Gaza and its territory, from [b]watchtower to fortified city.

9 Now it came about in the fourth year of King Hezekiah, which was the seventh year of Hoshea son of Elah king of Israel, that [a]Shalmaneser king of Assyria came up against Samaria and besieged it.

10 And at the end of three years they captured it; in the sixth year of Hezekiah, which was [a]the ninth year of Hoshea king of Israel, Samaria was captured.

11 Then the king of Assyria carried Israel away into exile to Assyria, and put them in [a]Halah and on the Habor, the river of Gozan, and in the cities of the Medes,

12 because they [a]did not obey the voice of the LORD their God, but transgressed His covenant, even all that Moses the servant of the LORD commanded; they would neither listen, nor do *it*.

25 [a]2 Kin. 17:32-41
27 [1]Lit., *exile from there* [2]Lit., *them*
29 [a]1 Kin. 12:31; 13:32
30 [a]2 Kin. 17:24
31 [a]2 Kin. 17:17 [b]2 Kin. 19:37 [c]2 Kin. 17:24
32 [1]Lit., *made for themselves from among* [a]Zeph. 1:5 [b]1 Kin. 12:31
34 [1]Lit., *do according to* [a]Gen. 32:28; 35:10
35 [a]Judg. 6:10 [b]Ex. 20:5 [c]Deut. 5:9
36 [a]Ex. 14:15-30 [b]Ex. 6:6; 9:15 [c]Lev. 19:32; Deut. 6:13
37 [a]Deut. 5:32
38 [a]Deut. 4:23; 6:12
41 [1]Or, *graven images* [a]Zeph. 1:5; Matt. 6:24
1 [a]2 Kin. 16:2; 17:1 [b]2 Chr. 28:27
2 [a]2 Chr. 29:1, 2
3 [a]2 Kin. 20:3; 2 Chr. 31:20
4 [1]I.e., a wooden symbol of a female deity [2]I.e., a piece of bronze [a]2 Kin. 18:22; 2 Chr. 31:1 [b]Num. 21:8, 9
5 [a]2 Kin. 19:10 [b]2 Kin. 23:25
6 [a]Deut. 10:20; Josh. 23:8
7 [a]Gen. 39:2, 3; 1 Sam. 18:14 [b]2 Kin. 16:7
8 [1]Lit., *smote* [a]2 Chr. 28:18; Is. 14:29 [b]2 Kin. 17:9
9 [a]2 Kin. 17:3-7
10 [a]2 Kin. 17:6
11 [a]1 Chr. 5:26
12 [a]1 Kin. 9:6; Dan. 9:6, 10

Invasion of Judah

13 [a]Now in the fourteenth year of
King Hezekiah, Sennacherib king of
Assyria came up against all the fortified
cities of Judah and seized them.
14 Then Hezekiah king of Judah sent
to the king of Assyria at Lachish, saying,
"[a]I have done wrong. [1]Withdraw from
me; whatever you [2]impose on me I will
bear." So the king of Assyria [3]required
of Hezekiah king of Judah three hundred
talents of silver and thirty talents of
gold.
15 And [a]Hezekiah gave *him* all the
silver which was found in the house of
the LORD, and in the treasuries of the
king's house.
16 At that time Hezekiah cut off *the
gold from* the doors of the temple of the
LORD, and *from* the doorposts which
Hezekiah king of Judah had overlaid,
and gave it to the king of Assyria.
17 Then the king of Assyria sent [a]Tar-
tan and Rab-saris and Rabshakeh from
Lachish to King Hezekiah with a large
army to Jerusalem. So they went up and
came to Jerusalem. And when they went
up, they came and stood by the [b]conduit
of the upper pool, which is on the
highway of the [1]fuller's field.
18 When they called to the king, [a]Elia-
kim the son of Hilkiah, who was over the
household, and [b]Shebnah the scribe and
Joah the son of Asaph the recorder,
came out to them.
19 Then Rabshakeh said to them,
"Say now to Hezekiah, 'Thus says the
great king, the king of Assyria, "[a]What is
this confidence that you [1]have?
20 "You say (but *they are* [1]only empty
words), '*I have* counsel and strength for
the war.' Now on whom do you rely,
[a]that you have rebelled against me?
21 "Now behold, you [1a]rely on the staff
of this crushed reed, *even* on Egypt; on
which if a man leans, it will go into his
[2]hand and pierce it. So is Pharaoh king
of Egypt to all who rely on him.
22 "But if you say to me, 'We trust in
the LORD our God,' is it not He whose
high places and [a]whose altars Hezekiah
has taken away, and has said to Judah
and to Jerusalem, 'You shall worship
before this altar in Jerusalem'?
23 "Now therefore, [1]come, make a
bargain with my master the king of
Assyria, and I will give you two thousand horses, if you are able on your part
to set riders on them.
24 "How then can you [1]repulse one
[2]official of the least of my master's
servants, and [3]rely on Egypt for chariots
and for horsemen?
25 "Have I now come up [1]without the
LORD's approval against this place to
destroy it? The LORD said to me, 'Go up
against this land and destroy it.' " ' "
26 Then Eliakim the son of Hilkiah,
and Shebnah and Joah, said to Rabshakeh, "Speak now to your servants in
Aramaic, for we [1]understand *it;* and do
not speak with us in [2a]Judean, in the
hearing of the people who are on the
wall."
27 But Rabshakeh said to them, "Has
my master sent me only to your master
and to you to speak these words, *and* not
to the men who sit on the wall, *doomed*
to eat their own dung and drink their
own urine with you?"
28 Then Rabshakeh stood and cried
with a loud voice in Judean, [1]saying,
"Hear the word of the great king, the
king of Assyria.
29 "Thus says the king, '[a]Do not let
Hezekiah deceive you, for he will not be
able to deliver you from [1]my hand;
30 nor let Hezekiah make you trust in
the LORD, saying, "The LORD will surely
deliver us, and this city shall not be
given into the hand of the king of Assyria."
31 'Do not listen to Hezekiah, for thus
says the king of Assyria, "[1]Make your
peace with me and come out to me, and
eat [a]each of his vine and each of his fig
tree and drink each of the waters of his
own cistern,
32 until I come and take you away [a]to
a land like your own land, a land of
grain and new wine, a land of bread and
vineyards, a land of olive trees and
honey, that you may live and not die."
But do not listen to Hezekiah, when he
misleads you, saying, "The LORD will
deliver us."
33 '[a]Has any one of the gods of the
nations delivered his land from the hand
of the king of Assyria?
34 '[a]Where are the gods of Hamath
and [b]Arpad? Where are the gods of
Sepharvaim, Hena and [1c]Ivvah? Have
they delivered Samaria from my hand?
35 'Who among all the gods of the
lands [1]have delivered their land from my
hand, [a]that the LORD should deliver
Jerusalem from my hand?' "
36 But the people were silent and
answered him not a word, for the king's
commandment was, "Do not answer
him."
37 Then [a]Eliakim the son of Hilkiah,
who was over the household, and
Shebna the scribe and Joah the son of
Asaph, the recorder, came to Hezekiah
[b]with their clothes torn and told him the
words of Rabshakeh.

Isaiah Encourages Hezekiah

19 [a]AND when King Hezekiah heard
it, he [b]tore his clothes, [c]covered
himself with sackcloth and entered the
house of the LORD.
2 Then he sent Eliakim who was over
the household with Shebna the scribe
and the elders of the priests, [a]covered
with sackcloth, to [b]Isaiah the prophet
the son of Amoz.
3 And they said to him, "Thus says
Hezekiah, 'This day is a day of distress,
rebuke, and rejection; for children have
come to birth, and there is no strength to
deliver.

---

13 [a]2 Chr. 32:1; Is. 36:1-39:8

14 [1]Lit., *Return* [2]Lit., *give* [3]Lit., *put on* [a]2 Kin. 18:7

15 [a]1 Kin. 15:18, 19; 2 Kin. 12:18; 16:8

17 [1]I.e., launderer's [a]Is. 20:1 [b]2 Kin. 20:20; Is. 7:3

18 [a]2 Kin. 19:2; Is. 22:20 [b]Is. 22:15

19 [1]Lit., *trust* [a]2 Chr. 32:10

20 [1]Lit., *a word of the lips* [a]2 Kin. 18:7

21 [1]Lit., *rely for yourself* [2]Lit., *palm* [a]Is. 30:2, 3, 7; Ezek. 29:6, 7

22 [a]2 Kin. 18:4; 2 Chr. 31:1

23 [1]Lit., *please exchange pledges*

24 [1]Lit., *turn away the face of* [2]Or, *governor* [3]Lit., *rely for yourself*

25 [1]Lit., *without the LORD*

26 [1]Lit., *hear* [2]I.e., Hebrew [a]Ezra 4:7; Dan. 2:4

28 [1]Lit., *and spoke, saying,*

29 [1]Heb., *his* [a]2 Chr. 32:15

31 [1]Lit., *Make with me a blessing* [a]1 Kin. 4:20, 25

32 [a]Deut. 8:7-9; 11:12

33 [a]2 Kin. 19:12; Is. 10:10, 11

34 [1]In 2 Kin. 17:24, *Avva* [a]2 Kin. 19:13 [b]Is. 10:9 [c]2 Kin. 17:24

35 [1]Lit., *who have* [a]Ps. 2:1-3; 59:7

37 [a]2 Kin. 18:26 [b]2 Kin. 6:30

1 [a]2 Chr. 32:20-22; Is. 37:1 [b]2 Kin. 18:37 [c]1 Kin. 21:27

2 [a]2 Sam. 3:31 [b]Is. 1:1; 2:1

4 '[a]Perhaps the LORD your God will hear all the words of Rabshakeh, whom his master the king of Assyria has sent [b]to reproach the living God, and will rebuke the words which the LORD your God has heard. Therefore, offer a prayer for [c]the remnant that is left.' "

5 So the servants of King Hezekiah came to Isaiah.

6 And Isaiah said to them, "Thus you shall say to your master, 'Thus says the LORD, "Do not be afraid because of the words that you have heard, with which the [a]servants of the king of Assyria [b]have blasphemed Me.

7 "Behold, I will put a spirit in him so that [a]he shall hear a rumor and return to his own land. And [b]I will make him fall by the sword in his own land." ' "

Sennacherib Defies God

8 Then Rabshakeh returned and found the king of Assyria fighting against [a]Libnah, for he had heard that [1]the king had left [b]Lachish.

9 When he heard *them* say concerning Tirhakah king of [1]Cush, "Behold, he has come out to fight against you," he sent messengers again to Hezekiah saying,

10 "Thus you shall say to Hezekiah king of [1]Judah, 'Do not [a]let your God in whom you trust deceive you saying, "[b]Jerusalem shall not be given into the hand of the king of Assyria."

11 'Behold, you have heard what the kings of Assyria have done to all the lands, destroying them completely. So will you be [1]spared?

12 '[a]Did the gods of [1]those nations which my fathers destroyed deliver them, *even* [b]Gozan and [c]Haran and Rezeph and [d]the sons of Eden who *were* in Telassar?

13 '[a]Where is the king of Hamath, the king of Arpad, the king of the city of Sepharvaim, and *of* Hena and Ivvah?' "

Hezekiah's Prayer

14 Then [a]Hezekiah took the [1]letter from the hand of the messengers and read it, and he went up to the house of the LORD and [2]spread it out before the LORD.

15 And Hezekiah prayed before the LORD and said, "O LORD, the God of Israel, [a]who art [1]enthroned *above* the cherubim, [b]Thou art the God, Thou alone, of all the kingdoms of the earth. Thou hast made heaven and earth.

16 "[a]Incline Thine ear, O LORD, and hear; [b]open Thine eyes, O LORD, and see; and listen to the words of Sennacherib, which he has sent [c]to reproach the living God.

17 "Truly, O LORD, the kings of Assyria have devastated the nations and their lands

18 and have cast their gods into the fire, [a]for they were not gods but the work of men's hands, wood and stone. So they have destroyed them.

19 "And now, O LORD our God, I pray, deliver us from his hand [a]that all the kingdoms of the earth may know that Thou alone, O [b]LORD, art God."

God's Answer through Isaiah

20 Then Isaiah the son of Amoz sent to Hezekiah saying, "Thus says the LORD, the God of Israel, 'Because you have prayed to Me about Sennacherib king of Assyria, [a]I have heard *you*.'

21 "This is the word that the LORD has spoken against him:

'She has despised you and mocked you,
[a]The virgin daughter of Zion;
She [b]has shaken *her* head behind you,
The daughter of Jerusalem!

22 'Whom have you [a]reproached and [b]blasphemed?
And against whom have you raised *your* voice,
And [1]haughtily lifted up your eyes?
Against the [c]Holy One of Israel!

23 '[a]Through your messengers you have reproached the Lord,
And you have said, "With my many chariots
I came up to the heights of the mountains,
To the remotest parts of Lebanon;
And I [1]cut down its tall cedars *and* its choice cypresses.
And I [1]entered its farthest lodging place, its [b]thickest forest.

24 "I dug *wells* and drank foreign waters,
And with the sole of my feet I [1a]dried up
All the rivers of [2]Egypt."

25 '[a]Have you not heard?
Long ago I did it;
From ancient times I planned it.
[b]Now I have brought it to pass,
That you should turn fortified cities into ruinous heaps.

26 'Therefore their inhabitants were short of strength,
They were dismayed and put to shame;
They were [a]as the vegetation of the field and as the green herb,
As grass on the housetops is scorched before it is grown up.

27 'But [a]I know your sitting down,
And your going out and your coming in,
And your raging against Me.

28 'Because of your raging against Me,
And because your [1]arrogance has come up to My ears,
Therefore I [a]will put My hook in your nose,
And My bridle in your lips,
And [b]I will turn you back by the way which you came.

4 [a]Josh. 14:12; 2 Sam. 16:12 [b]2 Kin. 18:35 [c]Is. 1:9

6 [a]2 Kin. 18:17 [b]2 Kin. 18:22-25; 30:35

7 [a]2 Kin. 7:6 [b]2 Kin. 19:37

8 [1]Lit., *he* [a]Josh. 10:29 [b]2 Kin. 18:14

9 [1]Or, *Ethiopia*

10 [1]Lit., *Judah, saying,* [a]2 Kin. 18:5 [b]2 Kin. 18:30

11 [1]Lit., *delivered*

12 [1]Lit., *the* [a]2 Kin. 18:33 [b]2 Kin. 17:6 [c]Gen. 11:31 [d]Is. 37:12

13 [a]2 Kin. 18:34

14 [1]Lit., *letters . . . read them* [2]Lit., *Hezekiah spread* [a]Is. 37:14

15 [1]Lit., *seated* [a]Ex. 25:22; Is. 37:14 [b]2 Kin. 5:15

16 [a]Ps. 31:2; Is. 37:17 [b]1 Kin. 8:29; 2 Chr. 6:40 [c]2 Kin. 19:4

18 [a]Is. 44:9-20; Acts 17:29

19 [a]1 Kin. 8:42, 43 [b]2 Kin. 19:15

20 [a]2 Kin. 20:5

21 [a]Jer. 14:17; Lam. 2:13 [b]Ps. 109:25; Matt. 27:39

22 [1]Lit., *on high* [a]2 Kin. 19:4 [b]2 Kin. 19:6 [c]Is. 5:24; 30:11-15

23 [1]So with some ancient versions; M.T., *will cut . . . will enter* [a]2 Kin. 18:17 [b]2 Chr. 26:10; Is. 10:18

24 [1]So with some ancient versions; M.T., *will dry up* [2]Lit., *the besieged place* [a]Is. 19:6

25 [a]Is. 45:7 [b]Is. 10:5

26 [a]Ps. 129:6

27 [a]Ps. 139:1

28 [1]Lit., *complacency* [a]Ezek. 19:9; 29:4 [b]2 Kin. 19:33, 36

29 'Then this shall be [a]the sign for you:
[1]you shall eat this year what grows of
itself, in the second year what springs
from the same, and in the third year sow,
reap, plant vineyards, and eat their fruit.
30 '[a]And the surviving remnant of the
house of Judah shall again take root
downward and bear fruit upward.
31 'For out of Jerusalem shall go forth
a remnant, and [a]out of Mount Zion
[1]survivors. [b]The zeal of [2]the LORD shall
perform this.
32 'Therefore thus says the LORD concerning the king of Assyria, "[a]He shall
not come to this city or shoot an arrow
there; neither shall he come before it
with a shield, nor throw up a mound
against it.
33 "[a]By the way that he came, by the
same he shall return, and he shall not
come to this city," ' declares the LORD.
34 '[a]For I will defend this city to save
it for My own sake and [b]for My servant
David's sake.' "
35 [a]Then it happened that night that
the angel of the LORD went out, and
struck 185,000 in the camp of the Assyrians; and when [1]men rose early in the
morning, behold, all of them were [2]dead.
36 So [a]Sennacherib king of Assyria
departed and returned *home,* and lived
at [b]Nineveh.
37 And it came about as he was worshiping in the house of Nisroch his god,
that [1a]Adrammelech and Sharezer killed
him with the sword; and they escaped
into [b]the land of Ararat. And [c]Esarhad-
don his son became king in his place.

Hezekiah's Illness and Recovery

20 [a]IN those days Hezekiah became
[1]mortally ill. And Isaiah the
prophet the son of Amoz came to him
and said to him, "Thus says the LORD,
'[b]Set your house in order, for you shall
die and not live.' "
2 Then he turned his face to the wall,
and prayed to the LORD, saying,
3 "[a]Remember now, O LORD, I beseech Thee, [b]how I have walked before
Thee in truth and with a whole heart,
and have done what is good in Thy
sight." And [c]Hezekiah wept [1]bitterly.
4 And it came about before Isaiah
had gone out of the middle court, that
the word of the LORD came to him,
saying,
5 "Return and say to [a]Hezekiah the
leader of My people, 'Thus says the
LORD, the God of your father David, "[b]I
have heard your prayer, [c]I have seen
your tears; behold, I will heal you. On
the third day you shall go up to the
house of the LORD.
6 "And I will add fifteen years to your
[1]life, and I will deliver you and this city
from the hand of the king of Assyria;
and [a]I will defend this city for My own
sake and for My servant David's
sake." ' "
7 Then Isaiah said, "Take a cake of
figs." And they took and laid *it* on the
boil, and he recovered.
8 Now Hezekiah said to Isaiah,
"What will be the sign that the LORD
will heal me, and that I shall go up to the
house of the LORD the third day?"
9 And Isaiah said, "[a]This shall be the
sign to you from the LORD, that the
LORD will do the thing that He has
spoken: shall the shadow go forward ten
steps or go back ten steps?"
10 So Hezekiah [1]answered, "It is easy
for the shadow to decline ten steps; no,
but let the shadow turn backward ten
steps."
11 And Isaiah the prophet cried to the
LORD, and [a]He brought the shadow on
the [1]stairway back ten steps by which it
had gone down on the [1]stairway of
Ahaz.

Hezekiah Shows Babylon His Treasures

12 [a]At that time [1]Berodach-baladan a
son of Baladan, king of Babylon, sent
letters and a present to Hezekiah, for he
heard that Hezekiah had been sick.
13 And Hezekiah listened to them,
and showed them [a]all his treasure house,
the silver and the gold and the spices
and the precious oil and the house of
his armor and all that was found in his
treasuries. There was nothing in his
house, nor in all his dominion, that
Hezekiah did not show them.
14 Then Isaiah the prophet came to
King Hezekiah and said to him, "What
did these men say, and from where have
they come to you?" And Hezekiah said,
"They have come from a far country,
from Babylon."
15 And he said, "What have they seen
in your house?" So Hezekiah [1]answered,
"They have seen all that is in my house;
there is nothing among my treasuries
that I have not shown them."
16 Then Isaiah said to Hezekiah,
"Hear the word of the LORD.
17 'Behold, the days are coming when
[a]all that is in your house, and all that
your fathers have laid up in store to this
day shall be carried to Babylon; nothing
shall be left,' says the LORD.
18 'And some [a]of your sons who shall
issue from you, whom you shall beget,
shall be taken away; and they shall
become [b]officials in the palace of the
king of Babylon.' "
19 Then Hezekiah said to Isaiah, "The
word of the LORD which you have spoken is [a]good." For he [1]thought, "Is it not
so, if there shall be peace and truth in
my days?"
20 [a]Now the rest of the acts of Hezekiah and all his might, and how he
[b]made the pool and the conduit, and
brought water into the city, are they not
written in the Book of the Chronicles of
the Kings of Judah?
21 [a]So Hezekiah slept with his fathers,
and Manasseh his son became king in
his place.

29 [1]Lit., *eating* [a]Ex. 3:12; 2 Kin. 20:8, 9
30 [a]2 Kin. 19:4; 2 Chr. 32:22, 23
31 [1]Lit., *those who escape* [2]Some ancient mss. read *the LORD of hosts* [a]Is. 10:20 [b]Is. 9:7
32 [a]Is. 8:7-10
33 [a]2 Kin. 19:28
34 [a]2 Kin. 20:6; Is. 31:5 [b]1 Kin. 11:12, 13
35 [1]Lit., *they* [2]Lit., *dead bodies* [a]2 Sam. 24:16; 2 Chr. 32:21
36 [a]2 Kin. 19:7, 28, 33 [b]Jon. 1:2
37 [1]Some ancient mss. read *Adrammelech and Sharezer his sons smote him* [a]2 Kin. 19:17, 31 [b]Gen. 8:4; Jer. 51:27 [c]Ezra 4:2
1 [1]Lit., *sick to the point of death* [a]2 Chr. 32:24; Is. 38:1-22 [b]2 Sam. 17:23
3 [1]Lit., *great weeping* [a]Neh. 5:19; 13:14, 22, 31 [b]2 Kin. 18:3-6 [c]2 Sam. 12:21, 22
5 [a]1 Sam. 9:16; 10:1 [b]2 Kin. 19:20 [c]Ps. 39:12
6 [1]Lit., *days* [a]2 Kin. 19:34
9 [a]Is. 38:7
10 [1]Lit., *said*
11 [1]Lit., *steps* [a]Josh. 10:12-14; Is. 38:8
12 [1]Many mss. and ancient versions read *Merodach-baladan;* cf. Is. 39:1 [a]2 Chr. 32:31; Is. 39:1-8
13 [a]2 Chr. 32:27
15 [1]Lit., *said*
17 [a]2 Kin. 24:13; 25:13-15; 2 Chr. 36:10; Jer. 52:17-19
18 [a]2 Kin. 24:12; 2 Chr. 33:11 [b]Dan. 1:3-7
19 [1]Lit., *said* [a]1 Sam. 3:18
20 [a]2 Chr. 32:32 [b]Neh. 3:16
21 [a]2 Chr. 32:33

Manasseh Succeeds Hezekiah

21 [a]MANASSEH was twelve years
old when he became king, and he
reigned fifty-five years in Jerusalem; and
his mother's name was Hephzibah.
2 And [a]he did evil in the sight of the
LORD, [b]according to the abominations
of the nations whom the LORD dispossessed before the sons of Israel.
3 For [a]he rebuilt the high places
which Hezekiah his father had destroyed; and [b]he erected altars for Baal
and made an [1]Asherah, as Ahab king of
Israel had done, and [c]worshiped all the
host of heaven and served them.
4 And [a]he built altars in the house of
the LORD, of which the LORD had said,
"[b]In Jerusalem I will put My name."
5 For he built altars for [a]all the host
of heaven in [b]the two courts of the house
of the LORD.
6 And [a]he made his son pass through
the fire, [b]practiced witchcraft and used
divination, and dealt with mediums and
spiritists. He did much evil in the sight
of the LORD provoking *Him to anger.*
7 Then [a]he set the carved image of
Asherah that he had made, in the house
of which the LORD said to David and to
his son Solomon, "[b]In this house and in
Jerusalem, which I have chosen from all
the tribes of Israel, I will put My name
forever.
8 "And I [a]will not make the feet of
Israel wander anymore from the land
which I gave their fathers, if only they
will observe to do according to all that I
have commanded them, and according
to all the law that My servant Moses
commanded them."
9 But they did not listen, and Manasseh [a]seduced them to do evil more than
the nations whom the LORD destroyed
before the sons of Israel.

The King's Idolatries Rebuked

10 Now the LORD spoke through His
servants the prophets, saying,
11 "[a]Because Manasseh king of Judah
has done these abominations, [b]having
done wickedly more than all the Amorites did who *were* before him, and [c]has
also made Judah sin [d]with his idols;
12 therefore thus says the LORD, the
God of Israel, 'Behold, I am bringing
such calamity on Jerusalem and Judah,
that whoever hears of it, [a]both his ears
shall tingle.
13 '[a]And I will stretch over Jerusalem
the line of Samaria and the plummet of
the house of Ahab, and I will wipe
Jerusalem as one wipes a dish, wiping it
and turning it upside down.
14 'And I will abandon the remnant of
My inheritance and deliver them into the
hand of their enemies, and they shall
become as plunder and spoil to all their
enemies;
15 because they have done evil in My
sight, and have been provoking Me to
anger, since the day their fathers came
from Egypt, even to this day.' "
16 [a]Moreover, Manasseh shed very
much innocent blood until he had filled
Jerusalem from one end to another;
besides his sin [b]with which he made
Judah sin, in doing evil in the sight of
the LORD.
17 [a]Now the rest of the acts of Manasseh and all that he did and his sin which
he [1]committed, are they not written in
the Book of the Chronicles of the Kings
of Judah?
18 [a]And Manasseh slept with his fathers and was buried in the garden of his
own house, [b]in the garden of Uzza, and
Amon his son became king in his place.

Amon Succeeds Manasseh

19 [a]Amon was twenty-two years old
when he became king, and he reigned
two years in Jerusalem; and his mother's
name *was* Meshullemeth the daughter of
Haruz of Jotbah.
20 And he did evil in the sight of the
LORD, [a]as Manasseh his father had
done.
21 For he walked in all the way that
his father had walked, and served the
idols that his father had served and
worshiped them.
22 So [a]he forsook the LORD, the God
of his fathers, and did not walk in the
way of the LORD.
23 And [a]the servants of Amon conspired against him and killed the king in
his own house.
24 Then [a]the people of the land [1]killed
all those who had conspired against
King Amon, and the people of the land
made Josiah his son king in his place.
25 Now the rest of the acts of Amon
which he did, are they not written in the
Book of the Chronicles of the Kings of
Judah?
26 And he was buried in his grave [a]in
the garden of Uzza, and Josiah his son
became king in his place.

Josiah Succeeds Amon

22 [a]JOSIAH was eight years old
when he became king, and he
reigned thirty-one years in Jerusalem;
and his mother's name *was* Jedidah the
daughter of Adaiah of [b]Bozkath.
2 And he did right in the sight of the
LORD and walked in all the way of his
father David, nor did he [a]turn aside to
the right or to the left.
3 Now [a]it came about in the eighteenth year of King Josiah that the king
sent Shaphan, the son of Azaliah the son
of Meshullam the scribe, to the house of
the LORD saying,
4 "[a]Go up to Hilkiah the high priest
that he may [1]count the money brought
in to the house of the LORD which the
doorkeepers have gathered from the
people.
5 "[a]And let them deliver it into the
hand of the workmen who have the
oversight of the house of the LORD, and
let them give it to the workmen who are
in the house of the LORD to repair the
[1]damages of the house,

1 [a]2 Chr. 33:1-9
2 [a]Jer. 15:4 [b]2 Kin. 16:3
3 [1]I.e., a wooden symbol of a female deity [a]2 Kin. 18:4 [b]1 Kin. 16:31-33 [c]Deut. 17:2-5; 2 Kin. 17:16; 23:5
4 [a]2 Kin. 16:10-16 [b]2 Sam. 7:13; 1 Kin. 8:29
5 [a]2 Kin. 23:4, 5 [b]1 Kin. 7:12; 2 Kin. 23:12
6 [a]Lev. 18:21; 2 Kin. 16:3; 17:17 [b]Lev. 19:26, 31; Deut. 18:10-14
7 [a]Deut. 16:21; 2 Kin. 23:6 [b]1 Kin. 8:29; 9:3; 2 Chr. 7:12, 16
8 [a]2 Sam. 7:10; 2 Kin. 18:11, 12
9 [a]Prov. 29:12
11 [a]2 Kin. 21:2; 24:3, 4 [b]Gen. 15:16; 1 Kin. 21:26 [c]2 Kin. 21:16 [d]2 Kin. 21:21
12 [a]1 Sam. 3:11; Jer. 19:3
13 [a]Is. 34:11; Amos 7:7, 8
16 [a]2 Kin. 24:4 [b]2 Kin. 21:11
17 [1]Lit., *sinned* [a]2 Chr. 33:11-19
18 [a]2 Chr. 33:20 [b]2 Kin. 21:26
19 [a]2 Chr. 33:21-23
20 [a]2 Kin. 21:2-6, 11, 16
22 [a]2 Kin. 22:17; 1 Chr. 28:9
23 [a]2 Kin. 12:20; 14:19
24 [1]Lit., *smote* [a]2 Kin. 14:5
26 [a]2 Kin. 21:18
1 [a]2 Chr. 34:1 [b]Josh. 15:39
2 [a]Deut. 5:32; Josh. 1:7
3 [a]2 Chr. 34:8
4 [1]Or, *total* [a]2 Kin. 12:4, 9, 10
5 [1]Lit., *breach* [a]2 Kin. 12:11-14

6 to the carpenters and the builders and the masons and for buying timber and hewn stone to repair the house.

7"Only [a]no accounting shall be made with them for the money delivered into their hands, for they deal faithfully."

The Lost Book

8 Then Hilkiah the high priest said to Shaphan the scribe, "[a]I have found the book of the law in the house of the LORD." And Hilkiah gave the book to Shaphan who read it.

9 And Shaphan the scribe came to the king and brought back word to the king and said, "Your servants have emptied out the money that was found in the house, and have delivered it into the hand of the workmen who have the oversight of the house of the LORD."

10 Moreover, Shaphan the scribe told the king saying, "Hilkiah the priest has given me a book." And Shaphan read it in the presence of the king.

11 And it came about when the king heard the words of the book of the law, that [a]he tore his clothes.

12 Then the king commanded Hilkiah the priest, [a]Ahikam the son of Shaphan, [1b]Achbor the son of Micaiah, Shaphan the scribe, and Asaiah the king's servant saying,

13"Go, inquire of the LORD for me and the people and all Judah concerning the words of this book that has been found, for [a]great is the wrath of the LORD that burns against us, because our fathers have not listened to the words of this book, to do according to all that is written concerning us."

Huldah Predicts

14 So Hilkiah the priest, Ahikam, Achbor, Shaphan, and Asaiah went to Huldah the prophetess, the wife of Shallum the son of [1a]Tikvah, the son of Harhas, keeper of the wardrobe (now she lived in Jerusalem in the [b]Second Quarter); and they spoke to her.

15 And she said to them, "Thus says the LORD God of Israel, 'Tell the man who sent you to me,

16 thus says the LORD, "Behold, I [a]bring evil on this place and on its inhabitants, *even* all the words of the book which the king of Judah has read.

17"[a]Because they have forsaken Me and have burned incense to other gods that they might provoke Me to anger with all the work of their hands, therefore My wrath burns against this place, and it shall not be quenched."'

18"But to [a]the king of Judah who sent you to inquire of the LORD thus shall you say to him, 'Thus says the LORD God of Israel, "*Regarding* the words which you have heard,

19 [a]because your heart was tender and [b]you humbled yourself before the LORD when you heard what I spoke against this place and against its inhabitants that they should become [c]a desolation and a [d]curse, and you have [e]torn your clothes and wept before Me, I truly have heard you," declares the LORD.

20"Therefore, behold, I will gather you to your fathers, and [a]you shall be gathered to your grave in peace, neither shall your eyes see all the evil which I will bring on this place."'" So they brought back word to the king.

Josiah's Covenant

23 [a]THEN the king sent, and they gathered to him all the elders of Judah and of Jerusalem.

2 And the king went up to the house of the LORD and all the men of Judah and all the inhabitants of Jerusalem with him, and the priests and the prophets and all the people, both small and great; and [a]he read in their hearing all the words of the book of the covenant, [b]which was found in the house of the LORD.

3 And [a]the king stood by the pillar and made a covenant before the LORD, [b]to walk after the LORD, and to keep His commandments and His testimonies and His statutes with all *his* heart and all *his* soul, to carry out the words of this covenant that were written in this book. And all the people [1]entered into the covenant.

Reforms under Josiah

4 Then the king commanded Hilkiah the high priest and [a]the priests of the second order and the [1]doorkeepers, [b]to bring out of the temple of the LORD all the vessels that were made for Baal, for [2]Asherah, and for all the host of heaven; and [c]he burned them outside Jerusalem in the fields of the Kidron, and carried their ashes to Bethel.

5 And he did away with the idolatrous priests whom the kings of Judah had appointed to burn incense in the high places in the cities of Judah and in the surrounding area of Jerusalem, also those who burned incense to Baal, to the sun and to the moon and to the constellations and to all the [a]host of heaven.

6 And he brought out the Asherah from the house of the LORD outside Jerusalem to the brook Kidron, and burned it at the brook Kidron, and [a]ground *it* to dust, and [b]threw its dust on the graves of the [1]common people.

7 He also broke down the houses of the [a]*male* cult prostitutes which *were* in the house of the LORD, where [b]the women were weaving [1]hangings for the Asherah.

8 Then he brought all the priests from the cities of Judah, and defiled the high places where the priests had burned incense, from [a]Geba to Beersheba; and he broke down the high places of the gates which *were* at the entrance of the gate of Joshua the governor of the city, which *were* on one's left at the city gate.

9 Nevertheless [a]the priests of the high places did not go up to the altar of the LORD in Jerusalem, but they ate unleavened bread among their brothers.

---

7 [a]2 Kin. 12:15; 1 Cor. 4:2

8 [a]Deut. 31:24-26; 2 Chr. 34:14, 15

11 [a]Gen. 37:34; Josh. 7:6

12 [1]In 2 Chr. 34:20, *Abdon, son of Micah* [a]2 Kin. 25:22; Jer. 26:24 [b]2 Chr. 34:20

13 [a]Deut. 29:23-28; 31:17, 18

14 [1]In 2 Chr. 34:22, *Tokhath, son of Hasrah* [a]2 Chr. 34:22 [b]Zeph. 1:10

16 [a]Deut. 29:27; Dan. 9:11-14

17 [a]Deut. 29:25, 26; 2 Kin. 21:22

18 [a]2 Chr. 34:26

19 [a]1 Sam. 24:5; Ps. 51:17 [b]Ex. 10:3; 1 Kin. 21:29 [c]Lev. 26:31 [d]Jer. 26:6 [e]2 Kin. 22:11

20 [a]2 Kin. 23:30

1 [a]2 Chr. 34:29-32

2 [a]Deut. 31:10-13 [b]2 Kin. 22:8

3 [1]Lit., *took a stand in* [a]2 Kin. 11:14, 17 [b]Deut. 13:4

4 [1]Lit., *keepers of the threshold* [2]I.e., a wooden symbol of a female deity, and so throughout the ch. [a]2 Kin. 25:18; Jer. 52:24 [b]2 Kin. 21:3?; 2 Chr. 33:3 [c]2 Kin. 23:15

5 [a]2 Kin. 21:3

6 [1]Lit., *sons of the people* [a]2 Kin. 23:15 [b]2 Chr. 34:4

7 [1]Or, *tents;* lit., *houses* [a]1 Kin. 14:24; 15:12 [b]Ex. 35:25, 26; Ezek. 16:16

8 [a]Josh. 21:17; 1 Kin. 15:22

9 [a]Ezek. 44:10-14

10 [a]He also defiled [1]Topheth, which is in the valley of the son of Hinnom, [b]that no man might make his son or his daughter pass through the fire for [c]Molech.

11 And he did away with the horses which the kings of Judah had given to the [a]sun, at the entrance of the house of the LORD, by the chamber of Nathan-melech the official, which *was* in the precincts; and he burned the chariots of the sun with fire.

12 And [a]the altars which *were* on the roof, the upper chamber of Ahaz, which the kings of Judah had made, and [b]the altars which Manasseh had made in the two courts of the house of the LORD, the king broke down; and he [1]smashed them there, and [c]threw their dust into the brook Kidron.

13 And the high places which *were* before Jerusalem, which *were* on the right of [a]the mount of destruction which Solomon the king of Israel had built for [b]Ashtoreth the abomination of the Sidonians, and for [c]Chemosh the abomination of Moab, and for Milcom the abomination of the sons of Ammon, the king defiled.

14 And [a]he broke in pieces the *sacred* pillars and cut down the Asherim and [b]filled their places with human bones.

15 Furthermore, [a]the altar that *was* at Bethel *and* the [b]high place which Jeroboam the son of Nebat, who made Israel sin, had made, even that altar and the high place he broke down. Then he [1c]demolished its stones, ground them to dust, and burned the Asherah.

16 Now when Josiah turned, he saw the graves that *were* there on the mountain, and he sent and took the bones from the graves and burned *them* on the altar and defiled it [a]according to the word of the LORD which the man of God proclaimed, who proclaimed these things.

17 Then he said, "What is this monument that I see?" And the men of the city told him, "[a]It is the grave of the man of God who came from Judah and proclaimed these things which you have done against the altar of Bethel."

18 And he said, "Let him alone; let no one disturb his bones." So they [1]left his bones undisturbed [a]with the bones of the prophet who came from Samaria.

19 And Josiah also removed all the houses of the high places which *were* [a]in the cities of Samaria, which the kings of Israel had made provoking [1]the LORD; and he did to them [2]just as he had done in Bethel.

20 And all the priests of the high places who *were* there [a]he slaughtered on the altars and burned human bones on them; then he returned to Jerusalem.

Passover Reinstituted

21 Then the king commanded all the people saying, "[a]Celebrate the Passover to the LORD your God [b]as it is written in this book of the covenant."

22 [a]Surely such a Passover had not been celebrated from the days of the judges who judged Israel, nor in all the days of the kings of Israel and of the kings of Judah.

23 But in the eighteenth year of King Josiah, this Passover was observed to the LORD in Jerusalem.

24 Moreover, Josiah [1]removed [a]the mediums and the spiritists and the [b]teraphim and [c]the idols and all the abominations that were seen in the land of Judah and in Jerusalem, [d]that he might [2]confirm the words of the law which were written [e]in the book that Hilkiah the priest found in the house of the LORD.

25 And before him there was no king [a]like him who turned to the LORD with all his heart and with all his soul and with all his might, according to all the law of Moses; nor did any like him arise after him.

26 However, the LORD did not turn from the fierceness of His great wrath with which His anger burned against Judah, [a]because of all the provocations with which Manasseh had provoked Him.

27 And the LORD said, "I will remove Judah also from My sight, [a]as I have removed Israel. And [b]I will cast off Jerusalem, this city which I have chosen, and the [1]temple of which I said, 'My name shall be there.' "

Jehoahaz Succeeds Josiah

28 Now the rest of the acts of Josiah and all that he did, are they not written in the Book of the Chronicles of the Kings of Judah?

29 [a]In his days [b]Pharaoh Neco king of Egypt went up to the king of Assyria to the river Euphrates. And King Josiah went to meet him, and when *Pharaoh Neco* saw him he killed him at [c]Megiddo.

30 And [a]his servants drove [1]his body in a chariot from Megiddo, and brought him to Jerusalem and buried him in his own tomb. [b]Then the people of the land took Jehoahaz the son of Josiah and anointed him and made him king in place of his father.

31 [a]Jehoahaz was twenty-three years old when he became king, and he reigned three months in Jerusalem; and his mother's name was [b]Hamutal the daughter of Jeremiah of Libnah.

32 And he did evil in the sight of the LORD, [a]according to all that his fathers had done.

33 And [a]Pharaoh Neco imprisoned him at [b]Riblah in the land of [c]Hamath, that he might not reign in Jerusalem; and he imposed on the land a fine of one hundred talents of silver and a talent of gold.

Jehoiakim Made King by Pharaoh

34 And Pharaoh Neco made [a]Eliakim the son of Josiah king in the place of Josiah his father, and [b]changed his name to Jehoiakim. But he took Jehoahaz away and [1c]brought *him* to Egypt, and he died there.

10 [1]I.e., place of burning [a]Is. 30:33; Jer. 7:31, 32; 19:4-6 [b]Lev. 18:21 [c]1 Kin. 11:7

11 [a]Deut. 4:19; Job 31:26; Ezek. 8:16

12 [1]Or, *ran from there* [a]Jer. 19:13; Zeph. 1:5 [b]2 Kin. 21:5; 2 Chr. 33:5 [c]2 Kin. 23:4, 6

13 [a]1 Kin. 11:7 [b]1 Kin. 11:5 [c]Num. 21:29

14 [a]Deut. 7:5, 25 [b]2 Kin. 23:16

15 [1]So the Gr.; Heb., *burned the high place* [a]1 Kin. 13:1 [b]1 Kin. 12:28-33 [c]2 Kin. 23:6

16 [a]1 Kin. 13:2

17 [a]1 Kin. 13:1, 30, 31

18 [1]Lit., *let his bones escape with* [a]1 Kin. 13:11, 31

19 [1]So with ancient versions [2]Lit., *according to all the acts* [a]2 Chr. 34:6, 7

20 [a]2 Kin. 10:25; 11:18

21 [a]2 Chr. 35:1-17 [b]Num. 9:2-4; Deut. 16:2-8

22 [a]2 Chr. 35:18, 19

24 [1]Lit., *consumed* [2]Or, *perform* [a]Lev. 19:31; 2 Kin. 21:6 [b]Gen. 31:19 mg. [c]2 Kin. 21:11, 21 [d]Deut. 18:10-22 [e]2 Kin. 22:8

25 [a]2 Kin. 18:5

26 [a]2 Kin. 21:11-13; Jer. 15:4

27 [1]Lit., *house* [a]2 Kin. 18:11 [b]2 Kin. 21:13, 14

29 [a]2 Chr. 35:20-24 [b]Jer. 46:2 [c]Judg. 5:19

30 [1]Lit., *him, dead* [a]2 Kin. 9:28 [b]2 Chr. 36:1-4

31 [a]1 Chr. 3:15; Jer. 22:11 [b]2 Kin. 24:18

32 [a]2 Kin. 21:2-7

33 [a]2 Kin. 23:29 [b]2 Kin. 25:6 [c]1 Kin. 8:65

34 [1]So with Gr.; Heb., *he came* [a]1 Chr. 3:15 [b]2 Kin. 24:17; 2 Chr. 36:4 [c]Jer. 22:11, 12; Ezek. 19:3, 4

35 So Jehoiakim [a]gave the silver and
gold to Pharaoh, but he taxed the land in
order to give the money at the [1]com-
mand of Pharaoh. He exacted the silver
and gold from the people of the land,
each according to his valuation, to give it
to Pharaoh Neco.
36 [a]Jehoiakim was twenty-five years
old when he became king, and he
reigned eleven years in Jerusalem; and
his mother's name *was* Zebidah the
daughter of Pedaiah of Rumah.
37 And he did evil in the sight of the
LORD, [a]according to all that his fathers
had done.

Babylon Controls Jehoiakim

24 [a]IN his days Nebuchadnezzar
king of Babylon came up, and
Jehoiakim became his servant *for* three
years; then he turned and rebelled
against him.
2 And the LORD sent against him
[a]bands of Chaldeans, [b]bands of Arameans, [c]bands of Moabites, and bands of
Ammonites. So He sent them against
Judah to destroy it, [d]according to the
word of the LORD, which He had spoken
through His servants the prophets.
3 [a]Surely at the [1]command of the
LORD it came upon Judah, to remove
them from His sight [b]because of the sins
of Manasseh, according to all that he
had done,
4 and [a]also for the innocent blood
which he shed, for he filled Jerusalem
with innocent blood; and the LORD
would not forgive.
5 Now the rest of the acts of Jehoiakim and all that he did, are they not
written in the Book of the Chronicles of
the Kings of Judah?

Jehoiachin Reigns

6 So [a]Jehoiakim slept with his fathers, and Jehoiachin his son became
king in his place.
7 And [a]the king of Egypt did not
come out of his land again, [b]for the king
of Babylon had taken all that belonged
to the king of Egypt from [c]the brook of
Egypt to the river Euphrates.
8 [a]Jehoiachin was [b]eighteen years old
when he became king, and he reigned
three months in Jerusalem; and his
mother's name *was* Nehushta the daughter of Elnathan of Jerusalem.
9 And he did evil in the sight of the
LORD, [a]according to all that his father
had done.

Deportation to Babylon

10 At that time the servants of Nebuchadnezzar king of Babylon went up to
Jerusalem, and the city came under
siege.
11 And Nebuchadnezzar the king of
Babylon came to the city, while his
servants were besieging it.
12 And [a]Jehoiachin the king of Judah
went out to the king of Babylon, he and
his mother and his servants and his
captains and his officials. So [b]the king of
Babylon took him captive in the eighth
year of his reign.
13 And [a]he carried out from there all
the treasures of the house of the LORD,
and the treasures of the king's house,
and [b]cut in pieces all the vessels of gold
[c]which Solomon king of Israel had made
in the temple of the LORD, just as the
LORD had said.
14 Then [a]he led away into exile all
Jerusalem and all the captains and all
the mighty men of valor, [b]ten thousand
captives, and [c]all the craftsmen and the
smiths. None remained [d]except the
poorest people of the land.
15 So [a]he led Jehoiachin away into
exile to Babylon; also the king's mother
and the king's wives and his officials and
the leading men of the land, he led away
into exile from Jerusalem to Babylon.
16 And all the men of valor, [a]seven
thousand, and the craftsmen and the
smiths, one thousand, all strong and fit
for war, and these the king of Babylon
brought into exile to Babylon.

Zedekiah Made King

17 [a]Then the king of Babylon made
[1]his uncle Mattaniah, king in his place,
and changed his name to Zedekiah.
18 [a]Zedekiah was twenty-one years
old when he became king, and he
reigned eleven years in Jerusalem; and
his mother's name *was* [b]Hamutal the
daughter of Jeremiah of Libnah.
19 And he did evil in the sight of the
LORD, [a]according to all that Jehoiakim
had done.
20 For [a]through the anger of the
LORD *this* came about in Jerusalem and
Judah until He cast them out from His
presence. And [b]Zedekiah rebelled
against the king of Babylon.

Nebuchadnezzar Besieges Jerusalem

25 [a]NOW it came about in the ninth
year of his reign, on the tenth day
of the tenth month, that [b]Nebuchadnez-
zar king of Babylon came, he and all his
army, against Jerusalem, camped against
it, and [c]built a siege wall all around [1]it.
2 So the city was under siege until
the eleventh year of King Zedekiah.
3 On the ninth day of the *fourth*
month [a]the famine was so severe in the
city that there was no food for the
people of the land.
4 [a]Then the city was broken into,
and all the men of war *fled* by night by
way of the gate between the two walls
beside [b]the king's garden, though the
Chaldeans were all around the city. And
[1]they went by way of the Arabah.
5 But the army of the Chaldeans
pursued the king and overtook him in
the plains of Jericho and all his army
was scattered from him.
6 Then [a]they captured the king and
[b]brought him to the king of Babylon at
[c]Riblah, and [1]he passed sentence on
him.

---

35 [1]Lit., *mouth* [a]2 Kin. 23:33
36 [a]2 Chr. 36:5; Jer. 22:18, 19; 26:1
37 [a]2 Kin. 23:32
1 [a]2 Chr. 36:6; Jer. 25:1; Dan. 1:1, 2
2 [a]Jer. 35:11f. [b]2 Kin. 6:23 [c]2 Kin. 13:20 [d]2 Kin. 23:27
3 [1]Lit., *mouth* [a]2 Kin. 18:25 [b]2 Kin. 23:26
4 [a]2 Kin. 21:16
6 [a]Jer. 22:18, 19
7 [a]Jer. 37:5-7 [b]Jer. 46:2 [c]Gen. 15:18
8 [a]1 Chr. 3:16 [b]2 Chr. 36:9
9 [a]2 Kin. 21:2-7
12 [a]Jer. 22:24-30; 24:1; 29:1, 2 [b]2 Chr. 36:10
13 [a]2 Kin. 20:17; Is. 39:6 [b]2 Kin. 25:13-15 [c]1 Kin. 7:48-50
14 [a]Jer. 24:1 [b]2 Kin. 24:16; Jer. 52:28 [c]Jer. 24:1; 29:2 [d]2 Kin. 25:12
15 [a]2 Chr. 36:10; Jer. 22:24-28; Ezek. 17:12
16 [a]2 Kin. 24:14
17 [1]I.e., Jehoiachin's uncle [a]2 Chr. 36:10-13; Jer. 37:1
18 [a]Jer. 27:1; 28:1; 52:1 [b]2 Kin. 23:31
19 [a]2 Kin. 23:37
20 [a]Deut. 4:24; 29:27; 2 Kin. 23:26 [b]2 Chr. 36:13; Ezek. 17:15
1 [1]Lit., *against it* [a]2 Chr. 36:17-20; Jer. 39:1-7 [b]Jer. 21:2; 34:1, 2; Ezek. 24:2 [c]Ezek. 21:22
3 [a]2 Kin. 6:24, 25; Lam. 4:9, 10
4 [1]So some ancient mss. and versions; M.T., *he* [a]Ezek. 33:21 [b]Neh. 3:15
6 [1]Lit., *they spoke judgment with him* [a]Jer. 34:21, 22 [b]Jer. 32:4 [c]2 Kin. 23:33

7 And [a]they slaughtered the sons of Zedekiah before his eyes, then [b]put out the eyes of Zedekiah and bound him with bronze fetters and brought him to Babylon.

Jerusalem Burned and Plundered

8 [a]Now on the seventh day of the [b]fifth month, which was the nineteenth year of King Nebuchadnezzar, king of Babylon, Nebuzaradan the captain of the guard, a servant of the king of Babylon, came to Jerusalem.

9 And [a]he burned the house of the LORD, [b]the king's house, and all the houses of Jerusalem; even every great house he burned with fire.

10 So all the army of the Chaldeans who *were with* the captain of the guard [a]broke down the walls around Jerusalem.

11 Then [a]the rest of the people who were left in the city and the deserters who had deserted to the king of Babylon and the rest of the multitude, Nebuzaradan the captain of the guard carried away into exile.

12 But the captain of the guard left some of [a]the poorest of the land to be vinedressers and plowmen.

13 [a]Now the bronze pillars which were in the house of the LORD, and the stands and [b]the bronze sea which were in the house of the LORD, the Chaldeans broke in pieces and carried the [1]bronze to Babylon.

14 [a]And they took away the pots, the shovels, the snuffers, the spoons, and all the bronze vessels which were used in *temple* service.

15 The captain of the guard also took away the firepans and the basins, what was fine gold and what was fine silver.

16 The two pillars, the one sea, and the stands which Solomon had made for the house of the LORD—[a]the bronze of all these vessels was beyond weight.

17 [a]The height of the one pillar was eighteen [1]cubits, and a bronze capital was on it; the height of the capital was three [1]cubits, with a network and pomegranates on the capital all around, all of bronze. And the second pillar was like these with network.

18 Then the captain of the guard took [a]Seraiah the chief priest and [b]Zephaniah the second priest, with the three [1]officers of the temple.

19 And from the city he took one official who was overseer of the men of war, and [a]five [1]of the king's advisers who were found in the city; and the [2]scribe of the captain of the army, who mustered the people of the land; and sixty men of the people of the land who were found in the city.

20 And Nebuzaradan the captain of the guard took them and brought them to the king of Babylon at [a]Riblah.

21 Then the king of Babylon struck them down and put them to death at Riblah in the land of Hamath. [a]So Judah was led away into exile from its land.

Gedaliah Made Governor

22 Now *as for* the people who were left in the land of Judah, whom Nebuchadnezzar king of Babylon had left, he appointed [a]Gedaliah the son of Ahikam, the son of Shaphan over them.

23 [a]When all the captains of the forces, they and *their* men, heard that the king of Babylon had appointed Gedaliah *governor,* they came to Gedaliah to [b]Mizpah, namely, Ishmael the son of Nethaniah, and Johanan the son of Kareah, and Seraiah the son of Tanhumeth the Netophathite, and Jaazaniah the son of the Maacathite, they and their men.

24 And Gedaliah swore to them and their men and said to them, "Do not be afraid of the servants of the Chaldeans; live in the land and serve the king of Babylon, and it will be well with you."

25 [a]But it came about in the seventh month, that Ishmael the son of Nethaniah, the son of Elishama, of the royal [1]family, came [2]with ten men and struck Gedaliah down so that he died along with the Jews and the Chaldeans who were with him at Mizpah.

26 [a]Then all the people, both small and great, and the captains of the forces arose and went to Egypt; for they were afraid of the Chaldeans.

27 [a]Now it came about in the thirty-seventh year of [b]the exile of Jehoiachin king of Judah, in the twelfth month, on the twenty-seventh *day* of the month, that Evil-merodach king of Babylon, in the year that he became king, [1c]released Jehoiachin king of Judah from prison;

28 and he [a]spoke kindly to him and set his throne above the throne of the kings who *were* with him in Babylon.

29 And [1]Jehoiachin changed his prison clothes, and [2a]had his meals in [3]the king's presence regularly all the days of his life;

30 and for his [a]allowance, a regular allowance was given him by the king, a portion for each day, all the days of his life.

7 [a]Jer. 39:6, 7 [b]Ezek. 12:13
8 [a]Jer. 52:12 [b]Jer. 39:8-12
9 [a]1 Kin. 9:8; 2 Chr. 36:19; Ps. 74:3-7 [b]Amos 2:5
10 [a]2 Kin. 14:13; Neh. 1:3
11 [a]2 Chr. 36:20
12 [a]2 Kin. 24:14; Jer. 40:7
13 [1]Lit., *bronze of them* [a]1 Kin. 7:15-22; 2 Kin. 20:17; 2 Chr. 3:15-17; 36:18 [b]1 Kin. 7:23-26; 2 Chr. 4:2-4
14 [a]Ex. 27:3; 1 Kin. 7:47-50; 2 Chr. 4:16
16 [a]1 Kin. 7:47
17 [1]I.e., One cubit equals approx. 18 in. [a]1 Kin. 7:15-22
18 [1]Lit., *keepers of the door* [a]1 Chr. 6:14; Ezra 7:1 [b]Jer. 21:1; 29:25, 29
19 [1]Lit., *men of those seeing the king's face* [2]Or, *scribe, a captain* [a]Esth. 1:14
20 [a]2 Kin. 23:33
21 [a]Deut. 28:64; 2 Kin. 23:27
22 [a]Jer. 39:14; 40:7-9
23 [a]Jer. 40:7-9 [b]Josh. 18:26
25 [1]Lit., *seed* [2]Lit., *and ten men with him* [a]Jer. 41:1, 2
26 [a]Jer. 43:4-7
27 [1]Lit., *lifted up the head of* [a]Jer. 52:31-34 [b]2 Kin. 24:12, 15 [c]Gen. 40:13, 20
28 [a]Dan. 2:37; 5:18, 19
29 [1]Lit., *he* [2]Lit., *ate bread* [3]Lit., *his presence* [a]2 Sam. 9:7
30 [a]Neh. 11:23; 12:47

THE FIRST BOOK OF THE
CHRONICLES

Genealogy from Adam

1 [a]ADAM, Seth, Enosh,
2 Kenan, Mahalalel, Jared,
3 Enoch, Methuselah, Lamech,
4 Noah, Shem, Ham and Japheth.
5 [a]The sons of Japheth *were* Gomer,
Magog, Madai, Javan, Tubal, Meshech,
and Tiras.
6 And the sons of Gomer *were* Ash-
kenaz, [1]Diphath, and Togarmah.
7 And the sons of Javan *were* Elishah, Tarshish, Kittim, and [1]Rodanim.
8 The sons of Ham *were* Cush, Mizraim, Put, and Canaan.
9 And the sons of Cush *were* Seba,
Havilah, Sabta, Raama, and Sabteca;
and the sons of Raamah *were* Sheba and
Dedan.
10 And Cush [1]became the father of
Nimrod; he began to be a mighty one in
the earth.
11 [a]And Mizraim became the father of
the people of Lud, Anam, Lehab, Naph-
tuh,
12 Pathrus, Casluh, from which the
[1]Philistines came, and Caphtor.
13 And Canaan became the father of
Sidon, his first-born, Heth,
14 and the Jebusites, the Amorites, the
Girgashites,
15 the Hivites, the Arkites, the Sinites,
16 the Arvadites, the Zemarites, and
the Hamathites.
17 [a]The sons of Shem *were* Elam,
Asshur, Arpachshad, Lud, Aram, Uz,
Hul, Gether, and [1]Meshech.
18 And Arpachshad became the father
of Shelah and Shelah became the father
of Eber.
19 And two sons were born to Eber,
the name of the one was Peleg, for in his
days the earth was divided, and his
brother's name was Joktan.
20 And Joktan became the father of
Almodad, Sheleph, Hazarmaveth, Jerah,
21 Hadoram, Uzal, Diklah,
22 [1]Ebal, Abimael, Sheba,
23 Ophir, Havilah, and Jobab; all
these *were* the sons of Joktan.
24 [a]Shem, Arpachshad, Shelah,
25 Eber, Peleg, Reu,
26 Serug, Nahor, Terah,

Descendants of Abraham

27 Abram, that is Abraham.
28 The sons of Abraham *were* Isaac
and Ishmael.
29 [a]These are their genealogies: the
first-born of Ishmael *was* Nebaioth, then
Kedar, Adbeel, Mibsam,
30 Mishma, Dumah, Massa, Hadad,
Tema,
31 Jetur, Naphish and Kedemah;
these *were* the sons of Ishmael.
32 [a]And the sons of Keturah, Abraham's concubine, *whom* she bore, *were*
Zimran, Jokshan, Medan, Midian, Ishbak, and Shuah. And the sons of Jokshan *were* Sheba and Dedan.
33 And the sons of Midian *were*
Ephah, Epher, Hanoch, Abida, and
Eldaah. All these were the sons of Keturah.
34 And [a]Abraham became the father
of Isaac. The sons of Isaac *were* [b]Esau
and Israel.
35 [a]The sons of Esau *were* Eliphaz,
Reuel, Jeush, Jalam, and Korah.
36 The sons of Eliphaz *were* Teman,
Omar, [1]Zephi, Gatam, Kenaz, Timna,
and Amalek.
37 The sons of Reuel *were* Nahath,
Zerah, Shammah, and Mizzah.
38 [a]And the sons of Seir *were* Lotan,
Shobal, Zibeon, Anah, Dishon, Ezer,
and Dishan.
39 And the sons of Lotan *were* Hori
and [1]Homam; and Lotan's sister *was*
Timna.
40 The sons of Shobal *were* [1]Alian,
Manahath, Ebal, [2]Shephi, and Onam.
And the sons of Zibeon *were* Aiah and
Anah.
41 The [1]son of Anah *was* Dishon. And
the sons of Dishon *were* [2]Hamran, Eshban, Ithran, and Cheran.
42 The sons of Ezer *were* Bilhan,
Zaavan and [1]Jaakan. The sons of Dishan
were Uz and Aran.
43 [a]Now these are the kings who
reigned in the land of Edom before any
king of the sons of Israel reigned. Bela
was the son of Beor, and the name of his
city was Dinhabah.
44 When Bela died, Jobab the son of
Zerah of [a]Bozrah became king in his
place.
45 When Jobab died, Husham of the
land of [a]the Temanites became king in
his place.
46 When Husham died, Hadad the
son of Bedad, who [1]defeated Midian in
the field of Moab, became king in his
place; and the name of his city *was*
Avith.
47 When Hadad died, Samlah of Masrekah became king in his place.
48 When Samlah died, Shaul of Rehoboth by the River became king in his
place.
49 When Shaul died, Baal-hanan the
son of Achbor became king in his place.
50 When Baal-hanan died, [1]Hadad
became king in his place; and the name
of his city was [2]Pai, and his wife's name
was Mehetabel, the daughter of Matred,
the daughter of Mezahab.
51 Then Hadad died. Now the chiefs
of Edom were: chief Timna, chief
[1]Aliah, chief Jetheth,
52 chief Oholibamah, chief Elah, chief
Pinon,
53 chief Kenaz, chief Teman, chief
Mibzar,
54 chief Magdiel, chief Iram. These
were the chiefs of Edom.

1 [a]Gen. 4:25-5:32
5 [a]Gen. 10:2-4
6 [1]In Gen. 10:3, *Riphath*
7 [1]In Gen. 10:4, *Dodanim*
10 [1]Lit., *begot*, and so throughout the ch.
11 [a]Gen. 10:13-18
12 [1]Or, *people of Pelisht*
17 [1]In Gen. 10:23, *Mash* [a]Gen. 10:22-29
22 [1]In Gen. 10:28, *Obal*
24 [a]Gen. 11:10-26; Luke 3:34-36
29 [a]Gen. 25:13-16
32 [a]Gen. 25:1-4
34 [a]1 Chr. 1:28 [b]Gen. 25:25, 26; 32:28
35 [a]Gen. 36:4-10
36 [1]In Gen. 36:11, *Zepho*
38 [a]Gen. 36:20-28
39 [1]In Gen. 36:22, *Hemam*
40 [1]In Gen. 36:23, *Alvan* [2]In Gen. 36:23, *Shepho*
41 [1]Lit., *sons* [2]In Gen. 36:26, *Hemdan*
42 [1]Or, *Akan*, as in Gen. 36:27
43 [a]Gen. 36:31-43
44 [a]Is. 34:6
45 [a]Job 2:11
46 [1]Lit., *smote*
50 [1]In Gen. 36:39, *Hadar* [2]In Gen. 36:39, *Pau*
51 [1]In Gen. 36:40, *Alvah*

Genealogy: Twelve Sons of Jacob (Israel)

2 [a]THESE are the sons of Israel: Reuben, Simeon, Levi, Judah, Issachar, Zebulun,

2 Dan, Joseph, Benjamin, Naphtali, Gad, and Asher.

3 [a]The sons of Judah *were* Er, Onan, and Shelah; *these* three were born to him by Bath-shua the Canaanitess. And Er, Judah's first-born, was wicked in the sight of the LORD, so He put him to death.

4 And [a]Tamar his daughter-in-law bore him Perez and Zerah. Judah had five sons in all.

5 The sons of Perez *were* Hezron and Hamul.

6 And the sons of Zerah *were* [1]Zimri, Ethan, Heman, Calcol, and [2]Dara; five of them in all.

7 And the [1]son of Carmi *was* [2a]Achar, the troubler of Israel, who violated the ban.

8 And the [1]son of Ethan *was* Azariah.

9 Now the sons of Hezron, who were born to him *were* Jerahmeel, Ram, and Chelubai.

10 And Ram [1]became the father of Amminadab, and Amminadab became the father of Nahshon, leader of the sons of Judah;

11 Nahshon became the father of Salma, Salma became the father of Boaz,

Genealogy of David

12 Boaz became the father of Obed, and Obed became the father of Jesse;

13 and Jesse became the father of Eliab his first-born, then Abinadab the second, [1]Shimea the third,

14 Nethanel the fourth, Raddai the fifth,

15 Ozem the sixth, David the seventh;

16 and their sisters *were* Zeruiah and Abigail. And the three sons of Zeruiah *were* [1]Abshai, Joab, and Asahel.

17 And Abigail bore Amasa, and the father of Amasa was [1]Jether the Ishmaelite.

18 Now Caleb the son of Hezron had sons by Azubah *his* wife, and by Jerioth; and these were her sons: Jesher, Shobab, and Ardon.

19 When Azubah died, Caleb married Ephrath, who bore him Hur.

20 And Hur became the father of Uri, and Uri became the father of Bezalel.

21 Afterward Hezron went in to the daughter of Machir the father of Gilead, whom he married when he was sixty years old; and she bore him Segub.

22 And Segub became the father of Jair, who had twenty-three cities in the land of Gilead.

23 But Geshur and Aram took [1]the towns of Jair from them, with Kenath and its villages, *even* sixty cities. All these were the sons of Machir, the father of Gilead.

24 And after the death of Hezron in Caleb-ephrathah, Abijah, Hezron's wife, bore him Ashhur the father of Tekoa.

25 Now the sons of Jerahmeel the first-born of Hezron *were* Ram the first-born, then Bunah, Oren, Ozem, *and* Ahijah.

26 And Jerahmeel had another wife, whose name was Atarah; she was the mother of Onam.

27 And the sons of Ram, the first-born of Jerahmeel, were Maaz, Jamin, and Eker.

28 And the sons of Onam were Shammai and Jada. And the sons of Shammai *were* Nadab and Abishur.

29 And the name of Abishur's wife *was* Abihail, and she bore him Ahban and Molid.

30 And the sons of Nadab *were* Seled and Appaim, and Seled died without sons.

31 And the [1]son of Appaim *was* Ishi. And the [1]son of Ishi *was* Sheshan. And the [1]son of Sheshan *was* Ahlai.

32 And the sons of Jada the brother of Shammai *were* Jether and Jonathan, and Jether died without sons.

33 And the sons of Jonathan *were* Peleth and Zaza. These were the sons of Jerahmeel.

34 Now Sheshan had no sons, only daughters. And Sheshan had an Egyptian servant whose name was Jarha.

35 And Sheshan gave his daughter to Jarha his servant in marriage, and she bore him Attai.

36 And Attai became the father of Nathan, and Nathan became the father of Zabad,

37 and Zabad became the father of Ephlal, and Ephlal became the father of Obed,

38 and Obed became the father of Jehu, and Jehu became the father of Azariah,

39 and Azariah became the father of Helez, and Helez became the father of Eleasah,

40 and Eleasah became the father of Sismai, and Sismai became the father of Shallum,

41 and Shallum became the father of Jekamiah, and Jekamiah became the father of Elishama.

42 Now the sons of Caleb, the brother of Jerahmeel, *were* Mesha his first-born, who was the father of Ziph; and [1]his son was Mareshah, the father of Hebron.

43 And the sons of Hebron *were* Korah and Tappuah and Rekem and Shema.

44 And Shema became the father of Raham, the father of Jorkeam; and Rekem became the father of Shammai.

45 And the son of Shammai was Maon, and Maon *was* the father of Bethzur.

46 And Ephah, Caleb's concubine, bore Haran, Moza, and Gazez; and Haran became the father of Gazez.

1 [a]Gen. 35:22-26; 46:8-25

3 [a]Gen. 38:2-10

4 [a]Gen. 38:13-30

6 [1]In Josh. 7:1, *Zabdi* [2]In 1 Kin. 4:31, *Darda*

7 [1]Lit., *sons* [2]In Josh. 7:18, *Achan* [a]Josh. 7:1

8 [1]Lit., *sons*

10 [1]Lit., *begot,* and so throughout the ch.

13 [1]In 1 Sam. 16:9, *Shammah;* in 2 Sam. 13:3, *Shimeah*

16 [1]In 2 Sam. 2:18, *Abishai*

17 [1]In 2 Sam. 17:25, *Ithra the Israelite*

23 [1]Or, *Havvoth-jair*

31 [1]Lit., *sons*

42 [1]Lit., *the sons of*

47 And the sons of Jahdai *were* Re-
gem, Jotham, Geshan, Pelet, Ephah, and
Shaaph.
48 Maacah, Caleb's concubine, bore
Sheber and Tirhanah.
49 She also bore Shaaph the father of
Madmannah, Sheva the father of Mach-
bena and the father of Gibea; and the
daughter of Caleb *was* Achsah.
50 These were the sons of Caleb.
The [1]sons of Hur, the first-born of
Ephrathah, *were* Shobal the father of
Kiriath-jearim,
51 Salma the father of Bethlehem *and*
Hareph the father of Beth-gader.
52 And Shobal the father of Kiriath-
jearim had sons: Haroeh, half of the
Manahathites,
53 and the families of Kiriath-jearim:
the Ithrites, the Puthites, the Shumath-
ites, and the Mishraites; from these
came the Zorathites and the Eshtaolites.
54 The sons of Salma *were* Bethlehem
and the Netophathites, Atroth-beth-joab
and half of the Manahathites, the Zo-
rites.
55 And the families of scribes who
lived at Jabez *were* the Tirathites, the
Shimeathites, *and* the Sucathites. Those
are the Kenites who came from Ham-
math, the father of the house of Rechab.

Family of David

3 [a]NOW these were the sons of David
who were born to him in Hebron:
the first-born *was* Amnon, by Ahinoam
the Jezreelitess; the second *was* Daniel,
by Abigail the Carmelitess;
2 the third *was* Absalom the son of
Maacah, the daughter of Talmai king of
Geshur; the fourth *was* Adonijah the son
of Haggith;
3 the fifth *was* Shephatiah, by Abital;
the sixth *was* Ithream, by his wife Eglah.
4 Six were born to him in Hebron,
and [a]there he reigned seven years and six
months. And in Jerusalem he reigned
thirty-three years.
5 [a]And these were born to him in
Jerusalem: Shimea, Shobab, Nathan,
and [b]Solomon, four, by [c]Bath-shua the
daughter of Ammiel;
6 and Ibhar, Elishama, Eliphelet,
7 Nogah, Nepheg, and Japhia,
8 Elishama, Eliada, and Eliphelet,
nine.
9 All *these were* the sons of David,
besides the sons of the concubines; and
[a]Tamar *was* their sister.
10 Now Solomon's son *was* Rehoboam, Abijah *was* his son, Asa his son,
Jehoshaphat his son,
11 Joram his son, Ahaziah his son,
Joash his son,
12 Amaziah his son, Azariah his son,
Jotham his son,
13 Ahaz his son, Hezekiah his son,
Manasseh his son,
14 Amon his son, Josiah his son.
15 And the sons of Josiah *were* Johanan the first-born, and the second *was*
Jehoiakim, the third Zedekiah, the
fourth Shallum.

50 [1]Lit., *son*

1 [a]2 Sam. 3:2-5

4 [a]2 Sam. 2:11; 5:4, 5; 1 Kin. 2:11; 1 Chr. 29:27

5 [a]2 Sam. 5:14-16; 1 Chr. 14:4-7 [b]2 Sam. 12:24, 25 [c]2 Sam. 11:3

9 [a]2 Sam. 13:1

19 [1]Lit., *son*

21 [1]Lit., *son*

22 [1]Lit., *sons*

23 [1]Lit., *son*

1 [a]1 Chr. 2:3

2 [1]Lit., *begot*, and so throughout the ch.

3 [1]So with some ancient versions; Heb., *father*

7 [1]Another reading is *Zohar*

12 [1]Or, *the city of Nahash*

13 [1]Lit., *sons*

16 And the sons of Jehoiakim *were*
Jeconiah his son, Zedekiah his son.
17 And the sons of Jeconiah, the
prisoner, *were* Shealtiel his son,
18 and Malchiram, Pedaiah, Shenaz-
zar, Jekamiah, Hoshama, and Nedabiah.
19 And the sons of Pedaiah *were* Zerubbabel and Shimei. And the [1]sons of
Zerubbabel *were* Meshullam and Hananiah, and Shelomith *was* their sister;
20 and Hashubah, Ohel, Berechiah,
Hasadiah, and Jushab-hesed, five.
21 And the [1]sons of Hananiah *were*
Pelatiah and Jeshaiah, the sons of Rephaiah, the sons of Arnan, the sons of
Obadiah, the sons of Shecaniah.
22 And the [1]son of Shecaniah *was*
Shemaiah, and the sons of Shemaiah
were Hattush, Igal, Bariah, Neariah, and
Shaphat, six.
23 And the [1]sons of Neariah *were*
Elioenai, Hizkiah, and Azrikam, three.
24 And the sons of Elioenai *were*
Hodaviah, Eliashib, Pelaiah, Akkub,
Johanan, Delaiah, and Anani, seven.

Line of Hur, Asher

4 [a]THE sons of Judah *were* Perez,
Hezron, Carmi, Hur, and Shobal.
2 And Reaiah the son of Shobal
[1]became the father of Jahath, and Jahath
became the father of Ahumai and La-
had. These *were* the families of the
Zorathites.
3 And these *were* the [1]sons of Etam:
Jezreel, Ishma, and Idbash; and the
name of their sister *was* Hazzelelponi.
4 And Penuel *was* the father of Gedor, and Ezer the father of Hushah.
These *were* the sons of Hur, the first-
born of Ephrathah, the father of Bethlehem.
5 And Ashhur, the father of Tekoa,
had two wives, Helah and Naarah.
6 And Naarah bore him Ahuzzam,
Hepher, Temeni, and Haahashtari.
These were the sons of Naarah.
7 And the sons of Helah *were* Zereth,
[1]Izhar and Ethnan.
8 And Koz became the father of
Anub and Zobebah, and the families of
Aharhel the son of Harum.
9 And Jabez was more honorable
than his brothers, and his mother named
him Jabez saying, "Because I bore *him*
with pain."
10 Now Jabez called on the God of
Israel, saying, "Oh that Thou wouldst
bless me indeed, and enlarge my border,
and that Thy hand might be with me,
and that Thou wouldst keep *me* from
harm, that *it* may not pain me!" And
God granted him what he requested.
11 And Chelub the brother of Shuhah
became the father of Mehir, who was the
father of Eshton.
12 And Eshton became the father of
Beth-rapha and Paseah, and Tehinnah
the father of [1]Ir-nahash. These are the
men of Recah.
13 Now the sons of Kenaz *were* Othniel and Seraiah. And the [1]son of Othniel *was* Hathath.

14 And Meonothai became the father of Ophrah, and Seraiah became the father of Joab the father of [1]Ge-harashim, for they were craftsmen.

15 And the sons of Caleb the son of Jephunneh *were* Iru, Elah and Naam; and the [1]son of Elah *was* [2]Kenaz.

16 And the sons of Jehallelel *were* Ziph and Ziphah, Tiria and Asarel.

17 And the [1]sons of Ezrah *were* Jether, Mered, Epher, and Jalon. ([2]And these are the sons of Bithia the daughter of Pharaoh, whom Mered took) and she conceived *and bore* Miriam, Shammai, and Ishbah the father of Eshtemoa.

18 And his Jewish wife bore Jered the father of Gedor, and Heber the father of Soco, and Jekuthiel the father of Zanoah.

19 And the sons of the wife of Hodiah, the sister of Naham, *were* the [1]fathers of Keilah the Garmite and Eshtemoa the Maacathite.

20 And the sons of Shimon *were* Amnon and Rinnah, Benhanan and Tilon. And the sons of Ishi *were* Zoheth and Ben-zoheth.

21 The sons of Shelah the son of Judah *were* Er the father of Lecah and Laadah the father of Mareshah, and the families of the house of the linen workers at Beth-ashbea;

22 and Jokim, the men of Cozeba, Joash, Saraph, who ruled in Moab, and Jashubi-lehem. And the [1]records are ancient.

23 These were the potters and the inhabitants of Netaim and Gederah; they lived there with the king for his work.

Descendants of Simeon

24 The sons of Simeon *were* [1]Nemuel and Jamin, [2]Jarib, [3]Zerah, Shaul;

25 Shallum his son, Mibsam his son, Mishma his son.

26 And the sons of Mishma *were* Hammuel his son, Zaccur his son, Shimei his son.

27 Now Shimei had sixteen sons and six daughters; but his brothers did not have many sons, nor did all their family multiply like the sons of Judah.

28 And they lived at Beersheba, Moladah, and Hazar-shual,

29 at Bilhah, Ezem, Tolad,

30 Bethuel, Hormah, Ziklag,

31 Beth-marcaboth, Hazar-susim, Beth-biri, and Shaaraim. These *were* their cities until the reign of David.

32 And their villages *were* Etam, Ain, Rimmon, Tochen, and Ashan, five cities;

33 and all their villages that *were* around the same cities as far as [1]Baal. These *were* their settlements, and they have their genealogy.

34 And Meshobab and Jamlech and Joshah the son of Amaziah,

35 and Joel and Jehu the son of Joshibiah, the son of Seraiah, the son of Asiel,

36 and Elioenai, Jaakobah, Jeshohaiah, Asaiah, Adiel, Jesimiel, Benaiah,

37 Ziza the son of Shiphi, the son of Allon, the son of Jedaiah, the son of Shimri, the son of Shemaiah;

38 these mentioned by name *were* leaders in their families; and their fathers' houses increased greatly.

39 And they went to the entrance of Gedor, even to the east side of the valley, to seek pasture for their flocks.

40 And they found rich and good pasture, and [a]the land was broad and quiet and peaceful; for those who lived there formerly *were* Hamites.

41 And [a]these, recorded by name, came in the days of Hezekiah king of Judah, and [1]attacked their tents, and the Meunites who were found there, and destroyed them utterly to this day, and lived in their place; because there was pasture there for their flocks.

42 And from them, from the sons of Simeon, five hundred men went to [a]Mount Seir, with Pelatiah, Neariah, Rephaiah, and Uzziel, the sons of Ishi, as their leaders.

43 And [a]they [1]destroyed the remnant of the Amalekites who escaped, and have lived there to this day.

Genealogy from Reuben

5 NOW the sons of Reuben the first-born of Israel (for [a]he was the first-born, but because [b]he defiled his father's bed, [c]his birthright was given to the sons of Joseph the son of Israel; so that he is not enrolled in the genealogy according to the birthright.

2 [a]Though Judah prevailed over his brothers, and [b]from him *came* the leader, yet the birthright belonged to Joseph),

3 [a]the sons of Reuben the first-born of Israel *were* Hanoch and Pallu, Hezron and Carmi.

4 The sons of Joel *were* Shemaiah his son, Gog his son, [a]Shimei his son,

5 Micah his son, Reaiah his son, Baal his son,

6 Beerah his son, whom [1]Tilgath-pilneser king of Assyria carried away into exile; he was leader of the Reubenites.

7 And his [1]kinsmen by their families, [a]in the genealogy of their generations, *were* Jeiel the chief, then Zechariah

8 and Bela the son of Azaz, the son of Shema, the son of Joel, who lived in [a]Aroer, even to Nebo and Baal-meon.

9 And to the east he settled as far as the entrance of the wilderness from the river Euphrates, [a]because their cattle had increased in the land of Gilead.

10 And in the days of Saul [a]they made war with the Hagrites, who fell by their hand, so that they [1]occupied their tents throughout [2]all the land east of Gilead.

11 Now the sons of Gad lived opposite them in the land of [a]Bashan as far as [b]Salecah.

12 Joel *was* the chief, and Shapham the second, then Janai and Shaphat in Bashan.

13 And their [1]kinsmen of their fathers' households *were* Michael, Meshullam,

14 [1]Or, *valley of craftsmen*
15 [1]Lit., *sons* [2]Lit., *and Kenaz*
17 [1]Lit., *son* [2]In the Heb. the words in ( ) are at the end of v. 18
19 [1]Lit., *father*
22 [1]Lit., *words*
24 [1]In Num. 26:12, *Jemuel* [2]In Num. 26:12, *Jachin* [3]In Gen. 46:10 and Ex. 6:15, *Zohar*
33 [1]In Josh. 19:8, *Baalath*
40 [a]Judg. 18:7-10
41 [1]Lit., *smote* [a]1 Chr. 4:33-38
42 [a]Gen. 36:8, 9
43 [1]Lit., *smote* [a]1 Sam. 15:7, 8; 30:17
1 [a]Gen. 29:32; 1 Chr. 2:1 [b]Gen. 35:22; 49:4 [c]Gen. 48:15-22
2 [a]Gen. 49:8-10; Ps. 60:7; 108:8 [b]Mic. 5:2; Matt. 2:6
3 [a]Gen. 46:9; Ex. 6:14; Num. 26:5-9
4 [a]1 Chr. 5:8
6 [1]In 2 Kin. 15:29, *Tiglath-pileser*
7 [1]Lit., *brothers* [a]1 Chr. 5:17
8 [a]Num. 32:34; Josh. 12:2
9 [a]Josh. 22:8, 9
10 [1]Lit., *dwelt in* [2]Lit., *all the face of the east* [a]1 Chr. 5:18-21
11 [a]Josh. 13:11 [b]Deut. 3:10
13 [1]Lit., *brother*

Sheba, Jorai, Jacan, Zia, and Eber,
seven.
14 These *were* the sons of Abihail, the
son of Huri, the son of Jaroah, the son of
Gilead, the son of Michael, the son of
Jeshishai, the son of Jahdo, the son
of Buz;
15 Ahi the son of Abdiel, the son of
Guni, *was* head of their fathers' households.
16 And they lived in Gilead, in Bashan and in its towns, and in all the
pasture lands of [a]Sharon, as far as their
[1]borders.
17 All of these were enrolled in the
genealogies in the days of [a]Jotham king
of Judah and in the days of [b]Jeroboam
king of Israel.
18 The sons of Reuben and the Gadites and the half-tribe of Manasseh,
consisting of valiant men, men who bore
shield and sword and shot with bow, and
were skillful in battle, *were* 44,760, who
[a]went to war.
19 And they made war against [a]the
Hagrites, [b]Jetur, Naphish, and Nodab.
20 And they were helped against
them, and the Hagrites and all who *were*
with them were given into their hand;
for [a]they cried out to God in the battle,
and He was entreated for them, because
[b]they trusted in Him.
21 And they took away their cattle:
their 50,000 camels, 250,000 sheep, 2,000
donkeys, and 100,000 [1]men.
22 For many fell slain, because [a]the
war *was* of God. And [b]they settled in
their place until the [c]exile.
23 Now the sons of the half-tribe of
Manasseh lived in the land; from Bashan to Baal-hermon and [a]Senir and
Mount Hermon they were numerous.
24 And these were the heads of their
fathers' households, even Epher, Ishi,
Eliel, Azriel, Jeremiah, Hodaviah, and
Jahdiel, mighty men of valor, famous
men, heads of their fathers' households.
25 But they [a]acted treacherously
against the God of their fathers, and
[b]played the harlot [c]after the gods of the
peoples of the land, whom God had
destroyed before them.
26 So the God of Israel stirred up the
spirit of [a]Pul, king of Assyria, even the
spirit of [1]Tilgath-pilneser king of Assyria, and he [b]carried them away into
exile, namely the Reubenites, the Gadites, and the half-tribe of Manasseh, and
brought them to Halah, Habor, Hara,
and to the river of Gozan, to this day.

Genealogy: The Priestly Line

6 [1a]THE sons of Levi *were* [2]Gershon,
Kohath and Merari.
2 And the sons of Kohath *were* Amram, Izhar, Hebron, and Uzziel.
3 And the children of Amram *were*
Aaron, Moses, and Miriam. And the
sons of Aaron *were* Nadab, Abihu, Eleazar, and Ithamar.
4 Eleazar [1]became the father of
Phinehas, *and* Phinehas became the
father of Abishua,
5 and Abishua became the father of
Bukki, and Bukki became the father of
Uzzi,
6 and Uzzi became the father of
Zerahiah, and Zerahiah became the
father of Meraioth,
7 Meraioth became the father of
Amariah, and Amariah became the father of Ahitub,
8 and [a]Ahitub became the father of
Zadok, and Zadok [b]became the father of
Ahimaaz,
9 and Ahimaaz became the father of
Azariah, and Azariah became the father
of Johanan,
10 and Johanan became the father of
Azariah ([a]it was he who served as the
priest in the house [b]which Solomon built
in Jerusalem),
11 and [a]Azariah became the father of
Amariah, and Amariah became the father of Ahitub,
12 and Ahitub became the father of
Zadok, and Zadok became the father of
[1]Shallum,
13 and Shallum became the father of
Hilkiah, and Hilkiah became the father
of Azariah,
14 and Azariah became the father of
[a]Seraiah, and Seraiah became the father
of Jehozadak;
15 and Jehozadak went *along* when
the LORD carried Judah and Jerusalem
away into exile [1]by Nebuchadnezzar.
16 [1a]The sons of Levi *were* [2]Gershom,
Kohath, and Merari.
17 And these are the names of the
sons of Gershom: Libni and Shimei.
18 And the sons of Kohath *were* Amram, Izhar, Hebron, and Uzziel.
19 The sons of [a]Merari *were* Mahli
and Mushi. And these are the families of
the Levites according to their fathers'
households.
20 Of Gershom: Libni his son, Jahath
his son, Zimmah his son,
21 Joah his son, Iddo his son, Zerah
his son, Jeatherai his son.
22 The sons of Kohath *were* Amminadab his son, Korah his son, Assir his son,
23 Elkanah his son, Ebiasaph his son,
and Assir his son,
24 Tahath his son, Uriel his son, Uzziah his son, and Shaul his son.
25 And the sons of Elkanah *were*
Amasai and Ahimoth.
26 *As for* Elkanah, the sons of Elkanah *were* Zophai his son and Nahath his
son,
27 Eliab his son, Jeroham his son,
Elkanah his son.
28 And the sons of Samuel *were* [a]Joel,
the first-born and Abijah, the second.
29 The sons of Merari *were* Mahli,
Libni his son, Shimei his son, Uzzah his
son,
30 Shimea his son, Haggiah his son,
Asaiah his son.
31 [a]Now these are those whom David
appointed over the service of song in the
house of the LORD, [b]after the ark rested
there.

---

16 [1]Lit., *goings out* [a]1 Chr. 27:29; Song 2:1; Is. 35:2; 65:10
17 [a]2 Kin. 15:5, 32 [b]2 Kin. 14:16, 28
18 [a]Num. 1:3
19 [a]1 Chr. 5:10 [b]Gen. 25:15; 1 Chr. 1:31
20 [a]2 Chr. 14:11-13 [b]Ps. 9:10; 20:7, 8; 22:4, 5
21 [1]Lit., *souls of men*
22 [a]Josh. 23:10; 2 Chr. 32:8; Rom. 8:31 [b]1 Chr. 4:41 [c]2 Kin. 15:29; 17:6
23 [a]Deut. 3:9
25 [a]Deut. 32:15-18 [b]Ex. 34:15 [c]2 Kin. 17:7
26 [1]In 2 Kin. 15:29, *Tiglath-pileser* [a]2 Kin. 15:19, 29; 2 Chr. 28:20 [b]2 Kin. 17:6
1 [1]Ch. 5:27 in Heb. [2]In v. 16, *Gershom* [a]Gen. 46:11; Ex. 6:16-25
4 [1]Lit., *begot*, and so throughout the ch.
8 [a]2 Sam. 8:17 [b]2 Sam. 15:27
10 [a]2 Chr. 26:17 [b]1 Kin. 6:1; 2 Chr. 3:1
11 [a]Ezra 7:3
12 [1]In ch. 9:11, *Meshullam*
14 [a]Neh. 11:11
15 [1]Lit., *by the hand of*
16 [1]Ch. 6:1 in Heb. [2]In v. 1, *Gershon* [a]Gen. 46:11; Ex. 6:16
19 [a]Num. 3:33; 1 Chr. 23:21
28 [a]1 Sam. 8:2; 1 Chr. 6:33
31 [a]1 Chr. 15:16-22, 27; 16:4-6 [b]2 Sam. 6:17; 1 Kin. 8:4; 1 Chr. 15:25-16:1

32 And they ministered with song before the tabernacle of the tent of meeting, until Solomon had built the house of the LORD in Jerusalem; and they [1]served in their office according to their order.

33 And these are those who [1]served with their sons. From the sons of the Kohathites *were* Heman the singer, the son of Joel, the son of Samuel,

34 the son of Elkanah, the son of Jeroham, the son of Eliel, the son of Toah,

35 the son of Zuph, the son of Elkanah, the son of Mahath, the son of Amasai,

36 the son of Elkanah, the son of Joel, the son of Azariah, the son of Zephaniah,

37 the son of Tahath, the son of Assir, the son of Ebiasaph, the son of Korah,

38 the son of Izhar, the son of Kohath, the son of Levi, the son of Israel.

39 And *Heman's* brother Asaph stood at his right hand, even Asaph the son of Berechiah, the son of Shimea,

40 the son of Michael, the son of Baaseiah, the son of Malchijah,

41 the son of Ethni, the son of Zerah, the son of Adaiah,

42 the son of Ethan, the son of Zimmah, the son of Shimei,

43 the son of Jahath, the son of Gershom, the son of Levi.

44 And on the left hand *were* their [1]kinsmen the sons of Merari: Ethan the son of Kishi, the son of Abdi, the son of Malluch,

45 the son of Hashabiah, the son of Amaziah, the son of Hilkiah,

46 the son of Amzi, the son of Bani, the son of Shemer,

47 the son of Mahli, the son of Mushi, the son of Merari, the son of Levi.

48 And their [1]kinsmen the Levites were [2]appointed for all the service of the tabernacle of the house of God.

49 But Aaron and his sons [1a]offered on the altar of burnt offering and [b]on the altar of incense, for all the work of the most holy place, and [c]to make atonement for Israel, according to all that Moses the servant of God had commanded.

50 [a]And these are the sons of Aaron: Eleazar his son, Phinehas his son, Abishua his son,

51 Bukki his son, Uzzi his son, Zerahiah his son,

52 Meraioth his son, Amariah his son, Ahitub his son,

53 Zadok his son, Ahimaaz his son.

54 Now these are their settlements according to their camps within their borders. To the sons of Aaron of the families of the Kohathites (for theirs was the [a]*first* lot),

55 to them they gave [a]Hebron in the land of Judah, and its pasture lands around it;

56 [a]but the fields of the city and its villages, they gave to Caleb the son of Jephunneh.

57 And [a]to the sons of Aaron they gave the *following* cities of refuge: Hebron, Libnah also with its pasture lands, Jattir, Eshtemoa with its pasture lands,

58 [1]Hilen with its pasture lands, Debir with its pasture lands,

59 [1]Ashan with its pasture lands, and Beth-shemesh with its pasture lands;

60 and from the tribe of Benjamin: Geba with its pasture lands, [1]Allemeth with its pasture lands, and Anathoth with its pasture lands. All their cities throughout their families were thirteen cities.

61 [a]Then to the rest of the sons of Kohath *were given* by lot, from the family of the tribe, from the half-tribe, the half of Manasseh, ten cities.

62 And to the sons of Gershom, according to their families, *were given* from the tribe of Issachar and from the tribe of Asher, the tribe of Naphtali, and the tribe of Manasseh, thirteen cities in Bashan.

63 [a]To the sons of Merari *were given* by lot, according to their families, from the tribe of Reuben, the tribe of Gad, and the tribe of Zebulun, twelve cities.

64 [a]So the sons of Israel gave to the Levites the cities with their pasture lands.

65 And they gave by lot from the tribe of the sons of Judah, the tribe of the sons of Simeon, and the tribe of the sons of Benjamin, [a]these cities which are mentioned by name.

66 [a]Now some of the families of the sons of Kohath had cities of their territory from the tribe of Ephraim.

67 And they gave to them the *following* cities of refuge: Shechem in the hill country of Ephraim with its pasture lands, Gezer also with its pasture lands,

68 Jokmeam with its pasture lands, Beth-horon with its pasture lands,

69 Aijalon with its pasture lands, and Gath-rimmon with its pasture lands;

70 and from the half-tribe of Manasseh: Aner with its pasture lands and Bileam with its pasture lands, for the rest of the family of the sons of Kohath.

71 To the sons of Gershom *were given,* from the family of the half-tribe of Manasseh: Golan in Bashan with its pasture lands and Ashtaroth with its pasture lands;

72 and from the tribe of Issachar: Kedesh with its pasture lands, Daberath with its pasture lands,

73 and Ramoth with its pasture lands, Anem with its pasture lands;

74 and from the tribe of Asher: Mashal with its pasture lands, Abdon with its pasture lands,

75 Hukok with its pasture lands, and Rehob with its pasture lands;

76 and from the tribe of Naphtali: Kedesh in Galilee with its pasture lands, Hammon with its pasture lands, and Kiriathaim with its pasture lands.

77 To the rest of *the Levites,* the sons of Merari, *were given,* from the tribe of

32 [1]Lit., *stood over*
33 [1]Lit., *stood*
44 [1]Lit., *brothers*
48 [1]Lit., *brothers* [2]Lit., *given*
49 [1]Lit., *offered up in smoke* [a]Ex. 27:1-8 [b]Ex. 30:1-7 [c]Ex. 30:10-16
50 [a]1 Chr. 6:4-8; Ezra 7:5
54 [a]Josh. 21:4, 10
55 [a]Josh. 14:13; 21:11f.
56 [a]Josh. 15:13
57 [a]Josh. 21:13, 19
58 [1]In Josh. 21:15, *Holon*
59 [1]In Josh. 21:16, *Ain*
60 [1]In Josh. 21:18, *Almon*
61 [a]Josh. 21:5; 1 Chr. 6:66-70
63 [a]Josh. 21:7, 34-40
64 [a]Num. 35:1-8; Josh. 21:3, 41, 42
65 [a]1 Chr. 6:57-60
66 [a]Josh. 21:20-26

Zebulun: Rimmono with its pasture
lands, Tabor with its pasture lands;
78 and beyond the Jordan at Jericho,
on the east side of the Jordan, *were given*
them, from the tribe of Reuben: Bezer in
the wilderness with its pasture lands,
Jahzah with its pasture lands,
79 Kedemoth with its pasture lands,
and Mephaath with its pasture lands;
80 and from the tribe of Gad: Ramoth
in Gilead with its pasture lands, Mahanaim with its pasture lands,
81 Heshbon with its pasture lands,
and Jazer with its pasture lands.

Genealogy from Issachar

7 NOW the sons of Issachar *were*
four: Tola, [1]Puah, [2]Jashub, and
Shimron.
2 And the sons of Tola *were* Uzzi,
Rephaiah, Jeriel, Jahmai, Ibsam, and
Samuel, heads of their fathers' households. *The sons* of Tola *were* mighty men
of valor in their generations; [a]their
number in the days of David was 22,600.
3 And the [1]son of Uzzi *was* Izrahiah.
And the sons of Izrahiah *were* Michael,
Obadiah, Joel, Isshiah; all five of them
were [a]chief men.
4 And with them by their generations
according to their fathers' households
were 36,000 [1]troops of the army for war,
for they had many wives and sons.
5 And their [1]relatives among all the
families of Issachar *were* mighty men of
valor, enrolled by genealogy, in all
87,000.

Descendants of Benjamin

6 [a]*The sons of* Benjamin *were* three:
Bela and Becher and Jediael.
7 And the sons of Bela were five:
Ezbon, Uzzi, Uzziel, Jerimoth, and Iri.
They *were* heads of fathers' households,
mighty men of valor, and were 22,034
enrolled by genealogy.
8 And the sons of Becher *were* Zemi-
rah, Joash, Eliezer, Elioenai, Omri, Jeremoth, Abijah, Anathoth, and Alemeth.
All these *were* the sons of Becher.
9 And they were enrolled by genealogy, according to their generations,
heads of their fathers' households,
20,200 mighty men of valor.
10 And the [1]son of Jediael *was* Bilhan.
And the sons of Bilhan *were* Jeush,
Benjamin, Ehud, Chenaanah, Zethan,
Tarshish, and Ahishahar.
11 All these *were* sons of Jediael,
according to the heads of their fathers'
households, 17,200 mighty men of valor,
who were [1]ready to go out with the army
to war.
12 And [1]Shuppim and [2]Huppim *were*
the sons of [3]Ir; Hushim *was* the [4]son of
[5]Aher.

Sons of Naphtali

13 The sons of Naphtali *were* [1]Jahziel,
Guni, Jezer, and [2]Shallum, the sons of
Bilhah.

Descendants of Manasseh

14 The sons of Manasseh *were* Asriel,
whom his Aramean concubine bore; she
bore Machir the father of Gilead.
15 And Machir took a wife for Huppim and Shuppim, [1]whose sister's name
was Maacah. And the name of the second was Zelophehad, and Zelophehad
had daughters.
16 And Maacah the wife of Machir
bore a son, and she named him Peresh;
and the name of his brother *was* Sheresh,
and his sons *were* Ulam and Rakem.
17 And the [1]son of Ulam *was* Bedan.
These *were* the sons of Gilead the son of
Machir, the son of Manasseh.
18 And his sister Hammolecheth bore
Ishhod and [1]Abiezer and Mahlah.
19 And the sons of Shemida were
Ahian and Shechem and Likhi and
Aniam.

Descendants of Ephraim

20 And [a]the sons of Ephraim *were*
Shuthelah and [1]Bered his son, Tahath
his son, Eleadah his son, Tahath his son,
21 Zabad his son, Shuthelah his son,
and Ezer and Elead whom the men of
Gath who were born in the land killed,
because they came down to take their
livestock.
22 And their father Ephraim
[a]mourned many days, and his relatives
[b]came to comfort him.
23 Then he went in to his wife, and
she conceived and bore a son, and he
named him [1]Beriah, because misfortune
had come upon his house.
24 And his daughter was Sheerah,
[a]who built lower and upper Beth-horon,
also Uzzen-sheerah.
25 And Rephah was his son *along* with
Resheph, Telah his son, Tahan his son,
26 Ladan his son, Ammihud his son,
Elishama his son,
27 [1]Non his son, and [a]Joshua his son.
28 And [a]their possessions and settlements *were* Bethel with its towns, and to
the east [1]Naaran, and to the west Gezer
with its towns, and Shechem with its
towns as far as [2]Ayyah with its towns,
29 and along the borders of the sons
of Manasseh, Beth-shean with its towns,
Taanach with its towns, Megiddo with
its towns, Dor with its towns. In these
lived the [a]sons of Joseph the son of
Israel.

Descendants of Asher

30 [a]The sons of Asher *were* Imnah,
Ishvah, Ishvi and Beriah, and Serah their
sister.
31 And the sons of Beriah *were* Heber
and Malchiel, who was the father of
Birzaith.
32 And Heber [1]became the father of
Japhlet, [2]Shomer and Hotham, and Shua
their sister.
33 And the sons of Japhlet *were* Pa-
sach, Bimhal, and Ashvath. These were
the sons of Japhlet.

1 [1]In Gen. 46:13, *Puvvah;* in Num. 26:23, *Puvah* [2]In Gen. 46:13, *Iob*

2 [a]2 Sam. 24:1-9

3 [1]Lit., *sons* [a]1 Chr. 5:24

4 [1]Or, *bands*

5 [1]Lit., *brothers,* and so throughout the ch.

6 [a]1 Chr. 8:1-40

10 [1]Lit., *sons*

11 [1]Lit., *going out*

12 [1]In Num. 26:39, *Shephupham* [2]In Num. 26:39, *Hupham* [3]In v. 7, *Iri* [4]Lit., *sons* [5]In Num. 26:38, *Ahiram*

13 [1]In Gen. 46:24, *Jahzeel* [2]In Gen. 46:24 and Num. 26:49, *Shillem*

15 [1]Lit., *and his*

17 [1]Lit., *sons*

18 [1]In Num. 26:30, *Iezer*

20 [1]In Num. 26:35, *Becher* [a]Num. 26:35, 36

22 [a]Gen. 37:34 [b]Job 2:11; John 11:19

23 [1]I.e., on misfortune

24 [a]Josh. 16:3, 5; 2 Chr. 8:5

27 [1]In Ex. 33:11, *Nun* [a]Ex. 17:9-14; 24:13

28 [1]In Josh. 16:7, *Naarah* [2]Many mss. read *Azzah* [a]Josh. 16:2

29 [a]Judg. 1:22-29

30 [a]Gen. 46:17; Num. 26:44-46

32 [1]Lit., *begot* [2]In v. 34, *Shemer*

34 And the sons of [1]Shemer *were* Ahi
and Rohgah, Jehubbah and Aram.
35 And the [1]sons of his brother Helem
were Zophah, Imna, Shelesh, and Amal.
36 The sons of Zophah *were* Suah,
Harnepher, Shual, Beri, and Imrah,
37 Bezer, Hod, Shamma, Shilshah,
Ithran, and Beera.
38 And the sons of Jether *were* Jephunneh, Pispa, and Ara.
39 And the sons of Ulla *were* Arah,
Hanniel, and Rizia.
40 All these *were* the sons of Asher,
heads of the fathers' houses, choice and
mighty men of valor, heads of the
princes. And the number of them enrolled by genealogy for service in war
was 26,000 men.

Genealogy from Benjamin

8 AND [a]Benjamin [1]became the father
of Bela his first-born, Ashbel the
second, [b]Aharah the third,
2 Nohah the fourth, and Rapha the
fifth.
3 And Bela had sons: [1]Addar, Gera,
Abihud,
4 Abishua, Naaman, Ahoah,
5 Gera, Shephuphan, and Huram.
6 And these are the sons of Ehud:
these are the heads of fathers' *households*
of the inhabitants of Geba, and they
carried them into exile to Manahath,
7 namely, Naaman, Ahijah, and
Gera—he carried them into exile; and he
became the father of Uzza and Ahihud.
8 And Shaharaim became the father
of children in the [1]country of Moab,
after he had [2]sent away Hushim and
Baara his wives.
9 And by Hodesh his wife he became
the father of Jobab, Zibia, Mesha, Malcam,
10 Jeuz, Sachia, Mirmah. These were
his sons, heads of fathers' *households.*
11 And by Hushim he became the
father of Abitub and Elpaal.
12 And the sons of Elpaal *were* Eber,
Misham, and Shemed, who built Ono
and Lod, with its towns;
13 and Beriah and Shema, who were
heads of fathers' *households* of the inhabitants of Aijalon, who put to flight
the inhabitants of Gath;
14 and [1]Ahio, Shashak, and Jeremoth.
15 And Zebadiah, Arad, Eder,
16 Michael, Ishpah, and Joha *were* the
sons of Beriah.
17 And Zebadiah, Meshullam, Hizki,
Heber,
18 Ishmerai, Izliah, and Jobab *were*
the sons of Elpaal.
19 And Jakim, Zichri, Zabdi,
20 Elienai, Zillethai, Eliel,
21 Adaiah, Beraiah, and Shimrath
were the sons of [1]Shimei.
22 And Ishpan, Eber, Eliel,
23 Abdon, Zichri, Hanan,
24 Hananiah, Elam, Anthothijah,
25 Iphdeiah, and Penuel *were* the sons
of Shashak.
26 And Shamsherai, Shehariah, Athaliah,
27 Jaareshiah, Elijah, and Zichri *were*
the sons of Jeroham.
28 These were heads of the fathers'
households according to their generations, chief men, [1]who lived in Jerusalem.
29 [a]Now in Gibeon, *Jeiel,* the father of
Gibeon lived, and his wife's name was
Maacah;
30 and his first-born son *was* Abdon,
then Zur, Kish, Baal, Nadab,
31 Gedor, Ahio, and [1]Zecher.
32 And Mikloth became the father of
[1]Shimeah. And they also lived with their
[2]relatives in Jerusalem opposite their
other [2]relatives.

Genealogy from King Saul

33 [a]And Ner became the father of
Kish, and Kish became the father
of Saul, and Saul became the father of
Jonathan, Malchi-shua, [1]Abinadab, and
[2]Eshbaal.
34 And the son of Jonathan *was*
[1]Merib-baal, and Merib-baal became the
father of Micah.
35 And the sons of Micah *were* Pithon, Melech, [1]Tarea, and Ahaz.
36 And Ahaz became the father of
[1]Jehoaddah, and Jehoaddah became the
father of Alemeth, Azmaveth, and
Zimri; and Zimri became the father of
Moza.
37 And Moza became the father of
Binea; [1]Raphah *was* his son, Eleasah his
son, Azel his son.
38 And Azel had six sons, and these
were their names: Azrikam, Bocheru,
Ishmael, Sheariah, Obadiah and Hanan.
All these *were* the sons of Azel.
39 And the sons of Eshek his brother
were Ulam his first-born, Jeush the
second, and Eliphelet the third.
40 And the sons of Ulam were mighty
men of valor, archers, and had many
sons and grandsons, 150 *of them.* All
these *were* of the sons of Benjamin.

People of Jerusalem

9 SO all Israel was enrolled by genealogies; and behold, they are written
in the Book of the Kings of Israel. And
[a]Judah was carried away into exile to
Babylon for their unfaithfulness.
2 [a]Now the first who lived in their
possessions in their cities *were* Israel, the
priests, the Levites and [b]the [1]temple
servants.
3 And some of the sons of Judah, of
the sons of Benjamin, and of the sons of
Ephraim and Manasseh lived in [a]Jerusa-
lem:
4 Uthai the son of Ammihud, the son
of Omri, the son of Imri, the son of Bani,
from the sons of Perez the [a]son of Judah.
5 And from the Shilonites *were* Asaiah the first-born and his sons.
6 And from the sons of Zerah *were*
Jeuel and their [1]relatives, 690 *of them.*
7 And from the sons of Benjamin
were Sallu the son of Meshullam, the son
of Hodaviah, the son of Hassenuah,

34 [1]In v. 32, *Shomer*
35 [1]Lit., *son*
1 [1]Lit., *begot,* and so throughout the ch. [a]Gen. 46:21; 1 Chr. 7:6-12 [b]1 Chr. 7:12
3 [1]In Gen. 46:21 and Num. 26:40, *Ard*
8 [1]Lit., *field* [2]Lit., *sent them away*
14 [1]Or, *his brothers*
21 [1]In v. 13, *Shema*
28 [1]Lit., *these*
29 [a]1 Chr. 9:35-38
31 [1]In ch. 9:37, *Zechariah*
32 [1]In ch. 9:38, *Shimeam* [2]Lit., *brothers*
33 [1]1 Sam. 14:49, *Ishvi* [2]In 2 Sam. 2:8, *Ish-bosheth* [a]1 Chr. 9:39-44
34 [1]In 2 Sam. 4:4, *Mephibosheth*
35 [1]In 9:41, *Tahrea*
36 [1]In 9:42, *Jarah*
37 [1]In 9:43, *Rephaiah*
1 [a]1 Chr. 5:25, 26
2 [1]Heb., *Nethinim* [a]Ezra 2:70; Neh. 7:73; 11:3-22 [b]Ezra 2:43, 58; 8:20
3 [a]Neh. 11:1
4 [a]Gen. 46:12; Num. 26:20
6 [1]Lit., *brothers,* and so throughout the ch.

8 and Ibneiah the son of Jeroham, and Elah the son of Uzzi, the son of Michri, and Meshullam the son of Shephatiah, the son of Reuel, the son of Ibnijah;

9 and their relatives according to their generations, [a]956. All these *were* heads of fathers' *households* according to their fathers' houses.

10 [a]And from the priests *were* Jedaiah, Jehoiarib, Jachin,

11 and [1]Azariah the son of Hilkiah, the son of Meshullam, the son of Zadok, the son of Meraioth, the son of Ahitub, [a]the chief officer of the house of God;

12 and Adaiah the son of Jeroham, the son of Pashhur, the son of Malchijah, and Maasai the son of Adiel, the son of Jahzerah, the son of Meshullam, the son of Meshillemith, the son of Immer;

13 and their relatives, heads of their fathers' households, 1,760 very able men for the work of the service of the house of God.

14 [a]And of the Levites *were* Shemaiah the son of Hasshub, the son of Azrikam, the son of Hashabiah, of the sons of Merari;

15 and Bakbakkar, Heresh and Galal and Mattaniah the son of Mica, the son of [1]Zichri, the son of Asaph,

16 and [1]Obadiah the son of [2]Shemaiah, the son of Galal, the son of Jeduthun, and Berechiah the son of Asa, the son of Elkanah, who lived in the villages of the Netophathites.

17 Now the gatekeepers *were* [1]Shallum and Akkub and Talmon and Ahiman and their relatives (Shallum the chief

18 *being stationed* until now at [a]the king's gate to the east). These *were* the gatekeepers for the camp of the sons of Levi.

19 And Shallum the son of Kore, the son of [1]Ebiasaph, the son of Korah, and his relatives, of his father's house, the Korahites, *were* over the work of the service, keepers of the thresholds of the tent; and their fathers had been over the camp of the LORD, keepers of the entrance.

20 And [a]Phinehas the son of Eleazar was ruler over them previously, *and* the LORD was with him.

21 [a]Zechariah the son of Meshelemiah was gatekeeper of the entrance of the tent of meeting.

22 All these who were chosen to be gatekeepers in the thresholds were 212. These were enrolled by genealogy in their villages, [a]whom David and Samuel the seer appointed [b]in their office of trust.

23 So they and their sons [1]had charge of the gates of the house of the LORD, *even* the house of the tent, as guards.

24 The gatekeepers were [1]on the four sides, to the east, west, north, and south.

25 And their relatives in their villages [a]*were* to come in every seven days from time to time *to be* with [1]them;

26 for the four chief gatekeepers who *were* Levites, were in an office of trust, and were over the chambers and over the treasuries in the house of God.

27 And they spent the night around the house of God, [a]because the watch was [1]committed to them; and they *were* [2]in charge of opening *it* morning by morning.

28 Now some of them [1]had charge of the utensils of service, for [2]they counted them when they brought them in and when they took them out.

29 Some of them also were appointed over the furniture and over all the utensils of the sanctuary and [a]over the fine flour and the wine and the oil and the frankincense and the spices.

30 And some of [a]the sons of the priests prepared the mixing of the spices.

31 And Mattithiah, one of the Levites, who was the first-born of Shallum the Korahite, had [a]the [1]responsibility over the things which were baked in pans.

32 And some of their relatives of the sons of the Kohathites [a]*were* over the showbread to prepare it every sabbath.

33 Now these are [a]the singers, heads of fathers' *households* of the Levites, *who lived* in the chambers *of the temple* free *from other service;* for they were [1]engaged [b]in their work day and night.

34 These were heads of fathers' *households* of the Levites according to their generations, chief men, [1]who lived in Jerusalem.

Ancestry and Descendants of Saul

35 [a]And in Gibeon Jeiel the father of Gibeon lived, and his wife's name was Maacah,

36 and his first-born son *was* Abdon, then Zur, Kish, Baal, Ner, Nadab,

37 Gedor, Ahio, Zechariah, and Mikloth.

38 And Mikloth became the father of Shimeam. And they also lived with their relatives in Jerusalem opposite their *other* relatives.

39 [a]And Ner became the father of Kish, and Kish became the father of Saul, and Saul became the father of Jonathan, Malchi-shua, Abinadab, and Eshbaal.

40 And the son of Jonathan *was* Merib-baal; and Merib-baal became the father of Micah.

41 And the sons of Micah *were* Pithon, Melech, Tahrea, [a]*and Ahaz.*

42 And Ahaz became the father of Jarah, and Jarah became the father of Alemeth, Azmaveth, and Zimri; and Zimri became the father of Moza,

43 and Moza became the father of Binea and Rephaiah his son, Eleasah his son, Azel his son.

44 And Azel had six sons whose names are these: Azrikam, Bocheru and Ishmael and Sheariah and Obadiah and Hanan. These were the sons of Azel.

---

9 [a]Neh. 11:8

10 [a]Neh. 11:10-14

11 [1]In Neh. 11:11, *Seraiah* [a]Jer. 20:1

14 [a]Neh. 11:15-19

15 [1]In Neh. 11:17, *Zabdi*

16 [1]In Neh. 11:17, *Abda* [2]In Neh. 11:17, *Shammua*

17 [1]In v. 21, *Meshelemiah;* in 26:14, *Shelemiah;* in Neh. 12:25, *Meshullam*

18 [a]Ezek. 44:1; 46:1, 2

19 [1]In Ex. 6:24, *Abiasaph*

20 [a]Num. 25:7-13

21 [a]1 Chr. 26:2, 14

22 [a]1 Chr. 26:1 [b]2 Chr. 31:15, 18

23 [1]Lit., *were over the gates*

24 [1]Lit., *to the four winds*

25 [1]Lit., *these* [a]2 Kin. 11:5, 7; 2 Chr. 23:8

27 [1]Lit., *on them* [2]Lit., *over the opening* [a]1 Chr. 23:30-32

28 [1]Lit., *were over the* [2]Lit., *by count they brought them in and by count they took them out*

29 [a]1 Chr. 23:29

30 [a]Ex. 30:23-25

31 [1]Lit., *office of trust* [a]1 Chr. 9:22

32 [a]Lev. 24:5-8

33 [1]Lit., *over them in the work* [a]1 Chr. 6:31-47; 25:1 [b]Ps. 134:1

34 [1]Lit., *these*

35 [a]1 Chr. 8:29-32

39 [a]1 Chr. 8:33-38

41 [a]1 Chr. 8:35-37

Defeat and Death of Saul and His Sons

10 [a]NOW the Philistines fought
against Israel; and the men of
Israel fled before the Philistines, and fell
slain on Mount Gilboa.
2 And the Philistines closely pursued
Saul and his sons, and the Philistines
struck down Jonathan, [1a]Abinadab and
Malchi-shua, the sons of Saul.
3 And the battle became heavy
against Saul, and the archers [1]overtook
him; and he was wounded by the archers.
4 Then Saul said to his armor bearer,
"Draw your sword and thrust me
through with it, lest these uncircumcised
come and abuse me." But his armor
bearer would not, for he was greatly
afraid. [a]Therefore Saul took his sword
and fell on it.
5 And when his armor bearer saw
that Saul was dead, he likewise fell on
his sword and died.
6 [a]Thus Saul died with his three sons,
and all *those* of his house died together.
7 When all the men of Israel who
were in the valley saw that they had fled,
and that Saul and his sons were dead,
they forsook their cities and fled; and
the Philistines came and lived in them.
8 And it came about the next day,
when the Philistines came to strip the
slain, that they found Saul and his sons
fallen on Mount Gilboa.
9 [a]So they stripped him and took his
head and his armor and sent *messengers*
around the land of the Philistines, to
carry the good news to their idols and to
the people.
10 And they put his armor in the
house of their gods and fastened his
head in the house of Dagon.

Jabesh-gilead's Tribute to Saul

11 When all Jabesh-gilead heard all
that the Philistines had done to Saul,
12 [a]all the valiant men arose and took
away the body of Saul and the bodies of
his sons, and brought them to Jabesh
and buried their bones under the oak in
Jabesh, and fasted seven days.
13 [a]So Saul died for his trespass which
he committed against the LORD, because
of the word of the LORD which he did
not keep; and also [b]because he asked
counsel of a medium, making inquiry *of*
it,
14 and did not inquire of the LORD.
Therefore He killed him, and [a]turned the
kingdom to David the son of Jesse.

David Made King over All Israel

11 [a]THEN all Israel gathered to David at Hebron [1]and said, "Behold, we are your bone and your flesh.
2 "In times past, even when Saul was
king, you *were* the one who led out and
brought in Israel; and the LORD your
God said to you, '[a]You shall shepherd
My people Israel, and you shall be
prince over My people Israel.' "
3 So all the elders of Israel came to
the king at Hebron, and David made a
covenant with them in Hebron before
the LORD; and [a]they anointed David
king over Israel, [b]according to the word
of the LORD through Samuel.

Jerusalem, Capital City

4 Then David and all Israel went to
Jerusalem ([a]that is, Jebus); and the
Jebusites, the inhabitants of the land,
were there.
5 And the inhabitants of Jebus said
to David, "You shall not enter here."
Nevertheless David captured the stronghold of Zion (that is, the city of David).
6 Now David had said, "Whoever
strikes down a Jebusite first shall be
chief and commander." [a]And Joab the
son of Zeruiah went up first, so he
became chief.
7 Then David dwelt in the stronghold; therefore it was called the city of
David.
8 And he [1]built the city all around,
from the [2]Millo even to the surrounding
area; and Joab [3]repaired the rest of the
city.
9 And [a]David became greater and
greater, for the LORD of hosts *was* with
him.

David's Mighty Men

10 [a]Now these are the heads of the
mighty men whom David had, who gave
him strong support in his kingdom,
together with all Israel, to make him
king, [b]according to the word of the
LORD concerning Israel.
11 And these *constitute* the list of the
mighty men whom David had: [a]Jasho-
beam, the son of a Hachmonite, [b]the
chief of the thirty; he lifted up his spear
against three hundred [1]whom he killed
at one time.
12 And after him was Eleazar the son
of [a]Dodo, the Ahohite, who *was* [1]one of
the three mighty men.
13 He was with David at [1]Pasdammim
[a]when the Philistines were gathered
together there to battle, and there was a
plot of ground full of barley; and the
people fled before the Philistines.
14 And they took their stand in the
midst of the plot, and defended it, and
struck down the Philistines; and the
LORD saved them by a great [1]victory.
15 Now three of the thirty chief men
went down to the rock to David, into the
cave of Adullam, while [a]the army of the
Philistines was camping in the valley of
Rephaim.
16 And David was then in the stronghold, while [a]the garrison of the Philistines *was* then in Bethlehem.
17 And David had a craving and said,
"Oh that someone would give me water
to drink from the well of Bethlehem,
which is by the gate!"
18 So the three broke through the
camp of the Philistines, and drew water
from the well of Bethlehem which *was* by
the gate, and took *it* and brought *it* to

---

1 [a]1 Sam. 31:1-13
2 [1]In 1 Sam. 14:49, *Ishvi* [a]1 Sam. 31:2
3 [1]Lit., *found him*
4 [a]1 Sam. 31:4
6 [a]1 Sam. 31:6
9 [a]1 Sam. 31:9
12 [a]1 Sam. 31:12f.
13 [a]1 Sam. 13:13, 14; 15:23 [b]Lev. 19:31; 20:6; 1 Sam. 28:7
14 [a]1 Sam. 15:28; 1 Chr. 12:23

1 [1]Lit., *saying* [a]2 Sam. 5:1, 3, 6-10
2 [a]2 Sam. 5:2; 7:7
3 [a]2 Sam. 2:4; 5:3, 5 [b]1 Sam. 16:1, 3, 12, 13
4 [a]Josh. 15:8, 63; Judg. 1:21
6 [a]2 Sam. 8:16
8 [1]Or, *fortified* [2]I.e., citadel [3]Lit., *revived*
9 [a]2 Sam. 3:1
10 [a]2 Sam. 23:8-39 [b]1 Chr. 11:3
11 [1]Lit., *slain ones* [a]2 Sam. 23:8 [b]1 Chr. 12:18
12 [1]Lit., *among* [a]1 Chr. 27:4
13 [1]In 1 Sam. 17:1, *Ephesdammim* [a]2 Sam. 23:11, 12
14 [1]Or, *salvation*
15 [a]1 Chr. 14:9
16 [a]1 Sam. 10:5

David; nevertheless David would not
drink it, but poured it out to the LORD;
19 and he said, "Be it far from me
before my God that I should do this.
Shall I drink the blood of these men *who*
went [1]at the risk of their lives? For at the
risk of their lives they brought it."
Therefore he would not drink it. These
things the three mighty men did.
20 As for [1]Abshai the brother of Joab,
he was chief of the [2]thirty, and he swung
his spear against three hundred [3]and
killed them; and he had a name as well
as the [2]thirty.
21 Of the three in the second *rank* he
was the most honored, and became their
commander; however, he did not attain
to the *first* three.
22 [a]Benaiah the son of Jehoiada, the
son of a valiant man of Kabzeel, mighty
in deeds, struck down the [1]two *sons of*
Ariel of Moab. He also went down and
[2]killed a lion inside a pit on a snowy
day.
23 And he [1]killed an Egyptian, a man
of *great* stature five [2]cubits tall. Now in
the Egyptian's hand *was* [a]a spear like a
weaver's beam, but he went down to him
with a club and snatched the spear from
the Egyptian's hand, and [1]killed him
with his own spear.
24 These *things* Benaiah the son of
Jehoiada did, and had a name as well as
the three mighty men.
25 Behold, he was honored among the
thirty, but he did not attain to the three;
and David appointed him over his
guard.
26 Now the mighty men of the armies
were Asahel the brother of Joab, Elhanan the son of Dodo of Bethlehem,
27 [1]Shammoth the Harorite, Helez the
[2]Pelonite,
28 Ira the son of Ikkesh the Tekoite,
Abiezer the Anathothite,
29 [1]Sibbecai the Hushathite, [2]Ilai the
Ahohite,
30 Maharai the Netophathite, [1]Heled
the son of Baanah the Netophathite,
31 Ithai the son of Ribai of Gibeah of
the sons of Benjamin, Benaiah the Pirathonite,
32 [1]Hurai of the brooks of Gaash,
[2]Abiel the Arbathite,
33 Azmaveth the Baharumite, Eliahba
the Shaalbonite,
34 the sons of [1]Hashem the Gizonite,
Jonathan the son of Shagee the Hararite,
35 Ahiam the son of [1]Sacar the Hararite, [2]Eliphal the son of Ur,
36 Hepher the Mecherathite, Ahijah
the Pelonite,
37 Hezro the Carmelite, [1]Naarai the
son of Ezbai,
38 Joel the brother of Nathan, Mibhar
the son of Hagri,
39 Zelek the Ammonite, Naharai the
Berothite, the armor bearer of Joab the
son of Zeruiah,
40 Ira the Ithrite, Gareb the Ithrite,
41 Uriah the Hittite, Zabad the son of
Ahlai,
42 Adina the son of Shiza the Reuben-
ite, a chief of the Reubenites, and thirty
with him,
43 Hanan the son of Maacah and
Joshaphat the Mithnite,
44 Uzzia the Ashterathite, Shama and
Jeiel the sons of Hotham the Aroerite,
45 Jediael the son of Shimri and Joha
his brother, the Tizite,
46 Eliel the Mahavite and Jeribai and
Joshaviah, the sons of Elnaam, and
Ithmah the Moabite,
47 Eliel and Obed and Jaasiel the
Mezobaite.

David's Supporters in Ziklag

12 [a]NOW these are the ones who
came to David at Ziklag, while he
was still restricted because of Saul the
son of Kish; and they were among the
mighty men who helped *him* in war.
2 They were equipped with bows,
[a]using both the right hand and the left *to*
sling stones and *to shoot* arrows from the
bow; [b]*they were* Saul's kinsmen from
Benjamin.
3 The chief was Ahiezer, then Joash,
the sons of Shemaah the Gibeathite; and
Jeziel and Pelet, the sons of Azmaveth,
and Beracah and Jehu the Anathothite,
4 and Ishmaiah the Gibeonite, a
mighty man among the thirty, and over
the thirty. [1]Then Jeremiah, Jahaziel,
Johanan, Jozabad the Gederathite,
5 [1]Eluzai, Jerimoth, Bealiah, Shemariah, Shephatiah the Haruphite,
6 Elkanah, Isshiah, Azarel, Joezer,
Jashobeam, the Korahites,
7 and Joelah and Zebadiah, the sons
of Jeroham of Gedor.
8 And from the Gadites there [1]came
over to David in the stronghold in the
wilderness, mighty men of valor, men
trained for war, who could handle shield
and spear, and whose faces were like the
faces of lions, and [a]*they were* as swift as
the gazelles on the mountains.
9 Ezer *was* the first, Obadiah the
second, Eliab the third,
10 Mishmannah the fourth, Jeremiah
the fifth,
11 Attai the sixth, Eliel the seventh,
12 Johanan the eighth, Elzabad the
ninth,
13 Jeremiah the tenth, Machbannai
the eleventh.
14 These of the sons of Gad were
[1]captains of the army; [a]he who was least
was equal to a hundred and the greatest
to a thousand.
15 [a]These are the ones who crossed
the Jordan in the first month when it was
overflowing all its banks and they put to
flight all those in the valleys, both to the
east and to the west.
16 Then some of the sons of Benjamin
and Judah came to the stronghold to
David.
17 And David went out to meet them,
and answered and said to them, "If you
come peacefully to me to help me, my
heart shall be united with you; but if to
betray me to my adversaries, since there

19 [1]Lit., *with their souls*

20 [1]In 2 Sam. 23:18, *Abishai* [2]So Syriac; M.T., *three* [3]Lit., *slain ones*

22 [1]Or, *two lion-like heroes* of [2]Lit., *smote* [a]2 Sam. 8:18

23 [1]Lit., *smote* [2]I.e., One cubit equals approx. 18 in. [a]1 Sam. 17:7

27 [1]In 2 Sam. 23:25, *Shammah the Harodite* [2]In 2 Sam. 23:26, *Paltite*

29 [1]In 2 Sam. 23:27, *Mebunnai* [2]In 2 Sam. 23:28, *Zalmon*

30 [1]In 2 Sam. 23:29, *Heleb*

32 [1]In 2 Sam. 23:30, *Hiddai* [2]In 2 Sam. 23:31, *Abi-albon*

34 [1]In 2 Sam. 23:32, *Jashen*

35 [1]In 2 Sam. 23:33, *Sharar* [2]In 2 Sam. 23:34, *Eliphelet the son of Ahasbai*

37 [1]In 2 Sam. 23:35, *Paarai the Arbite*

1 [a]1 Sam. 27:2-6

2 [a]Judg. 3:15; 20:16 [b]1 Chr. 12:29

4 [1]In Heb. the beginning of v. 5, making 41 vv. in ch.

5 [1]V. 6 in Heb.

8 [1]Lit., *separated themselves* [a]2 Sam. 2:18

14 [1]Or, *chiefs* [a]Deut. 32:30

15 [a]Josh. 3:15; 4:18

is no [1]wrong in my hands, may the God of our fathers look on *it* and decide."

18 Then [a]the Spirit [1]came upon [b]Amasai, who was the chief of the thirty, *and he said,*

"*We* are yours, O David,
And with you, O son of Jesse!
[c]Peace, peace to you,
And peace to him who helps you;
Indeed, your God helps you!"

Then David received them and made them [2]captains of the band.

19 [a]From Manasseh also some defected to David, when he was about to go to battle with the Philistines against Saul. But they did not help them, for the lords of the Philistines after consultation sent him away, saying, "At *the cost of* our heads he may defect to his master Saul."

20 As he went to Ziklag, there defected to him from Manasseh: Adnah, Jozabad, Jediael, Michael, Jozabad, Elihu, and Zillethai, [1]captains of thousands who belonged to Manasseh.

21 And they helped David against [a]the band of raiders, for they were all mighty men of valor, and were captains in the army.

22 For day by day *men* came to David to help him, until there was a great army [a]like the army of God.

Supporters Gathered at Hebron

23 Now these are the numbers of the [1]divisions equipped for war, [a]who came to David at Hebron, [b]to turn the kingdom of Saul to him, [c]according to the [2]word of the LORD.

24 The sons of Judah who bore shield and spear *were* 6,800, equipped for war.

25 Of the sons of Simeon, mighty men of valor for war, 7,100.

26 Of the sons of Levi 4,600.

27 Now Jehoiada was the leader of *the house of* Aaron, and with him were 3,700,

28 also [a]Zadok, a young man mighty of valor, and of his father's house twenty-two captains.

29 And of the sons of Benjamin, [a]Saul's kinsmen, 3,000; for until now [b]the greatest part of them had kept their allegiance to the house of Saul.

30 And of the sons of Ephraim 20,800, mighty men of valor, famous men in their fathers' households.

31 And of the half-tribe of Manasseh 18,000, who were designated by name to come and make David king.

32 And of the sons of Issachar, [a]men who understood the times, with knowledge of what Israel should do, their chiefs were two hundred; and all their kinsmen were at their command.

33 Of Zebulun, there were 50,000 who went out in the army, who could draw up in battle formation with all kinds of weapons of war and helped *David* [1]with [a]an undivided heart.

34 And of Naphtali *there were* 1,000 captains, and with them 37,000 with shield and spear.

35 And of the Danites who could draw up in battle formation, *there were* 28,600.

36 And of Asher *there were* 40,000 who went out in the army to draw up in battle formation.

37 And from the other side of the Jordan, of the Reubenites and the Gadites and of the half-tribe of Manasseh, *there were* 120,000 with all *kinds* of weapons of war for the battle.

38 All these, being men of war, who could draw up in battle formation, came to Hebron with [a]a perfect heart, to make David king over all Israel; and all the rest also of Israel were of one mind to make David king.

39 And they were there with David three days, eating and drinking; for their kinsmen had prepared for them.

40 Moreover those who were near to them, *even* as far as Issachar and Zebulun and Naphtali, [a]brought food on donkeys, camels, mules, and on oxen, great quantities of flour cakes, fig cakes and bunches of raisins, wine, oil, oxen and sheep. There was joy indeed in Israel.

Peril in Transporting the Ark

13 THEN David consulted with the captains of the thousands and the hundreds, even with every leader.

2 And David said to all the assembly of Israel, "If it seems good to you, and if it is from the LORD our God, let us send everywhere to our kinsmen who remain in all the land of Israel, also to the priests and Levites who are with them in their cities with pasture lands, that they may meet with us;

3 and let us bring back the ark of our God to us, [a]for we did not seek it in the days of Saul."

4 Then all the assembly said that they would do so, for the thing was right in the eyes of all the people.

5 [a]So David assembled all Israel together, from the Shihor of Egypt even to the entrance of Hamath, [b]to bring the ark of God from Kiriath-jearim.

6 [a]And David and all Israel went up to [b]Baalah, *that is,* to Kiriath-jearim, which belongs to Judah, to bring up from there the ark of God, the LORD [c]who is enthroned *above* the cherubim, where His name is called.

7 And they [1]carried the ark of God on a new cart from [a]the house of Abinadab, and Uzza and Ahio drove the cart.

8 And David and all Israel were celebrating before God with all *their* might, [a]even with songs and with lyres, harps, tambourines, cymbals, and with trumpets.

9 When they came to [a]the threshing floor of Chidon, Uzza put out his hand to hold the ark, because the oxen nearly upset *it.*

10 And the anger of the LORD burned against Uzza, so He struck him down [a]because he put out his hand to the ark; [b]and he died there before God.

17 [1]Lit., *violence*
18 [1]Lit., *clothed* [2]Or, *chiefs* [a]Judg. 3:10; 6:34 [b]1 Chr. 2:17 [c]1 Sam. 25:5, 6
19 [a]1 Sam. 29:2-9
20 [1]Or, *chiefs*
21 [a]1 Sam. 30:1
22 [a]Gen. 32:2; Josh. 5:13-15
23 [1]Lit., *heads* [2]Lit., *mouth* [a]2 Sam. 2:3, 4 [b]1 Chr. 10:14 [c]1 Chr. 11:10
28 [a]2 Sam. 8:17; 1 Chr. 6:8, 53
29 [a]1 Chr. 12:2 [b]2 Sam. 2:8, 9
32 [a]Esth. 1:13
33 [1]Lit., *not of double heart* [a]Ps. 12:2
38 [a]2 Sam. 5:1-3; 1 Chr. 12:33
40 [a]1 Sam. 25:18
3 [a]1 Sam. 7:1, 2
5 [a]2 Sam. 6:1; 1 Kin. 8:65; 1 Chr. 15:3 [b]1 Sam. 6:21; 7:1
6 [a]2 Sam. 6:2-11 [b]Josh. 15:9 [c]Ex. 25:22; 2 Kin. 19:15
7 [1]Lit., *caused to ride* [a]1 Sam. 7:1
8 [a]1 Chr. 15:16
9 [a]2 Sam. 6:6
10 [a]1 Chr. 15:13, 15 [b]Lev. 10:2

11 Then David became angry because [1]of the LORD's outburst against Uzza; and he called that place [2]Perez-uzza to this day.

12 And David was afraid of God that day, saying, "How can I bring the ark of God *home* to me?"

13 So David did not take the ark with him to the city of David, but took it aside [a]to the house of Obed-edom the Gittite.

14 Thus the ark of God remained with the family of Obed-edom in his house three months; and [a]the LORD blessed the family of Obed-edom with all that he had.

David's Family Enlarged

14 [a]NOW Hiram king of Tyre sent messengers to David with cedar trees, masons, and carpenters, to build a house for him.

2 And David realized that the LORD had established him as king over Israel, *and* that his kingdom was highly exalted, for the sake of His people Israel.

3 Then David took more wives at Jerusalem, and David [1]became the father of more sons and daughters.

4 [a]And these are the names of the children [1]born *to him* in Jerusalem: Shammua, Shobab, Nathan, Solomon,

5 Ibhar, Elishua, Elpelet,

6 Nogah, Nepheg, Japhia,

7 Elishama, Beeliada and Eliphelet.

Philistines Defeated

8 When the Philistines heard that David had been anointed king over all Israel, all the Philistines went up in search of David; and David heard of it and went out against them.

9 Now the Philistines had come and [a]made a raid in the valley of Rephaim.

10 And David inquired of God, saying, "Shall I go up against the Philistines? And wilt Thou give them into my hand?" Then the LORD said to him, "Go up, for I will give them into your hand."

11 So they came up to Baal-perazim, and David [1]defeated them there; and David said, "God has broken through my enemies by my hand, like the breakthrough of waters." Therefore they named that place [2]Baal-perazim.

12 And they abandoned their gods there; so David gave the order and they were burned with fire.

13 And the Philistines made [a]yet another raid in the valley.

14 And David inquired again of God, and God said to him, "You shall not go up after them; circle around [1]behind them, and come at them in front of the [2]balsam trees.

15 "And it shall be when you hear the sound of marching in the tops of the balsam trees, then you shall go out to battle, for God will have gone out before you to strike the army of the Philistines."

16 And David did just as God had commanded him, and they struck down the army of the Philistines from [1]Gibeon even as far as Gezer.

17 Then the fame of David went out into all the lands; and [a]the LORD brought the fear of him on all the nations.

Plans to Move the Ark to Jerusalem

15 NOW *David* built houses for himself in the city of David; and he prepared a place for the ark of God, and [a]pitched a tent for it.

2 Then David said, "[a]No one is to carry the ark of God but the Levites; for the LORD chose them to carry the ark of God, and to minister to Him forever."

3 And [a]David assembled all Israel at Jerusalem, to bring up the ark of the LORD [b]to its place, which he had prepared for it.

4 And David gathered together the sons of Aaron, and [a]the Levites:

5 of the sons of Kohath, Uriel the chief, and 120 of his [1]relatives;

6 of the sons of Merari, Asaiah the chief, and 220 of his relatives;

7 of the sons of Gershom, Joel the chief, and 130 of his relatives;

8 of the sons of Elizaphan, Shemaiah the chief, and 200 of his relatives;

9 of the sons of Hebron, Eliel the chief, and 80 of his relatives;

10 of the sons of Uzziel, Amminadab the chief, and 112 of his relatives.

11 Then David called for [a]Zadok and [b]Abiathar the priests, and for the Levites, for Uriel, Asaiah, Joel, Shemaiah, Eliel, and Amminadab,

12 and said to them, "You are the heads of the fathers' *households* of the Levites; [a]consecrate yourselves both you and your relatives, that you may bring up the ark of the LORD God of Israel, [b]to *the place* that I have prepared for it.

13 "[a]Because you did not *carry it* at the first, the LORD our God made an outburst on us, for we did not seek Him according to the ordinance."

14 [a]So the priests and the Levites consecrated themselves to bring up the ark of the LORD God of Israel.

15 And the sons of [a]the Levites carried the ark of God on their shoulders, with the poles thereon as Moses had commanded according to the word of the LORD.

16 Then David spoke to the chiefs of the Levites [a]to appoint their relatives the singers, with instruments of music, harps, lyres, loud-sounding cymbals, to raise sounds of joy.

17 So [a]the Levites appointed Heman the son of Joel, and from his relatives, Asaph the son of Berechiah; and from the sons of Merari their relatives, Ethan the son of Kushaiah,

18 and with them their relatives of the second rank, Zechariah, [1]Ben, Jaaziel, Shemiramoth, Jehiel, Unni, Eliab, Benaiah, Maaseiah, Mattithiah, Eliphelehu, Mikneiah, Obed-edom, and Jeiel, the gatekeepers.

---

11 [1]Lit., *the LORD had broken through a breakthrough* [2]I.e., the breakthrough of Uzza

13 [a]1 Chr. 15:25

14 [a]1 Chr. 26:4, 5

1 [a]2 Sam. 5:11

3 [1]Lit., *begot*

4 [1]Lit., *were to* [a]1 Chr. 3:5-8

9 [a]1 Chr. 11:15; 14:13

11 [1]Lit., *smote* [2]I.e., the master of breakthrough

13 [a]1 Chr. 14:9

14 [1]Lit., *from upon* [2]Or, *baka shrubs*

16 [1]In 2 Sam. 5:25, *Geba*

17 [a]Ex. 15:14-16; Deut. 2:25

1 [a]1 Chr. 15:3; 16:1; 17:1-5

2 [a]Num. 4:15; Deut. 10:8

3 [a]1 Kin. 8:1; 1 Chr. 13:5 [b]Ex. 40:20f.; 2 Sam. 6:12, 17; 1 Chr. 15:1, 12

4 [a]1 Chr. 6:16-30; 12:26

5 [1]Lit., *brothers;* i.e., fellow tribesmen, and so throughout the ch.

11 [a]1 Chr. 12:28 [b]1 Sam. 22:20-23; 1 Kin. 2:26, 35

12 [a]Ex. 19:14, 15; 2 Chr. 35:6 [b]1 Chr. 15:1, 3

13 [a]2 Sam. 6:3; 1 Chr. 13:7

14 [a]1 Chr. 15:12

15 [a]Ex. 25:14; Num. 4:5f.

16 [a]1 Chr. 13:8; 25:1

17 [a]1 Chr. 25:1

18 [1]Omitted in Gr. and many mss.

19 So the singers, Heman, Asaph, and
Ethan *were appointed* to sound aloud
cymbals of bronze;
20 and Zechariah, Aziel, Shemiramoth, Jehiel, Unni, Eliab, Maaseiah,
and Benaiah, with [1]harps *tuned* to [a]ala-
moth;
21 and Mattithiah, Eliphelehu, Mikneiah, Obed-edom, Jeiel, and Azaziah, to
lead with [1]lyres tuned to [a]the sheminith.
22 And Chenaniah, chief of the Levites, was *in charge of* the singing; he
gave instruction in singing because he
was skillful.
23 And Berechiah and Elkanah were
gatekeepers for the ark.
24 And Shebaniah, Joshaphat, Nethanel, Amasai, Zechariah, Benaiah, and
Eliezer, the priests, [a]blew the trumpets
before the ark of God. Obed-edom and
Jehiah also *were* gatekeepers for the ark.
25 [a]So *it was* David, with the elders of
Israel and the captains over thousands,
who went to bring up the ark of the
covenant of the LORD from [b]the house of
Obed-edom with joy.
26 And it came about because God
was helping the Levites who were carrying the ark of the covenant of the LORD,
that they sacrificed [a]seven bulls and
seven rams.
27 Now David was clothed with a
robe of fine linen with all the Levites
who were carrying the ark, and the
singers and Chenaniah the leader of the
singing *with* the singers. [a]David also
wore an ephod of linen.
28 Thus all Israel brought up the ark
of the covenant of the LORD with shouting, and with sound of the horn, with
trumpets, with loud-sounding cymbals,
with harps and lyres.
29 And it happened when the ark of
the covenant of the LORD came to the
city of David, that [a]Michal the daughter
of Saul looked out of the window, and
saw King David leaping and making
merry; and she despised him in her
heart.

A Tent for the Ark

16 AND they brought in the ark of
God and [a]placed it inside the tent
which David had pitched for it, and they
offered burnt offerings and peace offerings before God.
2 When David had finished offering
the burnt offering and the peace offerings, he blessed the people in the name
of the LORD.
3 And he distributed to everyone of
Israel, both man and woman, to everyone a loaf of bread and a portion *of meat*
and a raisin cake.
4 And he appointed some of the
Levites *as* ministers before the ark of the
LORD, even to celebrate and to thank
and praise the LORD God of Israel:
5 Asaph the chief, and second to him
Zechariah, *then* [1]Jeiel, Shemiramoth,
Jehiel, Mattithiah, Eliab, Benaiah,
Obed-edom, and Jeiel, with musical
instruments, harps, lyres; also Asaph
played loud-sounding cymbals,
6 and Benaiah and Jahaziel the
priests *blew* trumpets continually before
the ark of the covenant of God.
7 Then on that day David [a]first assigned [1]Asaph and his [2]relatives to give
thanks to the LORD.

Psalm of Thanksgiving

8 [a]Oh give thanks to the LORD, call
upon His name;
[b]Make known His deeds among the
peoples.
9 Sing to Him, sing praises to Him;
[1]Speak of all His [2]wonders.
10 [1]Glory in His holy name;
Let the heart of those who seek the
LORD be glad.
11 [a]Seek the LORD and His strength;
Seek His face continually.
12 [a]Remember His wonderful deeds
which He has done,
[b]His marvels and the judgments
from His mouth,
13 O seed of Israel His servant,
Sons of Jacob, His chosen ones!
14 He is the LORD our God;
[a]His judgments are in all the earth.
15 Remember His covenant forever,
The word which He commanded to
a thousand generations,
16 [a]*The covenant* which He made with
Abraham,
And His oath to Isaac.
17 [a]He also confirmed it to Jacob for a
statute,
To Israel as an everlasting covenant,
18 Saying, "[a]To you I will give the
land of Canaan,
As the portion of your inheritance."
19 [a]When they were only a few in
number,
Very few, and strangers in it,
20 And they wandered about from
nation to nation,
And from *one* kingdom to another
people,
21 He permitted no man to oppress
them,
And [a]He reproved kings for their
sakes, *saying,*
22 "Do not touch My anointed ones,
And [a]do My prophets no harm."
23 [a]Sing to the LORD, all the earth;
Proclaim good tidings of His salvation from day to day.
24 Tell of His glory among the nations,
His wonderful deeds among all the
peoples.
25 For [a]great is the LORD, and greatly
to be praised;
He also is [b]to be feared above all
gods.
26 For all the gods of the peoples are
[1a]idols,
[b]But the LORD made the heavens.
27 Splendor and majesty are before
Him,
Strength and joy are in His place.

20 [1]Or, *harps of maiden-like tone* [a]Ps. 46:title
21 [1]Or, *octave harps* [a]Ps. 6:title
24 [a]1 Chr. 15:28; 16:6
25 [a]2 Sam. 6:12, 15 [b]1 Chr. 13:13
26 [a]Num. 23:1-4, 29
27 [a]2 Sam. 6:14
29 [a]2 Sam. 3:13f.; 6:16
1 [a]1 Chr. 15:1
5 [1]In 1 Chr. 15:18, *Jaaziel*
7 [1]Lit., *by the hand of Asaph* [2]Lit., *brothers* [a]2 Sam. 22:1; 23:1
8 [a]1 Chr. 16:8-36; Ps. 105:1-15 [b]1 Kin. 8:43; 2 Kin. 19:19
9 [1]Or, *Meditate on* [2]I.e., wonderful acts
10 [1]Or, *Boast*
11 [a]Ps. 24:6
12 [a]Ps. 103:2 [b]Ps. 78:43-68
14 [a]Ps. 48:10
16 [a]Gen. 12:7; 17:2; 22:16-18; 26:3
17 [a]Gen. 35:11, 12
18 [a]Gen. 13:15
19 [a]Gen. 34:30; Deut. 7:7
21 [a]Gen. 12:17; 20:3; Ex. 7:15-18
22 [a]Gen. 20:7
23 [a]Ps. 96:1-13
25 [a]Ps. 144:3-6 [b]Ps. 89:7
26 [1]Or, *non-existent things* [a]Lev. 19:4 [b]Ps. 102:25

28 Ascribe to the LORD, O families of
the peoples,
Ascribe to the LORD glory and
strength.
29 Ascribe to the LORD the glory due
His name;
Bring an [1]offering, and come before
Him;
[a]Worship the LORD in [2]holy array.
30 Tremble before Him, all the earth;
Indeed, the world is firmly established, it will not be moved.
31 [a]Let the heavens be glad, and let
the earth rejoice;
And let them say among the nations, "[b]The LORD reigns."
32 [a]Let the sea [1]roar, and [2]all it contains;
Let the field exult, and all that is in
it.
33 Then the trees of the forest will
sing for joy before the LORD;
For He is coming to judge the
earth.
34 [a]O give thanks to the LORD, for *He*
is good;
For His lovingkindness is everlasting.
35 [a]Then say, "Save us, O God of our
salvation,
And gather us and deliver us from
the nations,
To give thanks to Thy holy name,
And [1]glory in Thy praise."
36 [a]Blessed be the LORD, the God of
Israel,
From everlasting even to everlasting.
Then all the people [b]said, "Amen," and
praised the LORD.

Worship before the Ark

37 So he left Asaph and his [1]relatives
there [a]before the ark of the covenant of
the LORD, to minister before the ark
continually, [b]as every day's work required;
38 and [a]Obed-edom with [1]his 68 relatives; Obed-edom, also the son of Jeduthun, and [b]Hosah as gatekeepers.
39 And *he left* [a]Zadok the priest and
his [1]relatives the priests [b]before the
[2]tabernacle of the LORD in the high
place which *was* at Gibeon,
40 to offer burnt offerings to the LORD
on the altar of burnt offering continually
morning and evening, [a]even according to
all that is written in the law of the LORD,
which He commanded Israel.
41 And with them *were* [a]Heman and
Jeduthun, and [b]the rest who were chosen, who were designated by name, to
[c]give thanks to the LORD, because His
lovingkindness is everlasting.
42 And with them *were* Heman and
Jeduthun *with* trumpets and cymbals for
those who should sound aloud, and *with*
instruments *for* [a]the songs of God, and
the sons of Jeduthun for the gate.
43 [a]Then all the people departed each
to his house, and David returned to bless
his household.

God's Covenant with David

17 [a]AND it came about, when David
dwelt in his house, that David
said to Nathan the prophet, "Behold, I
am dwelling in a house of cedar, but the
ark of the covenant of the LORD is under
curtains."
2 Then Nathan said to David, "Do
all that is in your heart, for God is with
you."
3 And it came about the same night,
that the word of God came to Nathan,
saying,
4 "Go and tell David My servant,
'Thus says the LORD, [a]"You shall not
build a house for Me to dwell in;
5 for I have not dwelt in a house
since the day that I brought up Israel to
this day, [a]but I have [1]gone from tent to
tent and from *one* dwelling place *to*
another.
6 "In all places where I have walked
with all Israel, have I spoken a word
[a]with any of the judges of Israel, whom I
commanded to shepherd My people,
saying, 'Why have you not built for Me a
house of cedar?' " '
7 "Now, therefore, thus shall you say
to My servant David, 'Thus says the
LORD of hosts, "I took you from the
pasture, from following the sheep, that
you should be leader over My people
Israel.
8 "And I have been with you wherever
you have gone, and have cut off all your
enemies from before you; and I will
make you a name like the name of the
great ones who are in the earth.
9 "And I will appoint a place for My
people Israel, and will plant them, that
they may dwell in their own place and be
moved no more; neither shall the
[1]wicked waste them anymore as formerly,
10 even from the day that I commanded judges *to be* over My people
Israel. And I will subdue all your enemies. Moreover, I tell you that the
LORD will build a house for you.
11 "And it shall come about when your
days are fulfilled that you must go *to be*
with your fathers, that I will set up *one of*
your [1]descendants after you, who shall
be of your sons; and I will establish his
kingdom.
12 "He shall build for Me a house, and
I will establish his throne forever.
13 "[a]I will be his father, and he shall be
My son; and I will not take My lovingkindness away from him, [b]as I took it
from him who was before you.
14 "But I will settle him in My house
and in My kingdom forever, and his
throne shall be established forever." ' "
15 According to all these words and
according to all this vision, so Nathan
spoke to David.

David's Prayer in Response

16 Then David the king went in and
sat before the LORD and said, "[a]Who am

29 [1]Or, *a grain offering* [2]Or, *the splendor of holiness* [a]Ps. 29:2
31 [a]Is. 44:23; 49:13 [b]Ps. 93:1; 96:10
32 [1]Or, *thunder* [2]Lit., *its fulness* [a]Ps. 98:7
34 [a]2 Chr. 5:13; 7:3; Ezra 3:11; Ps. 106:1; 136:1; Jer. 33:11
35 [1]Lit., *boast* [a]Ps. 106:47, 48
36 [a]1 Kin. 8:15, 56; Ps. 72:18 [b]Deut. 27:15; Neh. 8:6
37 [1]Lit., *brothers* [a]1 Chr. 16:4, 5 [b]2 Chr. 8:14; Ezra 3:4
38 [1]Lit., *their brothers, 68* [a]1 Chr. 13:14 [b]1 Chr. 26:10
39 [1]Lit., *brothers* [2]Lit., *dwelling place* [a]1 Chr. 15:11 [b]1 Kin. 3:4
40 [a]Ex. 29:38-42; Num. 28:3, 4
41 [a]1 Chr. 6:33 [b]1 Chr. 25:1-6 [c]2 Chr. 5:13
42 [a]1 Chr. 25:7; 2 Chr. 7:6; 29:27
43 [a]2 Sam. 6:19
1 [a]2 Sam. 7:1-29
4 [a]1 Chr. 28:2, 3
5 [1]Lit., *been* [a]Ex. 40:2, 3; 2 Sam. 7:6
6 [a]2 Sam. 7:7
9 [1]Lit., *sons of wickedness*
11 [1]Lit., *seed*
13 [a]2 Cor. 6:18; Heb. 1:5 [b]1 Chr. 10:14
16 [a]2 Sam. 7:18

I, O LORD God, and what is my house
that Thou hast brought me this far?
17 "And this was a small thing in Thine
eyes, O God; but Thou hast spoken of
Thy servant's house for a great while to
come, and hast regarded me according
to the standard of a man of high degree,
O LORD God.
18 "What more can David still *say* to
Thee concerning the honor *bestowed* on
Thy servant? For Thou knowest Thy
servant.
19 "O LORD, [a]for Thy servant's sake,
and according to Thine own heart, Thou
hast wrought all this greatness, to make
known all these great things.
20 "O LORD, there is none like Thee,
neither is there any God besides Thee,
according to all that we have heard with
our ears.
21 "And what one nation in the earth is
like Thy people Israel, whom God went
to redeem for Himself *as* a people, to
make Thee a name by great and terrible
things, in driving out nations from before Thy people, whom Thou didst redeem out of Egypt?
22 "[a]For Thy people Israel Thou didst
make Thine own people forever, and
Thou, O LORD, didst become their God.
23 "And now, O LORD, let the word
that Thou hast spoken concerning Thy
servant and concerning his house, be
established forever, and do as Thou hast
spoken.
24 "And let Thy name be established
and magnified forever, saying, 'The
LORD of hosts is the God of Israel, *even*
a God to Israel; and the house of David
Thy servant is established before Thee.'
25 "For Thou, O my God, hast revealed to Thy servant that Thou wilt
build for him a house; therefore Thy
servant hath found *courage* to pray
before Thee.
26 "And now, O LORD, Thou art God,
and hast [1]promised this good thing to
Thy servant.
27 "And now it hath pleased Thee to
bless the house of Thy servant, that it
may [1]continue forever before Thee; for
Thou, O LORD, hast blessed, and it is
blessed forever."

David's Kingdom Strengthened

18 NOW after this [a]it came about
that David [1]defeated the Philistines and subdued them and took Gath
and its towns from the hand of the
Philistines.
2 And he defeated Moab, and the
Moabites became servants to David,
bringing tribute.
3 David also defeated Hadadezer
king of Zobah *as far as* Hamath, as he
went to establish his [1]rule to the Euphrates River.
4 And David took from him 1,000
chariots and 7,000 horsemen and 20,000
foot soldiers, and David hamstrung all
the chariot horses, but reserved *enough*
of them for 100 chariots.
5 When the Arameans of [1]Damascus
came to help Hadadezer king [a]of Zobah,
David [2]killed 22,000 men of the Arameans.
6 Then David put *garrisons* among
the Arameans of [1]Damascus; and the
Arameans became servants to David,
bringing tribute. And the LORD helped
David wherever he went.
7 And David took the shields of gold
which were [1]carried by the servants of
Hadadezer, and brought them to Jerusalem.
8 Also from [1]Tibhath and from Cun,
cities of Hadadezer, David took a very
large amount of bronze, with which
[a]Solomon made the bronze sea and the
pillars and the bronze utensils.
9 Now when [1]Tou king of Hamath
heard that David had [2]defeated all the
army of Hadadezer king of Zobah,
10 he sent [1]Hadoram his son to King
David, to [2]greet him and to bless him,
because he had fought against Hadadezer and had [3]defeated him; for Hadadezer had been at war with Tou. And
Hadoram brought all kinds of articles of
gold and silver and bronze.
11 King David also dedicated these to
the LORD with the silver and the gold
which he had carried away from all the
nations: from Edom, Moab, the sons of
Ammon, the Philistines, and from Amalek.
12 Moreover Abishai the son of
Zeruiah [1]defeated 18,000 Edomites in
the Valley of Salt.
13 Then he put garrisons in Edom,
and all the Edomites became servants to
David. And the LORD helped David
wherever he went.
14 So David reigned over all Israel;
and he [1]administered justice and righteousness for all his people.
15 And [a]Joab the son of Zeruiah *was*
over the army, and Jehoshaphat the son
of Ahilud *was* recorder;
16 and Zadok the son of Ahitub and
Abimelech the son of Abiathar *were*
priests, and Shavsha *was* secretary;
17 and Benaiah the son of Jehoiada
was over the Cherethites and the Pelethites, and the sons of David *were* chiefs
at the king's side.

David's Messengers Abused

19 [a]NOW it came about after this,
that Nahash the king of the sons
of Ammon died, and his son became
king in his place.
2 Then David said, "I will show
kindness to Hanun the son of Nahash,
because his father showed kindness to
me." So David sent messengers to console him concerning his father. And
David's servants came into the land of
the sons of Ammon to Hanun, to console him.
3 But the princes of the sons of
Ammon said to Hanun, "[1]Do you think
that David is honoring your father, in
that he has sent comforters to you? Have
not his servants come to you to search

19 [a]2 Sam. 7:21; Is. 37:35
22 [a]Ex. 19:5, 6
26 [1]Lit., *said*
27 [1]Lit., *be*
1 [1]Lit., *smote*, and so in vv. 1-3 [a]2 Sam. 8:1-18
3 [1]Lit., *hand*
5 [1]Heb., *Darmeseq* [2]Lit., *smote* [a]1 Chr. 19:6
6 [1]Heb., *Darmeseq*
7 [1]Lit., *on*
8 [1]In 2 Sam. 8:8, *Betah* [a]1 Kin. 7:40-47; 2 Chr. 4:11-18
9 [1]In 2 Sam. 8:9, *Toi* [2]Lit., *smitten*
10 [1]In 2 Sam. 8:10, *Joram* [2]Lit., *ask him of his welfare* [3]Lit., *smitten*
12 [1]Lit., *smote*
14 [1]Lit., *was doing*
15 [a]1 Chr. 11:6
1 [a]2 Sam. 10:1-19
3 [1]Lit., *In your eyes is David honoring your father because*

and to overthrow and to spy out the
land?"
4 So Hanun took David's servants
and shaved them, and cut off their
garments in the middle as far as their
hips, and sent them away.
5 Then *certain persons* went and told
David about the men. And he sent to
meet them, for the men were greatly
humiliated. And the king said, "[1]Stay at
Jericho until your beards grow, and *then*
return."
6 When the sons of Ammon saw that
they had made themselves odious to
David, Hanun and the sons of Ammon
sent 1,000 talents of silver to hire for
themselves chariots and horsemen from
Mesopotamia, from Aram-maacah, and
[a]from Zobah.
7 So they hired for themselves 32,000
chariots, and the king of Maacah and his
people, who came and camped before
[a]Medeba. And the sons of Ammon gathered together from their cities and came
to battle.
8 When David heard *of it,* he sent
Joab and all the army, the mighty men.
9 And the sons of Ammon came out
and drew up in battle array at the
entrance of the city, and the kings who
had come were by themselves in the
field.

Ammon and Aram Defeated

10 Now when Joab saw that the [1]bat-
tle was set against him in front and in
the rear, he selected from all the choice
men of Israel and they arrayed themselves against the Arameans.
11 But the remainder of the people he
placed in the hand of [1]Abshai his
brother; and they arrayed themselves
against the sons of Ammon.
12 And he said, "If the Arameans are
too strong for me, then you shall help
me; but if the sons of Ammon are too
strong for you, then I will help you.
13 "Be strong, and let us show ourselves courageous for the sake of our
people and for the cities of our God; and
may the LORD do what is good in His
sight."
14 So Joab and the people who were
with him drew near to the battle against
the Arameans, and they fled before him.
15 When the sons of Ammon saw that
the Arameans fled, they also fled before
Abshai his brother, and entered the city.
Then Joab came to Jerusalem.
16 When the Arameans saw that they
had been [1]defeated by Israel, they sent
messengers, and brought out the Arameans who were beyond the [2]River, with
Shophach the commander of the army of
Hadadezer [3]leading them.
17 When it was told David, he gathered all Israel together and crossed the
Jordan, and came upon them and drew
up in formation against them. And when
David drew up in battle array against
the Arameans, they fought against him.

5 [1]Lit., *Return to*

6 [a]1 Chr. 18:5, 9

7 [a]Num. 21:30; Josh. 13:9, 16

10 [1]Lit., *the face of the battle*

11 [1]In 2 Sam. 10:10, *Abishai*

16 [1]Lit., *smitten before* [2]I.e., Euphrates [3]Lit., *before*

19 [1]Lit., *smitten before*

1 [1]Lit., *at the return of the year* [a]2 Sam. 11:1 [b]2 Sam. 12:26

2 [1]In Zeph. 1:5, *Malcam* [a]2 Sam. 12:30, 31

3 [a]2 Sam. 12:31

4 [1]Lit., *stood up* [2]In 2 Sam. 21:18, *Gob* [3]Lit., *smote* [4]Heb., *Raphah,* and so in vv. 6, 8 [a]2 Sam. 21:18-22

5 [1]Lit., *smote* [a]2 Sam. 21:19 [b]1 Sam. 17:7; 1 Chr. 11:23

7 [1]Lit., *smote*

1 [a]2 Sam. 24:1-25

2 [a]1 Chr. 27:23, 24

3 [a]Deut. 1:11

18 And the Arameans fled before Israel, and David killed of the Arameans
7,000 charioteers and 40,000 foot soldiers, and put to death Shophach the
commander of the army.
19 So when the servants of Hadadezer
saw that they were [1]defeated by Israel,
they made peace with David and served
him. Thus the Arameans were not willing to help the sons of Ammon anymore.

War with Philistine Giants

20 [a]THEN it happened [1]in the
spring, at the time when kings go
out *to battle,* that Joab led out the army
and ravaged the land of the sons of
Ammon, and came and besieged Rabbah. But David stayed at Jerusalem.
And [b]Joab struck Rabbah and overthrew it.
2 [a]And David took the crown of
[1]their king from his head, and he found
it to weigh a talent of gold, and there
was a precious stone in it; and it was
placed on David's head. And he brought
out the spoil of the city, a very great
amount.
3 And he brought out the people who
were in it, [a]and cut *them* with saws and
with sharp instruments and with axes.
And thus David did to all the cities of
the sons of Ammon. Then David and all
the people returned *to* Jerusalem.
4 [a]Now it came about after this, that
war [1]broke out at [2]Gezer with the Philistines; then Sibbecai the Hushathite
[3]killed Sippai, one of the descendants of
the [4]giants, and they were subdued.
5 And there was war with the Philistines again, and Elhanan the son of [a]Jair
[1]killed Lahmi the brother of Goliath the
Gittite, the [b]shaft of whose spear *was*
like a weaver's beam.
6 And again there was war at Gath,
where there was a man of *great* stature
who had twenty-four fingers and toes,
six *fingers on each hand* and six *toes on
each foot;* and he also was descended
from the giants.
7 And when he taunted Israel, Jonathan the son of Shimea, David's brother,
[1]killed him.
8 These were descended from the
giants in Gath, and they fell by the hand
of David and by the hand of his servants.

Census Brings Pestilence

21 [a]THEN Satan stood up against
Israel and moved David to number Israel.
2 So David said to Joab and to the
princes of the people, "[a]Go, number
Israel from Beersheba even to Dan, and
bring me *word* that I may know their
number."
3 And Joab said, "[a]May the LORD
add to His people a hundred times as
many as they are! But, my lord the king,
are they not all my lord's servants? Why
does my lord seek this thing? Why
should he be a cause of guilt to Israel?"

4 Nevertheless, the king's word prevailed against Joab. Therefore, Joab departed and went throughout all Israel, and came to Jerusalem.

5 And Joab gave the number of the [1]census of *all* the people to David. And [a]all Israel were 1,100,000 men who drew the sword; and Judah *was* 470,000 men who drew the sword.

6 [a]But he did not [1]number Levi and Benjamin among them, for the king's [2]command was abhorrent to Joab.

7 And [1]God was displeased with this thing, so He struck Israel.

8 And David said to God, "I have sinned greatly, in that I have done this thing. [a]But now, please take away the iniquity of Thy servant, for I have done very foolishly."

9 And the LORD spoke to [a]Gad, David's [b]seer, saying,

10 "Go and speak to David, saying, 'Thus says the LORD, "I [1]offer you three things; choose for yourself one of them, that I may do *it* to you." ' "

11 So Gad came to David and said to him, "Thus says the LORD, 'Take for yourself

12 [a]either three years of famine, or three months to be swept away before your foes, while the sword of your enemies overtakes *you,* or else three days of the sword of the LORD, even pestilence in the land, and the angel of the LORD destroying throughout all the territory of Israel.' Now, therefore, consider what answer I shall return to Him who sent me."

13 And David said to Gad, "I am in great distress; please let me fall into the hand of the LORD, [a]for His mercies are very great. But do not let me fall into the hand of man."

14 [a]So the LORD [1]sent a pestilence on Israel; 70,000 men of Israel fell.

15 And God sent an angel to Jerusalem to destroy it; but as he was about to destroy *it,* the LORD saw and [a]was sorry over the calamity, and said to the destroying angel, "It is enough; now relax your hand." And the angel of the LORD was standing by the threshing floor of [1]Ornan the Jebusite.

16 Then David lifted up his eyes and saw the angel of the LORD standing between earth and heaven, with his drawn sword in his hand stretched out over Jerusalem. Then David and the elders, [a]covered with sackcloth, fell on their faces.

17 And David said to God, "Is it not I who [1]commanded to count the people? Indeed, I am the one who has sinned and done very wickedly, [a]but these sheep, what have they done? O LORD my God, please let Thy hand be against me and my father's household, but not against Thy people that they should be plagued."

David's Altar

18 [a]Then the angel of the LORD [1]commanded Gad to say to David, that David should go up and build an altar to the LORD on the threshing floor of Ornan the Jebusite.

19 So David went up at the word of Gad, which he spoke in the name of the LORD.

20 Now Ornan turned back and saw the angel, and his four sons *who were* with him hid themselves. And Ornan was threshing wheat.

21 And as David came to Ornan, Ornan looked and saw David, and went out from the threshing floor, and prostrated himself [1]before David with his face to the ground.

22 Then David said to Ornan, "Give me the [1]site of *this* threshing floor, that I may build on it an altar to the LORD; for the full price you shall give it to me, that the plague may be restrained from the people."

23 And Ornan said to David, "Take *it* for yourself; and let my lord the king do what is good in his sight. See, I will give the oxen for burnt offerings and the threshing sledges for wood and the wheat for the grain offering; I will give *it* all."

24 But King David said to Ornan, "No, but I will surely buy *it* for the full price; for I will not take what is yours for the LORD, or offer a burnt offering [1]which costs me nothing."

25 So [a]David gave Ornan 600 shekels of gold by weight for the [1]site.

26 Then David built an altar to the LORD there, and offered burnt offerings and peace offerings. And he called to the LORD and [a]He answered him with fire from heaven on the altar of burnt offering.

27 And the LORD commanded the angel, and he put his sword back in its sheath.

28 At that time, when David saw that the LORD had answered him on the threshing floor of Ornan the Jebusite, he offered sacrifice there.

29 [a]For the tabernacle of the LORD, which Moses had made in the wilderness, and the altar of burnt offering *were* in the high place at Gibeon at that time.

30 But David could not go before it to inquire of God, for he was terrified by the sword of the angel of the LORD.

David Prepares for Temple Building

22 THEN David said, "[a]This is the house of the LORD God, and this is the altar of burnt offering for Israel."

2 So David [1]gave orders to gather [a]the foreigners who were in the land of Israel, and [b]he set stonecutters to hew out stones to build the house of God.

3 And David [a]prepared large quantities of iron [1]to make the nails for the doors of the gates and for the clamps, and more [b]bronze than could be weighed;

4 and timbers of cedar logs beyond number, for [a]the Sidonians and Tyrians brought large quantities of cedar timber to David.

---

5 [1]Lit., *muster* [a]2 Sam. 24:9
6 [1]Lit., *muster* [2]Lit., *word* [a]1 Chr. 27:24
7 [1]Lit., *it was evil in the sight of God*
8 [a]2 Sam. 12:13
9 [a]2 Sam. 24:11; 1 Chr. 29:29 [b]1 Sam. 9:9
10 [1]Lit., *stretch out to*
12 [a]2 Sam. 24:13
13 [a]Ps. 51:1; 130:4, 7
14 [1]Lit., *gave* [a]1 Chr. 27:24
15 [1]In 2 Sam. 24:16, *Araunah* [a]Ex. 32:14; 1 Sam. 15:11; Jon. 3:10
16 [a]1 Kin. 21:27
17 [1]Lit., *said* [a]2 Sam. 7:8; Ps. 74:1
18 [1]Lit., *said to* [a]2 Chr. 3:1
21 [1]Lit., *to*
22 [1]Lit., *place*
24 [1]Lit., *gratuitously*
25 [1]Lit., *place* [a]2 Sam. 24:24
26 [a]Lev. 9:24; Judg. 6:21
29 [a]1 Kin. 3:4; 1 Chr. 16:39
1 [a]1 Chr. 21:18-28; 2 Chr. 3:1
2 [1]Lit., *said to* [a]1 Kin. 9:20, 21; 2 Chr. 2:17 [b]1 Kin. 5:17, 18
3 [1]Lit., *for* [a]1 Chr. 29:2, 7 [b]1 Chr. 22:14
4 [a]1 Kin. 5:6-10

5 And David said, "My son [a]Solomon is young and inexperienced, and the house that is to be built for the LORD shall be exceedingly magnificent, famous and glorious throughout all lands. *Therefore* now I will make preparation for it." So David made ample preparations before his death.

Solomon Charged with the Task

6 Then [a]he called for his son Solomon, and charged him to build a house for the LORD God of Israel.

7 And David said to Solomon, "[a]My son, [1]I had intended to build a house to the name of the LORD my God.

8 "But the word of the LORD came to me, saying, '[a]You have shed much blood, and have [1]waged great wars; you shall not build a house to My name, because you have shed *so* much blood on the earth before Me.

9 'Behold, a son shall be born to you, who shall be a man of rest; and [a]I will give him rest from all his enemies on every side; for [b]his name shall be [1]Solomon, and I will give peace and quiet to Israel in his days.

10 '[a]He shall build a house for My name, and he shall be My son, and I will be his father; and I will establish the throne of his kingdom over Israel forever.'

11 "Now, my son, [a]the LORD be with you that you may be successful, and build the house of the LORD your God just as He has spoken concerning you.

12 "[a]Only the LORD give you discretion and understanding, and give you charge over Israel, so that you may [b]keep the law of the LORD your God.

13 "[a]Then you shall prosper, if you are careful to observe the statutes and the ordinances which the LORD commanded Moses concerning Israel. [b]Be strong and courageous, do not fear nor be dismayed.

14 "Now behold, [1]with great pains I have prepared for the house of the LORD [a]100,000 talents of gold and 1,000,000 talents of silver, and [b]bronze and iron beyond weight, for [2]they are in great quantity; also timber and stone I have prepared, and you may add to them.

15 "Moreover, there are many workmen with you, stonecutters and masons of stone and carpenters, and all men who are skillful in every kind of work.

16 "Of the gold, the silver and the bronze and the iron, there is no limit. Arise and work, and may [a]the LORD be with you."

17 [a]David also commanded all the leaders of Israel to help his son Solomon, *saying,*

18 "Is not the LORD your God with you? And [a]has He not given you rest on every side? For He has given the inhabitants of the land into my hand, and the land is subdued before the LORD and before His people.

19 "Now [a]set your heart and your soul to seek the LORD your God; arise, therefore, and build the sanctuary of the LORD God, [b]so that you may bring the ark of the covenant of the LORD, and the holy vessels of God into the house that is to be built [c]for the name of the LORD."

Solomon Reigns

23 [a]NOW when David [1]reached old age, [b]he made his son Solomon king over Israel.

2 And he gathered together all the leaders of Israel with the priests and the Levites.

Offices of the Levites

3 And [a]the Levites were numbered from thirty years old and upward, and [b]their number by [1]census of men was 38,000.

4 Of these, 24,000 were [a]to oversee the work of the house of the LORD; and 6,000 *were* [b]officers and judges,

5 and 4,000 *were* gatekeepers, and [a]4,000 *were* praising the LORD with the instruments which [1]David made for giving praise.

6 And David divided them into divisions [a]according to the sons of Levi: Gershon, Kohath, and Merari.

Gershonites

7 Of the Gershonites *were* [1]Ladan and Shimei.

8 The sons of Ladan *were* Jehiel the first and Zetham and Joel, three.

9 The sons of Shimei *were* Shelomoth and Haziel and Haran, three. These were the heads of the fathers' *households* of Ladan.

10 And the sons of Shimei *were* Jahath, [1]Zina, Jeush, and Beriah. These four *were* the sons of Shimei.

11 And Jahath was the first, and Zizah the second; but Jeush and Beriah did not have many sons, so they became a father's household, one [1]class.

Kohathites

12 The sons of Kohath were four: Amram, Izhar, Hebron and Uzziel.

13 [a]The sons of Amram were Aaron and Moses. And [b]Aaron was set apart to sanctify him as most holy, he and his sons forever, [c]to burn incense before the LORD, to minister to Him and to bless in His name forever.

14 But *as for* [a]Moses the man of God, his sons were named among the tribe of Levi.

15 The sons of Moses *were* Gershom and Eliezer.

16 The [1]son of Gershom *was* [2]Shebuel the chief.

17 And the [1]son of Eliezer was Rehabiah the chief; and Eliezer had no other sons, but the sons of Rehabiah were very many.

18 The [1]son of Izhar was [2]Shelomith the chief.

19 The sons of Hebron *were* Jeriah the first, Amariah the second, Jahaziel the third and Jekameam the fourth.

---

5 [a]1 Kin. 3:7; 1 Chr. 29:1
6 [a]1 Kin. 2:1
7 [1]Lit., *as for me, it was in my heart* [a]2 Sam. 7:2, 3; 1 Chr. 17:1
8 [1]Lit., *made* [a]1 Chr. 28:3
9 [1]I.e., peaceful [a]1 Kin. 4:20, 25 [b]2 Sam. 12:24, 25
10 [a]2 Sam. 7:13, 14; 1 Chr. 17:12
11 [a]1 Chr. 22:16
12 [a]1 Kin. 3:9-12; 2 Chr. 1:10 [b]1 Kin. 2:3
13 [a]1 Chr. 28:7 [b]Josh. 1:6-9
14 [1]Lit., *in my affliction* [2]Lit., *it is* [a]1 Chr. 29:4 [b]1 Chr. 22:3
16 [a]1 Chr. 22:11
17 [a]1 Chr. 28:1-6
18 [a]1 Chr. 22:9; 23:25
19 [a]1 Chr. 28:9 [b]1 Kin. 8:6, 21; 2 Chr. 5:7 [c]1 Chr. 22:7

1 [1]Lit., *became old and sated with days* [a]1 Chr. 29:28 [b]1 Kin. 1:1-40; 2:12; 1 Chr. 28:5; 29:22
3 [1]Lit., *their heads* [a]Num. 4:3-49 [b]Num. 4:48; 1 Chr. 23:24
4 [a]Ezra 3:8, 9 [b]1 Chr. 26:29
5 [1]Lit., *I made* [a]1 Chr. 15:16
6 [a]1 Chr. 6:1
7 [1]In Ex. 6:17, *Libni*
10 [1]In v. 11, *Zizah*
11 [1]Lit., *mustering*
13 [a]Ex. 6:20 [b]Ex. 28:1 [c]Ex. 30:6-10
14 [a]Deut. 33:1; Ps. 90:title
16 [1]Lit., *sons* [2]In ch. 24:20, *Shubael*
17 [1]Lit., *sons . . . were*
18 [1]Lit., *sons* [2]In ch. 24:22, *Shelomoth*

20 The sons of Uzziel *were* Micah the
first and Isshiah the second.

Merarites

21 The sons of Merari were Mahli and
Mushi. The sons of Mahli *were* Eleazar
and Kish.
22 And Eleazar died and had no sons,
but daughters only, so their brothers, the
sons of Kish, took them *as wives.*
23 The sons of Mushi *were* three:
Mahli, Eder, and Jeremoth.

Duties Revised

24 [a]These were the sons of Levi according to their fathers' households, *even*
the heads of the fathers' *households* of
those of them who were [1]counted, in the
number of names by their [2]census, doing
the work for the service of the house of
the LORD, [b]from twenty years old and
upward.
25 For David said, "The LORD God of
Israel [a]has given rest to His people, and
He dwells in Jerusalem forever.
26 "And also, [a]the Levites will no
longer need to carry the tabernacle and
all its utensils for its service."
27 For by the last words of David the
sons of Levi *were* numbered, from
twenty years old and upward.
28 For their office is [1]to assist the sons
of Aaron with the service of the house of
the LORD, in the courts and in the
chambers and in the purifying of all holy
things, even the work of the service of
the house of God,
29 [a]and with the showbread, and [b]the
fine flour for a grain offering, and unleavened wafers, or [c]*what is baked in* the
pan, or [d]what is well-mixed, and [e]all
measures of volume and size.
30 And they are to stand every morning to thank and to praise the LORD, and
likewise at evening,
31 and to offer all burnt offerings to
the LORD, [a]on the sabbaths, the new
moons and [b]the fixed festivals in the
number *set* by the ordinance concerning
them, continually before the LORD.
32 Thus [a]they are to keep charge of
the tent of meeting, and charge of the
holy place, and [b]charge of the sons of
Aaron their [1]relatives, for the service of
the house of the LORD.

Divisions of Levites

24 NOW the divisions of the [1]de-
scendants of Aaron *were these:*
[a]the sons of Aaron *were* Nadab, Abihu,
Eleazar, and Ithamar.
2 [a]But Nadab and Abihu died before
their father and had no [1]sons. So Eleazar
and Ithamar served as priests.
3 And David, with [a]Zadok of the
sons of Eleazar and Ahimelech of the
sons of Ithamar, divided them according
to their offices [1]for their ministry.
4 Since more chief men were found
from the [1]descendants of Eleazar than
the [1]descendants of Ithamar, they divided them thus: *there were* sixteen
heads of fathers' households of the
[1]descendants of Eleazar, and eight of the
[1]descendants of Ithamar according to
their fathers' households.
5 [a]Thus they were divided by lot, the
one as the other; for they were officers of
the sanctuary and officers of God, both
from the [1]descendants of Eleazar and
the [1]descendants of Ithamar.
6 And Shemaiah, the son of Nethanel the scribe, from the Levites,
recorded them in the presence of the
king, the princes, Zadok the priest,
[a]Ahimelech the son of Abiathar, and the
heads of the fathers' *households* of the
priests and of the Levites; one father's
household taken for Eleazar and one
taken for Ithamar.
7 Now the first lot came out for
Jehoiarib, the second for Jedaiah,
8 the third for Harim, the fourth for
Seorim,
9 the fifth for Malchijah, the sixth for
Mijamin,
10 the seventh for Hakkoz, the eighth
for [a]Abijah,
11 the ninth for Jeshua, the tenth for
Shecaniah,
12 the eleventh for Eliashib, the
twelfth for Jakim,
13 the thirteenth for Huppah, the
fourteenth for Jeshebeab,
14 the fifteenth for Bilgah, the sixteenth for Immer,
15 the seventeenth for Hezir, the eighteenth for Happizzez,
16 the nineteenth for Pethahiah, the
twentieth for Jehezkel,
17 the twenty-first for Jachin, the
twenty-second for Gamul,
18 the twenty-third for Delaiah, the
twenty-fourth for Maaziah.
19 [a]These were their offices for their
ministry, when *they* came in to the house
of the LORD according to the ordinance
given to them through Aaron their father, just as the LORD God of Israel had
commanded him.
20 Now for the rest of the sons of
Levi: of the sons of Amram, [1]Shubael;
of the sons of Shubael, Jehdeiah.
21 Of Rehabiah: of the sons of Rehabiah, Isshiah the first.
22 Of the Izharites, [1]Shelomoth; of
the sons of Shelomoth, Jahath.
23 And the sons [a]*of Hebron:* Jeriah *the
first,* Amariah the second, Jahaziel the
third, Jekameam the fourth.
24 *Of* the sons of Uzziel, Micah; of the
sons of Micah, Shamir.
25 The brother of Micah, Isshiah; of
the sons of Isshiah, Zechariah.
26 The sons of Merari, Mahli and
Mushi; the sons of Jaaziah, Beno.
27 The sons of Merari: by Jaaziah
were Beno, Shoham, Zaccur, and Ibri.
28 By Mahli: Eleazar, who had no
sons.
29 By Kish: the sons of Kish, Jerahmeel.
30 And the sons of Mushi: Mahli,
Eder, and Jerimoth. These *were* the sons
of the Levites according to their fathers'
households.

24 [1]Lit., *mustered* [2]Lit., *heads* [a]Num. 10:17, 21 [b]1 Chr. 23:3
25 [a]1 Chr. 22:18
26 [a]Num. 4:5, 15; 7:9; Deut. 10:8
28 [1]Lit., *at the hand of*
29 [a]Lev. 24:5-9 [b]Lev. 6:20 [c]1 Chr. 9:31 [d]Lev. 6:21 [e]Lev. 19:35, 36
31 [a]Is. 1:13, 14 [b]Lev. 23:2-4
32 [1]Lit., *brothers* [a]Num. 1:53; 1 Chr. 9:27 [b]Num. 3:6-9, 38
1 [1]Lit., *sons* [a]Ex. 6:23
2 [1]Or, *children* [a]Lev. 10:2
3 [1]Lit., *in their service* [a]1 Chr. 6:8
4 [1]Lit., *sons*
5 [1]Lit., *sons* [a]1 Chr. 24:31
6 [a]1 Chr. 18:16
10 [a]Neh. 12:4; Luke 1:5
19 [a]1 Chr. 9:25
20 [1]In 23:16, *Shebuel*
22 [1]In 23:18, *Shelomith*
23 [a]1 Chr. 23:19

31 [a]These also cast lots just as their
[1]relatives the sons of Aaron in the presence of David the king, [b]Zadok, Ahimelech, and the heads of the fathers' *households* of the priests and of the Levites—
the head of fathers' *households* as well as
those of his younger brother.

Number and Services of Musicians

25 MOREOVER, David and the
commanders of the army set
apart for the service *some* of the sons of
[a]Asaph and of Heman and of Jeduthun,
who *were* to [b]prophesy with lyres,
[c]harps, and cymbals; and the number of
[1]those who performed their service was:
2 Of the sons of Asaph: Zaccur,
Joseph, Nethaniah, and [1]Asharelah; the
sons of Asaph *were* under the [2]direction
of Asaph, who prophesied under the
[2]direction of the king.
3 [a]Of Jeduthun, the sons of Jeduthun: Gedaliah, [1]Zeri, Jeshaiah, [2]Shimei,
Hashabiah, and Mattithiah, six, under
the [3]direction of their father Jeduthun
with the harp, who prophesied in giving
thanks and praising the LORD.
4 Of Heman, the sons of Heman:
Bukkiah, Mattaniah, [1]Uzziel, [2]Shebuel
and Jerimoth, Hananiah, Hanani, Eliathah, Giddalti and Romamti-ezer, Josh-
bekashah, Mallothi, Hothir, Mahazioth.
5 All these *were* the sons of Heman
[a]the king's seer to [1]exalt him according
to the words of God, for God gave
fourteen sons and three daughters to
Heman.
6 All these were under the [1]direction
of their father to sing in the house of the
LORD, [a]with cymbals, harps and lyres,
for the service of the house of God.
[b]Asaph, Jeduthun and Heman *were* under the [1]direction of the king.
7 And their number who were
trained in singing to the LORD, with
their [1]relatives, all who were skillful, *was*
[a]288.

Divisions of Musicians

8 And [a]they cast lots for their duties,
all alike, the small as well as the great,
the teacher *as well* as the pupil.
9 Now the first lot came out for
Asaph to Joseph, the second for Gedaliah, he with his relatives and sons *were*
twelve;
10 the third to Zaccur, his sons and
his relatives, twelve;
11 the fourth to [1]Izri, his sons and his
relatives, twelve;
12 the fifth to Nethaniah, his sons and
his relatives, twelve;
13 the sixth to Bukkiah, his sons and
his relatives, twelve;
14 the seventh to [1]Jesharelah, his sons
and his relatives, twelve;
15 the eighth to Jeshaiah, his sons and
his relatives, twelve;
16 the ninth to Mattaniah, his sons
and his relatives, twelve;
17 the tenth to Shimei, his sons and
his relatives, twelve;
18 the eleventh to Azarel, his sons and
his relatives, twelve;
19 the twelfth to Hashabiah, his sons
and his relatives, twelve;
20 for the thirteenth, Shubael, his sons
and his relatives, twelve;
21 for the fourteenth, Mattithiah, his
sons and his relatives, twelve;
22 for the fifteenth to Jeremoth, his
sons and his relatives, twelve;
23 for the sixteenth to Hananiah, his
sons and his relatives, twelve;
24 for the seventeenth to Joshbeka-
shah, his sons and his relatives, twelve;
25 for the eighteenth to Hanani, his
sons and his relatives, twelve;
26 for the nineteenth to Mallothi, his
sons and his relatives, twelve;
27 for the twentieth to Eliathah, his
sons and his relatives, twelve;
28 for the twenty-first to Hothir, his
sons and his relatives, twelve;
29 for the twenty-second to Giddalti,
his sons and his relatives, twelve;
30 for the twenty-third to Mahazioth,
his sons and his relatives, twelve;
31 for the twenty-fourth to Romamti-
ezer, his sons and his relatives, twelve.

Divisions of the Gatekeepers

26 FOR the divisions of the gatekeepers *there were* of the Korahites, [1]Meshelemiah the son of Kore, of
the sons of [2]Asaph.
2 And Meshelemiah had sons:
Zechariah the first-born, Jediael the
second, Zebadiah the third, Jathniel the
fourth,
3 Elam the fifth, Johanan the sixth,
Eliehoenai the seventh.
4 And [a]Obed-edom had sons:
Shemaiah the first-born, Jehozabad the
second, Joah the third, Sacar the fourth,
Nethanel the fifth,
5 Ammiel the sixth, Issachar the
seventh, *and* Peullethai the eighth; God
had indeed blessed him.
6 Also to his son Shemaiah sons were
born who ruled over the house of their
father, for they were mighty men of
valor.
7 The sons of Shemaiah *were* Othni,
Rephael, Obed, and Elzabad, whose
brothers, Elihu and Semachiah, were
valiant men.
8 All these *were* of the sons of Obed-
edom; they and their sons and their
[1]relatives *were* able men with strength
for the service, 62 from Obed-edom.
9 And Meshelemiah had sons and
relatives, 18 valiant men.
10 Also [a]Hosah, *one* of the sons of
Merari had sons: Shimri the first (although he was not the first-born, his
father made him first),
11 Hilkiah the second, Tebaliah the
third, Zechariah the fourth; all the sons
and relatives of Hosah *were* 13.
12 To these divisions of the gatekeepers, the chief men, *were given* duties like
their relatives to minister in the house of
the LORD.

31 [1]Lit., *brothers* [a]1 Chr. 24:5, 6 [b]1 Chr. 24:6

1 [1]Lit., *workmen according to their service* [a]1 Chr. 6:33, 39 [b]2 Kin. 3:15 [c]1 Chr. 15:16

2 [1]In v. 14, *Jesharelah* [2]Lit., *hand*(s)

3 [1]In v. 11, *Izri* [2]So with mss. and ancient versions, cf. v. 17 [3]Lit., *hands* [a]1 Chr. 16:41, 42

4 [1]In v. 18, *Azarel* [2]In v. 20, *Shubael*

5 [1]Lit., *lift up the horn* [a]2 Sam. 24:11; 1 Chr. 21:9

6 [1]Lit., *hands* [a]1 Chr. 15:16 [b]1 Chr. 15:19

7 [1]Lit., *brothers*, and so throughout the ch. [a]1 Chr. 23:5

8 [a]1 Chr. 26:13

11 [1]In v. 3, *Zeri*

14 [1]In v. 2, *Asherelah*

1 [1]In v. 14, *Shelemiah* [2]In 9:19, *Ebiasaph*

4 [a]2 Sam. 6:11; 1 Chr. 13:14

8 [1]Lit., *brothers*, and so throughout the ch.

10 [a]1 Chr. 16:38

13 [a]And they cast lots, the small and
the great alike, according to their fathers' households, for every gate.
14 And the lot to the east fell to
[1]Shelemiah. Then they cast lots *for* his
son Zechariah, a counselor with insight,
and his lot came out to the north.
15 For Obed-edom *it fell* to the south,
and to his sons went the storehouse.
16 For Shuppim and Hosah *it was* to
the west, by the gate of Shallecheth, on
the ascending highway. Guard corre-
sponded to guard.
17 On the east there were six Levites,
on the north four daily, on the south
four daily, and at the storehouse two by
two.
18 At the [1a]Parbar on the west *there
were* four at the highway and two at the
Parbar.
19 These were the divisions of the
gatekeepers of the sons of Korah and of
the sons of Merari.

Keepers of the Treasure

20 [1]And the Levites, their relatives,
[2]had [a]charge of the treasures of the
house of God, and of the treasures of the
dedicated gifts.
21 The sons of Ladan, the sons of the
Gershonites belonging to Ladan, *namely,*
the Jehielites, *were* the heads of the
fathers' *households,* belonging to Ladan
the Gershonite.
22 The sons of Jehieli, Zetham and
Joel his brother, [1]had charge of the
treasures of the house of the LORD.
23 As for the Amramites, the Izharites, the Hebronites, and the Uzzielites,
24 Shebuel the son of Gershom, the
son of Moses, was officer over the treasures.
25 And his relatives by Eliezer *were*
Rehabiah his son, Jeshaiah his son,
Joram his son, Zichri his son, and Shelomoth his son.
26 This Shelomoth and his relatives
[1]had charge of all the treasures of the
dedicated gifts, [a]which King David and
the heads of the fathers' *households,* the
commanders of thousands and hundreds, and commanders of the army, had
dedicated.
27 They dedicated [1]part of the spoil
won in battles to repair the house of the
LORD.
28 And all that Samuel the seer had
dedicated and Saul the son of Kish,
Abner the son of Ner and Joab the son
of Zeruiah, everyone who had dedicated
anything, all of this was [1]in the care of
[2]Shelomoth and his relatives.

Outside Duties

29 As for the Izharites, Chenaniah
and his sons [a]were *assigned* to outside
duties for Israel, as [b]officers and judges.
30 As for the Hebronites, [a]Hashabiah
and his relatives, 1,700 capable men, had
charge of the affairs of Israel [1]west of the
Jordan, for all the work of the LORD and
the service of the king.
31 As for the Hebronites, [a]Jerijah the
chief [1](these Hebronites were investigated according to their genealogies and
fathers' *households,* in the fortieth year of
David's reign, and men of outstanding
capability were found among them at
[b]Jazer of Gilead)
32 and his relatives, capable men, *were*
2,700 in number, heads of fathers' *households.* And King David made them overseers of the Reubenites, the Gadites and
the half-tribe of the Manassites [a]con-
cerning [1]all the affairs of God and of the
king.

Commanders of the Army

27 NOW *this is* the enumeration of
the sons of Israel, the heads
of fathers' *households,* the commanders
of thousands and of hundreds, and their
officers who served the king in all the
affairs of the divisions which came in
and went out month by month throughout all the months of the year, each
division *numbering* 24,000.
2 Jashobeam the son of Zabdiel
[1a]had charge of the first division for the
first month; and in his division *were*
24,000.
3 *He was* from the sons of Perez, *and
was* chief of all the commanders of the
army for the first month.
4 Dodai the Ahohite and his division
had charge of the division for the second
month, Mikloth *being* the chief officer;
and in his division *were* 24,000.
5 The third commander of the army
for the third month *was* Benaiah, the son
of Jehoiada the priest, *as* chief; and in
his division *were* 24,000.
6 This Benaiah *was* the mighty man
of the thirty, and had charge of thirty;
and over his division was Ammizabad
his son.
7 The fourth for the fourth month
was Asahel the brother of Joab, and
Zebadiah his son after him; and in his
division *were* 24,000.
8 The fifth for the fifth month *was*
the commander Shamhuth the Izrahite;
and in his division *were* 24,000.
9 The sixth for the sixth month *was*
Ira the son of Ikkesh the Tekoite; and in
his division *were* 24,000.
10 The seventh for the seventh month
was Helez the Pelonite of the sons of
Ephraim; and in his division *were*
24,000.
11 The eighth for the eighth month
was Sibbecai the Hushathite of the Zerahites; and in his division *were* 24,000.
12 The ninth for the ninth month *was*
Abiezer the Anathothite of the Benjamites; and in his division *were* 24,000.
13 The tenth for the tenth month *was*
Maharai the Netophathite of the Zerahites; and in his division *were* 24,000.
14 The eleventh for the eleventh
month *was* Benaiah the Pirathonite of
the sons of Ephraim; and in his division
were 24,000.

13 [a]1 Chr. 24:5, 31; 25:8

14 [1]In 9:17, *Shallum*

18 [1]Possibly *court* or *colonnade* [a]2 Kin. 23:11

20 [1]So Gr.; Heb., *As for the Levites, Ahijah had* [2]Lit., *were over* [a]1 Chr. 26:22, 24, 26; 28:12; Ezra 2:69

22 [1]Lit., *were over*

26 [1]Lit., *were over* [a]2 Sam. 8:11

27 [1]Heb., *from the battles and from the spoil*

28 [1]Lit., *under the hand* [2]Heb., *Shelomith*

29 [a]Neh. 11:16 [b]1 Chr. 23:4

30 [1]Lit., *beyond the Jordan westward* [a]1 Chr. 27:17

31 [1]Heb., *according to the Hebronites . . . father's households* [a]1 Chr. 23:19 [b]1 Chr. 6:81

32 [1]Lit., *every matter of God and matter of the king.* [a]2 Chr. 19:11

2 [1]Lit., *was over,* and so throughout the ch. [a]2 Sam. 23:8-30; 1 Chr. 11:11-31

15 The twelfth for the twelfth month *was* Heldai the Netophathite of Othniel; and in his division *were* 24,000.

Chief Officers of the Tribes

16 Now in charge of the tribes of Israel: chief officer for the Reubenites was Eliezer the son of Zichri; for the Simeonites, Shephatiah the son of Maacah;

17 for Levi, Hashabiah the son of Kemuel; for Aaron, Zadok;

18 for Judah, Elihu, *one* of David's brothers; for Issachar, Omri the son of Michael;

19 for Zebulun, Ishmaiah the son of Obadiah; for Naphtali, Jeremoth the son of Azriel;

20 for the sons of Ephraim, Hoshea the son of Azaziah; for the half-tribe of Manasseh, Joel the son of Pedaiah;

21 for the half-tribe of Manasseh in Gilead, Iddo the son of Zechariah; for Benjamin, Jaasiel the son of Abner;

22 for Dan, Azarel the son of Jeroham. [a]These *were* the princes of the tribes of Israel.

23 But David did not [1]count those twenty years of age and under, [a]because the LORD had said He would multiply Israel [b]as the stars of heaven.

24 Joab the son of Zeruiah had begun to count *them,* but did not finish; and because of [a]this, wrath came upon Israel, and the number was not included in the account of the chronicles of King David.

Various Overseers

25 Now Azmaveth the son of Adiel had charge of the king's storehouses. And Jonathan the son of Uzziah had charge of the storehouses in the country, in the cities, in the villages, and in the towers.

26 And Ezri the son of Chelub had charge of the [1]agricultural workers who tilled the soil.

27 And Shimei the Ramathite had charge of the vineyards; and Zabdi the Shiphmite had charge of the [1]produce of the vineyards *stored* in the wine cellars.

28 And Baal-hanan the Gederite had charge of the olive and [a]sycamore trees in the [1]Shephelah; and Joash had charge of the stores of oil.

29 And Shitrai the Sharonite had charge of the cattle which were grazing in [a]Sharon; and Shaphat the son of Adlai had charge of the cattle in the valleys.

30 And Obil the Ishmaelite had charge of the camels; and Jehdeiah the Meronothite had charge of the donkeys.

31 And Jaziz the [a]Hagrite had charge of the flocks. All these were [1]overseers of the property which belonged to King David.

Counselors

32 Also Jonathan, David's uncle, *was* a counselor, a man of understanding, and a scribe; and Jehiel the son of Hachmoni [1]tutored the king's sons.

33 And [a]Ahithophel was counselor to the king; and [b]Hushai the Archite was the king's friend.

34 And Jehoiada the son of [a]Benaiah, and [b]Abiathar [1]succeeded Ahithophel; and Joab was the [c]commander of the king's army.

David's Address about the Temple

28 NOW [a]David assembled at Jerusalem all the officials of Israel, the princes of the tribes, and the commanders of the divisions that served the king, and the commanders of thousands, and the commanders of hundreds, and the overseers of all the property and livestock belonging to the king and his sons, with the officials and [b]the mighty men, even all the valiant men.

2 Then King David rose to his feet and said, "Listen to me, my brethren and my people; I [a]*had* [1]intended to build a [2]permanent home for the ark of the covenant of the LORD and for [b]the footstool of our God. So I had made preparations to build *it.*

3 "But God said to me, '[a]You shall not build a house for My name because you are a man of war and have shed blood.'

4 "Yet, the LORD, the God of Israel, [a]chose me from all the house of my father to be king over Israel [b]forever. For [c]He has chosen Judah to be a leader; and [d]in the house of Judah, my father's house, and among the sons of my father He took pleasure in me to make *me* king over all Israel.

5 "And [a]of all my sons (for the LORD has given me many sons), [b]He has chosen my son Solomon to sit on the throne of the kingdom of the LORD over Israel.

6 "And He said to me, 'Your son [a]Solomon is the one who shall build My house and My courts; for I have chosen him to be a son to Me, and I will be a father to him.

7 'And I will establish his kingdom forever, [a]if he resolutely performs My commandments and My ordinances, as [1]is done now.'

8 "So now, in the sight of all Israel, the assembly of the LORD, and in the hearing of our God, observe and seek after all the commandments of the LORD your God in order that you may possess the good land and bequeath *it* to your sons after you forever.

9 "As for you, my son Solomon, know the God of your father, and [a]serve Him with [1]a whole heart and a willing [2]mind; [b]for the LORD searches all hearts, and understands every intent of the thoughts. [c]If you seek Him, He will let you find Him; but if you forsake Him, He will reject you forever.

10 "Consider now, for the LORD has chosen you to build a house for the sanctuary; [a]be courageous and act."

22 [a]1 Chr. 28:1

23 [1]Lit., *take their number from* [a]1 Chr. 21:2-5 [b]Gen. 15:5; 22:17; 26:4

24 [a]2 Sam. 24:12-15; 1 Chr. 21:1-7

26 [1]Lit., *doers of the work of the field for the tilling of . . .*

27 [1]Lit., *what was in the vineyards of the storehouses of wine*

28 [1]Or, *lowlands* [a]1 Kin. 10:27; 2 Chr. 1:15

29 [a]1 Chr. 5:16

31 [1]Or, *rulers* [a]1 Chr. 5:10

32 [1]Lit., *was with*

33 [a]2 Sam. 15:12 [b]2 Sam. 15:32, 37

34 [1]Lit., *after* [a]1 Chr. 27:5 [b]1 Kin. 1:7 [c]1 Chr. 11:6

1 [a]1 Chr. 23:2; 27:1-31 [b]1 Chr. 11:10-47

2 [1]Lit., *in my heart* [2]Lit., *house of rest* [a]1 Chr. 17:1, 2 [b]Ps. 132:7; Is. 66:1

3 [a]1 Chr. 22:8

4 [a]1 Sam. 16:6-13 [b]1 Chr. 17:23, 27 [c]Gen. 49:8-10; 1 Chr. 5:2 [d]1 Sam. 16:1

5 [a]1 Chr. 3:1-9; 14:3-7 [b]1 Chr. 22:9, 10

6 [a]2 Sam. 7:13, 14

7 [1]Lit., *at this day* [a]1 Chr. 22:13

9 [1]Or, *the same* [2]Lit., *soul* [a]1 Kin. 8:61; 1 Chr. 29:17-19 [b]1 Sam. 16:7 [c]2 Chr. 15:2; Jer. 29:13

10 [a]1 Chr. 22:13

11 Then David gave to his son Solomon [a]the plan of [b]the porch *of the temple,* its buildings, its storehouses, its upper rooms, its inner rooms, and [c]the room for the mercy seat;

12 and the plan of all that he had in [1]mind, for the courts of the house of the LORD, and for all the surrounding rooms, for [a]the storehouses of the house of God, and for the storehouses of the dedicated things;

13 also for [a]the divisions of the priests and [b]the Levites and for all the work of the service of the house of the LORD and for all the utensils of service in the house of the LORD;

14 for the golden *utensils,* the weight of gold for all utensils for every kind of service; for the silver utensils, the weight *of silver* for all utensils for every kind of service;

15 and the weight *of gold* for the [a]golden lampstands and their golden lamps, with the weight of each lampstand and its lamps; and *the weight of silver* for the silver lampstands, with the weight of each lampstand and its lamps according to the use of each lampstand;

16 and the gold by weight for the tables of showbread, for each table; and silver for the silver tables;

17 and the forks, the basins, and the pitchers of pure gold; and for the golden bowls with the weight for each bowl; and for the silver bowls with the weight for each bowl;

18 and for [a]the altar of incense refined gold by weight; and gold for the model of the chariot, *even* [b]the cherubim, that spread out *their wings,* and covered the ark of the covenant of the LORD.

19 "All *this,*" *said David,* "the LORD made me understand in writing by His hand upon me, [a]all the [1]details of this pattern."

20 Then David said to his son Solomon, "[a]Be strong and courageous, and act; do not fear nor be dismayed, for the LORD God, my God, is with you. [b]He will not fail you nor forsake you until all the work for the service of the house of the LORD is finished.

21 "Now behold, [a]*there are* the divisions of the priests and the Levites for all the service of the house of God, and [b]every willing man of any skill will be with you in all the work for all kinds of service. The officials also and all the people will be entirely at your command."

Offerings for the Temple

29 THEN King David said to the entire assembly, "My son Solomon, whom alone God has chosen, [a]is still young and inexperienced and the work is great; for [b]the [1]temple is not for man, but for the LORD God.

2 "Now [a]with all my ability I have provided for the house of my God the gold for the *things of* gold, and the silver for the *things of* silver, and the bronze for the *things of* bronze, the iron for the *things of* iron, and wood for the *things of* wood, onyx stones and inlaid *stones,* stones of antimony, and stones of various colors, and all kinds of precious stones, and alabaster in abundance.

3 "And moreover, in my delight in the house of my God, the treasure I have of gold and silver, I give to the house of my God, over and above all that I have already provided for the holy [1]temple,

4 *namely,* [a]3,000 talents of gold, of [b]the gold of Ophir, and 7,000 talents of refined silver, to overlay the walls of the [1]buildings;

5 of gold for the *things of* gold, and of silver for the *things of* silver, that is, for all the work [1]done by the craftsmen. Who then is willing [2]to consecrate himself this day to the LORD?"

6 Then [a]the rulers of the fathers' *households,* and the princes of the tribes of Israel, and the commanders of thousands and of hundreds, with [b]the overseers over the king's work, offered willingly;

7 and for the service for the house of God they gave 5,000 talents and 10,000 [a]darics of gold, and 10,000 talents of silver, and 18,000 talents of brass, and 100,000 talents of iron.

8 And [1]whoever possessed *precious* stones gave them to the treasury of the house of the LORD, [2]in care of [a]Jehiel the Gershonite.

9 Then the people rejoiced because they had offered so willingly, for they made their offering to the LORD [a]with a whole heart, and King David also rejoiced greatly.

David's Prayer

10 So David blessed the LORD in the sight of all the assembly; and David said, "Blessed art Thou, O LORD God of Israel our father, forever and ever.

11 "[a]Thine, O LORD, is the greatness and the power and the glory and the victory and the majesty, indeed everything that is in the heavens and the earth; Thine is the dominion, O LORD, and Thou dost exalt Thyself as head over all.

12 "[a]Both riches and honor *come* from Thee, and Thou dost rule over all, and [b]in Thy hand is power and might; and it lies in Thy hand to make great, and to strengthen everyone.

13 "Now therefore, our God, we thank Thee, and praise Thy glorious name.

14 "But who am I and who are my people that we should [1]be able to offer as generously as this? For all things come from Thee, and from Thy hand we have given Thee.

15 "For [a]we are sojourners before Thee, and tenants, as all our fathers were; [b]our days on the earth are like a shadow, and there is no hope.

16 "O LORD our God, all this abundance that we have provided to build

---

11 [a]Ex. 25:40; 1 Chr. 28:12, 19 [b]1 Kin. 6:3 [c]Ex. 25:17-22
12 [1]Lit., *the spirit with him* [a]1 Chr. 26:20, 28
13 [a]1 Chr. 24:1 [b]1 Chr. 23:6
15 [a]Ex. 25:31-39
18 [a]Ex. 30:1-10 [b]Ex. 25:18-22
19 [1]Lit., *works* [a]1 Chr. 28:11, 12
20 [a]1 Chr. 22:13 [b]Josh. 1:5; Heb. 13:5
21 [a]1 Chr. 28:13 [b]Ex. 35:25-35; 36:1, 2

1 [1]Lit., *palace* [a]1 Chr. 22:5 [b]1 Chr. 29:19
2 [a]1 Chr. 22:3-5
3 [1]Lit., *house*
4 [1]Lit., *houses* [a]1 Chr. 22:14 [b]1 Kin. 9:28
5 [1]Lit., *by the hand of the craftsmen* [2]Lit., *to fill his hand*
6 [a]1 Chr. 27:1; 28:1 [b]1 Chr. 27:25-31
7 [a]Ezra 2:69; Neh. 7:70
8 [1]Lit., *those with whom were found* [2]Lit., *under the hand of* [a]1 Chr. 23:8
9 [a]1 Kin. 8:61; 2 Cor. 9:7
11 [a]Matt. 6:13; Rev. 5:13
12 [a]2 Chr. 1:12 [b]2 Chr. 20:6
14 [1]Lit., *retain strength*
15 [a]Lev. 25:23 [b]Job 14:2, 10-12

Thee a house for Thy holy name, it is
from Thy hand, and all is Thine.
17 "Since I know, O my God, that
[a]Thou triest the heart and [b]delightest in
uprightness, I, in the integrity of my
heart, have willingly offered all these
things; so now with joy I have seen Thy
people, who are present here, make *their*
offerings willingly to Thee.
18 "O LORD, the God of Abraham,
Isaac, and Israel, our fathers, preserve
this forever in the [1]intentions of the
heart of Thy people, and direct their
heart to Thee;
19 "and [a]give to my son Solomon a
perfect heart to keep Thy commandments, Thy testimonies, and Thy statutes, and to do *them* all, and [b]to build
the [1]temple, for which I have made
provision."
20 Then David said to all the assembly, "Now bless the LORD your God."
And [a]all the assembly blessed the LORD,
the God of their fathers, and [b]bowed low
and did homage to the LORD and to the
king.

Sacrifices

21 And on the next day [a]they [1]made
sacrifices to the LORD and offered burnt
offerings to the LORD, 1,000 bulls, 1,000
rams *and* 1,000 lambs, with their libations and sacrifices in abundance for all
Israel.
22 So they ate and drank that day
before the LORD with great gladness.

Solomon Again Made King

And they made Solomon the son of
David king [a]a second time, and they
[b]anointed *him* as ruler for the LORD and
Zadok as priest.
23 Then [a]Solomon sat on the throne
of the LORD as king instead of David his
father; and he prospered, and all Israel
obeyed him.
24 And all the officials, the mighty
men, and also all the sons of King David
[1]pledged allegiance to King Solomon.
25 And [a]the LORD highly exalted
Solomon in the sight of all Israel, and
[b]bestowed on him royal majesty which
had not been on any king before him in
Israel.
26 Now [a]David the son of Jesse
reigned over all Israel.
27 [a]And the period which he reigned
over Israel *was* forty years; he reigned in
Hebron seven years and [1]in Jerusalem
thirty-three *years.*

Death of David

28 Then he died in [a]a [1]ripe old age,
[b]full of days, riches and honor; and his
son Solomon reigned in his place.
29 Now the acts of King David, from
first to last, are written in the chronicles
of [a]Samuel the seer, in the chronicles of
[b]Nathan the prophet, and in the chronicles of [c]Gad the seer,
30 with all his reign, his power, and
the circumstances which came on him,
on Israel, and on all the kingdoms of the
lands.

17 [a]1 Chr. 28:9 [b]Ps. 15:2

18 [1]Lit., *intent of the thoughts of the heart*

19 [1]Lit., *palace* [a]1 Chr. 28:9; Ps. 72:1 [b]1 Chr. 29:1, 2

20 [a]Josh. 22:33 [b]Ex. 4:31

21 [1]Lit., *sacrificed* [a]1 Kin. 8:62, 63

22 [a]1 Chr. 23:1 [b]1 Kin. 1:33-39

23 [a]1 Kin. 2:12

24 [1]Lit., *put a hand under Solomon*

25 [a]2 Chr. 1:1 [b]1 Kin. 3:13; 2 Chr. 1:12

26 [a]1 Chr. 18:14

27 [1]Lit., *he reigned in* [a]2 Sam. 5:4, 5; 1 Kin. 2:11; 1 Chr. 3:4

28 [1]Lit., *good* [a]Gen. 15:15; Acts 13:36 [b]1 Chr. 23:1

29 [a]1 Sam. 9:9 [b]2 Sam. 7:2-4; 12:1-7 [c]1 Sam. 22:5

THE SECOND BOOK OF THE
CHRONICLES

Solomon Worships at Gibeon

1 NOW [a]Solomon the son of David
established himself securely over his
kingdom, and the LORD his God *was*
with him and [b]exalted him greatly.
2 And Solomon spoke to all Israel,
[a]to the commanders of thousands and of
hundreds and to the judges and to every
leader in all Israel, the heads of the
fathers' *households.*
3 Then Solomon, and all the assembly with him, went to [a]the high place
which was at Gibeon; [b]for God's tent of
meeting was there, which Moses the
servant of the LORD had made in the
wilderness.
4 However, David had brought up
[a]the ark of God from Kiriath-jearim [1]to
[b]the place he had prepared for it; for he
had pitched a tent for it in Jerusalem.
5 Now [a]the bronze altar, which Bezalel the son of Uri, the son of Hur, had
made, [1]was there before the tabernacle
of the LORD, and Solomon and the
assembly sought it out.
6 And Solomon went up there before
the LORD to the bronze altar which *was*
at the tent of meeting, and [a]offered a
thousand burnt offerings on it.
7 [a]In that night God appeared to
Solomon and said to him, "Ask what I
shall give you."

Solomon's Prayer for Wisdom

8 And Solomon said to God, "Thou
hast dealt with my father David with
great lovingkindness, and [a]hast made me
king in his place.
9 "Now, O LORD God, [a]Thy [1]promise
to my father David is fulfilled; for Thou
hast made me king over [b]a people as
numerous as the dust of the earth.
10 "[a]Give me now wisdom and knowledge, [b]that I may go out and come in
before this people; for who can rule this
great people of Thine?"
11 [a]And God said to Solomon, "Because [1]you had this in mind, and did not
ask for riches, wealth, or honor, or the
life of those who hate you, nor have you
even asked for long life, but you have
asked for yourself wisdom and knowledge, that you may rule My people, over
whom I have made you king,
12 wisdom and knowledge have been
granted to you. And [a]I will give you
riches and wealth and honor, [1]such as
none of the kings who were before you
has possessed, nor those who will [2]come
after you."
13 [a]So Solomon went [1]from the high
place which was at Gibeon, from the
tent of meeting, to Jerusalem, and he
reigned over Israel.

Solomon's Wealth

14 [a]And Solomon amassed chariots
and horsemen. [b]He had 1,400 chariots,
and 12,000 horsemen, and he stationed
them in [c]the chariot cities and with the
king at Jerusalem.
15 And [a]the king made [b]silver and
gold as plentiful in Jerusalem as stones,
and he made cedars as plentiful as
sycamores in the [1]lowland.
16 And Solomon's [a]horses were imported from Egypt and from Kue; the
king's traders procured them from Kue
for a price.
17 And they [1]imported chariots from
Egypt for 600 *shekels* of silver apiece,
and horses for 150 apiece, and [2]by the
same means they [3]exported them to all
the kings of the Hittites and the kings of
Aram.

Solomon Will Build a Temple and Palace

2 [1a]NOW Solomon [2]decided to build a
house for the name of the LORD,
and a [3]royal palace for himself.
2 [1]So [a]Solomon [2]assigned 70,000
men to carry loads, and 80,000 men to
quarry *stone* in the mountains, and 3,600
to supervise them.
3 [a]Then Solomon sent *word* to [1]Hu-
ram the king of Tyre, saying, "[b]As you
dealt with David my father, and sent
him cedars to build him a house to dwell
in, so do for me.
4 "Behold, I am about to build a
house for the name of the LORD my
God, dedicating it to Him, [a]to burn
fragrant incense before Him, and *to set*
out [b]the showbread continually, and to
offer [c]burnt offerings morning and evening, [d]on sabbaths and on new moons
and on the appointed feasts of the LORD
our God, this *being required* forever in
Israel.
5 "And the house which I am about to
build *will be* great; for [a]greater is our
God than all the gods.
6 "But [a]who is able to build a house
for Him, for the heavens and the highest
heavens cannot contain Him? So who
am I, that I should build a house for
Him, except to [1]burn *incense* before
Him?
7 "And now [a]send me a skilled man to
work in gold, silver, brass and iron, and
in purple, crimson and violet *fabrics,* and
who knows how to make engravings, to
work with the skilled men [1b]whom I have
in Judah and Jerusalem, whom David
my father provided.
8 "[a]Send me also cedar, cypress and
algum timber from Lebanon, for I know
that your servants know how to cut
timber of Lebanon; and indeed, [b]my
servants *will work* with your servants,
9 to prepare timber in abundance for
me, for the house which I am about to
build *will be* great and wonderful.
10 "Now behold, [a]I will give to your
servants, the woodsmen who cut the
timber, 20,000 [1]kors of crushed wheat,
and 20,000 [1]kors of barley, and 20,000
baths of wine, and 20,000 baths of oil."

1 [a]1 Kin. 2:12, 46 [b]1 Chr. 29:25
2 [a]1 Chr. 28:1
3 [a]1 Kin. 3:4 [b]Ex. 36:8
4 [1]Lit., *where David had prepared for it* [a]1 Chr. 15:25-28 [b]2 Chr. 6:2
5 [1]Lit., *he put* [a]Ex. 31:9; 38:1-7
6 [a]1 Kin. 3:4
7 [a]1 Kin. 3:5-14
8 [a]1 Chr. 28:5
9 [1]Lit., *word* [a]2 Sam. 7:12-16 [b]Gen. 13:16; 22:17; 28:14
10 [a]1 Kin. 3:9 [b]Num. 27:17; 2 Sam. 5:2
11 [1]Lit., *this was in your heart* [a]1 Kin. 3:11
12 [1]Lit., *which was not so to the kings who were before you* [2]Lit., *be* [a]1 Chr. 29:25; 2 Chr. 9:22
13 [1]Lit., *to* [a]2 Chr. 1:3
14 [a]1 Kin. 10:26-29 [b]1 Kin. 4:26 [c]1 Kin. 9:19
15 [1]Heb., *shephelah* [a]1 Kin. 10:27 [b]Deut. 17:17
16 [a]Deut. 17:16
17 [1]Lit., *brought up and brought out* [2]Lit., *and in like manner by their hand* [3]Lit., *brought out*

1 [1]Ch. 1:18 in Heb. [2]Lit., *said* [3]Lit., *house for his royalty* [a]1 Kin. 5:5
2 [1]Ch. 2:1 in Heb. [2]Lit., *numbered* [a]1 Kin. 5:15, 16; 2 Chr. 2:18
3 [1]In 1 Kin. 5:18, *Hiram* [a]1 Kin. 5:2-11 [b]1 Chr. 14:1
4 [a]Ex. 30:7 [b]Ex. 25:30 [c]Ex. 29:38-42 [d]Num. 28:9, 10
5 [a]Ex. 15:11; 1 Chr. 16:25
6 [1]Lit., *offer up in smoke* [a]1 Kin. 8:27; 2 Chr. 6:18
7 [1]Lit., *who are with me* [a]Ex. 31:3-5; 2 Chr. 2:13, 14 [b]1 Chr. 22:15
8 [a]1 Kin. 5:6 [b]2 Chr. 9:10, 11
10 [1]I.e., A kor equals approx. 10 bu. [a]1 Kin. 5:11

Huram to Assist

11 Then Huram, king of Tyre, [1]an-
swered in a letter sent to Solomon:
"[a]Because the LORD loves His people,
He has made you king over them."
12 Then Huram [1]continued, "Blessed
be [a]the LORD, the God of Israel, who has
made heaven and earth, who has given
King David a wise son, [2]endowed with
discretion and understanding, [b]who will
build a house for the LORD and a [3]royal
palace for himself.
13 "And now I am sending a skilled
man, [1]endowed with understanding,
Huram-abi,
14 [a]the son of a [1]Danite woman and
[2]a Tyrian father, who knows how to
work in gold, silver, bronze, iron, stone
and wood, *and* in purple, violet, linen
and crimson fabrics, and *who knows how*
to make all kinds of engravings and to
[3]execute any design which may be assigned to him, *to work* with your skilled
men, and with [4]those of my lord David
your father.
15 "Now then, let my lord send to his
servants wheat and barley, oil and wine,
of [a]which he has spoken.
16 "And [a]we will cut whatever timber
you need from Lebanon, and bring it to
you on rafts by sea to Joppa, so that you
may carry it up to Jerusalem."
17 And Solomon numbered all the
aliens who *were* in the land of Israel,
[a]following the [1]census which his father
David had [2]taken; and 153,600 were
found.
18 [a]And he appointed 70,000 of them
to carry loads, and 80,000 to quarry
stones in the mountains, and 3,600 supervisors to make the people work.

The Temple Construction in Jerusalem

3 [a]THEN Solomon began to build the
house of the LORD in Jerusalem on
Mount Moriah, where *the LORD* had
appeared to his father David, at the
place that David had prepared, [b]on the
threshing floor of [1]Ornan the Jebusite.
2 And he began to build on the
second *day* in the second month [1]of the
fourth year of his reign.

Dimensions and Materials of the Temple

3 Now these are the [1]foundations
which [a]Solomon laid for building the
house of God. The length in [2]cubits,
according to the old standard *was* sixty
cubits, and the width twenty cubits.
4 And the porch which was in front
of the house [a]was as long as the width of
the house, twenty cubits, and the height
120; and inside he overlaid it with pure
gold.
5 And he overlaid [a]the [1]main room
with cypress wood and overlaid it with
fine gold, and [2]ornamented it with palm
trees and chains.
6 Further, he [1]adorned the house
with precious stones; and the gold was
gold from [2]Parvaim.
7 [a]He also overlaid the house with
gold—the beams, the thresholds, and its
walls, and its doors; and he [b]carved
cherubim on the walls.
8 Now he made [a]the [1]room of the
holy of holies: its length, across the
width of the house, *was* twenty cubits,
and its width *was* twenty cubits; and he
overlaid it with fine gold, *amounting* to
600 talents.
9 And the weight of the nails was
fifty shekels of gold. He also overlaid
[a]the upper rooms with gold.
10 [a]Then he made two [1]sculptured
cherubim in the room of the holy of
holies and overlaid them with gold.
11 And the wingspan of the cherubim
was twenty cubits; the wing of one, of
five cubits, touched the wall of the
house, and *its* other wing, of five cubits,
touched the wing of the other cherub.
12 And the wing of the other cherub,
of five cubits, touched the wall of the
house; and *its* other wing of five cubits,
was attached to the wing of the [1]first
cherub.
13 The wings of these cherubim extended twenty cubits, and they stood on
their feet [1]facing the *main* room.
14 [a]And he made the veil of violet,
purple, crimson and fine linen, and he
worked cherubim on it.
15 [a]He also made two pillars for the
front of the house, thirty-five cubits
[1]high, and the capital on the top of each
was five cubits.
16 And he made chains in the inner
sanctuary, and placed *them* on the tops
of the pillars; and he made one hundred
pomegranates and placed *them* on the
chains.
17 [a]And he erected the pillars in front
of the temple, one on the right and the
other on the left, and named the one on
the right Jachin and the one on the left
Boaz.

Furnishings of the Temple

4 THEN [a]he made a bronze altar,
twenty cubits in length and twenty
cubits in width and ten cubits in height.
2 [a]Also he made the cast *metal* sea,
ten cubits from brim to brim, circular in
form, and its height *was* five cubits and
[1]its circumference thirty cubits.
3 Now figures like oxen *were* under it
and all around it, ten cubits, entirely
encircling the sea. The oxen *were* in two
rows, cast [1]in one piece.
4 It stood on twelve oxen, three
facing the north, three facing west, three
facing south, and three facing east; and
the sea *was set* on top of them, and all
their hindquarters turned inwards.
5 And it was a handbreadth thick,
and its brim was made like the brim of a
cup, *like* a lily blossom; it [a]could hold
3,000 baths.
6 [a]He also made ten basins in which
to wash, and he set five on the right side
and five on the left, [1]to rinse things for
the burnt offering; but the sea *was* for
the priests to wash in.

11 [1]Lit., *said . . . and he sent* [a]1 Kin. 10:9; 2 Chr. 9:8
12 [1]Lit., *said* [2]Lit., *knowing discretion* [3]Lit., *house for his royalty* [a]Ps. 33:6; 102:25 [b]2 Chr. 2:1
13 [1]Lit., *knowing understanding*
14 [1]Lit., *a woman of the daughters of Dan* [2]Lit., *whose father is a Tyrian man* [3]Lit., *devise any device* [4]Lit., *skilled men* [a]1 Kin. 7:14
15 [a]2 Chr. 2:10
16 [a]1 Kin. 5:8, 9
17 [1]Lit., *numbering* [2]Lit., *numbered of them* [a]1 Chr. 22:2
18 [a]2 Chr. 2:2

1 [1]In 2 Sam. 24:18, *Araunah* [a]1 Kin. 6:1 [b]1 Chr. 21:18
2 [1]Lit., *in*
3 [1]Lit., *founding of Solomon to build* [2]I.e., One cubit equals approx. 18 in. [a]1 Kin. 6:2
4 [a]1 Kin. 6:3
5 [1]Lit., *great house* [2]Lit., *put on it palm trees* [a]1 Kin. 6:17
6 [1]Lit., *overlaid . . . for beauty* [2]Or, *country of gold*
7 [a]1 Kin. 6:20-22 [b]1 Kin. 6:29-35
8 [1]Lit., *house* [a]Ex. 26:33; 1 Kin. 6:16
9 [a]1 Chr. 28:11
10 [1]Lit., *cherubim of sculptured work* [a]Ex. 25:18-20; 1 Kin. 6:23-28
12 [1]Lit., *other*
13 [1]Lit., *and their faces to*
14 [a]Ex. 26:31
15 [1]Lit., *long* [a]1 Kin. 7:15-20
17 [a]1 Kin. 7:21

1 [a]Ex. 27:1, 2; 2 Kin. 16:14
2 [1]Lit., *a line of 30 cubits encircling it round about* [a]1 Kin. 7:23-26
3 [1]Lit., *in its casting*
5 [a]1 Kin. 7:26
6 [1]Lit., *in which to* [a]Ex. 30:17-21; 1 Kin. 7:38, 40

7 Then [a]he made the ten golden lampstands in the way prescribed for them, and he set them in the temple, five on the right side and five on the left.

8 He also made [a]ten tables and placed them in the temple, five on the right side and five on the left. And he made one hundred golden bowls.

9 Then he made [a]the court of the priests and [b]the great court and doors for the court, and overlaid their doors with bronze.

10 And [a]he set the sea on the right [1]side *of the house* toward the southeast.

11 [a]Huram also made the pails, the shovels, and the bowls. So Huram finished doing the work which he performed for King Solomon in the house of God:

12 the two pillars, the bowls and the two capitals on top of the pillars, and the two networks to cover the two bowls of the capitals which were on top of the pillars,

13 and [a]the four hundred pomegranates for the two networks, two rows of pomegranates for each network to cover the two bowls of the capitals which were on the pillars.

14 [a]He also made the stands and he made the basins on the stands,

15 *and* the one sea with the twelve oxen under it.

16 And the pails, the shovels, the forks, and all its utensils, [a]Huram-abi made of polished bronze for King Solomon for the house of the LORD.

17 On the plain of the Jordan the king cast them, in the clay ground between Succoth and Zeredah.

18 [a]Thus Solomon made all these utensils in great quantities, for the weight of the bronze could not be found out.

19 Solomon also made all the things that *were* in the house of God: even the golden altar, [a]the tables with the bread of the Presence on them,

20 the lampstands with their lamps of pure gold, [a]to burn in front of the inner sanctuary in the way prescribed;

21 the flowers, the lamps, and the tongs of gold, of purest gold;

22 and the snuffers, the bowls, the spoons, and the firepans of pure gold; and the entrance of the house, its inner doors for the holy of holies, and the doors of the house, *that is,* of the nave, of gold.

The Ark Is Brought into the Temple

5 [a]THUS all the work that Solomon performed for the house of the LORD was finished. And Solomon brought in the [1][b]things that David his father had dedicated, even the silver and the gold and all the utensils, *and* put *them* in the treasuries of the house of God.

2 [a]Then Solomon assembled to Jerusalem the elders of Israel and all the heads of the tribes, the leaders of the

4:7 [a]Ex. 25:31-40; 1 Kin. 7:49
8 [a]1 Kin. 7:48
9 [a]1 Kin. 6:36 [b]2 Kin. 21:5
10 [1]Lit., *shoulder* [a]1 Kin. 7:39
11 [a]1 Kin. 7:40-51
13 [a]1 Kin. 7:20
14 [a]1 Kin. 7:27-43
16 [a]1 Kin. 7:14; 2 Chr. 2:13
18 [a]1 Kin. 7:47
19 [a]2 Chr. 4:8
20 [a]Ex. 25:31-37; 2 Chr. 5:7
5:1 [1]Lit., *dedicated things of David,* [a]1 Kin. 7:51 [b]2 Sam. 8:11; 1 Chr. 18:11
2 [a]1 Kin. 8:1-9 [b]2 Sam. 6:12-15; 1 Chr. 15:25-28; 2 Chr. 1:4
3 [a]1 Kin. 8:2 [b]2 Chr. 7:8-10
4 [a]Josh. 3:6; 2 Chr. 5:7
6 [1]Lit., *sheep. . . numbered for multitude*
8 [1]Lit., *poles above*
9 [1]Lit., *it is* [a]1 Kin. 8:8, 9
10 [a]Deut. 10:2-5; Heb. 9:4
11 [a]1 Chr. 24:1-5
12 [a]1 Chr. 25:1-4 [b]1 Chr. 13:8; 15:16, 24 [c]2 Chr. 7:6
13 [a]1 Chr. 16:42 [b]1 Chr. 16:34; 2 Chr. 7:3; Ezra 3:11; Ps. 100:5; Jer. 33:11
14 [a]Ex. 40:35; 1 Kin. 8:11
6:1 [a]1 Kin. 8:12-50

fathers' *households* of the sons of Israel, [b]to bring up the ark of the covenant of the LORD out of the city of David, which is Zion.

3 And [a]all the men of Israel assembled themselves to the king at [b]the feast, that is *in* the seventh month.

4 Then all the elders of Israel came, and [a]the Levites took up the ark.

5 And they brought up the ark and the tent of meeting and all the holy utensils which *were* in the tent; the Levitical priests brought them up.

6 And King Solomon and all the congregation of Israel who were assembled with him before the ark were sacrificing [1]so many sheep and oxen, that they could not be counted or numbered.

7 Then the priests brought the ark of the covenant of the LORD to its place, into the inner sanctuary of the house, to the holy of holies, under the wings of the cherubim.

8 For the cherubim spread their wings over the place of the ark, so that the cherubim made a covering over the ark and its [1]poles.

9 And the poles were so long that [a]the ends of the poles of the ark could be seen in front of the inner sanctuary, but they could not be seen outside; and [1]they are there to this day.

10 [a]There was nothing in the ark except the two tablets which Moses put *there* at Horeb, where the LORD made a covenant with the sons of Israel, when they came out of Egypt.

The Glory of God Fills the Temple

11 And when the priests came forth from the holy place (for all the priests who were present had sanctified themselves, without regard [a]to divisions),

12 and all the Levitical singers, [a]Asaph, Heman, Jeduthun, and their sons and kinsmen, clothed in fine linen, [b]with cymbals, harps, and lyres, standing east of the altar, and with them one hundred and twenty priests [c]blowing trumpets

13 in unison when the trumpeters and the singers were to make themselves heard with one voice to praise and to glorify the LORD, and when they lifted up their voice [a]accompanied by trumpets and cymbals and instruments of music, and when they praised the LORD *saying,* "[b]*He* indeed is good for His lovingkindness is everlasting," then the house, the house of the LORD, was filled with a cloud,

14 so that the priests could not stand to minister because of the cloud, for [a]the glory of the LORD filled the house of God.

Solomon's Dedication

6 [a]THEN Solomon said,
"The LORD has said that He would dwell in the thick cloud.

2 "I have built Thee a lofty house,
And a place for Thy dwelling forever."

3 Then the king [1]faced about and
blessed all the assembly of Israel, while
all the assembly of Israel was standing.
4 And he said, "Blessed be the LORD,
the God of Israel, who spoke with His
mouth to my father David and has
fulfilled *it* with His hands, saying,
5 'Since the day that I brought My
people from the land of Egypt, I did not
choose a city out of all the tribes of
Israel *in which* to build a house that My
name might be there, nor did I choose
any man for a leader over My people
Israel;
6 but [a]I have chosen Jerusalem that
My name might be there, and I [b]have
chosen David to be over My people
Israel.'
7 "[a]Now it was [1]in the heart of my
father David to build a house for the
name of the LORD, the God of Israel.
8 "But the LORD said to my father
David, 'Because it was [1]in your heart to
build a house for My name, you did well
that it was [1]in your heart.
9 'Nevertheless you shall not build
the house, but your son who [1]shall be
born to you, he shall build the house for
My name.'
10 "Now the LORD has fulfilled His
word which He spoke; for I have risen in
the place of my father David and sit on
the throne of Israel, as the LORD [1]prom-
ised, and have built the house for the
name of the LORD, the God of Israel.
11 "And there I have set the ark, [a]in
which is the covenant of the LORD,
which He made with the sons of Israel."

Solomon's Prayer of Dedication

12 Then he stood before the altar of
the LORD in the presence of all the
assembly of Israel and spread out his
hands.
13 [a]Now Solomon had made a bronze
platform, five cubits long, five cubits
wide, and three cubits high, and had set
it in the midst of the court; and he stood
on it, [b]knelt on his knees in the presence
of all the assembly of Israel, and spread
out his hands toward heaven.
14 And he said, "O LORD, the God of
Israel, [a]there is no god like Thee in
heaven or on earth, [b]keeping covenant
and *showing* lovingkindness to Thy servants who walk before Thee with all
their heart;
15 [a]who has kept with Thy servant
David, my father, that which Thou hast
[1]promised him; indeed, Thou hast spoken with Thy mouth, and hast fulfilled it
with Thy hand, as it is this day.
16 "Now therefore, O LORD, the God
of Israel, keep with Thy servant David,
my father, that which Thou hast [1]prom-
ised him, saying, '[2a]You shall not lack a
man to sit on the throne of Israel, if only
your sons take heed to their way, to walk
in My law as you have walked before
Me.'
17 "Now therefore, O LORD, the God
of Israel, let Thy word be confirmed
which Thou hast spoken to Thy servant
David.
18 "But [a]will God indeed dwell with
mankind on the earth? Behold, [b]heaven
and the [1]highest heaven cannot contain
Thee; how much less this house which I
have built.
19 "Yet have regard to the prayer of
Thy servant and to his supplication, O
LORD my God, to listen to the cry and to
the prayer which Thy servant prays
before Thee;
20 that Thine [a]eyes may be open
toward this house day and night, toward
[b]the place of which Thou hast said that
Thou wouldst put Thy name there, to
listen to the prayer which Thy servant
shall pray toward this place.
21 "And listen to the supplications of
Thy servant and of Thy people Israel,
when they pray toward this place; hear
Thou from Thy dwelling place, from
heaven; [a]hear Thou and forgive.
22 "If a man sins against his neighbor,
and is made to take an oath, and he
comes *and* takes an oath before Thine
altar in this house,
23 then hear Thou from heaven and
act and judge Thy servants, [1a]punishing
the wicked by bringing his way on his
own head and justifying the righteous by
giving him according to his righteousness.
24 "And if Thy people Israel [1]are defeated before an enemy, because [a]they
have sinned against Thee, and they
return *to Thee* and confess Thy name,
and pray and make supplication before
Thee in this house,
25 then hear Thou from heaven and
forgive the sin of Thy people Israel, and
bring them back to the land which Thou
hast given to them and to their fathers.
26 "When the [a]heavens are shut up and
there is no rain because they have sinned
against Thee, and they pray toward this
place and confess Thy name, and turn
from their sin when Thou dost afflict
them;
27 then hear Thou in heaven and
forgive the sin of Thy servants and Thy
people Israel, indeed, [a]teach them the
good way in which they should walk.
And send rain on Thy land, which Thou
hast given to Thy people for an inheritance.
28 "If there is [a]famine in the land, if
there is pestilence, if there is blight or
mildew, if there is locust or grasshopper,
if their enemies besiege them in the land
of their [1]cities, whatever plague or whatever sickness *there is*,
29 whatever prayer or supplication is
made by any man or by all Thy people
Israel, [1]each knowing his own affliction
and his own pain, and spreading his
hands toward this house,
30 then hear Thou from heaven Thy
dwelling place, and forgive, and render
to each according to all his ways, whose
heart Thou knowest [a]for Thou alone
dost know the hearts of the sons of men,

3 [1]Lit., *turned his face about*
6 [a]2 Chr. 12:13 [b]1 Chr. 28:4
7 [1]Lit., *with* [a]1 Kin. 5:3; 1 Chr. 28:2
8 [1]Lit., *with*
9 [1]Lit., *is to come forth from your loins*
10 [1]Lit., *spoke*
11 [a]2 Chr. 5:7, 10
13 [a]Neh. 8:4 [b]1 Kin. 8:54
14 [a]Ex. 15:11; Deut. 3:24 [b]Deut. 7:9
15 [1]Lit., *spoken to* [a]1 Chr. 22:9, 10
16 [1]Lit., *spoken to* [2]Lit., *There shall not be cut off to you a man from before Me* [a]1 Kin. 2:4; 2 Chr. 7:18
18 [1]Lit., *heaven of heavens* [a]Ps. 113:5, 6 [b]2 Chr. 2:6; Is. 66:1; Acts 7:49
20 [a]Ps. 33:18; 34:15 [b]Deut. 12:11
21 [a]Is. 43:25; 44:22; Mic. 7:18
23 [1]Lit., returning [a]Is. 3:11; Rom. 2:8, 9
24 [1]Lit., *smitten* [a]Ps. 51:4
26 [a]1 Kin. 17:1
27 [a]Ps. 94:12
28 [1]Lit., *gates* [a]2 Chr. 20:9
29 [1]Lit., *whoever shall know*
30 [a]1 Sam. 16:7; 1 Chr. 28:9

31 that they may [1]fear Thee, to walk
in Thy ways [2]as long as they live in the
land which Thou hast given to our
fathers.
32"Also concerning [a]the foreigner who
is not from Thy people Israel, when he
comes from a far country for Thy great
name's sake and Thy mighty hand and
Thine outstretched arm, when they come
and pray toward this house,
33 then hear Thou from heaven, from
Thy dwelling place, and do according to
all for which the foreigner calls to Thee,
in order that all the peoples of the earth
may know Thy name, and [1]fear Thee, as
do Thy people Israel, and that they may
know that [2]this house which I have built
is [a]called by Thy name.
34"When Thy people go out to battle
against their enemies, by whatever way
Thou shalt send them, and they pray to
Thee toward this city which Thou hast
chosen, and the house which I have built
for Thy name,
35 then hear Thou from heaven their
prayer and their supplication, and maintain their cause.
36"When they sin against Thee ([a]for
there is no man who does not sin) and
Thou art angry with them and dost
deliver them to an enemy, so that [1]they
take them away captive to a land far off
or near,
37 if they [1]take thought in the land
where they are taken captive, and repent
and make supplication to Thee in the
land of their captivity, saying, 'We have
sinned, we have committed iniquity, and
have acted wickedly';
38 [a]if they return to Thee with all their
heart and with all their soul in the land
of their captivity, where they have been
taken captive, and pray toward their
land which Thou hast given to their
fathers, and the city which Thou hast
chosen, and toward the house which I
have built for Thy name,
39 then hear from heaven, from Thy
dwelling place, their prayer and supplications, and maintain their cause, and
forgive Thy people who have sinned
against Thee.
40"Now, O my God, I pray Thee, [a]let
Thine eyes be open, and [b]Thine ears
attentive to the prayer *offered* in this
place.
41"[a]Now therefore arise, O LORD
God, to Thy resting place, Thou and the
ark of Thy might; let Thy priests, O
LORD God, be clothed with salvation,
and let Thy godly ones rejoice in what is
good.
42"O LORD God, do not turn away the
face of Thine anointed; [a]remember *Thy*
lovingkindness to Thy servant David."

The Shekinah Glory

7 [a]NOW when Solomon had finished
praying, [b]fire came down from
heaven and consumed the burnt offering
and the sacrifices; and the glory of the
LORD filled the house.
2 And [a]the priests could not enter
into the house of the LORD, because the
glory of the LORD filled the LORD's
house.
3 And all the sons of Israel, seeing
the fire come down and the glory of the
LORD upon the house, bowed down on
the pavement with their faces to the
ground, and they worshiped and gave
praise to the LORD, *saying,* "[a]Truly He is
good, truly His lovingkindness is everlasting."

Sacrifices Offered

4 [a]Then the king and all the people
offered sacrifice before the LORD.
5 And King Solomon offered a sacrifice of 22,000 oxen, and 120,000 sheep.
Thus the king and all the people dedicated the house of God.
6 And the priests stood at their posts
and [a]the Levites, with the instruments of
music to the LORD, which King David
had made for giving praise to the
LORD—"for His lovingkindness is everlasting"—whenever [1]he gave praise by
their [2]means, while [b]the priests on the
other side blew trumpets; and all Israel
was standing.
7 [a]Then Solomon consecrated the
middle of the court that *was* before the
house of the LORD, for there he offered
the burnt offerings and the fat of the
peace offerings, because the bronze altar
which Solomon had made was not able
to contain the burnt offering, the grain
offering, and the fat.

The Feast of Dedication

8 So [a]Solomon observed the feast at
that time for seven days, and all Israel
with him, a very great assembly, *who
came* from the entrance of Hamath to
the [b]brook of Egypt.
9 And on the eighth day they held [a]a
solemn assembly, for the dedication of
the altar they observed seven days, and
the feast seven days.
10 Then on the twenty-third day of
the seventh month he sent the people to
their tents, rejoicing and happy of heart
because of the goodness that the LORD
had shown to David and to Solomon
and to His people Israel.

God's Promise and Warning

11 [a]Thus Solomon finished the house
of the LORD and the king's palace, and
successfully completed all that [1]he had
planned on doing in the house of the
LORD and in his palace.
12 Then the LORD appeared to Solomon at night and said to him, "I have
heard your prayer, and [a]have chosen this
place for Myself as a house of sacrifice.
13"[a]If I shut up the heavens so that
there is no rain, or if I command the
locust to devour the land, or if I send
pestilence among My people,
14 [a]and My people [1]who are called by
My name humble themselves and pray,
and seek My face and turn from their

31 [1]Or, *reverence* [2]Lit., *all the days that they live on the face of the land*
32 [a]Is. 56:3-8
33 [1]Or, *reverence* [2]Lit., *Thy name is called upon this house* [a]2 Chr. 7:14
36 [1]Lit., *their captors take them captive* [a]Job 15:14-16; James 3:2; 1 John 1:8-10
37 [1]Lit., *return to their heart*
38 [a]Jer. 29:12, 13
40 [a]2 Chr. 7:15; Neh. 1:6, 11 [b]Ps. 17:1
41 [a]Ps. 132:8, 9
42 [a]Ps. 89:24, 28; 132:10-12; Is. 55:3
1 [a]1 Kin. 8:54 [b]Lev. 9:23f.; 1 Kin. 18:24, 38
2 [a]2 Chr. 5:14
3 [a]2 Chr. 5:13; 20:21
4 [a]1 Kin. 8:62, 63
6 [1]Lit., *David* [2]Lit., *hand* [a]1 Chr. 15:16-21 [b]2 Chr. 5:12
7 [a]1 Kin. 8:64-66
8 [a]1 Kin. 8:65 [b]Gen. 15:18
9 [a]Lev. 23:36
11 [1]Lit., *came upon the heart of Solomon to do* [a]1 Kin. 9:1-9
12 [a]Deut. 12:5, 11
13 [a]2 Chr. 6:26-28
14 [1]Lit., *over whom My name is called* [a]2 Chr. 6:37-39; James 4:10

wicked ways, then I will hear from
heaven, will forgive their sin, and will
heal their land.
15 "[a]Now My eyes shall be open and
My ears attentive to the [1]prayer *offered*
in this place.
16 "For [a]now I have chosen and consecrated this house that My name may be
there forever, and My eyes and My heart
will be there perpetually.
17 "And as for you, if you walk before
Me as your father David walked even to
do according to all that I have commanded you and will keep My statutes
and My ordinances,
18 then I will establish your royal
throne as I covenanted with your father
David, saying, '[1a]You shall not lack a
man *to be* ruler in Israel.'
19 "[a]But if you turn away and forsake
My statutes and My commandments
which I have set before you and shall go
and serve other gods and worship them,
20 [a]then I will uproot you from My
land which I have given [1]you, and this
house which I have consecrated for My
name I will cast out of My sight, and I
will make it [b]a proverb and a byword
among all peoples.
21 "As for this house, which was exalted, everyone who passes by it will be
astonished and say, '[a]Why has the LORD
done thus to this land and to this house?'
22 "And they will say, 'Because [a]they
forsook the LORD, the God of their
fathers, who brought them from the land
of Egypt, and they adopted other gods
and worshiped them and served them,
therefore He has brought all this adversity on them.' "

Solomon's Activities and Accomplishments

8 [a]NOW it came about at the end of
the twenty years in which Solomon
had built the house of the LORD and his
own house
2 that he built the cities which Huram had given to [1]him, and settled the
sons of Israel there.
3 Then Solomon went to Hamath-
zobah and captured it.
4 And he built Tadmor in the wilderness and all the storage cities which he
had built in Hamath.
5 He also built upper [a]Beth-horon
and lower Beth-horon, [b]fortified cities
with walls, gates, and bars;
6 and Baalath and all the storage
cities that Solomon had, and all the
cities for [1]his chariots and cities for [1]his
horsemen, and all that it pleased Solomon to build in Jerusalem, in Lebanon,
and in all the land [2]under his rule.
7 [a]All of the people who were left of
the Hittites, the Amorites, the Perizzites,
the Hivites, and the Jebusites, who were
not of Israel,
8 namely, from their descendants
who were left after them in the land
whom the sons of Israel had not destroyed, [a]them Solomon raised as forced
laborers to this day.
9 But Solomon did not make slaves
for his work from the sons of Israel; they
were men of war, his chief captains, and
commanders of his chariots and his
horsemen.
10 And these were the chief [1]officers
of King Solomon, two hundred and fifty
who ruled over the people.
11 [a]Then Solomon brought Pharaoh's
daughter up from the city of David to
the house which he had built for her; for
he said, "My wife shall not dwell in the
house of David king of Israel, because
[1]the places are holy where the ark of the
LORD has entered."
12 Then Solomon offered burnt offerings to the LORD on [a]the altar of the
LORD which he had built before the
porch;
13 and [a]*did so* according to the daily
rule, offering *them* up [b]according to the
commandment of Moses, for [c]the sabbaths, [d]the new moons, and the [e]three
annual feasts—the Feast of Unleavened
Bread, the Feast of Weeks, and the Feast
of Booths.
14 Now according to the ordinance of
his father David, he appointed [a]the
divisions of the priests for their service,
and [b]the Levites for their duties of praise
and ministering before the priests according to the daily rule, and [c]the gatekeepers by their divisions at every gate;
for [d]David the man of God had so
commanded.
15 And they did not depart from the
commandment of the king to the priests
and Levites in any manner or concerning
the storehouses.
16 Thus all the work of Solomon was
carried out [1]from the day of the foundation of the house of the LORD, and until
it was finished. So the house of the LORD
was completed.
17 Then Solomon went to [a]Ezion-
geber and to [b]Eloth on the seashore in
the land of Edom.
18 And Huram by his servants sent
him ships and servants who knew the
sea; and they went with Solomon's
servants to Ophir, and [a]took from there
four hundred and fifty talents of gold,
and brought them to King Solomon.

Visit of the Queen of Sheba

9 [a]NOW when the queen of Sheba
heard of the fame of Solomon, she
came to Jerusalem to test Solomon with
difficult questions. She had a very large
retinue, with camels carrying spices, and
a large amount of gold and precious
stones; and when she came to Solomon,
she spoke with him about all that was on
her heart.
2 And Solomon [1]answered all her
questions; nothing was hidden from
Solomon which he did not [2]explain to
her.
3 And when the queen of Sheba had
seen the wisdom of Solomon, the house
which he had built,

15 [1]Lit., *prayer of this place* [a]2 Chr. 6:20, 40
16 [a]2 Chr. 7:12
18 [1]Lit., *There shall not be cut off to you a man* [a]1 Kin. 2:4; 2 Chr. 6:16
19 [a]Lev. 26:14, 33; Deut. 28:15
20 [1]Ancient versions and Heb. read *them* [a]Deut. 29:28; 1 Kin. 14:15 [b]Deut. 28:37
21 [a]Deut. 29:24-27
22 [a]Judg. 2:13
1 [a]1 Kin. 9:10-28
2 [1]Lit., *Solomon*
5 [a]1 Chr. 7:24 [b]2 Chr. 14:7
6 [1]Lit., *the* [2]Lit., *of*
7 [a]Gen. 15:18-21; 1 Kin. 9:20
8 [a]1 Kin. 4:6; 9:21
10 [1]Or, *deputies*
11 [1]Lit., *they are* [a]1 Kin. 3:1; 7:8
12 [a]2 Chr. 4:1
13 [a]Ex. 29:38-42 [b]Num. 28:3 [c]Num. 28:9, 10 [d]Num. 28:11 [e]Ex. 23:14-17; 34:22, 23; Deut. 16:16
14 [a]1 Chr. 24:1 [b]1 Chr. 25:1 [c]1 Chr. 26:1 [d]Neh. 12:24, 36
16 [1]So ancient versions; M.T., *as far as*
17 [a]1 Kin. 9:26 [b]2 Kin. 14:22
18 [a]2 Chr. 9:10, 13
1 [a]1 Kin. 10:1-13; Matt. 12:42; Luke 11:31
2 [1]Lit., *told her all her words* [2]Lit., *tell*

4 the food at his table, the seating of his servants, the attendance of his ministers and their attire, his cupbearers and their attire, and [1]his stairway by which he went up to the house of the LORD, she was breathless.

5 Then she said to the king, "It was a true report which I heard in my own land about your words and your wisdom.

6 "Nevertheless I did not believe their reports until I came and my eyes had seen it. And behold, the half of the greatness of your wisdom was not told me. You surpass the report that I heard.

7 "How [1]blessed are your men, how [1]blessed are these your servants who stand before you continually and hear your wisdom.

8 "Blessed be the LORD your God who delighted in you, [a]setting you on His throne as king for the LORD your God; [b]because your God loved Israel establishing them forever, therefore He made you king over them, to do justice and righteousness."

9 Then she gave the king one hundred and twenty talents of gold, and a very great *amount of* spices and precious stones; there had never been spice like that which the queen of Sheba gave to King Solomon.

10 And the servants of Huram and the servants of Solomon [a]who brought gold from Ophir, also brought algum trees and precious stones.

11 And from the algum the king made steps for the house of the LORD and for the king's palace, and lyres and harps for the singers; and none like that was seen before in the land of Judah.

12 And King Solomon gave to the queen of Sheba all her desire which she requested besides *a return for* what she had brought to the king. Then she turned and went to her own land with her servants.

Solomon's Wealth and Power

13 [a]Now the weight of gold which came to Solomon in one year was 666 talents of gold,

14 besides that which the traders and merchants brought; and all [a]the kings of Arabia and the governors of the country brought gold and silver to Solomon.

15 And King Solomon made 200 large shields of beaten gold, [1]using 600 *shekels of* beaten gold on each large shield.

16 And *he made* 300 shields of beaten gold, [1]using three hundred shekels of gold on each shield, and the king put them in the house of the forest of Lebanon.

17 Moreover, the king made a great throne of ivory and overlaid it with pure gold.

18 And *there were* six steps to the throne and a footstool in gold attached to the throne, and [1]arms [2]on each side of the seat, and two lions standing beside the [1]arms.

19 And twelve lions were standing there on the six steps on the one side and on the other; nothing like *it* was made for any *other* kingdom.

20 And all King Solomon's drinking vessels *were* of gold, and all the vessels of the house of the forest of Lebanon *were* of pure gold; silver was not considered [1]valuable in the days of Solomon.

21 [a]For the king had ships which went to Tarshish with the servants of Huram; once every three years the ships of Tarshish came bringing gold and silver, ivory and apes and peacocks.

22 [a]So King Solomon became greater than all the kings of the earth in riches and wisdom.

23 And all the kings of the earth were seeking the presence of Solomon, to hear his wisdom which God had put in his heart.

24 And [a]they brought every man his gift, articles of silver and gold, garments, weapons, spices, horses, and mules, so much year by year.

25 Now Solomon had [a]4,000 stalls for horses and chariots and 12,000 horsemen, and he stationed them in the chariot cities and with the king in Jerusalem.

26 [a]And he was the ruler over all the kings from the Euphrates River even to the land of the Philistines, and as far as the border of Egypt.

27 [a]And the king made silver *as common* as stones in Jerusalem, and he made cedars as plentiful as sycamore trees that are in the [1]lowland.

28 [a]And they were bringing horses for Solomon from Egypt and from all countries.

29 [a]Now the rest of the acts of Solomon, from first to last, [b]are they not written in the [1]records of Nathan the prophet, and in the prophecy of Ahijah the Shilonite, and in the visions of [2]Iddo the seer concerning Jeroboam the son of Nebat?

30 And [a]Solomon reigned forty years in Jerusalem over all Israel.

Death of Solomon

31 And Solomon slept with his fathers and was buried in [a]the city of his father David; and his son Rehoboam reigned in his place.

Rehoboam's Reign of Folly

10 [a]THEN Rehoboam went to Shechem, for all Israel had come to Shechem to make him king.

2 And it came about when Jeroboam the son of Nebat heard *of it* (for [a]he was in Egypt where he had fled from the presence of King Solomon), that Jeroboam returned from Egypt.

3 So they sent and summoned him. When Jeroboam and all Israel came, they spoke to Rehoboam, saying,

4 "Your father made our [a]yoke hard; now therefore lighten the hard service of your father and his heavy yoke which he put on us, and we will serve you."

4 [1]Or, *his burnt offering which he offered*

7 [1]Or, *happy*

8 [a]1 Chr. 28:5; 29:23 [b]Deut. 7:8; 2 Chr. 2:11

10 [a]1 Kin. 10:11; 2 Chr. 8:18

13 [a]1 Kin. 10:14-28

14 [a]Ps. 68:29; 72:10

15 [1]Lit., *he brought up*

16 [1]Lit., *he brought up*

18 [1]Lit., *hands* [2]Lit., *on this side and on this at the place of the seat*

20 [1]Lit., *anything*

21 [a]2 Chr. 20:36, 37

22 [a]1 Kin. 3:13; 2 Chr. 1:12

24 [a]Ps. 72:10

25 [a]Deut. 17:16; 1 Kin. 4:26; 10:26; 2 Chr. 1:14

26 [a]Gen. 15:18; 1 Kin. 4:21, 24

27 [1]Heb., *shephelah* [a]2 Chr. 1:15-17

28 [a]2 Chr. 1:16

29 [1]Lit., *words* [2]Heb., *Jedo* [a]1 Kin. 11:41-43 [b]1 Chr. 29:29

30 [a]1 Kin. 11:42, 43

31 [a]1 Kin. 2:10

1 [a]1 Kin. 12:1-20

2 [a]1 Kin. 11:40

4 [a]1 Kin. 5:13-16

5 And he said to them, "Return to me again in three days." So the people departed.

6 Then King Rehoboam [a]consulted with the elders who had [1]served his father Solomon while he was still alive, saying, "How do you counsel *me* to answer this people?"

7 And they spoke to him, saying, "If you will be kind to this people and please them and [a]speak good words to them, then they will be your servants forever."

8 But he [a]forsook the counsel of the elders which they had given him, and consulted with the young men who grew up with him [1]and served him.

9 So he said to them, "What counsel do you give that we may answer this people, who have spoken to me, saying, 'Lighten the yoke which your father put on us'?"

10 And the young men who grew up with him spoke to him, saying, "Thus you shall say to the people who spoke to you, saying, 'Your father made our yoke heavy, but you make it lighter for us.' Thus you shall say to them, 'My little finger is thicker than my father's loins!

11 'Whereas my father loaded you with a heavy yoke, I will add to your yoke; my father disciplined you with whips, but I *will discipline you* with scorpions.'"

12 So Jeroboam and all the people came to Rehoboam on the third day as the king had [1]directed, saying, "Return to me on the third day."

13 And the king answered them harshly, and King Rehoboam forsook the counsel of the elders.

14 And he spoke to them according to the advice of the young men, saying, "[1]My father made your yoke heavy, but I will add to it; my father disciplined you with whips, but I *will discipline you* with scorpions."

15 So the king did not listen to the people, [a]for it was a turn *of events* from God [b]that the LORD might establish His word, which He spoke through Ahijah the Shilonite to Jeroboam the son of Nebat.

16 And when all Israel *saw* that the king did not listen to them the people answered the king, saying,

"[a]What portion do we have in David?
We have no inheritance in the son of Jesse.
Every man to your tents, O Israel;
Now look after your own house, David."

[b]So all Israel departed to their tents.

17 But as for the sons of Israel who lived in the cities of Judah, Rehoboam reigned over them.

18 Then King Rehoboam sent Hadoram, who was [a]over the forced labor, and the sons of Israel stoned him [1]to death. And King Rehoboam made haste to mount his chariot to flee to Jerusalem.

19 So [a]Israel has been in rebellion against the house of David to this day.

6 [1]Lit., *stood before* [a]Job 8:8, 9; 32:7
7 [a]Prov. 15:1
8 [1]Lit., *who stood before* [a]2 Sam. 17:14; Prov. 13:20
12 [1]Lit., *spoken*
14 [1]Many mss. read *I have made*
15 [a]2 Chr. 25:16-20 [b]1 Kin. 11:29-39
16 [a]2 Sam. 20:1 [b]2 Chr. 10:19
18 [1]Lit., *with stones that he died* [a]1 Kin. 4:6; 5:14
19 [a]1 Kin. 12:19
1 [a]1 Kin. 12:21-24
2 [a]2 Chr. 12:5-7, 15
4 [1]Lit., *brothers* [a]2 Chr. 28:8-11 [b]2 Chr. 10:15
5 [a]2 Chr. 8:2-6; 11:23
14 [a]Num. 35:2-5 [b]1 Kin. 12:28-33; 2 Chr. 13:9
15 [a]1 Kin. 12:31; 13:33
16 [1]Lit., *came after* [a]2 Chr. 15:9
17 [a]2 Chr. 12:1
18 [a]1 Sam. 16:6
20 [1]In 1 Kin. 15:2, *Abishalom* [a]1 Kin. 15:2; 2 Chr. 13:2
21 [a]Deut. 17:17

Rehoboam Reigns over Judah and Builds Cities

11 [a]NOW when Rehoboam had come to Jerusalem, he assembled the house of Judah and Benjamin, 180,000 chosen men who were warriors, to fight against Israel to restore the kingdom to Rehoboam.

2 But the word of the LORD came to [a]Shemaiah the man of God, saying,

3 "Speak to Rehoboam the son of Solomon, king of Judah, and to all Israel in Judah and Benjamin, saying,

4 'Thus says the LORD, "You shall not go up or fight against [a]your [1]relatives; return every man to his house, [b]for this thing is from Me."'" So they listened to the words of the LORD and returned from going against Jeroboam.

5 Rehoboam lived in Jerusalem and [a]built cities for defense in Judah.

6 Thus he built Bethlehem, Etam, Tekoa,

7 Beth-zur, Soco, Adullam,

8 Gath, Mareshah, Ziph,

9 Adoraim, Lachish, Azekah,

10 Zorah, Aijalon, and Hebron, which are fortified cities in Judah and in Benjamin.

11 He also strengthened the fortresses and put officers in them and stores of food, oil and wine.

12 And *he put* shields and spears in every city and strengthened them greatly. So he held Judah and Benjamin.

13 Moreover, the priests and the Levites who were in all Israel stood with him from all their districts.

Jeroboam Appoints False Priests

14 For [a]the Levites left their pasture lands and their property and came to Judah and Jerusalem, for [b]Jeroboam and his sons had excluded them from serving as priests to the LORD.

15 And [a]he set up priests of his own for the high places, for the satyrs, and for the calves which he had made.

16 And [a]those from all the tribes of Israel who set their hearts on seeking the LORD God of Israel, [1]followed them to Jerusalem to sacrifice to the LORD God of their fathers.

17 [a]And they strengthened the kingdom of Judah and supported Rehoboam the son of Solomon for three years, for they walked in the way of David and Solomon for three years.

Rehoboam's Family

18 Then Rehoboam took as a wife Mahalath the daughter of Jerimoth the son of David *and of* Abihail the daughter of [a]Eliab the son of Jesse,

19 and she bore him sons: Jeush, Shemariah, and Zaham.

20 And after her he took [a]Maacah the daughter of [1]Absalom, and she bore him Abijah, Attai, Ziza, and Shelomith.

21 And Rehoboam loved Maacah the daughter of Absalom more than all his *other* wives and concubines. For [a]he had

taken eighteen wives and sixty concubines and fathered twenty-eight sons
and sixty daughters.
22 And [a]Rehoboam appointed Abijah
the son of Maacah as head and leader
among his brothers, for he *intended* to
make him king.
23 And he acted wisely and distributed [1]some of his sons through all the
territories of Judah and Benjamin to all
the fortified cities, and he gave them
food in abundance. And he sought many
wives *for them.*

Shishak of Egypt Invades Judah

12 IT took place [a]when the kingdom
of Rehoboam was established
and strong that [b]he and all Israel with
him forsook the law of the LORD.
2 [a]And it came about in King Rehoboam's fifth year, because they had been
unfaithful to the LORD, that [b]Shishak
king of Egypt came up against Jerusalem
3 with 1,200 chariots and 60,000
horsemen. And the people who came
with him from Egypt were without number: [a]the Lubim, the Sukkiim, and the
Ethiopians.
4 And he captured [a]the fortified
cities of Judah and came as far as Jerusalem.
5 Then [a]Shemaiah the prophet came
to Rehoboam and the princes of Judah
who had gathered at Jerusalem because
of Shishak, and he said to them, "Thus
says the LORD, '[b]You have forsaken Me,
so I also have forsaken you [1]to Shishak.' "
6 So the princes of Israel and the
king humbled themselves and said, "The
[a]LORD is righteous."
7 And when the LORD saw that they
humbled themselves, the word of the
LORD came to Shemaiah, saying, "[a]They
have humbled themselves so I will not
destroy them, but I will grant them some
measure of deliverance, and [b]My wrath
shall not be poured out on Jerusalem by
means of Shishak.
8 "But they will become his slaves so
[a]that they may learn *the difference between* My service and the service of the
kingdoms of the countries."

Plunder Impoverishes Judah

9 [a]So Shishak king of Egypt came up
against Jerusalem, and took the treasures of the house of the LORD and the
treasures of the king's palace. He took
everything; [b]he even took the golden
shields which Solomon had made.
10 Then King Rehoboam made
shields of bronze in their place, and
committed them to the [1]care of the
commanders of the [2]guard who guarded
the door of the king's house.
11 And it happened as often as the
king entered the house of the LORD, the
[1]guards came and carried them and *then*
brought them back into the [1]guards'
room.
12 And [a]when he humbled himself,
the anger of the LORD turned away from
him, so as not to destroy *him* completely; and also conditions [b]were good
in Judah.
13 [a]So King Rehoboam strengthened
himself in Jerusalem, and reigned. Now
Rehoboam was forty-one years old when
he began to reign, and he reigned seventeen years in Jerusalem, the city which
the LORD had chosen from all the tribes
of Israel, to put His name there. And his
mother's name was Naamah the Ammonitess.
14 And he did evil [a]because he did not
set his heart to seek the LORD.
15 [a]Now the acts of Rehoboam, from
first to last, are they not written in the
[1]records of [b]Shemaiah the prophet and
of [c]Iddo the seer, according to genealogical enrollment? And *there were* wars
between Rehoboam and Jeroboam continually.
16 And Rehoboam slept with his fathers, and was buried in the city of
David; and his son [a]Abijah became king
in his place.

Abijah Succeeds Rehoboam

13 [a]IN the eighteenth year of King
Jeroboam, Abijah became king
over Judah.
2 He reigned three years in Jerusalem; and his mother's name was Micaiah
the daughter of Uriel of Gibeah. [a]And
there was war between Abijah and Jeroboam.
3 And Abijah began the battle with
an army of valiant warriors, 400,000
chosen men, while Jeroboam drew up in
battle formation against him with
800,000 chosen men *who were* valiant
warriors.

Civil War

4 Then Abijah stood on Mount
[a]Zemaraim, which is in the hill country
of Ephraim, and said, "Listen to me,
Jeroboam and all Israel:
5 "Do you not know that [a]the LORD
God of Israel gave the rule over Israel
forever to David [1]and his sons by [b]a
covenant of salt?
6 "Yet [a]Jeroboam the son of Nebat,
the servant of Solomon the son of David,
rose up and rebelled against his [1]master,
7 and worthless men gathered about
him, scoundrels, who proved too strong
for Rehoboam, the son of Solomon,
when [1a]he was young and timid and
could not hold his own against them.
8 "So now you intend to resist the
kingdom of the LORD [1]through the sons
of David, [2]being a great multitude and
having with you [a]the golden calves which
Jeroboam made for gods for you.
9 "[a]Have you not driven out the
priests of the LORD, the sons of Aaron
and the Levites, and made for yourselves
priests like the peoples of *other* lands?
Whoever comes [b]to consecrate himself
with a young bull and seven rams, even
he may become a priest of *what are* [c]no
gods.

22 [a]Deut. 21:15-17
23 [1]Lit., *from all*

1 [a]2 Chr. 11:17; 12:13 [b]2 Chr. 26:13-16
2 [a]1 Kin. 14:25 [b]1 Kin. 11:40
3 [a]2 Chr. 16:8; Nah. 3:9
4 [a]2 Chr. 11:5-12
5 [1]Lit., *in the hand of* [a]2 Chr. 11:2 [b]Deut. 28:15; 2 Chr. 15:2
6 [a]Ex. 9:27; Dan. 9:14
7 [a]1 Kin. 21:29 [b]2 Chr. 34:25-27; Ps. 78:38
8 [a]Deut. 28:47, 48
9 [a]1 Kin. 14:26-28 [b]1 Kin. 10:16, 17; 2 Chr. 9:15, 16
10 [1]Lit., *hands* [2]Lit., *runners*
11 [1]Lit., *runners*
12 [a]2 Chr. 12:6, 7 [b]2 Chr. 19:3
13 [a]1 Kin. 14:21
14 [a]2 Chr. 19:3
15 [1]Lit., *words* [a]1 Kin. 14:29 [b]2 Chr. 12:5 [c]2 Chr. 9:29
16 [a]2 Chr. 11:20

1 [a]1 Kin. 15:1, 2
2 [a]1 Kin. 15:7
4 [a]Josh. 18:22
5 [1]Lit., *to him and to his sons* [a]2 Sam. 7:12-16 [b]Lev. 2:13; Num. 18:19
6 [1]Or, *lord* [a]1 Kin. 11:26
7 [1]Lit., *Rehoboam* [a]2 Chr. 12:13
8 [1]Lit., *in the hands of* [2]Lit., *and you are a* [a]1 Kin. 12:28; 2 Chr. 11:15
9 [a]2 Chr. 11:14, 15 [b]Ex. 29:29-33 [c]Jer. 2:11; 5:7

10"But as for us, the LORD is our God,
and we have not forsaken Him; and the
sons of Aaron are ministering to the
LORD as priests, and the Levites [1]attend
to their work.
11"And every morning and evening
[a]they [1]burn to the LORD burnt offerings
and fragrant incense, and [b]the showbread is *set* on the clean table, and the
golden lampstand with its lamps is *ready*
to light every evening; for we keep the
charge of the LORD our God, but you
have forsaken Him.
12"Now behold, God is with us at *our*
head and [a]His priests with the signal
trumpets to sound the alarm against
you. O sons of Israel, do not fight
against the LORD God of your fathers,
for you will not succeed."
13 But Jeroboam [a]had set an ambush
to come from the rear, so that *Israel* was
in front of Judah, and the ambush was
behind them.
14 When Judah turned around, behold, [1]they were attacked both front and
rear; so [a]they cried to the LORD, and the
priests blew the trumpets.
15 Then the men of Judah raised a
war cry, and when the men of Judah
raised the war cry, then it was that God
[1a]routed Jeroboam and all Israel before
Abijah and Judah.
16 And when the sons of Israel fled
before Judah, [a]God gave them into their
hand.
17 And Abijah and his people defeated them with a great slaughter, so
that 500,000 chosen men of Israel fell
slain.
18 Thus the sons of Israel were subdued at that time, and the sons of Judah
[1]conquered [a]because they trusted in the
LORD, the God of their fathers.
19 And Abijah pursued Jeroboam,
and captured from him *several* cities,
Bethel with its villages, Jeshanah with its
villages, and [1]Ephron with its villages.

Death of Jeroboam

20 And Jeroboam did not again recover strength in the days of Abijah; and
the [a]LORD struck him and [b]he died.
21 But Abijah became powerful, and
took fourteen wives to himself; and
became the father of twenty-two sons
and sixteen daughters.
22 Now the rest of the acts of Abijah,
and his ways and his words are written
in [a]the [1]treatise of [b]the prophet Iddo.

Asa Succeeds Abijah in Judah

14 [1a]SO Abijah slept with his fathers,
and they buried him in the city of
David, and his son Asa became king in
his place. The land was undisturbed for
ten years during his days.
2 [1]And Asa did good and right in the
sight of the LORD his God,
3 for he removed [a]the foreign altars
and [b]high places, tore down the *sacred*
pillars, cut down the [1c]Asherim,
4 and commanded Judah to seek the
LORD God of their fathers and to observe the law and the commandment.
5 He also removed the high places
and the [a]incense altars from all the cities
of Judah. And the kingdom was undisturbed under him.
6 And [a]he built fortified cities in
Judah, since the land was undisturbed,
and [1]there was no one at war with him
during those years, [b]because the LORD
had given him rest.
7 For he said to Judah, "[a]Let us
build these cities and surround *them*
with walls and towers, gates and bars.
The land is still [1]ours, because we have
sought the LORD our God; we have
sought Him, and He has given us rest on
every side." So they built and prospered.
8 Now Asa had an army of [a]300,000
from Judah, bearing large shields and
spears, and 280,000 from Benjamin,
bearing shields and wielding bows; all of
them were valiant warriors.
9 Now Zerah the Ethiopian [a]came
out against them with an army of a
million men and 300 chariots, and he
came to [b]Mareshah.
10 So Asa went out [1]to meet him, and
they drew up in battle formation in the
valley of Zephathah at Mareshah.
11 Then Asa [a]called to the LORD his
God, and said, "LORD, there is no one
besides Thee to help *in the battle* between the powerful and those who have
no strength; so help us, O LORD our
God, [b]for we trust in Thee, and in Thy
name have come against this multitude.
O LORD, Thou art our God; let not man
prevail against Thee."
12 So [a]the LORD [1]routed the Ethiopians before Asa and before Judah, and
the Ethiopians fled.
13 And Asa and the people who *were*
with him pursued them as far as [a]Gerar;
and so many Ethiopians fell that [1]they
could not recover, for they were shattered before the LORD, and before His
army. And they carried away very much
plunder.
14 And they [1]destroyed all the cities
around Gerar, [a]for the dread of the
LORD had fallen on them; and they
despoiled all the cities, for there was
much plunder in them.
15 They also struck down [1]those who
owned livestock, and they carried away
large numbers of sheep and camels.
Then they returned to Jerusalem.

The Prophet Azariah Warns Asa

15 NOW [a]the Spirit of God came on
Azariah the son of Oded,
2 and he went out [1]to meet Asa and
said to him, "Listen to me, Asa, and all
Judah and Benjamin: [a]the LORD is with
you when you are with Him. And [b]if you
seek Him, He will let you find Him; but
if you forsake Him, He will forsake you.
3"And [a]for many days Israel was
without the true God and without [b]a
teaching priest and without law.

10 [1]Lit., *in the work*

11 [1]Lit., *offer up in smoke* [a]Ex. 29:38; 2 Chr. 2:4 [b]Ex. 25:30-39; Lev. 24:5-9

12 [a]Num. 10:8, 9

13 [a]Josh. 8:4-9

14 [1]Lit., *the battle was before and behind them* [a]2 Chr. 14:11

15 [1]Lit., *smote* [a]2 Chr. 14:12

16 [a]2 Chr. 16:8

18 [1]Lit., *were strong* [a]2 Chr. 14:11

19 [1]Another reading is *Ephrain*

20 [a]1 Sam. 25:38 [b]1 Kin. 14:20

22 [1]Heb., *midrash* [a]2 Chr. 24:27 [b]2 Chr. 9:29

1 [1]Ch. 13:23 in Heb. [a]1 Kin. 15:8

2 [1]Ch. 14:1 in Heb.

3 [1]I.e., wooden symbols of a female deity [a]Deut. 7:5 [b]1 Kin. 15:12-14 [c]Ex. 34:13

5 [a]2 Chr. 34:4, 7

6 [1]Lit., *there was not with him war* [a]2 Chr. 11:5 [b]2 Chr. 15:15

7 [1]Lit., *before us* [a]2 Chr. 8:5

8 [a]2 Chr. 13:3

9 [a]2 Chr. 12:2, 3; 16:8 [b]2 Chr. 11:8

10 [1]Lit., *before him*

11 [a]2 Chr. 13:14 [b]2 Chr. 13:18

12 [1]Lit., *struck* [a]2 Chr. 13:15

13 [1]Or, *there was none left alive* [a]Gen. 10:19

14 [1]Lit., *smote* [a]2 Chr. 17:10

15 [1]Lit., *tents of livestock*

1 [a]2 Chr. 20:14; 24:20

2 [1]Lit., *before Asa* [a]2 Chr. 20:17 [b]2 Chr. 15:4, 15

3 [a]1 Kin. 12:28-33 [b]Lev. 10:8-11; 2 Chr. 17:9

4"But [a]in their distress they turned to
the LORD God of Israel, and they sought
Him, and He let them find Him.
5"[a]And in those times there was no
peace to him who went out or to him
who came in, for many disturbances
[1]afflicted all the inhabitants of the lands.
6"And [a]nation was crushed by nation, and city by city, for God troubled
them with every kind of distress.
7"But you, [a]be strong and do not
[1]lose courage, for there is [b]reward for
your work."

Asa's Reforms

8 Now when Asa heard these words
and the [1]prophecy which Azariah the
son of Oded the prophet spoke, he took
courage and removed the abominable
idols from all the land of Judah and
Benjamin and from [a]the cities which he
had captured in the hill country of
Ephraim. [b]He then restored the altar of
the LORD which was in front of the
porch of the LORD.
9 And he gathered all Judah and
Benjamin and those from Ephraim, Manasseh, and Simeon [a]who resided with
them, for many defected to him from
Israel when they saw that the LORD his
God was with him.
10 So they assembled at Jerusalem in
the third month of the fifteenth year of
Asa's reign.
11 And [a]they sacrificed to the LORD
that day 700 oxen and 7,000 sheep from
the spoil they had brought.
12 And [a]they entered into the covenant to seek the LORD God of their
fathers with all their heart and soul;
13 and whoever would not seek the
LORD God of Israel [a]should be put to
death, whether small or great, man or
woman.
14 Moreover, they made an oath to
the LORD with a loud voice, with shouting, with trumpets, and with horns.
15 And all Judah rejoiced concerning
the oath, for they had sworn with their
whole heart and had sought Him [1]ear-
nestly, and He let them find Him. So
[a]the LORD gave them rest on every side.
16 [a]And he also removed Maacah, the
mother of King Asa, from the *position of*
queen mother, because she had made a
horrid image [1]as [b]an Asherah, and [c]Asa
cut down her horrid image, crushed *it*
and burned *it* at the brook Kidron.
17 But the high places were not removed from Israel; nevertheless Asa's
heart was blameless all his days.
18 And he brought into the house of
God the dedicated things of his father
and his own dedicated things: silver and
gold and utensils.
19 And there was no more war until
the thirty-fifth year of Asa's reign.

Asa Wars against Baasha

16 IN the thirty-sixth year of Asa's
reign [a]Baasha king of Israel came
up against Judah and [1]fortified Ramah
in order to prevent *anyone* from going
out or coming in to Asa king of Judah.
2 Then Asa brought out silver and
gold from the treasuries of the house of
the LORD and the king's house, and sent
them to Ben-hadad king of Aram, who
lived in Damascus, saying,
3"*Let there be* a treaty between [1]you
and me, *as* between my father and your
father. Behold, I have sent you silver and
gold; go, break your treaty with Baasha
king of Israel so that he will withdraw
from me."
4 So Ben-hadad listened to King Asa
and sent the commanders of his armies
against the cities of Israel, and they
[1]conquered Ijon, Dan, Abel-maim, and
all [a]the [2]store cities of Naphtali.
5 And it came about when Baasha
heard *of it* that he ceased [1]fortifying
Ramah and stopped his work.
6 Then King Asa brought all Judah,
and they carried away the stones of
Ramah and its timber with which Baasha had been building, and with them
he [1]fortified Geba and Mizpah.

Asa Imprisons the Prophet

7 At that time [a]Hanani the seer came
to Asa king of Judah and said to him,
"[b]Because you have relied on the king of
Aram and have not relied on the LORD
your God, therefore the army of the king
of Aram has escaped out of your hand.
8"Were not [a]the Ethiopians and the
Lubim [b]an immense army with very
many chariots and horsemen? Yet, [c]be-
cause you relied on the LORD, He delivered them into your hand.
9"For [a]the eyes of the LORD move to
and fro throughout the earth that He
may strongly support those [b]whose heart
is completely His. You have acted foolishly in this. Indeed, from now on you
will surely have wars."
10 Then Asa was angry with the seer
and put him in [1]prison, for he was
enraged at him for this. And Asa oppressed some of the people at the same
time.
11 [a]And now, the acts of Asa from
first to last, behold, they are written in
the Book of the Kings of Judah and
Israel.
12 And in the thirty-ninth year of his
reign Asa became diseased in his feet.
His disease was severe, yet even in his
disease he [a]did not seek the LORD, but
the physicians.
13 So Asa slept with his fathers, [1]hav-
ing died in the forty-first year of his
reign.
14 And they buried him in his own
tomb which he had cut out for himself in
the city of David, and they laid him in
the resting place which he had filled
[a]with spices of various kinds blended by
the perfumers' art; and [b]they made a
very great fire for him.

Jehoshaphat Succeeds Asa

17 [a]JEHOSHAPHAT his son then
became king in his place, and
made his position over Israel firm.

4 [a]Deut. 4:29
5 [1]Lit., *were on* [a]Judg. 5:6
6 [a]Matt. 24:7
7 [1]Lit., *let your hands drop* [a]Josh. 1:7, 9 [b]Ps. 58:11
8 [1]With several ancient versions; Heb., *the prophecy, Oded the prophet* [a]2 Chr. 13:19 [b]2 Chr. 4:1; 8:12
9 [a]2 Chr. 11:16
11 [a]2 Chr. 14:13-15
12 [a]2 Chr. 23:16
13 [a]Ex. 22:20; Deut. 13:6-9
15 [1]Lit., *with their whole desire* [a]2 Chr. 14:7
16 [1]Or, for *Asherah* [a]1 Kin. 15:13-15 [b]Ex. 34:13 [c]2 Chr. 14:2-5
1 [1]Lit., *built* [a]1 Kin. 15:17-22
3 [1]Lit., *me and you*
4 [1]Lit., *smote* [2]Lit., *storage places of the cities* [a]Ex. 1:11
5 [1]Lit., *building*
6 [1]Lit., *built*
7 [a]1 Kin. 16:1; 2 Chr. 19:2 [b]2 Chr. 14:11; 32:7, 8
8 [a]2 Chr. 14:9 [b]2 Chr. 12:3 [c]2 Chr. 13:16, 18
9 [a]Prov. 15:3; Jer. 16:17; Zech. 4:10 [b]2 Chr. 15:17
10 [1]Lit., *the house of the stocks*
11 [a]1 Kin. 15:23, 24
12 [a]Jer. 17:5
13 [1]Lit., *and*
14 [a]Gen. 50:2; John 19:39, 40 [b]2 Chr. 21:19
1 [a]1 Kin. 15:24

2 He placed troops in all [a]the fortified cities of Judah, and set garrisons in the land of Judah, and in the cities of Ephraim [b]which Asa his father had captured.

His Good Reign

3 And the LORD was with Jehoshaphat because he [1]followed the example of his father David's earlier days and did not seek the Baals,

4 but sought the God of his father, [1]followed His commandments, [a]and did not act as Israel did.

5 So the LORD established the kingdom in his [1]control, and all Judah brought tribute to Jehoshaphat, and [a]he had great riches and honor.

6 And [1]he took great pride in the ways of the LORD and again [a]removed the high places and the Asherim from Judah.

7 Then in the third year of his reign he sent his officials, Ben-hail, Obadiah, Zechariah, Nethanel, and Micaiah, [a]to teach in the cities of Judah;

8 and with them [a]the Levites, Shemaiah, Nethaniah, Zebadiah, Asahel, Shemiramoth, Jehonathan, Adonijah, Tobijah, and Tobadonijah, the Levites; and with them Elishama and Jehoram, the priests.

9 And they taught in Judah, *having* [a]the book of the law of the LORD with them; and they went throughout all the cities of Judah and taught among the people.

10 Now [a]the dread of the LORD was on all the kingdoms of the lands which *were* around Judah, so that they did not make war against Jehoshaphat.

11 And some of the Philistines [a]brought gifts and silver as tribute to Jehoshaphat; the Arabians also brought him flocks, 7,700 rams and 7,700 male goats.

12 So Jehoshaphat grew greater and greater, and he built fortresses and store cities in Judah.

13 And he had large supplies in the cities of Judah, and warriors, valiant men, in Jerusalem.

14 And this was their muster according to their fathers' households: of Judah, commanders of thousands, Adnah *was* the commander, and with him 300,000 valiant warriors;

15 and next to him *was* Johanan the commander, and with him 280,000;

16 and next to him Amasiah the son of Zichri, [a]who volunteered for the LORD, and with him 200,000 valiant warriors;

17 and of Benjamin, Eliada a valiant warrior, and with him 200,000 armed with bow and shield;

18 and next to him Jehozabad, and with him 180,000 equipped for war.

19 These are they who served the king, apart from [a]those whom the king put in the fortified cities through all Judah.

Jehoshaphat Allies with Ahab

18 NOW [a]Jehoshaphat had great riches and honor; and he allied himself by marriage with Ahab.

2 [a]And some years later he went down to *visit* Ahab at Samaria. And Ahab slaughtered many sheep and oxen for him and the people who were with him, and induced him to go up against Ramoth-gilead.

3 And Ahab king of Israel said to Jehoshaphat king of Judah, "Will you go with me *against* Ramoth-gilead?" And he said to him, "I am as you are, and my people as your people, and *we will be* with you in the battle."

4 Moreover, Jehoshaphat said to the king of Israel, "Please inquire [1]first for the word of the LORD."

5 Then the king of Israel assembled the prophets, four hundred men, and said to them, "Shall we go against Ramoth-gilead to battle, or shall I refrain?" And they said, "Go up, for God will give *it* into the hand of the king."

6 But Jehoshaphat said, "Is there not yet a prophet of the LORD here that we may inquire of him?"

7 And the king of Israel said to Jehoshaphat, "There is yet one man by whom we may inquire of the LORD, but I hate him, for he never prophesies good concerning me but always evil. He is Micaiah, son of Imla." But Jehoshaphat said, "Let not the king say so."

Ahab's False Prophets Assure Victory

8 Then the king of Israel called an officer and said, "[1]Bring quickly Micaiah, Imla's son."

9 Now the king of Israel and Jehoshaphat the king of Judah were sitting each on his throne, arrayed in *their* robes, and *they* were sitting [a]at the threshing floor at the entrance of the gate of Samaria; and all the prophets were prophesying before them.

10 And Zedekiah the son of Chenaanah made horns of iron for himself and said, "Thus says the LORD, 'With these you shall gore the Arameans, until they are consumed.' "

11 And all the prophets were prophesying thus, saying, "Go up to Ramoth-gilead and succeed, for the LORD will give *it* into the hand of the king."

Micaiah Brings Word from God

12 Then the messenger who went to summon Micaiah spoke to him saying, "Behold, the words of the prophets are uniformly favorable to the king. So please let your word be like one of them and speak favorably."

13 But Micaiah said, "As the LORD lives, [a]what my God says, that I will speak."

14 And when he came to the king, the king said to him, "Micaiah, shall we go to Ramoth-gilead to battle, or shall I refrain?" He said, "Go up and succeed, for they will be given into your hand."

---

2 [a]2 Chr. 11:5 [b]2 Chr. 15:8
3 [1]Lit., *walked in the earlier ways of his father*
4 [1]Lit., *walked in* [a]1 Kin. 12:28
5 [1]Lit., *hand* [a]2 Chr. 18:1
6 [1]Lit., *his heart was high* [a]2 Chr. 15:17
7 [a]2 Chr. 15:3; 35:3
8 [a]2 Chr. 19:8
9 [a]Deut. 6:4-9
10 [a]2 Chr. 14:14
11 [a]2 Chr. 9:14; 26:8
16 [a]Judg. 5:2, 9; 1 Chr. 29:9
19 [a]2 Chr. 17:2

1 [a]2 Chr. 17:5
2 [a]1 Kin. 22:2-35
4 [1]Lit., *as the day*
8 [1]Lit., *Hasten*
9 [a]Ruth 4:1
13 [a]Num. 22:18-20, 35

15 Then the king said to him, "How
many times must I adjure you to speak
to me nothing but the truth in the name
of the LORD?"
16 So he said,
"I saw all Israel
Scattered on the mountains,
[a]Like sheep which have no shepherd;
And the LORD said,
'These have no master.
Let each of them return to his
house in peace.'"
17 Then the king of Israel said to
Jehoshaphat, "Did I not tell you that he
would not prophesy good concerning
me, but evil?"
18 And Micaiah said, "Therefore, hear
the word of the LORD. [a]I saw the LORD
sitting on His throne, and all the host of
heaven standing on His right and on His
left.
19"And the LORD said, 'Who will
entice Ahab king of Israel to go up and
fall at Ramoth-gilead?' And one said
this while another said that.
20"Then a [a]spirit came forward and
stood before the LORD and said, 'I will
entice him.' And the LORD said to him,
'How?'
21"And he said, 'I will go and be [a]a
deceiving spirit in the mouth of all his
prophets.' Then He said, 'You are to
entice *him* and prevail also. Go and do
so.'
22"Now therefore, behold, [a]the LORD
has put a deceiving spirit in the mouth of
these your prophets; for the LORD has
proclaimed disaster against you."
23 Then Zedekiah the son of Chenaanah came near and [a]struck Micaiah on
the cheek and said, "[1]How did the Spirit
of the LORD pass from me to speak to
you?"
24 And Micaiah said, "Behold, you
shall see on that day, when you enter an
inner room to hide yourself."
25 Then the king of Israel said, "[a]Take
Micaiah and return him to Amon [b]the
governor of the city, and to Joash the
king's son;
26 and say, 'Thus says the king, "[a]Put
this *man* in prison, and feed him [1]spar-
ingly with bread and water until I return
safely."'"
27 And Micaiah said, "If you indeed
return safely, the LORD has not spoken
by me." And he said, "[a]Listen, all you
people."

Ahab's Defeat and Death

28 So the king of Israel and Jehoshaphat king of Judah went up against
Ramoth-gilead.
29 And the king of Israel said to
Jehoshaphat, "I will disguise myself and
go into battle, but you put on your
robes." So the king of Israel disguised
himself, and they went into battle.
30 Now the king of Aram had commanded the captains of his chariots,
saying, "Do not fight with small or great,
but with the king of Israel alone."
31 So it came about when the captains
of the chariots saw Jehoshaphat, that
they said, "It is the king of Israel," and
they turned aside to fight against him.
But Jehoshaphat [a]cried out, and the
LORD helped him, and God diverted
them from him.
32 Then it happened when the captains of the chariots saw that it was not
the king of Israel, that they turned back
from pursuing him.
33 And a certain man drew his bow at
random and struck the king of Israel [1]in
a joint of the armor. So he said to the
driver of the chariot, "Turn [2]around,
and take me out of the [3]fight; for I am
severely wounded."
34 And the battle raged that day, and
the king of Israel propped himself up in
his chariot in front of the Arameans
until the evening; and at sunset he died.

Jehu Rebukes Jehoshaphat

19 THEN Jehoshaphat the king of
Judah returned in safety to his
house in Jerusalem.
2 And [a]Jehu the son of Hanani the
seer went out to meet him and said to
King Jehoshaphat, "[b]Should you help
the wicked and love those who hate the
LORD and [1c]so *bring* wrath on yourself
from the LORD?
3"But [1a]there is *some* good in you, for
[b]you have removed the [2]Asheroth from
the land and you [c]have set your heart to
seek God."
4 So Jehoshaphat lived in Jerusalem
and went out again among the people
from Beersheba to the hill country of
Ephraim and [a]brought them back to the
LORD, the God of their fathers.

Reforms Instituted

5 And he appointed [a]judges in the
land in all the fortified cities of Judah,
city by city.
6 And he said to the judges, "Consider what you are doing, for [a]you do
not judge for man but for the LORD who
is with you [1]when you render judgment.
7"Now then let the fear of the LORD
be upon you; [1]be very careful what you
do, for [2]the LORD our God will [a]have no
part in unrighteousness, [b]or partiality, or
the taking of a bribe."
8 And in Jerusalem also Jehoshaphat
appointed some [a]of the Levites and
priests, and some of the heads of the
fathers' *households* of Israel, for the
judgment of the LORD and to judge
[1]disputes among the inhabitants of Jerusalem.
9 Then he charged them saying,
"Thus you shall do in the fear of the
LORD, faithfully and wholeheartedly.
10"[a]And whenever any dispute comes
to you from your brethren who live in
their cities, between blood and blood,
between law and commandment, statutes and ordinances, you shall warn
them that they may not be guilty before
the LORD, and [b]wrath may *not* come on

16 [a]Num. 27:17; 1 Kin. 22:17; Ezek. 34:5; 35:4-8; Matt. 9:36; Mark 6:34

18 [a]Is. 6:1-5; Dan. 7:9, 10

20 [a]Job 1:6; 2 Thess. 2:9

21 [a]John 8:44

22 [a]Is. 19:14; Ezek. 14:9

23 [1]Lit., *Which way* [a]Jer. 20:2; Mark 14:65; Acts 23:2

25 [a]2 Chr. 18:8 [b]2 Chr. 34:8

26 [1]Lit., *with bread of affliction and water of affliction* [a]2 Chr. 16:10

27 [a]Mic. 1:2

31 [a]2 Chr. 13:14, 15

33 [1]Lit., *between the scale-armor and the breastplate* [2]Lit., *your hand* [3]Lit., *camp*

2 [1]Lit., *by this* [a]1 Kin. 16:1; 2 Chr. 20:34 [b]2 Chr. 18:1, 3 [c]2 Chr. 24:18

3 [1]Lit., *good things are found* [2]I.e., wooden pillars [a]2 Chr. 12:12 [b]2 Chr. 17:6 [c]2 Chr. 12:14

4 [a]2 Chr. 15:8-13

5 [a]Deut. 16:18-20

6 [1]Lit., *in the word of judgment* [a]Lev. 19:15; Deut. 1:17

7 [1]Lit., *be careful and do* [2]Lit., *there is not with the LORD God* [a]Gen. 18:25; Deut. 32:4 [b]Deut. 10:17, 18

8 [1]So the versions; Heb. reads *disputes. And they returned to Jerusalem.* Or, *And they lived in Jerusalem* [a]2 Chr. 17:8, 9

10 [a]Deut. 17:8 [b]2 Chr. 19:2

you and your brethren. Thus you shall
do and you will not be guilty.
11 "And behold, Amariah the chief
priest will be over you in [1a]all that
pertains to the LORD; and Zebadiah the
son of Ishmael, the ruler of the house of
Judah, in [1]all that pertains to the king.
Also the Levites shall be officers before
you. [2b]Act resolutely, and the LORD be
with the upright."

Judah Invaded

20 NOW it came about after this
that the sons of Moab and the
sons of Ammon, together with some of
the [1a]Meunites, came to make war
against Jehoshaphat.
2 Then some came and reported to
Jehoshaphat, saying, "A great multitude
is coming against you from beyond the
sea, out of [1]Aram and behold, they are
in [a]Hazazon-tamar (that is Engedi)."
3 And Jehoshaphat was afraid and
[1a]turned his attention to seek the LORD;
and [b]proclaimed a fast throughout all
Judah.
4 So Judah gathered together to
[a]seek help from the LORD; they even
came from all the cities of Judah to seek
the LORD.
5 Then Jehoshaphat stood in the
assembly of Judah and Jerusalem, in the
house of the LORD before the new court,

Jehoshaphat's Prayer

6 and he said, "O LORD, the God of
our fathers, [a]art Thou not God in the
heavens? And [b]art Thou not ruler over
all the kingdoms of the nations? Power
and might are in Thy hand so that no
one can stand against Thee.
7 "Didst Thou not, O our God, drive
out the inhabitants of this land before
Thy people Israel, and [a]give it to the
descendants of [b]Abraham Thy friend
forever?
8 "And they lived in it, and have built
Thee a sanctuary there for Thy name,
saying,
9 '[a]Should evil come upon us, the
sword, *or* judgment, or pestilence, or
famine, we will stand before this house
and before Thee (for [b]Thy name is in
this house) and cry to Thee in our
distress, and Thou wilt hear and deliver
us.'
10 "And now behold, [a]the sons of
Ammon and Moab and [1]Mount Seir,
[b]whom Thou didst not let Israel invade
when they came out of the land of Egypt
(they turned aside from them and did
not destroy them),
11 behold *how* they are rewarding us,
by [a]coming to drive us out from Thy
possession which Thou hast given us as
an inheritance.
12 "O our God, [a]wilt Thou not judge
them? For we are powerless before this
great multitude who are coming against
us; nor do we know what to do, but [b]our
eyes are on Thee."
13 And all Judah was standing before

11 [1]Lit., *every matter of* [2]Lit., *Be strong and do* [a]2 Chr. 19:8 [b]1 Chr. 28:20
1 [1]So with Gr.; Heb., *Ammonites* [a]1 Chr. 4:41; 2 Chr. 26:7
2 [1]Another reading is *Edom* [a]Gen. 14:7
3 [1]Lit., *set his face* [a]2 Chr. 19:3 [b]1 Sam. 7:6; Ezra 8:21
4 [a]Joel 1:14
6 [a]Deut. 4:39 [b]1 Chr. 29:11
7 [a]Is. 41:8 [b]James 2:23
9 [a]2 Chr. 6:28-30 [b]2 Chr. 6:20
10 [1]I.e., Edom [a]2 Chr. 20:1, 22 [b]Num. 20:17-21
11 [a]Ps. 83:12
12 [a]Judg. 11:27 [b]Ps. 25:15; 121:1, 2
14 [a]2 Chr. 15:1; 24:20
15 [a]Ex. 14:13; Deut. 20:1-4; 2 Chr. 32:7, 8 [b]1 Sam. 17:47
17 [a]Ex. 14:13 [b]2 Chr. 15:2
18 [a]Ex. 4:31
20 [a]Is. 7:9
21 [a]1 Chr. 16:29; Ps. 29:2 [b]1 Chr. 16:34
22 [1]Lit., *struck down* [a]2 Chr. 13:13 [b]2 Chr. 20:10
23 [a]Judg. 7:22; 1 Sam. 14:20
25 [1]So several ancient mss.; others read *corpses*

the LORD, with their infants, their wives,
and their children.

Jahaziel Answers the Prayer

14 Then in the midst of the assembly
[a]the Spirit of the LORD came upon
Jahaziel the son of Zechariah, the son
of Benaiah, the son of Jeiel, the son of
Mattaniah, the Levite of the sons of
Asaph;
15 and he said, "Listen, all Judah and
the inhabitants of Jerusalem and King
Jehoshaphat: thus says the LORD to you,
'[a]Do not fear or be dismayed because of
this great multitude, for [b]the battle is not
yours but God's.
16 'Tomorrow go down against them.
Behold, they will come up by the ascent
of Ziz, and you will find them at the end
of the valley in front of the wilderness of
Jeruel.
17 'You *need* not fight in this *battle;*
station yourselves, [a]stand and see the
salvation of the LORD on your behalf, O
Judah and Jerusalem.' Do not fear or be
dismayed; tomorrow go out to face
them, [b]for the LORD is with you."
18 And Jehoshaphat [a]bowed his head
with *his* face to the ground, and all
Judah and the inhabitants of Jerusalem
fell down before the LORD, worshiping
the LORD.
19 And the Levites, from the sons of
the Kohathites and of the sons of the
Korahites, stood up to praise the LORD
God of Israel, with a very loud voice.

Enemies Destroy Themselves

20 And they rose early in the morning
and went out to the wilderness of Tekoa;
and when they went out, Jehoshaphat
stood and said, "Listen to me, O Judah
and inhabitants of Jerusalem, [a]put your
trust in the LORD your God, and you
will be established. Put your trust in His
prophets and succeed."
21 And when he had consulted with
the people, he appointed those who sang
to the LORD and those who [a]praised *Him*
in holy attire, as they went out before
the army and said, "[b]Give thanks to the
LORD, for His lovingkindness is everlasting."
22 And when they began singing and
praising, the LORD [a]set ambushes
against the sons of [b]Ammon, Moab, and
Mount Seir, who had come against Judah; so they were [1]routed.
23 For the sons of Ammon and Moab
rose up against the inhabitants of Mount
Seir destroying *them* completely, and
when they had finished with the inhabitants of Seir, [a]they helped to destroy one
another.
24 When Judah came to the lookout
of the wilderness, they looked toward
the multitude; and behold, they *were*
corpses lying on the ground, and no one
had escaped.
25 And when Jehoshaphat and his
people came to take their spoil, they
found much among them, *including*
goods, [1]garments, and valuable things

which they took for themselves, more than they could carry. And they were three days taking the spoil because there was so much.

Triumphant Return to Jerusalem

26 Then on the fourth day they assembled in the valley of Beracah, for there they blessed the LORD. Therefore they have named that place "The Valley of [1]Beracah" until today.

27 And every man of Judah and Jerusalem returned with Jehoshaphat at their head, returning to Jerusalem with joy, [a]for the LORD had made them to rejoice over their enemies.

28 And they came to Jerusalem with harps, lyres, and trumpets to the house of the LORD.

29 And [a]the dread of God was on all the kingdoms of the lands when they heard that the LORD had fought against the enemies of Israel.

30 So the kingdom of Jehoshaphat was at peace, [a]for his God gave him rest on all sides.

31 [a]Now Jehoshaphat reigned over Judah. He *was* thirty-five years old when he became king, and he reigned in Jerusalem twenty-five years. And his mother's name *was* Azubah the daughter of Shilhi.

32 And he walked in the way of his father Asa and did not depart from it, doing right in the sight of the LORD.

33 [a]The high places, however, were not removed; [b]the people had not yet directed their hearts to the God of their fathers.

34 Now the rest of the acts of Jehoshaphat, first [1]to last, behold, they are written in the annals of [a]Jehu the son of Hanani, which is [2]recorded in the Book of the Kings of Israel.

Alliance Displeases God

35 [a]And after this Jehoshaphat king of Judah allied himself with Ahaziah king of Israel. He acted wickedly [1]in so doing.

36 So he allied himself with him to make ships to go [a]to Tarshish, and they made the ships in Ezion-geber.

37 Then Eliezer the son of Dodavahu of Mareshah prophesied against Jehoshaphat saying, "Because you have allied yourself with Ahaziah, the LORD has destroyed your works." So the ships were broken and could not go to Tarshish.

Jehoram Succeeds Jehoshaphat in Judah

21 [a]THEN Jehoshaphat slept with his fathers and was buried with his fathers in the city of David, and Jehoram his son became king in his place.

2 And he had brothers, the sons of Jehoshaphat: Azariah, Jehiel, Zechariah, [1]Azaryahu, Michael, and Shephatiah. All these *were* the sons of Jehoshaphat king [a]of Israel.

3 And their father gave them many gifts of silver, gold and precious things, [a]with fortified cities in Judah, but he gave the kingdom to Jehoram because he was the first-born.

4 Now when Jehoram had [1]taken over the kingdom of his father and made himself [2]secure, he [a]killed all his brothers with the sword, and some of the rulers of Israel also.

5 [a]Jehoram *was* thirty-two years old when he became king, and he reigned eight years in Jerusalem.

6 [a]And he walked in the way of the kings of Israel, just as the house of Ahab did ([b]for Ahab's daughter was his wife), and he did evil in the sight of the LORD.

7 Yet the LORD was not willing to destroy the house of David because of the covenant which He had made with David, [a]and since He had promised to give a lamp to him and his sons forever.

Revolt against Judah

8 In his days [a]Edom revolted [1]against the rule of Judah, and set up a king over themselves.

9 Then Jehoram crossed over with his commanders and all his chariots with him. And it came about that he arose by night and struck down the Edomites who were surrounding him and the commanders of the chariots.

10 So Edom revolted [1]against Judah to this day. Then Libnah revolted at the same time [2]against his rule, because he had forsaken the LORD God of his fathers.

11 Moreover, [a]he made high places in the mountains of Judah, and caused the inhabitants of Jerusalem [b]to play the harlot and led Judah astray.

12 Then a letter came to him from Elijah the prophet saying, "Thus says the LORD God of your father David, 'Because [a]you have not walked in the ways of Jehoshaphat your father [b]and the ways of Asa king of Judah,

13 but [a]have walked in the way of the kings of Israel, and have caused Judah and the inhabitants of Jerusalem to play the harlot [b]as the house of Ahab played the harlot, and you [c]have also killed your brothers, [1]your own family, who were better than you,

14 behold, the LORD is going to strike your people, your sons, your wives, and all your possessions with a great [1]calamity;

15 and [a]you will suffer [1]severe sickness, a disease of your bowels, until your bowels come out because of the sickness, day by day.' "

16 Then [a]the LORD stirred up against Jehoram the spirit of the Philistines and [b]the Arabs who [1]bordered the Ethiopians;

17 and they came against Judah and invaded it, and carried away all the possessions found in the king's house together with his sons and his wives, so that no son was left to him except [1a]Jehoahaz, the youngest of his sons.

26 [1]I.e., *blessing*
27 [a]Neh. 12:43
29 [a]2 Chr. 14:14; 17:10
30 [a]2 Chr. 14:6, 7; 15:15
31 [a]1 Kin. 22:41-43
33 [a]2 Chr. 17:6 [b]2 Chr. 19:3
34 [1]Lit., *and* [2]Lit., *taken up* [a]2 Chr. 19:2
35 [1]Lit., *to do* [a]1 Kin. 22:48, 49
36 [a]2 Chr. 9:21
1 [a]1 Kin. 22:50
2 [1]Or, *Azariah* [a]2 Chr. 12:6; 23:2
3 [a]2 Chr. 11:5
4 [1]Lit., *risen up* [2]Lit., *strong* [a]Gen. 4:8; Judg. 9:5
5 [a]2 Kin. 8:17-22
6 [a]1 Kin. 12:28-30 [b]2 Chr. 18:1
7 [a]2 Sam. 7:12-17; 1 Kin. 11:13, 36
8 [1]Lit., *from under the hand of* [a]2 Chr. 20:22, 23; 21:10
10 [1]Lit., *from under the hand of* [2]Lit., *from under his hand*
11 [a]1 Kin. 11:7 [b]Lev. 20:5
12 [a]2 Chr. 17:3, 4 [b]2 Chr. 14:2-5
13 [1]Lit., *your father's house* [a]2 Chr. 21:6 [b]1 Kin. 16:31-33 [c]2 Chr. 21:4
14 [1]Lit., *blow*
15 [1]Lit., *in many sicknesses* [a]2 Chr. 21:18, 19
16 [1]Lit., *were at the hand of* [a]2 Chr. 33:11 [b]2 Chr. 17:11; 22:1
17 [1]In 2 Chr. 22:1, *Ahaziah* [a]2 Chr. 25:23

18 So after all this the LORD smote him [a]in his bowels with an incurable sickness.

19 Now it came about in the course of time, at the end of two years, that his bowels came out because of his sickness and he died in great pain. And his people made no fire for him like [a]the fire for his fathers.

20 He was thirty-two years old when he became king, and he reigned in Jerusalem eight years; and he departed [1a]with no one's regret, and they buried him in the city of David, [b]but not in the tombs of the kings.

Ahaziah Succeeds Jehoram in Judah

22 [a]THEN the inhabitants of Jerusalem made [1]Ahaziah, his youngest son, king in his place, for the band of men who came with [b]the Arabs to the camp had slain all the older *sons.* So Ahaziah the son of Jehoram king of Judah began to reign.

2 Ahaziah *was* [1]twenty-two years old when he became king, and he reigned one year in Jerusalem. And his mother's name was Athaliah, the [2]granddaughter of Omri.

3 He also walked in the ways of the house of Ahab, for his mother was his counselor to do wickedly.

4 And he did evil in the sight of the LORD like the house of Ahab, for they were his counselors after the death of his father, to [a]his destruction.

Ahaziah Allies with Jehoram of Israel

5 He also walked according to their counsel, and went with Jehoram the son of Ahab king of Israel to wage war against Hazael king of Aram at Ramoth-gilead. But the [1a]Arameans [2]wounded [3]Joram.

6 So he returned to be healed in Jezreel of the wounds [1]which they had inflicted on him at Ramah, when he fought against Hazael king of Aram. And [2]Ahaziah, the son of Jehoram king of Judah, went down to see Jehoram the son of Ahab in Jezreel, because he was sick.

7 Now [a]the destruction of Ahaziah was from God, in that [1]he went to Joram. For when he came, [b]he went out with Jehoram against Jehu the son of Nimshi, [c]whom the LORD had anointed to cut off the house of Ahab.

Jehu Murders Princes of Judah

8 [a]And it came about when Jehu was executing judgment on the house of Ahab, he found the princes of Judah and the sons of Ahaziah's brothers, ministering to Ahaziah, and slew them.

9 [a]He also sought Ahaziah, and they caught him while he was hiding in Samaria; they brought him to Jehu, put him to death, [b]and buried him. For they said, "He is the son of Jehoshaphat, [c]who sought the LORD with all his heart." So there was no one of the house of Ahaziah to retain the power of the kingdom.

10 [a]Now when Athaliah the mother of Ahaziah saw that her son was dead, she rose and destroyed all the royal [1]offspring of the house of Judah.

11 But Jehoshabeath the king's daughter took Joash the son of Ahaziah, and stole him from among the king's sons who were being put to death, and placed him and his nurse in the bedroom. So Jehoshabeath, the daughter of King Jehoram, the wife of Jehoiada the priest (for she was the sister of Ahaziah), hid him from Athaliah so that she would not put him to death.

12 And he was hidden with them in the house of God six years while Athaliah reigned over the land.

Jehoiada Sets Joash on the Throne of Judah

23 [a]NOW in the seventh year Jehoiada strengthened himself, and took captains of hundreds: Azariah the son of Jeroham, Ishmael the son of Johanan, Azariah the son of Obed, Maaseiah the son of Adaiah, and Elishaphat the son of Zichri, *and they entered* into a covenant with him.

2 And they went throughout Judah and gathered the Levites from all the cities of Judah, and the heads of the fathers' *households* of [a]Israel, and they came to Jerusalem.

3 Then all the assembly made a covenant with the king in the house of God. And [1]Jehoiada said to them, "Behold, the king's son shall reign, [a]as the LORD has spoken concerning the sons of David.

4 "This is the thing which you shall do: one third of you, of the priests and Levites [a]who come in on the sabbath, *shall be* gatekeepers,

5 and one third *shall be* at the king's house, and a third at the Gate of the Foundation; and all the people *shall be* in the courts of the house of the LORD.

6 "But let no one enter the house of the LORD except the priests and [a]the ministering Levites; they may enter, for they are holy. And let all the people keep the charge of the LORD.

7 "And the Levites will surround the king, each man with his weapons in his hand; and whoever enters the house, let him be killed. Thus be with the king when he comes in and when he goes out."

8 So the Levites and all Judah did according to all that Jehoiada the priest commanded. And each one of them took his men who were to come in on the sabbath, with those who were to go out on the sabbath, for Jehoiada the priest did not dismiss *any of* [a]the divisions.

9 Then Jehoiada the priest gave to the captains of hundreds the spears and the large and small shields which had been King David's, which *were* in the house of God.

---

18 [a]2 Chr. 21:15

19 [a]2 Chr. 16:14

20 [1]Lit., *without desire* [a]Jer. 22:18, 28 [b]2 Chr. 24:25; 28:27

1 [1]In 2 Chr. 21:17, *Jehoahaz* [a]2 Kin. 8:24-29 [b]2 Chr. 21:16

2 [1]So some versions and 2 Kin. 8:26; Heb., *42 years* [2]Lit., *daughter*

4 [a]Prov. 13:20

5 [1]Heb., *archers* [2]Lit., *smote* [3]I.e., Jehoram [a]2 Kin. 8:28

6 [1]Lit., *with which . . . smitten* [2]So with 2 Kin. 8:29; Heb., *Azariah*

7 [1]Lit., *to go* [a]2 Chr. 10:15 [b]2 Kin. 9:21 [c]2 Kin. 9:6, 7

8 [a]2 Kin. 10:11-14

9 [a]2 Kin. 9:27 [b]2 Kin. 9:28 [c]2 Chr. 17:4

10 [1]Lit., *seed* [a]2 Kin. 11:1-3

1 [a]2 Kin. 11:4-20

2 [a]2 Chr. 11:13-17; 21:2

3 [1]Lit., *he* [a]2 Sam. 7:12; 2 Chr. 21:7

4 [a]1 Chr. 9:25

6 [a]1 Chr. 23:28-32

8 [a]1 Chr. 24:1

10 And he stationed all the people,
each man with his weapon in his hand,
from the right [1]side of the house to the
left [1]side of the house, by the altar and
by the house, around the king.
11 Then they brought out the king's
son and put the crown on him, and *gave
him* [a]the testimony, and made him king.
And Jehoiada and his sons anointed him
and said, "[b]*Long* live the king!"

Athaliah Murdered

12 When Athaliah heard the noise of
the people running and praising the
king, she came into the house of the
LORD to the people.
13 And she looked, and behold, the
king was standing by his pillar at
the entrance, and the captains and the
[1]trumpeters *were* beside the king. And
all the people of the land rejoiced and
blew trumpets, the singers with *their*
musical instruments [2]leading the praise.
Then Athaliah tore her clothes and said,
"Treason! Treason!"
14 And Jehoiada the priest brought
out the captains of hundreds who were
appointed over the army, and said to
them, "Bring her out [1]between the
ranks; and whoever follows her, put to
death with the sword." For the priest
said, "Let her not be put to death in the
house of the LORD."
15 So they [1]seized her, and when she
arrived at the entrance of [a]the Horse
Gate of the king's house, they [b]put her
to death there.

Reforms Carried Out

16 Then [a]Jehoiada made a covenant
between himself and all the people and
the king, that they should be the LORD's
people.
17 And all the people went to the
house of Baal, and tore it down, and
they broke in pieces his altars and his
images, and [a]killed Mattan the priest of
Baal before the altars.
18 Moreover, Jehoiada placed the
offices of the house of the LORD under
the [1]authority of [a]the Levitical priests,
[b]whom David had assigned over the
house of the LORD, to offer the burnt
offerings of the LORD, as it is written in
the law of Moses—[c]with rejoicing and
singing according to the [2]order of David.
19 And he stationed [a]the gatekeepers
of the house of the LORD, so that no one
should enter *who was* in any way unclean.
20 And [a]he took the captains of hundreds, the nobles, the rulers of the
people, and all the people of the land,
and brought the king down from the
house of the LORD, and came through
the upper gate to the king's house. And
they placed the king upon the royal
throne.
21 So [a]all of the people of the land
rejoiced and the city was quiet. For they
had put Athaliah to death with the
sword.

10 [1]Lit., *shoulder*
11 [a]Ex. 25:16, 21 [b]1 Sam. 10:24
13 [1]Lit., *trumpets* [2]Lit., *and leading for praising*
14 [1]Lit., *from within*
15 [1]Lit., *placed hands to her* [a]Neh. 3:28; Jer. 31:40 [b]2 Chr. 22:10
16 [a]2 Kin. 11:17
17 [a]Deut. 13:6-9; 1 Kin. 18:40
18 [1]Lit., *hand* [2]Lit., *hands of* [a]2 Chr. 5:5 [b]1 Chr. 23:6, 25-31 [c]1 Chr. 25:1
19 [a]1 Chr. 9:22
20 [a]2 Kin. 11:19
21 [a]2 Kin. 11:20
1 [a]2 Kin. 11:21; 12:1-15
2 [a]2 Chr. 26:4, 5
4 [1]Lit., *was with a heart* [a]2 Chr. 24:7
5 [1]Lit., *to strengthen* [2]Lit., *from year to year* [a]2 Chr. 21:2
6 [a]Ex. 30:12-16 [b]Num. 1:50
7 [1]Lit., *made* [a]2 Chr. 21:17
8 [a]2 Kin. 12:9
9 [a]2 Chr. 36:22 [b]2 Chr. 24:6
10 [1]Lit., *threw*
11 [a]2 Kin. 12:10
12 [1]Lit., *to strengthen*
13 [1]Lit., *set up* [2]Lit., *upon its proportion*

Young Joash Influenced by Jehoiada

24 [a]JOASH *was* seven years old when
he became king, and he reigned
forty years in Jerusalem; and his mother's name *was* Zibiah from Beersheba.
2 And [a]Joash did what was right in
the sight of the LORD all the days of
Jehoiada the priest.
3 And Jehoiada took two wives for
him, and he became the father of sons
and daughters.

Faithless Priests

4 Now it came about after this that
Joash [1]decided [a]to restore the house of
the LORD.
5 And he gathered the priests and
Levites, and said to them, "Go out to the
cities of Judah, and collect money from
all [a]Israel to [1]repair the house of your
God [2]annually, and you shall do the
matter quickly." But the Levites did not
act quickly.
6 So the king summoned Jehoiada
the chief *priest* and said to him, "Why
have you not required the Levites to
bring in from Judah and from Jerusalem
[a]the levy *fixed by* Moses the servant of
the LORD on the congregation of Israel
[b]for the tent of the testimony?"
7 For [a]the sons of the wicked Athaliah had broken into the house of God
and even [1]used the holy things of the
house of the LORD for the Baals.

Temple Repaired

8 So the king commanded, and [a]they
made a chest and set it outside by the
gate of the house of the LORD.
9 And [a]they made a proclamation in
Judah and Jerusalem to bring to the
LORD [b]the levy *fixed by* Moses the servant of God on Israel in the wilderness.
10 And all the officers and all the
people rejoiced and brought in their
levies and [1]dropped *them* into the chest
until they had finished.
11 And it came about whenever the
chest was brought in to the king's officer
by the Levites, and when [a]they saw that
there was much money, then the king's
scribe and the chief priest's officer would
come, empty the chest, take it, and
return it to its place. Thus they did daily
and collected much money.
12 And the king and Jehoiada gave it
to those who did the work of the service
of the house of the LORD; and they hired
masons and carpenters to restore the
house of the LORD, and also workers in
iron and bronze to [1]repair the house of
the LORD.
13 So the workmen labored, and the
repair work progressed in their hands,
and they [1]restored the house of God
[2]according to its specifications, and
strengthened it.
14 And when they had finished, they
brought the rest of the money before the
king and Jehoiada; and it was made into
utensils for the house of the LORD,
utensils for the service and the burnt

offering, and pans and utensils of gold and silver. And they offered burnt offerings in the house of the LORD continually all the days of Jehoiada.

15 Now when Jehoiada [1]reached a ripe old age he died; he was one hundred and thirty years old at his death.

16 And they buried him [a]in the city of David among the kings, because he had done well in [b]Israel and [1]to God and His house.

17 But after the death of Jehoiada the officials of Judah came and bowed down to the king, and the king listened to them.

18 And they abandoned [a]the house of the LORD, the God of their fathers, and [b]served the [1]Asherim and the idols; so [c]wrath came upon Judah and Jerusalem for this their guilt.

19 Yet [a]He sent prophets to them to bring them back to the LORD; though they testified against them, they would not listen.

Joash Murders Son of Jehoiada

20 [a]Then the Spirit of God [1]came on Zechariah the son of Jehoiada the priest; and he stood above the people and said to them, "Thus God has said, '[b]Why do you transgress the commandments of the LORD and do not prosper? [c]Because you have forsaken the LORD, He has also forsaken you.' "

21 So [a]they conspired against him and at the command of the king they stoned him [1]to death in the court of the house of the LORD.

22 Thus Joash the king did not remember the kindness which his father Jehoiada had shown him, but he murdered his son. And as he died he said, "May [a]the LORD see and [1]avenge!"

Aram Invades and Defeats Judah

23 Now it came about at the turn of the year that [a]the army of the Arameans came up against him; and they came to Judah and Jerusalem, destroyed all the officials of the people from among the people, and sent all their spoil to the king of Damascus.

24 Indeed the army of the Arameans came with a small number of men; yet [a]the LORD delivered a very great army into their hands, [b]because they had forsaken the LORD, the God of their fathers. Thus they executed judgment on Joash.

25 [a]And when they had departed from him (for they left him very sick), his own servants conspired against him because of the blood of the [1]son of Jehoiada the priest, and murdered him on his bed. So he died, and they buried him in the city of David, but they did not bury him in the tombs of the kings.

26 Now these are those who conspired against him: Zabad the son of Shimeath the Ammonitess, and Jehozabad the son of Shimrith the Moabitess.

27 As to his sons and the many [1]oracles against him and [a]the [2]rebuilding of the house of God, behold, they are written in the [3b]treatise of the Book of the Kings. Then Amaziah his son became king in his place.

Amaziah Succeeds Joash in Judah

25 [a]AMAZIAH was twenty-five years old when he became king, and he reigned twenty-nine years in Jerusalem. And his mother's name was Jehoaddan of Jerusalem.

2 And he did right in the sight of the LORD, [a]yet not with a whole heart.

3 Now [a]it came about as soon as the kingdom was [1]firmly in his grasp, that he killed his servants who had slain his father the king.

4 However, he did not put their children to death, but *did* as it is written in the law in the book of Moses, which the LORD commanded, saying, "[a]Fathers shall not be put to death for sons, nor sons be put to death for fathers, but each shall be put to death for his own sin."

Amaziah Defeats Edomites

5 Moreover, Amaziah assembled Judah and appointed them according to *their* fathers' households under commanders of thousands and commanders of hundreds throughout Judah and Benjamin; and he [1]took a census of those [a]from twenty years old and upward, and found them to be [b]300,000 choice men, *able* to go to war *and* handle spear and shield.

6 He hired also 100,000 valiant warriors out of Israel for one hundred talents of silver.

7 But [a]a man of God came to him saying, "O king, do not let the army of Israel go with you, for the LORD is not with Israel *nor with* any of the sons of Ephraim.

8 "But if you do go, do *it,* be strong for the battle; *yet* God will [1]bring you down before the enemy, [a]for God has power to help and to [1]bring down."

9 And Amaziah said to the man of God, "But what *shall we* do for the hundred talents which I have given to the troops of Israel?" And the man of God answered, "[a]The LORD has much more to give you than this."

10 Then Amaziah [1]dismissed them, the troops which came to him from Ephraim, to go home; so their anger burned against Judah and they returned [2]home in fierce anger.

11 ¶ Now Amaziah strengthened himself, and led his people forth, and went to [a]the Valley of Salt, and struck down 10,000 of the sons of Seir.

12 The sons of Judah also captured 10,000 alive and brought them to the top of the cliff, and threw them down from the top of the cliff so that they were all dashed to pieces.

13 But the [1]troops whom Amaziah sent back from going with him to battle,

15 [1]Lit., *became old and satisfied with days*

16 [1]Lit., *with* [a]2 Chr. 21:20 [b]2 Chr. 21:2

18 [1]I.e., wooden symbols of a female deity [a]2 Chr. 24:4 [b]Ex. 34:12-14 [c]Josh. 22:20

19 [a]Jer. 7:25

20 [1]Lit., *clothed* [a]2 Chr. 20:14 [b]Num. 14:41 [c]2 Chr. 15:2

21 [1]Lit., *with stones* [a]Neh. 9:26; Matt. 23:34, 35

22 [1]Lit., *seek,* or *require* [a]Gen. 9:5

23 [a]2 Kin. 12:17

24 [a]2 Chr. 16:7, 8 [b]2 Chr. 24:20

25 [1]So some ancient versions; Heb., *sons* [a]2 Kin. 12:20, 21

27 [1]Or, *burdens upon* [2]Lit., *founding* [3]Heb., *midrash* [a]2 Chr. 24:12 [b]2 Chr. 13:22

1 [a]2 Kin. 14:1-6

2 [a]2 Chr. 25:14

3 [1]Lit., *firm upon him* [a]2 Kin. 14:5

4 [a]Deut. 24:16

5 [1]Lit., *mustered* [a]Num. 1:3 [b]2 Chr. 26:13

7 [a]2 Kin. 4:9

8 [1]Lit., *cause to stumble* [a]2 Chr. 14:11; 20:6

9 [a]Deut. 8:18; Prov. 10:22

10 [1]Lit., *separated* [2]Lit., *to their own place*

11 [a]2 Kin. 14:7

13 [1]Lit., *sons of the troops*

raided the cities of Judah, from Samaria
to Beth-horon, and struck down 3,000 of
them, and plundered much spoil.

Amaziah Rebuked for Idolatry

14 Now it came about after Amaziah
came from slaughtering the Edomites
that [a]he brought the gods of the sons of
Seir, set them up as his gods, bowed
down before them, and burned incense
to them.
15 Then the anger of the LORD burned
against Amaziah, and He sent him a
prophet who said to him, "Why have
you sought the gods of the people [a]who
have not delivered their own people
from your hand?"
16 And it came about as he was talking with him that [1]the king said to him,
"Have we appointed you a royal counselor? Stop! Why should you be struck
down?" Then the prophet stopped and
said, "I know that God has planned to
destroy you, because you have done this,
and have not listened to my counsel."

Amaziah Defeated by Joash of Israel

17 [a]Then Amaziah king of Judah took
counsel and sent to Joash the son of
Jehoahaz the son of Jehu, the king of
Israel, saying, "Come, let us face each
other."
18 And Joash the king of Israel sent to
Amaziah king of Judah, saying, "[a]The
thorn bush which was in Lebanon sent
to the cedar which was in Lebanon,
saying, 'Give your daughter to my son in
marriage.' But there passed by a wild
beast that was in Lebanon, and trampled
the thorn bush.
19 "You said, 'Behold, you have [1]de-
feated Edom.' And [a]your heart has
[2]become proud in boasting. Now stay at
home; for why should you provoke
trouble that you, even you, should fall
and Judah with you?"
20 But Amaziah would not listen, for
it was from God, that He might deliver
them into the hand *of Joash* because they
had sought the gods of Edom.
21 So Joash king of Israel went up,
and he and Amaziah king of Judah faced
each other at Beth-shemesh, which belonged to Judah.
22 And Judah was defeated [1]by Israel,
and they fled each to his tent.
23 Then Joash king of Israel captured
Amaziah king of Judah, the son of Joash
the son of [a]Jehoahaz, at Beth-shemesh,
and brought him to Jerusalem, and tore
down the wall of Jerusalem from the
Gate of Ephraim to the Corner Gate,
400 [1]cubits.
24 And *he took* all the gold and silver,
and all the utensils which were found in
the house of God with [a]Obed-edom, and
the treasures of the king's house, the
hostages also, and returned to Samaria.
25 [a]And Amaziah, the son of Joash
king of Judah, lived fifteen years after
the death of Joash, son of Jehoahaz, king
of Israel.
26 Now the rest of the acts of Amaziah, from first to last, behold, are they
not written in the Book of the Kings of
Judah and Israel?
27 And from the time that Amaziah
turned away from following the LORD
they conspired against him in Jerusalem,
and he fled to Lachish; but they sent
after him to Lachish and killed him
there.
28 Then they brought him on horses
and buried him with his fathers in the
city of Judah.

Uzziah Succeeds Amaziah in Judah

26 AND all the people of Judah
took [1]Uzziah, who *was* sixteen
years old, and made him king in the
place of his father Amaziah.
2 He built Eloth and restored it to
Judah after the king slept with his fathers.
3 Uzziah was [a]sixteen years old when
he became king, and he reigned fifty-two
years in Jerusalem; and his mother's
name was [1]Jechiliah of Jerusalem.
4 And he did right in the sight of the
LORD according to all that his father
Amaziah had done.
5 And [a]he continued to seek God in
the days of Zechariah, [b]who had understanding [1]through the vision of God;
and [2c]as long as he sought the LORD,
God prospered him.

Uzziah Succeeds in War

6 Now he went out and [a]warred
against the Philistines, and broke down
the wall of Gath and the wall of Jabneh
and the wall of Ashdod; and he built
cities in *the area of* Ashdod and among
the Philistines.
7 And [a]God helped him against the
Philistines, and against the Arabians
who lived in Gur-baal, and the Meunites.
8 The Ammonites also gave [a]tribute
to Uzziah, and his [1]fame extended to the
border of Egypt, for he became very
strong.
9 Moreover, Uzziah built towers in
Jerusalem at [a]the Corner Gate and at the
[b]Valley Gate and at the corner buttress
and fortified them.
10 And he built towers in the wilderness and [a]hewed many cisterns, for he
had much livestock, both in the [1]lowland
and in the plain. *He also had* plowmen
and vinedressers in the hill country and
the fertile fields, for he loved the soil.
11 Moreover, Uzziah had an army
ready for battle, which [1]entered combat
by divisions, according to the number of
their muster, [2]prepared by Jeiel the
scribe and Maaseiah the official, under
the direction of Hananiah, one of the
king's officers.
12 The total number of the heads of
the [1]households, of valiant warriors, was
2,600.

14 [a]2 Chr. 28:23
15 [a]2 Chr. 25:11, 12
16 [1]Lit., *he*
17 [a]2 Kin. 14:8-14
18 [a]Judg. 9:8-15
19 [1]Lit., *smitten* [2]Lit., *lifted you up to boast* [a]2 Chr. 26:16; 32:25
22 [1]Lit., *before*
23 [1]I.e., One cubit equals approx. 18 in. [a]2 Chr. 21:17; 22:1
24 [a]1 Chr. 26:15
25 [a]2 Kin. 14:17-22
1 [1]In 2 Kin. 14:21, *Azariah*
3 [1]In 2 Kin. 15:2, *Jecoliah* [a]2 Kin. 15:2, 3
5 [1]Many mss. read *in the fear of God* [2]Lit., *in the days of his seeking* [a]2 Chr. 24:2 [b]Dan. 1:17 [c]2 Chr. 15:2
6 [a]Is. 14:29
7 [a]2 Chr. 21:16
8 [1]Lit., *name went to the entering of Egypt* [a]2 Chr. 17:11
9 [a]2 Chr. 25:23 [b]Neh. 2:13, 15; 3:13
10 [1]Heb., *shephelah* [a]Gen. 26:18-21
11 [1]Lit., *goes out to* [2]Lit., *by the hand of*
12 [1]Lit., *fathers*

13 And under their direction was an [1]elite army of [a]307,500, who could wage war with great power, to help the king against the enemy.

14 Moreover, Uzziah prepared [1]for all the army shields, spears, helmets, body armor, bows and sling stones.

15 And in Jerusalem he made engines *of war* invented by skillful men to be on the towers and on the corners, for the purpose of shooting arrows and great stones. Hence his [1]fame spread afar, for he was marvelously helped until he *was* strong.

Pride Is Uzziah's Undoing

16 But [a]when he became strong, his heart was so [1]proud that he acted corruptly, and he was unfaithful to the LORD his God, for [b]he entered the temple of the LORD to burn incense on the altar of incense.

17 Then [a]Azariah the priest entered after him and with him eighty priests of the LORD, valiant men.

18 And [a]they opposed Uzziah the king and said to him, "[b]It is not for you, Uzziah, to burn incense to the LORD, [c]but for the priests, the sons of Aaron who are consecrated to burn incense. Get out of the sanctuary, for you have been unfaithful, and will have no honor from the LORD God."

19 But Uzziah, with a censer in his hand for burning incense, was enraged; and while he was enraged with the priests, [a]the leprosy broke out on his forehead before the priests in the house of the LORD, beside the altar of incense.

20 And Azariah the chief priest and all the priests looked at him, and behold, he *was* leprous on his forehead; and they hurried him out of there, and he himself also hastened to get out because the LORD had smitten him.

21 [a]And King Uzziah was a leper to the day of his death; and he lived in [b]a separate house, being a leper, for he was cut off from the house of the LORD. And Jotham his son *was* over the king's house judging the people of the land.

22 Now the rest of the acts of Uzziah, first to last, the prophet [a]Isaiah, the son of Amoz, has written.

23 So Uzziah slept with his fathers, and they buried him with his fathers [a]in the field of the grave which belonged to the kings, for they said, "He is a leper." And Jotham his son became king in his place.

Jotham Succeeds Uzziah in Judah

27 [a]JOTHAM was twenty-five years old when he became king, and he reigned sixteen years in Jerusalem. And his mother's name was Jerushah the daughter of Zadok.

2 And he did right in the sight of the LORD, according to all that his father Uzziah had done; [a]however he did not enter the temple of the LORD. But the people continued acting corruptly.

3 He built the upper gate of the house of the LORD, and he built extensively the wall of [a]Ophel.

4 Moreover, he built [a]cities in the hill country of Judah, and he built fortresses and towers on the wooded *hills.*

5 He fought also with the king of the Ammonites and prevailed over them so that the Ammonites gave him during that year one hundred talents of silver, ten thousand [1]kors of wheat and ten thousand of barley. The Ammonites also paid him this *amount* in the second and in the third year.

6 [a]So Jotham became mighty because he ordered his ways before the LORD his God.

7 [a]Now the rest of the acts of Jotham, even all his wars and his acts, behold, they are written in the Book of the Kings of Israel and Judah.

8 He was [a]twenty-five years old when he became king, and he reigned sixteen years in Jerusalem.

9 And Jotham slept with his fathers, and they buried him in the city of David; and Ahaz his son became king in his place.

Ahaz Succeeds Jotham in Judah

28 [a]AHAZ *was* twenty years old when he became king, and he reigned sixteen years in Jerusalem; and [b]he did not do right in the sight of the LORD as David his father *had done.*

2 [a]But he walked in the ways of the kings of Israel; he also [b]made molten images for the Baals.

3 Moreover, [a]he burned incense in the valley of Ben-hinnom, and [b]burned his sons in fire, [c]according to the abominations of the nations whom the LORD had driven out before the sons of Israel.

4 And he sacrificed and [a]burned incense on the high places, on the hills, and under every green tree.

Judah Is Invaded

5 Wherefore, [a]the LORD his God delivered him into the hand of the king of Aram; and they [1]defeated him and carried away from him a great number of captives, and brought *them* to Damascus. And he was also delivered into the hand of the king of Israel, who [2]inflicted him with heavy casualties.

6 For [a]Pekah the son of Remaliah slew in Judah 120,000 in one day, all valiant men, because they had forsaken the LORD God of their fathers.

7 And Zichri, a mighty man of Ephraim, slew Maaseiah the king's son, and Azrikam the ruler of the house and Elkanah the second to the king.

8 And [a]the sons of Israel carried away captive of [b]their brethren 200,000 women, sons, and daughters; and [1]took also a great deal of spoil from them, and they brought the spoil to Samaria.

13 [1]Lit., *powerful* [a]2 Chr. 25:5
14 [1]Lit., *for them, for all*
15 [1]Lit., *name*
16 [1]Lit., *lifted up* [a]Deut. 32:15; 2 Chr. 25:19 [b]1 Kin. 13:1-4
17 [a]1 Chr. 6:10
18 [a]2 Chr. 19:2 [b]Num. 3:10; 16:39, 40 [c]Ex. 30:7, 8
19 [a]2 Kin. 5:25-27
21 [a]2 Kin. 15:5-7 [b]Lev. 13:46
22 [a]Is. 1:1
23 [a]2 Chr. 21:20; 28:27; Is. 6:1
1 [a]2 Kin. 15:33-35
2 [a]2 Chr. 26:16
3 [a]2 Chr. 33:14; Neh. 3:26
4 [a]2 Chr. 11:5
5 [1]I.e., A kor equals approx. 10 bu.
6 [a]2 Chr. 26:5
7 [a]2 Kin. 15:36
8 [a]2 Chr. 27:1
1 [a]2 Kin. 16:2-4 [b]2 Chr. 27:2
2 [a]2 Chr. 22:3 [b]Ex. 34:17
3 [a]Josh. 15:8 [b]Lev. 18:21; 2 Chr. 33:6 [c]2 Chr. 33:2
4 [a]2 Chr. 28:25
5 [1]Lit., *smote* [2]Lit., *smote him with a great smiting* [a]2 Kin. 16:5; 2 Chr. 24:24; Is. 7:1
6 [a]2 Kin. 16:5
8 [1]Lit., *plundered* [a]Deut. 28:25, 41 [b]2 Chr. 11:4

9 But a prophet of the LORD was there, whose name *was* Oded; and [a]he went out to meet the army which came to Samaria and said to them, "Behold, because the LORD, the God of your fathers, [b]was angry with Judah, He has delivered them into your hand, and you have slain them in a rage [c]*which* has even reached heaven.

10 "And now you are proposing to [a]subjugate for yourselves the people of Judah and Jerusalem for male and female slaves. Surely, *do* you not *have* transgressions of your own against the LORD your God?

11 "Now therefore, listen to me and return the captives [a]whom you captured from your brothers, [b]for the burning anger of the LORD is against you."

12 Then some of the heads of the sons of Ephraim—Azariah the son of Johanan, Berechiah the son of Meshillemoth, Jehizkiah the son of Shallum, and Amasa the son of Hadlai—arose against those who were coming from the battle,

13 and said to them, "You must not bring the captives in here, for you are proposing *to bring* upon us guilt against the LORD adding to our sins and our guilt; for our guilt is great so that *His* burning anger is against Israel."

14 So the armed men left the captives and the spoil before the officers and all the assembly.

15 Then [a]the men who were designated by name arose, took the captives, and they clothed all their naked ones from the spoil; and they gave them clothes and sandals, fed them and [b]gave them drink, anointed them *with oil,* led all their feeble ones on donkeys, and brought them to Jericho, [c]the city of palm trees, to their brothers; then they returned to Samaria.

Compromise with Assyria

16 [a]At that time King Ahaz sent to the [1]kings of Assyria for help.

17 [a]For again the Edomites had come and attacked Judah, and carried away captives.

18 [a]The Philistines also had invaded the cities of the [1]lowland and of the Negev of Judah, and had taken Beth-shemesh, Aijalon, Gederoth, and Soco with its villages, Timnah with its villages, and Gimzo with its villages, and they settled there.

19 For the LORD humbled Judah because of Ahaz king of [a]Israel, for he had brought about a lack of restraint in Judah and was very unfaithful to the LORD.

20 So [a]Tilgath-pilneser king of Assyria came against him and afflicted him instead of strengthening him.

21 [a]Although Ahaz took a portion out of the house of the LORD and out of the palace of the king and of the princes, and gave *it* to the king of Assyria, it did not help him.

22 Now in the time of his distress this

9 [a]2 Chr. 25:15 [b]Is. 47:6 [c]Ezra 9:6; Rev. 18:5
10 [a]Lev. 25:39
11 [a]2 Chr. 28:8 [b]James 2:13
15 [a]2 Chr. 28:12 [b]2 Kin. 6:22; Prov. 25:21, 22 [c]Deut. 34:3
16 [1]Ancient versions read *king* [a]2 Kin. 16:7
17 [a]Obad. 10, 14
18 [1]Heb., *shephelah* [a]Ezek. 16:57
19 [a]2 Chr. 21:2
20 [a]1 Chr. 5:26
21 [a]2 Kin. 16:8, 9
22 [a]Is. 1:5; Jer. 5:3; Rev. 16:11
23 [1]Lit., *smitten* [2]Lit., *stumbling* [a]2 Chr. 25:14 [b]Jer. 44:17, 18
24 [a]2 Kin. 16:17 [b]2 Chr. 29:7 [c]2 Chr. 30:14; 33:3-5
26 [a]2 Kin. 16:19, 20
27 [a]2 Kin. 16:20; 2 Chr. 24:25; Is. 14:28 [b]2 Chr. 21:2
1 [a]2 Kin. 18:1-3
2 [a]2 Chr. 28:1; 34:2
3 [a]2 Chr. 28:24; 29:7
5 [a]2 Chr. 29:15, 34; 35:6
6 [1]Lit., *given* [a]Ezek. 8:16
7 [a]2 Chr. 28:24
8 [a]2 Chr. 24:20 [b]Jer. 25:9, 18
9 [a]2 Chr. 28:5-8, 17

same King Ahaz [a]became yet more unfaithful to the LORD.

23 [a]For he sacrificed to the gods of Damascus which had [1]defeated him, and said, "[b]Because the gods of the kings of Aram helped them, I will sacrifice to them that they may help me." But they became the [2]downfall of him and all Israel.

24 Moreover, when Ahaz gathered together the utensils of the house of God, he [a]cut the utensils of the house of God in pieces; and he [b]closed the doors of the house of the LORD, and [c]made altars for himself in every corner of Jerusalem.

25 And in every city of Judah he made high places to burn incense to other gods, and provoked the LORD, the God of his fathers, to anger.

26 [a]Now the rest of his acts and all his ways, from first to last, behold, they are written in the Book of the Kings of Judah and Israel.

27 [a]So Ahaz slept with his fathers, and they buried him in the city, in Jerusalem, for they did not bring him into the tombs of the kings of [b]Israel; and Hezekiah his son reigned in his place.

Hezekiah Succeeds Ahaz in Judah

29 [a]HEZEKIAH became king *when he was* twenty-five years old; and he reigned twenty-nine years in Jerusalem. And his mother's name *was* Abijah, the daughter of Zechariah.

2 And [a]he did right in the sight of the LORD, according to all that his father David had done.

3 In the first year of his reign, in the first month, he [a]opened the doors of the house of the LORD and repaired them.

4 And he brought in the priests and the Levites, and gathered them into the square on the east.

Reforms Begun

5 Then he said to them, "Listen to me, O Levites. [a]Consecrate yourselves now, and consecrate the house of the LORD, the God of your fathers, and carry the uncleanness out from the holy place.

6 "For our fathers have been unfaithful and have done evil in the sight of the LORD our God, and have forsaken Him and [a]turned their faces away from the dwelling place of the LORD, and have [1]turned *their* backs.

7 "They have also [a]shut the doors of the porch and put out the lamps, and have not burned incense or offered burnt offerings in the holy place to the God of Israel.

8 "Therefore [a]the wrath of the LORD was against Judah and Jerusalem, and He has made them an object of terror, of horror, and of [b]hissing, as you see with your own eyes.

9 "For behold, [a]our fathers have fallen by the sword, and our sons and our daughters and our wives are in captivity for this.

10 "Now it is in my heart [a]to make a
covenant with the LORD God of Israel,
that His burning anger may turn away
from us.
11 "My sons, do not be negligent now,
for [a]the LORD has chosen you to stand
before Him, to minister to Him, and to
be His ministers and burn incense."
12 Then the Levites arose: [a]Mahath,
the son of Amasai and Joel the son of
Azariah, from the sons of [b]the Kohathites; and from the sons of Merari, Kish
the son of Abdi and Azariah the son of
Jehallelel; and from the Gershonites,
Joah the son of Zimmah and Eden the
son of Joah;
13 and from the sons of Elizaphan,
Shimri and [1]Jeiel; and from the sons of
Asaph, Zechariah and Mattaniah;
14 and from the sons of Heman, [1]Je-
hiel and Shimei; and from the sons of
Jeduthun, Shemaiah and Uzziel.
15 And they assembled their brothers,
[a]consecrated themselves, and went in [b]to
cleanse the house of the LORD, according to the commandment of the king [c]by
the words of the LORD.
16 So the priests went in to the inner
part of the house of the LORD to cleanse
it, and every unclean thing which they
found in the temple of the LORD they
brought out to the court of the house of
the LORD. Then the Levites received *it* to
carry out to [a]the Kidron [1]valley.
17 Now they began [1]the consecration
[a]on the first *day* of the first month, and
on the eighth day of the month they
entered the porch of the LORD. Then
they consecrated the house of the LORD
in eight days, and finished on the sixteenth day of the first month.
18 Then they went in to King Hezekiah and said, "We have cleansed the
whole house of the LORD, the altar of
burnt offering with all of its utensils, and
the table of showbread with all of its
utensils.
19 "Moreover, [a]all the utensils which
King Ahaz had discarded during his
reign in his unfaithfulness, we have
prepared and consecrated; and behold,
they are before the altar of the LORD."

Hezekiah Restores Temple Worship

20 Then King Hezekiah arose early
and assembled the princes of the city
and went up to the house of the LORD.
21 And they brought seven bulls,
seven rams, seven lambs, and seven male
goats [a]for a sin offering for the kingdom,
the sanctuary, and Judah. And he ordered the priests, the sons of Aaron, to
offer *them* on the altar of the LORD.
22 So they slaughtered the bulls, and
the priests took the blood and sprinkled
it on the altar. They also slaughtered the
rams and sprinkled the blood on the
altar; they slaughtered the lambs also
and [a]sprinkled the blood on the altar.
23 Then they brought the male goats
of the sin offering before the king and
the assembly, and [a]they laid their hands
on them.

10 [a]2 Chr. 23:16
11 [a]Num. 3:6; 8:6
12 [a]2 Chr. 31:13 [b]Num. 3:19, 20
13 [1]Or, *Jeuel*
14 [1]Or, *Jehuel,* 1 Chr. 15:18, 20
15 [a]2 Chr. 29:5 [b]1 Chr. 23:28 [c]2 Chr. 30:12
16 [1]Or, *wadi* [a]2 Chr. 15:16
17 [1]Lit., *to consecrate* [a]2 Chr. 29:3
19 [a]2 Chr. 28:24
21 [a]Lev. 4:3-14
22 [a]Lev. 4:18
23 [a]Lev. 4:15
24 [a]Lev. 4:26
25 [a]1 Chr. 25:6 [b]2 Chr. 8:14 [c]2 Sam. 24:11 [d]2 Sam. 7:2
26 [a]1 Chr. 23:5 [b]2 Chr. 5:12
27 [1]Lit., *and according to the authority of the instruments* [a]2 Chr. 23:18
29 [a]2 Chr. 20:18
30 [a]Ps. 100:1; 106:12
31 [1]Lit., *filled your hands* [2]Lit., *willing of heart* [a]2 Chr. 13:9 [b]Ex. 35:5, 22
34 [1]Lit., *upright of heart* [a]2 Chr. 35:11 [b]2 Chr. 30:3
35 [1]Lit., *the burnt offerings to an abundance* [a]2 Chr. 29:32 [b]Lev. 3:16 [c]Num. 15:5-10

24 And the priests slaughtered them
and purged the altar with their blood [a]to
atone for all Israel, for the king ordered
the burnt offering and the sin offering
for all Israel.
25 [a]He then stationed the Levites in
the house of the LORD with cymbals,
with harps, and with lyres, [b]according to
the command of David and of [c]Gad the
king's seer, and of [d]Nathan the prophet;
for the command was from the LORD
through His prophets.
26 And the Levites stood with [a]the
musical instruments of David, and [b]the
priests with the trumpets.
27 Then Hezekiah gave the order to
offer the burnt offering on the altar.
When the burnt offering began, [a]the
song to the LORD also began with the
trumpets, [1]*accompanied* by the instruments of David, king of Israel.
28 While the whole assembly worshiped, the singers also sang and the
trumpets sounded; all this *continued*
until the burnt offering was finished.
29 Now at the completion of the burnt
offerings, [a]the king and all who were
present with him bowed down and worshiped.
30 Moreover, King Hezekiah and the
officials ordered the Levites to sing
praises to the LORD with the words of
David and Asaph the seer. [a]So they sang
praises with joy, and bowed down and
worshiped.
31 Then Hezekiah answered and said,
"[a]Now *that* you have [1]consecrated yourselves to the LORD, come near and bring
sacrifices and thank offerings to the
house of the LORD." And the assembly
brought sacrifices and thank offerings,
and [b]all those who were [2]willing *brought*
burnt offerings.
32 And the number of the burnt offerings which the assembly brought was 70
bulls, 100 rams, and 200 lambs; all these
were for a burnt offering to the LORD.
33 And the consecrated things were
600 bulls and 3,000 sheep.
34 But the priests were too few, so
that they were unable to skin all the
burnt offerings; [a]therefore their brothers
the Levites helped them until the work
was completed, and until the *other*
priests had consecrated themselves. For
[b]the Levites were more [1]conscientious to
consecrate themselves than the priests.
35 And there *were* also [1a]many burnt
offerings with [b]the fat of the peace
offerings and with [c]the libations for the
burnt offerings. Thus the service of the
house of the LORD was established
again.
36 Then Hezekiah and all the people
rejoiced over what God had prepared for
the people, because the thing came
about suddenly.

All Israel Invited to the Passover

30 NOW Hezekiah sent to all Israel
and Judah and wrote letters also
to Ephraim and Manasseh, that they
should come to the house of the LORD at

Jerusalem to [1]celebrate the Passover to
the LORD God of Israel.
2 For the king and his princes and all
the assembly in Jerusalem had decided
[a]to celebrate the Passover in the second
month,
3 since they could not celebrate it [a]at
that time, because the priests had not
consecrated themselves in sufficient
numbers, nor had the people been gathered to Jerusalem.
4 Thus the thing was right in the
sight of the king and [1]all the assembly.
5 So they established a decree to
circulate a [1]proclamation throughout all
Israel [a]from Beersheba even to Dan, that
they should come to celebrate the Passover to the LORD God of Israel at
Jerusalem. For they had not celebrated *it*
in great numbers as it was [2]prescribed.
6 And [a]the [1]couriers went throughout all Israel and Judah with the letters
from the hand of the king and his
princes, even according to the command
of the king, saying, "O sons of Israel,
return to the LORD God of Abraham,
Isaac, and Israel, that He may return to
those of you who escaped *and* are left
from [b]the [2]hand of the kings of Assyria.
7 "[a]And do not be like your fathers
and your brothers, who were unfaithful
to the LORD God of their fathers, so that
[b]He made them a horror, as you see.
8 "Now do not [a]stiffen your neck like
your fathers, but [1]yield to the LORD and
enter His sanctuary which He has consecrated forever, and serve the LORD your
God, [b]that His burning anger may turn
away from you.
9 "For [a]if you return to the LORD,
your brothers and your sons *will find*
compassion before those who led them
captive, and will return to this land. [b]For
the LORD your God is gracious and
compassionate, and will not turn *His*
face away from you if you return to
Him."
10 So the [1]couriers passed from city to
city through the country of Ephraim and
Manasseh, and as far as Zebulun, but
[a]they laughed them to scorn, and
mocked them.
11 Nevertheless [a]some men of Asher,
Manasseh, and Zebulun humbled themselves and came to Jerusalem.
12 The [a]hand of God was also on
Judah to give them one heart to do what
the king and the princes commanded by
the word of the LORD.

Passover Reinstituted

13 Now many people were gathered at
Jerusalem to celebrate the Feast of
Unleavened Bread [a]in the second month,
a very large assembly.
14 And they arose and removed the
altars which *were* in Jerusalem; they also
[a]removed all the incense altars and [b]cast
them into the brook Kidron.
15 Then [a]they slaughtered the Passover *lambs* on the fourteenth of the
second month. And [b]the priests and
Levites were ashamed of themselves and
consecrated themselves, and brought
burnt offerings to the house of the LORD.
16 And [a]they stood at their stations
after their custom, according to the law
of Moses the man of God; the priests
sprinkled the blood *which they received*
from the hand of the Levites.
17 For *there were* many in the assembly who had not consecrated themselves;
therefore, [a]the Levites *were* over the
slaughter of the Passover *lambs* for
everyone who *was* unclean, in order to
consecrate *them* to the LORD.
18 For a multitude of the people,
[a]*even* many from Ephraim and Manasseh, Issachar and Zebulun, had not
purified themselves, [b]yet they ate the
Passover [c]otherwise than [1]prescribed.
For Hezekiah prayed for them, saying,
"May the good LORD pardon
19 [a]everyone who prepares his heart
to seek God, the LORD God of his
fathers, though not according to the
purification *rules* of the sanctuary."
20 So the LORD heard Hezekiah and
[a]healed the people.
21 And the sons of Israel present in
Jerusalem [a]celebrated the Feast of Unleavened Bread *for* seven days with great
joy, and the Levites and the priests
praised the LORD day after day with
loud instruments to the LORD.
22 Then Hezekiah [a]spoke [1]encourag-
ingly to all the Levites who showed good
insight *in the things* of the LORD. So they
ate for the appointed seven days, sacrificing peace offerings and [b]giving thanks
to the LORD God of their fathers.
23 Then the whole assembly [a]decided
to celebrate *the feast* another seven days,
so they celebrated the seven days with
joy.
24 For [a]Hezekiah king of Judah had
contributed to the assembly 1,000 bulls
and 7,000 sheep, and the princes had
contributed to the assembly 1,000 bulls
and 10,000 sheep; and [b]a large number
of priests consecrated themselves.
25 And all the assembly of Judah
rejoiced, with the priests and the Levites,
and [a]all the assembly that came from
Israel, both the sojourners who came
from the land of Israel and those living
in Judah.
26 So there was great joy in Jerusalem,
because there was nothing like this in
Jerusalem [a]since the days of Solomon
the son of David, king of Israel.
27 Then [a]the Levitical priests arose
and [b]blessed the people; and their voice
was heard and their prayer came to [c]His
holy dwelling place, to heaven.

Idols Are Destroyed

31 NOW when all this was finished,
all Israel who were present went
out to the cities of Judah, [a]broke the
pillars in pieces, cut down the [1]Asherim,
and pulled down the high places and the
altars throughout all Judah and Benjamin, as well as in Ephraim and Manasseh, [2]until they had destroyed them all.

1 [1]Lit., *do*, so in vv. 2, 3, 5, 13, 21, 23
2 [a]Num. 9:10, 11; 2 Chr. 30:13, 15
3 [a]2 Chr. 29:17, 34
4 [1]Lit., *in the sight of all*
5 [1]Lit., *voice* [2]Lit., *written* [a]Judg. 20:1
6 [1]Lit., *runners* [2]Lit., *palm* [a]Esth. 8:14; Job 9:25; Jer. 51:31 [b]2 Chr. 28:20
7 [a]Ezek. 20:13 [b]2 Chr. 29:8
8 [1]Lit., *give a hand* [a]Ex. 32:9 [b]2 Chr. 29:10
9 [a]Deut. 30:2 [b]Ex. 34:6, 7; Mic. 7:18
10 [1]Lit., *runners* [a]2 Chr. 36:16
11 [a]2 Chr. 30:18, 21, 25
12 [a]2 Cor. 3:5; Phil. 2:13; Heb. 13:20, 21
13 [a]2 Chr. 30:2
14 [a]2 Chr. 28:24 [b]2 Chr. 29:16
15 [a]2 Chr. 30:2, 3 [b]2 Chr. 29:34
16 [a]2 Chr. 35:10, 15
17 [a]2 Chr. 29:34
18 [1]Lit., *written* [a]2 Chr. 30:11, 25 [b]Num. 9:10 [c]Ex. 12:43-49
19 [a]2 Chr. 19:3
20 [a]James 5:16
21 [a]Ex. 12:15; 13:6
22 [1]Lit., *to the heart of* [a]2 Chr. 32:6 [b]Ezra 10:11
23 [a]1 Kin. 8:65
24 [a]2 Chr. 35:7, 8 [b]2 Chr. 29:34; 30:3
25 [a]2 Chr. 30:11, 18
26 [a]2 Chr. 7:8-10
27 [a]2 Chr. 23:18 [b]Num. 6:23 [c]Deut. 26:15; Ps. 68:5
1 [1]I.e., wooden symbols of a female deity [2]Lit., *even to completion* [a]2 Kin. 18:4

Then all the sons of Israel returned to
their cities, each to his possession.
2 And Hezekiah appointed [a]the divisions of the priests and the Levites by
their divisions, each according to his
service, *both* the priests and the Levites,
[b]for burnt offerings and for peace offerings, to minister and to give thanks and
to praise in the gates of the camp of the
LORD.

Reforms Continued

3 *He* also *appointed* [a]the king's portion of his goods for the burnt offerings,
namely, for the morning and evening
burnt offerings, and the burnt offerings
for the sabbaths and for the new moons
and for the fixed festivals, [b]as it is
written in the law of the LORD.
4 Also he [1]commanded the people
who lived in Jerusalem to give [a]the
portion due to the priests and the Levites, that they might devote themselves
to [b]the law of the LORD.
5 And as soon as the [1]order spread,
the sons of Israel provided in abundance
the first fruits of grain, new wine, oil,
honey, and of all the produce of the
field; and they brought in abundantly
[a]the tithe of all.
6 And the sons of Israel and Judah
who lived in the cities of Judah, also
brought in the tithe of oxen and sheep,
and [a]the tithe of [1]sacred gifts which were
consecrated to the LORD their God, and
placed *them* in heaps.
7 In the third month they began to
[1]make the heaps, and finished *them* by
the seventh month.
8 And when Hezekiah and the rulers
came and saw the heaps, they blessed the
LORD and [a]His people Israel.
9 Then Hezekiah questioned the
priests and the Levites concerning the
heaps.
10 And Azariah the chief priest [a]of
the house of Zadok said to [1]him, "[b]Since
the contributions began to be brought
into the house of the LORD, we have had
enough to eat with plenty left over, for
the LORD has blessed His people, and
this great quantity is left over."
11 Then Hezekiah commanded *them*
to prepare [a]rooms in the house of the
LORD, and they prepared *them.*
12 And they faithfully brought in
the contributions and the tithes and the
consecrated things; and Conaniah the
Levite *was* the officer in charge [a]of them
and his brother Shimei *was* second.
13 And Jehiel, Azaziah, Nahath, Asahel, Jerimoth, Jozabad, Eliel, Ismachiah,
Mahath, and Benaiah *were* overseers
[1]under the authority of Conaniah and
Shimei his brother by the appointment
of King Hezekiah, and [a]Azariah *was* the
chief officer of the house of God.
14 And Kore the son of Imnah the
Levite, the keeper of the eastern *gate,*
was over the freewill offerings of God, to
apportion the contributions for the
LORD and the most holy things.

15 And [1]under his authority *were*
[a]Eden, Miniamin, Jeshua, Shemaiah,
Amariah, and Shecaniah in [b]the cities of
the priests, to distribute faithfully *their*
portions to their brothers by divisions,
whether great or small,
16 without regard to their genealogical
enrollment, to the males from [1a]thirty
years old and upward—everyone who
entered the house of the LORD [b]for his
daily obligations—for their work in their
duties according to their divisions;
17 as well as the priests who were
enrolled genealogically according to
their fathers' households, and the Levites
[a]from twenty years old and upwards, by
their duties *and* their divisions.
18 And the genealogical enrollment
included [1]all their little children, their
wives, their sons, and their daughters,
for the whole assembly, for they consecrated themselves [2]faithfully in holiness.
19 Also for the sons of Aaron the
priests *who were* in [a]the pasture lands of
their cities, or in each and every city,
[b]*there were* men who were designated by
name to distribute portions to every
male among the priests and to everyone
genealogically enrolled among the Levites.
20 And thus Hezekiah did throughout
all Judah; and [a]he did what *was* good,
right, and true before the LORD his God.
21 And every work which he began in
the service of the house of God in law
and in commandment, seeking his God,
he did with all his heart and [a]prospered.

Sennacherib Invades Judah

32 AFTER these [1]acts of faithfulness [a]Sennacherib king of Assyria
came and invaded Judah and besieged
the fortified cities, and [2]thought to break
into them for himself.
2 Now when Hezekiah saw that Sennacherib had come, and that [1]he intended to make war on Jerusalem,
3 he decided with his officers and his
warriors to cut off the *supply of* water
from the springs which *were* outside the
city, and they helped him.
4 So many people assembled [a]and
stopped up all the springs and [b]the
stream which flowed [1]through the region, saying, "Why should the kings of
Assyria come and find abundant water?"
5 And he took courage and [a]rebuilt
all the wall that had been broken down,
and [1]erected towers on it, and *built*
[b]another outside wall, and strengthened
the [c]Millo *in* the city of David, and made
weapons and shields in great number.
6 And he appointed military officers
over the people, and gathered them to
him in the square at the city gate, and
[a]spoke [1]encouragingly to them, saying,
7 "[a]Be strong and courageous, do not
fear or be dismayed because of the king
of Assyria, nor because of all the multitude which is with him; [b]for the one with
us is greater than the one with him.

2 [a]1 Chr. 24:1 [b]1 Chr. 23:28-31
3 [a]2 Chr. 35:7 [b]Num. 28:1-29:40
4 [1]Lit., *said to* [a]Num. 18:8 [b]Mal. 2:7
5 [1]Lit., *word* [a]Neh. 13:12
6 [1]Lit., *consecrated things* [a]Lev. 27:30; Deut. 14:28
7 [1]Lit., *found*
8 [a]Deut. 33:29; Ps. 33:12; 144:15
10 [1]Lit., *him, and he said* [a]1 Chr. 6:8, 9 [b]Mal. 3:10
11 [a]1 Kin. 6:5, 8
12 [a]2 Chr. 35:9
13 [1]Lit., *from the hand of* [a]2 Chr. 31:10
15 [1]Lit., *under his hand* [a]2 Chr. 29:12 [b]Josh. 21:9-19
16 [1]Heb., *three* [a]1 Chr. 23:3 [b]Ezra 3:4
17 [a]1 Chr. 23:24
18 [1]Lit., *with all* [2]Lit., *in their faithfulness*
19 [a]Lev. 25:34; Num. 35:2-5 [b]2 Chr. 31:12-15
20 [a]2 Kin. 20:3; 22:2
21 [a]Deut. 29:9; Prov. 3:9, 10
1 [1]Lit., *things and this faithfulness* [2]Lit., *said* [a]2 Kin. 18:13-19, 37; Is. 36:1-37:38
2 [1]Lit., *his face for war against*
4 [1]Lit., *in the midst of the land* [a]2 Kin. 20:20 [b]2 Chr. 32:30
5 [1]Lit., *raised on the towers* [a]2 Chr. 25:23 [b]2 Kin. 25:4 [c]1 Kin. 9:24
6 [1]Lit., *upon their hearts* [a]2 Chr. 30:22
7 [a]1 Chr. 22:13 [b]2 Kin. 6:16

8"With him is *only* [a]an arm of flesh,
but [b]with us is the LORD our God to
help us and to fight our battles." And
the people relied on the words of Hezekiah king of Judah.

Sennacherib Undermines Hezekiah

9 After this [a]Sennacherib king of
Assyria sent his servants to Jerusalem
while he *was* [1]besieging Lachish with all
his forces with him, against Hezekiah
king of Judah and against all Judah who
were at Jerusalem, saying,
10"Thus says Sennacherib king of
Assyria, 'On what are you trusting that
you are remaining in Jerusalem under
siege?
11 'Is not Hezekiah misleading you to
give yourselves over to die by hunger
and by thirst, saying, "The LORD our
God will deliver us from the [1]hand of
the king of Assyria"?
12 '[a]Has not the same Hezekiah taken
away His high places and His altars, and
said to Judah and [1]Jerusalem, "You
shall worship before one altar, and on it
you shall [2]burn incense"?
13 'Do you not know what I and my
fathers have done to all the peoples of
the lands? [a]Were the gods of the nations
of the lands able at all to deliver their
land from my hand?
14 '[a]Who *was there* among all the gods
of those nations which my fathers utterly
destroyed who could deliver his people
out of my hand, that your God should
be able to deliver you from my hand?
15 'Now therefore, do not let Hezekiah
deceive you or mislead you like this, and
do not believe him, for [a]no god of any
nation or kingdom was able to deliver
his people from my hand or from the
hand of my fathers. How much less shall
your God deliver you from my hand?' "
16 And his servants spoke further
against the LORD God and against His
servant Hezekiah.
17 He also wrote letters to insult the
LORD God of Israel, and to speak
against Him, saying, "[a]As the gods of
the nations of the lands [1]have not delivered their people from my hand, so the
God of Hezekiah shall not deliver His
people from my hand."
18 And [a]they called this out with a
loud voice in the language of Judah to
the people of Jerusalem who were on the
wall, to frighten and terrify them, so that
they might take the city.
19 And they spoke [1]of the God of
Jerusalem as of [a]the gods of the peoples
of the earth, the work of men's hands.

Hezekiah's Prayer Is Answered

20 But King Hezekiah and Isaiah the
prophet, the son of Amoz, prayed about
this and cried out to heaven.
21 And the LORD sent an angel who
destroyed every mighty warrior, commander and officer in the camp of the
king of Assyria. So he returned [1]in
shame to his own land. And when he
had entered the temple of his god, some
of his own children killed him there with
the sword.
22 So the LORD [a]saved Hezekiah and
the inhabitants of Jerusalem from the
hand of Sennacherib the king of Assyria,
and from the hand of all *others,* and
[1]guided them on every side.
23 And [a]many were bringing gifts to
the LORD at Jerusalem and choice presents to Hezekiah king of Judah, so that
[b]he was exalted in the sight of all nations
thereafter.
24 [a]In those days Hezekiah became
[1]mortally ill; and he prayed to the LORD,
and [2]the LORD spoke to him and gave
him a sign.
25 But Hezekiah gave no return for
the benefit [1]he received, [a]because his
heart was [2]proud; [b]therefore wrath came
on him and on Judah and Jerusalem.
26 However, [a]Hezekiah [1]humbled the
pride of his heart, both he
and the inhabitants of Jerusalem, so that
the wrath of the LORD did not come on
them in the days of Hezekiah.
27 Now Hezekiah had immense riches
and honor; and he made for himself
treasuries for silver, gold, precious
stones, spices, shields and all kinds of
valuable articles,
28 storehouses also for the produce of
grain, wine and oil, pens for all kinds of
cattle and [1]sheepfolds for the flocks.
29 And he made cities for himself, and
acquired flocks and herds in abundance;
for [a]God had given him very great
[1]wealth.
30 It was Hezekiah who [a]stopped the
upper outlet of the waters of [b]Gihon and
directed them to the west side of the city
of David. And Hezekiah prospered in all
that he did.
31 And even *in the matter of* [a]the
envoys of the rulers of Babylon, who
sent to him to inquire of [b]the wonder
that had happened in the land, God left
him *alone only* [c]to test him, that He
might know all that was in his heart.
32 Now the rest of the acts of Hezekiah and his deeds of devotion, behold,
they are written in the vision of Isaiah
the prophet, the son of Amoz, in the
Book of the Kings of Judah and Israel.
33 So Hezekiah slept with his fathers,
and they buried him in the [1]upper section of the tombs of the sons of David;
and all Judah and the inhabitants of
Jerusalem [a]honored him at his death.
And his son Manasseh became king in
his place.

Manasseh Succeeds Hezekiah in Judah

33 [a]MANASSEH was twelve years
old when he became king, and he
reigned fifty-five years in Jerusalem.
2 And [a]he did evil in the sight of the
LORD according to the abominations of
the nations whom the LORD dispossessed before the sons of Israel.

8 [a]Jer. 17:5 [b]2 Chr. 20:17

9 [1]Lit., *against* [a]2 Kin. 18:17

11 [1]Lit., *palm*

12 [1]Lit., *Jerusalem, saying,* [2]Lit., *offer up in smoke* [a]2 Chr. 31:1

13 [a]2 Kin. 18:33-35

14 [a]Is. 10:9-11

15 [a]Ex. 5:2; Is. 36:18-20; Dan. 3:15

17 [1]Lit., *who have* [a]2 Chr. 32:14

18 [a]2 Kin. 18:28

19 [1]Lit., *to* [a]Ps. 115:4-8

21 [1]Lit., *in shame of face*

22 [1]Another reading is *gave them rest* [a]Is. 31:5

23 [a]2 Sam. 8:10 [b]2 Chr. 1:1

24 [1]Lit., *sick to the point of death* [2]Lit., *He* [a]2 Kin. 20:1-11; Is. 38:1-8

25 [1]Lit., *to him* [2]Lit., *high* [a]2 Chr. 26:16; 32:31 [b]2 Chr. 24:18

26 [1]Lit., *humbled himself in* [a]Jer. 26:18, 19

28 [1]So ancient versions; Heb., *flocks for the sheepfolds*

29 [1]Lit., *possessions, property* [a]1 Chr. 29:12

30 [a]2 Kin. 20:20 [b]1 Kin. 1:33

31 [a]2 Kin. 20:12; Is. 39:1 [b]2 Chr. 32:24; Is. 38:7, 8 [c]Deut. 8:16

33 [1]Or, *ascent to* [a]Ps. 112:6; Prov. 10:7

1 [a]2 Kin. 21:1-9

2 [a]2 Chr. 28:3; Jer. 15:4

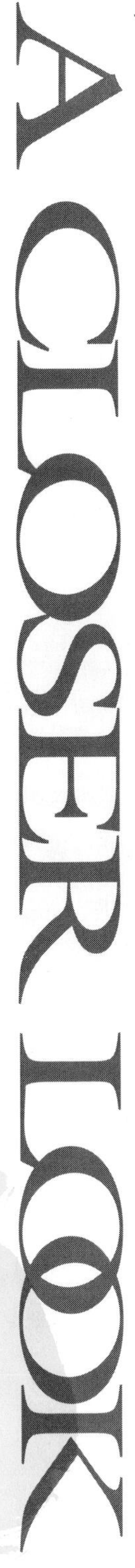

LIGHTING

Lighting for houses was provided by the oil lamp. Originally this consisted of an open earthenware saucer containing olive oil. Part of the saucer was *"pinched"* in manufacture, so as to provide a place for a flaxen wick. Such lamps obviously had problems arising from spillage, and closed containers were therefore developed with two holes–one for the wick and one to put oil in. When the oil began to run low, the flax would smoulder and the lamp would need to be refilled from a container (see Matthew 25:8).

Later, larger glazed and decorated lamps were made with handles and with multiple wicks to provide additional light. The higher the lamp, the better the light. Lamps were therefore put on a projection from the wall, hung from the ceiling, or placed on a simple lampstand (a thick tree branch pushed into the earthen floor). If nothing else was available, the lamp was put on an upturned measure or even on the floor.

THE TENT

The tent of the sand-dweller was made from a long piece of goatshair cloth about five or six feet wide. It was erected on a series of poles to provide a long awning, the two ends being pegged to the ground with tent nails (see Judges 4:21). The black colour of the tent is alluded to in Song of Songs 1:5. The strip was made on a loom pegged out on the ground; patches were inserted, like a huge darn, by the same method.

BRICK HOUSES

When the seminomadic Israelites under Joshua took over the Canaanite towns and villages, domestic architecture had developed a long way from the shelters used when the cave dwellers moved out into the open. Homes had developed from the mud brick, beehive-shaped dwelling, where the floor was at a lower level than the ground outside, to the single rectangular room that is still typical today.

Initially homes were made with sun-dried mud bricks, but technology advanced until it was possible to fire the bricks in a kiln, and until rough stones and rubble houses were being built. Not until the time of the settled kingdom under Solomon was squared stone used for domestic building. This was made possible because of the availability of iron tools to dress (or finish) the stone. In Galilee, the stone was normally black basalt, and on the coast, yellow sandstone; but for most of the country in the limestone area the stone was white.

HOUSE CONSTRUCTION

Houses, too, were looked upon as the gift of God, and when a house was first built there was an act of dedication (Deuteronomy 20:5). The basic house for the poorest members of the community living in the country was a single room, about ten feet (three metres) square. The walls were thick, of mud brick or of rough stone and rubble, and contained niches for the storage of food and utensils. A single window was small and high and sometimes had a wooden lattice (Proverbs 7:6) to keep out intruders.

HOMES FOR THE WEALTHY

The difference between the homes of the wealthy and of the poor lay in the provision of a courtyard. At the lowest level this was simply an enclosure added onto the house. But the courtyard made immediate differences. Animals could be kept outside the house, cooking could be done in a corner, there would be no problems of security over access to the roof because the stairway from the roof would come into the courtyard, windows could open onto the courtyard to let in more light, and the door of the enclosure could always be kept shut. A cistern now became a possibility.

People with greater wealth would build two or three rooms round the courtyard, and rooms would sometimes be built to provide an upper story (2 Kings 4:10, Mark 14:12-16; Acts 9:36-41). It was a home that was at once secluded and open to the sky — a flashback to the seminomadic experience of Abraham's time.

Really wealthy people could add courtyards with buildings around them by providing a porchway through what was one of the original rooms of the house. Pillars supported the roof beams so that the size of the room could be extended. Pillars were built parallel to the walls of the buildings so that colonnades or verandas could be made. Decorations were added in the form of carved lintels, capitals, and doorpost bases. Walls could be plastered and decorated and floors covered with tiles, and, later, mosaics of pebbles and of cut tiles. The courtyards themselves could be made into gardens.

HANNAH - *prayerful*

Hannah was an attractive girl, the favorite wife of her husband Elkanah. Yet for years her heart's desire, a child, was not granted. She longed for a child, but she continuously looked to the Lord to give her what she desired. Though she was young, her belief in the Lord was solid and mature.

Year after year she went to the temple at Shiloh and prayed fervently for a child. She did not sit around bemoaning her lack with others, or spend time feeling sorry for herself. She did not stop asking after years of no results. She continued to seek God until she had her answer.

Hannah was not satisfied to pray one time, she continued in prayer. And she prayed in a reverent and humble attitude. She was not disrespectful or demanding in her attitude. Yet she persevered in prayer, unwilling to give up. She believed God had the power to grant her request and that He loved her and wanted to bless her. Yet when God moved to answer her prayer, she gave up her beloved son to service in the temple despite his very young age. How could she give up what she had longed for? Because she had dedicated Samuel to serving God before he was even conceived.

Hannah did not make a bargain with God to get what she wanted. But she did vow to God what she would do with His gift. Giving Samuel to the Lord's service was her ultimate expression of joy and gratitude for what God had done in her life. The power and depth of her belief in God and her happiness are obvious in I Samuel 2:1-10.

Her joy and prayerfulness can help us to greater depths of belief. Note too that Hannah did not quit praying when she got what she wanted. Her prayer of triumph is as well-known as her petition.

Hannah's prayer life was her strength and the focal point of her relationship with God. Because of it, she was able to stand firm in her belief that her desire would be fulfilled. And she was able to withstand the teasing and humiliation that her barrenness brought.

Later in her life, God blessed Hannah with other children. Her strong belief in prayer and sacrificial mothering have stood as an example for generations.

QUESTIONS

1. Do you find power in your prayers, and the strength to continue believing in God's desire and ability to bless you? if not, how can you strengthen your prayer life?

2. Though Hannah's barrenness caused her ridicule and humiliation, she was not provoked. When have you trusted God for the strength to endure in peace?

3. Hannah took her problems to God and privately poured out her feelings. Too often we are inclined to first seek another person for sympathy or a shoulder to cry on. How have you denied God an opportunity to be your comfort?

4. Because Hannah's life was devoted to God, even the thing she most wanted—her son—was simply an extension of her loving service to God. What can you release in your life to God's service?

3 For [a]he rebuilt the high places
which Hezekiah his father had broken
down; [b]he also erected altars for the
Baals and made [1]Asherim, and worshiped all the host of heaven and served
them.
4 And [a]he built altars in the house of
the LORD of which the LORD had said,
"My name shall be [b]in Jerusalem forever."
5 For he built altars for all the host
of heaven in [a]the two courts of the house
of the LORD.
6 And [a]he made his sons pass
through the fire in the valley of Ben-
hinnom; and he practiced witchcraft,
used divination, practiced sorcery, and
[b]dealt with mediums and spiritists. He
did much evil in the sight of the LORD,
provoking Him *to anger.*
7 Then he put [a]the carved image of
the idol which he had made in the house
of God, of which God had said to David
and to Solomon his son, "[b]In this house
and in Jerusalem, which I have chosen
from all the tribes of Israel, I will put
My name forever;
8 and I will not again remove the
foot of Israel from the land [a]which I
have appointed for your fathers, if only
they will observe to do all that I have
commanded them according to all the
law, the statutes, and the ordinances
given through Moses."
9 Thus Manasseh misled Judah and
the inhabitants of Jerusalem to do more
evil than the nations whom the LORD
destroyed before the sons of Israel.

Manasseh's Idolatry Rebuked

10 And the LORD spoke to Manasseh
and his people, but [a]they paid no attention.
11 [a]Therefore the LORD brought the
commanders of the army of the king of
Assyria against them, and they captured
Manasseh with [1]hooks, [b]bound him with
bronze *chains,* and took him to Babylon.
12 And when [a]he was in distress, he
entreated the LORD his God and [b]hum-
bled himself greatly before the God of
his fathers.
13 When he prayed to Him, [a]He was
moved by his entreaty and heard his
supplication, and brought him again to
Jerusalem to his kingdom. Then Manasseh [b]knew that the LORD *was* God.
14 Now after this he built the outer
wall of the city of David on the west side
of [a]Gihon, in the valley, even to the
entrance of the [b]Fish Gate; and he
encircled the [c]Ophel *with it* and made it
very high. Then he put army commanders in all the fortified cities of Judah.
15 He also [a]removed the foreign gods
and the idol from the house of the LORD,
as well as all the altars which he had
built on the mountain of the house of the
LORD and in Jerusalem, and he threw
them outside the city.
16 And he set up the altar of the LORD
and sacrificed [a]peace offerings and thank
offerings on it; and he ordered Judah to
serve the LORD God of Israel.
17 Nevertheless [a]the people still sacrificed in the high places, *although* only to
the LORD their God.
18 Now the rest of the acts of Manasseh even [a]his prayer to his God, and the
words of [b]the seers who spoke to him in
the name of the LORD God of Israel,
behold, they are among the records of
the kings of [c]Israel.
19 His prayer also and [a]*how God* was
entreated by him, and all his sin, his
unfaithfulness, and [b]the sites on which
he built high places and erected the
Asherim and the carved images, before
he humbled himself, behold, they are
written in the records of the [1]Hozai.
20 So Manasseh slept with his fathers,
and they buried him in his own house.
And Amon his son became king in his
place.

Amon Becomes King in Judah

21 [a]Amon *was* twenty-two years old
when he became king, and he reigned
two years in Jerusalem.
22 And he did evil in the sight of the
LORD as Manasseh his father [a]had done,
and Amon sacrificed to all [b]the carved
images which his father Manasseh had
made, and he served them.
23 Moreover, he did not humble himself before the LORD [a]as his father
Manasseh had [1]done, but Amon multiplied guilt.
24 Finally [a]his servants conspired
against him and put him to death in his
own house.
25 But the people of the land [1]killed
all the conspirators against King Amon,
and the people of the land made Josiah
his son king in his place.

Josiah Succeeds Amon in Judah

34 [a]JOSIAH *was* eight years old
when he became king, and he
reigned thirty-one years in Jerusalem.
2 And [a]he did right in the sight of the
LORD, and walked in the ways of his
father David and did not turn aside to
the right or to the left.
3 For in the eighth year of his reign
while he was still a youth, he began to
[a]seek the God of his father David; and
in the twelfth year he began [b]to purge
Judah and Jerusalem of the high places,
the Asherim, the carved images, and the
molten images.
4 And they tore down the altars of
the Baals in his presence, and [a]the
incense altars that were high above them
he chopped down; also the Asherim, the
carved images, and the molten images he
broke in pieces and [b]ground to powder
and scattered *it* on the graves of those
who had sacrificed to them.
5 Then [a]he burned the bones of the
priests on their altars, and purged Judah
and Jerusalem.
6 And [a]in the cities of Manasseh,
Ephraim, Simeon, even as far as Naphtali, in their surrounding ruins,

3 [1]I.e., wooden symbols of a female deity [a]2 Chr. 31:1 [b]Deut. 16:21; 2 Kin. 23:5, 6
4 [a]2 Chr. 28:24 [b]2 Sam. 7:13; 2 Chr. 7:16
5 [a]2 Chr. 4:9
6 [a]2 Chr. 28:3 [b]Lev. 19:31; 20:27
7 [a]2 Chr. 33:15 [b]1 Kin. 9:3-5; 2 Chr. 7:16; 33:4
8 [a]2 Sam. 7:10
10 [a]Neh. 9:29; Jer. 25:4
11 [1]I.e., thongs put through the nose [a]Deut. 28:36 [b]2 Chr. 36:6
12 [a]Ps. 118:5; 120:1; 130:1, 2 [b]2 Chr. 32:26
13 [a]1 Chr. 5:20; Ezra 8:23 [b]Dan. 4:32
14 [a]1 Kin. 1:33 [b]Neh. 3:3 [c]2 Chr. 27:3
15 [a]2 Chr. 33:3-7
16 [a]Lev. 7:11-18
17 [a]2 Chr. 32:12
18 [a]2 Chr. 33:12, 13 [b]2 Chr. 33:10 [c]2 Chr. 21:2
19 [1]Gr. reads *seers* [a]2 Chr. 33:13 [b]2 Chr. 33:3
21 [a]2 Kin. 21:19-24
22 [a]2 Chr. 33:2-7 [b]2 Chr. 34:3, 4
23 [1]Lit., *humbled himself* [a]2 Chr. 33:12, 19
24 [a]2 Chr. 25:27
25 [1]Lit., *smote*
1 [a]2 Kin. 22:1, 2; Jer. 1:2; 3:6
2 [a]2 Chr. 29:2
3 [a]2 Chr. 15:2; Prov. 8:17 [b]1 Kin. 13:2; 2 Chr. 33:22
4 [a]2 Kin. 23:4, 5, 11 [b]Ex. 32:20
5 [a]1 Kin. 13:2; 2 Kin. 23:20
6 [a]2 Kin. 23:15, 19

7 he also tore down the altars and [a]beat the Asherim and the carved images into powder, and chopped down all the incense altars throughout the land of Israel. Then he returned to Jerusalem.

Josiah Repairs the Temple

8 [a]Now in the eighteenth year of his reign, when he had purged the land and the house, he sent Shaphan the son of Azaliah, and Maaseiah [b]an official of the city, and Joah the son of Joahaz the recorder, to repair the house of the LORD his God.

9 And they came to [a]Hilkiah the high priest and delivered the money that was brought into the house of God, which the Levites, the [1]doorkeepers, had collected [2]from [b]Manasseh and Ephraim, and from all the remnant of Israel, and from all Judah and Benjamin and the inhabitants of Jerusalem.

10 Then they gave *it* into the hands of the workmen who had the oversight of the house of the LORD, and the workmen who were working in the house of the LORD [1]used it to restore and repair the house.

11 They in turn gave *it* to the carpenters and to the builders to buy quarried stone and timber for couplings and to make beams for the houses [a]which the kings of Judah had let go to ruin.

12 And [a]the men did the work faithfully with foremen over them to supervise: Jahath and Obadiah, the Levites of the sons of Merari, Zechariah and Meshullam of the sons of the Kohathites, and [b]the Levites, all who were skillful with musical instruments.

13 *They were* also over [a]the burden bearers, and supervised all the workmen from job to job; and *some* of the Levites *were* scribes and officials and gatekeepers.

Hilkiah Discovers Lost Book of the Law

14 When they were bringing out the money which had been brought into the house of the LORD, [a]Hilkiah the priest found the book of the law of the LORD *given* by Moses.

15 And Hilkiah responded and said to Shaphan the scribe, "I have found the book of the law in the house of the LORD." And Hilkiah gave the book to Shaphan.

16 Then Shaphan brought the book to the king and [1]reported further word to the king, saying, "Everything that was [2]entrusted to your servants they are doing.

17 "They have also emptied out the money which was found in the house of the LORD, and have delivered it into the hands of the supervisors and the workmen."

18 Moreover, Shaphan the scribe told the king saying, "Hilkiah the priest gave me a book." And Shaphan read from it in the presence of the king.

19 And it came about when the king heard [a]the words of the law that [b]he tore his clothes.

20 Then the king commanded Hilkiah, Ahikam the son of Shaphan, [1]Abdon the son of Micah, Shaphan the scribe, and Asaiah the king's servant, saying,

21 "Go, inquire of the LORD for me and for those who are left in Israel and in Judah, concerning the words of the book which has been found; for [a]great is the wrath of the LORD which is poured out on us because our fathers have not observed the word of the LORD, to do according to all that is written in this book."

Huldah, the Prophetess, Speaks

22 So Hilkiah and *those* whom the king [1]had told went to Huldah the prophetess, the wife of Shallum the son of [2]Tokhath, the son of Hasrah, the keeper of the wardrobe (now she lived in Jerusalem in the Second Quarter); and they spoke to her regarding this.

23 And she said to them, "Thus says the LORD, the God of Israel, 'Tell the man who sent you to Me,

24 thus says the LORD, "Behold, [a]I am bringing evil on this place and on its inhabitants, *even* all [b]the curses written in the book which they have read in the presence of the king of Judah.

25 "[a]Because they have forsaken Me and have burned incense to other gods, that they might provoke Me to anger with all the works of their hands, therefore My wrath will be poured out on this place, and it shall not be quenched." '

26 "But to the king of Judah who sent you to inquire of the LORD, thus you will say to him, 'Thus says the LORD God of Israel *regarding* the words which you have heard,

27 "[a]Because your heart was tender and you humbled yourself before God, when you heard His words against this place and against its inhabitants, and *because* you humbled yourself before Me, tore your clothes, and wept before Me, I truly have heard you," declares the LORD.

28 "Behold, I will gather you to your fathers and you shall be gathered to your grave in peace, so your eyes shall not see all the evil which I will bring on this place and on its inhabitants." ' " And they brought back word to the king.

29 [a]Then the king sent and gathered all the elders of Judah and Jerusalem.

30 And the king went up to the house of the LORD and [a]all the men of Judah, the inhabitants of Jerusalem, the priests, the Levites, and all the people, from the greatest to the least; and he read in their hearing all the words of the book of the covenant which was found in the house of the LORD.

Josiah's Good Reign

31 Then the king [a]stood in his place and [b]made a covenant before the LORD to walk after the LORD, and to keep His commandments and His testimonies and

7 [a]2 Chr. 31:1
8 [a]2 Kin. 22:3-20 [b]2 Chr. 18:25
9 [1]Lit., *guardians of the threshold* [2]Lit., *from the hand of* [a]2 Chr. 35:8 [b]2 Chr. 30:10, 18
10 [1]Lit., *gave*
11 [a]2 Chr. 33:4-7
12 [a]2 Kin. 12:15 [b]1 Chr. 25:1
13 [a]Neh. 4:10
14 [a]2 Chr. 34:9
16 [1]Lit., *returned* [2]Lit., *given into the hand of*
19 [a]Deut. 28:3-68 [b]Josh. 7:6
20 [1]In 2 Kin. 22:12, *Achbor, son of Micaiah*
21 [a]2 Chr. 29:8
22 [1]So with Gr. [2]In 2 Kin. 22:14 *Tikvah, son of Harhas*
24 [a]2 Chr. 36:14-20 [b]Deut. 28:15-68
25 [a]2 Chr. 33:3
27 [a]2 Kin. 22:19; 2 Chr. 12:7; 32:26
29 [a]2 Kin. 23:1-3
30 [a]Neh. 8:1-3
31 [a]2 Kin. 11:14; 23:3; 2 Chr. 30:16 [b]2 Chr. 23:16; 29:10

His statutes with all his heart and with
all his soul, to perform the words of the
covenant written in this book.
32 Moreover, he made all who were
present in Jerusalem and Benjamin to
stand *with him.* So the inhabitants of
Jerusalem did according to the covenant
of God, the God of their fathers.
33 And Josiah [a]removed all the
abominations from all the lands belonging to the sons of Israel, and made all
who were present in Israel to serve the
LORD their God. Throughout his [1]life-
time they did not turn from following
the LORD God of their fathers.

The Passover Observed Again

35 THEN Josiah [a]celebrated the
Passover to the LORD in Jerusalem, and [b]they slaughtered the Passover
animals on the fourteenth *day* of the first
month.
2 And he set the priests in their
offices and [a]encouraged them in the
service of the house of the LORD.
3 He also said to [a]the Levites who
taught all Israel *and* who were holy to
the LORD, "Put the holy ark in the house
which Solomon the son of David king of
Israel built; [b]it will be a burden on *your*
shoulders no longer. Now serve the
LORD your God and His people Israel.
4 "And [a]prepare *yourselves* by your
fathers' households in your divisions,
according to the writing of David king of
Israel and [b]according to the writing of
his son Solomon.
5 "Moreover, [a]stand in the holy place
according to the sections of the fathers'
households of your brethren the [1]lay
people, and according to the Levites, by
division of a father's household.
6 "Now [a]slaughter the Passover *animals,* [b]sanctify yourselves, and prepare
for your brethren to do according to the
word of the LORD by Moses."
7 And Josiah contributed to the lay
people, to all who were present, flocks of
lambs and kids, all for the Passover
offerings, numbering 30,000 plus 3,000
bulls; these were from the king's possessions.
8 His officers also contributed a freewill offering to the people, the priests,
and the Levites. Hilkiah and Zechariah
and Jehiel, [a]the officials of the house of
God, gave to the priests for the Passover
offerings 2,600 *from the flocks* and 300
bulls.
9 [a]Conaniah also, and Shemaiah and
Nethanel, his brothers, and Hashabiah
and Jeiel and Jozabad, the officers of the
Levites, contributed to the Levites for
the Passover offerings 5,000 *from the
flocks* and 500 bulls.
10 So the service was prepared, and
[a]the priests stood at their stations and
the Levites by their divisions according
to the king's command.
11 And [1a]they slaughtered the Passover *animals,* and while [b]the priests
sprinkled [2]the blood *received* from their
hand, [c]the Levites skinned *them.*

33 [1]Lit., *days*
[a]2 Chr. 34:3-7

1 [a]2 Kin. 23:21
[b]Ex. 12:6; Num. 9:3

2 [a]2 Chr. 29:11

3 [a]2 Chr. 17:8, 9;
Neh. 8:7 [b]1 Chr.
23:26

4 [a]1 Chr. 9:10-13
[b]2 Chr. 8:14

5 [1]Lit., *sons of the
people,* and so
throughout the ch.
[a]Ezra 6:18

6 [a]2 Chr. 35:1
[b]2 Chr. 29:5

8 [a]2 Chr. 31:13

9 [a]2 Chr. 31:12

10 [a]2 Chr. 35:5

11 [1]I.e., the Levites
[2]So with Gr.
[a]2 Chr. 35:1, 6
[b]2 Chr. 29:22
[c]2 Chr. 29:34

13 [a]Ex. 12:8, 9
[b]Lev. 6:28

15 [a]1 Chr. 25:1
[b]1 Chr. 26:12-19

17 [a]Ex. 12:1-20;
2 Chr. 30:21

18 [a]2 Kin. 23:21;
2 Chr. 30:5

20 [1]Lit., *house*
[a]2 Kin. 23:29, 30
[b]Is. 10:9; Jer. 46:2

21 [1]Lit., *he*
[a]2 Chr. 25:19

22 [1]Lit., *his face*
[a]2 Chr. 18:29
[b]2 Chr. 35:21 [c]Judg.
5:19

24 [1]Lit., *and*
[a]Zech. 12:11

12 Then they removed the burnt offerings that *they* might give them to the
sections of the fathers' households of the
lay people to present to the LORD, as it is
written in the book of Moses. *They did*
this also with the bulls.
13 So [a]they roasted the Passover *animals* on the fire according to the ordinance, and they boiled [b]the holy things
in pots, in kettles, in pans, and carried
them speedily to all the lay people.
14 And afterwards they prepared for
themselves and for the priests, because
the priests, the sons of Aaron, *were*
offering the burnt offerings and the fat
until night; therefore the Levites prepared for themselves and for the priests,
the sons of Aaron.
15 The singers, the sons of Asaph,
were also at their stations [a]according to
the command of David, Asaph, Heman,
and Jeduthun the king's seer; and [b]the
gatekeepers at each gate did not have to
depart from their service, because the
Levites their brethren prepared for them.
16 So all the service of the LORD was
prepared on that day to celebrate the
Passover, and to offer burnt offerings on
the altar of the LORD according to the
command of King Josiah.
17 Thus [a]the sons of Israel who were
present celebrated the Passover at that
time, and the Feast of Unleavened Bread
seven days.
18 And [a]there had not been celebrated
a Passover like it in Israel since the days
of Samuel the prophet; nor had any of
the kings of Israel celebrated such a
Passover as Josiah did with the priests,
the Levites, all Judah and Israel who
were present, and the inhabitants of
Jerusalem.
19 In the eighteenth year of Josiah's
reign this Passover was celebrated.

Josiah Dies in Battle

20 [a]After all this, when Josiah had set
the [1]temple in order, Neco king of Egypt
came up to make war at [b]Carchemish on
the Euphrates, and Josiah went out to
engage him.
21 But [1]Neco sent messengers to him,
saying, "[a]What have we to do with each
other, O King of Judah? *I am* not *coming*
against you today but against the house
with which I am at war, and God has
ordered me to hurry. Stop for your own
sake from *interfering with* God who is
with me, that He may not destroy you."
22 However, Josiah would not turn
[1]away from him, but [a]disguised himself
in order to make war with him; nor did
he listen to the words of Neco [b]from the
mouth of God, but came to make war on
the plain of [c]Megiddo.
23 And the archers shot King Josiah,
and the king said to his servants, "Take
me away, for I am badly wounded."
24 So his servants took him out of the
chariot and carried him in the second
chariot which he had, and brought him
to Jerusalem [1]where he died and was
buried in the tombs of his fathers. [a]And

all Judah and Jerusalem mourned for
Josiah.
25 Then [a]Jeremiah chanted a lament
for Josiah. And all the male and female
singers speak about Josiah in their lamentations to this day. And they made
them an ordinance in Israel; behold,
they are also written in the Lamentations.
26 Now the rest of the acts of Josiah
and his deeds of devotion as written in
the law of the LORD,
27 and his acts, first to last, behold,
they are written in the Book of the Kings
of Israel and Judah.

Jehoahaz, Jehoiakim, then Jehoiachin Rule

36 [a]THEN the people of the land
took [1b]Joahaz the son of Josiah,
and made him king in place of his father
in Jerusalem.
2 Joahaz was twenty-three years old
when he became king, and he reigned
three months in Jerusalem.
3 Then the king of Egypt deposed
him at Jerusalem, and imposed on the
land a fine of one hundred talents of
silver and one talent of gold.
4 And the king of Egypt made Eliakim his brother king over Judah and
Jerusalem, and changed his name to
Jehoiakim. But [a]Neco took Joahaz his
brother and brought him to Egypt.
5 [a]Jehoiakim was twenty-five years
old when he became king, and he
reigned eleven years in Jerusalem; and
he did evil in the sight of the LORD his
God.
6 Nebuchadnezzar king of Babylon
came up [a]against him and [b]bound him
with bronze *chains* to take him to Babylon.
7 [a]Nebuchadnezzar also brought
some of the articles of the house of the
LORD to Babylon and put them in his
temple at Babylon.
8 [a]Now the rest of the acts of Jehoiakim and [1]the abominations which he
did, and what was found against him,
behold, they are written in the Book of
the Kings of Israel and Judah. And
Jehoiachin his son became king in his
place.
9 [a]Jehoiachin was eight years old
when he became king, and he reigned
three months and ten days in Jerusalem,
and he did evil in the sight of the LORD.

Captivity in Babylon Begun

10 And [a]at the turn of the year King
Nebuchadnezzar sent and brought him
to Babylon with the valuable articles of
the house of the LORD, and he made his
kinsman [b]Zedekiah king over Judah and
Jerusalem.

Zedekiah Rules in Judah

11 [a]Zedekiah was twenty-one years
old when he became king, and he
reigned eleven years in Jerusalem.
12 And he did evil in the sight of the
LORD his God; [a]he did not humble
himself [b]before Jeremiah the prophet
[1]who spoke for the LORD.
13 And [a]he also rebelled against King
Nebuchadnezzar who had made him
swear *allegiance* by God. But [b]he stiffened his neck and hardened his heart
against turning to the LORD God of
Israel.
14 Furthermore, all the officials of the
priests and the people were very unfaithful *following* all the abominations of the
nations; and they defiled the house of
the LORD which He had sanctified in
Jerusalem.
15 And the LORD, the God of their
fathers, [a]sent *word* to them again and
again by His messengers, because He
had compassion on His people and on
His dwelling place;
16 but they *continually* [a]mocked the
messengers of God, [b]despised His words
and scoffed at His prophets, [c]until the
wrath of the LORD arose against His
people, until there was no remedy.
17 [a]Therefore He brought up against
them the king of the Chaldeans who slew
their young men with the sword in the
house of their sanctuary, and had no
compassion on young man or virgin, old
man or infirm; He gave *them* all into his
hand.
18 And [a]all the articles of the house of
God, great and small, and the treasures
of the house of the LORD, and the
treasures of the king and of his officers,
he brought *them* all to Babylon.
19 Then [a]they burned the house of
God, and broke down the wall of Jerusalem and burned all its fortified buildings
with fire, and destroyed all its valuable
articles.
20 And those who had escaped from
the sword he [a]carried away to Babylon;
and [b]they were servants to him and to
his sons until the rule of the kingdom of
Persia,
21 [a]to fulfill the word of the LORD by
the mouth of Jeremiah, until [b]the land
had enjoyed its sabbaths. [c]All the days
of its desolation it kept sabbath [1d]until
seventy years were complete.

Cyrus Permits Return

22 [a]Now in the first year of Cyrus king
of Persia—in order to fulfill the word of
the LORD [b]by the mouth of Jeremiah—
the LORD [c]stirred up the spirit of Cyrus
king of Persia, so that he sent a proclamation throughout his kingdom, and
also *put it* in writing, saying,
23 "Thus says Cyrus king of Persia,
'The LORD, the God of heaven, has given
me all the kingdoms of the earth, and He
has appointed me to build Him a house
in Jerusalem, which is in Judah. Whoever there is among you of all His
people, may the LORD his God be with
him, and let him go up!' "

25 [a]Jer. 22:10; Lam. 4:20
1 [1]I.e., short form of Jehoahaz [a]2 Kin. 23:30-34 [b]Jer. 22:11
4 [a]Jer. 22:10-12
5 [a]2 Kin. 23:36, 37; Jer. 22:13-19; 26:1; 35:1
6 [a]2 Kin. 24:1; Jer. 25:1-9 [b]2 Chr. 33:11
7 [a]2 Kin. 24:13
8 [1]Lit., *his* [a]2 Kin. 24:5
9 [a]2 Kin. 24:8-17
10 [a]2 Sam. 11:1; Jer. 22:25; 24:1; 29:1; Ezek. 17:12 [b]Jer. 37:1
11 [a]2 Kin. 24:18-20; Jer. 27:1; 28:1; 52:1
12 [1]Lit., *from the mouth of the LORD* [a]2 Chr. 33:23 [b]Jer. 21:3-7
13 [a]Jer. 52:3; Ezek. 17:15 [b]2 Chr. 30:8
15 [a]Jer. 7:13; 25:3
16 [a]2 Chr. 30:10; Jer. 5:12, 13 [b]Prov. 1:24-32 [c]Ezra 5:12
17 [a]2 Kin. 25:1-7; Jer. 21:1-10
18 [a]2 Chr. 36:7, 10
19 [a]1 Kin. 9:8; 2 Kin. 25:9; Jer. 52:13
20 [a]2 Kin. 25:11 [b]Jer. 27:7
21 [1]Lit., *to fulfill seventy years* [a]Jer. 29:10 [b]Lev. 26:34 [c]Lev. 25:4 [d]Jer. 25:11
22 [a]Ezra 1:1-3 [b]Jer. 25:12; 29:10 [c]Is. 44:28

THE BOOK OF EZRA

Cyrus' Proclamation

1 [a]NOW in the first year of Cyrus king
of Persia, in order to fulfill the word
of the LORD by the mouth of Jeremiah,
the LORD stirred up the spirit of Cyrus
king of Persia, so that he [b]sent a proclamation throughout all his kingdom, and
also *put it* in writing, saying,
2 "Thus says Cyrus king of Persia,
'The LORD, the God of heaven, has given
me all the kingdoms of the earth, and
[a]He has appointed me to build Him a
house in Jerusalem, which is in Judah.
3 'Whoever there is among you of all
His people, may his God be with him!
Let him go up to Jerusalem which is in
Judah, and rebuild the house of the
LORD, the God of Israel; [a]He is the God
who is in Jerusalem.
4 'And every survivor, at whatever
place he may [1]live, let the men of [2]that
place support him with silver and gold,
with goods and cattle, together with a
freewill offering for the house of God
which is in Jerusalem.' "

Holy Vessels Restored

5 Then the heads of fathers' *households* of Judah and Benjamin and the
priests and the Levites arose, [a]even
everyone whose spirit God had stirred to
go up and rebuild the house of the LORD
which is in Jerusalem.
6 And all those about them [1a]en-
couraged them with articles of silver,
with gold, with goods, with cattle, and
with valuables, aside from all that was
given as a freewill offering.
7 [a]Also King Cyrus brought out the
articles of the house of the LORD, [b]which
Nebuchadnezzar had carried away from
Jerusalem and put in the house of his
gods;
8 and Cyrus, king of Persia, had
them brought out by the hand of Mithredath the treasurer, and he counted them
out to [a]Sheshbazzar, the prince of Judah.
9 Now this *was* their number: 30
[a]gold dishes, 1,000 silver dishes, 29
[1]duplicates;
10 30 gold bowls, 410 silver bowls of a
second *kind, and* 1,000 other articles.
11 All the articles of gold and silver
numbered 5,400. Sheshbazzar brought
them all up with the exiles who went up
from Babylon to Jerusalem.

Number of Those Returning

2 [a]NOW these are the [1]people of the
province who came up out of the
captivity of the exiles whom Nebuchadnezzar the king of Babylon had carried
away to Babylon, and returned to Jerusalem and Judah, each to his city.
2 [1]These came with Zerubbabel,
Jeshua, Nehemiah, [2]Seraiah, [3]Reelaiah,
Mordecai, Bilshan, [4]Mispar, Bigvai,
[5]Rehum, and Baanah.
The number of the men of the people
of Israel:
3 the sons of Parosh, 2,172;
4 the sons of Shephatiah, 372;
5 the sons of [a]Arah, 775;
6 the sons of [a]Pahath-moab of the
sons of Jeshua *and* Joab, 2,812;
7 the sons of Elam, 1,254;
8 the sons of Zattu, 945;
9 the sons of Zaccai, 760;
10 the sons of [1]Bani, 642;
11 the sons of Bebai, 623;
12 the sons of Azgad, 1,222;
13 the sons of [a]Adonikam, 666;
14 the sons of Bigvai, 2,056;
15 the sons of Adin, 454;
16 the sons of Ater of Hezekiah, 98;
17 the sons of Bezai, 323;
18 the sons of [1]Jorah, 112;
19 the sons of Hashum, 223;
20 the sons of [1]Gibbar, 95;
21 the [1]men of [a]Bethlehem, 123;
22 the men of Netophah, 56;
23 the men of Anathoth, 128;
24 the sons of [1]Azmaveth, 42;
25 the sons of [1]Kiriath-arim, Chephirah, and Beeroth, 743;
26 the sons of [a]Ramah and Geba, 621;
27 the men of Michmas, 122;
28 the men of Bethel and Ai, 223;
29 the sons of Nebo, 52;
30 the sons of Magbish, 156;
31 the sons of the other Elam, 1,254;
32 the sons of Harim, 320;
33 the sons of Lod, Hadid, and Ono,
725;
34 the [1]men of [a]Jericho, 345;
35 the sons of Senaah, 3,630.

Priests Returning

36 [a]The priests: the sons of Jedaiah of
the house of Jeshua, 973;
37 the sons of [a]Immer, 1,052;
38 [a]the sons of Pashhur, 1,247;
39 the sons of [a]Harim, 1,017.

Levites Returning

40 The Levites: the sons of Jeshua and
Kadmiel, of the sons of [1]Hodaviah, 74.
41 The singers: the sons of Asaph,
128.
42 The sons of the gatekeepers: the
sons of Shallum, the sons of Ater, the
sons of Talmon, the sons of Akkub,
the sons of Hatita, the sons of Shobai, in
all 139.
43 The [a]temple servants: the sons of
Ziha, the sons of Hasupha, the sons
of Tabbaoth,
44 the sons of Keros, the sons of
[1]Siaha, the sons of Padon,
45 the sons of Lebanah, the sons
of Hagabah, the sons of Akkub,
46 the sons of Hagab, the sons of
Shalmai, the sons of Hanan,
47 the sons of Giddel, the sons of
Gahar, the sons of Reaiah,
48 the sons of Rezin, the sons of
Nekoda, the sons of Gazzam,

---

1 [a]2 Chr. 36:22; Jer. 25:12; 29:10 [b]Ezra 5:13
2 [a]Is. 44:28; 45:1, 12, 13
3 [a]1 Kin. 8:23; 18:39; Is. 37:16; Dan. 6:26
4 [1]Or, *reside as an alien* [2]Lit., *his*
5 [a]Ezra 1:1, 2
6 [1]Lit., *strengthened their hands* [a]Neh. 6:9; Is. 35:3
7 [a]Ezra 5:14; 6:5 [b]2 Kin. 24:13; 2 Chr. 36:7
8 [a]Ezra 5:14
9 [1]Heb. obscure; other possible meanings are *knives, censers* [a]Ezra 8:27

1 [1]Lit., *sons* [a]2 Kin. 24:14-16; 25:11; 2 Chr. 36:20; Neh. 7:6-73
2 [1]Lit., *who* [2]In Neh. 7:7, *Azariah* [3]In Neh. 7:7, *Raamiah* [4]In Neh. 7:7, *Mispereth* [5]In Neh. 7:7, *Nehum*
5 [a]Neh. 7:10
6 [a]Neh. 7:11
10 [1]In Neh. 7:15, *Binnui*
13 [a]Ezra 8:13
18 [1]In Neh. 7:24, *Hariph*
20 [1]In Neh. 7:25, *Gibeon*
21 [1]Lit., *sons* [a]Gen. 35:19; Matt. 2:6
24 [1]In Neh. 7:28, *Beth-azmaveth*
25 [1]In Neh. 7:29, *Kiriath-jearim*
26 [a]Josh. 18:25
34 [1]Lit., *sons* [a]1 Kin. 16:34; 2 Chr. 28:15
36 [a]1 Chr. 24:7-18
37 [a]1 Chr. 24:14
38 [a]1 Chr. 9:12
39 [a]1 Chr. 24:8
40 [1]In Ezra 3:9, *Judah;* in Neh. 7:43, *Hodevah*
43 [a]1 Chr. 9:2
44 [1]In Neh. 7:47, *Sia*

49 the sons of Uzza, the sons of Paseah, the sons of Besai,
50 the sons of Asnah, the sons of
Meunim, the sons of [1]Nephisim,
51 the sons of Bakbuk, the sons of
Hakupha, the sons of Harhur,
52 the sons of [1]Bazluth, the sons of
Mehida, the sons of Harsha,
53 the sons of Barkos, the sons of
Sisera, the sons of Temah,
54 the sons of Neziah, the sons of
Hatipha.
55 The sons of [a]Solomon's servants:
the sons of Sotai, the sons of [1]Hassophe-
reth, the sons of [2]Peruda,
56 the sons of Jaalah, the sons of
Darkon, the sons of Giddel,
57 the sons of Shephatiah, the sons of
Hattil, the sons of Pochereth-hazzebaim,
the sons of [1]Ami.
58 All the [a]temple servants, and the
sons of [b]Solomon's servants, were 392.
59 Now these are those who came up
from Tel-melah, Tel-harsha, Cherub,
[1]Addan, *and* Immer, but they were not
able to [2]give evidence of their fathers'
households, and their [3]descendants,
whether they were of Israel:
60 the sons of Delaiah, the sons of
Tobiah, the sons of Nekoda, 652.

Priests Removed

61 And of the sons of the priests: the
sons of [1]Habaiah, the sons of Hakkoz,
the sons of [a]Barzillai, who took a wife
from the daughters of Barzillai the Gileadite, and he was called by their name.
62 These searched *among* their ancestral registration, but they could not be
located; [a]therefore they were considered
unclean *and excluded* from the priesthood.
63 And the [1]governor said to them
[a]that they should not eat from the most
holy things until a priest stood up with
[b]Urim and Thummim.
64 The whole assembly [1]numbered
42,360,
65 besides their male and female servants, [1]who numbered 7,337; and they
had 200 [a]singing men and women.
66 Their horses were 736; their mules,
245;
67 their camels, 435; *their* donkeys,
6,720.
68 And some of the heads of fathers'
households, when they arrived at the
house of the LORD which is in Jerusalem,
offered willingly for the house of God to
[1]restore it on its foundation.
69 According to their ability they gave
[a]to the treasury for the work 61,000 gold
drachmas, and 5,000 silver minas, and
100 priestly [1]garments.
70 [a]Now the priests and the Levites,
some of the people, the singers, the
gatekeepers, and the temple servants
lived in their cities, and all Israel in their
cities.

Altar and Sacrifices Restored

3 NOW when the seventh month
came, and [a]the sons of Israel *were* in
the cities, the people gathered together
as one man to Jerusalem.
2 Then [a]Jeshua the son of Jozadak
and his brothers the priests, and [b]Zerub-
babel the son [c]of Shealtiel, and his
brothers arose and [d]built the altar of the
God of Israel, to offer burnt offerings on
it, [e]as it is written in the law of Moses,
the man of God.
3 So they set up the altar on its
foundation, for [1a]they were terrified
because of the peoples of the lands; and
they [b]offered burnt offerings on it to the
LORD, burnt offerings morning and evening.
4 And they celebrated the [a]Feast of
[1]Booths, [b]as it is written, and *offered*
[2]the fixed number of burnt offerings
daily, [c]according to the ordinance, as
each day required;
5 and afterward *there was* a [a]contin-
ual burnt offering, also [b]for the new
moons and [c]for all the fixed festivals of
the LORD that were consecrated, and
from everyone who offered a freewill
offering to the LORD.
6 From the first day of the seventh
month they began to offer burnt offerings to the LORD, but the foundation of
the temple of the LORD had not been
laid.
7 Then they gave money to the masons and carpenters, and [a]food, drink,
and oil to the Sidonians and to the
Tyrians, [b]to bring cedar wood from
Lebanon to the sea at [c]Joppa, according
to the permission they had [1]from [d]Cyrus
king of Persia.

Temple Restoration Begun

8 Now in the second year of their
coming to the house of God at Jerusalem
in the second month, [a]Zerubbabel the
son of Shealtiel and Jeshua the son of
Jozadak and the rest of their brothers
the priests and the Levites, and all who
came from the captivity to Jerusalem,
began *the work* and [b]appointed the
Levites from twenty years and older to
oversee the work of the house of the
LORD.
9 Then [a]Jeshua *with* his sons and
brothers stood united *with* Kadmiel and
his sons, the sons of [1]Judah *and* the sons
of Henadad *with* their sons and brothers
the Levites, to oversee the workmen in
the temple of God.
10 Now when the builders had [a]laid
the foundation of the temple of the
LORD, [1]the priests stood in their apparel
with trumpets, and the Levites, the sons
of Asaph, with cymbals, to praise the
LORD [b]according to the [2]directions of
King David of Israel.
11 And [a]they sang, praising and giving
thanks to the LORD, *saying,* "[b]For He is
good, for His lovingkindness is upon
Israel forever." And all the people
shouted with a great shout when they
praised the LORD because the foundation of the house of the LORD was laid.

50 [1]In Neh. 7:52, *Nephushesim*

52 [1]In Neh. 7:54, *Bazlith*

55 [1]In Neh. 7:57, *Sophereth* [2]In Neh. 7:57, *Perida* [a]1 Kin. 9:21

57 [1]In Neh. 7:59, *Amon*

58 [a]1 Chr. 9:2 [b]1 Kin. 9:21

59 [1]In Neh. 7:61, *Addon* [2]Lit., *tell* [3]Lit., *seed*

61 [1]In Neh. 7:63, *Hobaiah* [a]2 Sam. 17:27; 1 Kin. 2:7

62 [a]Num. 16:39, 40

63 [1]Heb., *Tirshatha,* a Persian title [a]Lev. 2:3, 10 [b]Ex. 28:30; Num. 27:21

64 [1]Lit., *together was*

65 [1]Lit., *they were* [a]2 Chr. 35:25

68 [1]Lit., *establish*

69 [1]Or, *tunics* [a]Ezra 8:25-34

70 [a]1 Chr. 9:2; Neh. 11:3

1 [a]Neh. 7:73; 8:1

2 [a]Neh. 12:1, 8 [b]Ezra 2:2; Hag. 1:1; 2:2 [c]1 Chr. 3:17 [d]Ex. 27:1 [e]Deut. 12:5, 6

3 [1]Lit., *terror was upon them* [a]Ezra 4:4 [b]Num. 28:2

4 [1]Or, *Tabernacles* [2]Lit., *by number* [a]Neh. 8:14; Zech. 14:16 [b]Ex. 23:16 [c]Num. 29:12

5 [a]Ex. 29:38; Num. 28:3 [b]Num. 28:11 [c]Num. 29:39

7 [1]Lit., *of* [a]2 Chr. 2:10; Acts 12:20 [b]2 Chr. 2:16 [c]Acts 9:36 [d]Ezra 1:2; 6:3

8 [a]Ezra 3:2; 4:3 [b]1 Chr. 23:4, 24

9 [1]In Ezra 2:40, *Hodaviah* [a]Ezra 2:40

10 [1]So with the Gr. and some mss.; M.T., *they set the priests* [2]Lit., *hands* [a]Zech. 4:6-10 [b]1 Chr. 6:31; 25:1

11 [a]2 Chr. 7:3; Neh. 12:24, 40 [b]1 Chr. 16:34; 2 Chr. 5:13; Ps. 100:5; 106:1; 107:1; 118:1; 131:1; Jer. 33:11

12 Yet many of the priests and Levites
and heads of fathers' *households,* [a]the old
men who had seen the first [1]temple, wept
with a loud voice when the foundation of
this house was laid before their eyes,
while many shouted aloud for joy;
13 so that the people could not distinguish the sound of the shout of joy from
the sound of the weeping of the people,
for the people shouted with a loud shout,
and the sound was heard far away.

Adversaries Hinder the Work

4 NOW when [a]the enemies of Judah
and Benjamin heard that [b]the people of the exile were building a temple to
the LORD God of Israel,
2 they approached Zerubbabel and
the heads of fathers' *households,* and said
to them, "Let us build with you, for we,
like you, seek your God; [a]and we have
been sacrificing to Him since the days of
[b]Esarhaddon king of Assyria, who
brought us up here."
3 But Zerubbabel and Jeshua and the
rest of the heads of fathers' *households* of
Israel said to them, "[a]You have nothing
in common with us in building a house
to our God; but we ourselves will together build to the LORD God of Israel,
[b]as King Cyrus, the king of Persia has
commanded us."
4 Then [a]the people of the land [1]dis-
couraged the people of Judah, and
frightened them from building,
5 and hired counselors against them
to frustrate their counsel all the days of
Cyrus king of Persia, even until the reign
of Darius king of Persia.
6 Now in the reign of [1a]Ahasuerus, in
the beginning of his reign, they wrote an
accusation against the inhabitants of
Judah and Jerusalem.
7 And in the days of [1]Artaxerxes,
Bishlam, Mithredath, Tabeel, and the
rest of his colleagues, wrote to Artaxerxes king of Persia; and the [2]text of the
letter was written in Aramaic and translated [a]*from* Aramaic.

The Letter to King Artaxerxes

8 [1]Rehum the commander and Shimshai the scribe wrote a letter against
Jerusalem to King Artaxerxes, as follows—
9 then *wrote* Rehum the commander
and Shimshai the scribe and [a]the rest of
their colleagues, the judges and [b]the
lesser governors, the officials, the secretaries, the men of Erech, the Babylonians, the men of Susa, that is, the
Elamites,
10 and the rest of the nations which
the great and honorable [1]Osnappar
deported and settled in the city of Samaria, and in the rest of the region
beyond the [2]River. [a]And now
11 this is the copy of the letter which
they sent to him: "To King Artaxerxes:
Your servants, the men in the region
beyond the River, and now
12 let it be known to the king, that the
Jews who came up from you have come
to us at Jerusalem; they are rebuilding
[a]the rebellious and evil city, and [b]are
finishing the walls and repairing the
foundations.
13 "Now let it be known to the king,
that if that city is rebuilt and the walls
are finished, [a]they will not pay tribute,
custom, or toll, and it will damage the
revenue of the kings.
14 "Now because we [1]are in the service
of the palace, and it is not fitting for us
to see the king's dishonor, therefore we
have sent and informed the king,
15 so that a search may be made in the
record books of your fathers. And you
will discover in the record books, and
learn that that city is a rebellious city
and damaging to kings and provinces,
and that they have incited revolt within
it in past days; therefore that city was
laid waste.
16 "We inform the king that, if that city
is rebuilt and the walls finished, as a
result you will have no possession in *the*
province beyond the River."

The King Replies and Work Stops

17 *Then* the king sent an answer to
Rehum the commander, to Shimshai the
scribe, and to the rest of their colleagues
who live in Samaria and in the rest of *the*
provinces beyond the River: "Peace. And
now
18 the document which you sent to us
has been [1a]translated and read before
me.
19 "And a decree has been [1]issued by
me, and a search has been made and it
has been discovered that that city has
risen up against the kings in past days,
that rebellion and revolt have been
perpetrated in it,
20 [a]that mighty kings have [1]ruled over
Jerusalem, governing all *the provinces*
[b]beyond the River, and that [c]tribute,
custom, and toll were paid to them.
21 "So, now issue a decree to make
these men stop *work,* that the city may
not be rebuilt until a decree is issued by
me.
22 "And beware of being negligent in
carrying out this *matter;* why should
damage increase to the detriment of the
kings?"
23 Then as soon as the copy of King
Artaxerxes' document was read before
Rehum and Shimshai the scribe and
their colleagues, they went in haste to
Jerusalem to the Jews and stopped them
by force of arms.
24 Then work on the house of God in
Jerusalem ceased, and it was stopped
until the second year of the reign of
Darius king of Persia.

Temple Work Resumed

5 WHEN the prophets, [a]Haggai the
prophet and [b]Zechariah the son of
Iddo, prophesied to the Jews who were
in Judah and Jerusalem, in the name of
the God of Israel, who was over them,

12 [1]Lit., *house* [a]Hag. 2:3
1 [a]Ezra 4:7-10 [b]Ezra 1:11
2 [a]2 Kin. 17:32 [b]2 Kin. 19:37
3 [a]Neh. 2:20 [b]Ezra 1:1, 2
4 [1]Lit., *weakened the hands of* [a]Ezra 3:3
6 [1]Or, *Xerxes;* Heb., *Ahash-verosh* [a]Esth. 1:1; Dan. 9:1
7 [1]Heb., *Artah-shashta* [2]Lit., *writing* [a]2 Kin. 18:26; Dan. 2:4
8 [1]Ch. 4:8-6:18 is in Aram.
9 [a]2 Kin. 17:24 [b]Ezra 5:6; 6:6
10 [1]I.e., probably Ashurbanipal [2]I.e., Euphrates River, and so throughout the ch. [a]Ezra 4:11, 17; 7:12
12 [a]2 Chr. 36:13 [b]Ezra 5:3, 9
13 [a]Ezra 4:20; 7:24
14 [1]Lit., *eat the salt*
18 [1]Lit., *plainly read before* [a]Neh. 8:8
19 [1]Lit., *put* forth
20 [1]Lit., *been* [a]1 Kin. 4:21; 1 Chr. 18:3 [b]Gen. 15:18; Josh. 1:4 [c]Ezra 4:13; 7:24
1 [a]Hag. 1:1 [b]Zech. 1:1

2 then [a]Zerubbabel the son of Shealtiel and Jeshua the son of Jozadak arose
and began to rebuild the house of God
which is in Jerusalem; and [b]the prophets
of God were with them supporting them.
3 At that time [a]Tattenai, the governor of *the province* beyond the [1]River,
and Shethar-bozenai and their colleagues came to them and spoke to them
thus, "[b]Who issued you a decree to
rebuild this [2]temple and to finish this
structure?"
4 [a]Then we told them accordingly
what the names of the men were who
were reconstructing this building.
5 But [a]the eye of their God was on
the elders of the Jews, and they did not
stop them until a report should come to
Darius, and then a written reply be
returned concerning it.

Adversaries Write to Darius

6 *This is* the copy of the letter which
[a]Tattenai, the governor of *the province*
beyond the River, and Shethar-bozenai
and his colleagues [b]the officials, who
were beyond the River, sent to Darius
the king.
7 They sent a report to him in which
it was written thus: "To Darius the king,
all peace.
8 "Let it be known to the king, that we
have gone to the province of Judah, to
the house of the great God, which is
being built with huge stones, and [1]beams
are being laid in the walls; and this work
is going on with great care and is succeeding in their hands.
9 "Then we asked those elders and
said to them thus, 'Who issued you a
decree to rebuild this temple and to
finish this structure?'
10 "We also asked them their names so
as to inform you, and that we might
write down the names of the men who
were at their head.
11 "And thus they [1]answered us, saying, 'We are the servants of the God of
heaven and earth and are rebuilding the
temple that was built many years ago,
[a]which a great king of Israel built and
finished.
12 'But [a]because our fathers had provoked the God of heaven to wrath, [b]He
gave them into the hand of Nebuchadnezzar king of Babylon, the Chaldean,
who destroyed this temple and deported
the people to Babylon.
13 'However, [a]in the first year of Cyrus
king of Babylon, King Cyrus [b]issued a
decree to rebuild this house of God.
14 'And also [a]the gold and silver utensils of the house of God which Nebuchadnezzar had taken from the temple
[1]in Jerusalem, and brought them to the
temple of Babylon, these King Cyrus
took from the temple of Babylon, and
they were given to one [b]whose name was
Sheshbazzar, whom he had appointed
governor.
15 'And he said to him, "Take these
utensils, go *and* deposit them in the
temple [1]in Jerusalem, and let the house
of God be rebuilt in its place."
16 'Then that Sheshbazzar came *and*
[a]laid the foundations of the house of
God [1]in Jerusalem; and from then until
now it has been under construction, and
it is [b]not *yet* completed.'
17 "And now, if it pleases the king [a]let
a search be conducted in the king's
treasure house, which is there in Babylon, if it be that a decree was issued by
King Cyrus to rebuild this house of God
at Jerusalem; and let the king send to us
his decision concerning this *matter*."

Darius Finds Cyrus' Decree

6 THEN King Darius issued a decree,
and [a]search was made in the [1]ar-
chives, where the treasures were stored
in Babylon.
2 And in [1]Ecbatana in the fortress,
which is [a]in the province of Media, a
scroll was found and there was written
in it as follows: "Memorandum—
3 "[a]In the first year of King Cyrus,
Cyrus the king issued a decree: '*Concerning* the house of God at Jerusalem,
let the temple, the place where sacrifices
are offered, be rebuilt and let its foundations be [1]retained, its height being 60
cubits and its width 60 cubits;
4 [a]with three layers of huge stones,
and [1]one layer of timbers. And let the
cost be paid from the [2]royal treasury.
5 'And also let [a]the gold and silver
utensils of the temple of God, which
Nebuchadnezzar took from the temple
in Jerusalem and brought to Babylon, be
returned and [1]brought to their places in
the temple in Jerusalem; and you shall
put *them* in the house of God.'
6 "Now *therefore,* [a]Tattenai, governor
of *the province* beyond the [1]River, Shethar-bozenai, and [2]your colleagues, the
officials of *the provinces* beyond the
[1]River, [3]keep away from there.
7 "Leave this work on the house of
God alone; let the governor of the Jews
and the elders of the Jews rebuild this
house of God on its site.
8 "Moreover, [a]I issue a decree concerning what you are to do for these
elders of Judah in the rebuilding of this
house of God: the full cost is to be paid
to these people from the royal treasury
out of the taxes of *the provinces* beyond
the River, and that without delay.
9 "And whatever is needed, both
young bulls, rams, and lambs for a burnt
offering to the God of heaven, and
wheat, salt, wine, and anointing oil, as
the priests in Jerusalem request, *it* is to
be given to them daily without fail,
10 that they may offer [1]acceptable
sacrifices to the God of heaven and
[a]pray for the life of the king and his
sons.
11 "And I issued a decree that [a]any
man who violates this edict, a timber
shall be drawn from his house and
he shall be impaled on it and [b]his house
shall be made a refuse heap on account
of this.

2 [a]Ezra 3:2; Hag. 1:12; Zech. 4:6-9 [b]Ezra 6:14; Hag. 2:4; Zech. 3:1

3 [1]I.e., Euphrates River, and so throughout the ch. [2]Lit., *house,* and so in vv. 9, 11, 12 [a]Ezra 6:6, 13 [b]Ezra 1:3; 5:9

4 [a]Ezra 5:10

5 [a]Ezra 7:6, 28

6 [a]Ezra 5:3 [b]Ezra 4:9

8 [1]Lit., *timber is*

11 [1]Lit., *returned us the word* [a]1 Kin. 6:1, 38

12 [a]2 Chr. 36:16, 17 [b]2 Kin. 25:8-11; Jer. 52:12-15

13 [a]Ezra 1:1 [b]Ezra 1:1-4

14 [1]Lit., *that was in* [a]Ezra 1:7; 6:5; Dan. 5:2 [b]Ezra 1:8; 5:16

15 [1]Lit., *that is in*

16 [1]Lit., *that is in* [a]Ezra 3:8, 10 [b]Ezra 6:15

17 [a]Ezra 6:1, 2

1 [1]Lit., *house of the books* [a]Ezra 5:17

2 [1]Aram., *Achmetha* [a]2 Kin. 17:6

3 [1]Or, *fixed, laid* [a]Ezra 1:1; 5:13

4 [1]So Gr.; Aram., *a layer of new timber* [2]Lit., *king's house* [a]1 Kin. 6:36

5 [1]Lit., *go* [a]Ezra 1:7; 5:14

6 [1]I.e., Euphrates River, and so throughout the ch. [2]Aram., *their* [3]Lit., *be distant* [a]Ezra 5:3; 6:13

8 [a]Ezra 6:4; 7:14-22

10 [1]Lit., *pleasing;* or, *sweet-smelling sacrifices* [a]Ezra 7:23; Jer. 29:7; 1 Tim. 2:1, 2

11 [a]Ezra 7:26 [b]Dan. 2:5; 3:29

12“And may the God who [a]has caused
His name to dwell there overthrow any
king or people who [1]attempts to change
it, so as to destroy this house of God in
Jerusalem. I, Darius, have issued *this*
decree, let *it* be carried out with all
diligence!”

The Temple Completed and Dedicated

13 Then [a]Tattenai, the governor of *the*
province beyond the River, Shethar-
bozenai, and their colleagues carried out
the decree with all diligence, just as King
Darius had sent.
14 And [a]the elders of the Jews [1]were
successful in building through the
prophesying of Haggai the prophet and
Zechariah the son of Iddo. And [2]they
finished building according to the command of the God of Israel and the
decree [b]of Cyrus, [c]Darius, and [d]Artax-
erxes king of Persia.
15 And this temple was completed [1]on
the third day of the [a]month Adar; it was
the sixth year of the reign of King
Darius.
16 And the sons of Israel, the priests,
the Levites, and the rest of the [1]exiles,
[a]celebrated the dedication of this house
of God with joy.
17 And they offered for the dedication
of this temple of God 100 bulls, 200
rams, 400 lambs, and as a sin offering for
all Israel [a]12 male goats, corresponding
to the number of the tribes of Israel.
18 Then they appointed the priests to
[a]their divisions and the Levites in [b]their
orders for the service of God [1]in Jerusalem, [c]as it is written in the book of
Moses.

The Passover Observed

19 And [a]the exiles observed the Passover on [b]the fourteenth of the first
month.
20 [a]For the priests and the Levites had
purified themselves together; all of them
were pure. Then [b]they slaughtered the
Passover *lamb* for all the exiles, both for
their brothers the priests and for themselves.
21 And the sons of Israel who returned from exile and [a]all those who had
separated themselves from [b]the impurity
of the nations of the land to *join* them, to
seek the LORD God of Israel, ate *the*
Passover.
22 And [a]they observed the Feast of
Unleavened Bread seven days with joy,
for the LORD had caused them to rejoice,
and [b]had turned the heart of [c]the king of
Assyria toward them to [1]encourage them
in the work of the house of God, the
God of Israel.

Ezra Journeys from Babylon to Jerusalem

7 [a]NOW after these things, in the reign
of [b]Artaxerxes king of Persia, *there*
went up Ezra son of Seraiah, son of
Azariah, son of Hilkiah,
2 son of Shallum, son of Zadok, son
of Ahitub,

12 [1]Lit., *sends his hand* [a]Deut. 12:5, 11; 1 Kin. 9:3
13 [a]Ezra 6:6
14 [1]Lit., *were building and succeeding* [2]Lit., *built and finished* [a]Ezra 5:1, 2 [b]Ezra 1:1; 5:13 [c]Ezra 4:24; 6:12 [d]Ezra 7:1
15 [1]Lit., *until* [a]Esth. 3:7
16 [1]Lit., *sons of the captivity* [a]1 Kin. 8:63; 2 Chr. 7:5
17 [a]Ezra 8:35
18 [1]Lit., *which is in* [a]1 Chr. 24:1; 2 Chr. 35:5 [b]1 Chr. 23:6 [c]Num. 3:6; 8:9
19 [a]Ezra 1:11 [b]Ex. 12:6
20 [a]2 Chr. 29:34; 30:15 [b]2 Chr. 35:11
21 [a]Neh. 9:2; 10:28 [b]Ezra 9:11
22 [1]Lit., *strengthen their hands* [a]Ex. 12:15 [b]Ezra 7:27; Prov. 21:1 [c]Ezra 1:1; 6:1
1 [a]1 Chr. 6:4-14 [b]Ezra 7:12, 21; Neh. 2:1
6 [1]Lit., *his request* [a]Ezra 7:11, 12, 21 [b]Ezra 7:9, 28; 8:22
7 [a]Ezra 8:1-20
9 [1]Lit., *was the foundation* [a]Ezra 7:6; Neh. 2:8
10 [1]Lit., *seek* [a]Deut. 33:10; Ezra 7:25; Neh. 8:1
11 [1]Lit., *the scribe of*
12 [1]Ch. 7:12-26 is in Aram. [a]Ezek. 26:7; Dan. 2:37
13 [a]Ezra 6:1
14 [1]Lit., *from before* [a]Ezra 7:15, 28; 8:25
15 [a]2 Chr. 6:2; Ezra 6:12; Ps. 135:21
16 [a]Ezra 8:25 [b]Ezra 1:4, 6 [c]1 Chr. 29:6
17 [a]Num. 15:4-13 [b]Deut. 12:5-11

3 son of Amariah, son of Azariah,
son of Meraioth,
4 son of Zerahiah, son of Uzzi, son of
Bukki,
5 son of Abishua, son of Phinehas,
son of Eleazar, son of Aaron the chief
priest.
6 This Ezra went up from Babylon,
and he was a [a]scribe skilled in the law of
Moses, which the LORD God of Israel
had given; and the king granted him all
[1]he requested [b]because the hand of the
LORD his God *was* upon him.
7 And [a]some of the sons of Israel and
some of the priests, the Levites, the
singers, the gatekeepers, and the temple
servants went up to Jerusalem in the
seventh year of King Artaxerxes.
8 And he came to Jerusalem in the
fifth month, which was in the seventh
year of the king.
9 For on the first of the first month
[1]he began to go up from Babylon; and
on the first of the fifth month he came to
Jerusalem, [a]because the good hand of his
God *was* upon him.
10 For Ezra had set his heart to [1]study
the law of the LORD, and to practice *it,*
and [a]to teach *His* statutes and ordinances in Israel.

King's Decree on Behalf of Ezra

11 Now this is the copy of the decree
which King Artaxerxes gave to Ezra the
priest, the scribe, [1]learned in the words
of the commandments of the LORD and
His statutes to Israel:
12“[1]Artaxerxes, [a]king of kings, to Ezra
the priest, the scribe of the law of the
God of heaven, perfect *peace.* And now
13 [a]I have issued a decree that any of
the people of Israel and their priests and
the Levites in my kingdom who are
willing to go to Jerusalem, may go with
you.
14“Forasmuch as you are sent [1]by the
king and his [a]seven counselors to inquire
concerning Judah and Jerusalem according to the law of your God which is in
your hand,
15 and to bring the silver and gold,
which the king and his counselors have
freely offered to the God of Israel,
[a]whose dwelling is in Jerusalem,
16 with [a]all the silver and gold which
you shall find in the whole province of
Babylon, along [b]with the freewill offering of the people and of the priests, who
[c]offered willingly for the house of their
God which is in Jerusalem;
17 with this money, therefore, you
shall diligently buy bulls, rams, and
lambs, [a]with their grain offerings and
their libations and [b]offer them on the
altar of the house of your God which is
in Jerusalem.
18“And whatever seems good to you
and to your brothers to do with the rest
of the silver and gold, you may do
according to the will of your God.
19“Also the utensils which are given to
you for the service of the house of your

God, deliver in full before the God of
Jerusalem.
20 "And the rest of the needs for the
house of your God, for which you may
have occasion to provide, [a]provide *for it*
from the royal treasury.
21 "And I, even I King Artaxerxes,
issue a decree to all the treasurers who
are *in the provinces* beyond the [1]River,
that whatever Ezra the priest, [a]the scribe
of the law of the God of heaven, may
require of you, it shall be done diligently,
22 *even* up to 100 talents of silver, 100
[1]kors of wheat, 100 baths of wine, 100
baths of oil, and salt [2]as needed.
23 "Whatever is [1]commanded by the
God of heaven, let it be done with zeal
for the house of the God of heaven, [a]lest
there be wrath against the kingdom of
the king and his sons.
24 "We also inform you that [a]it is not
allowed to [1]impose tax, tribute or toll
[b]*on* any of the priests, Levites, singers,
doorkeepers, Nethinim, or servants of
this house of God.
25 "And you, Ezra, according to the
wisdom of your God which is in your
hand, [a]appoint magistrates and judges
that they may judge all the people who
are in *the province* beyond the River,
even all those who know the laws of your
God; and you may [b]teach anyone who is
ignorant *of them.*
26 "And [a]whoever will not observe the
law of your God and the law of the king,
let judgment be executed upon him
strictly, whether for death or for [1]ban-
ishment or for confiscation of goods or
for imprisonment."

The King's Kindness

27 Blessed be the LORD, the God of
our fathers, [a]who has put *such a thing* as
this in the king's heart, to adorn the
house of the LORD which is in Jerusalem,
28 and [a]has extended lovingkindness
to me before the king and his counselors
and before all the king's mighty princes.
Thus I was strengthened according to
[b]the hand of the LORD my God upon
me, and I gathered [1]leading men from
Israel to go up with me.

People Who Went with Ezra

8 NOW these are the heads of their
fathers' *households* and the genealogical enrollment of those who went up
with me from Babylon in the reign of
King Artaxerxes:
2 of the sons of Phinehas, Gershom;
of the sons of Ithamar, Daniel; of the
sons of David, [a]Hattush;
3 of the sons of Shecaniah *who was* of
the sons of [a]Parosh, Zechariah and with
him 150 males *who were in* the genealogical list;
4 of the sons of Pahath-moab, Eliehoenai the son of Zerahiah and 200
males with him;
5 of the sons of Shecaniah, the son of
Jahaziel and 300 males with him;
6 and of the sons of [a]Adin, Ebed the
son of Jonathan and 50 males with him;
7 and of the sons of Elam, Jeshaiah
the son of Athaliah and 70 males with
him;
8 and of the sons of Shephatiah,
Zebadiah the son of Michael and 80
males with him;
9 of the sons of Joab, Obadiah the
son of Jehiel and 218 males with him;
10 and of the sons of Shelomith, the
son of Josiphiah and 160 males with
him;
11 and of the sons of Bebai, Zechariah
the son of Bebai and 28 males with him;
12 and of the sons of Azgad, Johanan
the son of Hakkatan and 110 males with
him;
13 and of the sons of Adonikam, the
last ones, these being their names, Eliphelet, Jeuel, and Shemaiah and 60 males
with them;
14 and of the sons of Bigvai, Uthai
and [1]Zabbud and 70 males with [2]them.

Ezra Sends for Levites

15 Now I assembled them at [a]the river
that runs to Ahava, where we camped
for three days; and when I observed the
people and the priests, I [b]did not find
any Levites there.
16 So I sent for Eliezer, Ariel, Shemaiah, Elnathan, Jarib, Elnathan, Nathan,
Zechariah, and Meshullam, [1]leading
men, and for Joiarib and Elnathan,
teachers.
17 And I sent them to Iddo the [1]lead-
ing man at the place Casiphia; and I
[2]told them what to say to [3]Iddo *and* his
brothers, [a]the temple servants at the
place Casiphia, *that is,* to bring ministers
to us for the house of our God.
18 And [a]according to the good hand
of our God upon us they brought us a
[b]man of insight of the sons of Mahli, the
son of Levi, the son of Israel, namely
Sherebiah, and his sons and brothers, 18
men;
19 and Hashabiah and [1]Jeshaiah of
the sons of Merari, with his brothers and
their sons, 20 men;
20 and 220 of [a]the temple servants,
whom David and the princes had given
for the service of the Levites, all of them
designated by name.

Protection of God Invoked

21 Then I proclaimed [a]a fast there at
[b]the river of Ahava, that we might
[c]humble ourselves before our God to
seek from Him a [1]safe journey for us,
our little ones, and all our possessions.
22 For I was ashamed to request from
the king troops and horsemen to [1]pro-
tect us from the enemy on the way,
because we had said to the king, "[a]The
hand of our God is [2]favorably disposed
to all those who seek Him, but [b]His
power and His anger are against all
those who [c]forsake Him."
23 So we fasted and sought our God
concerning this *matter,* and He [1a]listened
to our entreaty.

20 [a]Ezra 6:4
21 [1]I.e., Euphrates River, and so throughout the ch. [a]Ezra 7:6
22 [1]I.e., One kor equals approx. ten bu. [2]Lit., *without prescription*
23 [1]Lit., *from the decree of* [a]Ezra 6:10
24 [1]Lit., *throw on them* [a]Ezra 4:13, 20 [b]Ezra 7:7
25 [a]Ex. 18:21; Deut. 16:18 [b]Ezra 7:10; Mal. 2:7; Col. 1:28
26 [1]Lit., *rooting out* [a]Ezra 6:11, 12
27 [a]Ezra 6:22
28 [1]Lit., *heads* [a]Ezra 9:9 [b]Ezra 5:5
2 [a]1 Chr. 3:22
3 [a]Ezra 2:3
6 [a]Ezra 2:15; Neh. 7:20; 10:16
14 [1]Or, *Zakkur* [2]Or, *him*
15 [a]Ezra 8:21, 31 [b]Ezra 7:7; 8:2
16 [1]Lit., *heads*
17 [1]Lit., *head* [2]Lit., *put words in their mouth to say* [3]So Gr.; Heb., *Iddo his brother* [a]Ezra 2:43
18 [a]Ezra 7:6, 28 [b]2 Chr. 30:22
19 [1]So Gr.; Heb., *with him Jeshaiah*
20 [a]Ezra 2:43; 7:7
21 [1]Lit., *straight way* [a]1 Sam. 7:6; 2 Chr. 20:3 [b]Ezra 8:15, 31 [c]Lev. 16:29; 23:29; Is. 58:3, 5
22 [1]Lit., *help* [2]Lit., *upon all . . . for good* [a]Ezra 7:6, 9, 28 [b]Josh. 22:16 [c]2 Chr. 15:2
23 [1]Lit., *was entreated by us* [a]1 Chr. 5:20; 2 Chr. 33:13

24 Then I set apart twelve of the
leading priests, [a]Sherebiah, Hashabiah,
and with them ten of their brothers;
25 and I [a]weighed out to them [b]the
silver, the gold, and the utensils, the
offering for the house of our God which
the king and [c]his counselors and his
princes, and all Israel present *there,* had
offered.
26 [a]Thus I weighed into their hands
650 talents of silver, and silver utensils
worth 100 talents, *and* 100 gold talents,
27 and 20 gold bowls, *worth* 1,000
darics; and two utensils of fine shiny
bronze, precious as gold.
28 Then I said to them, "[a]You are
holy to the LORD, and the [b]utensils are
holy; and the silver and the gold are a
freewill offering to the LORD God of
your fathers.
29 "Watch and keep *them* [a]until you
weigh *them* before the leading priests,
the Levites, and the heads of the fathers'
households of Israel at Jerusalem, *in* the
chambers of the house of the LORD."
30 So the priests and the Levites [a]ac-
cepted the weighed out silver and gold
and the utensils, to bring *them* to Jerusalem to the house of our God.
31 Then we journeyed from [a]the river
Ahava on [b]the twelfth of the first month
to go to Jerusalem; and [c]the hand of our
God was over us, and He delivered us
from the hand of the enemy and the
ambushes by the way.
32 [a]Thus we came to Jerusalem and
remained there three days.

Treasure Placed in the Temple

33 And on the fourth day the silver
and the gold and the utensils [a]were
weighed out in the house of our God
into the hand of [b]Meremoth the son of
Uriah the priest, and with him *was*
Eleazar the son of Phinehas; and with
them *were* the Levites, Jozabad the son
of Jeshua and Noadiah the son of Binnui.
34 Everything *was* numbered and
weighed, and all the weight was recorded
at that time.
35 [a]The exiles who had come from the
captivity offered burnt offerings to the
God of Israel: [b]12 bulls for all Israel, 96
rams, 77 lambs, 12 male goats for a sin
offering, all as a burnt offering to the
LORD.
36 Then [a]they delivered the king's
edicts to [b]the king's satraps, and to the
governors *in the provinces* beyond the
[1]River, and they supported the people
and the house of God.

Mixed Marriages

9 NOW when these things had been
completed, the princes approached
me, saying, "The people of Israel and the
priests and the Levites have not [a]sepa-
rated themselves from the peoples of the
lands, [b]according to their abominations,
those of the Canaanites, the Hittites, the
Perizzites, the Jebusites, the Ammonites,
the Moabites, the Egyptians, and the
Amorites.
2 "For [a]they have taken some of their
daughters *as wives* for themselves and
for their sons, so that [b]the holy [1]race has
[c]intermingled with the peoples of the
lands; indeed, the hands of the princes
and the rulers have been foremost in this
unfaithfulness."
3 And when I heard about this matter, I [a]tore my garment and my robe,
and pulled some of the hair from my
head and my beard, and [b]sat down
appalled.
4 Then [a]everyone who trembled at
the words of the God of Israel on account of the unfaithfulness of the exiles
gathered to me, and I sat appalled until
[b]the evening offering.

Prayer of Confession

5 But at the evening offering I arose
from my [1]humiliation, even with my
garment and my robe torn, and I fell on
my knees and [a]stretched out my [2]hands
to the LORD my God;
6 and I said, "O my God, I am
ashamed and embarrassed to lift up my
face to Thee, my God, for our iniquities
have [1]risen above our heads, and our
[a]guilt has grown even to the heavens.
7 "[a]Since the days of our fathers to
this day we *have been* in great guilt, and
on account of our iniquities we, our
kings *and* our priests have been given
into the hand of the kings of the lands,
to the sword, to captivity, and to plunder
and to [1b]open shame, as *it is* this day.
8 "But now for a brief moment grace
has been *shown* from the LORD our God,
[a]to leave us an escaped remnant and to
give us a [b]peg in His holy place, that our
God may [c]enlighten our eyes and grant
us a little reviving in our bondage.
9 "[a]For we are slaves; yet in our
bondage, our God has not forsaken us,
but [b]has extended lovingkindness to us
in the sight of the kings of Persia, to give
us reviving to raise up the house of our
God, to restore its ruins, and to give us a
wall in Judah and Jerusalem.
10 "And now, our God, what shall we
say after this? For we have forsaken Thy
commandments,
11 which Thou hast commanded by
Thy servants the prophets, saying, 'The
land which you are entering to possess is
an unclean land with the uncleanness of
the peoples of the lands, with their
abominations which have filled it from
end to end *and* [a]with their impurity.
12 'So now do not [a]give your daughters
to their sons nor take their daughters to
your sons, and [b]never seek their peace or
their prosperity, that you may be strong
and eat the good *things* of the land and
[c]leave *it* as an inheritance to your sons
forever.'
13 "And after all that has come upon
us for our evil deeds and [a]our great guilt,
since Thou our God hast requited *us* less
than our iniquities *deserve,* and hast
given us [b]an escaped remnant as this,

24 [a]Ezra 8:18, 19
25 [a]Ezra 8:33 [b]Ezra 7:15, 16 [c]Ezra 7:14
26 [a]Ezra 1:9-11
28 [a]Lev. 21:6-8 [b]Lev. 22:2, 3
29 [a]Ezra 8:33, 34
30 [a]Ezra 1:9
31 [a]Ezra 8:15, 21 [b]Ezra 7:9 [c]Ezra 8:22
32 [a]Neh. 2:11
33 [a]Ezra 8:30 [b]Neh. 3:4, 21
35 [a]Ezra 2:1 [b]Ezra 6:17
36 [1]I.e., Euphrates River [a]Ezra 7:21-24 [b]Ezra 4:7; 5:6
1 [a]Ezra 6:21; Neh. 9:2 [b]Lev. 18:24-30
2 [1]Lit., *seed* [a]Deut. 7:3; Ezra 10:2, 18 [b]Ex. 22:31; Deut. 14:2; 2 Cor. 6:14 [c]Neh. 13:3
3 [a]2 Kin. 18:37 [b]Neh. 1:4
4 [a]Ezra 10:3; Is. 66:2 [b]Ex. 29:39
5 [1]Or, *fasting* [2]Lit., *palms* [a]Ex. 9:29
6 [1]Lit., *multiplied over the head* [a]2 Chr. 28:9; Ezra 9:13, 15; Rev. 18:5
7 [1]Lit., *shame of faces* [a]2 Chr. 29:6; Ps. 106:6 [b]Dan. 9:7
8 [a]Ezra 9:13-15 [b]Is. 22:23 [c]Ps. 13:3
9 [a]Neh. 9:36 [b]Ezra 7:28
11 [a]Ezra 6:21
12 [a]Ex. 34:15, 16; Deut. 7:3; Ezra 9:2 [b]Deut. 23:6 [c]Prov. 13:22
13 [a]Ezra 9:6, 7 [b]Ezra 9:8

14 [a]shall we again break Thy commandments and intermarry with the
peoples [1]who commit these abominations? [b]Wouldst Thou not be angry with
us [2]to the point of destruction, until
there is no remnant nor any who escape?
15"O LORD God of Israel, [a]Thou art
righteous, for we have been left an
escaped remnant, as *it is* this day; behold, we are before Thee in [b]our guilt,
for [c]no one can stand before Thee because of this."

Reconciliation with God

10 NOW [a]while Ezra was praying
and making confession, weeping
and prostrating himself [b]before the
house of God, a very large assembly,
men, women, and children, gathered to
him from Israel; for the people wept
bitterly.
2 And Shecaniah the son of Jehiel,
one of the sons of Elam, answered and
said to Ezra, "[a]We have been unfaithful
to our God, and have [1]married foreign
women from the peoples of the land; yet
now there is hope for Israel in spite of
this.
3"So now [a]let us make a covenant
with our God to put away all the wives
and [1b]their children, according to the
counsel of [2]my lord and of [c]those who
tremble at the commandment of our
God; and let it be done [d]according to
the law.
4"Arise! For *this* matter is [1]your
responsibility, but we will be with you;
[a]be courageous and act."
5 Then Ezra rose and [a]made the
leading priests, the Levites, and all
Israel, take oath that they would do
according to this [1]proposal; so they took
the oath.
6 Then Ezra [a]rose from before the
house of God and went into the chamber
of Jehohanan the son of Eliashib. Although he went there, [b]he did not eat
bread, nor drink water, for he was
mourning over the unfaithfulness of the
exiles.
7 And they made a proclamation
throughout Judah and Jerusalem to all
the exiles, that they should assemble at
Jerusalem,
8 and that whoever would not come
within three days, according to the
counsel of the leaders and the elders, all
his possessions should be forfeited and
he himself excluded from the assembly
of the exiles.
9 So all the men of Judah and Benjamin assembled at Jerusalem within the
three days. It was the ninth month on
the twentieth of the month, and all the
people sat in the open square *before* the
house of God, [a]trembling because of this
matter and the heavy rain.
10 Then Ezra the priest stood up and
said to them, "You have been unfaithful
and have married foreign wives adding
to the guilt of Israel.
11"Now, therefore, [a]make confession
to the LORD God of your fathers, and

14 [1]Lit., *of these abominations* [2]Lit., *to destroy* [a]Ezra 9:2 [b]Deut. 9:8, 14
15 [a]Neh. 9:33; Dan. 9:7 [b]Ezra 9:6 [c]Job 9:2; Ps. 130:3
1 [a]Dan. 9:4, 20 [b]2 Chr. 20:9
2 [1]Lit., *given dwelling to* [a]Ezra 9:2; Neh. 13:27
3 [1]Lit., *that which is born of them* [2]Or, *the Lord* [a]2 Chr. 34:31 [b]Ezra 10:44 [c]Ezra 9:4 [d]Deut. 7:2, 3
4 [1]Lit., *upon you* [a]1 Chr. 28:10
5 [1]Lit., *word, thing* [a]Neh. 5:12; 13:25
6 [a]Ezra 10:1 [b]Deut. 9:18
9 [a]1 Sam. 12:18; Ezra 9:4; 10:3
11 [a]Lev. 26:40; Prov. 28:13 [b]Rom. 12:2 [c]Ezra 10:3
12 [1]Lit., *upon us*
14 [1]Lit., *stand for* [a]2 Kin. 23:26; 2 Chr. 28:11-13; 29:10; 30:8
15 [1]Lit., *stood against*
16 [1]Heb. reads *there were set apart Ezra the priest, men . . .* [2]Lit., *sat*
18 [a]Ezra 5:2; Hag. 1:1, 12; 2:4; Zech. 3:1; 6:11
19 [1]Lit., *gave their hand* [a]Lev. 5:15; 6:6
25 [a]Ezra 2:3; 8:3; Neh. 7:8
27 [a]Ezra 2:8; Neh. 7:13

[b]do His will; and [c]separate yourselves
from the peoples of the land and from
the foreign wives."
12 Then all the assembly answered
and said with a loud voice, "That's right!
As you have said, so it is [1]our duty to do.
13"But there are many people, it is the
rainy season, and we are not able to
stand in the open. Nor *can* the task *be
done* in one or two days, for we have
transgressed greatly in this matter.
14"Let our leaders [1]represent the
whole assembly and let all those in our
cities who have married foreign wives
come at appointed times, together with
the elders and judges of each city, until
the [a]fierce anger of our God on account
of this matter is turned away from us."
15 Only Jonathan the son of Asahel
and Jahzeiah the son of Tikvah [1]opposed
this, with Meshullam and Shabbethai
the Levite supporting them.
16 But the exiles did so. And [1]Ezra the
priest selected men *who were* heads of
fathers' *households* for *each of* their
father's households, all of them by name.
So they [2]convened on the first day of the
tenth month to investigate the matter.
17 And they finished *investigating* all
the men who had married foreign wives
by the first of the first month.

List of Offenders

18 And among the sons of the priests
who had married foreign wives were
found of the sons of [a]Jeshua the son of
Jozadak, and his brothers: Maaseiah,
Eliezer, Jarib, and Gedaliah.
19 And they [1]pledged to put away
their wives, and being guilty, *[a]they offered* a ram of the flock for their offense.
20 And of the sons of Immer *there
were* Hanani and Zebadiah;
21 and of the sons of Harim: Maaseiah, Elijah, Shemaiah, Jehiel, and Uzziah;
22 and of the sons of Pashhur: Elioenai, Maaseiah, Ishmael, Nethanel, Jozabad, and Elasah.
23 And of Levites *there were* Jozabad,
Shimei, Kelaiah (that is, Kelita), Pethahiah, Judah, and Eliezer.
24 And of the singers *there was* Eliashib; and of the gatekeepers: Shallum,
Telem, and Uri.
25 And of Israel, of the sons of [a]Pa-
rosh *there were* Ramiah, Izziah, Malchijah, Mijamin, Eleazar, Malchijah, and
Benaiah;
26 and of the sons of Elam: Mattaniah, Zechariah, Jehiel, Abdi, Jeremoth,
and Elijah;
27 and of the sons of [a]Zattu: Elioenai,
Eliashib, Mattaniah, Jeremoth, Zabad,
and Aziza;
28 and of the sons of Bebai: Jehohanan, Hananiah, Zabbai, *and* Athlai;
29 and of the sons of Bani: Meshullam, Malluch, and Adaiah, Jashub,
Sheal, *and* Jeremoth;
30 and of the sons of Pahath-moab:
Adna, Chelal, Benaiah, Maaseiah, Mattaniah, Bezalel, Binnui, and Manasseh;

31 and *of* the sons of Harim: Eliezer, Isshijah, [a]Malchijah, Shemaiah, Shimeon,

32 Benjamin, Malluch, *and* Shemariah;

33 of the sons of Hashum: Mattenai, Mattattah, Zabad, Eliphelet, Jeremai, Manasseh, *and* Shimei;

34 of the sons of Bani: Maadai, Amram, Uel,

35 Benaiah, Bedeiah, Cheluhi,

36 Vaniah, Meremoth, Eliashib,

37 Mattaniah, Mattenai, Jaasu,

38 Bani, Binnui, Shimei,

39 Shelemiah, Nathan, Adaiah,

40 Machnadebai, Shashai, Sharai,

41 Azarel, Shelemiah, Shemariah,

42 Shallum, Amariah, *and* Joseph.

43 Of the sons of [a]Nebo *there were* Jeiel, Mattithiah, Zabad, Zebina, Jaddai, Joel, *and* Benaiah.

44 All these had married [a]foreign wives, and some of them had wives *by whom* they had children.

31 [a]Neh. 3:11
43 [a]Num. 32:38; Ezra 2:29
44 [a]1 Kin. 11:1-3; Ezra 10:3

THE BOOK OF NEHEMIAH

Nehemiah's Grief for the Exiles

1 THE words of [a]Nehemiah the son of Hacaliah.

Now it happened in [b]the month Chislev, [c]*in* the twentieth year, while I was in [d]Susa the [1]capitol,

2 that [a]Hanani, one of my brothers, and [1]some men from Judah came; and I asked them concerning the Jews who had escaped *and* had survived the captivity, and about Jerusalem.

3 And they said to me, "The remnant there in the [a]province who survived the captivity are in great distress and [b]reproach, and [c]the wall of Jerusalem is broken down and [d]its gates are burned with fire."

4 Now it came about when I heard these words, [a]I sat down and wept and mourned for days; and I was fasting and praying before [b]the God of heaven.

5 And I said, "I beseech Thee, O LORD God of heaven, [a]the great and awesome God, [b]who preserves the covenant and lovingkindness for those who love Him and keep His commandments,

6 [a]let Thine ear now be attentive and Thine eyes open to hear the prayer of Thy servant which I am praying before Thee now, day and night, on behalf of the sons of Israel Thy servants, [b]confessing the sins of the sons of Israel which we have sinned against Thee; [c]I and my father's house have sinned.

7 "[a]We have acted very corruptly against Thee and have not kept the commandments, nor the statutes, nor the ordinances [b]which Thou didst command Thy servant Moses.

8 "Remember the word which Thou didst command Thy servant Moses, saying, '[a]If you are unfaithful I will scatter you among the peoples;

9 [a]but if you return to Me and keep My commandments and do them, though those of you who have been scattered were in the most remote part of the heavens, I [b]will gather them from there and will bring them [c]to the place where I have chosen to cause My name to dwell.'

10 "And [a]they are Thy servants and Thy people whom Thou didst redeem by Thy great power and by Thy strong hand.

11 "O Lord, I beseech Thee, [a]may Thine ear be attentive to the prayer of Thy servant and the prayer of Thy servants who delight to [1]revere Thy name, and make Thy servant successful today, and grant him compassion before this man."

Now I was the [b]cupbearer to the king.

Nehemiah's Prayer Answered

2 AND it came about in the month Nisan, [a]in the twentieth year of King [b]Artaxerxes, that wine *was* before him, and [c]I took up the wine and gave it to the king. Now I had not been sad in his presence.

2 So the king said to me, "Why is your face sad though you are not sick? [a]This is nothing but sadness of heart." Then I was very much afraid.

3 And I said to the king, "[a]Let the king live forever. Why should my face not be sad [b]when the city, the place of my fathers' tombs, lies desolate and its gates have been consumed by fire?"

4 Then the king said to me, "What would you request?" [a]So I prayed to the God of heaven.

5 And I said to the king, "If it please the king, and if your servant has found favor before you, send me to Judah, to the city of my fathers' tombs, that I may rebuild it."

6 Then the king said to me, the queen sitting beside him, "How long will your journey be, and when will you return?" So it pleased the king to send me, and [a]I gave him a definite time.

7 And I said to the king, "If it please the king, let letters be given me [a]for the governors *of the provinces* beyond the River, that they may allow me to pass through until I come to Judah,

8 and a letter to Asaph the keeper of the king's [a]forest, that he may give me timber to make beams for the gates of [b]the fortress which is by the [1]temple, for the wall of the city, and for the house to which I will go." And the king granted *them* to me because [c]the good hand of my God *was* on me.

1 [1]Or, *palace* or *citadel* [a]Neh. 10:1 [b]Zech. 7:1 [c]Neh. 2:1 [d]Esth. 1:2; Dan. 8:2
2 [1]Lit., *he and some* [a]Neh. 7:2
3 [a]Neh. 7:6 [b]Neh. 2:17 [c]Neh. 2:17 [d]Neh. 2:3
4 [a]Ezra 9:3; 10:1 [b]Neh. 2:4
5 [a]Neh. 4:14; 9:32; Dan. 9:4 [b]Ex. 20:6; Ps. 89:2, 3
6 [a]Dan. 9:17 [b]Ezra 10:1; Dan. 9:20 [c]2 Chr. 29:6
7 [a]Dan. 9:5 [b]Deut. 28:14
8 [a]Lev. 26:33
9 [a]Deut. 30:2, 3 [b]Deut. 30:4 [c]Deut. 12:5
10 [a]Ex. 32:11; Deut. 9:29
11 [1]Or, *fear* [a]Neh. 1:6 [b]Gen. 40:21; Neh. 2:1

1 [a]Neh. 1:1 [b]Ezra 7:1 [c]Neh. 1:11
2 [a]Prov. 15:13
3 [a]Dan. 2:4 [b]2 Kin. 25:8-10; 2 Chr. 36:19; Neh. 1:3; Jer. 52:12-14
4 [a]Neh. 1:4
6 [a]Neh. 13:6
7 [a]Ezra 7:21; 8:36
8 [1]Lit., *house* [a]Eccl. 2:5, 6 [b]Neh. 7:2 [c]Ezra 7:6; Neh. 2:18

9 Then I came to [a]the governors *of*
the provinces beyond the River and gave
them the king's letters. Now [b]the king
had sent with me officers of the army
and horsemen.
10 And when [a]Sanballat the Horonite
and Tobiah the Ammonite [1]official
heard *about it,* it was very displeasing to
them that someone had come to seek the
welfare of the sons of Israel.

Nehemiah Inspects Jerusalem's Walls

11 So I [a]came to Jerusalem and was
there three days.
12 And I arose in the night, I and a
few men with me. I did not tell anyone
what my God was putting into my
[1]mind to do for Jerusalem and there was
no animal with me except the animal on
which I was riding.
13 So I went out at night by [a]the
Valley Gate in the direction of the
Dragon's Well and *on* to the [1]Refuse
Gate, inspecting the walls of Jerusalem
[b]which were broken down and its [c]gates
which were consumed by fire.
14 Then I passed on to [a]the Fountain
Gate and [b]the King's Pool, but there was
no place for [1]my mount to pass.
15 So I went up at night by the [a]ravine
and inspected the wall. Then I entered
the Valley Gate again and returned.
16 And the officials did not know
where I had gone or what I had done;
nor had I as yet told the Jews, the
priests, the nobles, the officials, or the
rest who did the work.
17 Then I said to them, "You see the
bad situation we are in, that [a]Jerusalem
is desolate and its gates burned by fire.
Come, let us rebuild the wall of Jerusalem that we may no longer be a reproach."
18 And I told them how the hand of
my God had been favorable to me, and
also about the king's words which he
had spoken to me. Then they said, "Let
us arise and build." [a]So they put their
hands to the good *work.*
19 But when Sanballat the Horonite,
and Tobiah the Ammonite [1]official, and
[a]Geshem the Arab heard *it,* [b]they
mocked us and despised us and said,
"What is this thing you are doing? [c]Are
you rebelling against the king?"
20 So I answered them and said to
them, "[a]The God of heaven will give us
success; therefore we His servants will
arise and build, [b]but you have no portion, right, or memorial in Jerusalem."

Builders of the Walls

3 THEN [a]Eliashib the high priest
arose with his brothers the priests
and built [b]the Sheep Gate; they consecrated it and [c]hung its doors. They
consecrated [1]the wall to [d]the Tower of
the Hundred *and* [e]the Tower of Hananel.
2 And next to him [a]the men of Jericho built, and next to [1]them Zaccur the
son of Imri built.

9 [a]Neh. 2:7 [b]Ezra 8:22

10 [1]Lit., *servant* [a]Neh. 2:19; 4:1

11 [a]Ezra 8:32

12 [1]Lit., *heart*

13 [1]Lit., *Gate of Ash-heaps* [a]Neh. 3:13 [b]Neh. 1:3 [c]Neh. 2:3, 17

14 [1]Lit., *the animal under me* [a]Neh. 3:15 [b]2 Kin. 20:20

15 [a]John 18:1

17 [a]Neh. 1:3

18 [a]2 Sam. 2:7

19 [1]Lit., *servant* [a]Neh. 6:6 [b]Neh. 4:1 [c]Neh. 6:6

20 [a]Ezra 4:3 [b]Neh. 2:4; Acts 8:21

1 [1]Lit., *it* [a]Neh. 3:20; 13:28 [b]Neh. 3:32; 12:39 [c]Neh. 6:1; 7:1 [d]Neh. 12:39 [e]Jer. 31:38

2 [1]Lit., *him* [a]Neh. 7:36

3 [a]Neh. 12:39

4 [1]Lit., *them*

5 [1]Lit., *them* [2]Lit., *bring their neck to*

6 [a]Neh. 12:39

7 [1]Or, *which was under the jurisdiction of the governor* of the province *beyond the River, also made repairs* [a]Neh. 2:7

8 [a]Neh. 3:31, 32 [b]Neh. 12:38

9 [a]Neh. 3:12, 17

11 [a]Neh. 12:38

12 [a]Neh. 3:9

13 [1]Lit., *Gate of Ash-heaps* [a]Neh. 2:13

14 [1]Lit., *Gate of Ash-heaps* [a]Jer. 6:1 [b]Neh. 2:13

15 [a]Neh. 2:17 [b]2 Kin. 25:4 [c]Neh. 12:37

16 [a]Neh. 3:9, 12, 17 [b]2 Kin. 20:20; Is. 7:3

3 Now the sons of Hassenaah built
[a]the Fish Gate; they laid its beams and
hung its doors with its bolts and bars.
4 And next to them Meremoth the
son of Uriah the son of Hakkoz made
repairs. And next to him Meshullam the
son of Berechiah the son of Meshezabel
made repairs. And next to [1]him Zadok
the son of Baana also made repairs.
5 Moreover, next to [1]him the Tekoites made repairs, but their nobles did
not [2]support the work of their masters.
6 And Joiada the son of Paseah and
Meshullam the son of Besodeiah repaired [a]the Old Gate; they laid its beams
and hung its doors, with its bolts and its
bars.
7 Next to them Melatiah the Gibeonite and Jadon the Meronothite, the men
of Gibeon and of Mizpah, [1]also made
repairs for the official seat of the [a]gover-
nor *of the province* beyond the River.
8 Next to him Uzziel the son of
Harhaiah of the [a]goldsmiths made repairs. And next to him Hananiah, one of
the perfumers, made repairs, and they
restored Jerusalem as far as [b]the Broad
Wall.
9 And next to them Rephaiah the
son of Hur, [a]the official of half the
district of Jerusalem, made repairs.
10 Next to them Jedaiah the son of
Harumaph made repairs opposite his
house. And next to him Hattush the son
of Hashabneiah made repairs.
11 Malchijah the son of Harim and
Hasshub the son of Pahath-moab repaired another section and [a]the Tower of
Furnaces.
12 And next to him Shallum the son
of Hallohesh, [a]the official of half the
district of Jerusalem, made repairs, he
and his daughters.
13 Hanun and the inhabitants of Zanoah repaired [a]the Valley Gate. They
built it and hung its doors with its bolts
and its bars, and a thousand cubits of
the wall to the [1]Refuse Gate.
14 And Malchijah the son of Rechab,
the official of the district of [a]Beth-
haccherem repaired the [1b]Refuse Gate.
He built it and hung its doors with its
bolts and its bars.
15 Shallum the son of Col-hozeh, the
official of the district of Mizpah, [a]re-
paired the Fountain Gate. He built it,
covered it, and hung its doors with its
bolts and its bars, and the wall of the
Pool of Shelah at [b]the king's garden as
far as [c]the steps that descend from the
city of David.
16 After him Nehemiah the son of
Azbuk, [a]official of half the district of
Beth-zur, made repairs as far as *a point*
opposite the tombs of David, and as far
as [b]the artificial pool and the house of
the mighty men.
17 After him the Levites carried out
repairs *under* Rehum the son of Bani.
Next to him Hashabiah, the official of
half the district of Keilah, carried out
repairs for his district.

18 After him their brothers carried out
repairs *under* Bavvai the son of Henadad, official of *the other* half of the
district of Keilah.
19 And next to him Ezer the son of
Jeshua, [a]the official of Mizpah, repaired
[1]another section, in front of the ascent of
the armory [b]at the Angle.
20 After him Baruch the son of Zabbai zealously repaired another section,
from the Angle to the doorway of the
house of [a]Eliashib the high priest.
21 After him Meremoth the son of
Uriah the son of Hakkoz repaired another section, from the doorway of
Eliashib's house even as far as the end of
[1]his house.
22 And after him the priests, [a]the men
of the [1]valley, carried out repairs.
23 After [1]them Benjamin and Hasshub carried out repairs in front of their
house. After [1]them Azariah the son of
Maaseiah, son of Ananiah carried out
repairs beside his house.
24 After him Binnui the son of Henadad repaired another section, from the
house of Azariah as far as [a]the Angle
and as far as the corner.
25 Palal the son of Uzai *made repairs*
in front of the Angle and the tower
projecting from the upper house of the
king, which is by [a]the court of the guard.
After him Pedaiah the son of Parosh
made repairs.
26 And [a]the temple servants living in
[b]Ophel *made repairs* as far as the front of
[c]the Water Gate toward the east and the
projecting tower.
27 After him [a]the Tekoites repaired
another section in front of the great
projecting tower and as far as the wall of
Ophel.
28 Above [a]the Horse Gate the priests
carried out repairs, each in front of his
house.
29 After [1]them Zadok the son of Immer carried out repairs in front of his
house. And after him Shemaiah the son
of Shecaniah, the keeper of the East
Gate, carried out repairs.
30 After him Hananiah the son of
Shelemiah, and Hanun the sixth son of
Zalaph, repaired another section. After
him Meshullam the son of Berechiah
carried out repairs in front of his own
[1]quarters.
31 After him Malchijah [1]one of [a]the
goldsmiths, carried out repairs as far as
the house of the temple servants and of
the merchants, in front of the [2]Inspec-
tion Gate and as far as the upper room
of the corner.
32 And between the upper room of
the corner and [a]the Sheep Gate the
goldsmiths and the merchants carried
out repairs.

Work Is Ridiculed

4 1 NOW it came about that when
[a]Sanballat heard that we were rebuilding the wall, he became furious and
very angry and mocked the Jews.
2 And he spoke in the presence of his
brothers and [a]the [1]wealthy *men* of Samaria and said, "What are these feeble
Jews doing? Are they going to restore *it*
for themselves? Can they offer sacrifices?
Can they finish in a day? Can they revive
the stones from the [2b]dusty rubble even
the burned ones?"
3 Now Tobiah the Ammonite *was*
near him and he said, "Even what they
are building—[a]if a fox should [1]jump on
it, he would break their stone wall
down!"
4 [a]Hear, O our God, how we are
despised! [b]Return their reproach on
their own heads and give them up for
plunder in a land of captivity.
5 Do not [1a]forgive their iniquity and
let not their sin be blotted out before
Thee, for they have [2]demoralized the
builders.
6 So we built the wall and the whole
wall was joined together to half its
height, for the people had a [1]mind to
work.
7 [1]Now it came about when Sanballat, Tobiah, the Arabs, the Ammonites,
and the Ashdodites heard that the [2]re-
pair of the walls of Jerusalem went on,
and that the breaches began to be closed,
they were very angry.
8 And all of them [a]conspired together to come *and* fight against Jerusalem and to cause a disturbance in it.

Discouragement Overcome

9 But we prayed to our God, and
because of them we [a]set up a guard
against them day and night.
10 Thus [1]in Judah it was said,
"The strength of the burden bearers is failing,
Yet there is much [2]rubbish;
And we ourselves are unable
To rebuild the wall."
11 And our enemies said, "They will
not know or see until we come among
them, kill them, and put a stop to the
work."
12 And it came about when the Jews
who lived near them came and told us
ten times, "[1]They will come up against
us from every place where you may
turn,"
13 then I stationed *men* in the lowest
parts of the space behind the wall, the
[1]exposed places, and I [a]stationed the
people in families with their swords,
spears, and bows.
14 When I saw *their fear,* I rose and
spoke to the nobles, the officials, and the
rest of the people: "[a]Do not be afraid of
them; remember the Lord who is great
and awesome, and [b]fight for your brothers, your sons, your daughters, your
wives, and your houses."
15 And it happened when our enemies
heard that it was known to us, and that
[a]God had frustrated their plan, then all
of us returned to the wall, each one to
his work.

19 [1]Lit., *a second measure,* and so in vv. 20, 21, 24, 30 [a]Neh. 3:15 [b]2 Chr. 26:9
20 [a]Neh. 3:1
21 [1]Lit., *Eliashib's*
22 [1]Lit., *circle;* i.e., lower Jordan valley [a]Neh. 12:28
23 [1]Lit., *him*
24 [a]Neh. 3:19
25 [a]Jer. 32:2
26 [a]Neh. 7:46 [b]Neh. 11:21 [c]Neh. 8:1
27 [a]Neh. 3:5
28 [a]2 Kin. 11:16; 2 Chr. 23:15; Jer. 31:40
29 [1]Lit., *him*
30 [1]Or, *cell*
31 [1]Lit., *son of* [2]Or, *Mustering* [a]Neh. 3:8, 32
32 [a]Neh. 3:1; 12:39

1 [1]Ch. 3:33 in Heb. [a]Neh. 2:10
2 [1]Or, *army* [2]Lit., *heaps of dust* [a]Ezra 4:9, 10 [b]Neh. 4:10
3 [1]Lit., *go up* [a]Lam. 5:18
4 [a]Ps. 123:3, 4 [b]Ps. 79:12
5 [1]Lit., *cover* [2]Lit., *offended against* [a]Ps. 69:27, 28; Jer. 18:23
6 [1]Lit., *heart*
7 [1]Ch. 4:1 in Heb. [2]Lit., *healing*
8 [a]Ps. 83:3
9 [a]Neh. 4:11
10 [1]Lit., *Judah said* [2]Lit., *dust*
12 [1]So Gr.; Heb. omits *they . . . up*
13 [1]Lit., *bare* [a]Neh. 4:17, 18
14 [a]Num. 14:9; Deut. 1:29, 30 [b]2 Sam. 10:12
15 [a]2 Sam. 17:14

16 And it came about from that day on, that half of my servants carried on the work while half of them held the spears, the shields, the bows, and the breastplates; and the captains *were* behind the whole house of Judah.

17 Those who were rebuilding the wall and those who carried burdens took *their* load with one hand doing the work and the other holding a weapon.

18 As for the builders, each *wore* his sword girded at his side as he built, while [1]the trumpeter *stood* near me.

19 And I said to the nobles, the officials, and the rest of the people, "The work is great and extensive, and we are separated on the wall far from one another.

20 "At whatever place you hear the sound of the trumpet, [1]rally to us there. [a]Our God will fight for us."

21 So we carried on the work with half of them holding spears from [1]dawn until the stars [2]appeared.

22 At that time I also said to the people, "Let each man with his servant spend the night within Jerusalem so that they may be a guard for us by night and a laborer by day."

23 So neither I, my brothers, my servants, nor the men of the guard who followed me, none of us removed our clothes, each *took* his weapon *even to* the water.

Usury Abolished

5 NOW [a]there was a great outcry of the people and of their wives against their [b]Jewish brothers.

2 For there were those who said, "We, our sons and our daughters, are many; therefore let us [a]get grain that we may eat and live."

3 And there were others who said, "We are mortgaging our fields, our vineyards, and our houses that we might get grain because of the famine."

4 Also there were those who said, "We have borrowed money [a]for the king's tax *on* our fields and our vineyards.

5 "And now [a]our flesh is like the flesh of our brothers, our children like their children. Yet behold, [b]we are forcing our sons and our daughters to be slaves, and some of our daughters are forced into bondage *already,* and [1]we are helpless because our fields and vineyards belong to others."

6 Then I was very [a]angry when I had heard their outcry and these words.

7 And I consulted with myself, and contended with the nobles and the rulers and said to them, "[a]You are exacting usury, each from his brother!" Therefore, I held a great assembly against them.

8 And I said to them, "We according to our ability [a]have [1]redeemed our Jewish brothers who were sold to the nations; now would you even sell your brothers that they may be sold to us?" Then they were silent and could not find a word *to say.*

9 Again I said, "The thing which you are doing is not good; should you not walk in the fear of our God because of [a]the reproach of the nations, our enemies?

10 "And likewise I, my brothers and my servants, are lending them money and grain. Please, let us leave off this usury.

11 "Please, give back to them this very day their fields, their vineyards, their olive groves, and their houses, also the hundredth *part* of the money and of the grain, the new wine, and the oil that you are exacting from them."

12 Then they said, "We [a]will give *it* back and [b]will require nothing from them; we will do exactly as you say." So I called the priests and [c]took an oath from them that they would do according to this [1]promise.

13 I [a]also shook out the [1]front of my garment and said, "Thus may God shake out every man from his house and from his possessions who does not fulfill this [2]promise; even thus may he be shaken out and emptied." And [b]all the assembly said, "Amen!" And they praised the LORD. Then the people did according to this [2]promise.

Nehemiah's Example

14 Moreover, from the day that I was appointed to be their governor in the land of Judah, from [a]the twentieth year to the [b]thirty-second year of King Artaxerxes, *for* twelve years, neither I nor my [1]kinsmen have eaten the governor's food *allowance.*

15 But the former governors who were before me [1]laid burdens on the people and took from them bread and wine besides forty shekels of silver; even their servants domineered the people. But I did not do so [a]because of the fear of God.

16 And I also [1]applied myself to the work on this wall; we did not buy any land, and all my servants were gathered there for the work.

17 Moreover, [a]*there were* at my table one hundred and fifty Jews and officials, besides those who came to us from the nations that were around us.

18 Now [a]that which was prepared for each day was one ox *and* six choice sheep, also birds were prepared for me; and once in ten days all sorts of wine *were furnished* in abundance. Yet for all this [b]I did not demand the governor's food *allowance,* because the servitude was heavy on this people.

19 [a]Remember me, O my God, for good, *according to* all that I have done for this people.

The Enemy's Plot

6 NOW it came about when it was reported to Sanballat, Tobiah, to Geshem the Arab, and to the rest of our enemies that I had rebuilt the wall, and

18 [1]Lit., *he who sounded the trumpet*
20 [1]Lit., *assemble yourselves* [a]Ex. 14:14; Deut. 1:30
21 [1]Lit., *rising of the dawn* [2]Lit., *came out*
1 [a]Lev. 25:35 [b]Deut. 15:7
2 [a]Hag. 1:6
4 [a]Ezra 4:13; 7:24
5 [1]Lit., *there is not the power in our hands* [a]Gen. 37:27 [b]Lev. 25:39
6 [a]Ex. 11:8
7 [a]Ex. 22:25; Lev. 25:36; Deut. 23:19, 20
8 [1]Lit., *bought* [a]Lev. 25:48
9 [a]Neh. 4:4
12 [1]Lit., *word* [a]2 Chr. 28:15 [b]Neh. 10:31 [c]Ezra 10:5
13 [1]Lit., *bosom* [2]Lit., *word* [a]Acts 18:6 [b]Neh. 8:6
14 [1]Lit., *brothers* [a]Neh. 1:1 [b]Neh. 13:6
15 [1]Lit., *made heavy* [a]Neh. 5:9; Job 31:23
16 [1]Or, *held fast*
17 [a]1 Kin. 18:19
18 [a]1 Kin. 4:22, 23 [b]2 Thess. 3:8
19 [a]Neh. 13:14, 22, 31

that no breach remained in it, [a]although
at that time I had not set up the doors in
the gates,
2 that Sanballat and Geshem sent *a*
message to me, saying, "Come, let us
meet together at [1]Chephirim in the plain
of [a]Ono." But they were planning to
[2]harm me.
3 So I sent messengers to them,
saying, "I am doing a great work and I
cannot come down. Why should the
work stop while I leave it and come
down to you?"
4 And they sent *messages* to me four
times in this manner, and I answered
them in the same way.
5 Then Sanballat sent his servant to
me in the same manner a fifth time with
an open letter in his hand.
6 In it was written, "It is reported
among the nations, and [1]Gashmu says,
that [a]you and the Jews are planning to
rebel; therefore you are rebuilding the
wall. And you are to be their king,
according to these reports.
7 "And you have also appointed
prophets to proclaim in Jerusalem concerning [1]you, 'A king is in Judah!' And
now it will be reported to the king
according to these reports. So come now,
let us take counsel together."
8 Then I sent *a message* to him saying, "Such things as you are saying have
not been done, but you are [a]inventing
them [1]in your own mind."
9 For all of them were *trying* to
frighten us, [1]thinking, "[2]They will become discouraged with the work and it
will not be done." But now, [a]*O God,*
strengthen my hands.
10 And when I entered the house of
Shemaiah the son of Delaiah, son of
Mehetabel, [a]who was [1]confined at home,
he said, "Let us meet together in the
house of God, within the temple, and let
us close the doors of the temple, for they
are coming to kill you, and they are
coming to kill you at night."
11 But I said, "[a]Should a man like me
flee? And could one such as I go into the
temple [1]to save his life? I will not go in."
12 Then I perceived [1]that surely God
had not sent him, but he uttered *his*
prophecy against me because Tobiah
and Sanballat had hired him.
13 He was hired for this reason, [a]that
I might become frightened and act accordingly and sin, so that they might
have an evil report in order that they
could reproach me.
14 [a]Remember, O my God, Tobiah
and Sanballat according to these works
of theirs, and also Noadiah [b]the prophetess and the rest of the prophets who
were *trying* to frighten me.

The Wall Is Finished

15 So [a]the wall was completed on the
twenty-fifth of *the month* Elul, in fifty-
two days.
16 And it came about [a]when all our
enemies heard *of it,* and all the nations
surrounding us saw *it,* they [1]lost their
confidence; for [b]they recognized that
this work had been accomplished [2]with
the help of our God.
17 Also in those days many letters
went from the nobles of Judah to Tobiah, and Tobiah's *letters* came to them.
18 For many in Judah were bound by
oath to him because he was the son-in-
law of Shecaniah the son of Arah, and
his son Jehohanan had married the
daughter of Meshullam the son of Berechiah.
19 Moreover, they were speaking
about his good deeds in my presence and
reported my words to him. Then Tobiah
sent letters to frighten me.

Census of First Returned Exiles

7 NOW it came about when [a]the wall
was rebuilt and I had set up the
doors, and the gatekeepers and the
singers and the Levites were appointed,
2 that I put [a]Hanani my brother, and
[b]Hananiah the commander of [c]the fortress, in charge of Jerusalem, for he was
[d]a faithful man and feared God more
than many.
3 Then I said to them, "Do not let
the gates of Jerusalem be opened until
the sun is hot, and while they are standing *guard,* let them shut and bolt the
doors. Also appoint guards from the
inhabitants of Jerusalem, each at his
post, and each in front of his own
house."
4 Now the city was large and spacious, but the people in it were few and
the houses were not built.
5 [a]Then my God put it into my heart
to assemble the nobles, the officials, and
the people to be enrolled by genealogies.
Then I found the book of the genealogy
of those who came up first [1]in which I
found the following record:
6 [a]These are the [1]people of the province who came up from the captivity of
the exiles whom Nebuchadnezzar the
king of Babylon had carried away, and
who returned to Jerusalem and Judah,
each to his city,
7 who came with Zerubbabel,
Jeshua, Nehemiah, [1]Azariah, [2]Raamiah,
Nahamani, Mordecai, Bilshan, [3]Mispe-
reth, Bigvai, [4]Nehum, Baanah.
The number of men of the people of
Israel:
8 the sons of Parosh, 2,172;
9 the sons of Shephatiah, 372;
10 the sons of Arah, 652;
11 the sons of Pahath-moab of the
sons of Jeshua and Joab, 2,818;
12 the sons of Elam, 1,254;
13 the sons of Zattu, 845;
14 the sons of Zaccai, 760;
15 the sons of [1]Binnui, 648;
16 the sons of Bebai, 628;
17 the sons of Azgad, 2,322;
18 the sons of Adonikam, 667;
19 the sons of Bigvai, 2,067;
20 the sons of Adin, 655;
21 the sons of Ater, of Hezekiah, 98;
22 the sons of Hashum, 328;
23 the sons of Bezai, 324;

1 [a]Neh. 3:1, 3
2 [1]Another reading is, one of *the villages* [2]Lit., *do evil to me* [a]1 Chr. 8:12
6 [1]In v. 1 and elsewhere, *Geshem* [a]Neh. 2:19
7 [1]Lit., *you, saying*
8 [1]Lit., *from your heart* [a]Job 13:4; Ps. 52:2
9 [1]Lit., *saying,* [2]Lit., *Their hands will drop from* [a]Ps. 138:3
10 [1]Lit., *shut up* [a]Jer. 36:5
11 [1]Lit., *and live* [a]Prov. 28:1
12 [1]Lit., *and behold God*
13 [a]Neh. 6:6
14 [a]Neh. 13:29 [b]Ezek. 13:17
15 [a]Neh. 4:1, 2
16 [1]Lit., *fell exceedingly in their own eyes* [2]Lit., *from our God* [a]Neh. 2:10; 4:1, 7 [b]Ex. 14:25
1 [a]Neh. 6:1, 15
2 [a]Neh. 1:2 [b]Neh. 10:23 [c]Neh. 2:8 [d]Neh. 13:13
5 [1]Lit., *and I found written in it* [a]Prov. 2:6; 3:6
6 [1]Lit., *sons* [a]Ezra 2:1-70
7 [1]In Ezra 2:2, *Seraiah* [2]In Ezra 2:2, *Reelaiah* [3]In Ezra 2:2, *Mispar* [4]In Ezra 2:2, *Rehum*
15 [1]In Ezra 2:10, *Bani*

24 the sons of [1]Hariph, 112;
25 the sons of [1]Gibeon, 95;
26 the men of Bethlehem and Netophah, 188;
27 the men of Anathoth, 128;
28 the men of [1]Beth-azmaveth, 42;
29 the men of [1]Kiriath-jearim, Chephirah, and Beeroth, 743;
30 the men of Ramah and Geba, 621;
31 the men of Michmas, 122;
32 the men of Bethel and Ai, 123;
33 the men of the other Nebo, 52;
34 the sons of the other Elam, 1,254;
35 the sons of Harim, 320;
36 the [1]men of Jericho, 345;
37 the sons of Lod, Hadid, and Ono,
721;
38 the sons of Senaah, 3,930.
39 The priests: the sons of Jedaiah of
the house of Jeshua, 973;
40 the sons of Immer, 1,052;
41 the sons of Pashhur, 1,247;
42 the sons of Harim, 1,017.
43 The Levites: the sons of Jeshua, of
Kadmiel, of the sons of [1]Hodevah, 74.
44 The singers: the sons of Asaph,
148.
45 The gatekeepers: the sons of Shallum, the sons of Ater, the sons of Talmon, the sons of Akkub, the sons of
Hatita, the sons of Shobai, 138.
46 The temple servants: the sons of
Ziha, the sons of Hasupha, the sons of
Tabbaoth,
47 the sons of Keros, the sons of [1]Sia,
the sons of Padon,
48 the sons of Lebana, the sons of
Hagaba, the sons of Shalmai,
49 the sons of Hanan, the sons of
Giddel, the sons of Gahar,
50 the sons of Reaiah, the sons of
Rezin, the sons of Nekoda,
51 the sons of Gazzam, the sons of
Uzza, the sons of Paseah,
52 the sons of Besai, the sons of Meunim, the sons of [1]Nephushesim,
53 the sons of Bakbuk, the sons of
Hakupha, the sons of Harhur,
54 the sons of [1]Bazlith, the sons of
Mehida, the sons of Harsha,
55 the sons of Barkos, the sons of
Sisera, the sons of Temah,
56 the sons of Neziah, the sons of
Hatipha.
57 The sons of Solomon's servants:
the sons of Sotai, the sons of [1]Sophereth,
the sons of [2]Perida,
58 the sons of Jaala, the sons of Darkon, the sons of Giddel,
59 the sons of Shephatiah, the sons of
Hattil, the sons of Pochereth-hazzebaim,
the sons of [1]Amon.
60 All the temple servants and the
sons of Solomon's servants *were* 392.
61 And these *were* they who came up
from Tel-melah, Tel-harsha, Cherub,
[1]Addon, and Immer; but they could not
show their fathers' houses or their [2]de-
scendants, whether they were of Israel:
62 the sons of Delaiah, the sons of
Tobiah, the sons of Nekoda, 642.
63 And of the priests: the sons of
[1]Hobaiah, the sons of Hakkoz, the sons
of Barzillai, who took a wife of the
daughters of Barzillai, the Gileadite, and
was named after them.
64 These searched *among* their ancestral registration, but it could not be
located; therefore they were considered
unclean *and excluded* from the priesthood.
65 And [a]the [1]governor said to them
that they should not eat from the most
holy things until a priest arose with
[b]Urim and Thummim.

Total of People and Gifts

66 The whole assembly together *was*
42,360,
67 besides their male and their female
servants, [1]of whom *there were* 7,337; and
they had 245 male and female singers.
68 [1a]Their horses were 736; their
mules, 245;
69 *their* camels, 435; *their* donkeys,
6,720.
70 And some from among the heads
of fathers' *households* gave to the work.
The [1a]governor gave to the treasury
1,000 gold drachmas, 50 basins, 530
priests' garments.
71 And some of the heads of fathers'
households gave into the treasury of the
work 20,000 gold drachmas, and 2,200
silver minas.
72 And that which the rest of the
people gave was 20,000 gold drachmas
and 2,000 silver minas, and 67 priests'
garments.
73 Now [a]the priests, the Levites, the
gatekeepers, the singers, some of the
people, the temple servants, and all
Israel, lived in their cities.
[b]And when the seventh month came,
the sons of Israel *were* in their cities.

Ezra Reads the Law

8 AND all the people gathered as one
man at the square which was in
front of [a]the Water Gate, and they
[1]asked [b]Ezra the scribe to bring [c]the
book of the law of Moses which the
LORD had [2]given to Israel.
2 Then [a]Ezra the priest brought the
law before the assembly of men, women,
and all who *could* listen with understanding, on [b]the first day of the seventh
month.
3 And he read from it before the
square which was in front of [a]the Water
Gate from [1]early morning until midday,
in the presence of men and women,
those who could understand; and all the
people were attentive to the book of the
law.
4 And Ezra the scribe stood at a
wooden podium which they had made
for the purpose. And beside him stood
Mattithiah, Shema, Anaiah, Uriah, Hilkiah, and Maaseiah on his right hand;
and Pedaiah, Mishael, Malchijah, Hashum, Hashbaddanah, Zechariah, *and*
Meshullam on his left hand.

24 [1]In Ezra 2:18, *Jorah*
25 [1]In Ezra 2:20, *Gibbar*
28 [1]In Ezra 2:24, *Azmaveth*
29 [1]In Ezra 2:25, *Kiriath-arim*
36 [1]Lit., *sons*
43 [1]In Ezra 2:40, *Hodaviah*
47 [1]In Ezra 2:44, *Siaha*
52 [1]In Ezra 2:50, *Nephisim*
54 [1]In Ezra 2:52, *Bazluth*
57 [1]In Ezra 2:55, *Hassophereth* [2]In Ezra 2:55, *Peruda*
59 [1]In Ezra 2:57, *Ami*
61 [1]In Ezra 2:59, *Addan* [2]Lit., *seed*
63 [1]In Ezra 2:61, *Habaiah*
65 [1]Heb., *Tirshatha,* a Persian title [a]Neh. 8:9; 10:1 [b]Ex. 28:30; Deut. 33:8
67 [1]Lit., *these*
68 [1]So with some ancient mss. and Gr. [a]Ezra 2:66
70 [1]Heb., *Tirshatha,* a Persian title [a]Neh. 7:65; 8:9
73 [a]1 Chr. 9:2 [b]Ezra 3:1
1 [1]Lit., *said to* [2]Lit., *commanded* [a]Neh. 3:26 [b]Ezra 7:6 [c]2 Chr. 34:15
2 [a]Deut. 31:9-11; Neh. 8:9 [b]Lev. 23:24
3 [1]Lit., *the light* [a]Neh. 8:1

5 And Ezra opened [a]the book in the
sight of all the people for he was standing above all the people; and when he
opened it, all the people [b]stood up.
6 Then Ezra blessed the LORD the
great God. And all the people answered,
"[a]Amen, Amen!" while lifting up their
hands; then [b]they bowed low and worshiped the LORD with *their* faces to the
ground.
7 Also Jeshua, Bani, Sherebiah, Jamin, Akkub, Shabbethai, Hodiah, Maaseiah, Kelita, Azariah, Jozabad, Hanan,
Pelaiah, and the Levites, explained the
law to the people while the people
remained in their place.
8 And they read from the book, from
the law of God, [1]translating to give the
sense so that they understood the reading.

"This Day Is Holy"

9 Then Nehemiah, who was the
[1][a]governor, and Ezra [b]the priest *and*
scribe, and the Levites who taught the
people said to all the people, "[c]This day
is holy to the LORD your God; [d]do not
mourn or weep." For all the people were
weeping when they heard the words of
the law.
10 Then he said to them, "Go, eat of
the fat, drink of the sweet, and [a]send
portions to him who has nothing prepared; for this day is holy to our Lord.
Do not be grieved, for the joy of the
LORD is your strength."
11 So the Levites calmed all the people, saying, "Be still, for the day is holy;
do not be grieved."
12 And all the people went away to
eat, to drink, [a]to send portions and to
[1]celebrate a great festival, [b]because they
understood the words which had been
made known to them.

Feast of Booths Restored

13 Then on the second day the heads
of fathers' *households* of all the people,
the priests, and the Levites were gathered to Ezra the scribe that they might
gain insight into the words of the law.
14 And they found written in the law
how the LORD had commanded through
Moses that the sons of Israel [a]should live
in booths during the feast of the seventh
month.
15 [1][a]So they proclaimed and circulated a proclamation in all their cities
and [b]in Jerusalem, saying, "[c]Go out to
the hills, and bring olive branches, and
[2]wild olive branches, myrtle branches,
palm branches, and branches of *other*
leafy trees, to make booths, as it is
written."
16 So the people went out and
brought *them* and made booths for
themselves, each [a]on his roof, and in
their courts, and in the courts of the
house of God, and in the square at
[b]the Water Gate, and in the square at
[c]the Gate of Ephraim.
17 And the entire assembly of those
who had returned from the captivity

5 [a]Neh. 8:3 [b]Judg. 3:20; 1 Kin. 8:12-14

6 [a]Neh. 5:13 [b]Ex. 4:31

8 [1]Or, *explaining*

9 [1]Heb., *Tirshatha,* a Persian title [a]Neh. 7:65, 70 [b]Neh. 12:26 [c]Neh. 8:2 [d]Deut. 12:7, 12

10 [a]Deut. 26:11-13

12 [1]Lit., *make a great rejoicing* [a]Neh. 8:10 [b]Neh. 8:7, 8

14 [a]Lev. 23:34, 40, 42

15 [1]Lit., *And that they will cause to be heard* [2]Lit., *oil tree,* species unknown [a]Lev. 23:4 [b]Deut. 16:16 [c]Lev. 23:40

16 [a]Jer. 32:29 [b]Neh. 8:1 [c]2 Kin. 14:13; Neh. 12:39

17 [1]Lit., *the booths* [a]2 Chr. 7:8; 8:13 [b]2 Chr. 30:21

18 [a]Deut. 31:11 [b]Lev. 23:36 [c]Num. 29:35

1 [a]Neh. 8:2 [b]Ezra 8:23 [c]1 Sam. 4:12

2 [1]Lit., *seed* [a]Ezra 10:11; Neh. 13:3 [b]Prov. 28:13; Jer. 3:13

3 [a]Neh. 8:4

4 [a]Neh. 8:7

6 [a]Deut. 6:4; 2 Kin. 19:15 [b]Gen. 1:1 [c]Col. 1:16f.

7 [a]Gen. 12:1 [b]Gen. 11:31 [c]Gen. 17:5

8 [1]Lit., *seed* [a]Gen. 15:6, 18-21 [b]Josh. 21:43-45

9 [1]Lit., *Sea of Reeds* [a]Ex. 3:7 [b]Ex. 14:10-14, 31

made booths and lived in [1]them. The
sons of Israel [a]had indeed not done so
from the days of Joshua the son of Nun
to that day. And [b]there was great rejoicing.
18 And [a]he read from the book of the
law of God daily, from the first day to
the last day. And they [b]celebrated the
feast seven days, and on [c]the eighth day
there was a solemn assembly according
to the ordinance.

The People Confess Their Sin

9 NOW on the twenty-fourth day of
[a]this month the sons of Israel assembled [b]with fasting, in sackcloth, and with
[c]dirt upon them.
2 And the [1][a]descendants of Israel
separated themselves from all foreigners,
and stood and [b]confessed their sins and
the iniquities of their fathers.
3 While [a]they stood in their place,
they read from the book of the law of the
LORD their God for a fourth of the day;
and for *another* fourth they confessed
and worshiped the LORD their God.
4 [a]Now on the Levites' platform
stood Jeshua, Bani, Kadmiel, Shebaniah,
Bunni, Sherebiah, Bani, *and* Chenani,
and they cried with a loud voice to the
LORD their God.
5 Then the Levites, Jeshua, Kadmiel,
Bani, Hashabneiah, Sherebiah, Hodiah,
Shebaniah, *and* Pethahiah, said, "Arise,
bless the LORD your God forever and
ever!

O may Thy glorious name be blessed
And exalted above all blessing and praise!
6 "[a]Thou alone art the LORD.
[b]Thou hast made the heavens,
The heaven of heavens with all their host,
The earth and all that is on it,
The seas and all that is in them.
[c]Thou dost give life to all of them
And the heavenly host bows down before Thee.
7 "Thou art the LORD God,
[a]Who chose Abram
And brought him out from [b]Ur of the Chaldees,
And [c]gave him the name Abraham.
8 "And Thou didst find [a]his heart faithful before Thee,
And didst make a covenant with him
To give *him* the land of the Canaanite,
Of the Hittite and the Amorite,
Of the Perizzite, the Jebusite, and the Girgashite—
To give *it* to his [1]descendants.
And Thou [b]hast fulfilled Thy promise,
For Thou art righteous.

9 "[a]Thou didst see the affliction of our fathers in Egypt,
And didst [b]hear their cry by the [1]Red Sea.

10"Then Thou didst perform [a]signs
and wonders against Pharaoh,
Against all his servants and all the
people of his land;
For Thou didst know that [b]they
acted arrogantly toward them,
And [c]didst make a name for Thyself as *it is* this day.
11"And [a]Thou didst divide the sea
before them,
So they passed through the midst
of the sea on dry ground;
And [b]their pursuers Thou didst
hurl into the depths,
Like a stone into [1]raging waters.
12"And with a pillar of cloud [a]Thou
didst lead them by day,
And with a pillar of fire by night
To light for them the way
In which they were to go.
13"Then [a]Thou didst come down on
Mount Sinai,
And didst [b]speak with them from
heaven;
Thou didst give to them [c]just ordinances and true laws,
Good statutes and commandments.
14"So Thou didst make known to
them [a]Thy holy sabbath,
And didst lay down for them commandments, statutes, and law,
Through Thy servant Moses.
15"Thou didst [a]provide bread from
heaven for them for their hunger,
Thou didst [b]bring forth water from
a rock for them for their thirst,
And Thou didst [c]tell them to enter
in order to possess
The land which Thou didst [1]swear
to give them.

16"But they, our fathers, [a]acted arrogantly;
They [1b]became stubborn and
would not listen to Thy commandments.
17"And they refused to listen,
And [a]did not remember Thy wondrous deeds which Thou hadst
performed among them;
So they became stubborn and [b]ap-
pointed a leader to return to
their slavery [1]in Egypt.
But Thou art a God [c]of forgiveness,
Gracious and compassionate,
Slow to anger, and abounding in
lovingkindness;
And Thou didst not forsake them.
18"Even when they [a]made for themselves
A calf of molten metal
And said, 'This is your God
Who brought you up from Egypt,'
And committed great [1]blasphe-
mies,
19 [a]Thou, in Thy great compassion,
Didst not forsake them in the wilderness;
[b]The pillar of cloud did not leave
them by day,
To guide them on their way,
Nor the pillar of fire by night, to
light for them the way in which
they were to go.
20"And [a]Thou didst give Thy good
Spirit to instruct them,
Thy manna Thou didst not withhold from their mouth,
And Thou didst give them water
for their thirst.
21"Indeed, [a]forty years Thou didst
provide for them in the wilderness *and* they were not in want;
Their clothes did not wear out, nor
did their feet swell.
22"Thou didst also give them kingdoms and peoples,
And Thou didst allot *them* to them
as a [1]boundary.
[a]And they took possession of the
land of Sihon [2]the king of Heshbon,
And the land of Og the king of
Bashan.
23"And Thou didst make their sons
numerous as [a]the stars of
heaven,
And Thou didst bring them into
the land
Which Thou hadst told their fathers to enter and possess.
24"[a]So their sons entered and possessed the land.
And [b]Thou didst subdue before
them the inhabitants of the land,
the Canaanites,
And Thou didst give them into
their hand, with their kings, and
the peoples of the land,
To do with them [1]as they desired.
25"And [a]they captured fortified cities
and a [1b]fertile land.
They took possession of [c]houses
full of every good thing,
Hewn cisterns, vineyards, olive
groves,
Fruit trees in abundance.
So they ate, were filled, and [d]grew
fat,
And [e]reveled in Thy great goodness.

26"[a]But they became disobedient and
rebelled against Thee,
And [b]cast Thy law behind their
backs
And [c]killed Thy prophets who had
[d]admonished them
So that they might return to Thee,
And [e]they committed great [1]blas-
phemies.
27"Therefore Thou didst [a]deliver them
into the hand of their oppressors
who oppressed them,
But when they cried to Thee [b]in the
time of their distress,
Thou didst hear from heaven, and
according to Thy great compassion
Thou didst [c]give them deliverers
who delivered them from the
hand of their oppressors.

10 [a]Ex. 7:8-12:32 [b]Ex. 5:2 [c]Ex. 9:16

11 [1]Lit., *strong, mighty* [a]Ex. 14:21 [b]Ex. 15:1, 5, 10

12 [a]Ex. 13:21, 22

13 [a]Ex. 19:11, 18-20 [b]Ex. 20:1 [c]Ps. 19:7-9

14 [a]Ex. 16:23; 20:8

15 [1]Lit., *lift up Thy hand* [a]Ex. 16:4, 14, 15 [b]Ex. 17:6; Num. 20:7-13 [c]Deut. 1:8, 21

16 [1]Lit., *stiffened their neck;* so also v. 17 [a]Neh. 9:10 [b]Deut. 1:26-33; 31:27; Neh. 9:29

17 [1]So Gr. and some Heb. mss.; Heb. reads *in their rebellion* [a]Ps. 78:11, 42-55 [b]Num. 14:4 [c]Ex. 34:6, 7; Num. 14:18

18 [1]Lit., *acts of contempt* [a]Ex. 32:4-8, 31

19 [a]Deut. 8:2-4; Neh. 9:27, 31 [b]Neh. 9:12

20 [a]Num. 11:17; Neh. 9:30; Is. 63:11-14

21 [a]Deut. 2:7

22 [1]Lit., *side, corner* [2]So the Gr. and the Latin; Heb. reads *and the land of the king of Heshbon* [a]Num. 21:21-35

23 [a]Gen. 15:5; 22:17

24 [1]Lit., *according to their desire* [a]Josh. 11:23; 21:43 [b]Josh. 18:1

25 [1]Lit., *fat* [a]Deut. 3:5 [b]Num. 13:27 [c]Deut. 6:11 [d]Deut. 32:15 [e]1 Kin. 8:66

26 [1]Lit., *acts of contempt* [a]Judg. 2:11 [b]1 Kin. 14:9 [c]2 Chr. 36:16 [d]Neh. 9:30 [e]Neh. 9:18

27 [a]Judg. 2:14 [b]Deut. 4:29 [c]Judg. 2:16

28 "But [a]as soon as they had rest, they
did evil again before Thee;
Therefore Thou didst abandon
them to the hand of their enemies,
so that they ruled over
them.
When they cried again to Thee,
Thou didst hear from heaven,
And [b]many times Thou didst rescue
them according to Thy compassion,
29 And [a]admonished them in order to
turn them back to Thy law.
Yet [b]they acted arrogantly and did
not listen to Thy commandments
but sinned against Thine
ordinances,
By [c]which if a man observes them
he shall live.
And they [1d]turned a stubborn
shoulder and stiffened their
neck, and would not listen.
30 "[a]However, Thou didst bear with
them for many years,
And [b]admonished them by [c]Thy
Spirit through Thy prophets,
Yet they would not give ear.
Therefore Thou didst give them
into the hand of the peoples of
the lands.
31 "Nevertheless, in Thy great compassion
Thou [a]didst not make an
end of them or forsake them,
For Thou art [b]a gracious and compassionate
God.

32 "Now therefore, our God, [a]the great,
the mighty, and the awesome
God, who dost keep covenant
and lovingkindness,
Do not let all the hardship seem
insignificant before Thee,
Which has come upon us, our
kings, our princes, our priests,
our prophets, our fathers, and
on all Thy people,
[b]From the days of the kings of
Assyria to this day.
33 "However, [a]Thou art just in all that
has come upon us;
For Thou hast dealt faithfully, but
we have acted wickedly.
34 "For our kings, our leaders, our
priests, and our fathers have not
kept Thy law
Or paid attention to Thy commandments
and Thine [1]admonitions
with which Thou hast [2]admonished
them.
35 "But [a]they, in their own kingdom,
[b]With Thy great goodness which
Thou didst give them,
With the broad and rich land which
Thou didst set before them,
Did not serve Thee or turn from
their evil deeds.
36 "Behold, [a]we are slaves today,
And as to the land which Thou
didst give to our fathers to eat of
its fruit and its bounty,
Behold, we are slaves on it.
37 "And [a]its abundant produce is for
the kings

28 [a]Judg. 3:11 [b]Ps. 106:43
29 [1]Lit., *gave* [a]Neh. 9:26, 30 [b]Neh. 9:10, 16 [c]Lev. 18:5 [d]Zech. 7:11
30 [a]Ps. 95:10; Acts 13:18 [b]2 Kin. 17:13-18; 2 Chr. 36:15, 16; Neh. 9:26, 29 [c]Neh. 9:20
31 [a]Jer. 4:27 [b]Neh. 9:17
32 [a]Neh. 1:5 [b]2 Kin. 15:19, 29; 2 Kin. 17:3-6; Ezra 4:2, 10
33 [a]Gen. 18:25; Jer. 12:1
34 [1]Lit., *testimonies* [2]Or, *witnessed*
35 [a]Deut. 28:47 [b]Neh. 9:25
36 [a]Deut. 28:48
37 [a]Deut. 28:33
38 [1]Ch. 10:1 in Heb. [a]Neh. 10:29 [b]Neh. 10:1
1 [1]Ch. 10:2 in Heb. [2]Heb., *Tirshatha*, a Persian title [a]Neh. 9:38
28 [a]Ezra 2:36-58 [b]Neh. 9:2
29 [1]Lit., *brothers* [2]Lit., *entering into a* [3]Heb., *YHWH*, usually rendered *LORD* [a]Neh. 5:12
30 [a]Ex. 34:16; Deut. 7:3

Whom Thou hast set over us because
of our sins;
They also rule over our bodies
And over our cattle as they please,
So we are in great distress.

A Covenant Results

38 "[1]Now because of all this
[a]We are making an agreement in
writing;
And on the [b]sealed document *are
the names of* our leaders, our
Levites *and* our priests."

Signers of the Document

10 [1]NOW on the [a]sealed document
were the names of: Nehemiah the
[2]governor, the son of Hacaliah, and
Zedekiah,
2 Seraiah, Azariah, Jeremiah,
3 Pashhur, Amariah, Malchijah,
4 Hattush, Shebaniah, Malluch,
5 Harim, Meremoth, Obadiah,
6 Daniel, Ginnethon, Baruch,
7 Meshullam, Abijah, Mijamin,
8 Maaziah, Bilgai, Shemaiah. These
were the priests.
9 And the Levites: Jeshua the son of
Azaniah, Binnui of the sons of Henadad,
Kadmiel;
10 also their brothers Shebaniah, Hodiah,
Kelita, Pelaiah, Hanan,
11 Mica, Rehob, Hashabiah,
12 Zaccur, Sherebiah, Shebaniah,
13 Hodiah, Bani, Beninu.
14 The leaders of the people: Parosh,
Pahath-moab, Elam, Zattu, Bani,
15 Bunni, Azgad, Bebai,
16 Adonijah, Bigvai, Adin,
17 Ater, Hezekiah, Azzur,
18 Hodiah, Hashum, Bezai,
19 Hariph, Anathoth, Nebai,
20 Magpiash, Meshullam, Hezir,
21 Meshezabel, Zadok, Jaddua,
22 Pelatiah, Hanan, Anaiah,
23 Hoshea, Hananiah, Hasshub,
24 Hallohesh, Pilha, Shobek,
25 Rehum, Hashabnah, Maaseiah,
26 Ahiah, Hanan, Anan,
27 Malluch, Harim, Baanah.

Obligations of the Document

28 Now [a]the rest of the people, the
priests, the Levites, the gatekeepers, the
singers, the temple servants, and [b]all
those who had separated themselves
from the peoples of the lands to the law
of God, their wives, their sons and their
daughters, all those who had knowledge
and understanding,
29 are joining with their [1]kinsmen,
their nobles, and are [2a]taking on themselves
a curse and an oath to walk in
God's law, which was given through
Moses, God's servant, and to keep and
to observe all the commandments of
[3]GOD our Lord, and His ordinances and
His statutes;
30 and [a]that we will not give our
daughters to the peoples of the land or
take their daughters for our sons.

31 As [a]for the peoples of the land who
bring wares or any grain on the sabbath
day to sell, we will not buy from them on
the sabbath or a holy day; and we will
forego *the crops* the [b]seventh year and
the [c]exaction of every debt.
32 We also [1]placed ourselves under
obligation to contribute yearly [a]one
third of a shekel for the service of the
house of our God:
33 for the [a]showbread, for the continual grain offering, for the continual
burnt offering, the sabbaths, the new
moon, for the appointed times, for the
holy things and for the sin offerings to
make atonement for Israel, and all the
work of the house of our God.
34 Likewise [a]we cast lots [b]for the
supply of wood *among* the priests, the
Levites, and the people in order that
they might bring it to the house of our
God, according to our fathers' households, at fixed times annually, to burn
on the altar of the LORD our God as it is
written in the law;
35 and in order that they might bring
the first fruits of our ground and [a]the
first fruits of all the fruit of every tree to
the house of the LORD annually,
36 and [a]bring to the house of our God
the first-born of our sons and of our
cattle, and the first-born of our herds
and our flocks as it is written in the law,
for the priests who are ministering in the
house of our God.
37 [a]We will also bring the first of our
[1]dough, our contributions, the fruit of
every tree, the new wine and the oil [b]to
the priests at the chambers of the house
of our God, and the [c]tithe of our ground
to the Levites, for the Levites are they
who receive the tithes in all the rural
towns.
38 And [a]the priest, the son of Aaron,
shall be with the Levites when the Levites receive tithes, and the Levites shall
bring up the tenth of the tithes to the
house of our God, to the chambers of
[b]the storehouse.
39 For the sons of Israel and the sons
of Levi shall bring the [a]contribution of
the grain, the new wine and the oil, to
the chambers; there are the utensils
of the sanctuary, the priests who are
ministering, the gatekeepers, and the
singers. Thus [b]we will not [1]neglect the
house of our God.

Time Passes
Heads of Provinces

11 NOW [a]the leaders of the people
lived in Jerusalem, but the rest of
the people [b]cast lots to bring one out of
ten to live in Jerusalem, [c]the holy city,
while nine-tenths *remained* in the *other*
cities.
2 And the people blessed all the men
who [a]volunteered to live in Jerusalem.
3 [a]Now these are the heads of the
provinces who lived in Jerusalem, but in
the cities of Judah [b]each lived on his
own property in their cities—the [1]Israel-

31 [a]Neh. 13:15-22 [b]Ex. 23:10, 11; Lev. 25:1-7 [c]Deut. 15:1, 2
32 [1]Lit., *imposed commandments on us* [a]Ex. 30:11-16; Matt. 17:24
33 [a]Lev. 24:5, 6; 2 Chr. 2:4
34 [a]Neh. 11:1 [b]Neh. 13:31
35 [a]Ex. 23:19; 34:26; Deut. 26:2
36 [a]Ex. 13:2
37 [1]Or, *coarse meal* [a]Lev. 23:17 [b]Neh. 13:5, 9 [c]Lev. 27:30; Num. 18:21
38 [a]Num. 18:26 [b]Neh. 13:12, 13
39 [1]Lit., *forsake* [a]Deut. 12:6 [b]Neh. 13:10, 11
1 [a]Neh. 7:4 [b]Neh. 10:34 [c]Neh. 11:18; Is. 48:2
2 [a]Judg. 5:9
3 [1]Lit., *Israel* [2]Heb., *Nethinim* [3]Lit., *sons* [a]1 Chr. 9:2-34 [b]Neh. 7:73; 11:20 [c]Ezra 2:43 [d]Neh. 7:57
9 [1]Lit., *over*
12 [1]Lit., *brothers,* and so throughout the ch. [2]Lit., *house*
14 [1]Or, *the great ones*
16 [1]Lit., *heads* [2]Lit., *over* [a]1 Chr. 26:29
17 [1]In 1 Chr. 9:15, *Zichri* [2]Lit., *head* [3]In 1 Chr. 9:16, *Obadiah* [4]In 1 Chr. 9:16, *Shemaiah*
18 [a]Neh. 11:1
20 [a]Neh. 11:3

ites, the priests, the Levites, the [2][c]temple
servants and the [3][d]descendants of Solomon's servants.
4 And some of the sons of Judah and
some of the sons of Benjamin lived in
Jerusalem. From the sons of Judah:
Athaiah the son of Uzziah, the son of
Zechariah, the son of Amariah, the son
of Shephatiah, the son of Mahalalel, of
the sons of Perez;
5 and Maaseiah the son of Baruch,
the son of Col-hozeh, the son of Haza-
iah, the son of Adaiah, the son of Joiarib, the son of Zechariah, the son of the
Shilonite.
6 All the sons of Perez who lived in
Jerusalem were 468 able men.
7 Now these are the sons of Benjamin: Sallu the son of Meshullam, the son
of Joed, the son of Pedaiah, the son of
Kolaiah, the son of Maaseiah, the
son of Ithiel, the son of Jeshaiah;
8 and after him Gabbai *and* Sallai,
928.
9 And Joel the son of Zichri was
their overseer, and Judah the son of
Hassenuah was second [1]in command of
the city.
10 From the priests: Jedaiah the son
of Joiarib, Jachin,
11 Seraiah the son of Hilkiah, the son
of Meshullam, the son of Zadok, the son
of Meraioth, the son of Ahitub, the
leader of the house of God,
12 and their [1]kinsmen who performed
the work of the [2]temple, 822; and Adaiah the son of Jeroham, the son of
Pelaliah, the son of Amzi, the son of
Zechariah, the son of Pashhur, the
son of Malchijah,
13 and his kinsmen, heads of fathers'
households, 242; and Amashsai the son
of Azarel, the son of Ahzai, the son of
Meshillemoth, the son of Immer,
14 and their brothers, valiant warriors,
128. And their overseer was Zabdiel, the
son of [1]Haggedolim.
15 Now from the Levites: Shemaiah
the son of Hasshub, the son of Azrikam,
the son of Hashabiah, the son of Bunni;
16 and Shabbethai and Jozabad, from
the [1]leaders of the Levites, who were [2]in
charge of [a]the outside work of the house
of God;
17 and Mattaniah the son of Mica, the
son of [1]Zabdi, the son of Asaph, who
was the [2]leader in beginning the thanksgiving at prayer, and Bakbukiah, the
second among his brethren; and [3]Abda
the son of [4]Shammua, the son of Galal,
the son of Jeduthun.
18 All the Levites in [a]the holy city
were 284.
19 Also the gatekeepers, Akkub, Talmon, and their brethren, who kept watch
at the gates, *were* 172.

Outside Jerusalem

20 And the rest of Israel, of the
priests, *and* of the Levites, *were* in all the
cities of Judah, each [a]on his own inheritance.

21 But [a]the temple servants were living in Ophel, and Ziha and Gishpa were
[1]in charge of the temple servants.
22 Now [a]the overseer of the Levites in
Jerusalem was Uzzi the son of Bani, the
son of Hashabiah, the son of Mattaniah,
the son of Mica, from the sons of Asaph,
who were the singers for the [1]service of
the house of God.
23 [a]For *there was* a commandment
from the king concerning them and a
firm regulation for the song leaders [b]day
by day.
24 And Pethahiah the son of Meshezabel, of the sons [a]of Zerah the son of
Judah, was the [b]king's [1]representative in
all matters concerning the people.
25 Now as for the villages with their
fields, some of the sons of Judah lived in
[a]Kiriath-arba and its [1]towns, in [b]Dibon
and its [1]towns, and in Jekabzeel and its
villages,
26 and in Jeshua, in Moladah and
Beth-pelet,
27 and in Hazar-shual, in Beersheba
and its towns,
28 and in Ziklag, in Meconah and in
its towns,
29 and in En-rimmon, in Zorah and in
Jarmuth,
30 Zanoah, Adullam, and their villages, Lachish and its fields, Azekah and
its towns. So they encamped from Beersheba as far as the valley of Hinnom.
31 The sons of Benjamin also *lived*
from Geba *onward,* at Michmash and
Aija, at Bethel and its towns,
32 at Anathoth, Nob, Ananiah,
33 Hazor, Ramah, Gittaim,
34 Hadid, Zeboim, Neballat,
35 Lod and Ono, the valley of craftsmen.
36 And from the Levites, *some* divisions in Judah belonged to Benjamin.

Priests and Levites Who Returned to Jerusalem with Zerubbabel

12 NOW these are [a]the priests and
the Levites who came up with
Zerubbabel the son of Shealtiel, and
Jeshua: Seraiah, Jeremiah, Ezra,
2 Amariah, Malluch, Hattush,
3 Shecaniah, Rehum, Meremoth,
4 Iddo, Ginnethoi, Abijah,
5 Mijamin, Maadiah, Bilgah,
6 Shemaiah and Joiarib, Jedaiah,
7 Sallu, Amok, Hilkiah, and Jedaiah.
These were the heads of the priests and
their [1]kinsmen in the days of Jeshua.
8 And the Levites *were* Jeshua, Binnui,
Kadmiel, Sherebiah, Judah, *and* Mattaniah *who was* [1]in charge of the songs of
thanksgiving, he and his brothers.
9 Also Bakbukiah and Unni, their
brothers, stood opposite them [a]in *their*
service divisions.
10 And Jeshua [1]became the father of
Joiakim, and Joiakim [1]became the father
of Eliashib, and Eliashib [1]became the
father of Joiada,
11 and Joiada became the father of
Jonathan, and Jonathan became the
father of Jaddua.
12 Now in the days of Joiakim the
priests, the heads of fathers' *households*
were: of Seraiah, Meraiah; of Jeremiah,
Hananiah;
13 of Ezra, Meshullam; of Amariah,
Jehohanan;
14 of [1]Malluchi, Jonathan; of Shebaniah, Joseph;
15 of Harim, Adna; of Meraioth, Hel-
kai;
16 of Iddo, Zechariah; of Ginnethon,
Meshullam;
17 of Abijah, Zichri; of Miniamin, of
Moadiah, Piltai;
18 of Bilgah, Shammua; of Shemaiah,
Jehonathan;
19 of Joiarib, Mattenai; of Jedaiah,
Uzzi;
20 of Sallai, Kallai; of Amok, Eber;
21 of Hilkiah, Hashabiah; of Jedaiah,
Nethanel.

The Chief Levites

22 As for the Levites, the heads of
fathers' *households* were registered in the
days of Eliashib, Joiada, and Johanan,
and Jaddua; so *were* the priests in the
reign of Darius the Persian.
23 The sons of Levi, the heads of
fathers' *households,* were registered in the
Book of the Chronicles up to the days of
Johanan the son of Eliashib.
24 And the heads of the Levites *were*
Hashabiah, Sherebiah, and Jeshua the
son of Kadmiel, with their brothers
opposite them, [a]to praise *and* give
thanks, [1]as prescribed by David the man
of God, [b]division corresponding to division.
25 Mattaniah, and Bakbukiah, Obadiah, Meshullam, Talmon, *and* Akkub
were gatekeepers keeping watch at [a]the
storehouses of the gates.
26 These *served* in the days of Joiakim
the son of Jeshua, the son of Jozadak,
and in the days of [a]Nehemiah the governor and of Ezra the priest *and* scribe.

Dedication of the Wall

27 Now at the dedication of the wall
of Jerusalem they sought out the Levites
from all their places, to bring them to
Jerusalem so that they might celebrate
the dedication with gladness, with
hymns of thanksgiving and with songs
[a]*to the accompaniment* of cymbals, harps,
and lyres.
28 So the sons of the singers were
assembled from the district around Jerusalem, and from [a]the villages of the
Netophathites,
29 from Beth-gilgal, and from *their*
fields in Geba and Azmaveth, for the
singers had built themselves villages
around Jerusalem.
30 And the priests and the Levites
[a]purified themselves; they also purified
the people, the gates, and the wall.

Procedures for the Temple

31 Then I had the leaders of Judah
come up on top of the wall, and I

21 [1]Lit., *over* [a]Neh. 3:26
22 [1]Or, *work* [a]Neh. 11:9, 14
23 [a]Ezra 6:8; 7:20 [b]Neh. 12:47
24 [1]Lit., *hand* [a]Gen. 38:30 [b]1 Chr. 18:17
25 [1]Lit., *daughters,* and so throughout the ch. [a]Josh. 14:15 [b]Josh. 13:9, 17
1 [a]Ezra 2:1; 7:7
7 [1]Lit., *brothers*
8 [1]Lit., *over*
9 [a]Neh. 12:24
10 [1]Lit., *begot,* and so in vv. 11, 12
14 [1]In Neh. 12:2, *Malluch*
24 [1]Lit., *in the commandment of* [a]Neh. 11:17 [b]Neh. 12:9
25 [a]1 Chr. 26:15
26 [a]Neh. 8:9
27 [a]1 Chr. 15:16, 28
28 [a]1 Chr. 9:16
30 [a]Neh. 13:22, 30

appointed two great [1]choirs, [2a]the first proceeding to the right on top of the wall toward [b]the Refuse Gate.

32 Hoshaiah and half of the leaders of Judah followed them,

33 with Azariah, Ezra, Meshullam,

34 Judah, Benjamin, Shemaiah, Jeremiah,

35 and some of the sons of the priests with trumpets; *and* Zechariah the son of Jonathan, the son of Shemaiah, the son of Mattaniah, the son of Micaiah, the son of Zaccur, the son of Asaph,

36 and his [1]kinsmen, Shemaiah, Azarel, Milalai, Gilalai, Maai, Nethanel, Judah *and* Hanani, [a]with the musical instruments of David the man of God. And Ezra the scribe went before them.

37 And at [a]the Fountain Gate they went directly up [b]the steps of the city of David by the stairway of the wall above the house of David to [c]the Water Gate on the east.

38 [a]The second [1]choir proceeded to the [2]left, while I followed them with half of the people on the wall, [b]above the Tower of Furnaces, to [c]the Broad Wall,

39 and above [a]the Gate of Ephraim, by [b]the Old Gate, by the [c]Fish Gate, [d]the Tower of Hananel, and the Tower of the Hundred, as far as the Sheep Gate, and they stopped at [e]the Gate of the Guard.

40 Then the two choirs took their stand in the house of God. So did I and half of the officials with me;

41 and the priests, Eliakim, Maaseiah, Miniamin, Micaiah, Elioenai, Zechariah, and Hananiah, with the trumpets;

42 and Maaseiah, Shemaiah, Eleazar, Uzzi, Jehohanan, Malchijah, Elam, and Ezer. And the singers [1]sang, with Jezrahiah *their* leader,

43 and on that day they offered great sacrifices and rejoiced because [a]God had given them great joy, even the women and children rejoiced, so that the joy of Jerusalem was heard from afar.

44 On that day [a]men were also appointed over the chambers for the stores, the contributions, the first fruits, and the tithes, to gather into them from the fields of the cities the portions required by the law for the priests and Levites; for Judah rejoiced over the priests and Levites who [1]served.

45 For they performed the [1]worship of their God and the service of purification, together with the singers and the gatekeepers [a]in accordance with the command of David *and* of his son Solomon.

46 For in the days of David and [a]Asaph, in ancient times, *there were* [1b]leaders of the singers, songs of praise and hymns of thanksgiving to God.

47 And so all Israel in the days of Zerubbabel and Nehemiah gave the portions due the singers and the gatekeepers [a]as each day required, and [b]set apart the consecrated *portion* for the Levites, and the Levites set apart the consecrated *portion* for the sons of Aaron.

31 [1]Lit., *thanksgiving choirs* [2]Heb., *and processions to the right* [a]Neh. 12:38 [b]Neh. 2:13
36 [1]Lit., *brothers* [a]Neh. 12:24
37 [a]Neh. 2:14 [b]Neh. 3:15 [c]Neh. 3:26
38 [1]Lit., *thanksgiving choir* [2]Lit., *front* [a]Neh. 12:31 [b]Neh. 3:11 [c]Neh. 3:8
39 [a]Neh. 8:16 [b]Neh. 3:6 [c]Neh. 3:3 [d]Neh. 3:1 [e]Neh. 3:25
42 [1]Lit., *caused their voices to be heard*
43 [a]Ps. 9:2; 92:4
44 [1]Lit., *stood* [a]Neh. 13:4, 5, 12, 13
45 [1]Lit., *service* [a]1 Chr. 25:1
46 [1]Lit., *heads* [a]2 Chr. 29:30 [b]1 Chr. 9:33
47 [a]Neh. 11:23 [b]Num. 18:21
1 [a]Neh. 9:3 [b]Deut. 23:3-5; Neh. 13:23
2 [a]Num. 22:3-11 [b]Deut. 23:5
3 [a]Neh. 9:2; 10:28 [b]Ex. 12:38
4 [1]Lit., *close to* [a]Neh. 12:44 [b]Neh. 2:10; 6:1, 17, 18
5 [1]Or, *chamber* [2]Lit., *heave offerings* [a]Num. 18:21
6 [a]Neh. 5:14 [b]Ezra 6:22
7 [1]Or, *understood* [2]Or, *chamber*, and so in vv. 8, 9 [a]Neh. 13:5
8 [a]John 2:13-16
9 [a]2 Chr. 29:5, 15, 16
10 [1]Or, *knew* [2]Lit., *fled* [a]Deut. 12:19; Neh. 10:37 [b]Neh. 12:28, 29
11 [1]Or, *contended with* [a]Neh. 13:17, 25 [b]Neh. 10:39
12 [a]Neh. 10:37; 12:44; Mal. 3:10
13 [1]Lit., *on them to* [2]Lit., *brothers* [a]Neh. 7:2
14 [a]Neh. 5:19; 13:22, 31

Foreigners Excluded

13 ON that day [a]they read aloud from the book of Moses in the hearing of the people; and there was found written in it that [b]no Ammonite or Moabite should ever enter the assembly of God,

2 because they did not meet the sons of Israel with bread and water, but [a]hired Balaam against them to curse them. However, [b]our God turned the curse into a blessing.

3 So it came about, that when they heard the law, [a]they excluded [b]all foreigners from Israel.

Tobiah Expelled and the Temple Cleansed

4 Now prior to this, Eliashib the priest, [a]who was appointed over the chambers of the house of our God, being [1]related to [b]Tobiah,

5 had prepared a large [1]room for him, where formerly they put the grain offerings, the frankincense, the utensils, and the tithes of grain, wine and oil [a]prescribed for the Levites, the singers and the gatekeepers, and the [2]contributions for the priests.

6 But during all this *time* I was not in Jerusalem, for in [a]the thirty-second year of [b]Artaxerxes king of Babylon I had gone to the king. After some time, however, I asked leave from the king,

7 and I came to Jerusalem and [1]learned about the evil that Eliashib had done for Tobiah, [a]by preparing a [2]room for him in the courts of the house of God.

8 And it was very displeasing to me, so I [a]threw all of Tobiah's household goods out of the room.

9 Then I gave an order and [a]they cleansed the rooms; and I returned there the utensils of the house of God with the grain offerings and the frankincense.

Tithes Restored

10 I also [1]discovered that [a]the portions of the Levites had not been given *them*, so that the Levites and the singers who performed the service had [2]gone away, [b]each to his own field.

11 So I [1a]reprimanded the officials and said, "[b]Why is the house of God forsaken?" Then I gathered them together and restored them to their posts.

12 All Judah then brought [a]the tithe of the grain, wine, and oil into the storehouses.

13 And in charge of the storehouses I appointed Shelemiah the priest, Zadok the scribe, and Pedaiah of the Levites, and in addition to them was Hanan the son of Zaccur, the son of Mattaniah; for [a]they were considered reliable, and it was [1]their task to distribute to their [2]kinsmen.

14 [a]Remember me for this, O my God, and do not blot out my loyal deeds which I have performed for the house of my God and its services.

Sabbath Restored

15 In those days I saw in Judah some who were treading wine presses [a]on the sabbath, and bringing in sacks of grain and loading *them* on donkeys, as well as wine, grapes, figs, and all kinds of loads, [b]and they brought *them* into Jerusalem on the sabbath day. So [c]I admonished *them* on the day they sold food.

16 Also men of Tyre were living [1]there *who* imported fish and all kinds of merchandise, and sold *them* to the sons of Judah on the sabbath, even in Jerusalem.

17 Then [a]I [1]reprimanded the nobles of Judah and said to them, "What is this evil thing you are doing, [2]by profaning the sabbath day?

18 "[a]Did not your fathers do the same so that our God brought on us, and on this city, all this trouble? Yet you are adding to the wrath on Israel by profaning the sabbath."

19 [a]And it came about that just as it grew dark at the gates of Jerusalem before the sabbath, I commanded that the doors should be shut [1]and that they should not open them until after the sabbath. Then I stationed some of my servants at the gates *that* no load should enter on the sabbath day.

20 Once or twice the traders and merchants of every kind of merchandise spent the night outside Jerusalem.

21 Then [a]I [1]warned them and said to them, "Why do you spend the night in front of the wall? If you do so again, I will [2]use force against you." From that time on they did not come on the sabbath.

22 And I commanded the Levites that [a]they should purify themselves and come as gatekeepers to sanctify the sabbath day. *For* this also [b]remember me, O my God, and have compassion on me according to the greatness of Thy lovingkindness.

Mixed Marriages Forbidden

23 In those days I also saw that the Jews had [1a]married women from [b]Ashdod, [c]Ammon, *and* Moab.

24 As for their children, half spoke in the language of Ashdod, and none of them was able to speak the language of Judah, but [1]the language of his own people.

25 So [a]I contended with them and cursed them and [b]struck some of them and pulled out their hair, and [c]made them swear by God, "You shall not give your daughters to their sons, nor take of their daughters for your sons or for yourselves.

26 "[a]Did not Solomon king of Israel sin regarding these things? [b]Yet among the many nations there was no king like him, and [c]he was loved by his God, and God made him king over all Israel; nevertheless the foreign women caused even him to sin.

27 "[1]Do we then hear about you that you have committed all this great evil [a]by acting unfaithfully against our God by [2]marrying foreign women?"

28 Even one of the sons of Joiada, the son of Eliashib the high priest, was a son-in-law of [a]Sanballat the Horonite, so I drove him away from me.

29 [a]Remember them, O my God, [1]because they have defiled the priesthood and the [b]covenant of the priesthood and the Levites.

30 [a]Thus I purified them from everything foreign and appointed duties for the priests and the Levites, each in his task,

31 and *I arranged* [a]for the supply of wood at appointed times and for the first fruits. [b]Remember me, O my God, for good.

15 [a]Ex. 20:8; 34:21; Deut. 5:12-14; Jer. 17:22 [b]Neh. 10:31; Jer. 17:21 [c]Neh. 9:29; 13:21
16 [1]Lit., *in it*
17 [1]Or, *contended with* [2]Lit., *and* [a]Neh. 13:11, 25
18 [a]Ezra 9:13; Jer. 17:21
19 [1]Lit., *and commanded* [a]Lev. 23:32
21 [1]Lit., *witnessed against* [2]Lit., *send a hand against* [a]Neh. 13:15
22 [a]1 Chr. 15:12; Neh. 12:30 [b]Neh. 13:14, 31
23 [1]Lit., *given dwelling to* [a]Ex. 34:11-16; Deut. 7:1-5; Ezra 9:2; Neh. 10:30 [b]Neh. 4:7 [c]Ezra 9:1; Neh. 13:1
24 [1]Lit., *according to the tongue of people and people*
25 [a]Neh. 13:11, 17 [b]Deut. 25:2 [c]Neh. 10:29, 30
26 [a]1 Kin. 11:1 [b]1 Kin. 3:13; 2 Chr. 1:12 [c]2 Sam. 12:24, 25
27 [1]Or, *Is it reported* [2]Lit., *giving dwelling to* [a]Ezra 10:2; Neh. 13:23
28 [a]Neh. 2:10, 19; 4:1
29 [1]Lit., *for the defilings of* [a]Neh. 6:14 [b]Num. 25:13
30 [a]Neh. 10:30
31 [a]Neh. 10:34 [b]Neh. 13:14, 22

THE BOOK OF
ESTHER

The Banquets of the King

1 NOW it took place in the days of
[a]Ahasuerus, the Ahasuerus who
reigned [b]from India to [1]Ethiopia over
[c]127 provinces,
2 in those days as King Ahasuerus
[a]sat on his royal throne which *was* in
[b]Susa the capital,
3 in the third year of his reign, [a]he
gave a banquet for all his princes and
attendants, the army *officers* of Persia
and Media, the nobles, and the princes
of his provinces being in his presence.
4 [1]And he displayed the riches of his
royal glory and the splendor of his great
majesty for many days, 180 days.
5 And when these days were completed, the king gave a banquet lasting
seven days for all the people who were
present in Susa the capital, from the
greatest to the least, in the court of [a]the
garden of the king's palace.
6 *There were hangings of* fine white
and violet linen held by cords of fine
purple linen on silver rings and marble
columns, *and* [a]couches of gold and silver
on a mosaic pavement of porphyry,
marble, mother-of-pearl, and precious
stones.
7 Drinks were served in golden vessels of various kinds, and the royal wine
was plentiful [a]according to the king's
[1]bounty.
8 And the drinking was *done* according to the law, there was no compulsion,
for so the king had given orders to each
official of his household that he should
do according to the desires of each
person.
9 Queen Vashti also gave a banquet
for the women in the [1]palace which
belonged to King Ahasuerus.

Queen Vashti's Refusal

10 On the seventh day, when the heart
of the king was [a]merry with wine, he
commanded Mehuman, Biztha, Har-
bona, Bigtha, Abagtha, Zethar, and
Carkas, the seven eunuchs who served in
the presence of King Ahasuerus,
11 to bring Queen Vashti before the
king with *her* royal [a]crown in order to
display her beauty to the people and the
princes, for she was beautiful.
12 But Queen Vashti refused to come
at the king's command delivered by the
eunuchs. Then the king became very
angry and his wrath burned within him.
13 Then the king said to [a]the wise men
[b]who understood the times—for it was
the custom of the king so *to speak* before
all who knew law and justice,
14 and were close to him: Carshena,
Shethar, Admatha, Tarshish, Meres,
Marsena, and Memucan, the seven
princes of Persia and Media [a]who [1]had
access to the king's presence and sat in
the first place in the kingdom—
15 "According to law, what is to be
done with Queen Vashti, because she did
not [1]obey the command of King Ahasuerus *delivered* by the eunuchs?"
16 And in the presence of the king and
the princes, Memucan said, "Queen
Vashti has wronged not only the king
but *also* all the princes, and all the
peoples who are in all the provinces of
King Ahasuerus.
17 "For the queen's conduct will [1]be-
come known to all the women causing
them [2]to look with contempt on their
husbands by saying, 'King Ahasuerus
commanded Queen Vashti to be brought
in to his presence, but she did not come.'
18 "And this day the ladies of Persia
and Media who have heard of the
queen's conduct will speak in *the same
way* to all the king's princes, and there
will be plenty of contempt and anger.
19 "If it pleases the king, let a royal
[1]edict be issued by him and let it be
written in the laws of Persia and Media
so [a]that it cannot [2]be repealed, that
Vashti should come no more into the
presence of King Ahasuerus, and let the
king give her royal position to [3]another
who is more worthy than she.
20 "And when the king's edict which he
shall make is heard throughout all his
kingdom, [1]great as it is, then [a]all women
will give honor to their husbands, great
and small."
21 And *this* word pleased the king and
the princes, and the king did [1]as Memucan proposed.
22 So he sent letters to all the king's
provinces, [a]to each province according
to its script and to every people according to their language, that every man
should [b]be the master in his own house
and the one who speaks in the language
of his own people.

Vashti's Successor Sought

2 AFTER these things [a]when the anger of King Ahasuerus had subsided, he remembered Vashti and what
she had done and [b]what had been decreed against her.
2 Then the king's attendants, who
served him, said, "[a]Let beautiful young
virgins be sought for the king.
3 "And let the king appoint overseers
in [a]all the provinces of his kingdom that
they may gather every beautiful young
virgin to Susa the capital, to the harem,
into the custody of [b]Hegai, the king's
eunuch, who was in charge of the
women; and [c]let their cosmetics be given
them.
4 "Then let the young lady who
pleases the king be queen in place of
Vashti." And the matter pleased the
king, and he did accordingly.
5 *Now* there was a Jew in Susa the
capital whose name was [a]Mordecai, the
son of Jair, the son of Shimei, the son of
Kish, a Benjamite,

---

1 [1]Lit., *Cush* [a]Ezra 4:6; Dan. 9:1 [b]Esth. 8:9 [c]Esth. 9:30
2 [a]1 Kin. 1:46 [b]Neh. 1:1; Dan. 8:2
3 [a]Esth. 2:18
4 [1]Lit., *When*
5 [a]Esth. 7:7, 8
6 [a]Ezek. 23:41; Amos 6:4
7 [1]Lit., *hand* [a]Esth. 2:18
9 [1]Lit., *royal house*
10 [a]Judg. 16:25
11 [a]Esth. 2:17; 6:8
13 [a]Jer. 10:7; Dan. 2:2 [b]1 Chr. 12:32
14 [1]Lit., *saw the face of the king* [a]2 Kin. 25:19; Matt. 18:10
15 [1]Lit., *do*
17 [1]Lit., *go forth* [2]Lit., *to despise . . . in their eyes*
19 [1]Lit., *word go forth from* [2]Lit., *pass away* [3]Lit., *her neighbor* [a]Esth. 8:8; Dan. 6:8
20 [1]Lit., *for great is it* [a]Eph. 5:22; Col. 3:18
21 [1]Lit., *according to the word of*
22 [a]Esth. 3:12; 8:9 [b]Eph. 5:22-24

1 [a]Esth. 7:10 [b]Esth. 1:19, 20
2 [a]1 Kin. 1:2
3 [a]Esth. 1:1, 2 [b]Esth. 2:8, 15 [c]Esth. 2:9, 12
5 [a]Esth. 3:2

6 [a]who had been taken into exile from Jerusalem with the captives who had been exiled with Jeconiah king of Judah, whom Nebuchadnezzar the king of Babylon had exiled.

7 And he was bringing up Hadassah, that is [a]Esther, his uncle's daughter, for she had neither father nor mother. Now the young lady was beautiful of form and [1]face, and when her father and her mother died, Mordecai took her as his own daughter.

Esther Finds Favor

8 So it came about when the command and decree of the king were heard and [a]many young ladies were gathered to Susa the capital into the custody of [b]Hegai, that Esther was taken to the king's [1]palace into the custody of Hegai, who was in charge of the women.

9 Now the young lady pleased him and found favor with him. So he quickly provided her with her [a]cosmetics and [1]food, gave her seven choice maids from the king's palace, and transferred her and her maids to the best place in the harem.

10 [a]Esther did not make known her people or her kindred, for Mordecai had instructed her that she should not make *them* known.

11 And every day Mordecai walked back and forth in front of the court of the harem to learn how Esther was and how she fared.

12 Now when the turn of each young lady came to go in to King Ahasuerus, after the end of her twelve months under the regulations for the women—for the days of their beautification were completed as follows: six months with oil of myrrh and six months with spices and the cosmetics for women—

13 the young lady would go in to the king in this way: anything that she [1]desired was given her to take with her from the harem to the king's palace.

14 In the evening she would go in and in the morning she would return to the second harem, to the [1]custody of Shaashgaz, the king's eunuch who was in charge of the concubines. She would not again go in to the king unless the king delighted in her and she was summoned by name.

15 Now when the turn of Esther, [a]the daughter of Abihail the uncle of Mordecai who had taken her as his daughter, came to go in to the king, she did not request anything except what [b]Hegai, the king's eunuch who was in charge of the women, [1]advised. And Esther found favor in the eyes of all who saw her.

16 So Esther was taken to King Ahasuerus to his royal palace in the tenth month which is the month Tebeth, in the seventh year of his reign.

Esther Becomes Queen

17 And the king loved Esther more than all the women, and she found favor and kindness with him more than all the virgins, so that [a]he set the royal crown on her head and made her queen instead of Vashti.

18 Then [a]the king gave a great banquet, Esther's banquet, for all his princes and his servants; he also made a holiday for the provinces and gave gifts [b]according to the king's bounty.

19 And [a]when the virgins were gathered together the second time, then Mordecai [b]was sitting at the king's gate.

20 [a]Esther had not yet made known her kindred or her people, even as Mordecai had commanded her, for Esther did [1]what Mordecai told her as she had done [b]when under his care.

Mordecai Saves the King

21 In those days, while Mordecai was sitting at the king's gate, [a]Bigthan and Teresh, two of the king's officials from those who guarded the door, became angry and sought to [1]lay hands on King Ahasuerus.

22 But the [1]plot became known to Mordecai, and [a]he told Queen Esther, and Esther [2]informed the king in Mordecai's name.

23 Now when the plot was investigated and found *to be so,* they were both hanged on a [1]gallows; and it was written in [a]the Book of the Chronicles in the king's presence.

Haman's Plot against the Jews

3 AFTER these events King Ahasuerus [a]promoted Haman, the son of Hammedatha [b]the Agagite, and [c]advanced him and [1]established his authority over all the princes who *were* with him.

2 And all the king's servants who were at the king's gate bowed down [1]and paid homage to Haman; for so the king had commanded concerning him. But [a]Mordecai neither bowed down nor paid homage.

3 Then the king's servants who were at [a]the king's gate said to Mordecai, "[b]Why are you transgressing the king's command?"

4 Now it was when they had spoken daily to him and he would not listen to them, that they told Haman to see whether Mordecai's reason would stand; for he had told them that he was a Jew.

5 When Haman saw that [a]Mordecai neither bowed down nor paid homage to him, Haman was filled with rage.

6 But he [1]disdained to [2]lay hands on Mordecai alone, for they had told him *who* the people of Mordecai *were;* therefore Haman [a]sought to destroy all the Jews, the people of Mordecai, who *were* throughout the whole kingdom of Ahasuerus.

7 In the first month, which is the month Nisan, in the twelfth year of King Ahasuerus, [1]Pur, that is the lot, was [a]cast before Haman from day to day and from month *to month,* [2]until the twelfth month, that is [b]the month Adar.

6 [a]2 Kin. 24:14, 15; 2 Chr. 36:10

7 [1]Lit., *good of appearance* [a]Esth. 2:15

8 [1]Lit., *house* [a]Esth. 2:3 [b]Esth. 2:3, 15

9 [1]Lit., *portions* [a]Esth. 2:3, 12

10 [a]Esth. 2:20

13 [1]Lit., *said*

14 [1]Lit., *hand*

15 [1]Lit., *said* [a]Esth. 2:7; 9:29 [b]Esth. 2:3, 8

17 [a]Esth. 1:11

18 [a]Esth. 1:3 [b]Esth. 1:7

19 [a]Esth. 2:3, 4 [b]Esth. 2:21; 3:2

20 [1]Lit., *the word of Mordecai* [a]Esth. 2:10 [b]Esth. 2:7

21 [1]Lit., *send a hand against* [a]Esth. 6:2

22 [1]Lit., *matter,* so also v. 23 [2]Lit., *told* [a]Esth. 6:1, 2

23 [1]Lit., *tree* [a]Esth. 10:2

1 [1]Lit., *set his seat* [a]Esth. 5:11 [b]Esth. 3:10; 8:3 [c]Esth. 5:11

2 [1]Lit., *and prostrated themselves before* [a]Esth. 2:19; 5:9

3 [a]Esth. 2:19 [b]Esth. 3:2

5 [a]Esth. 5:9

6 [1]Lit., *despised in his eyes* [2]Lit., *send a hand against* [a]Ps. 83:4

7 [1]Lit., *he cast Pur . . . before* [2]Gr., *and the lot fell on the thirteenth day of* [a]Esth. 9:24-26 [b]Ezra 6:15

8 Then Haman said to King Ahasuerus, "There is a certain people scattered and dispersed among the peoples in all the provinces of your kingdom; [a]their laws are different from *those* of all *other* people, and they do not observe the king's laws, so it is not in the king's interest to let them remain.

9 "If it is pleasing to the king, let it be [1]decreed that they be destroyed, and I will pay ten thousand talents of silver into the hands of those who carry on the *king's* business, to put into the king's treasuries."

10 Then [a]the king took his signet ring from his hand and gave it to Haman, the son of Hammedatha [b]the Agagite, [c]the enemy of the Jews.

11 And the king said to Haman, "The silver is [1]yours, and the people *also,* to do with them as you please."

12 [a]Then the king's scribes were summoned on the thirteenth day of the first month, and it was written just as Haman commanded to [b]the king's satraps, to the governors who were over each province, and to the princes of each people, each province according to its script, each people according to its language, being written [c]in the name of King Ahasuerus and sealed with the king's signet ring.

13 And letters were sent by [a]couriers to all the king's provinces [b]to destroy, to kill, and to annihilate all the Jews, both young and old, women and children, [c]in one day, the thirteenth *day* of the twelfth month, which is the month Adar, and to [d]seize their possessions as plunder.

14 [a]A copy of the edict to be [1]issued as law in every province was published to all the peoples so that they should be ready for this day.

15 The couriers went out impelled by the king's command while the decree was [1]issued in Susa the capital; and while the king and Haman sat down to drink, [a]the city of Susa was in confusion.

Esther Learns of Haman's Plot

4 WHEN Mordecai learned [a]all that had been done, [1]he tore his clothes, put on sackcloth and ashes, and went out into the midst of the city and wailed loudly and bitterly.

2 And he went as far as the king's gate, for no one was to enter the king's gate clothed in sackcloth.

3 And in each and every province where the command and decree of the king came, there was great mourning among the Jews, with [a]fasting, weeping, and wailing; and many lay on sackcloth and ashes.

4 Then Esther's maidens and her eunuchs came and told her, and the queen writhed in great anguish. And she sent garments to clothe Mordecai that he might remove his sackcloth from him, but he did not accept *them.*

5 Then Esther summoned Hathach from the king's eunuchs, whom [1]the king had appointed to attend her, and ordered him *to go* to Mordecai to learn what this *was* and why it *was.*

6 So Hathach went out to Mordecai to the city square in front of the king's gate.

7 And Mordecai told him all that had happened to him, and [a]the exact amount of money that Haman had promised to pay to the king's treasuries for the destruction of the Jews.

8 He also gave him [a]a copy of the text of the edict which had been issued in Susa for their destruction, that he might show Esther and inform her, and to order her to go in to the king to implore his favor and to plead with him for her people.

9 And Hathach came back and related Mordecai's words to Esther.

10 Then Esther spoke to Hathach and ordered him *to reply* to Mordecai:

11 "All the king's servants and the people of the king's provinces know that for any man or woman who [a]comes to the king to the inner court who is not summoned, [b]he has but one law, that he be put to death, unless the king holds out [c]to him the golden scepter so that he may live. And I have not been summoned to come to the king for these thirty days."

12 And they related Esther's words to Mordecai.

13 Then Mordecai told *them* to reply to Esther, "Do not imagine that you in the king's palace can escape any more than all the Jews.

14 "For if you remain silent at this time, relief and [a]deliverance will arise for the Jews from another place and you and your father's house will perish. And who knows whether you have not attained royalty for such a time as this?"

Esther Plans to Intercede

15 Then Esther told *them* to reply to Mordecai,

16 "Go, assemble all the Jews who are found in Susa, and fast for me; [a]do not eat or drink for [b]three days, night or day. I and my maidens also will fast in the same way. And thus I will go in to the king, which is not according to the law; and if I perish, I perish."

17 So Mordecai went away and did just as Esther had commanded him.

Esther Plans a Banquet

5 NOW it came about [a]on the third day that Esther put on her royal robes and stood [b]in the inner court of the king's palace in front of the king's [1]rooms, and the king was sitting on his royal throne in the [2]throne room, opposite the entrance to the palace.

2 And it happened when the king saw Esther the queen standing in the court, [a]she obtained favor in his sight; and [b]the king extended to Esther the golden scepter which was in his hand. So Esther came near and touched the top of the scepter.

8 [a]Ezra 4:12-15; Acts 16:20, 21
9 [1]Lit., *written*
10 [a]Gen. 41:42; Esth. 8:2 [b]Esth. 3:1 [c]Esth. 7:6
11 [1]Lit., *given to you*
12 [a]Esth. 8:9 [b]Ezra 8:36 [c]1 Kin. 21:8; Esth. 8:8, 10
13 [a]2 Chr. 30:6; Esth. 8:10, 14 [b]Esth. 7:4 [c]Esth. 8:12 [d]Esth. 8:11; 9:10
14 [1]Lit., *given* [a]Esth. 8:13, 14
15 [1]Lit., *given* [a]Esth. 8:15
1 [1]Lit., *Mordecai* [a]2 Sam. 1:11; Esth. 3:8-10; Jon. 3:5,6
3 [a]Esth. 4:16
5 [1]Lit., *he*
7 [a]Esth. 3:9
8 [a]Esth. 3:14
11 [a]Esth. 5:1; 6:4 [b]Dan. 2:9 [c]Esth. 5:2; 8:4
14 [a]Lev. 26:42; 2 Kin. 13:5
16 [a]Joel 1:14; 2:12 [b]Esth. 5:1
1 [1]Lit., *house* [2]Lit., *royal house* [a]Esth. 4:16 [b]Esth. 4:11; 6:4
2 [a]Esth. 2:9 [b]Esth. 4:11; 8:4

3 Then the king said to her, "What is *troubling* you, Queen Esther? And what is your request? [a]Even to half of the kingdom it will be given to you."
4 And Esther said, "If it please the king, may the king and Haman come this day to the banquet that I have prepared for him."
5 Then the king said, "[a]Bring Haman quickly that we may do [1]as Esther desires." So the king and Haman came to the banquet which Esther had prepared.
6 And, [1]as they drank their wine at the banquet, [a]the king said to Esther, "[b]What is your petition, for it shall be granted to you. And what is your request? Even to half of the kingdom it shall be done."
7 So Esther answered and said, "My petition and my request is:
8 [a]if I have found favor in the sight of the king, and if it please the king to grant my petition and do [1]what I request, may the king and Haman come to [b]the banquet which I shall prepare for them, and tomorrow I will do [2]as the king says."

Haman's Pride

9 Then Haman went out that day glad and pleased of heart; but when Haman saw Mordecai [a]in the king's gate, and [b]that he did not stand up or [1]tremble before him, Haman was filled with anger against Mordecai.
10 Haman controlled himself, however, went to his house, and [1]sent for his friends and his wife [a]Zeresh.
11 Then Haman recounted to them the glory of his riches, and the [1a]number of his sons, and every *instance* where the king had magnified him, and how he had [2b]promoted him above the princes and servants of the king.
12 Haman also said, "Even Esther the queen let no one but me come with the king to the banquet which she had prepared; and [a]tomorrow also I am [1]invited by her with the king.
13 "Yet all of this [1]does not satisfy me every time I see Mordecai the Jew sitting at [a]the king's gate."
14 Then Zeresh his wife and all his friends said to him, "[a]Have a [1]gallows fifty cubits high made and in the morning ask the king to have Mordecai hanged on it, then go joyfully with the king to the banquet." And the [2]advice pleased Haman, so he had the gallows made.

The King Plans to Honor Mordecai

6 DURING that night [1]the king [a]could not sleep so he gave an order to bring [b]the book of records, the chronicles, and they were read before the king.
2 And it was found written what [a]Mordecai had reported concerning Bigthana and Teresh, two of the king's eunuchs who were doorkeepers, that they had sought to lay hands on King Ahasuerus.
3 And the king said, "What honor or dignity has been bestowed on Mordecai for this?" Then the king's servants who attended him said, "Nothing has been done for him."
4 So the king said, "Who is in the court?" Now Haman had just [a]entered the outer court of the king's palace in order to speak to the king about [b]hanging Mordecai on the gallows which he had prepared for him.
5 And the king's servants said to him, "Behold, Haman is standing in the court." And the king said, "Let him come in."
6 So Haman came in and the king said to him, "What is to be done for the man [a]whom the king desires to honor?" And Haman said [1]to himself, "Whom would the king desire to honor more than me?"
7 Then Haman said to the king, "For the man whom the king desires to honor,
8 let them bring a royal robe which the king has worn, and [a]the horse on which the king has ridden, and on whose head [b]a royal crown has been placed;
9 and let the robe and the horse be handed over to one of the king's most noble princes and let them array the man whom the king desires to honor and lead him on horseback through the city square, [a]and proclaim before him, 'Thus it shall be done to the man whom the king desires to honor.' "

Haman Must Honor Mordecai

10 Then the king said to Haman, "Take quickly the robes and the horse as you have said, and do so for Mordecai the Jew, who is sitting at the king's gate; do not fall short in anything of all that you have said."
11 So Haman took the robe and the horse, and arrayed Mordecai, and led him *on horseback* through the city square, and proclaimed before him, "Thus it shall be done to the man whom the king desires to honor."
12 Then Mordecai returned to the king's gate. But Haman hurried home, mourning, [a]with *his* head covered.
13 And Haman recounted [a]to Zeresh his wife and all his friends everything that had happened to him. Then his wise men and Zeresh his wife said to him, "If Mordecai, before whom you have begun to fall, is [1]of Jewish origin, you will not overcome him, but will surely fall before him."
14 While they were still talking with him, the king's eunuchs arrived and hastily [a]brought Haman to the banquet which Esther had prepared.

Esther's Plea

7 NOW the king and Haman came to drink *wine* with Esther the queen.
2 And the king said to Esther on the

3 [a]Esth. 7:2; Mark 6:23
5 [1]Lit., *the word of Esther* [a]Esth. 6:14
6 [1]Lit., *at the banquet of wine* [a]Esth. 7:2 [b]Esth. 5:3
8 [1]Lit., *my request* [2]Lit., *according to the word of the king* [a]Esth. 7:3; 8:5 [b]Esth. 6:14
9 [1]Or, *move for* [a]Esth. 2:19 [b]Esth. 3:5
10 [1]Lit., *sent and brought* [a]Esth. 6:13
11 [1]Lit., *multitude* [2]Lit., *lifted* [a]Esth. 9:7-10 [b]Esth. 3:1
12 [1]Lit., *summoned to her* [a]Esth. 5:8
13 [1]Lit., *is not suitable to me* [a]Esth. 5:9
14 [1]Lit., *tree* [2]Lit., *thing* [a]Esth. 6:4; 7:9, 10
1 [1]Lit., *the king's sleep fled* [a]Dan. 6:18 [b]Esth. 2:23; 10:2
2 [a]Esth. 2:21, 22
4 [a]Esth. 4:11 [b]Esth. 5:14
6 [1]Lit., *in his heart* [a]Esth. 6:7, 9, 11
8 [a]1 Kin. 1:33 [b]Esth. 1:11; 2:17
9 [a]Gen. 41:43
12 [a]2 Sam. 15:30
13 [1]Lit., *from the seed of the Jews* [a]Esth. 5:10
14 [a]Esth. 5:8

second day also [1]as they drank their
wine at the banquet, "[a]What is your
petition, Queen Esther? It shall be
granted you. And what is your request?
[b]Even to half of the kingdom it shall be
done."
3 Then Queen Esther answered and
said, "[a]If I have found favor in your
sight, O king, and if it please the king, let
my life be given me as my petition, and
my people as my request;
4 for [a]we have been sold, I and my
people, to be destroyed, [b]to be killed and
to be annihilated. Now if we had only
been sold as slaves, men and women, I
would have remained silent, for the
[1]trouble would not be commensurate
with the [2]annoyance to the king."
5 Then King Ahasuerus [1]asked
Queen Esther, "Who is he, and where is
he, [2]who would presume to do thus?"
6 And Esther said, "[a]A foe and an
enemy, is this wicked Haman!" Then
Haman became terrified before the king
and queen.

Haman Is Hanged

7 And the king arose [a]in his anger
from [1]drinking wine *and went* into [b]the
palace garden; but Haman stayed to beg
for his life from Queen Esther, for he
saw that harm had been determined
against him by the king.
8 Now when the king returned from
the palace garden into the [1]place where
they were drinking wine, Haman was
falling on [a]the couch where Esther was.
Then the king said, "Will he even assault
the queen with me in the house?" As the
word went out of the king's mouth, they
covered Haman's face.
9 Then Harbonah, one of the eunuchs who *were* before the king said,
"Behold indeed, [a]the gallows standing at
Haman's house fifty cubits high, which
Haman made for Mordecai [b]who spoke
good on behalf of the king!" And the
king said, "Hang him on it."
10 [a]So they hanged Haman on the
[1]gallows which he had prepared for
Mordecai, [b]and the king's anger subsided.

Mordecai Promoted

8 ON that day King Ahasuerus gave
the house of Haman, [a]the enemy of
the Jews, to Queen Esther; and Mordecai came before the king, for Esther had
disclosed [b]what he was to her.
2 [a]And the king took off his signet
ring which he had taken away from
Haman, and gave it to Mordecai. And
Esther set Mordecai over the house of
Haman.
3 Then Esther spoke again to the
king, fell at his feet, wept, and implored
him to avert the evil *scheme* of Haman
the Agagite and his plot which he had
devised against the Jews.
4 [a]And the king extended the golden
scepter to Esther. So Esther arose and
stood before the king.
5 Then she said, "[a]If it pleases the
king and if I have found favor before
him and the matter *seems* proper to the
king and I am pleasing in his sight, let it
be written to revoke the [b]letters devised
by Haman, the son of Hammedatha the
Agagite, which he wrote to destroy the
Jews who are in all the king's provinces.
6 "For [a]how can I endure to see the
calamity which shall befall my people,
and how can I endure to see the destruction of my kindred?"
7 So King Ahasuerus said to Queen
Esther and to Mordecai the Jew, "Behold, [a]I have given the house of Haman
to Esther, and him they have hanged on
the gallows because he had stretched out
his hands against the Jews.

The King's Decree Avenges the Jews

8 "Now you write to the Jews [1]as you
see fit, in the king's name, and [a]seal *it*
with the king's signet ring; for a decree
which is written in the name of the king
and sealed with the king's signet ring
[b]may not be revoked."
9 [a]So the king's scribes were called at
that time in the third month (that is, the
month Sivan), on the twenty-third [1]day;
and it was written according to all that
Mordecai commanded to the Jews, the
satraps, the governors, and the princes
of the provinces which *extended* [b]from
India to [2]Ethiopia, 127 provinces, to
[c]every province according to its script,
and to every people according to their
language, as well as to the Jews according to their script and their language.
10 And he wrote in the name of King
Ahasuerus, and sealed it with the king's
signet ring, and sent letters by couriers
on [a]horses, riding on steeds sired by the
royal stud.
11 [1]In them the king granted the Jews
who were in each and every city *the right*
[a]to assemble and to defend their lives,
[b]to destroy, to kill, and to annihilate the
entire army of any people or province
which might attack them, including
children and women, and [c]to plunder
their spoil,
12 on [a]one day in all the provinces of
King Ahasuerus, the thirteenth *day* of
the twelfth month (that is, the month
Adar).
13 [a]A copy of the edict to be [1]issued
as law in each and every province, was
published to all the peoples, so that the
Jews should be ready for this day to
avenge themselves on their enemies.
14 The couriers, hastened and impelled by the king's command, went out,
riding on the royal steeds; and the
decree was given out in Susa the capital.
15 Then Mordecai went out from the
presence of the king [a]in royal robes of
[1]blue and white, with a large crown of
gold and [b]a garment of fine linen and
purple; and [c]the city of Susa shouted
and rejoiced.
16 For the Jews there was [a]light and
gladness and joy and honor.

2 [1]Lit., *at the banquet of wine* [a]Esth. 5:6; 9:12 [b]Esth. 5:3

3 [a]Esth. 5:8; 8:5

4 [1]Or, *enemy could not compensate for the loss* [2]Or, *damage* [a]Esth. 3:9 [b]Esth. 3:13

5 [1]Lit., *said and said to* [2]Lit., *whose heart has been filled*

6 [a]Esth. 3:10

7 [1]Lit., *the banquet of wine* [a]Esth. 1:12 [b]Esth. 1:5

8 [1]Lit., *house of the banquet of wine* [a]Esth. 1:6

9 [a]Esth. 5:14 [b]Esth. 2:22

10 [1]Lit., *tree* [a]Ps. 7:16; 94:23 [b]Esth. 7:7, 8

1 [a]Esth. 7:6 [b]Esth. 2:7, 15

2 [a]Esth. 3:10

4 [a]Esth. 4:11; 5:2

5 [a]Esth. 5:8; 7:3 [b]Esth. 3:13

6 [a]Esth. 7:4; 9:1

7 [a]Esth. 8:1

8 [1]Lit., *according to the good in your eyes* [a]Esth. 3:12; 8:10 [b]Esth. 1:19

9 [1]Lit., *in it* [2]Lit., *Cush* [a]Esth. 3:12 [b]Esth. 1:1 [c]Esth. 1:22; 3:12

10 [a]1 Kin. 4:28

11 [1]Lit., *Which* [a]Esth. 9:2 [b]Esth. 3:13 [c]Esth. 9:10

12 [a]Esth. 3:13; 9:1

13 [1]Lit., *given* [a]Esth. 3:14

15 [1]Or, *violet* [a]Esth. 5:11 [b]Gen. 41:42 [c]Esth. 3:15

16 [a]Ps. 97:11; 112:4

17 And in each and every province.
and in each and every city, wherever the
king's commandment and his decree
arrived, there was gladness and joy for
the Jews, a feast and a [1a]holiday. And
[b]many among the peoples of the land
became Jews, for the dread of the Jews
had fallen on them.

The Jews Destroy Their Enemies

9 NOW [a]in the twelfth month (that is,
the month Adar), on [b]the thirteenth
[1]day [c]when the king's command and
edict [2]were about to be executed, on the
day when the enemies of the Jews hoped
to gain the mastery over them, it was
turned to the contrary so that the Jews
themselves gained the mastery over
those who hated them.
2 [a]The Jews assembled in their cities
throughout all the provinces of King
Ahasuerus to lay hands on those who
sought their harm; and no one could
stand before them, [b]for the dread of
them had fallen on all the peoples.
3 Even all the princes of the provinces, [a]the satraps, the governors, and
those who were doing the king's business
[1]assisted the Jews, because the dread of
Mordecai had fallen on them.
4 Indeed, Mordecai was great in the
king's house, and his fame spread
throughout all the provinces; for the
man Mordecai [a]became greater and
greater.
5 Thus [a]the Jews struck all their
enemies with [1]the sword, killing and
destroying; and they did what they
pleased to those who hated them.
6 And in Susa the capital the Jews
killed and destroyed five hundred men,
7 and Parshandatha, Dalphon, Aspa-
tha,
8 Poratha, Adalia, Aridatha,
9 Parmashta, Arisai, Aridai, and
Vaizatha,
10 [a]the ten sons of Haman the son of
Hammedatha, the Jews' enemy; but
[b]they did not lay their hands on the
plunder.
11 On that day the number of those
who were killed in Susa the capital [1]was
reported to the king.
12 And the king said to Queen Esther,
"The Jews have killed and destroyed five
hundred men and the ten sons of Haman
in Susa the capital. What then have they
done in the rest of the king's provinces!
[a]Now what is your petition? It shall even
be granted you. And what is your further
request? It shall also be done."
13 Then said Esther, "If it pleases the
king, [a]let tomorrow also be granted to
the Jews who are in Susa to do according
to the edict of today; and let Haman's
ten sons be hanged on the gallows."
14 So the king commanded that it
should be done so; and an edict was
issued in Susa, and Haman's ten sons
were hanged.
15 And the Jews who were in Susa
assembled also on the fourteenth day of
the month Adar and killed [a]three hundred men in Susa, but [b]they did not lay
their hands on the plunder.
16 Now [a]the rest of the Jews who *were*
in the king's provinces [b]assembled, to
defend their lives and [1]rid themselves of
their enemies, and kill 75,000 of those
who hated them; but they did not lay
their hands on the plunder.
17 *This was done* on [a]the thirteenth
day of the month Adar, and [b]on the
fourteenth [1]day they rested and made it
a day of feasting and rejoicing.
18 But the Jews who were in Susa
[a]assembled on the thirteenth and [b]the
fourteenth [1]of the same month, and they
rested on the fifteenth [1]day and made it
a day of feasting and rejoicing.
19 Therefore the Jews of the rural
areas, who live in [a]the rural towns, make
the fourteenth day of the month Adar *a*
[1b]holiday for rejoicing and feasting and
[c]sending portions *of food* to one another.

The Feast of Purim Instituted

20 Then Mordecai recorded these
events, and he sent letters to all the Jews
who were in all the provinces of King
Ahasuerus, both near and far,
21 obliging them to celebrate the fourteenth day of the month Adar, and the
fifteenth day [1]of the same month, annually,
22 because on those days the Jews [1]rid
themselves of their enemies, and *it was a*
month which was [a]turned for them from
sorrow into gladness and from mourning
into a [2]holiday; that they should make
them days of feasting and rejoicing and
[b]sending portions *of food* to one another
and gifts to the poor.
23 Thus the Jews undertook what they
had started to do, and what Mordecai
had written to them.
24 For Haman the son of Hammedatha, the Agagite, the adversary of all
the Jews, had schemed against the Jews
to destroy them, and [a]had cast Pur, that
is the lot, to disturb them and destroy
them.
25 But [a]when it came [1]to the king's
attention, he commanded by letter [b]that
his wicked scheme which he had [2]de-
vised against the Jews, [c]should return on
his own head, and that he and his sons
should be hanged on the [3]gallows.
26 Therefore they called these days
Purim after the name of Pur. [1]And
[a]because of the instructions in this letter,
both what they had seen in this regard
and what had happened to them,
27 the Jews established and [1]made a
custom for themselves, and for their
[2]descendants, and for [a]all those who
allied themselves with them, so that
[3]they should not fail [b]to celebrate these
two days according to their [4]regulation,
and according to their appointed time
annually.
28 So these days were to be remembered and celebrated throughout every
generation, every family, every province,
and every city; and these days of Purim

17 [1]Lit., *good day* [a]Esth 9:19 [b]Esth. 9:27

1 [1]Lit., *day in it* [2]Lit., *drew near* [a]Esth. 8:12 [b]Esth. 9:17 [c]Esth. 3:13

2 [a]Esth. 8:11; 9:15-18 [b]Esth. 8:17

3 [1]Lit., *lifted up* [a]Ezra 8:36

4 [a]2 Sam. 3:1; 1 Chr. 11:9

5 [1]Lit., *the stroke of* [a]Esth. 3:13

10 [a]Esth. 5:11 [b]Esth. 8:11

11 [1]Lit., *came*

12 [a]Esth. 5:6; 7:2

13 [a]Esth. 8:11; 9:15

15 [a]Esth. 9:12 [b]Esth. 9:10

16 [1]Lit., *have rest from* [a]Esth. 9:2 [b]Lev. 26:7, 8; Esth. 8:11

17 [1]Lit., *in it* [a]Esth. 9:1 [b]Esth. 9:21

18 [1]Lit., *in it* [a]Esth. 8:11; 9:2 [b]Esth. 9:21

19 [1]Lit., *rejoicing and feasting and a good day and sending* [a]Deut. 3:5; Zech. 2:4 [b]Esth. 9:22 [c]Neh. 8:10

21 [1]Lit., *in it*

22 [1]Lit., *had rest from* [2]Lit., *good day* [a]Ps. 30:11 [b]Neh. 8:12

24 [a]Esth. 3:7

25 [1]Lit., *before the king, he* [2]Lit., *schemed* [3]Lit., *tree* [a]Esth. 7:4-10 [b]Esth. 3:6-15 [c]Ps. 7:16

26 [1]Lit., *Therefore because of all the words* [a]Esth. 9:20

27 [1]Lit., *received* [2]Lit., *seed* [3]Lit., *it should not pass away* [4]Lit., *writing* [a]Esth. 8:17 [b]Esth. 9:20, 21

were not to [1]fail from among the Jews,
or their memory [2]fade from their [3]de-
scendants.
29 Then Queen Esther, [a]daughter of
Abihail, with Mordecai the Jew, wrote
with full authority to confirm [b]this
second letter about Purim.
30 And he sent letters to all the Jews,
[a]to the 127 provinces of the kingdom of
Ahasuerus, namely, words of peace and
truth,
31 to establish these days of Purim at
their appointed times, just as Mordecai
the Jew and Queen Esther had established for them, and just as they had
established for themselves and for their
[1]descendants with [2]instructions [a]for
their times of fasting and their lamentations.
32 And the command of Esther established these [1]customs for [a]Purim, and it
was written in the book.

Mordecai's Greatness

10 NOW King Ahasuerus laid a
tribute on the land and on the
[a]coastlands of the sea.
2 And all the [1]accomplishments of
his authority and strength, and the full
account of the greatness of Mordecai,
[a]to which the king [2]advanced him, are
they not written in [b]the Book of the
Chronicles of the Kings of Media and
Persia?
3 For Mordecai the Jew was [a]second
only to King Ahasuerus and great among
the Jews, and in favor with the multitude
of his kinsmen, [b]one who sought the
good of his people and one who spoke
for the welfare of his whole nation.

28 [1]Lit., *pass away* [2]Lit., *end* [3]Lit., *seed*
29 [a]Esth. 2:15 [b]Esth. 9:20, 21
30 [a]Esth. 1:1
31 [1]Lit., *seed* [2]Lit., *words* [a]Esth. 4:3
32 [1]Lit., *words* [a]Esth. 9:26
1 [a]Is. 11:11; 24:15
2 [1]Lit., *doings* [2]Lit., *made him great* [a]Esth. 8:15; 9:4 [b]Esth. 2:23
3 [a]Gen. 41:43, 44 [b]Neh. 2:10

THE BOOK OF JOB

Job's Character and Wealth

1 THERE was a man in the [a]land of
Uz, whose name was [b]Job, and that
man was [c]blameless, upright, [d]fearing
God, and [e]turning away from evil.
2 [a]And seven sons and three daughters were born to him.
3 [a]His possessions also were 7,000
sheep, 3,000 camels, 500 yoke of oxen,
500 female donkeys, and very many
servants; and that man was [b]the greatest
of all the [1]men of the east.
4 And his sons used to go and hold a
feast in the house of each one on his day,
and they would send and invite their
three sisters to eat and drink with them.
5 And it came about, when the days
of feasting had completed their cycle,
that Job would send and consecrate
them, rising up early in the morning and
offering [a]burnt offerings *according to* the
number of them all; for Job said, "[b]Per-
haps my sons have sinned and [c]cursed
God in their hearts." Thus Job did
continually.
6 [a]Now there was a day when the
[b]sons of God came to present themselves
before the LORD, and [1]Satan also came
among them.
7 And the LORD said to Satan,
"From where do you come?" Then Satan
answered the LORD and said, "[a]From
roaming about on the earth and walking
around on it."
8 And the LORD said to Satan,
"Have you [1]considered [a]My servant
Job? For there is no one like him on the
earth, [b]a blameless and upright man,
[2]fearing God and turning away from
evil."
9 Then [a]Satan answered the [1]LORD,
"Does Job fear God for nothing?
10 "[a]Hast Thou not made a hedge
about him and his house and all that he
has, on every side? [b]Thou hast blessed
the work of his hands, and his [c]posses-
sions have increased in the land.
11 "[a]But put forth Thy hand now and
[b]touch all that he has; he will surely
curse Thee to Thy face."
12 Then the LORD said to Satan, "Behold, all that he has is in your [1]power,
only do not put forth your hand on
him." So Satan departed from the presence of the LORD.

Satan Allowed to Test Job

13 Now it happened on the day when
his sons and his daughters were eating
and drinking wine in their oldest brother's house,
14 that a messenger came to Job and
said, "The oxen were plowing and the
[1]donkeys feeding beside them,
15 and [1]the [a]Sabeans [2]attacked and
took them. They also [3]slew the servants
with the edge of the sword, and [4]I alone
have escaped to tell you."
16 While he was still speaking, another also came and said, "[a]The fire of
God fell from heaven and burned up the
sheep and the servants and consumed
them, and I alone have escaped to tell
you."
17 While he was still speaking, another also came and said, "The [a]Chalde-
ans formed three bands and made a raid
on the camels and took them and [1]slew
the servants with the edge of the sword;
and I alone have escaped to tell you."
18 While he was still speaking, another also came and said, "Your sons
and your daughters were eating and
drinking wine in their oldest brother's
house,
19 and behold, a great wind came
from across the wilderness and struck
the four corners of the house, and it fell

1 [a]Jer. 25:20; Lam. 4:21 [b]Ezek. 14:14, 20; James 5:11 [c]Gen. 6:9; 17:1; Deut. 18:13 [d]Gen. 22:12; 42:18; Ex. 18:21; Prov. 8:13 [e]Job 28:28
2 [a]Job 42:13
3 [1]Lit., *sons* [a]Job 42:12 [b]Job 29:25
5 [a]Gen. 8:20; Job 42:8 [b]Job 8:4 [c]1 Kin. 21:10, 13
6 [1]I.e., the adversary, and so throughout chs. 1 and 2 [a]Job 2:1 [b]Job 38:7
7 [a]1 Pet. 5:8
8 [1]Lit., *set your heart to* [2]Or, *revering* [a]Num. 12:7; Josh. 1:2, 7; Job 42:7, 8 [b]Job 1:1
9 [1]Lit., *LORD and said* [a]Rev. 12:9f.
10 [a]Job 29:2-6; Ps. 34:7 [b]Job 31:25 [c]Job 1:3; 31:25
11 [a]Job 2:5 [b]Job 19:21
12 [1]Lit., *hand*
14 [1]Lit., *female donkeys*
15 [1]Lit., *Sheba* [2]Lit., *fell upon* [3]Lit., *smote* [4]Lit., *only I alone*, and so also vv. 16, 17, 19 [a]Gen. 10:7; Job 6:19
16 [a]Gen. 19:24; Lev. 10:2; Num. 11:1-3
17 [1]Lit., *smote* [a]Gen. 11:28, 31

on the young people and they died; and
I alone have escaped to tell you."
20 Then Job arose and [a]tore his robe
and shaved his head, and he fell to the
ground and worshiped.
21 And he said,
"[a]Naked I came from my mother's
womb,
And naked I shall return there.
The [b]LORD gave and the LORD
has taken away.
Blessed be the name of the
LORD."
22 [a]Through all this Job did not sin
nor did he [1]blame God.

Job Loses His Health

2 [a]AGAIN there was a day when the
sons of God came to present themselves before the LORD, and Satan also
came among them to present himself
before the LORD.
2 And the LORD said to Satan,
"Where have you come from?" Then
Satan answered the LORD and said,
"From roaming about on the earth, and
walking around on it."
3 And the LORD said to Satan,
"Have you [1]considered My servant Job?
For there is no one like him on the earth,
a blameless and upright man [2]fearing
God and turning away from evil. And he
still [a]holds fast his integrity, although
you incited Me against him, to [3]ruin him
without cause."
4 And Satan answered the LORD and
said, "Skin for skin! Yes, all that a man
has he will give for his life.
5 "[a]However, put forth Thy hand,
now, and [b]touch his bone and his flesh;
he will curse Thee to Thy face."
6 So the LORD said to Satan, "Behold, he is in your [1]power, only spare his
life."
7 Then Satan went out from the
presence of the LORD, and smote Job
with [a]sore boils from the sole of his foot
to the crown of his head.
8 And he took a potsherd to scrape
himself while [a]he was sitting among the
ashes.
9 Then his wife said to him, "Do you
still hold fast your integrity? Curse God
and die!"
10 But he said to her, "You speak as
one of the foolish women speaks. [a]Shall
we indeed accept good from God and
not accept adversity?" [b]In all this Job
did not sin with his lips.
11 Now when Job's three friends
heard of all this adversity that had come
upon him, they came each one from his
own place, Eliphaz the [a]Temanite, Bildad the [b]Shuhite, and Zophar the Naamathite; and they made an appointment
together to come to [c]sympathize with
him and comfort him.
12 And when they lifted up their eyes
at a distance, and did not recognize him,
they raised their voices and wept. And
each of them [a]tore his robe, and they
[b]threw dust over their heads toward the
sky.
13 [a]Then they sat down on the ground
with him for seven days and seven nights
with no one speaking a word to him, for
they saw that *his* pain was very great.

Job's Lament

3 AFTERWARD Job opened his
mouth and cursed [1]the day of his
birth.
2 And Job [1]said,
3 "[a]Let the day perish on which I was
to be born,
And the night *which* said, 'A [1]boy is
conceived.'
4 "May that day be darkness;
Let not God above care for it,
Nor light shine on it.
5 "Let [a]darkness and black gloom
claim it;
Let a cloud settle on it;
Let the blackness of the day terrify
it.
6 "*As for* that night, let darkness seize
it;
Let it not rejoice among the days of
the year;
Let it not come into the number of
the months.
7 "Behold, let that night be barren;
Let no joyful shout enter it.
8 "Let those curse it who curse the
day,
Who are [1]prepared to [a]rouse Levia-
than.
9 "Let the stars of its twilight be
darkened;
Let it wait for light but have none,
Neither let it see the [1]breaking
dawn;
10 Because it did not shut the opening
of my *mother's* womb,
Or hide trouble from my eyes.

11 "[a]Why did I not die [1]at birth,
Come forth from the womb and
expire?
12 "Why did the knees receive me,
And why the breasts, that I should
suck?
13 "For now I [a]would have lain down
and been quiet;
I would have slept then, I would
have been at rest,
14 With [a]kings and *with* [b]counselors
of the earth,
Who rebuilt [c]ruins for themselves;
15 Or with [a]princes [b]who had gold,
Who were filling their houses *with*
silver.
16 "Or like a miscarriage which is
[1]discarded, I would not be,
As infants that never saw light.
17 "There the wicked cease from raging,
And there the [1]weary are at [a]rest.
18 "The prisoners are at ease together;
They do not hear the voice of the
taskmaster.
19 "The small and the great are there,
And the slave is free from his
master.

20 [a]Gen. 37:29, 34; Josh. 7:6
21 [a]Eccl. 5:15 [b]1 Sam. 2:7, 8; Job 2:10
22 [1]Lit., *ascribe unseemliness to* [a]Job 2:10
1 [a]Job 1:6-8
3 [1]Lit., *set your heart to* [2]Or, *revering* [3]Lit., *swallow him up* [a]Job 27:5, 6
5 [a]Job 1:11 [b]Job 19:20
6 [1]Lit., *hand*
7 [a]Deut. 28:35; Job 7:5; 13:28; 30:17, 18, 30
8 [a]Job 42:6; Jer. 6:26; Ezek. 27:30; Jon. 3:6
10 [a]Job 1:21 [b]Job 1:22; Ps. 39:1; James 1:12
11 [a]Gen. 36:11; Job 6:19; Jer. 49:7 [b]Gen. 25:2 [c]Job 42:11; Rom. 12:15
12 [a]Job 1:20 [b]Josh. 7:6; Neh. 9:1; Lam. 2:10; Ezek. 27:30
13 [a]Gen. 50:10; Ezek. 3:15
1 [1]Lit., *his day*
2 [1]Lit., *answered and said*
3 [1]Lit., *man-child* [a]Jer. 20:14-18
5 [a]Jer. 13:16
8 [1]Or, *skillful* [a]Job 41:1, 25
9 [1]Lit., *eyelids*
11 [1]Lit., *from the womb* [a]Job 10:18, 19
13 [a]Job 3:13-19; 7:8-10, 21; 10:21, 22; 14:10-15, 20-22; 16:22; 17:13-16; 19:25-27; 21:13, 23-26; 24:19, 20; 26:5, 6; 34:22
14 [a]Job 12:18 [b]Job 12:17 [c]Job 15:28; Is. 58:12
15 [a]Job 12:21 [b]Job 27:16, 17
16 [1]Lit., *hidden*
17 [1]Lit., *weary of strength* [a]Job 17:16

20 "Why is [a]light given to him who suffers,
And life to the bitter of soul;
21 Who [1a]long for death, but there is none,
And dig for it more than for [b]hidden treasures;
22 Who rejoice greatly,
They exult when they find the grave?
23 "*Why is light given* to a man [a]whose way is hidden,
And whom [b]God has hedged in?
24 "For [a]my groaning comes at the sight of my food,
And [b]my cries pour out like water.
25 "For [1a]what I fear comes upon me,
And what I dread befalls me.
26 "I [a]am not at ease, nor am I quiet,
And I am not at rest, but turmoil comes."

Eliphaz: Innocent Do Not Suffer

4 THEN Eliphaz the Temanite [1]answered,
2 "If one ventures a word with you, will you become impatient?
But [a]who can refrain [1]from speaking?
3 "Behold [a]you have admonished many,
And you have strengthened weak hands.
4 "Your words have [1]helped the tottering to stand,
And you have strengthened [2]feeble knees.
5 "But now it has come to you, and you [a]are impatient;
It [b]touches you, and you are dismayed.
6 "Is not your [1a]fear *of God* [b]your confidence,
And the integrity of your ways your hope?

7 "Remember now, [a]who *ever* perished being innocent?
Or where were the upright destroyed?
8 "According to what I have seen, [a]those who plow iniquity
And those who sow trouble harvest it.
9 "By [a]the breath of God they perish,
And [b]by the [1]blast of His anger they come to an end.
10 "The [a]roaring of the lion and the voice of the *fierce* lion,
And the teeth of the young lions are broken.
11 "The [a]lion perishes for lack of prey,
And the [b]whelps of the lioness are scattered.

12 "Now a word [a]was brought to me stealthily,
And my ear received a [b]whisper of it.
13 "Amid disquieting [a]thoughts from the visions of the night,
When deep sleep falls on men,
14 Dread came upon me, and trembling,
And made [1]all my bones shake.
15 "Then a [1]spirit passed by my face;
The hair of my flesh bristled up.
16 "It stood still, but I could not discern its appearance;
A form *was* before my eyes;
There was silence, then I heard a voice:
17 'Can [a]mankind be just [1]before God?
Can a man be pure [1]before his [b]Maker?
18 '[a]He puts no trust even in His servants;
And against His angels He charges error.
19 'How much more those who dwell in [a]houses of clay,
Whose [b]foundation is in the dust,
Who are crushed before the moth!
20 '[a]Between morning and evening they are broken in pieces;
Unobserved, they [b]perish forever.
21 'Is not their [a]tent-cord plucked up within them?
They die, yet [b]without wisdom.'

God Is Just

5 "CALL now, is there anyone who will answer you?
And to which of the [a]holy ones will you turn?
2 "For [a]vexation slays the foolish man,
And anger kills the simple.
3 "I have seen the [a]foolish taking root,
And I [b]cursed his abode immediately.
4 "His [a]sons are far from safety,
They are even [1]oppressed in the gate,
Neither is there a deliverer.
5 "[1]His harvest the hungry devour,
And take it to a *place of* thorns;
And the [2a]schemer is eager for their wealth.
6 "For [a]affliction does not come from the dust,
Neither does trouble sprout from the ground,
7 For [a]man is born for trouble,
As sparks fly upward.

8 "But as for me, I would [a]seek God,
And I would place my cause before God;
9 Who [a]does great and unsearchable things,
[1]Wonders without number.
10 "He [a]gives rain on the earth,
And sends water on the fields,
11 So that [a]He sets on high those who are lowly,
And those who mourn are lifted to safety.
12 "He [a]frustrates the plotting of the shrewd,
So that their hands cannot attain success.
13 "He [a]captures the wise by their own shrewdness

---

20 aJer. 20:18
21 1Lit., *wait* aRev. 9:6 bProv. 2:4
23 aJob 19:6, 8, 12 bJob 19:8; Ps. 88:8; Lam. 3:7
24 aJob 6:7; 33:20 bJob 30:16; Ps. 42:4
25 1Lit., *the fear I fear and* aJob 9:28; 30:15
26 aJob 7:13, 14

1 1Lit., *answered and said*
2 1Lit., *in words* aJob 32:18-20
3 aJob 4:3, 4; 29:15, 16, 21, 25
4 1Lit., *caused* 2Lit., *bowing*
5 aJob 6:14 bJob 19:21
6 1Or, *reverence* aJob 1:1 bProv. 3:26
7 aJob 8:20; 36:6, 7; Ps. 37:25
8 aJob 15:31, 35; Prov. 22:8; Hos. 10:13; Gal. 6:7
9 1Lit., *wind* aJob 15:30; Is. 11:4; 30:33; 2 Thess. 2:8 bJob 40:11-13
10 aJob 5:15; Ps. 58:6
11 aJob 29:17; Ps. 34:10 bJob 5:4; 20:10; 27:14
12 aJob 4:12-17; 33:15-18 bJob 26:14
13 aJob 33:15
14 1Lit., *the multitude of*
15 1Or, *breath passed over*
17 1Lit., *from* aJob 9:2; 25:4 bJob 31:15; 32:22; 35:10; 36:3
18 aJob 15:15
19 aJob 10:9; 33:6 bGen. 2:7; 3:19; Job 22:16
20 aJob 14:2 bJob 14:20; 20:7
21 aJob 8:22 bJob 18:21; 36:12

1 aJob 15:15
2 aProv. 12:16; 27:3
3 aJer. 12:2 bJob 24:18; 31:30
4 1Lit., *crushed* aJob 4:11
5 1Lit., *Whose* 2Ancient versions read *thirsty* aJob 18:8-10; 22:10
6 aJob 15:35
7 aJob 14:1
8 aJob 13:2, 3; Ps. 50:15
9 1Or, *Miracles* aJob 9:10; 37:14, 16; 42:3
10 aJob 36:27-29; 37:6-11; 38:26
11 aJob 22:29; 36:7
12 aPs. 33:10
13 aJob 37:24; 1 Cor. 3:19

And the advice of the cunning is quickly thwarted.
14"By day they [a]meet with darkness,
And grope at noon as in the night.
15"But He saves from [a]the sword of their mouth,
And [b]the poor from the hand of the mighty.
16"So the helpless has hope,
And [a]unrighteousness must shut its mouth.

17"Behold, how [a]happy is the man whom God reproves,
So do not despise the [b]discipline of [1]the Almighty.
18"For [a]He inflicts pain, and [1]gives relief;
He wounds, and His hands *also* heal.
19"[1]From six troubles [a]He will deliver you,
Even in seven [b]evil will not touch you.
20"In [a]famine He will redeem you from death,
And [b]in war from the power of the sword.
21"You will be [a]hidden from the scourge of the tongue,
[b]Neither will you be afraid of violence when it comes.
22"You will [a]laugh at violence and famine,
[b]Neither will you be afraid of [1]wild beasts.
23"For you will be in league with the stones of the field;
And [a]the beasts of the field will be at peace with you.
24"And you will know that your [a]tent is secure,
For you will visit your abode and fear no loss.
25"You will know also that your [1a]descendants will be many,
And [b]your offspring as the grass of the earth.
26"You will [a]come to the grave in full vigor,
Like the stacking of grain in its season.
27"Behold this, we have investigated it, thus it is;
Hear it, and know for yourself."

Job's Friends Are No Help

6 THEN Job [1]answered,
2"[a]Oh that my vexation were actually weighed,
And laid in the balances together with my iniquity!
3"For then it would be [a]heavier than the sand of the seas,
Therefore my words have been rash.
4"For the [a]arrows of the Almighty are within me;
[1]Their [b]poison my spirit drinks;
The [c]terrors of God are arrayed against me.
5"Does the [a]wild donkey bray over *his* grass,
Or does the ox low over his fodder?
6"Can something tasteless be eaten without salt,
Or is there any taste in the [1]white of an egg?
7"My soul [a]refuses to touch *them;*
They are like loathsome food to me.

8"Oh that my request might come to pass,
And that God would grant my longing!
9"Would that God were [a]willing to crush me;
That He would loose His hand and cut me off!
10"But it is still my consolation,
And I rejoice in unsparing pain,
That I [a]have not [1]denied the words of the Holy One.
11"What is my strength, that I should wait?
And what is my end, that I should [1a]endure?
12"Is my strength the strength of stones,
Or is my flesh bronze?
13"Is it that my [a]help is not within me,
And that [1b]deliverance is driven from me?

14"For the [a]despairing man *there should be* kindness from his friend;
Lest he [b]forsake the [1]fear of the Almighty.
15"My brothers have acted [a]deceitfully like a [1]wadi,
Like the torrents of [1]wadis which vanish,
16 Which are turbid because of ice,
And into which the snow [1]melts.
17"When [a]they become waterless, they [1]are silent,
When it is hot, they vanish from their place.
18"The [1]paths of their course wind along,
They go up into nothing and perish.
19"The caravans of [a]Tema looked,
The travelers of [b]Sheba hoped for them.
20"They [a]were [1]disappointed for they had trusted,
They came there and were confounded.
21"Indeed, you have now become such,
[a]You see a terror and are afraid.
22"Have I said, 'Give me *something,*'
Or, 'Offer a bribe for me from your wealth,'
23 Or, 'Deliver me from the hand of the adversary,'
Or, 'Redeem me from the hand of the tyrants'?

24"Teach me, and [a]I will be silent;
And show me how I have erred.

---

14 [a]Job 12:25; 15:30; 18:18; 20:26; 24:13
15 [a]Job 4:10, 11; Ps. 35:10 [b]Job 29:17; 34:28; 36:6, 15; 38:15
16 [a]Ps. 107:42
17 [1]Heb., *Shaddai,* and so throughout ch. 6 [a]Ps. 94:12 [b]Job 36:15, 16; Prov. 3:11; Heb. 12:5-11; James 1:12
18 [1]Lit., *binds* [a]Deut. 32:39; 1 Sam. 2:6; Is. 30:26; Hos. 6:1
19 [1]Lit., *In* [a]Ps. 34:19 [b]Ps. 91:10
20 [a]Ps. 33:19; 37:19 [b]Ps. 144:10
21 [a]Job 5:15; Ps. 31:20 [b]Ps. 91:5, 6
22 [1]Lit., *beasts of the earth* [a]Job 8:21 [b]Ps. 91:13; Ezek. 34:25; Hos. 2:18
23 [a]Is. 11:6-9; 65:25
24 [a]Job 8:6
25 [1]Lit., *seed* [a]Ps. 112:2 [b]Is. 44:3, 4; 48:19
26 [a]Job 42:17

1 [1]Lit., *answered and said*
2 [a]Job 31:6
3 [a]Job 23:2
4 [1]Lit., *Whose* [a]Job 16:13; Ps. 38:2 [b]Job 20:16; 21:20 [c]Job 30:15
5 [a]Job 39:5-8
6 [1]Heb., *hallamuth,* meaning uncertain. Perhaps the juice of a plant.
7 [a]Job 3:24; 33:20
9 [a]Num. 11:15; 1 Kin. 19:4; Job 7:16; 9:21; 10:1
10 [1]Lit., *hidden* [a]Job 22:22; 23:11, 12
11 [1]Lit., *prolong my soul* [a]Job 21:4
13 [1]So ancient versions [a]Job 26:2 [b]Job 26:3
14 [1]Or, *reverence* [a]Job 4:5 [b]Job 1:5; 15:4
15 [1]Or, *brooks* [a]Jer. 15:18
16 [1]Lit., *hides itself*
17 [1]Or, *cease* [a]Job 24:19
18 [1]Or, *caravans turn from their course, they go up into the waste and perish.*
19 [a]Gen. 25:15; Is. 21:14; Jer. 25:23 [b]Job 1:15
20 [1]Lit., *ashamed* [a]Jer. 14:3
21 [a]Ps. 38:11
24 [a]Ps. 39:1

25"How painful are honest words!
But what does your argument prove?
26"Do you intend to reprove *my* words,
When the [a]words of one in despair belong to the wind?
27"You would even [a]cast *lots* for [b]the orphans,
And [c]barter over your friend.
28"And now please look at me,
And *see* if I [a]lie to your face.
29"Desist now, let there be no injustice;
Even desist, [a]my righteousness is yet in it.
30"Is there injustice on my tongue?
Cannot [a]my palate discern [1]calamities?

Job's Life Seems Futile

7 "[1]IS not man [a]forced to labor on earth,
And *are not* his days like the days of [b]a hired man?
2"As a slave who pants for the shade,
And as a hired man who eagerly waits for his wages,
3 So am I allotted months of vanity,
And [a]nights of trouble are appointed me.
4"When I [a]lie down I say,
'When shall I arise?'
But the night continues,
And I am [1]continually tossing until dawn.
5"My [a]flesh is clothed with worms and a crust of dirt;
My skin hardens and runs.
6"My days are [a]swifter than a weaver's shuttle,
And come to an end [b]without hope.

7"Remember that my life [a]is *but* breath,
My eye will [b]not again see good.
8"The [a]eye of him who sees me will behold me no more;
Thine eyes *will be* on me, but [b]I will not be.
9"When a [a]cloud vanishes, it is gone,
So [b]he who goes down to [c]Sheol does not come up.
10"He will not return again to his house,
Nor will [a]his place know him anymore.

11"Therefore, [a]I will not restrain my mouth;
I will speak in the anguish of my spirit,
I will complain in the bitterness of my soul.
12"Am I the sea, or [a]the sea monster,
That Thou dost set a guard over me?
13"If I say, '[a]My bed will comfort me,
My couch will [1]ease my complaint,'
14 Then Thou dost frighten me with dreams
And terrify me by visions;
15 So that my soul would choose suffocation,
Death rather than my [1]pains.
16"I [1][a]waste away; I will not live forever.
Leave me alone, [b]for my days are *but* a breath.
17"[a]What is man that Thou dost magnify him,
And that Thou [1]art concerned about him,
18 That [a]Thou dost examine him every morning,
And try him every moment?
19"[1][a]Wilt Thou never turn Thy gaze away from me,
Nor let me alone until I swallow my spittle?
20"[a]Have I sinned? What have I done to Thee,
O [b]watcher of men?
Why hast Thou set me as Thy target,
So that I am a burden to myself?
21"Why then [a]dost Thou not pardon my transgression
And take away my iniquity?
For now I will [b]lie down in the dust;
And Thou wilt seek me, [c]but I will not be."

Bildad Says God Rewards the Good

8 THEN Bildad the Shuhite [1]answered,
2"How long will you say these *things,*
And the [a]words of your mouth be a mighty wind?
3"Does [a]God pervert justice
Or does [1]the Almighty pervert what is right?
4"[a]If your sons sinned against Him,
Then He delivered them into the [1]power of their transgression.
5"If you would [a]seek God
And implore the compassion of [1]the Almighty,
6 If you are pure and upright,
Surely now [a]He would rouse Himself for you
And restore your righteous [1]estate.
7"Though your beginning was insignificant,
Yet your [a]end will increase greatly.

8"Please [a]inquire of past generations,
And consider the things searched out by their fathers.
9"For we are *only* of yesterday and know nothing,
Because [a]our days on earth are as a shadow.
10"Will they not teach you *and* tell you,
And bring forth words from their minds?

11"Can the papyrus grow up without marsh?
Can the rushes grow without water?

26 [a]Job 8:2; 15:2; 16:3
27 [a]Joel 3:3; Nah. 3:10 [b]Job 22:9; 24:3, 9 [c]2 Pet. 2:3
28 [a]Job 27:4; 33:3; 36:4
29 [a]Job 13:18; 19:6; 23:10; 27:5, 6; 34:5; 42:1-6
30 [1]Or, *words* [a]Job 12:11

1 [1]Lit., *Has not man compulsory labor* [a]Job 5:7; 10:17; 14:1, 14 [b]Job 14:6
3 [a]Job 16:7
4 [1]Lit., *sated with* [a]Deut. 28:67; Job 7:13, 14
5 [a]Job 2:7; 17:14
6 [a]Job 9:25 [b]Job 13:15; 14:19; 17:15, 16; 19:10
7 [a]Job 7:16; Ps. 78:39; James 4:14 [b]Job 9:25
8 [a]Job 8:18; 20:9 [b]Job 7:21
9 [a]Job 30:15 [b]Job 3:13-19 [c]2 Sam. 12:23; Job 11:8; 14:13; 17:13, 16
10 [a]Job 8:18; 20:9; 27:21, 23
11 [a]Job 10:1; 21:4; 23:2; Ps. 40:9
12 [a]Ezek. 32:2, 3
13 [1]Lit., *bear* [a]Job 7:4; Ps. 6:6
15 [1]Lit., *bones*
16 [1]Or, *loathe* [a]Job 6:9; 9:21; 10:1 [b]Job 7:7
17 [1]Lit., *shouldst set Thy heart on* [a]Job 22:2; Ps. 8:4; 144:3; Heb. 2:6
18 [a]Job 14:3
19 [1]Lit., *How long wilt Thou not* [a]Job 9:18; 10:20; 14:6
20 [a]Job 35:3, 6 [b]Ps. 36:6
21 [a]Job 9:28; 10:14 [b]Job 10:9 [c]Job 7:8

1 [1]Lit., *answered and said*
2 [a]Job 6:26
3 [1]Heb., *Shaddai* [a]Gen. 18:25; Deut. 32:4; 2 Chr. 19:7; Job 34:10, 12; 36:23; 37:23; Rom. 3:5
4 [1]Lit., *hand* [a]Job 1:5, 18, 19
5 [1]Heb., *Shaddai* [a]Job 5:17-27
6 [1]Lit., *place* [a]Job 22:27; 34:28; Ps. 7:6 [b]Job 5:24
7 [a]Job 42:12
8 [a]Deut. 4:32; 32:7; Job 15:18; 20:4
9 [a]Job 14:2

12 "While it is still green *and* not cut down,
Yet it withers before any *other* [1]plant.
13 "So are the paths of [a]all who forget God,
And the [b]hope of the godless will perish,
14 Whose confidence is fragile,
And whose trust a [a]spider's [1]web.
15 "He [1]trusts in his [a]house, but it does not stand;
He holds fast to it, but it does not endure.
16 "He [1a]thrives before the sun,
And his [b]shoots spread out over his garden.
17 "His roots wrap around a rock pile,
He [1]grasps a house of stones.
18 "If he is [1]removed from [a]his place,
Then it will deny him, *saying,* '[b]I never saw you.'
19 "Behold, [a]this is the joy of His way;
And out of the dust others will spring.
20 "Lo, [a]God will not reject *a man of* integrity,
Nor [b]will He [1]support the evildoers.
21 "He will yet fill [a]your mouth with laughter,
And your lips with shouting.
22 "Those who hate you will be [a]clothed with shame;
And the [b]tent of the wicked will be no more."

Job Says There Is No Arbitrator between God and Man

9 THEN Job [1]answered,
2 "In truth I know that this is so,
But how can a [a]man be in the right [1]before God?
3 "If one wished to [a]dispute with Him,
He could not answer Him once in a thousand *times.*
4 "[a]Wise in heart and [b]mighty in strength,
Who has [1c]defied Him [2]without harm?
5 "[a]*It is God* who removes the mountains, they know not *how,*
When He overturns them in His anger;
6 Who [a]shakes the earth out of its place,
And its [b]pillars tremble;
7 Who commands the [a]sun [1]not to shine,
And sets a seal upon the stars;
8 Who alone [a]stretches out the heavens,
And [1b]tramples down the waves of the sea;
9 Who makes the [a]Bear, Orion, and the Pleiades,
And the [b]chambers of the south;
10 Who [a]does great things, [1]unfathomable,
And wondrous works without number.
11 "Were He to pass by me, [a]I would not see Him;
Were He to move past *me,* I would not perceive Him.
12 "Were He to snatch away, who could [a]restrain Him?
Who could say to Him, '[b]What art Thou doing?'

13 "God will not turn back His anger;
Beneath Him crouch the helpers of [a]Rahab.
14 "How then can [a]I [1]answer Him,
And choose my words [2]before Him?
15 "For [a]though I were right, I could not [1]answer;
I would have to [b]implore the mercy of my judge.
16 "If I called and He answered me,
I could not believe that He was listening to my voice.
17 "For He [a]bruises me with a tempest,
And multiplies my wounds without cause.
18 "He will [a]not allow me to get my breath,
But saturates me with [b]bitterness.
19 "If *it is a matter* of power, [a]behold, *He is* the strong one!
And if *it is a matter* of justice, who can summon [1]Him?
20 "[a]Though I am righteous, my mouth will [b]condemn me;
Though I am guiltless, He will declare me guilty.
21 "I am [a]guiltless;
I do not take notice of myself;
I [b]despise my life.
22 "It is *all* one; therefore I say,
'He [a]destroys the guiltless and the wicked.'
23 "If the scourge kills suddenly,
He [a]mocks the despair of the innocent.
24 "The earth [a]is given into the hand of the wicked;
He [b]covers the faces of its judges.
If *it is* not *He,* then who is it?

25 "Now [a]my days are swifter than a runner;
They flee away, [b]they see no good.
26 "They slip by like [a]reed boats,
Like an [b]eagle that swoops on [1]its prey.
27 "Though I say, 'I will forget [a]my complaint,
I will leave off my *sad* countenance and be cheerful,'
28 I am [a]afraid of all my pains,
I know that [b]Thou wilt not acquit me.
29 "I am accounted [a]wicked,
Why then should I toil in vain?
30 "If I should [a]wash myself with snow
And cleanse [b]my hands with lye,
31 Yet Thou wouldst plunge me into the pit,
And my own clothes would abhor me.

12 [1]Lit., *reed*
13 [a]Ps. 9:17 [b]Job 11:20; 13:16; 15:34; 20:5; 27:8
14 [1]Lit., *house* [a]Is. 59:5, 6
15 [1]Lit., *leans on* [a]Job 8:22; 27:18; Ps. 49:11
16 [1]Lit., *is lush* [a]Ps. 37:35; Jer. 11:16 [b]Ps. 80:11
17 [1]Heb., *sees*
18 [1]Lit., *swallowed up* [a]Job 7:10 [b]Job 7:8
19 [a]Job 20:5
20 [1]Lit., *strengthen the hand of* [a]Job 4:7 [b]Job 21:30
21 [a]Job 5:22; Ps. 126:1, 2
22 [a]Ps. 132:18 [b]Job 8:15; 15:34; 18:14; 21:28

1 [1]Lit., *answered and said*
2 [1]Lit., *with* [a]Job 4:17; 25:4
3 [a]Job 10:2; 13:19; 23:6; 40:2
4 [1]Lit., *stiffened his neck against* [2]Lit., *and remained safe* [a]Job 11:6; 12:13; 28:23; 38:36, 37 [b]Job 9:19; 23:6 [c]2 Chr. 13:12; Prov. 29:1
5 [a]Job 9:5-10; 26:6-14; 41:11
6 [a]Is. 2:19, 21; 13:13; Hag. 2:6 [b]Ps. 75:3
7 [1]Lit., *and it does not shine* [a]Is. 13:10; Ezek. 32:7, 8
8 [1]Lit., *treads upon the heights of* [a]Gen. 1:1; Job 37:18; Ps. 104:2; Is. 40:22 [b]Job 38:16; Ps. 77:19
9 [a]Job 38:31, 32; Amos 5:8 [b]Job 37:9
10 [1]Lit., *until there is no searching out* [a]Job 5:9
11 [a]Job 23:8, 9; 35:14
12 [a]Job 10:7; 11:10 [b]Is. 45:9
13 [a]Job 26:12; Ps. 89:10; Is. 30:7; 51:9
14 [1]Or, *plead my case* [2]Lit., *with* [a]Job 9:3, 32
15 [1]Or, *plead my case* [a]Job 9:20, 21; 10:15 [b]Job 8:5
17 [a]Job 16:12, 14; 30:22
18 [a]Job 7:19; 10:20 [b]Job 13:26; 27:2
19 [1]So with Gr.; Heb., *me* [a]Job 9:4
20 [a]Job 9:15 [b]Job 9:29; 15:6
21 [a]Job 1:1; 12:4; 13:18 [b]Job 7:16
22 [a]Job 10:7, 8
23 [a]Job 24:12
24 [a]Job 10:3; 12:6; 16:11 [b]Job 12:17
25 [a]Job 7:6 [b]Job 7:7
26 [1]Lit., *food* [a]Is. 18:2 [b]Job 39:29; Hab. 1:8
27 [a]Job 7:11
28 [a]Job 3:25 [b]Job 7:21; 10:14
29 [a]Job 10:2; Ps. 37:33
30 [a]Jer. 2:22 [b]Job 31:7

32 "For [a]*He is* not a man as I am that [b]I may answer Him,
That we may go to [1]court together.
33 "There is no [a]umpire between us,
Who may lay his hand upon us both.
34 "Let Him [a]remove His rod from me,
And let not dread of Him terrify me.
35 "*Then* I [a]would speak and not fear Him;
But I am not like that in myself.

Job Despairs of God's Dealings

10 "[1a]I LOATHE my own life;
I will give full vent to [b]my complaint;
I will speak in the bitterness of my soul.
2 "I will say to God, '[a]Do not condemn me;
Let me know why Thou dost contend with me.
3 'Is it [1]right for Thee indeed to [a]oppress,
To reject [b]the labor of Thy hands,
And [2]to look favorably on [c]the schemes of the wicked?
4 'Hast Thou eyes of flesh?
Or dost Thou [a]see as a man sees?
5 'Are Thy days as the days of a mortal,
Or [a]Thy years as man's years,
6 That [a]Thou shouldst seek for my guilt,
And search after my sin?
7 'According to Thy knowledge [a]I am indeed not guilty;
Yet there is [b]no deliverance from Thy hand.

8 '[a]Thy hands fashioned and made me [1]altogether,
[b]And wouldst Thou destroy me?
9 'Remember now, that Thou hast made me as [a]clay;
And wouldst Thou [b]turn me into dust again?
10 'Didst Thou not pour me out like milk,
And curdle me like cheese;
11 Clothe me with skin and flesh,
And knit me together with bones and sinews?
12 'Thou hast [a]granted me life and lovingkindness;
And Thy care has preserved my spirit.
13 'Yet [a]these things Thou hast concealed in Thy heart;
I know that this is within Thee:
14 If I sin, then Thou wouldst [a]take note of me,
And [b]wouldst not acquit me of my guilt.
15 'If [a]I am wicked, woe to me!
And [b]if I am righteous, I dare not lift up my head.
I am sated with disgrace and [1]conscious of my misery.
16 'And should *my head* be lifted up,
[a]Thou wouldst hunt me like a lion;
And again Thou wouldst show Thy [b]power against me.
17 'Thou dost renew [a]Thy witnesses against me,
And increase Thine anger toward me,
[1b]Hardship after hardship is with me.

18 '[a]Why then hast Thou brought me out of the womb?
Would that I had died and no eye had seen me!
19 'I should have been as though I had not been,
Carried from womb to tomb.'
20 "Would He not let [a]my few days alone?
[1b]Withdraw from me that I may have a little cheer
21 Before I go—[a]and I shall not return—
[b]To the land of darkness and [c]deep shadow;
22 The land of utter gloom as darkness *itself,*
Of deep shadow without order,
And which shines as the darkness."

Zophar Rebukes Job

11 THEN Zophar the Naamathite [1]answered,
2 "Shall a multitude of words go unanswered,
And a [a]talkative man be acquitted?
3 "Shall your boasts silence men?
And shall you [a]scoff and none rebuke?
4 "For [a]you have said, 'My teaching is pure,
And [b]I am innocent in your eyes.'
5 "But would that God might speak,
And open His lips against you,
6 And show you the secrets of wisdom!
For sound wisdom [1a]has two sides.
Know then that God [2]forgets a part of [b]your iniquity.

7 "[a]Can you discover the depths of God?
Can you discover the limits of the Almighty?
8 "*They are* [a]high as [1]the heavens, what can you do?
Deeper than [2b]Sheol, what can you know?
9 "Its measure is longer than the earth,
And broader than the sea.
10 "If He passes by or shuts up,
Or calls an assembly, [a]who can restrain Him?
11 "For [a]He knows false men,
And He [b]sees iniquity [1]without investigating.
12 "And [1a]an idiot will become intelligent
When the [2]foal of a [b]wild donkey is born a man.

32 [1]Lit., *judgment* [a]Eccl. 6:10 [b]Job 9:3; Rom. 9:20
33 [a]1 Sam. 2:25; Job 9:19; Is. 1:18
34 [a]Job 13:21
35 [a]Job 13:22

1 [1]Lit., *My soul loathes* [a]Job 7:16 [b]Job 7:11
2 [a]Job 9:29
3 [1]Lit., *good* [2]Lit., *you shine forth* [a]Job 9:22-24; 16:11; 19:6; 27:2 [b]Job 10:8; 14:15; Ps. 138:8; Is. 64:8 [c]Job 21:16; 22:18
4 [a]1 Sam. 16:7; Job 28:24; 34:21
5 [a]Job 36:26
6 [a]Job 14:16
7 [a]Job 9:21; 13:18 [b]Job 9:12; 23:13; 27:22
8 [1]Lit., *together round about* [a]Job 10:3; Ps. 119:73 [b]Job 9:22
9 [a]Job 4:19; 33:6 [b]Job 7:21
12 [a]Job 33:4
13 [a]Job 23:13
14 [a]Job 7:20 [b]Job 7:21; 9:28
15 [1]Lit., *see* [a]Job 10:7; Is. 3:11 [b]Job 6:29
16 [a]Is. 38:13; Lam. 3:10; Hos. 13:7 [b]Job 5:9
17 [1]Lit., *Changes and warfare are with me* [a]Ruth 1:21; Job 16:8 [b]Job 7:1
18 [a]Job 3:11-13
20 [1]Lit., *Put* [a]Job 14:1 [b]Job 7:16, 19
21 [a]2 Sam. 12:23; Job 3:13-19; 16:22 [b]Ps. 88:12 [c]Job 10:22; 34:22; 38:17; Ps. 23:4

1 [1]Lit., *answered and said*
2 [a]Job 8:2; 15:2; 18:2
3 [a]Job 17:2; 21:3
4 [a]Job 6:10 [b]Job 10:7
6 [1]Lit., *is double* [2]Lit., *causes to be forgotten for you* [a]Job 9:4 [b]Job 15:5; 22:5
7 [a]Job 33:12, 13; 36:26; 37:5, 23; Rom. 11:33
8 [1]Lit., *the heights of heaven* [2]I.e., the nether world [a]Job 22:12; 35:5 [b]Job 26:6; 38:17
10 [a]Job 9:12
11 [1]Or, *even He does not consider* [a]Job 34:21-23 [b]Job 24:23; 28:24; 31:4
12 [1]Lit., *a hollow man* [2]Lit., *donkey* [a]Ps. 39:5, 11; 62:9; 144:4; Eccl. 1:2; 11:10 [b]Job 39:5

13 "[a]If you would [b]direct your heart right,
And [c]spread out your hand to Him;
14 If iniquity is in your hand, [a]put it far away,
And do not let wickedness dwell in your tents.
15 "Then, indeed, you could [a]lift up your face without *moral* defect,
And you would be steadfast and [b]not fear.
16 "For you would [a]forget *your* trouble,
As [b]waters that have passed by, you would remember *it.*
17 "And your [1]life would be [2a]brighter than noonday;
Darkness would be like the morning.
18 "Then you would trust, because there is hope;
And you would look around and rest securely.
19 "You would [a]lie down and none would disturb *you,*
And many would [b]entreat your [1]favor.
20 "But the [a]eyes of the wicked will fail,
And [1]there will [b]be no escape for them;
And their [c]hope is [2d]to breathe their last."

Job Chides His Accusers

12 THEN Job [1]responded,
2 "Truly then [a]you are the people,
And with you wisdom will die!
3 "But [a]I have intelligence as well as you;
I am not inferior to you.
And [1]who does not know such things as these?
4 "I am a [a]joke to [1]my friends.
The one who called on God, and He answered him;
The just *and* [b]blameless *man* is a joke.
5 "[1]He who is at ease holds calamity in contempt,
As prepared for those whose feet slip.
6 "The [a]tents of the destroyers prosper,
And those who provoke God [b]are secure,
[1]Whom God brings [c]into [2]their power.

7 "But now ask the beasts, and let them teach you;
And the birds of the heavens, and let them tell you.
8 "Or speak to the earth, and let it teach you;
And let the fish of the sea declare to you.
9 "Who among all these does not know
That [a]the hand of the LORD has done this,
10 [a]In whose hand is the life of every living thing,
And [b]the breath of all mankind?
11 "Does not [a]the ear test words,
As the palate [1]tastes its food?
12 "Wisdom is with [a]aged men,
With [1]long life is understanding.

Job Speaks of the Power of God

13 "With Him are [a]wisdom and [b]might;
To Him belong counsel and [c]understanding.
14 "Behold, He [a]tears down, and it cannot be rebuilt;
He [1b]imprisons a man, and [2]there can be no release.
15 "Behold, He [a]restrains the waters, and they dry up;
And He [b]sends them out, and they [1]inundate the earth.
16 "With Him are strength and sound wisdom,
The [a]misled and the misleader belong to Him.
17 "He makes [a]counselors walk [1]barefoot,
And makes fools of [b]judges.
18 "He [a]loosens the [1]bond of kings,
And binds their loins with a girdle.
19 "He makes priests walk [1]barefoot,
And overthrows [a]the secure ones.
20 "He deprives the trusted ones of speech,
And [a]takes away the discernment of the elders.
21 "He [a]pours contempt on nobles,
And [b]loosens the belt of the strong.
22 "He [a]reveals mysteries from the darkness,
And brings the deep darkness into light.
23 "He [a]makes the nations great, then destroys them;
He [1]enlarges the nations, then leads them away.
24 "He [a]deprives of intelligence the chiefs of the earth's people,
And makes them wander in a pathless waste.
25 "They [a]grope in darkness with no light,
And He makes them [b]stagger like a drunken man.

Job Says His Friends' Proverbs Are Ashes

13 "[a]BEHOLD, my eye has seen all *this,*
My ear has heard and understood it.
2 "[a]What you know I also know.
I am not inferior to you.

3 "But [a]I would speak to [1]the Almighty,
And I desire to [b]argue with God.
4 "But you [a]smear with lies;
You are all [b]worthless physicians.
5 "O that you would [a]be completely silent,

13 [a]Job 5:17-27; 11:13-20 [b]1 Sam. 7:3; Ps. 78:8 [c]Job 22:27; Ps. 88:9; 143:6
14 [a]Job 22:23
15 [a]Job 22:26 [b]Ps. 27:3; 46:2
16 [a]Is. 65:16 [b]Job 22:11
17 [1]Lit., *duration of life* [2]Lit., *above noonday* [a]Job 22:26
19 [1]Lit., *face* [a]Lev. 26:6; Is. 17:2; Mic. 4:4; Zeph. 3:13 [b]Is. 45:14
20 [1]Lit., *escape has perished from them* [2]Lit., *the expiring of the soul* [a]Deut. 28:65; Job 17:5 [b]Job 27:22; 34:22 [c]Job 8:13 [d]Job 6:9

1 [1]Lit., *answered and said*
2 [a]Job 17:10
3 [1]Lit., *with whom is there not like these?* [a]Job 13:2
4 [1]Lit., *his* [a]Job 17:6; 30:1, 9, 10; 34:7 [b]Job 6:29
5 [1]Lit., *Contempt for calamity is the thought of him who is at ease*
6 [1]Or, *He who brings God into his hand* [a]Job 9:24; 21:7-9 [b]Job 24:23 [c]Job 22:18
9 [a]Is. 41:20
10 [a]Acts 17:28 [b]Job 27:3; 33:4
11 [1]Lit., *tastes food for itself* [a]Job 34:3
12 [1]Lit., *length of days* [a]Job 15:10; 32:7
13 [a]Job 9:4 [b]Job 9:4 [c]Job 11:6; 26:12; 32:8; 36:5; 38:36
14 [1]Lit., *shuts against* [2]Lit., *it is not opened* [a]Job 19:10; Is. 25:2 [b]Job 37:7
15 [1]Lit., *overturn* [a]Deut. 11:17; 1 Kin. 8:35; 17:1 [b]Gen. 7:11-24
16 [a]Job 13:7, 9
17 [1]Or, *stripped* [a]Job 3:14 [b]Job 9:24
18 [1]Or, *discipline* [a]Ps. 116:16
19 [1]Or, *stripped* [a]Job 24:22; 34:24-28; 35:9
20 [a]Job 17:4; 32:9
21 [a]Job 34:19; Ps. 107:40 [b]Job 12:18
22 [a]Dan. 2:22; 1 Cor. 4:5
23 [1]Or, *spreads out* [a]Is. 9:3; 26:15
24 [a]Job 12:20
25 [a]Job 5:14 [b]Is. 24:20

1 [a]Job 12:9
2 [a]Job 12:3
3 [1]Heb., *Shaddai* [a]Job 13:22; 23:4 [b]Job 13:15
4 [a]Ps. 119:69 [b]Jer. 23:32
5 [a]Job 13:13; 21:5; Prov. 17:28

And that it would become your
wisdom!
6 "Please hear my argument,
And listen to the contentions of my
lips.
7 "Will you [a]speak what is unjust for
God,
And speak what is deceitful for
Him?
8 "Will you [a]show partiality for Him?
Will you contend for God?
9 "Will it be well when He examines
you?
Or [a]will you deceive Him as one
deceives a man?
10 "He will surely reprove you,
If you secretly [a]show partiality.
11 "Will not [a]His [1]majesty terrify you,
And the dread of Him fall on you?
12 "Your memorable sayings are proverbs of ashes,
Your defenses are defenses of clay.

Job Is Sure He Will Be Vindicated

13 "[a]Be silent before me so that I may
speak;
Then let come on me what may.
14 "Why should I take my flesh in my
teeth,
And [a]put my life in my [1]hands?
15 "[a]Though He slay me,
I will hope in Him.
Nevertheless I [b]will argue my ways
[1]before Him.
16 "This also will be my [a]salvation,
For [b]a godless man may not come
before His presence.
17 "Listen carefully to my speech,
And let my declaration *fill* your
ears.
18 "Behold now, I have [a]prepared my
case;
I know that [b]I will be vindicated.
19 "[a]Who will contend with me?
For then I would be silent and [b]die.

20 "Only two things do not do to me,
Then I will not hide from Thy face:
21 [a]Remove Thy [1]hand from me,
And let not the dread of Thee
terrify me.
22 "Then call, and [a]I will answer;
Or let me speak, then reply to me.
23 "[a]How many are my iniquities and
sins?
Make known to me my [1]rebellion
and my sin.
24 "Why dost Thou [a]hide Thy face,
And consider me [b]Thine enemy?
25 "Wilt Thou cause a [a]driven leaf to
tremble?
Or wilt Thou pursue the dry
[b]chaff?
26 "For Thou dost write [a]bitter things
against me,
And dost [b]make me to inherit the
iniquities of my youth.
27 "Thou [a]dost put my feet in the
stocks,
And dost watch all my paths;

7 [a]Job 27:4
8 [a]Lev. 19:15; Prov. 24:23
9 [a]Job 12:16
10 [a]Job 13:8; 32:21; 34:19
11 [1]Lit., *exaltation* [a]Job 31:23
13 [a]Job 13:5
14 [1]Lit., *palm* [a]Ps. 119:109
15 [1]Lit., *to His face* [a]Job 7:6 [b]Job 27:5
16 [a]Job 23:7; Is. 12:1, 2 [b]Job 34:21-23
18 [a]Job 23:4 [b]Job 9:21; 10:7; 12:4
19 [a]Is. 50:8 [b]Job 7:21; 10:8
21 [1]Lit., *palm* [a]Job 9:34; Ps. 39:10
22 [a]Job 9:16; 14:15
23 [1]Or, *transgression* [a]Job 7:21
24 [a]Ps. 13:1; 44:24; 88:14; Is. 8:17 [b]Job 19:11; 33:10; Lam. 2:5
25 [a]Lev. 26:36 [b]Job 21:18
26 [a]Job 9:18 [b]Ps. 25:7
27 [1]Lit., *carve for* [a]Job 33:11
28 [1]Lit., *he is* [a]Job 2:7

1 [1]Lit., *short of days* [a]Job 5:7 [b]Eccl. 2:23
2 [a]Ps. 90:5, 6; 103:15; Is. 40:6, 7; James 1:10; 1 Pet. 1:24 [b]Job 8:9
3 [1]So with some ancient versions; M.T., *me* [a]Ps. 8:4; 144:3 [b]Ps. 143:2
4 [a]Job 15:14; 25:4; Ps. 51:5
5 [1]Lit., *made* [a]Job 21:21
6 [1]Lit., *cease* [2]Lit., *makes acceptable* [a]Job 7:19; Ps. 39:13
7 [1]Or, *cease*
10 [a]Job 3:13; 14:10-15 [b]Job 13:9
11 [1]Lit., *disappears* [a]Is. 19:5
12 [1]Lit., *They* [2]Lit., *their* [a]Job 3:13
13 [1]I.e., the nether world [a]Is. 26:20
15 [a]Job 10:3
16 [a]Job 31:4; 34:21; Ps. 139:1-3; Prov. 5:21 [b]Job 10:6
17 [1]Lit., *plaster;* or, *glue together* [a]Deut. 32:32-34

Thou dost [1]set a limit for the soles
of my feet,
28 While [1]I am decaying like a [a]rotten
thing,
Like a garment that is moth-eaten.

Job Speaks of the Finality of Death

14 "[a]MAN, who is born of woman,
Is [1]short-lived and [b]full of turmoil.
2 "[a]Like a flower he comes forth and
withers.
He also flees like [b]a shadow and
does not remain.
3 "Thou also dost [a]open Thine eyes on
him,
And [b]bring [1]him into judgment
with Thyself.
4 "[a]Who can make the clean out of the
unclean?
No one!
5 "Since his days are determined,
The [a]number of his months is with
Thee,
And his limits Thou hast [1]set so
that he cannot pass.
6 "[a]Turn Thy gaze from him that he
may [1]rest,
Until he [2]fulfills his day like a hired
man.

7 "For there is hope for a tree,
When it is cut down, that it will
sprout again,
And its shoots will not [1]fail.
8 "Though its roots grow old in the
ground,
And its stump dies in the dry soil,
9 At the scent of water it will flourish
And put forth sprigs like a plant.
10 "But [a]man dies and lies prostrate.
Man [b]expires, and where is he?
11 "*As* [a]water [1]evaporates from the sea,
And a river becomes parched and
dried up,
12 So [a]man lies down and does not
rise.
Until the heavens be no more,
[1]He will not awake nor be aroused
out of [2]his sleep.

13 "Oh that Thou wouldst hide me in
[1]Sheol,
That Thou wouldst conceal me
[a]until Thy wrath returns *to Thee,*
That Thou wouldst set a limit for
me and remember me!
14 "If a man dies, will he live *again?*
All the days of my struggle I will
wait,
Until my change comes.
15 "Thou wilt call, and I will answer
Thee;
Thou wilt long for [a]the work of Thy
hands.
16 "For now Thou dost [a]number my
steps,
Thou dost not [b]observe my sin.
17 "My transgression is [a]sealed up in a
bag,
And Thou dost [1]wrap up my iniquity.

18"But the falling mountain [1]crumbles away,
And the rock moves from its place;
19 Water wears away stones,
Its torrents wash away the dust of the earth;
So Thou dost [a]destroy man's hope.
20"Thou dost forever overpower him and he [a]departs;
Thou dost change his appearance and send him away.
21"His sons achieve honor, but [a]he does not know *it;*
Or they become insignificant, but he does not perceive it.
22"But his [1]body pains him,
And he mourns only for himself."

Eliphaz Says Job Presumes Much

15 THEN Eliphaz the Temanite [1]responded,
2"Should a wise man answer with windy knowledge,
[a]And fill [1]himself with the east wind?
3"Should he argue with useless talk,
Or with words which are not profitable?
4"Indeed, you do away with [1]reverence,
And hinder meditation before God.
5"For [a]your guilt teaches your mouth,
And you choose the language of [b]the crafty.
6"Your [a]own mouth condemns you, and not I;
And your own lips testify against you.

7"Were you the first man to be born,
Or [a]were you brought forth before the hills?
8"Do you hear the [a]secret counsel of God,
And limit wisdom to yourself?
9"[a]What do you know that we do not know?
What do you understand that [1]we do not?
10"Both the [a]gray-haired and the aged are among us,
Older than your father.
11"Are [a]the consolations of God too small for you,
Even the [b]word *spoken* gently with you?
12"Why does your [a]heart carry you away?
And why do your eyes flash,
13 That you should turn your spirit against God,
And allow *such* words to go out of your mouth?
14"What is man, that [a]he should be pure,
Or [b]he who is born of a woman, that he should be righteous?
15"Behold, He puts no trust in His [a]holy ones,
And the [b]heavens are not pure in His sight;
16 How much less one who is [a]detestable and corrupt,
Man, who [b]drinks iniquity like water!

What Eliphaz Has Seen of Life

17"I will tell you, listen to me;
And what I have seen I will also declare;
18 What wise men have told,
And have not concealed from [a]their fathers,
19 To whom alone the land was given,
And no alien passed among them.
20"The wicked man writhes [a]in pain all *his* days,
And [1]numbered are the years [b]stored up for the ruthless.
21"[1]Sounds of [a]terror are in his ears,
[b]While at peace the destroyer comes upon him.
22"He does not believe that he will [a]return from darkness,
And he is destined for [b]the sword.
23"He wanders about for food, saying, 'Where is it?'
He knows that a day of [a]darkness is [1]at hand.
24"Distress and anguish terrify him,
They overpower him like a king ready for the attack,
25 Because he has stretched out his hand against God,
And conducts himself [a]arrogantly against [1]the Almighty.
26"He rushes [1]headlong at Him
With [2]his massive shield.
27"For he has [a]covered his face with his fat,
And made his thighs heavy with flesh.
28"And he has [a]lived in desolate cities,
In houses no one would inhabit,
Which are destined to become [1]ruins.
29"He [a]will not become rich, nor will his wealth endure;
And his grain will not bend down to the ground.
30"He will [a]not [1]escape from darkness;
The [b]flame will wither his shoots,
And by [c]the breath of His mouth he will go away.
31"Let him not [a]trust in emptiness, deceiving himself;
For emptiness will be his [1]reward.
32"It will be accomplished [a]before his time,
And his palm [b]branch will not be green.
33"He will drop off his unripe grape like the vine,
And will [a]cast off his flower like the olive tree.
34"For the company of [a]the godless is barren,
And fire consumes [b]the tents of [1]the corrupt.
35"They [a]conceive [1]mischief and bring forth iniquity,
And their [2]mind prepares deception."

18 [1]Lit., *withers*
19 [a]Job 7:6
20 [a]Job 4:20; 20:7
21 [a]Eccl. 9:5
22 [1]Lit., *flesh*
1 [1]Lit., *answered and said*
2 [1]Lit., *his belly* [a]Job 6:26
4 [1]Lit., *fear*
5 [a]Job 22:5 [b]Job 5:12, 13
6 [a]Job 18:7
7 [a]Job 38:4, 21; Prov. 8:25
8 [a]Job 29:4; Rom. 11:34; 1 Cor. 2:11
9 [1]Lit., *is not within us?* [a]Job 12:3; 13:2
10 [a]Job 12:12; 32:6, 7
11 [a]Job 5:17-19; 36:15, 16 [b]Job 6:10; 23:12
12 [a]Job 11:13; 36:13
14 [a]Job 14:4; Prov. 20:9; Eccl. 7:20 [b]Job 25:4
15 [a]Job 5:1 [b]Job 25:5
16 [a]Ps. 14:1 [b]Job 34:7; Prov. 19:28
18 [a]Job 8:8; 20:4
20 [1]Lit., *the number of years are* [a]Job 15:24 [b]Job 24:1; 27:13
21 [1]Lit., *A sound of terrors is* [a]Job 15:24; 18:11; 20:25; 24:17; 27:20 [b]Job 20:21; 1 Thess. 5:3
22 [a]Job 15:30 [b]Job 19:29; 27:14; 33:18; 36:12
23 [1]Lit., *ready at his hand* [a]Job 15:22, 30
25 [1]Heb., *Shaddai* [a]Job 36:9
26 [1]Lit., *with a stiff neck* [2]Lit., *the thick-bossed shields*
27 [a]Ps. 73:7; 119:70
28 [1]Or, *heaps* [a]Job 3:14; Is. 5:8, 9
29 [a]Job 27:16, 17
30 [1]Lit., *turn aside* [a]Job 5:14; 15:22 [b]Job 15:34; 20:26; 22:20; 31:12 [c]Job 4:9
31 [1]Lit., *exchange* [a]Job 35:13; Is. 59:4
32 [a]Job 22:16; Eccl. 7:17 [b]Job 18:16
33 [a]Job 14:2
34 [1]Lit., *a bribe* [a]Job 8:13 [b]Job 8:22
35 [1]Or, *pain* [2]Lit., *belly* [a]Ps. 7:14; Is. 59:4

Job Says Friends Are Sorry Comforters

16 THEN Job [1]answered,
2"I have heard many such things;
[1a]Sorry comforters are you all.
3"Is there *no* limit to [a]windy words?
Or what plagues you that you answer?
4"I too could speak like you,
If [1]I were in your place.
I could compose words against you,
And [a]shake my head at you.
5"I could strengthen you with my mouth,
And the solace of my lips could lessen *your pain.*

Job Says God Shattered Him

6"If I speak, [a]my pain is not lessened,
And if I hold back, what has left me?
7"But now He has [a]exhausted me;
Thou hast laid [b]waste all my company.
8"And Thou hast shriveled me up,
[a]It has become a witness;
And my [b]leanness rises up against me,
It testifies to my face.
9"His anger has [a]torn me and [1]hunted me down,
He has [b]gnashed at me with His teeth;
My [c]adversary [2]glares at me.
10"They have [a]gaped at me with their mouth,
They have [1b]slapped me on the cheek with contempt;
They have [c]massed themselves against me.
11"God hands me over to ruffians,
And tosses me into the hands of the wicked.
12"I was at ease, but [a]He shattered me,
And He has grasped me by the neck and shaken me to pieces;
He has also set me up as His [b]target.
13"His [a]arrows surround me.
Without mercy He splits my kidneys open;
He pours out [b]my gall on the ground.
14"He [a]breaks through me with breach after breach;
He [b]runs at me like a warrior.
15"I have sewed [a]sackcloth over my skin,
And [b]thrust my horn in the dust.
16"My face is flushed from [a]weeping,
[b]And deep darkness is on my eyelids,
17 Although there is no [a]violence in my hands,
And [b]my prayer is pure.

18"O earth, do not cover my blood,
And let there be no *resting* place for my cry.
19"Even now, behold, [a]my witness is in heaven,
And my [1]advocate is [b]on high.
20"My friends are my scoffers;
[a]My eye [1]weeps to God.
21"O that a man might plead with God
As a man with his neighbor!
22"For when a few years are past,
I shall go the way [a]of no return.

Job Says He Has Become a Byword

17 "MY spirit is broken, my days are extinguished,
The [1a]grave is *ready* for me.
2"[a]Surely mockers are with me,
And my eye [1]gazes on their provocation.

3"Lay down, now, a pledge [a]for me with Thyself;
Who is there that will [1]be my guarantor?
4"For Thou hast [1a]kept their heart from understanding;
Therefore Thou wilt not exalt *them.*
5"He who [a]informs against friends for a share *of the spoil,*
The [b]eyes of his children also shall languish.

6"But He has made me a [a]byword of the people,
And I am [1]one at whom men [b]spit.
7"My eye has also grown [a]dim because of grief,
And all my [b]members are as a shadow.
8"The upright shall be appalled at this,
And the [a]innocent shall stir up himself against the godless.
9"Nevertheless [a]the righteous shall hold to his way,
And [b]he who has clean hands shall grow stronger and stronger.
10"But come again all of [1]you now,
For I [a]do not find a wise man among you.
11"My [a]days are past, my plans are torn apart,
Even the wishes of my heart.
12"They make night into day, *saying,*
'The light is near,' in the presence of darkness.
13"If I look for [a]Sheol as my home,
I [1]make my bed in the darkness;
14 If I call to the [a]pit, 'You are my father';
To the [b]worm, 'my mother and my sister';
15 Where now is [a]my hope?
And who regards my hope?
16"[1]Will it go down with me to Sheol?
Shall we together [a]go down into the dust?"

Bildad Speaks of the Wicked

18 THEN Bildad the Shuhite [1]responded,
2"How long will you hunt for words?
Show understanding and then we can talk.
3"Why are we [a]regarded as beasts,
As stupid in your eyes?

16:1 [1]Lit., *answered and said*
2 [1]Lit., *Comforters of trouble* [a]Job 13:4; 21:34
3 [a]Job 6:26
4 [1]Lit., *your soul were in place of my soul* [a]Ps. 22:7; 109:25; Zeph. 2:15; Matt. 27:39
6 [a]Job 9:27, 28
7 [a]Job 7:3 [b]Job 16:20; 19:13-15
8 [a]Job 10:17 [b]Job 19:20; Ps. 109:24
9 [1]Lit., *borne a grudge against me* [2]Lit., *sharpens his eyes* [a]Job 19:11; Hos. 6:1 [b]Ps. 35:16; Lam. 2:16; Acts 7:54 [c]Job 13:24; 33:10
10 [1]Lit., *struck* [a]Ps. 22:13 [b]Is. 50:6; Lam. 3:30; Acts 23:2 [c]Job 30:12; Ps. 35:15
12 [a]Job 9:17 [b]Job 7:20; Lam. 3:12
13 [a]Job 6:4; 19:12; 25:3 [b]Job 20:25
14 [a]Job 9:17 [b]Joel 2:7
15 [a]Gen. 37:34; Ps. 69:11 [b]Ps. 7:5
16 [a]Job 16:20 [b]Job 24:17
17 [a]Is. 59:6; Jon. 3:8 [b]Job 27:4
19 [1]Or, *witness* [a]Gen. 31:50; Job 19:25-27; Rom. 1:9; Phil. 1:8; 1 Thess. 2:5 [b]Job 31:2
20 [1]Or, *drips* [a]Job 17:7
22 [a]Job 3:13

17:1 [1]Lit., *graves* [a]Ps. 88:3, 4
2 [1]Lit., *lodges* [a]Job 12:4; 17:6
3 [1]Lit., *strike hands with me* [a]Ps. 119:122; Is. 38:14
4 [1]Lit., *hidden* [a]Job 12:20
5 [a]Lev. 19:13, 16 [b]Job 11:20
6 [1]Lit., *a spitting to the faces* [a]Job 17:2 [b]Job 30:10
7 [a]Job 16:16 [b]Job 16:8
8 [a]Job 22:19
9 [a]Prov. 4:18 [b]Job 22:30; 31:7
10 [1]With some ancient mss. and versions; M.T., *them* [a]Job 12:2
11 [a]Job 7:6
13 [1]Lit., *spread out* [a]Job 3:13
14 [a]Job 7:5; 13:28; 30:30 [b]Job 21:26; 25:6
15 [a]Job 7:6
16 [1]So the Gr.; Heb. possibly, *Let my limbs sink down to Sheol, since there is rest in the dust for all.* [a]Job 3:17; 21:33

18:1 [1]Lit., *answered and said*
3 [a]Ps. 73:22

4"O [1]you who tear yourself in your anger—
For your sake is the earth to be abandoned,
Or the rock to be moved from its place?

5"Indeed, the [a]light of the wicked goes out,
And the [1]flame of his fire gives no light.
6"The light in his tent is [a]darkened,
And his lamp goes out above him.
7"His [1]vigorous stride is shortened,
And his [a]own scheme brings him down.
8"For he is [a]thrown into the net by his own feet,
And he steps on the webbing.
9"A snare seizes *him* by the heel,
And a trap snaps shut on him.
10"A noose for him is hidden in the ground,
And a trap for him on the path.
11"All around [a]terrors frighten him,
And [b]harry him at every step.
12"His strength is [a]famished,
And calamity is ready at his side.
13"[1]His skin is devoured by disease,
The first-born of death [a]devours his [2]limbs.
14"He is [a]torn from [1]the security of his tent,
And [2]they march him before the king of [b]terrors.
15"[1]There dwells in his tent nothing of his;
[a]Brimstone is scattered on his habitation.
16"His [a]roots are dried below,
And his [b]branch is cut off above.
17"[a]Memory of him perishes from the earth,
And he has no name abroad.
18"[1]He is driven from light [a]into darkness,
And [b]chased from the inhabited world.
19"He has no [a]offspring or posterity among his people,
Nor any survivor where he sojourned.
20"Those [1]in the west are appalled at [a]his [2]fate,
And those [3]in the east are seized with horror.
21"Surely such are the [a]dwellings of the wicked,
And this is the place of him who does not know God."

Job Feels Insulted

19 THEN Job [1]responded,
2"How long will you torment [1]me,
And crush me with words?
3"These ten times you have insulted me,
You are not ashamed to wrong me.
4"Even if I have truly erred,
My error lodges with me.
5"If indeed you [a]vaunt yourselves against me,
And prove my disgrace to me,
6 Know then that [a]God has wronged me,
And has closed [b]His net around me.

Everything Is against Him

7"Behold, [a]I cry, 'Violence!' but I get no answer;
I shout for help, but there is no justice.
8"He has [a]walled up my way so that I cannot pass;
And He has put [b]darkness on my paths.
9"He has [a]stripped my honor from me,
And removed the [b]crown from my head.
10"He [a]breaks me down on every side, and I am gone;
And He has uprooted my [b]hope [c]like a tree.
11"He has also [a]kindled His anger against me,
And [b]considered me as His enemy.
12"His [a]troops come together,
And [b]build up their [1]way against me,
And camp around my tent.

13"He has [a]removed my brothers far from me,
And my [b]acquaintances are completely estranged from me.
14"My relatives have failed,
And my [a]intimate friends have forgotten me.
15"Those who live in my house and my maids consider me a stranger.
I am a foreigner in their sight.
16"I call to my servant, but he does not answer,
I have to implore him with my mouth.
17"My breath is [1]offensive to my wife,
And I am loathsome to my own brothers.
18"Even young children despise me;
I rise up and they speak against me.
19"All [1]my [a]associates abhor me,
And those I love have turned against me.
20"My [a]bone clings to my skin and my flesh,
And I have escaped *only* by the skin of my teeth.
21"Pity me, pity me, O you my friends,
For the [a]hand of God has struck me.
22"Why do you [a]persecute me as God *does,*
And are not satisfied with my flesh?

Job Says, "My Redeemer Lives"

23"Oh that my words were written!
Oh that they were [a]inscribed in a book!

4 [1]Lit., *he . . . tears himself . . . his*
5 [1]Lit., *spark* [a]Job 21:17; Prov. 13:9; 20:20; 24:20
6 [a]Job 12:25
7 [1]Lit., *steps of his strength* [a]Job 15:6
8 [a]Job 22:10; Ps. 9:15; 35:8; Is. 24:17, 18
11 [a]Job 15:21 [b]Job 18:18; 20:8
12 [a]Is. 8:21
13 [1]Heb., *It eats parts of his skin* [2]Or, *parts* [a]Zech. 14:12
14 [1]Lit., *his tent his trust* [2]Or, *you or she shall march* [a]Job 8:22; 18:6 [b]Job 15:21
15 [1]A suggested reading is *Fire dwells in his tent* [a]Ps. 11:6
16 [a]Is. 5:24; Hos. 9:16; Amos 2:9; Mal. 4:1 [b]Job 15:30, 32
17 [a]Job 24:20; Ps. 34:16; Prov. 10:7
18 [1]Lit., *They drive him . . . And chase him* [a]Job 5:14; Is. 8:22; 15:30 [b]Job 20:8; 27:21-23
19 [a]Job 27:14, 15; Is. 14:22
20 [1]Lit., *who come after* [2]Lit., *day* [3]Lit., *who have gone before* [a]Ps. 37:13; Jer. 50:27; Obad. 12
21 [a]Job 21:28

1 [1]Lit., *answered and said*
2 [1]Lit., *my soul*
5 [a]Ps. 35:26; 38:16; 55:12, 13
6 [a]Job 16:11; 27:2 [b]Job 18:8-10; Ps. 66:11; Lam. 1:13
7 [a]Job 9:24; 30:20, 24; Hab. 1:2
8 [a]Job 3:23; Lam. 3:7, 9 [b]Job 30:26
9 [a]Job 12:17, 19; Ps. 89:44 [b]Job 16:15; Ps. 89:39; Lam. 5:16
10 [a]Job 12:14 [b]Job 7:6 [c]Job 24:20
11 [a]Job 16:9 [b]Job 13:24; 33:10
12 [1]I.e., siegework [a]Job 16:13 [b]Job 30:12
13 [a]Job 16:7; Ps. 69:8 [b]Job 16:20; Ps. 88:8, 18
14 [a]Job 19:19
17 [1]Lit., *strange*
19 [1]Lit., *the men of my council* [a]Ps. 38:11; 55:12, 13
20 [a]Job 16:8; 33:21; Ps. 102:5; Lam. 4:8
21 [a]Job 1:11; Ps. 38:2
22 [a]Job 13:24, 25; 16:11; 19:6; Ps. 69:26
23 [a]Is. 30:8; Jer. 36:2

24 "That with an iron stylus and lead
They were engraved in the rock
forever!
25 "And as for me, I know that [a]my
[1]Redeemer lives,
And [2]at the last He will take His
stand on the [3]earth.
26 "Even after my skin [1]is destroyed,
Yet from my flesh I shall [a]see God;
27 Whom I [1]myself shall behold,
And whom my eyes shall see and
not another.
My [2]heart [a]faints [3]within me.
28 "If you say, 'How shall we [a]persecute him?'
And '[1]What pretext for a case
against him can we find?'
29 *Then* be afraid of [a]the sword for
yourselves,
For wrath *brings* the punishment of
the sword,
So that you may know [b]there is
judgment."

Zophar Says, "The Triumph of the Wicked Is Short"

20 THEN Zophar the Naamathite
[1]answered,
2 "Therefore my disquieting thoughts
make me [1]respond,
Even because of my [2]inward agitation.
3 "I listened to [a]the reproof which
insults me,
And the spirit of my understanding
makes me answer.
4 "Do you know this from [a]of old,
From the establishment of man on
earth,
5 That the [a]triumphing of the wicked
is short,
And [b]the joy of the godless momentary?
6 "Though his loftiness [1a]reaches the
heavens,
And his head touches the clouds,
7 He [a]perishes forever like his refuse;
Those who have seen him [b]will say,
'Where is he?'
8 "He flies away like a [a]dream, and
they cannot find him;
Even like a vision of the night he is
[b]chased away.
9 "The [a]eye which saw him sees him
no more,
And [b]his place no longer beholds
him.
10 "His [a]sons [1]favor the poor,
And his hands [b]give back his
wealth.
11 "His [a]bones are full of his youthful
vigor,
But it lies down with him [1]in the
dust.

12 "Though [a]evil is sweet in his mouth,
And he hides it under his tongue,
13 *Though* he [1]desires it and will not
let it go,
But holds it [a]in his [2]mouth,
14 *Yet* his food in his stomach is
changed
To the [1]venom of cobras within
him.
15 "He swallows riches,
But will [a]vomit them up;
God will expel them from his belly.
16 "He sucks [a]the poison of cobras;
The viper's tongue slays him.
17 "He does not look at [a]the streams,
The rivers flowing with honey and
curds.
18 "He [a]returns what he has attained
And cannot swallow *it;*
As to the riches of his trading,
He cannot even enjoy *them.*
19 "For he has [a]oppressed *and* forsaken
the poor;
He has seized a house which he has
not built.

20 "Because he knew no quiet [1]within
him
He does [a]not retain anything he
desires.
21 "Nothing remains [1]for him to devour,
Therefore [a]his prosperity does not
endure.
22 "In the fulness of his plenty he will
be cramped;
The [a]hand of everyone who suffers
will come *against* him.
23 "When he [a]fills his belly,
God will send His fierce anger on
him
And will [b]rain *it* on him [1]while he
is eating.
24 "He may [a]flee from the iron weapon,
But the bronze bow will pierce him.
25 "It is drawn forth and comes out of
his back,
Even the glittering point from [a]his
gall.
[b]Terrors come upon him,
26 Complete [a]darkness is held in reserve for his treasures,
And unfanned [b]fire will devour
him;
It will consume the survivor in his
tent.
27 "The [a]heavens will reveal his iniquity,
And the earth will rise up against
him.
28 "The [a]increase of his house will
depart;
His possessions will flow away [b]in
the day of His anger.
29 "This is the wicked man's [a]portion
from God,
Even the heritage decreed to him
by God."

Job Says God Will Deal with the Wicked

21 THEN Job [1]answered,
2 "Listen carefully to my speech,
And let this be your *way of* consolation.
3 "Bear with me that I may speak;
Then after I have spoken, you may
[a]mock.

25 [1]Or, *Vindicator, defender;* lit., *kinsman* [2]Or, *as the Last* [3]Lit., *dust* [a]Job 16:19; Ps. 78:35; Prov. 23:11; Is. 43:14; Jer. 50:34
26 [1]Lit., *which they have cut off* [a]Ps. 17:15; Matt. 5:8; 1 Cor. 13:12; 1 John 3:2
27 [1]Or, *on my side* [2]Lit., *kidneys* [3]Lit., *in my loins* [a]Ps. 73:26
28 [1]Or, *the root of the matter is found in him* [a]Job 19:22
29 [a]Job 15:22 [b]Job 22:4; Ps. 1:5; 9:7; Eccl. 12:14

1 [1]Lit., *answered and said*
2 [1]Lit., *return* [2]Lit., *haste within me*
3 [a]Job 19:3
4 [a]Job 8:8
5 [a]Job 8:12, 13; Ps. 37:35, 36 [b]Job 8:13
6 [1]Lit., *goes up to* [a]Is. 14:13, 14; Obad. 3, 4
7 [a]Job 4:20; 14:20 [b]Job 7:10; 8:18
8 [a]Ps. 73:20; 90:5 [b]Job 18:18; 27:21-23
9 [a]Job 7:8; 8:18 [b]Job 7:10
10 [1]Or, *seek the favor of* [a]Job 5:4; 27:14 [b]Job 20:18; 27:16, 17
11 [1]Lit., *on* [a]Job 21:23, 24
12 [a]Job 15:16
13 [1]Lit., *has compassion on* [2]Lit., *palate* [a]Num. 11:18-20, 33; Job 20:23
14 [1]Lit., *gall*
15 [a]Job 20:10, 20, 21
16 [a]Deut. 32:24, 33
17 [a]Deut. 32:13, 14; Job 29:6
18 [a]Job 20:10, 15
19 [a]Job 24:2-4; 35:9
20 [1]Lit., *in his belly* [a]Eccl. 5:13-15
21 [1]Or, *of what he devours* [a]Job 15:29
22 [a]Job 5:5
23 [1]Or, *as his food* [a]Job 20:13, 14 [b]Num. 11:18-20, 33; Ps. 78:30, 31
24 [a]Is. 24:18; Amos 5:19
25 [a]Job 16:13 [b]Job 18:11, 14
26 [a]Job 18:18 [b]Job 15:30; Ps. 21:9
27 [a]Deut. 31:28; Is. 26:21
28 [a]Deut. 28:31 [b]Job 20:15; 21:30
29 [a]Job 27:13; 31:2, 3

1 [1]Lit., *answered and said*
3 [a]Job 11:3; 17:2

4 "As for me, is [a]my complaint [1]to man?
And [b]why should [2]I not be impatient?
5 "Look at me, and be astonished,
And [a]put *your* hand over *your* mouth.
6 "Even when I remember, I am disturbed,
And [a]horror takes hold of my flesh.
7 "Why [a]do the wicked *still* live,
Continue on, also become very [b]powerful?
8 "Their [1][a]descendants are established with them in their sight,
And their offspring before their eyes,
9 Their houses [a]are safe from fear,
Neither is the rod of God on them.
10 "His ox mates [1]without fail;
His cow calves and does not abort.
11 "They send forth their little ones like the flock,
And their children skip about.
12 "They [1]sing to the timbrel and harp
And rejoice at the sound of the flute.
13 "They [a]spend their days in prosperity,
And [1]suddenly they go down to [2]Sheol.
14 "And they say to God, '[a]Depart from us!
We do not even desire the knowledge of Thy ways.
15 '[1]Who is [2]the Almighty, that we should serve Him,
And [a]what would we gain if we entreat Him?'
16 "Behold, their prosperity is not in their hand;
The [a]counsel of the wicked is far from me.

17 "How often is [a]the lamp of the wicked put out,
Or *does* their [b]calamity fall on them?
Does [1]God apportion destruction in His anger?
18 "Are they as [a]straw before the wind,
And like [b]chaff which the storm carries away?
19 "*You say,* '[a]God stores away [1]a man's iniquity for his sons.'
Let [2]God repay him so that he may know *it.*
20 "Let his [a]own eyes see his decay,
And let him [b]drink of the wrath of [1]the Almighty.
21 "For what does he care for his household [1]after him,
When the number of his months is cut off?
22 "Can anyone [a]teach God knowledge,
In that He [b]judges those on high?
23 "One [a]dies in his full strength,
Being wholly at ease and [1]satisfied;
24 His [1]sides are filled out with fat,
And the [a]marrow of his bones is moist,
25 While another dies with a bitter soul,
Never even [1]tasting *anything* good.
26 "Together they [a]lie down in the dust,
And [b]worms cover them.

27 "Behold, I know your thoughts,
And the plans by which you would wrong me.
28 "For you say, 'Where is the house of [a]the nobleman,
And where is the [b]tent, the dwelling places of the wicked?'
29 "Have you not asked wayfaring men,
And do you not recognize their [1]witness?
30 "For the [a]wicked is reserved for the day of calamity;
They will be led forth at [b]the day of fury.
31 "Who will [1]confront him with his actions,
And who will repay him for what he has done?
32 "While he is carried to the grave,
Men will keep watch over *his* tomb.
33 "The [a]clods of the valley will [1]gently cover him;
Moreover, [b]all men will [2]follow after him,
While countless ones *go* before him.
34 "How then will you vainly [a]comfort me,
For your answers remain *full of* [1]falsehood?"

Eliphaz Accuses and Exhorts Job

22 THEN Eliphaz the Temanite [1]responded,
2 "Can a vigorous [a]man be of use to God,
Or a wise man be useful to himself?
3 "Is there any pleasure to [1]the Almighty if you are righteous,
Or profit if you make your ways perfect?
4 "Is it because of your [1]reverence that He reproves you,
That He [a]enters into judgment against you?
5 "Is not [a]your wickedness great,
And your iniquities without end?
6 "For you have [a]taken pledges of your brothers without cause,
And [b]stripped [1]men naked.
7 "To the weary you have [a]given no water to drink,
And from the hungry you have [b]withheld bread.
8 "But the earth [a]belongs to the [b]mighty man,
And [c]the honorable man dwells in it.
9 "You have sent [a]widows away empty,
And the [1]strength of the [b]orphans has been crushed.
10 "Therefore [a]snares surround you,
And sudden [b]dread terrifies you,

4 [1]Or, *against* [2]Lit., *my spirit* [a]Job 7:11 [b]Job 6:11
5 [a]Judg. 18:19; Job 13:5; 29:9; 40:4
6 [a]Ps. 55:5
7 [a]Job 9:24; Ps. 73:3; Jer. 12:1; Hab. 1:13 [b]Job 12:19
8 [1]Lit., *seed* [a]Ps. 17:14
9 [a]Job 12:6
10 [1]Lit., *and does not fail*
12 [1]Lit., *lifted up the voice*
13 [1]So with most versions; M.T., *are shattered by Sheol.* [2]I.e., the nether world [a]Job 21:23; 36:11
14 [a]Job 22:17
15 [1]Lit., *What* [2]Heb., *Shaddai* [a]Job 22:17; 34:9
16 [a]Job 22:18
17 [1]Lit., *He* [a]Job 18:5, 6 [b]Job 31:2, 3
18 [a]Job 13:25; Ps. 83:13 [b]Ps. 1:4; 35:5; Is. 17:13; Hos. 13:3
19 [1]Lit., *his* [2]Lit., *Him* [a]Ex. 20:5; Jer. 31:29; Ezek. 18:2
20 [1]Heb., *Shaddai* [a]Num. 14:28-32; Jer. 31:30; Ezek. 18:4 [b]Ps. 60:3; Is. 51:17; Jer. 25:15; Rev. 14:10
21 [1]I.e., after he dies
22 [a]Job 35:11; 36:22; Is. 40:14; Rom. 11:34 [b]Job 4:18; 15:15; Ps. 82:1
23 [1]Or, *quiet* [a]Job 20:11; 21:13
24 [1]So with Syr.; Heb. uncertain. Some render as, *his pails are full of milk* [a]Prov. 3:8
25 [1]Lit., *eating*
26 [a]Job 3:13; 20:11; Eccl. 9:2 [b]Job 24:20; Is. 14:11
28 [a]Job 1:3; 31:37 [b]Job 8:22; 18:21
29 [1]Lit., *signs*
30 [a]Job 20:29; Prov. 16:4; 2 Pet. 2:9 [b]Job 21:17, 20; 40:11
31 [1]Lit., *declare his way to his face*
33 [1]Lit., *be sweet to him* [2]Lit., *draw* [a]Job 3:22; 17:16 [b]Job 3:19; 24:24
34 [1]Or, *faithlessness* [a]Job 16:2

1 [1]Lit., *answered and said*
2 [a]Job 35:7; Luke 17:10
3 [1]Heb., *Shaddai*
4 [1]Or, *fear* [a]Job 14:3; 19:29
5 [a]Job 11:6; 15:5
6 [1]Lit., *clothing of the naked* [a]Ex. 22:26; Deut. 24:6, 17; Job 24:3, 9; Ezek. 18:16 [b]Job 31:19, 20
7 [a]Job 31:16, 17 [b]Job 31:31
8 [a]Job 9:24 [b]Job 12:19 [c]Is. 3:3; 9:15
9 [1]Lit., *arms* [a]Job 24:3, 21; 29:13; 31:16, 18 [b]Job 6:27
10 [a]Job 18:8 [b]Job 15:21

11 Or [a]darkness, so that you cannot see,
And an [b]abundance of water covers you.

12 "Is not God [a]*in* the height of heaven?
Look also at the [1]distant stars, how high they are!
13 "And you say, '[a]What does God know?
Can He judge through the thick darkness?
14 '[a]Clouds are a hiding place for Him, so that He cannot see;
And He walks on the [1]vault of heaven.'
15 "Will you keep to the ancient path
Which [a]wicked men have trod,
16 Who were snatched away [a]before their time,
Whose [b]foundations were [1]washed away by a river?
17 "They [a]said to God, 'Depart from us!'
And 'What can [1]the Almighty do to them?'
18 "Yet He [a]filled their houses with good *things;*
But [b]the counsel of the wicked is far from me.
19 "The [a]righteous see and are glad,
And the innocent mock them,
20 *Saying,* 'Truly our adversaries are cut off,
And their [1]abundance [a]the fire has consumed.'

21 "[1a]Yield now and be at peace with Him;
Thereby good will come to you.
22 "Please receive [1a]instruction from His mouth,
And establish His words in your heart.
23 "If you [a]return to [1]the Almighty, you will be [2]restored;
If you [b]remove unrighteousness far from your tent,
24 And [a]place *your* [1]gold in the dust,
And *the gold of* Ophir among the stones of the brooks,
25 Then [1]the Almighty will be your [2]gold
And choice silver to you.
26 "For then you will [a]delight in [1]the Almighty,
And lift up your face to God.
27 "You will [a]pray to Him, and [b]He will hear you;
And you will pay your vows.
28 "You will also decree a thing, and it will be established for you;
And [a]light will shine on your ways.
29 "When [1]you are cast down, you will speak with [2]confidence
And the [3a]humble person He will save.
30 "He will deliver one who is not innocent,
And he will be [a]delivered through the cleanness of your hands."

Job Says He Longs for God

23 THEN Job [1]replied,
2 "Even today my [a]complaint is rebellion;
[1]His hand is [b]heavy despite my groaning.
3 "Oh that I knew where I might find Him,
That I might come to His seat!
4 "I would [a]present *my* case before Him
And fill my mouth with arguments.
5 "I would learn the words *which* He would [1]answer,
And perceive what He would say to me.
6 "Would He contend with me by [a]the greatness of *His* power?
No, surely He would pay attention to me.
7 "There the upright would [a]reason with Him;
And I [1]would be [b]delivered forever from my Judge.

8 "Behold, I go forward but He is not *there,*
And backward, but I [a]cannot perceive Him;
9 When He acts on the left, I cannot behold *Him;*
He turns on the right, I cannot see Him.
10 "But He knows the [1]way I take;
When He has [a]tried me, I shall come forth as gold.
11 "My foot has [a]held fast to His path;
I have kept His way and not turned aside.
12 "I have not departed from the command of His lips;
I have treasured the [a]words of His mouth [1]more than my [2]necessary food.
13 "But He is unique and who can turn Him?
And *what* His soul desires, that He does.
14 "For He performs what is appointed for me,
And many such *decrees* are with Him.
15 "Therefore, I would be dismayed at His presence;
When I consider, I am terrified of Him.
16 "*It is* God *who* has made my [a]heart faint,
And the Almighty *who* has dismayed me,
17 But I [a]am not silenced by the darkness,
Nor [b]deep gloom *which* covers *me.*

Job Says God Seems to Ignore Wrongs

24 "[a]WHY are [1]times not stored up by the Almighty,
And why do those who know Him not see [b]His days?
2 "[1]Some [a]remove the landmarks;
They seize and [2]devour flocks.

11 [a]Job 5:14 [b]Job 38:34; Ps. 69:2; 124:5; Lam. 3:54
12 [1]Lit., *head, topmost* [a]Job 11:7-9
13 [a]Ps. 10:11; 59:7; 64:5; 94:7; Is. 29:15; Ezek. 8:12
14 [1]Lit., *circle* [a]Job 26:9
15 [a]Job 34:36
16 [1]Lit., *poured out* [a]Job 15:32; 21:13, 18 [b]Job 14:19; Ps. 90:5; Is. 28:2; Matt. 7:26, 27
17 [1]Heb., *Shaddai* [a]Job 21:14, 15
18 [a]Job 12:6 [b]Job 21:16
19 [a]Ps. 52:6; 58:10; 107:42
20 [1]Or, *excess* [a]Job 15:30
21 [1]Or, *Know intimately* [a]Ps. 34:10
22 [1]Or, *law* [a]Job 6:10; 23:12; Prov. 2:6
23 [1]Heb., *Shaddai* [2]Lit., *built up* [a]Job 8:5; 11:13; Is. 19:22; 31:6; Zech. 1:3 [b]Job 11:14
24 [1]Lit., *ore* [a]Job 31:24, 25
25 [1]Heb., *Shaddai* [2]Lit., *ore*
26 [1]Heb., *Shaddai* [a]Job 27:10; Ps. 37:4; Is. 58:14
27 [a]Job 11:13; 33:26; Is. 58:9 [b]Job 34:28
28 [a]Job 11:17; Ps. 112:4
29 [1]Lit., *they cast you down* [2]Lit., *pride* [3]Lit., *lowly of eyes* [a]Job 5:11; 36:7; Matt. 23:12; James 4:6; 1 Pet. 5:5
30 [a]Job 42:7, 8; Ps. 18:20; 24:3, 4

1 [1]Lit., *answered and said*
2 [1]So with Gr. and Syr.; M.T., *My* [a]Job 7:11 [b]Job 6:2, 3; Ps. 32:4
4 [a]Job 13:18
5 [1]Lit., *answer me*
6 [a]Job 9:4
7 [1]Or, *bring forth my justice forever* [a]Job 13:3 [b]Job 13:16; 23:10
8 [a]Job 9:11; 35:14
10 [1]Lit., *way with me* [a]Job 7:18; Ps. 7:9; 11:5; 66:10; Zech. 13:9; 1 Pet. 1:7
11 [a]Job 31:7; Ps. 17:5; 44:18
12 [1]Or, with some versions, *in my breast* [2]Lit., *prescribed portion* [a]Job 6:10; 22:22
16 [a]Deut. 20:3; Job 27:2; Jer. 51:46
17 [a]Job 10:18, 19 [b]Job 19:8

1 [1]I.e., times of judgment [a]Acts 1:7 [b]Is. 2:12; Jer. 46:10; Obad. 15; Zeph. 1:7
2 [1]Lit., *They* [2]Or, *pasture* [a]Deut. 19:14; 27:17; Prov. 23:10

3 "They drive away the donkeys of the [a]orphans;
They take the [b]widow's ox for a pledge.
4 "They push [a]the needy aside from the road;
The [b]poor of the land are made to hide themselves altogether.
5 "Behold, as [a]wild donkeys in the wilderness
They [b]go forth seeking food in their activity,
As [1]bread for *their* children in the desert.
6 "They harvest their fodder in the field,
And they glean the vineyard of the wicked.
7 "[a]They spend the night naked, without clothing,
And have no covering against the cold.
8 "They are wet with the mountain rains,
And they hug the rock for want of a shelter.
9 "[1]Others snatch the [a]orphan from the breast,
And against the poor they take a pledge.
10 "They cause *the poor* to go about naked without clothing,
And they take away the sheaves from the hungry.
11 "Within the walls they produce oil;
They tread wine presses but thirst.
12 "From the city men groan,
And the souls of the wounded cry out;
Yet God [a]does not pay attention to folly.

13 "[1]Others have been with those who rebel against the light;
They do not want to know its ways,
Nor abide in its paths.
14 "The murderer [a]arises at dawn;
He [b]kills the poor and the needy,
And at night he is as a thief.
15 "And the eye of the [a]adulterer waits for the twilight,
Saying, 'No eye will see me.'
And he [1]disguises his face.
16 "In the dark they [a]dig into houses,
They [b]shut themselves up by day;
They do not know the light.
17 "For the morning is the same to him as thick darkness,
For he is familiar with the [a]terrors of thick darkness.

18 "They are [1a]insignificant on the surface of the water;
Their portion is [b]cursed on the earth.
They do not turn [2]toward the [c]vineyards.
19 "Drought and heat [1a]consume the snow waters,
So does [2b]Sheol *those who* have sinned.

3 [a]Job 6:27 [b]Deut. 24:17; Job 22:9
4 [a]Job 24:14; 29:16; 30:25; 31:19 [b]Job 29:12; Ps. 41:1; Prov. 14:31; 28:28; Amos 8:4
5 [1]Lit., *his bread* [a]Job 39:5-8 [b]Ps. 104:23
7 [a]Ex. 22:26; Job 22:6
9 [1]Lit., *They* [a]Job 6:27
12 [a]Job 9:23, 24
13 [1]Lit., *They*
14 [a]Mic. 2:1 [b]Ps. 10:8
15 [1]Or, *puts a covering on his face* [a]Prov. 7:9
16 [a]Ex. 22:2; Matt. 6:19 [b]John 3:20
17 [a]Job 15:21
18 [1]Or, *light* or *swift* [2]Lit., *to the path of* [a]Job 22:11, 16; 27:20 [b]Job 5:3 [c]Job 24:6, 11
19 [1]Lit., *seize* [2]I.e., nether world [a]Job 6:16, 17 [b]Job 21:13
20 [1]Lit., *womb* [a]Is. 49:15 [b]Job 21:26 [c]Job 18:17; Ps. 34:16; Prov. 10:7 [d]Job 19:10; Dan. 4:14
21 [1]Lit., *barren who does not bear* [a]Job 22:9
22 [a]Job 9:4 [b]Job 18:20
23 [a]Job 12:6 [b]Job 10:4; 11:11
24 [a]Ps. 37:10 [b]Job 14:21
25 [a]Job 6:28; 27:4

1 [1]Lit., *answered and said*
2 [1]Lit., *are with Him* [a]Job 9:4; 36:5, 22; 37:23; 42:2 [b]Job 16:19; 31:2
3 [a]Job 16:13
4 [a]Job 4:17; 9:2 [b]Job 14:4
5 [a]Job 31:26 [b]Job 15:15
6 [a]Job 7:17 [b]Job 17:14

1 [1]Lit., *responded and said*
2 [1]Lit., *no power* [a]Job 6:11, 12 [b]Ps. 71:9
3 [1]Lit., *made known*
4 [1]Lit., *breath has gone forth*
5 [1]Or, *shades;* Heb., *Rephaim* [a]Job 3:13; Ps. 88:10
6 [1]I.e., the nether world [2]I.e., place of destruction [a]Job 9:5-10; 26:6-14; 38:17; 41:11 [b]Job 28:22; 31:12
7 [a]Job 9:8
8 [a]Job 37:11; Prov. 30:4

20 "A [1a]mother will forget him;
The [b]worm feeds sweetly till he is remembered [c]no more.
And wickedness will be broken [d]like a tree.
21 "He wrongs the [1]barren woman,
And does no good for [a]the widow.
22 "But He drags off the valiant by [a]His power;
He rises, but [b]no one has assurance of life.
23 "He provides them [a]with security, and they are supported;
And His [b]eyes are on their ways.
24 "They are exalted a [a]little while, then they are gone;
Moreover, they are [b]brought low and like everything gathered up;
Even like the heads of grain they are cut off.
25 "Now if it is not so, [a]who can prove me a liar,
And make my speech worthless?"

Bildad Says Man Is Inferior

25 THEN Bildad the Shuhite [1]answered,
2 "[a]Dominion and awe [1]belong to Him
Who establishes peace in [b]His heights.
3 "Is there any number to [a]His troops?
And upon whom does His light not rise?
4 "How then can a man be [a]just with God?
Or how can he be [b]clean who is born of woman?
5 "If even [a]the moon has no brightness
And the [b]stars are not pure in His sight,
6 How much less [a]man, *that* [b]maggot,
And the son of man, *that* worm!"

Job Rebukes Bildad

26 THEN Job [1]responded,
2 "What a help you are to [1a]the weak!
How you have saved the arm [b]without strength!
3 "What counsel you have given to *one* without wisdom!
What helpful insight you have abundantly [1]provided!
4 "To whom have you uttered words?
And whose [1]spirit was expressed through you?

The Greatness of God

5 "The [1a]departed spirits tremble
Under the waters and their inhabitants.
6 "Naked is [1a]Sheol before Him
And [2b]Abaddon has no covering.
7 "He [a]stretches out the north over empty space,
And hangs the earth on nothing.
8 "He [a]wraps up the waters in His clouds;

And the cloud does not burst under them.
9"He [1a]obscures the face of the [2]full moon,
And spreads His cloud over it.
10"He has inscribed a [a]circle on the surface of the waters,
At the [b]boundary of light and darkness.
11"The pillars of heaven tremble,
And are amazed at His rebuke.
12"He [a]quieted the sea with His power,
And by His [b]understanding He shattered [c]Rahab.
13"By His breath the [a]heavens are [1]cleared;
His hand has pierced [b]the fleeing serpent.
14"Behold, these are the fringes of His ways;
And how faint [a]a word we hear of Him!
But His mighty [b]thunder, who can understand?"

Job Affirms His Righteousness

27 THEN Job [1]continued his [a]discourse and said,
2"As God lives, [a]who has taken away my right,
And the Almighty, [b]who has embittered my soul,
3 For as long as [1]life is in me,
And the [2a]breath of God is in my nostrils,
4 My lips certainly will not speak unjustly,
Nor will [a]my tongue mutter deceit.
5"Far be it from me that I should declare you right;
Till I die [a]I will not put away my integrity from me.
6"I [a]hold fast my righteousness and will not let it go.
My heart does not reproach any of my days.

The State of the Godless

7"May my enemy be as the wicked,
And [1]my opponent as the unjust.
8"For what is [a]the hope of the godless [1]when he is cut off,
When God requires [b]his [2]life?
9"Will God [a]hear his cry,
When [b]distress comes upon him?
10"Will he take [a]delight in the Almighty,
Will he call on God at all times?
11"I will instruct you in the [1]power of God;
What is with the Almighty I will not conceal.
12"Behold, all of you have seen *it;*
Why then do you [1]act foolishly?

13"This is [a]the portion of a wicked man from God,
And the inheritance *which* [b]tyrants receive from the Almighty.
14"Though his sons are many, [1]they are destined [a]for the sword;
And his [b]descendants will not be satisfied with bread.
15"His survivors will be buried because of the plague,
And [1]their [a]widows will not be able to weep.
16"Though he piles up silver like dust,
And prepares garments as *plentiful as* the clay;
17 He may prepare *it,* [a]but the just will wear *it,*
And the innocent will divide the silver.
18"He has built his [a]house like the [1]spider's web,
Or as a hut *which* the watchman has made.
19"He lies down rich, but never [1]again;
He opens his eyes, and [a]it is no more.
20"[a]Terrors overtake him like a flood;
A tempest steals him away [b]in the night.
21"The east [a]wind carries him away, and he is gone,
For it whirls him [b]away from his place.
22"For it will hurl at him [a]without sparing;
He will surely try to [b]flee from its [1]power.
23"*Men* will clap their hands at him,
And will [a]hiss him from his place.

Job Tells of Earth's Treasures

28 "SURELY there is a [1]mine for silver,
And a place [2]where they refine gold.
2"Iron is taken from the dust,
And from rock copper is smelted.
3"*Man* puts an end to darkness,
And [a]to the farthest limit he searches out
The rock in gloom and deep shadow.
4"He [1]sinks a shaft far from [2]habitation,
Forgotten by the foot;
They hang and swing to and fro far from men.
5"The earth, from it comes food,
And underneath it is turned up as fire.
6"Its rocks are the [1]source of sapphires,
And its dust *contains* gold.
7"The path no bird of prey knows,
Nor has the falcon's eye caught sight of it.
8"The [1]proud beasts have not trodden it,
Nor has the *fierce* lion passed over it.
9"He puts his hand on the flint;
He overturns the mountains at the [1]base.
10"He hews out channels through the rocks;
And his eye sees anything precious.

---

9 [1]Lit., *covers* [2]Or, *throne* [a]Job 22:14; Ps. 97:2; 105:39
10 [a]Job 38:1-11; Prov. 8:29 [b]Job 38:19, 20, 24
12 [a]Is. 51:15; Jer. 31:35 [b]Job 12:13 [c]Job 9:13
13 [1]Lit., *made beautiful* [a]Job 9:8 [b]Is. 27:1
14 [a]Job 4:12 [b]Job 36:29; 37:4, 5

1 [1]Or, *again took up* [a]Job 13:12; 29:1
2 [a]Job 16:11; 34:5 [b]Job 9:18
3 [1]Lit., *breath* [2]Or, *spirit* [a]Job 32:8; 33:4
4 [a]Job 6:28; 33:3
5 [a]Job 6:29
6 [a]Job 2:3; 13:18
7 [1]Lit., *he who rises up against me*
8 [1]Or, *though he gains* [2]Lit., *soul* [a]Job 8:13; 11:20 [b]Job 12:10
9 [a]Job 35:12, 13; Ps. 18:41; Prov. 1:28; Is. 1:15; Jer. 14:12; Mic. 3:4 [b]Prov. 1:27
10 [a]Job 22:26, 27; Ps. 37:4; Is. 58:14
11 [1]Lit., *hand*
12 [1]Or, *speak vanity*
13 [a]Job 20:29 [b]Job 15:20
14 [1]Lit., *the sword is for them* [a]Job 15:22; 18:19 [b]Job 20:10
15 [1]So ancient versions; Heb., *his* [a]Ps. 78:64
17 [a]Job 20:18-21
18 [1]So ancient versions; Heb., *moth* [a]Job 8:15; 18:14
19 [1]So ancient versions; Heb., *will be gathered* [a]Job 7:8, 21; 20:7
20 [a]Job 15:21 [b]Job 20:8; 34:20
21 [a]Job 21:18 [b]Job 7:10
22 [1]Lit., *hand* [a]Jer. 13:14; Ezek. 5:11; 24:14 [b]Job 11:20
23 [a]Job 18:18; 20:8

1 [1]Or, *source* [2]Lit., *for gold they refine*
3 [a]Eccl. 1:13
4 [1]Lit., *breaks open* [2]Lit., *sojourning*
6 [1]Or, *place*
8 [1]Lit., *sons of pride*
9 [1]Lit., *roots*

11 "He dams up the streams from [1]flowing;
And what is hidden he brings out to the light.

The Search for Wisdom Is Harder

12 "But [a]where can wisdom be found?
And where is the place of understanding?
13 "[a]Man does not know its value,
Nor is it found in the land of the living.
14 "The deep says, 'It is not in me';
And the sea says, 'It is not with me.'
15 "[a]Pure gold cannot be given in exchange for it,
Nor can silver be weighed as its price.
16 "It cannot be valued in the gold of Ophir,
In precious onyx, or sapphire.
17 "[a]Gold or glass cannot equal it,
Nor can it be exchanged for articles of fine gold.
18 "Coral and crystal are not to be mentioned;
And the acquisition of [a]wisdom is above *that of* pearls.
19 "The topaz of Ethiopia cannot equal it,
Nor can it be valued in [a]pure gold.
20 "[a]Where then does wisdom come from?
And where is the place of understanding?
21 "Thus it is hidden from the eyes of all living,
And concealed from the birds of the sky.
22 "[1a]Abaddon and Death say,
'With our ears we have heard a report of it.'

23 "[a]God understands its way;
And He knows its place.
24 "For He [a]looks to the ends of the earth,
And sees everything under the heavens.
25 "When He imparted [a]weight to the wind,
And [b]meted out the waters by measure,
26 When He set a [a]limit for the rain,
And a course for the [b]thunderbolt,
27 Then He saw it and declared it;
He established it and also searched it out.
28 "And to man He said, 'Behold, the [a]fear of the Lord, that is wisdom;
And to depart from evil is understanding.' "

Job's Past Was Glorious

29 AND Job again took up his [a]discourse and said,
2 "Oh that I were as in months gone by,
As in the days when God [a]watched over me;
3 When [a]His lamp shone over my head,
And [b]by His light I walked through darkness;
4 As I was in [1]the prime of my days,
When the [2a]friendship of God *was* over my tent;
5 When [1]the Almighty was yet with me,
And my children were around me;
6 When my steps were bathed in [a]butter,
And the [b]rock poured out for me streams of oil!
7 "When I went out to [a]the gate of the city,
When I [1]took my seat in the square;
8 The young men saw me and hid themselves,
And the old men arose *and* stood.
9 "The princes [a]stopped talking,
And [b]put *their* hands on their mouths;
10 The voice of the nobles was [1a]hushed,
And their [b]tongue stuck to their palate.
11 "For when [a]the ear heard, it called me blessed;
And when the eye saw, it gave witness of me,
12 Because I delivered [a]the poor who cried for help,
And the [b]orphan who had no helper.
13 "The blessing of the one [a]ready to perish came upon me,
And I made the [b]widow's heart sing for joy.
14 "I [a]put on righteousness, and it clothed me;
My justice was like a robe and a turban.
15 "I was [a]eyes to the blind,
And feet to the lame.
16 "I was a father to [a]the needy,
And I investigated the case which I did not know.
17 "And I [a]broke the jaws of the wicked,
And snatched the prey from his teeth.
18 "Then I [1]thought, 'I shall die [2]in my nest,
And I shall multiply *my* days as the sand.
19 'My [a]root is spread out to the waters,
And [b]dew lies all night on my branch.
20 'My glory is *ever* new with me,
And my [a]bow is renewed in my hand.'

21 "To me [a]they listened and waited,
And kept silent for my counsel.
22 "After my words they did not [a]speak again,
And [b]my speech dropped on them.
23 "And they waited for me as for the rain,

11 [1]Lit., *weeping*
12 [a]Job 28:23, 28; Eccl. 7:24
13 [a]Matt. 13:44-46
15 [a]Prov. 3:13, 14; 8:10, 11; 16:16
17 [a]Prov. 8:10; 16:16
18 [a]Prov. 8:11
19 [a]Prov. 8:19
20 [a]Job 28:23, 28
22 [1]I.e., Destruction [a]Job 26:6; Prov. 8:32-36
23 [a]Job 9:4; Prov. 8:22-36
24 [a]Ps. 11:4; 33:13, 14; 66:7; Prov. 15:3
25 [a]Ps. 135:7 [b]Job 12:15; 38:8-11
26 [a]Job 37:6, 11, 12; 38:26-28 [b]Job 37:3; 38:25
28 [a]Ps. 111:10; Prov. 1:7; 9:10; Eccl. 12:13

1 [a]Num. 23:7; 24:3; Job 13:12; 27:1
2 [a]Jer. 31:28
3 [a]Job 18:6 [b]Job 11:17
4 [1]Lit., *the days of my autumn* [2]Lit., *counsel* [a]Job 15:8; Ps. 25:14; Prov. 3:32
5 [1]Heb., *Shaddai*
6 [a]Deut. 32:14; Job 20:17 [b]Deut. 32:13; Ps. 81:16
7 [1]Lit., *set up* [a]Job 31:21
9 [a]Job 29:21 [b]Job 21:5
10 [1]Lit., *hidden* [a]Job 29:22 [b]Ps. 137:6
11 [a]Job 4:3, 4
12 [a]Job 24:4, 9; 34:28; Ps. 72:12; Prov. 21:13 [b]Job 31:17, 21
13 [a]Job 31:19 [b]Job 22:9
14 [a]Job 27:5, 6; Ps. 132:9; Is. 59:17; 61:10; Eph. 6:14
15 [a]Num. 10:31
16 [a]Job 24:4; Prov. 29:7
17 [a]Ps. 3:7
18 [1]Lit., *said* [2]Lit., *with*
19 [a]Jer. 17:8 [b]Hos. 14:5
20 [a]Gen. 49:24; Ps. 18:34
21 [a]Job 4:3; 29:9
22 [a]Job 29:10 [b]Deut. 32:2

And opened their mouth as for the
spring rain.
24"I smiled on them when they did not
believe,
And the light of my face they did
not cast down.
25"I chose a way for them and sat as
[a]chief,
And dwelt as a king among the
troops,
As one who [b]comforted the mourners.

Job's Present State Is Humiliating

30 "BUT now those younger than I
[a]mock me,
Whose fathers I disdained to put
with the dogs of my flock.
2"Indeed, what *good was* the strength
of their hands to me?
Vigor had perished from them.
3"From want and famine they are
gaunt
Who gnaw the dry ground by night
in waste and desolation,
4 Who pluck [1]mallow by the bushes,
And whose food is the root of the
broom shrub.
5"They are driven from the community;
They shout against them as *against*
a thief,
6 So that they dwell in dreadful
[1]valleys,
In holes of the earth and of the
rocks.
7"Among the bushes they [1]cry out;
Under the nettles they are gathered
together.
8"[1]Fools, even [2]those without a
name,
They were scourged from the land.

9"And now I have become their
[1a]taunt,
I have even become a [b]byword to
them.
10"They abhor me *and* stand aloof
from me,
And they do not [1]refrain from
[a]spitting at my face.
11"Because [1]He has loosed [2]His [3]bow-
string and [a]afflicted me,
They have cast off [b]the bridle before me.
12"On the right hand their [1]brood
arises;
They [a]thrust aside my feet [b]and
build up against me their ways
of destruction.
13"They [a]break up my path,
They profit [1]from my destruction,
No one restrains them.
14"As *through* a wide breach they
come,
[1]Amid the tempest they roll on.
15"[a]Terrors are turned against me,
They pursue my [1]honor as the
wind,
And my [2]prosperity has passed
away [b]like a cloud.
16"And now [a]my soul is poured out
[1]within me;
Days of affliction have seized me.
17"At night it pierces [a]my bones
[1]within me,
And my gnawing *pains* take no rest.
18"By a great force my garment is
[a]distorted;
It binds me about as the collar of
my coat.
19"He has cast me into the [a]mire,
And I have become like dust and
ashes.
20"I [a]cry out to Thee for help, but
Thou dost not answer me;
I stand up, and Thou dost turn Thy
attention against me.
21"Thou hast [1]become cruel to me;
With the might of Thy hand Thou
dost [a]persecute me.
22"Thou dost [a]lift me up to the wind
and cause me to ride;
And Thou dost dissolve me in a
storm.
23"For I know that Thou [a]wilt bring
me to death
And to the [b]house of meeting for
all living.

24"Yet does not one in a heap of ruins
stretch out *his* hand,
Or in his disaster therefore [a]cry out
for help?
25"Have I not [a]wept for the [1]one
whose life is hard?
Was not my soul grieved for [b]the
needy?
26"When I [a]expected good, then evil
came;
When I waited for light, [b]then
darkness came.
27"[1]I am seething [a]within, and cannot
relax;
Days of affliction confront me.
28"I go about [1a]mourning without
comfort;
I stand up in the assembly *and* [b]cry
out for help.
29"I have become a brother to [a]jack-
als,
And a companion of ostriches.
30"My [a]skin turns black [1]on me,
And my [b]bones burn with [2]fever.
31"Therefore my [a]harp [1]is turned to
mourning,
And my flute to the sound of those
who weep.

Job Asserts His Integrity

31 "I HAVE made a covenant with
my [a]eyes;
How then could I gaze at a virgin?
2"And what is [a]the portion of God
from above
Or the heritage of the Almighty
from on high?
3"Is it not [a]calamity to the unjust,
And disaster to [b]those who work
iniquity?
4"Does He not [a]see my ways,
And [b]number all my steps?

25 [a]Job 1:3; 31:37 [b]Job 4:4; 16:5
1 [a]Job 12:4
4 [1]I.e., plant of the salt marshes
6 [1]Or, *wadis*
7 [1]Or, *bray*
8 [1]Lit., *Sons of fools* [2]Lit., *sons*
9 [1]Lit., *song* [a]Job 12:4 [b]Job 17:6; Ps. 69:11; Lam. 3:14, 63
10 [1]Lit., *withhold spit from my face* [a]Num. 12:14; Deut. 25:9; Job 17:6; Is. 50:6; Matt. 26:67
11 [1]Or, *they* [2]Some mss. read *my* [3]Or, *cord* [a]Ruth 1:21; Ps. 88:7 [b]Ps. 32:9
12 [1]Possibly, *sprout or offspring* [a]Ps. 140:4, 5 [b]Job 19:12
13 [1]Lit., *for* [a]Is. 3:12
14 [1]Lit., *Under*
15 [1]Or, *nobility* [2]Or, *welfare* [a]Job 3:25; 31:23; Ps. 55:3-5 [b]Job 7:9; Hos. 13:3
16 [1]Lit., *upon* [a]1 Sam. 1:15; Job 3:24; Ps. 22:14; 42:4; Is. 53:12
17 [1]Lit., *from upon* [a]Job 30:30
18 [a]Job 2:7
19 [a]Ps. 69:2, 14
20 [a]Job 19:7
21 [1]Lit., *turned to be* [a]Job 10:3; 16:9, 14; 19:6, 22
22 [a]Job 9:17; 27:21
23 [a]Job 9:22; 10:8 [b]Job 3:19; Eccl. 12:5
24 [a]Job 19:7
25 [1]Lit., *hard of day* [a]Ps. 35:13, 14; Rom. 12:15 [b]Job 24:4
26 [a]Job 3:25, 26; Jer. 8:15 [b]Job 19:8
27 [1]Lit., *My inward parts are boiling* [a]Lam. 2:11
28 [1]Or, *blackened, but not by the heat of the sun* [a]Job 30:31; Ps. 38:6; 42:9; 43:2 [b]Job 19:7
29 [a]Ps. 44:19; Mic. 1:8
30 [1]Lit., *from upon* [2]Lit., *heat* [a]Job 2:7 [b]Ps. 102:3
31 [1]Lit., *becomes* [a]Is. 24:8
1 [a]Matt. 5:28
2 [a]Job 20:29
3 [a]Job 18:12; 21:30 [b]Job 34:22
4 [a]2 Chr. 16:9; Job 24:23; 28:24; 34:21; 36:7; Prov. 5:21; 15:3 [b]Job 14:16; 31:37

5 "If I have [a]walked with falsehood,
And my foot has hastened after deceit,
6 Let Him [a]weigh me with [1]accurate scales,
And let God know [b]my integrity.
7 "If my step has [a]turned from the way,
Or my heart [1]followed my eyes,
Or if any [b]spot has stuck to my hands,
8 Let me [a]sow and another eat,
And let my [1b]crops be uprooted.

9 "If my heart has been [a]enticed by a woman,
Or I have lurked at my neighbor's doorway,
10 May my wife [a]grind for another,
And let [b]others [1]kneel down over her.
11 "For that would be a [a]lustful crime;
Moreover, it would be [b]an iniquity *punishable by* judges.
12 "For it would be [a]fire that consumes to [1b]Abaddon,
And would [c]uproot all my [2]increase.

13 "If I have [a]despised the claim of my male or female slaves
When they filed a complaint against me,
14 What then could I do when God arises,
And when He calls me to account, what will I answer Him?
15 "Did not [a]He who made me in the womb make him,
And the same one fashion us in the womb?

16 "If I have kept [a]the poor from *their* desire,
Or have caused the eyes of [b]the widow to fail,
17 Or have [a]eaten my morsel alone,
And [b]the orphan has not [1]shared it
18 (But from my youth he grew up with me as with a father,
And from [1]infancy I guided her),
19 If I have seen anyone perish [a]for lack of clothing,
Or that [b]the needy had no covering,
20 If his loins have not [1]thanked me,
And if he has not been warmed with the fleece of my sheep,
21 If I have lifted up my hand against [a]the orphan,
Because I saw [1]I had support [b]in the gate,
22 Let my shoulder fall from the [1]socket,
And my [a]arm be broken off [2]at the elbow.
23 "For [a]calamity from God is a terror to me,
And because of [b]His [1]majesty I can do nothing.

24 "If I have put my confidence *in* [a]gold,
And called fine gold my trust,
25 If I have [a]gloated because my wealth was great,
And because my hand had secured *so* much;
26 If I have [a]looked at the [1]sun when it shone,
Or the moon going in splendor,
27 And my heart became secretly enticed,
And my hand [1]threw a kiss from my mouth,
28 That too would have been [a]an iniquity *calling for* [1]judgment,
For I would have [b]denied God above.

29 "Have I [a]rejoiced at the extinction of my enemy,
Or [1]exulted when evil befell him?
30 "[1]No, [a]I have not [2]allowed my mouth to sin
By asking for his life in [b]a curse.
31 "Have the men of my tent not said,
'Who can [1]find one who has not been [a]satisfied with his meat'?
32 "The alien has not lodged outside,
For I have opened my doors to the [1]traveler.
33 "Have I [a]covered my transgressions like [1]Adam,
By hiding my iniquity in my bosom,
34 Because I [a]feared the great multitude,
And the contempt of families terrified me,
And kept silent and did not go out of doors?
35 "Oh that I had one to hear me!
Behold, here is my [1]signature;
[a]Let the Almighty answer me!
And the indictment which my [b]adversary has written,
36 Surely I would carry it on my shoulder;
I would bind it to myself like a crown.
37 "I would declare to Him [a]the number of my steps;
Like [b]a prince I would approach Him.

38 "If my [a]land cries out against me,
And its furrows weep together;
39 If I have [a]eaten its [1]fruit without money,
Or have [b]caused [2]its owners to lose their lives,
40 Let [a]briars [1]grow instead of wheat,
And stinkweed instead of barley."
The words of Job are ended.

Elihu in Anger Rebukes Job

32 THEN these three men ceased answering Job, because he was [a]righteous in his own eyes.

1 aJob 10:7; 13:18; 27:5, 6; 31:6

5 aJob 15:31; Mic. 2:11
6 1Lit., *just* aJob 6:2, 3 bJob 23:10; 27:5, 6
7 1Lit., *walked after* aJob 23:11 bJob 9:30
8 1Or, *offspring* aLev. 26:16; Job 20:18; Mic. 6:15 bJob 31:12
9 aJob 24:15; 31:1
10 1I.e., sexual relations aIs. 47:2 bDeut. 28:30; Jer. 8:10
11 aLev. 20:10; Deut. 22:24 bJob 31:28
12 1I.e., place of destruction 2Or, *yield* aJob 15:30 bJob 26:6 cJob 20:28; 31:8
13 aDeut. 24:14, 15
15 aJob 10:3
16 aJob 5:16; 20:19 bEx. 22:22-24; Job 22:9
17 1Lit., *eaten from it* aJob 22:7 bJob 29:12
18 1Lit., *my mother's womb*
19 aJob 22:6; 29:13 bJob 24:4
20 1Lit., *blessed*
21 1Lit., *my help* aJob 29:12; 31:17 bJob 29:7
22 1Lit., *shoulder;* or, *back* 2Lit., *from the bone of the upper arm* aJob 38:15
23 1Lit., *exaltation* aJob 31:3 bJob 13:11
24 aJob 22:24; Mark 10:23-25
25 aJob 1:3, 10; Ps. 62:10
26 1Lit., *light* aDeut. 4:19; 17:3; Ezek. 8:16
27 1Lit., *kissed my mouth*
28 1Lit., *judges* aDeut. 17:2-7; Job 31:11 bJosh. 24:27; Is. 59:13
29 1Lit., *lifted myself up* aProv. 17:5; 24:17; Obad. 12
30 1Lit., *And* 2Lit., *given my palate* aPs. 7:4 bJob 5:3
31 1Lit., *give* aJob 22:7
32 1M.T., *way*
33 1Or, *mankind* aGen. 3:10; Prov. 28:13
34 aEx. 23:2
35 1Lit., *mark* aJob 19:7; 30:20, 24, 28; 35:14 bJob 27:7
37 aJob 31:4 bJob 1:3; 29:25
38 aJob 24:2
39 1Lit., *strength* 2Lit., *the soul of its owners to expire* aJob 24:6, 10-12; James 5:4 b1 Kin. 21:19
40 1Lit., *come forth* aJob 32:13; Is. 5:6

2 But the anger of Elihu the son of
Barachel the [a]Buzite, of the family of
Ram burned; against Job his anger
burned, [b]because he justified himself
[1c]before God.
3 And his anger burned against his
three friends because they had found no
answer, and yet had condemned Job.
4 Now Elihu had waited [1]to speak to
Job because they were years older than
he.
5 And when Elihu saw that there was
no answer in the mouth of the three men
his anger burned.
6 So Elihu the son of Barachel the
Buzite [1]spoke out and said,

"I am young in years and you are
[a]old;
Therefore I was shy and afraid to
tell you [2]what I think.
7"I [1]thought [2a]age should speak,
And [3]increased years should teach
wisdom.
8"But it is a spirit in man,
And the [a]breath of the Almighty
gives them [b]understanding.
9"The [1]abundant *in years* may not be
wise,
Nor may [a]elders understand justice.
10"So I [1]say, 'Listen to me,
I too will tell [2]what I think.'

11"Behold, I waited for your words,
I listened to your reasonings,
While you [1]pondered what to say.
12"I even paid close attention to you,
[1]Indeed, there was no one who
refuted Job,
Not one of you who answered his
words.
13"[1]Do not say,
'[a]We have found wisdom;
God will [2]rout him, not man.'
14"For he has not arranged *his* words
against me;
Nor will I reply to him with your
[1]arguments.

15"They are dismayed, they answer no
more;
Words have [1]failed them.
16"And shall I wait, because they do
not speak,
Because they [1]stop *and* answer no
more?
17"I too will answer my share,
I also will tell my opinion.
18"For I am full of words;
The spirit within me constrains me.
19"Behold, my belly is like unvented
wine,
Like new wineskins it is about to
burst.
20"Let me speak that I may get relief;
Let me open my lips and answer.
21"Let me now [a]be partial to no one;
Nor flatter *any* man.
22"For I do not know how to flatter,
Else my Maker would soon take me
away.

Elihu Claims to Speak for God

33 "HOWEVER now, Job, please
[a]hear my speech,
And listen to all my words.
2"Behold now, I open my mouth,
My tongue in my [1]mouth speaks.
3"My words are *from* the uprightness
of my heart;
And my lips speak [a]knowledge
sincerely.
4"The [a]Spirit of God has made me,
And the [b]breath of [1]the Almighty
gives me life.
5"[a]Refute me if you can;
Array yourselves before me, take
your stand.
6"Behold, I belong to God like you;
I too have been [1]formed out of the
[a]clay.
7"Behold, [a]no fear of me should
terrify you,
Nor should my pressure weigh
heavily on you.

8"Surely you have spoken in my
hearing,
And I have heard the sound of *your*
words:
9 'I am [a]pure, [b]without transgression;
I am innocent and there [c]is no guilt
in me.
10 'Behold, He [1]invents pretexts
against me;
He [a]counts me as His enemy.
11 'He [a]puts my feet in the stocks;
He watches all my paths.'
12"Behold, let me [1]tell you, [a]you are
not right in this,
For God is greater than man.

13"Why do you [a]complain against
Him,
That He does not give an account
of all His doings?
14"Indeed [a]God speaks once,
Or twice, *yet* no one notices it.
15"In a [a]dream, a vision of the night,
When sound sleep falls on men,
While they slumber in their beds,
16 Then [a]He opens the ears of men,
And seals their instruction,
17 That He may turn man aside *from*
his conduct,
And [1]keep man from pride;
18 He [a]keeps back his soul from the
pit,
And his life from [1]passing over
[b]into Sheol.

19"[1]Man is also chastened with [a]pain
on his bed,
And with unceasing complaint in
his bones;
20 So that his life [a]loathes bread,
And his soul favorite food.
21"His [a]flesh wastes away from sight,
And his [b]bones which were not
seen stick out.
22"Then [a]his soul draws near to the
pit,
And his life to those who bring
death.

2 [1]Or, *more than* [a]Gen. 22:21 [b]Job 27:5, 6 [c]Job 30:21
4 [1]Lit., *for Job with words;* or possibly, *while they were speaking with Job*
6 [1]Lit., *answered* [2]Lit., *my knowledge* [a]Job 15:10
7 [1]Lit., *said* [2]Lit., *days* [3]Lit., *many* [a]Job 8:8, 9
8 [a]Job 33:4 [b]Job 38:36
9 [1]Or, *nobles* [a]Job 32:7
10 [1]Or, *said* [2]Lit., *my knowledge*
11 [1]Lit., *searched out words*
12 [1]Lit., *Behold*
13 [1]Lit., *Lest you say* [2]Lit., *drive away* [a]Jer. 9:23
14 [1]Lit., *words*
15 [1]Lit., *moved away from*
16 [1]Lit., *stand*
21 [a]Lev. 19:15; Job 13:8, 10; 34:19

1 [a]Job 13:6
2 [1]Lit., *palate*
3 [a]Job 6:28; 27:4; 36:4
4 [1]Heb., *Shaddai* [a]Gen. 2:7; Job 10:3; 32:8 [b]Job 27:3
5 [a]Job 33:32
6 [1]Lit., *cut out of* [a]Job 4:19
7 [a]Job 13:21
9 [a]Job 9:21; 10:7; 13:18; 16:17 [b]Job 7:21; 13:23; 14:17 [c]Job 10:14
10 [1]Lit., *finds* [a]Job 13:24
11 [a]Job 13:27
12 [1]Lit., *answer* [a]Eccl. 7:20
13 [a]Job 40:2; Is. 45:9
14 [a]Job 33:29; 40:5; Ps. 62:11
15 [a]Job 4:12-17; 33:15-18
16 [a]Job 36:10, 15
17 [1]Lit., *hide*
18 [1]M.T., *perishing by the sword* [a]Job 33:22, 24, 28, 30 [b]Job 15:22
19 [1]Lit., *He* [a]Job 30:17
20 [a]Job 3:24; 6:7; Ps. 107:18
21 [a]Job 16:8 [b]Job 19:20; Ps. 22:17; 102:5
22 [a]Job 33:18, 28

23 "If there is an angel *as* [a]mediator for him,
One out of a thousand,
To remind a man what is [1]right for him,
24 Then let him be gracious to him, and say,
'Deliver him from [a]going down to the pit,
I have found a [b]ransom';
25 Let his flesh become fresher than in youth,
Let him return to the days of his youthful vigor;
26 Then he will [a]pray to God, and He will accept him,
That [b]he may see His face with joy,
And He may restore His righteousness to man.
27 "He will sing to men and say,
'I [a]have sinned and perverted what is right,
And it is not [b]proper for me.
28 'He has redeemed my soul from going to the pit,
And my life shall [a]see the light.'

29 "Behold, God does [a]all these [1]oftentimes with men,
30 To [a]bring back his soul from the pit,
That he may be enlightened with the light of life.
31 "Pay attention, O Job, listen to me;
Keep silent and let me speak.
32 "*Then* if [1]you have anything to say, answer me;
Speak, for I desire to justify you.
33 "If not, [a]listen to me;
Keep silent, and I will teach you wisdom."

Elihu Vindicates God's Justice

34 THEN Elihu continued and said,
2 "Hear my words, you wise men,
And listen to me, you who know.
3 "For [a]the ear tests words,
As the palate tastes food.
4 "Let us choose for ourselves what is right;
Let us know among ourselves what is good.
5 "For Job has said, '[a]I am righteous,
But [b]God has taken away my right;
6 [1]Should I lie concerning my right?
My [2a]wound is incurable, *though I am* without transgression.'
7 "What man is like Job,
Who [a]drinks up derision like water,
8 Who goes [a]in company with the workers of iniquity,
And walks with wicked men?
9 "For he has said, '[a]It profits a man nothing
When he [1]is pleased with God.'

10 "Therefore, listen to me, you men of understanding.
Far be it from God to [a]do wickedness,
And from the Almighty to do wrong.
11 "For He pays a man according to [a]his work,
And makes [1]him find it according to his way.
12 "Surely, [a]God will not act wickedly,
And the Almighty will not pervert justice.
13 "Who [a]gave Him authority over the earth?
And who [b]has laid *on Him* the whole world?
14 "If He should [1]determine to do so,
If He should [a]gather to Himself His spirit and His breath,
15 All [a]flesh would perish together,
And man would [b]return to dust.

16 "But if *you have* understanding, hear this;
Listen to the sound of my words.
17 "Shall [a]one who hates justice rule?
And [b]will you condemn a righteous mighty one,
18 Who says to a king, 'Worthless one,'
To nobles, 'Wicked ones';
19 Who shows no [a]partiality to princes,
Nor regards the rich above the poor,
For they all are the [b]work of His hands?
20 "In a moment they die, and [a]at midnight
People are shaken and pass away,
And [b]the mighty are taken away without a hand.

21 "For [a]His eyes are upon the ways of a man,
And He sees all his steps.
22 "There is [a]no darkness or deep shadow
Where the workers of iniquity may hide themselves.
23 "For He does not [a]*need to* consider a man further,
That he should go before God in judgment.
24 "He breaks in pieces [a]mighty men without inquiry,
And sets others in their place.
25 "Therefore He [a]knows their works,
And [b]He overthrows *them* in the night,
And they are crushed.
26 "He [a]strikes them like the wicked
[1]In a public place,
27 Because they [a]turned aside from following Him,
And [b]had no regard for any of His ways;
28 So that they caused [a]the cry of the poor to come to Him,
And that He might [b]hear the cry of the afflicted—
29 When He keeps quiet, who then can condemn?
And when He hides His face, who then can behold Him,
That is, in regard to both nation and man?—

23 [1]Lit., *his uprightness* [a]Gen. 40:8
24 [a]Job 33:18, 28; Is. 38:17 [b]Job 36:18; Ps. 49:7
26 [a]Job 22:27; 34:28; Ps. 50:14, 15 [b]Job 22:26
27 [a]2 Sam. 12:13; Luke 15:21 [b]Rom. 6:21
28 [a]Job 22:28
29 [1]Lit., *twice, three times* [a]Eph. 1:11; Phil. 2:13
30 [a]Job 33:18; Zech. 9:11
32 [1]Lit., *there are words*
33 [a]Ps. 34:11

3 [a]Job 12:11
5 [a]Job 13:18; 33:9 [b]Job 27:2
6 [1]Or, *Although I am right I am accounted a liar* [2]Lit., *arrow* [a]Job 6:4
7 [a]Job 15:16
8 [a]Job 22:15
9 [1]Or, *takes delight in God* [a]Job 21:15; 35:3; Ps. 50:18
10 [a]Gen. 18:25; Deut. 32:4; Job 8:3; 34:12; Rom. 9:14
11 [1]Lit., *a man* [a]Job 34:25; Ps. 62:12; Prov. 24:12; Jer. 32:19; Ezek. 33:20; Matt. 16:27; Rom. 2:6; 2 Cor. 5:10; Rev. 22:12
12 [a]Job 34:10
13 [a]Job 38:4 [b]Job 38:5
14 [1]Lit., *set His mind on Himself* [a]Job 12:10; Ps. 104:29; Eccl. 12:7
15 [a]Gen. 7:21; Job 9:22 [b]Gen. 3:19; Job 10:9
17 [a]2 Sam. 23:3; Job 34:30 [b]Job 40:8
19 [a]Lev. 19:15; Deut. 10:17; 2 Chr. 19:7; Acts 10:34; Rom. 2:11; Gal. 2:6; Eph. 6:9; Col. 3:25; 1 Pet. 1:17 [b]Job 10:3
20 [a]Ex. 12:29; Job 34:25; 36:20 [b]Job 12:19
21 [a]Job 24:23; 31:4; Prov. 5:21; 15:3; Jer. 16:17
22 [a]Ps. 139:11, 12; Amos 9:2, 3
23 [a]Job 11:11
24 [a]Job 12:19
25 [a]Job 34:11 [b]Job 34:20
26 [1]Lit., *In the place of the ones seeing* [a]Ps. 9:5; 11:5
27 [a]1 Sam. 15:11 [b]Job 21:14
28 [a]Job 35:9; James 5:4 [b]Ex. 22:23; Job 22:27

30 So that [a]godless men should not rule,
Nor be snares of the people.

31 "For has anyone said to God,
'I have borne *chastisement;*
I will not offend *anymore;*
32 Teach Thou me what I do not see;
If I have [a]done iniquity,
I will do it no more'?
33 "Shall He [a]recompense on your terms, because you have rejected *it?*
For you must choose, and not I;
Therefore declare what you know.
34 "Men of understanding will say to me,
And a wise man who hears me,
35 'Job [a]speaks without knowledge,
And his words are without wisdom.
36 'Job ought to be tried [1]to the limit,
Because he answers [a]like wicked men.
37 'For he adds [a]rebellion to his sin;
He [b]claps his hands among us,
And multiplies his words against God.' "

Elihu Sharply Reproves Job

35 THEN Elihu continued and said,
2 "Do you think this is according to [a]justice?
Do you say, 'My righteousness is more than God's'?
3 "For you say, '[a]What advantage will it be to [1]You?
[b]What profit shall I have, more than if I had sinned?'
4 "I will answer you,
And your friends with you.
5 "[a]Look at the heavens and see;
And behold [b]the clouds—they are higher than you.
6 "If you have sinned, [a]what do you accomplish against Him?
And if your transgressions are many, what do you do to Him?
7 "If you are righteous, [a]what do you give to Him?
Or what does He receive from your hand?
8 "Your wickedness is for a man like yourself,
And your righteousness is for a son of man.

9 "Because of the [a]multitude of oppressions they cry out;
They cry for help because of the arm [b]of the mighty.
10 "But [a]no one says, 'Where is God my Maker,
Who [b]gives songs in the night,
11 Who [a]teaches us more than the beasts of the earth,
And makes us wiser than the birds of the heavens?'
12 "There [a]they cry out, but He does not answer
Because of the pride of evil men.
13 "Surely [a]God will not listen to [1]an empty *cry,*
Nor will the Almighty regard it.

30 [a]Job 5:15; 20:5; 34:17; Prov. 29:2-12
32 [a]Job 33:27
33 [a]Job 41:11
35 [a]Job 35:16; 38:2
36 [1]Or, *to the end* [a]Job 22:15
37 [a]Job 23:2 [b]Job 27:23
2 [a]Job 27:2
3 [1]Or, *you* [a]Job 34:9 [b]Job 9:30, 31
5 [a]Gen. 15:5; Ps. 8:3 [b]Job 22:12
6 [a]Job 7:20; Prov. 8:36; Jer. 7:19
7 [a]Job 22:2, 3; Prov. 9:12; Luke 17:10; Rom. 11:35
9 [a]Ex. 2:23 [b]Job 12:19
10 [a]Job 21:14; 27:10; 36:13; Is. 51:13 [b]Job 8:21; Ps. 42:8; 77:6; 149:5; Acts 16:25
11 [a]Job 36:22; Ps. 94:12; Jer. 32:33
12 [a]Prov. 1:28
13 [1]Or, *falsehood* [a]Job 27:9; Prov. 15:29; Is. 1:15; Jer. 11:11; Mic. 3:4
14 [a]Job 9:11; 23:8, 9 [b]Job 31:35
15 [1]Or, *arrogance*
16 [1]Lit., *vainly* [a]Job 34:35; 38:2
2 [1]Lit., *are yet words for God*
3 [a]Job 8:3; 37:23
4 [a]Job 33:3 [b]Job 37:16
5 [a]Ps. 22:24; 69:33; 102:17 [b]Job 12:13
6 [a]Job 8:22; 34:26 [b]Job 5:15
7 [a]Ps. 33:18; 34:15 [b]Job 5:11; Ps. 113:8
8 [a]Job 36:15, 21
9 [a]Job 15:25
10 [a]Job 33:16; 36:15 [b]2 Kin. 17:13; Job 36:21; Jon. 3:8
11 [a]1 Tim. 4:8 [b]Ps. 16:11
12 [1]Lit., *pass away* [a]Job 15:22 [b]Job 4:21
14 [1]Or, *Their soul dies* [a]Deut. 23:17
15 [1]Lit., *his* [2]Or, *in adversity* [a]Job 36:8, 21 [b]Job 36:10
16 [1]Or, *rich food* [a]Hos. 2:14

14 "How much less when [a]you say you do not behold Him,
The [b]case is before Him, and you must wait for Him!
15 "And now, because He has not visited *in* His anger,
Nor has He acknowledged [1]transgression well,
16 So Job opens his mouth [1]emptily;
He multiplies words [a]without knowledge."

Elihu Speaks of God's Dealings with Men

36 THEN Elihu continued and said,
2 "Wait for me a little, and I will show you
That there [1]is yet more to be said in God's behalf.
3 "I will fetch my knowledge from afar,
And I will ascribe [a]righteousness to my Maker.
4 "For truly [a]my words are not false;
One who is [b]perfect in knowledge is with you.
5 "Behold, God is mighty but does not [a]despise *any;*
He is [b]mighty in strength of understanding.
6 "He does not [a]keep the wicked alive,
But gives justice to [b]the afflicted.
7 "He does not [a]withdraw His eyes from the righteous;
But [b]with kings on the throne
He has seated them forever, and they are exalted.
8 "And if they are bound in fetters,
And are caught in the cords of [a]affliction,
9 Then he declares to them their work
And their transgressions, that they have [a]magnified themselves.
10 "And [a]He opens their ear to instruction,
And [b]commands that they return from evil.
11 "If they hear and serve *Him,*
They shall [a]end their days in prosperity,
And their years in [b]pleasures.
12 "But if they do not hear, they shall [1]perish [a]by the sword,
And they shall [b]die without knowledge.
13 "But the godless in heart lay up anger;
They do not cry for help when He binds them.
14 "[1]They die in youth,
And their life *perishes* among the [a]cult prostitutes.
15 "He delivers the afflicted in [1]their [a]affliction,
And [b]opens their ear [2]in *time of* oppression.
16 "Then indeed, He [a]enticed you from the mouth of distress,
Instead of it, a broad place with no constraint;
And that which was set on your table was full of [1]fatness.

17 "But you were full of [a]judgment on
the wicked;
Judgment and justice take hold *of*
you.
18 "*Beware* lest [a]wrath entice you to
scoffing;
And do not let the greatness of the
[b]ransom turn you aside.
19 "Will your [1]riches keep *you* from
distress,
Or all the forces of *your* strength?
20 "Do not long for [a]the night,
When people [1]vanish in their place.
21 "Be careful, do [a]not turn to evil;
For you have preferred this to
[b]affliction.
22 "Behold, God is exalted in His
power;
Who is a [a]teacher like Him?
23 "Who has appointed Him His way,
And who has said, '[a]Thou hast
done wrong'?

24 "Remember that you should [a]exalt
His work,
Of which men have [b]sung.
25 "All men have seen it;
Man beholds from afar.
26 "Behold, God is [a]exalted, and [b]we
do not know *Him;*
The [c]number of His years is unsearchable.
27 "For [a]He draws up the drops of
water,
They distill rain from [1]the [2]mist,
28 Which the clouds pour down,
They drip upon man abundantly.
29 "Can anyone understand the
[a]spreading of the clouds,
The [b]thundering of His [1]pavilion?
30 "Behold, He spreads His [1]lightning
about Him,
And He covers the depths of the
sea.
31 "For by these He [a]judges peoples;
He [b]gives food in abundance.
32 "He covers *His* hands with the
[1]lightning,
And [a]commands it to strike the
mark.
33 "Its [a]noise declares [1]His presence;
The cattle also, concerning what is
coming up.

Elihu Says God Is Back of the Storm

37 "AT this also my heart trembles,
And leaps from its place.
2 "Listen closely to the [a]thunder of
His voice,
And the rumbling that goes out
from His mouth.
3 "Under the whole heaven He lets it
loose,
And His [1]lightning to the [a]ends of
the earth.
4 "After it, a voice roars;
He thunders with His majestic
voice;
And He does not restrain [1]the
lightnings when His voice is
heard.
5 "God [a]thunders with His voice wondrously,
Doing [b]great things which we cannot comprehend.
6 "For to [a]the snow He says, 'Fall on
the earth,'
And to the [1b]downpour and the
rain, 'Be strong.'
7 "He [a]seals the hand of every man,
That [b]all men may know His work.
8 "Then the beast goes into its [a]lair,
And remains in its [1]den.
9 "Out of the [1a]south comes the
storm,
And out of the [2]north the cold.
10 "From the breath of God [a]ice is
made,
And the expanse of the waters is
frozen.
11 "Also with moisture He [a]loads the
thick cloud;
He [b]disperses [c]the cloud of His
[1]lightning.
12 "And it changes direction, turning
around by His guidance,
That [1]it may do whatever He [a]com-
mands [2]it
On the [b]face of the inhabited earth.
13 "Whether for [1a]correction, or for
[b]His world,
Or for [c]lovingkindness, He causes
it to [2]happen.

14 "Listen to this, O Job,
Stand and consider the wonders of
God.
15 "Do you know how God establishes
them,
And makes the [1]lightning of His
cloud to shine?
16 "Do you know about the layers of
the thick clouds,
The [a]wonders of one [b]perfect in
knowledge,
17 You whose garments are hot,
When the land is still because of
the south wind?
18 "Can you, with Him, [a]spread out the
skies,
Strong as a molten mirror?
19 "Teach us what we shall say to Him;
We [a]cannot arrange *our case* because of darkness.
20 "Shall it be told Him that I would
speak?
[1]Or should a man say that he
would be swallowed up?

21 "And now [1]men do not see the light
which is bright in the skies;
But the wind has passed and
cleared them.
22 "Out of the north comes golden
splendor;
Around God is awesome majesty.
23 "The Almighty—[a]we cannot find
Him;
He is [b]exalted in power;
And [c]He will not do violence [d]to
justice and abundant righteousness.
24 "Therefore men [a]fear Him;
He does not [b]regard any who are
wise of heart."

17 [a]Job 22:5, 10, 11
18 [a]Jon. 4:4, 9 [b]Job 33:24
19 [1]Or, *cry*
20 [1]Lit., *go up* [a]Job 34:20, 25
21 [a]Job 36:10; Ps. 31:6; 66:18 [b]Job 36:8, 15; Heb. 11:25
22 [a]Job 35:11
23 [a]Deut. 32:4; Job 8:3
24 [a]Ps. 92:5; Rev. 15:3 [b]Ex. 15:1; Judg. 5:1; 1 Chr. 16:9; Ps. 59:16; 138:5
26 [a]Job 11:7-9; 37:23 [b]1 Cor. 13:12 [c]Job 10:5; Ps. 90:2; 102:24, 27; Heb. 1:12
27 [1]Lit., *its* [2]Or, *flood* [a]Job 5:10; 36:26-29; 37:6, 11; 38:28; Ps. 147:8
29 [1]Lit., *booth* [a]Job 37:11, 16 [b]Job 26:14
30 [1]Lit., *light*
31 [a]Job 37:13 [b]Ps. 104:27; 136:25; Acts 14:17
32 [1]Lit., *light* [a]Job 37:11, 12, 15
33 [1]Lit., *concerning Him* [a]Job 37:2

2 [a]Job 36:33; 37:4, 5; Ps. 29:3-9
3 [1]Lit., *light* [a]Job 28:24; 37:11, 12; 38:13
4 [1]Lit., *them*
5 [a]Job 26:14 [b]Job 5:9; 37:14, 16, 23
6 [1]Lit., *shower of rain and shower of rains* [a]Job 38:22 [b]Job 36:27
7 [a]Job 12:14 [b]Ps. 111:2
8 [1]Lit., *dens* [a]Job 38:40; Ps. 104:21, 22
9 [1]Lit., *chamber* [2]Lit., *scattering winds* [a]Job 9:9
10 [a]Job 38:29; Ps. 147:17
11 [1]Lit., *light* [a]Job 36:27 [b]Job 36:29 [c]Job 37:15
12 [1]Lit., *they* [2]Lit., *them* [a]Job 36:32; Ps. 148:8 [b]Is. 14:21; 27:6
13 [1]Lit., *the rod* [2]Lit., *be found* [a]Ex. 9:18, 23; 1 Sam. 12:18, 19 [b]Job 38:26, 27 [c]1 Kin. 18:41-46
15 [1]Lit., *light*
16 [a]Job 37:5, 14, 23 [b]Job 36:4
18 [a]Job 9:8; Ps. 104:2; Is. 44:24; 45:12; Jer. 10:12; Zech. 12:1
19 [a]Job 9:14; Rom. 8:26
20 [1]Or, *If a man speak, surely he shall be swallowed up*
21 [1]Lit., *they*
23 [a]Job 11:7, 8; Rom. 11:33; 1 Tim. 6:16 [b]Job 9:4; 36:5 [c]Is. 63:9; Lam. 3:33; Ezek. 18:23, 32; 33:11 [d]Job 8:3

24 [a]Matt. 10:28 [b]Job 5:13; Matt. 11:25; 1 Cor. 1:26

God Speaks Now to Job

38 THEN the LORD [a]answered Job
out of the whirlwind and said,
2 "Who is this that [a]darkens counsel
By words without knowledge?
3 "Now [a]gird up your loins like a
man,
And [b]I will ask you, and you instruct Me!
4 "Where were you [a]when I laid the
foundation of the earth?
Tell *Me,* if you [1]have understanding,
5 Who set its [a]measurements, since
you know?
Or who stretched the line on it?
6 "On what [a]were its bases sunk?
Or who laid its cornerstone,
7 When the morning stars sang together,
And all the [a]sons of God shouted
for joy?

8 "Or *who* [a]enclosed the sea with
doors,
When, bursting forth, it went out
from the womb;
9 When I made a cloud its garment,
And thick darkness its swaddling
band,
10 And I [1a]placed boundaries on it,
And I set a bolt and doors,
11 And I said, 'Thus far you shall
come, but no farther;
And here shall your proud waves
stop'?

God's Mighty Power

12 "Have you [1]ever in your life commanded the morning,
And caused the dawn to know its
place;
13 That it might take hold of [a]the ends
of the earth,
And [b]the wicked be shaken out of
it?
14 "It is changed like clay *under* the
seal;
And they stand forth like a garment.
15 "And [a]from the wicked their light is
withheld,
And the [b]uplifted arm is broken.

16 "Have you entered into [a]the springs
of the sea?
Or have you walked [1]in the recesses
of the deep?
17 "Have the gates of death been revealed to you?
Or have you seen the gates of [a]deep
darkness?
18 "Have you understood the [1]expanse
of [a]the earth?
Tell *Me,* if you know all this.

19 "Where is the way to the dwelling of
light?
And darkness, where is its place,
20 That you may take it to [a]its territory,
And that you may discern the
paths to its [1]home?
21 "You know, for [a]you were born
then,
And the number of your days is
great!
22 "Have you entered the storehouses
[a]of the snow,
Or have you seen the storehouses of
the [b]hail,
23 Which I have reserved for the time
of distress,
For the day of war and battle?
24 "Where is the way that [a]the light is
divided,
Or the east wind scattered on the
earth?

25 "Who has cleft a channel for the
flood,
Or a way for the thunderbolt;
26 To bring [a]rain on a land without
[1]people,
On a desert without a man in it,
27 To [a]satisfy the waste and desolate
land,
And to make the [1]seeds of grass to
sprout?
28 "Has [a]the rain a father?
Or who has begotten the drops of
dew?
29 "From whose womb has come the
[a]ice?
And the frost of heaven, who has
given it birth?
30 "Water [1]becomes hard like stone,
And the surface of the deep is
imprisoned.

31 "Can you bind the chains of the
[a]Pleiades,
Or loose the cords of Orion?
32 "Can you lead forth a [1]constellation
in its season,
And guide the Bear with her [2]satel-
lites?
33 "Do you know the [a]ordinances of
the heavens,
Or fix their rule over the earth?

34 "Can you lift up your voice to the
clouds,
So that an [a]abundance of water
may cover you?
35 "Can you [a]send forth lightnings that
they may go
And say to you, 'Here we are'?
36 "Who has [a]put wisdom in the innermost being,
Or has given [b]understanding to the
[1]mind?
37 "Who can count the clouds by wisdom,
Or [a]tip the water jars of the heavens,
38 When the dust hardens into a mass,
And the clods stick together?

39 "Can you hunt the [a]prey for the
lion,
Or satisfy the appetite of the young
lions,

1 [a]Job 40:6
2 [a]Job 35:16; 42:3
3 [a]Job 40:7 [b]Job 42:4
4 [1]Lit., *know understanding* [a]Job 15:7; Ps. 104:5; Prov. 8:29; 30:4
5 [a]Prov. 8:29; Is. 40:12
6 [a]Job 26:7
7 [a]Job 1:6
8 [a]Gen. 1:9; Ps. 104:6-9; Prov. 8:29; Jer. 5:22
10 [1]Lit., *broke My decree on it* [a]Gen. 1:9; Ps. 33:7; 104:9; Prov. 8:29; Jer. 5:22
12 [1]Lit., *from your days*
13 [a]Job 28:24; 37:3 [b]Job 34:25, 26; 36:6
15 [a]Job 5:14 [b]Num. 15:30; Ps. 10:15; 37:17
16 [1]Or, *in search of* [a]Gen. 7:11; 8:2; Prov. 8:24, 28
17 [a]Job 10:21; 26:6; 34:22
18 [1]Or, *width* [a]Job 28:24
20 [1]Lit., *house* [a]Job 26:10
21 [a]Job 15:7
22 [a]Job 37:6 [b]Ex. 9:18; Josh. 10:11; Is. 30:30; Ezek. 13:11, 13; Rev. 16:21
24 [a]Job 26:10
26 [1]Lit., *man* [a]Job 36:27
27 [1]Or, *growth* [a]Ps. 104:13, 14; 107:35
28 [a]Job 36:27, 28; Ps. 147:8; Jer. 14:22
29 [a]Job 37:10; Ps. 147:17
30 [1]Lit., *hides itself*
31 [a]Job 9:9; Amos 5:8
32 [1]Heb., *Mazzaroth* [2]Lit., *sons*
33 [a]Ps. 148:6; Jer. 31:35, 36
34 [a]Job 22:11; 36:27, 28; 38:37
35 [a]Job 36:32; 37:3
36 [1]Or, *cock* [a]Job 9:4; Ps. 51:6; Eccl. 2:26 [b]Job 32:8
37 [a]Job 38:34
39 [a]Ps. 104:21

40 When they [a]crouch in *their* dens,
And lie in wait in *their* lair?
41 “Who prepares for [a]the raven its nourishment,
When its young cry to God,
And wander about without food?

God Speaks of Nature and Its Beings

39 “DO you know the time the [1][a]mountain goats give birth?
Do you observe the calving of the [b]deer?
2 “Can you count the months they fulfill,
Or do you know the time they give birth?
3 “They kneel down, they bring forth their young,
They get rid of their labor pains.
4 “Their offspring become strong, they grow up in the open field;
They leave and do not return to them.

5 “Who sent out the [a]wild donkey free?
And who loosed the bonds of the swift donkey,
6 To whom I gave [a]the wilderness for a home,
And the salt land for his dwelling place?
7 “He scorns the tumult of the city,
The shoutings of the driver he does not hear.
8 “He explores the mountains for his pasture,
And he searches after every green thing.
9 “Will the [a]wild ox consent to serve you?
Or will he spend the night at your manger?
10 “Can you bind the wild ox in a furrow with [1]ropes?
Or will he harrow the valleys after you?
11 “Will you trust him because his strength is great
And leave your labor to him?
12 “Will you have faith in him that he will return your [1]grain,
And gather *it from* your threshing floor?

13 “The ostriches’ wings flap joyously
With the pinion and plumage of [1]love,
14 For she abandons her eggs to the earth,
And warms them in the dust,
15 And she forgets that a foot may crush [1]them,
Or that a wild beast may trample [1]them.
16 “She treats her young [a]cruelly, as if *they* were not hers;
Though her labor be in vain, *she* is [1]unconcerned;
17 Because God has made her forget wisdom,
And has not given her a share of understanding.
18 “When she lifts herself [1]on high,
She laughs at the horse and his rider.

19 “Do you give the horse *his* might?
Do you clothe his neck with a mane?
20 “Do you make him [a]leap like the locust?
His majestic [b]snorting is terrible.
21 “[1]He paws in the valley, and rejoices in *his* strength;
He [a]goes out to meet the weapons.
22 “He laughs at fear and is not dismayed;
And he does not turn back from the sword.
23 “The quiver rattles against him,
The flashing spear and javelin.
24 “With shaking and rage he [1]races over the ground;
And he does not stand still at the voice of the trumpet.
25 “As often as the trumpet *sounds* he says, ‘Aha!’
And he scents the battle from afar,
And thunder of the captains, and the war cry.

26 “Is it by your understanding that the hawk soars,
Stretching his wings toward the south?
27 “Is it at your [1]command that the eagle mounts up,
And makes [a]his nest on high?
28 “On the cliff he dwells and lodges,
Upon the rocky crag, an inaccessible place.
29 “From there he [a]spies out food;
His eyes see *it* from afar.
30 “His young ones also suck up blood;
And [a]where the slain are, there is he.”

Job: What Can I Say?

40 THEN the LORD said to Job,
2 “Will the faultfinder [a]contend with the Almighty?
Let him who [b]reproves God answer it.”

3 Then Job answered the LORD and
said,
4 “Behold, I am insignificant; what can I reply to Thee?
I [a]lay my hand on my mouth.
5 “Once I have spoken, and [a]I will not answer;
Even twice, and I will add no more.”

God Questions Job

6 Then the [a]LORD answered Job out
of the storm, and said,
7 “Now [a]gird up your loins like a man;
I will [b]ask you, and you instruct Me.
8 “Will you really [a]annul My judgment?
Will you [b]condemn Me [c]that you may be justified?

40 [a]Job 37:8
41 [a]Ps. 147:9; Matt. 6:26; Luke 12:24
1 [1]Lit., *goats of the rock* [a]Deut. 14:5; 1 Sam. 24:2; Ps. 104:18 [b]Ps. 29:9
5 [a]Job 6:5; 11:12; 24:5; Ps. 104:11
6 [a]Job 24:5; Jer. 2:24; Hos. 8:9
9 [a]Num. 23:22; Deut. 33:17; Ps. 22:21; 29:6; 92:10; Is. 34:7
10 [1]Lit., *his rope*
12 [1]Lit., *seed*
13 [1]Or, *a stork*
15 [1]Lit., *it*
16 [1]Lit., *without fear* [a]Lam. 4:3
18 [1]Or, *to flee*
20 [a]Joel 2:5 [b]Jer. 8:16
21 [1]Lit., *They paw* [a]Jer. 8:6
24 [1]Or, *swallows up*
27 [1]Lit., *mouth* [a]Jer. 49:16; Obad. 4
29 [a]Job 9:26
30 [a]Matt. 24:28; Luke 17:37
2 [a]Job 9:3; 10:2; 33:13; Is. 45:9 [b]Job 13:3; 23:4; 31:35
4 [a]Job 21:5; 29:9
5 [a]Job 9:3, 15
6 [a]Job 38:1
7 [a]Job 38:3 [b]Job 38:3; 42:4
8 [a]Rom. 3:4 [b]Job 10:3, 7; 16:11; 19:6; 27:2 [c]Job 13:18; 27:6

9 "Or do you have an arm like God,
And can you [a]thunder with a voice like His?

10 "[a]Adorn yourself with eminence and dignity;
And clothe yourself with honor and majesty.
11 "Pour out [a]the overflowings of your anger;
And look on everyone who is [b]proud, and make him low.
12 "Look on everyone who is proud, *and* [a]humble him;
And [b]tread down the wicked [1]where they stand.
13 "[a]Hide them in the dust together;
Bind [1]them in the hidden *place.*
14 "Then I will also [1]confess to you,
That your own right hand can save you.

God's Power Shown in Creatures

15 "Behold now, [1]Behemoth, which [a]I made [2]as well as you;
He eats grass like an ox.
16 "Behold now, his strength in his loins,
And his power in the muscles of his belly.
17 "He bends his tail like a cedar;
The sinews of his thighs are knit together.
18 "His bones are tubes of bronze;
His [1]limbs are like bars of iron.

19 "He is the [a]first of the ways of God;
Let his [b]maker bring near his sword.
20 "Surely the mountains [a]bring him food,
And all the beasts of the field [b]play there.
21 "Under the lotus plants he lies down,
In the covert of the reeds and the marsh.
22 "The lotus plants cover him with [1]shade;
The willows of the brook surround him.
23 "If a river [1]rages, he is not alarmed;
He is confident, though the [a]Jordan rushes to his mouth.
24 "Can anyone capture him [1]when he is on watch,
With [2]barbs can anyone pierce *his* nose?

God's Power Shown in Creatures

41 "[1]CAN you draw out [2][a]Leviathan with a fishhook?
Or press down his tongue with a cord?
2 "Can you [a]put a [1]rope in his nose?
Or pierce his jaw with a [2]hook?
3 "Will he make many supplications to you?
Or will he speak to you soft words?
4 "Will he make a covenant with you?
Will you take him for a servant forever?
5 "Will you play with him as with a bird?
Or will you bind him for your maidens?
6 "Will the [1]traders bargain over him?
Will they divide him among the merchants?
7 "Can you fill his skin with harpoons,
Or his head with fishing spears?
8 "Lay your hand on him;
Remember the battle; [1]you will not do it again!
9 "[1]Behold, [2]your expectation is false;
Will [3]you be laid low even at the sight of him?
10 "No one is so fierce that he dares to [a]arouse him;
Who then is he that can stand before Me?
11 "Who has [1][a]given to Me that I should repay *him?*
Whatever is [b]under the whole heaven is Mine.

12 "I will not keep silence concerning his limbs,
Or his mighty strength, or his [1]orderly frame.
13 "Who can [1]strip off his outer armor?
Who can come within his double [2]mail?
14 "Who can open the doors of his face?
Around his teeth there is terror.
15 "*His* [1]strong scales are *his* pride,
Shut up *as with* a tight seal.
16 "One is so near to another,
That no air can come between them.
17 "They are joined one to another;
They clasp each other and cannot be separated.
18 "His sneezes flash forth light,
And his eyes are like the [a]eyelids of the morning.
19 "Out of his mouth go burning torches;
Sparks of fire leap forth.
20 "Out of his nostrils smoke goes forth,
As *from* a boiling pot and *burning* rushes.
21 "His breath kindles coals,
And a flame goes forth from his mouth.
22 "In his neck lodges strength,
And dismay leaps before him.
23 "The folds of his flesh are joined together,
Firm on him and immovable.
24 "His heart is as hard as a stone;
Even as hard as a lower millstone.
25 "When he raises himself up, the [1]mighty fear;
Because of the crashing they are bewildered.
26 "The sword that reaches him cannot avail;
Nor the spear, the dart, or the javelin.
27 "He regards iron as straw,
Bronze as rotten wood.

9 [a]Job 37:5; Ps. 29:3
10 [a]Ps. 93:1; 104:1
11 [a]Is. 42:25; Nah. 1:6, 8 [b]Is. 2:12; Dan. 4:37
12 [1]Lit., *under them* [a]1 Sam. 2:7; Is. 2:12; 13:11; Dan. 4:37 [b]Is. 63:3
13 [1]Or, *their faces* [a]Is. 2:10-12
14 [1]Or, *praise you*
15 [1]Or, *the hippopotamus* [2]Lit., *with* [a]Job 40:19
18 [1]Lit., *bones*
19 [a]Job 41:33 [b]Job 40:15
20 [a]Ps. 104:14 [b]Ps. 104:26
22 [1]Lit., *his shade*
23 [1]Or, *oppresses* [a]Gen. 13:10
24 [1]Lit., *in his eyes* [2]Lit., *snares*
1 [1]Ch. 40:25 in Heb. [2]Or, *the crocodile* [a]Job 3:8; Ps. 74:14; 104:26; Is. 27:1
2 [1]Lit., *rope of rushes* [2]Or, *thorn* or *ring* [a]2 Kin. 19:28; Is. 37:29
6 [1]Lit., *partners*
8 [1]Lit., *do not add*
9 [1]Ch. 41:1 in Heb. [2]Lit., *his* [3]Lit., *he*
10 [a]Job 3:8
11 [1]Lit., *anticipated* [a]Rom. 11:35 [b]Ex. 19:5; Deut. 10:14; Job 9:5-10; 26:6-14; 28:24; Ps. 24:1; 50:12; 1 Cor. 10:26
12 [1]Or, *graceful*
13 [1]Lit., *uncover the face of his garment* [2]So Gr.; Heb., *bridle*
15 [1]Lit., *rows of shields*
18 [a]Job 3:9
25 [1]Or, *gods*

28 "The [1]arrow cannot make him flee;
Slingstones are turned into stubble for him.
29 "Clubs are regarded as stubble;
He laughs at the rattling of the javelin.
30 "His underparts are *like* sharp potsherds;
He [1]spreads out *like* a threshing sledge on the mire.
31 "He makes the depths boil like a pot;
He makes the sea like a jar of ointment.
32 "Behind him he makes a wake to shine;
One would think the deep to be gray-haired.
33 "[a]Nothing on [1]earth is like him,
One made without fear.
34 "[1]He looks on everything that is high;
He is king over all the [a]sons of pride."

Job's Confession

42 THEN Job answered the LORD, and said,
2 "I know that [a]Thou canst do all things,
And that no purpose of Thine can be thwarted.
3 'Who is this that [a]hides counsel without knowledge?'
"Therefore I have declared that which I did not understand,
Things [b]too wonderful for me, which I did not know."
4 'Hear, now, and I will speak;
I will [a]ask Thee, and do Thou instruct me.'
5 "I have [a]heard of Thee by the hearing of the ear;
But now my [b]eye sees Thee;
6 Therefore I retract,
And I repent in dust and ashes."

God Displeased with Job's Friends

7 And it came about after the LORD
had spoken these words to Job, that the
LORD said to Eliphaz the Temanite, "My
wrath is kindled against you and against
your two friends, because you have not
spoken of Me what is right [a]as My
servant Job has.
8 "Now therefore, take for yourselves
[a]seven bulls and seven rams, and go to
My servant Job, and offer up a [b]burnt
offering for yourselves, and My servant
Job will [c]pray for you. [d]For I will [1]accept him so that I may not do with you
according to your folly, because you have
not spoken of Me what is right, as My
servant Job has."
9 So Eliphaz the Temanite and
Bildad the Shuhite *and* Zophar the Naamathite went and did as the LORD told
them; and the LORD [1]accepted Job.

God Restores Job's Fortunes

10 And the LORD [a]restored the fortunes of Job when he prayed for his
friends, and the LORD increased all that
Job had twofold.
11 Then all his [a]brothers, and all his
sisters, and all who had known him
before, came to him, and they ate bread
with him in his house; and they [b]consoled him and comforted him for all the
evil that the LORD had brought on him.
And each one gave him one [1]piece of
money, and each a ring of gold.
12 [a]And the LORD blessed the latter
days of Job more than his beginning,
[b]and he had 14,000 sheep, and 6,000
camels, and 1,000 yoke of oxen, and
1,000 female donkeys.
13 And [a]he had seven sons and three
daughters.
14 And he named the first Jemimah,
and the second Keziah, and the third
Keren-happuch.
15 And in all the land no women were
found so fair as Job's daughters; and
their father gave them inheritance
among their brothers.
16 And after this Job lived 140 years,
and saw his sons, and his grandsons,
four generations.
17 [a]And Job died, an old man and full
of days.

28 [1]Lit., *son of the bow*
30 [1]Or, *moves across*
33 [1]Lit., *dust* [a]Job 40:19
34 [1]Ch. 41:26 in Heb. [a]Job 28:8
2 [a]Gen. 18:14; Matt. 19:26
3 [a]Job 38:2 [b]Ps. 40:5; 131:1; 139:6
4 [a]Job 38:3; 40:7
5 [a]Job 26:14; Rom. 10:17 [b]Is. 6:5; Eph. 1:17, 18
7 [a]Job 40:3-5; 42:1-6
8 [1]Lit., *lift up his face* [a]Num. 23:1 [b]Job 1:5 [c]Gen. 20:17; James 5:16; 1 John 5:16 [d]Job 22:30
9 [1]Lit., *lifted up the face of*
10 [a]Deut. 30:3; Job 1:2, 3; Ps. 14:7; 85:1-3; 126:1-6
11 [1]Heb., *qesitah* [a]Job 19:13 [b]Job 2:11
12 [a]Job 1:10; 8:7; James 5:11 [b]Job 1:3
13 [a]Job 1:2
17 [a]Gen. 15:15; 25:8; Job 5:26

THE PSALMS

The following expressions occur often in the Psalms:

Selah	May mean *Pause, Crescendo* or *Musical Interlude*
Maskil	Possibly, *Contemplative*, or *Didactic*, or *Skillful Psalm*
Mikhtam	Possibly, *Epigrammatic Poem*, or *Atonement Psalm*
Sheol	The nether world

BOOK 1

PSALM 1

The Righteous and the Wicked Contrasted.

HOW blessed is the man who [a]does not walk in the [b]counsel of the wicked,
Nor stand in the [1c]path of sinners,
Nor [d]sit in the seat of scoffers!
2 But his [a]delight is [b]in the law of the LORD,
And in His law he meditates [c]day and [d]night.
3 And he will be like [a]a tree *firmly* planted by [1]streams of water,
Which yields its fruit in its season,
And its [2]leaf does not wither;
And [3]in whatever he does, [b]he prospers.

4 The wicked are not so,
But they are like [a]chaff which the wind drives away.
5 Therefore [a]the wicked will not stand in the [b]judgment,
Nor sinners in [c]the assembly of the righteous.
6 For the LORD [1a]knows the way of the righteous,
But the way of [b]the wicked will perish.

PSALM 2

The Reign of the LORD'S Anointed.

WHY are [a]the [1]nations in an uproar,
And the peoples [b]devising a vain thing?
2 The [a]kings of the earth take their stand,
And the rulers take counsel together
[b]Against the LORD and against His [1c]Anointed:
3 "Let us [a]tear their fetters apart,
And cast away their cords from us!"

4 He who [1]sits in the heavens [a]laughs,
The Lord [b]scoffs at them.
5 Then He will speak to them in His [a]anger
And [b]terrify them in His fury:
6 "But as for Me, I have [1]installed [a]My King
Upon Zion, [b]My holy mountain."

7 "I will surely tell of the [1]decree of the LORD:
He said to Me, 'Thou art [a]My Son,
Today I have begotten Thee.
8 'Ask of Me, and [a]I will surely give [b]the [1]nations as Thine inheritance,
And the *very* [c]ends of the earth as Thy possession.
9 'Thou shalt [1a]break them with a [2]rod of iron,
Thou shalt [b]shatter them like [3]earthenware.' "

10 Now therefore, O kings, [a]show discernment;
Take warning, O [1]judges of the earth.
11 [1]Worship the LORD with [2a]reverence,
And rejoice with [b]trembling.
12 [1]Do homage to [a]the Son, lest He become angry, and you perish *in* the way,
For [b]His wrath may [2]soon be kindled.
How blessed are all who [c]take refuge in Him!

PSALM 3

Morning Prayer of Trust in God.

A Psalm of David, when [+]he fled from Absalom his son.

O LORD, how [a]my adversaries have increased!
Many are rising up against me.
2 Many are saying [1]of my soul,
"There is no [2a]deliverance for him in God." [[3]Selah.

3 But Thou, O LORD, art [a]a shield about me,
My [b]glory, and the One who [c]lifts my head.
4 I was crying to the LORD with my voice,
And He [a]answered me from [b]His holy [1]mountain. [Selah.
5 [1]I [a]lay down and slept;
I awoke, for the LORD sustains me.
6 I will [a]not be afraid of ten thousands of people
Who have [b]set themselves against me round about.

7 [a]Arise, O LORD; [b]save me, O my God!
For Thou [1]hast [c]smitten all my enemies on the [2]cheek;
Thou [3]hast [d]shattered the teeth of the wicked.

1 [1]Or, *way* [a]Prov. 4:14 [b]Ps. 5:9, 10; 10:2-11; 36:1-4 [c]Ps. 17:4; 119:104 [d]Ps. 26:4, 5; Jer. 15:17
2 [a]Ps. 119:14, 16, 35 [b]Josh. 1:8 [c]Ps. 25:5 [d]Ps. 63:5, 6
3 [1]Or, *canals* [2]Or, *foliage* [3]Or, *all that he does prospers* [a]Ps. 92:12-14; Jer. 17:8; Ezek. 19:10 [b]Gen. 39:2, 3, 23; Ps. 128:2
4 [a]Job 21:18; Ps. 35:5; Is. 17:13
5 [a]Ps. 5:5 [b]Ps. 9:7, 8, 16 [c]Ps. 89:5, 7
6 [1]Or, *approves* or *has regard to* [a]Ps. 37:18; Nah. 1:7; John 10:14; 2 Tim. 2:19 [b]Ps. 9:5, 6; 11:6

1 [1]Or, *Gentiles* [a]Ps. 46:6; 83:2-5; Acts 4:25, 26 [b]Ps. 21:11
2 [1]Or, *Messiah* [a]Ps. 48:4-6 [b]Ps. 74:18, 23 [c]John 1:41
3 [a]Jer. 5:5
4 [1]Or, *is enthroned* [a]Ps. 37:13 [b]Ps. 59:8
5 [a]Ps. 21:8, 9; 76:7 [b]Ps. 78:49, 50
6 [1]Or, *consecrated* [a]Ps. 45:6 [b]Ps. 48:1, 2
7 [1]Or, *decree: The LORD said to Me* [a]Acts 13:33; Heb. 1:5; 5:5
8 [1]Or, *Gentiles* [a]Ps. 21:1, 2 [b]Ps. 22:27 [c]Ps. 67:7
9 [1]Another reading is *rule* [2]Or, *scepter* or *staff* [3]Lit., *potter's ware* [a]Ps. 89:23; 110:5, 6; Rev. 2:26, 27; 12:5; 19:15 [b]Ps. 28:5; 52:5; 72:4
10 [1]Or, *leaders* [a]Prov. 8:15; 27:11
11 [1]Or, *Serve* [2]Or, *fear* [a]Ps. 5:7 [b]Ps. 119:119, 120
12 [1]Lit., *Kiss;* some ancient versions read *Do homage purely*, or, *Lay hold of instruction* [2]Or, *quickly, suddenly, easily* [a]Ps. 2:7 [b]Rev. 6:16, 17 [c]Ps. 5:11; 34:22

+ 2 Sam. 15:13-17, 29
1 [a]2 Sam. 15:12; Ps. 69:4
2 [1]Or, *to* [2]Or, *salvation* [3]*Selah* may mean: *Pause, Crescendo* or *Musical interlude* [a]Ps. 22:7, 8; 71:11
3 [a]Ps. 5:12; 28:7 [b]Ps. 62:7 [c]Ps. 9:13; 27:6
4 [1]Or, *hill* [a]Ps. 4:3; 34:4 [b]Ps. 2:6; 15:1; 43:3
5 [1]Or, *As for me, I* [a]Lev. 26:6; Ps. 4:8; Prov. 3:24
6 [a]Ps. 23:4; 27:3 [b]Ps. 118:10-13
7 [1]Or, *dost smite* [2]Or, *jaw* [3]Or, *dost shatter* [a]Ps. 7:6 [b]Ps. 6:4; 22:21 [c]Job 16:10 [d]Ps. 57:4; 58:6

8 [1a]Salvation belongs to the LORD;
Thy [b]blessing [2]*be* upon Thy people! [Selah.

PSALM 4

Evening Prayer of Trust in God.

[+]For the choir director; on stringed instruments.
A Psalm of David.

[a]ANSWER me when [b]I call, O God [1]of my righteousness!
Thou hast [2c]relieved me in my distress;
Be [d]gracious to me and [e]hear my prayer.

2 O sons of men, how long will [a]my [1]honor become [b]a reproach?
How long will you love [c]what is worthless and aim at [d]deception? [[2]Selah.
3 But know that the LORD has [1a]set apart the [b]godly man for Himself;
The LORD [c]hears when I call to Him.

4 [1a]Tremble, [2b]and do not sin;
[3c]Meditate in your heart upon your bed, and be still. [Selah.
5 Offer [1]the [a]sacrifices of righteousness,
And [b]trust in the LORD.

6 Many are saying, "[a]Who will show us *any* good?"
[b]Lift up the light of Thy countenance upon us, O LORD!
7 Thou hast put [a]gladness in my heart,
More than when their grain and new wine abound.
8 In peace I will [1]both [a]lie down and sleep,
For Thou alone, O LORD, dost make me to [b]dwell in safety.

PSALM 5

Prayer for Protection from the Wicked.

For the choir director; for [+]flute accompaniment.
A Psalm of David.

[a]GIVE ear to my words, O LORD,
Consider my [1b]groaning.
2 Heed [a]the sound of my cry for help, [b]my King and my God,
For to Thee do I pray.
3 In the morning, O LORD, [1]Thou wilt hear my voice;
In the [a]morning I will order *my* [2]*prayer* to Thee and *eagerly* [b]watch.

4 For Thou art not a God [a]who takes pleasure in wickedness;
[b]No evil [1]dwells with Thee.
5 The [a]boastful shall not [b]stand before Thine eyes;
Thou [c]dost hate all who do iniquity.
6 Thou [a]dost destroy those who speak falsehood;
The LORD abhors [b]the man of bloodshed and deceit.
7 But as for me, [a]by Thine abundant lovingkindness I will enter Thy house,
[1]At Thy holy temple I will [b]bow in [c]reverence for Thee.

8 O LORD, [a]lead me [b]in Thy righteousness [c]because of [1]my foes;
Make Thy way [2]straight before me.
9 There is [a]nothing [1]reliable in [2]what they say;
Their [b]inward part is destruction *itself*;
Their [c]throat is an open grave;
They [3]flatter with their tongue.
10 Hold them guilty, O God;
[a]By their own devices let them fall!
In the multitude of their transgressions [b]thrust them out,
For they are [c]rebellious against Thee.

11 But let all who [a]take refuge in Thee [b]be glad,
Let them ever sing for joy;
And [1]mayest Thou [c]shelter them,
That those who [d]love Thy name may exult in Thee.
12 For it is Thou who dost [a]bless the righteous man, O LORD,
Thou dost [b]surround him with favor as with a shield.

PSALM 6

Prayer for Mercy in Time of Trouble.

For the choir director; with stringed instruments,
[+]upon an eight-stringed lyre.
A Psalm of David.

O LORD, [a]do not rebuke me in Thine anger,
Nor chasten me in Thy wrath.
2 Be gracious to me, O LORD, for I *am* [a]pining away;
[b]Heal me, O LORD, for [c]my bones are dismayed.
3 And my [a]soul is greatly dismayed;
But Thou, O LORD—[b]how long?

4 Return, O LORD, [a]rescue my [1]soul;
Save me because of Thy lovingkindness.
5 For [a]there is no [1]mention of Thee in death;
In [2]Sheol who will give Thee thanks?

6 I am [a]weary with my sighing;
Every night I make my bed swim,
I dissolve my couch with [b]my tears.

8 [1]Or, *Deliverance* [2]Or, *is* [a]Ps. 28:8; 35:3; Is. 43:11 [b]Ps. 29:11
+ I.e., Belonging to the choir director's anthology
1 [1]I.e., who maintainest my right [2]Lit., *made room for* [a]Ps. 3:4; 17:6 [b]Ps. 18:6 [c]Ps. 18:18, 19 [d]Ps. 25:16 [e]Ps. 17:6; 39:12
2 [1]Or, *glory* [2]*Selah* may mean: *Pause, Crescendo* or *Musical interlude* [a]Ps. 3:3 [b]Ps. 69:7-10, 19, 20 [c]Ps. 12:2; 31:6 [d]Ps. 31:18
3 [1]Another reading is *dealt wonderfully with* [a]Ps. 135:4 [b]Ps. 31:23; 50:5; 79:2 [c]Ps. 6:8, 9; 17:6
4 [1]I.e., with anger or fear [2]Or, *but* [3]Lit., *Speak* [a]Ps. 99:1 [b]Ps. 119:11; Eph. 4:26 [c]Ps. 77:6
5 [1]Or, *righteous sacrifices* [a]Deut. 33:19; Ps. 51:19 [b]Ps. 37:3, 5; 62:8
6 [a]Job 7:7; 9:25 [b]Num. 6:26; Ps. 80:3, 7, 19
7 [a]Ps. 97:11, 12; Is. 9:3; Acts 14:17
8 [1]Or, *at the same time* [a]Job 11:19; Ps. 3:5 [b]Lev. 25:18; Deut. 12:10; Ps. 16:9
+ Heb., *Nehiloth*
1 [1]Or, *meditation* [a]Ps. 54:2 [b]Ps. 104:34
2 [a]Ps. 140:6 [b]Ps. 84:3
3 [1]Or, *mayest Thou hear* [2]Or, *sacrifice* [a]Ps. 88:13 [b]Ps. 130:5
4 [1]Lit., *sojourns* [a]Ps. 11:5; 34:16 [b]Ps. 92:15
5 [a]Ps. 73:3; 75:4 [b]Ps. 1:5 [c]Ps. 11:5; 45:7
6 [a]Ps. 52:4, 5 [b]Ps. 55:23
7 [1]Or, *Toward* [a]Ps. 69:13 [b]Ps. 138:2 [c]Ps. 115:11, 13
8 [1]Or, *those who lie in wait for me* [2]Or, *smooth* [a]Ps. 31:3 [b]Ps. 31:1 [c]Ps. 27:11
9 [1]Or, *true* [2]Lit., *his mouth* [3]Or, *make their tongue smooth* [a]Ps. 52:3 [b]Ps. 7:14 [c]Rom. 3:13
10 [a]Ps. 9:16 [b]Ps. 36:12 [c]Ps. 107:10, 11
11 [1]Or, *Thou dost shelter* [a]Ps. 2:12 [b]Ps. 33:1; 64:10 [c]Ps. 12:7 [d]Ps. 69:36
12 [a]Ps. 29:11 [b]Ps. 32:7, 10
+ Or, *according to a lower octave* (Heb., *Sheminith*)
1 [a]Ps. 38:1; 118:18

2 [a]Ps. 102:4, 11 [b]Ps. 41:4; 147:3; Hos. 6:1 [c]Ps. 22:14; 31:10
3 [a]Ps. 88:3; John 12:27 [b]Ps. 90:13
4 [1]Or, *life* [a]Ps. 17:13
5 [1]Or, *remembrance* [2]I.e., the nether world [a]Ps. 30:9; 88:10-12; 115:17; Eccl. 9:10; Is. 38:18
6 [a]Ps. 69:3 [b]Ps. 42:3

7 My [a]eye has wasted away with grief;
It has become old because of all my adversaries.

8 [a]Depart from me, all you who do iniquity,
For the LORD [b]has heard the voice of my weeping.
9 The LORD [a]has heard my supplication,
The LORD [b]receives my prayer.
10 All my enemies shall [a]be ashamed and greatly dismayed;
They shall [1]turn back, they shall [b]suddenly be ashamed.

PSALM 7

The LORD Implored to Defend the Psalmist against the Wicked.

A +Shiggaion of David, which he sang to the Lord •concerning Cush, a Benjamite.

O LORD my God, [a]in Thee I have taken refuge;
Save me from all those who pursue me, and [b]deliver me,
2 Lest he tear [1]my soul [a]like a lion,
[2]Dragging me away, while there is none to deliver.

3 O LORD my God, if I have done this,
If there is [a]injustice in my hands,
4 If I have [a]rewarded evil to [1]my friend,
Or have [b]plundered [2]him who without cause was my adversary,
5 Let the enemy pursue [1]my soul and overtake [2]*it;*
And let him trample my life down to the ground,
And lay my glory in the dust. [[3]Selah.

6 [a]Arise, O LORD, in Thine anger;
[b]Lift up Thyself against [c]the rage of my adversaries,
And [d]arouse Thyself [1]for me; Thou hast appointed judgment.
7 And let the assembly of the [a]peoples encompass Thee;
And over [1]them return Thou on high.
8 The LORD [a]judges the peoples;
[1b]Vindicate me, O LORD, according to my righteousness and my integrity that is in me.
9 O let [a]the evil of the wicked come to an end, but [b]establish the righteous;
For the righteous God [c]tries the hearts and [1]minds.
10 My [a]shield is [1]with God,
Who [b]saves the upright in heart.
11 God is a [a]righteous judge,
And a God who has [b]indignation every day.

12 If [1]a man [a]does not repent, He will [b]sharpen His sword;
He has [c]bent His bow and [2]made it ready.
13 He has also prepared [1]for Himself deadly weapons;
He makes His [a]arrows fiery shafts.
14 Behold, he travails with wickedness,
And he [a]conceives mischief, and brings forth falsehood.
15 He has dug a pit and hollowed it out,
And has [a]fallen into the hole which he made.
16 His [a]mischief will return upon his own head,
And his [b]violence will descend upon [1]his own pate.

17 I will give thanks to the LORD [a]according to His righteousness,
And will [b]sing praise to the name of the LORD Most High.

PSALM 8

The LORD'S Glory and Man's Dignity.

For the choir director; on the Gittith. A Psalm of David.

O LORD, our Lord,
How majestic is Thy name in all the earth,
Who hast [1a]displayed Thy splendor above the heavens!
2 [a]From the mouth of infants and nursing babes Thou hast established [1b]strength,
Because of Thine adversaries,
To make [c]the enemy and the revengeful cease.

3 When I [1a]consider [b]Thy heavens, the work of Thy fingers,
The [c]moon and the stars, which Thou hast [2]ordained;
4 [a]What is man, that Thou [1]dost take thought of him?
And the son of man, that Thou dost care for him?
5 Yet Thou hast made him a [a]little lower than [1]God,
And [b]dost crown him with [c]glory and majesty!
6 Thou dost make him to [a]rule over the works of Thy hands;
Thou hast [b]put all things under his feet,
7 All sheep and oxen,
And also the [1]beasts of the field,
8 The birds of the heavens, and the fish of the sea,
Whatever passes through the paths of the seas.

9 [a]O LORD, our Lord,
How majestic is Thy name in all the earth!

7 [a]Job 17:7; Ps. 31:9; 38:10
8 [a]Ps. 119:115; Matt. 7:23; Luke 13:27 [b]Ps. 3:4; 28:6
9 [a]Ps. 116:1 [b]Ps. 66:19, 20
10 [1]Or, *again be ashamed suddenly* [a]Ps. 71:13, 24 [b]Ps. 73:19

+ I.e., Dithyrambic rhythm; or, wild passionate song
• Or, *concerning the words of*
1 [a]Ps. 31:1; 71:1 [b]Ps. 31:15
2 [1]Or, *me* [2]Or, *Rending it in pieces, while* [a]Ps. 57:4; Is. 38:13
3 [a]1 Sam. 24:11
4 [1]Lit., *him who was at peace with me* [2]Or, *my adversary without cause* [a]Ps. 109:4, 5 [b]1 Sam. 24:7; 26:9
5 [1]Or, *me* [2]Or, me [3]*Selah* may mean: *Pause, Crescendo* or *Musical interlude*
6 [1]One ancient version reads *O my God* [a]Ps. 3:7 [b]Ps. 94:2 [c]Ps. 138:7 [d]Ps. 35:23; 44:23
7 [1]Lit., *it* [a]Ps. 22:27
8 [1]Lit., *Judge* [a]Ps. 96:13; 98:9 [b]Ps. 18:20; 26:1; 35:24; 43:1
9 [1]Lit., *kidneys,* figurative for inner man [a]Ps. 34:21; 94:23 [b]Ps. 37:23; 40:2 [c]Ps. 11:4, 5; Jer. 11:20; Rev. 2:23
10 [1]Lit., *upon* [a]Ps. 18:2, 30 [b]Ps. 97:10, 11; 125:4
11 [a]Ps. 50:6 [b]Ps. 90:9
12 [1]Lit., *he* [2]Lit., *fixed it* [a]Ps. 58:5 [b]Deut. 32:41 [c]Ps. 64:7
13 [1]Or, *His deadly weapons* [a]Ps. 18:14; 45:5
14 [a]Job 15:35; Is. 59:4; James 1:15
15 [a]Job 4:8; Ps. 57:6
16 [1]I.e., the crown of his own head [a]Esth. 9:25; Ps. 140:9 [b]Ps. 140:11
17 [a]Ps. 71:15, 16 [b]Ps. 9:2; 66:1, 2, 4

1 [1]Or, *set* [a]Ps. 57:5, 11; 113:4; 148:13
2 [1]Or, *a bulwark* [a]Matt. 21:16; 1 Cor. 1:27 [b]Ps. 29:1; 118:14 [c]Ps. 44:16
3 [1]Or, *see* [2]Or, *appointed, fixed* [a]Ps. 111:2 [b]Ps. 89:11; 144:5 [c]Ps. 136:9
4 [1]Or, *dost remember him* [a]Job 7:17; Ps. 144:3; Heb. 2:6-8
5 [1]Or, *the angels;* Heb., *Elohim* [a]Gen. 1:26; Ps. 82:6 [b]Ps. 103:4 [c]Ps. 21:5
6 [a]Gen. 1:26, 28 [b]1 Cor. 15:27; Eph. 1:22; Heb. 2:8
7 [1]Or, *animals*
9 [a]Ps. 8:1

PSALM 9

A Psalm of Thanksgiving for God's Justice.

For the choir director; on +Muth-labben. A Psalm of David.

I WILL give thanks to the LORD with all [a]my heart;
I will [b]tell of all Thy [1]wonders.
2 I will be glad and [a]exult in Thee;
I will [b]sing praise to Thy name, O [c]Most High.

3 When my enemies turn back,
They stumble and [a]perish before Thee.
4 For Thou hast [a]maintained [1]my just cause;
Thou dost sit on the throne [2b]judging righteously.
5 Thou hast [a]rebuked the nations; Thou hast destroyed the wicked;
Thou hast [b]blotted out their name forever and ever.
6 [1]The enemy has come to an end in perpetual ruins,
And Thou hast uprooted the cities;
The very [a]memory of them has perished.

7 But the [a]LORD [1]abides forever;
He has established His [b]throne for judgment,
8 And He will [a]judge the world in righteousness;
He will execute judgment for the peoples with equity.
9 [1]The LORD also will be a [a]stronghold for the oppressed,
A stronghold in times of trouble,
10 And [1]those who [a]know Thy name will put their trust in Thee;
For Thou, O LORD, hast not [b]forsaken those who seek Thee.

11 Sing praises to the LORD, who [a]dwells in Zion;
[b]Declare among the peoples His deeds.
12 For [a]He who [1]requires blood remembers them;
He does not forget [b]the cry of the afflicted.
13 Be gracious to me, O LORD;
Behold my affliction from those [a]who hate me,
Thou who [b]dost lift me up from the gates of death;
14 That I may tell of [a]all Thy praises,
That in the gates of the daughter of Zion
I may [b]rejoice in Thy [1]salvation.
15 The nations have sunk down [a]in the pit which they have made;
In the [b]net which they hid, their own foot has been caught.
16 The LORD has [a]made Himself known;
He has [b]executed judgment.
In the work of his own hands the wicked is snared. [[1]Higgaion [2]Selah.

17 The wicked will [1a]return to [2]Sheol,
Even all the nations who [b]forget God.
18 For the [a]needy will not always be forgotten,
Nor the [b]hope of the afflicted perish forever.
19 [a]Arise, O LORD, do not let man prevail;
Let the nations be [b]judged before Thee.
20 Put them [a]in fear, O LORD;
Let the nations know that they are [b]but men. [Selah.

PSALM 10

A Prayer for the Overthrow of the Wicked.

WHY [a]dost Thou stand afar off, O LORD?
Why [b]dost Thou hide [1]*Thyself* in times of trouble?
2 In [a]pride the wicked [1]hotly pursue the afflicted;
[2]Let them be [b]caught in the plots which they have devised.

3 For the wicked [a]boasts of his [b]heart's desire,
And [1]the greedy man curses *and* [c]spurns the LORD.
4 The wicked, in the haughtiness of his countenance, [a]does not seek *Him*.
All his [1]thoughts are, "[b]There is no God."

5 His ways [1a]prosper at all times;
Thy judgments are on high, [b]out of his sight;
As for all his adversaries, he snorts at them.
6 He says to himself, "[a]I shall not be moved;
[1]Throughout all generations [b]I shall not be in adversity."
7 His [a]mouth is full of curses and deceit and [b]oppression;
[c]Under his tongue is mischief and wickedness.
8 He sits in the [a]lurking places of the villages;
In the hiding places he [b]kills the innocent;
His eyes [1]stealthily watch for the [2c]unfortunate.
9 He lurks in a hiding place as [a]a lion in his [1]lair;
He [b]lurks to catch [c]the afflicted;
He catches the afflicted when he draws him into his [d]net.
10 He [1]crouches, he [2]bows down,
And the [3]unfortunate fall [4]by his mighty ones.
11 He [a]says to himself, "God has forgotten;
He has hidden His face; He will never see it."

+ I.e., "Death to the Son"
1 [1]Or, *miracles* [a]Ps. 86:12 [b]Ps. 26:7
2 [a]Ps. 5:11; 104:34 [b]Ps. 66:2, 4 [c]Ps. 83:18; 92:1
3 [a]Ps. 27:2
4 [1]Lit., *my right and my cause* [2]Or, *a righteous Judge* [a]Ps. 140:12 [b]Ps. 50:6
5 [a]Ps. 119:21 [b]Ps. 69:28; Prov. 10:7
6 [1]Or, *O enemy, desolations are finished forever; And their cities Thou hast plucked up.* [a]Ps. 34:16
7 [1]Or, *sits* as king [a]Ps. 10:16 [b]Ps. 89:14
8 [a]Ps. 96:13; 98:9
9 [1]Or, *Let the LORD also be* [a]Ps. 32:7; 59:9, 16, 17
10 [1]Or, *let those . . . name put* [a]Ps. 91:14 [b]Ps. 37:28; 94:14
11 [a]Ps. 76:2 [b]Ps. 105:1; 107:22
12 [1]I.e., avenges bloodshed [a]Gen. 9:5; Ps. 72:14 [b]Ps. 9:18
13 [a]Ps. 38:19 [b]Ps. 30:3; 86:13
14 [1]Or, *deliverance* [a]Ps. 106:2 [b]Ps. 13:5; 20:5; 35:9; 51:12
15 [a]Ps. 7:15, 16 [b]Ps. 57:6
16 [1]Perhaps, resounding music or meditation [2]*Selah* may mean: *Pause, Crescendo* or *Musical interlude* [a]Ex. 7:5 [b]Ps. 9:4
17 [1]Or, *turn* [2]I.e., the nether world [a]Ps. 49:14 [b]Job 8:13; Ps. 50:22
18 [a]Ps. 9:12; 12:5 [b]Ps. 62:5; 71:5; Prov. 23:18
19 [a]Num. 10:35 [b]Ps. 9:5
20 [a]Ps. 14:5 [b]Ps. 62:9

1 [1]Or, Thine eyes [a]Ps. 22:1 [b]Ps. 13:1; 55:1
2 [1]Lit., *burn* [2]Or, *They will be caught* [a]Ps. 73:6, 8 [b]Ps. 7:16; 9:16
3 [1]Or, *blesses the greedy man* [a]Ps. 49:6; 94:3, 4 [b]Ps. 112:10 [c]Ps. 10:13
4 [1]Or, *plots* [a]Ps. 10:13; 36:2 [b]Ps. 14:1; 36:1
5 [1]Lit., *are strong* [a]Ps. 52:7 [b]Ps. 28:5
6 [1]Lit., *To* [a]Ps. 49:11; Eccl. 8:11 [b]Rev. 18:7
7 [a]Rom. 3:14 [b]Ps. 73:8 [c]Job 20:12; Ps. 140:3
8 [1]Lit., *lie in wait* [2]Or, *poor* [a]Ps. 11:2 [b]Ps. 94:6 [c]Ps. 72:12
9 [1]Or, *thicket* [a]Ps. 17:12 [b]Ps. 59:3; Mic. 7:2 [c]Ps. 10:2 [d]Ps. 140:5
10 [1]Or, *is crushed* [2]Or, *is bowed down* [3]Or, *poor* [4]Or, *into his claws*
11 [a]Ps. 10:4

12 Arise, O LORD; O God, [a]lift up Thy hand.
[b]Do not forget the afflicted.
13 Why has the wicked [a]spurned God?
He has said to himself, "Thou wilt not require *it*."
14 Thou hast seen *it*, for Thou hast beheld [a]mischief and vexation to [1]take it into Thy hand.
The [2b]unfortunate commits *himself* to Thee;
Thou hast been the [c]helper of the orphan.
15 [a]Break the arm of the wicked and the evildoer,
[1b]Seek out his wickedness until Thou dost find none.

16 The LORD is [a]King forever and ever;
[b]Nations have perished from His land.
17 O LORD, Thou hast heard the [a]desire of the [1]humble;
Thou wilt [b]strengthen their heart, [c]Thou wilt incline Thine ear
18 To [1]vindicate the [a]orphan and the [b]oppressed,
That man who is of the earth may cause [c]terror no more.

PSALM 11

The LORD a Refuge and Defense.

For the choir director. *A Psalm* of David.

IN the LORD I [a]take refuge;
How can you say to my soul, "Flee *as* a bird to your [b]mountain;
2 For, behold, the wicked [a]bend the bow,
They [1b]make ready their arrow upon the string,
To [c]shoot in darkness at the upright in heart.
3 If the [a]foundations are destroyed,
What can the righteous do?"

4 The LORD is in His [a]holy temple; the [1]LORD's [b]throne is in heaven;
His [c]eyes behold, His eyelids test the sons of men.
5 The LORD [a]tests the righteous and [b]the wicked,
And the one who loves violence His soul hates.
6 Upon the wicked He will [a]rain [1]snares;
[b]Fire and brimstone and [c]burning wind will be the portion of [d]their cup.
7 For the LORD is [a]righteous; [b]He loves [1]righteousness;
The upright will [c]behold His face.

PSALM 12

God, a Helper against the Treacherous.

For the choir director; [+]upon an eight-stringed lyre. A Psalm of David.

HELP, LORD, for [a]the godly man ceases to be,

12 [a]Ps. 17:7; Mic. 5:9 [b]Ps. 9:12
13 [a]Ps. 10:3
14 [1]Lit., *put, give* [2]Or, *poor* [a]Ps. 10:7 [b]Ps. 22:11 [c]Ps. 68:5
15 [1]Or, *Mayest Thou seek* [a]Ps. 37:17 [b]Ps. 140:11
16 [a]Ps. 29:10 [b]Deut. 8:20
17 [1]Or, *afflicted* [a]Ps. 9:18 [b]1 Chr. 29:18 [c]Ps. 34:15
18 [1]Lit., *judge* [a]Ps. 146:9 [b]Ps. 9:9; 74:21 [c]Is. 29:20

1 [a]Ps. 2:12 [b]Ps. 121:1
2 [1]Or, *fixed* [a]Ps. 7:12; 37:14 [b]Ps. 64:3 [c]Ps. 64:4
3 [a]Ps. 82:5; 87:1; 119:152
4 [1]Lit., *LORD, His throne* [a]Ps. 18:6; Mic. 1:2; Hab. 2:20 [b]Ps. 103:19; Is. 66:1; Matt. 5:34; Rev. 4:2 [c]Ps. 33:18; 34:15, 16
5 [a]Gen. 22:1; Ps. 34:19; James 1:12 [b]Ps. 5:5
6 [1]Or, *coals of fire* [a]Ps. 18:13, 14 [b]Gen. 19:24; Ezek. 38:22 [c]Jer. 4:11, 12 [d]Ps. 75:8
7 [1]Or, *righteous deeds* [a]Ps. 7:9, 11 [b]Ps. 33:5; 45:7 [c]Ps. 16:11; 17:15

[+] Or, *according to a lower octave* (Heb., *Sheminith*)
1 [a]Is. 57:1; Mic. 7:2
2 [1]Or, *emptiness* [2]Lit., *lip* [a]Ps. 10:7; 41:6 [b]Ps. 28:3; 55:21; Jer. 9:8; Rom. 16:18
3 [a]Dan. 7:8; Rev. 13:5
4 [1]Lit., *with us* [a]Ps. 73:8, 9
5 [a]Ps. 9:9; 10:18 [b]Is. 33:10 [c]Ps. 34:6; 35:10
6 [a]2 Sam. 22:31; Ps. 18:30; 19:8, 10; 119:140 [b]Prov. 30:5
7 [a]Ps. 37:28; 97:10
8 [1]Or, *worthlessness* [a]Ps. 55:10, 11 [b]Is. 32:5

1 [a]Ps. 44:24 [b]Job 13:24; Ps. 89:46
2 [a]Ps. 42:4 [b]Ps. 42:9
3 [a]Ps. 5:1 [b]1 Sam. 14:29; Ezra 9:8; Job 33:30; Ps. 18:28 [c]Jer. 51:39
4 [a]Ps. 12:4 [b]Ps. 25:2; 38:16
5 [a]Ps. 52:8 [b]Ps. 9:14
6 [a]Ps. 96:1, 2 [b]Ps. 116:7; 119:17; 142:7

1 [1]Lit., *doings* [a]Ps. 10:4; 53:1 [b]Ps. 14:1-3; 130:3; Rom. 3:10-12

For the faithful disappear from among the sons of men.
2 They [a]speak [1]falsehood to one another;
With [b]flattering [2]lips and with a double heart they speak.
3 May the LORD cut off all flattering lips,
The tongue that [a]speaks great things;
4 Who [a]have said, "With our tongue we will prevail;
Our lips are [1]our own; who is lord over us?"
5 "Because of the [a]devastation of the afflicted, because of the groaning of the needy,
Now [b]I will arise," says the LORD;
"I will [c]set him in the safety for which he longs."

6 The [a]words of the LORD are pure words;
As silver [b]tried in a furnace on the earth, refined seven times.
7 Thou, O LORD, wilt keep them;
Thou wilt [a]preserve him from this generation forever.
8 The [a]wicked strut about on every side,
When [1b]vileness is exalted among the sons of men.

PSALM 13

Prayer for Help in Trouble.

For the choir director. A Psalm of David.

HOW long, O LORD? Wilt Thou [a]forget me forever?
How long [b]wilt Thou hide Thy face from me?
2 How long shall I [a]take counsel in my soul,
Having [b]sorrow in my heart all the day?
How long will my enemy be exalted over me?

3 [a]Consider *and* answer me, O LORD, my God;
[b]Enlighten my eyes, lest I [c]sleep the *sleep of* death,
4 Lest my enemy [a]say, "I have overcome him,"
Lest [b]my adversaries rejoice when I am shaken.

5 But I have [a]trusted in Thy lovingkindness;
My heart shall [b]rejoice in Thy salvation.
6 I will [a]sing to the LORD,
Because He has [b]dealt bountifully with me.

PSALM 14

Folly and Wickedness of Men.

For the choir director. *A Psalm* of David.

THE fool has [a]said in his heart, "There is no God."
They are corrupt, they have committed abominable [1]deeds;
There is [b]no one who does good.

THE WOMAN OF SHUNEM

2 Kings 4:24. That the great woman of Shunem saddled a donkey and went to visit Elisha, was unusual, because it was normal for a man to ride and a woman to walk. It gives us some idea of her status that she was able to do this. If Mary rode the donkey and Joseph walked alongside, which is traditional in Christian art, then Joseph would have been a laughingstock to fellow travelers.

THE EYE OF THE NEEDLE

Matthew 19:24; 23:24. Many stories have been told to indicate that the *"eye of the needle"* is a small postern gate that was opened at night when the city gate had been shut, and that a camel could get through it provided it had been fully unloaded. It is a nice story but not true in biblical terms. The eye of the needle is a surgeon's needle. In both Matthew 19 and Matthew 23, the point was that the camel was the largest animal with which people of the day were familiar. Jesus was using the term much as we should use the word elephant as the largest creature in our experience. Jesus may also have used the camel as an illustration because it was ritually unclean.

THE ROOM IN THE INN

Luke 2:7. The *"inn"* where there was no room for Mary and Joseph was not a *khan*. The Greek word is *kataluma*, which means a *"temporary shelter."* The Romans erected large marquees for shelter when there was insufficient accommodation for people and shelter was needed. They were erected around Jerusalem, for instance, at Passover time. The *kataluma* was a noisy place, bustling with animals and people, and sometimes the odd cooking fire. No *"innkeepers"* were at hand. Since there was no room there for Mary and Joseph, then it is more than likely that Jesus was born either outside (the idea of the writer of the carol *"Away in a Manger" — "The stars in the bright sky look down where he lay")* or in a shepherd's cave. This last is more likely. Such a cave has been shown from antiquity as the birthplace of Jesus. It is now under the Church of Nativity in Bethlehem.

THE EYES OF A SHIP

Acts 27:15. Ships were often personified, and eyes were painted on each side of the bow. This seems to have been done to the ship Paul was on, because the literal meaning of the original is *"when we could not look the wind in the face."*

WATER FOR KING DAVID

2 Samuel 23:13-18. David longed for water from the well of Bethlehem, and three of his men fought their way to the well to get it. Instead of drinking the water, David poured it out *"to the Lord."* This story is often not understood. It is based on two things. First, it is sometimes possible to give a person something so expensive that he says, *"I'm sorry, I really cannot accept it."* David felt that way about the risks his men had taken and the blood that had possibly been spilled. The water was too precious for him to accept. Second, a person's most precious things were offered to God. David was giving to God the most precious thing he had.

A CITY AMIDST HILLS

Psalm 121:1. Jerusalem is on a ridge surrounded by hills. It was easy for the defenders of Jerusalem to feel that their city was safe because of those hills. The psalmist was challenging that attitude when he wrote, *"I will lift up my eyes to the hills–where does my help come from?"* The writer knew that his help came from God and so he wrote, *"My help comes from the Lord."* One of the hills overlooking Jerusalem on the west is Kiriath Jearim. It was there that David brought the Ark and let it rest so that it could overlook Jerusalem. He was too afraid at that time to bring the Ark into the city because the Temple was not yet built and because of the problems the Ark had caused on the way from the Philistines. Above Jerusalem to the west was the Mount of Olives. It was there that Jesus looked down on the city and wept, and it was there that he told his disciples of the coming end of the world.

JESUS' YOKE

Matthew 11:28. It is commonly thought that Jesus was talking here about the yoke that harnessed animals together when they were pulling a plough or a load. He was instead referring to a piece of wood that was fitted over one's shoulders so that loads could be hung on it. The device was similar to the yoke used by the milkmaid of a byegone age when she was carrying two pails. The reference in Matthew 11 is to a porter. Often he was asked to carry loads impossible for a human being, but when he was given a yoke, the burden became much easier. Jesus does not say that he will take our burdens away but that he will give us the means of carrying them so that they are not too much for us.

FOLLOWING AFTER JESUS

Matthew 16:24. In our culture, to *"follow after"* a person means to put oneself in a secondary position, but the phrase did not mean that in Bible times. The streets were so narrow that if two people went together they had to go single file. To follow after a person was to go *with* them. We would therefore say, *"If anyone comes with me..."*

DAVID - *confidence*

The battle lines were drawn.

The Philistine army camped on one hill. The Israelite army camped on the other hill. Everyday for forty days the Philistine champion stepped out into the valley between the two armies to mock and taunt the Israelites. And the Israelites were afraid.

When they looked at the Philistine champion, they saw a warrior standing over nine feet tall. They saw a warrior encased in armor. They saw an unbeatable opponent. They saw certain defeat. When the Israelites looked at themselves, their own weapons and their own strength, they decided not one of their own men could defeat the Philistine warrior. And they lost heart.

One day a teenage shepherd boy arrived in the Israelite camp to bring food to his brothers. This teenager, David, also heard the taunts of the Philistine, but instead of becoming afraid, he became angry, because this warrior mocked God's people, and by doing so, mocked God himself. Eventually, David went to King Saul and asked permission to fight the Philistine. David's request surprised Saul, since David was only a young shepherd, and had no formal military training. But even though he as young, David had something that nobody in the entire Israelite army had.

David had confidence in God.

All of the Israelites were afraid because they trusted in their own strength and in their own weapons. But David trusted God. He was confident that by depending on God and not on his own resources the Philistine could be defeated. David even refused to wear Saul's armor, knowing that the protection of God was much more powerful.

So David faced the warrior fully confident that the victory would come from God. Using only a slingshot, David hurled a stone at the mighty warrior, which struck him between the eyes and killed him instantly. God, using David, had defeated the Philistine champion. David and his slingshot had not defeated his enemy, God had. God could have used any one of the Israelite warriors to defeat the Philistine. But all of the Israelites took one look at the Philistine warrior and lost confidence in God.

And so God used a young shepherd to teach the entire Israelite army a lesson in misplaced confidence, a lesson expressed centuries later by the apostle Paul who said, *"We walk by faith, not by sight"* (2 Cor. 5:7).

QUESTIONS

1. **Why did the Israelites lose confidence in God?**

2. **How did David walk by faith? How can you walk by faith in your own life?**

3. **It's easy to lose your perspective on life when you face what appears to be an overwhelming problem. What could you do to trust God more instead of trusting yourself?**

4. **What made David stronger than the entire Israelite army? Why?**

2 The LORD has [a]looked down from
heaven upon the sons of men,
To see if there are any who [1b]understand,
Who [c]seek after God.
3 They have all [a]turned aside; together they have become corrupt;
There is [b]no one who does good,
not even one.

4 Do all the workers of wickedness
[a]not know,
Who [b]eat up my people *as* they eat
bread,
And [c]do not call upon the Lord?
5 There they are in great dread,
For God is with the [a]righteous
generation.
6 You would put to shame the counsel of the afflicted,
But the LORD is his [a]refuge.

7 Oh, that [a]the salvation of Israel
[1]would come out of Zion!
When the LORD [2b]restores His captive people,
Jacob will rejoice, Israel will be
glad.

PSALM 15

Description of a Citizen of Zion.
A Psalm of David.

O LORD, who may [1]abide [a]in Thy
tent?
Who may dwell on Thy [b]holy hill?
2 He who [a]walks with integrity, and
works righteousness,
And [b]speaks truth in his heart.
3 He [a]does not slander [1]with his
tongue,
Nor [b]does evil to his neighbor,
Nor [c]takes up a reproach against
his friend;
4 In [1]whose eyes a reprobate is despised,
But [2]who [a]honors those who fear
the LORD;
He [b]swears to his own hurt, and
does not change;
5 He [a]does not put out his money [1]at
interest,
Nor [b]does he take a bribe against
the innocent.
[c]He who does these things will
never be shaken.

PSALM 16

The LORD the Psalmist's Portion in Life and Deliverer in Death.
A [+]Mikhtam of David.

[a]PRESERVE me, O God, for [b]I take
refuge in Thee.
2 [1]I said to the LORD, "Thou art [2]my
Lord;
I [a]have no good besides Thee."
3 As for the [1a]saints who are in the
earth,
[2]They are the majestic ones [b]in
whom is all my delight.

2 [1]Or, *act wisely* [a]Ps. 33:13, 14; 102:19 [b]Ps. 92:6 [c]1 Chr. 22:19
3 [a]Ps. 58:3 [b]Ps. 143:2
4 [a]Ps. 82:5 [b]Ps. 27:2; Jer. 10:25; Mic. 3:3 [c]Ps. 79:6; Is. 64:7
5 [a]Ps. 73:15; 112:2
6 [a]Ps. 9:9; 40:17; 46:1; 142:5
7 [1]Lit., *would be* [2]Or, *restores the fortunes of His people* [a]Ps. 53:6 [b]Ps. 85:1, 2

1 [1]Lit., *sojourn* [a]Ps. 27:5, 6; 61:4 [b]Ps. 24:3
2 [a]Ps. 24:4; Is. 33:15 [b]Zech. 8:16; Eph. 4:25
3 [1]Lit., *according to* [a]Ps. 50:20 [b]Ps. 28:3 [c]Ex. 23:1
4 [1]Lit., *his* [2]Lit., *he* [a]Acts 28:10 [b]Judg. 11:35
5 [1]I.e., to a fellow Israelite [a]Ex. 22:25; Lev. 25:36; Deut. 23:20; Ezek. 18:8 [b]Ex. 23:8; Deut. 16:19 [c]2 Pet. 1:10

+ Possibly, *Epigrammatic Poem* or *Atonement Psalm*
1 [a]Ps. 17:8 [b]Ps. 7:1
2 [1]Or, O my soul, *you said* [2]Or, *the Lord* [a]Ps. 73:25
3 [1]Lit., *holy ones;* i.e., the godly [2]Lit., *And the majestic ones . . . delight* [a]Ps. 101:6 [b]Ps. 119:63
4 [1]I.e., sorrows due to idolatry [2]Or, *hastened to* [a]Ps. 32:10 [b]Ps. 106:37, 38 [c]Ex. 23:13; Josh. 23:7
5 [a]Ps. 73:26; 119:57; 142:5; Lam. 3:24 [b]Ps. 23:5 [c]Ps. 125:3 mg.
6 [a]Ps. 78:55 [b]Jer. 3:19
7 [1]Lit., *kidneys,* figurative for inner man [a]Ps. 73:24 [b]Ps. 77:6
8 [a]Ps. 16:8-11; Acts 2:25-28 [b]Ps. 27:8; 123:1, 2 [c]Ps. 73:23; 110:5; 121:5 [d]Ps. 112:6
9 [a]Ps. 4:7; 13:5 [b]Ps. 30:12; 57:8; 108:1 [c]Ps. 4:8
10 [1]I.e., the nether world [2]Lit., *give* [3]Or, *godly one* [4]Or, *see corruption* or *the pit* [a]Ps. 49:15; 86:13 [b]Acts 13:35
11 [a]Ps. 139:24; Matt. 7:14 [b]Ps. 21:6; 43:4 [c]Job 36:11; Ps. 36:7, 8; 46:4

1 [a]Ps. 9:4 [b]Ps. 61:1; 142:6 [c]Ps. 88:2 [d]Is. 29:13

4 The [1a]sorrows of those who have
[2]bartered for another *god* will be
multiplied;
I shall not pour out their libations
of [b]blood,
Nor shall I [c]take their names upon
my lips.

5 The LORD is the [a]portion of my
inheritance and my [b]cup;
Thou dost support my [c]lot.
6 The [a]lines have fallen to me in
pleasant places;
Indeed, my heritage is [b]beautiful to
me.

7 I will bless the LORD who has
[a]counseled me;
Indeed, my [1b]mind instructs me in
the night.
8 [a]I have [b]set the LORD continually
before me;
Because He is [c]at my right hand, [d]I
will not be shaken.
9 Therefore [a]my heart is glad, and
[b]my glory rejoices;
My flesh also will [c]dwell securely.
10 For Thou [a]wilt not abandon my
soul to [1]Sheol;
Neither wilt Thou [2b]allow Thy
[3]Holy One to [4]undergo decay.
11 Thou wilt make known to me [a]the
path of life;
In [b]Thy presence is fulness of joy;
In Thy right hand there are [c]pleasures forever.

PSALM 17

Prayer for Protection against Oppressors.
A Prayer of David.

HEAR a [a]just cause, O LORD, [b]give
heed to my cry;
[c]Give ear to my prayer, which is
not from [d]deceitful lips.
2 Let [a]my [1]judgment come forth
from Thy presence;
Let Thine eyes look with [b]equity.
3 Thou hast [a]tried my heart;
Thou hast visited *me* by night;
Thou hast [b]tested me and [c]dost
find [1]nothing;
I have [d]purposed that my mouth
will not transgress.
4 As for the deeds of men, [a]by the
word of Thy lips
I have kept from the [b]paths of the
violent.
5 My [a]steps have held fast to Thy
[1]paths.
My [b]feet have not slipped.

6 I have [a]called upon Thee, for Thou
wilt answer me, O God;
[b]Incline Thine ear to me, hear my
speech.

2 [1]I.e., vindication [a]Ps. 103:6 [b]Ps. 98:9; 99:4
3 [1]Or, *no evil device in me; My mouth* [a]Ps. 26:1, 2 [b]Job 23:10; Ps. 66:10; Zech. 13:9; 1 Pet. 1:7 [c]Jer. 50:20 [d]Ps. 39:1
4 [a]Ps. 119:9, 101 [b]Ps. 10:5-11
5 [1]Lit., *tracks* [a]Job 23:11; Ps. 44:18; 119:133 [b]Ps. 18:36; 37:31
6 [a]Ps. 86:7; 116:2 [b]Ps. 88:2

7 [a]Wondrously show Thy lovingkindness,
O [b]Savior of those who take refuge [1]at Thy right hand
From those who rise up *against them.*
8 Keep me as [1]the [a]apple of the eye;
Hide me [b]in the shadow of Thy wings,
9 From the [a]wicked who despoil me,
My [b]deadly enemies, who surround me.
10 They have [a]closed their [1]unfeeling *heart*;
With their mouth they [b]speak proudly.
11 They have now [a]surrounded us in our steps;
They set their eyes [b]to cast *us* down to the ground.
12 He is [a]like a lion that is eager to tear,
And as a young lion [b]lurking in hiding places.

13 [a]Arise, O LORD, confront him, [b]bring him low;
[c]Deliver my soul from the wicked with [d]Thy sword,
14 From men with [a]Thy hand, O LORD,
From men [1]of the world, [b]whose portion is in *this* life;
And whose belly Thou [c]dost fill with Thy treasure;
They are satisfied with children,
And leave their abundance to their babes.
15 As for me, I shall [a]behold Thy face in righteousness;
[b]I will be satisfied [1]with Thy [c]likeness when I awake.

PSALM 18

The LORD Praised for Giving Deliverance.

For the choir director. *A Psalm* of David the servant of the LORD, +who spoke to the LORD the words of this song in the day that the LORD delivered him from the hand of all his enemies and from the hand of Saul. And he said,

"I LOVE Thee, O LORD, [a]my strength."
2 The LORD is [a]my [1]rock and [b]my fortress and my [c]deliverer,
My God, my rock, in whom I take refuge;
My [d]shield and the [e]horn of my salvation, my [f]stronghold.
3 I call upon the LORD, who is [a]worthy to be praised,
And I am [b]saved from my enemies.

4 The [a]cords of death encompassed me,
And the [b]torrents of [1]ungodliness [2]terrified me.
5 The [a]cords of [1]Sheol surrounded me;
The snares of death confronted me.
6 In my [a]distress I called upon the LORD,
And cried to my God for help;
He heard my voice [b]out of His temple,
And my [c]cry for help before Him came into His ears.

7 Then the [a]earth shook and quaked;
And the [b]foundations of the mountains were trembling
And were shaken, because He was angry.
8 Smoke went up [1]out of His nostrils,
And [a]fire from His mouth devoured;
Coals were kindled by it.
9 He [a]bowed the heavens also, and came down
With thick [b]darkness under His feet.
10 And He rode upon a [a]cherub and flew;
And He sped upon the [b]wings of the wind.
11 He made [a]darkness His hiding place, [b]His [1]canopy around Him,
Darkness of waters, thick clouds of the skies.
12 From the [a]brightness before Him passed His thick clouds,
Hailstones and [b]coals of fire.
13 The LORD also [a]thundered in the heavens,
And the Most High uttered His voice,
Hailstones and coals of fire.
14 And He [a]sent out His arrows, and scattered them,
And lightning flashes in abundance, and [1]routed them.
15 Then the [a]channels of water appeared,
And the foundations of the world were [1]laid bare
At Thy [b]rebuke, O LORD,
At the blast of the [c]breath of Thy nostrils.

16 He [a]sent from on high, He took me;
He drew me out of [b]many waters.
17 He [a]delivered me from my strong enemy,
And from those who hated me, for they were [b]too mighty for me.
18 They confronted me in [a]the day of my calamity,
But [b]the LORD was my stay.
19 He brought me forth also into a [a]broad place;
He rescued me, because [b]He delighted in me.

20 The LORD has [a]rewarded me according to my righteousness;
According to the [b]cleanness of my hands He has recompensed me.

7 [1]Or, *from those who rise up . . . at Thy right hand* [a]Ps. 31:21 [b]Ps. 20:6
8 [1]Lit., *the pupil, the daughter of the eye* [a]Deut. 32:10; Zech. 2:8 [b]Ruth 2:12; Ps. 36:7; 57:1; 61:4; 63:7; 91:1, 4
9 [a]Ps. 31:20 [b]Ps. 27:12
10 [1]Lit., *fat* [a]Job 15:27; Ps. 73:7 [b]1 Sam. 2:3; Ps. 31:18; 73:8
11 [a]Ps. 88:17 [b]Ps. 37:14
12 [a]Ps. 7:2 [b]Ps. 10:9
13 [a]Ps. 3:7 [b]Ps. 55:23 [c]Ps. 22:20 [d]Ps. 7:12
14 [1]Or, *whose portion in life is of the world* [a]Ps. 17:7 [b]Ps. 73:3-7; Luke 16:25 [c]Ps. 49:6
15 [1]Or, *with* beholding [a]Ps. 11:7; 16:11; 140:13; 1 John 3:2 [b]Ps. 4:6, 7 [c]Num. 12:8

+ 2 Sam. 22:1-51
1 [a]Ps. 59:17
2 [1]Or, *crag* [a]Deut. 32:18; 1 Sam. 2:2; Ps. 18:31, 46; 28:1; 31:3; 42:9; 71:3; 78:15 [b]Ps. 144:2 [c]Ps. 19:14 [d]Ps. 28:7; 33:20; 59:11; 84:9, 11; Prov. 30:5 [e]Ps. 75:10 [f]Ps. 59:9
3 [a]Ps. 48:1; 96:4; 145:3 [b]Ps. 34:6
4 [1]Or, *destruction;* Heb., *Belial* [2]Or, *were assailing* or *terrifying* [a]Ps. 116:3 [b]Ps. 69:2; 124:3, 4
5 [1]I.e., the nether world [a]Ps. 116:3
6 [a]Ps. 50:15; 120:1 [b]Ps. 3:4 [c]Ps. 34:15
7 [a]Judg. 5:4; Ps. 68:7, 8; Is. 13:13; Hag. 2:6 [b]Ps. 114:4, 6
8 [1]Or, *in His wrath* [a]Ps. 50:3
9 [a]Ps. 144:5 [b]Ps. 97:2
10 [a]Ps. 80:1; 99:1 [b]Ps. 104:3
11 [1]Or, *pavilion* [a]Deut. 4:11 [b]Ps. 97:2
12 [a]Ps. 104:2 [b]Ps. 97:3; 140:10; Hab. 3:4
13 [a]Ps. 29:3; 104:7
14 [1]Lit., *confused* [a]Ps. 144:6; Hab. 3:11
15 [1]Or, *uncovered* [a]Ps. 106:9 [b]Ps. 76:6 [c]Ps. 18:8
16 [a]Ps. 144:7 [b]Ps. 32:6
17 [a]Ps. 59:1 [b]Ps. 35:10; 142:6
18 [a]Ps. 59:16 [b]Ps. 16:8
19 [a]Ps. 4:1; 31:8; 118:5 [b]Ps. 37:23; 41:11
20 [a]1 Sam. 24:19; Job 33:26; Ps. 7:8 [b]Job 22:30; Ps. 24:4

21 For I have [a]kept the ways of the LORD,
And have [b]not wickedly departed from my God.
22 For all [a]His ordinances were before me,
And I did not put away His [b]statutes from me.
23 I was also [1a]blameless with Him,
And I [b]kept myself from my iniquity.
24 Therefore the LORD has [a]recompensed me according to my righteousness,
According to the cleanness of my hands in His eyes.

25 With [a]the kind Thou dost show Thyself kind;
With the [1]blameless [b]Thou dost show Thyself blameless;
26 With the pure Thou dost show Thyself [a]pure;
And with the crooked [b]Thou dost show Thyself [1]astute.
27 For Thou dost [a]save an afflicted people;
But [b]haughty eyes Thou dost abase.
28 For Thou dost [a]light my lamp;
The LORD my God [b]illumines my darkness.
29 For by Thee I can [1a]run upon a troop;
And by my God I can [b]leap over a wall.

30 As for God, His way is [1a]blameless;
The [b]word of the LORD is tried;
He is a [c]shield to all who take refuge in Him.
31 For [a]who is God, but the LORD?
And who is a [b]rock, except our God,
32 The God who [a]girds me with strength,
And [1]makes my way [2b]blameless?
33 He [a]makes my feet like hinds' *feet*,
And [b]sets me upon my high places.
34 He [a]trains my hands for battle,
So that my arms can [b]bend a bow of bronze.
35 Thou hast also given me [a]the shield of Thy salvation,
And Thy [b]right hand upholds me;
And [c]Thy [1]gentleness makes me great.
36 Thou dost [a]enlarge my steps under me,
And my [1b]feet have not slipped.

37 I [a]pursued my enemies and overtook them,
And I did not turn back [b]until they were consumed.
38 I shattered them, so that they were [a]not able to rise;
They fell [b]under my feet.
39 For Thou hast [a]girded me with strength for battle;
Thou hast [1b]subdued under me those who rose up against me.
40 Thou hast also made my enemies [a]turn their backs to me,
And I [1b]destroyed those who hated me.
41 They cried for help, but there was [a]none to save,
Even to the LORD, but [b]He did not answer them.
42 Then I beat them fine as the [a]dust before the wind;
I emptied them out as the mire of the streets.

43 Thou hast delivered me from the [a]contentions of the people;
Thou hast placed me as [b]head of the nations;
A [c]people whom I have not known serve me.
44 As soon as they hear, they obey me;
Foreigners [1a]submit to me.
45 Foreigners [a]fade away,
And [b]come trembling out of their [1]fortresses.

46 The LORD [a]lives, and blessed be [b]my rock;
And exalted be [c]the God of my salvation,
47 The God who [a]executes vengeance for me,
And [b]subdues peoples under me.
48 He [a]delivers me from my enemies;
Surely Thou [b]dost lift me above those who rise up against me;
Thou dost rescue me from the [c]violent man.
49 Therefore I will [a]give thanks to Thee among the nations, O LORD,
And I will [b]sing praises to Thy name.
50 He gives great [1a]deliverance to His king,
And shows lovingkindness to [b]His anointed,
To David and [c]his [2]descendants forever.

PSALM 19

The Works and the Word of God.

For the choir director. A Psalm of David.

THE [a]heavens are telling of the glory of God;
And their [b]expanse is declaring the work of His hands.
2 Day to [a]day pours forth speech,
And [b]night to night reveals knowledge.
3 There is no speech, nor are there words;
Their voice is not heard.
4 Their [1a]line has gone out through all the earth,
And their utterances to the end of the world.
In them He has [b]placed a tent for the sun,

21 [a]Ps. 37:34; 119:33; Prov. 8:32 [b]2 Chr. 34:33; Ps. 119:102
22 [a]Ps. 119:30 [b]Ps. 119:83
23 [1]Lit., *complete;* or, *having integrity;* or, *perfect* [a]Ps. 18:32 [b]Ps. 19:12, 13; 25:11; 66:18
24 [a]1 Sam. 26:23; Ps. 18:20
25 [1]V. 23, note 1 [a]1 Kin. 8:32; Ps. 62:12; Matt. 5:7 [b]Ps. 18:30
26 [1]Lit., *twisted* [a]Job 25:5; Hab. 1:13 [b]Lev. 26:23, 24, 27, 28; Prov. 3:34
27 [a]Ps. 72:12 [b]Ps. 101:5; Prov. 6:17
28 [a]1 Kin. 15:4; Job 18:6; Ps. 132:17 [b]Ps. 27:1
29 [1]Or, *crush a troop* [a]Ps. 118:10-12 [b]Ps. 18:33; 40:2
30 [1]V. 23, note 1 [a]Deut. 32:4; Ps. 19:7; 145:17; Rev. 15:3 [b]Ps. 12:6 [c]Ps. 17:7; 91:4
31 [a]Deut. 32:39; 1 Sam. 2:2; Ps. 86:8-10; Is. 45:5 [b]Deut. 32:31; Ps. 18:2; 62:2
32 [1]Or, *has made* [2]Lit., *complete;* or, *having integrity* [a]Ps. 18:39; Is. 45:5 [b]Ps. 18:23
33 [a]Hab. 3:19 [b]Deut. 32:13
34 [a]Ps. 144:1 [b]Job 29:20
35 [1]Or, *condescension* [a]Ps. 33:20 [b]Ps. 63:8; 119:117 [c]Ps. 138:6
36 [1]Lit., *ankles* [a]Ps. 18:33 [b]Ps. 66:9; Prov. 4:12
37 [a]Ps. 44:5 [b]Ps. 37:20
38 [a]Ps. 36:12 [b]Ps. 47:3
39 [1]Lit., *caused to bow down* [a]Ps. 18:32 [b]Ps. 18:47
40 [1]Or, *silenced* [a]Ps. 21:12 [b]Ps. 94:23
41 [a]Ps. 50:22 [b]Job 27:9; Prov. 1:28
42 [a]Ps. 83:13
43 [a]2 Sam. 3:1; 19:9; Ps. 35:1 [b]2 Sam. 8:1-18; Ps. 89:27 [c]Is. 55:5
44 [1]Lit., *deceive me;* i.e., give feigned obedience [a]Ps. 66:3
45 [1]Lit., *fastnesses* [a]Ps. 37:2 [b]Mic. 7:17
46 [a]Job 19:25 [b]Ps. 18:2 [c]Ps. 51:14
47 [a]Ps. 94:1 [b]Ps. 18:43; 47:3; 144:2
48 [a]Ps. 3:7 [b]Ps. 27:6; 59:1 [c]Ps. 11:5
49 [a]Rom. 15:9 [b]Ps. 108:1
50 [1]I.e., victories; lit., *salvations* [2]Lit., *seed* [a]Ps. 21:1; 144:10 [b]Ps. 28:8 [c]Ps. 89:4

1 [a]Ps. 8:1; 50:6; Rom. 1:19, 20 [b]Gen. 1:6, 7
2 [a]Ps. 74:16 [b]Ps. 139:12

4 [1]Another reading is *sound* [a]Rom. 10:18 [b]Ps. 104:2

5 Which is as a bridegroom coming out of his chamber;
It rejoices as a strong man to run his course.
6 Its [a]rising is from [1]one end of the heavens,
And its circuit to the [2]other end of them;
And there is nothing hidden from its heat.

7 [a]The law of the LORD is [1b]perfect, [c]restoring the soul;
The testimony of the LORD is [d]sure, making [e]wise the simple.
8 The precepts of the LORD are [a]right, [b]rejoicing the heart;
The commandment of the LORD is [c]pure, [d]enlightening the eyes.
9 The fear of the LORD is clean, enduring forever;
The judgments of the LORD are [a]true; they are [b]righteous altogether.
10 They are more desirable than [a]gold, yes, than much fine gold;
[b]Sweeter also than honey and the drippings of the honeycomb.
11 Moreover, by them [a]Thy servant is warned;
In keeping them there is great [b]reward.
12 Who can [a]discern *his* errors? [b]Acquit me of [c]hidden *faults.*
13 Also keep back Thy servant [a]from presumptuous *sins*;
Let them not [b]rule over me;
Then I shall be [1c]blameless,
And I shall be acquitted of [d]great transgression.
14 Let the words of my mouth and [a]the meditation of my heart
Be acceptable in Thy sight,
O LORD, [b]my rock and my [c]Redeemer.

PSALM 20

Prayer for Victory over Enemies.

For the choir director. A Psalm of David.

MAY the LORD answer you [a]in the day of trouble!
May the [b]name of the [c]God of Jacob set you *securely* on high!
2 May He send you help [a]from the sanctuary,
And [b]support you from Zion!
3 May He [a]remember all your meal offerings,
And [b]find your burnt offering [1]acceptable! [[2]Selah.

4 May He grant you your [a]heart's desire,
And [b]fulfill all your [1]counsel!
5 [1]We will [a]sing for joy over your [2]victory,
And in the name of our God we will [b]set up our banners.
May the LORD [c]fulfill all your petitions.

6 Now [a]I know that the LORD saves His anointed;
He will [b]answer him from His holy heaven,
With the [1c]saving strength of His right hand.
7 Some [1]*boast* in chariots, and some in [a]horses;
But [b]we [2]will boast in the name of the LORD, our God.
8 They have [a]bowed down and fallen;
But we have [b]risen and stood upright.
9 [1a]Save, O LORD;
May the [b]King answer us in the day we call.

PSALM 21

Praise for Deliverance.

For the choir director. A Psalm of David.

O LORD, in Thy strength the king will [a]be glad,
And in Thy [1]salvation how greatly he will rejoice!
2 Thou hast [a]given him his heart's desire,
And Thou hast not withheld the request of his lips. [[1]Selah.
3 For Thou [a]dost meet him with the blessings of good things;
Thou dost set a [b]crown of fine gold on his head.
4 He asked life of Thee,
Thou [a]didst give it to him,
[b]Length of days forever and ever.
5 His [a]glory is great through Thy [1]salvation,
[b]Splendor and majesty Thou dost place upon him.
6 For Thou dost make him [1]most [a]blessed forever;
Thou dost make him joyful [b]with gladness in Thy presence.

7 For the king [a]trusts in the LORD,
And through the lovingkindness of the Most High [b]he will not be shaken.
8 Your hand will [a]find out all your enemies;
Your right hand will find out those who hate you.
9 You will make them [a]as a fiery oven in the time [1]of your anger;
The LORD will [b]swallow them up in His wrath,
And [c]fire will devour them.
10 Their [1]offspring Thou wilt destroy from the earth,
And their [2a]descendants from among the sons of men.
11 Though they [1a]intended evil against Thee,
And [b]devised a plot,
They will not succeed.
12 For Thou wilt [a]make them turn their back;
Thou wilt [1]aim [b]with Thy bowstrings at their faces.

---

6 [1]Lit., *the* [2]Lit., *the ends* [a]Ps. 113:3; Eccl. 1:5
7 [1]I.e., blameless [a]Ps. 111:7 [b]Ps. 119:160 [c]Ps. 23:3 [d]Ps. 93:5 [e]Ps. 119:98-100
8 [a]Ps. 119:128 [b]Ps. 119:14 [c]Ps. 12:6 [d]Ps. 36:9
9 [a]Ps. 119:142 [b]Ps. 119:138
10 [a]Ps. 119:72, 127 [b]Ps. 119:103
11 [a]Ps. 17:4 [b]Ps. 24:5, 6; Prov. 29:18
12 [a]Ps. 40:12; 139:6 [b]Ps. 51:1, 2 [c]Ps. 90:8; 139:23, 24
13 [1]Lit., *complete* [a]Num. 15:30 [b]Ps. 119:133 [c]Ps. 18:32 [d]Ps. 25:11
14 [a]Ps. 104:34 [b]Ps. 18:2 [c]Ps. 31:5; Is. 47:4

1 [a]Ps. 50:15 [b]Ps. 91:14 [c]Ps. 46:7, 11
2 [a]Ps. 3:4 [b]Ps. 110:2
3 [1]Lit., *fat* [2]*Selah* may mean: *Pause, Crescendo* or *Musical interlude* [a]Acts 10:4 [b]Ps. 51:19
4 [1]Or, *purpose* [a]Ps. 21:2 [b]Ps. 145:19
5 [1]Or, *Let us sing* [2]Or, *salvation* [a]Ps. 9:14 [b]Ps. 60:4 [c]1 Sam. 1:17
6 [1]Or, *mighty deeds of the victory of His right hand* [a]Ps. 41:11 [b]Is. 58:9 [c]Ps. 28:8
7 [1]Or, praise *chariots,* or, trust, or, are strong *through* [2]Lit., *make mention of;* or, *praise the name* [a]Ps. 33:17 [b]2 Chr. 32:8
8 [a]Is. 2:11, 17 [b]Ps. 37:24; Mic. 7:8
9 [1]Or, *O LORD, save the king; answer us* [a]Ps. 3:7 [b]Ps. 17:6

1 [1]Or, *victory* [a]Ps. 59:16, 17
2 [1]*Selah* may mean: *Pause, Crescendo* or *Musical interlude* [a]Ps. 20:4; 37:4
3 [a]Ps. 59:10 [b]2 Sam. 12:30
4 [a]Ps. 61:6; 133:3 [b]Ps. 91:16
5 [1]Or, *victory* [a]Ps. 9:14; 20:5 [b]Ps. 8:5; 96:6
6 [1]Lit., *blessings* [a]1 Chr. 17:27 [b]Ps. 43:4
7 [a]Ps. 125:1 [b]Ps. 112:6
8 [a]Is. 10:10
9 [1]Or, *of your presence* [a]Mal. 4:1 [b]Lam. 2:2 [c]Ps. 50:3
10 [1]Lit., *fruit* [2]Lit., *seed* [a]Ps. 37:28
11 [1]Lit., *stretched out* [a]Ps. 2:1-3 [b]Ps. 10:2
12 [1]Lit., *make ready* [a]Ps. 18:40 [b]Ps. 7:12, 13

13 Be Thou exalted, O LORD, in Thy strength;
We will [a]sing and praise Thy power.

PSALM 22

A Cry of Anguish and a Song of Praise.

For the choir director; upon +Aijeleth Hashshahar. A Psalm of David.

[a]MY God, my God, why hast Thou forsaken me?
[1b]Far from my deliverance are the words of my [2c]groaning.
2 O my God, I [a]cry by day, but Thou dost not answer;
And by night, but [1]I have no rest.
3 Yet [a]Thou art holy,
O Thou who [1]art enthroned upon [b]the praises of Israel.
4 In Thee our fathers [a]trusted;
They trusted, and Thou didst [b]deliver them.
5 To Thee they cried out, and were delivered;
[a]In Thee they trusted, and were not [1]disappointed.

6 But I am a [a]worm, and not a man,
A [b]reproach of men, and [c]despised by the people.
7 All who see me [1a]sneer at me;
They [2]separate with the lip, they [b]wag the head, *saying,*
8 "[1]Commit *yourself* to the LORD; [a]let Him deliver him;
Let Him rescue him, because He delights in him."

9 Yet Thou art He who [a]didst bring me forth from the womb;
Thou didst make me trust *when* upon my mother's breasts.
10 Upon Thee I was cast [a]from [1]birth;
Thou hast been my God from my mother's womb.

11 [a]Be not far from me, for [1]trouble is near;
For there is [b]none to help.
12 Many [a]bulls have surrounded me;
Strong *bulls* of [b]Bashan have encircled me.
13 They [a]open wide their mouth at me,
As a ravening and a roaring [b]lion.
14 I am [a]poured out like water,
And all my [b]bones are out of joint;
My [c]heart is like wax;
It is melted within [1]me.
15 My [a]strength is dried up like a potsherd,
And [b]my tongue cleaves to my jaws;
And Thou dost [c]lay me [1]in the dust of death.
16 For [a]dogs have surrounded me;
[1]A band of evildoers has encompassed me;
[2]They [b]pierced my hands and my feet.
17 I can count all my bones.
[a]They look, they stare at me;
18 They [a]divide my garments among them,
And for my clothing they cast lots.

19 But Thou, O LORD, [a]be not far off;
O Thou my help, [b]hasten to my assistance.
20 Deliver my [1]soul from [a]the sword,
My [b]only *life* from the [2]power of the dog.
21 Save me from the [a]lion's mouth;
And from the horns of the [b]wild oxen Thou dost [c]answer me.

22 I will [a]tell of Thy name to my brethren;
In the midst of the assembly I will praise Thee.
23 [a]You who fear the LORD, praise Him;
All you [1]descendants of Jacob, [b]glorify Him,
And [c]stand in awe of Him, all you [1]descendants of Israel.
24 For He has [a]not despised nor abhorred the affliction of the afflicted;
Neither has He [b]hidden His face from him;
But [c]when he cried to Him for help, He heard.

25 From Thee *comes* [a]my praise in the great assembly;
I shall [b]pay my vows before those who fear Him.
26 The [1]afflicted shall eat and [a]be satisfied;
Those who seek Him will [b]praise the LORD.
Let your [c]heart live forever!
27 All the [a]ends of the earth will remember and turn to the LORD,
And all the [b]families of the nations will worship before [1]Thee.
28 For the [a]kingdom is the LORD's,
And He [b]rules over the nations.
29 All the [1a]prosperous of the earth will eat and worship,
All those who [b]go down to the dust will bow before Him,
Even he who [2c]cannot keep his soul alive.
30 [1a]Posterity will serve Him;
It will be told of the Lord to [b]the *coming* generation.
31 They will come and [a]will declare His righteousness
To a people [b]who will be born, that He has performed *it.*

13 [a]Ps. 59:16; 81:1
+ Lit., *the hind of the morning*
1 [1]Or, Why art Thou so *far from helping me,* and from *the words of my groaning?* [2]Lit., *roaring* [a]Matt. 27:46; Mark 15:34 [b]Ps. 10:1 [c]Job 3:24; Ps. 6:6; 32:3; 38:8
2 [1]Lit., *there is no silence for me* [a]Ps. 42:3; 88:1
3 [1]Or, *dost inhabit the praises* [a]Ps. 99:9 [b]Deut. 10:21; Ps. 148:14
4 [a]Ps. 78:53 [b]Ps. 107:6
5 [1]Or, *ashamed* [a]Is. 49:23
6 [a]Job 25:6; Is. 41:14 [b]Ps. 31:11 [c]Is. 49:7; 53:3
7 [1]Or, *mock me* [2]I.e., make mouths at me [a]Ps. 79:4; Is. 53:3; Luke 23:35 [b]Matt. 27:39; Mark 15:29
8 [1]Lit., *Roll;* another reading is *He committed* himself [a]Ps. 91:14; Matt. 27:43
9 [a]Ps. 71:5, 6
10 [1]Lit., a *womb* [a]Is. 46:3; 49:1
11 [1]Or, *distress* [a]Ps. 71:12 [b]2 Kin. 14:26; Ps. 72:12; Is. 63:5
12 [a]Ps. 22:21; 68:30 [b]Deut. 32:14; Amos 4:1
13 [a]Job 16:10; Ps. 35:21; Lam. 2:16; 3:46 [b]Ps. 10:9; 17:12
14 [1]Lit., *my inward parts* [a]Job 30:16 [b]Ps. 31:10; Dan. 5:6 [c]Josh. 7:5; Job 23:16; Ps. 73:26; Nah. 2:10
15 [1]Lit., *to* [a]Ps. 38:10 [b]John 19:28 [c]Ps. 104:29
16 [1]Or, *An assembly* [2]Another reading is *Like a lion, my . . .* [a]Ps. 59:6, 7 [b]Matt. 27:35; John 20:25
17 [a]Luke 23:27, 35
18 [a]Matt. 27:35; Mark 15:24; Luke 23:34; John 19:24
19 [a]Ps. 22:11 [b]Ps. 70:5
20 [1]Or, *life* [2]Lit., *paw* [a]Ps. 37:14 [b]Ps. 35:17
21 [a]Ps. 22:13 [b]Ps. 22:12 [c]Ps. 34:4; 118:5; 120:1
22 [a]Ps. 40:10; Heb. 2:12
23 [1]Lit., *seed* [a]Ps. 135:19, 20 [b]Ps. 86:12 [c]Ps. 33:8
24 [a]Ps. 69:33 [b]Ps. 27:9; 69:17; 102:2 [c]Ps. 31:22; Heb. 5:7
25 [a]Ps. 35:18; 40:9, 10 [b]Ps. 61:8; Eccl. 5:4

26 [1]Or, *poor* [a]Ps. 107:9 [b]Ps. 40:16 [c]Ps. 69:32
27 [1]Some versions read *Him* [a]Ps. 2:8; 82:8 [b]Ps. 86:9
28 [a]Ps. 47:7; Obad. 21; Zech. 14:9; Matt. 6:13 [b]Ps. 47:8
29 [1]Lit., *fat ones* [2]Or, *did not* [a]Ps. 17:10; 45:12; Hab. 1:16 [b]Ps. 28:1; Is. 26:19 [c]Ps. 89:48
30 [1]Lit., *A seed* [a]Ps. 102:28 [b]Ps. 102:18
31 [a]Ps. 40:9; 71:18 [b]Ps. 78:6

PSALM 23

The LORD, the Psalmist's Shepherd.

A Psalm of David.

THE LORD is my [a]shepherd,
I [1]shall [b]not want.
2 He makes me lie down in [a]green pastures;
He [b]leads me beside [1c]quiet waters.
3 He [a]restores my soul;
He [b]guides me in the [1c]paths of righteousness
For His name's sake.

4 Even though I [a]walk through the [1]valley of the shadow of death,
I [b]fear no [2]evil; for [c]Thou art with me;
Thy [d]rod and Thy staff, they comfort me.
5 Thou dost [a]prepare a table before me in the presence of my enemies;
Thou [1]hast [b]anointed my head with oil;
My [c]cup overflows.
6 [1]Surely [a]goodness and lovingkindness will follow me all the days of my life,
And I will [2b]dwell in the house of the LORD [3]forever.

PSALM 24

The King of Glory Entering Zion.

A Psalm of David.

THE [a]earth is the LORD'S, and [1]all it contains,
The [b]world, and those who dwell in it.
2 For He has [a]founded it upon the seas,
And established it upon the rivers.
3 Who may [a]ascend into the [b]hill of the LORD?
And who may stand in His holy [c]place?
4 He who has [a]clean hands and a [b]pure heart,
Who has not [c]lifted up his soul [1]to falsehood,
And has not [d]sworn deceitfully.
5 He shall receive a [a]blessing from the LORD
And [1b]righteousness from the God of his salvation.
6 [1]This is the generation of those who [a]seek Him,
Who seek Thy face—*even* Jacob. [[2]Selah.

7 [a]Lift up your heads, O gates,
And be lifted up, O [1]ancient doors,
That the King of [b]glory may come in!
8 Who is the King of glory?
The LORD [a]strong and mighty,
The LORD [b]mighty in battle.
9 Lift up your heads, O gates,
And lift *them* up, O [1]ancient doors,
That the King of [a]glory may come in!

1 [1]Or, *do*
[a]Ps. 78:52; 80:1; Is. 40:11; Jer. 31:10; Ezek. 34:11-13; John 10:11; 1 Pet. 2:25 [b]Ps. 34:9, 10; Phil. 4:19
2 [1]Lit., *waters of rest*
[a]Ps. 65:11-13; Ezek. 34:14 [b]Rev. 7:17 [c]Ps. 36:8; 46:4
3 [1]Lit., *tracks*
[a]Ps. 19:7 [b]Ps. 5:8; 31:3 [c]Ps. 85:13; Prov. 4:11; 8:20
4 [1]Or, *valley of deep darkness* [2]Or, *harm*
[a]Job 10:21, 22; Ps. 107:14 [b]Ps. 3:6; 27:1 [c]Ps. 16:8; Is. 43:2 [d]Mic. 7:14
5 [1]Or, *dost anoint*
[a]Ps. 78:19 [b]Ps. 92:10; Luke 7:46 [c]Ps. 16:5
6 [1]Or, *Only* [2]Another reading is *return to* [3]Lit., *for length of days*
[a]Ps. 25:7, 10 [b]Ps. 27:4-6

1 [1]Lit., *its fulness*
[a]1 Cor. 10:26 [b]Ps. 89:11
2 [a]Ps. 104:3, 5; 136:6
3 [a]Ps. 15:1 [b]Ps. 2:6 [c]Ps. 65:4
4 [1]Or, *in vain*
[a]Job 17:9; Ps. 22:30; 26:6 [b]Ps. 51:10; 73:1; Matt. 5:8 [c]Ezek. 18:15 [d]Ps. 15:4
5 [1]I.e., as vindicated
[a]Ps. 115:13 [b]Ps. 36:10
6 [1]Or, *Such* [2]*Selah* may mean: *Pause, Crescendo* or *Musical interlude*
[a]Ps. 27:4, 8
7 [1]Lit., *everlasting*
[a]Ps. 118:20; Is. 26:2 [b]Ps. 29:2, 9; 97:6; Acts 7:2; 1 Cor. 2:8
8 [a]Deut. 4:34; Ps. 96:7 [b]Ex. 15:3, 6; Ps. 76:3-6
9 [1]Lit., *everlasting*
[a]Ps. 26:8; 57:11
10 [a]Gen. 32:2; Josh. 5:14; 2 Sam. 5:10; Neh. 9:6

1 [a]Ps. 86:4; 143:8
2 [a]Ps. 31:1 [b]Ps. 25:20; 31:1 [c]Ps. 13:4; 41:11
3 [1]Or, *Let those . . be ashamed*
[a]Ps. 37:9; 40:1; Is. 49:23 [b]Ps. 119:158; Is. 21:2; Hab. 1:13
4 [a]Ex. 33:13; Ps. 27:11; 86:11
5 [a]Ps. 25:10; 43:3 [b]Ps. 79:9 [c]Ps. 40:1
6 [1]Or, *everlasting*
[a]Ps. 98:3 [b]Ps. 103:17
7 [a]Job 13:26; 20:11 [b]Ps. 51:1 [c]Ps. 31:19
8 [a]Ps. 86:5 [b]Ps. 92:15 [c]Ps. 32:8
9 [1]Or, *afflicted*
[a]Ps. 23:3 [b]Ps. 27:11
10 [a]Ps. 40:11 [b]Ps. 103:18
11 [a]Ps. 31:3; 79:9 [b]Ex. 34:9

10 Who is this King of glory?
The LORD of [a]hosts,
He is the King of glory. [Selah.

PSALM 25

Prayer for Protection, Guidance and Pardon.

A Psalm of David.

TO Thee, O LORD, I [a]lift up my soul.
2 O my God, in Thee [a]I trust,
Do not let me [b]be ashamed;
Do not let my [c]enemies exult over me.
3 Indeed, [a]none of those who wait for Thee will be ashamed;
[1]Those who [b]deal treacherously without cause will be ashamed.

4 [a]Make me know Thy ways, O LORD;
Teach me Thy paths.
5 Lead me in [a]Thy truth and teach me,
For Thou art the [b]God of my salvation;
For Thee I [c]wait all the day.
6 [a]Remember, O LORD, Thy compassion and Thy lovingkindnesses,
For they have been [1b]from of old.
7 Do not remember the [a]sins of my youth or my transgressions;
[b]According to Thy lovingkindness remember Thou me,
For Thy [c]goodness' sake, O LORD.

8 [a]Good and [b]upright is the LORD;
Therefore He [c]instructs sinners in the way.
9 He [a]leads the [1]humble in justice,
And He [b]teaches the [1]humble His way.
10 All the paths of the LORD are [a]lovingkindness and truth
To [b]those who keep His covenant and His testimonies.
11 For [a]Thy name's sake, O LORD,
[b]Pardon my iniquity, for it is great.

12 Who is the man who [a]fears the LORD?
He will [b]instruct him in the way he should choose.
13 His soul will [a]abide in [1]prosperity,
And his [2]descendants will [b]inherit the [3]land.
14 The [1a]secret of the LORD is for those who fear Him,
[2]And He will [b]make them know His covenant.
15 My [a]eyes are continually toward the LORD,
For He will [1b]pluck my feet out of the net.

12 [a]Ps. 31:19 [b]Ps. 25:8; 37:23
13 [1]Lit., *good* [2]Lit., *seed* [3]Or, *earth* [a]Prov. 1:33; Jer. 23:6 [b]Ps. 37:11; 69:36; Matt. 5:5
14 [1]Or, *counsel* or *intimacy* [2]Or, *And His covenant, to make them know it.* [a]Prov. 3:32; John 7:17 [b]Gen. 17:1, 2
15 [1]Lit., *bring out*
[a]Ps. 123:2; 141:8 [b]Ps. 31:4; 124:7

16 [a]Turn to me and be gracious to me,
For I am [b]lonely and afflicted.
17 [1]The [a]troubles of my heart are enlarged;
Bring me [b]out of my distresses.
18 [a]Look upon my affliction and my [1]trouble,
And [b]forgive all my sins.
19 Look upon my enemies, for they [a]are many;
And they [b]hate me with violent hatred.
20 [a]Guard my soul and deliver me;
Do not let me [b]be ashamed, for I take refuge in Thee.
21 Let [a]integrity and uprightness preserve me,
For [b]I wait for Thee.
22 [a]Redeem Israel, O God,
Out of all his troubles.

PSALM 26

Protestation of Integrity and Prayer for Protection.

A Psalm of David.

[1a]VINDICATE me, O LORD, for I have [b]walked in my integrity;
And I have [c]trusted in the LORD [2d]without wavering.
2 [a]Examine me, O LORD, and try me;
[b]Test my [1]mind and my heart.
3 For Thy [a]lovingkindness is before my eyes,
And I have [b]walked in Thy [1]truth.
4 I do not [a]sit with [1]deceitful men,
Nor will I go with [2b]pretenders.
5 I [a]hate the assembly of evildoers,
And I will not sit with the wicked.
6 I shall [a]wash my hands in innocence,
And I will go about [b]Thine altar, O LORD,
7 That I may proclaim with the voice of [a]thanksgiving,
And declare all Thy [1]wonders.

8 O LORD, I [a]love the habitation of Thy house,
And the place [1]where Thy [b]glory dwells.
9 [a]Do not [1]take my soul away *along* with sinners,
Nor my life with [b]men of bloodshed,
10 In whose hands is a [a]wicked scheme,
And whose right hand is full of [b]bribes.
11 But as for me, I shall [a]walk in my integrity;
[b]Redeem me, and be gracious to me.
12 [a]My foot stands on a [b]level place;
In the [c]congregations I shall bless the LORD.

16 [a]Ps. 69:16 [b]Ps. 143:4
17 [1]Some commentators read *Relieve the troubles of my heart* [a]Ps. 40:12 [b]Ps. 107:6
18 [1]Lit., *toil* [a]2 Sam. 16:12; Ps. 31:7 [b]Ps. 103:3
19 [a]Ps. 3:1 [b]Ps. 9:13
20 [a]Ps. 86:2 [b]Ps. 25:2
21 [a]Ps. 41:12 [b]Ps. 25:3
22 [a]Ps. 130:8

1 [1]Lit., *Judge* [2]Lit., *I do not slide* [a]Ps. 7:8 [b]2 Kin. 20:3; Prov. 20:7 [c]Ps. 13:5; 28:7 [d]Heb. 10:23
2 [1]Lit., *kidneys,* figurative for inner man [a]Ps. 17:3; 139:23 [b]Ps. 7:9
3 [1]Or, *faithfulness* [a]Ps. 48:9 [b]2 Kin. 20:3; Ps. 86:11
4 [1]Or, *worthless men;* lit., *men of falsehood* [2]Or, *dissemblers, hypocrites* [a]Ps. 1:1 [b]Ps. 28:3
5 [a]Ps. 31:6; 139:21
6 [a]Ps. 73:13 [b]Ps. 43:3, 4
7 [1]Or, *miracles* [a]Ps. 9:1
8 [1]Lit., *of the tabernacle of Thy glory* [a]Ps. 27:4 [b]Ps. 24:7
9 [1]Lit., *gather* [a]Ps. 28:3 [b]Ps. 139:19
10 [a]Ps. 37:7 [b]Ps. 15:5
11 [a]Ps. 26:1 [b]Ps. 44:26; 69:18
12 [a]Ps. 40:2 [b]Ps. 27:11 [c]Ps. 22:22

1 [1]Or, *refuge* [a]Ps. 18:28; Is. 60:20; Mic. 7:8 [b]Ex. 15:2; Ps. 62:7; 118:14; Is. 33:2; Jon. 2:9 [c]Ps. 28:8 [d]Ps. 118:6
2 [a]Ps. 14:4 [b]Ps. 9:3
3 [1]Lit., *am confident* [a]Ps. 3:6 [b]Job 4:6
4 [1]Lit., *delightfulness* [2]Lit., *inquire* [a]Ps. 26:8 [b]Ps. 23:6 [c]Ps. 90:17 [d]Ps. 18:6
5 [1]Or, *shelter* [a]Ps. 50:15 [b]Ps. 31:20 [c]Ps. 17:8 [d]Ps. 40:2
6 [1]Lit., *of shouts* [a]Ps. 3:3 [b]Ps. 107:22 [c]Ps. 13:6
7 [a]Ps. 4:3; 61:1 [b]Ps. 13:3
8 [a]Ps. 105:4; Amos 5:6 [b]Ps. 34:4
9 [a]Ps. 69:17 [b]Ps. 6:1 [c]Ps. 40:17 [d]Ps. 94:14 [e]Ps. 37:28
10 [1]Or, *If my father . . . forsake me, Then the LORD* [a]Is. 49:15 [b]Is. 40:11

PSALM 27

A Psalm of Fearless Trust in God.

A Psalm of David.

THE LORD is my [a]light and my [b]salvation;
Whom shall I fear?
The LORD is the [1c]defense of my life;
[d]Whom shall I dread?
2 When evildoers came upon me to [a]devour my flesh,
My adversaries and my enemies, they [b]stumbled and fell.
3 Though a [a]host encamp against me,
My heart will not fear;
Though war arise against me,
In *spite of* this I [1]shall be [b]confident.

4 [a]One thing I have asked from the LORD, that I shall seek:
That I may [b]dwell in the house of the LORD all the days of my life,
To behold [c]the [1]beauty of the LORD,
And to [2d]meditate in His temple.
5 For in the [a]day of trouble He will [b]conceal me in His [1]tabernacle;
In the secret place of His tent He will [c]hide me;
He will [d]lift me up on a rock.
6 And now [a]my head will be lifted up above my enemies around me;
And I will offer in His tent [b]sacrifices [1]with shouts of joy;
I will [c]sing, yes, I will sing praises to the LORD.

7 [a]Hear, O LORD, when I cry with my voice,
And be gracious to me and [b]answer me.
8 *When Thou didst say,* "[a]Seek My face," my heart said to Thee,
"Thy face, O LORD, [b]I shall seek."
9 [a]Do not hide Thy face from me,
Do not turn Thy servant away in [b]anger;
Thou hast been [c]my help;
[d]Do not abandon me nor [e]forsake me,
O God of my salvation!
10 [1]For my father and [a]my mother have forsaken me,
But [b]the LORD will take me up.

11 [a]Teach me Thy way, O LORD,
And lead me in a [b]level path,
Because of [1]my foes.
12 Do not deliver me over to the [1a]desire of my adversaries;
For [b]false witnesses have risen against me,
And such as [c]breathe out violence.

11 [1]Or, *those who lie in wait for me* [a]Ps. 25:4; 86:11 [b]Ps. 5:8; 26:12
12 [1]Lit., *soul* [a]Ps. 41:2 [b]Deut. 19:18; Ps. 35:11; Matt. 26:60 [c]Acts 9:1

13 [1]*I would have despaired* unless I had believed that I would see the [a]goodness of the LORD
In the [b]land of the living.
14 [a]Wait for the LORD;
Be [b]strong, and let your heart take courage;
Yes, wait for the LORD.

PSALM 28

A Prayer for Help, and Praise for Its Answer.

A Psalm of David.

TO Thee, O LORD, I call;
My [a]rock, do not be deaf to me,
Lest, if Thou [b]be silent to me,
I become like those who [c]go down to the pit.
2 Hear the [a]voice of my supplications when I cry to Thee for help,
When I [b]lift up my hands [c]toward [1]Thy holy [d]sanctuary.
3 [a]Do not drag me away with the wicked
And with those who work iniquity;
Who [b]speak peace with their neighbors,
While evil is in their hearts.
4 Requite them [a]according to their work and according to the evil of their practices;
Requite them according to the deeds of their hands;
Repay them their [1]recompense.
5 Because they [a]do not regard the works of the LORD
Nor the deeds of His hands,
He will tear them down and not build them up.

6 Blessed be the LORD,
Because He [a]has heard the voice of my supplication.
7 The LORD is my [a]strength and my [b]shield;
My heart [c]trusts in Him, and I am helped;
Therefore [d]my heart exults,
And with [e]my song I shall thank Him.
8 The LORD is [1]their [a]strength,
And He is a [2b]saving defense to His anointed.
9 [a]Save Thy people, and bless [b]Thine inheritance;
Be their [c]shepherd also, and [d]carry them forever.

PSALM 29

The Voice of the LORD in the Storm.

A Psalm of David.

[a]ASCRIBE to the LORD, O [1]sons of the mighty,
Ascribe to the LORD glory and strength.
2 Ascribe to the LORD the glory [1]due to His name;
Worship the LORD [a]in [2]holy array.

3 The [a]voice of the LORD is upon the waters;

13 [1]Or, *Surely I believed* [a]Ps. 31:19 [b]Job 28:13; Ps. 52:5; 116:9; 142:5; Is. 38:11; Jer. 11:19; Ezek. 26:20
14 [a]Ps. 25:3; 37:34; 40:1; 62:5; 130:5; Prov. 20:22; Is. 25:9 [b]Ps. 31:24

1 [a]Ps. 18:2 [b]Ps. 35:22; 39:12; 83:1 [c]Ps. 88:4; 143:7; Prov. 1:12
2 [1]Lit., *the innermost place of Thy sanctuary* [a]Ps. 140:6 [b]Ps. 134:2; 141:2; Lam. 2:19; 1 Tim. 2:8 [c]Ps. 5:7; 138:2 [d]1 Kin. 6:5
3 [a]Ps. 26:9 [b]Ps. 12:2; 55:21; 62:4; Jer. 9:8
4 [1]Or, *dealings* [a]Ps. 62:12; 2 Tim. 4:14; Rev. 18:6; 22:12
5 [a]Is. 5:12
6 [a]Ps. 28:2
7 [a]Ps. 18:2; 59:17 [b]Ps. 3:3 [c]Ps. 13:5; 112:7 [d]Ps. 16:9 [e]Ps. 40:3; 69:30
8 [1]A few mss. and ancient versions read *the strength of His people* [2]Or, *refuge of salvation* [a]Ps. 20:6; 89:17 [b]Ps. 27:1; 140:7
9 [a]Ps. 106:47 [b]Deut. 9:29; 32:9; 1 Kin. 8:51; Ps. 33:12; 106:40 [c]Ps. 80:1 [d]Deut. 1:31; Is. 40:11; 46:3; 63:9

1 [1]Or, *sons of gods* [a]1 Chr. 16:28, 29; Ps. 96:7-9
2 [1]Lit., *of His name* [2]Or, *the majesty of holiness* [a]2 Chr. 20:21; Ps. 110:3
3 [1]Or, *great* [a]Ps. 104:7 [b]Job 37:4, 5; Ps. 18:13 [c]Ps. 18:16; 107:23
4 [a]Ps. 68:33
5 [a]Judg. 9:15; 1 Kin. 5:6; Ps. 104:16; Is. 2:13; 14:8
6 [a]Ps. 114:4, 6 [b]Deut. 3:9
7 [1]I.e., lightning
8 [1]Or, *causes . . . to whirl* [a]Num. 13:26
9 [a]Job 39:1 [b]Ps. 26:8
10 [a]Gen. 6:17 [b]Ps. 10:16
11 [1]Or, *May the LORD give* [2]Or, *May the LORD bless* [a]Ps. 28:8; 68:35; Is. 40:29 [b]Ps. 37:11; 72:3

1 [a]Ps. 118:28; 145:1 [b]Ps. 3:3 [c]Ps. 25:2; 35:19, 24
2 [a]Ps. 88:13 [b]Ps. 6:2; 103:3; Is. 53:5

The God of glory [b]thunders,
The LORD is over [1c]many waters.
4 The voice of the LORD is [a]powerful,
The voice of the LORD is majestic.
5 The voice of the LORD breaks the cedars;
Yes, the LORD breaks in pieces [a]the cedars of Lebanon.
6 And He makes Lebanon [a]skip like a calf,
And [b]Sirion like a young wild ox.
7 The voice of the LORD hews out [1]flames of fire.
8 The voice of the LORD [1]shakes the wilderness;
The LORD shakes the wilderness of [a]Kadesh.
9 The voice of the LORD makes [a]the deer to calve,
And strips the forests bare,
And [b]in His temple everything says, "Glory!"

10 The LORD sat *as King* at the [a]flood;
Yes, the LORD sits as [b]King forever.
11 [1]The LORD will give [a]strength to His people;
[2]The LORD will bless His people with [b]peace.

PSALM 30

Thanksgiving for Deliverance from Death.

A Psalm; a Song at the Dedication of the House.

A Psalm of David.

I WILL [a]extol Thee, O LORD, for Thou hast [b]lifted me up,
And hast not let my [c]enemies rejoice over me.
2 O LORD my God,
I [a]cried to Thee for help, and Thou didst [b]heal me.
3 O LORD, Thou hast [a]brought up my soul from [1]Sheol;
Thou hast kept me alive, [2]that I should not [b]go down to the pit.
4 [a]Sing praise to the LORD, you [b]His godly ones,
And [c]give thanks to His holy [1d]name.
5 For [a]His anger is but for a moment,
His [b]favor is for a lifetime;
Weeping may [c]last for the night,
But a shout of joy *comes* in the morning.

6 Now as for me, I said in my prosperity,
"I will [a]never be moved."
7 O LORD, by Thy favor Thou hast made my mountain to stand strong;

3 [1]I.e., the nether world [2]Some mss. read *from among those who go down* [a]Ps. 86:13 [b]Ps. 28:1
4 [1]Lit., *memorial* [a]Ps. 149:1 [b]Ps. 50:5 [c]Ps. 97:12 [d]Ex. 3:15; Ps. 135:13; Hos. 12:5
5 [a]Ps. 103:9; Is. 26:20; 54:7, 8 [b]Ps. 118:1 [c]Ps. 126:5; 2 Cor. 4:17
6 [a]Ps. 10:6; 62:2, 6

Thou didst [a]hide Thy face, I was dismayed.
8 To Thee, O LORD, I called,
And to the LORD I made supplication:
9 "What profit is there in my blood, if I [a]go down to the pit?
Will the [b]dust praise Thee? Will it declare Thy faithfulness?

10 "[a]Hear, O LORD, and be gracious to me;
O LORD, be Thou my [b]helper."
11 Thou hast turned for me [a]my mourning into dancing;
Thou hast [b]loosed my sackcloth and girded me with [c]gladness;
12 That *my* [1a]soul may sing praise to Thee, and not be silent.
O LORD my God, I will [b]give thanks to Thee forever.

PSALM 31

A Psalm of Complaint and of Praise.

For the choir director. A Psalm of David.

[a]IN Thee, O LORD, I have taken refuge;
Let me never [b]be ashamed;
[c]In Thy righteousness deliver me.
2 [a]Incline Thine ear to me, rescue me quickly;
Be Thou to me a [b]rock of [1]strength,
A stronghold to save me.
3 For Thou art my [1]rock and [a]my fortress;
For [b]Thy name's sake Thou wilt lead me and guide me.
4 Thou wilt [a]pull me out of the net which they have secretly laid for me;
For Thou art my [b]strength.
5 [a]Into Thy hand I commit my spirit;
Thou hast [b]ransomed me, O LORD, [c]God of [1]truth.

6 I hate those who [a]regard [1]vain idols;
But I [b]trust in the LORD.
7 I will [a]rejoice and be glad in Thy lovingkindness,
Because Thou hast [b]seen my affliction;
Thou hast known the troubles of my soul,
8 And Thou hast not [a]given me over into the hand of the enemy;
Thou hast set my feet in a large place.

9 Be gracious to me, O LORD, for [a]I am in distress;
My [b]eye is wasted away from grief, [c]my soul and my body *also.*
10 For my life is spent with [a]sorrow,
And my years with sighing;
My [b]strength has failed because of my iniquity,
And [c]my [1]body has wasted away.
11 Because of all my adversaries, I have become a [a]reproach,
Especially to my [b]neighbors,
And an object of dread to my acquaintances;
Those who see me in the street flee from me.
12 I am [a]forgotten as a dead man, out of mind,
I am like a broken vessel.
13 For I have heard the [1a]slander of many,
[b]Terror is on every side;
While they [c]took counsel together against me,
They [d]schemed to take away my life.

14 But as for me, I trust in Thee, O LORD,
I say, "[a]Thou art my God."
15 My [a]times are in Thy hand;
[b]Deliver me from the hand of my enemies, and from those who persecute me.
16 Make Thy [a]face to shine upon Thy servant;
[b]Save me in Thy lovingkindness.
17 Let me not be [a]put to shame, O LORD, for I call upon Thee;
Let the [b]wicked be put to shame, let them [c]be silent in [1]Sheol.
18 Let the [a]lying lips be dumb,
Which [b]speak arrogantly against the righteous
With pride and contempt.

19 How great is Thy [a]goodness,
Which Thou hast stored up for those who fear Thee,
Which Thou hast wrought for those who [b]take refuge in Thee,
[c]Before the sons of men!
20 Thou dost hide them in the [a]secret place of Thy presence from the [b]conspiracies of man;
Thou dost keep them secretly in a [1]shelter from the [c]strife of tongues.
21 [a]Blessed be the LORD,
For He has made [b]marvelous His lovingkindness to me in a besieged [c]city.
22 As for me, [a]I said in my alarm,
"I am [b]cut off from before Thine eyes";
Nevertheless Thou didst [c]hear the voice of my supplications
When I cried to Thee.

23 O love the LORD, all you [a]His godly ones!
The LORD [b]preserves the faithful,
And fully [c]recompenses the proud doer.
24 [a]Be strong, and let your heart take courage,
All you who [1]hope in the LORD.

PSALM 32

Blessedness of Forgiveness and of Trust in God.

A Psalm of David. A [+]Maskil.

[a]HOW blessed is he whose transgression is forgiven,
Whose sin is covered!

---

7 [a]Deut. 31:17; Ps. 104:29; 143:7
9 [a]Ps. 28:1 [b]Ps. 6:5
10 [a]Ps. 4:1; 27:7 [b]Ps. 27:9; 54:4
11 [a]Eccl. 3:4; Jer. 31:4, 13 [b]Is. 20:2 [c]Ps. 4:7
12 [1]Lit., *glory* [a]Ps. 16:9; 57:8; 108:1 [b]Ps. 44:8

1 [a]Ps. 31:1-3; 71:1-3 [b]Ps. 25:2 [c]Ps. 143:1
2 [1]Or, *refuge, protection* [a]Ps. 17:6; 71:2; 86:1; 102:2 [b]Ps. 18:2; 71:3
3 [1]Or, *crag* [a]Ps. 18:2 [b]Ps. 23:3; 25:11
4 [a]Ps. 25:15 [b]Ps. 46:1
5 [1]Or, *faithfulness* [a]Luke 23:46; Acts 7:59 [b]Ps. 55:18; 71:23 [c]Deut. 32:4; Ps. 71:22
6 [1]Lit., *empty vanities* [a]Jon. 2:8 [b]Ps. 52:8
7 [a]Ps. 90:14 [b]Ps. 10:14
8 [a]Deut. 32:30; Ps. 37:33
9 [a]Ps. 66:14; 69:17 [b]Ps. 6:7 [c]Ps. 63:1
10 [1]Or, *bones, substance* [a]Ps. 13:2 [b]Ps. 39:11 [c]Ps. 32:3; 38:3; 102:3
11 [a]Ps. 69:19 [b]Job 19:13; Ps. 38:11; 88:8, 18
12 [a]Ps. 88:5
13 [1]Lit., *whispering* [a]Ps. 50:20; Jer. 20:10 [b]Lam. 2:22 [c]Ps. 62:4; Matt. 27:1 [d]Ps. 41:7
14 [a]Ps. 140:6
15 [a]Job 14:5; 24:1 [b]Ps. 143:9
16 [a]Num. 6:25; Ps. 4:6; 80:3 [b]Ps. 6:4
17 [1]I.e., the nether world [a]Ps. 25:2, 20 [b]Ps. 25:3 [c]1 Sam. 2:9; Ps. 94:17; 115:17
18 [a]Ps. 109:2; 120:2 [b]1 Sam. 2:3; Ps. 94:4; Jude 15
19 [a]Ps. 65:4; 145:7; Is. 64:4; Rom. 2:4; 11:22 [b]Ps. 5:11 [c]Ps. 23:5
20 [1]Or, *pavilion* [a]Ps. 27:5 [b]Ps. 37:12 [c]Job 5:21; Ps. 31:13
21 [a]Ps. 28:6 [b]Ps. 17:7 [c]1 Sam. 23:7; Ps. 87:5
22 [a]Ps. 116:11 [b]Ps. 88:5; Is. 38:11, 12; Lam. 3:54 [c]Ps. 18:6; 66:19; 145:19
23 [a]Ps. 30:4; 37:28; 50:5 [b]Ps. 145:20; Rev. 2:10 [c]Deut. 32:41; Ps. 94:2
24 [1]Or, *wait for* [a]Ps. 27:14

+ Possibly, *Contemplative,* or *Didactic,* or *Skillful Psalm*
1 [a]Ps. 85:2; 103:3; Rom. 4:7, 8

2 How blessed is the man to whom the LORD [a]does not impute iniquity,
And in whose spirit there is [b]no deceit!

3 When [a]I kept silent *about my sin*, [b]my [1]body wasted away
Through my [2c]groaning all day long.
4 For day and night [a]Thy hand was heavy upon me;
My [1b]vitality was drained away *as* with the fever heat of summer. [[2]Selah.
5 I [a]acknowledged my sin to Thee,
And my iniquity I [b]did not hide;
I said, "[c]I will confess my transgressions to the LORD";
And Thou [d]didst forgive the [1]guilt of my sin. [Selah.
6 Therefore, let everyone who is godly pray to Thee [1a]in a time when Thou mayest be found;
Surely [b]in a flood of great waters they shall not reach him.
7 Thou art [a]my hiding place; Thou [b]dost preserve me from trouble;
Thou dost surround me with [1c]songs of deliverance. [Selah.

8 I will [a]instruct you and teach you in the way which you should go;
I will counsel you [b]with My eye upon you.
9 Do not be [a]as the horse or as the mule which have no understanding,
Whose trappings include bit and bridle to hold them in check,
Otherwise they will not come near to you.
10 Many are the [a]sorrows of the wicked;
But [b]he who trusts in the LORD, lovingkindness shall surround him.
11 Be [a]glad in the LORD and rejoice, you righteous ones,
And shout for joy, all you who are [b]upright in heart.

PSALM 33

Praise to the Creator and Preserver.

[a]SING for joy in the LORD, O you righteous ones;
Praise is [b]becoming to the upright.
2 Give thanks to the LORD with the [a]lyre;
Sing praises to Him with a [b]harp of ten strings.
3 Sing to Him a [a]new song;
Play skillfully with [b]a shout of joy.
4 For the word of the LORD [a]is upright;
And all His work is *done* [b]in faithfulness.
5 He [a]loves righteousness and justice;
The [b]earth is full of the lovingkindness of the LORD.

6 By the [a]word of the LORD the heavens were made,
And [b]by the breath of His mouth [c]all their host.
7 He gathers the [a]waters of the sea together [1]as a heap;
He lays up the deeps in storehouses.
8 Let [a]all the earth fear the LORD;
Let all the inhabitants of the world [b]stand in awe of Him.
9 For [a]He spoke, and it was done;
He commanded, and it [1]stood fast.
10 The LORD [a]nullifies the counsel of the nations;
He frustrates the plans of the peoples.
11 The [a]counsel of the LORD stands forever,
The [b]plans of His heart from generation to generation.
12 Blessed is the [a]nation whose God is the LORD,
The people whom He has [b]chosen for His own inheritance.

13 The LORD [a]looks from heaven;
He [b]sees all the sons of men;
14 From [a]His dwelling place He looks out
On all the inhabitants of the earth,
15 He who [a]fashions [1]the hearts of them all,
He who [b]understands all their works.
16 [a]The king is not saved by a mighty army;
A warrior is not delivered by great strength.
17 A [a]horse is a false hope for victory;
Nor does it deliver anyone by its great strength.

18 Behold, [a]the eye of the LORD is on those who fear Him,
On those who [1b]hope for His lovingkindness,
19 To [a]deliver their soul from death,
And to keep them alive [b]in famine.
20 Our soul [a]waits for the LORD;
He is our [b]help and our shield.
21 For our [a]heart rejoices in Him,
Because we trust in His holy name.
22 Let Thy lovingkindness, O LORD, be upon us,
According as we have [1]hoped in Thee.

PSALM 34

The LORD a Provider and Deliverer.

A Psalm of David when he +feigned madness before •Abimelech, who drove him away and he departed.

I WILL [a]bless the LORD at all times;
His [b]praise shall continually be in my mouth.

2 [a]2 Cor. 5:19 [b]John 1:47
3 [1]Or, *bones, substance* [2]Lit., *roaring* [a]Ps. 39:2, 3 [b]Ps. 31:10 [c]Ps. 38:8
4 [1]Lit., *life juices were turned into the drought of summer* [2]*Selah* may mean: *Pause, Crescendo* or *Musical interlude* [a]1 Sam. 5:6; Job 23:2; 33:7; Ps. 38:2; 39:10 [b]Ps. 22:15
5 [1]Or, *iniquity* [a]Lev. 26:40 [b]Job 31:33 [c]Ps. 38:18; Prov. 28:13; 1 John 1:9 [d]Ps. 103:12
6 [1]Lit., *in a time of finding out* [a]Ps. 69:13; Is. 55:6 [b]Ps. 46:1-3; 69:1; 124:5; 144:7; Is. 43:2
7 [1]Or, *shouts* [a]Ps. 9:9; 31:20; 91:1; 119:114 [b]Ps. 121:7 [c]Ex. 15:1; Judg. 5:1; Ps. 40:3
8 [a]Ps. 25:8 [b]Ps. 33:18
9 [a]Prov. 26:3
10 [a]Ps. 16:4; Prov. 13:21; Rom. 2:9 [b]Ps. 5:11, 12; Prov. 16:20
11 [a]Ps. 64:10; 68:3; 97:12 [b]Ps. 7:10; 64:10

1 [a]Ps. 32:11; Phil. 3:1; 4:4 [b]Ps. 92:1; 147:1
2 [a]Ps. 71:22; 147:7 [b]Ps. 144:9
3 [a]Ps. 40:3; 96:1; 98:1; 144:9; Is. 42:10; Rev. 5:9 [b]Ps. 98:4
4 [a]Ps. 19:8 [b]Ps. 119:90
5 [a]Ps. 11:7; 37:28 [b]Ps. 119:64
6 [a]Gen. 1:6; Ps. 148:5; Heb. 11:3 [b]Ps. 104:30 [c]Gen. 2:1
7 [1]Some versions read *in a water skin;* i.e., container [a]Ex. 15:8; Josh. 3:16; Ps. 78:13
8 [a]Ps. 67:7 [b]Ps. 96:9
9 [1]Or, *stood forth* [a]Gen. 1:3; Ps. 148:5
10 [a]Ps. 2:1-3; Is. 8:10; 19:3
11 [a]Job 23:12; Prov. 19:21 [b]Ps. 40:5; 92:5; 139:17; Is. 55:8
12 [a]Ps. 144:15 [b]Ex. 19:5; Deut. 7:6; Ps. 28:9
13 [a]Job 28:24; Ps. 14:2 [b]Ps. 11:4
14 [a]1 Kin. 8:39, 43; Ps. 102:19
15 [1]Or, *their heart together* [a]Job 10:8; Ps. 119:73 [b]2 Chr. 16:9; Job 34:21; Jer. 32:19
16 [a]Ps. 44:6; 60:11
17 [a]Ps. 20:7; 147:10; Prov. 21:31
18 [1]Or, *wait* [a]Job 36:7; Ps. 32:8; 34:15; 1 Pet. 3:12 [b]Ps. 32:10; 147:11
19 [a]Ps. 56:13; Acts 12:11 [b]Job 5:20; Ps. 37:19
20 [a]Ps. 62:1; 130:6; Is. 8:17 [b]Ps. 115:9
21 [a]Ps. 13:5; 28:7; Zech. 10:7; John 16:22
22 [1]Or, *waited for*

+ Or, *changed his behavior*
• *Possibly a title of King Achish of Gath. See 1 Sam. 21:10-15*
1 [a]Eph. 5:20; 1 Thess. 5:18 [b]Ps. 71:6

2 My soul shall [a]make its boast in the LORD;
The [b]humble shall hear it and rejoice.
3 O [a]magnify the LORD with me,
And let us [b]exalt His name together.

4 I [a]sought the LORD, and He answered me,
And [b]delivered me from all my fears.
5 They [a]looked to Him and were radiant,
And their faces shall [b]never be ashamed.
6 This [1]poor man cried and [a]the LORD heard him,
And saved him out of all his troubles.
7 The [a]angel of the LORD encamps around those who fear Him,
And rescues them.

8 O [a]taste and see that the LORD is good;
How [b]blessed is the man who takes refuge in Him!
9 O fear the LORD, you [a]His saints;
For to those who fear Him, there is [b]no want.
10 The young lions do lack and suffer hunger;
But they who seek the LORD shall [a]not be in want of any good thing.
11 [a]Come, you children, listen to me;
[b]I will teach you [c]the fear of the LORD.
12 [a]Who is the man who desires life,
And loves *length of* days that he may [b]see good?
13 Keep [a]your tongue from evil,
And your lips from speaking [b]deceit.
14 [a]Depart from evil, and do good;
Seek peace, and [b]pursue it.

15 The [a]eyes of the LORD are toward the righteous,
And His ears are *open* to their cry.
16 The [a]face of the LORD is against evildoers,
To [b]cut off the memory of them from the earth.
17 *The righteous* [a]cry and the LORD hears,
And delivers them out of all their troubles.
18 The LORD [a]is near to the [b]brokenhearted,
And saves those who are [1c]crushed in spirit.

19 [a]Many are the [b]afflictions of the righteous;
But the LORD [c]delivers him out of them all.
20 He keeps all his bones;
[a]Not one of them is broken.
21 [a]Evil shall slay the wicked;
And those who hate the righteous will be [1]condemned.
22 The LORD [a]redeems the soul of His servants;
And none of those who [b]take refuge in Him will be [1]condemned.

PSALM 35

Prayer for Rescue from Enemies.
A Psalm of David.

CONTEND, O LORD, with those who [a]contend with me;
Fight against those who [b]fight against me.
2 Take hold of [1a]buckler and shield,
And rise up for [b]my help.
3 Draw also the spear and [1]the battle-axe to meet those who pursue me;
Say to my soul, "I am [a]your salvation."
4 Let those be [a]ashamed and dishonored who seek my [1]life;
Let those be [b]turned back and humiliated who devise evil against me.
5 Let them be [a]like chaff before the wind,
With the angel of the LORD driving *them* on.
6 Let their way be dark and [a]slippery,
With the angel of the LORD pursuing them.
7 For [a]without cause they [b]hid their net for me;
Without cause they dug a [1]pit for my soul.
8 Let [a]destruction come upon him unawares;
And [b]let the net which he hid catch himself;
Into that very [c]destruction let him fall.

9 And my soul shall [a]rejoice in the LORD;
It shall [b]exult in His salvation.
10 All my [a]bones will say, "LORD, [b]who is like Thee,
Who delivers the afflicted from him [c]who is too strong for him,
And [d]the afflicted and the needy from him who robs him?"
11 [a]Malicious witnesses rise up;
They ask me of things that I do not know.
12 They [a]repay me evil for good,
To the bereavement of my soul.
13 But as for me, [a]when they were sick, my [b]clothing was sackcloth;
I [c]humbled my soul with fasting;
And my [d]prayer kept returning to my bosom.
14 I went about as though it were my friend or brother;
I [a]bowed down [1]mourning, as one who sorrows for a mother.

---

2 [a]Ps. 44:8; Jer. 9:24; 1 Cor. 1:31 [b]Ps. 69:32
3 [a]Ps. 35:27; 69:30; Luke 1:46 [b]Ps. 18:46
4 [a]2 Chr. 15:2; Ps. 9:10; Matt. 7:7 [b]Ps. 34:6, 17, 19
5 [a]Ps. 36:9; Is. 60:5 [b]Ps. 25:3
6 [1]Or, *afflicted* [a]Ps. 34:4
7 [a]Ps. 91:11; Dan. 6:22
8 [a]Ps. 119:103; Heb. 6:5; 1 Pet. 2:3 [b]Ps. 2:12
9 [a]Ps. 31:23 [b]Ps. 23:1
10 [a]Ps. 84:11
11 [a]Ps. 66:16 [b]Ps. 32:8 [c]Ps. 111:10
12 [a]Ps. 34:12-16; 1 Pet. 3:10-12 [b]Eccl. 3:13
13 [a]Ps. 141:3; Prov. 13:3; James 1:26 [b]1 Pet. 2:22
14 [a]Ps. 37:27; Is. 1:16, 17 [b]Rom. 14:19; Heb. 12:14
15 [a]Job 36:7; Ps. 33:18
16 [a]Lev. 17:10; Jer. 44:11; Amos 9:4 [b]Job 18:17; Ps. 9:6; 109:15; Prov. 10:7
17 [a]Ps. 34:6; 145:19
18 [1]Or, *contrite* [a]Ps. 145:18 [b]Ps. 147:3; Is. 61:1 [c]Ps. 51:17; Is. 57:15
19 [a]Prov. 24:16 [b]Ps. 71:20; 2 Tim. 3:11f. [c]Ps. 34:4, 6, 17
20 [a]John 19:33, 36
21 [1]Or, *held guilty* [a]Ps. 94:23; 140:11; Prov. 24:16
22 [1]V. 21, note 1 [a]1 Kin. 1:29; Ps. 71:23 [b]Ps. 37:40

1 [a]Ps. 18:43; Is. 49:25 [b]Ps. 56:2
2 [1]I.e., small shield [a]Ps. 91:4 [b]Ps. 44:26
3 [1]Or, *close up the path against those* [a]Ps. 62:2
4 [1]Or, *soul* [a]Ps. 70:2 [b]Ps. 40:14; 129:5
5 [a]Job 21:18; Ps. 83:13; Is. 29:5
6 [a]Ps. 73:18; Jer. 23:12
7 [1]*Pit* has been transposed from line above [a]Ps. 69:4; 109:3; 140:5 [b]Ps. 9:15
8 [a]Ps. 55:23; Is. 47:11; 1 Thess. 5:3 [b]Ps. 9:15 [c]Ps. 73:18
9 [a]Is. 61:10 [b]Ps. 9:14; 13:5; Luke 1:47
10 [a]Ps. 51:8 [b]Ex. 15:11; Ps. 86:8; Mic. 7:18 [c]Ps. 18:17 [d]Ps. 37:14; 109:16
11 [a]Ps. 27:12
12 [a]Ps. 38:20; 109:5; Jer. 18:20; John 10:32
13 [a]Job 30:25 [b]Ps. 69:11 [c]Ps. 69:10 [d]Matt. 10:13; Luke 10:6
14 [1]Or, *dressed in black* [a]Ps. 38:6

15 But [a]at my [1]stumbling they rejoiced, and gathered themselves together;
The [2b]smiters whom I did not know gathered together against me,
They [3c]slandered me without ceasing.
16 Like godless jesters at a feast,
They [a]gnashed at me with their teeth.

17 Lord, [a]how long wilt Thou look on?
Rescue my soul [b]from their ravages,
My [c]only *life* from the lions.
18 I will [a]give Thee thanks in the great congregation;
I will [b]praise Thee among a mighty throng.
19 [a]Do not let those who are wrongfully [b]my enemies rejoice over me;
Neither let those [c]who hate me without cause [1d]wink maliciously.
20 For they do not speak peace,
But they devise [a]deceitful words against those who are quiet in the land.
21 And they [a]opened their mouth wide against me;
They said, "[b]Aha, aha, our eyes have seen it!"

22 [a]Thou hast seen it, O LORD, [b]do not keep silent;
O Lord, [c]do not be far from me.
23 [a]Stir up Thyself, and awake to my right,
And to my cause, my God and my Lord.
24 [a]Judge me, O LORD my God, according to Thy righteousness;
And [b]do not let them rejoice over me.
25 Do not let them say in their heart, "[a]Aha, our desire!"
Do not let them say, "We have [b]swallowed him up!"
26 Let [a]those be ashamed and humiliated altogether who rejoice at my distress;
Let those be [b]clothed with shame and dishonor who [c]magnify themselves over me.

27 Let them [a]shout for joy and rejoice, who favor [b]my vindication;
And [c]let them say continually, "The LORD be magnified,
Who [d]delights in the prosperity of His servant."
28 And [a]my tongue shall declare Thy righteousness
And Thy praise all day long.

15 [1]Or, *limping* [2]Or, *smitten ones* [3]Lit., *tore* [a]Obad. 12 [b]Job 30:1, 8, 12 [c]Ps. 7:2
16 [a]Job 16:9; Ps. 37:12; Lam. 2:16
17 [a]Ps. 13:1; Hab. 1:13 [b]Ps. 35:7 [c]Ps. 22:20, 21
18 [a]Ps. 22:22 [b]Ps. 22:25
19 [1]Or, *wink the eye* [a]Ps. 13:4; 30:1; 38:16 [b]Ps. 38:19; 69:4 [c]John 15:25 [d]Prov. 6:13; 10:10
20 [a]Ps. 55:21; Jer. 9:8; Mic. 6:12
21 [a]Job 16:10; Ps. 22:13 [b]Ps. 40:15; 70:3
22 [a]Ex. 3:7; Ps. 10:14 [b]Ps. 28:1 [c]Ps. 10:1; 22:11; 38:21; 71:12
23 [a]Ps. 7:6; 44:23; 59:4; 80:2
24 [a]Ps. 9:4; 26:1; 43:1 [b]Ps. 35:19
25 [a]Ps. 35:21 [b]Ps. 56:1; 124:3; Prov. 1:12; Lam. 2:16
26 [a]Ps. 40:14 [b]Ps. 109:29 [c]Job 19:5; Ps. 38:16
27 [a]Ps. 32:11 [b]Ps. 9:4 [c]Ps. 40:16; 70:4 [d]Ps. 147:11; 149:4
28 [a]Ps. 51:14; 71:15, 24

1 [1]Another reading is *my heart* [a]Rom. 3:18
2 [1]Or, *he flatters himself* [a]Deut. 29:19; Ps. 10:11; 49:18
3 [1]Or, *understand to do good* [a]Ps. 10:7; 12:2 [b]Ps. 94:8; Jer. 4:22
4 [a]Prov. 4:16; Mic. 2:1 [b]Is. 65:2 [c]Ps. 52:3; Rom. 12:9
5 [1]Lit., *is in* [a]Ps. 57:10; 103:11; 108:4
6 [1]Or, *mighty mountains* [a]Ps. 71:19 [b]Job 11:8; Ps. 77:19; Rom. 11:33 [c]Neh. 9:6; Ps. 104:14, 15; 145:16
7 [a]Ps. 40:5; 139:17 [b]Ruth 2:12; Ps. 17:8; 57:1; 91:4
8 [1]Lit., *fatness* [a]Ps. 63:5; 65:4; Is. 25:6; Jer. 31:12-14 [b]Job 20:17; Ps. 46:4; Rev. 22:1
9 [a]Jer. 2:13
10 [a]Jer. 22:16 [b]Ps. 24:5
12 [a]Ps. 140:10; Is. 26:14

1 [a]Prov. 23:17; 24:19 [b]Ps. 73:3; Prov. 3:31
2 [a]Job 14:2; Ps. 90:6; 92:7; James 1:11 [b]Ps. 129:6

PSALM 36

Wickedness of Men and Lovingkindness of God.

For the choir director. *A Psalm* of David the servant of the LORD.

TRANSGRESSION speaks to the ungodly within [1]his heart;
There is [a]no fear of God before his eyes.
2 For [1]it [a]flatters him in his *own* eyes,
Concerning the discovery of his iniquity *and* the hatred *of it.*
3 The [a]words of his mouth are wickedness and deceit;
He has [b]ceased to [1]be wise *and* to do good.
4 He [a]plans wickedness upon his bed;
He sets himself on a [b]path that is not good;
He [c]does not despise evil.

5 Thy [a]lovingkindness, O LORD, [1]extends to the heavens,
Thy faithfulness *reaches* to the skies.
6 Thy [a]righteousness is like the [1]mountains of God;
Thy [b]judgments are *like* a great deep.
O LORD, Thou [c]preservest man and beast.
7 How [a]precious is Thy lovingkindness, O God!
And the children of men [b]take refuge in the shadow of Thy wings.
8 They [a]drink their fill of the [1]abundance of Thy house;
And Thou dost give them to drink of the [b]river of Thy delights.
9 For with Thee is the [a]fountain of life;
In Thy light we see light.

10 O continue Thy lovingkindness to [a]those who know Thee,
And Thy [b]righteousness to the upright in heart.
11 Let not the foot of pride come upon me,
And let not the hand of the wicked drive me away.
12 There the doers of iniquity have fallen;
They have been thrust down and [a]cannot rise.

PSALM 37

Security of Those Who Trust in the LORD, and Insecurity of the Wicked.

A Psalm of David.

[a]DO not fret because of evildoers,
Be not [b]envious toward wrongdoers.
2 For they will [a]wither quickly like the grass,
And [b]fade like the green herb.

3 [a]Trust in the LORD, and do good;
[b]Dwell in the land and [1c]cultivate faithfulness.
4 [a]Delight yourself in the LORD;
And He will [b]give you the desires of your heart.
5 [a]Commit your way to the LORD,
Trust also in Him, and He will do it.
6 And He will bring forth [a]your righteousness as the light,
And your judgment [b]as the noonday.

7 [1]Rest in the LORD and [a]wait [2]patiently for Him;
[b]Do not fret because of him who [c]prospers in his way,
Because of the man who carries out wicked schemes.
8 Cease from anger, and [a]forsake wrath;
Do not fret, *it leads* only to evildoing.
9 For [a]evildoers will be cut off,
But those who wait for the LORD, they will [b]inherit the land.
10 Yet [a]a little while and the wicked man will be no more;
And you will look carefully for [b]his place, and he will not be *there.*
11 But [a]the humble will inherit the land,
And will delight themselves in [b]abundant prosperity.

12 The wicked [a]plots against the righteous,
And [b]gnashes at him with his teeth.
13 The Lord [a]laughs at him;
For He sees [b]his day is coming.
14 The wicked have drawn the sword and [a]bent their bow,
To cast down the [b]afflicted and the needy,
To [c]slay those who are upright in conduct.
15 Their sword will enter their own heart,
And their [a]bows will be broken.

16 [a]Better is the little of the righteous
Than the abundance of many wicked.
17 For the [a]arms of the wicked will be broken;
But the LORD [b]sustains the righteous.
18 The LORD [a]knows the days of the [1]blameless;
And their [b]inheritance will be forever.
19 They will not be ashamed in the time of evil;
And [a]in the days of famine they will have abundance.
20 But the [a]wicked will perish;
And the enemies of the LORD will be like the [1]glory of the pastures,
They vanish—[b]like smoke they vanish away.

3 [1]Or, *feed securely* or *feed on His faithfulness*
[a]Ps. 62:8 [b]Deut. 30:20 [c]Is. 40:11; Ezek. 34:13, 14
4 [a]Job 22:26; Ps. 94:19; Is. 58:14 [b]Ps. 21:2; 145:19; Matt. 7:7, 8
5 [a]Ps. 55:22; Prov. 16:3; 1 Pet. 5:7
6 [a]Ps. 97:11; Is. 58:8, 10; Mic. 7:9 [b]Job 11:17
7 [1]Or, *Be still* [2]Or, *longingly*
[a]Ps. 40:1; 62:5; Lam. 3:26 [b]Ps. 37:1, 8 [c]Jer. 12:1
8 [a]Eph. 4:31; Col. 3:8
9 [a]Ps. 37:2, 22 [b]Ps. 25:13; Prov. 2:21; Is. 57:13; 60:21; Matt. 5:5
10 [a]Job 24:24 [b]Job 7:10; Ps. 37:35, 36
11 [a]Matt. 5:5 [b]Ps. 72:7
12 [a]Ps. 31:13, 20 [b]Ps. 35:16
13 [a]Ps. 2:4 [b]1 Sam. 26:10; Job 18:20
14 [a]Ps. 11:2; Lam. 2:4 [b]Ps. 35:10; 86:1 [c]Ps. 11:2
15 [a]1 Sam. 2:4; Ps. 46:9
16 [a]Prov. 15:16; 16:8
17 [a]Job 38:15; Ps. 10:15; Ezek. 30:21 [b]Ps. 71:6; 145:14
18 [1]Lit., *complete;* or, *perfect*
[a]Ps. 1:6; 31:7 [b]Ps. 37:27, 29
19 [a]Job 5:20; Ps. 33:19
20 [1]I.e., flowers
[a]Ps. 73:27 [b]Ps. 68:2; 102:3
21 [a]Ps. 112:5, 9
22 [a]Prov. 3:33 [b]Ps. 37:9 [c]Job 5:3
23 [a]1 Sam. 2:9; Ps. 40:2; 66:9; 119:5 [b]Ps. 147:11
24 [1]Or, *who sustains him with His hand*
[a]Ps. 145:14; Prov. 24:16; Mic. 7:8 [b]Ps. 147:6
25 [1]Lit., *seed*
[a]Ps. 37:28; Is. 41:17; Heb. 13:5 [b]Ps. 109:10
26 [1]Lit., *seed*
[a]Deut. 15:8; Ps. 37:21 [b]Ps. 147:13
27 [1]Or, *And dwell forever*
[a]Ps. 34:14 [b]Ps. 37:18; 102:28
28 [1]Lit., *judgment* [2]Lit., *seed*
[a]Ps. 11:7; 33:5 [b]Ps. 37:25 [c]Ps. 31:23 [d]Ps. 21:10; 37:9; Prov. 2:22; Is. 14:20
29 [a]Ps. 37:9; Prov. 2:21 [b]Ps. 37:18
30 [a]Ps. 49:3; Prov. 10:13 [b]Ps. 101:1; 119:13
31 [a]Deut. 6:6; Ps. 40:8; 119:11; Is. 51:7; Jer. 31:33 [b]Ps. 26:1; 37:23
32 [a]Ps. 10:8; 17:11 [b]Ps. 37:14
33 [a]Ps. 31:8; 2 Pet. 2:9 [b]Ps. 34:22; 109:31

21 The wicked borrows and does not pay back,
But the righteous [a]is gracious and gives.
22 For [a]those blessed by Him will [b]inherit the land;
But those [c]cursed by Him will be cut off.

23 [a]The steps of a man are established by the LORD;
And He [b]delights in his way.
24 When [a]he falls, he shall not be hurled headlong;
Because [b]the LORD is the One [1]who holds his hand.
25 I have been young, and now I am old;
Yet [a]I have not seen the righteous forsaken,
Or [b]his [1]descendants begging bread.
26 All day long [a]he is gracious and lends;
And [b]his [1]descendants are a blessing.

27 [a]Depart from evil, and do good,
[1]So you will abide [b]forever.
28 For the LORD [a]loves [1]justice,
And [b]does not forsake His godly ones;
They are [c]preserved forever;
But the [2d]descendants of the wicked will be cut off.
29 The righteous will [a]inherit the land,
And [b]dwell in it forever.
30 The mouth of the righteous [a]utters wisdom,
And his tongue [b]speaks justice.
31 The [a]law of his God is in his heart;
His [b]steps do not slip.
32 The [a]wicked spies upon the righteous,
And [b]seeks to kill him.
33 The LORD will [a]not leave him in his hand,
Or [b]let him be condemned when he is judged.
34 [a]Wait for the LORD, and keep His way,
And He will exalt you to inherit the land;
When the [b]wicked are cut off, you will see it.

35 I have [a]seen a violent, wicked man
Spreading himself like a [b]luxuriant [1]tree in its native soil.
36 Then [1]he passed away, and lo, he [a]was no more;
I sought for him, but he could not be found.
37 Mark the [1a]blameless man, and behold the [b]upright;
For the man of peace will have a [2c]posterity.

34 [a]Ps. 27:14; 37:9 [b]Ps. 52:5, 6; 91:8
35 [1]Lit., *native;* Heb. obscure [a]Job 5:3; Jer. 12:2 [b]Job 8:16
36 [1]Ancient versions read *I passed by* [a]Job 20:5; Ps. 37:10
37 [1]Lit., *complete;* or, *perfect* [2]Lit., *an end* [a]Ps. 37:18 [b]Ps. 7:10 [c]Is. 57:1, 2

38 But transgressors will be altogether
[a]destroyed;
The [1]posterity of the wicked will be
[b]cut off.
39 But the [a]salvation of the righteous
is from the LORD;
He is their strength [b]in time of
trouble.
40 And [a]the LORD helps them, and
delivers them;
He [b]delivers them from the wicked,
and saves them,
Because they [c]take refuge in Him.

PSALM 38

Prayer of a Suffering Penitent.

A Psalm of David, for a memorial.

O LORD, [a]rebuke me not in Thy
wrath;
And chasten me not in Thy burning anger.
2 For Thine [a]arrows have sunk deep
into me,
And [b]Thy hand has pressed down
on me.
3 There is [a]no soundness in my flesh
[b]because of Thine indignation;
There is no health [c]in my bones
because of my sin.
4 For my [a]iniquities are gone over
my head;
As a heavy burden they weigh too
much for me.
5 My [1]wounds grow foul *and* fester.
Because of [a]my folly,
6 I am bent over and [a]greatly bowed
down;
I [b]go mourning all day long.
7 For my loins are filled with [a]burning;
And there is [b]no soundness in my
flesh.
8 I am [a]benumbed and [1]badly
crushed;
I [2b]groan because of the [3]agitation
of my heart.

9 Lord, all [a]my desire is [1]before
Thee;
And my [b]sighing is not hidden
from Thee.
10 My heart throbs, [a]my strength fails
me;
And the [b]light of my eyes, even
[1]that [2]has gone from me.
11 My [1a]loved ones and my friends
stand aloof from my plague;
And my kinsmen [b]stand afar off.
12 Those who [a]seek my life [b]lay snares
for me;
And those who [c]seek to injure me
have [1]threatened destruction,
And they [d]devise treachery all day
long.

13 But I, like a deaf man, do not hear;
And I am like a [a]dumb man who
does not open his mouth.
14 Yes, I am like a man who does not
hear,
And in whose mouth are no arguments.
15 For [a]I [1]hope in Thee, O LORD;
Thou [b]wilt answer, O Lord my
God.
16 For I said, "May they not rejoice
over me,
Who, when my foot slips, [a]would
magnify themselves against me."
17 For I am [a]ready to fall,
And [b]my [1]sorrow is continually
before me.
18 For I [1a]confess my iniquity;
I am full of [b]anxiety because of my
sin.
19 But my [a]enemies are vigorous *and*
[1]strong;
And many are those who [b]hate me
wrongfully.
20 And those who [a]repay evil for
good,
They [b]oppose me, because I follow
what is good.
21 Do not forsake me, O LORD;
O my God, [a]do not be far from me!
22 Make [a]haste to help me,
O Lord, [b]my salvation!

PSALM 39

The Vanity of Life.

For the choir director, for [+]Jeduthun.
A Psalm of David.

I SAID, "I will [a]guard my ways,
That I [b]may not sin with my
tongue;
I will guard [c]my mouth as with a
muzzle,
While the wicked are in my presence."
2 I was [a]dumb [1]and silent,
I [2]refrained *even* from good;
And my [3]sorrow grew worse.
3 My [a]heart was hot within me;
While I was musing the fire
burned;
Then I spoke with my tongue:
4 "LORD, make me to know [a]my end,
And what is the extent of my days,
Let me know how [b]transient I am.
5 "Behold, Thou hast made [a]my days
as handbreadths,
And my [b]lifetime as nothing in Thy
sight,
Surely every man [1]at his best is [2]a
mere [c]breath. [[3]Selah.
6 "Surely every man [a]walks about as
[1]a phantom;
Surely they make an [b]uproar for
nothing;
He [c]amasses *riches*, and does not
know who will gather them.

7 "And now, Lord, for what do I wait?
My [a]hope is in Thee.
8 "[a]Deliver me from all my transgressions;
Make me not the [b]reproach of the
foolish.
9 "I have become [a]dumb, I do not
open my mouth,
Because it is [b]Thou who hast done
it.

38 [1]Lit., *end* [a]Ps. 1:4-6; 37:20, 28 [b]Ps. 37:9; 73:17
39 [a]Ps. 3:8; 62:1 [b]Ps. 9:9; 37:19
40 [a]Ps. 54:4 [b]Ps. 22:4; Is. 31:5; Dan. 3:17; 6:23 [c]1 Chr. 5:20; Ps. 34:22

1 [a]Ps. 6:1
2 [a]Job 6:4 [b]Ps. 32:4
3 [a]Is. 1:6 [b]Ps. 102:10 [c]Job 33:19; Ps. 6:2; 31:10
4 [a]Ezra 9:6; Ps. 40:12
5 [1]Or, *stripes* [a]Ps. 69:5
6 [a]Ps. 35:14 [b]Job 30:28; Ps. 42:9; 43:2
7 [a]Ps. 102:3 [b]Ps. 38:3
8 [1]Or, *greatly* [2]Lit., *roar* [3]Lit., *growling* [a]Lam. 1:13, 20f.; 2:11; 5:17 [b]Job 3:24; Ps. 22:1; 32:3
9 [1]Or, known *to Thee* [a]Ps. 10:17 [b]Ps. 6:6; 102:5
10 [1]Lit., *they have* [2]Lit., *is not with me* [a]Ps. 31:10 [b]Ps. 6:7; 69:3; 88:9
11 [1]Or, *lovers* [a]Ps. 31:11; 88:18 [b]Luke 23:49
12 [1]Lit., *spoken* [a]Ps. 54:3 [b]Ps. 140:5 [c]Ps. 35:4 [d]Ps. 35:20
13 [a]Ps. 39:2, 9
15 [1]Or, *wait for* [a]Ps. 39:7 [b]Ps. 17:6
16 [a]Ps. 35:26
17 [1]Lit., *pain* [a]Ps. 35:15 [b]Ps. 13:2
18 [1]Or, *declare* [a]Ps. 32:5 [b]2 Cor. 7:9, 10
19 [1]Or, *numerous* [a]Ps. 18:17 [b]Ps. 35:19
20 [a]Ps. 35:12 [b]Ps. 109:5; 1 John 3:12
21 [a]Ps. 22:19; 35:22
22 [a]Ps. 40:13, 17 [b]Ps. 27:1

+ 1 Chr. 16:41
1 [a]1 Kin. 2:4; 2 Kin. 10:31; Ps. 119:9 [b]Job 2:10; Ps. 34:13; James 3:5-12 [c]Ps. 141:3; James 3:2
2 [1]Lit., *with silence* [2]Lit., *kept silence* [3]Lit., *pain* [a]Ps. 38:13
3 [a]Ps. 32:4; Jer. 20:9; Luke 24:32
4 [a]Job 6:11; Ps. 90:12; 119:84 [b]Ps. 78:39; 103:14
5 [1]Lit., *standing firm* [2]Or, *altogether vanity* [3]*Selah* may mean: *Pause, Crescendo* or *Musical interlude* [a]Ps. 89:47 [b]Ps. 144:4 [c]Job 14:2; Ps. 62:9; Eccl. 6:12
6 [1]Lit., *an image* [a]1 Cor. 7:31; James 1:10, 11; 1 Pet. 1:24 [b]Ps. 127:2; Eccl. 5:17 [c]Ps. 49:10; Eccl. 2:26; 5:14; Luke 12:20
7 [a]Ps. 38:15
8 [a]Ps. 51:9, 14; 79:9 [b]Ps. 44:13; 79:4; 119:22

9 [a]Ps. 39:2 [b]2 Sam. 16:10; Job 2:10

10 "[a]Remove Thy plague from me;
Because of [b]the opposition of Thy hand, I am [1]perishing.
11 "With [a]reproofs Thou dost chasten a man for iniquity;
Thou dost [b]consume as a moth what is precious to him;
Surely [c]every man is a mere breath. [Selah.

12 "[a]Hear my prayer, O LORD, and give ear to my cry;
Do not be silent [b]at my tears;
For I am [c]a stranger with Thee,
A [d]sojourner like all my fathers.
13 "[a]Turn Thy gaze away from me, that I may [1]smile *again*,
Before I depart and am no more."

PSALM 40

God Sustains His Servant.

For the choir director. A Psalm of David.

I [a]WAITED [1]patiently for the LORD;
And He inclined to me, and [b]heard my cry.
2 He brought me up out of the [a]pit of destruction, out of the [1]miry clay;
And [b]He set my feet upon a rock [c]making my footsteps firm.
3 And He put a [a]new song in my mouth, a song of praise to our God;
Many will [b]see and fear,
And will trust in the LORD.

4 How [a]blessed is the man who has made the LORD his trust,
And [b]has not [1]turned to the proud, nor to those who [c]lapse into falsehood.
5 Many, O LORD my God, are [a]the wonders which Thou hast done,
And Thy [b]thoughts toward us;
There is none to compare with Thee;
If I would declare and speak of them,
They [c]would be too numerous to count.

6 [1a]Sacrifice and meal offering Thou hast not desired;
My ears Thou hast [2]opened;
Burnt offering and sin offering Thou hast not required.
7 Then I said, "Behold, I come;
In the scroll of the book it is [1]written of me;
8 [a]I delight to do Thy will, O my God;
[b]Thy Law is within my heart."

9 I have [a]proclaimed glad tidings of righteousness in the great congregation;
Behold, I will [b]not restrain my lips,
O LORD, [c]Thou knowest.
10 I have [a]not hidden Thy righteousness within my heart;
I have [b]spoken of Thy faithfulness and Thy salvation;
I have not concealed Thy lovingkindness and Thy truth from the great congregation.

11 Thou, O LORD, wilt not withhold Thy compassion from me;
[1]Thy [a]lovingkindness and Thy truth will continually preserve me.
12 For evils beyond number have [a]surrounded me;
My [b]iniquities have overtaken me, so that I am not able to see;
They are [c]more numerous than the hairs of my head;
And my [d]heart has [1]failed me.

13 [a]Be pleased, O LORD, to deliver me;
Make [b]haste, O LORD, to help me.
14 Let those be [a]ashamed and humiliated together
Who [b]seek my [1]life to destroy it;
Let those be turned back and dishonored
Who delight [2]in my hurt.
15 Let those [a]be [1]appalled because of their shame
Who [b]say to me, "Aha, aha!"
16 [a]Let all who seek Thee rejoice and be glad in Thee;
Let those who love Thy salvation [b]say continually,
"The LORD be magnified!"
17 Since [a]I am afflicted and needy,
[1b]Let the Lord be mindful of me;
Thou art my help and my deliverer;
Do not delay, O my God.

PSALM 41

The Psalmist in Sickness Complains of Enemies and False Friends.

For the choir director. A Psalm of David.

HOW blessed is he who [a]considers the [1]helpless;
The LORD will deliver him [b]in a day of [2]trouble.
2 The LORD will [a]protect him, and keep him alive,
And he shall [1]be called [b]blessed upon the earth;
And [c]do not give him over to the desire of his enemies.
3 The LORD will sustain him upon his sickbed;
In his illness, Thou dost [1]restore him to health.

4 As for me, I said, "O LORD, be gracious to me;
[a]Heal my soul, for [b]I have sinned against Thee."
5 My enemies [a]speak evil against me,
"When will he die, and his name perish?"
6 And [1]when he comes to see *me*, he [a]speaks [2]falsehood;
His heart gathers wickedness to itself;
When he goes outside, he tells it.
7 All who hate me whisper together against me;

---

10 [1]Or, *wasting away* [a]Job 9:34; 13:21 [b]Ps. 32:4
11 [a]Ezek. 5:15; 2 Pet. 2:16 [b]Job 13:28; Ps. 90:7; Is. 50:9 [c]Ps. 39:5
12 [a]Ps. 102:1; 143:1 [b]2 Kin. 20:5; Ps. 56:8 [c]Lev. 25:23; 1 Chr. 29:15; Ps. 119:19; Heb. 11:13; 1 Pet. 2:11 [d]Gen. 47:9
13 [1]Or, *become cheerful* [a]Job 7:19; 10:20, 21; 14:6; Ps. 102:24

1 [1]Or, *intently* [a]Ps. 25:5; 27:14; 37:7 [b]Ps. 34:15
2 [1]Lit., *mud of the mire* [a]Ps. 69:2, 14; Jer. 38:6 [b]Ps. 27:5 [c]Ps. 37:23
3 [a]Ps. 32:7; 33:3 [b]Ps. 52:6; 64:9
4 [1]Lit., *regard* [a]Ps. 34:8; 84:12 [b]Job 37:24 [c]Ps. 125:5
5 [a]Job 5:9; Ps. 136:4 [b]Ps. 139:17; Is. 55:8 [c]Ps. 71:15; 139:18
6 [1]I.e., Blood sacrifice [2]Lit., *dug*; or possibly, *pierced* [a]1 Sam. 15:22; Ps. 51:16; Is. 1:11; Jer. 6:20; 7:22, 23; Amos 5:22; Mic. 6:6-8; Heb. 10:5-7
7 [1]Or, *prescribed for*
8 [a]John 4:34 [b]Ps. 37:31; Jer. 31:33; 2 Cor. 3:3
9 [a]Ps. 22:22, 25 [b]Ps. 119:13 [c]Josh. 22:22; Ps. 139:4
10 [a]Acts 20:20, 27 [b]Ps. 89:1
11 [1]Or, *May . . . preserve* [a]Ps. 43:3; 57:3; 61:7; Prov. 20:28
12 [1]Lit., *forsaken* [a]Ps. 18:5; 116:3 [b]Ps. 38:4; 65:3 [c]Ps. 69:4 [d]Ps. 73:26
13 [a]Ps. 70:1 [b]Ps. 22:19; 71:12
14 [1]Or, *soul* [2]Or, *to injure me* [a]Ps. 35:4, 26; 70:2; 71:13 [b]Ps. 63:9
15 [1]Or, *desolated* [a]Ps. 70:3 [b]Ps. 35:21; 70:3
16 [a]Ps. 70:4 [b]Ps. 35:27
17 [1]Or, *The Lord is mindful* [a]Ps. 70:5; 86:1; 109:22 [b]Ps. 40:5; 1 Pet. 5:7

1 [1]Or, *poor* [2]Or, *evil* [a]Ps. 82:3, 4; Prov. 14:21 [b]Ps. 27:5; 37:19
2 [1]Or, *be blessed* [a]Ps. 37:28 [b]Ps. 37:22 [c]Ps. 27:12
3 [1]Lit., *turn all his bed*
4 [a]Ps. 6:2; 103:3; 147:3 [b]Ps. 51:4
5 [a]Ps. 38:12
6 [1]Or, *if he* [2]Or, *emptiness* [a]Ps. 12:2; 62:4; Prov. 26:24-26

Against me they [a]devise my hurt, *saying,*
8 "A wicked thing is poured out [1]upon him,
That when he lies down, he will [a]not rise up again."
9 Even my [a]close friend, in whom I trusted,
Who ate my bread,
Has lifted up his heel against me.

10 But Thou, O LORD, be gracious to me, and [a]raise me up,
That I may repay them.
11 By this I know that [a]Thou art pleased with me,
Because [b]my enemy does not shout in triumph over me.
12 As for me, [a]Thou dost uphold me in my integrity,
And Thou dost set me [b]in Thy presence forever.

13 [a]Blessed be the LORD, the God of Israel,
From everlasting to everlasting.
Amen, and Amen.

BOOK 2

PSALM 42

Thirsting for God in Trouble and Exile.

For the choir director.
A +Maskil of the sons of Korah.

AS the deer [1]pants for the water brooks,
So my soul [1a]pants for Thee, O God.
2 My soul [a]thirsts for God, for the [b]living God;
When shall I come and [1c]appear before God?
3 My [a]tears have been my food day and night,
While *they* [b]say to me all day long, "Where is your God?"
4 These things I remember, and I [a]pour out my soul within me.
For I [b]used to go along with the throng *and* [1]lead them in procession to the house of God,
With the voice of [c]joy and thanksgiving, a multitude keeping festival.

5 [a]Why are you [1b]in despair, O my soul?
And *why* have you become [c]disturbed within me?
[2d]Hope in God, for I shall [3]again praise [4]Him
For the [5e]help of His presence.
6 O my God, my soul is [1]in despair within me;
Therefore I [a]remember Thee from [b]the land of the Jordan,
And the [2]peaks of [c]Hermon, from Mount Mizar.
7 Deep calls to deep at the sound of Thy waterfalls;
All Thy [a]breakers and Thy waves have rolled over me.

7 [a]Ps. 56:5
8 [1]Or, *within* [a]Ps. 71:10, 11
9 [a]2 Sam. 15:12; Job 19:13, 19; Ps. 55:12, 13, 20; Jer. 20:10; Mic. 7:5; Matt. 26:23; Luke 22:21; John 13:18
10 [a]Ps. 3:3
11 [a]Ps. 37:23; 147:11 [b]Ps. 25:2
12 [a]Ps. 18:32; 37:17; 63:8 [b]Job 36:7; Ps. 21:6
13 [a]Ps. 72:18, 19; 89:52; 106:48; 150:6

+ Possibly, *Contemplative,* or *Didactic,* or *Skillful Psalm*
1 [1]Lit., *longs for* [a]Ps. 119:131
2 [1]Some mss. read *see the face of God* [a]Ps. 63:1; 84:2; 143:6 [b]Josh. 3:10; Ps. 84:2; Jer. 10:10; Dan. 6:26; Matt. 26:63; Rom. 9:26; 1 Thess. 1:9 [c]Ex. 23:17; Ps. 43:4; 84:7
3 [a]Ps. 80:5; 102:9 [b]Ps. 79:10; 115:2; Joel 2:17; Mic. 7:10
4 [1]Or, *move slowly with them* [a]1 Sam. 1:15; Job 30:16; Ps. 62:8; Lam. 2:19 [b]Ps. 55:14; 122:1; Is. 30:29 [c]Ps. 100:4
5 [1]Or, *sunk down* [2]Or, *Wait for* [3]Or, *still* [4]Some ancient versions read *Him, the help of my countenance and my God* [5]Or, *saving acts of* [a]Ps. 42:11; 43:5 [b]Ps. 38:6; Matt. 26:38 [c]Ps. 77:3 [d]Ps. 71:14; Lam. 3:24 [e]Ps. 44:3
6 [1]Or, *sunk down* [2]Lit., *Hermons* [a]Ps. 61:2 [b]2 Sam. 17:22 [c]Deut. 3:8
7 [a]Ps. 69:1, 2; 88:7; Jon. 2:3
8 [a]Ps. 57:3; 133:3 [b]Job 35:10; Ps. 16:7; 63:6; 77:6; 149:5 [c]Eccl. 5:18; 8:15
9 [1]Or, *while the enemy oppresses* [a]Ps. 18:2 [b]Ps. 38:6 [c]Ps. 17:9
10 [a]Ps. 42:3; Joel 2:17
11 [1]Or, *sunk down* [2]Or, *Wait for* [3]Or, *saving acts of* [a]Ps. 42:5; 43:5

1 [1]Or, *Mayest Thou* [a]Ps. 26:1; 35:24 [b]1 Sam. 24:15; Ps. 35:1 [c]Ps. 5:6; 38:12
2 [1]Or, *while the enemy oppresses* [a]Ps. 18:1; 28:7; 31:4 [b]Ps. 44:9; 88:14 [c]Ps. 42:9
3 [a]Ps. 36:9 [b]Ps. 2:6; 3:4; 42:4; 46:4 [c]Ps. 84:1
4 [1]Lit., *the gladness of my joy* [a]Ps. 26:6 [b]Ps. 21:6 [c]Ps. 33:2; 49:4; 57:8; 71:22

8 The LORD will [a]command His lovingkindness in the daytime;
And His song will be with me [b]in the night,
A prayer to [c]the God of my life.
9 I will say to God [a]my rock, "Why hast Thou forgotten me?
Why do I go [b]mourning [1]because of the [c]oppression of the enemy?"
10 As a shattering of my bones, my adversaries revile me,
While they [a]say to me all day long, "Where is your God?"
11 [a]Why are you [1]in despair, O my soul?
And why have you become disturbed within me?
[2]Hope in God, for I shall yet praise Him,
The [3]help of my countenance, and my God.

PSALM 43

Prayer for Deliverance.

[a]VINDICATE me, O God, and [b]plead my case against an ungodly nation;
[1]O deliver me from [c]the deceitful and unjust man!
2 For Thou art the [a]God of my strength; why hast Thou [b]rejected me?
Why do I go [c]mourning [1]because of the oppression of the enemy?

3 O send out Thy [a]light and Thy truth, let them lead me;
Let them bring me to Thy [b]holy hill,
And to Thy [c]dwelling places.
4 Then I will go to [a]the altar of God,
To God [1]my exceeding [b]joy;
And upon the [c]lyre I shall praise Thee, O God, my God.

5 [a]Why are you [1]in despair, O my soul?
And why are you disturbed within me?
[2]Hope in God, for I shall [3]again praise Him,
The [4]help of my countenance, and my God.

PSALM 44

Former Deliverances and Present Troubles.

For the choir director.
A +Maskil of the sons of Korah.

O GOD, we have heard with our ears,
Our [a]fathers have told us,
The [b]work that Thou didst in their days,
In the [c]days of old.

5 [1]Or, *sunk down* [2]Or, *Wait for* [3]Or, *still* [4]Or, *saving acts of* [a]Ps. 42:5, 11

+ Possibly, *Contemplative,* or *Didactic,* or *Skillful Psalm*
1 [a]Ex. 12:26, 27; Deut. 6:20; Judg. 6:13; Ps. 78:3 [b]Ps. 78:12 [c]Deut. 32:7; Ps. 77:5; Is. 51:9; 63:9

2 Thou with Thine own hand didst
[a]drive out the nations;
Then Thou didst [b]plant them;
Thou didst [c]afflict the peoples,
Then Thou didst [d]spread them
abroad.
3 For by their own sword they [a]did
not possess the land;
And their own arm did not save
them;
But Thy right hand, and Thine
[b]arm, and the [c]light of Thy presence,
For Thou didst [d]favor them.

4 Thou art [a]my King, O God;
[b]Command [1]victories for Jacob.
5 Through Thee we will [a]push back
our adversaries;
Through Thy name we will [b]tram-
ple down those who rise up
against us.
6 For I will [a]not trust in my bow,
Nor will my sword save me.
7 But Thou [a]hast saved us from our
adversaries,
And Thou hast [b]put to shame those
who hate us.
8 In God we have [a]boasted all day
long,
And we will [b]give thanks to Thy
name forever. [[1]Selah.

9 Yet Thou [a]hast rejected *us* and
brought us to [b]dishonor,
And [c]dost not go out with our
armies.
10 Thou dost cause us to [a]turn back
from the adversary;
And those who hate us [b]have taken
spoil for themselves.
11 Thou dost give us as [a]sheep [1]to be
eaten,
And hast [b]scattered us among the
nations.
12 Thou dost [a]sell Thy people
[1]cheaply,
And hast not [2]profited by their
sale.
13 Thou dost make us a [a]reproach to
our neighbors,
A scoffing and a [b]derision to those
around us.
14 Thou dost make us [a]a byword
among the nations,
A [1b]laughingstock among the peoples.
15 All day long my dishonor is before
me,
And [1]my [a]humiliation has overwhelmed me,
16 Because of the voice of him who
[a]reproaches and reviles,
Because of the presence of the
[b]enemy and the avenger.

17 All this has come upon us, but we
have [a]not forgotten Thee,
And we have not [b]dealt falsely with
Thy covenant.
18 Our heart has not [a]turned back,
And our steps [b]have not deviated
from Thy way,

2 [a]Josh. 3:10; Neh. 9:24; Ps. 78:55; 80:8 [b]Ex. 15:17; 2 Sam. 7:10; Jer. 24:6; Amos 9:15 [c]Ps. 135:10-12 [d]Ps. 80:9-11; Zech. 2:6
3 [a]Deut. 8:17, 18; Josh. 24:12 [b]Ps. 77:15 [c]Ps. 4:6; 89:15 [d]Deut. 4:37; 7:7, 8; 10:15; Ps. 106:4
4 [1]Lit., *salvation* [a]Ps. 74:12 [b]Ps. 42:8
5 [a]Deut. 33:17; Ps. 60:12; Dan. 8:4 [b]Ps. 108:13; Zech. 10:5
6 [a]1 Sam. 17:47; Ps. 33:16; Hos. 1:7
7 [a]Ps. 136:24 [b]Ps. 53:5
8 [1]*Selah* may mean: *Pause, Crescendo* or *Musical interlude* [a]Ps. 34:2 [b]Ps. 30:12
9 [a]Ps. 43:2; 60:1, 10; 74:1; 89:38; 108:11 [b]Ps. 69:19 [c]Ps. 60:10; 108:11
10 [a]Lev. 26:17; Josh. 7:8, 12; Ps. 89:43 [b]Ps. 89:41
11 [1]Lit., *for food* [a]Ps. 44:22; Rom. 8:36 [b]Lev. 26:33; Deut. 4:27; 28:64; Ps. 106:27; Ezek. 20:23
12 [1]Lit., *for no wealth* [2]Or, *set a high price on them* [a]Deut. 32:30; Judg. 2:14; 3:8; Is. 52:3, 4; Jer. 15:13
13 [a]Deut. 28:37; Ps. 79:4; 89:41 [b]Ps. 80:6; Ezek. 23:32
14 [1]Lit., *shaking of the head* [a]Job 17:6; Ps. 69:11; Jer. 24:9 [b]2 Kin. 19:21; Ps. 109:25
15 [1]Lit., *the shame of my face has covered me* [a]2 Chr. 32:21; Ps. 69:7
16 [a]Ps. 74:10 [b]Ps. 8:2
17 [a]Ps. 78:7; 119:61, 83, 109, 141, 153, 176 [b]Ps. 78:57
18 [a]Ps. 78:57 [b]Job 23:11; Ps. 119:51, 157
19 [a]Ps. 51:8; 94:5 [b]Job 30:29; Is. 13:22; Jer. 9:11 [c]Job 3:5; Ps. 23:4
20 [1]Lit., *palms* [a]Ps. 78:11 [b]Deut. 6:14; Ps. 81:9
21 [a]Ps. 139:1, 2; Jer. 17:10
22 [a]Rom. 8:36 [b]Is. 53:7; Jer. 12:3
23 [a]Ps. 7:6 [b]Ps. 78:65 [c]Ps. 77:7
24 [a]Job 13:24; Ps. 88:14 [b]Ps. 42:9; Lam. 5:20
25 [a]Ps. 119:25
26 [a]Ps. 35:2 [b]Ps. 6:4; 25:22

\+ Or possibly, *Lilies*
• Possibly, *Contemplative*, or *Didactic*, or *Skillful Psalm*

19 Yet Thou hast [a]crushed us in a
place of [b]jackals,
And covered us with [c]the shadow
of death.

20 If we had [a]forgotten the name of
our God,
Or extended our [1]hands to [b]a
strange god;
21 Would not God [a]find this out?
For He knows the secrets of the
heart.
22 But [a]for Thy sake we are killed all
day long;
We are considered as [b]sheep to be
slaughtered.
23 [a]Arouse Thyself, why [b]dost Thou
sleep, O Lord?
Awake, [c]do not reject us forever.
24 Why dost Thou [a]hide Thy face,
And [b]forget our affliction and our
oppression?
25 For our [a]soul has sunk down into
the dust;
Our body cleaves to the earth.
26 [a]Rise up, be our help,
And [b]redeem us for the sake of Thy
lovingkindness.

PSALM 45

A Song Celebrating the King's Marriage.

For the choir director; according to the +Shoshannim. A •Maskil of the sons of Korah. A Song of Love.

MY heart [1]overflows with a good
theme;
I [2]address my [3]verses to the [4]King;
My tongue is the pen of [a]a ready
writer.
2 Thou art fairer than the sons of
men;
[a]Grace is poured [1]upon Thy lips;
Therefore God has [b]blessed Thee
forever.

3 Gird [a]Thy sword on *Thy* thigh, O
[1b]Mighty One,
In Thy splendor and Thy majesty!
4 And in Thy majesty ride on victori-
ously,
For the cause of truth and [a]meek-
ness *and* righteousness;
Let Thy [b]right hand teach Thee
[1]awesome things.
5 Thine [a]arrows are sharp;
The [b]peoples fall under Thee;
Thine arrows are [c]in the heart of the
King's enemies.

6 [a]Thy throne, O God, is forever and
ever;
A scepter of [b]uprightness is the
scepter of Thy kingdom.

1 [1]Lit., *is astir* [2]Lit., *am saying* [3]Lit., *works* [4]Probably refers to Solomon as a type of Christ. [a]Ezra 7:6
2 [1]Or, *through* [a]Luke 4:22 [b]Ps. 21:6
3 [1]Or, *warrior* [a]Heb. 4:12; Rev. 1:16 [b]Is. 9:6
4 [1]Or, *fearful* [a]Zeph. 2:3 [b]Ps. 21:8
5 [a]Ps. 18:14; 120:4; Is. 5:28; 7:13 [b]Ps. 92:9 [c]2 Sam. 18:14
6 [a]Ps. 93:2; Heb. 1:8, 9 [b]Ps. 98:9

7 Thou hast [a]loved righteousness,
and hated wickedness;
Therefore God, Thy God, has
[b]anointed Thee
With the oil of joy above Thy
fellows.
8 All Thy garments are *fragrant with*
[a]myrrh and aloes *and* cassia;
Out of ivory palaces [b]stringed instruments have made Thee glad.
9 Kings' daughters are among [a]Thy
noble ladies;
At Thy [b]right hand stands the
queen in [c]gold from Ophir.

10 Listen, O daughter, give attention
and incline your ear;
[a]Forget your people and your father's house;
11 Then the King will desire your
beauty;
Because He is your [a]Lord, [b]bow
down to Him.
12 And the daughter of [a]Tyre *will*
come with a gift;
The [b]rich among the people will
entreat your favor.

13 The King's daughter is all glorious
within;
Her clothing is [a]interwoven with
gold.
14 She will be [a]led to the King [b]in
embroidered work;
The [c]virgins, her companions who
follow her,
Will be brought to Thee.
15 They will be led forth with gladness
and rejoicing;
They will enter into the King's
palace.

16 In place of your fathers will be
your sons;
You shall make them princes in all
the earth.
17 I will cause [a]Thy name to be remembered in all generations;
Therefore the peoples [b]will give
Thee thanks forever and ever.

PSALM 46

God the Refuge of His People.

For the choir director. *A Psalm* of the sons
of Korah, +set to Alamoth. A Song.

GOD is our [a]refuge and strength,
[1]A very [b]present help [c]in [2]trouble.
2 Therefore we will [a]not fear, though
[b]the earth should change,
And though [c]the mountains slip
into the heart of the [1]sea;
3 Though its [a]waters roar *and* foam,
Though the mountains quake at its
swelling pride. [[1]Selah.

4 There is a [a]river whose streams
make glad the [b]city of God,
The holy [c]dwelling places of the
Most High.

7 [a]Ps. 11:7; 33:5 [b]Ps. 2:2
8 [a]Song 4:14; John 19:39 [b]Ps. 150:4
9 [a]Song 6:8 [b]1 Kin. 2:19 [c]1 Kin. 9:28; Is. 13:12
10 [a]Deut. 21:13; Ruth 1:16, 17
11 [a]Gen. 18:12; 1 Pet. 3:6 [b]Eph. 5:33
12 [a]Ps. 87:4 [b]Ps. 22:29; 68:29; 72:10, 11; Is. 49:23
13 [a]Ex. 39:2, 3
14 [a]Song 1:4 [b]Judg. 5:30; Ezek. 16:10 [c]Ps. 45:9
17 [a]Mal. 1:11 [b]Ps. 138:4

+ Possibly, *for soprano voices*
1 [1]Or, *Abundantly available for help* [2]Or, *tight places* [a]Ps. 14:6; 62:7, 8 [b]Deut. 4:7; Ps. 145:18 [c]Ps. 9:9
2 [1]Lit., *seas* [a]Ps. 23:4; 27:1 [b]Ps. 82:5 [c]Ps. 18:7
3 [1]*Selah* may mean: *Pause, Crescendo* or *Musical interlude* [a]Ps. 93:3, 4; Jer. 5:22
4 [a]Ps. 36:8; 65:9; Is. 8:6; Rev. 22:1 [b]Ps. 48:1; 87:3; 101:8; Is. 60:14; Rev. 3:12 [c]Ps. 43:3
5 [1]Lit., *at the turning of the morning* [a]Deut. 23:14; Is. 12:6; Ezek. 43:7, 9; Hos. 11:9; Joel 2:27; Zech. 2:5 [b]Ps. 37:40; Is. 41:14; Luke 1:54
6 [1]Or, *Gentiles* [2]Lit., *gave forth* [a]Ps. 2:1, 2 [b]Ps. 18:13; 68:33; Jer. 25:30; Joel 2:11; Amos 1:2 [c]Amos 9:5; Mic. 1:4; Nah. 1:5
7 [a]Num. 14:9; 2 Chr. 13:12 [b]Ps. 9:9; 48:3
8 [1]Or, *Which He has wrought as desolations* [a]Ps. 66:5 [b]Is. 61:4; Jer. 51:43
9 [a]Is. 2:4; Mic. 4:3 [b]1 Sam. 2:4; Ps. 76:3 [c]Is. 9:5; Ezek. 39:9
10 [1]Or, *Let go, relax* [2]Or, *Gentiles* [a]Ps. 100:3 [b]Is. 2:11, 17

1 [1]Or, *a ringing cry* [a]Ps. 98:8 [b]Ps. 106:47
2 [a]Deut. 7:21; Neh. 1:5; Ps. 66:3, 5; 68:35 [b]Mal. 1:14
3 [a]Ps. 18:47
4 [1]*Selah* may mean: *Pause, Crescendo* or *Musical interlude* [a]1 Pet. 1:4 [b]Amos 6:8; 8:7; Nah. 2:2

5 God is [a]in the midst of her, she will
not be moved;
God will [b]help her [1]when morning
dawns.
6 The [1]nations [a]made an uproar, the
kingdoms tottered;
He [2b]raised His voice, the earth
[c]melted.
7 The LORD of hosts [a]is with us;
The God of Jacob is [b]our stronghold. [Selah.

8 Come, [a]behold the works of the
LORD,
[1]Who has wrought [b]desolations in
the earth.
9 He [a]makes wars to cease to the end
of the earth;
He [b]breaks the bow and cuts the
spear in two;
He [c]burns the chariots with fire.
10 "[1]Cease *striving* and [a]know that I
am God;
I will be [b]exalted among the [2]na-
tions, I will be exalted in the
earth."
11 The LORD of hosts is with us;
The God of Jacob is our stronghold. [Selah.

PSALM 47

God the King of the Earth.

For the choir director.
A Psalm of the sons of Korah.

O [a]CLAP your hands, all peoples;
[b]Shout to God with the voice of
[1]joy.
2 For the LORD Most High is to be
[a]feared,
A [b]great King over all the earth.
3 He [a]subdues peoples under us,
And nations under our feet.
4 He chooses our [a]inheritance for us,
The [b]glory of Jacob whom He
loves. [[1]Selah.

5 God has [a]ascended [1]with a shout,
The LORD, [1]with the [b]sound of a
trumpet.
6 [a]Sing praises to God, sing praises;
Sing praises to [b]our King, sing
praises.
7 For God is the [a]King of all the
earth;
Sing praises [b]with a [1]skillful psalm.
8 God [a]reigns over the nations,
God [1]sits on [b]His holy throne.
9 The [1a]princes of the people have
assembled themselves *as* the
[b]people of the God of Abraham;
For the [c]shields of the earth belong
to God;
He [2]is [d]highly exalted.

5 [1]Or, *amid* [a]Ps. 68:18 [b]Ps. 98:6
6 [a]Ps. 68:4 [b]Ps. 89:18
7 [1]Heb., *Maskil* [a]Zech. 14:9 [b]1 Cor. 14:15
8 [1]Or, *has taken His seat* [a]1 Chr. 16:31; Ps. 22:28 [b]Ps. 97:2
9 [1]Or, *nobles* [2]Lit., *has greatly exalted Himself* [a]Ps. 72:11; 102:22; Is. 49:7, 23 [b]Rom. 4:11, 12 [c]Ps. 89:18 [d]Ps. 97:9

PSALM 48

The Beauty and Glory of Zion.

A Song; a Psalm of the sons of Korah.

[a]GREAT is the LORD, and greatly to be praised,
In the [b]city of our God, His [c]holy mountain.
2 [a]Beautiful in elevation, [b]the joy of the whole earth,
Is Mount Zion *in* the far north,
The [c]city of the great King.
3 God, in her palaces,
Has made Himself known as a [a]stronghold.

4 For, lo, the [a]kings assembled themselves,
They passed by together.
5 They saw *it*, then they were amazed;
They were [a]terrified, they [1]fled in alarm.
6 [1]Panic seized them there,
Anguish, as of [a]a woman in childbirth.
7 With the [a]east wind
Thou [b]dost break the [c]ships of Tarshish.
8 As we have heard, so have we seen
In the city of the LORD of hosts, in the city of our God;
God will [a]establish her forever. [[1]Selah.

9 We have thought on [a]Thy lovingkindness, O God,
In the midst of Thy temple.
10 As is Thy [a]name, O God,
So is Thy [b]praise to the ends of the earth;
Thy [c]right hand is full of righteousness.
11 Let Mount [a]Zion be glad,
Let the [a]daughters of Judah rejoice,
Because of Thy judgments.
12 Walk about Zion, and go around her;
Count her [a]towers;
13 Consider her [a]ramparts;
Go through her palaces;
That you may [b]tell *it* to the next generation.
14 For [1]such is God,
Our God forever and ever;
He will [a]guide us [2]until death.

PSALM 49

The Folly of Trusting in Riches.

For the choir director.
A Psalm of the sons of Korah.

[a]HEAR this, all peoples;
Give ear, all [b]inhabitants of the world,
2 Both [a]low and high,
Rich and poor together.
3 My mouth will [a]speak wisdom;
And the meditation of my heart *will be* [b]understanding.
4 I will incline my ear to [a]a proverb;
[b]I will [1]express my [c]riddle on the harp.

5 Why should I [a]fear in days of adversity,
When the iniquity of my [1]foes surrounds me,
6 Even those who [a]trust in their wealth,
And boast in the abundance of their riches?
7 No man can by any means [a]redeem *his* brother,
Or give to God a [b]ransom for him—
8 For [a]the redemption of [1]his soul is costly,
And he should cease *trying* forever—
9 That he should [a]live on eternally;
That he should not [1b]undergo decay.

10 For he sees *that even* [a]wise men die;
The [b]stupid and the senseless alike perish,
And [c]leave their wealth to others.
11 Their [1a]inner thought is, *that* their houses [b]are forever,
And their dwelling places to all generations;
They have [c]called their lands after their own names.
12 But [a]man in *his* [1]pomp will not endure;
He is like the [2]beasts that [3]perish.

13 This is the [a]way of those who are foolish,
And of those after them who [b]approve their words. [[1]Selah.
14 As sheep they are appointed [a]for [1]Sheol;
Death shall be their shepherd;
And the [b]upright shall rule over them in the morning;
And their form shall be for [1]Sheol [c]to consume,
[2]So that they have no habitation.
15 But God will [a]redeem my soul from the [1]power of [2]Sheol;
For [b]He will receive me. [Selah.

16 Do not be afraid [a]when a man becomes rich,
When the [1]glory of his house is increased;
17 For when he dies he will [a]carry nothing away;
His [1]glory will not descend after him.
18 Though while he lives he [a]congratulates [1]himself—
And though *men* praise you when you do well for yourself—
19 [1]He shall [a]go to the generation of his fathers;
They shall never see [b]the light.

Psalm 48: 1 [a]1 Chr. 16:25; Ps. 96:4; 145:3 [b]Ps. 46:4 [c]Ps. 2:6; 87:1; Is. 2:3; Mic. 4:1; Zech. 8:3
2 [a]Ps. 50:2 [b]Lam. 2:15 [c]Matt. 5:35
3 [a]Ps. 46:7
4 [a]2 Sam. 10:6-19
5 [1]Lit., *were hurried away* [a]Ex. 15:15
6 [1]Lit., *Trembling* [a]Is. 13:8
7 [a]Jer. 18:17 [b]1 Kin. 22:48 [c]1 Kin. 10:22; Ezek. 27:25
8 [1]*Selah* may mean: *Pause, Crescendo* or *Musical interlude* [a]Ps. 87:5
9 [a]Ps. 26:3; 40:10
10 [a]Deut. 28:58; Josh. 7:9; Mal. 1:11 [b]Ps. 65:1, 2; 100:1 [c]Is. 41:10
11 [a]Ps. 97:8
12 [a]Neh. 3:1, 11, 25-27
13 [a]Ps. 122:7 [b]Ps. 78:5-7
14 [1]Lit., *this* [2]Lit., *upon;* some mss. and the Gr. read *forever.* [a]Ps. 23:4; Is. 58:11

Psalm 49: 1 [a]Ps. 78:1; Is. 1:2; Mic. 1:2 [b]Ps. 33:8
2 [a]Ps. 62:9
3 [a]Ps. 37:30 [b]Ps. 119:130
4 [1]Lit., *open up* [a]Ps. 78:2 [b]2 Kin. 3:15 [c]Num. 12:8
5 [1]Lit., *supplanters* [a]Ps. 23:4; 27:1
6 [a]Job 31:24; Ps. 52:7; Prov. 11:28; Mark 10:24
7 [a]Matt. 25:8, 9 [b]Job 36:18, 19
8 [1]Lit., *their* [a]Matt. 16:26
9 [1]Or, *see corruption* or *the pit* [a]Ps. 22:29 [b]Ps. 16:10; 89:48
10 [a]Eccl. 2:16 [b]Ps. 92:6; 94:8 [c]Ps. 39:6; Eccl. 2:18, 21; Luke 12:20
11 [1]Some versions read *graves are their houses* [a]Ps. 64:6 [b]Ps. 10:6 [c]Gen. 4:17; Deut. 3:14
12 [1]Lit., *honor* [2]Or, *animals* [3]Lit., *are destroyed* [a]Ps. 49:20
13 [1]*Selah* may mean: *Pause, Crescendo* or *Musical interlude* [a]Jer. 17:11 [b]Ps. 49:18
14 [1]I.e., the nether world [2]Lit., *Away from his habitation* [a]Ps. 9:17 [b]Dan. 7:18; Mal. 4:3; 1 Cor. 6:2; Rev. 2:26 [c]Job 24:19
15 [1]Lit., *hand* [2]I.e., the nether world [a]Ps. 16:10; 56:13; Hos. 13:14 [b]Gen. 5:24; Ps. 16:11; 73:24
16 [1]Or, *wealth* [a]Ps. 37:7
17 [1]Or, *wealth* [a]Ps. 17:14; 1 Tim. 6:7
18 [1]Lit., *his soul* [a]Deut. 29:19; Ps. 10:3, 6; Luke 12:19
19 [1]Lit., *You;* or, *It* [a]Gen. 15:15 [b]Job 33:30; Ps. 56:13

20 [a]Man in *his* [1]pomp, yet without understanding,
Is [b]like the [2]beasts that [3]perish.

PSALM 50

God the Judge of the Righteous and the Wicked.

A Psalm of +Asaph.

[a]THE Mighty One, God, the LORD, has spoken,
And summoned the earth [b]from the rising of the sun to its setting.
2 Out of Zion, [a]the perfection of beauty,
God [b]has shone forth.
3 May our God [a]come and not keep silence;
[b]Fire devours before Him,
And it is very [c]tempestuous around Him.
4 He [a]summons the heavens above,
And the earth, to judge His people:
5 "Gather My [a]godly ones to Me,
Those who have made a [b]covenant with Me by [c]sacrifice."
6 And the [a]heavens declare His righteousness,
For [b]God Himself is judge. [[1]Selah.

7 "[a]Hear, O My people, and I will speak;
O Israel, I will testify [1]against you;
I am God, [b]your God.
8 "I do [a]not reprove you for your sacrifices,
And your burnt offerings are continually before Me.
9 "I shall take no [a]young bull out of your house,
Nor male goats out of your folds.
10 "For [a]every beast of the forest is Mine,
The cattle on a thousand hills.
11 "I know every [a]bird of the mountains,
And everything that moves in the field is [1]Mine.
12 "If I were hungry, I would not tell you;
For the [a]world is Mine, and [1]all it contains.
13 "Shall I eat the flesh of [1a]bulls,
Or drink the blood of male goats?
14 "Offer to God [a]a sacrifice of thanksgiving,
And [b]pay your vows to the Most High;
15 And [a]call upon Me in the day of trouble;
I shall [b]rescue you, and you will [c]honor Me."

16 But to the wicked God says,
"What right have you to tell of My statutes,
And to take [a]My covenant in your mouth?
17 "For you [a]hate discipline,
And you [b]cast My words behind you.
18 "When you see a thief, you [1a]are pleased with him,
And [2]you [b]associate with adulterers.
19 "You [1a]let your mouth loose in evil,
And your [b]tongue frames deceit.
20 "You sit and [a]speak against your brother;
You slander your own mother's son.
21 "These things you have done, and [a]I kept silence;
You thought that I was just like you;
I will [b]reprove you, and state *the case* in order before your eyes.

22 "Now consider this, you who [a]forget God,
Lest I [b]tear *you* in pieces, and there be none to deliver.
23 "He who [a]offers a sacrifice of thanksgiving honors Me;
And to him who [1]orders *his* way *aright*
I shall [c]show the salvation of God."

PSALM 51

A Contrite Sinner's Prayer for Pardon.

For the choir director. A Psalm of David, when +Nathan the prophet came to him, after he had gone in to Bathsheba.

[a]BE gracious to me, O God, according to Thy lovingkindness;
According to the greatness of [b]Thy compassion [c]blot out my transgressions.
2 [a]Wash me thoroughly from my iniquity,
And [b]cleanse me from my sin.
3 For [1]I [a]know my transgressions,
And my sin is ever before me.
4 [a]Against Thee, Thee only, I have sinned,
And done what is [b]evil in Thy sight,
So that [c]Thou [1]art justified [2]when Thou dost speak,
And [3]blameless when Thou dost judge.

5 Behold, I was [a]brought forth in iniquity,
And in sin my mother conceived me.
6 Behold, Thou dost desire [a]truth in the [1]innermost being,
And in the hidden part Thou wilt [b]make me know wisdom.
7 [1]Purify me [a]with hyssop, and I shall be clean;
[2]Wash me, and I shall be [b]whiter than snow.

20 [1]Lit., *honor* [2]Or, *animals* [3]Lit., *are destroyed* [a]Ps. 49:12 [b]Eccl. 3:19

+1 Chr. 15:17; 2 Chr. 29:30

1 [a]Josh. 22:22 [b]Ps. 113:3

2 [a]Ps. 48:2; Lam. 2:15 [b]Deut. 33:2; Ps. 80:1; 94:1

3 [a]Ps. 96:13 [b]Lev. 10:2; Num. 16:35; Ps. 97:3; Dan. 7:10 [c]Ps. 18:12, 13

4 [a]Deut. 4:26; 31:28; 32:1; Is. 1:2

5 [a]Ps. 30:4; 37:28; 52:9 [b]Ex. 24:7; 2 Chr. 6:11; Ps. 25:10 [c]Ps. 50:8

6 [1]*Selah* may mean: *Pause, Crescendo* or *Musical interlude* [a]Ps. 89:5; 97:6 [b]Ps. 75:7; 96:13

7 [1]Or, *to* [a]Ps. 49:1; 81:8 [b]Ex. 20:2; Ps. 48:14

8 [a]Ps. 40:6; 51:16; Is. 1:11; Hos. 6:6

9 [a]Ps. 69:31

10 [a]Ps. 104:24

11 [1]Or, *in My mind;* lit., *with Me* [a]Matt. 6:26

12 [1]Lit., *its fulness* [a]Ex. 19:5; Deut. 10:14; Ps. 24:1; 1 Cor. 10:26

13 [1]Lit., *strong ones* [a]Ps. 50:9

14 [a]Ps. 27:6; 69:30; 107:22; 116:17; Hos. 14:2; Rom. 12:1; Heb. 13:15 [b]Num. 30:2; Deut. 23:21; Ps. 22:25; 56:12; 61:8; 65:1; 76:11

15 [a]Ps. 91:15; 107:6, 13; Zech. 13:9 [b]Ps. 81:7 [c]Ps. 22:23

16 [a]Is. 29:13

17 [a]Prov. 5:12; 12:1; Rom. 2:21, 22 [b]1 Kin. 14:9; Neh. 9:26

18 [1]Some ancient versions read *run together* [2]Lit., *your part is with* [a]Rom. 1:32 [b]1 Tim. 5:22

19 [1]Lit., *send* [a]Ps. 10:7 [b]Ps. 36:3; 52:2

20 [a]Job 19:18; Matt. 10:21

21 [a]Eccl. 8:11; Is. 42:14; 57:11 [b]Ps. 90:8

22 [a]Job 8:13; Ps. 9:17 [b]Ps. 7:2

23 [1]Lit., *sets* [a]Ps. 50:14 [b]Ps. 85:13 [c]Ps. 91:16

+ 2 Sam. 12:1

1 [a]Ps. 4:1; 109:26 [b]Ps. 69:16; 106:45 [c]Ps. 51:9; Is. 43:25; 44:22; Acts 3:19; Col. 2:14

2 [a]Ps. 51:7; Is. 1:16; 4:4; Jer. 4:14; Acts 22:16; Rev. 1:5 [b]Jer. 33:8; Ezek. 36:33; Heb. 9:14; 1 John 1:7, 9

3 [1]Or, *I myself know* [a]Is. 59:12

4 [1]Or, *mayest be in the right* [2]Many mss. read *in Thy words* [3]Lit., *pure* [a]Gen. 20:6; 39:9; 2 Sam. 12:13; Ps. 41:4 [b]Luke 15:21 [c]Rom. 3:4

5 [a]Job 14:4; 15:14; Ps. 58:3; Eph. 2:3

6 [1]Or, *inward parts* [a]Job 38:36; Ps. 15:2 [b]Prov. 2:6; Eccl. 2:26; James 1:5

7 [1]Or, *Mayest Thou purify . . . that I may be clean* [2]Or, *Mayest Thou wash* [a]Ex. 12:22; Lev. 14:4; Num. 19:18; Heb. 9:19 [b]Is. 1:18

8 [1]Make me to hear [a]joy and gladness,
Let the [b]bones which Thou hast broken rejoice.
9 [a]Hide Thy face from my sins,
And blot out all my iniquities.

10 [a]Create [1]in me a [b]clean heart, O God,
And renew [2]a [c]steadfast spirit within me.
11 [a]Do not cast me away from Thy presence,
And do not take Thy [b]Holy Spirit from me.
12 Restore to me the [a]joy of Thy salvation,
And sustain me with a [b]willing spirit.
13 *Then* I will [a]teach transgressors Thy ways,
And sinners will [1]be [b]converted to Thee.

14 Deliver me from [a]bloodguiltiness, O God, Thou [b]God of my salvation;
Then my [c]tongue will joyfully sing of Thy righteousness.
15 O Lord, [1a]open my lips,
That my mouth may [b]declare Thy praise.
16 For Thou [a]dost not delight in sacrifice, otherwise I would give it;
Thou art not pleased with burnt offering.
17 The sacrifices of God are a [a]broken spirit;
A broken and a contrite heart, O God, Thou wilt not despise.

18 [a]By Thy favor do good to Zion;
[1b]Build the walls of Jerusalem.
19 Then Thou wilt delight in [1a]righteous sacrifices,
In [b]burnt offering and whole burnt offering;
Then [2]young bulls will be offered on Thine altar.

PSALM 52

Futility of Boastful Wickedness.

For the choir director. A +Maskil of David, •when Doeg the Edomite came and told Saul, and said to him, "David has come to the house of Ahimelech."

WHY do you [a]boast in evil, O mighty man?
The [b]lovingkindness of God *endures* all day long.
2 Your tongue devises [a]destruction,
Like a [b]sharp razor, [c]O worker of deceit.
3 You [a]love evil more than good,
[b]Falsehood more than speaking what is right. [[1]Selah.
4 You love all words that devour,
O [a]deceitful tongue.

5 [1]But God will break you down forever;
He will snatch you up, and [a]tear you away from *your* tent,
And [b]uproot you from the [c]land of the living. [Selah.
6 And the righteous will [a]see and fear,
And will [b]laugh at him, *saying,*
7 "Behold, the man who would not make God his refuge,
But [a]trusted in the abundance of his riches,
And [b]was strong in [1]his *evil* desire."
8 But as for me, I am like a [a]green olive tree in the house of God;
I [b]trust in the lovingkindness of God forever and ever.
9 I will [a]give Thee thanks forever, because Thou hast done *it,*
And I will wait on Thy name, [b]for *it is* good, in the presence of Thy godly ones.

PSALM 53

Folly and Wickedness of Men.

For the choir director; according to +Mahalath. A •Maskil of David.

[a]THE fool has said in his heart, "There is no God,"
They are corrupt, and have committed abominable injustice;
[b]There is no one who does good.
2 God has looked down from heaven upon the sons of men,
To see if there is [a]anyone who [1]understands,
Who [b]seeks after God.
3 [a]Every one of them has turned aside; together they have become corrupt;
There is no one who does good, not even one.

4 Have the workers of wickedness [a]no knowledge,
Who eat up My people *as though* they ate bread,
And have not called upon God?
5 There they were in great [1]fear [a]*where* no [1]fear had been;
For God [b]scattered the bones of [2]him who encamped against you;
You [c]put *them* to shame, because [d]God had rejected them.
6 Oh, that [a]the salvation of Israel [1]would come out of Zion!
When God [2]restores His captive people,
[3]Let Jacob rejoice, let Israel be glad.

PSALM 54

Prayer for Defense against Enemies.

For the choir director; on stringed instruments. A +Maskil of David, •when the Ziphites came and said to Saul, "Is not David hiding himself among us?"

SAVE me, O God, by [a]Thy name,
And [1]vindicate me by [b]Thy power.

+ Possibly, *Contemplative,* or *Didactic,* or *Skillful Psalm*
• 1 Sam. 23:19; 26:1
1 [1]Lit., *judge* [a]Ps. 20:1 [b]2 Chr. 20:6

---

8 [1]Or, *Mayest Thou make* [a]Is. 35:10; Joel 1:16 [b]Ps. 35:10
9 [a]Jer. 16:17
10 [1]Lit., *for* [2]Or, *an upright* [a]Ezek. 18:31; Eph. 2:10 [b]Ps. 24:4; Matt. 5:8; Acts 15:9 [c]Ps. 78:37
11 [a]2 Kin. 13:23; 24:20; Jer. 7:15 [b]Is. 63:10, 11
12 [a]Ps. 13:5 [b]Ps. 110:3
13 [1]Or, *turn back* [a]Acts 9:21, 22 [b]Ps. 22:27
14 [a]2 Sam. 12:9; Ps. 26:9 [b]Ps. 25:5 [c]Ps. 35:28; 71:15
15 [1]Or, *mayest Thou open* [a]Ex. 4:15 [b]Ps. 9:14
16 [a]1 Sam. 15:22; Ps. 40:6
17 [a]Ps. 34:18
18 [1]Or, *Mayest Thou build* [a]Ps. 69:35; Is. 51:3 [b]Ps. 102:16; 147:2
19 [1]Or, *sacrifices of righteousness* [2]Lit., *they will offer young bulls* [a]Ps. 4:5 [b]Ps. 66:13, 15

+ Possibly, *Contemplative,* or *Didactic,* or *Skillful Psalm*
• 1 Sam. 22:9
1 [a]Ps. 94:4 [b]Ps. 52:8
2 [a]Ps. 5:9 [b]Ps. 57:4; 59:7 [c]Ps. 101:7
3 [1]*Selah* may mean: *Pause, Crescendo* or *Musical interlude* [a]Ps. 36:4 [b]Ps. 58:3; Jer. 9:5
4 [a]Ps. 120:3
5 [1]Or, *Also* [a]Is. 22:18, 19 [b]Prov. 2:22 [c]Ps. 27:13
6 [a]Ps. 37:34; 40:3 [b]Job 22:19
7 [1]Or, *his destruction* [a]Ps. 49:6 [b]Ps. 10:6
8 [a]Ps. 92:12; 128:3; Jer. 11:16 [b]Ps. 13:5
9 [a]Ps. 30:12 [b]Ps. 54:6

+ I.e., sickness, a sad tone
• Possibly, *Contemplative,* or *Didactic,* or *Skillful Psalm*
1 [a]Ps. 10:4; 14:1-7; 53:1-6 [b]Rom. 3:10
2 [1]Or, *acts wisely* [a]Rom. 3:11 [b]2 Chr. 15:2
3 [a]Rom. 3:12
4 [a]Jer. 4:22
5 [1]Or, *dread* [2]Or possibly, *those* [a]Lev. 26:17, 36; Prov. 28:1 [b]Ps. 141:7; Jer. 8:1, 2; Ezek. 6:5 [c]Ps. 44:7 [d]2 Kin. 17:20; Jer. 6:30; Lam. 5:22
6 [1]Lit., *would be* [2]Or, *restores the fortunes of His people* [3]Or, *Jacob will rejoice, Israel will be glad* [a]Ps. 14:7

2 [a]Hear my prayer, O God;
[b]Give ear to the words of my mouth.
3 For strangers have [a]risen against me,
And [b]violent men have [c]sought my [1]life;
They have [d]not set God before them. [[2]Selah.

4 Behold, [a]God is my helper;
The Lord is [1]the [b]sustainer of my soul.
5 [1]He will [a]recompense the evil to [2]my foes;
[3b]Destroy them [c]in Thy [4]faithfulness.

6 [1a]Willingly I will sacrifice to Thee;
I will give [b]thanks to Thy name, O LORD, for it is good.
7 For [1]He has [a]delivered me from all [2]trouble;
And my eye has [b]looked *with satisfaction* upon my enemies.

PSALM 55

Prayer for the Destruction of the Treacherous.

For the choir director; on stringed instruments. A +Maskil of David.

[a]GIVE ear to my prayer, O God;
And [b]do not hide Thyself from my supplication.
2 Give [a]heed to me, and answer me;
I am restless in my [b]complaint and [1c]am surely distracted,
3 Because of the voice of the enemy,
Because of the [a]pressure of the wicked;
For they [b]bring down [1]trouble upon me,
And in anger they [c]bear a grudge against me.

4 My [a]heart is in anguish within me,
And the terrors of [b]death have fallen upon me.
5 Fear and [a]trembling come upon me;
And [1b]horror has overwhelmed me.
6 And I said, "Oh, that I had wings like a dove!
I would fly away and [1a]be at rest.
7 "Behold, I would wander far away,
I would [a]lodge in the wilderness. [[1]Selah.
8 "I would hasten to my place of refuge
From the [a]stormy wind *and* tempest."

9 [1]Confuse, O Lord, [a]divide their tongues,
For I have seen [b]violence and strife in the city.
10 Day and night they go around her upon her walls;
And iniquity and mischief are in her midst.
11 [a]Destruction is in her midst;
[b]Oppression and deceit do not depart from her [1]streets.

12 For it is [a]not an enemy who reproaches me,
Then I could bear *it*;
Nor is it one who hates me who [b]has exalted himself against me,
Then I could hide myself from him.
13 But it is you, a man [1]my equal,
My [a]companion and my [2b]familiar friend.
14 We who had sweet [1]fellowship together,
[a]Walked in the house of God in the throng.
15 Let [1]death come [a]deceitfully upon them;
Let them [b]go down alive to [2]Sheol,
For evil is in their dwelling, in their midst.

16 As for me, I shall [a]call upon God,
And the LORD will save me.
17 [a]Evening and [b]morning and at [c]noon, I will complain and murmur,
And He will hear my voice.
18 He will [a]redeem my soul in peace [1]from the battle *which is* against me,
For they are [b]many *who strive* with me.
19 God will [a]hear and [1]answer them—
Even the one [b]who [2]sits enthroned from of old— [Selah.
With whom there [3]is no change,
And who [c]do not fear God.
20 He has put forth his hands against [a]those who were at peace with him;
He has [1b]violated his covenant.
21 His [1]speech was [a]smoother than butter,
But his heart was war;
His words were [a]softer than oil,
Yet they were drawn [b]swords.

22 [a]Cast [1]your burden upon the LORD, and He will sustain you;
[b]He will never allow the righteous to [2c]be shaken.
23 But Thou, O God, wilt bring them down to the [1a]pit of destruction;
[b]Men of bloodshed and deceit will [c]not live out half their days.
But I will [d]trust in Thee.

2 [a]Ps. 17:6; 55:1 [b]Ps. 5:1
3 [1]Or, *soul* [2]*Selah* may mean: *Pause, Crescendo* or *Musical interlude* [a]Ps. 86:14 [b]Ps. 18:48; 86:14; 140:1, 4, 11 [c]1 Sam. 20:1; 25:29; Ps. 40:14; 63:9; 70:2 [d]Ps. 36:1
4 [1]Lit., *as those who sustain* [a]Ps. 30:10; 37:40; 118:7 [b]Ps. 37:17, 24; 41:12; 51:12; 145:14; Is. 41:10
5 [1]Lit., *The evil will return* [2]Or, *those who lie in wait for me* [3]Or, *Put to silence* [4]Or, *truth* [a]Ps. 94:23 [b]Ps. 143:12 [c]Ps. 89:49; 96:13; Is. 42:3
6 [1]Or, *With a freewill offering* [a]Num. 15:3; Ps. 116:17 [b]Ps. 50:14
7 [1]Or, *it;* i.e., His name [2]Or, *distress* [a]Ps. 34:6 [b]Ps. 59:10; 92:11; 112:8; 118:7

+ Possibly, *Contemplative,* or *Didactic,* or *Skillful Psalm*
1 [a]Ps. 54:2; 61:1; 86:6 [b]Ps. 27:9
2 [1]Or, *I must moan* [a]Ps. 66:19; 86:6, 7 [b]1 Sam. 1:16; Job 9:27; Ps. 64:1; 77:3; 142:2 [c]Is. 38:14; 59:11; Ezek. 7:16
3 [1]Or, *wickedness* [a]Ps. 17:9 [b]2 Sam. 16:7, 8 [c]Ps. 71:11; 143:3
4 [a]Ps. 38:8 [b]Ps. 18:4, 5; 116:3
5 [1]Lit., *shuddering* [a]Ps. 119:120 [b]Job 21:6; Is. 21:4; Ezek. 7:18
6 [1]Lit., *settle down* [a]Job 3:13
7 [1]*Selah* may mean: *Pause, Crescendo* or *Musical interlude* [a]1 Sam. 23:14
8 [a]Is. 4:6; 25:4; 29:6
9 [1]Lit., *Swallow up* [a]Gen. 11:9 [b]Ps. 11:5; Jer. 6:7
11 [1]Or, *plaza* [a]Ps. 5:9 [b]Ps. 10:7; 17:9
12 [a]Ps. 41:9 [b]Ps. 35:26
13 [1]Lit., *according to my valuation* [2]Or, *acquaintance* [a]2 Sam. 15:12 [b]Job 19:14; Ps. 41:9
14 [1]Lit., *counsel;* or, *intimacy* [a]Ps. 42:4
15 [1]Another reading is *desolations be upon them* [2]I.e., the nether world [a]Ps. 64:7; Prov. 6:15; Is. 47:11; 1 Thess. 5:3 [b]Num. 16:30, 33
16 [a]Ps. 57:2, 3
17 [a]Ps. 141:2; Dan. 6:10; Acts 3:1; 10:3, 30 [b]Ps. 5:3; 88:13; 92:2 [c]Acts 10:9

18 [1]Or, *so that none may approach me* [a]Ps. 103:4 [b]Ps. 56:2
19 [1]Or, *afflict* [2]Or, *abides from* [3]Lit., *are no changes* [a]Ps. 78:59 [b]Deut. 33:27; Ps. 90:2; 93:2 [c]Ps. 36:1
20 [1]Lit., *profaned* [a]Ps. 7:4; 120:7 [b]Num. 30:2; Ps. 89:34
21 [1]Lit., *mouth* [a]Ps. 12:2; 28:3; Prov. 5:3, 4 [b]Ps. 57:4; 59:7
22 [1]Or, *what He has given you* [2]Or, *totter* [a]Ps. 37:5; 1 Pet. 5:7 [b]Ps. 37:24 [c]Ps. 15:5; 112:6
23 [1]Or, *lowest pit* [a]Ps. 73:18; Is. 38:17; Ezek. 28:8 [b]Ps. 5:6 [c]Job 15:32; Prov. 10:27 [d]Ps. 25:2; 56:3

PSALM 56

Supplication for Deliverance, and Grateful Trust in God.

For the choir director; according to +Jonath elem rehokim. A •Mikhtam of David, ∆when the Philistines seized him in Gath.

BE gracious, O God, for man has
[1a]trampled upon me;
[2]Fighting all day long he [b]oppresses me.
2 My foes have [1a]trampled upon me all day long,
For [2]they are many who [b]fight proudly against me.
3 [1]When I am [a]afraid,
[2]I will [b]put my trust in Thee.
4 [a]In God, whose word I praise,
In God I have put my trust;
I shall not be afraid.
[b]What can *mere* [1]man do to me?
5 All day long they [1a]distort my words;
All their [2b]thoughts are against me for evil.
6 They [1a]attack, they lurk,
They [b]watch my [2]steps,
As they have [c]waited *to take* my [3]life.
7 Because of wickedness, [1a]cast them forth,
In anger [b]put down the peoples, O God!

8 Thou [a]hast taken account of my wanderings;
Put my [b]tears in Thy bottle;
Are *they* not in [c]Thy book?
9 Then my enemies will [a]turn back [b]in the day when I call;
This I know, [1]that [c]God is for me.
10 In God, *whose* word I praise,
In the LORD, *whose* word I praise,
11 In God I have put my [1]trust, I shall not be afraid.
What can man do to me?
12 Thy [a]vows are *binding* upon me, O God;
I will render thank offerings to Thee.
13 For Thou hast [a]delivered my soul from death,
[1]Indeed [b]my feet from stumbling,
So that I may [c]walk before God
In the [d]light of the [2]living.

PSALM 57

Prayer for Rescue from Persecutors.

For the choir director; *set to* +Al-tashheth. A •Mikhtam of David, ∆when he fled from Saul, in the cave.

BE gracious to me, O God, be gracious to me,
For my soul [a]takes refuge in Thee;
And in the [b]shadow of Thy wings I will take refuge,
Until destruction [c]passes by.
2 I will cry to God Most High,
To God who [a]accomplishes *all things* for me.
3 He will [a]send from heaven and save me;
He reproaches him who [1b]tramples upon me. [[2]Selah.
God will send forth His [c]lovingkindness and His [3]truth.

4 My soul is among [a]lions;
I must lie among those who breathe forth fire,
Even the sons of men, whose [b]teeth are spears and arrows,
And their [c]tongue a sharp sword.
5 [a]Be exalted above the heavens, O God;
Let Thy glory *be* above all the earth.
6 They have [1]prepared a [a]net for my steps;
My soul is [b]bowed down;
They [c]dug a pit before me;
They *themselves* have [d]fallen into the midst of it. [Selah.

7 [a]My [b]heart is steadfast, O God, my heart is steadfast;
I will sing, yes, I will sing praises!
8 Awake, [a]my glory;
Awake, [b]harp and lyre,
I will awaken the dawn!
9 [a]I will give thanks to Thee, O Lord, among the peoples;
I will sing praises to Thee among the [1]nations.
10 For Thy [a]lovingkindness is great to the heavens,
And Thy [1]truth to the clouds.
11 [a]Be exalted above the heavens, O God;
Let Thy glory *be* above all the earth.

PSALM 58

Prayer for the Punishment of the Wicked.

For the choir director; *set to* +Al-tashheth. A •Mikhtam of David.

DO you indeed [1]speak righteousness, O [2]gods?
Do you [a]judge [3]uprightly, O sons of men?
2 No, in heart you [a]work unrighteousness;
On earth you [b]weigh out the violence of your hands.
3 The wicked are estranged [a]from the womb;
These who speak lies [b]go astray from [1]birth.
4 They have venom like the [a]venom of a serpent;
Like a deaf cobra that stops up its ear,

+ Or, *The silent dove of those who are far off*, or, *The dove of the distant terebinths.*
• Possibly, *Epigrammatic Poem*, or *Atonement Psalm*
∆ 1 Sam. 21:10, 11
1 [1]Or, *snapped at* [2]Or, *A fighting man* [a]Ps. 57:3 [b]Ps. 17:9
2 [1]Or, *snapped at* [2]Or, *many are fighting* [a]Ps. 35:25; 57:3; 124:3 [b]Ps. 35:1
3 [1]Lit., *In the day* [2]Or, *I am one who puts* [a]Ps. 55:4, 5 [b]Ps. 11:1
4 [1]Lit., *flesh* [a]Ps. 56:10, 11 [b]Ps. 118:6; Heb. 13:6
5 [1]Or, *trouble my affairs* [2]Or, *purposes* [a]2 Pet. 3:16 [b]Ps. 41:7
6 [1]Or, *stir up strife* [2]Lit., *heels* [3]Lit., *soul* [a]Ps. 59:3; 140:2; Is. 54:15 [b]Ps. 17:11 [c]Ps. 71:10
7 [1]Or, *will they have escape?* [a]Ps. 36:12; Prov. 19:5; Ezek. 17:15; Rom. 2:3 [b]Ps. 55:23
8 [a]Ps. 139:3 [b]2 Kin. 20:5; Ps. 39:12 [c]Mal. 3:16
9 [1]Or, *because* [a]Ps. 9:3 [b]Ps. 102:2 [c]Ps. 41:11; 118:6; Rom. 8:31
11 [1]Or, *trust without fear*
12 [a]Ps. 50:14
13 [1]Or, *Hast Thou not delivered* [2]Or, *life* [a]Ps. 33:19; 49:15; 86:13 [b]Ps. 116:8 [c]Ps. 116:9 [d]Job 33:30

+ Lit., *Do Not Destroy*
• Possibly, *Epigrammatic Poem* or *Atonement Psalm*
∆ 1 Sam. 22:1; 24:3
1 [a]Ps. 2:12; 34:22 [b]Ruth 2:12; Ps. 17:8; 36:7; 63:7; 91:4 [c]Is. 26:20
2 [a]Ps. 138:8
3 [1]Or, *snaps at* [2]*Selah* may mean: *Pause, Crescendo* or *Musical interlude* [3]Or, *faithfulness* [a]Ps. 18:16; 144:5, 7 [b]Ps. 56:2 [c]Ps. 25:10; 40:11
4 [a]Ps. 35:17; 58:6 [b]Prov. 30:14 [c]Ps. 55:21; 59:7; 64:3; Prov. 12:18
5 [a]Ps. 57:11; 108:5
6 [1]Or, *spread* [a]Ps. 10:9; 31:4; 35:7; 140:5 [b]Ps. 145:14 [c]Ps. 7:15 [d]Prov. 26:27; 28:10; Eccl. 10:8
7 [a]Ps. 57:7-11; 108:1-5 [b]Ps. 112:7
8 [a]Ps. 16:9; 30:12 [b]Ps. 150:3
9 [1]Lit., *peoples* [a]Ps. 108:3
10 [1]Or, *faithfulness* [a]Ps. 36:5; 103:11; 108:4
11 [a]Ps. 57:5; 108:5

+ Lit., *Do Not Destroy*
• Possibly, *Epigrammatic Poem* or *Atonement Psalm*
1 [1]Another reading is *speak righteousness in silence* [2]Or, *mighty ones* or *judges* [3]Or, *uprightly the sons of men* [a]Ps. 82:2
2 [a]Mal. 3:15 [b]Ps. 94:20; Is. 10:1
3 [1]Lit., *the womb* [a]Ps. 51:5; Is. 48:8 [b]Ps. 53:3
4 [a]Deut. 32:33; Ps. 140:3

5 So that it [a]does not hear the voice
of [1b]charmers,
Or a skillful caster of spells.

6 O God, [a]shatter their teeth in their
mouth;
Break out the fangs of the young
lions, O LORD.
7 Let them [a]flow away like water that
runs off;
When he [1b]aims his arrows, let
them be as [2]headless shafts.
8 *Let them be* as a snail which [1]melts
away as it goes along,
Like the [a]miscarriages of a woman
which never see the sun.
9 Before your [a]pots can feel *the fire of*
thorns,
He will [b]sweep them away with a
whirlwind, the [1]green and the
burning alike.

10 The [a]righteous will rejoice when he
[b]sees the vengeance;
He will [c]wash his feet in the blood
of the wicked.
11 And men will say, "Surely there is
a [1a]reward for the righteous;
Surely there is a God who [b]judges
[2]on earth!"

PSALM 59

Prayer for Deliverance from Enemies.

For the choir director; *set to* +Al-tashheth. A •Mikhtam of David, ^Δ^when Saul sent *men,* and they watched the house in order to kill him.

[a]DELIVER me from my enemies, O
my God;
[1b]Set me *securely* on high away
from those who rise up against
me.
2 Deliver me from [a]those who do
iniquity,
And save me from [b]men of bloodshed.
3 For behold, they [a]have [1]set an
ambush for my [2]life;
[3]Fierce men [4a]launch an attack
against me,
[b]Not for my transgression nor for
my sin, O LORD,
4 [1a]For no guilt of *mine,* they run
and set themselves against me.
[b]Arouse Thyself to [2]help me, and
see!
5 And Thou, [a]O LORD God of hosts,
the God of Israel,
Awake to [1b]punish all the nations;
[c]Do not be gracious to any *who are*
treacherous in iniquity. [[2]Selah.
6 They [a]return at evening, they howl
like a [b]dog,
And go around the city.
7 Behold, they [a]belch forth with their
mouth;
[b]Swords are in their lips,
For, *they say,* "[c]Who hears?"
8 But Thou, O LORD, dost [a]laugh at
them;
Thou dost [b]scoff at all the nations.

9 *Because of* [1]his [a]strength I will
watch for Thee,
For God is my [b]stronghold.
10 [1]My God [a]in His lovingkindness
will meet me;
God will let me [b]look *triumphantly*
upon [2]my foes.
11 Do not slay them, [a]lest my people
forget;
[1b]Scatter them by Thy power, and
bring them down,
O Lord, [c]our shield.
12 [1]*On account of* the [a]sin of their
mouth *and* the words of their
lips,
Let them even be [b]caught in their
pride,
And on account of [c]curses and [2]lies
which they utter.
13 [1a]Destroy *them* in wrath, [1]destroy
them, that they may be no more;
That *men* may [b]know that God
[2]rules in Jacob,
To the ends of the earth. [Selah.
14 And they [a]return at evening, they
howl like a dog,
And go around the city.
15 They [a]wander about [1]for food,
And [2]growl if they are not satisfied.

16 But as for me, I shall [a]sing of Thy
strength;
Yes, I shall [b]joyfully sing of Thy
lovingkindness in the [c]morning,
For Thou hast been my [d]strong-
hold,
And a [e]refuge in the day of my
distress.
17 [a]O my strength, I will sing praises
to Thee;
For God is my [b]stronghold, the
[1]God who shows me lovingkindness.

PSALM 60

Lament over Defeat in Battle, and Prayer for Help.

For the choir director; according to +Shushan Eduth. A •Mikhtam of David, to teach; ^Δ^when he struggled with Aram-naharaim and with Aram-zobah, and Joab returned, and smote twelve thousand of Edom in the Valley of Salt.

O GOD, [a]Thou hast rejected us. Thou
hast [1b]broken us;
Thou hast been [c]angry; O, [d]restore
us.
2 Thou hast made the [1a]land quake,
Thou hast split it open;
[b]Heal its breaches, for it totters.

5 [1]Or, *whisperers* [a]Jer. 8:17 [b]Eccl. 10:11
6 [a]Job 4:10; Ps. 3:7
7 [1]Lit., *bends* [2]Lit., *though they were cut off* [a]Josh. 2:11; 7:5; Ps. 112:10; Is. 13:7; Ezek. 21:7 [b]Ps. 64:3
8 [1]I.e., secretes slime [a]Job 3:16; Eccl. 6:3
9 [1]Lit., *living* [a]Ps. 118:12; Eccl. 7:6 [b]Job 27:21; Ps. 83:15; Prov. 10:25
10 [a]Job 22:19; Ps. 32:11; 64:10; 107:42 [b]Deut. 32:43; Ps. 91:8; Jer. 11:20; 20:12 [c]Ps. 68:23
11 [1]Lit., *fruit* [2]Or, *in* [a]Ps. 18:20; 19:11; Is. 3:10; Luke 6:23, 35 [b]Ps. 9:8; 67:4; 75:7; 94:2

+ Lit., *Do Not Destroy*
• Possibly, *Epigrammatic Poem* or *Atonement Psalm*
Δ 1 Sam. 19:11
1 [1]Or, *Mayest Thou put me in an inaccessibly high place* [a]Ps. 143:9 [b]Ps. 20:1; 69:29
2 [a]Ps. 28:3; 36:12; 53:4; 92:7; 94:16 [b]Ps. 26:9; 139:19; Prov. 29:10
3 [1]Or, *lain in wait* [2]Lit., *soul* [3]Or, *Strong* [4]Or, *stir up strife* [a]Ps. 56:6 [b]1 Sam. 24:11; Ps. 7:3, 4; 69:4
4 [1]Lit., *Without guilt* [2]Lit., *meet* [a]Ps. 35:19 [b]Ps. 7:6; 35:23
5 [1]Lit., *visit* [2]*Selah* may mean: *Pause, Crescendo* or *Musical interlude* [a]Ps. 69:6; 80:4; 84:8 [b]Ps. 9:5; Is. 26:14 [c]Is. 2:9; Jer. 18:23
6 [a]Ps. 59:14 [b]Ps. 22:16
7 [a]Ps. 94:4; Prov. 15:2, 28 [b]Ps. 57:4; Prov. 12:18 [c]Job 22:13; Ps. 10:11; 73:11; 94:7
8 [a]Ps. 37:13; Prov. 1:26 [b]Ps. 2:4
9 [1]Many mss. and some ancient versions read *My strength* [a]Ps. 18:17 [b]Ps. 9:9; 62:2
10 [1]Many mss. and some ancient versions read *The God of my lovingkindness* [2]Lit., *those who lie in wait for me* [a]Ps. 21:3 [b]Ps. 54:7
11 [1]Or, *Make them wander* [a]Deut. 4:9; 6:12 [b]Ps. 106:27; 144:6; Is. 33:3 [c]Ps. 84:9
12 [1]Or, *The sin of their mouth is the word of their lips,* [2]Lit., *lying* [a]Prov. 12:13 [b]Zeph. 3:11 [c]Ps. 10:7
13 [1]Lit., *Bring to an end* [2]Or, *is Ruler* [a]Ps. 104:35 [b]Ps. 83:18
14 [a]Ps. 59:6
15 [1]Or, *to devour* [2]Another reading is *tarry all night* [a]Job 15:23
16 [a]Ps. 21:13 [b]Ps. 101:1 [c]Ps. 5:3; 88:13 [d]Ps. 59:9 [e]2 Sam. 22:3; Ps. 46:1
17 [1]Lit., *God of my lovingkindness* [a]Ps. 59:9 [b]Ps. 59:10

+ Lit., *The lily of testimony*
• Possibly, *Epigrammatic Poem* or *Atonement Psalm*
Δ 2 Sam. 8:3, 13; 1 Chr. 18:3, 12
1 [1]Or, *broken out upon us* [a]Ps. 44:9 [b]2 Sam. 5:20 [c]Ps. 79:5 [d]Ps. 80:3
2 [1]Or, *earth* [a]Ps. 18:7 [b]2 Chr. 7:14; Is. 30:26

3 Thou hast [1a]made Thy people experience hardship;
Thou hast given us [2]wine to [b]drink that makes us stagger.
4 Thou hast given a [a]banner to those who fear Thee,
That it may be displayed because of the truth. [[1]Selah.
5 [a]That Thy [b]beloved may be delivered,
[c]Save with Thy right hand, and answer [1]us!

6 God has spoken in His [1a]holiness:
"I will exult, I will portion out [b]Shechem and measure out the valley of [c]Succoth.
7 "[a]Gilead is Mine, and Manasseh is Mine;
[b]Ephraim also is the [1]helmet of My head;
Judah is My [2c]scepter.
8 "[a]Moab is My washbowl;
Over [b]Edom I shall throw My shoe;
Shout loud, O [c]Philistia, because of Me!"

9 Who will bring me into the besieged city?
Who [1]will lead me to Edom?
10 Hast not Thou Thyself, O God, [a]rejected us?
And [b]wilt Thou not go forth with our armies, O God?
11 O give us help against the adversary,
For [a]deliverance [1]by man is in vain.
12 [1]Through God we shall [a]do valiantly,
And it is He who will [b]tread down our adversaries.

PSALM 61

Confidence in God's Protection.

For the choir director; on a stringed instrument. *A Psalm* of David.

[a]HEAR my cry, O God;
[b]Give heed to my prayer.
2 From the [a]end of the earth I call to Thee, when my heart is [b]faint;
Lead me to [c]the rock that is higher than I.
3 For Thou hast been a [a]refuge for me,
A [b]tower of strength [1]against the enemy.
4 Let me [1a]dwell in Thy tent forever;
Let me [b]take refuge in the shelter of Thy wings. [[2]Selah.

5 For Thou hast heard my [a]vows, O God;
Thou hast given *me* the inheritance of those who [b]fear Thy name.
6 Thou wilt [1a]prolong the king's [2]life;
His years will be as many generations.

3 [1]Lit., *caused Thy people to see* [2]Lit., *wine of staggering* [a]Ps. 66:12; 71:20 [b]Ps. 75:8; Is. 51:17, 22; Jer. 25:15
4 [1]*Selah* may mean: *Pause, Crescendo* or *Musical interlude* [a]Ps. 20:5; Is. 5:26; 11:12; 13:2
5 [1]Some authorities read *me* [a]Ps. 60:5-12; 108:6-13 [b]Deut. 33:12; Ps. 127:2; Is. 5:1; Jer. 11:15 [c]Ps. 17:7
6 [1]Or, *sanctuary* [a]Ps. 89:35 [b]Gen. 12:6; 33:18; Josh. 17:7 [c]Gen. 33:17; Josh. 13:27
7 [1]Lit., *protection* [2]Or, *lawgiver* [a]Josh. 13:31 [b]Deut. 33:17 [c]Gen. 49:10
8 [a]2 Sam. 8:2 [b]2 Sam. 8:14 [c]2 Sam. 8:1
9 [1]Or, *has led*
10 [a]Ps. 60:1; 108:11 [b]Josh. 7:12; Ps. 44:9
11 [1]Lit., *of* [a]Ps. 146:3
12 [1]Or, *In* or *With* [a]Num. 24:18; Ps. 118:16 [b]Ps. 44:5; Is. 63:3

1 [a]Ps. 64:1 [b]Ps. 86:6
2 [a]Ps. 42:6 [b]Ps. 77:3 [c]Ps. 18:2; 94:22
3 [1]Lit., *from* [a]Ps. 62:7 [b]Ps. 59:9; Prov. 18:10
4 [1]Or, *sojourn* [2]*Selah* may mean: *Pause, Crescendo* or *Musical interlude* [a]Ps. 23:6; 27:4 [b]Ps. 17:8; 91:4
5 [a]Job 22:27; Ps. 56:12 [b]Deut. 28:58; Neh. 1:11; Ps. 86:11; 102:15; Is. 59:19; Mal. 2:5; 4:2
6 [1]Lit., *add days to* [2]Lit., *days* [a]Ps. 21:4
7 [1]Or, *sit enthroned* [a]Ps. 41:12 [b]Ps. 40:11
8 [a]Judg. 5:3; Ps. 30:4; 33:2; 71:22 [b]Ps. 65:1; Is. 19:21

+ Cf. 1 Chr. 16:41; 25:1; Ps. 39 and 77 titles
1 [a]Ps. 33:20 [b]Ps. 37:39
2 [a]Ps. 89:26 [b]Ps. 59:17; 62:6
3 [a]Is. 30:13
4 [1]Lit., *his* [2]*Selah* may mean: *Pause, Crescendo* or *Musical interlude* [a]Ps. 4:2 [b]Ps. 28:3; 55:21
5 [a]Ps. 62:1
6 [a]Ps. 62:2
7 [a]Ps. 85:9; Jer. 3:23 [b]Ps. 46:1
8 [a]Ps. 37:3, 5; 52:8; Is. 26:4 [b]1 Sam. 1:15; Ps. 42:4; Lam. 2:19
9 [a]Ps. 49:2 [b]Job 7:16; Ps. 39:5; Is. 40:17 [c]Ps. 116:11 [d]Is. 40:15

7 He will [1]abide [a]before God forever;
Appoint [b]lovingkindness and truth, that they may preserve him.
8 So I will [a]sing praise to Thy name forever,
That I may [b]pay my vows day by day.

PSALM 62

God Alone a Refuge from Treachery and Oppression.

For the choir director; +according to Jeduthun. A Psalm of David.

[a]MY soul *waits* in silence for God only;
From Him [b]is my salvation.
2 He only is my [a]rock and my salvation,
My [b]stronghold; I shall not be greatly shaken.

3 How long will you assail a man,
That you may murder *him,* all of you,
Like a [a]leaning wall, like a tottering fence?
4 They have counseled only to thrust him down from his high position;
They [a]delight in falsehood;
They [b]bless with [1]their mouth,
But inwardly they curse. [[2]Selah.

5 My soul, [a]wait in silence for God only,
For my hope is from Him.
6 He only is [a]my rock and my salvation,
My stronghold; I shall not be shaken.
7 On God my [a]salvation and my glory *rest;*
The rock of my strength, my [b]refuge is in God.
8 [a]Trust in Him at all times, O people;
[b]Pour out your heart before Him;
God is a refuge for us. [Selah.

9 Men of [a]low degree are only [b]vanity, and men of rank are a [c]lie;
In the [d]balances they go up;
They are together lighter than breath.
10 [a]Do not trust in oppression,
And do not [1]vainly hope in [b]robbery;
If riches increase, [c]do not set *your* heart *upon them.*

11 [1]Once God has [a]spoken;
[2]Twice I have heard this:
That [b]power belongs to God;

10 [1]Lit., *become vain in robbery* [a]Is. 30:12 [b]Is. 61:8; Ezek. 22:29; Nah. 3:1 [c]Job 31:25; Ps. 49:6; 52:7; Mark 10:24; Luke 12:15; 1 Tim. 6:10
11 [1]Or, *One thing* [2]Or, *These two things I have heard* [a]Job 33:14; 40:5 [b]Ps. 59:17; Rev. 19:1

12 And lovingkindness [a]is Thine, O Lord,
For Thou [b]dost recompense a man according to his work.

PSALM 63

The Thirsting Soul Satisfied in God.

A Psalm of David, [+]when he was in the wilderness of Judah.

O GOD, [a]Thou art my God; I shall seek Thee [1]earnestly;
My soul [b]thirsts for Thee, my flesh [2]yearns for Thee,
In a [c]dry and weary land where there is no water.
2 Thus I have [a]beheld Thee in the sanctuary,
To see Thy power and Thy glory.
3 Because Thy [a]lovingkindness is better than life,
My lips will praise Thee.
4 So I will bless Thee [a]as long as I live;
I will [b]lift up my hands in Thy name.
5 My soul is [a]satisfied as with [1]marrow and fatness,
And my mouth offers [b]praises with joyful lips.

6 When I remember Thee [a]on my bed,
I meditate on Thee in the [b]night watches,
7 For [a]Thou hast been my help,
And in the [b]shadow of Thy wings I sing for joy.
8 My soul [a]clings [1]to Thee;
Thy [b]right hand upholds me.

9 But those who [a]seek my [1]life, to destroy it,
Will go into the [2b]depths of the earth.
10 [1]They will be [2a]delivered over to the power of the sword;
They will be a [3b]prey for foxes.
11 But the [a]king will rejoice in God;
Everyone who [b]swears by Him will glory,
For the [c]mouths of those who speak lies will be stopped.

PSALM 64

Prayer for Deliverance from Secret Enemies.

For the choir director. A Psalm of David.

HEAR my voice, O God, in [a]my [1]complaint;
[b]Preserve my life from dread of the enemy.
2 Hide me from the [a]secret counsel of evildoers,
From the tumult of [b]those who do iniquity,
3 Who [a]have sharpened their tongue like a sword.
They [b]aimed bitter speech *as* their arrow,
4 To [a]shoot [1]from concealment at the blameless;
Suddenly they shoot at him, and [b]do not fear.
5 They [1]hold fast to themselves an evil purpose;
They [2]talk of [a]laying snares secretly;
They say, "[b]Who can see them?"
6 They [1]devise injustices, *saying,*
"We are [2]ready with a well-conceived plot";
For the [3a]inward thought and the heart of a man are [4]deep.

7 But [a]God [1]will shoot at them with an arrow;
Suddenly [2]they will be wounded.
8 So [1]they [2]will [a]make him stumble;
[b]Their own tongue is against them;
All who see them will [c]shake the head.
9 Then all men [1]will [a]fear,
And [2]will [b]declare the work of God,
And [3]will consider [4]what He has done.
10 The righteous man will be [a]glad in the LORD, and will [b]take refuge in Him;
And all the upright in heart will glory.

PSALM 65

God's Abundant Favor to Earth and Man.

For the choir director. A Psalm of David. A Song.

THERE will be silence [1]before Thee, *and* praise in Zion, O God;
And to Thee the [a]vow will be performed.
2 O Thou who dost hear prayer,
To Thee [a]all [1]men come.
3 [1a]Iniquities prevail against me;
As for our transgressions, Thou dost [2b]forgive them.
4 How [a]blessed is the one whom Thou dost [b]choose, and bring near *to Thee,*
To dwell in Thy courts.
We will be [c]satisfied with the goodness of Thy house,
Thy holy temple.

5 By [a]awesome *deeds* Thou dost answer us in righteousness, O [b]God of our salvation,
Thou who art the trust of all the [c]ends of the earth and of the farthest [1d]sea;
6 Who dost [a]establish the mountains by His strength,
Being [b]girded with might;
7 Who dost [a]still the roaring of the seas,
The roaring of their waves,
And the [b]tumult of the peoples.

12 [a]Ps. 86:5; 103:8; 130:7 [b]Job 34:11; Ps. 28:4; Jer. 17:10; Matt. 16:27; Rom. 2:6; 1 Cor. 3:8; Rev. 2:23

\+ 1 Sam. 22:5; 23:14
1 [1]Lit., *early* [2]Lit., *faints*
[a]Ps. 118:28 [b]Ps. 42:2; 84:2; Matt. 5:6 [c]Ps. 143:6
2 [a]Ps. 27:4
3 [a]Ps. 69:16
4 [a]Ps. 104:33; 146:2 [b]Ps. 28:2; 143:6
5 [1]Lit., *fat*
[a]Ps. 36:8 [b]Ps. 71:23
6 [a]Ps. 4:4 [b]Ps. 16:7; 42:8; 119:55
7 [a]Ps. 27:9 [b]Ps. 17:8
8 [1]Lit., *after*
[a]Num. 32:12; Deut. 1:36; Hos. 6:3 [b]Ps. 18:35; 41:12
9 [1]Lit., *soul* [2]Lit., *lowest places*
[a]Ps. 40:14 [b]Ps. 55:15
10 [1]Lit., *They will pour him out* [2]Lit., *poured out by* [3]Lit., *portion*
[a]Jer. 18:21; Ezek. 35:5 [b]Lam. 5:18
11 [a]Ps. 21:1 [b]Deut. 6:13; Is. 45:23; 65:16 [c]Job 5:16; Ps. 107:42; Rom. 3:19

1 [1]Or, *concern*
[a]Ps. 55:2 [b]Ps. 140:1
2 [a]Ps. 56:6 [b]Ps. 59:2
3 [a]Ps. 140:3 [b]Ps. 58:7
4 [1]Lit., *in*
[a]Ps. 10:8; 11:2 [b]Ps. 55:19
5 [1]Lit., *make firm* [2]Lit., *tell of*
[a]Ps. 140:5 [b]Job 22:13; Ps. 10:11
6 [1]Or, *search out* [2]Lit., *complete* [3]Or, *inward part* [4]Or, *unsearchable*
[a]Ps. 49:11
7 [1]Or, *shot* [2]Or, *they were wounded;* lit., *their wounds occurred*
[a]Ps. 7:12, 13
8 [1]Or, *they make their tongue a stumbling for themselves* [2]Or, *made*
[a]Ps. 9:3 [b]Prov. 12:13; 18:7 [c]Ps. 22:7; 44:14; Jer. 18:16; 48:27; Lam. 2:15
9 [1]Or, *feared* [2]Or, *declared* [3]Or, *considered* [4]Lit., *His work*
[a]Ps. 40:3 [b]Jer. 51:10
10 [a]Job 22:19; Ps. 32:11 [b]Ps. 11:1; 25:20

1 [1]Lit., *to*
[a]Ps. 116:18
2 [1]Lit., *flesh*
[a]Ps. 86:9; 145:21; Is. 66:23
3 [1]Lit., *Words of iniquities* [2]Lit., *cover over, atone for*
[a]Ps. 38:4; 40:12 [b]Ps. 79:9
4 [a]Ps. 33:12; 84:4 [b]Ps. 4:3 [c]Ps. 36:8

5 [1]Or, *seas* [a]Ps. 45:4; 66:3 [b]Ps. 85:4 [c]Ps. 22:27; 48:10 [d]Ps. 107:23
6 [a]Ps. 95:4 [b]Ps. 93:1
7 [a]Ps. 89:9; 93:3, 4; 107:29; Matt. 8:26 [b]Ps. 2:1; 74:23; Is. 17:12, 13

8 And they who dwell in the [a]ends *of the earth* stand in awe of Thy signs;
Thou dost make the [1]dawn and the sunset shout for joy.

9 Thou dost visit the earth, and [a]cause it to overflow;
Thou dost greatly [b]enrich it;
The [1c]stream of God is full of water;
Thou dost prepare their [d]grain, for thus Thou dost prepare [2]the earth.
10 Thou dost water its furrows abundantly;
Thou dost [1]settle its ridges;
Thou dost soften it [a]with showers;
Thou dost bless its growth.
11 Thou hast crowned the year [1]with Thy [2a]bounty,
And Thy [3]paths [b]drip *with* fatness.
12 [a]The pastures of the wilderness drip,
And the [b]hills gird themselves with rejoicing.
13 The meadows are [a]clothed with flocks,
And the valleys are [b]covered with grain;
They [c]shout for joy, yes, they sing.

PSALM 66

Praise for God's Mighty Deeds and for His Answer to Prayer.

For the choir director. A Song. A Psalm.

[a]SHOUT joyfully to God, all the earth;
2 Sing the [a]glory of His name;
Make His [b]praise glorious.
3 Say to God, "How [a]awesome are Thy works!
Because of the greatness of Thy power Thine enemies will [1b]give feigned obedience to Thee.
4 "[a]All the earth will worship Thee,
And will [b]sing praises to Thee;
They will sing praises to Thy name." [[1]Selah.

5 [a]Come and see the works of God,
Who is [b]awesome in *His* deeds toward the sons of men.
6 He [a]turned the sea into dry land;
They passed through [b]the river on foot;
There let us [c]rejoice in Him!
7 He [a]rules by His might forever;
His [b]eyes keep watch on the nations;
Let not the rebellious [c]exalt themselves. [Selah.

8 Bless our God, O peoples,
And [1a]sound His praise abroad,
9 Who [1a]keeps us in life,
And [b]does not allow our feet to [2]slip.
10 For Thou hast [a]tried us, O God;
Thou hast [b]refined us as silver is refined.
11 Thou [a]didst bring us into the net;
Thou didst lay an oppressive burden upon our loins.
12 Thou didst make men [a]ride over our heads;
We went through [b]fire and through water;
Yet Thou [c]didst bring us out into *a place of* abundance.
13 I shall [a]come into Thy house with burnt offerings;
I shall [b]pay Thee my vows,
14 Which my lips uttered
And my mouth spoke when I was [a]in distress.
15 I shall [a]offer to Thee burnt offerings of fat beasts,
With the smoke of [b]rams;
I shall make *an offering of* [1]bulls with male goats. [Selah.

16 [a]Come *and* hear, all who [1]fear God,
And I will [b]tell of what He has done for my soul.
17 I cried to Him with my mouth,
And [1]He was [a]extolled with my tongue.
18 If I [1a]regard wickedness in my heart,
The [b]Lord [2]will not [3]hear;
19 But certainly [a]God has heard;
He has given heed to the voice of my prayer.
20 [a]Blessed be God,
Who [b]has not turned away my prayer,
Nor His lovingkindness from me.

PSALM 67

The Nations Exhorted to Praise God.

For the choir director; with stringed instruments. A Psalm. A Song.

GOD be gracious to us and [a]bless us,
And [b]cause His face to shine [1]upon us— [[2]Selah.
2 That [a]Thy way may be known on the earth,
[b]Thy salvation among all nations.
3 Let the [a]peoples praise Thee, O God;
Let all the peoples praise Thee.
4 Let the [a]nations be glad and sing for joy;
For Thou wilt [b]judge the peoples with uprightness,
And [c]guide the nations on the earth. [Selah.
5 Let the [a]peoples praise Thee, O God;
Let all the peoples praise Thee.
6 The [a]earth has yielded its produce;
God, our God, [b]blesses us.
7 God blesses us,
[1]That [a]all the ends of the earth may fear Him.

8 [1]Lit., *the outgoings of the morning and evening* [a]Ps. 2:8; 139:9; Is. 24:16
9 [1]Or, *channel* [2]Lit., *it* [a]Lev. 26:4; Job 5:10; Ps. 68:9; 104:13; 147:8; Jer. 5:24 [b]Ps. 104:24 [c]Ps. 46:4 [d]Ps. 104:14; 147:14
10 [1]Or, *smooth* [a]Deut. 32:2; Ps. 72:6; 147:8
11 [1]Lit., *of* [2]Or, *goodness* [3]I.e., wagon tracks [a]Ps. 104:28 [b]Job 36:28; Ps. 147:14
12 [a]Job 38:26, 27; Joel 2:22 [b]Ps. 98:8; Is. 55:12
13 [a]Ps. 144:13; Is. 30:23 [b]Ps. 72:16 [c]Ps. 98:8; Is. 44:23; 55:12

1 [a]Ps. 81:1; 95:1; 98:4; 100:1
2 [a]Ps. 79:9; Is. 42:8 [b]Is. 42:12
3 [1]Lit., *deceive* [a]Ps. 47:2; 65:5; 145:6 [b]Ps. 18:44; 81:15
4 [1]*Selah* may mean: *Pause, Crescendo* or *Musical interlude* [a]Ps. 22:27; 67:7; 86:9; 117:1; Zech. 14:16 [b]Ps. 67:4
5 [a]Ps. 46:8 [b]Ps. 106:22
6 [a]Ex. 14:21; Ps. 106:9 [b]Josh. 3:16; Ps. 114:3 [c]Ps. 105:43
7 [a]Ps. 145:13 [b]Ps. 11:4 [c]Ps. 140:8
8 [1]Lit., *cause to hear the sound of His praise* [a]Ps. 98:4
9 [1]Lit., *puts our soul in life* [2]Or, *dodder, stumble* [a]Ps. 30:3 [b]Ps. 121:3
10 [a]Job 23:10; Ps. 7:9; 17:3; 26:2 [b]Is. 48:10; Zech. 13:9; Mal. 3:3; 1 Pet. 1:7
11 [a]Lam. 1:13; Ezek. 12:13
12 [a]Is. 51:23 [b]Ps. 78:21; Is. 43:2 [c]Ps. 18:19
13 [a]Ps. 96:8; Jer. 17:26 [b]Ps. 22:25; 116:14; Eccl. 5:4
14 [a]Ps. 18:6
15 [1]Or, *cattle* [a]Ps. 51:19 [b]Num. 6:14
16 [1]Or, *revere* [a]Ps. 34:11 [b]Ps. 71:15, 24
17 [1]Or, *praise was under my tongue* [a]Ps. 30:1
18 [1]Or, *had regarded* [2]Or, *would* [3]Or, *have heard* [a]Job 36:21; John 9:31 [b]Job 27:9; Ps. 18:41; Prov. 1:28; 28:9; Is. 1:15; James 4:3
19 [a]Ps. 18:6; 116:1, 2
20 [a]Ps. 68:35 [b]Ps. 22:24

1 [1]Lit., *with* [2]*Selah* may mean: *Pause, Crescendo* or *Musical interlude* [a]Num. 6:25 [b]Ps. 4:6; 31:16; 80:3, 7, 19; 119:135
2 [a]Ps. 98:2; Acts 18:25; Titus 2:11 [b]Is. 52:10
3 [a]Ps. 66:4
4 [a]Ps. 100:1, 2 [b]Ps. 9:8; 96:10, 13; 98:9 [c]Ps. 47:8
5 [a]Ps. 67:3
6 [a]Lev. 26:4; Ps. 85:12; Ezek. 34:27; Zech. 8:12 [b]Ps. 29:11; 115:12
7 [1]Or, *And let all . . . earth fear Him* [a]Ps. 22:27; 33:8

PSALM 68

The God of Sinai and of the Sanctuary.

For the choir director. A Psalm of David. A Song.

1 LET [a]God arise, [2]let His enemies be scattered;
And [3]let those who hate Him flee before Him.
2 As [a]smoke is driven away, *so* drive *them* away;
As [b]wax melts before the fire,
So let the [c]wicked perish before God.
3 But let the [a]righteous be glad; let them exult before God;
Yes, let them rejoice with gladness.
4 Sing to God, [a]sing praises to His name;
[1b]Lift up *a song* for Him who [c]rides through the deserts,
Whose [d]name is [2]the LORD, and exult before Him.

5 A [a]father of the fatherless and a [b]judge [1]for the widows,
Is God in His [c]holy habitation.
6 God [1a]makes a home for the lonely;
He [b]leads out the prisoners into prosperity,
Only [c]the rebellious dwell in a parched land.

7 O God, when Thou [a]didst go forth before Thy people,
When Thou didst [b]march through the wilderness, [[1]Selah.
8 The [a]earth quaked;
The [b]heavens also dropped *rain* at the presence of God;
[1c]Sinai itself *quaked* at the presence of God, the God of Israel.
9 Thou didst [a]shed abroad a plentiful rain, O God;
Thou didst confirm Thine inheritance, when it was [1]parched.
10 Thy creatures settled in it;
Thou didst [a]provide in Thy goodness for the poor, O God.

11 The Lord gives the [1]command;
The [a]women who proclaim the *good* tidings are a great host:
12 "[a]Kings of armies flee, they flee,
And she who remains at home will [b]divide the spoil!"
13 [1]When you lie down [a]among the [2]sheepfolds,
You are like the wings of a dove covered with silver,
And its pinions with glistening gold.
14 When the Almighty [a]scattered the kings [1]there,
It was snowing in [b]Zalmon.

15 A [1a]mountain of God is the mountain of Bashan;
A mountain *of many* peaks is the mountain of Bashan.
16 Why do you look with envy, O mountains with *many* peaks,

1 [1]Or, *God shall* [2]Or, *His enemies shall* [3]Or, *those who hate Him shall* [a]Num. 10:35; Ps. 12:5; 132:8
2 [a]Ps. 37:20; Is. 9:18; Hos. 13:3 [b]Ps. 22:14; 97:5; Mic. 1:4 [c]Ps. 9:3; 37:20; 80:16
3 [a]Ps. 32:11; 64:10; 97:12
4 [1]Or, *Cast up a highway* [2]Heb., *YAH* [a]Ps. 66:2 [b]Is. 57:14; 62:10 [c]Deut. 33:26; Ps. 18:10; 68:33; Is. 40:3 [d]Ex. 6:3; Ps. 83:18
5 [1]Lit., *of* [a]Ps. 10:14; 146:9 [b]Deut. 10:18 [c]Deut. 26:15
6 [1]Lit., *makes the solitary to dwell in a house* [a]Ps. 107:4-7; 113:9 [b]Ps. 69:33; 102:20; 107:10, 14; 146:7; Acts 12:7; 16:26 [c]Ps. 78:17; 107:34, 40
7 [1]*Selah* may mean: *Pause, Crescendo* or *Musical interlude* [a]Ex. 13:21; Ps. 78:14; Hab. 3:13 [b]Judg. 5:4; Ps. 78:52
8 [1]Lit., *This is Sinai* which [a]Ex. 19:18; Judg. 5:4; 2 Sam. 22:8; Ps. 77:18; Jer. 10:10 [b]Judg. 5:4; Ps. 18:9; Is. 45:8 [c]Ex. 19:18; Judg. 5:5
9 [1]Lit., *weary* [a]Lev. 26:4; Deut. 11:11; Job 5:10; Ezek. 34:26
10 [a]Ps. 65:9; 74:19; 78:20; 107:9
11 [1]Lit., *word* [a]Ex. 15:20; 1 Sam. 18:6
12 [a]Josh. 10:16; Judg. 5:19; Ps. 135:11 [b]Judg. 5:30; 1 Sam. 30:24
13 [1]Lit., *If* [2]Or, *cooking stones* or *saddle bags* [a]Gen. 49:14; Judg. 5:16
14 [1]Lit., *in it* [a]Josh. 10:10 [b]Judg. 9:48
15 [1]Or, *mighty mountain is* [a]Ps. 36:6
16 [a]Deut. 12:5; Ps. 87:1, 2; 132:13 [b]Ps. 132:14
17 [1]Lit., *twice ten thousand* [2]Another reading is *The Lord came from Sinai into the sanctuary* [a]2 Kin. 6:17; Hab. 3:8 [b]Deut. 33:2; Dan. 7:10
18 [1]Heb., *YAH* [a]Ps. 7:7; 47:5; Eph. 4:8 [b]Judg. 5:12
19 [a]Ps. 55:22; Is. 46:4 [b]Ps. 65:5
20 [1]Heb., *YHWH,* usually rendered *LORD* [2]I.e., in view of; lit., *for* [a]Ps. 106:43 [b]Deut. 32:39; Ps. 49:15; 56:13
21 [a]Ps. 110:6; Hab. 3:13

At the mountain which God has [a]desired for His abode?
Surely, [b]the LORD will dwell *there* forever.
17 The [a]chariots of God are [1]myriads, [b]thousands upon thousands;
[2]The Lord is among them *as at* Sinai, in holiness.
18 Thou hast [a]ascended on high, Thou hast [b]led captive *Thy* captives;
Thou hast received gifts among men,
Even *among* the rebellious also, that [1]the LORD God may dwell *there.*

19 Blessed be the Lord, who daily [a]bears our burden,
[b]The God *who* is our salvation. [Selah.
20 God is to us a [a]God of deliverances;
And [b]to [1]GOD the Lord belong escapes [2]from death.
21 Surely God will [a]shatter the head of His enemies,
The hairy crown of him who goes on in his guilty deeds.
22 The Lord [1]said, "[a]I will bring *them* back from Bashan.
I will bring *them* back from the depths of the sea;
23 That [1a]your foot may shatter *them* in blood,
The tongue of your [b]dogs *may have* its portion from *your* enemies."

24 They have seen [a]Thy [1]procession, O God,
The [1]procession of my God, my King, [2b]into the sanctuary.
25 The [a]singers went on, the musicians after *them,*
[1]In the midst of the [b]maidens beating tambourines.
26 [a]Bless God in the congregations,
Even the LORD, *you who are* of the [b]fountain of Israel.
27 There is [a]Benjamin, the [1]youngest, [2]ruling them,
The princes of Judah *in* their throng,
The princes of [b]Zebulun, the princes of Naphtali.

28 [1]Your God has [a]commanded your strength;
Show Thyself strong, O God, [b]who hast acted [2]on our behalf.

22 [1]Or, *says* [a]Num. 21:33; Amos 9:1-3
23 [1]Some versions render, you may *bathe your foot in blood* [a]Ps. 58:10 [b]1 Kin. 21:19; Jer. 15:3
24 [1]Lit., *goings* [2]Lit., *in the sanctuary;* or, *in holiness* [a]Ps. 77:13 [b]Ps. 63:2
25 [1]Or, *The maidens in the midst* [a]1 Chr. 13:8; 15:6; Ps. 47:6 [b]Ex. 15:20; Judg. 11:34
26 [a]Ps. 22:22, 23; 26:12 [b]Deut. 33:28; Is. 48:1
27 [1]Or, *smallest* [2]Or, *their ruler* [a]Judg. 5:14; 1 Sam. 9:21 [b]Judg. 5:18
28 [1]Some mss. read *Command, God* [2]Lit., *for us* [a]Ps. 29:11; 44:4 [b]Is. 26:12

29 [1]Because of Thy temple at Jerusalem
[a]Kings will bring gifts to Thee.
30 Rebuke the [a]beasts [1]in the reeds,
The herd of [b]bulls with the calves of the peoples,
Trampling under foot the pieces of silver;
He has [c]scattered the peoples who delight in war.
31 Envoys will come out of [a]Egypt;
[1b]Ethiopia will quickly stretch out her hands to God.

32 Sing to God, O [a]kingdoms of the earth;
[b]Sing praises to the Lord, [Selah.
33 To Him who [a]rides upon the [1b]highest heavens, which are from ancient times;
Behold, [c]He [2]speaks forth with His voice, a [d]mighty voice.
34 [a]Ascribe strength to God;
His majesty is over Israel,
And [b]His strength is in the [1]skies.
35 [1]O God, *Thou art* [a]awesome from Thy [2]sanctuary.
The God of Israel Himself [b]gives strength and power to the people.
[c]Blessed be God!

PSALM 69

A Cry of Distress and Imprecation on Adversaries.

For the choir director; according to [+]Shoshannim. *A Psalm* of David.

SAVE me, O God,
For the [a]waters have [1]threatened my life.
2 I have sunk in deep [a]mire, and there is no foothold;
I have come into deep waters, and a [1b]flood overflows me.
3 I am [a]weary with my crying; my throat is parched;
My [b]eyes fail while I wait for my God.
4 Those [a]who hate me without a cause are more than the hairs of my head;
Those who would [1]destroy me [b]are powerful, being wrongfully my enemies,
[c]What I did not steal, I then have to restore.

5 O God, it is Thou who dost know [a]my folly,
And [b]my wrongs are not hidden from Thee.
6 May those who wait for Thee not [a]be ashamed through me, O Lord [1]GOD of hosts;
May those who seek Thee not be dishonored through me, O God of Israel,
7 Because [a]for Thy sake I have borne reproach;
[b]Dishonor has covered my face.
8 I have become [a]estranged [1]from my brothers,
And an alien to my mother's sons.
9 For [a]zeal for Thy house has consumed me,
And [b]the reproaches of those who reproach Thee have fallen on me.
10 When I wept [a]in my soul with fasting,
It became my reproach.
11 When I made [a]sackcloth my clothing,
I became [b]a byword to them.
12 Those who [a]sit in the gate talk about me,
And I *am* the [1b]song of the drunkards.

13 But as for me, my prayer is to Thee, O LORD, [a]at an acceptable time;
O God, in the [b]greatness of Thy lovingkindness,
Answer me with [1]Thy saving truth.
14 Deliver me from the [a]mire, and do not let me sink;
May I be [b]delivered from [1]my foes, and from the [2c]deep waters.
15 May the [1a]flood of water not overflow me,
And may the deep not swallow me up,
And may the [b]pit not shut its mouth on me.

16 Answer me, O LORD, for [a]Thy lovingkindness is good;
[b]According to the greatness of Thy compassion, [c]turn to me,
17 And [a]do not hide Thy face from Thy servant,
For I am [b]in distress; answer me quickly.
18 Oh draw near to my soul *and* [a]redeem it;
[b]Ransom me because of my enemies!
19 Thou dost know my [a]reproach and my shame and my dishonor;
All my adversaries are [1]before Thee.

20 Reproach has [a]broken my heart, and I am so sick.
And [b]I looked for sympathy, but there was none,
And for [c]comforters, but I found none.
21 They also gave me [1a]gall [2]for my food,
And for my thirst they [b]gave me vinegar to drink.

22 May [a]their table before them become a snare;
And [1b]when they are in peace, *may it become* a trap.

29 [1]Or, *From Thy temple* [a]1 Kin. 10:10, 25; 2 Chr. 32:23; Ps. 45:12; 72:10; Is. 18:7
30 [1]Lit., *of* [a]Job 40:21; Ezek. 29:3 [b]Ps. 22:12 [c]Ps. 18:14; 89:10
31 [1]Lit., *Cush* [a]Is. 19:19, 21 [b]Is. 45:14; Zeph. 3:10
32 [a]Ps. 102:22 [b]Ps. 67:4
33 [1]Lit., *heaven of heavens of old* [2]Lit., *gives forth* [a]Deut. 33:26; Ps. 18:10; 104:3 [b]Deut. 10:14; 1 Kin. 8:27 [c]Ps. 46:6 [d]Ps. 29:4
34 [1]Lit., *clouds* [a]Ps. 29:1 [b]Ps. 150:1
35 [1]Or, *Awesome is God from your sanctuary* [2]Lit., *holy places* [a]Deut. 7:21; 10:17; Ps. 47:2; 66:5 [b]Ps. 29:11; Is. 40:29 [c]Ps. 66:20; 2 Cor. 1:3

+ Or possibly, *Lilies*
1 [1]Lit., *come to the soul* [a]Job 22:11; Ps. 32:6; 42:7; 69:14, 15; Jon. 2:5
2 [1]Lit., *flowing stream* [a]Ps. 40:2 [b]Jon. 2:3
3 [a]Ps. 6:6 [b]Deut. 28:32; Ps. 38:10; 119:82, 123; Is. 38:14
4 [1]Or, *silence* [a]Ps. 35:19; John 15:25 [b]Ps. 35:19; 38:19; 59:3 [c]Ps. 35:11; Jer. 15:10
5 [a]Ps. 38:5 [b]Ps. 44:21
6 [1]Heb., *YHWH, usually rendered LORD* [a]2 Sam. 12:14
7 [a]Jer. 15:15 [b]Ps. 44:15; Is. 50:6; Jer. 51:51
8 [1]Lit., *to* [a]Job 19:13-15; Ps. 31:11; 38:11
9 [a]Ps. 119:139; John 2:17 [b]Ps. 89:41, 50; Rom. 15:3
10 [a]Ps. 35:13
11 [a]1 Kin. 20:31; Ps. 35:13 [b]1 Kin. 9:7; Job 17:6; Ps. 44:14; Jer. 24:9
12 [1]Lit., *songs* [a]Gen. 19:1; Ruth 4:1 [b]Job 30:9
13 [1]Or, *the faithfulness of Thy salvation* [a]Ps. 32:6; Is. 49:8; 2 Cor. 6:2 [b]Ps. 51:1
14 [1]Lit., *those who hate me* [2]Lit., *deep places of water* [a]Ps. 69:2 [b]Ps. 144:7 [c]Ps. 69:2
15 [1]Lit., *stream* [a]Ps. 124:4, 5 [b]Num. 16:33; Ps. 28:1; 141:7
16 [a]Ps. 63:3; 109:21 [b]Ps. 51:1; 106:45 [c]Ps. 25:16; 86:16

17 [a]Ps. 27:9; 102:2; 143:7 [b]Ps. 31:9; 66:14
18 [a]2 Sam. 4:9; Ps. 26:11; 49:15 [b]Ps. 119:134
19 [1]Or, known *to Thee* [a]Ps. 22:6; 31:11
20 [a]Jer. 23:9 [b]Ps. 142:4; Is. 63:5 [c]Job 16:2
21 [1]Or, *poison* [2]Or, *in* [a]Deut. 29:18 [b]Matt. 27:34, 48; Mark 15:23, 36; Luke 23:36; John 19:28-30
22 [1]Lit., *for those who are secure* [a]Rom. 11:9, 10 [b]1 Thess. 5:3

23 May their [a]eyes grow dim so that they cannot see,
And make their [b]loins shake continually.
24 [a]Pour out Thine indignation on them,
And may Thy burning anger overtake them.
25 May their [1a]camp be desolate;
May none dwell in their tents.
26 For they have [a]persecuted him whom [b]Thou Thyself hast smitten,
And they tell of the pain of those whom [c]Thou hast [1]wounded.
27 Do Thou add [a]iniquity to their iniquity,
And [b]may they not come into [c]Thy righteousness.
28 May they be [a]blotted out of the [b]book of life,
And may they not be [1c]recorded with the righteous.

29 But I am [a]afflicted and in pain;
[1]May Thy salvation, O God, [b]set me *securely* on high.
30 I will [a]praise the name of God with song,
And shall [b]magnify Him with [c]thanksgiving.
31 And it will [a]please the LORD better than an ox
Or a young bull with horns and hoofs.
32 The [a]humble [1]have seen *it and* are glad;
You who seek God, [b]let your heart [2]revive.
33 For [a]the LORD hears the needy,
And [b]does not despise His *who are* prisoners.

34 Let [a]heaven and earth praise Him,
The seas and [b]everything that moves in them.
35 For God will [a]save Zion and [b]build the cities of Judah,
That they may dwell there and [c]possess it.
36 And the [1a]descendants of His servants will inherit it,
And those who love His name [b]will dwell in it.

PSALM 70

Prayer for Help against Persecutors.

For the choir director. *A Psalm* of David; for a memorial.

[a]O GOD, *hasten* to deliver me;
O LORD, hasten to my help!
2 [a]Let those be ashamed and humiliated
Who seek my [1]life;
Let those be turned back and dishonored
Who delight [2]in my hurt.
3 [a]Let those be [1]turned back because of their shame
Who say, "Aha, aha!"
4 Let all who seek Thee rejoice and be glad in Thee;
And let those who love Thy salvation say continually,
"Let God be magnified."
5 But [a]I am afflicted and needy;
[b]Hasten to me, O God!
Thou art my help and my deliverer;
O LORD, do not delay.

PSALM 71

Prayer of an Old Man for Deliverance.

[a]IN Thee, O LORD, I have taken refuge;
Let me never be ashamed.
2 [a]In Thy righteousness deliver me, and rescue me;
[b]Incline Thine ear to me, and save me.
3 [a]Be Thou to me a rock of [b]habitation, to which I may continually come;
Thou hast given [c]commandment to save me,
For Thou art [d]my [1]rock and my fortress.
4 [a]Rescue me, O my God, out of the hand of the wicked,
Out of the [1]grasp of the wrongdoer and ruthless man,
5 For Thou art my [a]hope;
O Lord [1]GOD, *Thou art* my [b]confidence from my youth.
6 [1]By Thee I have been [a]sustained from *my* birth;
Thou art He who [b]took me from my mother's womb;
My [c]praise is continually [2]of Thee.

7 I have become a [a]marvel to many;
For Thou art [b]my strong refuge.
8 My [a]mouth is filled with Thy praise,
And with [b]Thy glory all day long.
9 Do not cast me off in the [a]time of old age;
Do not forsake me when my strength fails.
10 For my enemies have spoken [1]against me;
And those who [a]watch for my [2]life [b]have consulted together,
11 Saying, "[a]God has forsaken him;
Pursue and seize him, for there is [b]no one to deliver."

12 O God, [a]do not be far from me;
O my God, [b]hasten to my help!
13 Let those who are adversaries of my soul be [a]ashamed *and* consumed;
Let them be [b]covered with reproach and dishonor, who [c]seek [1]to injure me.

23 [a]Is. 6:10 [b]Dan. 5:6
24 [a]Ps. 79:6; Jer. 10:25; Ezek. 20:8; Hos. 5:10
25 [1]Lit., *encampment* [a]Matt. 23:38; Luke 13:35; Acts 1:20
26 [1]Lit., *pierced* [a]2 Chr. 28:9; Zech. 1:15 [b]Is. 53:4 [c]Ps. 109:22
27 [a]Neh. 4:5; Ps. 109:14; Rom. 1:28 [b]Is. 26:10 [c]Ps. 103:17
28 [1]Lit., *written* [a]Ex. 32:32, 33; Rev. 3:5 [b]Phil. 4:3; Rev. 13:8; 17:8; 20:15 [c]Ps. 87:6; Ezek. 13:9; Luke 10:20; Heb. 12:23
29 [1]Or, *Thy salvation, O God, will set . . .* [a]Ps. 70:5 [b]Ps. 20:1; 59:1
30 [a]Ps. 28:7 [b]Ps. 34:3 [c]Ps. 50:14
31 [a]Ps. 50:13, 14; 51:16
32 [1]Some mss. and ancient versions read *will see* [2]Or, *live* [a]Ps. 34:2 [b]Ps. 22:26
33 [a]Ps. 12:5 [b]Ps. 68:6
34 [a]Ps. 96:11; 98:7; 148:1-13; Is. 44:23; 49:13 [b]Is. 55:12
35 [a]Ps. 46:5; 51:18 [b]Ps. 147:2; Is. 44:26 [c]Obad. 17
36 [1]Lit., *seed* [a]Ps. 25:13; 102:28 [b]Ps. 37:29

1 [a]Ps. 40:13-17; 70:1-5
2 [1]Or, *soul* [2]Or, *to injure me* [a]Ps. 35:4, 26
3 [1]Some mss. read *appalled* [a]Ps. 40:15
5 [a]Ps. 40:17 [b]Ps. 141:1

1 [a]Ps. 25:2, 3; 31:1-3; 71:1-3
2 [a]Ps. 31:1 [b]Ps. 17:6
3 [1]Or, *crag* [a]Ps. 31:2, 3 [b]Deut. 33:27; Ps. 90:1; 91:9 [c]Ps. 7:6; 42:8 [d]Ps. 18:2
4 [1]Lit., *palm* [a]Ps. 140:1, 4
5 [1]Heb., *YHWH*, usually rendered *LORD* [a]Ps. 39:7; Jer. 14:8; 17:7, 13, 17; 50:7 [b]Ps. 22:9
6 [1]Lit., *Upon Thee I have been supported* [2]Lit., *in* [a]Ps. 22:10; Is. 46:3 [b]Job 10:18; Ps. 22:9 [c]Ps. 34:1
7 [a]Is. 8:18; 1 Cor. 4:9 [b]Ps. 61:3
8 [a]Ps. 35:28; 63:5 [b]Ps. 96:6; 104:1
9 [a]Ps. 71:18; 92:14; Is. 46:4
10 [1]Lit., *with reference to* [2]Lit., *soul* [a]Ps. 56:6 [b]Ps. 31:13; 83:3; Matt. 27:1
11 [a]Ps. 3:2 [b]Ps. 7:2
12 [a]Ps. 10:1; 22:11; 35:22; 38:21 [b]Ps. 38:22; 40:13; 70:1, 5
13 [1]Lit., *my injury* [a]Ps. 35:4, 26; 40:14 [b]Ps. 109:29 [c]Esth. 9:2; Ps. 71:24

14 But as for me, I will [a]hope continually,
And will [1b]praise Thee yet more and more.
15 My [a]mouth shall tell of Thy righteousness,
And of [b]Thy salvation all day long;
For I [c]do not know the [1]sum *of them.*
16 I will come [a]with the mighty deeds of the Lord [1]GOD;
I will [b]make mention of Thy righteousness, Thine alone.

17 O God, Thou [a]hast taught me from my youth;
And I still [b]declare Thy wondrous deeds.
18 And even when *I am* [a]old and gray, O God, do not forsake me,
Until I [b]declare Thy [1]strength to *this* generation,
Thy power to all who are to come.
19 [1]For Thy [a]righteousness, O God, *reaches* to the [2]heavens,
Thou who hast [b]done great things;
O God, [c]who is like Thee?
20 Thou, who hast [a]shown [1]me many troubles and distresses,
Wilt [b]revive [1]me again,
And wilt bring [1]me up again [c]from the depths of the earth.
21 Mayest Thou increase my [a]greatness,
And turn *to* [b]comfort me.

22 I will also praise Thee with [1a]a harp,
Even Thy [2]truth, O my God;
To Thee I will sing praises with the [b]lyre,
O Thou [c]Holy One of Israel.
23 My lips will [a]shout for joy when I sing praises to Thee;
And my [b]soul, which Thou hast redeemed.
24 My [a]tongue also will utter Thy righteousness all day long;
For they are [b]ashamed, for they are humiliated who seek [1]my hurt.

PSALM 72

The Reign of the Righteous King.
A Psalm of Solomon.

GIVE the king [a]Thy judgments, O God,
And [b]Thy righteousness to the king's son.
2 [1]May [2]he [a]judge Thy people with righteousness,
And [3b]Thine afflicted with justice.
3 [1]Let the mountains bring [2a]peace to the people,
And the hills in righteousness.
4 [1]May he [a]vindicate the [2]afflicted of the people,
Save the children of the needy,
And crush the oppressor.

5 [1]Let them fear Thee [a]while the sun endures,
And [2]as long as the moon, throughout all generations.
6 [1]May he come down [a]like rain upon the mown grass,
Like [b]showers that water the earth.
7 In his days [1]may the [a]righteous flourish,
And [b]abundance of peace till the moon is no more.

8 May he also rule [a]from sea to sea,
And from the River to the ends of the earth.
9 [1]Let [a]the nomads of the desert [b]bow before him;
And his enemies [c]lick the dust.
10 [1]Let the kings of [a]Tarshish and of the [2b]islands bring presents;
The kings of [c]Sheba and [d]Seba [e]offer [3]gifts.
11 [1]And let all [a]kings bow down before him,
All [b]nations serve him.

12 For he will [a]deliver the needy when he cries for help,
The [1]afflicted also, and him who has no helper.
13 He will have [a]compassion on the poor and needy,
And the [1]lives of the needy he will save.
14 He will [1a]rescue their [2]life from oppression and violence;
And their blood will be [b]precious in his sight;
15 So may he live; and may the [a]gold of Sheba be given to him;
And let [1]them pray for him continually;
Let [1]them bless him all day long.

16 May there be abundance of grain in the earth on top of the mountains;
Its fruit will wave like *the cedars of* [a]Lebanon;
And may those from the city flourish like [b]vegetation of the earth.
17 May his [a]name endure forever;
May his name [1]increase [2b]as long as the sun *shines*;
And let *men* [c]bless themselves by him;
[d]Let all nations call him blessed.

18 [a]Blessed be the LORD God, the God of Israel,
Who alone [b]works wonders.

14 [1]Lit., *add upon all Thy praise* [a]Ps. 130:7 [b]Ps. 71:8
15 [1]Lit., *numbers* [a]Ps. 35:28 [b]Ps. 96:2 [c]Ps. 40:5
16 [1]Heb., *YHWH,* usually rendered *LORD* [a]Ps. 106:2 [b]Ps. 51:14
17 [a]Deut. 4:5; 6:7 [b]Ps. 26:7; 40:5; 119:27
18 [1]Lit., *arm* [a]Ps. 71:9 [b]Ps. 22:31; 78:4, 6
19 [1]Or, *And* [2]Lit., *height* [a]Ps. 36:6; 57:10 [b]Ps. 126:2; Luke 1:49 [c]Deut. 3:24; Ps. 35:10
20 [1]Another reading is *us* [a]Ps. 60:3 [b]Ps. 80:18; 85:6; 119:25; 138:7; Hos. 6:1, 2 [c]Ps. 86:13
21 [a]Ps. 18:35 [b]Ps. 23:4; 86:17; Is. 12:1; 49:13
22 [1]Lit., *an instrument of a harp* [2]Or, *faithfulness* [a]Ps. 33:2; 81:2; 92:1-3; 144:9 [b]Ps. 33:2; 147:7 [c]2 Kin. 19:22; Ps. 78:41; 89:18; Is. 1:4
23 [a]Ps. 5:11; 32:11; 132:9, 16 [b]Ps. 34:22; 55:18; 103:4
24 [1]Or, *to injure me* [a]Ps. 35:28 [b]Ps. 71:13

1 [a]1 Kin. 3:9; 1 Chr. 22:13 [b]Ps. 24:5
2 [1]Or, *He will judge* [2]Many of the pronouns in this Psalm may be rendered *He* since the typical reference is to the Messiah. [3]Or, *Thy humble* [a]Is. 9:7; 11:2-5; 32:1 [b]Ps. 82:3
3 [1]Or, *The mountains will bring* [2]Or, *prosperity* [a]Is. 2:4; 9:5, 6; Mic. 4:3, 4; Zech. 9:10
4 [1]Or, *He will vindicate* [2]Or, *humble* [a]Is. 11:4
5 [1]Or, *They will fear* [2]Lit., *before the moon* [a]Ps. 72:17; 89:36, 37
6 [1]Or, *He will come down* [a]Deut. 32:2; 2 Sam. 23:4; Hos. 6:3 [b]Ps. 65:10
7 [1]Or, *the righteous will flourish* [a]Ps. 92:12 [b]Is. 2:4
8 [a]Ex. 23:31; Zech. 9:10
9 [1]Or, *The nomads . . . will bow* [a]Ps. 74:14; Is. 23:13 [b]Ps. 22:29 [c]Is. 49:23; Mic. 7:17
10 [1]Or, *The kings . . . will bring* [2]Or, *coastlands* [3]Or, *tribute* [a]2 Chr. 9:21; Ps. 48:7 [b]Ps. 97:1; Is. 42:4, 10; Zeph. 2:11 [c]1 Kin. 10:1; Job 6:19; Is. 60:6 [d]Gen. 10:7; Is. 43:3 [e]Ps. 45:12; 68:29

11 [1]Or, *All kings will bow down* [a]Ps. 138:4; Is. 49:23 [b]Ps. 86:9
12 [1]Or, *humble* [a]Job 29:12; Ps. 72:4
13 [1]Lit., *souls* [a]Prov. 19:17; 28:8
14 [1]Lit., *redeem* [2]Lit., *soul* [a]Ps. 69:18 [b]1 Sam. 26:21; Ps. 116:15
15 [1]Lit., *him* [a]Is. 60:6
16 [a]Ps. 104:16 [b]Job 5:25
17 [1]Or, *sprout forth* [2]Lit., *before the sun* [a]Ex. 3:15; Ps. 135:13 [b]Ps. 89:36 [c]Gen. 12:3; 22:18 [d]Luke 1:48
18 [a]1 Chr. 29:10; Ps. 41:13; 89:52; 106:48 [b]Ex. 15:11; Job 5:9; Ps. 77:14; 86:10; 136:4

19 And blessed be His [a]glorious name
forever;
And may the whole [b]earth be filled
with His glory.
[c]Amen, and Amen.

20 The prayers of David the son of
Jesse are ended.

BOOK 3

PSALM 73

The End of the Wicked Contrasted with That of the Righteous.

A Psalm of Asaph.

SURELY God is [a]good to Israel,
To those who are [b]pure in heart!
2 But as for me, [a]my feet came close
to stumbling;
My steps [1]had almost slipped.
3 For I was [a]envious of the [1]arro-
gant,
As I saw the [b]prosperity of the
wicked.
4 For there are no pains in their
death;
And their [1]body is fat.
5 They are [a]not [1]in trouble *as other*
[2]men;
Nor are they [b]plagued [3]like mankind.
6 Therefore pride is [a]their necklace;
The [b]garment of violence covers
them.
7 Their eye [1]bulges from [a]fatness;
The imaginations of *their* heart
[2]run riot.
8 They [a]mock, and [1]wickedly speak
of oppression;
They [b]speak from on high.
9 They have [a]set their mouth [1]against
the heavens,
And their tongue [2]parades through
the earth.

10 Therefore [1]his people return to this
place;
And waters of [a]abundance are
[2]drunk by them.
11 And they say, "[a]How does God
know?
And is there knowledge [1]with the
Most High?"
12 Behold, [a]these are the wicked;
And always [b]at ease, they have
increased *in* wealth.
13 Surely [a]in vain I have [1]kept my
heart pure,
And [b]washed my hands in innocence;
14 For I have been stricken [a]all day
long,
And [1b]chastened every morning.

15 If I had said, "I will speak thus,"
Behold, I should have betrayed the
[a]generation of Thy children.
16 When I [a]pondered to understand
this,
It was [1]troublesome in my sight

17 Until I came into the [1a]sanctuary
of God;
Then I perceived their [b]end.
18 Surely Thou dost set them in [a]slip-
pery places;
Thou dost cast them down to [1b]de-
struction.
19 How they are [1a]destroyed in a
moment!
They are utterly swept away by
[b]sudden terrors!
20 Like a [a]dream when one awakes,
O Lord, when [b]aroused, Thou wilt
[c]despise their [1]form.

21 When my [a]heart was embittered,
And I was [b]pierced [1]within,
22 Then I was [a]senseless and ignorant;
I was *like* [1]a [b]beast [2]before Thee.
23 Nevertheless [a]I am continually
with Thee;
Thou hast taken hold of my right
hand.
24 With Thy counsel Thou wilt [a]guide
me,
And afterward [b]receive me [1]to
glory.

25 [a]Whom have I in heaven *but Thee*?
And [1]besides Thee, I desire nothing
on earth.
26 My [a]flesh and my heart may fail,
But God is the [1]strength of my
heart and my [b]portion forever.
27 For, behold, [a]those who are far
from Thee will [b]perish;
Thou hast [1]destroyed all those who
[2c]are unfaithful to Thee.
28 But as for me, [a]the nearness of God
is my good;
I have made the Lord [1]GOD my
[b]refuge,
That I may [c]tell of all Thy works.

PSALM 74

An Appeal against the Devastation of the Land by the Enemy.

A +Maskil of Asaph.

O GOD, why hast Thou [a]rejected *us*
forever?
Why does Thine anger [b]smoke
against the [c]sheep of Thy [1]pas-
ture?
2 Remember Thy congregation,
which Thou hast [a]purchased of
old,
Which Thou hast [b]redeemed to be
the [c]tribe of Thine inheritance;
And this Mount [d]Zion, where Thou
hast dwelt.

19 aNeh. 9:5; Ps. 96:8 bNum. 14:21 cPs. 41:13
1 aPs. 86:5 bPs. 24:4; 51:10; Matt. 5:8
2 1Lit., *were caused to slip* aPs. 94:18
3 1Or, *boasters* aPs. 37:1; Prov. 23:17 bJob 21:7; Ps. 37:7; Jer. 12:1
4 1Or, *belly*
5 1Lit., *in the trouble of men* 2Or, *mortals* 3Lit., *with* aJob 21:9; Ps. 73:12 bPs. 73:14
6 aGen. 41:42; Prov. 1:9 bPs. 109:18
7 1Lit., *goes forth* 2Lit., *overflow* aJob 15:27; Ps. 17:10; Jer. 5:28
8 1Or, *they speak in wickedness; From on high they speak of oppression.* aPs. 1:1 bPs. 17:10; 2 Pet. 2:18; Jude 16
9 1Or, *in* 2Lit., *walks* aRev. 13:6
10 1Or, *His* 2Lit., *drained out* aPs. 23:5
11 1Lit., *in* aJob 22:13
12 aPs. 49:6; 52:7 bJer. 49:31; Ezek. 23:42
13 1Or, *cleansed my heart* aJob 21:15; 34:9; 35:3 bPs. 26:6
14 1Lit., *my chastening* aPs. 38:6 bJob 33:19; Ps. 118:18
15 aPs. 14:5
16 1Lit., *labor, trouble* aEccl. 8:17
17 1Lit., *sanctuaries* aPs. 27:4; 77:13 bPs. 37:38
18 1Lit., *ruins* aPs. 35:6 bPs. 35:8; 36:12
19 1Lit., *become a desolation* aNum. 16:21; Is. 47:11 bJob 18:11
20 1Or, *image* aJob 20:8 bPs. 78:65 c1 Sam. 2:30
21 1Lit., *in my kidneys* aJudg. 10:16 bActs 2:37
22 1Or, *an animal* 2Lit., *with Thee* aPs. 49:10; 92:6 bJob 18:3; Ps. 49:20; Eccl. 3:18
23 aPs. 16:8
24 1Or, *with honor* aPs. 32:8; 48:14; Is. 58:11 bGen. 5:24; Ps. 49:15
25 1Or, *with* aPs. 16:2; Phil. 3:8
26 1Lit., *rock* aPs. 38:10; 40:12; 84:2; 119:81 bPs. 16:5
27 1Or, *silenced* 2Lit., *go to a whoring from* aPs. 119:155 bPs. 37:20 cEx. 34:15; Num. 15:39; Ps. 106:39; Hos. 4:12; 9:1

28 1Heb., *YHWH*, usually rendered *LORD* aPs. 65:4; Heb. 10:22; James 4:8 bPs. 14:6; 71:7 cPs. 40:5; 107:22; 118:17

+ Possibly, *Contemplative*, or *Didactic*, or *Skillful Psalm*
1 1Or, *pasturing* aPs. 44:9; 77:7 bDeut. 29:20; Ps. 18:8; 89:46 cPs. 79:13; 95:7; 100:3
2 aEx. 15:16; Deut. 32:6 bEx. 15:13; Ps. 77:15; 106:10; Is. 63:9 cDeut. 32:9; Is. 63:17; Jer. 10:16; 51:19 dPs. 9:11; 68:16

3 [1]Turn Thy footsteps toward the
[a]perpetual ruins;
The enemy [b]has damaged everything within the sanctuary.
4 Thine adversaries have [a]roared in
the midst of Thy meeting place;
They have set up their [b]own [1]stan-
dards [c]for signs.
5 It seems as if one had lifted up
His [1a]axe in a [2]forest of trees.
6 And now [1]all its [a]carved work
They smash with hatchet and
[2]hammers.
7 They have [1a]burned Thy sanctuary
[2]to the ground;
They have [b]defiled the dwelling
place of Thy name.
8 They [a]said in their heart, "Let us
[1]completely [2]subdue them."
They have burned all the meeting
places of God in the land.
9 We do not see our [a]signs;
There is [b]no longer any prophet,
Nor is there any among us who
knows [c]how long.
10 How long, O God, will the adversary [a]revile,
And the enemy [b]spurn Thy name
forever?
11 Why [a]dost Thou withdraw Thy
hand, even Thy right hand?
From within Thy bosom, [b]destroy
them!

12 Yet God is [a]my king from of old,
Who works deeds of deliverance in
the midst of the earth.
13 [1]Thou didst [a]divide the sea by Thy
strength;
[1]Thou [b]didst break the heads of the
[c]sea monsters [2]in the waters.
14 [1]Thou didst crush the heads of
[2a]Leviathan;
[1]Thou didst give him as food for
the [3]creatures [b]of the wilderness.
15 [1]Thou didst [a]break open springs
and torrents;
[1]Thou didst [b]dry up ever-flowing
streams.
16 Thine is the day, Thine also is the
night;
[1]Thou hast [a]prepared the [2]light and
the sun.
17 [1]Thou hast [a]established all the
boundaries of the earth;
[1]Thou hast [2]made [b]summer and
winter.

18 Remember this, [1]O LORD, that the
enemy has [a]reviled;
And a [b]foolish people has spurned
Thy name.
19 Do not deliver the soul of Thy
[a]turtledove to the wild beast;
[b]Do not forget the life of Thine
afflicted forever.
20 Consider the [a]covenant;
For the [b]dark places of the land are
full of the habitations of violence.

3 [1]Lit., *Lift up* [a]Is. 61:4 [b]Ps. 79:1
4 [1]Lit., *signs* [a]Lam. 2:7 [b]Num. 2:2 [c]Ps. 74:9
5 [1]Lit., *axes* [2]Lit., *thicket* [a]Jer. 46:22
6 [1]Lit., *altogether* [2]Or, *axes* [a]1 Kin. 6:18, 29, 32, 35
7 [1]Lit., *set on fire* [2]Or, *To the ground they . . .* [a]2 Kin. 25:9 [b]Ps. 89:39; Lam. 2:2
8 [1]Lit., *altogether* [2]Or, *oppress* [a]Ps. 83:4
9 [a]Ps. 78:43 [b]1 Sam. 3:1; Lam. 2:9; Ezek. 7:26; Amos 8:11 [c]Ps. 6:3; 79:5; 80:4
10 [a]Ps. 44:16; 79:12; 89:51 [b]Lev. 24:16
11 [a]Lam. 2:3 [b]Ps. 59:13
12 [a]Ps. 44:4
13 [1]Or, *Thou Thyself* [2]Lit., *on* [a]Ex. 14:21; Ps. 78:13 [b]Is. 51:9 [c]Ps. 148:7; Jer. 51:34
14 [1]Or, *Thou Thyself* [2]Or, *sea monster* [3]Lit., *people* [a]Job 41:1; Ps. 104:26; Is. 27:1 [b]Ps. 72:9
15 [1]Or, *Thou Thyself* [a]Ex. 17:5, 6; Num. 20:11; Ps. 78:15; 105:41; 114:8; Is. 48:21 [b]Ex. 14:21, 22; Josh. 2:10; 3:13; Ps. 114:3
16 [1]Or, *Thou Thyself* [2]Or, *luminary* [a]Gen. 1:14-18; Ps. 104:19; 136:7, 8
17 [1]Or, *Thou Thyself* [2]Or, *formed* [a]Deut. 32:8; Acts 17:26 [b]Gen. 8:22; Ps. 147:16-18
18 [1]Or, *that the enemy has reviled the LORD* [a]Ps. 74:10 [b]Deut. 32:6; Ps. 14:1; 39:8; 53:1
19 [a]Song 2:14 [b]Ps. 9:18
20 [a]Gen. 17:7; Ps. 106:45 [b]Ps. 88:6; 143:3
21 [a]Ps. 103:6 [b]Ps. 35:10; Is. 41:17
22 [1]Lit., *Thy reproach from the foolish man* [a]Ps. 43:1; Is. 3:13; 43:26; Ezek. 20:35 [b]Ps. 14:1; 53:1; 74:18
23 [a]Ps. 74:10 [b]Ps. 65:7

+ Lit., *Do Not Destroy*
1 [a]Ps. 79:13 [b]Ps. 145:18 [c]Ps. 26:7; 44:1; 71:17
2 [a]Ps. 102:13 [b]Ps. 9:8; 67:4; Is. 11:4
3 [1]Or, *totter* [2]*Selah* may mean: *Pause, Crescendo* or *Musical interlude* [a]Ps. 46:6; Is. 24:19 [b]1 Sam. 2:8

21 Let not the [a]oppressed return dis-
honored;
Let the [b]afflicted and needy praise
Thy name.

22 Do arise, O God, *and* [a]plead Thine
own cause;
Remember [1]how the [b]foolish man
reproaches Thee all day long.
23 Do not forget the voice of Thine
[a]adversaries,
The [b]uproar of those who rise
against Thee which ascends continually.

PSALM 75

God Abases the Proud, but Exalts the Righteous.

For the choir director; *set to* +Al-tashheth.
A Psalm of Asaph, a Song.

WE [a]give thanks to Thee, O God, we
give thanks,
For Thy name is [b]near;
Men declare [c]Thy wondrous works.
2 "When I select an [a]appointed time,
It is I who [b]judge with equity.
3 "The [a]earth and all who dwell in it
[1]melt;
It is I who have firmly set its [b]pil-
lars. [[2]Selah.
4 "I said to the boastful, 'Do not
boast,'
And to the wicked, '[a]Do not lift up
the horn;
5 Do not lift up your horn on high,
[a]Do not speak with insolent
[1]pride.' "

6 For not from the east, nor from the
west,
Nor from the [1a]desert *comes* exaltation;
7 But [a]God is the Judge;
He [b]puts down one, and exalts
another.
8 For a [a]cup is in the hand of the
LORD, and the wine foams;
It is [1b]well mixed, and He pours
out of this;
Surely all the wicked of the earth
must drain *and* [c]drink down its
dregs.

9 But as for me, I will [a]declare *it*
forever;
I will sing praises to the God of
Jacob.
10 And all the [a]horns of the wicked
[1]He will cut off,
But [b]the horns of the righteous will
be lifted up.

4 [a]Zech. 1:21
5 [1]Lit., *neck* [a]1 Sam. 2:3; Ps. 94:4
6 [1]Or, *mountainous desert* [a]Ps. 3:3
7 [a]Ps. 50:6 [b]1 Sam. 2:7; Ps. 147:6; Dan. 2:21
8 [1]Lit., *full of mixture* [a]Job 21:20; Ps. 11:6; 60:3; Jer. 25:15 [b]Prov. 23:30 [c]Obad. 16
9 [a]Ps. 22:22; 40:10
10 [1]Heb., *I* [a]Ps. 101:8; Jer. 48:25 [b]1 Sam. 2:1; Ps. 89:17; 92:10; 148:14

PSALM 76

The Victorious Power of the God of Jacob.

For the choir director; on stringed instruments.
A Psalm of Asaph, a Song.

GOD is [a]known in Judah;
His name is [b]great in Israel.
2 And His [1a]tabernacle is in [b]Salem;
His [c]dwelling place also is in Zion.
3 There He [a]broke the [1]flaming arrows,
The shield, and the sword, and the [2]weapons of war. [[3]Selah.

4 Thou art resplendent,
[1]More majestic than the mountains of prey.
5 The [a]stouthearted were plundered;
[1]They sank into sleep;
And none of the [2]warriors could use his hands.
6 At Thy [a]rebuke, O God of Jacob,
Both [1b]rider and horse were cast into a dead sleep.
7 Thou, even Thou, art [a]to be feared;
And [b]who may stand in Thy presence when once [1]Thou art angry?

8 Thou didst cause judgment to be heard from heaven;
The earth [a]feared, and was still,
9 When God [a]arose to judgment,
To save all the humble of the earth. [Selah.
10 For the [1a]wrath of man shall praise Thee;
With a remnant of wrath Thou shalt gird Thyself.

11 [a]Make vows to the LORD your God and [b]fulfill *them*;
Let all who are around Him [c]bring gifts to Him who is to be feared.
12 He will cut off the spirit of princes;
He is [1a]feared by the kings of the earth.

PSALM 77

Comfort in Trouble from Recalling God's Mighty Deeds.

For the choir director; [+]according to Jeduthun.
A Psalm of Asaph.

MY voice *rises* to God, and I will [a]cry aloud;
My voice *rises* to God, and He will hear me.
2 In the [a]day of my trouble I sought the Lord;
[b]In the night my [c]hand was stretched out [1]without weariness;
My soul [d]refused to be comforted.
3 *When* I remember God, then I am [a]disturbed;
When I [b]sigh, then [c]my spirit grows faint. [[1]Selah.

1 [a]Ps. 48:3 [b]Ps. 99:3
2 [1]Lit., *shelter* [a]Ps. 27:5; Lam. 2:6 [b]Gen. 14:18 [c]Ps. 9:11; 132:13; 135:21
3 [1]Lit., *fiery shafts of the bow* [2]Lit., *battle* [3]*Selah* may mean: *Pause, Crescendo* or *Musical interlude* [a]Ps. 46:9
4 [1]Or, *Majestic from the mountains*
5 [1]Lit., *They slumbered their sleep* [2]Lit., *men of might have found their hands* [a]Is. 10:12; 46:12
6 [1]Lit., *chariot* [a]Ps. 80:16 [b]Ex. 15:1, 21; Ps. 78:53
7 [1]Lit., *Thine anger is* [a]1 Chr. 16:25; Ps. 89:7; 96:4 [b]Ezra 9:15; Ps. 130:3; Nah. 1:6; Mal. 3:2; Rev. 6:17
8 [a]1 Chr. 16:30; 2 Chr. 20:29, 30; Ps. 33:8
9 [a]Ps. 9:7, 8; 74:22; 82:8
10 [1]Lit., *wraths* [a]Ex. 9:16; Rom. 9:17
11 [a]Eccl. 5:4-6 [b]Ps. 50:14 [c]2 Chr. 32:23; Ps. 68:29
12 [1]Lit., *awesome to* [a]Ps. 47:2

+ 1 Chr. 16:41
1 [a]Ps. 3:4; 142:1
2 [1]Lit., *and did not grow numb* [a]Ps. 50:15; 86:7 [b]Ps. 63:6; Is. 26:9 [c]Job 11:13; Ps. 88:9 [d]Gen. 37:35
3 [1]*Selah* may mean: *Pause, Crescendo* or *Musical interlude* [a]Ps. 42:5, 11; 43:5 [b]Ps. 55:2; 142:2 [c]Ps. 61:2; 143:4
4 [a]Ps. 39:9
5 [a]Deut. 32:7; Ps. 44:1; 143:5; Is. 51:9
6 [1]Lit., *searched* [a]Ps. 42:8 [b]Ps. 4:4
7 [a]Ps. 44:9 [b]Ps. 85:1, 5
8 [1]Lit., *word* [2]Lit., *from generation to generation* [a]Ps. 89:49 [b]2 Pet. 3:9
9 [1]Lit., *shut up* [a]Is. 49:15 [b]Ps. 25:6; 40:11; 51:1
10 [1]Or, *infirmity, the years of the right hand of the Most High* [a]Ps. 31:22; 73:14 [b]Ps. 44:2, 3
11 [1]Heb., *YAH* [a]Ps. 105:5; 143:5
12 [a]Ps. 145:5
13 [a]Ps. 63:2; 73:17 [b]Ex. 15:11; Ps. 71:19; 86:8
14 [a]Ps. 72:18 [b]Ps. 106:8
15 [1]Lit., *arm* [a]Ex. 6:6; Deut. 9:29; Ps. 74:2; 78:42 [b]Ps. 80:1

4 Thou hast held my eyelids *open*;
I am so troubled that I [a]cannot speak.
5 I have considered the [a]days of old,
The years of long ago.
6 I will remember my [a]song in the night;
I [b]will meditate with my heart;
And my spirit [1]ponders.

7 Will the Lord [a]reject forever?
And will He [b]never be favorable again?
8 Has His [a]lovingkindness ceased forever?
Has *His* [1b]promise come to an end [2]forever?
9 Has God [a]forgotten to be gracious?
Or has He in anger [1]withdrawn His [b]compassion? [Selah.
10 Then I said, "[a]It is my [1]grief,
That the [b]right hand of the Most High has changed."

11 I shall remember the [a]deeds of [1]the LORD;
Surely I will [a]remember Thy wonders of old.
12 I will [a]meditate on all Thy work,
And muse on Thy deeds.
13 Thy way, O God, is [a]holy;
[b]What god is great like our God?
14 Thou art the [a]God who workest wonders;
Thou hast [b]made known Thy strength among the peoples.
15 Thou hast by Thy [1]power [a]redeemed Thy people,
The sons of Jacob and [b]Joseph. [Selah.

16 The [a]waters saw Thee, O God;
The waters saw Thee, they were in anguish;
The deeps also trembled.
17 The [a]clouds poured out water;
The skies [b]gave forth a sound;
Thy [c]arrows [1]flashed here and there.
18 The [a]sound of Thy thunder was in the whirlwind;
The [b]lightnings lit up the world;
The [c]earth trembled and shook.
19 Thy [a]way was in the sea,
And Thy paths in the mighty waters,
And Thy footprints may not be known.
20 Thou [a]didst lead Thy people like a flock,
By the hand of [b]Moses and Aaron.

16 [a]Ex. 14:21; Ps. 114:3; Hab. 3:8, 10
17 [1]Lit., *went* [a]Judg. 5:4 [b]Ps. 68:33 [c]Ps. 18:14
18 [a]Ps. 18:13; 104:7 [b]Ps. 97:4 [c]Judg. 5:4; Ps. 18:7
19 [a]Is. 51:10; Hab. 3:15
20 [a]Ex. 13:21; 14:19; Ps. 78:52; 80:1; Is. 63:11-13 [b]Ex. 6:26; Ps. 105:26

PSALM 78

God's Guidance of His People in Spite of Their Unfaithfulness.

A [+]Maskil of Asaph.

[a]LISTEN, O my people, to my [1]instruction;
[b]Incline your ears to the words of my mouth.
2 I will [a]open my mouth in a parable;
I will utter [b]dark sayings of old,
3 Which we have heard and known,
And [a]our fathers have told us.
4 We will [a]not conceal them from their children,
But [b]tell to the generation to come the praises of the LORD,
And His strength and His [c]wondrous works that He has done.

5 For He established a [a]testimony in Jacob,
And appointed a [b]law in Israel,
Which He [c]commanded our fathers,
That they should [1d]teach them to their children,
6 [a]That the generation to come might know, *even* [b]the children *yet* to be born,
That they may arise and [c]tell *them* to their children,
7 That they should put their confidence in God,
And [a]not forget the works of God,
But [b]keep His commandments,
8 And [a]not be like their fathers,
A [b]stubborn and rebellious generation,
A generation that [c]did not [1]prepare its heart,
And whose spirit was not [d]faithful to God.

9 The sons of Ephraim [1]were [a]archers equipped with bows,
Yet [b]they turned back in the day of battle.
10 They [a]did not keep the covenant of God,
And refused to [b]walk in His law;
11 And they [a]forgot His deeds,
And His [1]miracles that He had shown them.
12 [a]He wrought wonders before their fathers,
In the land of Egypt, in the [b]field of Zoan.
13 He [a]divided the sea, and caused them to pass through;
And He made the waters stand [b]up like a heap.
14 Then He led them with the cloud by [a]day,
And all the night with a [b]light of fire.
15 He [a]split the rocks in the wilderness,
And gave *them* abundant drink like the ocean depths.

+ Possibly, *Contemplative,* or *Didactic,* or *Skillful Psalm*
1 [1]Or, *law, teaching* [a]Is. 51:4 [b]Is. 55:3
2 [a]Ps. 49:4; Matt. 13:35 [b]Prov. 1:6
3 [a]Ps. 44:1
4 [a]Ex. 12:26; Deut. 6:7; 11:19; Job 15:18; Ps. 145:4; Is. 38:19; Joel 1:3 [b]Ex. 13:8, 14; Ps. 22:30 [c]Job 37:16; Ps. 26:7; 71:17
5 [1]Lit., *make them known* [a]Ps. 19:7; 81:5; Is. 8:20 [b]Ps. 147:19 [c]Deut. 6:4-9 [d]Deut. 4:9
6 [a]Ps. 102:18 [b]Ps. 22:31 [c]Deut. 11:19
7 [a]Deut. 4:9; 6:12; 8:14 [b]Deut. 4:2; 5:1, 29; 27:1; Josh. 22:5
8 [1]Or, *put right* [a]2 Kin. 17:14; 2 Chr. 30:7; Ezek. 20:18 [b]Ex. 32:9; Deut. 9:7, 24; 31:27; Judg. 2:19; Is. 30:9 [c]Job 11:13; Ps. 78:37 [d]Ps. 51:10
9 [1]Or, *being* [a]1 Chr. 12:2 [b]Judg. 20:39; Ps. 78:57
10 [a]Judg. 2:20; 1 Kin. 11:11; 2 Kin. 17:15; 18:12 [b]Ps. 119:1; Jer. 32:23; 44:10, 23
11 [1]Or, *wonderful works* [a]Ps. 106:13
12 [a]Ex. chs. 7-12; Ps. 106:22 [b]Num. 13:22; Ps. 78:43; Is. 19:11; 30:4; Ezek. 30:14
13 [a]Ex. 14:21; Ps. 74:13; 136:13 [b]Ex. 15:8; Ps. 33:7
14 [a]Ex. 13:21; Ps. 105:39 [b]Ex. 14:24
15 [a]Ex. 17:6; Num. 20:11; Ps. 105:41; 114:8; Is. 48:21; 1 Cor. 10:4
16 [a]Num. 20:8, 10, 11
17 [a]Deut. 9:22; Is. 63:10; Heb. 3:16
18 [a]Ex. 17:6; Deut. 6:16; Ps. 78:41, 56; 95:9; 106:14; 1 Cor. 10:9 [b]Num. 11:4
19 [a]Ex. 16:3; Num. 11:4; 20:3; 21:5; Ps. 23:5
20 [1]Lit., *flesh* [a]Num. 20:11; Ps. 78:15, 16 [b]Num. 11:18
21 [1]Or, *became infuriated* [a]Num. 11:1
22 [a]Deut. 1:32; 9:23; Heb. 3:18
23 [a]Gen. 7:11; Mal. 3:10
24 [1]Lit., *grain* [a]Ex. 16:4 [b]Ps. 105:40; John 6:31
25 [1]Lit., *mighty ones* [2]Or, *provision* [3]Lit., *to satiation* [a]Ex. 16:3
26 [1]Or, *strength* [a]Num. 11:31
27 [1]Lit., *flesh* [a]Ex. 16:13; Ps. 105:40

16 He [a]brought forth streams also from the rock,
And caused waters to run down like rivers.

17 Yet they still continued to sin against Him,
To [a]rebel against the Most High in the desert.
18 And in their heart they [a]put God to the test
By asking [b]food according to their desire.
19 Then they spoke against God;
They said, "[a]Can God prepare a table in the wilderness?
20 "Behold, He [a]struck the rock, so that waters gushed out,
And streams were overflowing;
Can He give bread also?
Will He provide [1b]meat for His people?"

21 Therefore the LORD heard and [1]was [a]full of wrath,
And a fire was kindled against Jacob,
And anger also mounted against Israel;
22 Because they [a]did not believe in God,
And did not trust in His salvation.
23 Yet He commanded the clouds above,
And [a]opened the doors of heaven;
24 And He [a]rained down manna upon them to eat,
And gave them [1b]food from heaven.
25 Man did eat the bread of [1]angels;
He sent them [2]food [3a]in abundance.
26 He [a]caused the east wind to blow in the heavens;
And by His [1]power He directed the south wind.
27 When He rained [1]meat upon them like the dust,
Even [a]winged fowl like the sand of the seas,
28 Then He let *them* fall in the midst of [1]their camp,
Round about their dwellings.
29 So they [a]ate and were well filled;
And their desire He gave to them.
30 [1]Before they had satisfied their desire,
[a]While their food was in their mouths,
31 The [a]anger of God rose against them,
And killed [1]some of their [b]stoutest ones,
And [2]subdued the choice men of Israel.
32 In spite of all this they [a]still sinned,
And [b]did not believe in His wonderful works.

28 [1]Lit., *His*
29 [a]Num. 11:19, 20
30 [1]Lit., *They were not estranged from* [a]Num. 11:33
31 [1]Lit., *among their fat ones* [2]Lit., *caused to bow down* [a]Num. 11:33, 34; Job 20:23 [b]Is. 10:16
32 [a]Num. chs. 14, 16, 17 [b]Num. 14:11; Ps. 78:11

33 So He brought [a]their days to an end in [1]futility,
And their years in sudden terror.

34 When He killed them, then they [a]sought Him,
And returned and searched [b]diligently for God;
35 And they remembered that God was their [a]rock,
And the Most High God their [b]Redeemer.
36 But they [a]deceived Him with their mouth,
And [b]lied to Him with their tongue.
37 For their heart was not [a]steadfast toward Him,
Nor were they faithful in His covenant.
38 But He, being [a]compassionate, [1b]forgave *their* iniquity, and did not destroy *them*;
And often He [2c]restrained His anger,
And did not arouse all His wrath.
39 Thus [a]He remembered that they were but [b]flesh,
A [1c]wind that passes and does not return.

40 How often they [a]rebelled against Him in the wilderness,
And [b]grieved Him in the [c]desert!
41 And again and again they [1a]tempted God,
And pained the [b]Holy One of Israel.
42 They [a]did not remember [b]His [1]power,
The day when He [c]redeemed them from the adversary,
43 When He performed His [a]signs in Egypt,
And His [b]marvels in the field of Zoan,
44 And [a]turned their rivers to blood,
And their streams, they could not drink.
45 He sent among them swarms of [a]flies, which devoured them,
And [b]frogs which destroyed them.
46 He gave also their crops to the [a]grasshopper,
And the product of their labor to the [b]locust.
47 He [1]destroyed their vines with [a]hailstones,
And their sycamore trees with frost.
48 He gave over their [a]cattle also to the hailstones,
And their herds to bolts of lightning.
49 He [a]sent upon them His burning anger,
Fury, and indignation, and trouble,
[1]A band of destroying angels.
50 He leveled a path for His anger;
He did not spare their soul from death,
But [a]gave over their life to the plague,
51 And [a]smote all the first-born in Egypt,
The [b]first *issue* of their virility in the tents of [c]Ham.
52 But He [a]led forth His own people like sheep,
And guided them in the wilderness [b]like a flock;
53 And He led them [a]safely, so that they did not fear;
But [b]the sea engulfed their enemies.

54 So [a]He brought them to His holy [1]land,
To this [2b]hill country [c]which His right hand had gained.
55 He also [a]drove out the nations before them,
And He [b]apportioned them for an inheritance by measurement,
And made the tribes of Israel dwell in their tents.
56 Yet they [1a]tempted and [b]rebelled against the Most High God,
And did not keep His testimonies,
57 But turned back and [a]acted treacherously like their fathers;
They [b]turned aside like a treacherous bow.
58 For they [a]provoked Him with their [b]high places,
And [c]aroused His jealousy with their [d]graven images.
59 When God heard, He [1]was filled with [a]wrath,
And greatly [b]abhorred Israel;
60 So that He [a]abandoned the [b]dwelling place at Shiloh,
The tent [1]which He had pitched among men,
61 And gave up His [a]strength to captivity,
And His glory [b]into the hand of the adversary.
62 He also [a]delivered His people to the sword,
And [1]was filled with wrath at His inheritance.
63 [a]Fire devoured [1]His young men;
And [1]His [b]virgins had no wedding songs.
64 [1]His [a]priests fell by the sword;
And [1]His [b]widows could not weep.

65 Then the Lord [a]awoke as *if from* sleep,
Like a [b]warrior [1]overcome by wine.
66 And He [1a]drove His adversaries backward;
He put on them an everlasting reproach.

33 [1]Lit., *vanity, a mere breath* [a]Num. 14:29, 35
34 [a]Num. 21:7; Hos. 5:15 [b]Ps. 63:1
35 [a]Deut. 32:4 [b]Ex. 15:13; Deut. 9:26; Ps. 74:2; Is. 41:14
36 [a]Ex. 24:7, 8; Ezek. 33:31 [b]Ex. 32:7, 8; Is. 57:11
37 [a]Ps. 51:10; 78:8; Acts 8:21
38 [1]Lit., *covered over, atoned for* [2]Lit., *turned away* [a]Ex. 34:6 [b]Num. 14:18-20 [c]Is. 48:9
39 [1]Or, *breath* [a]Job 10:9; Ps. 103:14 [b]Gen. 6:3 [c]Job 7:7, 16; Ps. 103:14; James 4:14
40 [a]Ps. 95:8, 9; 106:43; 107:11; Heb. 3:16 [b]Ps. 95:10; Is. 63:10; Eph. 4:30 [c]Ps. 106:14
41 [1]Or, *put God to the test* [a]Num. 14:22 [b]2 Kin. 19:22; Ps. 89:18
42 [1]Lit., *hand* [a]Judg. 8:34 [b]Ps. 44:3 [c]Ps. 106:10
43 [a]Ps. 105:27 [b]Ex. 4:21; 7:3
44 [a]Ex. 7:20; Ps. 105:29
45 [a]Ex. 8:24; Ps. 105:31 [b]Ex. 8:6; Ps. 105:30
46 [a]1 Kin. 8:37; Ps. 105:34 [b]Ex. 10:14
47 [1]Lit., *was killing* [a]Ex. 9:23-25; Ps. 105:32
48 [a]Ex. 9:19
49 [1]Lit., *A deputation of angels of evil* [a]Ex. 15:7
50 [a]Ex. 12:29, 30
51 [a]Ex. 12:29; Ps. 105:36; 135:8; 136:10 [b]Gen. 49:3 [c]Ps. 105:23, 27; 106:22
52 [a]Ex. 15:22 [b]Ps. 77:20
53 [a]Ex. 14:19, 20 [b]Ex. 14:27, 28; Ps. 106:11
54 [1]Lit., *border, territory* [2]Or, *mountain* [a]Ex. 15:17 [b]Ps. 68:16; Is. 11:9 [c]Ps. 44:3
55 [a]Josh. 11:16-23; Ps. 44:2 [b]Josh. 13:7; 23:4; Ps. 105:11; 135:12
56 [1]Or, *put to the test* [a]Ps. 78:18 [b]Judg. 2:11-13; Ps. 78:40
57 [a]Ezek. 20:27, 28 [b]Hos. 7:16
58 [a]Deut. 4:25; Judg. 2:12; 1 Kin. 14:9; Is. 65:3 [b]Lev. 26:30; 1 Kin. 3:2; 2 Kin. 16:4; Jer. 17:3 [c]Deut. 32:16, 21; 1 Kin. 14:22 [d]Ex. 20:4; Lev. 26:1; Deut. 4:25
59 [1]Or, *became infuriated* [a]Deut. 1:34; 9:19; Ps. 106:40 [b]Lev. 26:30; Deut. 32:19; Amos 6:8

60 [1]Some ancient versions read *where He dwelt* [a]1 Sam. 4:11; Ps. 78:67; Jer. 7:12, 14; 26:6 [b]Josh. 18:1
61 [a]Ps. 63:2; 132:8 [b]1 Sam. 4:17
62 [1]Or, *became infuriated* [a]Judg. 20:21; 1 Sam. 4:10
63 [1]Or, *their* [a]Num. 11:1; 21:28; Is. 26:11; Jer. 48:45 [b]Jer. 7:34; 16:9; Lam. 2:21
64 [1]Or, *their* [a]1 Sam. 4:17; 22:18 [b]Job 27:15; Ezek. 24:23
65 [1]Or, *sobered up from* [a]Ps. 44:23; 73:20 [b]Is. 42:13
66 [1]Lit., *smote* [a]1 Sam. 5:6

67 He also [a]rejected the tent of Joseph,
And did not choose the tribe of Ephraim,
68 But chose the tribe of Judah,
Mount [a]Zion which He loved.
69 And He [a]built His sanctuary like the heights,
Like the earth which He has founded forever.
70 He also [a]chose David His servant,
And took him from the sheepfolds;
71 From [1a]the care of the [2]ewes [b]with suckling lambs He brought him,
To [c]shepherd Jacob His people,
And Israel [d]His inheritance.
72 So he shepherded them according to the [a]integrity of his heart,
And guided them with his skillful hands.

PSALM 79

A Lament over the Destruction of Jerusalem, and Prayer for Help.

A Psalm of Asaph.

O GOD, the [a]nations have [1]invaded [b]Thine inheritance;
They have defiled Thy [c]holy temple;
They have [d]laid Jerusalem in ruins.
2 They have given the [a]dead bodies of Thy servants for food to the birds of the heavens,
The flesh of Thy godly ones to the beasts of the earth.
3 They have poured out their blood like water round about Jerusalem;
And there was [a]no one to bury them.
4 We have become a [a]reproach to our neighbors,
A scoffing and derision to those around us.
5 [a]How long, O LORD? Wilt Thou be angry forever?
Will Thy [b]jealousy [c]burn like fire?
6 [a]Pour out Thy wrath upon the nations which [b]do not know Thee,
And upon the kingdoms which [c]do not call upon Thy name.
7 For they have [a]devoured Jacob,
And [b]laid waste his [1]habitation.

8 [a]Do not remember [1]the iniquities of *our* forefathers against us;
Let Thy compassion come quickly to [b]meet us;
For we are [c]brought very low.
9 [a]Help us, O God of our salvation, for the glory of [b]Thy name;
And deliver us, and [1c]forgive our sins, [d]for Thy name's sake.
10 [a]Why should the nations say, "Where is their God?"
Let there be known among the nations in our sight,
[b]Vengeance for the blood of Thy servants, which has been shed.

67 [a]Ps. 78:60
68 [a]Ps. 87:2; 132:13
69 [a]1 Kin. 6:1-38
70 [a]1 Sam. 16:11, 12
71 [1]Lit., *following* [2]Lit., *ewes which gave suck, He . . .* [a]2 Sam. 7:8; Is. 40:11 [b]Gen. 33:13 [c]2 Sam. 5:2; 1 Chr. 11:2; Ps. 28:9 [d]1 Sam. 10:1
72 [a]1 Kin. 9:4
1 [1]Lit., *come into* [a]Lam. 1:10 [b]Ps. 74:2 [c]Ps. 74:3, 7 [d]2 Kin. 25:9, 10; 2 Chr. 36:17-19; Jer. 26:18; 52:12-14; Mic. 3:12
2 [a]Deut. 28:26; Jer. 7:33; 16:4; 19:7; 34:20
3 [a]Jer. 14:16; 16:4
4 [a]Ps. 44:13; 80:6; Dan. 9:16
5 [a]Ps. 13:1; 74:1, 9, 10; 85:5; 89:46 [b]Deut. 29:20; Ezek. 36:5; 38:19 [c]Ps. 89:46; Zeph. 3:8
6 [a]Ps. 69:24; Jer. 10:25; Ezek. 21:31; Zeph. 3:8 [b]1 Thess. 4:5; 2 Thess. 1:8 [c]Ps. 14:4; 53:4
7 [1]Lit., *pasture* [a]Ps. 53:4 [b]2 Chr. 36:19; Jer. 39:8
8 [1]Or, our *former iniquities* [a]Ps. 106:6; Is. 64:9 [b]Ps. 21:3 [c]Deut. 28:43; Ps. 116:6; 142:6; Is. 26:5
9 [1]Lit., *cover over, atone for* [a]2 Chr. 14:11 [b]Ps. 31:3 [c]Ps. 25:11; 65:3 [d]Jer. 14:7
10 [a]Ps. 42:10; 115:2 [b]Ps. 94:1, 2
11 [1]Lit., *arm* [2]Lit., *the children of death* [a]Ps. 102:20
12 [1]Lit., *Their* [a]Gen. 4:15; Lev. 26:21, 28; Ps. 12:6; 119:164; Prov. 6:31; 24:16; Is. 30:26 [b]Ps. 35:13; Is. 65:6, 7; Jer. 32:18; Luke 6:38 [c]Ps. 74:10, 18, 22
13 [1]Or, *pasturing* [a]Ps. 74:1; 95:7; 100:3 [b]Ps. 44:8 [c]Ps. 89:1; Is. 43:21

+ Possibly, *to the Lilies*
• *Lit., A testimony*
1 [a]Ps. 23:1 [b]Ps. 77:15; 78:67; Amos 5:15 [c]Ex. 25:22; 1 Sam. 4:4; 2 Sam. 6:2; Ps. 99:1
2 [a]Num. 2:18-24 [b]Ps. 35:23
3 [1]Or, *that we may* [a]Ps. 60:1; 80:7, 19; 85:4; 126:1; Lam. 5:21 [b]Num. 6:25; Ps. 4:6; 31:16
4 [1]Lit., *smoke against* [a]Ps. 59:5; 84:8 [b]Ps. 79:5; 85:5
5 [1]Lit., *a third part of a* [a]Ps. 42:3; 102:9; Is. 30:20
6 [1]Lit., *a strife to* [a]Ps. 44:13; 79:4

11 Let [a]the groaning of the prisoner come before Thee;
According to the greatness of Thy [1]power preserve [2]those who are [a]doomed to die.
12 And return to our neighbors [a]sevenfold [b]into their bosom
[1]The [c]reproach with which they have reproached Thee, O Lord.
13 So we Thy people and the [a]sheep of Thy [1]pasture
Will [b]give thanks to Thee forever;
To all generations we will [c]tell of Thy praise.

PSALM 80

God Implored to Rescue His People from Their Calamities.

For the choir director; *set to* +El Shoshannim; •Eduth. A Psalm of Asaph.

OH, give ear, [a]Shepherd of Israel,
Thou who dost lead [b]Joseph like a flock;
Thou who [c]art enthroned *above* the cherubim, shine forth!
2 Before [a]Ephraim and Benjamin and Manasseh, [b]stir up Thy power,
And come to save us!
3 O God, [a]restore us,
And [b]cause Thy face to shine *upon us*, [1]and we will be saved.

4 O [a]LORD God *of* hosts,
[b]How long wilt Thou [1]be angry with the prayer of Thy people?
5 Thou hast fed them with the [a]bread of tears,
And Thou hast made them to drink tears in [1]large measure.
6 Thou dost make us [1]an object of contention [a]to our neighbors;
And our enemies laugh among themselves.
7 O God *of* hosts, restore us,
And cause Thy face to shine *upon us*, [1]and we will be saved.

8 Thou didst remove a [a]vine from Egypt;
Thou didst [b]drive out the [1]nations, and didst [c]plant it.
9 Thou didst [a]clear *the ground* before it,
And it [b]took deep root and filled the land.
10 The mountains were covered with its shadow;
And [1]the cedars of God with its [a]boughs.
11 It was sending out its branches [a]to the sea,
And its shoots to the River.
12 Why hast Thou [a]broken down its [1]hedges,

7 [1]Or, *that we may*
8 [1]Or, *Gentiles* [a]Ps. 80:15; Is. 5:1, 2, 7; Jer. 2:21; 12:10; Ezek. 17:6; 19:10 [b]Josh. 13:6; 2 Chr. 20:7; Ps. 44:2; Acts 7:45 [c]Jer. 11:17; 32:41; Ezek. 17:23; Amos 9:15
9 [a]Ex. 23:28; Josh. 24:12; Is. 5:2 [b]Hos. 14:5
10 [1]Or, *its boughs are like the cedars of God* [a]Gen. 49:22
11 [a]Ps. 72:8
12 [1]Or, *walls, fences* [a]Ps. 89:40; Is. 5:5

So that all who pass *that* way pick
its *fruit*?
13 A boar from the forest [a]eats it
away,
And whatever moves in the field
feeds on it.

14 O God *of* hosts, [a]turn again now,
we beseech Thee;
[b]Look down from heaven and see,
and take care of this vine,
15 Even the [1a]shoot which Thy right
hand has planted,
And on the [2]son whom Thou hast
[3]strengthened for Thyself.
16 It is [a]burned with fire, it is cut
down;
They perish at the [b]rebuke of Thy
countenance.
17 Let [a]Thy hand be upon the man of
Thy right hand,
Upon the son of man whom Thou
[b]didst make strong for Thyself.
18 Then we shall not [a]turn back from
Thee;
[b]Revive us, and we will call upon
Thy name.
19 O LORD God of hosts, [a]restore us;
Cause Thy face to shine *upon us*,
[1]and we will be saved.

PSALM 81

God's Goodness and Israel's Waywardness.

For the choir director; [+]on the Gittith.
A Psalm of Asaph.

[a]SING for joy to God our [b]strength;
Shout [c]joyfully to the [d]God of
Jacob.
2 Raise a song, strike [a]the timbrel,
The sweet sounding [b]lyre with the
[c]harp.
3 Blow the trumpet at the [a]new
moon,
At the full moon, on our [b]feast day.
4 For it is a statute for Israel,
An ordinance of the God of Jacob.
5 He established it for a testimony in
Joseph,
When he [1a]went throughout the
land of Egypt.
I heard a [b]language that I did not
know:

6"I [1a]relieved his shoulder of the
burden,
His hands were freed from the
[2]basket.
7"You [a]called in trouble, and I rescued you;
I [b]answered you in the hiding place
of thunder;
I proved you at the [c]waters of
Meribah. [[1]Selah.
8"[a]Hear, O My people, and I will
[1]admonish you;
O Israel, if you [b]would listen to
Me!
9"Let there be no [a]strange god among
you;
Nor shall you worship any foreign
god.
10"[a]I, the LORD, am your God,
Who brought you up from the land
of Egypt;
[b]Open your mouth wide and I will
[c]fill it.

11"But My people [a]did not listen to
My voice;
And Israel did not [1]obey Me.
12"So I [a]gave [1]them over to the stubbornness of their heart,
To walk in their own devices.
13"Oh that My people [a]would listen to
Me,
That Israel would [b]walk in My
ways!
14"I would quickly [a]subdue their enemies,
And [b]turn My hand against their
adversaries.
15"[a]Those who hate the LORD would
[b]pretend obedience to Him;
And their time *of punishment* would
be forever.
16"[1]But I would feed you with the
[2a]finest of the wheat;
And with [b]honey from the rock I
would satisfy you."

PSALM 82

Unjust Judgments Rebuked.

A Psalm of Asaph.

GOD takes His [a]stand in [1]His own
congregation;
He [b]judges in the midst of the
[2c]rulers.
2 How long will you [a]judge unjustly,
And [b]show partiality to the
wicked? [[1]Selah.
3 [a]Vindicate the weak and fatherless;
Do justice to the afflicted and destitute.
4 [a]Rescue the weak and needy;
Deliver *them* out of the hand of the
wicked.

5 They [a]do not know nor do they
understand;
They [b]walk about in darkness;
All the [c]foundations of the earth
are shaken.
6 [1]I [a]said, "You are gods,
And all of you are [b]sons of the
Most High.
7"Nevertheless [a]you will die like men,
And fall like *any* [b]one of the
princes."
8 [a]Arise, O God, [b]judge the earth!
For it is Thou who dost [c]possess all
the nations.

13 [a]Jer. 5:6
14 [a]Ps. 90:13 [b]Ps. 102:19; Is. 63:15
15 [1]Or, *root* [2]Or, *figuratively: branch* [3]Or, *secured* [a]Ps. 80:8
16 [a]2 Chr. 36:19; Ps. 74:8; Jer. 52:13 [b]Ps. 39:11; 76:6
17 [a]Ps. 89:21 [b]Ps. 80:15
18 [a]Is. 50:5 [b]Ps. 71:20
19 [1]Or, *that we may* [a]Ps. 80:3

[+] Or, *according to*
1 [a]Ps. 51:14; 59:16; 95:1 [b]Ps. 46:1 [c]Ps. 66:1; 95:2; 98:4 [d]Ps. 84:8
2 [a]Ex. 15:20; Ps. 149:3 [b]Ps. 92:3; 98:5; 147:7 [c]Ps. 108:2; 144:9
3 [a]Num. 10:10 [b]Lev. 23:24
5 [1]Lit., *went out over* [a]Ex. 11:4 [b]Deut. 28:49; Ps. 114:1; Jer. 5:15
6 [1]Lit., *removed his shoulder from* [2]Or, *brick load* [a]Is. 9:4; 10:27
7 [1]*Selah* may mean: *Pause, Crescendo* or *Musical interlude* [a]Ex. 2:23; 14:10; Ps. 50:15 [b]Ex. 19:19; 20:18 [c]Ex. 17:6, 7; Num. 20:13; Ps. 95:8
8 [1]Or, *bear witness against* [a]Ps. 50:7 [b]Ps. 95:7
9 [a]Ex. 20:3; Deut. 5:7; 32:12; Ps. 44:20; Is. 43:12
10 [a]Ex. 20:2; Deut. 5:6 [b]Job 29:23 [c]Ps. 37:4; 78:25; 107:9
11 [1]Lit., *yield to* [a]Deut. 32:15; Ps. 106:25
12 [1]Lit., *him* [a]Job 8:4; Acts 7:42; Rom. 1:24, 26
13 [a]Deut. 5:29; Ps. 81:8; Is. 48:18 [b]Ps. 128:1; Is. 42:24; Jer. 7:23
14 [a]Ps. 18:47; 47:3 [b]Amos 1:8
15 [a]Rom. 1:30 [b]Ps. 18:44; 66:3
16 [1]Lit., *He would feed him* [2]Lit., *fat* [a]Deut. 32:14; Ps. 147:14 [b]Deut. 32:13

1 [1]Lit., *the congregation of God* [2]Lit., *gods* [a]Is. 3:13 [b]2 Chr. 19:6; Ps. 58:11 [c]Ex. 21:6; 22:8, 28
2 [1]*Selah* may mean: *Pause, Crescendo* or *Musical interlude* [a]Ps. 58:1 [b]Deut. 1:17; Prov. 18:5
3 [a]Deut. 24:17; Ps. 10:18; Is. 11:4; Jer. 22:16
4 [a]Job 29:12

5 [a]Ps. 14:4; Jer. 4:22; Mic. 3:1 [b]Prov. 2:13; Is. 59:9; Jer. 23:12 [c]Ps. 11:3
6 [1]Lit., *I, on my part* [a]Ps. 82:1; John 10:34 [b]Ps. 89:26
7 [a]Job 21:32; Ps. 49:12; Ezek. 31:14 [b]Ps. 83:11
8 [a]Ps. 12:5 [b]Ps. 58:11; 96:13 [c]Ps. 2:8; Rev. 11:15

PSALM 83

God Implored to Confound His Enemies.

A Song, a Psalm of Asaph.

O GOD, [a]do not remain quiet;
[b]Do not be silent and, O God, do not be still.
2 For, behold, Thine enemies [a]make an uproar;
And [b]those who hate Thee have [1c]exalted themselves.
3 They [a]make shrewd plans against Thy people,
And [1]conspire together against [b]Thy [2]treasured ones.
4 They have said, "Come, and [a]let us wipe them out [1]as a nation,
That the [b]name of Israel be remembered no more."
5 For they have [1a]conspired together with one mind;
Against Thee do they make a covenant:
6 The tents of [a]Edom and the [b]Ishmaelites;
[c]Moab, and the [d]Hagrites;
7 [a]Gebal, and [b]Ammon, and [c]Amalek;
[d]Philistia with the inhabitants of [e]Tyre;
8 [a]Assyria also has joined with them;
They have become [1]a help to the [b]children of Lot. [[2]Selah.

9 Deal with them [a]as with Midian,
As [b]with Sisera *and* Jabin, at the torrent of Kishon,
10 Who were destroyed at En-dor,
Who [a]became as dung for the ground.
11 Make their nobles like [a]Oreb and Zeeb,
And all their princes like [b]Zebah and Zalmunna,
12 Who said, "[a]Let us possess for ourselves
The [b]pastures of God."

13 O my God, make them like the [1a]whirling dust;
Like [b]chaff before the wind.
14 Like [a]fire that burns the forest,
And like a flame that [b]sets the mountains on fire,
15 So pursue them [a]with Thy tempest,
And terrify them with Thy storm.
16 [a]Fill their faces with dishonor,
That they may seek Thy name, O LORD.
17 Let them be [a]ashamed and dismayed forever;
And let them be humiliated and perish,
18 That they may [a]know that [b]Thou alone, whose name is the LORD,
Art the [c]Most High over all the earth.

1 [a]Ps. 28:1; 35:22 [b]Ps. 109:1
2 [1]Lit., *lifted up the head* [a]Ps. 2:1; Is. 17:12 [b]Ps. 81:15 [c]Judg. 8:28; Zech. 1:21
3 [1]Or, *consult* [2]Or, *hidden ones* [a]Ps. 64:2; Is. 29:15 [b]Ps. 27:5; 31:20
4 [1]Lit., *from* [a]Esth. 3:6; Ps. 74:8; Jer. 48:2 [b]Ps. 41:5; Jer. 11:19
5 [1]Or, *consulted* [a]Ps. 2:2; Dan. 6:7
6 [a]2 Chr. 20:10; Ps. 137:7 [b]Gen. 25:12-16 [c]2 Chr. 20:10 [d]1 Chr. 5:10
7 [a]Josh. 13:5; Ezek. 27:9 [b]2 Chr. 20:10 [c]1 Sam. 15:2 [d]1 Sam. 4:1; 29:1 [e]Ezek. 27:3; Amos 1:9
8 [1]Lit., *an arm* [2]*Selah* may mean: *Pause, Crescendo* or *Musical interlude* [a]2 Kin. 15:19 [b]Deut. 2:9
9 [a]Judg. 7:1-24 [b]Judg. 4:7, 15, 21-24
10 [a]Zeph. 1:17
11 [a]Judg. 7:25 [b]Judg. 8:12, 21
12 [a]2 Chr. 20:11 [b]Ps. 132:13
13 [1]Or, *tumbleweed* [a]Is. 17:13 [b]Job 21:18; Ps. 35:5; Is. 40:24; Jer. 13:24
14 [a]Is. 9:18 [b]Ex. 19:18; Deut. 32:22
15 [a]Job 9:17; Ps. 58:9
16 [a]Job 10:15; Ps. 109:29; 132:18
17 [a]Ps. 35:4; 70:2
18 [a]Ps. 59:13 [b]Ps. 86:10; Is. 45:21 [c]Ps. 9:2; 18:13; 97:9

+ Or, *according to*
1 [a]Ps. 43:3; 132:5
2 [a]Ps. 42:1, 2; 63:1 [b]Ps. 42:2
3 [a]Ps. 43:4 [b]Ps. 5:2
4 [1]*Selah* may mean: *Pause, Crescendo* or *Musical interlude* [a]Ps. 65:4 [b]Ps. 42:5, 11
5 [1]Lit., *their* [a]Ps. 81:1 [b]Ps. 86:11; 122:1; Jer. 31:6
6 [1]Probably, *Weeping;* or, *Balsam trees* [2]Or, *place of springs* [a]Ps. 107:35; Joel 2:23
7 [1]Some ancient versions read *The God of gods will be seen in Zion.* [a]Prov. 4:18; Is. 40:31; John 1:16; 2 Cor. 3:18 [b]Ex. 34:23; Deut. 16:16; Ps. 42:2
8 [a]Ps. 59:5; 80:4; 84:1 [b]Ps. 81:1
9 [a]Gen. 15:1; Ps. 3:3; 28:7; 59:11; 115:9-11 [b]1 Sam. 16:6; 2 Sam. 19:21; Ps. 2:2; 132:17
10 [a]Ps. 27:4

PSALM 84

Longing for the Temple Worship.

For the choir director; +on the Gittith.
A Psalm of the sons of Korah.

HOW lovely are Thy [a]dwelling places, O LORD of hosts!
2 My [a]soul longed and even yearned for the courts of the LORD;
My heart and my flesh sing for joy to the [b]living God.
3 The bird also has found a house,
And the swallow a nest for herself, where she may lay her young,
Even Thine [a]altars, O LORD of hosts,
[b]My King and my God.
4 How [a]blessed are those who dwell in Thy house!
They are [b]ever praising Thee. [[1]Selah.

5 How blessed is the man whose [a]strength is in Thee;
In [1]whose heart are the [b]highways *to Zion*!
6 Passing through the valley of [1]Baca, they make it a [2]spring,
The [a]early rain also covers it with blessings.
7 They [a]go from strength to strength,
[1]*Every one of them* [b]appears before God in Zion.

8 O [a]LORD God of hosts, hear my prayer;
Give ear, O [b]God of Jacob! [Selah.
9 Behold our [a]shield, O God,
And look upon the face of [b]Thine anointed.
10 For [a]a day in Thy courts is better than a thousand *outside.*
I would rather stand at the threshold of the house of my God,
Than dwell in the tents of wickedness.
11 For the LORD God is [a]a sun and [b]shield;
The LORD gives grace and [c]glory;
[d]No good thing does He withhold [1]from those who walk [2]uprightly.
12 O LORD of hosts,
How [a]blessed is the man who trusts in Thee!

PSALM 85

Prayer for God's Mercy upon the Nation.

For the choir director.
A Psalm of the sons of Korah.

O LORD, Thou didst show [a]favor to Thy land;
Thou didst [1b]restore the captivity of Jacob.

11 [1]Lit., *with regard to* [2]Lit., *with integrity* [a]Is. 60:19, 20; Mal. 4:2; Rev. 21:23 [b]Gen. 15:1 [c]Ps. 85:9 [d]Ps. 34:9, 10
12 [a]Ps. 2:12; 40:4

1 [1]Or, *restore the fortunes* [a]Ps. 77:7; 106:4 [b]Ezra 1:11; Ps. 14:7; 126:1; Jer. 30:18; Ezek. 39:25; Hos. 6:11; Joel 3:1

2 Thou didst [a]forgive the iniquity of Thy people;
Thou didst [b]cover all their sin. [[1]Selah.
3 Thou didst [a]withdraw all Thy fury;
Thou didst [b]turn away from Thy burning anger.

4 [a]Restore us, O God of our salvation,
And [b]cause Thine indignation toward us to cease.
5 Wilt [a]Thou be angry with us forever?
Wilt Thou prolong Thine anger to [1]all generations?
6 Wilt Thou not Thyself [1a]revive us again,
That Thy people may [b]rejoice in Thee?
7 Show us Thy lovingkindness, O LORD,
And [a]grant us Thy salvation.

8 [1]I will hear what God the LORD will say;
For He will [a]speak peace to His people, [2]to His godly ones;
But let them not [b]turn back to [3]folly.
9 Surely [a]His salvation is near to those who [1]fear Him,
That [b]glory may dwell in our land.
10 [a]Lovingkindness and [1]truth have met together;
[b]Righteousness and peace have kissed each other.
11 [1]Truth [a]springs from the earth;
And righteousness looks down from heaven.
12 Indeed, [a]the LORD will give what is good;
And our [b]land will yield its produce.
13 [a]Righteousness will go before Him,
And will make His footsteps into a way.

PSALM 86

A Psalm of Supplication and Trust.

A Prayer of David.

[a]INCLINE Thine ear, O LORD, *and* answer me;
For I am [b]afflicted and needy.
2 [a]Do preserve my [1]soul, for I am a [b]godly man;
O Thou my God, save Thy servant who [c]trusts in Thee.
3 Be [a]gracious to me, O Lord,
For [b]to Thee I cry all day long.
4 Make glad the soul of Thy servant,
For to Thee, O Lord, [a]I lift up my soul.
5 For Thou, Lord, art [a]good, and [b]ready to forgive,
And [c]abundant in lovingkindness to all who call upon Thee.
6 [a]Give ear, O LORD, to my prayer;
And give heed to the voice of my supplications!

2 [1]*Selah* may mean: *Pause, Crescendo* or *Musical interlude* [a]Num. 14:19; 1 Kin. 8:34; Ps. 78:38; 103:3; Jer. 31:34 [b]Ps. 32:1
3 [a]Ps. 78:38; 106:23 [b]Ex. 32:12; Deut. 13:17; Ps. 106:23; Jon. 3:9
4 [a]Ps. 80:3,7 [b]Dan. 9:16
5 [1]Lit., *generation and generation* [a]Ps. 74:1; 79:5; 80:4
6 [1]Or, *bring to life* [a]Ps. 71:20; 80:18 [b]Ps. 33:1; 90:14; 149:2
7 [a]Ps. 106:4
8 [1]Or, *Let me hear* [2]Lit., *even to* [3]Or, *stupidity* [a]Ps. 29:11; Hag. 2:9; Zech. 9:10 [b]Ps. 78:57; 2 Pet. 2:21
9 [1]Or, *reverence* [a]Ps. 34:18; Is. 46:13 [b]Ps. 84:11; Hag. 2:7; Zech. 2:5; John 1:14
10 [1]Or, *faithfulness* [a]Ps. 25:10; 89:14; Prov. 3:3 [b]Ps. 72:3; Is. 32:17
11 [1]Or, *Faithfulness* [a]Is. 45:8
12 [a]Ps. 84:11; James 1:17 [b]Lev. 26:4; Ps. 67:6; Ezek. 34:27; Zech. 8:12
13 [a]Ps. 89:14

1 [a]Ps. 17:6; 31:2; 71:2 [b]Ps. 40:17; 70:5
2 [1]Or, *life* [a]Ps. 25:20 [b]Ps. 4:3; 50:5 [c]Ps. 25:2; 31:14; 56:4
3 [a]Ps. 4:1; 57:1 [b]Ps. 25:5; 88:9
4 [a]Ps. 25:1; 143:8
5 [a]Ps. 25:8 [b]Ps. 130:4 [c]Ex. 34:6; Neh. 9:17; Ps. 103:8; 145:8; Joel 2:13; Jon. 4:2
6 [a]Ps. 55:1
7 [a]Ps. 50:15; 77:2 [b]Ps. 17:6
8 [a]Ex. 15:11; 2 Sam. 7:22; 1 Kin. 8:23; Ps. 89:6; Jer. 10:6 [b]Deut. 3:24
9 [a]Ps. 22:27; 66:4; Is. 66:23; Rev. 15:4
10 [1]Or, *miracles* [a]Ps. 77:13 [b]Ex. 15:11; Ps. 72:18; 77:14; 136:4 [c]Deut. 6:4; 32:39; Ps. 83:18; Is. 37:16; 44:6, 8; Mark 12:29; 1 Cor. 8:4
11 [a]Ps. 25:5 [b]Jer. 32:39
12 [a]Ps. 111:1
13 [1]Lit., *lowest Sheol* [2]I.e., the nether world [a]Ps. 30:3
14 [1]Or, *an assembly* [2]Lit., *soul* [a]Ps. 54:3
15 [1]Or, *faithfulness* [a]Ps. 86:5
16 [a]Ps. 25:16 [b]Ps. 68:35 [c]Ps. 116:16
17 [a]Judg. 6:17; Ps. 119:122 [b]Ps. 112:10

1 [a]Ps. 78:69; Is. 28:16
2 [a]Ps. 78:67, 68

7 In [a]the day of my trouble I shall call upon Thee,
For [b]Thou wilt answer me.
8 There is [a]no one like Thee among the gods, O Lord;
Nor are there any works [b]like Thine.
9 [a]All nations whom Thou hast made shall come and worship before Thee, O Lord;
And they shall glorify Thy name.
10 For Thou art [a]great and [b]doest [1]wondrous deeds;
Thou alone [c]art God.

11 [a]Teach me Thy way, O LORD;
I will walk in Thy truth;
[b]Unite my heart to fear Thy name.
12 I will [a]give thanks to Thee, O Lord my God, with all my heart,
And will glorify Thy name forever.
13 For Thy lovingkindness toward me is great,
And Thou hast [a]delivered my soul from the [1]depths of [2]Sheol.

14 O God, arrogant men have [a]risen up against me,
And [1]a band of violent men have sought my [2]life,
And they have not set Thee before them.
15 But Thou, O Lord, art a God [a]merciful and gracious,
Slow to anger and abundant in lovingkindness and [1]truth.
16 [a]Turn to me, and be gracious to me;
Oh [b]grant Thy strength to Thy servant,
And save the [c]son of Thy handmaid.
17 [a]Show me a sign for good,
That those who hate me may [b]see *it*, and be ashamed,
Because Thou, O LORD, [c]hast helped me and comforted me.

PSALM 87

The Privileges of Citizenship in Zion.

A Psalm of the sons of Korah. A Song.

HIS [a]foundation is in the holy mountains.
2 The LORD [a]loves the gates of Zion
More than all the *other* dwelling places of Jacob.
3 [a]Glorious things are spoken of you,
O [b]city of God. [[1]Selah.
4 "I shall mention [1a]Rahab and Babylon [2]among those who know Me;
Behold, Philistia and [b]Tyre with [3c]Ethiopia:
'This one was born there.' "

3 [1]*Selah* may mean: *Pause, Crescendo* or *Musical interlude* [a]Is. 60:1 [b]Ps. 46:4; 48:8
4 [1]I.e., Egypt [2]Or, *as* [3]Lit., *Cush* [a]Job 9:13; Ps. 89:10; Is. 19:23-25 [b]Ps. 45:12 [c]Ps. 68:31

5 But of Zion it shall be said, "This one and that one were born in her";
And the Most High Himself will [a]establish her.
6 The LORD shall count when He [a]registers the peoples,
"This one was born there." [Selah.
7 Then those who [a]sing as well as those who [1b]play the flutes *shall say,*
"All my [c]springs *of joy* are in you."

PSALM 88

A Petition to Be Saved from Death.

A Song. A Psalm of the sons of Korah. For the choir director; according to Mahalath Leannoth. A •Maskil of Heman +the Ezrahite.

O LORD, the [a]God of my salvation,
I have [b]cried out by day and in the night before Thee.
2 Let my prayer [a]come before Thee;
[b]Incline Thine ear to my cry!
3 For my [a]soul has [1]had enough troubles,
And [b]my life has drawn near to [2]Sheol.
4 I am reckoned among those who [a]go down to the pit;
I have become like a man [b]without strength,
5 [1]Forsaken [a]among the dead,
Like the slain who lie in the grave,
Whom Thou dost remember no more,
And they are [b]cut off from Thy hand.
6 Thou hast put me in [a]the lowest pit,
In [b]dark places, in the [c]depths.
7 Thy wrath [a]has rested upon me,
And Thou hast afflicted me with [b]all Thy waves. [[1]Selah.
8 Thou hast removed [a]my acquaintances far from me;
Thou hast made me an [1b]object of loathing to them;
I am [c]shut up and cannot go out.
9 My [a]eye has wasted away because of affliction;
I have [b]called upon Thee every day, O LORD;
I have [c]spread out my [1]hands to Thee.

10 Wilt Thou perform wonders for the dead?
Will [a]the [1]departed spirits rise *and* praise Thee? [Selah.
11 Will Thy lovingkindness be declared in the grave,
Thy faithfulness in [1]Abaddon?
12 Will Thy wonders be made known in the [a]darkness?
And Thy [1]righteousness in the land of forgetfulness?

13 But I, O LORD, have cried out [a]to Thee for help,
And [b]in the morning my prayer comes before Thee.
14 O LORD, why [a]dost Thou reject my soul?
Why dost Thou [b]hide Thy face from me?
15 I was afflicted and [a]about to die from my youth on;
I suffer [b]Thy terrors; I am [1]overcome.
16 Thy [a]burning anger has passed over me;
Thy terrors have [1b]destroyed me.
17 They have [a]surrounded me [b]like water all day long;
They have [c]encompassed me altogether.
18 Thou hast removed [a]lover and friend far from me;
My acquaintances are *in* darkness.

PSALM 89

The LORD'S Covenant with David, and Israel's Afflictions.

A •Maskil of ΔEthan +the Ezrahite.

I WILL [a]sing of the lovingkindness of the LORD forever;
To all generations I will [b]make known Thy [c]faithfulness with my mouth.
2 For I have said, "[a]Lovingkindness will be built up forever;
In the heavens Thou wilt establish Thy [b]faithfulness."
3 "I have made a covenant with [a]My chosen;
I have [b]sworn to David My servant,
4 I will establish your [a]seed forever,
And build up your [b]throne to all generations." [[1]Selah.

5 And the [a]heavens will praise Thy wonders, O LORD;
Thy faithfulness also [b]in the assembly of the [c]holy ones.
6 For [a]who in the skies is comparable to the LORD?
Who among the [1b]sons of the mighty is like the LORD,
7 A God [a]greatly feared in the council of the [b]holy ones,
And [c]awesome above all those who are around Him?
8 O LORD God of hosts, [a]who is like Thee, O mighty [1]LORD?
Thy faithfulness also surrounds Thee.
9 Thou dost rule the swelling of the sea;
When its waves rise, Thou [a]dost still them.

5 [a]Ps. 48:8
6 [a]Ps. 69:28; Is. 4:3; Ezek. 13:9
7 [1]Or, *dance* [a]Ps. 68:25; 149:3 [b]2 Sam. 6:14; Ps. 30:11 [c]Ps. 36:9

• Possibly, *Contemplative,* or *Didactic,* or *Skillful Psalm*
+ 1 Kin. 4:31; 1 Chr. 2:6; Ps. 89:title
1 [a]Ps. 24:5; 27:9 [b]Ps. 22:2; 86:3; Luke 18:7
2 [a]Ps. 18:6 [b]Ps. 31:2; 86:1
3 [1]Or, *been satisfied with* [2]I.e., the nether world [a]Ps. 107:26 [b]Ps. 107:18; 116:3
4 [a]Ps. 28:1; 143:7 [b]Job 29:12; Ps. 22:11
5 [1]Lit., *A freed one among the dead* [a]Ps. 31:12 [b]Ps. 31:22; Is. 53:8
6 [a]Ps. 86:13; Lam. 3:55 [b]Ps. 143:3 [c]Ps. 69:15
7 [1]*Selah* may mean: *Pause, Crescendo* or *Musical interlude* [a]Ps. 32:4; 39:10 [b]Ps. 42:7
8 [1]Lit., *abomination to them* [a]Job 19:13, 19; Ps. 31:11; 142:4 [b]Job 30:10 [c]Ps. 142:7; Jer. 32:2; 36:5
9 [1]Lit., *palms* [a]Ps. 6:7; 31:9 [b]Ps. 22:2; 86:3 [c]Job 11:13; Ps. 143:6
10 [1]Or, *ghosts, shades* [a]Ps. 6:5; 30:9
11 [1]I.e., place of destruction
12 [1]I.e., faithfulness to His gracious promises [a]Job 10:21; Ps. 88:6
13 [a]Ps. 30:2 [b]Ps. 5:3; 119:147
14 [a]Ps. 43:2; 44:9 [b]Job 13:24; Ps. 13:1; 44:24
15 [1]Or, *embarrassed* [a]Prov. 24:11 [b]Job 6:4; 31:23
16 [1]Or, *silenced* [a]2 Chr. 28:11; Is. 13:13; Lam. 1:12 [b]Lam. 3:54; Ezek. 37:11
17 [a]Ps. 118:10-12 [b]Ps. 124:4 [c]Ps. 17:11; 22:12, 16
18 [a]Job 19:13; Ps. 88:8; 31:11; 38:11

• Possibly, *Contemplative,* or *Didactic,* or *Skillful Psalm*
Δ *1 Kin. 4:31*
+ Ps. 88: title
1 [a]Ps. 59:16; 101:1 [b]Ps. 40:10 [c]Ps. 36:5; 88:11; 89:5, 8, 24, 33, 49; 92:2; 119:90; Is. 25:1; Lam. 3:23
2 [a]Ps. 103:17 [b]Ps. 36:5; 119:90
3 [a]1 Kin. 8:16 [b]Ps. 132:11
4 [1]*Selah* may mean: *Pause, Crescendo* or *Musical interlude* [a]2 Sam. 7:16 [b]2 Sam. 7:13; Is. 9:7; Luke 1:33
5 [a]Ps. 19:1; 97:6 [b]Ps. 149:1 [c]Job 5:1
6 [1]Or, *sons of gods* [a]Ps. 86:8; 113:5 [b]Ps. 29:1; 82:1
7 [a]Ps. 47:2; 68:35; 76:7, 11 [b]Ps. 89:5 [c]Ps. 96:4
8 [1]Heb., *YAH* [a]Ps. 35:10; 71:19
9 [a]Ps. 65:7; 107:29

10 Thou Thyself didst crush [1a]Rahab like one who is slain;
Thou didst [b]scatter Thine enemies with [2]Thy mighty arm.

11 The [a]heavens are Thine, the earth also is Thine;
The [b]world and [1]all it contains, Thou hast founded them.
12 The [a]north and the south, Thou hast created them;
[b]Tabor and [c]Hermon [d]shout for joy at Thy name.
13 Thou hast [1]a strong arm;
Thy hand is mighty, Thy [a]right hand is exalted.
14 [a]Righteousness and justice are the foundation of Thy throne;
[b]Lovingkindness and [1]truth go before Thee.
15 How blessed are the people who know the [1a]joyful sound!
O LORD, they walk in the [b]light of Thy countenance.
16 In [a]Thy name they rejoice all the day,
And by Thy righteousness they are exalted.
17 For Thou art the glory of [a]their strength,
And by Thy favor [1]our [b]horn is exalted.
18 For our [a]shield belongs to the LORD,
[1]And our king to the [b]Holy One of Israel.

19 [1]Once Thou didst speak in vision to Thy godly [2]ones,
And didst say, "I have [3]given help to one who is [a]mighty;
I have exalted one [b]chosen from the people.
20 "I have [a]found David My servant;
With My holy [b]oil I have anointed him,
21 With whom [a]My hand will be established;
My arm also will [b]strengthen him.
22 "The enemy will not [1]deceive him,
Nor the [2a]son of wickedness afflict him.
23 "But I shall [a]crush his adversaries before him,
And strike those who hate him.
24 "And My [a]faithfulness and My lovingkindness will be with him,
And in My name his [b]horn will be exalted.
25 "I shall also set his hand [a]on the sea,
And his right hand on the rivers.
26 "He will cry to Me, 'Thou art [a]my Father,
My God, and the [b]rock of my salvation.'
27 "I also shall make him *My* [a]firstborn,
The [b]highest of the kings of the earth.
28 "My [a]lovingkindness I will keep for him forever,
And My [b]covenant shall be confirmed to him.

10 [1]I.e., Egypt [2]Lit., *the arm of Thy might* [a]Ps. 87:4; Is. 30:7; 51:9 [b]Ps. 18:14; 68:1; 144:6
11 [1]Lit., *its fulness* [a]Gen. 1:1; 1 Chr. 29:11; Ps. 96:5 [b]Ps. 24:1
12 [a]Job 26:7 [b]Josh. 19:22; Judg. 4:6; Jer. 46:18 [c]Deut. 3:8; Josh. 11:17; 12:1; Ps. 133:3; Song 4:8 [d]Ps. 98:8
13 [1]Lit., *an arm with strength* [a]Ps. 98:1; 118:16
14 [1]Or, *faithfulness* [a]Ps. 97:2 [b]Ps. 85:13
15 [1]Or, *blast of the trumpet, shout of joy* [a]Lev. 23:24; Num. 10:10; Ps. 98:6 [b]Ps. 4:6; 44:3; 67:1; 80:3; 90:8
16 [a]Ps. 105:3
17 [1]Another reading is *Thou dost exalt our horn* [a]Ps. 28:8 [b]Ps. 75:10; 92:10; 148:14
18 [1]Or, *Even to the Holy One of Israel our King* [a]Ps. 47:9 [b]Ps. 71:22; 78:41
19 [1]Or, *At that time* [2]Some mss. read *one* [3]Lit., *placed help upon* [a]2 Sam. 17:10 [b]1 Kin. 11:34; Ps. 78:70
20 [a]1 Sam. 13:14; 16:1-12; Acts 13:22 [b]1 Sam. 16:13
21 [a]Ps. 18:35; 80:17 [b]Ps. 18:32
22 [1]Or, *exact usury from him* [2]Or, *wicked man* [a]2 Sam. 7:10; Ps. 125:3
23 [a]2 Sam. 7:9; Ps. 18:40
24 [a]Ps. 89:1 [b]Ps. 132:17
25 [a]Ps. 72:8
26 [a]2 Sam. 7:14; 1 Chr. 22:10; Jer. 3:19 [b]2 Sam. 22:47; Ps. 95:1
27 [a]Ex. 4:22; Ps. 2:7; Jer. 31:9; Col. 1:15, 18 [b]Num. 24:7; Ps. 72:11; Rev. 19:16
28 [a]Ps. 89:33 [b]Ps. 89:3, 34
29 [1]Lit., *seed* [a]Ps. 18:50; 89:4, 36 [b]1 Kin. 2:4; Ps. 89:4; 132:12; Is. 9:7; Jer. 33:17 [c]Deut. 11:21
30 [a]2 Sam. 7:14; Ps. 119:53
31 [1]Lit., *profane*
32 [a]Job 9:34; 21:9
33 [a]2 Sam. 7:15
34 [1]Lit., *profane* [2]Lit., *that which goes forth* [a]Deut. 7:9; Jer. 33:20, 21 [b]Num. 23:19
35 [1]Or, *One thing* [a]Ps. 60:6; Amos 4:2
36 [1]Lit., *seed* [a]Ps. 89:29; Luke 1:33 [b]Ps. 72:5 [c]Ps. 72:17

29 "So I will establish his [1a]descendants forever,
And his [b]throne [c]as the days of heaven.

30 "If his sons [a]forsake My law,
And do not walk in My judgments,
31 If they [1]violate My statutes,
And do not keep My commandments,
32 Then I will visit their transgression with the [a]rod,
And their iniquity with stripes.
33 "But I will not break off [a]My lovingkindness from him,
Nor deal falsely in My faithfulness.
34 "My [a]covenant I will not [1]violate,
Nor will I [b]alter [2]the utterance of My lips.
35 "[1]Once I have [a]sworn by My holiness;
I will not lie to David.
36 "His [1a]descendants shall endure forever,
And his [b]throne [c]as the sun before Me.
37 "It shall be established forever [a]like the moon,
And the [b]witness in the sky is faithful." [[1]Selah.

38 But Thou hast [a]cast off and [b]rejected,
Thou hast been full of wrath [1]against Thine [c]anointed.
39 Thou hast [a]spurned the covenant of Thy servant;
Thou hast [b]profaned [c]his crown [1]in the dust.
40 Thou hast [a]broken down all his walls;
Thou hast [b]brought his strongholds to ruin.
41 [a]All who pass along the way plunder him;
He has become a [b]reproach to his neighbors.
42 Thou hast [a]exalted the right hand of his adversaries;
Thou hast [b]made all his enemies rejoice.
43 Thou dost also turn back the edge of his sword,
And hast [a]not made him stand in battle.
44 Thou hast made his [1a]splendor to cease,
And cast his throne to the ground.
45 Thou hast [a]shortened the days of his youth;
Thou hast [b]covered him with shame. [Selah.

37 [1]*Selah* may mean: *Pause, Crescendo* or *Musical interlude* [a]Ps. 72:5 [b]Job 16:19
38 [1]Lit., *with* [a]Ps. 44:9 [b]Deut. 32:19; 1 Chr. 28:9 [c]Ps. 20:6; 89:20, 51
39 [1]Lit., *to the ground* [a]Ps. 78:59; Lam. 2:7 [b]Ps. 74:7 [c]Lam. 5:16
40 [a]Ps. 80:12 [b]Lam. 2:2, 5
41 [a]Ps. 80:12 [b]Ps. 44:13; 69:9, 19; 79:4
42 [a]Ps. 13:2 [b]Ps. 80:6
43 [a]Ps. 44:10
44 [1]Lit., *clearness, luster* [a]Ezek. 28:7
45 [a]Ps. 102:23 [b]Ps. 44:15; 71:13; 109:29

46 [a]How long, O LORD?
Wilt Thou hide Thyself forever?
Will Thy [b]wrath burn like fire?
47 [a]Remember [1]what my span of life is;
For what [b]vanity [2]Thou hast created all the sons of men!
48 What man can live and not [a]see death?
Can he [b]deliver his soul from the [1]power of [2]Sheol? [Selah.

49 Where are Thy former lovingkindnesses, O Lord,
Which Thou didst [a]swear to David in Thy faithfulness?
50 Remember, O Lord, the [a]reproach of Thy servants;
[1]How I do bear in my bosom *the reproach of* all the many peoples,
51 With which [a]Thine enemies have reproached, O LORD,
With which they have reproached the footsteps of [b]Thine anointed.

52 [a]Blessed be the LORD forever!
Amen and Amen.

BOOK 4

PSALM 90

God's Eternity and Man's Transitoriness.

A Prayer of +Moses the man of God.

LORD, Thou hast been our [1a]dwelling place in all generations.
2 Before [a]the mountains were born,
[1]Or Thou [b]didst give birth to the earth and the world,
Even [c]from everlasting to everlasting, Thou art God.

3 Thou dost [a]turn man back into dust,
And dost say, "Return, O children of men."
4 For [a]a thousand years in Thy sight
Are like [b]yesterday when it passes by,
[1]Or *as* a [c]watch in the night.
5 Thou [a]hast [1]swept them away like a flood, they [2b]fall asleep;
In the morning they are like [c]grass which [3]sprouts anew.
6 In the morning it [a]flourishes, and [1]sprouts anew;
Toward evening it [b]fades, and [c]withers away.

7 For we have been [a]consumed by Thine anger,
And by Thy wrath we have been [1]dismayed.
8 Thou hast [a]placed our iniquities before Thee,
Our [b]secret *sins* in the light of Thy presence.
9 For [a]all our days have declined in Thy fury;
We have finished our years like a [1]sigh.

46 [a]Ps. 13:1; 44:24 [b]Ps. 79:5; 80:4
47 [1]Lit., *of what duration I am* [2]Or, *hast Thou . . . men?* [a]Job 7:7; 10:9; 14:1 [b]Ps. 39:5; 62:9; Eccl. 1:2; 2:11
48 [1]Lit., *hand* [2]I.e., the nether world [a]Ps. 22:29; 49:9 [b]Ps. 49:15
49 [a]2 Sam. 7:15; Jer. 30:9; Ezek. 34:23
50 [1]Lit., *My bearing in my bosom* [a]Ps. 69:9; 74:18, 22
51 [a]Ps. 74:10, 18, 22 [b]Ps. 89:38
52 [a]Ps. 41:13; 72:19; 106:48

+ Deut. 33:1
1 [1]Or, *hiding place;* some ancient mss. read *place of refuge* [a]Deut. 33:27; Ps. 71:3; 91:1; Ezek. 11:16
2 [1]Or, *And* [a]Job 15:7; Prov. 8:25 [b]Gen. 1:1; Ps. 102:25; 104:5 [c]Ps. 93:2; 102:24, 27; Jer. 10:10
3 [a]Gen. 3:19; Job 34:14, 15; Ps. 104:29
4 [1]Or, *And* [a]2 Pet. 3:8 [b]Ps. 39:5 [c]Ex. 14:24; Judg. 7:19
5 [1]Or, *flooded* [2]Lit., *become asleep* [3]Or, *passes away* [a]Job 22:16; 27:20 [b]Job 14:12; 20:8; Ps. 76:5 [c]Ps. 103:15; Is. 40:6
6 [1]Or, *passes away* [a]Job 14:2 [b]Ps. 92:7; Matt. 6:30 [c]James 1:11
7 [1]Or, *terrified* [a]Ps. 39:11
8 [a]Ps. 50:21; Jer. 16:17 [b]Ps. 19:12; Eccl. 12:14
9 [1]Or, *whisper* [a]Ps. 78:33
10 [1]Lit., *years* [2]Lit., *in them are* [a]2 Kin. 19:35 [b]Eccl. 12:2-7; Jer. 20:18 [c]Job 20:8; Ps. 78:39
11 [1]Or, *knows* [2]Lit., *of Thee* [a]Ps. 76:7 [b]Neh. 5:9
12 [1]Or, *gain, bring in* [a]Deut. 32:29; Ps. 39:4 [b]Prov. 2:1-6
13 [1]Or, *repent in regard to* [a]Ps. 6:4; 80:14 [b]Ps. 6:3; 74:10 [c]Ex. 32:12; Deut. 32:36; Ps. 106:45; 135:14; Amos 7:3, 6; Jon. 3:9
14 [a]Ps. 36:8; 65:4; 103:5; Jer. 31:14 [b]Ps. 31:7; 85:6
15 [1]Or, *as many days as* [2]Or, *trouble* [a]Ps. 86:4 [b]Deut. 2:14-16; Ps. 31:10
16 [1]Or, *upon* [a]Deut. 32:4; Ps. 44:1; 77:12; 92:4; Hab. 3:2 [b]1 Kin. 8:11; Is. 6:3
17 [1]Or, *give permanence to* [a]Ps. 27:4 [b]Ps. 37:23; Is. 26:12; 1 Cor. 3:7

10 As for the days of our [1]life, [2]they contain seventy years,
Or if due to strength, [a]eighty years,
Yet their pride is *but* [b]labor and sorrow;
For soon it is gone and we [c]fly away.
11 Who [1]understands the [a]power of Thine anger,
And Thy fury, according to the [b]fear [2]that is due Thee?
12 So [a]teach us to number our days,
That we may [1b]present to Thee a heart of wisdom.

13 Do [a]return, O LORD; [b]how long *will it be*?
And [1]be [c]sorry for Thy servants.
14 O [a]satisfy us in the morning with Thy lovingkindness,
That we may [b]sing for joy and be glad all our days.
15 [a]Make us glad [1]according to the days Thou hast afflicted us,
And the [b]years we have seen [2]evil.
16 Let Thy [a]work appear to Thy servants,
And Thy [b]majesty [1]to their children.
17 And let the [a]favor of the Lord our God be upon us;
And do [1b]confirm for us the work of our hands;
Yes, [1]confirm the work of our hands.

PSALM 91

Security of the One Who Trusts in the LORD.

HE who dwells in the [a]shelter of the Most High
Will abide in the [b]shadow of the Almighty.
2 I will say to the LORD, "My [a]refuge and my [b]fortress,
My God, in whom I [c]trust!"
3 For it is He who delivers you from the [a]snare of the trapper,
And from the deadly [b]pestilence.
4 He will [a]cover you with His pinions,
And [b]under His wings you may seek refuge;
His [c]faithfulness is a [d]shield and bulwark.

5 You [a]will not be afraid of the [b]terror by night,
Or of the [c]arrow that flies by day;
6 Of the [a]pestilence that [1]stalks in darkness,
Or of the [b]destruction that lays waste at noon.

1 [a]Ps. 27:5; 31:20; 32:7 [b]Ps. 17:8; 121:5; Is. 25:4; 32:2
2 [a]Ps. 14:6; 91:9; 94:22; 142:5 [b]Ps. 18:2; 31:3; Jer. 16:19 [c]Ps. 25:2; 56:4
3 [a]Ps. 124:7; Prov. 6:5 [b]1 Kin. 8:37; 2 Chr. 20:9; Ps. 91:6
4 [a]Is. 51:16 [b]Ps. 17:8; 36:7; 57:1; 63:7 [c]Ps. 40:11 [d]Ps. 35:2
5 [a]Job 5:19-23; Ps. 23:4; 27:1 [b]Song 3:8 [c]Ps. 64:4
6 [1]Or, *walks* [a]2 Kin. 19:35; Ps. 91:10 [b]Job 5:22

7 A thousand may fall at your side,
And ten thousand at your right hand;
But [a]it shall not approach you.
8 You will only look on with your eyes,
And [a]see the recompense of the wicked.
9 [1]For you have made the LORD, [a]my refuge,
Even the Most High, [b]your dwelling place.
10 [a]No evil will befall you,
Nor will any plague come near your [1]tent.

11 For He will give [a]His angels charge concerning you,
To guard you in all your ways.
12 They will [a]bear you up in their hands,
Lest you strike your foot against a stone.
13 You will [a]tread upon the lion and cobra,
The young lion and the [1]serpent you will trample down.

14 "[a]Because he has loved Me, therefore I will deliver him;
I will [b]set him *securely* on high, because he has [c]known My name.
15 "He will [a]call upon Me, and I will answer him;
I will be with him in [1]trouble;
I will rescue him, and [b]honor him.
16 "With [1]a [a]long life I will satisfy him,
And [2b]let him behold My salvation."

PSALM 92

Praise for the LORD'S Goodness.

A Psalm, a Song for the Sabbath day.

IT is [a]good to give thanks to the LORD,
And to [b]sing praises to Thy name, O Most High;
2 To [a]declare Thy lovingkindness in the morning,
And Thy [b]faithfulness [1]by night,
3 [1]With the [a]ten-stringed lute, and [1]with the [a]harp;
[1]With resounding music [2]upon the [a]lyre.
4 For Thou, O LORD, hast made me glad by [1]what Thou [a]hast done,
I will [b]sing for joy at the [c]works of Thy hands.

5 How [a]great are Thy works, O LORD!
Thy [1b]thoughts are very [c]deep.
6 A [a]senseless man has no knowledge;
Nor does a [a]stupid man understand this:
7 That when the wicked [a]sprouted up like grass,
And all [b]who did iniquity flourished,

7 [a]Gen. 7:23; Josh. 14:10
8 [a]Ps. 37:34; 58:10
9 [1]Or, *For Thou O LORD art my Refuge; You have made the Most High your dwelling place.* [a]Ps. 91:2 [b]Ps. 90:1
10 [1]Or, *dwelling* [a]Prov. 12:21
11 [a]Ps. 34:7; Matt. 4:6; Luke 4:10, 11; Heb. 1:14
12 [a]Matt. 4:6; Luke 4:11
13 [1]Or, *dragon* [a]Judg. 14:6; Dan. 6:22; Luke 10:19
14 [a]Ps. 145:20 [b]Ps. 59:1 [c]Ps. 9:10
15 [1]Or, *distress* [a]Job 12:4; Ps. 50:15 [b]1 Sam. 2:30; John 12:26
16 [1]Lit., *length of days* [2]Or, *cause him to feast his eyes on* [a]Deut. 6:2; Ps. 21:4; Prov. 3:1, 2 [b]Ps. 50:23

1 [a]Ps. 147:1 [b]Ps. 135:3
2 [1]Lit., *nights* [a]Ps. 59:16 [b]Ps. 89:1
3 [1]Lit., *Upon* [2]Lit., *by means of* [a]1 Sam. 10:5; 1 Chr. 13:8; Neh. 12:27; Ps. 33:2
4 [1]Lit., *Thy working* [a]Ps. 40:5; 90:16 [b]Ps. 106:47 [c]Ps. 8:6; 111:7; 143:5
5 [1]Or, *purposes* [a]Ps. 40:5; 111:2; Rev. 15:3 [b]Ps. 33:11; 40:5; 139:17 [c]Ps. 36:6; Rom. 11:33
6 [a]Ps. 49:10; 73:22; 94:8
7 [a]Job 12:6; Ps. 90:5 [b]Ps. 94:4 [c]Ps. 37:38
8 [a]Ps. 83:18; 93:4; 113:5
9 [a]Ps. 37:20 [b]Ps. 68:1; 89:10
10 [1]Or, *become moist* [a]Ps. 75:10; 89:17; 112:9 [b]Ps. 23:5; 45:7
11 [1]Or, *those who lie in wait for me* [a]Ps. 54:7; 91:8
12 [1]Lit., *sprout* [a]Num. 24:6; Ps. 1:3; 52:8; 72:7; Jer. 17:8; Hos. 14:5, 6 [b]Ps. 104:16; Ezek. 31:3
13 [a]Ps. 80:15; Is. 60:21 [b]Ps. 100:4; 116:19
14 [1]Or, *thrive in* [2]Lit., *fat and* [a]Prov. 11:30; Is. 37:31; John 15:2; James 3:18
15 [1]Or, *show forth* [a]Job 34:10; Ps. 25:8 [b]Deut. 32:4; Ps. 18:2; 94:22 [c]Rom. 9:14

It *was only* that they might be [c]destroyed forevermore.
8 But Thou, O LORD, art [a]on high forever.
9 For, behold, Thine enemies, O LORD,
For, behold, [a]Thine enemies will perish;
All who do iniquity will be [b]scattered.

10 But Thou hast exalted my [a]horn like *that of* the wild ox;
I have [1]been [b]anointed with fresh oil.
11 And my eye has [a]looked *exultantly* upon [1]my foes,
My ears hear of the evildoers who rise up against me.
12 The [a]righteous man will [1]flourish like the palm tree,
He will grow like a [b]cedar in Lebanon.
13 [a]Planted in the house of the LORD,
They will flourish [b]in the courts of our God.
14 They will still [1a]yield fruit in old age;
They shall be [2]full of sap and very green,
15 To [1]declare that [a]the LORD is upright;
He is my [b]rock, and there is [c]no unrighteousness in Him.

PSALM 93

The Majesty of the LORD.

[a]THE LORD [1]reigns, He is [b]clothed with majesty;
The LORD has [c]clothed and girded Himself with strength;
Indeed, the [d]world is firmly established, it will not be moved.
2 Thy [a]throne is established from of old;
Thou [b]art from everlasting.

3 The [a]floods have lifted up, O LORD,
The floods have lifted up their voice;
The floods lift up their pounding waves.
4 More than the sounds of many waters,
Than the mighty breakers of the sea,
The LORD [a]on high is mighty.
5 Thy [a]testimonies are fully confirmed;
[b]Holiness befits Thy house,
O LORD, [1]forevermore.

1 [1]Or, *has assumed kingship* [a]Ps. 96:10; 97:1; 99:1 [b]Ps. 104:1 [c]Ps. 65:6; Is. 51:9 [d]Ps. 96:10
2 [a]Ps. 45:6; Lam. 5:19 [b]Ps. 90:2
3 [a]Ps. 96:11; 98:7, 8
4 [a]Ps. 65:7; 89:6, 9; 92:8
5 [1]Lit., *for length of days* [a]Ps. 19:7 [b]Ps. 29:2; 96:9; 1 Cor. 3:17

PSALM 94

The LORD Implored to Avenge His People.

O LORD, God of [1a]vengeance;
God of [1]vengeance, [2b]shine forth!
2 [a]Rise up, O [b]Judge of the earth;
Render recompense [c]to the proud.
3 How long shall the wicked, O LORD,
How long shall the [a]wicked exult?
4 They pour forth *words*, they [a]speak arrogantly;
All who do wickedness [b]vaunt themselves.
5 They [a]crush Thy people, O LORD,
And [b]afflict Thy heritage.
6 They [a]slay the widow and the [1]stranger,
And murder the orphans.
7 And [a]they have said, "[1]The LORD does not see,
Nor does the God of Jacob pay heed."

8 Pay heed, you [a]senseless among the people;
And when will you understand, [a]stupid ones?
9 He who [a]planted the ear, [1]does He not hear?
He who formed the eye, [1]does He not see?
10 He who [1a]chastens the nations, will He not rebuke,
Even He who [b]teaches man knowledge?
11 The LORD [a]knows the thoughts of man,
[1]That they are a *mere* breath.

12 Blessed is the man whom [a]Thou dost chasten, O [1]LORD,
And [b]dost teach out of Thy law;
13 That Thou mayest grant him [a]relief from the [b]days of adversity,
Until [c]a pit is dug for the wicked.
14 For [a]the LORD will not abandon His people,
Nor will He [b]forsake His inheritance.
15 For [1a]judgment [2]will again be righteous;
And all the upright in heart [3]will follow it.
16 Who will [a]stand up for me against evildoers?
Who will take his stand for me [b]against those who do wickedness?

17 If [a]the LORD had not been my help,
My soul would soon have dwelt in *the abode of* silence.
18 If I should say, "[a]My foot has slipped,"
Thy lovingkindness, O LORD, will hold me up.
19 When my anxious thoughts [1]multiply within me,
Thy [a]consolations delight my soul.
20 Can a [1a]throne of destruction be allied with Thee,
One [b]which devises [2]mischief by decree?
21 They [a]band themselves together against the [1]life of the righteous,
And [b]condemn [2]the innocent to death.
22 But the LORD has been my [a]stronghold,
And my God the [b]rock of my refuge.
23 And He has [a]brought back their wickedness upon them,
And will [1b]destroy them in their evil;
The LORD our God will [1]destroy them.

PSALM 95

Praise to the LORD, and Warning against Unbelief.

O COME, let us [a]sing for joy to the LORD;
Let us shout joyfully to [b]the rock of our salvation.
2 Let us [a]come before His presence [b]with [1]thanksgiving;
Let us shout joyfully to Him [c]with [2]psalms.
3 For the LORD is a [a]great God,
And a great King [b]above all gods,
4 In whose hand are the [a]depths of the earth;
The peaks of the mountains are His also.
5 [1]The sea is His, for it was He [a]who made it;
And His hands formed the dry land.

6 Come, let us [a]worship and bow down;
Let us [b]kneel before the LORD our [c]Maker.
7 For He is our God,
And [a]we are the people of His [1b]pasture, and the sheep of His hand.
[c]Today, [2]if you would hear His voice,
8 Do not harden your hearts, as at [1a]Meribah,
As in the day of [2b]Massah in the wilderness;
9 "When your fathers [a]tested Me,
They tried Me, though they had seen My work.
10 "For [a]forty years I loathed *that* generation,
And said they are a people who err in their heart,
And they do not know My ways.

1 [1]Or, *avenging acts* [2]Or, *has shone forth* [a]Deut. 32:35; Is. 35:4; Nah. 1:2; Rom. 12:19 [b]Ps. 50:2; 80:1
2 [a]Ps. 7:6 [b]Gen. 18:25 [c]Ps. 31:23
3 [a]Job 20:5
4 [a]Ps. 31:18; 75:5 [b]Ps. 10:3; 52:1
5 [a]Is. 3:15 [b]Ps. 79:1
6 [1]Or, *sojourner* [a]Is. 10:2
7 [1]Heb., YAH [a]Job 22:13; Ps. 10:11
8 [a]Ps. 92:6
9 [1]Or, *can* [a]Ex. 4:11; Prov. 20:12
10 [1]Or, *instructs* [a]Ps. 44:2 [b]Job 35:11; Is. 28:26
11 [1]Or, *For* [a]Job 11:11; 1 Cor. 3:20
12 [1]Heb., YAH [a]Deut. 8:5; Job 5:17; Ps. 119:71; Prov. 3:11, 12; Heb. 12:5, 6 [b]Ps. 119:171
13 [a]Job 34:29; Hab. 3:16 [b]Ps. 49:5 [c]Ps. 9:15; 55:23
14 [a]1 Sam. 12:22; Lam. 3:31; Rom. 11:2 [b]Ps. 37:28
15 [1]I.e., administration of justice [2]Lit., *will return to righteousness* [3]Lit., *will be after it* [a]Ps. 97:2; Is. 42:3; Mic. 7:9
16 [a]Num. 10:35; Is. 28:21; 33:10 [b]Ps. 17:13; 59:2
17 [a]Ps. 124:1, 2
18 [a]Ps. 38:16; 73:2
19 [1]Or, *are many* [a]Is. 57:18; 66:13
20 [1]Or, *tribunal* [2]Or, *trouble, misfortune* [a]Amos 6:3 [b]Ps. 50:16; 58:2
21 [1]Or, *soul* [2]Lit., *innocent blood* [a]Ps. 56:6; 59:3 [b]Ex. 23:7; Ps. 106:38; Prov. 17:15; Matt. 27:4
22 [a]Ps. 9:9; 59:9 [b]Ps. 18:2; 71:7
23 [1]Or, *silence* [a]Ps. 7:16; 140:9, 11 [b]Gen. 19:15

1 [a]Ps. 66:1; 81:1 [b]Ps. 89:26
2 [1]Or, *a song of thanksgiving* [2]Or, *songs* (with instrumental accompaniment) [a]Mic. 6:6 [b]Ps. 100:4; 147:7; Jon. 2:9 [c]Ps. 81:2; Eph. 5:19; James 5:13
3 [a]Ps. 48:1; 135:5; 145:3 [b]Ps. 96:4; 97:9
4 [a]Ps. 135:6
5 [1]Lit., *Who has the sea* [a]Gen. 1:9, 10; Ps. 146:6; Jon. 1:9
6 [a]Ps. 96:9; 99:5, 9 [b]2 Chr. 6:13; Dan. 6:10; Phil. 2:10 [c]Ps. 100:3; 149:2; Is. 17:7; Hos. 8:14
7 [1]Lit., *pasturing* [2]Or, *O that you would obey* [a]Ps. 79:13 [b]Ps. 74:1 [c]Heb. 3:7-11, 15; 4:7
8 [1]Or, *place of strife* [2]Or, *temptation* [a]Ex. 17:2-7; Num. 20:13 [b]Ex. 17:7; Deut. 6:16
9 [a]Num. 14:22; Ps. 78:18; 1 Cor. 10:9
10 [a]Acts 7:36; 13:18; Heb. 3:10, 17

11 "Therefore I [a]swore in My anger,
Truly they shall not enter into My [b]rest."

PSALM 96

A Call to Worship the LORD the Righteous Judge.

[a]SING to the LORD a [b]new song;
Sing to the LORD, all the earth.
2 Sing to the LORD, bless His name;
[a]Proclaim good tidings of His salvation from day to day.
3 Tell of [a]His glory among the nations,
His wonderful deeds among all the peoples.
4 For [a]great is the LORD, and [b]greatly to be praised;
He is to be [c]feared [d]above all gods.
5 For [a]all the gods of the peoples are [1]idols,
But [b]the LORD made the heavens.
6 [a]Splendor and majesty are before Him,
Strength and beauty are in His sanctuary.

7 [1]Ascribe to the LORD, O [a]families of the peoples,
[1b]Ascribe to the LORD glory and strength.
8 [1]Ascribe to the LORD the [a]glory of His name;
Bring an [2b]offering, and come into His courts.
9 [a]Worship the LORD in [1]holy attire;
[b]Tremble before Him, all the earth.
10 Say among the nations, "[a]The LORD reigns;
Indeed, the [a]world is firmly established, it will not be moved;
He will [b]judge the peoples with [1]equity."

11 Let the [a]heavens be glad, and let the [b]earth rejoice;
Let [c]the sea [1]roar, and [2]all it contains;
12 Let the [a]field exult, and all that is in it.
Then all the [b]trees of the forest will sing for joy
13 Before the LORD, [a]for He is coming;
For He is coming to judge the earth.
[b]He will judge the world in righteousness,
And the peoples in His faithfulness.

PSALM 97

The LORD'S Power and Dominion.

[a]THE LORD [1]reigns; let the [b]earth rejoice;
Let the many [2c]islands be glad.
2 [a]Clouds and thick darkness surround Him;
[b]Righteousness and justice are the foundation of His throne.

11 [a]Num. 14:23, 28-30; Deut. 1:35; Heb. 4:3, 5 [b]Deut. 12:9

1 [a]1 Chr. 16:23-33 [b]Ps. 40:3
2 [a]Ps. 71:15
3 [a]Ps. 145:12
4 [a]Ps. 48:1; 145:3 [b]Ps. 18:3 [c]Ps. 89:7 [d]Ps. 95:3
5 [1]Or, *non-existent things* [a]1 Chr. 16:26; Jer. 10:11 [b]Ps. 115:15; Is. 42:5
6 [a]Ps. 104:1
7 [1]Lit., *Give* [a]Ps. 22:27 [b]1 Chr. 16:28,29; Ps. 29:1,2
8 [1]Lit., *Give* [2]Or, *meal offering* [a]Ps. 79:9; 115:1 [b]Ps. 45:12; 72:10
9 [1]Or, *the splendor of holiness* [a]1 Chr. 16:29; 2 Chr. 20:21; Ps. 29:2; 110:3 [b]Ps. 33:8; 114:7
10 [1]Or, *uprightness* [a]Ps. 93:1; 97:1 [b]Ps. 9:8; 58:11; 67:4; 98:9
11 [1]Or, *thunder* [2]Lit., *its fulness* [a]Ps. 69:34; Is. 49:13 [b]Ps. 97:1 [c]Ps. 98:7
12 [a]Ps. 65:13; Is. 35:1; 55:12, 13 [b]Is. 44:23
13 [a]Ps. 98:9 [b]Rev. 19:11

1 [1]Or, *has assumed Kingship* [2]Or, *coastlands* [a]Ps. 96:10 [b]Ps. 96:11 [c]Is. 42:10, 12
2 [a]Ex. 19:9; Deut. 4:11; 1 Kin. 8:12; Ps. 18:11 [b]Ps. 89:14
3 [a]Ps. 18:8; 50:3; Dan. 7:10; Hab. 3:5 [b]Mal. 4:1; Heb. 12:29
4 [a]Ex. 19:16; Ps. 77:18 [b]Ps. 96:9; 104:32
5 [a]Ps. 46:6; Amos 9:5; Mic. 1:4; Nah. 1:5 [b]Josh. 3:11
6 [a]Ps. 19:1; 50:6 [b]Ps. 98:2; Is. 6:3; 40:5; 66:18
7 [1]Or, *All the gods have worshiped Him* [2]Or, *supernatural powers* [a]Ps. 78:58; Is. 42:17; 44:9, 11; Jer. 10:14 [b]Ps. 106:36; Jer. 50:2; Hab. 2:18 [c]Heb. 1:6
8 [1]Or possibly, *hears and is glad* [a]Ps. 48:11; Zeph. 3:14
9 [1]Or, *supernatural powers* [a]Ps. 83:18 [b]Ex. 18:11; Ps. 95:3; 96:4; 135:5
10 [a]Ps. 34:14; Prov. 8:13; Amos 5:15; Rom. 12:9 [b]Ps. 31:23; 145:20; Prov. 2:8 [c]Ps. 37:40; Jer. 15:21; Dan. 3:28

3 [a]Fire goes before Him,
And [b]burns up His adversaries round about.
4 His [a]lightnings lit up the world;
The earth saw and [b]trembled.
5 The mountains [a]melted like wax at the presence of the LORD,
At the presence of the [b]Lord of the whole earth.
6 The [a]heavens declare His righteousness,
And [b]all the peoples have seen His glory.

7 Let all those be ashamed who serve [a]graven images,
Who boast themselves of [b]idols;
[1c]Worship Him, all you [2]gods.
8 Zion [1]heard *this* and [a]was glad,
And the daughters of Judah have rejoiced
Because of Thy judgments, O LORD.
9 For Thou art the LORD [a]Most High over all the earth;
Thou art exalted far [b]above all [1]gods.

10 [a]Hate evil, you who love the LORD,
Who [b]preserves the souls of His godly ones;
He [c]delivers them from the hand of the wicked.
11 [a]Light is sown *like seed* for the righteous,
And [b]gladness for the upright in heart.
12 Be [a]glad in the LORD, you righteous ones;
And [b]give thanks [1]to His holy name.

PSALM 98

A Call to Praise the LORD for His Righteousness.

A Psalm.

O SING to the LORD a [a]new song,
For He has done [b]wonderful things,
His [c]right hand and His [d]holy arm have [1]gained the victory for Him.
2 [a]The LORD has made known His salvation;
He has [b]revealed His [1]righteousness in the sight of the nations.
3 He has [a]remembered His lovingkindness and His faithfulness to the house of Israel;
[b]All the ends of the earth have seen the salvation of our God.

11 [a]Job 22:28; Ps. 112:4; Prov. 4:18 [b]Ps. 64:10
12 [1]Lit., *for the memory of His holiness* [a]Ps. 32:11 [b]Ps. 30:4

1 [1]Or, *accomplished salvation* [a]Ps. 33:3 [b]Ps. 40:5; 96:3 [c]Ex. 15:6 [d]Is. 52:10
2 [1]I.e., faithfulness to His gracious promises [a]Is. 52:10 [b]Is. 62:2; Rom. 3:25
3 [a]Luke 1:54, 72 [b]Ps. 22:27

4 [a]Shout joyfully to the LORD, all the earth;
[b]Break forth and sing for joy and sing praises.
5 Sing praises to the LORD with the [a]lyre;
With the lyre and the [1b]sound of melody.
6 With [a]trumpets and the sound of the horn
[b]Shout joyfully before [c]the King, the LORD.

7 Let the [a]sea roar and [1]all it contains,
The [b]world and those who dwell in it.
8 Let the [a]rivers clap their hands;
Let the [b]mountains sing together for joy
9 Before the LORD; for He is coming to [a]judge the earth;
He will judge the world with righteousness,
And [b]the peoples with [1]equity.

PSALM 99

Praise to the LORD for His Fidelity to Israel.

[a]THE LORD reigns, let the peoples tremble;
He [1b]is enthroned *above* the cherubim, let the earth shake!
2 The LORD [1]is [a]great in Zion,
And He is [b]exalted above all the peoples.
3 Let them praise Thy [a]great and awesome name;
[b]Holy is [1]He.
4 And the [1]strength of the King [a]loves [2]justice;
Thou hast established [3b]equity;
Thou hast [c]executed [2]justice and righteousness in Jacob.
5 [1a]Exalt the LORD our God,
And [b]worship at His footstool;
[c]Holy is He.

6 [a]Moses and Aaron were among His [b]priests,
And [c]Samuel was among those who [d]called on His name;
They [e]called upon the LORD, and He answered them.
7 He [a]spoke to them in the pillar of cloud;
They [b]kept His testimonies,
And the statute that He gave them.
8 O LORD our God, Thou didst [a]answer them;
Thou wast a [b]forgiving God to them,
And *yet* an [c]avenger of their *evil* deeds.
9 Exalt the LORD our God,
And worship at His holy hill;
For holy is the LORD our God.

4 [a]Ps. 100:1 [b]Is. 44:23
5 [1]Or, *voice of song* (accompanied by music) [a]Ps. 92:3 [b]Is. 51:3
6 [a]Num. 10:10; 2 Chr. 15:14 [b]Ps. 66:1 [c]Ps. 47:7
7 [1]Lit., *its fulness* [a]Ps. 96:11 [b]Ps. 24:1
8 [a]Ps. 93:3; Is. 55:12 [b]Ps. 65:12; 89:12
9 [1]Or, *uprightness* [a]Ps. 96:13 [b]Ps. 96:10

1 [1]Lit., *sits* [a]Ps. 97:1 [b]Ex. 25:22; 1 Sam. 4:4; Ps. 80:1
2 [1]Or, *in Zion is great* [a]Ps. 48:1; Is. 12:6 [b]Ps. 97:9; 113:4
3 [1]Or, *it* [a]Deut. 28:58; Ps. 76:1 [b]Lev. 19:2; Josh. 24:19; 1 Sam. 2:2; Ps. 22:3; Is. 6:3
4 [1]Or, *Thou hast established in equity the strength of the King who loves justice* [2]Or, *judgment* [3]Or, *uprightness* [a]Ps. 11:7; 33:5 [b]Ps. 17:2; 98:9 [c]Ps. 103:6; 146:7; Jer. 23:5
5 [1]The verb is plural. [a]Ps. 34:3; 107:32; 118:28 [b]Ps. 132:7 [c]Ps. 99:3
6 [a]Jer. 15:1 [b]Ex. 24:6-8; 29:26; 40:23-27; Lev. 8:1-30 [c]Jer. 15:1 [d]1 Sam. 7:9; 12:18; Ps. 22:4, 5 [e]Ex. 15:25; 32:30-34
7 [a]Ex. 33:9; Num. 12:5 [b]Ps. 105:28
8 [a]Ps. 106:44 [b]Num. 14:20; Ps. 78:38 [c]Ex. 32:28; Num. 20:12; Ps. 95:11; 107:12

+ Or, *thank offering*
1 [a]Ps. 95:1; 98:4, 6
2 [a]Deut. 12:11, 12; 28:47 [b]Ps. 95:2
3 [1]Or, *He* [2]Some mss. read *His we are* [a]Deut. 4:35; 1 Kin. 18:39; Ps. 46:10 [b]Job 10:3, 8; Ps. 95:6; 119:73 [c]Ps. 74:1, 2; 95:7; Is. 40:11; Ezek. 34:30, 31
4 [1]Or, *a thank offering* [a]Ps. 95:2; 116:17 [b]Ps. 96:2
5 [a]1 Chr. 16:34; 2 Chr. 5:13; 7:3; Ezra 3:11; Ps. 25:8; 86:5; 106:1; 107:1; 118:1; Jer. 33:11; Nah. 1:7 [b]Ps. 136:1 [c]Ps. 119:90

1 [1]Or, *judgment* [a]Ps. 51:14; 89:1; 145:7
2 [1]Or, *behave prudently in* [2]Or, *way of integrity* [3]Or, *blamelessness* [a]1 Sam. 18:5, 14 [b]1 Kin. 9:4

PSALM 100

All Men Exhorted to Praise God.

A Psalm for +Thanksgiving.

[a]SHOUT joyfully to the LORD, all the earth.
2 [a]Serve the LORD with gladness;
[b]Come before Him with joyful singing.
3 Know that [a]the LORD [1]Himself is God;
It is He who has [b]made us, and [2]not we ourselves;
We are [c]His people and the sheep of His pasture.

4 Enter His gates [a]with [1]thanksgiving,
And His courts with praise.
Give thanks to Him; [b]bless His name.
5 For [a]the LORD is good;
[b]His lovingkindness is everlasting,
And His [c]faithfulness to all generations.

PSALM 101

The Psalmist's Profession of Uprightness.

A Psalm of David.

I WILL [a]sing of lovingkindness and [1]justice,
To Thee, O LORD, I will sing praises.
2 I will [1a]give heed to the [2]blameless way.
When wilt Thou come to me?
I will walk within my house in the [3b]integrity of my heart.
3 I will set no [a]worthless thing before my eyes;
I hate the [1]work of those who [b]fall away;
It shall not fasten its grip on me.
4 A [a]perverse heart shall depart from me;
I will know no evil.
5 Whoever secretly [a]slanders his neighbor, him I will [1]destroy;
No one who has a [b]haughty look and an arrogant heart will I endure.

6 My eyes shall be upon the faithful of the land, that they may dwell with me;
He who walks in a [1a]blameless way is the one who will minister to me.
7 He who [a]practices deceit shall not dwell within my house;
He who speaks falsehood [b]shall not [1]maintain his position before me.

3 [1]Or, *practice of apostasy* [a]Deut. 15:9 [b]Josh. 23:6; Ps. 40:4
4 [a]Prov. 11:20
5 [1]Or, *silence* [a]Ps. 50:20; Jer. 9:4 [b]Ps. 10:4; 18:27; Prov. 6:17
6 [1]Or, *way of integrity* [a]Ps. 119:1
7 [1]Lit., *be established before my eyes* [a]Ps. 43:1; 52:2 [b]Ps. 52:4, 5

8 [a]Every morning I will [1b]destroy all
the wicked of the land,
So as to [c]cut off from the [d]city of
the LORD all those who do iniquity.

PSALM 102

Prayer of an Afflicted Man for Mercy on Himself and on Zion.

A Prayer of the Afflicted, when he is faint, and +pours out his complaint before the LORD.

[a]HEAR my prayer, O LORD!
And let my cry for help [b]come to
Thee.
2 [a]Do not hide Thy face from me in
the day of my distress;
[b]Incline Thine ear to me;
In the day when I call [c]answer me
quickly.
3 For my days [a]have been [1]con-
sumed in smoke,
And my [b]bones have been scorched
like a hearth.
4 My heart [a]has been smitten like
[1]grass and has [b]withered away,
Indeed, I [c]forget to eat my bread.
5 Because of the [1]loudness of my
groaning
My [a]bones [2]cling to my flesh.
6 I [1]resemble a [a]pelican of the wilderness;
I have become like an owl of the
waste places.
7 I [a]lie awake,
I have become like a lonely bird on
a housetop.

8 My enemies [a]have reproached me
all day long;
Those who [1b]deride me [2]have used
my *name* as a [c]curse.
9 For I have eaten ashes like bread,
And [a]mingled my drink with weeping,
10 [a]Because of Thine indignation and
Thy wrath;
For Thou hast [b]lifted me up and
cast me away.
11 My days are like a [1a]lengthened
shadow;
And [2]I [b]wither away like [3]grass.

12 But Thou, O LORD, dost [1a]abide
forever;
And Thy [2b]name to all generations.
13 Thou wilt [a]arise *and* have [b]compas-
sion on Zion;
For [c]it is time to be gracious to her,
For the [d]appointed time has come.
14 Surely Thy servants [1]find pleasure
in her stones,
And feel pity for her dust.
15 [1]So the [2a]nations will fear the name
of the LORD,
And [b]all the kings of the earth Thy
glory.
16 For the LORD has [a]built up Zion;
He has [b]appeared in His glory.
17 He has [a]regarded the prayer of the
[1]destitute,
And has not despised their prayer.
18 [1]This will be [a]written for the [b]gen-
eration to come;
[2]That [c]a people yet to be created
[3]may praise [4]the LORD.
19 For He [a]looked down from His
holy height;
[b]From heaven the LORD gazed
[1]upon the earth,
20 To hear the [a]groaning of the prisoner;
To [b]set free [1]those who were
doomed to death;
21 That *men* may [a]tell of the name of
the LORD in Zion,
And His praise in Jerusalem;
22 When [a]the peoples are gathered
together,
And the kingdoms, to serve the
LORD.

23 He has weakened my strength in
the way;
He has [a]shortened my days.
24 I say, "O my God, [a]do not take me
away in the [1]midst of my days,
Thy [b]years are throughout all generations.
25 "Of old Thou didst [a]found the
earth;
And the [b]heavens are the work of
Thy hands.
26 "[1]Even they will [a]perish, but Thou
dost endure;
And all of them will wear out like a
garment;
Like clothing Thou wilt change
them, and they will be changed.
27 "But Thou art [1a]the same,
And Thy years will not come to an
end.
28 "The [a]children of Thy servants will
continue,
And their [1b]descendants will be
established before Thee."

PSALM 103

Praise for the LORD'S Mercies.

A Psalm of David.

[a]BLESS the LORD, O my soul;
And all that is within me, *bless* His
[b]holy name.
2 Bless the LORD, O my soul,
And [a]forget none of His benefits;
3 Who [a]pardons all your iniquities;
Who [b]heals all your diseases;
4 Who [a]redeems your life from the
pit;
Who [b]crowns you with lovingkindness and compassion;
5 Who [a]satisfies your [1]years with
good things,
So that your youth is [b]renewed like
the eagle.

8 [1]Or, *silence* [a]Jer. 21:12 [b]Ps. 75:10 [c]Ps. 118:10-12 [d]Ps. 46:4; 48:2, 8
+ Ps. 142:2
1 [a]Ps. 39:12; 61:1 [b]Ex. 2:23; 1 Sam. 9:16
2 [a]Ps. 69:17 [b]Ps. 31:2 [c]Ps. 69:17
3 [1]Or, *finished* [a]Ps. 37:20; James 4:14 [b]Job 30:30; Lam. 1:13
4 [1]Lit., *herbage* [a]Ps. 90:5, 6 [b]Ps. 37:2; Is. 40:7 [c]1 Sam. 1:7; 2 Sam. 12:17; Ezra 10:6; Job 33:20
5 [1]Lit., *voice* [2]Lit., *have cleaved* [a]Job 19:20; Lam. 4:8
6 [1]Lit., *have become similar to* [a]Is. 34:11; Zeph. 2:14
7 [a]Ps. 77:4
8 [1]Or, *made a fool of* [2]Lit., *have sworn by me* [a]Ps. 31:11 [b]Acts 26:11 [c]2 Sam. 16:5; Is. 65:15; Jer. 29:22
9 [a]Ps. 42:3; 80:5
10 [a]Ps. 38:3 [b]Job 27:21; 30:22
11 [1]Lit., *stretched out* [2]Or, *as for me, I* [3]Lit., *herbage* [a]Job 14:2; Ps. 109:23 [b]Ps. 102:4
12 [1]Or, *sit enthroned* [2]Lit., *memorial* [a]Ps. 9:7; 10:16; Lam. 5:19 [b]Ex. 3:15; Ps. 135:13
13 [a]Ps. 12:5; 44:26 [b]Is. 60:10; Zech. 1:12 [c]Ps. 119:126 [d]Ps. 75:2; Dan. 8:19
14 [1]Or, *have found*
15 [1]Or, *And* [2]Or, *Gentiles, heathen* [a]1 Kin. 8:43; Ps. 67:7 [b]Ps. 138:4
16 [a]Ps. 147:2 [b]Is. 60:1, 2
17 [1]Or, *naked* [a]Neh. 1:6; Ps. 22:24
18 [1]Or, *Let this be written* [2]Or, *And* [3]Or, *will* [4]Heb., *YAH* [a]Deut. 31:19; Rom. 15:4; 1 Cor. 10:11 [b]Ps. 22:30; 48:13 [c]Ps. 22:31; 78:6f.
19 [1]Lit., *toward* [a]Deut. 26:15; Ps. 14:2; 53:2 [b]Ps. 33:13
20 [1]Lit., *the sons of death* [a]Ps. 79:11 [b]Ps. 146:7
21 [a]Ps. 22:22
22 [a]Ps. 22:27; 86:9; Is. 49:22, 23; 60:3; Zech. 8:20-23
23 [a]Ps. 39:5
24 [1]Lit., *half* [a]Ps. 39:13; Is. 38:10 [b]Job 36:26; Ps. 90:2; 102:12; Hab. 1:12
25 [a]Gen. 1:1; Neh. 9:6; Heb. 1:10-12 [b]Ps. 96:5
26 [1]Lit., *They themselves* [a]Is. 34:4; 51:6; Matt. 24:35; 2 Pet. 3:10; Rev. 20:11

27 [1]Lit., *He* [a]Is. 41:4; 43:10; Mal. 3:6; James 1:17
28 [1]Lit., *seed* [a]Ps. 69:36 [b]Ps. 89:4

1 [a]Ps. 104:1, 35 [b]Ps. 33:21; 105:3; 145:21; Ezek. 36:21; 39:7
2 [a]Deut. 6:12; 8:11
3 [a]Ex. 34:7; Ps. 86:5; 130:8; Is. 43:25 [b]Ex. 15:26; Ps. 30:2; Jer. 30:17
4 [a]Ps. 49:15 [b]Ps. 5:12
5 [1]Or, *desire* [a]Ps. 107:9; 145:16 [b]Is. 40:31

6 The LORD [a]performs [1]righteous deeds,
And judgments for all who are [b]oppressed.
7 He [a]made known His ways to Moses,
His [b]acts to the sons of Israel.
8 The LORD is [a]compassionate and gracious,
[b]Slow to anger and abounding in lovingkindness.
9 He [a]will not always strive *with us*;
Nor will He [b]keep *His anger* forever.
10 He has [a]not dealt with us according to our sins,
Nor rewarded us according to our iniquities.
11 For as high [a]as the heavens are above the earth,
So great is His lovingkindness toward those who [1]fear Him.
12 As far as the east is from the west,
So far has He [a]removed our transgressions from us.
13 Just [a]as a father has compassion on *his* children,
So the LORD has compassion on those who [1]fear Him.
14 For [a]He Himself knows [1]our frame;
He [b]is mindful that we are *but* [c]dust.
15 As for man, his days are [a]like grass;
As a [b]flower of the field, so he flourishes.
16 When the [a]wind has passed over it, it is no more;
And its [b]place acknowledges it no longer.
17 But the [a]lovingkindness of the LORD is from everlasting to everlasting on those who [1]fear Him,
And His [2]righteousness [b]to children's children,
18 To [a]those who keep His covenant,
And who remember His precepts to do them.
19 The LORD has established His [a]throne in the heavens;
And His [1b]sovereignty rules over [2]all.
20 Bless the LORD, you [a]His angels,
[b]Mighty in strength, who [c]perform His word,
[d]Obeying the voice of His word!
21 Bless the LORD, all you [a]His hosts,
You [b]who serve Him, doing His will.
22 Bless the LORD, [a]all you works of His,
In all places of His dominion;
Bless the LORD, O my soul!

PSALM 104

The LORD's Care over All His Works.

[a]BLESS the LORD, O my soul!
O LORD my God, Thou art very great;
Thou art [b]clothed with splendor and majesty,
2 Covering Thyself with [a]light as with a cloak,
[b]Stretching out heaven like a *tent* curtain.
3 [1]He [a]lays the beams of His upper chambers in the waters;
[1]He makes the [b]clouds His chariot;
[1]He walks upon the [c]wings of the wind;
4 [1]He makes [2a]the winds His messengers,
[3]Flaming [b]fire His ministers.

5 He [a]established the earth upon its foundations,
So that it will not [1]totter forever and ever.
6 Thou [a]didst cover it with the deep as with a garment;
The waters were standing above the mountains.
7 At Thy [a]rebuke they fled;
At the [b]sound of Thy thunder they hurried away.
8 The mountains rose; the valleys sank down
To the [a]place which Thou didst establish for them.
9 Thou didst set a [a]boundary that they may not pass over;
That they may not return to cover the earth.

10 [1]He sends forth [a]springs in the valleys;
They flow between the mountains;
11 They [a]give drink to every beast of the field;
The [b]wild donkeys quench their thirst.
12 [1]Beside them the birds of the heavens [a]dwell;
They [2]lift up *their* voices among the branches.
13 [1]He [a]waters the mountains from His upper chambers;
[b]The earth is satisfied with the fruit of His works.

14 [1]He causes the [a]grass to grow for the [2]cattle,
And [b]vegetation for the [3]labor of man,
So that [4]he may bring forth [5]food [c]from the earth,
15 And [a]wine which makes man's heart glad,
[b]So that he may make *his* face glisten with oil,
And [1]food which [c]sustains man's heart.
16 The trees of the LORD [1]drink their fill,
The cedars of Lebanon which He planted,

6 [1]Or, *deeds of vindication* [a]Ps. 99:4; 146:7 [b]Ps. 12:5
7 [a]Ex. 33:13; Ps. 99:7; 147:19 [b]Ps. 78:11; 106:22
8 [a]Ex. 34:6; Num. 14:18; Neh. 9:17; Ps. 86:15; Jon. 4:2; James 5:11 [b]Ps. 145:8; Joel 2:13; Nah. 1:3
9 [a]Ps. 30:5; Is. 57:16 [b]Jer. 3:5, 12; Mic. 7:18
10 [a]Ezra 9:13; Lam. 3:22
11 [1]Or, *revere* [a]Ps. 36:5; 57:10
12 [a]2 Sam. 12:13; Is. 38:17; 43:25; Zech. 3:9; Heb. 9:26
13 [1]Or, *revere* [a]Mal. 3:17
14 [1]I.e., what we are made of [a]Is. 29:16 [b]Ps. 78:39 [c]Gen. 3:19; Eccl. 12:7
15 [a]Ps. 90:5; Is. 40:6; 1 Pet. 1:24 [b]Job 14:2; James 1:10, 11
16 [a]Is. 40:7 [b]Job 7:10; 8:18; 20:9
17 [1]Or, *revere* [2]I.e., faithfulness to His gracious promises [a]Ps. 25:6 [b]Ex. 20:6; Deut. 5:10; Ps. 105:8
18 [a]Deut. 7:9; Ps. 25:10
19 [1]Or, *kingdom* [2]I.e., the universe [a]Ps. 11:4 [b]Ps. 47:2, 8; Dan. 4:17, 25
20 [a]Ps. 148:2 [b]Ps. 29:1; 78:25 [c]Matt. 6:10 [d]Ps. 91:11; Heb. 1:14
21 [a]1 Kin. 22:19; Neh. 9:6; Ps. 148:2; Luke 2:13 [b]Ps. 104:4
22 [a]Ps. 145:10

1 [a]Ps. 103:22 [b]Ps. 93:1
2 [a]Dan. 7:9 [b]Is. 40:22
3 [1]Lit., *The one who* [a]Amos 9:6 [b]Is. 19:1 [c]Ps. 18:10
4 [1]Lit., *Who* [2]Or, *His angels, spirits* [3]Or, *His ministers flames of fire* [a]Ps. 148:8; Heb. 1:7 [b]2 Kin. 2:11; 6:17
5 [1]Or, *move out of place* [a]Job 38:4; Ps. 24:2
6 [a]Gen. 1:2
7 [a]Ps. 18:15; 106:9; Is. 50:2 [b]Ps. 29:3; 77:18
8 [a]Ps. 33:7
9 [a]Job 38:10, 11; Jer. 5:22
10 [1]Lit., *The one who sends* [a]Ps. 107:35; Is. 41:18
11 [a]Ps. 104:13 [b]Job 39:5
12 [1]Or, *Over, Above* [2]Lit., *give forth* [a]Matt. 8:20
13 [1]Lit., *Who* [a]Ps. 65:9; 147:8 [b]Jer. 10:13

14 [1]Lit., *Who* [2]Or, *beasts* [3]Or, *cultivation by* or *service of* [4]Or, *He* [5]Lit., *bread* [a]Job 38:27; Ps. 147:8 [b]Gen. 1:29 [c]Job 28:5
15 [1]Lit., *bread* [a]Judg. 9:13; Prov. 31:6; Eccl. 10:19 [b]Ps. 23:5; 92:10; 141:5; Luke 7:46 [c]Gen. 18:5; Judg. 19:5, 8
16 [1]Lit., *are satisfied*

17 Where the [a]birds build their nests,
And the [b]stork, whose home is the [1]fir trees.

18 The high mountains are for the [a]wild goats;
The [b]cliffs are a refuge for the [c]rock badgers.
19 He made the moon [a]for the seasons;
The [b]sun knows the place of its setting.
20 Thou [a]dost appoint darkness and it becomes night,
In which all the [b]beasts of the forest [1]prowl about.
21 The [a]young lions roar after their prey,
[1]And [b]seek their food from God.
22 *When* the sun rises they withdraw,
And lie down in their [a]dens.
23 Man goes forth to [a]his work
And to his labor until evening.

24 O LORD, how [a]many are Thy works!
[1]In [b]wisdom Thou hast made them all;
The [c]earth is full of Thy [2]possessions.
25 [1]There is the [a]sea, great and [2]broad,
In which are swarms without number,
Animals both small and great.
26 There the [a]ships move along,
And [1b]Leviathan, which Thou hast formed to sport in it.

27 They all [a]wait for Thee,
To [b]give them their food in [1]due season.
28 Thou dost give to them, they gather *it* up;
Thou [a]dost open Thy hand, they are satisfied with good.
29 Thou [a]dost hide Thy face, they are dismayed;
Thou [b]dost take away their [1]spirit, they expire,
And [c]return to their dust.
30 Thou dost send forth Thy [1a]Spirit, they are created;
And Thou dost renew the face of the ground.

31 Let the [a]glory of the LORD endure forever;
Let the LORD [b]be glad in His works;
32 [1]He [a]looks at the earth, and it [b]trembles;
He [c]touches the mountains, and they smoke.
33 [1]I will sing to the LORD [2a]as long as I live;
[1]I will [b]sing praise to my God [3]while I have my being.
34 Let my [a]meditation be pleasing to Him;
As for me, I shall [b]be glad in the LORD.

35 Let sinners be [a]consumed from the earth,
And let the [b]wicked be no more.
[c]Bless the LORD, O my soul.
[1d]Praise [2]the LORD!

PSALM 105

The LORD'S *Wonderful Works in Behalf of Israel.*

OH [a]give thanks to the LORD, [b]call upon His name;
[c]Make known His deeds among the peoples.
2 Sing to Him, [a]sing praises to Him;
[1b]Speak of all His [2]wonders.
3 [1]Glory in His holy name;
Let the [a]heart of those who seek the LORD be glad.
4 Seek the LORD and [a]His strength;
[b]Seek His face continually.
5 Remember His [1a]wonders which He has done,
His marvels, and the [b]judgments [2]uttered by His mouth,
6 O seed of [a]Abraham, His servant,
O sons of [b]Jacob, His [c]chosen ones!
7 He is the LORD our God;
His [a]judgments are in all the earth.

8 He has [a]remembered His covenant forever,
The word which He commanded to a [b]thousand generations,
9 *The* [a]*covenant* which He made with Abraham,
And His [b]oath to Isaac.
10 Then He [a]confirmed it to Jacob for a statute,
To Israel as an everlasting covenant,
11 Saying, "[a]To you I will give the land of Canaan
As the [1b]portion of your inheritance,"
12 When they were only a [a]few men in number,
Very few, and [b]strangers in it.
13 And they wandered about from nation to nation,
From *one* kingdom to another people.
14 He [a]permitted no man to oppress them,
And He [b]reproved kings for their sakes:
15 "[a]Do not touch My anointed ones,
And do My prophets no harm."

16 And He [a]called for a famine upon the land;
He [b]broke the whole staff of bread.
17 He [a]sent a man before them,
Joseph, *who* was [b]sold as a slave.
18 They afflicted his [a]feet with fetters,
[1]He himself was laid in irons;

17 [1]Or, *cypress* [a]Ps. 104:12 [b]Lev. 11:19
18 [a]Job 39:1 [b]Prov. 30:26 [c]Lev. 11:5
19 [a]Gen. 1:14 [b]Ps. 19:6
20 [1]Lit., *creep* [a]Ps. 74:16; Is. 45:7 [b]Ps. 50:10; Is. 56:9; Mic. 5:8
21 [1]Lit., *And to seek* [a]Job 38:39 [b]Ps. 145:15; Joel 1:20
22 [a]Job 37:8
23 [a]Gen. 3:19
24 [1]Or, *With* [2]Or, *creatures* [a]Ps. 40:5 [b]Ps. 136:5; Prov. 3:19; Jer. 10:12; 51:15 [c]Ps. 65:9
25 [1]Or, *This* [2]Or, *broad of dimensions* (lit., *hands*) [a]Ps. 8:8; 69:34
26 [1]Or, *a sea monster* [a]Ps. 107:23; Ezek. 27:9 [b]Job 41:1; Ps. 74:14; Is. 27:1
27 [1]Lit., *its appointed time* [a]Ps. 145:15 [b]Job 36:31; 38:41; Ps. 136:25; 147:9
28 [a]Ps. 145:16
29 [1]Or, *breath* [a]Deut. 31:17; Ps. 30:7 [b]Job 34:14, 15; Ps. 146:4; Eccl. 12:7 [c]Gen. 3:19; Job 10:9; Ps. 90:3
30 [1]Or, *breath* [a]Job 33:4; Ezek. 37:9
31 [a]Ps. 86:12; 111:10 [b]Gen. 1:31
32 [1]Lit., *The one who* [a]Judg. 5:5; Ps. 97:4, 5; 114:7 [b]Hab. 3:10 [c]Ex. 19:18; Ps. 144:5
33 [1]Or, *Let me sing* [2]Lit., *in my lifetime* [3]Lit., *while I still am* [a]Ps. 63:4 [b]Ps. 146:2
34 [a]Ps. 19:14 [b]Ps. 9:2
35 [1]Or, *Hallelujah!* [2]Heb., *YAH* [a]Ps. 59:13 [b]Ps. 37:10 [c]Ps. 104:1 [d]Ps. 105:45; 106:48

1 [a]1 Chr. 16:8-22, 34; Ps. 106:1; Is. 12:4 [b]Ps. 99:6 [c]Ps. 145:12
2 [1]Or, *Meditate on* [2]I.e., wonderful acts [a]Ps. 96:1; 98:5 [b]Ps. 77:12; 119:27; 145:5
3 [1]Or, *Boast* [a]Ps. 33:21
4 [a]Ps. 63:2 [b]Ps. 27:8
5 [1]I.e., wonderful acts [2]Lit., *of His mouth* [a]Ps. 40:5; 77:11 [b]Ps. 119:13
6 [a]Ps. 105:42 [b]Ps. 135:4 [c]1 Chr. 16:13; Ps. 106:5; 135:4
7 [a]Is. 26:9
8 [a]Ps. 105:42; 106:45; Luke 1:72 [b]Deut. 7:9
9 [a]Gen. 12:7; 17:2, 8; 22:16-18; Gal. 3:17 [b]Gen. 26:3
10 [a]Gen. 28:13-15

11 [1]Lit., *measuring line* [a]Gen. 13:15; 15:18 [b]Josh. 23:4; Ps. 78:55
12 [a]Gen. 34:30; Deut. 7:7 [b]Gen. 23:4; Heb. 11:9
14 [a]Gen. 20:7; 35:5 [b]Gen. 12:17; 20:3, 7
15 [a]Gen. 26:11
16 [a]Gen. 41:54 [b]Lev. 26:26; Is. 3:1; Ezek. 4:16
17 [a]Gen. 45:5 [b]Gen. 37:28, 36; Acts 7:9
18 [1]Lit., *His soul came into* [a]Gen. 39:20; 40:15

19 Until the time that his [a]word came to pass,
The word of the LORD [1b]tested him.
20 The [a]king sent and released him,
The ruler of peoples, and set him free.
21 He [a]made him lord of his house,
And ruler over all his possessions,
22 To [1]imprison his princes [2a]at will,
That he might teach his elders wisdom.
23 [a]Israel also came into Egypt;
Thus Jacob [b]sojourned in the land of Ham.
24 And He [a]caused His people to be very fruitful,
And made them stronger than their adversaries.

25 He [a]turned their heart to hate His people,
To [b]deal craftily with His servants.
26 He [a]sent Moses His servant,
And [b]Aaron whom He had chosen.
27 They [1a]performed His wondrous acts among them,
And miracles in the land of Ham.
28 He [a]sent darkness and made *it* dark;
And they did not [b]rebel against His words.
29 He [a]turned their waters into blood,
And caused their fish to die.
30 Their land swarmed with [a]frogs
Even in the [b]chambers of their kings.
31 He spoke, and there came a [a]swarm of flies
And [b]gnats in all their territory.
32 He [1]gave them [a]hail for rain,
And flaming fire in their land.
33 He [a]struck down their vines also and their fig trees,
And shattered the trees of their territory.
34 He spoke, and [a]locusts came,
And young locusts, even without number,
35 And ate up all vegetation in their land,
And ate up the fruit of their ground.
36 He also [a]struck down all the first-born in their land,
The [b]first fruits of all their vigor.

37 Then He brought them out with [a]silver and gold;
And among His tribes there was not one who stumbled.
38 Egypt was [a]glad when they departed;
For the [b]dread of them had fallen upon them.
39 He spread a [a]cloud for a [1]covering,
And [b]fire to illumine by night.
40 [1]They [a]asked, and He brought [b]quail,
And satisfied them with the [2c]bread of heaven.
41 He opened the [1]rock, and [a]water flowed out;
[2]It ran in the dry places *like* a river.
42 For He [a]remembered His holy word
With Abraham His servant;
43 And He brought forth His people with joy,
His chosen ones with a joyful [a]shout.
44 He [a]gave them also the lands of the [1]nations,
That they [b]might take possession of *the fruit of* the peoples' labor,
45 So that they might [a]keep His statutes,
And observe His laws,
[1]Praise [2]the LORD!

PSALM 106

Israel's Rebelliousness and the LORD'S Deliverances.

1 PRAISE [2]the LORD!
Oh [a]give thanks to the LORD, for He [b]is good;
For [c]His lovingkindness is everlasting.
2 Who can speak of the [a]mighty deeds of the LORD,
Or can show forth all His praise?
3 How blessed are those who keep [1]justice,
[2]Who [a]practice righteousness at all times!

4 Remember me, O LORD, in *Thy* [a]favor [1]toward Thy people;
Visit me with Thy salvation,
5 That I may see the [a]prosperity of Thy chosen ones,
That I may [b]rejoice in the gladness of Thy nation,
That I may [c]glory with Thine [1]inheritance.

6 [a]We have sinned [1b]like our fathers,
We have committed iniquity, we have behaved wickedly.
7 Our fathers in Egypt did not understand Thy [1]wonders;
They [a]did not remember [2]Thine abundant kindnesses,
But [b]rebelled by the sea, at the [3]Red Sea.
8 Nevertheless He saved them [a]for the sake of His name,
That He might [b]make His power known.
9 Thus He [a]rebuked the [1]Red Sea and it [b]dried up;
And He [c]led them through the deeps, as through the wilderness.
10 So He [a]saved them from the [1]hand of the one who hated *them,*
And [b]redeemed them from the [1]hand of the enemy.

19 [1]Or, *refined* [a]Gen. 40:20, 21 [b]Ps. 66:10
20 [a]Gen. 41:14
21 [a]Gen. 41:40-44
22 [1]Lit., *bind* [2]Lit., *at his* [a]Gen. 41:44
23 [a]Gen. 46:6; Acts 7:15 [b]Acts 13:17
24 [a]Ex. 1:7, 9
25 [a]Ex. 1:8; 4:21 [b]Ex. 1:10; Acts 7:19
26 [a]Ex. 3:10; 4:12 [b]Ex. 4:14; Num. 16:5; 17:5-8
27 [1]Lit., *set the words of His signs* [a]Ps. 78:43-51; 105:27-36
28 [a]Ex. 10:21, 22 [b]Ps. 99:7
29 [a]Ex. 7:20, 21
30 [a]Ex. 8:6 [b]Ex. 8:3
31 [a]Ex. 8:21 [b]Ex. 8:16, 17
32 [1]Or, *made their rain hail* [a]Ex. 9:23-25
33 [a]Ps. 78:47
34 [a]Ex. 10:12-15
36 [a]Ex. 12:29; 13:15; Ps. 135:8; 136:10 [b]Gen. 49:3
37 [a]Ex. 12:35, 36
38 [a]Ex. 12:33 [b]Ex. 15:16
39 [1]Or, *curtain* [a]Ex. 13:21; Neh. 9:12; Ps. 78:14; Is. 4:5 [b]Ex. 40:38
40 [1]Or, *One* [2]Or, *food* [a]Ex. 16:12; Ps. 78:18 [b]Ex. 16:13; Num. 11:31; Ps. 78:27 [c]Ex. 16:15; Neh. 9:15; Ps. 78:24; John 6:31
41 [1]Or, *boulder* [2]Lit., *They went* [a]Ex. 17:6; Num. 20:11; Ps. 78:15; 114:8; Is. 48:21; 1 Cor. 10:4
42 [a]Gen. 15:13, 14; Ps. 105:8
43 [a]Ex. 15:1; Ps. 106:12
44 [1]Or, *Gentiles* [a]Josh. 11:16-23; 13:7; Ps. 78:55 [b]Deut. 6:10, 11
45 [1]Or, *Hallelujah!* [2]Heb., *YAH* [a]Deut. 4:1, 40

1 [1]Or, *Hallelujah!* [2]Heb., *YAH* [a]Ps. 105:1; 107:1; 118:1; 136:1; Jer. 33:11 [b]2 Chr. 5:13; 7:3; Ezra 3:11; Ps. 100:5 [c]1 Chr. 16:34, 41
2 [a]Ps. 145:4, 12; 150:2
3 [1]Or, *judgment* [2]Many Heb. mss. read *The one who performs* [a]Ps. 15:2
4 [1]Lit., *of* [a]Ps. 44:3; 119:132
5 [1]I.e., people [a]Ps. 1:3 [b]Ps. 118:15 [c]Ps. 105:3
6 [1]Lit., *with* [a]1 Kin. 8:47; Ezra 9:7; Neh. 1:7; Jer. 3:25; Dan. 9:5 [b]2 Chr. 30:7; Neh. 9:2; Ps. 78:8, 57; Zech. 1:4

7 [1]I.e., wonderful acts [2]Lit., *the multitude of Thy lovingkindnesses* [3]Lit., *Sea of Reeds* [a]Judg. 3:7; Ps. 78:11, 42 [b]Ex. 14:11, 12; Ps. 78:17
8 [a]Ezek. 20:9 [b]Ex. 9:16
9 [1]Lit., *Sea of Reeds* [a]Ps. 18:15; 78:13; Is. 50:2; Nah. 1:4 [b]Ex. 14:21; Is. 51:10 [c]Is. 63:11-13
10 [1]Or, *power* [a]Ex. 14:30 [b]Ps. 78:42; 107:2

11 And [a]the waters covered their adversaries;
Not one of them was left.
12 Then they [a]believed His words;
They [b]sang His praise.

13 They quickly [a]forgot His works;
They [b]did not wait for His counsel,
14 But [a]craved intensely in the wilderness,
And [1b]tempted God in the desert.
15 So He [a]gave them their request,
But [b]sent a [1]wasting disease among them.

16 When they became [a]envious of Moses in the camp,
And of Aaron, the holy one of the LORD,
17 The [a]earth opened and swallowed up Dathan,
And engulfed the [1]company of Abiram.
18 And a [a]fire blazed up in their [1]company;
The flame consumed the wicked.

19 They [a]made a calf in Horeb,
And worshiped a molten image.
20 Thus they [a]exchanged their glory
For the image of an ox that eats grass.
21 They [a]forgot God their Savior,
Who had done [b]great things in Egypt,
22 [1a]Wonders in the land of Ham,
And awesome things by the [2]Red Sea.
23 Therefore [a]He said that He would destroy them,
Had not [b]Moses His chosen one stood in the breach before Him,
To turn away His wrath from destroying *them.*
24 Then they [a]despised the [b]pleasant land;
They [c]did not believe in His word,
25 But [a]grumbled in their tents;
They did not listen to the voice of the LORD.
26 Therefore He [1a]swore to them,
That He would cast them down in the wilderness,
27 And that He would [a]cast their seed among the nations,
And [b]scatter them in the lands.

28 They [a]joined themselves also to [1]Baal-peor,
And ate [b]sacrifices offered to the dead.
29 Thus they [a]provoked *Him* to anger with their deeds;
And the plague broke out among them.
30 Then Phinehas [a]stood up and interposed;
And so the [b]plague was stayed.
31 And it was [a]reckoned to him for righteousness,
To all generations forever.

32 They also [a]provoked *Him* to wrath at the waters of [1]Meribah,
So that it [b]went hard with Moses on their account;
33 Because they [a]were rebellious against [1]His Spirit,
He spoke rashly with his lips.

34 They [a]did not destroy the peoples,
As [b]the LORD commanded them,
35 But [a]they mingled with the nations,
And learned their [1]practices,
36 And [a]served their idols,
[b]Which became a snare to them.
37 They even [a]sacrificed their sons and their daughters to the [b]demons,
38 And shed [a]innocent blood,
The blood of their [b]sons and their daughters,
Whom they sacrificed to the idols of Canaan;
And the land was [c]polluted with the blood.
39 Thus they became [a]unclean in their [1]practices,
And [b]played the harlot in their deeds.

40 Therefore the [a]anger of the LORD was kindled against His people,
And He [b]abhorred His [1c]inheritance.
41 Then [a]He gave them into the hand of the [1]nations;
And those who hated them ruled over them.
42 Their enemies also [a]oppressed them,
And they were subdued under their [1]power.
43 Many times He would [a]deliver them;
They, however, were rebellious in their [b]counsel,
And *so* [c]sank down in their iniquity.

44 Nevertheless He looked upon their distress,
When He [a]heard their cry;
45 And He [a]remembered His covenant for their sake,
And [1b]relented [c]according to the greatness of His lovingkindness.
46 He also made them [a]*objects* of compassion
In the presence of all their captors.

47 [a]Save us, O LORD our God,
And [b]gather us from among the nations,
To give thanks to Thy holy name,
And [1c]glory in Thy praise.

11 [a]Ex. 14:27, 28; 15:5; Ps. 78:53
12 [a]Ex. 14:31 [b]Ex. 15:1-21; Ps. 105:43
13 [a]Ex. 15:24; 16:2; 17:2 [b]Ps. 107:11
14 [1]Or, *put God to the test* [a]Num. 11:4; Ps. 78:18; 1 Cor. 10:6 [b]Ex. 17:2; 1 Cor. 10:9
15 [1]Or, *leanness into their soul* [a]Num. 11:31; Ps. 78:29 [b]Is. 10:16
16 [a]Num. 16:1-3
17 [1]Or, *assembly, band* [a]Num. 16:32; Deut. 11:6
18 [1]Or, *assembly, band* [a]Num. 16:35
19 [a]Ex. 32:4; Deut. 9:8; Acts 7:41
20 [a]Jer. 2:11; Rom. 1:23
21 [a]Ps. 78:11; 106:7, 13 [b]Deut. 10:21
22 [1]I.e., Wonderful acts [2]Lit., *Sea of Reeds* [a]Ps. 105:27
23 [a]Ex. 32:10; Deut. 9:14; Ezek. 20:8, 13 [b]Ex. 32:11-14; Deut. 9:25-29
24 [a]Num. 14:31 [b]Deut. 8:7; Jer. 3:19; Ezek. 20:6 [c]Deut. 1:32; 9:23; Heb. 3:19
25 [a]Num. 14:2; Deut. 1:27
26 [1]Lit., *lifted up His hand* [a]Num. 14:28-35; Ps. 95:11; Ezek. 20:15; Heb. 3:11
27 [a]Deut. 4:27 [b]Lev. 26:33; Ps. 44:11
28 [1]Or, *Baal of Peor* [a]Num. 25:3; Deut. 4:3; Hos. 9:10 [b]Num. 25:2
29 [a]Num. 25:4
30 [a]Num. 25:7 [b]Num. 25:8
31 [a]Gen. 15:6; Num. 25:11-13
32 [1]Lit., *strife* [a]Num. 20:2-13; Ps. 81:7; 95:9 [b]Num. 20:12
33 [1]Or, *his spirit* [a]Num. 20:3, 10; Ps. 78:40; 107:11
34 [a]Judg. 1:21, 27-36 [b]Deut. 7:2, 16
35 [1]Lit., *works* [a]Judg. 3:5, 6
36 [a]Judg. 2:12 [b]Deut. 7:16
37 [a]Deut. 12:31; 32:17; 2 Kin. 16:3; 17:17; Ezek. 16:20, 21; 1 Cor. 10:20 [b]Lev. 17:7
38 [a]Ps. 94:21 [b]Deut. 18:10 [c]Num. 35:33; Is. 24:5; Jer. 3:1, 2
39 [1]Lit., *works* [a]Lev. 18:24; Ezek. 20:18 [b]Lev. 17:7; Num. 15:39; Judg. 2:17; Hos. 4:12
40 [1]I.e., people [a]Judg. 2:14; Ps. 78:59 [b]Lev. 26:30; Deut. 32:19 [c]Deut. 9:29; 32:9

41 [1]Or, *Gentiles* [a]Judg. 2:14; Neh. 9:27
42 [1]Lit., *hand* [a]Judg. 4:3; 10:12
43 [a]Judg. 2:16-18 [b]Ps. 81:12 [c]Judg. 6:6
44 [a]Judg. 3:9; 6:7; 10:10
45 [1]Lit., *was sorry* [a]Lev. 26:42; Ps. 105:8 [b]Judg. 2:18 [c]Ps. 69:16
46 [a]1 Kin. 8:50; 2 Chr. 30:9; Ezra 9:9; Neh. 1:11; Jer. 42:12
47 [1]Lit., *boast* [a]1 Chr. 16:35, 36 [b]Ps. 147:2 [c]Ps. 47:1

48 [a]Blessed be the LORD, the God of
Israel,
From everlasting even to everlasting.
And let all the people say, "Amen."
[1]Praise [2]the LORD!

BOOK 5

PSALM 107

The LORD Delivers Men from Manifold Troubles.

OH [a]give thanks to the LORD, for [b]He
is good;
For His lovingkindness is everlasting.
2 Let [a]the redeemed of the LORD say
so,
Whom He has [b]redeemed from the
hand of the adversary,
3 And [a]gathered from the lands,
From the east and from the west,
From the north and from the
[1]south.

4 They [a]wandered in the wilderness
in a [1]desert region;
They did not find a way to [2]an
inhabited [b]city.
5 *They were* hungry [1]and thirsty;
Their [a]soul fainted within them.
6 Then they [a]cried out to the LORD
in their trouble;
He delivered them out of their
distresses.
7 He led them also by a [1a]straight
way,
To go to [2b]an inhabited city.
8 [a]Let them give thanks to the LORD
for His lovingkindness,
And for His [1]wonders to the sons
of men!
9 For He has [a]satisfied the [1]thirsty
soul,
And the [b]hungry soul He has filled
with what is good.

10 There were those who [a]dwelt in
darkness and in the shadow of
death,
[b]Prisoners in [1]misery and [2]chains,
11 Because they had [a]rebelled against
the words of God,
And [b]spurned the [c]counsel of the
Most High.
12 Therefore He humbled their heart
with labor;
They stumbled and there was [a]none
to help.
13 Then they [a]cried out to the LORD
in their trouble;
He saved them out of their distresses.
14 He [a]brought them out of darkness
and the shadow of death,
And [b]broke their bands apart.
15 [a]Let them give thanks to the LORD
for His lovingkindness,
And for His [1]wonders to the sons
of men!
16 For He has [a]shattered gates of
bronze,
And cut bars of iron asunder.

17 Fools, because of [1]their rebellious
way,
And [a]because of their iniquities,
were afflicted.
18 Their [a]soul abhorred all kinds of
food;
And they [b]drew near to the [c]gates
of death.
19 Then they cried out to the LORD in
their trouble;
He saved them out of their distresses.
20 He [a]sent His word and [b]healed
them,
And [c]delivered *them* from their
[1]destructions.
21 [a]Let them give thanks to the LORD
for His lovingkindness,
And for His [1]wonders to the sons
of men!
22 Let them also offer [a]sacrifices of
thanksgiving,
And [b]tell of His works with joyful
singing.

23 Those who [a]go down to the sea in
ships,
Who do business on great waters;
24 They have seen the works of the
LORD,
And His [1]wonders in the deep.
25 For He [a]spoke and raised up a
[b]stormy wind,
Which [c]lifted up the waves [1]of the
sea.
26 They rose up to the heavens, they
went down to the depths;
Their soul [a]melted away in *their*
misery.
27 They reeled and [a]staggered like a
drunken man,
And [1]were at their wits' end.
28 Then they cried to the LORD in
their trouble,
And He brought them out of their
distresses.
29 He [a]caused the storm to be still,
So that the waves [1]of the sea were
hushed.
30 Then they were glad because they
were quiet;
So He guided them to their desired
haven.
31 [a]Let them give thanks to the LORD
for His lovingkindness,
And for His [1b]wonders to the sons
of men!
32 Let them [a]extol Him also [b]in the
congregation of the people,
And [c]praise Him at the seat of the
elders.

48 [1]Or, *Hallelujah!* [2]Heb., *YAH* [a]Ps. 41:13; 72:18; 89:52
1 [a]1 Chr. 16:34; Ps. 106:1; 118:1; 136:1; Jer. 33:11 [b]2 Chr. 5:13; 7:3; Ezra 3:11; Ps. 100:5
2 [a]Is. 35:9, 10; 62:12; 63:4 [b]Ps. 78:42; 106:10
3 [1]Lit., *sea* [a]Deut. 30:3; Neh. 1:9; Ps. 106:47; Is. 11:12; 43:5; 56:8; Ezek. 11:17; 20:34
4 [1]Lit., *waste* [2]Or, *a habitable city;* lit., *a city of habitation* [a]Num. 14:33; 32:13; Deut. 2:7; 32:10; Josh. 5:6; 14:10 [b]Ps. 107:7, 36
5 [1]Lit., *also* [a]Ps. 77:3
6 [a]Ps. 50:15; 107:13, 19, 28
7 [1]Or, *level* [2]Or, *a habitable city;* lit., *a city of habitation* [a]Ezra 8:21; Ps. 5:8; Jer. 31:9 [b]Ps. 107:4, 36
8 [1]I.e., wonderful acts [a]Ps. 107:15, 21, 31
9 [1]Or, *parched* [a]Ps. 22:26; 34:10; 63:5; 103:5 [b]Ps. 146:7; Matt. 5:6; Luke 1:53
10 [1]Lit., *affliction* [2]Lit., *irons* [a]Ps. 143:3; Is. 42:7; Mic. 7:8; Luke 1:79 [b]Job 36:8; Ps. 102:20
11 [a]Ps. 78:40; 106:7; Lam. 3:42 [b]Num. 15:31; 2 Chr. 36:16; Prov. 1:25; Is. 5:24 [c]Ps. 73:24
12 [a]Ps. 22:11; 72:12
13 [a]Ps. 107:6
14 [a]Ps. 86:13; 107:10 [b]Ps. 116:16; Jer. 2:20; 30:8; Nah. 1:13; Luke 13:16; Acts 12:7
15 [1]I.e., wonderful acts [a]Ps. 107:8, 21, 31
16 [a]Is. 45:1, 2
17 [1]Lit., *the way of their transgression* [a]Is. 65:6, 7; Jer. 30:14, 15; Lam. 3:39; Ezek. 24:23
18 [a]Job 33:20; Ps. 102:4 [b]Job 33:22; Ps. 88:3 [c]Job 38:17; Ps. 9:13
20 [1]Or, *pits* [a]Ps. 147:15, 18; Matt. 8:8 [b]2 Kin. 20:5; Ps. 30:2; 103:3; 147:3 [c]Job 33:28, 30; Ps. 30:3; 49:15; 56:13; 103:4
21 [1]I.e., wonderful acts [a]Ps. 107:8, 15, 31
22 [a]Lev. 7:12; Ps. 50:14; 116:17 [b]Ps. 9:11; 73:28; 118:17
23 [a]Is. 42:10; Jon. 1:3
24 [1]I.e., wonderful acts
25 [1]Lit., *of it* [a]Ps. 105:31, 34 [b]Ps. 148:8; Jon. 1:4 [c]Ps. 93:3, 4
26 [a]Ps. 22:14; 119:28
27 [1]Lit., *all their wisdom was swallowed up* [a]Job 12:25; Is. 24:20
29 [1]Lit., *of it* [a]Ps. 65:7; 89:9; Matt. 8:26; Luke 8:24
31 [1]I.e., wonderful acts [a]Ps. 107:8, 15, 21 [b]Ps. 78:4; 111:4
32 [a]Ps. 34:3; 99:5; Is. 25:1 [b]Ps. 22:22, 25 [c]Ps. 35:18

33 He [1a]changes rivers into a [2]wilderness,
And springs of water into a thirsty ground;
34 A [a]fruitful land into a [b]salt waste,
Because of the wickedness of those who dwell in it.
35 He [1a]changes a [2]wilderness into a pool of water,
And a dry land into springs of water;
36 And there He makes the hungry to dwell,
So that they may establish [1a]an inhabited city,
37 And sow fields, and [a]plant vineyards,
And [1]gather a fruitful harvest.
38 Also He blesses them and they [a]multiply greatly;
And He [b]does not let their cattle decrease.

39 When they are [a]diminished and [b]bowed down
Through oppression, misery, and sorrow,
40 He [a]pours contempt upon [1]princes,
And [b]makes them wander [c]in a pathless waste.
41 But He [a]sets the needy [1]securely on high away from affliction,
And [b]makes *his* families like a flock.
42 The [a]upright see it, and are glad;
But all [b]unrighteousness shuts its mouth.
43 Who is [a]wise? Let him give heed to these things;
And consider the [b]lovingkindnesses of the LORD.

PSALM 108

God Praised and Supplicated to Give Victory.

A Song, a Psalm of David.

[a]MY heart is steadfast, O God;
I will sing, I will sing praises, even with my [1]soul.
2 Awake, harp and lyre;
I will awaken the dawn!
3 I will give thanks to Thee, O LORD, among the peoples;
And I will sing praises to Thee among the nations.
4 For Thy [a]lovingkindness is great [b]above the heavens;
And Thy truth *reaches* to the skies.
5 [a]Be exalted, O God, above the heavens,
And Thy glory above all the earth.
6 [a]That Thy beloved may be delivered,
Save with Thy right hand, and answer me!

7 God has spoken in His [1]holiness:
"I will exult, I will portion out Shechem,
And measure out the valley of Succoth.
8 "Gilead is Mine, Manasseh is Mine;
Ephraim also is the [1]helmet of My head;
[a]Judah is My [2]scepter.
9 "Moab is My washbowl;
Over Edom I shall throw My shoe;
Over Philistia I will shout aloud."

10 [a]Who will bring me into the besieged city?
Who [1]will lead me to Edom?
11 Hast not Thou Thyself, O God, [a]rejected us?
And wilt Thou not go forth with our armies, O God?
12 Oh give us help against the adversary,
For [a]deliverance [1]by man is in vain.
13 [1]Through God we shall do valiantly;
And [a]it is He who will tread down our adversaries.

PSALM 109

Vengeance Invoked upon Adversaries.

For the choir director. A Psalm of David.

O [a]GOD of my praise,
[b]Do not be silent!
2 For they have opened the [1]wicked and [a]deceitful mouth against me;
They have spoken [2]against me with a [b]lying tongue.
3 They have also surrounded me with words of hatred,
And fought against me [a]without cause.
4 In return [a]for my love they act as my accusers;
But [b]I am *in* prayer.
5 Thus they have [1a]repaid me evil for good,
And [b]hatred for my love.

6 Appoint a wicked man over him;
And let an [1a]accuser stand at his right hand.
7 When he is judged, let him [a]come forth guilty;
And let his [b]prayer become sin.
8 Let [a]his days be few;
Let [b]another take his office.
9 Let his [a]children be fatherless,
And his [b]wife a widow.
10 Let his [a]children wander about and beg;
And let them [b]seek *sustenance* [1]far from their ruined homes.
11 Let [a]the creditor [1]seize all that he has;
And let [b]strangers plunder the product of his labor.
12 Let there be none to [1a]extend lovingkindness to him,
Nor [b]any to be gracious to his fatherless children.
13 Let his [a]posterity be [1]cut off;
In a following generation let their [b]name be blotted out.

107:33 [1]Or, *turns* [2]Or, *desert* [a]1 Kin. 17:1, 7; Ps. 74:15; Is. 42:15; 50:2
34 [a]Gen. 13:10; 14:3; 19:24, 25; Deut. 29:23 [b]Job 39:6; Jer. 17:6
35 [1]Or, *turns* [2]Or, *desert* [a]Ps. 105:41; 114:8; Is. 35:6, 7; 41:18
36 [1]Or, *a habitable city;* lit., *a city of habitation* [a]Ps. 107:4, 7
37 [1]Lit., *acquire fruits of yield* [a]2 Kin. 19:29; Is. 65:21; Amos 9:14
38 [a]Gen. 12:2; 17:20; Ex. 1:7; Deut. 1:10 [b]Deut. 7:14
39 [a]2 Kin. 10:32; Ezek. 5:11; 29:15 [b]Ps. 38:6; 44:25; 57:6
40 [1]Or, *nobles* [a]Job 12:21 [b]Job 12:24 [c]Deut. 32:10
41 [1]Lit., *in an inaccessibly high place* [a]1 Sam. 2:8; Ps. 59:1; 113:7, 8 [b]Job 21:11; Ps. 78:52; 113:9
42 [a]Job 22:19; Ps. 52:6 [b]Job 5:16; Ps. 63:11; Rom. 3:19
43 [a]Ps. 64:9; Jer. 9:12; Hos. 14:9 [b]Ps. 107:1

108:1 [1]Lit., *glory* [a]Ps. 57:7-11; 108:1-5
4 [a]Num. 14:18; Deut. 7:9; Ps. 36:5; 100:5; Mic. 7:18-20 [b]Ps. 113:4
5 [a]Ps. 57:5
6 [a]Ps. 60:5-12; 108:6-13
7 [1]Or, *sanctuary*
8 [1]Lit., *protection* [2]Or, *lawgiver* [a]Gen. 49:10
10 [1]Or, *has led* [a]Ps. 60:9
11 [a]Ps. 44:9
12 [1]Lit., *of* [a]Is. 30:3
13 [1]Or, *In* or *With* [a]Is. 60:12; 63:1-4

109:1 [a]Deut. 10:21 [b]Ps. 28:1; 83:1
2 [1]Lit., *wicked mouth and the deceitful* [2]Lit., *with* [a]Ps. 10:7; 52:4 [b]Ps. 120:2
3 [a]Ps. 35:7; 69:4; John 15:25
4 [a]Ps. 38:20 [b]Ps. 69:13; 141:5
5 [1]Lit., *laid upon me* [a]Ps. 35:12; 38:20 [b]John 7:7; 10:32
6 [1]Or, *adversary, Satan* [a]Zech. 3:1
7 [a]Ps. 1:5 [b]Prov. 28:9
8 [a]Ps. 55:23 [b]Acts 1:20
9 [a]Ex. 22:24 [b]Jer. 18:21
10 [1]Or, *out of their desolate places* [a]Gen. 4:12; Job 30:5-8; Ps. 59:15 [b]Ps. 37:25
11 [1]Lit., *ensnare, strike at* [a]Neh. 5:7; Job 5:5; 20:15 [b]Is. 1:7; Lam. 5:2; Ezek. 7:21
12 [1]Lit., *continue* [a]Ezra 7:28; 9:9 [b]Job 5:4; Is. 9:17
13 [1]Lit., *for cutting off* [a]Job 18:19; Ps. 21:10; 37:28 [b]Ps. 9:5; Prov. 10:7

14 Let [a]the iniquity of his fathers be remembered [1]before the LORD,
And do not let the sin of his mother be [b]blotted out.
15 Let [a]them be before the LORD continually,
That He may [b]cut off their memory from the earth;
16 Because he did not remember to show lovingkindness,
But persecuted the [a]afflicted and needy man,
And the [b]despondent in heart, to [c]put *them* to death.
17 He also loved cursing, so [a]it came to him;
And he did not delight in blessing, so it was far from him.
18 But he [a]clothed himself with cursing as with his garment,
And it [b]entered into [1]his body like water,
And like oil into his bones.
19 Let it be to him as [a]a garment with which he covers himself,
And for a belt with which he constantly [b]girds himself.
20 [1]Let this be the [a]reward of my accusers from the LORD,
And of those who [b]speak evil against my soul.

21 But Thou, O [1]GOD, the Lord, deal *kindly* with me [a]for Thy name's sake;
Because [b]Thy lovingkindness is good, deliver me;
22 For [a]I am afflicted and needy,
And [1]my heart is [b]wounded within me.
23 I am passing [a]like a shadow when it lengthens;
I am shaken off [b]like the locust.
24 My [a]knees [1]are weak from [b]fasting;
And my flesh has grown lean, without fatness.
25 I also have become a [a]reproach to them;
When they see me, they [b]wag their head.

26 [a]Help me, O LORD my God;
Save me according to Thy lovingkindness.
27 [1]And let them [a]know that this is Thy hand;
Thou, LORD, hast done it.
28 [a]Let them curse, but do Thou bless;
When they arise, they shall be ashamed,
But Thy [b]servant shall be glad.
29 [1]Let [a]my accusers be clothed with dishonor,
And [2]let them [b]cover themselves with their own shame as with a robe.

30 With my mouth I will give thanks abundantly to the LORD;
And in the midst of many [a]I will praise Him.
31 For He stands [a]at the right hand of the needy,
To save him from those who [b]judge his soul.

PSALM 110

The LORD Gives Dominion to the King.

A Psalm of David.

[a]THE LORD says to my Lord:
"[b]Sit at My right hand,
Until I make [c]Thine enemies a footstool for Thy feet."
2 The LORD will stretch forth Thy strong [a]scepter from Zion, *saying,*
"[b]Rule in the midst of Thine enemies."
3 Thy [a]people [1]will volunteer freely in the day of Thy [2]power;
[b]In [3]holy array, from the womb of the dawn,
[4]Thy youth are to Thee *as* the [c]dew.

4 [a]The LORD has sworn and will [b]not [1]change His mind,
"Thou art a [c]priest forever
According to the order of Melchizedek."
5 The Lord is [a]at Thy right hand;
He [1]will [b]shatter kings in the [c]day of His wrath.
6 He will [a]judge among the nations,
He [1]will fill *them* with [b]corpses,
He [2]will [c]shatter the [3]chief men over a broad country.
7 He will [a]drink from the brook by the wayside;
Therefore He will [b]lift up *His* head.

PSALM 111

The LORD Praised for His Goodness.

[1]PRAISE [2]the LORD!
I [a]will give thanks to the LORD with all *my* heart,
In the [b]company of the upright and in the assembly.
2 [a]Great are the works of the LORD;
They are [1b]studied by all who delight in them.
3 [1a]Splendid and majestic is His work;
And [b]His righteousness endures forever.
4 He has made His [1]wonders [2]to be remembered;
The LORD is [a]gracious and compassionate.

14 [1]Lit., *to* [a]Ex. 20:5; Num. 14:18; Is. 65:6, 7; Jer. 32:18 [b]Neh. 4:5; Jer. 18:23
15 [a]Ps. 90:8; Jer. 16:17 [b]Job 18:17; Ps. 34:16
16 [a]Ps. 37:14 [b]Ps. 34:18 [c]Ps. 37:32; 94:6
17 [a]Prov. 14:14; Ezek. 35:9; Matt. 7:2
18 [1]Lit., *his inward parts* [a]Ps. 73:6; 109:29; Ezek. 7:27 [b]Num. 5:22
19 [a]Ps. 73:6; 109:29; Ezek. 7:27 [b]2 Sam. 22:40; Ps. 30:11; Is. 11:5
20 [1]Lit., *This is* [a]Ps. 54:5; 94:23; Is. 3:11; 2 Tim. 4:14 [b]Ps. 41:5; 71:10
21 [1]Heb., *YHWH,* usually rendered *LORD* [a]Ps. 23:3; 25:11; 79:9; 106:8; Ezek. 36:22 [b]Ps. 69:16
22 [1]Lit., *one has pierced my heart within me* [a]Ps. 40:17; 86:1 [b]Job 24:12; Ps. 143:4; Prov. 18:14
23 [a]Ps. 102:11 [b]Ex. 10:19; Job 39:20
24 [1]Or, *totter* [a]Heb. 12:12 [b]Ps. 35:13
25 [a]Ps. 22:6 [b]Ps. 22:7; Jer. 18:16; Lam. 2:15; Matt. 27:39; Mark 15:29
26 [a]Ps. 119:86
27 [1]Or, *That they may know* [a]Job 37:7
28 [a]2 Sam. 16:11, 12 [b]Is. 65:14
29 [1]Or, *My accusers will be* [2]Or, *they will cover* [a]Job 8:22; Ps. 132:18 [b]Job 8:22; Ps. 35:26
30 [a]Ps. 22:22; 35:18; 111:1
31 [a]Ps. 16:8; 73:23; 110:5; 121:5 [b]Ps. 37:33

1 [a]Matt. 22:44; Mark 12:36; Luke 20:42, 43; Acts 2:34, 35; Heb. 1:13 [b]Matt. 26:64; Eph. 1:20; Col. 3:1; Heb. 1:3; 8:1; 10:12; 12:2 [c]1 Cor. 15:25; Eph. 1:22
2 [a]Ps. 45:6; Jer. 48:17; Ezek. 19:14 [b]Ps. 2:9; 72:8; Dan. 7:13, 14
3 [1]Lit., *will be freewill offerings* [2]Or, *army* [3]Or, *the splendor of holiness* [4]Or, *The dew of Thy youth is Thine.* [a]Judg. 5:2; Neh. 11:2 [b]1 Chr. 16:29; Ps. 96:9 [c]2 Sam. 17:12; Mic. 5:7
4 [1]Lit., *be sorry* [a]Heb. 7:21 [b]Num. 23:19 [c]Zech. 6:13; Heb. 5:6, 10; 6:20; 7:17, 21

5 [1]Or, *has shattered* [a]Ps. 16:8; 109:31 [b]Ps. 68:14; 76:12 [c]Ps. 2:5, 12; Rom. 2:5; Rev. 6:17
6 [1]Or, *has filled* [2]Or, *has shattered* [3]Lit., *head over* [a]Is. 2:4; Joel 3:12; Mic. 4:3 [b]Is. 66:24 [c]Ps. 68:21
7 [a]Judg. 7:5, 6 [b]Ps. 27:6

1 [1]Or, *Hallelujah! I will* [2]Heb., *YAH* [a]Ps. 35:18; 138:1 [b]Ps. 89:7; 149:1
2 [1]Lit., *sought out* [a]Ps. 92:5 [b]Ps. 143:5
3 [1]Lit., *Splendor and majesty* [a]Ps. 96:6; 145:5 [b]Ps. 112:3, 9; 119:142
4 [1]I.e., wonderful acts [2]Lit., *a memorial* [a]Ps. 86:5, 15; 103:8; 145:8

5 He has [a]given [1]food to those who
[2]fear Him;
He will [b]remember His covenant
forever.
6 He has made known to His people
the power of His works,
In giving them the heritage of the
nations.

7 The works of His hands are [1a]truth
and justice;
All His precepts [b]are [2]sure.
8 They are [a]upheld forever and ever;
They are performed in [1b]truth and
uprightness.
9 He has sent [a]redemption to His
people;
He has [1]ordained His covenant
forever;
[b]Holy and [2]awesome is His name.
10 The [1a]fear of the LORD is the beginning of wisdom;
A [b]good understanding have all
those who [2]do *His commandments*;
His [c]praise endures forever.

PSALM 112

Prosperity of the One Who Fears the LORD.

[1]PRAISE [2]the LORD!
How [a]blessed is the man who [3]fears
the LORD,
Who greatly [b]delights in His commandments.
2 His [1a]descendants will be mighty
[2]on earth;
The generation of the [b]upright will
be blessed.
3 [a]Wealth and riches are in his house,
And his righteousness endures forever.
4 Light arises in the darkness [a]for the
upright;
He is [b]gracious and compassionate
and righteous.
5 It is well with the man who [a]is
gracious and lends;
He will [1]maintain his cause in
judgment.
6 For he will [a]never be shaken;
The [b]righteous will be [1]remem-
bered forever.

7 He will not fear [a]evil tidings;
His [b]heart is steadfast, [c]trusting in
the LORD.
8 His [a]heart is upheld, he [b]will not
fear,
Until he [c]looks *with satisfaction* on
his adversaries.
9 [1]He [a]has given freely to the poor;
His righteousness endures forever;
His [b]horn will be exalted in honor.

10 The [a]wicked will see it and be
[1]vexed;
He will [b]gnash his teeth and [c]melt
away;
The [d]desire of the wicked will perish.

5 [1]Lit., *prey* [2]Or, *revere* [a]Matt. 6:31-33 [b]Ps. 105:8
7 [1]Or, *faithfulness* [2]Or, *trustworthy* [a]Rev. 15:3 [b]Ps. 19:7; 93:5
8 [1]Or, *faithfulness* [a]Ps. 119:160; Is. 40:8; Matt. 5:18 [b]Ps. 19:9
9 [1]Lit., *commanded* [2]I.e., inspiring reverence [a]Luke 1:68 [b]Ps. 99:3; Luke 1:49
10 [1]Or, *reverence for* [2]Lit., *do* them [a]Job 28:28; Prov. 1:7; 9:10; Eccl. 12:13 [b]Ps. 119:98; Prov. 3:4 [c]Ps. 145:2

1 [1]Or, *Hallelujah! Blessed* [2]Heb., *YAH* [3]Or, *reveres* [a]Ps. 128:1 [b]Ps. 1:2; 119:14, 16
2 [1]Lit., *seed* [2]Or, *in the land* [a]Ps. 102:28; 127:4 [b]Ps. 128:4
3 [a]Prov. 3:16; 8:18; Matt. 6:33
4 [a]Job 11:17; Ps. 97:11 [b]Ps. 37:26
5 [1]Or, *conduct his affairs with justice* [a]Ps. 37:21
6 [1]Lit., *for an eternal remembrance* [a]Ps. 15:5; 55:22 [b]Prov. 10:7
7 [a]Prov. 1:33 [b]Ps. 57:7; 108:1 [c]Ps. 56:4
8 [a]Heb. 13:9 [b]Ps. 27:1; 56:11; Prov. 1:33; 3:24; Is. 12:2 [c]Ps. 54:7; 59:10
9 [1]Lit., *He has scattered, he has given to. . .* [a]2 Cor. 9:9 [b]Ps. 75:10; 89:17; 92:10; 148:14
10 [1]Or, *angry* [a]Ps. 86:17 [b]Ps. 35:16; 37:12; Matt. 8:12; 25:30; Luke 13:28 [c]Ps. 58:7 [d]Job 8:13; Prov. 10:28; 11:7

1 [1]Or, *Hallelujah! Praise* [2]Heb., *YAH* [a]Ps. 135:1 [b]Ps. 34:22; 69:36; 79:10; 90:13
2 [a]Ps. 145:21; Dan. 2:20
3 [a]Ps. 50:1; Is. 59:19; Mal. 1:11 [b]Ps. 18:3; 48:1, 10
4 [a]Ps. 97:9; 99:2 [b]Ps. 8:1; 57:11; 148:13
5 [a]Ex. 15:11; Ps. 35:10; 89:6 [b]Ps. 103:19
6 [1]Or, *looks far below in the heavens and on the earth?* [a]Ps. 11:4; 138:6; Is. 57:15
7 [a]1 Sam. 2:8; Ps. 107:41
8 [1]Or, *nobles* [a]Job 36:7
9 [1]Or, *Hallelujah!* [2]Heb., *YAH* [a]1 Sam. 2:5; Ps. 68:6; Is. 54:1

1 [a]Ex. 12:51; 13:3 [b]Ps. 81:5
2 [a]Ex. 15:17; 29:45, 46; Ps. 78:68, 69 [b]Ex. 19:6

PSALM 113

The LORD Exalts the Humble.

[1]PRAISE [2]the LORD!
[a]Praise, O [b]servants of the LORD.
Praise the name of the LORD.
2 [a]Blessed be the name of the LORD
From this time forth and forever.
3 [a]From the rising of the sun to its
setting
The [b]name of the LORD is to be
praised.
4 The LORD is [a]high above all nations;
His [b]glory is above the heavens.

5 [a]Who is like the LORD our God,
Who [b]is enthroned on high,
6 Who [1a]humbles Himself to behold
The things that are in heaven and in
the earth?
7 He [a]raises the poor from the dust,
And lifts the needy from the ash
heap,
8 To make *them* [a]sit with [1]princes,
With the [1]princes of His people.
9 He [a]makes the barren woman
abide in the house
As a joyful mother of children.
[1]Praise [2]the LORD!

PSALM 114

God's Deliverance of Israel from Egypt.

WHEN Israel went forth [a]from
Egypt,
The house of Jacob from a people
of [b]strange language,
2 Judah became [a]His sanctuary,
Israel, [b]His dominion.

3 The [a]sea looked and fled;
The [b]Jordan turned back.
4 The mountains [a]skipped like rams,
The hills, like lambs.
5 What [a]ails you, O sea, that you
flee?
O Jordan, that you turn back?
6 O mountains, that you skip like
rams?
O hills, like lambs?

7 [a]Tremble, O earth, before the Lord,
Before the God of Jacob,
8 Who [a]turned the rock into a [b]pool
of water,
The [c]flint into a fountain of water.

PSALM 115

Heathen Idols Contrasted with the LORD.

[a]NOT to us, O LORD, not to us,
But [b]to Thy name give glory
Because of Thy lovingkindness,
because of Thy [1]truth.

3 [a]Ex. 14:21; Ps. 77:16 [b]Josh. 3:13, 16
4 [a]Ex. 19:18; Judg. 5:5; Ps. 18:7; 29:6; Hab. 3:6
5 [a]Hab. 3:8
7 [a]Ps. 96:9
8 [a]Ex. 17:6; Num. 20:11; Ps. 78:15; 105:41 [b]Ps. 107:35 [c]Deut. 8:15

1 [1]Or, *faithfulness* [a]Is. 48:11; Ezek. 36:22 [b]Ps. 29:2; 96:8

2 [a]Why should the nations say,
"[b]Where, now, is their God?"
3 But our [a]God is in the heavens;
He [b]does whatever He pleases.
4 Their [a]idols are silver and gold,
The [b]work of man's hands.
5 They have mouths, but they [a]cannot speak;
They have eyes, but they cannot see;
6 They have ears, but they cannot hear;
They have noses, but they cannot smell;
7 [1]They have hands, but they cannot feel;
[2]They have feet, but they cannot walk;
They cannot make a sound with their throat.
8 [a]Those who make them [1]will become like them,
Everyone who trusts in them.

9 O [a]Israel, [b]trust in the LORD;
He is their [c]help and their shield.
10 O house of [a]Aaron, trust in the LORD;
He is their help and their shield.
11 You who [1a]fear the LORD, trust in the LORD;
He is their help and their shield.
12 The LORD [a]has been mindful of us;
He will bless *us*;
He will bless the house of Israel;
He will bless the house of Aaron.
13 He will [a]bless those who [1]fear the LORD,
[b]The small together with the great.
14 May the LORD [a]give you increase,
You and your children.
15 May you be blessed of the LORD,
[a]Maker of heaven and earth.

16 The heavens are [a]the heavens of the LORD;
But [b]the earth He has given to the sons of men.
17 The [a]dead do not praise [1]the LORD,
Nor *do* any who go down into [b]silence;
18 But as for us, we will [a]bless [1]the LORD
From this time forth and forever.
[2]Praise [1]the LORD!

PSALM 116

Thanksgiving for Deliverance from Death.

[a]I LOVE the LORD, because He [b]hears
My voice *and* my supplications.
2 Because He has [a]inclined His ear to me,
Therefore I shall call *upon Him* as long as I live.
3 The [a]cords of death encompassed me,
And the [1]terrors of [2]Sheol [3]came upon me;
I found distress and sorrow.
4 Then [a]I called upon the name of the LORD:
"O LORD, I beseech Thee, [1b]save my life!"

5 [a]Gracious is the LORD, and [b]righteous;
Yes, our God is [c]compassionate.
6 The LORD preserves [a]the simple;
I was [b]brought low, and He saved me.
7 Return to your [a]rest, O my soul,
For the LORD has [b]dealt bountifully with you.
8 For Thou hast [a]rescued my soul from death,
My eyes from tears,
My feet from stumbling.
9 I shall walk before the LORD
In the [1a]land of the living.
10 I [a]believed when I said,
"I am [b]greatly afflicted."
11 I [a]said in my alarm,
"[b]All men are liars."

12 What shall I [a]render to the LORD
For all His [b]benefits [1]toward me?
13 I shall lift up the [a]cup of salvation,
And [b]call upon the name of the LORD.
14 I shall [a]pay my vows to the LORD,
Oh *may it be* [b]in the presence of all His people.
15 [a]Precious in the sight of the LORD
Is the death of His godly ones.
16 O LORD, [1]surely I am [a]Thy servant,
I am Thy servant, the [b]son of Thy handmaid,
Thou hast [c]loosed my bonds.
17 To Thee I shall offer [a]a sacrifice of thanksgiving,
And [b]call upon the name of the LORD.
18 I shall [a]pay my vows to the LORD,
Oh *may it be* in the presence of all His people,
19 In the [a]courts of the LORD's house,
In the midst of you, O [b]Jerusalem.
[1]Praise [2]the LORD!

PSALM 117

A Psalm of Praise.

[a]PRAISE the LORD, all nations;
Laud Him, all peoples!
2 For His [a]lovingkindness [1]is great toward us,
And the [2b]truth of the LORD is everlasting.
[3]Praise [4]the LORD!

Psalm 115: 2 [a]Ps. 79:10 [b]Ps. 42:3, 10
3 [a]Ps. 103:19 [b]Ps. 135:6; Dan. 4:35
4 [a]Ps. 115:4-8; 135:15-18; Jer. 10:4 [b]Deut. 4:28; 2 Kin. 19:18; Is. 37:19; 44:10, 20; Jer. 10:3
5 [a]Jer. 10:5
7 [1]Lit., *Their hands* [2]Lit., *Their feet*
8 [1]Or, *are like them* [a]Ps. 135:18; Is. 44:9-11
9 [a]Ps. 118:2; 135:19 [b]Ps. 37:3; 62:8 [c]Ps. 33:20
10 [a]Ps. 118:3; 135:19
11 [1]Or, *revere* [a]Ps. 22:23; 103:11; 135:20
12 [a]Ps. 98:3
13 [1]Or, *revere* [a]Ps. 103:11; 112:1; 128:1 [b]Rev. 11:18; 19:5
14 [a]Deut. 1:11
15 [a]Gen. 1:1; Neh. 9:6; Ps. 96:5; 102:25; 121:2; 124:8; 134:3; 146:6; Acts 14:15; Rev. 14:7
16 [a]Ps. 89:11 [b]Ps. 8:6
17 [1]Heb., *YAH* [a]Ps. 6:5; 88:10-12; Is. 38:18 [b]Ps. 31:17
18 [1]Heb., *YAH* [2]Or, *Hallelujah!* [a]Ps. 113:2; Dan. 2:20

Psalm 116: 1 [a]Ps. 18:1 [b]Ps. 6:8; 66:19; Is. 37:17; Dan. 9:18
2 [a]Ps. 17:6; 31:2; 40:1
3 [1]Lit., *straits* [2]I.e., the nether world [3]Lit., *found me* [a]Ps. 18:4, 5
4 [1]Or, *deliver my soul* [a]Ps. 18:6; 118:5 [b]Ps. 17:13; 22:20
5 [a]Ps. 86:15; 103:8 [b]Ezra 9:15; Neh. 9:8; Ps. 119:137; 145:17; Jer. 12:1; Dan. 9:14 [c]Ex. 34:6
6 [a]Ps. 19:7; Prov. 1:4 [b]Ps. 79:8; 142:6
7 [a]Jer. 6:16; Matt. 11:29 [b]Ps. 13:6; 142:7
8 [a]Ps. 49:15; 56:13; 86:13
9 [1]Lit., *lands* [a]Ps. 27:13
10 [a]2 Cor. 4:13 [b]Ps. 88:7
11 [a]Ps. 31:22 [b]Ps. 62:9; Rom. 3:4
12 [1]Lit., *upon* [a]2 Chr. 32:25; 1 Thess. 3:9 [b]Ps. 103:2
13 [a]Ps. 16:5 [b]Ps. 80:18; 105:1
14 [a]Ps. 50:14; 116:18 [b]Ps. 22:25
15 [a]Ps. 72:14
16 [1]Or, *because* [a]Ps. 86:16; 119:125; 143:12 [b]Ps. 86:16 [c]Ps. 107:14
17 [a]Lev. 7:12; Ps. 50:14 [b]Ps. 116:13
18 [a]Ps. 116:14
19 [1]Or, *Hallelujah!* [2]Heb., *YAH* [a]Ps. 92:13; 96:8; 135:2 [b]Ps. 102:21

Psalm 117: 1 [a]Rom. 15:11
2 [1]Lit., *prevails over us* [2]Or, *faithfulness* [3]Or, *Hallelujah!* [4]Heb., *YAH* [a]Ps. 103:11 [b]Ps. 100:5; 146:6

PSALM 118

Thanksgiving for the LORD'S Saving Goodness.

[a]GIVE thanks to the LORD, for [b]He is good;
For His lovingkindness is everlasting.
2 Oh let [a]Israel say,
"His lovingkindness is everlasting."
3 Oh let the [a]house of Aaron say,
"His lovingkindness is everlasting."
4 Oh let those [a]who [1]fear the LORD say,
"His lovingkindness is everlasting."

5 From *my* [a]distress I called upon [1]the LORD;
[1]The LORD answered me *and* [b]*set me* in a large place.
6 The LORD is [a]for me; I will [b]not fear;
[c]What can man do to me?
7 The LORD is for me [a]among those who help me;
Therefore I shall [b]look *with satisfaction* on those who hate me.
8 It is [a]better to take refuge in the LORD
Than to trust in man.
9 It is [a]better to take refuge in the LORD
Than to trust in princes.

10 All nations [a]surrounded me;
In the name of the LORD I will surely [b]cut them off.
11 They [a]surrounded me, yes, they surrounded me;
In the name of the LORD I will surely cut them off.
12 They surrounded me [a]like bees;
They were extinguished as a [b]fire of thorns;
In the name of the LORD I will surely cut them off.
13 You [a]pushed me violently so that I [1]was falling,
But the LORD [b]helped me.
14 [1a]The LORD is my strength and song,
And He has become [b]my salvation.

15 The sound of [a]joyful shouting and salvation is in the tents of the righteous;
The [b]right hand of the LORD does valiantly.
16 The [a]right hand of the LORD is exalted;
The right hand of the LORD does valiantly.
17 I [a]shall not die, but live,
And [b]tell of the works of [1]the LORD.
18 [1]The LORD has [a]disciplined me severely,
But He has [b]not given me over to death.

19 [a]Open to me the gates of righteousness;
I shall enter through them, I shall give thanks to [1]the LORD.
20 This is the gate of the LORD;
The [a]righteous will enter through it.
21 I shall give thanks to Thee, for Thou hast [a]answered me;
And Thou hast [b]become my salvation.

22 The [a]stone which the builders rejected
Has become the chief corner *stone*.
23 This is [1]the LORD's doing;
It is marvelous in our eyes.
24 This is the day which the LORD has made;
Let us [a]rejoice and be glad in it.
25 O LORD, [a]do save, we beseech Thee;
O LORD, we beseech Thee, do send [b]prosperity!
26 [a]Blessed is the one who comes in the name of the LORD;
We have [b]blessed you from the house of the LORD.
27 [a]The LORD is God, and He has given us [b]light;
Bind the festival sacrifice with cords [1]to the [c]horns of the altar.
28 [a]Thou art my God, and I give thanks to Thee;
Thou art my God, [b]I extol Thee.
29 [a]Give thanks to the LORD, for He is good;
For His lovingkindness is everlasting.

PSALM 119

Meditations and Prayers Relating to the Law of God.

א ALEPH.

HOW blessed are those whose way is [1a]blameless,
Who [b]walk in the law of the LORD.
2 How blessed are those who [a]observe His testimonies,
Who [b]seek Him [c]with all *their* heart.
3 They also [a]do no unrighteousness;
They walk in His ways.
4 Thou hast [1a]ordained Thy precepts,
[2]That we should keep *them* diligently.
5 Oh that my [a]ways may be established
To [b]keep Thy statutes!
6 Then I [a]shall not be ashamed
When I look [1]upon all Thy commandments.
7 I shall [a]give thanks to Thee with uprightness of heart,
When I learn Thy righteous judgments.
8 I shall keep Thy statutes;
Do not [a]forsake me utterly!

1 [a]1 Chr. 16:8, 34; Ps. 106:1; 107:1; Jer. 33:11 [b]2 Chr. 5:13; 7:3; Ezra 3:11; Ps. 100:5; 136:1-26
2 [a]Ps. 115:9
3 [a]Ps. 115:10
4 [1]Or, *revere* [a]Ps. 115:11
5 [1]Heb., *YAH* [a]Ps. 18:6; 86:7; 120:1 [b]Ps. 18:19
6 [a]Job 19:27; Ps. 56:9; Heb. 13:6 [b]Ps. 23:4; 27:1 [c]Ps. 56:4, 11
7 [a]Ps. 54:4 [b]Ps. 54:7; 59:10
8 [a]2 Chr. 32:7, 8; Ps. 40:4; 108:12; Is. 31:1, 3; 57:13; Jer. 17:5
9 [a]Ps. 146:3
10 [a]Ps. 3:6; 88:17 [b]Ps. 18:40
11 [a]Ps. 88:17
12 [a]Deut. 1:44 [b]Ps. 58:9; Nah. 1:10
13 [1]Or, *fell* [a]Ps. 140:4 [b]Ps. 86:17
14 [1]Heb., *YAH* [a]Ex. 15:2; Is. 12:2 [b]Ps. 27:1
15 [a]Ps. 68:3 [b]Ex. 15:6; Ps. 89:13; Luke 1:51
16 [a]Ex. 15:6; Ps. 89:13
17 [1]Heb., *YAH* [a]Ps. 6:5; 116:8, 9; Hab. 1:12 [b]Ps. 73:28; 107:22
18 [1]Heb., *YAH* [a]Ps. 73:14; Jer. 31:18; 1 Cor. 11:32; 2 Cor. 6:9 [b]Ps. 86:13
19 [1]Heb., *YAH* [a]Is. 26:2
20 [a]Ps. 15:1, 2; 24:3-6; 140:13; Is. 35:8; Rev. 22:14
21 [a]Ps. 116:1; 118:5 [b]Ps. 118:14
22 [a]Matt. 21:42; Mark 12:10, 11; Luke 20:17; Acts 4:11; Eph. 2:20; 1 Pet. 2:7
23 [1]Lit., *from the LORD*
24 [a]Ps. 31:7
25 [a]Ps. 106:47 [b]Ps. 122:6, 7
26 [a]Matt. 21:9; 23:39; Mark 11:9; Luke 13:35; 19:38; John 12:13 [b]Ps. 129:8
27 [1]Lit., *unto* [a]1 Kin. 18:39 [b]Esth. 8:16; Ps. 18:28; 27:1; 1 Pet. 2:9 [c]Ex. 27:2
28 [a]Ps. 63:1; 140:6 [b]Ex. 15:2; Is. 25:1
29 [a]Ps.118:1

1 [1]Lit., *complete;* or, *having integrity* [a]Ps. 101:2, 6; Prov. 11:20; 13:6 [b]Ps. 128:1; Ezek. 11:20; 18:17; Mic. 4:2
2 [a]Ps. 25:10; 99:7; 119:22, 168 [b]Deut. 4:29; Ps. 119:10 [c]Deut. 6:5; 10:12; 11:13; 13:3; 30:2
3 [a]1 John 3:9; 5:18
4 [1]Lit., *commanded* [2]Lit., *To keep* [a]Deut. 4:13; Neh. 9:13
5 [a]Ps. 40:2; Prov. 4:26 [b]Deut. 12:1; 2 Chr. 7:17
6 [1]Lit., *to* [a]Job 22:26; Ps. 119:80
7 [a]Ps. 119:62
8 [a]Ps. 38:21; 71:9, 18

ב Beth.

9 How can a young man keep his way pure?
By [a]keeping *it* according to Thy word.
10 With [a]all my heart I have sought Thee;
Do not let me [b]wander from Thy commandments.
11 Thy word I have [a]treasured in my heart,
That I may not sin against Thee.
12 Blessed art Thou, O LORD;
[a]Teach me Thy statutes.
13 With my lips I have [a]told of
All the [b]ordinances of Thy mouth.
14 I have [a]rejoiced in the way of Thy testimonies,
[1]As much as in all riches.
15 I will [a]meditate on Thy precepts,
And [1]regard [b]Thy ways.
16 I shall [1a]delight in Thy statutes;
I shall [b]not forget Thy word.

ג Gimel.

17 [a]Deal bountifully with Thy servant,
That I may live and keep Thy word.
18 Open my eyes, that I may behold
Wonderful things from Thy law.
19 I am a [a]stranger in the earth;
Do not hide Thy commandments from me.
20 My soul is crushed [1a]with longing
After Thine ordinances at all times.
21 Thou dost [a]rebuke the arrogant, [1]the [b]cursed,
Who [c]wander from Thy commandments.
22 [a]Take away reproach and contempt from me,
For I [b]observe Thy testimonies.
23 Even though [a]princes sit and talk against me,
Thy servant [b]meditates on Thy statutes.
24 Thy testimonies also are my [a]delight;
They are [1]my counselors.

ד Daleth.

25 My [a]soul cleaves to the dust;
[b]Revive me [c]according to Thy word.
26 I have told of my ways, and Thou hast answered me;
[a]Teach me Thy statutes.
27 Make me understand the way of Thy precepts,
So I will [a]meditate on Thy wonders.
28 My [a]soul [1]weeps because of grief;
[b]Strengthen me according to Thy word.
29 Remove the false way from me,
And graciously grant me Thy law.
30 I have chosen the faithful way;
I have [1]placed Thine ordinances *before me.*
31 I [a]cleave to Thy testimonies;
O LORD, do not put me to shame!
32 I shall run the way of Thy commandments,
For Thou wilt [a]enlarge my heart.

ה He.

33 [a]Teach me, O LORD, the way of Thy statutes,
And I shall observe it to the end.
34 [a]Give me understanding, that I may [b]observe Thy law,
And keep it [c]with all *my* heart.
35 Make me walk in the [a]path of Thy commandments,
For I [b]delight in it.
36 [a]Incline my heart to Thy testimonies,
And not to [b]*dishonest* gain.
37 Turn away my [a]eyes from looking at vanity,
And [b]revive me in Thy ways.
38 [a]Establish Thy [1]word to Thy servant,
[2]As that which produces reverence for Thee.
39 [a]Turn away my reproach which I dread,
For Thine ordinances are good.
40 Behold, I [a]long for Thy precepts;
Revive me through Thy righteousness.

ו Vav.

41 May Thy [a]lovingkindnesses also come to me, O LORD,
Thy salvation [b]according to Thy [1]word;
42 So I shall have an [a]answer for him who [b]reproaches me,
For I trust in Thy word.
43 And do not take the word of truth utterly out of my mouth,
For I [1a]wait for Thine ordinances.
44 So I will [a]keep Thy law continually,
Forever and ever.
45 And I will [a]walk [1]at liberty,
For I [b]seek Thy precepts.
46 I will also speak of Thy testimonies [a]before kings,
And shall not be ashamed.
47 And I shall [1a]delight in Thy commandments,
Which I [b]love.
48 And I shall lift up my hands to Thy commandments,
Which I [a]love;
And I will [b]meditate on Thy statutes.

ז Zayin.

49 Remember the word to Thy servant,
[1]In which Thou hast made me hope.
50 This is my [a]comfort in my affliction,
That Thy word has [1]revived me.

9 [a]1 Kin. 2:4; 8:25; 2 Chr. 6:16
10 [a]2 Chr. 15:15; Ps. 119:2, 145 [b]Ps. 119:21, 118
11 [a]Ps. 37:31; 40:8; Luke 2:19, 51
12 [a]Ps. 119:26, 64, 108, 124, 135, 171
13 [a]Ps. 40:9 [b]Ps. 119:72
14 [1]Lit., *As over all* [a]Ps. 119:111, 162
15 [1]Or, *look upon* [a]Ps. 1:2; 119:23, 48, 78, 97, 148 [b]Ps. 25:4; 27:11; Is. 58:2
16 [1]Lit., *delight myself* [a]Ps. 1:2; 119:24, 35, 47, 70, 77, 92, 143, 174 [b]Ps. 119:93
17 [a]Ps. 13:6; 116:7
19 [a]Gen. 47:9; Lev. 25:23; 1 Chr. 29:15; Ps. 39:12; 119:54; Heb. 11:13
20 [1]Lit., *for* [a]Ps. 42:1, 2; 63:1; 84:2; 119:40, 131
21 [1]Or, *Cursed are those who wander*… [a]Ps. 68:30 [b]Deut. 27:26; Ps. 37:22 [c]Ps. 119:10, 118
22 [a]Ps. 39:8; 119:39 [b]Ps. 119:2
23 [a]Ps. 119:161 [b]Ps. 119:15
24 [1]Lit., *the men of my counsel* [a]Ps. 119:16
25 [a]Ps. 44:25 [b]Ps. 119:37, 40, 88, 93, 107, 149, 154, 156, 159; 143:11 [c]Ps. 119:65
26 [a]Ps. 25:4; 27:11; 86:11; 119:12
27 [a]Ps. 105:2; 145:5
28 [1]Lit., *drops* [a]Ps. 22:14; 107:26 [b]Ps. 20:2; 1 Pet. 5:10
30 [1]Or, *accounted Thine ordinances worthy*
31 [a]Deut. 11:22
32 [a]1 Kin. 4:29; Is. 60:5; 2 Cor. 6:11, 13
33 [a]Ps. 119:5, 12
34 [a]Ps. 119:27, 73, 125, 144, 169 [b]1 Chr. 22:12; Ezek. 44:24 [c]Ps. 119:2, 69
35 [a]Ps. 25:4; Is. 40:14 [b]Ps. 112:1; 119:16
36 [a]1 Kin. 8:58 [b]Ezek. 33:31; Mark 7:21, 22; Luke 12:15; Heb. 13:5
37 [a]Is. 33:15 [b]Ps. 71:20; 119:25
38 [1]Or, *promise* [2]Lit., *Which is for the fear of Thee* [a]2 Sam. 7:25
39 [a]Ps. 119:22
40 [a]Ps. 119:20
41 [1]Or, *promise* [a]Ps. 119:77 [b]Ps. 119:58, 76, 116, 170
42 [a]Prov. 27:11 [b]Ps. 102:8; 119:39
43 [1]Or, *hope in* [a]Ps. 119:49, 74, 81, 114, 147
44 [a]Ps. 119:33
45 [1]Lit., *in a wide place* [a]Prov. 4:12 [b]Ps. 119:94, 155
46 [a]Matt. 10:18; Acts 26:1, 2
47 [1]Lit., *delight myself* [a]Ps. 119:16 [b]Ps. 119:97, 127, 159
48 [a]Ps. 119:97, 127, 159 [b]Ps. 119:15
49 [1]Lit., *On*
50 [1]Or, *preserved me alive* [a]Job 6:10; Rom. 15:4

51 The arrogant [a]utterly deride me,
Yet I do not [b]turn aside from Thy law.
52 I have [a]remembered Thine ordinances from [1]of old, O LORD,
And comfort myself.
53 Burning [a]indignation has seized me because of the wicked,
Who [b]forsake Thy law.
54 Thy statutes are my songs
In the house of my [a]pilgrimage.
55 O LORD, I [a]remember Thy name [b]in the night,
And keep Thy law.
56 This has become mine,
[1]That I [a]observe Thy precepts.

ח HETH.

57 The LORD is my [a]portion;
I have [1]promised to [b]keep Thy words.
58 I [a]entreated Thy favor [b]with all *my* heart;
[c]Be gracious to me [d]according to Thy [1]word.
59 I [a]considered my ways,
And turned my feet to Thy testimonies.
60 I hastened and did not delay
To keep Thy commandments.
61 The [a]cords of the wicked have encircled me,
But I have [b]not forgotten Thy law.
62 At [a]midnight I shall rise to give thanks to Thee
Because of Thy [b]righteous ordinances.
63 I am a [a]companion of all those who [1]fear Thee,
And of those who keep Thy precepts.
64 [a]The earth is full of Thy lovingkindness, O LORD;
[b]Teach me Thy statutes.

ט TETH.

65 Thou hast dealt well with Thy servant,
O LORD, according to Thy word.
66 Teach me good [1a]discernment and knowledge,
For I believe in Thy commandments.
67 [a]Before I was afflicted I went astray,
But now I keep Thy word.
68 Thou art [a]good and [b]doest good;
[c]Teach me Thy statutes.
69 The arrogant [1]have [a]forged a lie against me;
With all *my* heart I will [b]observe Thy precepts.
70 Their heart is [1a]covered with fat,
But I [b]delight in Thy law.
71 It is [a]good for me that I was afflicted,
That I may learn Thy statutes.
72 The [a]law of Thy mouth is better to me
Than thousands of gold and silver *pieces*.

51 [a]Job 30:1; Jer. 20:7 [b]Job 23:11; Ps. 44:18; 119:157
52 [1]Or, *everlasting* [a]Ps. 103:18
53 [a]Ex. 32:19; Ezra 9:3; Neh. 13:25; Ps. 119:158 [b]Ps. 89:30
54 [a]Gen. 47:9; Ps. 119:19
55 [a]Ps. 63:6 [b]Ps. 42:8; 92:2; 119:62; Is. 26:9; Acts 16:25
56 [1]Or, *Because* [a]Ps. 119:22, 69, 100
57 [1]Lit., *said that I would keep* [a]Ps. 16:5; Lam. 3:24 [b]Deut. 33:9
58 [1]Or, *promise* [a]1 Kin. 13:6 [b]Ps. 119:2 [c]Ps. 41:4; 56:1; 57:1 [d]Ps. 119:41
59 [a]Mark 14:72; Luke 15:17
61 [a]Job 36:8; Ps. 140:5 [b]Ps. 119:83, 141, 153, 176
62 [a]Ps. 119:55 [b]Ps. 119:7
63 [1]Or, *revere* [a]Ps. 101:6
64 [a]Ps. 33:5 [b]Ps. 119:12
66 [1]Or, *judgment* [a]Phil. 1:9
67 [a]Ps. 119:71, 75; Jer. 31:18, 19; Heb. 12:5-11
68 [a]Ps. 86:5; 100:5; 106:1; 107:1; Matt. 19:17 [b]Deut. 8:16; 28:63; 30:5; Ps. 125:4 [c]Ps. 119:12
69 [1]Lit., *besmear me with lies* [a]Job 13:4; Ps. 109:2 [b]Ps. 119:56
70 [1]Lit., *gross like fat* [a]Deut. 32:15; Job 15:27; Ps. 17:10; Is. 6:10; Jer. 5:28; Acts 28:27 [b]Ps. 119:16
71 [a]Ps. 119:67, 75
72 [a]Ps. 19:10; 119:127; Prov. 8:10, 11, 19
73 [1]Lit., *established* [a]Job 10:8; 31:15; Ps. 100:3; 138:8; 139:15, 16 [b]Ps. 119:34
74 [1]Or, *revere* [2]Or, *hope in* [a]Ps. 34:2; 35:27; 107:42 [b]Ps. 119:43
75 [a]Ps. 119:138 [b]Heb. 12:10
76 [1]Lit., *be for my comfort* [2]Or, *promise*
77 [a]Ps. 119:41 [b]Ps. 119:16
78 [a]Jer. 50:32 [b]Ps. 119:86 [c]Ps. 119:15
79 [1]Or, *revere*
80 [1]Lit., *complete;* or, *having integrity* [a]Ps. 119:1 [b]Ps. 119:46
81 [1]Or, *hope in* [a]Ps. 84:2 [b]Ps. 119:43
82 [1]Or, *promise* [2]Lit., *Saying* [a]Ps. 69:3; 119:123; Is. 38:14; Lam. 2:11
83 [a]Job 30:30 [b]Ps. 119:61
84 [a]Ps. 39:4 [b]Rev. 6:10
85 [1]Lit., *according to Thy law* [a]Ps. 7:15; 35:7; 57:6; Jer. 18:22

י YODH.

73 [a]Thy hands made me and [1]fashioned me;
[b]Give me understanding, that I may learn Thy commandments.
74 May those who [1]fear Thee [a]see me and be glad,
Because I [2b]wait for Thy word.
75 I know, O LORD, that Thy judgments are [a]righteous,
And that [b]in faithfulness Thou hast afflicted me.
76 O may Thy lovingkindness [1]comfort me,
According to Thy [2]word to Thy servant.
77 May [a]Thy compassion come to me that I may live,
For Thy law is my [b]delight.
78 May [a]the arrogant be ashamed, for they subvert me [b]with a lie;
But I shall [c]meditate on Thy precepts.
79 May those who [1]fear Thee turn to me,
Even those who know Thy testimonies.
80 May my heart be [1a]blameless in Thy statutes,
That I may not [b]be ashamed.

כ KAPH.

81 My [a]soul languishes for Thy salvation;
I [1b]wait for Thy word.
82 My [a]eyes fail *with longing* for Thy [1]word,
[2]While I say, "When wilt Thou comfort me?"
83 Though I have [a]become like a wineskin in the smoke,
I do [b]not forget Thy statutes.
84 How many are the [a]days of Thy servant?
When wilt Thou [b]execute judgment on those who persecute me?
85 The arrogant have [a]dug pits for me,
Men who are not [1]in accord with Thy law.
86 All Thy commandments are [a]faithful;
They have [b]persecuted me with a lie; [c]help me!
87 They almost destroyed me [1]on earth,
But as for me, I [a]did not forsake Thy precepts.
88 Revive me according to Thy lovingkindness,
So that I may keep the testimony of Thy mouth.

ל LAMEDH.

89 [a]Forever, O LORD,
Thy word [1]is settled in heaven.

86 [a]Ps. 119:138 [b]Ps. 35:19; 119:78, 161 [c]Ps. 109:26
87 [1]Lit., *in the earth* [a]Is. 58:2
89 [1]Lit., *stands firm* [a]Ps. 89:2; 119:160; Is. 40:8; Matt. 24:35; 1 Pet. 1:25

90 Thy [a]faithfulness *continues* [1]throughout all generations;
Thou didst [b]establish the earth, and it [c]stands.
91 They stand this day according to Thine [a]ordinances,
For [b]all things are Thy servants.
92 If Thy law had not been my [a]delight,
Then I would have perished [b]in my affliction.
93 I will [a]never forget Thy precepts,
For by them Thou hast [1b]revived me.
94 I am Thine, [a]save me;
For I have [b]sought Thy precepts.
95 The wicked [a]wait for me to destroy me;
I shall diligently consider Thy testimonies.
96 I have seen [1]a limit to all perfection;
Thy commandment is exceedingly broad.

מ Mem.

97 O how I [a]love Thy law!
It is my [b]meditation all the day.
98 Thy [a]commandments make me wiser than my enemies,
For they are ever [1]mine.
99 I have more insight than all my teachers,
For Thy testimonies are my [a]meditation.
100 I understand [a]more than the aged,
Because I have [b]observed Thy precepts.
101 I have [a]restrained my feet from every evil way,
That I may keep Thy word.
102 I have not [a]turned aside from Thine ordinances,
For Thou Thyself hast taught me.
103 How [a]sweet are Thy [1]words to my [2]taste!
Yes, sweeter than honey to my mouth!
104 From Thy precepts I [a]get understanding;
Therefore I [b]hate every false way.

נ Nun.

105 Thy word is a [a]lamp to my feet,
And a light to my path.
106 I have [a]sworn, and I will confirm it,
That I will keep Thy righteous ordinances.
107 I am exceedingly [a]afflicted;
[1b]Revive me, O Lord, according to Thy word.
108 O accept the [a]freewill offerings of my mouth, O Lord,
And [b]teach me Thine ordinances.
109 My [1a]life is continually [2]in my hand,
Yet I do not [b]forget Thy law.
110 The wicked have [a]laid a snare for me,
Yet I have not [b]gone astray from Thy precepts.

91 [a]Jer. 31:35; 33:25 [b]Ps. 104:2-4
92 [a]Ps. 119:16 [b]Ps. 119:50
93 [1]Or, *kept me alive* [a]Ps. 119:16, 83 [b]Ps. 119:25
94 [a]Ps. 119:146 [b]Ps. 119:45
95 [a]Ps. 40:14; Is. 32:7
96 [1]Lit., *an end of*
97 [a]Ps. 119:47, 48, 127, 163, 165 [b]Ps. 1:2; 119:15
98 [1]Or, *with me* [a]Deut. 4:6; Ps. 119:130
99 [a]Ps. 119:15
100 [a]Job 32:7-9 [b]Ps. 119:22, 56
101 [a]Prov. 1:15
102 [a]Deut. 17:20; Josh. 23:6; 1 Kin. 15:5
103 [1]Or, *promises* [2]Lit., *palate* [a]Ps. 19:10; Prov. 8:11; 24:13, 14
104 [a]Ps. 119:130 [b]Ps. 119:128
105 [a]Prov. 6:23
106 [a]Neh. 10:29
107 [1]Or, *Keep me alive* [a]Ps. 119:25, 50 [b]Ps. 119:25
108 [a]Hos. 14:2; Heb. 13:15 [b]Ps. 119:12
109 [1]Lit., *soul* [2]I.e., in danger [a]Judg. 12:3; Job 13:14 [b]Ps. 119:16
110 [a]Ps. 91:3; 140:5; 141:9 [b]Ps. 119:10
111 [a]Deut. 33:4 [b]Ps. 119:14, 162
112 [a]Ps. 119:36 [b]Ps. 119:33
113 [a]1 Kin. 18:21; James 1:8; 4:8 [b]Ps. 119:47
114 [1]Or, *hope in* [a]Ps. 31:20; 32:7; 61:4; 91:1 [b]Ps. 84:9 [c]Ps. 119:74
115 [a]Ps. 6:8; 139:19; Matt. 7:23 [b]Ps. 119:22
116 [1]Or, *promise* [2]Lit., *put to shame because of* [a]Ps. 37:17, 24; 54:4 [b]Ps. 25:2, 20; 31:1, 17; Rom. 5:5; 9:33; Phil. 1:20
117 [a]Ps. 12:5; Prov. 29:25 [b]Ps. 119:6, 15
118 [1]Lit., *made light of* [2]Lit., *falsehood* [a]Ps. 119:10, 21
119 [1]Lit., *caused to cease* [a]Is. 1:22, 25; Ezek. 22:18, 19 [b]Ps. 119:47
120 [1]Lit., *bristles up from* [a]Job 4:14; Hab. 3:16 [b]Ps. 119:161

111 I have [a]inherited Thy testimonies forever,
For they are the [b]joy of my heart.
112 I have [a]inclined my heart to perform Thy statutes
Forever, *even* [b]to the end.

ס Samekh.

113 I hate those who are [a]double-minded,
But I love Thy [b]law.
114 Thou art my [a]hiding place and my [b]shield;
I [1c]wait for Thy word.
115 [a]Depart from me, evildoers,
That I may [b]observe the commandments of my God.
116 [a]Sustain me according to Thy [1]word, that I may live;
And [b]do not let me be [2]ashamed of my hope.
117 Uphold me that I may be [a]safe,
That I may [b]have regard for Thy statutes continually.
118 Thou hast [1]rejected all those [a]who wander from Thy statutes,
For their deceitfulness is [2]useless.
119 Thou hast [1]removed all the wicked of the earth *like* [a]dross;
Therefore I [b]love Thy testimonies.
120 My flesh [1a]trembles for fear of Thee,
And I am [b]afraid of Thy judgments.

ע Ayin.

121 I have [a]done justice and righteousness;
Do not leave me to my oppressors.
122 Be [a]surety for Thy servant for good;
Do not let the arrogant [b]oppress me.
123 My [a]eyes fail *with longing* for Thy salvation,
And for Thy righteous [1]word.
124 Deal with Thy servant [a]according to Thy lovingkindness,
And [b]teach me Thy statutes.
125 [a]I am Thy servant; [b]give me understanding,
That I may know Thy testimonies.
126 It is time for the Lord to [a]act,
For they have broken Thy law.
127 Therefore I [a]love Thy commandments
Above gold, yes, above fine gold.
128 Therefore I esteem right all *Thy* [a]precepts concerning everything,
I [b]hate every false way.

פ Pe.

129 Thy testimonies are [a]wonderful;
Therefore my soul [b]observes them.

121 [a]2 Sam. 8:15; Job 29:14
122 [a]Job 17:3; Heb. 7:22 [b]Ps. 119:134
123 [1]Or, *promise* [a]Ps. 119:82
124 [a]Ps. 51:1; 106:45; 109:26; 119:88, 149, 159 [b]Ps. 119:12
125 [a]Ps. 116:16 [b]Ps. 119:27
126 [a]Jer. 18:23; Ezek. 31:11
127 [a]Ps. 19:10; 119:47
128 [a]Ps. 19:8 [b]Ps. 119:104
129 [a]Ps. 119:18 [b]Ps. 119:22

130 The [a]unfolding of Thy words gives light;
It gives [b]understanding to the simple.
131 I [a]opened my mouth wide and [b]panted,
For I [c]longed for Thy commandments.
132 [a]Turn to me and be gracious to me,
After Thy manner [1]with those who love Thy name.
133 Establish my [a]footsteps in Thy [1]word,
And do not let any iniquity [b]have dominion over me.
134 [a]Redeem me from the oppression of man,
That I may keep Thy precepts.
135 [a]Make Thy face shine upon Thy servant,
And [b]teach me Thy statutes.
136 My eyes [1]shed [a]streams of water,
Because they [b]do not keep Thy law.

צ TSADHE.

137 [a]Righteous art Thou, O LORD,
And upright are Thy judgments.
138 Thou hast commanded Thy testimonies in [a]righteousness
And exceeding [b]faithfulness.
139 My [a]zeal has [1]consumed me,
Because my adversaries have forgotten Thy words.
140 Thy [1a]word is very [2]pure,
Therefore Thy servant [b]loves it.
141 I am small and [a]despised,
Yet I do not [b]forget Thy precepts.
142 Thy righteousness is an everlasting righteousness,
And [a]Thy law is truth.
143 Trouble and anguish have [1]come upon me;
Yet Thy commandments are my [a]delight.
144 Thy [a]testimonies are righteous forever;
[b]Give me understanding that I may live.

ק QOPH.

145 I cried [a]with all my heart; answer me, O LORD!
I will [b]observe Thy statutes.
146 I cried to Thee; [a]save me,
And I shall keep Thy testimonies.
147 I [1a]rise before dawn and cry for help;
I [2]wait for Thy words.
148 My eyes anticipate the [a]night watches,
That I may [b]meditate on Thy [1]word.
149 Hear my voice [a]according to Thy lovingkindness;
[b]Revive me, O LORD, according to Thine ordinances.
150 Those who follow after wickedness draw near;
They are far from Thy law.
151 Thou art [a]near, O LORD,
And all Thy commandments are [b]truth.
152 Of old I have [a]known from Thy testimonies,
That Thou hast founded them [b]forever.

ר RESH.

153 [a]Look upon my [b]affliction and rescue me,
For I do not [c]forget Thy law.
154 [a]Plead my cause and [b]redeem me;
Revive me according to Thy [1]word.
155 Salvation is [a]far from the wicked,
For they [b]do not seek Thy statutes.
156 [1a]Great are Thy mercies, O LORD;
Revive me according to Thine ordinances.
157 Many are my [a]persecutors and my adversaries,
Yet I do not [b]turn aside from Thy testimonies.
158 I behold the [a]treacherous and [b]loathe *them*,
Because they do not keep Thy [1]word.
159 Consider how I [a]love Thy precepts;
[b]Revive me, O LORD, according to Thy lovingkindness.
160 The [a]sum of Thy word is [b]truth,
And every one of Thy righteous ordinances [c]is everlasting.

ש SHIN.

161 [a]Princes persecute me without cause,
But my heart [b]stands in awe of Thy words.
162 I [a]rejoice at Thy [1]word,
As one who [b]finds great spoil.
163 I [a]hate and despise falsehood,
But I [b]love Thy law.
164 Seven times a day I praise Thee,
Because of Thy [a]righteous ordinances.
165 Those who love Thy law have [a]great peace,
And [1b]nothing causes them to stumble.
166 I [a]hope for Thy salvation, O LORD,
And do Thy commandments.
167 My [a]soul keeps Thy testimonies,
And I [b]love them exceedingly.
168 I [a]keep Thy precepts and Thy testimonies,
For all my [b]ways are before Thee.

ת TAV.

169 Let my [a]cry [1]come before Thee, O LORD;
[b]Give me understanding [c]according to Thy word.
170 Let my [a]supplication come before Thee;
[b]Deliver me according to Thy [1]word.

130 aProv. 6:23 bPs. 19:7
131 aJob 29:23; Ps. 81:10 bPs. 42:1 cPs. 119:20
132 1Lit., *to* aPs. 25:16; 106:4
133 1Or, *promise* aPs. 17:5 bPs. 19:13; Rom. 6:12
134 aPs. 119:84; 142:6; Luke 1:74
135 aNum. 6:25; Ps. 4:6; 31:16; 67:1; 80:3, 7, 19 bPs. 119:12
136 1Lit., *run down* aJer. 9:1, 18; 14:17; Lam. 3:48 bPs. 119:158
137 aEzra 9:15; Neh. 9:33; Ps. 116:5; 129:4; 145:17; Jer. 12:1; Lam. 1:18; Dan. 9:7, 14
138 aPs. 19:7-9; 119:144, 172 bPs. 119:86, 90
139 1Lit., *put an end to* aPs. 69:9; John 2:17
140 1Or, *promise* 2Lit., *refined* aPs. 12:6; 19:8 bPs. 119:47
141 aPs. 22:6 bPs. 119:61
142 aPs. 19:9; 119:151, 160
143 1Lit., *found me* aPs. 119:24
144 aPs. 19:9 bPs. 119:27
145 aPs. 119:10 bPs. 119:22, 55
146 aPs. 3:7
147 1Lit., *anticipate the dawn* 2Or, *hope in* aPs. 5:3; 57:8; 108:2
148 1Or, *promise* aPs. 63:6 bPs. 119:15
149 aPs. 119:124 bPs. 119:25
151 aPs. 34:18; 145:18; Is. 50:8 bPs. 119:142
152 aPs. 119:125 bPs. 119:89; Luke 21:33
153 aLam. 5:1 bPs. 119:50 cPs. 119:16; Prov. 3:1; Hos. 4:6
154 1Or, *promise* a1 Sam. 24:15; Ps. 35:1; Mic. 7:9 bPs. 119:134
155 aJob 5:4 bPs. 119:45, 94
156 1Or, *Many* a2 Sam. 24:14
157 aPs. 7:1; 119:86, 161 bPs. 119:51
158 1Or, *promise* aIs. 21:2; 24:16 bPs. 139:21
159 aPs. 119:47 bPs. 119:25
160 aPs. 139:17 bPs. 119:142 cPs. 119:89, 152
161 a1 Sam. 24:11; 26:18; Ps. 119:23 bPs. 119:120
162 1Or, *promise* aPs. 119:14, 111 b1 Sam. 30:16; Is. 9:3
163 aPs. 31:6; 119:104, 128; Prov. 13:5 bPs. 119:47
164 aPs. 119:7, 160

165 1Lit., *they have no stumbling block* aPs. 37:11; Prov. 3:2; Is. 26:3; 32:17 bProv. 3:23; Is. 63:13; 1 John 2:10
166 aGen. 49:18; Ps. 119:81, 174
167 aPs. 119:129 bPs. 119:47
168 aPs. 119:22 bJob 24:23; Ps. 139:3; Prov. 5:21
169 1Lit., *come near before* aJob 16:18; Ps. 18:6; 102:1 bPs. 119:27, 144 cPs. 119:65, 154
170 1Or, *promise* aPs. 28:2; 130:2; 140:6; 143:1 bPs. 22:20; 31:2; 59:1

171 Let my [a]lips utter praise,
For Thou [b]dost teach me Thy statutes.
172 Let my [a]tongue sing of Thy [1]word,
For all Thy [b]commandments are righteousness.
173 Let Thy [a]hand be [1]ready to help me,
For I have [b]chosen Thy precepts.
174 I [a]long for Thy salvation, O LORD,
And Thy law is my [b]delight.
175 Let my [a]soul live that it may praise Thee,
And let Thine ordinances help me.
176 I have [a]gone astray like a lost sheep; seek Thy servant,
For I do [b]not forget Thy commandments.

PSALM 120

Prayer for Deliverance from the Treacherous.

A Song of [+]Ascents.

[a]IN my trouble I cried to the LORD,
And He answered me.
2 Deliver my soul, O LORD, from [a]lying lips,
From a [b]deceitful tongue.
3 What shall be given to you, and what more shall be done to you,
You [a]deceitful tongue?
4 [a]Sharp arrows of the warrior,
With the *burning* [b]coals of the broom tree.

5 Woe is me, for I sojourn in [a]Meshech,
For I dwell among the [b]tents of [c]Kedar!
6 Too long has my soul had its dwelling
With those who [a]hate peace.
7 I [a]am *for* peace, but when I speak,
They are [b]for war.

PSALM 121

The LORD the Keeper of Israel.

A Song of Ascents.

I WILL [a]lift up my eyes to [b]the mountains;
From whence shall my help come?
2 My [a]help *comes* from the LORD,
Who [b]made heaven and earth.
3 He will not [a]allow your foot to slip;
He who [b]keeps you will not slumber.
4 Behold, He who keeps Israel
Will neither slumber nor sleep.

5 The LORD is your [a]keeper;
The LORD is your [b]shade on your right hand.
6 The [a]sun will not smite you by day,
Nor the moon by night.
7 The LORD will [1a]protect you from all evil;
He will keep your soul.
8 The LORD will [1a]guard your going out and your coming in
[b]From this time forth and forever.

171 [a]Ps. 51:15; 63:3 [b]Ps. 94:12; 119:12; Is. 2:3; Mic. 4:2
172 [1]Or, *promise* [a]Ps. 51:14 [b]Ps. 119:138
173 [1]Lit., *to help me* [a]Ps. 37:24; 73:23 [b]Josh. 24:22; Luke 10:42
174 [a]Ps. 119:166 [b]Ps. 119:16, 24
175 [a]Is. 55:3
176 [a]Is. 53:6; Jer. 50:6; Matt. 18:12; Luke 15:4 [b]Ps. 119:16

+ Ex. 34:24; 1 Kin. 12:27
1 [a]Ps. 18:6; 66:14; 102:2; Jon. 2:2
2 [a]Ps. 109:2; Prov. 12:22 [b]Ps. 52:4; Zeph. 3:13
3 [a]Ps. 52:4; Zeph. 3:13
4 [a]Ps. 45:5; Prov. 25:18; Is. 5:28 [b]Ps. 140:10
5 [a]Gen. 10:2; 1 Chr. 1:5; Ezek. 27:13; 38:2, 3; 39:1 [b]Song 1:5 [c]Gen. 25:13; Is. 21:16; 60:7; Jer. 2:10; 49:28; Ezek. 27:21
6 [a]Ps. 35:20
7 [a]Ps. 109:4 [b]Ps. 55:21

1 [a]Ps. 123:1; Is. 40:26 [b]Ps. 87:1
2 [a]Ps. 124:8 [b]Ps. 115:15
3 [a]1 Sam. 2:9; Ps. 66:9 [b]Ps. 41:2; 127:1; Is. 27:3
5 [a]Ps. 91:4 [b]Ps. 16:8; 91:1; Is. 25:4
6 [a]Ps. 91:5; Is. 49:10; Jon. 4:8; Rev. 7:16
7 [1]Or, *keep* [a]Ps. 41:2; 91:10-12
8 [1]Or, *keep* [a]Deut. 28:6 [b]Ps. 113:2; 115:18

1 [a]Ps. 42:4; Is. 2:3; Mic. 4:2; Zech. 8:21
2 [a]Ps. 9:14; 87:2; 116:19; Jer. 7:2
3 [a]Ps. 48:13; 147:2 [b]2 Sam. 5:9; Neh. 4:6
4 [1]Heb., *YAH* [2]Or, *A testimony* [a]Ex. 23:17; Deut. 16:16; Ps. 84:5
5 [a]Deut. 17:8; 2 Chr. 19:8; Ps. 89:29
6 [a]Ps. 29:11; Jer. 29:7 [b]Ps. 102:14
7 [a]Ps. 51:18; Is. 62:6 [b]Ps. 48:3, 13; Jer. 17:27
8 [a]Ps. 133:1 [b]1 Sam. 25:6; John 20:19
9 [a]Neh. 2:10; Esth. 10:3

1 [a]Ps. 121:1; 141:8 [b]Ps. 2:4; 11:4
2 [a]Prov. 27:18; Mal. 1:6 [b]Ps. 25:15
3 [a]Ps. 4:1; 51:1 [b]Neh. 4:4; Ps. 119:22

PSALM 122

Prayer for the Peace of Jerusalem.

A Song of Ascents, of David.

I WAS glad when they said to me,
"Let us [a]go to the house of the LORD."
2 Our feet are standing
Within your [a]gates, O Jerusalem,
3 Jerusalem, that is [a]built
As a city that is [b]compact together;
4 To which the tribes [a]go up, even the tribes of [1]the LORD—
[2]An ordinance for Israel—
To give thanks to the name of the LORD.
5 For there [a]thrones were set for judgment,
The thrones of the house of David.

6 Pray for the [a]peace of Jerusalem:
"May they prosper who [b]love you.
7 "May peace be within your [a]walls,
And prosperity within your [b]palaces."
8 For the sake of my [a]brothers and my friends,
I will now say, "[b]May peace be within you."
9 For the sake of the house of the LORD our God
I will [a]seek your good.

PSALM 123

Prayer for the LORD'S Help.

A Song of Ascents.

TO Thee I [a]lift up my eyes,
O Thou who [b]art enthroned in the heavens!
2 Behold, as the eyes of [a]servants *look* to the hand of their master,
As the eyes of a maid to the hand of her mistress;
So our [b]eyes *look* to the LORD our God,
Until He shall be gracious to us.

3 [a]Be gracious to us, O LORD, be gracious to us;
For we are greatly filled [b]with contempt.
4 Our soul is greatly filled
With the [a]scoffing of [b]those who are at ease,
And with the [c]contempt of the proud.

PSALM 124

Praise for Rescue from Enemies.

A Song of Ascents, of David.

"[a]HAD it not been the LORD who was on our side,"
[b]Let Israel now say,
2 "Had it not been the LORD who was on our side,
When men rose up against us;

4 [a]Neh. 2:19; Ps. 79:4 [b]Job 12:5; Is. 32:9, 11; Amos 6:1 [c]Neh. 4:4; Ps. 119:22

1 [a]Ps. 94:17 [b]Ps. 129:1

3 Then they would have [a]swallowed
us alive,
When their [b]anger was kindled
against us;
4 Then the [a]waters would have engulfed us,
The stream would have [1]swept over
our soul;
5 Then the [a]raging waters would
have [1]swept over our soul."

6 Blessed be the LORD,
Who has not given us [1]to be [a]torn
by their teeth.
7 Our soul has [a]escaped [b]as a bird
out of the [c]snare of the trapper;
The snare is broken and we have
escaped.
8 Our [a]help is in the name of the
LORD,
Who [b]made heaven and earth.

PSALM 125

The LORD Surrounds His People.

A Song of Ascents.

THOSE who trust in the LORD
Are as Mount Zion, which [a]cannot
be moved, but [b]abides forever.
2 As the mountains surround Jerusalem,
So [a]the LORD surrounds His people
[b]From this time forth and forever.
3 For the [a]scepter of wickedness
shall not rest upon the [1]land of
the righteous;
That the righteous [b]may not put
forth their hands to do wrong.

4 [a]Do good, O LORD, to those who
are good,
And to those who are [b]upright in
their hearts.
5 But as for those who [a]turn aside to
their [b]crooked ways,
The LORD will lead them away with
the [c]doers of iniquity.
[d]Peace be upon Israel.

PSALM 126

Thanksgiving for Return from Captivity.

A Song of Ascents.

WHEN the LORD [a]brought back [1]the
captive ones of Zion,
We were [b]like those who dream.
2 Then our [a]mouth was filled with
laughter,
And our [b]tongue with joyful shouting;
Then they said among the nations,
"The LORD has [c]done great things
for them."
3 The LORD has done great things for
us;
We are [a]glad.

4 Restore our captivity, O LORD,
As the [1a]streams in the [2]South.
5 Those who sow in [a]tears shall reap
with [b]joyful shouting.
6 He who goes to and fro weeping,
carrying *his* bag of seed,
Shall indeed come again with a
shout of joy, bringing his
sheaves *with him.*

PSALM 127

Prosperity Comes from the LORD.

A Song of Ascents, of Solomon.

UNLESS the LORD [a]builds the house,
They labor in vain who build it;
Unless the LORD [b]guards the city,
The watchman keeps awake in
vain.
2 It is vain for you to rise up early,
To [1]retire late,
To [a]eat the bread of [2]painful la-
bors;
For He gives to His [b]beloved [c]*even
in his* sleep.

3 Behold, [a]children are a [1]gift of the
LORD;
The [b]fruit of the womb is a reward.
4 Like arrows in the hand of a [a]war-
rior,
So are the children of one's youth.
5 How [a]blessed is the man whose
quiver is full of them;
[b]They shall not be ashamed,
When they [c]speak with their enemies [d]in the gate.

PSALM 128

Blessedness of the Fear of the LORD.

A Song of Ascents.

[a]HOW blessed is everyone who fears
the LORD,
Who [b]walks in His ways.
2 When you shall [a]eat of the [1b]fruit
of your hands,
You will be happy and [c]it will be
well with you.
3 Your wife shall be like a [a]fruitful
vine,
[1]Within your house,
Your children like [b]olive plants
Around your table.
4 Behold, for thus shall the man be
blessed
Who fears the LORD.

5 [a]The LORD bless you [b]from Zion,
And may you see the prosperity of
Jerusalem all the days of your
life.
6 Indeed, may you see your [a]chil-
dren's children.
[b]Peace be upon Israel!

PSALM 129

Prayer for the Overthrow of Zion's Enemies.

A Song of Ascents.

"[1]MANY times they have [2a]per-
secuted me from my [b]youth
up,"
[c]Let Israel now say,

3 [a]Num. 16:30; Ps. 35:25; 56:1; 57:3; Prov. 1:12 [b]Gen. 39:19; Ps. 138:7
4 [1]Or, *passed over* [a]Job 22:11; Ps. 18:16; 32:6; 69:2; 144:7
5 [1]Or, *passed over* [a]Job 38:11
6 [1]Lit., *as a prey to* [a]Ps. 27:2; Prov. 30:14
7 [a]Ps. 141:10; 2 Cor. 11:33; Heb. 11:34 [b]Prov. 6:5 [c]Ps. 91:3; Hos. 9:8
8 [a]Ps. 121:2 [b]Gen. 1:1; Ps. 134:3

1 [a]Ps. 46:5 [b]Ps. 61:7; Eccl. 1:4
2 [a]Zech. 2:5 [b]Ps. 121:8
3 [1]Lit., *lot* [a]Ps. 89:22; Prov. 22:8; Is. 14:5 [b]1 Sam. 24:10; Ps. 55:20; Acts 12:1
4 [a]Ps. 119:68 [b]Ps. 7:10; 11:2; 32:11; 36:10; 94:15
5 [a]Job 23:11; Ps. 40:4; 101:3 [b]Prov. 2:15; Is. 59:8 [c]Ps. 92:7; 94:4 [d]Ps. 128:6; Gal. 6:16

1 [1]Or, *those who returned to* [a]Ps. 85:1; Jer. 29:14; Hos. 6:11 [b]Acts 12:9
2 [a]Job 8:21 [b]Ps. 51:14; Is. 35:6 [c]1 Sam. 12:24; Ps. 71:19; Luke 1:49
3 [a]Is. 25:9; Zeph. 3:14
4 [1]Lit., *stream-beds* [2]Heb., *Negev* [a]Is. 35:6; 43:19
5 [a]Ps. 80:5; Jer. 31:9, 16; Lam. 1:2 [b]Is. 35:10; 51:11; 61:7; Gal. 6:9

1 [a]Ps. 78:69 [b]Ps. 121:4
2 [1]Lit., *delay sitting* [2]Lit., *toils* [a]Gen. 3:17, 19 [b]Ps. 60:5 [c]Job 11:18, 19; Prov. 3:24; Eccl. 5:12
3 [1]Or, *heritage* [a]Gen. 33:5; 48:4; Josh. 24:3, 4; Ps. 113:9 [b]Deut. 7:13; 28:4; Is. 13:18
4 [a]Ps. 112:2; 120:4
5 [a]Ps. 128:2, 3 [b]Prov. 27:11 [c]Is. 29:21; Amos 5:12 [d]Gen. 34:20

1 [a]Ps. 112:1; 119:1 [b]Ps. 119:3
2 [1]Lit., *labor* [a]Is. 3:10 [b]Ps. 109:11; Hag. 2:17 [c]Eccl. 8:12; Eph. 6:3
3 [1]Lit., *In the innermost parts of* [a]Ezek. 19:10 [b]Ps. 52:8; 144:12
5 [a]Ps. 134:3 [b]Ps. 20:2; 135:21
6 [a]Gen. 48:11; 50:23; Job 42:16; Ps. 103:17; Prov. 17:6 [b]Ps. 125:5

1 [1]Lit., *Much* [2]Lit., *showed hostility toward* [a]Ex. 1:11; Judg. 3:8; Ps. 88:15 [b]Is. 47:12; Jer. 2:2; 22:21; Ezek. 16:22; Hos. 2:15; 11:1 [c]Ps. 124:1

A LAW FOR SOCIETY

Leviticus 4:22-31; 19:10; 23:22. Leviticus 4 is an example of a law that was not immediately applicable to contemporary society because in the clan life of people involved in the Exodus there were no such distinctions in society. Leviticus 19 and 23 were written before the Jews had fields and vineyards. It is common to read in many books about the text of the Old Testament that such laws really belonged to a later period of Israel's history and were *"written back"* into this period. I prefer to believe that God prepared for the development of society by giving laws in advance.

It is interesting to compare laws in Exodus 20 with those in Deuteronomy and then those in Leviticus because they correspond to three successive periods of development in Jewish history. The laws of liberty for a slave are interesting in this respect. in Deuteronomy 15:12-18, slaves were to be released after seven years, and when King Zedekiah did not release slaves, Jeremiah referred him to this seven-year law (Jeremiah 34:8-14). the law in Leviticus 25:40 seems to be for a later period, because the short terms for slavery did not work. Jeremiah did not quote it as appropriate for his time.

WAS DAVID ELHANAN?

2 Samuel 21:19. Elhanan the son of a Bethlehemite killed Goliath the Gittite, the shaft of whose spear was like a weaver's rod. This is so similar to David son of an Ephrathite of Bethlehem who killed Goliath of Gath, whose spear was like a weaver's rod (I Samuel 17:7), that some people wonder if David was the coronation name and Elhanan the original name.

OPENING AND SHUTTING

Isaiah 22:22. This verse describes the authority of the master of the palace. Eliakim was to have the key of the house of David, and what Eliakim would open no one else could shut, and what he shut no one else could open. These words are used of Christ in Revelation 3:7. because Christ has such authority in the kingdom of heaven. This is quite distinct from what Jesus tells Peter in Matthew 16:9. the binding and loosing Peter was given was also given to the other disciples (Matthew 18:18). When a person acts in accordance with God's Word, it can be declared that he is bound or free by someone who knows that Word.

RIGHTS OF CITIZENSHIP

Acts 22:25-29. When Paul was bound and an attempt was made to scourge him, there was consternation when it was realized that he was a Roman citizen, because such treatment of a citizen was contrary to the law. The tribune, who was the officer commanding the unit in Jerusalem, had apparently purchased his own citizenship at a time when it was put up for sale. If Paul was free born and came from Tarsus in Cilicia, his father probably had performed some service for the republic (not the Empire) for which citizenship had been conferred on himself and his family.

ENTERING MANHOOD

Luke 2. The Jewish boy was recognized as entering manhood at thirteen years of age, but it is not certain when this practice began. By New Testament times a boy of thirteen became a *"son of the lay."* The significance of the account of Jesus' being left behind at the Temple is that it showed he was leaving his childhood (Luke 2:41-49). It was the last time he would attend Passover as a child. Only after age thirteen did the child qualify to become one of the ten men who could constitute a synagogue.

DIVISIONS IN SOCIETY

There were no divisions within society during the period of the patriarches (Abraham, Isaac, and Jacob) because everyone was a member of a family. Even slaves were looked upon as members of the family, so that Abraham could expect his slave Eliezer to inherit his possessions (Genesis 15:2-3). Even when clans developed from the families there were still no social divisions, because a clan is simply a family that has settled to form a village. In such a society the laws were upheld by the clan elders, who presided over village affairs. There were seventy-seven elders at Succoth in Gideon's time (Judges 7:14). By the time the monarchy arrived the term elder was used for the ruling class. The servants of Amon who killed him were elders (2 Kings 21:23) and Zedekiah was concerned that Jeremiah should not repeat their conversaticn to the princes, or elders (Jeremiah 38:24-25).

ELISHA - *commitment*

When God called Elisha through Elijah to serve Him, his response was immediate and complete. He was plowing his fields with his oxen. He responded by slaughtering his oxen and burning them with the wood from his plow. Elisha gave them as a burnt offering to the Lord. They represented his material wealth and his livelihood. There would be no going back — he was committed to God's call on his life.

Elisha lived during a time of Bal worship and sin in Israel. The house of Ahab was still in power. Elijah had worked to defeat these enemies of God and cleanse Israel. Elisha was called to carry on this work. He served with Elijah for six years before Elijah was taken up in a chariot. After such training, Elisha knew what God wanted him to do. He had attained a position of respect among the others faithful to God in Israel. He knew his work would be difficult and he asked for a special gift to get the job done: a double portion of Elijah's spirit!

Elisha did not ask lightly or in an untimely way. He stayed with Elijah on his final journey, despite Elijah's repeated requests to go on alone. He knew, as did Elijah, what was going to happen at journey's end. Yet he stayed with Elijah until he finally asked Elisha what he could do for him before being taken up. Thus Elisha was able to ask appropriately.

Elijah had performed miracles and defeated false gods through the power of the spirit of God. And Elisha asked for a double portion of that same spirit! Why did he have the nerve to ask such a thing? From what he had seen, that was what would be needed to get the job done. Why did he receive what he asked? Because he proven he was committed to seeing God's will fulfilled in his life.

QUESTIONS

1. **Elisha gave everything he had to the Lord as a sacrifice. How has the Lord led you to make sacrifices?**

2. **Elisha, through his double portion of the the spirit, led a triumphant life of service of God. When has God's spirit brought victory in your life?**

3. **Elisha was known for his commitment. Do you have trouble keeping commitments? How could you strengthen your depth of commitment?**

4. **Even on his deathbed, Elisha advised a king, still full of God's power. Why do you think this was possible?**

2 "[1]Many times they have [2]persecuted me from my youth up;
Yet they have [a]not prevailed against me.
3 "The plowers plowed upon my back;
They lengthened their furrows."
4 The LORD [a]is righteous;
He has cut in two the [b]cords of the wicked.

5 May all who [a]hate Zion,
Be [b]put to shame and turned backward,
6 Let them be like [a]grass upon the housetops,
Which withers before it [1]grows up;
7 With which the reaper does not fill his [1]hand,
Or the binder of sheaves his [a]bosom;
8 Nor do those who pass by say,
"The [a]blessing of the LORD be upon you;
We bless you in the name of the LORD."

PSALM 130

Hope in the LORD'S Forgiving Love.

A Song of Ascents.

OUT of the [a]depths I have cried to Thee, O LORD.
2 Lord, [a]hear my voice!
Let [b]Thine ears be attentive
To the [c]voice of my supplications.
3 If Thou, [1]LORD, shouldst mark iniquities,
O Lord, who could [a]stand?
4 But there is [a]forgiveness with Thee,
That Thou mayest be [b]feared.

5 I wait for the LORD, my [a]soul does wait,
And [1b]in His word do I hope.
6 My soul *waits* for the Lord
More than the watchmen [a]for the morning;
Indeed, more than the watchmen for the morning.
7 O Israel, [a]hope in the LORD;
For with the LORD there is [b]lovingkindness,
And with Him is [c]abundant redemption.
8 And He will [a]redeem Israel
From all his iniquities.

PSALM 131

Childlike Trust in the LORD.

A Song of Ascents, of David.

O LORD, my heart is not [a]proud, nor my eyes [1b]haughty;
Nor do I [2]involve myself in [c]great matters,
Or in things [d]too [3]difficult for me.
2 Surely I have [a]composed and quieted my soul;
Like a weaned [b]child *rests* [1]against his mother,
My soul is like a weaned child [1]within me.

2 [1]Lit., *Much* [2]Lit., *showed hostility toward* [a]Jer. 1:19; 15:20; 20:11; Matt. 16:18; 2 Cor. 4:8, 9
4 [a]Ps. 119:137 [b]Ps. 140:5
5 [a]Mic. 4:11 [b]Ps. 70:3; 71:13
6 [1]Lit., *draws out* [a]2 Kin. 19:26; Ps. 37:2; Is. 37:27
7 [1]Lit., *palm* [a]Ps. 79:12
8 [a]Ruth 2:4; Ps. 118:26

1 [a]Ps. 42:7; 69:2; Lam. 3:55
2 [a]Ps. 64:1; 119:149 [b]2 Chr. 6:40; Neh. 1:6, 11 [c]Ps. 28:2; 140:6
3 [1]Heb., *YAH* [a]Ps. 76:7; 143:2; Nah. 1:6; Mal. 3:2; Rev. 6:17
4 [a]Ex. 34:7; Neh. 9:17; Ps. 86:5; Is. 55:7; Dan. 9:9 [b]1 Kin. 8:39, 40; Jer. 33:8, 9
5 [1]Lit., *for* [a]Ps. 27:14; 33:20; 40:1; 62:1, 5; Is. 8:17; 26:8 [b]Ps. 119:74, 81
6 [a]Ps. 63:6; 119:147
7 [a]Ps. 131:3 [b]Ps. 86:5; 103:4 [c]Ps. 111:9; Rom. 3:24; Eph. 1:7
8 [a]Ps. 103:3, 4; Luke 1:68; Titus 2:14

1 [1]Or, *lofty* [2]Lit., *go after, walk* [3]Or, *marvelous* [a]2 Sam. 22:28; Ps. 101:5; Is. 2:12; Zeph. 3:11 [b]Prov. 30:13; Is. 5:15 [c]Jer. 45:5; Rom. 12:16 [d]Job 42:3; Ps. 139:6
2 [1]Or, *upon* [a]Ps. 62:1 [b]Matt. 18:3; 1 Cor. 14:20
3 [a]Ps. 130:7 [b]Ps. 113:2

1 [a]Gen. 49:24; 2 Sam. 16:12
2 [a]Gen. 49:24; Is. 49:26; 60:16
3 [1]Lit., *come into the tabernacle of* [2]Lit., *go up into the couch of* [a]Job 21:28
4 [a]Prov. 6:4
5 [1]Lit., *Dwelling places* [a]1 Kin. 8:17; 1 Chr. 22:7; Ps. 26:8; Acts 7:46 [b]Ps. 132:2
6 [1]Or, *the wood* [a]Gen. 35:19; 1 Sam. 17:12 [b]1 Sam. 7:1
7 [1]Lit., *dwelling places* [a]Ps. 43:3 [b]Ps. 5:7; 99:5 [c]1 Chr. 28:2
8 [a]Num. 10:35; 2 Chr. 6:41; Ps. 68:1 [b]Ps. 132:14 [c]Ps. 78:61
9 [a]Job 29:14 [b]Ps. 30:4; 132:16; 149:5
10 [a]Ps. 2:2; 132:17
11 [a]Ps. 89:3, 35 [b]2 Sam. 7:12-16; 1 Chr. 17:11-14; 2 Chr. 6:16; Ps. 89:4; Acts 2:30

3 O Israel, [a]hope in the LORD
[b]From this time forth and forever.

PSALM 132

Prayer for the LORD'S Blessing upon the Sanctuary.

A Song of Ascents.

REMEMBER, O LORD, on David's behalf,
All [a]his affliction;
2 How he swore to the LORD,
And vowed to [a]the Mighty One of Jacob,
3 "Surely I will not [1]enter [a]my house,
Nor [2]lie on my bed;
4 I will not [a]give sleep to my eyes,
Or slumber to my eyelids;
5 Until I find a [a]place for the LORD,
[1]A dwelling place for [b]the Mighty One of Jacob."

6 Behold, we heard of it in [a]Ephrathah;
We found it in the [b]field of [1]Jaar.
7 Let us go into His [1a]dwelling place;
Let us [b]worship at His [c]footstool.
8 [a]Arise, O LORD, to Thy [b]resting place;
Thou and the ark of Thy [c]strength.
9 Let Thy priests be [a]clothed with righteousness;
And let Thy [b]godly ones sing for joy.

10 For the sake of David Thy servant,
Do not turn away the face of Thine [a]anointed.
11 The LORD has [a]sworn to David,
A truth from which He will not turn back;
"[b]Of the fruit of your body I will set upon your throne.
12 "If your sons will keep My covenant,
And My testimony which I will teach them,
Their sons also shall [a]sit upon your throne forever."

13 For the LORD has [a]chosen Zion;
He has [b]desired it for His habitation.
14 "This is My [a]resting place forever;
Here I will [b]dwell, for I have desired it.
15 "I will abundantly [a]bless her provision;
I will [b]satisfy her needy with bread.
16 "Her [a]priests also I will clothe with salvation;
And her [a]godly ones will sing aloud for joy.
17 "There I will cause the [a]horn of David to spring forth;
I have prepared a [b]lamp for Mine anointed.

12 [a]Luke 1:32; Acts 2:30
13 [a]Ps. 48:1, 2; 78:68 [b]Ps. 68:16
14 [a]Ps. 132:8 [b]Ps. 68:16; Matt. 23:21
15 [a]Ps. 147:14 [b]Ps. 107:9
16 [a]2 Chr. 6:41; Ps. 132:9
17 [a]Ezek. 29:21; Luke 1:69 [b]1 Kin. 11:36; 15:4; 2 Kin. 8:19; 2 Chr. 21:7; Ps. 18:28

18 “His enemies I will [a]clothe with shame;
But upon himself his [b]crown shall shine.”

PSALM 133

The Excellency of Brotherly Unity.

A Song of Ascents, of David.

BEHOLD, how good and how pleasant it is
For [a]brothers to dwell together in unity!
2 It is like the precious [a]oil upon the head,
Coming down upon the beard,
Even Aaron’s beard,
Coming down upon the [b]edge of his robes.
3 It is like the [a]dew of [b]Hermon,
Coming down upon the [c]mountains of Zion;
For there the LORD [d]commanded the blessing—[e]life forever.

PSALM 134

Greetings of Night Watchers.

A Song of Ascents.

BEHOLD, [a]bless the LORD, all [b]servants of the LORD,
Who [1c]serve [d]by night in the house of the LORD!
2 [a]Lift up your hands to the [b]sanctuary,
And bless the LORD.
3 May the LORD [a]bless you from Zion,
He who [b]made heaven and earth.

PSALM 135

Praise the LORD’S Wonderful Works. Vanity of Idols.

[1a]PRAISE [2]the LORD!
Praise the name of the LORD;
Praise *Him,* O [b]servants of the LORD,
2 You who stand in the house of the LORD,
In the [a]courts of the house of our God!
3 [1]Praise [2]the LORD, for [a]the LORD is good;
[b]Sing praises to His name, [c]for it is lovely.
4 For [1]the LORD has [a]chosen Jacob for Himself,
Israel for His [2b]own possession.

5 For I know that [a]the LORD is great,
And that our Lord is [b]above all gods.
6 [a]Whatever the LORD pleases, He does,
In heaven and in earth, in the seas and in all deeps.
7 [1]He [a]causes the [2]vapors to ascend from the ends of the earth;
Who [b]makes lightnings for the rain;
Who [c]brings forth the wind from His treasuries.
8 [1]He [a]smote the first-born of Egypt,
[2]Both of man and beast.
9 [1]He sent [a]signs and wonders into your midst, O Egypt,
Upon [b]Pharaoh and all his servants.
10 [1a]He [b]smote many nations,
And slew mighty kings,
11 [a]Sihon, king of the Amorites,
And [b]Og, king of Bashan,
And [c]all the kingdoms of Canaan;
12 And He [a]gave their land as a heritage,
A heritage to Israel His people.
13 Thy [a]name, O LORD, is everlasting,
Thy [1]remembrance, O LORD, [2]throughout all generations.
14 For the LORD will [a]judge His people,
And [b]will have compassion on His servants.
15 The [a]idols of the nations are *but* silver and gold,
The work of man’s hands.
16 They have mouths, but they do not speak;
They have eyes, but they do not see;
17 They have ears, but they do not hear;
Nor is there any breath at all in their mouths.
18 Those who make them will be like them,
Yes, everyone who trusts in them.

19 O house of [a]Israel, bless the LORD;
O house of Aaron, bless the LORD;
20 O house of Levi, bless the LORD;
You [a]who [1]revere the LORD, bless the LORD.
21 Blessed be the LORD [a]from Zion,
Who [b]dwells in Jerusalem.
[1]Praise [2]the LORD!

PSALM 136

Thanks for the LORD’S Goodness to Israel.

[a]GIVE thanks to the LORD, for [b]He is good;
For [c]His lovingkindness is everlasting.
2 Give thanks to the [a]God of gods,
For His lovingkindness is everlasting.
3 Give thanks to the [a]Lord of lords,
For His lovingkindness is everlasting.
4 To Him who [a]alone does great [1]wonders,
For His lovingkindness is everlasting;
5 To Him who [a]made the heavens [1b]with skill,
For His lovingkindness is everlasting;

18 [a]Job 8:22; Ps. 35:26; 109:29 [b]Ps. 21:3
1 [a]Gen. 13:8; Heb. 13:1
2 [a]Ex. 29:7; 30:25, 30; Lev. 8:12 [b]Ex. 28:33; 39:24
3 [a]Prov. 19:12; Hos. 14:5; Mic. 5:7 [b]Deut. 3:9; 4:48 [c]Ps. 48:2; 74:2; 78:68 [d]Lev. 25:21; Deut. 28:8; Ps. 42:8 [e]Ps. 21:4
1 [1]Lit., *stand* [a]Ps. 103:21 [b]Ps. 135:1, 2 [c]Deut. 10:8; 1 Chr. 23:30; 2 Chr. 29:11 [d]1 Chr. 9:33
2 [a]Ps. 28:2; 1 Tim. 2:8 [b]Ps. 63:2
3 [a]Ps. 128:5 [b]Ps. 124:8
1 [1]Or, *Hallelujah!* [2]Heb., *YAH* [a]Ps. 113:1 [b]Ps. 134:1
2 [a]Ps. 92:13; 116:19
3 [1]Or, *Hallelujah!* [2]Heb., *YAH* [a]Ps. 100:5; 119:68 [b]Ps. 68:4 [c]Ps. 147:1
4 [1]Heb., *YAH* [2]Or, *special treasure* [a]Deut. 7:6; 10:15; Ps. 105:6 [b]Ex. 19:5; Mal. 3:17; Titus 2:14; 1 Pet. 2:9
5 [a]Ps. 48:1; 95:3; 145:3 [b]Ps. 97:9
6 [a]Ps. 115:3
7 [1]Lit., *The one who* [2]I.e., clouds [a]Jer. 10:13; 51:16 [b]Job 28:25, 26; 38:25, 26; Zech. 10:1 [c]Jer. 10:13; 51:16
8 [1]Lit., *The one who* [2]Lit., *From man to beast* [a]Ex. 12:12; Ps. 78:51; 105:36
9 [1]Lit., *The one who* [a]Ex. 7:10; Deut. 6:22; Ps. 78:43 [b]Ps. 136:15
10 [1]Lit., *The one who* [a]Num. 21:24; Ps. 135:10-12; 136:17-21 [b]Ps. 44:2
11 [a]Num. 21:21-26; Deut. 29:7 [b]Num. 21:33-35 [c]Josh. 12:7-24
12 [a]Deut. 29:8; Ps. 78:55; 136:21, 22
13 [1]Or, *memorial* [2]Lit., *to* [a]Ex. 3:15; Ps. 102:12
14 [a]Deut. 32:36; Ps. 50:4 [b]Ps. 90:13; 106:46
15 [a]Ps. 115:4-8; 135:15-18
19 [a]Ps. 115:9
20 [1]Lit., *fear* [a]Ps. 118:4
21 [1]Or, *Hallelujah!* [2]Heb., *YAH* [a]Ps. 128:5; 134:3 [b]Ps. 132:14

1 [a]1 Chr. 16:34; Ps. 106:1; 107:1; 118:1; Jer. 33:11 [b]2 Chr. 5:13; 7:3; Ezra 3:11; Ps. 100:5 [c]1 Chr. 16:41; 2 Chr. 20:21; Ps. 118:1-4
2 [a]Deut. 10:17
3 [a]Deut. 10:17
4 [1]I.e., wonderful acts [a]Deut. 6:22; Job 9:10; Ps. 72:18
5 [1]Lit., *with understanding* [a]Gen. 1:1 [b]Ps. 104:24; Prov. 3:19; Jer. 10:12; 51:15

6 To Him who [a]spread out the earth above the waters,
For His lovingkindness is everlasting;
7 To Him who [a]made *the* great lights,
For His lovingkindness is everlasting:
8 The [a]sun to rule [1]by day,
For His lovingkindness is everlasting,
9 The [a]moon and stars to rule [1]by night,
For His lovingkindness is everlasting.

10 To Him who [a]smote [1]the Egyptians in their first-born,
For His lovingkindness is everlasting,
11 And [a]brought Israel out from their midst,
For His lovingkindness is everlasting,
12 With a [a]strong hand and an [b]outstretched arm,
For His lovingkindness is everlasting;
13 To Him who [a]divided the [1]Red Sea [2]asunder,
For His lovingkindness is everlasting,
14 And [a]made Israel pass through the midst of it,
For His lovingkindness is everlasting;
15 But [a]He [1]overthrew Pharaoh and his army in the [2]Red Sea,
For His lovingkindness is everlasting.
16 To Him who [a]led His people through the wilderness,
For His lovingkindness is everlasting;
17 To Him who [a]smote great kings,
For His lovingkindness is everlasting,
18 And [a]slew [1]mighty kings,
For His lovingkindness is everlasting:
19 [a]Sihon, king of the Amorites,
For His lovingkindness is everlasting,
20 And [a]Og, king of Bashan,
For His lovingkindness is everlasting,
21 And [a]gave their land as a heritage,
For His lovingkindness is everlasting,
22 Even a heritage to Israel His [a]servant,
For His lovingkindness is everlasting.

23 Who [a]remembered us in our low estate,
For His lovingkindness is everlasting,
24 And has [a]rescued us from our adversaries,
For His lovingkindness is everlasting;

6 [a]Gen. 1:2, 6, 9; Ps. 24:2; Is. 42:5; 44:24; Jer. 10:12
7 [a]Gen. 1:14-18; Ps. 74:16
8 [1]Or, *over the* [a]Gen. 1:16
9 [1]Or, *over the* [a]Gen. 1:16
10 [1]Lit., *Egypt* [a]Ex. 12:29; Ps. 78:51; 135:8
11 [a]Ex. 12:51; 13:3; Ps. 105:43
12 [a]Ex. 6:1; 13:9; 1 Kin. 8:42; Neh. 1:10; Ps. 44:3; Jer. 32:21 [b]Ex. 6:6; Deut. 4:34; 5:15; 7:19; 9:29; 11:2; 2 Kin. 17:36; 2 Chr. 6:32; Jer. 32:17
13 [1]Lit., *Sea of Reeds* [2]Lit., *in parts* [a]Ex. 14:21; Ps. 66:6; 78:13
14 [a]Ex. 14:22; Ps. 106:9
15 [1]Lit., *shook off* [2]Lit., *Sea of Reeds* [a]Ex. 14:27; Ps. 78:53; 106:11
16 [a]Ex. 13:18; 15:22; Deut. 8:15; Ps. 78:52
17 [a]Ps. 135:10-12; 136:17-22
18 [1]Lit., *majestic* [a]Deut. 29:7
19 [a]Num. 21:21-24
20 [a]Num. 21:33-35
21 [a]Josh. 12:1
22 [a]Ps. 105:6; Is. 41:8; 44:1; 45:4
23 [a]Ps. 9:12; 103:14; 106:45
24 [a]Judg. 6:9; Neh. 9:28; Ps. 107:2
25 [a]Ps. 104:27; 145:15
26 [a]Gen. 24:3, 7; 2 Chr. 36:23; Ezra 1:2; 5:11; Neh. 1:4

1 [a]Ezek. 1:1, 3 [b]Neh. 1:4
2 [1]Or, *poplars* [2]Lit., *lyres* [a]Lev. 23:40; Is. 44:4 [b]Job 30:31; Is. 24:8; Ezek. 26:13
3 [1]Lit., *asked* [2]Lit., *words of song* [a]Ps. 80:6 [b]Is. 49:17
4 [a]2 Chr. 29:27; Neh. 12:46
5 [1]I.e., become lame [a]Is. 65:11
6 [1]Lit., *cause to ascend* [a]Job 29:10; Ps. 22:15; Ezek. 3:26 [b]Neh. 2:3
7 [a]Ps. 83:4-8; Is. 34:5, 6; Jer. 49:7-22; Lam. 4:21; Ezek. 25:12-14; 35:2; Amos 1:11; Obad. 10-14 [b]Ps. 74:7; Hab. 3:13
8 [1]Or, *devastator* [2]Lit., *your recompense* [a]Is. 13:1-22; 47:1-15; Jer. 25:12; 50:1-46; 51:1-64 [b]Jer. 50:15; 51:24, 35, 36, 49; Rev. 18:6
9 [a]2 Kin. 8:12; Is. 13:16; Hos. 13:16; Nah. 3:10

1 [a]Ps. 111:1 [b]Ps. 95:3; 96:4; 97:7

25 Who [a]gives food to all flesh,
For His lovingkindness is everlasting.
26 Give thanks to the [a]God of heaven,
For His lovingkindness is everlasting.

PSALM 137

An Experience of the Captivity.

BY the [a]rivers of Babylon,
There we sat down and [b]wept,
When we remembered Zion.
2 Upon the [1a]willows in the midst of it
We [b]hung our [2]harps.
3 For there our captors [1a]demanded of us [2]songs,
And [b]our tormentors mirth, *saying,*
"Sing us one of the songs of Zion."

4 How can we sing [a]the LORD's song
In a foreign land?
5 If I [a]forget you, O Jerusalem,
May my right hand [1]forget *her skill.*
6 May my [a]tongue cleave to the roof of my mouth,
If I do not remember you,
If I do not [1b]exalt Jerusalem
Above my chief joy.

7 Remember, O LORD, against the sons of [a]Edom
The day of Jerusalem,
Who said, "Raze it, raze it,
[b]To its very foundation."
8 O daughter of Babylon, you [1a]devastated one,
How blessed will be the one who [b]repays you
With [2]the recompense with which you have repaid us.
9 How blessed will be the one who seizes and [a]dashes your little ones
Against the rock.

PSALM 138

Thanksgiving for the LORD'S Favor.
A Psalm of David.

[a]I WILL give Thee thanks with all my heart;
I will sing praises to Thee before the [b]gods.
2 I will bow down [a]toward Thy holy temple,
And [b]give thanks to Thy name for Thy lovingkindness and Thy [1]truth;
For Thou hast [c]magnified Thy [2]word [3]according to all Thy name.
3 On the day I [a]called Thou didst answer me;
Thou didst make me bold with [b]strength in my soul.

4 [a]All the kings of the earth will give thanks to Thee, O LORD,

2 [1]Or, *faithfulness* [2]Or, *promise* [3]Or, *together with* [a]I Kin. 8:29; Ps. 5:7; 28:2 [b]Ps. 140:13 [c]Is. 42:21
3 [a]Ps. 118:5 [b]Ps. 28:7; 46:1
4 [a]Ps. 72:11; 102:15

When they have heard the words of
Thy mouth.
5 And they will [a]sing of the ways of
the LORD.
For [b]great is the glory of the LORD.
6 For [a]though the LORD is exalted,
Yet He [b]regards the lowly;
But the [c]haughty He knows from
afar.

7 Though I [a]walk in the midst of
trouble, Thou wilt [1b]revive me;
Thou wilt [c]stretch forth Thy hand
against the wrath of my enemies,
And Thy right hand will [d]save me.
8 The LORD will [a]accomplish what
concerns me;
Thy [b]lovingkindness, O LORD, is
everlasting;
[c]Do not forsake the [d]works of Thy
hands.

PSALM 139

God's Omnipresence and Omniscience.

For the choir director. A Psalm of David.

O LORD, Thou hast [a]searched me
and known *me*.
2 Thou [a]dost know [1]when I sit down
and [2]when I rise up;
Thou [b]dost understand my thought
from afar.
3 Thou [a]dost [1]scrutinize my [2]path
and my lying down,
And art intimately acquainted with
all my ways.
4 [1]Even before there is a word on my
tongue,
Behold, O LORD, Thou [a]dost know
it all.
5 Thou hast [a]enclosed me behind
and before,
And [b]laid Thy hand upon me.
6 *Such* [a]knowledge is [b]too wonderful
for me;
It is *too* high, I cannot attain to it.

7 [a]Where can I go from Thy Spirit?
Or where can I flee from Thy presence?
8 [a]If I ascend to heaven, Thou art
there;
If I make my bed in [1]Sheol, behold,
[b]Thou art there.
9 If I take the wings of the dawn,
If I dwell in the remotest part of
the sea,
10 Even there Thy hand will [a]lead me,
And Thy right hand will lay hold of
me.
11 If I say, "Surely the [a]darkness will
[1]overwhelm me,
And the light around me will be
night,"
12 Even the [a]darkness is not dark [1]to
Thee,
And the night is as bright as the
day.
[b]Darkness and light are alike *to
Thee.*

13 For Thou didst [a]form my [1]inward
parts;
Thou didst [b]weave me in my mother's womb.
14 I will give thanks to Thee, for [1]I am
fearfully and wonderfully made;
[a]Wonderful are Thy works,
And my soul knows it very well.
15 My [1a]frame was not hidden from
Thee,
When I was made in secret,
And skillfully wrought in the
[b]depths of the earth.
16 Thine [a]eyes have seen my unformed substance;
And in [b]Thy book they were all
written,
The [c]days that were ordained *for
me*,
When as yet there was not one of
them.

17 How precious also are Thy
[a]thoughts to me, O God!
How vast is the sum of them!
18 If I should count them, they would
[a]outnumber the sand.
When [b]I awake, I am still with
Thee.

19 O that Thou wouldst [a]slay the
wicked, O God;
[b]Depart from me, therefore, [c]men
of bloodshed.
20 For they [a]speak [1]against Thee
wickedly,
And Thine enemies [2b]take *Thy
name* in vain.
21 Do I not [a]hate those who hate
Thee, O LORD?
And do I not [b]loathe those who rise
up against Thee?
22 I hate them with the utmost hatred;
They have become my enemies.

23 [a]Search me, O God, and know my
heart;
[b]Try me and know my anxious
thoughts;
24 And see if there be any [1a]hurtful
way in me,
And [b]lead me in the [c]everlasting
way.

PSALM 140

Prayer for Protection against the Wicked.

For the choir director. A Psalm of David.

[a]RESCUE me, O LORD, from evil men;
Preserve me from [b]violent men,
2 Who [a]devise evil things in *their*
hearts;
They [b]continually stir up wars.
3 They [a]sharpen their tongues as a
serpent;
[b]Poison of a viper is under their
lips. [[1]Selah.

4 [a]Keep me, O LORD, from the hands
of the wicked;
[b]Preserve me from violent men,
Who have [1]purposed to [2c]trip up
my feet.

3 [1]*Selah* may mean: *Pause, Crescendo* or *Musical interlude* [a]Ps. 57:4; 64:3 [b]Ps. 58:4; Rom. 3:13; James 3:8
4 [1]Or, *devised* [2]Lit., *push violently* [a]Ps. 71:4 [b]Ps. 140:1 [c]Ps. 36:11

5 [a]Ps. 145:7 [b]Ps. 21:5
6 [a]Ps. 113:4-7 [b]Prov. 3:34; Is. 57:15; Luke 1:48; James 4:6; 1 Pet. 5:5 [c]Ps. 40:4; 101:5
7 [1]Or, *keep me alive* [a]Ps. 23:4; 143:11 [b]Ezra 9:8, 9; Ps. 71:20; Is. 57:15 [c]Ex. 7:5; 15:12; Is. 5:25; Jer. 51:25; Ezek. 6:14; 25:13 [d]Ps. 20:6; 60:5
8 [a]Ps. 57:2; Phil. 1:6 [b]Ps. 136:1 [c]Job 10:8; Ps. 27:9; 71:9; 119:8 [d]Job 10:3; 14:15; Ps. 100:3

1 [a]Ps. 17:3; 44:21; Jer. 12:3
2 [1]Lit., *my sitting* [2]Lit., *my rising* [a]2 Kin. 19:27 [b]Ps. 94:11; Is. 66:18; Matt. 9:4
3 [1]Lit., *winnow* [2]Or, *journeying* [a]Job 14:16; 31:4
4 [1]Lit., *For there is not* [a]Heb. 4:13
5 [a]Ps. 34:7; 125:2 [b]Job 9:33
6 [a]Rom. 11:33 [b]Job 42:3
7 [a]Jer. 23:24
8 [1]I.e., the nether world [a]Amos 9:2-4 [b]Job 26:6; Prov. 15:11
10 [a]Ps. 23:2, 3
11 [1]Lit., *bruise;* some commentators read *cover* [a]Job 22:13
12 [1]Lit., *from* [a]Job 34:22; Dan. 2:22 [b]1 John 1:5
13 [1]Lit., *kidneys* [a]Ps. 119:73; Is. 44:24 [b]Job 10:11
14 [1]Some ancient versions read *Thou art fearfully wonderful* [a]Ps. 40:5
15 [1]Lit., *bones were* [a]Job 10:8-10; Eccl. 11:5 [b]Ps. 63:9
16 [a]Job 10:8-10; Eccl. 11:5 [b]Ps. 56:8 [c]Job 14:5
17 [a]Ps. 40:5; 92:5
18 [a]Ps. 40:5 [b]Ps. 3:5
19 [a]Is. 11:4 [b]Ps. 6:8; 119:115 [c]Ps. 5:6; 26:9
20 [1]Or, *of* [2]Some mss. read *lift themselves up* against Thee [a]Jude 15 [b]Ex. 20:7; Deut. 5:11
21 [a]2 Chr. 19:2; Ps. 26:5; 31:6 [b]Ps. 119:158
23 [a]Job 31:6; Ps. 26:2 [b]Ps. 7:9; Prov. 17:3; Jer. 11:20; 1 Thess. 2:4
24 [1]Lit., *way of pain* [a]Ps. 146:9; Prov. 15:9; 28:10; Jer. 25:5; 36:3 [b]Ps. 5:8; 143:10 [c]Ps. 16:11

1 [a]Ps. 17:13; 59:2; 71:4 [b]Ps. 18:48; 86:14; 140:11
2 [a]Ps. 7:14; 36:4; 52:2; Prov. 6:14; Is. 59:4; Hos. 7:15 [b]Ps. 56:6

5 The proud have [a]hidden a trap for
me, and cords;
They have spread a [b]net by the
[1]wayside;
They have set [c]snares for me. [Selah.

6 I [a]said to the LORD, "Thou art my
God;
[b]Give ear, O LORD, to the [c]voice of
my supplications.
7 "O [1]GOD the Lord, [a]the strength of
my salvation,
Thou hast [b]covered my head in the
day of [2]battle.
8 "Do not grant, O LORD, the [a]desires
of the wicked;
Do not promote [b]his *evil* device,
lest they be exalted. [Selah.

9 "As for the head of those who surround me,
May the [a]mischief of their lips
cover them.
10 "May [a]burning coals fall upon
them;
May they be [b]cast into the fire,
Into [1]deep pits from which they
[c]cannot rise.
11 "May a [1]slanderer not be established in the earth;
[a]May evil hunt the violent man
[2]speedily."

12 I know that the LORD will [a]main-
tain the cause of the afflicted,
And [b]justice for the poor.
13 Surely the [a]righteous will give
thanks to Thy name;
The [b]upright will dwell in Thy
presence.

PSALM 141

An Evening Prayer for Sanctification and Protection.

A Psalm of David.

O LORD, I call upon Thee; [a]hasten
to me!
[b]Give ear to my voice when I call
to Thee!
2 May my prayer be [1]counted as
[a]incense before Thee;
The [b]lifting up of my hands as the
[c]evening offering.
3 Set a [a]guard, O LORD, [1]over my
mouth;
Keep watch over the [b]door of my
lips.
4 [a]Do not incline my heart to any
evil thing,
To practice deeds [1]of wickedness
With men who [b]do iniquity;
And [c]do not let me eat of their
delicacies.

5 Let the [a]righteous smite me [1]in
kindness and reprove me;
It is [b]oil upon the head;
Do not let my head refuse it,
[2]For still my prayer [c]is [3]against
their wicked deeds.
6 Their judges are [a]thrown down by
the sides of the rock,

5 [1]Lit., *track* [a]Job 18:9; Ps. 35:7; 141:9; 142:3 [b]Ps. 31:4; 57:6; Lam. 1:13 [c]Ps. 141:9; Is. 8:14; Amos 3:5
6 [a]Ps. 16:2; 31:14 [b]Ps. 143:1 [c]Ps. 116:1; 130:2
7 [1]Heb., *YHWH,* usually rendered *LORD* [2]Lit., *weapons* [a]Ps. 28:8; 118:14 [b]Ps. 144:10
8 [a]Ps. 112:10 [b]Esth. 9:25; Ps. 10:2, 3
9 [a]Ps. 7:16; Prov. 18:7
10 [1]Lit., *watery* [a]Ps. 11:6 [b]Ps. 21:9; Matt. 3:10 [c]Ps. 36:12
11 [1]Lit., *man of tongue* [2]Lit., *thrust upon thrust* [a]Ps. 34:21
12 [a]1 Kin. 8:45, 49; Ps. 9:4; 18:27; 82:3 [b]Ps. 12:5; 35:10
13 [a]Ps. 97:12 [b]Ps. 11:7; 16:11; 17:15

1 [a]Ps. 22:19; 38:22; 70:5 [b]Ps. 5:1; 143:1
2 [1]Lit., *fixed* [a]Ex. 30:8; Luke 1:10; Rev. 5:8; 8:3, 4 [b]1 Tim. 2:8 [c]Ex. 29:39, 41; 1 Kin. 18:29, 36; Dan. 9:21
3 [1]Lit., *to* [a]Ps. 34:13; 39:1; Prov. 13:3; 21:23 [b]Mic. 7:5
4 [1]Lit., *in* [a]Ps. 119:36 [b]Is. 32:6; Hos. 6:8; Mal. 3:15 [c]Prov. 23:6
5 [1]Or, *lovingly* [2]Lit., *And my prayer* [3]Or, *in spite of their calamities* [a]Prov. 9:8; 19:25; 25:12; 27:6; Eccl. 7:5; Gal. 6:1 [b]Ps. 23:5; 133:2 [c]Ps. 35:14
6 [a]2 Chr. 25:12
7 [1]I.e., the nether world [a]Ps. 129:3 [b]Ps. 53:5 [c]Num. 16:32, 33; Ps. 88:3-5
8 [1]Heb., *YHWH,* usually rendered *LORD* [2]Lit., *pour out my soul* [a]Ps. 25:15; 123:2 [b]Ps. 2:12; 11:1 [c]Ps. 27:9
9 [1]Lit., *hands of the trap* [a]Ps. 38:12; 64:5; 91:3; 119:110 [b]Ps. 140:5
10 [1]Lit., *altogether* [a]Ps. 7:15; 35:8; 57:6 [b]Ps. 124:7

+ Possibly, *Contemplative,* or *Didactic,* or *Skillful Psalm*
• 1 Sam. 22:1; 24:3
1 [a]Ps. 77:1 [b]Ps. 30:8
2 [a]Ps. 102:title [b]Ps. 77:2
3 [1]Lit., *fainted* [a]Ps. 77:3; 143:4 [b]Ps. 140:5
4 [1]Lit., *Escape has perished from me* [a]Ps. 31:11; 88:8, 18 [b]Job 11:20; Jer. 25:35 [c]Jer. 30:17

And they hear my words, for they
are pleasant.
7 As when one [a]plows and breaks
open the earth,
Our [b]bones have been scattered at
the [c]mouth of [1]Sheol.

8 For my [a]eyes are toward Thee, O
[1]GOD, the Lord;
In Thee I [b]take refuge; [c]do not
[2]leave me defenseless.
9 Keep me from the [1a]jaws of the
trap which they have set for me,
And from the [b]snares of those who
do iniquity.
10 Let the wicked [a]fall into their own
nets,
While I pass by [1b]safely.

PSALM 142

Prayer for Help in Trouble.

+Maskil of David, when he was •in the cave. A Prayer.

I [a]CRY aloud with my voice to the
LORD;
I [b]make supplication with my voice
to the LORD.
2 I [a]pour out my complaint before
Him;
I declare my [b]trouble before Him.
3 When [a]my spirit [1]was overwhelmed
within me,
Thou didst know my path.
In the way where I walk
They have [b]hidden a trap for me.
4 Look to the right and see;
For there is [a]no one who regards
me;
[1]There is no [b]escape for me;
[c]No one cares for my soul.

5 I cried out to Thee, O LORD;
I said, "Thou art [a]my refuge,
My [b]portion in the [c]land of the
living.
6 "[a]Give heed to my cry,
For I am [b]brought very low;
Deliver me from my persecutors,
For they are too [c]strong for me.
7 "[a]Bring my soul out of prison,
So that I may give thanks to Thy
name;
The righteous will surround me,
For Thou wilt [b]deal bountifully
with me."

PSALM 143

Prayer for Deliverance and Guidance.

A Psalm of David.

HEAR my prayer, O LORD,
[a]Give ear to my supplications!
Answer me in Thy [b]faithfulness, in
Thy [c]righteousness!
2 And [a]do not enter into judgment
with Thy servant,
For in Thy sight [b]no man living is
righteous.

5 [a]Ps. 91:2, 9 [b]Ps. 16:5; 73:26 [c]Ps. 27:13
6 [a]Ps. 17:1 [b]Ps. 79:8; 116:6 [c]Ps. 18:17
7 [a]Ps. 143:11; 146:7 [b]Ps. 13:6

1 [a]Ps. 140:6 [b]Ps. 89:1, 2 [c]Ps. 71:2
2 [a]Job 14:3; 22:4 [b]1 Kin. 8:46; Job 4:17; 9:2; 25:4; Ps. 130:3; Eccl. 7:20; Rom. 3:10, 20; Gal. 2:16

3 For the enemy has persecuted my soul;
He has crushed my life [a]to the ground;
He [b]has made me dwell in dark places, like those who have long been dead.
4 Therefore [a]my spirit [1]is overwhelmed within me;
My heart is [2b]appalled within me.

5 I [a]remember the days of old;
I [b]meditate on all Thy doings;
I [c]muse on the work of Thy hands.
6 I [a]stretch out my hands to Thee;
My [b]soul *longs* for Thee, as a [1]parched land. [[2]Selah.

7 [a]Answer me quickly, O LORD, my [b]spirit fails;
[c]Do not hide Thy face from me,
Lest I become like [d]those who go down to the pit.
8 Let me hear Thy [a]lovingkindness [b]in the morning;
For I trust [c]in Thee;
Teach me the [d]way in which I should walk;
For to Thee I [e]lift up my soul.
9 [a]Deliver me, O LORD, from my enemies;
[1]I take refuge in Thee.

10 [a]Teach me to do Thy will,
For Thou art my God;
Let [b]Thy good Spirit [c]lead me on level [1]ground.
11 [a]For the sake of Thy name, O LORD, [b]revive me.
[c]In Thy righteousness bring my soul out of trouble.
12 And in Thy lovingkindness [1a]cut off my enemies,
And [b]destroy all those who afflict my soul;
For [c]I am Thy servant.

PSALM 144

Prayer for Rescue and Prosperity.

A Psalm of David.

BLESSED be the LORD, [a]my rock,
Who [b]trains my hands for war,
And my fingers for battle;
2 My lovingkindness and [a]my fortress,
My [b]stronghold and my deliverer;
My [c]shield and He in whom I take refuge;
Who [d]subdues [1]my people under me.
3 O LORD, [a]what is man, that Thou dost take knowledge of him?
Or the son of man, that Thou dost think of him?
4 [a]Man is like a mere breath;
His [b]days are like a passing shadow.

5 [a]Bow Thy heavens, O LORD, and [b]come down;
[c]Touch the mountains, that they may smoke.
6 Flash forth [a]lightning and scatter them;
Send out Thine [b]arrows and confuse them.
7 Stretch forth Thy hand [a]from on high;
Rescue me and [b]deliver me out of great waters,
Out of the hand of [c]aliens
8 Whose mouths [a]speak deceit,
And whose [b]right hand is a right hand of falsehood.

9 I will sing a [a]new song to Thee, O God;
Upon a [b]harp of ten strings I will sing praises to Thee,
10 Who dost [a]give salvation to kings;
Who [b]dost rescue David His servant from the evil sword.
11 Rescue me, and deliver me out of the hand of [a]aliens,
Whose mouth [b]speaks deceit,
And whose [c]right hand is a right hand of falsehood.

12 Let our sons in their youth be as [a]grown-up plants,
And our daughters as [b]corner pillars [1]fashioned as for a palace;
13 *Let* our [a]garners be full, furnishing every kind of produce,
And our flocks bring forth thousands and ten thousands in our [1]fields;
14 *Let* our [a]cattle [1]bear,
Without [2b]mishap and without [3c]loss,
Let there be no [d]outcry in our streets!
15 How blessed are the people who are so situated;
How [a]blessed are the people whose God is the LORD!

PSALM 145

The LORD *Extolled for His Goodness.*

A Psalm of Praise, of David.

I WILL [a]extol Thee, [b]my God, O King;
And I will [c]bless Thy name forever and ever.
2 Every day I will bless Thee,
And I will [a]praise Thy name forever and ever.
3 [a]Great is the LORD, and highly to be praised;
And His [b]greatness is unsearchable.
4 One [a]generation shall praise Thy works to another,
And shall declare Thy mighty acts.
5 On the [a]glorious [1]splendor of Thy majesty,
And [b]on Thy wonderful works, I will meditate.
6 And men shall speak of the [1]power of Thine [a]awesome acts;
And I will [b]tell of Thy greatness.

3 [a]Ps. 44:25 [b]Ps. 88:6; Lam. 3:6
4 [1]Lit., *faints* [2]Or, *desolate* [a]Ps. 77:3; 142:3 [b]Lam. 3:11
5 [a]Ps. 77:5, 10, 11 [b]Ps. 77:12 [c]Ps. 105:2
6 [1]Lit., *weary* [2]*Selah* may mean: *Pause, Crescendo* or *Musical interlude* [a]Job 11:13; Ps. 88:9 [b]Ps. 42:2; 63:1
7 [a]Ps. 69:17 [b]Ps. 73:26; 84:2; Jer. 8:18; Lam. 1:22 [c]Ps. 27:9; 69:17; 102:2 [d]Ps. 28:1; 88:4
8 [a]Ps. 90:14 [b]Ps. 46:5 [c]Ps. 25:2 [d]Ps. 27:11; 32:8; 86:11 [e]Ps. 25:1; 86:4
9 [1]Lit., *To Thee have I hidden* [a]Ps. 31:15; 59:1
10 [1]Lit., *land* [a]Ps. 25:4, 5; 119:12 [b]Neh. 9:20 [c]Ps. 23:3
11 [a]Ps. 25:11 [b]Ps. 119:25 [c]Ps. 31:1; 71:2
12 [1]Or, *silence* [a]Ps. 54:5 [b]Ps. 52:5 [c]Ps. 116:16

1 [a]Ps. 18:2 [b]2 Sam. 22:35; Ps. 18:34
2 [1]Another reading is *peoples* [a]Ps. 18:2; 91:2 [b]Ps. 59:9 [c]Ps. 3:3; 28:7; 84:9 [d]Ps. 18:39
3 [a]Job 7:17; Ps. 8:4; Heb. 2:6
4 [a]Ps. 39:11 [b]Job 8:9; 14:2; Ps. 102:11; 109:23
5 [a]Ps. 18:9 [b]Is. 64:1 [c]Ps. 104:32
6 [a]Ps. 18:14 [b]Ps. 7:13; 58:7; Hab. 3:11; Zech. 9:14
7 [a]Ps. 18:16 [b]Ps. 69:1, 14 [c]Ps. 18:44; 54:3
8 [a]Ps. 12:2; 41:6 [b]Gen. 14:22; Deut. 32:40; Ps. 106:26; Is. 44:20
9 [a]Ps. 33:3; 40:3 [b]Ps. 33:2
10 [a]Ps. 18:50 [b]2 Sam. 18:7; Ps. 140:7
11 [a]Ps. 18:44; 54:3 [b]Ps. 12:2; 41:6 [c]Gen. 14:22; Deut. 32:40; Ps. 106:26; Is. 44:20
12 [1]Lit., *cut after the pattern of* [a]Ps. 92:12-14; 128:3 [b]Song 4:4; 7:4
13 [1]Lit., *outside* [a]Prov. 3:9, 10
14 [1]Lit., *be laden* [2]Lit., *bursting forth* [3]Lit., *going out* [a]Prov. 14:4 [b]2 Kin. 25:10, 11 [c]Amos 5:3 [d]Is. 24:11; Jer. 14:2
15 [a]Ps. 33:12

1 [a]Ps. 30:1; 66:17 [b]Ps. 5:2 [c]Ps. 34:1
2 [a]Ps. 71:6
3 [a]Ps. 48:1; 86:10; 147:5 [b]Job 5:9; 9:10; 11:7; Is. 40:28; Rom. 11:33
4 [a]Ps. 22:30, 31; Is. 38:19
5 [1]Or, *majesty of Thy splendor* [a]Ps. 145:12 [b]Ps. 119:27

6 [1]Or, *strength* [a]Deut. 10:21; Ps. 66:3; 106:22 [b]Deut. 32:3

7 They shall [1]eagerly utter the memory of Thine [a]abundant goodness,
And shall [b]shout joyfully of Thy righteousness.

8 The LORD is [a]gracious and merciful;
Slow to anger and great in lovingkindness.
9 The LORD is [a]good to all,
And His [b]mercies are over all His works.
10 [a]All Thy works shall give thanks to Thee, O LORD,
And Thy [b]godly ones shall bless Thee.
11 They shall speak of the [a]glory of Thy kingdom,
And talk of Thy power;
12 To [a]make known to the sons of men [1]Thy mighty acts,
And the [b]glory of the majesty of [1]Thy kingdom.
13 Thy kingdom is [1]an [a]everlasting kingdom,
And Thy dominion *endures* throughout all generations.

14 The LORD [a]sustains all who fall,
And [b]raises up all who are bowed down.
15 The eyes of all [1]look to Thee,
And Thou [a]dost give them their food in due time.
16 Thou [a]dost open Thy hand,
And dost satisfy the desire of every living thing.

17 The LORD is [a]righteous in all His ways,
And kind in all His deeds.
18 The LORD is [a]near to all who call upon Him,
To all who call upon Him [b]in truth.
19 He will [a]fulfill the desire of those who fear Him;
He will also [b]hear their cry and will save them.
20 The LORD [a]keeps all who love Him;
But all the [b]wicked, He will destroy.
21 My [a]mouth will speak the praise of the LORD;
And [b]all flesh will [c]bless His holy name forever and ever.

PSALM 146

The LORD an Abundant Helper.

1 PRAISE [2]the LORD!
[a]Praise the LORD, O my soul!
2 I will praise the LORD [a]while I live;
I will [b]sing praises to my God while I have my being.
3 [a]Do not trust in princes,
In [1]mortal [b]man, in whom there is [c]no salvation.
4 His [a]spirit departs, he [b]returns to [1]the earth;
In that very day his [c]thoughts perish.

7 [1]Or, *bubble over with* [a]Ps. 31:19; Is. 63:7 [b]Ps. 51:14
8 [a]Ex. 34:6; Num. 14:18; Ps. 86:5, 15; 103:8
9 [a]Ps. 100:5; 136:1; Jer. 33:11; Nah. 1:7; Matt. 19:17; Mark 10:18 [b]Ps. 145:15
10 [a]Ps. 19:1; 103:22 [b]Ps. 68:26
11 [a]Jer. 14:21
12 [1]Lit., *His* [a]Ps. 105:1 [b]Ps. 145:5; Is. 2:10, 19, 21
13 [1]Lit., *a kingdom of all ages* [a]Ps. 10:16; 29:10; 1 Tim. 1:17; 2 Pet. 1:11
14 [a]Ps. 37:24 [b]Ps. 146:8
15 [1]Lit., *wait;* or, *hope for* [a]Ps. 104:27; 136:25
16 [a]Ps. 104:28
17 [a]Ps. 116:5
18 [a]Deut. 4:7; Ps. 34:18; 119:151 [b]John 4:24
19 [a]Ps. 21:2; 37:4 [b]Ps. 10:17; Prov. 15:29; 1 John 5:14
20 [a]Ps. 31:23; 91:14; 97:10 [b]Ps. 9:5; 37:38
21 [a]Ps. 71:8 [b]Ps. 65:2; 150:6 [c]Ps. 145:1, 2

1 [1]Or, *Hallelujah!* [2]Heb., *YAH* [a]Ps. 103:1
2 [a]Ps. 63:4 [b]Ps. 104:33
3 [1]Lit., *a son of a man* [a]Ps. 118:9 [b]Ps. 118:8; Is. 2:22 [c]Ps. 60:11; 108:12
4 [1]Lit., *his earth* [a]Ps. 104:29 [b]Eccl. 12:7 [c]Ps. 33:10; 1 Cor. 2:6
5 [a]Ps. 144:15; Jer. 17:7 [b]Ps. 71:5
6 [1]Or, *truth* [a]Ps. 115:15; Rev. 14:7 [b]Acts 14:15 [c]Ps. 117:2
7 [a]Ps. 103:6 [b]Ps. 107:9; 145:15 [c]Ps. 68:6; Is. 61:1
8 [a]Matt. 9:30; John 9:7 [b]Ps. 145:14 [c]Ps. 11:7
9 [1]Or, *keeps* [2]Or, *sojourners* [3]Or, *relieves* [4]Lit., *makes crooked* [a]Ex. 22:21; Lev. 19:34 [b]Deut. 10:18; Ps. 68:5 [c]Ps. 147:6
10 [1]Or, *Hallelujah!* [2]Heb., *YAH* [a]Ex. 15:18; Ps. 10:16

1 [1]Or, *Hallelujah!* [2]Heb., *YAH* [3]Or, *He is gracious* [a]Ps. 92:1; 135:3 [b]Ps. 33:1
2 [a]Ps. 51:18; 102:16 [b]Deut. 30:3; Ps. 106:47; Is. 11:12; 56:8; Ezek. 39:28
3 [1]Lit., *sorrows* [a]Ps. 34:18; 51:17; Is. 61:1 [b]Job 5:18; Is. 30:26; Ezek. 34:16

5 How [a]blessed is he whose help is the God of Jacob,
Whose [b]hope is in the LORD his God;
6 Who [a]made heaven and earth,
The [b]sea and all that is in them;
Who [c]keeps [1]faith forever;
7 Who [a]executes justice for the oppressed;
Who [b]gives food to the hungry.
The LORD [c]sets the prisoners free.

8 The LORD [a]opens *the eyes of* the blind;
The LORD [b]raises up those who are bowed down;
The LORD [c]loves the righteous;
9 The LORD [1a]protects the [2]strangers;
He [3b]supports the fatherless and the widow;
But He [4]thwarts [c]the way of the wicked.
10 The LORD will [a]reign forever,
Thy God, O Zion, to all generations.
[1]Praise [2]the LORD!

PSALM 147

Praise for Jerusalem's Restoration and Prosperity.

1 PRAISE [2]the LORD!
For [a]it is good to sing praises to our God;
For [3]it is pleasant *and* praise is [b]becoming.
2 The LORD [a]builds up Jerusalem;
He [b]gathers the outcasts of Israel.
3 He heals the [a]brokenhearted,
And [b]binds up their [1]wounds.
4 He [a]counts the number of the stars;
He [1b]gives names to all of them.
5 [a]Great is our Lord, and abundant in strength;
His [b]understanding is [1]infinite.
6 The LORD [1a]supports the afflicted;
He brings down the wicked to the ground.

7 [a]Sing to the LORD with thanksgiving;
Sing praises to our God on the lyre,
8 Who [a]covers the heavens with clouds,
Who [b]provides rain for the earth,
Who [c]makes grass to [1]grow on the mountains.
9 He [a]gives to the beast its food,
And to the [b]young ravens which cry.
10 He does not delight in the strength of the [a]horse;
He [b]does not take pleasure in the legs of a man.

4 [1]Or, *calls them all by* their *names* [a]Gen. 15:5 [b]Is. 40:26
5 [1]Lit., *innumerable* [a]Ps. 48:1; 145:3 [b]Is. 40:28
6 [1]Or, *relieves* [a]Ps. 37:24; 146:8, 9
7 [a]Ps. 33:2; 95:1, 2
8 [1]Lit., *spring forth* [a]Job 26:8 [b]Job 5:10; 38:26; Ps. 104:13 [c]Job 38:27; Ps. 104:14
9 [a]Ps. 104:27, 28; 145:15 [b]Job 38:41; Matt. 6:26
10 [a]Ps. 33:17 [b]1 Sam. 16:7

11 The LORD [a]favors those who fear Him,
[b]Those who wait for His lovingkindness.

12 Praise the LORD, O Jerusalem!
Praise your God, O Zion!
13 For He has strengthened the [a]bars of your gates;
He has [b]blessed your sons within you.
14 He [a]makes [1]peace in your borders;
He [b]satisfies you with [c]the [2]finest of the wheat.
15 He sends forth His [a]command to the earth;
His [b]word runs very swiftly.
16 He gives [a]snow like wool;
He scatters the [b]frost like ashes.
17 He casts forth His [a]ice as fragments;
Who can stand before His [b]cold?
18 He [a]sends forth His word and melts them;
He [b]causes His wind to blow and the waters to flow.
19 He [a]declares His words to Jacob,
His [b]statutes and His ordinances to Israel.
20 He [a]has not dealt thus with any nation;
And as for His ordinances, they have [b]not known them.
[1]Praise [2]the LORD!

PSALM 148

The Whole Creation Invoked to Praise the LORD.

1 PRAISE [2]the LORD!
Praise the LORD [a]from the heavens;
Praise Him [b]in the heights!
2 Praise Him, [a]all His angels;
Praise Him, [b]all His hosts!
3 Praise Him, sun and moon;
Praise Him, all stars of light!
4 Praise Him, [1a]highest heavens,
And the [b]waters that are above the heavens!
5 Let them praise the name of the LORD,
For [a]He commanded and they were created.
6 He has also [a]established them forever and ever;
He has made a [b]decree which will not pass away.

7 Praise the LORD from the earth,
[a]Sea monsters and all [b]deeps;
8 [a]Fire and hail, [b]snow and [c]clouds;
[d]Stormy wind, [e]fulfilling His word;
9 [a]Mountains and all hills;
Fruit [b]trees and all cedars;
10 [a]Beasts and all cattle;
[b]Creeping things and winged fowl;
11 [a]Kings of the earth and all peoples;
Princes and all judges of the earth;
12 Both young men and virgins;
Old men and children.

13 Let them praise the name of the LORD,
For His [a]name alone is exalted;
His [b]glory is above earth and heaven.
14 And He has [a]lifted up a horn for His people,
[b]Praise for all His godly ones;
Even for the sons of Israel, a people [c]near to Him.
[1]Praise [2]the LORD!

PSALM 149

Israel Invoked to Praise the LORD.

1 PRAISE [2]the LORD!
Sing to the LORD a [a]new song,
And His praise [b]in the congregation of the godly ones.
2 Let Israel be glad in [a]his Maker;
Let the sons of Zion rejoice in their [b]King.
3 Let them praise His name with [a]dancing;
Let them sing praises to Him with [b]timbrel and lyre.
4 For the LORD [a]takes pleasure in His people;
He will [b]beautify the afflicted ones with salvation.

5 Let the [a]godly ones exult in glory;
Let them [b]sing for joy on their beds.
6 *Let* the [a]high praises of God *be* in their [1]mouth,
And a [b]two-edged [c]sword in their hand,
7 To [a]execute vengeance on the nations,
And punishment on the peoples;
8 To bind their kings [a]with chains,
And their [b]nobles with fetters of iron;
9 To [a]execute on them the judgment written;
This is an [b]honor for all His godly ones.
[1]Praise [2]the LORD!

PSALM 150

A Psalm of Praise.

1 PRAISE [2]the LORD!
Praise God in His [a]sanctuary;
Praise Him in His mighty [3b]expanse.
2 Praise Him for His [a]mighty deeds;
Praise Him according to His excellent [b]greatness.

3 Praise Him with [a]trumpet sound;
Praise Him with [b]harp and lyre.
4 Praise Him with [a]timbrel and dancing;
Praise Him with [b]stringed instruments and [c]pipe.
5 Praise Him with loud [a]cymbals;
Praise Him with resounding cymbals.
6 Let [a]everything that has breath praise [1]the LORD.
[2]Praise [1]the LORD!

11 [a]Ps. 149:4 [b]Ps. 33:18
13 [a]Neh. 3:3; 7:3 [b]Ps. 37:26
14 [1]Lit., *your borders peace* [2]Lit., *fat* [a]Ps. 29:11; Is. 54:13; 60:17, 18 [b]Ps. 132:15 [c]Deut. 32:14; Ps. 81:16
15 [a]Job 37:12; Ps. 148:5 [b]Ps. 104:4
16 [a]Job 37:6; Ps. 148:8 [b]Job 38:29
17 [a]Job 37:10 [b]Job 37:9
18 [a]Ps. 33:9; 107:20; 147:15 [b]Ps. 107:25
19 [a]Deut. 33:3, 4 [b]Mal. 4:4
20 [1]Or, *Hallelujah!* [2]Heb., *YAH* [a]Deut. 4:7, 8, 32-34; Rom. 3:1, 2 [b]Ps. 79:6; Jer. 10:25
1 [1]Or, *Hallelujah!* [2]Heb., *YAH* [a]Ps. 69:34 [b]Job 16:19; Ps. 102:19; Matt. 21:9
2 [a]Ps. 103:20 [b]Ps. 103:21
4 [1]Lit., *heavens of heavens* [a]Deut. 10:14; 1 Kin. 8:27; Neh. 9:6; Ps. 68:33 [b]Gen. 1:7
5 [a]Gen. 1:1; Ps. 33:6, 9
6 [a]Ps. 89:37; Jer. 31:35, 36; 33:20, 25 [b]Job 38:33
7 [a]Gen. 1:21; Ps. 74:13 [b]Gen. 1:2; Deut. 33:13; Hab. 3:10
8 [a]Ps. 18:12 [b]Ps. 147:16 [c]Ps. 135:7 [d]Ps. 107:25 [e]Job 37:12; Ps. 103:20
9 [a]Is. 44:23; 49:13 [b]Is. 55:12
10 [a]Is. 43:20 [b]Hos. 2:18
11 [a]Ps. 102:15
13 [a]Is. 12:4 [b]Ps. 8:1; 113:4
14 [1]Or, *Hallelujah!* [2]Heb., *YAH* [a]1 Sam. 2:1; Ps. 75:10 [b]Deut. 10:21; Ps. 109:1; Jer. 17:14 [c]Lev. 10:3; Eph. 2:17
1 [1]Or, *Hallelujah!* [2]Heb., *YAH* [a]Ps. 33:3 [b]Ps. 35:18; 89:5
2 [a]Ps. 95:6 [b]Judg. 8:23; Ps. 47:6; Zech. 9:9
3 [a]2 Sam. 6:14; Ps. 150:4 [b]Ex. 15:20; Ps. 81:2
4 [a]Job 36:11; Ps. 16:11; 35:27; 147:11 [b]Ps. 132:16; Is. 61:3
5 [a]Ps. 132:16 [b]Job 35:10; Ps. 42:8
6 [1]Lit., *throat* [a]Ps. 66:17 [b]Heb. 4:12 [c]Neh. 4:17
7 [a]Ezek. 25:17; Mic. 5:15
8 [a]Job 36:8 [b]Nah. 3:10
9 [1]Or, *Hallelujah!* [2]Heb., *YAH* [a]Deut. 7:12; Ezek. 28:26 [b]Ps. 112:9; 148:14

1 [1]Or, *Hallelujah!* [2]Heb., *YAH* [3]Or, *firmament* [a]Ps. 73:17; 102:19 [b]Ps. 19:1
2 [a]Ps. 145:12 [b]Deut. 3:24; Ps. 145:3
3 [a]Ps. 98:6 [b]Ps. 33:2
4 [a]Ps. 149:3 [b]Ps. 45:8; Is. 38:20 [c]Gen. 4:21; Job 21:12
5 [a]2 Sam. 6:5; 1 Chr. 13:8; 15:16; Ezra 3:10; Neh. 12:27
6 [1]Heb., *YAH* [2]Or, *Hallelujah!* [a]Ps. 103:22; 145:21

THE PROVERBS

The Usefulness of Proverbs

1 THE [a]proverbs of Solomon [b]the son of David, king of Israel:
2 To know [a]wisdom and instruction,
To discern the sayings of [b]understanding,
3 To [a]receive instruction in wise behavior,
[b]Righteousness, justice and equity;
4 To give [a]prudence to the [1]naive,
To the youth [b]knowledge and discretion,
5 A wise man will hear and [a]increase in learning,
And a [b]man of understanding will acquire wise counsel,
6 To understand a proverb and a figure,
The words of the wise and their [a]riddles.

7 [a]The fear of the LORD is the beginning of knowledge;
Fools despise wisdom and instruction.

The Enticement of Sinners

8 [a]Hear, my son, your father's instruction,
And [b]do not forsake your mother's teaching;
9 Indeed, they are a [a]graceful wreath to your head,
And [1b]ornaments about your neck.
10 My son, if sinners [a]entice you,
[b]Do not consent.
11 If they say, "Come with us,
Let us [a]lie in wait for blood,
Let us [b]ambush the innocent without cause;
12 Let us [a]swallow them alive like Sheol,
Even whole, as those who [b]go down to the pit;
13 We shall find all *kinds* of precious wealth,
We shall fill our houses with spoil;
14 Throw in your lot [1]with us,
We shall all have one purse,"
15 My son, [a]do not walk in the way with them.
[b]Keep your feet from their path,
16 For [a]their feet run to evil,
And they hasten to shed blood.
17 Indeed, it is [1]useless to spread the net
In the eyes of any [2]bird;
18 But they [a]lie in wait for their own blood;
They ambush their own lives.
19 So are the ways of everyone who [a]gains by violence;
It takes away the life of its possessors.

Wisdom Warns

20 [a]Wisdom shouts in the street,
She [1]lifts her voice in the square;
21 At the head of the noisy *streets* she cries out;
At the entrance of the gates in the city, she utters her sayings:
22 "How long, O [1a]naive ones, will you love [2]simplicity?
And [b]scoffers delight themselves in scoffing,
And fools [c]hate knowledge?
23 "Turn to my reproof,
Behold, I will [a]pour out my spirit on you;
I will make my words known to you.
24 Because [a]I called, and you [b]refused;
I [c]stretched out my hand, and no one paid attention;
25 And you [a]neglected all my counsel,
And did not [b]want my reproof;
26 I will even [a]laugh at your [b]calamity;
I will mock when your [c]dread comes,
27 When your dread comes like a storm,
And your calamity comes on like a [a]whirlwind,
When distress *and* anguish come on you.
28 "Then they will [a]call on me, but I will not answer;
They will [b]seek me diligently, but they shall not find me,
29 Because they [a]hated knowledge,
And did not choose the fear of the LORD.
30 "They [a]would not accept my counsel,
They spurned all my reproof.
31 "So they shall [a]eat of the fruit of their own way,
And be [b]satiated with their own devices.
32 "For the [a]waywardness of the [1]naive shall kill them,
And the complacency of fools shall destroy them.
33 "But [a]he who listens to me shall [1]live securely,
And shall be at ease from the dread of evil."

The Pursuit of Wisdom Brings Security

2 MY son, if you will [a]receive my sayings,
And [b]treasure my commandments within you,
2 [a]Make your ear attentive to wisdom,
Incline your heart to understanding;
3 For if you cry for discernment,
[1]Lift your voice for understanding;
4 If you seek her as [a]silver,
And search for her as for [b]hidden treasures;
5 Then you will discern the [a]fear of the LORD,
And discover the knowledge of God.
6 For [a]the LORD gives wisdom;
From His mouth *come* knowledge and understanding.

1 a1 Kin. 4:32; Prov. 10:1; 25:1; Eccl. 12:9 bEccl. 1:1
2 aProv. 15:33 bProv. 4:1
3 aProv. 2:1; 19:20 bProv. 2:9
4 1Lit., *simple ones* aProv. 8:5, 12 bProv. 2:10, 11; 3:21
5 aProv. 9:9 bProv. 14:6; Eccl. 9:11
6 aNum. 12:8; Ps. 49:4; 78:2; Dan. 8:23
7 aJob 28:28; Ps. 111:10; Prov. 9:10; 15:33; Eccl. 12:13
8 aProv. 4:1 bProv. 6:20
9 1Lit., *necklaces* aProv. 4:9 bGen. 41:42; Dan. 5:29
10 aProv. 16:29 bGen. 39:7-10; Deut. 13:8; Ps. 50:18; Eph. 5:11
11 aProv. 12:6; Jer. 5:26 bPs. 10:8; Prov. 1:18
12 aPs. 124:3 bPs. 28:1
14 1Lit., *in the midst of us*
15 aPs. 1:1; Prov. 4:14 bPs. 119:101
16 aProv. 6:17, 18; Is. 59:7
17 1Lit., *in vain* 2Lit., *possessor of wing*
18 aProv. 11:19
19 aProv. 15:27
20 1Lit., *gives* aProv. 8:1-3; 9:3
22 1Lit., *simple ones* 2Or, *naivete* aProv. 1:4, 32; 8:5; 9:4; 22:3 bPs. 1:1 cProv. 1:29; 5:12
23 aIs. 32:15; Joel 2:28; John 7:39
24 aIs. 65:12; 66:4; Jer. 7:13 bZech. 7:11 cIs. 65:2; Rom. 10:21
25 aPs. 107:11; Luke 7:30 bProv. 15:10
26 aPs. 2:4 bProv. 6:15 cProv. 10:24
27 aProv. 10:25
28 a1 Sam. 8:18; Job 27:9; 35:12; Ps. 18:41; Is. 1:15; Jer. 11:11; 14:12; Ezek. 8:18; Mic. 3:4; Zech. 7:13; James 4:3 bProv. 8:17
29 aJob 21:14; Prov. 1:22
30 aPs. 81:11; Prov. 1:25
31 aJob 4:8; Prov. 5:22, 23; 22:8; Is. 3:11; Jer. 6:19 bProv. 14:14
32 1Lit., *simple ones* aJer. 2:19
33 1Lit., *dwell* aPs. 25:12, 13; Prov. 3:24-26

1 aProv. 4:10 bProv. 3:1
2 aProv. 22:17
3 1Lit., *Give*
4 aProv. 3:14 bJob 3:21; Matt. 13:44
5 aProv. 1:7
6 a1 Kin. 3:12; Job 32:8; James 1:5

7 He stores up sound wisdom for the
upright;
He is a [a]shield to those who walk in
integrity,
8 Guarding the paths of justice,
And He [a]preserves the way of His
godly ones.
9 Then you will discern [a]righteous-
ness and justice
And equity *and* every [b]good course.
10 For [a]wisdom will enter your heart,
And [b]knowledge will be pleasant to
your soul;
11 Discretion will [a]guard you,
Understanding will watch over
you,
12 To [a]deliver you from the way of
evil,
From the man who speaks [b]per-
verse things;
13 From those who [a]leave the paths of
uprightness,
To walk in the [b]ways of darkness;
14 Who [a]delight in doing evil,
And rejoice in the perversity of
evil;
15 Whose paths are [a]crooked,
And who are devious in their ways;
16 To [a]deliver you from the strange
woman,
From the [1][b]adulteress who flatters
with her words;
17 That leaves the [a]companion of her
youth,
And forgets the [b]covenant of her
God;
18 For [a]her house [1]sinks down to
death,
And her tracks *lead* to the [2]dead;
19 None [a]who go to her return again,
Nor do they reach the [b]paths of
life.
20 So you will [a]walk in the way of
good men,
And keep to the [b]paths of the
righteous.
21 For [a]the upright will [1]live in the
land,
And [b]the blameless will remain in
it;
22 But [a]the wicked will be cut off from
the land,
And [b]the treacherous will be [c]up-
rooted from it.

The Rewards of Wisdom

3 MY son, [a]do not forget my [1]teach-
ing,
But let your heart [b]keep my commandments;
2 For [a]length of days and years of
life,
And peace they will add to you.
3 Do not let [a]kindness and truth
leave you;
[b]Bind them around your neck,
[c]Write them on the tablet of your
heart.
4 So you will [a]find favor and [b]good
[1]repute
In the sight of God and man.
5 [a]Trust in the LORD with all your
heart,
And [b]do not lean on your own
understanding.
6 In all your ways [a]acknowledge
Him,
And He will [b]make your paths
straight.
7 [a]Do not be wise in your own eyes;
[b]Fear the LORD and turn away
from evil.
8 It will be [a]healing to your [1]body,
And [b]refreshment to your bones.
9 [a]Honor the LORD from your
wealth,
And from the [b]first of all your
produce;
10 So your [a]barns will be filled with
plenty,
And your [b]vats will overflow with
new wine.
11 [a]My son, do not reject the [1]disci-
pline of the LORD,
Or loathe His reproof,
12 For [a]whom the LORD loves He
reproves,
Even [b]as a father, the son in whom
he delights.

13 [a]How blessed is the man who finds
wisdom,
And the man who gains understanding.
14 For its [a]profit is better than the
profit of silver,
And its gain than fine gold.
15 She is [a]more precious than [1]jewels;
And nothing you desire compares
with her.
16 [1][a]Long life is in her right hand;
In her left hand are [b]riches and
honor.
17 Her [a]ways are pleasant ways,
And all her paths are [b]peace.
18 She is a [a]tree of life to those who
take hold of her,
And happy are all who hold her
fast.
19 The LORD [a]by wisdom founded the
earth;
By understanding He [b]established
the heavens.
20 By His knowledge the [a]deeps were
broken up,
And the [b]skies drip with dew.
21 My son, [a]let them not depart from
your sight;
Keep sound wisdom and discretion,
22 So they will be [a]life to your soul,
And [b]adornment to your neck.
23 Then you will [a]walk in your way
securely,
And your foot will not [b]stumble.
24 When you [a]lie down, you will not
be afraid;

7 [a]Ps. 84:11; Prov. 30:5
8 [a]1 Sam. 2:9; Ps. 66:9
9 [a]Prov. 8:20 [b]Prov. 4:18
10 [a]Prov. 14:33 [b]Prov. 22:18
11 [a]Prov. 4:6; 6:22
12 [a]Prov. 28:26 [b]Prov. 6:12
13 [a]Prov. 21:16 [b]Ps. 82:5; Prov. 4:19; John 3:19, 20
14 [a]Prov. 10:23; Jer. 11:15
15 [a]Ps. 125:5; Prov. 21:8
16 [1]Lit., *strange woman* [a]Prov. 6:24; 7:5 [b]Prov. 23:27
17 [a]Mal. 2:14, 15 [b]Gen. 2:24
18 [1]Lit., *bows down* [2]Lit., *departed spirits* [a]Prov. 7:27
19 [a]Eccl. 7:26 [b]Ps. 16:11; Prov. 5:6
20 [a]Heb. 6:12 [b]Prov. 4:18
21 [1]Or, *dwell* [a]Ps. 37:9, 29; Prov. 10:30 [b]Prov. 28:10
22 [a]Ps. 37:38; Prov. 10:30 [b]Prov. 11:3 [c]Deut. 28:63; Ps. 52:5

1 [1]Or, *law* [a]Ps. 119:61; Prov. 4:5 [b]Ex. 20:6; Deut. 30:16
2 [a]Ps. 91:16; Prov. 3:16; 4:10; 9:11; 10:27
3 [a]2 Sam. 15:20; Prov. 14:22 [b]Deut. 6:8; 11:18; Prov. 1:9; 6:21 [c]Prov. 7:3; Jer. 17:1; 2 Cor. 3:3
4 [1]Lit., *understanding* [a]1 Sam. 2:26; Prov. 8:35; Luke 2:52 [b]Ps. 111:10
5 [a]Ps. 37:3, 5; Prov. 22:19 [b]Prov. 23:4; Jer. 9:23
6 [a]1 Chr. 28:9; Prov. 16:3; Phil. 4:6; James 1:5 [b]Is. 45:13; Jer. 10:23
7 [a]Rom. 12:16 [b]Job 1:1; 28:28; Prov. 8:13; 16:6
8 [1]Lit., *navel* [a]Prov. 4:22 [b]Job 21:24
9 [a]Is. 43:23 [b]Ex. 23:19; Deut. 26:2; Mal. 3:10
10 [a]Deut. 28:8 [b]Joel 2:24
11 [1]Or, *instruction* [a]Job 5:17; Heb. 12:5, 6
12 [a]Rev. 3:19 [b]Deut. 8:5; Prov. 13:24
13 [a]Prov. 8:32, 34
14 [a]Job 28:15-19; Prov. 8:10, 19; 16:16
15 [1]Lit., *corals* [a]Job 28:18; Prov. 8:11
16 [1]Lit., *Length of days* [a]Prov. 3:2 [b]Prov. 8:18; 22:4
17 [a]Matt. 11:29 [b]Ps. 119:165; Prov. 16:7
18 [a]Gen. 2:9; Prov. 11:30; 13:12; 15:4; Rev. 2:7

19 [a]Ps. 104:24; Prov. 8:27 [b]Prov. 8:27, 28
20 [a]Gen. 7:11 [b]Deut. 33:28; Job 36:28
21 [a]Prov. 4:21
22 [a]Deut. 32:47; Prov. 4:22; 8:35; 16:22; 21:21 [b]Prov. 1:9
23 [a]Prov. 4:12; 10:9 [b]Ps. 91:12; Is. 5:27; 63:13
24 [a]Job 11:19; Ps. 3:5; Prov. 1:33; 6:22

When you lie down, your sleep will be sweet.
25 [a]Do not be afraid of sudden fear,
Nor of the [1b]onslaught of the wicked when it comes;
26 For the LORD will be [1]your confidence,
And will [a]keep your foot from being caught.

27 [a]Do not withhold good from [1]those to whom it is due,
When it is in your power to do *it.*
28 [a]Do not say to your neighbor, "Go, and come back,
And tomorrow I will give *it,*"
When you have it with you.
29 [a]Do not devise harm against your neighbor,
While he lives in security beside you.
30 [a]Do not contend with a man without cause,
If he has done you no harm.
31 [a]Do not envy a man of violence,
And do not choose any of his ways.
32 For the [a]crooked *man* is an abomination to the LORD;
But [1]He is [b]intimate with the upright.
33 The [a]curse of the LORD is on the house of the wicked,
But He [b]blesses the dwelling of the righteous.
34 Though [a]He scoffs at the scoffers,
Yet [b]He gives grace to the afflicted.
35 [a]The wise will inherit honor,
But fools [1]display dishonor.

A Father's Instruction

4 HEAR, *O* sons, the [a]instruction of a father,
And [b]give attention that you may [1]gain understanding,
2 For I give you [1]sound [a]teaching;
[b]Do not abandon my [2]instruction.
3 When I was a son to my father,
[a]Tender and [b]the only son in the sight of my mother,
4 Then he [a]taught me and said to me,
"Let your heart [b]hold fast my words;
[c]Keep my commandments and live;
5 [a]Acquire wisdom! [b]Acquire understanding!
Do not forget, nor turn away from the words of my mouth.
6 "Do not forsake her, and she will guard you;
[a]Love her, and she will watch over you.
7 "[a]The [1]beginning of wisdom *is:*
[b]Acquire wisdom;
And with all your acquiring, get understanding.
8 "[a]Prize her, and she will exalt you;
She will honor you if you embrace her.
9 "She will place [a]on your head a garland of grace;
She will present you with a crown of beauty."
10 Hear, my son, and [a]accept my sayings,
And the [b]years of your life will be many.
11 I have [a]directed you in the way of wisdom;
I have led you in upright paths.
12 When you walk, your [a]steps will not be impeded;
And if you run, you [b]will not stumble.
13 [a]Take hold of instruction; do not let go.
Guard her, for she is your [b]life.
14 [a]Do not enter the path of the wicked,
And do not proceed in the way of evil men.
15 Avoid it, do not pass by it;
Turn away from it and pass on.
16 For they [a]cannot sleep unless they do evil;
And [1]they are robbed of sleep unless they make *someone* stumble.
17 For they [a]eat the bread of wickedness,
And drink the wine of violence.
18 But the [a]path of the righteous is like the [b]light of dawn,
That [c]shines brighter and brighter until the [d]full day.
19 The [a]way of the wicked is like darkness;
They do not know over what they [1b]stumble.

20 My son, [a]give attention to my words;
[b]Incline your ear to my sayings.
21 [a]Do not let them depart from your sight;
[b]Keep them in the midst of your heart.
22 For they are [a]life to those who find them,
And [b]health to all [1]their whole body.
23 Watch over your heart with all diligence,
For [a]from it *flow* the springs of life.
24 Put away from you a [a]deceitful mouth,
And [b]put devious lips far from you.
25 Let your eyes look directly ahead,
And let your [1]gaze be fixed straight in front of you.
26 [a]Watch the path of your feet,
And all your [b]ways will be established.
27 [a]Do not turn to the right nor to the left;
[b]Turn your foot from evil.

Pitfalls of Immorality

5 MY son, [a]give attention to my wisdom,
[b]Incline your ear to my understanding;

25 [1]Lit., *storm* [a]Ps. 91:5; 1 Pet. 3:14 [b]Job 5:21
26 [1]Or, *at your side* [a]1 Sam. 2:9
27 [1]Lit., *its owners* [a]Rom. 13:7; Gal. 6:10
28 [a]Lev. 19:13; Deut. 24:15
29 [a]Prov. 6:14; 14:22
30 [a]Prov. 26:17; Rom. 12:18
31 [a]Ps. 37:1; Prov. 24:1
32 [1]Lit., *His private counsel is* [a]Prov. 11:20 [b]Job 29:4; Ps. 25:14
33 [a]Lev. 26:14, 16; Deut. 11:28; Zech. 5:3, 4; Mal. 2:2 [b]Job 8:6; Ps. 1:3
34 [a]James 4:6 [b]1 Pet. 5:5
35 [1]Lit., *raise high* [a]Dan. 12:3

1 [1]Lit., *know* [a]Ps. 34:11; Prov. 1:8 [b]Prov. 1:2; 2:2
2 [1]Lit., *good* [2]Or, *law* [a]Deut. 32:2; Job 11:4 [b]Ps. 89:30; 119:87; Prov. 3:1
3 [a]1 Chr. 22:5; 29:1 [b]Zech. 12:10
4 [a]Eph. 6:4 [b]Ps. 119:168 [c]Prov. 7:2
5 [a]Prov. 4:7 [b]Prov. 16:16
6 [a]2 Thess. 2:10
7 [1]Or, *the primary thing is wisdom* [a]Prov. 8:23 [b]Prov. 23:23
8 [a]1 Sam. 2:30
9 [a]Prov. 1:9
10 [a]Prov. 2:1 [b]Prov. 3:2
11 [a]1 Sam. 12:23
12 [a]Job 18:7; Ps. 18:36 [b]Ps. 91:11; Prov. 3:23
13 [a]Prov. 3:18 [b]Prov. 3:22; John 6:63
14 [a]Ps. 1:1; Prov. 1:15
16 [1]Lit., *their sleep is robbed* [a]Ps. 36:4; Mic. 2:1
17 [a]Prov. 13:2
18 [a]Is. 26:7; Matt. 5:14; Phil. 2:15 [b]2 Sam. 23:4 [c]Dan. 12:3 [d]Job 11:17
19 [1]Or, *may stumble* [a]Job 18:5, 6; Prov. 2:13; Is. 59:9, 10; Jer. 23:12; John 12:35 [b]John 11:10
20 [a]Prov. 5:1 [b]Prov. 2:2
21 [a]Prov. 3:21 [b]Prov. 7:1, 2
22 [1]Lit., *his* [a]Prov. 3:22 [b]Prov. 3:8; 12:18
23 [a]Matt. 12:34; 15:18, 19; Mark 7:21; Luke 6:45
24 [a]Prov. 6:12; 10:32 [b]Prov. 19:1
25 [1]Or, *eyelids*
26 [a]Prov. 5:21; Heb. 12:13 [b]Ps. 119:5
27 [a]Deut. 5:32; 28:14 [b]Prov. 1:15; Is. 1:16

1 [a]Prov. 4:20 [b]Prov. 22:17

2 That you may [a]observe discretion,
And your [b]lips may reserve knowledge.
3 For the lips of an [1a]adulteress [b]drip honey,
And [c]smoother than oil is her [2]speech;
4 But in the end she is [a]bitter as wormwood,
[b]Sharp as a two-edged sword.
5 Her feet [a]go down to death,
Her steps lay hold of Sheol.
6 [1]She does not ponder the [a]path of life;
Her ways are [b]unstable, she [c]does not know *it*.

7 [a]Now then, *my* sons, listen to me,
And [b]do not depart from the words of my mouth.
8 [a]Keep your way far from her,
And do not go near the [b]door of her house,
9 Lest you give your vigor to others,
And your years to the cruel one;
10 Lest strangers be filled with your strength,
And your hard-earned goods *go* to the house of an alien;
11 And you groan at your latter end,
When your flesh and your body are consumed;
12 And you say, "How I have [a]hated instruction!
And my heart [b]spurned reproof!
13 "And I have not listened to the voice of my [a]teachers,
Nor inclined my ear to my instructors!
14 "I was almost in utter ruin
In the midst of the assembly and congregation."

15 Drink water from your own cistern,
And [1]fresh water from your own well.
16 Should your [a]springs be dispersed abroad,
Streams of water in the streets?
17 Let them be yours alone,
And not for strangers with you.
18 Let your [a]fountain be blessed,
And [b]rejoice in the [c]wife of your youth.
19 *As* a loving [a]hind and a graceful doe,
Let her breasts satisfy you at all times;
Be [1]exhilarated always with her love.
20 For why should you, my son, be exhilarated with an [1a]adulteress,
And embrace the bosom of a [b]foreigner?
21 For the [a]ways of a man are before the eyes of the LORD,
And He [b]watches all his paths.
22 His [a]own iniquities will capture the wicked,
And he will be held with the cords of his sin.
23 He will [a]die for lack of instruction,
And in the greatness of his folly he will go astray.

Parental Counsel

6 MY son, if you have become [a]surety for your neighbor,
Have [1]given a pledge for a stranger,
2 *If* you have been snared with the words of your mouth,
Have been caught with the words of your mouth,
3 Do this then, my son, and deliver yourself;
Since you have come into the [1]hand of your neighbor,
Go, humble yourself, and importune your neighbor.
4 Do not give [a]sleep to your eyes,
Nor slumber to your eyelids;
5 Deliver yourself like a gazelle from *the hunter's* hand,
And like a [a]bird from the hand of the fowler.

6 Go to the [a]ant, O [b]sluggard,
Observe her ways and be wise,
7 Which, having [a]no chief,
Officer or ruler,
8 Prepares her food [a]in the summer,
And gathers her provision in the harvest.
9 How long will you lie down, O sluggard?
When will you arise from your sleep?
10 "[a]A little sleep, a little slumber,
A little folding of the hands to [1]rest"—
11 [a]And your poverty will come in like a [1]vagabond,
And your need like [2]an armed man.

12 A [a]worthless person, a wicked man,
Is the one who walks with a [b]false mouth,
13 Who [a]winks with his eyes, who [1]signals with his feet,
Who [2]points with his fingers;
14 Who *with* [a]perversity in his heart
[b]devises evil continually,
Who [1c]spreads strife.
15 Therefore [a]his calamity will come suddenly;
[b]Instantly he will be broken, and there will be [c]no healing.

16 There are six things which the LORD hates,
Yes, seven which are an abomination [1]to Him:
17 [a]Haughty eyes, a [b]lying tongue,
And hands that [c]shed innocent blood,
18 A heart that devises [a]wicked plans,
[b]Feet that run rapidly to evil,
19 A [a]false witness *who* utters lies,
And one who [1b]spreads strife among brothers.

2 [a]Prov. 3:21 [b]Mal. 2:7
3 [1]Lit., *strange woman* [2]Lit., *palate* [a]Prov. 2:16; 5:20; 7:5; 22:14 [b]Song 4:11 [c]Ps. 55:21
4 [a]Eccl. 7:26 [b]Ps. 57:4; Heb. 4:12
5 [a]Prov. 7:27
6 [1]Lit., *Lest she watch* [a]Prov. 4:26; 5:21 [b]2 Pet. 2:14 [c]Prov. 30:20
7 [a]Prov. 7:24 [b]Ps. 119:102
8 [a]Prov. 7:25 [b]Prov. 9:14
12 [a]Prov. 1:7, 22, 29 [b]Prov. 1:25; 12:1
13 [a]Prov. 1:8
15 [1]Lit., *flowing*
16 [a]Prov. 5:18; 9:17; Song 4:12, 15
18 [a]Prov. 9:17; Song 4:12, 15 [b]Eccl. 9:9 [c]Mal. 2:14
19 [1]Lit., *intoxicated* [a]Song 2:9, 17; 4:5; 7:3
20 [1]Lit., *strange woman* [a]Prov. 5:3 [b]Prov. 2:16; 6:24; 7:5; 23:27
21 [a]Job 14:16; 31:4; 34:21; Ps. 119:168; Prov. 15:3; Jer. 16:17; 32:19; Hos. 7:2; Heb. 4:13 [b]Prov. 4:26
22 [a]Num. 32:23; Ps. 7:15; 9:15; 40:12; Prov. 1:31, 32
23 [a]Job 4:21; 36:12

1 [1]Lit., *clapped your palms* [a]Prov. 11:15; 17:18; 20:16; 22:26; 27:13
3 [1]Lit., *palm*
4 [a]Ps. 132:4
5 [a]Ps. 91:3; 124:7
6 [a]Prov. 30:24, 25 [b]Prov. 6:9; 10:26; 13:4; 20:4; 26:16
7 [a]Prov. 30:27
8 [a]Prov. 10:5
10 [1]Lit., *lie down* [a]Prov. 24:33
11 [1]Lit., *one who walks* [2]Lit., *a man with a shield* [a]Prov. 24:34
12 [a]Prov. 16:27 [b]Prov. 4:24; 10:32
13 [1]Lit., *scrapes* [2]Lit., *instructs with* [a]Job 15:12; Ps. 35:19; Prov. 10:10
14 [1]Lit., *sends out* [a]Prov. 17:20 [b]Prov. 3:29; Mic. 2:1 [c]Prov. 6:19; 16:28
15 [a]Prov. 24:22 [b]Is. 30:13, 14; Jer. 19:11 [c]2 Chr. 36:16
16 [1]Lit., *of His soul*
17 [a]Ps. 18:27; 101:5; Prov. 21:4; 30:13 [b]Ps. 31:18; 120:2; Prov. 12:22; 17:7 [c]Deut. 19:10; Prov. 28:17; Is. 1:15; 59:7
18 [a]Gen. 6:5; Prov. 24:2 [b]Prov. 1:16; Is. 59:7; Rom. 3:15
19 [1]Lit., *sends out* [a]Ps. 27:12; Prov. 12:17; 19:5, 9; 21:28 [b]Prov. 6:14

20 [a]My son, observe the commandment of your father,
And do not forsake the [1]teaching of your mother;
21 [a]Bind them continually on your heart;
Tie them around your neck.
22 When you [a]walk about, [1]they will guide you;
When you sleep, [1]they will watch over you;
And when you awake, [1]they will talk to you.
23 For [a]the commandment is a lamp, and the [1]teaching is light;
And reproofs for discipline are the way of life,
24 To [a]keep you from the evil woman,
From the smooth tongue of the [1]adulteress.
25 [a]Do not desire her beauty in your heart,
Nor let her catch you with her [b]eyelids.
26 For [a]on account of a harlot *one is reduced* to a loaf of bread,
And [1]an adulteress [b]hunts for the precious life.
27 Can a man [1]take fire in his bosom,
And his clothes not be burned?
28 Or can a man walk on hot coals,
And his feet not be scorched?
29 So is the one who [a]goes in to his neighbor's wife;
Whoever touches her [b]will not [1]go unpunished.
30 [1]Men do not despise a thief if he steals
To [a]satisfy [2]himself when he is hungry;
31 But when he is found, he must [a]repay sevenfold;
He must give all the [1]substance of his house.
32 The one who commits adultery with a woman is [a]lacking [1]sense;
He who would [b]destroy [2]himself does it.
33 Wounds and disgrace he will find,
And his reproach will not be blotted out.
34 For [a]jealousy [1]enrages a man,
And he will not spare in the [b]day of vengeance.
35 He will not [1]accept any ransom,
Nor will he be [2]content though you give many [3]gifts.

The Wiles of the Harlot

7 MY son, [a]keep my words,
And treasure my commandments within you.
2 [a]Keep my commandments and live,
And my [1]teaching [b]as the [2]apple of your eye.
3 [a]Bind them on your fingers;
[b]Write them on the tablet of your heart.
4 Say to wisdom, "You are my sister,"
And call understanding *your* intimate friend;
5 That they may keep you from an [1]adulteress,
From the foreigner who [2]flatters with her words.

6 For [a]at the window of my house
I looked out [b]through my lattice,
7 And I saw among the [1a]naive,
I discerned among the [2]youths,
A young man [b]lacking [3]sense,
8 Passing through the street near [a]her corner;
And he [1]takes the way to [b]her house,
9 In the [a]twilight, in the [1]evening,
In the [2]middle of the night and *in* the darkness.
10 And behold, a woman *comes* to meet him,
[a]Dressed as a harlot and cunning of heart.
11 She is [a]boisterous and rebellious;
Her [b]feet do not remain at home;
12 *She is* now in the streets, now [a]in the squares,
And [b]lurks by every corner.
13 So she seizes him and kisses him,
[1]And with a [a]brazen face she says to him:
14 "[1]I was due to offer [a]peace offerings;
Today I have [b]paid my vows.
15 "Therefore I have come out to meet you,
To seek your presence earnestly, and I have found you.
16 "I have spread my couch with [a]coverings,
With colored [b]linens of Egypt.
17 "I have sprinkled my bed
With [a]myrrh, aloes and [b]cinnamon.
18 "Come, let us drink our fill of love until morning;
Let us delight ourselves with caresses.
19 "For [1]the man is not at home,
He has gone on a long journey;
20 He has taken a [a]bag of money [1]with him,
At full moon he will come home."
21 With her many persuasions she entices him;
With her [1a]flattering lips she seduces him.
22 Suddenly he follows her,
As an ox goes to the slaughter,
Or as [1]*one in* fetters to the discipline of a fool,
23 Until an arrow pierces through his liver;
As a [a]bird hastens to the snare,
So he does not know that it *will cost him* his life.

24 Now therefore, *my* sons, [a]listen to me,
And pay attention to the words of my mouth.

20 [1]Or, *law*
[a]Eph. 6:1
21 [a]Prov. 3:3
22 [1]Lit., *she*
[a]Prov. 3:23
23 [1]Or, *law*
[a]Ps. 19:8; 119:105
24 [1]Lit., *foreign woman*
[a]Prov. 5:3; 7:5, 21
25 [a]Matt. 5:28
[b]2 Kin. 9:30; Jer. 4:30; Ezek. 23:40
26 [1]Lit., *a man's wife*
[a]Prov. 5:9, 10; 29:3
[b]Prov. 7:23; Ezek. 13:18
27 [1]Lit., *snatch up*
29 [1]Lit., *be innocent*
[a]Ezek. 18:6; 33:26
[b]Prov. 16:5
30 [1]Lit., *They do not;* or, *Do not men . . . ?* [2]Lit., *his soul*
[a]Job 38:39
31 [1]Or, *wealth*
[a]Ex. 22:1-4
32 [1]Lit., *heart* [2]Lit., *his soul*
[a]Prov. 7:7; 9:4, 16; 10:13, 21; 11:12; 12:11 [b]Prov. 7:22, 23
34 [1]Lit., *is the rage of*
[a]Prov. 27:4; Song 8:6 [b]Prov. 11:4
35 [1]Lit., *lift up the face of any* [2]Lit., *willing* [3]Or, *bribes*

1 [a]Prov. 2:1; 6:20
2 [1]Or, *law* [2]Lit., *pupil*
[a]Prov. 4:4 [b]Deut. 32:10; Ps. 17:8; Zech. 2:8
3 [a]Deut. 6:8; 11:18; Prov. 6:21 [b]Prov. 3:3
5 [1]Lit., *strange woman* [2]Lit., *is smooth*
6 [a]Judg. 5:28 [b]Song 2:9
7 [1]Lit., *simple ones* [2]Lit., *sons* [3]Lit., *heart*
[a]Prov. 1:22 [b]Prov. 6:32; 9:4
8 [1]Lit., *steps*
[a]Prov. 7:12 [b]Prov. 7:27
9 [1]Lit., *evening of the day* [2]Lit., *pupil* (of the eye)
[a]Job 24:15
10 [a]Gen. 38:14, 15; 1 Tim. 2:9
11 [a]Prov. 9:13 [b]1 Tim. 5:13; Titus 2:5
12 [a]Prov. 9:14 [b]Prov. 23:28
13 [1]Lit., *She makes bold her face and says*
[a]Prov. 21:29
14 [1]Lit., *Sacrifices of peace offerings are with me*
[a]Lev. 7:11 [b]Lev. 7:16
16 [a]Prov. 31:22 [b]Is. 19:9; Ezek. 27:7
17 [a]Ps. 45:8 [b]Ex. 30:23
19 [1]I.e., my husband
20 [1]Lit., *in his hand*
[a]Gen. 42:35
21 [1]Lit., *smooth*
[a]Prov. 5:3; 6:24

22 [1]Or, *as a stag goes into a trap;* so some ancient versions
23 [a]Eccl. 9:12
24 [a]Prov. 5:7

25 Do not let your heart [a]turn aside to her ways,
Do not stray into her paths.
26 For many are the [1]victims she has cast down,
And [a]numerous are all her slain.
27 Her [a]house is the way to Sheol,
Descending to the chambers of death.

The Commendation of Wisdom

8 DOES not [a]wisdom call,
And understanding [1]lift up her voice?
2 On top of [a]the heights beside the way,
Where the paths meet, she takes her stand;
3 Beside the [a]gates, at the opening to the city,
At the entrance of the doors, she cries out:
4 "To you, O men, I call,
And my voice is to the sons of men.
5 "O [1a]naive ones, discern prudence;
And, O [b]fools, discern [2]wisdom.
6 "Listen, for I shall speak [a]noble things;
And the opening of my lips *will produce* [b]right things.
7 "For my [a]mouth will utter truth;
And wickedness is an abomination to my lips.
8 "All the utterances of my mouth are in righteousness;
There is nothing [a]crooked or perverted in them.
9 "They are all [a]straightforward to him who understands,
And right to those who [b]find knowledge.
10 "Take my [a]instruction, and not silver,
And knowledge rather than choicest gold.
11 "For wisdom is [a]better than [1]jewels;
And [b]all desirable things can not compare with her.

12 "I, wisdom, [a]dwell with prudence,
And I find [b]knowledge *and* discretion.
13 "The [a]fear of the LORD is to hate evil;
[b]Pride and arrogance and [c]the evil way,
And the [d]perverted mouth, I hate.
14 "[a]Counsel is mine and [b]sound wisdom;
I am understanding, [c]power is mine.
15 "By me [a]kings reign,
And rulers decree justice.
16 "By me princes rule, and nobles,
All who judge rightly.
17 "I [a]love those who love me;
And [b]those who diligently seek me will find me.
18 "[a]Riches and honor are with me,
Enduring [b]wealth and righteousness.
19 "My fruit is [a]better than gold, even pure gold,
And my yield than [b]choicest silver.
20 "I walk in the way of righteousness,
In the midst of the paths of justice,
21 To endow those who love me with wealth,
That I may [a]fill their treasuries.

22 "The LORD possessed me [a]at the beginning of His way,
Before His works [1]of old.
23 "From everlasting I was [1a]established,
From the beginning, [b]from the earliest times of the earth.
24 "When there were no [a]depths I was [1]brought forth,
When there were no springs abounding with water.
25 "[a]Before the mountains were settled,
Before the hills I was [1]brought forth;
26 While He had not yet made the earth and the [1]fields,
Nor the first dust of the world.
27 "When He [a]established the heavens, I was there,
When [b]He inscribed a circle on the face of the deep,
28 When He made firm the skies above,
When the springs of the deep became [1]fixed,
29 When [a]He set for the sea its boundary,
So that the water should not transgress His [1]command,
When He marked out [b]the foundations of the earth;
30 Then [a]I was beside Him, *as* a master workman;
And I was daily *His* delight,
[1]Rejoicing always before Him,
31 [1]Rejoicing in the world, His earth,
And *having* [a]my delight in the sons of men.

32 "Now therefore, *O* sons, [a]listen to me,
For [b]blessed are they who keep my ways.
33 "[a]Heed instruction and be wise,
And do not neglect *it*.
34 "[a]Blessed is the man who listens to me,
Watching daily at my gates,
Waiting at my doorposts.
35 "For [a]he who finds me finds life,
And [b]obtains favor from the LORD.
36 "But he who [1]sins against me [a]injures himself;
All those who [b]hate me [c]love death."

Wisdom's Invitation

9 WISDOM has [a]built her house,
She has hewn out her seven pillars;

25 [a]Prov. 5:8
26 [1]Lit., *mortally wounded* [a]Prov. 9:18
27 [a]Prov. 2:18; 5:5; 9:18; 1 Cor. 6:9, 10; Rev. 22:15

1 [1]Lit., *give* [a]Prov. 1:20, 21; 8:1-3; 9:3; 1 Cor. 1:24
2 [a]Prov. 9:3, 14
3 [a]Job 29:7
5 [1]Lit., *simple* [2]Lit., *heart* [a]Prov. 1:4 [b]Prov. 1:22, 32; 3:35
6 [a]Prov. 22:20 [b]Prov. 23:16
7 [a]Ps. 37:30; John 8:14; Rom. 15:8
8 [a]Deut. 32:5; Prov. 2:15; Phil. 2:15
9 [a]Prov. 14:6 [b]Prov. 3:13
10 [a]Prov. 3:14, 15; 8:19
11 [1]Lit., *corals* [a]Job 28:15, 18; Ps. 19:10 [b]Prov. 3:15
12 [a]Prov. 8:5 [b]Prov. 1:4
13 [a]Prov. 3:7; 16:6 [b]1 Sam. 2:3; Prov. 16:18; Is. 13:11 [c]Prov. 15:9 [d]Prov. 6:12
14 [a]Prov. 1:25; 19:20; Is. 28:29; Jer. 32:19 [b]Prov. 2:7; 3:21; 18:1 [c]Eccl. 7:19; 9:16
15 [a]2 Chr. 1:10; Prov. 29:4; Dan. 2:21; Matt. 28:18; Rom. 13:1
17 [a]1 Sam. 2:30; Prov. 4:6; John 14:21 [b]Prov. 2:4, 5; John 7:37; James 1:5
18 [a]Prov. 3:16 [b]Ps. 112:3; Matt. 6:33
19 [a]Job 28:15; Prov. 3:14 [b]Prov. 10:20
21 [a]Prov. 24:4
22 [1]Lit., *from then* [a]Job 28:26-28; Ps. 104:24; Prov. 3:19
23 [1]Or, *consecrated* [a]John 1:1-3 [b]John 17:5
24 [1]Or, *born* [a]Gen. 1:2; Ex. 15:5; Job 38:16; Prov. 3:20
25 [1]Or, *born* [a]Job 15:7; Ps. 90:2
26 [1]Lit., *outside places*
27 [a]Prov. 3:19 [b]Job 26:10
28 [1]Lit., *strong*
29 [1]Lit., *mouth* [a]Job 38:10; Ps. 104:9 [b]Job 38:6; Ps. 104:5
30 [1]Or, *Playing* [a]John 1:2, 3
31 [1]Or, *Playing* [a]Ps. 16:3; John 13:1
32 [a]Prov. 5:7; 7:24 [b]Ps. 119:1, 2; 128:1; Prov. 29:18; Luke 11:28
33 [a]Prov. 4:1
34 [a]Prov. 3:13, 18
35 [a]Prov. 4:22; John 17:3 [b]Prov. 3:4; 12:2
36 [1]Or, *misses me* [a]Prov. 1:31, 32; 15:32 [b]Prov. 5:12; 12:1 [c]Prov. 21:6

1 [a]1 Cor. 3:9, 10; Eph. 2:20-22; 1 Pet. 2:5

2 She has [1a]prepared her food, she has [b]mixed her wine;
She has also [c]set her table;
3 She has [a]sent out her maidens, she [b]calls
From the [c]tops of the heights of the city:
4 "[a]Whoever is [1]naive, let him turn in here!"
To him who [b]lacks [2]understanding she says,
5 "Come, [a]eat of my food,
And drink of the wine I have mixed.
6 "[1]Forsake *your* folly and [a]live,
And [b]proceed in the way of understanding."

7 He who [a]corrects a scoffer gets dishonor for himself,
And he who reproves a wicked man *gets* [1]insults for himself.
8 [a]Do not reprove a scoffer, lest he hate you,
[b]Reprove a wise man, and he will love you.
9 Give *instruction* to a wise man, and he will be still wiser,
Teach a righteous man, and he will [a]increase *his* learning.
10 The [a]fear of the LORD is the beginning of wisdom,
And the knowledge of the Holy One is understanding.
11 For [a]by me your days will be multiplied,
And years of life will be added to you.
12 If you are wise, you are wise [a]for yourself,
And if you [b]scoff, you alone will bear it.

13 The [1]woman of folly is [a]boisterous,
She is [2]naive, and [b]knows nothing.
14 And she sits at the doorway of her house,
On a seat by [a]the high places of the city,
15 Calling to those who pass by,
Who are making their paths straight:
16 "[a]Whoever is [1]naive, let him turn in here,"
And to him who lacks [2]understanding she says,
17 "Stolen water is sweet;
And [a]bread *eaten* in secret is pleasant."
18 But he does not know that the [1]dead are there,
That her guests are in the [a]depths of Sheol.

Contrast of the Righteous and the Wicked

10 THE [a]proverbs of Solomon.
[b]A wise son makes a father glad,
But [c]a foolish son is a grief to his mother.
2 [1a]Ill-gotten gains do not profit,
But righteousness delivers from death.
3 The LORD [a]will not allow the [1]righteous to hunger,
But He [b]will thrust *aside* the craving of the wicked.
4 Poor is he who works with a negligent hand,
But the [a]hand of the diligent makes rich.
5 He who gathers in summer is a son who acts wisely,
But he who sleeps in harvest is a son who acts shamefully.
6 [a]Blessings are on the head of the righteous,
But [b]the mouth of the wicked conceals violence.
7 The [a]memory of the righteous is blessed,
But [b]the name of the wicked will rot.
8 The [a]wise of heart will receive commands,
But [1]a babbling fool will be thrown down.
9 He [a]who walks in integrity walks securely,
But [b]he who perverts his ways will be found out.
10 He [a]who winks the eye causes trouble,
And [1b]a babbling fool will be thrown down.
11 The [a]mouth of the righteous is a fountain of life,
But [b]the mouth of the wicked conceals violence.
12 Hatred stirs up strife,
But [a]love covers all transgressions.
13 On [a]the lips of the discerning, wisdom is found,
But [b]a rod is for the back of him who lacks [1]understanding.
14 Wise men [a]store up knowledge,
But with [b]the mouth of the foolish, ruin is at hand.
15 The [a]rich man's wealth is his [1]fortress,
The [b]ruin of the poor is their poverty.
16 The [1a]wages of the righteous is life,
The income of the wicked, punishment.
17 He [a]is *on* the path of life who heeds instruction,
But he who forsakes reproof goes astray.
18 He [a]who conceals hatred *has* lying lips,
And he who spreads slander is a fool.
19 When there are [a]many words, transgression is unavoidable,
But [b]he who restrains his lips is wise.
20 The tongue of the righteous is *as* [a]choice silver,
The heart of the wicked is *worth* little.

2 [1]Lit., *slaughtered her slaughter* [a]Matt. 22:4 [b]Song 8:2 [c]Luke 14:16, 17
3 [a]Ps. 68:11; Matt. 22:3 [b]Prov. 8:1, 2 [c]Prov. 9:14
4 [1]Lit., *simple* [2]Lit., *heart* [a]Prov. 8:5; 9:16 [b]Prov. 6:32
5 [a]Song 5:1; Is. 55:1; John 6:27
6 [1]Or, *Forsake the simple ones* [a]Prov. 8:35; 9:11 [b]Ezek. 11:20; 37:24
7 [1]Lit., *a blemish* [a]Prov. 23:9
8 [a]Prov. 15:12; Matt. 7:6 [b]Ps. 141:5; Prov. 10:8
9 [a]Prov. 1:5
10 [a]Job 28:28; Ps. 111:10; Prov. 1:7
11 [a]Prov. 3:16; 10:27
12 [a]Job 22:2; Prov. 14:14 [b]Prov. 19:29
13 [1]Or, *foolish woman* [2]Lit., *simple* [a]Prov. 7:11 [b]Prov. 5:6
14 [a]Prov. 9:3
16 [1]Lit., *simple* [2]Lit., *heart* [a]Prov. 9:4
17 [a]Prov. 20:17
18 [1]Lit., *departed spirits* [a]Prov. 7:27

1 [a]Prov. 1:1 [b]Prov. 15:20; 29:3 [c]Prov. 17:25; 29:15
2 [1]Lit., *Treasures of wickedness* [a]Ps. 49:7; Prov. 11:4; 21:6; Ezek. 7:19; Luke 12:19, 20
3 [1]Lit., *soul of the righteous* [a]Ps. 34:9, 10; 37:25; Prov. 28:25; Matt. 6:33 [b]Ps. 112:10; Prov. 28:9
4 [a]Prov. 13:4; 21:5
6 [a]Prov. 28:20 [b]Prov. 10:11; Obad. 10
7 [a]Ps. 112:6 [b]Ps. 9:5, 6; 109:13; Eccl. 8:10
8 [1]Lit., *the foolish of lips* [a]Prov. 9:8; Matt. 7:24
9 [a]Ps. 23:4; Prov. 3:23; 28:18; Is. 33:15, 16 [b]Prov. 26:26; Matt. 10:26; 1 Tim. 5:25
10 [1]Lit., *the foolish of lips* [a]Ps. 35:19; Prov. 6:13 [b]Prov. 10:8
11 [a]Ps. 37:30; Prov. 13:14; 18:4 [b]Prov. 10:6
12 [a]Prov. 17:9; 1 Cor. 13:4-7; James 5:20; 1 Pet. 4:8
13 [1]Lit., *heart* [a]Prov. 10:31 [b]Prov. 19:29; 26:3
14 [a]Prov. 9:9 [b]Prov. 10:8, 10; 13:3; 18:7
15 [1]Lit., *strong city* [a]Job 31:24; Ps. 52:7; Prov. 18:11 [b]Prov. 19:7
16 [1]Or, *work* [a]Prov. 11:18, 19
17 [a]Prov. 6:23
18 [a]Prov. 26:24
19 [a]Job 11:2; Prov. 18:21; Eccl. 5:3 [b]Prov. 17:27; James 1:19; 3:2
20 [a]Prov. 8:19

21 The [a]lips of the righteous feed many,
But fools [b]die for lack of [1]understanding.
22 It is the [a]blessing of the LORD that makes rich,
And He adds no sorrow to it.
23 Doing wickedness is like [a]sport to a fool;
And *so is* wisdom to a man of understanding.
24 What [a]the wicked fears will come upon him,
And the [b]desire of the righteous will be granted.
25 When the [a]whirlwind passes, the wicked is no more,
But the [b]righteous *has* an everlasting foundation.
26 Like vinegar to the teeth and smoke to the eyes,
So is the [a]lazy one to those who send him.
27 The [a]fear of the LORD prolongs [1]life,
But the [b]years of the wicked will be shortened.
28 The [a]hope of the righteous is gladness,
But the [b]expectation of the wicked perishes.
29 The [a]way of the LORD is a stronghold to the upright,
But [b]ruin to the workers of iniquity.
30 The [a]righteous will never be shaken,
But [b]the wicked will not dwell in the land.
31 The [a]mouth of the righteous flows with wisdom,
But the [b]perverted tongue will be cut out.
32 The lips of the righteous bring forth [a]what is acceptable,
But the [b]mouth of the wicked, what is perverted.

Contrast the Upright and the Wicked

11 A [a]FALSE balance is an abomination to the LORD,
But a [b]just weight is His delight.
2 When [a]pride comes, then comes dishonor,
But with the humble is wisdom.
3 The [a]integrity of the upright will guide them,
But the [b]falseness of the treacherous will destroy them.
4 [a]Riches do not profit in the day of wrath,
But [b]righteousness delivers from death.
5 The [a]righteousness of the blameless will smooth his way,
But [b]the wicked will fall by his own wickedness.
6 The righteousness of the upright will deliver them,
But the treacherous will [a]be caught by *their own* greed.
7 When a wicked man dies, *his* [a]expectation will perish,
And the [b]hope of strong men perishes.
8 The righteous is delivered from trouble,
But the wicked [1]takes his place.
9 With *his* [a]mouth the godless man destroys his neighbor,
But through knowledge the [b]righteous will be delivered.
10 When it [a]goes well with the righteous, the city rejoices,
And when the wicked perish, there is glad shouting.
11 By the blessing of the upright a city is exalted,
But by the mouth of the wicked it is torn down.
12 He who despises his neighbor lacks [1]sense,
But a man of understanding keeps silent.
13 He [a]who goes about as a talebearer reveals secrets,
But he who is [1]trustworthy [b]conceals a matter.
14 Where there is no [a]guidance, the people fall,
But in abundance of counselors there is [1]victory.
15 He who is [a]surety for a stranger will surely suffer for it,
But he who hates [1]going surety is safe.
16 A [a]gracious woman attains honor,
And violent men attain riches.
17 The [a]merciful man does [1]himself good,
But the cruel man [2]does himself harm.
18 The wicked earns deceptive wages,
But he who [a]sows righteousness *gets* a true reward.
19 He who is steadfast in [a]righteousness *will attain* to life,
And [b]he who pursues evil *will bring about* his own death.
20 The perverse in heart are an abomination to the LORD,
But the [a]blameless in *their* [1]walk are His [b]delight.
21 [1]Assuredly, the evil man will not go unpunished,
But the [2]descendants of the righteous will be delivered.
22 *As* a [a]ring of gold in a swine's snout,
So is a beautiful woman who lacks [1]discretion.
23 The desire of the righteous is only good,
But the [a]expectation of the wicked is wrath.
24 There is one who scatters, yet increases all the more,
And there is one who withholds what is justly due, but *it results* only in want.
25 The [1][a]generous man will be [2]prosperous,
And he who [b]waters will himself be watered.

21 [1]Lit., *heart* [a]Prov. 10:11 [b]Prov. 5:23; Hos. 4:6
22 [a]Gen. 24:35; 26:12; Deut. 8:18; Prov. 8:21
23 [a]Prov. 2:14; 15:21
24 [a]Job 15:21; Prov. 1:27; Is. 66:4 [b]Ps. 145:19; Prov. 15:8; Matt. 5:6; 1 John 5:14, 15
25 [a]Job 21:18; Ps. 58:9; Prov. 12:7 [b]Ps. 15:5; Prov. 12:3; Matt. 7:24, 25
26 [a]Prov. 26:6
27 [1]Lit., *days* [a]Prov. 3:2; 9:11; 14:27 [b]Job 15:32, 33; 22:16; Ps. 55:23
28 [a]Prov. 11:23 [b]Job 8:13; 11:20; Prov. 11:7
29 [a]Prov. 13:6 [b]Prov. 21:15
30 [a]Ps. 37:29; 125:1; Prov. 2:21 [b]Prov. 2:22
31 [a]Ps. 37:30; Prov. 10:13 [b]Prov. 17:20
32 [a]Eccl. 12:10 [b]Prov. 2:12; 6:12

1 [a]Lev. 19:35, 36; Deut. 25:13-16; Prov. 20:10, 23; Mic. 6:11 [b]Prov. 16:11
2 [a]Prov. 16:18; 18:12; 29:23
3 [a]Prov. 13:6 [b]Prov. 19:3; 22:12
4 [a]Prov. 10:2; Ezek. 7:19; Zeph. 1:18 [b]Gen. 7:1
5 [a]Prov. 3:6 [b]Prov. 5:22
6 [a]Ps. 7:15, 16; 9:15; Eccl. 10:8
7 [a]Prov. 10:28 [b]Job 8:13, 14
8 [1]Lit., *enters*
9 [a]Prov. 16:29 [b]Prov. 11:6
10 [a]Prov. 28:12
12 [1]Lit., *heart*
13 [1]Lit., *faithful of spirit* [a]Lev. 19:16; Prov. 20:19; 1 Tim. 5:13 [b]Prov. 19:11
14 [1]Lit., *deliverance* [a]Prov. 15:22; 20:18; 24:6
15 [1]Lit., *those who strike hands* [a]Prov. 6:1; 27:13
16 [a]Prov. 31:28, 30
17 [1]Lit., *good to his own soul* [2]Lit., *troubles his flesh* [a]Matt. 5:7; 25:34-36
18 [a]Hos. 10:12; Gal. 6:8, 9; James 3:18
19 [a]Prov. 10:16; 12:28; 19:23 [b]Prov. 21:16; Rom. 6:23; James 1:15
20 [1]Lit., *way* [a]Ps. 119:1; Prov. 13:6 [b]1 Chr. 29:17
21 [1]Lit., *Hand to hand* [2]Lit., *seed*
22 [1]Lit., *taste* [a]Gen. 24:47
23 [a]Prov. 10:28; Rom. 2:8, 9
25 [1]Lit., *soul of blessing* [2]Lit., *made fat* [a]Prov. 3:9, 10; 2 Cor. 9:6, 7 [b]Matt. 5:7

26 He who withholds grain, the [a]people will curse him,
But [b]blessing will be on the head of him who [c]sells *it.*
27 He who diligently seeks good seeks favor,
But [a]he who searches after evil, it will come to him.
28 He who [a]trusts in his riches will fall,
But [b]the righteous will flourish like the *green* leaf.
29 He who [a]troubles his own house will [b]inherit wind,
And [c]the foolish will be servant to the wisehearted.
30 The fruit of the righteous is [a]a tree of life,
And [b]he who is wise [1]wins souls.
31 If [a]the righteous will be rewarded in the earth,
How much more the wicked and the sinner!

Contrast the Upright and the Wicked

12 WHOEVER loves [1]discipline loves knowledge,
But he who hates reproof is stupid.
2 A [a]good man will obtain favor from the LORD,
But He will condemn a man [1]who devises evil.
3 A man will [a]not be established by wickedness,
But the root of the [b]righteous will not be moved.
4 An [1a]excellent wife is the crown of her husband,
But she who shames *him* is as [b]rottenness in his bones.
5 The thoughts of the righteous are just,
But the counsels of the wicked are deceitful.
6 The [a]words of the wicked lie in wait for blood,
But the [b]mouth of the upright will deliver them.
7 The [a]wicked are overthrown and are no more,
But the [b]house of the righteous will stand.
8 A man will be praised according to his insight,
But one of perverse [1]mind will be despised.
9 Better is he who is lightly esteemed and has a servant,
Than he who honors himself and lacks bread.
10 A [a]righteous man has regard for the life of his beast,
But the compassion of the wicked is cruel.
11 He [a]who tills his land will have plenty of bread,
But he who pursues vain *things* lacks [1]sense.
12 The [a]wicked desires the [1]booty of evil men,
But the root of the righteous [b]yields *fruit.*
13 [1]An evil man is ensnared by the transgression of his lips,
But the [a]righteous will escape from trouble.
14 A man will be [a]satisfied with good by the fruit of his [1]words,
And the [b]deeds of a man's hands will return to him.
15 The [a]way of a fool is right in his own eyes,
But a wise man is he who listens to counsel.
16 A [a]fool's vexation is known at once,
But a prudent man conceals dishonor.
17 He who [1]speaks truth tells what is right,
But a false witness, deceit.
18 There is one who [a]speaks rashly like the thrusts of a sword,
But the [b]tongue of the wise brings healing.
19 Truthful lips will be established forever,
But a [a]lying tongue is only for a moment.
20 Deceit is in the heart of those who devise evil,
But counselors of peace have joy.
21 [a]No harm befalls the righteous,
But the wicked are filled with trouble.
22 [a]Lying lips are an abomination to the LORD,
But those who deal faithfully are His delight.
23 A [a]prudent man conceals knowledge,
But the heart of fools proclaims folly.
24 The hand of the diligent will rule,
But the [1]slack *hand* will be [a]put to forced labor.
25 [a]Anxiety in the heart of a man weighs it down,
But a [b]good word makes it glad.
26 The righteous is a guide to his neighbor,
But the way of the wicked leads them astray.
27 A [1]slothful man does not [2]roast his prey,
But the [a]precious possession of a man *is* diligence.
28 [a]In the way of righteousness is life,
And in *its* pathway there is no death.

Contrast the Upright and the Wicked

13 A [a]WISE son *accepts his* father's discipline,
But a [b]scoffer does not listen to rebuke.
2 From the fruit of a man's mouth he [1a]enjoys good,
But the [2]desire of the treacherous is [b]violence.
3 The one who [a]guards his mouth preserves his life;
The one who [b]opens wide his lips [1]comes to ruin.

26 [a]Prov. 24:24 [b]Job 29:13 [c]Gen. 42:6
27 [a]Esth. 7:10; Ps. 7:15, 16; 57:6
28 [a]Ps. 49:6; Mark 10:25; 1 Tim. 6:17 [b]Ps. 1:3; 92:12; Jer. 17:8
29 [a]Prov. 15:27 [b]Eccl. 5:16 [c]Prov. 14:19
30 [1]Lit., *takes* [a]Prov. 3:18 [b]Prov. 14:25; Dan. 12:3; 1 Cor. 9:19-22; James 5:20
31 [a]2 Sam. 22:21, 25; Prov. 13:21; 1 Pet. 4:18

1 [1]Or, *instruction*
2 [1]Lit., *of evil devices* [a]Prov. 3:4; 8:35
3 [a]Prov. 11:5 [b]Prov. 10:25
4 [1]Or, *virtuous* [a]Prov. 31:11; 1 Cor. 11:7 [b]Prov. 14:30; Hab. 3:16
6 [a]Prov. 1:11, 16 [b]Prov. 14:3
7 [a]Job 34:25; Prov. 10:25 [b]Matt. 7:24-27
8 [1]Lit., *heart*
10 [a]Deut. 25:4
11 [1]Lit., *heart* [a]Prov. 28:19
12 [1]Lit., *net* [a]Prov. 21:10 [b]Prov. 11:30
13 [1]Lit., *In the transgression of the lips is an evil snare* [a]Prov. 11:8; 21:23; 2 Pet. 2:9
14 [1]Lit., *mouth* [a]Prov. 13:2; 15:23; 18:20 [b]Job 34:11; Prov. 1:31; 24:12; Is. 3:10, 11; Hos. 4:9
15 [a]Prov. 14:12; 16:2; 21:2
16 [a]Prov. 14:33; 27:3; 29:11
17 [1]Lit., *breathes*
18 [a]Ps. 57:4 [b]Prov. 4:22; 15:4
19 [a]Ps. 52:4, 5; Prov. 19:9
21 [a]Ps. 91:10; 121:7; Prov. 1:33; 1 Pet. 3:13
22 [a]Rev. 22:15
23 [a]Prov. 10:14; 11:13; 13:16; 15:2; 29:11
24 [1]Lit., *slackness* [a]Gen. 49:15; Judg. 1:28; 1 Kin. 9:21
25 [a]Prov. 15:13 [b]Is. 50:4
27 [1]Lit., *slackness* [2]Or, *catch* [a]Prov. 10:4; 13:4
28 [a]Deut. 30:15f.; 32:46f.; Jer. 21:8

1 [a]Prov. 10:1; 15:20 [b]Prov. 9:7, 8; 15:12
2 [1]Lit., *eats* [2]Lit., *soul* [a]Prov. 12:14 [b]Prov. 1:31; Hos. 10:13
3 [1]Lit., *ruin is his* [a]Prov. 18:21; 21:23; James 3:2 [b]Prov. 18:7; 20:19

4 The soul of the sluggard craves and *gets* nothing,
But the soul of the diligent is made fat.
5 A righteous man [a]hates falsehood,
But a wicked man [1b]acts disgustingly and shamefully.
6 Righteousness [a]guards the [1]one whose way is blameless,
But wickedness subverts the [2]sinner.
7 There is one who [a]pretends to be rich, but has nothing;
Another [1]pretends to be [b]poor, but has great wealth.
8 The ransom of a man's life is his riches,
But the poor hears no rebuke.
9 The [a]light of the righteous [1]rejoices,
But the [b]lamp of the wicked goes out.
10 Through presumption [1]comes nothing but strife,
But with those who receive counsel is wisdom.
11 Wealth *obtained* by [1]fraud dwindles,
But the one who gathers [2]by labor increases *it.*
12 Hope deferred makes the heart sick,
But desire [1]fulfilled is a tree of life.
13 The one who [a]despises the word will be [1]in debt to it,
But the one who fears the commandment will be [b]rewarded.
14 The [1]teaching of the wise is a [a]fountain of life,
To turn aside from the [b]snares of death.
15 [a]Good understanding produces favor,
But the way of the treacherous is hard.
16 Every [a]prudent man acts with knowledge,
But a fool [1]displays folly.
17 A wicked messenger falls into adversity,
But [a]a faithful envoy *brings* healing.
18 Poverty and shame *will come* to him who [a]neglects [1]discipline,
But he who regards reproof will be honored.
19 Desire realized is sweet to the soul,
But it is an abomination to fools to depart from evil.
20 [a]He who walks with wise men will be wise,
But the companion of fools will suffer harm.
21 [a]Adversity pursues sinners,
But the [b]righteous will be rewarded with prosperity.
22 A good man [a]leaves an inheritance to his [1]children's children,
And the [b]wealth of the sinner is stored up for the righteous.
23 [a]Abundant food *is in* the fallow ground of the poor,
But [1]it is swept away by injustice.

5 [1]Lit., *causes a bad odor and causes shame* [a]Col. 3:9 [b]Prov. 3:35
6 [1]Lit., *blamelessness of way* [2]Lit., *sin* [a]Prov. 11:3
7 [1]Lit., *impoverishes himself* [a]Prov. 11:24; Luke 12:20, 21 [b]Luke 12:33; 2 Cor. 6:10; James 2:5
9 [1]I.e., shines brightly [a]Job 29:3; Prov. 4:18 [b]Job 18:5; Prov. 24:20
10 [1]Lit., *gives*
11 [1]Lit., *vanity* [2]Or, *gradually;* lit., *on the hand*
12 [1]Lit., *coming*
13 [1]Lit., *pledged to it* [a]Num. 15:31; 2 Chr. 36:16 [b]Prov. 13:21
14 [1]Or, *law* [a]Prov. 10:11; 14:27 [b]Ps. 18:5
15 [a]Ps. 111:10; Prov. 3:4
16 [1]Lit., *spreads out* [a]Prov. 12:23
17 [a]Prov. 25:13
18 [1]Or, *instruction* [a]Prov. 15:5, 32
20 [a]Prov. 2:20; 15:31
21 [a]Ps. 32:10; 54:5; Is. 47:11 [b]Prov. 11:31; 13:13; Is. 3:10
22 [1]Lit., *sons' sons* [a]Ezra 9:12; Ps. 37:25 [b]Job 27:16, 17; Prov. 28:8; Eccl. 2:26
23 [1]Lit., *there is what is swept* [a]Prov. 12:11
24 [1]Lit., *seeks him diligently with discipline* [a]Prov. 19:18; 22:15; 23:13, 14; 29:15, 17 [b]Deut. 8:5; Prov. 3:12; Heb. 12:7
25 [1]Lit., *eats to the satisfaction of his soul* [a]Ps. 34:10; 103:5; 132:15; Prov. 10:3 [b]Prov. 13:18; Luke 15:14

1 [a]Ruth 4:11; Prov. 31:10-27
2 [a]Prov. 19:1; 28:6 [b]Prov. 2:15
3 [1]Lit., *of pride* [a]Prov. 12:6
5 [1]Lit., *breathes out* [a]Rev. 1:5; 3:14 [b]Ex. 23:1; Deut. 19:16; Prov. 6:19; 12:17 [c]Prov. 19:5
7 [1]Lit., *know* [2]Lit., *lips* [a]Prov. 23:9
8 [a]1 Cor. 3:19
9 [1]Lit., *guilt* [2]Or, the *favor* of God [a]Prov. 3:34; 11:20
10 [a]1 Sam. 1:10; Job 21:25
11 [a]Job 8:15
12 [a]Prov. 12:15; 16:25 [b]Rom. 6:21
13 [a]Eccl. 2:1, 2
14 [1]Lit., *from himself* [a]Prov. 1:31; 12:21 [b]Prov. 12:14; 18:20

24 He who [a]spares his rod hates his son,
But he who loves him [1b]disciplines him diligently.
25 The [a]righteous [1]has enough to satisfy his appetite,
But the stomach of the [b]wicked is in want.

Contrast the Upright and the Wicked

14 THE [a]wise woman builds her house,
But the foolish tears it down with her own hands.
2 He who [a]walks in his uprightness fears the LORD,
But he who is [b]crooked in his ways despises Him.
3 In the mouth of the foolish is a rod [1]for *his* back,
But [a]the lips of the wise will preserve them.
4 Where no oxen are, the manger is clean,
But much increase *comes* by the strength of the ox.
5 A [a]faithful witness will not lie,
But a [b]false witness [1c]speaks lies.
6 A scoffer seeks wisdom, and *finds* none,
But knowledge is easy to him who has understanding.
7 Leave the [a]presence of a fool,
Or you will not [1]discern [2]words of knowledge.
8 The wisdom of the prudent is to understand his way,
But [a]the folly of fools is deceit.
9 Fools mock at [1]sin,
But [a]among the upright there is [2]good will.
10 The heart knows its own [a]bitterness,
And a stranger does not share its joy.
11 The [a]house of the wicked will be destroyed,
But the tent of the upright will flourish.
12 There [a]is a way *which seems* right to a man,
But its [b]end is the way of death.
13 Even in laughter the heart may be in pain,
And the [a]end of joy may be grief.
14 The backslider in heart will have his [a]fill of his own ways,
But a good man will [b]*be satisfied* [1]with his.
15 The [1]naive believes everything,
But the prudent man considers his steps.
16 A wise man [1]is cautious and [a]turns away from evil,
But a fool is arrogant and careless.
17 A quick-tempered man acts foolishly,
And a man of evil devices is hated.

15 [1]Lit., *simple*
16 [1]Lit., *fears* [a]Job 28:28; Ps. 34:14; Prov. 3:7; 22:3

18 The [1]naive inherit folly,
But the prudent are crowned with knowledge.
19 The [a]evil will bow down before the good,
And the wicked at the gates of the righteous.
20 The [a]poor is hated even by his neighbor,
But those who love the rich are many.
21 He who [a]despises his neighbor sins,
But [b]happy is he who is gracious to the [1]poor.
22 Will they not go astray who [a]devise evil?
But kindness and truth *will be to* those who devise good.
23 In all labor there is profit,
But [1]mere talk *leads* only to poverty.
24 The [a]crown of the wise is their riches,
But the folly of fools is foolishness.
25 A truthful witness saves lives,
But he who [1a]speaks lies is [2]treacherous.
26 In the [1a]fear of the LORD there is strong confidence,
And [2]his children will have refuge.
27 The [1]fear of the LORD is a fountain of life,
That one may avoid the snares of death.
28 In a multitude of people is a king's glory,
But in the dearth of people is a prince's ruin.
29 He who is [a]slow to anger has great understanding,
But he who is [1]quick-tempered exalts folly.
30 A [a]tranquil heart is life to the body,
But passion is [b]rottenness to the bones.
31 He [a]who oppresses the poor reproaches [b]his Maker,
But he who is gracious to the needy honors Him.
32 The wicked is [a]thrust down by his [1]wrongdoing,
But the [b]righteous has a refuge when he dies.
33 Wisdom rests in the heart of one who has understanding,
But in the [1]bosom of fools it is made known.
34 Righteousness exalts a nation,
But sin is a disgrace to *any* people.
35 The king's favor is toward a [a]servant who acts wisely,
But his anger is toward him who acts shamefully.

Contrast the Upright and the Wicked

15 A [a]GENTLE answer turns away wrath,
But a [1b]harsh word stirs up anger.
2 The [a]tongue of the wise makes knowledge [1]acceptable,
But the [b]mouth of fools spouts folly.
3 The [a]eyes of the LORD are in every place,
Watching the evil and the good.
4 A [1]soothing tongue is a tree of life,
But perversion in it [2]crushes the spirit.
5 A fool [1]rejects his father's discipline,
But he who regards reproof is prudent.
6 Much wealth is *in* the house of the [a]righteous,
But trouble is in the income of the wicked.
7 The lips of the wise spread knowledge,
But the hearts of fools are not so.
8 The [a]sacrifice of the wicked is an abomination to the LORD,
But [b]the prayer of the upright is His delight.
9 The way of the wicked is an abomination to the LORD,
But He loves him who [a]pursues righteousness.
10 Stern discipline is for him who forsakes the way;
He who hates reproof will die.
11 [1a]Sheol and [2]Abaddon *lie open* before the LORD,
How much more the [b]hearts of [3]men!
12 A [a]scoffer does not love one who reproves him,
He will not go to the wise.
13 A [a]joyful heart makes a [1]cheerful face,
But [2]when the heart is [b]sad, the [c]spirit is broken.
14 The [a]mind of the intelligent seeks knowledge,
But the mouth of fools feeds on folly.
15 All the days of the afflicted are bad,
But a [1]cheerful heart *has* a continual feast.
16 [a]Better is a little with the [1]fear of the LORD,
Than great treasure and turmoil with it.
17 [a]Better is a [1]dish of [2]vegetables where love is,
Than a [b]fattened ox and hatred with it.
18 A [a]hot-tempered man stirs up strife,
But the [b]slow to anger [c]pacifies contention.
19 The way of the sluggard is as a hedge of thorns,
But the path of the upright is a highway.
20 A [a]wise son makes a father glad,
But a foolish man [b]despises his mother.
21 Folly is joy to him who lacks [1]sense,
But a man of understanding [a]walks straight.

18 [1]Lit., *simple*
19 [a]1 Sam. 2:36; Prov. 11:29
20 [a]Prov. 19:7
21 [1]Or, *afflicted* [a]Prov. 11:12 [b]Ps. 41:1; Prov. 19:17; 28:8
22 [a]Ps. 36:4; Prov. 3:29; 12:2; Mic. 2:1
23 [1]Lit., *word of lips*
24 [a]Prov. 10:22; 13:8; 21:20
25 [1]Lit., *breathes out* [2]Lit., *treachery* [a]Prov. 14:5
26 [1]Or, *reverence* [2]Or, *His* [a]Prov. 18:10; 19:23; Is. 33:6
27 [1]Or, *reverence*
29 [1]Lit., *short of spirit* [a]Prov. 16:32; 19:11; Eccl. 7:9; James 1:19
30 [a]Prov. 15:13 [b]Prov. 12:4; Hab. 3:16
31 [a]Prov. 17:5; Matt. 25:40; 1 John 3:17 [b]Job 31:15; Prov. 22:2
32 [1]Or, *calamity* [a]Prov. 6:15; 24:16 [b]Gen. 49:18; Ps. 16:11; 17:15; 37:37; 73:24; 2 Cor. 1:9; 5:8; 2 Tim. 4:18
33 [1]Lit., *midst*
35 [a]Matt. 24:45, 47; 25:21, 23

1 [1]Lit., *painful* [a]Judg. 8:1-3; Prov. 15:18; 25:15 [b]1 Sam. 25:10-13
2 [1]Lit., *good* [a]Prov. 15:7 [b]Prov. 12:23; 13:16; 15:28
3 [a]2 Chr. 16:9; Job 31:4; Jer. 16:17; Zech. 4:10; Heb. 4:13
4 [1]Lit., *healing* [2]Lit., *is the crushing of the spirit*
5 [1]Or, *despises*
6 [a]Prov. 8:21
8 [a]Prov. 21:27; Eccl. 5:1; Is. 1:11; Jer. 6:20; Mic. 6:7 [b]Prov. 15:29
9 [a]1 Tim. 6:11
11 [1]I.e., the nether world [2]I.e., place of destruction [3]Lit., *sons of Adam* [a]Job 26:6; Ps. 139:8 [b]1 Sam. 16:7; 2 Chr. 6:30; Ps. 44:21; Acts 1:24
12 [a]Prov. 13:1; Amos 5:10
13 [1]Lit., *good* [2]Lit., *in sadness of heart* [a]Prov. 17:22 [b]Prov. 12:25 [c]Prov. 17:22; 18:14
14 [a]Prov. 18:15
15 [1]Lit., *good*
16 [1]Or, *reverence* [a]Ps. 37:16; Prov. 16:8; Eccl. 4:6; 1 Tim. 6:6
17 [1]Or, *portion* [2]Or, *herbs* [a]Prov. 17:1 [b]Matt. 22:4; Luke 15:23
18 [a]Prov. 16:28; 26:21; 29:22 [b]Prov. 14:29 [c]Gen. 13:8; Prov. 16:14; Eccl. 10:4
20 [a]Prov. 10:1; 29:3 [b]Prov. 30:17
21 [1]Lit., *heart* [a]Prov. 14:8; Eph. 5:15

22 Without consultation, plans are frustrated,
But with many counselors they [1]succeed.
23 A [a]man has joy in an [1]apt answer,
And how delightful is a timely [b]word!
24 The [a]path of life *leads* upward for the wise,
That he may keep away from [1]Sheol below.
25 The LORD will [a]tear down the house of the proud,
But He will [b]establish the boundary of the [c]widow.
26 Evil plans are an abomination to the LORD,
But pleasant words are pure.
27 He who [a]profits illicitly troubles his own house,
But he who [b]hates bribes will live.
28 The heart of the righteous [a]ponders how to answer,
But the [b]mouth of the wicked pours out evil things.
29 The LORD is [a]far from the wicked,
But He [b]hears the prayer of the righteous.
30 [1]Bright eyes gladden the heart;
Good news puts fat on the bones.
31 He whose ear listens to the life-giving reproof
Will dwell among the wise.
32 He who [a]neglects discipline [b]despises himself,
But he who [c]listens to reproof acquires [1]understanding.
33 The [1]fear of the LORD is the instruction for wisdom,
And before honor *comes* humility.

Contrast the Upright and the Wicked

16 THE [a]plans of the heart belong to man,
But the answer of the tongue is from the LORD.
2 All the ways of a man are clean in his own sight,
But the [a]LORD weighs the [1]motives.
3 [1a]Commit your works to the LORD,
And your plans will be established.
4 The LORD [a]has made everything for [1]its own purpose,
Even the [b]wicked for the day of evil.
5 Everyone who is proud in heart is an abomination to the LORD;
Assuredly, he will not be unpunished.
6 By [a]lovingkindness and truth iniquity is atoned for,
And by the [1b]fear of the LORD one keeps away from evil.
7 When a man's ways are pleasing to the LORD,
He [a]makes even his enemies to be at peace with him.
8 Better is a little with righteousness
Than great income with injustice.
9 The mind of [a]man plans his way,
But [b]the LORD directs his steps.
10 A divine [a]decision is in the lips of the king;
His mouth should not [1]err in judgment.
11 A [a]just balance and scales belong to the LORD;
All the [1]weights of the bag are His [2]concern.
12 It is an abomination for kings to commit wickedness,
For a [a]throne is established on righteousness.
13 Righteous lips are the delight of kings,
And he who speaks right is loved.
14 The wrath of a king is *as* messengers of death,
But a wise man will appease it.
15 In the light of a king's face is life,
And his favor is like a cloud with the [1a]spring rain.
16 How much [a]better it is to get wisdom than gold!
And to get understanding is to be chosen above silver.
17 The [a]highway of the upright is to depart from evil;
He who watches his way preserves his [1]life.
18 [a]Pride *goes* before destruction,
And a haughty spirit before stumbling.
19 It is better to be of a [a]humble spirit with the lowly,
Than to [b]divide the spoil with the proud.
20 He who gives attention to the word shall [a]find good,
And [b]blessed is he who trusts in the LORD.
21 The [a]wise in heart will be called discerning,
And sweetness of [1]speech [b]increases [2]persuasiveness.
22 Understanding is a fountain of life to him who has it,
But the discipline of fools is folly.
23 The [a]heart of the wise teaches his mouth,
And adds [1]persuasiveness to his lips.
24 [a]Pleasant words are a honeycomb,
Sweet to the soul and [b]healing to the bones.
25 [a]There is a way *which seems* right to a man,
But its end is the way of death.
26 A worker's appetite works for him,
For his [1]hunger urges him *on*.
27 A [a]worthless man digs up evil,
While [1]his words are as a [b]scorching fire.
28 A perverse man spreads strife,
And a slanderer separates intimate friends.
29 A man of violence [a]entices his neighbor,
And leads him in a way that is not good.
30 He who winks his eyes *does so* to devise perverse things;
He who compresses his lips brings evil to pass.

---

22 [1]Or, *are established*
23 [1]Lit., *answer of his mouth* [a]Prov. 12:14 [b]Prov. 25:11; Is. 50:4
24 [1]I.e., the nether world [a]Prov. 4:18
25 [a]Prov. 12:7; 14:11 [b]Deut. 19:14; Prov. 23:10 [c]Ps. 68:5; 146:9
27 [a]Prov. 1:19; 28:25; 1 Tim. 6:10 [b]Ex. 23:8; Deut. 16:19; 1 Sam. 12:3; Is. 33:15
28 [a]1 Pet. 3:15 [b]Prov. 10:32; 15:2
29 [a]Ps. 18:41; Prov. 1:28 [b]Ps. 145:18, 19
30 [1]Lit., *The light of the eyes gladdens*
32 [1]Lit., *heart* [a]Prov. 1:7; 8:33 [b]Prov. 8:36 [c]Prov. 15:5
33 [1]Or, *reverence*

1 [a]Prov. 16:9; 19:21
2 [1]Lit., *spirits* [a]1 Sam. 16:7; Dan. 5:27
3 [1]Lit., *Roll* [a]Ps. 37:5; 55:22; Prov. 3:6; 1 Pet. 5:7
4 [1]Or, *His* [a]Gen. 1:31; Eccl. 3:11 [b]Rom. 9:22
6 [1]Or, *reverence* [a]Dan. 4:27; Luke 11:41 [b]Prov. 8:13; 14:16
7 [a]Gen. 33:4; 2 Chr. 17:10
9 [a]Prov. 16:1; 19:21 [b]Ps. 37:23; Prov. 20:24; Jer. 10:23
10 [1]Lit., *be unfaithful* [a]1 Kin. 3:28
11 [1]Lit., *stones* [2]Lit., *work* [a]Prov. 11:1
12 [a]Prov. 25:5
15 [1]Lit., *latter* [a]Job 29:23
16 [a]Prov. 8:10, 19
17 [1]Lit., *soul* [a]Is. 35:8
18 [a]Prov. 11:2; 18:12; Jer. 49:16; Obad. 3, 4
19 [a]Prov. 3:34; 29:23; Is. 57:15 [b]Ex. 15:9; Judg. 5:30; Prov. 1:13, 14
20 [a]Prov. 19:8 [b]Ps. 2:12; 34:8; Jer. 17:7
21 [1]Lit., *lips* [2]Or, *learning* [a]Hos. 14:9 [b]Prov. 16:23
23 [1]Or, *learning* [a]Ps. 37:30; Prov. 15:28; Matt. 12:34
24 [a]Ps. 19:10; Prov. 15:26; 24:13, 14 [b]Prov. 4:22; 17:22
25 [a]Prov. 12:15; 14:12
26 [1]Lit., *mouth*
27 [1]Lit., *on his lips* [a]Prov. 6:12, 14, 18 [b]James 3:6
29 [a]Prov. 1:10; 12:26

31 A [a]gray head is a crown of glory;
It [b]is found in the way of righteousness.
32 He who is slow to anger is better than the mighty,
And he who rules his spirit, than he who captures a city.
33 The [a]lot is cast into the lap,
But its every [b]decision is from the LORD.

Contrast the Upright and the Wicked

17 [a]BETTER is a dry morsel and quietness with it
Than a house full of [1]feasting with strife.
2 A servant who acts wisely will rule over a son who acts shamefully,
And will share in the inheritance among brothers.
3 The [a]refining pot is for silver and the furnace for gold,
But [b]the LORD tests hearts.
4 An [a]evildoer listens to wicked lips,
A [1]liar pays attention to a destructive tongue.
5 He who mocks the [a]poor reproaches his Maker;
He who [b]rejoices at calamity will not go unpunished.
6 [a]Grandchildren are the crown of old men,
And the [b]glory of sons is their fathers.
7 [1][a]Excellent speech is not fitting for a fool;
Much less are [b]lying lips to a prince.
8 A [a]bribe is a [1]charm in the sight of its owner;
Wherever he turns, he prospers.
9 He who [a]covers a transgression seeks love,
But he who repeats a matter [b]separates intimate friends.
10 A rebuke goes deeper into one who has understanding
Than a hundred blows into a fool.
11 A rebellious man seeks only evil,
So a cruel messenger will be sent against him.
12 Let a [a]man meet a [b]bear robbed of her cubs,
Rather than a fool in his folly.
13 He who [a]returns evil for good,
[b]Evil will not depart from his house.
14 The beginning of strife is *like* letting out water,
So [a]abandon the quarrel before it breaks out.
15 He who [a]justifies the wicked, and he who condemns the righteous,
Both of them alike are an abomination to the LORD.
16 Why is there a price in the hand of a fool to [a]buy wisdom,
When [1]he has no sense?
17 A [a]friend loves at all times,
And a brother is born for adversity.
18 A man lacking in [1]sense [2][a]pledges,
And becomes surety in the presence of his neighbor.
19 He who [a]loves transgression loves strife;
He who [b]raises his door seeks destruction.
20 He who has a crooked [1]mind [a]finds no good,
And he who is [b]perverted in his language falls into evil.
21 He who [a]begets a fool *does so* to his sorrow,
And the father of a fool has no joy.
22 A [a]joyful heart [1]is good medicine,
But a broken spirit [b]dries up the bones.
23 A wicked man receives a [a]bribe from the bosom
To [b]pervert the ways of justice.
24 Wisdom is in the presence of the one who has understanding,
But the [a]eyes of a fool are on the ends of the earth.
25 A [a]foolish son is a grief to his father,
And [b]bitterness to her who bore him.
26 It is also not good to [a]fine the righteous,
Nor to strike the noble for *their* uprightness.
27 He who [a]restrains his words [1]has knowledge,
And he who has a [b]cool spirit is a man of understanding.
28 Even a fool, when he [a]keeps silent, is considered wise;
When he closes his lips, he is *counted* prudent.

Contrast the Upright and the Wicked

18 HE who separates himself seeks *his own* desire,
He [1][a]quarrels against all sound wisdom.
2 A fool does not delight in understanding,
But only [a]in revealing his own [1]mind.
3 When a wicked man comes, contempt also comes,
And with dishonor *comes* reproach.
4 The words of a man's mouth are [a]deep waters;
[1]The fountain of wisdom is a bubbling brook.
5 To [a]show partiality to the wicked is not good,
Nor to [b]thrust aside the righteous in judgment.
6 A fool's lips [1]bring strife,
And his mouth calls for [a]blows.
7 A [a]fool's mouth is his ruin,
And his lips are the snare of his soul.
8 The words of a whisperer are like dainty morsels,
And they go down into the [1]innermost parts of the body.
9 He also who is [a]slack in his work
[b]Is brother to him who destroys.

31 [a]Prov. 20:29 [b]Prov. 3:1, 2
33 [a]Prov. 18:18 [b]Prov. 29:26

1 [1]Lit., *sacrifices of strife* [a]Prov. 15:17
3 [a]Prov. 27:21 [b]1 Chr. 29:17; Ps. 26:2; Prov. 15:11; Jer. 17:10; Mal. 3:3
4 [1]Lit., *falsehood* [a]Prov. 14:15
5 [a]Prov. 14:31 [b]Job 31:29; Prov. 24:17; Obad. 12
6 [a]Gen. 48:11; Prov. 13:22 [b]Ex. 20:12; Mal. 1:6
7 [1]Lit., *A lip of abundance* [a]Prov. 24:7 [b]Ps. 31:18; Prov. 12:22
8 [1]Lit., *stone of favor* [a]Prov. 21:14; Is. 1:23; Amos 5:12
9 [a]Prov. 10:12; James 5:20; 1 Pet. 4:8 [b]Prov. 16:28
12 [a]Prov. 29:9 [b]2 Sam. 17:8; Hos. 13:8
13 [a]Ps. 35:12; 109:5; Jer. 18:20 [b]2 Sam. 12:10; 1 Kin. 21:22; Prov. 13:21
14 [a]Prov. 20:3; 25:8; 1 Thess. 4:11
15 [a]Ex. 23:7; Prov. 18:5; 24:24; Is. 5:23
16 [1]Lit., *there is no heart* [a]Prov. 23:23
17 [a]Ruth 1:16; Prov. 18:24
18 [1]Lit., *heart* [2]Lit., *shakes hands* [a]Prov. 6:1; 11:15; 22:26
19 [a]Prov. 29:22 [b]Prov. 16:18; 29:23
20 [1]Lit., *heart* [a]Prov. 24:20 [b]James 3:8
21 [a]Prov. 10:1; 17:25; 19:13
22 [1]Lit., *causes good healing* [a]Prov. 15:13 [b]Ps. 22:15
23 [a]Prov. 17:8 [b]Ex. 23:8; Mic. 3:11; 7:3
24 [a]Eccl. 2:14
25 [a]Prov. 19:13 [b]Prov. 10:1
26 [a]Prov. 17:15; 18:5
27 [1]Lit., *knows* [a]Prov. 10:19; James 1:19 [b]Prov. 14:29
28 [a]Job 13:5

1 [1]Lit., *breaks out* [a]Prov. 3:21; 8:14
2 [1]Lit., *heart* [a]Prov. 12:23; 13:16; Eccl. 10:3
4 [1]Or, *A bubbling brook, a fountain of wisdom* [a]Prov. 20:5
5 [a]Lev. 19:15; Deut. 1:17; 16:19; Ps. 82:2; Prov. 17:15; 24:23; 28:21 [b]Ex. 23:2, 6; Prov. 17:26; 31:5; Mic. 3:9
6 [1]Lit., *come with* [a]Prov. 19:29
7 [a]Ps. 64:8; 140:9; Prov. 10:14; 12:13; 13:3; Eccl. 10:12
8 [1]Lit., *chambers of the belly*
9 [a]Prov. 10:4 [b]Prov. 28:24

10 The [a]name of the LORD is a [b]strong
tower;
The righteous runs into it and [c]is
[1]safe.
11 A [a]rich man's wealth is his strong
city,
And like a high wall in his own
imagination.
12 [a]Before destruction the heart of
man is haughty,
But [b]humility *goes* before honor.
13 He who [a]gives an answer before he
hears,
It is folly and shame to him.
14 The [a]spirit of a man can endure his
sickness,
But a [b]broken spirit who can bear?
15 The [1a]mind of the prudent acquires
knowledge,
And the [b]ear of the wise seeks
knowledge.
16 A man's [a]gift makes room for him,
And brings him before great men.
17 The first [1]to plead his case *seems*
just,
Until [2]another comes and examines
him.
18 The [a]lot puts an end to contentions,
And [1]decides between the mighty.
19 A brother offended *is harder to be*
won than a strong city,
And contentions are like the bars
of a castle.
20 With the [1a]fruit of a man's mouth
his stomach will be satisfied;
[b]He will be satisfied *with* the product of his lips.
21 [a]Death and life are in the [1]power of
the tongue,
And those who love it will eat its
[b]fruit.
22 He who finds a [a]wife finds a good
thing,
And [b]obtains favor from the LORD.
23 The [a]poor man utters supplications,
But the [b]rich man [c]answers
roughly.
24 A man of *many* friends *comes* to
[1]ruin,
But there is [a]a [2]friend who sticks
closer than a brother.

On Life and Conduct

19 [a]BETTER is a poor man who
[b]walks in his integrity
Than he who is perverse in [1]speech
and is a fool.
2 Also it is not good for a person to
be without knowledge,
And he who makes [a]haste with his
feet [1]errs.
3 The [a]foolishness of man subverts
his way,
And his heart [b]rages against the
LORD.
4 [a]Wealth adds many friends,
But a poor man is separated from
his friend.
5 A [a]false witness will not go unpunished,

10 [1]Lit., *set on high* [a]Ex. 3:15 [b]2 Sam. 22:2, 3, 33; Ps. 18:2; 61:3; 91:2; 144:2 [c]Prov. 29:25
11 [a]Prov. 10:15
12 [a]Prov. 11:2; 16:18; 29:23 [b]Prov. 15:33
13 [a]Prov. 20:25; John 7:51
14 [a]Prov. 17:22 [b]Prov. 15:13
15 [1]Lit., *heart* [a]Prov. 15:14; Eph. 1:17 [b]Prov. 15:31
16 [a]Gen. 32:20; 1 Sam. 25:27
17 [1]Lit., *in his plea* [2]Lit., *his neighbor*
18 [1]Lit., *makes a division* [a]Prov. 16:33
20 [1]I.e., speech [a]Prov. 12:14 [b]Prov. 14:14
21 [1]Lit., *hand* [a]Prov. 12:13; 13:3; Matt. 12:37 [b]Prov. 13:2; Is. 3:10; Hos. 10:13
22 [a]Gen. 2:18; Prov. 12:4; 19:14; 31:10-31 [b]Prov. 8:35
23 [a]Prov. 19:7 [b]James 2:3, 6 [c]1 Kin. 12:13; 2 Chr. 10:13
24 [1]Lit., *be broken in pieces* [2]Or, *lover* [a]Prov. 17:17; John 15:14, 15

1 [1]Lit., *his lips* [a]Prov. 28:6 [b]Ps. 26:11; Prov. 14:2; 20:7
2 [1]Lit., *sins* [a]Prov. 21:5; 28:20; 29:20
3 [a]Prov. 11:3 [b]Is. 8:21
4 [a]Prov. 14:20
5 [1]Lit., *breathes* [a]Ex. 23:1; Deut. 19:16-19; Prov. 19:9; 21:28 [b]Prov. 6:19
6 [1]Or, *noble* [a]Prov. 29:26 [b]Prov. 18:16; 21:14
7 [1]Lit., *not* [a]Ps. 38:11 [b]Prov. 18:23
8 [1]Lit., *heart* [a]Prov. 16:20
9 [1]Lit., *breathes* [a]Prov. 19:5; Dan. 6:24
10 [a]Prov. 17:7; 26:1; Eccl. 10:6, 7 [b]Prov. 30:22
11 [a]Prov. 14:29; 16:32 [b]Matt. 5:44; Eph. 4:32; Col. 3:13
12 [a]Prov. 16:14 [b]Gen. 27:28; Deut. 33:28; Ps. 133:3; Hos. 14:5; Mic. 5:7
13 [a]Prov. 17:25 [b]Prov. 21:9, 19; 27:15
14 [a]2 Cor. 12:14
15 [1]Lit., *soul* [a]Prov. 6:9, 10; 24:33
16 [1]Lit., *despises* [a]Prov. 13:13; 16:17; Luke 10:28; 11:28
17 [1]Or, *benefits* [a]Deut. 15:7, 8; Prov. 14:31; 28:27; Eccl. 11:1, 2; Matt. 10:42; 25:40; 2 Cor. 9:6-8; Heb. 6:10 [b]Prov. 12:14; Luke 6:38

And he who [1b]tells lies will not
escape.
6 [a]Many will entreat the favor of a
[1]generous man,
And every man is a friend to him
who [b]gives gifts.
7 All the brothers of a poor man hate
him;
How much more do his [a]friends go
far from him!
He [b]pursues *them with* words, *but*
they are [1]gone.
8 He who gets [1]wisdom loves his own
soul;
He who keeps understanding will
[a]find good.
9 A [a]false witness will not go unpunished,
And he who [1]tells lies will perish.
10 Luxury is [a]not fitting for a fool;
Much less for a [b]slave to rule over
princes.
11 A man's [a]discretion makes him
slow to anger,
And it is his glory [b]to overlook a
transgression.
12 The [a]king's wrath is like the roaring
of a lion,
But his favor is like [b]dew on the
grass.
13 A [a]foolish son is destruction to his
father,
And the [b]contentions of a wife are
a constant dripping.
14 House and wealth are an [a]inheri-
tance from fathers,
But a prudent wife is from the
LORD.
15 [a]Laziness casts into a deep sleep,
And an idle [1]man will suffer hunger.
16 He who [a]keeps the commandment
keeps his soul,
But he who [1]is careless of his ways
will die.
17 He who [a]is gracious to a poor man
lends to the LORD,
And He will repay him for his
[1b]good deed.
18 [a]Discipline your son while there is
hope,
And do not desire [1]his death.
19 *A man of* great anger shall bear the
penalty,
For if you rescue *him,* you will only
have to do it again.
20 [a]Listen to counsel and accept discipline,
That you may be wise [1]the rest of
your days.
21 Many are the [a]plans in a man's
heart,
But the [b]counsel of the LORD, it
will stand.
22 What is desirable in a man is his
[1]kindness,
And *it is* better to be a poor man
than a liar.

18 [1]Lit., *causing him to die* [a]Prov. 13:24; 23:13; 29:15, 17
20 [1]Lit., *in your latter end* [a]Prov. 4:1; 8:33; 12:15
21 [a]Prov. 16:1, 9 [b]Ps. 33:10, 11; Is. 14:26, 27
22 [1]Or, *loyalty*

23 The [1a]fear of the LORD *leads* to life,
So that one may sleep [b]satisfied, [2c]untouched by evil.
24 The [a]sluggard buries his hand [b]in the dish,
And will not even bring it back to his mouth.
25 [a]Strike a scoffer and the [1]naive may become shrewd,
But [b]reprove one who has understanding and he will [2]gain knowledge.
26 He [a]who assaults *his* father *and* drives *his* mother away
Is a shameful and disgraceful son.
27 Cease listening, my son, to discipline,
And you will stray from the words of knowledge.
28 A rascally witness makes a mockery of justice,
And the mouth of the wicked [1a]spreads iniquity.
29 [1]Judgments are prepared for [a]scoffers,
And [b]blows for the back of fools.

On Life and Conduct

20 [a]WINE is a mocker, [b]strong drink a brawler,
And whoever [1]is intoxicated by it is not wise.
2 The terror of a king is like the growling of a lion;
He who provokes him to anger [1a]forfeits his own life.
3 [1a]Keeping away from strife is an honor for a man,
But any fool will [2]quarrel.
4 The [a]sluggard does not plow after the autumn,
So he [1]begs during the harvest and has nothing.
5 A plan in the heart of a man is *like* deep water,
But a man of understanding draws it out.
6 Many a man [a]proclaims his own loyalty,
But who can find a [b]trustworthy man?
7 A righteous man who [a]walks in his integrity—
[b]How blessed are his sons after him.
8 [a]A king who sits on the throne of justice
[1]Disperses all evil with his eyes.
9 [a]Who can say, "I have cleansed my heart,
I am pure from my sin"?
10 [1a]Differing weights and differing measures,
Both of them are abominable to the LORD.
11 It is by his deeds that a lad [1a]distinguishes himself
If his conduct is pure and right.
12 The hearing [a]ear and the seeing eye,
The LORD has made both of them.
13 [a]Do not love sleep, lest you become poor;
Open your eyes, *and* you will be satisfied with [1]food.
14 "Bad, bad," says the buyer;
But when he goes his way, then he boasts.
15 There is gold, and an abundance of [1]jewels;
But the lips of knowledge are a more precious thing.
16 Take his garment when he becomes surety for a stranger;
And for foreigners, hold him in pledge.
17 [a]Bread obtained by falsehood is sweet to a man,
But afterward his mouth will be filled with gravel.
18 Prepare [a]plans by consultation,
And [b]make war by wise guidance.
19 He who [a]goes about as a slanderer reveals secrets,
Therefore do not associate with [1b]a gossip.
20 He who [a]curses his father or his mother,
His [b]lamp will go out in [1]time of darkness.
21 An inheritance gained hurriedly at the beginning,
Will not be blessed in the end.
22 [a]Do not say, "I will repay evil";
[b]Wait for the LORD, and He will save you.
23 [1a]Differing weights are an abomination to the LORD,
And a [2b]false scale is not good.
24 [a]Man's steps are *ordained* by the LORD,
How then can man understand his way?
25 It is a snare for a man to say rashly, "It is holy!"
And [a]after the vows to make inquiry.
26 A [a]wise king winnows the wicked,
And [1]drives the [b]*threshing* wheel over them.
27 The [1a]spirit of man is the lamp of the LORD,
Searching all the [2]innermost parts of his being.
28 [1]Loyalty and [a]truth preserve the king,
And he upholds his throne by [1]righteousness.
29 The glory of young men is their strength,
And the [1a]honor of old men is their gray hair.
30 [a]Stripes that wound scour away evil,
And strokes *reach* the [1]innermost parts.

23 [1]Or, *reverence* [2]Lit., *not visited* [a]Prov. 14:27; 1 Tim. 4:8 [b]Ps. 25:13 [c]Ps. 91:10; Prov. 12:21
24 [a]Prov. 26:15 [b]Matt. 26:23; Mark 14:20
25 [1]Lit., *simple* [2]Lit., *discern* [a]Prov. 21:11 [b]Prov. 9:8
26 [a]Prov. 28:24
28 [1]Or, *swallows* [a]Job 15:16; 20:12, 13; 34:7
29 [1]Gr., *Rods* [a]Ps. 1:1; Prov. 9:12 [b]Prov. 10:13; 18:6; 26:3

1 [1]Lit., *errs* [a]Gen. 9:21; Prov. 23:29, 30; Is. 28:7; Hos. 4:11 [b]Prov. 31:4; Is. 5:22; 56:12
2 [1]Lit., *sins against* [a]Num. 16:38; 1 Kin. 2:23; Prov. 8:36; Hab. 2:10
3 [1]Lit., *Ceasing* [2]Lit., *burst out* [a]Gen. 13:7f.; Prov. 17:14
4 [1]Lit., *asks* [a]Prov. 13:4; 21:25
6 [a]Prov. 25:14; Matt. 6:2; Luke 18:11 [b]Ps. 12:1; Luke 18:8
7 [a]Prov. 19:1 [b]Ps. 37:26; 112:2
8 [1]Or, *Sifts* [a]Prov. 20:26; 25:5
9 [a]1 Kin. 8:46; 2 Chr. 6:36; Job 14:4; Eccl. 7:20; Rom. 3:9; 1 John 1:8
10 [1]Lit., *A stone and a stone, an ephah and an ephah* [a]Prov. 11:1; 20:23
11 [1]Or, *makes himself known* [a]Matt. 7:16
12 [a]Ex. 4:11; Ps. 94:9
13 [1]Lit., *bread* [a]Prov. 6:9, 10; 19:15; 24:33
15 [1]Or, *corals*
17 [a]Prov. 9:17
18 [a]Prov. 11:14; 15:22 [b]Prov. 24:6; Luke 14:31
19 [1]Lit., *one who opens his lips* [a]Prov. 11:13 [b]Prov. 13:3
20 [1]Lit., *pupil* (of eye) [a]Ex. 21:17; Lev. 20:9; Prov. 30:11; Matt. 15:4 [b]Job 18:5; Prov. 13:9; 24:20
22 [a]Prov. 24:29; Matt. 5:39; Rom. 12:17, 19; 1 Thess. 5:15; 1 Pet. 3:9 [b]Ps. 27:14
23 [1]Lit., *A stone and a stone* [2]Lit., *balance of deceit* [a]Prov. 20:10 [b]Prov. 11:1
24 [a]Prov. 16:9
25 [a]Eccl. 5:4, 5
26 [1]Lit., *turns* [a]Prov. 20:8 [b]Is. 28:27
27 [1]Lit., *breath* [2]Lit., *chambers of the body* [a]1 Cor. 2:11
28 [1]Lit., *Covenant loyalty* [a]Prov. 29:14
29 [1]Or, *splendor* [a]Prov. 16:31
30 [1]Lit., *chambers of the body* [a]Ps. 89:32; Prov. 22:15; Is. 53:5; 1 Pet. 2:24

On Life and Conduct

21 THE king's heart is *like* channels of water in the hand of the LORD;
He [a]turns it wherever He wishes.
2 [a]Every man's way is right in his own eyes,
But the LORD [b]weighs the hearts.
3 To do [a]righteousness and justice
Is desired by the LORD rather than sacrifice.
4 Haughty eyes and a proud heart,
The [a]lamp of the wicked, is sin.
5 The plans of the [a]diligent *lead* surely to advantage,
But everyone [b]who is hasty *comes* surely to poverty.
6 The [a]getting of treasures by a lying tongue
Is a fleeting vapor, the [1]pursuit of [b]death.
7 The violence of the wicked will drag them away,
Because they [a]refuse to act with justice.
8 The way of a guilty man is [a]crooked,
But as for the pure, his conduct is upright.
9 It is better to live in a corner of a roof,
Than [1]in a house shared with a contentious woman.
10 The soul of the wicked desires evil;
His [a]neighbor finds no favor in his eyes.
11 When the [a]scoffer is punished, the [1]naive becomes wise;
But when the wise is instructed, he receives knowledge.
12 The righteous one considers the house of the wicked,
Turning the [a]wicked to ruin.
13 He who [a]shuts his ear to the cry of the poor
Will also cry himself and not be [b]answered.
14 A [a]gift in secret subdues anger,
And a bribe in the bosom, strong wrath.
15 The execution of justice is joy for the righteous,
But is [a]terror to the workers of iniquity.
16 A man who wanders from the way of understanding
Will [a]rest in the assembly of the [1]dead.
17 He who [a]loves pleasure *will become* a poor man;
He who loves wine and oil will not become rich.
18 The wicked is a [a]ransom for the righteous,
And the [b]treacherous is in the place of the upright.
19 [a]It is better to live in a desert land,
Than with a contentious and vexing woman.
20 There is precious [a]treasure and oil in the dwelling of the wise,
But a foolish man [b]swallows it up.
21 He who [a]pursues righteousness and loyalty
Finds life, righteousness and honor.
22 A [a]wise man scales the city of the mighty,
And brings down the [1]stronghold in which they trust.
23 He who [a]guards his mouth and his tongue,
Guards his soul from troubles.
24 "Proud," "Haughty," "[a]Scoffer," are his names,
Who acts with [b]insolent pride.
25 The [a]desire of the sluggard puts him to death,
For his hands refuse to work;
26 All day long he [1]is craving,
While the righteous [a]gives and does not hold back.
27 The [a]sacrifice of the wicked is an abomination,
How much more when he brings it with evil intent!
28 A [a]false witness will perish,
But the man who listens *to the truth* will speak forever.
29 A wicked man [1a]shows a bold face,
But as for the [b]upright, he makes his way sure.
30 There is [a]no wisdom and no understanding
And no counsel against the LORD.
31 The [a]horse is prepared for the day of battle,
But [b]victory belongs to the LORD.

On Life and Conduct

22 A [a]*GOOD* name is to be more desired than great riches,
Favor is better than silver and gold.
2 The rich and the poor [1]have a common bond,
The LORD is the [a]maker of them all.
3 The [a]prudent sees the evil and hides himself,
But the [1]naive go on, and are punished for it.
4 The reward of humility *and* the [1]fear of the LORD
Are riches, honor and life.
5 [a]Thorns *and* snares are in the way of the perverse;
He who guards himself will be far from them.
6 [a]Train up a child [1]in the way he should go,
Even when he is old he will not depart from it.
7 The [a]rich rules over the poor,
And the borrower *becomes* the lender's slave.
8 He who [a]sows iniquity will reap vanity,
And the [b]rod of his fury will perish.
9 He who [1]is [a]generous will be blessed,
For he [b]gives some of his food to the poor.

1 [a]Ezra 6:22
2 [a]Prov. 16:2 [b]Prov. 16:2; 24:12; Luke 16:15
3 [a]1 Sam. 15:22; Prov. 15:8; Is. 1:11, 16, 17; Hos. 6:6; Mic. 6:7, 8
4 [a]Prov. 24:20; Luke 11:34
5 [a]Prov. 10:4; 13:4 [b]Prov. 28:22
6 [1]Lit., *seekers* [a]Prov. 13:11; 20:21 [b]Prov. 8:36
7 [a]Amos 5:7; Mic. 3:9
8 [a]Prov. 2:15
9 [1]Lit., *with a woman of contentions and a house of association*
10 [a]Ps. 52:3; Prov. 2:14; 14:21
11 [1]Lit., *simple* [a]Prov. 19:25
12 [a]Prov. 14:11
13 [a]Matt. 18:30-34; 1 John 3:17 [b]James 2:13
14 [a]Prov. 18:16; 19:6
15 [a]Prov. 10:29
16 [1]Lit., *departed spirits* [a]Ps. 49:14
17 [a]Prov. 23:21
18 [a]Is. 43:3 [b]Prov. 11:8
19 [a]Prov. 21:9
20 [a]Ps. 112:3; Prov. 8:21; 22:4 [b]Job 20:15, 18
21 [a]Prov. 15:9; Matt. 5:6; 1 Cor. 15:58
22 [1]Lit., *strength of trust* [a]2 Sam. 5:6-9; Prov. 24:5; Eccl. 7:19; 9:15, 16
23 [a]Prov. 12:13; 13:3; 18:21; James 3:2
24 [a]Ps. 1:1; Prov. 1:22; 3:34; 24:9; Is. 29:20 [b]Is. 16:6; Jer. 48:29
25 [a]Prov. 13:4
26 [1]Lit., *desires desire* [a]Ps. 37:26; 112:5, 9; Matt. 5:42; Eph. 4:28
27 [a]Prov. 15:8; Is. 66:3; Jer. 6:20; Amos 5:22
28 [a]Prov. 19:5, 9
29 [1]Lit., *makes firm with his face* [a]Eccl. 8:1 [b]Ps. 119:5; Prov. 11:5
30 [a]Jer. 9:23; Acts 5:38, 39; 1 Cor. 3:19, 20
31 [a]Ps. 20:7; 33:17; Is. 31:1 [b]Ps. 3:8; Jer. 3:23; 1 Cor. 15:57

1 [a]Prov. 10:7; Eccl. 7:1
2 [1]Lit., *meet together* [a]Job 31:15; Prov. 14:31
3 [1]Lit., *simple* [a]Prov. 14:16; 27:12; Is. 26:20
4 [1]Or, *reverence*
5 [a]Prov. 15:19
6 [1]Lit., *according to his way* [a]Eph. 6:4
7 [a]Prov. 18:23; James 2:6
8 [a]Job 4:8 [b]Ps. 125:3
9 [1]Lit., *has a good eye* [a]Prov. 19:17; 2 Cor. 9:6 [b]Luke 14:13

10 [a]Drive out the scoffer, and contention will go out,
Even strife and dishonor will cease.
11 He who loves [a]purity of heart
And [1]whose speech is [b]gracious, the king is his friend.
12 The eyes of the LORD preserve knowledge,
But He overthrows the words of the treacherous man.
13 The [a]sluggard says, "There is a lion outside;
I shall be slain in the streets!"
14 The mouth of [1a]an adulteress is a deep pit;
He who is [b]cursed of the LORD will fall [2]into it.
15 Foolishness is bound up in the heart of a child;
The [a]rod of discipline will remove it far from him.
16 He [a]who oppresses the poor to make much for himself
Or who gives to the rich, [b]*will* only *come to* poverty.

17 [a]Incline your ear and hear the words of the wise,
And apply your mind to my knowledge;
18 For it will be [a]pleasant if you keep them within you,
[1]That they may be ready on your lips.
19 So that your [a]trust may be in the LORD,
I have [1]taught you today, even you.
20 Have I not written to you [1a]excellent things
Of counsels and knowledge,
21 To make you [a]know the [1]certainty of the words of truth
That you may [2b]correctly answer to him who sent you?

22 [a]Do not rob the poor because he is poor,
Or [b]crush the afflicted at the gate;
23 For the LORD will [a]plead their case,
And [1]take the life of those who rob them.

24 Do not associate with a man *given* to anger;
Or go with a [a]hot-tempered man,
25 Lest you [a]learn his ways,
And [1]find a snare for yourself.

26 Do not be among those who [a]give [1]pledges,
Among those who become sureties for debts.
27 If you have nothing with which to pay,
Why should he [a]take your bed from under you?

28 [a]Do not move the ancient boundary
Which your fathers have set.

29 Do you see a man skilled in his work?
He will [a]stand before kings;
He will not stand before obscure men.

On Life and Conduct

23 WHEN you sit down to dine with a ruler,
Consider carefully [1]what is before you;
2 And put a knife to your throat,
If you are a [a]man of *great* appetite.
3 Do not [a]desire his delicacies,
For it is deceptive food.

4 [a]Do not weary yourself to gain wealth,
[b]Cease from your [1]consideration *of it.*
5 [1]When you set your eyes on it, it is gone.
For [a]*wealth* certainly makes itself wings,
Like an eagle that flies *toward* the heavens.

6 [a]Do not eat the bread of [1]a [b]selfish man,
Or desire his delicacies;
7 For as he [1]thinks within himself, so he is.
He says to you, "Eat and drink!"
But [a]his heart is not with you.
8 You will [a]vomit up [1]the morsel you have eaten,
And waste your [2]compliments.

9 [a]Do not speak in the [1]hearing of a fool,
For he will [b]despise the wisdom of your words.

10 Do not move the ancient boundary,
Or [a]go into the fields of the fatherless;
11 For their [a]Redeemer is strong;
[b]He will plead their case against you.
12 Apply your heart to discipline,
And your ears to words of knowledge.

13 [a]Do not hold back discipline from the child,
Although you [1]beat him with the rod, he will not die.
14 You shall [1]beat him with the rod,
And [a]deliver his soul from Sheol.

15 My son, if your heart is [a]wise,
My own heart also will be glad;
16 And my [1]inmost being will rejoice,
When your lips speak [a]what is right.

17 [a]Do not let your heart envy sinners,
But *live* in the [1b]fear of the LORD [2]always.
18 Surely there is a [1a]future,
And your [b]hope will not be cut off.

10 aGen. 21:9, 10; Prov. 18:6; 26:20
11 1Lit., *has grace on his lips* aPs. 24:4; Matt. 5:8 bProv. 14:35; 16:13
13 aProv. 26:13
14 1Lit., *strange woman* 2Lit., *there* aProv. 2:16; 5:3; 7:5; 23:27 bEccl. 7:26
15 aProv. 13:24; 23:14
16 aEccl. 5:8; James 2:13 bProv. 28:22
17 aProv. 5:1
18 1Lit., *They together* aProv. 2:10
19 1Lit., *made you know* aProv. 3:5
20 1Or, *previous* aProv. 8:6
21 1Lit., *truth* 2Lit., *return words of truth* aLuke 1:3, 4 bProv. 25:13; 1 Pet. 3:15
22 aEx. 23:6; Job 31:16; Prov. 22:16 bZech. 7:10; Mal. 3:5
23 1Lit., *rob the soul* a1 Sam. 25:39; Ps. 12:5; 35:10; 140:12; Prov. 23:11; Jer. 51:36
24 aProv. 29:22
25 1Lit., *take* a1 Cor. 15:33
26 1Lit., *strike hands* aProv. 17:18
27 aEx. 22:26; Prov. 20:16
28 aDeut. 19:14; 27:17; Job 24:2; Prov. 23:10
29 aGen. 41:46; 1 Kin. 10:8

1 1Or, *who*
2 aProv. 23:20
3 aPs. 141:4; Prov. 23:6; Dan. 1:5, 8, 13, 15, 16
4 1Or, *understanding* aProv. 15:27; 28:20; Matt. 6:19; 1 Tim. 6:9; Heb. 13:5 bProv. 3:5, 7
5 1Lit., *Will your eyes fly upon it and it is not?* aProv. 27:24; 1 Tim. 6:17
6 1Lit., *an evil eye* aPs. 141:4 bDeut. 15:9; Prov. 28:22
7 1Lit., *reckons in his soul* aProv. 26:24, 25
8 1Lit., *your* 2Lit., *pleasant words* aProv. 25:16
9 1Lit., *ears* aMatt. 7:6 bProv. 1:7
10 aJer. 22:3; Zech. 7:10
11 aJob 19:25; Jer. 50:34 bProv. 22:23
13 1Lit., *smite* aProv. 13:24; 19:18
14 1Lit., *smite* a1 Cor. 5:5
15 aProv. 23:24f.; 27:11; 29:3
16 1Lit., *kidneys* aProv. 8:6
17 1Or, *reverence* 2Lit., *all the day* aPs. 37:1; Prov. 24:1, 19 bProv. 28:14
18 1Lit., *latter end* aPs. 19:11; 58:11; Prov. 24:14 bPs. 9:18

19 Listen, my son, and [a]be wise,
And [b]direct your heart in the way.
20 Do not be with [a]heavy drinkers of
wine,
Or with [b]gluttonous eaters of meat;
21 For the [a]heavy drinker and the
glutton will come to poverty,
And [b]drowsiness will clothe *a man*
with rags.

22 [a]Listen to your father who begot
you,
And [b]do not despise your mother
when she is old.
23 [a]Buy truth, and do not sell *it,*
Get wisdom and instruction and
understanding.

24 The father of the righteous will
greatly rejoice,
And [a]he who begets a wise son will
be glad in him.
25 Let your [a]father and your mother
be glad,
And let her rejoice who gave birth
to you.

26 [a]Give me your heart, my son,
And let your eyes [1b]delight in my
ways.
27 For a harlot is a [a]deep pit,
And an [1b]adulterous woman is a
narrow well.
28 Surely she [a]lurks as a robber,
And increases the [1]faithless among
men.

29 Who has [a]woe? Who has sorrow?
Who has contentions? Who has
complaining?
Who has wounds without cause?
Who has redness of eyes?
30 Those who [a]linger long over wine,
Those who go to [1]taste [b]mixed
wine.
31 Do not look on the wine when it is
red,
When it [1]sparkles in the cup,
When it [a]goes down smoothly;
32 At the last it [a]bites like a serpent,
And stings like a [b]viper.
33 Your eyes will see strange things,
And your [1]mind will [a]utter perverse things.
34 And you will be like one who lies
down in the [1]middle of the sea,
Or like one who lies down on the
top of a [2]mast.
35 "They [a]struck me, *but* I did not
become ill;
They beat me, *but* I did not know
it.
When shall I awake?
I will [b]seek [1]another drink."

Precepts and Warnings

24 DO not be [a]envious of evil men,
Nor desire to [b]be with them;
2 For their [1]minds devise [a]violence,
And their lips [b]talk of trouble.

3 [a]By wisdom a house is built,
And by understanding it is established;
4 And by knowledge the rooms are
[a]filled
With all precious and pleasant
riches.

5 A [a]wise man is [1]strong,
And a man of knowledge [2]increases
power.
6 For [a]by wise guidance you will
[1]wage war,
And [b]in abundance of counselors
there is victory.

7 Wisdom is [a]too high for a fool,
He does not open his mouth [b]in the
gate.

8 He who [a]plans to do evil,
Men will call him a [1]schemer.
9 The [a]devising of folly is sin,
And the scoffer is an abomination
to men.

10 If you [a]are slack in the day of
distress,
Your strength is limited.

11 [a]Deliver those who are being taken
away to death,
And those who are staggering to
slaughter, O hold *them* back.
12 If you say, "See, we did not know
this,"
Does He not [a]consider *it* [b]who
weighs the hearts?
And [c]does He not know *it* who
[d]keeps your soul?
And will He not [1e]render to man
according to his work?

13 My son, eat [a]honey, for it is good,
Yes, the [b]honey from the comb is
sweet to your taste;
14 Know *that* [a]wisdom is thus for your
soul;
If you find *it,* then there will be a
[1b]future,
And your hope will not be cut off.

15 [a]Do not lie in wait, O wicked man,
against the dwelling of the righteous;
Do not destroy his resting place;
16 For a [a]righteous man falls seven
times, and rises again,
But the [b]wicked stumble in *time of*
calamity.

17 [a]Do not rejoice when your enemy
falls,
And do not let your heart be glad
when he stumbles;
18 Lest the LORD see *it* and [1]be displeased,
And He turn away His anger from
him.

19 [a]Prov. 6:6 [b]Prov. 4:23; 9:6
20 [a]Prov. 20:1; 23:29, 30; Is. 5:22; Matt. 24:49; Luke 21:34; Rom. 13:13; Eph. 5:18 [b]Deut. 21:20; Prov. 28:7
21 [a]Prov. 21:17 [b]Prov. 6:10, 11
22 [a]Prov. 1:8; Eph. 6:1 [b]Prov. 15:20; 30:17
23 [a]Prov. 4:7; 18:15; Matt. 13:44
24 [a]Prov. 10:1; 15:20; 29:3
25 [a]Prov. 27:11
26 [1]Another reading is *observe* [a]Prov. 3:1; 4:4 [b]Ps. 1:2; 119:24
27 [1]Lit., *strange* [a]Prov. 22:14 [b]Prov. 5:20
28 [1]Lit., *treacherous* [a]Prov. 6:26; 7:12; Eccl. 7:26
29 [a]Is. 5:11, 22
30 [1]Or, *search out* [a]1 Sam. 25:36; Prov. 20:1; Is. 5:11; 28:7; Eph. 5:18 [b]Ps. 75:8
31 [1]Lit., *gives its eye* [a]Song 7:9
32 [a]Job 20:16; Prov. 20:1; Eph. 5:18 [b]Ps. 91:13; Is. 11:8
33 [1]Lit., *heart* [a]Prov. 2:12
34 [1]Lit., *heart* [2]Or, *lookout*
35 [1]Lit., *it yet again* [a]Prov. 27:22; Jer. 5:3 [b]Prov. 26:11; Is. 56:12

1 [a]Ps. 37:1; Prov. 3:31; 23:17; 24:19 [b]Ps. 1:1; Prov. 1:15
2 [1]Lit., *hearts* [a]Is. 30:12; Jer. 22:17 [b]Job 15:35; Ps. 10:7; 38:12
3 [a]Prov. 9:1; 14:1
4 [a]Prov. 8:21
5 [1]Lit., *in strength* [2]Lit., *strengthens power* [a]Prov. 21:22
6 [1]Lit., *make battle for yourself* [a]Prov. 20:18 [b]Prov. 11:14
7 [a]Ps. 10:5; Prov. 14:6; 17:16 [b]Job 5:4; Ps. 127:5
8 [1]Or, *deviser of evil* [a]Prov. 6:14; 14:22; Rom. 1:30
9 [a]Matt. 15:19; Acts 8:22
10 [a]Deut. 20:8; Job 4:5; Jer. 51:46; Heb. 12:3
11 [a]Ps. 82:4; Is. 58:6, 7
12 [1]Lit., *bring back* [a]Eccl. 5:8 [b]1 Sam. 16:7; Prov. 21:2 [c]Ps. 94:9-11 [d]Ps. 121:3-8 [e]Job 34:11; Prov. 12:14
13 [a]Ps. 19:10; 119:103; Prov. 25:16; Song 5:1 [b]Prov. 16:24; 27:7; Song 4:11
14 [1]Lit., *latter end* [a]Prov. 2:10 [b]Prov. 23:18
15 [a]Ps. 10:9, 10
16 [a]Job 5:19; Ps. 37:24; Mic. 7:8 [b]Prov. 6:15; 14:32; 24:22; Jer. 18:17
17 [a]Job 31:29; Ps. 35:15, 19; Prov. 17:5; Obad. 12
18 [1]Lit., *it is evil in His eyes*

19 [a]Do not fret because of evildoers,
Or be [b]envious of the wicked;
20 For [a]there will be no [1b]future for the evil man;
The [c]lamp of the wicked will be put out.

21 My son, [1a]fear the LORD and the king;
Do not associate with those who are given to change;
22 For their [a]calamity will rise suddenly,
And who knows the ruin *that comes* from both of them?

23 These also are [a]sayings of the wise.
To [1b]show partiality in judgment is not good.
24 He [a]who says to the wicked, "You are righteous,"
[b]Peoples will curse him, nations will abhor him;
25 But [a]to those who rebuke the *wicked* will be delight,
And a good blessing will come upon them.
26 He kisses the lips
Who gives [1]a right answer.

27 Prepare your work outside,
And [a]make it ready for yourself in the field;
Afterwards, then, build your house.

28 Do not be a [a]witness against your neighbor without cause,
And [b]do not deceive with your lips.
29 [a]Do not say, "Thus I shall do to him as he has done to me;
I will [1]render to the man according to his work."

30 I passed by the field of the sluggard,
And by the vineyard of the man [a]lacking [1]sense;
31 And behold, it was completely [a]overgrown with thistles,
Its surface was covered with [1b]nettles,
And its stone [c]wall was broken down.
32 When I saw, I [1]reflected upon it;
I looked, *and* received instruction.
33 "[a]A little sleep, a little slumber,
A little folding of the hands to rest,"
34 Then your poverty will come *as* [1]a robber,
And your want like [2]an armed man.

Similitudes, Instructions

25 THESE also are [a]proverbs of Solomon which the men of Hezekiah, king of Judah, transcribed.
2 It is the glory of God to [a]conceal a matter,
But the glory of [b]kings is to search out a matter.
3 *As* the heavens for height and the earth for depth,
So the heart of kings is unsearchable.
4 Take away the [a]dross from the silver,
And there comes out a vessel for the [b]smith;
5 Take away the [a]wicked *from* before the king,
And his [b]throne will be established in righteousness.
6 Do not claim honor in the presence of the king,
And do not stand in the place of great men;
7 For [a]it is better that it be said to you, "Come up here,"
Than that you should be put lower in the presence of the prince,
Whom your eyes have seen.

8 Do not go out [a]hastily to [1]argue *your case;*
[2]Otherwise, what will you do in [3]the end,
When your neighbor puts you to shame?
9 [1a]Argue your case with your neighbor,
And [b]do not reveal the secret of another,
10 Lest he who hears *it* reproach you,
And the evil report about you not [1]pass away.

11 *Like* apples of gold in settings of silver
Is a [a]word spoken in [1]right circumstances.
12 *Like* [1]an [a]earring of gold and an [b]ornament of [c]fine gold
Is a wise reprover to a [d]listening ear.
13 Like the cold of snow in the [1]time of harvest
Is a [a]faithful messenger to those who send him,
For he refreshes the soul of his masters.
14 *Like* [a]clouds and [b]wind without rain
Is a man who boasts [1]of his gifts falsely.
15 By [1a]forbearance a ruler may be persuaded,
And a soft tongue breaks the bone.
16 Have you [a]found honey? Eat *only* [1]what you need,
Lest you have it in excess and vomit it.
17 Let your foot rarely be in your neighbor's house,
Lest he become [1]weary of you and hate you.
18 *Like* a club and a [a]sword and a sharp [b]arrow
Is a man who bears [c]false witness against his neighbor.
19 *Like* a bad tooth and [1]an unsteady foot
Is confidence in a [a]faithless man in time of trouble.

19 [a]Ps. 37:1 [b]Prov. 23:17; 24:1
20 [1]Lit., *latter end* [a]Job 15:31 [b]Prov. 23:18 [c]Job 18:5, 6; 21:17; Prov. 13:9; 20:20
21 [1]Or, *reverence* [a]Rom. 13:1-7; 1 Pet. 2:17
22 [a]Prov. 24:16
23 [1]Lit., *regard the face* [a]Prov. 1:6; 22:17 [b]Prov. 18:5; 28:21
24 [a]Prov. 17:15; Is. 5:23 [b]Prov. 11:26
25 [a]Prov. 28:23
26 [1]Or, *an honest*
27 [a]Prov. 27:23-27
28 [a]Prov. 25:18 [b]Lev. 6:2, 3; 19:11; Eph. 4:25
29 [1]Lit., *bring back* [a]Prov. 20:22; Matt. 5:39; Rom. 12:17
30 [1]Lit., *heart* [a]Prov. 6:32
31 [1]I.e., a kind of weed [a]Gen. 3:18 [b]Job 30:7 [c]Is. 5:5
32 [1]Lit., *set my heart*
33 [a]Prov. 6:10
34 [1]Or, *a vagabond;* lit., *one who walks* [2]Lit., *a man with a shield*

1 [a]Prov. 1:1
2 [a]Deut. 29:29; Rom. 11:33 [b]Ezra 6:1
4 [a]Prov. 26:23; Ezek. 22:18 [b]Mal. 3:2, 3
5 [a]Prov. 20:8 [b]Prov. 16:12
7 [a]Luke 14:7-11
8 [1]Lit., *contend* [2]Lit., *Lest* [3]Lit., *its* [a]Prov. 17:14; Matt. 5:25
9 [1]Lit., *Contend* [a]Matt. 18:15 [b]Prov. 11:13
10 [1]Lit., *return*
11 [1]Lit., *its* [a]Prov. 15:23
12 [1]Or, *a nose ring* [a]Ex. 32:2; 35:22; Ezek. 16:12 [b]2 Sam. 1:24 [c]Job 28:17 [d]Prov. 15:31; 20:12
13 [1]Lit., *day* [a]Prov. 13:17
14 [1]Lit., *in a gift of falsehood* [a]Jude 12 [b]Jer. 5:13; Mic. 2:11
15 [1]Lit., *length of anger* [a]Gen. 32:4; 1 Sam. 25:24; Eccl. 10:4
16 [1]Lit., *your sufficiency* [a]Judg. 14:8; 1 Sam. 14:25
17 [1]Lit., *surfeited with*
18 [a]Ps. 57:4; Prov. 12:18 [b]Jer. 9:8 [c]Ex. 20:16; Prov. 24:28
19 [1]Lit., *a slipping foot* [a]Job 6:15; Is. 36:6

20 *Like* one who takes off a garment on a cold day, *or like* vinegar on [1]soda,
Is he who sings songs to [2]a troubled heart.
21 [a]If [1]your enemy is hungry, give him food to eat;
And if he is thirsty, give him water to drink;
22 For you will [1]heap burning coals on his head,
And [a]the LORD will reward you.
23 The north wind brings forth rain,
And a [1a]backbiting tongue, an angry countenance.
24 It is [a]better to live in a corner of the roof
Than [1]in a house shared with a contentious woman.
25 *Like* cold water to a weary soul,
So is [a]good news from a distant land.
26 *Like* a [a]trampled spring and a [1]polluted well
Is a righteous man who gives way before the wicked.
27 It is not good to eat much honey,
Nor is it glory to [a]search out [1]one's own glory.
28 *Like* a [a]city that is broken into *and* without walls
Is a man [b]who has no control over his spirit.

Similitudes, Instructions

26 LIKE snow in summer and like [a]rain in harvest,
So honor is not [b]fitting for a fool.
2 Like a [a]sparrow in *its* [1]flitting, like a swallow in *its* flying,
So a [b]curse without cause does not [2]alight.
3 A [a]whip is for the horse, a bridle for the donkey,
And a [b]rod for the back of fools.
4 [a]Do not answer a fool according to his folly,
Lest you also be like him.
5 [a]Answer a fool as his folly *deserves,*
Lest he be [b]wise in his own eyes.
6 He cuts off *his own* feet, *and* drinks violence
Who sends a message by the hand of a fool.
7 *Like* the legs *which* hang down from the lame,
So is a proverb in the mouth of fools.
8 Like [1]one who binds a stone in a sling,
So is he who gives honor to a fool.
9 *Like* a thorn *which* [1]falls into the hand of a drunkard,
So is a proverb in the mouth of fools.
10 [1]*Like* an archer who wounds everyone,
So is he who hires a fool or who hires those who pass by.
11 Like [a]a dog that returns to its vomit
Is a fool who [b]repeats [1]his folly.
12 Do you see a man [a]wise in his own eyes?
[b]There is more hope for a fool than for him.
13 The [a]sluggard says, "There is a lion in the road!
A lion is [1]in the open square!"
14 *As* the door turns on its hinges,
So *does* the [a]sluggard on his bed.
15 The [a]sluggard buries his hand in the dish;
He is weary of bringing it to his mouth again.
16 The sluggard is [a]wiser in his own eyes
Than seven men who can [1]give a discreet answer.
17 *Like* one who takes a dog by the ears
Is he who passes by *and* [1]meddles with [a]strife not belonging to him.
18 Like a madman who throws
[a]Firebrands, arrows and death,
19 So is the man who [a]deceives his neighbor,
And says, "[b]Was I not joking?"
20 For lack of wood the fire goes out,
And where there is no [a]whisperer, [b]contention quiets down.
21 *Like* charcoal to hot embers and wood to fire,
So is a [a]contentious man to kindle strife.
22 The [a]words of a whisperer are like dainty morsels,
And they go down into the [1]innermost parts of the body.
23 *Like* an earthen [a]vessel overlaid with silver [b]dross
Are burning lips and a wicked heart.
24 He who [a]hates disguises *it* with his lips,
But he lays up [b]deceit in his [1]heart.
25 When [1]he [a]speaks graciously, do not believe him,
For there are seven abominations in his heart.
26 *Though his* hatred [a]covers itself with guile,
His wickedness will be [b]revealed before the assembly.
27 He who [a]digs a pit will fall into it,
And he who rolls a stone, it will come back on him.
28 A lying tongue hates [1]those it crushes,
And a [a]flattering mouth works ruin.

Warnings and Instructions

27 [a]DO not boast about tomorrow,
For you [b]do not know what a day may bring forth.
2 Let [a]another praise you, and not your own mouth;
A stranger, and not your own lips.
3 A stone is heavy and the sand weighty,

20 [1]I.e., natron [2]Lit., *an evil*
21 [1]Lit., *one who hates you* [a]Ex. 23:4, 5; 2 Kin. 6:22; 2 Chr. 28:15; Matt. 5:44; Rom. 12:20
22 [1]Lit., *snatch up* [a]2 Sam. 16:12; Matt. 6:4, 6
23 [1]Lit., *tongue of secrecy* [a]Ps. 101:5
24 [1]Lit., *with a woman of contentions and a house of association* [a]Prov. 21:9
25 [a]Prov. 15:30
26 [1]Lit., *ruined* [a]Ezek. 32:2; 34:18, 19
27 [1]Lit., *their* [a]Prov. 27:2; Luke 14:11
28 [a]Prov. 16:32 [b]2 Chr. 32:5; Neh. 1:3

1 [a]1 Sam. 12:17 [b]Prov. 17:7
2 [1]Lit., *wandering* [2]Lit., *come* [a]Prov. 27:8; Is. 16:2 [b]Num. 23:8; Deut. 23:5; 2 Sam. 16:12
3 [a]Ps. 32:9 [b]Prov. 10:13; 19:29
4 [a]Prov. 23:9; 29:9; Is. 36:21; Matt. 7:6
5 [a]Matt. 16:1-4; 21:24-27 [b]Prov. 3:7; 28:11; Rom. 12:16
8 [1]Lit., *the binding of*
9 [1]Lit., *goes up*
10 [1]Or, *A master workman produces all things, But he who hires a fool is* like *one who hires those who pass by.*
11 [1]Lit., *with his* [a]2 Pet. 2:22 [b]Ex. 8:15
12 [a]Prov. 3:7; 26:5 [b]Prov. 29:20
13 [1]Lit., *within* [a]Prov. 22:13
14 [a]Prov. 6:9
15 [a]Prov. 19:24
16 [1]Lit., *return discreetly* [a]Prov. 27:11
17 [1]Lit., *infuriates himself* [a]Prov. 3:30
18 [a]Is. 50:11
19 [a]Prov. 24:28 [b]Eph. 5:4
20 [a]Prov. 16:28 [b]Prov. 22:10
21 [a]Prov. 15:18; 29:22
22 [1]Lit., *chambers of the belly* [a]Prov. 18:8
23 [a]Matt. 23:27; Luke 11:39 [b]Prov. 25:4
24 [1]Lit., *inward part* [a]Ps. 41:6; Prov. 10:18 [b]Prov. 12:20
25 [1]Lit., *his voice is gracious* [a]Ps. 28:3; Prov. 26:23; Jer. 9:8
26 [a]Matt. 23:28 [b]Luke 8:17
27 [a]Esth. 7:10; Prov. 28:10
28 [1]Lit., *its crushed ones* [a]Prov. 29:5

1 [a]James 4:13-16 [b]Luke 12:19, 20; James 4:14
2 [a]Prov. 25:27; 2 Cor. 10:12, 18; 12:11

But the provocation of a fool is
heavier than both of them.
4 Wrath is fierce and anger is a flood,
But [a]who can stand before jealousy?
5 Better is [a]open rebuke
Than love that is concealed.
6 Faithful are the [a]wounds of a
friend,
But [1]deceitful are the [b]kisses of an
enemy.
7 A sated [1]man [2]loathes honey,
But to a famished [1]man any bitter
thing is sweet.
8 Like a [a]bird that wanders from her
nest,
So is a man who [b]wanders from his
[1]home.
9 [a]Oil and perfume make the heart
glad,
So a [1]man's counsel is sweet to his
friend.
10 Do not forsake your own [a]friend or
[b]your father's friend,
And do not go to your brother's
house in the day of your calamity;
Better is a neighbor who is near
than a brother far away.
11 [a]Be wise, my son, and make my
heart glad,
That I may [b]reply to him who
reproaches me.
12 A prudent man sees evil *and* hides
himself,
The [1]naive proceed *and* pay the
penalty.
13 [a]Take his garment when he becomes
surety for a stranger;
And for an [1]adulterous woman
hold him in pledge.
14 [a]He who blesses his friend with a
loud voice early in the morning,
It will be reckoned a curse to him.
15 A [a]constant dripping on a day of
steady rain
And a contentious woman are
alike;
16 He who would [1]restrain her [1]restrains
the wind,
And [2]grasps oil with his right hand.
17 Iron sharpens iron,
So one man sharpens another.
18 He who tends the [a]fig tree will eat
its fruit;
And he who [b]cares for his master
will be honored.
19 As in water face *reflects* face,
So the heart of man *reflects* man.
20 [1][a]Sheol and [2]Abaddon are [b]never
satisfied,
Nor are the [c]eyes of man ever
satisfied.
21 The [a]crucible is for silver and the
furnace for gold,
And a man [b]*is tested* by the praise
accorded him.
22 Though you [a]pound a fool in a
mortar with a pestle along with
crushed grain,
Yet his folly will not depart from
him.
23 [a]Know well the [1]condition of your
flocks,
And pay attention to your herds;
24 For riches are not forever,
Nor does a [a]crown *endure* to all
generations.
25 *When* the grass disappears, the new
growth is seen,
And the herbs of the mountains are
[a]gathered in,
26 The lambs *will be* for your clothing,
And the goats *will bring* the price of
a field,
27 And *there will be* goats' milk
enough for your food,
For the food of your household,
And sustenance for your maidens.

Warnings and Instructions

28 THE wicked [a]flee when no one is
pursuing,
But the righteous are [1]bold as a
lion.
2 By the transgression of a land
[a]many are its princes,
But [b]by a man of understanding
and knowledge, so it endures.
3 A [a]poor man who oppresses the
lowly
Is *like* a driving rain [1]which leaves
no food.
4 Those who forsake the law [a]praise
the wicked,
But those who keep the law [b]strive
with them.
5 Evil men [a]do not understand justice,
But those who seek the LORD [b]understand
all things.
6 [a]Better is the poor who walks in his
integrity,
Than he who is [1]crooked though he
be rich.
7 He who keeps the law is a discerning
son,
But he who is a companion of
[a]gluttons humiliates his father.
8 He who increases his wealth by
[a]interest and usury,
Gathers it [b]for him who is gracious
to the poor.
9 He who turns away his ear from
listening to the law,
Even his [a]prayer is an abomination.
10 He who leads the upright astray in
an evil way
Will [a]himself fall into his own pit,
But the [b]blameless will inherit
good.
11 The rich man is [a]wise in his own
eyes,
But the poor who has understanding
[1]sees through him.
12 When the [a]righteous triumph, there
is great glory,
But [b]when the wicked rise, men
[1]hide themselves.
13 He who [a]conceals his transgressions
will not prosper,
But he who [b]confesses and forsakes
them will find compassion.

4 [a]Prov. 6:34; 1 John 3:12
5 [a]Prov. 28:23; Gal. 2:14
6 [1]Or, *excessive* [a]Ps. 141:5; Prov. 20:30 [b]Matt. 26:49
7 [1]Lit., *soul* [2]Lit., *tramples on*
8 [1]Lit., *place* [a]Prov. 26:2; Is. 16:2 [b]Gen. 21:14
9 [1]Lit., *soul's* [a]Ps. 23:5; 141:5
10 [a]Prov. 18:24 [b]1 Kin. 12:6-8; 2 Chr. 10:6-8
11 [a]Prov. 10:1; 23:15; 29:3 [b]Ps. 119:42
12 [1]Lit., *simple*
13 [1]Lit., *strange* [a]Prov. 20:16
14 [a]Ps. 12:2
15 [a]Prov. 19:13
16 [1]Lit., *hide(s)* [2]Lit., *encounters*
18 [a]2 Kin. 18:31; Song 8:12; Is. 36:16; 1 Cor. 3:8; 9:7; 2 Tim. 2:6 [b]Luke 12:42-44; 19:17
20 [1]I.e., The nether world [2]I.e., the place of destruction [a]Job 26:6; Prov. 15:11 [b]Prov. 30:15, 16; Hab. 2:5 [c]Eccl. 1:8; 4:8
21 [a]Prov. 17:3 [b]Luke 6:26
22 [a]Prov. 23:35; 26:11; Jer. 5:3
23 [1]Lit., *face* [a]Jer. 31:10; Ezek. 34:12; John 10:3
24 [a]Job 19:9; Ps. 89:39; Jer. 13:18; Lam. 5:16; Ezek. 21:26
25 [a]Is. 17:5; Jer. 40:10, 12

1 [1]Lit., *confident* [a]Lev. 26:17, 36; Ps. 53:5
2 [a]1 Kin. 16:8-28; 2 Kin. 15:8-15 [b]Prov. 11:11
3 [1]Lit., *and there is no bread* [a]Matt. 18:28
4 [a]Ps. 49:18; Rom. 1:32 [b]1 Kin. 18:18; Neh. 13:11, 15; Matt. 3:7; 14:4; Eph. 5:11
5 [a]Ps. 92:6; Is. 6:9; 44:18 [b]Ps. 119:100; Prov. 2:9; John 7:17; 1 Cor. 2:15; 1 John 2:20, 27
6 [1]Lit., *perverse of two ways* [a]Prov. 19:1
7 [a]Prov. 23:20
8 [a]Ex. 22:25; Lev. 25:36 [b]Job 27:17; Prov. 13:22; 14:31
9 [a]Ps. 66:18; 109:7; Prov. 15:8; 21:27
10 [a]Ps. 7:15; Prov. 26:27 [b]Matt. 6:33; Heb. 6:12; 1 Pet. 3:9
11 [1]Lit., *examines him* [a]Prov. 3:7; 26:5, 12
12 [1]Lit., *will be searched for* [a]Prov. 11:10; 29:2 [b]Prov. 28:28; Eccl. 10:5, 6
13 [a]Job 31:33; Ps. 32:3 [b]Ps. 32:5; 1 John 1:9

14 How blessed is the man who [a]fears always,
But he who [b]hardens his heart will fall into calamity.
15 *Like* a [a]roaring lion and a rushing bear
Is a [b]wicked ruler over a poor people.
16 A [a]leader who is a great oppressor lacks understanding,
But he who hates unjust gain will prolong *his* days.
17 A man who is [a]laden with the guilt of human blood
Will [1]be a fugitive until death; let no one support him.
18 He who walks blamelessly will be delivered,
But he who is [1a]crooked will fall all at once.
19 [a]He who tills his land will [b]have plenty of food,
But he who follows empty *pursuits* will have poverty in plenty.
20 A [a]faithful man will abound with blessings,
But he who [b]makes haste to be rich will not go unpunished.
21 To [1a]show partiality is not good,
[b]Because for a piece of bread a man will transgress.
22 A man with an [a]evil eye [b]hastens after wealth,
And does not know that want will come upon him.
23 He who [a]rebukes a man will afterward find *more* favor
Than he who [b]flatters with the tongue.
24 He who [a]robs his father or his mother,
And says, "It is not a transgression,"
Is the [b]companion of a man who destroys.
25 An [1]arrogant man [a]stirs up strife,
But he who [b]trusts in the LORD [c]will [2]prosper.
26 He who [a]trusts in his own heart is a fool,
But he who walks wisely will be delivered.
27 He who [a]gives to the poor will never want,
But he who [1]shuts his eyes will have many curses.
28 When the wicked rise, men hide themselves;
But when they perish, the righteous increase.

Warnings and Instructions

29 A MAN who hardens *his* neck after [a]much reproof
Will [b]suddenly be broken [1]beyond remedy.
2 When the [a]righteous [1]increase, the people rejoice,
But when a wicked man rules, people groan.
3 A man who [a]loves wisdom makes his father glad,
But he who [b]keeps company with harlots wastes *his* wealth.
4 The [a]king gives stability to the land by justice,
But a man who takes bribes overthrows it.
5 A man who [a]flatters his neighbor
Is spreading a net for his steps.
6 By transgression an evil man is [a]ensnared,
But the righteous [b]sings and rejoices.
7 The [a]righteous [1]is concerned for the rights of the poor,
The wicked does not understand *such* [2]concern.
8 Scorners [a]set a city aflame,
But [b]wise men turn away anger.
9 When a wise man has a controversy with a foolish man,
[1]The foolish man either rages or laughs, and there is no rest.
10 Men of [a]bloodshed hate the blameless,
But the upright [1]are concerned for his life.
11 A [a]fool [1]always loses his temper,
But a [b]wise man holds it back.
12 If a [a]ruler pays attention to falsehood,
All his ministers *become* wicked.
13 The [a]poor man and the oppressor [1]have this in common:
The LORD gives [b]light to the eyes of both.
14 If a [a]king judges the poor with truth,
His [b]throne will be established forever.
15 The [a]rod and reproof give wisdom,
But a child [1]who gets his own way [b]brings shame to his mother.
16 When the wicked [1]increase, transgression increases;
But the [a]righteous will see their fall.
17 [a]Correct your son, and he will give you comfort;
He will also [1b]delight your soul.
18 Where there is [a]no [1]vision, the people [b]are unrestrained,
But [c]happy is he who keeps the law.
19 A slave will not be instructed by words *alone;*
For though he understands, there will be no response.
20 Do you see a man who is [a]hasty in his words?
There is [b]more hope for a fool than for him.
21 He who pampers his slave from childhood
Will in the end find him to be a son.
22 An [a]angry man stirs up strife,
And a hot-tempered man abounds in transgression.

14 [a]Prov. 23:17 [b]Ps. 95:8; Rom. 2:5
15 [a]Prov. 19:12; 1 Pet. 5:8 [b]Ex. 1:14; Prov. 29:2; Matt. 2:16
16 [a]Eccl. 10:16; Is. 3:12
17 [1]Lit., *flee to the pit* [a]Gen. 9:6; Ex. 21:14
18 [1]Lit., *perverse of two ways* [a]Prov. 10:27
19 [a]Prov. 12:11 [b]Prov. 20:13
20 [a]Prov. 10:6; Matt. 24:45; 25:21 [b]Prov. 20:21; 28:22; 1 Tim. 6:9
21 [1]Lit., *regard the face* [a]Prov. 24:23 [b]Ezek. 13:19
22 [a]Prov. 23:6 [b]Prov. 21:5
23 [a]Prov. 27:5, 6 [b]Prov. 29:5
24 [a]Prov. 19:26 [b]Prov. 18:9
25 [1]Lit., *broad soul* [2]Lit., *be made fat* [a]Prov. 15:18 [b]Prov. 29:25; 1 Tim. 6:6 [c]Prov. 11:25
26 [a]Prov. 3:5
27 [1]Lit., *hides* [a]Prov. 11:24; 19:17

1 [1]Lit., *and there is no remedy* [a]1 Sam. 2:25; 2 Chr. 36:16; Prov. 1:24-31 [b]Prov. 6:15
2 [1]Or, *become great* [a]Esth. 8:15; Prov. 11:10; 28:12
3 [a]Prov. 10:1; 15:20; 27:11; 28:7 [b]Prov. 5:10; 6:26; Luke 15:30
4 [a]2 Chr. 9:8; Prov. 8:15; 29:14
5 [a]Ps. 5:9
6 [a]Prov. 22:5; Eccl. 9:12 [b]Ex. 15:1
7 [1]Lit., *knows the cause* [2]Lit., *knowledge* [a]Job 29:16; Ps. 41:1; Prov. 31:8, 9
8 [a]Prov. 11:11 [b]Prov. 16:14
9 [1]Lit., *He*
10 [1]Lit., *seek his soul* [a]Gen. 4:5-8; 1 John 3:12
11 [1]Lit., *sends forth all his spirit* [a]Prov. 12:16; 14:33 [b]Prov. 19:11
12 [a]1 Kin. 12:14
13 [1]Lit., *meet together* [a]Prov. 22:2 [b]Ezra 9:8; Ps. 13:3
14 [a]Ps. 72:4; Is. 11:4 [b]Prov. 16:12; 25:5
15 [1]Lit., *left to himself* [a]Prov. 13:24; 22:15 [b]Prov. 10:1; 17:25
16 [1]Or, *become great* [a]Ps. 37:34, 36; 58:10; 91:8; 92:11; Prov. 21:12
17 [1]Lit., *give delight to* [a]Prov. 13:24; 29:15 [b]Prov. 10:1

18 [1]Or, *revelation* [a]1 Sam. 3:1; Ps. 74:9; Amos 8:11, 12 [b]Ex. 32:25 [c]Ps. 1:1, 2; 106:3; 119:2; Prov. 8:32; John 13:17
20 [a]James 1:19 [b]Prov. 26:12
22 [a]Prov. 15:18; 26:21

23 A man's [a]pride will bring him low,
But a [b]humble spirit will obtain honor.
24 He who is a partner with a thief hates his own life;
He [a]hears the oath but tells nothing.
25 The [a]fear of man [1]brings a snare,
But he who [b]trusts in the LORD will be exalted.
26 [a]Many seek the ruler's [1]favor,
But [b]justice for man *comes* from the LORD.
27 An [a]unjust man is abominable to the righteous,
And he who is [b]upright in the way is abominable to the wicked.

The Words of Agur

30 THE words of Agur the son of Jakeh, the [1]oracle.
The man declares to Ithiel, to Ithiel and Ucal:
2 Surely I am more [a]stupid than any man,
And I do not have the understanding of a man.
3 Neither have I learned wisdom,
Nor do I have the [a]knowledge of the Holy One.
4 Who has [a]ascended into heaven and descended?
Who has gathered the [b]wind in His fists?
Who has [c]wrapped the waters in [1]His garment?
Who has [d]established all the ends of the earth?
What is His [e]name or His son's name?
Surely you know!

5 Every [a]word of God is tested;
He is a [b]shield to those who take refuge in Him.
6 [a]Do not add to His words
Lest He reprove you, and you be proved a liar.

7 Two things I asked of Thee,
Do not refuse me before I die:
8 Keep deception and [1]lies far from me,
Give me neither poverty nor riches;
Feed me with the [a]food that is my portion,
9 Lest I be [a]full and deny [b]*Thee* and say, "Who is the LORD?"
Or lest I be [c]in want and steal,
And [d]profane the name of my God.

10 Do not slander a slave to his master,
Lest he [a]curse you and you be found guilty.

11 There is a [1]kind of *man* who [a]curses his father,
And does not bless his mother.
12 There is a [1]kind who is [a]pure in his own eyes,
Yet is not washed from his filthiness.
13 There is a [1]kind—oh how [a]lofty are his eyes!
And his eyelids are raised *in arrogance.*
14 There is a [1]kind of *man* whose [a]teeth are *like* swords,
And his [b]jaw teeth *like* knives,
To [c]devour the afflicted from the earth,
And the needy from among men.

15 The leech has two daughters,
"Give," "Give."
There are three things that will not be satisfied,
Four that will not say, "Enough":
16 [1a]Sheol, and the [b]barren womb,
Earth that is never satisfied with water,
And fire that never says, "Enough."
17 The eye that [a]mocks a father,
And [1b]scorns a mother,
The [c]ravens of the valley will pick it out,
And the young [c]eagles will eat it.

18 There are three things which are too wonderful for me,
Four which I do not understand:
19 The way of an [a]eagle in the sky,
The way of a serpent on a rock,
The way of a ship in the middle of the sea,
And the way of a man with a maid.
20 This is the way of an [a]adulterous woman:
She eats and wipes her mouth,
And says, "I have done no wrong."

21 Under three things the earth quakes,
And under four, it cannot bear up:
22 Under a [a]slave when he becomes king,
And a fool when he is satisfied with food,
23 Under an unloved woman when she gets a husband,
And a maidservant when she supplants her mistress.

24 Four things are small on the earth,
But they are exceedingly wise:
25 The [a]ants are not a strong folk,
But they prepare their food in the summer;
26 The [a]badgers are not mighty folk,
Yet they make their houses in the rocks;
27 The locusts have no king,
Yet all of them go out in [a]ranks;
28 The lizard you may grasp with the hands,
Yet it is in kings' palaces.

29 There are three things which are stately in *their* march,
Even four which are stately when they walk:
30 The lion *which* is [a]mighty among beasts
And does not [1b]retreat before any,

23 [a]Prov. 11:2; 16:18; Dan. 4:30, 31; Matt. 23:12; James 4:6 [b]Prov. 15:33; 18:12; 22:4; Is. 66:2; Luke 14:11; 18:14; James 4:10
24 [a]Lev. 5:1
25 [1]Lit., *gives* [a]Gen. 12:12; 20:2; Luke 12:4; John 12:42, 43 [b]Ps. 91:1-16; Prov. 18:10; 28:25
26 [1]Lit., *face* [a]Prov. 19:6 [b]Is. 49:4; 1 Cor. 4:4
27 [a]Ps. 6:8; 139:21, 22; Prov. 12:8 [b]Ps. 69:4; Prov. 29:10; Matt. 10:22; 24:9; John 15:18; 17:14; 1 John 3:13
1 [1]Or, *burden*
2 [a]Ps. 49:10; 73:22; Prov. 12:1
3 [a]Prov. 9:10
4 [1]Lit., *the* [a]Ps. 68:18; John 3:13; Eph. 4:8 [b]Ex. 15:10; Ps. 135:7 [c]Job 26:8; 38:8, 9 [d]Ps. 24:2; Is. 45:18 [e]Rev. 19:12
5 [a]Ps. 12:6; 18:30 [b]Ps. 3:3; 84:11; Prov. 2:7
6 [a]Deut. 4:2; 12:32; Rev. 22:18
8 [1]Lit., *words of falsehood* [a]Job 23:12; Matt. 6:11
9 [a]Deut. 8:12; 31:20; Neh. 9:25; Hos. 13:6 [b]Josh. 24:27; Job 31:28 [c]Prov. 6:30 [d]Ex. 20:7
10 [a]Eccl. 7:21
11 [1]Or, *generation* [a]Ex. 21:17; Prov. 20:20
12 [1]Or, *generation* [a]Prov. 16:2; Is. 65:5; Luke 18:11; Titus 1:15, 16
13 [1]Or, *generation* [a]Prov. 6:17; Is. 2:11; 5:15
14 [1]Or, *generation* [a]Ps. 57:4 [b]Job 29:17 [c]Ps. 14:4; Amos 8:4
16 [1]I.e., The nether world [a]Prov. 27:20 [b]Gen. 30:1
17 [1]Lit., *despises to obey* [a]Gen. 9:22 [b]Prov. 15:20 [c]Deut. 28:26
19 [a]Deut. 28:49; Jer. 48:40; 49:22
20 [a]Prov. 5:6
22 [a]Prov. 19:10; Eccl. 10:7
25 [a]Prov. 6:6
26 [a]Lev. 11:5; Ps. 104:18
27 [a]Joel 2:7
30 [1]Lit., *turn back* [a]Judg. 14:18; 2 Sam. 1:23 [b]Mic. 5:8

31 The [1]strutting cock, the male goat
also,
And a king *when his* army is with
him.

32 If you have been foolish in exalting
yourself
Or if you have plotted *evil,* [a]*put
your* hand on your mouth.
33 For the [1]churning of milk produces
butter,
And pressing the nose brings forth
blood;
So the [1]churning of [a]anger produces strife.

The Words of Lemuel

31 THE words of King Lemuel, the
[1]oracle which his mother taught
him.
2 What, O my son?
And what, O [a]son of my womb?
And what, O son of my [b]vows?
3 [a]Do not give your strength to
women,
Or your ways to that which [b]de-
stroys kings.
4 It is not for [a]kings, O Lemuel,
It is not for kings to [b]drink wine,
Or for rulers to desire strong drink,
5 Lest they drink and forget what is
decreed,
And [a]pervert the [1]rights of all the
[2]afflicted.
6 Give strong drink to him who is
[a]perishing,
And wine to him [1b]whose life is
bitter.
7 Let him drink and forget his poverty,
And remember his trouble no
more.
8 [a]Open your mouth for the dumb,
For the [1]rights of all the [2]unfortu-
nate.
9 Open your mouth, [a]judge righteously,
And [1]defend the [b]rights of the
afflicted and needy.

Description of a Worthy Woman

10 An [a]excellent wife, who can find?
For her worth is far [b]above jewels.
11 The heart of her husband trusts in
her,
And he will have no lack of gain.
12 She does him good and not evil
All the days of her life.
13 She looks for wool and flax,
And works with her [1]hands [2]in
delight.
14 She is like [a]merchant ships;
She brings her food from afar.
15 She [a]rises also while it is still night,
And [b]gives food to her household,
And [1]portions to her maidens.
16 She considers a field and buys it;
From [1]her earnings she plants a
vineyard.
17 She [a]girds [1]herself with strength,
And makes her arms strong.
18 She senses that her gain is good;
Her lamp does not go out at night.
19 She stretches out her hands to the
distaff,
And her [1]hands grasp the spindle.
20 She [1a]extends her hand to the poor;
And she stretches out her hands to
the needy.
21 She is not afraid of the snow for
her household,
For all her household are [a]clothed
with scarlet.
22 She makes [a]coverings for herself;
Her clothing is [b]fine linen and
[c]purple.
23 Her husband is known [a]in the
gates,
When he sits among the elders of
the land.
24 She makes [a]linen garments and
sells *them,*
And [1]supplies belts to the [2]trades-
men.
25 Strength and [a]dignity are her clothing,
And she smiles at the [1]future.
26 She [a]opens her mouth in wisdom,
And the [1]teaching of kindness is on
her tongue.
27 She looks well to the ways of her
household,
And does not eat the [a]bread of
idleness.
28 Her children rise up and bless her;
Her husband *also,* and he praises
her, *saying:*
29 "Many daughters have done nobly,
But you excel them all."
30 Charm is deceitful and beauty is
vain,
But a woman who [1a]fears the
LORD, she shall be praised.
31 Give her the [1]product of her hands,
And let her works praise her in the
gates.

31 [1]Lit., *girt in the loins*
32 [a]Job 21:5; 40:4; Mic. 7:16
33 [1]Lit., *pressing* [a]Prov. 10:12; 29:22

1 [1]Or, *burden*
2 [a]Is. 49:15 [b]1 Sam. 1:11
3 [a]Prov. 5:9 [b]Deut. 17:17; 1 Kin. 11:1; Neh. 13:26
4 [a]Eccl. 10:17 [b]Prov. 20:1; Is. 5:22; Hos. 4:11
5 [1]Lit., *judgment* [2]Lit., *sons of affliction* [a]Ex. 23:6; Deut. 16:19; Prov. 17:15
6 [1]Lit., *bitter of soul* [a]Job 29:13 [b]Job 3:20; Is. 38:15
8 [1]Lit., *judgment* [2]Lit., *sons of passing away* [a]Job 29:12-17; Ps. 82
9 [1]Lit., *judge the afflicted* [a]Lev. 19:15; Deut. 1:16 [b]Is. 1:17; Jer. 22:16
10 [a]Ruth 3:11; Prov. 12:4; 19:14 [b]Job 28:18; Prov. 8:11
13 [1]Lit., *palms* [2]Or, *willingly*
14 [a]Ezek. 27:25
15 [1]Or, *prescribed tasks* [a]Prov. 20:13; Rom. 12:11 [b]Luke 12:42
16 [1]Lit., *the fruit of her palms*
17 [1]Lit., *her loins* [a]1 Kin. 18:46; 2 Kin. 4:29; Job 38:3
19 [1]Lit., *palms*
20 [1]Lit., *spreads out her palm* [a]Deut. 15:11; Job 31:16-20; Prov. 22:9; Rom. 12:13; Eph. 4:28
21 [a]2 Sam. 1:24
22 [a]Prov. 7:16 [b]Gen. 41:42; Rev. 19:8, 14 [c]Judg. 8:26; Luke 16:19
23 [a]Deut. 16:18; Ruth 4:1, 11
24 [1]Lit., *gives* [2]Lit., *Canaanite* [a]Judg. 14:12
25 [1]Lit., *latter days* [a]1 Tim. 2:9, 10
26 [1]Or, *law* [a]Prov. 10:31
27 [a]Prov. 19:15
30 [1]Or, *reverences* [a]Ps. 112:1; Prov. 22:4
31 [1]Lit., *fruit*

THE BOOK OF
ECCLESIASTES

The Futility of All Endeavor

1 THE words of the [a]Preacher, the son of David, king in Jerusalem.

2 "[1a]Vanity of vanities," says the
Preacher,
"[1]Vanity of vanities! All is [2]vanity."

3 [a]What advantage does man have in
all his work
Which he does under the sun?
4 A generation goes and a generation
comes,
But the [a]earth [1]remains forever.
5 Also, [a]the sun rises and the sun
sets;
And [1]hastening to its place it rises
there *again.*
6 [1a]Blowing toward the south,
Then turning toward the north,
The wind continues [2]swirling
along;
And on its circular courses the
wind returns.
7 All the rivers [1]flow into the sea,
Yet the sea is not full.
To the place where the rivers [1]flow,
There they [1]flow again.
8 All things are wearisome;
Man is not able to tell *it.*
[a]The eye is not satisfied with seeing,
Nor is the ear filled with hearing.
9 [a]That which has been is that which
will be,
And that which has been done is
that which will be done.
So, there is nothing new under the
sun.
10 Is there anything of which one
might say,
"See this, it is new"?
Already it has existed for ages
Which were before us.
11 There is [a]no remembrance of [1]earlier things;
And also of the [2]later things which
will occur,
There will be for them no remembrance
Among those who will come [2]later
still.

The Futility of Wisdom

12 I, the [a]Preacher, have been king over Israel in Jerusalem.

13 And I [a]set my [1]mind to seek and [b]explore by wisdom concerning all that has been done under heaven. *It* is [2]a grievous [c]task *which* God has given to the sons of men to be afflicted with.

14 I have seen all the works which have been done under the sun, and behold, all is [1a]vanity and striving after wind.

15 What is [a]crooked cannot be straightened, and what is lacking cannot be counted.

16 I [1]said to myself, "Behold, I have magnified and increased [a]wisdom more than all who were over Jerusalem before me; and my [2]mind has observed [3]a wealth of wisdom and knowledge."

17 And I [a]set my [1]mind to know wisdom and to [b]know madness and folly; I realized that this also is [c]striving after wind.

18 Because [a]in much wisdom there is much grief, and increasing knowledge *results in* increasing pain.

The Futility of Pleasure and Possessions

2 I SAID [1]to myself, "Come now, I will test you with [a]pleasure. So [2]enjoy yourself." And behold, it too was futility.

2 [a]I said of laughter, "It is madness," and of pleasure, "What does it accomplish?"

3 I explored with my [1]mind *how* to [a]stimulate my body with wine while my [1]mind was guiding *me* wisely, and how to take hold of [b]folly, until I could see [c]what good there is for the sons of men [2]to do under heaven the [3]few years of their lives.

4 I enlarged my works: I [a]built houses for myself, I planted [b]vineyards for myself;

5 I made [a]gardens and [b]parks for myself, and I planted in them all kinds of fruit trees;

6 I made [a]ponds of water for myself from which to irrigate a forest of growing trees.

7 I bought male and female slaves, and I had [1a]homeborn slaves. Also I possessed flocks and [b]herds larger than all who preceded me in Jerusalem.

8 Also, I collected for myself silver and [a]gold, and the treasure of kings and provinces. I provided for myself [b]male and female singers and the pleasures of men—many concubines.

9 Then I became [a]great and increased more than all who preceded me in Jerusalem. My wisdom also stood by me.

10 And [a]all that my eyes desired I did not refuse them. I did not withhold my heart from any pleasure, for my heart was pleased because of all my labor and this was my [b]reward for all my labor.

11 Thus I considered all my activities which my hands had done and the labor which I had [1]exerted, and behold all was [2a]vanity and striving after wind and there was [b]no profit under the sun.

Wisdom Excels Folly

12 So I turned to [a]consider wisdom, madness and folly, for what *will* the man *do* who will come after the king *except* [b]what has already been done?

13 And I saw that [a]wisdom excels folly as light excels darkness.

14 The wise man's eyes are in his head, but the [a]fool walks in darkness. And yet I know that [b]one fate befalls them both.

---

1 [a]Eccl. 1:12; 7:27; 12:8-10
2 [1]Or, *Futility of futilities* [2]Or, *futile* [a]Ps. 39:5, 6; 62:9; 144:4; Eccl. 12:8; Rom. 8:20
3 [a]Eccl. 2:11; 3:9; 5:16
4 [1]Lit., *stands* [a]Ps. 104:5; 119:90
5 [1]Lit., *panting* [a]Ps. 19:6
6 [1]Lit., *Going* [2]Lit., *turning* [a]Eccl. 11:5; John 3:8
7 [1]Lit., *go*
8 [a]Prov. 27:20; Eccl. 4:8
9 [a]Eccl. 1:10; 2:12; 3:15; 6:10
11 [1]Lit., *first* or *former* [2]Lit., *latter* or *after* [a]Eccl. 2:16; 9:5
12 [a]Eccl. 1:1; 7:27; 12:8-10
13 [1]Lit., *heart* [2]Lit., *an evil* [a]Eccl. 1:17 [b]Eccl. 3:10, 11; 7:25; 8:17 [c]Eccl. 2:23, 26; 3:10; 4:8
14 [1]Or, *futility* [a]Eccl. 2:11, 17; 4:4; 6:9
15 [a]Eccl. 7:13
16 [1]Lit., *spoke with my heart, saying* [2]Lit., *heart* [3]Lit., *an abundance* [a]1 Kin. 3:12; 4:30; 10:23; Eccl. 2:9
17 [1]Lit., *heart* [a]Eccl. 1:13; 7:25 [b]Eccl. 2:12; 7:25 [c]Eccl. 1:14; 2:11, 17, 28; 4:4, 6, 16; 6:9
18 [a]Eccl. 2:23; 12:12

1 [1]Lit., *in my heart* [2]Lit., *consider with goodness* [a]Eccl. 7:4; 8:15
2 [a]Prov. 14:13; Eccl. 7:3, 6
3 [1]Lit., *heart* [2]Lit., *which they do* [3]Lit., *days* [a]Judg. 9:13; Ps. 104:15; Eccl. 10:19 [b]Eccl. 7:25 [c]Eccl. 2:24; 3:12, 13; 5:18; 6:12; 8:15; 12:13
4 [a]1 Kin. 7:1-12 [b]Song 8:11
5 [a]Song 4:16; 5:1 [b]Neh. 2:8
6 [a]Neh. 2:14; 3:15, 16
7 [1]Lit., *sons of the house* [a]Gen. 14:14; 15:3 [b]1 Kin. 4:23
8 [a]1 Kin. 9:28; 10:10, 14, 21 [b]2 Sam. 19:35
9 [a]1 Chr. 29:25; Eccl. 1:16
10 [a]Eccl. 6:2 [b]Eccl. 3:22; 5:18; 9:9
11 [1]Lit., *labored to do* [2]Or, *futility*, and so throughout the ch. [a]Eccl. 1:14; 2:22, 23 [b]Eccl. 1:3; 3:9; 5:16
12 [a]Eccl. 1:17 [b]Eccl. 1:9, 10; 3:15
13 [a]Eccl. 7:11, 12, 19; 9:18; 10:10

14 [a]1 John 2:11 [b]Ps. 49:10; Eccl. 3:19; 6:6; 7:2; 9:2, 3

15 Then I said [1]to myself, "[a]As is the
fate of the fool, it will also befall me.
[b]Why then have I been extremely wise?"
So [2]I said to myself, "This too is vanity."
16 For there is [a]no [1]lasting remembrance of the wise man *as* with the fool,
inasmuch as *in* the coming days all will
be forgotten. And [b]how the wise man
and the fool alike die!
17 So I [a]hated life, for the work which
had been done under the sun was [1]griev-
ous to me; because everything is futility
and striving after wind.

The Futility of Labor

18 Thus I hated [a]all the fruit of my
labor for which I had labored under the
sun, for I must [b]leave it to the man who
will come after me.
19 And who knows whether he will be
a wise man or [a]a fool? Yet he will have
[1]control over all the fruit of my labor for
which I have labored by acting wisely
under the sun. This too is [b]vanity.
20 Therefore I [1]completely despaired
of all the fruit of my labor for which I
had labored under the sun.
21 When there is a man who has
labored with wisdom, knowledge and
[a]skill, then he [b]gives his [1]legacy to one
who has not labored with them. This too
is vanity and a great evil.
22 For what does a man get in [a]all his
labor and in [1]his striving with which he
labors under the sun?
23 Because all his days his task is
painful and [a]grievous; even at night his
[1]mind [b]does not rest. This too is vanity.
24 There is [a]nothing better for a man
than to eat and drink and [1]tell himself
that his labor is good. This also I have
seen, that it is [b]from the hand of God.
25 For who can eat and who can have
enjoyment without [1]Him?
26 For to a person who is good in His
sight [a]He has given wisdom and knowledge and joy, while to the sinner He has
given the task of gathering and collect-
ing so that he may [b]give to one who is
good in God's sight. This too is [c]vanity
and striving after wind.

A Time for Everything

3 THERE is an appointed time for
everything. And there is a [a]time for
every [1]event under heaven—

2 A time to give birth, and a [a]time to die;
A time to plant, and a time to uproot what is planted.
3 A [a]time to kill, and a time to heal;
A time to tear down, and a time to build up.
4 A time to [a]weep, and a time to [b]laugh;
A time to mourn, and a time to [c]dance.
5 A time to throw stones, and a time to gather stones;
A time to embrace, and a time to shun embracing.
6 A time to search, and a time to give up as lost;
A time to keep, and a time to throw away.
7 A time to tear apart, and a time to sew together;
A time to [a]be silent, and a time to speak.
8 A time to love, and a time to [a]hate;
A time for war, and a time for peace.

9 [a]What profit is there to the worker
from that in which he toils?
10 I have seen the [a]task which God
has given the sons of men with which to
occupy themselves.

God Set Eternity in the Heart of Man

11 He has [a]made everything [1]appro-
priate in its time. He has also set eternity
in their heart, [2]yet so that man [b]will not
find out the work which God has done
from the beginning even to the end.
12 I know that there is [a]nothing better
for them than to rejoice and to do good
in one's lifetime;
13 moreover, that every man who eats
and drinks sees good in all his labor—it
is the [a]gift of God.
14 I know that everything God does
will remain forever; there is nothing to
add to it and there is nothing to take
from it, for God has *so* worked that men
should [1][a]fear Him.
15 That [a]which is has been already,
and that which will be has already been,
for God seeks what has passed by.
16 Furthermore, I have seen under the
sun *that* in the place of justice there is
[a]wickedness, and in the place of righteousness there is wickedness.
17 I said [1]to myself, "[a]God will judge
both the righteous man and the wicked
man," for a [b]time for every [2]matter and
for every deed is there.
18 I said [1]to myself concerning the
sons of men, "God has surely tested
them in order for them to see that they
are but [a]beasts."
19 [a]For the fate of the sons of men
and the fate of beasts [1]is the same. As
one dies so dies the other; indeed, they
all have the same breath and there is no
advantage for man over beast, for all is
[2]vanity.
20 All go to the same place. All came
from the [a]dust and all return to the dust.
21 Who knows that the [a]breath of
man ascends upward and the breath of
the beast descends downward to the
earth?
22 And I have seen that [a]nothing is
better than that man should be happy in
his activities, for that is his lot. For who
will bring him to see [b]what will occur
after him?

15 [1]Lit., *in my heart* [2]Lit., *I spoke in heart* [a]Eccl. 2:16 [b]Eccl. 6:8, 11
16 [1]Lit., *forever* [a]Eccl. 1:11; 9:5 [b]Eccl. 2:14
17 [1]Lit., *evil* [a]Eccl. 4:2, 3
18 [a]Eccl. 1:3; 2:11 [b]Ps. 39:6; 49:10
19 [1]Lit., *dominion* [a]1 Kin. 12:13 [b]1 Tim. 6:10
20 [1]Lit., *turned aside my heart to despair*
21 [1]Lit., *share* [a]Eccl. 4:4 [b]Eccl. 2:18
22 [1]Lit., *the striving of his heart* [a]Eccl. 1:3; 2:11
23 [1]Lit., *heart* [a]Job 5:7; 14:1; Eccl. 1:18; 5:17 [b]Ps. 127:2
24 [1]Lit., *cause his soul to see good in his labor* [a]Eccl. 2:3; 3:12, 13, 22; 5:18; 6:12; 8:15; 9:7; Is. 56:12; Luke 12:19; 1 Cor. 15:32; 1 Tim. 6:17 [b]Eccl. 3:13
25 [1]So Gr.; Heb., *me*
26 [a]Job 32:8; Prov. 2:6 [b]Job 27:16, 17; Prov. 13:22 [c]Eccl. 1:14

1 [1]Lit., *delight* [a]Eccl. 3:17; 8:6
2 [a]Job 14:5; Heb. 9:27
3 [a]Gen. 9:6; 1 Sam. 2:6; Hos. 6:1, 2
4 [a]Rom. 12:15 [b]Ps. 126:2 [c]Ex. 15:20
7 [a]Amos 5:13
8 [a]Ps. 101:3; Prov. 13:5
9 [a]Eccl. 1:3; 2:11; 5:16
10 [a]Eccl. 1:13; 2:26
11 [1]Lit., *beautiful* [2]Or, *without which man* [a]Gen. 1:31 [b]Job 5:9; Eccl. 7:23; 8:17; Rom. 11:33
12 [a]Eccl. 2:24
13 [a]Eccl. 2:24; 5:19
14 [1]Or, *be in awe before Him* [a]Eccl. 5:7; 7:18; 8:12, 13; 12:13
15 [a]Eccl. 1:9; 6:10
16 [a]Eccl. 4:1; 5:8; 8:9
17 [1]Lit., *in my heart* [2]Or, *delight* [a]Gen. 18:25; Ps. 96:13; 98:9; Eccl. 11:9; Matt. 16:27; Rom. 2:6-10; 2 Thess. 1:6-9 [b]Eccl. 3:1; 8:6
18 [1]Lit., *in my heart* [a]Ps. 49:12, 20; 73:22
19 [1]Lit., *and they have one fate* [2]Or, *futility* [a]Ps. 49:12; Eccl. 9:12
20 [a]Gen. 3:19; Ps. 103:14; Eccl. 12:7
21 [a]Eccl. 12:7
22 [a]Eccl. 2:24 [b]Eccl. 2:18; 6:12; 8:7; 10:14

The Evils of Oppression

4 THEN I looked again at all the acts of [a]oppression which were being done under the sun. And behold *I saw* the tears of the oppressed and *that* they had [b]no one to comfort *them;* and on the side of their oppressors was power, but they had no one to comfort *them.*

2 So [a]I congratulated the dead who are already dead more than the living who are still living.

3 But [a]better *off* than both of them is the one who has never existed, who has never seen the evil activity that is done under the sun.

4 And I have seen that every labor and every [a]skill which is done is *the result of* rivalry between a man and his neighbor. This too is [1b]vanity and striving after wind.

5 The fool [a]folds his hands and [b]consumes his own flesh.

6 One hand full of rest is [a]better than two fists full of labor and striving after wind.

7 Then I looked again at vanity under the sun.

8 There was a certain man without a [1]dependent, having neither a son nor a brother, yet there was no end to all his labor. Indeed, [a]his eyes were not satisfied with riches *and he never asked,* "And [b]for whom am I laboring and depriving myself of pleasure?" This too is vanity and it is a [c]grievous task.

9 Two are better than one because they have a good return for their labor.

10 For if [1]either of them falls, the one will lift up his companion. But woe to the one who falls when there is not [2]another to lift him up.

11 Furthermore, if two lie down together they [1]keep warm, but [a]how can one be warm *alone?*

12 And if [1]one can overpower him who is alone, two can resist him. A cord of three *strands* is not quickly torn apart.

13 A [a]poor, yet wise lad is better than an old and foolish king who no longer knows *how* to receive [1]instruction.

14 For he has come [a]out of prison to become king, even though he was born poor in his kingdom.

15 I have seen all the living under the sun throng to the side of the second lad who [1]replaces him.

16 There is no end to all the people, to all who were before them, and even the ones who will come later will not be happy with him, for this too is [a]vanity and striving after wind.

Your Attitude Toward God

5 [1a]GUARD your steps as you go to the house of God, and draw near to listen rather than to offer the [b]sacrifice of fools; for they do not know they are doing evil.

2 [1]Do not be [a]hasty [2]in word or [3]impulsive in thought to bring up a matter in the presence of God. For God is in heaven and you are on the earth; therefore let your [b]words be few.

3 For the dream comes through much [1]effort, and the voice of a [a]fool through many words.

4 When you [a]make a vow to God, do not be late in paying it, for *He takes* no delight in fools. [b]Pay what you vow!

5 It is [a]better that you should not vow than that you should vow and not pay.

6 Do not let your [1]speech cause [2]you to sin and do not say in the presence of the messenger *of God* that it was a [a]mistake. Why should God be angry on account of your voice and destroy the work of your hands?

7 For in many dreams and in many words there is [1]emptiness. Rather, [2a]fear God.

8 If you see [a]oppression of the poor and [b]denial of justice and righteousness in the province, do not be [c]shocked at the [1]sight, for one [2]official watches over another [2]official, and there are higher [3]officials over them.

9 After all, a king who cultivates the field is an advantage to the land.

The Folly of Riches

10 [a]He who loves money will not be satisfied with money, nor he who loves abundance *with its* income. This too is [1]vanity.

11 [a]When good things increase, those who consume them increase. So what is the advantage to their owners except to [1]look on?

12 The sleep of the working man is [a]pleasant, whether he eats little or much. But the [1]full stomach of the rich man does not allow him to sleep.

13 There is a grievous evil *which* I have seen under the sun: [a]riches being [1]hoarded by their owner to his hurt.

14 When those riches were lost through [1]a bad investment and he had fathered a son, then there was nothing [2]to support him.

15 [a]As he had come naked from his mother's womb, so will he return as he came. He will [b]take nothing from the fruit of his labor that he can carry in his hand.

16 And this also is a grievous evil—exactly as a man [1]is born, thus will he [2]die. So, [a]what is the advantage to him who [b]toils for the wind?

17 Throughout his life [a]*he* also eats in darkness with [b]great vexation, sickness and anger.

18 Here is what I have seen to be [a]good and [1]fitting: to eat, to drink and [2]enjoy oneself in all one's labor in which he toils under the sun *during* the few [3]years of his life which God has given him; for this is his [4b]reward.

19 Furthermore, as for every man to whom [a]God has given riches and wealth, He has also [b]empowered him to eat from them and to receive his [1]reward and rejoice in his labor; this is the [c]gift of God.

---

1 [a]Job 35:9; Ps. 12:5; Eccl. 3:16; 5:8; Is. 5:7 [b]Jer. 16:7; Lam. 1:9
2 [a]Job 3:11-26; Eccl. 2:17; 7:1
3 [a]Job 3:11-22; Eccl. 6:3; Luke 23:29
4 [1]Or, *futility,* and so throughout the ch. [a]Eccl. 2:21 [b]Eccl. 1:14
5 [a]Prov. 6:10; 24:33 [b]Is. 9:20
6 [a]Prov. 15:16, 17; 16:8
8 [1]Lit., *second* [a]Prov. 27:20; Eccl. 1:8; 5:10 [b]Eccl. 2:21 [c]Eccl. 1:13
10 [1]Lit., *they fall* [2]Lit., *a second*
11 [1]Lit., *have warmth* [a]1 Kin. 1:1-4
12 [1]Lit., *he*
13 [1]Or, *warning* [a]Eccl. 7:19; 9:15
14 [a]Gen. 41:14, 41-43
15 [1]Lit., *stands in his stead*
16 [a]Eccl. 1:14

1 [1]Ch. 4:17 in Heb. [a]Ex. 3:5; 30:18-20; Is. 1:12 [b]1 Sam. 15:22; Prov. 15:8; 21:27
2 [1]Ch. 5:1 in Heb. [2]Lit., *with your mouth* [3]Lit., *hurry your heart* [a]Prov. 20:25 [b]Prov. 10:19; Matt. 6:7
3 [1]Lit., *task* [a]Job 11:2; Prov. 15:2; Eccl. 10:14
4 [a]Num. 30:2; Ps. 50:14; 76:11 [b]Ps. 66:13, 14
5 [a]Prov. 20:25; Acts 5:4
6 [1]Lit., *mouth* [2]Lit., *your body* [a]Lev. 4:2, 22; Num. 15:25
7 [1]Lit., *vanity* [2]Or, *revere* [a]Eccl. 3:14; 7:18; 8:12, 13; 12:13
8 [1]Lit., *delight* [2]Lit., *high one* [3]Lit., *ones* [a]Eccl. 4:1 [b]Ezek. 18:18 [c]1 Pet. 4:12
10 [1]Or, *futility* [a]Eccl. 1:8; 2:10, 11; 4:8
11 [1]Lit., *see with their eyes* [a]Eccl. 2:9
12 [1]Lit., *satiety* [a]Prov. 3:24
13 [1]Lit., *guarded* [a]Eccl. 6:2
14 [1]Lit., *an evil task* [2]Lit., *in his hand*
15 [a]Job 1:21 [b]Ps. 49:17; 1 Tim. 6:7
16 [1]Lit., *comes* [2]Lit., *go* [a]Eccl. 1:3; 2:11; 3:9 [b]Prov. 11:29
17 [a]Ps. 127:2 [b]Eccl. 2:23
18 [1]Lit., *beautiful* [2]Lit., *see good* [3]Or, *days* [4]Or, *share* [a]Eccl. 2:24 [b]Eccl. 2:10
19 [1]Or, *share* [a]2 Chr. 1:12; Eccl. 6:2 [b]Eccl. 6:2 [c]Eccl. 3:13

20 For he will not often [1]consider the
[2]years of his life, because [a]God keeps
[3]him occupied with the gladness of his
heart.

The Futility of Life

6 THERE is an [a]evil which I have
seen under the sun and it is prevalent [1]among men—
2 a man to whom God has [a]given
riches and wealth and honor so that his
soul [b]lacks nothing of all that he desires,
but God has not empowered him to eat
from them, for a foreigner [1]enjoys them.
This is [2]vanity and a severe affliction.
3 If a man fathers a hundred *children*
and lives many years, however many
[1]they be, but his soul is not satisfied with
good things, and he does not even have a
proper [a]burial, *then* I say, "Better [b]the
miscarriage than he,
4 for it comes in futility and goes
into obscurity; and its name is covered
in obscurity.
5 "It never sees the sun and it never
knows *anything;* [1]it is better off than he.
6 "Even if the *other* man lives a thousand years twice and does not [1]enjoy
good things—[a]do not all go to one
place?"
7 [a]All a man's labor is for his mouth
and yet the [1]appetite is not [2]satisfied.
8 For [a]what advantage does the wise
man have over the fool? What *advantage*
does the poor man have, knowing *how* to
walk before the living?
9 What the eyes [a]see is better than
what the soul [1]desires. This too is [b]futil-
ity and a striving after wind.
10 Whatever [a]exists has already been
named, and it is known what man is; for
he [b]cannot dispute with him who is
stronger than he is.
11 For there are many words which
increase futility. What *then* is the advantage to a man?
12 For who knows what is good for a
man during *his* lifetime, *during* the few
[1]years of his futile life? He will [2]spend
them like a shadow. For who can tell a
man [a]what will be after him under the
sun?

Wisdom and Folly Contrasted

7 A [a]GOOD name is better than a good ointment,
And the [b]day of *one's* death is better than the day of one's birth.
2 It is better to go to a house of mourning
Than to go to a house of feasting,
Because [1]that is the [a]end of every man,
And the living [2b]takes *it* to [3]heart.
3 [a]Sorrow is better than laughter,
For [b]when a face is sad a heart may be happy.
4 The [1]mind of the wise is in the house of mourning,
While the [1]mind of fools is in the house of pleasure.
5 It is better to [a]listen to the rebuke of a wise man
Than for one to listen to the song of fools.
6 For as the [1]crackling of [a]thorn bushes under a pot,
So is the [b]laughter of the fool,
And this too is futility.
7 For [a]oppression makes a wise man mad,
And a [b]bribe [1]corrupts the heart.
8 The [a]end of a matter is better than its beginning;
[b]Patience of spirit is better than haughtiness of spirit.
9 Do not be [1a]eager in your heart to be angry,
For anger resides in the bosom of fools.
10 Do not say, "Why is it that the former days were better than these?"
For it is not from wisdom that you ask about this.
11 Wisdom along with an inheritance is good
And an [a]advantage to those who see the sun.
12 For [a]wisdom is [1]protection *just as* money is [1]protection.
But the advantage of knowledge is that [b]wisdom preserves the lives of its possessors.
13 Consider the [a]work of God,
For who is [b]able to straighten what He has bent?
14 [a]In the day of prosperity be happy,
But [b]in the day of adversity consider—
God has made the one as well as the other
So that man may [c]not discover anything *that will be* after him.

15 I have seen everything during my
[1a]lifetime of futility; there is [b]a righteous
man who perishes in his righteousness,
and there is [c]a wicked man who prolongs
his life in his wickedness.
16 Do not be excessively [a]righteous,
and do not [b]be overly wise. Why should
you ruin yourself?
17 Do not be excessively wicked, and
do not be a fool. Why should you [a]die
before your time?
18 It is good that you grasp one thing,
and also not [1]let go of the other; for the
one who [a]fears God comes forth with
[2]both of them.
19 [a]Wisdom strengthens a wise man
more than ten rulers who are in a city.
20 Indeed, [a]there is not a righteous
man on earth who *continually* does good
and who never sins.
21 Also, do not [1]take seriously all
words which are spoken, lest you hear
your servant [a]cursing you.
22 For [1]you also have realized that
you likewise have many times cursed
others.

20 [1]Lit., *remember* [2]Or, *days* [3]So with Gr.
[a]Ex. 23:25

1 [1]Lit., *upon*
[a]Eccl. 5:13
2 [1]Lit., *eats from them* [2]Or, *futility*
[a]1 Kin. 3:13 [b]Ps. 17:14; 73:7; Eccl. 2:10
3 [1]Lit., *the days of his years*
[a]Is. 14:20; Jer. 8:2; 22:19 [b]Job 3:16; Eccl. 4:3
5 [1]Lit., *more rest has this one than that*
6 [1]Lit., *see*
[a]Eccl. 2:14
7 [1]Lit., *soul* [2]Lit., *filled*
[a]Prov. 16:26
8 [a]Eccl. 2:15
9 [1]Lit., *goes after*
[a]Eccl. 11:9 [b]Eccl. 1:14
10 [a]Eccl. 1:9; 3:15
[b]Job 9:32; 40:2; Prov. 21:30; Is. 45:9
12 [1]Lit., *days* [2]Lit., *do*
[a]Eccl. 3:22

1 [a]Prov. 22:1
[b]Eccl. 4:2; 7:8
2 [1]I.e., death [2]Lit., *gives* [3]Lit., *his heart*
[a]Eccl. 2:14, 16; 3:19, 20; 6:6; 9:2, 3 [b]Ps. 90:12
3 [a]Eccl. 2:2
[b]2 Cor. 7:10
4 [1]Lit., *heart*
5 [a]Ps. 141:5; Prov. 6:23; 13:18; 15:31, 32; 25:12; Eccl. 9:17
6 [1]Lit., *voice*
[a]Ps. 58:9; 118:12
[b]Eccl. 2:2
7 [1]Lit., *destroys*
[a]Eccl. 4:1; 5:8 [b]Ex. 23:8; Deut. 16:19; Prov. 17:8, 23
8 [a]Eccl. 7:1 [b]Prov. 14:29; 16:32; Gal. 5:22; Eph. 4:2
9 [1]Lit., *hasty in your spirit*
[a]Prov. 14:17; James 1:19
11 [a]Prov. 8:10, 11; Eccl. 2:13
12 [1]Lit., *in a shadow*
[a]Eccl. 7:19; 9:18
[b]Prov. 3:18; 8:35
13 [a]Eccl. 3:11; 8:17
[b]Eccl. 1:15
14 [a]Deut. 26:11; Eccl. 3:22; 9:7; 11:9
[b]Deut. 8:5; Job 2:10
[c]Eccl. 3:22
15 [1]Lit., *days*
[a]Eccl. 6:12; 9:9
[b]Eccl. 8:14 [c]Eccl. 8:12, 13
16 [a]Prov. 25:16; Phil. 3:6 [b]Rom. 12:3
17 [a]Job 22:16; Ps. 55:23; Prov. 10:27
18 [1]Lit., *rest your hand* [2]Lit., *all*
[a]Eccl. 3:14; 5:7; 8:12, 13; 12:13
19 [a]Eccl. 7:12; 9:13-18
20 [a]1 Kin. 8:46; 2 Chr. 6:36; Ps. 143:2; Prov. 20:9; Rom. 3:23
21 [1]Lit., *give your heart to*
[a]Prov. 30:10
22 [1]Lit., *your heart knows also*

23 I tested all this with wisdom, *and* I
said, “I will be wise,” [a]but it was far
from me.
24 What has been is remote and [a]ex-
ceedingly [1]mysterious. [b]Who can discover it?
25 I [1a]directed my [2]mind to know, to
investigate, and to seek wisdom and an
explanation, and to know the evil of
folly and the foolishness of madness.
26 And I discovered more [a]bitter than
death the woman whose heart is [b]snares
and nets, whose hands are chains. [c]One
who is pleasing to God will escape from
her, but [d]the sinner will be captured by
her.
27 “Behold, I have discovered this,”
says the Preacher, “*adding* one thing to
another to find an explanation,
28 which [1]I am still seeking but have
not found. I have found one man among
a thousand, but I have not found a
[a]woman among all these.
29 “Behold, I have found only this, that
[a]God made men upright, but they have
sought out many devices.”

Obey Rulers

8 WHO is like the wise man and who
knows the interpretation of a matter? A man's wisdom [a]illumines [1]him
and causes his [b]stern face to [2]beam.
2 I say, “Keep the [1]command of the
king because of the [a]oath [2]before God.
3 “Do not be in a hurry [1a]to leave
him. Do not join in an evil matter, for he
will do whatever he pleases.”
4 Since the word of the king is au-
thoritative, [a]who will say to him, “What
are you doing?”
5 He who [a]keeps a *royal* command
[b]experiences no [1]trouble, for a wise heart
knows the proper time and procedure.
6 For [a]there is a proper time and
procedure for every delight, when a
man's trouble is heavy upon him.
7 If no one [a]knows what will happen,
who can tell him when it will happen?
8 [a]No man has authority to restrain
the wind with the wind, or authority
over the day of death; and there is no
discharge in the time of war, and [b]evil
will not deliver [1]those who practice it.
9 All this I have seen and applied my
[1]mind to every deed that has been done
under the sun wherein a man has exer-
cised [a]authority over *another* man to his
hurt.
10 So then, I have seen the wicked
buried, those who used to go in and out
from the holy place, and they are [a]*soon*
forgotten in the city where they did thus.
This too is futility.
11 Because the [a]sentence against an
evil deed is not executed quickly, therefore [b]the hearts of the sons of men
among them are given fully to do evil.
12 Although a sinner does evil a hundred *times* and may [a]lengthen his *life,*
still I know that it will be [b]well for those
who fear God, who fear [1]Him openly.
13 But it will [a]not be well for the evil
man and he will not lengthen his days
like a [b]shadow, because he does not fear
God.
14 There is futility which is done on
the earth, that is, there are [a]righteous
men to whom it [1]happens according to
the deeds of the wicked. On the other
hand, there are [b]evil men to whom it
[1]happens according to the deeds of the
righteous. I say that this too is futility.
15 So I commended pleasure, for there
is nothing good for [a]a man under the sun
except to eat and to drink and to be
merry, and this will stand by him in his
[1]toils *throughout* the days of his life
which God has given him under the sun.
16 When I [a]gave my heart to know
wisdom and to see the task which has
been done on the earth (even though one
should [1b]never sleep day or night),
17 and I saw every work of God, *I
concluded* that [a]man cannot discover the
work which has been done under the
sun. Even though man should seek labo-
riously, he will not discover; and
[b]though the wise man should say, “I
know,” he cannot discover.

Men Are in the Hand of God

9 FOR I have taken all this to my
heart and explain [1]it that righteous
men, wise men, and their deeds are [a]in
the hand of God. [b]Man does not know
whether *it will be* [c]love or hatred; anything [2]awaits him.
2 [a]It is the same for all. There is [b]one
fate for the righteous and for the wicked;
for the good, for the clean, and for the
unclean; for the man who offers a sacrifice and for the one who does not sacrifice. As the good man is, so is the sinner;
as the swearer is, so is the one who [1]is
afraid to swear.
3 This is an evil in all that is done
under the sun, that there is [a]one fate for
all men. Furthermore, [b]the hearts of the
sons of men are full of evil, and [c]insanity
is in their hearts throughout their lives.
Afterwards they *go* to the dead.
4 For whoever is joined with all the
living, there is hope; surely a live dog is
better than a dead lion.
5 For the living know they will die;
but the dead [a]do not know anything, nor
have they any longer a reward, for their
[b]memory is forgotten.
6 Indeed their love, their hate, and
their zeal have already perished, and
they will no longer have a [a]share in all
that is done under the sun.
7 Go *then,* [a]eat your bread in happiness, and drink your wine with a cheerful heart; for God has already approved
your works.
8 Let your [a]clothes be white all the
time, and let not [b]oil be lacking on your
head.
9 Enjoy life with the woman whom
you love all the days of your [1a]fleeting
life which He has given to you under the
sun; for this is your [b]reward in life, and
in your toil in which you have labored
under the sun.

23 [a]Eccl. 3:11; 8:17
24 [1]Lit., *deep* [a]Rom. 11:33 [b]Job 11:7; 37:23; Eccl. 8:17
25 [1]Lit., *turned about* [2]Lit., *heart* [a]Eccl. 1:15, 17; 10:13
26 [a]Prov. 5:4 [b]Prov. 7:23 [c]Prov. 6:23, 24 [d]Prov. 22:14
28 [1]Lit., *my soul still seeks* [a]1 Kin. 11:3
29 [a]Gen. 1:27

1 [1]Lit., *his face* [2]Or, *change* [a]Ex. 34:29, 30 [b]Deut. 28:50
2 [1]Lit., *mouth* [2]Lit., *of* [a]Ex. 22:11; 2 Sam. 21:7; Ezek. 17:18
3 [1]Lit., *to go out from his presence* [a]Eccl. 10:4
4 [a]Job 9:12; Dan. 4:35
5 [1]Lit., *evil thing* [a]Eccl. 12:13 [b]Prov. 12:21
6 [a]Eccl. 3:1, 17
7 [a]Eccl. 3:22; 6:12; 7:14; 9:12
8 [1]Lit., *its possessors* [a]Ps. 49:7 [b]Eccl. 8:13
9 [1]Lit., *heart* [a]Eccl. 4:1; 5:8; 7:7
10 [a]Eccl. 1:11; 2:16; 9:5, 15
11 [a]Ex. 34:6; Ps. 86:15; Rom. 2:4; 2 Pet. 3:9 [b]Eccl. 9:3
12 [1]Lit., *before Him* [a]Eccl. 7:15 [b]Deut. 4:40; 12:25; Ps. 37:11; Prov. 1:33; Is. 3:10
13 [a]Eccl. 8:8; Is. 3:11 [b]Job 14:2; Eccl. 6:12
14 [1]Lit., *strikes* [a]Ps. 73:14; Eccl. 7:15 [b]Job 21:7; Ps. 73:3, 12; Jer. 12:1; Mal. 3:15
15 [1]Lit., *labor* [a]Eccl. 2:24; 3:12, 13; 5:18; 9:7
16 [1]Lit., *see no sleep in his eyes* [a]Eccl. 1:13, 14 [b]Eccl. 2:23
17 [a]Eccl. 3:11 [b]Ps. 73:16; Eccl. 7:23; Rom. 11:33

1 [1]Lit., *all this* [2]Lit., *is before them* [a]Deut. 33:3; Job 12:10; Ps. 119:109 [b]Eccl. 10:14 [c]Eccl. 9:6
2 [1]Lit., *fears an oath* [a]Job 9:22; Eccl. 9:11 [b]Eccl. 2:14; 3:19; 6:6; 7:2
3 [a]Eccl. 9:2; Jer. 17:10 [b]Eccl. 8:11 [c]Eccl. 1:17
5 [a]Job 14:21 [b]Ps. 88:12; Eccl. 1:11; 2:16; 8:10; Is. 26:14
6 [a]Eccl. 2:10; 3:22
7 [a]Eccl. 2:24; 8:15
8 [a]Rev. 3:4 [b]Ps. 23:5
9 [1]Lit., *life of vanity* [a]Eccl. 6:12; 7:15 [b]Eccl. 2:10

Whatever Your Hand Finds to Do

10 Whatever your hand finds to do,
verily, [a]do *it* with all your might; for
there is no [b]activity or planning or
wisdom in [c]Sheol where you are going.
11 I again saw under the sun that the
[a]race is not to the swift, and the [b]battle
is not to the warriors, and neither is
bread to the wise, nor [c]wealth to the
discerning, nor favor to men of ability;
for time and [d]chance overtake them all.
12 Moreover, man does not [a]know his
time: like fish caught in a treacherous
net, and [b]birds trapped in a snare, so the
sons of men are [c]ensnared at an evil time
when it [d]suddenly falls on them.
13 Also this I came to see as wisdom
under the sun, and [1]it impressed me.
14 There [a]was a small city with few
men in it and a great king came to it,
surrounded it, and constructed large
siegeworks against it.
15 But there was found in it a [a]poor
wise man and he [1]delivered the city [b]by
his wisdom. Yet [c]no one remembered
that poor man.
16 So I said, "[a]Wisdom is better than
strength." But the wisdom of the poor
man is despised and his words are not
heeded.
17 The [a]words of the wise heard in
quietness are *better* than the shouting of
a ruler among fools.
18 [a]Wisdom is better than weapons of
war, but [b]one sinner destroys much
good.

A Little Foolishness

10 DEAD flies make a [a]perfumer's
oil stink, so a little foolishness is
weightier than wisdom *and* honor.
2 A wise man's heart *directs him*
toward the right, but the foolish [a]man's
heart *directs him* toward the left.
3 Even when the fool walks along the
road his [1]sense is lacking, and he [2a]dem-
onstrates to everyone *that* he is a fool.
4 If the ruler's [1]temper rises against
you, [a]do not abandon your position,
because [b]composure allays great offenses.
5 There is an evil I have seen under
the sun, like an error which goes forth
from the ruler—
6 [a]folly is set in many exalted places
while rich men sit in humble places.
7 I have seen [a]slaves *riding* [b]on
horses and princes walking like slaves on
the land.
8 [a]He who digs a pit may fall into it,
and a [b]serpent may bite him who breaks
through a wall.
9 He who quarries stones may be
hurt by them, and he who splits logs may
be endangered by them.
10 If the [1]axe is dull and he does not
sharpen *its* edge, then he must [2]exert
more strength. Wisdom has the advantage of giving success.
11 If the serpent bites [1a]before being
charmed, there is no profit for the
charmer.
12 [a]Words from the mouth of a wise
man are gracious, while the lips of a
[b]fool consume him;
13 the beginning of [1]his talking is
folly, and the end of [2]it is wicked [a]mad-
ness.
14 Yet the [a]fool multiplies words. No
man knows what will happen, and who
can tell him [b]what will come after him?
15 The toil of [1]a fool *so* wearies him
that he does not *even* know how to go to
a city.
16 Woe to you, O land, whose [a]king is
a lad and whose princes [1]feast in the
morning.
17 Blessed are you, O land, whose
king is of nobility and whose princes eat
at the appropriate time—for strength,
and not for [a]drunkenness.
18 Through [a]indolence the rafters sag,
and through slackness the house leaks.
19 *Men* prepare a meal for enjoyment,
and [a]wine makes life merry, and [b]money
[1]is the answer to everything.
20 Furthermore, [a]in your bedchamber
do not [b]curse a king, and in your sleeping rooms do not curse a rich man, for a
bird of the heavens will carry the sound,
and the winged creature will make the
matter known.

Cast Your Bread on the Waters

11 CAST your bread on the surface
of the waters, for you [a]will find it
[1]after many days.
2 [a]Divide your portion to seven, or
even to eight, for you do not know what
[b]misfortune may occur on the earth.
3 If the clouds are full, they pour out
rain upon the earth; and whether a tree
falls toward the south or toward the
north, wherever the tree falls, there it
[1]lies.
4 He who watches the wind will not
sow and he who looks at the clouds will
not reap.
5 Just as you do not [a]know [1]the path
of the wind and [b]how bones *are formed*
in the womb of the [2]pregnant woman, so
you do not [c]know the activity of God
who makes all things.
6 Sow your seed [a]in the morning, and
do not [1]be idle in the evening, for you do
not know whether [2]morning or evening
sowing will succeed, or whether both of
them alike will be good.
7 The light is pleasant, and *it is* good
for the eyes to [a]see the sun.
8 Indeed, if a man should live many
years, let him [a]rejoice in them all, and let
him remember the [b]days of darkness, for
they shall be many. Everything that is to
come *will be* futility.
9 Rejoice, young man, during your
childhood, and let your heart be pleasant
during the days of young manhood. And
follow the [1]impulses of your heart and
the [2a]desires of your eyes. Yet know that
[b]God will bring you to judgment for all
these things.

10 [a]Eccl. 11:6; Rom. 12:11; Col. 3:23 [b]Eccl. 9:5 [c]Gen. 37:35; Job 21:13; Is. 38:10
11 [a]Amos 2:14, 15 [b]2 Chr. 20:15; Ps. 76:5; Zech. 4:6 [c]Deut. 8:17, 18 [d]1 Sam. 6:9
12 [a]Eccl. 8:7 [b]Prov. 7:23 [c]Prov. 29:6; Is. 24:18; Hos. 9:8 [d]Luke 21:34, 35
13 [1]Lit., *great it was to me*
14 [a]2 Sam. 20:16-22
15 [1]Or, *might have delivered* [a]Eccl. 4:13 [b]2 Sam. 20:22 [c]Eccl. 2:16; 8:10
16 [a]Prov. 21:22; Eccl. 7:12, 19
17 [a]Eccl. 7:5; 10:12
18 [a]Eccl. 9:16 [b]Josh. 7:1-26; 2 Kin. 21:2-17

1 [a]Ex. 30:25
2 [a]Matt. 6:33; Col. 3:1
3 [1]Lit., *heart* [2]Lit., *says* [a]Prov. 13:16; 18:2
4 [1]Lit., *spirit* [a]Eccl. 8:3 [b]1 Sam. 25:24-33; Prov. 25:15
6 [a]Esth. 3:1, 5f.; Prov. 28:12; 29:2
7 [a]Prov. 19:10 [b]Esth. 6:8-10
8 [a]Ps. 7:15; Prov. 26:27 [b]Amos 5:19
10 [1]Lit., *iron* [2]Lit., *strengthen*
11 [1]Lit., *without enchantment* [a]Ps. 58:4, 5; Jer. 8:17
12 [a]Prov. 10:32; 22:11; Luke 4:22 [b]Prov. 10:14; 18:7; Eccl. 4:5
13 [1]Lit., *the words of his mouth* [2]Lit., *his mouth* [a]Eccl. 7:25
14 [a]Prov. 15:2; Eccl. 5:3 [b]Eccl. 3:22; 6:12; 7:14; 8:7
15 [1]Lit., *fools*
16 [1]Lit., *eat* [a]Is. 3:4, 12
17 [a]Prov. 31:4; Is. 5:11
18 [a]Prov. 24:30-34
19 [1]Lit., *answers all* [a]Judg. 9:13; Ps. 104:15; Eccl. 2:3 [b]Eccl. 7:12
20 [a]2 Kin. 6:12; Luke 12:3 [b]Ex. 22:28; Acts 23:5

1 [1]Lit., *in, within* [a]Deut. 15:10; Prov. 19:17; Matt. 10:42; Gal. 6:9; Heb. 6:10
2 [a]Ps. 112:9; Matt. 5:42; Luke 6:30; 1 Tim. 6:18, 19 [b]Eccl. 11:8; 12:1
3 [1]Lit., *is*
5 [1]Or, with many mss., *how the spirit enters the bones in the womb* [2]Lit., *full* [a]John 3:8 [b]Ps. 139:13-16 [c]Eccl. 1:13; 3:10, 11; 8:17
6 [1]Lit., *let down your hand* [2]Lit., *this or that* [a]Eccl. 9:10

7 [a]Eccl. 6:5; 7:11
8 [a]Eccl. 9:7 [b]Eccl. 12:1
9 [1]Lit., *ways* [2]Lit., *sights* [a]Num. 15:39; Job 31:7; Eccl. 2:10 [b]Eccl. 3:17; 12:14; Rom. 14:10

10 So, remove vexation from your
heart and put away [1a]pain from your
body, because childhood and the prime
of life are fleeting.

Remember God in Your Youth

12 [a]REMEMBER also your Creator
in the days of your youth, before
the [b]evil days come and the years draw
near when you will say, "I have no
delight in them";
2 before the [a]sun, the light, the
moon, and the stars are darkened, and
clouds return after the rain;
3 in the day that the watchmen of the
house tremble, and mighty men [a]stoop,
the grinding ones stand idle because they
are few, and [b]those who look through
[1]windows grow dim;
4 and the doors on the street are shut
as the [a]sound of the grinding mill is low,
and one will arise at the sound of the
bird, and all the [b]daughters of song will
[1]sing softly.
5 Furthermore, [1]men are afraid of a
high place and of terrors on the road;
the almond tree blossoms, the grasshopper drags himself along, and the caper-
berry is ineffective. For man goes to his
eternal [a]home while [b]mourners go about
in the street.
6 *Remember Him* before the silver
cord is [1]broken and the [a]golden bowl is
crushed, the pitcher by the well is shattered and the wheel at the cistern is
crushed;
7 then the [a]dust will return to the
earth as it was, and the [1b]spirit will
return to [c]God who gave it.
8 "[a]Vanity of vanities," says the
Preacher, "all is vanity!"

Purpose of the Preacher

9 In addition to being a wise man,
the Preacher also taught the people
knowledge; and he pondered, searched
out and arranged [a]many proverbs.
10 The Preacher sought to find [a]de-
lightful words and to write [b]words of
truth correctly.
11 The [a]words of wise men are like
[b]goads, and masters of *these* collections
are like [1]well-driven [c]nails; they are
given by one Shepherd.
12 But beyond this, my son, be
warned: the [1]writing of [a]many books is
endless, and excessive [b]devotion *to books*
is wearying to the body.
13 The conclusion, when all has been
heard, *is:* [a]fear God and [b]keep His
commandments, because this *applies to*
[c]every person.
14 For [a]God will bring every act to
judgment, everything which is hidden,
whether it is good or evil.

10 [1]Lit., *evil* [a]2 Cor. 7:1; 2 Tim. 2:22
1 [a]Deut. 8:18; Neh. 4:14; Ps. 63:6; 119:55 [b]Eccl. 11:8
2 [a]Is. 5:30; 13:10; Ezek. 32:7, 8; Joel 3:15; Matt. 24:29
3 [1]Or, *holes* [a]Ps. 35:14; 38:6 [b]Gen. 27:1; 48:10; 1 Sam. 3:2
4 [1]Lit., *be brought low* [a]Jer. 25:10; Rev. 18:22 [b]2 Sam. 19:35
5 [1]Lit., *they* [a]Job 17:13; 30:23 [b]Gen. 50:10; Jer. 9:17
6 [1]So with Gr.; Heb., *removed* [a]Zech. 4:2, 3
7 [1]Or, *breath* [a]Gen. 3:19; Job 34:15; Ps. 104:29; Eccl. 3:20 [b]Job 34:14; Eccl. 3:21; Luke 23:46; Acts 7:59 [c]Num. 16:22; 27:16; Is. 57:16; Zech. 12:1
8 [a]Eccl. 1:2
9 [a]1 Kin. 4:32
10 [a]Prov. 10:32 [b]Prov. 22:20, 21
11 [1]Lit., *planted* [a]Prov. 1:6; 22:17; Eccl. 7:5; 10:12 [b]Acts 2:37 [c]Ezra 9:8; Is. 22:23
12 [1]Lit., *making* [a]1 Kin. 4:32 [b]Eccl. 1:18

13 [a]Eccl. 3:14; 5:7; 7:18; 8:12 [b]Deut. 4:2; Eccl. 8:5 [c]Deut. 10:12; Mic. 6:8
14 [a]Eccl. 3:17; 11:9; Matt. 10:26; Rom. 2:16; 1 Cor. 4:5

THE SONG OF SOLOMON

The Young Shulammite Bride and Jerusalem's Daughters

1 THE [1]Song of [a]Songs, which is
Solomon's.

2 "[1]May he kiss me with the kisses of
his mouth!
For your [a]love is better than wine.
3 "Your [a]oils have a pleasing fragrance,
Your [b]name is *like* [1]purified oil;
Therefore the [2c]maidens love you.
4 "Draw me after you *and* let us run
together!
The [a]king has brought me into his
chambers."

"[1]We will rejoice in you and be glad;
We will [2]extol your [b]love more
than wine.
Rightly do they love you."

5 "[1]I am black but [a]lovely,
O [b]daughters of Jerusalem,
Like the [c]tents of [d]Kedar,
Like the curtains of Solomon.
6 "Do not stare at me because I am
[1]swarthy,
For the sun has burned me.
My [a]mother's sons were angry with
me;
They made me [b]caretaker of the
vineyards,
But I have not taken care of my
own vineyard.
7 "Tell me, O you [a]whom my soul
loves,
Where do you [b]pasture *your flock,*
Where do you make *it* [c]lie down at
noon?
For why should I be like one who
[1]veils herself
Beside the flocks of your [d]compan-
ions?"

Solomon, the Lover, Speaks

8 "[1]If you yourself do not know,
[a]Most beautiful among women,
Go forth on the trail of the flock,
And pasture your young goats
By the tents of the shepherds.

9 "[1]To me, [a]my darling, you are like
My [b]mare among the chariots of
Pharaoh.
10 "Your [a]cheeks are lovely with orna-
ments,
Your neck with strings of [b]beads."

1 [1]Or, *Best of the Songs* [a]1 Kin. 4:32
2 [1]BRIDE [a]Song 1:4; 4:10
3 [1]Lit., *oil which is emptied* (from one vessel to another) [2]Or, *virgins* [a]Song 4:10; John 12:3 [b]Eccl. 7:1 [c]Ps. 45:14
4 [1]CHORUS [2]Lit., *mention with praise* [a]Ps. 45:14, 15 [b]Song 1:4; 4:10
5 [1]BRIDE [a]Song 2:14; 4:3; 6:4 [b]Song 2:7; 3:5, 10; 5:8, 16; 8:4 [c]Ps. 120:5 [d]Is. 60:7
6 [1]Or, *black* [a]Ps. 69:8 [b]Song 8:11
7 [1]Some versions read *wanders* [a]Song 3:1-4 [b]Song 2:16; 6:3 [c]Is. 13:20; Jer. 33:12 [d]Song 8:13
8 [1]BRIDEGROOM [a]Song 5:9; 6:1
9 [1]Lit., *I have compared you to* [a]Song 1:15; 2:2, 10, 13 [b]2 Chr. 1:16, 17
10 [a]Song 5:13 [b]Gen. 24:53; Is. 61:10

11“[1]We will make for you ornaments of gold
With beads of silver.”

12“[1]While the king was at his [2]table,
My [3][a]perfume gave forth its fragrance.
13“My beloved is to me a pouch of [a]myrrh
Which lies all night between my breasts.
14“My beloved is to me a cluster of [a]henna blossoms
In the vineyards of [b]Engedi.”

15“[1,2][a]How beautiful you are, my darling,
[2]How beautiful you are!
Your [b]eyes are *like* doves.”

16“[1,2]How handsome you are, [a]my beloved,
And so pleasant!
Indeed, our couch is luxuriant!
17“The beams of our houses are [a]cedars,
Our rafters, [1][b]cypresses.

The Bride's Admiration

2 “[1]I AM the [2][a]rose of [b]Sharon,
The [c]lily of the valleys.”

2“[1]Like a lily among the thorns,
So is [a]my darling among the [2]maidens.”

3“[1]Like an [2][a]apple tree among the trees of the forest,
So is my beloved among the [3]young men.
In his shade I took great delight and sat down,
And his [b]fruit was sweet to my [4]taste.
4“He has [a]brought me to *his* [1]banquet hall,
And his [b]banner over me is love.
5“Sustain me with [a]raisin cakes,
Refresh me with [1][b]apples,
Because [c]I am lovesick.
6“*Let* [a]his left hand be under my head
And [a]his right hand [b]embrace me.”

7“[1]I [a]adjure you, O [b]daughters of Jerusalem,
By the [c]gazelles or by the [d]hinds of the field,
[a]That you will not arouse or awaken *my* love,
Until [2]she pleases.”

8“[1]Listen! My beloved!
Behold, he is coming,
Climbing [a]on the mountains,
Leaping on the hills!
9“My beloved is like a [a]gazelle or a [b]young [1]stag.
Behold, he is standing behind our wall,
He is looking through the windows,
He is peering [c]through the lattice.
10“My beloved responded and said to me,
‘[a]Arise, my darling, my beautiful one,
And come along.
11 ‘For behold, the winter is past,
The rain is over *and* gone.
12 ‘The flowers have *already* appeared in the land;
The time has arrived for [1]pruning *the vines,*
And the voice of the [a]turtledove has been heard in our land.
13 ‘The [a]fig tree has ripened its figs,
And the [b]vines in blossom have given forth *their* fragrance.
Arise, my darling, my beautiful one,
And come along!’ ”
14“[1]O [a]my dove, [b]in the clefts of the [2]rock,
In the secret place of the steep [3]pathway,
Let me see your [4]form,
[c]Let me hear your voice;
For your voice is sweet,
And your [4]form is [d]lovely.”

15“[1][a]Catch the foxes for us,
The [2]little foxes that are ruining the vineyards,
While our [b]vineyards are in blossom.”
16“[1][a]My beloved is mine, and I am his;
He [b]pastures *his flock* among the lilies.
17“[a]Until [1]the cool of the day when the shadows flee away,
Turn, my beloved, and be like a [b]gazelle
Or a young stag [c]on the mountains of [2]Bether.”

The Bride's Troubled Dream

3 “[1]ON my bed night after night I sought him
[a]Whom my soul loves;
I [b]sought him but did not find him.
2 ‘I must arise now and [1]go about the city;
In the [a]streets and in the squares
[2]I must seek him whom my soul loves.’
I sought him but did not find him.
3“[a]The watchmen who make the rounds in the city found me,
And I said, ‘Have you seen him whom my soul loves?’
4“[a]Scarcely had I [1]left them
When I found him whom my soul loves;
I [b]held on to him and would not let him go,
Until I had [c]brought him to my mother's house,
And into the room of her who conceived me.”

11 [1]CHORUS
12 [1]BRIDE [2]Or, *couch* [3]Lit., *nard* [a]Song 4:14; Mark 14:3; John 12:3
13 [a]Ps. 45:8; John 19:39
14 [a]Song 4:13 [b]1 Sam. 23:29
15 [1]BRIDEGROOM [2]Lit., *Behold* [a]Song 1:16; 2:10, 13; 4:1, 7; 6:4, 10 [b]Song 4:1; 5:12
16 [1]BRIDE [2]Lit., *Behold* [a]Song 2:3, 9, 17; 5:2, 5, 6, 8
17 [1]Or, *junipers* [a]1 Kin. 6:9, 10; Jer. 22:14 [b]2 Chr. 3:5

1 [1]BRIDE [2]Lit., *crocus* [a]Is. 35:1 [b]Is. 33:9; 35:2 [c]Song 5:13; 7:2; Hos. 14:5
2 [1]BRIDEGROOM [2]Lit., *daughters* [a]Song 1:9
3 [1]BRIDE [2]Or, *apricot* [3]Lit., *sons* [4]Lit., *palate* [a]Song 8:5 [b]Song 4:13, 16; 8:11, 12
4 [1]Lit., *house of wine* [a]Song 1:4 [b]Ps. 20:5
5 [1]Or, *apricots* [a]2 Sam. 6:19; 1 Chr. 16:3; Hos. 3:1 [b]Song 7:8 [c]Song 5:8
6 [a]Song 8:3 [b]Prov. 4:8
7 [1]BRIDEGROOM [2]Or, *it* [a]Song 3:5; 5:8, 9; 8:4 [b]Song 1:5 [c]Prov. 6:5; Song 2:9, 17; 3:5; 8:14 [d]Gen. 49:21; Ps. 18:33; Hab. 3:19
8 [1]BRIDE [a]Song 2:17; Is. 52:7
9 [1]Lit., *of the stags* [a]Prov. 6:5; Song 2:17; 3:5; 8:14 [b]Song 2:17; 8:14 [c]Judg. 5:28
10 [a]Song 2:13
12 [1]Or, *singing* [a]Gen. 15:9; Ps. 74:19; Jer. 8:7
13 [a]Matt. 24:32 [b]Song 7:12
14 [1]BRIDEGROOM [2]Or, *crag* [3]Or, *cliff* [4]Lit., *appearance* [a]Song 5:2; 6:9 [b]Jer. 48:28 [c]Song 8:13 [d]Song 1:5
15 [1]CHORUS [2]Or, *young* [a]Ezek. 13:4; Luke 13:32 [b]Song 2:13
16 [1]BRIDE [a]Song 6:3; 7:10 [b]Song 4:5; 6:2, 3
17 [1]Lit., *the day blows* [2]Or, *cleavage* or *a kind of spice* [a]Song 4:6 [b]Song 2:9 [c]Song 2:8

1 [1]BRIDE [a]Song 1:7 [b]Song 5:6
2 [1]Or, *Let me arise* [2]Or, *Let me seek* [a]Jer. 5:1
3 [a]Song 5:7; Is. 21:6-8, 11, 12
4 [1]Lit., *passed* [a]Prov. 8:17 [b]Prov. 4:13; Rom. 8:35, 39 [c]Song 8:2

5"[1]I [a]adjure you, O daughters of Jerusalem,
By the [b]gazelles or by the hinds of the field,
That you will not arouse or awaken *my* love,
Until [2]she pleases."

Solomon's Wedding Day

6"[1,2][a]What is this coming up from the wilderness
Like [b]columns of smoke,
Perfumed with [c]myrrh and [d]frankincense,
With all scented powders of the merchant?
7"Behold, it is the *traveling* couch of Solomon;
Sixty mighty men around it,
Of the mighty men of Israel.
8"All of them are wielders of the sword,
[a]Expert in war;
Each man has his [b]sword at his side,
Guarding against the [1c]terrors of the night.
9"King Solomon has made for himself a sedan chair
From the timber of Lebanon.
10"He made its posts of silver,
Its [1]back of gold
And its seat of purple fabric,
With its interior lovingly fitted out
By the [a]daughters of Jerusalem.
11"Go forth, O [a]daughters of Zion,
And gaze on King Solomon with the [1]crown
With which his mother has crowned him
On the [b]day of his wedding,
And on the day of his gladness of heart."

Solomon's Love Expressed

4 "[1,2]HOW beautiful [a]you are, my darling,
[2]How beautiful you are!
Your [b]eyes are *like* doves [c]behind your veil;
Your [d]hair is like a flock of goats
That have descended from Mount [e]Gilead.
2"Your [a]teeth are like a flock of *newly* shorn ewes
Which have come up from *their* washing,
All of which bear twins,
And not one among them has [1]lost her young.
3"Your lips are like a [a]scarlet thread,
And your [b]mouth is lovely.
Your [c]temples are like a slice of a pomegranate
Behind your veil.
4"Your [a]neck is like the tower of David
Built [1]with rows of stones,
On which are [b]hung a thousand shields,
All the round [c]shields of the mighty men.
5"Your [a]two breasts are like two fawns,
Twins of a gazelle,
Which [b]feed among the lilies.
6"[a]Until [1]the cool of the day
When the shadows flee away,
I will go my way to the mountain of [b]myrrh
And to the hill of [b]frankincense.

7"[a]You are altogether beautiful, my darling,
And there is no blemish in you.
8"*Come* with me from [a]Lebanon, *my* [b]bride,
May you come with me from Lebanon.
[1]Journey down from the summit of [c]Amana,
From the summit of [d]Senir and Hermon,
From the dens of lions,
From the mountains of leopards.
9"You have made my heart beat faster, [a]my sister, *my* bride;
You have made my heart beat faster with a single *glance* of your eyes,
With a single strand of your [b]necklace.
10"[a]How beautiful is your love, my sister, *my* bride!
How much [b]better is your love than wine,
And the [c]fragrance of your oils
Than all *kinds* of [1]spices!
11"Your lips, *my* bride, [a]drip [b]honey;
Honey and milk are under your tongue,
And the fragrance of your garments is like the [c]fragrance of Lebanon.
12"A garden locked is my sister, *my* bride,
A [1]rock garden locked, a [a]spring [b]sealed up.
13"Your shoots are an [1a]orchard of [b]pomegranates
With [c]choice fruits, [d]henna with nard plants,
14 [a]Nard and saffron, calamus and [b]cinnamon,
With all the trees of [c]frankincense,
[d]Myrrh and aloes, along with all the finest [1]spices.
15"*You are* a garden spring,
A well of [1a]fresh water,
And streams *flowing* from Lebanon."

16"[1]Awake, O north *wind*,
And come, *wind of* the south;
Make my [a]garden breathe out *fragrance*,
Let its [2]spices [3]be wafted abroad.
May [b]my beloved come into his garden
And eat its [c]choice fruits!"

---

5 [1]BRIDEGROOM [2]Or, *it* [a]Song 2:7; 5:8; 8:4 [b]Song 2:7
6 [1]CHORUS [2]Lit., *Who* [a]Song 8:5 [b]Ex. 13:21; Joel 2:30 [c]Song 1:13; 4:6, 14; Matt. 2:11 [d]Ex. 30:34; Rev. 18:13
8 [1]Lit., *terror in the nights* [a]Jer. 50:9 [b]Ps. 45:3 [c]Ps. 91:5
10 [1]Or, *support* [a]Song 1:5
11 [1]Or, *wreath* [a]Is. 3:16, 17; 4:4 [b]Is. 62:5

1 [1]BRIDEGROOM [2]Lit., *Behold* [a]Song 1:15 [b]Song 1:15; 5:12 [c]Song 6:7 [d]Song 6:5 [e]Mic. 7:14
2 [1]Or, *miscarried* [a]Song 6:6
3 [a]Josh. 2:18 [b]Song 5:16 [c]Song 6:7
4 [1]Or, *for an arsenal* [a]Song 7:4 [b]Ezek. 27:10, 11 [c]2 Sam. 1:21
5 [a]Song 7:3 [b]Song 2:16; 6:2, 3
6 [1]Lit., *the day blows* [a]Song 2:17 [b]Song 4:14
7 [a]Song 1:15; Eph. 5:27
8 [1]Or, *Look* [a]1 Kin. 4:33; Ps. 72:16 [b]Song 5:1; Is. 62:5 [c]2 Kin. 5:12 [d]Deut. 3:9; 1 Chr. 5:23; Ezek. 27:5
9 [a]Song 4:10, 12; 5:1, 2 [b]Gen. 41:42; Prov. 1:9; Ezek. 16:11; Dan. 5:7
10 [1]Or, *balsam odors* [a]Song 7:6 [b]Song 1:2, 4 [c]Song 1:3
11 [a]Prov. 5:3 [b]Ps. 19:10; Prov. 24:13 [c]Gen. 27:27; Hos. 14:6
12 [1]Lit., *stone heap* [a]Prov. 5:15-18 [b]Gen. 29:3
13 [1]Or, *park* or *paradise* [a]Eccl. 2:5 [b]Song 6:11; 7:12 [c]Song 2:3; 4:16; 7:13 [d]Song 1:14
14 [1]Or, *balsam odors* [a]Song 1:12 [b]Ex. 30:23 [c]Song 4:6 [d]Ps. 45:8; Song 3:6; John 19:39
15 [1]Lit., *living* [a]Zech. 14:8; John 4:10
16 [1]BRIDE [2]Or, *balsam odors* [3]Lit., *flow forth* [a]Song 5:1; 6:2 [b]Song 1:13; 2:3, 8; 6:2 [c]Song 4:13

The Torment of Separation

5 "[1]I HAVE [a]come into my garden, [b]my sister, *my* bride;
I have gathered my [c]myrrh along with my balsam.
I have eaten my honeycomb [2]and my [d]honey;
I have [e]drunk my wine [2]and my milk.
Eat, [f]friends;
Drink and [3]imbibe deeply, O lovers."

2 "[1]I was asleep, but my heart was awake.
A voice! My beloved was knocking:
'Open to me, [a]my sister, my darling,
[b]My dove, my perfect one!
For my head is [2]drenched with dew,
My [c]locks with the [3]damp of the night.'
3 "I have [a]taken off my dress,
How can I put it on *again?*
I have [b]washed my feet,
How can I dirty them *again?*
4 "My beloved extended his hand through the opening,
And my [1a]feelings were aroused for him.
5 "I arose to open to my beloved;
And my hands [a]dripped with myrrh,
And my fingers with [1]liquid myrrh,
On the handles of the bolt.
6 "I opened to my beloved,
But my beloved had [a]turned away *and* had gone!
My [1]heart went out *to him* as he [b]spoke.
I [c]searched for him, but I did not find him;
I [d]called him, but he did not answer me.
7 "The [a]watchmen who make the rounds in the city found me,
They struck me *and* wounded me;
The guardsmen of the walls took away my shawl from me.
8 "I [a]adjure you, O daughters of Jerusalem,
If you find my beloved,
As to what you will tell him:
For [b]I am lovesick."

9 "[1,2]What kind of beloved is your beloved,
O [a]most beautiful among women?
[2]What kind of beloved is your beloved,
That thus you adjure us?"

Admiration by the Bride

10 "[1]My beloved is dazzling and [a]ruddy,
[2b]Outstanding among ten thousand.
11 "His head is *like* gold, pure gold;
His [a]locks are *like* clusters of dates,
And black as a raven.

1 [1]BRIDEGROOM [2]Lit., *with* [3]Or, *become drunk* [a]Song 6:2 [b]Song 4:9 [c]Song 1:13; 4:14 [d]Song 4:11 [e]Prov. 9:5; Is. 55:1 [f]Judg. 14:11, 20; John 3:29
2 [1]BRIDE [2]Lit., *filled* [3]Lit., *drops* [a]Song 4:9 [b]Song 2:14; 6:9 [c]Song 5:11
3 [a]Luke 11:7 [b]Gen. 19:2
4 [1]Lit., *bowels* [a]Jer. 31:20
5 [1]Lit., *passing* [a]Song 5:13
6 [1]Lit., *soul* [a]Song 6:1 [b]Song 5:2 [c]Song 3:1 [d]Prov. 1:28
7 [a]Song 3:3
8 [a]Song 2:7; 3:5 [b]Song 2:5
9 [1]CHORUS [2]Or, *What is your beloved more than another beloved* [a]Song 1:8; 6:1
10 [1]BRIDE [2]Lit., *Lifted up banner* [a]1 Sam. 16:12 [b]Ps. 45:2
11 [a]Song 5:2
12 [1]Lit., *sitting upon* [a]Song 1:15; 4:1 [b]Ex. 25:7
13 [a]Song 6:2 [b]Song 2:1 [c]Song 5:5
14 [1]Lit., *lapis lazuli* [a]Ex. 28:20; 39:13; Ezek. 1:16; Dan. 10:6 [b]Ex. 24:10; 28:18; Job 28:16; Is. 54:11
15 [a]Song 7:4 [b]1 Kin. 4:33; Ps. 80:10; Ezek. 17:23; 31:8
16 [1]Lit., *palate* [a]Song 7:9 [b]2 Sam. 1:23

1 [1]CHORUS [a]Song 5:6 [b]Song 1:8
2 [1]BRIDE [a]Song 4:16; 5:1 [b]Song 5:13 [c]Song 1:7 [d]Song 2:1; 5:13
3 [a]Song 2:16; 7:10 [b]Song 2:16; 4:5
4 [1]BRIDEGROOM [2]Lit., *bannered ones* [a]Song 1:15 [b]1 Kin. 14:17 [c]Song 1:5 [d]Ps. 48:2; 50:2 [e]Song 6:10
5 [a]Song 4:1
6 [1]Or, *miscarried* [a]Song 4:2
7 [a]Song 4:3
8 [1]Or, *virgins* [a]1 Kin. 11:3 [b]Song 1:3
9 [1]Lit., *one* [2]Lit., *daughters* [a]Song 2:14; 5:2 [b]Gen. 30:13 [c]1 Kin. 11:3

12 "His [a]eyes are like doves,
Beside streams of water,
Bathed in milk,
And [1]reposed in *their* [b]setting.
13 "His cheeks are like a [a]bed of balsam,
Banks of sweet-scented herbs;
His lips are [b]lilies,
[c]Dripping with liquid myrrh.
14 "His hands are rods of gold
Set with [a]beryl;
His abdomen is carved ivory
Inlaid with [1b]sapphires.
15 "His legs are pillars of alabaster
Set on pedestals of pure gold;
His appearance is like [a]Lebanon,
Choice as the [b]cedars.
16 "His [1a]mouth is *full of* sweetness.
And he is wholly [b]desirable.
This is my beloved and this is my friend,
O daughters of Jerusalem."

Mutual Delight in Each Other

6 "[1a]WHERE has your beloved gone,
O [b]most beautiful among women?
Where has your beloved turned,
That we may seek him with you?"

2 "[1]My beloved has gone down to his [a]garden,
To the [b]beds of balsam,
To [c]pasture *his flock* in the gardens
And gather [d]lilies.
3 "[a]I am my beloved's and my beloved is mine,
He who [b]pastures *his flock* among the lilies."

4 "[1a]You are as beautiful as [b]Tirzah, my darling,
As [c]lovely as [d]Jerusalem,
As [e]awesome as [2]an army with banners.
5 "Turn your eyes away from me,
For they have confused me;
[a]Your hair is like a flock of goats
That have descended from Gilead.
6 "[a]Your teeth are like a flock of ewes
Which have come up from *their* washing,
All of which bear twins,
And not one among them has [1]lost her young.
7 "[a]Your temples are like a slice of a pomegranate
Behind your veil.
8 "There are sixty [a]queens and eighty concubines,
And [1b]maidens without number;
9 *But* [a]my dove, my perfect one, is [1]unique:
She is her mother's [1]only *daughter;*
She is the pure *child* of the one who bore her.
The [2b]maidens saw her and called her blessed,
The [c]queens and the concubines *also,* and they praised her, *saying,*

10 'Who is this that [1]grows like the dawn,
As beautiful as the full [a]moon,
As pure [b]as the sun,
As [c]awesome as [2]an army with banners?'
11 "I went down to the orchard of nut trees
To see the blossoms of the valley,
To see whether [a]the vine had budded
Or the [b]pomegranates had bloomed.
12 "Before I was aware, my soul set me
Over the chariots of [1]my noble people."

13 "[1,2]Come back, come back, O Shulammite;
Come back, come back, that we may gaze at you!"

"[3]**W**hy should you gaze at the Shulammite,
As at the [a]dance of [4b]the two companies?

Admiration by the Bridegroom

7 "[1]HOW beautiful are your [2]feet in sandals,
O [3a]prince's daughter!
The curves of your hips are like [4]jewels,
The work of the hands of an artist.
2 "Your navel is *like* a round goblet
Which never lacks mixed wine;
Your belly is like a heap of wheat
Fenced about with lilies.
3 "Your [a]two breasts are like two fawns,
Twins of a gazelle.
4 "Your [a]neck is like a tower of ivory,
Your eyes *like* the pools in [b]Heshbon
By the gate of Bath-rabbim;
Your nose is like the tower of Lebanon,
Which faces toward Damascus.
5 "Your head [1]crowns you like [a]Carmel,
And the flowing locks of your head are like purple threads;
The king is captivated by *your* tresses.
6 "How [a]beautiful and how delightful you are,
[1]*My* love, with *all* your charms!
7 "[1]Your stature is like a palm tree,
And your breasts are *like its* clusters.
8 "I said, 'I will climb the palm tree,
I will take hold of its fruit stalks.'
Oh, may your breasts be like clusters of the vine,
And the fragrance of your [1]breath like [2a]apples,
9 And your [1a]mouth like the best wine!"

"[2]**I**t [b]goes *down* smoothly for my beloved,
Flowing gently *through* the lips of those who fall asleep.

The Union of Love

10 "[a]I am my beloved's,
And his [b]desire is for me.
11 "Come, my beloved, let us go out into the [1]country,
Let us spend the night in the villages.
12 "Let us rise early *and go* to the vineyards;
Let us [a]see whether the vine has budded
And its blossoms have opened,
And whether the pomegranates have bloomed.
There I will give you my love.
13 "The [a]mandrakes have given forth fragrance;
And over our doors are all [b]choice *fruits,*
Both new and old,
Which I have saved up for you, my beloved.

The Lovers Speak

8 "OH that you were like a brother to me
Who nursed at my mother's breasts.
If I found you outdoors, I would kiss you;
No one would despise me, either.
2 "I would lead you *and* [a]bring you
Into the house of my mother, who used to instruct me;
I would give you spiced wine to drink from the juice of my pomegranates.
3 "Let [a]his left hand be under my head,
And his right hand embrace me."

4 "[1a]I want you to swear, O daughters of Jerusalem,
[2]Do not arouse or awaken *my* love,
Until [3]she pleases."

5 "[1a]Who is this coming up from the wilderness,
Leaning on her beloved?"

"[2]**B**eneath the [3b]apple tree I awakened you;
There your mother was in labor with you,
There she was in labor *and* gave you birth.
6 "Put me like a [1]seal over your heart,
Like a [a]seal on your arm.
For love is as strong as death,
[2b]Jealousy is as severe as Sheol;
Its flashes are flashes of fire,
[3]The *very* flame of the LORD.
7 "Many waters cannot quench love,
Nor will rivers overflow it;
[a]If a man were to give all the riches of his house for love,
It would be utterly despised."

8 "[1]We have a little sister,
And she [a]has no breasts;
What shall we do for our sister
On the day when she is spoken for?

10 [1]Lit., *looks down* [2]Lit., *bannered ones* [a]Job 31:26 [b]Matt. 17:2; Rev. 1:16 [c]Song 6:4

11 [a]Song 7:12 [b]Song 4:13

12 [1]Another reading is *Amminadib*

13 [1]CHORUS [2]Ch. 7:1 in Heb. [3]BRIDEGROOM [4]Or, *Mahanaim* [a]Judg. 21:21 [b]Gen. 32:2; 2 Sam. 17:24

1 [1]Ch. 7:2 in Heb. [2]Lit., *footsteps* [3]Or, *nobleman's* [4]Or, *ornaments* [a]Ps. 45:13

3 [a]Song 4:5

4 [a]Song 4:4 [b]Num. 21:26

5 [1]Lit., *is upon* [a]Is. 35:2

6 [1]Or, With *love among your delights* [a]Song 1:15, 16; 4:10

7 [1]Lit., *This stature of yours*

8 [1]Lit., *nose* [2]Or, *apricots* [a]Song 2:5

9 [1]Lit., *palate* [2]BRIDE [a]Song 5:16 [b]Prov. 23:31

10 [a]Song 2:16; 6:3 [b]Ps. 45:11; Gal. 2:20

11 [1]Lit., *field*

12 [a]Song 6:11

13 [a]Gen. 30:14 [b]Song 2:3; 4:13, 16; Matt. 13:52

2 [a]Song 3:4

3 [a]Song 2:6

4 [1]BRIDEGROOM [2]Or, *Why should you arouse* [3]Or, *it* [a]Song 2:7; 3:5

5 [1]CHORUS [2]BRIDEGROOM [3]Or, *apricot* [a]Song 3:6 [b]Song 2:3

6 [1]Or, *signet* [2]Or, Its *ardor is as inflexible* [3]Another reading is *A vehement flame* [a]Is. 49:16; Jer. 22:24; Hag. 2:23 [b]Prov. 6:34

7 [a]Prov. 6:35

8 [1]CHORUS [a]Ezek. 16:7

9"If she is a wall,
We shall build on her a battlement of silver;
But if she is a door,
We shall barricade her with [a]planks of cedar."

10"[1]I was a wall, and [a]my breasts were like towers;
Then I became in his eyes as one who finds peace.
11"Solomon had a [a]vineyard at Baal-hamon;
He [b]entrusted the vineyard to [c]caretakers;
Each one was to bring a [d]thousand *shekels* of silver for its [e]fruit.
12"My very own vineyard is [1]at my disposal;
The thousand *shekels* are for you, Solomon,
And two hundred are for those who take care of its fruit."
13"[1]O you who sit in the gardens,
My [a]companions are listening for your voice—
[b]Let me hear it!"
14"[1,2]Hurry, my beloved,
And be [a]like a gazelle or a young [3]stag
On the [b]mountains of spices."

9 [a]1 Kin. 6:15
10 [1]BRIDE [a]Ezek. 16:7
11 [a]Eccl. 2:4 [b]Matt. 21:33 [c]Song 1:6 [d]Is. 7:23 [e]Song 2:3; 8:12
12 [1]Lit., *before me*
13 [1]BRIDEGROOM [a]Song 1:7 [b]Song 2:14
14 [1]BRIDE [2]Lit., *Flee* [3]Lit., *of the stags* [a]Song 2:7, 9, 17 [b]Song 4:6

THE BOOK OF ISAIAH

Rebellion of God's People

1 THE vision of Isaiah the son of
Amoz, concerning [a]Judah and Jerusalem which he saw during the [1]reigns of
[b]Uzziah, [c]Jotham, [d]Ahaz, *and* [e]Hez-
ekiah, kings of Judah.
2 [a]Listen, O heavens, and hear, O [b]earth;
For the LORD speaks,
"[c]Sons I have reared and brought up,
But they have [d]revolted against Me.
3"An ox knows its owner,
And a donkey its master's manger,
But Israel [a]does not know,
My people [b]do not understand."

4 Alas, sinful nation,
People weighed down with iniquity,
[1a]Offspring of evildoers,
Sons who [b]act corruptly!
They have [c]abandoned the LORD,
They have [d]despised the Holy One of Israel,
They have turned away [2]from Him.

5 Where will you be stricken again,
As you [a]continue in *your* rebellion?
The whole head is [b]sick,
And the whole heart is faint.
6 [a]From the sole of the foot even to the head
There is [b]nothing sound in it,
Only bruises, welts, and raw wounds,
[c]Not pressed out or bandaged,
Nor softened with oil.

7 Your [a]land is desolate,
Your cities are burned with fire,
Your fields—strangers are devouring them in your presence;
[1]It is desolation, as overthrown by strangers.
8 And the daughter of Zion is left like a shelter in a vineyard,
Like a watchman's hut in a cucumber field, like a besieged city.
9 [a]Unless the LORD of hosts
Had left us a few [b]survivors,
We would be like [c]Sodom,
We would be like Gomorrah.

God Has Had Enough

10 Hear [a]the word of the LORD,
You rulers of [b]Sodom;
Give ear to the instruction of our God,
You people of Gomorrah.
11"[a]What are your multiplied sacrifices to Me?"
Says the LORD.
"I [1]have had enough of burnt offerings of rams,
And the fat of fed cattle.
And I take no pleasure in the blood of bulls, lambs, or goats.
12"When you come [a]to appear before Me,
Who requires [1]of you this trampling of My courts?
13"Bring your worthless offerings no longer,
[a]Incense is an abomination to Me.
[b]New moon and sabbath, the [c]calling of assemblies—
I cannot [d]endure iniquity and the solemn assembly.
14"I hate your new moon *festivals* and your [a]appointed feasts,
They have become a burden to Me.
I am [b]weary of bearing *them.*
15"So when you [a]spread out your hands *in prayer,*
[b]I will hide My eyes from you,
Yes, even though you [c]multiply prayers,
I will not listen.
[d]Your hands are [1]covered with blood.

16"[a]Wash yourselves, [b]make yourselves clean;
[c]Remove the evil of your deeds from My sight.
[d]Cease to do evil,

1 [1]Lit., *days* [a]Is. 2:1; 40:9 [b]2 Kin. 15:1-7, 13; 2 Chr. 26:1-23 [c]2 Kin. 15:32-38; 2 Chr. 27:1-9 [d]2 Kin. 16:1-20; 2 Chr. 28:1-27; Is. 7:1 [e]2 Kin. 18:1-20:21; 2 Chr. 29:1-32:33
2 [a]Deut. 32:1 [b]Mic. 1:2 [c]Jer. 3:22 [d]Is. 30:1, 9; 65:2
3 [a]Jer. 9:3, 6 [b]Is. 44:18
4 [1]Lit., *Seed* [2]Lit., *backward* [a]Is. 14:20 [b]Neh. 1:7 [c]Is. 1:28 [d]Is. 5:24
5 [a]Is. 31:6 [b]Is. 33:24; Ezek. 34:4, 16
6 [a]Job 2:7 [b]Ps. 38:3 [c]Jer. 8:22
7 [1]Lit., *And* [a]Lev. 26:33; Jer. 44:6
9 [a]Rom. 9:29 [b]Is. 10:20-22; 11:11, 16; 37:4, 31, 32; 46:3 [c]Gen. 19:24
10 [a]Is. 8:20; 28:14 [b]Is. 3:9; Ezek. 16:49; Rom. 9:29; Rev. 11:8
11 [1]Or, *am sated with* [a]Ps. 50:8; Jer. 6:20; Amos 5:21, 22; Mal. 1:10
12 [1]Lit., *of your hand* [a]Ex. 23:17
13 [a]Is. 66:3 [b]1 Chr. 23:31 [c]Ex. 12:16 [d]Jer. 7:9, 10
14 [a]Is. 29:1, 2 [b]Is. 7:13; 43:24
15 [1]Lit., *full of* [a]1 Kin. 8:22; Lam. 1:17 [b]Is. 8:17; 59:2 [c]Mic. 3:4 [d]Is. 59:3
16 [a]Ps. 26:6 [b]Is. 52:11 [c]Is. 55:7 [d]Jer. 25:5

17 Learn to do good;
[a]Seek justice,
Reprove the ruthless;
[1b]Defend the orphan,
Plead for the widow.

"Let Us Reason"

18 "Come now, and [a]let us reason together,"
Says the LORD,
"[b]Though your sins are as scarlet,
They will be as white as snow;
Though they are red like crimson,
They will be like wool.
19 "[a]If you consent and obey,
You will [b]eat the best of the land;
20 "But if you refuse and rebel,
You will be [a]devoured by the sword."
Truly, [b]the mouth of the LORD has spoken.

Zion Corrupted, to be Redeemed

21 How the faithful city has become a [a]harlot,
She *who* was full of justice!
Righteousness once lodged in her,
But now murderers.
22 Your silver has become dross,
Your drink diluted with water.
23 Your [a]rulers are rebels,
And companions of thieves;
Everyone [b]loves a bribe,
And chases after rewards.
They [c]do not [1]defend the [2]orphan,
Nor does the widow's plea come before them.

24 Therefore the Lord [1]GOD of hosts,
The [a]Mighty One of Israel declares,
"Ah, I will be relieved of My adversaries,
And [b]avenge Myself on My foes.
25 "I will also turn My hand against you,
And will [a]smelt away your dross as with lye,
And will remove all your alloy.
26 "Then I will restore your [a]judges as at the first,
And your counselors as at the beginning;
After that you will be called the [b]city of righteousness,
A faithful city."

27 Zion will be [a]redeemed with justice,
And her [1]repentant ones with righteousness.
28 But [1]transgressors and sinners will be [a]crushed together,
And those who forsake the LORD shall come to an end.
29 Surely, [1]you will be ashamed of the [2a]oaks which you have desired,
And you will be embarrassed at the [b]gardens which you have chosen.
30 For you will be like an [1]oak whose [a]leaf fades away,
Or as a garden that has no water.
31 And the strong man will become tinder,
His work also a spark.
Thus they shall both [a]burn together,
And there will be [b]none to quench *them*.

God's Universal Reign

2 THE word which [a]Isaiah the son of Amoz saw concerning Judah and Jerusalem.
2 Now it will come about that
[a]In the last days,
The [b]mountain of the house of the LORD
Will be established [1]as the chief of the mountains,
And will be raised above the hills;
And [c]all the nations will stream to it.
3 And many peoples will come and say,
"Come, let us go up to the mountain of the LORD,
To the house of the God of Jacob;
That He may teach us [1]concerning His ways,
And that we may walk in His paths."
For the [2]law will go forth [a]from Zion,
And the word of the LORD from Jerusalem.
4 And He will judge between the nations,
And will [1]render decisions for many peoples;
And [a]they will hammer their swords into plowshares, and their spears into pruning hooks.
[b]Nation will not lift up sword against nation,
And never again will they learn war.

5 Come, [a]house of Jacob, and let us walk in the [b]light of the LORD.
6 For Thou hast [a]abandoned Thy people, the house of Jacob,
Because they are filled *with influences* from the east,
And *they are* soothsayers [b]like the Philistines,
And they [c]strike *bargains* with the children of foreigners.
7 Their land has also been filled with silver and gold,
And there is no end to their treasures;
Their land has also been filled with [a]horses,
And there is no end to their chariots.
8 Their land has also been [a]filled with idols;
They worship the [b]work of their hands,
That which their fingers have made.
9 So [a]the *common* man has been humbled,
And the man *of importance* has been abased,
But [b]do not forgive them.

17 [1]Or, *Vindicate the fatherless* [a]Jer. 22:3; Zeph. 2:3 [b]Ps. 82:3

18 [a]Is. 41:1, 21; 43:26; Mic. 6:2 [b]Ps. 51:7; Is. 43:25; 44:22; Rev. 7:14

19 [a]Deut. 28:1; 30:15, 16 [b]Is. 55:2

20 [a]Is. 3:25; 65:12 [b]Is. 40:5; 58:14; Mic. 4:4; Titus 1:2

21 [a]Is. 57:3-9; Jer. 2:20

23 [1]Or, *vindicate* [2]Or, *fatherless* [a]Hos. 5:10; Mic. 7:3 [b]Ex. 23:8; Mic. 7:3 [c]Is. 10:2; Jer. 5:28; Ezek. 22:7; Zech. 7:10

24 [1]Heb., *YHWH*, usually rendered *LORD* [a]Ps. 132:2; Is. 49:26; 60:16 [b]Deut. 28:63; Is. 35:4; 59:18; 61:2; 63:4

25 [a]Ezek. 22:19-22; Mal. 3:3

26 [a]Is. 60:17 [b]Is. 33:5; 60:14; 62:1, 2; Zech. 8:3

27 [1]Or, *returnees* [a]Is. 35:9f.; 62:12; 63:4

28 [1]Lit., the *crushing of transgressors and sinners shall be together* [a]Ps. 9:5; Is. 66:24; 2 Thess. 1:8, 9

29 [1]So with some mss.; M.T., *they* [2]Or, *terebinths* [a]Is. 57:5 [b]Is. 65:3; 66:17

30 [1]Or, *terebinth* [a]Is. 64:6

31 [a]Is. 5:24; 9:19; 26:11; 33:11-14 [b]Is. 66:24; Matt. 3:12; Mark 9:43

1 [a]Is. 1:1

2 [1]Lit., *on* [a]Mic. 4:1-3 [b]Is. 27:13; 66:20 [c]Is. 56:7

3 [1]Or, *some of* [2]Or, *instruction* [a]Is. 51:4, 5; Luke 24:47

4 [1]Or, *reprove many* [a]Is. 32:17, 18; Joel 3:10 [b]Is. 9:5, 7; 11:6-9; Hos. 2:18; Zech. 9:10

5 [a]Is. 58:1 [b]Is. 60:1, 2, 19, 20; 1 John 1:5

6 [a]Deut. 31:17 [b]2 Kin. 1:2 [c]2 Kin. 16:7, 8; Prov. 6:1

7 [a]Deut. 17:16; Is. 30:16; 31:1; Mic. 5:10

8 [a]Is. 10:11 [b]Ps. 115:4-8; Is. 17:8; 37:19; 40:19; 44:17

9 [a]Ps. 49:2; 62:9; Is. 5:15 [b]Neh. 4:5

10 [a]Enter the rock and hide in the dust
[b]From the terror of the LORD and from the splendor of His majesty.
11 The [1a]proud look of man will be abased,
And the [b]loftiness of man will be humbled,
And the LORD alone will be exalted in that day.

A Day of Reckoning Coming

12 For the LORD of hosts will have a day of reckoning
Against [a]everyone who is proud and lofty,
And against everyone who is lifted up,
That he may be abased.
13 And *it will be* against all the cedars of Lebanon that are lofty and lifted up,
Against all the [a]oaks of Bashan,
14 Against all the [a]lofty mountains,
Against all the hills that are lifted up,
15 Against every [a]high tower,
Against every fortified wall,
16 Against all the [a]ships of Tarshish,
And against all the beautiful craft.
17 And the pride of man will be humbled,
And the loftiness of men will be abased,
And the LORD alone will be exalted in that day.
18 But the [a]idols will completely vanish.
19 And *men* will [a]go into caves of the rocks,
And into holes of the [1]ground
Before the terror of the LORD,
And before the splendor of His majesty,
When He arises [b]to make the earth tremble.
20 In that day men will [a]cast away to the moles and the [b]bats
Their idols of silver and their idols of gold,
Which they made for themselves to worship,
21 In order to [a]go into the caverns of the rocks and the clefts of the cliffs,
Before the terror of the LORD and the splendor of His majesty,
When He arises to make the earth tremble.
22 [1a]Stop regarding man, whose breath *of life* is in his nostrils;
For [2b]why should he be esteemed?

God Will Remove the Leaders

3 FOR behold, the Lord [1]GOD of hosts [a]is going to remove from Jerusalem and Judah
Both [2]supply and support, the whole [2]supply of bread,
And the whole [2]supply of water;
2 [a]The mighty man and the warrior,
The judge and the prophet,
The diviner and the elder,
3 The captain of fifty and the honorable man,
The counselor and the expert artisan,
And the skillful enchanter.
4 And I will make mere [a]lads their princes
And [1]capricious children will rule over them,
5 And the people will be [a]oppressed,
Each one by another, and each one by his [b]neighbor;
The youth will storm against the elder,
And the inferior against the honorable.
6 When a man [a]lays hold of his brother in his father's house, *saying,*
"You have a cloak, you shall be our ruler,
And these ruins will be under your [1]charge,"
7 On that day will he [1]protest, saying,
"I will not be *your* [2a]healer,
For in my house there is neither bread nor cloak;
You should not appoint me ruler of the people."
8 For [a]Jerusalem has stumbled, and Judah has fallen,
Because their [1b]speech and their actions are against the LORD,
To [c]rebel against [2]His glorious presence.
9 [1]The expression of their faces bears witness against them.
And they display their sin like [a]Sodom;
They do not *even* conceal *it.*
Woe to [2]them!
For they have [b]brought evil on themselves.
10 Say to the [a]righteous that *it will go* well *with them,*
For they will eat the fruit of their actions.
11 Woe to the wicked! *It will go* badly *with him,*
For [1a]what he deserves will be done to him.
12 O My people! Their oppressors [1]are [a]children,
And women rule over them.
O My people! [b]Those who guide you lead *you* astray,
And confuse the direction of your paths.

God Will Judge

13 [a]The LORD arises to contend,
And stands to judge the people.
14 The LORD [a]enters into judgment with the elders and princes of His people,
"It is you who have [b]devoured the vineyard;
The [c]plunder of the poor is in your houses.

10 [a]Is. 2:19, 21; Rev. 6:15, 16 [b]2 Thess. 1:9
11 [1]Lit., *eyes of the loftiness of men* [a]Is. 5:15; 37:23 [b]Ps. 18:27; Is. 13:11; 23:9; 2 Cor. 10:5
12 [a]Job 40:11, 12; Is. 24:4, 21; Mal. 4:1
13 [a]Zech. 11:2
14 [a]Is. 40:4
15 [a]Is. 25:12
16 [a]1 Kin. 10:22; Is. 23:1, 14; 60:9
18 [a]Is. 21:9; Mic. 1:7
19 [1]Lit., *dust* [a]Is. 2:10 [b]Ps. 18:7; Is. 2:21; 13:13; 24:1, 19, 20; Hag. 2:6, 7; Heb. 12:26
20 [a]Is. 30:22; 31:7 [b]Lev. 11:19
21 [a]Is. 2:19
22 [1]Lit., *Cease from man* [2]Lit., *in what* [a]Ps. 146:3; Jer. 17:5 [b]Ps. 8:4; 144:3, 4; Is. 40:15, 17; James 4:14

1 [1]Heb., *YHWH,* usually rendered *LORD* [2]Lit., *staff* [a]Lev. 26:26; Is. 5:13; 9:20; Ezek. 4:16
2 [a]2 Kin. 24:14; Is. 9:14, 15; Ezek. 17:12, 13
4 [1]Lit., *arbitrary power will rule* [a]Eccl. 10:16
5 [a]Mic. 7:3-6 [b]Is. 9:19; Jer. 9:3-8
6 [1]Lit., *hand* [a]Is. 4:1
7 [1]Lit., *lift up his voice* [2]Lit., *binder of wounds* [a]Ezek. 34:4; Hos. 5:13
8 [1]Lit., *tongue* [2]Lit., *the eyes of His glory* [a]Is. 1:7; 6:11 [b]Ps. 73:9-11; Is. 9:17; 59:3 [c]Is. 65:3
9 [1]Or, *Their partiality bears* [2]Lit., *their soul* [a]Gen. 13:13; Is. 1:10-15 [b]Prov. 8:36; 15:32; Rom. 6:23
10 [a]Deut. 28:1-14; Eccl. 8:12; Is. 54:17
11 [1]Lit., *the dealing of his hands* [a]Deut. 28:15-68; Is. 65:6, 7
12 [1]Or, *deal severely* [a]Is. 3:4 [b]Is. 9:16; 28:14, 15
13 [a]Is. 66:16; Hos. 4:1; Mic. 6:2
14 [a]Job 22:4; Ps. 143:2; Ezek. 20:35, 36 [b]Ps. 14:4; Mic. 3:3 [c]Job 24:9, 14; Ps. 10:9; Prov. 30:14; Is. 10:1, 2; Ezek. 18:12; James 2:6

15 "What do you mean by [a]crushing My people,
And grinding the face of the poor?"
Declares the Lord [1]GOD of hosts.

Judah's Women Denounced

16 Moreover, the LORD said, "Because the [a]daughters of Zion are proud,
And walk with [1]heads held high and seductive eyes,
And go along with mincing steps,
And tinkle the bangles on their feet,
17 Therefore the Lord will afflict the scalp of the daughters of Zion with scabs,
And the LORD will make their foreheads bare."
18 In that day the Lord will take away
the beauty of *their* anklets, headbands,
[a]crescent ornaments,
19 dangling earrings, bracelets, veils,
20 [a]headdresses, ankle chains, sashes,
perfume boxes, amulets,
21 [1]finger rings, [a]nose rings,
22 festal robes, outer tunics, cloaks,
money purses,
23 hand mirrors, undergarments, turbans, and veils.
24 Now it will come about that instead of [1]sweet [a]perfume there will be putrefaction;
Instead of a belt, a rope;
Instead of [b]well-set hair, a [c]plucked-out scalp;
Instead of fine clothes, a [d]donning of sackcloth;
And branding instead of beauty.
25 Your men will [a]fall by the sword,
And your [1]mighty ones in battle.
26 And her [1a]gates will lament and mourn;
And deserted she will [b]sit on the ground.

A Remnant Prepared

4 FOR seven women will take hold of
[a]one man in that day, saying, "We
will eat our own bread and wear our own
clothes, only let us be called by your
name; [b]take away our reproach!"
2 In that day the [a]Branch of the
LORD will be beautiful and glorious, and
the [b]fruit of the earth *will* be the pride
and the adornment of the [c]survivors of
Israel.
3 And it will come about that he who
is [a]left in Zion and remains in Jerusalem
will be called [b]holy—everyone who is
[c]recorded for life in Jerusalem.
4 When the Lord has washed away
the filth of the [a]daughters of Zion, and
[1]purged the [b]bloodshed of Jerusalem
from her midst, by the [c]spirit of judgment and the [d]spirit of burning,
5 then the LORD will create over the
whole area of Mount Zion and over her
assemblies [a]a cloud by day, even smoke,
and the brightness of a flaming fire by
night; for over all the [b]glory will be a
canopy.
6 And there will be a [a]shelter to *give*
shade from the heat by day, and refuge
and [1]protection from the storm and the
rain.

Parable of the Vineyard

5 LET me sing now for my well-beloved
A song of my beloved concerning His vineyard.
My well-beloved had a [a]vineyard on [1]a fertile hill.
2 And He dug it all around, removed its stones,
And planted it with [1]the [a]choicest vine.
And He built a tower in the middle of it,
And hewed out a [2]wine vat in it;
Then He [b]expected *it* to produce *good* grapes,
But it produced *only* [3]worthless ones.

3 "And now, O inhabitants of Jerusalem and men of Judah,
[a]Judge between Me and My vineyard.
4 "[a]What more was there to do for My vineyard [1]that I have not done in it?
Why, when I expected *it* to produce *good* grapes did it produce [2]worthless ones?
5 "So now let Me tell you what I am going to do to My vineyard:
I will [a]remove its hedge and it will be consumed;
I will [b]break down its wall and it will become [c]trampled ground.
6 "And I will [a]lay it waste;
It will not be pruned or hoed,
But briars and thorns will come up.
I will also charge the clouds to [b]rain no rain on it."

7 For the [a]vineyard of the LORD of hosts is the house of Israel,
And the men of Judah His delightful plant.
Thus He looked for justice, but behold, [b]bloodshed;
For righteousness, but behold, a cry of distress.

Woes for the Wicked

8 Woe to those who [a]add house to house *and* join field to field,
Until there is no more room,
So that you have to live alone in the midst of the land!
9 In my ears the LORD of hosts *has sworn,* "Surely, [a]many houses shall become [b]desolate,
Even great and fine ones, without occupants.
10 "For [a]ten acres of vineyard will yield *only* one [1]bath *of wine,*
And a [b]homer of seed will yield *but* an [2]ephah of grain."
11 Woe to those who rise early in the morning that they may pursue [a]strong drink;

---

15 [1]Heb., *YHWH,* usually rendered LORD [a]Ps. 94:5
16 [1]Lit., *outstretched necks* [a]Song 3:11; Is. 3:16-4:1, 4; 32:9-15
18 [a]Judg. 8:21, 26
20 [a]Ex. 39:28
21 [1]Or, *signet rings* [a]Gen. 24:47; Ezek. 16:12
24 [1]Or, *balsam oil* [a]Esth. 2:12 [b]1 Pet. 3:3 [c]Is. 22:12; Ezek. 27:31; Amos 8:10 [d]Is. 15:3; Lam. 2:10
25 [1]Lit., *strength* [a]Is. 1:20; 65:12
26 [1]Lit., *entrances* [a]Jer. 14:2; Lam. 1:4 [b]Lam. 2:10

1 [a]Is. 13:12 [b]Gen. 30:23; Is. 54:4
2 [a]Is. 11:1; 53:2; Jer. 23:5; 33:15; Zech. 3:8; 6:12 [b]Ps. 72:16 [c]Is. 10:20; 37:31, 32; Joel 2:32; Obad. 17
3 [a]Is. 28:5; 46:3; Rom. 11:4, 5 [b]Is. 52:1; 62:12 [c]Ex. 32:32; Ps. 69:28; Luke 10:20
4 [1]Lit., *rinsed away* [a]Is. 3:16 [b]Is. 1:15 [c]Is. 28:6 [d]Is. 1:31; 9:19; Matt. 3:11
5 [a]Ex. 13:21, 22; 24:16; Num. 9:15-23 [b]Is. 60:1, 2
6 [1]Lit., *a hiding place* [a]Ps. 27:5; Is. 25:4; 32:1, 2

1 [1]Lit., *a horn, the son of fatness* [a]Ps. 80:8; Jer. 12:10; Matt. 21:33; Mark 12:1; Luke 20:9
2 [1]Lit., *a bright red grape* [2]Or, *wine press* [3]Or, *wild grapes* [a]Jer. 2:21 [b]Matt. 21:19; Mark 11:13; Luke 13:6
3 [a]Matt. 21:40
4 [1]Lit., *and I have not done* [2]Or, *wild grapes* [a]2 Chr. 36:16; Jer. 2:5; 7:25, 26; Mic. 6:3; Matt. 23:37
5 [a]Ps. 89:40 [b]Ps. 80:12 [c]Is. 10:6; 28:18; Lam. 1:15; Luke 21:24; Rev. 11:2
6 [a]2 Chr. 36:19-21; Is. 7:19-25; 24:1, 3; Jer. 25:11 [b]1 Kin. 8:35; 17:1; Jer. 14:1-22
7 [a]Ps. 80:8-11 [b]Is. 3:14, 15; 30:12; 59:13
8 [a]Jer. 22:13-17; Mic. 2:2; Hab. 2:9-12
9 [a]Is. 6:11, 12 [b]Matt. 23:38
10 [1]I.e., Approx. 10½ gal. [2]I.e., Approx. one bu. [a]Lev. 26:26; Is. 7:23; Hag. 1:6; 2:16 [b]Ezek. 45:11
11 [a]Prov. 23:29, 30; Eccl. 10:16, 17; Is. 5:22; 22:13; 28:1, 3, 7, 8

Who stay up late in the evening
that wine may inflame them!
12 And their banquets are *accompanied* by lyre and [a]harp, by tambourine and flute, and by wine;
But they [b]do not pay attention to the deeds of the LORD,
Nor do they consider the work of His hands.

13 Therefore My people go into exile for their [a]lack of knowledge;
And [1]their [b]honorable men are famished,
And their multitude is parched with thirst.
14 Therefore [a]Sheol has enlarged its [1]throat and opened its mouth without measure;
And [2]Jerusalem's splendor, her multitude, her din *of revelry*, and the jubilant within her, descend *into it*.
15 So the *common* man will be humbled, and the man of *importance* abased,
[a]The eyes of the proud also will be abased.
16 But the [a]LORD of hosts will be [b]exalted in judgment,
And the holy God will show Himself [c]holy in righteousness.
17 [a]Then the lambs will graze as in their pasture,
And strangers will eat in the waste places of the [1]wealthy.

18 Woe to those who drag [a]iniquity with the cords of [1]falsehood,
And sin as if with cart ropes;
19 [a]Who say, "Let Him make speed, let Him hasten His work, that we may see *it;*
And let the purpose of the Holy One of Israel draw near
And come to pass, that we may know *it!*"
20 Woe to those who [a]call evil good, and good evil;
Who [1b]substitute darkness for light and light for darkness;
Who [1]substitute bitter for sweet, and sweet for bitter!
21 Woe to those who are [a]wise in their own eyes,
And clever in their own sight!
22 [a]Woe to those who are heroes in drinking wine,
And valiant men in mixing strong drink;
23 [a]Who justify the wicked for a bribe,
And [b]take away the [1]rights of the ones who are in the right!

24 Therefore, [a]as a tongue of fire consumes stubble,
And dry grass collapses into the flame,
So their [b]root will become [c]like rot and their blossom [1]blow away as dust;
For they have [d]rejected the law of the LORD of hosts,
And despised the word of the Holy One of Israel.
25 On this account the [a]anger of the LORD has burned against His people,
And He has stretched out His hand against them and struck them down,
And the [b]mountains quaked; and their [c]corpses [1]lay like refuse in the middle of the streets.
[d]For all this His anger [2]is not spent,
But His [e]hand is still stretched out.

26 He will also lift up a [a]standard to the [1]distant nation,
And will [b]whistle for it [c]from the ends of the earth;
And behold, it will [d]come with speed swiftly.
27 [a]No one in it is weary or stumbles,
None slumbers or sleeps;
Nor is the [b]belt at its waist undone,
Nor its sandal strap broken.
28 [1a]Its arrows are sharp, and all its bows are bent;
The hoofs of its horses [2]seem like flint, and its *chariot* [b]wheels like a whirlwind.
29 Its [a]roaring is like a lioness, and it roars like young lions;
It growls as it [b]seizes the prey,
And carries *it* off with [c]no one to deliver *it*.
30 And it shall [a]growl over it in that day like the roaring of the sea.
If one [b]looks to the land, behold, there is darkness *and* distress;
Even the light is darkened by its clouds.

Isaiah's Vision

6 IN the year of [a]King Uzziah's death,
[b]I saw the Lord sitting on a throne,
lofty and exalted, with the train of His
robe filling the temple.
2 Seraphim stood above Him, [a]each
having six wings; with two he covered
his face, and with two he covered his
feet, and with two he flew.
3 And one called out to another and
said,
"[a]Holy, Holy, Holy, is the LORD of hosts,
The [1b]whole earth is full of His glory."
4 And the [1]foundations of the thresholds trembled at the voice of him who
called out, while the [2a]temple was filling
with smoke.
5 Then I said,
"[a]Woe is me, for I am ruined!
Because I am a man of [b]unclean lips,
And I live among a [c]people of unclean lips;
For my eyes have seen the [d]King, the LORD of hosts."
6 Then one of the seraphim flew to
me, with a burning coal in his hand

12 [a]Amos 6:5, 6 [b]Job 34:27; Ps. 28:5
13 [1]Lit., *their glory are men of famine* [a]Is. 1:3; 27:11; Hos. 4:6 [b]Is. 3:3
14 [1]Or, *appetite* [2]Lit., *her* [a]Prov. 30:16; Hab. 2:5
15 [a]Is. 2:11; 10:33
16 [a]Is. 28:17; 30:18; 61:8 [b]Is. 2:11, 17; 33:5, 10 [c]Is. 8:13; 29:23; 1 Pet. 3:15
17 [1]Lit., *the fat* [a]Is. 7:25; Mic. 2:12; Zeph. 2:6
18 [1]Or, *worthlessness* [a]Is. 59:4-8; Jer. 23:10-14
19 [a]Ezek. 12:22; 2 Pet. 3:4
20 [1]Lit., *set* [a]Prov. 17:15; Amos 5:7 [b]Job 17:12; Matt. 6:22, 23; Luke 11:34, 35
21 [a]Prov. 3:7; Rom. 12:16; 1 Cor. 3:18-20
22 [a]Prov. 23:20; Is. 5:11; 56:12; Hab. 2:15
23 [1]Lit., *righteousness* [a]Ex. 23:8; Is. 1:23; 10:1, 2; Mic. 3:11; 7:3 [b]Ps. 94:21; James 5:6
24 [1]Lit., *ascend* [a]Is. 9:18, 19; Joel 2:5 [b]Job 18:16 [c]Hos. 5:12 [d]Is. 8:6; 30:9, 12; Acts 13:41
25 [1]Lit., *were* [2]Lit., *has not turned away* [a]2 Kin. 22:13, 17; Is. 66:15 [b]Ps. 18:7; Is. 64:3; Jer. 4:24; Nah. 1:5 [c]2 Kin. 9:37; Is. 14:19; Jer. 16:4 [d]Is. 9:12, 17, 19, 21; 10:4; Jer. 4:8; Dan. 9:16 [e]Ex. 7:19; Is. 23:11
26 [1]Lit., *nations;* probably Assyria [a]Is. 13:2, 3 [b]Is. 7:18; Zech. 10:8 [c]Deut. 28:49 [d]Is. 13:4, 5
27 [a]Joel 2:7, 8 [b]Job 12:18
28 [1]Lit., *Which, its arrows* [2]Lit., *are regarded as* [a]Ps. 7:12, 13; 45:5; Is. 13:18 [b]Is. 21:1; Jer. 4:13
29 [a]Jer. 51:38; Zeph. 3:3; Zech. 11:3 [b]Is. 10:6; 49:24, 25; Mic. 5:8 [c]Is. 42:22
30 [a]Is. 17:12; Jer. 6:23; Luke 21:25 [b]Is. 8:22; Jer. 4:23-28; Joel 2:10; Luke 21:25, 26

1 [a]2 Kin. 15:7; 2 Chr. 26:23; Is. 1:1 [b]John 12:41; Rev. 4:2, 3; 20:11
2 [a]Rev. 4:8
3 [1]Lit., *fulness of the whole earth is His glory* [a]Rev. 4:8 [b]Num. 14:21; Ps. 72:19
4 [1]Lit., *door sockets* [2]Lit., *house* [a]Rev. 15:8
5 [a]Ex. 33:20; Luke 5:8 [b]Ex. 6:12, 30 [c]Is. 59:3; Jer. 9:3-8 [d]Jer. 51:57

which he had taken from the [a]altar with
tongs.
7 And he [a]touched my mouth *with it*
and said, "Behold, this has touched your
lips; and [b]your iniquity is taken away,
and your sin is [1]forgiven."

Isaiah's Commission

8 Then I heard the [a]voice of the
Lord, saying, "Whom shall I send, and
who will go for Us?" Then [b]I said, "Here
am I. Send me!"
9 And He said, "Go, and tell this
people:
'Keep on [a]listening, but do not
perceive;
Keep on looking, but do not understand.'
10 "[a]Render the hearts of this people
[1b]insensitive,
Their ears [2]dull,
And their eyes [3]dim,
[c]Lest they see with their eyes,
Hear with their ears,
Understand with their hearts,
And return and be healed."
11 Then I said, "Lord, [a]how long?"
And He answered,
"Until [b]cities are devastated *and*
without inhabitant,
Houses are without people,
And the land is utterly desolate,
12 "The LORD has [a]removed men far
away,
And the [1b]forsaken places are
many in the midst of the land.
13 "Yet there will be a tenth portion in
it,
And it will again be *subject* to
burning,
Like a terebinth or an [a]oak
Whose stump remains when it is
felled.
The [b]holy seed is its stump."

War against Jerusalem

7 NOW it came about in the days of
[a]Ahaz, the son of Jotham, the son of
Uzziah, king of Judah, that [b]Rezin the
king of Aram and [c]Pekah the son of
Remaliah, king of Israel, went up to
Jerusalem to *wage* war against it, but
[d]could not [1]conquer it.
2 When it was reported to the [a]house
of David, saying, "The Arameans [1b]have
camped in [c]Ephraim," his heart and the
hearts of his people shook as the trees of
the forest shake [2]with the wind.
3 Then the LORD said to Isaiah, "Go
out now to meet Ahaz, you and your son
[1]Shear-jashub, at the end of the [a]conduit
of the upper pool, on the highway to the
[2]fuller's field,
4 and say to him, 'Take care, and be
[a]calm, have no [b]fear and [c]do not be
fainthearted because of these two stubs
of smoldering [d]firebrands, on account of
the fierce anger of Rezin and Aram, and
the [e]son of Remaliah.
5 'Because [a]Aram, *with* Ephraim and
the son of Remaliah, has planned evil
against you, saying,
6 'Let us go up against Judah and
[1]terrorize it, and make for ourselves a
breach in [2]its walls, and set up the son of
Tabeel as king in the midst of it,"
7 thus says the Lord [1]GOD, "[a]It shall
not stand nor shall it come to pass.
8 "For the head of Aram is [a]Damas-
cus and the head of Damascus is Rezin
(now within another 65 years Ephraim
will be shattered, *so that it is* no longer a
people),
9 and the head of Ephraim is Samaria and the head of Samaria is the son
of Remaliah. [a]If you will not believe,
you surely shall not [1]last."'"

The Child Immanuel

10 Then the LORD spoke again to
Ahaz, saying,
11 "Ask a [a]sign for yourself from the
LORD your God; [1]make *it* deep as Sheol
or high as [2]heaven."
12 But Ahaz said, "I will not ask, nor
will I test the LORD!"
13 Then he said, "Listen now, O
[a]house of David! Is it too slight a thing
for you to try the patience of men, that
you will [b]try the patience of [c]my God as
well?
14 "Therefore the Lord Himself will
give you a sign: Behold, [a]a [1]virgin will be
with child and bear a son, and she will
call His name [2b]Immanuel.
15 "He will eat [a]curds and honey [1]at
the time He knows *enough* to refuse evil
and choose good.
16 "[a]For before the boy will know
enough to refuse evil and choose good,
[b]the land whose two kings you dread
will be forsaken.

Trials to Come for Judah

17 "The LORD will bring on you, on
your people, and on your father's house
such days as have never come since the
day that [a]Ephraim separated from Judah, the [b]king of Assyria."
18 And it will come about in that day,
that the LORD will [a]whistle for the fly
that is in the [1b]remotest part of the rivers
of Egypt, and for the bee that is in the
land of Assyria.
19 And they will all come and settle
on the steep [1]ravines, on the [a]ledges of
the cliffs, [b]on all the thorn bushes, and
on all the [2]watering places.
20 In that day the Lord will [a]shave
with a [b]razor, [c]hired from regions beyond [d]the [1]Euphrates (*that is,* with the
king of Assyria), the head and the hair of
the legs; and it will also remove the
beard.
21 Now it will come about in that day
that a man may keep alive a [a]heifer and
a pair of sheep;

6 [a]Rev. 8:3
7 [1]Lit., *atoned for* [a]Jer. 1:9; Dan. 10:16 [b]Is. 40:2; 53:5, 6, 11; 1 John 1:7
8 [a]Ezek. 10:5; Acts 9:4 [b]Acts 26:19
9 [a]Is. 43:8; Matt. 13:14; Mark 4:12; Luke 8:10; John 12:40; Acts 28:26; Rom. 11:8
10 [1]Lit., *fat* [2]Lit., *heavy* [3]Lit., *besmeared* [a]Matt. 13:15 [b]Deut. 31:20; 32:15 [c]Jer. 5:21
11 [a]Ps. 79:5 [b]Lev. 26:31; Is. 1:7; 3:8, 26
12 [1]Or, *forsakenness will be great* [a]Deut. 28:64 [b]Jer. 4:29
13 [a]Job 14:7 [b]Deut. 7:6; Ezra 9:2

1 [1]Lit., *fight against* [a]2 Kin. 16:1; Is. 1:1 [b]2 Kin. 15:37 [c]2 Kin. 15:25; 2 Chr. 28:6 [d]Is. 7:6, 7
2 [1]Lit., *has settled down on* [2]Lit., *from before* [a]Is. 7:13; 22:22 [b]Is. 8:12 [c]Is. 9:9
3 [1]I.e., a remnant shall return [2]I.e., laundryman's [a]2 Kin. 18:17; Is. 36:2
4 [a]Ex. 14:13; Is. 30:15; Lam. 3:26 [b]Is. 10:24; Matt. 24:6 [c]Deut. 20:3; 1 Sam. 17:32; Is. 35:4 [d]Amos 4:11; Zech. 3:2 [e]Is. 7:1, 9
5 [a]Is. 7:2
6 [1]Lit., *cause it a sickening dread* [2]Lit., *it*
7 [1]Heb., *YHWH,* usually rendered *LORD* [a]Is. 8:10; 28:18; Acts 4:25, 26
8 [a]Gen. 14:15; Is. 17:1-3
9 [1]Or, *be established* [a]2 Chr. 20:20; Is. 5:24; 8:6-8; 30:12-14
11 [1]So with the versions; M.T., *make the request deep or high* [2]Lit., *heights* [a]2 Kin. 19:29; Is. 37:30; 38:7, 8; 55:13
13 [a]Is. 7:2 [b]Is. 1:14; 43:24 [c]Is. 25:1
14 [1]Or, *maiden* [2]I.e., God is with us [a]Matt. 1:23 [b]Is. 8:8, 10
15 [1]Lit., *with respect to his knowing* [a]Is. 7:22
16 [a]Is. 8:4 [b]Is. 8:14; 17:3; Jer. 7:15; Hos. 5:3, 9, 14; Amos 1:3-5
17 [a]1 Kin. 12:16 [b]2 Chr. 28:20; Is. 8:7, 8; 10:5, 6
18 [1]Or, *mouth of the rivers;* i.e., the Nile Delta [a]Is. 5:26 [b]Is. 13:5
19 [1]Or, *wadis* [2]Or, *pastures* [a]Is. 2:19; Jer. 16:16 [b]Is. 7:24, 25
20 [1]Lit., *River* [a]2 Kin. 18:13-16; Is. 24:1 [b]Ezek. 5:1-4 [c]Is. 10:5, 15 [d]Is. 8:7; 11:15; Jer. 2:18
21 [a]Is. 14:30; 27:10; Jer. 39:10

22 and it will happen that because of
the abundance of the milk produced he
will eat curds, for everyone that is left
within the land will eat [a]curds and
honey.
23 And it will come about in that day,
[a]that every place where there used to be
a thousand vines, *valued* at a thousand
shekels of silver, will become [b]briars and
thorns.
24 *People* will come there with bows
and arrows because all the land will be
briars and thorns.
25 And as for all the hills which used
to be cultivated with the hoe, you will
not go there for fear of briars and
thorns; but they will become a place for
[1a]pasturing oxen and for sheep to trample.

Damascus and Samaria Fall

8 THEN the LORD said to me, "Take
for yourself a large tablet and [a]write
on it [1]in ordinary letters: [2b]Swift is the
booty, speedy is the prey.
2 "And [1]I will take to Myself faithful
witnesses for testimony, [a]Uriah the
priest and Zechariah the son of Jebere-
chiah."
3 So I approached the prophetess,
and she conceived and gave birth to a
son. Then the LORD said to me, "Name
him [1a]Maher-shalal-hash-baz;
4 for [a]before the boy knows how to
cry out 'My father' or 'My mother,' the
wealth of [b]Damascus and the spoil of
Samaria will be carried away before the
king of Assyria."
5 And again the LORD spoke to me
further, saying,
6 "Inasmuch as these people have
[a]rejected the gently flowing waters of Shiloah,
And rejoice in [b]Rezin and the son
of Remaliah;
7 "Now therefore, behold, the Lord
is about to bring on them the
[a]strong and abundant waters of
the [1b]Euphrates,
Even the [c]king of Assyria and all
his glory;
And it will [d]rise up over all its
channels and go over all its
banks.
8 "Then [a]it will sweep on into Judah,
it will overflow and pass
through,
It will [b]reach even to the neck;
And the spread of its wings will
[1]fill the breadth of [2]your land, O
[c]Immanuel.

A Believing Remnant

9 "[a]Be broken, O peoples, and be
[1b]shattered;
And give ear, all remote places of
the earth.
Gird yourselves, yet be [1]shat-
tered;
Gird yourselves, yet be [1]shattered.
10 "[a]Devise a plan but it will be
thwarted;
State a [1]proposal, but [b]it will not
stand,
For [2c]God is with us."
11 For thus the LORD spoke to me
[1]with [a]mighty power and instructed me
[b]not to walk in the way of this people,
saying,
12 "You are not to say, '*It is* a [a]con-
spiracy!'
In regard to all that this people
call a conspiracy,
And [b]you are not to fear [1]what
they fear or be in dread of *it.*
13 "It is the [a]LORD of hosts [b]whom
you should regard as holy.
And He shall be your fear,
And He shall be your dread.
14 "Then He shall become a [a]sanctu-
ary;
But to both the houses of Israel, a
[b]stone to strike and a rock to
stumble over,
And a snare and a [c]trap for the
inhabitants of Jerusalem.
15 "And many [a]will stumble over
them,
Then they will fall and be broken;
They will even be snared and
caught."
16 [a]Bind up the testimony, [b]seal the
[1]law among [c]my disciples.
17 And I will [a]wait for the LORD [b]who
is hiding His face from the house of
Jacob; I will even look eagerly for Him.
18 [a]Behold, I and the children whom
the LORD has given me are for [b]signs
and wonders in Israel from the LORD of
hosts, who [c]dwells on Mount Zion.
19 And when they say to you, "[a]Con-
sult the mediums and the spiritists who
whisper and mutter," should not a people [b]consult their God? *Should they*
[c]consult the dead on behalf of the living?
20 To the [1a]law and to the testimony!
If they do not speak according to this
word, it is because [b]they have no dawn.
21 And they will pass through [1]the
land [a]hard-pressed and famished, and it
will turn out that when they are hungry,
they will be enraged and curse [2]their
king and their God as they face upward.
22 Then they will [a]look to the earth,
and behold, distress and darkness, the
gloom of anguish; and *they will be*
[b]driven away into darkness.

Birth and Reign of the Prince of Peace

9 [1]BUT there will be no *more* [a]gloom
for her who was in anguish; in
earlier times He [b]treated the [c]land of
Zebulun and the land of Naphtali with
contempt, but later on He shall make *it*
glorious, by the way of the sea, on the
other side of Jordan, Galilee of the
[2]Gentiles.
2 [1a]The people who walk in darkness
Will see a great light;
Those who live in a dark land,
The light will shine on them.

22 [a]Is. 8:15
23 [a]Is. 5:10; 32:13, 14 [b]Is. 5:6
25 [1]Lit., *sending* [a]Is. 5:17

1 [1]Lit., *with the stylus of man* [2]Heb., *Maher-shalal-hash-baz* [a]Is. 30:8; Hab. 2:2 [b]Is. 8:3
2 [1]Another reading is *take for me* [a]2 Kin. 16:10, 11, 15, 16
3 [1]I.e., swift is the booty, speedy is the prey [a]Is. 8:1
4 [a]Is. 7:16 [b]Is. 7:8, 9
6 [a]Is. 1:20; 5:24; 7:9; 30:12 [b]Is. 7:1
7 [1]Lit., *River* [a]Is. 17:12, 13 [b]Is. 7:20; 11:15 [c]Is. 7:17; 10:5 [d]Amos 8:8; 9:5
8 [1]Lit., *be the fulness of* [2]Or, *Your* [a]Is. 10:6 [b]Is. 30:28 [c]Is. 7:14
9 [1]Or, *dismayed* [a]Is. 17:12-14 [b]Dan. 2:34, 35
10 [1]Lit., *word* [2]Heb., *Immanu-el* [a]Job 5:12; Is. 28:18 [b]Is. 7:7 [c]Is. 8:8; Rom. 8:31
11 [1]Lit., *with strength of the hand* [a]Ezek. 3:14 [b]Ezek. 2:8
12 [1]Lit., *their fear* [a]Is. 7:2; 30:1 [b]1 Pet. 3:14, 15
13 [a]Is. 5:16; 29:23 [b]Num. 20:12
14 [a]Is. 4:6; 25:4; Ezek. 11:16 [b]Luke 2:34; Rom. 9:33; 1 Pet. 2:8 [c]Is. 24:17, 18
15 [a]Is. 28:13; 59:10; Luke 20:18; Rom. 9:32
16 [1]Or, *teaching* [a]Is. 8:1, 2; 29:11, 12 [b]Dan. 12:4 [c]Is. 50:4
17 [a]Is. 25:9; 30:18; Hab. 2:3 [b]Deut. 31:17; Is. 1:15; 45:15; 54:8
18 [a]Heb. 2:13 [b]Luke 2:34 [c]Ps. 9:11; Zech. 8:3
19 [a]Lev. 20:6; 2 Kin. 21:6; 23:24; Is. 19:3; 29:4; 47:12, 13 [b]Is. 30:2; 45:11 [c]1 Sam. 28:8-11
20 [1]Or, *teaching* [a]Is. 1:10; 8:16; Luke 16:29 [b]Is. 8:22; Mic. 3:6
21 [1]Lit., *it* [2]Or, *by their king* [a]Is. 9:20, 21
22 [a]Is. 5:30; 59:9; Jer. 13:16; Amos 5:18, 20; Zeph. 1:14, 15 [b]Is. 8:20

1 [1]Ch. 8:23 in Heb. [2]Or, *nations* [a]Is. 8:22 [b]2 Kin. 15:29; 2 Chr. 16:4 [c]Matt. 4:15, 16
2 [1]Ch. 9:1 in Heb. [a]Matt. 4:16; Luke 1:79; Eph. 5:8

3 [a]Thou shalt multiply the nation,
Thou [b]shalt [1]increase [2]their gladness;
They will be glad in Thy presence
As with the gladness [3]of harvest,
As [4c]men rejoice when they divide the spoil.
4 For [a]Thou shalt break the yoke of their burden and the staff on their shoulders,
The rod of their [b]oppressor, as [1]at the battle of [c]Midian.
5 For every boot of the booted warrior in the *battle* tumult,
And cloak rolled in blood, will be for burning, fuel for the fire.
6 For a [a]child will be born to us, a [b]son will be given to us;
And the [c]government will [1]rest [d]on His shoulders;
And His name will be called [e]Wonderful Counselor, [f]Mighty God,
Eternal [g]Father, Prince of [h]Peace.
7 There will be [a]no end to the increase of *His* government or of peace,
On the [b]throne of David and over his kingdom,
To establish it and to uphold it with [c]justice and righteousness
From then on and forevermore.
[d]The zeal of the LORD of hosts will accomplish this.

God's Anger with Israel's Arrogance

8 The Lord sends a [1]message against Jacob,
And it falls on Israel.
9 And all the people know *it,*
That is, [a]Ephraim and the inhabitants of Samaria,
Asserting in pride and in [b]arrogance of heart:
10 "The bricks have fallen down,
But we will [a]rebuild with smooth stones;
The sycamores have been cut down,
But we will replace *them* with cedars."
11 Therefore the LORD raises against them adversaries from [a]Rezin,
And spurs their enemies on,
12 The Arameans on the east and the [a]Philistines on the west;
And they [b]devour Israel with [1]gaping jaws.
[c]In *spite of* all this His anger does not turn away,
And His hand is still stretched out.

13 Yet the people [a]do not turn back to Him who struck them,
Nor do they [b]seek the LORD of hosts.
14 So the LORD cuts off [a]head and tail from Israel,
Both palm branch and bulrush [b]in a single day.
15 The head is [a]the elder and honorable man,
And the prophet who teaches [b]falsehood is the tail.
16 [a]For those who guide this people are leading *them* astray;
And those who are guided by them are [1]brought to confusion.
17 Therefore the Lord does [a]not take pleasure in their young men,
[b]Nor does He have pity on their [1]orphans or their widows;
For every one of them is [c]godless and an [d]evildoer,
And every [e]mouth is speaking foolishness.
[f]In *spite of* all this His anger does not turn away,
And His hand is still stretched out.

18 [a]For wickedness burns like a fire;
It consumes briars and thorns;
It even sets the thickets of the forest aflame,
And they roll upward in a column of smoke.
19 By the [a]fury of the LORD of hosts the [b]land is burned up,
And the [c]people are like fuel for the fire;
No [d]man spares his brother.
20 And [1]they slice off *what is* on the right hand but *still* are [a]hungry,
And [2]they eat *what is* on the left hand but they are not satisfied;
Each of them eats the [b]flesh of his own arm.
21 Manasseh *devours* Ephraim, and Ephraim Manasseh,
[a]*And* together they are against Judah.
[b]In *spite of* all this His anger does not turn away,
And His hand is still stretched out.

Assyria Is God's Instrument

10 WOE to those who [a]enact evil statutes,
And to those who constantly record [1]unjust decisions,
2 So as [a]to [1]deprive the needy of justice,
And rob the poor of My people of *their* rights,
In order [b]that widows may be their spoil,
And that they may plunder the [2]orphans.
3 Now [a]what will you do in the [b]day of punishment,
And in the devastation which will come [c]from afar?
[d]To whom will you flee for help?
And where will you leave your [1]wealth?
4 Nothing *remains* but to crouch [1]among the [a]captives
Or fall [1]among the [b]slain.
[c]In *spite of* all this His anger does not turn away,
And His hand is still stretched out.

5 Woe to [a]Assyria, the [b]rod of My anger
And the staff in whose hands is [c]My indignation,

3 [1]Another reading is *not increase* [2]Lit., *the* [3]Lit., *in* [4]Lit., *they* [a]Is. 26:15 [b]Is. 35:10; 65:14, 18, 19; 66:10 [c]1 Sam. 30:16
4 [1]Lit., *in the day of Midian* [a]Is. 10:27; 14:25 [b]Is. 14:4; 49:26; 51:13; 54:14 [c]Judg. 7:25; Is. 10:26
6 [1]Lit., *be* [a]Is. 7:14; 11:1, 2; 53:2; Luke 2:11 [b]John 3:16 [c]Matt. 28:18; 1 Cor. 15:25 [d]Is. 22:22 [e]Is. 28:29 [f]Deut. 10:17; Neh. 9:32; Is. 10:21 [g]Is. 63:16; 64:8 [h]Is. 26:3, 12; 54:10; 66:12
7 [a]Dan. 2:44; Luke 1:32, 33 [b]Is. 16:5 [c]Is. 11:4, 5; 32:1; 42:3, 4; 63:1 [d]Is. 37:32; 59:17
8 [1]Lit., *word*
9 [a]Is. 7:8, 9; 28:1, 3 [b]Is. 46:12
10 [a]Mal. 1:4
11 [a]Is. 7:1, 8
12 [1]Lit., *the whole mouth* [a]2 Chr. 28:18 [b]Ps. 79:7; Jer. 10:25 [c]Is. 5:25
13 [a]Jer. 5:3; Hos. 7:10 [b]Is. 31:1; Hos. 3:5
14 [a]Is. 19:15 [b]Rev. 18:8
15 [a]Is. 3:2, 3 [b]Is. 28:15; 59:3, 4; Jer. 23:14, 32; Matt. 24:24
16 [1]Or, *swallowed up* [a]Is. 3:12; Matt. 15:14; 23:16, 24
17 [1]Or, *fatherless* [a]Jer. 18:21; Amos 4:10; 8:13 [b]Is. 27:11 [c]Is. 10:6; 32:6 [d]Is. 1:4; 14:20; 31:2 [e]Matt. 12:34 [f]Is. 5:25
18 [a]Ps. 83:14; Is. 1:7; Nah. 1:10; Mal. 4:1
19 [a]Is. 10:6; 13:9, 13; 42:25 [b]Joel 2:3 [c]Is. 1:31; 24:6 [d]Mic. 7:2, 6
20 [1]Lit., *he slices* [2]Lit., *he eats* [a]Is. 8:21, 22 [b]Is. 49:26
21 [a]2 Chr. 28:6, 8; Is. 11:13 [b]Is. 5:25

1 [1]Lit., *mischief* or *misfortune* [a]Ps. 94:20; Is. 29:21; 59:4, 13
2 [1]Lit., *turn aside from* [2]Or, *fatherless* [a]Is. 5:23 [b]Is. 1:23; 3:14, 15
3 [1]Lit., *glory* [a]Job 31:14 [b]Is. 13:6; 26:14, 21; 29:6; Jer. 9:9; Hos. 9:7; Luke 19:44 [c]Is. 5:26 [d]Is. 20:6; 30:5, 7; 31:3
4 [1]Lit., *under* [a]Is. 24:22 [b]Is. 22:2; 34:3; 66:16 [c]Is. 5:25
5 [a]Is. 7:17; 8:7; 14:24-27; Zeph. 2:13-15 [b]Jer. 51:20 [c]Is. 13:5; 30:30; 34:2; 66:14

6 I send it against a [a]godless nation
And commission it against the [b]people of My fury
To capture booty and [c]to seize plunder,
And to [1]trample them down like [d]mud in the streets.
7 Yet it [a]does not so intend
Nor does [1]it plan so in its heart,
But rather it is [2]its purpose to destroy,
And to cut off [3]many nations.
8 For it says, "Are not my princes [1]all kings?
9 "Is not [a]Calno like [b]Carchemish,
Or [c]Hamath like Arpad,
Or [d]Samaria like [e]Damascus?
10 "As my hand has reached to the [a]kingdoms of the idols,
Whose graven images *were* greater than those of Jerusalem and Samaria,
11 Shall I not [1]do to Jerusalem and her images
Just as I have done to Samaria and [a]her idols?"

12 So it will be that when the Lord has
completed all His [a]work on Mount Zion
and on Jerusalem, *He will say,* "I will
[1]punish the fruit of the arrogant heart of
the king of Assyria and [b]the pomp of
[2]his haughtiness."

13 For [a]he has said,
"By the power of my hand and by my wisdom I did *this,*
For I have understanding;
And I [b]removed the boundaries of the peoples,
And plundered their treasures,
And like a mighty man I brought down [1]*their* inhabitants,
14 And my hand reached to the riches of the peoples like a [a]nest,
And as one gathers abandoned eggs, I gathered all the earth;
And there was not one that flapped its wing or opened *its* beak or chirped."

15 Is the [a]axe to [b]boast itself over the one who chops with it?
Is the saw to exalt itself over the one who wields it?
That would be like [c]a [1]club wielding those who lift it,
Or like [d]a rod lifting *him who* is not wood.
16 Therefore the Lord, the [1]GOD of hosts, will send a [a]wasting disease among his [b]stout warriors;
And under his [c]glory a fire will be kindled like a burning flame.
17 And the [a]light of Israel will become a fire and his [b]Holy One a flame,
And it will [c]burn and devour his thorns and his briars in a single day.
18 And He will [a]destroy the glory of his forest and of his fruitful garden, both soul and body;
And it will be as when a sick man wastes away.
19 And the [a]rest of the trees of his forest will be so small in number
That a child could write them down.

A Remnant Will Return

20 Now it will come about in that day
that the [a]remnant of Israel, and those of
the house of Jacob [b]who have escaped,
will never again rely on the one who
struck them, but will truly [c]rely on the
LORD, the Holy One of Israel.

21 A [a]remnant will return, the remnant of Jacob, to the [b]mighty God.
22 For [a]though your people, O Israel, may be like the sand of the sea,
Only a remnant within them will return;
A [b]destruction is determined, overflowing with righteousness.

23 For a complete destruction, one
that is decreed, [a]the Lord [1]GOD of hosts
will execute in the midst of the whole
land.

24 Therefore thus says the Lord [1]GOD
of hosts, "O My people who dwell in
[a]Zion, [b]do not fear the Assyrian [2]who
[c]strikes you with the rod and lifts up his
staff against you, the way Egypt *did.*
25 "For in a very [a]little while [b]My
indignation *against you* will be spent,
and My anger *will be directed* to their
destruction."

26 And the LORD of hosts will [a]arouse
a scourge against him like the slaughter
of [b]Midian at the rock of Oreb; and His
[c]staff will be over the sea, and He will lift
it up [d]the way *He did* in Egypt.

27 So it will be in that day, that [1]his
[a]burden will be removed from your
shoulders and his yoke from your neck,
and the yoke will be broken because [b]of
fatness.

28 He has come against Aiath,
He has passed through [a]Migron;
At [b]Michmash he deposited his [c]baggage.
29 They have gone through [a]the pass, *saying,*
"[b]Geba will be our lodging place."
[c]Ramah is terrified, and [d]Gibeah of Saul has fled away.
30 Cry aloud with your voice, O daughter of [a]Gallim!
Pay attention, Laishah *and* [1]wretched [b]Anathoth!
31 Madmenah has fled.
The inhabitants of Gebim have sought refuge.
32 Yet today he will halt at [a]Nob;
He [b]shakes his fist at the mountain of the [1][c]daughter of Zion, the hill of Jerusalem.

6 [1]Lit., *make them a trampled place* [a]Is. 9:17 [b]Is. 9:19 [c]Is. 5:29 [d]Is. 5:25
7 [1]Lit., *its heart so plan* [2]Lit., *in its heart* [3]Lit., *not a few* [a]Gen. 50:20; Mic. 4:11, 12; Acts 2:23, 24
8 [1]Lit., *altogether*
9 [a]Gen. 10:10; Amos 6:2 [b]2 Chr. 35:20 [c]Num. 34:8 [d]2 Kin. 17:6 [e]2 Kin. 16:9
10 [a]2 Kin. 19:17, 18
11 [1]Lit., *do thus* [a]Is. 2:8
12 [1]Lit., *visit* [2]Lit., *haughtiness of his eyes* [a]2 Kin. 19:31; Is. 28:21, 22; 29:14; 65:7 [b]Is. 37:23
13 [1]Or, *those who sit* on thrones [a]2 Kin. 19:22-24; Is. 37:24-27; Ezek. 28:4; Dan. 4:30 [b]Hab. 2:6-11
14 [a]Jer. 49:16; Obad. 4
15 [1]Lit., *staff* [a]Jer. 51:20 [b]Is. 29:16; 45:9; Rom. 9:20, 21 [c]Is. 10:5 [d]Is. 10:5
16 [1]Heb., *YHWH,* usually rendered LORD [a]Ps. 106:15 [b]Is. 17:4 [c]Is. 8:7; 10:18
17 [a]Is. 30:33; 31:9 [b]Is. 37:23 [c]Num. 11:1-3; Is. 27:4; 33:12; Jer. 4:4; 7:20
18 [a]Is. 10:33, 34
19 [a]Is. 21:17
20 [a]Is. 1:9; 11:11, 16; 46:3 [b]Is. 4:2; 37:31, 32 [c]2 Chr. 14:11; Is. 17:7, 8; 50:10
21 [a]Is. 7:3 [b]Is. 9:6
22 [a]Rom. 9:27, 28 [b]Is. 28:22; Dan. 9:27; Rom. 9:28
23 [1]Heb., *YHWH,* usually rendered LORD [a]Is. 28:22; Dan. 9:27; Rom. 9:28
24 [1]Heb., *YHWH,* usually rendered LORD [2]Lit., *he* [a]Ps. 87:5, 6 [b]Is. 7:4; 12:2; 37:6 [c]Ex. 5:14-16
25 [a]Is. 17:14; Hag. 2:6 [b]Is. 10:5; 26:20; Dan. 11:36
26 [a]Is. 37:36-38 [b]Judg. 7:25; Is. 9:4 [c]Ex. 14:16 [d]Ex. 14:27
27 [1]I.e., the Assyrian [a]Is. 9:4; 14:25 [b]Is. 30:23; 55:2
28 [a]1 Sam. 14:2 [b]1 Sam. 13:2, 5 [c]Judg. 18:21; 1 Sam. 17:22
29 [a]1 Sam. 13:23 [b]Josh. 21:17; 1 Sam. 13:16 [c]Josh. 18:25; 1 Sam. 7:17 [d]1 Sam. 10:26

30 [1]An ancient version reads *Answer her, O Anathoth* [a]1 Sam. 25:44 [b]Josh. 21:18; Jer. 1:1
32 [1]Another reading is *house of* [a]1 Sam. 21:1; 22:9 [b]Is. 19:16; Zech. 2:9 [c]Is. 1:8; Jer. 6:23

33 Behold, the Lord, the [1]GOD of hosts, will lop off the boughs with a terrible crash;
Those also who are [a]tall in stature will be cut down,
And those who are lofty will be abased.
34 And He will cut down the thickets of the forest with an iron *axe*,
And [a]Lebanon will fall [1]by the Mighty One.

Righteous Reign of the Branch

11 THEN a [a]shoot will spring from the [b]stem of Jesse,
And a [c]branch from [d]his roots will bear fruit.
2 And the [a]Spirit of the LORD will rest on Him,
The spirit of [b]wisdom and understanding,
The spirit of counsel and [c]strength,
The spirit of knowledge and the fear of the LORD.
3 And He will delight in the fear of the LORD,
And He will not judge by what His eyes [a]see,
Nor make a decision by what His ears hear;
4 But with [a]righteousness He will judge the [b]poor,
And decide with fairness for the [c]afflicted of the earth;
And He will strike the earth with the [d]rod of His mouth,
And with the [e]breath of His lips He will slay the wicked.
5 Also [a]righteousness will be the belt about His loins,
And [b]faithfulness the belt about His waist.

6 And the [a]wolf will dwell with the lamb,
And the leopard will lie down with the kid,
And the calf and the young lion [1]and the fatling together;
And a little boy will lead them.
7 Also the cow and the bear will graze;
Their young will lie down together;
And the [a]lion will eat straw like the ox.
8 And the nursing child will play by the hole of the cobra,
And the weaned child will put his hand on the viper's den.
9 They will [a]not hurt or destroy in all My holy mountain,
For the [b]earth will be full of the knowledge of the LORD
As the waters cover the sea.

10 Then it will come about in that day
That the [a]nations will resort to the [b]root of Jesse,
Who will stand as a [1c]signal for the peoples;
And His [d]resting place will be [2]glorious.

The Restored Remnant

11 Then it will happen on that day that the Lord
Will again recover the second time with His hand
The [a]remnant of His people, who will remain,
From [b]Assyria, [c]Egypt, Pathros, Cush, [d]Elam, Shinar, Hamath,
And from the [1e]islands of the sea.
12 And He will lift up a [a]standard for the nations,
And will [b]assemble the banished ones of Israel,
And will gather the dispersed of Judah
From the four corners of the earth.
13 Then the [a]jealousy of Ephraim will depart,
And those who harass Judah will be cut off;
Ephraim will not be jealous of Judah,
And Judah will not harass Ephraim.
14 And they will [a]swoop down on the slopes of the Philistines on the [b]west;
Together they will [c]plunder the sons of the east;
[1]They will possess [d]Edom and [e]Moab;
And the sons of Ammon will be [2]subject to them.
15 And the LORD will [1a]utterly destroy
The tongue of the [2]Sea of Egypt;
And He will [b]wave His hand over the [3c]River
With His scorching wind;
And He will strike it into seven streams,
And make *men* walk over [4]dry-shod.
16 And there will be a [a]highway from Assyria
For the [b]remnant of His people who will be left,
Just as there was for Israel
In [c]the day that they came up out of the land of Egypt.

Thanksgiving Expressed

12 THEN you will say on that day,
"[a]I will give thanks to Thee, O LORD;
For [b]although Thou wast angry with me,
Thine anger is turned away,
And Thou dost comfort me.
2 "Behold, [a]God is my salvation,
I will [b]trust and not be afraid;
For [c]the LORD GOD is my strength and song,
And He has become my salvation."
3 Therefore you will joyously [a]draw water
From the [b]springs of salvation.

33 [1]Heb., *YHWH*, usually rendered *LORD* [a]Is. 37:24, 36-38; Ezek. 31:3; Amos 2:9
34 [1]Or, *as a mighty one* [a]Is. 2:13; 33:9; 37:24

1 [a]Is. 4:2; 53:2 [b]Is. 9:7; 11:10; Acts 13:23 [c]Is. 6:13; Jer. 23:5; Zech. 3:8 [d]Rev. 5:5; 22:16
2 [a]Is. 42:1; 48:16; 61:1; Matt. 3:16; John 1:32 [b]John 16:13; 1 Cor. 1:30; Eph. 1:17, 18 [c]2 Tim. 1:7
3 [a]John 2:25; 7:24
4 [a]Is. 9:7; 16:5; 32:1 [b]Ps. 72:2, 13, 14; Is. 3:14 [c]Is. 29:19; 32:7; 61:1 [d]Ps. 2:9; Is. 49:2; Mal. 4:6 [e]Job 4:9; Is. 30:28, 33; 2 Thess. 2:8
5 [a]Eph. 6:14 [b]Is. 25:1
6 [1]Some versions read *will feed together* [a]Is. 65:25
7 [a]Is. 65:25
9 [a]Job 5:23; Is. 65:25; Ezek. 34:25; Hos. 2:18 [b]Ps. 98:2, 3; Is. 45:6; 52:10; 66:18-23; Hab. 2:14
10 [1]Or, *standard* [2]Lit., *glory* [a]Luke 2:32; Acts 11:18 [b]Is. 11:1; Rom. 15:12 [c]Is. 11:12; 49:22; 62:10; John 3:14, 15; 12:32 [d]Is. 14:3; 28:12; 32:17, 18
11 [1]Or, *coastlands* [a]Is. 10:20-22; 37:4, 31, 32; 46:3 [b]Is. 19:23-25; Hos. 11:11; Zech. 10:10 [c]Is. 19:21, 22; Mic. 7:12 [d]Gen. 10:22; 14:1 [e]Is. 24:15; 42:4, 10, 12; 49:1; 51:5; 60:9; 66:19
12 [a]Is. 11:10 [b]Is. 56:8; Zeph. 3:10; Zech. 10:6
13 [a]Is. 9:21; Jer. 3:18; Ezek. 37:16, 17, 22; Hos. 1:11
14 [1]Lit., *Edom and Moab will be the outstretching of their hand* [2]Lit., *their obedience* [a]Jer. 48:40; 49:22; Hab. 1:8 [b]Is. 9:12 [c]Jer. 49:28 [d]Is. 63:1; Dan. 11:41; Joel 3:19; Amos 9:12 [e]Is. 16:14; 25:10
15 [1]Another reading is *dry up the tongue* [2]Perhaps the Red Sea [3]I.e., Euphrates [4]Lit., *in sandals* [a]Is. 43:16; 44:27; 50:2; 51:10, 11 [b]Is. 19:16 [c]Is. 7:20; 8:7; Rev. 16:12
16 [a]Is. 19:23; 35:8; 40:3; 62:10 [b]Is. 11:11 [c]Ex. 14:26-29

1 [a]Ps. 9:1; Is. 25:1 [b]Ps. 30:5; Is. 40:1, 2; 54:7-10
2 [a]Is. 32:2; 45:17; 62:11 [b]Is. 26:3 [c]Ex. 15:2; Ps. 118:14
3 [a]John 4:10; 7:37, 38 [b]Is. 41:18; Jer. 2:13

4 And in that day you will [a]say,
“[b]Give thanks to the LORD, call on
His name.
[c]Make known His deeds among the
peoples;
[1]Make *them* remember that His
name is exalted.”
5 [a]Praise the LORD in song, for He
has done [1]excellent things;
Let this be known throughout the
earth.
6 [a]Cry aloud and shout for joy, O
inhabitant of Zion,
For [b]great in your midst is the
Holy One of Israel.

Prophecies about Babylon

13 THE [1a]oracle concerning [b]Baby-
lon which [c]Isaiah the son of
Amoz saw.
2 [a]Lift up a standard on the [1b]bare
hill,
Raise your voice to them,
[c]Wave the hand that they may
[d]enter the doors of the nobles.
3 I have commanded My consecrated
ones,
I have even called My [a]mighty
warriors,
My proudly exulting ones,
To *execute* My anger.
4 A [a]sound of tumult on the mountains,
Like that of many people!
A sound of the uproar of kingdoms,
Of nations gathered together!
The LORD of hosts is mustering the
army for battle.
5 They are coming from a far country
From the [1a]farthest horizons,
The LORD and His instruments of
[b]indignation,
To [c]destroy the whole land.

Judgment on the Day of the LORD

6 Wail, for the [a]day of the LORD is
near!
It will come as [b]destruction from
[1]the Almighty.
7 Therefore [a]all hands will fall limp,
And every man’s [b]heart will melt.
8 And they will be [a]terrified,
Pains and anguish will take hold of
them;
They will [b]writhe like a woman in
labor,
They will look at one another in
astonishment,
Their faces aflame.
9 Behold, [a]the day of the LORD is
coming,
Cruel, with fury and burning anger,
To make the land a desolation;
And He will exterminate its sinners
from it.
10 For the [a]stars of heaven and their
constellations
Will not flash forth their light;
The [b]sun will be dark when it rises,
And the moon will not shed its
light.
11 Thus I will [a]punish the world for its
evil,
And the [b]wicked for their iniquity;
I will also put an end to the [c]arro-
gance of the proud,
And abase the [d]haughtiness of the
[1e]ruthless.
12 I will make mortal man [1a]scarcer
than pure gold,
And mankind than the [b]gold of
Ophir.
13 Therefore I shall make the [a]heav-
ens tremble,
And [b]the earth will be shaken from
its place
At the fury of the LORD of hosts
In [c]the day of His burning anger.
14 And it will be that like a hunted
gazelle,
Or like [a]sheep with none to gather
them,
They will each turn to his own
people,
And each one flee to his own land.
15 Anyone who is found will be
[a]thrust through,
And anyone who is captured will
fall by the sword.
16 Their [a]little ones also will be
dashed to pieces
Before their eyes;
Their houses will be plundered
And their wives ravished.

Babylon Will Fall to the Medes

17 Behold, I am going to [a]stir up the
Medes against them,
Who will not value silver or [b]take
pleasure in gold,
18 And *their* bows will [1]mow down
the [a]young men,
They will not even have compassion on the fruit of the womb,
Nor will their [b]eye pity [2]children.
19 And [a]Babylon, the [b]beauty of kingdoms, the glory of the Chalde-
ans’ pride,
Will be as when God [c]overthrew
Sodom and Gomorrah.
20 It will [a]never be inhabited or lived
in from generation to genera-
tion;
Nor will the [b]Arab pitch *his* tent
there,
Nor will shepherds make *their*
flocks lie down there.
21 But [a]desert creatures will lie down
there,
And their houses will be full of
[1]owls,
Ostriches also will live there, and
[2]shaggy goats will frolic there.

4 [1]Or, *Proclaim* to them *that* [a]Is. 24:15; 42:12; 48:20 [b]Ps. 105:1 [c]Ps. 145:4
5 [1]Or, *gloriously* [a]Ex. 15:1; Ps. 98:1; Is. 24:14; 42:10, 11; 44:23
6 [a]Is. 52:9; 54:1; Zeph. 3:14 [b]Is. 1:24; 49:26; 60:16; Zeph. 3:15-17; Zech. 2:5, 10, 11

1 [1]Or, *burden of* [a]Is. 14:28; 15:1 [b]Is. 13:19; 14:4; 47:1-15; Jer. 24:1; 50:1-51:64; Matt. 1:11; Rev. 14:8 [c]Is. 1:1
2 [1]Or, *wind-swept mountain* [a]Is. 5:26; Jer. 50:2 [b]Jer. 51:25 [c]Is. 10:32; 19:16 [d]Is. 45:1-3; Jer. 51:58
3 [a]Joel 3:11
4 [a]Is. 5:30; 17:12; Joel 3:14
5 [1]Lit., *end of heaven* [a]Is. 5:26; 7:18 [b]Is. 10:5 [c]Is. 24:1
6 [1]Heb., *Shaddai* [a]Is. 2:12; 10:3; 13:9; 34:2, 8; 61:2; Ezek. 30:3; Amos 5:18; Zeph. 1:7 [b]Is. 10:25; 14:23; Joel 1:15
7 [a]Ezek. 7:17 [b]Is. 19:1; Ezek. 21:7; Nah. 2:10
8 [a]2 Kin. 19:26; Is. 21:3; Jer. 46:5 [b]Is. 26:17; Jer. 4:31; John 16:21
9 [a]Is. 13:6
10 [a]Is. 5:30; Ezek. 32:7; Joel 2:10; Matt. 24:29; Mark 13:24; Luke 21:25; Rev. 6:13; 8:12 [b]Is. 24:23; 50:3; Ezek. 32:7; Acts 2:20; Rev. 6:12
11 [1]Or, *tyrants, despots* [a]Is. 26:21 [b]Is. 3:11; 11:4; 14:5 [c]Is. 2:11; 23:9; Dan. 5:22, 23 [d]Jer. 48:29 [e]Is. 25:3; 29:5, 20
12 [1]Lit., *more precious* [a]Is. 4:1; 6:11, 12 [b]1 Kin. 9:28; Job 28:16; Ps. 45:9
13 [a]Is. 34:4; 51:6 [b]Ps. 18:7; Is. 2:19; 24:1, 19, 20; Hag. 2:6 [c]Lam. 1:12
14 [a]1 Kin. 22:17; Matt. 9:36; Mark 6:34; 1 Pet. 2:25
15 [a]Is. 14:19; Jer. 50:25; 51:3, 4
16 [a]Ps. 137:8, 9; Is. 13:18; 14:21; Hos. 10:14; Nah. 3:10
17 [a]Jer. 51:11; Dan. 5:28 [b]Prov. 6:34, 35
18 [1]Lit., *dash in pieces* [2]Lit., *sons* [a]2 Kin. 8:12; 2 Chr. 36:17 [b]Ezek. 9:5, 10
19 [a]Is. 21:9; 48:14 [b]Dan. 4:30; Rev. 18:11-16, 19, 21 [c]Gen. 19:24; Deut. 29:23; Jer. 49:18; Amos 4:11
20 [a]Is. 14:23; 34:10-15; Jer. 51:37-43 [b]2 Chr. 17:11
21 [1]Or, *howling creatures* [2]Or, *goat demons* [a]Is. 34:11-15; Zeph. 2:14; Rev. 18:2

22 And [1]hyenas will howl in their fortified towers
And jackals in their luxurious [a]palaces.
Her *fateful* time also [2]will soon come
And her days will not be prolonged.

Israel's Taunt

14 WHEN the LORD will [a]have compassion on Jacob, and again
[b]choose Israel, and settle them in their
own land, then [c]strangers will join them
and attach themselves to the house of
Jacob.
2 And the peoples will take them
along and bring them to their place, and
the [a]house of Israel will possess them as
an inheritance in the land of the LORD
[b]as male servants and female servants;
and [1]they will take their captors captive,
and will rule over their oppressors.
3 And it will be in the day when the
LORD gives you [a]rest from your pain and
turmoil and harsh service in which you
have been enslaved,
4 that you will [a]take up this [1]taunt
against the king of Babylon, and say,

"How [b]the oppressor has ceased,
And how [2]fury has ceased!
5"The LORD has broken the staff of the wicked,
The scepter of rulers
6 [a]Which used to strike the peoples in fury with unceasing strokes,
Which [1]subdued the nations in anger with unrestrained persecution.
7"The whole earth is at rest *and* is quiet;
They [a]break forth into shouts of joy.
8"Even the [a]cypress trees rejoice over you, *and* the cedars of Lebanon, *saying,*
'Since you were laid low, no *tree* cutter comes up against us.'
9"[a]Sheol from beneath is excited over you to meet you when you come;
It arouses for you the [1]spirits of the dead, all the [2]leaders of the earth;
It raises all the kings of the nations from their thrones.
10"[a]They will all respond and say to you,
'Even you have been made weak as we,
You have become like us.
11 'Your [a]pomp *and* the music of your harps
Have been brought down to Sheol;
Maggots are spread out *as your bed* beneath you,
And worms are your covering.'
12"How you have [a]fallen from heaven,
O [1b]star of the morning, son of the dawn!
You have been cut down to the earth,
You who have weakened the nations!
13"But you said in your heart,
'I will [a]ascend to heaven;
I will [b]raise my throne above the stars of God,
And I will sit on the mount of assembly
In the recesses of the north.
14 'I will ascend above the heights of the clouds;
[a]I will make myself like the Most High.'
15"Nevertheless you [a]will be thrust down to Sheol,
To the recesses of the pit.
16"Those who see you will gaze at you,
They will [1]ponder over you, *saying,*
'Is this the man who made the earth tremble,
Who shook kingdoms,
17 Who made the world like a [a]wilderness
And overthrew its cities,
Who [b]did not [1]allow his prisoners to *go* home?'
18"All the kings of the nations lie in glory,
Each in his own [1]tomb.
19"But you have been [a]cast out of your tomb
Like [1]a rejected branch,
[2]Clothed with the slain who are pierced with a sword,
Who go down to the stones of the [b]pit,
Like a [c]trampled corpse.
20"You will not be united with them in burial,
Because you have ruined your country,
You have slain your people.
May the [a]offspring of evildoers not be mentioned forever.
21"Prepare for his sons a place of slaughter
Because of the [a]iniquity of their fathers.
They must not arise and take possession of the earth
And fill the face of the world with cities."

22"And I will rise up against them,"
declares the LORD of hosts, "and will cut
off from Babylon [a]name and survivors,
[b]offspring and posterity," declares the
LORD.
23"I will also make it a possession for
the [a]hedgehog, and swamps of water,
and I will sweep it with the broom of
[b]destruction," declares the LORD of
hosts.

Judgment on Assyria

24 The LORD of hosts has sworn saying, "Surely, [a]just as I have intended so
it has happened, and just as I have
planned so it will stand,
25 to [a]break Assyria in My land, and I
will trample him on My mountains.
Then his [b]yoke will be removed from

---

22 [1]Or, *howling creatures* [2]Lit., *is near to come* [a]Is. 25:2; 32:14; 34:13

1 [a]Ps. 102:13; Is. 49:13, 15; 54:7, 8 [b]Is. 41:8, 9; 44:1; 49:7; Zech. 1:17; 2:12 [c]Is. 56:3, 6; Eph. 2:12-19

2 [1]Lit., *the captors will become their captives* [a]Is. 45:14; 49:23; 54:3 [b]Is. 60:10; 61:5; Dan. 7:18, 27

3 [a]Ezra 9:8, 9; Is. 11:10; 40:2; Jer. 30:10; 46:27

4 [1]Or, *proverb* [2]Amended from the meaningless *medhebah* to *marhebah* [a]Hab. 2:6 [b]Is. 9:4; 16:4; 49:26; 51:13; 54:14

6 [1]Or, *ruled* [a]Is. 10:14; 47:6

7 [a]Ps. 47:1-3; 98:1-9; 126:1-3

8 [a]Is. 55:12; Ezek. 31:16

9 [1]Or, *shades* (Heb., *Repha'im*) [2]Lit., *male goats* [a]Is. 5:14

10 [a]Ezek. 32:21

11 [a]Is. 5:14

12 [1]Heb., *Helel;* i.e., shining one [a]Is. 34:4; Luke 10:18; Rev. 8:10; 9:1 [b]2 Pet. 1:19; Rev. 2:28; 22:16

13 [a]Ezek. 28:2 [b]Dan. 5:22, 23; 8:10; 2 Thess. 2:4

14 [a]Is. 47:8; 2 Thess. 2:4

15 [a]Ezek. 28:8; Matt. 11:23; Luke 10:15

16 [1]Lit., *show themselves attentive to*

17 [1]Lit., *open* [a]Joel 2:3 [b]Is. 45:13

18 [1]Lit., *house*

19 [1]Lit., *an abhorred branch* [2]Or, *As the clothing of those who are slain* [a]Is. 22:16-18 [b]Jer. 41:7, 9 [c]Is. 5:25

20 [a]Job 18:16, 19; Ps. 21:10; 37:28; Is. 1:4; 31:2

21 [a]Ex. 20:5; Lev. 26:39; Is. 13:16; Matt. 23:35

22 [a]Prov. 10:7 [b]Job 18:19; Is. 47:9

23 [a]Is. 34:11; Zeph. 2:14 [b]1 Kin. 14:10; Is. 13:6

24 [a]Job 23:13; Is. 46:11; 55:8, 9; Acts 4:28

25 [a]Is. 10:12; 30:31; 31:8 [b]Is. 9:4; 10:27; Nah. 1:13

them, and his burden removed from
their shoulder.
26"This is the [a]plan [1]devised against
the whole earth; and this is the [b]hand
that is stretched out against all the
nations.
27"For [a]the LORD of hosts has
planned, and who can frustrate *it*? And
as for His stretched-out hand, who can
turn it back?"
28 In the [a]year that King Ahaz died
this [1b]oracle came:

Judgment on Philistia

29"Do not rejoice, O [a]Philistia, all of you,
Because the rod that [b]struck you is broken;
For from the serpent's root a [c]viper will come out,
And its fruit will be a [d]flying serpent.
30"And [1]those who are most [a]helpless will eat,
And the needy will lie down in security;
I will [2]destroy your root with [b]famine,
And it will kill off your survivors.
31"Wail, O [a]gate; cry, O city;
[1]Melt away, O [b]Philistia, all of you;
For smoke comes from the [c]north,
And [d]there is no straggler in his ranks.
32"How then will one answer the [a]messengers of the nation?
That [b]the LORD has founded Zion,
And [c]the afflicted of His people will seek refuge in it."

Judgment on Moab

15 THE [1]oracle concerning [a]Moab.
Surely in a night [b]Ar of Moab is devastated *and* ruined;
Surely in a night Kir of Moab is devastated *and* ruined.
2 They have gone up to the [1]temple and *to* [a]Dibon, *even* to the high places to weep.
Moab wails over Nebo and Medeba;
Everyone's head is [b]bald *and* every beard is cut off.
3 In their streets they have girded themselves with [a]sackcloth;
[b]On their housetops and in their squares
Everyone is wailing, [1c]dissolved in tears.
4 [a]Heshbon and Elealeh also cry out,
Their voice is heard all the way to Jahaz;
Therefore the [1]armed men of Moab cry aloud;
His soul trembles within him.
5 My heart cries out for Moab;
His fugitives are as far as [a]Zoar *and* Eglath-shelishiyah,
For they go up the [b]ascent of Luhith weeping;
Surely on the road to Horonaim they raise a cry of distress [c]over *their* ruin.
6 For the [a]waters of Nimrim are [1]desolate.
Surely the grass is withered, the tender grass [2]died out,
There is [b]no green thing.
7 Therefore the [a]abundance *which* they have acquired and stored up
They carry off over the brook of [1]Arabim.
8 For the cry of distress has gone around the territory of Moab,
Its wail *goes* as far as Eglaim and its wailing even to Beer-elim.
9 For the waters of Dimon are full of [1]blood;
Surely I will bring added *woes* upon Dimon,
A [a]lion upon the fugitives of Moab and upon the remnant of the land.

Prophecy of Moab's Devastation

16 [a]SEND the *tribute* lamb to the ruler of the land,
From [1b]Sela by way of the wilderness to the [c]mountain of the daughter of Zion.
2 Then, like [1a]fleeing birds *or* scattered [2]nestlings,
The daughters of [b]Moab will be at the fords of the [c]Arnon.
3"[1]Give *us* advice, make a decision;
[2]Cast your [a]shadow like night [3]at high noon;
[b]Hide the outcasts, do not betray the fugitive.
4"Let the [1]outcasts of Moab stay with you;
Be a hiding place to them from the destroyer."
For the extortioner has come to an end, destruction has ceased,
[a]Oppressors have completely *disappeared* from the land.
5 A [a]throne will even be established in lovingkindness,
And a judge will sit on it in faithfulness in the tent of [b]David;
Moreover, he will seek justice
And be prompt in righteousness.

6 [a]We have heard of the pride of Moab, an excessive pride;
Even of his arrogance, pride, and fury;
[b]His idle boasts are [1]false.
7 Therefore Moab shall wail; everyone of Moab shall wail.
You shall moan for the [a]raisin cakes of [b]Kir-hareseth
As those who are utterly stricken.
8 For the fields of [a]Heshbon have [1]withered, the vines of [b]Sibmah *as well*;
The lords of the nations have trampled down its choice clusters
Which reached as far as Jazer *and* wandered to the deserts;
[c]Its tendrils spread themselves out *and* passed over the sea.

26 [1]Lit., *planned* [a]Is. 23:9; Zeph. 3:6, 8 [b]Ex. 15:12
27 [a]2 Chr. 20:6; Is. 43:13; Dan. 4:31, 35
28 [1]Or, *burden* [a]2 Kin. 16:20; 2 Chr. 28:27 [b]Is. 13:1
29 [a]Is. 2:6; 11:14; Jer. 47:1-7; Ezek. 25:15-17; Joel 3:4-8; Amos 1:6-8; Zeph. 2:4-7; Zech. 9:5-7 [b]2 Chr. 26:6 [c]Is. 11:8 [d]Is. 30:6
30 [1]Lit., *the firstborn of the helpless* [2]Lit., *put to death* [a]Is. 3:14, 15; 7:21, 22; 11:4 [b]Is. 8:21; 9:20; 51:19
31 [1]Or, *Become demoralized* [a]Is. 3:26; 24:12; 45:2 [b]Is. 14:29 [c]Jer. 1:14 [d]Is. 34:16
32 [a]Is. 37:9 [b]Ps. 87:1, 5; 102:16; Is. 28:16; 44:28; 54:11 [c]Is. 4:6; 25:4; 57:13; Zeph. 3:12; Heb. 11:10; James 2:5

1 [1]Or, *burden of* [a]Is. 11:14; 25:10; Jer. 48:1; Ezek. 25:8-11; Amos 2:1-3; Zeph. 2:8-11 [b]Num. 21:28
2 [1]Lit., *house* [a]Jer. 48:18, 22 [b]Lev. 21:5; Jer. 48:37
3 [1]Lit., *going down in weeping* [a]Jon. 3:6-8 [b]Jer. 48:38 [c]Is. 22:4
4 [1]Another reading is *the loins of* [a]Num. 21:28; 32:3; Jer. 48:34
5 [a]Jer. 48:34 [b]Jer. 48:5 [c]Is. 59:7; Jer. 4:20
6 [1]Lit., *desolations* [2]Lit., *come to an end* [a]Is. 19:5-7; Jer. 48:34 [b]Joel 1:10-12; 2:3
7 [1]Or, *the poplars* [a]Is. 30:6; Jer. 48:36
9 [1]Heb., *dam* (a wordplay) [a]2 Kin. 17:25; Jer. 50:17

1 [1]I.e., Petra in Edom [a]2 Kin. 3:4; Ezra 7:17 [b]2 Kin. 14:7; Is. 42:11 [c]Is. 10:32
2 [1]Or, *fluttering* [2]Lit., *nest* [a]Prov. 27:8 [b]Jer. 48:20, 46 [c]Num. 21:13, 14
3 [1]Lit., *Bring* [2]Lit., *Set* [3]Lit., *in the midst of the noon* [a]Is. 25:4; 32:2 [b]1 Kin. 18:4
4 [1]So the versions; M.T., *My outcasts, as for Moab* [a]Is. 9:4; 14:4; 49:26; 51:13; 54:14
5 [a]Is. 9:6, 7; 32:1; 55:4; Dan. 7:14; Mic. 4:7; Luke 1:33 [b]Is. 9:7
6 [1]Lit., *not so* [a]Jer. 48:29; Amos 2:1; Obad. 3, 4; Zeph. 2:8, 10 [b]Jer. 48:30
7 [a]1 Chr. 16:3 [b]2 Kin. 3:25; Jer. 48:31

8 [1]Or, *languished* [a]Is. 15:4 [b]Num. 32:38 [c]Jer. 48:32

9 Therefore I will [a]weep bitterly for
Jazer, for the vine of Sibmah;
I will drench you with my tears, O
[b]Heshbon and Elealeh;
For the shouting over your [c]summer fruits and your harvest has
fallen away.
10 And [a]gladness and joy are taken
away from the fruitful field;
In the [b]vineyards also there will be
no cries of joy or jubilant shouting,
No [c]treader treads out wine in the
presses,
For I have made the shouting to
cease.
11 Therefore my [1a]heart intones like a
harp for Moab,
And my [2]inward feelings for Kir-hareseth.
12 So it will come about when Moab
[a]presents himself,
When he [b]wearies himself upon *his*
[c]high place,
And comes to his sanctuary to
pray,
That he will not prevail.
13 This is the word which the LORD
spoke earlier concerning Moab.
14 But now the LORD speaks, saying,
"Within three years, as [1a]a hired man
would count them, the glory of [b]Moab
will be degraded along with all *his* great
population, and *his* remnant will be very
small *and* [2]impotent."

Prophecy about Damascus

17 THE [1a]oracle concerning [b]Damascus.
"Behold, Damascus is about to be
[c]removed from being a city,
And it will become a [d]fallen ruin.
2 "The cities [1]of [a]Aroer are forsaken;
They will be for [b]flocks [2]to lie
down in,
And there will be [c]no one to
frighten *them*.
3 "The [1a]fortified city will disappear
from Ephraim,
And [2]sovereignty from Damascus
And the remnant of Aram;
They will be like the [b]glory of the
sons of Israel,"
Declares the LORD of hosts.

4 Now it will come about in that day
that the [a]glory of Jacob will
[1]fade,
And [b]the fatness of his flesh will
become lean.
5 It will be [a]even like the [1]reaper
gathering the standing grain,
As his arm harvests the ears,
Or it will be like one gleaning ears
of grain
In the [b]valley of Rephaim.
6 Yet [a]gleanings will be left in it like
the [1]shaking of an olive tree,
Two *or* three olives on the topmost
bough,
Four *or* five on the branches of a
fruitful tree,
Declares the LORD, the God of
Israel.
7 In that day man will [a]have regard
for his Maker,
And his eyes will look to the Holy
One of Israel.
8 And he will not have regard for the
[a]altars, the work of his hands,
Nor will he look to that which his
[b]fingers have made,
Even the [1c]Asherim and [2]incense
stands.
9 In that day [1]their strong cities will
be like [2]forsaken places in the
forest,
Or like [3]branches which they abandoned before the sons of Israel;
And [4]the land will be a desolation.
10 For [a]you have forgotten the [b]God
of your salvation
And have not remembered the
[c]rock of your refuge.
Therefore you plant delightful
plants
And set them with vine slips of a
strange *god*.
11 In the day that you plant *it* you
carefully fence *it* in,
And in the [a]morning you bring
your seed to blossom;
But the harvest will [b]be a heap
In a day of sickliness and incurable
pain.

12 Alas, the uproar of many peoples
[a]Who roar like the roaring of the
seas,
And the rumbling of nations
Who rush on like the [b]rumbling of
mighty waters!
13 The [a]nations rumble on like the
rumbling of many waters,
But He will [b]rebuke them and they
will flee far away,
And be chased [c]like chaff in the
mountains before the wind,
Or like whirling dust before a gale.
14 At evening time, behold, *there is*
terror!
Before morning [a]they are no more.
[1]Such *will be* the portion of those
who plunder us,
And the lot of those who pillage us.

Message to Ethiopia

18 ALAS, oh land of whirring wings
Which lies beyond the rivers of
[1a]Cush,
2 Which sends envoys by the sea,
Even in [a]papyrus vessels on the
surface of the waters.
Go, swift messengers, to a nation
[1b]tall and smooth,
To a people [c]feared [2]far and wide,
A powerful and oppressive nation
Whose land the rivers divide.

9 [a]Jer. 48:32 [b]Is. 15:4 [c]Jer. 40:10, 12; 48:32
10 [a]Is. 24:8; Jer. 48:33 [b]Judg. 9:27; Is. 24:7; Amos 5:11, 17 [c]Job 24:11; Amos 9:13
11 [1]Lit., *entrails murmur* [2]Lit., *inward part* [a]Is. 15:5; 63:15; Jer. 48:36; Hos. 11:8; Phil. 2:1
12 [a]Num. 22:39-41; Jer. 48:35 [b]1 Kin. 18:29 [c]Is. 15:2
14 [1]Lit., *the years of a hireling* [2]Lit., *not mighty* [a]Job 7:1; 14:6; Is. 21:16 [b]Is. 25:10; Jer. 48:42

1 [1]Or, *burden of* [a]Is. 13:1 [b]Gen. 14:15; 15:2; 2 Kin. 16:9; Jer. 49:23; Amos 1:3-5; Zech. 9:1; Acts 9:2 [c]Is. 7:16; 8:4; 10:9 [d]Is. 25:2; Jer. 49:2; Mic. 1:6
2 [1]Gr. reads *forever and ever* [2]Lit., *and they will lie down* [a]Num. 32:34 [b]Is. 7:21, 22; Ezek. 25:5; Zeph. 2:6 [c]Mic. 4:4
3 [1]Or, *fortification* [2]Or, *royal power, kingdom* [a]Is. 7:8, 16; 8:4 [b]Is. 17:4; Hos. 9:11
4 [1]Lit., *become thin* [a]Is. 10:3 [b]Is. 10:16
5 [1]Lit., *gathering of the harvest, the standing grain* [a]Is. 17:11; Jer. 51:33; Joel 3:13; Matt. 13:30 [b]2 Sam. 5:18, 22
6 [1]Lit., *striking* [a]Deut. 4:27; Is. 24:13; 27:12; Obad. 5
7 [a]Is. 10:20; Hos. 3:5; 6:1; Mic. 7:7
8 [1]I.e., wooden symbols of a female deity [2]Or, *sun pillars* [a]2 Chr. 34:7; Is. 27:9 [b]Is. 2:8, 20; 30:22; 31:7 [c]Ex. 34:13; Deut. 7:5; Mic. 5:14
9 [1]I.e., man's [2]Gr. reads *the deserted places of the Amorites and the Hivites which they abandoned* [3]Or, *the treetop* [4]Lit., *it*
10 [a]Is. 51:13 [b]Ps. 68:19; Is. 12:2; 33:2; 61:10; 62:11 [c]Deut. 32:4, 18, 31; Is. 26:4; 30:29; 44:8
11 [a]Ps. 90:6 [b]Job 4:8; Hos. 8:7; 10:13
12 [a]Is. 5:30; Jer. 6:23; Ezek. 43:2; Luke 21:25 [b]Ps. 18:4
13 [a]Is. 33:3 [b]Ps. 9:5; Is. 41:11 [c]Job 21:18; Ps. 1:4; 83:13; Is. 29:5; 41:15, 16

14 [1]Lit., *This* [a]2 Kin. 19:35; Is. 41:12

1 [1]Or, *Ethiopia* [a]2 Kin. 19:9; Is. 20:3-5; Ezek. 30:4, 5, 9; Zeph. 2:12; 3:10
2 [1]Lit., *drawn out* [2]Lit., *from it and beyond* [a]Ex. 2:3 [b]Is. 18:7 [c]Gen. 10:8, 9; 2 Chr. 12:2-4; 14:9; 16:8

3 [a]All you inhabitants of the world and dwellers on earth,
As soon as a standard is raised on the mountains, [b]you will see *it,*
And as soon as the trumpet is blown, you will hear *it.*
4 For thus the LORD has told me,
"I will look [1]from My [a]dwelling place quietly
Like dazzling heat in the [2b]sunshine,
Like a cloud of [c]dew in the heat of harvest."
5 For [a]before the harvest, as soon as the bud [1]blossoms
And the flower becomes a ripening grape,
Then He will cut off the sprigs with pruning knives
And remove *and* cut away the spreading branches.
6 They will be left together for mountain birds [a]of prey,
And for the beasts of the earth;
And the birds of prey will spend the summer *feeding* on them,
And all the beasts of the earth will spend harvest time on them.
7 At that time a gift of homage will be brought to the LORD of hosts
[1]From a [a]people [2]tall and smooth,
Even from a people feared [3]far and wide,
A powerful and oppressive nation,
Whose land the rivers divide—
To the [b]place of the name of the LORD of hosts, *even* Mount Zion.

Message to Egypt

19 THE [1a]oracle concerning [b]Egypt.
Behold, the LORD is [c]riding on a swift cloud, and is about to come to Egypt;
The [d]idols of Egypt will tremble at His presence,
And the [e]heart of the Egyptians will melt within them.
2 "So I will incite Egyptians against Egyptians;
And they will [a]each fight against his brother, and each against his neighbor,
City against city, *and* kingdom against kingdom.
3 "Then the spirit of the Egyptians will be demoralized within them;
And I will confound their strategy,
So that [a]they will resort to idols and ghosts of the dead,
And to [1]mediums and spiritists.
4 "Moreover, I will deliver the Egyptians into the hand of a [a]cruel master,
And a [1]mighty king will rule over them," declares the Lord [2]GOD of hosts.

5 [a]And the waters from the sea will dry up,
And the river will be parched and dry.
6 And the [1a]canals will emit a stench,
The [2b]streams of Egypt will thin out and dry up;
[c]The reeds and rushes will rot away.
7 The bulrushes by the [a]Nile, by the [1]edge of the Nile
And all the sown fields by the Nile
Will become dry, be driven away, and be no more.
8 And the [a]fishermen will lament,
And all those who cast a [1]line into the Nile will mourn,
And those who spread nets on the waters will [2]pine away.
9 Moreover, the manufacturers of linen made from combed flax
And the weavers of white [a]cloth will be [1]utterly dejected.
10 And [1]the [a]pillars *of Egypt* will be crushed;
All the hired laborers will be grieved in soul.

11 The princes of [1a]Zoan are mere fools;
The advice of Pharaoh's wisest advisers has become [2]stupid.
How can you *men* say to Pharaoh,
"I am a son of the [b]wise, a son of ancient kings"?
12 Well then, where are your wise men?
Please let them tell you,
And let them [1]understand what the LORD of hosts
Has [a]purposed against Egypt.
13 The princes of [1]Zoan have acted foolishly,
The princes of [a]Memphis are deluded;
Those who are the [b]cornerstone of her tribes
Have [2]led Egypt astray.
14 The LORD has mixed within her a spirit of [a]distortion;
[b]They have led Egypt astray in all [1]that it does,
As a [c]drunken man [2]staggers in his vomit.
15 And there will be no work for Egypt
[a]Which *its* head or tail, *its* palm branch or bulrush, may do.
16 In that day the Egyptians will become like women, and they will tremble and be in [a]dread because of the [b]waving of the hand of the LORD of hosts, which He is going to wave over them.
17 And the land of Judah will become a [1]terror to Egypt; everyone [2]to whom it is mentioned will be in dread of it, because of the [a]purpose of the LORD of hosts which He is purposing against them.

3 [a]Ps. 49:1; Mic. 1:2 [b]Is. 26:11
4 [1]Lit., *in* [2]Lit., *light* [a]Is. 26:21; Hos. 5:15 [b]2 Sam. 23:4 [c]Prov. 19:12; Is. 26:19; Hos. 14:5
5 [1]Lit., *is finished* [a]Is. 17:10, 11; Ezek. 17:6-10
6 [a]Is. 46:11; 56:9; Jer. 7:33; Ezek. 32:4-6; 39:17-20
7 [1]So with some ancient versions and DSS; M.T. implies *Consisting of a people* [2]Lit., *drawn out* [3]Lit., *from it and beyond* [a]Ps. 68:31; Is. 45:14; Zeph. 3:10; Acts 8:27-38 [b]Zech. 14:16, 17

1 [1]Or, *burden of* [a]Is. 13:1 [b]Joel 3:19 [c]Ps. 18:9, 10; 104:3; Matt. 26:64; Rev. 1:7 [d]Ex. 12:12; Jer. 43:12; 44:8 [e]Josh. 2:11; Is. 13:7
2 [a]Judg. 7:22; 1 Sam. 14:20; 2 Chr. 20:23; Matt. 10:21, 36
3 [1]Or, *ghosts and spirits* [a]1 Chr. 10:13; Is. 8:19; Dan. 2:2
4 [1]Or, *fierce* [2]Heb., *YHWH,* usually rendered *LORD* [a]Is. 20:4; Jer. 46:26; Ezek. 29:19
5 [a]Is. 50:2; Jer. 51:36; Ezek. 30:12
6 [1]Lit., *rivers* [2]Or, *Nile branches;* i.e., the delta [a]Ex. 7:18 [b]Is. 37:25 [c]Ex. 2:3; Job 8:11; Is. 15:6
7 [1]Or, *mouth* [a]Is. 23:3, 10
8 [1]Lit., *hook* [2]Or, *languish* [a]Ezek. 47:10; Hab. 1:15
9 [1]Lit., *ashamed* [a]Prov. 7:16; Ezek. 27:7
10 [1]Lit., *her pillars* or, *her weavers* [a]Ps. 11:3
11 [1]Or, *Tanis* [2]Or, *brutish* [a]Num. 13:22; Ps. 78:12, 43; Is. 30:4 [b]Gen. 41:38, 39; 1 Kin. 4:30; Acts 7:22
12 [1]Or, *know* [a]Is. 14:24; Rom. 9:17
13 [1]Or, *Tanis* [2]Or, *have caused Egypt to stagger* [a]Jer. 2:16; 46:14, 19; Ezek. 30:13 [b]Zech. 10:4
14 [1]Lit., *its work* [2]Or, *goes astray* [a]Prov. 12:8; Matt. 17:17 [b]Is. 3:12; 9:16 [c]Is. 28:7
15 [a]Is. 9:14, 15
16 [a]2 Cor. 5:11; Heb. 10:31 [b]Is. 11:15

17 [1]Or, *cause of shame* [2]Lit., *who mentions it will be in dread to it* [a]Is. 14:24; Dan. 4:35

18 In that day five cities in the land of
Egypt will be speaking the language of
Canaan and [a]swearing *allegiance* to the
LORD of hosts; one will be called the
City of [1]Destruction.
19 In that day there will be an [a]altar
to the LORD in the midst of the land of
Egypt, and a [b]pillar to the LORD near its
border.
20 And it will become a sign and a
witness to the LORD of hosts in the land
of Egypt; for they will cry to the LORD
because of oppressors, and He will send
them a [a]Savior and a [1b]Champion, and
He will deliver them.
21 Thus the LORD will make Himself
known to Egypt, and the Egyptians will
know the LORD in that day. They will
even worship with [a]sacrifice and offering, and will make a vow to the LORD
and perform it.
22 And the LORD will strike Egypt,
striking but [a]healing; so they will [b]return
to the LORD, and He will respond to
them and will heal them.
23 In that day there will be a [a]highway
from Egypt to Assyria, and the Assyrians will come into Egypt and the Egyptians into Assyria, and the Egyptians
will [b]worship with the Assyrians.
24 In that day Israel will be the third
party with Egypt and Assyria, a blessing
in the midst of the earth,
25 whom the LORD of hosts has
blessed, saying, "Blessed is [a]Egypt My
people, and Assyria [b]the work of My
hands, and Israel My inheritance."

Prophecy about Egypt and Ethiopia

20 IN the year that the [1a]com-
mander came to [b]Ashdod, when
Sargon the king of Assyria sent him and
he fought against Ashdod and captured
it,
2 at that time the LORD spoke
through [a]Isaiah the son of Amoz, saying,
"Go and loosen the [b]sackcloth from
your hips, and take your [c]shoes off your
feet." And he did so, going [d]naked and
barefoot.
3 And the LORD said, "Even as My
servant Isaiah has gone naked and barefoot three years as a [1a]sign and token
against Egypt and [2b]Cush,
4 so the [a]king of Assyria will lead
away the captives of Egypt and the exiles
of Cush, [b]young and old, naked and
barefoot with buttocks uncovered, to the
[1]shame of Egypt.
5 "Then they shall be [a]dismayed and
ashamed because of Cush their hope and
Egypt their [b]boast.
6 "So the inhabitants of this coastland
will say in that day, 'Behold, such is our
hope, where we fled [a]for help to be
delivered from the king of Assyria; and
we, [b]how shall we escape?' "

God Commands That Babylon Be Taken

21 THE [1a]oracle concerning the
[2b]wilderness of the sea.
As [c]windstorms in the [3]Negev
sweep on,

18 [1]Some ancient mss. and versions read *the Sun* [a]Is. 45:23; 65:16
19 [a]Is. 56:7; 60:7 [b]Gen. 28:18; Ex. 24:4; Josh. 22:10, 26, 27
20 [1]Lit., *Mighty One* [a]Is. 43:3, 11; 45:15, 21; 49:26; 60:16; 63:8 [b]Is. 49:25
21 [a]Is. 56:7; 60:7; Zech. 14:16-18
22 [a]Deut. 32:39; Is. 30:26; 57:18; Heb. 12:11 [b]Is. 27:13; 45:14; Hos. 14:1
23 [a]Is. 11:16; 35:8; 49:11; 62:10 [b]Is. 27:13
25 [a]Is. 45:14 [b]Ps. 100:3; Is. 29:23; 45:11; 60:21; 64:8; Eph. 2:10

1 [1]Heb., *Tartan* [a]2 Kin. 18:17 [b]1 Sam. 5:1
2 [a]Is. 1:1; 13:1 [b]Zech. 13:4; Matt. 3:4 [c]Ezek. 24:17, 23 [d]1 Sam. 19:24; Mic. 1:8
3 [1]Or, *wonder* [2]Or, *Ethiopia,* so in vv. 4, 5 [a]Is. 8:18 [b]Is. 37:9; 43:3
4 [1]Lit., *nakedness* [a]Is. 19:4 [b]Is. 47:2, 3
5 [a]2 Kin. 18:21; Is. 30:3-5; 31:1; Ezek. 29:6, 7 [b]Jer. 9:23, 24; 17:5; 1 Cor. 3:21
6 [a]Is. 10:3; 30:7; 31:3; Jer. 30:1, 7, 15-17; 31:1-3 [b]Matt. 23:33; 1 Thess. 5:3; Heb. 2:3

1 [1]Or, *burden of* [2]Or, *sandy wastes, sea country* [3]I.e., South country [a]Is. 13:1 [b]Is. 13:20-22; 14:23; Jer. 51:42 [c]Zech. 9:14
2 [1]Lit., *her groaning* [a]Ps. 60:3 [b]Is. 24:16; 33:1 [c]Is. 22:6; Jer. 49:34
3 [a]Is. 13:8; 16:11 [b]Ps. 48:6; Is. 13:8; 26:17; 1 Thess. 5:3
4 [1]Lit., *heart has wandered* [2]Lit., *shuddering* [a]Deut. 28:67
5 [1]Or, *spread out the rugs* or possibly, *they arranged the seating* [a]Jer. 51:39, 57; Dan. 5:1-4
6 [a]2 Kin. 9:17-20
7 [a]Is. 21:9
8 [1]So DSS; M.T., *he called* like *a lion* [a]Hab. 2:1
9 [1]Lit., *he has shattered to the earth* [a]Is. 13:19; 47:5, 9; 48:14; Jer. 51:8; Rev. 14:8; 18:2 [b]Is. 46:1; Jer. 50:2; 51:44
10 [1]Lit., *son* [a]Jer. 51:33; Mic. 4:13

It comes from the wilderness, from
a terrifying land.
2 A [a]harsh vision has been shown to
me;
The [b]treacherous one still deals
treacherously, *and* the destroyer
still destroys.
Go up, [c]Elam, lay siege, Media;
I have made an end of all [1]the
groaning she has caused.
3 For this reason my [a]loins are full of
anguish;
Pains have seized me like the pains
of a [b]woman in labor.
I am so bewildered I cannot hear,
so terrified I cannot see.
4 My [1]mind reels, [2]horror over-
whelms me;
The twilight I longed for has been
[a]turned for me into trembling.
5 They [a]set the table, they [1]spread
out the cloth, they eat, they
drink;
"Rise up, captains, oil the shields,"
6 For thus the Lord says to me,
"Go, station the lookout, let him
[a]report what he sees.
7 "When he sees [a]riders, horsemen in
pairs,
A train of donkeys, a train of camels,
Let him pay close attention, very
close attention."
8 Then [1]the lookout called,
"[a]O Lord, I stand continually by day
on the watchtower,
And I am stationed every night at
my guard post.
9 "Now behold, here comes a troop of
riders, horsemen in pairs."
And one answered and said,
"[a]Fallen, fallen is Babylon;
And all the [b]images of her gods
[1]are shattered on the ground."
10 O my [a]threshed *people,* and my
[1]afflicted of the threshing floor!
What I have heard from the LORD
of hosts,
The God of Israel, I make known
to you.

Oracles about Edom and Arabia

11 The [1]oracle concerning [2a]Edom.
One keeps calling to me from [b]Seir,
"Watchman, [3]how far gone is the
night?
Watchman, [3]how far gone is the
night?"
12 The watchman says,
"Morning comes but also night.
If you would inquire, inquire;
Come back again."

13 The [1]oracle about [a]Arabia.
In the thickets of Arabia you [2]must
spend the night,
O caravans of [b]Dedanites.

11 [1]Or, *burden* [2]So the Gr.; Heb., *Dumah, silence* [3]Lit., *what* is the time *of the night?* [a]Gen. 25:14 [b]Gen. 32:3
13 [1]Or, *burden* [2]Or, *will spend* [a]Jer. 25:23, 24; 49:28 [b]Gen. 10:7; Ezek. 27:15

14 Bring water [1]for the thirsty,
O inhabitants of the land of [a]Tema,
Meet the fugitive with bread.
15 For they have [a]fled from the swords,
From the drawn sword, and from the bent bow,
And from the press of battle.
16 For thus the Lord said to me, "In a
[a]year, as [1]a hired man would count it, all
the splendor of [b]Kedar will terminate;
17 and the [a]remainder of the number
of bowmen, the mighty men of the
sons of Kedar, will be few; for the LORD
God of Israel [b]has spoken."

The Valley of Vision

22 THE [1]oracle concerning the [a]valley of vision.
What is the matter with you now,
that you have all gone up to the [b]housetops?
2 You who were full of noise,
You boisterous town, you [a]exultant city;
Your slain were [b]not slain with the sword,
Nor [1]did they die in battle.
3 [a]All your rulers have fled together,
And have been captured [1]without the bow;
All of you who were found were taken captive together,
[2]Though they had fled far away.
4 Therefore I say, "Turn your eyes away from me,
Let me [a]weep bitterly,
Do not [1]try to comfort me concerning the destruction of the daughter of my people."
5 [a]For the Lord [1]GOD of hosts has a [b]day of panic, [c]subjugation, and confusion
[d]In the valley of vision,
A breaking down of walls
And a crying [2]to the mountain.
6 And [a]Elam took up the quiver
With the chariots, [1]infantry, *and* horsemen;
And [b]Kir uncovered the shield.
7 Then your choicest valleys were full of chariots,
And the horsemen took up fixed positions at the gate.
8 And He removed the [1]defense of Judah.
In that day you [2]depended on the weapons of the [a]house of the forest,
9 And you saw that the breaches
In the *wall* of the city of David were many;
And you [a]collected the waters of the lower pool.
10 Then you counted the houses of Jerusalem,
And you tore down houses to fortify the wall.
11 And you made a reservoir [a]between the two walls
For the waters of the [b]old pool.
But you did not [1]depend on Him who made it,
Nor did you [2]take into consideration Him who planned it long ago.

12 Therefore in that day the Lord [1]GOD of hosts, called *you* to [a]weeping, to wailing,
To [b]shaving the head, and to wearing sackcloth.
13 Instead, there is [a]gaiety and gladness,
Killing of cattle and slaughtering of sheep,
Eating of meat and drinking of wine:
"[b]Let us eat and drink, for tomorrow we may die."
14 But the LORD of hosts revealed Himself [1]to me,
"Surely this [a]iniquity [b]shall not be [2]forgiven you
[c]Until you die," says the Lord [3]GOD of hosts.

15 Thus says the Lord [1]GOD of hosts,
"Come, go to this steward,
To [a]Shebna, who is in charge of the *royal* household,
16 'What right do you have here,
And whom do you have here,
That you have [a]hewn a tomb for yourself here,
You who hew a tomb on the height,
You who carve a resting place for [1]yourself in the rock?
17 'Behold, the LORD is about to hurl you headlong, O man.
And He is about to grasp you firmly,
18 *And* roll you tightly like a ball,
To be [a]*cast* into a vast country;
There you will die,
And there your splendid chariots will be,
You shame of your master's house.'
19 "And I will [a]depose you from your office,
And [1]I will pull you down from your station.
20 "Then it will come about in that day,
That I will summon My servant [a]Eliakim the son of Hilkiah
21 And I will clothe him with your tunic,
And tie your sash securely about him,
I will entrust him with your [1]authority,
And he will become a [a]father to the inhabitants of Jerusalem and to the house of Judah.
22 "Then I will set [a]the key of the [b]house of David on his shoulder,
When he opens no one will shut,
When he shuts no one will [c]open.
23 "And I will drive him *like* a [a]peg in a firm place,
And he will become a [b]throne of glory to his father's house.

14 [1]Lit., *to meet* [a]Gen. 25:15; Job 6:19
15 [a]Is. 13:14, 15; 17:13
16 [1]Lit., *the years of a hireling* [a]Is. 16:14 [b]Ps. 120:5; Song 1:5; Is. 42:11; 60:7; Ezek. 27:21
17 [a]Is. 10:19 [b]Num. 23:19; Zech. 1:6

1 [1]Or, *burden of* [a]Ps. 125:2; Jer. 21:13; Joel 3:12, 14 [b]Is. 15:3
2 [1]Lit., *dead in battle* [a]Is. 23:7; 32:13 [b]Jer. 14:18; Lam. 2:20
3 [1]Lit., *from a bow* [2]So with ancient versions; Heb., *They fled far away* [a]Is. 21:15
4 [1]Lit., *insist* [a]Is. 15:3; Jer. 9:1; Luke 19:41
5 [1]Heb., *YHWH,* usually rendered *LORD* [2]Or, *against* [a]Lam. 1:5; 2:2 [b]Is. 37:3 [c]Is. 10:6; 63:3 [d]Is. 22:1
6 [1]Lit., *man* [a]Is. 21:2; Jer. 49:35 [b]2 Kin. 16:9; Amos 1:5; 9:7
8 [1]Lit., *screen, covering* [2]Or, *looked to, considered* [a]1 Kin. 7:2; 10:17
9 [a]2 Kin. 20:20; Neh. 3:16
11 [1]Or, *look to, consider* [2]Lit., *see . . . Him* [a]2 Kin. 25:4; Jer. 39:4 [b]2 Kin. 20:20; 2 Chr. 32:3, 4
12 [1]Heb., *YHWH,* usually rendered *LORD* [a]Is. 32:11; Joel 1:13; 2:17 [b]Mic. 1:16
13 [a]Is. 5:11, 22; 28:7, 8; Luke 17:26-29 [b]Is. 56:12; 1 Cor. 15:32
14 [1]Lit., *in my ears* [2]Lit., *atoned for* [3]Heb., *YHWH,* usually rendered *LORD* [a]Is. 13:11; 26:21; 30:13; 65:7 [b]1 Sam. 3:14; Ezek. 24:13 [c]Is. 65:20
15 [1]Heb., *YHWH,* usually rendered *LORD* [a]2 Kin. 18:18, 26, 37; Is. 36:3, 11, 22; 37:2
16 [1]Lit., *himself* [a]2 Sam. 18:18; 2 Chr. 16:14; Matt. 27:60
18 [a]Job 18:18; Is. 17:13
19 [1]So with many ancient versions; Heb., *He* [a]Job 40:11, 12; Ezek. 17:24
20 [a]2 Kin. 18:18; Is. 36:3, 22; 37:2
21 [1]Lit., *rule* [a]Gen. 45:8; Job 29:16
22 [a]Rev. 3:7 [b]Is. 7:2, 13 [c]Job 12:14

23 [a]Ezra 9:8; Zech. 10:4 [b]1 Sam. 2:8; Job 36:7

24 "So they will hang on him all the
glory of his father's house, offspring and
[1]issue, all the least of vessels, from bowls
to all the jars.
25 "In that day," declares the LORD of
hosts, "the [a]peg driven in a firm place
will give way; it will even [b]break off and
fall, and the load hanging on it will be
cut off, for the [c]LORD has spoken."

The Fall of Tyre

23 THE [1]oracle concerning [a]Tyre.
Wail, O [b]ships of [c]Tarshish,
For *Tyre* is destroyed, without
house *or* [2][d]harbor;
It is reported to them from the land
of [3][e]Cyprus.
2 [a]Be silent, you inhabitants of the
coastland,
You merchants of Sidon;
[1]Your messengers crossed the sea
3 And *were* on many waters.
[a]The grain of the [1][b]Nile, the harvest of the River was her revenue;
And she was the [c]market of nations.
4 Be ashamed, O [a]Sidon;
For the sea speaks, the stronghold
of the sea, saying,
"I have neither travailed nor given
birth,
I have neither brought up young
men *nor* reared virgins."
5 When the report *reaches* Egypt,
They will be in [a]anguish at the
report of Tyre.
6 Pass over to [a]Tarshish;
Wail, O inhabitants of the coastland.
7 Is this your [a]jubilant *city*,
Whose origin is from antiquity,
Whose feet used to carry her to
[1]colonize distant places?

8 Who has planned this against Tyre,
[a]the bestower of crowns,
Whose merchants were princes,
whose traders were the honored
of the earth?
9 [a]The LORD of hosts has planned it
to [b]defile the pride of all beauty,
To despise all the [c]honored of the
earth.
10 [1]Overflow your land like the Nile,
O daughter of Tarshish,
There is no more [2]restraint.
11 He has [a]stretched His hand out
[b]over the sea,
He has [c]made the kingdoms tremble;
The LORD has given a command
concerning Canaan to [d]demolish its strongholds.
12 And He has said, "[a]You shall exult
no more, O crushed virgin
daughter of Sidon.
Arise, pass over to [1][b]Cyprus; even
there you will find no rest."
13 Behold, the land of the Chaldeans—this is the people *which* was not;
[a]Assyria appointed it for [b]desert creatures—they erected their siege towers,
they stripped its palaces, [c]they made it a
ruin.
14 Wail, O [a]ships of Tarshish,
For your stronghold is destroyed.
15 Now it will come about in that day
that Tyre will be forgotten for [a]seventy
years like the days of one king. At the
end of seventy years it will happen to
Tyre as *in* the song of the harlot:
16 Take *your* harp, walk about the
city,
O forgotten harlot;
Pluck the strings skillfully, sing
many songs,
That you may be remembered.
17 And it will come about at [a]the end
of seventy years that the LORD will visit
Tyre. Then she will go back to her
harlot's wages, and will [b]play the harlot
with all the kingdoms [1]on the face of the
earth.
18 And her [a]gain and her harlot's
wages will be [b]set apart to the LORD; it
will not be stored up or hoarded, but her
gain will become sufficient food and
choice attire for those who dwell in the
presence of the LORD.

Judgment on the Earth

24 BEHOLD, the LORD [a]lays the
earth waste, devastates it, distorts
its surface, and scatters its inhabitants.
2 And the people will be like the
priest, the servant like his master,
the maid like her mistress, the buyer like
the seller, the lender like the borrower, the [a]creditor like the debtor.
3 The earth will be completely laid
waste and completely despoiled, for the
LORD has spoken this word.
4 The [a]earth mourns *and* withers, the
world fades *and* withers, the [b]exalted of
the people of the earth fade away.
5 The earth is also [a]polluted [1]by its
inhabitants, for they transgressed laws,
violated statutes, [b]broke the everlasting
covenant.
6 Therefore, a [a]curse devours the
earth, and those who live in it are held
guilty. Therefore, the [b]inhabitants of the
earth are burned, and few men are left.
7 The [a]new wine mourns,
The vine decays,
All the merry-hearted sigh.
8 The [a]gaiety of tambourines ceases,
The noise of revelers stops,
The gaiety of the harp ceases.
9 They do not drink wine with song;
[a]Strong drink is [b]bitter to those
who drink it.
10 The [a]city of chaos is broken down;
[b]Every house is shut up so that
none may enter.
11 There is an [a]outcry in the streets
concerning the wine;
[b]All joy [1]turns to gloom.
The gaiety of the earth is banished.
12 Desolation is left in the city,
And the [a]gate is battered to ruins.

24 [1]Or perhaps, *leaf*
25 [a]Is. 22:23 [b]Esth. 9:24, 25 [c]Is. 46:11; Mic. 4:4

1 [1]Or, *burden of* [2]Lit., *entering* [3]Heb., *Kittim*
[a]Josh. 19:29; 1 Kin. 5:1; Jer. 25:22; 47:4; Ezek. 26:1-27:36; Joel 3:4-8; Amos 1:9; Zech. 9:2-4 [b]Is. 2:16 [c]Gen. 10:4; 1 Kin. 10:22 [d]Is. 24:10 [e]Gen. 10:4; Is. 23:12; Ezek. 27:6
2 [1]So DSS; M.T., *Who passed over the sea, they replenished you.*
[a]Is. 47:5
3 [1]Heb., *Shihor*
[a]Is. 19:7-9 [b]Josh. 13:3; 1 Chr. 13:5; Jer. 2:18 [c]Ezek. 27:3-23
4 [a]Gen. 10:15, 19; Josh. 11:8; Judg. 10:6; Jer. 25:22; 27:3; 47:4; Ezek. 28:21, 22
5 [a]Ex. 15:14-16; Josh. 2:9-11
6 [a]Is. 23:1
7 [1]Lit., *sojourn afar off*
[a]Is. 22:2; 32:13
8 [a]Ezek. 28:2
9 [a]Is. 2:11; 13:11 [b]Job 40:11, 12; Dan. 4:37 [c]Is. 5:13; 9:15
10 [1]Lit., *Pass over* [2]Perhaps *girdle* or *shipyard*
11 [a]Ex. 14:21; Is. 14:26 [b]Is. 19:5; 50:2 [c]Is. 13:13 [d]Is. 25:2; Zech. 9:3, 4
12 [1]Heb., *Kittim*
[a]Ezek. 26:13, 14; Rev. 18:22 [b]Is. 23:1
13 [a]Is. 10:5 [b]Is. 13:21; 18:6 [c]Is. 10:7
14 [a]Is. 2:16; Ezek. 27:25, 26
15 [a]Jer. 25:11, 22
17 [1]Lit., *of the earth on the face of the land*
[a]Is. 23:15 [b]Ezek. 16:25-29; Nah. 3:4
18 [a]Ps. 72:10, 11; Is. 60:5-9; Mic. 4:13 [b]Ex. 28:36; Zech. 14:20

1 [a]Is. 2:19; 13:13; 24:19, 20; 30:32; 33:9
2 [a]Lev. 25:36, 37; Deut. 23:19, 20
4 [a]Is. 33:9 [b]Is. 2:12; 24:21
5 [1]Lit., *under*
[a]Gen. 3:17; Num. 35:33; Is. 9:17; 10:6 [b]Is. 33:8
6 [a]Josh. 23:15; Is. 34:5; 43:28; Zech. 5:3, 4 [b]Is. 1:31; 5:24; 9:19
7 [a]Is. 16:10; Joel 1:10, 12
8 [a]Is. 5:12, 14; Ezek. 26:13; Hos. 2:11; Rev. 18:22
9 [a]Is. 5:11, 22 [b]Is. 5:20
10 [a]Is. 34:11 [b]Is. 23:1
11 [1]Lit., is *darkened*
[a]Jer. 14:2; 46:12 [b]Is. 16:10; 32:13
12 [a]Is. 14:31; 45:2

13 For [a]thus it will be in the midst of
the earth among the peoples,
As the [1]shaking of an olive tree,
As the gleanings when the grape
harvest is over.
14 [a]They raise their voices, they shout
for joy.
They cry out from the [1]west concerning the majesty of the
LORD.
15 Therefore [a]glorify the LORD in the
[1]east,
The [b]name of the LORD, the God of
Israel
In the [2c]coastlands of the sea.
16 From the [a]ends of the earth we
hear songs, "[b]Glory to the
Righteous One,"
But I say, "[1c]Woe to me! [1]Woe to
me! Alas for me!
The [d]treacherous deal treacherously,
And the treacherous deal very
treacherously."
17 [a]Terror and pit and snare
[1]Confront you, O inhabitant of the
earth.
18 Then it will be that he who flees the
[1]report of disaster will fall into
the pit,
And he who [2]climbs out of the pit
will be caught in the snare;
For the [a]windows [3]above are
opened, and the [b]foundations of
the earth shake.
19 [a]The earth is broken asunder,
The earth is [b]split through,
The earth is shaken violently.
20 The earth [a]reels to and fro like a
drunkard,
And it totters like a [1]shack,
For its [b]transgression is heavy
upon it,
And it will fall, [c]never to rise again.
21 So it will happen in that day,
That the LORD will [a]punish the
host of [1]heaven, on high,
And the [b]kings of the earth, on
earth.
22 And they will be gathered together
Like [a]prisoners in the [1]dungeon,
And will be confined in prison;
And after many days they will [b]be
punished.
23 Then the [a]moon will be abashed
and the sun ashamed,
For the [b]LORD of hosts will reign
on [c]Mount Zion and in Jerusalem,
And *His* glory will be before His
elders.

Song of Praise for God's Favor

25 O LORD, Thou art [a]my God;
I will exalt Thee, I will give
thanks to Thy name;
For Thou hast [b]worked wonders,
[c]Plans *formed* long ago, with perfect faithfulness.
2 For Thou hast made a city into a
[a]heap,
A [b]fortified city into a ruin;
A [c]palace of strangers is a city no
more,
It will never be rebuilt.
3 Therefore a strong people will
[a]glorify Thee;
[b]Cities of ruthless nations will revere Thee.
4 For Thou hast been a [a]defense for
the helpless,
A defense for the needy in his
distress,
A [b]refuge from the storm, a shade
from the heat;
For the breath of the [c]ruthless
Is like a *rain* storm *against* a wall.
5 Like heat in drought, Thou dost
subdue the [a]uproar of aliens;
Like heat by the shadow of a cloud,
the song of the ruthless is [1]silenced.

6 And [a]the LORD of hosts will prepare a [1]lavish banquet for [b]all
peoples on this mountain;
A banquet of [2]aged wine, [3]choice
pieces with marrow,
And [4]refined, aged wine.
7 And on this mountain He will
swallow up the [1a]covering which
is over all peoples,
Even the veil which is [2]stretched
over all nations.
8 He will [a]swallow up death for all
time,
And the Lord [1]GOD will [b]wipe
tears away from all faces,
And He will remove the [c]reproach
of His people from all the earth;
For the LORD has spoken.
9 And it will be said in that day,
"Behold, [a]this is our God for whom
we have [b]waited that [c]He might
save us.
This is the LORD for whom we have
waited;
[d]Let us rejoice and be glad in His
salvation."
10 For the hand of the LORD will rest
on this mountain,
And [a]Moab will be trodden down
in his place
As straw is trodden down in the
water of a manure pile.
11 And he will [a]spread out his hands
in the middle of it
As a swimmer spreads out *his
hands* to swim,
But *the Lord* will [b]lay low his pride
together with the trickery of his
hands.
12 And the [a]unassailable fortifications
of your walls He will bring
down,
Lay low, *and* cast to the ground,
even to the dust.

13 [1]Lit., *striking* [a]Is. 17:6; 27:12
14 [1]Lit., *sea* [a]Is. 12:6; 48:20; 52:8; 54:1
15 [1]Lit., *region of light* [2]Or, *islands* [a]Is. 25:3 [b]Mal. 1:11 [c]Is. 11:11; 42:4, 10, 12; 49:1; 51:5; 60:9; 66:19
16 [1]Lit., *Wasting to me!* [a]Is. 11:12; 42:10 [b]Is. 28:5; 60:21 [c]Lev. 26:39 [d]Is. 21:2; 33:1; Jer. 3:20; 5:11
17 [1]Lit., *Are upon you* [a]Jer. 48:43; Amos 5:19
18 [1]Lit., *sound of terror* [2]Lit., *goes up from the midst of* [3]Lit., *from the height;* i.e., heaven [a]Gen. 7:11 [b]Ps. 18:7; 46:2; Is. 2:19, 21; 13:13
19 [a]Is. 24:1 [b]Num. 16:31, 32; Deut. 11:6
20 [1]Or, *hut* [a]Is. 19:14; 24:1; 28:7 [b]Is. 1:28; 43:27; 66:24 [c]Dan. 11:19; Amos 8:14
21 [1]Lit., *the height in the height* [a]Is. 10:12; 13:11 [b]Ps. 76:12
22 [1]Lit., *pit* [a]Is. 10:4; 42:22 [b]Ezek. 38:8; Zech. 9:11, 12
23 [a]Is. 13:10 [b]Is. 60:19, 20; Zech. 14:6, 7; Rev. 21:23; 22:5 [c]Mic. 4:7; Heb. 12:22

1 [a]Ex. 15:2; Ps. 118:28; Is. 7:13; 49:4, 5; 61:10 [b]Ps. 40:5; 98:1 [c]Eph. 1:11
2 [a]Is. 17:1; 26:5; 27:10; 32:19 [b]Is. 17:3; 25:12 [c]Is. 13:22; 32:14; 34:13
3 [a]Is. 24:15 [b]Is. 13:11
4 [a]Is. 14:32; 17:10; 27:5; 33:16 [b]Is. 4:6; 32:2 [c]Is. 29:5, 20; 49:25
5 [1]Lit., *humbled* [a]Jer. 51:54-56
6 [1]Lit., *feast of fat things;* i.e., abundance [2]Lit., *wine on the lees* [3]Lit., *fat pieces* [4]Lit., *wine refined on the lees* [a]Is. 1:19 [b]Is. 2:2-4; 56:7
7 [1]Lit., *face of the covering* [2]Lit., *woven* [a]2 Cor. 3:15, 16; Eph. 4:18
8 [1]Heb., *YHWH,* usually rendered *LORD* [a]Hos. 13:14; 1 Cor. 15:54 [b]Is. 30:19; 35:10; 51:11; 65:19; Rev. 7:17; 21:4 [c]Ps. 69:9; 89:50, 51; Is. 51:7; 54:4; Matt. 5:11; 1 Pet. 4:14
9 [a]Is. 35:2; 40:9; 52:10 [b]Is. 8:17; 30:18; 33:2 [c]Is. 33:22; 35:4; 49:25, 26; 60:16 [d]Ps. 20:5; Is. 35:1, 2, 10; 65:18; 66:10
10 [a]Is. 16:14; Jer. 48:1-47; Ezek. 25:8-11; Amos 2:1-3; Zeph. 2:9
11 [a]Is. 5:25; 14:26 [b]Job 40:11; Is. 2:10-12, 15-17; 16:6, 14
12 [a]Is. 15:1; 25:2; 26:5

Song of Trust in God's Protection

26 [a]IN that day this song will be sung in the land of Judah:
"We have a [b]strong city;
He sets up walls and ramparts for [1c]security.
2 "Open the [a]gates, that the [b]righteous nation may enter,
The one that [1]remains faithful.
3 "The steadfast of mind Thou wilt keep in perfect [a]peace,
Because he trusts in Thee.
4 "[a]Trust in the LORD forever,
For in [1]GOD the LORD, *we have* an everlasting [b]Rock.
5 "For He has brought low those who dwell on high, the [a]unassailable city;
[b]He lays it low, He lays it low to the ground, He casts it to the dust.
6 "[a]The foot will trample it,
The feet of the [b]afflicted, the steps of the helpless."

7 The [a]way of the righteous is smooth;
O Upright One, [b]make the path of the righteous level.
8 Indeed, *while following* the way of [a]Thy judgments, O LORD,
We have waited for Thee eagerly;
[b]Thy name, even Thy [c]memory, is the desire of *our* souls.
9 [a]At night [1]my soul longs for Thee,
Indeed, [2]my spirit within me [b]seeks Thee diligently;
For when the earth [3]experiences Thy judgments
The inhabitants of the world [c]learn righteousness.
10 *Though* the wicked is shown favor,
He does not [a]learn righteousness;
He [b]deals unjustly in the land of uprightness,
And does not perceive the majesty of the LORD.

11 O LORD, Thy hand is lifted up *yet* they [a]do not see it.
[1]They see [b]*Thy* zeal for the people and are put to shame;
Indeed, [2c]fire will devour Thine enemies.
12 LORD, Thou wilt establish [a]peace for us,
Since Thou hast also performed for us all our works.
13 O LORD our God, [a]other masters besides Thee have ruled us;
But through Thee alone we [1b]confess Thy name.
14 [a]The dead will not live, the [1]departed spirits will not rise;
Therefore Thou hast [b]punished and destroyed them,
And Thou hast wiped out all remembrance of them.
15 [a]Thou hast increased the nation, O LORD,
Thou hast increased the nation, Thou art glorified;
Thou hast [b]extended all the borders of the land.
16 O LORD, they sought Thee [a]in distress;
They [1]could only whisper a prayer,
Your chastening was upon them.
17 [a]As the pregnant woman approaches *the time* to give birth,
She writhes *and* cries out in her labor pains,
Thus were we before Thee, O LORD.
18 We were pregnant, we writhed *in labor*,
We [a]gave birth, as it were, *only* to wind.
We could not accomplish deliverance for the earth
Nor were [b]inhabitants of the world [1]born.
19 Your [a]dead will live;
[1]Their corpses will rise.
You who lie in the dust, [b]awake and shout for joy,
For your dew is as the dew of the [2]dawn,
And the earth will [3]give birth to the [4]departed spirits.

20 Come, my people, [a]enter into your rooms,
And close your doors behind you;
Hide for a little [1b]while,
Until [c]indignation [2]runs *its* course.
21 For behold, the LORD is about to [a]come out from His place
To [b]punish the inhabitants of the earth for their iniquity;
And the earth will [c]reveal her bloodshed,
And will no longer cover her slain.

The Deliverance of Israel

27 IN that day [a]the LORD will punish [1b]Leviathan the fleeing serpent,
With His fierce and great and mighty sword,
Even [1]Leviathan the twisted serpent;
And [c]He will kill the dragon who *lives* in the sea.

2 In that day,
"A [1a]vineyard of wine, sing of it!
3 "I, the LORD, am its keeper;
[a]I water it every moment.
Lest anyone [1]damage it,
I [b]guard it night and day.
4 "I have no wrath.
Should [1]someone give Me [a]briars *and* thorns in battle,
Then I would step on them, [b]I would burn them [2]completely.
5 "Or let him [1a]rely on My protection,
Let him make peace with Me,
Let him [b]make peace with Me."

1 [1]Or, *salvation* [a]Is. 4:2; 12:1 [b]Is. 14:31; 31:5, 9; 33:5, 6, 20-24 [c]Is. 60:18
2 [1]Lit., *keeps faithfulness* [a]Is. 60:11, 18; 62:10 [b]Is. 45:25; 54:14, 17; 58:8; 60:21; 61:3; 62:1, 2
3 [a]Is. 26:12; 27:5; 57:19; 66:12
4 [1]Heb., *YAH*, usually rendered *LORD* [a]Is. 12:2; 50:10; 51:5 [b]Is. 17:10; 30:29; 44:8
5 [a]Is. 25:12 [b]Job 40:11-13
6 [a]Is. 28:3 [b]Is. 3:14, 15; 11:4; 29:19
7 [a]Is. 57:2 [b]Ps. 25:4, 5; 27:11; Is. 42:16; 52:12
8 [a]Is. 51:4; 56:1 [b]Is. 12:4; 24:15; 25:1; 26:13 [c]Ex. 3:15
9 [1]Lit., with *my soul I long* [2]Lit., with *my spirit . . . I seek* [3]Lit., *has* [a]Ps. 63:5, 6; 77:2; 119:62; Is. 50:10; Luke 6:12 [b]Ps. 63:1; 78:34; Matt. 6:33 [c]Is. 55:6; Hos. 5:15
10 [a]Is. 22:12, 13; 32:6, 7 [b]Hos. 11:7; John 5:37, 38
11 [1]Or, *Let them see . . . and be* [2]Or, *let the fire for Thine adversaries devour them* [a]Is. 44:9, 18 [b]Is. 9:7; 37:32; 59:17 [c]Is. 5:24; 9:18, 19; 10:17; 66:15, 24; Heb. 10:27
12 [a]Is. 26:3
13 [1]Or, *cause to be remembered* [a]Is. 2:8; 10:11 [b]Is. 63:7
14 [1]Or, *shades* [a]Deut. 4:28; Ps. 135:17; Is. 8:19; Hab. 2:19 [b]Is. 10:3
15 [a]Is. 9:3 [b]Is. 33:17; 54:2, 3
16 [1]Lit., *sound forth a whisper* [a]Is. 37:3; Hos. 5:15
17 [a]Is. 13:8; 21:3; John 16:21
18 [1]Lit., *fallen* [a]Is. 33:11; 59:4 [b]Ps. 17:14
19 [1]So with some ancient versions; Heb., *My* [2]Lit., *lights* [3]Lit., *cause to fall* [4]Or, *shades* [a]Is. 25:8; Ezek. 37:1-14; Dan. 12:2; Hos. 13:14 [b]Eph. 5:14
20 [1]Lit., *moment* [2]Lit., *passes over* [a]Ex. 12:22, 23; Ps. 91:1, 4 [b]Ps. 30:5; Is. 54:7, 8; 2 Cor. 4:17 [c]Is. 10:5, 25; 13:5; 34:2; 66:14
21 [a]Mic. 1:3; Jude 14 [b]Is. 13:11; 30:12-14; 65:6, 7 [c]Job 16:18; Luke 11:50

1 [1]Or, *sea monster* [a]Is. 66:16 [b]Job 3:8; 41:1; Ps. 74:14; 104:26 [c]Is. 51:9
2 [1]Some mss. read *a vineyard of delight* [a]Ps. 80:8; Is. 5:7; Jer. 2:21
3 [1]Lit., *punish* [a]Is. 58:11 [b]1 Sam. 2:9; Is. 31:5; John 10:28
4 [1]Lit., *who* [2]Lit., *altogether* [a]2 Sam. 23:6; Is. 10:17 [b]Is. 33:12; Matt. 3:12; Heb. 6:8
5 [1]Lit., *take hold of* [a]Is. 12:2; 25:4 [b]Job 22:21; Is. 26:3, 12; Rom. 5:1; 2 Cor. 5:20

6 [1]In the days to come Jacob [a]will take root,
Israel will [b]blossom and sprout;
And they will fill the [2]whole world with [c]fruit.

7 Like the striking of Him who has struck them, has [a]He struck them?
Or like the slaughter of His slain, [1]have they been slain?
8 Thou didst contend with them [1]by banishing them, by [a]driving them away.
With His fierce wind He has expelled *them* on the day of the [b]east wind.
9 Therefore through this Jacob's iniquity will be [a]forgiven;
And this will be [1]the full price of the [2b]pardoning of his sin:
When he makes all the [c]altar stones like pulverized chalk stones;
When [3]Asherim and incense altars will not stand.
10 For the fortified city is [a]isolated,
A [1]homestead forlorn and forsaken like the desert;
[b]There the calf will graze,
And there it will lie down and [2]feed on its branches.
11 When its [a]limbs are dry, they are broken off;
Women come *and* make a fire with them.
For they are not a people of [b]discernment,
Therefore [c]their Maker [d]will not have compassion on them.
And their Creator will not be gracious to them.
12 And it will come about in that day,
that the LORD [a]will start *His* threshing
from the flowing stream of the [b]Euphra-
tes to the brook of Egypt; and you will
be [c]gathered up one by one, O sons of
Israel.
13 It will come about also in that day
that a great [a]trumpet will be blown; and
those who were perishing in the land of
[b]Assyria and who were scattered in the
land of Egypt will come and [c]worship
the LORD in the holy mountain at Jerusalem.

Ephraim's Captivity Predicted

28 WOE to the proud crown of the [a]drunkards of [b]Ephraim,
And to the fading flower of its glorious beauty,
Which is at the head of the [1]fertile valley
Of those who are [2]overcome with wine!
2 Behold, the Lord has a strong and [a]mighty *agent;*
As a storm of [b]hail, a tempest of destruction,
Like a storm of [c]mighty overflowing waters,
He has cast *it* down to the earth with *His* hand.
3 The proud crown of the drunkards of Ephraim is [a]trodden under foot.
4 And the fading flower of its glorious beauty,
Which is at the head of the [1]fertile valley,
Will be like the [a]first-ripe fig prior to summer;
Which [2]one sees,
And [3]as soon as it is in his [4]hand,
He swallows it.
5 In that day the [a]LORD of hosts will become a beautiful [b]crown
And a glorious diadem to the remnant of His people;
6 A [a]spirit of justice for him who sits in judgment,
A [b]strength to those who repel the [1]onslaught at the gate.
7 And these also [a]reel with wine and stagger from strong drink:
[b]The priest and [c]the prophet reel with strong drink,
They are confused by wine, they stagger from [d]strong drink;
They reel while [1]having [e]visions,
They totter *when rendering* judgment.
8 For all the tables are full of filthy [a]vomit, without a *single clean* place.

9 "To [a]whom would He teach knowledge?
And to whom would He interpret the message?
Those *just* [b]weaned from milk?
Those *just* taken from the breast?
10 "For *He says,*
'[1a]Order on order, order on order,
Line on line, line on line,
A little here, a little there.' "
11 Indeed, He will speak to this people
Through [a]stammering lips and a foreign tongue,
12 He who said to them, "Here is [a]rest, give rest to the weary,"
And, "Here is repose," but they would not listen.
13 So the word of the LORD to them will be,
"[1]Order on order, order on order,
Line on line, line on line,
A little here, a little there,"
That they may go and [a]stumble backward, be broken, snared, and taken captive.

Judah Is Warned

14 Therefore, [a]hear the word of the LORD, O [b]scoffers,
Who rule this people who are in Jerusalem,

6 [1]Lit., *Those coming* [2]Lit., *face of* [a]Is. 37:31 [b]Is. 35:1, 2; Hos. 14:5, 6 [c]Is. 4:2
7 [1]Lit., *he was slain* [a]Is. 10:12, 17; 30:31-33; 31:8, 9; 37:36-38
8 [1]Some ancient versions read *by exact measure* [a]Is. 50:1; 54:7 [b]Jer. 4:11; Ezek. 19:12; Hos. 13:15
9 [1]Lit., *all the fruit* [2]Lit., *removing* [3]I.e., wooden symbols of a female deity [a]Is. 1:25; 48:10; Dan. 11:35 [b]Rom. 11:27 [c]Ex. 34:13; Deut. 12:3; 2 Kin. 10:26; Is. 17:8
10 [1]Lit., *pasture* [2]Lit., *consume* [a]Is. 32:13, 14 [b]Is. 17:2
11 [a]Is. 18:5 [b]Deut. 32:28; Is. 1:3; 5:13; Jer. 8:7 [c]Deut. 32:18; Is. 43:1, 7; 44:2, 21, 24 [d]Is. 9:17
12 [a]Is. 11:11; 17:6; 24:13; 56:8 [b]Gen. 15:18 [c]Deut. 30:3, 4; Neh. 1:9
13 [a]Lev. 25:9; 1 Chr. 15:24; Matt. 24:31; Rev. 11:15 [b]Is. 19:24, 25 [c]Is. 19:21, 23; 49:7; 66:23; Zech. 14:16; Heb. 12:22

1 [1]Lit., *valley of fatness* [2]Lit., *smitten* [a]Is. 28:7; Hos. 7:5 [b]Is. 9:9
2 [a]Is. 8:7; 40:10 [b]Is. 28:17; 30:30; 32:19; Ezek. 13:11 [c]Is. 8:6, 7; 30:28; Nah. 1:8
3 [a]Is. 26:6; 28:18
4 [1]Lit., *valley of fatness* [2]Lit., *the one seeing sees* [3]Lit., *while it is yet* [4]Lit., *palm* [a]Hos. 9:10; Mic. 7:1; Nah. 3:12
5 [a]Is. 41:16; 45:25; 60:1, 19 [b]Is. 62:3
6 [1]Lit., *battle* [a]1 Kin. 3:28; Is. 11:2; 32:15, 16; John 5:30 [b]2 Chr. 32:6-8; Is. 25:4
7 [1]Lit., *seeing* [a]Is. 5:11, 22; 22:13; 56:12; Hos. 4:11 [b]Is. 24:2 [c]Is. 9:15 [d]Hab. 2:15, 16 [e]Is. 29:11
8 [a]Jer. 48:26
9 [a]Is. 2:3; 28:26; 30:20; 48:17; 50:4; 54:13 [b]Ps. 131:2
10 [1]Heb., *Sav lasav, sav lasav, Kav lakav, kav lakav, Ze'er sham, ze'er sham.* These Hebrew monosyllables, imitating the babbling of a child, mock the prophet's preaching [a]2 Chr. 36:15; Neh. 9:30
11 [a]Is. 33:19; 1 Cor. 14:21
12 [a]Is. 11:10; 30:15; 32:17, 18; Jer. 6:16; Matt. 11:28, 29
13 [1]V. 10, note 1. The LORD responds to their scoffing by imitating their mockery, to represent the unintelligible language of a conqueror. [a]Is. 8:15; Matt. 21:44
14 [a]Is. 1:10; 28:22 [b]Is. 29:20

A PERFECT SACRIFICE

Numbers 19:2. The law said that oxen could be sacrificed only if they had not been yoked. This is because a bull that had been ploughing had been castrated and would therefore be imperfect for sacrifice.

SWORDS INTO PLOUGHSHARES

Joel 3:10. Joel speaks of people preparing for war who beat their ploughs into swords and their pruninghooks into spears. Isaiah 2:4 and Micah 4:3 speak of peace where people beat their swords into ploughshares and their spears into pruninghooks. Metal was so scarce at the time that there was a need for change of use.

LIFE-CYCLE OF FIG TREES

Song of songs 2:13; Jeremiah 24:2; 29:17; Matthew 21:18. It is not easy to relate the biblical references to the life cycle of the fig tree. The reference in the Song of Songs is probably to the first-ripe figs because they are ready at the time that the vines are in blossom. The bad figs seen by Jeremiah may be the inedible male caprifigs, which house the fig wasps while they develop. Jesus may have been looking either for remaining winter figs or for first-ripe figs. Whichever was missing indicated that the tree was infertile and would not give a main crop at *"the time of figs."* Jesus confirmed its uselessness by causing its death.

ST PETER'S FISH

Matthew 17:24-27. The fish concerned was the *tilapa* (nowadays called *"St. Peter's fish"*). Tilapa carry their eggs and later the young fish within their mouths. Even when they go in search of food for themselves, the young still return to the protection of the mother's mouth. When the mother fish wishes to keep them out she will pick up an object (a bright one, preferably) and will keep it in her mouth to prevent their return. In this case the fish has picked up a shekel piece.

"QUIET! BE STILL!"

Mark 4:39. When Jesus said, *"Quiet! Be still!"* he used the word *phimothete*, which would normally be used to exorcise evil spirits. Jesus recognized the devil's attempt on his life in the storm and spoke accordingly.

THE FIRST SMITHS

Genesis 4:15. Metalwork was taken up by the Jews so that metalsmiths became the elite of all craftsmen and were taken into captivity by the Babylonians (2 Kings 24:15-16). Solomon used his metalsmiths to create the implements for use in the Temple (1 Kings 7:45-47). It is not clear, however, where the Jews learned the craft.

Some scholars believe that they learned it form traveling metalsmiths of the Kenite clan, whose people traveled throughout the land with their bellows strapped onto donkeys. The traveling smith was recognized by a metal cross worn on his forehead. It has been suggested that this was the *"mark of Cain"* given by God to indicate that the descendents of Cain (which means *"smith"*) should be artisans, not rulers of tribes.

HEALTH LAWS

God gave the Jewish people a number of commandments and their medical significance has been appreciated only in recent years. Deuteronomy 23:13 ensured that the soldier carried a spade so that all human excrement could be buried. Leviticus 13 ensured isolation for people who had leprosy. It has been suggested that the insistence on circumcision has led to a very low incidence of cancer of the cervix among Jewish women, and that the forbidden degrees of marriage were given to control a number of hereditary diseases.

JEWELRY MAKING

Exodus 28:9-14. The Jews developed the craft of jewelry making and engraving. Ivory was carved and used for inlay (1 Kings 10:22; 22:39; Amos 2:15). Small cylinders were engraved and were used as personal seals. This craft developed naturally because as nomads it was not possible to carry a lot of material around.

UNGLAZED POTS

Matthew 10:42. Unglazed pottery was extremely important. As water evaporated through the clay, it cooled the liquid inside. This lies behind the description of water as *cold* water.

DESIGNATION OF MONEY

The terms used for money in the New Testament illustrate the problems Bible translators actually face. If they use the original term, it might be meaningless to the reader. If they substitute the name of a current coin, or a monetary value, then inflation might make the substitute completely out of date in a short time. *"Pieces of silver"* or a *"day's wages"* does not always indicate the value of the coinage because amounts vary in different societies.

ESTHER - *courage*

Despite the fact that Esther was very young, God used her to save the entire Jewish population from death. Had she not boldly risked her own life on behalf of her people, they would have been massacred. Her own cousin, Mordecai, remarked that she might have been born for just that purpose. Yet all this responsibility rested on the shoulders of a young maiden.

King Ahasuerus had already cast aside his first queen, Vashti, because of her disobedience to him. He had then called for all the beautiful young maidens to be gathered so he could choose a new queen. Esther was an orphan raised raised by her cousin, Mordecai, a devout Jew. He sent her to this assembly but advised her not to disclose she was a Jew. The king loved her more than any other woman and made her the queen. Her knowledge of God must have given her the strength she would need in her life as the queen of the Persian Empire.

When she learned of the plot against the Jews, she determined she would see the the king, even though it would mean disobeying him. She went saying *"If I perish, I perish,"* (Esther 4:16). She put her people's lives ahead of her own.

Because of Esther's fearlessness in this crises, she was able to think clearly. Her actions showed great wit and strategy, as well as caution and great judgement in timing. Her intelligent actions saved the lives of her people and gave them permanent protection through the right to defend themselves against their enemies. For twenty-four centuries Jews have celebrated the Feast of Purim, to remember the courage of this brave young woman.

QUESTIONS

1. Esther believed God would be her protection and thus carried out His will bravely. Where can you believe God to protect you so you can live more courageously for Him?

2. Esther put others' safety and well-being before her own, though it could have cost her life. Think about incidents when you have put yourself first. How might you have acted more generously?

3. Esther listened to wise counsel and made intelligent decisions. How can you take advantage of helpful advice in your own own life?

4. Mordecai believed Esther had been born to rescue her people. Do you have a sense of God's purpose for your life? What can you do to see that purpose fulfilled?

15 Because you have said, "We have
made a [a]covenant with death,
And with [1]Sheol we have made a
[2]pact.
[b]The overwhelming [3]scourge will
not reach us when it passes by,
For we have made [c]falsehood our
refuge and we have [d]concealed
ourselves with deception."
16 Therefore thus says the Lord
[1]GOD,
"[a]Behold, I am laying in Zion a
stone, a tested [b]stone,
A costly cornerstone *for* the foundation, [2]firmly placed.
He who believes *in it* will not be
[3]disturbed.
17 "And I will make [a]justice the measuring line,
And righteousness the level;
Then [b]hail shall sweep away the
refuge of lies,
And the waters shall overflow the
secret place.
18 "And your [a]covenant with death
shall be [1b]canceled,
And your pact with Sheol shall not
stand;
When the [c]overwhelming scourge
passes through,
Then you become its [d]trampling
place.
19 "As [a]often as it passes through, it
will [1]seize you.
For [b]morning after morning it will
pass through, *anytime* during the
day or night.
And it will be [2]sheer [c]terror to
understand [3]what it means."
20 The bed is too short on which to
stretch out,
And the [a]blanket is too [1]small to
wrap oneself in.
21 For the LORD will rise up as *at*
Mount [a]Perazim,
He will be stirred up as in the
valley of [b]Gibeon;
To do His [c]task, His [1d]unusual
task,
And to work His work, His
[2]extraordinary work.
22 And now do not carry on as [a]scoff-
ers,
Lest your fetters be made stronger;
For I have heard from the Lord
[1]GOD of hosts,
Of decisive [b]destruction on all the
earth.

23 Give ear and hear my voice,
Listen and hear my words.
24 Does the [1]farmer plow [2]continually
to plant seed?
Does he *continually* [3]turn and harrow the ground?
25 Does he not level its surface,
And sow dill and scatter [a]cummin,
And [1]plant [b]wheat in rows,
Barley in its place, and rye within
its [2]area?
26 For his God instructs and teaches
him properly.
27 For dill is not threshed with a
[a]threshing sledge,
Nor is the cartwheel [1]driven over
cummin;
But dill is beaten out with a rod,
and cummin with a club.
28 *Grain for* bread is crushed,
Indeed, he does not continue to
thresh it forever.
Because the wheel of *his* cart and
his horses *eventually* [1]damage *it,*
He does not thresh it longer.
29 This also comes from the LORD of
hosts,
Who has made *His* counsel [a]won-
derful and *His* wisdom [b]great.

Jerusalem Is Warned

29 WOE, O [1]Ariel, [1]Ariel the city
where David *once* [a]camped!
Add year to year, [2b]observe *your*
feasts on schedule.
2 And I will bring distress to Ariel,
And she shall be *a city of* lamenting
and [a]mourning;
And she shall be like an Ariel to
me.
3 And I will [a]camp against you [1]en-
circling *you,*
And I will set siegeworks against
you,
And I will raise up battle towers
against you.
4 Then you shall [a]be brought low;
From the earth you shall speak,
And from the dust *where* you are
prostrate,
Your words *shall come.*
Your voice shall also be like that of
a [1]spirit from the ground,
And your speech shall whisper
from the dust.

5 But the multitude of your [1]enemies
shall become like fine [a]dust,
And the multitude of the [b]ruthless
ones like the chaff which [2]blows
away;
And it shall happen [c]instantly,
suddenly.
6 From the LORD of hosts you will be
[a]punished with [b]thunder and
earthquake and loud noise,
With whirlwind and tempest and
the flame of a consuming fire.
7 And the [a]multitude of all the nations who wage war against
[1]Ariel,
Even all who wage war against her
and her stronghold, and who
distress her,
Shall be like a dream, a [b]vision of
the night.
8 And it will be as when a hungry
man dreams—
And behold, he is eating;
But when he awakens, his [1]hunger
is not satisfied,
Or as when a thirsty man dreams—
And behold, he is drinking,
But when he awakens, behold, he is
faint,

15 [1]I.e., the nether world [2]So some ancient versions; Heb., *seer* [3]Or, *flood* [a]Is. 28:18 [b]Is. 8:8; 28:2; 30:28; Dan. 11:22 [c]Is. 9:15; 30:9; 44:20; 59:3, 4; Ezek. 13:22 [d]Is. 29:15
16 [1]Heb., *YHWH,* usually rendered *LORD* [2]Lit., *well-laid* [3]Lit., *in a hurry* [a]Rom. 9:33; 10:11; 1 Pet. 2:6 [b]Ps. 118:22; Is. 8:14, 15; Matt. 21:42; Mark 12:10; Luke 20:17; Acts 4:11; Eph. 2:20
17 [a]2 Kin. 21:13; Is. 5:16; 30:18; 61:8; Amos 7:7-9 [b]Is. 28:2
18 [1]Lit., *covered over* [a]Is. 28:15 [b]Is. 7:7; 8:10 [c]Is. 28:15 [d]Is. 28:3; Dan. 8:13
19 [1]Lit., *take* [2]Lit., *only* [3]Lit., *the report,* or, *the message* [a]2 Kin. 24:2 [b]Is. 50:4 [c]Job 6:4; 18:11; 24:17; Ps. 55:4; 88:15; Lam. 2:22
20 [1]Lit., *narrow* [a]Is. 59:6
21 [1]Lit., *task is strange* [2]Lit., *work is alien* [a]2 Sam. 5:20; 1 Chr. 14:11 [b]Josh. 10:10, 12; 2 Sam. 5:25; 1 Chr. 14:16 [c]Is. 10:12; 29:14; 65:7 [d]Lam. 2:15; 3:33; Luke 19:41-44
22 [1]Heb., *YHWH,* usually rendered *LORD* [a]Is. 28:14 [b]Is. 10:22, 23
24 [1]Lit., *plowman* [2]Lit., *all day* [3]Lit., *open*
25 [1]Lit., *put* [2]Lit., *region* [a]Matt. 23:23 [b]Ex. 9:32
27 [1]Lit., *rolled* [a]Amos 1:3
28 [1]Lit., *discomfit*
29 [a]Is. 9:6 [b]Is. 31:2; Rom. 11:33

1 [1]I.e., Lion of God, or, Jerusalem [2]Lit., *let your feasts run their round* [a]2 Sam. 5:9 [b]Is. 1:14; 5:12; 22:12, 13; 29:9, 13
2 [a]Is. 3:26; Lam. 2:5
3 [1]Lit., *like a circle* [a]Luke 19:43, 44
4 [1]Or, *ghost* [a]Is. 8:19
5 [1]Lit., *strangers* [2]Lit., *passes away* [a]Is. 17:13; 41:15, 16 [b]Is. 13:11; 25:3; 29:20 [c]Is. 17:14; 30:13; 47:11; 1 Thess. 5:3
6 [a]Is. 10:3; 26:14, 21 [b]1 Sam. 2:10; Matt. 24:7; Mark 13:8; Luke 21:11; Rev. 11:13, 19; 16:18
7 [1]V. 1, note 1 [a]Mic. 4:11, 12; Zech. 12:9 [b]Job 20:8; Ps. 73:20; Is. 17:14

And his [1]thirst is not quenched.
[a]Thus the multitude of all the nations shall be,
Who wage war against Mount Zion.

9 [a]Be delayed and wait.
Blind yourselves and be blind.
They [b]become drunk, but not with wine;
They stagger, but not with strong drink.
10 For the LORD has poured over you a spirit of deep [a]sleep,
He has [b]shut your eyes, the prophets;
And He has covered your heads, the seers.
11 And the entire vision shall be to
you like the words of a sealed [1a]book,
which when they give it to the one who
[2]is literate, saying, "Please read this," he
will say, "I cannot, for it is sealed."
12 Then the [1]book will be given to the
one who [2]is illiterate, saying, "Please
read this." And he will say, "I [3]cannot
read."
13 Then the Lord said,
"Because [a]this people draw near with their [1]words
And honor Me with their [2]lip service,
But they remove their hearts far from Me,
And their [3]reverence for Me [4]consists of [5]tradition learned *by rote,*
14 Therefore behold, I will once again deal [a]marvelously with this people, wondrously marvelous;
And [b]the wisdom of their wise men shall perish,
And the discernment of their discerning men shall be concealed.

15 Woe to those who deeply [a]hide their [1]plans from the LORD,
And whose [b]deeds are *done* in a dark place,
And they say, "[c]Who sees us?" or "Who knows us?"
16 You turn *things* around!
Shall the potter be considered [1]as equal with the clay,
That [a]what is made should say to its maker, "He did not make me";
Or what is formed say to him who formed it, "He has no understanding"?

Blessing after Discipline

17 Is it not yet just a little while
[1]Before Lebanon will be turned into a [a]fertile field,
And the fertile field will be considered as a forest?
18 And on that day the [a]deaf shall hear [b]words of a book,
And out of *their* gloom and darkness the [c]eyes of the blind shall see.

8 [1]Lit., *soul* [a]Is. 54:17
9 [a]Is. 29:1 [b]Is. 51:17, 21, 22; 63:6
10 [a]Ps. 69:23; Is. 6:9, 10; Mic. 3:6; Rom. 11:8 [b]Is. 44:18; 2 Thess. 2:9-12
11 [1]Or, *scroll* [2]Lit., *knows books* [a]Is. 8:16; Dan. 12:4, 9; Matt. 13:11
12 [1]Or, *scroll* [2]Lit., *does not know books* [3]Lit., *do not know books*
13 [1]Lit., *mouth* [2]Lit., *lips* [3]Lit., *fear of Me* [4]Lit., *is* [5]Lit., *commandment of rulers* [a]Ezek. 33:31; Matt. 15:8, 9; Mark 7:6, 7
14 [a]Is. 6:9, 10; 28:21; 65:7; Hab. 1:5 [b]Is. 44:25; Jer. 8:9; 49:7; 1 Cor. 1:19
15 [1]Lit., *counsel* [a]Ps. 10:11, 13; Is. 28:15; 30:1 [b]Job 22:13; Is. 57:12; Ezek. 8:12 [c]Ps. 94:7; Is. 47:10; Mal. 2:17
16 [1]Lit., *like* [a]Is. 45:9; 64:8; Jer. 18:1-6; Rom. 9:19-21
17 [1]Lit., *And* [a]Ps. 84:6; 107:33, 35; Is. 32:15
18 [a]Is. 35:5; 42:18, 19; 43:8; Matt. 11:5; Mark 7:37 [b]Is. 29:11 [c]Ps. 119:18; Prov. 20:12; Is. 32:3
19 [a]Ps. 25:9; 37:11; Is. 11:4; 61:1; Matt. 5:5; 11:29 [b]Is. 3:14, 15; 11:4; 14:30, 32; 25:4; 26:6; Matt. 11:5; James 1:9; 2:5
20 [1]Lit., *watch evil* [a]Is. 29:5 [b]Is. 28:14 [c]Is. 59:4; Mic. 2:1
21 [1]Lit., *bring a person under condemnation* [2]Lit., *turn aside* [3]Lit., *confusion* [a]Amos 5:10 [b]Is. 32:7; Amos 5:12
22 [a]Is. 41:8; 51:2; 63:16 [b]Is. 45:17; 49:23; 50:7; 54:4
23 [1]Or, *his children see* [a]Is. 49:20-26 [b]Is. 26:12; 45:11; Eph. 2:10 [c]Is. 5:16; 8:13
24 [1]Lit., *spirit* [2]Lit., *understanding* [3]Lit., *murmur* [4]Lit., *learn* [a]Is. 30:21; Heb. 5:2 [b]Is. 41:20; 60:16 [c]Is. 54:13

1 [1]Lit., *pour out a drink offering* [a]Is. 1:2, 23; 30:9; 65:2 [b]Is. 29:15 [c]Is. 8:11, 12
2 [1]Lit., *My mouth* [a]Is. 31:1; Jer. 43:7 [b]Is. 8:19 [c]Is. 36:9
3 [a]Is. 20:5, 6; 36:6; Jer. 42:18, 22
4 [a]Is. 19:11
5 [a]Jer. 2:36 [b]Is. 10:3; 30:7; 31:3

19 The [a]afflicted also shall increase their gladness in the LORD,
And the [b]needy of mankind shall rejoice in the Holy One of Israel.
20 For the [a]ruthless will come to an end, and the [b]scorner will be finished,
Indeed [c]all who [1]are intent on doing evil will be cut off;
21 Who [1]cause a person to be indicted by a word,
And [a]ensnare him who adjudicates at the gate,
And [2b]defraud the one in the right with [3]meaningless arguments.
22 Therefore thus says the LORD, who
redeemed [a]Abraham, concerning the
house of Jacob,
"Jacob [b]shall not now be ashamed, nor shall his face now turn pale;
23 But when [1]he sees his [a]children, the [b]work of My hands, in his midst,
They will sanctify My name;
Indeed, they will [c]sanctify the Holy One of Jacob,
And will stand in awe of the God of Israel.
24 "And those who [a]err in [1]mind will [b]know [2]the truth,
And those who [3]criticize will [4c]accept instruction.

Judah Warned against Egyptian Alliance

30 "WOE to the [a]rebellious children," declares the LORD,
"Who [b]execute a plan, but not Mine,
And [1c]make an alliance, but not of My Spirit,
In order to add sin to sin;
2 Who [a]proceed down to Egypt,
Without [b]consulting [1]Me,
[c]To take refuge in the safety of Pharaoh,
And to seek shelter in the shadow of Egypt!
3 "Therefore the safety of Pharaoh will be [a]your shame,
And the shelter in the shadow of Egypt, your humiliation.
4 "For [a]their princes are at Zoan,
And their ambassadors arrive at Hanes.
5 "Everyone will be [a]ashamed because of a people who cannot profit them,
Who are [b]not for help or profit, but for shame and also for reproach."

6 The [1]oracle concerning the [a]beasts of the [b]Negev.
Through a land of [c]distress and anguish,
From [2]where *come* lioness and lion, viper and [d]flying serpent,
They [e]carry their riches on the [3]backs of young donkeys
And their treasures on [f]camels' humps,

6 [1]Or, *burden of* [2]Lit., *them* [3]Lit., *shoulders* [a]Is. 46:1, 2 [b]Gen. 12:9 [c]Ex. 5:10, 21; Deut. 4:20; 8:15; Is. 5:30; 8:22; Jer. 11:4 [d]Deut. 8:15; Is. 14:29 [e]Is. 15:7; 46:1, 2 [f]1 Kin. 10:2

To a people who cannot profit
them;
7 Even Egypt, whose [a]help is vain
and empty.
Therefore, I have called [1]her
"[2b]Rahab who has been exterminated."
8 Now go, [a]write it on a tablet before
them
And inscribe it on a scroll,
That it may [1]serve in the time to
come
[2]As a witness forever.
9 For this is a [a]rebellious people,
[b]false sons,
Sons who [1]refuse to [c]listen
To the [2]instruction of the LORD;
10 Who say to the [a]seers, "You must
not see *visions*";
And to the prophets, "You must
not [b]prophesy to us what is
right,
[c]Speak to us [1]pleasant words,
Prophesy illusions.
11 "Get out of the way, [a]turn aside
from the path,
[1b]Let us hear no more about the
Holy One of Israel."
12 Therefore thus says the Holy One
of Israel,
"[a]Since you have rejected this word,
And have put your trust in [b]oppression and guile, and have
relied on them,
13 Therefore this [a]iniquity will be to
you
Like a [b]breach about to fall,
A bulge in a high wall,
Whose collapse comes [c]suddenly in
an instant.
14 "And whose collapse is like the
smashing of a [a]potter's jar;
[1]So ruthlessly shattered
That a sherd will not be found
among its pieces
To [2]take fire from a hearth,
Or to scoop water from a cistern."
15 For thus the Lord [1]GOD, the Holy
One of Israel, has said,
"In [2]repentance and [a]rest you shall
be saved,
In [b]quietness and trust is your
strength."
But you were not willing,
16 And you said, "No, for we will flee
on [a]horses,"
Therefore you shall flee!
"And we will ride on swift *horses,*"
Therefore those who pursue you
shall be swift.
17 [a]One thousand *shall flee* at the
threat of one *man,*
You shall flee at the threat of five;
Until you are left as a [1]flag on a
mountain top,
And as a signal on a hill.

God Is Gracious and Just

18 Therefore the LORD [1a]longs to be
gracious to you,
And therefore He [2]waits on [b]high
to have compassion on you.
For the LORD is a [c]God of justice;
How blessed are all those who
[3d]long for Him.

19 [1]O people in Zion, [a]inhabitant in Jerusalem, you will [b]weep no longer. He will surely be gracious to you at the sound of your cry; when He hears it, He will [c]answer you.

20 Although the Lord has given you [a]bread of privation and water of oppression, *He,* your Teacher will no longer [b]hide Himself, but your eyes will behold your Teacher.

21 And your ears will hear a word behind you, [1]"This is the [a]way, walk in it," whenever you [b]turn to the right or to the left.

22 And you will defile your graven [a]images, overlaid with silver, and your molten [a]images plated with gold. You will scatter them as an impure thing; *and* say to [1]them, "[b]Be gone!"

23 Then He will [a]give *you* rain for [1]the seed which you will sow in the ground, and bread *from* the yield of the ground, and it will be [2]rich and [3]plenteous; on that day [b]your livestock will graze in a roomy pasture.

24 Also the oxen and the donkeys which work the ground will eat salted fodder, which [1]has been [a]winnowed with shovel and fork.

25 And on every lofty mountain and on [a]every high hill there will be [1]streams running with water on the day of the great [b]slaughter, when the towers fall.

26 And [a]the light of the moon will be as the light of the sun, and the light of the sun will be seven times *brighter,* like the light of seven days, on the day [b]the LORD binds up the [c]fracture of His people and [d]heals the bruise [1]He has inflicted.

27 Behold, [a]the name of the LORD
comes from a [1]remote place;
[b]Burning is His anger, and [2]dense
is *His* [3]smoke;
His lips are filled with [c]indignation,
And His tongue is like a [d]consuming fire;
28 And His [a]breath is like an overflowing torrent,
Which [b]reaches to the neck,
To [c]shake the nations back and
forth in a [1]sieve,
And to *put* in the jaws of the peoples [d]the bridle which [2]leads to
ruin.
29 You will have [1]songs as in the night
when you keep the festival;
And gladness of heart as when one
marches to *the sound of* the flute,
To go to the mountain of the LORD,
to the Rock of Israel.

7 [1]Lit., *this* one [2]M.T. reads *They are Rahab* (or *arrogance*), *to remain* [a]Is. 30:5 [b]Job 9:13; Ps. 87:4; 89:10; Is. 51:9
8 [1]Lit., *be* [2]So the versions; Heb., *Forever and ever* [a]Is. 8:1
9 [1]Lit., *are not willing* [2]Or, *law* [a]Is. 30:1 [b]Is. 28:15; 59:3, 4 [c]Is. 1:10; 5:24; 24:5
10 [1]Lit., *smooth things* [a]Is. 29:10 [b]Is. 5:20; Jer. 11:21; Amos 2:12; 7:13 [c]1 Kin. 22:8, 13; Jer. 6:14; 23:17, 26; Ezek. 13:7; Rom. 16:18; 2 Tim. 4:3, 4
11 [1]Lit., *Cause to cease from our presence* the [a]Acts 13:8 [b]Job 21:14
12 [a]Is. 5:24; 7:9; 8:6 [b]Is. 3:14, 15; 5:7; 59:13
13 [a]Is. 26:21 [b]1 Kin. 20:30; Ps. 62:4; Is. 58:12 [c]Is. 29:5; 47:11
14 [1]Lit., *Crushed, it will not be spared* [2]Lit., *snatch up* [a]Ps. 2:9; Jer. 19:10, 11
15 [1]Heb., *YHWH,* usually rendered *LORD* [2]Lit., *returning* [a]Ps. 116:7; Is. 28:12 [b]Is. 7:4; 32:17
16 [a]Is. 2:7; 31:1, 3
17 [1]Lit., *pole* [a]Lev. 26:36; Deut. 28:25; 32:30; Josh. 23:10; Prov. 28:1
18 [1]Lit., *waits* [2]Lit., *is on high* [3]Lit., *wait* [a]Is. 42:14, 16; 48:9; Jon. 3:4, 10; 2 Pet. 3:9, 15 [b]Is. 2:11, 17; 33:5 [c]Is. 5:16; 28:17; 61:8 [d]Is. 8:17; 25:9; 26:8; 33:2
19 [1]M.T. reads *A people will inhabit Zion, Jerusalem.* [a]Is. 65:9; Ezek. 37:25, 28 [b]Is. 25:8; 60:20; 61:1-3 [c]Ps. 50:15; Is. 58:9; 65:24; Matt. 7:7-11
20 [a]1 Kin. 22:27; Ps. 80:5 [b]Ps. 74:9; Amos 8:11
21 [1]Lit., *saying, "This* [a]Ps. 25:8, 9; Prov. 3:6; Is. 35:8, 9; 42:16 [b]Is. 29:24
22 [1]Lit., *it "Go out"* [a]Ex. 32:2, 4; Judg. 17:3, 4; Is. 46:6 [b]Matt. 4:10
23 [1]Lit., *your* [2]Lit., *fatness* [3]Lit., *fat* [a]Ps. 65:9-13; 104:13, 14 [b]Ps. 144:13; Is. 32:20; Hos. 4:16
24 [1]Lit., *one winnows* [a]Matt. 3:12; Luke 3:17
25 [1]Lit., *canals, streams of water* [a]Is. 35:6, 7; 41:18; 43:19, 20 [b]Is. 34:2
26 [1]Lit., *of His blow* [a]Is. 24:23; 60:19, 20; Rev. 21:23; 22:5 [b]Is. 61:1 [c]Is. 1:6; 30:13, 14 [d]Deut. 32:39; Job 5:18; Is. 33:24; Jer. 33:6; Hos. 6:1, 2
27 [1]Lit., *distance* [2]Lit., *heaviness* [3]Lit., *uplifting* [a]Is. 59:19 [b]Is. 10:17 [c]Is. 10:5; 13:5; 66:14 [d]Is. 66:15
28 [1]Lit., *sifting of the worthless* [2]Lit., *misleads* [a]Is. 11:4; 30:33; 2 Thess. 2:8 [b]Is. 8:8 [c]Amos 9:9 [d]2 Kin. 19:28; Is. 37:29
29 [1]Lit., *the song*

30 And the LORD will cause [1]His voice of authority to be heard.
And the [2]descending of His arm to be seen in fierce anger,
And *in* the flame of a consuming fire,
In cloudburst, downpour, and hailstones.
31 For [a]at the voice of the LORD [b]Assyria will be terrified,
When He strikes with the [c]rod.
32 And every [1]blow of the [2a]rod of punishment,
Which the LORD will lay on him,
Will be with *the music of* [b]tambourines and lyres;
And in battles, [c]brandishing weapons, He will fight them.
33 For [1a]Topheth has long been ready,
Indeed, it has been prepared for the king.
He has made it deep and large,
[2]A pyre of fire with plenty of wood;
The [b]breath of the LORD, like a torrent of [c]brimstone, sets it afire.

Help Not in Egypt but in God

31 WOE to those who go down to [a]Egypt for help,
And [b]rely on horses,
And trust in chariots because they are many,
And in horsemen because they are very strong,
But they do not [c]look to the [d]Holy One of Israel, nor seek the LORD!
2 Yet He also is [a]wise and will [b]bring disaster,
And does [c]not retract His words,
But will arise against the house of [d]evildoers,
And against the help of the [e]workers of iniquity.
3 Now the Egyptians are [a]men, and not God,
And their [b]horses are flesh and not spirit;
So the LORD will [c]stretch out His hand,
And [d]he who helps will stumble
And he who is helped will fall,
And all of them will come to an end together.

4 For thus says the LORD to me,
"As the [a]lion or the young lion growls over his prey,
Against which a band of shepherds is called out,
Will not be terrified at their voice, nor disturbed at their noise,
So will the LORD of hosts come down to wage [b]war on Mount Zion and on its hill."
5 Like [1]flying [a]birds so the LORD of hosts will protect Jerusalem.
He will [b]protect and deliver *it;*
He will pass over and rescue *it.*
6 [a]Return to Him from whom [1]you
have [b]deeply defected, O sons of Israel.

30 [1]Lit., *the majesty of His voice* [2]Lit., *descent*
31 [a]Is. 11:4 [b]Is. 10:12; 14:25; 31:8 [c]Is. 10:26; 11:4
32 [1]Lit., *passing* [2]Lit., *staff of foundation* [a]Is. 10:24 [b]1 Sam. 18:6; Jer. 31:4 [c]Ezek. 32:10
33 [1]I.e., the place of human sacrifice to Molech [2]Lit., *Its pile* [a]2 Kin. 23:10; Jer. 7:31; 19:6 [b]Is. 11:4; 30:28 [c]Gen. 19:24; Is. 34:9

1 [a]Is. 30:2, 7; 36:6 [b]Deut. 17:16; Ps. 20:7; 33:17; Is. 2:7; 30:16 [c]Is. 9:13; Dan. 9:13; Amos 5:4-8 [d]Is. 10:17; 43:15; Hos. 11:9; Hab. 1:12; 3:3
2 [a]Is. 28:29; Rom. 16:27 [b]Is. 45:7 [c]Num. 23:19; Jer. 44:29 [d]Is. 1:4; 9:17; 14:20 [e]Is. 22:14; 32:6
3 [a]Ezek. 28:9; 2 Thess. 2:4 [b]Is. 36:9 [c]Is. 9:17; Jer. 15:6; Ezek. 20:33, 34 [d]Is. 30:5, 7; Matt. 15:14
4 [a]Num. 24:9; Hos. 11:10; Amos 3:8 [b]Is. 42:13; Zech. 12:8
5 [1]Or, *hovering* [a]Deut. 32:11; Ps. 91:4 [b]Is. 37:35; 38:6
6 [1]Lit., *they* [a]Is. 44:22; 55:7; Jer. 3:10, 14, 22; Ezek. 18:31, 32 [b]Is. 1:2, 5
7 [a]Is. 2:20; 30:22 [b]1 Kin. 12:30
8 [1]Lit., *flee* [a]Is. 10:12; 14:25; 30:31-33; 37:7, 36-38 [b]Is. 66:16 [c]Is. 21:15 [d]Gen. 49:15; Is. 14:2
9 [a]Deut. 32:31, 37 [b]Is. 5:26; 13:2; 18:3 [c]Is. 10:16, 17; 30:33; Zech. 2:5

1 [a]Ps. 72:1-4; Is. 9:6, 7; 11:4, 5; Jer. 23:5; 33:15; Ezek. 37:24; Zech. 9:9
2 [1]Lit., *canals* [2]Lit., *heavy* [3]Lit., *an exhausted* [a]Is. 4:6; 25:4 [b]Is. 35:6; 41:18; 43:19, 20
3 [1]Or, *turned away* [a]Is. 29:18
4 [1]Lit., *heart* [2]Lit., *knowledge* [a]Is. 29:24
5 [a]1 Sam. 25:25
6 [1]Or, *does* [2]Lit., *make empty the hungry soul* [3]Lit., *he causes to lack* [a]Prov. 19:3; 24:7-9; Is. 59:7, 13 [b]Is. 9:17; 10:6 [c]Is. 3:15; 10:2
7 [1]Lit., *words of falsehood* [2]Lit., *justly* [a]Jer. 5:26-28; Mic. 7:3 [b]Is. 11:4; 61:1 [c]Is. 5:23
8 [a]Prov. 11:25
9 [a]Is. 47:8; Amos 6:1; Zeph. 2:15 [b]Is. 28:23

7 For in that day every man will
[a]cast away his silver idols and his gold
idols, which your hands have made as [b]a
sin.
8 And the [a]Assyrian will fall by a sword not of man,
And a [b]sword not of man will devour him.
So he will [1c]not escape the sword,
And his young men will become [d]forced laborers.
9 "And his [a]rock will pass away because of panic,
And his princes will be terrified at the [b]standard,"
Declares the LORD, whose [c]fire is in Zion and whose furnace is in Jerusalem.

The Glorious Future

32 BEHOLD, a [a]king will reign righteously,
And princes will rule justly.
2 And each will be like a [a]refuge from the wind,
And a shelter from the storm,
Like [1b]streams of water in a dry country,
Like the [a]shade of a [2]huge rock in [3]a parched land.
3 Then [a]the eyes of those who see will not be [1]blinded,
And the ears of those who hear will listen.
4 And the [1]mind of the [a]hasty will discern the [2]truth,
And the tongue of the stammerers will hasten to speak clearly.
5 No longer will the [a]fool be called noble,
Or the rogue be spoken of *as* generous.
6 For a fool speaks nonsense,
And his heart [1a]inclines toward wickedness,
To practice [b]ungodliness and to speak error against the LORD,
To [2c]keep the hungry person unsatisfied
And [3]to withhold drink from the thirsty.
7 As for a rogue, his weapons are evil;
He [a]devises wicked schemes
To [b]destroy *the* afflicted with [1]slander,
[c]Even though *the* needy one speaks [2]what is right.
8 But [a]the noble man devises noble plans;
And by noble plans he stands.

9 Rise up you [a]women who are at ease,
And hear my voice;
[b]Give ear to my word,
You complacent daughters.
10 Within a year and *a few* days,
You will be troubled, O complacent *daughters;*

[a]For the vintage is ended,
And the *fruit* gathering will not come.
11 Tremble, you *women* who are at ease;
[a]Be troubled, you complacent *daughters;*
[b]Strip, undress, and put *sackcloth* on *your* waist,
12 [a]Beat your breasts for the pleasant fields, for the fruitful vine,
13 [a]For the land of my people *in which* thorns *and* briars shall come up;
Yea, for all the joyful houses, *and for* the [b]jubilant city.
14 Because [a]the palace has been abandoned, the [1]populated [b]city forsaken.
[2]Hill and watch-tower have become [c]caves forever,
A delight for [d]wild donkeys, a pasture for flocks;
15 Until the [a]Spirit is poured out upon us from on high,
And the wilderness becomes a [b]fertile field
And the fertile field is considered as a forest.
16 Then [a]justice will dwell in the wilderness,
And righteousness will abide in the fertile field.
17 And the [a]work of righteousness will be peace,
And the service of righteousness, [b]quietness and [1]confidence forever.
18 Then my people will live in a [a]peaceful habitation,
And in secure dwellings and in undisturbed [b]resting places;
19 And it will [a]hail when the [b]forest comes down,
And [c]the city will be utterly laid low.
20 How [a]blessed will you be, you who sow beside all waters,
Who [1]let out freely the ox and the donkey.

The Judgment of God

33 WOE [a]to you, O destroyer,
While you were not destroyed;
And he [b]who is treacherous, while *others* did not deal treacherously with him.
As soon as you shall finish destroying, [c]you shall be destroyed;
As soon as you shall cease to deal treacherously, *others* shall [d]deal treacherously with you.
2 O LORD, [a]be gracious to us; we have [b]waited for Thee.
Be Thou [1]their [2c]strength every morning,
Our salvation also in the [d]time of distress.
3 At the sound of the tumult [a]peoples flee;
At the [b]lifting up of Thyself nations disperse.
4 And your spoil is gathered *as* the caterpillar gathers;
As locusts rushing about, men rush about on it.
5 The LORD is [a]exalted, for He dwells on high;
He has [b]filled Zion with justice and righteousness.
6 And He shall be the [1a]stability of your times,
A [b]wealth of salvation, wisdom, and [c]knowledge;
The [d]fear of the LORD is his treasure.
7 Behold, their brave men cry in [1]the streets,
The [2a]ambassadors of peace weep bitterly.
8 The highways are desolate, [1]the [a]traveler has ceased,
He has [b]broken the covenant, he has despised the cities,
He has no regard for man.
9 [a]The land mourns and pines away,
[b]Lebanon is shamed and withers;
[c]Sharon is like a desert plain,
And Bashan and Carmel [1]lose *their foliage.*
10 "Now [a]I will arise," says the LORD,
"Now I will be exalted, now I will be lifted up.
11 "You have [a]conceived [1]chaff, you will give birth to stubble;
[2]My [b]breath will consume you like a fire.
12 "And the peoples will be burned to lime,
[a]Like cut thorns which are burned in the fire.

13 "You who are far away, [a]hear what I have done;
And you who are near, [1]acknowledge My might."
14 [a]Sinners in Zion are terrified;
[b]Trembling has seized the godless.
"Who among us can live with [c]the consuming fire?
Who among us can live with [1]continual [d]burning?"
15 He who [a]walks righteously, and speaks with sincerity,
He who rejects [1]unjust gain,
And shakes his hands so that they hold no bribe;
He who stops his ears from hearing about bloodshed,
And [b]shuts his eyes from looking upon evil;
16 He will dwell on the heights;
[a]His refuge will be the [1]impregnable rock;
[b]His bread will be given *him;*
His water will be sure.

17 Your eyes will see [a]the King in His beauty;
They will behold [b]a far-distant land.

10 [a]Is. 5:5, 6; 7:23; 24:7
11 [a]Is. 22:12 [b]Is. 47:2
12 [a]Nah. 2:7
13 [a]Is. 5:6, 10, 17; 27:10 [b]Is. 22:2; 23:9
14 [1]Lit., *multitude of the* [2]Or, *Ophel* [a]Is. 13:22; 25:2; 34:13 [b]Is. 6:11; 22:2; 24:10, 12 [c]Is. 13:21; 34:13 [d]Ps. 104:11; Jer. 14:6
15 [a]Is. 11:2; 44:3; 59:21; Ezek. 39:29; Joel 2:28 [b]Ps. 107:35; Is. 29:17; 35:1, 2
16 [a]Is. 33:5; Zech. 8:3
17 [1]Or, *security* [a]Ps. 72:2, 3; 85:8; 119:165; Is. 2:4; Rom. 14:17; James 3:18 [b]Is. 30:15
18 [a]Is. 26:3, 12 [b]Is. 11:10; 14:3; 30:15; Hos. 2:18-23; Zech. 2:5; 3:10
19 [a]Is. 28:2, 17; 30:30 [b]Is. 10:18, 19, 34 [c]Is. 24:10, 12; 26:5; 27:10; 29:4
20 [1]Lit., *send out the foot of the ox* [a]Eccl. 11:1; Is. 30:23, 24

1 [a]Is. 10:6; 21:2 [b]Is. 24:16; 48:8 [c]Is. 10:12; 14:25; 31:8; Hab. 2:8 [d]Jer. 25:12-14; Matt. 7:2
2 [1]Some versions read *our* [2]Lit., *arm* [a]Is. 30:18, 19 [b]Is. 25:9 [c]Is. 40:10; 51:5; 59:16 [d]Is. 37:3
3 [a]Is. 17:13; 21:15 [b]Is. 10:33; 17:13; 59:16-18; Jer. 25:30, 31
5 [a]Ps. 97:9 [b]Is. 1:26; 28:6; 32:16
6 [1]Or, *faithfulness* [a]Is. 33:20 [b]Is. 45:17; 51:6 [c]Is. 11:9 [d]2 Kin. 18:7; Ps. 112:1-3; Is. 11:3; Matt. 6:33
7 [1]Lit., *the outside* [2]Lit., *messengers* [a]2 Kin. 18:18, 37
8 [1]Lit., *he who passes along the way* [a]Is. 35:8 [b]Is. 24:5
9 [1]Lit., *shake off* [a]Is. 3:26; 24:4; 29:2 [b]Is. 2:13; 10:34 [c]Is. 35:2; 65:10
10 [a]Ps. 12:5; Is. 2:19, 21
11 [1]Lit., *dry grass* [2]So one ancient version; M.T. reads *Your breath will* [a]Ps. 7:14; Is. 26:18; 59:4; James 1:15 [b]Is. 1:31
12 [a]2 Sam. 23:6, 7; Is. 10:17; 27:4
13 [1]Lit., *know* [a]Ps. 48:10; Is. 49:1
14 [1]Lit., *everlasting* [a]Is. 1:28 [b]Is. 32:11 [c]Is. 30:27, 30; Heb. 12:29 [d]Is. 9:18, 19; 10:16; 47:14
15 [1]Lit., *gain of extortioners* [a]Ps. 15:2; 24:4; Is. 58:6-11 [b]Ps. 119:37
16 [1]Lit., *stronghold of rock* [a]Is. 25:4 [b]Is. 49:10
17 [a]Is. 6:5; 24:23; 33:21, 22 [b]Is. 26:15

18 Your heart will meditate on [a]terror:
"Where is [b]he who counts?
Where is he who weighs?
Where is he who counts the towers?"
19 You will no longer see a fierce people,
A people of [1a]unintelligible speech [2]which no one comprehends,
Of a stammering tongue [3]which no one understands.
20 [a]Look upon Zion, the city of our appointed feasts;
Your eyes shall see Jerusalem an [b]undisturbed habitation,
[c]A tent which shall not be folded,
Its stakes shall never be pulled up
Nor any of its cords be torn apart.
21 But there the majestic *One,* the LORD, shall be for us
A place of [a]rivers *and* wide canals,
On which no boat with oars shall go,
And on which no mighty ship shall pass—
22 For the LORD is our [a]judge,
The LORD is [b]our lawgiver,
The LORD is [c]our king;
[d]He will save us—
23 Your tackle hangs slack;
It cannot hold the base of its mast firmly,
Nor spread out the sail.
Then the [a]prey of an abundant spoil will be divided;
[b]The lame will take the plunder.
24 And no resident will say, "I am [a]sick";
The people who dwell [1]there will be [b]forgiven *their* iniquity.

God's Wrath against Nations

34 DRAW near, [a]O nations, to hear; and listen, O peoples!
[b]Let the earth and [1]all it contains hear, and the world and all that springs from it.
2 For the LORD's [a]indignation is against all the nations,
And *His* wrath against all their armies;
He has [1b]utterly destroyed them,
He has given them over to [c]slaughter.
3 So their slain will be [a]thrown out,
And their corpses [1]will give off their [b]stench,
And the mountains will [2]be drenched with their [c]blood.
4 And [a]all the host of heaven will [1]wear away,
And the [b]sky will be rolled up like a scroll;
All their hosts will also wither away
As a leaf withers from the vine,
Or as *one* withers from the fig tree.
5 For [a]My sword is satiated in heaven,
Behold it shall descend for judgment upon [b]Edom,
And upon the people whom I have [c]devoted to destruction.
6 The sword of the LORD is filled with blood,
It is [1]sated with fat, with the blood of lambs and goats,
With the fat of the kidneys of rams.
For the LORD has a sacrifice in [a]Bozrah,
And a great slaughter in the land of [b]Edom.
7 [a]Wild oxen shall also [1]fall with them,
And [b]young bulls with strong ones;
Thus their land shall be [c]soaked with blood,
And their dust [2]become greasy with fat.
8 For the LORD has a day of [a]vengeance,
A year of recompense for the [1]cause of Zion.
9 And [1]its streams shall be turned into pitch,
And its loose earth into [a]brimstone,
And its land shall become burning pitch.
10 It shall [a]not be quenched night or day;
Its [b]smoke shall go up forever;
From [c]generation to generation it shall be desolate;
[d]None shall pass through it forever and ever.
11 But [1a]pelican and hedgehog shall possess it,
And [2]owl and raven shall dwell in it;
And He shall stretch over it the [b]line of [3]desolation
And the [4]plumb line of emptiness.
12 Its nobles—there is [a]no one there
Whom they may proclaim king—
And all its princes shall be [b]nothing.
13 And thorns shall come up in its [a]fortified towers,
Nettles and thistles in its fortified cities;
It shall also be a haunt of [b]jackals
And an abode of ostriches.
14 And the desert [a]creatures shall meet with the [1]wolves,
The [2b]hairy goat also shall cry to its kind;
Yes, the [3]night monster shall settle there
And shall find herself a resting place.
15 The tree snake shall make its nest and lay *eggs* there,
And it will hatch and gather *them* under its [1]protection.
Yes, [a]the [2]hawks shall be gathered there,
Every one with its kind.

16 Seek from the [a]book of the LORD, and read:
Not one of these will be missing;
None will lack its mate.
For [1b]His mouth has commanded,
And His Spirit has gathered them.

18 [a]Is. 17:14 [b]1 Cor. 1:20
19 [1]Lit., *deepness of lip* [2]Lit., *from hearing* [3]Lit., *there is no understanding* [a]Deut. 28:49, 50; Is. 28:11; Jer. 5:15
20 [a]Ps. 48:12 [b]Ps. 46:5; 125:1, 2; Is. 32:18 [c]Is. 54:2
21 [a]Is. 41:18; 43:19, 20; 48:18; 66:12
22 [a]Is. 2:4; 11:4; 16:5; 51:5 [b]Is. 1:10; 51:4, 7; James 4:12 [c]Ps. 89:18; Is. 33:17; Zech. 9:9 [d]Is. 25:9; 35:4; 49:25, 26; 60:16
23 [a]2 Kin. 7:16 [b]2 Kin. 7:8; Is. 35:6
24 [1]Lit., *in it* [a]Is. 30:26; 58:8; Jer. 30:17 [b]Is. 40:2; 44:22; Jer. 50:20; Mic. 7:18, 19; 1 John 1:7-9

1 [1]Lit., *its fulness* [a]Ps. 49:1; Is. 41:1; 43:9 [b]Deut. 32:1; Is. 1:2
2 [1]Lit., *put under the ban* [a]Is. 26:20 [b]Is. 13:5; 24:1 [c]Is. 30:25; 63:6; 65:12
3 [1]Lit., *their stench will go up* [2]Lit., *dissolve* [a]Is. 14:19 [b]Joel 2:20; Amos 4:10 [c]Ezek. 14:19; 35:6; 38:22
4 [1]Lit., *rot* [a]Is. 13:13; 51:6; Ezek. 32:7, 8; Joel 2:31; Matt. 24:29; 2 Pet. 3:10 [b]Rev. 6:12-14
5 [a]Deut. 32:41, 42; Jer. 46:10; Ezek. 21:3-5 [b]Is. 63:1; Jer. 49:7, 8, 20; Ezek. 25:12-14; 35:1-15; Amos 1:11, 12; Obad. 1-14; Mal. 1:4 [c]Is. 24:6; 43:28
6 [1]Lit., *made fat* [a]Is. 63:1; Jer. 49:13 [b]Is. 63:1
7 [1]Lit., *go down* [2]Lit., *made fat* [a]Num. 23:22; Ps. 22:21 [b]Ps. 68:30; Jer. 50:27 [c]Is. 63:6
8 [1]Or, *controversy* [a]Is. 13:6; 35:4; 47:3; 61:2; 63:4
9 [1]I.e., Edom's [a]Deut. 29:23; Ps. 11:6; Is. 30:33
10 [a]Is. 1:31; 66:24 [b]Rev. 14:11; 19:3 [c]Is. 13:20-22; 24:1; 34:10-15; Mal. 1:3, 4 [d]Ezek. 29:11
11 [1]Or, *owl* or *jackdaw* [2]Or, *great horned owl* [3]Or, *formlessness* [4]Lit., *stones of void* [a]Zeph. 2:14 [b]2 Kin. 21:13; Is. 24:10; Lam. 2:8
12 [a]Jer. 27:20; 39:6 [b]Is. 41:11, 12
13 [a]Is. 13:22; 25:2; 32:13 [b]Ps. 44:19; Jer. 9:11; 10:22
14 [1]Or, *howling creatures* [2]Or, *demon* [3]Heb., *Lilith* [a]Is. 13:21 [b]Is. 13:21
15 [1]Lit., *shade* [2]Or, *kites* [a]Deut. 14:13
16 [1]So DSS; M.T., *My* [a]Is. 30:8 [b]Is. 1:20; 40:5; 58:14

17 And He has cast the [a]lot for them,
And His hand has divided it to them by [b]line.
They shall possess it forever;
From [c]generation to generation they shall dwell in it.

Zion's Happy Future

35 THE [a]wilderness and the desert will be glad,
And the [1b]Arabah will rejoice and blossom;
Like the crocus
2 It will [a]blossom profusely
And [b]rejoice with rejoicing and shout of joy.
The [c]glory of Lebanon will be given to it,
The majesty of [d]Carmel and Sharon.
They will see the [e]glory of the LORD,
The majesty of our God.
3 [a]Encourage the [1]exhausted, and strengthen the [2]feeble.
4 Say to those with [a]anxious heart,
"Take courage, fear not.
Behold, your God will come *with* [b]vengeance;
The [c]recompense of God will come,
But He will [d]save you."
5 Then the [a]eyes of the blind will be opened,
And the ears of the deaf will be unstopped.
6 Then the [a]lame will leap like a deer,
And the [b]tongue of the dumb will shout for joy.
For waters will break forth in the [c]wilderness
And streams in the [1]Arabah.
7 And the [1]scorched land will become a pool,
And the thirsty ground [a]springs of water;
In the [b]haunt of jackals, its resting place,
Grass *becomes* reeds and rushes.
8 And [a]a highway will be there, [b]a roadway,
And it will be called the Highway of [c]Holiness.
The unclean will not travel on it,
But it *will* be for him who walks *that* way,
And [d]fools will not wander *on it.*
9 No [a]lion will be there,
Nor will any vicious beast go up on it;
[1]These will not be found there.
But [b]the redeemed will walk *there,*
10 And [a]the ransomed of the LORD will return,
And come with joyful shouting to Zion,
With everlasting joy upon their heads.
They will [1]find gladness and joy,
And [b]sorrow and sighing will flee away.

17 [a]Is. 17:13, 14; Jer. 13:25 [b]Is. 34:11 [c]Is. 34:10
1 [1]Or, *desert* [a]Is. 6:11; 7:21-25; 27:10; 41:18; 55:12, 13 [b]Is. 41:19; 51:3
2 [a]Is. 27:6; 32:15 [b]Is. 25:9; 35:10; 55:12, 13; 66:10, 14 [c]Is. 60:13 [d]Song 7:5 [e]Is. 25:9
3 [1]Lit., *slack hands* [2]Lit., *tottering knees* [a]Job 4:3, 4; Heb. 12:12
4 [a]Is. 32:4 [b]Is. 1:24; 47:3; 61:2; 63:4 [c]Is. 34:8; 59:18 [d]Ps. 145:19; Is. 33:22; 35:4
5 [a]Is. 29:18; 32:3, 4; 42:7, 16; 50:4; Matt. 11:5; John 9:6, 7
6 [1]Or, *desert* [a]Matt. 15:30; John 5:8, 9; Acts 3:8 [b]Matt. 9:32; Luke 11:14 [c]Is. 35:1; 41:18; 43:19; 49:10; 51:3; John 7:38
7 [1]Or, *mirage* [a]Is. 49:10 [b]Is. 13:22; 34:13
8 [a]Is. 11:16; 19:23; 40:3; 49:11; 62:10 [b]Is. 30:21; 51:10 [c]Is. 4:3; 52:1; Matt. 7:13, 14; 1 Pet. 1:15, 16 [d]Is. 33:8
9 [1]Lit., *It* [a]Is. 5:29; 30:6 [b]Is. 51:10; 62:12; 63:4
10 [1]Lit., *overtake* [a]Is. 1:27; 51:11 [b]Is. 25:8; 30:19; 65:19; Rev. 7:17; 21:4

1 [a]2 Kin. 18:13 [b]2 Chr. 32:1
2 [1]I.e., launderer's [a]2 Kin. 18:17-20:11; 2 Chr. 32:9-24; Is. 36:2-38:8 [b]Is. 7:3
3 [a]Is. 22:20 [b]Is. 22:15
4 [1]Lit., *trust* [a]2 Kin. 18:19
5 [1]Lit., *words of lips* [a]2 Kin. 18:7
6 [1]Lit., *palm* [a]Ezek. 29:6, 7 [b]Ps. 146:3; Is. 30:3, 5, 7
7 [a]Deut. 12:2-5; 2 Kin. 18:4, 5
8 [1]Lit., *please exchange pledges*
9 [1]Lit., *turn away the face of* [2]Or, *governor* [3]Lit., *rely on for yourself* [a]Is. 20:5; 30:2-5, 7; 31:3
10 [1]Lit., *without the LORD* [a]1 Kin. 13:18; 22:6, 12
11 [1]Lit., *hear* [2]I.e., Hebrew [a]Ezra 4:7; Dan. 2:4 [b]Is. 36:13
13 [a]2 Chr. 32:18
14 [a]Is. 37:10
15 [a]Is. 36:18, 20; 37:10, 11

Sennacherib Invades Judah

36 [a]NOW it came about in the fourteenth year of King Hezekiah, [b]Sennacherib king of Assyria came up against all the fortified cities of Judah and seized them.

2 And the [a]king of Assyria sent Rabshakeh from Lachish to Jerusalem to King Hezekiah with a large army. And he stood by the [b]conduit of the upper pool on the highway of the [1]fuller's field.

3 Then [a]Eliakim the son of Hilkiah, who was over the household, and [b]Shebna the scribe, and Joah the son of Asaph, the recorder, came out to him.

4 Then [a]Rabshakeh said to them, "Say now to Hezekiah, 'Thus says the great king, the king of Assyria, "What is this confidence that you [1]have?

5 "I say, 'Your counsel and strength for the war are only [1]empty words.' Now on whom do you rely, that [a]you have rebelled against me?

6 "Behold, you rely on the [a]staff of this crushed reed, *even* on Egypt; on which if a man leans, it will go into his [1]hand and pierce it. [b]So is Pharaoh king of Egypt to all who rely on him.

7 "But if you say to me, 'We trust in the LORD our God,' is it not He [a]whose high places and whose altars Hezekiah has taken away, and has said to Judah and to Jerusalem, 'You shall worship before this altar'?

8 "Now therefore, [1]come make a bargain with my master the king of Assyria, and I will give you two thousand horses, if you are able on your part to set riders on them.

9 "How then can you [1]repulse one [2]official of the least of my master's servants, and [3]rely on Egypt for chariots and for horsemen?

10 "And have I now come up [1]without the LORD's approval against this land to destroy it? [a]The LORD said to me, 'Go up against this land, and destroy it.' " ' "

11 Then Eliakim and Shebna and Joah said to Rabshakeh, "Speak now to your servants in [a]Aramaic, for we [1]understand *it;* and do not speak with us in [2b]Judean, in the hearing of the people who are on the wall."

12 But Rabshakeh said, "Has my master sent me only to your master and to you to speak these words, *and* not to the men who sit on the wall, *doomed* to eat their own dung and drink their own urine with you?"

13 Then Rabshakeh stood and [a]cried with a loud voice in Judean, and said, "Hear the words of the great king, the king of Assyria.

14 "Thus says the king, 'Do not let Hezekiah [a]deceive you, for he will not be able to deliver you;

15 nor let Hezekiah make you [a]trust in the LORD, saying, "The LORD will surely deliver us, this city shall not be given into the hand of the king of Assyria."

16 'Do not listen to Hezekiah,' for thus
says the king of Assyria, '[1]Make your
peace with me and come out to me, and
eat each of his [a]vine and each of his fig
tree and drink each of the [b]waters of his
own cistern,
17 until I come and take you away to
a land like your own land, a land of
grain and new wine, a land of bread and
vineyards.
18 '*Beware* lest Hezekiah misleads you,
saying, "[a]The LORD will deliver us." Has
any one of the gods of the nations
delivered his land from the hand of the
king of Assyria?
19 'Where are the gods of [a]Hamath
and Arpad? Where are the gods of
[a]Sepharvaim? And when have they [b]de-
livered Samaria from my hand?
20 'Who among all the [a]gods of these
lands have delivered their land from my
hand, that the [b]LORD should deliver
Jerusalem from my hand?' "
21 But they were silent and [a]answered
him not a word; for the king's commandment was, "Do not answer him."
22 Then [a]Eliakim the son of Hilkiah,
who was over the household, and
[b]Shebna the scribe and Joah the son of
Asaph, the recorder, came to Hezekiah
with their clothes torn and told him the
words of Rabshakeh.

Hezekiah Seeks Isaiah's Help

37 AND [a]when King Hezekiah
heard *it*, he tore his clothes, covered himself with sackcloth and entered
the house of the LORD.
2 Then he sent [a]Eliakim who was
over the household with [b]Shebna the
scribe and the elders of the priests,
covered with sackcloth, to [c]Isaiah the
prophet, the son of Amoz.
3 And they said to him, "Thus says
Hezekiah, 'This day is a [a]day of distress,
rebuke, and rejection; for [b]children have
come to birth, and there is no strength to
[1]deliver.
4 'Perhaps the LORD your God will
hear the words of Rabshakeh, whom his
master the king of Assyria has sent to
[a]reproach the living God, and will rebuke the words which the LORD your
God has heard. Therefore, offer a prayer
for [b]the remnant that is left.' "
5 So the servants of King Hezekiah
came to Isaiah.
6 And Isaiah said to them, "Thus
you shall say to your master, 'Thus says
the LORD, "[a]Do not be afraid because of
the words that you have heard, with
which the servants of the king of Assyria
have blasphemed Me.
7 "Behold, I will put a spirit in him so
that he shall [a]hear a rumor and [b]return
to his own land. And I will make him
fall by the sword in his own land." ' "
8 Then Rabshakeh returned and
found the king of Assyria fighting
against [a]Libnah, for he had heard that
[1]the king had left [b]Lachish.
9 When he [a]heard *them* say concerning Tirhakah king of [1][b]Cush, "He has
come out to fight against you," and
when he heard *it* he sent messengers to
Hezekiah, saying,
10 "Thus you shall say to Hezekiah
king of [1]Judah, '[a]Do not let your God in
whom you trust deceive you, saying,
"Jerusalem shall not be given into the
hand of the king of Assyria."
11 '[a]Behold, you have heard what the
kings of Assyria have done to all the
lands, destroying them completely. So
will you be [1]spared?
12 'Did the gods of [1]those nations
which my fathers have destroyed deliver
them, *even* [a]Gozan and [b]Haran and
Rezeph and the sons of Eden who *were*
in Telassar?
13 'Where is the king of Hamath, the
king of Arpad, the king of the city of
Sepharvaim, *and of* Hena and Ivvah?' "

Hezekiah's Prayer in the Temple

14 Then Hezekiah took the [1]letter
from the hand of the messengers and
read it, and he went up to the house of
the LORD and [2]spread it out before the
LORD.
15 And Hezekiah prayed to the LORD
saying,
16 "O LORD of hosts, the God of Israel,
[a]who art enthroned *above* the cherubim,
Thou art the [b]God, Thou alone, of all
the kingdoms of the earth. [c]Thou hast
made heaven and earth.
17 "[a]Incline Thine ear, O LORD, and
hear; open Thine eyes, O LORD, and see;
and [b]listen to all the words of Sennacherib, who sent *them* to [c]reproach the
living God.
18 "Truly, O LORD, the [a]kings of Assyria have devastated all the countries
and their lands,
19 and have cast their gods into the
fire, for they were not gods but the [a]work
of men's hands, wood and stone. So they
have [b]destroyed them.
20 "And now, O LORD our God, [a]de-
liver us from his hand that [b]all the
kingdoms of the earth may know that
Thou alone, LORD, [1]art God."

God Answers through Isaiah

21 Then [a]Isaiah the son of Amoz sent
word to Hezekiah, saying, "Thus says the
LORD, the God of Israel, 'Because you
have prayed to Me about Sennacherib
king of Assyria,
22 this is the word that the LORD has
spoken against him:
"She has despised you and mocked you,
The [a]virgin [b]daughter of Zion;
She has [c]shaken *her* head behind you,
The daughter of Jerusalem!
23 "Whom have you [a]reproached and blasphemed?
And against whom have you raised *your* voice,
And [1]haughtily [b]lifted up your eyes?
Against the [c]Holy One of Israel!

---

16 [1]Lit., *Make with me a blessing* [a]1 Kin. 4:25; Mic. 4:4; Zech. 3:10 [b]Prov. 5:15
18 [a]Is. 36:15
19 [a]Is. 10:9-11; 37:11-13; Jer. 49:23 [b]2 Kin. 17:6
20 [a]1 Kin. 20:23, 28 [b]Is. 36:15
21 [a]Prov. 9:7, 8; 26:4
22 [a]Is. 22:20; 36:3 [b]Is. 22:15

1 [a]2 Kin. 19:1-37; Is. 37:1-38
2 [a]Is. 22:20 [b]Is. 22:15 [c]Is. 1:1; 20:2
3 [1]Lit., *give birth* [a]Is. 22:5; 26:16; 33:2 [b]Is. 26:17, 18; 66:9; Hos. 13:13
4 [a]Is. 36:13-15, 18, 20 [b]Is. 1:9; 10:20-22; 37:31, 32; 46:3
6 [a]Is. 7:4; 35:4
7 [a]Is. 37:9 [b]Is. 37:37, 38
8 [1]Lit., *he* [a]Num. 33:20; Josh. 10:29 [b]Josh. 10:31, 32
9 [1]Or, *Ethiopia* [a]Is. 37:7 [b]Is. 18:1; 20:5
10 [1]Lit., *Judah, saying* [a]Is. 36:15
11 [1]Lit., *delivered* [a]Is. 10:9-11; 36:18-20
12 [1]Lit., *the* [a]2 Kin. 17:6; 18:11 [b]Gen. 11:31; 12:1-4; Acts 7:2
14 [1]Lit., *letters* [2]Lit., *Hezekiah spread*
16 [a]Ex. 25:22; 1 Sam. 4:4; Ps. 80:1; 99:1 [b]Deut. 10:17; Ps. 86:10; 136:2, 3 [c]Is. 42:5; 45:12; Jer. 10:12
17 [a]2 Chr. 6:40; Ps. 17:6; Dan. 9:18 [b]Ps. 74:22 [c]Is. 37:4
18 [a]2 Kin. 15:29; 16:9; 17:6, 24; 1 Chr. 5:26
19 [a]Is. 2:8; 17:8; 41:24, 29 [b]Is. 26:14
20 [1]So DSS and 2 Kin. 19:19; M.T. omits *God* [a]Is. 25:9; 33:22; 35:4 [b]1 Kin. 18:36, 37; Ps. 46:10; Is. 37:16; Ezek. 36:23
21 [a]Is. 37:2
22 [a]Jer. 14:17; Lam. 2:13 [b]Ps. 9:14; Zeph. 3:14; Zech. 2:10 [c]Job 16:4
23 [1]Lit., *on high* [a]Is. 37:4 [b]Is. 2:11; 5:15, 21 [c]Ezek. 39:7; Hab. 1:12

24 "Through your servants you have reproached the Lord,
And you have said, 'With my many chariots I came up to the heights of the mountains,
To the remotest parts of [a]Lebanon;
And I cut down its tall [b]cedars *and* its choice cypresses.
And I will go to its [1]highest peak, its thickest [c]forest.
25 'I dug *wells* and drank waters,
And [a]with the sole of my feet I dried up
All the rivers of [1]Egypt.'
26 "[a]Have you not heard?
Long ago I did it,
From ancient times I [b]planned it.
Now [c]I have brought it to pass,
That [d]you should turn fortified cities into [e]ruinous heaps.
27 "Therefore their inhabitants were short of strength,
They were dismayed and put to shame;
They were *as* the [a]vegetation of the field and *as* the green herb,
As [b]grass on the housetops [1]is scorched before it is grown up.
28 "But I [a]know your sitting down,
And your going out and your coming in,
And your raging against Me.
29 "Because of your raging against Me,
And because your [1a]arrogance has come up to My ears,
Therefore I will put My [b]hook in your nose,
And My [c]bridle in your lips,
And I will turn you back [d]by the way which you came.

30 "Then this shall be the sign for you: [1]you shall eat this year what [a]grows of itself, in the second year what springs from the same, and in the third year sow, reap, plant vineyards, and eat their fruit.
31 "And the [a]surviving [b]remnant of the house of Judah shall again [c]take root downward and bear fruit upward.
32 "For out of Jerusalem shall go forth a [a]remnant, and out of Mount Zion [1]survivors. The [b]zeal of the LORD of hosts shall perform this." '
33 "Therefore, thus says the LORD concerning the king of Assyria, 'He shall not come to this city, or shoot an arrow there; neither shall he come before it with a shield, nor throw up a [a]mound against it.
34 '[a]By the way that he came, by the same he shall return, and he shall not come to this city,' declares the LORD.
35 'For I will [a]defend this city to save it [b]for My own sake and for My servant David's sake.' "

Assyrians Destroyed

36 Then the [a]angel of the LORD went out, and struck 185,000 in the camp of the Assyrians; and when [1]men arose early in the morning, behold, all of these were [2]dead.
37 So Sennacherib, king of Assyria, departed and [1]returned *home*, and lived at [a]Nineveh.
38 And it came about as he was worshiping in the house of Nisroch his god, that Adrammelech and Sharezer his sons killed him with the sword; and they escaped into the land of [a]Ararat. And [b]Esarhaddon his son became king in his place.

Hezekiah Healed

38 [a]IN those days Hezekiah became [1]mortally ill. And [b]Isaiah the prophet the son of Amoz came to him and said to him, "Thus says the LORD, '[c]Set your house in order, for you shall die and not live.' "
2 Then Hezekiah turned his face to the wall, and prayed to the LORD,
3 and said, "[a]Remember now, O LORD, I beseech Thee, how I have [b]walked before Thee in truth and with a [c]whole heart, and [d]have done what is good in Thy sight." And Hezekiah [e]wept [1]bitterly.
4 Then the word of the LORD came to Isaiah, saying,
5 "Go and say to Hezekiah, 'Thus says the LORD, the God of your father David, "I have heard your prayer, I have seen your tears; behold, I will add [a]fifteen years to your [1]life.
6 "And I will [a]deliver you and this city from the hand of the king of Assyria; and I will defend this city." '
7 "And this shall be the [a]sign to you from the LORD, that the LORD will do this thing that He has spoken:
8 "Behold, I will [a]cause the shadow on the stairway, which has gone down with the sun on the stairway of Ahaz, to go back ten steps." So the [b]sun's *shadow* went back ten steps on the stairway on which it had gone down.
9 A writing of Hezekiah king of Judah, after his illness and [1]recovery:
10 I said, "[a]In the middle of my [1]life
I am to enter the [b]gates of Sheol;
I am to be [c]deprived of the rest of my years."
11 I said, "I shall not see the LORD,
The LORD [a]in the land of the living;
I shall look on man no more among the inhabitants of the world.
12 "Like a shepherd's [a]tent my dwelling is pulled up and removed from me;
As a [b]weaver I [c]rolled up my life.
He [d]cuts me off from the loom;
From [e]day until night Thou dost make an end of me.
13 "I composed *my soul* until morning.
[a]Like a lion—so He [b]breaks all my bones,
From [c]day until night Thou dost make an end of me.

24 [1]Lit., *farthest height* [a]Is. 10:33, 34 [b]Is. 14:8 [c]Is. 10:18
25 [1]Or, *the besieged place* [a]Deut. 11:10; 1 Kin. 20:10
26 [a]Is. 40:21, 28 [b]Acts 2:23; 4:27, 28; 1 Pet. 2:8 [c]Is. 46:11 [d]Is. 10:6 [e]Is. 17:1; 25:2
27 [1]So DSS and 2 Kin. 19:26; M.T., as *a plowed field* [a]Is. 40:7 [b]Ps. 129:6
28 [a]Ps. 139:1
29 [1]Lit., *complacency* [a]Is. 10:12 [b]Ezek. 29:4; 38:4 [c]Is. 30:28 [d]Is. 37:34
30 [1]Lit., *eating* [a]Lev. 25:5, 11
31 [a]Is. 4:2; 10:20 [b]Is. 37:4 [c]Is. 27:6
32 [1]Lit., *those who escape* [a]Is. 37:4 [b]2 Kin. 19:31; Is. 9:7; 59:17; Joel 2:18; Zech. 1:14
33 [a]Jer. 6:6; 32:24
34 [a]Is. 37:29
35 [a]2 Kin. 20:6; Is. 31:5; 38:6 [b]Is. 43:25; 48:9, 11
36 [1]Lit., *they* [2]Lit., *dead bodies* [a]2 Kin. 19:35; Is. 10:12, 33, 34
37 [1]Lit., *went and returned* [a]Gen. 10:11; Jon. 1:2; 3:3; 4:11; Zeph. 2:13
38 [a]Gen. 8:4; Jer. 51:27 [b]Ezra 4:2

1 [1]Lit., *sick to the point of death* [a]2 Kin. 20:1-6, 9-11; 2 Chr. 32:24; Is. 38:1-8 [b]Is. 1:1; 37:2 [c]2 Sam. 17:23
3 [1]Lit., *great weeping* [a]Neh. 13:14 [b]2 Kin. 18:5, 6; Ps. 26:3 [c]1 Chr. 28:9; 29:19 [d]Deut. 6:18 [e]Ps. 6:6-8
5 [1]Lit., *days* [a]2 Kin. 18:2, 13
6 [a]Is. 31:5; 37:35
7 [a]Judg. 6:17, 21, 36-40; Is. 7:11, 14; 37:30
8 [a]2 Kin. 20:9-11 [b]Josh. 10:12-14
9 [1]Lit., *he lived after his illness*
10 [1]Lit., *days* [a]Ps. 102:24 [b]Ps. 107:18 [c]Job 17:11, 15; 2 Cor. 1:9
11 [a]Ps. 27:13; 116:9
12 [a]2 Cor. 5:1, 4; 2 Pet. 1:13, 14 [b]Job 7:6 [c]Heb. 1:12 [d]Job 6:9 [e]Job 4:20; Ps. 73:14
13 [a]Job 10:16 [b]Ps. 51:8; Dan. 6:24 [c]Ps. 32:4

14 “[a]Like a swallow, *like* a crane, so I twitter;
I [b]moan like a dove;
My [c]eyes look wistfully to the heights;
O Lord, I am oppressed, be my [d]security.

15 “[a]What shall I say?
[1]For He has spoken to me, and He Himself has done it;
I shall [b]wander about all my years because of the [c]bitterness of my soul.
16 “O Lord, [a]by *these* things *men* live;
And in all these is the life of my spirit;
[1][b]O restore me to health, and [c]let me live!
17 “Lo, for *my own* welfare I had great bitterness;
It is Thou who hast [1][a]kept my soul from the pit of [2]nothingness,
For Thou hast [b]cast all my sins behind Thy back.
18 “For [a]Sheol cannot thank Thee,
Death cannot praise Thee;
Those who go down [b]to the pit cannot hope for Thy faithfulness.
19 “It is the [a]living who give thanks to Thee, as I do today;
A [b]father tells his sons about Thy faithfulness.
20 “The LORD will surely save me;
So we will [a]play my songs on stringed instruments
[b]All *the* days of our life [c]at the house of the LORD.”
21 Now [a]Isaiah had said, “Let them
take a cake of figs, and apply it to the
boil, that he may recover.”
22 Then Hezekiah had said, “What is
the [a]sign that I shall go up to the house
of the LORD?”

Hezekiah Shows His Treasures

39 [a]AT that time Merodach-baladan
son of Baladan, king of Babylon,
sent letters and a present to Hezekiah,
for he heard that he had been sick and
had recovered.
2 And Hezekiah [1]was [a]pleased, and
showed them all his treasure house, the
[b]silver and the gold and the spices and
the precious oil and his whole armory
and all that was found in his treasuries.
There was nothing in his house, nor in
all his dominion, that Hezekiah did not
show them.
3 Then Isaiah the [a]prophet came to
King Hezekiah and said to him, “What
did these men say, and from where have
they come to you?” And Hezekiah said,
“They have come to me from a far
[b]country, from Babylon.”
4 And he said, “What have they seen
in your house?” So Hezekiah [1]answered,
“They have seen all that is in my house;
there is nothing among my treasuries
that I have not shown them.”
5 Then Isaiah said to Hezekiah,
“Hear the [a]word of the LORD of hosts,
6 ‘Behold, the days are coming when
[a]all that is in your house, and all that
your fathers have laid up in store to this
day shall be carried to Babylon; nothing
shall be left,’ says the LORD.
7 ‘And *some* of your sons who shall
issue from you, whom you shall beget,
[a]shall be taken away; and [b]they shall
become officials in the palace of the king
of Babylon.’ ”
8 [a]Then Hezekiah said to Isaiah,
“The word of the LORD which you have
spoken is good.” For he [1]thought, “For
there will be peace and truth [b]in my
days.”

The Greatness of God

40 “[a]COMFORT, O comfort My people,” says your God.
2 “[a]Speak [1]kindly to Jerusalem;
And call out to her, that her [2][b]warfare has ended,
That her [3][c]iniquity has been removed,
That she has received of the LORD’s hand
[d]Double for all her sins.”

3 [a]A voice [1]is calling,
“[b]Clear the way for the LORD in the wilderness;
Make smooth in the desert a highway for our God.
4 “Let every valley be lifted up,
And every mountain and hill be made low;
And let the rough ground become a plain,
And the rugged terrain a broad valley;
5 [1]Then the [a]glory of the LORD will be revealed,
And [b]all flesh will see *it* together;
For the [c]mouth of the LORD has spoken.”
6 A voice says, “Call out.”
Then [1]he answered, “What shall I call out?”
[a]All flesh is grass, and all its [2]loveliness is like the flower of the field.
7 The [a]grass withers, the flower fades,
[1]When the [b]breath of the LORD blows upon it;
Surely the people are grass.
8 The grass withers, the flower fades,
But [a]the word of our God stands forever.

9 Get yourself up on a [a]high mountain,
O Zion, bearer of [b]good news,
Lift up your voice mightily,
O Jerusalem, bearer of good news;
Lift *it* up, do not fear.
Say to the [c]cities of Judah,
“[d]Here is your God!”

14 [a]Job 30:29; Ps. 102:6 [b]Is. 59:11; Ezek. 7:16; Nah. 2:7 [c]Ps. 119:123 [d]Job 17:3; Ps. 119:122
15 [1]Targum and DSS read *And what shall I say for He* [a]Ps. 39:9 [b]1 Kin. 21:27 [c]Job 7:11; 10:1; Is. 38:17
16 [1]Lit., *Thou wilt* [a]Ps. 119:71, 75 [b]Ps. 39:13 [c]Ps. 119:25
17 [1]So some versions; Heb., *loved* [2]Or, *destruction* [a]Ps. 30:3; 86:13; Jon. 2:6 [b]Is. 43:25; Jer. 31:34; Mic. 7:19
18 [a]Ps. 6:5; 30:9; 88:11; Eccl. 9:10 [b]Num. 16:33; Ps. 28:1
19 [a]Ps. 118:17; 119:175 [b]Deut. 6:7; 11:19; Ps. 78:5-7
20 [a]Ps. 33:1-3; 68:24-26 [b]Ps. 104:33; 116:2; 146:2 [c]Ps. 116:17-19
21 [a]2 Kin. 20:7, 8
22 [a]Is. 38:7

1 [a]2 Kin. 20:12-19; 2 Chr. 32:31; Is. 39:1-8
2 [1]Lit., *rejoiced over them* [a]2 Chr. 32:25, 31; Job 31:25 [b]2 Kin. 18:15, 16
3 [a]2 Sam. 12:1; 2 Chr. 16:7 [b]Deut. 28:49; Jer. 5:15
4 [1]Lit., *said*
5 [a]1 Sam. 13:13, 14; 15:16
6 [a]2 Kin. 24:13; 25:13-15; Jer. 20:5
7 [a]2 Kin. 24:10-16; 2 Chr. 36:10 [b]Dan. 1:1-7
8 [1]Lit., *said* [a]2 Chr. 32:26 [b]2 Chr. 34:28

1 [a]Is. 12:1; 49:13; 51:3, 12; 52:9; 61:2; 66:13; Jer. 31:10-14; Zeph. 3:14-17; 2 Cor. 1:4
2 [1]Lit., *to the heart of* [2]Or, *hard service* [3]Or, *penalty of iniquity accepted as paid off* [a]Is. 35:4; Zech. 1:13 [b]Is. 41:11-13; 49:25; 54:15, 17 [c]Is. 33:24; 53:5, 6, 11 [d]Jer. 16:18; Zech. 9:12; Rev. 18:6
3 [1]Or, *of one calling out* [a]Matt. 3:3; Mark 1:3; Luke 3:4-6; John 1:23 [b]Mal. 3:1; 4:5, 6
5 [1]Or, *In order that the* [a]Is. 6:3; Hab. 2:14 [b]Is. 52:10; Joel 2:28 [c]Is. 1:20; 34:16; 58:14
6 [1]Another reading is *I said* [2]Or, *constancy* [a]Job 14:2; Ps. 102:11; 103:15; 1 Pet. 1:24, 25
7 [1]Or, *Because* [a]Ps. 90:5, 6; James 1:10, 11 [b]Job 4:9; 41:21; Is. 11:4; 40:24
8 [a]Is. 55:11; 59:21; Matt. 5:18

9 [a]Is. 52:7 [b]Is. 61:1 [c]Is. 44:26 [d]Is. 25:9; 35:2

10 Behold, the Lord [1]GOD will come [a]with might,
With His [b]arm ruling for Him.
Behold, His [c]reward is with Him,
And His recompense before Him.
11 Like a shepherd He will [a]tend His flock,
In His arm He will gather the lambs,
And carry *them* in His bosom;
He will gently lead the nursing *ewes.*

12 Who has [a]measured the [1]waters in the hollow of His hand,
And marked off the heavens by the [2]span,
And [3]calculated the dust of the earth by the measure,
And weighed the mountains in a balance,
And the hills in a pair of scales?
13 [a]Who has [1]directed the Spirit of the LORD,
Or as His [b]counselor has informed Him?
14 [a]With whom did He consult and *who* [b]gave Him understanding?
And *who* taught Him in the path of justice and taught Him knowledge,
And informed Him of the way of understanding?
15 Behold, the [a]nations are like a drop from a bucket,
And are regarded as a speck of [b]dust on the scales;
Behold, He lifts up the [1]islands like fine dust.
16 Even Lebanon is not enough to burn,
Nor its [a]beasts enough for a burnt offering.
17 [a]All the nations are as nothing before Him,
They are regarded by Him as less than nothing and [1]meaningless.

18 [a]To whom then will you liken God?
Or what likeness will you compare with Him?
19 *As for* the [1a]idol, a craftsman casts it,
A goldsmith [b]plates it with gold,
And a silversmith *fashions* chains of silver.
20 He who is too impoverished for *such* an offering
Selects a [a]tree that does not rot;
He seeks out for himself a skillful craftsman
To [1]prepare [2]an idol that [b]will not totter.

21 [a]Do you not know? Have you not heard?
Has it not been declared to you from the beginning?
Have you not understood [b]from the foundations of the earth?
22 It is He who [1]sits above the [2a]vault of the earth,
And its inhabitants are like [b]grasshoppers,
Who [c]stretches out the heavens like a [d]curtain
And spreads them out like a [e]tent to dwell in.
23 He *it is* who reduces [a]rulers to nothing,
Who [b]makes the judges of the earth [1]meaningless.
24 [1]Scarcely have they been planted,
[1]Scarcely have they been sown,
[1]Scarcely has their stock taken root in the earth,
But He merely blows on them, and they wither,
And the [a]storm carries them away like stubble.
25 "[a]To whom then will you liken Me
That I should be *his* equal?" says the Holy One.
26 [a]Lift up your eyes on high
And see [b]who has created these *stars,*
The [c]One who leads forth their host by number,
He calls them all by name;
Because of the [d]greatness of His might and the [1]strength of *His* power
[e]Not one *of them* is missing.

27 [a]Why do you say, O Jacob, and assert, O Israel,
"My way is [b]hidden from the LORD,
And the [c]justice due me [1]escapes the notice of [d]my God"?
28 [a]Do you not know? Have you not heard?
The [b]Everlasting God, the LORD, the Creator of the ends of the earth
Does not become weary or tired.
His understanding is [c]inscrutable.
29 He gives strength to the [a]weary,
And to *him who* lacks might He [b]increases power.
30 Though [a]youths grow weary and tired,
And vigorous [b]young men stumble badly,
31 Yet those who [1]wait for the LORD
Will [a]gain new strength;
They will [2b]mount up *with* [3]wings like eagles,
They will run and not get tired,
They will walk and not become weary.

Israel Encouraged

41 "[a]COASTLANDS, listen to Me [b]in silence,
And let the peoples [c]gain new strength;
[d]Let them come forward, then let them speak;
[e]Let us come together for judgment.

10 [1]Heb., *YHWH,* usually rendered *LORD* [a]Is. 9:6, 7 [b]Is. 59:16, 18 [c]Is. 62:11; Rev. 22:12
11 [a]Jer. 31:10; Ezek. 34:12-14, 23, 31; Mic. 5:4; John 10:11, 14-16
12 [1]DSS reads *waters of the sea* [2]Or, *half cubit;* i.e., 9 in. [3]Lit., *contained* or *comprehended* [a]Job 38:8-11; Ps. 102:25, 26; Is. 48:13; Heb. 1:10-12
13 [1]Or, *measured, marked off* [a]Rom. 11:34; 1 Cor. 2:16 [b]Is. 41:28
14 [a]Job 38:4 [b]Job 21:22; Col. 2:3
15 [1]Or, *coastlands* [a]Jer. 10:10 [b]Is. 17:13; 29:5
16 [a]Ps. 50:9-11; Mic. 6:6, 7; Heb. 10:5-9
17 [1]Or, *void* [a]Is. 29:7
18 [a]Ex. 8:10; 15:11; 1 Sam. 2:2; Is. 40:25; 46:5; Mic. 7:18; Acts 17:29
19 [1]Or, *graven image* [a]Ps. 115:4-8; Is. 41:7; 44:10; Hab. 2:18, 19 [b]Is. 2:20; 30:22
20 [1]Or, *set up* [2]Or, *a graven image* [a]Is. 44:14 [b]1 Sam. 5:3, 4; Is. 41:7; 46:7
21 [a]Ps. 19:1; 50:6; Is. 37:26; Acts 14:17; Rom. 1:19 [b]Is. 48:13; 51:13
22 [1]Or, *is enthroned* [2]Or, *circle* [a]Job 22:14; Prov. 8:27 [b]Num. 13:33 [c]Job 9:8; Is. 37:16; 42:5; 44:24 [d]Ps. 104:2 [e]Job 36:29; Ps. 18:11; 19:4
23 [1]Or, *void* [a]Job 12:21; Ps. 107:40; Is. 34:12 [b]Is. 5:21; Jer. 25:18-27
24 [1]Or, *Not even* [a]Is. 17:13; 41:16
25 [a]Is. 40:18
26 [1]So DSS and ancient versions; M.T., *strong* [a]Is. 51:6 [b]Is. 42:5; 48:12, 13 [c]Ps. 147:4 [d]Ps. 89:11-13 [e]Is. 34:16; 48:13
27 [1]Lit., *passes by my God* [a]Is. 49:4, 14 [b]Is. 54:8 [c]Job 27:2; 34:5; Luke 18:7, 8 [d]Is. 25:1
28 [a]Is. 40:21 [b]Gen. 21:33; Ps. 90:2 [c]Ps. 147:5; Rom. 11:33
29 [a]Is. 50:4; Jer. 31:25 [b]Is. 41:10
30 [a]Jer. 6:11; 9:21 [b]Is. 9:17
31 [1]Or, *hope in* [2]Or, *sprout wings* [3]Or, *pinions* [a]Job 17:9; Ps. 103:5; 2 Cor. 4:8-10, 16 [b]Ex. 19:4; Deut. 32:11; Luke 18:1; 2 Cor. 4:1, 16; Gal. 6:9; Heb. 12:3

1 [a]Is. 11:11 [b]Hab. 2:20; Zech. 2:13 [c]Is. 40:31 [d]Is. 34:1; 48:16 [e]Is. 1:18; 43:26; 50:8

2"[a]Who has aroused one from the
east
Whom He [b]calls in righteousness to
His [1]feet?
He [c]delivers up nations before him,
And subdues kings.
He makes them like [d]dust with his
sword,
As the wind-driven [e]chaff with his
bow.
3"He pursues them, passing on in
safety,
By a way he had not been [1]travers-
ing with his feet.
4"[a]Who has performed and accomplished *it,*
Calling forth the generations from
the beginning?
'[b]I, the LORD, am the first, and with
the last. [c]I am He.' "

5 The [a]coastlands have seen and are
afraid;
The [b]ends of the earth tremble;
They have drawn near and have
come.
6 Each one helps his neighbor,
And says to his brother, "Be
strong!"
7 So the [a]craftsman encourages the
[b]smelter,
And he who smooths *metal* with the
hammer *encourages* him who
beats the anvil,
Saying of the soldering, "It is
good";
And he fastens it with nails,
[c]*That* it should not totter.
8"But you, Israel, [a]My servant,
Jacob whom I have chosen,
Descendant of [b]Abraham My
[c]friend,
9"You whom I have [1a]taken from the
ends of the earth,
And called from its [b]remotest
parts,
And said to you, 'You are [c]My
servant,
I have [d]chosen you and not rejected
you.
10 'Do not [a]fear, for I am with you;
Do not anxiously look about you,
for I am your God.
I will strengthen you, surely [b]I will
help you,
Surely I will uphold you with My
righteous [c]right hand.'
11"Behold, [a]all those who are angered
at you will be shamed and dishonored;
[b]Those who contend with you will
be as nothing, and will perish.
12"[a]You will seek those who quarrel
with you, but will not find them,
Those who war with you will be as
nothing, and non-existent.
13"For I am the LORD your God, [a]who
upholds your right hand,
Who says to you, '[b]Do not fear, I
will help you.'
14"Do not fear, you [a]worm Jacob, you
men of Israel;

2 [1]Lit., *foot*
[a]Is. 41:25; 45:1-3; 46:11 [b]Is. 42:6 [c]2 Chr. 36:23; Ezra 1:2 [d]2 Sam. 22:43 [e]Is. 40:24
3 [1]Lit., *going*
4 [a]Is. 41:26; 44:7; 46:10 [b]Is. 43:10; 44:6; Rev. 1:8, 17; 22:13 [c]Is. 43:13; 46:4; 48:12
5 [a]Is. 41:1; Ezek. 26:15, 16 [b]Josh. 5:1; Ps. 67:7
7 [a]Is. 44:12, 13 [b]Is. 40:19 [c]Is. 40:20; 46:7
8 [a]Is. 42:19; 43:10; 44:1, 2, 21 [b]Is. 29:22; 51:2; 63:16 [c]2 Chr. 20:7; James 2:23
9 [1]Or, *taken hold of*
[a]Is. 11:11 [b]Is. 43:5-7 [c]Is. 42:1; 44:1 [d]Deut. 7:6; 14:2; Ps. 135:4
10 [a]Deut. 20:1; 31:6; Josh. 1:9; Ps. 27:1; Is. 41:13, 14; 43:2, 5; Rom. 8:31 [b]Is. 41:14; 44:2; 49:8 [c]Ps. 89:13, 14
11 [a]Is. 45:24 [b]Is. 17:13; 29:5, 7, 8
12 [a]Job 20:7-9; Ps. 37:35, 36; Is. 17:14
13 [a]Is. 42:6; 45:1 [b]Is. 41:10
14 [1]Or, *even your Redeemer, the Holy One*
[a]Job 25:6; Ps. 22:6 [b]Is. 35:10; 43:14; 44:6, 22-24
15 [a]Mic. 4:13; Hab. 3:12 [b]Is. 42:15; 64:1; Jer. 9:10; Ezek. 33:28
16 [a]Jer. 51:2 [b]Is. 25:9; 35:10; 51:3; 61:10
17 [1]Or, *poor*
[a]Is. 43:20; 44:3; 49:10; 55:1 [b]Is. 30:19; 65:24 [c]Is. 42:16; 62:12
18 [a]Is. 30:25; 43:19 [b]Ps. 107:35; Is. 35:6, 7
19 [1]Or, *oleaster*
[a]Is. 35:1; 55:13; 60:13
20 [a]Is. 40:5; 43:10 [b]Job 12:9; Is. 66:14
21 [1]Lit., *Bring near*
[a]Is. 44:6
22 [a]Is. 44:7; 45:21; 46:10 [b]Is. 43:9
23 [a]Is. 42:9; 44:7, 8; 45:3; John 13:19 [b]Jer. 10:5
24 [1]Lit., *nothing*
[a]Ps. 115:8; Is. 44:9; 1 Cor. 8:4 [b]Is. 37:19; 41:29 [c]Prov. 3:32; 28:9

I will help you," declares the LORD,
"[1]and [b]your Redeemer is the
Holy One of Israel.
15"Behold, I have made you a new,
sharp threshing sledge with double edges;
[a]You will thresh the [b]mountains,
and pulverize *them,*
And will make the hills like chaff.
16"You will [a]winnow them, and the
wind will carry them away,
And the storm will scatter them;
But you will [b]rejoice in the LORD,
You will glory in the Holy One of
Israel.

17"The [1]afflicted and needy are seeking [a]water, but there is none,
And their tongue is parched with
thirst;
I, the LORD, [b]will answer them
Myself,
As the God of Israel I [c]will not
forsake them.
18"I will open [a]rivers on the bare
heights,
And springs in the midst of the
valleys;
I will make [b]the wilderness a pool
of water,
And the dry land fountains of
water.
19"I will put the cedar in the wilderness,
The acacia, and the [a]myrtle, and
the [1]olive tree;
I will place the [a]juniper in the
desert,
Together with the box tree and the
cypress,
20 That [a]they may see and recognize,
And consider and gain insight as
well,
That the [b]hand of the LORD has
done this,
And the Holy One of Israel has
created it.

21"[1]Present your case," the LORD says.
"Bring forward your strong *arguments,*"
The [a]King of Jacob says.
22 [a]Let them bring forth and declare
to us what is going to take
place;
As for the [b]former *events,* declare
what they *were,*
That we may consider them, and
know their outcome;
Or announce to us what is coming.
23 [a]Declare the things that are going
to come afterward,
That we may know that you are
gods;
Indeed, [b]do good or evil, that we
may anxiously look about us
and fear together.
24 Behold, [a]you are of [1]no account,
And [b]your work amounts to nothing;
He who chooses you is an [c]abomi-
nation.

25“I have aroused [a]one from the north, and he has come;
From the rising of the sun he will call on My name;
And he will come upon rulers as *upon* [b]mortar,
Even as the potter treads clay.”
26 Who has [a]declared *this* from the beginning, that we might know?
Or from former times, that we may say, “*He is* right!”?
Surely there was [b]no one who declared,
Surely there was no one who proclaimed,
Surely there was no one who heard your words.
27“[a]Formerly *I said* to Zion, ‘Behold, here they are.’
And to Jerusalem, ‘I will give a [b]messenger of good news.’
28“But [a]when I look, there is no one,
And there is no [b]counselor [1]among them
Who, if I ask, can [c]give an answer.
29“Behold, all of them are [1]false;
Their [a]works are [b]worthless,
Their molten images are [c]wind and emptiness.

God's Promise concerning His Servant

42 “[a]BEHOLD, My [b]Servant, whom I [1]uphold;
My [c]chosen one *in whom* My [d]soul delights.
I have put My [e]Spirit upon Him;
He will bring forth [f]justice to the [2]nations.
2“He will not cry out or raise *His voice,*
Nor make His voice heard in the street.
3“A bruised reed He will not break,
And a dimly burning wick He will not extinguish;
He will faithfully bring forth [a]justice.
4“He will not be [a]disheartened or crushed,
Until He has established justice in the earth;
And the [b]coastlands will wait expectantly for His [1]law.”

5 Thus says God the LORD,
Who [a]created the heavens and [b]stretched them out,
Who spread out the [c]earth and its [1]offspring,
Who [d]gives breath to the people on it,
And spirit to those who walk in it,
6“I am the LORD, I have [a]called you in righteousness,
I will also [b]hold you by the hand and [c]watch over you,
And I will appoint you as a [d]covenant to the people,
As a [e]light to the nations,
7 To [a]open blind eyes,
To [b]bring out prisoners from the dungeon,
And those who dwell in darkness from the prison.
8“[a]I am the LORD, that is [b]My name;
I will not give My [c]glory to another,
Nor My praise to [1]graven images.
9“Behold, the [a]former things have come to pass,
Now I declare [b]new things;
Before they spring forth I proclaim *them* to you.”

10 Sing to the LORD a [a]new song,
Sing His praise from the [b]end of the earth!
[c]You who go down to the sea, and [d]all that is in it.
You [e]islands and those who dwell on them.
11 Let the [a]wilderness and its cities lift up *their voices,*
The settlements where [b]Kedar inhabits.
Let the inhabitants of [c]Sela sing aloud,
Let them shout for joy from the tops of the [d]mountains.
12 Let them [a]give glory to the LORD,
And declare His praise in the [b]coastlands.
13 [a]The LORD will go forth like a warrior,
He will arouse *His* [b]zeal like a man of war.
He will utter a shout, yes, He will raise a war cry.
He will [c]prevail against His enemies.

The Blindness of the People

14“[a]I have kept silent for a long time,
I have kept still and restrained Myself.
Now like a woman in labor I will groan,
I will both gasp and pant.
15“I will [a]lay waste the mountains and hills,
And wither all their vegetation;
I will [b]make the rivers into coastlands,
And dry up the ponds.
16“And I will [a]lead the blind by a way they do not know,
In paths they do not know I will guide them.
I will [b]make darkness into light before them
And [c]rugged places into plains.
These are the things I will do,
And I will [d]not leave them undone.”
17 They shall be turned back and be [a]utterly put to shame,
Who trust in [1]idols,
Who say to molten images,
“You are our gods.”

18 [a]Hear, you deaf!
And look, you blind, that you may see.

25 [a]Is. 41:2; Jer. 50:3 [b]2 Sam. 22:43; Is. 10:6; Mic. 7:10; Zech. 10:5
26 [a]Is. 41:22; 44:7; 45:21 [b]Hab. 2:18, 19
27 [a]Is. 48:3-8 [b]Is. 40:9; 44:28; 52:7; Nah. 1:15
28 [1]Lit., *out of those*
[a]Is. 50:2; 59:16; 63:5 [b]Is. 40:13, 14 [c]Is. 46:7
29 [1]Another reading is *nothing*
[a]Is. 2:8; 17:8; 41:24 [b]Is. 44:9 [c]Jer. 5:13

1 [1]Or, *hold fast*
[2]Or, *Gentiles*
[a]Matt. 12:18-21 [b]Is. 41:8; 43:10; 49:3-6; 52:13; 53:11; Matt. 12:18-21; Phil. 2:7 [c]Luke 9:35; 1 Pet. 2:4, 6 [d]Matt. 3:17; 17:5; Mark 1:11; Luke 3:22 [e]Is. 11:2; 59:21; 61:1; Matt. 3:16; Luke 4:18, 19, 21 [f]Is. 2:4
3 [a]Ps. 72:2, 4; 96:13
4 [1]Or, *instruction*
[a]Is. 40:28 [b]Is. 11:11; 24:15; 42:10, 12; 49:1; 51:5; 60:9; 66:19
5 [1]Or, *vegetation*
[a]Ps. 102:25, 26; Is. 45:18 [b]Ps. 104:2; Is. 40:22 [c]Ps. 24:1, 2; 136:6 [d]Job 12:10; 33:4; Is. 57:16; Dan. 5:23; Acts 17:25
6 [a]Is. 41:2; Jer. 23:5, 6 [b]Is. 41:13; 45:1 [c]Is. 26:3; 27:3 [d]Is. 49:8 [e]Is. 49:6; 51:4; 60:1, 3; Luke 2:32; Acts 13:47; 26:23
7 [a]Is. 29:18; 35:5 [b]Is. 49:9; 61:1
8 [1]Or, *idols*
[a]Is. 43:3, 11, 15 [b]Ex. 3:15; Ps. 83:18 [c]Ex. 20:3-5; Is. 48:11
9 [a]Is. 48:3 [b]Is. 43:19; 48:6
10 [a]Ps. 33:3; 40:3; 98:1 [b]Is. 49:6; 62:11 [c]Ps. 65:5; 107:23 [d]Ex. 20:11; 1 Chr. 16:32; Ps. 96:11 [e]Is. 42:4
11 [a]Is. 32:16; 35:1, 6 [b]Is. 21:16; 60:7 [c]Is. 16:1 [d]Is. 52:7; Nah. 1:15
12 [a]Is. 24:15 [b]Is. 42:4
13 [a]Ex. 15:3 [b]Is. 9:7; 26:11; 37:32; 59:17 [c]Is. 66:14-16
14 [a]Ps. 50:21; Is. 57:11
15 [a]Is. 2:12-16; Ezek. 38:19, 20 [b]Is. 44:27; 50:2; Nah. 1:4-6
16 [a]Is. 29:18; 30:21; 32:3; Jer. 31:8, 9; Luke 1:78, 79 [b]Is. 29:18; Eph. 5:8 [c]Is. 40:4; Luke 3:5 [d]Josh. 1:5; Ps. 94:14; Is. 41:17; Heb. 13:5
17 [1]Or, *graven images*
[a]Ps. 97:7; Is. 1:29; 44:9, 11; 45:16
18 [a]Is. 29:18; 35:5

19 Who is blind but My [a]servant,
Or so deaf as My [b]messenger whom
I send?
Who is so blind as he that is [1c]at
peace *with Me,*
Or so blind as the servant of the
LORD?
20 [a]You have seen many things, but
you do not observe *them;*
Your ears are open, but none hears.
21 The LORD was pleased for His
righteousness' sake
To make the law [a]great and glori-
ous.
22 But this is a people plundered and
despoiled;
All of them are [a]trapped in [1]caves,
Or are [b]hidden away in prisons;
They have become a prey with
none to deliver *them,*
And a spoil, with none to say,
"Give *them* back!"

23 Who among you will give ear to
this?
Who will give heed and listen here-
after?
24 Who gave Jacob up for spoil, and
Israel to plunderers?
Was it not the LORD, against whom
we have sinned,
And in whose ways they [a]were not
willing to walk,
And whose law they did not [b]obey?
25 So He poured out on him the heat
of His anger
And the [a]fierceness of battle;
And it set him aflame all around,
Yet he did not recognize *it;*
And it burned him, but he [1b]paid
no attention.

Israel Redeemed

43 BUT now, thus says the LORD,
your [a]Creator, O Jacob,
And He who [b]formed you, O Israel,
"Do not [c]fear, for I have [d]redeemed
you;
I have [e]called you by name; you are
[f]Mine!
2 "When you [a]pass through the waters, [b]I will be with you;
And through the rivers, they will
not overflow you.
When you [c]walk through the fire,
you will not be scorched,
Nor will the flame burn you.
3 "For [a]I am the LORD your God,
The Holy One of Israel, your [b]Sav-
ior;
I have given Egypt as your ransom,
[1c]Cush and Seba in your place.
4 "Since you are [a]precious in My
sight,
Since you are [b]honored and I [c]love
you,
I will give *other* men in your place
and *other* peoples in exchange
for your life.
5 "Do not fear, for [a]I am with you;
I will bring [b]your offspring from
the east,
And [c]gather you from the west.

19 [1]Or, *the devoted one* [a]Is. 41:8 [b]Is. 44:26 [c]Is. 26:3; 27:5
20 [a]Rom. 2:21
21 [a]Is. 42:4; 51:4
22 [1]Or, *holes* [a]Is. 24:18 [b]Is. 24:22
24 [a]Is. 30:15 [b]Is. 48:18; 57:17
25 [1]Lit., *did not lay it to heart* [a]Is. 5:25; 9:19 [b]Is. 29:13; 47:7; 57:1; Hos. 7:9
1 [a]Is. 43:15 [b]Is. 43:7, 21; 44:2, 21, 24 [c]Is. 43:5 [d]Is. 44:22, 23; 48:20 [e]Gen. 32:28; Is. 43:7; 45:3, 4 [f]Is. 43:21
2 [a]Ps. 66:12; Is. 8:7, 8 [b]Deut. 31:6, 8 [c]Is. 29:6; 30:27-29; Dan. 3:25, 27
3 [1]Or, *Ethiopia* [a]Ex. 20:2 [b]Is. 19:20; 43:11; 45:15, 21; 49:26; 60:16; 63:8 [c]Is. 20:3-5
4 [a]Ex. 19:5, 6 [b]Is. 49:5 [c]Is. 63:9
5 [a]Is. 8:10; 43:2 [b]Is. 41:8; 49:12; 61:9 [c]Is. 49:12
6 [a]Ps. 107:3 [b]2 Cor. 6:18 [c]Is. 45:22
7 [a]Is. 56:5; 62:2; James 2:7 [b]Ps. 100:3; Is. 29:23; Eph. 2:10 [c]Is. 44:23; 46:13 [d]Is. 43:1
8 [a]Is. 6:9; 42:19; Ezek. 12:2
9 [a]Is. 34:1; 41:1 [b]Is. 41:22, 23, 26 [c]Is. 44:9 [d]Is. 43:26
10 [a]Is. 44:8 [b]Is. 41:8 [c]Is. 41:4 [d]Is. 45:5, 6
11 [a]Is. 43:3; 45:21; Hos. 13:4 [b]Is. 44:6, 8
12 [a]Deut. 32:16; Ps. 81:9
13 [1]So with Gr.; Heb., *from the day* [a]Ps. 90:2; Is. 48:16 [b]Is. 41:4 [c]Ps. 50:22 [d]Job 9:12; Is. 14:27
14 [1]Another reading is *As for the Chaldeans, their rejoicing is turned into lamentations* [2]Lit., *of their rejoicing* [a]Is. 41:14 [b]Is. 23:13 [c]Jer. 51:13
15 [a]Is. 43:1 [b]Is. 41:20; 44:6
16 [a]Ex. 14:21, 22; Ps. 77:19; Is. 11:15; 44:27; 50:2; 51:10; 63:11, 12

6 "I will say to the [a]north, 'Give *them*
up!'
And to the south, 'Do not hold
them back.'
Bring My [b]sons from afar,
And My daughters from the [c]ends
of the earth,
7 Everyone who is [a]called by My
name,
And whom I have [b]created for My
[c]glory,
[d]Whom I have formed, even whom
I have made."

Israel Is God's Witness

8 Bring out the people who are
[a]blind, even though they have
eyes,
And the deaf, even though they
have ears.
9 All the nations have [a]gathered
together
In order that the peoples may be
assembled.
Who among them can [b]declare this
And proclaim to us the former
things?
Let them present [c]their witnesses
[d]that they may be justified,
Or let them hear and say, "It is
true."
10 "You are [a]My witnesses," declares
the LORD,
"And [b]My servant whom I have
chosen,
In order that you may know and
believe Me,
And understand that [c]I am He.
[d]Before Me there was no God
formed,
And there will be none after Me.
11 "I, even I, am the LORD;
And there is no [a]savior [b]besides
Me.
12 "It is I who have declared and saved
and proclaimed,
And there was no [a]strange *god*
among you;
So you are My witnesses," declares
the LORD,
"And I am God.
13 "Even [1a]from eternity [b]I am He;
And there is [c]none who can deliver
out of My hand;
[d]I act and who can reverse it?"

Babylon to Be Destroyed

14 Thus says the LORD your [a]Re-
deemer, the Holy One of Israel,
"For your sake I have sent to Babylon,
And will bring them all down as
fugitives,
[1]Even the [b]Chaldeans, into the
[c]ships [2]in which they rejoice.
15 "I am the LORD, your Holy One,
[a]The Creator of Israel, your
[b]King."
16 Thus says the LORD,
Who [a]makes a way through the sea
And a path through the mighty
waters,

17 Who brings forth the [a]chariot and
the horse,
The army and the mighty man
(They will lie down together *and*
not rise again;
They have been [b]quenched *and*
extinguished like a wick):
18 "[a]Do not call to mind the former
things,
Or ponder things of the past.
19 "Behold, I will do something [a]new,
Now it will spring forth;
Will you not be aware of it?
I will even [b]make a roadway in the
wilderness,
Rivers in the desert.
20 "The beasts of the field will glorify
Me;
The [a]jackals and the ostriches;
Because I have [b]given waters in the
wilderness
And rivers in the desert,
To give drink to My chosen people.
21 "The people whom [a]I formed for
Myself,
[b]Will declare My praise.

The Shortcomings of Israel

22 "Yet you have not called on Me, O
Jacob;
But you have become [a]weary of
Me, O Israel.
23 "You have [a]not brought to Me the
sheep of your burnt offerings;
Nor have you [b]honored Me with
your sacrifices.
I have not [c]burdened you with
[1]offerings,
Nor wearied you with [d]incense.
24 "You have bought Me no [1a]sweet
cane with money,
Neither have you [2]filled Me with
the fat of your sacrifices;
Rather you have burdened Me with
your sins,
You have [b]wearied Me with your
iniquities.

25 "I, even I, am the one who [a]wipes
out your transgressions [b]for My
own sake;
And I will [c]not remember your
sins.
26 "[1]Put Me in remembrance; [a]let us
argue our case together,
State your *cause,* [b]that you may be
proved right.
27 "Your [a]first [1]forefather sinned,
And your [2b]spokesmen have [3]trans-
gressed against Me.
28 "So I will [1]pollute the [2]princes of the
sanctuary;
And I will consign Jacob to the
[a]ban, and Israel to [b]revilement.

The Blessings of Israel

44 "BUT now listen, O Jacob, My
[a]servant;
And Israel, whom I have chosen:
2 Thus says the LORD who made you
And [a]formed you from the womb,
who [b]will help you,
'[c]Do not fear, O Jacob My servant;
And you [d]Jeshurun whom I have
chosen.
3 'For [a]I will pour out water on [1]the
thirsty *land*
And streams on the dry ground;
I will [b]pour out My Spirit on your
[c]offspring,
And My blessing on your descendants;
4 And they will spring up [1]among the
grass
Like [a]poplars by streams of water.'
5 "This one will say, 'I am the
LORD'S';
And that one [1]will call on the name
of Jacob;
And another will [a]write [2]*on* his
hand, 'Belonging to the LORD,'
And will name Israel's name with
honor.

6 "Thus says the LORD, the [a]King of
Israel
And his [b]Redeemer, the LORD of
hosts:
'I am the [c]first and I am the last,
And there is no God [d]besides Me.
7 'And who is like Me? [a]Let him
proclaim and declare it;
Yes, let him recount it to Me in
order,
[1]From the time that I established
the ancient [2]nation.
And let them declare to them the
things that are coming
And the events that are going to
take place.
8 'Do not tremble and do not be
afraid;
[a]Have I not long since announced
it to you and declared it?
And [b]you are My witnesses.
Is there any God [c]besides Me,
Or is there any *other* [d]Rock?
I know of none.' "

The Folly of Idolatry

9 Those who fashion [1]a graven image
are all of them futile, and their precious
things are of no profit; even their own
witnesses fail to see or know, so that
they will be [a]put to shame.
10 Who has fashioned a god or cast
[1]an idol to [a]no profit?
11 Behold, all his companions will be
[a]put to shame, for the craftsmen themselves are mere men. Let them all assemble themselves, let them stand up, let
them tremble, let them together be put
to shame.
12 The [a]man shapes iron into a cutting tool, and does his work over the
coals, [1]fashioning it with hammers, and
working it with his strong arm. He also
gets hungry and [2]his strength fails; he
drinks no water and becomes weary.

17 [a]Ex. 15:19 [b]Ps. 118:12; Is. 1:31
18 [a]Is. 65:17; Jer. 23:7
19 [a]Is. 42:9; 48:6; 2 Cor. 5:17 [b]Ex. 17:6; Num. 20:11; Deut. 8:15; Ps. 78:16; Is. 35:1, 6; 41:18, 19; 49:10; 51:3
20 [a]Is. 13:22; 35:7 [b]Is. 41:17, 18; 48:21
21 [a]Is. 43:1 [b]Ps. 102:18; Is. 42:12; Luke 1:74, 75; 1 Pet. 2:9
22 [a]Mic. 6:3; Mal. 1:13; 3:14
23 [1]Or, *a meal offering* [a]Amos 5:25 [b]Zech. 7:5, 6; Mal. 1:6-8 [c]Jer. 7:21-26 [d]Ex. 30:34; Lev. 2:1; 24:7
24 [1]Or, *calamus* [2]Or, *saturated* [a]Ex. 30:23; Jer. 6:20 [b]Ps. 95:10; Is. 1:14; 7:13; Ezek. 6:9; Mal. 2:17
25 [a]Is. 44:22; 55:7; Jer. 50:20 [b]Is. 37:35; 48:9, 11; Ezek. 36:22 [c]Is. 38:17; Jer. 31:34
26 [1]Or, *Report to Me* [a]Is. 1:18; 41:1; 50:8 [b]Is. 43:9
27 [1]Lit., *father* [2]Or, *interpreters* [3]Or, *rebelled* [a]Is. 51:2; Ezek. 16:3 [b]Is. 9:15; 28:7; 29:10; Jer. 5:31
28 [1]Or, *pierce through* [2]Or, *holy princes* [a]Is. 24:6; 34:5; Jer. 24:9; Dan. 9:11; Zech. 8:13 [b]Ps. 79:4; Ezek. 5:15

1 [a]Is. 41:8; Jer. 30:10; 46:27, 28
2 [a]Is. 44:21, 24 [b]Is. 41:10 [c]Is. 43:5 [d]Deut. 32:15; 33:5, 26
3 [1]Or, *him who is thirsty* [a]Is. 41:17; Ezek. 34:26; Joel 3:18 [b]Is. 32:15; Joel 2:28 [c]Is. 61:9; 65:23
4 [1]Another reading is *like grass among the waters* [a]Lev. 23:40; Job 40:22
5 [1]Another reading is *will be called by the name of Jacob* [2]Or, *with* [a]Ex. 13:9; Neh. 9:38
6 [a]Is. 41:21; 43:15 [b]Is. 41:14; 43:1, 14 [c]Is. 41:4; 43:10; 48:12; Rev. 1:8, 17; 22:13 [d]Is. 43:11; 44:8; 45:5, 6, 21
7 [1]Lit., *From My establishing of* [2]Or, *people* [a]Is. 41:22, 26
8 [a]Is. 42:9; 48:5 [b]Is. 43:10 [c]Deut. 4:35, 39; 1 Sam. 2:2; Is. 45:5; Joel 2:27 [d]Is. 17:10; 26:4; 30:29
9 [1]Or, *an idol* [a]Ps. 97:7; Is. 42:17; 44:11; 45:16

10 [1]Or, *a graven image* [a]Is. 41:29; Jer. 10:5; Hab. 2:18; Acts 19:26
11 [a]Ps. 97:7; Is. 42:17; 44:9; 45:16
12 [1]Lit., *and fashions* [2]Lit., *there is no strength* [a]Is. 40:19, 20; 41:6, 7; 46:6, 7; Jer. 10:3-5; Hab. 2:18

13 [a]*Another* shapes wood, he extends a measuring line; he outlines it with red chalk. He works it with planes, and outlines it with a compass, and makes it like the form of a man, like the beauty of [b]man, so that it may sit in a [c]house.
14 Surely he cuts cedars for himself, and takes a [1]cypress or an oak, and [2]raises *it* for himself among the trees of the forest. He plants a fir, and the rain makes it grow.
15 Then it becomes *something* for a man to burn, so he takes one of them and warms himself; he also makes a fire to bake bread. He also [a]makes a god and worships it; he makes it a graven image, and [b]falls down before it.
16 Half of it he burns in the fire; over *this* half he eats meat as he roasts a roast, and is satisfied. He also warms himself and says, "Aha! I am warm, I have seen the fire."
17 But the rest of it he [a]makes into a god, his graven image. He falls down before it and worships; he also [b]prays to it and says, "Deliver me, for thou art my god."
18 They do not [a]know, nor do they understand, for He has [b]smeared over their eyes so that they cannot see and their hearts so that they cannot comprehend.
19 And no one [1]recalls, nor is there [a]knowledge or understanding to say, "I have burned half of it in the fire, and also have baked bread over its coals. I roast meat and eat *it.* Then [2]I make the rest of it into an [b]abomination, [3]I fall down before a block of wood!"
20 He [1a]feeds on ashes; a [b]deceived heart has turned him aside. And he cannot deliver [2]himself, nor say, "[c]Is there not a lie in my right hand?"

God Forgives and Redeems

21 "[a]Remember these things, O Jacob,
And Israel, for you are [b]My servant;
I have formed you, you are My servant,
O Israel, you will [c]not be forgotten by Me.
22 "I have [a]wiped out your transgressions like a thick cloud,
And your sins like a [1]heavy mist.
[b]Return to Me, for I have [c]redeemed you."
23 [a]Shout for joy, O heavens, for the LORD has done *it!*
Shout joyfully, you lower parts of the earth;
[b]Break forth into a shout of joy, you mountains,
O forest, and every tree in it;
For [c]the LORD has redeemed Jacob
And in Israel He [d]shows forth His glory.

24 Thus says the LORD, your [a]Redeemer, and the one who [b]formed you from the womb,
"I, the LORD, am the maker of all things,
[c]Stretching out the heavens by Myself,
And spreading out the earth [1]all alone,
25 [a]Causing the [1]omens of boasters to fail,
[2]Making fools out of diviners,
[b]Causing wise men to draw back,
And [3]turning their knowledge into foolishness,
26 [a]Confirming the word of His servant,
And [1]performing the purpose of His messengers.
It is I who says of Jerusalem, 'She shall be inhabited!'
And of the [b]cities of Judah, '[c]They shall be built.'
And I will raise up her ruins *again.*
27 "*It is I* who says to the depth of the sea, 'Be dried up!'
And I will make your rivers [a]dry.
28 "*It is I* who says of [a]Cyrus, '*He is* My shepherd!
And he will perform all My desire.'
And [1]he declares of Jerusalem, '[b]She will be built,'
And of the temple, '[2]Your foundation will be laid.' "

God Uses Cyrus

45 THUS says the LORD to [a]Cyrus His anointed,
Whom I have taken by the right [b]hand,
To [c]subdue nations before him,
And [1]to [d]loose the loins of kings;
To open doors before him so that gates will not be shut:
2 "I will go before you and [a]make the [1]rough places smooth;
I will [b]shatter the doors of bronze, and cut through their iron [c]bars.
3 "And I will give you the [1a]treasures of darkness,
And hidden wealth of secret places,
In order that you may know that it is I,
The LORD, the God of Israel, who [b]calls you by your name.
4 "For the sake of [a]Jacob My servant,
And Israel My chosen *one,*
I have also [b]called you by your name;
I have given you a title of honor
Though you have [c]not known Me.
5 "I am the LORD, and [a]there is no other;
[b]Besides Me there is no God.
I will [1c]gird you, though you have not known Me;
6 That [1a]men may know from the rising to the setting of the sun
That there is [b]no one besides Me.
I am the LORD, and there is no other,

13 [a]Is. 41:7 [b]Ps. 115:5-7 [c]Judg. 17:4, 5; Ezek. 8:10, 11
14 [1]Or, *holm-oak* [2]Lit., *makes strong*
15 [a]Is. 44:17 [b]2 Chr. 25:14
17 [a]Is. 44:15 [b]1 Kin. 18:26, 28; Is. 45:20
18 [a]Is. 1:3; Jer. 10:8, 14 [b]Ps. 81:12; Is. 6:9, 10; 29:10
19 [1]Lit., *returns to his heart* [2]Or, *shall I make . . .?* [3]Or, *shall I fall . . .?* [a]Is. 5:13; 44:18, 19; 45:20 [b]Deut. 27:15; 1 Kin. 11:5, 7; 2 Kin. 23:13, 14
20 [1]Or, *is a companion of ashes* [2]Lit., *his soul* [a]Ps. 102:9 [b]Job 15:31; Hos. 4:12; Rom. 1:21, 22; 2 Thess. 2:11; 2 Tim. 3:13 [c]Is. 57:11; 59:3, 4, 13; Rom. 1:25
21 [a]Is. 46:8; Zech. 10:9 [b]Is. 44:1, 2 [c]Is. 49:15
22 [1]Or, *cloud* [a]Ps. 51:1, 9; Is. 43:25; Acts 3:19 [b]Is. 31:6; 55:7 [c]Is. 43:1; 48:20; 1 Cor. 6:20; 1 Pet. 1:18, 19
23 [a]Ps. 69:34; 96:11, 12; Is. 42:10; 49:13 [b]Ps. 98:7, 8; 148:7, 9; Is. 55:12 [c]Is. 43:1 [d]Is. 49:3; 61:3
24 [1]Or, *who was with Me?* [a]Is. 41:14; 43:14 [b]Is. 44:2 [c]Is. 40:22; 42:5; 45:12, 18; 51:13
25 [1]Lit., *signs* [2]Lit., *He makes* [3]Lit., *He turns* [a]Is. 47:13 [b]2 Sam. 15:31; Job 5:12-14; Ps. 33:10; Is. 29:14; Jer. 51:57; 1 Cor. 1:20, 27
26 [1]Lit., *He performs* [a]Zech. 1:6; Matt. 5:18 [b]Is. 40:9 [c]Jer. 32:15, 44
27 [a]Is. 42:15; 50:2; Jer. 50:38; 51:36
28 [1]Lit., *to say* [2]Lit., *You will be founded* [a]Is. 45:1 [b]2 Chr. 36:22, 23; Ezra 1:1; Is. 14:32; 45:13; 54:11

1 [1]Lit., *I will loose* [a]Is. 44:28 [b]Ps. 73:23; Is. 41:13; 42:6 [c]Is. 41:2, 25; Jer. 50:3, 35; 51:11, 20, 24 [d]Job 12:21; Is. 45:5
2 [1]Another reading is *mountains* [a]Is. 40:4 [b]Ps. 107:16 [c]Jer. 51:30
3 [1]Or, *hoarded treasures* [a]Jer. 41:8; 50:37 [b]Ex. 33:12, 17; Is. 43:1; 49:1
4 [a]Is. 41:8, 9; 44:1 [b]Is. 43:1 [c]Acts 17:23
5 [1]Or, *arm* [a]Is. 45:6, 14, 18, 21; 46:9 [b]Is. 44:6, 8 [c]Ps. 18:39
6 [1]Lit., *they* [a]Ps. 102:15; Mal. 1:11 [b]Is. 45:5

7 The One [a]forming light and [b]creating darkness,
Causing [1]well-being and [c]creating calamity;
I am the LORD who does all these.

God's Supreme Power

8 "[a]Drip down, O heavens, from above,
And let the clouds pour down righteousness;
Let the [b]earth open up and salvation bear fruit,
[c]And righteousness spring up with it.
I, the LORD, have created it.

9 "Woe to *the one* who [a]quarrels with his [1]Maker—
An earthenware vessel [2]among the vessels of earth!
Will the [b]clay say to the [1]potter, 'What are you doing?'
Or the thing you are making *say,* 'He has no hands'?
10 "Woe to him who says to a father, 'What are you begetting?'
Or to a woman, 'To what are you [1]giving birth?' "

11 Thus says the [a]LORD, the Holy One of Israel, and his [1b]Maker:
"[2c]Ask Me about the things to come [3]concerning My [d]sons,
And you shall commit to Me [e]the work of My hands.
12 "It is I who [a]made the earth, and created man upon it.
I [b]stretched out the heavens with My hands,
And I [1]ordained [c]all their host.
13 "I have aroused him in [a]righteousness,
And I will [b]make all his ways smooth;
He will [c]build My city, and will let My exiles go [d]free,
Without any payment or reward," says the LORD of hosts.

14 Thus says the LORD,
"The [1]products of [a]Egypt and the merchandise of [2b]Cush
And the Sabeans, men of stature,
Will [c]come over to you and will be yours;
They will walk behind you, they will come over in [d]chains
And will [e]bow down to you;
They will make supplication to you:
'[3]Surely, [f]God is [4]with you, and [g]there is none else,
No other God.' "
15 Truly, Thou art a God who [a]hides Himself,
O God of Israel, [b]Savior!
16 They will be [a]put to shame and even humiliated, all of them;
The [b]manufacturers of idols will go away together in humiliation.
17 Israel has been saved by the LORD
With an [a]everlasting salvation;
You [b]will not be put to shame or humiliated
To all eternity.

18 For thus says the LORD, who [a]created the heavens
(He is the God who [b]formed the earth and made it,
He established it and did not create it [1]a [c]waste place,
But formed it to be [d]inhabited),
"I am the LORD, and [e]there is none else.
19 "[a]I have not spoken in secret,
In [1]some dark land;
I did not say to the [2b]offspring of Jacob,
'[c]Seek Me in [3]a waste place';
I, the LORD, [d]speak righteousness
[e]Declaring things that are upright.

20 "[a]Gather yourselves and come;
Draw near together, you fugitives of the nations;
[b]They have no knowledge,
Who [c]carry about [1]their wooden idol,
And [d]pray to a god who cannot save.
21 "[a]Declare and set forth *your case;*
Indeed, let them consult together.
[b]Who has announced this from of old?
Who has long since declared it?
Is it not I, the LORD?
And there is [c]no other God besides Me,
A righteous God and a [d]Savior;
There is none except Me.
22 "[a]Turn to Me, and [b]be saved, all the ends of the earth;
For I am God, and there is no other.
23 "[a]I have sworn by Myself,
The [b]word has gone forth from My mouth in righteousness
And will not turn back,
That to Me [c]every knee will bow, every tongue will [d]swear *allegiance.*
24 "They will say of Me, 'Only [a]in the LORD are righteousness and strength.'
Men will come to Him,
And [b]all who were angry at Him shall be put to shame.
25 "In the LORD all the offspring of Israel
Will be [a]justified, and will [b]glory."

Babylon's Idols and the True God

46 [a]BEL has bowed down, Nebo stoops over;
Their images are *consigned* to the beasts and the cattle.
The things [1]that you carry are burdensome,
A load for the weary *beast.*

1 [1]Lit., *carried by you* [a]Is. 2:18; 21:9; Jer. 50:2-4; 51:44

7 [1]Or, *peace* [a]Is. 42:16 [b]Ps. 104:20; 105:28 [c]Is. 31:2; 47:11; Amos 3:6
8 [a]Ps. 72:6; Hos. 10:12; 14:5; Joel 3:18 [b]Ps. 85:11 [c]Is. 60:21; 61:11
9 [1]Lit., *Fashioner* [2]Lit., *with* [a]Job 15:25; 40:8, 9; Ps. 2:2, 3; Prov. 21:30; Jer. 50:24 [b]Is. 29:16; 64:8; Jer. 18:6; Rom. 9:20, 21
10 [1]Lit., *in labor pains with*
11 [1]Lit., *Fashioner* [2]Or, *Will you ask* [3]Or, *upon* [a]Is. 43:15; 48:17; Ezek. 39:7 [b]Is. 44:2; 54:5 [c]Is. 8:19 [d]Jer. 31:9 [e]Is. 19:25; 29:23; 60:21; 64:8
12 [1]Or, *commanded* [a]Is. 42:5; 45:18; Jer. 27:5 [b]Ps. 104:2; Is. 42:5; 44:24 [c]Gen. 2:1; Neh. 9:6
13 [a]Is. 41:2 [b]Is. 45:2 [c]2 Chr. 36:22, 23; Is. 44:28 [d]Is. 52:3
14 [1]Lit., *labor* [2]Or, *Ethiopia* [3]Or, *God is with you alone* [4]Or, *in* [a]Ps. 68:31; Is. 19:21 [b]Is. 18:1; 43:3 [c]Is. 14:1, 2; 49:23; 54:3 [d]Ps. 149:8 [e]Is. 49:23; 60:14 [f]Jer. 16:19; Zech. 8:20-23; 1 Cor. 14:25 [g]Is. 45:5
15 [a]Ps. 44:24; Is. 1:15; 8:17; 57:17 [b]Is. 43:3
16 [a]Is. 42:17; 44:9 [b]Is. 44:11
17 [a]Is. 26:4; 51:6; Rom. 11:26 [b]Is. 49:23; 50:7; 54:4
18 [1]Or, *in vain* [a]Is. 42:5 [b]Is. 45:12 [c]Gen. 1:2 [d]Gen. 1:26; Ps. 115:16 [e]Is. 45:5
19 [1]Lit., *a place of a land of darkness* [2]Lit., *seed* [3]Or, *vain* [a]Is. 48:16 [b]Is. 45:25; 65:9 [c]2 Chr. 15:2; Ps. 78:34; Jer. 29:13, 14 [d]Ps. 19:8; Is. 45:23; 63:1 [e]Is. 43:12; 44:8
20 [1]Lit., *the wood of their graven image* [a]Is. 43:9 [b]Is. 44:18, 19; 48:5-7 [c]Is. 46:1, 7; Jer. 10:5 [d]Is. 44:17; 46:6, 7
21 [a]Is. 41:23; 43:9 [b]Is. 41:26; 44:7; 48:14 [c]Is. 45:5 [d]Is. 43:3, 11
22 [a]Num. 21:8, 9; 2 Chr. 20:12; Mic. 7:7; Zech. 12:10 [b]Is. 30:15; 49:6, 12; 52:10
23 [a]Gen. 22:16; Is. 62:8; Heb. 6:13 [b]Is. 55:11 [c]Rom. 14:11; Phil. 2:10 [d]Deut. 6:13; Ps. 63:11; Is. 19:18; 65:16
24 [a]Jer. 33:16 [b]Is. 41:11
25 [a]1 Kin. 8:32; Is. 53:11 [b]Is. 41:16; 60:19

2 They stooped over, they have bowed down together;
They could not rescue the burden,
But [1]have themselves [a]gone into captivity.

3 "[a]Listen to Me, O house of Jacob,
And all [b]the remnant of the house of Israel,
You who have been [c]borne by Me from [1]birth,
And have been carried from the womb;
4 Even to your old age, [a]I [1]shall be the same,
And even to your [2b]graying years I shall bear *you!*
I have [3]done *it,* and I shall carry *you;*
And I shall bear *you,* and I shall deliver *you.*

5 "[a]To whom would you liken Me,
And make Me equal and compare Me,
That we should be alike?
6 "Those who [a]lavish gold from the purse
And weigh silver on the scale
Hire a goldsmith, and he makes it *into* a god;
They [b]bow down, indeed they worship it.
7 "They [a]lift it upon the shoulder and carry it;
They set it in its place and it stands *there.*
[b]It does not move from its place.
Though one may cry to it, it [c]cannot answer;
It [d]cannot deliver him from his distress.

8 "[a]Remember this, and be [1]assured;
[b]Recall it to [2]mind, you [c]transgressors.
9 "Remember the [a]former things long past,
For I am God, and there is [b]no other;
I am God, and there is [c]no one like Me,
10 Declaring the end from the beginning
And from ancient times things which have not been done,
Saying, '[a]My purpose will be established,
And I will accomplish all My good pleasure';
11 Calling a [a]bird of prey from the [b]east,
The man of [1]My purpose from a far country.
Truly I have [c]spoken; truly I will bring it to pass.
I have planned *it, surely* I will do it.

12 "[a]Listen to Me, you [b]stubborn-minded,
Who are [c]far from righteousness.
13 "I [a]bring near My righteousness, it is not far off;
And My salvation will not delay.
And I will grant [b]salvation in Zion,
And My [c]glory for Israel.

Lament for Babylon

47 "[a]COME down and sit in the dust,
O [b]virgin [c]daughter of Babylon;
Sit on the ground without a throne,
O daughter of the Chaldeans.
For you shall no longer be called [d]tender and delicate.
2 "Take the [a]millstones and [b]grind meal.
Remove your [c]veil, [d]strip off the skirt,
Uncover the leg, cross the rivers.
3 "Your [a]nakedness will be uncovered,
Your shame also will be exposed;
I will [b]take vengeance and will not [1]spare a man."
4 Our [a]Redeemer, the LORD of hosts is His name,
The Holy One of Israel.
5 "[a]Sit silently, and go into [b]darkness,
O daughter of the Chaldeans;
For you will no more be called
The [c]queen of [d]kingdoms.
6 "I was angry with My people,
I profaned My heritage,
And gave them into your hand.
You did not show mercy to them,
On the [a]aged you made your yoke very heavy.
7 "Yet you said, 'I shall be a [a]queen forever.'
These things you did not [b]consider,
Nor remember the [c]outcome of [1]them.

8 "Now, then, hear this, you [a]sensual one,
Who [b]dwells securely,
Who says in [1]your heart,
'[c]I am, and there is no one besides me.
I shall [d]not sit as a widow,
Nor shall I know loss of children.'
9 "But these [a]two things shall come on you [b]suddenly in one day:
Loss of children and widowhood.
They shall come on you in full measure
In spite of your many [c]sorceries,
In spite of the great power of your spells.
10 "And you felt [a]secure in your wickedness and said,
'[b]No one sees me,'
Your [c]wisdom and your knowledge, [1]they have deluded you;
For you have said in your heart,
'[d]I am, and there is no one besides me.'
11 "But [a]evil will come on you
Which you will not know how to charm away;
And disaster will fall on you
For which you cannot atone,
And [b]destruction about which you do not know
Will come on you [c]suddenly.

2 [1]Or, *their soul has* [a]Judg. 18:17, 18, 24; 2 Sam. 5:21; Jer. 43:12, 13; 48:7; Hos. 10:5, 6
3 [1]Lit., *the belly* [a]Is. 46:12 [b]Is. 10:21, 22 [c]Ps. 71:6; Is. 49:1
4 [1]Lit., *I am He* [2]Lit., *gray hairs* [3]Or, *made* you [a]Is. 41:4; 43:13; 48:12 [b]Ps. 71:18
5 [a]Is. 40:18, 25
6 [a]Is. 40:19; 41:7; 44:12-17; Jer. 10:4 [b]Is. 44:15, 17
7 [a]Is. 45:20; 46:1; Jer. 10:5 [b]Is. 40:20; 41:7 [c]Is. 41:28 [d]Is. 45:20
8 [1]Lit., *firm* [2]Lit., *heart* [a]Is. 44:21 [b]Is. 44:19 [c]Is. 50:1
9 [a]Deut. 32:7; Is. 42:9; 65:17 [b]Is. 45:5, 21 [c]Is. 41:26, 27
10 [a]Ps. 33:11; Prov. 19:21; Is. 14:24; 25:1; 40:8; Acts 5:39
11 [1]Lit., *His* [a]Is. 18:6 [b]Is. 41:2 [c]Num. 23:19; Is. 14:24; 37:26
12 [a]Is. 46:3 [b]Ps. 76:5; Is. 48:4; Zech. 7:11, 12; Mal. 3:13 [c]Ps. 119:150; Is. 48:1; Jer. 2:5
13 [a]Is. 51:5; 61:11; Rom. 3:21 [b]Is. 61:3; 62:11; Joel 3:17; 1 Pet. 2:6 [c]Is. 43:7; 44:23

1 [a]Is. 3:26; Jer. 48:18 [b]Is. 23:12; 37:22; Jer. 46:11 [c]Ps. 137:8; Jer. 50:42; 51:33; Zech. 2:7 [d]Deut. 28:56
2 [a]Ex. 11:5; Jer. 25:10 [b]Job 31:10; Eccl. 12:4; Matt. 24:41 [c]Gen. 24:65; Is. 3:23; 1 Cor. 11:5 [d]Is. 32:11
3 [1]Lit., *meet* [a]Ezek. 16:37; Nah. 3:5 [b]Is. 34:8; 63:4
4 [a]Is. 41:14
5 [a]Is. 23:2; Jer. 8:14; Lam. 2:10 [b]Is. 13:10 [c]Is. 47:7 [d]Is. 13:19; Dan. 2:37
6 [a]Deut. 28:50
7 [1]Lit., *it* [a]Is. 47:5 [b]Is. 42:25; 57:11 [c]Deut. 32:29; Jer. 5:31; Ezek. 7:2, 3
8 [1]Lit., *her* [a]Is. 22:13; 32:9; Jer. 50:11 [b]Is. 32:9, 11; Zeph. 2:15 [c]Is. 45:5, 6, 18; 47:10; Zeph. 2:15 [d]Rev. 18:7
9 [a]Is. 13:16, 18; 14:22 [b]Ps. 73:19; 1 Thess. 5:3; Rev. 18:8, 10 [c]Is. 47:13; Nah. 3:4; Rev. 18:23
10 [1]Lit., *it has* [a]Ps. 52:7; 62:10; Is. 59:4 [b]Is. 29:15; Ezek. 8:12; 9:9 [c]Is. 5:21; 44:20 [d]Is. 47:8
11 [a]Is. 57:1 [b]Is. 13:6; Jer. 51:8, 43; Luke 17:27; 1 Thess. 5:3 [c]Is. 47:9

12"Stand *fast* now in your [a]spells
And in your many sorceries
With which you have labored from your youth;
Perhaps you will be able to profit,
Perhaps you may cause trembling.
13"You are [a]wearied with your many counsels;
Let now the [b]astrologers,
Those who prophesy by the stars,
Those who predict by the new moons,
Stand up and [c]save you from what will come upon you.
14"Behold, they have become [a]like stubble,
[b]Fire burns them;
They cannot deliver themselves from the power of the flame;
There will be [c]no coal to warm by,
Nor a fire to sit before!
15"So have those become to you with whom you have labored,
Who have [a]trafficked with you from your youth;
Each has wandered in his own [1]way.
There is [b]none to save you.

Israel's Obstinacy

48 "[a]HEAR this, O house of Jacob, who are named Israel
And who came forth from the [1][b]loins of Judah,
Who [c]swear by the name of the LORD
And invoke the God of Israel,
But not in truth nor in [d]righteousness.
2"For they call themselves after the [a]holy city,
And [b]lean on the God of Israel;
The LORD of hosts is His name.
3"I [a]declared the former things long ago
And they went forth from My mouth, and I proclaimed them.
[b]Suddenly I acted, and they [c]came to pass.
4"Because I know that you are [1][a]obstinate,
And your [b]neck is an iron sinew,
And your [c]forehead bronze,
5 Therefore I declared *them* to you long ago,
Before [1]they took place I proclaimed *them* to you,
Lest you should say, 'My [a]idol has done them,
And my graven image and my molten image have commanded them.'
6"You have heard; look at all this.
And you, will you not declare it?
I proclaim to you [a]new things from this time,
Even hidden things which you have not known.
7"They are created now and not long ago;

12 [a]Is. 47:9
13 [a]Jer. 51:58, 64 [b]Is. 8:19; 44:25; 47:9; Dan. 2:2, 10 [c]Is. 47:15
14 [a]Is. 5:24; Nah. 1:10; Mal. 4:1 [b]Is. 10:17; Jer. 51:30, 32, 58 [c]Is. 44:16
15 [1]Lit., *side, region* [a]Rev. 18:11 [b]Is. 5:29; 43:13; 46:7

1 [1]Lit., *waters* [a]Is. 46:12 [b]Num. 24:7; Deut. 33:28; Ps. 68:26 [c]Deut. 6:13; Is. 45:23; 65:16 [d]Is. 58:2; Jer. 4:2
2 [a]Is. 52:1; 64:10 [b]Is. 10:20; Jer. 7:4; 21:2; Mic. 3:11; Rom. 2:17
3 [a]Is. 41:22; 42:9; 43:9; 44:7, 8; 45:21; 46:10 [b]Is. 29:5; 30:13 [c]Josh. 21:45; Is. 42:9
4 [1]Or, *harsh* [a]Ex. 32:9; Deut. 31:27; Ezek. 2:4; 3:7 [b]2 Chr. 36:13; Prov. 29:1; Acts 7:51 [c]Ezek. 3:7-9
5 [1]Lit., *it* [a]Jer. 44:15-18
6 [a]Is. 42:9; 43:19
8 [1]Or, *transgressor* [2]Lit., *the belly* [a]Is. 42:25; 47:11; Hos. 7:9 [b]Deut. 9:7, 24; Ps. 58:3; Is. 46:8
9 [a]Is. 48:11 [b]Neh. 9:30, 31; Ps. 78:38; 103:8-10; Is. 30:18; 65:8
10 [a]Jer. 9:7; Ezek. 22:18-22 [b]Deut. 4:20; 1 Kin. 8:51; Jer. 11:4
11 [a]1 Sam. 12:22; Ps. 25:11; 106:8; Is. 37:35; 43:25; Jer. 14:7; Ezek. 20:9, 14, 22, 44; Dan. 9:17-19 [b]Deut. 32:26, 27; Is. 42:8
12 [1]Lit., *My called one* [a]Is. 41:4; 43:10-13; 46:4 [b]Is. 44:6; Rev. 1:17; 22:13
13 [a]Ex. 20:11; Ps. 102:25; Is. 42:5; 45:12, 18; Heb. 1:10-12 [b]Is. 40:26
14 [a]Is. 43:9; 45:20 [b]Is. 45:21 [c]Is. 46:10, 11 [d]Is. 13:4, 5, 17-19; Jer. 50:21-29; 51:24
15 [a]Is. 41:2; 45:1, 2
16 [1]Heb., *YHWH*, usually rendered *LORD* [a]Is. 34:1; 41:1; 57:3 [b]Is. 45:19 [c]Is. 43:13 [d]Zech. 2:9, 11
17 [a]Is. 41:14; 43:14; 49:7, 26; 54:5, 8 [b]Ps. 32:8; Is. 30:21; 49:9, 10
18 [1]Or, *peace* [a]Deut. 5:29; 32:29; Ps. 81:13-16 [b]Ps. 119:165; Is. 32:16-18; 66:12 [c]Is. 45:8; 61:10, 11; 62:1; Hos. 10:12; Amos 5:24

And before today you have not heard them,
Lest you should say, 'Behold, I knew them.'
8"You have not [a]heard, you have not known.
Even from long ago your ear has not been open,
Because I knew that you would deal very treacherously;
And you have been called a [1][b]rebel from [2]birth.
9"[a]For the sake of My name I [b]delay My wrath,
And *for* My praise I restrain *it* for you,
In order not to cut you off.
10"Behold, I have refined you, but [a]not as silver;
I have tested you in the [b]furnace of affliction.
11"[a]For My own sake, for My own sake, I will act;
For how can *My name* be profaned?
And My [b]glory I will not give to another.

Deliverance Promised

12"Listen to Me, O Jacob, even Israel [1]whom I called;
[a]I am He, [b]I am the first, I am also the last.
13"Surely My hand [a]founded the earth,
And My right hand spread out the heavens;
When I [b]call to them, they stand together.
14"[a]Assemble, all of you, and listen!
[b]Who among them has declared these things?
The LORD loves him; he shall [c]carry out His good pleasure on [d]Babylon,
And His arm *shall be against* the Chaldeans.
15"I, even I, have spoken; indeed I have [a]called him,
I have brought him, and He will make his ways successful.
16"[a]Come near to Me, listen to this:
From the first I have [b]not spoken in secret,
[c]From the time it took place, I was there.
And now [d]the Lord [1]GOD has sent Me, and His Spirit."

17 Thus says the LORD, your [a]Redeemer, the Holy One of Israel;
"I am the LORD your God, who teaches you to profit,
Who [b]leads you in the way you should go.
18"If only you had [a]paid attention to My commandments!
Then your [1][b]well-being would have been like a river,
And your [c]righteousness like the waves of the sea.

19"Your [1a]descendants would have
been like the sand,
And [2]your offspring like its grains;
[b]Their name would never be cut off
or destroyed from My presence."

20 [a]Go forth from Babylon! Flee from
the Chaldeans!
Declare with the sound of [b]joyful
shouting, proclaim this,
[c]Send it out to the end of the earth;
Say, "[d]The LORD has redeemed His
servant Jacob."
21 And they did not [a]thirst when He
led them through the deserts.
He [b]made the water flow out of the
rock for them;
He split the rock, and [c]the water
gushed forth.
22"[a]There is no peace for the wicked,"
says the LORD.

Salvation Reaches to the End of the Earth

49 LISTEN to Me, O [a]islands,
And pay attention, you peoples
from afar.
[b]The LORD called Me from the
womb;
From the [1]body of My mother He
named Me.
2 And He has made My [a]mouth like
a sharp sword;
In the [b]shadow of His hand He has
concealed Me,
And He has also made Me a [1]select
[c]arrow;
He has hidden Me in His quiver.
3 And He said to Me, "[a]You are My
Servant, Israel,
[b]In Whom I will [1]show My glory."
4 But I said, "I have [a]toiled in vain,
I have spent My strength for nothing and vanity;
Yet surely the justice *due* to Me is
with the LORD,
And My [b]reward with My God."

5 And now says [a]the LORD, who
formed Me from the womb to be
His Servant,
To bring Jacob back to Him, in
order that [b]Israel might be gathered to Him
(For I am [c]honored in the sight of
the LORD,
And My God is My [d]strength),
6 He says, "It is too [1]small a thing
that You should be My Servant
To raise up the tribes of Jacob, and
to restore the [a]preserved ones of
Israel;
I will also make You a [b]light [2]of
the nations
So that My salvation may [3]reach to
the [c]end of the earth."
7 Thus says the LORD, the [a]Redeemer of Israel, *and* its Holy
One,
To the [b]despised One,
To the One abhorred by the nation,
To the Servant of rulers,
"[c]Kings shall see and arise,
Princes shall also [d]bow down;
Because of the LORD who is faithful, the Holy One of Israel who
has chosen You."

8 Thus says the LORD, "In a [a]favorable time I have answered You,
And in a day of salvation I have
helped You;
And I will [b]keep You and [c]give
You for a covenant of the people,
To [1d]restore the land, to make *them*
inherit the desolate heritages;
9 Saying to those who are [a]bound,
'Go forth,'
To those who are in darkness,
'Show yourselves.'
Along the roads they will feed,
And their pasture will be on all
[b]bare heights.
10"They will [a]not hunger or thirst,
Neither will the scorching [b]heat or
sun strike them down;
For [c]He who has compassion on
them will [d]lead them,
And will guide them to [e]springs of
water.
11"And I will make all [a]My mountains
a road,
And My [b]highways will be raised
up.
12"Behold, these shall come [a]from
afar;
And lo, these *will come* from the
[b]north and from the west,
And these from the land of Sinim."
13 [a]Shout for joy, O heavens! And
rejoice, O earth!
Break forth into joyful shouting, O
mountains!
For the [b]LORD has comforted His
people,
And will [c]have compassion on His
afflicted.

Promise to Zion

14 But Zion said, "The LORD has
forsaken me,
And the Lord has forgotten me."
15"Can a woman forget her nursing
child,
And have no compassion on the
son of her womb?
Even these may forget, but [a]I will
not forget you.
16"Behold, I have [a]inscribed you on
the palms *of My hands;*
Your [b]walls are continually before
Me.
17"Your [1]builders hurry;
Your [a]destroyers and devastators
Will depart from you.
18"[a]Lift up your eyes and look
around;
[b]All of them gather together, [c]they
come to you.
[d]As I live," declares the LORD,
"You shall surely [e]put on all of them
as [1]jewels, and bind them on as
a bride.

19 [1]Lit., *seed* [2]Lit., *the offspring of your inward parts*
[a]Gen. 22:17; Is. 10:22; 44:3, 4; 54:3; Jer. 33:22 [b]Is. 56:5; 66:22

20 [a]Jer. 50:8; 51:6, 45; Zech. 2:6, 7; Rev. 18:4 [b]Is. 42:10; 49:13; 52:9 [c]Is. 62:11; Jer. 31:10; 50:2 [d]Is. 43:1; 52:9; 63:9

21 [a]Is. 30:25; 35:6, 7; 41:17, 18; 43:19, 20; 49:10 [b]Ex. 17:6; Ps. 78:15, 16 [c]Ps. 78:20; 105:41

22 [a]Is. 57:21

1 [1]Lit., *inward parts*
[a]Is. 42:4 [b]Is. 44:2, 24; 46:3; Jer. 1:5

2 [1]Or, *sharpened*
[a]Is. 11:4; Heb. 4:12; Rev. 1:16; 2:12, 16 [b]Is. 51:16 [c]Hab. 3:11

3 [1]Or, *glorify Myself*
[a]Zech. 3:8 [b]Is. 44:23

4 [a]Is. 65:23 [b]Is. 35:4; 59:18

5 [a]Is. 44:2 [b]Is. 11:12; 27:12 [c]Is. 43:4 [d]Is. 12:2

6 [1]Lit., *light* [2]Or, *to* [3]Lit., *be*
[a]Ps. 37:28; 97:10 [b]Is. 42:6; 51:4; Luke 2:32; Acts 13:47; 26:23 [c]Is. 48:20

7 [a]Is. 48:17 [b]Ps. 22:6-8; 69:7-9; Is. 53:3 [c]Is. 52:15 [d]Is. 19:21, 23; 27:13; 66:23

8 [1]Lit., *establish*
[a]Ps. 69:13; 2 Cor. 6:2 [b]Is. 26:3; 27:3; 42:6 [c]Is. 42:6 [d]Is. 44:26

9 [a]Is. 42:7; 61:1; Luke 4:18 [b]Is. 41:18

10 [a]Is. 33:16; 48:21; Rev. 7:16 [b]Ps. 121:6 [c]Is. 14:1 [d]Ps. 23:2; Is. 40:11 [e]Is. 35:7; 41:17

11 [a]Is. 40:4 [b]Is. 11:16; 19:23; 35:8; 62:10

12 [a]Is. 49:1; 60:4 [b]Is. 43:5, 6

13 [a]Is. 44:23 [b]Is. 40:1; 51:3, 12 [c]Is. 54:7, 8, 10

15 [a]Is. 44:21

16 [a]Song 8:6; Hag. 2:23 [b]Ps. 48:12, 13; Is. 62:6, 7

17 [1]So ancient versions and DSS; M.T. reads *sons*
[a]Is. 10:6; 37:18

18 [1]Lit., *an ornament*
[a]Is. 60:4; John 4:35 [b]Is. 43:5; 54:7; 60:4 [c]Is. 49:12 [d]Is. 45:23; 54:9 [e]Is. 52:1; 61:10

19 "For [a]your waste and desolate places, and your destroyed land—
Surely now you will be [b]too cramped for the inhabitants,
And those who [c]swallowed you will be far away.
20 "The [a]children of [1]whom you were bereaved will yet say in your ears,
'The place is too cramped for me;
Make room for me that I may live *here.*'
21 "Then you will [a]say in your heart,
'Who has begotten these for me,
Since I have been bereaved of my children,
And am [b]barren, an [c]exile and a wanderer?
And who has reared these?
Behold, I was [d]left alone;
[1e]From where did these come?' "

22 Thus says the Lord [1]GOD,
"Behold, I will lift up My hand to the nations,
And set up My [a]standard to the peoples;
And they will [b]bring your sons in *their* bosom,
And your daughters will be carried on *their* shoulders.
23 "And [a]kings will be your guardians,
And their princesses your nurses.
They will [b]bow down to you with their faces to the earth,
And [c]lick the dust of your feet;
And *you* will [d]know that I am the LORD;
Those who hopefully [e]wait for Me will [f]not be put to shame.

24 "[a]Can the prey be taken from the mighty man,
Or the captives of [1]a tyrant be rescued?"
25 Surely, thus says the LORD,
"Even the [a]captives of the mighty man will be taken away,
And the prey of the tyrant will be rescued;
For I will contend with the one who contends with you,
And I will [b]save your sons.
26 "And I will feed your [a]oppressors with their [b]own flesh,
And they will become drunk with their own blood as with sweet wine;
And [c]all flesh will know that I, the LORD, am your [d]Savior,
And your [e]Redeemer, the Mighty One of Jacob."

God Helps His Servant

50 THUS says the LORD,
"Where is the [a]certificate of divorce,
By which I have [b]sent your mother away?
Or to whom of My creditors did I [c]sell you?

19 [a]Is. 1:7; 3:8; 5:6; 51:3 [b]Is. 54:1, 2; Zech. 10:10 [c]Ps. 56:1, 2
20 [1]Lit., *your bereavement* [a]Is. 54:1-3
21 [1]Lit., *These, where are they?* [a]Is. 29:23; 54:6, 7 [b]Is. 27:10; Lam. 1:1 [c]Is. 5:13 [d]Is. 1:8 [e]Is. 60:8
22 [1]Heb., *YHWH,* usually rendered *LORD* [a]Is. 11:10, 12; 18:3; 62:10 [b]Is. 14:2; 43:6; 60:4
23 [a]Is. 14:1, 2; 60:3, 10, 11 [b]Is. 45:14; 60:14 [c]Ps. 72:9; Mic. 7:17 [d]Is. 41:20; 43:10; 60:16 [e]Ps. 37:9; Is. 25:9; 26:8 [f]Ps. 25:3; Is. 45:17; Joel 2:27
24 [1]So ancient versions and DSS; M.T. reads *the righteous,* cf. v. 25 [a]Matt. 12:29; Luke 11:21
25 [a]Is. 10:6; 14:1, 2; Jer. 50:33, 34 [b]Is. 25:9; 33:22; 35:4
26 [a]Is. 9:4; 14:4; 16:4; 51:13; 54:14 [b]Is. 9:20 [c]Is. 45:6; Ezek. 39:7 [d]Is. 43:3 [e]Is. 49:7

1 [a]Deut. 24:1, 3; Jer. 3:8 [b]Is. 54:6, 7 [c]Deut. 32:30; 2 Kin. 4:1; Neh. 5:5 [d]Is. 52:3; 59:2 [e]Is. 1:28; 43:27 [f]Jer. 3:8
2 [a]Is. 41:28; 59:16; 66:4 [b]Gen. 18:14; Num. 11:23; Is. 59:1 [c]Ex. 14:21; Is. 19:5; 43:16; 44:27 [d]Josh. 3:16; Is. 42:15
3 [a]Is. 13:10; Rev. 6:12
4 [1]Heb., *YHWH,* usually rendered *LORD,* and so throughout the ch. [a]Is. 8:16; 54:13 [b]Is. 57:19; Jer. 31:25 [c]Ps. 5:3; 88:13; 119:147; 143:8
5 [a]Ps. 40:6; Is. 35:5 [b]Matt. 26:39; John 8:29; 14:31; 15:10; Acts 26:19; Phil. 2:8; Heb. 5:8; 10:7
6 [a]Matt. 26:67; 27:30; Mark 14:65; 15:19; Luke 22:63
7 [a]Is. 42:1; 49:8 [b]Is. 45:17; 54:4 [c]Ezek. 3:8; 9
8 [a]Is. 45:25; Rom. 8:33, 34 [b]Is. 1:18; 41:1; 43:26
9 [a]Is. 41:10 [b]Is. 54:17 [c]Job 13:28; Is. 51:8
10 [a]Is. 49:2, 3; 50:4 [b]Is. 9:2; 26:9; Eph. 5:8 [c]Is. 12:2; 26:4
11 [1]Lit., *gird* [a]Prov. 26:18; Is. 9:18; James 3:6 [b]Is. 8:22; 65:13-15; Amos 4:9, 10

Behold, you were sold for your [d]iniquities,
And for your [e]transgressions your mother [f]was sent away.
2 "Why was there [a]no man when I came?
When I called, *why* was there none to answer?
Is My [b]hand so short that it cannot ransom?
Or have I no power to deliver?
Behold, I [c]dry up the sea with My rebuke,
I [d]make the rivers a wilderness;
Their fish stink for lack of water,
And die of thirst.
3 "I [a]clothe the heavens with blackness,
And I make sackcloth their covering."

4 The Lord [1]GOD has given Me the tongue of [a]disciples,
That I may know how to [b]sustain the weary one with a word.
He awakens *Me* [c]morning by morning,
He awakens My ear to listen as a disciple.
5 The Lord GOD has [a]opened My ear;
And I was [b]not disobedient,
Nor did I turn back.
6 I [a]gave My back to those who strike *Me,*
And My cheeks to those who pluck out the beard;
I did not cover My face from humiliation and spitting.
7 For the Lord GOD [a]helps Me,
Therefore, I am [b]not disgraced;
Therefore, I have set My face like [c]flint,
And I know that I shall not be ashamed.
8 He who [a]vindicates Me is near;
Who will contend with Me?
Let us [b]stand up to each other;
Who has a case against Me?
Let him draw near to Me.
9 Behold, [a]the Lord GOD helps Me;
[b]Who is he who condemns Me?
Behold, [c]they will all wear out like a garment;
The moth will eat them.
10 Who is among you that fears the LORD,
That obeys the voice of His [a]servant,
That [b]walks in darkness and has no light?
Let him [c]trust in the name of the LORD and rely on his God.
11 Behold, all you who [a]kindle a fire,
Who [1]encircle yourselves with firebrands,
Walk in the light of your fire
And among the brands you have set ablaze.
This you will have from My hand;
And you will [b]lie down in torment.

Israel Exhorted

51 "[a]LISTEN to me, you who [b]pursue righteousness,
Who seek the LORD:
Look to the [c]rock from which you were hewn,
And to the [1]quarry from which you were dug.
2 "Look to [a]Abraham your father,
And to Sarah who gave birth to you in pain;
When *he* [b]*was* one I called him,
Then I blessed him and multiplied him."
3 Indeed, [a]the LORD will comfort Zion;
He will comfort all her [b]waste places.
And her [c]wilderness He will make like [d]Eden,
And her desert like the [e]garden of the LORD;
[f]Joy and gladness will be found in her,
Thanksgiving and sound of a melody.

4 "[a]Pay attention to Me, O My people;
And give ear to Me, O My [1]nation;
For a [b]law will go forth from Me,
And I will [2]set My [c]justice for a [d]light of the peoples.
5 "My [a]righteousness is near, My salvation has gone forth,
And My [b]arms will judge the peoples;
The [c]coastlands will wait for Me,
And for My [d]arm they will wait expectantly.
6 "[a]Lift up your eyes to the sky,
Then look to the earth beneath;
For the [b]sky will vanish like smoke,
And the [b]earth will wear out like a garment,
And its inhabitants will die [1]in like manner,
But My [c]salvation shall be forever,
And My righteousness shall not [2]wane.
7 "[a]Listen to Me, you who know righteousness,
A people in whose [b]heart is My law;
Do not fear the [c]reproach of man,
Neither be dismayed at their revilings.
8 "For the [a]moth will eat them like a garment,
And the [b]grub will eat them like wool.
But My [c]righteousness shall be forever,
And My salvation to all generations."

9 [a]Awake, awake, put on strength, O arm of the LORD;
Awake as in the [b]days of old, the generations of long ago.
[c]Was it not Thou who cut Rahab in pieces,
Who pierced the [d]dragon?
10 Was it not Thou who [a]dried up the sea,
The waters of the great deep;
Who made the depths of the sea a pathway
For the [b]redeemed to cross over?
11 So the [a]ransomed of the LORD will return,
And come with joyful shouting to Zion;
And [b]everlasting joy *will be* on their heads.
They will obtain gladness and joy,
And [c]sorrow and sighing will flee away.

12 "I, even I, am He who [a]comforts you.
Who are you that you are afraid of [b]man who dies,
And of the son of man who is made [c]like grass;
13 That you have [a]forgotten the LORD your Maker,
Who [b]stretched out the heavens,
And laid the foundations of the earth;
That you [c]fear continually all day long because of the fury of the oppressor,
As he makes ready to destroy?
But where is the fury of the [d]oppressor?
14 "The [1a]exile will soon be set free,
and will not die in the dungeon, [b]nor
will his bread be lacking.
15 "For I am the LORD your God, who
[a]stirs up the sea and its waves roar (the
LORD of hosts is His name).
16 "And I have [a]put My words in your
mouth, and have [b]covered you with the
shadow of My hand, to [1c]establish the
heavens, to found the earth, and to say
to Zion, 'You are My people.' "
17 [a]Rouse yourself! Rouse yourself! Arise, O Jerusalem,
You who have [b]drunk from the LORD's hand the cup of His anger;
The [1]chalice of reeling you have [2]drained to the dregs.
18 There is [a]none to guide her among all the sons she has borne;
Nor is there one to take her by the hand among all the sons she has reared.
19 These two things have befallen you;
Who will mourn for you?
The [a]devastation and destruction, famine and sword;
How shall I comfort you?
20 Your sons have fainted,
They [a]lie *helpless* at the head of every street,
Like an [b]antelope in a net,
Full of the wrath of the LORD,
The [c]rebuke of your God.

21 Therefore, please hear this, you [a]afflicted,
Who are [b]drunk, but not with wine:

1 [1]Lit., *excavation of a pit* [a]Is. 46:3; 48:12; 51:7 [b]Ps. 94:15; Prov. 15:9 [c]Gen. 17:15-17
2 [a]Is. 29:22; 41:8; 63:16 [b]Gen. 12:1; 15:5; Deut. 1:10; Ezek. 33:24
3 [a]Is. 40:1; 49:13 [b]Is. 52:9 [c]Is. 35:1; 41:19 [d]Gen. 2:8; Joel 2:3 [e]Gen. 13:10 [f]Is. 25:9; 41:16; 65:18; 66:10
4 [1]Or, *people* [2]Lit., *cause to rest* [a]Ps. 50:7; 78:1 [b]Deut. 18:18; Is. 2:3; Mic. 4:2 [c]Is. 1:27; 42:4 [d]Is. 42:6; 49:6
5 [a]Is. 46:13; 54:17 [b]Is. 40:10 [c]Is. 42:4; 60:9 [d]Is. 59:16; 63:5
6 [1]Or, *like gnats* [2]Lit., *be broken* [a]Is. 40:26 [b]Ps. 102:25, 26; Is. 13:13; 34:4; Matt. 24:35; Heb. 1:10-12; 2 Pet. 3:10 [c]Is. 45:17; 51:8
7 [a]Is. 51:1 [b]Ps. 37:31 [c]Is. 25:8; 54:4; Matt. 5:11; Acts 5:41
8 [a]Is. 50:9 [b]Is. 14:11; 66:24 [c]Is. 51:6
9 [a]Is. 51:17; 52:1 [b]Ex. 6:6; Deut. 4:34 [c]Job 26:12; Ps. 89:10; Is. 30:7 [d]Ps. 74:13; Is. 27:1
10 [a]Is. 11:15, 16; 50:2; 63:11, 12 [b]Ex. 15:13; Ps. 106:10; Is. 63:9
11 [a]Is. 35:10; Jer. 31:11, 12 [b]Is. 60:19; 61:7 [c]Is. 25:8; 60:20; 65:19; Rev. 7:17; 21:1, 4; 22:3
12 [a]Is. 51:3 [b]Ps. 118:6; Is. 2:22 [c]Is. 40:6, 7; 1 Pet. 1:24
13 [a]Deut. 6:12; 8:11; Is. 17:10 [b]Job 9:8; Ps. 104:2; Is. 40:22; 45:12, 18; 48:13 [c]Is. 7:4; 10:24 [d]Is. 49:26; 54:14
14 [1]Lit., *one in chains* [a]Is. 48:20; 52:2 [b]Is. 33:6; 49:10
15 [a]Ps. 107:25; Jer. 31:35
16 [1]Lit., *plant* [a]Deut. 18:18; Is. 59:21 [b]Ex. 33:22; Is. 49:2 [c]Is. 66:22
17 [1]Lit., *bowl of the cup of reeling* [2]Lit., *drunk* [a]Is. 51:9; 52:1 [b]Job 21:20; Is. 29:9; 63:6; Jer. 25:15; Rev. 14:10; 16:19
18 [a]Ps. 88:18; 142:4; Is. 49:21
19 [a]Is. 8:21; 9:20; 14:30
20 [a]Is. 5:25; Jer. 14:16 [b]Deut. 14:5 [c]Is. 66:15
21 [a]Is. 54:11 [b]Is. 29:9; 51:17; 63:6

22 Thus says your Lord, the LORD, even your God
Who [a]contends for His people,
"Behold, I have taken out of your hand the [b]cup of reeling;
The [1]chalice of My anger,
You will never drink it again.
23 "And I will [a]put it into the hand of your tormentors,
Who have said to [1]you, '[b]Lie down that we may walk over you.'
You have even made your back like the ground,
And like the street for those who walk over *it*."

Cheer for Prostrate Zion

52 [a]AWAKE, awake,
Clothe yourself in your strength, O Zion;
Clothe yourself in your [b]beautiful garments,
O Jerusalem, the [c]holy city.
For the uncircumcised and the [d]unclean
Will no more come into you.
2 Shake yourself [a]from the dust, [b]rise up,
O captive Jerusalem;
[c]Loose yourself from the chains around your neck,
O captive daughter of Zion.
3 For thus says the LORD, "You were
[a]sold for nothing and you will be [b]re-
deemed [c]without money."
4 For thus says the Lord [1]GOD, "My
people [a]went down at the first into
Egypt to reside there, then the Assyrian
oppressed them without cause.
5 "Now therefore, what do I have
here," declares the LORD, "seeing that
My people have been taken away without cause?" *Again* the LORD declares,
"Those who rule over them howl, and
My [a]name is continually blasphemed all
day long.
6 "Therefore My people shall [a]know
My name; therefore in that day I am the
one who is speaking, 'Here I am.' "
7 How lovely on the mountains
Are the feet of him who brings [a]good news,
Who announces [1]peace
And brings good news of [2]happiness,
Who announces salvation,
And says to Zion, "Your [b]God [3]reigns!"
8 Listen! Your watchmen lift up *their* [a]voices,
They shout joyfully together;
For they will see [1]with their own eyes
When the LORD restores Zion.
9 [a]Break forth, shout joyfully together,
You [b]waste places of Jerusalem;
For the LORD has comforted His people,
He has [c]redeemed Jerusalem.
10 The LORD has bared His holy [a]arm
In the sight of all the nations,
[1]That [b]all the ends of the earth may see
The salvation of our God.

11 [a]Depart, depart, go out from there,
[b]Touch nothing unclean;
Go out of the midst of her, [c]purify yourselves,
You who carry the vessels of the LORD.
12 But you will not go out in [a]haste,
Nor will you go [1]as fugitives;
For the [b]LORD will go before you,
And [c]the God of Israel *will be* your rear guard.

The Exalted Servant

13 Behold, My [a]servant will prosper,
He will be high and lifted up, and [1]greatly [b]exalted.
14 Just as many were astonished at you, *My people,*
So His [a]appearance was marred more than any man,
And His form more than the sons of men.
15 Thus He will [a]sprinkle many nations,
Kings will [b]shut their mouths on account of Him;
For [c]what had not been told them they will see,
And what they had not heard they will understand.

The Suffering Servant

53 [a]WHO has believed our message?
And to whom has the arm of the LORD been revealed?
2 For He grew up before Him like a [a]tender [1]shoot,
And like a root out of parched ground;
He has [b]no *stately* form or majesty
That we should look upon Him,
Nor appearance that we should [2]be attracted to Him.
3 He was [a]despised and forsaken of men,
A man of [1]sorrows, and [b]acquainted with [2]grief;
And like one from whom men hide their face,
He was [c]despised, and we did not [d]esteem Him.

4 Surely our [1]griefs He Himself [a]bore,
And our [2]sorrows He carried;
Yet we ourselves esteemed Him stricken,
[3]Smitten of [b]God, and afflicted.
5 But He was [1]pierced through for [a]our transgressions,
He was crushed for [b]our iniquities;
The [c]chastening for our [2]well-being *fell* upon Him,
And by [d]His scourging we are healed.

22 [1]Lit., *bowl of the cup of* [a]Is. 3:12, 13; 49:25; Jer. 50:34 [b]Is. 51:17
23 [1]Lit., *your soul* [a]Is. 49:26; Jer. 25:15-17, 26, 28; Zech. 12:2 [b]Josh. 10:24

1 [a]Is. 51:9, 17 [b]Ex. 28:2, 40; 1 Chr. 16:29; Ps. 110:3; Is. 49:18; 61:3, 10; Zech. 3:4 [c]Neh. 11:1; Is. 48:2; 64:10; Zech. 14:20, 21; Matt. 4:5; Rev. 21:2-27 [d]Is. 35:8
2 [a]Is. 29:4 [b]Is. 60:1 [c]Is. 9:4; 10:27; 14:25; Zech. 2:7
3 [a]Ps. 44:12; Jer. 15:13 [b]Is. 1:27; 62:12; 63:4 [c]Is. 45:13
4 [1]Heb., *YHWH,* usually rendered *LORD* [a]Gen. 46:6
5 [a]Ezek. 36:20, 23; Rom. 2:24
6 [a]Is. 49:23
7 [1]Or, *well-being* [2]Lit., *good* [3]Or, *is King* [a]Is. 40:9; 61:1; Nah. 1:15; Rom. 10:15; Eph. 6:15 [b]Ps. 93:1; Is. 24:23
8 [1]Lit., *eye to eye* [a]Is. 62:6
9 [a]Ps. 98:4; Is. 44:23 [b]Is. 44:26; 51:3; 61:4 [c]Is. 43:1; 48:20
10 [1]Lit., *And . . . earth will see* [a]Ps. 98:1-3; Is. 51:9; 66:18, 19 [b]Is. 45:22; 48:20
11 [a]Is. 48:20; Jer. 50:8; Zech. 2:6, 7; 2 Cor. 6:17 [b]Num. 19:11, 16 [c]Lev. 22:2; Is. 1:16
12 [1]Lit., *in flight* [a]Ex. 12:11, 33; Deut. 16:3 [b]Is. 26:7; 42:16; 49:10, 11 [c]Ex. 14:19, 20; Is. 58:8
13 [1]Or, *very high* [a]Is. 42:1; 49:1-7; 53:11 [b]Is. 57:15; Phil. 2:9
14 [a]Is. 53:2, 3
15 [a]Num. 19:18-21; Ezek. 36:25 [b]Job 21:5 [c]Rom. 15:21; Eph. 3:5

1 [a]John 12:38; Rom. 10:16
2 [1]Lit., *suckling* [2]Lit., *desire* [a]Is. 11:1 [b]Is. 52:14
3 [1]Or, *pains* [2]Or, *sickness* [a]Ps. 22:6; Is. 49:7; Luke 18:31-33 [b]Is. 53:10 [c]Mark 10:33, 34 [d]John 1:10, 11
4 [1]Or, *sickness* [2]Or, *pains* [3]Or, *Struck down by* [a]Matt. 8:17 [b]John 19:7
5 [1]Or, *wounded* [2]Or, *peace* [a]Is. 53:8; Heb. 9:28 [b]Is. 53:10; Rom. 4:25; 1 Cor. 15:3 [c]Deut. 11:2; Heb. 5:8 [d]1 Pet. 2:24, 25

6 All of us like sheep have gone astray,
Each of us has turned to his own way;
But the LORD has caused the iniquity of us all
To [1]fall on Him.

7 He was oppressed and He was afflicted,
Yet He did not [a]open His mouth;
[b]Like a lamb that is led to slaughter,
And like a sheep that is silent before its shearers,
So He did not open His mouth.
8 By oppression and judgment He was taken away;
And as for His generation, who considered
That He was cut off out of the land of the [1]living,
[a]For the transgression of my people to whom the stroke *was due?*
9 His grave was assigned with wicked men,
Yet He was with a [a]rich man in His death,
[b]Because He had [c]done no violence,
Nor was there any deceit in His mouth.

10 But the LORD was pleased
To [a]crush Him, [1b]putting *Him* to grief;
If [2]He would render Himself *as* a guilt [c]offering,
He will see [d]*His* [3]offspring,
He will prolong *His* days,
And the [4]good [e]pleasure of the LORD will prosper in His hand.
11 As a result of the [1]anguish of His soul,
He will [a]see [2]*it* and be satisfied;
By His [b]knowledge the Righteous One,
My Servant, will justify the many,
As He will [c]bear their iniquities.
12 Therefore, I will allot Him a [a]portion with the great,
And He will divide the booty with the strong;
Because He poured out [1b]Himself to death,
And was [c]numbered with the transgressors;
Yet He Himself [d]bore the sin of many,
And interceded for the transgressors.

The Fertility of Zion

54 "[a]SHOUT for joy, O barren one, you who have borne no *child;*
Break forth into joyful shouting and cry aloud, you who have not travailed;
For the sons of the [b]desolate one *will be* [c]more numerous
Than the sons of the married woman," says the LORD.
2 "[a]Enlarge the place of your tent;
[1]Stretch out the curtains of your dwellings, spare not;
Lengthen your [b]cords,
And strengthen your [b]pegs.
3 "For you will [a]spread abroad to the right and to the left.
And your [1]descendants will [b]possess nations,
And they will [c]resettle the desolate cities.

4 "Fear not, for you will [a]not be put to shame;
Neither feel humiliated, for you will not be disgraced;
But you will forget the [b]shame of your youth,
And the [c]reproach of your widowhood you will remember no more.
5 "For your [a]husband is your Maker,
Whose name is the LORD of hosts;
And your [b]Redeemer is the Holy One of Israel,
Who is called the [c]God of all the earth.
6 "For the LORD has called you,
Like a wife [a]forsaken and grieved in spirit,
Even like a wife of *one's* youth when she is rejected,"
Says your God.
7 "[1]For a [a]brief moment I forsook you,
But with great compassion I will [b]gather you.
8 "In an [1a]outburst of anger
I hid My face from you for a moment;
But with everlasting [b]lovingkindness I will [c]have compassion on you,"
Says the LORD your [d]Redeemer.

9 "For [1]this is like the days of Noah to Me;
When I swore that the waters of Noah
Should [a]not [2]flood the earth again,
So I have sworn that I will [b]not be angry with you,
Nor will I rebuke you.
10 "For the [a]mountains may be removed and the hills may shake,
But My lovingkindness will not be removed from you,
And My [b]covenant of peace will not be shaken,"
Says [c]the LORD who has compassion on you.

11 "O [a]afflicted one, storm-tossed, and [b]not comforted,
Behold, I will set your stones in antimony,
And your foundations I will [c]lay in [1d]sapphires.
12 "Moreover, I will make your battlements of [1]rubies,
And your gates of [2]crystal,
And your entire [3]wall of precious stones.

6 [1]Lit., *encounter Him*

7 [a]Matt. 26:63; 27:12-14; Mark 14:61; 15:5; Luke 23:9; John 19:9 [b]Acts 8:32, 33; Rev. 5:6

8 [1]Or, *life* [a]Is. 53:5, 12

9 [a]Matt. 27:57-60 [b]Is. 42:1-3 [c]1 Pet. 2:22

10 [1]Lit., *He made Him sick* [2]Lit., *His soul* [3]Lit., *seed* [4]Or, *will of* [a]Is. 53:5 [b]Is. 53:3, 4 [c]Is. 53:6, 12; John 1:29 [d]Ps. 22:30; Is. 54:3; 61:9; 66:22 [e]Is. 46:10

11 [1]Or, *toilsome labor* [2]Another reading is *light* [a]John 10:14-18 [b]Is. 45:25; Rom. 5:18, 19 [c]Is. 53:5, 6

12 [1]Lit., *His soul* [a]Is. 52:13; Phil. 2:9-11 [b]Matt. 26:38, 39, 42 [c]Mark 15:28; Luke 22:37 [d]Is. 53:6, 11; 2 Cor. 5:21

1 [a]Gal. 4:27 [b]Is. 62:4 [c]1 Sam. 2:5; Is. 49:20

2 [1]Lit., *Let them stretch out* [a]Is. 33:20; 49:19, 20 [b]Ex. 35:18; 39:40

3 [1]Lit., *seed* [a]Gen. 28:14; Is. 43:5, 6; 60:3 [b]Is. 14:1, 2 [c]Is. 49:19

4 [a]Is. 45:17 [b]Jer. 31:19 [c]Is. 4:1; 25:8; 51:7

5 [a]Jer. 3:14; Hos. 2:19 [b]Is. 43:14; 48:17 [c]Is. 6:3; 11:9; 65:16

6 [a]Is. 49:14-21; 50:1, 2; 62:4

7 [1]Lit., *in* [a]Is. 26:20 [b]Is. 11:12; 43:5; 49:18

8 [1]Lit., *overflowing* [a]Is. 60:10 [b]Is. 54:10; 63:7 [c]Is. 49:10, 13 [d]Is. 54:5

9 [1]Some mss. read *the waters of Noah this is to me* [2]Lit., *cross over* [a]Gen. 9:11 [b]Is. 12:1; Ezek. 39:29

10 [a]Ps. 102:26; Is. 51:6 [b]2 Sam. 23:5; Ps. 89:34; Is. 55:3; 59:21; 61:8 [c]Is. 54:8

11 [1]Or, *lapis lazuli* [a]Is. 51:21 [b]Is. 51:18, 19 [c]Is. 14:32; 28:16; 44:28 [d]Job 28:16; Rev. 21:19

12 [1]I.e., bright red [2]Or, *carbuncles* [3]Lit., *border, boundary*

13 "And [a]all your sons will be [1]taught
of the LORD;
And the well-being of your sons
will be [b]great.
14 "In [a]righteousness you will be established;
You will be far from [b]oppression,
for you will [c]not fear;
And from [d]terror, for it will not
come near you.
15 "If anyone fiercely assails *you* it will
not be from Me.
[a]Whoever assails you will fall because of you.
16 "Behold, I Myself have created the
smith who blows the fire of
coals,
And brings out a weapon for its
work;
And I have created the destroyer to
ruin.
17 "[a]No weapon that is formed against
you shall prosper;
And [b]every tongue that [1]accuses
you in judgment you will condemn.
This is the heritage of the servants
of the LORD,
And their [c]vindication is from Me,"
declares the LORD.

The Free Offer of Mercy

55 "HO! Every one who [a]thirsts,
come to the waters;
And you who have [b]no [1]money
come, buy and eat.
Come, buy [c]wine and milk
[d]Without money and without cost.
2 "Why do you [1]spend money for
what is [a]not bread,
And your wages for what does not
satisfy?
Listen carefully to Me, and [b]eat
what is good,
And [c]delight yourself in abundance.
3 "[a]Incline your ear and come to Me.
Listen, that [1]you may [b]live;
And I will make [c]an everlasting
covenant with you,
According to the [d]faithful mercies
[2]shown to David.
4 "Behold, I have made [a]him a witness
to the peoples,
A [b]leader and commander for the
peoples.
5 "Behold, you will call a [a]nation you
do not know,
And a nation which knows you not
will [b]run to you,
Because of the LORD your God,
even the Holy One of Israel;
For He has [c]glorified you."

6 [a]Seek the LORD while He may be
found;
[b]Call upon Him while He is near.
7 [a]Let the wicked forsake his way,
And the unrighteous man his
[b]thoughts;
And let him [c]return to the LORD,
And He will have [d]compassion on
him;
And to our God,
For He will [e]abundantly pardon.
8 "For My thoughts are not [a]your
thoughts,
Neither are [b]your ways My ways,"
declares the LORD.
9 "For [a]*as* the heavens are higher than
the earth,
So are My ways higher than your
ways,
And My thoughts than your
thoughts.
10 "For as the [a]rain and the snow come
down from heaven,
And do not return there without
watering the earth,
And making it bear and sprout,
And furnishing [b]seed to the sower
and bread to the eater;
11 So shall My [a]word be which goes
forth from My mouth;
It shall [b]not return to Me empty,
Without [c]accomplishing what I
desire,
And without succeeding *in the matter* for which I sent it.
12 "For you will go out with [a]joy,
And be led forth with [b]peace;
The [c]mountains and the hills will
break forth into shouts of joy
before you,
And all the [d]trees of the field will
clap *their* hands.
13 "Instead of the [a]thorn bush the
[b]cypress will come up;
And instead of the [c]nettle the myrtle will come up;
And [1]it will be a [2][d]memorial to the
LORD,
For an everlasting [e]sign which [f]will
not be cut off."

Rewards for Obedience to God

56 THUS says the LORD,
"[a]Preserve justice, and do righteousness,
For My [b]salvation is about to come
And My righteousness to be revealed.
2 "How [a]blessed is the man who does
this,
And the son of man who [b]takes
hold of it;
Who [c]keeps from profaning the
sabbath,
And keeps his hand from doing any
evil."
3 Let not the [a]foreigner who has
joined himself to the LORD say,
"The LORD will surely separate me
from His people."
Neither let the [b]eunuch say, "Behold, I am a dry tree."
4 For thus says the LORD,
"To the eunuchs who [a]keep My
sabbaths,
And choose what pleases Me,
And [b]hold fast My covenant,

13 [1]Or, *disciples* [a]John 6:45 [b]Is. 48:18; 66:12
14 [a]Is. 1:26, 27; 9:7; 62:1 [b]Is. 9:4; 14:4 [c]Is. 54:4 [d]Is. 33:18
15 [a]Is. 41:11-16
17 [1]Lit., *rises against* [a]Is. 17:12-14; 29:8 [b]Is. 50:8, 9 [c]Is. 45:24; 46:13

1 [1]Lit., *silver* [a]Ps. 42:1, 2; 63:1; 143:6; Is. 41:17; 44:3; John 4:14; 7:37; Rev. 21:6 [b]Lam. 5:4 [c]Song 5:1; Joel 3:18 [d]Hos. 14:4; Matt. 10:8
2 [1]Lit., *weigh out silver* [a]Eccl. 6:2; Hos. 8:7 [b]Ps. 22:26; Is. 1:19; 62:8, 9 [c]Is. 25:6; Jer. 31:14
3 [1]Lit., *your soul* [2]Lit., *of David* [a]Is. 51:4 [b]Lev. 18:5; Rom. 10:5 [c]Is. 61:8 [d]Acts 13:34
4 [a]Ps. 18:43; Jer. 30:9; Hos. 3:5 [b]Ezek. 34:24; 37:24, 25; Dan. 9:25; Mic. 5:2
5 [a]Is. 45:14, 22-24; 49:6, 12, 23 [b]Zech. 8:22 [c]Is. 60:9
6 [a]Ps. 32:6; Is. 45:19, 22; 49:8; Amos 5:6 [b]Is. 58:9; 65:24
7 [a]Is. 1:16, 19; 58:6 [b]Is. 32:7; 59:7 [c]Is. 31:6; 44:22 [d]Is. 14:1; 54:8, 10 [e]Is. 1:18; 40:2; 43:25; 44:22
8 [a]Is. 65:2; 66:18 [b]Is. 53:6
9 [a]Ps. 103:11
10 [a]Is. 30:23 [b]2 Cor. 9:10
11 [a]Is. 45:23; Matt. 24:35 [b]Is. 44:26; 59:21 [c]Is. 46:10; 53:10
12 [a]Ps. 105:43; Is. 51:11; 52:9 [b]Is. 54:10, 13; Jer. 29:11 [c]Is. 44:23; 49:13 [d]1 Chr. 16:33
13 [1]I.e., the transformation of the desert [2]Lit., *name* [a]Is. 7:19 [b]Is. 60:13 [c]Is. 5:6; 7:24; 32:13 [d]Is. 63:12, 14; Jer. 33:9 [e]Is. 19:20 [f]Is. 56:5

1 [a]Is. 1:17; 33:5; 61:8 [b]Ps. 85:9; Is. 46:13; 51:5
2 [a]Ps. 112:1; 119:1, 2 [b]Is. 56:4, 6 [c]Ex. 20:8-11; 31:13-17; Is. 56:6; 58:13; Jer. 17:21, 22; Ezek. 20:12, 20
3 [a]Is. 14:1; 56:6 [b]Deut. 23:1; Jer. 38:7; Acts 8:27
4 [a]Is. 56:2, 6 [b]Is. 56:6

5 To them I will give in My [a]house
and within My [b]walls a memorial,
And a name better than that of
sons and daughters;
I will give [1]them an everlasting
[c]name which [d]will not be cut off.

6 "Also the [a]foreigners who join themselves to the LORD,
To minister to Him, and to love the
name of the LORD,
To be His servants, every one who
[b]keeps from profaning the sabbath,
And holds fast My covenant;
7 Even [a]those I will bring to My
[b]holy mountain,
And [c]make them joyful in My
house of prayer.
Their burnt offerings and their
sacrifices will be acceptable on
[d]My altar;
For [e]My house will be called a
house of prayer for all the peoples."
8 The Lord [1]GOD, who [a]gathers the
dispersed of Israel, declares,
"Yet [b]*others* I will gather to [2]them,
to those *already* gathered."

9 All you [a]beasts of the field,
All you beasts in the forest,
Come to eat.
10 His [a]watchmen are [b]blind,
All of them know nothing.
All of them are dumb dogs unable
to bark,
[1]Dreamers lying down, who love to
slumber;
11 And the dogs are [1a]greedy, they
[2]are not satisfied.
And they are shepherds who have
[b]no understanding;
They have all [c]turned to their own
way,
Each one to his unjust gain, to the
last one.
12 "Come," *they say,* "let [1]us get [a]wine,
and let us drink heavily of
strong drink;
And [b]tomorrow will be like today,
only more so."

Evil Leaders Rebuked

57 THE righteous man perishes, and
no man [a]takes it to heart;
And devout men are taken away,
while no one understands.
For the righteous man is taken
away from [b]evil,
2 He enters into peace;
They rest in their [1]beds,
Each one who [a]walked in his upright way.
3 "But come here, you sons of a [a]sorceress,
[b]Offspring of an adulterer and [1]a
[c]prostitute.
4 "Against whom do you jest?
Against whom do you open wide
your mouth
And stick out your tongue?
Are you not children of [a]rebellion,
Offspring of deceit,
5 *Who* inflame yourselves among the
[1a]oaks,
[b]Under every luxuriant tree,
Who [c]slaughter the children in the
[2]ravines,
Under the clefts of the crags?
6 "Among the [1a]smooth *stones* of the
[2]ravine
Is your portion, [3]they are your lot;
Even to them you have [b]poured out
a libation,
You have made a grain offering.
Shall I [4c]relent concerning these
things?
7 "Upon a [a]high and lofty mountain
You have [b]made your bed.
You also went up there to offer
sacrifice.
8 "And behind the door and the doorpost
You have set up your sign;
Indeed, far removed from Me, you
have [a]uncovered yourself;
And have gone up and made your
bed wide.
And you have made an agreement
for yourselves with them,
You have loved their [1]bed,
You have looked on *their* [2]manhood.
9 "And you have journeyed to the
king with oil
And increased your perfumes;
You have [a]sent your envoys a great
distance,
And made *them* go down to [1]Sheol.
10 "You were tired out by the length of
your road,
Yet you did not say, '[a]It is hopeless.'
You found [1]renewed strength,
Therefore you did not [2]faint.

11 "Of [a]whom were you worried and
fearful,
When you lied, and did [b]not remember Me,
[1]Nor [c]give *Me* a thought?
Was I not silent even for a long
time
So you do not fear Me?
12 "I will [a]declare your righteousness
and your [b]deeds,
But they will not profit you.
13 "When you cry out, [a]let your collection *of idols* deliver you.
But the wind will carry all of them
up,
And a breath will take *them away.*
But he who [b]takes refuge in Me
shall [c]inherit the land,
And shall [d]possess My holy mountain."

14 And it shall be said,
"[a]Build up, build up, prepare the
way,
Remove *every* obstacle out of the
way of My people."

5 [1]So DSS; M.T. reads *him* [a]Is. 2:2, 3; 56:7; 66:20 [b]Is. 26:1; 60:18 [c]Is. 62:2 [d]Is. 48:19; 55:13
6 [a]Is. 56:3; 60:10; 61:5 [b]Is. 56:2, 4
7 [a]Is. 2:2, 3; 60:11; Mic. 4:1, 2 [b]Is. 11:9; 65:25 [c]Is. 61:10 [d]Is. 60:7 [e]Matt. 21:13; Mark 11:17; Luke 19:46
8 [1]Heb., *YHWH,* usually rendered *LORD* [2]Lit., *him* [a]Is. 11:12 [b]Is. 60:3-11; 66:18-21; John 10:16
9 [a]Is. 18:6; 46:11
10 [1]So DSS; M. T., *Ravers* [a]Ezek. 3:17 [b]Is. 29:9-14; Jer. 14:13, 14
11 [1]Lit., *strong of soul/appetite* [2]Lit., *do not know satisfaction* [a]Is. 28:7; Ezek. 13:19; Mic. 3:5, 11 [b]Is. 1:3 [c]Is. 57:17; Jer. 22:17
12 [1]So DSS and many versions; M. T., *me* [a]Is. 5:11, 12, 22 [b]Ps. 10:6; Luke 12:19, 20

1 [a]Is. 42:25; 47:7 [b]2 Kin. 22:20; Is. 47:11; Jer. 18:11
2 [1]I.e., graves [a]Is. 26:7
3 [1]So ancient versions; Heb., *she prostitutes herself* [a]Mal. 3:5 [b]Is. 1:4; Matt. 16:4 [c]Is. 1:21; 57:7-9
4 [a]Is. 48:8
5 [1]Or, *terebinths* [2]Or, *wadis* [a]Is. 1:29 [b]2 Kin. 16:4; Jer. 2:20; 3:13 [c]2 Kin. 23:10; Ps. 106:37, 38; Jer. 7:31
6 [1]I.e., symbols of fertility gods [2]Or, *wadi* [3]Lit., *they, they* [4]Or, *repent* [a]Jer. 3:9; Hab. 2:19 [b]Jer. 7:18 [c]Jer. 5:9, 29; 9:9
7 [a]Jer. 3:6; Ezek. 16:16 [b]Ezek. 23:41
8 [1]Or, *lying down* [2]Lit., *hand* [a]Ezek. 23:18
9 [1]I.e., the nether world [a]Ezek. 23:16, 40
10 [1]Lit., *the life of your hand* [2]Or, *become sick* [a]Jer. 2:25; 18:12
11 [1]Lit., *You did not set it upon your heart* [a]Prov. 29:25; Is. 51:12, 13 [b]Jer. 2:32; 3:21 [c]Ps. 50:21; Is. 42:14
12 [a]Is. 58:1, 2 [b]Is. 29:15; 59:6; 65:7; 66:18; Mic. 3:2-4
13 [a]Jer. 22:20; 30:14 [b]Ps. 37:3, 9; Is. 25:4 [c]Is. 49:8; 60:21 [d]Is. 65:9
14 [a]Is. 62:10; Jer. 18:15

15 For thus says the [a]high and exalted One
Who [1b]lives forever, whose name is Holy,
"I [c]dwell *on* a high and holy place,
And *also* with the [d]contrite and lowly of spirit
In order to [e]revive the spirit of the lowly
And to revive the heart of the contrite.
16 "For I will [a]not contend forever,
[b]Neither will I always be angry;
For the spirit would grow faint before Me,
And the [c]breath *of those whom* I have made.
17 "Because of the iniquity of his [a]unjust gain I was angry and struck him;
I hid *My face* and was angry,
And he went on [b]turning away, in the way of his heart.
18 "I have seen his ways, but I will [a]heal him;
I will [b]lead him and [c]restore comfort to him and to his mourners,
19 Creating the [1a]praise of the lips.
[b]Peace, peace to him who is [c]far and to him who is near,"
Says the LORD, "and I will heal him."
20 But the [a]wicked are like the tossing sea,
For it cannot be quiet,
And its waters toss up refuse and mud.
21 "[a]There is no peace," says [b]my God, "for the wicked."

Observances of Fasts

58 "[a]CRY loudly, do not hold back;
Raise your voice like a trumpet,
And declare to My people their [b]transgression,
And to the house of Jacob their sins.
2 "Yet they [a]seek Me day by day, and delight to know My ways,
As a nation that has done [b]righteousness,
And [c]has not forsaken the ordinance of their God.
They ask Me *for* just decisions,
They delight [d]in the nearness of God.
3 'Why have we [a]fasted and Thou dost not see?
Why have we humbled ourselves and Thou dost not [1]notice?'
Behold, on the [b]day of your fast you find *your* desire,
And drive hard all your workers.
4 "Behold, you fast for contention and [a]strife and to strike with a wicked fist.
You do not fast like *you do* today to [b]make your voice heard on high.
5 "Is it a fast like this which I choose, a day for a man to humble himself?

15 [1]Or, *dwells in eternity*
[a]Is. 52:13 [b]Deut. 33:27; Is. 40:28 [c]Is. 33:5; 66:1 [d]Ps. 34:18; 51:17; Is. 66:2 [e]Ps. 147:3; Is. 61:1-3
16 [a]Gen. 6:3 [b]Ps. 85:5; 103:9; Mic. 7:18 [c]Is. 42:5
17 [a]Is. 2:7; 56:11; Jer. 6:13 [b]Is. 1:4; Jer. 3:14, 22
18 [a]Is. 19:22; 30:26; 53:5 [b]Is. 52:12 [c]Is. 61:1-3
19 [1]Lit., *fruit of the lips*
[a]Is. 6:7; 51:16; 59:21; Heb. 13:15 [b]Is. 26:12; 32:17 [c]Acts 2:39; Eph. 2:17
20 [a]Job 18:5-14; Is. 3:9, 11
21 [a]Is. 48:22; 59:8 [b]Is. 49:4

1 [a]Is. 40:6 [b]Is. 43:27; 50:1; 59:12
2 [a]Is. 1:11; Titus 1:16 [b]Is. 48:1; Jer. 7:9, 10 [c]Is. 1:4, 28; 59:13 [d]Ps. 119:150; Is. 29:13; 57:3; James 4:8
3 [1]Lit., *know*
[a]Mal. 3:14; Luke 18:12 [b]Is. 22:12, 13; Zech. 7:5, 6
4 [a]Is. 3:14, 15; 59:6 [b]Is. 1:15; 59:2; Joel 2:12-14
5 [1]Lit., *his*
[a]1 Kin. 21:27 [b]Is. 49:8; 61:2
6 [a]Neh. 5:10-12; Jer. 34:8 [b]Is. 1:17 [c]Is. 58:9
7 [1]Lit., *for*
[a]Job 31:19, 20; Is. 58:10; Ezek. 18:7, 16 [b]Is. 16:3, 4; Heb. 13:2 [c]Matt. 25:35, 36; Luke 3:11 [d]Deut. 22:1-4; Luke 10:31, 32
8 [a]Is. 58:10 [b]Is. 30:26; 33:24; Jer. 30:17; 33:6 [c]Ps. 85:13; Is. 62:1 [d]Ex. 14:19; Is. 52:12
9 [1]Lit., *sending out*
[a]Ps. 50:15; Is. 55:6; 65:24 [b]Is. 58:6 [c]Prov. 6:13 [d]Ps. 12:2; Is. 59:13
10 [1]Lit., *furnish*
[2]Or, *soul*
[a]Deut. 15:7; Is. 58:7 [b]Job 11:17; Ps. 37:6; Is. 42:16; 58:8
11 [1]Or, *soul* [2]Or, *deceive*
[a]Is. 49:10; 57:18 [b]Ps. 107:9; Is. 41:17 [c]Is. 66:14 [d]Song 4:15; Is. 27:3; Jer. 31:12 [e]John 4:14; 7:38
12 [1]Lit., *paths*
[a]Is. 49:8; 61:4; Ezek. 36:10 [b]Is. 44:28 [c]Is. 30:13; Amos 9:11
13 [a]Ex. 31:16, 17; 35:2, 3; Is. 56:2, 4, 6; Jer. 17:21-27 [b]Ps. 27:4; 42:4; 84:2, 10 [c]Is. 55:8 [d]Is. 59:13

Is it for bowing [1]one's head like a reed,
And for spreading out [a]sackcloth and ashes as a bed?
Will you call this a fast, even an [b]acceptable day to the LORD?
6 "Is this not the fast which I choose,
To [a]loosen the bonds of wickedness,
To undo the bands of the yoke,
And to [b]let the oppressed go free,
And [c]break every yoke?
7 "Is it not to [a]divide your bread [1]with the hungry,
And [b]bring the homeless poor into the house;
When you see the [c]naked, to cover him;
And not to [d]hide yourself from your own flesh?
8 "Then your [a]light will break out like the dawn,
And your [b]recovery will speedily spring forth;
And your [c]righteousness will go before you;
The glory of the [d]LORD will be your rear guard.
9 "Then you will [a]call, and the LORD will answer;
You will cry, and He will say, 'Here I am.'
If you [b]remove the yoke from your midst,
The [1c]pointing of the finger, and [d]speaking wickedness,
10 And if you [1a]give yourself to the hungry,
And satisfy the [2]desire of the afflicted,
Then your [b]light will rise in darkness,
And your gloom *will become* like midday.
11 "And the [a]LORD will continually guide you,
And [b]satisfy your [1]desire in scorched places,
And [c]give strength to your bones;
And you will be like a [d]watered garden,
And like a [e]spring of water whose waters do not [2]fail.
12 "And those from among you will [a]rebuild the ancient ruins;
You will [b]raise up the age-old foundations;
And you will be called the repairer of the [c]breach,
The restorer of the [1]streets in which to dwell.

Keeping the Sabbath

13 "If because of the sabbath, you [a]turn your foot
From doing your *own* pleasure on My holy day,
And call the sabbath a [b]delight, the holy *day* of the LORD honorable,
And shall honor it, desisting from your [c]*own* ways,
From seeking your *own* pleasure,
And [d]speaking *your own* word,

14 Then you will take [a]delight in the
LORD,
And I will make you ride [b]on the
heights of the earth;
And I will feed you *with* the heri-
tage of Jacob your father,
For the [c]mouth of the LORD has
spoken."

Separation from God

59 BEHOLD, [a]the LORD'S hand is
not so short
That it cannot save;
[b]Neither is His ear so dull
That it cannot hear.
2 But your [a]iniquities have made a
separation between you and
your God,
And your sins have hidden *His*
[1]face from you, so that He does
[b]not hear.
3 For your [a]hands are defiled with
blood,
And your fingers with iniquity;
Your lips have spoken [b]falsehood,
Your tongue mutters wickedness.
4 [a]No one sues righteously and [b]no
one pleads [1]honestly.
They [c]trust in confusion, and speak
lies;
They [d]conceive mischief, and bring
forth iniquity.
5 They hatch adders' eggs and
[a]weave the spider's web;
He who eats of their eggs dies,
And *from* that which is crushed a
snake breaks forth.
6 Their webs will not become clothing,
Nor will they [a]cover themselves
with their works;
Their [b]works are works of iniquity,
And an [c]act of violence is in their
[1]hands.
7 [a]Their feet run to evil,
And they hasten to shed innocent
blood;
[b]Their thoughts are thoughts of
iniquity;
Devastation and destruction are in
their highways.
8 They do not know the [a]way of
peace,
And there is [b]no justice in their
tracks;
They have made their paths
crooked;
[c]Whoever treads on [1]them does not
know peace.

A Confession of Wickedness

9 Therefore, [a]justice is far from us,
And righteousness does not overtake us;
We [b]hope for light, but behold,
darkness;
For brightness, but we walk in
gloom.
10 We [a]grope along the wall like blind
men,
We grope like those who have no
eyes;
We [b]stumble at midday as in the
twilight,
Among those who are vigorous we
are [c]like dead men.
11 All of us growl like bears,
And [a]moan sadly like doves;
We hope for [b]justice, but there is
none,
For salvation, *but* it is far from us.
12 For our [a]transgressions are multi-
plied before Thee,
And our [b]sins [1]testify against us;
For our transgressions are with us,
And [2]we know our iniquities:
13 Transgressing and [a]denying the
LORD,
And turning away from our God,
Speaking [b]oppression and revolt,
Conceiving *in* and [c]uttering from
the heart lying words.
14 And [a]justice is turned back,
And [b]righteousness stands far
away;
For truth has stumbled in the
street,
And uprightness cannot enter.
15 Yes, truth is lacking;
And he who turns aside from evil
[a]makes himself a prey.

Now the LORD saw,
And it was [1]displeasing in His sight
[b]that there was no justice.
16 And He saw that there was [a]no
man,
And was astonished that there was
no one to intercede;
Then His [b]own arm brought salvation to Him;
And His righteousness upheld
Him.
17 And He put on [a]righteousness like
a breastplate,
And a [b]helmet of salvation on His
head;
And He put on [c]garments of vengeance for clothing,
And wrapped Himself with [d]zeal as
a mantle.
18 [a]According to *their* [1]deeds, [2]so He
will repay,
Wrath to His adversaries, recompense to His enemies;
To the coastlands He will [3]make
recompense.
19 So they will fear the name of the
LORD from the [a]west
And His glory from the [b]rising of
the sun,
For He will [c]come like a [1]rushing
stream,
Which the wind of the LORD drives.
20 "And a [a]Redeemer will come to
Zion,
And to those who [b]turn from transgression in Jacob," declares the
LORD.

14 [a]Job 22:26; Is. 61:10 [b]Deut. 32:13; 33:29; Is. 33:16; Hab. 3:19 [c]Is. 1:20; 40:5

1 [a]Num. 11:23; Is. 50:2; Jer. 32:17 [b]Is. 58:9; 65:24; Ezek. 8:18

2 [1]So versions; M. T., *faces*
[a]Is. 1:15; 50:1 [b]Is. 58:4

3 [a]Is. 1:15, 21; Jer. 2:30, 34; Ezek. 7:23; Hos. 4:2 [b]Is. 28:15; 30:9; 59:13

4 [1]Lit., *in truth*
[a]Is. 5:7; 59:14 [b]Is. 59:14, 15 [c]Is. 30:12; Jer. 7:4, 8 [d]Job 15:35; Ps. 7:14; Is. 33:11

5 [a]Job 8:14

6 [1]Lit., *palms*
[a]Is. 28:20 [b]Is. 57:12; Jer. 6:7 [c]Is. 58:4; Ezek. 7:11

7 [a]Prov. 1:16; 6:17; Rom. 3:15-17 [b]Is. 65:2; 66:18; Mark 7:21, 22

8 [1]Lit., *it*
[a]Luke 1:79 [b]Is. 59:9, 11; Hos. 4:1 [c]Is. 57:20, 21

9 [a]Is. 59:14 [b]Is. 5:30; 8:21, 22

10 [a]Deut. 28:29; Job 5:14 [b]Is. 8:14, 15; 28:13 [c]Lam. 3:6

11 [a]Is. 38:14; Ezek. 7:16 [b]Is. 59:9, 14

12 [1]Lit., *answer*
[2]Lit., *our iniquities we know them*
[a]Ezra 9:6; Is. 58:1 [b]Is. 3:9; Jer. 14:7; Hos. 5:5

13 [a]Josh. 24:27; Prov. 30:9; Matt. 10:33; Titus 1:16 [b]Is. 5:7; 30:12; Jer. 9:3, 4 [c]Is. 59:3, 4; Mark 7:21, 22

14 [a]Is. 1:21; 5:7 [b]Is. 46:12; Hab. 1:4

15 [1]Or, *evil*
[a]Is. 5:23; 10:2; 29:21; 32:7 [b]Is. 1:21-23

16 [a]Is. 41:28; 63:5; Ezek. 22:30 [b]Ps. 98:1; Is. 52:10; 63:5

17 [a]Eph. 6:14 [b]Eph. 6:17; 1 Thess. 5:8 [c]Is. 63:2, 3 [d]Is. 9:7; 37:32; Zech. 1:14

18 [1]Lit., *recompense* [2]Lit., *accordingly* [3]Lit., *repay*
[a]Job 34:11; Is. 65:6, 7; 66:6; Jer. 17:10

19 [1]Lit., *narrow*
[a]Is. 49:12 [b]Ps. 113:3 [c]Is. 30:28; 66:12

20 [a]Rom. 11:26 [b]Ezek. 18:30, 31; Acts 2:38, 39

21 "And as for Me, this is My [a]cov-
enant with them," says the LORD: "My
[b]Spirit which is upon you, and My
[c]words which I have put in your mouth,
shall not depart from your mouth, nor
from the mouth of your [1]offspring, nor
from the mouth of your [1]offspring's
offspring," says the LORD, "from now
and forever."

A Glorified Zion

60 "[a]ARISE, shine; for your [b]light
has come,
And the [c]glory of the LORD has
risen upon you.
2 "For behold, [a]darkness will cover
the earth,
And deep darkness the peoples;
But the LORD will rise upon you,
And His [b]glory will appear upon
you.
3 "And [a]nations will come to your
light,
And kings to the brightness of your
rising.

4 "[a]Lift up your eyes round about,
and see;
They all gather together, they
[b]come to you.
Your sons will come from afar,
And your [c]daughters will be [1]car-
ried in the arms.
5 "Then you will see and be [a]radiant,
And your heart will [1]thrill and
rejoice;
Because the [b]abundance of the sea
will be turned to you,
The [c]wealth of the nations will
come to you.
6 "A multitude of camels will cover
you,
The young camels of Midian and
[a]Ephah;
All those from [b]Sheba will come;
They will bring [c]gold and frankincense,
And will [d]bear good news of the
praises of the LORD.
7 "All the flocks of [a]Kedar will be
gathered together to you,
The rams of Nebaioth will minister
to you;
They will go up with acceptance on
My [b]altar,
And I shall [1c]glorify My [2]glorious
house.
8 "[a]Who are these who fly like a
cloud,
And like the doves to their [1]lat-
tices?
9 "Surely the [a]coastlands will wait for
Me;
And the [b]ships of Tarshish *will
come* first,
To [c]bring your sons from afar,
Their silver and their gold with
them,
For the name of the LORD your
God,
And for the Holy One of Israel
because He has [1d]glorified you.
10 "And [a]foreigners will build up your
walls,
And their [b]kings will minister to
you;
For in My [c]wrath I struck you,
And in My favor I have had compassion on you.
11 "And your [a]gates will be open continually;
They will not be closed day or
night,
So that *men* may [b]bring to you the
wealth of the nations,
With [c]their kings led in procession.
12 "For the [a]nation and the kingdom
which will not serve you will
perish,
And the nations will be utterly
ruined.
13 "The [a]glory of Lebanon will come to
you,
The [b]juniper, the box tree, and the
cypress together,
To beautify the place of My sanctuary;
And I shall make the [c]place of My
feet glorious.
14 "And the [a]sons of those who afflicted you will come bowing to
you,
And all those who despised you
will bow themselves at the soles
of your feet;
And they will call you the [b]city of
the LORD,
The [c]Zion of the Holy One of
Israel.

15 "Whereas you have been [a]forsaken
and [b]hated
With no one passing through,
I will make you an everlasting
[c]pride,
A joy from generation to genera-
tion.
16 "You will also [a]suck the milk of
nations,
And will suck the breast of kings;
Then you will know that I, the
LORD, am your [b]Savior,
And your [c]Redeemer, the Mighty
One of Jacob.
17 "Instead of bronze I will bring gold,
And instead of iron I will bring
silver,
And instead of wood, bronze,
And instead of stones, iron.
And I will make peace your admin-
istrators,
And righteousness your overseers.
18 "[a]Violence will not be heard again in
your land,
Nor [b]devastation or destruction
within your borders;
But you will call your [c]walls salva-
tion, and your [d]gates praise.
19 "No longer will you have the [a]sun
for light by day,
Nor for brightness will the moon
give you light;
But you will have the [b]LORD for an
everlasting light,
And your [c]God for your [1]glory.

21 [1]Lit., *seed* [a]Jer. 31:31-34; Rom. 11:27 [b]Is. 11:2; 32:15; 44:3 [c]Is. 55:11

1 [a]Is. 52:2 [b]Is. 60:19, 20 [c]Is. 24:23; 35:2; 58:8

2 [a]Is. 58:10; Jer. 13:16; Col. 1:13 [b]Is. 4:5

3 [a]Is. 2:3; 45:14, 22-25; 49:23

4 [1]Lit., *nursed upon the side* [a]Is. 11:12; 49:18 [b]Is. 49:20-22 [c]Is. 43:6; 49:22

5 [1]Lit., *tremble and be enlarged* [a]Ps. 34:5 [b]Is. 23:18; 24:14 [c]Is. 61:6

6 [a]Gen. 25:4 [b]Gen. 25:3; Ps. 72:10 [c]Is. 60:9; Matt. 2:11 [d]Is. 42:10

7 [1]Or, *beautify* [2]Or, *beautiful* [a]Gen. 25:13 [b]Is. 19:19; 56:7 [c]Is. 60:13; Hag. 2:7, 9

8 [1]Or, *dovecotes, windows* [a]Is. 49:21

9 [1]Lit., *beautified* [a]Is. 11:11; 24:15; 42:4, 10, 12; 49:1; 51:5; 66:19 [b]Ps. 48:7; Is. 2:16 [c]Is. 14:2; 43:6; 49:22 [d]Is. 55:5

10 [a]Is. 14:1, 2; 61:5; Zech. 6:15 [b]Is. 49:23; Rev. 21:24 [c]Is. 54:8

11 [a]Is. 26:2; 60:18; 62:10; Rev. 21:25, 26 [b]Is. 60:5 [c]Ps. 149:8; Is. 24:21

12 [a]Is. 14:2; Zech. 14:17

13 [a]Is. 35:2 [b]Is. 41:19 [c]1 Chr. 28:2; Ps. 99:5; 132:7

14 [a]Is. 14:1, 2; 45:14, 23; 49:23; Rev. 3:9 [b]Is. 1:26 [c]Heb. 12:22

15 [a]Is. 1:7-9; 6:11-13; Jer. 30:17 [b]Is. 66:5 [c]Is. 4:2; 65:18

16 [a]Is. 66:11 [b]Is. 19:20; 43:3, 11; 45:15, 21; 63:8 [c]Is. 59:20; 63:16

18 [a]Is. 54:14 [b]Is. 51:19 [c]Is. 26:1 [d]Is. 60:11

19 [1]Or, *beauty* [a]Rev. 21:23; 22:5 [b]Is. 2:5; 9:2 [c]Is. 41:16; 45:25; Zech. 2:5

20 "Your [a]sun will set no more,
Neither will your moon wane;
For you will have the LORD for an everlasting light,
And the days of your [b]mourning will be finished.
21 "Then all your [a]people *will be* righteous;
They will [b]possess the land forever,
The branch of [1]My planting,
The [c]work of My hands,
That I may be [d]glorified.
22 "The [a]smallest one will become a [1]clan,
And the least one a mighty nation.
I, the LORD, will hasten it in its time."

Exaltation of the Afflicted

61 THE [a]Spirit of the Lord [1]GOD is upon me,
Because the LORD has anointed me
To [b]bring good news to the [2c]afflicted;
He has sent me to [d]bind up the brokenhearted,
To [e]proclaim liberty to captives,
And [3]freedom to prisoners;
2 To [a]proclaim the favorable year of the LORD,
And the [b]day of vengeance of our God;
To [c]comfort all who mourn,
3 To [a]grant those who mourn *in* Zion,
Giving them a garland instead of ashes,
The [b]oil of gladness instead of mourning,
The mantle of praise instead of a spirit of fainting.
So they will be called [1c]oaks of righteousness,
The planting of the LORD, that He may be glorified.

4 Then they will [a]rebuild the ancient ruins,
They will raise up the former devastations,
And they will repair the ruined cities,
The desolations of many generations.
5 And [a]strangers will stand and pasture your flocks,
And [1]foreigners will be your farmers and your vinedressers.
6 But you will be called the [a]priests of the LORD;
You will be spoken of *as* [b]ministers of our God.
You will eat the [c]wealth of nations,
And in their [1]riches you will boast.
7 Instead of your [a]shame *you will have a* [b]double *portion,*
And *instead of* humiliation they will shout for joy over their portion.
Therefore they will possess a double *portion* in their land,
[c]Everlasting joy will be theirs.
8 For I, the LORD, [a]love justice,
I hate robbery [1]in the burnt offering;
And I will faithfully give them their recompense,
And I will make an [b]everlasting covenant with them.
9 Then their offspring will be known among the nations,
And their descendants in the midst of the peoples.
All who see them will recognize them
Because they are the [a]offspring *whom* the LORD has blessed.

10 I will [a]rejoice greatly in the LORD,
My soul will exult in [b]my God;
For He has [c]clothed me with garments of salvation,
He has wrapped me with a robe of righteousness,
As a bridegroom decks himself with a garland,
And [d]as a bride adorns herself with her jewels.
11 For as the [a]earth brings forth its sprouts,
And as a garden causes the things sown in it to spring up,
So the Lord [1]GOD will [b]cause [c]righteousness and praise
To spring up before all the nations.

Zion's Glory and New Name

62 FOR Zion's sake I will not keep silent,
And for Jerusalem's sake I will not keep quiet,
Until her [a]righteousness goes forth like brightness,
And her [b]salvation like a torch that is burning.
2 And the [a]nations will see your righteousness,
And all kings your glory;
And you will be called by a new [b]name,
Which the mouth of the LORD will designate.
3 You will also be a [a]crown of beauty in the hand of the LORD,
And a royal [1]diadem in the hand of your God.
4 It will no longer be said to you, "[1a]Forsaken,"
Nor to your land will it any longer be said, "[2]Desolate";
But you will be called, "[3]My delight is in her,"
And your land, "[4b]Married";
For the [c]LORD delights in you,
And *to Him* your land will be married.
5 For *as* a young man marries a virgin,
So your sons will marry you;
And *as* the [1]bridegroom rejoices over the bride,
So your [a]God will rejoice over you.

20 [a]Is. 30:26 [b]Is. 35:10; 65:19; Rev. 21:4
21 [1]Lit., *His* [a]Is. 45:24, 25; 52:1 [b]Ps. 37:11, 22; Is. 57:13; 61:7 [c]Is. 19:25; 29:23; 45:11; 64:8 [d]Is. 61:3
22 [1]Or, *thousand* [a]Is. 10:22; 51:2
1 [1]Heb., *YHWH,* usually rendered *LORD* [2]Or, *humble* [3]Lit., *opening to those who are bound* [a]Is. 11:2; 48:16; Luke 4:18 [b]Matt. 11:5; Luke 7:22 [c]Is. 11:4; 29:19; 32:7 [d]Is. 57:15 [e]Is. 42:7; 49:9
2 [a]Is. 49:8; 60:10 [b]Is. 2:12; 13:6; 34:2, 8 [c]Is. 57:18; Jer. 31:13; Matt. 5:4
3 [1]Or, *terebinths* [a]Is. 60:20 [b]Ps. 23:5; 45:7; 104:15 [c]Is. 60:21; Jer. 17:7, 8
4 [a]Is. 49:8; 58:12; Ezek. 36:33; Amos 9:14
5 [1]Lit., *sons of the foreigner* [a]Is. 14:2; 60:10
6 [1]Or, *glory* [a]Is. 66:21 [b]Is. 56:6 [c]Is. 60:5, 11
7 [a]Is. 54:4 [b]Is. 40:2; Zech. 9:12 [c]Ps. 16:11
8 [1]Or, *with iniquity* [a]Is. 5:16; 28:17; 30:18 [b]Gen. 17:7; Ps. 105:10; Is. 55:3; Jer. 32:40
9 [a]Is. 44:3
10 [a]Is. 12:1, 2; 25:9; 41:16; 51:3 [b]Is. 49:4 [c]Is. 49:18; 52:1 [d]Rev. 21:2
11 [1]Heb., *YHWH,* usually rendered *LORD* [a]Is. 4:2; 55:10 [b]Is. 45:23, 24; 60:18, 21 [c]Ps. 72:3; 85:11
1 [a]Is. 1:26; 58:8; 61:11 [b]Is. 46:13; 52:10
2 [a]Is. 60:3 [b]Is. 56:5; 62:4, 12; 65:15
3 [1]Lit., *turban* [a]Is. 28:5; Zech. 9:16; 1 Thess. 2:19
4 [1]I.e., Azubah [2]I.e., Shemamah [3]I.e., Hephzibah [4]I.e., Beulah [a]Is. 54:6, 7; 60:15, 18 [b]Hos. 2:19, 20 [c]Jer. 32:41; Zeph. 3:17
5 [1]Lit., *exultation of the bridegroom* [a]Is. 65:19

6 On your walls, O Jerusalem, I have
appointed [a]watchmen;
All day and all night they will
never keep silent.
You who [b]remind the LORD, take
no rest for yourselves;
7 And [a]give Him no rest until He
establishes
And makes [b]Jerusalem a praise in
the earth.
8 [a]The LORD has sworn by His right
hand and by His strong arm,
"I will [b]never again give your grain
as food for your enemies;
Nor will [1]foreigners drink your new
wine, for which you have labored."
9 But those who [a]garner it will eat it,
and praise the LORD;
And those who gather it will drink
it in the courts of My sanctuary.

10 Go through, [a]go through the gates;
Clear the way [1]for the people;
[b]Build up, build up the [c]highway;
Remove the stones, lift up a [d]stan-
dard over the peoples.
11 Behold, the LORD has proclaimed
to the [a]end of the earth,
[b]Say to the daughter of Zion, "Lo,
your [c]salvation comes;
[d]Behold His reward is with Him,
and His recompense before
Him."
12 And they will call them, "[a]The holy
people,
The [b]redeemed of the LORD";
And you will be called, "Sought
out, a city [c]not forsaken."

God's Vengeance on the Nations

63 WHO is this who comes from
[a]Edom,
With [b]garments of [1]glowing colors
from [c]Bozrah,
This One who is majestic in His
apparel,
[2]Marching in the greatness of His
strength?
"It is I who speak in righteousness,
[d]mighty to save."
2 Why is Your apparel red,
And Your garments like the one
who [a]treads in the wine press?
3 "[a]I have trodden the wine trough
alone,
And from the peoples there was no
man with Me.
I also [b]trod them in My anger,
And [c]trampled them in My wrath;
And [d]their [1]lifeblood is sprinkled
on My garments,
And I [2]stained all My raiment.
4 "For the [a]day of vengeance was in
My heart,
And My year of redemption has
come.
5 "And I looked, and there was [a]no
one to help,
And I was astonished and there
was no one to uphold;

6 [a]Is. 52:8; Jer. 6:17; Ezek. 3:17; 33:7 [b]Ps. 74:2; Jer. 14:21; Lam. 5:1, 20
7 [a]Luke 18:1-8 [b]Is. 60:18; Jer. 33:9; Zeph. 3:19, 20
8 [1]Lit., *sons of foreigners*
[a]Is. 45:23; 54:9 [b]Lev. 26:16; Deut. 28:31, 33; Judg. 6:3-6; Is. 1:7; Jer. 5:17
9 [a]Is. 65:13, 21-23
10 [1]Lit., *of*
[a]Is. 26:1; 60:11, 18 [b]Is. 57:14 [c]Is. 11:16; 19:23; 35:8; 49:11 [d]Is. 11:10, 12; 49:22
11 [a]Is. 42:10; 49:6 [b]Matt. 21:5; Zech. 9:9 [c]Is. 51:5 [d]Is. 40:10; Rev. 22:12
12 [a]Deut. 7:6; Is. 4:3; 1 Pet. 2:9 [b]Is. 35:9; 51:10 [c]Is. 41:17; 42:16; 62:4

1 [1]Or, *crimson* [2]Lit., *Inclining*
[a]Ps. 137:7; Is. 34:5, 6; Ezek. 25:12-14; 35:1-15; Obad. 1-14; Mal. 1:2-5 [b]Is. 63:2 [c]Is. 34:6; Jer. 49:13; Amos 1:12 [d]Zeph. 3:17
2 [a]Rev. 19:13, 15
3 [1]Lit., *juice* [2]Lit., *defiled*
[a]Rev. 14:20; 19:15 [b]Is. 22:5; 28:3 [c]Mic. 7:10 [d]Rev. 19:13
4 [a]Is. 34:8; 35:4; 61:2; Jer. 51:6
5 [a]Is. 59:16 [b]Ps. 44:3; Is. 40:10; 52:10
6 [1]Lit., *brought down their juice to the earth*
[a]Is. 22:5; 34:2; 65:12 [b]Is. 29:9; 51:17, 21
7 [a]Ps. 25:6; 92:2; Is. 54:8, 10 [b]1 Kin. 8:66; Neh. 9:25, 35 [c]Ps. 51:1; 86:5, 15; Is. 54:7, 8; Eph. 2:4
8 [a]Ex. 6:7; Is. 3:15; 51:4 [b]Is. 60:16
9 [1]Another reading is *He was not an adversary.*
[a]Judg. 10:16 [b]Ex. 23:20-23; 33:14, 15 [c]Deut. 7:7, 8 [d]Is. 43:1; 52:9 [e]Deut. 1:31; 32:10-12; Is. 46:3
10 [a]Ps. 78:40; 106:33; Acts 7:51; Eph. 4:30 [b]Ps. 51:11; Is. 63:11
11 [1]Some mss. read *shepherd* [2]Lit., *him*
[a]Ps. 106:44, 45 [b]Is. 51:10 [c]Num. 11:17, 25, 29; Hag. 2:5
12 [a]Ex. 6:6; 15:16 [b]Ex. 14:21, 22; Is. 11:15; 51:10
13 [a]Jer. 31:9
14 [1]Lit., *him*
[a]Josh. 21:44; 23:1 [b]Deut. 32:12
15 [a]Deut. 26:15; Ps. 80:14 [b]Ps. 68:5; 123:1 [c]Is. 9:7; 26:11; 37:32; 42:13; 59:17 [d]Jer. 31:20; Hos. 11:8

So My [b]own arm brought salvation
to Me;
And My wrath upheld Me.
6 "And I [a]trod down the peoples in
My anger,
And made them [b]drunk in My
wrath,
And I [1]poured out their lifeblood
on the earth."

God's Ancient Mercies Recalled

7 I shall make mention of the [a]lov-
ingkindnesses of the LORD, the
praises of the LORD,
According to all that the LORD has
granted us,
And the great [b]goodness toward
the house of Israel,
Which He has granted them according to His [c]compassion,
And according to the multitude of
His lovingkindnesses.
8 For He said, "Surely, they are [a]My
people,
Sons who will not deal falsely."
So He became their [b]Savior.
9 In all their affliction [1a]He was
afflicted,
And the [b]angel of His presence
saved them;
In His [c]love and in His mercy He
[d]redeemed them;
And He [e]lifted them and carried
them all the days of old.
10 But they [a]rebelled
And grieved His [b]Holy Spirit;
Therefore, He turned Himself to
become their enemy,
He fought against them.
11 Then [a]His people remembered the
days of old, of Moses.
Where is [b]He who brought them up
out of the sea with the [1]shep-
herds of His flock?
Where is He who [c]put His Holy
Spirit in the midst of [2]them,
12 Who caused His [a]glorious arm to
go at the right hand of Moses,
Who [b]divided the waters before
them to make for Himself an
everlasting name,
13 Who led them through the depths?
Like the horse in the wilderness,
they did not [a]stumble;
14 As the cattle which go down into
the valley,
The Spirit of the [a]LORD gave [1]them
rest.
So didst Thou [b]lead Thy people,
To make for Thyself a glorious
name.

"Thou Art Our Father"

15 [a]Look down from heaven, and see
from Thy holy and glorious
[b]habitation;
Where are Thy [c]zeal and Thy
mighty deeds?
The [d]stirrings of Thy heart and Thy
compassion are restrained
toward me.

16 For Thou art our [a]Father, though
[b]Abraham does not know us,
And Israel does not recognize us.
Thou, O LORD, art our Father,
Our [c]Redeemer from of old is Thy
name.
17 Why, O LORD, dost Thou [a]cause us
to stray from Thy ways,
And [b]harden our heart from fearing Thee?
[c]Return for the sake of Thy servants, the tribes of Thy heritage.
18 Thy holy people possessed Thy
sanctuary for a little while,
Our adversaries have [a]trodden *it*
down.
19 We have become *like* those over
whom Thou hast never ruled,
Like those who were not called by
Thy name.

Prayer for Mercy and Help

64 [1]OH, that Thou wouldst rend the
heavens *and* [a]come down,
That the mountains might [b]quake
at Thy presence—
2 [1]As fire kindles the brushwood, *as*
fire causes water to boil—
To make Thy name known to
Thine adversaries,
That the [a]nations may tremble at
Thy presence!
3 When Thou didst [a]awesome things
which we did not expect,
Thou didst come down, the mountains quaked at Thy presence.
4 For from of old [a]they have not
heard nor perceived by ear,
Neither has the eye seen a God
besides Thee,
Who acts in behalf of the one who
[b]waits for Him.
5 Thou dost [a]meet him who rejoices
in [b]doing righteousness,
Who [c]remembers Thee in Thy
ways.
Behold, [d]Thou wast angry, for we
sinned,
We continued in them a long time;
And shall we be saved?
6 For all of us have become like one
who is [a]unclean,
And all our [b]righteous deeds are
like a filthy garment;
And all of us [c]wither like a leaf,
And our [d]iniquities, like the wind,
take us away.
7 And there is [a]no one who calls on
Thy name,
Who arouses himself to take hold
of Thee;
For Thou hast [b]hidden Thy face
from us,
And hast [1]delivered us into the
power of our iniquities.

8 But now, O LORD, [a]Thou art our
Father,
We are the [b]clay, and Thou our
potter;
And all of us are the [c]work of Thy
hand.

16 [a]Is. 1:2; 64:8 [b]Is. 29:22; 41:8; 51:2 [c]Is. 41:14; 44:6; 60:16

17 [a]Is. 30:28; Ezek. 14:7-9 [b]Is. 29:13, 14 [c]Num. 10:36

18 [a]Ps. 74:3-7; Is. 64:11

1 [1]Ch. 63:19b in Heb. [a]Ex. 19:18; Ps. 18:9; 144:5; Mic. 1:3, 4; Hab. 3:13 [b]Judg. 5:5; Ps. 68:8; Nah. 1:5

2 [1]Ch. 64:1 in Heb. [a]Ps. 99:1; Jer. 5:22; 33:9

3 [a]Ps. 65:5; 66:3, 5; 106:22

4 [a]1 Cor. 2:9 [b]Is. 25:9; 30:18; 40:31

5 [a]Ex. 20:24 [b]Is. 56:1 [c]Is. 26:13; 63:7 [d]Is. 12:1

6 [a]Is. 6:5 [b]Is. 46:12; 48:1 [c]Ps. 90:5, 6; Is. 1:30 [d]Is. 50:1

7 [1]Reading with the DSS and versions; M.T., *melted* [a]Is. 59:4; Ezek. 22:30 [b]Deut. 31:18; Is. 1:15; 54:8

8 [a]Is. 63:16 [b]Is. 29:16; 45:9 [c]Ps. 100:3; Is. 60:21

9 [a]Is. 57:17; 60:10 [b]Is. 43:25; Mic. 7:18 [c]Ps. 79:13; Is. 63:8

10 [a]Is. 48:2; 52:1 [b]Is. 1:7; 6:11

11 [a]2 Kin. 25:9; Ps. 74:5-7; Is. 63:18 [b]Lam. 1:7, 10, 11

12 [a]Ps. 74:10, 11, 18, 19; Is. 42:14; 63:15

1 [a]Rom. 9:24-26; 10:20 [b]Is. 63:19; Hos. 1:10

2 [1]Lit., *after* [a]Rom. 10:21 [b]Is. 1:2, 23; 30:1, 9 [c]Ps. 81:11, 12; Is. 59:7; 66:18

3 [a]Job 1:11; 2:5; Is. 3:8 [b]Is. 1:29; 66:17 [c]Is. 66:3

4 [a]Lev. 11:7; Is. 66:3, 17

5 [1]Lit., *nose* [a]Matt. 9:11; Luke 7:39; 18:9-12

6 [a]Ps. 50:3, 21; Is. 42:14; 64:12 [b]Jer. 16:18

7 [1]Lit., *your* [a]Is. 13:11; 22:14; 26:21; 30:13, 14 [b]Is. 57:7; Hos. 2:13 [c]Ezek. 20:27, 28 [d]Jer. 5:29; 13:25

8 [1]Lit., *blessing* [2]Lit., *the whole* [a]Is. 1:9; 10:21, 22; 48:9

9 Do not be [a]angry beyond measure,
O LORD,
[b]Neither remember iniquity forever;
Behold, look now, all of us are [c]Thy
people.
10 Thy [a]holy cities have become a
[b]wilderness,
Zion has become a wilderness,
Jerusalem a desolation.
11 Our holy and beautiful [a]house,
Where our fathers praised Thee,
Has been burned *by* fire;
And [b]all our precious things have
become a ruin.
12 Wilt Thou [a]restrain Thyself at
these things, O LORD?
Wilt Thou keep silent and afflict us
beyond measure?

A Rebellious People

65 "I PERMITTED Myself to be
sought by [a]those who did not
ask *for Me;*
I permitted Myself to be found by
those who did not seek Me.
I said, 'Here am I, here am I,'
To a nation which [b]did not call on
My name.
2 "[a]I have spread out My hands all
day long to a [b]rebellious people,
Who walk *in* the way which is not
good, [1]following their own
[c]thoughts,
3 A people who continually [a]provoke
Me to My face,
Offering sacrifices in [b]gardens and
[c]burning incense on bricks;
4 Who sit among graves, and spend
the night in secret places;
Who [a]eat swine's flesh,
And the broth of unclean meat is *in*
their pots.
5 "Who say, '[a]Keep to yourself, do not
come near me,
For I am holier than you!'
These are smoke in My [1]nostrils,
A fire that burns all the day.
6 "Behold, it is written before Me,
I will [a]not keep silent, but [b]I will
repay;
I will even repay into their bosom,
7 Both [1]their own [a]iniquities and the
iniquities of their fathers together," says the LORD.
"Because they have [b]burned incense
on the mountains,
And [c]scorned Me on the hills,
Therefore I will [d]measure their
former work into their bosom."

8 Thus says the LORD,
"As the new wine is found in the
cluster,
And one says, 'Do not destroy it,
for there is [1]benefit in it,'
So I will act on behalf of My servants
In order [a]not to destroy [2]all of
them.

9"And I will bring forth [a]offspring
from Jacob,
And an [b]heir of My mountains
from Judah;
Even [c]My chosen ones shall inherit
it,
And [d]My servants shall dwell there.
10"And [a]Sharon shall be a pasture
land for flocks,
And the [b]valley of Achor a resting
place for herds,
For My people who [c]seek Me.
11"But you who [a]forsake the LORD,
Who forget My [b]holy mountain,
Who set a table for [1]Fortune,
And who fill *cups* with mixed wine
for [2]Destiny,
12 I will destine you for the [a]sword,
And all of you shall bow down to
the [b]slaughter.
Because I called, but you [c]did not
answer;
I spoke, but you did not hear.
And you did evil in My sight,
And chose that in which I did not
delight."

13 Therefore, thus says the Lord
[1]GOD,
"Behold, My servants shall [a]eat, but
you shall be [b]hungry.
Behold, My servants shall [c]drink,
but you shall be [d]thirsty.
Behold, My servants shall [e]rejoice,
but you shall be [f]put to shame.
14"Behold, My servants shall [a]shout
joyfully with a glad heart,
But you shall [b]cry out with a
[1]heavy heart,
And you shall wail with a broken
spirit.
15"And you will leave your name for a
[a]curse to My chosen ones,
And the Lord [1]GOD will slay you.
But [2]My servants will be called by
[b]another name.
16"Because he who [1]is blessed in the
earth
Shall [1]be blessed by the [a]God of
truth;
And he who swears in the earth
Shall [b]swear by the God of truth;
Because the former troubles are
forgotten,
And because they are hidden from
My sight!

New Heavens and a New Earth

17"For behold, I create [a]new heavens
and a new earth;
And the [b]former things shall not be
remembered or come to [1]mind.
18"But be [a]glad and rejoice forever in
what I create;
For behold, I create Jerusalem *for*
rejoicing,
And her people *for* gladness.
19"I will also [a]rejoice in Jerusalem,
and be glad in My people;

9 [a]Is. 45:19, 25; Jer. 31:36, 37 [b]Is. 49:8; 60:21; Amos 9:11-15 [c]Is. 57:13 [d]Is. 32:18
10 [a]Is. 33:9; 35:2 [b]Josh. 7:24, 26; Hos. 2:15 [c]Is. 51:1; 55:6
11 [1]Heb., *Gad* [2]Heb., *Meni* [a]Deut. 29:24, 25; Is. 1:4, 28 [b]Is. 2:2, 3; 66:20
12 [a]Is. 27:1; 34:5, 6; 66:16 [b]Is. 63:6 [c]2 Chr. 36:15, 16; Prov. 1:24; Is. 41:28; 50:2; 66:4; Jer. 7:13
13 [1]Heb., *YHWH, usually rendered LORD* [a]Is. 1:19 [b]Is. 8:21 [c]Is. 41:17, 18; 49:10 [d]Is. 5:13 [e]Is. 61:7; 66:14 [f]Is. 42:17; 44:9, 11; 66:5
14 [1]Lit., *pain of* [a]Ps. 66:4; Is. 51:11; James 5:13 [b]Is. 13:6; Matt. 8:12
15 [1]Heb., *YHWH, usually rendered LORD* [2]So with Gr.; Heb., *He will call His servants* [a]Jer. 24:9; 25:18; Zech. 8:13 [b]Is. 62:2
16 [1]Or, *bless(es) himself* [a]Ex. 34:6; Ps. 31:5 [b]Is. 19:18; 45:23
17 [1]Lit., *heart* [a]Is. 66:22; 2 Pet. 3:13; Rev. 21:1 [b]Is. 43:18; Jer. 3:16
18 [a]Ps. 98; Is. 12:1, 2; 25:9; 35:10; 41:16; 51:3; 61:10
19 [a]Is. 62:4, 5; Jer. 32:41 [b]Is. 25:8; 30:19; 35:10; 51:11; Rev. 7:17; 21:4
20 [1]Lit., *from there* [2]Lit., *fill out* [3]Lit., *one who misses the mark* [a]Deut. 4:40; Job 5:26; Ps. 34:12 [b]Eccl. 8:12, 13; Is. 3:11; 22:14
21 [a]Is. 32:18; Amos 9:14 [b]Is. 30:23; 37:30; Jer. 31:5
22 [1]Lit., *days* [a]Is. 62:8, 9 [b]Ps. 92:12-14 [c]Ps. 21:4; 91:16
23 [1]Lit., *seed* [a]Deut. 28:3-12; Is. 55:2 [b]Is. 61:9; Jer. 32:38, 39; Acts 2:39
24 [a]Ps. 91:15; Is. 55:6; 58:9; Dan. 9:20-23; 10:12
25 [a]Is. 11:6 [b]Is. 11:7 [c]Gen. 3:14; Mic. 7:17 [d]Is. 11:9; Mic. 4:3 [e]Is. 65:11

1 [1]Lit., *is My resting place?* [a]1 Kin. 8:27; Ps. 11:4; Matt. 5:34, 35; 23:22 [b]2 Sam. 7:5-7; Jer. 7:4; John 4:20, 21; Acts 7:48-50
2 [a]Is. 40:26 [b]Ps. 34:18; Is. 57:15; Matt. 5:3, 4; Luke 18:13, 14 [c]Ps. 119:120; Is. 66:5
3 [1]Lit., *offers a memorial of incense* [a]Is. 65:4 [b]Lev. 2:2; Is. 1:13 [c]Is. 57:17; 65:2 [d]Is. 44:19

And there will no longer be heard
in her
The voice of [b]weeping and the
sound of crying.
20"No longer will there be [1]in it an
infant *who lives but a few* days,
Or an old man who does [a]not [2]live
out his days;
For the youth will die at the age of
one hundred
And the [3b]one who does not reach
the age of one hundred
Shall be *thought* accursed.
21"And they shall [a]build houses and
inhabit *them;*
They shall also [b]plant vineyards
and eat their fruit.
22"They shall not build, and [a]another
inhabit,
They shall not plant, and another
eat;
For [b]as the [1]lifetime of a tree, *so
shall be* the days of My people,
And My chosen ones shall [c]wear
out the work of their hands.
23"They shall [a]not labor in vain,
Or bear *children* for calamity;
For they are the [1b]offspring of
those blessed by the LORD,
And their descendants with them.
24"It will also come to pass that before
they call, I will [a]answer; and while they
are still speaking, I will hear.
25"The [a]wolf and the lamb shall graze
together, and the [b]lion shall eat straw
like the ox; and [c]dust shall be the serpent's food. They shall [d]do no evil or
harm in all My [e]holy mountain," says
the LORD.

Heaven Is God's Throne

66 THUS says the LORD,
"[a]Heaven is My throne, and the
earth is My footstool.
Where then is a [b]house you could
build for Me?
And where is a place that [1]I may
rest?
2"For [a]My hand made all these
things,
Thus all these things came into
being," declares the LORD.
"But to this one I will look,
To him who is humble and [b]con-
trite of spirit, and who [c]trembles
at My word.

Hypocrisy Rebuked

3"*But* he who kills an ox is *like* one
who slays a man;
He who sacrifices a lamb is *like* the
one who breaks a dog's neck;
He who offers a grain offering *is
like one who offers* [a]swine's
blood;
He who [1b]burns incense is *like* the
one who blesses an idol.
As they have chosen their [c]own
ways,
And their soul delights in their
[d]abominations,

4 So I will [a]choose their [1]punishments,
And I will [b]bring on them what they dread.
Because I called, but [c]no one answered;
I spoke, but they did not listen.
And they did [d]evil in My sight,
And chose that in which I did not delight."
5 Hear the word of the LORD, you who [a]tremble at His word:
"Your brothers who [b]hate you, who [c]exclude you for My name's sake,
Have said, 'Let the LORD be glorified, that we may see your joy.'
But [d]they will be put to shame.
6 "A voice of uproar from the city, a voice from the temple,
The voice of the LORD who is [a]rendering recompense to His enemies.

7 "Before she travailed, [a]she brought forth;
Before her pain came, [b]she gave birth to a boy.
8 "[a]Who has heard such a thing? Who has seen such things?
Can a land be [1]born in one day?
Can a nation be brought forth all at once?
As soon as Zion travailed, she also brought forth her sons.
9 "Shall I bring to the point of birth, and [a]not give delivery?" says the LORD.
"Or shall I who gives delivery shut *the womb?*" says your God.

Joy in Jerusalem's Future

10 "Be [a]joyful with Jerusalem and rejoice for her, all you who [b]love her;
Be exceedingly [c]glad with her, all you who mourn over her,
11 That you may nurse and [a]be satisfied with her comforting breasts,
That you may suck and be delighted with her [b]bountiful bosom."
12 For thus says the LORD, "Behold, I extend [a]peace to her like a river,
And the [b]glory of the nations like an overflowing stream;
And you shall [1]be nursed, you shall be [c]carried on the [2]hip and fondled on the knees.
13 "As one whom his mother comforts, so I will [a]comfort you;
And you shall be comforted in Jerusalem."
14 Then you shall [a]see *this,* and your [b]heart shall be glad,
And your [c]bones shall flourish like the new grass;
And the [d]hand of the LORD shall be made known to His servants,
But He shall be [e]indignant toward His enemies.
15 For behold, the LORD will come in [a]fire
And His [b]chariots like the whirlwind,
To render His anger with fury,
And His rebuke with flames of fire.
16 For the LORD will execute judgment by [a]fire
And by His [b]sword on all flesh,
And those slain by the LORD will be many.
17 "Those who sanctify and purify themselves *to go* to the [a]gardens,
[1]Following one in the center,
Who eat [b]swine's flesh, detestable things, and mice,
Shall [c]come to an end altogether," declares the LORD.
18 "For I [1]know their works and their
[a]thoughts; [2]the time is coming to [b]gather
all nations and tongues. And they shall
come and see My glory.
19 "And I will set a [a]sign among them
and will send survivors from them to the
nations: [b]Tarshish, [1]Put, [c]Lud, [2]Me-
shech, Rosh, [d]Tubal, and [3]Javan, to the
distant [e]coastlands that have neither
heard My fame nor seen My glory. And
they will [f]declare My glory among the
nations.
20 "Then they shall [a]bring all your
brethren from all the nations as a grain
offering to the LORD, on horses, in
chariots, in litters, on mules, and on
camels, to My [b]holy mountain Jerusalem," says the LORD, "just as the sons of
Israel bring their grain offering in a
[c]clean vessel to the house of the LORD.
21 "I will also take some of them for
[a]priests *and* for Levites," says the LORD.
22 "For just as the [a]new heavens and the new earth
Which I make will endure before Me," declares the LORD,
"So your [b]offspring and your [c]name will endure.
23 "And it shall be from [a]new moon to new moon
And from sabbath to sabbath,
All [1]mankind will come to [b]bow down before Me," says the LORD.
24 "Then they shall go forth and look
On the [a]corpses of the men
Who have [1b]transgressed against Me.
For their [c]worm shall not die,
[d]And their fire shall not be quenched;
And they shall be an [e]abhorrence to all [2]mankind."

4 [1]Lit., *ill treatments* [a]Prov. 1:31, 32; Is. 65:7 [b]Prov. 10:24 [c]Prov. 1:24; Is. 65:12; Jer. 7:13 [d]2 Kin. 21:2, 6; Is. 59:7; 65:12; Jer. 7:30
5 [a]Is. 66:2 [b]Ps. 38:20; Is. 60:15 [c]Matt. 5:10-12; 10:22; John 9:34; 15:18-20 [d]Luke 13:17
6 [a]Is. 59:18; 65:6; Joel 3:7
7 [a]Is. 37:3; 54:1 [b]Rev. 12:5
8 [1]Lit., *travailed with* [a]Is. 64:4
9 [a]Is. 37:3
10 [a]Deut. 32:43; Is. 65:18; Rom. 15:10 [b]Ps. 26:8; 122:6 [c]Ps. 137:6
11 [a]Is. 49:23; 60:16; Joel 3:18 [b]Is. 60:1, 2; 62:2
12 [1]Lit., *nurse* [2]Lit., *side* [a]Ps. 72:3, 7; Is. 48:18 [b]Is. 60:5; 61:6 [c]Is. 60:4
13 [a]Is. 12:1; 40:1, 2; 49:13; 51:3; 2 Cor. 1:3, 4
14 [a]Is. 33:20 [b]Zech. 10:7 [c]Prov. 3:8; Is. 58:11 [d]Ezra 7:9; 8:31 [e]Is. 10:5; 13:5; 34:2
15 [a]Is. 10:17; 30:27, 33; 31:9 [b]Ps. 68:17; Is. 5:28; Hab. 3:8
16 [a]Is. 30:30; Ezek. 38:22 [b]Is. 65:12; Ezek. 38:21
17 [1]Lit., *After* [a]Is. 1:29; 65:3 [b]Lev. 11:7; Is. 65:4 [c]Is. 1:28, 31
18 [1]So with Gr.; Heb. omits *know* [2]Lit., *it is coming* [a]Is. 59:7; 65:2 [b]Is. 45:22-25; Jer. 3:17
19 [1]So with Gr.; Heb., *Pul* [2]So with Gr.; Heb., *those who draw the bow* [3]I.e., Greece [a]Is. 11:10, 12; 49:22; 62:10 [b]Is. 2:16; 60:9 [c]Ezek. 27:10 [d]Gen. 10:2 [e]Is. 11:11; 24:15; 60:9 [f]1 Chr. 16:24; Is. 42:12
20 [a]Is. 43:6; 49:22; 60:4 [b]Is. 2:2, 3; 11:9; 56:7; 65:11, 25 [c]Is. 52:11
21 [a]Ex. 19:6; Is. 61:6; 1 Pet. 2:5, 9
22 [a]Is. 65:17; Heb. 12:26, 27; 2 Pet. 3:13; Rev. 21:1 [b]Is. 61:8, 9; 65:22, 23; John 10:27-29; 1 Pet. 1:4, 5 [c]Is. 56:5
23 [1]Lit., *flesh* [a]Is. 1:13, 14; Ezek. 46:1, 6 [b]Is. 19:21, 23; 27:13; 49:7
24 [1]Or, *rebelled* [2]Lit., *flesh* [a]Is. 5:25; 34:3 [b]Is. 1:28; 24:20 [c]Is. 14:11; Mark 9:48 [d]Is. 1:31; Matt. 3:12 [e]Dan. 12:2

THE BOOK OF
JEREMIAH

Jeremiah's Call and Commission

1 THE words of [a]Jeremiah, the son of
Hilkiah, of the priests who were in
[b]Anathoth in the land of Benjamin,
2 to whom the word of the LORD
came in the days of [a]Josiah, the son of
[b]Amon, king of Judah, in the [c]thirteenth
year of his reign.
3 It came also in the days of [a]Jehoia-
kim, the son of Josiah, king of Judah,
until the end of the eleventh year of
[b]Zedekiah, the son of Josiah, king of
Judah, until the exile of Jerusalem in the
fifth month.
4 Now the word of the LORD came to
me saying,
5 "Before I [a]formed you in the womb
I knew you,
And [b]before you were born I consecrated you;
I have [c]appointed you a prophet to
the nations."
6 Then [a]I said, "Alas, Lord [1]GOD!
Behold, I do not know how to
speak,
Because [b]I am a youth."
7 But the LORD said to me,
"Do not say, 'I am a youth,'
[a]Because everywhere I send you,
you shall go,
And [b]all that I command you, you
shall speak.
8 "[a]Do not be afraid of them,
For [b]I am with you to deliver you,"
declares the LORD.
9 Then the LORD stretched out His
hand and [a]touched my mouth, and the
LORD said to me,
"Behold, I have [b]put My words in
your mouth.
10 "See, [a]I have appointed you this day
over the nations and over the
kingdoms,
[b]To pluck up and to break down,
To destroy and to overthrow,
[c]To build and to plant."

The Almond Rod and Boiling Pot

11 And the word of the LORD came to
me saying, "What do you see, [a]Jere-
miah?" And I said, "I see a rod of an
[1]almond tree."
12 Then the LORD said to me, "You
have seen well, for [a]I am [1]watching over
My word to perform it."
13 And the word of the LORD came to
me a second time saying, "[a]What do you
see?" And I said, "I see a boiling [b]pot,
facing away from the north."
14 Then the LORD said to me, "[a]Out
of the north the evil [1]will break forth on
all the inhabitants of the land.
15 "For, behold, I am calling [a]all the
families of the kingdoms of the north,"
declares the LORD; "and they will come,
and they will [b]set each one his throne at
the entrance of the gates of Jerusalem,
and against all its walls round about,
and against all the [c]cities of Judah.
16 "And I will [1]pronounce My judgments on them concerning all their
wickedness, whereby they have [a]for-
saken Me and have [2b]offered sacrifices to
other gods, and worshiped the [c]works of
their own hands.
17 "Now, [a]gird up your loins, and arise,
and speak to them all which I command
you. [b]Do not be dismayed before them,
lest I dismay you before them.
18 "Now behold, I have made you
today as a fortified city, and as a pillar of
iron and as walls of bronze against the
whole land, to the kings of Judah, to its
princes, to its priests and to the people
of the land.
19 "And they will fight against you, but
they will not overcome you, for [a]I am
with you to deliver you," declares the
LORD.

Judah's Apostasy

2 NOW the word of the LORD came to
me saying,
2 "Go and [a]proclaim in the ears of
Jerusalem, saying, 'Thus says the LORD,
"I remember concerning you the
[1b]devotion of your youth,
The love of your betrothals,
[c]Your following after Me in the
wilderness,
Through a land not sown.
3 "Israel was [a]holy to the LORD,
The [b]first of His harvest;
[c]All who ate of it became guilty;
Evil came upon them," declares the
LORD.' "
4 Hear the word of the LORD, O
house of Jacob, and all the families of
the house of Israel.
5 Thus says the LORD,
"[a]What injustice did your fathers
find in Me,
That they went far from Me
And walked after [b]emptiness and
became empty?
6 "And they did not say, 'Where is the
LORD
Who [a]brought us up out of the land
of Egypt,
Who [b]led us through the wilderness,
Through a land of deserts and of
pits,
Through a land of drought and of
[1]deep darkness,
Through a land that no one crossed
And where no man dwelt?'
7 "And I brought you into the [a]fruit-
ful land,
To eat its fruit and its good things.
But you came and [b]defiled My
land,
And My inheritance you made an
abomination.

---

1 [a]2 Chr. 35:25; 36:12, 21, 22; Ezra 1:1; Dan. 9:2; Matt. 2:17; 16:14; 27:9 [b]Josh. 21:18; 1 Kin. 2:26; 1 Chr. 6:60; Is. 10:30; Jer. 11:21; 32:7
2 [a]1 Kin. 13:2; 2 Kin. 21:24; 22:3; 2 Chr. 34:1; Jer. 3:6; 36:2 [b]2 Kin. 21:18, 24 [c]Jer. 25:3
3 [a]2 Kin. 23:34; 1 Chr. 3:15; 2 Chr. 36:5-8; Jer. 25:1 [b]2 Kin. 24:17; 1 Chr. 3:15; 2 Chr. 36:11-13; Jer. 39:2
5 [a]Ps. 139:15, 16 [b]Is. 49:1, 5; Luke 1:15 [c]Jer. 1:10; 25:15-26
6 [1]Heb., *YHWH,* usually rendered *LORD* [a]Ex. 4:10 [b]1 Kin. 3:7
7 [a]Ezek. 2:3, 4 [b]Num. 22:20; Jer. 1:17
8 [a]Ex. 3:12; Deut. 31:6; Josh. 1:5; Jer. 15:20 [b]Ezek. 2:6
9 [a]Is. 6:7; Mark 7:33-35 [b]Ex. 4:11-16; Deut. 18:18; Is. 51:16
10 [a]Rev. 11:3-6 [b]Jer. 18:7-10; Ezek. 32:18; 2 Cor. 10:4 [c]Is. 44:26-28; Jer. 24:6; 31:28, 40
11 [1]Heb., *shaqed* [a]Jer. 24:3; Amos 7:8
12 [1]Heb., *shoqed* [a]Jer. 31:28
13 [a]Zech. 4:2 [b]Ezek. 11:3, 7
14 [1]Lit., *will be opened* [a]Is. 41:25; Jer. 4:6; 10:22
15 [a]Jer. 25:9 [b]Is. 22:7; Jer. 39:3 [c]Jer. 4:16; 9:11
16 [1]Lit., *speak* [2]Or, *burned incense* [a]Deut. 28:20 [b]Jer. 7:9; 19:4; 44:17 [c]Is. 2:8; 37:19; Jer. 10:3-5
17 [a]1 Kin. 18:46; Job 38:3 [b]Ezek. 2:6; 3:16-18
19 [a]Num. 14:9; Jer. 1:8; 20:11

2 [1]Or, *lovingkindness* [a]Is. 58:1; Jer. 7:2; 11:6 [b]Ezek. 16:8; Hos. 2:15 [c]Deut. 2:7; Jer. 2:6
3 [a]Ex. 19:5, 6; Deut. 7:6; 14:2 [b]James 1:18; Rev. 14:4 [c]Is. 41:11; Jer. 30:16; 50:7
5 [a]Is. 5:4; Mic. 6:3 [b]2 Kin. 17:15; Jer. 8:19; Rom. 1:21
6 [1]Or, *the shadow of death* [a]Ex. 20:2; Is. 63:11 [b]Deut. 8:15; 32:10
7 [a]Deut. 8:7-9; 11:10-12 [b]Ps. 106:38; Jer. 3:2; 16:18

8"The [a]priests did not say, 'Where is
the LORD?'
And those who handle the law [b]did
not know Me;
The [1]rulers also transgressed
against Me,
And the [c]prophets prophesied by
Baal
And walked after [d]things that did
not profit.

9"Therefore I will yet [a]contend with
you," declares the LORD,
"And with your sons' sons I will
contend.
10"For [a]across to the coastlands of
[1]Kittim and see,
And send to [b]Kedar and observe
closely,
And see if there has been such *a*
thing as this!
11"Has a nation changed gods,
When [a]they were not gods?
But My people have [b]changed their
glory
For that which does not profit.
12"Be appalled, [a]O heavens, at this,
And shudder, be very desolate,"
declares the LORD.
13"For My people have committed
two evils:
They have forsaken Me,
The [a]fountain of living waters,
To hew for themselves [b]cisterns,
Broken cisterns,
That can hold no water.

14"Is Israel [a]a slave? Or is he a home-
born servant?
Why has he become a prey?
15"The young [a]lions have roared at
him,
They have [1]roared loudly.
And they have [b]made his land a
waste;
His cities have been destroyed,
without inhabitant.
16"Also the [1]men of [a]Memphis and
Tahpanhes
Have [2]shaved the [b]crown of your
head.
17"Have you not [a]done this to yourself,
By your forsaking the LORD your
God,
When He [a]led you in the way?
18"But now what are you doing [a]on
the road to Egypt,
To drink the waters of the [1b]Nile?
Or what are you doing on the road
to Assyria,
To drink the waters of the [2]Euphra-
tes?
19"[a]Your own wickedness will correct
you,
And your [b]apostasies will reprove
you;
Know therefore and see that it is
evil and [c]bitter
For you to forsake the LORD your
God,
And [d]the dread of Me is not in
you," declares the Lord [1]GOD of
hosts.

20"For long ago [1a]I broke your yoke
And tore off your bonds;
But you said, 'I will not serve!'
For on every [b]high hill
And under every green tree
You have lain down as a harlot.
21"Yet I [a]planted you a choice vine,
A completely faithful seed.
How then have you turned yourself
before Me
Into the [b]degenerate shoots of a
foreign vine?
22"Although you [a]wash yourself with
lye
And [1]use much soap,
The [b]stain of your iniquity is before
Me," declares the Lord [2]GOD.
23"[a]How can you say, 'I am not de-
filed,
I have not gone after the [b]Baals'?
Look at your way in the [c]valley!
Know what you have done!
You are a swift young camel [d]en-
tangling her ways,
24 A [a]wild donkey accustomed to the
wilderness,
That sniffs the wind in her passion.
In *the time of* her [1]heat who can
turn her away?
All who seek her will not become
weary;
In her month they will find her.
25"Keep your feet from being unshod
And your throat from thirst;
But you said, '[a]It is [1]hopeless!
No! For I have [b]loved strangers,
And after them I will walk.'

26"As the [a]thief is shamed when he is
discovered,
So the house of Israel is shamed;
They, their kings, their princes,
And their priests, and their proph-
ets,
27 Who say to a tree, 'You are my
father,'
And to a stone, 'You gave me
birth.'
For they have turned *their* [a]back to
Me,
And not *their* face;
But in the [b]time of their [1]trouble
they will say,
'Arise and save us.'
28"But where are your [a]gods
Which you made for yourself?
Let them arise, if they can [b]save
you
In the time of your [1]trouble;
For [c]*according to* the number of
your cities
Are your gods, O Judah.

29"Why do you contend with Me?
You have [a]all transgressed against
Me," declares the LORD.

8 [1]Lit., *shepherds* [a]Jer. 10:21 [b]Jer. 4:22; Mal. 2:7, 8 [c]Jer. 23:13 [d]Jer. 16:19; Hab. 2:18

9 [a]Jer. 2:35; Ezek. 20:35, 36

10 [1]I.e., Cyprus and other islands [a]Is. 23:12 [b]Ps. 120:5; Is. 21:16; Jer. 49:28

11 [a]Is. 37:19; Jer. 5:7; 16:20 [b]Ps. 106:20; Rom. 1:23

12 [a]Is. 1:2; Jer. 4:23

13 [a]Ps. 36:9; Jer. 17:13; John 4:14 [b]Jer. 14:3

14 [a]Jer. 5:19; 17:4

15 [1]Lit., *given their voice* [a]Jer. 50:17 [b]Jer. 4:7

16 [1]Or, *sons* [2]Lit., *grazed* [a]Is. 19:13; Jer. 44:1; Hos. 9:6 [b]Deut. 33:20; Jer. 48:45

17 [a]Deut. 32:10; Jer. 4:18

18 [1]Heb., *Shihor* [2]Lit., *River* [a]Is. 30:2 [b]Josh. 13:3

19 [1]Heb., *YHWH,* usually rendered *LORD* [a]Is. 3:9; Jer. 4:18; Hos. 5:5 [b]Jer. 3:6, 8, 11, 14; Hos. 11:7 [c]Job 20:12-16; Amos 8:10 [d]Ps. 36:1; Jer. 5:24

20 [1]Or, *you* [a]Lev. 26:13 [b]Deut. 12:2; Is. 57:5, 7; Jer. 3:2, 6; 17:2

21 [a]Ex. 15:17; Ps. 44:2; 80:8; Is. 5:2 [b]Is. 5:4

22 [1]Lit., *cause to be great to you* [2]Heb., *YHWH,* usually rendered *LORD* [a]Jer. 4:14 [b]Job 14:17; Hos. 13:12

23 [a]Prov. 30:12 [b]Jer. 9:14 [c]Jer. 7:31 [d]Jer. 2:33, 36; 31:22

24 [1]Lit., *occasion* [a]Jer. 14:6

25 [1]Or, *desperate* [a]Jer. 18:12 [b]Deut. 32:16; Jer. 14:10

26 [a]Jer. 48:27

27 [1]Or, *evil* [a]Jer. 18:17; 32:33 [b]Judg. 10:10; Is. 26:16

28 [1]Or, *evil* [a]Deut. 32:37; Judg. 10:14; Is. 45:20; Jer. 1:16 [b]Jer. 11:12 [c]2 Kin. 17:30, 31; Jer. 11:13

29 [a]Jer. 5:1; 6:13; Dan. 9:11

30"[a]In vain I have struck your sons;
They accepted no chastening.
Your [b]sword has devoured your prophets
Like a destroying lion.
31"O generation, heed the word of the LORD.
Have I been a wilderness to Israel,
Or a [a]land of thick darkness?
Why do My people say, '[b]We *are free to* roam;
We will come no more to Thee'?
32"Can a virgin forget her ornaments,
Or a bride her attire?
Yet My people have [a]forgotten Me
Days without number.
33"How well you prepare your way
To seek love!
Therefore even [1]the wicked women
You have taught your ways.
34"Also on your skirts is found
The [a]lifeblood of the innocent poor;
You did not find them [b]breaking in.
But in spite of all these things,
35 Yet you said, 'I am innocent;
Surely His anger is turned away from me.'
Behold, I will [a]enter into judgment with you
Because you [b]say, 'I have not sinned.'
36"Why do you [a]go around so much
Changing your way?
Also, [b]you shall be put to shame by Egypt
As you were put to shame by [c]Assyria.
37"From this *place* also you shall go out
With [a]your hands on your head;
For the LORD has rejected [b]those in whom you trust,
And you shall not prosper with them."

The Polluted Land

3 GOD [1]says, "[a]If a husband divorces his wife,
And she goes from him,
And belongs to another man,
Will he still return to her?
Will not that land be completely [2]polluted?
But you [b]are a harlot *with* many [3]lovers;
Yet you [c]turn to Me," declares the LORD.
2"Lift up your eyes to the [a]bare heights and see;
Where have you not been violated?
By the roads you have [b]sat for them
Like an Arab in the desert,
And you have [c]polluted a land
With your harlotry and with your wickedness.
3"Therefore the [a]showers have been withheld,
And there has been no spring rain.
Yet you had a [b]harlot's forehead;
You refused to be ashamed.

30 [a]Is. 1:5; Jer. 5:3; 7:28 [b]Neh. 9:26; Jer. 26:20-24; Acts 7:52; 1 Thess. 2:15
31 [a]Is. 45:19 [b]Deut. 32:15; Jer. 2:20, 25
32 [a]Ps. 106:21; Is. 17:10; Jer. 3:21; 13:25; Hos. 8:14
33 [1]Or, *in wickedness*
34 [a]2 Kin. 21:16; 24:4; Ps. 106:38; Jer. 7:6; 19:4 [b]Ex. 22:2
35 [a]Jer. 25:31 [b]Prov. 28:13; 1 John 1:8, 10
36 [a]Jer. 2:23; 31:22; Hos. 12:1 [b]Is. 30:3 [c]2 Chr. 28:16, 20, 21
37 [a]2 Sam. 13:19; Jer. 14:3, 4 [b]Jer. 37:7-10
1 [1]Lit., *saying* [2]Or, *alienated* [3]Lit., *companions* [a]Deut. 24:1-4 [b]Jer. 2:20; Ezek. 16:26, 28, 29 [c]Jer. 4:1; Zech. 1:3
2 [a]Deut. 12:2; Jer. 2:20; 3:21; 7:29 [b]Gen. 38:14; Ezek. 16:25 [c]Jer. 2:7
3 [a]Lev. 26:19; Jer. 14:3-6 [b]Jer. 6:15; 8:12
4 [1]Lit., *leader* [a]Jer. 3:19; 31:9 [b]Ps. 71:17; Prov. 2:17 [c]Jer. 2:2; Hos. 2:15
5 [1]Lit., *keep it* [2]Lit., *been able* [a]Ps. 103:9; Is. 57:16; Jer. 3:12
6 [a]Jer. 17:2; Ezek. 23:4-10
7 [1]Lit., *said* [a]2 Kin. 17:13 [b]Jer. 3:11; Ezek. 16:47
8 [a]Deut. 24:1, 3; Is. 50:1 [b]Ezek. 16:46, 47; 23:11
9 [a]Jer. 2:7; 3:2 [b]Is. 57:6; Jer. 2:27; 10:8
10 [a]Jer. 12:2; Hos. 7:14
11 [a]Ezek. 16:51, 52; 23:11
12 [1]Lit., *cause My countenance to fall* [a]Jer. 3:14, 22; Ezek. 33:11 [b]Jer. 3:5 [c]Ps. 86:15; Jer. 12:15; 31:20; 33:26
13 [1]Lit., *know* [2]Lit., *ways* [a]Deut. 30:1-3; Jer. 3:25; 14:20; 1 John 1:9 [b]Jer. 2:20, 25; 3:2, 6 [c]Deut. 12:2
14 [a]Jer. 31:32; Hos. 2:19 [b]Jer. 31:6, 12
15 [a]Jer. 23:4; 31:10; Ezek. 34:23; Eph. 4:11 [b]Acts 20:28
16 [a]Is. 65:17

4"Have you not just now called to Me,
'[a]My Father, Thou art the [1b]friend of my [c]youth?
5 '[a]Will He be angry forever?
Will He [1]be indignant to the end?'
Behold, you have spoken
And have done evil things,
And you have [2]had your way."

Faithless Israel

6 Then the LORD said to me in the
days of Josiah the king, "Have you seen
what faithless Israel did? She [a]went up
on every high hill and under every green
tree, and she was a harlot there.
7"And [a]I [1]thought, 'After she has
done all these things, she will return to
Me'; but she did not return, and her
[b]treacherous sister Judah saw it.
8"And I saw that for all the adulteries
of faithless Israel, I had sent her away
and [a]given her a writ of divorce, yet her
[b]treacherous sister Judah did not fear;
but she went and was a harlot also.
9"And it came about because of the
lightness of her harlotry, that she [a]polluted the land and committed adultery
with [b]stones and trees.
10"And yet in spite of all this her
treacherous sister Judah did not return
to Me with all her heart, but rather in
[a]deception," declares the LORD.

God Invites Repentance

11 And the LORD said to me, "[a]Faithless Israel has proved herself more righteous than treacherous Judah.
12"Go, and proclaim these words
toward the north and say,
'[a]Return, faithless Israel,' declares the LORD;
'[b]I will not [1]look upon you in anger.
For I am [c]gracious,' declares the LORD;
'I will not be angry forever.
13 'Only [1a]acknowledge your iniquity,
That you have transgressed against the LORD your God
And have [b]scattered your [2]favors to the strangers [c]under every green tree,
And you have not obeyed My voice,' declares the LORD.
14 'Return, O faithless sons,' declares the LORD;
'For I am a [a]master to you,
And I will take you one from a city and two from a family,
And [b]I will bring you to Zion.'
15"Then I will give you [a]shepherds
after My own heart, who will [b]feed you
on knowledge and understanding.
16"And it shall be in those days when
you are multiplied and increased in the
land," declares the LORD, "they shall
[a]say no more, 'The ark of the covenant
of the LORD.' And it shall not come to
mind, nor shall they remember it, nor
shall they miss *it,* nor shall it be made
again.

17"At that time they shall call Jerusalem 'The [a]Throne of the LORD,' and [b]all
the nations will be gathered to it, to
Jerusalem, for the [c]name of the LORD;
nor shall they [d]walk anymore after the
stubbornness of their evil heart.
18"[a]In those days the house of Judah
will walk with the house of Israel, and
they will come together [b]from the land
of the north to the [c]land that I gave your
fathers as an inheritance.
19"Then I said,
'How I would set you among [1]My sons,
And give you a pleasant land,
The most [a]beautiful inheritance of the nations!'
And I said, 'You shall call Me, [b]My Father,
And not turn away from following Me.'
20"Surely, as a woman treacherously departs from her [1]lover,
So you have [a]dealt treacherously with Me,
O house of Israel," declares the LORD.

21 A voice is heard on the [a]bare heights,
The weeping *and* the supplications of the sons of Israel;
Because they have perverted their way,
They have [b]forgotten the LORD their God.
22"Return, O faithless sons,
[a]I will heal your faithlessness."
"Behold, we come to Thee;
For Thou art the LORD our God.
23"Surely, [a]the hills are a deception,
A tumult *on* the mountains.
Surely, in the [b]LORD our God
Is the salvation of Israel.
24"But [a]the shameful thing has consumed the labor of our fathers since our
youth, their flocks and their herds, their
sons and their daughters.
25"Let us lie down in our [a]shame, and
let our humiliation cover us; for we have
sinned against the LORD our God, we
and our fathers, [b]since our youth even to
this day. And we have not obeyed the
voice of the LORD our God."

Judah Threatened with Invasion

4 "IF you will [a]return, O Israel," declares the LORD,
"*Then* you should return to Me.
And [b]if you will put away your detested things from My presence,
And will not waver,
2 And you will [a]swear, 'As the LORD lives,'
[b]In truth, in justice, and in righteousness;
Then the [c]nations will bless themselves in Him,
And [d]in Him they will glory."

3 For thus says the LORD to the men
of Judah and to Jerusalem,
"[1][a]Break up your fallow ground,
And [b]do not sow among thorns.
4"[a]Circumcise yourselves to the LORD
And remove the foreskins of your heart,
Men of Judah and inhabitants of Jerusalem,
Lest My [b]wrath go forth like fire
And burn with [c]none to quench it,
Because of the evil of your deeds."

5 Declare in Judah and proclaim in Jerusalem, and say,
"[a]Blow the trumpet in the land;
Cry aloud and say,
'[b]Assemble yourselves, and let us go
Into the fortified cities.'
6"Lift up a [a]standard toward Zion!
Seek refuge, do not stand *still,*
For I am bringing [b]evil from the north,
And great destruction.
7"A [a]lion has gone up from his thicket,
And a [b]destroyer of nations has set out;
He has gone out from his place
To [c]make your land a waste.
Your cities will be ruins
Without inhabitant.
8"For this, [a]put on sackcloth,
Lament and wail;
For the [b]fierce anger of the LORD
Has not turned back from us."
9"And it shall come about in that
day," declares the LORD, "that the [a]heart
of the king and the heart of the princes
will fail; and the priests will be appalled,
and the [b]prophets will be astounded."
10 Then I said, "Ah, Lord [1]GOD!
Surely Thou hast utterly [a]deceived this
people and Jerusalem, saying, '[b]You will
have peace'; whereas a sword touches
the [2]throat."
11 In that time it will be said to this
people and to Jerusalem, "A [a]scorching
wind from the bare heights in the wilderness in the direction of the daughter of
My people—not to winnow, and not to
cleanse,
12 a wind too strong for [1]this—will
come [2]at My command; now I will also
pronounce judgments against them.
13"Behold, he [a]goes up like clouds,
And his [b]chariots like the whirlwind;
His horses are [c]swifter than eagles.
Woe to us, for [d]we are ruined!"

14 Wash your heart from evil, O Jerusalem,
That you may be saved.
How long will your [a]wicked thoughts
Lodge within you?
15 For a voice declares from [a]Dan,
And proclaims wickedness from Mount Ephraim.
16"Report *it* to the nations, now!
Proclaim over Jerusalem,

---

17 [a]Jer. 17:12; Ezek. 43:7 [b]Jer. 3:19; 4:2; 12:15, 16; 16:19 [c]Is. 60:9 [d]Jer. 11:8
18 [a]Is. 11:13; Jer. 50:4, 5; Hos. 1:11 [b]Jer. 16:15; 31:8 [c]Amos 9:15
19 [1]Lit., *the* [a]Ps. 16:6 [b]Is. 63:16; Jer. 3:4
20 [1]Or, *companion* [a]Is. 48:8
21 [a]Is. 15:2; Jer. 3:2; 7:29 [b]Is. 17:10; Jer. 2:32; 13:25
22 [a]Jer. 30:17; 33:6; Hos. 6:1; 14:4
23 [a]Jer. 17:2 [b]Ps. 3:8; Jer. 17:14; 31:7
24 [a]Hos. 9:10
25 [a]Ezra 9:6, 7 [b]Jer. 22:21
1 [a]Jer. 3:22; 15:19; Joel 2:12 [b]Jer. 7:3, 7; 35:15
2 [a]Deut. 10:20; Is. 45:23; 65:16; Jer. 12:16 [b]Is. 48:1 [c]Gen. 22:18; Jer. 3:17; 12:15, 16; Gal. 3:8 [d]Is. 45:25; Jer. 9:24; 1 Cor. 1:31
3 [1]Lit., *Plow for yourselves plowed ground* [a]Hos. 10:12 [b]Matt. 13:7
4 [a]Deut. 10:16; 30:6; Jer. 9:25, 26; Rom. 2:28, 29; Col. 2:11 [b]Is. 30:27, 33; Jer. 21:12; Zeph. 2:2 [c]Amos 5:6; Mark 9:43, 48
5 [a]Jer. 6:1; Hos. 8:1 [b]Josh. 10:20; Jer. 8:14
6 [a]Is. 62:10; Jer. 4:21; 50:2 [b]Jer. 1:14, 15; 6:1, 22
7 [a]Jer. 5:6; 25:38; 50:17 [b]Jer. 25:9; Ezek. 26:7-10 [c]Is. 1:7; 6:11; Jer. 2:15
8 [a]Is. 22:12; Jer. 6:26 [b]Is. 5:25; 10:4; Jer. 30:24
9 [a]Is. 22:3-5; Jer. 48:41 [b]Is. 29:9, 10; Ezek. 13:9-16
10 [1]Heb., *YHWH,* usually rendered *LORD* [2]Or, *life* [a]Ezek. 14:9; 2 Thess. 2:11 [b]Jer. 5:12; 14:13
11 [a]Jer. 13:24; 51:1; Ezek. 17:10; Hos. 13:15
12 [1]Lit., *these* [2]Lit., *for Me*
13 [a]Is. 19:1; Nah. 1:3 [b]Is. 5:28; 66:15 [c]Lam. 4:19; Hab. 1:8 [d]Is. 3:8
14 [a]Prov. 1:22; Jer. 6:19; 13:27; James 4:8
15 [a]Jer. 8:16

'Besiegers come from a [a]far country,
And [b]lift their voices against the cities of Judah.
17 'Like watchmen of a field they are [a]against her round about,
Because she has [b]rebelled against Me,' declares the LORD.
18 "Your [a]ways and your deeds
Have [1]brought these things to you.
This is your evil. How [b]bitter!
How it has touched your heart!"

Lament over Judah's Devastation

19 [a]My [1]soul, my [1]soul! I am in anguish! [2]Oh, my heart!
My [b]heart is pounding in me;
I cannot be silent,
Because [3]you have heard, O my soul,
The [c]sound of the trumpet,
The alarm of war.
20 [a]Disaster on disaster is proclaimed,
For the [b]whole land is devastated;
Suddenly my [c]tents are devastated,
My curtains in an instant.
21 How long must I see the standard,
And hear the sound of the trumpet?
22 "[a]For My people are foolish,
They know Me not;
They are stupid children,
And they have no understanding.
They are shrewd to [b]do evil,
But to do good they do not know."

23 I looked on the earth, and behold, *it was* [1a]formless and void;
And to the heavens, and they had no light.
24 I looked on the mountains, and behold, they were [a]quaking,
And all the hills [1]moved to and fro.
25 I looked, and behold, there was no man,
And all the [a]birds of the heavens had fled.
26 I looked, and behold, [1]the [a]fruitful land was a wilderness,
And all its cities were pulled down
Before the LORD, before His fierce anger.

27 For thus says the LORD,
"The [a]whole land shall be a desolation,
Yet I will [b]not execute a complete destruction.
28 "For this the [a]earth shall mourn,
And the [b]heavens above be dark,
Because I have [c]spoken, I have purposed,
And I will not [1]change My mind, nor will I turn from it."
29 At the sound of the horseman and bowman [a]every city flees;
They [b]go into the thickets and climb among the rocks;
[c]Every city is forsaken,
And no man dwells in them.
30 And you, O desolate one, [a]what will you do?
Although you dress in scarlet,

16 [a]Is. 39:3; Jer. 5:15 [b]Ezek. 21:22
17 [a]2 Kin. 25:1, 4 [b]Is. 1:20, 23; Jer. 5:23
18 [1]Lit., *done* [a]Ps. 107:17; Is. 50:1; Jer. 2:17, 19 [b]Jer. 2:19
19 [1]Lit., *inward parts* [2]Lit., *The walls of my heart* [3]Or, *I, my soul, heard* [a]Is. 15:5; 16:11; 21:3; 22:4; Jer. 9:1, 10; 20:9 [b]Hab. 3:16 [c]Num. 10:9
20 [a]Ps. 42:7; Ezek. 7:26 [b]Jer. 4:27 [c]Jer. 10:20
22 [a]Jer. 5:4, 21; 10:8; Rom. 1:22 [b]Jer. 9:3; 13:23; Rom. 16:19; 1 Cor. 14:20
23 [1]Or, *a waste and emptiness* [a]Gen. 1:2; Is. 24:19
24 [1]Lit., *moved lightly* [a]Is. 5:25; Jer. 10:10; Ezek. 38:20
25 [a]Jer. 9:10; 12:4; Zeph. 1:3
26 [1]Or, *Carmel* [a]Jer. 9:10
27 [a]Jer. 12:11, 12; 25:11 [b]Jer. 5:10, 18; 30:11; 46:28
28 [1]Lit., *be sorry* [a]Jer. 12:4, 11; 14:2; Hos. 4:3 [b]Is. 5:30; 50:3; Joel 2:30, 31 [c]Num. 23:19; Jer. 23:20; 30:24
29 [a]2 Kin. 25:4 [b]Is. 2:19-21; Jer. 16:16 [c]Jer. 4:7
30 [1]Lit., *paramours* [a]Is. 10:3; 20:6; Jer. 13:21 [b]2 Kin. 9:30; Ezek. 23:40 [c]Jer. 22:20, 22; Lam. 1:2, 19; Ezek. 23:9, 10, 22
31 [1]Lit., *sound* [2]Lit., *palms* [3]Lit., *my soul faints* [a]Is. 42:14 [b]Is. 1:15; Lam. 1:17

1 [1]Lit., *faithfulness* [a]2 Chr. 16:9; Dan. 12:4 [b]Ezek. 22:30 [c]Gen. 18:26, 32
2 [a]Is. 48:1; Titus 1:16
3 [1]Lit., *faithfulness* [2]Or, *become sick* [a]2 Chr. 16:9 [b]Is. 1:5; 9:13; Jer. 2:30 [c]Jer. 7:28; 8:5; Zeph. 3:2 [d]Jer. 7:26; 19:15; Ezek. 3:8
4 [a]Is. 27:11; Jer. 8:7; Hos. 4:6
5 [a]Mic. 3:1 [b]Ex. 32:25; Ps. 2:3; Jer. 2:20
6 [a]Jer. 4:7 [b]Ezek. 22:27; Hab. 1:8; Zeph. 3:3 [c]Hos. 13:7 [d]Jer. 30:14, 15
7 [a]Josh. 23:7; Jer. 12:16; Zeph. 1:5 [b]Deut. 32:21; Jer. 2:11; Gal. 4:8 [c]Jer. 7:9

Although you decorate *yourself with* ornaments of gold,
Although you [b]enlarge your eyes with paint,
In vain you make yourself beautiful;
Your [1c]lovers despise you;
They seek your life.
31 For I heard a [1]cry as of a woman in labor,
The anguish as of one giving birth to her first child,
The [1]cry of the daughter of Zion [a]gasping for breath,
[b]Stretching out her [2]hands, *saying,*
"Ah, woe is me, for [3]I faint before murderers."

Jerusalem's Godlessness

5 "[a]ROAM to and fro through the streets of Jerusalem,
And look now, and take note.
And seek in her open squares,
If you can [b]find a man,
[c]If there is one who does justice, who seeks [1]truth,
Then I will pardon her.
2 "And [a]although they say, 'As the LORD lives,'
Surely they swear falsely."
3 O LORD, do not [a]Thine eyes look for [1]truth?
Thou hast [b]smitten them,
But they did not [2]weaken;
Thou hast consumed them,
But they [c]refused to take correction.
They have [d]made their faces harder than rock;
They have refused to repent.

4 Then I said, "They are only the poor,
They are foolish;
For they [a]do not know the way of the LORD
Or the ordinance of their God.
5 "I will go to the great
And will speak to them,
For [a]they know the way of the LORD,
And the ordinance of their God."
But they too, with one accord, have [b]broken the yoke
And burst the bonds.
6 Therefore [a]a lion from the forest shall slay them,
A [b]wolf of the deserts shall destroy them,
A [c]leopard is watching their cities.
Everyone who goes out of them shall be torn in pieces,
Because their [d]transgressions are many,
Their apostasies are numerous.

7 "Why should I pardon you?
Your sons have forsaken Me
And [a]sworn by those who are [b]not gods.
When I had fed them to the full,
They [c]committed adultery
And trooped to the harlot's house.

8"They were well-fed lusty horses,
Each one neighing after his [a]neighbor's wife.
9"Shall I not punish [1]these *people,*"
declares the LORD,
"And on a nation such as this
[a]Shall I not avenge Myself?

10"Go up through her vine rows and destroy,
But do not execute a complete destruction;
Strip away her branches,
For they are not the LORD's.
11"For the [a]house of Israel and the house of Judah
Have dealt very treacherously with Me," declares the LORD.
12 They have [a]lied about the LORD
And said, "[1b]Not He;
Misfortune will [c]not come on us;
And we [d]will not see sword or famine.
13"And the [a]prophets are *as* wind,
And the word is not in them.
Thus it will be done to them!"

Judgment Proclaimed

14 Therefore, thus says the LORD, the
God of hosts,
"Because you have spoken this word,
Behold, I am [a]making My words in your mouth fire
And this people wood, and it will consume them.
15"Behold, I am [a]bringing a nation against you from afar, O house of Israel," declares the LORD.
"It is an enduring nation,
It is an ancient nation,
A nation whose [b]language you do not know,
Nor can you understand what they say.
16"Their [a]quiver is like an [b]open grave,
All of them are mighty men.
17"And they will [a]devour your harvest and your food;
They will devour your sons and your daughters;
They will devour your flocks and your herds;
They will devour your [b]vines and your fig trees;
They will demolish with the sword your [c]fortified cities in which you trust.
18"Yet even in those days," declares
the LORD, "I will not make you a complete destruction.
19"And it shall come about [a]when
[1]they say, 'Why has the LORD our God
done all these things to us?' then you
shall say to them, 'As you have forsaken
Me and served foreign gods in your land,
so you shall [b]serve strangers in a land
that is not yours.'
20"Declare this in the house of Jacob
And proclaim it in Judah, saying,
21 'Hear this, O foolish and [1]senseless people,
Who have [a]eyes, but see not;
Who have ears, but hear not.
22 'Do you not [a]fear Me?' declares the LORD.
'Do you not tremble in My presence?
For I have [b]placed the sand as a boundary for the sea,
An eternal decree, so it cannot cross over it.
Though the waves toss, yet they cannot prevail;
Though they roar, yet they cannot cross over it.
23 'But this people has a [a]stubborn and rebellious heart;
They have turned aside and departed.
24 'They do not say in their heart,
"Let us now fear the LORD our God,
Who [a]gives rain in its season,
Both [b]the autumn rain and the spring rain,
Who keeps for us
The [c]appointed weeks of the harvest."
25 'Your [a]iniquities have turned these away,
And your sins have withheld good from you.
26 'For wicked men are found among My people,
They [a]watch like fowlers [1]lying in wait;
They set a trap,
They catch men.
27 'Like a cage full of birds,
So their houses are full of [a]deceit;
Therefore they have become great and rich.
28 'They are [a]fat, they are sleek,
They also [1]excel in deeds of wickedness;
They do not plead the cause,
The cause of the [2b]orphan, that they may prosper;
And they do not [3]defend the rights of the poor.
29 '[a]Shall I not punish [1]these *people?*'
declares the LORD,
'On a nation such as this
Shall I not avenge Myself?'

30"An appalling and [a]horrible thing
Has happened in the land:
31 The [a]prophets prophesy falsely,
And the priests rule [1]on their *own* authority;
And My people [b]love it so!
But what will you do at the end of it?

Destruction of Jerusalem Impending

6 "FLEE for safety, O sons of [a]Benjamin,
From the midst of Jerusalem!
Now blow a trumpet in Tekoa,
And raise a signal over [1b]Beth-haccerem;
For evil looks down from the [c]north,

8 [a]Jer. 13:27; 29:23; Ezek. 22:11
9 [1]Or, *for these things* [a]Jer. 9:9
11 [a]Jer. 3:6, 7, 20
12 [1]Lit., *He is not* [a]2 Chr. 36:16 [b]Prov. 30:9; Jer. 14:22; 43:1-4 [c]Jer. 23:17 [d]Jer. 14:13
13 [a]Job 8:2; Jer. 14:13, 15; 22:22
14 [a]Is. 24:6; Jer. 1:9; 23:29; Hos. 6:5; Zech. 1:6
15 [a]Deut. 28:49; Is. 5:26; Jer. 4:16 [b]Is. 28:11
16 [a]Is. 5:28; 13:18 [b]Ps. 5:9
17 [a]Lev. 26:16; Deut. 28:31, 33; Jer. 8:16; 50:7, 17 [b]Jer. 8:13 [c]Hos. 8:14
19 [1]Or, *you* [a]Deut. 29:24-26; 1 Kin. 9:8, 9; Jer. 13:22; 16:10-13 [b]Deut. 28:48; Jer. 16:13
21 [1]Lit., *without heart* [a]Is. 6:9; 43:8; Ezek. 12:2; Matt. 13:14; Mark 8:18; John 12:40; Acts 28:26; Rom. 11:8
22 [a]Deut. 28:58; Ps. 119:120; Jer. 2:19; 10:7; Rev. 15:4 [b]Job 38:8-11; Ps. 104:9; Prov. 8:29
23 [a]Deut. 21:18; Ps. 78:8; Jer. 4:17; 6:28
24 [a]Ps. 147:8; Jer. 3:3; Matt. 5:45; Acts 14:17 [b]Joel 2:23 [c]Gen. 8:22
25 [a]Jer. 2:17; 4:18
26 [1]Perhaps, *crouching down* [a]Ps. 10:9; Prov. 1:11; Jer. 18:22; Hab. 1:15
27 [a]Jer. 9:6
28 [1]Lit., *pass over,* or, *overlook deeds* [2]Or, *fatherless* [3]Lit., *judge* [a]Deut. 32:15 [b]Is. 1:23; Jer. 7:6; 22:3; Zech. 7:10
29 [1]Or, *for these things* [a]Jer. 5:9; Mal. 3:5
30 [a]Jer. 23:14; Hos. 6:10
31 [1]Lit., *over their own hands* [a]Ezek. 13:6 [b]Mic. 2:11
1 [1]I.e., house of the vineyard [a]Josh. 18:28 [b]Neh. 3:14 [c]Jer. 1:14; 4:6; 6:22

And a great destruction.
2 "The comely and [a]dainty one, [b]the daughter of Zion, I will cut off.
3 "[a]Shepherds and their flocks will come to her,
They will [b]pitch *their* tents [1]around her,
They will pasture each in his [2]place.
4 "[1a]Prepare war against her;
Arise, and let us [2]attack at [b]noon.
Woe to us, for the day declines,
For the shadows of the evening lengthen!
5 "Arise, and let us [1]attack by night
And [a]destroy her [2]palaces!"
6 For thus says the LORD of hosts,
"[a]Cut down her trees,
And cast up a [b]siege against Jerusalem.
This is the city to be punished,
In whose midst there is only [c]oppression.
7 "[a]As a well [1]keeps its waters fresh,
So she [1]keeps fresh her wickedness.
[b]Violence and destruction are heard in her;
[c]Sickness and wounds are ever before Me.
8 "[a]Be warned, O Jerusalem,
Lest [1b]I be alienated from you;
Lest I make you a desolation,
A land not inhabited."

9 Thus says the LORD of hosts,
"They will [a]thoroughly glean as the vine the [b]remnant of Israel;
Pass your hand again like a grape gatherer
Over the branches."
10 To whom shall I speak and give warning,
That they may hear?
Behold, their [a]ears are [1]closed,
And they cannot listen.
Behold, [b]the word of the LORD has become a reproach to them;
They have no delight in it.
11 But I am [a]full of the wrath of the LORD:
I am [b]weary with holding *it* in.
"[c]Pour *it* out on the children in the street,
And on the [1]gathering of young men together;
For both husband and wife shall be taken,
The aged [2]and the very old.
12 "And their [a]houses shall be turned over to others,
Their fields and their wives together;
For I will [b]stretch out My hand
Against the inhabitants of the land," declares the LORD.
13 "For [a]from the least of them even to the greatest of them,
Everyone is [b]greedy for gain,
And from the prophet even to the priest
Everyone [1]deals falsely.
14 "And they have [a]healed the brokenness of My people superficially,
Saying, 'Peace, peace,'
But there is no peace.
15 "Were they [a]ashamed because of the abomination they have done?
They were not even ashamed at all;
They did not even know how to blush.
Therefore they shall fall among those who fall;
At the time that I punish them,
They shall be cast down," says the LORD.

16 Thus says the LORD,
"Stand by the ways and see and ask for the [a]ancient paths,
Where the good way is, and walk in it;
And [b]you shall find rest for your souls.
But they said, 'We will not walk *in it.*'
17 "And I set [a]watchmen over you, *saying,*
'Listen to the sound of the trumpet!'
But they said, 'We will not listen.'
18 "Therefore hear, O nations,
And know, O congregation, what is among them.
19 "[a]Hear, O earth: behold, I am bringing disaster on this people,
The [b]fruit of their [1]plans,
Because they have not listened to My words,
And as for My law, they have [c]rejected it also.
20 "[a]For what purpose does [b]frankincense come to Me from Sheba,
And the [1c]sweet cane from a distant land?
[d]Your burnt offerings are not acceptable,
And your sacrifices are not pleasing to Me."
21 Therefore, thus says the LORD,
"Behold, [a]I am [1]laying stumbling blocks before this people.
And they will stumble against them,
[b]Fathers and sons together;
Neighbor and [2]friend will perish."

The Enemy from the North

22 Thus says the LORD,
"Behold, [a]a people is coming from the north land,
And a great nation will be aroused from the [b]remote parts of the earth.
23 "They seize [a]bow and spear;
They are [b]cruel and have no mercy;
Their voice [c]roars like the sea,
And they ride on horses,
Arrayed as a man for the battle
Against you, O daughter of Zion!"
24 We have [a]heard the report of it;
Our hands are limp.
[b]Anguish has seized us,
Pain as of a woman in childbirth.

---

2 [a]Deut. 28:56 [b]Is. 1:8; Jer. 4:31

3 [1]Lit., *against her round about* [2]Lit., *hand* [a]Jer. 12:10 [b]2 Kin. 25:1; Jer. 4:17; Luke 19:43

4 [1]Lit., *Sanctify* [2]Lit., *go up* [a]Jer. 6:23; Joel 3:9 [b]Jer. 15:8; Zeph. 2:4

5 [1]Lit., *go up* [2]Or, *fortified towers* [a]Is. 32:14; Jer. 52:13

6 [a]Deut. 20:19, 20 [b]Jer. 32:24; 33:4 [c]Jer. 22:17

7 [1]Lit., *keeps cold* [a]James 3:11f. [b]Jer. 20:8; Ezek. 7:11, 23 [c]Jer. 30:12, 13

8 [1]Lit., *my soul* [a]Jer. 7:28; 17:23 [b]Ezek. 23:18; Hos. 9:12

9 [a]Jer. 16:16; 49:9; Obad. 5, 6 [b]Jer. 8:3; 11:23

10 [1]Lit., *uncircumcised* [a]Jer. 5:21; 7:26; Acts 7:51 [b]Jer. 20:8

11 [1]Lit., *council* [2]Lit., *with fulness of days* [a]Job 32:18, 19; Mic. 3:8 [b]Jer. 15:6; 20:9 [c]Jer. 7:20; 9:21

12 [a]Deut. 28:30; Jer. 8:10; 38:22, 23 [b]Jer. 15:6

13 [1]Or, *makes lies* [a]Jer. 8:10 [b]Is. 56:11; 57:17; Jer. 8:10; 22:17

14 [a]Jer. 8:11; Ezek. 13:10

15 [a]Jer. 3:3; 8:12

16 [a]Is. 8:20; Jer. 12:16; 18:15; 31:21; Mal. 4:4; Luke 16:29 [b]Matt. 11:29

17 [a]Is. 21:11; 58:1; Jer. 25:4; Ezek. 3:17; Hab. 2:1

19 [1]Or, *devices* [a]Is. 1:2; Jer. 19:3, 15; 22:29 [b]Prov. 1:31 [c]Jer. 8:9

20 [1]Lit., *good* [a]Ps. 50:7-9; Is. 1:11; 66:3; Mic. 6:6 [b]Is. 60:6 [c]Ex. 30:23 [d]Ps. 40:6; Amos 5:22

21 [1]Lit., *giving* [2]Lit., *his friend* [a]Is. 8:14; Jer. 13:16 [b]Is. 9:14-17; Jer. 9:21, 22

22 [a]Jer. 1:15; 10:22; 50:41-43 [b]Neh. 1:9

23 [a]Is. 13:18; Jer. 4:29 [b]Jer. 50:42 [c]Is. 5:30

24 [a]Is. 28:19; Jer. 4:19-21 [b]Is. 21:3; Jer. 4:31; 13:21; 30:6; 49:24; 50:43

25 [a]Do not go out into the field,
And [b]do not walk on the road,
For the enemy has a sword,
[c]Terror is on every side.
26 O daughter of my people, [a]put on
sackcloth
And [b]roll in ashes;
[1c]Mourn as for an only son,
A lamentation most bitter.
For suddenly the destroyer
Will come upon us.

27 "I have [a]made you an assayer *and* a
tester among My people,
That you may know and assay their
way."
28 All of them are stubbornly rebellious,
[a]Going about as a talebearer.
They are [b]bronze and iron;
They, all of them, are corrupt.
29 The bellows blow fiercely,
The lead is consumed by the fire;
In vain the refining goes on,
But the [a]wicked are not [1]separated.
30 [a]They call them rejected silver,
Because the [b]LORD has rejected
them.

Message at the Temple Gate

7 THE word that came to Jeremiah
from the LORD, saying,
2 "[a]Stand in the gate of the LORD'S
house and proclaim there this word, and
say, 'Hear the word of the LORD, all you
of Judah, who enter by these gates to
worship the LORD!' "
3 Thus says the LORD of hosts, the
God of Israel, "[a]Amend your ways and
your deeds, and I will let you dwell in
this place.
4 "[a]Do not trust in deceptive words,
saying, '[1]This is the temple of the LORD,
the temple of the LORD, the temple of
the LORD.'
5 "For [a]if you truly amend your ways
and your deeds, if you truly [b]practice
justice between a man and his neighbor,
6 *if* you do not oppress the alien, the
[1a]orphan, or the widow, and do not shed
[b]innocent blood in this place, nor [c]walk
after other gods to your own ruin,
7 then I will let you [a]dwell in this
place, in the [b]land that I gave to your
fathers forever and ever.
8 "Behold, you are trusting in [a]decep-
tive words to no avail.
9 "Will you steal, murder, and commit
adultery, and swear falsely, and [1a]offer
sacrifices to Baal, and walk after [b]other
gods that you have not known,
10 then [a]come and stand before Me in
[b]this house, which is called by My name,
and say, 'We are delivered!'—that you
may do all these abominations?
11 "Has [a]this house, which is called by
My name, become a [b]den of robbers in
your sight? Behold, [c]I, even I, have seen
it," declares the LORD.
12 "But go now to My place which was
in [a]Shiloh, where I [b]made My name
dwell at the first, and [c]see what I did to
it because of the wickedness of My
people Israel.
13 "And now, because you have done
all these things," declares the LORD,
"and I spoke to you, [a]rising up early and
[b]speaking, but you did not hear, and I
[c]called you but you did not answer,
14 therefore, I will do to the [a]house
which is called by My name, [b]in which
you trust, and to the place which I gave
you and your fathers, as I [c]did to Shiloh.
15 "And I will [a]cast you out of My
sight, as I have cast out all your brothers, all the [1]offspring of [b]Ephraim.
16 "As for you, [a]do not pray for this
people, and do not lift up cry or prayer
for them, and do not intercede with Me;
for I do not hear you.
17 "Do you not see what they are doing
in the cities of Judah and in the streets of
Jerusalem?
18 "The [1]children gather wood, and the
fathers kindle the fire, and the women
knead dough to make cakes for the
queen of heaven; and *they* [a]pour out
libations to other gods in order to [b]spite
Me.
19 "[a]Do they spite Me?" declares the
LORD. "Is it not themselves *they spite,* to
[1]their own [b]shame?"
20 Therefore thus says the Lord
[1]GOD, "Behold, My [a]anger and My
wrath will be poured out on this place,
on man and on beast and on the [b]trees
of the field and on the fruit of the
ground; and it will burn and not be
quenched."
21 Thus says the LORD of hosts, the
God of Israel, "Add your [a]burnt offerings to your sacrifices and [b]eat flesh.
22 "For I did not [a]speak to your fathers, or command them in the day that
I brought them out of the land of Egypt,
concerning burnt offerings and sacrifices.
23 "But this is [1]what I commanded
them, saying, '[a]Obey My voice, and [b]I
will be your God, and you will be My
people; and you will walk in all the way
which I command you, that it may [c]be
well with you.'
24 "Yet they [a]did not obey or incline
their ear, but walked in *their own* counsels *and* in the stubbornness of their evil
heart, and [1b]went backward and not
forward.
25 "Since the day that your fathers
came out of the land of Egypt until this
day, I have [a]sent you all My servants the
prophets, daily rising early and sending
them.
26 "Yet they did not listen to Me or
incline their ear, but [a]stiffened their
neck; they [b]did evil more than their
fathers.
27 "And you shall [a]speak all these
words to them, but they will not listen to
you; and you shall call to them, but they
will [b]not answer you.

25 [a]Jer. 14:18 [b]Judg. 5:6 [c]Jer. 20:10; 46:5; 49:29
26 [1]Lit., *Make for yourself mourning* [a]Jer. 4:8 [b]Jer. 25:34; Mic. 1:10 [c]Amos 8:10; Zech. 12:10
27 [a]Jer. 1:18; 15:20
28 [a]Jer. 9:4 [b]Ezek. 22:18
29 [1]Or, *drawn off* [a]Jer. 15:19
30 [a]Ps. 119:119; Is. 1:22 [b]Jer. 7:29; Hos. 9:17; Zech. 11:8

2 [a]Jer. 17:19; 26:2
3 [a]Jer. 4:1; 7:5; 18:11; 26:13
4 [1]Lit., *They are* [a]Jer. 7:8; Mic. 3:11
5 [a]Is. 1:19; Jer. 4:1, 2 [b]1 Kin. 6:12; Jer. 21:12; 22:3
6 [1]Or, *fatherless* [a]Ex. 22:21-24; Jer. 5:28 [b]Jer. 2:34; 19:4 [c]Deut. 6:14, 15; 8:19; 11:28; Jer. 13:10
7 [a]Deut. 4:40 [b]Jer. 3:18
8 [a]Jer. 7:4; 28:15
9 [1]Or, *burn incense* [a]Jer. 11:13, 17 [b]Ex. 20:3; Jer. 7:6; 19:4
10 [a]Ezek. 23:39 [b]Jer. 7:11, 14, 30; 32:34
11 [a]Is. 56:7 [b]Matt. 21:13; Mark 11:17; Luke 19:46 [c]Jer. 29:23
12 [a]Judg. 18:31; Jer. 26:6 [b]Josh. 18:1, 10 [c]1 Sam. 4:10, 11, 22; Ps. 78:60-64
13 [a]Jer. 7:25 [b]Jer. 35:17 [c]Prov. 1:24; Is. 65:12; 66:4
14 [a]Deut. 12:5; 1 Kin. 9:7 [b]Jer. 7:4 [c]Jer. 7:12
15 [1]Lit., *seed* [a]Jer. 15:1; 52:3 [b]Ps. 78:67; Hos. 7:13; 9:13; 12:1
16 [a]Ex. 32:10; Deut. 9:14; Jer. 11:14
18 [1]Lit., *sons* [a]Jer. 19:13 [b]Deut. 32:16, 21; 1 Kin. 14:9; 16:2; Jer. 11:17; Ezek. 8:17
19 [1]Lit., *their faces'* [a]Job 35:6; 1 Cor. 10:22 [b]Jer. 9:19; 15:9; 22:22
20 [1]Heb., *YHWH,* usually rendered *LORD* [a]Is. 42:25; Jer. 6:11, 12; 42:18; Lam. 2:3-5; 4:11 [b]Jer. 8:13; 11:16
21 [a]Is. 1:11; Jer. 6:20; 14:12; Amos 5:22 [b]Ezek. 33:25; Hos. 8:13
22 [a]1 Sam. 15:22; Ps. 51:16; Hos. 6:6
23 [1]Lit., *the word which* [a]Ex. 15:26; 16:32; Deut. 6:3 [b]Ex. 19:5, 6; Lev. 26:12; Jer. 11:4; 13:11 [c]Is. 3:10; Jer. 38:20; 42:6
24 [1]Lit., *they were* [a]Deut. 29:19; Ps. 81:11; Jer. 11:8; Ezek. 20:8, 13, 16, 21 [b]Jer. 15:6

25 [a]2 Chr. 36:15; Jer. 25:4; 29:19; Luke 11:49
26 [a]Neh. 9:16; Jer. 17:23; 19:15 [b]Jer. 16:12; Matt. 23:32
27 [a]Jer. 1:7; 26:2; Ezek. 2:7 [b]Is. 50:2; 65:12; Zech. 7:13

28"And you shall say to them, 'This is
the nation that [a]did not obey the voice
of the LORD their God or accept correction; [1][b]truth has perished and has been
cut off from their mouth.
29 '[a]Cut off [1]your hair and cast *it*
away,
And [b]take up a lamentation on the
bare heights;
For the LORD has [c]rejected and
forsaken
The generation of His wrath.'
30"For the sons of Judah have done
that which is evil in My sight," declares
the LORD, "they have [a]set their detestable things in the house which is called
by My name, to defile it.
31"And they have [a]built the high
places of Topheth, which is in the valley
of the son of Hinnom, to [b]burn their
sons and their daughters in the fire,
which I [c]did not command, and it did
not come into My [1]mind.
32"[a]Therefore, behold, days are coming," declares the LORD, "when it will no
more be called Topheth, or the valley of
the son of Hinnom, but the valley of the
Slaughter; for they will [b]bury in Topheth
[1]because there is no *other* place.
33"And the [a]dead bodies of this people will be food for the birds of the sky,
and for the beasts of the earth; and no
one will frighten *them away.*
34"Then I will make to [a]cease from the
cities of Judah and from the streets of
Jerusalem the voice of joy and the voice
of gladness, the voice of the bridegroom
and the voice of the bride; for the [b]land
will become a ruin.

The Sin and Treachery of Judah

8 "AT that time," declares the LORD,
"they will [a]bring out the bones of
the kings of Judah, and the bones of its
princes, and the bones of the priests, and
the bones of the prophets, and the bones
of the inhabitants of Jerusalem from
their graves.
2"And they will spread them out to
the sun, the moon, and to all the [a]host of
heaven, which they have loved, and
which they have served, and which they
have gone after, and which they have
sought, and which they have worshiped.
They will not be gathered [b]or buried;
[c]they will be as dung on the face of the
ground.
3"And [a]death will be chosen rather
than life by all the remnant that remains
of this evil family, that remains in all the
[b]places to which I have driven them,"
declares the LORD of hosts.
4"And you shall say to them, 'Thus
says the LORD,
"Do *men* [a]fall and not get up again?
Does one turn away and not [1]re-
pent?
5"Why then has this people, Jerusalem,
[a]Turned away in continual apostasy?
They [b]hold fast to deceit,
They [c]refuse to return.

28 [1]Lit., *faithfulness* [a]Jer. 6:17; 11:10 [b]Is. 59:14, 15; Jer. 9:5
29 [1]Lit., *your crown* [a]Job 1:20; Is. 15:2; 22:12; Jer. 16:6; Mic. 1:16 [b]Jer. 3:21; 9:17, 18 [c]Jer. 6:30; 14:19
30 [a]2 Kin. 21:3f.; 2 Chr. 33:3-5, 7; Jer. 32:34, 35; Ezek. 7:20; Dan. 9:27; 11:31
31 [1]Lit., *heart* [a]2 Kin. 23:10; Jer. 19:5; 32:35 [b]Lev. 18:21; 2 Kin. 17:17; Ps. 106:38 [c]Deut. 17:3
32 [1]Or, *until there is no place left* [a]Jer. 19:6, 11 [b]2 Kin. 23:10
33 [a]Deut. 28:26; Ps. 79:2; Jer. 12:9; 19:7
34 [a]Is. 24:7, 8; Jer. 16:9; 25:10; Ezek. 26:13; Hos. 2:11; Rev. 18:23 [b]Lev. 26:33; Is. 1:7; Jer. 4:27

1 [a]Ezek. 6:5
2 [a]2 Kin. 23:5; Jer. 19:13; Zeph. 1:5; Acts 7:42 [b]Jer. 22:19; 36:30 [c]2 Kin. 9:37; Ps. 83:10; Jer. 9:22
3 [a]Job 3:21, 22; 7:15, 16; Jon. 4:3; Rev. 9:6 [b]Deut. 30:1, 4; Jer. 23:3, 8; 29:14
4 [1]Lit., *turn back* [a]Prov. 24:16; Amos 5:2; Mic. 7:8
5 [a]Jer. 5:6; 7:24 [b]Jer. 5:27; 9:6 [c]Jer. 5:3
6 [a]Ps. 14:2; Mal. 3:16 [b]Ezek. 22:30; Mic. 7:2; Rev. 9:20 [c]Job 39:21-25
7 [1]Lit., *coming* [a]Prov. 6:6-8; Is. 1:3 [b]Song 2:12 [c]Jer. 5:4
8 [a]Job 5:12, 13; Jer. 4:22; Rom. 1:22
9 [a]Is. 19:11; Jer. 6:15; 1 Cor. 1:27 [b]Jer. 6:19
10 [1]Lit., *possessing ones* [a]Deut. 28:30; Jer. 6:12, 13; 38:22f. [b]Is. 56:11; 57:17; Jer. 6:13
11 [a]Jer. 6:14; 14:13, 14; Lam. 2:14; Ezek. 13:10
12 [a]Ps. 52:1, 7; Is. 3:9; Jer. 3:3; 6:15; Zeph. 3:5 [b]Is. 9:14; Jer. 6:21; Hos. 4:5 [c]Deut. 32:35; Jer. 10:15
13 [a]Jer. 14:12; Ezek. 22:20, 21 [b]Jer. 5:17; 7:20; Joel 1:7 [c]Matt. 21:19; Luke 13:6
14 [a]Jer. 4:5 [b]2 Sam. 20:6; Jer. 35:11 [c]Deut. 29:18; Ps. 69:21; Jer. 9:15; 23:15; Lam. 3:19; Matt. 27:34 [d]Jer. 3:25; 14:20

6"I [a]have listened and heard,
They have spoken what is not
right;
[b]No man repented of his wickedness,
Saying, 'What have I done?'
Everyone turned to his course,
Like a [c]horse charging into the
battle.
7"Even the stork in the sky
[a]Knows her seasons;
And the [b]turtledove and the swift
and the thrush
Observe the time of their [1]migra-
tion;
But [c]My people do not know
The ordinance of the LORD.

8"[a]How can you say, 'We are wise,
And the law of the LORD is with
us'?
But behold, the lying pen of the
scribes
Has made *it* into a lie.
9"The wise men are [a]put to shame,
They are dismayed and caught;
Behold, they have [b]rejected the
word of the LORD,
And what kind of wisdom do they
have?
10"Therefore I will [a]give their wives to
others,
Their fields to [1]new owners;
Because from the least even to the
greatest
Everyone is [b]greedy for gain;
From the prophet even to the priest
Everyone practices deceit.
11"And they [a]heal the brokenness of
the daughter of My people su-
perficially,
Saying, 'Peace, peace,'
But there is no peace.
12"Were they [a]ashamed because of the
abomination they had done?
They certainly were not ashamed,
And they did not know how to
blush;
Therefore they shall [b]fall among
those who fall;
At the [c]time of their punishment
they shall be brought down,"
Declares the LORD.

13"I will [a]surely snatch them away,"
declares the LORD;
"There will be [b]no grapes on the
vine,
And [c]no figs on the fig tree,
And the leaf shall wither;
And what I have given them shall
pass away."'"
14 Why are we sitting still?
[a]Assemble yourselves, and let us
[b]go into the fortified cities,
And let us perish there,
Because the LORD our God has
doomed us
And given us [c]poisoned water to
drink,
For [d]we have sinned against the
LORD.

15 *We* [a]waited for peace, but no good *came;*
For a time of healing, but behold, terror!
16 From [a]Dan is heard the snorting of his horses;
At the sound of the neighing of his [b]stallions
The whole land quakes;
For they come and [c]devour the land and its fulness,
The city and its inhabitants.
17 "For behold, I am [a]sending serpents against you,
Adders, for which there is [b]no charm,
And they will bite you," declares the LORD.

18 [1]My [a]sorrow is beyond healing,
My [b]heart is faint *within me!*
19 Behold, listen! The cry of the daughter of my people from a [a]distant land:
"Is the LORD not in Zion? Is her King not within her?"
"Why have they [b]provoked Me with their graven images, with foreign [1c]idols?"
20 "Harvest is past, summer is ended,
And we are not saved."
21 For the [a]brokenness of the daughter of my people I am broken;
I [b]mourn, dismay has taken hold of me.
22 Is there no [a]balm in Gilead?
Is there no physician there?
[b]Why then has not the [1]health of the daughter of my people [2]been restored?

A Lament over Zion

9 [1a]OH, that my head were waters,
And my eyes a fountain of tears,
That I might weep day and night
For the slain of the [b]daughter of my people!
2 [1a]O that I had in the desert
A wayfarers' lodging place;
That I might leave my people,
And go from them!
For all of them are [b]adulterers,
An assembly of [c]treacherous men.
3 "And they [a]bend their tongue *like* their bow;
Lies and not truth prevail in the land;
For they [b]proceed from evil to evil,
And they [c]do not know Me," declares the LORD.
4 "Let everyone [a]be on guard against his neighbor,
And [b]do not trust any brother;
Because every [c]brother deals [1]craftily,
And every neighbor [d]goes about as a slanderer.
5 "And everyone [a]deceives his neighbor,
And does not speak the truth,
They have taught their tongue to speak lies;
They [b]weary themselves committing iniquity.
6 "Your [a]dwelling is in the midst of deceit;
Through deceit they [b]refuse to know Me," declares the LORD.

7 Therefore thus says the LORD of hosts,
"Behold, I will refine them and [a]assay them;
For [b]what *else* can I do, because of the daughter of My people?
8 "Their [a]tongue is a deadly arrow;
It speaks deceit;
With his mouth one [b]speaks peace to his neighbor,
But inwardly he [c]sets an ambush for him.
9 "[a]Shall I not punish them for these things?" declares the LORD.
"On a nation such as this
Shall I not avenge Myself?

10 "For the [a]mountains I will take up a weeping and wailing,
And for the pastures of the [b]wilderness a dirge,
Because they are [c]laid waste, so that no one passes through,
And the lowing of the cattle is not heard;
Both the [d]birds of the sky and the beasts have fled; they are gone.
11 "And I will make Jerusalem a [a]heap of ruins,
A haunt of [b]jackals;
And I will make the cities of Judah a [c]desolation, without inhabitant."
12 Who is the [a]wise man that may
understand this? And *who is* he to whom
[b]the mouth of the LORD has spoken, that
he may declare it? [c]Why is the land
ruined, laid waste like a desert, so that
no one passes through?
13 And the LORD said, "Because they
have [a]forsaken My law which I set
before them, and have not obeyed My
voice nor walked according to it,
14 but have [a]walked after the stubbornness of their heart and after the
[b]Baals, as their [c]fathers taught them,"
15 therefore thus says the LORD of
hosts, the God of Israel, "behold, [a]I will
feed them, this people, with wormwood
and give them [b]poisoned water to drink.
16 "And I will [a]scatter them among the
nations, whom neither they nor their
fathers have known; and I will send the
[b]sword after them until I have annihilated them."
17 Thus says the LORD of hosts,
"Consider and call for the [a]mourning women, that they may come;
And send for the [1b]wailing women, that they may come!
18 "And let them make haste, and take up a wailing for us,
That our [a]eyes may shed tears,
And our eyelids flow with water.

15 aJer. 8:11; 14:19
16 aJudg. 18:29; Jer. 4:15 bJudg. 5:22 cJer. 3:24; 10:25
17 aNum. 21:6; Deut. 32:24 bPs. 58:4, 5
18 1So Gr. and versions aIs. 22:4; Lam. 1:16, 17 bJer. 23:9; Lam. 5:17
19 1Lit., *vanities* aIs. 13:5; 39:3; Jer. 4:16; 9:16 bDeut. 32:21; Jer. 7:19 cPs. 31:6
21 aJer. 4:19; 9:1; 14:17 bJer. 14:2; Joel 2:6; Nah. 2:10
22 1Or, *healing* 2Lit., *gone up* aGen. 37:25; Jer. 46:11 bJer. 14:19; 30:13

1 1Ch. 8:23 in Heb. aIs. 22:4; Jer. 8:18; 13:17; Lam. 2:18 bJer. 6:26; 8:21, 22
2 1Ch. 9:1 in Heb. aPs. 55:6, 7; 120:5, 6 bJer. 5:7, 8; 23:10; Hos. 4:2 cJer. 5:11; 12:1, 6
3 aPs. 64:3; Is. 59:4; Jer. 9:8 bJer. 4:22 cJudg. 2:10; 1 Sam. 2:12; Jer. 4:22; 5:4, 5; Hos. 4:1; 1 Cor. 15:34
4 1I.e., like Jacob (a play on words) aPs. 12:2; Prov. 26:24, 25; Jer. 9:8; Mic. 7:5, 6 bJer. 12:6 cGen. 27:35 dPs. 15:3; Prov. 10:18; Jer. 6:28
5 aMic. 6:12 bJer. 12:13; 51:58, 64
6 aPs. 120:5, 6; Jer. 5:27; 8:5 bJob 21:14, 15; Prov. 1:24; Jer. 11:10; 13:10; John 3:19, 20
7 aIs. 1:25; Jer. 6:27; Mal. 3:3 bHos. 11:8
8 aJer. 9:3 bPs. 28:3 cJer. 5:26
9 aIs. 1:24; Jer. 5:9, 29
10 aJer. 4:24; 7:29 bJer. 4:26; Hos. 4:3 cJer. 12:4, 10; Ezek. 14:15; 29:11; 33:28 dJer. 4:25; 12:4; Hos. 4:3
11 aIs. 25:2; Jer. 51:37 bIs. 13:22; 34:13 cJer. 4:27; 26:9
12 aPs. 107:43; Is. 42:23; Hos. 14:9 bJer. 9:20; 23:16 cPs. 107:34; Jer. 23:10
13 a2 Chr. 7:19; Ps. 89:30; Jer. 5:19; 22:9
14 aJer. 7:24; 11:8; Rom. 1:21-24 bJer. 2:8, 23; 23:27 cGal. 1:14; 1 Pet. 1:18
15 aPs. 80:5 bDeut. 29:18; Jer. 8:14; 23:15; Lam. 3:15
16 aLev. 26:33; Deut. 28:64; Jer. 13:24 bJer. 44:27; Ezek. 5:2, 12
17 1Lit., *skilled* a2 Chr. 35:25; Eccl. 12:5 bAmos 5:16
18 aIs. 22:4; Jer. 9:1; 14:17

19 "For a voice of [a]wailing is heard
from Zion,
'[b]How are we ruined!
We are put to great shame,
For we have [c]left the land,
Because they have cast down our
dwellings.' "
20 Now hear the word of the LORD, O
you [a]women,
And let your ear receive the word
of His mouth;
Teach your daughters wailing,
And everyone her neighbor a dirge.
21 For [a]death has come up through
our windows;
It has entered our palaces
To cut off the [b]children from the
streets,
The young men from the town
squares.
22 Speak, "Thus declares the LORD,
'The corpses of men will fall [a]like
dung on the open field,
And like the sheaf after the reaper,
But no one will gather *them.*' "
23 Thus says the LORD, "[a]Let not a
wise man boast of his wisdom, and let
not the [b]mighty man boast of his might,
let not a [c]rich man boast of his riches;
24 but let him who boasts [a]boast of
this, that he understands and knows Me,
that I am the LORD who [b]exercises
lovingkindness, justice, and righteousness on earth; for I [c]delight in these
things," declares the LORD.
25 "Behold, the days are coming,"
declares the LORD, "that I will punish all
who are circumcised and yet [a]uncircum-
cised—
26 Egypt, and Judah, and Edom, and
the sons of Ammon, and Moab, and [a]all
those inhabiting the desert who clip the
hair on their temples; for all the nations
are uncircumcised, and all the house of
Israel are [b]uncircumcised of heart."

A Satire on Idolatry

10 HEAR the word which the LORD
speaks to you, O house of Israel.
2 Thus says the LORD,
"[a]Do not learn the way of the nations,
And do not be terrified by the signs
of the heavens
Although the nations are terrified
by them;
3 For the customs of the peoples are
[1a]delusion;
Because [b]it is wood cut from the
forest,
The work of the hands of a craftsman with a cutting tool.
4 "They [a]decorate *it* with silver and
with gold;
They [b]fasten it with nails and with
hammers
So that it will not totter.
5 "Like a scarecrow in a cucumber
field are they,
And they [a]cannot speak;
They must be [b]carried,
Because they cannot walk!
Do not fear them,
For they [c]can do no harm,
Nor can they do any good."

6 [a]There is none like Thee, O LORD;
Thou art [b]great, and great is Thy
name in might.
7 [a]Who would not fear Thee, O
[b]King of the nations?
Indeed it is Thy due!
For among all the [c]wise men of the
nations,
And in all their kingdoms,
There is none like Thee.
8 But they are altogether [a]stupid and
foolish
In their discipline of [1]delusion—
[2]their idol is wood!
9 Beaten [a]silver is brought from
[b]Tarshish,
And [c]gold from Uphaz,
The work of a craftsman and of the
hands of a goldsmith;
Violet and purple are their clothing;
They are all the [d]work of skilled
men.
10 But the LORD is the [a]true God;
He is the [b]living God and the
[c]everlasting King.
At His wrath the [d]earth quakes,
And the nations cannot [e]endure
His indignation.
11 [1]Thus you shall say to them, "The
[a]gods that did not make the heavens and
the earth shall [b]perish from the earth
and from under the [2]heavens."
12 *It is* [a]He who made the earth by
His power,
Who [b]established the world by His
wisdom;
And by His understanding He has
[c]stretched out the heavens.
13 When He utters His [a]voice, *there is*
a tumult of waters in the heav-
ens,
And He causes the [b]clouds to ascend from the end of the earth;
He makes lightning for the rain,
And brings out the [c]wind from His
storehouses.
14 Every man is [a]stupid, devoid of
knowledge;
Every goldsmith is put to shame by
his [1]idols;
For his molten images are deceitful,
And there is no breath in them.
15 They are [a]worthless, a work of
mockery;
In the [b]time of their punishment
they will perish.
16 The [a]portion of Jacob is not like
these;
For the [1b]Maker of all is He,
And [c]Israel is the tribe of His
inheritance;
The [d]LORD of hosts is His name.

17 [a]Pick up your bundle from the
ground,
You who dwell under siege!

19 [a]Jer. 7:29; Ezek. 7:16-18 [b]Deut. 28:29; Jer. 4:13 [c]Jer. 7:15; 15:1
20 [a]Is. 32:9
21 [a]2 Chr. 36:17; Jer. 15:7; 18:21; Ezek. 9:5, 6; Amos 6:9, 10 [b]Jer. 6:11
22 [a]Ps. 83:10; Is. 5:25; Jer. 8:2; 16:4; 25:33
23 [a]Eccl. 9:11; Is. 47:10; Ezek. 28:3-7 [b]1 Kin. 20:10, 11; Is. 10:8-12 [c]Job 31:24, 25; Ps. 49:6-9
24 [a]Ps. 20:7; 44:8; Is. 41:16; Jer. 4:2; 1 Cor. 1:31; 2 Cor. 10:17; Gal. 6:14 [b]Ex. 34:6, 7; Ps. 36:5, 7; 51:1 [c]Is. 61:8; Mic. 7:18
25 [a]Jer. 4:4; Rom. 2:28, 29
26 [a]Jer. 25:23 [b]Lev. 26:41; Jer. 4:4; 6:10; Ezek. 44:7; Rom. 2:28
2 [a]Lev. 18:3; 20:23; Deut. 12:30
3 [1]Lit., *vanity* [a]Jer. 14:22 [b]Is. 44:9-20
4 [a]Is. 40:19 [b]Is. 40:20; 41:7
5 [a]Ps. 115:5; Is. 46:7; Jer. 10:14; 1 Cor. 12:2 [b]Ps. 115:7; Is. 46:1, 7 [c]Is. 41:23, 24
6 [a]Ex. 15:11; Deut. 33:26; Ps. 86:8, 10; Jer. 10:16 [b]Ps. 48:1; 96:4; Is. 12:6; Jer. 32:18
7 [a]Rev. 15:4 [b]Ps. 22:28 [c]Dan. 2:27, 28; 1 Cor. 1:19, 20
8 [1]Lit., *vanities,* or *idols* [2]Lit., *it is* [a]Jer. 4:22; 5:4; 10:8
9 [a]Is. 40:19 [b]Ps. 72:10; Is. 23:6 [c]Dan. 10:5 [d]Ps. 115:4
10 [a]Is. 65:16 [b]Jer. 4:2 [c]Ps. 10:16; 29:10 [d]Jer. 4:24; 50:46 [e]Ps. 76:7
11 [1]This verse is in Aram. [2]Or, *these heavens* [a]Ps. 96:5 [b]Is. 2:18; Zeph. 2:11
12 [a]Gen. 1:1, 6; Job 38:4-7; Ps. 136:5; 148:4, 5; Jer. 51:15, 19 [b]Ps. 78:69; Is. 45:18 [c]Job 9:8; Is. 40:22
13 [a]Ps. 29:3-9 [b]Job 36:27-29 [c]Ps. 135:7
14 [1]Or, *graven image* [a]Jer. 10:8; 51:17, 18
15 [a]Is. 41:24; Jer. 8:19; 14:22 [b]Jer. 8:12; 51:18
16 [1]Lit., *Fashioner* [a]Ps. 16:5; 73:26; 119:57; Jer. 51:19; Lam. 3:24 [b]Is. 45:7; Jer. 10:12 [c]Deut. 32:9; Ps. 74:2 [d]Jer. 31:35; 32:18
17 [a]Ezek. 12:3-12

18 For thus says the LORD,
"Behold, I am [a]slinging out the inhabitants of the land
At this time,
And will cause them distress,
That they may [1]be found."

19 [a]Woe is me, because of my [1]injury!
My [b]wound is incurable.
But I said, "Truly this is a sickness,
And I [c]must bear it."
20 My [a]tent is destroyed,
And all my ropes are broken;
My [b]sons have gone from me and are no more.
There is [c]no one to stretch out my tent again
Or to set up my curtains.
21 For the shepherds have become stupid
And [a]have not sought the LORD;
Therefore they have not prospered,
And [b]all their flock is scattered.
22 The sound of a [a]report! Behold, it comes—
A great commotion [b]out of the land of the north—
To [c]make the cities of Judah
A desolation, a haunt of jackals.

23 I know, O LORD, that [a]a man's way is not in himself;
[b]Nor is it in a man who walks to direct his steps.
24 [a]Correct me, O LORD, but with justice;
Not with Thine anger, lest Thou [1]bring me to nothing.
25 [a]Pour out Thy wrath on the nations that [b]do not know Thee,
And on the families that [c]do not call Thy name;
For they have devoured Jacob;
They have [d]devoured him and consumed him,
And have laid waste his [1]habitation.

The Broken Covenant

11 THE word which came to Jeremiah from the LORD, saying,

2 "[a]Hear the words of this [b]covenant, and speak to the men of Judah and to the inhabitants of Jerusalem;

3 and say to them, 'Thus says the LORD, the God of Israel, "[a]Cursed is the man who does not heed the words of this covenant

4 which I commanded your forefathers in the [a]day that I brought them out of the land of Egypt, from the [b]iron furnace, saying, '[c]Listen to My voice, and [1]do according to all which I command you; so you shall be [d]My people, and I will be your God,'

5 in order to confirm the [a]oath which I swore to your forefathers, to give them a land flowing with milk and honey, as *it is* this day." ' " Then I answered and said, "[b]Amen, O LORD."

6 And the LORD said to me, "[a]Proclaim all these words in the cities of Judah and in the streets of Jerusalem, saying, '[b]Hear the words of this covenant and [c]do them.

7 'For I solemnly [a]warned your fathers in the [b]day that I brought them up from the land of Egypt, even to this day, [1c]warning persistently, saying, "[d]Listen to My voice."

8 'Yet they [a]did not obey or incline their ear, but walked, each one, in the stubbornness of his evil heart; therefore I brought on them all the [b]words of this covenant, which I commanded *them* to do, but they did not.' "

9 Then the LORD said to me, "A [a]conspiracy has been found among the men of Judah and among the inhabitants of Jerusalem.

10 "They have [a]turned back to the iniquities of their [1]ancestors who [b]refused to hear My words, and they [c]have gone after other gods to serve them; the house of Israel and the house of Judah have [d]broken My covenant which I made with their fathers."

11 Therefore thus says the LORD, "Behold I am [a]bringing disaster on them which they will [b]not be able to escape; though they will [c]cry to Me, yet I will not listen to them.

12 "Then the cities of Judah and the inhabitants of Jerusalem will [a]go and cry to the gods to whom they burn incense, but they surely will not save them in the time of their disaster.

13 "For your gods are [1a]as many as your cities, O Judah; and [1]as many as the streets of Jerusalem are the altars you have set up to the [b]shameful thing, altars to [c]burn incense to Baal.

14 "Therefore [a]do not pray for this people, nor lift up a cry or prayer for them; for I will [b]not listen when they call to Me because of their disaster.

15 "What right has My [a]beloved in My house
When [b]she has done many vile deeds?
Can the sacrificial flesh take away from you your disaster,
[1]So *that* you can rejoice?"
16 The LORD called your name,
"A [a]green olive tree, beautiful in fruit and form";
With the [b]noise of a great tumult
He has [c]kindled fire on it,
And its branches are worthless.

17 And the LORD of hosts, who [a]planted you, has [b]pronounced evil against you because of the evil of the house of Israel and of the house of Judah, which they have [1]done to provoke Me by [2c]offering up sacrifices to Baal.

Plots against Jeremiah

18 Moreover, the LORD [a]made it known to me and I knew it;
Then Thou didst show me their deeds.

18 [1]Lit., *find* [a]1 Sam. 25:29
19 [1]Lit., *breaking* [a]Jer. 4:31 [b]Jer. 14:17 [c]Mic. 7:9
20 [a]Jer. 4:20; Lam. 2:4 [b]Jer. 31:15; Lam. 1:5 [c]Is. 51:18
21 [a]Jer. 2:8 [b]Jer. 23:2
22 [a]Jer. 4:15 [b]Jer. 1:14; 25:9 [c]Jer. 9:11; 49:33
23 [a]Prov. 16:1; 20:24 [b]Is. 26:7
24 [1]Lit., *diminish me* [a]Ps. 6:1; 38:1
25 [1]Or, *pasture* [a]Ps. 79:6, 7; Zeph. 3:8 [b]Job 18:21; 1 Thess. 4:5; 2 Thess. 1:8 [c]Zeph. 1:6 [d]Jer. 8:16; 50:7, 17

2 [a]Jer. 11:6 [b]Ex. 19:5
3 [a]Deut. 27:26; Jer. 17:5; Gal. 3:10
4 [1]Lit., *do them* [a]Ex. 24:3-8; Jer. 31:32 [b]Deut. 4:20; 1 Kin. 8:51 [c]Lev. 26:3; Deut. 11:27; Jer. 7:23; 26:13 [d]Jer. 24:7; Zech. 8:8
5 [a]Ex. 13:5; Deut. 7:12; Ps. 105:9; Jer. 32:22 [b]Jer. 28:6
6 [a]Jer. 3:12; 7:2 [b]Jer. 11:2 [c]John 13:17; Rom. 2:13; James 1:22
7 [1]Lit., *rising early and warning* [a]1 Sam. 8:9 [b]Jer. 11:4 [c]Ex. 15:26; 2 Chr. 36:15; Jer. 7:25 [d]Jer. 11:7
8 [a]Jer. 7:24; 9:14; 35:15; Ezek. 20:8 [b]Lev. 26:14-43
9 [a]Ezek. 22:25; Hos. 6:9
10 [1]Lit., *former fathers* [a]1 Sam. 15:11; Jer. 3:10, 11; Ezek. 20:18 [b]Deut. 9:7; Ps. 78:8-10; Jer. 13:10 [c]Judg. 2:11-13 [d]Jer. 3:6-11; Ezek. 16:59
11 [a]2 Kin. 22:16; Jer. 6:19; 11:17 [b]Is. 24:17; Jer. 25:35 [c]Ps. 18:41; Prov. 1:28; Is. 1:15; Jer. 11:14; 14:12; Ezek. 8:18; Mic. 3:4; Zech. 7:13
12 [a]Deut. 32:37; Jer. 44:17
13 [1]Lit., *the number of* [a]2 Kin. 23:13; Jer. 2:28 [b]Jer. 3:24 [c]Jer. 7:9
14 [a]Ex. 32:10; Jer. 7:16; 14:11; 1 John 5:16 [b]Ps. 66:18; Jer. 11:11; Hos. 5:6
15 [1]Lit., *Then* [a]Jer. 13:27 [b]Ezek. 16:25
16 [a]Ps. 52:8; Rom. 11:17 [b]Ps. 83:2 [c]Ps. 80:16; Is. 27:11; Jer. 21:14
17 [1]Or, *done for themselves* [2]Or, *burning incense* [a]Is. 5:2; Jer. 2:21; 12:2 [b]Jer. 1:14; 16:10; 19:15 [c]Jer. 7:9; 11:13; 32:29

18 [a]1 Sam. 23:11, 12; 2 Kin. 6:9, 10; Ezek. 8:6

19 But I was like a gentle [a]lamb led to
the slaughter;
And I did not know that they had
[b]devised plots against me, *saying*,
"Let us destroy the tree with its
[1]fruit,
And [c]let us cut him off from the
[d]land of the living,
That his [e]name be remembered no
more."
20 But, O LORD of hosts, who [a]judges
righteously,
Who [b]tries the [1]feelings and the
heart,
Let me see Thy vengeance on them,
For to Thee have I [2]committed my
cause.
21 Therefore thus says the LORD concerning the men of [a]Anathoth, who
[b]seek your life, saying, "[c]Do not prophesy in the name of the LORD, that you
might not [d]die at our hand";
22 therefore, thus says the LORD of
hosts, "Behold, I am about to [a]punish
them! The [b]young men will die by the
sword, their sons and daughters will die
by famine;
23 and a remnant [a]will not be left to
them, for I will [b]bring disaster on the
men of Anathoth—[c]the year of their
punishment."

Jeremiah's Prayer

12 [a]RIGHTEOUS art Thou, O
LORD, that I would plead *my*
case with Thee;
Indeed I would [b]discuss matters of
justice with Thee:
Why has the [c]way of the wicked
prospered?
Why are all those who [d]deal in
treachery at ease?
2 Thou hast [a]planted them, they have
also taken root;
They grow, they have even produced fruit.
Thou art [b]near [1]to their lips
But far from their [2]mind.
3 But Thou [a]knowest me, O LORD;
Thou seest me;
And Thou dost [b]examine my
heart's *attitude* toward Thee.
Drag them off like sheep for the
slaughter
And [1]set them apart for a [c]day of
carnage!
4 How long is the [a]land to mourn
And the [b]vegetation of the countryside to wither?
For the [c]wickedness of those who
dwell in it,
[d]Animals and birds have been
snatched away,
Because *men* have said, "He will
not see our latter [e]ending."

5 "If you have run with footmen and
they have tired you out,
Then how can you compete with
horses?
If you fall down in a land of peace,
How will you do in the [1a]thicket of
the Jordan?
6 "For even your [a]brothers and the
household of your father,
Even they have dealt treacherously
with you,
Even they have cried aloud after
you.
Do not believe them, although they
may say [b]nice things to you."

God's Answer

7 "I have [a]forsaken My house,
I have abandoned My inheritance;
I have given the [b]beloved of My
soul
Into the hand of her enemies.
8 "My inheritance has become to Me
Like a lion in the forest;
She has [1a]roared against Me;
Therefore I have come to [b]hate her.
9 "Is My inheritance like a speckled
bird of prey to Me?
Are the [a]birds of prey against her
on every side?
Go, gather all the [b]beasts of the
field,
Bring them to devour!
10 "Many [a]shepherds have ruined My
[b]vineyard,
They have [c]trampled down My
field;
They have made My [d]pleasant field
A desolate wilderness.
11 "[1]It has been made a desolation,
Desolate, it [a]mourns [2]before Me;
The [b]whole land has been made
desolate,
Because no man [c]lays it to heart.
12 "On all the [1a]bare heights in the
wilderness
Destroyers have come,
For a [b]sword of the LORD is devouring
From one end of the land even to
the [2]other;
There is [c]no peace for [3]anyone.
13 "They have [a]sown wheat and have
reaped thorns,
They have [b]strained themselves [1]to
no profit.
But be ashamed of your [2c]harvest
Because of the [d]fierce anger of the
LORD."
14 Thus says the LORD concerning all
My [a]wicked neighbors who [b]strike at the
inheritance with which I have endowed
My people Israel, "Behold I am about to
uproot them from their land and will
[c]uproot the house of Judah from among
them.
15 "And it will come about that after I
have uprooted them, I will [a]again have
compassion on them; and I will [b]bring
them back, each one to his inheritance
and each one to his land.
16 "Then it will come about that if they
will really [a]learn the ways of My people,
to [b]swear by My name, 'As the LORD
lives,' even as they taught My people to
[c]swear by Baal, then they will be [d]built
up in the midst of My people.

19 [1]Lit., *bread* [a]Is. 53:7 [b]Jer. 18:18; 20:10 [c]Ps. 83:4; Is. 53:8 [d]Job 28:13; Ps. 52:5 [e]Ps. 109:13
20 [1]Lit., *kidneys* [2]Lit., *revealed* [a]Gen. 18:25; Ps. 7:8; Jer. 20:12 [b]1 Sam. 16:7; Ps. 7:9; Jer. 17:10
21 [a]Jer. 1:1 [b]Jer. 12:5, 6; 20:10 [c]Amos 2:12 [d]Jer. 26:8; 38:4
22 [a]Jer. 21:14 [b]2 Chr. 36:17; Jer. 18:21
23 [a]Jer. 6:9 [b]Jer. 23:12; Hos. 9:7; Mic. 7:4 [c]Luke 19:44

1 [a]Ezra 9:15; Ps. 51:4; 129:4; Jer. 11:20 [b]Job 13:3 [c]Job 12:6; Jer. 5:27, 28; Hab. 1:4; Mal. 3:15 [d]Jer. 3:7, 20; 5:11
2 [1]Lit., *in their mouth* [2]Lit., *kidneys* [a]Jer. 11:17; 45:4; Ezek. 17:5-10 [b]Is. 29:13; Jer. 3:10; Ezek. 33:31; Titus 1:16
3 [1]Lit., *sanctify them* [a]Ps. 139:1-4 [b]Ps. 7:9; 11:5; Jer. 11:20 [c]Jer. 17:18; 50:27; James 5:5
4 [a]Jer. 4:28; 9:10; 23:10 [b]Joel 1:10-17 [c]Ps. 107:34 [d]Jer. 4:25; 7:20; 9:10; Hos. 4:3; Hab. 3:17 [e]Jer. 5:31; Ezek. 7:2
5 [1]Lit., *pride* [a]Jer. 49:19; 50:44
6 [a]Gen. 37:4-11; Job 6:15; Ps. 69:8; Jer. 9:4, 5 [b]Ps. 12:2; Prov. 26:25
7 [a]Is. 2:6; Jer. 7:29; 23:39 [b]Jer. 11:15; Hos. 11:1-8
8 [1]Lit., *raised her voice* [a]Is. 59:13 [b]Hos. 9:15; Amos 6:8
9 [a]2 Kin. 24:2; Ezek. 23:22-25 [b]Is. 56:9; Jer. 7:33; 15:3; 34:20
10 [a]Jer. 6:3; 23:1 [b]Ps. 80:8-16; Is. 5:1-7 [c]Is. 63:18 [d]Jer. 3:19
11 [1]Lit., *One has made it* [2]Or, *upon* [a]Jer. 12:4; 14:2; 23:10 [b]Jer. 4:20, 27; 25:11 [c]Is. 42:25
12 [1]Or, *caravan trails* [2]Lit., *other end of the land* [3]Lit., *all flesh* [a]Jer. 3:2, 21 [b]Is. 34:6; Jer. 47:6; Amos 9:4 [c]Jer. 16:5; 30:5
13 [1]Lit., *they do not profit* [2]Lit., *products* [a]Lev. 26:16; Deut. 28:38; Mic. 6:15; Hag. 1:6 [b]Is. 55:2; Jer. 9:5 [c]Jer. 17:10 [d]Jer. 4:26; 25:37, 38
14 [a]Jer. 49:1, 7; Zeph. 2:8-10 [b]Jer. 2:3; 50:11, 12; Zech. 2:8 [c]Deut. 30:3; Ps. 106:47; Is. 11:11-16
15 [a]Jer. 48:47; 49:6, 39 [b]Amos 9:14

16 [a]Is. 42:6; 49:6 [b]Jer. 4:2; Zeph. 1:5 [c]Josh. 23:7; Jer. 5:7 [d]Jer. 3:17; 4:2; 16:19

17"But if they will not listen, then I
will [a]uproot that nation, uproot and
destroy it," declares the LORD.

The Ruined Waistband

13 THUS the LORD said to me, "Go
and [a]buy yourself a linen waistband, and put it around your waist, but
do not put it in water."
2 So I bought the waistband in accordance with the [a]word of the LORD
and put it around my waist.
3 Then the word of the LORD came
to me a second time, saying,
4"Take the waistband that you have
bought, which is around your waist, and
arise, go to [1]the [a]Euphrates and hide it
there in a crevice of the rock."
5 So I went and hid it by the Euphrates, [a]as the LORD had commanded me.
6 And it came about after many days
that the LORD said to me, "Arise, go to
the Euphrates and take from there the
waistband which I commanded you to
hide there."
7 Then I went to the Euphrates and
dug, and I took the waistband from the
place where I had hidden it; and lo, the
waistband was ruined, it was totally
worthless.
8 Then the word of the LORD came
to me, saying,
9"Thus says the LORD, 'Just so will I
destroy the [a]pride of Judah and the great
pride of Jerusalem.
10 'This wicked people, who [a]refuse to
listen to My words, who [b]walk in the
stubbornness of their hearts and have
gone after other gods to serve them and
to bow down to them, let them be just
like this waistband, which is totally
worthless.
11 'For as the waistband clings to the
waist of a man, so I made the whole
household of Israel and the whole household of Judah [a]cling to Me,' declares the
LORD, 'that they might be for Me a
people, for [1b]renown, for [c]praise, and for
glory; but they [d]did not listen.'

Captivity Threatened

12"Therefore you are to speak this
word to them, 'Thus says the LORD, the
God of Israel, "Every jug is to be filled
with wine."' And when they say to you,
'Do we not very well know that every jug
is to be filled with wine?'
13 then say to them, 'Thus says the
LORD, "Behold I am about to fill all the
inhabitants of this land—the kings that
sit for David on his throne, the priests,
the prophets and all the inhabitants of
Jerusalem—with [a]drunkenness!
14"And I will [a]dash them against each
other, both the [b]fathers and the sons
together," declares the LORD. "I will
[c]not show pity nor be sorry nor have
compassion that I should not destroy
them."'"
15 Listen and give heed, do not be
[a]haughty,
For the LORD has spoken.

16 [a]Give glory to the LORD your God,
Before He brings [b]darkness
And before your [c]feet stumble
On the dusky mountains,
And while you are hoping for light
He makes it into [d]deep darkness,
And turns *it* into gloom.
17 But [a]if you will not listen to it,
My soul will [b]sob in secret for *such*
pride;
And my eyes will bitterly weep
And flow down with tears,
Because the [c]flock of the LORD has
been taken captive.
18 Say to the [a]king and the queen
mother,
"[b]Take a lowly seat,
For your beautiful [c]crown
Has come down from your head."
19 The [a]cities of the Negev have been
locked up,
And there is no one to open *them*;
All [b]Judah has been carried into
exile,
Wholly carried into exile.

20"Lift up your eyes and see
Those coming [a]from the north.
Where is the [b]flock that was given
you,
Your beautiful sheep?
21"What will you say when He appoints over you—
And you yourself had taught
them—
Former [1a]companions to be head
over you?
Will not [b]pangs take hold of you,
Like a woman in childbirth?
22"And if you [a]say in your heart,
'[b]Why have these things happened
to me?'
Because of the [c]magnitude of your
iniquity
[d]Your skirts have been removed,
And your heels have [1]been exposed.
23"[a]Can the Ethiopian change his skin
Or the leopard his spots?
Then you also can [b]do good
Who are accustomed to do evil.
24"Therefore I will [a]scatter them like
drifting straw
To the desert [b]wind.
25"This is your [a]lot, the portion measured to you
From Me," declares the LORD,
"Because you have [b]forgotten Me
And trusted in falsehood.
26"So I Myself have also [a]stripped
your skirts off over your face,
That your shame may be seen.
27"As for your [a]adulteries and your
lustful neighings,
The [b]lewdness of your prostitution
On the [c]hills in the field,
I have seen your abominations.
Woe to you, O Jerusalem!
[d]How long will you remain unclean?"

17 aPs. 2:8-12; Is. 60:12

1 aJer. 13:11

2 aIs. 20:2; Ezek. 2:8

4 1Or, *Parah,* cf. Josh. 18:23; so through v. 7 aJer. 51:63

5 aEx. 39:42, 43; 40:16

9 aLev. 26:19; Is. 2:10-17; 23:9; Jer. 13:15-17; Zeph. 3:11

10 aNum. 14:11; 2 Chr. 36:15, 16; Jer. 11:10 bJer. 9:14; 11:8; 16:12

11 1Lit., *a name* aEx. 19:5, 6; Deut. 32:10, 11 bJer. 32:20 cIs. 43:21; Jer. 33:9 dPs. 81:11; Jer. 7:13, 24, 26

13 aPs. 60:3; 75:8; Is. 51:17; 63:6; Jer. 25:27; 51:7, 57

14 aIs. 9:20, 21; Jer. 19:9-11 bJer. 6:21; Ezek. 5:10 cDeut. 29:20; Is. 27:11; Jer. 16:5; 21:7

15 aProv. 16:5; Is. 28:14-22

16 aJosh. 7:19; Ps. 96:8 bIs. 5:30; 8:22; 59:9; Amos 5:18; 8:9 cProv. 4:19; Jer. 23:12 dPs. 44:19; 107:10, 14; Jer. 2:6

17 aMal. 2:2 bPs. 119:136; Jer. 9:1; 14:17; Luke 19:41, 42 cPs. 80:1; Jer. 23:1, 2

18 a2 Kin. 24:12, 15; Jer. 22:26 b2 Chr. 33:12, 19 cEx. 39:28; Is. 3:20; Ezek. 24:17, 23; 44:18

19 aJer. 32:44 bJer. 20:4; 52:27-30

20 aJer. 1:15; 6:22; Hab. 1:6 bJer. 13:17; 23:2

21 1Or, *chieftains* aJer. 2:25; 38:22 bIs. 13:8; Jer. 4:31

22 1Or, *suffered violence* aDeut. 7:17 bJer. 5:19; 16:10 cJer. 2:17-19; 9:2-9 dIs. 47:2; Ezek. 16:37; Nah. 3:5

23 aProv. 27:22; Is. 1:5 bJer. 4:22; 9:5

24 aLev. 26:33; Jer. 9:16; Ezek. 5:2, 12 bJer. 4:11; 18:17

25 aJob 20:29; Ps. 11:6; Matt. 24:51 bPs. 9:17; Jer. 2:32; 3:21

26 aLam. 1:8; Ezek. 23:29; Hos. 2:10

27 aJer. 5:7, 8 bJer. 11:15 cIs. 65:7; Jer. 2:20; Ezek. 6:13 dProv. 1:22; Hos. 8:5

Drought and a Prayer for Mercy

14 THAT which came as the word of the LORD to Jeremiah in regard to the [a]drought:

2 "Judah mourns,
And [a]her gates languish
They sit on the ground [b]in mourning,
And the [c]cry of Jerusalem has ascended.
3 "And their nobles have [a]sent their [1]servants for water;
They have come to the [b]cisterns and found no water.
They have returned with their vessels empty;
They have been [c]put to shame and humiliated,
And they [d]cover their heads.
4 "Because the [a]ground is [1]cracked,
For there has been [b]no rain on the land;
The [c]farmers have been put to shame,
They have covered their heads.
5 "For even the doe in the field has given birth only to abandon *her young,*
Because there is [a]no grass.
6 "And the [a]wild donkeys stand on the bare heights;
They pant for air like jackals,
Their eyes fail
For there is [b]no vegetation.
7 "Although our [a]iniquities testify against us,
O LORD, act [b]for Thy name's sake!
Truly our [c]apostasies have been many,
We have [d]sinned against Thee.
8 "Thou [a]Hope of Israel,
Its [b]Savior in [c]time of distress,
Why art Thou like a stranger in the land
Or like a traveler who has pitched his *tent* for the night?
9 "Why art Thou like a man dismayed,
Like a mighty man who [a]cannot save?
Yet [b]Thou art in our midst, O LORD,
And we are [c]called by Thy name;
Do not forsake us!"

10 Thus says the LORD to this people, "Even so they have [a]loved to wander; they have not [b]kept their feet in check. Therefore the LORD does [c]not accept them; now He will [d]remember their iniquity and call their sins to account."

11 So the LORD said to me, "[a]Do not pray for the welfare of this people.

12 "When they fast, I am [a]not going to listen to their cry; and when they offer [b]burnt offering and grain offering, I am not going to accept them. Rather I am going to [c]make an end of them by the [d]sword, famine and pestilence."

False Prophets

13 But, "Ah, Lord [1]GOD!" I said, "Look, the prophets are telling them, 'You [a]will not see the sword nor will you have famine, but I will give you [2]lasting [b]peace in this place.' "

14 Then the LORD said to me, "The [a]prophets are prophesying falsehood in My name. [b]I have neither sent them nor commanded them nor spoken to them; they are prophesying to you a [c]false vision, divination, futility and the deception of their own [1]minds.

15 "Therefore thus says the LORD concerning the prophets who are prophesying in My name, although it was not I who sent them—yet they keep saying, 'There shall be no sword or famine in this land'—[a]by sword and famine those prophets shall [1]meet their end!

16 "The people also to whom they are prophesying will be [a]thrown out into the streets of Jerusalem because of the famine and the sword; and there will be no one to [b]bury them—*neither* them, *nor* their wives, nor their sons, nor their daughters—for I shall [c]pour out their *own* wickedness on them.

17 "And you will say this word to them,
'[a]Let my eyes flow down with tears night and day,
And let them not cease;
For the virgin [b]daughter of my people has been crushed with a mighty blow,
With a sorely [c]infected wound.
18 'If I [a]go out to the country,
Behold, those [1]slain with the sword!
Or if I enter the city,
Behold, diseases of famine!
For [b]both prophet and priest
Have [2]gone roving about in the land that they do not know.' "

19 Hast Thou completely [a]rejected Judah?
Or hast [1]Thou loathed Zion?
Why hast Thou stricken us so that we [b]are beyond healing?
We [c]waited for peace, but nothing good *came;*
And for a time of healing, but behold, terror!
20 We [a]know our wickedness, O LORD,
The iniquity of our fathers, for [b]we have sinned against Thee.
21 Do not despise *us,* [a]for Thine own name's sake;
Do not disgrace the [b]throne of Thy glory;
Remember *and* do not annul Thy covenant with us.
22 Are there any among the [1][a]idols of the nations who [b]give rain?
Or can the heavens grant showers?
Is it not Thou, O LORD our God?
Therefore we [2][c]hope in Thee,
For Thou art the one who hast done all these things.

1 [a]Jer. 17:8
2 [a]Is. 3:26 [b]Jer. 8:21 [c]1 Sam. 5:12; Jer. 11:11; 46:12; Zech. 7:13
3 [1]Lit., *little ones* [a]1 Kin. 18:5 [b]2 Kin. 18:31; Jer. 2:13 [c]Job 6:20; Ps. 40:14 [d]2 Sam. 15:30
4 [1]Lit., *shattered* [a]Joel 1:19, 20 [b]Jer. 3:3 [c]Joel 1:11
5 [a]Is. 15:6
6 [a]Job 39:5, 6; Jer. 2:24 [b]Joel 1:18
7 [a]Is. 59:12; Hos. 5:5 [b]Ps. 25:11; Jer. 14:21 [c]Jer. 5:6; 8:5 [d]Jer. 3:25; 8:14; 14:20
8 [a]Jer. 17:13 [b]Is. 43:3; 63:8 [c]Ps. 9:9; 50:15
9 [a]Num. 11:23; Is. 50:2; 59:1 [b]Ex. 29:45; Ps. 46:5; Jer. 8:19 [c]Is. 63:19; Jer. 15:16
10 [a]Jer. 2:25; 3:13 [b]Ps. 119:101 [c]Jer. 6:20; Amos 5:22 [d]Jer. 44:21-23; Hos. 8:13; 9:9
11 [a]Ex. 32:10; Jer. 7:16; 11:14
12 [a]Prov. 1:28; Is. 1:15; Jer. 11:11; Ezek. 8:18; Mic. 3:4; Zech. 7:13 [b]Jer. 6:20; 7:21 [c]Jer. 8:13 [d]Jer. 21:9
13 [1]Heb., *YHWH,* usually rendered *LORD* [2]Lit., *peace of truth* [a]Jer. 5:12; 23:17 [b]Jer. 6:14; 8:11
14 [1]Lit., *hearts* [a]Jer. 5:31; 23:25 [b]Jer. 23:21 [c]Jer. 23:16, 26; 27:9, 10; Ezek. 12:24
15 [1]Lit., *be finished* [a]Jer. 23:15; Ezek. 14:10
16 [a]Ps. 79:2, 3; Jer. 7:33; 15:2, 3 [b]Jer. 8:1, 2 [c]Prov. 1:31; Jer. 13:22-25
17 [a]Jer. 9:1; 13:17; Lam. 1:16 [b]Is. 37:22; Jer. 8:21; Lam. 1:15; 2:13 [c]Jer. 10:19; 30:14
18 [1]Lit., *pierced* [2]Or, *gone around trading* [a]Jer. 6:25; Lam. 1:20; Ezek. 7:15 [b]Jer. 6:13; 8:10
19 [1]Lit., *Thy soul* [a]Jer. 6:30; 7:29; 12:7; Lam. 5:22 [b]Jer. 30:13 [c]Job 30:26; Jer. 8:15; 1 Thess. 5:3
20 [a]Neh. 9:2; Ps. 32:5; Jer. 3:25 [b]Jer. 8:14; 14:7; Dan. 9:8
21 [a]Ps. 25:11; Jer. 14:7 [b]Jer. 3:17; 17:12
22 [1]Lit., *vanities* [2]Or, *wait for* [a]Is. 41:29; Jer. 10:3 [b]1 Kin. 17:1; Jer. 5:24 [c]Lam. 3:26

Judgment Must Come

15 THEN the LORD said to me,
"Even [a]though [b]Moses and [c]Sam-
uel were to [d]stand before Me, My [1]heart
would not be [2]with this people; [e]send
them away from My presence and let
them go!
2 "And it shall be that when they say
to you, 'Where should we go?' then you
are to tell them, 'Thus says the LORD:
"Those *destined* [a]for death, to death;
And those *destined* for the sword, to the sword;
And those *destined* for famine, to famine;
And those *destined* for captivity, to captivity." '
3 "And I shall [a]appoint over them
four kinds *of doom*," declares the LORD:
"the sword to slay, the [b]dogs to drag off,
and the [c]birds of the sky and the beasts
of the earth to devour and destroy.
4 "And I shall [a]make them an object
of horror among all the kingdoms of the
earth because of [b]Manasseh, the son of
Hezekiah, the king of Judah, for what he
did in Jerusalem.
5 "Indeed, who will have [a]pity on you, O Jerusalem,
Or who will [b]mourn for you,
Or who will turn aside to ask about your welfare?
6 "You who have [a]forsaken Me," declares the LORD,
"You keep [b]going backward.
So I will [c]stretch out My hand against you and destroy you;
I am [d]tired of relenting!
7 "And I will [a]winnow them with a winnowing fork
At the gates of the land;
I will [b]bereave *them* of children, I will destroy My people;
[c]They did not [1]repent of their ways.
8 "Their [a]widows will be more numerous before Me
Than the sand of the seas;
I will bring against them, against the mother of a young man,
A [b]destroyer at noonday;
I will suddenly bring down on her
Anguish and dismay.
9 "She who [a]bore seven *sons* pines away;
[1]Her breathing is labored.
Her [b]sun has set while it was yet day;
She has been [c]shamed and humiliated.
So I shall [d]give over their survivors to the sword
Before their enemies," declares the LORD.

10 [a]Woe to me, my mother, that you have borne me
As a [b]man of strife and a man of contention to all the land!
I have neither [c]lent, nor have men lent money to me,
Yet everyone curses me.
11 The LORD said, "Surely I will [a]set you free for *purposes of* good;
Surely I will cause the [b]enemy to make supplication to you
In a time of disaster and a time of distress.

12 "Can anyone smash iron,
[a]Iron from the north, or bronze?
13 "Your [a]wealth and your treasures
I will give for booty [b]without cost,
Even for all your sins
And within all your borders.
14 "Then I will cause your enemies to bring [1]*it*
Into a [a]land you do not know;
For a [b]fire has been kindled in My anger,
It will burn upon you."

Jeremiah's Prayer and God's Answer

15 [a]Thou who knowest, O LORD,
Remember me, take notice of me,
And [b]take vengeance for me on my persecutors.
Do *not,* in view of Thy patience, take me away;
Know that [c]for Thy sake I endure reproach.
16 Thy words were found and I [a]ate them,
And Thy [b]words became for me a joy and the delight of my heart;
For I have been [c]called by Thy name,
O LORD God of hosts.
17 I [a]did not sit in the circle of merrymakers,
Nor did I exult.
Because of Thy hand *upon me* I sat [b]alone,
For Thou didst [c]fill me with indignation.
18 Why has my pain been perpetual
And my [a]wound incurable, refusing to be healed?
Wilt Thou indeed be to me [b]like a deceptive *stream*
With water that is unreliable?

19 Therefore, thus says the LORD,
"[a]If you return, then I will restore you—
[b]Before Me you will stand;
And [c]if you extract the precious from the worthless,
You will become [1]My spokesman.
They for their part may turn to you,
But as for you, you must not turn to them.
20 "Then I will [a]make you to this people
A fortified wall of bronze;
And though they fight against you,
They will not prevail over you;
For [b]I am with you to save you
And deliver you," declares the LORD.

1 [1]Lit., *soul* [2]Lit., *toward* [a]Ps. 99:6; Ezek. 14:14, 20 [b]Ex. 32:11-14; Num. 14:13-20; Ps. 99:6; 106:23 [c]1 Sam. 7:9; 12:23 [d]Jer. 15:19; 18:20; 35:19 [e]2 Kin. 17:20; Jer. 7:15; 10:18; 52:3
2 [a]Jer. 14:12; 24:10; 43:11; Ezek. 5:2, 12; Zech. 11:9; Rev. 13:10
3 [a]Lev. 26:16, 22, 25; Ezek. 14:21 [b]1 Kin. 21:23, 24 [c]Deut. 28:26; Is. 18:6; Jer. 7:33
4 [a]Lev. 26:33; Jer. 24:9; 29:18; Ezek. 23:46 [b]2 Kin. 21:1-18; 23:26, 27; 24:3, 4; 2 Chr. 33:1-9
5 [a]Ps. 69:20; Is. 51:19; Jer. 13:14; 21:7 [b]Nah. 3:7
6 [a]Jer. 6:19; 8:9 [b]Is. 1:4; Jer. 7:24 [c]Jer. 6:12; Zeph. 1:4 [d]Jer. 6:11; 7:16
7 [1]Lit., *turn back from* [a]Ps. 1:4; Jer. 51:2 [b]Jer. 18:21; Hos. 9:12-16 [c]Is. 9:13
8 [a]Is. 3:25, 26; 4:1 [b]Jer. 22:7
9 [1]Or, *She has breathed out her soul* [a]1 Sam. 2:5; Is. 47:9 [b]Jer. 6:4; Amos 8:9 [c]Jer. 50:12 [d]Jer. 21:7
10 [a]Job 3:1, 3; Jer. 20:14 [b]Jer. 1:18, 19; 15:20; 20:7, 8 [c]Ex. 22:25; Lev. 25:36, 37; Deut. 23:19
11 [a]Ps. 138:3; Is. 41:10 [b]Jer. 21:2; 37:3; 38:14; 42:2
12 [a]Jer. 28:14
13 [a]Jer. 17:3; 20:5 [b]Ps. 44:12; Is. 52:3
14 [1]I. e., your possessions [a]Deut. 28:36, 64; Jer. 16:13 [b]Deut. 32:22; Ps. 21:9; Jer. 17:4
15 [a]Jer. 12:3 [b]Jer. 11:20 [c]Ps. 44:22; 69:7-9; Jer. 20:8
16 [a]Ezek. 3:3 [b]Job 23:12; Ps. 119:103 [c]Jer. 14:9
17 [a]Ps. 1:1; Jer. 16:8; 2 Cor. 6:17 [b]Ps. 102:7; Jer. 13:17; Lam. 3:28; Ezek. 3:24, 25 [c]Jer. 6:11
18 [a]Job 34:6; Jer. 30:12, 15; Mic. 1:9 [b]Job 6:15, 20; Jer. 14:3
19 [1]Lit., *as My mouth* [a]Jer. 4:1; Zech. 3:7 [b]1 Kin. 17:1; Jer. 15:1; 35:19 [c]Jer. 6:29; Ezek. 22:26; 44:23
20 [a]Jer. 1:18, 19; Ezek. 3:9 [b]Ps. 46:7; Is. 41:10; Jer. 1:8, 19; 15:15; 20:11

21 “So I will [a]deliver you from the hand of the wicked,
And I will [b]redeem you from the [1]grasp of the violent.”

Distresses Foretold

16 THE word of the LORD also came to me saying,

2 “You shall not take a wife for yourself nor have sons or daughters in this place.”

3 For thus says the LORD concerning the sons and daughters born in this place, and concerning their [a]mothers who bear them, and their [b]fathers who beget them in this land:

4 “They will [a]die of deadly diseases, they [b]will not be lamented or buried; they will be as [c]dung on the surface of the ground and come to an end by sword and famine, and their carcasses will become food for the [d]birds of the sky and for the beasts of the earth.”

5 For thus says the LORD, “Do not enter a house of [1a]mourning, or go to lament or to console them; for I have [b]withdrawn My peace from this people,” declares the LORD, “*My* [c]lovingkindness and compassion.

6 “Both [a]great men and small will die in this land; they will not be buried, they will not be lamented, nor will anyone [b]gash himself or [c]shave his head for them.

7 “Neither will men [a]break *bread* in mourning for them, to comfort anyone for the dead, nor give them a cup of consolation to drink for anyone’s father or mother.

8 “Moreover you shall [a]not go into a house of feasting to sit with them to eat and drink.”

9 For thus says the LORD of hosts, the God of Israel: “Behold, I am going to [1a]eliminate from this place, before your eyes and in your time, the voice of rejoicing and the voice of gladness, the voice of the groom and the voice of the bride.

10 “Now it will come about when you tell this people all these words that they will say to you, ‘[a]For what reason has the LORD declared all this great calamity against us? And what is our iniquity, or what is our sin which we have committed against the LORD our God?’

11 “Then you are to say to them, ‘*It is* [a]because your forefathers have forsaken Me,’ declares the LORD, ‘and have followed [b]other gods and served them and bowed down to them; but Me they have forsaken and have not kept My law.

12 ‘You too have done evil, *even* [a]more than your forefathers; for behold, you are each one walking according to the [b]stubbornness of his own [c]evil heart, without listening to Me.

13 ‘So I will [a]hurl you out of this land into the [b]land which you have not known, neither you nor your fathers; and there you will [c]serve other gods day and night, for I shall grant you no favor.’

God Will Restore Them

14 “[a]Therefore behold, days are coming,” declares the LORD, “when it will no longer be said, ‘As the LORD lives, who [b]brought up the sons of Israel out of the land of Egypt,’

15 but, ‘As the LORD lives, who brought up the sons of Israel from the [a]land of the north and from all the countries where He had banished them.’ For I will restore them to their own land which I gave to their fathers.

16 “Behold, I am going to send for many [a]fishermen,” declares the LORD, “and they will fish for them; and afterwards I shall send for many hunters, and they will [b]hunt them [c]from every mountain and every hill, and from the clefts of the rocks.

17 “[a]For My eyes are on all their ways; they are not hidden from My face, [b]nor is their iniquity concealed from My eyes.

18 “And I will first [a]doubly repay their iniquity and their sin, because they have [b]polluted My land; they have filled My inheritance with the carcasses of their [c]detestable idols and with their abominations.”

19 O LORD, my [a]strength and my stronghold,
And my [b]refuge in the day of distress,
To Thee the [c]nations will come
From the ends of the earth and say,
“Our fathers have inherited nothing but [d]falsehood,
Futility and [1e]things of no profit.”
20 Can man make gods for himself?
Yet they are [a]not gods!

21 “Therefore behold, I am going to make them know—
This time I will [a]make them know
My [1]power and My might;
And they shall [b]know that My name is the LORD.”

The Deceitful Heart

17 THE [a]sin of Judah is written down with an [b]iron stylus;
With a diamond point it is [c]engraved upon the tablet of their heart,
And on the horns of [1]their altars,
2 As they remember their [a]children,
So they *remember* their altars and their [1b]Asherim
By [c]green trees on the high hills.
3 O [a]mountain of Mine in the countryside,
I will [b]give over your wealth and all your treasures for booty,
Your high places for sin throughout your borders.

21 [1]Lit., *palm* [a]Ps. 37:40; Is. 49:25; Jer. 20:13; 39:11, 12 [b]Gen. 48:16; Is. 49:26; 60:16; Jer. 31:11; 50:34

3 [a]Jer. 15:8 [b]Jer. 6:21

4 [a]Jer. 15:2 [b]Jer. 25:33 [c]Ps. 83:10; Jer. 9:22; 25:33 [d]Ps. 79:2; Is. 18:6; Jer. 15:3; 34:20

5 [1]Or, *banqueting* [a]Ezek. 24:16-23 [b]Jer. 12:12; 15:1-4 [c]Ps. 25:6; Is. 27:11; Jer. 13:14

6 [a]2 Chr. 36:17; Ezek. 9:6 [b]Deut. 14:1; Jer. 41:5; 47:5 [c]Is. 22:12

7 [a]Deut. 26:14; Ezek. 24:17; Hos. 9:4

8 [a]Eccl. 7:2-4; Is. 22:12-14; Jer. 15:17; Amos 6:4-6

9 [1]Lit., *cause to cease* [a]Jer. 7:34; 25:10; Ezek. 26:13; Hos. 2:11; Rev. 18:23

10 [a]Deut. 29:24; 1 Kin. 9:8; Jer. 5:19; 13:22; 22:8

11 [a]Deut. 29:25; 1 Kin. 9:9; 2 Chr. 7:22; Neh. 9:26-29; Jer. 22:9 [b]Deut. 29:26; 1 Kin. 9:9; Ps. 106:35-41; Jer. 5:7-9; 8:2; Ezek. 11:21; 1 Pet. 4:3

12 [a]Jer. 7:26 [b]1 Sam. 15:23; Jer. 7:24; 9:14; 13:10 [c]Eccl. 9:3; Mark 7:21

13 [a]Deut. 4:26, 27; 2 Chr. 7:20; Jer. 15:1 [b]Jer. 15:14; 17:4 [c]Deut. 4:28; 28:36; Jer. 5:19

14 [a]Is. 43:18; Jer. 23:7 [b]Ex. 20:2; Deut. 15:15

15 [a]Ps. 106:47; Is. 11:11-16; 14:1; Jer. 3:18; 23:8; 24:6

16 [a]Amos 4:2; Hab. 1:14, 15 [b]1 Sam. 26:20; Mic. 7:2 [c]Is. 2:21; Amos 9:3

17 [a]2 Chr. 16:9; Job 34:21; Ps. 90:8; Prov. 5:21; 15:3; Jer. 23:24; 32:19; Zech. 4:10; Luke 12:2; 1 Cor. 4:5; Heb. 4:13 [b]Jer. 2:22

18 [a]Jer. 17:18; Rev. 18:6 [b]Num. 35:33, 34; Jer. 2:7; 3:9 [c]Jer. 7:30; Ezek. 11:18, 21

19 [1]Lit., *there is nothing profitable in them* [a]Ps. 18:1, 2; Is. 25:4 [b]Nah. 1:7 [c]Ps. 22:27; Is. 2:2; Jer. 3:17; 4:2 [d]Is. 44:20; Hab. 2:18 [e]Is. 44:10

20 [a]Ps. 115:4-8; Is. 37:19; Jer. 2:11; 5:7; Hos. 8:4-6; Gal. 4:8

21 [1]Lit., *hand* [a]Ps. 9:16 [b]Ps. 83:18; Is. 43:3; Jer. 33:2; Amos 5:8

1 [1]So ancient versions; M.T., *your* [a]Jer. 2:22; 4:14 [b]Job 19:24 [c]Prov. 3:3; 7:3; Is. 49:16; 2 Cor. 3:3

2 [1]I.e., wooden symbols of a female deity [a]Jer. 7:18 [b]Ex. 34:13; 2 Chr. 24:18; 33:3; Is. 17:8 [c]Jer. 3:6

3 [a]Jer. 26:18; Mic. 3:12 [b]2 Kin. 24:13; Is. 39:4-6; Jer. 15:13; 20:5

4 And you will, even of yourself, [a]let
go of your inheritance
That I gave you;
And I will make you serve your
[b]enemies
In the [c]land which you do not
know;
For you have [d]kindled a fire in My
anger
Which will burn forever.

5 Thus says the LORD,
"[a]Cursed is the man who trusts in
mankind
And makes [b]flesh his [1]strength,
And whose heart turns away from
the LORD.
6 "For he will be like a [a]bush in the
desert
And will not see when prosperity
comes,
But will live in stony wastes in the
wilderness,
A [b]land of salt [1]without inhabitant.
7 "[a]Blessed is the man who trusts in
the LORD
And whose [b]trust is the LORD.
8 "For he will be like a [a]tree planted
by the water,
That extends its roots by a stream
And will not fear when the heat
comes;
But its leaves will be green,
And it will not be anxious in a year
of [b]drought
Nor cease to yield fruit.

9 "The [a]heart is more [b]deceitful than
all else
And is desperately [c]sick;
Who can understand it?
10 "I, the LORD, [a]search the heart,
I test the [1]mind,
Even [b]to give to each man according
to his ways,
According to the [2]results of his
deeds.
11 "As a partridge that hatches eggs
which it has not laid,
So is he who [a]makes a fortune, but
unjustly;
In the midst of his days it will
forsake him,
And in [1]the end he will be a [b]fool."

12 [a]A glorious throne on high from
the beginning
Is the place of our sanctuary.
13 O LORD, the [a]hope of Israel,
All who [b]forsake Thee will be put
to shame.
Those who turn [1]away on earth will
be [c]written down,
Because they have forsaken the
fountain of living water, even
the LORD.
14 [a]Heal me, O LORD, and I will be
healed;
[b]Save me and I will be saved,
For Thou art my [c]praise.
15 Look, they keep [a]saying to me,
"Where is the word of the LORD?
Let it come now!"

4 [a]Jer. 12:7; Lam. 5:2 [b]Deut. 28:48; Is. 14:3; Jer. 15:14; 27:12, 13 [c]Jer. 16:13 [d]Is. 5:25; Jer. 7:20; 15:14
5 [1]Lit., *arm* [a]Ps. 146:3; Is. 2:22; 30:1; Ezek. 29:7 [b]2 Chr. 32:8; Is. 31:3
6 [1]Lit., *and is not inhabited* [a]Jer. 48:6 [b]Deut. 29:23; Job 39:6
7 [a]Ps. 2:12; 34:8; 84:12; Prov. 16:20 [b]Ps. 40:4
8 [a]Ps. 1:3; 92:12-14; Ezek. 31:3-9 [b]Jer. 14:1-6
9 [a]Eccl. 9:3; Mark 7:21, 22 [b]Rom. 7:11; Eph. 4:22 [c]Is. 1:5, 6; 6:10; Matt. 13:15; Mark 2:17; Rom. 1:21
10 [1]Lit., *kidneys* [2]Lit., *fruit* [a]1 Sam. 16:7; 1 Chr. 28:9; Ps. 139:23; Prov. 17:3; Jer. 11:20; 20:12; Rom. 8:27; Rev. 2:23 [b]Ps. 62:12; Jer. 32:19; Rom. 2:6
11 [1]Lit., *his* [a]Jer. 6:13; 8:10; 22:13, 17 [b]Luke 12:20
12 [a]Jer. 3:17; 14:21
13 [1]Lit., *away from Me* [a]Jer. 14:8; 50:7 [b]Is. 1:28 [c]Luke 10:20
14 [a]Jer. 30:17; 33:6 [b]Ps. 54:1; 60:5 [c]Deut. 10:21; Ps. 109:1
15 [a]Is. 5:19; 2 Pet. 3:4
16 [a]Jer. 12:3
17 [a]Ps. 88:15 [b]Jer. 16:19; Nah. 1:7
18 [a]Ps. 35:4, 26; Jer. 17:13; 20:11 [b]Jer. 1:17 [c]Ps. 35:8
19 [1]Lit., *gate of the sons of the people*
20 [a]Ezek. 2:7 [b]Ps. 49:1, 2; Jer. 19:3, 4
21 [a]Deut. 4:9, 15, 23; Mark 4:24 [b]Num. 15:32-36; Neh. 13:15-21; John 5:9-12
22 [1]Lit., *fathers* [a]Ex. 16:23-29; 20:8-10; Deut. 5:12-14; Is. 56:2-6; 58:13 [b]Ex. 31:13-17; Ezek. 20:12; Zech. 1:4
23 [a]Jer. 7:24, 28; 11:10 [b]Prov. 29:1; Jer. 7:26; 19:15
24 [a]Ex. 15:26; Deut. 11:13; Is. 21:7; 55:2 [b]Jer. 17:21, 22 [c]Ex. 20:8-11; Ezek. 20:20
25 [a]Jer. 22:4 [b]2 Sam. 7:16; Is. 9:7; Jer. 33:15, 17, 21; Luke 1:32 [c]Ps. 132:13, 14; Heb. 12:22
26 [a]Jer. 32:44; 33:13 [b]Zech. 7:7 [c]Ps. 107:22; Jer. 33:11
27 [a]Is. 1:20; Jer. 22:5; 26:4; Zech. 7:11-14 [b]Lam. 4:11 [c]2 Kin. 25:9; Jer. 39:8; Amos 2:5 [d]Jer. 7:20; Ezek. 20:47

16 But as for me, I have not hurried
away from *being* a shepherd
after Thee,
Nor have I longed for the woeful
day;
[a]Thou Thyself knowest the utterance
of my lips
Was in Thy presence.
17 Do not be a [a]terror to me;
Thou art my [b]refuge in the day of
disaster.
18 Let those who persecute me be [a]put
to shame, but as for me, [b]let me
not be put to shame;
Let them be dismayed, but let me
not be dismayed.
[c]Bring on them a day of disaster,
And crush them with twofold destruction!

The Sabbath Must Be Kept

19 Thus the LORD said to me, "Go
and stand in the [1]public gate, through
which the kings of Judah come in and go
out, as well as in all the gates of Jerusalem;
20 and say to them, '[a]Listen to the
word of the LORD, [b]kings of Judah, and
all Judah, and all inhabitants of Jerusalem,
who come in through these gates:
21 'Thus says the LORD, "[a]Take heed
for yourselves, and [b]do not carry any
load on the sabbath day or bring anything
in through the gates of Jerusalem.
22 "And you shall not bring a load out
of your houses on the sabbath day [a]nor
do any work, but keep the sabbath day
holy, as I [b]commanded your [1]forefathers.
23 "Yet they [a]did not listen or incline
their ears, but [b]stiffened their necks in
order not to listen or take correction.
24 "But it will come about, if you
[a]listen attentively to Me," declares the
LORD, "to [b]bring no load in through the
gates of this city on the sabbath day,
[c]but to keep the sabbath day holy by
doing no work on it,
25 [a]then there will come in through
the gates of this city kings and princes
[b]sitting on the throne of David, riding in
chariots and on horses, they and their
princes, the men of Judah, and the
inhabitants of Jerusalem; and this [c]city
will be inhabited forever.
26 "They will come in from the [a]cities
of Judah and from the environs of Jerusalem,
from the land of Benjamin, from
the [b]lowland, from the hill country, and
from the [c]Negev, bringing burnt offerings,
sacrifices, grain offerings and incense,
and bringing sacrifices of thanksgiving
to the house of the LORD.
27 "But [a]if you do not listen to Me to
keep the sabbath day holy by not carrying
a load and coming in through the
gates of Jerusalem on the sabbath day,
then [b]I shall kindle a fire in its gates, and
it will [c]devour the palaces of Jerusalem
and [d]not be quenched." ' "

The Potter and the Clay

18 THE word which came to Jeremiah from the LORD saying,
2 "Arise and [a]go down to the potter's
house, and there I shall announce My
words to you."
3 Then I went down to the potter's
house, and there he was, making something on the [1]wheel.
4 But the vessel that he was making
of clay was spoiled in the hand of the
potter; so he remade it into another
vessel, as it pleased the potter to make.
5 Then the word of the LORD came
to me saying,
6 "Can I not, O house of Israel, deal
with you as this potter *does?*" declares
the LORD. "Behold, like the [a]clay in the
potter's hand, so are you in My hand, O
house of Israel.
7 "At one moment I might speak
concerning a nation or concerning a
kingdom to [a]uproot, to pull down, or to
destroy *it;*
8 [a]if that nation against which I have
spoken turns from its evil, I will [1b]relent
concerning the calamity I planned to
bring on it.
9 "Or at another moment I might
speak concerning a nation or concerning
a kingdom to [a]build up or to plant *it;*
10 if it does [a]evil in My sight by not
obeying My voice, then I will [1b]think
better of the good with which I had
promised to [2]bless it.
11 "So now then, speak to the men of
Judah and against the inhabitants of
Jerusalem saying, 'Thus says the LORD,
"Behold, I am [a]fashioning calamity
against you and devising a plan against
you. Oh [b]turn back, each of you from his
evil way, and [1]reform your ways and
your deeds." '
12 "But [a]they will say, 'It's hopeless!
For we are going to follow our own
plans, and each of us will act according
to the [b]stubbornness of his evil heart.'
13 "Therefore thus says the LORD,
'[a]Ask now among the nations,
Who ever heard the like of [1]this?
The [b]virgin of Israel
Has done a most [c]appalling thing.
14 'Does the snow of Lebanon forsake
the rock of the open country?
Or is the cold flowing water *from* a
foreign *land* ever snatched
away?
15 'For [a]My people have forgotten Me,
[b]They burn incense [1]to worthless
gods
And they [2]have stumbled [3]from
their ways,
[3]From the [c]ancient paths,
To walk in bypaths,
Not on a [d]highway,
16 To make their land a [a]desolation,
An object of perpetual [b]hissing;
Everyone who passes by it will be
astonished
And [c]shake his head.
17 'Like an [a]east wind I will [b]scatter
them
Before the enemy;
I will [1]show them [c]My back and
not *My* face
[d]In the day of their calamity.' "
18 Then they said, "Come and let us
[a]devise plans against Jeremiah. Surely
the [b]law is not going to be lost to the
priest, nor [c]counsel to the sage, nor the
divine [d]word to the prophet! Come on
and let us [e]strike at him with *our* tongue,
and let us [f]give no heed to any of his
words."
19 Do give heed to me, O LORD,
And listen to [1]what my opponents
are saying!
20 [a]Should good be repaid with evil?
For they have [b]dug a pit for [1]me.
Remember how I [c]stood before
Thee
To speak good on their behalf,
So as to turn away Thy wrath from
them.
21 Therefore, [a]give their children over
to famine,
And deliver them up to the [1]power
of the sword;
And let their wives become [b]childless and [c]widowed.
Let their men also be smitten to
death,
Their [d]young men struck down by
the sword in battle.
22 May an [a]outcry be heard from their
houses,
When Thou suddenly bringest raiders upon them;
[b]For they have dug a pit to capture
me
And [c]hidden snares for my feet.
23 Yet Thou, O LORD, knowest
All their [1]deadly designs against
me;
[a]Do not [2]forgive their iniquity
Or blot out their sin from Thy
sight.
But may they be [3b]overthrown before Thee;
Deal with them in the [c]time of
Thine anger!

The Broken Jar

19 THUS says the LORD, "Go and
buy a [a]potter's earthenware [b]jar,
and *take* some of the [c]elders of the
people and some of the [1d]senior priests.
2 "Then go out to the [a]valley of Ben-hinnom, which is by the entrance of the
potsherd gate; and [b]proclaim there the
words that I shall tell you,
3 and say, 'Hear the word of the
LORD, O [a]kings of Judah and inhabitants of Jerusalem: thus says the LORD
of hosts, the God of Israel, "Behold I am
about to bring a [b]calamity upon this
place, at which the [c]ears of everyone that
hears of it will tingle.

2 [a]Jer. 19:1, 2
3 [1]Lit., *pair of stone discs*
6 [a]Is. 45:9; 64:8; Matt. 20:15; Rom. 9:21
7 [a]Jer. 1:10
8 [1]Lit., *repent of* [a]Jer. 7:3-7; 12:16; Ezek. 18:21 [b]Ps. 106:45; Jer. 26:3, 13, 19; Hos. 11:8; Joel 2:13, 14; Jon. 3:10
9 [a]Jer. 1:10; 31:28; Amos 9:11-15
10 [1]Lit., *repent* [2]Lit., *do it good* [a]Ps. 125:5; Jer. 7:24-28; Ezek. 33:18 [b]1 Sam. 2:30; 13:13
11 [1]Lit., *make good* [a]Is. 5:5; Jer. 4:6; 11:11 [b]2 Kin. 17:13; Is. 1:16-19; Jer. 4:1; Acts 26:20
12 [a]Is. 57:10; Jer. 2:25 [b]Deut. 29:19; Jer. 7:24; 16:12
13 [1]Lit., *these* [a]Is. 66:8; Jer. 2:10, 11 [b]Jer. 14:17; 31:4 [c]Jer. 5:30; 23:14; Hos. 6:10
15 [1]Lit., *to worthlessness* [2]So ancient versions; Heb., *caused them to* [3]Or, *in* [a]Jer. 2:32; 3:21 [b]Is. 65:7; Jer. 7:9; 10:15; 44:17 [c]Jer. 6:16 [d]Is. 57:14; 62:10
16 [a]Jer. 25:9; 49:13; 50:13; Ezek. 33:28, 29 [b]1 Kin. 9:8; Lam. 2:15; Mic. 6:16 [c]Ps. 22:7; Is. 37:22; Jer. 48:27
17 [1]So ancient versions; M.T. reads *look them in the back and not in the face* [a]Ps. 48:7 [b]Job 27:21; Jer. 13:24 [c]Jer. 2:27; 32:33 [d]Jer. 46:21
18 [a]Jer. 11:19; 18:11 [b]Jer. 2:8; Mal. 2:7 [c]Job 5:13; Jer. 8:8 [d]Jer. 5:13 [e]Ps. 52:2; Jer. 20:10 [f]Jer. 43:2
19 [1]Lit., *the voice of my opponents*
20 [1]Lit., *my soul* [a]Ps. 109:4 [b]Ps. 35:7; 57:6; Jer. 5:26; 18:22 [c]Ps. 106:23
21 [1]Lit., *hands of* [a]Ps. 109:9-20; Jer. 11:22; 14:16 [b]1 Sam. 15:33; Is. 13:18 [c]Jer. 15:8; Ezek. 22:25 [d]Jer. 9:21; 11:22
22 [a]Jer. 6:26; 25:34, 36 [b]Jer. 18:20 [c]Ps. 140:5
23 [1]Lit., *unto death* [2]Lit., *cover over, atone for* [3]Lit., *ones made to stumble* [a]Neh. 4:5; Ps. 109:14; Is. 2:9 [b]Jer. 6:15, 21 [c]Jer. 7:20; 17:4

1 [1]Or, *elders of* [a]Jer. 18:2 [b]Jer. 19:10 [c]Num. 11:16 [d]2 Kin. 19:2; Ezek. 8:11
2 [a]Josh. 15:8; 2 Kin. 23:10; Jer. 7:31, 32; 32:35 [b]Prov. 1:20
3 [a]Jer. 17:20 [b]Jer. 6:19; 19:15 [c]1 Sam. 3:11

4 "Because they have [a]forsaken Me and have [b]made this an alien place and have burned [1]sacrifices in it to [c]other gods that neither they nor their forefathers nor the kings of Judah had *ever* known, and *because* they have filled this place with the [d]blood of the innocent

5 and have built the [a]high places of Baal to burn their [b]sons in the fire as burnt offerings to Baal, a thing which I never commanded or spoke of, nor did it *ever* enter My [1]mind;

6 therefore, behold, [a]days are coming," declares the LORD, "when this place will no longer be called [b]Topheth or [c]the valley of Ben-hinnom, but rather the valley of Slaughter.

7 "And I shall [a]make void the counsel of Judah and Jerusalem in this place, and [b]I shall cause them to fall by the sword before their enemies and by the hand of those who seek their life; and I shall give over their [c]carcasses as food for the birds of the sky and the beasts of the earth.

8 "I shall also make this city a [a]desolation and an *object of* hissing; [b]everyone who passes by it will be astonished and hiss because of all its [1]disasters.

9 "And I shall make them [a]eat the flesh of their sons and the flesh of their daughters, and they will eat one another's flesh in the siege and in the distress with which their enemies and those who seek their life will distress them." '

10 "Then you are to break the [a]jar in the sight of the men who accompany you

11 and say to them, 'Thus says the LORD of hosts, "Just so shall I [a]break this people and this city, even as one breaks a potter's vessel, which cannot again be repaired; and they will [b]bury in Topheth [1]because there is no *other* place for burial.

12 "This is how I shall treat this place and its inhabitants," declares the LORD, "so as to make this city like Topheth.

13 "And the [a]houses of Jerusalem and the houses of the kings of Judah will be [b]defiled like the place Topheth, because of all the [c]houses on whose rooftops they burned [1]sacrifices to [d]all the heavenly host and [e]poured out libations to other gods." ' "

14 Then Jeremiah came from Topheth, where the LORD had sent him to prophesy; and he stood in the [a]court of the LORD's house and said to all the people:

15 "Thus says the LORD of hosts, the God of Israel, 'Behold, I am about to bring on this city and all its towns the entire calamity that I have declared against it, because they have [a]stiffened their necks so [b]as not to heed My words.' "

Pashhur Persecutes Jeremiah

20 WHEN Pashhur the priest, the son of [a]Immer, who was [b]chief officer in the house of the LORD, heard Jeremiah prophesying these things,

2 Pashhur had Jeremiah the prophet [a]beaten, and put him in the [b]stocks that were at the upper [c]Benjamin Gate, which was by the house of the LORD.

3 Then it came about on the next day, when Pashhur released Jeremiah from the stocks, that Jeremiah said to him, "Pashhur is not the name the LORD has [a]called you, but rather [1b]Magor-missabib.

4 "For thus says the LORD, 'Behold, I am going to make you a [a]terror to yourself and to all your friends; and while [b]your eyes look on, they will fall by the sword of their enemies. So I shall [c]give over all Judah to the hand of the king of Babylon, and he will carry them away as [d]exiles to Babylon and will slay them with the sword.

5 'I shall also give over all the [a]wealth of this city, all its produce, and all its costly things; even all the treasures of the kings of Judah I shall give over to the [b]hand of their enemies, and they will plunder them, take them away, and bring them to Babylon.

6 'And you, [a]Pashhur, and all who live in your house will go into captivity; and you will enter Babylon, and there you will die, and there you will be buried, you and all your [b]friends to whom you have [c]falsely prophesied.' "

Jeremiah's Complaint

7 O LORD, Thou hast deceived me and I was deceived;
Thou hast [a]overcome me and prevailed.
I have become a [b]laughingstock all day long;
Everyone [c]mocks me.
8 For each time I speak, I cry aloud;
I [a]proclaim violence and destruction,
Because for me the [b]word of the LORD has [1]resulted
In reproach and derision all day long.
9 But if I say, "I will not [a]remember Him
Or speak anymore in His name,"
Then in [b]my heart it becomes like a burning fire
Shut up in my bones;
And I am weary of holding *it* in,
And [c]I cannot endure *it.*
10 For [a]I have heard the whispering of many,
"[b]Terror on every side!
[c]Denounce *him;* yes, let us denounce him!"
[1]All my [d]trusted friends,
Watching for my fall, say:
"Perhaps he will be [2]deceived, so that we may [e]prevail against him
And take our revenge on him."

4 [1]Or, *incense* [a]Deut. 28:20; Is. 65:11; Jer. 2:13, 17, 19; 17:13 [b]Ezek. 7:22; Dan. 11:31 [c]Jer. 7:9; 11:13 [d]2 Kin. 21:6, 16; Jer. 2:34; 7:6
5 [1]Lit., *heart* [a]Num. 22:41; Jer. 32:35 [b]Lev. 18:21; 2 Kin. 17:17; Ps. 106:37, 38
6 [a]Jer. 7:32 [b]Is. 30:33 [c]Josh. 15:8
7 [a]Ps. 33:10, 11; Is. 28:17, 18; Jer. 8:8, 9 [b]Lev. 26:17; Deut. 28:25; Jer. 15:2, 9 [c]Ps. 79:2; Jer. 16:4
8 [1]Lit., *blows* [a]Jer. 18:16; 49:13; 50:13 [b]1 Kin. 9:8; 2 Chr. 7:21
9 [a]Lev. 26:29; Deut. 28:53, 55; Is. 9:20; Lam. 4:10; Ezek. 5:10
10 [a]Jer. 19:1
11 [1]Or, *until there is no place* left *to bury* [a]Ps. 2:9; Is. 30:14; Lam. 4:2; Rev. 2:27 [b]Jer. 7:32
13 [1]Or, *incense* [a]Jer. 52:13 [b]2 Kin. 23:10; Ps. 74:7; 79:1; Ezek. 7:21, 22 [c]Jer. 32:29; Zeph. 1:5 [d]Deut. 4:19; 2 Kin. 17:16; Jer. 8:2 [e]Jer. 7:18; 44:18; Ezek. 20:28
14 [a]2 Chr. 20:5; Jer. 26:2
15 [a]Neh. 9:17, 29; Jer. 7:26; 17:23 [b]Ps. 58:4

1 [a]1 Chr. 24:14; Ezra 2:37, 38 [b]2 Kin. 25:18
2 [a]1 Kin. 22:27; 2 Chr. 16:10; 24:21; Jer. 1:19; Amos 7:10-13 [b]Job 13:27; 33:11 [c]Jer. 37:13; 38:7; Zech. 14:10
3 [1]I.e., terror on every side [a]Is. 8:3; Hos. 1:4, 9 [b]Jer. 6:25; 20:10
4 [a]Job 18:11-21; Jer. 6:25; 46:5; Ezek. 26:21 [b]Jer. 29:21; 39:6, 7 [c]Jer. 21:4-10; 25:9 [d]Jer. 13:10; 52:27
5 [a]Jer. 15:13; 17:3 [b]2 Kin. 20:17, 18; 2 Chr. 36:10; Jer. 27:21, 22
6 [a]Jer. 20:1 [b]Jer. 20:4; 29:21 [c]Jer. 14:14, 15; Lam. 2:14
7 [a]Ezek. 3:14 [b]Job 12:4; Lam. 3:14 [c]Ps. 22:7; Jer. 38:19
8 [1]Lit., *become* [a]Jer. 6:7 [b]2 Chr. 36:16; Jer. 6:10
9 [a]1 Kin. 19:3, 4; Jon. 1:2, 3 [b]Job 32:18-20; Ps. 39:3; Jer. 4:19; 23:9; Ezek. 3:14; Acts 4:20 [c]Job 32:18-20

10 [1]Lit., *Every man of my peace* [2]Or, *persuaded* [a]Ps. 31:13 [b]Jer. 6:25 [c]Neh. 6:6-13; Is. 29:21; Jer. 18:18 [d]Ps. 41:9 [e]1 Kin. 19:2

11 But the [a]LORD is with me like a
dread champion;
Therefore my [b]persecutors will
stumble and not prevail.
They will be utterly ashamed, because they have [1]failed,
With an [c]everlasting disgrace that
will not be forgotten.
12 Yet, O LORD of hosts, Thou who
dost [a]test the righteous,
Who seest the [1]mind and the heart;
Let me [b]see Thy vengeance on
them;
For [c]to Thee I have set forth my
cause.
13 [a]Sing to the LORD, praise the
LORD!
For He has [b]delivered the soul of
the needy one
From the hand of evildoers.

14 Cursed be the [a]day when I was
born;
Let the day not be blessed when my
mother bore me!
15 Cursed be the man who brought
the news
To my father, saying,
"A [1a]baby boy has been born to
you!"
And made him very happy.
16 But let that man be like the cities
Which the LORD [a]overthrew without [1]relenting,
And let him hear an [b]outcry in the
morning
And a [2]shout of alarm at noon;
17 Because he did not [a]kill me [1]before
birth,
So that my mother would have
been my grave,
And her womb ever pregnant.
18 Why did I ever come forth from the
womb
To [a]look on trouble and sorrow,
So that my [b]days have been spent
in [c]shame?

Jeremiah's Message for Zedekiah

21 THE word which came to Jeremiah from the LORD when [a]King
Zedekiah sent to him [b]Pashhur the son
of Malchijah, and [c]Zephaniah the priest,
the son of Maaseiah, saying,
2 "Please [a]inquire of the LORD on our
behalf, for [b]Nebuchadnezzar king of
[c]Babylon is warring against us; perhaps
the LORD will deal with us [d]according to
all His [1]wonderful acts, that *the enemy*
may withdraw from us."
3 Then Jeremiah said to them, "You
shall say to Zedekiah as follows:
4 'Thus says the LORD God of Israel,
"Behold, I am about to [a]turn back the
weapons of war which are in your hands,
with which you are warring against the
king of Babylon and the Chaldeans who
are besieging you outside the wall; and I
shall [b]gather them into the center of this
city.
5 "And I [a]Myself shall war against
you with an [b]outstretched hand and a
mighty arm, even in [c]anger and wrath
and great indignation.
6 "I shall also strike down the inhabitants of this city, both man and beast;
they will die of a great [a]pestilence.
7 "Then afterwards," declares the
LORD, "[a]I shall give over Zedekiah king
of Judah and his servants and the people, even those who survive in this city
from the pestilence, the sword, and the
famine, into the hand of Nebuchadnezzar king of Babylon, and into the hand
of their foes, and into the hand of those
who seek their lives; and he will strike
them down with the edge of the sword.
He [b]will not spare them nor have pity
nor compassion."'
8 "You shall also say to this people,
'Thus says the LORD, "Behold, I [a]set
before you the way of life and the way of
death.
9 "He who [a]dwells in this city will die
by the [b]sword and by famine and by
pestilence; but he who goes out and falls
away to the Chaldeans who are besieging
you will live, and he will have his own
life as booty.
10 "For I have [a]set My face against this
city for [1]harm and not for good," declares the LORD. "It will be [b]given into
the hand of the king of Babylon, and he
will [c]burn it with fire."'
11 "Then *say* to the household of the
[a]king of Judah, 'Hear the word of the
LORD,
12 O [a]house of David, thus says the
LORD:
"[b]Administer justice [1]every [c]morn-
ing;
And deliver the *person* who has
been robbed from the [2]power of
his oppressor,
[d]That My wrath may not go forth
like fire
And [e]burn with none to extinguish
it,
Because of the evil of their deeds.

13 "Behold, [a]I am against you, O [b]val-
ley dweller,
O [1]rocky plain," declares the
LORD,
"You men who say, '[c]Who will come
down against us?
Or who will enter into our habitations?'
14 "But I shall punish you [a]according
to the [1]results of your deeds,"
declares the LORD,
"And I shall [b]kindle a fire in its
forest
That it may devour all its environs."'"

Warning of Jerusalem's Fall

22 THUS says the LORD, "Go down
to the house of the king of Judah,
and there speak this word,

11 [1]Lit., *not succeeded;* or, *not acted wisely* [a]Jer. 1:8; 15:20; Rom. 8:31 [b]Deut. 32:35, 36; Jer. 15:15, 20; 17:18 [c]Jer. 23:40
12 [1]Lit., *kidneys* [a]Ps. 7:9; 11:5; 17:3; 139:23; Jer. 11:20; 17:10 [b]Ps. 54:7; 59:10; Jer. 11:20 [c]Ps. 62:8
13 [a]Jer. 31:7 [b]Ps. 34:6; 69:33; Jer. 15:21
14 [a]Job 3:3-6; Jer. 15:10
15 [1]Lit., *male child* [a]Gen. 21:6, 7
16 [1]Lit., *being sorry* [2]Or, *trumpet blast* [a]Gen. 19:25 [b]Jer. 18:22; 48:3, 4
17 [1]Lit., *from the womb* [a]Job 3:10, 11, 16; 10:18, 19
18 [a]Job 3:20; 5:7; 14:1; Jer. 15:10; Lam. 3:1 [b]Ps. 90:9; 102:3 [c]Ps. 69:19; Jer. 3:25; 1 Cor. 4:9-13

18; Jer. 32:1-3; 37:1; 52:1-3 [b]1 Chr. 9:12; Jer. 38:1 [c]2 Kin. 25:18; Jer. 29:25, 29; 37:3; 52:24
2 [1]Or, *miracles* [a]Ex. 9:28; Jer. 37:3, 17; Ezek. 14:7; 20:1-3 [b]2 Kin. 25:1 [c]Gen. 10:10; 2 Kin. 17:24 [d]Ps. 44:1-3; Jer. 32:17
4 [a]Jer. 32:5; 33:5; 37:8-10; 38:2, 3, 17, 18 [b]Is. 5:5; 13:4; Jer. 39:3; Lam. 2:5, 7; Zech. 14:2
5 [a]Is. 63:10 [b]Ex. 6:6; Deut. 4:34; Jer. 6:12 [c]Is. 5:25; Jer. 32:37
6 [a]Jer. 14:12; 32:24
7 [a]2 Kin. 25:5-7, 18-21; Jer. 37:17; 39:5-9; 52:9 [b]2 Chr. 36:17; Jer. 13:14; Ezek. 7:9; Hab. 1:6-10
8 [a]Deut. 30:15, 19; Is. 1:19, 20
9 [a]Jer. 38:2, 17-23; 39:18; 45:5 [b]Jer. 14:12; 24:10
10 [1]Lit., *evil* [a]Lev. 17:10; Jer. 44:11, 27; Amos 9:4 [b]Jer. 32:28, 29; 38:3 [c]2 Chr. 36:19; Jer. 34:2; 37:10; 38:18; 39:8; 52:13
11 [a]Jer. 17:20
12 [1]Or, *in the* [2]Lit., *hand* [a]Is. 7:2, 13 [b]Ps. 72:1; Is. 1:17; Jer. 7:5; 22:3; Zech. 7:9, 10 [c]Ps. 101:8; Zeph. 3:5 [d]Jer. 4:4; 17:4; Ezek. 20:47, 48; Nah. 1:6 [e]Is. 1:31; Jer. 7:20
13 [1]Lit., *rock of the level place* [a]Jer. 23:30-32; Ezek. 13:8 [b]Ps. 125:2; Is. 22:1 [c]2 Sam. 5:6, 7; Jer. 49:4; Lam. 4:12; Obad. 3, 4

14 [1]Lit., *fruit* [a]Is. 3:10, 11; Jer. 17:10; 32:19 [b]2 Chr. 36:19; Is. 10:16, 18; Jer. 11:16; 17:27; 52:13; Ezek. 20:47, 48

2 and say, 'Hear the word of the
LORD, O king of Judah, who [a]sits on
David's throne, you and your servants
and your people who enter these gates.
3 'Thus says the LORD, "[a]Do justice
and righteousness, and deliver the one
who has been robbed from the power of
his [b]oppressor. Also [c]do not mistreat *or*
do violence to the stranger, the orphan,
or the widow; and do not [d]shed innocent
blood in this place.
4 "For if you men will indeed perform
this thing, then [a]kings will enter the
gates of this house, sitting [1]in David's
place on his throne, riding in chariots
and on horses, *even the king* himself and
his servants and his people.
5 "[a]But if you will not obey these
words, I [b]swear by Myself," declares the
LORD, "that this house will become a
desolation." ' "
6 For thus says the LORD concerning
the house of the king of Judah:

"You are *like* [a]Gilead to Me,
Like the summit of Lebanon;
Yet most assuredly I shall make
you like a [b]wilderness,
Like cities which are not inhabited.
7 "For I shall set apart [a]destroyers
against you,
Each with his weapons;
And they will [b]cut down your
choicest cedars
And [c]throw *them* on the fire.

8 "And many nations will pass by this
city; and they will [a]say to one another,
'Why has the LORD done thus to this
great city?'
9 "Then they will [1]answer, 'Because
they [a]forsook the covenant of the LORD
their God and bowed down to other
gods and served them.' "

10 [a]Do not weep for the dead or
mourn for him,
But weep continually for the one
who goes away;
For [b]he will never return
Or see his native land.

11 For thus says the LORD in regard to
[1a]Shallum the son of Josiah, king of
Judah, who became king in the place of
Josiah his father, who went forth from
this place, "He will never return there;
12 but in the place where they led him
captive, there he will [a]die and not see
this land again.

Messages about the Kings

13 "Woe to him who builds his house
[a]without righteousness
And his [1]upper rooms without justice,
Who uses his neighbor's services
without pay
And [b]does not give him his wages,
14 Who says, 'I will [a]build myself a
roomy house
With spacious [1]upper rooms,
And cut out its windows,
[2]Paneling *it* with [b]cedar and painting *it* [3]bright red.'
15 "Do you become a king because you
are competing in cedar?
Did not your father eat and drink,
And [a]do justice and righteousness?
Then it was [b]well with him.
16 "He pled the cause of the [a]afflicted
and needy;
Then it was well.
[b]Is not that what it means to know
Me?"
Declares the LORD.
17 "But your eyes and your heart
Are *intent* only upon your own
[a]dishonest gain,
And on [b]shedding innocent blood
And on practicing oppression and
extortion."

18 Therefore thus says the LORD in
regard to [a]Jehoiakim the son of Josiah,
king of Judah,

"They will not [b]lament for him:
'[c]Alas, my brother!' or, 'Alas, sister!'
They will not lament for him:
'Alas for the master!' or, 'Alas for
his splendor!'
19 "He will be [a]buried with a donkey's
burial,
Dragged off and thrown out beyond the gates of Jerusalem.
20 "Go up to Lebanon and cry out,
And lift up your voice in Bashan;
Cry out also from [a]Abarim,
For all your [b]lovers have been
crushed.
21 "I spoke to you in your prosperity;
But [a]you said, 'I will not listen!'
[b]This has been your practice [c]from
your youth,
That you have not obeyed My
voice.
22 "The wind will sweep away all your
[a]shepherds,
And your [b]lovers will go into captivity;
Then you will surely be [c]ashamed
and humiliated
Because of all your wickedness.
23 "You who dwell in Lebanon,
Nested in the cedars,
How you will groan when pangs
come upon you,
[a]Pain like a woman in childbirth!

24 "As I live," declares the LORD,
"even though [1a]Coniah the son of Jehoiakim king of Judah were a [b]signet
ring on My right hand, yet I would pull
[1]you [2]off;
25 and I shall [a]give you over into the
hand of those who are seeking your life,
yes, into the hand of those whom you
dread, even into the hand of Nebuchadnezzar king of Babylon, and into the
hand of the Chaldeans.
26 "I shall [a]hurl you and your [b]mother
who bore you into another country
where you were not born, and there you
will die.
27 "But as for the land to which they
desire to return, they will not return to
it.

2 [a]Is. 9:7; Jer. 22:4, 30; 17:25; Luke 1:32
3 [a]Is. 58:6, 7; Jer. 7:5, 23; 21:12; Mic. 6:8; Zech. 7:9; 8:16; Matt. 23:23 [b]Ps. 72:4 [c]Ex. 22:21-24 [d]Jer. 7:6; 19:4; 22:17
4 [1]Lit., *for David* [a]Jer. 17:25
5 [a]Jer. 17:27; 26:4 [b]Gen. 22:16; Amos 6:8; Heb. 6:13
6 [a]Gen. 37:25; Num. 32:1; Song 4:1 [b]Ps. 107:34; Is. 6:11; Jer. 7:34; Mic. 3:12
7 [a]Is. 10:3-6; Jer. 4:6, 7 [b]Is. 10:33, 34; 37:24 [c]Jer. 21:14
8 [a]Deut. 29:24-26; 1 Kin. 9:8, 9; 2 Chr. 7:20-22; Jer. 16:10
9 [1]Lit., *say* [a]2 Kin. 22:17; 2 Chr. 34:25; Jer. 11:3
10 [a]Eccl. 4:2; Is. 57:1; Jer. 16:7; 22:18 [b]Jer. 25:27; 44:14
11 [1]I.e., Jehoahaz [a]2 Kin. 23:30-34; 1 Chr. 3:15; 2 Chr. 36:1-4
12 [a]2 Kin. 23:34; Jer. 22:18
13 [1]Or, *roof chambers* [a]Jer. 17:11; Mic. 3:10; Hab. 2:9 [b]Lev. 19:13; James 5:4
14 [1]Or, *roof chambers* [2]Or, *Paneled* [3]Or, *vermilion* [a]Is. 5:8 [b]2 Sam. 7:2; Hag. 1:4
15 [a]2 Kin. 23:25; Jer. 7:5; 21:12 [b]Ps. 128:2; Is. 3:10; Jer. 42:6
16 [a]Ps. 72:1-4, 12, 13 [b]1 Chr. 28:9; Jer. 9:24
17 [a]Jer. 6:13; 8:10; Luke 12:15-20 [b]2 Kin. 24:4; Jer. 22:3
18 [a]2 Kin. 23:36-24:6; 2 Chr. 36:5 [b]Jer. 22:10; 34:5 [c]1 Kin. 13:30
19 [a]1 Kin. 21:23, 24; Jer. 36:30
20 [a]Num. 27:12; Deut. 32:49 [b]Jer. 2:25; 3:1
21 [a]Jer. 13:10; 19:15 [b]Jer. 3:25 [c]Jer. 3:24; 32:30
22 [a]Jer. 23:1 [b]Jer. 30:14 [c]Is. 65:13; Jer. 20:11
23 [a]Jer. 4:31; 6:24
24 [1]I.e., Jehoiachin [2]Lit., *off from there* [a]2 Kin. 24:6; 1 Chr. 3:16; 2 Chr. 36:9; Jer. 37:1 [b]Song 8:6; Is. 49:16; Hag. 2:23
25 [a]2 Kin. 24:15, 16; Jer. 21:7; 34:20, 21
26 [a]2 Kin. 24:15; Jer. 10:18; 16:13 [b]2 Kin. 24:8

28 "Is this man Coniah a despised, shattered jar?
Or is he an [a]undesirable vessel?
Why have he and his descendants been [b]hurled out
And cast into a [c]land that they had not known?
29 "[a]O land, land, land,
Hear the word of the LORD!
30 "Thus says the LORD,
'Write this man down [a]childless,
A man who will [b]not prosper in his days;
For no man of his [c]descendants will prosper
Sitting on the throne of David
Or ruling again in Judah.' "

The Coming Messiah: the Righteous Branch

23 "[a]WOE to the shepherds who are [b]destroying and scattering the [c]sheep of My pasture!" declares the LORD.

2 Therefore thus says the LORD God of Israel concerning the shepherds who are [1]tending My people: "You have scattered My flock and driven them away, and have not attended to them; behold, I am about to [a]attend to you for the [b]evil of your deeds," declares the LORD.

3 "Then I Myself shall [a]gather the remnant of My flock out of all the countries where I have driven them and shall bring them back to their pasture; and they will be fruitful and multiply.

4 "I shall also raise up [a]shepherds over them and they will [1]tend them; and they will [b]not be afraid any longer, nor be terrified, [c]nor will any be missing," declares the LORD.

5 "Behold, *the* [a]days are coming,"
declares the LORD,
"When I shall raise up for David a righteous [1b]Branch;
And He will [c]reign as king and [2]act wisely
And [d]do justice and righteousness in the land.
6 "In His days Judah will be saved,
And [a]Israel will dwell securely;
And this is His [b]name by which He will be called,
'The [c]LORD our righteousness.'

7 "[a]Therefore behold, *the* days are coming," declares the LORD, "when they will no longer say, 'As the LORD lives, who brought up the sons of Israel from the land of Egypt,'

8 [a]but, 'As the LORD lives, who [b]brought up and led back the descendants of the household of Israel from *the* north land and from all the countries where I had driven them.' Then they will live on their own soil."

False Prophets Denounced

9 As for the prophets:
My [a]heart is broken within me,
All my bones tremble;
I have become like a drunken man,
Even like a man overcome with wine,
Because of the LORD
And because of His holy words.
10 For the land is full of [a]adulterers;
For the land [b]mourns because of the curse.
The [c]pastures of the wilderness have dried up.
Their course also is evil,
And their might is not right.
11 "For [a]both prophet and priest are polluted;
Even in My house I have found their wickedness," declares the LORD.
12 "Therefore their way will be like [a]slippery paths to them,
They will be driven away into the [b]gloom and fall down in it;
For I shall bring [c]calamity upon them,
The year of their punishment," declares the LORD.

13 "Moreover, among the prophets of Samaria I saw an [a]offensive thing:
They [b]prophesied by Baal and [c]led My people Israel astray.
14 "Also among the prophets of Jerusalem I have seen a [a]horrible thing:
The committing of [b]adultery and walking in falsehood;
And they strengthen the hands of [c]evildoers,
So that no one has turned back from his wickedness.
All of them have become to Me like [d]Sodom,
And her inhabitants like Gomorrah.
15 "Therefore thus says the LORD of hosts concerning the prophets,
'Behold, I am going to [a]feed them wormwood
And make them drink poisonous water,
For from the prophets of Jerusalem
Pollution has gone forth into all the land.' "

16 Thus says the LORD of hosts,
"[a]Do not listen to the words of the prophets who are prophesying to you.
They are [b]leading you into futility;
They speak a [c]vision of their own [1]imagination,
Not [d]from the mouth of the LORD.
17 "They keep saying to those who [a]despise Me,
'The LORD has said, "[b]You will have peace" ';
And as for everyone who walks in the [c]stubbornness of his own heart,
They say, '[d]Calamity will not come upon you.'

28 aPs. 31:12; Jer. 48:38; Hos. 8:8 bJer. 15:1 cJer. 17:4
29 aDeut. 4:26; Jer. 6:19; Mic. 1:2
30 a1 Chr. 3:17; Matt. 1:12 bJer. 2:37; 10:21 cPs. 94:20; Jer. 36:30
1 aEzek. 13:3; 34:2; Zech. 11:17 bIs. 56:9-12; Jer. 10:21; 50:6 cEzek. 34:31
2 1Lit., *shepherding* aEx. 32:34 bJer. 21:12; 44:22
3 aIs. 11:11, 12, 16; Jer. 31:7, 8; 32:37
4 1Or, *shepherd* aJer. 3:15; 31:10; Ezek. 34:23 bJer. 30:10; 46:27, 28 cJohn 6:39; 10:28; 1 Pet. 1:5
5 1Lit., *Sprout* 2Or, *succeed* aJer. 33:14 bIs. 4:2; 11:1-5; 53:2; Jer. 30:9; 33:15, 16; Zech. 3:8; 6:12, 13 cIs. 9:7; 52:13; Luke 1:32, 33 dPs. 72:2; Is. 9:7; 32:1; Dan. 9:24
6 aDeut. 33:28; Jer. 30:10; Zech. 14:11 bIs. 7:14; 9:6; Matt. 1:21-23 cIs. 45:24; Jer. 33:16; Dan. 9:24; Rom. 3:22; 1 Cor. 1:30
7 aIs. 43:18, 19; Jer. 16:14, 15
8 aJer. 16:15 bIs. 43:5, 6; Ezek. 34:13; Amos 9:14, 15
9 aJer. 8:18; Hab. 3:16
10 aJer. 9:2; Hos. 4:2, 3; Mal. 3:5 bJer. 12:4 cPs. 107:34; Jer. 9:10
11 aJer. 6:13; Zeph. 3:4
12 aPs. 35:6; Prov. 4:19; Jer. 13:16 bIs. 8:22; John 12:35 cJer. 11:23
13 aHos. 9:7, 8 b1 Kin. 18:18-21; Jer. 2:8; 23:32 cIs. 9:16
14 aJer. 5:30 bJer. 29:23 cJer. 23:22; Ezek. 13:22, 23 dGen. 18:20; Deut. 32:32; Is. 1:9, 10; Jer. 20:16; 49:18; Matt. 11:24
15 aDeut. 29:18; Jer. 8:14; 9:15
16 1Lit., *heart* aJer. 27:9, 10, 14-17; 1 John 4:1 bMatt. 7:15; 2 Cor. 11:13-15; Gal. 1:8, 9 cJer. 14:14; Ezek. 13:3, 6 dJer. 9:12, 20
17 aMic. 2:11 bJer. 8:11; Ezek. 13:10 cJer. 13:10; 18:12 dJer. 5:12; Amos 9:10; Mic. 3:11

18 "But [a]who has stood in the council of the LORD,
That he should see and hear His word?
Who has given [b]heed to [1]His word and listened?
19 "Behold, the [a]storm of the LORD has gone forth in wrath,
Even a whirling tempest;
It will swirl down on the head of the wicked.
20 "The [a]anger of the LORD will not turn back
Until He has [b]performed and carried out the purposes of His heart;
[c]In the last days you will clearly understand it.
21 "[a]I did not send *these* prophets,
But they ran.
I did not speak to them,
But they prophesied.
22 "But if they had [a]stood in My council,
Then they would have [b]announced My words to My people,
And would have turned them back from their evil way
And from the evil of their deeds.

23 "Am I a God who is [a]near," declares the LORD,
"And not a God far off?
24 "Can a man [a]hide himself in hiding places,
So I do not see him?" declares the LORD.
"[b]Do I not fill the heavens and the earth?" declares the LORD.

25 "I have [a]heard what the prophets have said who [b]prophesy falsely in My name, saying, 'I had a [c]dream, I had a dream!'

26 "How long? Is there *anything* in the hearts of the prophets who prophesy falsehood, even *these* prophets of the [a]deception of their own heart,

27 who intend to [a]make My people forget My name by their dreams which they relate to one another, just as their fathers [b]forgot My name because of Baal?

28 "The prophet who has a dream may relate *his* dream, but let him who has [a]My word speak My word in truth. [b]What does straw have *in common* with grain?" declares the LORD.

29 "Is not My word like [a]fire?" declares the LORD, "and like a [b]hammer which shatters a rock?

30 "Therefore behold, [a]I am against the prophets," declares the LORD, "who steal My words from each other.

31 "Behold, I am against the prophets," declares the LORD, "who use their tongues and declare, '*The Lord* declares.'

32 "Behold, I am against those who have prophesied [a]false dreams," declares the LORD, "and related them, and led My people astray by their falsehoods and [b]reckless boasting; yet [c]I did not send them or command them, nor do they [d]furnish this people the slightest benefit," declares the LORD.

18 [1]Another reading is *My*
[a]Job 15:8, 9; Jer. 23:22; 1 Cor. 2:16 [b]Job 33:31
19 [a]Jer. 25:32; 30:23; Amos 1:14
20 [a]2 Kin. 23:26, 27; Jer. 30:24 [b]Is. 55:11; Zech. 1:6 [c]Gen. 49:1
21 [a]Jer. 14:14; 23:32; 27:15
22 [a]Jer. 9:12; 23:18 [b]Jer. 35:15; Zech. 1:4
23 [a]Ps. 139:1-10
24 [a]Job 22:13, 14; 34:21, 22; Ps. 139:7-12; Is. 29:15; Jer. 49:10; Heb. 4:13 [b]1 Kin. 8:27; 2 Chr. 2:6; Is. 66:1
25 [a]Jer. 8:6; 1 Cor. 4:5 [b]Jer. 14:14 [c]Num. 12:6; Jer. 23:28, 32; 29:8; Joel 2:28
26 [a]1 Tim. 4:1, 2
27 [a]Deut. 13:1-3; Jer. 29:8 [b]Judg. 3:7; 8:33, 34
28 [a]Jer. 9:12, 20 [b]1 Cor. 3:12, 13
29 [a]Jer. 5:14; 20:9 [b]2 Cor. 10:4, 5
30 [a]Deut. 18:20; Ps. 34:16; Jer. 14:14, 15; Ezek. 13:8
32 [a]Deut. 13:1, 2; Jer. 23:25 [b]Zeph. 3:4 [c]Jer. 23:21; Lam. 3:37 [d]Jer. 7:8; Lam. 2:14
33 [1]Or, *burden,* and so throughout the ch.
[a]Is. 13:1; Nah. 1:1; Hab. 1:1; Zech. 9:1; Mal. 1:1 [b]Jer. 12:7; 23:39
34 [a]Lam. 2:14; Zech. 13:3
35 [a]Jer. 33:3; 42:4
36 [a]Gal. 1:7, 8; 2 Pet. 3:16 [b]2 Kin. 19:4; Jer. 10:10
39 [a]Jer. 7:14, 15; 23:33; Ezek. 8:18
40 [a]Jer. 20:11; 42:18; Ezek. 5:14, 15

1 [a]2 Kin. 24:10-16; 2 Chr. 36:10; Jer. 27:20; 29:1, 2 [b]Amos 8:1
2 [a]Mic. 7:1; Nah. 3:12 [b]Is. 5:4, 7; Jer. 29:17
3 [a]Jer. 1:11, 13; Amos 8:2; Zech. 4:2
5 [a]Nah. 1:7; Zech. 13:9
6 [a]Jer. 12:15; 29:10; 32:37; Ezek. 11:17 [b]Jer. 31:4; 32:41; 33:7; 42:10 [c]Jer. 32:41
7 [a]Deut. 30:6; Jer. 31:33; 32:40; Ezek. 11:19; 36:26 [b]Is. 51:16; Jer. 7:23; 30:22; 31:33; 32:38; Ezek. 14:11; Zech. 8:8; Heb. 8:10 [c]1 Sam. 7:3; Ps. 119:2; Jer. 29:13

33 "Now when this people or the prophet or a priest asks you saying, 'What is the [1a]oracle of the LORD?' then you shall say to them, 'What [1]oracle?' The LORD declares, 'I shall [b]abandon you.'

34 "Then as for the prophet or the priest or the people who say, 'The [a]oracle of the LORD,' I shall bring punishment upon that man and his household.

35 "Thus shall each of you say to his neighbor and to his brother, '[a]What has the LORD answered?' or, 'What has the LORD spoken?'

36 "For you will no longer remember the oracle of the LORD, because every man's own word will become the oracle, and you have [a]perverted the words of the [b]living God, the LORD of hosts, our God.

37 "Thus you will say to *that* prophet, 'What has the LORD answered you?' and, 'What has the LORD spoken?'

38 "For if you say, 'The oracle of the LORD!' surely thus says the LORD, 'Because you said this word, "The oracle of the LORD!" I have also sent to you, saying, "You shall not say, 'The oracle of the LORD!' " '

39 "Therefore behold, [a]I shall surely forget you and cast you away from My presence, along with the city which I gave you and your fathers.

40 "And I will put an everlasting [a]reproach on you and an everlasting humiliation which will not be forgotten."

Baskets of Figs and the Returnees

24 AFTER [a]Nebuchadnezzar king of Babylon had carried away captive Jeconiah the son of Jehoiakim, king of Judah, and the officials of Judah with the craftsmen and smiths from Jerusalem and had brought them to Babylon, the LORD showed me: behold, two [b]baskets of figs set before the temple of the LORD!

2 One basket had very good figs, like [a]first-ripe figs; and the other basket had [b]very bad figs, which could not be eaten due to rottenness.

3 Then the LORD said to me, "[a]What do you see, Jeremiah?" And I said, "Figs, the good figs, very good; and the bad *figs,* very bad, which cannot be eaten due to rottenness."

4 Then the word of the LORD came to me, saying,

5 "Thus says the LORD God of Israel, 'Like these good figs, so I will regard [a]as good the captives of Judah, whom I have sent out of this place *into* the land of the Chaldeans.

6 'For I will set My eyes on them for good, and I will [a]bring them again to this land; and I will [b]build them up and not overthrow them, and I will [c]plant them and not pluck *them* up.

7 'And I will give them a [a]heart to know Me, for I am the LORD; and they will be [b]My people, and I will be their God, for they will [c]return to Me with their whole heart.

8 'But like the [a]bad figs which cannot be eaten due to rottenness—indeed, thus says the LORD—so I will [1]abandon [b]Zedekiah king of Judah and his officials, and the [c]remnant of Jerusalem who remain in this land, and the ones who dwell in the land of [d]Egypt.

9 'And I will [a]make them a terror *and an* evil for all the kingdoms of the earth, as a [b]reproach and a proverb, a taunt and a [c]curse in all places where I shall scatter them.

10 'And I will send the [a]sword, the famine, and the pestilence upon them until they are destroyed from the land which I gave to them and their forefathers.' "

Prophecy of the Captivity

25 THE word that came to Jeremiah concerning all the people of Judah, in the [a]fourth year of [b]Jehoiakim the son of Josiah, king of Judah (that was the [c]first year of Nebuchadnezzar king of Babylon),

2 which Jeremiah the prophet spoke to all the [a]people of Judah and to all the inhabitants of Jerusalem, saying,

3 "From the [a]thirteenth year of [b]Josiah the son of Amon, king of Judah, even to this day, [1]these [c]twenty-three years the word of the LORD has come to me, and I have spoken to you [2d]again and again, but you have not listened.

4 "And the LORD has sent to you all His [a]servants the prophets [1]again and again, but you have not listened nor inclined your ear to hear,

5 saying, '[a]Turn now everyone from his evil way and from the evil of your deeds, and dwell on the land which the LORD has given to you and your forefathers [b]forever and ever;

6 and [a]do not go after other gods to [1]serve them and to [2]worship them, and do not provoke Me to anger with the work of your hands, and I will do you no harm.'

7 "Yet you have not listened to Me," declares the LORD, "in order that you might [a]provoke Me to anger with the work of your hands to your own harm.

8 "Therefore thus says the LORD of hosts, 'Because you have not obeyed My words,

9 behold, I will [a]send and take all the families of the north,' declares the LORD, 'and *I will send* to Nebuchadnezzar king of Babylon, [b]My servant, and will bring them against this land, and against its inhabitants, and against all these nations round about; and I will [1]utterly destroy them, and [c]make them a horror, and a hissing, and an everlasting desolation.

10 'Moreover, I will [1a]take from them the voice of joy and the voice of gladness, the voice of the bridegroom and the voice of the bride, the [b]sound of the millstones and the light of the lamp.

11 'And [a]this whole land shall be a desolation and a horror, and these nations shall serve the king of Babylon [b]seventy years.

Babylon Will Be Judged

12 'Then it will be [a]when seventy years are completed I will [b]punish the king of Babylon and that nation,' declares the LORD, 'for their iniquity, and the land of the Chaldeans; and [c]I will make it an everlasting desolation.

13 'And I will bring upon that land all My words which I have pronounced against it, all that is written in [a]this book, which Jeremiah has prophesied against [b]all the nations.

14 '([1]For [a]many nations and great kings shall make slaves of them, even them; and I will [b]recompense them according to their deeds, and according to the work of their hands.)' "

15 For thus the LORD, the God of Israel, says to me, "Take this [a]cup of the wine of wrath from My hand, and cause all the nations, to whom I send you, to drink it.

16 "And they shall [a]drink and stagger and go mad because of the sword that I will send among them."

17 Then I took the cup from the LORD's hand, and [a]made all the nations drink, to whom the LORD sent me:

18 [a]Jerusalem and the cities of Judah, and its kings *and* its princes, to make them a ruin, a horror, a hissing, and a curse, as it is this day;

19 [a]Pharaoh king of Egypt, his servants, his princes, and all his people;

20 and all the [1a]foreign people, all the kings of the [b]land of Uz, all the kings of the land of the [c]Philistines (even Ashkelon, Gaza, Ekron, and the remnant of [d]Ashdod);

21 [a]Edom, [b]Moab, and the sons of [c]Ammon;

22 and all the kings of [a]Tyre, all the kings of Sidon, and the kings of [b]the coastlands which are beyond the sea;

23 and [a]Dedan, Tema, [b]Buz, and all who [c]cut the corners *of their hair;*

24 and all the kings of [a]Arabia and all the kings of the [1b]foreign people who dwell in the desert;

25 and all the kings of Zimri, all the kings of [a]Elam, and all the kings of [b]Media;

26 and all the kings of the north, near and far, one with another; and [a]all the kingdoms of the earth which are upon the face of the ground, and the king of [1b]Sheshach shall drink after them.

27 "And you shall say to them, 'Thus says the LORD of hosts, the God of Israel, "[a]Drink, be drunk, vomit, fall, and rise no more because of the [b]sword which I will send among you." '

28 "And it will be, if they [a]refuse to take the cup from your hand to drink, then you will say to them, 'Thus says the LORD of hosts: "[b]You shall surely drink!

8 [1]Lit., *give up* [a]Jer. 29:17 [b]Jer. 39:5; Ezek. 12:12, 13 [c]Jer. 39:9 [d]Jer. 44:1, 26-30
9 [a]Jer. 15:4; 29:18; 34:17 [b]1 Kin. 9:7; Ps. 44:13, 14 [c]Is. 65:15
10 [a]Is. 51:19; Jer. 21:9; 27:8; Ezek. 5:12-17

1 [a]Jer. 36:1; 46:2 [b]2 Kin. 24:1, 2; 2 Chr. 36:4-6; Dan. 1:1, 2 [c]Jer. 32:1
2 [a]Jer. 18:11
3 [1]Lit., *this* [2]Lit., *rising early and speaking* [a]Jer. 1:2 [b]2 Chr. 34:1-3, 8 [c]Jer. 36:2 [d]Jer. 7:25; 11:7; 26:5
4 [1]Lit., *rising early and sending* [a]2 Chr. 36:15; Jer. 26:5
5 [a]2 Kin. 17:13; Is. 55:6, 7; Jer. 4:1; 35:15; Ezek. 18:30; Jon. 3:8-10 [b]Gen. 17:8; Jer. 7:7; 17:25
6 [1]Or, *worship* [2]Or, *bow down to* [a]Deut. 6:14; 8:19; 2 Kin. 17:35; Jer. 35:15
7 [a]2 Kin. 17:17; 21:15; Jer. 7:19; 32:30-33
9 [1]Or, *put them under the ban* [a]Jer. 1:15; 6:22, 23 [b]Is. 13:3; Jer. 27:6; 43:10 [c]1 Kin. 9:7, 8; Jer. 18:16; 25:18
10 [1]Lit., *cause to perish* [a]Is. 24:8-11; Jer. 7:34; 16:9; Ezek. 26:13; Rev. 18:23 [b]Eccl. 12:4; Is. 47:2
11 [a]Jer. 4:27; 12:11, 12 [b]2 Chr. 36:21; Jer. 29:10; Dan. 9:2; Zech. 7:5
12 [a]Ezra 1:1; Jer. 29:10; Dan. 9:2 [b]Is. 13:14; Jer. ch. 50, 51 [c]Is. 13:19
13 [a]Jer. 36:4, 29, 32 [b]Jer. 1:5, 10; 36:2
14 [1]Or, *For they have served many nations and great kings* [a]Jer. 27:7; 50:9, 41; 51:27, 28 [b]Jer. 51:6, 24, 56
15 [a]Job 21:20; Ps. 75:8; Is. 51:17, 22; Jer. 51:7
16 [a]Nah. 3:11
17 [a]Jer. 1:10; 25:28
18 [a]Ps. 60:3; Is. 51:17
19 [a]Jer. 46:2-28; Nah. 3:8-10
20 [1]Or, *mixed multitude* [a]Jer. 25:24; 50:37; Ezek. 30:5 [b]Job 1:1; Lam. 4:21 [c]Jer. 47:1-7 [d]Is. 20:1
21 [a]Ps. 137:7; Jer. 49:7-22 [b]Jer. 48:1-47; Amos 2:1-3 [c]Jer. 49:1-6; Amos 1:13-15
22 [a]Jer. 47:4; Zech. 9:2-4 [b]Jer. 31:10
23 [a]Is. 21:13; Jer. 49:7, 8 [b]Gen. 22:21 [c]Jer. 9:26; 49:32

24 [1]Or, *mixed multitude* [a]2 Chr. 9:14 [b]Jer. 25:20; 50:37; Ezek. 30:5
25 [a]Gen. 10:22; Is. 11:11; Jer. 49:34 [b]Is. 13:17; Jer. 51:11, 28
26 [1]Cryptic name for Babylon [a]Jer. 25:9; 50:9 [b]Jer. 51:41
27 [a]Jer. 25:16; Hab. 2:16 [b]Ezek. 21:4, 5
28 [a]Job 34:33 [b]Jer. 49:12

29"For behold, I am [a]beginning to
work calamity in *this* city which is
[b]called by My name, and shall you be
completely free from punishment? You
will not be free from punishment; for [c]I
am summoning a sword against all the
inhabitants of the earth," declares the
LORD of hosts.'
30"Therefore you shall prophesy
against them all these words, and you
shall say to them,

'The [a]LORD will [b]roar from on high,
And utter His voice from His holy habitation;
He will roar mightily against His [1]fold.
He will shout like those who tread *the grapes,*
Against all the inhabitants of the earth.
31 'A clamor has come to the end of the earth,
Because the LORD has [a]a controversy with the nations.
He is entering into [b]judgment with all flesh;
As for the wicked, He has given them to the sword,' declares the LORD."

32 Thus says the LORD of hosts,
"Behold, evil is going forth
From [a]nation to nation,
And a great [b]storm is being stirred up
From the remotest parts of the earth.

33"And those [a]slain by the LORD on
that day shall be from one end of the
earth to the [1]other. They shall [b]not be
lamented, gathered, or buried; they shall
be like [c]dung on the face of the ground.

34"Wail, you shepherds, and cry;
And [a]wallow *in ashes,* you masters of the flock;
For the days of your [b]slaughter and your dispersions [1]have come,
And you shall fall like a choice vessel.
35"[a]Flight shall perish from the shepherds,
And escape from the masters of the flock.
36"*Hear* the sound of the cry of the shepherds,
And the wailing of the masters of the flock!
For the LORD is destroying their pasture,
37"And the peaceful [1a]folds are made silent
Because of the [b]fierce anger of the LORD.
38"He has left His hiding place [a]like the lion;
For their land has become a horror
Because of the fierceness of the [1]oppressing *sword,*
And because of His fierce anger."

Cities of Judah Warned

26 IN the beginning of the reign of
[a]Jehoiakim the son of Josiah,
king of Judah, this word came from the
LORD, saying,
2"Thus says the LORD, '[a]Stand in the
court of the LORD's house, and speak to
all the cities of Judah, who have [b]come
to worship *in* the LORD's house, [c]all the
words that I have commanded you to
speak to them. [d]Do not omit a word!
3 '[a]Perhaps they will listen and everyone will turn from his evil way, that [b]I
may repent of the calamity which I am
planning to do to them because of the
evil of their deeds.'
4"And you will say to them, 'Thus
says the LORD, "[a]If you will not listen to
Me, to [b]walk in My law, which I have set
before you,
5 to listen to the words of [a]My servants the prophets, whom I have been
sending to you [1]again and again, but you
have not listened;
6 then I will make this house like
[a]Shiloh, and this city I will make a
[b]curse to all the nations of the earth." ' "

A Plot to Murder Jeremiah

7 And the [a]priests and the prophets
and all the people heard Jeremiah speaking these words in the house of the
LORD.
8 And when Jeremiah finished speaking all that the LORD had commanded
him to speak to all the people, the priests
and the prophets and all the people
seized him, saying, "[a]You must die!
9"Why have you prophesied in the
name of the LORD saying, 'This house
will be like Shiloh, and this city will be
[a]desolate, without inhabitant'?" And [b]all
the people gathered about Jeremiah in
the house of the LORD.
10 And when the [a]princes of Judah
heard these things, they came up from
the king's house to the house of the
LORD and sat in the [b]entrance of the
New Gate of the LORD's *house.*
11 Then the priests and the prophets
[a]spoke to the officials and to all the
people, saying, "A [b]death sentence for
this man! For he has prophesied [c]against
this city as you have heard in your
hearing."
12 Then Jeremiah spoke to all the
officials and to all the people, saying,
"[a]The LORD sent me to prophesy against
this house and against this city all the
words that you have heard.
13"Now therefore [a]amend your ways
and your deeds, and obey the voice of
the LORD your God; and the LORD will
[1]change His mind about the misfortune
which He has pronounced against you.
14"But as for me, behold, [a]I am in
your hands; do with me as is good and
right in your sight.
15"Only know for certain that if you
put me to death, you will bring [a]inno-
cent blood on yourselves, and on this
city, and on its inhabitants; for truly the
LORD has sent me to you to speak all
these words in your hearing."

29 [a]Prov. 11:31; Is. 10:12; Jer. 13:13; Ezek. 9:6; 1 Pet. 4:17 [b]1 Kin. 8:43 [c]Ezek. 38:21

30 [1]Or, *pasture* [a]Is. 42:13; Jer. 25:38 [b]Joel 2:11; 3:16; Amos 1:2

31 [a]Hos. 4:1; Mic. 6:2 [b]Is. 66:16; Ezek. 20:35, 36; Joel 3:2

32 [a]2 Chr. 15:6; Is. 34:2 [b]Is. 30:30; Jer. 23:19

33 [1]Lit., *other end of the earth* [a]Is. 34:2, 3; 66:16 [b]Ps. 79:3; Jer. 16:4; Ezek. 39:4, 17 [c]Is. 5:25

34 [1]Lit., *are full* [a]Jer. 6:26; Ezek. 27:30 [b]Is. 34:6, 7; Jer. 50:27

35 [a]Job 11:20; Jer. 11:11; Amos 2:14

37 [1]Or, *pastures* [a]Is. 27:10, 11; Jer. 5:17; 13:20 [b]Ps. 97:1-3; Is. 66:15; Heb. 12:29

38 [1]Or, *oppressor* [a]Jer. 4:7; 5:6; Hos. 5:14; 13:7, 8

1 [a]2 Kin. 23:36; 2 Chr. 36:4, 5

2 [a]2 Chr. 24:20, 21; Jer. 7:2; 19:14 [b]Deut. 12:5 [c]Jer. 1:17; 42:4; Matt. 28:20; Acts 20:20, 27 [d]Deut. 4:2

3 [a]Is. 1:16-19; Jer. 36:3-7 [b]Jer. 18:8; Jon. 3:8

4 [a]Lev. 26:14; 1 Kin. 9:6; Is. 1:20; Jer. 17:27; 22:5 [b]Jer. 32:23; 44:10, 23

5 [1]Lit., *rising early and sending* [a]2 Kin. 9:7; Ezra 9:11; Jer. 7:13; 25:3, 4

6 [a]Josh. 18:1; 1 Sam. 4:12; Ps. 78:60, 61; Jer. 7:12, 14 [b]2 Kin. 22:19; Is. 65:15; Jer. 24:9; 25:18

7 [a]Jer. 5:31; Mic. 3:11

8 [a]Jer. 11:19; 18:23; Lam. 4:13, 14; Matt. 21:35, 36; 23:34, 35; 27:20

9 [a]Jer. 9:11; 33:10 [b]Acts 3:11; 5:12

10 [a]Jer. 26:21 [b]Jer. 36:10

11 [a]Jer. 18:23 [b]Deut. 18:20; Matt. 26:66 [c]Jer. 38:4; Acts 6:11-14

12 [a]Jer. 1:17, 18; 26:15; Amos 7:15; Acts 4:19; 5:29

13 [1]Lit., *be sorry for* [a]Jer. 7:3, 5; 18:8, 11; 26:3; 35:15; Joel 2:14; Jon. 3:9; 4:2

14 [a]Jer. 38:5

15 [a]Num. 35:33; Prov. 6:16, 17; Jer. 7:6

Jeremiah Is Spared

16 Then the officials and all the people
[a]said to the priests and to the prophets,
"No [b]death sentence for this man! For
he has spoken to us in the name of the
LORD our God."
17 Then [a]some of the elders of the
land rose up and spoke to all the assembly of the people, saying,
18 "[1a]Micah of Moresheth prophesied
in the days of Hezekiah king of Judah;
and he spoke to all the people of Judah,
saying, 'Thus the LORD of hosts has said,
"[b]Zion will be plowed *as* a field,
And Jerusalem will become ruins,
And the [c]mountain of the house as
the [2]high places of a forest." '
19 "Did Hezekiah king of Judah and all
Judah put him to death? Did he not
[a]fear the LORD and entreat the favor of
the LORD, and [b]the LORD [1]changed His
mind about the misfortune which He
had pronounced against them? But we
are [c]committing a great evil against
ourselves."
20 Indeed, there was also a man who
prophesied in the name of the LORD,
Uriah the son of Shemaiah from [a]Kiri-
ath-jearim; and he prophesied against
this city and against this land words
similar to all those of Jeremiah.
21 When King Jehoiakim and all his
mighty men and all the officials heard
his words, then the [a]king sought to put
him to death; but Uriah heard *it,* and he
was afraid and [b]fled, and went to Egypt.
22 Then King Jehoiakim sent men to
Egypt: [a]Elnathan the son of Achbor and
certain men with him *went* into Egypt.
23 And they brought Uriah from
Egypt and led him to King Jehoiakim,
who [a]slew him with a sword, and cast his
dead body into the [1]burial place of the
[2]common people.
24 But the hand of [a]Ahikam the son of
Shaphan was with Jeremiah, so that he
was [b]not given into the hands of the
people to put him to death.

The Nations to Submit to Nebuchadnezzar

27 IN the beginning of the reign of
[1a]Zedekiah the son of Josiah,
king of Judah, this word came to Jeremiah from the LORD, saying—
2 thus says the LORD to me—"Make
for yourself [a]bonds and [b]yokes and put
them on your neck,
3 and send [1]word to the king of
[a]Edom, to the king of [a]Moab, to the king
of the sons of [a]Ammon, to the king of
[a]Tyre, and to the king of [a]Sidon [2]by the
messengers who come to Jerusalem to
Zedekiah king of Judah.
4 "And command them *to go* to their
masters, saying, 'Thus says the LORD of
hosts, the God of Israel, thus you shall
say to your masters,
5 "[a]I have made the earth, the men
and the beasts which are on the face of
the earth [b]by My great power and by My
outstretched arm, and I will [c]give it to
the one who is [1]pleasing in My sight.
6 "And now I [a]have given all these
lands into the hand of Nebuchadnezzar
king of Babylon, [b]My servant, and I
have given him also the [c]wild animals of
the field to serve him.
7 "And [a]all the nations shall serve
him, and his son, and his grandson,
[b]until the time of his own land comes;
then [c]many nations and great kings will
[1]make him their servant.
8 "And it will be, *that* the nation or
the kingdom which [a]will not serve him,
Nebuchadnezzar king of Babylon, and
which will not put its neck under the
yoke of the king of Babylon, I will
punish that nation with the [b]sword, with
famine, and with pestilence," declares
the LORD, "until I have destroyed [1]it by
his hand.
9 "But as for you, [a]do not listen to
your prophets, your diviners, your
[1]dreamers, your soothsayers, or your
sorcerers, who speak to you, saying,
'You shall not serve the king of Babylon.'
10 "For they prophesy a [a]lie to you, in
order to [b]remove you far from your
land; and I will drive you out, and you
will perish.
11 "But the nation which will [a]bring its
neck under the yoke of the king of
Babylon and serve him, I will [b]let remain
on its land," declares the LORD, "and
they will till it and dwell in it." ' "
12 And I spoke words like all these to
[a]Zedekiah king of Judah, saying, "Bring
your necks under the yoke of the king of
Babylon, and serve him and his people,
and live!
13 "Why will you [a]die, you and your
people, by the sword, famine, and pestilence, as the LORD has spoken to that
nation which will not serve the king of
Babylon?
14 "So [a]do not listen to the words of
the prophets who speak to you, saying,
'You shall not serve the king of Babylon,' for they prophesy a [b]lie to you;
15 for [a]I have not sent them," declares
the LORD, "but they [b]prophesy falsely in
My name, in order that I may [c]drive you
out, and that you may perish, [d]you and
the prophets who prophesy to you."
16 *Then* I spoke to the priests and to
all this people, saying, "Thus says the
LORD: Do not listen to the words of
your prophets who prophesy to you,
saying, 'Behold, the [a]vessels of the
LORD's house will now shortly be
brought again from Babylon'; for they
are prophesying a [b]lie to you.
17 "Do not listen to them; serve the
king of Babylon, and live! Why should
this city [a]become a ruin?
18 "But [a]if they are prophets, and if the
word of the LORD is with them, let them
now [b]entreat the LORD of hosts, that the
vessels which are left in the house of the
LORD, in the house of the king of Judah,
and in Jerusalem, may not go to Babylon.

16 [a]Jer. 26:11; 36:19, 25; 38:7, 13 [b]Acts 5:34-39; 23:9, 29; 25:25; 26:31
17 [a]Acts 5:34
18 [1]Lit., *Micaiah the Morasthite* [2]Or, *a wooded height* [a]Mic. 1:1 [b]Neh. 4:2; Ps. 79:1; Jer. 9:11; Mic. 3:12 [c]Is. 2:2, 3; Jer. 17:3; Mic. 4:1; Zech. 8:3
19 [1]Lit., *was sorry for* [a]2 Chr. 29:6-11; 32:26; Is. 37:1, 4, 15-20 [b]Ex. 32:14; 2 Sam. 24:16 [c]Jer. 44:7; Hab. 2:10
20 [a]Josh. 9:17; 1 Sam. 6:21; 7:2
21 [a]2 Chr. 16:10; 24:21; Jer. 36:26; Matt. 14:5 [b]1 Kin. 19:2-4; Matt. 10:23
22 [a]Jer. 36:12
23 [1]Lit., *graves* [2]Lit., *sons of the people* [a]Jer. 2:30
24 [a]2 Kin. 22:12-14; Jer. 39:14; 40:5-7 [b]1 Kin. 18:4; Jer. 1:18, 19

1 [1]Many mss. read *Jehoiakim* [a]2 Kin. 24:18-20; 2 Chr. 36:11-13
2 [a]Jer. 30:8 [b]Jer. 28:10, 13
3 [1]Lit., *them* [2]Lit., *by the hand of* [a]Jer. 25:21, 22
5 [1]Or, *upright* [a]Ps. 96:5; 146:5, 6; Is. 42:5; 45:12; Jer. 10:12; 51:15 [b]Deut. 9:29; Jer. 32:17; Dan. 4:17 [c]Ps. 115:15, 16; Acts 17:26
6 [a]Jer. 21:7; 22:25; Ezek. 29:18-20 [b]Is. 44:28; Jer. 25:9; 43:10 [c]Jer. 28:14; Dan. 2:38
7 [1]Or, *enslave him* [a]2 Chr. 36:20; Jer. 44:30; 46:13 [b]Dan. 5:26; Zech. 2:8, 9 [c]Is. 14:4-6; Jer. 25:12
8 [1]Lit., *them* [a]Jer. 38:17-19; 42:15, 16; Ezek. 17:19-21 [b]Jer. 24:10; 27:13; 29:17, 18; Ezek. 14:21
9 [1]Lit., *dreams* [a]Ex. 22:18; Deut. 18:10; Prov. 19:27; Is. 8:19; Mal. 3:5; Eph. 5:6
10 [a]Jer. 23:25 [b]Jer. 8:19; 32:31
11 [a]Jer. 27:2, 8, 12 [b]Jer. 21:9; 38:2; 40:9-12; 42:10, 11
12 [a]Jer. 27:3; 28:1; 38:17
13 [a]Prov. 8:36; Jer. 27:8; 38:23; Ezek. 18:31
14 [a]Jer. 27:9; 2 Cor. 11:13-15 [b]Jer. 14:14; 23:21; 27:10; 29:8, 9; Ezek. 13:22
15 [a]Jer. 23:21; 29:9 [b]Jer. 23:25 [c]2 Chr. 25:16; Jer. 27:10 [d]Jer. 6:13-15; 14:15, 16
16 [a]2 Kin. 24:13; 2 Chr. 36:7, 10; Jer. 28:3; Dan. 1:2 [b]Jer. 27:10
17 [a]Jer. 7:34
18 [a]1 Kin. 18:24 [b]1 Sam. 7:8; 12:19, 23; Jer. 18:20

19 "For thus says the LORD of hosts concerning the [a]pillars, concerning the sea, concerning the stands, and concerning the rest of the vessels that are left in this city,

20 which Nebuchadnezzar king of Babylon did not take when he [a]carried into exile Jeconiah the son of Jehoiakim, king of Judah, from Jerusalem to Babylon, and all the nobles of Judah and Jerusalem.

21 "Yes, thus says the LORD of hosts, the God of Israel, concerning the vessels that are left in the house of the LORD, and in the house of the king of Judah, and in Jerusalem,

22 'They shall be [a]carried to Babylon, and they shall be there until the [b]day I visit them,' declares the LORD. 'Then I will [c]bring them [1]back and restore them to this place.' "

Hananiah's False Prophecy

28 NOW it came about in the same year, [a]in the beginning of the reign of [b]Zedekiah king of Judah, in the fourth year, in the fifth month, that [c]Hananiah the son of Azzur, the prophet, who was from [d]Gibeon, spoke to me in the house of the LORD in the presence of the priests and all the people, saying,

2 "[a]Thus says the LORD of hosts, the God of Israel, 'I have broken the yoke of the king of Babylon.

3 'Within two years I am going to bring back to this place [a]all the vessels of the LORD's house, which Nebuchadnezzar king of Babylon took away from this place and carried to Babylon.

4 'I am [a]also going to bring back to this place [b]Jeconiah the son of Jehoiakim, king of Judah, and all the [c]exiles of Judah who went to Babylon,' declares the LORD, 'for I will break the [d]yoke of the king of Babylon.' "

5 Then the prophet Jeremiah spoke to the prophet Hananiah in the presence of the priests and in the presence of all the people who were standing in the [a]house of the LORD,

6 and the prophet Jeremiah said, "[a]Amen! May the LORD do so; may the LORD [1]confirm your words which you have prophesied to bring back the vessels of the LORD's house and all the exiles, from Babylon to this place.

7 "Yet [a]hear now this word which I am about to speak in your hearing and in the hearing of all the people!

8 "The prophets who were before me and before you from ancient times [a]prophesied against many lands and against great kingdoms, of war and of calamity and of pestilence.

9 "The prophet who prophesies of peace, [a]when the word of the prophet shall come to pass, then that prophet will be known *as* one whom the LORD has truly sent."

10 Then Hananiah the prophet took the [a]yoke from the neck of Jeremiah the prophet and broke it.

11 And Hananiah spoke in the presence of all the people, saying, "[a]Thus says the LORD, 'Even so will I break within two full years, the yoke of Nebuchadnezzar king of Babylon from the neck of all the nations.' " Then the prophet Jeremiah went his way.

12 And the [a]word of the LORD came to Jeremiah, after Hananiah the prophet had broken the yoke from off the neck of the prophet Jeremiah, saying,

13 "Go and speak to Hananiah, saying, 'Thus says the LORD, "You have broken the yokes of wood, but you have made instead of them [a]yokes of iron."

14 'For thus says the LORD of hosts, the God of Israel, "I have put a [a]yoke of iron on the neck of all these nations, that they may serve Nebuchadnezzar king of Babylon; and they shall [b]serve him. And [c]I have also given him the beasts of the field." ' "

15 Then Jeremiah the prophet said to Hananiah the prophet, "Listen now, Hananiah, the LORD has not sent you, and [a]you have made this people trust in a lie.

16 "Therefore thus says the LORD, '[a]Behold, I am about to [1]remove you from the face of the earth. This year you are going to [b]die, because you have [2c]counseled rebellion against the LORD.' "

17 So Hananiah the prophet died in the same year in the seventh month.

Message to the Exiles

29 NOW these are the words of the [a]letter which Jeremiah the prophet sent from Jerusalem to the rest of the elders of the exile, the priests, the prophets, and all the people whom Nebuchadnezzar had taken into exile from Jerusalem to Babylon.

2 (This was after King [a]Jeconiah and the [b]queen mother, the court officials, the princes of Judah and Jerusalem, the craftsmen and the smiths had departed from Jerusalem.)

3 *The letter was sent* by the hand of Elasah the son of Shaphan, and Gemariah the son of [a]Hilkiah, whom Zedekiah king of Judah sent to Babylon to Nebuchadnezzar king of Babylon, saying,

4 "Thus says the LORD of hosts, the God of Israel, to all the exiles whom I have [a]sent into exile from Jerusalem to Babylon,

5 '[a]Build houses and live *in them;* and plant gardens, and eat their [1]produce.

6 'Take [a]wives and [1]become the fathers of sons and daughters, and take wives for your sons and give your daughters to husbands, that they may bear sons and daughters; and multiply there and do not decrease.

7 'And [a]seek the [1]welfare of the city where I have sent you into exile, and [b]pray to the LORD on its behalf; for in its [1]welfare you will have [1]welfare.'

19 [a]1 Kin. 7:15; 2 Kin. 25:13, 17; Jer. 52:17-23
20 [a]2 Kin. 24:12, 14-16; 2 Chr. 36:10, 18; Jer. 22:28; 24:1
22 [1]Lit., *up* [a]Jer. 34:2, 3 [b]Jer. 25:11, 12; 27:7; 29:10; 32:5 [c]Ezra 1:7-11; 5:13-15; 7:19
1 [a]Jer. 27:1; 49:34 [b]2 Kin. 24:18-20; 2 Chr. 36:11-13; Jer. 27:3, 12 [c]Jer. 28:17 [d]Josh. 9:3; 10:12; 1 Kin. 3:4
2 [a]Jer. 27:12; 28:11
3 [a]2 Kin. 24:13; 2 Chr. 36:10; Jer. 27:16; Dan. 1:2
4 [a]Jer. 22:26, 27 [b]2 Kin. 25:27; Jer. 22:24; 24:1 [c]Jer. 22:10 [d]Jer. 27:8
5 [a]Jer. 28:1
6 [1]Or, *fulfill* [a]1 Kin. 1:36; Ps. 41:13; Jer. 11:5
7 [a]1 Kin. 22:28
8 [a]Lev. 26:14-39; 1 Kin. 14:15; 17:1; 22:17; Is. 5:5-7; Joel 1:20; Amos 1:2; Nah. 1:2
9 [a]Deut. 18:22
10 [a]Jer. 27:2
11 [a]Jer. 14:14; 27:10; 28:15
12 [a]Jer. 1:2
13 [a]Ps. 107:16; Is. 45:2
14 [a]Deut. 28:48; Jer. 27:8 [b]Jer. 25:11 [c]Jer. 27:6
15 [a]Jer. 20:6; 29:31; Lam. 2:14; Ezek. 13:2, 3, 22; 22:28; Zech. 13:3
16 [1]Lit., *send you away* [2]Lit., *spoken* [a]Gen. 7:4; Ex. 32:12; Deut. 6:15; 1 Kin. 13:34 [b]Jer. 20:6 [c]Deut. 13:5; Jer. 29:32
1 [a]2 Chr. 30:1, 6; Esth. 9:20; Jer. 29:25, 29
2 [a]2 Kin. 24:12-16; 2 Chr. 36:9, 10; Jer. 22:24-28; 24:1; 27:20 [b]2 Kin. 24:12, 15; Jer. 13:18; 22:26
3 [a]1 Chr. 6:13
4 [a]Jer. 24:5
5 [1]Lit., *fruit* [a]Jer. 29:28
6 [1]Lit., *beget* [a]Jer. 16:2-4
7 [1]Or, *peace* [a]Dan. 4:27; 6:4, 5 [b]Ezra 6:10; 7:23; Dan. 4:19; 1 Tim. 2:1, 2

8 "For thus says the LORD of hosts,
the God of Israel, 'Do not let your
[a]prophets who are in your midst and
your diviners [b]deceive you, and do not
listen to [1][c]the dreams which [2]they
dream.
9 'For they [a]prophesy falsely to you
in My name; [b]I have not sent them,'
declares the LORD.
10 "For thus says the LORD, 'When
[a]seventy years have been completed for
Babylon, I will visit you and fulfill My
[b]good word to you, to bring you back to
this place.
11 'For I know the [a]plans that I [1]have
for you,' declares the LORD, 'plans for
[b]welfare and not for calamity to give you
a future and a [c]hope.
12 'Then you will [a]call upon Me and
come and pray to Me, and I will [b]listen
to you.
13 'And you will [a]seek Me and find
Me, when you [b]search for Me with all
your heart.
14 'And I will be [a]found by you,'
declares the LORD, 'and I will [b]restore
your [1]fortunes and will [c]gather you from
all the nations and from all the places
where I have driven you,' declares the
LORD, 'and I will [d]bring you back to the
place from where I sent you into exile.'
15 "Because you have said, 'The LORD
has raised up [a]prophets for us in Babylon'—
16 for thus says the LORD concerning
the king who sits on the throne of David,
and concerning all the people who dwell
in this city, your brothers who did [a]not
go with you into exile—
17 thus says the LORD of hosts, 'Behold, I am sending upon them the
[a]sword, famine, and pestilence, and I
will make them like [b]split-open figs that
cannot be eaten due to rottenness.
18 'And I will pursue them with the
sword, with famine and with pestilence;
and I will [a]make them a terror to all the
kingdoms of the earth, to be a [b]curse,
and a horror, and a [c]hissing, and a
reproach among all the nations where I
have driven them,
19 because they have [a]not listened to
My words,' declares the LORD, 'which I
sent to them again and again by [b]My
servants the prophets; but you did not
listen,' declares the LORD.
20 "You, therefore, hear the word of
the LORD, all you exiles, whom I have
[a]sent away from Jerusalem to Babylon.
21 "Thus says the LORD of hosts, the
God of Israel, concerning Ahab the son
of Kolaiah and concerning Zedekiah the
son of Maaseiah, who are [a]prophesying
to you falsely in My name, 'Behold, I
will deliver them into the hand of Nebuchadnezzar king of Babylon, and he
shall slay them before your eyes.
22 'And because of them a [a]curse shall
be [1]used by all the exiles from Judah
who are in Babylon, saying, "May the
LORD make you like Zedekiah and like
Ahab, whom the king of Babylon
[b]roasted in the fire,
23 because they have [a]acted foolishly
in Israel, and [b]have committed adultery
with their neighbors' wives, and have
[c]spoken words in My name falsely,
which I did not command them; and I
am He who [d]knows, and am a witness,"
declares the LORD.' "
24 And to [a]Shemaiah the Nehelamite
you shall speak, saying,
25 "Thus says the LORD of hosts, the
God of Israel, 'Because you have sent
[a]letters in your own name to all the
people who are in Jerusalem, and to
[b]Zephaniah the son of Maaseiah, the
priest, and to all the priests, saying,
26 "The LORD has made you priest
instead of Jehoiada the priest, to be the
[1][a]overseer in the house of the LORD over
every [b]madman who [c]prophesies, to [d]put
him in the stocks and in the iron collar,
27 now then, why have you not rebuked Jeremiah of [a]Anathoth who
prophesies to you?
28 "For he has [a]sent to us in Babylon,
saying, '*The exile* will be [b]long; [c]build
houses and live *in them* and plant gardens and eat their [1]produce.' " ' "
29 And [a]Zephaniah the priest read
this letter [1]to Jeremiah the prophet.
30 Then came the word of the LORD
to Jeremiah, saying,
31 "Send to [a]all the exiles, saying,
'Thus says the LORD concerning
[b]Shemaiah the Nehelamite, "Because
Shemaiah has [c]prophesied to you, although I did not send him, and he has
[d]made you trust in a lie,"
32 therefore thus says the LORD, "Behold, I am about to [a]punish Shemaiah
the Nehelamite and his [1]descendants; he
shall [b]not have anyone living among this
people, [c]and he shall not see the good
that I am about to do to My people,"
declares the LORD, "because he has
[2][d]preached rebellion against the
LORD." ' "

Deliverance from Captivity Promised

30 THE word which came to Jeremiah from the LORD, saying,
2 "Thus says the LORD, the God of
Israel, '[a]Write all the words which I have
spoken to you in a book.
3 'For, behold, [a]days are coming,'
declares the LORD, 'when I will [b]restore
the [1]fortunes of My people [c]Israel and
Judah.' The LORD says, 'I will also
[d]bring them back to the land that I gave
to their forefathers, and they shall possess it.' "
4 Now these are the words which the
LORD spoke concerning Israel and concerning Judah,
5 "For thus says the LORD,
'[1]I have heard a sound of [a]terror,
Of dread, and there is no peace.

8 [1]Lit., *your* [2]Lit., *you*
[a]Jer. 27:9; 29:1 [b]Jer. 14:14; 23:21; 27:14, 15; 28:15; Eph. 5:6 [c]Jer. 23:25, 27
9 [a]Jer. 27:15; 29:21 [b]Jer. 29:31
10 [a]2 Chr. 36:21-23; Jer. 25:12; 27:22; Dan. 9:2; Zech. 7:5 [b]Jer. 24:6, 7; Zeph. 2:7
11 [1]Lit., *am planning*
[a]Ps. 40:5; Jer. 23:5, 6; 30:9, 10 [b]Is. 40:9-11; Jer. 30:18-22 [c]Jer. 31:17; Hos. 2:15
12 [a]Ps. 50:15; Jer. 33:3; Dan. 9:3 [b]Ps. 145:19
13 [a]Deut. 4:29; Ps. 32:6; Matt. 7:7 [b]1 Chr. 22:19; 2 Chr. 22:9; Jer. 24:7
14 [1]Or, *captivity*
[a]Deut. 30:1-10; Ps. 32:6; Is. 55:6 [b]Jer. 30:3; 32:37-41 [c]Is. 43:5, 6; Jer. 23:8; 32:37 [d]Jer. 3:14; 12:15; 16:15
15 [a]Jer. 29:21, 24
16 [a]Jer. 38:2, 3, 17-23
17 [a]Jer. 27:8; 29:18; 32:24 [b]Jer. 24:3, 8-10
18 [a]Deut. 28:25; 2 Chr. 29:8; Jer. 15:4; 24:9; 34:17; Ezek. 12:15 [b]Is. 65:15; Jer. 42:18 [c]Jer. 25:9; Lam. 2:15, 16
19 [a]Jer. 6:19 [b]Jer. 25:4; 26:5; 35:15
20 [a]Jer. 24:5; Ezek. 11:9; Mic. 4:10
21 [a]Jer. 14:14, 15; 29:8, 9; Lam. 2:14; 2 Pet. 2:1
22 [1]Lit., *taken*
[a]Is. 65:15 [b]Dan. 3:6, 21
23 [a]Gen. 34:7; 2 Sam. 13:12 [b]Jer. 5:8; 23:14 [c]Jer. 29:8, 9, 21 [d]Prov. 5:21; Jer. 7:11; 16:17; Mal. 3:5; Heb. 4:13
24 [a]Jer. 29:31, 32
25 [a]Jer. 29:1
[b]2 Kin. 25:18; Jer. 21:1; 29:29; 37:3; 52:24
26 [1]Lit., *overseers*
[a]Jer. 20:1 [b]2 Kin. 9:11; Hos. 9:7; Mark 3:21; John 10:20; Acts 26:24, 25; 2 Cor. 5:13 [c]Deut. 13:1-5; Zech. 13:1-5 [d]Jer. 20:1, 2; Acts 16:24
27 [a]Jer. 1:1
28 [1]Lit., *fruit*
[a]Jer. 29:1 [b]Jer. 29:10 [c]Jer. 29:5
29 [1]Lit., *in the ears of*
[a]Jer. 29:25
31 [a]Jer. 29:20 [b]Jer. 29:24 [c]Jer. 14:14, 15; 29:9, 23; Ezek. 13:8-16, 22, 23 [d]Jer. 28:15
32 [1]Lit., *seed* [2]Lit., *spoken*
[a]Jer. 36:31 [b]1 Sam. 2:30-34; Jer. 22:30 [c]2 Kin. 7:2, 19, 20; Jer. 17:6; 29:10 [d]Deut. 13:5; Jer. 28:16

2 [a]Is. 30:8; Jer. 25:13; 36:4, 28, 32; Hab. 2:2
3 [1]Or, *captivity* [a]Jer. 29:10 [b]Ps. 53:6; Jer. 29:14; 30:18; 32:44; Ezek. 39:25; Amos 9:14; Zeph. 3:20 [c]Jer. 3:18 [d]Jer. 16:15; 23:7, 8; Ezek. 20:42; 36:24
5 [1]Lit., *We* [a]Is. 5:30; Jer. 6:25; 8:16; Amos 5:16-18

6 'Ask now, and see,
If a male can give birth.
Why do I see every man
With his hands on his loins, [a]as a
woman in childbirth?
And *why* have all faces turned pale?
7 'Alas! for that [a]day is great,
There is [b]none like it;
And it is the time of Jacob's [c]dis-
tress,
But he will be [d]saved from it.
8 'And it shall come about on that
day,' declares the LORD of hosts, 'that I
will [a]break his yoke from off [1]their neck,
and will tear off [1]their [b]bonds; and
strangers shall no longer [c]make [2]them
their slaves.
9 'But they shall serve the LORD their
God, and [a]David their king, whom I will
raise up for them.
10 '[a]And fear not, O Jacob My servant,' declares the LORD,
'And do not be dismayed, O Israel;
For behold, I will save you [b]from
afar,
And your [1]offspring from the land
of their captivity.
And Jacob shall return, and shall
be [c]quiet and at ease,
And [d]no one shall make him afraid.
11 'For [a]I am with you,' declares the
LORD, 'to save you;
For I will [b]destroy completely all
the nations where I have scattered you,
Only I will [c]not destroy you completely.
But I will [d]chasten you justly,
And will by no means leave you
unpunished.'

12 "For thus says the LORD,
'Your wound is incurable,
And your [a]injury is serious.
13 'There is no one to plead your
cause;
No healing for *your* sore,
[a]No recovery for you.
14 'All your [a]lovers have forgotten
you,
They do not seek you;
For I have [b]wounded you with the
wound of an enemy,
With the [c]punishment of a [d]cruel
one,
Because your [e]iniquity is great
And your [f]sins are numerous.
15 'Why do you cry out over your
injury?
Your pain is incurable.
Because your iniquity is great
And your sins are numerous,
I have done these things to you.
16 'Therefore all who [a]devour you
shall be devoured;
And all your adversaries, every one
of them, [b]shall go into captivity;
And those who plunder you shall
be for plunder,
And all who prey upon you I will
give for prey.
17 'For I will [1]restore you to [2a]health
And I will heal you of your
wounds,' declares the LORD,
'Because they have called you an
[b]outcast, saying:
"It is Zion; no one [3]cares for her." '

Restoration of Jacob

18 "Thus says the LORD,
'Behold, I will [a]restore the [1]fortunes
of the tents of Jacob
And [b]have compassion on his
dwelling places;
And the [c]city shall be rebuilt on its
ruin,
And the [d]palace shall stand on its
rightful place.
19 'And from them shall proceed
[a]thanksgiving
And the voice of those who [1b]make
merry;
And I will [c]multiply them, and they
shall not be diminished;
I will also [d]honor them, and they
shall not be insignificant.
20 '[1]Their children also shall be as
formerly,
And [2]their congregation shall be
[a]established before Me;
And I will punish all [2]their oppressors.
21 'And [1]their [a]leader shall be one of
them,
And [1]their ruler shall come forth
from [1]their midst;
And I will [b]bring him near, and he
shall approach Me;
For [2]who would dare to risk his life
to [c]approach Me?' declares the
LORD.
22 'And you shall be [a]My people,
And I will be your God.' "

23 Behold, the [a]tempest of the LORD!
Wrath has gone forth,
A [1]sweeping tempest;
It will burst on the head of the
wicked.
24 The [a]fierce anger of the LORD will
not turn back,
Until He has performed, and until
He has accomplished
The intent of His heart;
In the [b]latter days you will under-
stand this.

Israel's Mourning Turned to Joy

31 "AT that time," declares the
LORD, "I will be the [a]God of all
the [b]families of Israel, and they shall be
My people."
2 Thus says the LORD,
"The people who survived the sword
[a]Found grace in the wilderness—
Israel, when it went to [b]find its
rest."
3 The LORD appeared to [1]him from
afar, *saying*,
"I have [a]loved you with an everlasting love;
Therefore I have drawn you with
[b]lovingkindness.

6 [a]Jer. 4:31; 6:24; 22:23
7 [a]Is. 2:12; Hos. 1:11; Joel 2:11; Amos 5:18; Zeph. 1:14 [b]Lam. 1:12; Dan. 9:12; 12:1 [c]Jer. 2:27, 28; 14:8 [d]Jer. 30:10; 50:19
8 [1]So Gr.; Heb., *your* [2]Lit., *him their slave*
[a]Is. 9:4; Jer. 2:20; Ezek. 34:27 [b]Jer. 27:2 [c]Ezek. 34:27
9 [a]Is. 55:3-5; Ezek. 34:23, 24; 37:24, 25; Hos. 3:5; Luke 1:69; Acts 2:30; 13:23, 34
10 [1]Lit., *seed*
[a]Is. 41:13; 43:5; 44:2; Jer. 46:27, 28 [b]Is. 60:4; Jer. 23:3, 8; 29:14 [c]Is. 35:9; Jer. 33:16; Hos. 2:18 [d]Mic. 4:4
11 [a]Jer. 1:8, 19 [b]Jer. 46:28; Amos 9:8 [c]Jer. 4:27; 5:10, 18 [d]Ps. 6:1; Jer. 10:24
12 [a]2 Chr. 36:16; Jer. 15:18; 30:15
13 [a]Jer. 14:19; 46:11
14 [a]Jer. 22:20, 22; Lam. 1:2 [b]Lam. 2:4, 5 [c]Job 30:21 [d]Jer. 6:23; 50:42 [e]Jer. 32:30-35; 44:22 [f]Jer. 5:6
16 [a]Jer. 2:3; 8:16; 10:25 [b]Is. 14:2; Joel 3:8
17 [1]Lit., *cause to go up* [2]Or, *healing* [3]Lit., *is seeking*
[a]Ex. 15:26; Ps. 107:20; Is. 30:26; Jer. 8:22; 33:6 [b]Is. 11:12; 56:8; Jer. 33:24
18 [1]Or, *captivity*
[a]Jer. 30:3; 31:23 [b]Ps. 102:13 [c]Jer. 31:4, 38-40 [d]1 Chr. 29:1, 19; Ps. 48:3, 13; 122:7
19 [1]Or, *dance*
[a]Is. 12:1; 35:10; 51:3; Jer. 17:26; 33:11 [b]Ps. 126:1, 2; Is. 51:11; Jer. 31:4; Zeph. 3:14 [c]Jer. 33:22 [d]Is. 55:5; 60:9
20 [1]Lit., *His* [2]Lit., *his*
[a]Is. 54:14
21 [1]Lit., *his* [2]Lit., *who is he that gives his heart in pledge*
[a]Jer. 30:9; Ezek. 34:23, 24; 37:24 [b]Num. 16:5; Ps. 65:4 [c]Ex. 3:5; Jer. 50:44
22 [a]Ex. 6:7; Jer. 32:38; Ezek. 36:28; Hos. 2:23; Zech. 13:9
23 [1]Or, *raging*
[a]Jer. 23:19
24 [a]Jer. 4:8 [b]Jer. 23:20

1 [a]Jer. 30:22 [b]Gen. 17:7, 8; Is. 41:10; Rom. 11:26-28
2 [a]Num. 14:20 [b]Ex. 33:14; Num. 10:33; Deut. 1:33; Josh. 1:13
3 [1]Lit., *me*
[a]Deut. 4:37; 7:8; Mal. 1:2 [b]Ps. 25:6

THE SADDUCEES

The Sadducees were the successors of the Hellenists. Still the wealthy, ruling class, they were identified with the high priesthood and with Greek thought. Their group name, Sadducee, may be derived from Zadok, to indicate their high-priestly connection. They found the world a good place in which to live and were interested in the here-and-now rather than believing in a resurrection, a judgement, or an afterlife. They rejected ideas of resurrection in favour of the Greek idea of immortality of the soul and believed they could show that the idea of a bodily resurrection was ridiculous. They limited the canon of Scripture to the five books of Moses, which is why Jesus confined himself to those books in refuting their arguments against the resurrection (Matthew 22:23-32). The Sadducees rejected any belief in angels or spirits and followed *"common-sense"* morality—good and evil, they believed, resulted from personal action.

THE PHARISEES

The Pharisees followed a direct line from the Hasidim. Their name means *"those who separate themselves."* There were some six thousand of them at the time of Jesus. They were concerned, above all else, for their religious faith and believed that the Exile had been the result of their ancestors' breaking God's law. They wanted to be legally pure, separate from any form of defilement. They believed that the difference between being *"clean"* and *"unclean"* depended upon that law. What was *"clean"* was obedience to the law; what was *"unclean"* was disobedience to the law.

This position regarding the law created problems, however, for although there are six hundred and thirteen commandments in the Torah (the books of Moses), they were not always specific. If the Sabbath day is to be kept *"holy,"* then exactly what may be done and what may not? There were lengthy discussions on such subjects as whether or not it was lawful (or *"unclean"*) to eat an egg laid on the Sabbath.

THE HERODIANS

The Herodians supported the family of Herod as rulers. The Herods were originally an Edomite family, and they ruled the country for the Romans. The Edomites, after all, had some affinity with the Jews as descendants of Esau and the Jew believed that intermediary rule by the Herods was better than direct Roman rule. The Herodians accepted the good that Herod the Great had done for Jerusalem by providing a new Temple, although they sided with the Pharisees in objecting to paying taxes to Rome (Mark 12:13-14). They reacted against Jesus when he healed the man with the withered hand on the Sabbath day (Mark 3:5). Like the Sadducees, Herodian opposition to Jesus was probably because they believed he would upset the status quo and

A CLOSER LOOK

because his clear moral teaching was as big a challenge to their life-style as had been the teaching of John the Baptist.

THE ZEALOTS

The Zealots reacted to foreign influence by seeking to destroy the enemy. They believed that only when the Romans were driven from the soil would God redeem his people. The Zealots were founded by Judas of Galilee in AD 6. The Zealots held that paying taxes to the Roman Empire was treason against God. They took their name from the zeal shown by the Maccabeans when they threw off the Syrian yoke. The Romans referred to the Zealots as *"sicarii,"* or *"dagger men,"* because they were continually in action with this weapon.

THE ESSENES

The Essenes withdrew from the world into communities of their own — about four thousand of them in all. The last straw preceding their withdrawal came when a particular priest-king was deemed to be so evil that a *"Teacher of Righteousness"* led people away from the *"Wicked High Priest."* The Essenes undertook basic agricultural craft and spent much time together in the study of religious and moral questions and in interpreting the sacred books. All property was held in common, they held to a program that ensured ritual purity, were unmarried, and rejected animal sacrifice...

THE SAMARITANS

The Samartians took their name from the city of Samaria, the capital of the Northern Kingdom of Israel from the time of the kings Omri and Ahab (1 Kings 16:24). The city of Samaria were destroyed by the Assyrians in 721 BC, and about twenty-seven thousand people of the ruling classes and those who were useful artisans were deported to Assyria and dispersed (2 Kings 17:24). As part of Assyrian policy, leadership of the city was taken over by other subject peoples, so that lack of communication with the local working people combined with the new rulers' gratitude to the Assyrians for placing them in charge would result in a stable, peaceful situation.

Things did not go well — wild animals increased in the country at an alarming rate, killing many people. The newcomers believed these attacks to mean that they were not worshipping the God of Samaria in the right way. One of the priests in exile was sent back to teach the Jewish faith, and he set up a religious sanctuary at Bethel. As a result, a syncretistic religion was formed between the worship of Yahweh and the worship of the local gods from the original homes of the new rulers of Samaria (2 Kings 17:25-34)

JEREMIAH - *boldness*

Jeremiah was a well-known Old Testament prophet called at a very early age (Jer. 1:6). His ministry was not popular and his life was not easy. Yet he served God faithfully, boldly and without compromise.

Jeremiah was born into he priesthood, as was the Jewish tradition at that time. His family life and education prepared him for god's service. But god Himself called Jeremiah to speak of the sins in the lifestyles of God's people. His message was of condemnation and the coming fall of Jerusalem unless the people changed. None of this was good news and the people did not want to hear it. They reacted with hostility and anger toward Jeremiah. Yet Jeremiah spoke the message God had given him fearlessly.

Because Jeremiah continue to prophesy, he was beaten and even had to hid during the reign of Jehojakim. Eventually the people of Israel were defeated and taken into Babylon in captivity by King Nebuchadnezzar. They had continued to disobey God.

Jeremiah's name means "exalted of God" and there is a key to his boldness. God gave Jeremiah a special call, but He also gave him special protection. God knew how difficult Jeremiah's job would be. In Jer. 1:18 and 19, God said to Jeremiah, "I have made you today as a fortified city... they will not overcome you, for I am with you to deliver you." What a strength that message must have been to Jeremiah!

Another aspect of Jeremiah's message was that God loved His people. His desire was not to see them destroyed, but to be reconciled to them. Jeremiah cared deeply for the fate of his people. He is known as "the weeping prophet" because of his sorrow for Israel. He expressed some of these feelings in the book of Jeremiah and then more fully in Lamentations after the Jews had been taken into captivity. He knew terrible things were about to happen if Israel did not change, and he cared deeply about what was going to happen. His grasp of the urgency of God's message helped him to speak boldly to try to save his people.

QUESTIONS

1. Jeremiah's life was set apart for God's service from its beginning. Yet God has a plan for each of us to serve Him in our own way. What things in your life could be a hindrance to serving God? What things are helping you prepare for God's service? ______________________

2. God promised protection and deliverance to Jeremiah when he spoke what God told him. God you believe God offers the same powerful protection today to those He calls? Why or why not? ______________________

3. Jeremiah's message was not pleasant or well received. Does the possibility of an unpleasant reception keep you from sharing the Gospel of Jesus Christ? ______________________

4. Jeremiah's heart was deeply touched by the terrible fate of Israel. Today, all around us lost people die and spend eternity in hell. How do you feel about that? Does it stir you to speak boldly? ______________________

4"[a]Again I will build you, and you shall be rebuilt,
O virgin of Israel!
Again you shall [1]take up your [b]tambourines,
And go forth to the dances of the [c]merrymakers.
5"Again you shall [a]plant vineyards
On the [1]hills of Samaria;
The planters shall plant
And shall [2]enjoy *them*.
6"For there shall be a day when watchmen
On the hills of Ephraim shall call out,
'Arise, and [a]let us go up *to* Zion,
To the LORD our God.' "

7 For thus says the LORD,
"[a]Sing aloud with gladness for Jacob,
And shout among the [1b]chiefs of the nations;
Proclaim, give praise, and say,
'O LORD, [c]save Thy people,
The [d]remnant of Israel.'
8"Behold, I am [a]bringing them from the north country,
And I will [b]gather them from the remote parts of the earth,
Among them the [c]blind and the [d]lame,
The woman with child and she who is in labor with child, together;
A great [1]company, they shall return here.
9"[a]With weeping they shall come,
And by supplication I will lead them;
I will make them walk by [b]streams of waters,
On a straight path in which they shall [c]not stumble;
For I am a [d]father to Israel,
And Ephraim is [e]My first-born."

10 Hear the word of the LORD, O nations,
And declare in the [a]coastlands afar off,
And say, "He who scattered Israel will [b]gather him,
And keep him as a [c]shepherd keeps his flock."
11 For the LORD has [a]ransomed Jacob,
And redeemed him from the hand of him who was [b]stronger than he.
12"And they shall [a]come and shout for joy on the [b]height of Zion,
And they shall be [c]radiant over the [1]bounty of the LORD—
Over the [d]grain, and the new wine, and the oil,
And over the young of the [e]flock and the herd;
And their life shall be like a [f]watered garden,
And they shall [g]never languish again.
13"Then the virgin shall rejoice in the [a]dance,
And the young men and the old, together,
For I will [b]turn their mourning into joy,
And will comfort them, and give them [c]joy for their sorrow.
14"And I will [1]fill the soul of the priests with [2]abundance,
And My people shall be [a]satisfied with My goodness," declares the LORD.

15 Thus says the LORD,
"[a]A voice is heard in [b]Ramah,
Lamentation *and* bitter weeping.
Rachel is weeping for her children;
She [c]refuses to be comforted for her children,
Because [d]they are no more."
16 Thus says the LORD,
"[a]Restrain your voice from weeping,
And your eyes from tears;
For your [b]work shall be rewarded," declares the LORD,
"And they shall [c]return from the land of the enemy.
17"And there is [a]hope for your future," declares the LORD,
"And *your* children shall return to their own territory.
18"I have surely heard Ephraim [a]grieving,
'Thou hast [b]chastised me, and I was chastised,
Like an untrained [c]calf;
[d]Bring me back that I may be restored,
For Thou art the LORD my God.
19 'For after I turned back, I [a]repented;
And after I was instructed, I [b]smote on *my* thigh;
I was [c]ashamed, and also humiliated,
Because I bore the reproach of my youth.'
20"Is [a]Ephraim My dear son?
Is he a delightful child?
Indeed, as often as I have spoken against him,
I certainly *still* remember him;
Therefore My [1b]heart yearns for him;
I will surely [c]have mercy on him," declares the LORD.

21"Set up for yourself roadmarks,
Place for yourself guideposts;
[a]Direct your [1]mind to the highway,
The way by which you went.
[b]Return, O virgin of Israel,
Return to these your cities.
22"How long will you go here and there,
O [a]faithless daughter?
For the LORD has created a new thing in the earth—
A woman will encompass a man."
23 Thus says the LORD of hosts, the
God of Israel, "Once again they will
speak this word in the land of Judah and

4 [1]Or, *be adorned with* [a]Jer. 24:6; 33:7 [b]Is. 30:32 [c]Jer. 30:19
5 [1]Or, *mountains* [2]Lit., *defile* [a]Ps. 107:37; Is. 65:21; Ezek. 28:26; Amos 9:14
6 [a]Is. 2:3; Jer. 31:12; 50:4, 5; Mic. 4:2
7 [1]Lit., *heads* [a]Ps. 14:7; Jer. 20:13 [b]Deut. 28:13; Is. 61:9 [c]Ps. 28:9 [d]Is. 37:31; Jer. 23:3
8 [1]Or, *assembly* [a]Jer. 3:18; 23:8 [b]Deut. 30:4; Is. 43:6; Ezek. 34:13 [c]Is. 42:16 [d]Is. 40:11; Ezek. 34:16; Mic. 4:6
9 [a]Ps. 126:5; Jer. 50:4 [b]Is. 43:20; 49:10 [c]Is. 63:13 [d]Is. 64:8; Jer. 3:4, 19 [e]Ex. 4:22
10 [a]Is. 66:19; Jer. 25:22 [b]Jer. 50:19 [c]Is. 40:11; Ezek. 34:12
11 [a]Is. 44:23; 48:20; Jer. 15:21; 50:34 [b]Ps. 142:6
12 [1]Lit., *goodness* [a]Jer. 31:6, 7 [b]Ezek. 17:23 [c]Is. 2:2; Mic. 4:1 [d]Hos. 2:22; Joel 3:18 [e]Jer. 31:24; 33:12, 13 [f]Is. 58:11 [g]Is. 35:10; 60:20; 65:19; John 16:22; Rev. 21:4
13 [a]Judg. 21:21; Ps. 30:11; Zech. 8:4, 5 [b]Is. 61:3 [c]Is. 51:11
14 [1]Lit., *saturate* [2]Lit., *fatness* [a]Jer. 50:19
15 [a]Matt. 2:18 [b]Josh. 18:25; Judg. 4:5; Is. 10:29; Jer. 40:1 [c]Gen. 37:35; Ps. 77:2 [d]Gen. 5:24; 42:13, 36; Jer. 10:20
16 [a]Is. 25:8; 30:19 [b]Ruth 2:12; Heb. 6:10 [c]Jer. 30:3; Ezek. 11:17
17 [a]Jer. 29:11
18 [a]Jer. 3:21 [b]Job 5:17; Ps. 94:12 [c]Hos. 4:16 [d]Ps. 80:3, 7, 19; Jer. 17:14; Lam. 5:21; Acts 3:26
19 [a]Ezek. 36:31; Zech. 12:10 [b]Ezek. 21:12; Luke 18:13 [c]Jer. 3:25
20 [1]Lit., *inward parts* [a]Hos. 11:8 [b]Gen. 43:30; Judg. 10:16; Is. 63:15; Hos. 11:8 [c]Is. 55:7; 57:18; Hos. 14:4; Mic. 7:18
21 [1]Lit., *heart* [a]Jer. 50:5 [b]Is. 48:20; 52:11
22 [a]Jer. 3:6; 49:4

in its cities, when I [a]restore their [1]for-
tunes,
'The LORD bless you, O [b]abode of
righteousness,
O [c]holy hill!'
24"And Judah and all its cities will
[a]dwell together in it, the farmer and they
who go about with flocks.
25"[a]For I satisfy the weary ones and
[1]refresh everyone who languishes."
26 At this I [a]awoke and looked, and
my [b]sleep was pleasant to me.

A New Covenant

27"Behold, days are coming," declares
the LORD, "when I will [a]sow the house of
Israel and the house of Judah with the
seed of man and with the seed of beast.
28"And it will come about that as I
have [a]watched over them to [b]pluck up,
to break down, to overthrow, to destroy,
and to bring disaster, so I will watch
over them to [c]build and to plant,"
declares the LORD.
29"In those days they will not say
again,
'[a]The fathers have eaten sour
grapes,
And the children's teeth are [1]set on
edge.'
30"But [a]everyone will die for his own
iniquity; each man who eats the sour
grapes, his teeth will be [1]set on edge.
31"[a]Behold, days are coming," declares the LORD, "when I will make a
[b]new covenant with the house of Israel
and with the house of Judah,
32 not like the [a]covenant which I
made with their fathers in the day I
[b]took them by the hand to bring them
out of the land of Egypt, My [c]covenant
which they broke, although I was a
husband to them," declares the LORD.
33"But [a]this is the covenant which I
will make with the house of Israel after
those days," declares the LORD, "[b]I will
put My law within them, and on their
heart I will write it; and [c]I will be their
God, and they shall be My people.
34"And they shall [a]not teach again,
each man his neighbor and each man his
brother, saying, 'Know the LORD,' for
they shall all [b]know Me, from the least
of them to the greatest of them," declares the LORD, "for I will [c]forgive their
iniquity, and their [d]sin I will remember
no more."
35 Thus says the LORD,
Who [a]gives the sun for light by day,
And the [1]fixed order of the moon
and the stars for light by night,
Who [b]stirs up the sea so that its
waves roar;
[c]The LORD of hosts is His name:
36"[a]If [1]this fixed order departs
From before Me," declares the
LORD,
"Then the offspring of Israel also
shall [b]cease
From being a nation before Me
[2]forever."

23 [1]Or, *captivity* [a]Jer. 30:18; 32:44 [b]Is. 1:26; Jer. 50:7 [c]Ps. 48:1; 87:1; Zech. 8:3
24 [a]Jer. 31:12; Ezek. 36:10; Zech. 8:4-8
25 [1]Lit., *fill* [a]Ps. 107:9; Jer. 31:12, 14; Matt. 5:6; John 4:14
26 [a]Zech. 4:1 [b]Prov. 3:24
27 [a]Ezek. 36:9, 11; Hos. 2:23
28 [a]Jer. 44:27; Dan. 9:14 [b]Jer. 1:10; 18:7 [c]Jer. 24:6
29 [1]Or, *dull* [a]Lam. 5:7; Ezek. 18:2
30 [1]Or, *dull* [a]Deut. 24:16; Is. 3:11; Ezek. 18:4, 20
31 [a]Jer. 31:31-34; Heb. 8:8-12 [b]Jer. 32:40; 33:14; Ezek. 37:26; Luke 22:20; 1 Cor. 11:25; 2 Cor. 3:6; Heb. 8:8-12; 10:16, 17
32 [a]Ex. 19:5; 24:6-8; Deut. 5:2, 3 [b]Deut. 1:31; Is. 63:12 [c]Jer. 11:7, 8
33 [a]Jer. 32:40; Heb. 10:16 [b]Ps. 40:8; 2 Cor. 3:3 [c]Jer. 24:7; 30:22; 32:38
34 [a]1 Thess. 4:9; 1 John 2:27 [b]Is. 11:9; 54:13; Jer. 24:7; Hab. 2:14; John 6:45; 1 John 2:20 [c]Jer. 33:8; 50:20; Mic. 7:18; Rom. 11:27 [d]Is. 43:25; Heb. 10:17
35 [1]Lit., *statutes* [a]Gen. 1:14-18; Deut. 4:19; Ps. 19:1-6; 136:7-9 [b]Is. 51:15 [c]Jer. 10:16; 32:18; 50:34
36 [1]Lit., *these statutes* [2]Lit., *all the days* [a]Ps. 89:36, 37; 148:6; Is. 54:9, 10; Jer. 33:20-26 [b]Amos 9:8, 9
37 [a]Is. 40:12; Jer. 33:22 [b]Jer. 33:24-26; Rom. 11:2-5, 26, 27
38 [a]Jer. 30:18; 31:4 [b]Neh. 3:1; 12:39; Zech. 14:10 [c]2 Kin. 14:13; 2 Chr. 26:9
39 [a]Zech. 2:1
40 [a]Jer. 7:32; 8:2 [b]2 Sam. 15:23; 2 Kin. 23:6, 12; John 18:1 [c]2 Kin. 11:16; 2 Chr. 23:15; Neh. 3:28 [d]Joel 3:17; Zech. 14:20

1 [a]2 Kin. 25:1, 2; Jer. 39:1, 2
2 [a]Neh. 3:25; Jer. 33:1; 37:21; 38:6; 39:14
3 [a]2 Kin. 6:32 [b]Jer. 26:8, 9 [c]Jer. 21:3-7; 34:2, 3 [d]Jer. 21:4-7; 32:28, 29; 34:2, 3
4 [1]Lit., *mouth to mouth* [a]2 Kin. 25:4-7; Jer. 37:17; 38:18, 23; 39:4-7 [b]Jer. 39:5
5 [a]Jer. 27:22; 39:7; Ezek. 12:12, 13 [b]Ezek. 17:9, 10, 15

37 Thus says the LORD,
"[a]If the heavens above can be measured,
And the foundations of the earth
searched out below,
Then I will also [b]cast off all the
offspring of Israel
For all that they have done," declares the LORD.
38"Behold, days are coming," declares
the LORD, "when the [a]city shall be
rebuilt for the LORD from the [b]Tower of
Hananel to the [c]Corner Gate.
39"And the [a]measuring line shall go
out farther straight ahead to the hill
Gareb; then it will turn to Goah.
40"And [a]the whole valley of the dead
bodies and of the ashes, and all the fields
as far as the brook [b]Kidron, to the
corner of the [c]Horse Gate toward the
east, shall be [d]holy to the LORD; it shall
not be plucked up, or overthrown anymore forever."

Jeremiah Imprisoned

32 THE word that came to Jeremiah
from the LORD in the [a]tenth year
of Zedekiah king of Judah, which was
the eighteenth year of Nebuchadnezzar.
2 Now at that time the army of the
king of Babylon was besieging Jerusalem, and Jeremiah the prophet was shut
up in the [a]court of the guard, which was
in the house of the king of Judah,
3 because Zedekiah king of Judah
had [a]shut him up, saying, "Why do you
[b]prophesy, saying, '[c]Thus says the LORD,
"Behold, I am about to [d]give this city
into the hand of the king of Babylon,
and he will take it;
4 and Zedekiah king of Judah shall
[a]not escape out of the hand of the
Chaldeans, but he shall surely be given
into the hand of the king of Babylon,
and he shall [b]speak with him [1]face to
face, and see him eye to eye;
5 and he shall [a]take Zedekiah to
Babylon, and he shall be there until I
visit him," declares the LORD. "If you
fight against the Chaldeans, you shall
[b]not succeed" ' ? "
6 And Jeremiah said, "The word of
the LORD came to me, saying,
7 'Behold, Hanamel the son of Shallum your uncle is coming to you, saying,
"Buy for yourself my field which is at
[a]Anathoth, for you have the [b]right of
redemption to buy *it*." '
8"Then Hanamel my uncle's son
came to me in the [a]court of the guard
according to the word of the LORD, and
said to me, 'Buy my field, please, that is
at [b]Anathoth, which is in the land of
Benjamin; for you have the right of
possession and the redemption is yours;
buy *it* for yourself.' Then I knew that
this was the [c]word of the LORD.
9"And I bought the field which was
at Anathoth from Hanamel my uncle's

7 [a]Jer. 1:1; 11:21 [b]Lev. 25:25; Ruth 4:3, 4
8 [a]Jer. 32:2; 33:1 [b]Jer. 1:1; 32:7 [c]1 Sam. 9:16, 17; 10:3-7; 1 Kin. 22:25; Jer. 32:25

son, and I [a]weighed out the silver for him, seventeen [b]shekels of silver.

10 "And I [1a]signed and [b]sealed the deed, and [c]called in witnesses, and weighed out the silver on the scales.

11 "Then I took the deeds of purchase, both the sealed *copy containing* the [a]terms and conditions, and the open *copy;*

12 and I gave the deed of purchase to [a]Baruch the son of [b]Neriah, the son of Mahseiah, in the sight of Hanamel my uncle's *son,* and in the sight of the witnesses who signed the deed of purchase, before all the Jews who were sitting in the court of the guard.

13 "And I commanded Baruch in their presence, saying,

14 'Thus says the LORD of hosts, the God of Israel, "Take these deeds, this sealed deed of purchase, and this open deed, and put them in an earthenware jar, that they may [1]last a long time."

15 'For thus says the LORD of hosts, the God of Israel, "[a]Houses and fields and vineyards shall again be bought in this land." '

Jeremiah Prays and God Explains

16 "After I had given the deed of purchase to Baruch the son of Neriah, then I [a]prayed to the LORD, saying,

17 '[a]Ah Lord [1]GOD! Behold, Thou hast [b]made the heavens and the earth by Thy great power and by Thine outstretched arm! [c]Nothing is too difficult for Thee,

18 who [a]showest lovingkindness to thousands, but [b]repayest the iniquity of fathers into the bosom of their children after them, O [c]great and [d]mighty God. The [e]LORD of hosts is His name;

19 [a]great in counsel and mighty in deed, whose [b]eyes are open to all the ways of the sons of men, [c]giving to everyone according to his ways and according to the fruit of his deeds;

20 who hast [a]set signs and wonders in the land of Egypt, *and* even to this day both in Israel and among mankind; and Thou hast [b]made a name for Thyself, as at this day.

21 'And Thou didst [a]bring Thy people Israel out of the land of Egypt with signs and with wonders, and with a strong hand and with an outstretched arm, and with great terror;

22 and gavest them this land, which Thou didst [a]swear to their forefathers to give them, a land flowing with milk and honey.

23 'And they [a]came in and took possession of it, but they [b]did not obey Thy voice or [c]walk in Thy law; they have done nothing of all that Thou commandedst them to do; therefore Thou hast made [d]all this calamity come upon them.

24 'Behold, the [a]siege mounds have reached the city to take it; and the city is [b]given into the hand of the Chaldeans who fight against it, because of the [c]sword, the famine, and the pestilence; and what Thou hast spoken has [d]come to pass; and, behold, Thou seest *it.*

25 'And Thou hast said to me, O Lord [1]GOD, "Buy for yourself the field with money, and call in witnesses"—although the city is given into the hand of the Chaldeans.' "

26 Then the word of the LORD came to Jeremiah, saying,

27 "Behold, I am the LORD, the [a]God of all flesh; is anything [b]too difficult for Me?"

28 Therefore thus says the LORD, "Behold, I am about to [a]give this city into the hand of the Chaldeans and into the hand of Nebuchadnezzar king of Babylon, and he shall take it.

29 "And the Chaldeans who are fighting against this city shall enter and [a]set this city on fire and burn it, with the [b]houses where *people* have offered incense to Baal on their roofs and poured out libations to other gods to provoke Me to anger.

30 "Indeed the sons of Israel and the sons of Judah have been doing only [a]evil in My sight from their youth; for the sons of Israel have been only [b]provoking Me to anger by the work of their hands," declares the LORD.

31 "Indeed this city has been to Me *a* [a]*provocation of* My anger and My wrath from the day that they built it, even to this day, that it should be [b]removed from before My face,

32 because of all the evil of the sons of Israel and the sons of Judah, which they have done to provoke Me to anger—they, their [a]kings, their leaders, their priests, their prophets, the men of Judah, and the inhabitants of Jerusalem.

33 "And they have turned *their* back to Me, and not *their* face; though *I* taught them, [1a]teaching again and again, they would not listen [2]and receive instruction.

34 "But they [a]put their detestable things in the house which is called by My name, to defile it.

35 "And they built the [a]high places of Baal that are in the valley of Ben-hinnom to cause their sons and their daughters to pass through *the fire* to [b]Molech, which I had not commanded them nor had it [1]entered My mind that they should do this abomination, to cause Judah to sin.

36 "Now therefore thus says the LORD God of Israel concerning this city of which you say, 'It is [a]given into the hand of the king of Babylon by sword, by famine, and by pestilence.'

9 [a]Gen. 23:16; Zech. 11:12 [b]Gen. 24:22; Ex. 21:32; Neh. 5:15; Ezek. 4:10
10 [1]Or, *wrote . . . on the document* [a]Is. 44:5; Jer. 32:44 [b]Deut. 32:34; Job 14:17 [c]Ruth 4:1, 9; Is. 8:2
11 [a]Luke 2:27
12 [a]Jer. 32:16; 36:4, 5, 32; 43:3; 45:1 [b]Jer. 51:59
14 [1]Lit., *stand many days*
15 [a]Jer. 30:18; 31:5, 12, 24; 32:37, 43, 44; 33:12, 13; Amos 9:14, 15; Zech. 3:10
16 [a]Gen. 32:9-12; Jer. 12:1; Phil. 4:6, 7
17 [1]Heb., *YHWH,* usually rendered *LORD* [a]Jer. 1:6; 4:10 [b]2 Kin. 19:15; Ps. 102:25; Is. 40:26-29; Jer. 27:5 [c]Gen. 18:14; Jer. 32:27; Zech. 8:6; Matt. 19:26; Mark 10:27; Luke 1:37; 18:27
18 [a]Ex. 20:6; 34:6, 7; Deut. 5:9, 10; 7:9, 10 [b]1 Kin. 14:9, 10; 16:1-3; Matt. 23:32-36 [c]Ps. 145:3 [d]Ps. 50:1; Is. 9:6; Jer. 20:11 [e]Jer. 10:16; 31:35
19 [a]Is. 9:6; 28:29 [b]Job 34:21; Jer. 23:24 [c]Ps. 62:12; Jer. 17:10; 21:14; Matt. 16:27; John 5:29
20 [a]Ps. 78:43; 105:27 [b]Ex. 9:16; Is. 63:12, 14; Dan. 9:15
21 [a]Ex. 6:6; Deut. 4:34; 7:19; 26:8; 2 Sam. 7:23; 1 Chr. 17:21; Ps. 136:11
22 [a]Ex. 3:8, 17; 13:5; Deut. 1:8; Ps. 105:9-11; Jer. 11:5
23 [a]Ps. 44:2, 3; 78:54, 55; Jer. 2:7 [b]Neh. 9:26; Jer. 11:8; Dan. 9:10-14 [c]Ezra 9:7; Jer. 26:4; 44:10 [d]Lam. 1:18; Dan. 9:11, 12
24 [a]Jer. 33:4; Ezek. 21:22 [b]Jer. 20:5; 21:4-7; 32:5 [c]Jer. 14:12; 29:17, 18; 32:36; 34:17; Ezek. 14:21 [d]Deut. 4:26; Josh. 23:15, 16; Zech. 1:6
25 [1]Heb., *YHWH,* usually rendered *LORD*
27 [a]Num. 16:22; 27:16 [b]Jer. 32:17; Matt. 19:26
28 [a]2 Kin. 25:11; 2 Chr. 36:17-21; Jer. 19:7-12; 32:3, 24, 36; 34:2, 3
29 [a]2 Chr. 36:19; Jer. 21:10; 37:8, 10; 39:8 [b]Jer. 19:13; 44:17-19, 25; 52:13
30 [a]Deut. 9:7-12; Is. 63:10; Jer. 2:7; 7:22-26 [b]Jer. 8:19; 11:17; 25:7

31 [a]1 Kin. 11:7, 8; 2 Kin. 21:4-7, 16; Jer. 5:9-11; 6:6, 7; Matt. 23:37 [b]2 Kin. 23:27; 24:3, 4; Jer. 27:10
32 [a]Ezra 9:7; Is. 1:4-6, 23; Jer. 2:26; 44:17, 21; Dan. 9:8
33 [1]Lit., *rising up early and teaching* [2]Lit., *to* [a]2 Chr. 36:15, 16; Jer. 7:13; 25:3; 26:5; 35:15; John 8:2
34 [a]2 Kin. 21:1-7; Jer. 7:30; 19:4-6; Ezek. 8:5
35 [1]Lit., *come up into My heart* [a]2 Chr. 28:2, 3; 33:6; Jer. 7:31; 19:5 [b]Lev. 18:21; 20:2-5; 1 Kin. 11:7; 2 Kin. 23:10; Acts 7:43
36 [a]Jer. 32:24

37 "Behold, I will [a]gather them out of all the lands to which I have driven them in My anger, in My wrath, and in great indignation; and I will bring them back to this place and [b]make them dwell in safety.

38 "And they shall be [a]My people, and I will be their God;

39 and I will [a]give them one heart and one way, that they may fear Me always, for their own [b]good, and for *the good of* their children after them.

40 "And I will make an [a]everlasting covenant with them that I will [b]not turn away from them, to do them good; and I will [c]put the fear of Me in their hearts so that they will not turn away from Me.

41 "And I will [a]rejoice over them to do them good, and I will [1]faithfully [b]plant them in this land with [c]all My heart and with all My soul.

42 "For thus says the LORD, '[a]Just as I brought all this great disaster on this people, so I am going to [b]bring on them all the good that I am promising them.

43 'And [a]fields shall be bought in this land of which you say, "[b]It is a desolation, without man or beast; it is given into the hand of the Chaldeans."

44 'Men shall buy fields for money, [1a]sign and seal deeds, and call in witnesses in the [b]land of Benjamin, in the environs of Jerusalem, in the cities of Judah, in the cities of the hill country, in the cities of the lowland, and in the cities of the [2]Negev; for I will [c]restore their [3]fortunes,' declares the LORD."

Restoration Promised

33 THEN the word of the LORD came to Jeremiah the second time, while he was still [1a]confined in the court of the guard, saying,

2 "Thus says [a]the LORD who made [1]*the earth,* the LORD who formed it to establish it, the [b]LORD is His name,

3 '[a]Call to Me, and I will answer you, and I will tell you [b]great and mighty things, [c]which you do not know.'

4 "For thus says the LORD God of Israel concerning the [a]houses of this city, and concerning the houses of the kings of Judah, which are broken down *to make a defense* against the [b]siege mounds and against the sword,

5 'While *they* are coming to [a]fight with the Chaldeans, and to fill them with the corpses of men whom I have slain in My anger and in My wrath, and I have [b]hidden My face from this city because of all their wickedness:

6 'Behold, I will bring to it [a]health and healing, and I will heal them; and I will reveal to them an [b]abundance of peace and truth.

7 'And I will [a]restore the [1]fortunes of Judah and the fortunes of Israel, and I will [b]rebuild them as they were at first.

8 'And I will [a]cleanse them from all their iniquity by which they have sinned against Me, and I will pardon all their iniquities by which they have sinned against Me, and by which they have transgressed against Me.

9 'And [1]it shall be to Me a [a]name of joy, praise, and glory before [b]all the nations of the earth, which shall hear of all the [c]good that I do for them, and they shall [d]fear and tremble because of all the good and all the peace that I make for it.'

10 "Thus says the LORD, 'Yet again there shall be heard in this place, of which you say, "It is a [a]waste, without man and without beast," *that is,* in the cities of Judah and in the streets of Jerusalem that are [b]desolate, without man and without inhabitant and without beast,

11 the voice of [a]joy and the voice of gladness, the voice of the bridegroom and the voice of the bride, the voice of those who say,

"[b]Give thanks to the LORD of hosts,
For the LORD is good,
For His lovingkindness is everlasting";

and of those who bring a [c]thank offering into the house of the LORD. For I will restore the [1]fortunes of the land as they were at first,' says the LORD.

12 "Thus says the LORD of hosts, 'There shall again be in this place which is waste, [a]without man or beast, and in all its cities, a [1]habitation of shepherds who rest their [b]flocks.

13 'In the [a]cities of the hill country, in the cities of the lowland, in the cities of the Negev, in the land of Benjamin, in the environs of Jerusalem, and in the cities of Judah, the flocks shall again [b]pass under the hands of the one who numbers them,' says the LORD.

The Davidic Kingdom

14 'Behold, [a]days are coming,' declares the LORD, 'when I will [b]fulfill the good word which I have spoken concerning the house of Israel and the house of Judah.

15 'In those days and at that time I will cause a [a]righteous Branch of David to spring forth; and He shall execute [b]justice and righteousness on the earth.

16 'In those days [a]Judah shall be saved, and Jerusalem shall dwell in safety; and this is *the name* by which she shall be called: the [b]LORD is our righteousness.'

17 "For thus says the LORD, '[1]David shall [a]never lack a man to sit on the throne of the house of Israel;

32:37 [a]Deut. 30:3; Ps. 106:47; Is. 11:11-16; Jer. 16:14, 15; 23:3, 8; Ezek. 11:17; Hos. 1:11; Amos 9:14, 15 [b]Jer. 23:6; Ezek. 34:25, 28; Zech. 14:11
38 [a]Jer. 24:7
39 [a]2 Chr. 30:12; Jer. 31:33; Ezek. 11:19; John 17:21; Acts 4:32 [b]Deut. 11:18-21; Ezek. 37:25
40 [a]Is. 55:3; Jer. 31:33, 34; 50:5; Ezek. 37:26 [b]Deut. 31:6, 8; Ezek. 39:29 [c]Jer. 24:7; 31:33
41 [1]Or, *truly* [a]Deut. 30:9; Is. 62:5; 65:19 [b]Jer. 24:6; 31:28; Amos 9:15 [c]Hos. 2:19, 20
42 [a]Jer. 31:28; Zech. 8:14, 15 [b]Jer. 33:14
43 [a]Jer. 32:15, 25; Ezek. 37:11-14 [b]Jer. 33:10
44 [1]Or, *write . . . on the document* [2]I.e., South country [3]Or, *captivity* [a]Jer. 32:10 [b]Jer. 17:26; 33:13 [c]Jer. 31:23; 33:7, 11, 26

33:1 [1]Lit., *shut up* [a]Jer. 32:2, 8; 37:21; 38:28
2 [1]Lit., *it* [a]Jer. 51:19 [b]Ex. 3:15; 6:3; 15:3; Jer. 10:16
3 [a]Ps. 50:15; 91:15; Is. 55:6, 7; Jer. 29:12 [b]Jer. 32:17, 27 [c]Is. 48:6
4 [a]Is. 32:13, 14 [b]Jer. 32:24; Ezek. 4:2; 21:22; Hab. 1:10
5 [a]Jer. 21:4-7; 32:5 [b]Is. 8:17; Jer. 21:10; Mic. 3:4
6 [a]Jer. 17:14; 30:17; Hos. 6:1 [b]Is. 66:12; Gal. 5:22, 23
7 [1]Or, *captivity* [a]Ps. 85:1; Jer. 30:18; 32:44; 33:26; Amos 9:14 [b]Is. 1:26; Jer. 30:18; 31:4, 38; Amos 9:14, 15
8 [a]Ps. 51:2; Is. 44:22; Jer. 50:20; Ezek. 36:25, 33; Mic. 7:18, 19; Zech. 13:1; Heb. 9:11-14
9 [1]I.e., this city [a]Is. 62:2, 4, 7; Jer. 13:11 [b]Jer. 3:17, 19; 4:2; 16:19 [c]Jer. 24:6; 32:42 [d]Neh. 6:16; Ps. 40:3; Is. 60:5; Hos. 3:5
10 [a]Jer. 32:43 [b]Jer. 26:9; 34:22
11 [1]Or, *captivity* [a]Is. 35:10; 51:3, 11 [b]1 Chr. 16:8, 34; 2 Chr. 5:13; 7:3; Ezra 3:11; Ps. 100:4, 5; 106:1; 107:1; 118:1; 136:1 [c]Lev. 7:12, 13; Ps. 107:22; 116:17; Jer. 17:26; Heb. 13:15
12 [1]Or, *pasture* [a]Jer. 32:43; 36:29; 51:62 [b]Is. 65:10; Jer. 31:12; Ezek. 34:12-15; Zeph. 2:6, 7
13 [a]Jer. 17:26; 32:44 [b]Lev. 27:32; Luke 15:4
14 [a]Jer. 23:5 [b]Is. 32:1, 2; Jer. 29:10; 32:42; 33:9; Ezek. 34:23-25; Hag. 2:6-9
15 [a]Is. 4:2; 11:1-5; Jer. 23:5, 6; 30:9; Zech. 3:8; 6:12, 13 [b]Ps. 72:1-5
16 [a]Is. 45:17, 22; Jer. 23:6 [b]Is. 45:24, 25; Jer. 23:6; 1 Cor. 1:30; 2 Cor. 5:21; Phil. 3:9
17 [1]Lit., *There shall not be cut off for David* [a]2 Sam. 7:16; 1 Kin. 2:4; 8:25; 1 Chr. 17:11-14; Ps. 89:29-37

18 [1]and the [a]Levitical priests shall
never lack a man before Me to offer
burnt offerings, to burn grain offerings,
and to [b]prepare sacrifices [2]continu-
ally.' "
19 And the word of the LORD came to
Jeremiah, saying,
20 "Thus says the LORD, 'If you can
[a]break My covenant for the day, and My
covenant for the night, so that day and
night will not be at their appointed time,
21 then [a]My covenant may also be
broken with David My servant that he
shall not have a son to reign on his
throne, and with the Levitical priests,
My ministers.
22 'As the [a]host of heaven cannot be
counted, and the [b]sand of the sea cannot
be measured, so I will [c]multiply the
[1]descendants of David My servant and
the [d]Levites who minister to Me.' "
23 And the word of the LORD came to
Jeremiah, saying,
24 "Have you not observed what this
people have spoken, saying, 'The [a]two
families which the LORD chose, He has
[b]rejected them'? Thus they [c]despise My
people, no longer are they as a nation [1]in
their sight.
25 "Thus says the LORD, 'If My [a]cov-
enant *for* day and night *stand* not, *and*
the [1]fixed patterns of heaven and earth I
have [b]not established,
26 then I would [a]reject the [1]descend-
ants of Jacob and David My servant,
[2]not taking from his [1]descendants [b]rul-
ers over the [1]descendants of Abraham,
Isaac, and Jacob. But I will [c]restore their
[3]fortunes and will have [d]mercy on
them.' "

A Prophecy against Zedekiah

34 THE word which came to Jeremiah from the LORD, when
[a]Nebuchadnezzar king of Babylon and
all his army, with [b]all the kingdoms of
the earth that were under his dominion
and all the peoples, were fighting against
Jerusalem and against all its cities,
saying,
2 "Thus says the LORD God of Israel,
'[a]Go and speak to Zedekiah king of
Judah and say to him: "Thus says the
LORD, 'Behold, [b]I am giving this city
into the hand of the king of Babylon,
and [c]he will burn it with fire.
3 'And [a]you will not escape from his
hand, for you will surely be captured
and delivered into his hand; and you will
[b]see the king of Babylon eye to eye, and
he will speak with you [1]face to face, and
you will go to Babylon.' " '
4 "Yet hear the word of the LORD, O
Zedekiah king of Judah! Thus says the
LORD concerning you, 'You will not die
by the sword.
5 'You will die in peace; and as spices
were burned for your fathers, the former
kings who were before you, so they will
[a]burn spices for you; and [b]they will
lament for you, "Alas, lord!" ' For I
have spoken the word," declares the
LORD.
6 Then Jeremiah the prophet spoke
[a]all these words to Zedekiah king of
Judah in Jerusalem
7 when the army of the king of Babylon was fighting against Jerusalem and
against all the remaining cities of Judah,
that is, [a]Lachish and [b]Azekah, for they
alone remained as [c]fortified cities among
the cities of Judah.
8 The word which came to Jeremiah
from the LORD, after King Zedekiah had
[a]made a covenant with all the people
who were in Jerusalem to [b]proclaim
[1]release to them:
9 that each man should set free his
male servant and each man his female
servant, a [a]Hebrew man or a Hebrew
woman; so that [b]no one should keep
them, a Jew his brother, in bondage.
10 And all the [a]officials and all the
people obeyed, who had entered into the
covenant that each man should set free
his male servant and each man his
female servant, so that no one should
keep them any longer in bondage; they
obeyed, and set *them free.*
11 But afterward they turned around
and took back the male servants and the
female servants, whom they had set free,
and brought them into subjection for
male servants and for female servants.
12 Then the word of the LORD came
to Jeremiah from the LORD, saying,
13 "Thus says the LORD God of Israel,
'I [a]made a covenant with your forefathers in the day that I [b]brought them out
of the land of Egypt, from the house of
bondage, saying,
14 "[a]At the end of seven years each of
you shall set free his Hebrew brother,
who [1]has been sold to you and has
served you six years, you shall send him
out free from you; but your forefathers
[b]did not obey Me, or incline their ear to
Me.
15 "Although recently you *had* turned
and [a]done what is right in My sight, each
man proclaiming [1]release to his neighbor, and you had [b]made a covenant
before Me [c]in the house which is called
by My name.
16 "Yet you [a]turned and [b]profaned My
name, and each man [1]took back his male
servant and each man his female servant,
whom you had set free according to their
desire, and you brought them into subjection to be your male servants and
female servants." '
17 "Therefore thus says the LORD, 'You
have not obeyed Me in proclaiming
[1]release each man to his brother, and
each man to his neighbor. Behold, I am
[a]proclaiming a [1]release to you,' declares
the LORD, 'to the [b]sword, to the pestilence, and to the famine; and I will make
you a [c]terror to all the kingdoms of the
earth.

18 [1]Lit., *there shall not be cut off for the Levitical priests* [2]Lit., *all the days*
[a]Num. 3:5-10; Deut. 18:1; 24:8; Josh. 3:3; Ezek. 44:15
[b]Ezra 3:5; Heb. 13:15
20 [a]Ps. 89:37; 104:19-23; Is. 54:9, 10; Jer. 31:35-37; 33:25
21 [a]2 Sam. 23:5; 2 Chr. 7:18; 21:7
22 [1]Lit., *seed*
[a]Gen. 15:5; Jer. 31:37 [b]Gen. 22:17 [c]Ezek. 37:24-27 [d]Is. 66:21; Jer. 33:18
24 [1]Lit., *to their faces*
[a]Is. 7:17; 11:13; Jer. 3:7, 8, 10, 18; 33:26; Ezek. 37:22 [b]Jer. 30:17 [c]Neh. 4:2-4; Esth. 3:6, 8, 9; Ps. 44:13, 14; 83:4
25 [1]Lit., *statutes*
[a]Gen. 8:22; Jer. 31:35, 36; 33:20 [b]Ps. 74:16, 17
26 [1]Lit., *seed* [2]Lit., *from taking* [3]Or, *captivity*
[a]Jer. 31:37 [b]Gen. 49:10 [c]Jer. 33:7 [d]Is. 14:1; 54:8; Jer. 31:20; Ezek. 39:25; Hos. 1:7; 2:23

1 [a]2 Kin. 25:1; Jer. 32:2; 39:1; 52:4 [b]Jer. 1:15; 27:7; Dan. 2:37, 38
2 [a]2 Chr. 36:11, 12; Jer. 22:1, 2; 37:1, 2 [b]Jer. 21:10; 32:3; 34:22; 37:8-10 [c]Jer. 32:29
3 [1]Lit., *mouth to mouth*
[a]2 Kin. 25:4, 5; Jer. 21:7; 32:4; 34:21 [b]2 Kin. 25:6, 7; Jer. 39:6, 7
5 [a]2 Chr. 16:14; 21:19 [b]Jer. 22:18
6 [a]1 Sam. 3:18; 15:16-24
7 [a]Josh. 10:3, 5; 2 Kin. 14:19; 18:14; Is. 36:2 [b]Josh. 10:10; 2 Chr. 11:9 [c]2 Chr. 11:5-10
8 [1]Or, *liberty*
[a]2 Kin. 11:17; 23:2, 3 [b]Ex. 21:2; Lev. 25:10, 39-46; Neh. 5:1-13; Is. 58:6; Jer. 34:14, 17
9 [a]Gen. 14:13; Ex. 2:6 [b]Lev. 25:39
10 [a]Jer. 26:10, 16
13 [a]Ex. 24:3, 7, 8; Deut. 5:2, 3, 27; Jer. 31:32 [b]Ex. 20:2
14 [1]Or, *has sold himself*
[a]Ex. 21:2; Deut. 15:12; 1 Kin. 9:22 [b]1 Sam. 8:7, 8; 2 Kin. 17:13, 14
15 [1]Or, *liberty*
[a]Jer. 34:8 [b]2 Kin. 23:3; Neh. 10:29 [c]Jer. 7:10f.; 32:34
16 [1]Lit., *caused them to return*
[a]1 Sam. 15:11; Jer. 34:11; Ezek. 3:20; 18:24 [b]Ex. 20:7; Lev. 19:12
17 [1]Or, *liberty*
[a]Lev. 26:34, 35; Esth. 7:10; Dan. 6:24; Matt. 7:2 [b]Jer. 32:24; 38:2 [c]Deut. 28:25; Jer. 29:18

18 'And I will give the men who have [a]transgressed My covenant, who have not fulfilled the words of the covenant which they made before Me, *when* they [b]cut the calf in two and passed between its parts—

19 the [a]officials of Judah, and the officials of Jerusalem, the court officers, and the priests, and all the people of the land, who passed between the parts of the calf—

20 and I will give them into the hand of their enemies and into the hand of those who [a]seek their life. And their [b]dead bodies shall be food for the birds of the sky and the beasts of the earth.

21 'And [a]Zedekiah king of Judah and his officials I will give into the hand of their enemies, and into the hand of those who seek their life, and into the hand of the army of the king of Babylon which has [b]gone away from you.

22 'Behold, I am going to command,' declares the LORD, 'and I will bring them back to this city; and they shall fight against it and [a]take it and burn it with fire; and I will make the cities of Judah a [b]desolation [c]without inhabitant.' "

The Rechabites' Obedience

35 THE word which came to Jeremiah from the LORD in the days of [a]Jehoiakim the son of Josiah, king of Judah, saying,

2 "Go to the house of the [a]Rechabites, and speak to them, and bring them into the house of the LORD, into one of the [b]chambers, and give them wine to drink."

3 Then I took Jaazaniah the son of Jeremiah, son of Habazziniah, and his brothers, and all his sons, and the whole house of the Rechabites,

4 and I brought them into the house of the LORD, into the chamber of the sons of Hanan the son of Igdaliah, the [a]man of God, which was near the chamber of the officials, which was above the chamber of Maaseiah the son of Shallum, [b]the doorkeeper.

5 Then I set before the [1]men of the house of the Rechabites pitchers full of wine, and cups; and I said to them, "[a]Drink wine!"

6 But they said, "We will not drink wine, for [a]Jonadab the son of [b]Rechab, our father, commanded us, saying, 'You shall [c]not drink wine, you or your sons, forever.

7 'And you shall not build a house, and you shall not sow seed, and you shall not plant a vineyard or own one; but in [a]tents you shall dwell all your days, that you may live [b]many days in the land where you [c]sojourn.'

8 "And we have [a]obeyed the voice of Jonadab the son of Rechab, our father, in all that he commanded us, not to drink wine all our days, we, our wives, our sons, or our daughters,

9 nor to build ourselves houses to dwell in; and we [a]do not have vineyard or field or seed.

10 "We have only [a]dwelt in tents, and have obeyed, and have done according to all that [b]Jonadab our father commanded us.

11 "But it came about, when [a]Nebuchadnezzar king of Babylon came up against the land, that we said, 'Come and let us [b]go to Jerusalem before the army of the Chaldeans and before the army of the Arameans.' So we have dwelt in Jerusalem."

Judah Rebuked

12 Then the word of the LORD came to Jeremiah, saying,

13 "Thus says the LORD of hosts, the God of Israel, 'Go and say to the men of Judah and the inhabitants of Jerusalem, "[a]Will you not receive instruction by listening to My words?" declares the LORD.

14 "The [a]words of Jonadab the son of Rechab, which he commanded his sons not to drink wine, are observed. So they do not drink *wine* to this day, for they have obeyed their father's command. But I have spoken to you [1b]again and again; yet you have [c]not listened to Me.

15 "Also I have sent to you all My [a]servants the prophets, sending *them* [1]again and again, saying: '[b]Turn now every man from his evil way, and amend your deeds, and [c]do not go after other gods to worship them, then you shall [d]dwell in the land which I have given to you and to your forefathers; but you have not [e]inclined your ear or listened to Me.

16 'Indeed, the sons of Jonadab the son of Rechab have [a]observed the command of their father which he commanded them, but this people has not listened to Me.' " '

17 "Therefore thus says the LORD, the God of hosts, the God of Israel, 'Behold, [a]I am bringing on Judah and on all the inhabitants of Jerusalem all the disaster that I have pronounced against them; because I [b]spoke to them but they did not listen, and I have called them but they did not answer.' "

18 Then Jeremiah said to the house of the Rechabites, "Thus says the LORD of hosts, the God of Israel, 'Because you have [a]obeyed the command of Jonadab your father, kept all his commands, and done according to all that he commanded you;

19 therefore thus says the LORD of hosts, the God of Israel, "Jonadab the son of Rechab [a]shall not lack a man to [b]stand before Me [1]always." ' "

Jeremiah's Scroll Read in the Temple

36 AND it came about in the [a]fourth year of Jehoiakim the son of Josiah, king of Judah, that this word came to Jeremiah from the LORD, saying,

---

18 [a]Deut. 17:2; Hos. 6:7; 8:1; Rom. 2:8 [b]Gen. 15:10
19 [a]Jer. 34:10; Ezek. 22:27; Zeph. 3:3, 4
20 [a]Jer. 11:21; 21:7; 22:25 [b]Deut. 28:26; 1 Sam. 17:44, 46; 1 Kin. 14:11; 16:4; Ps. 79:2; Jer. 7:33; 16:4; 19:7
21 [a]2 Kin. 25:18-21; Jer. 32:3, 4; 39:6; 52:10, 24-27; Ezek. 17:16 [b]Jer. 37:5-11
22 [a]Jer. 34:2; 39:1, 2, 8; 52:7, 13 [b]Jer. 4:7; 9:11 [c]Jer. 33:10; 44:22

1 [a]2 Kin. 23:34-36; 24:1; 2 Chr. 36:5-7; Jer. 1:3; 27:20; Dan. 1:1
2 [a]2 Kin. 10:15; 1 Chr. 2:55 [b]1 Kin. 6:5, 8; 1 Chr. 9:26, 33
4 [a]Deut. 33:1; Josh. 14:6; 1 Kin. 12:22; 2 Kin. 1:9-13 [b]1 Chr. 9:18f.
5 [1]Lit., *sons* [a]Amos 2:12
6 [a]2 Kin. 10:15, 23 [b]1 Chr. 2:55 [c]Lev. 10:9; Num. 6:2-4; Judg. 13:7, 14; Luke 1:15
7 [a]Gen. 25:27; Heb. 11:9 [b]Ex. 20:12; Eph. 6:2, 3 [c]Gen. 36:7
8 [a]Prov. 1:8, 9; 4:1, 2, 10; 6:20; Eph. 6:1; Col. 3:20
9 [a]Ps. 37:16; Jer. 35:7; 1 Tim. 6:6
10 [a]Jer. 35:7 [b]Jer. 35:6
11 [a]2 Kin. 24:1, 2; Dan. 1:1, 2 [b]Jer. 4:5-7; 8:14
13 [a]Is. 28:9-12; Jer. 5:3; 6:8-10; 32:33
14 [1]Lit., *rising early and speaking* [a]Jer. 35:6-10 [b]2 Chr. 36:15; Jer. 7:13, 25; 11:7; 25:3, 4 [c]Is. 30:9; 50:2
15 [1]Lit., *rising early and speaking* [a]Jer. 7:25; 25:4; 26:5; 29:19; 32:33 [b]Is. 1:16, 17; Jer. 4:1; 18:11; 25:5f.; Ezek. 18:30-32; Acts 26:20 [c]Deut. 6:14; Jer. 7:6; 13:10; 25:6 [d]Jer. 7:7; 25:5, 6 [e]Jer. 7:24, 26; 11:8; 17:23; 34:14
16 [a]Jer. 35:14; Mal. 1:6
17 [a]Josh. 23:15; Jer. 19:3, 15; 21:4-10; Mic. 3:12 [b]Prov. 1:24, 25; Is. 65:12; 66:4; Jer. 7:13, 26, 27; 26:5; Luke 13:34, 35; Rom. 10:21
18 [a]Ex. 20:12; Eph. 6:1-3
19 [1]Lit., *all the days* [a]1 Chr. 2:55; Jer. 33:17 [b]Jer. 15:19; Luke 21:36

1 [a]2 Kin. 24:1; 2 Chr. 36:5-7; Jer. 25:1, 3; 45:1; 46:2; Dan. 1:1

2“Take a [1a]scroll and write on it all the [b]words which I have spoken to you concerning [c]Israel, and concerning Judah, and concerning all the [d]nations, from the [e]day I *first* spoke to you, from the days of Josiah, even to this day.

3“[a]Perhaps the house of Judah will hear all the calamity which I plan to bring on them, in order that every man will [b]turn from his evil way; then I will [c]forgive their iniquity and their sin.”

4 Then Jeremiah called [a]Baruch the son of Neriah, and Baruch wrote [1]at the dictation of Jeremiah all the words of the LORD, which He had spoken to him, on a [2b]scroll.

5 And Jeremiah commanded Baruch, saying, “I am [1a]restricted; I cannot go into the house of the LORD.

6“So you go and [a]read from the scroll which you have [b]written [1]at my dictation the words of the LORD [2]to the people in the LORD’s house on a [c]fast day. And also you shall read them [2]to all *the people of* Judah who come from their cities.

7“[a]Perhaps their supplication will [1]come before the LORD, and everyone will turn from his evil way, for [b]great is the anger and the wrath that the LORD has pronounced against this people.”

8 And Baruch the son of Neriah did according to all that Jeremiah the prophet commanded him, [a]reading from the book the words of the LORD in the LORD’s house.

9 Now it came about in the [a]fifth year of Jehoiakim the son of Josiah, king of Judah, in the [b]ninth month, that all the people in Jerusalem and all the people who [c]came from the cities of Judah to Jerusalem proclaimed a [d]fast before the LORD.

10 Then Baruch read from the book the words of Jeremiah in the house of the LORD in the [a]chamber of [b]Gemariah the son of Shaphan the [c]scribe, in the upper court, at the [d]entry of the New Gate of the LORD’s house, to all the people.

11 Now when [a]Micaiah the son of Gemariah, the son of Shaphan, had heard all the words of the LORD from the book,

12 he went down to the king’s house, into the scribe’s chamber. And, behold, all the officials were sitting there—[a]Elishama the scribe, and [b]Delaiah the son of Shemaiah, and [c]Elnathan the son of Achbor, and Gemariah the son of Shaphan, and Zedekiah the son of Hananiah, and all the *other* officials.

13 And Micaiah [a]declared to them all the words that he had heard, when Baruch read from the book to the people.

14 Then all the officials sent [a]Jehudi the son of Nethaniah, the son of Shelemiah, the son of Cushi, to Baruch, saying, “Take in your hand the scroll from which you have read to the people and come.” So Baruch the son of Neriah [b]took the scroll in his hand and went to them.

15 And they said to him, “Sit down please, and read it to us.” So Baruch [a]read it to them.

16 Now it came about when they had heard all the words, they turned in [a]fear one to another and said to Baruch, “We will surely [b]report all these words to the king.”

17 And they asked Baruch, saying, “Tell us please, [a]how did you write all these words? *Was it* [1]at his dictation?”

18 Then Baruch said to them, “He [a]dictated all these words to me, and I wrote them with ink on the book.”

19 Then the officials said to Baruch, “Go, [a]hide yourself, you and Jeremiah, and do not let anyone know where you are.”

The Scroll Is Burned

20 So they went to the [a]king in the court, but they had deposited the scroll in the chamber of [a]Elishama the scribe, and they reported all the words to the king.

21 Then the king sent Jehudi to get the scroll, and he took it out of the chamber of Elishama the scribe. And Jehudi [a]read it to the king as well as to all the officials who stood beside the king.

22 Now the king was sitting in the [a]winter house in the [b]ninth month, with *a fire* burning in the brazier before him.

23 And it came about, when Jehudi had read three or four columns, *the king* cut it with a scribe’s knife and [a]threw *it* into the fire that was in the brazier, until all the scroll was consumed in the fire that was in the brazier.

24 Yet the king and all his servants who heard all these words were [a]not afraid, nor did they [b]rend their garments.

25 Even though Elnathan and Delaiah and Gemariah [a]entreated the king not to burn the scroll, he would not listen to them.

26 And the king commanded Jerahmeel the king’s son, Seraiah the son of Azriel, and Shelemiah the son of Abdeel to [a]seize Baruch the scribe and Jeremiah the prophet, but the [b]LORD hid them.

The Scroll Is Replaced

27 Then the word of the LORD came to Jeremiah after the king had [a]burned the scroll and the words which [b]Baruch had written at the dictation of Jeremiah, saying,

28“[a]Take again another scroll and write on it all the former words that were [b]on the first scroll which Jehoiakim the king of Judah burned.

29“And concerning Jehoiakim king of Judah you shall say, ‘Thus says the

2 [1]Lit., *scroll of a book* [a]Ex. 17:14; Is. 8:1; Jer. 36:6, 23, 28; Zech. 5:1, 2 [b]Jer. 1:9, 10; 30:2; Hab. 2:2 [c]Jer. 3:3-10; 23:13, 14; 32:30-32 [d]Jer. 1:5, 10; 25:9-29; chs. 47-51 [e]Jer. 1:2, 3; 25:3
3 [a]Jer. 26:3; 36:7; Ezek. 12:3 [b]Deut. 30:2, 8; 1 Sam. 7:3; Is. 55:7; Jer. 18:8, 11; 35:15; Jon. 3:8 [c]Jon. 3:10; Mark 4:12; Acts 3:19
4 [1]Lit., *from the mouth of* [2]Lit., *scroll of a book* [a]Jer. 32:12; 36:18; 43:3; 45:1 [b]Jer. 36:14; Ezek. 2:9
5 [1]Lit., *shut up* [a]Jer. 32:2; 33:1; 2 Cor. 11:23
6 [1]Lit., *from my mouth* [2]Lit., *in the ears of,* and so throughout this context [a]Jer. 36:8 [b]Jer. 36:4 [c]Jer. 36:9; Zech. 8:19
7 [1]Lit., *fall* [a]1 Kin. 8:33; 2 Chr. 33:12, 13; Jer. 26:3; 36:3 [b]Deut. 28:15; 31:16, 17; 2 Kin. 22:13, 17; Jer. 4:4; 21:5; Lam. 4:11
8 [a]Jer. 1:17; 36:6
9 [a]Jer. 36:1 [b]Jer. 36:22 [c]Jer. 36:6 [d]Judg. 20:26; 1 Sam. 7:6; 2 Chr. 20:3; Esth. 4:16; Joel 1:14; 2:15; Jon. 3:5
10 [a]Jer. 35:4 [b]Jer. 36:11, 25 [c]2 Sam. 8:17; Jer. 52:25 [d]Jer. 26:10
11 [a]Jer. 36:13
12 [a]Jer. 36:20 [b]Jer. 36:25 [c]Jer. 26:22
13 [a]2 Kin. 22:10
14 [a]Jer. 36:21 [b]Jer. 36:2; Ezek. 2:7-10
15 [a]Jer. 36:21
16 [a]Jer. 36:24; Acts 24:25 [b]Jer. 13:18; Amos 7:10, 11
17 [1]Lit., *from his mouth,* and so throughout this context [a]John 9:10, 15, 26
18 [a]Jer. 36:4
19 [a]1 Kin. 17:3; 18:4, 10; Jer. 26:20-24; 36:26
20 [a]Jer. 36:12
21 [a]2 Kin. 22:10; 2 Chr. 34:18; Ezek. 2:4, 5
22 [a]Judg. 3:20; Amos 3:15 [b]Jer. 36:9
23 [a]1 Kin. 22:8, 27; Prov. 1:30; Is. 5:18, 19; 28:14, 22; Jer. 36:29
24 [a]Ps. 36:1; 64:5; Jer. 36:16 [b]Gen. 37:29, 34; 2 Sam. 1:11; 1 Kin. 21:27; 2 Kin. 19:1, 2; 22:11, 19; Is. 36:22; 37:1; Jon. 3:6
25 [a]Gen. 37:22, 26, 27; Acts 5:34-39
26 [a]1 Kin. 19:1-3, 10, 14; Matt. 23:34, 37 [b]Ps. 91:1

27 [a]Jer. 36:23 [b]Jer. 36:4, 18
28 [a]Zech. 1:5, 6 [b]Jer. 36:4, 23

LORD, "You have [a]burned this scroll,
saying, '[b]Why have you written on it
[1]that the [c]king of Babylon shall certainly
come and destroy this land, and shall
make man and beast to cease from it?' "
30 'Therefore thus says the LORD concerning Jehoiakim king of Judah, "He
shall have [a]no one to sit on the throne of
David, and his [b]dead body shall be cast
out to the heat of the day and the frost
of the night.
31 "I shall also [a]punish him and his
[1]descendants and his servants for their
iniquity, and I shall [b]bring on them and
the inhabitants of Jerusalem and the
men of Judah all the calamity that I have
declared to them—but they did not
listen." ' "
32 Then Jeremiah took another scroll
and gave it to Baruch the son of Ne-
raiah, the scribe, and he [a]wrote on it at
the dictation of Jeremiah all the words
of the book which Jehoiakim king of
Judah had burned in the fire; and many
[1]similar words were added to them.

Jeremiah Warns against Trust in Pharaoh

37 NOW [a]Zedekiah the son of Josiah whom Nebuchadnezzar king
of Babylon had [b]made king in the land
of Judah, reigned as king in place of
[c]Coniah the son of Jehoiakim.
2 But [a]neither he nor his servants nor
the people of the land listened to the
words of the LORD which He spoke
through Jeremiah the prophet.
3 Yet [a]King Zedekiah sent Jehucal
the son of Shelemiah, and [b]Zephaniah
the son of Maaseiah, the priest, to Jeremiah the prophet, saying, "[c]Please pray
to the LORD our God on our behalf."
4 Now Jeremiah was *still* coming in
and going out among the people, for
they had not *yet* [a]put him in the prison.
5 Meanwhile, [a]Pharaoh's army had
set out from Egypt; and when the Chaldeans who had been besieging Jerusalem
heard the report about them, they [b]lifted
the *siege* from Jerusalem.
6 Then the word of the LORD came
to Jeremiah the prophet, saying,
7 "Thus says the LORD God of Israel,
'[a]Thus you are to say to the king of
Judah, who sent you to Me to inquire of
Me: "Behold, [b]Pharaoh's army which
has come out for your assistance is going
to return to its own land of Egypt.
8 "The Chaldeans will also [a]return
and fight against this city, and they will
capture it and burn it with fire." '
9 "Thus says the LORD, 'Do not [a]de-
ceive yourselves, saying, "The Chaldeans
will surely go away from us," for they
will not go.
10 'For [a]even if you had defeated the
entire army of Chaldeans who were
fighting against you, and there were *only*
wounded men left among them, each
man in his tent, they would rise up and
[b]burn this city with fire.' "

29 [1]Lit., *saying* [a]Deut. 29:19; Job 15:24, 25; Is. 45:9 [b]Is. 29:21; 30:10; Jer. 26:9; 32:3 [c]Jer. 25:9-11
30 [a]2 Kin. 24:12-15; Jer. 22:30 [b]Jer. 22:19
31 [1]Lit., *seed* [a]Jer. 23:34 [b]Deut. 28:15; Prov. 29:1; Jer. 19:15; 35:17
32 [1]Lit., *like those* [a]Ex. 4:15, 16; 34:1; Jer. 36:4, 18, 23

1 [a]2 Kin. 24:17; 1 Chr. 3:15; 2 Chr. 36:10 [b]Ezek. 17:12-21 [c]2 Kin. 24:12; 1 Chr. 3:16; 2 Chr. 36:9, 10; Jer. 22:24, 28; 24:1; 52:31
2 [a]2 Kin. 24:19, 20; 2 Chr. 36:12-16; Prov. 29:12
3 [a]Jer. 21:1, 2 [b]Jer. 29:25; 52:24 [c]1 Kin. 13:6; Jer. 2:27; 15:11; 21:1, 2; 42:1-4, 20; Acts 8:24
4 [a]Jer. 32:2, 3; 37:15
5 [a]2 Kin. 24:7; Jer. 37:7; Ezek. 17:15 [b]Jer. 37:11
7 [a]2 Kin. 22:18; Jer. 21:1, 2; 37:3 [b]Is. 30:1-3; 31:1-3; Jer. 2:18, 36; Lam. 4:17; Ezek. 17:17
8 [a]Jer. 34:22; 38:23; 39:2-8
9 [a]Jer. 29:8; Obad. 3; Matt. 24:4, 5; Eph. 5:6
10 [a]Lev. 26:36-38; Is. 30:17; Jer. 21:4, 5 [b]Jer. 37:8
12 [1]Or, *part in a dividing* [a]Jer. 32:8
13 [1]Lit., *falling* [a]Jer. 38:7; Zech. 14:10 [b]Jer. 18:18; 20:10; Luke 23:2; Acts 6:11; 24:5-9, 13
14 [1]Lit., *falling* [a]Ps. 27:12; 52:1, 2; Jer. 40:4-6; Matt. 5:11, 12
15 [a]Jer. 18:23; 20:1-3; 26:16; Matt. 21:35 [b]Gen. 39:20; 2 Chr. 16:10; 18:26; Jer. 38:26; Acts 5:18
16 [1]Lit., *house of the cistern-pit* [a]Jer. 38:6
17 [a]1 Kin. 14:1-4; Jer. 38:5, 14-16, 24-27 [b]1 Kin. 22:15, 16; 2 Kin. 3:11, 12; Jer. 15:11; 21:1, 2; 37:3 [c]Jer. 21:7; 24:8; Ezek. 12:12, 13; 17:19, 20
18 [a]1 Sam. 24:9; 26:18; Dan. 6:22; John 10:32; Acts 25:8, 11, 25
19 [a]Deut. 32:37, 38; 2 Kin. 3:13; Jer. 2:28 [b]Jer. 27:14; 28:1-4, 10-17
20 [1]Lit., *fall* [a]Jer. 36:7; 38:26
21 [a]Jer. 32:2; 38:13, 28 [b]1 Kin. 17:6; Job 5:20; Ps. 33:18, 19; Is. 33:16 [c]2 Kin. 25:3; Jer. 38:9; 52:6

1 [a]Jer. 37:3 [b]Jer. 21:1

Jeremiah Imprisoned

11 Now it happened, when the army
of the Chaldeans had lifted *the siege*
from Jerusalem because of Pharaoh's
army,
12 that Jeremiah went out from Jerusalem to go to the land of Benjamin in
order to [a]take [1]possession of *some* property there among the people.
13 While he was at the [a]Gate of Benjamin, a captain of the guard whose name
was Irijah, the son of Shelemiah the son
of Hananiah was there; and he [b]arrested
Jeremiah the prophet, saying, "You are
[1]going over to the Chaldeans!"
14 But Jeremiah said, "[a]A lie! I am
not [1]going over to the Chaldeans"; yet
he would not listen to him. So Irijah
arrested Jeremiah and brought him to
the officials.
15 Then the officials were [a]angry at
Jeremiah and beat him, and they [b]put
him in jail in the house of Jonathan the
scribe, which they had made into the
prison.
16 For Jeremiah had come into the
[1a]dungeon, that is, the vaulted cell; and
Jeremiah stayed there many days.
17 Now King Zedekiah sent and took
him *out;* and in his palace the king
[a]secretly asked him and said, "Is there a
[b]word from the LORD?" And Jeremiah
said, "There is!" Then he said, "You will
be [c]given into the hand of the king of
Babylon!"
18 Moreover Jeremiah said to King
Zedekiah, "[a]*In* what *way* have I sinned
against you, or against your servants, or
against this people, that you have put me
in prison?
19 "[a]Where then are your prophets who
prophesied to you, saying, 'The [b]king of
Babylon will not come against you or
against this land'?
20 "But now, please listen, O my lord
the king; please let my [a]petition [1]come
before you, and do not make me return
to the house of Jonathan the scribe, that
I may not die there."
21 Then King Zedekiah gave commandment, and they committed Jeremiah to the [a]court of the guardhouse
and gave him a loaf of [b]bread daily from
the bakers' street, until all the bread in
the city was [c]gone. So Jeremiah remained in the court of the guardhouse.

Jeremiah Thrown into the Cistern

38 NOW Shephatiah the son of
Mattan, and Gedaliah the son of
Pashhur, and Jucal the [a]son of Shelemiah, and [b]Pashhur the son of Malchijah heard the words that Jeremiah was
speaking to all the people, saying,
2 "Thus says the LORD, 'He who
[a]stays in this city will die by the [b]sword
and by famine and by pestilence, but he
who goes out to the Chaldeans will live
and have his *own* [c]life as booty and stay
alive.'

2 [a]Jer. 21:9 [b]Jer. 34:17; 42:17 [c]Jer. 21:9; 39:18; 45:5

3 "Thus says the LORD, 'This city will
certainly be [a]given into the hand of the
army of the king of Babylon, and he will
capture it.' "
4 Then the [a]officials said to the king,
"Now let this man be put to death,
inasmuch as he is [1b]discouraging the
men of war who are left in this city and
[2]all the people, by speaking such words
to them; for this man [c]is not seeking the
well-being of this people, but rather their
harm."
5 So King Zedekiah said, "Behold,
he is in your [1]hands; for the king [a]can *do*
nothing against you."
6 Then they took Jeremiah and cast
him into the [a]cistern *of* Malchijah the
king's son, which was in the court of the
guardhouse; and they let Jeremiah down
with ropes. Now in the cistern there was
no water but only [b]mud, and Jeremiah
sank into the mud.
7 But [a]Ebed-melech the Ethiopian,
[1]a [b]eunuch, while he was in the king's
palace, heard that they had put Jeremiah
into the cistern. Now the king was sitting
in the [c]Gate of Benjamin;
8 and Ebed-melech went out from
the king's palace and spoke to the king,
saying,
9 "My lord the king, these men have
acted wickedly in all that they have done
to Jeremiah the prophet whom they have
cast into the cistern; and he [1]will die
right where he is because of the famine,
for there is [a]no more bread in the city."
10 Then the king commanded Ebed-
melech the Ethiopian, saying, "Take
thirty men from here [1]under your authority, and bring up Jeremiah the
prophet from the cistern before he dies."
11 So Ebed-melech took the men under his [1]authority and went into the
king's palace to *a place* beneath the
storeroom and took from there worn-out
clothes and worn-out rags and let them
down by ropes into the cistern to Jeremiah.
12 Then Ebed-melech the Ethiopian
said to Jeremiah, "Now put these worn-
out clothes and rags under your armpits
under the ropes"; and Jeremiah did so.
13 So they pulled Jeremiah up with
the ropes and lifted him out of the
cistern, and Jeremiah stayed in the
[a]court of the guardhouse.
14 Then King Zedekiah [a]sent and
[1]had Jeremiah the prophet brought to
him at the third entrance that is in the
house of the LORD; and the king said to
Jeremiah, "I am going to [b]ask you
something; do not hide anything from
me."
15 Then Jeremiah said to Zedekiah,
"[a]If I tell you, will you not certainly put
me to death? Besides, if I give you
advice, you will not listen to me."
16 But King Zedekiah swore to Jeremiah in [a]secret saying, "As the LORD
lives, who made this [1b]life for us, surely I
will not put you to death nor will I give
you over to the hand of [c]these men who
are seeking your [1]life."

Interview with Zedekiah

17 Then Jeremiah said to Zedekiah,
"Thus says the LORD [a]God of hosts, the
[b]God of Israel, 'If you will indeed [c]go
out to the officers of the king of Babylon,
then [1]you will live, this city will not be
burned with fire, and you and your
household will [2]survive.
18 'But if you will [a]not go out to the
officers of the king of Babylon, then this
city [b]will be given over to the hand of
the Chaldeans; and they will burn it
with fire, and [c]you yourself will not
escape from their hand.' "
19 Then King Zedekiah said to Jeremiah, "I [a]dread the Jews who have
[1b]gone over to the Chaldeans, lest they
give me over into their hand and they
[c]abuse me."
20 But Jeremiah said, "They will not
give you over. Please [1a]obey the LORD in
what I am saying to you, that it may go
[b]well with you and [2c]you may live.
21 "But if you keep refusing to go out,
this is the word which the LORD has
shown me:
22 'Then behold, all of the [a]women
who have been left in the palace of the
king of Judah are going to be brought
out to the [1]officers of the king of Babylon; and those women will say,

"[2]Your close friends
Have misled and overpowered you;
While your feet were sunk in the mire,
They turned back."

23 'They will also bring out all your
wives and your [a]sons to the Chaldeans,
and [b]you yourself will not escape from
their hand, but will be seized by the
hand of the king of Babylon, and [b]this
city will be burned with fire.' "
24 Then Zedekiah said to Jeremiah,
"Let no man know about these words
and you will not die.
25 "But if the [a]officials hear that I have
talked with you and come to you and say
to you, 'Tell us now what you said to the
king, and what the king said to you; do
not hide *it* from us, and we will not put
you to death,'
26 then you are to say to them, 'I was
[a]presenting my petition before the king,
not to make me return to the house of
Jonathan to die there.' "
27 Then all the officials came to Jeremiah and questioned him. So he reported to them in accordance with all
these words which the king had commanded; and they ceased speaking with
him, since the [1]conversation had not
been overheard.
28 So Jeremiah [a]stayed in the court of
the guardhouse until the day that Jerusalem was captured.

Jerusalem Captured

39 1 NOW it came about when Jerusalem was captured [2a]in the ninth
year of Zedekiah king of Judah, in the
tenth month, Nebuchadnezzar king of
Babylon and all his army came to Jerusalem and laid siege to it;

3 [a]Jer. 21:10; 32:3-5
4 [1]Lit., *weakening the hands of* [2]Lit., *the hands of all* [a]Jer. 18:23; 26:11, 21; 36:12 [b]Ex. 5:4; 1 Kin. 18:17, 18; 21:20; Neh. 6:9; Amos 7:10; Acts 16:20 [c]Jer. 29:7
5 [1]Lit., *hand* [a]2 Sam. 3:39
6 [a]Jer. 37:16, 21; Acts 16:24 [b]Ps. 40:2; 69:2, 14, 15; Jer. 38:22; Zech. 9:11
7 [1]Or, *an official* [a]Jer. 39:16 [b]Jer. 29:2; Acts 8:27 [c]Deut. 21:19; Job 29:7; Jer. 37:13; Amos 5:10
9 [1]M.T. reads *has died* [a]Jer. 37:21; 52:6
10 [1]Lit., *in your hand*
11 [1]Lit., *hand*
13 [a]Neh. 3:25; Jer. 32:2; 37:21; 38:6; 39:14, 15; Acts 23:35; 24:27; 28:16, 30
14 [1]Lit., *took Jeremiah the prophet to him* [a]Jer. 21:1, 2; 37:17 [b]1 Sam. 3:17, 18; 1 Kin. 22:16; Jer. 15:11; 42:2-5, 20
15 [a]Luke 22:67, 68
16 [1]Lit., *soul* [a]Jer. 37:17; John 3:2 [b]Num. 16:22; 27:16; Is. 42:5; 57:16; Zech. 12:1; Acts 17:25, 28 [c]Jer. 34:20; 38:4-6
17 [1]Lit., *your soul* [2]Lit., *live* [a]Ps. 80:7, 14; Amos 5:27 [b]1 Chr. 17:24; Ezek. 8:4 [c]2 Kin. 24:12; 25:27-30; Jer. 21:8-10; 27:12, 17; 38:2; 39:3
18 [a]Jer. 27:8 [b]2 Kin. 25:4-10; Jer. 24:8-10; 32:3-5; 37:8; 38:3 [c]Jer. 32:4; 34:3
19 [1]Lit., *fallen* [a]Is. 51:12, 13; 57:11; John 12:42; 19:12, 13 [b]Jer. 39:9 [c]2 Chr. 30:10; Neh. 4:1; Jer. 38:22
20 [1]Lit., *listen to the voice of* [2]Lit., *your soul* [a]2 Chr. 20:20; Jer. 11:4, 8; 26:13; Dan. 4:27; Acts 26:29 [b]Jer. 7:23 [c]Gen. 19:20; Is. 55:3
22 [1]Or, *princes* [2]Lit., *The men of your peace* [a]Jer. 6:12; 8:10; 43:6
23 [a]2 Kin. 25:7; Jer. 39:6; 41:10 [b]Jer. 38:18
25 [a]Jer. 38:4-6, 27
26 [a]Jer. 37:20
27 [1]Lit., *word*
28 [a]Ps. 23:4; Jer. 15:20, 21; 37:20, 21; 38:13; 39:13, 14

1 [1]Ch. 38:28-b in Heb. [2]Ch. 39:1 in Heb. [a]2 Kin. 25:1-12; Jer. 52:4; Ezek. 24:1, 2

2 in the eleventh year of Zedekiah, in
the fourth month, in the ninth *day* of the
month, the city *wall* was [a]breached.
3 Then all the [a]officials of the king of
Babylon came in and sat down at the
[b]Middle Gate: Nergal-sar-ezer, Samgar-
nebu, Sar-sekim the [1]Rab-saris, Nergal-
sar-ezer *the* [2]Rab-mag, and all the rest of
the officials of the king of Babylon.
4 And it came about, when Zedekiah
the king of Judah and all the men of war
saw them, that they [a]fled and went out
of the city at night by way of the king's
garden through the gate [b]between the
two walls; and he went out toward the
[1]Arabah.
5 But the army of the [a]Chaldeans
pursued them and overtook Zedekiah in
the [b]plains of Jericho; and they seized
him and brought him up to Nebuchadnezzar king of Babylon at [c]Riblah in the
land of Hamath, and he passed sentence
on him.
6 Then the [a]king of Babylon slew the
sons of Zedekiah [b]before his eyes at
Riblah; the king of Babylon also slew all
the [c]nobles of Judah.
7 He then [a]blinded Zedekiah's eyes
and bound him in [b]fetters of bronze to
bring him to [c]Babylon.
8 The Chaldeans also [a]burned with
fire the king's palace and the houses of
the people, and they [b]broke down the
walls of Jerusalem.
9 And as for the rest of the people
who were left in the city, the [1a]deserters
who had gone over to him and [b]the rest
of the people who remained, [c]Nebuzara-
dan the [d]captain of the bodyguard carried *them* into exile in Babylon.
10 But some of the [a]poorest people
who had nothing, [a]Nebuzaradan the
captain of the bodyguard left behind in
the land of Judah, and gave them vineyards and fields [1]at that time.

Jeremiah Spared

11 Now Nebuchadnezzar king of
Babylon gave orders about [a]Jeremiah
through Nebuzaradan the captain of the
bodyguard, saying,
12 "Take him and [1]look after him, and
[a]do nothing harmful to him; but rather
deal with him just as he tells you."
13 So Nebuzaradan the captain of the
bodyguard sent *word,* along with Nebu-
shazban the [1]Rab-saris, and Nergal-
sar-ezer the [2]Rab-mag, and all the leading officers of the king of Babylon;
14 they even sent and [a]took Jeremiah
out of the court of the guardhouse and
entrusted him to [b]Gedaliah, the son of
[c]Ahikam, the son of Shaphan, to take
him home. So he stayed among the
people.
15 Now the word of the LORD had
come to Jeremiah while he was [a]confined
in the court of the guardhouse, saying,
16 "Go and speak to [a]Ebed-melech the
Ethiopian, saying, 'Thus says the LORD
of hosts, the God of Israel, "Behold, I
am about to bring My words on this city
[b]for disaster and not for [1]prosperity;
and they will [c]take place before you on
that day.
17 "But I will [a]deliver you on that
day," declares the LORD, "and you shall
not be given into the hand of the men
whom you dread.
18 "For I will certainly rescue you, and
you will not fall by the sword; but you
will have your *own* [a]life as booty, because you have [b]trusted in Me," declares
the LORD.' "

Jeremiah Remains in Judah

40 THE word which came to Jeremiah from the LORD after [a]Nebu-
zaradan captain of the bodyguard had
released him from [b]Ramah, when he had
taken him bound in [c]chains, among all
the exiles of Jerusalem and Judah, who
were being exiled to Babylon.
2 Now the captain of the bodyguard
had taken Jeremiah and said to him,
"The [a]LORD your God promised this
calamity against this place;
3 and the LORD has brought *it* on
and done just as He promised. Because
you *people* [a]sinned against the LORD and
did not listen to His voice, therefore this
thing has happened to you.
4 "But now, behold, I am [a]freeing you
today from the chains which are on your
hands. If [1]you would prefer to come with
me to Babylon, come *along,* and I will
[2]look after you; but if [3]you would prefer
not to come with me to Babylon, [4]never
mind. Look, the [b]whole land is before
you; go wherever it seems good and right
for you to go."
5 As [1]Jeremiah was still not going
back, [2]*he said,* "Go on back then to
[a]Gedaliah the son of Ahikam, the son of
Shaphan, whom the king of Babylon has
[b]appointed over the cities of Judah, and
stay with him among the people; or else
go anywhere it seems right for you to
go." So the captain of the bodyguard
gave him a [c]ration and a [d]gift and let
him go.
6 Then Jeremiah went to [a]Mizpah to
[b]Gedaliah the son of Ahikam and stayed
with him among the people who were
left in the land.
7 [a]Now all the [1]commanders of the
forces that were in the field, they and
their men, heard that the king of Babylon had appointed Gedaliah the son of
Ahikam over the land and that he had
put him in charge of the men, women
and [2]children, those of the [b]poorest of
the land who had not been exiled to
Babylon.
8 So they came to Gedaliah at Mizpah, along with [a]Ishmael the son of
Nethaniah, and [b]Johanan and Jonathan
the sons of Kareah, and Seraiah the son
of Tanhumeth, and the sons of Ephai the
[c]Netophathite, and [d]Jezaniah the son of
the [e]Maacathite, *both* they and their
men.

---

2 [a]2 Kin. 25:4; Jer. 52:7
3 [1]I.e., chief official [2]I.e., title of a high official [a]Jer. 38:17 [b]Jer. 21:4
4 [1]I.e., Jordan valley [a]2 Kin. 25:4; Is. 30:16; Jer. 52:7; Amos 2:14 [b]2 Chr. 32:5
5 [a]Jer. 32:4, 5; 38:18, 23; 52:8 [b]Josh. 4:13; 5:10 [c]2 Kin. 23:33; Jer. 52:9, 26, 27
6 [a]2 Kin. 25:7; Jer. 52:10 [b]Deut. 28:34 [c]Jer. 21:7; 24:8-10; 34:19-21
7 [a]2 Kin. 25:7; Jer. 52:11; Ezek. 12:13 [b]Judg. 16:21 [c]Jer. 32:5
8 [a]2 Kin. 25:9; Jer. 21:10; 38:18; 52:13 [b]2 Kin. 25:10; Neh. 1:3; Jer. 52:14
9 [1]Lit., *fallers who had fallen* [a]Jer. 38:19; 52:15 [b]Jer. 24:8 [c]2 Kin. 25:11, 20; Jer. 39:13; 40:1; 52:12-16, 26 [d]Gen. 37:36
10 [1]Lit., *on that day* [a]2 Kin. 25:12; Jer. 52:16
11 [a]Job 5:15, 16; Jer. 1:8; 15:20, 21; Acts 24:23
12 [1]Lit., *set your eyes on* [a]Ps. 105:14, 15; Prov. 16:7; 21:1; 1 Pet. 3:13
13 [1]I.e., chief official [2]I.e., title of a high official
14 [a]Jer. 38:28; 40:1-6 [b]Jer. 40:5 [c]2 Kin. 22:12, 14; 2 Chr. 34:20; Jer. 26:24
15 [a]Jer. 38:28
16 [1]Lit., *good* [a]Jer. 38:7 [b]Jer. 21:10; Dan. 9:12; Zech. 1:6 [c]Ps. 91:8
17 [a]Ps. 41:1, 2; 50:15
18 [a]Jer. 21:9; 38:2; 45:5 [b]Ps. 34:22; Jer. 17:7, 8

1 [a]Jer. 39:9, 11 [b]Jer. 31:15 [c]Acts 12:6, 7; 21:13; 28:20; Eph. 6:20
2 [a]Lev. 26:14-38; Deut. 28:15-68; 29:24-28; 31:17; 32:19-25; Jer. 22:8, 9
3 [a]Jer. 50:7; Dan. 9:11; Rom. 2:5
4 [1]Lit., *it is good in your eyes* [2]Lit., *set my eyes on* [3]Lit., *it is evil in your eyes* [4]Lit., *refrain!* [a]Jer. 39:11, 12 [b]Gen. 13:9; 20:15; 47:6
5 [1]Lit., *he* [2]I.e., Nebuzaradan [a]Jer. 39:14 [b]2 Kin. 25:23 [c]Jer. 52:34 [d]2 Kin. 8:7-9
6 [a]Judg. 20:1; 21:1; 1 Sam. 7:5; 2 Chr. 16:6 [b]Jer. 39:14
7 [1]Or, *princes* [2]Lit., *infants* [a]2 Kin. 25:23 [b]Jer. 39:10; 52:16
8 [a]Jer. 40:14; 41:2 [b]Jer. 40:13, 15; 42:1; 43:2 [c]2 Sam. 23:28, 29; Ezra 2:22; Neh. 7:26 [d]Jer. 42:1 [e]Deut. 3:14; Josh. 12:5; 2 Sam. 10:6, 8

9 Then Gedaliah the son of Ahikam, the son of Shaphan, [a]swore to them and to their men, saying, "[b]Do not be afraid of serving the Chaldeans; stay in the land and serve the king of Babylon, that it may go well with you.

10 "Now as for me, behold, I am going to stay at Mizpah to [a]stand *for you* before the Chaldeans who come to us; but as for you, [b]gather in wine and [c]summer fruit and oil, and put *them* in your *storage* vessels, and live in your cities that you have taken over."

11 Likewise also all the Jews who were in [a]Moab and among the sons of [b]Ammon and in [c]Edom, and who were in all the *other* countries, heard that the king of Babylon had left a remnant for Judah and that he had appointed over them Gedaliah the son of Ahikam, the son of Shaphan.

12 Then all the Jews [a]returned from all the places to which they had been driven away and came to the land of Judah, to Gedaliah at Mizpah, and gathered in wine and summer fruit in great abundance.

13 Now Johanan the son of Kareah and all the commanders of the forces that were in the field came to Gedaliah at Mizpah,

14 and said to him, "Are you well aware that Baalis the king of the sons of [a]Ammon has sent Ishmael the son of Nethaniah to take your life?" But Gedaliah the son of Ahikam did not believe them.

15 Then Johanan the son of Kareah spoke secretly to Gedaliah in Mizpah, saying, "[a]Let me go and kill Ishmael the son of Nethaniah, and not a man will know! Why should he [b]take your life, so that all the Jews who are gathered to you should be scattered and the [c]remnant of Judah perish?"

16 But Gedaliah the son of Ahikam said to Johanan the son of Kareah, "[a]Do not do this thing, for you are telling a lie about Ishmael."

Gedaliah Is Murdered

41 NOW it [a]came about in the seventh month that [b]Ishmael the son of Nethaniah, the son of Elishama, of the royal [1]family and *one* of the chief officers of the king, along with ten men, came to Mizpah to [c]Gedaliah the son of Ahikam. While they [d]were eating bread together there in Mizpah,

2 Ishmael the son of Nethaniah and the ten men who were with him arose and [a]struck down Gedaliah the son of Ahikam, the son of Shaphan, with the sword and [b]put to death the one [c]whom the king of Babylon had appointed over the land.

3 Ishmael also struck down all the Jews who were with him, *that is* with Gedaliah at Mizpah, and the Chaldeans who were found there, the men of war.

4 Now it happened on the [1]next day after the killing of Gedaliah, when no one knew about *it*,

9 [a]1 Sam. 20:16, 17; 2 Kin. 25:24 [b]Jer. 27:11; 38:17-20

10 [a]Deut. 1:38; 1 Kin. 10:8; Jer. 35:19 [b]Deut. 16:13; Jer. 39:10 [c]Is. 16:9; Jer. 40:12; 48:32

11 [a]Num. 22:1; 25:1, 2; Is. 16:4; Jer. 9:26 [b]1 Sam. 11:1; 12:12 [c]Gen. 36:8; Is. 11:14

12 [a]Jer. 43:5

14 [a]1 Sam. 11:1-3; 2 Sam. 10:1-6; Jer. 25:21; 41:10

15 [a]1 Sam. 26:8 [b]2 Sam. 21:17 [c]Jer. 42:2

16 [a]Matt. 10:16; 1 Cor. 13:5

1 [1]Lit., *seed* [a]2 Kin. 25:25 [b]Jer. 40:8, 14 [c]Jer. 39:14; 40:5, 6 [d]Ps. 41:9; Jer. 40:13, 14

2 [a]2 Sam. 3:27; 20:9, 10; 2 Kin. 25:25; Ps. 41:9; 109:5; John 13:18 [b]2 Kin. 25:25 [c]Jer. 40:5

4 [1]Or, *second*

5 [1]Lit., *having cut themselves* [a]2 Kin. 10:13, 14 [b]Gen. 33:18; 37:12; Judg. 9:1; 1 Kin. 12:1, 25 [c]Josh. 18:1; Judg. 18:31; 1 Sam. 3:21; Ps. 78:60 [d]1 Kin. 16:24, 29 [e]Lev. 19:27; Deut. 14:1 [f]Deut. 14:1; Jer. 16:6 [g]1 Sam. 1:7; 2 Kin. 25:9

6 [a]2 Sam. 3:16; Jer. 50:4

7 [a]Ps. 55:23; Is. 59:7; Ezek. 22:27; 33:24, 26

8 [a]Is. 45:3

9 [1]Or, *by the side of* [a]1 Kin. 15:17-22; 2 Chr. 16:1-6 [b]Judg. 6:2; 1 Sam. 13:6; 2 Sam. 17:9; Heb. 11:38

10 [a]Jer. 40:11, 12 [b]Jer. 43:6 [c]Neh. 2:10, 19; 4:7; Jer. 40:14

11 [a]Jer. 40:7, 8, 13-16

12 [1]Lit., *waters* [a]Gen. 14:14-16; 1 Sam. 30:1-8, 18, 20 [b]2 Sam. 2:13

15 [a]1 Sam. 30:17; 1 Kin. 20:20; Job 21:30; Prov. 28:17

16 [1]Lit., *brought back* [2]Lit., *men of war* [3]Lit., *infants* [a]Jer. 42:8; 43:4-7

5 that eighty men [a]came from [b]Shechem, from [c]Shiloh, and from [d]Samaria with [e]their beards shaved off and their clothes torn and [1]their bodies [f]gashed, having grain offerings and incense in their hands to bring to the [g]house of the LORD.

6 Then Ishmael the son of Nethaniah went out from Mizpah to meet them, [a]weeping as he went; and it came about as he met them that he said to them, "Come to Gedaliah the son of Ahikam!"

7 Yet it turned out that as soon as they came inside the city, Ishmael the son of Nethaniah and the men that were with him [a]slaughtered them, *and cast them* into the cistern.

8 But ten men who were found among them said to Ishmael, "Do not put us to death; for we have [a]stores of wheat, barley, oil and honey hidden in the field." So he refrained and did not put them to death along with their companions.

9 Now as for the cistern where Ishmael had cast all the corpses of the men whom he had struck down [1]because of Gedaliah, it was the [a]one that King Asa had made on [b]account of Baasha, king of Israel; Ishmael the son of Nethaniah filled it with the slain.

10 Then Ishmael took captive all the [a]remnant of the people who were in Mizpah, the [b]king's daughters and all the people who were left in Mizpah, whom Nebuzaradan the captain of the bodyguard had put under the charge of Gedaliah the son of Ahikam; thus Ishmael the son of Nethaniah took them captive and proceeded to cross over to the sons of [c]Ammon.

Johanan Rescues the People

11 But Johanan the son of Kareah and all the [a]commanders of the forces that were with him heard of all the evil that Ishmael the son of Nethaniah had done.

12 So they took all the men and went to [a]fight with Ishmael the son of Nethaniah and they found him by the [b]great [1]pool that is in Gibeon.

13 Now it came about, as soon as all the people who were with Ishmael saw Johanan the son of Kareah and the commanders of the forces that were with him, they were glad.

14 So all the people whom Ishmael had taken captive from Mizpah turned around and came back, and went to Johanan the son of Kareah.

15 But Ishmael the son of Nethaniah [a]escaped from Johanan with eight men and went to the sons of Ammon.

16 Then Johanan the son of Kareah and all the commanders of the forces that were with him took from Mizpah [a]all the remnant of the people whom he had [1]recovered from Ishmael the son of Nethaniah, after he had struck down Gedaliah the son of Ahikam, *that is,* the men who were [2]soldiers, *the* women, *the* [3]children, and *the* eunuchs, whom he had brought back from Gibeon.

17 And they went and stayed in
[1a]Geruth Chimham, which is beside
Bethlehem, in order to [b]proceed into
Egypt
18 because of the Chaldeans; for they
were [a]afraid of them, since Ishmael the
son of Nethaniah had struck down
Gedaliah the son of Ahikam, whom [b]the
king of Babylon had appointed over the
land.

Warning against Going to Egypt

42 THEN all the [1]commanders of
the forces, [a]Johanan the son of
Kareah, Jezaniah the son of Hoshaiah,
and all the people [b]both small and great
approached
2 and said to Jeremiah the prophet,
"Please let our [a]petition [1]come before
you, and [b]pray for us to the LORD your
God, *that is* for all this remnant; because
we are left *but* a [c]few out of many, as
your own eyes *now* see us,
3 that the LORD your God may tell
us the [a]way in which we should walk and
the thing that we should do."
4 Then Jeremiah the prophet said to
them, "I have heard *you.* Behold, I am
going to [a]pray to the LORD your God in
accordance with your words; and it will
come about that the whole [1]message
which the [b]LORD will answer you I will
tell you. I will [c]not keep back a word
from you."
5 Then they said to Jeremiah, "May
the [a]LORD be a true and faithful witness
against us, if we do not act in accordance with the whole [1]message with
which the LORD your God will send you
to us.
6 "Whether *it* is [1]pleasant or [2]unpleas-
ant, we will [a]listen to the voice of the
LORD our God to whom we are sending
you, in order that it may go [b]well with us
when we listen to the voice of the LORD
our God."
7 Now it came about at the [a]end of
ten days that the word of the LORD came
to Jeremiah.
8 Then he called for Johanan the son
of Kareah, and all the [1]commanders of
the forces that were with him, and for all
the people both small and great,
9 and said to them, "Thus [a]says the
LORD the God of Israel, to whom you
sent me to present your petition before
Him:
10 'If you will indeed stay in this land,
then I will [a]build you up and not tear
you down, and I will plant you and not
uproot you; for I [1]shall [b]relent concerning the calamity that I have inflicted on
you.
11 '[a]Do not be afraid of the king of
Babylon, whom you are *now* fearing; do
not be afraid of him,' declares the LORD,
'for [b]I am with you to save you and
deliver you from his hand.
12 'I will also show you compassion, so
that [a]he will have compassion on you
and restore you to your own soil.
13 'But if you are going to say, "We
will [a]not stay in this land," so as not to
listen to the voice of the LORD your
God,
14 saying, "No, but we will [a]go to the
land of Egypt, where we shall not see
war or [b]hear the sound of a trumpet or
hunger for bread, and we will stay
there";
15 then [1]in that case listen to the word
of the LORD, O remnant of Judah. Thus
says the LORD of hosts, the God of
Israel, "If you really set your [2]mind to
enter [a]Egypt, and go in to reside there,
16 then it will come about that the
[a]sword, which you are afraid of will
overtake you there in the land of Egypt;
and the famine, about which you are
anxious, will follow closely after you
there *in* Egypt; and you will die there.
17 "So all the men who set their [1]mind
to go to Egypt to reside there will die by
the [a]sword, by famine, and by pestilence; and they will [b]have no survivors
or refugees from the calamity that I am
going to bring on them."' "
18 For thus says the LORD of hosts,
the God of Israel, "As My [a]anger and
wrath have been poured out on the
inhabitants of Jerusalem, so My wrath
will be poured out on you when you
enter Egypt. And you will become a
[b]curse, an object of horror, an imprecation, and a reproach; and [c]you will see
this place no more."
19 The LORD has spoken to you, O
remnant of Judah, "Do not [a]go into
Egypt!" You should clearly [b]understand
that today I have [c]testified against you.
20 For you have *only* [1a]deceived yourselves; for it is you who sent me to the
LORD your God, saying, "Pray for us to
the LORD our God; and whatever the
LORD our God says, tell us so, and we
will do it."
21 So, I have [a]told you today, but you
have [b]not [1]obeyed the LORD your God,
even in whatever He has sent me to *tell*
you.
22 Therefore you should now clearly
understand that you will [a]die by the
sword, by famine, and by pestilence, in
the [b]place where you wish to go to
reside.

In Egypt Jeremiah Warns of Judgment

43 BUT it came about, as soon as
Jeremiah whom the LORD their
God had sent, had [a]finished telling all
the people all the words of the LORD
their God—that is, all these words—
2 that Azariah the [a]son of Hoshaiah,
and Johanan the son of Kareah, and all
the arrogant men said to Jeremiah, "You
are [b]telling a lie! The LORD our God has
not sent you to say, 'You are not to enter
Egypt to reside there';
3 but [a]Baruch the son of Neriah is
inciting you against us to give us over

17 [1]Or, *the lodging place of Chimham* [a]2 Sam. 19:37, 38, 40 [b]Jer. 42:14
18 [a]Is. 51:12, 13; 57:11; Jer. 42:11, 16; 43:2, 3; Luke 12:4, 5 [b]Jer. 40:5

1 [1]Or, *princes* [a]Jer. 40:8, 13; 41:11, 18 [b]Jer. 6:13; 8:10; 42:8; 44:12; Acts 8:10
2 [1]Lit., *fall* [a]Jer. 36:7; 37:20 [b]Ex. 8:28; 1 Sam. 7:8; 12:19; 1 Kin. 13:6; Is. 37:4; Jer. 37:3; 42:20; Acts 8:24; James 5:16 [c]Lev. 26:22; Deut. 28:62; Is. 1:9; Lam. 1:1
3 [a]Ps. 86:11; Prov. 3:6; Jer. 6:16; Mic. 4:2
4 [1]Lit., *word* [a]Ex. 8:29; 1 Sam. 12:23 [b]1 Kin. 22:14; Jer. 23:28 [c]1 Sam. 3:17, 18; Ps. 40:10; Acts 20:20
5 [1]Lit., *word* [a]Gen. 31:50; Judg. 11:10; Jer. 43:2; Mic. 1:2; Mal. 2:14; 3:5
6 [1]Lit., *good* [2]Lit., *evil* [a]Ex. 24:7; Deut. 5:27; Josh. 24:24 [b]Deut. 5:29, 33; 6:3; Jer. 7:23
7 [a]Ps. 27:14; Is. 30:18
8 [1]Or, *princes*
9 [a]2 Kin. 19:4, 6, 20; 22:15
10 [1]Or, *shall have changed my mind about* [a]Jer. 24:6; 31:28; 33:7; Ezek. 36:36 [b]Jer. 18:7, 8; Hos. 11:8; Joel 2:13; Amos 7:3, 6; Jon. 3:10; 4:2
11 [a]Jer. 1:8; 27:12, 17; 41:18 [b]Num. 14:9; 2 Chr. 32:7, 8; Ps. 46:7, 11; 118:6; Is. 8:9, 10; 43:2, 5; Jer. 1:19; 15:20; Rom. 8:31
12 [a]Neh. 1:11; Ps. 106:46; Prov. 16:7
13 [a]Ex. 5:2; Jer. 44:16
14 [a]Is. 31:1; Jer. 41:17 [b]Ex. 16:3; Num. 11:4; Jer. 4:19, 21
15 [1]Lit., *now therefore* [2]Lit., *face* [a]Deut. 17:16; Jer. 42:17; 44:12-14
16 [a]Jer. 44:13, 27; Ezek. 11:8; Amos 9:1-4
17 [1]Lit., *face* [a]Jer. 24:10; 38:2; 42:22; 44:13 [b]Jer. 44:14, 28
18 [a]2 Chr. 36:16-19; Jer. 7:20; 33:5; 39:1-9 [b]Deut. 29:21; Is. 65:15; Jer. 18:16; 24:9; 29:18; 44:12 [c]Jer. 22:10, 27
19 [a]Deut. 17:16; Is. 30:1-7 [b]Ezek. 2:5 [c]Neh. 9:26, 29, 30
20 [1]Or, *acted errantly in your souls* [a]Jer. 43:2; Ezek. 14:3
21 [1]Lit., *listened to the voice of* [a]Deut. 11:26; Jer. 43:1; Ezek. 2:7; Zech. 7:11; Acts 20:26, 27 [b]Jer. 43:4
22 [a]Jer. 43:11; Ezek. 6:11 [b]Hos. 9:6

1 [a]Jer. 26:8; 51:63
2 [a]Jer. 42:1 [b]2 Chr. 36:13; Is. 7:9; Jer. 5:12, 13; 42:5
3 [a]Jer. 36:4, 10, 26, 32; 43:6; 45:1-3

into the hand of the Chaldeans, so they
may put us to death or exile us to
Babylon."
4 So [a]Johanan the son of Kareah and
all the [1]commanders of the forces, and
all the people, [b]did not obey the voice of
the LORD, so as to [c]stay in the land of
Judah.
5 But Johanan the son of Kareah and
all the [1]commanders of the forces took
the [a]entire remnant of Judah who had
returned from all the nations to which
they had been driven away, in order to
reside in the land of Judah—
6 the men, the women, the [1]children,
the [a]king's daughters and [b]every person
that Nebuzaradan the captain of the
bodyguard had left with Gedaliah the
son of Ahikam [2]and grandson of Shaphan,
together with [c]Jeremiah the
prophet and Baruch the son of Neriah—
7 and they entered the land of Egypt
(for they did not obey the voice of the
LORD) and went in as far as [a]Tahpanhes.
8 Then the word of the LORD came
to Jeremiah in [a]Tahpanhes, saying,
9 "Take *some* large stones in your
[1]hands and hide them in the mortar in
the [2]brick *terrace* which is at the entrance
of Pharaoh's [3]palace in Tahpanhes,
in the sight of [4]some *of the* Jews;
10 and say to them, 'Thus says the
LORD of hosts, the God of Israel, "Behold,
I am going to send and get [a]Nebuchadnezzar
the king of Babylon, [b]My
servant, and I am going to set his throne
right over these stones that I have hidden;
and he will spread his [c]canopy over
them.
11 "He will also come and [a]strike the
land of Egypt; those who are *meant* for
death *will be given over* to death, and
those for captivity to captivity, and
[b]those for the sword to the sword.
12 "And [1]I shall set fire to the temples
of the [a]gods of Egypt, and he will burn
them and take them captive. So he will
[b]wrap himself with the land of Egypt as
a shepherd wraps himself with his garment,
and he will depart from there
safely.
13 "He will also shatter the [1]obelisks of
[2]Heliopolis, which is in the land
of Egypt; and the temples of the gods of
Egypt he will burn with fire."'"

Conquest of Egypt Predicted

44 THE word that came to Jeremiah
for all the Jews living in the land
of Egypt, those who were living in [a]Migdol,
[b]Tahpanhes, [c]Memphis, and the
land of [d]Pathros, saying,
2 "Thus says the LORD of hosts, the
God of Israel, 'You yourselves have seen
all the calamity that I have brought on
Jerusalem and all the cities of Judah;
and behold, this day they are in [a]ruins
and no one lives in them,
3 [a]because of their wickedness which
they committed so as to [b]provoke Me to
anger by continuing to [c]burn [1]sacrifices
and to [d]serve other gods whom they had
not known, *neither* they, you, nor your
fathers.
4 'Yet I [a]sent you all My servants the
prophets, [1]again and again, saying, "Oh,
do not do this [b]abominable thing which
I hate."
5 'But [a]they did not listen or incline
their ears to turn from their wickedness,
so as not to burn [1]sacrifices to other
gods.
6 'Therefore My [a]wrath and My anger
were poured out and burned in the
[b]cities of Judah and in the streets of
Jerusalem, so they have become a ruin
and a [c]desolation as it is this day.
7 'Now then thus says the LORD God
of hosts, the God of Israel, "Why are
you [a]doing great harm to yourselves, so
as to [b]cut off from you man and woman,
child and infant, from among Judah,
leaving yourselves without remnant,
8 [a]provoking Me to anger with the
works of your hands, [b]burning [1]sacrifices
to other gods in the land of Egypt,
where you are entering to reside, so that
you might be cut off and become a
[c]curse and a reproach among all the
nations of the earth?
9 "Have you forgotten the [a]wickedness
of your fathers, the wickedness of
the kings of Judah, and the wickedness
of their wives, your own wickedness, and
the wickedness of your wives, which they
committed in the land of Judah and in
the streets of Jerusalem?
10 "But they [a]have not become [1]contrite
even to this day, nor have they
feared nor [b]walked in My law or My
statutes, which I have set before you and
before your fathers."'
11 "Therefore thus says the LORD of
hosts, the God of Israel, 'Behold, I am
going to [a]set My face against you for
[1]woe, even to cut off all Judah.
12 'And I will [a]take away the remnant
of Judah who have set their [1]mind on
entering the land of Egypt to reside
there, and they will all [2b]meet their end
in the land of Egypt; they will fall by the
sword *and* meet their end by famine.
Both small and great will die by the
sword and famine; and they will become
a [c]curse, an object of horror, an imprecation
and a reproach.
13 'And I will [a]punish those who live
in the land of Egypt, as I have punished
Jerusalem, with the sword, with famine,
and with pestilence.
14 'So there will be [a]no refugees or
survivors for the remnant of Judah who
have entered the land of Egypt to reside
there and then to return to the land of
Judah, to which they are [1b]longing to
return and live; for none will [c]return
except *a few* refugees.'"

4 [1]Or, *princes* [a]Jer. 42:8 [b]2 Chr. 25:16; Jer. 42:5, 6; 44:5 [c]Ps. 37:3; Jer. 42:10-12
5 [1]Or, *princes* [a]Jer. 40:11
6 [1]Lit., *infants* [2]Lit., *the son* [a]Jer. 41:10 [b]Jer. 39:10; 40:7 [c]Eccl. 9:1, 2; Lam. 3:1
7 [a]Jer. 2:16; 44:1
8 [a]Jer. 2:16; 44:1; 46:14; Ezek. 30:18
9 [1]Lit., *hand* [2]Or, *brickwork* [3]Lit., *house* [4]Lit., *men*
10 [a]Jer. 25:9, 11 [b]Is. 44:28; 45:1; Jer. 25:9; 27:6 [c]Ps. 18:11; 27:5; 31:20
11 [a]Is. 19:1-25; Jer. 25:15-19; 44:13; 46:1, 2, 13-26; Ezek. 29:19, 20 [b]Jer. 15:2
12 [1]Some ancient versions read *he will set* [a]Ex. 12:12; Is. 19:1; Jer. 46:25; Ezek. 30:13 [b]Ps. 104:2; 109:18, 19; Is. 49:18
13 [1]Or, *stone pillars* [2]Heb., *Beth-shemesh;* i.e., the house of the sun-god

1 [a]Ex. 14:2; Jer. 46:14 [b]Jer. 43:7; Ezek. 30:18 [c]Is. 19:13; Jer. 2:16; 46:14; Ezek. 30:13, 16; Hos. 9:6 [d]Is. 11:11; Ezek. 29:14; 30:14
2 [a]Is. 6:11; Jer. 4:7; 9:11; 34:22; Mic. 3:12
3 [1]Or, *incense* [a]Neh. 9:33; Jer. 2:17-19; 44:23; Ezek. 8:17, 18; Dan. 9:5 [b]Is. 3:8; Jer. 7:19; 32:30-32; 44:8 [c]Jer. 19:4 [d]Deut. 13:6; 29:26; 32:17
4 [1]Lit., *rising early and sending* [a]Jer. 7:13, 25; 25:4; 26:5; 29:19; 35:15; Zech. 7:7 [b]Jer. 16:18; 32:34, 35; Ezek. 8:10
5 [1]Or, *incense* [a]Jer. 11:8, 10; 13:10
6 [a]Is. 51:17-20; Jer. 42:18; Ezek. 8:18 [b]Jer. 7:17, 34 [c]Jer. 4:27; 34:22
7 [a]Num. 16:38; Jer. 26:19; Ezek. 33:11; Hab. 2:10 [b]Jer. 3:24; 9:21; 51:22
8 [1]Or, *incense* [a]2 Kin. 17:15-17; Jer. 25:6, 7; 44:3; 1 Cor. 10:21, 22 [b]Jer. 7:9; 11:12, 17; 44:3; Hos. 4:13; Hab. 1:16 [c]1 Kin. 9:7, 8; 2 Chr. 7:20; Jer. 42:18
9 [a]Jer. 7:9, 10, 17, 18; 44:17, 21
10 [1]Lit., *crushed* [a]Jer. 6:15; 8:12 [b]Jer. 26:4; 32:23; 44:23
11 [1]Lit., *evil* [a]Lev. 17:10; 20:5, 6; 26:17; Jer. 21:10; Amos 9:4

12 [1]Lit., *face* [2]Lit., *be finished* [a]Jer. 42:15-18, 22 [b]Is. 1:28; Jer. 16:4; 44:7 [c]Is. 65:15; Jer. 18:16; 24:9; 26:6; 29:18; 42:18; Zech. 8:13
13 [a]Jer. 11:22; 44:27, 28
14 [1]Lit., *lifting up their soul* [a]Jer. 22:10; 44:27 [b]Jer. 22:26, 27 [c]Is. 4:2; 10:20; Jer. 44:28; Rom. 9:27

15 Then [a]all the men who were aware that their wives were burning [1]sacrifices to other gods, along with all the women who were standing by, *as* a large assembly, [2]including all the people who were living in Pathros in the land of Egypt, responded to Jeremiah, saying,

16 "As for the [1a]message that you have spoken to us in the name of the LORD, [b]we are not going to listen to you!

17 "But rather we will certainly [a]carry out every word that has proceeded from our mouths, [1]by burning [2]sacrifices to the [b]queen of heaven and pouring out libations to her, just as [c]we ourselves, our forefathers, our kings and our princes did in the cities of Judah and in the streets of Jerusalem; for *then* we had [d]plenty of [3]food, and were well off, and saw no [4]misfortune.

18 "But since we stopped burning [1]sacrifices to the queen of heaven and pouring out libations to her, we have [a]lacked everything and have [2]met our end by the sword and by famine."

19 "And," *said the women,* "when we were [a]burning [1]sacrifices to the queen of heaven, and [2]were pouring out libations to her, was it [b]without our husbands that we made for her *sacrificial* cakes [3]in her image and poured out libations to her?"

Calamity for the Jews

20 Then Jeremiah said to all the people, to the men and women—even to all the people who were giving him *such* an answer—saying,

21 "As for the [1a]smoking sacrifices that you burned in the cities of Judah and in the [b]streets of Jerusalem, you and your forefathers, your kings and your princes, and the people of the land, did not the LORD [c]remember them, and did not *all this* come into His [2]mind?

22 "So the LORD was [a]no longer able to endure *it,* [b]because of the evil of your deeds, because of the abominations which you have committed; thus your land has become a [c]ruin, an object of horror and a curse, without an inhabitant, as *it is* this day.

23 "Because you have burned [1]sacrifices and have sinned against the LORD and [a]not obeyed the voice of the LORD or [b]walked in His law, His statutes or His testimonies, therefore this [c]calamity has befallen you, as *it has* this day."

24 Then Jeremiah said to all the people, including all the women, "[a]Hear the word of the LORD, all Judah who are [b]in the land of Egypt,

25 thus says the LORD of hosts, the God of Israel, as follows: 'As for you and your wives, you have spoken with your mouths and fulfilled *it* with your hands, saying, "We will [a]certainly perform our vows that we have vowed, to burn [1]sacrifices to the queen of heaven and pour out libations to her." [2b]Go ahead and confirm your vows, and certainly perform your vows!'

26 "[1]Nevertheless hear the word of the LORD, all Judah who are living in the land of Egypt, 'Behold, I have [a]sworn by My great name,' says the LORD, '[b]never shall My name be invoked again by the mouth of any man of Judah in all the land of Egypt, saying, "[c]As the Lord [2]GOD lives."

27 'Behold, I am watching over them [a]for harm and not for good, and [b]all the men of Judah who are in the land of Egypt will [1]meet their end by the sword and by famine until they [2]are completely gone.

28 '[a]And those who escape the sword will return out of the land of Egypt to the land of Judah [1b]few in number. Then all the remnant of Judah who have gone to the land of Egypt to reside there will know [c]whose word will stand, Mine or theirs.

29 'And this will be the [a]sign to you,' declares the LORD, 'that I am going to punish you in this place, so that you may know that [b]My words will surely stand against you for harm.'

30 "Thus says the LORD, 'Behold, I am going to give over [a]Pharaoh Hophra king of Egypt to the hand of his enemies, to the hand of those who seek his life, just as I gave over [b]Zedekiah king of Judah to the hand of Nebuchadnezzar king of Babylon, *who was* his enemy and was seeking his life.' "

Message to Baruch

45 *THIS is* the message which Jeremiah the prophet spoke to [a]Baruch the son of Neriah, when he had [b]written down these words in a book [1]at Jeremiah's dictation, in the [c]fourth year of Jehoiakim the son of Josiah, king of Judah, saying:

2 "Thus says the LORD the God of Israel to you, O Baruch:

3 'You said, "Ah, woe is me! For the LORD has added sorrow to my pain; I am [a]weary with my groaning and have found no rest." '

4 "Thus you are to say to him, 'Thus says the LORD, "Behold, [a]what I have built I am about to tear down, and what I have planted I am about to uproot, that is, the whole land."

5 'But you, are you [a]seeking great things for yourself? Do not seek *them;* for behold, I am going to [b]bring disaster on all flesh,' declares the LORD, 'but I will [c]give your life to you as booty in all the places where you may go.' "

Defeat of Pharaoh Foretold

46 THAT which came as the word of the LORD to Jeremiah the prophet [a]concerning the nations.

---

15 [1]Or, *incense* [2]Lit., *and* [a]Prov. 11:21; Is. 1:5; Jer. 5:1-5

16 [1]Lit., *word* [a]Jer. 43:2 [b]Prov. 1:24-27; Jer. 11:8, 10; 13:10

17 [1]Or, *so as to burn* [2]Or, *incense* [3]Lit., *bread* [4]Lit., *evil* [a]Num. 30:12; Deut. 23:23 [b]2 Kin. 17:16; Jer. 7:18 [c]Neh. 9:34; Jer. 32:32; 44:21 [d]Ex. 16:3; Hos. 2:5-9; Phil. 3:19

18 [1]Or, *incense* [2]Lit., *been finished* [a]Num. 11:5, 6; Jer. 40:12; Mal. 3:13-15

19 [1]Or, *incense* [2]Lit., *to pour* [3]Lit., *to make an image of her* [a]Jer. 7:18 [b]Num. 30:6, 7; Jer. 44:15

21 [1]Or, *incense* [2]Lit., *heart* [a]Ezek. 8:10, 11 [b]Jer. 11:13; 44:9, 17 [c]Ps. 79:8; Is. 64:9; Jer. 14:10; Hos. 7:2; Amos 8:7

22 [a]Is. 7:13; 43:24; Mal. 2:17 [b]Jer. 4:4; 21:12; 30:14 [c]Gen. 19:13; Ps. 107:33, 34; Jer. 25:11, 18, 38; 29:18; 42:18; 44:12

23 [1]Or, *incense* [a]Jer. 7:13-15; 40:3 [b]Jer. 44:10; Ps. 119:136, 150 [c]1 Kin. 9:9; Neh. 13:18; Jer. 44:2; Dan. 9:11, 12

24 [a]Jer. 42:15; 44:16 [b]Jer. 43:7; 44:15, 26

25 [1]Or, *incense* [2]Lit., *Surely cause to stand* [a]Jer. 44:17; Matt. 14:9; Acts 23:12 [b]Ezek. 20:39

26 [1]Lit., *Therefore* [2]Heb., *YHWH,* usually rendered *LORD* [a]Gen. 22:16; Deut. 32:40, 41; Jer. 22:5; Amos 6:8; Heb. 6:13 [b]Ps. 50:16; Ezek. 20:39 [c]Is. 48:1, 2; Jer. 5:2

27 [1]Lit., *be finished* [2]Lit., *come to an end* [a]Jer. 1:10; 31:28; 39:16 [b]2 Kin. 21:14; Jer. 44:14

28 [1]Lit., *men of number* [a]Jer. 44:14 [b]Is. 10:19; 27:12, 13 [c]Ps. 33:11; Is. 14:27; 46:10, 11; Zech. 1:6

29 [a]Is. 7:11, 14; 8:18; Jer. 44:30; Matt. 24:15, 16, 32 [b]Prov. 19:21; Is. 40:8

30 [a]Jer. 43:9-13; 46:25; Ezek. 29:3; 30:21 [b]2 Kin. 25:4-7; Jer. 34:21; 39:5-7

1 [1]Lit., *from the mouth of Jeremiah* [a]Jer. 32:12, 16; 43:3, 6 [b]Jer. 36:4, 18, 32 [c]2 Kin. 24:1; 2 Chr. 36:5-7; Jer. 25:1; 36:1; 46:2; Dan. 1:1

3 [a]Ps. 6:6; 69:3; 2 Cor. 4:1, 16; Gal. 6:9

4 [a]Is. 5:5; Jer. 1:10; 11:17; 18:7-10; 31:28

5 [a]1 Kin. 3:9, 11; 2 Kin. 5:26; Matt. 6:25, 32; Rom. 12:16 [b]Is. 66:16; Jer. 25:31 [c]Jer. 21:9; 38:2; 39:18

1 [a]Jer. 1:10; 25:15-38

2 To [a]Egypt, concerning the army of
[b]Pharaoh Neco king of Egypt, which was
by the Euphrates River at [c]Carchemish,
which Nebuchadnezzar king of Babylon
defeated in the [d]fourth year of Jehoiakim the son of Josiah, king of Judah:
3 "[a]Line up the shield and [1]buckler,
And draw near for the battle!
4 "Harness the horses,
And [1]mount the steeds,
And take your stand with helmets *on!*
[a]Polish the spears,
Put on the [b]scale-armor!
5 "Why have I seen *it?*
They are terrified,
They are [a]drawing back,
And their [b]mighty men are defeated
And have taken refuge in flight,
Without facing back;
[1c]Terror is on every side!"
Declares the LORD.
6 Let not the [a]swift man flee,
Nor the mighty man escape;
In the north beside the river Euphrates
They have [b]stumbled and fallen.
7 Who is this that [a]rises like the Nile,
Like the rivers whose waters surge about?
8 Egypt rises like the Nile,
Even like the rivers whose waters surge about;
And He has said, "I will [a]rise and cover *that* land;
I will surely [b]destroy the city and its inhabitants."
9 Go up, you horses, and [1a]drive madly, you chariots,
That the mighty men may [2]march forward:
Ethiopia and [3b]Put, that handle the shield,
And the [4c]Lydians, that handle *and* bend the bow.
10 For [a]that day belongs to the Lord [1]GOD of hosts,
A day of [b]vengeance, so as to avenge Himself on His foes;
And the [c]sword will devour and be satiated
And [2]drink its fill of their blood;
For there will be a [d]slaughter for the Lord [1]GOD of hosts,
In the land of the north by the river Euphrates.
11 Go [a]up to Gilead and obtain balm,
[b]O virgin daughter of Egypt!
In vain have you multiplied [1]remedies;
There is [c]no healing for you.
12 The nations have heard of your [a]shame,
And the earth is full of your [b]cry *of distress;*
For one [c]warrior has stumbled over [1]another,
And both of them have fallen down together.
13 *This is* the [1]message which the
LORD spoke to Jeremiah the prophet
about the [a]coming of Nebuchadnezzar
king of Babylon to [b]smite the land of
Egypt:
14 "Declare in Egypt and proclaim in [a]Migdol,
Proclaim also in Memphis and [b]Tahpanhes;
Say, 'Take your stand and get yourself ready,
For the [c]sword has devoured those around you.'
15 "Why have your [a]mighty ones become prostrate?
They do not stand because the LORD has [b]thrust them down.
16 "They have repeatedly [a]stumbled;
Indeed, they have fallen one against another.
Then they said, 'Get up! And [b]let us go back
To our own people and our native land
Away from the [1c]sword of the oppressor.'
17 "[1]They cried there, 'Pharaoh king of Egypt *is but* [a]a big noise;
He has let the appointed time pass by!'
18 "As I live," declares the [a]King
Whose name is the LORD of hosts,
"Surely one shall come *who looms up* like [b]Tabor among the mountains,
Or like [c]Carmel by the sea.
19 "Make your baggage ready for [a]exile,
O [b]daughter dwelling in Egypt,
For [c]Memphis will become a desolation;
It will even be burned down *and* [1]bereft of inhabitants.
20 "Egypt is a pretty [a]heifer,
But a [1]horsefly is coming [b]from the north—it is coming!
21 "Also her [a]mercenaries in her midst
Are like [1]fattened [b]calves,
For even they too have turned back *and* have fled away together;
They did not stand *their ground.*
For the day of their calamity has come upon them,
The time of their [c]punishment.
22 "Its sound moves along like a serpent;
For they move on [1]like an army
And come to her as woodcutters with axes.
23 "They have cut down her [a]forest," declares the LORD;
"Surely it will no *more* be found,
Even though [1]they are *now* more numerous than [b]locusts
And are without number.
24 "The daughter of Egypt has been put to shame,
Given over to the [1]power of the [a]people of the north."

2 [a]Jer. 46:14; Ezek. chs. 29-32 [b]2 Kin. 18:21; 23:29, 33-35; Jer. 25:19 [c]2 Chr. 35:20; Is. 10:9 [d]Jer. 45:1
3 [1]I.e., small shield [a]Is. 21:5; Jer. 51:11; Joel 3:9; Nah. 2:1; 3:14
4 [1]Or, *go up, you horsemen* [a]Ezek. 21:9-11 [b]1 Sam. 17:5, 38; 2 Chr. 26:14; Neh. 4:16; Jer. 51:3
5 [1]Heb., *Magor-missabib;* i.e., Terror is on every side [a]Is. 42:17; Jer. 46:21 [b]Is. 5:25; Ezek. 39:18 [c]Jer. 6:25; 20:3; 49:29
6 [a]Is. 30:16 [b]Jer. 46:12, 16; Dan. 11:19
7 [a]Jer. 47:2
8 [a]Is. 37:24 [b]Is. 10:13
9 [1]Lit., *act like madmen* [2]Lit., *go forth* [3]I.e., Libya (or Somaliland) [4]Heb., *Ludim* [a]Jer. 47:3; Nah. 2:4 [b]Nah. 3:9 [c]Is. 66:19
10 [1]Heb., *YHWH,* usually rendered *LORD* [2]Lit., *be saturated with* [a]Joel 1:15 [b]Jer. 50:15, 18 [c]Deut. 32:42; Is. 31:8; Jer. 12:12 [d]Is. 34:6; Zeph. 1:7
11 [1]Lit., *healings* [a]Jer. 8:22 [b]Is. 47:1; Jer. 31:4, 21 [c]Jer. 30:13; Mic. 1:9; Nah. 3:19
12 [1]Lit., *warrior* [a]Jer. 2:36; Nah. 3:8-10 [b]Jer. 14:2 [c]Is. 19:2
13 [1]Lit., *word* [a]Jer. 43:10-13 [b]Is. 19:1
14 [a]Jer. 44:1 [b]Jer. 43:8 [c]Is. 1:20; Jer. 2:30; 46:10; Nah. 2:13
15 [a]Is. 66:15, 16; Jer. 46:5 [b]Ps. 18:14, 39; 68:1, 2
16 [1]Lit., *oppressing sword* [a]Lev. 26:36, 37; Jer. 46:6 [b]Jer. 51:9 [c]Jer. 50:16
17 [1]Some ancient versions read *Call the name of Pharaoh a big noise* [a]Ex. 15:9, 10; 1 Kin. 20:10, 11; Is. 19:11-16
18 [a]Jer. 48:15; Mal. 1:14 [b]Josh. 19:22; Judg. 4:6; Ps. 89:12 [c]Josh. 12:22; 1 Kin. 18:42
19 [1]Lit., *without* [a]Is. 20:4 [b]Jer. 48:18 [c]Jer. 46:14; Ezek. 30:13
20 [1]Or possibly, *mosquito* [a]Hos. 10:11 [b]Jer. 1:14; 47:2
21 [1]Lit., *of the stall* [a]2 Sam. 10:6; 2 Kin. 7:6; Jer. 46:5 [b]Is. 34:7 [c]Jer. 48:44; Hos. 9:7; Obad. 13; Mic. 7:4

22 [1]Or, *in force*
23 [1]I.e., trees of the forest, the Egyptians [a]Jer. 21:14 [b]Judg. 6:5; 7:12; Joel 2:25
24 [1]Lit., *hand* [a]Jer. 1:15

25 The LORD of hosts, the God of
Israel, says, "Behold, I am going to
punish Amon of [a]Thebes, and [b]Pharaoh,
and Egypt along with her [c]gods and her
kings, even Pharaoh and those who
[d]trust in him.
26 "And I shall give them over to the
[1]power of those who are [a]seeking their
lives, even into the hand of Nebuchadnezzar king of Babylon and into the
hand of his [2]officers. [b]Afterwards, however, it will be inhabited as in the days of
old," declares the LORD.

27 "But as for you, O Jacob My servant, [a]do not fear,
Nor be dismayed, O Israel!
For, see, I am going to [b]save you from afar,
And your descendants from the land of their captivity;
And Jacob shall return and be [c]undisturbed
And secure, with no one making *him* tremble.
28 "O Jacob My servant, do not fear," declares the LORD,
"For [a]I am with you.
For I shall make a full end of all the nations
Where I have driven you,
Yet I shall [b]not make a full end of you;
But I shall [c]correct you properly
And by no means leave you unpunished."

Prophecy against Philistia

47

THAT which came as the word
of the LORD to Jeremiah the
prophet concerning the [a]Philistines,
before Pharaoh [1]conquered [b]Gaza.
2 Thus says the LORD:
"Behold, waters are going to rise from [a]the north
And become an overflowing torrent,
And [b]overflow the land and all its fulness,
The city and those who live in it;
And the men will [c]cry out,
And every inhabitant of the land will wail.
3 "Because of the noise of the [1]galloping hoofs of his [2]stallions,
The tumult of his chariots, *and* the rumbling of his wheels,
The fathers have not turned back for *their* children,
Because of the limpness of *their* hands,
4 On account of the day that is coming
To [a]destroy all the Philistines,
To cut off from [b]Tyre and Sidon
Every ally that is left;
For the LORD is going to destroy the Philistines,
The remnant of the coastland of [c]Caphtor.
5 "[a]Baldness has come upon Gaza;
[b]Ashkelon has been ruined.
O remnant of their valley,
How long will you [c]gash yourself?
6 "Ah, [a]sword of the LORD,
How long will you not be quiet?
Withdraw into your sheath;
Be at rest and stay still.
7 "How can [1]it be quiet,
When the LORD has [a]given it an order?
Against Ashkelon and against the seacoast—
There He has [b]assigned it."

Prophecy against Moab

48

CONCERNING [a]Moab.
Thus says the LORD of hosts, the God of Israel,
"Woe to [b]Nebo, for it has been destroyed;
[c]Kiriathaim has been put to shame, it has been captured;
The lofty stronghold has been put to shame and [1]shattered.
2 "There is praise for Moab no longer;
In [a]Heshbon they have devised calamity against her:
'Come and let us cut her off from *being* a nation!'
You too, [1]Madmen, will be silenced;
The sword will follow after you.
3 "The sound of an outcry from [a]Horonaim,
'Devastation and great destruction!'
4 "Moab is broken,
Her little ones have sounded out a cry *of distress*.
5 "For by the ascent of [a]Luhith
They will ascend with continual weeping;
For at the descent of Horonaim
They have heard the [1]anguished cry of destruction.
6 "[a]Flee, save your lives,
That you may be like a juniper in the wilderness.
7 "For because of your [a]trust in your own achievements and treasures,
Even you yourself will be captured;
And [b]Chemosh will go off into exile
Together with his priests and his princes.
8 "And a destroyer will come to every city,
So that no city will escape;
The valley also will be ruined,
And the [a]plateau will be destroyed,
As the LORD has said.
9 "Give [1a]wings to Moab,
For she will [2]flee away;
And her cities will become a [b]desolation,
Without inhabitants in them.
10 "[a]Cursed be the one who does the LORD's work [b]negligently,
And cursed be the one who restrains his [c]sword from blood.

25 [a]Ezek. 30:14-16; Nah. 3:8 [b]Jer. 44:30 [c]Ex. 12:12; Jer. 43:12, 13; Ezek. 30:13; Zeph. 2:11 [d]Is. 20:5
26 [1]Lit., *hand* [2]Lit., *servants* [a]Jer. 44:30; Ezek. 32:11 [b]Ezek. 29:8-14
27 [a]Is. 41:13, 14; Jer. 30:10, 11 [b]Is. 11:11; Jer. 23:3, 4; 29:14; Mic. 7:12 [c]Jer. 23:6; 50:19
28 [a]Ps. 46:7, 11; Is. 8:10; 43:2; Jer. 1:19 [b]Jer. 4:27; Amos 9:8, 9 [c]Jer. 10:24; Hab. 3:2

1 [1]Lit., *smote* [a]Jer. 25:20; Zech. 9:6 [b]Gen. 10:19; 1 Kin. 4:24; Jer. 25:20; Amos 1:6; Zeph. 2:4
2 [a]Is. 14:31; Jer. 1:14; 6:22; 46:20, 24 [b]Is. 8:7, 8 [c]Is. 15:2-5; Jer. 46:12
3 [1]Lit., *stamping of the* [2]Lit., *mighty ones* [a]Judg. 5:22; Jer. 8:16; Nah. 3:2
4 [a]Is. 14:31 [b]Is. 23:5; Jer. 25:22; Joel 3:4; Amos 1:9, 10; Zech. 9:2-4 [c]Gen. 10:14; Deut. 2:23; Amos 9:7
5 [a]Jer. 48:37; Mic. 1:16 [b]Judg. 1:18; Jer. 25:20; Amos 1:7, 8; Zeph. 2:4, 7; Zech. 9:5 [c]Jer. 16:6; 41:5
6 [a]Judg. 7:20; Jer. 12:12; Ezek. 21:3-5
7 [1]Lit., *you* [a]Is. 10:6; Ezek. 14:17 [b]Mic. 6:9

1 [1]Or, *dismayed* [a]Is. 15:1; Ezek. 25:9 [b]Num. 32:3, 38; Jer. 48:22 [c]Num. 32:37; Jer. 48:23; Ezek. 25:9
2 [1]I.e., a city of Moab [a]Num. 21:25; Jer. 48:34, 45; 49:3
3 [a]Is. 15:5; Jer. 48:5, 34
5 [1]Lit., *distresses of outcry* [a]Is. 15:5
6 [a]Jer. 51:6
7 [a]Ps. 52:7; Is. 59:4; Jer. 9:23 [b]Num. 21:29; 1 Kin. 11:33; Jer. 48:13, 46
8 [a]Josh. 13:9, 17, 21
9 [1]Or, *salt* [2]Or, *fall in ruins* [a]Ps. 11:1; Is. 16:2; Jer. 48:28 [b]Jer. 44:22
10 [a]Jer. 11:3 [b]1 Kin. 20:39, 40, 42; 2 Kin. 13:19 [c]Jer. 47:6, 7

11"Moab has been [a]at ease since his
youth;
He has also been [b]undisturbed on
his lees,
Neither has he been [c]emptied from
vessel to vessel,
Nor has he gone into exile.
Therefore [1]he retains his flavor,
And his aroma has not changed.
12"Therefore behold, the days are
coming," declares the LORD, "when I
shall send to him those who tip *vessels,*
and they will tip him over, and they will
empty his vessels and shatter [1]his jars.
13"And Moab will be [a]ashamed of
[b]Chemosh, as the house of Israel was
ashamed of [c]Bethel, their confidence.
14"How can you say, 'We are [a]mighty
warriors,
And men valiant for battle'?
15"Moab has been destroyed, and
[1]men have gone up to [2]his cities;
His choicest [3a]young men have also
gone down to the slaughter,"
Declares the [b]King, whose name is
the LORD of hosts.
16"The disaster of Moab will [a]soon
come,
And his calamity has swiftly hastened.
17"Mourn for him, all you who *live*
around him,
Even all of you who know his
name;
Say, 'How has the mighty [1a]scepter
been broken,
A staff of splendor!'
18"[a]Come down from your glory
And sit [1]on the parched ground,
O [b]daughter dwelling in [c]Dibon,
For the destroyer of Moab has
come up against you,
He has ruined your strongholds.
19"Stand by the road and keep watch,
O inhabitant of [a]Aroer;
[b]Ask him who flees and her who
escapes
And say, 'What has happened?'
20"Moab has been put to shame, for it
has been [1]shattered.
Wail and cry out;
Declare by the [a]Arnon
That Moab has been destroyed.
21"Judgment has also come upon the
plain, upon Holon, [a]Jahzah, and against
[b]Mephaath,
22 against Dibon, Nebo, and Beth-
diblathaim,
23 against Kiriathaim, Beth-gamul,
and [a]Beth-meon,
24 against [a]Kerioth, Bozrah, and all
the cities of the land of Moab, far and
near.
25"The [a]horn of Moab has been cut
off, and his [b]arm broken," declares the
LORD.
26"[a]Make him drunk, for he has [1]be-
come [b]arrogant toward the LORD; so
Moab will [2]wallow in his vomit, and he
also will become a laughingstock.
27"Now was not Israel a [a]laughing-
stock to you? Or was he [1b]caught among
thieves? For each time you speak about
him you [c]shake *your head in scorn.*
28"Leave the cities and dwell among
the [a]crags,
O inhabitants of Moab,
And be like a [b]dove that nests
Beyond the mouth of the chasm.
29"[a]We have heard of the pride of
Moab—he *is* very proud—
Of his haughtiness, his [b]pride, his
arrogance and [1]his self-exaltation.
30"I know his [a]fury," declares the
LORD,
"But it is futile;
His idle boasts have accomplished
nothing.
31"Therefore I shall [a]wail for Moab,
Even for all Moab shall I cry out;
[1]I will moan for the men of [b]Kir-
heres.
32"More than the [a]weeping for [b]Jazer
I shall weep for you, O vine of
Sibmah!
Your tendrils stretched across the
sea,
They reached to the sea of Jazer;
Upon your summer fruits and your
grape harvest
The destroyer has fallen.
33"So [a]gladness and joy are taken
away
From the fruitful field, even from
the land of Moab.
And I have made the wine to [b]cease
from the wine presses;
No one will tread *them* with shouting,
The shouting will not be shouts *of
joy.*
34"[a]From the outcry at Heshbon even
to [b]Elealeh, even to Jahaz they have
[1]raised their voice, from [c]Zoar even to
Horonaim *and to* Eglath-shelishiyah; for
even the waters of Nimrim will become
desolate.
35"And I shall make an end of Moab,"
declares the LORD, "the one who offers
sacrifice on the [a]high place and the one
who [1b]burns incense to his gods.
36"Therefore My [a]heart [1]wails for
Moab like flutes; My heart also [1]wails
like flutes for the men of Kir-heres.
Therefore they have [b]lost the abundance
it produced.
37"For [a]every head is bald and every
beard cut short; there are gashes on all
the hands and [b]sackcloth on the loins.
38"On all the [a]housetops of Moab and
in its streets [1]there is lamentation everywhere; for I have broken Moab like an
undesirable [b]vessel," declares the LORD.
39"How [1]shattered it is! *How* they
have wailed! How Moab has turned his
back—he is ashamed! So Moab will
become a laughingstock and an [a]object
of terror to all around him."
40 For thus says the LORD,
"Behold, one will [a]fly swiftly like an
eagle,
And [b]spread out his wings against
Moab.

11 [1]Lit., *his flavor has stayed in him* [a]Jer. 22:21; Ezek. 16:49; Zech. 1:15 [b]Zeph. 1:12 [c]Nah. 2:2
12 [1]Lit., *their*
13 [a]Is. 45:16; Jer. 48:39 [b]Judg. 11:24 [c]1 Kin. 12:29; Hos. 8:5, 6
14 [a]Ps. 33:16; Is. 10:13-16
15 [1]Lit., *one has* [2]Lit., *her* [3]I.e., warriors [a]Is. 40:30, 31; Jer. 50:27 [b]Jer. 46:18; 51:57; Mal. 1:14
16 [a]Is. 13:22
17 [1]Or, *rod* [a]Is. 9:4; 14:5
18 [1]Lit., *in thirst* [a]Is. 47:1 [b]Jer. 46:19 [c]Num. 21:30; Josh. 13:9, 17; Is. 15:2; Jer. 48:22
19 [a]Deut. 2:36; Josh. 12:2 [b]1 Sam. 4:13, 14, 16
20 [1]Or, *dismayed* [a]Num. 21:13
21 [a]Num. 21:23; Is. 15:4; Jer. 48:34 [b]Josh. 13:18
23 [a]Josh. 13:17
24 [a]Jer. 48:41; Amos 2:2
25 [a]Ps. 75:10; Zech. 1:19-21 [b]Job 22:9; Ps. 10:15
26 [1]Or, *magnified himself against* [2]Or, *splash into* [a]Jer. 25:15 [b]Ex. 5:2; Jer. 48:42; Dan. 5:23
27 [1]Or, *found* [a]Lam. 2:15-17; Mic. 7:8-10 [b]Jer. 2:26 [c]Job 16:4; Jer. 18:16
28 [a]Judg. 6:2; Is. 2:19; Jer. 49:16; Obad. 3 [b]Ps. 55:6; Song 2:14
29 [1]Lit., *elevation of his heart* [a]Is. 16:6; Zeph. 2:8 [b]Job 40:11, 12; Ps. 138:6
30 [a]Is. 37:28
31 [1]Another reading is *He* [a]Is. 15:5; 16:7, 11 [b]2 Kin. 3:25; Is. 16:7, 11; Jer. 48:36
32 [a]Is. 16:8, 9 [b]Num. 21:32
33 [a]Is. 16:10; Jer. 25:10; Joel 1:12 [b]Is. 5:10; Hag. 2:16
34 [1]Lit., *given forth* [a]Is. 15:4-6 [b]Num. 32:3, 37 [c]Gen. 13:10; 14:2; Is. 15:5, 6
35 [1]Or, *offers up in smoke* [a]Is. 15:2; 16:12 [b]Jer. 7:9; 11:13
36 [1]Lit., *sounds* [a]Is. 15:5; 16:11 [b]Is. 15:7
37 [a]Is. 15:2; Jer. 16:6; 41:5; 47:5 [b]Gen. 37:34; Is. 15:3; 20:2
38 [1]Lit., *all of it is lamentation* [a]Is. 22:1 [b]Jer. 19:10, 11; 22:28; 25:34
39 [1]Or, *dismayed* [a]Ezek. 26:16
40 [a]Deut. 28:49; Jer. 49:22; Hos. 8:1; Hab. 1:8 [b]Is. 8:8

41 "Kerioth has been captured
And the strongholds have been seized,
So the [a]hearts of the mighty men of Moab in that day
Will be like the heart of a [b]woman in labor.
42 "And Moab will be [a]destroyed from *being* a people
Because he has [1]become [b]arrogant toward the LORD.
43 "[a]Terror, pit, and snare are *coming* upon you,
O inhabitant of Moab," declares the LORD.
44 "The one who [a]flees from the terror
Will fall into the pit,
And the one who climbs up out of the pit
Will be caught in the snare;
For I shall bring upon her, *even* upon Moab,
The year of their [b]punishment," declares the LORD.

45 "In the shadow of Heshbon
The fugitives stand without strength;
For a fire has gone forth from Heshbon,
And a [a]flame from the midst of [b]Sihon,
And it has devoured the [c]forehead of Moab
And the scalps of the [1]riotous revelers.
46 "[a]Woe to you, Moab!
The people of [b]Chemosh have perished;
For your sons have been taken away captive,
And your daughters into captivity.
47 "Yet I will [a]restore the [1]fortunes of Moab
In the [2]latter days," declares the LORD.
Thus far the judgment on Moab.

Prophecy against Ammon

49 CONCERNING the sons of [a]Ammon.
Thus says the LORD:
"Does Israel have no sons?
Or has he no heirs?
Why then has [1]Malcam taken possession of Gad
And his people settled in its cities?
2 "Therefore behold, the days are coming," declares the LORD,
"That I shall cause a [1a]trumpet blast of war to be heard
Against [b]Rabbah of the sons of Ammon;
And it will become a desolate heap,
And her [c]towns will be set on fire.
Then Israel will take [d]possession of his possessors,"
Says the LORD.
3 "Wail, O [a]Heshbon, for [b]Ai has been destroyed!
Cry out, O daughters of Rabbah,
[c]Gird yourselves with sackcloth and lament,
And rush back and forth inside the walls;
For [1]Malcam will [d]go into exile
Together with his priests and his princes.
4 "How [a]boastful you are about the valleys!
Your valley is flowing *away,*
O [b]backsliding daughter
Who trusts in her [c]treasures, *saying,*
'[d]Who will come against me?'
5 "Behold, I am going to bring [a]terror upon you,"
Declares the Lord [1]GOD of hosts,
"From all *directions* around you;
And each of you will be [b]driven out [2]headlong,
With no one to gather the [c]fugitives together.
6 "But afterward I will [a]restore
The [1]fortunes of the sons of Ammon,"
Declares the LORD.

Prophecy against Edom

7 Concerning [a]Edom.
Thus says the LORD of hosts,
"Is there no longer any [b]wisdom in [c]Teman?
Has good counsel been lost to the prudent?
Has their wisdom decayed?
8 "Flee away, turn back, dwell in the depths,
O inhabitants of [a]Dedan,
For I [1]will bring the [b]disaster of Esau upon him
At the time I [2]punish him.
9 "[a]If grape gatherers came to you,
Would they not leave gleanings?
If thieves *came* by night,
They would destroy *only* [1]until they had enough.
10 "But I have [a]stripped Esau bare,
I have uncovered his hiding places
So that he will not be able to conceal himself;
His [1]offspring has been destroyed along with his [2]relatives
And his neighbors, and [b]he is no more.
11 "Leave your [1a]orphans behind, I will keep *them* alive;
And let your [b]widows trust in Me."
12 For thus says the LORD, "Behold, those [1]who were not sentenced to drink the [a]cup will certainly drink *it,* and are you the one who will be [b]completely acquitted? You will not be acquitted, but you will certainly drink *it.*
13 "For I have [a]sworn by Myself," declares the LORD, "that [b]Bozrah will become an [c]object of horror, a reproach, a ruin and a curse; and all its cities will become perpetual ruins."
14 I have [a]heard a message from the LORD,
And an [b]envoy is sent among the nations, *saying,*
"[c]Gather yourselves together and come against her,
And rise up for battle!"

41 [a]Jer. 49:22 [b]Is. 13:8; 21:3; Jer. 30:6; Mic. 4:9, 10
42 [1]Or, *magnified himself against* [a]Ps. 83:4; Jer. 48:2 [b]Is. 37:23; Jer. 48:26
43 [a]Is. 24:17, 18; Lam. 3:47
44 [a]1 Kin. 19:17; Is. 24:18; Amos 5:19 [b]Jer. 46:21
45 [1]Lit., *sons of tumult* [a]Num. 21:28, 29 [b]Num. 21:21, 26; Ps. 135:11 [c]Num. 24:17
46 [a]Num. 21:29 [b]Judg. 11:24; 1 Kin. 11:7; Jer. 48:7
47 [1]Or, *captivity* [2]Lit., *end of the days* [a]Jer. 12:14-17; 49:6, 39
1 [1]In 1 Kin. 11:5, 33 and Zeph. 1:5, *Milcom* [a]Deut. 23:3, 4; 2 Chr. 20:1; Ezek. 21:28-32; 25:2-10; Amos 1:13-15; Zeph. 2:8-11
2 [1]Or, *shout of* [a]Num. 10:9; Jer. 4:19 [b]Deut. 3:11; 2 Sam. 11:1; Ezek. 21:20 [c]Josh. 17:11, 16 [d]Is. 14:2
3 [1]Cf. v. 1 [a]Jer. 48:2 [b]Josh. 7:2-5; 8:1-29; Ezra 2:28 [c]Is. 32:11; Jer. 48:37 [d]Jer. 46:25; 48:7
4 [a]Jer. 9:23 [b]Jer. 31:22 [c]Ps. 62:10; Ezek. 28:4, 5; 1 Tim. 6:17 [d]Jer. 21:13
5 [1]Heb., *YHWH,* usually rendered *LORD* [2]Lit., *before him* [a]Jer. 48:43f.; 49:29 [b]Jer. 16:16; 46:5 [c]Lam. 4:15
6 [1]Or, *captivity* [a]Jer. 48:47; 49:39
7 [a]Gen. 25:30; 32:3; Is. 34:5, 6; Jer. 25:21; Ezek. 25:12; Amos 1:11; Obad. 1-21 [b]Job 2:11; Jer. 8:9 [c]Gen. 36:11, 15, 34; Jer. 49:20
8 [1]Or, *brought* [2]Or, *punished* [a]Is. 21:13; Jer. 25:23 [b]Jer. 46:21; Mal. 1:3, 4
9 [1]Lit., *their sufficiency* [a]Obad. 5
10 [1]Lit., *seed* [2]Lit., *brothers* [a]Jer. 13:26 [b]Is. 17:14
11 [1]Or, *fatherless* [a]Ps. 68:5; Hos. 14:3 [b]Ps. 68:5; Zech. 7:10
12 [1]Lit., *whose judgment was not to* [a]Jer. 25:15 [b]Jer. 25:28, 29; 1 Pet. 4:17
13 [a]Gen. 22:16; Is. 45:23; Jer. 44:26; Amos 6:8 [b]Gen. 36:33; 1 Chr. 1:44; Is. 34:6; 63:1; Amos 1:12 [c]Is. 34:9-15; Jer. 18:16
14 [a]Obad. 1-4 [b]Is. 18:2; 30:4 [c]Jer. 50:14

15"For behold, I have made you small
among the nations,
Despised among men.
16"As for the terror of you,
The arrogance of your heart has
deceived you,
O you who live in the clefts of [1]the
[a]rock,
Who occupy the height of the hill.
Though you make your nest as
[b]high as an eagle's,
I will [c]bring you down from there,"
declares the LORD.
17"And Edom will become an [a]object
of horror; everyone who passes by it will
be horrified and will [b]hiss at all its
wounds.
18"Like the [a]overthrow of Sodom and
Gomorrah with its neighbors," says the
LORD, "[b]no one will live there, nor will a
son of man reside in it.
19"[a]Behold, one will come up like a
lion from the [1b]thickets of the Jordan
against [2]a perennially watered pasture;
for in an instant I shall make him run
away from it, and whoever is [c]chosen I
shall appoint over it. For who is [d]like
Me, and who will summon Me *into
court?* And who then is the shepherd
[e]who can stand against Me?"
20 Therefore hear the [a]plan of the
LORD which He has planned against
Edom, and His purposes which He has
purposed against the inhabitants of
Teman: surely they will drag them off,
even the little ones of the flock; surely
He will make their [1]pasture [b]desolate
because of them.
21 The [a]earth has quaked at the noise
of their downfall. There is an outcry!
The noise of it has been heard at the
[1]Red Sea.
22 Behold, [1]He will mount up and
[a]swoop like an eagle, and spread out His
wings [2]against Bozrah; and the [b]hearts
of the mighty men of Edom in that day
will be like the heart of a woman in
labor.

Prophecy against Damascus

23 Concerning [a]Damascus.
"[b]Hamath and [c]Arpad are put to
shame,
For they have heard bad news;
They are [d]disheartened.
There is anxiety by the sea,
It [e]cannot be calmed.
24"Damascus has become helpless;
She has turned away to flee,
And panic has gripped her;
[a]Distress and pangs have taken
hold of her
Like a woman in childbirth.
25"How [1]the [a]city of praise has not
been deserted,
The town of My joy!
26"Therefore, her [a]young men will fall
in her streets,
And all the men of war will be
[1]silenced in that day," declares
the LORD of hosts.
27"And I shall [a]set fire to the wall of
Damascus,
And it will devour the [1]fortified
towers of [b]Ben-hadad."

Prophecy against Kedar and Hazor

28 Concerning [a]Kedar and the kingdoms of Hazor, which Nebuchadnezzar
king of Babylon defeated. Thus says the
LORD,
"Arise, go up to Kedar
And devastate the [1b]men of the
east.
29"They will take away their tents and
their flocks;
They will carry off for themselves
Their tent [a]curtains, all their goods,
and their [b]camels,
And they will call out to one another, '[c]Terror on every side!'
30"Run away, flee! Dwell in the
depths,
O inhabitants of Hazor," declares
the LORD;
"For [a]Nebuchadnezzar king of
Babylon has formed a plan
against you
And devised a scheme against you.
31"Arise, go up against a nation which
is [a]at ease,
Which lives securely," declares the
LORD.
"It has [b]no gates or bars;
They [c]dwell alone.
32"And their camels will become plunder,
And the multitude of their cattle
for booty,
And I shall [a]scatter to all the winds
those who [b]cut the corners *of
their hair;*
And I shall bring their disaster
from every side," declares the
LORD.
33"And Hazor will become a [a]haunt of
jackals,
A desolation forever;
No one will live there,
Nor will a son of man reside in it."

Prophecy against Elam

34 That which came as the word of the
LORD to Jeremiah the prophet concerning [a]Elam, [b]at the beginning of the reign
of Zedekiah king of Judah, saying,
35"Thus says the LORD of hosts,
'Behold, I am going to [a]break the
bow of Elam,
The [1]finest of their might.
36 'And I shall bring upon Elam the
[a]four winds
From the four ends of heaven,
And shall [b]scatter them to all these
winds;
And there will be no nation
To which the outcasts of Elam will
not go.

16 [1]Or, *Sela* [a]2 Kin. 14:7; Jer. 48:28 [b]Job 39:27; Is. 14:13-15 [c]Amos 9:2
17 [a]Jer. 18:16; 49:13; 50:13; Ezek. 35:7 [b]1 Kin. 9:8; Jer. 51:37
18 [a]Gen. 19:24, 25; Deut. 29:23; Jer. 50:40; Amos 4:11; Zeph. 2:9 [b]Job 18:15-18; Jer. 49:33
19 [1]Lit., *pride* [2]Or, *an enduring habitation* [a]Jer. 50:44 [b]Josh. 3:15; Jer. 12:5 [c]Num. 16:5 [d]Ex. 15:11; Is. 46:9 [e]Job 41:10
20 [1]Or, *habitation* [a]Is. 14:24, 27; Jer. 50:45 [b]Mal. 1:3, 4
21 [1]Lit., *Sea of Reeds* [a]Jer. 50:46; Ezek. 26:15, 18
22 [1]Or, *one* [2]Or, *over* [a]Jer. 4:13; 48:40; Hos. 8:1 [b]Is. 13:8; Jer. 30:6; 48:41
23 [a]Gen. 14:15; 15:2; 2 Kin. 5:12; 2 Chr. 16:2; Is. 7:8; 17:1; Amos 1:3; Acts 9:2 [b]Num. 13:21; Is. 10:9; Jer. 39:5; Amos 6:2 [c]2 Kin. 18:34; 19:13; Is. 10:9 [d]Ex. 15:15; Nah. 2:10 [e]Is. 57:20
24 [a]Is. 13:8
25 [1]Or, *deserted is the city of praise* [a]Jer. 33:9; 51:41
26 [1]Or, *destroyed* [a]Jer. 11:22; 50:30; Amos 4:10
27 [1]Or, *palaces* [a]Jer. 43:12; Amos 1:3-5 [b]1 Kin. 15:18-20; 2 Kin. 13:3
28 [1]Lit., *sons* [a]Gen. 25:13; Ps. 120:5; Is. 21:16, 17; Jer. 2:10; Ezek. 27:21 [b]Job 1:3; Is. 11:14
29 [a]Hab. 3:7 [b]1 Chr. 5:21 [c]Jer. 46:5
30 [a]Jer. 25:9; 27:6
31 [a]Judg. 18:7; Is. 47:8 [b]Is. 42:11 [c]Num. 23:9; Deut. 33:28; Mic. 7:14
32 [a]Ezek. 5:10; 12:14, 15 [b]Jer. 9:26; 25:23
33 [a]Is. 13:20-22; Jer. 9:11; 10:22; 51:37; Zeph. 2:9, 13-15; Mal. 1:3
34 [a]Gen. 10:22; 14:1, 9; Is. 11:11; Jer. 25:25; Ezek. 32:24; Dan. 8:2 [b]2 Kin. 24:17, 18; Jer. 28:1
35 [1]Lit., *first* [a]Ps. 46:9; Is. 22:6; Jer. 51:56
36 [a]Dan. 7:2; 8:8; Rev. 7:1 [b]Jer. 49:32; Ezek. 5:10; Amos 9:9

37 'So I shall [1]shatter Elam before their enemies
And before those who seek their lives;
And I shall [a]bring calamity upon them,
Even My [b]fierce anger,' declares the LORD,
'And I shall [c]send out the sword after them
Until I have consumed them.
38 'Then I shall set My throne in Elam,
And I shall destroy [1]out of it king and princes,'
Declares the LORD.
39 'But it will come about in the last days
That I shall [a]restore the [1]fortunes of Elam,' "
Declares the LORD.

Prophecy against Babylon

50 THE word which the LORD spoke
concerning [a]Babylon, the land of
the Chaldeans, through Jeremiah the
prophet:
2 "[a]Declare and proclaim among the nations.
Proclaim it and [b]lift up a standard.
Do not conceal *it but* say,
'[c]Babylon has been captured,
[d]Bel has been put to shame, [1]Marduk has been [2]shattered;
Her [e]images have been put to shame, her idols have been shattered.'
3 "For a nation has come up against
her out of the [a]north; it will make her
land [b]an object of horror, and there will
be [c]no inhabitant in it. Both man and
beast have wandered off, they have gone
away!
4 "In those days and at that time,"
declares the LORD, "the sons of Israel
will come, *both* they and the sons of
Judah [a]as well; they will go along [b]weeping as they go, and it will be [c]the LORD
their God they will seek.
5 "They will [a]ask for the way to Zion,
turning their faces [1]in its direction; [2]they
[3]will come that they may join themselves
to the LORD *in* an [b]everlasting covenant
that will not be forgotten.
6 "My people have become [a]lost sheep;
[b]Their shepherds have led them astray.
They have made them turn aside *on* the [c]mountains;
They have gone along from mountain to hill
And have forgotten their [d]resting place.
7 "All who came upon them have devoured them;
And their adversaries have said, '[a]We are not guilty,
Inasmuch as they have sinned against the LORD *who is* the [b]habitation of righteousness,
Even the LORD, the [c]hope of their fathers.'
8 "Wander away from the [a]midst of Babylon;
And [1]go forth from the land of the Chaldeans;
Be also like male goats [2]at the head of the flock.
9 "For behold, I am going to [a]arouse and bring up against Babylon
A horde of great nations from the land of the north,
And they will draw up *their* battle lines against her;
From there she will be taken captive.
Their arrows will be like [1]an expert warrior
Who does not return empty-handed.
10 "And [1a]Chaldea will become plunder;
All who plunder her will have enough," declares the LORD.

11 "Because you are glad, because you are jubilant,
O you who [a]pillage My heritage,
Because you skip about [1]like a threshing [b]heifer
And neigh like [2]stallions,
12 Your [a]mother [1]will be greatly ashamed,
She who gave you birth [1]will be humiliated.
Behold, *she will be* the least of the nations,
A [b]wilderness, a parched land, and a desert.
13 "Because of the indignation of the LORD she will [a]not be inhabited,
But she will be [b]completely desolate;
Everyone who passes by Babylon [c]will be horrified
And will hiss because of all her wounds.
14 "Draw up your battle lines against Babylon on every side,
All you who [1]bend the bow;
Shoot at her, do not be sparing with *your* arrows,
For she has [a]sinned against the LORD.
15 "Raise your battle cry against her on every side!
She has [a]given [1]herself up, her pillars have fallen,
Her [b]walls have been torn down.
For this is the [c]vengeance of the LORD:
Take vengeance on her;
[d]As she has done *to others, so* do to her.
16 "Cut off the [a]sower from Babylon,
And the one who wields the sickle at the time of harvest;
From before [1]the [b]sword of the oppressor
[c]They will each turn back to his own people,
And they will each flee to his own land.

37 [1]Or, *dismay* [a]Jer. 6:19 [b]Jer. 30:24 [c]Jer. 9:16; 48:2
38 [1]Or, *from there*
39 [1]Or, *captivity* [a]Jer. 48:47

1 [a]Gen. 10:10; 11:9; 2 Kin. 17:24; Is. 13:1; 47:1; Dan. 1:1; Rev. 14:8
2 [1]Heb., *Merodach* [2]Or, *dismayed* [a]Jer. 4:16 [b]Jer. 51:27 [c]Jer. 51:31 [d]Is. 46:1 [e]Jer. 51:47
3 [a]Is. 13:17; Jer. 50:9; 51:11, 27 [b]Is. 14:22, 23; Jer. 50:13 [c]Jer. 9:10, 11; Zeph. 1:3
4 [a]Is. 11:12, 13; Jer. 3:18; 31:31; 33:7; Hos. 1:11 [b]Ezra 3:12, 13; Ps. 126:5; Jer. 31:9 [c]Hos. 3:5
5 [1]Lit., *hither* [2]M.T. reads *come ye!* [3]Or, *will have come* [a]Is. 35:8; Jer. 6:16 [b]Is. 55:3; Jer. 32:40; Heb. 8:6-10
6 [a]Is. 53:6; Ezek. 34:15, 16; Matt. 9:36; 10:6 [b]Jer. 23:11-14 [c]Jer. 13:16; Ezek. 34:6 [d]Jer. 33:12; 50:19
7 [a]Jer. 2:3; Zech. 11:5 [b]Jer. 31:23; 40:2, 3 [c]Ps. 22:4; Jer. 14:8; 17:13
8 [1]Another reading is *let them go forth* [2]Or, *in front of* [a]Is. 48:20; Jer. 51:6; Rev. 18:4
9 [1]So some mss. and versions; M.T. reads *a warrior who makes childless* [a]Jer. 51:1
10 [1]Or, *the Chaldeans* [a]Jer. 51:24, 35; Ezek. 11:24
11 [1]Another reading is *in the grass* [2]Lit., *mighty ones* [a]Jer. 12:14 [b]Jer. 46:20
12 [1]Or, *has become* [a]Jer. 15:9 [b]Jer. 22:6; 51:43
13 [a]Jer. 34:22 [b]Jer. 51:26 [c]Jer. 18:16; 49:17
14 [1]Lit., *tread* (in order to string) [a]Hab. 2:8, 17
15 [1]Lit., *her hand* [a]1 Chr. 29:24; 2 Chr. 30:8; Lam. 5:6 [b]Jer. 50:44, 58; 51:58 [c]Jer. 46:10 [d]Ps. 137:8; Rev. 18:6
16 [1]Or, *the oppressing sword* [a]Joel 1:11 [b]Jer. 25:38; 46:16 [c]Is. 13:14

17 "Israel is a [a]scattered [1]flock, the [b]lions have driven *them* away. The first one *who* devoured him was the [c]king of Assyria, and this last one *who* has broken his bones is [d]Nebuchadnezzar king of Babylon.

18 "Therefore thus says the LORD of hosts, the God of Israel: 'Behold, I am going to punish the king of Babylon and his land, just as I [a]punished the king of Assyria.

19 'And I shall [a]bring Israel back to his pasture, and he will graze on Carmel and Bashan, and his [1]desire will be satisfied in the [b]hill country of Ephraim and Gilead.

20 'In those days and at that time,' declares the LORD, 'search will be made for the iniquity of Israel, but [a]there will be none; and for the sins of Judah, but they will not be found; for I shall pardon those [b]whom I leave as a remnant.'

21 "Against the land of [1]Merathaim, go up against it,
And against the inhabitants of [2a]Pekod.
Slay and [3]utterly destroy them," declares the LORD,
"And do according to all that I have commanded you.

22 "The [a]noise of battle is in the land,
And great destruction.

23 "How the [a]hammer of the whole earth
Has been cut off and broken!
How Babylon has become
An object of horror among the nations!

24 "I [a]set a snare for you, and you were also [b]caught, O Babylon,
While you yourself were not aware;
You have been found and also seized
Because you have engaged in [c]conflict with the LORD."

25 The LORD has opened His armory
And has brought forth the [a]weapons of His indignation,
For it is a [b]work of the Lord [1]GOD of hosts
In the land of the Chaldeans.

26 Come to her from the [1]farthest border;
[a]Open up her barns,
Pile her up like heaps
And [2b]utterly destroy her,
Let nothing be left to her.

27 [a]Put all her young bulls to the sword;
Let them [b]go down to the slaughter!
Woe be upon them, for their [c]day has come,
The time of their punishment.

28 There is a [a]sound of fugitives and refugees from the land of Babylon,
To declare in Zion the [b]vengeance of the LORD our God,
Vengeance for His [c]temple.

29 "Summon [1]many against Babylon,
All those who [2]bend the bow:
Encamp against her on every side,
Let there be no escape[3].
Repay her according to her work;
[a]According to all that she has done, *so* do to her;
For she has become [b]arrogant against the LORD,
Against the Holy One of Israel.

30 "Therefore her [a]young men will fall in her streets,
And all her men of war will be [1b]silenced in that day," declares the LORD.

31 "Behold, [a]I am against you, O [1]arrogant one,"
Declares the Lord [2]GOD of hosts,
"For your day has come,
The time [3]when I shall punish you.

32 "And the [1a]arrogant one will stumble and fall
With no one to raise him up;
And I shall [b]set fire to his cities,
And it will devour all his environs."

33 Thus says the LORD of hosts,
"The sons of Israel are oppressed,
And the sons of Judah as well;
And [a]all who took them captive have held them fast,
They have refused to let them go.

34 "Their [a]Redeemer is strong, [b]the LORD of hosts is His name;
He will vigorously [c]plead their case,
So that He may [d]bring rest to [1]the earth,
But turmoil to the inhabitants of Babylon.

35 "A [a]sword against the Chaldeans," declares the LORD,
"And against the inhabitants of Babylon,
And against her [b]officials and her [c]wise men!

36 "A sword against the [a]oracle priests, and they will become fools!
A sword against her [b]mighty men, and they will be [1c]shattered!

37 "A sword against [1]their [a]horses and against [1]their chariots,
And against all the [2b]foreigners who are in the midst of her,
And they will become [c]women!
A sword against her treasures, and they will be plundered!

38 "A [1a]drought on her waters, and they will be dried up!
For it is a land of [b]idols,
And they are mad over fearsome idols.

39 "Therefore the [a]desert creatures will live *there* along with the jackals;
The ostriches also will live in it,
And it will [b]never again be inhabited
Or dwelt in from generation to generation.

17 [1]Lit., *sheep* [a]Joel 3:2 [b]Jer. 2:15; 4:7 [c]2 Kin. 15:19; 17:6; 18:9-13 [d]2 Kin. 24:1, 10-12; 25:1-7
18 [a]Is. 10:12; Ezek. 31:3, 11, 12; Nah. 3:7, 18, 19
19 [1]Lit., *soul* [a]Is. 65:10; Jer. 31:10; 33:12; Ezek. 34:13 [b]Jer. 31:6
20 [a]Is. 43:25; Jer. 31:34; Mic. 7:19 [b]Is. 1:9
21 [1]Or, *Double Rebellion* [2]Or, *Punishment* [3]Lit., *put under the ban* [a]Ezek. 23:23
22 [a]Jer. 4:19-21; 51:54-56
23 [a]Jer. 51:20-24
24 [a]Jer. 48:43, 44 [b]Jer. 51:31; Dan. 5:30, 31 [c]Job 9:4; 40:2, 9
25 [1]Heb., *YHWH,* usually rendered *LORD* [a]Is. 13:5 [b]Jer. 50:15; 51:12, 25, 55
26 [1]Lit., *end* [2]Lit., *put under the ban* [a]Is. 45:3; Jer. 50:10 [b]Is. 14:23
27 [a]Is. 34:7 [b]Jer. 48:10 [c]Ps. 37:13; Jer. 46:21; 48:44; Ezek. 7:7
28 [a]Is. 48:20 [b]Ps. 149:6-9; Jer. 50:15; 51:10 [c]Lam. 1:10; 2:6, 7
29 [1]Another reading is *archers* [2]Lit., *tread* (in order to string) [3]Some mss. add *to her* [a]Ps. 137:8; Jer. 50:15; 51:56; 2 Thess. 1:6 [b]Ex. 10:3; Jer. 49:16; Dan. 4:37
30 [1]Or, *made lifeless* or *destroyed* [a]Is. 13:17, 18; Jer. 9:21; 18:21; 49:26; 51:4 [b]Jer. 51:57
31 [1]Lit., *arrogance* [2]Heb., *YHWH,* usually rendered *LORD* [3]Another reading is *of your punishment* [a]Jer. 21:13; Nah. 2:13
32 [1]Lit., *arrogance* [a]Is. 10:12-15 [b]Jer. 21:14; 49:27
33 [a]Is. 14:17; 58:6
34 [1]Or, their *land* [a]Prov. 23:11; Is. 43:14; Jer. 15:21; 31:11; Rev. 18:8 [b]Is. 47:4; Jer. 32:18; 51:19 [c]Jer. 51:36; Mic. 7:9 [d]Is. 14:3-7
35 [a]Jer. 47:6; Hos. 11:6 [b]Dan. 5:1, 2 [c]Dan. 5:7, 8
36 [1]Or, *dismayed* [a]Is. 44:25 [b]Jer. 49:22 [c]Nah. 3:13
37 [1]Lit., *his* [2]Lit., *mixed multitude* [a]Ps. 20:7, 8; Jer. 51:21, 22 [b]Jer. 25:20; Ezek. 30:5 [c]Jer. 48:41; 51:30; Nah. 3:13

38 [1]Another reading is *sword* [a]Is. 44:27; Jer. 51:32, 36; Rev. 16:12 [b]Is. 46:1, 6, 7
39 [a]Is. 13:21; 34:14; Rev. 18:2 [b]Is. 13:20; Jer. 25:12

40 "As when God overthrew [a]Sodom
And Gomorrah with its neighbors," declares the LORD,
"No man will live there,
Nor will *any* son of man reside in it.

41 "Behold, a people is coming [a]from the north,
And a great nation and many kings
Will be aroused from the remote parts of the earth.
42 "They [a]seize *their* bow and javelin;
They are [b]cruel and have no mercy.
Their [c]voice roars like the sea,
And they ride on [d]horses,
[e]Marshalled like a man for the battle
Against you, O daughter of Babylon.
43 "The [a]king of Babylon has heard the report about them,
And his hands hang limp;
[b]Distress has gripped him,
Agony like a woman in childbirth.
44 "[a]Behold, one will come up like a
lion from the [1]thicket of the Jordan to [2]a
perennially watered pasture; for in an
instant I shall make them run away from
it, and whoever is [b]chosen I shall appoint over it. For who is [c]like Me, and
who will summon Me *into court?* And
who then is the shepherd who can [d]stand
before Me?"
45 Therefore hear the [a]plan of the
LORD which He has planned against
Babylon, and His purposes which He
has purposed against the land of the
Chaldeans: [b]surely they will drag them
off, *even* the little ones of the flock;
surely He will make their [1]pasture desolate because of them.
46 At the [1]shout, "Babylon has been
seized!" the [a]earth is shaken, and an
[b]outcry is heard among the nations.

Babylon Judged for Sins against Israel

51 THUS says the LORD:
"Behold, I am going to arouse against Babylon
And against the inhabitants of [1]Leb-kamai
[2]The [a]spirit of a destroyer.
2 "And I shall dispatch [1]foreigners to Babylon that they may [a]winnow her
And may devastate her land;
For on every side they will be opposed to her
In the day of *her* calamity.
3 "[1]Let not [2]him who [3a]bends his bow [3]bend *it,*
[1]Nor let him rise up in his [b]scale-armor;
So do not spare her young men;
Devote all her army to destruction.
4 "And they will fall down [1]slain in the land of the Chaldeans,
And [a]pierced through in their streets."

5 For [a]neither Israel nor Judah has been [1]forsaken
By his God, the LORD of hosts,
Although their land is [b]full of guilt
[2]Before the Holy One of Israel.
6 [a]Flee from the midst of Babylon,
And each of you save his life!
Do not be [1b]destroyed in her [2]punishment,
For this is the [c]LORD's time of vengeance;
He is going to [d]render recompense to her.
7 Babylon has been a golden [a]cup in the hand of the LORD,
Intoxicating all the earth.
The [b]nations have drunk of her wine;
Therefore the nations are [c]going mad.
8 Suddenly [a]Babylon has fallen and been broken;
[b]Wail over her!
[c]Bring [1]balm for her pain;
Perhaps she may be healed.
9 We applied healing to Babylon, but she was not healed;
Forsake her and [a]let us each go to his own country,
For her judgment has [b]reached to heaven
And [1]towers up to the very skies.
10 The LORD has [a]brought [1]about our vindication;
Come and let us [b]recount in Zion
The work of the LORD our God!

11 [a]Sharpen the arrows, fill the quivers!
The LORD has aroused the spirit of the kings of the Medes,
Because His purpose is against Babylon to destroy it;
For it is the [b]vengeance of the LORD, vengeance for His temple.
12 [a]Lift up a [1]signal against the walls of Babylon;
Post a strong guard,
Station [2]sentries,
Place men in ambush!
For the LORD has both [b]purposed and performed
What He spoke concerning the inhabitants of Babylon.
13 O you who [a]dwell by many waters,
Abundant in [b]treasures,
Your end has come,
The [1]measure of your [2c]end.
14 The [a]LORD of hosts has sworn by Himself:
"Surely I will fill you with a [1]population like [b]locusts,
And they will cry out with [2]shouts of victory over you."

15 *It is* [a]He who made the earth by His power,
Who established the world by His wisdom,
And by His understanding He [b]stretched out the heavens.

40 [a]Gen. 19:24, 25; Is. 13:19; Jer. 49:18; Luke 17:28-30; 2 Pet. 2:6; Jude 7
41 [a]Is. 13:2-5; Jer. 6:22; 50:3, 9; 51:27, 28
42 [a]Jer. 6:23 [b]Is. 13:17, 18; 47:6 [c]Is. 5:30 [d]Jer. 8:16; 47:3; Hab. 1:8 [e]Jer. 50:9, 14; Joel 2:5
43 [a]Jer. 51:31 [b]Jer. 30:6; 49:24
44 [1]Lit., *pride* [2]Or, *an enduring habitation* [a]Jer. 49:19-21 [b]Num. 16:5 [c]Is. 46:9 [d]Job 41:10; Jer. 30:21
45 [1]Or, *habitation* [a]Ps. 33:11; Is. 14:24; Jer. 51:10, 11 [b]Jer. 49:20
46 [1]Lit., *voice* [a]Jer. 10:10; 49:21; Ezek. 26:18; 31:16 [b]Is. 5:7; 15:5; Jer. 46:12; 51:54; Ezek. 27:28

1 [1]Cryptic name for Chaldea; or, *the heart of those who rise up against Me* [2]Or, *a destroying wind* [a]Jer. 4:11, 12; 23:19; Hos. 13:15
2 [1]Some versions read *winnowers* [a]Is. 41:16; Jer. 15:7; Matt. 3:12
3 [1]M.T. reads *Against him who* [2]I.e., the Chaldean defender [3]Lit., *tread(s)* (in order to string) [a]Jer. 50:14, 29 [b]Jer. 46:4
4 [1]Or, *wounded* [a]Is. 13:15; 14:19; Jer. 49:26; 50:30, 37
5 [1]Lit., *widowed* [2]Lit., *From* [a]Is. 54:7, 8; Jer. 33:24-26 [b]Hos. 4:1, 2
6 [1]Or, *silenced* or *made lifeless* [2]Or, *penalty for iniquity* [a]Jer. 50:8, 28; Rev. 18:4 [b]Num. 16:26 [c]Jer. 50:15 [d]Jer. 25:14
7 [a]Jer. 25:15; Hab. 2:16; Rev. 14:8; 17:4 [b]Rev. 14:8; 18:3 [c]Jer. 25:16
8 [1]Or, *balsam resin* [a]Is. 21:9; Jer. 50:2; Rev. 14:8; 18:2 [b]Is. 13:6; Rev. 18:9 [c]Jer. 46:11
9 [1]Lit., *is lifted* [a]Is. 13:14; Jer. 46:16; 50:16 [b]Ezra 9:6; Rev. 18:5
10 [1]Lit., *forth* [a]Ps. 37:6; Mic. 7:9 [b]Is. 40:2; Jer. 50:28
11 [a]Jer. 46:4, 9; Joel 3:9, 10 [b]Jer. 50:28
12 [1]Or, *standard* [2]Or, *watchmen* [a]Is. 13:2; Jer. 50:2; 51:27 [b]Jer. 4:28; 23:20; 51:29
13 [1]Lit., *cubit* [2]Lit., *being cut off* [a]Rev. 17:1 [b]Is. 45:3 [c]Is. 57:17; Hab. 2:9-11
14 [1]Or, *mankind* [2]I.e., like the song of grape treaders [a]Jer. 49:13 [b]Jer. 51:27; Nah. 3:15
15 [a]Gen. 1:1; Jer. 10:12-16; 51:15-19 [b]Job 9:8; Ps. 146:5, 6; Jer. 32:17; Acts 14:15; Rom. 1:20

16 When He utters His [a]voice, *there is*
a tumult of waters in the heavens,
And He causes the [b]clouds to ascend from the end of the earth;
He makes lightning for the rain,
And brings forth the [c]wind from
His storehouses.
17 [a]All mankind is stupid, devoid of
knowledge;
Every goldsmith is put to shame by
his [1]idols,
For his molten images are [b]deceitful,
And there is no breath in them.
18 They are [a]worthless, a work of
mockery;
In the time of their punishment
they will perish.
19 The [a]portion of Jacob is not like
these;
For the [1]Maker of all is He,
And of the [2]tribe of His inheritance;
The [b]LORD of hosts is His name.
20 *He says,* "You are My [1a]war-club,
My weapon of war;
And with you I [b]shatter nations,
And with you I destroy kingdoms.
21 "And with you I [a]shatter the horse
and his rider,
22 And with you I shatter the [a]chariot
and its rider,
And with you I shatter [b]man and
woman,
And with you I shatter old man
and [c]youth,
And with you I shatter young man
and virgin,
23 And with you I shatter the shepherd and his flock,
And with you I shatter the farmer
and his team,
And with you I shatter governors
and prefects.
24 "But I will repay Babylon and all
the inhabitants of [a]Chaldea for [b]all their
evil that they have done in Zion before
your eyes," declares the LORD.
25 "Behold, [a]I am against you, [b]O
destroying mountain,
Who destroy the whole earth,"
declares the LORD,
"And I will stretch out My hand
against you,
And roll you down from the crags
And I will make you a [c]burnt out
mountain.
26 "And they will not take from you
even a stone for a corner
Nor a stone for foundations,
But you will be [a]desolate forever,"
declares the LORD.

27 [a]Lift up a [1]signal in the land,
Blow a trumpet among the nations!
Consecrate the nations against her,
Summon against her the [b]kingdoms
of [c]Ararat, Minni and [d]Ashkenaz;
Appoint a marshal against her,
Bring up the [e]horses like bristly
locusts.
28 Consecrate the nations against her,
The kings of the Medes,
[1]Their governors and all [1]their
[2]prefects,
And every land of [3]their dominion.
29 So the [a]land quakes and writhes,
For the purposes of the LORD
against Babylon stand,
To make the land of Babylon
[1]A [b]desolation without inhabitants.
30 The [a]mighty men of Babylon have
ceased fighting,
They stay in the strongholds;
[b]Their strength is [1]exhausted,
They are becoming [b]*like* women;
Their dwelling places are set on
fire,
The [c]bars of her *gates* are broken.
31 One [1a]courier runs to meet [1]another,
And one [2b]messenger to meet [2]another,
To tell the king of Babylon
That his city has been captured
from end *to end;*
32 The fords also have been seized,
And they have burned the marshes
with fire,
And the men of war are terrified.

33 For thus says the LORD of hosts,
the God of Israel:
"The daughter of Babylon is like a
[a]threshing floor
At the time [1]it is stamped firm;
Yet in a little while the time of
[b]harvest will come for her."

34 "Nebuchadnezzar king of Babylon
has [a]devoured me *and* crushed
me,
He has set me down *like* an [b]empty
vessel;
He has [c]swallowed me like a monster,
He has filled his stomach with my
delicacies;
He has washed me away.
35 "May the [a]violence *done* to me and
to my flesh be upon Babylon,"
The [1]inhabitant of Zion will say;
And, "May my blood be upon the
inhabitants of Chaldea,"
Jerusalem will say.
36 Therefore thus says the LORD,
"Behold, I am going to [a]plead your
case
And [b]exact full vengeance for you;
And [c]I shall dry up her [1]sea
And make her fountain dry.
37 "And [a]Babylon will become a heap
of ruins, a haunt of jackals,
An [b]object of horror and hissing,
without inhabitants.
38 "They will roar together like [a]young
lions,
They will growl like lions' cubs.
39 "When they become heated up, I
shall serve *them* their banquet
And [a]make them drunk, that they
may become jubilant
And may [b]sleep a perpetual sleep

16 aJob 37:2-6; Ps. 18:13 bPs. 135:7; Jer. 10:13 cJon. 1:4

17 1Or, *graven images* aIs. 44:18-20; Jer. 10:14 bHab. 2:18, 19

18 aJer. 18:15

19 1Lit., *Fashioner* 2Or, *Scepter;* cf. Num. 24:17 aPs. 73:26; Jer. 10:16 bJer. 50:34

20 1Lit., *shatterer* aIs. 10:5; 41:15, 16; Jer. 50:23 bIs. 8:9; 41:15, 16; Mic. 4:12, 13

21 aEx. 15:1

22 aEx. 15:4; Is. 43:17 b2 Chr. 36:17; Is. 13:15, 16 cIs. 13:18

24 aJer. 50:10 bJer. 50:15, 29

25 aJer. 50:31 bIs. 13:2; Zech. 4:7 cRev. 8:8

26 aIs. 13:19-22; 50:13; Jer. 51:29

27 1Or, *standard* aIs. 13:2-5; 18:3; Jer. 50:2; 51:12 bJer. 50:3, 9 cGen. 8:4; 2 Kin. 19:37; Is. 37:38 dGen. 10:3 eJer. 50:42

28 1Lit., *Her* 2I.e., lieutenant governors 3Lit., *his*

29 1Or, *An object of horror* aJer. 8:16; 10:10; 50:46; Amos 8:8 bIs. 13:19, 20; 47:11; Jer. 50:13; 51:26, 43

30 1Lit., *dried up* aPs. 76:5; Jer. 50:15, 36, 37 bIs. 13:7, 8; Nah. 3:13 cIs. 45:1, 2; Lam. 2:9; Amos 1:5; Nah. 3:13

31 1Lit., *runner* 2Lit., *announcer* a2 Chr. 30:6 b2 Sam. 18:19-31

33 1Lit., *of treading it* aIs. 21:10; 41:15, 16; Mic. 4:13 bIs. 17:5; Hos. 6:11; Joel 3:13; Rev. 14:15

34 aJer. 50:17 bIs. 24:1-3 cJob 20:15; Jer. 51:44

35 1Lit., *inhabitress* aPs. 137:8

36 1Or, *broad river* aPs. 140:12 bJer. 51:6, 11; Rom. 12:19 cJer. 50:38

37 aRev. 18:2 bJer. 25:9

38 aJer. 2:15

39 aJer. 25:27; 48:26; 51:57 bPs. 76:5

And not wake up," declares the
LORD.
40 "I shall bring them down like [1]lambs
[a]to the slaughter,
Like rams together with male goats.

41 "How [1a]Sheshak has been captured,
And [b]the praise of the whole earth
been seized!
How Babylon has become an object of horror among the nations!
42 "The [1a]sea has come up over Babylon;
She has been engulfed with its
tumultuous waves.
43 "Her cities have become an [a]object
of horror,
A parched land and a desert,
A land in which [b]no man lives,
And through which no son of man
passes.
44 "And [a]I shall punish Bel in Babylon,
And I shall make what he has
swallowed [b]come out of his
mouth;
And the nations will no longer
[c]stream to him.
Even the [d]wall of Babylon has
fallen down!

45 "[a]Come forth from her midst, My
people,
And each of you [b]save yourselves
From the fierce anger of the LORD.
46 "Now [a]lest your heart grow faint,
And you be afraid at the [b]report
that *will be* heard in the land—
For the report will come [1]one year,
And after that [2]another report in
[2]another year,
And violence *will be* in the land
With [c]ruler against ruler—
47 Therefore behold, days are coming
When I shall punish the [a]idols of
Babylon;
And her whole land will be [b]put to
shame,
And all her slain will fall in her
midst.
48 "Then [a]heaven and earth and all
that is in them
Will shout for joy over Babylon,
For [b]the destroyers will come to
her from the north,"
Declares the LORD.

49 [a]Indeed Babylon is to fall *for* the
slain of Israel,
As also for Babylon [b]the slain of all
the earth have fallen.
50 You [a]who have escaped the sword,
Depart! Do not stay!
[b]Remember the LORD from afar,
And let Jerusalem [1]come to your
mind.
51 [a]We are ashamed because we have
heard reproach;
Disgrace has covered our faces,
For [b]aliens have entered
The holy places of the LORD's
house.

40 [1]Or, *young rams* [a]Jer. 48:15; 50:27
41 [1]Cryptic name for Babylon [a]Jer. 25:26 [b]Jer. 49:25
42 [1]Or, *broad river* [a]Is. 8:7, 8; Jer. 51:55; Dan. 9:26
43 [a]Jer. 50:12 [b]Is. 13:20; Jer. 2:6
44 [a]Is. 46:1; Jer. 50:2 [b]Ezra 1:7, 8 [c]Is. 2:2 [d]Jer. 50:15; 51:58
45 [a]Is. 48:20; Jer. 50:8, 28; 51:6; Rev. 18:4 [b]Gen. 19:12-16; Acts 2:40
46 [1]Lit., *in the* [2]Lit., *the* [a]Is. 43:5; Jer. 46:27, 28 [b]2 Kin. 19:7; Is. 13:3-5 [c]Is. 19:2
47 [a]Is. 21:9; 46:1, 2; Jer. 50:2; 51:52 [b]Jer. 50:12, 35-37
48 [a]Is. 44:23; 48:20; 49:13; Rev. 18:20 [b]Jer. 50:3
49 [a]Ps. 137:8; Jer. 50:29 [b]Rev. 18:24
50 [1]Lit., *come upon your heart* [a]Jer. 44:28 [b]Deut. 4:29-31; Ps. 137:6
51 [a]Ps. 44:15 [b]Ps. 74:3-8; Lam. 1:10
52 [a]Jer. 50:38
53 [1]Lit., *the height of her strength* [a]Gen. 11:4; Job 20:6; Ps. 139:8-10; Is. 14:12-14; Jer. 49:16; Amos 9:2; Obad. 4 [b]Is. 13:3
54 [a]Jer. 48:3-5; 50:22, 46
55 [1]Or, *voice* [2]Lit., *is given* [a]Ps. 18:4; 69:2; 124:2, 4, 5; Jer. 51:42
56 [a]Jer. 51:48, 53; Hab. 2:8 [b]Ps. 46:9; 76:3 [c]Deut. 32:35; Ps. 94:1, 2; Jer. 51:6, 24
57 [a]Jer. 25:27 [b]Ps. 76:5, 6 [c]Jer. 46:18; 48:15
58 [a]Jer. 50:15 [b]Is. 45:1, 2 [c]Hab. 2:13 [d]Jer. 9:5; 51:64; Lam. 5:5
59 [1]Lit., *word* [a]Jer. 32:12; 36:4; 45:1 [b]Jer. 28:1; 52:1
60 [1]Or, *book* [a]Is. 30:8; Jer. 30:2, 3; 36:2, 4, 32
62 [1]Lit., *spoken* [2]Lit., *from man even to beast* [a]Is. 13:19-22; 14:22, 23; Jer. 50:3, 13, 39, 40 [b]Jer. 51:43; Ezek. 35:9
63 [1]Or, *book* [a]Jer. 19:10, 11; Rev. 18:21

52 "Therefore behold, the days are
coming," declares the LORD,
"When I shall punish her [a]idols,
And the mortally wounded will
groan throughout her land.
53 "Though Babylon should [a]ascend to
the heavens,
And though she should fortify [1]her
lofty stronghold,
From [b]Me destroyers will come to
her," declares the LORD.

54 The [a]sound of an outcry from
Babylon,
And of great destruction from the
land of the Chaldeans!
55 For the LORD is going to destroy
Babylon,
And He will make *her* loud [1]noise
vanish from her.
And their [a]waves will roar like
many waters;
The tumult of their voices [2]sounds
forth.
56 For the [a]destroyer is coming
against her, against Babylon,
And her mighty men will be captured,
Their [b]bows are shattered;
For the LORD is a God of [c]recompense,
He will fully repay.
57 "And I shall [a]make her princes and
her wise men drunk,
Her governors, her prefects, and
her mighty men,
That they may sleep a [b]perpetual
sleep and not wake up,"
[c]Declares the King, whose name is
the LORD of hosts.
58 Thus says the LORD of hosts,
"The broad [a]wall of Babylon will be
completely razed,
And her high [b]gates will be set on
fire;
So the peoples will [c]toil for nothing,
And the nations become [d]exhausted *only* for fire."
59 The [1]message which Jeremiah the
prophet commanded Seraiah the son of
[a]Neriah, the grandson of Mahseiah,
when he went with [b]Zedekiah the king of
Judah to Babylon in the fourth year of
his reign. (Now Seraiah was quartermaster.)
60 So Jeremiah [a]wrote in a single
[1]scroll all the calamity which would
come upon Babylon, *that is,* all these
words which have been written concerning Babylon.
61 Then Jeremiah said to Seraiah, "As
soon as you come to Babylon, then see
that you read all these words aloud,
62 and say, 'Thou, O LORD, hast
[1]promised concerning this place to [a]cut
it off, so that there will be [b]nothing
dwelling in it, [2]whether man or beast,
but it will be a perpetual desolation.'
63 "And it will come about as soon as
you finish reading this [1]scroll, you will
tie a stone to it and [a]throw it into the
middle of the Euphrates,

64 and say, 'Just so shall Babylon sink
down and [a]not rise again, because of the
calamity that I am going to bring upon
her; and they will become [b]exhausted.' "
[c]Thus far are the words of Jeremiah.

[a]Recount the Fall of Jerusalem

52 ZEDEKIAH was twenty-one
years old when he became king,
and he reigned eleven years in Jerusalem; and his mother's name was [1b]Ham-
utal the daughter of Jeremiah of [c]Lib-
nah.
2 And he did [a]evil in the sight of the
LORD like all that [b]Jehoiakim had done.
3 For through the [a]anger of the
LORD *this* came about in Jerusalem and
Judah until He cast them out from His
presence. And Zedekiah [b]rebelled
against the king of Babylon.
4 [a]Now it came about in the ninth
year of his reign, on the tenth day of the
tenth month, that Nebuchadnezzar king
of Babylon came, he and all his army,
against Jerusalem, camped against it,
and built a [b]siege wall all around [1]it.
5 [a]So the city was under siege until
the eleventh year of King Zedekiah.
6 On the ninth day of the [a]fourth
month the [b]famine was so severe in the
city that there was no food for the
people of the land.
7 Then the city was [a]broken into,
and all the [b]men of war fled and went
forth from the city at night by way of the
gate between the two walls which *was* by
the king's garden, though the Chaldeans
were [1c]all around the city. And they
went by way of the Arabah.
8 But the army of the Chaldeans
pursued the king and [a]overtook Zedekiah in the [1]plains of Jericho, and all his
army was scattered from him.
9 Then they captured the king and
[a]brought him up to the king of Babylon
at [b]Riblah in the land of [c]Hamath; and
he [1]passed sentence on him.
10 And the king of Babylon [a]slaugh-
tered the sons of Zedekiah before his
eyes, and he also slaughtered all the
[1]princes of Judah in Riblah.
11 Then he [a]blinded the eyes of Zedekiah; and the king of Babylon bound
him with bronze fetters and brought him
to Babylon, and put him in prison until
the day of his death.
12 [a]Now on the tenth day of the fifth
month, which was the [b]nineteenth year
of King Nebuchadnezzar, king of Babylon, [c]Nebuzaradan the captain of the
bodyguard, [1]who was in the service of
the king of Babylon, came to Jerusalem.
13 And he [a]burned the house of the
LORD, the [b]king's house, and all the
houses of Jerusalem; even every large
house he burned with fire.
14 So all the army of the Chaldeans
who *were* with the captain of the guard
[a]broke down all the walls around Jerusalem.
15 Then Nebuzaradan the captain of
the guard [a]carried away into exile some
of the poorest of the people, the rest of
the people who were left in the city, the
[1b]deserters who had deserted to the king
of Babylon, and the rest of the artisans.
16 But [a]Nebuzaradan the captain of
the guard left some of the poorest of the
land to be vinedressers and [1]plowmen.
17 Now the bronze [a]pillars which
belonged to the house of the LORD and
the [b]stands and the bronze [c]sea, which
were in the house of the LORD, the
Chaldeans broke in pieces and carried
all their bronze to Babylon.
18 And they also took away the [a]pots,
the shovels, the snuffers, the basins, the
[1]pans, and all the bronze vessels which
were used in *temple* service.
19 The captain of the guard also took
away the [a]bowls, the firepans, the basins,
the pots, the lampstands, the [1]pans and
the libation bowls, what was fine gold
and what was fine silver.
20 The two pillars, the one sea, and
the twelve bronze bulls that were under
[1]the sea, *and* the stands, which King
Solomon had made for the house of the
LORD—the bronze of all these vessels
was [a]beyond weight.
21 As for the pillars, the [a]height of
each pillar was eighteen [1]cubits, and [2]it
was twelve cubits in [a]circumference and
four fingers in thickness, *and* hollow.
22 Now a [a]capital of bronze was on it;
and the height of each capital was five
cubits, with network and [b]pomegranates
upon the capital all around, all of
bronze. And the second pillar was like
these, including pomegranates.
23 And there were ninety-six [1]exposed
pomegranates; all [a]the pomegranates
numbered a hundred on the network all
around.
24 Then the captain of the guard took
[a]Seraiah the chief priest and [b]Zephaniah
the second priest, with the three [1c]offi-
cers of the temple.
25 He also took from the city one
official who was overseer of the men of
war, and seven [1]of the [a]king's advisers
who were found in the city, and the
scribe of the commander of the army
who mustered the people of the land,
and sixty men of the people of the land
who were found in the midst of the city.
26 And Nebuzaradan the captain of
the guard took them and [a]brought them
to the king of Babylon at Riblah.
27 Then the king of Babylon [a]struck
them down and put them to death at
Riblah in the land of Hamath. So Judah
was [b]led away into exile from its land.

64 [a]Nah. 1:8, 9 [b]Jer. 51:58 [c]Job 31:40; Ps. 72:20
1 [1]Another reading is *Hamital* [a]2 Kin. 24:18; 2 Chr. 36:11 [b]2 Kin. 22:31; 24:18 [c]Josh. 10:29; 2 Kin. 8:22; Is. 37:8
2 [a]1 Kin. 14:22; 2 Kin. 24:19; 2 Chr. 36:12 [b]Jer. 36:30, 31
3 [a]2 Kin. 24:20; Is. 3:1, 4, 5 [b]2 Chr. 36:13; Ezek. 17:12-16
4 [1]Lit., *against it* [a]2 Kin. 25:1; Jer. 39:1; Ezek. 24:1, 2; Zech. 8:19 [b]Jer. 32:24
5 [a]2 Kin. 25:2
6 [a]Jer. 39:2 [b]2 Kin. 25:3; Is. 3:1; Jer. 38:9; Ezek. 4:16; 5:16; 14:13
7 [1]Lit., *against the city on every side* [a]2 Kin. 25:4; Jer. 39:2 [b]Jer. 39:4-7; 51:32 [c]Ezek. 33:21
8 [1]Lit., *Arabah* [a]Jer. 21:7; 32:4; 34:21; 37:17; 38:23
9 [1]Lit., *spoke judgments with* [a]2 Kin. 25:6; Jer. 32:4; 39:5 [b]Num. 34:11; Jer. 39:5 [c]Num. 13:21; Josh. 13:5
10 [1]Or, *commanders* [a]2 Kin. 25:7; Jer. 22:30; 39:6
11 [a]Jer. 39:7; Ezek. 12:13
12 [1]Lit., *stood before the king* [a]2 Kin. 25:8-21; Zech. 7:5; 8:19 [b]2 Kin. 24:12; 25:8; Jer. 52:29 [c]Jer. 39:9
13 [a]1 Kin. 9:8; 2 Kin. 25:9; 2 Chr. 36:19; Ps. 74:6-8; 79:1; Is. 64:10, 11; Lam. 2:7; Mic. 3:12 [b]Jer. 39:8
14 [a]2 Kin. 25:10; Neh. 1:3
15 [1]Lit., *fallers who had fallen* [a]2 Kin. 25:11 [b]Jer. 39:9
16 [1]Or, *unpaid laborers* [a]2 Kin. 25:12; Jer. 39:10; 40:2-6
17 [a]1 Kin. 7:15-22; 2 Kin. 25:13; Jer. 27:19-22; 52:20-23 [b]1 Kin. 7:27-37 [c]1 Kin. 7:23-26
18 [1]Or, *spoons* for incense [a]Ex. 27:3; 1 Kin. 7:40, 45; 2 Kin. 25:14
19 [1]Or, *spoons* for incense [a]1 Kin. 7:49, 50; 2 Kin. 25:15
20 [1]So Gr. and Syriac; Heb. omits *the sea* [a]1 Kin. 7:47; 2 Kin. 25:16
21 [1]I.e., One cubit equals approx. 18 in. [2]Lit., *a line of 12 cubits would encircle it* [a]1 Kin. 7:15; 2 Kin. 25:17; 2 Chr. 3:15

22 [a]1 Kin. 7:16; 2 Kin. 25:17 [b]1 Kin. 7:20, 42
23 [1]Lit., *windward* [a]1 Kin. 7:20
24 [1]Lit., *keepers of the door* [a]2 Kin. 25:18; 1 Chr. 6:14; Ezra 7:1 [b]2 Kin. 25:18; Jer. 21:1; 29:25, 29; 37:3 [c]1 Chr. 9:19; Jer. 35:4
25 [1]Lit., *men of those seeing the king's face* [a]2 Kin. 25:19; Esth. 1:14
26 [a]2 Kin. 25:20
27 [a]2 Kin. 25:21; Ezek. 8:11-18 [b]Is. 6:11, 12; 27:10; 32:13, 14; Jer. 13:19; 20:4; 25:9-11; 39:9; Ezek. 33:28; Mic. 4:10

28 These are the people whom [a]Nebu-
chadnezzar carried away into exile: in
the [1]seventh year 3,023 Jews;
29 in the eighteenth year of Nebuchadnezzar 832 persons from Jerusalem;
30 in the twenty-third year of Nebuchadnezzar, [a]Nebuzaradan the captain
of the guard carried into exile 745 Jewish
people; there were 4,600 persons in all.
31 [a]Now it came about in the thirty-
seventh year of the exile of Jehoiachin
king of Judah, in the twelfth month, on
the twenty-fifth of the month, that [1]Evil-
merodach king of Babylon, in the *first*
year of his reign, [2b]showed favor to

28 [1]Or possibly, *seventeenth* [a]2 Kin. 24:2, 3, 12-16; 2 Chr. 36:20; Ezra 2:1; Neh. 7:6; Dan. 1:1-3
30 [a]2 Kin. 25:11; Jer. 39:9
31 [1]Or, *Awil-Marduk* ("Man of Marduk") [2]Lit., *lifted up the head of* [a]2 Kin. 25:27 [b]Gen. 40:13, 20; Ps. 3:3; 27:6
32 [a]2 Kin. 25:28
33 [1]Lit., *he* [2]Lit., *ate* [3]Lit., *his presence* [a]Gen. 41:14, 42; 2 Kin. 25:29 [b]2 Sam. 9:7, 13; 1 Kin. 2:7

Jehoiachin king of Judah and brought
him out of prison.
32 [a]Then he spoke kindly to him and
set his throne above the thrones of the
kings who *were* with him in Babylon.
33 So [1]Jehoiachin [a]changed his prison
clothes, and [2b]had his meals in [3]the
king's presence regularly all the days of
his life.
34 And for his allowance, a [a]regular
allowance was given him by the king of
Babylon, a daily portion all the days of
his life until the day of his death.

34 [a]2 Sam. 9:10; 2 Kin. 25:30

THE LAMENTATIONS OF JEREMIAH

The Sorrows of Zion

1 HOW [a]lonely sits the city
That was [b]full of people!
She has become like a [c]widow
Who was *once* [d]great among the nations!
She who was a princess among the [1]provinces
Has become a [e]forced laborer!
2 She [a]weeps bitterly in the night,
And her tears are on her cheeks;
She has none to comfort her
Among all her [b]lovers.
All her friends have [c]dealt treacherously with her;
They have become her enemies.
3 [a]Judah has gone into exile [1]under affliction,
And [1]under [2]harsh servitude;
She dwells [b]among the nations,
But she has found no rest;
All [c]her pursuers have overtaken her
In the midst of [3]distress.
4 The roads [1]of Zion are in mourning
Because [a]no one comes to the appointed feasts.
All her gates are [b]desolate;
Her priests are groaning,
Her [c]virgins are afflicted,
And she herself [2]is [d]bitter.
5 Her adversaries have become [1]her masters,
Her enemies [2]prosper;
For the LORD has [a]caused her grief
Because of the multitude of her transgressions;
Her little ones have gone away
As captives before the adversary.
6 And all her [a]majesty
Has departed from the daughter of Zion;
Her princes have become like bucks
That have found no pasture;
And they have [1b]fled without strength
Before the pursuer.

1 [1]Or, *districts* [a]Is. 3:26 [b]Is. 22:2 [c]Is. 54:4 [d]1 Kin. 4:21; Ezra 4:20; Jer. 31:7 [e]2 Kin. 23:35; Jer. 40:9
2 [a]Ps. 6:6; 77:2-6; Lam. 1:16 [b]Jer. 2:25; 3:1; 22:20-22 [c]Job 19:13, 14; Ps. 31:11; Mic. 7:5
3 [1]Or, *by reason of* [2]Lit., *great* [3]Or, *narrow places* [a]Jer. 13:19 [b]Lev. 26:39; Deut. 28:64-67 [c]2 Kin. 25:4, 5
4 [1]Or, *to* [2]Or, *suffers bitterly* [a]Is. 24:4-6; Lam. 2:6, 7 [b]Jer. 9:11; 10:22 [c]Lam. 2:10, 21 [d]Joel 1:8-13
5 [1]Lit., *head* [2]Or, *are at ease* [a]Ps. 90:7, 8; Ezek. 8:17, 18; 9:9, 10
6 [1]Lit., *gone* [a]Jer. 13:18 [b]2 Kin. 25:4, 5
7 [1]Lit., *cessation* [a]Ps. 42:4; 77:5-9 [b]Jer. 37:7; Lam. 4:17 [c]Ps. 79:4; Jer. 48:27
8 [a]Is. 59:2-13; Lam. 1:5, 20 [b]Lam. 1:17 [c]Lam. 1:11, 21, 22
9 [1]Lit., *did not remember her latter end* [2]Lit., *come down* [a]Jer. 2:34; Ezek. 24:13 [b]Deut. 32:29; Is. 47:7 [c]Is. 3:8; Jer. 13:17, 18 [d]Eccl. 4:1; Jer. 16:7 [e]Ps. 25:18; 119:153 [f]Ps. 74:23; Zeph. 2:10
10 [a]Ps. 74:4-8; Is. 64:10, 11; Jer. 51:51 [b]Deut. 23:3
11 [1]Lit., *soul* [a]Jer. 38:9; 52:6 [b]1 Sam. 30:12 [c]Jer. 15:19
12 [1]Or, *sorrow* [a]Jer. 18:16; 48:27 [b]Jer. 30:23, 24 [c]Is. 13:13; Jer. 4:8

7 In the days of her affliction and homelessness
[a]Jerusalem remembers all her precious things
That were from the days of old
When her people fell into the hand of the adversary,
And [b]no one helped her.
The adversaries saw her,
They [c]mocked at her [1]ruin.
8 Jerusalem sinned [a]greatly,
Therefore [b]she has become an unclean thing.
All who honored her despise her
Because they have seen her nakedness;
Even [c]she herself groans and turns away.
9 Her [a]uncleanness was in her skirts;
She [1]did not consider her [b]future;
Therefore she has [2c]fallen astonishingly;
[d]She has no comforter.
"[e]See, O LORD, my affliction,
For the enemy has [f]magnified himself!"
10 The adversary has stretched out his hand
Over all her precious things,
For she has seen the [a]nations enter her sanctuary,
The ones whom Thou didst command
That they should [b]not enter into Thy congregation.
11 All her people groan [a]seeking bread;
They have given their precious things for food
To [b]restore their [1]lives themselves.
"See, O LORD, and look,
For I am [c]despised."
12 "Is [a]it nothing to all you who pass this way?
Look and see if there is any [1]pain like my [1]pain
Which was severely dealt out to me,
Which the [b]LORD inflicted on the day of His [c]fierce anger.

13"From on high He sent fire into my
[a]bones,
And it [1]prevailed *over them;*
He has spread a [b]net for my feet;
He has turned me back;
He has made me [c]desolate,
[2]Faint all day long.
14"The [a]yoke of my transgressions is
bound;
By His hand they are knit together;
They have [b]come upon my neck;
He has made my strength [1]fail;
The Lord [c]has given me into the
hands
Of *those against whom* I am not
able to stand.
15"The [a]Lord has rejected all my
strong men
In my midst;
He has called an appointed [1]time
against me
To crush my [b]young men;
The Lord has [c]trodden *as in* a wine
press
The virgin daughter of Judah.
16"For these things I [a]weep;
[1]My eyes run down with water;
Because far from me is a [b]comforter,
One who restores my soul;
My children are desolate
Because the enemy has prevailed."
17 Zion [a]stretches out her hands;
There is no one to comfort her;
The LORD has [b]commanded concerning Jacob
That the ones round about him
should be his adversaries;
[c]Jerusalem has become an unclean
thing among them.
18"The LORD is [a]righteous;
For I have [b]rebelled against His
[1]command;
Hear now, all peoples,
And [c]behold my [2]pain;
[d]My virgins and my young men
Have gone into captivity.
19"I [a]called to my lovers, *but* they
deceived me;
My [b]priests and my elders perished
in the city,
While they sought food to [c]restore
[1]their strength themselves.
20"See, O LORD, for I am in distress;
My [1a]spirit is greatly troubled;
My heart is overturned within me,
For I have been very [b]rebellious.
In the street the sword [2]slays;
In the house it is like death.
21"They have heard that I [a]groan;
There is no one to comfort me;
All my enemies have heard of my
[1]calamity;
They are [b]glad that Thou hast done
it.
Oh, that Thou wouldst bring the
day which Thou hast proclaimed,
That they may become [c]like me.
22"Let all their wickedness come before Thee;

13 [1]Or, *descended, overthrew* [2]Or, *Sick* [a]Job 30:30; Ps. 22:14; Hab. 3:16 [b]Job 19:6; Ps. 66:11 [c]Jer. 44:6

14 [1]Lit., *stumble* [a]Prov. 5:22; Is. 47:6 [b]Jer. 28:13, 14 [c]Jer. 32:3, 5; Ezek. 25:4, 7

15 [1]Or, *feast* [a]Is. 41:2; Jer. 13:24; 37:10 [b]Jer. 6:11; 18:21 [c]Mal. 4:3

16 [1]Lit., *My eye, my eye* [a]Jer. 14:17; Lam. 2:11, 18; 3:48, 49 [b]Ps. 69:20; Eccl. 4:1; Lam. 1:2

17 [a]Is. 1:15; Jer. 4:31 [b]2 Kin. 24:2-4; Jer. 12:9 [c]Lam. 1:8

18 [1]Lit., *mouth* [2]Or, *sorrow* [a]Ps. 119:75; Jer. 12:1 [b]1 Sam. 12:14, 15; Jer. 4:17 [c]Lam. 1:12 [d]Deut. 28:32, 41

19 [1]Lit., *their soul* [a]Job 19:13-19; Lam. 1:2 [b]Jer. 14:15; Lam. 2:20 [c]Lam. 1:11

20 [1]Lit., *inward parts are in ferment* [2]Lit., *bereaves* [a]Is. 16:11; Lam. 2:11 [b]Jer. 14:20

21 [1]Lit., *evil* [a]Lam. 1:4, 8, 22 [b]Ps. 35:15; Jer. 50:11; Lam. 2:15 [c]Is. 14:5, 6; 47:6, 11; Jer. 30:16

22 [a]Neh. 4:4, 5; Ps. 137:7, 8

1 [a]Ezek. 30:18 [b]Is. 14:12-15; Ezek. 28:14-16 [c]Is. 64:11 [d]Ps. 99:5; 132:7

2 [a]Ps. 21:9; Lam. 3:43 [b]Lam. 2:5; Mic. 5:11, 14 [c]Is. 25:12; 26:5 [d]Ps. 89:39, 40; Is. 43:28

3 [1]Lit., *Every horn* [a]Ps. 75:5, 10; Jer. 48:25 [b]Ps. 74:11; Jer. 21:4, 5 [c]Is. 42:25; Jer. 21:14

4 [a]Job 6:4; 16:13; Lam. 3:12, 13 [b]Ezek. 24:25 [c]Is. 42:25; Jer. 7:20

5 [a]Jer. 30:14 [b]Lam. 2:2 [c]Jer. 52:13; Lam. 2:2 [d]Jer. 9:17-20

6 [1]Lit., *booth* [2]Or, *feast* [a]Jer. 52:13 [b]Jer. 17:27; Lam. 1:4; Zeph. 3:18 [c]Lam. 4:16

7 [a]Ps. 78:59-61; Is. 64:11; Ezek. 7:20-22 [b]Jer. 33:4, 5; 52:13 [c]Ps. 74:3-8

And [a]deal with them as Thou hast
dealt with me
For all my transgressions;
For my groans are many, and my
heart is faint."

God's Anger over Israel

2 HOW the Lord has [a]covered the
daughter of Zion
With a cloud in His anger!
He has [b]cast from heaven to earth
The [c]glory of Israel,
And has not remembered His
[d]footstool
In the day of His anger.
2 The Lord has [a]swallowed up; He
has not spared
All the habitations of Jacob.
In His wrath He has [b]thrown down
The strongholds of the daughter of
Judah;
He has [c]brought *them* down to the
ground;
He has [d]profaned the kingdom and
its princes.
3 In fierce anger He has cut off
[1]All the [a]strength of Israel;
He has [b]drawn back His right hand
From before the enemy.
And He has [c]burned in Jacob like a
flaming fire
Consuming round about.
4 He has bent His [a]bow like an
enemy,
He has set His right hand like an
adversary
And slain all that were [b]pleasant to
the eye;
In the tent of the daughter of Zion
He has [c]poured out His wrath like
fire.
5 The Lord has become like an
[a]enemy.
He has [b]swallowed up Israel;
He has swallowed up all its [c]palaces;
He has destroyed its strongholds
And [d]multiplied in the daughter of
Judah
Mourning and moaning.
6 And He has violently treated His
[1]tabernacle like a garden *booth;*
He has [a]destroyed His appointed
[2]meeting place;
The LORD has [b]caused to be forgotten
The appointed feast and sabbath in
Zion,
And He has [c]despised king and
priest
In the indignation of His anger.
7 The Lord has [a]rejected His altar,
He has abandoned His sanctuary;
He [b]has delivered into the hand of
the enemy
The walls of her palaces.
They have made a [c]noise in the
house of the LORD
As in the day of an appointed feast.

8 The LORD [1]determined to destroy
The wall of the daughter of Zion.
He has [a]stretched out a line,
He has not restrained His hand from [2]destroying;
And He has [b]caused rampart and wall to lament;
They have languished together.
9 Her [a]gates have sunk into the ground,
He has destroyed and broken her bars.
Her king and her princes are among the nations;
The [b]law is no more;
Also, her prophets find
[c]No vision from the LORD.
10 The elders of the daughter of Zion
[a]Sit on the ground, they [b]are silent.
They have thrown [c]dust on their heads;
They have girded themselves with [d]sackcloth.
The [e]virgins of Jerusalem
Have bowed their heads to the ground.
11 My [a]eyes fail because of tears,
My [1b]spirit is greatly troubled;
My [2c]heart is poured out on the earth,
[d]Because of the [3]destruction of the daughter of my people,
When [e]little ones and infants faint
In the streets of the city.
12 They say to their mothers,
"[a]Where is grain and wine?"
As they faint like a wounded man
In the streets of the city,
As their [b]life is poured out
On their mothers' bosom.
13 How shall I admonish you?
To what [a]shall I compare you,
O daughter of Jerusalem?
To what shall I liken you as I comfort you,
O [b]virgin daughter of Zion?
For your [1]ruin is as vast as the sea;
Who can [c]heal you?
14 Your [a]prophets have seen for you
False and foolish *visions;*
And they have not [b]exposed your iniquity
So as to restore you from captivity,
But they have [c]seen for you false and misleading [1]oracles.
15 All who pass along the way
[a]Clap their hands *in derision* at you;
They [b]hiss and shake their heads
At the daughter of Jerusalem,
"Is this the city of which they said,
'[c]The perfection of beauty,
[d]A joy to all the earth'?"
16 All [a]your enemies
Have opened their mouths wide against you;
They hiss and [b]gnash *their* teeth.
They say, "We have [c]swallowed *her* up!
Surely this is the [d]day for which we waited;
We have reached *it,* we have seen *it.*"
17 The LORD has [a]done what He purposed;
He has accomplished His word
Which He commanded from days of old.
He has thrown down [b]without sparing,
And He has caused the enemy to [c]rejoice over you;
He has [d]exalted the [1]might of your adversaries.
18 Their [a]heart cried out to the Lord,
"O [b]wall of the daughter of Zion,
Let *your* [c]tears run down like a river day and night;
Give yourself no relief;
Let [1]your eyes have no rest.
19 "Arise, cry aloud in the [a]night
At the beginning of the night watches;
[b]Pour out your heart like water
Before the presence of the Lord;
Lift up your hands to Him
For the [c]life of your little ones
Who are [d]faint because of hunger
At the head of every street."
20 See, O LORD, and look!
With [a]whom hast Thou dealt thus?
Should women [b]eat their [1]offspring,
The little ones who were [2]born healthy?
Should [c]priest and prophet be slain
In the sanctuary of the Lord?
21 On the ground in the streets
Lie [a]young and old,
My [b]virgins and my young men
Have fallen by the sword.
Thou hast slain *them* in the day of Thine anger,
Thou hast slaughtered, [c]not sparing.
22 Thou didst call as in the day of an appointed feast
My [a]terrors on every side;
And there was [b]no one who escaped or survived
In the day of the LORD's anger.
Those [c]whom I [1]bore and reared,
My enemy annihilated them.

Jeremiah Shares Israel's Affliction

3 I AM the man who has [a]seen affliction
Because of the rod of His wrath.
2 He has driven me and made me walk
In [a]darkness and not in light.
3 Surely against me He has [a]turned His hand
Repeatedly all the day.
4 He has caused my [a]flesh and my skin to waste away,
He has [b]broken my bones.
5 He has [a]besieged and encompassed me with [b]bitterness and hardship.
6 In [a]dark places He has made me dwell,
Like those who have long been dead.

---

8 [1]Lit., *thought* [2]Lit., *swallowing up* [a]2 Kin. 21:13; Is. 34:11; Amos 7:7-9 [b]Is. 3:26; Jer. 14:2
9 [a]Neh. 1:3 [b]Hos. 3:4 [c]Jer. 14:14; 23:16; Ezek. 7:26
10 [a]Job 2:13; Is. 3:26; 47:1 [b]Amos 8:3 [c]Job 2:12; Ezek. 27:30 [d]Is. 15:3; Jon. 3:6-8 [e]Lam. 1:4
11 [1]Lit., *inward parts are in ferment* [2]Lit., *liver* [3]Lit., *breaking* [a]Lam. 1:16; 3:48, 51 [b]Jer. 4:19 [c]Job 16:13 [d]Is. 22:4; Lam. 4:10 [e]Jer. 44:7; Lam. 2:19
12 [a]Jer. 5:17 [b]Job 30:16; Ps. 42:4; 62:8
13 [1]Lit., *breaking* [a]Lam. 1:12 [b]Is. 37:22 [c]Jer. 8:22; 30:12-15
14 [1]Lit., *burdens* [a]Jer. 23:25-29; 29:8, 9 [b]Is. 58:1; Ezek. 23:36; Mic. 3:8 [c]Jer. 23:36; Ezek. 22:25, 28
15 [a]Job 27:23; Ezek. 25:6 [b]Ps. 22:7; Is. 37:22; Jer. 18:16; 19:8; Zeph. 2:15 [c]Ps. 50:2 [d]Ps. 48:2
16 [a]Job 16:10; Ps. 22:13; Lam. 3:46 [b]Job 16:9; Ps. 35:16; 37:12 [c]Ps. 56:2; 124:3; Jer. 51:34 [d]Obad. 12-15
17 [1]Lit., *horn* [a]Jer. 4:28 [b]Lam. 2:1, 2; Ezek. 5:11; 7:8, 9; 8:18 [c]Ps. 35:24, 26; 89:42; Is. 14:29 [d]Deut. 28:43, 44; Lam. 1:5
18 [1]Lit., *the daughter of your eye* [a]Ps. 119:145; Hos. 7:14 [b]Lam. 2:8; Hab. 2:11 [c]Ps. 119:136; Jer. 9:1; Lam. 1:2, 16; 3:48, 49
19 [a]Ps. 42:3; Is. 26:9 [b]1 Sam. 1:15; Ps. 42:4; 62:8 [c]Lam. 2:11 [d]Is. 51:20
20 [1]Lit., *fruit* [2]Or, *tenderly cared for* [a]Ex. 32:11; Deut. 9:26 [b]Jer. 19:9; Lam. 4:10 [c]Ps. 78:64; Jer. 14:15; 23:11, 12
21 [a]2 Chr. 36:17; Jer. 6:11 [b]Ps. 78:62, 63 [c]Jer. 13:14; Zech. 11:6
22 [1]Lit., *bore healthy* or, *tenderly cared for* [a]Ps. 31:13; Is. 24:17; Jer. 6:25 [b]Jer. 11:11 [c]Jer. 16:2-4; 44:7

1 [a]Ps. 88:7, 15, 16
2 [a]Job 30:26; Is. 59:9; Jer. 4:23
3 [a]Ps. 38:2; Is. 5:25
4 [a]Ps. 31:9, 10; 38:2-8; 102:3-5 [b]Ps. 51:8; Is. 38:13
5 [a]Job 19:8 [b]Jer. 23:15; Lam. 3:19
6 [a]Ps. 88:5, 6; 143:3

7 He has [a]walled *me* in so that I cannot go out;
He has made my [1b]chain heavy.
8 Even when I cry out and call for help,
He [a]shuts out my prayer.
9 He has [a]blocked my ways with hewn stone;
He has made my paths crooked.
10 He is to me like a bear lying in wait,
Like a lion in secret places.
11 He has turned aside my ways and [a]torn me to pieces;
He has made me desolate.
12 He [a]bent His bow
And [b]set me as a target for the arrow.
13 He made the [1]arrows of His [a]quiver
To enter into my [2]inward parts.
14 I have become a [a]laughingstock to all my people,
Their *mocking* [b]song all the day.
15 He has [a]filled me with bitterness,
He has made me drunk with wormwood.
16 And He has [a]broken my teeth with [b]gravel;
He has made me cower in the [c]dust.
17 And my soul has been rejected [a]from peace;
I have forgotten [1]happiness.
18 So I say, "My strength has perished,
And *so has* my [a]hope from the LORD."

Hope of Relief in God's Mercy

19 Remember my affliction and my [1]wandering, the [a]wormwood and bitterness.
20 Surely [a]my soul remembers
And is [b]bowed down within me.
21 This I recall to my mind,
Therefore I have [a]hope.
22 The LORD's [a]lovingkindnesses [1]indeed never cease,
[b]For His compassions never fail.
23 *They* are new [a]every morning;
Great is [b]Thy faithfulness.
24 "The LORD is my [a]portion," says my soul,
"Therefore I [b]have hope in Him."
25 The LORD is good to those who [a]wait for Him,
To the [1]person who [b]seeks Him.
26 *It is* good that he [a]waits silently
For the salvation of the LORD.
27 *It is* good for a man that he should bear
The yoke in his youth.
28 Let him [a]sit alone and be silent
Since He has laid *it* on him.
29 Let him [1]put his mouth in the [a]dust,
Perhaps there is [b]hope.
30 Let him give his [a]cheek to [1]the smiter;
Let him be filled with reproach.
31 For the Lord will [a]not reject forever,
32 For if He causes grief,
Then He will have [a]compassion
According to His abundant lovingkindness.
33 For He [a]does not afflict [1]willingly,
Or grieve the sons of men.
34 To crush under His feet
All the prisoners of the [1]land,
35 To [1]deprive a man of [a]justice
In the presence of the Most High,
36 To [1a]defraud a man in his lawsuit—
Of these things the Lord does not [2]approve.
37 Who is [1]there who speaks and it [a]comes to pass,
Unless the Lord has commanded *it*?
38 *Is it* not from the mouth of the Most High
That [1a]both good and ill go forth?

39 Why should *any* living [1]mortal, or *any* man,
Offer [a]complaint [2]in view of his sins?
40 Let us [a]examine and probe our ways,
And let us return to the LORD.
41 We [a]lift up our heart [1]and hands
Toward God in heaven;
42 We have [a]transgressed and rebelled,
Thou hast [b]not pardoned.
43 Thou hast covered *Thyself* with [a]anger
And [b]pursued us;
Thou hast slain *and* [c]hast not spared.
44 Thou hast [a]covered Thyself with a cloud
So that [b]no prayer can pass through.
45 *Mere* [a]offscouring and refuse Thou hast made us
In the midst of the peoples.
46 All our enemies have [a]opened their mouths against us.
47 [a]Panic and pitfall have befallen us,
Devastation and destruction;
48 My [1a]eyes run down with streams of water
Because of the destruction of the daughter of my people.
49 My eyes pour down [a]unceasingly,
Without stopping,
50 Until the LORD [a]looks down
And sees from heaven.
51 My eyes bring pain to my soul
Because of all the daughters of my city.
52 My enemies [a]without cause
Hunted me down [b]like a bird;
53 They have silenced [1]me [a]in the pit
And have [2b]placed a stone on me.

7 [1]Lit., *bronze piece* [a]Job 3:23; 19:8 [b]Jer. 40:4
8 [a]Job 30:20; Ps. 22:2
9 [a]Is. 63:17; Hos. 2:6
11 [a]Job 16:12, 13; Jer. 15:3; Hos. 6:1
12 [a]Ps. 7:12; Lam. 2:4 [b]Job 6:4; 7:20; Ps. 38:2
13 [1]Lit., *sons* [2]Lit., *kidneys* [a]Jer. 5:16
14 [a]Ps. 22:6, 7; 123:4; Jer. 20:7 [b]Job 30:9; Lam. 3:63
15 [a]Jer. 9:15
16 [a]Ps. 3:7; 58:6 [b]Prov. 20:17 [c]Jer. 6:26
17 [1]Lit., *good* [a]Is. 59:11; Jer. 12:12
18 [a]Job 17:15; Ezek. 37:11
19 [1]Or, *bitterness* [a]Jer. 9:15; Lam. 3:5, 15
20 [a]Job 21:6 [b]Ps. 42:5, 6, 11; 43:5; 44:25
21 [a]Ps. 130:7
22 [1]Or, *that we are not consumed* [a]Ps. 78:38; Jer. 3:12; 30:11 [b]Mal. 3:6
23 [a]Is. 33:2; Zeph. 3:5 [b]Heb. 10:23
24 [a]Ps. 16:5; 73:26 [b]Ps. 33:18
25 [1]Lit., *soul* [a]Ps. 27:14; Is. 25:9 [b]Is. 26:9
26 [a]Ps. 37:7
28 [a]Jer. 15:17
29 [1]Lit., *give* [a]Job 16:15; 40:4 [b]Jer. 31:17
30 [1]Lit., *his* [a]Job 16:10; Is. 50:6
31 [a]Ps. 77:7; 94:14; Is. 54:7-10
32 [a]Ps. 78:38; 106:43-45; Hos. 11:8
33 [1]Lit., *from His heart* [a]Ps. 119:67, 71, 75; Ezek. 33:11; Heb. 12:10
34 [1]Or, *earth*
35 [1]Or, *turn aside a man's case* [a]Ps. 140:12; Prov. 17:15
36 [1]Lit., *make crooked* [2]Lit., *see* [a]Jer. 22:3; Hab. 1:13
37 [1]Lit., *this* [a]Ps. 33:9-11
38 [1]Lit., *the evil things and the good* [a]Job 2:10; Is. 45:7; Jer. 32:42
39 [1]Or, *human being* [2]Or, *on the basis of* [a]Jer. 30:15; Mic. 7:9; Heb. 12:5, 6
40 [a]Ps. 119:59; 139:23, 24; 2 Cor. 13:5
41 [1]Lit., *toward* our [a]Ps. 25:1; 28:2; 141:2
42 [a]Neh. 9:26; Jer. 14:20; Dan. 9:5 [b]2 Kin. 24:4; Jer. 5:7, 9
43 [a]Lam. 2:21 [b]Ps. 83:15; Lam. 3:66 [c]Lam. 2:2, 17, 21
44 [a]Ps. 97:2 [b]Lam. 3:8; Zech. 7:13
45 [a]1 Cor. 4:13
46 [a]Job 30:9, 10; Ps. 22:6-8; Lam. 2:16
47 [a]Is. 24:17, 18; Jer. 48:43, 44
48 [1]Lit., *eye brings* [a]Ps. 119:136; Jer. 9:1, 18; Lam. 1:16; 2:11, 18
49 [a]Ps. 77:2; Jer. 14:17
50 [a]Ps. 80:14; Is. 63:15; Lam. 5:1
52 [a]Ps. 35:7, 19 [b]1 Sam. 26:20; Ps. 11:1; 124:7
53 [1]Lit., *my life* [2]Or, *cast stones* [a]Jer. 37:16; 38:6, 9 [b]Dan. 6:17

54 Waters flowed [a]over my head;
I said, "I am cut off!"
55 I [a]called on Thy name, O LORD,
Out of the lowest pit.
56 Thou hast [a]heard my voice,
"[b]Do not hide Thine ear from my
prayer for relief,
From my cry for help."
57 Thou didst [a]draw near when I
called on Thee;
Thou didst say, "[b]Do not fear!"
58 O Lord, Thou didst [a]plead my
soul's cause;
Thou hast [b]redeemed my life.
59 O LORD, Thou hast [a]seen my oppression;
[b]Judge my case.
60 Thou hast seen all their vengeance,
All their [a]schemes against me.
61 Thou hast heard their [a]reproach, O
LORD,
All their schemes against me.
62 The [a]lips of my assailants and their
whispering
Are against me all day long.
63 Look on their [a]sitting and their
rising;
[b]I am their mocking song.
64 Thou wilt [a]recompense them, O
LORD,
According to the work of their
hands.
65 Thou wilt give them [1a]hardness of
heart,
Thy curse will be on them.
66 Thou wilt [a]pursue them in anger
and destroy them
From under the [b]heavens of the
LORD!

Distress of the Siege Described

4 HOW [a]dark the gold has become,
How the pure gold has changed!
The sacred stones are poured out
At the [1]corner of every street.
2 The precious sons of Zion,
Weighed against fine gold,
How they are regarded as [a]earthen
jars,
The work of a potter's hands!
3 Even [a]jackals offer the breast,
They nurse their young;
But the daughter of my people has
become [b]cruel
Like [c]ostriches in the wilderness.
4 The [a]tongue of the infant cleaves
To the roof of its mouth because of
[b]thirst;
The little ones [c]ask for bread,
But no one breaks *it* for them.
5 Those who ate [a]delicacies
Are desolate in the streets;
Those [1]reared in purple
Embrace ash pits.
6 For the [1]iniquity of the daughter of
my people
Is greater than the [2a]sin of Sodom,
Which was [b]overthrown as in a
moment,
And no hands were [3]turned toward
her.
7 Her [1]consecrated ones were [a]purer
than snow,
They were whiter than milk;
They were more ruddy *in* [2]body
than corals,
Their polishing *was* like [3b]lapis
lazuli.
8 Their appearance is [a]blacker than
soot,
They are not recognized in the
streets;
Their [b]skin is shriveled on their
bones,
It is withered, it has become like
wood.
9 Better are those [1a]slain with the
sword
Than those [1]slain with hunger;
For they [2b]pine away, being
stricken
For lack of the fruits of [3]the field.
10 The hands of compassionate
women
[a]Boiled their own children;
They became [b]food for them
Because of the destruction of the
daughter of my people.
11 The LORD has [a]accomplished His
wrath,
He has poured out His fierce anger;
And He has [b]kindled a fire in Zion
Which has consumed its foundations.
12 The kings of the earth did not
believe,
Nor *did* any of [a]the inhabitants of
the world,
That the adversary and the enemy
Could [b]enter the gates of Jerusalem.
13 Because of the sins of her [a]prophets
And the iniquities of her priests,
Who have shed in her midst
The [b]blood of the righteous,
14 They wandered, [a]blind, in the
streets;
They were defiled with [b]blood
So that no one could touch their
[c]garments.
15 "Depart! [a]Unclean!" [1]they cried of
themselves.
"Depart, depart, do not touch!"
So they [b]fled and wandered;
Men among the nations said,
"They shall not continue to dwell
with us."
16 The presence of the LORD has
scattered them;
He will not continue to regard
them.
They did not [1a]honor the priests,
They did not favor the elders.
17 Yet our eyes failed;
Looking for [1]help was [a]useless.
In our watching we have watched
For a [b]nation that could not save.
18 They [a]hunted our steps
So that we could not walk in our
streets;
Our [b]end drew near,
Our days were [1]finished
For our end had come.

54 [a]Ps. 69:2; Jon. 2:3-5
55 [a]Ps. 130:1; Jon. 2:2
56 [a]Job 34:28 [b]Ps. 55:1
57 [a]Ps. 145:18 [b]Is. 41:10, 14
58 [a]Jer. 50:34 [b]Ps. 34:22
59 [a]Jer. 18:19, 20 [b]Ps. 26:1; 43:1
60 [a]Jer. 11:19
61 [a]Ps. 74:18; 89:50; Lam. 5:1; Zeph. 2:8
62 [a]Ps. 59:7, 12; 140:3; Ezek. 36:3
63 [a]Ps. 139:2 [b]Job 30:9; Lam. 3:14
64 [a]Ps. 28:4; Jer. 51:6, 24, 56
65 [1]Or, *insolence* [a]Ex. 14:8; Deut. 2:30; Is. 6:10
66 [a]Lam. 3:43 [b]Ps. 8:3

1 [1]Lit., *head* [a]Ezek. 7:19-22
2 [a]Is. 30:14; Jer. 19:1, 11
3 [a]Is. 13:22; 34:13 [b]Is. 49:15; Ezek. 5:10 [c]Job 39:14-17
4 [a]Ps. 22:15 [b]Jer. 14:3 [c]Lam. 2:12
5 [1]Lit., *established in crimson* [a]Jer. 6:2; Amos 6:3-7
6 [1]Or, *punishment for iniquity* [2]Or, *punishment for sin* [3]Or, *wrung over her* [a]Gen. 19:24 [b]Gen. 19:25; Jer. 20:16
7 [1]Or, *Nazirites* [2]Lit., *bones* [3]Heb., *sappir* [a]Ps. 51:7 [b]Ex. 24:10; Job 28:16
8 [a]Job 30:30; Lam. 5:10 [b]Job 19:20; Ps. 102:3-5
9 [1]Lit., *pierced* [2]Lit., *flow away* [3]Lit., *my fields* [a]Jer. 16:4 [b]Lev. 26:39; Ezek. 24:23
10 [a]Lev. 26:29; Deut. 28:57; 2 Kin. 6:29; Jer. 19:9; Lam. 2:20; Ezek. 5:10 [b]Deut. 28:53-55
11 [a]Jer. 7:20; Lam. 2:17; Ezek. 22:31 [b]Deut. 32:22; Jer. 17:27
12 [a]Deut. 29:24 [b]Jer. 21:13
13 [a]Jer. 5:31; 6:13; Lam. 2:14; Ezek. 22:26-28 [b]Jer. 2:30; 26:8, 9; Matt. 23:31
14 [a]Deut. 28:28, 29; Is. 29:10; 56:10; 59:9, 10 [b]Is. 1:15 [c]Jer. 2:34
15 [1]Or, *they* (men) *cried to them* [a]Lev. 13:45, 46 [b]Jer. 49:5
16 [1]Lit., *lift up the faces of* [a]Is. 9:14-16; Jer. 52:24-27
17 [1]Lit., *our help* [a]Jer. 37:7; Lam. 1:7 [b]Ezek. 29:6, 7, 16
18 [1]Lit., *full* [a]Jer. 16:16 [b]Jer. 5:31; Ezek. 7:2-12; Amos 8:2

19 Our pursuers were [a]swifter
Than the eagles of the sky.
They chased us on the mountains;
They waited in ambush for us in the wilderness.
20 The [a]breath of our nostrils, the [b]LORD's anointed,
Was [c]captured in their pits,
Of whom we had said, "Under his [d]shadow
We shall live among the nations."
21 Rejoice and be glad, O daughter of [a]Edom,
Who dwells in the land of Uz;
But the [b]cup will come around to you as well,
You will become drunk and make yourself naked.
22 *The punishment* of your iniquity has been [a]completed, O daughter of Zion;
He will exile you no longer.
But He [b]will punish your iniquity, O daughter of Edom;
He will expose your sins!

A Prayer for Mercy

5 REMEMBER, O LORD, what has befallen us;
Look, and see our [a]reproach!
2 Our inheritance has been turned over to [a]strangers,
Our [b]houses to aliens.
3 We have become orphans [a]without a father,
Our mothers are like widows.
4 [1]We have to pay for our drinking [a]water,
Our wood comes *to us* at a price.
5 [1]Our pursuers are at our necks;
We are worn out, there is [a]no rest for us.
6 We have [1]submitted to [a]Egypt *and* Assyria [2]to get enough bread.
7 Our [a]fathers sinned, *and* are no more;
It is we who have borne their iniquities.
8 [a]Slaves rule over us;
There is [b]no one to deliver us from their hand.
9 We get our bread [1]at the [a]risk of our lives
[2]Because of the sword in the wilderness.
10 Our skin has become as [a]hot as an oven,
Because of [1]the burning heat of famine.
11 They ravished the [a]women in Zion,
The virgins in the cities of Judah.
12 Princes were hung by their hands;
[1a]Elders were not respected.
13 Young men [1a]worked at the grinding mill;
And youths [b]stumbled under *loads* of wood.
14 Elders [1]are gone from the gate,
Young men from their [a]music.
15 The joy of our hearts has [a]ceased;
Our dancing has been turned into mourning.
16 The [a]crown has fallen from our head;
[b]Woe to us, for we have sinned!
17 Because of this our [a]heart is faint;
Because of these things our [b]eyes are dim;
18 Because of [a]Mount Zion which lies desolate,
[b]Foxes prowl in it.

19 [a]Thou, O LORD, dost [1]rule forever;
Thy [b]throne is from generation to generation.
20 Why dost Thou [a]forget us forever;
Why dost Thou forsake us [1]so long?
21 [a]Restore us to Thee, O LORD, that we may be restored;
Renew [b]our days as of old,
22 Unless [a]Thou hast utterly rejected us,
And art exceedingly [b]angry with us.

19 [a]Is. 5:26-28; 30:16, 17; Jer. 4:13; Hab. 1:8
20 [a]Gen. 2:7 [b]2 Sam. 1:14; 19:21 [c]Jer. 39:5; 52:9 [d]Dan. 4:12
21 [a]Ps. 137:7; Jer. 25:21 [b]Obad. 16
22 [a]Is. 40:2; Jer. 33:7, 8 [b]Jer. 49:10; Mal. 1:3, 4

1 [a]Ps. 44:13-16
2 [a]Is. 1:7; Hos. 8:7, 8 [b]Zeph. 1:13
3 [a]Ex. 22:24; Jer. 15:8; 18:21
4 [1]Lit., *We drink our water for silver* [a]Is. 3:1
5 [1]Lit., *We have been pursued upon* [a]Neh. 9:36, 37
6 [1]Lit., *given the hand to* [2]Lit., *to be satisfied with* [a]Hos. 9:3; 12:1
7 [a]Jer. 14:20; 16:12
8 [a]Neh. 5:15 [b]Ps. 7:2; Zech. 11:6
9 [1]Lit., *with our soul* [2]Or, *In the face of* [a]Jer. 40:9-12
10 [1]Or, *the ravages of hunger* [a]Job 30:30; Lam. 4:8
11 [a]Is. 13:16; Zech. 14:2
12 [1]Lit., *The faces of elders* [a]Is. 47:6; Lam. 4:16
13 [1]Lit., *carry* [a]Judg. 16:21 [b]Jer. 7:18
14 [1]Lit., *have ceased* [a]Is. 24:8; Jer. 7:34
15 [a]Jer. 25:10; Amos 8:10
16 [a]Job 19:9; Ps. 89:39; Jer. 13:18 [b]Is. 3:9-11
17 [a]Is. 1:5 [b]Job 17:7; Lam. 2:11
18 [a]Mic. 3:12 [b]Neh. 4:3
19 [1]Lit., *sit* [a]Ps. 102:12, 25-27 [b]Ps. 45:6

20 [1]Lit., *to length of days* [a]Ps. 13:1; 44:24
21 [a]Ps. 80:3; Jer. 31:18 [b]Is. 60:20-22
22 [a]Ps. 60:1, 2; Jer. 7:29 [b]Is. 64:9

THE BOOK OF
EZEKIEL

The Vision of Four Figures

1 NOW it came about in the thirtieth year, on the fifth *day* of the fourth month, while I was by the [a]river Chebar among the exiles, the [b]heavens were opened and I saw [1c]visions of God.

2 (On the fifth of the month [1]in the [a]fifth year of King Jehoiachin's exile,

3 the [a]word of the LORD came expressly to Ezekiel the priest, son of Buzi, in the [b]land of the Chaldeans by the river Chebar; and there [c]the hand of the LORD came upon him.)

4 And as I looked, behold, a [a]storm wind was coming from the north, a great cloud with fire flashing forth continually and a bright light around it, and in its midst something like [b]glowing metal in the midst of the fire.

5 And within it there were figures resembling [a]four living beings. And this was their appearance: they had human [b]form.

6 Each of them had [a]four faces and [b]four wings.

7 And their legs were straight and [1]their feet were like a calf's hoof, and they gleamed like [a]burnished bronze.

8 Under their wings on their [a]four sides *were* human [b]hands. As for the faces and wings of the four of them,

9 their wings touched one another; their *faces* did [a]not turn when they moved, each [b]went straight forward.

10 As for the [a]form of their faces, *each* had the [b]face of a man, [1]all four had the face of a lion on the right and the face of a bull on the left, and [1]all four had the face of an eagle.

11 Such were their faces. Their wings were spread out above; each had two touching another *being,* and [a]two covering their bodies.

12 And [a]each went straight forward; [b]wherever the spirit was about to go, they would go, without turning as they went.

13 [1]In the midst of the living beings there was something that looked like burning coals of [a]fire, [2]like torches darting back and forth among the living beings. The fire was bright, and lightning was [3]flashing from the fire.

14 And the living beings [a]ran to and fro like bolts of [b]lightning.

15 Now as I looked at the living beings, behold, there was one [a]wheel on the earth beside the living beings, [1]for *each of* the four of them.

16 The [a]appearance of the wheels and their workmanship *was* like [1]sparkling [b]beryl, and all four of them had the same form, their appearance and workmanship *being* as if [2]one wheel were within another.

17 Whenever they [1]moved, they [1]moved in any of their four [2]directions, without [a]turning as they [1]moved.

18 As for their rims they were lofty and awesome, and the rims of all four of them were [a]full of eyes round about.

19 And [a]whenever the living beings [1]moved, the wheels [1]moved with them. And whenever the living beings [b]rose from the earth, the wheels rose *also.*

20 [a]Wherever the spirit was about to go, they would go in that direction[1]. And the wheels rose close beside them; for the spirit of the living [2]beings *was* in the wheels.

21 [a]Whenever those went, these went; and whenever those stood still, these stood still. And whenever those rose from the earth, the wheels rose close beside them; for the spirit of the living [1]beings *was* in the wheels.

Vision of Divine Glory

22 Now [a]over the heads of the living [1]beings *there was* something like an expanse, like the awesome gleam of [2]crystal, extended over their heads.

23 And under the expanse their wings *were stretched out* straight, one toward the other; each one also had [a]two wings covering their bodies on the one side and on the other.

24 I also heard the sound of their wings like the [a]sound of abundant waters as they went, like the [b]voice of [1]the Almighty, a sound of tumult like the [c]sound of an army camp; whenever they stood still, they dropped their wings.

25 And there came a voice from above the [a]expanse that was over their heads; whenever they stood still, they dropped their wings.

26 Now [a]above the expanse that was over their heads there was something [b]resembling a throne, like [1c]lapis lazuli in appearance; and on that which resembled a throne, high up, *was* a figure with the appearance of a [d]man.

27 Then I [1]noticed from the appearance of His loins and upward something [a]like [2]glowing metal that looked like fire all around within it, and from the appearance of His loins and downward I saw something like fire; and *there was* a radiance around Him.

28 As the appearance of the [a]rainbow [1]in the clouds on a rainy day, so *was* the appearance of the surrounding radiance. Such *was* the appearance of the likeness of the [b]glory of the LORD. And when I saw *it,* I [c]fell on my face and heard a voice speaking.

1 [1]Some ancient mss. and versions read *a vision* [a]Ezek. 3:23; 10:15, 20 [b]Matt. 3:16; Mark 1:10; Luke 3:21; Acts 7:56; 10:11; Rev. 4:1; 19:11 [c]Ex. 24:10; Num. 12:6; Is. 1:1; 6:1; Ezek. 8:3; 11:24; 40:2; Dan. 8:1, 2
2 [1]Lit., *it was* [a]2 Kin. 24:12-15; Ezek. 8:1; 20:1
3 [a]2 Pet. 1:21 [b]Ezek. 12:13 [c]1 Kin. 18:46; 2 Kin. 3:15; Ezek. 3:14, 22
4 [a]Is. 21:1; Jer. 23:19; Ezek. 13:11, 13 [b]Ezek. 1:27; 8:2
5 [a]Ezek. 10:15, 17, 20; Rev. 4:6-8 [b]Ezek. 1:26
6 [a]Ezek. 1:10; 10:14, 21 [b]Ezek. 1:23
7 [1]Lit., *the soles of their feet* [a]Dan. 10:6; Rev. 1:15
8 [a]Ezek. 1:17; 10:11 [b]Ezek. 10:8, 21
9 [a]Ezek. 1:17 [b]Ezek. 1:12; 10:22
10 [1]Lit., *the four of them* [a]Rev. 4:7 [b]Ezek. 10:14
11 [a]Is. 6:2; Ezek. 1:23
12 [a]Ezek. 1:9 [b]Ezek. 1:20
13 [1]So with some ancient versions; Heb., *as the likeness of the living beings.* [2]Lit., *like the appearance of* [3]Lit., *coming out* [a]Ps. 104:4; Rev. 4:5
14 [a]Zech. 4:10 [b]Matt. 24:27; Luke 17:24
15 [1]Lit., *for his four faces* [a]Ezek. 1:19-21; 10:9
16 [1]Lit., *the look of beryl* [2]Lit., *the wheel in the midst of the wheel* [a]Ezek. 10:9-11 [b]Ezek. 10:9; Dan. 10:6
17 [1]Lit., *went* [2]Lit., *sides* [a]Ezek. 1:9, 12; 10:11
18 [a]Ezek. 10:12; Rev. 4:6, 8
19 [1]Lit., *went* [a]Ezek. 10:16 [b]Ezek. 10:19
20 [1]M.T. adds *the spirit to go* [2]M.T. reads *being* [a]Ezek. 1:12
21 [1]M.T. reads *being* [a]Ezek. 10:17
22 [1]So some ancient mss. and versions; M.T. reads *being* [2]Or, *ice* [a]Ezek. 10:1
23 [a]Ezek. 1:6, 11
24 [1]Heb., *Shaddai* [a]Ezek. 43:2; Rev. 1:15; 19:6 [b]Ezek. 10:5 [c]2 Kin. 7:6; Dan. 10:6

25 [a]Ezek. 1:22; 10:1
26 [1]Heb., *eben-sappir* [a]Ezek. 1:22; 10:1 [b]Is. 6:1; Ezek. 10:1; Dan. 7:9 [c]Ex. 24:10; Is. 54:11 [d]Ezek. 43:6, 7; Rev. 1:13
27 [1]Lit., *saw* [2]Or, *electrum* [a]Ezek. 1:4; 8:2
28 [1]Lit., *which occurs in* [a]Gen. 9:13; Rev. 4:3; 10:1 [b]Ex. 24:16; Ezek. 8:4; 11:22, 23; 43:4, 5 [c]Gen. 17:3; Ezek. 3:23; Dan. 8:17; Rev. 1:17

The Prophet's Call

2 THEN He said to me, "Son of man, [a]stand on your feet that I may speak with you!"

2 And as He spoke to me the [a]Spirit entered me and set me on my feet; and I heard *Him* speaking to me.

3 Then He said to me, "Son of man, I am sending you to the sons of Israel, to a rebellious people who have [a]rebelled against Me; [b]they and their fathers have transgressed against Me to this very day.

4 "And I am sending you to them who are [1a]stubborn and obstinate children; and you shall say to them, 'Thus says the Lord [2]GOD.'

5 "As for them, [a]whether they listen or [1]not—for they are a rebellious house—they will [b]know that a prophet has been among them.

6 "And you, son of man, [a]neither fear them nor fear their words, though [b]thistles and thorns are with you and you sit on scorpions; neither fear their words nor be dismayed at their presence, for they are a rebellious house.

7 "But you shall [a]speak My words to them [b]whether they listen or [1]not, for they are rebellious.

8 "Now you, son of man, listen to what I am speaking to you; do not be rebellious like that rebellious house. Open your mouth and [a]eat what I am giving you."

9 Then I looked, behold, a [a]hand was extended to me; and lo, a [1b]scroll *was* in it.

10 When He spread it out before me, it was written on the front and back; and written on it were lamentations, mourning and [a]woe.

Ezekiel's Commission

3 THEN He said to me, "Son of man, eat what you find; [a]eat this scroll, and go, speak to the house of Israel."

2 So I [a]opened my mouth, and He fed me this scroll.

3 And He said to me, "Son of man, feed your stomach, and [a]fill your [1]body with this scroll which I am giving you." Then I [b]ate it, and it was sweet as [c]honey in my mouth.

4 Then He said to me, "Son of man, [1]go to the house of Israel and speak with My words to them.

5 "For [a]you are not being sent to a people of [1b]unintelligible speech or difficult language, *but* to the house of Israel,

6 nor to many peoples of [1]unintelligible speech or difficult language, whose words you cannot understand. [2]But I have sent you to them [3]who should listen to you;

7 yet the house of Israel will not be willing to listen to you, since they are [a]not willing to listen to Me. Surely the whole house of Israel is [1]stubborn and obstinate.

8 "Behold, I have made your face as hard as their faces, and your forehead as hard as their foreheads.

9 "Like [1]emery harder than flint I have made your forehead. Do not be afraid of them or be dismayed before them, though they are a rebellious house."

10 Moreover, He said to me, "Son of man, take into your heart all My [a]words which I shall speak to you, and listen [1]closely.

11 "And [1]go to the exiles, to the sons of your people, and speak to them and tell them, whether they listen or [2]not, 'Thus says the Lord [3]GOD.' "

12 Then the [a]Spirit lifted me up, and I heard a great [b]rumbling sound behind me, "Blessed be the glory of the LORD [1]in His place."

13 And I *heard* the sound of the wings of the living beings touching one another, and the sound of the [a]wheels beside them, even a great rumbling sound.

14 So the Spirit lifted me up and took me away; and I went embittered in the rage of my spirit, and [a]the hand of the LORD was strong on me.

15 Then I came to the exiles who lived beside the river Chebar at Tel-abib, and I sat there [a]seven days where they were living, causing consternation among them.

16 Now it came about [a]at the end of seven days that the word of the LORD came to me, saying,

17 "Son of man, I have appointed you a [a]watchman to the house of Israel; whenever you hear a word from My mouth, [b]warn them from Me.

18 "When I say to the wicked, 'You shall surely die'; and you do not warn him or speak out to warn the wicked from his wicked way that he may live, that wicked man shall die in his iniquity, but his [a]blood I will require at your hand.

19 "Yet if you have [a]warned the wicked, and he does not turn from his wickedness or from his wicked way, he shall die in his iniquity; but you have [b]delivered yourself.

20 "Again, [a]when a righteous man turns away from his righteousness and commits iniquity, and I place an [b]obstacle before him, he shall die; since you have not warned him, he shall die in his sin, and his righteous deeds which he has done shall not be remembered; but his blood I will require at your hand.

21 "However, if you have [a]warned [1]the righteous man that the righteous should not sin, and he does not sin, he shall surely live because he took warning; and you have delivered yourself."

22 And the hand of the LORD was on me there, and He said to me, "Get up, go out to the plain, and there I will [a]speak to you."

1 aDan. 10:11; Acts 9:6
2 aEzek. 3:24; Dan. 8:18
3 a1 Sam. 8:7, 8; Jer. 3:25 bEzek. 20:18, 30
4 1Lit., *the sons, stiff-faced and hard-hearted* 2Heb., *YHWH*, usually rendered *LORD* aPs. 95:8; Is. 48:4; Jer. 5:3; 6:15; Ezek. 3:7
5 1Lit., *forbear* aEzek. 2:7; 3:11, 27; Matt. 10:12-15; Acts 13:46 bEzek. 33:33; Luke 10:10, 11; John 15:22
6 aIs. 51:12; Jer. 1:8, 17; Ezek. 3:9 b2 Sam. 23:6, 7; Ezek. 28:24; Mic. 7:4
7 1Lit., *forbear* aJer. 1:7, 17; Ezek. 3:10, 17 bEzek. 2:5
8 aJer. 15:16; Ezek. 3:3; Rev. 10:9
9 1Lit., *scroll of a book* aEzek. 8:3 bJer. 36:2; Ezek. 3:1; Rev. 5:1-5; 10:8-11
10 aIs. 3:11; Rev. 8:13

1 aEzek. 2:9
2 aJer. 25:17
3 1Lit., *inward parts* aJer. 6:11; 20:9 bJer. 15:16 cPs. 19:10; 119:103; Rev. 10:9, 10
4 1Lit., *go, come*
5 1Lit., *deepness of lip and heaviness of tongue* aJon. 1:2; Acts 14:11; 26:17 bIs. 28:11; 33:19
6 1Lit., *deepness of lip and heaviness of tongue* 2Or, *If I had sent you to them, they would listen to you.* 3Lit., *they*
7 1Lit., *of a hard forehead and a stiff heart* a1 Sam. 8:7
9 1Lit., *corundum*
10 1Lit., *with your ears* aJob 22:22; Ezek. 2:8; 3:1-3
11 1Lit., *go, come* 2Lit., *forbear* 3Heb., *YHWH*, usually rendered *LORD*
12 1Or, *from* aEzek. 3:14; 8:3; Acts 8:39 bActs 2:2
13 aEzek. 1:15; 10:16, 17
14 a2 Kin. 3:15
15 aJob 2:13
16 aJer. 42:7
17 aIs. 52:8; 56:10; 62:6; Jer. 6:17; Ezek. 33:7-9 b2 Chr. 19:10; Is. 58:1; Hab. 2:1
18 aEzek. 3:20; 33:6, 8
19 a2 Kin. 17:13, 14; Ezek. 33:3, 9 bEzek. 14:14, 20; Acts 18:6; 1 Tim. 4:16

20 aPs. 125:5; Ezek. 18:24; 33:18; Zeph. 1:6 bIs. 8:14; Jer. 6:21; Ezek. 14:3, 7-9
21 1Lit., *him, the righteous* aActs 20:31
22 aActs 9:6

23 So I got up and went out to the
plain; and behold, the [a]glory of the
LORD was standing there, like the glory
which [b]I saw by the river Chebar, and I
fell on my face.
24 The [a]Spirit then entered me and
made me stand on my feet, and He
spoke with me and said to me, "Go, shut
yourself up in your house.
25 "As for you, son of man, they will
[a]put ropes on you and bind you with
them, so that you cannot go out among
them.
26 "Moreover, [a]I will make your
tongue stick to [1]the roof of your mouth
so that you will be dumb, and cannot be
a man who rebukes them, for they are a
rebellious house.
27 "But [a]when I speak to you, I will
open your mouth, and you will say to
them, 'Thus says the Lord [1]GOD.' He
who hears, let him hear; and he who
refuses, let him refuse; [b]for they are a
rebellious house.

Siege of Jerusalem Predicted

4 "NOW you son of man, [a]get yourself a brick, place it before you, and
inscribe a city on it, Jerusalem.
2 "Then [a]lay siege against it, build a
siege wall, [1]raise up a ramp, pitch
camps, and place battering rams against
it all around.
3 "Then get yourself an iron plate and
set it up as an iron wall between you and
the city, and set your face toward it so
that [a]it is under siege, and besiege it.
This is a [b]sign to the house of Israel.
4 "As for you, lie down on your left
side, and lay the iniquity of the house of
Israel on it; you shall [a]bear their iniquity
for the number of days that you lie on it.
5 "For I have assigned you a number
of days corresponding to the years of
their iniquity, three hundred and ninety
days; thus [a]you shall bear the iniquity of
the house of Israel.
6 "When you have completed these,
you shall lie down a second time, *but* on
your right side, and bear the iniquity of
the house of Judah; I have assigned it to
you for forty days, a day for [a]each year.
7 "Then you shall set your face toward
the siege of Jerusalem with your arm
bared, and [a]prophesy against it.
8 "Now behold, I will [a]put ropes on
you so that you cannot turn from one
side to the other, until you have completed the days of your siege.

Defiled Bread

9 "But as for you, take wheat, barley,
beans, lentils, millet and [a]spelt, put them
in one vessel and make them into bread
for yourself; you shall eat it according to
the number of the days that you lie on
your side, three hundred and ninety
days.
10 "And your food which you eat *shall
be* [a]twenty shekels a day by weight; you
shall eat it from time to time.

23 [a]Ezek. 1:28; Acts 7:55 [b]Ezek. 1:1
24 [a]Ezek. 2:2
25 [a]Ezek. 4:8
26 [1]Lit., *your palate* [a]Luke 1:20, 22
27 [1]Heb., *YHWH*, usually rendered *LORD* [a]Ezek. 24:27; 33:22 [b]Ezek. 12:2, 3

1 [a]Is. 20:2; Jer. 13:1; 18:2; 19:1
2 [1]Lit., *cast* [a]Jer. 6:6; Ezek. 21:22
3 [a]Jer. 39:1, 2; Ezek. 5:2 [b]Is. 8:18; 20:3; Ezek. 12:6, 11; 24:24-27
4 [a]Lev. 10:17; 16:22; Num. 18:1
5 [a]Num. 14:34
6 [a]Num. 14:34; Dan. 9:24-26; 12:11, 12; Rev. 11:2, 3
7 [a]Ezek. 21:2
8 [a]Ezek. 3:25
9 [a]Ex. 9:32; Is. 28:25
10 [a]Ezek. 45:12
12 [a]Is. 36:12
13 [a]Dan. 1:8; Hos. 9:3
14 [1]Heb., *YHWH*, usually rendered *LORD* [a]Jer. 1:6; Ezek. 9:8; 20:49 [b]Acts 10:14 [c]Lev. 17:15; 22:8; Ezek. 44:31 [d]Deut. 14:3; Is. 65:4; 66:17
16 [a]Lev. 26:26; Is. 3:1; Ezek. 5:16; 14:13 [b]Ezek. 4:10, 11; 12:19 [c]Lam. 5:4; Ezek. 12:18, 19
17 [a]Lev. 26:39; Ezek. 24:23; 33:10

1 [1]Lit., *make it pass over your head* [2]Lit., *them* [a]Lev. 21:5; Is. 7:20; Ezek. 44:20 [b]Dan. 5:27
2 [1]Lit., *it* [a]Jer. 39:1, 2; Ezek. 4:2-8 [b]Lev. 26:33
3 [1]Lit., *there*
4 [1]Lit., *go out*
5 [1]Heb., *YHWH*, usually rendered *LORD*, and so throughout the ch. [a]Jer. 6:6; Ezek. 4:1 [b]Deut. 4:6; Lam. 1:1; Ezek. 16:14
6 [1]Lit., *in them, My statutes* [a]2 Kin. 17:8-20; Ezek. 16:47, 48, 51 [b]Neh. 9:16, 17; Ps. 78:10; Jer. 11:10; Zech. 7:11
7 [a]2 Kin. 21:9-11; 2 Chr. 33:9; Jer. 2:10, 11
8 [a]Jer. 21:5, 13; Ezek. 15:7; 21:3; Zech. 14:2 [b]Jer. 24:9; Ezek. 5:15; 11:9

11 "And the water you drink will be the
sixth part of a hin by measure; you shall
drink it from time to time.
12 "And you shall eat it as a barley
cake, having baked *it* in their sight over
human [a]dung."
13 Then the LORD said, "Thus shall
the sons of Israel eat their bread [a]un-
clean among the nations where I shall
banish them."
14 But I said, "[a]Ah, Lord [1]GOD!
Behold, I have [b]never been defiled; for
from my youth until now I have never
eaten what [c]died of itself or was torn by
beasts, nor has any [d]unclean meat ever
entered my mouth."
15 Then He said to me, "See, I shall
give you cow's dung in place of human
dung over which you will prepare your
bread."
16 Moreover, He said to me, "Son of
man, behold, I am going to [a]break the
staff of bread in Jerusalem, and they will
eat bread by [b]weight and with anxiety,
and drink water by [c]measure and in
horror,
17 because bread and water will be
scarce; and they will be appalled with
one another and [a]waste away in their
iniquity.

Jerusalem's Desolation Foretold

5 "AS for you, son of man, take a
[a]sharp sword; take and [1]use it *as* a
barber's razor on your head and beard.
Then take [b]scales for weighing and
divide [2]the hair.
2 "One third you shall burn in the fire
at the center of the city, when the [a]days
of the siege are completed. Then you
shall take one third and strike *it* with the
sword all around [1]the city, and one third
you shall scatter to the wind; and I will
[b]unsheathe a sword behind them.
3 "Take also a few in number from
[1]them and bind them in the edges of
your *robes*.
4 "And take again some of them and
throw them into the fire, and burn them
in the fire; from it a fire will [1]spread to
all the house of Israel.
5 "Thus says the Lord [1]GOD, 'This is
[a]Jerusalem; I have set her at the [b]center
of the nations, with lands around her.
6 'But she has rebelled against My
ordinances more wickedly than the nations and against My statutes [a]more
than the lands which surround her; for
they have [b]rejected My ordinances and
have not walked [1]in My statutes.'
7 "Therefore, thus says the Lord GOD,
'Because you have [a]more turmoil than
the nations which surround you, and
have not walked in My statutes, nor
observed My ordinances, nor observed
the ordinances of the nations which
surround you,'
8 therefore, thus says the Lord GOD,
'Behold, I, even I, am [a]against you, and I
will [b]execute judgments among you in
the sight of the nations.

9 'And because of all your abominations, I will do among you what I have [a]not done, and the like of which I will never do again.

10 'Therefore, [a]fathers will eat *their* sons among you, and sons will eat their fathers; for I will execute judgments on you, and [b]scatter all your remnant to every wind.

11 'So as I live,' declares the Lord GOD, 'surely, because you have [a]defiled My sanctuary with all your [b]detestable idols and with all your abominations, therefore I will also withdraw, and My eye shall have no pity and I will not spare.

12 'One third of you will die by [a]plague or be consumed by famine among you, one third will fall by the sword around you, and one third I will [b]scatter to every wind, and I will [c]unsheathe a sword behind them.

13 'Thus My anger will be spent, and I will [1]satisfy My wrath on them, and I shall be [2a]appeased; then they will know that I, the LORD, have [b]spoken in My zeal when I have spent My wrath upon them.

14 'Moreover, I will make you a desolation and a [a]reproach among the nations which surround you, in the sight of all who pass by.

15 'So [1]it will be a reproach, a reviling, a [a]warning and an object of horror to the nations who surround you, when I [b]execute judgments against you in anger, wrath, and raging rebukes. I, the LORD, have spoken.

16 'When I send against them the [1]deadly arrows of famine which [2]were for the destruction of those whom I shall send to destroy you, then I shall also intensify the famine upon you, and break the staff of bread.

17 'Moreover, [a]I will send on you famine and wild beasts, and they will bereave you of children; [b]plague and bloodshed also will pass through you, and I will bring the sword on you. I, the LORD, have spoken.' "

Idolatrous Worship Denounced

6 AND the word of the LORD came to me saying,

2 "Son of man, set your face toward the [a]mountains of Israel, and prophesy against them,

3 and say, 'Mountains of Israel, listen to the word of the Lord [1]GOD! Thus says the Lord [1]GOD to the mountains, the hills, the ravines and the valleys: "Behold, I Myself am going to bring a sword on you, and [a]I will destroy your high places.

4 "So your [a]altars will become desolate, and your incense altars will be smashed; and I shall make your slain fall in front of your idols.

5 "I shall also lay the dead bodies of the sons of Israel in front of their idols; and I shall scatter your [a]bones around your altars.

6 "In all your dwellings, [a]cities will become waste and the high places will be desolate, that your altars may become waste and [1]desolate, your [b]idols may be broken and brought to an end, your incense altars may be cut down, and your works may be blotted out.

7 "And the slain will fall among you, and you will know that I am the LORD.

8 "However, I shall leave a [a]remnant, for you will have those who [b]escaped the sword among the nations when you are scattered among the countries.

9 "Then those of you who escape will [a]remember Me among the nations to which they will be carried captive, how I have [1b]been hurt by their adulterous hearts which turned away from Me, and by their eyes, which played the harlot after their idols; and they will [c]loathe themselves in their own sight for the evils which they have committed, for all their abominations.

10 "Then they will know that I am the LORD; I have not said in vain [1]that I would inflict this disaster on them." '

11 "Thus says the Lord [1]GOD, 'Clap your hand, [a]stamp your foot, and say, "[b]Alas, because of all the evil abominations of the house of Israel, which will fall by [c]sword, famine, and plague!

12 "He who is [a]far off will die by the plague, and he who is near will fall by the sword, and he who remains and is besieged will die by the famine. Thus shall I [b]spend My wrath on them.

13 "Then you will know that I am the LORD, when their [a]slain are among their idols around their altars, on [b]every high hill, on all the tops of the mountains, under every green tree, and under every leafy oak—the places where they offered soothing aroma to all their idols.

14 "So throughout all their habitations I shall [a]stretch out My hand against them and make the land more desolate and waste than the wilderness toward Diblah; thus they will know that I am the LORD." ' "

Punishment for Wickedness Foretold

7 MOREOVER, the word of the LORD came to me saying,

2 "And you, son of man, thus says the Lord [1]GOD to the land of Israel, 'An [a]end! The end is coming on the four corners of the land.

3 'Now the end is upon you, and I shall send My anger against you; I shall judge you according to your ways, and I shall bring all your abominations upon you.

4 'For My eye will have no pity on you, nor shall I spare *you,* but I shall [a]bring your ways upon you, and your abominations will be among you; then you will [b]know that I am the LORD!'

5 "Thus says the Lord [1]GOD, 'A [a]disaster, unique disaster, behold it is coming!

6 'An end is coming; the end has come! It has [a]awakened against you; behold, it has come!

9 [a]Dan. 9:12; Amos 3:2; Matt. 24:21
10 [a]Lev. 26:29; Jer. 19:9; Lam. 4:10 [b]Ps. 44:11; Ezek. 5:2, 12; 6:8; 12:14; Amos 9:9; Zech. 2:6; 7:14
11 [a]Jer. 7:9-11; Ezek. 8:5, 6, 16 [b]Jer. 16:18; Ezek. 7:20
12 [a]Jer. 15:2; 21:9; Ezek. 5:17; 6:11, 12 [b]Ezek. 5:2, 10; Amos 9:9; Zech. 2:6 [c]Jer. 43:10, 11; 44:27; Ezek. 5:2; 12:14
13 [1]Lit., *cause to rest* [2]Lit., *comforted* [a]Is. 1:24 [b]Is. 59:17; Ezek. 36:5, 6; 38:19
14 [a]Ps. 74:3-10; 79:1-4; Ezek. 22:4
15 [1]Ancient versions read *you* [a]Is. 26:9; Jer. 22:8, 9; 1 Cor. 10:11 [b]Is. 66:15, 16; Ezek. 5:8; 25:17
16 [1]Lit., *evil* [2]Or, *are for destruction, which I will send*
17 [a]Lev. 26:22; Rev. 6:8 [b]Ezek. 38:22

2 [a]Ezek. 36:1
3 [1]Heb., *YHWH,* usually rendered *LORD* [a]Lev. 26:30
4 [a]Lev. 26:30; 2 Chr. 14:5; Is. 27:9; Ezek. 6:6
5 [a]2 Kin. 23:14, 16, 20; Jer. 8:1, 2
6 [1]So some ancient versions; Heb., *bear their guilt* [a]Lev. 26:31; Is. 6:11; Ezek. 5:14 [b]Ezek. 6:4; Mic. 1:7; Zech. 13:2
8 [a]Is. 6:13; Jer. 30:11 [b]Jer. 44:14, 28; Ezek. 7:16; 14:22
9 [1]Lit., *been broken,* or, *broken for Myself their* [a]Deut. 4:29; 30:2; Jer. 51:50 [b]Ps. 78:40; Is. 7:13; 43:24; Hos. 11:8 [c]Job 42:6; Ezek. 20:43; 36:31
10 [1]Lit., *to do this evil to*
11 [1]Heb., *YHWH,* usually rendered *LORD* [a]Ezek. 25:6 [b]Ezek. 9:4 [c]Ezek. 5:12; 7:15
12 [a]Dan. 9:7 [b]Lam. 4:11, 22; Ezek. 5:13
13 [a]Ezek. 6:4-7 [b]1 Kin. 14:23; 2 Kin. 16:4; Is. 57:5-7; Ezek. 20:28; Hos. 4:13
14 [a]Is. 5:25; 9:12; Ezek. 14:13; 20:33, 34

2 [1]Heb., *YHWH,* usually rendered *LORD* [a]Ezek. 7:3, 5, 6; 11:13; Amos 8:2, 10
4 [a]Ezek. 11:21; 22:31; Hos. 9:7 [b]Ezek. 6:7, 14; 7:27
5 [1]Heb., *YHWH,* usually rendered *LORD* [a]2 Kin. 21:12, 13; Nah. 1:9
6 [a]Zech. 13:7

7 'Your doom has come to you, O
inhabitant of the land. The [a]time has
come, the [b]day is near—tumult rather
than joyful shouting on the mountains.
8 'Now I will shortly [a]pour out My
wrath on you, and spend My anger
against you, [b]judge you according to
your ways, and bring on you all your
abominations.
9 'And My eye will show no pity, nor
will I spare. I will [1]repay you according
to your ways, while your abominations
are in your midst; then you will know
that I, the LORD, do the smiting.
10 'Behold, the day! Behold, it is coming! *Your* doom has gone forth; the [a]rod
has budded, arrogance has blossomed.
11 'Violence [1]has grown into a rod of
[a]wickedness. None of them *shall remain,*
none of their multitude, none of their
[b]wealth, nor anything eminent among
them.
12 'The [a]time has come, the day has
arrived. Let not the [b]buyer rejoice nor
the seller mourn; for [c]wrath is against all
their multitude.
13 'Indeed, the seller will not [1a]regain
[2]what he sold as long as [3]they *both* live;
for the vision regarding all their multitude will not [4]be averted, nor will any of
them maintain his life by his iniquity.
14 'They have [a]blown the trumpet and
made everything ready, but no one is
going to the battle; for My wrath is
against all [1]their multitude.
15 'The [a]sword is outside, and the
plague and the famine are within. He
who is in the field will die by the sword;
famine and the plague will also consume
those in the city.
16 'Even when their survivors [a]escape,
they will be on the mountains like
[b]doves of the valleys, all of them
[1c]mourning, each over his own iniquity.
17 'All [a]hands will hang limp, and all
knees will [1]become like water.
18 'And they will [a]gird themselves with
sackcloth, and [b]shuddering will overwhelm them; and shame *will be* on all
faces, and [c]baldness on all their heads.
19 'They shall [a]fling their silver into
the streets, and their gold shall become
an abhorrent thing; their [b]silver and
their gold shall not be able to deliver
them in the day of the wrath of the
LORD. They cannot satisfy their [1]appe-
tite, nor can they fill their stomachs, for
their iniquity has become an occasion of
stumbling.

The Temple Profaned

20 'And they transformed the beauty
of His ornaments into pride, and [a]they
made the images of their abominations
and their detestable things with it; therefore I will make it an abhorrent thing to
them.
21 'And I shall give it into the hands of
the [a]foreigners as plunder and to the
wicked of the earth as spoil, and they
will profane it.
22 'I shall also turn My [a]face from
them, and they will profane My secret
place; then robbers will enter and profane it.
23 '[a]Make the chain, for the land is full
of [1b]bloody crimes, and the city is [c]full
of violence.
24 'Therefore, I shall bring the worst of
the [a]nations, and they will possess their
houses. I shall also make the [b]pride of
the strong ones cease, and their [c]holy
places will be profaned.
25 'When anguish comes, they will
seek [a]peace, but there will be none.
26 '[a]Disaster will come upon disaster,
and [b]rumor will be *added* to rumor; then
they will seek a [c]vision from a prophet,
but the [d]law will be lost from the priest
and [e]counsel from the elders.
27 'The king will mourn, the prince
will be [a]clothed with horror, and the
hands of the people of the land will
[1]tremble. According to their conduct I
shall deal with them, and by their judgments I shall judge them. And they will
know that I am the LORD.' "

Vision of Abominations in Jerusalem

8 AND it came about in the sixth
year, on the fifth *day* of the sixth
month, as I was sitting in my house with
the elders of Judah sitting before me,
that the hand of the Lord [1]GOD fell on
me there.
2 Then I looked, and behold, a likeness as the appearance of [1]a man; from
His loins and downward *there was* the
[a]appearance of fire, and from His loins
and upward the appearance of brightness, like the appearance [b]of [2]glowing
metal.
3 And He stretched out the form of a
hand and caught me by a lock of my
head; and the [a]Spirit lifted me up between earth and heaven and brought me
in the visions of God to Jerusalem, to
the entrance of the [1]north gate of the
inner *court,* where the seat of the idol of
jealousy, which [b]provokes to jealousy,
was *located.*
4 And behold, the [a]glory of the God
of Israel *was* there, like the appearance
which I saw in the plain.
5 Then He said to me, "Son of man,
[a]raise your eyes, now, toward the north."
So I raised my eyes toward the north,
and behold, to the north of the altar gate
was this [b]idol of jealousy at the entrance.
6 And He said to me, "Son of man,
do you see what they are doing, the great
[a]abominations which the house of Israel
are committing here, that I should be far
from My sanctuary? But yet you will see
still greater abominations."
7 Then He brought me to the entrance of the court, and when I looked,
behold, a hole in the wall.
8 And He said to me, "Son of man,
now [a]dig through the wall." So I dug
through the wall, and behold, an entrance.

7 [a]Ezek. 7:12; 12:23-25, 28 [b]Is. 22:5
8 [a]Is. 42:25; Ezek. 9:8; 14:19; Nah. 1:6 [b]Ezek. 7:3; 33:20; 36:19
9 [1]Lit., *give*
10 [a]Ps. 89:32; Is. 10:5
11 [1]Lit., *has risen* [a]Ps. 73:8; 125:3; Is. 59:6-8 [b]Zeph. 1:18
12 [a]Ezek. 7:5-7, 10; 1 Cor. 7:29-31; James 5:8, 9 [b]Prov. 20:14; 1 Cor. 7:30 [c]Is. 5:13, 14; Ezek. 6:11, 12; 7:14
13 [1]Lit., *return to* [2]Lit., *thing sold,* i.e., his inherited land [3]Lit., *their life among the living ones* [4]Lit., *return* [a]Lev. 25:24-28, 31
14 [1]Lit., *her* [a]Num. 10:9; Jer. 4:5
15 [a]Jer. 14:18; Ezek. 5:12; 6:11, 12; 12:16
16 [1]Lit., *moaning* [a]Ezra 9:15; Is. 37:31; Ezek. 6:8; 14:22 [b]Is. 38:14 [c]Is. 59:11; Nah. 2:7
17 [1]Lit., *run with water* [a]Is. 13:7; Ezek. 21:7; 22:14; Heb. 12:12
18 [a]Is. 15:3; Ezek. 27:31; Amos 8:10 [b]Job 21:6; Ps. 55:5 [c]Ezek. 27:31
19 [1]Lit., *soul* [a]Is. 2:20; 30:22 [b]Prov. 11:4; Zeph. 1:18
20 [a]Jer. 7:30
21 [a]2 Kin. 24:13; Ps. 74:2-8; Jer. 52:13
22 [a]Jer. 18:17; Ezek. 39:23, 24
23 [1]Lit., *judgment of blood* [a]Jer. 27:2 [b]Ezek. 9:9; Hos. 4:2 [c]Ezek. 8:17
24 [a]Ezek. 21:31; 28:7 [b]Ezek. 33:28 [c]2 Chr. 7:20; Ezek. 24:21
25 [a]Ezek. 13:10, 16
26 [a]Is. 47:11; Jer. 4:20 [b]Ezek. 21:7 [c]Jer. 21:2; 37:17 [d]Ps. 74:9; Ezek. 22:26; Mic. 3:6 [e]Jer. 18:18; Ezek. 11:2
27 [1]Lit., *be terrified* [a]Job 8:22; Ps. 35:26; 109:18, 29; Ezek. 26:16

1 [1]Heb., *YHWH,* usually rendered LORD
2 [1]Lit., *fire* [2]Or, *electrum* [a]Ezek. 1:27 [b]Ezek. 1:4, 27
3 [1]Lit., *facing north* [a]Ezek. 3:12; 11:1 [b]Ex. 20:4; Deut. 32:16
4 [a]Ezek. 1:28; 3:22, 23
5 [a]Jer. 3:2; Zech. 5:5 [b]Ps. 78:58; Jer. 7:30; 32:34; Ezek. 8:3
6 [a]2 Kin. 23:4, 5; Ezek. 5:11; 8:9, 17
8 [a]Is. 29:15

9 And He said to me, "Go in and see the wicked abominations that they are committing here."

10 So I entered and looked, and behold, every form of creeping things and beasts *and* detestable things, with all the idols of the house of Israel, were carved on the wall all around.

11 And standing in front of them were [a]seventy [b]elders of the house of Israel, with Jaazaniah the son of Shaphan standing among them, each man with his [c]censer in his hand, and the fragrance of the cloud of incense rising.

12 Then He said to me, "Son of man, do you see what the elders of the house of Israel are committing in the dark, each man in the room of his carved images? For they say, '[a]The LORD does not see us; the LORD has [b]forsaken the land.' "

13 And He said to me, "Yet you will see still greater abominations which they are committing."

14 Then He brought me to the entrance of the [a]gate of the LORD's house which *was* toward the north; and behold, women were sitting there weeping for Tammuz.

15 And He said to me, "Do you see *this,* son of man? Yet you will see still greater abominations than these."

16 Then He brought me into the inner court of the LORD's house. And behold, at the entrance to the temple of the LORD, between the porch and the altar, *were* about twenty-five men with their [a]backs to the temple of the LORD and their faces toward the east; and [b]they were [1]prostrating themselves eastward toward the sun.

17 And He said to me, "Do you see *this,* son of man? Is it too light a thing for the house of Judah to commit the abominations which they have committed here, that they have [a]filled the land with violence and [b]provoked Me repeatedly? For behold, they are putting the twig to their nose.

18 "Therefore, I indeed shall deal in wrath. My eye will have no pity nor shall I spare; and [a]though they cry in My ears with a loud voice, yet I shall not listen to them."

The Vision of Slaughter

9 THEN He cried out in my hearing with a loud [a]voice saying, "Draw near, [1]O executioners of the city, each with his destroying weapon in his hand."

2 And behold, six men came from the direction of the upper gate which faces north, each with his shattering weapon in his hand; and among them was [a]a certain man clothed in linen with a [1]writing case at his loins. And they went in and stood beside the bronze altar.

3 Then the [a]glory of the God of Israel went up from the cherub on which it had been, to the threshold of the [1]temple. And He called to the man clothed in linen at whose loins was the writing case.

4 And the LORD said to him, "Go through the midst of the city, *even* through the midst of Jerusalem, and put a [a]mark on the foreheads of the men who [b]sigh and groan over all the abominations which are being committed in its midst."

5 But to the others He said in my hearing, "Go through the city after him and strike; do not let your eye have pity, and do not spare.

6 "[1]Utterly [a]slay old men, young men, maidens, little children, and women, but do not [b]touch any man on whom is the mark; and you shall [c]start from My sanctuary." So they started with the [2]elders who *were* before the [3]temple.

7 And He said to them, "[a]Defile the [1]temple and fill the courts with the slain. Go out!" Thus they went out and struck down *the people* in the city.

8 Then it came about as they were striking and I *alone* was left, that I [a]fell on my face and cried out [1]saying, "[b]Alas, Lord [2]GOD! Art Thou destroying the whole remnant of Israel [3]by pouring out Thy wrath on Jerusalem?"

9 Then He said to me, "The iniquity of the house of Israel and Judah is very, very great, and the land is [a]filled with blood, and the city is [b]full of perversion; for [c]they say, 'The LORD has forsaken the land, and the LORD does not see!'

10 "But as for Me, [a]My eye will have no pity nor shall I spare, but [b]I shall bring their conduct upon their heads."

11 Then behold, the man clothed in linen at whose loins was the [1]writing case [2]reported, saying, "I have done just as Thou hast commanded me."

Vision of God's Glory Departing from the Temple

10 THEN I looked, and behold, in the [1a]expanse that was over the heads of the cherubim something like a [b]sapphire stone, in appearance resembling a [c]throne, appeared above them.

2 And He spoke to the man clothed in linen and said, "Enter between the [a]whirling wheels under the [1]cherubim, and fill your hands with [b]coals of fire from between the cherubim, and scatter *them* over the city." And he entered in my sight.

3 Now the cherubim were standing on the right side of the [1]temple when the man entered, and the cloud filled the [a]inner court.

4 Then the [a]glory of the LORD went up from the cherub to the threshold of the temple, and the [b]temple was filled with the cloud, and the court was filled with the [c]brightness of the glory of the LORD.

5 Moreover, the sound of the wings of the cherubim was heard as far as the outer court, like the [a]voice of [1]God Almighty when He speaks.

11 [a]Num. 11:16, 25; Luke 10:1 [b]Jer. 19:1 [c]Num. 16:17, 35
12 [a]Ps. 14:1; Is. 29:15; Ezek. 9:9 [b]Ps. 10:11
14 [a]Ezek. 44:4; 46:9
16 [1]I.e., worshiping [a]2 Chr. 29:6; Jer. 2:27; Ezek. 23:39 [b]Deut. 4:19; 17:3; Job 31:26-28; Jer. 44:17
17 [a]Ezek. 7:11, 23; 9:9; Amos 3:10; Mic. 2:2 [b]Jer. 7:18, 19; Ezek. 16:26
18 [a]Is. 1:15; Jer. 11:11; Mic. 3:4; Zech. 7:13

1 [1]Lit., *you who punish* [a]Is. 6:8
2 [1]Or, *scribal inkhorn* [a]Lev. 16:4
3 [1]Lit., *house* [a]Ezek. 10:4; 11:22, 23
4 [a]Ex. 12:7, 13; Ezek. 9:6; 2 Cor. 1:22; 2 Tim. 2:19; Rev. 7:2, 3; 9:4; 14:1 [b]Ps. 119:53, 136; Jer. 13:17; Ezek. 6:11; 21:6
6 [1]Lit., To *destruction* [2]Or, *old men* [3]Lit., *house* [a]2 Chr. 36:17 [b]Ex. 12:23; Rev. 9:4 [c]Jer. 25:29; Amos 3:2; Luke 12:47
7 [1]Lit., *house* [a]2 Chr. 36:17; Ezek. 7:20-22
8 [1]Lit., *and said* [2]Heb., *YHWH,* usually rendered *LORD* [3]Lit., *pouring* [a]1 Chr. 21:16 [b]Ezek. 11:13; Amos 7:2-6
9 [a]2 Kin. 21:16; Jer. 2:34; Ezek. 7:23; 22:2, 3 [b]Ezek. 22:29; Mic. 3:1-3; 7:3 [c]Job 22:13; Ps. 10:11; 94:7; Is. 29:15; Ezek. 8:12
10 [a]Is. 65:6; Ezek. 8:18; 24:14 [b]Ezek. 7:4; 11:21; Hos. 9:7
11 [1]Or, *inkhorn* [2]Lit., *brought back word*

1 [1]Or, *firmament* [a]Ezek. 1:22, 26 [b]Ex. 24:10 [c]Rev. 4:2, 3
2 [1]So with Gr.; Heb., *cherub* [a]Ezek. 1:15-21; 10:13 [b]Ps. 18:10-13; Is. 6:6; Ezek. 1:13; Rev. 8:5
3 [1]Lit., *house,* and so throughout the ch. [a]Ezek. 8:3, 16
4 [a]Ezek. 9:3; 11:22, 23 [b]Ex. 40:34, 35; Is. 6:1-4 [c]Ezek. 1:28
5 [1]Heb., *El Shaddai* [a]Job 40:9; Ezek. 1:24; Rev. 10:3

6 And it came about when He commanded the man clothed in linen, saying, "Take fire from between the whirling wheels, from between the cherubim,"
he entered and stood beside a wheel.
7 Then the cherub stretched out his
hand from between the cherubim to the
fire which *was* between the cherubim,
took some and put it into the hands of
the one clothed in linen, who took *it* and
went out.
8 And the cherubim appeared to
have the form of a man's hand under
their wings.
9 Then I looked, and behold, [a]four
wheels beside the cherubim, one wheel
beside each cherub; and the appearance
of the wheels *was* like the gleam of a
[1b]Tarshish stone.
10 And as for their appearance, all
four of them had the same likeness, as if
one wheel were within another wheel.
11 When they moved, they went [a]in
any of their four [1]directions without
turning as they went; but they followed
in the direction which [2]they faced, without turning as they went.
12 And their [a]whole body, their backs,
their hands, their wings, and the [b]wheels
were full of eyes all around, the wheels
belonging to all four of them.
13 The wheels were called in my hearing, the whirling wheels.
14 And [a]each one had four faces. The
first face *was* the face of a cherub, the
second face *was* the face of a man, the
third the face of a lion, and the fourth
the face of an eagle.
15 Then the cherubim rose up. They
are the [a]living beings that I saw by the
river Chebar.
16 Now when the cherubim moved,
the wheels would go beside them; also
when the cherubim lifted up their wings
to rise from the ground, the wheels
would not turn from beside them.
17 When [1]the cherubim [a]stood still,
[1]the wheels would stand still; and when
they rose up, [1]the wheels would rise with
them; for the spirit of the living beings
was in them.
18 Then the glory of the LORD departed from the threshold of the temple
and stood [a]over the cherubim.
19 When [a]the cherubim departed, they
lifted their wings and rose up from the
earth in my sight with the wheels beside
them; and they stood still at the entrance of the east gate of the LORD's
house. And the glory of the God of
Israel [1]hovered over them.
20 These are the [a]living beings that I
saw beneath the God of Israel by [b]the
river Chebar; so I knew that they *were*
cherubim.
21 [a]Each one had four faces and each
one four wings, and beneath their wings
was the form of human hands.
22 As for the likeness of their faces,
they were the same faces whose appearance I had seen by the river Chebar.
Each one went straight ahead.

Evil Rulers to Be Judged

11 MOREOVER, the [a]Spirit lifted
me up and brought me to the east
gate of the LORD's house which faced
eastward. And behold, *there were*
twenty-five men at the entrance of the
gate, and among them I saw Jaazaniah
son of Azzur and [b]Pelatiah son of Benaiah, leaders of the people.
2 And He said to me, "Son of man,
these are the men who devise iniquity
and [a]give evil advice in this city,
3 who say, '[1]Is not *the time* near to
build houses? [2]This [a]*city* is the pot and
we are the flesh.'
4 "Therefore, [a]prophesy against them,
son of man, prophesy!"
5 Then the Spirit of the LORD fell
upon me, and He said to me, "Say, 'Thus
says the LORD, "So you think, house of
Israel, for [a]I know [1]your [b]thoughts.
6 "You have [a]multiplied your slain in
this city, filling its streets with [1]them."
7 'Therefore, thus says the Lord
[1]GOD, "Your [a]slain whom you have laid
in the midst of [2]the city are the flesh, and
this *city* is the pot; but [3]I shall [b]bring
you out of it.
8 "You have [a]feared a sword; so I will
[b]bring a sword upon you," the Lord
GOD declares.
9 "And I shall bring you out of the
midst of [1]the city, and I shall deliver you
into the hands of [a]strangers and [b]execute
judgments against you.
10 "You will [a]fall by the sword. I shall
judge you to the [b]border of Israel; so
you shall know that I am the LORD.
11 "This *city* will [a]not be a pot for you,
nor will you be flesh in the midst of it,
but I shall judge you to the border of
Israel.
12 "Thus you will know that I am the
LORD; for you have not walked in My
statutes nor have you [a]executed My
ordinances, but have acted according to
the ordinances of the [b]nations around
you." ' "
13 Now it came about as I prophesied,
that [a]Pelatiah son of Benaiah died. Then
I fell on my face and cried out with a
loud voice and said, "[b]Alas, Lord GOD!
Wilt Thou bring the remnant of Israel to
a complete end?"

Promise of Restoration

14 Then the word of the LORD came
to me, saying,
15 "Son of man, your brothers, your
[1]relatives, [2]your fellow exiles, and the
whole house of Israel, all of them, *are
those* to whom the inhabitants of Jerusalem have said, 'Go far from the LORD;
this land has been given [a]us as a possession.'
16 "Therefore say, 'Thus says the Lord
GOD, "Though I had removed them far
away among the nations, and though I
had scattered them among the countries,
yet I was a [a]sanctuary for them a little
while in the countries where they had
gone." '

9 [1]Perhaps, *beryl* [a]Ezek. 1:15-17 [b]Dan. 10:6; Rev. 21:20

11 [1]Lit., *sides* [2]Lit., *the head turned* [a]Ezek. 1:17

12 [a]Rev. 4:6, 8 [b]Ezek. 1:18

14 [a]1 Kin. 7:29, 36; Ezek. 1:6, 10; 10:21; Rev. 4:7

15 [a]Ezek. 1:3, 5

17 [1]Lit., *they* [a]Ezek. 1:21

18 [a]Ps. 18:10

19 [1]Lit., *over them from above* [a]Ezek. 11:22

20 [a]Ezek. 1:5, 22, 26; 10:15 [b]Ezek. 1:1

21 [a]Ezek. 1:6, 8; 10:14; 41:18, 19

1 [a]Ezek. 3:12, 14; 8:3; 11:24; 43:5 [b]Ezek. 11:13

2 [a]Ps. 2:1, 2; 52:2; Is. 30:1; Jer. 5:5; Mic. 2:1

3 [1]Or, The time *is not near* [2]Or, *This is* [a]Jer. 1:13; Ezek. 11:7, 11; 24:3, 6

4 [a]Ezek. 3:4, 17

5 [1]Lit., *what comes up in your spirit* [a]Jer. 11:20; 17:10 [b]Ezek. 38:10

6 [1]Lit., *the slain* [a]Is. 1:15; Ezek. 7:23; 22:2-6, 9, 12, 27

7 [1]Heb., *YHWH,* usually rendered *LORD,* and so throughout the ch. [2]Lit., *it* [3]So with Gr.; Heb., *he will bring you out* [a]Ezek. 24:3-13; Mic. 3:2, 3 [b]2 Kin. 25:18-22; Jer. 52:24-27; Ezek. 11:9

8 [a]Prov. 10:24; Is. 66:4 [b]Job 3:25; Is. 24:17, 18

9 [1]Lit., *it* [a]Deut. 28:36, 49, 50; Ps. 106:41 [b]Ezek. 5:8; 16:41

10 [a]Jer. 52:9, 10 [b]2 Kin. 14:25

11 [a]Ezek. 11:3, 7; 24:3, 6

12 [a]Ezek. 18:8, 9 [b]Ezek. 8:10, 14, 16

13 [a]Ezek. 11:1 [b]Ezek. 9:8

15 [1]Lit., *brothers* [2]So with Gr. and some ancient versions; Heb., *the men of your redemption* [a]Ezek. 33:24

16 [a]Ps. 31:20; 90:1; 91:9; Is. 8:14; Jer. 29:7, 11

17"Therefore say, 'Thus says the Lord
God, "I shall [a]gather you from the
peoples and assemble you out of the
countries among which you have been
scattered, and I shall give you the land
of Israel." '
18"When they come there, they will
[a]remove all its [b]detestable things and all
its abominations from it.
19"And I shall [a]give them one heart,
and shall put a new spirit within [1]them.
And I shall take the [b]heart of stone out
of their flesh and give them a [c]heart of
flesh,
20 that they may [a]walk in My statutes
and keep My ordinances, and do them.
Then they will be [b]My people, and I
shall be their God.
21"[1]But as for those whose hearts go
after their [a]detestable things and abominations, I shall [b]bring their conduct
down on their heads," declares the Lord
God.
22 Then the cherubim [a]lifted up their
wings with the wheels beside them, and
[b]the glory of the God of Israel [1]hovered
over them.
23 And the [a]glory of the Lord went
up from the midst of the city, and [b]stood
over the mountain which is east of the
city.
24 And the [a]Spirit lifted me up and
brought me in a vision by the Spirit of
God to the exiles [1]in Chaldea. So the
vision that I had seen [2b]left me.
25 Then I [a]told the exiles all the things
that the Lord had shown me.

Ezekiel Prepares for Exile

12 THEN the word of the Lord
came to me saying,
2"Son of man, you live in the [a]midst
of the [b]rebellious house, who [c]have eyes
to see but do not see, ears to hear but do
not hear; for they are a rebellious house.
3"Therefore, son of man, prepare for
yourself baggage for exile and go into
exile by day in their sight; even go into
exile from your place to another place in
their sight. [a]Perhaps they will [1]under-
stand though they are a rebellious house.
4"And bring your baggage out by day
in their sight, as baggage for exile. Then
you will go out [a]at evening in their sight,
as those going into exile.
5"Dig a hole through the wall in their
sight and [1]go out through it.
6"Load *the baggage* on *your* shoulder
in their sight, *and* carry *it* out in the
dark. You shall [a]cover your face so that
you can not see the land, for I have set
you as a [b]sign to the house of Israel."
7 And I [a]did so, as I had been commanded. By day I [b]brought out my
baggage like the baggage of an exile.
Then in the evening I dug through the
wall with my hands; I went out in the
dark *and* carried *the baggage* on *my*
shoulder in their sight.
8 And in the morning the word of the
Lord came to me, saying,
9"Son of man, has not the house of
Israel, the [a]rebellious house, said to you,
'[b]What are you doing?'
10"Say to them, 'Thus says the Lord
[1]God, "This [2a]burden *concerns* the
prince in Jerusalem, as well as all the
house of Israel who are [3]in it." '
11"Say, 'I am [1]a [a]sign to you. As I
have done, so it will be done to them;
they will [b]go into exile, into captivity.'
12"And the [a]prince who is among
them will load *his baggage* on *his* shoulder in the dark and go out. [1]They will
dig a hole through the wall to bring *it*
out. He will cover his face so that he can
not see the land with *his* eyes.
13"I shall also spread My [a]net over
him, and he will be caught in My snare.
And I shall bring him to Babylon in the
land of the Chaldeans; yet he will [b]not
see it, though he will die there.
14"And I shall [a]scatter to every wind
all who are around him, his helpers and
all his troops; and I shall draw out a
sword after them.
15"So they will [a]know that I am the
Lord when I scatter them among the
nations, and spread them among the
countries.
16"But I shall [1]spare a few of them
from the [a]sword, the famine, and the
pestilence that they may tell all their
abominations among the nations where
they go, and [2]may [b]know that I am the
Lord."
17 Moreover, the word of the Lord
came to me saying,
18"Son of man, [a]eat your bread with
trembling, and drink your water with
quivering and anxiety.
19"Then say to the people of the land,
'Thus says the Lord God concerning the
inhabitants of Jerusalem in the land of
Israel, "They will eat their bread with
anxiety and drink their water with horror, because [1]their land will be
[2a]stripped of its fulness on account of
the violence of all who live in it.
20"And the inhabited [a]cities will be
laid waste, and the [b]land will be a
desolation. So you will know that I am
the Lord." ' "
21 Then the word of the Lord came
to me saying,
22"Son of man, what is this [a]proverb
you *people* have concerning the land of
Israel, saying, 'The [b]days are long and
every [c]vision fails'?
23"Therefore say to them, 'Thus says
the Lord God, "I will make this proverb
cease so that they will no longer use it as
a proverb in Israel." But tell them, "[a]The
days draw near as well as the [1]fulfillment
of every vision.
24"For there will no longer be any
[1a]false vision or flattering divination
within the house of Israel.

17 [a]Is. 11:11-16; Jer. 3:12, 18; 24:5; Ezek. 20:41, 42; 28:25
18 [a]Ezek. 37:23 [b]Ezek. 5:11; 7:20
19 [1]So with Gr. and many mss.; Heb., *you* [a]Jer. 24:7; 32:39; Ezek. 18:31; 36:26 [b]Zech. 7:12; Rom. 2:4, 5 [c]2 Cor. 3:3
20 [a]Ps. 105:45; Ezek. 36:27 [b]Ezek. 14:11
21 [1]Lit., *And to the heart of their detestable things and their abomination their heart goes.* [a]Jer. 16:18; Ezek. 11:18 [b]Ezek. 9:10; 16:43
22 [1]Lit., *over them from above* [a]Ezek. 10:19 [b]Ezek. 43:2
23 [a]Ezek. 8:4 [b]Zech. 14:4
24 [1]I.e., Babylonia [2]Lit., *went up from* [a]Ezek. 8:3; 11:1; 37:1; 2 Cor. 12:2-4 [b]Acts 10:16
25 [a]Ezek. 2:7; 3:4, 17, 27

2 [a]Is. 6:5 [b]Ps. 78:40; Is. 1:23; Ezek. 2:7, 8 [c]Is. 6:9f.; 43:8; Jer. 5:21; Matt. 13:13, 14; Mark 4:12; 8:18; Luke 8:10; John 9:39-41; 12:40; Acts 28:26f.; Rom. 11:8
3 [1]Or, *see that they are* [a]Jer. 26:3; 36:3, 7; Luke 20:13; 2 Tim. 2:25
4 [a]2 Kin. 25:4; Jer. 39:4; Ezek. 12:12
5 [1]Lit., *bring it out*
6 [a]1 Sam. 28:8; Ezek. 12:12, 13 [b]Is. 8:18; 20:3; Ezek. 4:3; 12:11; 24:24
7 [a]Ezek. 24:18; 37:7, 10 [b]Ezek. 12:3-6
9 [a]Ezek. 2:5-8; 12:1-3 [b]Ezek. 17:12; 20:49; 24:19
10 [1]Heb., *YHWH*, usually rendered *LORD*, and so throughout the ch. [2]Or, *oracle* [3]Lit., *in their midst* [a]2 Kin. 9:25; Is. 13:1; Ezek. 12:3-8
11 [1]Lit., *your sign* [a]Ezek. 12:6 [b]Jer. 15:2; 52:15, 28-30; Ezek. 12:3
12 [1]I.e., the king's attendants [a]2 Kin. 25:4; Jer. 39:4; 52:7; Ezek. 12:6
13 [a]Is. 24:17, 18; Ezek. 17:20; 19:8; Hos. 7:12 [b]Jer. 39:7; 52:11
14 [a]2 Kin. 25:4, 5; Ezek. 5:2; 17:21
15 [a]Ezek. 6:7, 14; 12:16, 20
16 [1]Lit., *leave over* [2]Or, *they will know* [a]Ezek. 7:15; 14:21 [b]Jer. 22:8, 9
18 [a]Lam. 5:9; Ezek. 4:16
19 [1]Lit., *her* [2]Lit., *desolate* [a]Jer. 10:22; Ezek. 6:6, 7, 14; Mic. 7:13; Zech. 7:14
20 [a]Is. 3:26; Jer. 4:7; Ezek. 5:14 [b]Is. 7:23, 24; Jer. 25:9; Ezek. 36:3
22 [a]Ezek. 16:44; 18:2, 3 [b]Jer. 5:12; Ezek. 11:3; 12:27; Amos 6:3; 2 Pet. 3:4 [c]Ezek. 7:26
23 [1]Lit., *word* [a]Ps. 37:13; Joel 2:1; Zeph. 1:14
24 [1]Lit., *vain* [a]Jer. 14:13-16; Ezek. 13:6, 23; Zech. 13:2-4

25"For I the LORD shall speak, and whatever [a]word I speak will be performed. It will no longer be delayed, for in [b]your days, O [c]rebellious house, I shall speak the word and perform it," declares the Lord GOD.' "

26 Furthermore, the word of the LORD came to me saying,

27"Son of man, behold, the house of Israel is saying, 'The vision that he sees is for [a]many [1]years *from now,* and he prophesies of times far off.'

28"Therefore say to them, 'Thus says the Lord GOD, "None of My words will be delayed any longer. Whatever word I speak will be performed," ' " declares the Lord GOD.

False Prophets Condemned

13 THEN the word of the LORD came to me saying,

2"Son of man, prophesy against the [a]prophets of Israel who prophesy, and say to those who prophesy from their own [1]inspiration, '[b]Listen to the word of the LORD!

3 'Thus says the Lord [1]GOD, "Woe to the [a]foolish prophets who are following their own spirit and have [b]seen nothing.

4"O Israel, your prophets have been like foxes among ruins.

5"You have not [a]gone up into the [b]breaches, nor did you build the wall around the house of Israel to stand in the battle on the [c]day of the LORD.

6"They see [1a]falsehood and lying divination who are saying, 'The LORD declares,' when the LORD has not sent them; [b]yet they hope for the fulfillment of *their* word.

7"[a]Did you not see a false vision and speak a lying divination when you said, 'The LORD declares,' but it is not I who have spoken?" ' "

8 Therefore, thus says the Lord GOD, "Because you have spoken [1]falsehood and seen a lie, therefore behold, [a]I am against you," declares the Lord GOD.

9"So My hand will be against the [a]prophets who see false visions and utter lying divinations. They will [1]have no place in the council of My people, [b]nor will they be written down in the register of the house of Israel, nor will they enter the land of Israel, [2]that you may know that I am the Lord GOD.

10"It is definitely because they have [a]misled My people by saying, '[b]Peace!' when there is [c]no peace. And when anyone builds a wall, behold, they plaster it over with whitewash;

11 *so* tell those who plaster it over with whitewash, that it will fall. A [a]flooding rain will come, and you, O hailstones, will fall; and a violent wind will break out.

12"Behold, when the wall has fallen, will you not be asked, 'Where is the plaster with which you plastered *it*?' "

13 Therefore, thus says the Lord GOD, "I will make a violent wind break out in My wrath. There will also be in My anger a flooding rain and [a]hailstones to consume *it* in wrath.

14"So I shall tear down the wall which you plastered over with whitewash and bring it down to the ground, so that its [a]foundation is laid bare; and when it falls, you will be [b]consumed in its midst. And you will [c]know that I am the LORD.

15"Thus I shall spend My wrath on the wall and on those who have plastered it over with whitewash; and I shall say to you, 'The wall [1]is gone and its plasterers are gone,

16 *along with* the prophets of Israel who prophesy to Jerusalem, and who [a]see visions of peace for her when there is [b]no peace,' declares the Lord GOD.

17"Now you, son of man, set your face against the daughters of your people who are [a]prophesying [b]from their own [1]inspiration. Prophesy against them,

18 and say, 'Thus says the Lord GOD, "Woe to the women who sew *magic* bands on [1]all wrists, and make veils for the heads of *persons* of every stature to [a]hunt down [2]lives! Will you hunt down the [2]lives of My people, but preserve the [2]lives *of others* for yourselves?

19"And [a]for handfuls of barley and fragments of bread, you have profaned Me to My people to put to death [1]some who should not die and to [b]keep [1]others alive who should not live, by your lying to My people who listen to lies." ' "

20 Therefore, thus says the Lord GOD, "Behold, I am against your *magic* bands by which you hunt [1]lives there as [2]birds, and I will tear them off your arms; and I will let [1]them go, even those [1]lives whom you hunt as [2]birds.

21"I will also tear off your veils and [a]deliver My people from your hands, and they will no longer be in your hands to be hunted; and you will know that I am the LORD.

22"Because you [a]disheartened the righteous with falsehood when I did not cause him grief, but have [1b]encouraged the wicked not to [c]turn from his wicked way *and* preserve his life,

23 therefore, you women will no longer see [1a]false visions or practice divination, and I will [b]deliver My people out of your hand. Thus you will [c]know that I am the LORD."

Idolatrous Elders Condemned

14 THEN some [a]elders of Israel came to me and [b]sat down before me.

2 And the word of the LORD came to me saying,

3"Son of man, these men have [a]set up their idols in their hearts, and have [b]put right before their faces the stumbling block of their iniquity. Should I be [c]consulted by them at all?

25 [a]Num. 14:28-34; Is. 14:24; Ezek. 6:10; 12:28 [b]Jer. 16:9; Hab. 1:5 [c]Ezek. 12:2
27 [1]Lit., *days* [a]Ezek. 12:22; Dan. 10:14

2 [1]Lit., *heart* [a]Is. 9:15; Jer. 37:19; Ezek. 22:25, 28 [b]Is. 1:10; Amos 7:16
3 [1]Heb., *YHWH,* usually rendered *LORD,* and so throughout the ch. [a]Lam. 2:14; Hos. 9:7; Zech. 11:15 [b]Jer. 23:28-32
5 [a]Ps. 106:23; Jer. 23:22; Ezek. 22:30 [b]Is. 58:12 [c]Is. 13:6, 9; Ezek. 7:19
6 [1]Lit., *vanity* [a]Jer. 29:8; Ezek. 22:28 [b]Jer. 28:15; 37:19
7 [a]Ezek. 22:28
8 [1]Lit., *vanity* [a]Ezek. 5:8; 21:3; Nah. 2:13
9 [1]Lit., *not be in* [2]Or, *and you will know* [a]Jer. 20:3-6; 28:15-17 [b]Ps. 69:28; 87:6; Jer. 17:13; Dan. 12:1
10 [a]Jer. 23:32; 50:6 [b]Jer. 6:14; 8:11; 14:13 [c]Ezek. 7:25; 13:16
11 [a]Ezek. 38:22
13 [a]Ex. 9:24, 25; Ps. 18:12, 13; Is. 30:30; Rev. 11:19; 16:21
14 [a]Mic. 1:6; Hab. 3:13 [b]Jer. 6:15; 14:15 [c]Ezek. 13:9
15 [1]Lit., *is not . . . are not*
16 [a]Jer. 6:14; 8:11; Ezek. 13:10 [b]Is. 57:21
17 [1]Lit., *heart* [a]Judg. 4:4; 2 Kin. 22:14; Luke 2:36; Acts 21:9 [b]Ezek. 13:2; Rev. 2:20
18 [1]Lit., *all joints of the hand;* M.T. reads *of my hands* [2]Or, *souls* [a]2 Pet. 2:14
19 [1]Or, *souls* [a]Prov. 28:21; Mic. 3:5 [b]Jer. 23:14, 17
20 [1]Lit., *souls* [2]Or, *flying ones*
21 [a]Ps. 91:3; 124:7
22 [1]Lit., *strengthen the hands of* [a]Amos 5:12 [b]Jer. 23:14; 34:16, 22 [c]Ezek. 18:21, 27, 30-32; 33:14-16
23 [1]Lit., *vanity* [a]Ezek. 12:24; 13:6; Mic. 3:6; Zech. 13:3 [b]Ezek. 13:21; 34:10 [c]Ezek. 13:9, 21

1 [a]2 Kin. 6:32; Ezek. 8:1; 20:1 [b]Is. 29:13; Ezek. 33:31, 32
3 [a]Ezek. 20:16 [b]Ezek. 7:19; 14:4, 7; Zeph. 1:3 [c]Is. 1:15; Jer. 11:11; Ezek. 20:3, 31

4"Therefore speak to them and tell
them, 'Thus says the Lord [1]GOD, "Any
man of the house of Israel who sets up
his idols in his heart, puts right before
his face the stumbling block of his
iniquity, and *then* comes to the prophet,
I the LORD will be brought to give him
an answer in [2]the matter in view of the
[a]multitude of his idols,
5 in order to lay hold of [1a]the hearts
of the house of Israel who are [2]es-
tranged from Me through all their
idols." '
6"Therefore say to the house of Israel, 'Thus says the Lord GOD, "[a]Repent
and turn away from your idols, and turn
your faces away from all your [b]abomina-
tions.
7"For anyone of the house of Israel
or of the [a]immigrants who stay in Israel
who separates himself from Me, sets up
his idols in his heart, puts right before
his face the stumbling block of his
iniquity, and *then* comes to the prophet
to inquire of Me for himself, [b]I the LORD
will be brought to answer him in My
own person.
8"And I shall [a]set My face against
that man and make him a [b]sign and [1]a
proverb, and I shall cut him off from
among My people. So you will know
that I am the LORD.
9"But if the prophet is [1]prevailed
upon to speak a word, it is I, the LORD,
who have [1]prevailed upon that prophet,
and I will stretch out My hand against
him and [a]destroy him from among My
people Israel.
10"And they will bear *the punishment
of* their iniquity; as the iniquity of the
inquirer is, so the iniquity of the prophet
will be,
11 in order that the house of Israel
may no longer [a]stray from Me and no
longer [b]defile themselves with all their
transgressions. Thus they will be [c]My
people, and I shall be their God," '
declares the Lord GOD."

The City Will Not Be Spared

12 Then the word of the LORD came
to me saying,
13"Son of man, if a country sins
against Me by [a]committing unfaithfulness, and I stretch out My hand against
it, [1]destroy its [b]supply of bread, send
famine against it, and cut off from it
both man and beast,
14 even [a]*though* these three men,
[b]Noah, [c]Daniel, and [d]Job were in its
midst, by their *own* righteousness they
could *only* deliver [e]themselves," declares
the Lord GOD.
15"If I were to cause [a]wild beasts to
pass through the land, and they [1]de-
populated it, and it became desolate so
that no one would pass through it because of the beasts,
16 *though* these three men were in its
midst, as I live," declares the Lord GOD,
"they could not deliver either *their* sons
or *their* daughters. [a]They alone would be
delivered, but the country would be
desolate.
17"Or *if* I should [a]bring a sword on
that country and say, 'Let the sword
pass through the country and [b]cut off
man and beast from it,'
18 even *though* these three men were
in its midst, as I live," declares the Lord
GOD, "they could not deliver either *their*
sons or *their* daughters, but they alone
would be delivered.
19"Or *if* I should send a [a]plague
against that country and pour out My
wrath in blood on it, to cut off man and
beast from it,
20 even *though* Noah, Daniel, and Job
were in its midst, as I live," declares the
Lord GOD, "they could not deliver either
their son or *their* daughter. They would
deliver only themselves by their righteousness."
21 For thus says the Lord GOD, "How
much more when [a]I send My four [1]se-
vere judgments against Jerusalem:
sword, famine, wild beasts, and plague
to cut off man and beast from it!
22"Yet, behold, [1]survivors will be left
in it who will be brought out, *both* sons
and daughters. Behold, they are going to
come forth to you and you will [a]see their
conduct and actions; then you will be
[b]comforted for the calamity which I
have brought against Jerusalem for
everything which I have brought upon it.
23"Then they will comfort you when
you see their conduct and actions, for
you will know that I have not done [a]in
vain whatever I did [1]to it," declares the
Lord GOD.

Jerusalem like a Useless Vine

15 THEN the word of the LORD
came to me saying,
2"Son of man, how is the wood of the
[a]vine *better* than any wood of a branch
which is among the trees of the forest?
3"Can wood be taken from it to make
[1]anything, or can *men* take a peg from it
on which to hang any vessel?
4"[1]If it has been put into the [a]fire for
fuel, *and* the fire has consumed both of
its ends, and its middle part has been
charred, is it *then* useful for [2]anything?
5"Behold, while it is intact, it is not
made into [1]anything. How much less,
when the fire has consumed it and it is
charred, can it still be made into [1]any-
thing!
6"Therefore, thus says the Lord
[1]GOD, 'As the wood of the vine among
the trees of the forest, which I have given
to the fire for fuel, so have I given up the
inhabitants of Jerusalem;
7 and I [a]set My face against them.
Though they have [b]come out of the fire,
yet the fire will consume them. Then you
will know that I am the LORD, when I set
My face against them.
8 'Thus I will make the land desolate,
because they have [a]acted unfaithfully,' "
declares the Lord GOD.

4 [1]Heb., *YHWH,* usually rendered *LORD,* and so throughout the ch. [2]Lit., *it* [a]1 Kin. 21:20-24; 2 Kin. 1:16; Is. 66:4
5 [1]Lit., *their* [2]Or, *all estranged from Me through their idols* [a]Jer. 17:10; Zech. 7:12 [b]Is. 1:4; Jer. 2:11; Zech. 11:8
6 [a]1 Sam. 7:3; Neh. 1:9; Is. 2:20; 30:22; 55:6, 7; Ezek. 18:30 [b]Ezek. 8:6; 14:4
7 [a]Ex. 12:48; 20:10 [b]Ezek. 14:4
8 [1]Lit., *proverbs* [a]Jer. 44:11; Ezek. 15:7 [b]Is. 65:15; Ezek. 5:15
9 [1]Or, *enticed* [a]Jer. 6:14, 15; 14:15
11 [a]Ezek. 44:10, 15; 48:11 [b]Ezek. 11:18; 37:23 [c]Ezek. 11:20; 34:30; 36:28
13 [1]Lit., *break the staff* [a]Ezek. 15:8; 20:27 [b]Lev. 26:26; Is. 3:1; Ezek. 4:16
14 [a]Jer. 15:1 [b]Gen. 6:8; 7:1; Heb. 11:7 [c]Ezek. 28:3; Dan. 1:6; 9:21; 10:11 [d]Job 1:1, 5; 42:8, 9 [e]Ezek. 16:18, 20; 18:20
15 [1]Lit., *bereave of children* [a]Lev. 26:22; Num. 21:6; Ezek. 5:17; 14:21
16 [a]Gen. 19:29; Ezek. 18:20
17 [a]Lev. 26:25; Ezek. 5:12; 21:3, 4 [b]Ezek. 25:13; Zeph. 1:3
19 [a]Jer. 14:12; Ezek. 5:12; 14:21
21 [1]Lit., *evil* [a]Ezek. 5:17; 33:27; Amos 4:6-10; Rev. 6:8
22 [1]Lit., *escaped ones* [a]Ezek. 12:16; 36:20 [b]Ezek. 16:54; 31:16; 32:31
23 [1]Or, *in* [a]Jer. 22:8, 9

2 [a]Ps. 80:8-16; Is. 5:1-7; Hos. 10:1
3 [1]Lit., *a work*
4 [1]Or, *Behold* [2]Lit., *a work* [a]Is. 27:11; Ezek. 15:6; 19:14
5 [1]Lit., *a work*
6 [1]Heb., *YHWH,* usually rendered *LORD,* and so throughout the ch.
7 [a]Lev. 26:17; Ps. 34:16; Jer. 21:10; Ezek. 14:8 [b]1 Kin. 19:17; Is. 24:18; Amos 9:1-4
8 [a]Ezek. 14:13; 17:20

God's Grace to Unfaithful Jerusalem

16 THEN the word of the LORD
came to me saying,
2 “Son of man, [a]make known to Jerusalem her abominations,
3 and say, ‘Thus says the Lord [1]GOD
to Jerusalem, “Your origin and your
birth are from the land of the Canaanite,
your father was an Amorite and your
mother a Hittite.
4 “As for your birth, [a]on the day you
were born your navel cord was not cut,
nor were you washed with water for
cleansing; you were not rubbed with salt
or even wrapped in cloths.
5 “No eye looked with pity on you to
do any of these things for you, to have
compassion on you. Rather you were
thrown out into the [1a]open field, [2]for
you were abhorred on the day you were
born.
6 “When I passed by you and saw you
squirming in your blood, I said to you
while you were in your blood, ‘Live!’ I
said to you while you were in your
blood, ‘Live!’
7 “I [a]made you [1]numerous like plants
of the field. Then you grew up, became
tall, and reached the age for fine ornaments; *your* breasts were formed and
your hair had grown. Yet you were
naked and bare.
8 “Then I passed by you and saw you,
and behold, [1]you were at the time for
love; so I [a]spread My skirt over you and
covered your nakedness. I also [b]swore to
you and [c]entered into a covenant with
you so that you [d]became Mine,” declares
the Lord GOD.
9 “Then I bathed you with water,
washed off your blood from you, and
[a]anointed you with oil.
10 “I also clothed you with [a]embroi-
dered cloth, and put sandals of porpoise
skin on your feet; and I wrapped you
with fine linen and covered you with silk.
11 “And I adorned you with ornaments, put [a]bracelets on your hands, and
a [b]necklace around your neck.
12 “I also put a [a]ring in your nostril,
earrings in your ears, and a [b]beautiful
crown on your head.
13 “Thus you were adorned with [a]gold
and silver, and your dress was of fine
linen, silk, and embroidered cloth. You
ate fine flour, honey, and oil; so you
were exceedingly beautiful and advanced
to [b]royalty.
14 “Then your [a]fame went forth among
the nations on account of your beauty,
for it was [b]perfect because of My splendor which I bestowed on you,” declares
the Lord GOD.
15 “But you [a]trusted in your beauty
and [b]played the harlot because of your
fame, and you poured out your harlotries on every passer-by [1]who might be
willing.
16 “And you took some of your clothes,
made for yourself high places of various
colors, and played the harlot on them,
[1]which should never come about nor
happen.
17 “You also took your beautiful [1a]jew-
els *made* of My gold and of My silver,
which I had given you, and made for
yourself male images that you might
play the harlot with them.
18 “Then you took your embroidered
cloth and covered them, and offered My
oil and My incense before them.
19 “Also [a]My bread which I gave you,
fine flour, oil, and honey with which I
fed you, [1]you would offer before them
for a soothing aroma; so it happened,”
declares the Lord GOD.
20 “Moreover, you took your sons and
daughters whom you had borne to [a]Me,
and you [b]sacrificed them to [1]idols to be
devoured. Were your harlotries so small
a matter?
21 “You slaughtered [a]My children, and
offered them up to [1]idols by [b]causing
them to pass through *the fire*.
22 “And besides all your abominations
and harlotries you did not remember the
days of [a]your youth, when you were
naked and bare and squirming in your
blood.
23 “Then it came about after all your
wickedness (‘Woe, woe to you!’ declares
the Lord GOD),
24 that you built yourself a [a]shrine
and made yourself a [b]high place in every
square.
25 “You built yourself a high place at
the top of [a]every street, and made your
beauty abominable; and you spread
your legs to every passer-by to multiply
your harlotry.
26 “You also played the harlot with the
Egyptians, your [1]lustful neighbors, and
multiplied your harlotry to [a]make Me
angry.
27 “Behold now, I have stretched out
My hand against you and diminished
your rations. And I delivered you up to
the desire of those who hate you, the
[a]daughters of the Philistines, who are
ashamed of your lewd conduct.
28 “Moreover, you played the harlot
with the [a]Assyrians because you were
not satisfied; you even played the harlot
with them and still were not satisfied.
29 “You also multiplied your harlotry
with the land of merchants, Chaldea, yet
even with this you were not satisfied.” ’ ”
30 “How [a]languishing is your heart,”
declares the Lord GOD, “while you do
all these things, the actions of a [1b]bold-
faced harlot.
31 “When you built your shrine at the
beginning of every street and made your
high place in every square, in [a]disdaining
money, you were not like a harlot.
32 “You adulteress wife, who takes
strangers instead of her husband!
33 “[1]Men give gifts to all harlots, but
you [a]give your gifts to all your lovers to
bribe them to come to you from every
direction for your harlotries.

2 [a]Is. 58:1; Ezek. 20:4; 22:2
3 [1]Heb., *YHWH*, usually rendered *LORD*, and so throughout the ch.
4 [a]Hos. 2:3
5 [1]Lit., *surface* [2]Lit., *in the loathing of your soul* [a]Deut. 32:10
7 [1]Lit., *a myriad* [a]Ex. 1:7; Deut. 1:10
8 [1]Lit., *your time was* [a]Ruth 3:9; Jer. 2:2 [b]Gen. 22:16-18 [c]Ex. 24:7, 8 [d]Ex. 19:5; Ezek. 20:5; Hos. 2:19, 20
9 [a]Ruth 3:3
10 [a]Ex. 26:36; Ezek. 16:13, 18; 26:16; 27:7, 16
11 [a]Gen. 24:22, 47; Is. 3:19; Ezek. 23:42 [b]Gen. 41:42; Prov. 1:9
12 [a]Gen. 24:47; Is. 3:21 [b]Is. 28:5; Jer. 13:18; Ezek. 16:14
13 [a]Ps. 45:13, 14; Ezek. 16:17 [b]1 Sam. 10:1; 1 Kin. 4:21
14 [a]1 Kin. 10:1, 24 [b]Ps. 50:2; Lam. 2:15
15 [1]Lit., *to whom it might be* [a]Ezek. 16:25; 27:3 [b]Is. 57:8; Jer. 2:20
16 [1]Lit., *things which had not happened nor will it be*
17 [1]Lit., *articles of beauty* [a]Ezek. 16:11, 12
19 [1]Lit., *and you . . . offer it* [a]Hos. 2:8
20 [1]Lit., *them* [a]Ex. 13:2, 12; Deut. 29:11, 12 [b]Ps. 106:37, 38; Jer. 7:31; Ezek. 20:31; 23:37
21 [1]Lit., *them* [a]Ex. 13:2 [b]2 Kin. 17:17; Jer. 19:5
22 [a]Jer. 2:2
24 [a]Jer. 11:13; Ezek. 16:31, 39; 20:28, 29 [b]Ps. 78:58; Is. 57:7
25 [a]Prov. 9:14
26 [1]Lit., *great of flesh* [a]Jer. 7:18, 19; Ezek. 8:17
27 [a]Is. 9:12; Ezek. 16:57
28 [a]2 Kin. 16:7, 10-18; 2 Chr. 28:16, 20-23; Jer. 2:18, 36; Ezek. 23:12; Hos. 10:6
30 [1]Lit., *domineering* [a]Prov. 9:13; Is. 1:3; Jer. 4:22 [b]Is. 3:9; Jer. 3:3
31 [a]Is. 52:3
33 [1]Lit., *they* [a]Is. 57:9; Ezek. 16:41; Hos. 8:9, 10

34 "Thus you are different from those women in your harlotries, in that no one plays the harlot [1]as you do, because you give money and no money is given you; thus you are different."

35 Therefore, O harlot, hear the word of the LORD.

36 Thus says the Lord GOD, "Because your lewdness was poured out and your nakedness uncovered through your harlotries with your lovers and with all your detestable [a]idols, and because of the blood of your sons which you gave to [1]idols,

37 therefore, behold, I shall [a]gather all your lovers with whom you took pleasure, even all those whom you loved *and* all those whom you [b]hated. So I shall gather them against you from every direction and [c]expose your nakedness to them that they may see all your nakedness.

38 "Thus I shall [a]judge you, like women who commit adultery or shed blood are judged; and I shall bring on you the blood of [b]wrath and jealousy.

39 "I shall also give you into [1]the hands of your lovers, and they will tear down your shrines, demolish your high places, [a]strip you of your clothing, take away your [2]jewels, and will leave you naked and bare.

40 "They will [1]incite a [a]crowd against you, and they will stone you and cut you to pieces with their swords.

41 "And they will [a]burn your houses with fire and execute judgments on you in the sight of many women. Then I shall [b]stop you from playing the harlot, and you will also no longer pay [1]your lovers.

42 "So I [a]shall calm My fury against you, and My jealousy will depart from you, and I shall be pacified and angry [b]no more.

43 "Because you have [a]not remembered the days of your youth but [1]have [b]enraged Me by all these things, behold, I in turn will [c]bring your conduct down on your own head," declares the Lord GOD, "so that you will not commit this lewdness on top of all your *other* abominations.

44 "Behold, everyone who quotes [a]proverbs will quote *this* proverb concerning you, saying, '[1]Like mother, [1]like daughter.'

45 "You are the daughter of your mother, who loathed her husband and children. You are also the [a]sister of your sisters, who [b]loathed their husbands and children. Your mother was a Hittite and your father an Amorite.

46 "Now your [a]older sister is Samaria, who lives [1]north of you with her [2]daughters; and your younger sister, who lives [3]south of you, is [b]Sodom with her [2]daughters.

47 "Yet you have not merely walked in their ways or done according to their abominations; but, as if that were [a]too little, you acted [b]more corruptly in all your conduct than they.

48 "As I live," declares the Lord GOD, "Sodom, your sister, and her daughters, have [a]not done as you and your daughters have done.

49 "Behold, this was the guilt of your sister Sodom: she and her daughters had [a]arrogance, [b]abundant food, and [c]careless ease, but she did not [1]help the [d]poor and needy.

50 "Thus they were haughty and committed [a]abominations before Me. Therefore I [b]removed them [1]when I saw *it.*

51 "Furthermore, Samaria did not commit half of your sins, for you have multiplied your abominations more than they. Thus you have made your sisters appear [a]righteous by all your abominations which you have committed.

52 "Also bear your disgrace in that you have [1]made judgment favorable for your sisters. Because of your sins in which you acted [a]more abominably than they, they are more in the right than you. Yes, be also ashamed and bear your disgrace, in that you made your sisters appear righteous.

53 "Nevertheless, I will restore their captivity, the captivity of Sodom and her daughters, the captivity of Samaria and her daughters, and [1]along with them [2]your own captivity,

54 in order that you may bear your humiliation, and feel [a]ashamed for all that you have done when you become [b]a consolation to them.

55 "And your sisters, Sodom with her daughters and Samaria with her daughters, [1]will return to their former state, and you with your daughters will *also* return to your former state.

56 "As *the name of* your sister Sodom was not heard from your lips in your day of pride,

57 before your [a]wickedness was uncovered, [1]so now you have become the [b]reproach of the daughters of [2]Edom, and of all who are around her, of the daughters of the Philistines—those surrounding *you* who despise you.

58 "You have [a]borne *the penalty of* your lewdness and abominations," the LORD declares.

59 For thus says the Lord GOD, "I will also do with you as you have done, you who have [a]despised the oath by breaking the covenant.

The Covenant Remembered

60 "Nevertheless, I will remember My covenant with you in the days of your youth, and I will establish an [a]everlasting covenant with you.

61 "Then you will [a]remember your ways and be ashamed when you receive your sisters, *both* your older and your younger; and I will give them to you as daughters, but not because of your covenant.

34 [1]Lit., *after you*
36 [1]Lit., *them* [a]Jer. 19:5; Ezek. 20:31; 23:37
37 [a]Jer. 13:22, 26; Ezek. 23:9, 22; Hos. 2:3, 10; Nah. 3:5, 6 [b]Ezek. 23:17, 28 [c]Is. 47:3
38 [a]Ezek. 23:45 [b]Ps. 79:3, 5; Jer. 18:21; Ezek. 23:25; Zeph. 1:17
39 [1]Lit., *their hands, and they* [2]Lit., *articles of beauty* [a]Ezek. 23:26; Hos. 2:3
40 [1]Lit., *bring up an assembly* [a]Ezek. 23:47; Hab. 1:6-10
41 [1]Lit., *a harlot's hire* [a]2 Kin. 25:9; Jer. 39:8; 52:13 [b]Ezek. 23:48
42 [a]2 Sam. 24:25; Ezek. 5:13; 21:17; Zech. 6:8 [b]Is. 40:1, 2; 54:9, 10; Ezek. 39:29
43 [1]So with ancient versions; Heb., *are angry against* [a]Ps. 78:42; 106:13; Ezek. 16:22 [b]Is. 63:10; Ezek. 6:9 [c]Ezek. 11:21; 22:31
44 [1]Lit., *Her* [a]1 Sam. 24:13; Ezek. 12:22, 23; 18:2, 3
45 [a]Ezek. 23:2 [b]Is. 1:4; Ezek. 23:37-39; Zech. 11:8
46 [1]Lit., *on your left* [2]I.e., environs; so through v. 55 [3]Lit., *from your right* [a]Jer. 3:8-11; Ezek. 23:4 [b]Gen. 13:10-13; 18:20; Ezek. 16:48, 49, 53-56, 61
47 [a]1 Kin. 16:31 [b]2 Kin. 21:9; Ezek. 5:6; 16:48, 51
48 [a]Matt. 10:15; 11:23, 24
49 [1]Lit., *grasp the hand of* [a]Gen. 19:9; Ps. 138:6; Is. 3:9; Ezek. 28:2, 9, 17 [b]Gen. 13:10; Is. 22:13; Amos 6:4-6 [c]Luke 12:16-20; 16:19 [d]Ezek. 18:7, 12, 16
50 [1]Many ancient mss. and versions read *as you have seen* [a]Gen. 13:13; 18:20; 19:5 [b]Gen. 19:24, 25
51 [a]Jer. 3:8-11
52 [1]Lit., *mediated for* [a]Ezek. 16:47, 48, 51
53 [1]Lit., *in their midst* [2]Lit., *the captivity of your captivity*
54 [a]Jer. 2:26 [b]Ezek. 14:22, 23
55 [1]Heb. includes *will return . . . state* after Sodom also
57 [1]Lit., *as at the time of* [2]So with many mss. and one version; M.T., *Aram* [a]Ezek. 16:36, 37 [b]2 Kin. 16:5-7; 2 Chr. 28:5, 6, 18-23; Ezek. 5:14, 15; 22:4
58 [a]Ezek. 23:49
59 [a]Is. 24:5; Ezek. 17:19
60 [a]Is. 55:3; Jer. 32:38-41; Ezek. 37:26
61 [a]Jer. 50:4, 5; Ezek. 6:9

62“Thus I will [a]establish My covenant
with you, and you shall [b]know that I am
the LORD,
63 in order that you may [a]remember
and be ashamed, and [b]never open your
mouth anymore because of your humiliation, when I have [c]forgiven you for all
that you have done,” the Lord GOD
declares.

Parable of Two Eagles and a Vine

17 NOW the word of the LORD
came to me saying,
2“Son of man, propound a riddle,
and speak a [a]parable to the house of
Israel,
3 [1]saying, ‘Thus says the Lord [2]GOD,
“A great [a]eagle with [b]great wings, long
pinions and a full plumage of many
colors, came to [c]Lebanon and took away
the top of the cedar.
4“He plucked off the topmost of its
young twigs and brought it to a land of
merchants; he set it in a city of traders.
5“He also took some of the seed of
the land and planted it in [1a]fertile soil.
He [2]placed *it* beside abundant waters; he
set it *like* a [b]willow.
6“Then it sprouted and became a
low, spreading vine with its branches
turned toward him, but its roots remained under it. So it became a vine,
and yielded shoots and sent out
branches.
7“But there was [1]another great eagle
with great wings and much plumage;
and behold, this vine bent its roots
toward him and sent out its branches
toward him from the beds where it was
[a]planted, that he might water it.
8“It was planted in good [1]soil beside
abundant waters, that it might yield
branches and bear fruit, *and* become a
splendid vine.” ’
9“Say, ‘Thus says the Lord GOD,
“Will it thrive? Will he not pull up its
roots and cut off its fruit, so that it
withers—so that all its sprouting leaves
wither? And neither by great [1]strength
nor by many people can it be raised
from its roots *again*.
10“Behold, though it is planted, will it
thrive? Will it not [a]completely wither as
soon as the east wind strikes it—wither
on the beds where it grew?” ’ ”

Zedekiah’s Rebellion

11 Moreover, the word of the LORD
came to me saying,
12“Say now to the [a]rebellious house,
‘Do you not [b]know what these things
mean?’ Say, ‘Behold, the [c]king of Babylon came to Jerusalem, took its king and
princes, and brought them to him in
Babylon.
13 ‘And he took one of the royal
[1a]family and made a covenant with him,
[2]putting him under [b]oath. He also took
away the [c]mighty of the land,
14 that the kingdom might [a]be [1]in
subjection, not exalting itself, *but* keeping his covenant, that it might continue.
15 ‘But he [a]rebelled against him by
sending his envoys to Egypt that they
might give him horses and many [1]troops.
Will he succeed? Will he who does such
things [b]escape? Can he indeed break the
covenant and escape?
16 ‘As I live,’ declares the Lord GOD,
‘Surely in the [1]country of the king who
[2]put him on the throne, whose oath he
[a]despised, and whose covenant he broke,
[3b]in Babylon he shall die.
17 ‘And [a]Pharaoh with *his* mighty
army and great company will not [1]help
him in the war, when they cast up
mounds and build siege walls to cut off
many lives.
18 ‘Now he despised the oath by
breaking the covenant, and behold, he
[1a]pledged his allegiance, yet did all these
things; he shall not escape.’ ”
19 Therefore, thus says the Lord GOD,
“As I live, surely My oath which he
despised and My covenant which he
broke, I will [1]inflict on his head.
20“And I will spread My [a]net over
him, and he will be [b]caught in My snare.
Then I will bring him to Babylon and
[c]enter into judgment with him there
regarding the unfaithful act which he has
committed against Me.
21“And all the [1a]choice men in all his
troops will fall by the sword, and the
survivors will be scattered to every wind;
and you will know that I, the LORD,
have spoken.”
22 Thus says the Lord GOD, “I shall
also take *a sprig* from the lofty top of the
cedar and set *it* out; I shall pluck from
the topmost of its young twigs a tender
one, and I shall plant *it* on a [a]high and
lofty mountain.
23“On the high mountain of Israel I
shall plant it, that it may bring forth
boughs and bear fruit, and become a
stately [a]cedar. And birds of every [1]kind
will [2]nest under it; they will [2]nest in the
shade of its branches.
24“And all the [a]trees of the field will
know that I am the LORD; I bring down
the high tree, exalt the low tree, dry up
the green tree, and make the dry tree
[b]flourish. I am the LORD; I have spoken,
and I will perform *it*.”

God Deals Justly with Individuals

18 THEN the word of the LORD
came to me saying,
2“[a]What do you mean by using this
proverb concerning the land of Israel
saying,

‘[b]The fathers eat the sour grapes,
But the children’s teeth [1]are set on
edge’?

3“As I live,” declares the Lord [1]GOD,
“you are surely not going to use this
proverb in Israel anymore.
4“Behold, [a]all [1]souls are Mine; the
[2]soul of the father as well as the [2]soul of
the son is Mine. The [3]soul who [b]sins will
die.
5“But if a man is righteous, and
practices justice and righteousness,

---

62 [a]Ezek. 20:37; 34:25; 37:26 [b]Jer. 24:7; Ezek. 20:43, 44
63 [a]Ezek. 36:31, 32; Dan. 9:7, 8 [b]Ps. 39:9; Rom. 3:19 [c]Ps. 65:3; 78:38; 79:9

2 [a]Ezek. 20:49; 24:3
3 [1]Lit., *and you shall say* [2]Heb., *YHWH*, usually rendered *LORD*, and so throughout the ch.
[a]Jer. 48:40; Ezek. 17:12; Hos. 8:1 [b]Dan. 4:22 [c]Jer. 22:23
5 [1]Lit., *a field of seed* [2]Lit., *took* [a]Deut. 8:7-9 [b]Is. 44:4
7 [1]So with several ancient versions; M.T., *one* [a]Ezek. 31:4
8 [1]Lit., *field*
9 [1]Lit., *arm*
10 [a]Ezek. 19:14; Hos. 13:15
12 [a]Ezek. 2:3-5 [b]Ezek. 12:9-11; 24:19 [c]2 Kin. 24:11, 12, 15; Ezek. 1:2; 17:3
13 [1]Lit., *seed* [2]Lit., *and caused him to enter into an oath* [a]2 Kin. 24:17; Ezek. 17:5 [b]2 Chr. 36:13 [c]2 Kin. 24:15, 16
14 [1]Lit., *low* [a]Ezek. 29:14
15 [1]Lit., *people* [a]2 Kin. 24:20; 2 Chr. 36:13; Jer. 52:3; Ezek. 17:7 [b]Jer. 34:3; 38:18, 23; Ezek. 17:18
16 [1]Lit., *place* [2]Lit., *made him king* [3]Lit., *with him in Babylon* [a]2 Kin. 24:17, 20; Ezek. 16:59; 17:13, 18, 19 [b]Jer. 52:11; Ezek. 12:13
17 [1]Lit., *act with* [a]Is. 36:6; Jer. 37:5, 7; Ezek. 29:6, 7
18 [1]Lit., *gave his hand* [a]1 Chr. 29:24
19 [1]Lit., *give it*
20 [a]Ezek. 12:13; 32:3 [b]Jer. 39:5-7 [c]Jer. 2:35; Ezek. 20:35, 36
21 [1]So many ancient mss. and versions; M.T., *fugitives* [a]2 Kin. 25:5, 11; Ezek. 5:2, 10, 12-14
22 [a]Ps. 72:16; Ezek. 20:40; 37:22
23 [1]Lit., *wing* [2]Lit., *dwell* [a]Ps. 92:12
24 [a]Ps. 96:12; Is. 55:12 [b]Amos 9:11

2 [1]Lit., *become dull* [a]Is. 3:15 [b]Jer. 31:29; Lam. 5:7
3 [1]Heb., *YHWH*, usually rendered *LORD*, and so throughout the ch.
4 [1]Or, *lives* [2]Or, *life* [3]Or, *person* [a]Num. 16:22; 27:16; Is. 42:5; 57:16 [b]Ezek. 18:20; Rom. 6:23

6 and does not [a]eat at the mountain
shrines or [b]lift up his eyes to the idols of
the house of Israel, or [c]defile his neighbor's wife, or approach a woman during
her menstrual period—
7 if a man does not oppress anyone,
but [a]restores to the debtor his pledge,
[b]does not commit robbery, *but* [c]gives his
bread to the hungry, and covers the
naked with clothing,
8 if he does not lend *money* on [a]inter-
est or take [b]increase, *if* he keeps his hand
from iniquity, *and* [c]executes true justice
between man and man,
9 *if* he walks in [a]My statutes and My
ordinances so as to deal faithfully—[b]he
is righteous *and* will surely [c]live," declares the Lord GOD.
10"Then he may [1]have a violent son
who sheds blood, and who does any of
these things to a brother
11 (though he himself did not do any
of these things), that is, he even eats at
the mountain *shrines*, and [a]defiles his
neighbor's wife,
12 oppresses the [a]poor and needy,
[b]commits robbery, does not restore a
pledge, but lifts up his eyes to the idols,
and [c]commits abomination,
13 he [a]lends *money* on interest and
takes increase; will he live? He will not
live! He has committed all these abominations, he will surely be put to death;
his [b]blood will be [1]on his own head.
14"Now behold, he [1]has a son who has
observed all his father's sins which he
committed, and [a]observing does not do
likewise.
15"He does not eat at the mountain
shrines or lift up his eyes to the idols of
the house of Israel, or defile his neighbor's wife,
16 or oppress anyone, or retain a
pledge, or commit robbery, *but* he [a]gives
his bread to the hungry, and covers the
naked with clothing,
17 he keeps his hand from [1]the poor,
does not take interest or increase, *but*
executes My ordinances, and walks in
My statutes; [a]he will not die for his
father's iniquity, he will surely live.
18"As for his father, because he practiced extortion, robbed *his* brother, and
did what was not good among his people, behold, he will die for his iniquity.
19"Yet you say, '[a]Why should the son
not bear the punishment for the father's
iniquity?' When the son has practiced
[b]justice and righteousness, and has observed all My statutes and done them, he
shall surely live.
20"The person who [a]sins will die. The
[b]son will not bear the punishment for
the father's iniquity, nor will the father
bear the punishment for the son's iniquity; the [c]righteousness of the righteous
will be upon himself, and the wickedness
of the wicked will be upon himself.
21"But if the [a]wicked man turns from
all his sins which he has committed and
observes all My statutes and practices
justice and righteousness, he shall surely
live; he shall not die.
22"[a]All his transgressions which he has
committed will not be remembered
against him; because of his [b]righteous-
ness which he has practiced, he will live.
23"[a]Do I have any pleasure in the
death of the wicked," declares the Lord
GOD, "[1]rather than that he should [b]turn
from his ways and live?
24"But when a righteous man [a]turns
away from his righteousness, commits
iniquity, and does according to all the
abominations that a wicked man does,
will he live? [b]All his righteous deeds
which he has done will not be remembered for his [c]treachery which he has
committed and his sin which he has
committed; for them he will die.
25"Yet you say, '[a]The way of the Lord
is not right.' Hear now, O house of
Israel! Is [b]My way not right? Is it not
your ways that are not right?
26"When a righteous man turns away
from his righteousness, commits iniquity, and dies because of it, for his
iniquity which he has committed he will
die.
27"Again, when a wicked man turns
away [a]from his wickedness which he has
committed and practices justice and
righteousness, he will save his life.
28"Because he considered and turned
away from all his transgressions which
he had committed, he shall surely live;
he shall not die.
29"But the house of Israel says, 'The
way of the Lord is not right.' Are My
ways not right, O house of Israel? Is it
not your ways that are not right?
30"Therefore I will judge you, O house
of Israel, each according to his conduct,"
declares the Lord GOD. "[a]Repent and
turn away from all your transgressions,
so that iniquity may not become a stumbling block to you.
31"[a]Cast away from you all your
transgressions which you have committed, and make yourselves a [b]new
heart and a new spirit! For why will you
die, O house of Israel?
32"For I have [a]no pleasure in the
death of anyone who dies," declares the
Lord GOD. "Therefore, repent and live."

Lament for the Princes of Israel

19 "AS for you, take up a [a]lamenta-
tion for the [b]princes of Israel,
2 and say,
'[1]What was your mother?
A lioness among lions!
She lay down among young lions,
She reared her cubs.
3 'When she brought up one of her
cubs,
He became a lion,
And he learned to tear *his* prey;
He devoured men.
4 'Then nations heard about him;
He was captured in their pit,
And they [a]brought him with
hooks
To the land of Egypt.

6 [a]Ezek. 6:13; 18:15; 22:9 [b]Deut. 4:19; Ezek. 18:12, 15; 20:24; 33:25 [c]Ezek. 18:15; 22:11
7 [a]Deut. 24:13; Ezek. 33:15; Amos 2:8 [b]Lev. 19:13; Amos 3:10 [c]Deut. 15:11; Ezek. 18:16; Matt. 25:35-40; Luke 3:11
8 [a]Ex. 22:25; Deut. 23:19, 20 [b]Lev. 25:36 [c]Zech. 7:9; 8:16
9 [a]Lev. 18:5 [b]Rom. 8:1 [c]Amos 5:4; Hab. 2:4; Rom. 1:17
10 [1]Lit., *beget*
11 [a]1 Cor. 6:9
12 [a]Amos 4:1; Zech. 7:10 [b]Is. 59:6, 7; Jer. 22:3, 17; Ezek. 7:23; 18:7, 16, 18 [c]2 Kin. 21:11; Ezek. 8:6, 17
13 [1]Lit., *on him* [a]Ex. 22:25 [b]Ezek. 33:4, 5
14 [1]Lit., *begets* [a]2 Chr. 29:6-10; 34:21
16 [a]Job 31:16, 20; Ps. 41:1; Is. 58:7, 10; Ezek. 18:7
17 [1]So M.T.; Gr. reads *iniquity* as in v. 8 [a]Rom. 2:7
19 [a]Ex. 20:5; Jer. 15:4; Ezek. 18:2 [b]Ezek. 18:9; 20:18-20; Zech. 1:3-6
20 [a]2 Kin. 14:6; 22:18-20; Ezek. 18:4 [b]Deut. 24:16; Jer. 31:30 [c]1 Kin. 8:32; Is. 3:10, 11; Matt. 16:27; Rom. 2:6-9
21 [a]Ezek. 18:27, 28; 33:12, 19
22 [a]Is. 43:25; Jer. 50:20; Ezek. 18:24; 33:16; Mic. 7:19 [b]Ps. 18:20-24
23 [1]Lit., *is it not* [a]Ezek. 18:32; 33:11 [b]Ps. 147:11; Mic. 7:18
24 [a]1 Sam. 15:11; 2 Chr. 24:2, 17-22; Ezek. 3:20; 18:26; 33:18 [b]Ezek. 18:22; Gal. 3:3, 4 [c]Prov. 21:16; Ezek. 17:20; 20:27
25 [a]Ezek. 18:29; 33:17, 20; Mal. 2:17; 3:13-15 [b]Gen. 18:25; Jer. 12:1; Zeph. 3:5
27 [a]Is. 1:18; 55:7
30 [a]Ezek. 14:6; 33:11; Hos. 12:6
31 [a]Is. 1:16, 17; 55:7 [b]Ps. 51:10; Ezek. 11:19; 36:26
32 [a]Ezek. 18:23; 33:11

1 [a]Ezek. 2:10; 19:14 [b]2 Kin. 23:29, 30, 34; 24:6, 12; 25:5-7
2 [1]Or, *Why did your mother, a lioness, lie down among lions; among young lions rear her cubs?*
4 [a]2 Kin. 23:34; 2 Chr. 36:4, 6

5 'When she saw, as she waited,
That her hope was lost,
She took [1]another of her cubs
And made him a young lion.
6 'And he [a]walked about among the lions;
He became a young lion,
He learned to tear *his* prey;
He devoured men.
7 'And he [1]destroyed their [2]fortified towers
And laid waste their cities;
And the land and its fulness were appalled
Because of the sound of his roaring.
8 'Then [a]nations set against him
On every side from *their* provinces,
And they spread their net over him;
He was captured in their pit.
9 'And [a]they put him in a cage with hooks
And [b]brought him to the king of Babylon;
They brought him in hunting nets
So that his voice should be heard no more
On the mountains of Israel.
10 'Your mother was [a]like a vine in your [1]vineyard,
Planted by the waters;
It was fruitful and full of branches
Because of abundant waters.
11 'And it had [1a]strong branches *fit* for scepters of rulers,
And its [b]height was raised above the clouds
So that it was seen in its height with the mass of its branches.
12 'But it was [a]plucked up in fury;
It was [b]cast down to the ground;
And the [c]east wind dried up its fruit.
Its [1d]strong branch [2]was torn off
So that [3]it withered;
The fire consumed it.
13 'And now it is planted in the [a]wilderness,
In a dry and thirsty land.
14 'And [a]fire has gone out from *its* branch;
It has consumed its shoots *and* fruit,
So that there is not in it a [1]strong branch,
A scepter to rule.' "
This is a lamentation, and has become a lamentation.

God's Dealings with Israel Rehearsed

20 NOW it came about in the seventh year, in the fifth *month,* on the tenth of the month, that [1]certain of the [a]elders of Israel came to inquire of the LORD, and sat before me.
2 And the word of the LORD came to me saying,
3 "Son of man, speak to the elders of Israel, and say to them, 'Thus says the Lord [1]GOD, "Do you come to inquire of
Me? As I live," declares the Lord GOD,
"[a]I will not be inquired of by you." '
4 "Will you judge them, will you judge
them, son of man? [a]Make them know
the abominations of their fathers;
5 and say to them, 'Thus says the
Lord GOD, "On the day when I [a]chose
Israel and [1]swore to the [2]descendants of
the house of Jacob and made Myself
known to them in the land of Egypt,
when I [1]swore to them, saying, [b]I am the
LORD your God,
6 on that day I swore to them, [a]to
bring them out from the land of Egypt
into a land that I had [1]selected for them,
[b]flowing with milk and honey, which is
[c]the glory of all lands.
7 "And I said to them, '[a]Cast away,
each of you, the detestable things of his
eyes, and [b]do not defile yourselves with
the idols of Egypt; [c]I am the LORD your
God.'
8 "But they [a]rebelled against Me and
were not willing to listen to Me; [1]they
did not cast away the detestable things
of their eyes, nor did they forsake the
[b]idols of Egypt.
Then I [2]resolved to [c]pour out My
wrath on them, to accomplish My anger
against them in the midst of the land of
Egypt.
9 "But I acted [a]for the sake of My
name, that it should [b]not be profaned in
the sight of the nations among whom
they *lived,* in whose sight I made Myself
known to them by bringing them out of
the land of Egypt.
10 "So I took them out of the land of
Egypt and brought them into the [a]wilderness.
11 "And I gave them My [a]statutes and
informed them of My ordinances, by
[b]which, if a man [1]observes them, he will
live.
12 "And also I gave them My sabbaths
to be a [a]sign between Me and them, that
they might know that I am the LORD
who sanctifies them.
13 "But the house of Israel [a]rebelled
against Me in the wilderness. They did
not walk in My statutes, and they rejected My ordinances, [b]by which, if a
man [1]observes them, he will live; and
My [c]sabbaths they greatly profaned.
Then I [2]resolved to [d]pour out My wrath
on them in the wilderness, to annihilate
them.
14 "But I acted for the sake of My
name, that it should not be profaned in
the sight of the nations, before whose
sight I had brought them out.
15 "And also [a]I swore to them in the
wilderness that I would not bring them
into the land which I had given them,
flowing with milk and honey, which is
the glory of all lands,
16 because they rejected My ordinances, and as for My statutes, they did
not walk in them; they even profaned
My sabbaths, for their [a]heart continually
went after their idols.

5 [1]Lit., *one*
6 [a]2 Kin. 24:9; 2 Chr. 36:9
7 [1]So Targum; M.T., *knew* [2]Or, *widows*
8 [a]2 Kin. 24:11
9 [a]2 Chr. 36:6 [b]2 Kin. 24:15
10 [1]So with some ancient mss.; M.T., *blood* [a]Ps. 80:8-11
11 [1]Lit., *rods of strength* [a]Ps. 80:15 [b]Ezek. 31:3
12 [1]Lit., *rods of her strength* [2]So Gr.; M.T., *they were* [3]So Gr.; M.T., *they* [a]Jer. 31:28 [b]Lam. 2:1; Ezek. 28:17 [c]Ezek. 17:10; Hos. 13:15 [d]Is. 27:11; Ezek. 19:11
13 [a]2 Kin. 24:12-16; Ezek. 19:10; 20:35; Hos. 2:3
14 [1]Lit., *rod of strength* [a]Ezek. 15:4; 20:47, 48

1 [1]Lit., *men* [a]Ezek. 8:1, 11, 12
3 [1]Heb., *YHWH,* usually rendered *LORD,* and so throughout the ch. [a]Ezek. 14:3
4 [a]Ezek. 16:2; 22:2; Matt. 23:32
5 [1]Lit., *lifted up My hand,* and so throughout the ch. [2]Lit., *seed* [a]Ex. 6:6-8 [b]Ex. 6:2, 3
6 [1]Lit., *spied out* [a]Jer. 32:22 [b]Ex. 13:5; 33:3 [c]Ps. 48:2
7 [a]Ex. 20:4, 5; 22:20 [b]Lev. 18:3; Deut. 29:16-18 [c]Ex. 20:2
8 [1]Lit., *each one* [2]Lit., *said* [a]Deut. 9:7; Is. 63:10 [b]Ex. 32:1-9 [c]Ezek. 5:13; 7:8; 20:13, 21
9 [a]Ex. 32:11-14; Ezek. 20:14, 22; 36:21, 22 [b]Ezek. 39:7
10 [a]Ex. 19:1
11 [1]Lit., *does* [a]Ex. 20:1-23:33 [b]Lev. 18:5; Ezek. 20:13
12 [a]Ex. 31:13, 17; Ezek. 20:20
13 [1]Lit., *does* [2]Lit., *said* [a]Num. 14:11, 12, 22; Ezek. 20:8 [b]Lev. 18:5 [c]Is. 56:6; Ezek. 20:21 [d]Ex. 32:10; Deut. 9:8; Ezek. 20:8, 21
15 [a]Num. 14:30; Ps. 95:11; 106:26
16 [a]Ezek. 11:21; 14:3-7; 20:8

17“Yet My eye spared them rather
than destroying them, and I did not
cause their [a]annihilation in the wilderness.
18“And I said to their [1][a]children in the
wilderness, ‘[b]Do not walk in the statutes
of your fathers, or keep their ordinances,
or defile yourselves with their idols.
19 ‘[a]I am the LORD your God; [b]walk in
My statutes, and keep My ordinances,
and [1]observe them.
20 ‘And [a]sanctify My sabbaths; and
they shall be a sign between Me and you,
that you may know that I am the LORD
your God.’
21“But the [a]children rebelled against
Me; they did not walk in My statutes,
nor were they careful to observe My
ordinances, by which, *if* a man observes
them, he will live; they profaned My
sabbaths. So I [1]resolved to pour out My
wrath on them, to accomplish My anger
against them in the wilderness.
22“But I [a]withdrew My hand and
acted [b]for the sake of My name, that it
should not be profaned in the sight of
the nations in whose sight I had brought
them out.
23“Also I swore to them in the wilderness that I would [a]scatter them among
the nations and disperse them among the
lands,
24 because they had not observed My
ordinances, but had rejected My statutes, and had profaned My sabbaths,
and [a]their eyes were [1]on the idols of
their fathers.
25“And I also gave them statutes that
were [a]not good and ordinances by which
they could not live;
26 and I pronounced them [a]unclean
because of their gifts, in that they
[b]caused all [1]their first-born to pass
through *the fire* so that I might make
them desolate, in order that they might
[c]know that I am the LORD.” ’
27“Therefore, son of man, [a]speak to
the house of Israel, and say to them,
‘Thus says the Lord GOD, “Yet in this
your fathers have [b]blasphemed Me by
[c]acting treacherously against Me.
28“When I had [a]brought them into the
land which I swore to give to them, then
they saw every [b]high hill and every leafy
tree, and they offered there their sacrifices, and there they presented the
provocation of their offering. There also
they made their soothing aroma, and
there they poured out their libations.
29“Then I said to them, ‘What is the
high place to which you go?’ So its name
is called [1]Bamah to this day.” ’
30“Therefore, say to the house of
Israel, ‘Thus says the Lord GOD, “Will
you defile yourselves [1]after the manner
of your [a]fathers and play the harlot after
their detestable things?
31“And [1]when you offer your gifts,
when you [a]cause your sons to pass
through the fire, you are defiling yourselves with all your idols to this day.
And shall I be inquired of by you, O
house of Israel? As I live,” declares the
Lord GOD, “I will not be inquired of by
you.
32“And what [a]comes [1]into your mind
will not come about, when you say: ‘We
will be like the nations, like the tribes of
the lands, [b]serving wood and stone.’

God Will Restore Israel to Her Land

33“As I live,” declares the Lord GOD,
“surely with a mighty hand and with an
[a]outstretched arm and with wrath
poured out, I shall be [b]king over you.
34“And I shall [a]bring you out from the
peoples and gather you from the lands
where you are scattered, with a mighty
hand and with an outstretched arm and
with [b]wrath poured out;
35 and I shall bring you into the
[a]wilderness of the peoples, and there I
shall enter into judgment with you face
to face.
36“As I [a]entered into judgment with
your fathers in the [b]wilderness of the
land of Egypt, so I will enter into judgment with you,” declares the Lord GOD.
37“And I shall make you [a]pass under
the rod, and I shall bring you into the
bond of the covenant;
38 and I shall [a]purge from you the
rebels and those who transgress against
Me; I shall bring them out of the land
where they sojourn, but they will [b]not
enter the [1]land of Israel. Thus you will
know that I am the LORD.
39“As for you, O house of Israel,” thus
says the Lord GOD, “[a]Go, serve everyone his idols; [1]but later, you will surely
listen to Me, and My holy name you will
[b]profane no longer with your gifts and
with your idols.
40“For on My holy mountain, on the
high mountain of Israel,” declares the
Lord GOD, “there the whole house of
Israel, [a]all of them, will serve Me in the
land; there I shall [b]accept them, and
there I shall [1]seek your contributions
and the choicest of your gifts, with all
your holy things.
41“[1]As a soothing aroma I shall accept
you, when I [a]bring you out from the
peoples and gather you from the lands
where you are scattered; and I shall
prove Myself [b]holy among you in the
sight of the nations.
42“And [a]you will know that I am the
LORD, [b]when I bring you into the land
of Israel, into the [c]land which I swore to
give to your forefathers.
43“And there you will [a]remember your
ways and all your deeds, with which you
have defiled yourselves; and you will
[b]loathe yourselves in your own [1]sight for
all the evil things that you have done.
44“Then [a]you will know that I am the
LORD when I have dealt with you [b]for
My name’s sake, not according to your
evil ways or according to your corrupt

17 [a]Jer. 4:27; 5:18; Ezek. 11:13
18 [1]Lit., *sons* [a]Num. 14:31; Deut. 4:3-6 [b]Zech. 1:4
19 [1]Lit., *do* [a]Ex. 6:7; 20:2 [b]Deut. 5:32, 33; 6:1, 2; 8:1, 2; 11:1; 12:1
20 [a]Jer. 17:22
21 [1]Lit., *said* [a]Num. 21:5; 25:1-3
22 [a]Job 13:21; Ps. 78:38; Ezek. 20:17 [b]Is. 48:9-11; Jer. 14:7, 21; Ezek. 20:9, 14
23 [a]Lev. 26:33; Deut. 4:27; 28:64
24 [1]Lit., *after* [a]Ezek. 6:9
25 [a]Ps. 81:12; Is. 66:4; Rom. 1:21-25, 28
26 [1]Lit., *that which opens the womb* [a]Lev. 18:21; 20:2-5; Is. 63:17; Ezek. 20:30; Rom. 11:8 [b]Jer. 7:31; 19:4-9 [c]Ezek. 6:7; 20:12, 20
27 [a]Ezek. 2:7; 3:4, 11, 27 [b]Num. 15:30; Rom. 2:24 [c]Ezek. 18:24; 39:23, 26
28 [a]Josh. 23:3, 14; Neh. 9:22-26; Ps. 78:55; Jer. 2:7 [b]1 Kin. 14:23; Ps. 78:58; Is. 57:5-7; Jer. 3:6; Ezek. 6:13
29 [1]Or, *High Place*
30 [1]Lit., *in the way of* [a]Judg. 2:19; Jer. 7:26; 16:12
31 [1]Lit., *in your lifting up* [a]Ps. 106:37-39; Jer. 7:31; Ezek. 16:20; 20:26
32 [1]Lit., *upon your spirit* [a]Ezek. 11:5 [b]Jer. 2:25; 44:17
33 [a]Jer. 21:5 [b]Jer. 51:57
34 [a]Is. 27:12, 13; Ezek. 20:38; 34:16 [b]Jer. 42:18; 44:6; Lam. 2:4
35 [a]Ezek. 19:13; 20:36; Hos. 2:14
36 [a]Num. 11:1-35; Ps. 106:15; Ezek. 20:13, 21; 1 Cor. 10:5-10 [b]Deut. 32:10
37 [a]Lev. 27:32; Jer. 33:13
38 [1]Lit., *ground* or *soil* [a]Ezek. 34:17-22; Amos 9:9, 10; Zech. 13:8, 9; Mal. 3:3; 4:1-3 [b]Num. 14:29, 30; Ps. 95:11; Ezek. 13:9; 20:15, 16; Heb. 4:3
39 [1]Or, *and afterwards, if you will not listen to Me, but* [a]Jer. 44:25, 26 [b]Is. 1:13-15; Ezek. 23:38, 39; 43:7
40 [1]Or, *require* [a]Is. 66:23; Ezek. 37:22, 24 [b]Is. 56:7; 60:7; Ezek. 43:12, 27
41 [1]Lit., *With* [a]Is. 27:12, 13; Ezek. 11:17; 28:25 [b]Is. 5:16; Ezek. 28:25; 36:23

42 [a]Ezek. 36:23; 38:23 [b]Ezek. 11:17; 34:13; 36:24 [c]Ezek. 20:6, 15
43 [1]Lit., *faces* [a]Ezek. 6:9; 16:61, 63; Hos. 5:15 [b]Jer. 31:18; Ezek. 36:31; Zech. 12:10
44 [a]Ezek. 24:24 [b]Ezek. 36:22

deeds, O house of Israel," declares the
Lord GOD.' "
45 [1]Now the word of the LORD came
to me saying,
46 "Son of man, set your face toward
[1]Teman, and speak out against the
[a]south, and [b]prophesy against the [c]forest
[2]land of the Negev,
47 and say to the forest of the Negev,
'Hear the word of the LORD: thus says
the Lord GOD, "Behold, I am about to
[a]kindle a fire in you, and it shall consume every [1]green tree in you, as well as
every dry tree; the blazing flame will not
be quenched, and [2b]the whole surface
from south to north will be burned by it.
48 "And all flesh will see that I, the
LORD, have kindled it; it shall [a]not be
quenched." ' "
49 Then I said, "Ah Lord GOD! They
are saying of me, 'Is he not *just* speaking
[a]parables?' "

Parable of the Sword of the LORD

21 [1] AND the word of the LORD came
to me saying,
2 "Son of man, [a]set your face toward
Jerusalem, and [1b]speak against the sanctuaries, and prophesy against the land of
Israel;
3 and say to the land of Israel, 'Thus
says the LORD, "Behold, [a]I am against
you; and I shall draw My sword out of
its sheath and cut off from you the
[b]righteous and the wicked.
4 "Because I shall cut off from you the
righteous and the wicked, therefore My
sword shall go forth from its sheath
against [a]all flesh from south *to* north.
5 "Thus all flesh will know that I, the
LORD, have drawn My sword out of its
sheath. It will [a]not return *to its sheath*
again." '
6 "As for you, son of man, groan with
breaking [1]heart and bitter grief, groan in
their sight.
7 "And it will come about when they
say to you, 'Why do you groan?' that
you will say, 'Because of the [a]news that
is coming; and [b]every heart will melt, all
hands will be feeble, every spirit will
[1]faint, and all knees will [2]be weak as
water. Behold, it comes and it will
happen,' declares the Lord [3]GOD."
8 Again the word of the LORD came
to me saying,
9 "Son of man, prophesy and say,
'Thus says the LORD.' Say,
'[a]A sword, a sword sharpened
And also polished!
10 'Sharpened to make a [a]slaughter,
Polished [1]to flash like lightning!'
Or shall we rejoice, the [2]rod of My son
[b]despising every tree?
11 "And it is given to be polished, that
it may be handled; the sword is sharpened and polished, to give it into the
hand of the slayer.
12 "[a]Cry out and wail, son of man; for
it is against My people, it is against all
the [b]officials of Israel. They are delivered
over to the sword with My people,
therefore strike *your* thigh.
13 "For *there is* a testing; and what if
even the [1]rod which despises will be no
more?" declares the Lord GOD.
14 "You therefore, son of man, prophesy, and clap *your* hands together; and
let the sword be [a]doubled the third time,
the sword for the slain. It is the sword
for the great one slain, which surrounds
them,
15 that *their* [a]hearts may melt, and
many [b]fall at all their [c]gates. I have
given the glittering sword. Ah! It is made
for striking like lightning, it is wrapped
up *in readiness* for slaughter.
16 "[1]Show yourself sharp, go to the
right; set yourself; go to the left, wherever your [2]edge is appointed.
17 "I shall also clap My hands together,
and I shall [1a]appease My wrath; I, the
LORD, have spoken."

The Instrument of God's Judgment

18 And the word of the LORD came to
me saying,
19 "As for you, son of man, [1a]make two
ways for the sword of the king of Babylon to come; both of them will go out of
one land. And [2]make a signpost; [3]make
it at the head of the way to the city.
20 "You shall [1]mark a way for the
sword to come to [a]Rabbah of the sons of
Ammon, and to Judah into [b]fortified
Jerusalem.
21 "For the king of Babylon stands at
the [1]parting of the way, at the head of
the two ways, to use [a]divination; he
[b]shakes the arrows, he consults the
[2c]household idols, he looks at the liver.
22 "Into his right hand came the divination, 'Jerusalem,' to [a]set battering
rams, to open the mouth [1]for slaughter,
to lift up the voice with a battle cry, to
set battering rams against the gates, to
cast up mounds, to build a siege wall.
23 "And it will be to them like a false
divination in their eyes; [a]they have *sworn*
solemn oaths. But he [b]brings iniquity to
remembrance, that they may be seized.
24 "Therefore, thus says the Lord GOD,
'Because you have made your iniquity to
be remembered, in that your transgressions are uncovered, so that in all your
deeds your sins appear—because you
have come to remembrance, you will be
seized with the hand.
25 'And you, O slain, wicked one, the
prince of Israel, whose [a]day has come, in
the time of the [1]punishment of the end,'
26 thus says the Lord GOD, 'Remove
the turban, and take off the [a]crown; this
will *be* [1]no more the same. [b]Exalt that
which is low, and abase that which is
high.
27 '[a]A ruin, a ruin, a ruin, I shall make
it. This also will be no more, until [b]He
comes whose right it is; and I shall give
it *to Him*.'

45 [1]Ch. 21:1 in Heb.
46 [1]Or, *the South* [2]Lit., *of the field* [a]Jer. 13:19; Ezek. 21:4 [b]Ezek. 21:2; Amos 7:16 [c]Is. 30:6-11
47 [1]Lit., *moist* [2]Or, *all the faces* [a]Is. 9:18, 19; Jer. 21:14 [b]Is. 13:8
48 [a]Jer. 7:20; 17:27
49 [a]Ezek. 17:2; Matt. 13:13; John 16:25

1 [1]Ch. 21:6 in Heb.
2 [1]Lit., *flow* [a]Ezek. 20:46; 25:2; 28:21 [b]Job 29:22; Ezek. 20:46
3 [a]Jer. 21:13; Ezek. 5:8; Nah. 2:13; 3:5 [b]Is. 57:1
4 [a]Jer. 12:12; Ezek. 7:2; 20:47
5 [a]1 Sam. 3:12; Jer. 23:20; Ezek. 21:30; Nah. 1:9
6 [1]Lit., *loins*
7 [1]Lit., *be dim* [2]Lit., *flow* [3]Heb., *YHWH*, usually rendered *LORD*, and so throughout the ch. [a]Ezek. 7:26 [b]Is. 13:7; Nah. 2:10
9 [a]Deut. 32:41
10 [1]Lit., *lightning to be to her* [2]Or, *scepter* [a]Is. 34:5, 6 [b]Ps. 110:5, 6; Ezek. 20:47
12 [a]Ezek. 21:6; Joel 1:13 [b]Ezek. 21:25; 22:6
13 [1]Or, *scepter*
14 [a]Lev. 26:21, 24; 2 Kin. 24:1, 10-16; 25:1
15 [a]Josh. 2:11; 2 Sam. 17:10; Ps. 22:14; Ezek. 21:7 [b]Is. 59:10; Jer. 13:16; 18:15 [c]Jer. 17:27; Ezek. 21:19
16 [1]Or, *Unite yourself* [2]Lit., *face*
17 [1]Lit., *cause to rest* [a]Ezek. 5:13
19 [1]Or, *set for yourself* [2]Lit., *cut out a hand* [3]Lit., *cut it* [a]Jer. 1:10; Ezek. 4:1-3
20 [1]Lit., *set* [a]Deut. 3:11; Jer. 49:2; Ezek. 25:5; Amos 1:14 [b]Ps. 48:12, 13; 125:1, 2
21 [1]Lit., *mother* [2]Heb., *teraphim* [a]Num. 22:7; 23:23 [b]Prov. 16:33 [c]Gen. 31:19, 30; Judg. 17:5; 18:17, 20
22 [1]Lit., *in* [a]Ezek. 4:2; 26:9
23 [a]Ezek. 17:16, 18 [b]Num. 5:15; Ezek. 21:24; 29:16
25 [1]Or, *iniquity* [a]Ps. 37:13; Ezek. 7:2, 3, 7
26 [1]Lit., *not this* [a]Jer. 13:18; Ezek. 16:12 [b]Ps. 75:7; Ezek. 17:24
27 [a]Hag. 2:21, 22 [b]Ps. 2:6; 72:7, 10; Jer. 23:5, 6; Ezek. 34:24; 37:24

28"And you, son of man, prophesy and say, 'Thus says the Lord GOD concerning the sons of Ammon and concerning their [a]reproach,' and say: 'A sword, a sword is drawn, polished for the slaughter, to cause it [1]to [b]consume, that it may be like lightning—

29 while they see for you [a]false visions, while they divine lies for you—to place you on the necks of the wicked who are slain, whose day has come, in the [b]time of the [1]punishment of the end.

30 '[a]Return *it* to its sheath. In the [b]place where you were created, in the land of your origin, I shall judge you.

31 'And I shall [a]pour out My indignation on you; I shall [b]blow on you with the fire of My wrath, and I shall give you into the hand of brutal men, [1][c]skilled in destruction.

32 'You will be [1][a]fuel for the fire; your blood will be in the midst of the land. You will [b]not be remembered, for I, the LORD, have spoken.' "

The Sins of Israel

22 THEN the word of the LORD came to me saying,

2"And you, son of man, will you judge, will you judge the bloody city? Then cause her to know all her abominations.

3"And you shall say, 'Thus says the Lord [1]GOD, "A city [a]shedding blood in her midst, so that her time will come, and that makes idols, contrary to her *interest,* for defilement!

4"You have become [a]guilty by [1]the blood which you have shed, and defiled by your idols which you have made. Thus you have brought your [2]day near and have come to your years; therefore I have made you a [b]reproach to the nations, and a mocking to all the lands.

5"Those who are near and those who are far from you will mock you, you of ill repute, full of [a]turmoil.

6"Behold, the [a]rulers of Israel, each according to his [1]power, have been in you for the purpose of shedding blood.

7"They have [a]treated father and mother lightly within you. The [b]alien they have oppressed in your midst; the [c]fatherless and the widow they have wronged in you.

8"You have [a]despised My holy things and [b]profaned My sabbaths.

9"Slanderous men have been in you for the purpose of shedding blood, and in you they have eaten at the mountain *shrines.* In your midst they have [a]committed acts of lewdness.

10"In you [1]they have [a]uncovered *their* fathers' nakedness; in you they have humbled her who was [b]unclean in her menstrual impurity.

11"And one has committed abomination with his [a]neighbor's wife, and another has lewdly defiled his [b]daughter-in-law. And another in you has [c]humbled his sister, his father's daughter.

12"In you they have [a]taken bribes to shed blood; you have taken [b]interest and profits, and you have injured your neighbors for gain by [c]oppression, and you have [d]forgotten Me," declares the Lord GOD.

13"Behold, then, I smite My hand at your [a]dishonest gain which you have acquired and at [1]the bloodshed which is among you.

14"Can [a]your heart endure, or can your hands be strong, in the days that I shall deal with you? [b]I, the LORD, have spoken and shall act.

15"And I shall [a]scatter you among the nations, and I shall disperse you through the lands, and I shall [b]consume your uncleanness from you.

16"And you will profane yourself in the sight of the nations, and you will [a]know that I am the LORD." ' "

17 And the word of the LORD came to me saying,

18"Son of man, the house of Israel has become [a]dross to Me; all of them are [b]bronze and tin and iron and lead in the [c]furnace; they are the dross of silver.

19"Therefore, thus says the Lord GOD, 'Because all of you have become dross, therefore, behold, I am going to gather you into the midst of Jerusalem.

20 'As they gather silver and bronze and iron and lead and tin into the [a]furnace to blow fire on it in order to melt *it,* so I shall gather *you* in My anger and in My wrath, and I shall lay you *there* and melt you.

21 'And I shall gather you and blow on you with the fire of My wrath, and you will be melted in the midst of it.

22 'As silver is melted in the furnace, so you will be melted in the midst of it; and you will know that I, the LORD, have [a]poured out My wrath on you.' "

23 And the word of the LORD came to me saying,

24"Son of man, say to her, 'You are a land that is [a]not cleansed or rained on in the day of indignation.'

25"There is a [a]conspiracy of her prophets in her midst, like a roaring lion tearing the prey. They have [b]devoured lives; they have taken treasure and precious things; they have made many [c]widows in the midst of her.

26"Her [a]priests have done violence to My law and have [b]profaned My holy things; they have made no [c]distinction between the holy and the profane, and they have not taught the difference between the [d]unclean and the clean; and they hide their eyes from My sabbaths, and I am profaned among them.

27"Her princes within her are like wolves tearing the prey, by shedding blood *and* [a]destroying lives in order to get [b]dishonest gain.

28"And her prophets have smeared whitewash for them, seeing [a]false visions and divining lies for them, saying, 'Thus says the Lord GOD,' when the LORD has not spoken.

28 [1]Lit., *to finish* [a]Ezek. 36:15; Zeph. 2:8-10 [b]Is. 31:8; Jer. 12:12; 46:10, 14
29 [1]Or, *iniquity* [a]Jer. 27:9; Ezek. 13:6-9; 22:28 [b]Ezek. 21:25; 35:5
30 [a]Jer. 47:6, 7 [b]Ezek. 25:5
31 [1]Or, *artisans of* [a]Ezek. 14:19; 25:7; Nah. 1:6 [b]Ps. 18:15; Is. 30:33; Ezek. 22:20, 21; Hag. 1:9 [c]Jer. 4:7; 6:22, 23; 51:20-23; Hab. 1:6, 10
32 [1]Lit., *food* [a]Ezek. 20:47, 48; Mal. 4:1 [b]Ezek. 25:10

3 [1]Heb., *YHWH,* usually rendered *LORD,* and so throughout the ch. [a]Ezek. 22:6, 27; 23:37, 45
4 [1]Lit., *your* [2]Lit., *days* [a]2 Kin. 21:16; Ezek. 24:7, 8 [b]Ps. 44:13, 14; Ezek. 5:14, 15; 16:57
5 [a]Is. 22:2
6 [1]Lit., *arm* [a]Is. 1:23; Ezek. 22:27
7 [a]Ex. 20:12; Lev. 20:9; Deut. 5:16; 27:16 [b]Ex. 22:21f.; 23:9; Deut. 24:17; Jer. 7:6; Zech. 7:10 [c]Ex. 22:22; Ezek. 22:25; Mal. 3:5
8 [a]Ezek. 22:26 [b]Ezek. 20:13, 21, 24; 23:38, 39
9 [a]Ezek. 23:29; Hos. 4:2, 10, 14
10 [1]Lit., *he has* [a]Lev. 18:8 [b]Lev. 18:19; Ezek. 18:6
11 [a]Ezek. 18:11; 33:26 [b]Lev. 18:15 [c]2 Sam. 13:11-14
12 [a]Ex. 23:8; Deut. 16:19; 27:25; Mic. 7:2, 3 [b]Lev. 25:36; Deut. 23:19 [c]Lev. 19:13 [d]Ps. 106:21; Ezek. 23:35
13 [1]Lit., *your* [a]Is. 33:15; Amos 2:6-8; Mic. 2:2
14 [a]Ezek. 21:7 [b]Ezek. 17:24
15 [a]Deut. 4:27; Neh. 1:8; Ezek. 20:23; Zech. 7:14 [b]Ezek. 23:27, 48
16 [a]Ps. 83:18; Ezek. 6:7
18 [a]Ps. 119:119; Is. 1:22; Lam. 4:1 [b]Jer. 6:28-30 [c]Prov. 17:3; Is. 48:10
20 [a]Is. 1:25
22 [a]Ezek. 20:8, 33; Hos. 5:10
24 [a]Is. 9:13; Jer. 2:30; Ezek. 24:13; Zeph. 3:2
25 [a]Jer. 11:9; Hos. 6:9 [b]Jer. 2:34; Ezek. 13:19; 22:27 [c]Jer. 15:8; Ezek. 22:7
26 [a]Jer. 2:8, 26; Ezek. 7:26 [b]1 Sam. 2:12-17, 22; Ezek. 22:8 [c]Lev. 10:10; Ezek. 44:23 [d]Hag. 2:11-14
27 [a]Ezek. 22:25 [b]Ezek. 22:13
28 [a]Jer. 23:25-32; Ezek. 13:6

29 "The people of the land have practiced [a]oppression and committed robbery, and they have wronged the poor and needy and have [b]oppressed the sojourner without justice.

30 "And I [a]searched for a man among them who should [b]build up the wall and [c]stand in the gap before Me for the land, that I should not destroy it; but I found [1]no one.

31 "Thus I have poured out My [a]indignation on them; I have consumed them with the fire of My wrath; [b]their way I have brought upon their heads," declares the Lord GOD.

Oholah and Oholibah's Sin and Its Consequences

23 THE word of the LORD came to me again saying,

2 "Son of man, there were [a]two women, the daughters of one mother;

3 and they played the harlot in Egypt. They [a]played the harlot in their youth; there their breasts were pressed, and there their virgin bosom was handled.

4 "And their names were Oholah the elder and Oholibah her sister. And they became Mine, and they bore sons and daughters. And *as for* their names, Samaria is Oholah, and Jerusalem is Oholibah.

5 "And Oholah played the harlot [1]while she was Mine; and she lusted after her lovers, after the [a]Assyrians, *her* neighbors,

6 who were clothed in purple, [a]governors and officials, all of them desirable young men, horsemen riding on horses.

7 "And she bestowed her harlotries on them, all of whom *were* the choicest [1]men of Assyria; and with all whom she lusted after, with all their idols she [a]defiled herself.

8 "And she did not forsake her harlotries [a]from *the time in* Egypt; for in her youth [1]men had lain with her, and they handled her virgin bosom and poured out their [2]lust on her.

9 "Therefore, I gave her into the hand of her [a]lovers, into the hand of the [1]Assyrians, after whom she lusted.

10 "They [a]uncovered her nakedness; they took her sons and her daughters, but they slew her with the sword. Thus she became a [1]byword among women, and they executed judgments on her.

11 "Now her sister Oholibah saw *this,* yet she was [a]more corrupt in her lust than she, and her harlotries were more than the harlotries of her sister.

12 "She lusted after the [1a]Assyrians, governors and officials, the ones near, magnificently dressed, horsemen riding on horses, all of them desirable young men.

13 "And I saw that she had defiled herself; they both took [1]the same way.

14 "So she increased her harlotries. And she saw men [a]portrayed on the wall, images of the [b]Chaldeans portrayed with vermilion,

15 girded with belts on their loins, with flowing turbans on their heads, all of them looking like officers, [1]like the [2]Babylonians *in* Chaldea, the land of their birth.

16 "And [1]when she saw them she [a]lusted after them and sent messengers to them in Chaldea.

17 "And the [1a]Babylonians came to her to the bed of love, and they defiled her with their harlotry. And when she had been defiled by them, [2]she became disgusted with them.

18 "And she [a]uncovered her harlotries and uncovered her nakedness; then [1]I became [b]disgusted with her, as [1]I had become disgusted with her [c]sister.

19 "Yet she multiplied her harlotries, remembering the days of her youth, when she played the harlot in the land of Egypt.

20 "And she [a]lusted after their paramours, whose flesh is *like* the flesh of donkeys and whose issue is *like* the issue of horses.

21 "Thus you longed for the [a]lewdness of your youth, when [1]the Egyptians handled your bosom because of the breasts of your youth.

22 "Therefore, O Oholibah, thus says the Lord [1]GOD, 'Behold I will arouse your lovers against you, from whom [2]you were alienated, and I will bring them against you from every side:

23 the [1a]Babylonians and all the [b]Chaldeans, [c]Pekod and Shoa and Koa, *and* all the [2d]Assyrians with them; desirable young men, governors and officials all of them, officers and [3]men of renown, all of them riding on horses.

24 'And they will come against you with weapons, [a]chariots, and [1]wagons, and with a company of peoples. They will set themselves against you on every side with buckler and shield and helmet; and I shall commit the [b]judgment to them, and they will judge you according to their customs.

25 'And I will set My [a]jealousy against you, that they may deal with you in wrath. They will remove your nose and your ears; and your [1]survivors will fall by the sword. They will take your [b]sons and your daughters; and your [1]survivors will be consumed by the fire.

26 'They will also [a]strip you of your clothes and take away your [b]beautiful jewels.

27 'Thus [a]I shall make your lewdness and your harlotry *brought* from the land of Egypt to cease from you, so that you will not lift up your eyes to them or remember Egypt anymore.'

28 "For thus says the Lord GOD, 'Behold, I will give you into the hand of those whom you [a]hate, into the hand of those from whom [1]you were alienated.

---

29 [a]Is. 5:7; Ezek. 9:9; 22:7; Amos 3:10 [b]Ex. 23:9
30 [1]Lit., *not* [a]Is. 59:16; 63:5; Jer. 5:1 [b]Ezek. 13:5 [c]Ps. 106:23; Jer. 15:1
31 [a]Is. 10:5; 13:5; 30:27; Ezek. 22:20 [b]Ezek. 7:3, 8, 9; 9:10; 16:43; Rom. 2:8, 9
2 [a]Ezek. 16:46
3 [a]Lev. 17:7; Jer. 3:9
5 [1]Lit., *under Me* [a]2 Kin. 15:19; 16:7; 17:3; Ezek. 16:28; Hos. 5:13; 8:9, 10
6 [a]Ezek. 23:12, 13
7 [1]Lit., *sons of Asshur* [a]Ezek. 20:7; 22:3, 4; Hos. 5:3; 6:10
8 [1]Lit., *they* [2]Lit., *harlotry* [a]Ex. 32:4; 1 Kin. 12:28; 2 Kin. 10:29; 17:16; Ezek. 23:3, 19
9 [1]Lit., *sons of Asshur* [a]Ezek. 16:37; 23:22
10 [1]Lit., *name* [a]Ezek. 16:37, 41
11 [a]Jer. 3:8-11; Ezek. 16:51
12 [1]Lit., *sons of Asshur* [a]2 Kin. 16:7
13 [1]Lit., *one*
14 [a]Ezek. 8:10 [b]Ezek. 16:29
15 [1]Lit., *the likeness of* [2]Lit., *sons of Babel*
16 [1]Lit., *at the sight of her eyes* [a]Ezek. 23:20; Matt. 5:28
17 [1]Lit., *sons of Babel* [2]Lit., *her soul* [a]2 Kin. 24:17
18 [1]Lit., *My soul* [a]Jer. 8:12; Ezek. 21:24; 23:10 [b]Ps. 78:59; 106:40; Jer. 12:8 [c]Ezek. 23:9; Amos 5:21
20 [a]Ezek. 16:26; 17:15
21 [1]So two mss.; M.T., *from Egypt* [a]Jer. 3:9; Ezek. 23:3
22 [1]Heb., *YHWH,* usually rendered *LORD,* and so throughout the ch. [2]Lit., *your soul was alienated*
23 [1]Lit., *sons of Babylon* [2]Lit., *sons of Assyria* [3]Lit., *the called ones* [a]2 Kin. 20:14-17; Ezek. 21:19; 23:14-17 [b]2 Kin. 24:2; Job 1:17; Is. 23:13 [c]Jer. 50:21 [d]Gen. 2:14; 25:18; Ezra 6:22
24 [1]Lit., *wheels* [a]Jer. 47:3; Ezek. 26:10; Nah. 2:3, 4 [b]Jer. 39:5, 6; Ezek. 16:38; 23:45
25 [1]Lit., *remainder* [a]Ex. 34:14; Ezek. 5:13; 8:17, 18; Zeph. 1:18 [b]Ezek. 23:47; Hos. 2:4
26 [a]Jer. 13:22; Ezek. 16:39; 23:29 [b]Is. 3:18-23
27 [a]Ezek. 16:41
28 [1]Lit., *your soul was alienated* [a]Jer. 21:7-10; 34:20; Ezek. 16:37; 23:17, 22

29 'And they will [a]deal with you in
hatred, take all your property, and leave
you naked and bare. And the nakedness
of your harlotries shall be uncovered,
both your lewdness and your harlotries.
30 'These things will be done to you
because you have [a]played the harlot with
the nations, because you have defiled
yourself with their idols.
31 'You have walked in the way of
your sister; therefore I will give [a]her cup
into your hand.'
32 "Thus says the Lord GOD,
'You will [a]drink your sister's cup,
Which is deep and wide.
[1]You will be [b]laughed at and held
in derision;
It contains much.
33 'You will be filled with [a]drunken-
ness and sorrow,
The cup of horror and desolation,
The cup of your sister Samaria.
34 'And you will [a]drink it and drain
it.
Then you will gnaw its fragments
And tear your breasts;
for I have spoken,' declares the Lord
GOD.
35 "Therefore, thus says the Lord GOD,
'Because you have [a]forgotten Me and
[b]cast Me behind your back, bear now
the *punishment* of your lewdness and
your harlotries.'"
36 Moreover, the LORD said to me,
"Son of man, will you [a]judge Oholah
and Oholibah? Then [b]declare to them
their abominations.
37 "For they have committed adultery,
and blood is on their hands. Thus they
have committed adultery with their idols
and even caused their sons, [a]whom they
bore to Me, to pass through *the fire* to
[1]them as food.
38 "Again, they have done this to Me:
they have [a]defiled My sanctuary on the
same day and have [b]profaned My sabbaths.
39 "For when they had slaughtered
their children for their idols, they entered My [a]sanctuary on the same day to
profane it; and lo, thus they did within
My house.
40 "Furthermore, [1]they have even sent
for men who come from afar, to whom a
messenger was sent; and lo, they came—
for whom you bathed, [a]painted your
eyes, and [b]decorated yourselves with
ornaments;
41 and you sat on a splendid [a]couch
with a [b]table arranged before it, on
which you had set My [c]incense and My
[c]oil.
42 "And the sound of a [1a]carefree
multitude was with her; and [b]drunkards
were brought from the wilderness with
men of the [2]common sort. And they put
[c]bracelets on [3]the hands of the women
and beautiful crowns on their heads.
43 "Then I said concerning her who
was [a]worn out by adulteries, '[1]Will they
now commit adultery with her when she
is *thus*?'
44 "[1]But they went in to her as they
would go in to a harlot. Thus they went
in to Oholah and to Oholibah, the lewd
women.
45 "But they, righteous men, will
[a]judge them with the judgment of adulteresses, and with the judgment of
women who shed blood, because they
are adulteresses and blood is on their
hands.
46 "For thus says the Lord GOD, 'Bring
up a company against them, and give
them over to [a]terror and plunder.
47 'And the company will [a]stone them
with stones and cut them down with
their swords; they will slay their sons
and their daughters and [b]burn their
houses with fire.
48 'Thus I shall make lewdness cease
from the land, that all women may be
admonished and not commit [1]lewdness
as you have done.
49 'And your lewdness [1]will be [a]re-
quited upon you, and you will bear the
penalty of *worshiping* your idols; thus
you will know that I am the Lord
GOD.'"

Parable of the Boiling Pot

24 AND the word of the LORD came
to me in the ninth year, in the
tenth month, on the tenth of the month,
saying,
2 "Son of man, write the name of the
day, this very day. The king of Babylon
[1]has [a]laid siege to Jerusalem this very
day.
3 "And speak a [a]parable to the [b]rebel-
lious house, and say to them, 'Thus says
the Lord [1]GOD,
"Put on the [c]pot, put *it* on, and also
pour water in it;
4 [1a]Put in it the pieces,
Every good piece, the thigh, and
the shoulder;
Fill *it* with choice bones.
5 "Take the [a]choicest of the flock,
And also pile [1]wood under [2]the
pot.
Make it boil vigorously.
Also seethe its bones in it."

6 'Therefore, thus says the Lord
GOD,
"Woe to the [a]bloody city,
To the pot in which there is rust
And whose rust has not gone out
of it!
Take out of it piece after piece,
[1]Without making a choice.
7 "For her blood is in her midst;
She placed it on the bare rock;
She did not [a]pour it on the ground
To cover it with dust.
8 "That it may [a]cause wrath to come
up to take vengeance,
I have put her blood on the bare
rock,
That it may not be covered."
9 'Therefore, thus says the Lord
GOD,

29 [a]Deut. 28:48; Ezek. 23:25, 26, 45-47
30 [a]Ezek. 6:9
31 [a]2 Kin. 21:13; Jer. 7:14, 15; Ezek. 23:33
32 [1]Or, *It will be for jesting and deriding because of its great size* [a]Ps. 60:3; Is. 51:17; Jer. 25:15 [b]Ezek. 5:14, 15; 16:57; 22:4, 5
33 [a]Jer. 25:15, 16, 27; Hab. 2:16
34 [a]Ps. 75:8; Is. 51:17
35 [a]Is. 17:10; Jer. 3:21; Ezek. 22:12; Hos. 8:14; 13:6 [b]1 Kin. 14:9; Jer. 2:27; 32:33
36 [a]Jer. 1:10; Ezek. 20:4; 22:2 [b]Is. 58:1; Ezek. 16:2; Mic. 3:8
37 [1]I.e., idols [a]Ezek. 16:20; 20:26
38 [a]2 Kin. 21:4, 7; Ezek. 5:11; 7:20 [b]Jer. 17:27; Ezek. 20:13, 24
39 [a]Jer. 7:9-11
40 [1]Or, *you* (women) [a]2 Kin. 9:30; Jer. 4:30 [b]Is. 3:18-23; Ezek. 16:13-16
41 [a]Esth. 1:6; Is. 57:7; Amos 6:4 [b]Is. 65:11; Ezek. 44:16 [c]Jer. 44:17; Hos. 2:8
42 [1]Lit., *at ease* [2]Lit., *multitude of mankind* [3]Lit., *their hands* [a]Ezek. 16:49; Amos 6:3-6 [b]Jer. 51:7 [c]Gen. 24:30; Ezek. 16:11, 12
43 [1]Or, *Now they will commit adultery with her, and she with them.* [a]Ezek. 23:3
44 [1]Or, *And*
45 [a]Ezek. 16:38
46 [a]Jer. 15:4; 24:9; 29:18
47 [a]Lev. 20:10; Ezek. 16:40 [b]Jer. 39:8
48 [1]Lit., *according to your lewdness*
49 [1]Lit., *they will give* [a]Is. 59:18; Ezek. 7:4, 9; 9:10; 23:35

2 [1]Lit., *leaned on* [a]2 Kin. 25:1; Jer. 39:1; 52:4
3 [1]Heb., *YHWH*, usually rendered *LORD*, and so throughout the ch. [a]Ps. 78:2; Ezek. 17:2; 20:49 [b]Is. 1:2; 30:1, 9; Ezek. 2:3, 6, 8 [c]Jer. 1:13, 14; Ezek. 11:3, 7, 11; 24:6
4 [1]Lit., *Gather her pieces* [a]Mic. 3:2, 3
5 [1]Lit., *bones* [2]Lit., *it* [a]Jer. 39:6; 52:10, 24-27
6 [1]Lit., *No lot has fallen on it* [a]2 Kin. 24:3, 4; Ezek. 22:2, 3, 27; Mic. 7:2; Nah. 3:1
7 [a]Lev. 17:13; Deut. 12:16
8 [a]Is. 26:21

"[a]Woe to the bloody city!
I also shall make the pile great.
10 "Heap on the wood, kindle the fire,
[1]Boil the flesh well,
And mix in the spices,
And let the bones be burned.
11 "Then [a]set it empty on its coals,
So that it may be hot,
And its bronze may [1]glow,
And its [b]filthiness may be melted
in it,
Its rust consumed.
12 "She has [a]wearied *Me* with toil,
Yet her great rust has not gone
from her;
Let her rust *be* in the fire!
13 "In your filthiness is lewdness.
Because I *would* have cleansed
you,
Yet you are [a]not clean,
You will not be cleansed from
your filthiness again,
Until I have [1b]spent My wrath on
you.
14"I, the LORD, have spoken; it is
[a]coming and I shall act. I shall not
relent, and I shall not [b]pity, and I shall
not be sorry; [c]according to your ways
and according to your deeds [1]I shall
judge you," declares the Lord GOD.' "

Death of Ezekiel's Wife Is a Sign

15 And the word of the LORD came to
me saying,
16"Son of man, behold, I am about to
take from you the [a]desire of your eyes
with a [b]blow; but you shall not [c]mourn,
and you shall not weep, and your [d]tears
shall not come.
17"Groan silently; make [a]no mourning
for the dead. Bind on your turban, and
put your shoes on your feet, and do not
cover *your* mustache, and [b]do not eat the
bread of men."
18 So I spoke to the people in the
morning, and in the evening my wife
died. And in the morning I did as I was
commanded.
19 And the people said to me, "Will
you not tell us what these things that
you are doing mean for us?"
20 Then I said to them, "The word of
the LORD came to me saying,
21 'Speak to the house of Israel, "Thus
says the Lord GOD, 'Behold, I am about
to profane My sanctuary, the pride of
your power, the [a]desire of your eyes, and
the delight of your soul; and your [b]sons
and your daughters whom you have left
behind will fall by the sword.
22 'And you will do as I have done;
you will not cover *your* mustache, and
you will not eat the bread of men.
23 'And your turbans will be on your
heads and your shoes on your feet. You
[a]will not mourn, and you will not weep;
but [b]you will rot away in your iniquities,
and you will groan [1]to one another.
24 'Thus Ezekiel will be a [a]sign to you;
according to all that he has done you

9 [a]Ezek. 24:6; Hab. 2:12
10 [1]Lit., *Complete*
11 [1]Lit., *become hot* [a]Jer. 21:10; Mal. 4:1 [b]Ezek. 22:15; 23:27
12 [a]Jer. 9:5
13 [1]Lit., *caused to rest* [a]Jer. 6:28-30; Ezek. 22:24 [b]Ezek. 5:13; 8:18
14 [1]So with several ancient mss. and versions; M.T., *they* [a]Ps. 33:9; Is. 55:11 [b]Jer. 13:14; Ezek. 9:10 [c]Is. 3:11; Ezek. 18:30; 36:19
16 [a]Song 7:10; Ezek. 24:18 [b]Job 23:2 [c]Jer. 16:5; 22:10 [d]Jer. 13:17
17 [a]Lev. 21:10-12 [b]Jer. 16:7; Hos. 9:4
21 [a]Ps. 27:4; 84:1; Ezek. 24:16 [b]Jer. 6:11; 16:3, 4; Ezek. 23:25, 47
23 [1]Lit., *a man to his brother* [a]Job 27:15; Ps. 78:64 [b]Lev. 26:39; Ezek. 33:10
24 [a]Ezek. 4:3; Luke 11:29, 30
25 [1]Or, *beauty* [2]Lit., *the lifting up of their soul* [a]Ps. 48:2; 50:2; Ezek. 24:21
26 [a]1 Sam. 4:12; Job 1:15-19
27 [a]Ezek. 3:26; 33:22
2 [a]Jer. 49:1-6; Amos 1:13-15; Zeph. 2:9
3 [1]Heb., *YHWH*, usually rendered *LORD*, and so throughout the ch. [a]Ps. 70:2, 3; Ezek. 21:28; 25:6; 26:2; 36:2
4 [a]Judg. 6:3, 33; 1 Kin. 4:30 [b]Deut. 28:33, 51; Is. 1:7
5 [a]Deut. 3:11; 2 Sam. 12:26; Jer. 49:2; Ezek. 21:20
6 [a]Job 27:23; Nah. 3:19 [b]Obad. 12; Zeph. 2:8, 10
7 [a]Ezek. 25:13, 16; Zeph. 1:4 [b]Is. 33:4; Ezek. 26:5 [c]Ezek. 21:32 [d]Amos 1:14, 15 [e]Ezek. 6:14
8 [a]Is. 15:1; Jer. 48:1; Amos 2:1, 2
9 [1]Lit., *open* [2]Lit., *end* [a]Num. 33:49; Josh. 12:3; 13:20 [b]Num. 32:3, 38; Josh. 13:17; 1 Chr. 5:8; Jer. 48:23 [c]Num. 32:37; Josh. 13:19; Jer. 48:1, 23
10 [a]Ezek. 25:4

will do; when it comes, then you will
know that I am the Lord GOD.' "
25 'As for you, son of man, will *it* not
be on the day when I take from them
their [a]stronghold, the joy of their [1]pride,
the desire of their eyes, and [2]their heart's
delight, their sons and their daughters,
26 that on that day he who [a]escapes
will come to you with information for
your ears?
27 'On that day your [a]mouth will be
opened to him who escaped, and you
will speak and be dumb no longer. Thus
you will be a sign to them, and they will
know that I am the LORD.' "

Judgment on Gentile Nations—Ammon

25 AND the word of the LORD came
to me saying,
2"Son of man, set your face toward
the [a]sons of Ammon, and prophesy
against them,
3 and say to the sons of Ammon,
'Hear the word of the Lord [1]GOD! Thus
says the Lord GOD, "Because you said,
'[a]Aha!' against My sanctuary when it
was profaned, and against the land of
Israel when it was made desolate, and
against the house of Judah when they
went into exile,
4 therefore, behold, I am going to
give you to the [a]sons of the east for a
possession, and they will set their en-
campments among you and make their
dwellings among you; they will [b]eat your
fruit and drink your milk.
5"And I shall make [a]Rabbah a pasture for camels and the sons of Ammon
a resting place for flocks. Thus you will
know that I am the LORD."
6 'For thus says the Lord GOD, "Because you have [a]clapped your hands and
stamped your feet and [b]rejoiced with all
the scorn of your soul against the land of
Israel,
7 therefore, behold, I have [a]stretched
out My hand against you, and I shall
give you for [b]spoil to the nations. And I
shall [c]cut you off from the peoples and
[d]make you perish from the lands; I shall
destroy you. Thus you will [e]know that I
am the LORD."

Moab

8 'Thus says the Lord GOD, "Because
[a]Moab and Seir say, 'Behold, the house
of Judah is like all the nations,'
9 therefore, behold, I am going to
[1]deprive the flank of Moab of *its* cities,
of its cities which are on its [2]frontiers,
the glory of the land, [a]Beth-jeshimoth,
[b]Baal-meon, and [c]Kiriathaim,
10 and I will give it for a possession,
along with the sons of Ammon, to the
[a]sons of the east, that the sons of Ammon may not be remembered among the
nations.
11"Thus I will execute judgments on
Moab, and they will know that I am the
LORD."

Edom

12 'Thus says the Lord GOD, "Because
[a]Edom has acted against the house of
Judah by taking vengeance, and has
incurred grievous guilt, and avenged
themselves upon them,"
13 therefore, thus says the Lord GOD,
"I will also [a]stretch out My hand against
Edom and [b]cut off man and beast from
it. And I will lay it waste; from [c]Teman
even to [d]Dedan they will fall by the
sword.
14 "And [a]I will lay My vengeance on
Edom by the hand of My people Israel.
Therefore, they will act in Edom [b]ac-
cording to My anger and according to
My wrath; thus they will know My
vengeance," declares the Lord GOD.

Philistia

15 'Thus says the Lord GOD, "Because
the Philistines have acted in [a]revenge
and have taken vengeance with scorn of
soul to destroy with everlasting enmity,"
16 therefore, thus says the Lord GOD,
"Behold, I will [a]stretch out My hand
against the Philistines, even cut off the
[b]Cherethites and destroy the remnant of
the seacoast.
17 "And I will execute great vengeance
on them with wrathful rebukes; and they
will [a]know that I am the LORD when I
lay My vengeance on them." ' "

Judgment on Tyre

26 NOW it came about in the eleventh year, on the first of the
month, that the word of the LORD came
to me saying,
2 "Son of man, because [a]Tyre has said
concerning Jerusalem, 'Aha, the [b]gate-
way of the peoples is broken; it has
[1][c]opened to me. I shall be filled, *now that*
she is laid waste,'
3 therefore, thus says the Lord [1]GOD,
'Behold, I am against you, O Tyre, and I
will bring up [a]many nations against you,
as the [b]sea brings up its waves.
4 'And they will [a]destroy the walls of
Tyre and break down her towers; and I
will scrape her debris from her and make
her a bare rock.
5 'She will be a place for the spreading of nets in the midst of the sea, for I
have spoken,' declares the Lord GOD,
'and she will become [a]spoil for the
nations.
6 'Also her [a]daughters who are [1]on
the mainland will be slain by the sword,
and they will know that I am the
LORD.' "
7 For thus says the Lord GOD, "Behold, I will bring upon Tyre from the
north Nebuchadnezzar king of Babylon,
[a]king of kings, with horses, [b]chariots,
cavalry, and [1]a great army.
8 "He will slay your daughters [1]on the
mainland with the sword; and he will
make [a]siege walls against you, cast up a
[b]mound against you, and raise up a large
shield against you.
9 "And the blow of his battering rams
he will direct against your walls, and
with his [1]axes he will break down your
towers.
10 "Because of the multitude of his
[a]horses, the dust *raised by* them will
cover you; your walls will [b]shake at the
noise of cavalry and [1]wagons and chariots, when he [c]enters your gates as men
enter a city that is breached.
11 "With the hoofs of his [a]horses he
will trample all your streets. He will slay
your people with the sword; and your
strong pillars will [b]come down to the
ground.
12 "Also they will make a spoil of your
riches and a prey of your [a]merchandise,
[b]break down your walls and destroy
your [c]pleasant houses, and [1]throw your
stones and your timbers and your debris
[d]into the water.
13 "So I will [1]silence the sound of your
[a]songs, and the sound of your [b]harps
will be heard no more.
14 "And I will make you a bare rock;
you will be a place for the spreading of
nets. You will be [a]built no more, for I
the [b]LORD have spoken," declares the
Lord GOD.
15 Thus says the Lord GOD to Tyre,
"Shall not the [a]coastlands [b]shake at the
sound of your fall when the wounded
groan, when the slaughter occurs in your
midst?
16 "Then all the princes of the sea will
[a]go down from their thrones, remove
their robes, and strip off their embroidered garments. They will [b]clothe themselves with [1]trembling; they will sit on
the ground, [c]tremble every moment, and
be appalled at you.
17 "And they will take up a [a]lamenta-
tion over you and say to you,
'[b]How you have perished, O inhabited one,
From the seas, O renowned city,
Which was [c]mighty on the sea,
She and her inhabitants,
Who [1]imposed [2]her terror
On all her inhabitants!
18 'Now the [a]coastlands will tremble
On the day of your fall;
Yes, the coastlands which are by
the sea
Will be terrified at your [b]pass-
ing.' "
19 For thus says the Lord GOD,
"When I shall make you a desolate city,
like the cities which are not inhabited,
when I shall [a]bring up the deep over you,
and the great waters will cover you,
20 then I shall bring you down with
those who [a]go down to the pit, to the
people of old, and I shall make you
dwell in the [b]lower parts of the earth,
like the ancient waste places, with those
who go down to the pit, so that you will
not [1]be inhabited; but I shall set [c]glory
in the land of the living.

---

12 [a]2 Chr. 28:17; Ps. 137:7; Jer. 49:7-22
13 [a]Jer. 49:8, 13 [b]Ezek. 29:8; Mal. 1:3, 4 [c]Gen. 36:34; Jer. 49:7; Amos 1:12 [d]Jer. 25:23; 49:8
14 [a]Is. 11:14 [b]Ezek. 35:11
15 [a]Is. 14:29-31; Ezek. 25:6, 12; Joel 3:4
16 [a]Jer. 25:20; 47:1-7 [b]1 Sam. 30:14; Zeph. 2:5
17 [a]Ps. 9:16

2 [1]Lit., *turned* [a]2 Sam. 5:11; Is. 23:1; Jer. 25:22 [b]Is. 62:10 [c]Ezek. 25:8; 35:10
3 [1]Heb., *YHWH*, usually rendered *LORD*, and so throughout the ch. [a]Mic. 4:11 [b]Is. 5:30; Jer. 50:42; 51:42
4 [a]Is. 23:11; Ezek. 26:9; Amos 1:10
5 [a]Ezek. 25:7; 29:19
6 [1]Lit., *in the field* [a]Ezek. 16:46, 53; 26:8
7 [1]Lit., *an assembly, even many people* [a]Ezra 7:12; Is. 10:8; Jer. 52:32; Dan. 2:37, 47 [b]Ezek. 23:24; Nah. 2:3, 4
8 [1]Lit., *in the field* [a]Jer. 52:4; Ezek. 21:22 [b]Jer. 32:24
9 [1]Lit., *swords*
10 [1]Lit., *wheels* [a]Jer. 4:13; 47:3 [b]Ezek. 26:15; 27:28 [c]Jer. 39:3
11 [a]Is. 5:28; Hab. 1:8 [b]Is. 26:5; Jer. 43:13
12 [1]Lit., *put* [a]Is. 23:8, 18; Ezek. 27:3-27; Zech. 9:3 [b]Jer. 52:14 [c]2 Chr. 32:27; Amos 5:11 [d]Ezek. 27:27, 32, 34; 28:8
13 [1]Lit., *cause to cease* [a]Is. 23:16; 24:8, 9; Amos 6:5 [b]Is. 5:12; Rev. 18:22
14 [a]Deut. 13:16; Job 12:14; Mal. 1:4 [b]Is. 14:27
15 [a]Ezek. 26:18; 27:35 [b]Jer. 49:21; Ezek. 31:16
16 [1]Lit., *tremblings* [a]Jon. 3:6 [b]Job 8:22; Ps. 35:26; Ezek. 7:27; 1 Pet. 5:5 [c]Ezek. 32:10; Hos. 11:10
17 [1]Lit., *put* [2]Lit., *their* [a]Ezek. 19:1, 14; 27:2, 32; 32:2, 16 [b]Is. 14:12; Jer. 48:39; 50:23 [c]Ezek. 27:3, 10, 11; 28:2
18 [a]Is. 41:5; Ezek. 26:15; 27:35 [b]Is. 23:5-7, 10, 11
19 [a]Is. 8:7, 8; Ezek. 26:3
20 [1]Or, *return* [a]Is. 14:9, 10; Ezek. 32:30 [b]Ps. 88:6; Amos 9:2; Jon. 2:2, 6 [c]Jer. 33:9; Zech. 2:8

21 "I shall [1]bring [a]terrors on you, and
you will be no more; though you will be
sought, [b]you will never be found again,"
declares the Lord GOD.

Lament over Tyre

27 MOREOVER, the word of the
LORD came to me saying,
2 "And you, son of man, [a]take up a
lamentation over Tyre;
3 and say to Tyre, [a]who dwells at the
[1]entrance to the sea, [b]merchant of the
peoples to many coastlands, 'Thus says
the Lord [2]GOD,

"O Tyre, you have said, 'I am
perfect in beauty.'
4 "Your borders are in the heart of
the seas;
Your builders have perfected your
beauty.
5 "They have [1]made all *your* planks
of fir trees from [a]Senir;
They have taken a cedar from
Lebanon to make a mast for
you.
6 "Of [a]oaks from [b]Bashan they have
made your oars;
With ivory they have [1]inlaid your
deck of boxwood from the
coastlands of [c]Cyprus.
7 "Your sail was of fine embroidered
linen from Egypt
So that it became your [1]distinguishing mark;
Your [2]awning was [3a]blue and
purple from the coastlands of
[b]Elishah.
8 "The inhabitants of Sidon and
[a]Arvad were your rowers;
Your [b]wise men, O Tyre, were
[1]aboard; they were your pilots.
9 "The elders of [a]Gebal and her wise
men were with you repairing
your seams;
All the ships of the sea and their
sailors were with you in order to
deal in your merchandise.

10 "[a]Persia and [a]Lud and [a]Put were in
your army, your men of war. They hung
shield and helmet in you; they set forth
your splendor.
11 "The sons of Arvad and your army
were on your walls, *all* around, and the
[1]Gammadim were in your towers. They
hung their shields on your walls, *all*
around; they perfected your beauty.
12 "Tarshish was your customer because of the abundance of all *kinds* of
wealth; with silver, iron, tin, and lead,
they paid for your wares.
13 "[a]Javan, [a]Tubal, and [b]Meshech,
they were your traders; with the [c]lives of
men and vessels of bronze they paid for
your merchandise.
14 "Those from [a]Beth-togarmah gave
horses and war horses and mules for
your wares.
15 "The sons of [a]Dedan were your
traders. Many coastlands were [1]your
market; [b]ivory tusks and ebony they
brought as your payment.
16 "[a]Aram was your customer because
of the abundance of your [1]goods; they
paid for your wares with [b]emeralds,
purple, [c]embroidered work, fine linen,
coral, and rubies.
17 "Judah and the land of Israel, they
were your traders; with the wheat of
[a]Minnith, [1]cakes, honey, oil, and balm
they paid for your merchandise.
18 "[a]Damascus was your customer because of the abundance of your [1]goods,
because of the abundance of all *kinds* of
wealth, because of the wine of Helbon
and white wool.
19 "Vedan and Javan paid for your
wares [1]from Uzal; wrought iron, cassia,
and [2]sweet cane were among your merchandise.
20 "[a]Dedan traded with you in saddle-
cloths for riding.
21 "[a]Arabia and all the princes of
Kedar, they were [1]your customers for
[b]lambs, rams, and goats; for these they
were your customers.
22 "The traders of [a]Sheba and Raamah, they traded with you; they paid for
your wares with the best of all *kinds* of
[b]spices, and with all *kinds* of precious
stones, and gold.
23 "Haran, Canneh, [a]Eden, the traders
of Sheba, Asshur, *and* Chilmad traded
with you.
24 "They traded with you in choice
garments, in clothes of [1]blue and embroidered work, and in carpets of many
colors, *and* tightly wound cords, *which*
were among your merchandise.
25 "The [a]ships of Tarshish were [1]the
carriers for your merchandise.
And you were filled and were very
[2]glorious
In the heart of the seas.

26 "Your rowers have brought you
Into [a]great waters;
The [b]east wind has broken you
In the heart of the seas.
27 "Your wealth, your wares, your
merchandise,
Your sailors, and your pilots,
Your repairers of seams, your deal-
ers in merchandise,
And all your men of war who are in
you,
With all your company that is in
your midst,
Will fall into the heart of the seas
On the day of your overthrow.
28 "At the sound of the cry of your
pilots
The pasture lands will [a]shake.
29 "And all who handle the oar,
The [a]sailors, *and* all the pilots of
the sea
Will come down from their ships;
They will stand on the land,
30 And they will [a]make their voice
heard over you
And will cry bitterly.
They will [b]cast dust on their heads,
They will [c]wallow in ashes.

21 [1]Lit., *give you terrors* [a]Ezek. 26:15, 16; 27:36 [b]Rev. 18:21
2 [a]Jer. 9:10, 17-20; Ezek. 28:12
3 [1]Lit., *entrances* [2]Heb., *YHWH,* usually rendered *LORD,* and so throughout the ch. [a]Ezek. 28:2 [b]Is. 23:3
5 [1]Lit., *built* [a]Deut. 3:9; 1 Chr. 5:23; Song 4:8
6 [1]Lit., *made* [a]Is. 2:13; Zech. 11:2 [b]Num. 21:33; Is. 2:13; Jer. 22:20 [c]Gen. 10:4; Is. 23:1, 12; Jer. 2:10
7 [1]Or, *standard* [2]Lit., *covering* [3]Or, *violet* [a]Ex. 25:4; Jer. 10:9 [b]Gen. 10:4
8 [1]Lit., *in you* [a]Gen. 10:18; 1 Chr. 1:16; Ezek. 27:11 [b]1 Kin. 9:27
9 [a]Josh. 13:5; 1 Kin. 5:18
10 [a]Ezek. 30:5; 38:5
11 [1]Or, *valorous ones*
13 [a]Gen. 10:2; Is. 66:19; Ezek. 27:19 [b]Gen. 10:2; Ezek. 38:2; 39:1 [c]Joel 3:3; Rev. 18:13
14 [a]Gen. 10:3; Ezek. 38:6
15 [1]Lit., *the market of your hand* [a]Jer. 25:23; Ezek. 25:13; 27:20 [b]1 Kin. 10:22; Rev. 18:12
16 [1]Lit., *works* [a]Judg. 10:6; Is. 7:1-8; Ezek. 16:57 [b]Ezek. 28:13 [c]Ezek. 16:13, 18
17 [1]Heb., *pannag* [a]Judg. 11:33
18 [1]Lit., *works* [a]Gen. 14:15; Is. 7:8; Jer. 49:23; Ezek. 47:16-18
19 [1]Or, *with yarn* [2]Or, *calamus*
20 [a]Gen. 25:3
21 [1]Lit., *customers of your hand* [a]Is. 21:13 [b]Is. 60:7
22 [a]Gen. 10:7; Is. 60:6; Ezek. 38:13 [b]Gen. 43:11; 1 Kin. 10:2
23 [a]2 Kin. 19:12; Is. 37:12; Amos 1:5
24 [1]Or, *violet*
25 [1]Lit., *your travelers* [2]Lit., *honored* [a]Is. 2:16
26 [a]Ezek. 26:19 [b]Ps. 48:7; Jer. 18:17; Acts 27:14
28 [a]Ezek. 26:10, 15, 18
29 [a]Rev. 18:17-19
30 [a]Is. 23:1-6; Ezek. 26:17 [b]1 Sam. 4:12; 2 Sam. 1:2; Lam. 2:10; Rev. 18:19 [c]Jer. 6:26; Jon. 3:6

31 "Also they will make themselves [a]bald for you
And [b]gird themselves with sackcloth;
And they will [c]weep for you in bitterness of soul
With bitter mourning.
32 "Moreover, in their wailing they will take up a [a]lamentation for you
And lament over you:
'Who is like Tyre,
Like her who is silent in the midst of the sea?
33 'When your wares went out from the seas,
You satisfied many peoples;
With the [a]abundance of your wealth and your merchandise
You enriched the kings of earth.
34 '[1]Now that you are [a]broken by the seas
In the depths of the waters,
Your [b]merchandise and all your company
Have fallen in the midst of you.
35 'All the [a]inhabitants of the coastlands
Are appalled at you,
And their kings are horribly afraid;
They are troubled in countenance.
36 'The merchants among the peoples [a]hiss at you;
You have become [1]terrified,
And you [b]will be no more.' " ' "

Tyre's King Overthrown

28 THE word of the LORD came again to me saying,
2 "Son of man, say to the [1]leader of Tyre, 'Thus says the Lord [2]GOD,
"Because your heart is lifted up
And you have said, '[a]I am a god,
I sit in the seat of [3]gods,
In the heart of the seas';
Yet you are a [b]man and not God,
Although you make your heart like the heart of God—
3 Behold, you are wiser than [a]Daniel;
There is no secret that is a match for you.
4 "By your wisdom and understanding
You have acquired [a]riches for yourself,
And have acquired gold and silver for your treasuries.
5 "By your great wisdom, by your [a]trade
You have increased your riches,
And your [b]heart is lifted up because of your riches—
6 Therefore, thus says the Lord GOD,
'Because you have [a]made your heart
Like the heart of God,
7 Therefore, behold, I will bring [a]strangers upon you,
The [b]most ruthless of the nations.
And they will draw their swords
Against the beauty of your wisdom
And defile your splendor.
8 'They will bring you down to the pit,
And you will die the [a]death of those who are slain
In the heart of the seas.
9 'Will you still say, "I am a god,"
In the presence of your slayer,
Although you are a man and not God,
In the hands of those who wound you?
10 'You will die the death of the [a]uncircumcised
By the hand of strangers,
For I have spoken!' declares the Lord GOD!" ' "
11 Again the word of the LORD came to me saying,
12 "Son of man, [a]take up a lamentation over the king of Tyre, and say to him,
'Thus says the Lord GOD,
"You [1]had the seal of perfection,
Full of wisdom and perfect in beauty.
13 "You were in [a]Eden, the garden of God;
[b]Every precious stone was your covering:
The [c]ruby, the topaz, and the diamond;
The beryl, the onyx, and the jasper;
The lapis lazuli, the turquoise, and the emerald;
And the gold, the workmanship of your [1][d]settings and [2]sockets,
Was in you.
On the day that you were created
They were prepared.
14 "You were the [a]anointed cherub who [1]covers,
And I placed you *there.*
You were on the holy [b]mountain of God;
You walked in the midst of the [c]stones of fire.
15 "You were [a]blameless in your ways
From the day you were created,
Until [b]unrighteousness was found in you.
16 "By the [a]abundance of your trade
[1]You were internally [b]filled with violence,
And you sinned;
Therefore I have cast you as profane
From the mountain of God.
And I have destroyed you, O [2]covering cherub,
From the midst of the stones of fire.
17 "Your heart was lifted up because of your [a]beauty;
You [b]corrupted your wisdom by reason of your splendor.
I cast you to the ground;
I put you before [c]kings,
That they may see you.
18 "By the multitude of your iniquities,
In the unrighteousness of your trade,
You profaned your sanctuaries.

31 [a]Is. 15:2; Ezek. 29:18 [b]Is. 22:12; Ezek. 7:18 [c]Is. 16:9; 22:4
32 [a]Ezek. 26:17; 27:2; 28:12
33 [a]Ezek. 27:12, 18; 28:4, 5
34 [1]Lit., *The time* [a]Ezek. 26:12; 27:26, 27 [b]Zech. 9:3, 4
35 [a]Is. 23:6; Ezek. 26:16
36 [1]Lit., *terrors* [a]Jer. 18:16; 19:8; 49:17; 50:13; Zeph. 2:15 [b]Ps. 37:10, 36
2 [1]Or, *ruler, prince* [2]Heb., *YHWH,* usually rendered *LORD,* and so throughout the ch. [3]Or, *God* [a]Is. 14:14; 47:8; Ezek. 28:9; 2 Thess. 2:4 [b]Ps. 9:20; 82:6, 7; Is. 31:3; Ezek. 28:9
3 [a]Dan. 1:20; 2:20-23, 28; 5:11, 12
4 [a]Ezek. 27:33; Zech. 9:2, 3
5 [a]Ezek. 27:12; Hos. 12:7, 8 [b]Job 31:24, 25; Ps. 52:7; Ezek. 28:2; Hos. 13:6
6 [a]Ex. 9:17; Ezek. 28:2
7 [a]Ezek. 26:7 [b]Ezek. 30:11; 31:12; 32:12; Hab. 1:6-8
8 [a]Ezek. 27:26, 27, 34
10 [a]1 Sam. 17:26, 36; Ezek. 31:18; 32:30
12 [1]Lit., were *the one sealing a pattern* [a]Ezek. 19:1; 26:17; 27:2
13 [1]Or, *tambourines* [2]Or, *flutes* [a]Gen. 2:8; Is. 51:3; Ezek. 31:8, 9, 16; 36:35 [b]Ezek. 27:16, 22 [c]Ex. 28:17-20 [d]Is. 24:8; 30:32
14 [1]Or, *guards* [a]Ex. 25:17-20; 30:26; 40:9; Ezek. 28:16 [b]Ezek. 20:40; 28:16 [c]Ezek. 28:13, 16; Rev. 18:16
15 [a]Ezek. 27:3, 4; 28:3-6, 12 [b]Ezek. 28:17, 18
16 [1]Lit., *They filled your midst* [2]Or, *guardian* [a]Ezek. 27:12 [b]Ezek. 8:17; Hab. 2:8, 17
17 [a]Ezek. 27:3, 4; 28:7 [b]Is. 19:11 [c]Ezek. 26:16

Therefore I have brought [a]fire from
the midst of you;
It has consumed you,
And I have turned you to [b]ashes on
the earth
In the eyes of all who see you.
19"All who know you among the peoples
Are appalled at you;
You have become [1a]terrified,
And you will be [b]no more." ' "

Judgment of Sidon

20 And the word of the LORD came to
me saying,
21"Son of man, [a]set your face toward
[b]Sidon, prophesy against her,
22 and say, 'Thus says the Lord GOD,
"Behold, I am against you, O Sidon,
And I shall [1]be glorified in your
midst.
Then they will know that I am the
LORD, when I [a]execute judgments in her,
And I shall manifest My holiness in
her.
23"For [a]I shall send pestilence to her
And blood to her streets,
And the [b]wounded will [1]fall in her
midst
By the sword upon her on every
side;
Then they will know that I am the
LORD.
24"And there will be no more for the
house of Israel a [a]prickling brier or a
painful thorn from any round about
them who scorned them; then they will
know that I am the Lord GOD."

Israel Regathered

25 'Thus says the Lord GOD, "When I
[a]gather the house of Israel from the
peoples among whom they are scattered,
and shall manifest My holiness in them
in the sight of the nations, then they will
[b]live in their [1]land which I gave to My
servant Jacob.
26"And they will [a]live in it securely;
and they will [b]build houses, plant vineyards, and live securely, when I [c]execute
judgments upon all who scorn them
round about them. Then they will know
that I am the LORD their God." ' "

Judgment of Egypt

29 IN the [a]tenth year, in the tenth
month, on the twelfth of the
month, the word of the LORD came to
me saying,
2"Son of man, set your face against
[a]Pharaoh, king of Egypt, and prophesy
against him and against all [b]Egypt.
3"Speak and say, 'Thus says the Lord
[1]GOD,
"Behold, I am against you, Pharaoh,
king of Egypt,
The great [2a]monster that lies in the
midst of his [3]rivers,
That [b]has said, 'My Nile is mine,
and I myself have made it.'

18 [a]Amos 1:9, 10 [b]Mal. 4:3
19 [1]Lit., *terrors* [a]Ezek. 26:21; 27:36 [b]Jer. 51:64
21 [a]Ezek. 6:2; 25:2 [b]Gen. 10:15, 19; Is. 23:2, 4; Ezek. 27:8
22 [1]Or, *glorify Myself* [a]Ezek. 28:26; 30:19
23 [1]Or, *be judged* [a]Ezek. 38:22 [b]Jer. 51:52
24 [a]Num. 33:55; Josh. 23:13; Is. 55:13; Ezek. 2:6
25 [1]Lit., *ground* [a]Ps. 106:47; Is. 11:12, 13; Jer. 32:37; Ezek. 20:41; 34:13, 27 [b]Jer. 23:8; 27:11
26 [a]Jer. 23:6; Ezek. 34:25-28; 38:8 [b]Jer. 32:15, 43, 44; Amos 9:13, 14 [c]Ezek. 25:11; 28:22

1 [a]Ezek. 26:1; 29:17; 30:20
2 [a]Jer. 44:30 [b]Is. 19:1-17; Jer. 46:2-26; Ezek. 30:1-32:32
3 [1]Heb., *YHWH,* usually rendered *LORD,* and so throughout the ch. [2]Lit., *tannim* [3]Or, *Nile* [a]Is. 27:1; Ezek. 32:2 [b]Ezek. 29:9; 30:12
4 [1]Or, *Nile* [a]2 Kin. 19:28; Ezek. 38:4
5 [1]Or, *Nile* [2]Lit., *faces of the field* [3]Or, with several mss. and Targum, *buried* [a]Ezek. 32:4-6 [b]Jer. 8:2; 25:33 [c]Jer. 7:33; 34:20; Ezek. 39:4
6 [a]2 Kin. 18:21; Is. 36:6
7 [1]So with some ancient versions; M.T., *shoulders* [2]Lit., *stand* [a]2 Kin. 18:21; Is. 36:6; Ezek. 17:15-17
8 [a]Jer. 46:13; Ezek. 14:17
9 [1]Lit., *he* [a]Ezek. 29:10-12; 30:7, 8, 13-19 [b]Prov. 16:18; 18:12; Ezek. 29:3
10 [1]Or, *Nile* [2]Lit., *Cush* [a]Ezek. 13:8; 21:3; 26:3; 29:3
11 [a]Jer. 43:11, 12; 46:19; Ezek. 32:13
12 [a]Jer. 25:15-19; 27:6-11; Ezek. 30:7 [b]Jer. 46:19; Ezek. 30:23, 26
13 [1]Lit., *where* [a]Is. 19:22; Jer. 46:26
14 [a]Is. 11:11; Jer. 44:1, 15; Ezek. 30:14
15 [a]Ezek. 17:6, 14; 30:13; Zech. 10:11 [b]Ezek. 31:2; 32:2; Nah. 3:8-10
16 [1]Lit., *causing to remember* [2]Lit., *after them* [a]Is. 20:5; 30:1-3; 31:1; 36:6; Ezek. 17:15; 29:6, 7 [b]Is. 64:9; Jer. 14:10; Ezek. 21:23; Hos. 8:13

4"And I shall put [a]hooks in your
jaws,
And I shall make the fish of your
[1]rivers cling to your scales.
And I shall bring you up out of the
midst of your [1]rivers,
And all the fish of your [1]rivers will
cling to your scales.
5"And I shall [a]abandon you to the
wilderness, you and all the fish
of your [1]rivers;
You will fall on the [2]open field;
you will not be brought together
or [3b]gathered.
I have given you for [c]food to the
beasts of the earth and to the
birds of the sky.
6"Then all the inhabitants of Egypt
will know that I am the LORD,
Because they have been *only* a [a]staff
made of reed to the house of
Israel.
7"When they took hold of you with
the hand,
You [a]broke and tore all their
[1]hands;
And when they leaned on you,
You broke and made all their loins
[2]quake."
8 'Therefore, thus says the Lord GOD,
"Behold, I shall [a]bring upon you a
sword, and I shall cut off from you man
and beast.
9"And the [a]land of Egypt will become a desolation and waste. Then they
will know that I am the LORD.
Because [1]you [b]said, 'The Nile is mine,
and I have made *it,*'
10 therefore, behold, I am [a]against
you and against your [1]rivers, and I will
make the land of Egypt an utter waste
and desolation, from Migdol *to* Syene
and even to the border of [2]Ethiopia.
11"A man's foot will [a]not pass through
it, and the foot of a beast will not pass
through it, and it will not be inhabited
for forty years.
12"So I shall make the land of Egypt a
desolation in the [a]midst of desolated
lands. And her cities, in the midst of
cities that are laid waste, will be desolate
forty years; and I shall [b]scatter the
Egyptians among the nations and disperse them among the lands."
13 'For thus says the Lord GOD, "At
the end of forty years I shall [a]gather the
Egyptians from the peoples [1]among
whom they were scattered.
14"And I shall turn the fortunes of
Egypt and shall make them return to the
land of [a]Pathros, to the land of their
origin; and there they will be a lowly
kingdom.
15"It will be the [a]lowest of the kingdoms; and it will never again lift itself
up above the nations. And I shall make
them so small that they will not [b]rule
over the nations.
16"And it will never again be the
[a]confidence of the house of Israel,
[1b]bringing to mind the iniquity of their
having turned [2]to Egypt. Then they will
know that I am the Lord GOD." ' "

17 Now in the [a]twenty-seventh year,
in the first *month,* on the first of the
month, the word of the LORD came to
me saying,
18 "Son of man, [a]Nebuchadnezzar king
of Babylon made his army labor [1]hard
against Tyre; every head was made
[b]bald, and every shoulder was rubbed
bare. But he and his army had no wages
from Tyre for the labor that he had
[2]performed against it."
19 Therefore, thus says the Lord GOD,
"Behold, I [a]shall give the land of Egypt
to Nebuchadnezzar king of Babylon.
And he will carry off her [1b]wealth, and
capture her spoil and seize her plunder;
and it will be wages for his army.
20 "I have given him the land of Egypt
for his labor which he [1a]performed,
because they acted for Me," declares the
Lord GOD.
21 "On that day I shall make a [a]horn
sprout for the house of Israel, and I shall
[1b]open your mouth in their midst. Then
they will know that I am the LORD."

Lament over Egypt

30 THE word of the LORD came
again to me saying,
2 "Son of man, prophesy and say,
'Thus says the Lord [1]GOD,
"[a]Wail, 'Alas for the day!'
3 "For the day is near,
Even [a]the day of the LORD is near;
It will be a day of [b]clouds,
A time *of doom* for the nations.
4 "And a sword will come upon Egypt,
And anguish will be in [1]Ethiopia,
When the slain fall in Egypt,
They [a]take away her [2]wealth,
And her foundations are torn down.
5 "[1]Ethiopia, Put, Lud, all [2a]Arabia,
[3]Libya, and the [4]people of the land [5]that
is in league will fall with them by the
sword."
6 'Thus says the LORD,
"Indeed, those who support [a]Egypt will fall,
And the pride of her power will come down;
From Migdol *to* Syene
They will fall within her by the sword,"
Declares the Lord GOD.
7 "And they will be desolate
In the [a]midst of the desolated lands;
And her cities will be
In the midst of the devastated cities.
8 "And they will [a]know that I am the LORD,
When I set a [b]fire in Egypt
And all her helpers are broken.
9 "On that day [a]messengers will go
forth from Me in ships to frighten [b]se-
cure [1]Ethiopia; and [c]anguish will be on
them as on the day of Egypt; for, be-
hold, it comes!"
10 'Thus says the Lord GOD,
"[a]I will also make the [1]multitude of Egypt cease
By the hand of Nebuchadnezzar king of Babylon.
11 "He and his people with him,
[a]The most ruthless of the nations,
Will be brought in to destroy the land;
And they will draw their swords against Egypt
And fill the land with the slain.
12 "Moreover, I will make the [a]Nile canals dry
And [b]sell the land into the hands of evil men.
And I will make the land desolate,
And [1]all that is in it,
By the hand of strangers; I, the LORD, have spoken."

13 'Thus says the Lord GOD,
"I will also [a]destroy the idols
And make the [1]images cease from [2b]Memphis.
And there will no longer be a prince in the land of Egypt;
And I will put fear in the land of Egypt.
14 "And I will make [a]Pathros desolate,
Set a fire in [b]Zoan,
And execute judgments on [1c]Thebes.
15 "And I will pour out My wrath on [1]Sin,
The stronghold of Egypt;
I will also cut off the multitude of [2]Thebes.
16 "And I will set a fire in Egypt;
[1]Sin will writhe in anguish,
[2]Thebes will be breached,
And [3]Memphis *will have* [4]distresses daily.
17 "The young men of [1a]On and of Pi-beseth
Will fall by the sword,
And [2]the women will go into captivity.
18 "And in [a]Tehaphnehes the day will [1]be [b]dark
When I [c]break there the yoke bars of Egypt.
Then the pride of her power will cease in her;
A cloud will cover her,
And her daughters will go into captivity.
19 "Thus I will [a]execute judgments on Egypt,
And they will know that I am the LORD." ' "

Victory for Babylon

20 And it came about in the [a]eleventh
year, in the first *month,* on the seventh of
the month, that the word of the LORD
came to me saying,

17 [a]Ezek. 24:1; 26:1; 29:1; 30:20; 40:1
18 [1]Lit., *a great labor* [2]Lit., *labored* [a]Jer. 25:9; 27:6; Ezek. 26:7-12 [b]Jer. 48:37; Ezek. 27:31
19 [1]Or, *multitude* [a]Ezek. 30:10, 24, 25; 32:11 [b]Jer. 43:10-13; Ezek. 30:14
20 [1]Lit., *labored* [a]Is. 10:6, 7; 45:1-3; Jer. 25:9
21 [1]Lit., *give you an opening of the mouth* [a]1 Sam. 2:10; Ps. 92:10; 132:17 [b]Ezek. 3:27; 24:27; 33:22; Amos 3:7, 8; Luke 21:15

2 [1]Heb., *YHWH,* usually rendered *LORD,* and so throughout the ch. [a]Is. 13:6; 15:2; Ezek. 21:12; Joel 1:5, 11, 13
3 [a]Ezek. 7:19; 13:5; Joel 1:15; 2:1; Obad. 15 [b]Ezek. 30:18; 32:7; 34:12
4 [1]Lit., *Cush* [2]Or, *multitude* [a]Ezek. 29:19
5 [1]Lit., *Cush* [2]Or, *the mixed people* [3]Or, *Cub* [4]Lit., *sons* [5]Lit., *of the covenant* [a]Jer. 25:20, 24
6 [a]Is. 20:3-6
7 [a]Jer. 25:18-26; Ezek. 29:12
8 [a]Ps. 58:11; Ezek. 29:6, 9, 16 [b]Ezek. 22:31; 30:14, 16; Amos 1:4, 7, 10, 12, 14
9 [1]Lit., *Cush* [a]Is. 18:1, 2 [b]Is. 47:8; Ezek. 38:11; 39:6 [c]Is. 19:17; 23:5; Ezek. 32:9, 10
10 [1]Or, *wealth* [a]Ezek. 29:19
11 [a]Ezek. 28:7
12 [1]Lit., *her fulness* [a]Ezek. 29:3, 9 [b]Is. 19:4
13 [1]Or, *futile ones* [2]Or, *Noph* [a]Is. 2:18 [b]Is. 19:13; Jer. 2:16; 44:1; 46:14; Ezek. 30:16
14 [1]Or, *No* [a]Is. 11:11; Jer. 44:1, 15; Ezek. 29:14 [b]Ps. 78:12, 43; Is. 19:11, 13 [c]Jer. 46:25; Ezek. 30:15, 16; Nah. 3:8
15 [1]Or, *Pelusium* [2]Or, *No*
16 [1]Or, *Pelusium* [2]Or, *No* [3]Or, *Noph* [4]Or, *adversaries*
17 [1]Or, *Aven* [2]Lit., *they* [a]Gen. 41:45; 46:20
18 [1]So with many mss. and ancient versions; M.T., *restrain* [a]Jer. 43:8-13 [b]Ezek. 30:3 [c]Lev. 26:13; Is. 10:27; Jer. 27:2; 28:10, 13; 30:8; Ezek. 34:27
19 [a]Ps. 9:16; Ezek. 5:8, 15; 25:11; 30:14
20 [a]Ezek. 26:1; 29:1, 17; 31:1

21 "Son of man, I have [a]broken the arm of Pharaoh king of Egypt; and, behold, it has not been [b]bound up [1]for healing [2]or wrapped with a bandage, that it may be strong to hold the sword.

22 "Therefore, thus says the Lord GOD, 'Behold, I am [a]against Pharaoh king of Egypt and will break his arms, both the strong and the [b]broken; and I will make the sword [c]fall from his hand.

23 'And I will [a]scatter the Egyptians among the nations and disperse them among the lands.

24 'For I will [a]strengthen the arms of the king of Babylon and put [b]My sword in his hand; and I will break the arms of Pharaoh, so that he will groan before him with the groanings of a wounded man.

25 'Thus I will strengthen the arms of the king of Babylon, but the arms of Pharaoh will fall. Then they will know that I am the LORD, when I put My sword into the hand of the king of Babylon and he [a]stretches it out against the land of Egypt.

26 'When I scatter the Egyptians among the nations and disperse them among the lands, then they will know that I am the LORD.' "

Pharaoh Warned of Assyria's Fate

31 AND it came about in the [a]eleventh year, in the third *month,* on the first of the month, that the word of the LORD came to me saying,

2 "Son of man, say to Pharaoh king of Egypt, and to his [a]multitude,

'Whom are you like in your greatness?
3 'Behold, Assyria *was* a [a]cedar in Lebanon
With beautiful branches and forest shade,
And [1b]very high;
And its top was among the [2]clouds.
4 'The [a]waters made it grow, the [1]deep made it high.
With its rivers it continually [2]extended all around its planting place,
And it sent out its channels to all the trees of the field.
5 'Therefore [a]its height was loftier than all the trees of the field
And its boughs became many and its branches long
Because of [b]many waters [1]as it spread them out.
6 'All the [a]birds of the heavens nested in its boughs,
And under its branches all the beasts of the field gave birth,
And all great nations lived under its shade.
7 'So it was beautiful in its greatness, in the length of its branches;
For its [1]roots extended to many waters.
8 'The [a]cedars in [b]God's garden [1]could not match it;
The [2]cypresses [1]could not compare with its boughs,
And the plane trees [3]could not match its branches.
No tree in [b]God's garden [1]could compare with it in its beauty.
9 'I made it beautiful with the multitude of its branches,
And all the trees of [a]Eden, which were in the [a]garden of God, were jealous of it.

10 'Therefore, thus says the Lord [1]GOD, "Because [2]it is high in stature, and it has set its top among the [3]clouds, and its [a]heart is haughty in its loftiness,

11 therefore, I will give it into the hand of a [1a]despot of the nations; he will thoroughly deal with it. According to its wickedness I have [b]driven it away.

12 "And [a]alien [b]tyrants of the nations have cut it down and left it; on the [c]mountains and in all the valleys its branches have fallen, and its boughs have been broken in all the ravines of the land. And all the peoples of the earth have [d]gone down from its shade and left it.

13 "On its ruin all the [a]birds of the heavens will dwell. And all the beasts of the field will be on its *fallen* branches

14 in order that all the trees by the waters may not be exalted in their stature, nor set their top among the [1]clouds, nor their [2]well-watered mighty ones stand *erect* in their height. For they have all been given over to death, to the [a]earth beneath, among the sons of men, with those who go down to the pit."

15 'Thus says the Lord GOD, "On the day when it went down to Sheol I [a]caused lamentations; I closed the [1]deep over it and held back its rivers. And *its* many waters were stopped up, and I made Lebanon [2]mourn for it, and all the trees of the field wilted away on account of it.

16 "I made the nations [a]quake at the sound of its fall when I made it [b]go down to Sheol with those who go down to the pit; and all the [1]well-watered trees of Eden, the choicest and best of [c]Lebanon, were [d]comforted in the earth beneath.

17 "They also [a]went down with it to Sheol to those who were [b]slain by the sword; and those who were its [1]strength lived [c]under its shade among the nations.

18 "To which among the trees of Eden are you thus [1]equal in glory and greatness? Yet you will be brought down with the trees of Eden to the earth beneath; you will lie in the midst of the [a]uncircumcised, with those who were slain by the sword. [b]So is Pharaoh and all his multitude!" ' declares the Lord GOD."

21 [1]Lit., *to give healing* [2]Lit., *to put a bandage, to wrap it* [a]Ps. 10:15; 37:17; Ezek. 30:24 [b]Jer. 30:13; 46:11
22 [a]Jer. 46:25; Ezek. 29:3 [b]2 Kin. 24:7; Jer. 37:7 [c]Jer. 46:21
23 [a]Ezek. 29:12; 30:17, 18, 26
24 [a]Neh. 6:9; Is. 45:1, 5; Ezek. 30:10, 25; Zech. 10:12 [b]Ezek. 30:11, 25; Zeph. 2:12
25 [a]Josh. 8:18; 1 Chr. 21:16; Is. 5:25
1 [a]Jer. 52:5, 6; Ezek. 30:20; 32:1
2 [a]Ezek. 29:19; 30:10; Nah. 3:9
3 [1]Lit., *high of stature* [2]So Gr.; M.T., *thick boughs* [a]Is. 10:33, 34; Ezek. 17:3, 4, 22; 31:16; Dan. 4:10, 20-23 [b]Is. 10:33; Ezek. 31:5, 10
4 [1]I.e., subterranean waters [2]Lit., *was going* [a]Ezek. 17:5, 8; Rev. 17:1, 15
5 [1]Lit., *in its sending forth* [a]Dan. 4:11 [b]Ps. 1:3; Ezek. 17:5
6 [a]Ezek. 17:23; 31:13; Dan. 4:12, 21; Matt. 13:32
7 [1]Lit., *root was*
8 [1]Lit., *did* [2]Or, *Phoenician junipers* [3]Lit., *were not like* [a]Ps. 80:10; Ezek. 31:3 [b]Gen. 2:8, 9; 13:10; Is. 51:3; Ezek. 28:13; 31:16, 18
9 [a]Gen. 2:8, 9; 13:10; Is. 51:3; Ezek. 28:13; 31:16, 18
10 [1]Heb., *YHWH,* usually rendered *LORD,* and so throughout the ch. [2]Lit., *you are* [3]Or, *thick boughs* [a]2 Chr. 32:25; Is. 10:12; 14:13, 14; Ezek. 28:17; Dan. 5:20
11 [1]Or, *mighty one* [a]Ezek. 30:10, 11; 32:11, 12; Dan. 5:18, 19 [b]Deut. 18:12; Nah. 3:18
12 [a]Ezek. 7:21; 28:7; 30:12; Hab. 1:6 [b]Ezek. 28:7; 30:11; 32:12 [c]Ezek. 32:5; 35:8 [d]Ezek. 31:17; Dan. 4:14; Nah. 3:17, 18
13 [a]Is. 18:6; Ezek. 29:5; 31:6; 32:4
14 [1]Or, *thick boughs* [2]Lit., *drinkers of water* [a]Num. 16:30, 33; Ps. 63:9; Ezek. 26:20; 31:18; 32:24; Amos 9:2; Jon. 2:2, 6; Eph. 4:9
15 [1]I.e., subterranean waters [2]Lit., *be darkened* [a]Ezek. 32:7; Nah. 2:10
16 [1]Lit., *drinkers of water* [a]Ezek. 26:15; 27:28; Hag. 2:7 [b]Is. 14:15; Ezek. 32:18 [c]Is. 14:8; Hab. 2:17 [d]Ezek. 14:22, 23; 32:31
17 [1]Lit., *arm* [a]Ps. 9:17 [b]Ezek. 32:20f. [c]Ezek. 31:3, 6; Dan. 4:12
18 [1]Lit., *like* [a]Jer. 9:25, 26; Ezek. 28:10; 32:19, 21 [b]Ps. 52:7; Matt. 13:19

Lament over Pharaoh and Egypt

32 AND it came about in the
[a]twelfth year, in the twelfth
month, on the first of the month, that the
word of the LORD came to me saying,
2"Son of man, take up a [a]lamentation
over Pharaoh king of Egypt, and say to
him,

'You [1]compared yourself to a
young [b]lion of the nations,
Yet you are like the [c]monster in
the seas;
And you [d]burst forth in your
rivers,
And muddied the waters with
your feet,
And [2]fouled their rivers.' "

3 Thus says the Lord [1]GOD,
"Now I will [a]spread My net over
you
With a company of many peoples,
And they shall lift you up in My
net.
4 "And I will leave you on the land;
I will cast you on the [1]open field.
And I will cause all the [a]birds of
the heavens to dwell on you,
And I will satisfy the beasts of the
whole earth [2]with you.
5 "And I will lay your flesh [a]on the
mountains,
And fill the valleys with your
refuse.
6 "I will also make the land drink the
discharge of your [a]blood,
As far as the mountains,
And the ravines shall be full of
you.
7 "And when *I* [a]extinguish you,
I will [b]cover the heavens, and
darken their [c]stars;
I will cover the [d]sun with a cloud,
And the moon shall not give its
light.
8 "All the shining [a]lights in the
heavens
I will darken over you
And will set darkness on your
land,"
Declares the Lord GOD.

9"I will also [a]trouble the hearts of
many peoples, when I [b]bring your destruction among the nations, into lands
which you have not known.
10"And I will make many peoples
[a]appalled at you, and their kings shall be
horribly afraid of you when I brandish
My sword before them; and [b]they shall
tremble every moment, every man for his
own life, on the day of your fall."
11 For [a]thus says the Lord GOD, "The
sword of the king of Babylon shall come
upon you.
12"By the swords of the mighty ones I
will cause your multitude to fall; all of
them are [a]tyrants of the nations,

And they shall [b]devastate the
pride of Egypt,
And all its multitude shall be
destroyed.
13 "I will also destroy all its cattle
from beside many waters;
And [a]the foot of man shall not
muddy them anymore,
And the hoofs of beasts shall not
muddy them.
14 "Then I will make their waters
settle,
And will cause their rivers to run
like oil,"
Declares the Lord GOD.
15 "When I make the land of Egypt a
[a]desolation,
And the land is destitute of that
which filled it,
When I smite all those who live in
it,
Then they shall [b]know that I am
the LORD.

16"This is a [a]lamentation and they
shall [1]chant it. The daughters of the
nations shall [1]chant it. Over Egypt and
over all her multitude they shall [1]chant
it," declares the Lord GOD.
17 And it came about in the [a]twelfth
year, on the [a]fifteenth of the month, that
the word of the LORD came to me saying,
18"Son of man, [a]wail for the multitude
of Egypt, and [b]bring it down, her and
the daughters of the powerful nations, to
the [c]nether world, with those who go
down to the pit;

19 'Whom do you surpass in beauty?
Go down and make your bed with
the [a]uncircumcised.'

20"They shall fall in the midst of those
who are slain by the sword. [1]She is given
over to the sword; they have [a]drawn her
and all her multitudes away.
21"The [a]strong among the mighty ones
shall speak of him *and* his helpers from
the midst of Sheol, 'They have gone
down, they lie still, the uncircumcised,
slain by the sword.'
22"[a]Assyria is there and all her company; [1]her graves are round about [2]her.
All of them are slain, fallen by the
sword,
23 whose [a]graves are set in the remotest parts of the pit, and her company is
round about her grave. All of them are
slain, fallen by the sword, who [1]spread
terror in the land of the living.
24"[a]Elam is there and all her multitude
around her grave; all of them slain,
fallen by the sword, who went down
uncircumcised to the [b]lower parts of the
earth, who instilled their terror in the
[c]land of the living, and [d]bore their
disgrace with those who went down to
the pit.
25"They have made a [a]bed for her
among the slain with all her multitude.
Her graves are around it, they are all
uncircumcised, slain by the sword (although their terror was [1]instilled in the
land of the living), and they bore their
disgrace with those who go down to the
pit; [2]they were put in the midst of the
slain.

1 [a]Ezek. 30:20; 31:1; 32:17; 33:21
2 [1]Or, *were like* [2]Lit., *fouled by stamping* [a]Ezek. 19:1; 27:2; 28:12; 32:16 [b]Jer. 4:7; Ezek. 19:2-6; Nah. 2:11-13 [c]Is. 27:1; Ezek. 29:3 [d]Jer. 46:7, 8
3 [1]Heb., *YHWH,* usually rendered *LORD,* and so throughout the ch. [a]Ezek. 12:13
4 [1]Lit., *surface of the field* [2]Lit., *from* [a]Is. 18:6
5 [a]Ezek. 31:12
6 [a]Ex. 7:17; Is. 34:3, 7; Ezek. 35:6; Rev. 14:20
7 [a]Job 18:5, 6; Prov. 13:9 [b]Ex. 10:21-23; Is. 34:4; Ezek. 30:3, 18; 34:12 [c]Is. 13:10 [d]Joel 2:2, 31; 3:15; Amos 8:9; Matt. 24:29; Mark 13:24f.; Luke 21:25; Rev. 6:12; 8:12
8 [a]Gen. 1:14
9 [a]Ezek. 27:29-32; 28:19; Rev. 18:10-15 [b]Ex. 15:14-16
10 [a]Ezek. 27:35 [b]Ezek. 26:16
11 [a]Jer. 46:26
12 [a]Ezek. 28:7 [b]Ezek. 28:19
13 [a]Ezek. 29:11
15 [a]Ps. 107:33, 34; Ezek. 29:12, 19, 20 [b]Ex. 7:5; 14:4, 18; Ps. 9:16; 83:17, 18; Ezek. 6:7; 30:19, 26
16 [1]Or, *lament* [a]2 Sam. 1:17; 3:33, 34; 2 Chr. 35:25; Jer. 9:17; Ezek. 26:17; 32:2
17 [a]Ezek. 31:1; 32:1; 33:21
18 [a]Is. 16:9; Ezek. 21:6; 32:2, 16; Mic. 1:8 [b]Jer. 1:10; Ezek. 43:3; Hos. 6:5 [c]Ezek. 31:14, 16, 18; 32:24
19 [a]Jer. 9:25, 26; Ezek. 31:18; 32:21, 24, 29, 30
20 [1]Or, *The sword is given* [a]Ps. 28:3
21 [a]Is. 14:9-12; Ezek. 32:27
22 [1]Lit., *his* [2]Lit., *him* [a]Ezek. 27:23; 31:3, 16
23 [1]Lit., *gave,* and so throughout the ch. [a]Is. 14:15
24 [a]Gen. 10:22; 14:1; Is. 11:11; Jer. 25:25; 49:34-39 [b]Ezek. 26:20; 31:14, 18; 32:18 [c]Job 28:13; Ps. 27:13; 52:5; 142:5; Is. 38:11; Jer. 11:19 [d]Ezek. 16:52, 54; 32:25, 30
25 [1]Lit., *given* [2]So with ancient versions; M.T. reads *he was* [a]Ps. 139:8

26 "[a]Meshech, [b]Tubal and all their multitude are there; their graves [1]surround them. All of them were slain by the sword [c]uncircumcised, though they instilled their terror in the land of the living.

27 "[a]Nor do they lie beside the fallen [1][b]heroes of the uncircumcised, who went down to Sheol with their weapons of war, and whose swords were laid under their heads; but the punishment for their [c]iniquity rested on their bones, though the terror of *these* [1]heroes *was* once in the land of the living.

28 "But in the midst of the uncircumcised you will be broken and lie with those slain by the sword.

29 "There also is [a]Edom, its kings, and all its [1]princes, who [2]for *all* their might are laid with those slain by the sword; they will lie with the uncircumcised, and with those who go down to the pit.

30 "There also are the [1]chiefs of the [a]north, all of them, and all the [b]Sidonians, who in spite of the terror resulting from their might, in shame went down with the slain. So they lay down uncircumcised with those slain by the sword, and bore their disgrace with those who go down to the pit.

31 "These Pharaoh will see, and he will be [a]comforted for all his multitude slain by the sword, *even* Pharaoh and all his army," declares the Lord GOD.

32 "Though I instilled a terror of him in the land of the living, yet he will be made to lie down among *the* uncircumcised *along* with those slain by the sword, *even* Pharaoh and all his multitude," declares the Lord GOD.

The Watchman's Duty

33 AND the word of the LORD came to me saying,

2 "Son of man, speak to the [a]sons of your people, and say to them, 'If I bring a sword upon a land, and the people of the land take one man from among them and make him their watchman;

3 and he sees the sword coming upon the land, and he [a]blows on the trumpet and warns the people,

4 then he who hears the sound of the trumpet and [a]does not take warning, and a sword comes and takes him away, his [b]blood will be on his *own* head.

5 'He heard the sound of the trumpet, but did not take warning; his blood will be on himself. But had he taken warning, he would have [a]delivered his life.

6 'But if the watchman sees the sword coming and does not blow the trumpet, and the people are not warned, and a sword comes and takes a person from them, he is [a]taken away [1]in his iniquity; but his [b]blood I will require from the watchman's hand.'

7 "Now as for you, son of man, I have [1][a]appointed you a watchman for the house of Israel; so you will hear a [2]message from My mouth, and give them [b]warning from Me.

8 "When I say to the wicked, 'O wicked man, you shall [a]surely die,' and you do not speak to warn the wicked from his way, that wicked man shall die in his iniquity, but his blood I will require from your hand.

9 "But if you on your part warn a wicked man to turn from his way, and he [a]does not turn from his way, he will die in his iniquity; but you have [b]delivered your life.

10 "Now as for you, son of man, say to the house of Israel, 'Thus you have spoken, saying, "Surely our transgressions and our sins are upon us, and we are [a]rotting away in them; [b]how then can we [1]survive?" '

11 "Say to them, '[a]As I live!' declares the Lord [1]GOD, 'I take [b]no pleasure in the death of the wicked, but rather that the wicked [c]turn from his way and live. [d]Turn back, turn back from your evil ways! Why then will you die, O house of Israel?'

12 "And you, son of man, say to [1]your fellow citizens, 'The [a]righteousness of a righteous man will not deliver him in the day of his transgression, and as for the wickedness of the wicked, he will [b]not stumble because of it in the day when he turns from his wickedness; whereas a righteous man will not be able to live [2]by his righteousness on the day when he commits sin.'

13 "When I say to the righteous he will surely live, and he *so* trusts in his righteousness that he [a]commits iniquity, none of his righteous deeds will be remembered; but in that same iniquity of his which he has committed he will die.

14 "But when I say to the wicked, 'You will surely die,' and he [a]turns from his sin and practices [b]justice and righteousness,

15 *if a* wicked man restores a pledge, [a]pays back what he has taken by robbery, walks by the [b]statutes [1]which ensure life without committing iniquity, he will surely live; he shall not die.

16 "[a]None of his sins that he has committed will be remembered against him. He has practiced justice and righteousness; he will surely live.

17 "Yet [1]your fellow citizens say, 'The way of the Lord is not right,' when it is their own way that is not right.

18 "When the righteous turns from his righteousness and [a]commits iniquity, then he shall die in [1]it.

19 "But when the wicked turns from his wickedness and practices justice and righteousness, he will live by them.

20 "Yet you say, '[a]The way of the Lord is not right.' O house of Israel, I will judge each of you according to his ways."

26 [1]Lit., *are around him*
[a]Gen. 10:2; Ezek. 27:13; 38:2, 3; 39:1 [b]Gen. 10:2; Is. 66:19; Ezek. 27:13; 38:2, 3; 39:1 [c]Ezek. 32:19
27 [1]Or, *mighty ones*
[a]Is. 14:18, 19 [b]Job 3:13-15; Ezek. 32:21 [c]Job 20:11; Ps. 109:18
29 [1]Or, *leaders* [2]Or, *in*
[a]Is. 34:5-15; Jer. 49:7-22; Ezek. 25:13; 35:9, 15
30 [1]Or, *princes*
[a]Jer. 1:15; 25:26; Ezek. 38:6, 15; 39:2 [b]Jer. 25:22; Ezek. 28:21-23
31 [a]Ezek. 14:22; 31:16

2 [a]Ezek. 3:11; 33:12, 17, 30; 37:18
3 [a]Neh. 4:18-20; Is. 58:1; Ezek. 33:9; Hos. 8:1; Joel 2:1
4 [a]2 Chr. 25:16; Jer. 6:17; Zech. 1:4 [b]Ezek. 18:13; 33:5, 9; Acts 18:6
5 [a]Ex. 9:19-21; Heb. 11:7
6 [1]Or, *for,* and so throughout the ch.
[a]Ezek. 18:20, 24; 33:8, 9 [b]Ezek. 3:18, 20
7 [1]Or, *given* [2]Lit., *word*
[a]Is. 62:6; Ezek. 3:17-21 [b]Jer. 1:17; 26:2; Ezek. 2:7, 8; Acts 5:20
8 [a]Is. 3:11; Ezek. 18:4, 13, 18, 20; 33:14
9 [a]Acts 13:40, 41, 46 [b]Ezek. 3:19, 21; Acts 20:26
10 [1]Lit., *live*
[a]Lev. 26:39; Ezek. 4:17; 24:23 [b]Is. 49:14; Ezek. 37:11
11 [1]Heb., *YHWH,* usually rendered *LORD,* and so throughout the ch.
[a]Is. 49:18; Ezek. 5:11 [b]Ezek. 18:23, 32; Hos. 11:8 [c]Jer. 31:20; 1 Tim. 2:4; 2 Pet. 3:9 [d]Is. 55:6, 7; Jer. 3:22; Ezek. 18:30, 31; Hos. 14:1; Acts 3:19
12 [1]Lit., *the sons of your people* [2]Lit., *by it*
[a]Ezek. 3:18; 18:24; 33:20 [b]2 Chr. 7:14; Ezek. 18:21; 33:19
13 [a]Ezek. 18:26; Heb. 10:38; 2 Pet. 2:20, 21
14 [a]Is. 55:7; Jer. 18:7, 8; Ezek. 18:27; 33:8, 19; Hos. 14:1, 4 [b]Mic. 6:8
15 [1]Lit., *of life*
[a]Ex. 22:1-4; Lev. 6:4, 5; Luke 19:8 [b]Ps. 119:59; 143:8; Ezek. 20:11
16 [a]Is. 1:18; 43:25; Ezek. 18:22
17 [1]Lit., *the sons of your people*
18 [1]Lit., *them*
[a]Ezek. 3:20; 18:24; 33:12, 13
20 [a]Ezek. 18:25

Word of Jerusalem's Capture

21 Now it [a]came about in the [b]twelfth
year of our exile, on the fifth of the tenth
month, that the [1]refugees from Jerusalem came to me, saying, "[c]The city has
been [2]taken."
22 Now the [a]hand of the LORD had
been upon me in the evening, before the
[1]refugees came. And He [b]opened my
mouth [2]at the time *they* came to me in
the morning; so my mouth was [c]opened,
and I was no longer [3]speechless.
23 Then the word of the LORD came
to me saying,
24 "Son of man, they who [a]live in these
waste places in the land of Israel are
saying, '[b]Abraham was *only* one, yet he
possessed the land; so to [c]us who are
many the land has been given as a
possession.'
25 "Therefore, say to them, 'Thus says
the Lord GOD, "You eat *meat* with the
[a]blood *in it,* lift up your eyes to your
idols as you shed blood. [b]Should you
then possess the land?
26 "You [1a]rely on your sword, you
commit abominations, and each of
you defiles his neighbor's wife. Should
you then possess the land?" '
27 "Thus you shall say to them, 'Thus
says the Lord GOD, "As I live, surely
those who are in the waste places will
[a]fall by the sword, and whoever is in the
[1]open field I will give to the beasts to be
devoured, and those who are in the
strongholds and in the [b]caves will die of
pestilence.
28 "And I shall [a]make the land a desolation and a waste, and the [b]pride of her
power will cease; and the mountains of
Israel will be desolate, so that no one
will pass through.
29 "Then they will know that I am the
LORD, when I make the land a desolation and a waste because of all their
abominations which they have committed." '
30 "But as for you, son of man, [1]your
fellow citizens who talk about you by the
walls and in the doorways of the houses,
speak to one another, each to his
brother, saying, '[a]Come now, and hear
what the [2]message is which comes forth
from the LORD.'
31 "And they come to you as people
come, and sit before you *as* My people,
and hear your words, but they do not do
them, for they do the lustful desires
expressed by their [a]mouth, *and* their
heart goes after their [b]gain.
32 "And behold, you are to them like a
sensual song by one who has a [a]beautiful
voice and plays well on an instrument;
for they hear your words, but they do
not practice them.
33 "So when it [a]comes to pass—[1]as
surely it will—then they will know that a
prophet has been in their midst."

Prophecy against the Shepherds of Israel

34 THEN the word of the LORD
came to me saying,
2 "Son of man, prophesy against the
[a]shepherds of Israel. Prophesy and
say to [1]those shepherds, 'Thus says the
Lord [2]GOD, "Woe, shepherds of Israel
who have been [3b]feeding themselves!
Should not the shepherds [3c]feed the
flock?
3 "You [a]eat the fat and clothe yourselves with the wool, you [b]slaughter the
fat *sheep* without [1]feeding the flock.
4 "Those who are sickly you have not
strengthened, the [1]diseased you have not
healed, [a]the broken you have not bound
up, the scattered you have not brought
back, nor have you [b]sought for the lost;
but with force and with severity you
have dominated them.
5 "And they were [a]scattered for lack
of a shepherd, and they became [b]food
for every beast of the field and were
scattered.
6 "My flock [a]wandered through all the
mountains and on every high hill, and
[b]My flock was scattered over all the
surface of the earth; and there was [c]no
one to search or seek *for them.*" ' "
7 Therefore, you shepherds, hear the
word of the LORD:
8 "As I live," declares the Lord GOD,
"surely because My flock has become a
[a]prey, My flock has even become food
for all the beasts of the field for lack of a
shepherd, and My shepherds did not
search for My flock, but *rather* the
shepherds fed themselves and did not
feed My flock;
9 therefore, you shepherds, hear the
word of the LORD:
10 'Thus says the Lord GOD, "Behold,
I am [a]against the shepherds, and I shall
demand My [1]sheep [2]from them and
make them [b]cease from feeding [1]sheep.
So the shepherds will not [3]feed themselves anymore, but I shall [c]deliver My
flock from their mouth, that they may
not be food for them." ' "

The Restoration of Israel

11 For thus says the Lord GOD, "Behold, I Myself will [a]search for My sheep
and seek them out.
12 "[a]As a shepherd [1]cares for his herd
in the day when he is among his scattered [2]sheep, so I will [1b]care for My
[2]sheep and will deliver them from all the
places to which they were scattered on a
[c]cloudy and gloomy day.
13 "And I will bring them out from the
peoples and gather them from the countries and bring them to their own land;
and I will [a]feed them on the mountains
of Israel, by the [b]streams, and in all the
inhabited places of the land.
14 "I will feed them in a [a]good pasture,
and their grazing ground will be on the
mountain heights of Israel. There they
will lie down in good grazing ground,
and they will feed in [1b]rich pasture on
the mountains of Israel.

21 [1]Or, *refugee* [2]Lit., *smitten* [a]Ezek. 31:1; 32:1, 17 [b]Jer. 39:1, 2; 40:1; 52:4-7; Ezek. 24:1, 2 [c]2 Kin. 25:10; Jer. 39:8
22 [1]Lit., *refugee* [2]Lit., *until he came* [3]Or, *dumb* [a]Ezek. 1:3; 8:1; 37:1 [b]Ezek. 3:26, 27; 24:27 [c]Luke 1:64
24 [a]Jer. 39:10; 40:7; Ezek. 33:27 [b]Is. 51:2; Luke 3:8; Acts 7:5; Rom. 4:12 [c]Ezek. 11:15
25 [a]Lev. 17:10, 12, 14; Deut. 12:16, 23; 15:23 [b]Jer. 7:9, 10
26 [1]Lit., *stand* [a]Mic. 2:1, 2; Zeph. 3:3
27 [1]Lit., *surface of the field* [a]Jer. 15:2, 3; 42:22; Ezek. 5:12 [b]1 Sam. 13:6; Is. 2:19
28 [a]Ezek. 5:14; 6:14; Mic. 7:13 [b]Ezek. 7:24; 24:21; 30:6
30 [1]Lit., *the sons of your people* [2]Lit., *word* [a]Is. 29:13; 58:2; Ezek. 14:3; 20:3, 31
31 [a]Ps. 78:36, 37; Is. 29:13; 1 John 3:18 [b]Ezek. 22:13, 27; Luke 12:15
32 [a]Mark 6:20
33 [1]Lit., *behold, it is coming* [a]Jer. 28:9; Ezek. 33:29

2 [1]Lit., *them, the shepherds* [2]Heb., *YHWH,* usually rendered *LORD,* and so throughout the ch. [3]Lit., *pasturing, pasture* [a]Jer. 2:8; 3:15; 10:21; 12:10 [b]Jer. 23:1; Ezek. 22:25; 34:8-10; Mic. 3:1-3, 11 [c]Ps. 78:71, 72; Is. 40:11; Ezek. 34:14, 15; John 10:11; 21:15-17
3 [1]Lit., *pasturing* [a]Zech. 11:16 [b]Ezek. 22:25, 27
4 [1]Lit., *sick* [a]Zech. 11:16 [b]Matt. 9:36; 10:6; 18:12, 13; Luke 15:4
5 [a]Num. 27:17; 2 Chr. 18:16; Jer. 10:21; 23:2; 50:6, 7; Matt. 9:36; Mark 6:34 [b]Ezek. 34:8, 28
6 [a]Jer. 40:11, 12; Ezek. 7:16; 1 Pet. 2:25 [b]John 10:16 [c]Ps. 142:4
8 [a]Acts 20:29
10 [1]Or, (a) *flock* [2]Lit., *from their hand* [3]Lit., *pasture,* and so throughout the ch. [a]Jer. 21:13; Ezek. 5:8; 13:8; 34:2; Zech. 10:3 [b]1 Sam. 2:29, 30; Jer. 52:24-27 [c]Ps. 72:12-14; Ezek. 13:23
11 [a]Ezek. 11:17; 20:41

12 [1]Or, *seek(s) out* [2]Or, *flock* [a]Jer. 31:10 [b]Is. 40:11; 56:8; Jer. 23:3; 31:8; Luke 19:10; John 10:16 [c]Jer. 13:16; Ezek. 30:3; Joel 2:2
13 [a]Ezek. 34:23; 36:29, 30; Mic. 7:14 [b]Is. 30:25
14 [1]Lit., *fat* [a]Ps. 23:2; Jer. 31:12-14, 25; John 10:9 [b]Ezek. 28:25, 26; 36:29, 30

15 "I will [a]feed My flock and I will [1]lead them to rest," declares the Lord GOD.

16 "I will seek the lost, bring back the scattered, bind up the broken, and strengthen the sick; but the [a]fat and the strong I will destroy. I will [b]feed them with judgment.

17 "And as for you, My flock, thus says the Lord GOD, 'Behold, I will [a]judge between one [1]sheep and another, between the rams and the male goats.

18 'Is it too [a]slight a thing for you that you should feed in the good pasture, that you must tread down with your feet the rest of your pastures? Or that you should drink of the clear waters, that you must [1]foul the rest with your feet?

19 'And as for My flock, they must eat what you tread down with your feet, and they must drink what you [1]foul with your feet!' "

20 Therefore, thus says the Lord GOD to them, "Behold, I, even I, will judge between the fat sheep and the lean sheep.

21 "Because you push with side and with shoulder, and [a]thrust at all the [1]weak with your horns, until you have scattered them [2]abroad,

22 therefore, I will [a]deliver My flock, and they will no longer be a prey; and I will judge between one sheep and another.

23 "Then I will [a]set over them one [b]shepherd, My servant [c]David, and he will feed them; he will feed them himself and be their shepherd.

24 "And I, the LORD, will be their God, and My servant [a]David will be prince among them; I, the LORD, have spoken.

25 "And I will make a [a]covenant of peace with them and [b]eliminate harmful beasts from the land, so that they may [c]live securely in the wilderness and sleep in the woods.

26 "And I will make them and the places around My hill a [a]blessing. And I will cause [b]showers to come down in their season; they will be showers of [c]blessing.

27 "Also the tree of the field will yield its fruit, and the earth will yield its increase, and they will be [a]secure on their land. Then they will know that I am the LORD, when I have [b]broken the bars of their yoke and have delivered them from the hand of those who enslaved them.

28 "And they will no longer be a prey to the nations, and the beasts of the earth will not devour them; but they will [a]live securely, and no one will make *them* afraid.

29 "And I will establish for them a [a]renowned planting place, and they will [b]not again be [1]victims of famine in the land, and they will not [c]endure the insults of the nations anymore.

30 "Then they will know that [a]I, the LORD their God, am with them, and that they, the house of Israel, are My people," declares the Lord GOD.

31 "As for you, My [a]sheep, the [b]sheep of My pasture, you are men, and I am your God," declares the Lord GOD.

Prophecy against Mount Seir

35 MOREOVER, the word of the LORD came to me saying,

2 "Son of man, set your face against [a]Mount Seir, and prophesy against it,

3 and say to it, 'Thus says the Lord [1]GOD,

"Behold, I am against you, Mount Seir,
And I will [a]stretch out My hand against you,
And I will make you a [b]desolation and a waste.

4 "I will [a]lay waste your cities,
And you will become a desolation.
Then you will know that I am the LORD.

5 "Because you have had everlasting [a]enmity and have [1]delivered the sons of Israel to the power of the sword at the time of their calamity, at the time of the [2b]punishment of the end,

6 therefore, as I live," declares the Lord GOD, "I will [1]give you over to [a]bloodshed, and bloodshed will pursue you; since you have not hated bloodshed, therefore bloodshed will pursue you.

7 "And I will make Mount Seir a waste and a desolation, and I will cut off from it the one who passes through and returns.

8 "And I will [a]fill its mountains with its slain; on your hills and in your valleys and in all your ravines those slain by the sword will [1]fall.

9 "I will make you an everlasting [a]desolation, and your cities will not be inhabited. Then you will know that I am the LORD.

10 "Because you have [a]said, 'These two nations and these two lands will be mine, and we will possess [1]them,' although the [b]LORD was there,

11 therefore, as I live," declares the Lord GOD, "I will deal *with you* [a]according to your anger and according to your envy which you showed because of your hatred against them; so I will [b]make Myself known among them when I judge you.

12 "Then you will know [1]that I, the LORD, have heard all your revilings which you have spoken against the mountains of Israel saying, 'They are laid desolate; they are [a]given to us for food.'

13 "And you have [1a]spoken arrogantly against Me and have multiplied your words against Me; [b]I have heard."

14 'Thus says the Lord GOD, "As all the [a]earth rejoices, I will make you a desolation.

15 [1]Lit., *cause them to lie down* [a]Ps. 23:1, 2; Ezek. 34:23
16 [a]Is. 10:16 [b]Is. 49:26
17 [1]Or, *lamb* [a]Ezek. 20:38; 34:20-22; Mal. 4:1; Matt. 25:32
18 [1]Lit., *foul by trampling* [a]Num. 16:9, 13; 2 Sam. 7:19; Is. 7:13
19 [1]Lit., *foul by trampling*
21 [1]Or, *sick* [2]Lit., *to the outside* [a]Deut. 33:17; Dan. 8:4; Luke 13:14-16
22 [a]Ps. 72:12-14; Jer. 23:3; Ezek. 34:10
23 [a]Rev. 7:17 [b]Is. 40:11; John 10:11 [c]Jer. 30:9; Ezek. 37:24
24 [a]Is. 55:3; Jer. 30:9; Ezek. 37:24, 25; Hos. 3:5
25 [a]Ezek. 16:60; 20:37; 37:26 [b]Job 5:22, 23; Is. 11:6-9 [c]Jer. 33:16; Ezek. 28:26; 34:27, 28
26 [a]Gen. 12:2; Ezek. 34:14 [b]Deut. 11:13-15; 28:12 [c]Lev. 25:21; Is. 44:3
27 [a]Ezek. 38:8, 11 [b]Lev. 26:13; Is. 52:2, 3; Jer. 30:8
28 [a]Jer. 30:10; Ezek. 39:26
29 [1]Lit., *those gathered* [a]Is. 4:2; 60:21; 61:3 [b]Ezek. 34:26, 27; 36:29 [c]Ezek. 36:6, 15
30 [a]Ps. 46:7, 11; Ezek. 14:11; 36:28
31 [a]Ps. 78:52; 80:1; Ezek. 36:38 [b]Ps. 100:3; Jer. 23:1

2 [a]Gen. 36:8; Ezek. 25:12; 36:5
3 [1]Heb., *YHWH,* usually rendered *LORD,* and so throughout the ch. [a]Jer. 6:12; 15:6; Ezek. 25:13 [b]Jer. 49:13, 17, 18; Ezek. 35:7
4 [a]Ezek. 6:6; 35:9; Mal. 1:3, 4
5 [1]Lit., *poured* [2]Or, *iniquity* [a]Ps. 137:7; Ezek. 25:12, 15; 36:5; Amos 1:11; Obad. 10 [b]Ezek. 7:2; 21:25, 29
6 [1]Lit., *prepare you for* [a]Is. 63:2-6; Ezek. 16:38; 32:6
8 [1]Lit., *fall in them* [a]Is. 34:5, 6; Ezek. 31:12; 32:4, 5; 39:4, 5
9 [a]Jer. 49:13; Ezek. 25:13
10 [1]Lit., *it* [a]Ps. 83:4-12; Ezek. 36:2, 5 [b]Ps. 48:1-3; 132:13, 14; Is. 12:6; Ezek. 48:35; Zeph. 3:15
11 [a]Ps. 137:7; Ezek. 25:14; Amos 1:11 [b]Ps. 9:16; 73:17, 18

12 [1]Or, *that I am the LORD: I have heard* [a]Jer. 50:7; Ezek. 36:2
13 [1]Lit., *made great with your mouth* [a]Is. 10:13, 14; 36:20; Jer. 48:26, 42; Dan. 11:36 [b]Jer. 7:11; 29:23
14 [a]Is. 44:23; 49:13; Jer. 51:48

15 "As you [a]rejoiced over the inheritance of the house of Israel because it
was desolate, [b]so I will do to you. You
will be a [c]desolation, O Mount Seir, and
all Edom, all of it. Then they will know
that I am the LORD." '

The Mountains of Israel to Be Blessed

36 "AND you, son of man, prophesy to the mountains of Israel
and say, 'O mountains of Israel, hear the
word of the LORD.
2 'Thus says the Lord [1]GOD, "Because the enemy has spoken against you,
'Aha!' and, 'The everlasting [2a]heights
have become our possession,'
3 therefore, prophesy and say, 'Thus
says the Lord GOD, "[1]For good cause
they have made you [a]desolate and
crushed you from every side, that you
should become a possession of the rest
of the nations, and you have been taken
up in the [2b]talk and the whispering of
the people." ' "
4 'Therefore, O [a]mountains of Israel,
hear the word of the Lord GOD. Thus
says the Lord GOD to the mountains and
to the hills, to the ravines and to the
valleys, to the desolate wastes and to the
forsaken cities, which have become a
[b]prey and a derision to the rest of the
nations which are round about,
5 therefore, thus says the Lord GOD,
"Surely in the fire of My [a]jealousy I have
spoken against the [b]rest of the nations,
and against all Edom, who [1]appropri-
ated My land for themselves as a possession with wholehearted [c]joy *and* with
scorn of soul, to drive it out for a prey."
6 'Therefore, prophesy concerning the
land of Israel, and say to the mountains
and to the hills, to the ravines and to the
valleys, "Thus says the Lord GOD, 'Behold, I have spoken in My jealousy and
in My wrath because you have [a]endured
the insults of the nations.'
7 "Therefore, thus says the Lord GOD,
'I have [1]sworn that surely the nations
which are around you will themselves
endure their insults.
8 'But you, O mountains of Israel,
you will [a]put forth your branches and
bear your fruit for My people Israel; for
they will soon come.
9 'For, behold, I am for you, and I
will [a]turn to you, and you shall be
[b]cultivated and sown.
10 'And I will multiply men on you,
[a]all the house of Israel, all of it; and the
[b]cities will be inhabited, and the waste
places will be rebuilt.
11 'And I will multiply on you man
and beast; and they will increase and be
fruitful; and I will cause you to be
inhabited as you were [a]formerly and will
[1]treat you [b]better than at the first. Thus
you will know that I am the LORD.
12 'Yes, I will cause [a]men—My people
Israel—to walk on you and possess you,
so that you will become their [b]inheri-
tance and never again [c]bereave them of
children.'
13 "Thus says the Lord GOD, 'Because
they say to you, "You are a [a]devourer of
men and have bereaved your [1]nation of
children,"
14 therefore, you will no longer devour men, and no longer bereave your
nation of children,' declares the Lord
GOD.
15 "And I will not let you hear [a]insults
from the nations anymore, nor will you
bear [b]disgrace from the peoples any
longer, nor will you cause your nation to
[c]stumble any longer," declares the Lord
GOD.' "
16 Then the word of the LORD came
to me saying,
17 "Son of man, when the house of
Israel was living in their own land, they
[a]defiled it by their ways and their deeds;
their way before Me was like [b]the uncleanness of a woman in her impurity.
18 "Therefore, I [a]poured out My wrath
on them for the blood which they had
shed on the land, because they had
defiled it with their idols.
19 "Also I [a]scattered them among the
nations, and they were dispersed
throughout the lands. [b]According to
their ways and their deeds I judged
them.
20 "When they came to the nations
where they went, they [a]profaned My
holy name, because it was said of them,
'These are the [b]people of the LORD; yet
they have come out of His land.'
21 "But I had [1]concern for My [a]holy
name, which the house of Israel had
profaned among the nations where they
went.

Israel to Be Renewed for His Name's Sake

22 "Therefore, say to the house of
Israel, 'Thus says the Lord GOD, "It is
[a]not for your sake, O house of Israel,
that I am about to act, but for My holy
name, which you have profaned among
the nations where you went.
23 "And I will [a]vindicate the holiness
of My great name which has been profaned among the nations, which you
have profaned in their midst. Then the
[b]nations will know that I am the LORD,"
declares the Lord GOD, "when I prove
Myself holy among you in their sight.
24 "For I will [a]take you from the
nations, gather you from all the lands,
and bring you into your own land.
25 "Then I will [a]sprinkle clean water on
you, and you will be clean; I will cleanse
you from all your [b]filthiness and from all
your [c]idols.
26 "Moreover, I will give you a [a]new
heart and put a new spirit within you;
and I will remove the [b]heart of stone
from your flesh and give you a heart of
flesh.

15 aJer. 50:11; Lam. 4:21 bObad. 15 cIs. 34:5, 6; Ezek. 35:3, 4
2 1Heb., *YHWH,* usually rendered *LORD,* and so throughout the ch. 2Heb., *Bamoth* aDeut. 32:13; Ps. 78:69; Is. 58:14; Hab. 3:19
3 1Lit., *Because;* or, *By the cause* 2Lit., *lip of the tongue* aJer. 2:15 bPs. 44:13, 14; Jer. 18:16; Ezek. 35:13
4 aDeut. 11:11; Ezek. 36:1, 6, 8 bEzek. 34:8, 28
5 1Lit., *gave* aEzek. 5:13; 36:6; 38:19 bJer. 25:9, 15-29; Ezek. 36:3 cJer. 50:11; Ezek. 35:15; Mic. 7:8
6 aPs. 74:10; 123:3, 4; Ezek. 34:29
7 1Lit., *lifted up My hand*
8 aIs. 4:2; 27:6; Ezek. 17:23; 34:26-29
9 aLev. 26:9 bEzek. 28:26; 34:14; 36:34
10 aIs. 27:6; 49:17-23; Ezek. 37:21, 22 bJer. 31:27, 28; 33:12; Ezek. 36:33
11 1Lit., *cause good* aJer. 30:18; Ezek. 16:55; Mic. 7:14 bJob 42:12; Is. 51:3
12 aEzek. 34:13, 14 bEzek. 47:14 cJer. 15:7; Ezek. 22:12, 27
13 1Or, *nations,* and so throughout the ch. aNum. 13:32
15 aIs. 60:14; Ezek. 34:29; 36:7 bPs. 89:50; Is. 54:4; Ezek. 22:4 cIs. 63:13; Jer. 13:16; 18:15
17 aJer. 2:7 bLev. 15:19
18 a2 Chr. 34:21, 25; Lam. 2:4; 4:11; Ezek. 22:20, 22
19 aDeut. 28:64; Ezek. 5:12; 22:15; Amos 9:9 bEzek. 24:14; 39:24; Rom. 2:6
20 aIs. 52:5; Ezek. 12:16; Rom. 2:24 bJer. 33:24
21 1Lit., *compassion* aPs. 74:18; Is. 48:9; Ezek. 20:44
22 aDeut. 7:7, 8; 9:5, 6; Ezek. 36:32
23 aIs. 5:16; Ezek. 20:41; 38:23; 39:7, 25 bPs. 102:15; 126:2
24 aIs. 43:5, 6; Ezek. 34:13; 37:21
25 aNum. 19:17-19; Ps. 51:7; Titus 3:5, 6; Heb. 9:13, 19; 10:22 bIs. 4:4; Zech. 13:1 cIs. 2:18, 20; Hos. 14:3, 8
26 aPs. 51:10; Ezek. 11:19; 18:31; John 3:3, 5; 2 Cor. 5:17 bEzek. 11:19; Zech. 7:12

27"And I will [a]put My Spirit within you and cause you to walk in My statutes, and you will be careful to observe My ordinances.

28"And you will live in the land that I gave to your forefathers; so you will be [a]My people, and I will be your God.

29"Moreover, I will save you from all your uncleanness; and I will call for the grain and multiply it, and I [a]will not [1]bring a famine on you.

30"And I will [a]multiply the fruit of the tree and the produce of the field, that you may not receive again the disgrace of famine among the nations.

31"Then you will [a]remember your evil ways and your deeds that were not good, and you will loathe yourselves in your own sight for your iniquities and your abominations.

32"I am not doing *this* [a]for your sake," declares the Lord GOD, "let it be known to you. Be ashamed and confounded for your ways, O house of Israel!"

33 'Thus says the Lord GOD, "On the day that I cleanse you from all your iniquities, I will cause the [a]cities to be inhabited, and the [b]waste places will be rebuilt.

34"And the desolate land will be cultivated instead of being a desolation in the sight of everyone who passed by.

35"And they will say, 'This desolate land has become like the [a]garden of Eden; and the waste, desolate, and ruined cities are fortified *and* inhabited.'

36"Then the nations that are left round about you will know that I, the LORD, have rebuilt the ruined places *and* planted that which was desolate; I, the LORD, have spoken and [a]will do it."

37 'Thus says the Lord GOD, "This also I will let the house of Israel ask Me to do for them: I will increase their men like a flock.

38"Like the [a]flock [1]for sacrifices, like the flock at Jerusalem during her appointed feasts, so will the waste cities be filled with [b]flocks of men. Then they will know that I am the LORD." ' "

Vision of the Valley of Dry Bones

37 THE [a]hand of the LORD was upon me, and He [b]brought me out [1]by the Spirit of the LORD and set me down in the middle of the [c]valley; and it was full of bones.

2 And He caused me to pass among them round about, and behold, *there were* very many on the surface of the valley; and lo, *they were* very dry.

3 And He said to me, "Son of man, [a]can these bones live?" And I answered, "O Lord [1]GOD, [b]Thou knowest."

4 Again He said to me, "[a]Prophesy over these bones, and say to them, 'O dry bones, [b]hear the word of the LORD.'

5"Thus says the Lord GOD to these bones, 'Behold, I will cause [1a]breath to enter you that you may come to life.

6 'And I will put sinews on you, make flesh grow back on you, cover you with skin, and put breath in you that you may come alive; and you will [a]know that I am the LORD.' "

7 So I prophesied [a]as I was commanded; and as I prophesied, there was a [1]noise, and behold, a rattling; and the bones came together, bone to its bone.

8 And I looked, and behold, sinews were on them, and flesh grew, and skin covered them; but there was no breath in them.

9 Then He said to me, "Prophesy to the breath, prophesy, son of man, and say to the breath, 'Thus says the Lord GOD, "Come from the four winds, O breath, and [a]breathe on these slain, that they [b]come to life." ' "

10 So I prophesied as He commanded me, and the [a]breath came into them, and they came to life, and stood on their feet, an [b]exceedingly great army.

The Vision Explained

11 Then He said to me, "Son of man, these bones are the [a]whole house of Israel; behold, they say, 'Our [b]bones are dried up, and our hope has perished. We are [1]completely [c]cut off.'

12"Therefore prophesy, and say to them, 'Thus says the Lord GOD, "Behold, I will open your graves and [a]cause you to come up out of your graves, My people; and I will bring you into the land of Israel.

13"Then you will know that I am the LORD, when I have opened your graves and caused you to come up out of your graves, My people.

14"And I will [a]put My [1]Spirit within you, and you will come to life, and I will place you on your own land. Then you will know that I, the LORD, have spoken and done it," declares the LORD.' "

Reunion of Judah and Israel

15 The word of the LORD came again to me saying,

16"And you, son of man, take for yourself [a]one stick and write on it, 'For [b]Judah and for the sons of Israel, his companions'; then take another stick and write on it, 'For [c]Joseph, the stick of Ephraim and all the house of Israel, his companions.'

17"Then [a]join them for yourself one to another into one stick, that they may become one in your hand.

18"And when the sons of your people speak to you saying, 'Will you not declare to us [a]what you mean by these?'

19 say to them, 'Thus says the Lord GOD, "Behold, I will take the stick of Joseph, which is in the hand of Ephraim, and the tribes of Israel, his companions; and I will put them with it, with the stick of Judah, and make them one stick, and they will be one in My hand." '

20"And the sticks on which you write will be in your hand before their eyes.

21"And say to them, 'Thus says the Lord GOD, "Behold, I will [a]take the sons of Israel from among the nations where they have gone, and I will gather them

27 [a]Is. 44:3; 59:21; Ezek. 37:14; 39:29; Joel 2:28, 29
28 [a]Ezek. 14:11; 37:23, 27
29 [1]Lit., *put* [a]Ezek. 34:27, 29; Hos. 2:21-23
30 [a]Lev. 26:4; Ezek. 34:27
31 [a]Ezek. 16:61-63; 20:43
32 [a]Deut. 9:5
33 [a]Ezek. 36:10; Zech. 8:7, 8 [b]Is. 58:12
35 [a]Is. 51:3; Ezek. 31:9; Joel 2:3
36 [a]Ezek. 17:24; 22:14; 37:14; Hos. 14:4-9
38 [1]Lit., *of holy things* [a]1 Kin. 8:63; 2 Chr. 35:7-9; John 2:14 [b]Ps. 74:1; 100:3; Jer. 23:1; John 10:7, 9, 16

1 [1]Or, *in* [a]Ezek. 1:3; 33:22; 40:1 [b]Ezek. 8:3; 11:24; 43:5; Acts 8:39 [c]Jer. 7:32-8:2
3 [1]Heb., *YHWH,* usually rendered *LORD,* and so throughout the ch. [a]Ezek. 26:19 [b]Deut. 32:39; 1 Sam. 2:6
4 [a]Ezek. 37:9, 12 [b]Jer. 22:29; Ezek. 36:1
5 [1]Or, *spirit,* and so throughout the ch. [a]Gen. 2:7; Ps. 104:29, 30; Ezek. 37:9, 10, 14
6 [a]Is. 49:23; Ezek. 35:9; 38:23; 39:6; Joel 2:27; 3:17
7 [1]Lit., *voice;* or, *thunder* [a]Jer. 13:5-7
9 [a]Ps. 104:30 [b]Hos. 13:14
10 [a]Rev. 11:11 [b]Jer. 30:19; 33:22
11 [1]Lit., *cut off to ourselves* [a]Jer. 33:24; Ezek. 36:10; 39:25 [b]Ps. 141:7 [c]Ps. 88:5; Lam. 3:54
12 [a]Deut. 32:39; 1 Sam. 2:6; Is. 26:19; 66:14; Hos. 13:14
14 [1]Or, *breath* [a]Is. 32:15; Ezek. 11:19; 36:27; 37:6, 9; 39:29; Joel 2:28, 29; Zech. 12:10
16 [a]Num. 17:2, 3 [b]2 Chr. 10:17; 11:11-17; 15:9 [c]1 Kin. 12:16-20; 2 Chr. 10:19
17 [a]Is. 11:13; Jer. 50:4; Ezek. 37:22-24; Hos. 1:11; Zeph. 3:9
18 [a]Ezek. 12:9; 17:12; 20:49; 24:19
21 [a]Is. 43:5, 6; Jer. 29:14; Ezek. 36:24; 39:27; Amos 9:14, 15

SHEPHERD-KINGS

Micah 7:14. Micah looked forward to the time when kings would shepherd their people as a shepherd looked after the flock, *"Shepherd your people with your staff, the flock of your inheritance."* The rod symbolized the protection of the people and was eventually stylized into a sceptre.

TWO POUCHES

1 Samuel 25:29. Abigail made an interesting contrast between the two pouches used by the shepherd. *"Even though someone is pursuing you to take your life, the life of my Master will be bound securely in the bundle of the living by the Lord your God. But the lives of your enemies he will hurl away as from the pocket of a sling."* The bundle of the living is the pouch that held food; the hollow of a sling is the pouch that held the stone.

CARE OF THE SHEEP

"When you pass through the waters, I will be with you, and when you pass through the rivers, they will not sweep over you" probably refers to the care the shepherd has to take when he takes the flock through running water (Isaiah 43:2). Isaiah 40:11 utilizes the action of the shepherd's carrying the lambs and not pushing the ewes too hard when it is lambing time to demonstrate God's care for his people: *"He gathers the lambs in his arms and carries them close to his heart; he gently leads those that have young."* Any flesh wounds incurred by the sheep were anointed with olive oil (Psalm 23:5) — the same methods as was used for dealing with human wounds (Luke 10:34).

THE SCAPEGOAT

John 1:29. It is normally assumed that when John refers to the *"lamb of God who takes away the sin of the world"* that he was referring to Isaiah 53:7, *"a lamb to the slaughter."* However, because sheep and goats are the same so far as language is concerned, he may be referring to the scapegoat–Jesus taking away the world's sin when he died and left the world.

JESUS' BIRTHDAY

Luke 2:8. Nobody knows the exact birthday of Jesus. December 25 was chosen as the *"official"* birthday because it coincided with the Jewish festival of Hannukah (25th Chislev), which was a festival of light, and with many of the festivities that were invented to counteract the dark winters of the northern hemisphere. The fact that there were sheep on the Bethlehem hills indicates that Jesus was actually born about Passover time, because sheep were kept on the hillsides of Bethlehem to provide for the Passover lambs at Jerusalem. The fact that there was no room for Jesus to be born at a *kataluma*, a rough

A CLOSER LOOK

marquee for shelter that was also put up for pilgrims unable to find a bed in the city at Passover time, is additional evidence. Because God sent his son *"when the time had fully come"* (Galatians 4:4), and his whole life was bound up with the imagery of sheep, some people believe Passover would have been the most appropriate time for birth.

THE PASTOR

Ephesians 4:11. This verse describes one of the leaders in the church as a *"pastor."* The actual word is *shepherd.* The pastor is in relationship to the Chief Shepherd (1 Peter 5:4) as shepherds would have been to the king's stockmaster in the days of the kingdom of Israel.

THE SHEEPFOLD

At night the shepherd gathered his sheep to a safe place and kept watch (Luke 2:8). A shallow cave was a good place of safety, and a wall was often built partly across the cave mouth to form an enclosure in front of it. The wall was made of local stones and was topped with thorns. It was in such a cave the King Saul went to sleep (1 Samuel 24:3). If there was no cave, a pallisade of stones was made out in the open, thorns being substituted for stones if necessary (Ezekiel 34:14). The shepherd lay down across the one opening, effectively becoming a door for the sheep (John 10:7). It was a tough life. Jacob spelled out the thirst, the frost, and the lack of sleep (Genesis 31:40). Although the shepherd carried a tent with him (Song of Songs 1:8), it was no camping trip.

Sheepfolds were often set up in the home village at a sunny spot, so that when the flock returned t could be kept in safety. The sheepfold was a low, arched building with a drystone wall enclosure attached. The flock could be kept indoors or out of doors according to the weather. A watchman was set to guard the flock. Jesus referred to this kind of setting when he said that thieves and robbers do not use the door but climb over the wall (John 10:1-3, 10). The current criminal practice was to climb over the wall, slaughter as many sheep as possible before detection, and throw them to accomplices outside.

DANIEL - *uncompromising*

Daniel faced a tough decision.

The king of Babylon had ordered that anyone who prayed to any god other than the king would be thrown into a den of lions. Daniel was forced to decide. Would he compromise his faith and pray to the king in order to live or would he remain faithful by continuing to pray to God under penalty of death? The decision wasn't difficult.

Daniel chose God.

"Now when Daniel knew that the [king's order] had been signed, he entered his house... and he continued kneeling on his knees three times a day, praying and giving thanks before his God, as he had been previously" (Dan. 6:10).

Daniel was a very committed person. When he was carried off to Babylon, the Babylonians forced him to conform to their way of life. They changed his name, forced him to learn their language, and forced him to learn their literature. But he would only conform to their expectations to a point. He refused to compromise his faith by eating their food which would have defiled him, and he refused to compromise his faith by praying to their gods or to their king.

So when some of the king's administrators found out that Daniel still prayed to his God, true to the royal decree, they threw him into a den of lions. But because Daniel had been faithful to God, God was faithful to Daniel.

The next morning the king went to check on Daniel. After the king called out to Daniel in the lion's den, Daniel replied, *"My God sent His angel and shut the lion's mouths, and they have not harmed me, Inasmuch as I was found innocent before Him; and also toward you, O king, I have committed no crime"* (Dan. 6:22).

Because of Daniel's loyalty to God, God spared his life. God always looks favorably upon a person who, when faced with danger or temptation, stands up for his faith.

A person who is uncompromising.

A person like Daniel.

QUESTIONS

1. **What situations do you face every day that pressure you into compromising your faith?**

2. **What two things could be done to help you remain uncompromising in your faith?**

3. **Have you ever been faced with a situation that forced you to either compromise your faith or stand up for God? What was the outcome?**

4. **When is it acceptable and when is it not acceptable to conform to the expectations of others?**

from every side and bring them into
their own land;
22 and I will make them [a]one nation
in the land, on the mountains of Israel;
and [b]one king will be king for all of
them; and they will no longer be two
nations, and they will no longer be
divided into two kingdoms.
23 "And they will [a]no longer defile
themselves with their idols, or with their
detestable things, or with any of their
transgressions; but [b]I will deliver them
from all their [1]dwelling places in which
they have sinned, and will cleanse them.
And they will be My people, and I will
be their God.

The Davidic Kingdom

24 "And My servant [a]David will be
king over them, and they will all have
[b]one shepherd; and they will walk in My
ordinances, and keep My statutes, and
observe them.
25 "And they shall live on the land that
I gave to Jacob My servant, in which
your fathers lived; and they will live on
it, they, and their sons, and their sons'
sons, forever; and [a]David My servant
shall be their prince forever.
26 "And I will make a [a]covenant of
peace with them; it will be an [b]ever-
lasting covenant with them. And I will
place them and [c]multiply them, and will
set My [d]sanctuary in their midst forever.
27 "My [a]dwelling place also will be
with them; and [b]I will be their God, and
they will be My people.
28 "And the nations will know that I
am the LORD [a]who sanctifies Israel,
when My sanctuary is in their midst
forever." ' "

Prophecy about Gog and Future Invasion of Israel

38 AND the word of the LORD came
to me saying,
2 "Son of man, set your face toward
[a]Gog of the land of [b]Magog, the [1]prince
of [c]Rosh, [d]Meshech, and [d]Tubal, and
prophesy against him,
3 and say, 'Thus says the Lord [1]GOD,
"Behold, I am against you, O Gog,
[2]prince of Rosh, Meshech, and Tubal.
4 "And I will turn you about, and put
hooks into your jaws, and I will [a]bring
you out, and all your army, [b]horses and
horsemen, all of them [1]splendidly attired, a great company *with* buckler and
shield, all of them wielding swords;
5 [a]Persia, [1b]Ethiopia, and [c]Put with
them, all of them *with* shield and helmet;
6 [a]Gomer with all its troops; [b]Beth-
togarmah *from* the remote parts of the
north with all its troops—many peoples
with you.
7 "[a]Be prepared, and prepare yourself,
you and all your companies that are
assembled about you, and be a guard for
them.
8 "[a]After many days you will be summoned; in the latter years you will come
into the land that is restored from the
sword, *whose inhabitants* have been
[b]gathered from many [1]nations to the
[c]mountains of Israel which had been a
continual waste; but [2]its people were
brought out from the [1]nations, and they
are [d]living securely, all of them.
9 "And you will go up, you will come
[a]like a storm; you will be like a [b]cloud
covering the land, you and all your
troops, and many peoples with you."
10 'Thus says the Lord GOD, "It will
come about on that day, that [1]thoughts
will come into your mind, and you will
[a]devise an evil plan,
11 and you will say, 'I will go up
against the land of [1a]unwalled villages. I
will go against those who are [b]at rest,
that live securely, all of them living
without walls, and having no bars or
gates,
12 to [a]capture spoil and to seize plunder, to turn your hand against the waste
places which are *now* inhabited, and
against the people who are gathered
from the nations, who have acquired
cattle and goods, who live at the [1]center
of the world.'
13 "[a]Sheba, and [b]Dedan, and the merchants of [c]Tarshish, with all its [1]villages,
will say to you, 'Have you come to
capture spoil? Have you assembled your
company to seize plunder, to carry away
silver and gold, to take away cattle and
goods, to capture great [d]spoil?' " '
14 "Therefore, prophesy, son of man,
and say to Gog, 'Thus says the Lord
GOD, "On that day when My people
Israel are [a]living securely, will you not
know *it*?
15 "And [a]you will come from your
place out of the remote parts of the
north, you and many peoples with you,
all of them riding on horses, a great
assembly and a mighty army;
16 and you will come up against My
people Israel like a cloud to cover the
land. It will come about in the last days
that I shall bring you against My land, in
order that the nations may [a]know Me
when I shall be [b]sanctified through you
before their eyes, O Gog."
17 'Thus says the Lord GOD, "Are you
the one of whom I spoke in former days
through My servants the prophets of
Israel, who [a]prophesied in those days for
many years that I would bring you
against them?
18 "And it will come about on that day,
when Gog comes against the land of
Israel," declares the Lord GOD, "that
My fury will mount up in My [a]anger.
19 "And in My [a]zeal and in My blazing
wrath I declare *that* on that day there
will surely be a great [1b]earthquake in the
land of Israel.

22 [a]Jer. 3:18; 50:4, 5; Ezek. 36:10 [b]Ezek. 34:23, 24; 37:24
23 [1]Another reading is *backslidings* [a]Ezek. 36:25 [b]Ezek. 36:28, 29
24 [a]Jer. 30:9; Ezek. 34:24; 37:25; Hos. 3:5 [b]Ps. 78:71; Is. 40:11; Ezek. 34:23
25 [a]Is. 11:1; Ezek. 37:24; Zech. 6:12
26 [a]Ezek. 16:62; 20:37; 34:25 [b]Ps. 89:3, 4; Is. 55:3; 59:21; Ezek. 16:60 [c]Jer. 30:19; Ezek. 36:10, 11, 37 [d]Ezek. 20:40; 43:7
27 [a]John 1:14; Rev. 21:3 [b]Ezek. 37:23; 2 Cor. 6:16
28 [a]Ex. 31:13; Ezek. 20:12

2 [1]Or, *chief prince of Meshech* [a]Ezek. 38:3, 14, 16, 18; 39:1, 11; Rev. 20:8 [b]Gen. 10:2; Ezek. 39:6; Rev. 20:8 [c]Ezek. 38:3; 39:1 [d]Ezek. 27:13; 38:3; 39:1
3 [1]Heb., *YHWH*, usually rendered *LORD*, and so throughout the ch. [2]Or, *chief prince of Meshech*
4 [1]Or, *clothed in full armor* [a]Is. 43:17 [b]Ezek. 38:15; Dan. 11:40
5 [1]Lit., *Cush* [a]2 Chr. 36:20; Ezra 1:1; Ezek. 27:10; Dan. 8:20 [b]Gen. 10:6-8; Ezek. 30:4, 5 [c]Ezek. 27:10; 30:5
6 [a]Gen. 10:2, 3 [b]Gen. 10:3; Ezek. 27:14
7 [a]Is. 8:9
8 [1]Lit., *peoples* [2]Lit., *it was* [a]Is. 24:22 [b]Is. 11:11; Ezek. 36:24; 37:21; 38:12; 39:27, 28 [c]Ezek. 34:13; 36:1-8 [d]Ezek. 38:11, 14; 39:26
9 [a]Is. 5:28; 21:1; 25:4; 28:2; Jer. 4:13 [b]Ezek. 30:18; 38:16; Joel 2:2
10 [1]Lit., *words* [a]Ps. 36:4; Mic. 2:1
11 [1]Or, *open country* [a]Zech. 2:4 [b]Jer. 49:31
12 [1]Lit., *navel* [a]Is. 10:6; Ezek. 29:19
13 [1]Or, *young lions* [a]Ezek. 27:22, 23 [b]Ezek. 25:13; 27:15, 20 [c]Ezek. 27:12 [d]Is. 10:6; 33:23; Jer. 15:13
14 [a]Jer. 23:6; Ezek. 38:8, 11; Zech. 2:5, 8
15 [a]Ezek. 39:2
16 [a]Ps. 83:18; Ezek. 36:23; 38:23 [b]Is. 5:16; 8:13; 29:23; Ezek. 28:22
17 [a]Is. 5:26-29; 34:1-6; 63:1-6; 66:15, 16; Joel 3:9-14
18 [a]Ps. 18:8, 15
19 [1]Or, *shaking* [a]Deut. 32:22; Ps. 18:7, 8; Ezek. 5:13; 36:5, 6; Nah. 1:2; Heb. 12:29 [b]Joel 3:16; Hag. 2:6, 7, 21

20"[a]And the fish of the sea, the birds
of the heavens, the beasts of the field, all
the creeping things that creep on the
earth, and all the men who are on the
face of the earth will shake at My presence; the [b]mountains also will be thrown
down, the steep pathways will [1]collapse,
and every wall will fall to the ground.
21"And I shall call for a [a]sword
against [1]him on all My mountains,"
declares the Lord GOD. "[b]Every man's
sword will be against his brother.
22"And with pestilence and with blood
I shall enter into [a]judgment with him;
and I shall rain on him, and on his
troops, and on the many peoples who
are with him, [1]a torrential rain, with
[b]hailstones, fire, and brimstone.
23"And I shall magnify Myself, sanctify Myself, and [a]make Myself known in
the sight of many nations; and they will
know that I am the LORD."'

Prophecy against Gog—Invaders Destroyed

39 "AND [a]you, son of man, prophesy against Gog, and say, 'Thus
says the Lord [1]GOD, "Behold, I am
against you, O Gog, [2]prince of Rosh,
Meshech, and Tubal;
2 and I shall turn you around, drive
you on, take you up from the remotest
parts of the north, and bring you against
the mountains of Israel.
3"And I shall [a]strike your bow from
your left hand, and dash down your
arrows from your right hand.
4"You shall [a]fall on the mountains of
Israel, you and all your troops, and the
peoples who are with you; I shall give
you as [b]food to every [1]kind of predatory
bird and beast of the field.
5"You will fall on the [1]open field; for
it is I who have spoken," declares the
Lord GOD.
6"And I shall send [a]fire upon Magog
and those who inhabit the [b]coastlands in
safety; and they will know that I am the
LORD.
7"And My [a]holy name I shall make
known in the midst of My people Israel;
and I shall not let My holy name be
[b]profaned anymore. And the [c]nations
will know that I am the LORD, the [d]Holy
One in Israel.
8"Behold, it is coming and it shall be
done," declares the Lord GOD. "That is
the day of which I have spoken.
9"Then those who inhabit the cities
of Israel will [a]go out, and make [b]fires
with the weapons and burn *them,* both
shields and bucklers, bows and arrows,
war clubs and spears and for seven years
they will make fires of them.
10"And they will not take wood from
the field or gather firewood from the
forests, for they will make fires with the
weapons; and they will take the spoil of
those who despoiled them, and seize the
[a]plunder of those who plundered them,"
declares the Lord GOD.
11"And it will come about on that day
that I shall give Gog a burial ground
there in Israel, the valley of those who
pass by east of the sea, and it will block
off the passers-by. So they will bury Gog
there with all his multitude, and they
will call *it* the valley of [1]Hamon-gog.
12"For seven months the house of
Israel will be burying them in order to
[a]cleanse the land.
13"Even all the people of the land will
bury *them;* and it will be [1]to their [a]re-
nown *on* the day that I [b]glorify Myself,"
declares the Lord GOD.
14"And they will set apart men who
will constantly pass through the land,
[a]burying those who were passing
through, even those left on the surface of
the ground, in order to cleanse it. At the
end of seven months they will make a
search.
15"And as those who pass through the
land pass through and anyone sees a
man's bone, then he will [1]set up a
marker by it until the buriers have
buried it in the valley of [2]Hamon-gog.
16"And even *the* name of *the* city will
be Hamonah. So they will cleanse the
land."'
17"And as for you, son of man, thus
says the Lord GOD, 'Speak to every
[1]kind of [a]bird and to every [a]beast of the
field, "Assemble and come, gather from
every side to My sacrifice which I am
going to [b]sacrifice for you, as a great
sacrifice on the mountains of Israel, that
you may eat flesh and drink blood.
18"You shall [a]eat the flesh of mighty
men, and drink the blood of the princes
of the earth, as *though they were* [b]rams,
lambs, goats, and [c]bulls, all of them
fatlings of [d]Bashan.
19"So you will eat fat until you are
glutted, and drink blood until you are
drunk, from My sacrifice which I have
sacrificed for you.
20"And you will be glutted at My
table with [a]horses and charioteers, with
mighty men and all the men of war,"
declares the Lord GOD.
21"And I shall set My [a]glory among
the nations; and all the nations will see
My judgment which I have executed,
and My hand which I have laid on them.
22"And the house of Israel will [a]know
that I am the LORD their God from that
day onward.
23"And the nations will know that the
house of Israel went into exile for their
[a]iniquity because they acted treacherously against Me, and I [b]hid My face
from them; so I gave them into the hand
of their adversaries, and all of them fell
by the sword.
24"[a]According to their uncleanness
and according to their transgressions I
dealt with them, and I hid My face from
them."'"

Israel Restored

25 Therefore thus says the Lord GOD,
"Now I shall [1a]restore the fortunes of
Jacob, and have mercy on the whole
[b]house of Israel; and I shall be [c]jealous
for My holy name.

38:20 [1]Lit., *fall* [a]Jer. 4:24, 25; Hos. 4:3; Nah. 1:4-6 [b]Zech. 14:4
21 [1]I.e., Gog [a]Ezek. 14:17 [b]Judg. 7:22; 1 Sam. 14:20; 2 Chr. 20:23; Hag. 2:22
22 [1]Lit., *an overflowing* [a]Is. 66:16; Jer. 25:31 [b]Ps. 11:6; 18:12-14; Is. 28:17
23 [a]Ps. 9:16; Ezek. 37:28; 38:16

39:1 [1]Heb., *YHWH,* usually rendered *LORD,* and so throughout the ch. [2]Or, *chief prince of Meshech* [a]Ezek. 38:2
3 [a]Ps. 76:3; Jer. 21:4, 5; Ezek. 30:21-24; Hos. 1:5
4 [1]Lit., *wing* [a]Is. 14:24, 25; Ezek. 39:17-20 [b]Ezek. 29:5; 32:4, 5; 33:27
5 [1]Lit., *face of the*
6 [a]Ezek. 30:8, 16; 38:19, 22; Amos 1:4, 7, 10; Nah. 1:6 [b]Ps. 72:10; Is. 66:19; Jer. 25:22
7 [a]Ezek. 36:20-22; 39:25 [b]Ex. 20:7; Ezek. 20:9, 14, 39 [c]Ezek. 38:16, 23 [d]Is. 12:6; 43:3, 14; 55:5; 60:9, 14
9 [a]Is. 66:24; Mal. 1:5 [b]Josh. 11:6; Ps. 46:9
10 [a]Is. 14:2; 33:1; Mic. 5:8; Hab. 2:8
11 [1]Or, *the multitude of Gog*
12 [a]Deut. 21:23; Ezek. 39:14, 16
13 [1]Or, *a memorial for them* [a]Jer. 33:9; Zeph. 3:19, 20 [b]Ezek. 28:22
14 [a]Jer. 14:16
15 [1]Lit., *build* [2]Or, *the multitude of Gog*
17 [1]Lit., *wing* [a]Is. 56:9; Jer. 12:9; Ezek. 39:4; Rev. 19:17, 18 [b]Is. 34:6, 7; Jer. 46:10; Zeph. 1:7
18 [a]Ezek. 29:5; Rev. 19:18 [b]Jer. 51:40 [c]Jer. 50:27 [d]Ps. 22:12; Amos 4:1
20 [a]Ps. 76:5, 6; Ezek. 38:4; Hag. 2:22; Rev. 19:18
21 [a]Ex. 9:16; Is. 37:20; Ezek. 36:23; 38:16, 23; 39:13
22 [a]Jer. 24:7
23 [a]Jer. 22:8, 9; 44:22; Ezek. 36:18, 19 [b]Is. 1:15; 59:2; Ezek. 39:29
24 [a]2 Kin. 17:7; Jer. 2:17, 19; 4:18; Ezek. 36:19
25 [1]Or, *return the captivity* [a]Is. 27:12, 13; Jer. 33:7; Ezek. 34:13 [b]Jer. 31:1; Ezek. 36:10; 37:21, 22; Hos. 1:11 [c]Ex. 20:5; Nah. 1:2

26 "And they shall [1a]forget their disgrace and all their treachery which they
[2]perpetrated against Me, when they [b]live
securely on their *own* land with [c]no one
to make them afraid.
27 "When I [a]bring them back from the
peoples and gather them from the lands
of their enemies, then I shall be [b]sancti-
fied [1]through them in the sight of the
many nations.
28 "Then they will know that I am the
LORD their God because I made them go
into exile among the nations, and then
gathered them *again* to their own land;
and I will leave none of them there any
longer.
29 "And I will not hide My face from
them any longer, for I shall have [a]poured
out My Spirit on the house of Israel,"
declares the Lord GOD.

Vision of the Man with a Measuring Rod

40 IN the [a]twenty-fifth year of our
exile, at the beginning of the
year, on the tenth of the month, in the
fourteenth year after the [b]city was
[1]taken, on that same day the [c]hand of
the LORD was upon me and He brought
me there.
2 In the [a]visions of God He brought
me into the land of Israel, and set me on
a very [b]high mountain; and on it [c]to the
south *there was* a [d]structure like a city.
3 So He brought me there; and behold, there was a man whose appearance
was like the appearance of [a]bronze, with
a [b]line of flax and a [c]measuring [1]rod in
his hand; and he was standing in the
gateway.
4 And the man said to me, "[a]Son of
man, [b]see with your eyes, hear with your
ears, and give attention to all that I am
going to show you; for you have been
brought here in order to show *it* to you.
[c]Declare to the house of Israel all that
you see."

Measurements Relating to the Temple

5 And behold, there was a [a]wall on
the outside of the [1]temple all around,
and in the man's hand was a measuring
rod of six cubits, *each of which was* a
cubit and a [2]handbreadth. So he measured the thickness of the [3]wall, one rod;
and the height, one rod.
6 Then he went to the gate which
faced [a]east, went up its steps, and measured the threshold of the gate, one rod
[1]in width; and the other threshold *was*
one rod [1]in width.
7 And the [a]guardroom *was* one rod
long and one rod wide; and *there were*
five cubits between the guardrooms. And
the threshold of the gate by the porch of
the gate [1]facing inward *was* one rod.
8 Then he measured the porch of the
gate [1]facing inward, one rod.
9 And he measured the porch of the
gate, eight cubits; and its side pillars,
two cubits. And the porch of the gate
was [1]faced inward.
10 And the guardrooms of the gate
toward the east *numbered* three on each
side; the three of them had the same
measurement. The side pillars also had
the same measurement on each side.
11 And he measured the width of the
[1]gateway, ten cubits, and the length of
the gate, thirteen cubits.
12 And *there was* a [1]barrier *wall* one
cubit *wide* in front of the guardrooms on
each side; and the guardrooms *were* six
cubits *square* on each side.
13 And he measured the gate from the
roof of the one guardroom to the roof of
the other, a width of twenty-five cubits
from *one* door to *the* door opposite.
14 And he made the side pillars sixty
cubits *high;* the gate *extended* round
about to the side pillar of the [a]courtyard.
15 And *from* the front of the entrance
gate to the front of the inner porch of
the gate *was* fifty cubits.
16 And *there were* [1a]shuttered windows *looking* toward the guardrooms,
and toward their side pillars within the
gate all around, and likewise for the
porches. And *there were* windows all
around inside; and on *each* side pillar
were [b]palm tree ornaments.
17 Then he brought me into the [a]outer
court, and behold, *there were* [b]chambers
and a pavement, made for the court all
around; thirty chambers [1]faced the
pavement.
18 And the pavement (*that is,* the
lower pavement) *was* by the [1]side of
the gates, corresponding to the length of
the gates.
19 Then he measured the width from
the front of the [a]lower gate to the front
of the exterior of the inner court, a
[b]hundred cubits on the east and on the
north.
20 And *as for* the [a]gate of the outer
court which faced the north, he measured its length and its width.
21 And [1]it had three [a]guardrooms on
each side; and its [b]side pillars and its
porches [2]had the same measurement as
the first gate. Its length *was* [c]fifty cubits,
and the width [d]twenty-five cubits.
22 And its [a]windows, and its porches,
and its palm tree ornaments *had* the
same measurements as the [b]gate which
faced toward the east; and [1]it was
reached by seven [c]steps, and its [2]porch
was in front of them.
23 And the inner court had a gate
opposite the gate on the north as well as
the gate on the east; and he measured a
[a]hundred cubits from gate to gate.
24 Then he led me toward the south,
and behold, there was a [a]gate toward the
south; and he measured its [b]side pillars
and its porches according to [1]those same
measurements.
25 And [1]the gate and its porches had
[a]windows all around like [2]those other
windows; the length *was* [b]fifty cubits
and the width twenty-five cubits.

26 [1]Another reading is *bear* [2]Lit., *did treacherously* [a]Ezek. 16:63; 20:43; 36:31 [b]1 Kin. 4:25; Ezek. 34:25-28 [c]Is. 17:2; Mic. 4:4
27 [1]Lit., *in* [a]Ezek. 36:24; 37:21 [b]Ezek. 36:23; 38:16, 23
29 [a]Is. 32:15; Ezek. 36:27; 37:14; Joel 2:28

1 [1]Lit., *struck* [a]Ezek. 32:1, 17; 33:21 [b]2 Kin. 25:1-7; Jer. 39:1-9; 52:4-11; Ezek. 33:21 [c]Ezek. 1:3; 3:14, 22; 37:1
2 [a]Ezek. 1:1; 8:3; Dan. 7:1, 7 [b]Is. 2:2, 3; Ezek. 17:23; 20:40; 37:22; Mic. 4:1; Rev. 21:10 [c]Ps. 48:2; Is. 14:13 [d]1 Chr. 28:12, 19
3 [1]Lit., *reed,* and so throughout the ch. [a]Ezek. 1:7; Dan. 10:6; Rev. 1:15 [b]Ezek. 47:3; Zech. 2:1, 2 [c]Rev. 11:1; 21:15
4 [a]Ezek. 2:1, 3, 6, 8; 44:5 [b]Ezek. 2:7, 8; 44:5 [c]Is. 21:10; Jer. 26:2; Acts 20:27
5 [1]Lit., *house* [2]I.e., 20.4 in. [3]Lit., *building* [a]Is. 26:1; Ezek. 42:20
6 [1]Or, *in depth* [a]Ezek. 8:16; 11:1; 40:20; 43:1
7 [1]Lit., *from the house* [a]Ezek. 40:10-16, 21, 29, 33, 36
8 [1]Lit., *from the house*
9 [1]Lit., *from the house*
11 [1]Lit., *entrance of the gate*
12 [1]Lit., *border*
14 [a]Ex. 27:9; 1 Chr. 28:6; Ps. 100:4; Is. 62:9; Ezek. 8:7; 42:1
16 [1]Or, *beveled inwards* [a]1 Kin. 6:4; Ezek. 41:16, 26 [b]1 Kin. 6:29, 32, 35; 2 Chr. 3:5; Ezek. 40:22, 26, 31, 34, 37; 41:18-20, 25, 26
17 [1]Lit., *to* [a]Ezek. 10:5; 42:1; 46:21; Rev. 11:2 [b]2 Kin. 23:11; 1 Chr. 9:26; 23:28; 2 Chr. 31:11; Ezek. 40:38
18 [1]Lit., *shoulder*
19 [a]Ezek. 40:23, 27; 46:1, 2 [b]Ezek. 40:23, 27
20 [a]Ezek. 40:6
21 [1]Lit., *its guardrooms were three* [2]Lit., *were* [a]Ezek. 40:7 [b]Ezek. 40:16, 30 [c]Ezek. 40:15 [d]Ezek. 40:13
22 [1]Lit., *they were going up into it* [2]Or, *porches* [a]Ezek. 40:16 [b]Ezek. 40:6 [c]Ezek. 40:26, 31, 34, 37, 49
23 [a]Ezek. 40:19, 27

24 [1]Lit., *these measurements,* and so throughout the ch. [a]Ezek. 40:6, 20, 35; 46:9 [b]Ezek. 40:21
25 [1]Lit., *it* [2]Lit., *these windows* [a]Ezek. 40:16, 22, 29 [b]Ezek. 40:21, 33

26 And *there were* seven [a]steps going up to it, and its porches *were* in front of them; and it had [b]palm tree ornaments on its side pillars, one on each side.

27 And the inner court had a gate toward the [a]south; and he measured from gate to gate toward the south, a [b]hundred cubits.

28 Then he brought me to the inner court by the south gate; and he measured the south gate [a]according to those same measurements.

29 Its [a]guardrooms also, its side pillars, and its [b]porches *were* according to those same measurements. And [1]the gate and its porches had [b]windows all around; it *was* [c]fifty cubits long and twenty-five cubits wide.

30 And *there were* [a]porches all around, twenty-five cubits long and five cubits wide.

31 And its porches *were* toward the outer court; and [a]palm tree ornaments *were* on its side pillars, and its stairway had eight [b]steps.

32 And he brought me into the [a]inner court toward the east. And he measured the gate [b]according to those same measurements.

33 Its [a]guardrooms also, its side pillars, and its porches *were* according to those same measurements. And [1]the gate and its porches had [b]windows all around; it *was* [c]fifty cubits long and twenty-five cubits wide.

34 And its [a]porches *were* toward the outer court; and [a]palm tree ornaments *were* on its side pillars, on each side, and its stairway had eight [b]steps.

35 Then he brought me to the [a]north gate; and he measured *it* according to those same measurements,

36 *with* its [a]guardrooms, its side pillars, and its [b]porches. And [1]the gate had [b]windows all around; the length *was* [c]fifty cubits and the width twenty-five cubits.

37 And its side pillars *were* toward the outer court; and [a]palm tree ornaments *were* on its side pillars on each side, and its stairway had eight [b]steps.

38 And a [a]chamber with its doorway was by the side pillars at the gates; there they [b]rinse the burnt offering.

39 And in the porch of the gate *were* two [a]tables on each side, on which to slaughter the [b]burnt offering, the sin offering, and the guilt offering.

40 And on the outer [1]side, [2]as one went up to the [3]gateway toward the north, were two tables; and on the other [1]side of the porch of the gate *were* two tables.

41 Four [a]tables *were* on each side [1]next to the gate; *or,* eight tables on which they slaughter *sacrifices.*

42 And for the burnt offering *there were* four [a]tables of [b]hewn stone, a cubit and a half long, a cubit and a half wide, and one cubit high, on which they lay the instruments with which they slaughter the [c]burnt offering and the sacrifice.

43 And the double [1]hooks, one handbreadth in length, were installed [2]in the house all around; and on the tables *was* the flesh of the offering.

44 And from the outside to the [a]inner gate were [1b]chambers for the [c]singers in the inner court, *one of* which was at the [2]side of the north gate, with [3]its front toward the south, and one at the [2]side of the [4]east gate facing toward the north.

45 And he said to me, "This is the [a]chamber which faces toward the south, *intended* for the priests who [b]keep charge of the [1]temple;

46 but the [a]chamber which faces toward the north is for the priests who [b]keep charge of the altar. These are the [c]sons of Zadok, who from the sons of Levi [d]come near to the LORD to minister to Him."

47 And he measured the court, a *perfect* square, a [a]hundred cubits long and a hundred cubits wide; and the altar was in front of the [1]temple.

48 Then he brought me to the [a]porch of the [1]temple and measured *each* side pillar of the porch, five cubits on each side; and the width of the gate was three cubits on each side.

49 The length of the porch was twenty cubits, and the width eleven cubits; and at the [a]stairway by which it was ascended *were* [b]columns belonging to the side pillars, one on each side.

The Inner Temple

41 THEN he [a]brought me to the [1b]nave and measured the [c]side pillars; six cubits wide on each side *was* the width of the [2]side pillar.

2 And the width of the entrance *was* ten cubits, and the [1]sides of the entrance were five cubits on each side. And he measured [2]the length of the nave, [a]forty cubits, and the width, [a]twenty cubits.

3 Then he went [1a]inside and measured each [b]side pillar of the doorway, two cubits, and the doorway, six cubits *high;* and the width of the doorway, seven cubits.

4 And he measured its length, [a]twenty cubits, and the width, twenty cubits, before the [b]nave; and he said to me, "This is the [c]most holy *place.*"

5 Then he measured the wall of the [1]temple, six cubits; and the width of the [a]side chambers, four cubits, all around about the house on every side.

6 And [a]the side chambers were in three stories, [1]one above another, and [2]thirty in each story; and [3]the side chambers [b]extended to the wall which *stood* on [4]their inward side all around, that they might be fastened, and not be fastened into the wall of the temple *itself.*

5 [1]Lit., *house,* and so throughout the ch. [a]1 Kin. 6:5; Ezek. 41:6-11
6 [1]Lit., *chamber upon chamber* [2]Lit., *thirty times* [3]Lit., they were *coming* [4]Lit., *the inside of the side chambers* [a]1 Kin. 6:5-10 [b]1 Kin. 6:6, 10

26 [a]Ezek. 40:6, 22 [b]Ezek. 40:16
27 [a]Ezek. 40:23, 32 [b]Ezek. 40:19
28 [a]Ezek. 40:32, 35
29 [1]Lit., *it* [a]Ezek. 40:7, 10, 21 [b]Ezek. 40:16, 22, 25 [c]Ezek. 40:21
30 [a]Ezek. 40:16, 21
31 [a]Ezek. 40:16 [b]Ezek. 40:22, 26, 34, 37
32 [a]Ezek. 40:28-31, 35 [b]Ezek. 40:28
33 [1]Lit., *it* [a]Ezek. 40:29 [b]Ezek. 40:16 [c]Ezek. 40:21
34 [a]Ezek. 40:16 [b]Ezek. 40:22, 37
35 [a]Ezek. 40:27, 32; 44:4; 47:2
36 [1]Lit., *it* [a]Ezek. 40:7, 29 [b]Ezek. 40:16 [c]Ezek. 40:21
37 [a]Ezek. 40:16 [b]Ezek. 40:34
38 [a]1 Chr. 28:12; Neh. 13:5, 9; Jer. 35:4; 36:10; Ezek. 40:17; 41:10; 42:13 [b]2 Chr. 4:6
39 [a]Ezek. 40:42 [b]Lev. 1:3-17; Ezek. 46:2
40 [1]Lit., *shoulder* [2]Lit., *to the one going up* [3]Lit., *entrance of the gate*
41 [1]Lit., *by the shoulder of* [a]Ezek. 40:39, 40
42 [a]Ezek. 40:39 [b]Ex. 20:25 [c]Ezek. 40:39
43 [1]Or, *ledges* [2]Or, *inside*
44 [1]Gr. reads *in two chambers* [2]Lit., *shoulder* [3]Lit., *their* [4]Gr. reads *south* [a]Ezek. 40:23, 27 [b]Ezek. 40:17, 38 [c]1 Chr. 6:31, 32; 16:41-43; 25:1-7
45 [1]Or, *house* [a]Ezek. 40:17, 38 [b]1 Chr. 9:23; Ps. 134:1
46 [a]Ezek. 40:17, 38 [b]Lev. 6:12, 13; Ezek. 44:15 [c]1 Kin. 2:35; Ezek. 43:19; 48:11 [d]Lev. 10:3; Num. 16:5, 40; Ezek. 42:13; 45:4
47 [1]Lit., *house* [a]Ezek. 40:19, 23, 27
48 [1]Lit., *house* [a]1 Kin. 6:3; 2 Chr. 3:4
49 [a]Ezek. 40:31, 34, 37 [b]1 Kin. 7:15-22; 2 Chr. 3:17; Jer. 52:17-23; Rev. 3:12

1 [1]I.e., the main inner hall [2]Lit., *tent* [a]Ezek. 40:2, 3, 17 [b]Ezek. 41:21, 23 [c]Ezek. 40:9; 41:3
2 [1]Lit., *shoulders* [2]Lit., *its length,* [a]1 Kin. 6:2, 17; 2 Chr. 3:3
3 [1]I.e., of the inner sanctuary [a]Ezek. 40:16 [b]Ezek. 41:1
4 [a]1 Kin. 6:20 [b]1 Kin. 6:5 [c]Ex. 26:33, 34; 1 Kin. 6:16; 7:50; 8:6; 2 Chr. 5:7; Heb. 9:3-8

7 And the side chambers surrounding the temple were wider at each successive story. Because the [a]structure
surrounding the temple went upward by
stages on all sides of the temple, therefore the width of the temple *increased* as
it went higher; and thus one went up
from the lowest *story* to the highest by
way of the [1]second *story.*
8 I saw also that the house had a
raised [1]platform all around; the foundations of the side chambers were a full
rod of [a]six [2]long cubits *in height.*
9 The [1]thickness of the outer wall of
the side chambers was five cubits. But
the [a]free space between the side chambers belonging to the temple
10 and the *outer* [a]chambers *was*
twenty cubits in width all around the
temple on every side.
11 And the [1]doorways of the [2]side
chambers toward the [a]free space *consisted of* one doorway toward the north
and another doorway toward the south;
and the width of the [a]free space was five
cubits all around.
12 And the [a]building that *was* in front
of the [b]separate area at the side toward
the west *was* seventy cubits wide; and
the wall of the building was five cubits
[1]thick all around, and its length *was*
ninety cubits.
13 Then he measured the temple, a
[a]hundred cubits long; the [b]separate area
with the [c]building and its walls *were* also
a [a]hundred cubits long.
14 Also the width of the front of the
temple and *that of* the separate [1]areas
along the east *side totaled* a hundred
cubits.
15 And he measured the length of the
[a]building [1]along the front of the [b]sepa-
rate area behind it, with a [2c]gallery on
each side, a hundred cubits; *he* also
measured the inner nave and the porches
of the court.
16 The [a]thresholds, the [1b]latticed windows, and the [2c]galleries round about
their [d]three stories, opposite the threshold, were [e]paneled with wood all around,
and *from* the ground to the windows
(but the windows were covered),
17 over the entrance, and to the inner
house, and on the outside, and on all the
wall all around inside and outside, by
measurement.
18 And it was [1]carved with [a]cherubim
and [b]palm trees; and a palm tree was
between cherub and cherub, and every
cherub had two faces,
19 a [a]man's face toward the palm tree
on one side, and a young [a]lion's face
toward the palm tree on the other side;
they were [1]carved on all the house all
around.
20 From the ground to above the
entrance [a]cherubim and [a]palm trees
were [1]carved, as well as *on* the wall of
the nave.
21 The [a]doorposts of the [b]nave were
square; as for the front of the sanctuary,
the appearance of one doorpost was like
that of the other.
22 The [a]altar *was* of wood, three cubits high, and its length two cubits; its
corners, its [1]base, and its [2]sides *were* of
wood. And he said to me, "This is the
[b]table that is before the LORD."
23 And the [a]nave and the [b]sanctuary
each had a double [c]door.
24 And each of the doors had two
leaves, two [1a]swinging leaves; two *leaves*
for one door and two leaves for the
other.
25 Also there were [1]carved on them,
on the doors of the nave, [a]cherubim and
[a]palm trees like those [1]carved on the
walls; and *there was* a [2b]threshold of
wood on the front of the porch outside.
26 And *there were* [1a]latticed windows
and [b]palm trees on one side and on the
other, on the sides of the [c]porch; thus
were the [d]side chambers of the house
and the [2]thresholds.

Chambers of the Temple

42 THEN he [a]brought me out into
the [b]outer court, the way [c]toward
the north; and he brought me to the
[d]chamber which *was* opposite the [e]sepa-
rate area and opposite the [f]building
toward the north.
2 Along the length, *which was* a
[a]hundred cubits, *was* the north door; the
width *was* fifty cubits.
3 Opposite the [a]twenty *cubits* which
belonged to the inner court, and opposite the [b]pavement which belonged to
the outer court, *was* [1c]gallery corresponding to [1]gallery in three stories.
4 And before the [a]chambers *was* an
inner walk ten cubits wide, a way of one
hundred cubits; and their openings *were*
on the north.
5 Now the upper chambers *were*
[1]smaller because the [2a]galleries took
more *space* away from them than from
the lower and middle ones in the building.
6 For they *were* in [a]three stories and
had no pillars like the pillars of the
courts; therefore *the upper chambers*
were [1]set back from the ground upward,
more than the lower and middle ones.
7 As for the [a]outer wall by the side of
the chambers, toward the outer court
facing the chambers, its length *was* fifty
cubits.
8 For the length of the chambers
which *were* in the outer court *was* fifty
cubits; and behold, *the length of those*
facing the temple *was* a [a]hundred cubits.
9 And below these chambers *was* the
[a]entrance on the east side, as one enters
them from the outer court.
10 In the [1]thickness of the [a]wall of the
court toward the east, facing the [b]sepa-
rate area and facing the building, *there
were* [c]chambers.
11 And the [a]way in front of them *was*
like the appearance of the chambers
which *were* on the north, according to
their length so was their width; and all
their exits *were* both according to their
arrangements and openings.

7 [1]Lit., *middle* [a]1 Kin. 6:8
8 [1]Lit., *height* [2]Or, *to the joint* [a]Ezek. 40:5
9 [1]Lit., *width* [a]Ezek. 41:11
10 [a]Ezek. 40:17
11 [1]Lit., *doorway* [2]Lit., *side chamber* [a]Ezek. 41:9
12 [1]Lit., *wide* [a]Ezek. 41:13, 15; 42:1 [b]Ezek. 41:14; 42:10, 13
13 [a]Ezek. 40:47 [b]Ezek. 41:13-15; 42:1, 10, 13 [c]Ezek. 41:12
14 [1]Lit., *area*
15 [1]Lit., *to* [2]Or, *passageway* [a]Ezek. 41:12, 13; 42:1 [b]Ezek. 41:14; 42:1, 10, 13 [c]Ezek. 41:16; 42:3, 5
16 [1]Or, *framed* [2]Or, *passageways* [a]Is. 6:4; Ezek. 10:18; 40:6; 41:25 [b]1 Kin. 6:4; Ezek. 40:16, 25; 41:26 [c]Ezek. 41:15 [d]Ezek. 42:3 [e]1 Kin. 6:15
18 [1]Lit., *made* [a]1 Kin. 6:29, 32, 35; 7:36; Ezek. 41:20, 25 [b]2 Chr. 3:5; Ezek. 40:16
19 [1]Lit., *made* [a]Ezek. 1:10; 10:14
20 [1]Lit., *made* [a]Ezek. 41:18
21 [a]1 Kin. 6:33; Ezek. 40:9, 14, 16; 41:1 [b]Ezek. 41:1
22 [1]Lit., *length* [2]Lit., *walls* [a]Ex. 30:1-3; 1 Kin. 6:20; Rev. 8:3 [b]Ex. 25:23, 30; Lev. 24:6; Ezek. 23:41; 44:16; Mal. 1:7, 12
23 [a]Ezek. 41:1 [b]Ezek. 41:4 [c]1 Kin. 6:31-35
24 [1]Or, *turning* [a]1 Kin. 6:34
25 [1]Lit., *made* [2]Or, *canopy of wood over* [a]Ezek. 41:18 [b]Ezek. 41:16
26 [1]Or, *framed* [2]Or, *canopies* [a]Ezek. 41:16 [b]Ezek. 40:16 [c]Ezek. 40:9, 48 [d]Ezek. 41:5

1 [a]Ezek. 40:17, 28, 48; 41:1 [b]Ezek. 40:17, 20 [c]Ezek. 40:20 [d]Ezek. 40:17; 42:4 [e]Ezek. 41:12; 42:10, 13 [f]Ezek. 41:12
2 [a]Ezek. 41:13
3 [1]Or, *passageway* [a]Ezek. 41:10 [b]Ezek. 40:17 [c]Ezek. 41:15, 16; 42:5
4 [a]Ezek. 46:19
5 [1]Lit., *shorter* [2]Or, *passageways* [a]Ezek. 42:3
6 [1]Or, *reduced* [a]Ezek. 41:6
7 [a]Ezek. 42:10, 12
8 [a]Ezek. 41:13, 14
9 [a]Ezek. 44:5; 46:19
10 [1]Lit., *width* [a]Ezek. 42:7 [b]Ezek. 42:1, 13 [c]Ezek. 40:17
11 [a]Ezek. 42:4

12 And corresponding to the openings of the chambers which were toward the south was an opening at the head of the way, the way in front of the [a]wall toward the east, as one enters them.

13 Then he said to me, "The north chambers *and* the south chambers, which are opposite the [a]separate area, they are the [b]holy chambers where the priests who are [c]near to the LORD shall eat the [d]most holy things. There they shall lay the most holy things, the grain offering, the sin offering, and the guilt offering; for the place is holy.

14 "When the priests enter, then they shall not go out into the outer court from the sanctuary [1]without [a]laying there their [b]garments in which they minister, for they are holy. They shall put on other garments; then they shall approach that which is for the people."

15 Now when he had finished measuring the inner house, he brought me out by the way of the [a]gate which faced toward the east, and measured it all around.

16 He measured on the east side with the measuring reed five hundred reeds, by the [a]measuring reed.

17 He measured on the north side five hundred reeds by the measuring reed.

18 On the south side he measured five hundred reeds with the measuring reed.

19 He turned to the west side, *and* measured five hundred reeds with the measuring reed.

20 He measured it [1]on the four sides; it had a [a]wall all around, the [b]length five hundred and the [b]width five hundred, to [c]divide between the holy and the profane.

Vision of the Glory of God Filling the Temple

43 THEN he led me to the [a]gate, the gate facing toward the east;

2 and behold, the [a]glory of the God of Israel was coming from the way of the [b]east. And His [c]voice was like the sound of many waters; and the earth [d]shone with His glory.

3 And *it was* like the appearance of the vision which I saw, like the [a]vision which I saw when [1]He came to [b]destroy the city. And the visions *were* like the vision which I saw by the [c]river Chebar; and I [d]fell on my face.

4 And the glory of the LORD came into the house by the way of the gate facing toward the [a]east.

5 And the [a]Spirit lifted me up and brought me into the inner court; and behold, the [b]glory of the LORD filled the house.

6 Then I heard one speaking to me from the house, while a [a]man was standing beside me.

7 And He said to me, "Son of man, *this is* the place of My [a]throne and the place of the soles of My feet, where I will [b]dwell among the sons of Israel forever. And the house of Israel will not again defile My holy name, neither they nor their kings, by their harlotry and by the [1c]corpses of their kings [2]when they die,

8 by setting their threshold by My threshold, and their door post beside My door post, with *only* the wall between Me and them. And they have [a]defiled My holy name by their abominations which they have committed. So I have consumed them in My anger.

9 "Now let them [a]put away their harlotry and the [1]corpses of their kings far from Me; and I will [b]dwell among them forever.

10 "As for you, son of man, [1a]describe the [2]temple to the house of Israel, that they may be [b]ashamed of their iniquities; and let them measure the [3c]plan.

11 "And if they are ashamed of all that they have done, make known to them the [1]design of the house, its structure, its [a]exits, its entrances, all its designs, all its statutes[2], and all its laws. And write *it* [b]in their sight, so that they may observe its whole [1]design and all its statutes, and [c]do them.

12 "This is the [1]law of the house: its entire [2]area on the top of the [a]mountain all around *shall be* most holy. Behold, this is the [1]law of the house.

The Altar of Sacrifice

13 "And these are the measurements of the [a]altar by cubits (the [b]cubit being a cubit and a handbreadth): the [1]base *shall be* a cubit, and the width a cubit, and its border on its edge round about one span; and this *shall be* the *height of the* [2]base of the altar.

14 "And from the base on the ground to the lower [a]ledge *shall be* two cubits, and the width one cubit; and from the smaller ledge to the larger ledge *shall be* four cubits, and the width [1]one cubit.

15 "And the [1]altar hearth *shall be* four cubits; and from the [1]altar hearth shall extend upwards four [a]horns.

16 "Now the [1]altar hearth *shall be* twelve *cubits* long by twelve wide, [a]square in its four sides.

17 "And the ledge *shall be* fourteen *cubits* long by fourteen wide in its four sides, the border around it *shall be* half a cubit, and its base *shall be* a cubit round about; and its [a]steps shall [1b]face the east."

The Offerings

18 And He said to me, "[a]Son of man, thus says the Lord [1]GOD, 'These are the statutes for the altar on the day it is built, to offer [b]burnt offerings on it and to [c]sprinkle blood on it.

19 'And you shall give to the Levitical priests who are from the offspring of [a]Zadok, who draw [b]near to Me to minister to Me,' declares the Lord GOD, 'a [c]young bull for a [d]sin offering.

12 [a]Ezek. 42:7
13 [a]Ezek. 42:1, 10 [b]Ex. 29:31; Lev. 7:6; 10:13, 14, 17 [c]Lev. 10:3; Deut. 21:5; Ezek. 40:46 [d]Lev. 6:25, 29; 14:13; Num. 18:9, 10
14 [1]Lit., *but there they shall lay* [a]Ezek. 44:19 [b]Ex. 29:4-9; Lev. 8:7, 13; Is. 61:10; Zech. 3:4, 5
15 [a]Ezek. 40:6; 43:1
16 [a]Ezek. 40:3
20 [1]Lit., *toward the four winds* [a]Is. 60:18; Ezek. 40:5; Zech. 2:5 [b]Ezek. 45:2; Rev. 21:16 [c]Ezek. 22:26; 44:23; 48:15

1 [a]Ezek. 10:19; 40:6; 42:15; 43:4; 44:1; 46:1
2 [a]Is. 6:3; Ezek. 1:28; 3:23; 10:18, 19 [b]Ezek. 11:23 [c]Ezek. 1:24; Rev. 1:15; 14:2 [d]Ezek. 1:28; 10:4; Rev. 18:1
3 [1]So with some mss. and some ancient versions; M.T., *I* [a]Ezek. 1:4-28 [b]Jer. 1:10; Ezek. 9:1, 5; 32:18 [c]Ezek. 1:3; 10:20 [d]Ezek. 1:28; 3:23
4 [a]Ezek. 10:19; 11:23; 43:2
5 [a]Ezek. 3:14; 8:3; 11:1, 24; 2 Cor. 12:2-4 [b]Ezek. 10:4
6 [a]Ezek. 1:26; 40:3
7 [1]Or, *monuments* as in Ugaritic [2]Or, *in their high places* [a]Ps. 47:8; Ezek. 1:26 [b]Ezek. 37:26, 28 [c]Lev. 26:30; Ezek. 6:5, 13
8 [a]Ezek. 8:3, 16
9 [1]Or, *monuments* as in Ugaritic [a]Ezek. 18:30, 31 [b]Ezek. 37:26-28; 43:7
10 [1]Lit., *declare* [2]Lit., *house* [3]Lit., *perfection* or *pattern* [a]Ezek. 40:4 [b]Ezek. 16:61, 63; 43:11 [c]Ezek. 28:12
11 [1]Or, *form(s)* [2]M.T. repeats *and all its designs* after *statutes* [a]Ezek. 44:5 [b]Ezek. 12:3 [c]Ezek. 11:20; 36:27
12 [1]Or, *instruction for* [2]Lit., *border* [a]Ezek. 40:2
13 [1]Lit., *lap* [2]Or, *back* [a]Ex. 27:1-8; 2 Chr. 4:1 [b]Ezek. 40:5; 41:8
14 [1]Lit., *the* [a]Ezek. 43:17, 20; 45:19
15 [1]Or, *ariel* shall [a]Ex. 27:2; Lev. 9:9; 1 Kin. 1:50; Ps. 118:27
16 [1]Or, *ariel* shall [a]Ex. 27:1
17 [1]Or, *be on the east side* [a]Ex. 20:26 [b]Ezek. 40:6

18 [1]Heb., *YHWH*, usually rendered *LORD*, and so throughout the ch. [a]Ezek. 2:1 [b]Ex. 40:29 [c]Lev. 1:5, 11; Heb. 9:21, 22
19 [a]1 Kin. 2:35; Ezek. 40:46; 44:15 [b]Num. 16:5, 40 [c]Lev. 4:3; Ezek. 43:23; 45:18 [d]Ezek. 45:19; Heb. 7:27

20 'And you shall take some of its
blood, and put it on its four [a]horns, and
on the four corners of the [b]ledge, and on
the border round about; thus you shall
[c]cleanse it and make atonement for it.
21 'You shall also take the bull for the
sin offering; and it *shall be* [a]burned in
the appointed place of the house, outside
the sanctuary.
22 'And on the second day you shall
offer a [a]male goat without blemish for a
sin offering; and they shall [b]cleanse the
altar, as they cleansed *it* with the bull.
23 'When you have finished cleansing
it, you shall present a [a]young bull without blemish and a [b]ram without blemish
from the flock.
24 'And you shall present them before
the LORD, and the priests shall throw
[a]salt on them, and they shall offer them
up as a burnt offering to the LORD.
25 '[a]For seven days you shall prepare
daily a goat for a sin offering; also a
young bull and a ram from the flock,
without blemish, shall be prepared.
26 'For seven days they shall make
atonement for the altar and purify it; so
shall they [1]consecrate it.
27 'And when they have completed the
days, it shall be that on the [a]eighth day
and onward, the priests shall [1]offer your
burnt offerings on the altar, and your
[b]peace offerings; and I will [c]accept you,'
declares the Lord GOD."

Gate for the Prince

44 THEN He brought me back by
the way of the [a]outer gate of the
sanctuary, which faces the east; and it
was shut.
2 And the LORD said to me, "This
gate shall be shut; it shall not be opened,
and no one shall enter by it, for the
[a]LORD God of Israel has entered by it;
therefore it shall be shut.
3 "As for the [a]prince, he shall sit in it
as prince to [b]eat bread before the LORD;
he shall [c]enter by way of the [d]porch of
the gate, and shall go out [1]by the same
way."
4 Then He brought me by way of the
[a]north gate to the front of the house;
and I looked, and behold, the [b]glory of
the LORD filled the house of the LORD,
and I [c]fell on my face.
5 And the LORD said to me, "Son of
man, [1a]mark well, see with your eyes,
and hear with your ears all that I say to
you concerning all the [b]statutes of the
house of the LORD and concerning all its
laws; and [1]mark well the entrance of the
house, with all exits of the sanctuary.
6 "And you shall say to the [1a]rebel-
lious ones, to the house of Israel, 'Thus
says the Lord [2]GOD, "[b]Enough of all
your abominations, O house of Israel,
7 when you brought in [a]foreigners,
[b]uncircumcised in heart and uncircumcised in flesh, to be in My sanctuary to
profane it, *even* My house, when you
[c]offered My food, the fat and the blood;
for they [d]made My covenant void—*this*
in addition to all your abominations.
8 "And you have not [a]kept charge of
My holy things yourselves, but you have
set *foreigners* [1]to keep charge of My
sanctuary."
9 'Thus says the Lord GOD, "[a]No
foreigner, uncircumcised in heart and
uncircumcised in flesh, of all the foreigners who are among the sons of Israel,
shall enter My sanctuary.
10 "But the Levites who went far from
Me, when Israel went astray, who [a]went
astray from Me after their idols, shall
[b]bear the punishment for their iniquity.
11 "Yet they shall be [a]ministers in My
sanctuary, having [b]oversight at the gates
of the house and [c]ministering in the
house; they shall [d]slaughter the burnt
offering and the sacrifice for the people,
and they shall [e]stand before them to
minister to them.
12 "Because they ministered to them
[a]before their idols and became a [b]stum-
bling block of iniquity to the house of
Israel, therefore I have [1c]sworn against
them," declares the Lord GOD, "that
they shall [d]bear the punishment for their
iniquity.
13 "And they shall [a]not come near to
Me to serve as a priest to Me, nor come
near to any of My holy things, to the
things that are most holy; but they shall
[b]bear their shame and their abominations which they have committed.
14 "Yet I will [1]appoint them [2]to [a]keep
charge of the house, of all its service, and
of all that shall be done in it.

Ordinances for the Levites

15 "But the [a]Levitical priests, the sons
of [b]Zadok, who [c]kept charge of My
sanctuary when the sons of Israel [d]went
astray from Me, shall come near to Me
to minister to Me; and they shall [e]stand
before Me to offer Me the [f]fat and the
blood," declares the Lord GOD.
16 "They shall [a]enter My sanctuary;
they shall come near to My [b]table to
minister to Me and keep My charge.
17 "And it shall be that when they
enter at the gates of the inner court, they
shall be clothed with [a]linen garments;
and wool shall not [1]be on them while
they are ministering in the gates of the
inner court and in the house.
18 "Linen [a]turbans shall be on their
heads, and [b]linen undergarments shall
be on their loins; they shall not gird
themselves with *anything which makes
them* sweat.
19 "And when they go out into the
outer court, into the outer court to the
people, they shall [a]put off their garments
in which they have been ministering and
lay them in the holy chambers; then they
shall put on other garments that they
may [b]not transmit holiness to the people
with their garments.

20 [a]Lev. 8:15; 9:9; Ezek. 43:15 [b]Ezek. 43:14, 17 [c]Lev. 16:19; Ezek. 43:22, 26
21 [a]Ex. 29:14; Lev. 4:12; Heb. 13:11
22 [a]Ezek. 43:25 [b]Ezek. 43:20, 26
23 [a]Ex. 29:1, 10; Ezek. 45:18 [b]Ex. 29:1
24 [a]Lev. 2:13; Num. 18:19; Mark 9:49, 50; Col. 4:6
25 [a]Ex. 29:35-37; Lev. 8:33, 35
26 [1]Lit., *fill its hands*
27 [1]Lit., *make* [a]Lev. 9:1 [b]Lev. 3:1; 17:5 [c]Ezek. 20:40

1 [a]Ezek. 40:6, 17; 42:14
2 [a]Ezek. 43:2-4
3 [1]Lit., *by his way* [a]Ezek. 34:24; 37:25 [b]Gen. 31:54; Ex. 24:9-11 [c]Ezek. 46:2, 8-10 [d]Ezek. 40:9
4 [a]Ezek. 40:20, 40 [b]Is. 6:3, 4; Ezek. 1:28; 3:23; 43:4, 5; Hag. 2:7 [c]Ezek. 1:28; 43:3
5 [1]Lit., *set your heart on* [a]Deut. 32:46; Ezek. 40:4 [b]Deut. 12:32; Ezek. 43:10, 11
6 [1]Lit., *rebellion* [2]Heb., *YHWH,* usually rendered *LORD,* and so throughout the ch. [a]Ezek. 2:5-7; 3:9 [b]Ezek. 45:9; 1 Pet. 4:3
7 [a]Ex. 12:43-49 [b]Lev. 26:41; Deut. 10:16; Jer. 4:4; 9:26 [c]Lev. 22:25 [d]Gen. 17:14
8 [1]Lit., *as keepers of My charge in My* [a]Lev. 22:2; Num. 18:7
9 [a]Ezek. 44:7; Joel 3:17; Zech. 14:21
10 [a]2 Kin. 23:8, 9; Ezek. 22:26; 44:12 [b]Num. 18:23
11 [a]Num. 3:5-37; 4:1-33; 18:2-7 [b]1 Chr. 26:1-19 [c]Ezek. 40:45; 44:14 [d]2 Chr. 29:34; 30:17 [e]Num. 16:9
12 [1]Lit., *lifted up My hand* [a]2 Kin. 16:10-16 [b]Ezek. 14:3, 4 [c]Ezek. 20:15, 23 [d]Ezek. 44:10
13 [a]Num. 18:3 [b]Ezek. 16:61, 63; 39:26
14 [1]Lit., *give* [2]Lit., *keepers of the charge* [a]Num. 18:4; 1 Chr. 23:28-32; Ezek. 44:11
15 [a]Jer. 33:18-22 [b]Ezek. 40:46; 43:19; 48:11 [c]Num. 18:7; Ezek. 40:45 [d]Ezek. 44:10; 48:11 [e]Zech. 3:1, 7 [f]Lev. 3:16, 17; 17:5, 6; Ezek. 44:7
16 [a]Num. 18:5, 7, 8 [b]Ezek. 41:22; Mal. 1:7, 12
17 [1]Lit., *come upon* [a]Ex. 28:42, 43; 39:27-29; Rev. 19:8
18 [a]Ex. 28:40; Is. 3:20; Ezek. 24:17, 23 [b]Ex. 28:42; Lev. 16:4
19 [a]Lev. 6:10; 16:4, 23, 24; Ezek. 42:14 [b]Lev. 6:27; Ezek. 46:20

20"Also they shall [a]not shave their heads, yet they shall not [b]let their locks [1]grow long; they shall only trim *the hair of* their heads.

21"[a]Nor shall any of the priests drink wine when they enter the inner court.

22"And they shall not [1]marry a widow or a [a]divorced woman but shall [b]take virgins from the offspring of the house of Israel, or a widow who is the widow of a priest.

23"Moreover, they shall teach My people *the* [a]*difference* between the holy and the profane, and cause them to discern between the unclean and the clean.

24"And in a dispute [a]they shall take their stand to judge; they shall judge it according to My ordinances. They shall also keep My laws and My statutes in all My [b]appointed feasts, and [c]sanctify My sabbaths.

25"And [1a]they shall not go to a dead person to defile *themselves;* however, for father, for mother, for son, for daughter, for brother, or for a sister who has not had a husband, they may defile themselves.

26"And after he is [a]cleansed, seven days shall [1]elapse for him.

27"And on the day that he goes into the sanctuary, into the [a]inner court to minister in the sanctuary, he shall offer his [b]sin offering," declares the Lord GOD.

28"And it shall be with regard to an inheritance for them, *that* [a]I am their inheritance; and you shall give them no possession in Israel—I am their possession.

29"They shall [a]eat the grain offering, the sin offering, and the guilt offering; and every [1b]devoted thing in Israel shall be theirs.

30"And the first of all the [a]first fruits of every kind and every [1]contribution of every kind, from all your [1]contributions, shall be for the priests; you shall also give to the priest the [b]first of your [2]dough to cause a [c]blessing to rest on your house.

31"The priests shall not eat any bird or beast that has [a]died a natural death or has been torn to pieces.

The LORD's Portion of the Land

45 "AND when you shall [a]divide by lot the land for inheritance, you shall offer [1]an [b]allotment to the LORD, a [c]holy portion of the land; the length shall be the length of 25,000 [d]*cubits,* and the width shall be [2]10,000. It shall be holy within all its boundary round about.

2"Out of this there shall be for the holy place a square round about [a]five hundred by five hundred *cubits,* and fifty cubits for its [1b]open space round about.

3"And from this [1]area you shall measure a length of 25,000 *cubits,* and a width of 10,000 *cubits;* and in it shall be the sanctuary, the most holy place.

20 [1]Or, *hang loose* [a]Lev. 21:5 [b]Num. 6:5
21 [a]Lev. 10:9
22 [1]Lit., *take as wives for themselves* [a]Lev. 21:7, 14 [b]Lev. 21:13
23 [a]Lev. 10:10; Ezek. 22:26; Hos. 4:6; Mic. 3:9-11; Zeph. 3:4; Hag. 2:11-13; Mal. 2:6-8
24 [a]Deut. 17:8, 9; 19:17; 21:5; 1 Chr. 23:4; 2 Chr. 19:8-10 [b]Lev. 23:2, 4, 44 [c]Ezek. 20:12, 20
25 [1]Lit., *he* [a]Lev. 21:1-4
26 [1]Lit., *be counted* [a]Num. 19:13-19
27 [a]Ezek. 44:17 [b]Lev. 5:3, 6; Num. 6:9-11
28 [a]Num. 18:20; Deut. 10:9; 18:1, 2; Josh. 13:33
29 [1]Or, *dedicated* [a]Num. 18:9, 14; Josh. 13:14 [b]Lev. 27:21, 28; Num. 18:14
30 [1]Or, *heave offering(s)* [2]Or, *coarse meal* [a]Num. 18:12, 13; 2 Chr. 31:4-6, 10; Neh. 10:35-37 [b]Num. 15:20, 21 [c]Mal. 3:10
31 [a]Lev. 22:8; Deut. 14:21; Ezek. 4:14

1 [1]Or, *a contribution* [2]Or, with Gr., *20,000* [a]Num. 34:13; Josh. 13:7; 14:3; Ezek. 47:21; 48:29 [b]Ezek. 48:8, 9 [c]Zech. 14:20, 21 [d]Ezek. 42:16; 45:2
2 [1]Or, *pasture land* [a]Ezek. 42:20 [b]Ezek. 27:28
3 [1]Lit., *measure*
4 [a]Ezek. 48:10, 11 [b]Num. 16:5; Ezek. 40:45; 43:19
5 [1]So with Gr.; M.T., *twenty chambers* [a]Ezek. 48:13
6 [1]Or, *contribution* [a]Ezek. 48:15-18, 30-35
7 [1]Or, *contribution* [2]Lit., *possession* [a]Ezek. 34:24; 37:24; 46:16-18; 48:21
8 [a]Is. 11:3-5; Jer. 23:5; Ezek. 19:7; 22:27; 46:18 [b]Josh. 11:23
9 [1]Heb., *YHWH,* usually rendered *LORD,* and so throughout the ch. [a]Ezek. 44:6 [b]Jer. 6:7; Ezek. 7:11, 23; 8:17 [c]Jer. 22:3; Zech. 8:16 [d]Neh. 5:1-5
10 [a]Lev. 19:36; Deut. 25:15; Prov. 16:11; Amos 8:4-6; Mic. 6:10, 11 [b]Is. 5:10
11 [1]Lit., *one* [2]Lit., *its measure* [a]Is. 5:10

4"It shall be the holy portion of the land; it shall be for the [a]priests, the ministers of the sanctuary, who [b]come near to minister to the LORD, and it shall be a place for their houses and a holy place for the sanctuary.

5"And *an area* [a]25,000 *cubits* in length and 10,000 in width shall be for the Levites, the ministers of the house, *and* for their possession [1]cities to dwell in.

6"And you shall give the [a]city possession of *an area* 5,000 *cubits* wide and 25,000 *cubits* long, alongside the [1]allotment of the holy portion; it shall be for the whole house of Israel.

Portion for the Prince

7"And the [a]prince shall have *land* on either side of the holy [1]allotment and the [2]property of the city, adjacent to the holy [1]allotment and the [2]property of the city, on the west side toward the west and on the east side toward the east, and in length comparable to one of the portions, from the west border to the east border.

8"This shall be his land for a possession in Israel; so My princes shall no longer [a]oppress My people, but they shall give *the rest of* the land to the house of Israel [b]according to their tribes."

9 'Thus says the Lord [1]GOD, "[a]Enough, you princes of Israel; put away [b]violence and destruction, and [c]practice justice and righteousness. Stop your [d]expropriations from My people," declares the Lord GOD.

10"You shall have [a]just balances, a just [b]ephah, and a just [b]bath.

11"The ephah and the bath shall be [1]the same quantity, so that the bath may contain a tenth of a [a]homer, and the ephah a tenth of a homer; [2]their standard shall be according to the homer.

12"And the [a]shekel shall be twenty [a]gerahs; twenty shekels, twenty-five shekels, *and* fifteen shekels shall be your [1]maneh.

13"This is the offering that you shall offer: a sixth of an ephah from a homer of wheat; a sixth of an ephah from a homer of barley;

14 and the prescribed portion of oil (*namely,* the bath of oil), a tenth of a bath from *each* kor (*which is* ten baths *or* a homer, for ten baths are a homer);

15 and one sheep from *each* flock of two hundred from the watering places of Israel—for a [a]grain offering, for a burnt offering, and for peace offerings, to [b]make atonement for them," declares the Lord GOD.

16"[a]All the people of the land shall [1]give to this offering for the [b]prince in Israel.

12 [1]Or, *mina* [a]Ex. 30:13; Lev. 27:25; Num. 3:47
15 [a]Ezek. 45:17 [b]Lev. 1:4; 6:30
16 [1]Lit., *be* [a]Ex. 30:14, 15 [b]Is. 16:1

17"And it shall be the [a]prince's part *to*
provide the [b]burnt offerings, the grain
offerings, and the libations, at the
[c]feasts, on the [d]new moons, and on the
sabbaths, at all the appointed feasts of
the house of Israel; he shall provide the
sin offering, the grain offering, the burnt
offering, and the [e]peace offerings, to
make atonement for the house of Israel."
18 'Thus says the Lord GOD, "In the
[a]first *month,* on the first of the month,
you shall take a young bull [b]without
blemish and [c]cleanse the sanctuary.
19"And the priest shall take some of
the blood from the sin offering and put *it*
on the door posts of the house, on the
[a]four corners of the [b]ledge of the altar,
and on the posts of the gate of the inner
court.
20"And thus you shall do on the
seventh *day* of the month for everyone
who goes [a]astray or is [1]naive; so you
shall make [b]atonement for the house.
21"In the [a]first *month,* on the fourteenth day of the month, you shall have
the [b]Passover, a feast of seven days;
unleavened bread shall be eaten.
22"And on that day the prince shall
provide for himself and all the people of
the land a [a]bull for a sin offering.
23"And *during* the [a]seven days of the
feast he shall provide as a [b]burnt offering to the LORD [c]seven bulls and seven
rams without blemish on every day of
the seven days, and a male goat daily for
a sin offering.
24"And he shall provide as a [a]grain
offering an ephah [1]with a bull, an ephah
[1]with a ram, and a hin of oil [1]with an
ephah.
25"In the [a]seventh *month,* on the fifteenth day of the month, at the feast, he
shall provide like this, seven days [1]for
the sin offering, the burnt offering, the
grain offering, and the oil."

The Prince's Offerings

46 'THUS says the Lord [1]GOD,
"The [a]gate of the [b]inner court
facing east shall be [c]shut the six [d]work-
ing days; but it shall be opened on the
[e]sabbath day, and opened on the day of
the [f]new moon.
2"And the [a]prince shall enter by way
of the porch of the gate from outside and
stand by the [b]post of the gate. Then the
priests shall provide his burnt offering
and his peace offerings, and he shall
worship at the threshold of the gate and
then go out; but the gate shall not be
[c]shut until the evening.
3"The [a]people of the land shall also
worship at the doorway of that gate
before the LORD on the sabbaths and on
the [b]new moons.
4"And the [a]burnt offering which the
prince shall offer to the LORD on the
sabbath day shall be [b]six lambs without
blemish and a ram without blemish;
5 and the [a]grain offering shall be an
ephah [1]with the ram, and the grain
offering [1]with the lambs [2]as much as he
is [b]able to give, and a hin of oil [1]with an
ephah.
6"And on the day of the [a]new moon
he shall offer a young bull without blemish, also six lambs and a ram, *which* shall
be without blemish.
7"And he shall provide a [a]grain
offering, an ephah [1]with the bull, and an
ephah [1]with the ram, and [1]with the
lambs as [2]much as he is [b]able, and a hin
of oil [1]with an ephah.
8"And when the [a]prince enters, he
shall go in by way of the porch of the
gate and go out [1]by the same way.
9"But when the people of the land
come [a]before the LORD at the appointed
feasts, he who enters by way of the north
gate to worship shall go out by way of
the south gate. And he who enters by
way of the south gate shall go out by
way of the north gate. [1]No one shall
return by way of the gate by which he
entered but shall go straight out.
10"And when they go in, the prince
shall go in [a]among them; and when they
go out, [1]he shall go out.
11"And at the [a]festivals and the appointed feasts the [b]grain offering shall be
an ephah [1]with a bull and an ephah
[1]with a ram, and [1]with the lambs as
[2]much as one is able to give, and a hin of
oil [1]with an ephah.
12"And when the prince provides a
[a]freewill offering, a burnt offering, or
peace offerings *as* a freewill offering to
the LORD, the gate facing east shall be
[b]opened for him. And he shall provide
his burnt offering and his peace offerings
as he does on the [c]sabbath day. Then he
shall go out, and the gate shall be shut
after he goes out.
13"And you shall provide a [a]lamb a
year old without blemish for a burnt
offering to the LORD daily; [b]morning by
morning you shall provide it.
14"Also you shall provide a grain
offering with it morning by morning, a
[a]sixth of an ephah, and a third of a hin
of oil to moisten the fine flour, a grain
offering to the LORD continually by a
perpetual [1]ordinance.
15"Thus they shall provide the lamb,
the grain offering, and the oil, morning
by morning, for a [a]continual burnt
offering."
16 'Thus says the Lord GOD, "If the
prince gives a [a]gift *out of* his inheritance
to any of his sons, it shall belong to his
sons; it is their possession by inheritance.
17"But if he gives a gift from his
inheritance to one of his servants, it shall
be his until the [a]year of liberty; then it
shall return to the prince. His inheritance *shall be* only his sons'; it shall
belong to them.
18"And the prince shall [a]not take from
the people's inheritance, [1b]thrusting
them out of their possession; he shall
give his sons inheritance from his own
possession so that My people shall not
be scattered, anyone from his possession." ' "

17 [a]Ezek. 46:4-12 [b]1 Kin. 8:64; 1 Chr. 16:2; 2 Chr. 31:3 [c]Lev. 23:1-44; Num. 28:1-29:39 [d]Is. 66:23 [e]1 Kin. 8:63; Ezek. 43:27
18 [a]Ex. 12:2 [b]Lev. 22:20; Heb. 9:14 [c]Lev. 16:16, 33; Ezek. 43:22, 26
19 [a]Lev. 16:18-20; Ezek. 43:20 [b]Ezek. 43:14, 17, 20
20 [1]Lit., *simple* [a]Lev. 4:27; Ps. 19:12 [b]Lev. 16:20; Ezek. 45:15, 18
21 [a]Num. 28:16f. [b]Ex. 12:1-24; Lev. 23:5-8
22 [a]Lev. 4:14
23 [a]Lev. 23:8 [b]Num. 28:16-25 [c]Num. 23:1, 2; Job 42:8
24 [1]Lit., *for* [a]Num. 28:12-15; Ezek. 46:5-7
25 [1]Lit., *according to* [a]Lev. 23:33-43; Num. 29:12-38; 2 Chr. 5:3; 7:8, 10

1 [1]Heb., *YHWH,* usually rendered *LORD,* and so throughout the ch. [a]Ezek. 45:19 [b]Ezek. 8:16; 10:3 [c]Ezek. 44:1, 2 [d]Ex. 20:9 [e]Is. 66:23; Ezek. 45:17 [f]Ezek. 45:18; 46:3, 6
2 [a]Ezek. 44:3; 46:8 [b]Ezek. 45:19 [c]Ezek. 46:12
3 [a]Luke 1:10 [b]Ezek. 46:1
4 [a]Ezek. 45:17 [b]Num. 28:9
5 [1]Lit., *for* [2]Lit., *a gift of his hand* [a]Num. 28:12; Ezek. 45:24; 46:7, 11 [b]Ezek. 46:7
6 [a]Ezek. 46:1
7 [1]Lit., *for* [2]Lit., *his hand can reach* [a]Ezek. 46:5 [b]Lev. 14:21; Deut. 16:17; Ezek. 46:5
8 [1]Lit., *by its way* [a]Ezek. 44:3; 46:2
9 [1]Lit., *He shall not* [a]Ex. 34:23; Ps. 84:7; Mic. 6:6
10 [1]So with many mss. and the ancient versions; M.T., *they* [a]2 Sam. 6:14, 15; 1 Chr. 29:20, 22; 2 Chr. 6:3; 7:4; Ps. 42:4
11 [1]Lit., *for* [2]Lit., *a gift of his hand* [a]Ezek. 45:17 [b]Ezek. 46:5, 7
12 [a]Lev. 23:38; 2 Chr. 29:31 [b]Ezek. 44:3; 46:1, 2, 8 [c]Ezek. 45:17
13 [a]Num. 28:3-5 [b]Is. 50:4
14 [1]Lit., *statute* [a]Num. 28:5
15 [a]Ex. 29:42; Num. 28:6
16 [a]2 Chr. 21:3
17 [a]Lev. 25:10
18 [1]Lit., *oppressing* [a]Ezek. 45:8 [b]1 Kin. 21:19; Ezek. 22:27; Mic. 2:1, 2

The Boiling Places

19 Then he brought me through the [a]entrance, which *was* at the side of the gate, into the holy chambers for the priests, which faced north; and behold, there *was* a place at the extreme rear toward the west.

20 And he said to me, "This is the place where the priests shall boil the [a]guilt offering and the sin offering, *and* where they shall [b]bake the grain offering, in order that they may not bring *them* out into the outer court to transmit holiness to the people."

21 Then he brought me out into the outer court and led me across to the four corners of the court; and behold, in every corner of the court *there was* a *small* court.

22 In the four corners of the court *there were* enclosed courts, forty *cubits* long and thirty wide; these four in the corners *were* [1]the same size.

23 And *there was* a row *of masonry* round about in them, around the four of them, and boiling places were made under the rows round about.

24 Then he said to me, "These are the boiling [1]places where the ministers of the house shall boil the sacrifices of the people."

Water from the Temple

47 THEN he brought me back to the [a]door of the house; and behold, [b]water was flowing from under the threshold of the house toward the east, for the house faced east. And the water was flowing down from under, from the right side of the house, from south of the altar.

2 And he brought me out by way of the north gate and led me around [1]on the outside to the outer gate by way of *the gate* that faces east. And behold, water was trickling from the south side.

3 When the man went out toward the east with a line in his hand, he measured a thousand cubits, and he led me through the water, water *reaching* the ankles.

4 Again he measured a thousand and led me through the water, water *reaching* the knees. Again he measured a thousand and led me through *the water,* water *reaching* the loins.

5 Again he measured a thousand; *and it was* a river that I could not ford, for the water had risen, *enough* water to swim in, a [a]river that could not be forded.

6 And he said to me, "Son of man, have you [a]seen *this?*" Then he brought me [1]back to the bank of the river.

7 Now when I had returned, behold, on the bank of the river there *were* very many [a]trees on the one side and on the other.

8 Then he said to me, "These waters go out toward the eastern region and go down into the [a]Arabah; then they go toward the sea, being made to flow into the [b]sea, and the waters *of the sea* become [1]fresh.

9 "And it will come about that every living creature which swarms in every place where the [1]river goes, will live. And there will be very many fish, for these waters go there, and *the others* [2]become fresh; so [a]everything will live where the river goes.

10 "And it will come about that [a]fishermen will stand beside it; from [b]Engedi to Eneglaim there will be a place for the [c]spreading of nets. Their fish will be according to their kinds, like the fish of the [d]Great Sea, [e]very many.

11 "But its swamps and marshes will not become [1]fresh; they will be [2]left for [a]salt.

12 "And [a]by the river on its bank, on one side and on the other, will grow all *kinds of* [b]trees for food. Their [c]leaves will not wither, and their fruit will not fail. They will bear every month because their water flows from the sanctuary, and their fruit will be for food and their [d]leaves for healing."

Boundaries and Division of the Land

13 Thus says the Lord [1]GOD, "This *shall be* the [a]boundary by which you shall divide the land for an inheritance among the twelve tribes of Israel; Joseph *shall have two* [b]portions.

14 "And you shall divide it for an inheritance, each one [1]equally with the other; for I [2a]swore to give it to your forefathers, and this land shall fall to you [3]as an inheritance.

15 "And this *shall be* the boundary of the land: on the [a]north side, from the Great Sea *by* the way of Hethlon, to the entrance of [1b]Zedad;

16 [1a]Hamath, Berothah, Sibraim, which is between the border of [b]Damascus and the border of Hamath; Hazer-hatticon, which is by the border of Hauran.

17 "And the boundary shall [1]extend from the sea *to* [a]Hazar-enan *at* the border of Damascus, and on the north toward the north is the border of Hamath. This is the north side.

18 "And the [a]east side, from between Hauran, Damascus, [b]Gilead, and the land of Israel, *shall be* the [c]Jordan; from the *north* border to the eastern sea you shall measure. This is the east side.

19 "And the [a]south side toward the south *shall extend* from [b]Tamar as far as the waters of [c]Meribath-kadesh, to the [d]brook *of Egypt, and* to the [e]Great Sea. This is the south side toward the south.

20 "And the [a]west side *shall be* the Great Sea, from the *south* border to a point opposite [1b]Lebo-hamath. This is the west side.

21 "So you shall divide this land among yourselves according to the tribes of Israel.

---

19 [a]Ezek. 42:9; 44:5

20 [a]2 Chr. 35:13; Ezek. 44:29 [b]Lev. 2:4-7

22 [1]Lit., *one measure*

24 [1]Lit., *houses*

1 [a]Ezek. 41:2, 23-25 [b]Ps. 46:4; Is. 30:25; 55:1; Jer. 2:13; Joel 3:18; Zech. 13:1; 14:8; Rev. 22:1, 17

2 [1]Lit., *by way of*

5 [a]Is. 11:9; Hab. 2:14

6 [1]Lit., *and caused me to return* [a]Ezek. 8:6; 40:4; 44:5

7 [a]Is. 60:13, 21; 61:3; Ezek. 47:12

8 [1]Lit., *healed* [a]Deut. 3:17; Is. 35:6, 7; 41:17-19; 44:3 [b]Josh. 3:16

9 [1]Lit., *two rivers* [2]Lit., *are healed* [a]Is. 12:3; 55:1; John 4:14; 7:37, 38

10 [a]Matt. 4:19; 13:47; Luke 5:10 [b]Gen. 14:7; Josh. 15:62; 1 Sam. 23:29; 24:1; 2 Chr. 20:2 [c]Ezek. 26:5, 14 [d]Num. 34:6; Ps. 104:25; Ezek. 47:15; 48:28 [e]Luke 5:5-9; John 21:6

11 [1]Lit., *healed* [2]Lit., *given* [a]Deut. 29:23

12 [a]Ezek. 47:7; Rev. 22:2 [b]Gen. 2:9 [c]Ps. 1:3; Jer. 17:8 [d]Rev. 22:2

13 [1]Heb., *YHWH,* usually rendered *LORD,* and so throughout the ch. [a]Num. 34:2-12 [b]Gen. 48:5; Ezek. 48:4, 5

14 [1]Lit., *like his brother* [2]Lit., *lifted up My hand* [3]Lit., *in* [a]Deut. 1:8; Ezek. 20:6

15 [1]Or, *Hamath* [a]Num. 34:7-9 [b]Num. 34:8

16 [1]Or, *Zedad* [a]Num. 13:21; Is. 10:9; Ezek. 47:17, 20; 48:1; Zech. 9:2 [b]Gen. 14:15; Ezek. 47:17, 18; 48:1

17 [1]Lit., *be* [a]Num. 34:9

18 [a]Num. 34:10-12 [b]Gen. 37:25; Jer. 50:19 [c]Gen. 13:10, 11

19 [a]Num. 34:3-5 [b]Ezek. 48:28 [c]Deut. 32:51 [d]Num. 34:5; 1 Kin. 8:65; Is. 27:12 [e]Ezek. 47:10, 15

20 [1]Or, *entrance of Hamath* [a]Num. 34:6 [b]Judg. 3:3; 2 Chr. 7:8; Ezek. 48:1; Amos 6:14

22"And it will come about that you
shall divide it by [a]lot for an inheritance
among yourselves and among the [b]aliens
who stay in your midst, who bring forth
sons in your midst. And they shall be to
you as the native-born among the sons
of Israel; they shall be allotted an [c]inher-
itance with you among the tribes of
Israel.
23"And it will come about that in the
tribe with which the alien stays, there
you shall give *him* his inheritance,"
declares the Lord GOD.

Division of the Land

48 "NOW [a]these are the names of
the tribes: from the northern
extremity, [1]beside the way of Hethlon to
[2]Lebo-hamath, *as far as* Hazar-enan *at*
the border of Damascus, toward the
north [1]beside Hamath, [3]running from
east to west, [b]Dan, one *portion.*
2"And beside the border of Dan,
from the east side to the west side,
[a]Asher, one *portion.*
3"And beside the border of Asher,
from the east side to the west side,
[a]Naphtali, one *portion.*
4"And beside the border of Naphtali,
from the east side to the west side,
[a]Manasseh, one *portion.*
5"And beside the border of Manasseh, from the east side to the west side,
[a]Ephraim, one *portion.*
6"And beside the border of Ephraim,
from the east side to the west side,
[a]Reuben, one *portion.*
7"And beside the border of Reuben,
from the east side to the west side,
[a]Judah, one *portion.*
8"And beside the border of Judah,
from the east side to the west side, shall
be the [1]allotment which you shall [2]set
apart, 25,000 [3]*cubits* in width, and in
length like one of the portions, from the
east side to the west side; and the
[a]sanctuary shall be in the middle of it.
9"The allotment that you shall set
apart to the LORD *shall be* 25,000 *cubits*
in length, and 10,000 in width.

Portion for the Priests

10"And the holy allotment shall be for
these, *namely* for the [a]priests, toward the
north 25,000 *cubits in length,* toward the
west 10,000 in width, toward the east
10,000 in width, and toward the south
25,000 in length; and the sanctuary of
the LORD shall be in its midst.
11"*It shall be* for the priests who are
sanctified of the [a]sons of Zadok, who
have kept My charge, who did not go
astray when the sons of Israel went
astray, as the [b]Levites went astray.
12"And it shall be an allotment to
them from the allotment of the land, a
most holy place, by the border of the
Levites.
13"And alongside the border of the
priests the Levites *shall have* 25,000
cubits in length and 10,000 in width. The
whole length *shall be* 25,000 *cubits* and
the width 10,000.

22 [a]Num. 26:55, 56 [b]Is. 14:1; 56:6, 7 [c]Acts 11:18; 15:9; Eph. 2:12-14; 3:6; Col. 3:11

1 [1]Lit., *at the hand of* [2]Or, *the entrance of Hamath* [3]Lit., *and there shall be to it an east and west side* [a]Ex. 1:1 [b]Josh. 19:40-48

2 [a]Josh. 19:24-31

3 [a]Josh. 19:32-39

4 [a]Josh. 13:29-31; 17:1-11

5 [a]Josh. 16:5-9; 17:8-10, 14-18

6 [a]Josh. 13:15-21

7 [a]Josh. 15:1-63; 19:9

8 [1]Or, *contribution,* and so throughout the ch. [2]Lit., *offer* [3]Or possibly, *reeds,* and so throughout the ch. [a]Is. 12:6; 33:20-22; Ezek. 45:3, 4

10 [a]Ezek. 44:28; 45:4

11 [a]Ezek. 40:46; 44:15 [b]Ezek. 44:10, 12

14 [1]Lit., *first* or *first fruits* [a]Lev. 25:32-34; 27:10, 28, 33

15 [1]Lit., *in front* [2]Or, *pasture land* [a]Ezek. 42:20; 45:6

16 [a]Rev. 21:16

17 [1]Or, *pasture land*

18 [1]Or, *exactly as*

20 [1]Lit., *offer* [2]Lit., *fourth* [3]Or, *possession*

21 [1]Or, *possession* [a]Ezek. 34:24; 45:7; 48:22

22 [1]Or, *possession*

23 [a]Josh. 18:21-28

24 [a]Josh. 19:1-9

25 [a]Josh. 19:17-23

26 [a]Josh. 19:10-16

27 [a]Josh. 13:24-28

28 [a]Gen. 14:7; 2 Chr. 20:2; Ezek. 47:19 [b]Ezek. 47:10, 15, 19, 20

14"Moreover, they [a]shall not sell or
exchange any of it, or alienate this
[1]choice *portion* of land; for it is holy to
the LORD.
15"And the remainder, 5,000 *cubits* in
width and 25,000 [1]in length, shall be for
[a]common use for the city, for dwellings
and for [2]open spaces; and the city shall
be in its midst.
16"And these *shall be* its measurements: the north side 4,500 *cubits,* the
south side [a]4,500 *cubits,* the east side
4,500 *cubits,* and the west side 4,500
cubits.
17"And the city shall have [1]open
spaces: on the north 250 *cubits,* on the
south 250 *cubits,* on the east 250 *cubits,*
and on the west 250 *cubits.*
18"And the remainder of the length
alongside the holy allotment shall be
10,000 *cubits* toward the east, and 10,000
toward the west; and it shall be [1]along-
side the holy allotment. And its produce
shall be food for the workers of the city.
19"And the workers of the city, out of
all the tribes of Israel, shall cultivate it.
20"The whole allotment *shall be* 25,000
by 25,000 *cubits;* you shall [1]set apart the
holy allotment, a [2]square, with the
[3]property of the city.

Portion for the Prince

21"And the [a]remainder *shall be* for the
prince, on the one side and on the other
of the holy allotment and of the [1]prop-
erty of the city; in front of the 25,000
cubits of the allotment toward the east
border and westward in front of the
25,000 toward the west border, alongside
the portions, *it shall be* for the prince.
And the holy allotment and the sanctuary of the house shall be in the middle of
it.
22"And exclusive of the [1]property of
the Levites and the [1]property of the city,
which are in the middle of that which
belongs to the prince, *everything* between
the border of Judah and the border of
Benjamin shall be for the prince.

Portion for Other Tribes

23"As for the rest of the tribes: from
the east side to the west side, [a]Benjamin,
one *portion.*
24"And beside the border of Benjamin, from the east side to the west side,
[a]Simeon, one *portion.*
25"And beside the border of Simeon,
from the east side to the west side,
[a]Issachar, one *portion.*
26"And beside the border of Issachar,
from the east side to the west side,
[a]Zebulun, one *portion.*
27"And beside the border of Zebulun,
from the east side to the west side, [a]Gad,
one *portion.*
28"And beside the border of Gad, at
the south side toward the south, the
border shall be from [a]Tamar to the
waters of Meribath-kadesh, to the brook
of Egypt, to the [b]Great Sea.

29 "This is the [a]land which you shall divide by lot to the tribes of Israel for an inheritance, and these are their *several* portions," declares the Lord [1]GOD.

The City Gates

30 "And these are the exits of the city: on the [a]north side, 4,500 *cubits* by measurement,

31 [1]shall be the gates of the city, [2][a]named for the tribes of Israel, three gates toward the north: the gate of Reuben, one; the gate of Judah, one; the gate of Levi, one.

32 "And on the east side, 4,500 *cubits,* [1]shall be three gates: the gate of Joseph, one; the gate of Benjamin, one; the gate of Dan, one.

33 "And on the south side, 4,500 *cubits* by measurement, [1]shall be three gates: the gate of Simeon, one; the gate of Issachar, one; the gate of Zebulun, one.

34 "On the west side, 4,500 *cubits, shall be* three gates: the gate of Gad, one; the gate of Asher, one; the gate of Naphtali, one.

35 "*The city shall be* 18,000 *cubits* round about; and the [a]name of the city from *that* day *shall be,* '[1]The [b]LORD is there.' "

29 [1]Heb., *YHWH,* usually rendered *LORD* [a]Ezek. 47:13-20
30 [a]Ezek. 48:32-34
31 [1]Lit., *and* [2]Lit., *according to the names of* [a]Rev. 21:12, 13
32 [1]Lit., *and*
33 [1]Lit., *and*
35 [1]Heb., *YHWH-shammah* [a]Jer. 23:6; 33:16 [b]Is. 12:6; 14:32; 24:23; Jer. 3:17; 8:19; 14:9; Ezek. 35:10; Joel 3:21; Zech. 2:10; Rev. 21:3; 22:3

THE BOOK OF DANIEL

The Choice Young Men

1 IN the third year of the reign of [a]Jehoiakim king of Judah, [b]Nebuchadnezzar king of Babylon came to Jerusalem and besieged it.

2 And the [a]Lord gave Jehoiakim king of Judah into his hand, along with some of the [b]vessels of the house of God; and he brought them to the land of [c]Shinar, to the house of his [1]god, and he brought the vessels into the treasury of his [1][d]god.

3 Then the king [1]ordered Ashpenaz, the chief of his [2]officials, to bring in some of the sons of Israel, including some of the [3]royal [a]family and of the nobles,

4 youths in whom was [a]no defect, who were good-looking, showing [b]intelligence in every *branch of* wisdom, endowed with understanding, and discerning knowledge, and who had ability for [1]serving in the king's [2]court; and *he ordered him* to teach them the [3]literature and [c]language of the [d]Chaldeans.

5 And the king appointed for them a daily ration from the [a]king's choice food and from the wine which he drank, and *appointed* that they should be [1]educated three years, at the end of which they were to [2][b]enter the king's personal service.

6 Now among them from the sons of Judah were [a]Daniel, Hananiah, Mishael and Azariah.

7 Then the commander of the officials assigned *new* names to them; and to Daniel he assigned *the name* [a]Belteshazzar, to Hananiah [b]Shadrach, to Mishael [b]Meshach, and to Azariah [b]Abed-nego.

Daniel's Resolve

8 But Daniel [1]made up his mind that he would not [a]defile himself with the [b]king's choice food or with the [c]wine which he drank; so he sought *permission* from the commander of the officials that he might not defile himself.

9 Now God granted Daniel [1][a]favor and compassion in the sight of the commander of the officials,

10 and the commander of the officials said to Daniel, "I am afraid of my lord the king, who has appointed your food and your drink; for why should he see your faces looking more haggard than the youths who are your own age? Then you would [1]make me forfeit my head to the king."

11 But Daniel said to the overseer whom the commander of the officials had appointed over Daniel, Hananiah, Mishael and Azariah,

12 "Please test your servants for ten days, and let us be [a]given some vegetables to eat and water to drink.

13 "Then let our appearance be [1]observed in your presence, and the appearance of the youths who are eating the king's choice food; and deal with your servants according to what you see."

14 So he listened to them in this matter and tested them for ten days.

15 And at the end of ten days their appearance seemed [a]better and [1]they were fatter than all the youths who had been eating the king's choice food.

16 So the overseer continued to [1]withhold their choice food and the wine they were to drink, and kept [a]giving them vegetables.

17 And as for these four youths, [a]God gave them knowledge and intelligence in every *branch of* [1]literature and wisdom; Daniel even understood all *kinds of* [b]visions and dreams.

18 Then at the end of the days which the king had [1]specified [2]for presenting them, the commander of the officials [3]presented them before Nebuchadnezzar.

19 And the king talked with them, and out of them all not one was found like [a]Daniel, Hananiah, Mishael and Azariah; so they [1][b]entered the king's personal service.

1 [a]2 Kin. 24:1; 2 Chr. 36:5, 6 [b]Jer. 25:1; 52:12, 28-30
2 [1]Or, *gods* [a]Is. 42:24; Dan. 2:37, 38 [b]2 Chr. 36:7; Jer. 27:19, 20; Dan. 5:2 [c]Gen. 10:10; 11:2; Is. 11:11; Zech. 5:11 [d]Jer. 50:2; 51:44
3 [1]Or, *said to* [2]Or, *eunuchs,* and so throughout the ch. [3]Lit., *seed of the* [a]2 Kin. 24:15; Is. 39:7
4 [1]Lit., *standing* [2]Lit., *palace* [3]Or, *writing* [a]2 Sam. 14:25 [b]Dan. 1:17 [c]Is. 36:11; Jer. 5:15; Dan. 2:4 [d]Dan. 2:2, 4, 5, 10; 3:8; 4:7; 5:7, 11, 30; 9:1
5 [1]Or, *reared* [2]Lit., *stand before the king* [a]Dan. 1:8 [b]1 Sam. 16:22; Dan. 1:19
6 [a]Ezek. 14:14, 20; 28:3; Matt. 24:15
7 [a]Dan. 2:26; 4:8; 5:12 [b]Dan. 2:49; 3:12
8 [1]Lit., *set upon his heart* [a]Lev. 11:47; Ezek. 4:13, 14; Hos. 9:3, 4 [b]Ps. 141:4; Dan. 1:5 [c]Deut. 32:38; Dan. 5:4
9 [1]Lit., *lovingkindness* [a]Gen. 39:21; 1 Kin. 8:50; Job 5:15, 16; Ps. 106:46; Prov. 16:7
10 [1]Lit., *make my head guilty*
12 [a]Dan. 1:16
13 [1]Lit., *seen*
15 [1]Lit., *fat of flesh* [a]Ex. 23:25; Prov. 10:22
16 [1]Lit., *take away* [a]Dan. 1:12
17 [1]Or, *writing* [a]1 Kin. 3:12, 28; Job 32:8; Dan. 1:20; 2:21, 23; Acts 7:22 [b]Dan. 2:19; 7:1; 8:1
18 [1]Lit., *said* [2]Lit., *to bring them in* [3]Lit., *brought in*
19 [1]Lit., *stood before the king* [a]Dan. 1:6, 7 [b]Gen. 41:46; Dan. 1:5

20 And as for every matter of [a]wisdom
[1]and understanding about which the
king consulted them, he found them [b]ten
times [c]better than all the [2d]magicians
and conjurers who *were* in all his realm.
21 And Daniel [1]continued until the
[a]first year of Cyrus the king.

The King's Forgotten Dream

2 NOW in the second year of the
reign of Nebuchadnezzar, Nebuchadnezzar [1a]had dreams; and his spirit
was troubled and his [b]sleep [2]left him.
2 Then the king [1]gave orders to call
in the [2a]magicians, the conjurers, the
sorcerers and the [3]Chaldeans, to tell the
king his dreams. So they came in and
stood before the king.
3 And the king said to them, "I [1a]had
a dream, and my spirit [2]is anxious to
[3]understand the dream."
4 Then the Chaldeans spoke to the
king in [1a]Aramaic: "[b]O king, live forever! [c]Tell the dream to your servants,
and we will declare the interpretation."
5 The king answered and said to the
Chaldeans, "[1]The command from me is
firm: if you do not make known to me
the dream and its interpretation, you
will be [2a]torn limb from limb, and your
houses will be made a rubbish heap.
6 "But if you declare the dream and
its interpretation, you will receive from
me [a]gifts and a reward and great honor;
therefore declare to me the dream and
its interpretation."
7 They answered a second time and
said, "Let the king [a]tell the dream to his
servants, and we will declare the interpretation."
8 The king answered and said, "I
know for certain that you are [1]bargain-
ing for time, inasmuch as you have seen
that [2]the command from me is firm,
9 that if you do not make the dream
known to me, there is only [a]one [1]decree
for you. For you have agreed together to
speak lying and corrupt [2]words before
me until the [3]situation is changed; therefore tell me the dream, that I may [b]know
that you can declare to me its interpretation."
10 The Chaldeans answered [1]the king
and said, "There is not a man on earth
who could declare the matter [2]for the
king, inasmuch as no great king or ruler
has *ever* asked anything like this of any
[3a]magician, conjurer or Chaldean.
11 "Moreover, the thing which the king
demands is [1]difficult, and there is no one
else who could declare it [2]to the king
except [a]gods, whose [b]dwelling place is
not with *mortal* flesh."
12 Because of this the king became
[a]indignant and very furious, and gave
orders to destroy all the wise men of
Babylon.
13 So the [1]decree went forth that the
wise men should be slain; and they
looked for [a]Daniel and his friends to
[2]kill *them.*

20 [1]Lit., *of* [2]Or, *soothsayer priests* [a]1 Kin. 4:30, 31; Dan. 1:17 [b]Gen. 31:7; Num. 14:22; Neh. 4:12; Job 19:3 [c]Dan. 2:27, 28, 46, 48 [d]Is. 19:3; Dan. 2:2; 4:18; 5:7
21 [1]Lit., *was until* [a]Dan. 6:28; 10:1
1 [1]Lit., *dreamed dreams* [2]Lit., *was gone upon him* [a]Gen. 40:5-8; 41:1, 8; Job 33:15-17; Dan. 2:3; 4:5 [b]Esth. 6:1; Dan. 6:18
2 [1]Lit., *said to call* [2]Or, *soothsayer priests* [3]Or, *master astrologers,* and so throughout the ch. [a]Gen. 41:8; Ex. 7:11; Is. 47:12, 13; Dan. 1:20; 2:10, 27; 4:6; 5:7
3 [1]Lit., *dreamed* [2]Lit., *was troubled* [3]Lit., *know* [a]Gen. 40:8; 41:15; Dan. 4:5
4 [1]The text is in Aramaic from here through 7:28 [a]Ezra 4:7; Is. 36:11 [b]Dan. 3:9; 5:10 [c]Dan. 2:7
5 [1]Another reading is *The word has gone from me* [2]Lit., *made into limbs* [a]Ezra 6:11; Dan. 2:12; 3:29
6 [a]Dan. 2:48; 5:7, 16, 29
7 [a]Dan. 2:4
8 [1]Lit., *buying* [2]V. 5, note 1
9 [1]Or, *law* [2]Lit., *word* [3]Lit., *time* [a]Esth. 4:11; Dan. 3:15 [b]Is. 41:23
10 [1]Lit., *before the* [2]Lit., *of* [3]Or, *soothsayer priest* [a]Dan. 2:2, 27
11 [1]Or, *rare* [2]Lit., *before* [a]Gen. 41:39; Dan. 5:11 [b]Ex. 29:45; Is. 57:15
12 [a]Ps. 76:10; Dan. 2:5; 3:13, 19
13 [1]Or, *law* [2]Lit., *be killed* [a]Dan. 1:19, 20
14 [1]Or, *executioners* [a]Dan. 2:24
15 [1]Or, *law* [2]Or, *harsh*
16 [1]Or, *appoint a time for him*
17 [a]Dan. 1:6
18 [a]Esth. 4:15, 16; Is. 37:4; Jer. 33:3; Ezek. 36:37; Dan. 2:23 [b]Gen. 18:28; Mal. 3:18
19 [a]Num. 12:6; Job 33:15, 16; Dan. 1:17; 7:2, 7, 13
20 [a]Ps. 103:1, 2; 113:1, 2; 115:18; 145:1, 2, 21 [b]1 Chr. 29:11, 12; Job 12:13, 16-22; Dan. 2:21-23
21 [1]Or, *sets up* [2]Lit., *knowers* [a]Ps. 31:15; Dan. 2:9; 7:25 [b]Job 12:18; Ps. 75:6, 7; Dan. 4:17, 32 [c]1 Kin. 3:9, 10; 4:29; James 1:5

14 Then Daniel replied with discretion
and discernment to [a]Arioch, the captain
of the king's [1]bodyguard, who had gone
forth to slay the wise men of Babylon;
15 he answered and said to Arioch,
the king's commander, "For what reason
is the [1]decree from the king *so* [2]urgent?"
Then Arioch informed Daniel about the
matter.
16 So Daniel went in and requested of
the king that he would [1]give him time, in
order that he might declare the interpretation to the king.
17 Then Daniel went to his house and
informed his friends, [a]Hananiah, Mishael and Azariah, about the matter,
18 in order that they might [a]request
compassion from the God of heaven
concerning this mystery, so that Daniel
and his friends might not be [b]destroyed
with the rest of the wise men of Babylon.

The Secret Is Revealed to Daniel

19 Then the mystery was revealed to
Daniel in a night [a]vision. Then Daniel
blessed the God of heaven;
20 Daniel answered and said,
"Let the name of God be [a]blessed
forever and ever,
For [b]wisdom and power belong to
Him.
21 "And it is He who [a]changes the
times and the epochs;
He [b]removes kings and [1]estab-
lishes kings;
He gives [c]wisdom to wise men,
And knowledge to [2]men of understanding.
22 "It is He who [a]reveals the pro-
found and hidden things;
[b]He knows what is in the darkness,
And the [c]light dwells with Him.
23 "To Thee, O [a]God of my fathers, I
give thanks and praise,
For Thou hast given me [b]wisdom
and power;
Even now Thou hast made known
to me what we [c]requested of
Thee,
For Thou hast made known to us
the king's matter."
24 Therefore, Daniel went in to Arioch, whom the king had appointed to
destroy the wise men of Babylon; he
went and spoke to him as follows: "[a]Do
not destroy the wise men of Babylon!
Take me [1]into the king's presence, and I
will declare the interpretation to the
king."
25 Then Arioch hurriedly [a]brought
Daniel [1]into the king's presence and
spoke to him as follows: "I have found a
man among the [2b]exiles from Judah who
can make the interpretation known to
the king!"

22 [a]Job 12:22; Ps. 25:14; Dan. 2:19, 28 [b]Job 26:6; Ps. 139:12; Is. 45:7; Jer. 23:24; Heb. 4:13 [c]Ps. 36:9; Dan. 5:11, 14; James 1:17; 1 John 1:5
23 [a]Gen. 31:42; Ex. 3:15 [b]Dan. 1:17; 2:21 [c]Ps. 21:2, 4; Dan. 2:18, 29, 30
24 [1]Lit., *in before the king* [a]Dan. 2:12, 13; Acts 27:24
25 [1]Lit., *in before the king* [2]Lit., *sons of the exile of* [a]Gen. 41:14 [b]Dan. 1:6; 5:13; 6:13

26 The king answered and said to
Daniel, whose name was [a]Belteshazzar,
"Are you able to make known to me the
dream which I have seen and its interpretation?"
27 Daniel answered before the king
and said, "As for the mystery about
which the king has inquired, neither
[a]wise men, conjurers, [1]magicians, *nor*
diviners are able to declare *it* to the king.
28"However, there is a [a]God in heaven
who reveals mysteries, and He has made
known to King Nebuchadnezzar what
will take place in the [1b]latter days. This
was your dream and the [c]visions [2]in your
mind *while* on your bed.
29"As for you, O king, *while* on your
bed your thoughts [1]turned to what
would take place [2]in the future; and [a]He
who reveals mysteries has made known
to you what will take place.
30"But as for me, this mystery has not
been revealed to me for any [a]wisdom
[1]residing in me more than *in* any *other*
living man, but for the purpose of making the interpretation known to the king,
and that you may [2]understand the
[b]thoughts of your [3]mind.

The King's Dream

31"You, O king, were looking and
behold, there was a single great statue;
that statue, which was large and [1]of
extraordinary splendor, was standing in
front of you, and its appearance was
[a]awesome.
32"The [a]head of that statue *was made*
of fine gold, its breast and its arms of
silver, its belly and its thighs of bronze,
33 its legs of iron, its feet partly of
iron and partly of clay.
34"You [1]continued looking until a
[a]stone was cut out [b]without hands, and
it struck the statue on its feet of iron and
clay, and [c]crushed them.
35"Then the iron, the clay, the bronze,
the silver and the gold were crushed [1]all
at the same time, and became [a]like chaff
from the summer threshing floors; and
the wind carried them away so that [b]not
a trace of them was found. But the stone
that struck the statue became a great
[c]mountain and filled the whole earth.

The Interpretation—Babylon the First Kingdom

36"This *was* the dream; now we shall
tell [a]its interpretation before the king.
37"You, O king, are the [a]king of kings,
to whom the God of heaven has given
the [1]kingdom, the [b]power, the strength,
and the glory;
38 and wherever the sons of men
dwell, *or* the [a]beasts of the field, or the
birds of the sky, He has given *them* into
your hand and has caused you to rule
over them all. You are the head of gold.

Medo-Persia and Greece

39"And after you there will arise
another kingdom inferior to you, then
another third kingdom of bronze, which
will rule over all the earth.

Rome

40"Then there will be a [a]fourth kingdom as strong as iron; inasmuch as iron
crushes and shatters all things, so, like
iron that breaks in pieces, it will crush
and break all these in pieces.
41"And in that you saw the feet and
toes, partly of potter's clay and partly of
iron, it will be a divided kingdom; but it
will have in it the toughness of iron,
inasmuch as you saw the iron mixed
with [1]common clay.
42"And *as* the toes of the feet *were*
partly of iron and partly of pottery, *so*
some of the kingdom will be strong and
part of it will be brittle.
43"And in that you saw the iron mixed
with [1]common clay, they will combine
with one another [2]in the seed of men;
but they will not adhere to one another,
even as iron does not combine with
pottery.

The Divine Kingdom

44"And in the days of those kings the
[a]God of heaven will [b]set up a [c]kingdom
which will never be destroyed, and *that*
kingdom will not be [1]left for another
people; it will [d]crush and put an end to
all these kingdoms, but it will itself
endure forever.
45"Inasmuch as you saw that a [a]stone
was cut out of the mountain without
hands and that it crushed the iron, the
bronze, the clay, the silver, and the gold,
the [b]great God has made known to the
king what [c]will take place [1]in the future;
so the dream is true, and its interpretation is trustworthy."

Daniel Promoted

46 Then King Nebuchadnezzar fell on
his face and did [a]homage to Daniel, and
gave orders to present to him an offering
and [1b]fragrant incense.
47 The king answered Daniel and
said, "Surely [a]your God is a [b]God of
gods and a Lord of kings and a [c]revealer
of mysteries, since you have been able to
reveal this mystery."
48 Then the king [1a]promoted Daniel
and gave him many great gifts, and he
made him ruler over the whole [b]province
of Babylon and chief [2]prefect over all
the wise men of Babylon.
49 And Daniel made request of the
king, and he [a]appointed [b]Shadrach,
Meshach and Abed-nego over the administration of the province of Babylon,
while Daniel *was* at the king's [1c]court.

The King's Golden Image

3 NEBUCHADNEZZAR the king
made an [a]image of gold, the height
of which *was* sixty [1]cubits *and* its width
six [1]cubits; he set it up on the plain of
Dura in the [b]province of Babylon.
2 Then Nebuchadnezzar the king
sent *word* to assemble the [a]satraps, the
prefects and the governors, the counselors, the treasurers, the judges, the magistrates and all the rulers of the provinces to come to the dedication of the

26 [a]Dan. 1:7; 4:8; 5:12
27 [1]Or, *soothsayer priests* [a]Dan. 2:2, 10, 11; 5:7, 8
28 [1]Lit., *end of the days* [2]Lit., *of your head* [a]Gen. 40:8; 41:16; Dan. 2:22, 45 [b]Gen. 49:1; Is. 2:2; Dan. 10:14; Mic. 4:1 [c]Dan. 4:5
29 [1]Lit., *came up* [2]Lit., *after this* [a]Dan. 2:23, 47
30 [1]Lit., *which is* [2]Lit., *know* [3]Lit., *heart* [a]Gen. 41:16; Dan. 1:17 [b]Ps. 139:2; Amos 4:13
31 [1]Lit., *its splendor was surpassing* [a]Hab. 1:7
32 [a]Dan. 2:38
34 [1]Lit., *were* [a]Dan. 2:45 [b]Dan. 8:25; Zech. 4:6 [c]Ps. 2:9; Is. 60:12
35 [1]Lit., *like one* [a]Ps. 1:4; Is. 17:13; 41:15, 16; Hos. 13:3 [b]Ps. 37:10, 36 [c]Is. 2:2; Mic. 4:1
36 [a]Dan. 2:24
37 [1]Or, *sovereignty* [a]Is. 47:5; Jer. 27:6, 7; Ezek. 26:7 [b]Ps. 62:11
38 [a]Ps. 50:10, 11; Dan. 4:21, 22
40 [a]Dan. 7:23
41 [1]Lit., *clay of mud*
43 [1]Lit., *clay of mud* [2]Or, *with*
44 [1]Or, *passed on to* [a]Dan. 2:28, 37 [b]Is. 9:6, 7 [c]Ps. 145:13; Ezek. 37:25; Dan. 4:3, 34; 6:26; 7:14, 27; Mic. 4:7; Luke 1:32, 33 [d]Ps. 2:9; Is. 60:12; Dan. 2:34, 35
45 [1]Lit., *after this* [a]Dan. 2:34 [b]Deut. 10:17; 2 Sam. 7:22; Ps. 48:1; Jer. 32:18, 19; Dan. 2:29; Mal. 1:11 [c]Gen. 41:28, 32
46 [1]Lit., *sweet odors* [a]Dan. 3:5, 7; Acts 10:25; 14:13; Rev. 19:10; 22:8 [b]Lev. 26:31; Ezra 6:10
47 [a]Dan. 3:15; 4:25 [b]Deut. 10:17; Ps. 136:2, 3; Dan. 11:36 [c]Dan. 2:22, 30; Amos 3:7
48 [1]Lit., *made great* [2]Lit., *of the prefects* [a]Gen. 41:39-43; Dan. 2:6; 5:16, 29 [b]Dan. 3:1, 12, 30
49 [1]Lit., *gate* [a]Dan. 3:12 [b]Dan. 1:7 [c]Esth. 2:19, 21; Amos 5:15

1 [1]I.e., One cubit equals approx. 18 in. [a]1 Kin. 12:28; Is. 46:6; Jer. 16:20; Dan. 2:31; Hos. 2:8; 8:4; Hab. 2:19 [b]Dan. 2:48; 3:30
2 [a]Dan. 3:3, 27; 6:1-7

image that Nebuchadnezzar the king
had set up.
3 Then the satraps, the prefects and
the governors, the counselors, the treasurers, the judges, the magistrates and all
the rulers of the provinces were assembled for the dedication of the image that
Nebuchadnezzar the king had set up;
and they stood before the image that
Nebuchadnezzar had set up.
4 Then the herald loudly proclaimed:
"To you [1]the command is given, [a]O
peoples, nations and *men of every* [2]lan-
guage,
5 that at the moment you [a]hear the
sound of the horn, flute, [1]lyre, [2]trigon,
[3]psaltery, bagpipe, and all kinds of
music, you are to fall down and worship
the golden image that Nebuchadnezzar
the king has set up.
6 "But whoever does not fall down
and worship shall [1]immediately be [a]cast
into the midst of a [b]furnace of blazing
fire."
7 Therefore at that time, when all the
peoples heard the sound of the horn,
flute, [1]lyre, trigon, psaltery, bagpipe, and
all kinds of music, all the peoples, nations and *men of every* [2]language fell
down *and* worshiped the golden image
that Nebuchadnezzar the king had set
up.

Worship of the Image Refused

8 For this reason at that time certain
[a]Chaldeans came forward and [1b]brought
charges against the Jews.
9 They responded and said to Nebuchadnezzar the king: "[a]O king, live
forever!
10 "You yourself, O king, have [a]made a
decree that every man who hears the
sound of the horn, flute, [1]lyre, trigon,
psaltery, and bagpipe, and all kinds of
music, is to [b]fall down and worship the
golden image.
11 "But whoever does not fall down
and worship shall be cast into the midst
of a furnace of blazing fire.
12 "There are certain Jews whom you
have [a]appointed over the administration
of the province of Babylon, *namely*
Shadrach, Meshach and Abed-nego.
These men, O king, have disregarded
you; they do not serve your gods or
worship the golden image which you
have set up."
13 Then Nebuchadnezzar in [a]rage and
anger gave orders to bring Shadrach,
Meshach and Abed-nego; then these
men were brought before the king.
14 Nebuchadnezzar responded and
said to them, "Is it true, Shadrach,
Meshach and Abed-nego, that you do
not serve [a]my gods or worship the
golden image that I have set up?
15 "Now if you are ready, [a]at the
moment you hear the sound of the horn,
flute, [1]lyre, trigon, psaltery, and bagpipe,
and all kinds of music, to fall down and
worship the image that I have made, *very
well.* But if you will not worship, you will
[2]immediately be [b]cast into the midst of a
furnace of blazing fire; and [c]what god is
there who can deliver you out of my
hands?"
16 [a]Shadrach, Meshach and Abed-
nego answered and said to the king, "O
Nebuchadnezzar, we do not need to give
you an answer concerning this matter.
17 "[1]If it be *so,* our [a]God whom we
serve is able to deliver us from the
furnace of blazing fire; [2]and [b]He will
deliver us out of your hand, O king.
18 "[a]But *even* if *He does* not, [b]let it be
known to you, O king, that we are not
going to serve your gods or worship the
golden image that you have set up."

Daniel's Friends Protected

19 Then Nebuchadnezzar was filled
with [a]wrath, and his facial expression
was altered toward Shadrach, Meshach
and Abed-nego. He answered [1]by giving
orders to heat the furnace seven times
more than it was usually heated.
20 And he commanded certain valiant
warriors who *were* in his army to tie up
Shadrach, Meshach and Abed-nego, in
order to cast *them* into the furnace of
blazing fire.
21 Then these men were tied up in
their [1a]trousers, their [2]coats, their caps
and their *other* clothes, and were cast
into the midst of the furnace of blazing
fire.
22 For this reason, because the king's
[1]command *was* [2a]urgent and the furnace
had been made extremely hot, the flame
of the fire slew those men who carried up
Shadrach, Meshach and Abed-nego.
23 But these three men, Shadrach,
Meshach and Abed-nego, [a]fell into the
midst of the furnace of blazing fire *still*
tied up.
24 Then Nebuchadnezzar the king
was astounded and stood up in haste; he
responded and said to his high officials,
"Was it not three men we cast bound
into the midst of the fire?" They answered and said to the king, "Certainly,
O king."
25 He answered and said, "Look! I see
four men loosed *and* [a]walking *about* in
the midst of the fire [1]without harm, and
the appearance of the fourth is like a son
of *the* [b]gods!"
26 Then Nebuchadnezzar came near
to the door of the furnace of blazing fire;
he responded and said, "Shadrach, Meshach and Abed-nego, come out, you
servants of the [a]Most High God, and
come here!" Then Shadrach, Meshach
and Abed-nego [b]came out of the midst
of the fire.
27 And the [a]satraps, the prefects, the
governors and the king's high officials
gathered around *and* saw in regard to
these men that the [b]fire had no [1]effect on
[2]the bodies of these men nor was the
hair of their head singed, nor were their
[3c]trousers [4]damaged, nor had the smell
of fire *even* come upon them.

4 [1]Lit., *they command* [2]Lit., *tongue* [a]Dan. 3:7; 4:1; 6:25

5 [1]Or, *zither* [2]I.e., triangular lyre [3]Or, *a type of harp* [a]Dan. 3:7, 10, 15

6 [1]Or, *in the same hour* [a]Dan. 3:11, 15, 21; 6:7 [b]Jer. 29:22; Ezek. 22:18-22; Matt. 13:42, 50; Rev. 9:2; 14:11

7 [1]V. 5, notes 1, 2, 3 [2]Lit., *tongue*

8 [1]Lit., *ate the pieces of* [a]Dan. 2:2, 10; 4:7 [b]Ezra 4:12-16; Esth. 3:8, 9; Dan. 6:12, 13

9 [a]Dan. 2:4; 5:10; 6:6, 21

10 [1]V. 5, notes 1, 2, 3 [a]Esth. 3:12-14; Dan. 3:4-6; 6:12 [b]Dan. 3:5, 7, 15

12 [a]Dan. 2:49

13 [a]Dan. 2:12; 3:19

14 [a]Is. 46:1; Jer. 50:2; Dan. 3:1; 4:8

15 [1]V. 5, notes 1, 2, 3 [2]Or, *in the same hour* [a]Dan. 3:5 [b]Dan. 3:6 [c]Ex. 5:2; Is. 36:18-20; Dan. 2:47

16 [a]Dan. 1:7; 3:12

17 [1]Or, *If our God . . . is able* [2]Or, *then* [a]Job 5:19; Ps. 27:1, 2; Is. 26:3, 4; Jer. 1:8; 15:20, 21 [b]1 Sam. 17:37; Mic. 7:7; 2 Cor. 1:10

18 [a]Josh. 24:15; 1 Kin. 19:14, 18; Is. 51:12, 13; Dan. 3:28 [b]Heb. 11:25

19 [1]Lit., *and ordered to* [a]Esth. 7:7; Dan. 3:13

21 [1]Or, *leggings* [2]Or, *cloaks* [a]Dan. 3:27

22 [1]Lit., *word* [2]Or, *harsh* [a]Ex. 12:33; Dan. 2:15

23 [a]Is. 43:2

25 [1]Lit., *there is no injury in them* [a]Ps. 91:3-9; Is. 43:2 [b]Jer. 1:8, 19; 15:21

26 [a]Dan. 3:17; 4:2 [b]Deut. 4:20; 1 Kin. 8:51; Jer. 11:4

27 [1]Lit., *power over* [2]Lit., *their* [3]Or, *cloaks* [4]Lit., *changed* [a]Dan. 3:2, 3 [b]Is. 43:2; Heb. 11:34 [c]Dan. 3:21

28 Nebuchadnezzar responded and
said, "Blessed be the [a]God of Shadrach,
Meshach and Abed-nego, who has [b]sent
His angel and delivered His servants
who put their [c]trust in Him, [1]violating
the king's command, and yielded up
their bodies so as [d]not to serve or worship any god except their own God.
29 "Therefore, I [a]make a decree that
any people, nation or tongue that speaks
anything offensive against the God of
[b]Shadrach, Meshach and Abed-nego
shall be torn limb from limb and their
[c]houses reduced to a rubbish heap,
inasmuch as there is [d]no other god who
is able to deliver in this way."
30 Then the king [a]caused Shadrach,
Meshach and Abed-nego to prosper in
the province of Babylon.

The King Acknowledges God

4 [1]NEBUCHADNEZZAR the king to
all the peoples, nations, and *men of*
every [2]language that live in all the earth:
"May your [3a]peace abound!
2 "It has seemed good to me to declare the signs and wonders which the
[a]Most High God has done for me.
3 "How great are His [a]signs,
And how mighty are His wonders!
His [b]kingdom is an everlasting
kingdom,
And His dominion is from generation to generation.

The Vision of a Great Tree

4 "[1]I, Nebuchadnezzar, was at ease in
my house and [a]flourishing in my palace.
5 "I saw a [a]dream and it made me
fearful; and *these* fantasies *as I lay* on
my bed and the [b]visions [1]in my mind
kept alarming me.
6 "So I gave orders to [a]bring into my
presence all the wise men of Babylon,
that they might make known to me the
interpretation of the dream.
7 "Then the [1a]magicians, the conjurers, the [2]Chaldeans, and the diviners
came in, and I related the dream [3]to
them; but they could not make its [b]inter-
pretation known to me.
8 "But finally Daniel came in before
me, whose name is [a]Belteshazzar according to the name of my god, and in whom
is [1b]a spirit of the holy gods; and I
related the dream [2]to him, *saying,*
9 'O Belteshazzar, [a]chief of the magicians, since I know that [b]a spirit of the
holy gods is in you and [c]no mystery
baffles you, [d]tell *me* the visions of my
dream which I have seen, along with its
interpretation.
10 'Now *these were* the [a]visions [1]in my
mind *as I lay* on my bed: I was looking,
and behold, *there was* a [b]tree in the
midst of the [2]earth, and its height *was*
great.
11 'The tree grew large and became
strong,
And its height [a]reached to the sky,
And it *was* visible to the end of
the whole earth.
12 'Its foliage *was* [a]beautiful and its
fruit abundant,
And in it *was* food for all.
The [b]beasts of the field found
[c]shade under it,
And the [d]birds of the sky dwelt in
its branches,
And all [1]living creatures fed
themselves from it.
13 'I was looking in the [a]visions [1]in my
mind *as I lay* on my bed, and behold,
[b]an *angelic* watcher, a [c]holy one, descended from heaven.
14 'He shouted out and spoke as follows:
"[a]Chop down the tree and cut off
its branches,
Strip off its foliage and scatter its
fruit;
Let the [b]beasts flee from under it,
And the birds from its branches.
15 "Yet [a]leave the stump [1]with its
roots in the ground,
But with a band of iron and
bronze *around it*
In the new grass of the field;
And let him be drenched with the
dew of heaven,
And let [2]him share with the beasts
in the grass of the earth.
16 "Let his [1]mind be changed from
that of a man,
And let a beast's [1]mind be given
to him,
And let [a]seven [2]periods of time
pass over him.
17 "This sentence is by the decree of
the *angelic* watchers,
And the decision is a command of
the holy ones,
In order that the living may
[a]know
That the Most High is ruler over
the realm of mankind,
And [b]bestows it on whom He
wishes,
And sets over it the [c]lowliest of
men."
18 'This is the dream *which* I, King
Nebuchadnezzar, have seen. Now you,
Belteshazzar, tell *me* its interpretation,
inasmuch as none of the [a]wise men of
my kingdom is able to make known to
me the interpretation; but you are able,
for a [b]spirit of the holy gods is in you.'

Daniel Interprets the Vision

19 "Then Daniel, whose name is Belteshazzar, was appalled for a while as his
[a]thoughts alarmed him. The king responded and said, 'Belteshazzar, do not
[b]let the dream or its interpretation alarm
you.' Belteshazzar answered and said,
'[c]My lord, *if only* the dream applied to
those who hate you, and its interpretation to [d]your adversaries!
20 'The [a]tree that you saw, which
became large and grew strong, whose

28 [1]Lit., *and changed the king's word* [a]Dan. 2:47; 3:15-17 [b]Ps. 34:7, 8; Is. 37:36; Dan. 3:25; 6:22; Acts 5:19; 12:7 [c]Ps. 22:4, 5; 40:4; 84:12; Is. 12:2; 26:3, 4; 50:10; Jer. 17:7 [d]Dan. 3:16-18
29 [a]Dan. 6:26 [b]Dan. 1:7, 19; 2:17, 49; 3:12 [c]Ezra 6:11; Dan. 2:5 [d]Dan. 2:47; 3:15
30 [a]Dan. 2:49; 3:12
1 [1]Ch. 3:31 in Aram. [2]Lit., *tongue* [3]Or, *welfare* or *prosperity* [a]Ezra 4:17; Dan. 6:25
2 [a]Dan. 3:26; 4:17, 24, 25, 32, 34
3 [a]Ps. 77:19; 105:27; Is. 25:1; Dan. 6:27 [b]Dan. 2:44; 4:34; 6:26
4 [1]Ch. 4:1 in Aram. [a]Ps. 30:6; Is. 47:7, 8
5 [1]Lit., *of my head* [a]Dan. 2:3 [b]Dan. 2:1, 28; 4:10, 13
6 [a]Gen. 41:8; Dan. 2:2
7 [1]Or, *soothsayer priests,* and so throughout the ch. [2]Or, *master astrologers* [3]Lit., *before* [a]Gen. 41:8; Dan. 2:10, 27; 5:7 [b]Is. 44:25; Jer. 27:9, 10; Dan. 2:7
8 [1]Or possibly, *the Spirit of the holy God,* and so throughout the ch. [2]Lit., *before* [a]Dan. 1:7; 2:26; 5:12 [b]Dan. 4:9, 18; 5:11, 14
9 [a]Dan. 1:20; 2:48; 5:11 [b]Gen. 41:38; Dan. 4:8 [c]Ezek. 28:3; Dan. 2:47 [d]Gen. 41:15; Dan. 2:4, 5
10 [1]Lit., *of my head* [2]Or, *land,* and so throughout the ch. [a]Dan. 4:5 [b]Ezek. 31:3, 6
11 [a]Deut. 9:1; Dan. 4:21, 22
12 [1]Lit., *flesh* [a]Ezek. 31:7 [b]Jer. 27:6; Ezek. 31:6 [c]Lam. 4:20 [d]Ezek. 17:23; Matt. 13:32; Luke 13:19
13 [1]Lit., *of my head* [a]Dan. 7:1 [b]Dan. 4:17, 23 [c]Deut. 33:2; Ps. 89:7; Dan. 8:13
14 [a]Ezek. 31:10-14; Dan. 4:23; Matt. 3:10; 7:19; Luke 13:7-9 [b]Ezek. 31:12, 13; Dan. 4:12
15 [1]Lit., *of* [2]Lit., *his portion be with* [a]Job 14:7-9
16 [1]Lit., *heart* [2]I.e., *years* [a]Dan. 4:23, 25, 32
17 [a]Ps. 9:16; 83:18; Dan. 2:21; 5:21 [b]Jer. 27:5-7; Dan. 4:25; 5:18, 19 [c]1 Sam. 2:8; Dan. 11:21

18 [a]Gen. 41:8, 15; Dan. 4:7; 5:8, 15 [b]Dan. 4:8, 9
19 [a]Jer. 4:19; Dan. 7:15, 28; 8:27; 10:16, 17 [b]1 Sam. 3:17; Dan. 4:4, 5 [c]2 Sam. 18:31; Dan. 4:24; 10:16 [d]2 Sam. 18:32
20 [a]Dan. 4:10-12

height reached to the sky and was visible to all the earth,

21 and whose foliage *was* beautiful and its fruit abundant, and in which *was* food for all, under which the beasts of the field dwelt and in whose branches the birds of the sky lodged—

22 it is [a]you, O king; for you have become great and grown strong, and your [1]majesty has become great and reached to the sky and your [b]dominion to the end of the earth.

23 'And in that the king saw an *angelic* watcher, a holy one, descending from heaven and saying, "[a]Chop down the tree and destroy it; yet leave the stump [1]with its roots in the ground, but with a band of iron and bronze *around it* in the new grass of the field, and let him be drenched with the dew of heaven, and let [2]him share with the beasts of the field until [b]seven [3]periods of time pass over him";

24 this is the interpretation, O king, and this is the decree of the Most High, which has [a]come upon my lord the king:

25 that you be [a]driven away from mankind, and your dwelling place be with the beasts of the field, and you be given grass to eat like cattle and be drenched with the dew of heaven; and seven [1]periods of time will pass over you, until you recognize that the [b]Most High is ruler over the realm of mankind, and [c]bestows it on whomever He wishes.

26 'And in that it was commanded to [a]leave the stump [1]with the roots of the tree, your kingdom will be [2]assured to you after you recognize that *it is* [b]Heaven *that* rules.

27 'Therefore, O king, may my [a]advice be pleasing to you: [1b]break away now from your sins by *doing* righteousness, and from your iniquities by [c]showing mercy to *the* poor, in case there may be a [d]prolonging of your prosperity.'

The Vision Fulfilled

28 "All *this* [a]happened to Nebuchadnezzar the king.

29 "[a]Twelve months later he was walking on the *roof of* the royal palace of Babylon.

30 "The king [1]reflected and said, 'Is this not Babylon the [a]great, which I myself have built as a royal [2]residence by the might of my power and for the glory of my majesty?'

31 "While the word *was* in the king's mouth, a voice [1]came from heaven, *saying,* 'King Nebuchadnezzar, to you it is declared: [2]sovereignty has been removed from you,

32 and [a]you will be driven away from mankind, and your dwelling place *will be* with the beasts of the field. You will be given grass to eat like cattle, and [b]seven [1]periods of time will pass over you, until you recognize that the [c]Most High is ruler over the realm of mankind, and bestows it on whomever He wishes.'

33 "Immediately the word concerning Nebuchadnezzar was fulfilled; and he was [a]driven away from mankind and began eating grass like cattle, and his body was drenched with the dew of heaven, until his hair had grown like eagles' *feathers* and his nails like birds' *claws.*

34 "But at the end of [1]that period I, Nebuchadnezzar, raised my eyes toward heaven, and my [2]reason returned to me, and I blessed the [a]Most High and praised and honored [b]Him who lives forever;

For His dominion is an [c]everlasting dominion,
And His kingdom *endures* from generation to generation.

35 "And [a]all the inhabitants of the earth are accounted as nothing,
But [b]He does according to His will in the host of heaven
And *among* the inhabitants of earth;
And [c]no one can [1]ward off His hand
Or say to Him, '[d]What hast Thou done?'

36 "At that time my [1a]reason returned to me. And my majesty and [b]splendor were [2]restored to me for the glory of my kingdom, and my counselors and my nobles began seeking me out; so I was reestablished in my [3]sovereignty, and surpassing [c]greatness was added to me.

37 "Now I Nebuchadnezzar praise, exalt, and honor the King of [a]heaven, for [b]all His works are [1]true and His ways [2]just, and He is able to humble those who [c]walk in pride."

Belshazzar's Feast

5 BELSHAZZAR the king [1]held a great [a]feast for a thousand of his nobles, and he was drinking wine in the presence of the thousand.

2 When Belshazzar tasted the wine, he gave orders to bring the gold and silver [a]vessels which Nebuchadnezzar his [1]father had taken out of the temple which *was* in Jerusalem, in order that the king and his nobles, his wives, and his concubines might drink from them.

3 Then they brought the gold vessels that had been taken out of the temple, the house of God which *was* in Jerusalem; and the king and his nobles, his wives, and his concubines drank from them.

4 They [a]drank the wine and praised the gods of [b]gold and silver, of bronze, iron, wood, and stone.

5 Suddenly the fingers of a man's hand emerged and began writing opposite the lampstand on the plaster of the wall of the king's palace, and the king saw the [1]back of the hand that did the writing.

6 Then the king's [1a]face grew pale, and his thoughts alarmed him; and his [b]hip joints went slack, and his [c]knees began knocking together.

22 [1]Lit., *greatness* [a]2 Sam. 12:7; Dan. 2:37, 38 [b]Jer. 27:6, 7
23 [1]Lit., *of* [2]Lit., *his portion be with* [3]I.e., years [a]Dan. 4:14, 15 [b]Dan. 4:16
24 [a]Job 40:11, 12; Ps. 107:40
25 [1]I.e., years [a]Dan. 4:33; 5:21 [b]Ps. 83:18; Jer. 27:5; Dan. 4:2, 17 [c]Dan. 2:37; 4:17; 5:21
26 [1]Lit., *of* [2]Lit., *enduring* [a]Dan. 4:15, 23 [b]Dan. 2:18, 19, 28, 37, 44; 4:31
27 [1]Or, *redeem now your sins* [a]Gen. 41:33-37 [b]Prov. 28:13; Is. 55:6, 7; Ezek. 18:7, 21, 22; Acts 8:22 [c]Ps. 41:1-3; Is. 58:6, 7, 10 [d]1 Kin. 21:29; Jon. 3:9
28 [a]Num. 23:19; Zech. 1:6
29 [a]2 Pet. 3:9
30 [1]Lit., *answered* [2]Lit., *house* [a]Hab. 2:4
31 [1]Lit., *fell* [2]Or, *kingdom*
32 [1]I.e., years [a]Dan. 4:25 [b]Dan. 4:16 [c]Dan. 4:17
33 [a]Dan. 4:25; 5:21
34 [1]Lit., *the days* [2]Lit., *knowledge* [a]Dan. 4:2; 5:18, 21 [b]Ps. 102:24-27; Dan. 6:26; 12:7; Rev. 4:10 [c]Ps. 145:13; Jer. 10:10; Dan. 4:3; Mic. 4:7; Luke 1:33
35 [1]Lit., *strike against* [a]Ps. 39:5; Is. 40:15, 17 [b]Ps. 33:11; 115:3; 135:6; Dan. 6:27 [c]Job 42:2; Is. 43:13 [d]Job 9:12; Is. 45:9; Rom. 9:20
36 [1]Lit., *knowledge* [2]Lit., *returning* [3]Or, *kingdom* [a]2 Chr. 33:12, 13; Dan. 4:34 [b]Dan. 2:31 [c]Prov. 22:4; Dan. 4:22
37 [1]Lit., *truth* [2]Lit., *justice* [a]Dan. 4:26; 5:23 [b]Deut. 32:4; Ps. 33:4, 5; Is. 5:16 [c]Ex. 18:11; Job 40:11, 12; Dan. 5:20

1 [1]Lit., *made* [a]Esth. 1:3; Is. 22:12-14
2 [1]Or, *forefather,* and so throughout the ch. [a]2 Kin. 24:13; 25:15; Ezra 1:7-11; Dan. 1:2
4 [a]Is. 42:8; Dan. 5:23; Rev. 9:20 [b]Ps. 115:4; 135:15; Is. 40:19, 20; Dan. 3:1; Hab. 2:19
5 [1]Or, *palm*
6 [1]Lit., *brightness changed for him* [a]Dan. 5:9, 10; 7:28 [b]Ps. 69:23 [c]Ezek. 7:17; 21:7; Nah. 2:10

7 The king called aloud to bring in the [a]conjurers, the [1]Chaldeans and the diviners. The king spoke and said to the wise men of Babylon, "Any man who can read this inscription and explain its interpretation to me will be [b]clothed with purple, and *have* a [c]necklace of gold around his neck, and have authority as [2d]third *ruler* in the kingdom."

8 Then all the king's wise men came in, but [a]they could not read the inscription or make known its interpretation to the king.

9 Then King Belshazzar was greatly [a]alarmed, his [1b]face grew *even* paler, and his nobles were perplexed.

10 The queen entered the banquet [1]hall because of the words of the king and his nobles; the queen spoke and said, "[a]O king, live forever! Do not let your thoughts alarm you or your [2]face be pale.

11 "There is a [a]man in your kingdom in whom is [1]a [b]spirit of the holy gods; and in the days of your father, illumination, insight, and wisdom like the wisdom of the gods were found in him. And King Nebuchadnezzar, your father, your father [2c]the king, appointed him chief of the [3]magicians, conjurers, [4]Chaldeans, *and* diviners.

12 "*This was* because an [a]extraordinary spirit, knowledge and insight, interpretation of dreams, explanation of enigmas, and solving of difficult problems were found in this Daniel, whom the king named [b]Belteshazzar. Let Daniel now be summoned, and he will declare the interpretation."

Daniel Interprets Handwriting on the Wall

13 Then Daniel was brought in before the king. The king spoke and said to Daniel, "Are you that Daniel who is one of the [1a]exiles from Judah, whom my father the king [b]brought from Judah?

14 "Now I have heard about you that [1]a spirit of the gods is in you, and that illumination, insight, and extraordinary wisdom have been found in you.

15 "Just now the [a]wise men *and* the conjurers were brought in before me that they might read this inscription and make its interpretation known to me, but they [b]could not declare the interpretation of the [1]message.

16 "But I personally have heard about you, that you are able to give interpretations and solve difficult problems. Now if you are able to read the inscription and make its [a]interpretation known to me, you will be [b]clothed with purple and *wear* a necklace of gold around your neck, and you will have authority as the [1]third *ruler* in the kingdom."

17 Then Daniel answered and said before the king, "[1]Keep your [a]gifts for yourself, or give your rewards to someone else; however, I will read the inscription to the king and make the interpretation known to him.

18 "[1]O king, the [a]Most High God [b]granted [2]sovereignty, [c]grandeur, glory, and majesty to Nebuchadnezzar your father.

19 "And because of the grandeur which He bestowed on him, all the peoples, nations, and *men of every* [1]language feared and trembled before him; [a]whomever he wished he killed, and whomever he wished he spared alive; and whomever he wished he elevated, and whomever he wished he humbled.

20 "But when his heart was [a]lifted up and his spirit became so [1b]proud that he behaved arrogantly, he was [c]deposed from his royal throne, and *his* glory was taken away from him.

21 "He was also [a]driven away from [1]mankind, and his heart was made like *that of* beasts, and his dwelling place *was* with the [b]wild donkeys. He was given grass to eat like cattle, and his body was drenched with the dew of heaven, until he recognized that the [c]Most High God is ruler over the realm of mankind, and *that* He sets over it whomever He wishes.

22 "Yet you, his [1]son, Belshazzar, have [a]not humbled your heart, [2]even though you knew all this,

23 but you have [a]exalted yourself against the [b]Lord of heaven; and they have brought the vessels of His house before you, and you and your nobles, your wives and your concubines have been drinking wine from them; and you have praised the [c]gods of silver and gold, of bronze, iron, wood and stone, which do not see, hear or understand. But the God [d]in whose hand are your life-breath and your [e]ways, you have not glorified.

24 "Then the [1a]hand was sent from Him, and this inscription was written out.

25 "Now this is the inscription that was written out: '[1]MENĒ, [1]MENĒ, [2]TEKĒL, [3]UPHARSIN.'

26 "This is the interpretation of the [1]message: 'MENĒ'—God has numbered your kingdom and [a]put an end to it.

27 " 'TEKĒL'—you have been [a]weighed on the scales and found deficient.

28 " 'PERĒS'—your kingdom has been divided and given over to the [a]Medes and [1]Persians."

29 Then Belshazzar gave orders, and they [a]clothed Daniel with purple and *put* a necklace of gold around his neck, and issued a proclamation concerning him that he *now* had authority as the [1]third *ruler* in the kingdom.

30 That same night [a]Belshazzar the Chaldean king was [b]slain.

31 [1]So [a]Darius the Mede received the kingdom at about the age of sixty-two.

7 [1]Or, *master astrologers* [2]Or, *a triumvir*
[a]Is. 44:25; 47:13; Dan. 4:6, 7; 5:11, 15 [b]Gen. 41:42-44; Dan. 5:16, 29 [c]Ezek. 16:11 [d]Dan. 2:48; 5:16, 29; 6:2, 3
8 [a]Gen. 41:8; Dan. 2:27; 4:7; 5:15
9 [1]Lit., *brightness was changing upon him*
[a]Job 18:11; Is. 21:2-4; Jer. 6:24; Dan. 2:1; 5:6 [b]Is. 13:6-8
10 [1]Lit., *house* [2]Lit., *brightness be changed*
[a]Dan. 3:9; 6:6
11 [1]Or possibly, *the Spirit of the holy God* [2]Or, *O king* [3]Or, *soothsayer priests* [4]Or, *master astrologers*
[a]Gen. 41:11-15; Dan. 2:47 [b]Dan. 4:8, 9, 18; 5:14 [c]Dan. 2:48
12 [a]Dan. 5:14; 6:3 [b]Dan. 1:7; 4:8
13 [1]Lit., *sons of the exile*
[a]Ezra 4:1; 6:16, 19, 20; Dan. 2:25; 6:13 [b]Dan. 1:1, 2
14 [1]Or possibly, *the Spirit of God*
15 [1]Lit., *word*
[a]Dan. 5:7 [b]Is. 47:12f.; Dan. 5:8
16 [1]Or, *triumvir*
[a]Gen. 40:8 [b]Dan. 5:7, 29
17 [1]Lit., *Let . . . be for*
[a]2 Kin. 5:16
18 [1]Lit., *You, O king* [2]Or, *the kingdom*
[a]Dan. 4:2; 5:21 [b]Dan. 2:37, 38; 4:17 [c]Jer. 25:9; 27:5-7
19 [1]Lit., *tongue*
[a]Dan. 2:12, 13; 3:6; 11:3, 16, 36
20 [1]Lit., *strong*
[a]Ex. 9:17; Job 15:25; Is. 14:13-15; Dan. 4:30, 31 [b]2 Kin. 17:14; 2 Chr. 36:13 [c]Job 40:11, 12; Jer. 13:18
21 [1]Lit., *the sons of man*
[a]Job 30:3-7; Dan. 4:32, 33 [b]Job 39:5-8 [c]Ex. 9:14-16; Ps. 83:17, 18; Ezek. 17:24; Dan. 4:17, 34, 35
22 [1]Or, *descendant* [2]Lit., *inasmuch as you*
[a]Ex. 10:3; 2 Chr. 33:23; 36:12
23 [a]2 Kin. 14:10; Is. 2:12; 37:23; Jer. 50:29; Dan. 5:3, 4 [b]Dan. 4:37 [c]Ps. 115:4-8; Is. 37:19; Hab. 2:18, 19 [d]Job 12:10 [e]Job 31:4; Ps. 139:3; Prov. 20:24; Jer. 10:23
24 [1]Lit., *palm of the hand*
[a]Dan. 5:5
25 [1]Or, *a mina* (50 shekels) from verb "to number" [2]Or, *a shekel* from verb "to weigh" [3]Or, *and half-shekels* (sing.: *perēs*) from verb "to divide"

26 [1]Lit., *word* [a]Is. 13:6, 17-19; Jer. 50:41-43
27 [a]Job 31:6; Ps. 62:9
28 [1]Aram.: *Pāras* [a]Is. 13:17; 21:2; 45:1, 2; Dan. 5:31; 6:8, 28; Acts 2:9
29 [1]Or, *triumvir* [a]Dan. 5:7, 16
30 [a]Dan. 5:1, 2 [b]Is. 21:4-9; 47:9; Jer. 51:11, 31, 39, 57
31 [1]Ch. 6:1 in Aram. [a]Dan. 6:1; 9:1

Daniel Serves Darius

6 [1]IT seemed good to Darius to appoint 120 satraps over the kingdom, that they should be in charge of the whole kingdom,

2 and over them three commissioners (of whom [a]Daniel was one), that these satraps might be accountable to them, and that the king might not suffer [b]loss.

3 Then this Daniel began distinguishing himself [1]among the commissioners and satraps because [2]he possessed an [a]extraordinary spirit, and the king planned to appoint him over the [b]entire kingdom.

4 Then the commissioners and satraps began [a]trying to find a ground of accusation against Daniel in regard to [1]government affairs; but they could find [b]no ground of accusation or *evidence of* corruption, inasmuch as he was faithful, and no negligence or corruption was *to be* found in him.

5 Then these men said, "We shall not find any ground of accusation against this Daniel unless we find *it* against him with regard to the [a]law of his God."

6 Then these commissioners and satraps came [1]by agreement to the king and spoke to him as follows: "King Darius, [a]live forever!

7 "All the [a]commissioners of the kingdom, the prefects and the satraps, the high officials and the governors have [b]consulted together that the king should establish a statute and enforce an injunction that anyone who makes a petition to any god or man besides you, O king, for thirty days, shall [c]be cast into the lions' [1]den.

8 "Now, O king, [a]establish the injunction and sign the document so that it may not be changed, according to the [b]law of the Medes and Persians, which [1]may not be revoked."

9 Therefore King Darius [a]signed the document, that is, the injunction.

10 Now when Daniel knew that the document was signed, he entered his house (now in his roof chamber he had windows open [a]toward Jerusalem); and he continued [b]kneeling on his knees three times a day, [c]praying and [d]giving thanks before his God, [1]as he had been doing previously.

11 Then these men came [1a]by agreement and found Daniel making petition and supplication before his God.

12 Then they approached and [a]spoke before the king about the king's injunction, "Did you not sign an injunction that any man who makes a petition to any god or man besides you, O king, for thirty days, is to be cast into the lions' den?" The king answered and said, "The statement is true, according to the [b]law of the Medes and Persians, which [1]may not be revoked."

13 Then they answered and spoke before the king, "[a]Daniel, who is one of the [1]exiles from Judah, pays [b]no attention to you, O king, or to the injunction which you signed, but keeps making his petition three times a day."

14 Then, as soon as the king heard this statement, he was deeply [a]distressed and set *his* mind on delivering Daniel; and even until sunset he kept exerting himself to rescue him.

15 Then these men came [1]by agreement to the king and said to the king, "Recognize, O king, that it is a [a]law of the Medes and Persians that no injunction or statute which the king establishes may be changed."

Daniel in the Lions' Den

16 Then the king gave orders, and Daniel was brought in and [a]cast into the lions' den. The king spoke and said to Daniel, "[1b]Your God whom you constantly serve will Himself deliver you."

17 And a [a]stone was brought and laid over the mouth of the den; and the king sealed it with his own signet ring and with the signet rings of his nobles, so that nothing might be changed in regard to Daniel.

18 Then the king went off to his palace and spent the night [a]fasting, and no entertainment was brought before him; and his [b]sleep fled from him.

19 Then the king arose with the dawn, at the break of day, and went in haste to the lions' den.

20 And when he had come near the den to Daniel, he cried out with a troubled voice. The king spoke and said to Daniel, "Daniel, servant of the living God, has [a]your God, whom you constantly serve, been [b]able to deliver you from the lions?"

21 Then Daniel spoke [1]to the king, "[a]O king, live forever!

22 "My God [a]sent His angel and [b]shut the lions' mouths, and they have not harmed me, inasmuch as [1]I was found innocent before Him; and also [2]toward you, O king, I have committed no crime."

23 Then the king was very pleased and gave orders for Daniel to be taken up out of the den. So Daniel was taken up out of the den, and [a]no injury whatever was found on him, because he had [b]trusted in his God.

24 The king then gave orders, and they brought those men who had [1]maliciously accused Daniel, and they [a]cast them, their [b]children, and their wives into the lions' den; and they had not reached the bottom of the den before the lions overpowered them and crushed all their bones.

25 Then Darius the king wrote to all the [a]peoples, nations, and *men of every* [1]language who were living in all the land: "[b]May your [2]peace abound!

1 [1]Ch. 6:2 in Aram.
2 [a]Dan. 2:48, 49; 5:16, 29 [b]Ezra 4:22; Esth. 7:4
3 [1]Lit., *above* [2]Lit., *there was in him* [a]Dan. 5:12, 14; 9:23 [b]Gen. 41:40; Esth. 10:3
4 [1]Lit., *the kingdom* [a]Gen. 43:18; Judg. 14:4; Jer. 20:10; Dan. 3:8; Luke 20:20 [b]Dan. 6:22; Luke 20:26; 23:14, 15; Phil. 2:15; 1 Pet. 2:12; 3:16
5 [a]Acts 24:13-16, 20, 21
6 [1]Or, *thronging* [a]Neh. 2:3; Dan. 2:4; 5:10; 6:21
7 [1]Or, *pit*, and so throughout the ch. [a]Dan. 3:2, 27 [b]Ps. 59:3; 62:4; 64:2-6; 83:1-3 [c]Ps. 10:9; Dan. 3:6; 6:16
8 [1]Lit., *does not pass away* [a]Esth. 3:12; 8:10; Is. 10:1 [b]Esth. 1:19; 8:8; Dan. 6:12, 15
9 [a]Ps. 118:9; 146:3
10 [1]Or, *because* [a]1 Kin. 8:44, 48, 49; Ps. 5:7; Jon. 2:4 [b]Ps. 55:17; 95:6 [c]Dan. 9:4-19 [d]Ps. 34:1; Phil. 4:6; 1 Thess. 5:17, 18
11 [1]Or, *thronging* [a]Ps. 37:32, 33; Dan. 6:6
12 [1]Lit., *does not pass away* [a]Dan. 3:8-12; Acts 16:19-21 [b]Esth. 1:19; Dan. 6:8, 15
13 [1]Lit., *sons of the exile* [a]Dan. 2:25; 5:13 [b]Esth. 3:8; Dan. 3:12; Acts 5:29
14 [a]Mark 6:26
15 [1]Or, *thronging* [a]Esth. 8:8; Ps. 94:20, 21; Dan. 6:8, 12
16 [1]Or, *May your God . . . Himself deliver you* [a]2 Sam. 3:39; Jer. 38:5; Dan. 6:7 [b]Job 5:19; Ps. 37:39, 40; Is. 41:10; Dan. 3:17, 28; 6:20; 2 Cor. 1:10
17 [a]Lam. 3:53; Matt. 27:66
18 [a]2 Sam. 12:16, 17 [b]Esth. 6:1; Ps. 77:4; Dan. 2:1
20 [a]Dan. 6:16, 27 [b]Gen. 18:14; Num. 11:23; Jer. 32:17; Dan. 3:17
21 [1]Lit., *with* [a]Dan. 2:4; 6:6
22 [1]Lit., *innocence was found for me* [2]Lit., *before* [a]Num. 20:16; Is. 63:9; Dan. 3:28; Acts 12:11; Heb. 1:14 [b]Ps. 91:11-13; 2 Tim. 4:17; Heb. 11:33
23 [a]Dan. 3:25, 27 [b]1 Chr. 5:20; 2 Chr. 20:20; Ps. 118:8, 9; Is. 26:3; Dan. 3:17, 28

24 [1]Lit., *eaten the pieces of Daniel* [a]Deut. 19:18, 19; Esth. 7:10 [b]Deut. 24:16; 2 Kin. 14:6; Esth. 9:10
25 [1]Lit., *tongue* [2]Or, *welfare* or *prosperity* [a]Ezra 1:1, 2; Esth. 3:12; 8:9; Dan. 4:1 [b]Ezra 4:17; 1 Pet. 1:2

26“[1]I [a]make a decree that in all the
dominion of my kingdom men are to
fear and tremble before the God of
Daniel;
For He is the [b]living God and
[c]enduring forever,
And [d]His kingdom is one which
will not be destroyed,
And His dominion *will be* [2]forever.
27 “He delivers and rescues and performs
[a]signs and wonders
In heaven and on earth,
Who has *also* delivered Daniel
from the [1]power of the lions.”
28 So this [a]Daniel enjoyed success in
the reign of Darius and in the reign of
[b]Cyrus the Persian.

Vision of the Four Beasts

7 IN the first year of Belshazzar king
of Babylon Daniel saw a [a]dream
and visions [1]in his mind *as he lay* on his
bed; then he [b]wrote the dream down *and*
related the *following* [2]summary of [3]it.
2 Daniel [1]said, “I was [a]looking in my
vision by night, and behold, the [b]four
winds of heaven were stirring up the
great sea.
3“And four great [a]beasts were coming
up from the sea, different from one
another.
4“The first *was* [a]like a lion and had
the wings of an eagle. I kept looking
until its wings were plucked, and it was
lifted up from the ground and made to
stand on two feet like a man; a human
[1]mind also was given to it.
5“And behold, another beast, a second
one, resembling a bear. And it was
raised up on one side, and three ribs
were in its mouth between its teeth; and
thus they said to it, ‘Arise, devour much
meat!’
6“After this I kept looking, and
behold, another one, [a]like a leopard,
which had on its [1]back four wings of a
bird; the beast also had [b]four heads, and
dominion was given to it.
7“After this I kept looking in the
night visions, and behold, a [a]fourth
beast, dreadful and terrifying and extremely
strong; and it had large iron
teeth. It devoured and crushed, and
trampled down the remainder with its
feet; and it was different from all the
beasts that were before it, and it had
[b]ten horns.
8“While I was contemplating the
horns, behold, [a]another horn, a little
one, came up among them, and three of
the first horns were pulled out by the
roots before it; and behold, [1]this horn
possessed eyes like the eyes of a man,
and [b]a mouth uttering great *boasts.*

The Ancient of Days Reigns

9 “I kept looking
Until [a]thrones were set up,
And the Ancient of Days took *His*
seat;
His [b]vesture *was* like white snow,
And the [c]hair of His head like
pure wool.
His [d]throne *was* [1]ablaze with
flames,
Its [e]wheels *were* a burning fire.
10 “A river of [a]fire was flowing
And coming out from before
Him;
[b]Thousands upon thousands were
attending Him,
And myriads upon myriads were
standing before Him;
The [c]court sat,
And [d]the books were opened.
11“Then I kept looking because of the
sound of the [1]boastful words which the
horn was speaking; I kept looking until
the beast was slain, and its body was
destroyed and given to the [a]burning
[2]fire.
12“As for the rest of the beasts, their
dominion was taken away, but an extension
of life was granted to them for an
appointed period of time.

The Son of Man Presented

13 “I kept looking in the night visions,
And behold, with the clouds of
heaven
One like a [a]Son of Man was coming,
And He came up to the Ancient
of Days
And was presented before Him.
14 “And to Him was given [a]dominion,
Glory and [1b]a kingdom,
[c]That all the peoples, nations, and
men of every [2]language
Might serve Him.
[d]His dominion is an everlasting
dominion
Which will not pass away;
[e]And His kingdom is one
Which will not be destroyed.

The Vision Interpreted

15“As for me, Daniel, my spirit was
distressed [1]within me, and the [a]visions
[2]in my mind kept [b]alarming me.
16“I approached one of those who
were [a]standing by and began asking him
the [1]exact meaning of all this. So he
[b]told me and made known to me the
interpretation of these things:
17 ‘These great beasts, which are four
in number, are four kings *who* will arise
from the earth.
18 ‘But the [1a]saints of the Highest One
will [b]receive the kingdom and possess
the kingdom forever, [2]for all ages to
come.’
19“Then I desired to know the [1]exact
meaning of the [a]fourth beast, which was
different from all [2]the others, exceedingly
dreadful, with its teeth of iron and
its claws of bronze, *and which* devoured,
crushed, and trampled down the remainder
with its feet,
20 and *the meaning* of the ten horns
that *were* on its head, and the other *horn*
which came up, and before which three

26 [1]Lit., *From me a decree is made* [2]Lit., *to the end* [a]Ezra 6:8-12; 7:13, 21; Dan. 3:29 [b]Dan. 4:34; 6:20; Hos. 1:10; Rom. 9:26 [c]Ps. 93:1, 2; Mal. 3:6 [d]Dan. 2:44; 4:3; 7:14, 27; Luke 1:33
27 [1]Lit., *hand* [a]Dan. 4:2, 3
28 [a]Dan. 1:21 [b]2 Chr. 36:22, 23; Dan. 10:1

1 [1]Lit., *of his head* [2]Or, *beginning* [3]Lit., *words* [a]Job 33:14-16; Dan. 1:17; 2:1, 26-28; 4:5-9; Joel 2:28 [b]Jer. 36:4, 32
2 [1]Lit., *spoke and said* [a]Dan. 7:7, 13 [b]Rev. 7:1
3 [a]Dan. 7:17; Rev. 13:1; 17:8
4 [1]Lit., *heart* [a]Jer. 4:7
6 [1]Or, *sides* [a]Rev. 13:2 [b]Dan. 8:22
7 [a]Dan. 7:19, 20, 23 [b]Rev. 12:3; 13:1
8 [1]Lit., *in this horn* were *eyes* [a]Dan. 8:9 [b]Rev. 13:5, 6
9 [1]Lit., *flames of fire* [a]Rev. 20:4 [b]Mark 9:3 [c]Rev. 1:14 [d]Ezek. 1:13, 26 [e]Ezek. 10:2, 6
10 [a]Ps. 18:8; 50:3; 97:3; Is. 30:27, 33 [b]Deut. 33:2; 1 Kin. 22:19; Rev. 5:11 [c]Ps. 96:11-13; Dan. 7:22, 26 [d]Dan. 12:1; Rev. 20:11-15
11 [1]Lit., *great* [2]Lit., *of the fire* [a]Rev. 19:20; 20:10
13 [a]Matt. 24:30; 26:64; Mark 13:26; 14:62; Luke 21:27; Rev. 1:7, 13; 14:14
14 [1]Or, *sovereignty* [2]Lit., *tongue* [a]Dan. 7:27; John 3:35; 1 Cor. 15:27; Eph. 1:20-22; Phil. 2:9-11; Rev. 1:6; 11:15 [b]Dan. 2:37 [c]Ps. 72:11; 102:22 [d]Mic. 4:7; Luke 1:33 [e]Heb. 12:28
15 [1]Lit., *in the midst of* its *sheath* [2]Lit., *of my head* [a]Dan. 7:1 [b]Dan. 4:19; 7:28
16 [1]Lit., *truth concerning* [a]Zech. 1:9, 19; Rev. 5:5; 7:13, 14 [b]Dan. 8:16, 17; 9:22
18 [1]Lit., *holy ones* [2]Lit., *and unto the age of the ages* [a]Dan. 7:22, 25, 27 [b]Ps. 149:5-9; Is. 60:12-14; Dan. 7:14; Rev. 2:26, 27; 20:4; 22:5
19 [1]Lit., *truth concerning* [2]Lit., *of them* [a]Dan. 7:7, 8

of them fell, namely, that horn which had
eyes and a mouth uttering great *boasts,*
and [1]which was larger in appearance
than its associates.
21 "I kept looking, and that horn was
[a]waging war with the [1]saints and over-
powering them
22 until the Ancient of Days came,
and [a]judgment was [1]passed in favor of
the [2]saints of the Highest One, and the
time arrived when the [2]saints took possession of the kingdom.
23 "Thus he said: 'The fourth beast will
be a fourth kingdom on the earth, which
will be different from all the *other* kingdoms, and it will devour the whole earth
and tread it down and crush it.
24 'As for the [a]ten horns, out of this
kingdom ten kings will arise; and another will arise after them, and he will be
different from the previous ones and will
subdue three kings.
25 'And he will [a]speak [1]out against the
[b]Most High and [c]wear down the [2]saints
of the Highest One, and he will intend to
make [d]alterations in times and in law;
and [3]they will be given into his hand for
a [4e]time, [4]times, and half a [4]time.
26 'But the court will sit *for judgment,*
and his dominion will be [a]taken away,
[1]annihilated and destroyed [2]forever.
27 'Then the [1a]sovereignty, the dominion, and the greatness of *all* the kingdoms under the whole heaven will be
given to the people of the [2]saints of the
Highest One; His kingdom *will be* an
[b]everlasting kingdom, and all the dominions will [c]serve and obey Him.'
28 "[1]At this point the revelation ended.
As for me, Daniel, my thoughts were
[a]greatly alarming me and my [2]face grew
pale, but I [b]kept the matter [3]to myself."

Vision of the Ram and Goat

8 IN the third year of the reign of
Belshazzar the king a vision appeared to me, [1]Daniel, subsequent to the
one which appeared to me [2]previously.
2 And I [a]looked in the vision, and it
came about while I was looking, that I
was in the citadel of [b]Susa, which is in
the province of [c]Elam; and I looked in
the vision, and I myself was beside the
Ulai [1]Canal.
3 Then I lifted my gaze and looked,
and behold, a [a]ram which had two horns
was standing in front of the [1]canal. Now
the two horns *were* [2]long, but one *was*
[2]longer than the other, with the [2]longer
one coming up last.
4 I saw the ram [a]butting westward,
northward, and southward, and no *other*
beasts could stand before him, nor was
there anyone to rescue from his [1]power;
but [b]he did as he pleased and magnified
himself.
5 While I was observing, behold, a
male goat was coming from the west
over the surface of the whole earth
without touching the ground; and the
[1]goat *had* a [a]conspicuous horn between
his eyes.

20 [1]Lit., *its appearance was larger*
21 [1]Lit., *holy ones* [a]Rev. 11:7; 13:7
22 [1]Lit., *given for* [2]Lit., *holy ones* [a]Dan. 7:10; 1 Cor. 6:2, 3
24 [a]Dan. 7:7; Rev. 17:12
25 [1]Lit., *words* [2]Lit., *holy ones* [3]I.e., the saints [4]I.e., year(s) [a]Dan. 11:36; Rev. 13:6 [b]Dan. 3:26; 4:2, 17, 34 [c]Rev. 13:7; 18:24 [d]Dan. 2:21 [e]Dan. 12:7; Rev. 12:14
26 [1]Lit., *to annihilate and to destroy* [2]Lit., *to the end* [a]Rev. 17:14; 19:2
27 [1]Or, *kingdom* [2]Lit., *holy ones* [a]Is. 54:3; Dan. 7:14, 18, 22; Rev. 20:4 [b]Ps. 145:13; Is. 9:7; Dan. 2:44; 4:34; 7:14; Luke 1:33; Rev. 11:15; 22:5 [c]Ps. 2:6-12; 22:27; 72:11; 86:9; Is. 60:12; Rev. 11:1
28 [1]Lit., *To here the end of the word* [2]Lit., *brightness was changing upon me* [3]Lit., *in my heart* [a]Dan. 4:19 [b]Luke 2:19, 51

1 [1]Lit., *I, Daniel* [2]Lit., *at the beginning*
2 [1]Or, *river* [a]Num. 12:6; Dan. 7:2, 15; 8:3 [b]Neh. 1:1; Esth. 1:2; 2:8 [c]Gen. 10:22; 14:1; Is. 11:11; Jer. 25:25; Ezek. 32:24
3 [1]Or, *river* [2]Lit., *high(er)* [a]Dan. 8:20
4 [1]Lit., *hand* [a]Deut. 33:17; 1 Kin. 22:11; Ezek. 34:21 [b]Dan. 11:3
5 [1]Lit., *buck* [a]Dan. 8:8, 21; 11:3
6 [1]Or, *river*
7 [1]Lit., *hand*
8 [a]2 Chr. 26:16; Dan. 5:20 [b]Dan. 8:22 [c]Dan. 7:2; Rev. 7:1
9 [1]I.e., Palestine [a]Dan. 8:23 [b]Ps. 48:2; Dan. 11:16, 41
10 [a]Is. 14:13; Jer. 48:26; Rev. 12:4 [b]Dan. 7:7; 8:7
11 [1]Lit., *up to the* [2]Or, *Prince* [a]2 Kin. 19:22, 23; 2 Chr. 32:15-17; Is. 37:23; Dan. 8:25; 11:36, 37 [b]Ezek. 46:14; Dan. 11:31; 12:11
12 [a]Is. 59:14
13 [1]Or possibly, *and the transgression that horrifies* [2]Lit., *as a trampling* [a]Dan. 4:13, 23; 1 Pet. 1:12 [b]Ps. 74:10; 79:5; Is. 6:11; Dan. 12:6, 8; Rev. 6:10 [c]Is. 63:18; Jer. 12:10; Luke 21:24; Heb. 10:29; Rev. 11:2

6 And he came up to the ram that
had the two horns, which I had seen
standing in front of the [1]canal, and
rushed at him in his mighty wrath.
7 And I saw him come beside the
ram, and he was enraged at him; and he
struck the ram and shattered his two
horns, and the ram had no strength to
withstand him. So he hurled him to the
ground and trampled on him, and there
was none to rescue the ram from his
[1]power.
8 Then the male goat magnified *himself* exceedingly. But as soon as [a]he was
mighty, the [b]large horn was broken; and
in its place there came up four conspicu-
ous *horns* toward the [c]four winds of
heaven.

The Little Horn

9 And out of one of them came forth
a rather [a]small horn which grew exceedingly great toward the south, toward the
east, and toward the [1b]Beautiful *Land.*
10 And it grew up to the host of
heaven and caused some of the host and
some of the [a]stars to fall to the earth,
and it [b]trampled them down.
11 It even [a]magnified *itself* [1]to be
equal with the [2]Commander of the host;
and it removed the [b]regular sacrifice
from Him, and the place of His sanctuary was thrown down.
12 And on account of transgression
the host will be given over *to the horn*
along with the regular sacrifice; and it
will [a]fling truth to the ground and perform *its will* and prosper.
13 Then I heard a [a]holy one speaking,
and another holy one said to that particular one who was speaking, "[b]How
long will the vision *about* the regular
sacrifice apply, [1]while the transgression
causes horror, so as to allow both the
holy place and the host [2]to be [c]tram-
pled?"
14 And he said to me, "For [a]2,300
evenings *and* mornings; then the holy
place will be [1]properly restored."

Interpretation of the Vision

15 And it came about when [a]I, Daniel,
had seen the vision, that I sought [1]to
understand it; and behold, standing
before me was one [2]who looked like a
[b]man.
16 And I heard the voice of a man
between *the banks of* Ulai, and he called
out and said, "[a]Gabriel, give this *man* an
understanding of the vision."
17 So he came near to where I was
standing, and when he came I was
frightened and [a]fell on my face; but he
said to me, "Son of man, understand
that the vision pertains to the [b]time of
the end."

14 [1]Lit., *vindicated* [a]Dan. 7:25; 12:7, 11; Rev. 11:2, 3; 12:14; 13:5
15 [1]Lit., *understanding* [2]Lit., *like the appearance of a man* [a]Dan. 8:1 [b]Dan. 7:13; 10:16, 18
16 [a]Dan. 9:21; Luke 1:19, 26
17 [a]Ezek. 1:28; 44:4; Dan. 2:46; Rev. 1:17 [b]Dan. 8:19; 11:35, 40

18 Now while he was talking with me,
I [a]sank into a deep sleep with my face to
the ground; but he [b]touched me and
made me stand [1]upright.
19 And he said, "Behold, I am going
to [a]let you know what will occur at the
final period of the indignation, for *it*
pertains to the appointed time of the
end.

The Ram's Identity

20"The [a]ram which you saw with the
two horns represents the kings of Media
and Persia.

The Goat

21"And the shaggy [1]goat *represents* the
[2]kingdom of Greece, and the large horn
that is between his eyes is the first king.
22"And the [a]broken *horn* and the four
horns that arose in its place *represent*
four kingdoms *which* will arise from *his*
nation, although not with his power.

23 "And in the latter period of their
[1]rule,
When the transgressors have [2]run
their course,
A king will arise
[3]Insolent and skilled in [4]intrigue.
24 "And his power will be mighty, but
not by his *own* power,
And he will [1a]destroy to an
extraordinary degree
And prosper and perform *his will;*
He will [1]destroy mighty men and
[2]the holy people.
25 "And through his shrewdness
He will cause deceit to succeed by
his [1]influence;
And he will magnify *himself* in his
heart,
And he will [2]destroy many while
they are [3]at ease.
He will even [4a]oppose the Prince
of princes,
But he will be broken [b]without
[1]human agency.
26 "And the vision of the evenings
and mornings
Which has been told is [a]true;
But [b]keep the vision secret,
For *it* pertains to many [c]days *in
the future.*"

27 Then I, Daniel, was [1a]exhausted
and sick for days. Then I got up *again*
and [b]carried on the king's business; but
I was astounded at the vision, and there
was none to [2]explain *it.*

Daniel's Prayer for His People

9 IN the first year of [a]Darius the son
of Ahasuerus, of Median descent,
who was made king over the kingdom of
the Chaldeans—
2 in the first year of his reign I,
Daniel, observed in the books the number of the years which was *revealed as*
the word of the LORD to [a]Jeremiah the
prophet for the completion of the desolations of Jerusalem, *namely,* [a]seventy
years.
3 So I [1]gave my attention to the Lord
God to seek *Him by* prayer and supplications, with fasting, sackcloth, and
ashes.
4 And I prayed to the LORD my God
and confessed and said, "Alas, O Lord,
the [a]great and awesome God, who
[b]keeps His covenant and lovingkindness
for those who love Him and keep His
commandments,
5 [a]we have sinned, committed iniquity, acted wickedly, and [b]rebelled, even
[c]turning aside from Thy commandments
and ordinances.
6"Moreover, we have not [a]listened to
Thy servants the prophets, who spoke in
Thy name to our kings, our princes, our
fathers, and all the people of the land.
7"[a]Righteousness belongs to Thee, O
Lord, but to us [1b]open shame, as it is
this day—to the men of Judah, the
inhabitants of Jerusalem, and all Israel,
those who are nearby and those who are
far away in [c]all the countries to which
Thou hast driven them, because of their
unfaithful deeds which they have committed against Thee.
8"[1]Open shame belongs to us, O
Lord, to our kings, our princes, and our
fathers, because we have sinned against
Thee.
9"To the Lord our God belong [a]com-
passion and forgiveness, [1]for we have
[b]rebelled against Him;
10 nor have we obeyed the voice of the
LORD our God, to walk in His [1]teachings
which He [a]set before us through His
servants the prophets.
11"Indeed [a]all Israel has transgressed
Thy law and turned aside, not obeying
Thy voice; so the [b]curse has been poured
out on us, along with the oath which is
written in the law of Moses the servant
of God, for we have sinned against Him.
12"Thus He has [a]confirmed His words
which He had spoken against us and
against our [1b]rulers who ruled us, to
bring on us great calamity; for under the
whole heaven there has [c]not been done
anything like what was done to Jerusalem.
13"As it is written in the [a]law of
Moses, all this calamity has come on us;
yet we have [b]not [1]sought the favor of the
LORD our God by [c]turning from our
iniquity and [2]giving attention to Thy
truth.
14"Therefore, the LORD has [1a]kept the
calamity in store and brought it on us;
for the LORD our God is [b]righteous with
respect to all His deeds which He has
done, but we have not obeyed His voice.
15"And now, O Lord our God, who
hast [a]brought Thy people out of the land
of Egypt with a mighty hand and hast
[b]made a name for Thyself, as it is this
day—we have sinned, we have been
wicked.

18 [1]Lit., *on my standing* [a]Dan. 10:9; Luke 9:32 [b]Ezek. 2:2; Dan. 10:10, 16, 18
19 [a]Dan. 8:15-17
20 [a]Dan. 8:3
21 [1]Lit., *buck* [2]Lit., *king*
22 [a]Dan. 8:8
23 [1]Or, *kingdom* [2]Lit., *finished* [3]Lit., *Strong of face* [4]Or, *ambiguous speech*
24 [1]Or, *corrupt* [2]Lit., *people of the saints* [a]Dan. 8:11-13; 11:36; 12:7
25 [1]Lit., *hand* [2]Or, *corrupt* [3]Or, *secure* [4]Lit., *stand against* [a]Dan. 8:11 [b]Job 34:20; Dan. 2:34, 45
26 [a]Dan. 10:1 [b]Ezek. 12:27; Dan. 12:4, 9; Rev. 22:10 [c]Dan. 10:14
27 [1]Or, *done in* [2]Lit., *make* me *understand* [a]Dan. 7:28; 8:17; Hab. 3:16 [b]Dan. 2:48

1 [a]Dan. 5:31; 11:1
2 [a]2 Chr. 36:21; Ezra 1:1; Jer. 25:11, 12; 29:10; Zech. 7:5
3 [1]Lit., *set my face*
4 [a]Deut. 7:21; Neh. 9:32 [b]Deut. 7:9
5 [a]1 Kin. 8:48; Neh. 9:33; Ps. 106:6; Is. 64:5-7; Jer. 14:7 [b]Lam. 1:18, 20 [c]Ps. 119:176; Is. 53:6; Dan. 9:11
6 [a]2 Chr. 36:16; Jer. 44:4, 5
7 [1]Lit., *the shame of face* [a]Jer. 23:6; 33:16; Dan. 9:18 [b]Ps. 44:15; Jer. 2:26, 27; 3:25 [c]Deut. 4:27
8 [1]Lit., *The shame of face*
9 [1]Or, *though* [a]Neh. 9:17; Ps. 130:4 [b]Ps. 106:43; Jer. 14:7; Dan. 9:5, 6
10 [1]Or, *laws* [a]2 Kin. 17:13-15; 18:12
11 [a]Is. 1:3, 4; Jer. 8:5-10 [b]Deut. 27:15-26
12 [1]Lit., *judges who judged us* [a]Is. 44:26; Jer. 44:2-6; Lam. 2:17; Zech. 1:6 [b]Job 12:17; Ps. 82:2-7; 148:11 [c]Lam. 1:12; 2:13; Ezek. 5:9
13 [1]Lit., *softened the face of* [2]Or, *having insight into* [a]Lev. 26:14-45; Deut. 28:15-68; Dan. 9:11 [b]Job 36:13; Is. 9:13; Jer. 2:30; 5:3 [c]Jer. 31:18
14 [1]Lit., *watched over the evil* [a]Jer. 31:28; 44:27 [b]Ps. 51:14; Dan. 9:7
15 [a]Deut. 5:15 [b]Neh. 9:10; Jer. 32:20

16"O Lord, in accordance with all Thy
[1]righteous acts, let now Thine [a]anger
and Thy wrath turn away from Thy city
Jerusalem, Thy [b]holy mountain; for
because of our sins and the iniquities of
our fathers, Jerusalem and Thy people
have become a [c]reproach to all those
around us.
17"So now, our God, listen to the
prayer of Thy servant and to his supplications, and for [1]Thy sake, O Lord, [a]let
Thy face shine on Thy [b]desolate sanctuary.
18"O my God, [a]incline Thine ear and
hear! Open Thine eyes and [b]see our
desolations and the city which is [c]called
by Thy name; for we are not [1d]present-
ing our supplications before Thee on
account of [2]any merits of our own, but
on account of Thy great compassion.
19"O Lord, hear! O Lord, forgive! O
Lord, listen and take action! For Thine
own sake, O my God, [a]do not delay,
because Thy city and Thy people are
called by Thy name."

Gabriel Brings an Answer

20 Now while I was [a]speaking and
praying, and [b]confessing my sin and the
sin of my people Israel, and [1]presenting
my supplication before the LORD my
God in behalf of the holy mountain of
my God,
21 while I was still speaking in prayer,
then the man [a]Gabriel, whom I had seen
in the vision [1]previously, [2]came to me
[3]in *my* extreme weariness about the time
of the [b]evening offering.
22 And he gave *me* instruction and
talked with me, and said, "O Daniel, I
have now come forth to give you insight
with [a]understanding.
23"At the [a]beginning of your supplications the [1]command was issued, and I
have come to tell *you,* for you are
[2b]highly esteemed; so give heed to the
message and gain [c]understanding of the
vision.

Seventy Weeks and the Messiah

24"Seventy [1a]weeks have been decreed
for your people and your holy city, to
[2]finish the transgression, to [3]make an
end of sin, to [b]make atonement for
iniquity, to bring in [c]everlasting righteousness, to seal up vision and [4]proph-
ecy, and to anoint the most holy *place.*
25"So you are to know and discern
that from the issuing of a [1a]decree to
restore and rebuild Jerusalem until
[2b]Messiah the [c]Prince *there will be* seven
weeks and sixty-two weeks; it will be
built again, with [3]plaza and moat, even
in times of distress.
26"Then after the sixty-two weeks the
[1]Messiah will be [a]cut off and have [2]noth-
ing, and the people of the prince who is
to come will [b]destroy the city and the
sanctuary. And [3]its end *will come* with a
[c]flood; even to the end [4]there will be
war; desolations are determined.

16 [1]Lit., *righteousnesses* [a]Jer. 32:31, 32 [b]Ps. 87:1-3; Dan. 9:20; Joel 3:17; Zech. 8:3 [c]Ezek. 5:14
17 [1]Lit., *the sake of the Lord* [a]Num. 6:24-26; Ps. 80:3, 7, 19 [b]Lam. 5:18
18 [1]Lit., *causing to fall* [2]Lit., *our righteousnesses* [a]Is. 37:17 [b]Ps. 80:14 [c]Jer. 7:10-12 [d]Jer. 36:7
19 [a]Ps. 44:23; 74:10, 11
20 [1]Lit., *causing to fall* [a]Ps. 145:18; Is. 58:9; Dan. 9:3; 10:12 [b]Is. 6:5
21 [1]Lit., *at the beginning* [2]Lit., *was reaching;* or, *touching* [3]Lit., *wearied with weariness* [a]Dan. 8:16; Luke 1:19, 26 [b]Ex. 29:39; 1 Kin. 18:36; Ezra 9:4
22 [a]Dan. 8:16; 10:21; Zech. 1:9
23 [1]Lit., *word went out* [2]Lit., *desirable;* or, *precious* [a]Dan. 10:12 [b]Dan. 10:11, 19 [c]Matt. 24:15
24 [1]Or, *units of seven,* and so throughout the ch. [2]Or, *restrain* [3]Another reading is *seal up sins* [4]Lit., *prophet* [a]Lev. 25:8; Num. 14:34; Ezek. 4:5, 6 [b]2 Chr. 29:24; Is. 53:10; Rom. 5:10 [c]Is. 51:6, 8; 56:1; Jer. 23:5, 6; Rom. 3:21, 22
25 [1]Lit., *word* [2]Or, *an anointed one* [3]Or, *streets* [a]Ezra 4:24; 6:1-15; Neh. 2:1-8; 3:1 [b]John 1:41; 4:25 [c]Is. 9:6; Dan. 8:11, 25
26 [1]Or, *anointed one* [2]Or, *no one* [3]Or, *his* [4]Or, *war will be decreed for desolations* [a]Is. 53:8; Mark 9:12; Luke 24:26 [b]Matt. 24:2; Mark 13:2; Luke 19:43, 44 [c]Nah. 1:8
27 [1]Or, *detestable things* [2]Or, *causes horror* [a]Dan. 11:31; Matt. 24:15; Mark 13:14; Luke 21:20 [b]Is. 10:23; 28:22

1 [1]Lit., *word* [2]Or, *warfare* [a]Dan. 1:21; 6:28 [b]Dan. 1:7 [c]Dan. 8:26 [d]Dan. 1:17; 2:21
2 [a]Ezra 9:4, 5; Neh. 1:4
3 [1]Lit., *bread of desirability* [a]Dan. 6:18
4 [1]Heb., *Hiddekel* [a]Ezek. 1:3; Dan. 8:2
5 [a]Ezek. 9:2; Dan. 12:6, 7 [b]Rev. 1:13; 15:6 [c]Jer. 10:9

27"And he will make a firm covenant
with the many for one week, but in the
middle of the week he will put a stop to
sacrifice and grain offering; and on the
wing of [1a]abominations *will come* one
who [2]makes desolate, even until a [b]com-
plete destruction, one that is decreed, is
poured out on the one who [2]makes
desolate."

Daniel Is Terrified by a Vision

10 IN the third year of [a]Cyrus king
of Persia a [1]message was revealed
to [b]Daniel, who was named Belteshazzar; and the [1c]message was true and *one*
of great [2]conflict, but he understood the
[1]message and had an [d]understanding of
the vision.
2 In those days I, Daniel, had been
[a]mourning for three entire weeks.
3 I [a]did not eat any [1]tasty food, nor
did meat or wine enter my mouth, nor
did I use any ointment at all, until the
entire three weeks were completed.
4 And on the twenty-fourth day of
the first month, while I was by the bank
of the great [a]river, that is, the [1]Tigris,
5 I lifted my eyes and looked, and
behold, there was a certain man [a]dressed
in linen, whose waist was [b]girded with *a*
belt of pure [c]gold of Uphaz.
6 His body also was like [1]beryl, his
face [2]had the appearance of lightning,
[a]his eyes were like flaming torches, his
arms and feet like the gleam of polished
bronze, and the sound of his words like
the sound of a [3]tumult.
7 Now I, Daniel, [a]alone saw the
vision, while the [b]men who were with me
did not see the vision; nevertheless, a
great [c]dread fell on them, and they ran
away to hide themselves.
8 So I was [a]left alone and saw this
great vision; yet [b]no strength was left in
me, for my [1]natural color turned to [2]a
deathly pallor, and I retained no
strength.
9 But I heard the sound of his words;
and as soon as I heard the sound of his
words, I [a]fell into a deep sleep on my
face, with my face to the ground.

Daniel Comforted

10 Then behold, a hand [a]touched me
and set me trembling on my [1]hands and
knees.
11 And he said to me, "O [a]Daniel,
man of [1]high esteem, [b]understand the
words that I am about to tell you and
[c]stand [2]upright, for I have now been sent
to you." And when he had spoken this
word to me, I stood up [d]trembling.

6 [1]Or, *yellow serpentine* [2]Lit., *like* [3]Or, *roaring* [a]Rev. 1:14; 2:18; 19:12
7 [a]2 Kin. 6:17-20 [b]Acts 9:7 [c]Ezek. 12:18
8 [1]Lit., *splendor* [2]Lit., *corruption* [a]Gen. 32:24 [b]Dan. 7:28; 8:27; Hab. 3:16
9 [a]Gen. 15:12; Job 4:13; Dan. 8:18
10 [1]Lit., *knees and the palms of my hands* [a]Jer. 1:9; Dan 8:18
11 [1]Lit., *desirability;* or, *preciousness* [2]Lit., *upon your standing* [a]Dan. 10:19 [b]Dan. 8:16, 17 [c]Ezek. 2:1 [d]Job 4:14, 15

12 Then he said to me, "[a]Do not be
afraid, Daniel, for from the first day that
you set your heart on understanding *this*
and on [b]humbling yourself before your
God, your words were heard, and I have
come in response [c]to your words.
13 "But the prince of the kingdom of
Persia was [1]withstanding me for twenty-
one days; then behold, [a]Michael, one of
the chief princes, came to help me, for I
had been left there with the kings of
Persia.
14 "Now I have come to [a]give you an
understanding of what will happen to
your people in the [1b]latter days, for the
vision pertains to [c]the days yet *future*."
15 And when he had spoken to me
according to these words, I [1]turned my
face toward the ground and became
[a]speechless.
16 And behold, [1a]one who resembled
a human being was [b]touching my lips;
then I opened my mouth and spoke, and
said to him who was standing before me,
"O my lord, as a result of the vision
[2c]anguish has come upon me, and I have
retained no strength.
17 "For [a]how can such a servant of my
lord talk with such as my lord? As for
me, there remains just now [b]no strength
in me, nor has any breath been left in
me."
18 Then *this* one with human appearance touched me again and
[a]strengthened me.
19 And he said, "O man of [1]high
esteem, [a]do not be afraid. Peace [2]be with
you; take [b]courage and be courageous!"
Now as soon as he spoke to me, I
received strength and said, "May my
lord speak, for you have [c]strengthened
me."
20 Then he said, "Do you [1]understand
why I came to you? But I shall now
return to fight against the [2]prince of
Persia; so I am going forth, and behold,
the [2a]prince of [3]Greece is about to come.
21 "However, I will tell you what is
inscribed in the writing of [a]truth. Yet
there is no one who [1]stands firmly with
me against these *forces* except [b]Michael
your prince.

Conflicts to Come

11 "AND in the [a]first year of Darius
the Mede, [1]I arose to be [2]an
encouragement and a protection for him.
2 "And now I will tell you the [a]truth.
Behold, three more kings are going to
arise [1]in Persia. Then a fourth will gain
far more riches than all *of them;* as soon
as he becomes strong through his riches,
[2]he will arouse the whole *empire* against
the realm of [3b]Greece.
3 "And a [a]mighty king will arise, and
he will rule with great authority and [b]do
as he pleases.
4 "But as soon as he has arisen, his
kingdom will be broken up and parceled
out [a]toward the [b]four [1]points of the
compass, though not to his *own* descendants, nor according to his authority
which he wielded; for his sovereignty
will be [c]uprooted and *given* to others
besides [2]them.
5 "Then the [a]king of the South will
grow strong, [1]along with *one* of his
princes [2]who will gain ascendancy over
him and obtain dominion; his domain
will be a great dominion *indeed.*
6 "And after some years they will
form an alliance, and the daughter of the
king of the South will come to the [a]king
of the North to carry out [1]a peaceful
arrangement. But she will not retain her
[2]position of power, nor will he remain
with his [3]power, but she will be given up,
along with those who brought her in,
and the one who sired her, as well as he
who supported her in *those* times.
7 "But one of the [1]descendants of her
line will arise in his place, and he will
come against *their* army and enter the
[a]fortress of the king of the North, and he
will deal with them and display *great*
strength.
8 "And also their [a]gods with their
[1]metal images *and* their precious vessels
of silver and gold he will take into
captivity to Egypt, and he on his part
will [2]refrain from *attacking* the king of
the North for *some* years.
9 "Then [1]the latter will enter the
realm of the king of the South, but will
return to his *own* land.
10 "And his sons will [1]mobilize and
assemble a multitude of great forces;
and one of them will keep on coming
and [a]overflow and pass through, that he
may [2]again wage war up to his *very*
fortress.
11 "And the [a]king of the South will be
enraged and go forth and fight [1]with the
king of the North. Then the latter will
raise a great multitude, but *that* multitude will be given into [2]the hand of the
former.
12 "When the multitude is carried
away, his heart will be lifted up, and he
will cause tens of thousands to fall; yet
he will not prevail.
13 "For the king of the North will
again raise a greater multitude than the
former, and [1]after an [a]interval of some
years he will [2]press on with a great army
and much equipment.
14 "Now in those times many will rise
up against the king of the South; the
violent ones among your people will also
lift themselves up in order to fulfill the
vision, but they will [1]fall down.
15 "Then the king of the North will
come, cast up a [a]siege mound, and
capture a well-fortified city; and the
forces of the South will not stand *their
ground,* not even [1]their choicest troops,
for there will be no strength to make a
stand.

12 [a]Is. 41:10, 14; Dan. 10:19 [b]Dan. 9:20-23; 10:2, 3 [c]Acts 10:30, 31
13 [1]Lit., *standing opposite* [a]Dan. 10:21; 12:1; Jude 9; Rev. 12:7
14 [1]Lit., *end of the days* [a]Dan. 8:16; 9:22 [b]Deut. 31:29; Dan. 2:28 [c]Dan. 8:26; 12:4, 9
15 [1]Lit., *set* [a]Ezek. 3:26; 24:27; Luke 1:20
16 [1]Lit., *as a likeness of sons of man* [2]Lit., *my pains have* [a]Dan. 8:15 [b]Is. 6:7; Jer. 1:9 [c]Dan. 7:15, 28; 8:17, 27; 10:8, 9
17 [a]Ex. 24:10, 11; Is. 6:1-5 [b]Dan. 10:8
18 [a]Is. 35:3, 4
19 [1]Lit., *desirability;* or, *preciousness* [2]Lit., *to you* [a]Judg. 6:23; Is. 43:1; Dan. 10:12 [b]Josh. 1:6, 7, 9; Is. 35:4 [c]Ps. 138:3; 2 Cor. 12:9
20 [1]Lit., *know* [2]I.e., Satanic angel [3]Heb., *Javan* [a]Dan. 8:21; 11:2
21 [1]Lit., *shows himself strong* [a]Dan. 12:4 [b]Dan. 10:13; Rev. 12:7

1 [1]Lit., *my standing up* was [2]Lit., *for a strengthener* [a]Dan. 5:31; 9:1
2 [1]Lit., *for* [2]Or, they *all will stir up the realm of Greece* [3]Heb., *Javan* [a]Dan. 8:26; 10:1, 21 [b]Dan. 8:21; 10:20
3 [a]Dan. 8:5, 21 [b]Dan. 5:19; 8:4; 11:16, 36
4 [1]Lit., *winds of the heaven* [2]I.e., his descendants [a]Dan. 8:8, 22 [b]Jer. 49:36; Ezek. 37:9; Dan. 7:2; 8:8; Zech. 2:6; Rev. 7:1 [c]Jer. 12:15, 17; 18:7
5 [1]Lit., *and* [2]Lit., *and he* [a]Dan. 11:9, 11, 14, 25, 40
6 [1]Or, *an equitable agreement* [2]Lit., *strength of arm* [3]Lit., *arm* [a]Dan. 11:7, 13, 15, 40
7 [1]Lit., *branch of her roots* [a]Dan. 11:19, 38, 39
8 [1]Lit., *cast images* [2]Or, *stand against the king* [a]Is. 37:19; 46:1, 2; Jer. 43:12, 13
9 [1]Lit., *he will,* and so throughout the ch.
10 [1]Or, *wage war* [2]Or, *return and wage* [a]Is. 8:8; Jer. 46:7, 8; 51:42; Dan. 11:26, 40
11 [1]Lit., *with him, with* [2]Lit., *his hand* [a]Dan. 11:5
13 [1]Lit., *at the end of the times, years* [2]Or, *keep on coming* [a]Dan. 4:16; 12:7
14 [1]Lit., *stumble,* and so throughout the ch.
15 [1]Lit., *the people of its choice ones* [a]Jer. 6:6; Ezek. 4:2; 17:17

16"But he who comes against him will [a]do as he pleases, and [b]no one will *be able to* withstand him; he will also stay *for a time* in the [1c]Beautiful Land, with destruction in his hand.

17"And he will [a]set his face to come with the power of his whole kingdom, [1]bringing with him [2]a proposal of peace which he will put into effect; he will also give him the daughter of women to ruin it. But she will not take a stand *for him* or be [3]on his side.

18"Then he will turn his face to the [a]coastlands and capture many. But a commander will put a stop to his scorn against him; moreover, he will [b]repay him for his scorn.

19"So he will turn his face toward the fortresses of his own land, but he will [a]stumble and fall and be [b]found no more.

20"Then in his place one will arise who will [a]send an [1]oppressor through the [2]Jewel of *his* kingdom; yet within a few days he will be shattered, though neither in anger nor in battle.

21"And in his place a despicable person will arise, on whom the honor of kingship has not been conferred, but he will come in a time of tranquility and [a]seize the kingdom by intrigue.

22"And the overflowing [a]forces will be flooded away before him and shattered, and also the prince of the covenant.

23"And after an alliance is made with him he will practice deception, and he will go up and gain power with a small *force of* people.

24"[1]In a time of tranquility he will enter the [a]richest *parts* of the [2]realm, and he will accomplish what his fathers never did, nor his [3]ancestors; he will distribute plunder, booty, and possessions among them, and he will devise his schemes against strongholds, but *only* for a time.

25"And he will stir up his strength and [1]courage against the [a]king of the South with a large army; so the king of the South will mobilize an extremely large and mighty army for war; but he will not stand, for schemes will be devised against him.

26"And those who eat his choice food will [1]destroy him, and his army will [2a]overflow, but many will fall down slain.

27"As for both kings, their hearts will be *intent* on [a]evil, and they will [b]speak lies *to each other* at the same table; but it will not succeed, for the [c]end is still *to come* at the appointed time.

28"Then he will return to his land with much [1]plunder; but his heart will be *set* against the holy covenant, and he will take action and *then* return to his *own* land.

29"At the appointed time he will return and come into the South, but [1]this last time it will not turn out the way it did before.

30"For ships of [1a]Kittim will come against him; therefore he will be disheartened, and will return and become enraged at the holy covenant and take action; so he will come back and show regard for those who forsake the holy covenant.

31"And forces from him will arise, [a]desecrate the sanctuary fortress, and do away with the regular sacrifice. And they will set up the [b]abomination [1]of desolation.

32"And by [a]smooth *words* he will [1]turn to godlessness those who act wickedly toward the covenant, but the people who know their God will display [b]strength and take action.

33"And [1a]those who have insight among the people will give understanding to the many; yet they will [b]fall by sword and by flame, by captivity and by plunder, for *many* days.

34"Now when they fall they will be granted a little help, and many will [a]join with them in [b]hypocrisy.

35"And some of [1]those who have insight will fall, in order to [a]refine, [b]purge, and make them [2c]pure, until the [d]end time; because *it is* still *to come* at the appointed time.

36"Then the king will [a]do as he pleases, and he will exalt and [b]magnify himself above every god, and will [c]speak [1]monstrous things against the [d]God of gods; and he will prosper until the [e]indignation is finished, for that which is [f]decreed will be done.

37"And he will show no regard for the [1]gods of his fathers or for the desire of women, nor will he show regard for any *other* god; for he will magnify himself above *them* all.

38"But [1]instead he will honor a god of fortresses, a god whom his fathers did not know; he will honor *him* with gold, silver, costly stones, and treasures.

39"And he will take action against the strongest of fortresses with *the help of* a foreign god; he will give great honor to [1]those who acknowledge *him*, and he will cause them to rule over the many, and will parcel out land for a price.

40"And at the [a]end time the [b]king of the South will collide with him, and the [c]king of the North will [d]storm against him with chariots, with horsemen, and with many ships; and he will enter countries, [e]overflow *them*, and pass through.

41"He will also enter the [1a]Beautiful Land, and many *countries* will fall; but these will be rescued out of his hand: Edom, [b]Moab and the foremost of the sons of [c]Ammon.

42"Then he will stretch out his hand against *other* countries, and the land of Egypt will not escape.

16 [1]I.e., Palestine [a]Dan. 5:19; 11:3, 36 [b]Josh. 1:5 [c]Dan. 8:9; 11:41
17 [1]Lit., *and* [2]Lit., *equitable things* [3]Lit., *for him;* i.e., for her father [a]2 Kin. 12:17; Ezek. 4:3, 7
18 [a]Gen. 10:5; Is. 66:19; Jer. 2:10; 31:10; Zeph. 2:11 [b]Hos. 12:14
19 [a]Ps. 27:2; Jer. 46:6 [b]Job 20:8; Ps. 37:36; Ezek. 26:21
20 [1]Or, *exactor* of tribute [2]Lit., *adornment;* i.e., probably Jerusalem and its temple [a]Is. 60:17
21 [a]2 Sam. 15:6
22 [a]Dan. 9:26; 11:10
24 [1]Lit., *Into tranquility and the richest . . . ; he will enter* [2]Or, *province* [3]Lit., *fathers' fathers* [a]Num. 13:20; Neh. 9:25; Ezek. 34:14
25 [1]Lit., *heart* [a]Dan. 11:5
26 [1]Lit., *break* [2]Or, *be swept away, and many* [a]Dan. 11:10, 40
27 [a]Ps. 52:1; 64:6 [b]Ps. 12:2; Jer. 9:3-5; 41:1-3 [c]Dan. 8:19; 11:35, 40; Hab. 2:3
28 [1]Lit., *possessions*
29 [1]Lit., *it will not happen as the first and as the last*
30 [1]I.e., Cyprus [a]Gen. 10:4; Num. 24:24; Is. 23:1, 12; Jer. 2:10
31 [1]Lit., *that makes desolate;* or, *that causes horror* [a]Dan. 8:11-13; 12:11 [b]Dan. 9:27; Matt. 24:15; Mark 13:14
32 [1]Or, *pollute those* [a]Dan. 11:21, 34 [b]Mic. 5:7-9; Zech. 9:13-16; 10:3-6
33 [1]Or, *instructors of* the *people* [a]Mal. 2:7 [b]Matt. 24:9; John 16:2; Heb. 11:36-38
34 [a]Matt. 7:15; Acts 20:29, 30 [b]Dan. 11:21, 32; Rom. 16:18
35 [1]Or, *the instructors* [2]Lit., *white* [a]Deut. 8:16; Prov. 17:3; Dan. 12:10; Zech. 13:9; Mal. 3:2, 3 [b]John 15:2 [c]Rev. 7:14 [d]Dan. 11:27
36 [1]Lit., *extraordinary* [a]Dan. 5:19; 11:3, 16 [b]Is. 14:13; Dan. 5:20; 8:11, 25; 2 Thess. 2:4 [c]Rev. 13:5, 6 [d]Deut. 10:17; Ps. 136:2; Dan. 2:47 [e]Is. 10:25; 26:20; Dan. 8:19 [f]Dan. 9:27
37 [1]Or, *God*
38 [1]Lit., *in his place*

39 [1]Lit., *the one who acknowledges*
40 [a]Dan. 11:27, 35; 12:4, 9 [b]Dan. 11:11, 25 [c]Dan. 11:7, 13, 15 [d]Is. 5:28; Jer. 4:13 [e]Dan. 11:10, 26
41 [1]I.e., Palestine [a]Dan. 8:9; 11:16 [b]Jer. 48:47 [c]Jer. 49:6

43"But he will [1]gain control over the hidden treasures of gold and silver, and over all the precious things of Egypt; and [a]Libyans and [b]Ethiopians *will follow* at his [2]heels.

44"But rumors from the East and from the North will disturb him, and he will go forth with great wrath to destroy and [1]annihilate many.

45"And he will pitch the tents of his royal pavilion between the seas and the beautiful [a]Holy Mountain; yet he will come to his end, and no one will help him.

The Time of the End

12 "NOW at that time [a]Michael, the great prince who stands *guard* over the sons of your people, will arise. And there will be a [b]time of distress [c]such as never occurred since there was a nation until that time; and at that time your people, everyone who is found written in the [d]book, will be rescued.

2"And [a]many of those who sleep in the dust of the ground will awake, [b]these to everlasting life, but the others to disgrace *and* everlasting [1]contempt.

3"And [1]those who have [a]insight will [b]shine brightly like the brightness of the [2]expanse of heaven, and those who [c]lead the many to righteousness, like the stars forever and ever.

4"But as for you, Daniel, [a]conceal these words and [b]seal up the book until the [c]end of time; [d]many will go back and forth, and knowledge will increase."

5 Then I, Daniel, looked and behold, two others were standing, one on this bank of the river, and the other on that bank of the river.

6 And [a]one said to the man [b]dressed in linen, who was above the waters of the river, "[c]How long *will it be* until the end of *these* wonders?"

7 And I heard the man dressed in linen, who was above the waters of the river, [1]as he [a]raised his right hand and his left toward heaven, and swore by [b]Him who lives forever that it would be for a [2][c]time, [2]times, and half *a* [2]*time;* and as soon as [3]they finish [d]shattering the [4]power of the holy people, all these *events* will be completed.

8 As for me, I heard but could not understand; so I said, "My lord, what *will be* the [1]outcome of these *events?*"

9 And he said, "Go *your way,* Daniel, for *these* words are concealed and [a]sealed up until the end time.

10"[a]Many will be purged, [1]purified and refined; but the [b]wicked will act wickedly, and none of the wicked will understand, but [2]those who [c]have insight will understand.

11"And from the time that the regular sacrifice is abolished, and the [1][a]abomination of desolation is set up, *there will be* 1,290 days.

12"How [a]blessed is he who keeps waiting and attains to the [b]1,335 days!

13"But as for you, go *your way* to the [1]end; then you will enter into [a]rest and rise *again* for your [b]allotted portion at the end of the [2]age."

43 [1]Or, *rule over* [2]Lit., *footsteps* [a]2 Chr. 12:3; Nah. 3:9 [b]2 Chr. 12:3; Ezek. 30:4, 5; Nah. 3:9

44 [1]Lit., *devote to destruction*

45 [a]Is. 11:9; 27:13; 65:25; 66:20; Dan. 9:16, 20

1 [a]Dan. 10:13, 21; Rev. 12:7 [b]Rev. 7:14; 16:18 [c]Jer. 30:7; Ezek. 5:9; Dan. 9:12; Matt. 24:21; Mark 13:19 [d]Dan. 7:10; 10:21

2 [1]Lit., *abhorrence* [a]Is. 26:19; Ezek. 37:12-14 [b]Matt. 25:46; John 5:28, 29

3 [1]Or, *the instructors will* [2]Or, *firmament* [a]Dan. 11:33, 35; 12:10 [b]John 5:35 [c]Is. 53:11; Dan. 11:33

4 [a]Dan. 8:26; 12:9 [b]Is. 8:16; Dan. 12:9; Rev. 22:10 [c]Dan. 8:17; 12:9, 13 [d]Is. 11:9; 29:18, 19; Dan. 11:33

6 [a]Dan. 8:16; Zech. 1:12, 13 [b]Ezek. 9:2; Dan. 10:5 [c]Dan. 8:13; 12:8; Matt. 24:3; Mark 13:4

7 [1]Lit., *and* [2]I.e., year(s) [3]Lit., *to finish* [4]Lit., *hand* [a]Ezek. 20:5; Rev. 10:5, 6 [b]Dan. 4:34 [c]Dan. 7:25; Rev. 12:14 [d]Dan. 8:24; Luke 21:24

8 [1]Or, *final end*

9 [a]Dan. 12:4

10 [1]Lit., *made white* [2]Or, *the instructors will* [a]Zech. 13:9 [b]Is. 32:6, 7; Rev. 22:11 [c]Dan. 12:3; Hos. 14:9; John 7:17; 8:47

11 [1]Or, *horrible abomination* [a]Dan. 9:27; 11:31; Matt. 24:15; Mark 13:14

12 [a]Is. 30:18 [b]Dan. 8:14; Rev. 11:2; 12:6; 13:5

13 [1]I.e., end of your life [2]Lit., *days* [a]Is. 57:2; Rev. 14:13 [b]Ps. 16:5

THE BOOK OF
HOSEA

Hosea's Wife and Children

1 THE word of the LORD which came
to [a]Hosea the son of Beeri, during
the days of [b]Uzziah, [c]Jotham, [d]Ahaz,
and [e]Hezekiah, kings of Judah, and
during the days of [f]Jeroboam the son of
Joash, king of Israel.
2 When the LORD first spoke through
Hosea, the LORD said to Hosea, "[a]Go,
take to yourself a wife of harlotry, and
have children of harlotry; for [b]the land
commits flagrant harlotry, [1]forsaking the
LORD."
3 So he went and took Gomer the
daughter of Diblaim, and she conceived
and [a]bore him a son.
4 And the LORD said to him, "Name
him [a]Jezreel; for yet a little while, and [b]I
will [1]punish the house of Jehu for the
bloodshed of Jezreel, and [c]I will put an
end to the kingdom of the house of
Israel.
5 "And it will come about on that day,
that I will [a]break the bow of Israel in the
[b]valley of Jezreel."
6 Then she conceived again and gave
birth to a daughter. And [1]the LORD said
to him, "Name her [2]Lo-ruhamah, for I
will no longer [a]have compassion on the
house of Israel, that I should ever forgive
them.
7 "But I will have [a]compassion on the
house of Judah and [b]deliver them by the
LORD their God, and will not deliver
them by [c]bow, sword, battle, horses, or
horsemen."
8 When she had weaned Lo-ruhamah, she conceived and gave birth to a
son.
9 And [1]the LORD said, "Name him
[2]Lo-ammi, for you are not My people
and I am not [3]your God."

10 [1]Yet the number of the sons of
Israel
Will be like the [a]sand of the sea,
Which cannot be measured or
numbered;
And [b]it will come about that, in the
place
Where it is said to them,
"You are [c]not My people,"
It will be said to them,
"*You are* the [d]sons of the living
God."
11 And the [a]sons of Judah and the
sons of Israel will be [b]gathered
together,
And they will appoint for them-
selves [c]one leader,
And they will go up from the land,
For great will be the day of Jezreel.

Israel's Unfaithfulness Condemned

2 [1]SAY to your brothers, "[2]Ammi,"
and to your sisters, "[3]Ruhamah."
2 "Contend with your mother, [a]con-
tend,
For she is [b]not my wife, and I am
not her husband;
And let her put away her [c]harlotry
from her face,
And her adultery from between her
breasts,
3 Lest I strip her [a]naked
And expose her as on the [b]day
when she was born.
I will also [c]make her like a wilderness,
Make her like desert land,
And slay her with [d]thirst.
4 "Also, I will have no compassion on
her children,
Because they are [a]children of harlotry.
5 "For their mother has [a]played the
harlot;
She who conceived them has acted
shamefully.
For she said, 'I will go after my
lovers,
Who [b]give *me* my bread and my
water,
My wool and my flax, my [c]oil and
my drink.'
6 "Therefore, behold, I will [a]hedge up
[1]her way with [b]thorns,
And I will build [2]a wall against her
so that she cannot find her
[c]paths.
7 "And she will [a]pursue her lovers, but
she will not overtake them;
And she will seek them, but will
not find *them.*
Then she will say, '[b]I will go back
to my [c]first husband,
For it was [d]better for me then than
now!'

8 "For she does [a]not know that it was
[b]I who gave her the grain, the
new wine, and the oil,
And lavished on her silver and
gold,
Which they [1]used for Baal.
9 "Therefore, I will [a]take back My
grain at [1]harvest time
And My new wine in its season.
I will also take away My wool and
My flax
Given to cover her nakedness.
10 "And then I will [a]uncover her lewd-
ness
In the sight of her lovers,
And no one will rescue her out of
My hand.
11 "I will also [a]put an end to all her
gaiety,
Her [b]feasts, her [c]new moons, her
sabbaths,
And all her festal assemblies.
12 "And I will [a]destroy her vines and
fig trees,
Of which she said, 'These are my
wages
Which my lovers have given me.'
And I will [b]make them a forest,
And the [c]beasts of the field will
devour them.

---

1 [a]Rom. 9:25 [b]2 Chr. 26:1-23; Is. 1:1; Amos 1:1 [c]2 Kin. 15:5, 7, 32-38; 2 Chr. 27:1-9 [d]2 Kin. 16:1-20; 2 Chr. 28:1-27; Is. 1:1; 7:1-17; Mic. 1:1 [e]2 Kin. 18:1-20:21; 2 Chr. 29:1-32:33; Mic. 1:1 [f]2 Kin. 13:13; 14:23-29; Amos 1:1
2 [1]Lit., *from not following after* [a]Hos. 3:1 [b]Deut. 31:16; Jer. 3:1; Ezek. 23:3-21; Hos. 2:5; 5:3
3 [a]Ezek. 23:4
4 [1]Lit., *visit the bloodshed of Jezreel on the house of Jehu* [a]Hos. 2:22 [b]2 Kin. 10:11 [c]2 Kin. 15:8-10
5 [a]Jer. 49:35; Ezek. 39:3 [b]Josh. 17:16; Judg. 6:33
6 [1]Lit., *He* [2]I.e., she has not obtained compassion [a]Hos. 2:4
7 [a]2 Kin. 19:29-35; Is. 30:18 [b]Jer. 25:5, 6; Zech. 9:9, 10 [c]Ps. 44:3-7; Zech. 4:6
9 [1]Lit., *He* [2]I.e., not my people [3]Lit., *yours*
10 [1]Ch. 2:1 in Heb. [a]Gen. 22:17; 32:12; Jer. 33:22 [b]Rom. 9:26 [c]Is. 65:1; Hos. 1:9 [d]Is. 63:16; 64:8; John 1:12; 1 Pet. 2:10
11 [a]Is. 11:12 [b]Jer. 23:5, 6; 50:4, 5; Ezek. 37:21-24 [c]Jer. 30:21; Hos. 3:5

1 [1]Ch. 2:3 in Heb. [2]I.e., my people [3]I.e., she has obtained compassion
2 [a]Ezek. 23:45; Hos. 2:5; 4:5 [b]Is. 50:1 [c]Jer. 3:1, 9, 13
3 [a]Jer. 13:22; Ezek. 16:7, 22, 39 [b]Ezek. 16:4 [c]Is. 32:13, 14; Hos. 13:15 [d]Jer. 14:3; Amos 8:11-13
4 [a]Jer. 13:14
5 [a]Is. 1:21; Jer. 2:25; 3:1, 2; Hos. 3:1 [b]Jer. 44:17, 18; Hos. 2:12 [c]Hos. 2:8
6 [1]So with some ancient versions; Heb., *your* [2]Lit., *her wall so that* [a]Job 19:8; Lam. 3:7, 9 [b]Hos. 9:6; 10:8 [c]Jer. 18:15
7 [a]Hos. 5:13 [b]Luke 15:17, 18 [c]Jer. 2:2; 3:1; Ezek. 16:8; 23:4 [d]Jer. 14:22; Hos. 13:6
8 [1]Or, *made into the* [a]Is. 1:3 [b]Ezek. 16:19
9 [1]Lit., *its time* [a]Hos. 8:7; 9:2
10 [a]Ezek. 16:37
11 [a]Jer. 7:34; 16:9 [b]Hos. 3:4; Amos 5:21; 8:10 [c]Is. 1:13, 14
12 [a]Jer. 5:17; 8:13 [b]Is. 5:5; 7:23 [c]Hos. 13:8

13"And I will punish her for the [a]days of the Baals
When she used to [1][b]offer sacrifices to them
And [c]adorn herself with her [2]earrings and jewelry,
And follow her lovers, so that she [d]forgot Me," declares the LORD.

Restoration of Israel

14"Therefore, behold, I will allure her,
[a]Bring her into the wilderness,
And speak [1]kindly to her.
15"Then I will give her her [a]vineyards from there,
And [b]the valley of Achor as a door of hope.
And she will [1][c]sing there as in the days of her youth,
As in the [d]day when she came up from the land of Egypt.
16"And it will come about in that day," declares the LORD,
"That you will call Me [1][a]Ishi
And will no longer call Me [2]Baali.
17"For [a]I will remove the names of the Baals from her mouth,
So that they will be [1]mentioned by their names no more.
18"In that day I will also make a covenant for them
With the [a]beasts of the field,
The birds of the sky,
And the creeping things of the ground.
And I will [1][b]abolish the bow, the sword, and war from the land,
And will make them [c]lie down in safety.
19"And I will [a]betroth you to Me forever;
Yes, I will betroth you to Me in [b]righteousness and in justice,
In lovingkindness and in compassion,
20 And I will betroth you to Me in faithfulness.
Then you will [a]know the LORD.

21"And it will come about in that day that [a]I will respond," declares the LORD.
"I will respond to the heavens, and they will respond to the earth,
22 And the [a]earth will respond to the grain, to the new wine, and to the oil,
And they will respond to [1]Jezreel.
23"And I will [a]sow her for Myself in the land.
[b]I will also have compassion on [1]her who had not obtained compassion,
And [c]I will say to [2]those who were [d]not My people,
'You are My people!'
And [3]they will say, '*Thou art* my God!' "

Hosea's Second Symbolic Marriage

3 THEN the LORD said to me, "Go
again, love a [1]woman *who* is loved
by *her* [2]husband, yet an adulteress, even
[a]as the LORD loves the sons of Israel,
though they turn to other gods and love
raisin [b]cakes."
2 So I [a]bought her for myself for
fifteen *shekels* of silver and a homer and
a [1]half of barley.
3 Then I said to her, "You shall [a]stay
with me for many days. You shall not
play the harlot, nor shall you have a
[1]man; so I will also be toward you."
4 For the sons of Israel will remain
for many days [a]without king or prince,
[b]without sacrifice or *sacred* [c]pillar, and
without [d]ephod or [1][e]household idols.
5 Afterward the sons of Israel will
[a]return and seek the LORD their God
and [b]David their king; and [c]they will
come trembling to the LORD and to His
goodness in the last days.

God's Controversy with Israel

4 [a]LISTEN to the word of the LORD, O sons of Israel,
For the LORD has a [b]case against the inhabitants of the land,
Because there is [c]no [1]faithfulness or [2]kindness
Or [d]knowledge of God in the land.
2 *There is* [a]swearing, [b]deception, [c]murder, [d]stealing, and [e]adultery.
They employ violence, so that [f]bloodshed [1]follows bloodshed.
3 Therefore the land [a]mourns,
And everyone who lives in it languishes
Along with the beasts of the field and the birds of the sky;
And also the fish of the sea [1]disappear.

4 Yet let no one [1][a]find fault, and let none offer reproof;
For your people are like those who [b]contend with the priest.
5 So you will [a]stumble by day,
And the prophet also will stumble with you by night;
And I will destroy your [b]mother.
6 [a]My people are destroyed for lack of knowledge.
Because you have [b]rejected knowledge,
I also will [c]reject you from being My priest.
Since you have [d]forgotten the [e]law of your God,
I also will forget your children.

7 The more they [a]multiplied, the more they sinned against Me;
I will [b]change their glory into shame.
8 They [a]feed on the [1]sin of My people,
And [b]direct their desire toward their iniquity.

13 [1]Or, *burn incense* [2]Or, *nose rings* [a]Hos. 4:13; 11:2 [b]Jer. 7:9 [c]Ezek. 16:12, 17; 23:40 [d]Hos. 4:6; 8:14; 13:6
14 [1]Lit., *upon her heart* [a]Ezek. 20:33-38
15 [1]Or, *give answer* [a]Ezek. 28:25, 26 [b]Josh. 7:26 [c]Jer. 2:1-3; Ezek. 16:8-14 [d]Hos. 11:1; 12:9, 13; 13:4
16 [1]I.e., my husband [2]I.e., my master, or my Baal [a]Is. 54:5; Hos. 2:7
17 [1]Or, *remembered* [a]Ex. 23:13; Josh. 23:7; Ps. 16:4
18 [1]Lit., *break* [a]Job 5:23; Is. 11:6-9; Ezek. 34:25 [b]Is. 2:4; Ezek. 39:1-10 [c]Lev. 26:5; Jer. 23:6; Ezek. 34:25
19 [a]Is. 62:4, 5 [b]Is. 1:27; 54:6-8
20 [a]Jer. 31:33, 34; Hos. 6:6; 13:4
21 [a]Is. 55:10; Zech. 8:12; Mal. 3:10, 11
22 [1]I.e., God sows [a]Jer. 31:12; Joel 2:19
23 [1]Heb., *Lo-ruhamah* [2]Heb., *Lo-ammi* [3]Lit., *he* [a]Jer. 31:27 [b]Hos. 1:6 [c]Rom. 9:25; 1 Pet. 2:10 [d]Hos. 1:9

1 [1]I.e., Gomer [2]Lit., *companion* [a]Jer. 3:20 [b]2 Sam. 6:19; 1 Chr. 16:3; Song 2:5
2 [1]Heb., *lethech* [a]Ruth 4:10
3 [1]Or, *husband* [a]Deut. 21:13
4 [1]Heb., *teraphim* [a]Hos. 10:3; 13:10, 11 [b]Dan. 9:27; 11:31; 12:11; Hos. 2:11 [c]Hos. 10:1, 2 [d]Ex. 28:4-12; 1 Sam. 23:9-12 [e]Gen. 31:19, 34; Judg. 17:5; 18:14, 17; 1 Sam. 15:23
5 [a]Jer. 50:4, 5 [b]Jer. 30:9; Ezek. 34:24 [c]Is. 2:2, 3; Jer. 31:9

1 [1]Or, *truth* [2]Or, *loyalty* [a]Hos. 5:1 [b]Hos. 12:2; Mic. 6:2 [c]Is. 59:4; Jer. 7:28 [d]Jer. 4:22
2 [1]Lit., *touches* [a]Deut. 5:11; Hos. 10:4 [b]Hos. 7:3; 10:13; 11:12 [c]Gen. 4:8; Hos. 6:9 [d]Deut. 5:19; Hos. 7:1 [e]Deut. 5:18; Hos. 7:4 [f]Hos. 6:8; 12:14
3 [1]Lit., *are taken away* [a]Is. 24:4; 33:9; Amos 5:16; Zeph. 1:3
4 [1]Lit., *contend* [a]Ezek. 3:26; Amos 5:10, 13 [b]Deut. 17:12
5 [a]Ezek. 14:3, 7; Hos. 5:5 [b]Jer. 15:8; Hos. 2:2, 5
6 [a]Is. 5:13 [b]Hos. 4:14; Mal. 2:7, 8 [c]Zech. 11:8, 9, 15-17 [d]Hos. 2:13; 8:14; 13:6 [e]Hos. 8:1, 12
7 [a]Hos. 10:1; 13:6 [b]Hab. 2:16
8 [1]Or, *sin offering* [a]Hos. 10:13 [b]Is. 56:11; Mic. 3:11

9 And it will be, like people, [a]like priest;
So I will [b]punish them for their ways,
And repay them for their deeds.
10 And [a]they will eat, but not have enough;
They will [b]play the harlot, but not increase,
Because they have [1c]stopped giving heed to the LORD.

11 Harlotry, [a]wine, and new wine take away the [1]understanding.
12 My people [a]consult their wooden idol, and their *diviner's* wand informs them;
For a spirit of harlotry has led *them* astray,
And they have played the harlot, *departing* [1]from their God.
13 They offer sacrifices on the [a]tops of the mountains
And [1b]burn incense on the hills,
[c]Under oak, poplar, and terebinth,
Because their shade is pleasant.
Therefore your daughters play the harlot,
And your [2]brides commit adultery.
14 I will not punish your daughters when they play the harlot
Or your [1]brides when they commit adultery,
For *the men* themselves go apart with harlots
And offer sacrifices with [a]temple prostitutes;
So the people without understanding are [2]ruined.

15 Though you, Israel, play the harlot,
Do not let Judah become guilty;
Also do not go to [a]Gilgal,
Or go up to Beth-aven,
[b]And take the oath:
"As the LORD lives!"
16 Since Israel is [a]stubborn
Like a stubborn heifer,
[1]Can the LORD now [b]pasture them
Like a lamb in a large field?
17 Ephraim is joined to [a]idols;
[b]Let him alone.
18 Their liquor gone,
They play the harlot continually;
[a]Their [1]rulers dearly love shame.
19 [a]The wind wraps them in its wings,
And they will be ashamed because of their sacrifices.

The People's Apostasy Rebuked

5 HEAR this, O priests!
Give heed, O house of Israel!
Listen, O house of the king!
For the judgment applies to you,
For you have been a [a]snare at Mizpah,
And a net spread out on Tabor.
2 And the [a]revolters have [1b]gone deep in depravity,
But I will chastise all of them.
3 I [a]know Ephraim, and Israel is not hidden from Me;
For now, O Ephraim, you have played the harlot,
Israel has defiled itself.
4 Their deeds will not allow them
To return to their God.
For a [a]spirit of harlotry is within them,
And they [b]do not know the LORD.
5 Moreover, the [a]pride of Israel testifies against him,
And Israel and Ephraim stumble in their iniquity;
[b]Judah also has stumbled with them.
6 They will [a]go with their flocks and herds
To seek the LORD, but they will [b]not find *Him*;
He has [c]withdrawn from them.
7 They have [a]dealt treacherously against the LORD,
For they have borne [1b]illegitimate children.
Now the [c]new moon will devour them with their [2]land.

8 [a]Blow the horn in [b]Gibeah,
The trumpet in Ramah.
Sound an alarm at Beth-aven:
"[c]Behind you, Benjamin!"
9 Ephraim will become a [a]desolation in the [b]day of rebuke;
Among the tribes of Israel I [c]declare what is sure.
10 The princes of Judah have become like those who [a]move a boundary;
On them I will [b]pour out My wrath [c]like water.
11 Ephraim is [a]oppressed, crushed in judgment,
[b]Because he was determined to [1]follow *man's* command.
12 Therefore I am like a [a]moth to Ephraim,
And like rottenness to the house of Judah.
13 When Ephraim saw his sickness,
And Judah his [1]wound,
Then Ephraim went to [a]Assyria
And sent to [2b]King Jareb.
But he is [c]unable to heal you,
Or to cure you of your [1]wound.
14 For I *will be* [a]like a lion to Ephraim,
And like a young lion to the house of Judah.
[b]I, even I, will tear to pieces and go away,
I will carry away, and there will be [c]none to deliver.
15 I will go away *and* return to My place
Until they [1a]acknowledge their guilt and seek My face;
In their affliction they will earnestly [b]seek Me.

9 [a]Is. 24:2; Jer. 5:31 [b]Hos. 8:13; 9:9
10 [1]Lit., *forsaken giving heed;* or, *forsaken the LORD to practice* (v. 11) *harlotry.* [a]Lev. 26:26; Is. 65:13; Mic. 6:14 [b]Hos. 7:4 [c]Hos. 9:17
11 [1]Lit., *heart* [a]Prov. 20:1; Is. 5:12; 28:7
12 [1]Lit., *from under* [a]Is. 44:19; Jer. 2:27
13 [1]Or, *offer sacrifices* [2]Or, *daughters-in-law* [a]Jer. 3:6 [b]Hos. 2:13; 11:2 [c]Is. 1:29; Jer. 2:20
14 [1]Or, *daughters-in-law* [2]Lit., *thrust down* [a]Deut. 23:17
15 [a]Hos. 9:15; 12:11 [b]Jer. 5:2; 44:26; Amos 8:14
16 [1]Or, *Now the LORD will pasture . . . field.* [a]Ps. 78:8 [b]Is. 5:17; 7:25
17 [a]Hos. 13:2 [b]Ps. 81:12; Hos. 4:4
18 [1]Lit., *shields* [a]Mic. 3:11
19 [a]Hos. 12:1; 13:15

1 [a]Hos. 9:8
2 [1]Or, *waded deep in slaughter* [a]Hos. 9:15 [b]Is. 29:15; Hos. 4:2; 6:9
3 [a]Amos 3:2; 5:12
4 [a]Hos. 4:12 [b]Hos. 4:6, 14
5 [a]Hos. 7:10 [b]Ezek. 23:31-35
6 [a]Hos. 8:13; Mic. 6:6, 7 [b]Prov. 1:28; Is. 1:15; Jer. 14:12 [c]Ezek. 8:6
7 [1]Lit., *strange* [2]Lit., *portions* [a]Is. 48:8; Jer. 3:20; Hos. 6:7 [b]Hos. 2:4 [c]Is. 1:14; Hos. 2:11
8 [a]Joel 2:1 [b]Hos. 9:9; 10:9 [c]Judg. 5:14
9 [a]Is. 28:1-4; Hos. 9:11-17 [b]Is. 37:3 [c]Is. 46:10; Zech. 1:6
10 [a]Deut. 19:14; 27:17 [b]Ezek. 7:8 [c]Ps. 32:6; 93:3, 4
11 [1]Or, with some ancient versions, *follow nothingness* [a]Deut. 28:33 [b]Mic. 6:16
12 [a]Ps. 39:11; Is. 51:8
13 [1]Or, *ulcer* [2]Or, *the avenging king* or *the great king* [a]Hos. 7:11; 8:9; 12:1 [b]Hos. 10:6 [c]Jer. 30:12-15
14 [a]Ps. 7:2; Hos. 13:7, 8; Amos 3:4 [b]Ps. 50:22 [c]Mic. 5:8
15 [1]Or, *bear their punishment* [a]Is. 64:7-9; Jer. 3:13, 14 [b]Ps. 50:15; 78:34; Jer. 2:27; Hos. 3:5

The Response to God's Rebuke

6 "[a]COME, let us return to the LORD.
For [b]He has torn *us,* but [c]He will heal us;
He has [1]wounded *us,* but He will [d]bandage us.
2 "He will [a]revive us after two days;
He will [b]raise us up on the third day
That we may live before Him.
3 "So let us [a]know, let us press on to know the LORD.
His [b]going forth is as certain as the dawn;
And He will come to us like the [c]rain,
Like the spring rain watering the earth."

4 What shall I do with you, O [a]Ephraim?
What shall I do with you, O Judah?
For your [1]loyalty is like a [b]morning cloud,
And like the dew which goes away early.
5 Therefore I have [a]hewn *them* in pieces by the prophets;
I have slain them by the [b]words of My mouth;
And the judgments on you are *like* the light that goes forth.
6 For [a]I delight in loyalty [b]rather than sacrifice,
And in the knowledge of God rather than burnt offerings.
7 But [a]like [1]Adam they have [b]transgressed the covenant;
There they have [c]dealt treacherously against Me.
8 [a]Gilead is a city of wrongdoers,
Tracked with [b]bloody *footprints.*
9 And as [a]raiders wait for a man,
So a band of priests [b]murder on the way to Shechem;
Surely they have committed [1c]crime.
10 In the house of Israel I have seen a [a]horrible thing;
Ephraim's [b]harlotry is there, Israel has defiled itself.
11 Also, O Judah, there is a [a]harvest appointed for you,
When I [b]restore the fortunes of My people.

Ephraim's Iniquity

7 WHEN I [a]would heal Israel, The iniquity of Ephraim is uncovered,
And the evil deeds of Samaria,
For they deal [b]falsely;
The thief enters in,
[c]Bandits raid outside,
2 And they do not [1]consider in their hearts
That I [a]remember all their wickedness.
Now their [b]deeds are all around them;
They are before My face.
3 [a]With their wickedness they make the [b]king glad,
And the princes with their [c]lies.
4 They are [a]all adulterers
Like an oven heated by the baker,
Who ceases to stir up *the fire*
From the kneading of the dough until it is leavened.
5 On the [1]day of our king, the princes [a]became sick with the heat of wine;
He stretched out his hand with [b]scoffers,
6 For their hearts are like an [a]oven
As they approach their [1]plotting;
Their [2]anger [3]smolders all night,
In the morning it burns like a flaming fire.
7 All of them are hot like an oven,
And they consume their [a]rulers;
All their kings have fallen.
[b]None of them calls on Me.

8 Ephraim [a]mixes himself with the [1]nations;
Ephraim has become a cake not turned.
9 [a]Strangers devour his strength,
Yet he [b]does not know *it;*
Gray hairs also are sprinkled on him,
Yet he does not know *it.*
10 Though the [a]pride of Israel testifies against him,
Yet [b]they have neither returned to the LORD their God,
Nor have they sought Him, for all this.
11 So [a]Ephraim has become like a silly dove, [b]without [1]sense;
They call to [c]Egypt, they go to [d]Assyria.
12 When they go, I will [a]spread My net over them;
I will bring them down like the birds of the sky.
I will [b]chastise them in accordance with the [1]proclamation to their assembly.
13 [a]Woe to them, for they have [b]strayed from Me!
Destruction is theirs, for they have rebelled against Me!
I [c]would redeem them, but they speak lies against Me.
14 And [a]they do not cry to Me from their heart
When they wail on their beds;
For the sake of grain and new wine they [1b]assemble themselves,
They [c]turn away from Me.
15 Although I trained *and* strengthened their arms,
Yet they [a]devise evil against Me.
16 They turn, *but* not [1]upward,
They are like a [a]deceitful bow;
Their princes will fall by the sword
Because of the [2b]insolence of their tongue.
This *will be* their [c]derision in the land of Egypt.

1 [1]Lit., *struck* [a]Jer. 50:4, 5 [b]Deut. 32:39; Hos. 5:14 [c]Jer. 30:17; Hos. 14:4 [d]Is. 30:26
2 [a]Ps. 30:5 [b]1 Cor. 15:4
3 [a]Is. 2:3; Mic. 4:2 [b]Ps. 19:6; Mic. 5:2 [c]Job 29:23; Ps. 72:6; Joel 2:23
4 [1]Or, *lovingkindness* [a]Hos. 7:1; 11:8 [b]Ps. 78:34-37; Hos. 13:3
5 [a]1 Sam. 15:32, 33; Jer. 1:10; 5:14 [b]Jer. 23:29
6 [a]Matt. 9:13; 12:7 [b]Is. 1:11
7 [1]Or, *men* [a]Job 31:33 [b]Hos. 8:1 [c]Hos. 5:7
8 [a]Hos. 12:11 [b]Hos. 4:2
9 [1]Or, *lewdness* [a]Hos. 7:1 [b]Jer. 7:9, 10; Hos. 4:2 [c]Ezek. 22:9; 23:27; Hos. 2:10
10 [a]Jer. 5:30, 31; 23:14 [b]Hos. 5:3
11 [a]Jer. 51:33; Joel 3:13 [b]Zeph. 2:7

1 [a]Ezek. 24:13; Hos. 6:4; 7:13; 11:8 [b]Hos. 4:2 [c]Hos. 6:9
2 [1]Lit., *say to their heart* [a]Ps. 25:7; Jer. 14:10; 17:1; Hos. 8:13; 9:9; Amos 8:7 [b]Jer. 2:19; 4:18; Hos. 4:9
3 [a]Rom. 1:32 [b]Jer. 28:1-4; Hos. 7:5; Mic. 7:3 [c]Hos. 4:2; 11:12
4 [a]Jer. 9:2; 23:10
5 [1]I.e., a festive occasion [a]Is. 28:1, 7 [b]Is. 28:14
6 [1]Lit., *ambush* [2]So with some ancient versions; M.T., *baker* [3]Lit., *sleeps* [a]Ps. 21:9
7 [a]Hos. 13:10 [b]Is. 64:7
8 [1]Lit., *peoples* [a]Ps. 106:35
9 [a]Is. 1:7; Hos. 8:7 [b]Hos. 4:6
10 [a]Hos. 5:5 [b]Is. 9:13
11 [1]Lit., *heart* [a]Hos. 11:11 [b]Hos. 4:6, 11, 14; 5:4 [c]Hos. 8:13; 9:3, 6 [d]Hos. 5:13; 8:9; 12:1
12 [1]Lit., *report* [a]Ezek. 12:13 [b]Lev. 26:14-39; Deut. 28:15
13 [a]Hos. 9:12 [b]Jer. 14:10; Ezek. 34:6; Hos. 9:17 [c]Jer. 51:9; Hos. 7:1; Matt. 23:37
14 [1]Or, with Gr. and many ancient mss., *gash themselves* [a]Job 35:9-11; Hos. 8:2; Zech. 7:5 [b]Judg. 9:27; Amos 2:8; Mic. 2:11 [c]Hos. 13:16
15 [a]Nah. 1:9
16 [1]Or possibly, *to the Most High* [2]Lit., *indignation;* or, *cursing* [a]Ps. 78:57 [b]Ps. 12:3, 4; 17:10; 73:9; Dan. 7:25; Mal. 3:13, 14 [c]Ezek. 23:32; Hos. 9:3, 6

Israel Reaps the Whirlwind

8 [a]PUT the trumpet to your [1]lips!
[b]Like an eagle *the enemy comes* [c]against the house of the LORD,
Because they have [d]transgressed My covenant,
And rebelled against My [e]law.
2 [a]They cry out to Me,
"My God, [b]we of Israel know Thee!"
3 Israel has rejected the good;
The enemy will pursue him.
4 [a]They have set up kings, but not by Me;
They have appointed princes, but I did not know *it.*
With their [b]silver and gold they have made idols for themselves,
That [1]they might be cut off.
5 [1]He has rejected your [a]calf, O Samaria, saying,
"My anger burns against them!"
How long will they be incapable of [b]innocence?
6 For from Israel is even this!
A [a]craftsman made it, so it is not God;
Surely the calf of Samaria will be broken to [1]pieces.
7 For [a]they sow the wind,
And they reap the [b]whirlwind.
The standing grain has no [1]heads;
It yields [c]no [2]grain.
Should it yield, strangers would swallow it up.

8 Israel is [a]swallowed up;
They are now among the nations
Like a [b]vessel in which no one delights.
9 For they have gone up to [a]Assyria,
Like [b]a wild donkey all alone;
Ephraim has [c]hired [1]lovers.
10 Even though they hire *allies* among the nations,
Now I will [a]gather them up;
And they will begin [b]to [1]diminish
Because of the burden of the [c]king of princes.

11 Since Ephraim has [a]multiplied altars for sin,
They have become altars of sinning for him.
12 Though [a]I wrote for him ten thousand *precepts* of My [b]law,
They are regarded as a strange thing.
13 As for My [a]sacrificial gifts,
They [b]sacrifice the flesh and eat *it,*
But the LORD has taken no delight in them.
Now He will [c]remember their iniquity,
And [d]punish *them* for their sins;
They will return to [e]Egypt.
14 For Israel has [a]forgotten his Maker and [b]built palaces;
And Judah has multiplied fortified cities,
But I will send a [c]fire on its cities that it may consume its palatial dwellings.

Ephraim Punished

9 [a]DO not rejoice, O Israel, [1]with exultation like the [2]nations!
For you have [b]played the harlot, [3]forsaking your God.
You have loved *harlots'* earnings on [4]every threshing floor.
2 Threshing floor and wine press will [a]not feed them,
And the new wine will fail [1]them.
3 They will not remain in [a]the LORD's land,
But Ephraim will return to [b]Egypt,
And in [c]Assyria they will eat [d]unclean *food.*
4 They will not pour out libations of [a]wine to the LORD,
[b]Their sacrifices will not please Him.
Their bread will [1]*be* like [2]mourners' bread;
All who eat of it will be [c]defiled,
For their bread will be for [3]themselves *alone*;
It will not enter the house of the LORD.
5 [a]What will you do on the day of the appointed festival
And on the day of the [b]feast of the LORD?
6 For behold, they will go because of destruction;
Egypt will gather them up, [a]Memphis will bury them.
Weeds will take over their treasures of silver;
[b]Thorns *will be* in their tents.

7 The days of [a]punishment have come,
The days of [b]retribution have come;
[1]Let Israel know *this*!
The prophet is a [c]fool,
The [2]inspired man is [d]demented,
Because of the grossness of your [e]iniquity,
And *because* your hostility is *so* great.
8 Ephraim *was* a watchman with my God, a prophet;
Yet the snare of a bird catcher is in all his ways,
And there is *only* hostility in the house of his God.
9 They have gone [a]deep [1]in depravity
As in the days of [b]Gibeah;
He will [c]remember their iniquity,
He will punish their sins.

10 I found Israel like [a]grapes in the wilderness;
I saw your forefathers as the [b]earliest fruit on the fig tree in its first *season.*
But they came to [c]Baal-peor and devoted themselves to [1][d]shame,
And they became as [e]detestable as that which they loved.

---

1 [1]Lit., *palate* [a]Jer 4:13; Hos. 5:8 [b]Hab. 1:8 [c]Deut. 28:49 [d]Hos. 6:7 [e]Hos. 4:6
2 [a]Ps. 78:34; Hos. 7:14 [b]Titus 1:16
4 [1]Lit., *he* [a]2 Kin. 15:13, 17, 25; Hos. 13:10, 11 [b]Hos. 2:8; 13:1, 2
5 [1]Or, *Your calf has rejected you* [a]Hos. 10:5; 13:2 [b]Ps. 19:13; Jer. 13:27
6 [1]Or, *splinters* [a]Hos. 13:2
7 [1]Lit., *growth* [2]Or, *meal* [a]Prov. 22:8 [b]Is. 66:15; Nah. 1:3 [c]Hos. 2:9
8 [a]2 Kin. 17:6; Jer. 51:34 [b]Jer. 22:28; 25:34
9 [1]Lit., *loves* [a]Hos. 7:11 [b]Jer. 2:24 [c]Ezek. 16:33, 34
10 [1]Or, *suffer for awhile* [a]Ezek. 16:37; 22:20 [b]Jer. 42:2 [c]Is. 10:8
11 [a]Hos. 10:1
12 [a]Deut. 4:6, 8 [b]Hos. 4:6
13 [a]Hos. 5:6 [b]Jer. 6:20; 7:21 [c]Jer. 14:10; Hos. 7:2; Luke 12:2; 1 Cor. 4:5 [d]Hos. 4:9; 9:7 [e]Hos. 9:3, 6
14 [a]Deut. 32:18; Hos. 2:13; 4:6; 13:6 [b]Is. 9:9, 10 [c]Jer.

1 [1]Lit., *to* [2]Lit., *peoples* [3]Lit., *away from your God* [4]Lit., *all threshing floors of grain* [a]Is. 22:12, 13; Hos. 10:5 [b]Hos. 4:12
2 [1]Lit., *her* [a]Hos. 2:9
3 [a]Lev. 25:23; Jer. 2:7 [b]Hos. 7:16; 8:13 [c]Hos. 7:11 [d]Ezek. 4:13
4 [1]Lit., *be to them* [2]Or, *bread of misfortune* [3]Lit., *their appetite* [a]Ex. 29:40 [b]Jer. 6:20; Hos. 8:13 [c]Hag. 2:13, 14
5 [a]Is. 10:3; Jer. 5:31 [b]Hos. 2:11; Joel 1:13
6 [a]Is. 19:13; Jer. 2:16; 44:1; 46:14, 19; Ezek. 30:13, 16 [b]Is. 5:6; 7:23; Hos. 10:8
7 [1]Or, *Israel will know it* [2]Lit., *man of the spirit* [a]Is. 10:3; Jer. 10:15; Mic. 7:4; Luke 21:22 [b]Is. 34:8; Jer. 16:18; 25:14 [c]Lam. 2:14; Ezek. 13:3, 10 [d]Is. 44:25 [e]Ezek. 14:9, 10
9 [1]Lit., *they have corrupted* [a]Is. 31:6 [b]Judg. 19:12, 16-30; Hos. 10:9 [c]Hos. 7:2; 8:13
10 [1]I.e., Baal [a]Mic. 7:1 [b]Jer. 24:2 [c]Num. 25:1-5; Ps. 106:28, 29 [d]Jer. 11:13; Hos. 4:18 [e]Ps. 115:8; Ezek. 20:8

11 As for Ephraim, their [a]glory will fly away like a bird—
No birth, no pregnancy, and no conception!
12 Though they bring up their children,
Yet I will bereave them [1]until not a man is left.
Yes, [a]woe to them indeed when I depart from them!
13 Ephraim, as I have seen,
Is planted in a pleasant meadow like [a]Tyre;
But Ephraim will bring out his children for slaughter.
14 Give them, O LORD—what wilt Thou give?
Give them a [a]miscarrying womb and dry breasts.

15 All their evil is at [a]Gilgal;
Indeed, I came to hate them there!
Because of the [b]wickedness of their deeds
I will drive them out of My house!
I will love them no more;
All their princes are [c]rebels.
16 [a]Ephraim is stricken, their root is dried up,
They will bear [b]no fruit.
Even though they bear children,
I will slay the [c]precious ones of their womb.
17 My God will cast them away
Because they have [a]not listened to Him;
And they will be [b]wanderers among the nations.

Retribution for Israel's Sin

10 ISRAEL is a [1]luxuriant [a]vine;
He produces fruit for himself.
The more his fruit,
The more altars he [b]made;
The [2]richer his land,
The better [3]he made the *sacred* [c]pillars.
2 Their heart is [1a]faithless;
Now they must bear their [b]guilt.
[2]The LORD will [c]break down their altars
And destroy their *sacred* pillars.

3 Surely now they will say, "We have [a]no king,
For we do not revere the LORD.
As for the king, what can he do for us?"
4 They speak *mere* words,
[1]With [a]worthless oaths they make covenants;
And [b]judgment sprouts like poisonous weeds in the furrows of the field.
5 The inhabitants of Samaria will fear
For the [1a]calf of [b]Beth-aven.
Indeed, its people will mourn for it,
And its [c]idolatrous priests [2]will cry out over it,
Over its [d]glory, since it has departed from it.

11 [a]Hos. 4:7; 10:5
12 [1]Lit., *without a man* [a]Deut. 31:17; Hos. 7:13
13 [a]Ezek. 26:1-21
14 [a]Hos. 9:11
15 [a]Hos. 4:15; 12:11 [b]Hos. 4:9; 7:2; 12:2 [c]Is. 1:23; Hos. 5:2
16 [a]Hos. 5:11 [b]Hos. 8:7 [c]Ezek. 24:21
17 [a]Hos. 4:10 [b]Hos. 7:13
1 [1]Or, *degenerate* [2]Or, *better* [3]Lit., *they* [a]Is. 5:1-7; Ezek. 15:1-6 [b]Jer. 2:28; Hos. 8:11; 12:11 [c]1 Kin. 14:23; Hos. 3:4
2 [1]Lit., *smooth* [2]Lit., *He* [a]1 Kin. 18:21; Zeph. 1:5 [b]Hos. 13:16 [c]Hos. 10:8; Mic. 5:13
3 [a]Ps. 12:4; Is. 5:19
4 [1]Or, *Swearing falsely in making a covenant* [a]Ezek. 17:13-19; Hos. 4:2 [b]Deut. 31:16, 17; 2 Kin. 17:3, 4; Amos 5:7
5 [1]So with some ancient versions; Heb., *calves* [2]Or, who *used to rejoice over* [a]Hos. 8:5, 6 [b]Hos. 4:15; 5:8 [c]2 Kin. 23:5 [d]Hos. 9:11
6 [1]Or, *the avenging king* or *the great king* [2]Lit., *receive shame* [a]Hos. 11:5 [b]Hos. 5:13 [c]Hos. 4:7 [d]Is. 30:3; Jer. 7:24
7 [a]Hos. 13:11
8 [a]Hos. 4:13 [b]1 Kin. 12:28-30; 13:34 [c]Is. 32:13; Hos. 9:6; 10:2 [d]Is. 2:19; Luke 23:30; Rev. 6:16
10 [1]Or, *bind* [a]Ezek. 5:13 [b]Hos. 4:9 [c]Jer. 16:16
11 [a]Jer. 50:11; Hos. 4:16; Mic. 4:13 [b]Jer. 28:14
12 [1]Or, *loyalty* [2]Or, *teach* [a]Prov. 11:18 [b]Jer. 4:3 [c]Hos. 12:6 [d]Hos. 6:3 [e]Is. 44:3; 45:8
13 [a]Job 4:8; Prov. 22:8; Gal. 6:7, 8 [b]Hos. 4:2; 7:3; 11:12 [c]Ps. 33:16
14 [a]Is. 17:3 [b]Hos. 13:16
1 [a]Hos. 2:15; 12:9, 13; 13:4 [b]Ex. 4:22, 23; Matt. 2:15

6 The thing itself will be carried to [a]Assyria
As tribute to [1b]King Jareb;
Ephraim will [2]be [c]seized with shame,
And Israel will be ashamed of its [d]own counsel.
7 Samaria will be [a]cut off *with* her king,
Like a stick on the surface of the water.
8 Also the [a]high places of Aven, the [b]sin of Israel, will be destroyed;
[c]Thorn and thistle will grow on their altars,
Then they will [d]say to the mountains,
"Cover us!" And to the hills, "Fall on us!"
9 From the days of Gibeah you have sinned, O Israel;
There they stand!
Will not the battle against the sons of iniquity overtake them in Gibeah?
10 When it is My [a]desire, I will [1b]chastise them;
And [c]the peoples will be gathered against them
When they are bound for their double guilt.

11 And Ephraim is a trained [a]heifer that loves to thresh,
But I will [b]come over her fair neck *with a yoke*;
I will harness Ephraim,
Judah will plow, Jacob will harrow for himself.
12 [a]Sow with a view to righteousness,
Reap in accordance with [1]kindness;
[b]Break up your fallow ground,
For it is time to [c]seek the LORD
Until He [d]comes to [2e]rain righteousness on you.
13 You have [a]plowed wickedness, you have reaped injustice,
You have eaten the fruit of [b]lies.
Because you have trusted in your way, in your [c]numerous warriors,
14 Therefore, a tumult will arise among your people,
And all your [a]fortresses will be destroyed,
As Shalman destroyed Beth-arbel on the day of battle,
When [b]mothers were dashed in pieces with *their* children.
15 Thus it will be done to you at Bethel because of your great wickedness.
At dawn the king of Israel will be completely cut off.

God Yearns over His People

11 WHEN Israel *was* a youth I loved him,
And [a]out of Egypt I [b]called My son.

2 The more [1a]they called them,
The more they went from [1]them;
They kept [b]sacrificing to the Baals
And [c]burning incense to idols.
3 Yet it is I who taught Ephraim to walk,
[1]I [a]took them in My arms;
But they did not know that I [b]healed them.
4 I [a]led them with cords of a man, with bonds of love,
And [b]I became to them as one who lifts the yoke from their jaws;
And I bent down *and* [c]fed them.

5 [1]They will not return to the land of Egypt;
But Assyria—he will be [2]their king,
Because they [a]refused to return *to Me.*
6 And the [a]sword will whirl against [1]their cities,
And will demolish [1]their gate bars
And [b]consume *them* because of their [c]counsels.
7 So My people are bent on [a]turning from Me.
Though [1]they call [2]them to *the One* on high,
None at all exalts *Him.*

8 [a]How can I give you up, O Ephraim?
How can I surrender you, O Israel?
How can I [1]make you like [b]Admah?
How can I treat you like [b]Zeboiim?
My heart is turned over within Me,
[2]All my compassions are kindled.
9 I will [a]not execute My fierce anger;
I will not destroy Ephraim [b]again.
For [c]I am God and not man, the [d]Holy One in your midst,
And I will not come in [1]wrath.
10 They will [a]walk after the LORD,
He will [b]roar like a lion;
Indeed He will roar,
And *His* sons will come [c]trembling from the west.
11 They will come trembling like birds from [a]Egypt,
And like [b]doves from the land of [a]Assyria;
And I will [c]settle them in their houses, declares the LORD.

12 [1]Ephraim surrounds Me with [a]lies,
And the house of Israel with deceit;
Judah is also unruly against God,
Even against the Holy One who is faithful.

Ephraim Reminded

12 [1]EPHRAIM feeds on [a]wind,
And pursues the [b]east wind continually;
He multiplies lies and violence.
Moreover, [2]he makes a covenant with Assyria,
And oil is carried to Egypt.
2 The LORD also has a [a]dispute with Judah,
And will punish Jacob [b]according to his ways;

2 [1]I.e., God's prophets
[a]2 Kin. 17:13-15 [b]Hos. 2:13; 4:13 [c]Is. 65:7; Jer. 18:15
3 [1]So ancient versions; Heb., *He . . . His*
[a]Deut. 1:31; 32:10, 11 [b]Ps. 107:20; Jer. 30:17
4 [a]Jer. 31:2, 3 [b]Lev. 26:13 [c]Ex. 16:32; Ps. 78:25
5 [1]Lit., *He* [2]Lit., *his*
[a]Hos. 7:16
6 [1]Lit., *his*
[a]Hos. 13:16 [b]Lam. 2:9 [c]Hos. 4:16, 17
7 [1]I.e., God's prophets [2]Lit., *him;* i.e., Israel
[a]Jer. 3:6, 7; 8:5
8 [1]Lit., *give* [2]Lit., *Together*
[a]Hos. 6:4; 7:1 [b]Gen. 14:8; Deut. 29:23
9 [1]Lit., *excitement*
[a]Deut. 13:17 [b]Jer. 26:3; 30:11 [c]Num. 23:19 [d]Is. 5:24; 12:6; 41:14, 16
10 [a]Hos. 3:5; 6:1-3 [b]Is. 31:4; Joel 3:16; Amos 1:2 [c]Is. 66:2, 5
11 [a]Is. 11:11 [b]Is. 60:8; Hos. 7:11 [c]Ezek. 28:25, 26; 34:27, 28
12 [1]Ch. 12:1 in Heb.
[a]Hos. 4:2; 7:3

1 [1]Ch. 12:2 in Heb. [2]Lit., *they make*
[a]Jer. 22:22 [b]Gen. 41:6; Ezek. 17:10
2 [a]Hos. 4:1; Mic. 6:2 [b]Hos. 4:9; 7:2
3 [a]Gen. 25:26 [b]Gen. 32:28
4 [a]Gen. 32:26 [b]Gen. 28:13-19; 35:10-15
5 [1]Lit., *memorial*
[a]Ex. 3:15
6 [1]Or, *loyalty*
[a]Hos. 6:1-3; 10:12 [b]Mic. 6:8 [c]Mic. 7:7
7 [1]Or, *Canaanite*
[a]Prov. 11:1; Amos 8:5; Mic. 6:11
8 [a]Ps. 62:10; Hos. 13:6; Rev. 3:17 [b]Hos. 4:8; 14:1
9 [a]Lev. 23:42
10 [1]Lit., *multiplied the vision*
[a]2 Kin. 17:13; Jer. 7:25 [b]Ezek. 17:2; 20:49
11 [a]Hos. 8:11; 10:1, 2
12 [1]Lit., *field*
[a]Gen. 28:5 [b]Gen. 29:20
13 [a]Ex. 14:19-22; Is. 63:11-14
14 [a]2 Kin. 17:7-18 [b]Ezek. 18:10-13 [c]Dan. 11:18; Mic. 6:16

1 [1]Or, *spoke with trembling* [2]Or, *became guilty*
[a]Job 29:21, 22 [b]Judg. 8:1; 12:1 [c]Hos. 2:8-17; 11:2

He will repay him according to his deeds.
3 In the womb he [a]took his brother by the heel,
And in his maturity he [b]contended with God.
4 Yes, he wrestled with the angel and prevailed;
He wept and [a]sought His favor.
He found Him at [b]Bethel,
And there He spoke with us,
5 Even the LORD, the God of hosts;
The LORD is His [1a]name.
6 Therefore, [a]return to your God,
[b]Observe [1]kindness and justice,
And [c]wait for your God continually.
7 A [1]merchant, in whose hands are false [a]balances,
He loves to oppress.
8 And Ephraim said, "Surely I have become [a]rich,
I have found wealth for myself;
In all my labors they will find in me
[b]No iniquity, which *would be* sin."
9 But I *have been* the LORD your God since the land of Egypt;
I will make you [a]live in tents again,
As in the days of the appointed festival.
10 I have also spoken to the [a]prophets,
And I [1]gave numerous visions;
And through the prophets I gave [b]parables.
11 Is there iniquity *in* Gilead?
Surely they are worthless.
In Gilgal they sacrifice bulls,
Yes, [a]their altars are like the stone heaps
Beside the furrows of the field.

12 Now [a]Jacob fled to the [1]land of Aram,
And [b]Israel worked for a wife,
And for a wife he kept *sheep.*
13 But by a [a]prophet the LORD brought Israel from Egypt,
And by a prophet he was kept.
14 [a]Ephraim has provoked to bitter anger;
So his Lord will leave his [b]bloodguilt on him,
And bring back his [c]reproach to him.

Ephraim's Idolatry

13 [a]WHEN Ephraim [1]spoke, *there was* trembling.
He [b]exalted himself in Israel,
But through [c]Baal he [2]did wrong and died.
2 And now they sin more and more,
And make for themselves [a]molten images,
Idols [1b]skillfully made from their silver,
All of them the [c]work of craftsmen.
They say of them, "Let the [2]men who sacrifice kiss the [d]calves!"

2 [1]Or, *according to their own understanding* [2]Lit., *sacrificers of* (or, *among*) *mankind* [a]Is. 46:6; Jer. 10:4; Hos. 2:8 [b]Is. 44:17-20 [c]Hos. 8:6 [d]Hos. 8:5, 6; 10:5

3 Therefore, they will be like the [a]morning cloud,
And like dew which [1]soon disappears,
Like [b]chaff which is blown away from the threshing floor,
And like [c]smoke from a [2]chimney.

4 Yet I *have been* the [a]LORD your God
Since the land of Egypt;
And you were not to know [b]any god except Me,
For there is no savior [c]besides Me.
5 I [1a]cared for you in the wilderness,
[b]In the land of drought.
6 As *they had* their pasture, they became [a]satisfied,
And being satisfied, their [b]heart became proud;
Therefore, they [c]forgot Me.
7 So I will be [a]like a lion to them;
Like a [b]leopard I will [1]lie in wait by the wayside.
8 I will encounter them [a]like a bear robbed of her cubs,
And I will tear open [1]their chests;
There I will also [b]devour them like a lioness,
As a wild beast would tear them.

9 *It is* your destruction, O Israel,
[1]That *you are* [a]against Me, against your [b]help.
10 Where now is your [a]king
That he may save you in all your cities,
And your [b]judges of whom you [1]requested,
"Give me a king and princes"?
11 I [a]gave you a king in My anger,
And [b]took him away in My wrath.

12 The iniquity of Ephraim is bound up;
His sin is [a]stored up.
13 The pains of [a]childbirth come upon him;
He is [b]not a wise son,
For [1]it is not the time that he should [c]delay at the opening of the womb.
14 Shall I [a]ransom them from the [1]power of Sheol?
Shall I redeem them from death?
[b]O Death, where are your thorns?
O Sheol, where is your sting?
[c]Compassion will be hidden from My sight.

15 Though he [a]flourishes among the [1]reeds,
An [b]east wind will come,
The wind of the LORD coming up from the wilderness;
And his fountain will [c]become dry,
And his spring will be dried up;
It will [d]plunder *his* treasury of every precious article.

3 [1]Lit., *goes away early* [2]Lit., *window* [a]Hos. 6:4 [b]Ps. 1:4; Is. 17:13; Dan. 2:35 [c]Ps. 68:2
4 [a]Hos. 12:9 [b]Ex. 20:3; 2 Kin. 18:35 [c]Is. 43:11; 45:21, 22
5 [1]Or, *knew* [a]Deut. 2:7; 32:10 [b]Deut. 8:15
6 [a]Deut. 8:12, 14; 32:13-15; Jer. 5:7 [b]Hos. 7:14 [c]Hos. 2:13; 4:6; 8:14
7 [1]Or, *watch* [a]Lam. 3:10; Hos. 5:14 [b]Jer. 5:6
8 [1]Lit., *the enclosure of their heart* [a]2 Sam. 17:8 [b]Ps. 50:22
9 [1]Or, *But in Me is your help* [a]Jer. 2:17, 19; Mal. 1:12, 13 [b]Deut. 33:26, 29
10 [1]Lit., *said* [a]2 Kin. 17:4; Hos. 8:4 [b]1 Sam. 8:5, 6
11 [a]1 Sam. 8:7; 10:17-24 [b]1 Sam. 15:26; 1 Kin. 14:7-10; Hos. 10:7
12 [a]Deut. 32:34, 35; Job 14:17; Rom. 2:5
13 [1]Lit., *it is the time that he should not tarry at the breaking forth of children* [a]Is. 13:8; Mic. 4:9, 10 [b]Deut. 32:6; Hos. 5:4 [c]Is. 37:3; 66:9
14 [1]Lit., *hand* [a]Ps. 49:15; Ezek. 37:12, 13 [b]1 Cor. 15:55 [c]Jer. 20:16; 31:35-37
15 [1]Or, *brothers* [a]Gen. 49:22; Hos. 10:1 [b]Gen. 41:6; Jer. 4:11, 12; Ezek. 17:10; 19:12 [c]Jer. 51:36 [d]Jer. 20:5
16 [1]Ch. 14:1 in Heb. [a]Hos. 10:2 [b]Hos. 7:14 [c]2 Kin. 8:12 [d]Hos. 11:6 [e]Hos. 10:14 [f]2 Kin. 15:16

1 [1]Ch. 14:2 in Heb. [2]Or, *in* [a]Hos. 6:1; 10:12; 12:6; Joel 2:13 [b]Hos. 4:8; 5:5; 9:7
2 [1]Or, *accept that which is good* [2]So with ancient versions; M.T., *our lips as bulls* [a]Mic. 7:18, 19 [b]Ps. 51:16, 17; Hos. 6:6; Heb. 13:15
3 [1]Or, *fatherless* [a]Ps. 33:17; Is. 31:1 [b]Hos. 8:6; 13:2 [c]Hos. 4:12 [d]Ps. 10:14; 68:5
4 [a]Is. 57:18; Hos. 6:1 [b]Zeph. 3:17 [c]Is. 12:1
5 [1]Lit., *strike his roots* [a]Prov. 19:12; Is. 26:19 [b]Song 2:1; Matt. 6:28 [c]Is. 35:2

16 [1]Samaria will be held [a]guilty,
For she has [b]rebelled against her God.
[c]They will fall by the [d]sword,
Their little ones will be [e]dashed in pieces,
And their pregnant [f]women will be ripped open.

[1a]*Israel's Future Blessing*

14 RETURN, O Israel, to the LORD your God,
For you have stumbled [2]because of your [b]iniquity.
2 Take words with you and return to the LORD.
Say to Him, "[a]Take away all iniquity,
And [1]receive *us* graciously,
That we may [b]present [2]the fruit of our lips.
3 "Assyria will not save us,
We will [a]not ride on horses;
Nor will we say again, '[b]Our god,'
To the [c]work of our hands;
For in [d]Thee the [1]orphan finds mercy."

4 I will [a]heal their apostasy,
I will [b]love them freely,
For My anger has [c]turned away from them.
5 I will be like the [a]dew to Israel;
He will blossom like the [b]lily,
And he will [1]take root like *the cedars of* [c]Lebanon.
6 His shoots will [1]sprout,
And his [2]beauty will be like the [a]olive tree,
And his fragrance like *the cedars of* [b]Lebanon.
7 Those who [a]live in his shadow
Will [1]again raise [b]grain,
And they will blossom like the vine.
His renown *will be* like the wine of Lebanon.

8 O Ephraim, what more have I to do with [a]idols?
It is I who answer and look after [1]you.
I am like a luxuriant [b]cypress;
From [c]Me comes your fruit.

9 [a]Whoever is wise, let him understand these things;
Whoever is discerning, let him know them.
For the [b]ways of the LORD are right,
And the [c]righteous will walk in them,
But [d]transgressors will stumble in them.

6 [1]Lit., *go* [2]Or, *splendor* [a]Jer. 11:16 [b]Song 4:11
7 [1]Or, *return, they will raise grain* [a]Ezek. 17:23 [b]Hos. 2:21, 22
8 [1]Lit., *him* [a]Job 34:32; Hos. 14:3 [b]Is. 41:19 [c]Ezek. 17:23
9 [a]Ps. 107:43; Jer. 9:12 [b]Ps. 111:7, 8; Prov. 10:29; Zeph. 3:5 [c]Is. 26:7 [d]Is. 1:28

THE BOOK OF
JOEL

The Devastation of Locusts

1 THE [a]word of the LORD that came to [b]Joel, the son of Pethuel.
2 [a]Hear this, O [b]elders,
And listen, all inhabitants of the land.
[c]Has *anything like* this happened in your days
Or in your fathers' days?
3 [a]Tell your sons about it,
And *let* your sons *tell* their sons,
And their sons the next generation.

4 What the [a]gnawing locust has left, the swarming locust has eaten;
And what the [b]swarming locust has left, the creeping locust has eaten;
And what the creeping locust has left, the [c]stripping locust has eaten.
5 Awake, [a]drunkards, and weep;
And wail, all you wine drinkers,
On account of the sweet wine
That is [b]cut off from your mouth.
6 For a [a]nation has [1]invaded my land,
Mighty and without number;
[b]Its teeth are the teeth of a lion,
And it has the fangs of a lioness.
7 It has [a]made my vine a waste,
And my fig tree [1]splinters.
It has stripped them bare and cast *them* away;
Their branches have become white.

8 [a]Wail like a virgin [b]girded with sackcloth
For the bridegroom of her youth.
9 The [a]grain offering and the libation are cut off
From the house of the LORD.
The [b]priests mourn,
The ministers of the LORD.
10 The field is [a]ruined,
[b]The land mourns,
For the grain is ruined,
The new wine dries up,
Fresh oil [1]fails.
11 [1a]Be ashamed, O farmers,
Wail, O vinedressers,
For the wheat and the barley;
Because the [b]harvest of the field is destroyed.
12 The [a]vine dries up,
And the fig tree [1]fails;
The [b]pomegranate, the [c]palm also, and the [2d]apple tree,
All the trees of the field dry up.
Indeed, [e]rejoicing dries up
From the sons of men.

13 [a]Gird yourselves *with sackcloth*,
And lament, O priests;
[b]Wail, O ministers of the altar!
Come, [c]spend the night in sackcloth,
O ministers of my God,
For the grain offering and the libation
Are withheld from the house of your God.

Starvation and Drought

14 [a]Consecrate a fast,
Proclaim a [b]solemn assembly;
Gather the elders
And all the inhabitants of the land
To the house of the LORD your God,
And [c]cry out to the LORD.
15 [a]Alas for the day!
For the [b]day of the LORD is near,
And it will come as [c]destruction from the [1]Almighty.
16 Has not [a]food been cut off before our eyes,
Gladness and [b]joy from the house of our God?
17 The [1a]seeds shrivel under their [2]clods;
The storehouses are desolate,
The barns are torn down,
For the grain is dried up.
18 How [a]the beasts groan!
The herds of cattle wander aimlessly
Because there is no pasture for them;
Even the flocks of sheep [1]suffer.
19 [a]To Thee, O LORD, I cry;
For [b]fire has devoured the pastures of the wilderness,
And the flame has burned up all the trees of the field.
20 Even the beasts of the field [1a]pant for Thee;
For the [b]water brooks are dried up,
And fire has devoured the pastures of the wilderness.

The Terrible Visitation

2 [a]BLOW a trumpet in Zion,
And sound an alarm on My holy mountain!
Let all the inhabitants of the land tremble,
For the [b]day of the LORD is coming;
Surely it is near,
2 A day of [a]darkness and gloom,
A day of clouds and thick darkness.
As the dawn is spread over the mountains,
So there is a [b]great and mighty people;
There has [c]never been *anything* like it,
Nor will there be again after it
To the years of many generations.
3 A [a]fire consumes before them,
And behind them a flame burns.
The land is [b]like the garden of Eden before them,
But a [c]desolate wilderness behind them,
And nothing at all escapes them.
4 Their [a]appearance is like the appearance of horses;
And like war horses, so they run.

---

1 [a]Jer. 1:2; Ezek. 1:3; Hos. 1:1 [b]Acts 2:16
2 [a]Hos. 4:1; 5:1 [b]Job 8:8; Joel 1:14 [c]Jer. 30:7; Joel 2:2
3 [a]Ex. 10:2; Ps. 78:4
4 [a]Deut. 28:38; Joel 2:25; Amos 4:9 [b]Nah. 3:15, 16 [c]Is. 33:4
5 [a]Joel 3:3 [b]Is. 32:10
6 [1]Lit., *come up against* [a]Joel 2:2, 11, 25 [b]Rev. 9:8
7 [1]Or, *a stump* [a]Is. 5:6; Amos 4:9
8 [a]Is. 22:12 [b]Joel 1:13; Amos 8:10
9 [a]Hos. 9:4; Joel 1:13; 2:14 [b]Joel 2:17
10 [1]Lit., *wastes away* [a]Is. 24:4, 7 [b]Jer. 12:11
11 [1]Or, *The farmers are ashamed, The vinedressers wail* [a]Jer. 14:4; Amos 5:16 [b]Is. 17:11; Jer. 9:12
12 [1]Lit., *wastes away* [2]Or, *apricot* [a]Joel 1:10; Hab. 3:17 [b]Hag. 2:19 [c]Song 7:8 [d]Song 2:3 [e]Is. 16:10; 24:11; Jer. 48:33
13 [a]Jer. 4:8; Ezek. 7:18 [b]Jer. 9:10 [c]1 Kin. 21:27
14 [a]Joel 2:15, 16 [b]Lev. 23:36 [c]Jon. 3:8
15 [1]Heb., *Shaddai* [a]Is. 13:9; Jer. 30:7; Amos 5:16 [b]Joel 2:1, 11, 31 [c]Is. 13:6; Ezek. 7:2-12
16 [a]Is. 3:7; Amos 4:6 [b]Deut. 12:7; Ps. 43:4
17 [1]Or, *dried figs* [2]Or, *shovels* [a]Is. 17:10, 11
18 [1]Lit., *bear punishment* [a]1 Kin. 8:5; Jer. 12:4; 14:5, 6; Hos. 4:3
19 [a]Ps. 50:15; Mic. 7:7 [b]Jer. 9:10; Amos 7:4
20 [1]Lit., *long for* [a]Ps. 104:21; 147:9; Joel 1:18 [b]1 Kin. 17:7; 18:5

1 [a]Jer. 4:5; Joel 2:15; Zeph. 1:16 [b]Joel 1:15; 2:11, 31; 3:14; Obad. 15; Zeph. 1:14
2 [a]Joel 2:10, 31; Amos 5:18; Zeph. 1:15 [b]Joel 1:6; 2:11, 25 [c]Lam. 1:12; Dan. 9:12; 12:1; Joel 1:2
3 [a]Ps. 97:3; Is. 9:18, 19 [b]Is. 51:3; Ezek. 36:35 [c]Ex. 10:5, 15; Ps. 105:34, 35; Zech. 7:14
4 [a]Rev. 9:7

5 [1]With a [a]noise as of chariots
They leap on the tops of the mountains,
Like the [2]crackling of a [b]flame of fire consuming the stubble,
Like a mighty people arranged for battle.
6 Before them the people are in [a]anguish;
All [b]faces [1]turn pale.
7 They run like mighty men;
They climb the wall like soldiers;
And they each [a]march [1]in line,
Nor do they deviate from their paths.
8 They do not crowd each other;
They march everyone in his path.
When they [1]burst through the [2]defenses,
They do not break ranks.
9 They rush on the city,
They run on the wall;
They climb into the [a]houses,
They [b]enter through the windows like a thief.
10 Before them the earth [a]quakes,
The heavens tremble,
The [b]sun and the moon grow dark,
And the stars lose their brightness.
11 And the LORD [a]utters His voice before [b]His army;
Surely His camp is very great,
For [c]strong is he who carries out His word.
The [d]day of the LORD is indeed great and very awesome,
And [e]who can endure it?
12 "Yet even now," declares the LORD,
"[a]Return to Me with all your heart,
And with [b]fasting, weeping, and mourning;
13 And [a]rend your heart and not [b]your garments."
Now return to the LORD your God,
For He is [c]gracious and compassionate,
Slow to anger, abounding in lovingkindness,
And [d]relenting of evil.
14 Who knows [a]whether He will *not* turn and relent,
And leave a [b]blessing behind Him,
Even [c]a grain offering and a libation
For the LORD your God?
15 [a]Blow a trumpet in Zion,
[b]Consecrate a fast, proclaim a solemn assembly,
16 Gather the people, [a]sanctify the congregation,
Assemble the elders,
Gather the children and the nursing infants.
Let the [b]bridegroom come out of his room
And the bride out of her *bridal* chamber.
17 Let the priests, the LORD's ministers,
Weep [a]between the porch and the altar,
And let them say, "[b]Spare Thy people, O LORD,
And do not make Thine inheritance a [c]reproach,
A byword among the nations.
Why should they among the peoples say,
'[d]Where is their God?' "

Deliverance Promised

18 Then the LORD [1]will be [a]zealous for His land,
And [2]will have [b]pity on His people.
19 And the LORD [1]will answer and say to His people,
"Behold, I am going to [a]send you grain, new wine, and oil,
And you will be satisfied *in full* with [2]them;
And I will [b]never again make you a reproach among the nations.
20 "But I will remove the [a]northern *army* far from you,
And I will drive it into a parched and desolate land,
And its vanguard into the [b]eastern sea,
And its rear guard into the [c]western sea.
And its [d]stench will arise and its foul smell will come up,
For it has done great things."

21 [a]Do not fear, O land, rejoice and be glad,
For the LORD has done [b]great things.
22 Do not fear, beasts of the field,
For the [a]pastures of the wilderness have turned green,
For the tree has borne its fruit,
The fig tree and the vine have yielded [1]in full.
23 So rejoice, O [a]sons of Zion,
And [b]be glad in the LORD your God;
For He has [c]given you [1]the early rain for *your* vindication.
And He has poured down for you the rain,
The [2]early and [3][d]latter rain [4]as before.
24 And the threshing floors will be full of grain,
And the vats will [a]overflow with the new wine and oil.
25 "Then I will make up to you for the years
That the swarming [a]locust has eaten,
The creeping locust, the stripping locust, and the gnawing locust,
My great army which I sent among you.
26 "And you shall have plenty to [a]eat and be satisfied,
And [b]praise the name of the LORD your God,
Who has [c]dealt wondrously with you;
Then My people will [d]never be put to shame.

5 [1]Lit., *Like the noise of chariots* [2]Lit., *noise* [a]Rev. 9:9 [b]Is. 5:24; 30:30
6 [1]Or, *become flushed* [a]Is. 13:8; Nah. 2:10 [b]Jer. 30:6
7 [1]Lit., *in his ways* [a]Prov. 30:27
8 [1]Lit., *fall* [2]Lit., *weapon,* probably *javelin*
9 [a]Ex. 10:6 [b]Jer. 9:21; John 10:1
10 [a]Ps. 18:7; Joel 3:16; Nah. 1:5 [b]Is. 13:10; 34:4; Jer. 4:23; Ezek. 32:7, 8; Joel 2:31; 3:15; Matt. 24:29; Rev. 8:12
11 [a]Ps. 46:6; Is. 13:4; Jer. 25:30; Joel 3:16 [b]Joel 2:25 [c]Jer. 50:34; Rev. 18:8 [d]Jer. 30:7; Joel 1:15; 2:1, 31; 3:14; Zeph. 1:14, 15; Rev. 6:17 [e]Ezek. 22:14; Mal. 3:2
12 [a]Deut. 4:29; Jer. 4:1, 2; Ezek. 33:11; Hos. 12:6 [b]Dan. 9:3
13 [a]Ps. 34:18; 51:17; Is. 57:15 [b]Gen. 37:34; 2 Sam. 1:11; Job 1:20; Jer. 41:5 [c]Ex. 34:6 [d]Jer. 18:8; 42:10; Amos 7:3, 6
14 [a]Jer. 26:3; Jon. 3:9 [b]Hag. 2:19 [c]Joel 1:9, 13
15 [a]Num. 10:3; 2 Kin. 10:20 [b]Joel 1:14
16 [a]1 Sam. 16:5; 2 Chr. 29:5 [b]Ps. 19:5
17 [a]2 Chr. 8:12; Ezek. 8:16 [b]Ex. 32:11, 12; Is. 37:20; Amos 7:2, 5 [c]Ps. 44:13; 74:10 [d]Ps. 42:10; 79:10; 115:2
18 [1]Or, *was zealous* [2]Or, *had pity* [a]Zech. 1:14; 8:2 [b]Is. 60:10; 63:9, 15
19 [1]Or, *answered and said* [2]Lit., *it* [a]Jer. 31:12; Hos. 2:21, 22; Joel 1:10; Mal. 3:10 [b]Ezek. 34:29; 36:15
20 [a]Jer. 1:14, 15 [b]Zech. 14:8 [c]Deut. 11:24 [d]Is. 34:3; Amos 4:10
21 [a]Is. 54:4; Jer. 30:10; Zeph. 3:16, 17 [b]Ps. 126:3; Joel 2:26
22 [1]Lit., *their wealth* [a]Ps. 65:12, 13
23 [1]I.e., autumn; or possibly, *the teacher for righteousness* [2]I.e., autumn [3]I.e., spring [4]So with ancient versions; Heb., *in the first* [a]Ps. 149:2 [b]Is. 12:2-6 [c]Deut. 11:14; Is. 41:16; Jer. 5:24; Hab. 3:18; Zech. 10:7 [d]Lev. 26:4; Hos. 6:3; Zech. 10:1
24 [a]Lev. 26:10; Amos 9:13; Mal. 3:10
25 [a]Joel 1:4-7; 2:2-11

26 [a]Lev. 26:5; Deut. 11:15; Is. 62:9 [b]Deut. 12:7; Ps. 67:5-7 [c]Ps. 126:2, 3; Is. 25:1 [d]Is. 45:17

27 "Thus you will [a]know that I am in
the midst of Israel,
And that I am the LORD your God
And there is [b]no other;
And My people will never be [c]put
to shame.

The Promise of the Spirit

28 "[1a]And it will come about after this
That I will [b]pour out My Spirit on
all [2c]mankind;
And your sons and daughters will
prophesy,
Your old men will dream dreams,
Your young men will see visions.
29 "And even on the [a]male and female
servants
I will pour out My Spirit in those
days.

The Day of the LORD

30 "And I will [a]display wonders in the
sky and on the earth,
Blood, fire, and columns of smoke.
31 "The [a]sun will be turned into dark-
ness,
And the moon into blood,
Before the [b]great and awesome day
of the LORD comes.
32 "And it will come about that [a]who-
ever calls on the name of the
LORD
Will be delivered;
For [b]on Mount Zion and in Jerusa-
lem
There will be those who [c]escape,
As the LORD has said,
Even among the [d]survivors whom
the LORD calls.

The Nations Will Be Judged

3 "[1]FOR behold, [a]in those days and
at that time,
When I [b]restore the fortunes of
Judah and Jerusalem,
2 I will [a]gather all the nations,
And bring them down to the [b]val-
ley of [1]Jehoshaphat.
Then I will [c]enter into judgment
with them there
On behalf of My people and My
inheritance, Israel,
Whom they have [d]scattered among
the nations;
And they have [e]divided up My
land.
3 "They have also [a]cast lots for My
people,
[1b]Traded a boy for a harlot,
And sold a girl for wine that they
may drink.
4 "Moreover, what are you to Me, O
[a]Tyre, Sidon, and all the regions of
[b]Philistia? Are you rendering Me a
recompense? But if you do recompense
Me, swiftly and speedily I will [c]return
your recompense on your head.
5 "Since you have [a]taken My silver
and My gold, brought My precious
[1]treasures to your temples,

27 [a]Lev. 26:11, 12; Joel 3:17, 21 [b]Is. 45:5, 6 [c]Is. 49:23
28 [1]Ch. 3:1 in Heb. [2]Lit., *flesh* [a]Acts 2:17-21 [b]Is. 32:15; 44:3; Ezek. 39:29; Zech. 12:10 [c]Is. 40:5; 49:26
29 [a]1 Cor. 12:13; Gal. 3:28
30 [a]Matt. 24:29; Mark 13:24, 25; Luke 21:11, 25, 26; Acts 2:19
31 [a]Is. 13:10; 34:4; Joel 2:10; 3:15; Matt. 24:29; Mark 13:24; Luke 21:25; Acts 2:20; Rev. 6:12, 13 [b]Is. 13:9; Zeph. 1:14-16; Mal. 4:1, 5
32 [a]Jer. 33:3; Acts 2:21; Rom. 10:13 [b]Is. 46:13; Rom. 11:26 [c]Is. 4:2; Obad. 17 [d]Is. 11:11; Jer. 31:7; Mic. 4:7; Rom. 9:27

1 [1]Ch. 4:1 in Heb. [a]Jer. 30:3; Ezek. 38:14 [b]Jer. 16:15
2 [1]I.e., YHWH judges [a]Is. 66:18; Mic. 4:12; Zech. 14:2 [b]Joel 3:12, 14 [c]Is. 66:16; Jer. 25:31; Ezek. 38:22 [d]Jer. 50:17; Ezek. 34:6 [e]Ezek. 35:10; 36:1-5
3 [1]Lit., *Given* [a]Obad. 11; Nah. 3:10 [b]Amos 2:6
4 [a]Is. 23:1-18; Amos 1:9, 10; Zech. 9:2-4; Matt. 11:21, 22; Luke 10:13, 14 [b]Is. 14:29-31; Jer. 47:1-7; Ezek. 25:15-17; Amos 1:6-8; Zech. 9:5-7 [c]Is. 34:8; 59:18
5 [1]Lit., *goodly things* [a]2 Kin. 12:18; 2 Chr. 21:16, 17
6 [1]Lit., *sons of Javan* [a]Ezek. 27:13
7 [a]Is. 43:5, 6; Jer. 23:8; Zech. 9:13
8 [a]Is. 14:2; 60:14 [b]Job 1:15; Ps. 72:10; Ezek. 38:13
9 [a]Jer. 51:27 [b]Jer. 6:4; Ezek. 38:7; Mic. 3:5 [c]Is. 8:9, 10; Jer. 46:3, 4; Zech. 14:2, 3
10 [a]Is. 2:4; Mic. 4:3 [b]Zech. 12:8
11 [1]Or, *Lend aid* [a]Ezek. 38:15, 16 [b]Is. 13:3
12 [1]I.e., YHWH judges [a]Joel 3:2, 14 [b]Ps. 7:6; 96:13; 98:9; Is. 2:4; 3:13
13 [a]Rev. 14:14-19 [b]Jer. 51:33; Hos. 6:11 [c]Rev. 14:19, 20; 19:15 [d]Is. 63:3; Lam. 1:15 [e]Gen. 18:20
14 [1]I.e., God's verdict [a]Is. 34:2-8 [b]Joel 3:2, 12 [c]Joel 1:15; 2:1, 11, 31
15 [a]Joel 2:10, 31

6 and sold the [a]sons of Judah and
Jerusalem to the [1]Greeks in order to
remove them far from their territory,
7 behold, I am going to [a]arouse them
from the place where you have sold
them, and return your recompense on
your head.
8 "Also I will [a]sell your sons and your
daughters into the hand of the sons of
Judah, and they will sell them to the
[b]Sabeans, to a distant nation," for the
LORD has spoken.
9 [a]Proclaim this among the nations:
[b]Prepare a war; [c]rouse the mighty
men!
Let all the soldiers draw near, let
them come up!
10 [a]Beat your plowshares into swords,
And your pruning hooks into
spears;
[b]Let the weak say, "I am a mighty
man."
11 [1a]Hasten and come, all you surrounding nations,
And gather yourselves there.
Bring down, O LORD, Thy [b]mighty
ones.
12 Let the nations be aroused
And come up to the [a]valley of
[1]Jehoshaphat,
For there I will sit to [b]judge
All the surrounding nations.
13 [a]Put in the sickle, for the [b]harvest
is ripe.
Come, [c]tread, for the [d]wine press is
full;
The vats overflow, for their [e]wick-
edness is great.
14 [a]Multitudes, multitudes in the [b]val-
ley of [1]decision!
For the [c]day of the LORD is near in
the valley of [1]decision.
15 The [a]sun and moon grow dark,
And the stars lose their brightness.
16 And the LORD [a]roars from Zion
And [b]utters His voice from Jerusalem,
And the [c]heavens and the earth
tremble.
But the LORD is a [d]refuge for His
people
And a [e]stronghold to the sons of
Israel.
17 Then you will [a]know that I am the
LORD your God,
Dwelling in Zion My [b]holy mountain.
So Jerusalem will be [c]holy,
And [d]strangers will pass through it
no more.

Judah Will Be Blessed

18 And it will come about in that day
That the [a]mountains will drip with
[1]sweet wine,
And the hills will [b]flow with milk,
And all the [c]brooks of Judah will
flow with water;

16 [a]Hos. 11:10; Amos 1:2 [b]Joel 2:11 [c]Ezek. 38:19; Joel 2:10; Hag. 2:6 [d]Ps. 61:3; Is. 33:16; Jer. 17:17 [e]Jer. 16:19; Nah. 1:7
17 [a]Joel 2:27 [b]Is. 11:9; 56:7; Ezek. 20:40 [c]Is. 4:3; Obad. 17 [d]Is. 52:1; Nah. 1:15
18 [1]Lit., *freshly pressed out grape juice* [a]Amos 9:13 [b]Ex. 3:8 [c]Is. 30:25; 35:6

And a [d]spring will go out from the house of the LORD,
To water the valley of [2]Shittim.
19 Egypt will become a waste,
And Edom will become a desolate wilderness,
Because of the [a]violence [1]done to the sons of Judah,
In whose land they have shed innocent blood.
20 But Judah will be [a]inhabited forever,
And Jerusalem for all generations.
21 And I will [a]avenge their blood which I have not avenged,
For the LORD dwells in Zion.

18 [2]Or, *acacias* [d]Ezek. 47:1-12
19 [1]Lit., *of the sons* [a]Obad. 10
20 [a]Ezek. 37:25; Amos 9:15
21 [a]Is. 4:4

THE BOOK OF AMOS

Judgment on Neighbor Nations

1 THE words of Amos, who was among the [a]sheepherders from [b]Tekoa, which he [1]envisioned in visions concerning Israel in the days of [c]Uzziah king of Judah, and in the days of [d]Jeroboam son of Joash, king of Israel, two years before the [e]earthquake.
2 And he said,
"The [a]LORD roars from Zion,
And from Jerusalem He utters His voice;
And the shepherds' [b]pasture grounds mourn,
And the [1c]summit of Carmel dries up."

3 Thus says the LORD,
"For [a]three transgressions of [b]Damascus and for four
I will not [1]revoke its *punishment*,
Because they threshed Gilead with *implements* of sharp iron.
4 "So I will send fire upon the house of Hazael,
And it will consume the citadels of [a]Ben-hadad.
5 "I will also [a]break the *gate* bar of Damascus,
And cut off the inhabitant from the [1]valley of Aven,
And him who holds the scepter, from Beth-eden;
So the people of Aram will go exiled to [b]Kir,"
Says the LORD.

6 Thus says the LORD,
"For three transgressions of [a]Gaza and for four
I will not revoke its *punishment*,
Because they deported an entire population
To [b]deliver *it* up to Edom.
7 "So I will send fire upon the wall of Gaza,
And it will consume her citadels.
8 "I will also cut off the inhabitant from [a]Ashdod,
And him who holds the scepter, from [b]Ashkelon;
I will even [1]unleash My [2]power upon Ekron,
And the remnant of the [c]Philistines will perish,"
Says the Lord [3]GOD.

9 Thus says the LORD,
"For three transgressions of [a]Tyre and for four
I will not revoke its *punishment*,
Because they delivered up an entire population to Edom
And did not remember *the* covenant of [1b]brotherhood.
10 "So I will [a]send fire upon the wall of Tyre,
And it will consume her citadels."

11 Thus says the LORD,
"For three transgressions of [a]Edom and for four
I will not revoke its *punishment*,
Because he [b]pursued his brother with the sword,
While he [1]stifled his compassion;
His anger also [c]tore continually,
And he maintained his fury forever.
12 "So I will send fire upon [a]Teman,
And it will consume the citadels of Bozrah."

13 Thus says the LORD,
"For three transgressions of the sons of [a]Ammon and for four
I will not revoke its *punishment*,
Because they [b]ripped open the pregnant women of Gilead
In order to [c]enlarge their borders.
14 "So I will kindle a fire on the wall of [a]Rabbah,
And it will consume her citadels
Amid [1b]war cries on the day of battle
And a [c]storm on the day of tempest.
15 "Their [a]king will go into exile,
He and his princes together," says the LORD.

Judgment on Judah and Israel

2 THUS says the LORD,
"For three transgressions of [a]Moab and for four
I will not [1]revoke its *punishment*,
Because he [b]burned the bones of the king of Edom to lime.

1 [1]Lit., *saw concerning* [a]Amos 7:14 [b]2 Sam. 14:2; Jer. 6:1 [c]2 Chr. 26:1-23; Is. 1:1 [d]2 Kin. 14:23-29; Hos. 1:1; Amos 7:10, 11 [e]Zech. 14:5
2 [1]Lit., *head* [a]Is. 42:13; Jer. 25:30; Joel 3:16 [b]Jer. 12:4; Joel 1:18, 19 [c]Amos 9:3
3 [1]Lit., *cause it to turn back,* and so throughout the ch. [a]Amos 2:1, 4, 6 [b]Is. 8:4; 17:1-3; Jer. 49:23-27; Zech. 9:1
4 [a]1 Kin. 20:1; 2 Kin. 6:24
5 [1]Possibly, *Baalbek* [a]Jer. 51:30; Lam. 2:9 [b]2 Kin. 16:9; Amos 9:7
6 [a]1 Sam. 6:17; Jer. 47:1, 5; Zeph. 2:4 [b]Ezek. 35:5; Obad. 11
8 [1]Lit., *cause to return* [2]Lit., *hand* [3]Heb., *YHWH,* usually rendered LORD [a]2 Chr. 26:6; Amos 3:9; Zech. 9:6 [b]Jer. 47:5; Zeph. 2:4 [c]Is. 14:29-31; Jer. 47:1-7; Ezek. 25:16; Joel 3:4-8; Zeph. 2:4-7; Zech. 9:5-7
9 [1]Lit., *brothers* [a]Is. 23:1-18; Jer. 25:22; Ezek. 26:2-4; Joel 3:4-8; Zech. 9:1-4; Matt. 11:21, 22; Luke 10:13, 14 [b]1 Kin. 9:11-14
10 [a]Zech. 9:4
11 [1]Lit., *corrupted* [a]Is. 34:5, 6; 63:1-6; Jer. 49:7-22; Ezek. 25:12-14; 35:1-15; Obad. 1-14; Mal. 1:2-5 [b]Num. 20:14-21; 2 Chr. 28:17; Obad. 10-12 [c]Is. 57:16; Mic. 7:18
12 [a]Jer. 49:7, 20; Obad. 9
13 [a]Jer. 49:1-6; Ezek. 21:28-32; 25:2-7; Zeph. 2:8, 9 [b]2 Kin. 15:16; Hos. 13:16 [c]Is. 5:8; Ezek. 35:10
14 [1]Or, *shouts* [a]Deut. 3:11; 1 Chr. 20:1; Jer. 49:2 [b]Ezek. 21:22; Amos 2:2 [c]Is. 29:6; 30:30
15 [a]Jer. 49:3

1 [1]Lit., *cause it to turn back,* and so throughout the ch. [a]Is. 15:1-16:14; 25:10-12; Jer. 48:1-47; Ezek. 25:8-11; Zeph. 2:8, 9 [b]2 Kin. 3:26, 27

2 "So I will send fire upon Moab,
And it will consume the citadels of [a]Kerioth;
And Moab will die amid [b]tumult,
With [1]war cries and the sound of a trumpet.
3 "I will also cut off the [1a]judge from her midst,
And slay all her [b]princes with him," says the LORD.

4 Thus says the LORD,
"For three transgressions of [a]Judah and for four
I will not revoke its *punishment*,
Because they [b]rejected the law of the LORD
And have not kept His statutes;
Their [1c]lies also have led them astray,
Those after which their [d]fathers walked.
5 "So I will [a]send fire upon Judah,
And it will consume the citadels of Jerusalem."

6 Thus says the LORD,
"For three transgressions of [a]Israel and for four
I will not revoke its *punishment*,
Because they [b]sell the righteous for money
And the needy for a pair of sandals.
7 "These who [1]pant after the *very* dust of the earth on the head of the [a]helpless
Also [b]turn aside the way of the humble;
And a [c]man and his father [2]resort to the same [3]girl
In order to profane My holy name.
8 "And on garments [a]taken as pledges they stretch out beside [b]every altar,
And in the house of their God they [c]drink the wine of those who have been fined.

9 "Yet it was I who destroyed the [a]Amorite before them,
[1]Though his [b]height *was* like the height of cedars
And he *was* strong as the oaks;
I even destroyed his [c]fruit above and his root below.
10 "And it was I who [a]brought you up from the land of Egypt,
And I led you in the wilderness [b]forty years
[1]That you might take possession of the land of the [c]Amorite.
11 "Then I [a]raised up some of your sons to be prophets
And some of your young men to be [b]Nazirites.
Is this not so, O sons of Israel?" declares the LORD.
12 "But you made the Nazirites drink wine,
And you commanded the prophets saying, 'You [a]shall not prophesy!'
13 "Behold, I am [1a]weighted down beneath you
As a wagon [2]is weighted down when filled with sheaves.
14 "[1a]Flight will perish from the swift,
And the stalwart will not strengthen his power,
Nor the [b]mighty man save his [2]life.
15 "He who [a]grasps the bow will not stand *his ground*,
The swift of foot will not escape,
Nor will he who rides the [b]horse save his [1]life.
16 "Even the [1]bravest among the warriors will [a]flee naked in that day," declares the LORD.

All the Tribes Are Guilty

3 HEAR this word which the LORD
has spoken against you, sons of
Israel, against the entire [1a]family which
[2]He brought up from the land of Egypt,
2 "[a]You only have I [1]chosen among all the families of the earth;
Therefore, I will [2b]punish you for all your iniquities."
3 Do two men walk together unless they have made an [1]appointment?
4 Does a [a]lion roar in the forest when he has no prey?
Does a young lion [1]growl from his den unless he has captured *something*?
5 Does a bird fall into a trap on the ground when there is no [1]bait in it?
Does a trap spring up from the earth when it captures nothing at all?
6 If a [a]trumpet is blown in a city will not the people tremble?
If a [b]calamity occurs in a city has not the LORD done it?
7 [1]Surely the Lord GOD does nothing
Unless He [a]reveals His secret counsel
To His servants the prophets.
8 A [a]lion has roared! Who will not fear?
The [b]Lord [1]GOD has spoken! [c]Who can but prophesy?
9 Proclaim on the citadels in [a]Ash-
dod and on the citadels in the land of
Egypt and say, "Assemble yourselves on
the [b]mountains of Samaria and see *the*
great tumults within her and *the* [c]oppres-
sions in her midst.
10 "But they [a]do not know how to do
what is right," declares the LORD, "these
who [b]hoard up [1]violence and devastation in their citadels."
11 Therefore, thus says the Lord GOD,
"An [a]enemy, even one surrounding the land,
Will pull down your [1]strength from you
And your [b]citadels will be looted."

2 [1]Or, *shouts* [a]Jer. 48:24, 41 [b]Jer. 48:45
3 [1]Or, *executive officer* [a]Ps. 2:10; 141:6; Amos 5:7, 12; 6:12 [b]Job 12:21; Is. 40:23
4 [1]Or, *false gods* [a]2 Kin. 17:19; Hos. 12:2; Amos 3:2 [b]Judg. 2:17-20; 2 Kin. 22:11-17; Jer. 6:19; 8:9 [c]Is. 9:15, 16; 28:15; Jer. 16:19; Hab. 2:18 [d]Jer. 9:14; 16:11, 12; Ezek. 20:18, 24, 30
5 [a]Jer. 17:27; 21:10; Hos. 8:14
6 [a]2 Kin. 18:11, 12 [b]Joel 3:3; Amos 5:11, 12; 8:6
7 [1]Or, *trample* or, *snap at the head of the helpless on the dust* [2]Lit., *go* [3]Possibly a harlot, or a temple prostitute [a]Amos 8:4; Mic. 2:2, 9 [b]Amos 5:12 [c]Hos. 4:14
8 [a]Ex. 22:26 [b]Amos 3:14 [c]Amos 4:1; 6:6
9 [1]Lit., *Whose height* [a]Num. 21:23-25; Josh. 10:12 [b]Num. 13:32 [c]Ezek. 17:9; Mal. 4:1
10 [1]Lit., *To possess* [a]Ex. 12:51; 20:2; Amos 3:1; 9:7 [b]Deut. 2:7 [c]Ex. 3:8
11 [a]Deut. 18:18; Jer. 7:25 [b]Num. 6:2, 3; Judg. 13:5
12 [a]Is. 30:10; Jer. 11:21; Amos 7:13, 16; Mic. 2:6
13 [1]Or, *tottering* [2]Or, *totters* [a]Is. 1:14
14 [1]Or, *A place of refuge* [2]Lit., *soul* [a]Is. 30:16, 17 [b]Ps. 33:16; Jer. 9:23
15 [1]Lit., *soul* [a]Jer. 51:56; Ezek. 39:3 [b]Is. 31:3
16 [1]Lit., *stout of heart* [a]Judg. 4:17

1 [1]I.e., nation [2]Lit., *I* [a]Jer. 8:3; 13:11
2 [1]Lit., *known* [2]Lit., *visit* [a]Gen. 18:19; Ex. 19:5, 6; Deut. 4:32-37; 7:6 [b]Jer. 14:10; Ezek. 20:36; Dan. 9:12; Rom. 2:9
3 [1]Or, *agreement*
4 [1]Lit., *give his voice* [a]Ps. 104:21; Hos. 5:14; 11:10
5 [1]Or, *striker-bar set*
6 [a]Jer. 4:5, 19, 21; 6:1; Hos. 5:8; Zeph. 1:16 [b]Is. 14:24-27; 45:7
7 [1]Or, *For* [a]Gen. 6:13; 18:17; Jer. 23:22; Dan. 9:22; John 15:15
8 [1]Heb., *YHWH*, usually rendered *LORD*, and so throughout the ch. [a]Amos 1:2 [b]Jon. 1:1-3; 3:1-3 [c]Jer. 20:9; Acts 4:20
9 [a]1 Sam. 5:1 [b]Amos 4:1; 6:1 [c]Amos 5:11; 8:6
10 [1]I.e., the booty from violence [a]Ps. 14:4; Jer. 4:22; Amos 5:7; 6:12 [b]Hab. 2:8-10; Zeph. 1:9; Zech. 5:3, 4
11 [1]Or, *stronghold* [a]Amos 6:14 [b]Amos 2:5

12 Thus says the LORD,
"Just as the shepherd [1a]snatches
from the lion's mouth a couple
of legs or a piece of an ear,
So will the sons of Israel dwelling
in Samaria be [2]snatched away—
With *the* [b]corner of a bed and *the*
[3c]cover of a couch!
13 "Hear and [a]testify against the house
of Jacob,"
Declares the Lord GOD, the God of
hosts.
14 "For on the day that I punish Israel's transgressions,
I will also punish the altars of
[a]Bethel;
The horns of the altar will be cut
off,
And they will fall to the ground.
15 "I will also smite the [1a]winter house
together with the [b]summer
house;
The houses of [2c]ivory will also
perish
And the [d]great houses will come to
an end,"
Declares the LORD.

"Yet You Have Not Returned to Me"

4 HEAR this word, you cows of [a]Ba-
shan who are on the [b]mountain of
Samaria,
Who [c]oppress the poor, who crush
the needy,
Who say to [1]your husbands, "Bring
now, that we may [d]drink!"
2 The Lord [1]GOD has [a]sworn by His
[b]holiness,
"Behold, the days are coming upon
you
When [2]they will take you away
with [c]meat hooks,
And the last of you with [d]fish
hooks.
3 "You will [a]go out *through* breaches
in the walls,
Each one straight before her,
And you [1]will be cast to Harmon,"
declares the LORD.

4 "Enter Bethel and transgress;
In Gilgal multiply transgression!
[a]Bring your sacrifices every morn-
ing,
Your tithes every three days.
5 "[1]Offer a [a]thank offering also from
that which is leavened,
And proclaim [b]freewill offerings,
make them known.
For so you [c]love *to do,* you sons of
Israel,"
Declares the Lord GOD.

6 "But I gave you also [a]cleanness of
teeth in all your cities
And lack of bread in all your
places,
Yet you have [b]not returned to Me,"
declares the LORD.
7 "And furthermore, I [a]withheld the
rain from you
While *there were* still three months
until harvest.
Then I would send rain on one city
And on [b]another city I would not
send rain;
One part would be rained on,
While the part not rained on would
dry up.
8 "So two or three cities would stagger
to another city to drink [a]water,
But would [b]not be satisfied;
Yet you have [c]not returned to Me,"
declares the LORD.
9 "I [a]smote you with scorching *wind*
and mildew;
And the [b]caterpillar was devouring
Your many gardens and vineyards,
fig trees and olive trees;
Yet you have [c]not returned to Me,"
declares the LORD.
10 "I sent a [a]plague among you after
the manner of Egypt;
I [b]slew your young men by the
sword along with your [c]captured
horses,
And I made the [d]stench of your
camp rise up in your nostrils;
Yet you have [e]not returned to Me,"
declares the LORD.
11 "I overthrew you as [a]God overthrew
Sodom and Gomorrah,
And you were like a [b]firebrand
snatched from a blaze;
Yet you have [c]not returned to Me,"
declares the LORD.
12 "Therefore, thus I will do to you, O
Israel;
Because I shall do this to you,
Prepare to [a]meet your God, O
Israel."
13 For behold, He who [a]forms mountains and [b]creates the wind
And [c]declares to man what are His
thoughts,
He who [d]makes dawn into darkness
And [e]treads on the high places of
the earth,
[f]The LORD God of hosts is His
name.

"Seek Me that You May Live"

5 HEAR this word which I take up for
you as a [a]dirge, O house of Israel.
2 She has fallen, she will [a]not rise
again—
The [b]virgin Israel.
She *lies* neglected on her land;
There is [c]none to raise her up.
3 For thus says the Lord [1]GOD,
"The city which goes forth a thou-
sand *strong*
Will have a [a]hundred left,
And the one which goes forth a
hundred *strong*
Will have [b]ten left to the house of
Israel."

4 For thus says the LORD to the
house of Israel,
"[a]Seek Me [b]that you may live.

---

12 [1]Or, *delivers* [2]Or, *delivered* [3]Lit., *damask*
[a]1 Sam. 17:34-37 [b]Ps. 132:3 [c]Esth. 1:6; 7:8; Amos 6:4
13 [a]Ezek. 2:7
14 [a]2 Kin. 23:15; Hos. 10:5-8, 14, 15; Amos 4:4; 5:5, 6; 7:10, 13
15 [1]Or, *autumn* [2]I.e., ivory inlay
[a]Jer. 36:22 [b]Judg. 3:20 [c]1 Kin. 22:39; Ps. 45:8 [d]Amos 2:5; 6:11

1 [1]Lit., *their lords*
[a]Ps. 22:12; Ezek. 39:18 [b]Amos 3:9; 6:1 [c]Amos 5:11; 8:6 [d]Amos 2:8; 6:6
2 [1]Heb., *YHWH,* usually rendered *LORD,* and so throughout the ch. [2]Lit., *he*
[a]Amos 6:8; 8:7 [b]Ps. 89:35 [c]Is. 37:29; Ezek. 38:4 [d]Jer. 16:16; Ezek. 29:4; Hab. 1:15
3 [1]So Gr.; M.T. reads *will cast*
[a]Jer. 52:7
4 [a]Num. 28:3; Amos 5:21, 22
5 [1]Lit., *Offer up in smoke*
[a]Lev. 7:13 [b]Lev. 22:18-21 [c]Jer. 7:9, 10; Hos. 9:1, 10
6 [a]Is. 3:1; Jer. 14:18 [b]Is. 9:13; Jer. 5:3; Hag. 2:17
7 [a]Deut. 11:17; 2 Chr. 7:13; Is. 5:6 [b]Ex. 9:4, 26; 10:22, 23
8 [a]1 Kin. 18:5; Jer. 14:4 [b]Ezek. 4:16, 17; Hag. 1:6 [c]Jer. 3:7
9 [a]Deut. 28:22; Hag. 2:17 [b]Joel 1:4, 7; Amos 7:1, 2 [c]Jer. 3:10
10 [a]Ex. 9:3; Lev. 26:25; Deut. 28:27, 60; Ps. 78:50 [b]Jer. 11:22; 18:21; 48:15 [c]2 Kin. 13:3, 7 [d]Joel 2:20 [e]Is. 9:13
11 [a]Gen. 19:24, 25; Deut. 29:23; Is. 13:19 [b]Zech. 3:2 [c]Jer. 23:14
12 [a]Is. 32:11; 64:2; Jer. 5:22
13 [a]Job 38:4-7; Ps. 65:6; Is. 40:12 [b]Ps. 135:7; Jer. 10:13 [c]Dan. 2:28, 30 [d]Jer. 13:16; Joel 2:2; Amos 5:8 [e]Mic. 1:3 [f]Is. 47:4; Jer. 10:16; Amos 5:8, 27; 9:6

1 [a]Jer. 7:29; 9:10, 17; Ezek. 19:1
2 [a]Amos 8:14 [b]Jer. 14:17 [c]Is. 51:18; Jer. 50:32
3 [1]Heb., *YHWH,* usually rendered *LORD,* and so throughout the ch.
[a]Is. 6:13 [b]Amos 6:9
4 [a]Deut. 4:29; 32:46, 47; Jer. 29:13 [b]Is. 55:3

5"But do not [1]resort to [a]Bethel,
And do not come to [b]Gilgal,
Nor cross over to [c]Beersheba;
For Gilgal will certainly go into captivity,
And Bethel will [2]come to trouble.
6"[a]Seek the LORD that you may live,
Lest He break forth like a [b]fire, [1]O house of Joseph,
And it consume with none to quench *it* for Bethel,
7 *For* those who turn [a]justice into wormwood
And [1]cast righteousness down to the earth."

8 He who made the [a]Pleiades and Orion
And [b]changes deep darkness into morning,
[1]Who also [c]darkens day *into* night,
Who [d]calls for the waters of the sea
And pours them out on the surface of the earth,
The [e]LORD is His name.
9 It is He who [a]flashes forth *with* destruction upon the strong,
So that [b]destruction comes upon the fortress.

10 They hate him who [a]reproves in the [1]gate,
And they [b]abhor him who speaks *with* integrity.
11 Therefore, because you [1]impose heavy rent on the poor
And exact a tribute of grain from them,
Though you have built [a]houses of well-hewn stone,
Yet you will not live in them;
You have planted pleasant vineyards, yet you will [b]not drink their wine.
12 For I know your transgressions are many and your sins are great,
You who [a]distress the righteous *and* accept bribes,
And [1]turn aside the poor in the [2]gate.
13 Therefore, at [1]such a time the prudent person [a]keeps silent, for it is an evil time.

14 Seek good and not evil, that you may live;
And thus may the LORD God of hosts be with you,
[a]Just as you have said!
15 [a]Hate evil, love good,
And establish justice in the [1]gate!
Perhaps the LORD God of hosts
[b]May be gracious to the [c]remnant of Joseph.

16 Therefore, thus says the LORD God of hosts, the Lord,
"There is [a]wailing in all the plazas,
And in all the streets they say, 'Alas! Alas!'
They also call the [b]farmer to mourning
And [1c]professional mourners to lamentation.
17"And in all the [a]vineyards *there is* wailing,
Because I shall pass through the midst of you," says the LORD.

18 Alas, you who are longing for the [a]day of the LORD,
For what purpose *will* the day of the LORD *be* to you?
It *will be* [b]darkness and not light;
19 As when a man [a]flees from a lion,
And a bear meets him,
[1]Or goes home, leans his hand against the wall,
And a snake bites him.
20 *Will* not the day of the LORD *be* [a]darkness instead of light,
Even gloom with no brightness in it?

21"I hate, I [a]reject your festivals,
Nor do I [1b]delight in your solemn assemblies.
22"Even though you [a]offer up to Me burnt offerings and your grain offerings,
I will not accept *them*;
And I will not *even* look at the [b]peace offerings of your fatlings.
23"Take away from Me the noise of your songs;
I will not even listen to the sound of your harps.
24"But let [a]justice roll down like waters
And righteousness like an ever-flowing stream.
25"[1a]Did you present Me with sacrifices and grain offerings in the wilderness for forty years, O house of Israel?
26"[a]You also carried along [1]Sikkuth
your king and [2]Kiyyun, your images,
[3]the star of your gods which you made
for yourselves.
27"Therefore, I will make you go into
exile beyond Damascus," says the LORD,
whose name is the God of hosts.

"Those at Ease in Zion"

6 [a]WOE to those who are at ease in Zion,
And to those who *feel* secure in the mountain of Samaria,
The [b]distinguished men of the foremost of nations,
To whom the house of Israel comes.
2 Go over to [a]Calneh and look,
And go from there to [b]Hamath the great,
Then go down to [c]Gath of the Philistines.
Are [1]they better than these kingdoms,
Or is their territory greater than yours?

5 [1]Lit., *seek* [2]Or, *become iniquity* [a]1 Kin. 12:28, 29; Amos 3:14; 4:4; 7:10, 13 [b]1 Sam. 7:16; 11:14 [c]Gen. 21:31–33; Amos 8:14
6 [1]Or, in *the house* [a]Is. 55:3, 6, 7; Amos 5:14 [b]Deut. 4:24
7 [1]Lit., *they have put down* [a]Amos 2:3; 5:12; 6:12
8 [1]Lit., *And He darkened* [a]Job 9:9; 38:31 [b]Job 12:22; 38:12; Is. 42:16 [c]Ps. 104:20 [d]Ps. 104:6-9; Amos 9:6 [e]Amos 4:13
9 [a]Is. 29:5; Amos 2:14 [b]Mic. 5:11
10 [1]I.e., the place where court was held [a]Is. 29:21; Amos 5:15 [b]1 Kin. 22:8; Is. 59:15; Jer. 17:16-18
11 [1]Another reading is *trample upon* [a]Amos 3:15; 6:11 [b]Mic. 6:15
12 [1]Lit., *they turn* [2]I.e., the place where court was held [a]Is. 1:23; 5:23; Amos 2:6
13 [1]Lit., *that time* [a]Eccl. 3:7; Hos. 4:4
14 [a]Mic. 3:11
15 [1]I.e., the place where court was held [a]Ps. 97:10; Rom. 12:9 [b]Joel 2:14 [c]Mic. 5:3, 7, 8
16 [1]Lit., *those who know lamentation* [a]Jer. 9:10, 18-20; Amos 8:3 [b]Joel 1:11 [c]2 Chr. 35:25; Jer. 9:17
17 [a]Is. 16:10; Jer. 48:33
18 [a]Is. 5:19; Jer. 30:7; Joel 1:15; 2:1, 11, 31 [b]Is. 5:30; Joel 2:2
19 [1]Or, *Then* [a]Job 20:24; Is. 24:17, 18; Jer. 15:2, 3; 48:44
20 [a]Is. 13:10; Zeph. 1:15
21 [1]Lit., *like to smell* [a]Is. 1:11-16; 66:3; Amos 4:4, 5; 8:10 [b]Lev. 26:31; Jer. 14:12; Hos. 5:6
22 [a]Is. 66:3; Mic. 6:6, 7 [b]Lev. 7:11-15; Amos 4:5
24 [a]Jer. 22:3; Ezek. 45:9; Mic. 6:8
25 [1]Or, *You presented Me with the sacrifices and a grain offering* [a]Deut. 32:17; Josh. 24:14; Neh. 9:18–21; Acts 7:42, 43
26 [1]Or, *Sakkuth (Saturn)* or *shrine of your Moloch* [2]Or, *Kaiwan (Saturn)* or *stands of* [3]Or, *your star gods* [a]Acts 7:43

1 [a]Is. 32:9-11; Zeph. 1:12; Luke 6:24 [b]Ex. 19:5; Amos 3:2
2 [1]Or, *you* [a]Gen. 10:10; Is. 10:9 [b]1 Kin. 8:65; 2 Kin. 18:34; Is. 10:9 [c]1 Sam. 5:8; 2 Chr. 26:6

3 Do you [a]put off the day of calamity,
And would you [b]bring near the seat of violence?

4 Those who recline on beds of ivory
And sprawl on their [a]couches,
And [b]eat lambs from the flock
And calves from the midst of the stall,
5 Who improvise to the sound of the harp,
And like David have [1]composed [a]songs for themselves,
6 Who [a]drink wine from [1]sacrificial bowls
While they anoint themselves with the finest of oils,
Yet they have not [b]grieved over the ruin of Joseph.
7 Therefore, they will now [a]go into exile at the head of the exiles,
And the [b]sprawlers' [1]banqueting will [2]pass away.

8 The Lord [1]GOD has [a]sworn by Himself, the LORD God of hosts has declared:
"I [b]loathe the arrogance of Jacob,
And I [2]detest his [c]citadels;
Therefore, I will [d]deliver up *the* city and [3]all it contains."
9 And it will be, if [a]ten men are left
in one house, they will die.
10 Then one's [1]uncle, or his [2a]under-
taker, will lift him up to carry out *his*
bones from the house, and he will say to
the one who is in the innermost part of
the house, "Is anyone else with you?"
And that one will say, "No one." Then
he will [3]answer, "[b]Keep quiet. For [4]the
name of the LORD is [c]not to be mentioned."
11 For behold, the LORD is going to
[a]command that the [b]great house be
smashed to pieces and the small house to
fragments.
12 Do horses run on rocks?
Or does one plow [1]them with oxen?
Yet you have turned [a]justice into poison,
And the fruit of righteousness into [2]wormwood,
13 You who rejoice in [1a]Lo-debar,
[2]And say, "Have we not [b]by our *own* strength taken [3]Karnaim for ourselves?"
14 "For behold, [a]I am going to raise up a nation against you,
O house of Israel," declares the LORD God of hosts,
"And they will afflict you from the [b]entrance of Hamath
To the [b]brook of the Arabah.

Warning Through Visions

7 THUS the Lord [1]GOD showed me,
and behold, He was forming a [a]lo-
cust-swarm [2]when the spring crop began
to sprout. And behold, the spring crop
was after the king's [3]mowing.
2 And it came about, [1]when it had
[a]finished eating the vegetation of the
land, that I said,
"[b]Lord GOD, please pardon!
[2]How can Jacob stand,
For he is [c]small?"
3 The LORD [1a]changed His mind about this.
"It shall not be," said the LORD.
4 Thus the Lord GOD showed me,
and behold, the Lord GOD was calling to
contend *with them* by [a]fire, and it consumed the great deep and began to
consume the [1]farm land.
5 Then I said,
"[a]Lord GOD, please stop!
[b]How can Jacob stand, for he is small?"
6 The LORD [1a]changed His mind about this.
"This too shall not be," said the Lord GOD.
7 Thus He showed me, and behold,
the Lord was standing [1]by a [2]vertical
wall, with a plumb line in His hand.
8 And the LORD said to me, "[a]What
do you see, Amos?" And I said, "A
plumb line." Then the Lord said,
"Behold I am about to put a [b]plumb line
In the midst of My people Israel.
I will [1c]spare them no longer.
9 "The [a]high places of Isaac will be desolated
And the [b]sanctuaries of Israel laid waste.
Then shall I [c]rise up against the house of Jeroboam with the sword."

Amos Accused, Answers

10 Then Amaziah, the [a]priest of
Bethel, sent *word* to [b]Jeroboam, king of
Israel, saying, "Amos has [c]conspired
against you in the midst of the house of
Israel; the land is unable to endure all
his words.
11 "For thus Amos says, 'Jeroboam
will die by the sword and Israel will
certainly go from its land into exile.'"
12 Then Amaziah said to Amos, "[a]Go,
you seer, flee away to the land of Judah,
and there eat bread and there do your
prophesying!
13 "But [a]no longer prophesy at Bethel,
for it is a [b]sanctuary of the king and a
royal [1]residence."
14 Then Amos answered and said to
Amaziah, "I am not a prophet, nor am I
the [a]son of a prophet; for I am a herds-
man and a [1]grower of sycamore figs.
15 "But the LORD took me from [1]fol-
lowing the flock and the LORD said to
me, 'Go [a]prophesy to My people Israel.'

3 [a]Is. 56:12; Amos 9:10 [b]Amos 3:10
4 [a]Amos 3:12 [b]Ezek. 34:2, 3
5 [1]Or, *invented musical instruments* [a]1 Chr. 15:16; 23:5; Is. 5:12
6 [1]Lit., *sprinkling basins* [a]Amos 2:8; 4:1 [b]Ezek. 9:4
7 [1]Or, *cultic feasts* [2]Lit., *turn aside* [a]Amos 7:11, 17 [b]1 Kin. 20:16-21; Dan. 5:4-6, 30
8 [1]Heb., *YHWH,* usually rendered *LORD* [2]Lit., *hate* [3]Lit., *its fulness* [a]Gen. 22:16; Jer. 22:5; 51:14; Amos 4:2; 8:7 [b]Lev. 26:30; Deut. 32:19; Ps. 106:40; Amos 5:21 [c]Amos 3:10, 11 [d]Hos. 11:6
9 [a]Amos 5:3
10 [1]Or, *beloved one* [2]Lit., *one who burns him* [3]Lit., *say* [4]Lit., *not to make mention of the name of* [a]1 Sam. 31:12 [b]Amos 5:13; 8:3 [c]Jer. 44:26; Ezek. 20:39
11 [a]Is. 55:11 [b]2 Kin. 25:9; Amos 3:15; 5:11
12 [1]Another reading is *the sea with oxen* [2]I.e., bitterness [a]1 Kin. 21:7-13; Is. 59:13, 14; Hos. 10:4; Amos 5:7, 11, 12
13 [1]Lit., *a thing of nothing* [2]Lit., *Who* [3]Lit., *a pair of horns* [a]Job 8:14, 15; Ps. 2:2-4; Luke 12:19, 20 [b]Ps. 75:4, 5; Is. 28:14, 15
14 [a]Jer. 5:15 [b]Num. 34:7, 8; 1 Kin. 8:65; 2 Kin. 14:25

1 [1]Heb., *YHWH,* usually rendered *LORD,* and so throughout the ch. [2]Lit., *at the beginning of the coming up of* [3]Or, *shearings* [a]Joel 1:4; Amos 4:9; Nah. 3:15
2 [1]Lit., *if* [2]Lit., *As who* [a]Ex. 10:15 [b]Jer. 14:7, 20, 21; Ezek. 9:8; 11:13 [c]Is. 37:4; Jer. 42:2
3 [1]Or, *relented* [a]Deut. 32:36; Jer. 26:19; Hos. 11:8; Amos 5:15; Jon. 3:10
4 [1]Lit., *portion* [a]Deut. 32:22; Is. 66:15, 16; Amos 2:5
5 [a]Ps. 85:4; Joel 2:17 [b]Amos 7:2
6 [1]Or, *relented* [a]Ps. 106:45; Amos 7:3; Jon. 3:10
7 [1]Or, *upon* [2]Lit., *wall of a plumb line*

8 [1]Lit., *pass him by* [a]Jer. 1:11; Amos 8:2 [b]2 Kin. 21:13; Is. 28:17; 34:11; Lam. 2:8 [c]Jer. 15:6; Ezek. 7:4-9; Amos 8:2
9 [a]Gen. 46:1; Hos. 10:8; Mic. 1:5 [b]Lev. 26:31; Is. 63:18; Jer. 51:51; Amos 7:13 [c]2 Kin. 15:8-10; Amos 7:11
10 [a]1 Kin. 12:31, 32; 13:33 [b]2 Kin. 14:23, 24 [c]Jer. 26:8-11; 38:4
12 [a]Matt. 8:34
13 [1]Lit., *house* [a]Amos 2:12; Acts 4:18 [b]1 Kin. 12:29, 32; Amos 7:9
14 [1]Or, *nipper* [a]1 Kin. 20:35; 2 Kin. 2:3, 5; 4:38; 2 Chr. 19:2
15 [1]Lit., *behind* [a]Jer. 1:7; Ezek. 2:3, 4

16“And now hear the word of the
LORD: you are saying, ‘You [a]shall not
prophesy against Israel [b]nor shall you
[1]speak against the house of Isaac.’
17“Therefore, thus says the LORD,
‘Your [a]wife will become a harlot in the
city, your [b]sons and your daughters will
fall by the sword, your land will be
parceled up by a *measuring* line, and you
yourself will die [1]upon [c]unclean soil.
Moreover, Israel will certainly go from
its land into exile.’ ”

Basket of Fruit and Israel’s Captivity

8 THUS the Lord [1]GOD showed me,
and behold, *there was* a basket of
summer fruit.
2 And He said, “What do you see,
Amos?” And [a]I said, “A basket of summer fruit.” Then the LORD said to me,
“The [b]end has come for My people
Israel. I will [1c]spare them no longer.
3“[1]The [a]songs of the palace will turn
to [b]wailing in that day,” declares the
Lord GOD. “Many *will be* the [c]corpses;
in every place [2]they will cast them forth
[3]in silence.”
4 Hear this, you who [1a]trample the
needy, to do away with the humble of
the land,
5 saying,
“When will the [a]new moon [1]be over,
So that we may sell grain,
And the [b]sabbath, that we may open the wheat *market*,
To make the [2]bushel smaller and the shekel bigger,
And to [c]cheat with [3]dishonest scales,
6 So as to [a]buy the helpless for [1]money
And the needy for a pair of sandals,
And *that* we may sell the refuse of the wheat?”

7 The LORD has [a]sworn by the [b]pride of Jacob,
“Indeed, I will [c]never forget any of their deeds.
8“Because of this will not the land [a]quake
And everyone who dwells in it [b]mourn?
Indeed, all of it will [c]rise up like the Nile,
And it will be tossed about,
And subside like the Nile of Egypt.
9“And it will come about in that day,” declares the Lord GOD,
“That I shall make the [a]sun go down at noon
And [b]make the earth dark in [1]broad daylight.
10“Then I shall [a]turn your festivals into mourning
And all your songs into [1]lamentation;
And I will bring [b]sackcloth on everyone’s loins
And baldness on every head.
And I will make it [c]like *a time of* mourning for an only son,

16 [1]Lit., *flow* [a]Amos 2:12; 7:13 [b]Deut. 32:2; Ezek. 20:46; 21:2
17 [1]Or, *in an unclean land* [a]Hos. 4:13, 14 [b]Jer. 14:16 [c]2 Kin. 17:6; Ezek. 4:13; Hos. 9:3

1 [1]Heb., *YHWH*, usually rendered *LORD*, and so throughout the ch.
2 [1]Lit., *pass him by* [a]Jer. 24:3 [b]Ezek. 7:2, 3, 6 [c]Amos 7:8
3 [1]Or, *They will howl the palace songs* [2]Lit., *he has thrown* [3]Or, *hush!* [a]Amos 5:23; 6:4, 5; 8:10 [b]Amos 5:16 [c]Amos 6:8–10
4 [1]Or, *snap at* [a]Ps. 14:4; Prov. 30:14; Amos 2:7; 5:11, 12
5 [1]Lit., *pass by* [2]Lit., *ephah* [3]Lit., *balances of deception* [a]Num. 28:11; 2 Kin. 4:23 [b]Ex. 31:13-17; Neh. 13:15 [c]Hos. 12:7; Mic. 6:11
6 [1]Lit., *silver* [a]Amos 2:6
7 [a]Amos 4:2 [b]Deut. 33:26, 29; Ps. 68:34; Amos 6:8 [c]Ps. 10:11; Hos. 7:2; 8:13
8 [a]Ps. 18:7; 60:2; Is. 5:25 [b]Hos. 4:3 [c]Jer. 46:7, 8; Amos 9:5
9 [1]Lit., *a day of light* [a]Job 5:14; Is. 13:10; Jer. 15:9; Mic. 3:6 [b]Is. 59:9, 10; Amos 4:13; 5:8
10 [1]Or, *a dirge* [a]Job 20:23; Amos 5:21 [b]Is. 15:2, 3; Jer. 48:37; Ezek. 7:18; 27:31 [c]Jer. 6:26; Zech. 12:10
11 [a]1 Sam. 3:1; 2 Chr. 15:3; Ps. 74:9; Ezek. 7:26; Mic. 3:6
12 [a]Ezek. 20:3, 31
13 [a]Lam. 1:18; 2:21 [b]Is. 41:17; Hos. 2:3
14 [1]Or, *Ashimah* [a]Hos. 8:5 [b]1 Kin. 12:28, 29 [c]Amos 5:5 [d]Amos 5:2

1 [a]Amos 3:14 [b]Zeph. 2:14 [c]Ps. 68:21; Hab. 3:13 [d]Amos 7:17 [e]Jer. 11:11
2 [a]Ps. 139:8 [b]Jer. 51:53; Obad. 4
3 [a]Jer. 16:16 [b]Job 34:22; Ps. 139:9, 10 [c]Is. 27:1
4 [a]Lev. 26:33 [b]Lev. 17:10; Jer. 21:10; 39:16; 44:11
5 [1]Heb., *YHWH*, usually rendered *LORD*, and so throughout the ch. [a]Ps. 104:32; 144:5; Is. 64:1; Mic. 1:4 [b]Amos 8:8

And the end of it will be like a bitter day.

11“Behold, days are coming,” declares the Lord GOD,
“When I will send a famine on the land,
Not a famine for bread or a thirst for water,
But rather [a]for hearing the words of the LORD.
12“And people will stagger from sea to sea,
And from the north even to the east;
They will go to and fro to [a]seek the word of the LORD,
But they will not find *it*.
13“In that day the beautiful [a]virgins
And the young men will [b]faint from thirst.
14“*As for* those who swear by the [1a]guilt of Samaria,
Who say, ‘As your god lives, O [b]Dan,’
And, ‘As the way of [c]Beersheba lives,’
They will fall and [d]not rise again.”

God’s Judgment Unavoidable

9 I SAW the Lord standing beside the [a]altar, and He said,
“Smite the capitals so that the [b]thresholds will shake,
And [c]break them on the heads of them all!
Then I will [d]slay the rest of them with the sword;
They will [e]not have a fugitive who will flee,
Or a refugee who will escape.
2“Though they dig into [a]Sheol,
From there shall My hand take them;
And though they [b]ascend to heaven,
From there will I bring them down.
3“And though they hide on the summit of Carmel,
I will [a]search them out and take them from there;
And though they [b]conceal themselves from My sight on the floor of the sea,
From there I will command the [c]serpent and it will bite them.
4“And though they go into [a]captivity before their enemies,
From there I will command the sword that it slay them,
And I will [b]set My eyes against them for evil and not for good.”

5 And the Lord [1]GOD of hosts,
The One who [a]touches the land so that it melts,
And [b]all those who dwell in it mourn,
And all of it rises up like the Nile
And subsides like the Nile of Egypt;

6 The One who builds His [1a]upper chambers in the heavens,
And has founded His vaulted dome over the earth,
He who [b]calls for the waters of the sea
And [c]pours them out on the face of the earth,
[d]The LORD is His name.

7 "Are you not as the sons of [a]Ethiopia to Me,
O sons of Israel?" declares the LORD.
"Have I not brought up Israel from the land of Egypt,
And the [b]Philistines from Caphtor and the [c]Arameans from [d]Kir?
8 "Behold, the [a]eyes of the Lord GOD are on the sinful kingdom,
And I will [b]destroy it from the face of the earth;
Nevertheless, I will [c]not totally destroy the house of Jacob,"
Declares the LORD.
9 "For behold, I am commanding,
And I will [a]shake the house of Israel among all nations
As *grain* is shaken in a sieve,
But not a [1]kernel will fall to the ground.
10 "All the [a]sinners of My people will die by the sword,
Those who say, '[b]The calamity will not overtake or confront us.'

The Restoration of Israel

11 "In that day I will [a]raise up the fallen [1b]booth of David,
And wall up its [c]breaches;
I will also raise up its ruins,
And rebuild it as in the [d]days of old;
12 [a]That they may possess the remnant of [b]Edom
And all the [1]nations who are [c]called by My name,"
Declares the LORD who does this.

13 "Behold, days are coming," declares the LORD,
"When the [a]plowman will overtake the reaper
And the treader of grapes him who sows seed;
When the [b]mountains will drip sweet [c]wine,
And all the hills will be dissolved.
14 "Also I will [a]restore the [1]captivity of My people Israel,
And they will [b]rebuild the ruined cities and live *in them*,
They will also [c]plant vineyards and drink their wine,
And make gardens and eat their fruit.
15 "I will also plant them on their land,
And [a]they will not again be rooted out from their land
Which I have given them,"
Says the LORD your God.

6 [1]Or, *stairs* [a]Ps. 104:3, 13 [b]Amos 5:8 [c]Ps. 104:6 [d]Amos 4:13

7 [a]2 Chr. 14:9, 12; Is. 20:4; 43:3 [b]Deut. 2:23; Jer. 47:4 [c]Amos 1:5 [d]2 Kin. 16:9; Is. 22:6

8 [a]Jer. 44:27; Amos 9:4 [b]Amos 7:17; 9:10 [c]Jer. 5:10; 30:11; 31:35, 36; Joel 2:32; Amos 3:12; Obad. 17

9 [1]Or, *pebble* [a]Is. 30:28; Luke 22:31

10 [a]Is. 33:14; Zech. 13:8 [b]Amos 6:3

11 [1]Or, *shelter* or *tabernacle* [a]Acts 15:16-18 [b]Is. 16:5 [c]Ps. 80:12 [d]Is. 63:11; Jer. 46:26

12 [1]Or, *Gentiles* [a]Obad. 19 [b]Num. 24:18; Is. 11:14 [c]Is. 43:7

13 [a]Lev. 26:5 [b]Joel 3:18 [c]Gen. 49:11

14 [1]Or, *fortunes* [a]Ps. 53:6; Is. 60:4; Jer. 30:3, 18 [b]Is. 61:4; 65:21 [c]Jer. 24:6; 31:28

15 [a]Is. 60:21; Ezek. 34:28; 37:25

THE BOOK OF OBADIAH

Edom Will Be Humbled

1 THE vision of Obadiah.
Thus says the Lord [1]GOD concerning [a]Edom—
[b]We have heard a report from the LORD,
And an [c]envoy has been sent among the nations saying,
"[d]Arise and let us go against her for battle"—
2 "Behold, I will make you [a]small among the nations;
You are greatly despised.
3 "The [a]arrogance of your heart has deceived you,
You who live in the clefts of [1]the [b]rock,
In the loftiness of your dwelling place,
Who say in your heart,
'[c]Who will bring me down to earth?'
4 "Though you [a]build high like the eagle,
Though you set your nest among the [b]stars,
From there I will bring you down,"
declares the LORD.
5 "If [a]thieves came to you,
If [1]robbers by night—
O how you will be ruined!—
Would they not steal *only* [2]until they had enough?
If grape gatherers came to you,
[b]Would they not leave *some* gleanings?
6 "O how Esau will be [a]ransacked,
And his hidden treasures searched out!
7 "All the [a]men [1]allied with you
Will send you forth to the border,
And the men at peace with you
Will deceive you and overpower you.
They who eat your [b]bread
Will set an ambush for you.
(There is [c]no understanding [2]in him.)
8 "Will I not on that day," declares the LORD,
"[a]Destroy wise men from Edom
And understanding from the mountain of Esau?
9 "Then your [a]mighty men will be dismayed, O [b]Teman,
In order that everyone may be [c]cut

1 [1]Heb., *YHWH*, usually rendered *LORD* [a]Ps. 137:7; Is. 21:11, 12; 34:1-17; 63:1-6; Jer. 49:7-22; Ezek. 25:12-14; 35:15; Joel 3:19; Amos 1:11, 12; Mal. 1:4 [b]Jer. 49:14-16; Obad. 1-4 [c]Is. 18:2; 30:4 [d]Jer. 6:4, 5

2 [a]Num. 24:18; Is. 23:9

3 [1]Or, *Sela* [a]Is. 16:6; Jer. 49:16 [b]2 Kin. 14:7; 2 Chr. 25:11f. [c]Is. 14:13-15; Rev. 18:7

4 [a]Job 20:6, 7; Hab. 2:9 [b]Is. 14:12-15

5 [1]Lit., *devastators of* the *night* [2]Lit., *their sufficiency* [a]Jer. 49:9 [b]Deut. 24:21

6 [a]Jer. 49:10

7 [1]Lit., *of your covenant* [2]I.e., in Esau; or, *of it* [a]Jer. 30:14 [b]Ps. 41:9 [c]Is. 19:11; Jer. 49:7

8 [a]Job 5:12-14; Is. 29:14

9 [a]Jer. 49:22 [b]Gen. 36:11; 1 Chr. 1:45; Job 2:11; Jer. 49:7; Ezek. 25:13; Amos 1:12; Hab. 3:3 [c]Is. 34:5-8; 63:1-3; Obad. 5

off from the mountain of Esau
by slaughter.

10 "Because of [a]violence to your
brother Jacob,
[1]You will be covered *with* shame,
[b]And you will be cut off forever.
11 "On the day that you [a]stood aloof,
On the day that strangers carried
off his wealth,
And foreigners entered his gate
And [b]cast lots for Jerusalem—
[c]You too were as one of them.
12 "[a]Do not [1]gloat over your brother's
day,
The day of his misfortune.
And [b]do not rejoice over the sons
of Judah
In the day of their destruction;
Yes, [c]do not [2]boast
In the day of *their* distress.
13 "Do not enter the gate of My people
In the [a]day of their disaster.
Yes, you, do not [1]gloat over their
calamity
In the day of their disaster.
And do not [b]loot their wealth
In the day of their disaster.
14 "And do not [a]stand at the fork of
the road
To cut down their fugitives;
And do not imprison their survi-
vors
In the day of their distress.

The Day of the LORD *and the Future*

15 "For the [a]day of the LORD draws
near on all the nations.
[b]As you have done, it will be done
to you.
Your [c]dealings will return on your
own head.
16 "Because just as you [a]drank on [b]My
holy mountain,
All the nations [c]will drink continually.
They will drink and [1]swallow,
And become as if they had never
existed.
17 "But on Mount [a]Zion there will be
those who escape,
And it will be holy.
And the house of Jacob will [b]pos-
sess their possessions.
18 "Then the house of Jacob will be a
[a]fire
And the house of Joseph a flame;
But the house of Esau *will be* as
stubble.
And they will set [1]them on fire and
consume [1]them,
So that there will be [b]no survivor of
the house of Esau,"
For the LORD has spoken.
19 Then *those of* the [1]Negev will [a]pos-
sess the mountain of Esau,
And *those of* the [2]Shephelah the
[b]Philistine *plain*;
Also, they will [c]possess the terri-
tory of Ephraim and the territory of Samaria,
And Benjamin *will possess* Gilead.
20 And the exiles of this host of the
sons of Israel,
Who are *among* the Canaanites as
far as [a]Zarephath,
And the exiles of Jerusalem who
are in Sepharad
Will possess the [b]cities of the
Negev.
21 The [a]deliverers will ascend Mount
Zion
To judge the mountain of Esau,
And the [b]kingdom will be the
LORD'S.

10 [1]Lit., *Shame will cover you*
[a]Gen. 27:41; Ezek. 25:12; Joel 3:19; Amos 1:11 [b]Ezek. 35:9

11 [a]Ps. 83:5, 6; 137:7; Amos 1:6, 9 [b]Joel 3:3; Nah. 3:10 [c]Ezek. 35:10

12 [1]Lit., *look on* [2]Lit., *make your mouth large*
[a]Mic. 4:11; 7:10 [b]Prov. 17:5; Ezek. 35:15; 36:5 [c]Ps. 31:18; Ezek. 35:12

13 [1]Lit., *look on*
[a]Ezek. 35:5 [b]Ezek. 35:10; 36:2, 3

14 [a]Is. 16:3, 4

15 [a]Ezek. 30:3; Joel 1:15; 2:1, 11, 31; Amos 5:18, 20 [b]Jer. 50:29; 51:56; Hab. 2:8 [c]Ezek. 35:11

16 [1]Or, *stagger*
[a]Jer. 49:12 [b]Joel 3:17 [c]Is. 51:22, 23; Jer. 25:15, 16

17 [a]Is. 4:2, 3 [b]Is. 14:1, 2; Amos 9:11-15

18 [1]I.e., the people of Esau
[a]Is. 5:24; 9:18, 19; Zech. 12:6 [b]Jer. 11:23; Amos 1:8

19 [1]I.e., South country [2]I.e., the foothills
[a]Is. 11:14; Amos 9:12 [b]Is. 11:14 [c]Jer. 31:5; 32:44

20 [a]1 Kin. 17:9; Luke 4:26 [b]Jer. 32:44; 33:13

21 [a]Neh. 9:27 [b]Ps. 22:28; 47:7-9; 67:4; Zech. 14:9; Rev. 11:15

THE BOOK OF
JONAH

Jonah's Disobedience

1 THE word of the LORD came to
[a]Jonah the son of Amittai saying,
2 "Arise, go to [a]Nineveh the great
city, and [b]cry against it, for their [c]wick-
edness has come up before Me."
3 But Jonah rose up to flee to [a]Tar-
shish [b]from the presence of the LORD. So
he went down to [c]Joppa, found a ship
which was going to Tarshish, paid the
fare, and went down into it to go with
them to Tarshish from the presence of
the LORD.
4 And the [a]LORD hurled a great wind
on the sea and there was a great storm
on the sea so that the ship was about to
[1]break up.
5 Then the sailors became afraid, and
every man cried to [a]his god, and they
[b]threw the [1]cargo which was in the ship
into the sea to lighten *it* [2]for them. But
Jonah had gone below into the hold of
the ship, lain down, and fallen sound
asleep.
6 So the captain approached him and
said, "How is it that you are sleeping?
Get up, [a]call on your god. Perhaps *your*
[b]god will be concerned about us so that
we will not perish."
7 And each man said to his mate,
"Come, let us [a]cast lots so we may [1]learn
on whose account this calamity *has*
struck us." So they cast lots and the [b]lot
fell on Jonah.
8 Then they said to him, "[a]Tell us,
now! On whose account *has* this calamity *struck* us? What is your [b]occupation?
And where do you come from? What is
your country? From what people are
you?"
9 And he said to them, "I am a
[a]Hebrew, and I [b]fear the LORD [c]God of
heaven who [d]made the sea and the dry
land."
10 Then the men became extremely
frightened and they said to him, "[1]How
could you do this?" For the men knew
that he was [a]fleeing from the presence of
the LORD, because he had told them.
11 So they said to him, "What should
we do to you that the sea may become
calm [1]for us?"—for the sea was becoming increasingly stormy.
12 And he said to them, "Pick me up
and throw me into the sea. Then the sea
will become calm [1]for you, for I know
that [a]on account of me this great storm
has come upon you."
13 However, the men [1]rowed *desper-*
ately to return to land but they could
not, for the sea was becoming *even*
stormier against them.
14 Then they called on the [a]LORD and
said, "We earnestly pray, O LORD, do
not let us perish on account of this man's
life and do not put innocent blood on
us; for [b]Thou, O LORD, hast done as
Thou hast pleased."
15 So they picked up Jonah, threw
him into the sea, and the sea [a]stopped its
raging.
16 Then the men feared the LORD
greatly, and they offered a sacrifice to
the LORD and made [a]vows.
17 [1]And the LORD appointed a great
fish to swallow Jonah, and Jonah was in
the [a]stomach of the fish three days and
three nights.

Jonah's Prayer

2 [1]THEN Jonah prayed to the LORD
his God [a]from the stomach of the
fish,
2 and he said,
"I [a]called out of my distress to the
LORD,
And He answered me.
I cried for help from the [1]depth of
[b]Sheol;
Thou didst hear my voice.
3 "For Thou hadst [a]cast me into the
deep,
Into the heart of the seas,
And the current [1]engulfed me.
All Thy [b]breakers and billows
passed over me.
4 "So I said, 'I have been [a]expelled
from [1]Thy sight.
Nevertheless I will look again
[b]toward Thy holy temple.'
5 "[a]Water encompassed me to the
[1]point of death.
The great [b]deep [2]engulfed me,
Weeds were wrapped around my
head.
6 "I [a]descended to the roots of the
mountains.
The earth with its [b]bars *was* around
me forever,
But Thou hast [c]brought up my life
from [1]the pit, O LORD my God.
7 "While [1]I was [a]fainting away,
I [b]remembered the LORD;
And my [c]prayer came to Thee,
Into [d]Thy holy temple.
8 "Those who [a]regard [1]vain idols
Forsake their faithfulness,
9 But I will [a]sacrifice to Thee
With the voice of thanksgiving.
That which I have vowed I will
[b]pay.
[c]Salvation is from the LORD."
10 Then the LORD commanded the
[a]fish, and it vomited Jonah up onto the
dry land.

Nineveh Repents

3 NOW the word of the LORD came to
Jonah the second time, saying,
2 "Arise, go to [a]Nineveh the great city
and [b]proclaim to it the proclamation
which I am going to tell you."

1 [a]2 Kin. 14:25; Matt. 12:39-41; 16:4; Luke 11:29, 30, 32
2 [a]Gen. 10:11; 2 Kin. 19:36; Is. 37:37; Nah. 1:1; Zeph. 2:13 [b]Is. 58:1 [c]Gen. 18:20; Hos. 7:2
3 [a]Is. 23:1, 6, 10; Jer. 10:9 [b]Gen. 4:16; Ps. 139:7, 9, 10 [c]Josh. 19:46; 2 Chr. 2:16; Ezra 3:7; Acts 9:36, 43
4 [1]Lit., *be broken* [a]Ps. 107:23–28; 135:6, 7
5 [1]Lit., *vessels* [2]Lit., *from upon them* [a]1 Kin. 18:26 [b]Acts 27:18, 19, 38
6 [a]Ps. 107:28 [b]2 Sam. 12:22; Amos 5:15; Jon. 3:9
7 [1]Lit., *know* [a]Josh. 7:14–18; 1 Sam. 10:20, 21; 14:41, 42; Acts 1:23–26 [b]Num. 32:23; Prov. 16:33
8 [a]Josh. 7:19; 1 Sam. 14:43 [b]Gen. 47:3; 1 Sam. 30:13
9 [a]Gen. 14:13; Ex. 1:15; 2:13 [b]2 Kin. 17:25, 28, 32, 33 [c]Ezra 1:2; Neh. 1:4; Ps. 136:26; Dan. 2:18 [d]Neh. 9:6; Ps. 95:5; 146:6
10 [1]Lit., *What is this you have done* [a]Job 27:22; Jon. 1:3
11 [1]Lit., *from upon us*
12 [1]Lit., *from upon you* [a]2 Sam. 24:17; 1 Chr. 21:17
13 [1]Lit., *dug their oars into the water*
14 [a]Ps. 107:28; Jon. 1:16 [b]Ps. 115:3; 135:6; Dan. 4:34, 35
15 [a]Ps. 65:7; 93:3, 4; 107:29
16 [a]Ps. 50:14; 66:13, 14
17 [1]Ch. 2:1 in Heb. [a]Matt. 12:40; 16:4

1 [1]Ch. 2:2 in Heb. [a]Job 13:15; Ps. 130:1, 2; Lam. 3:53-56
2 [1]Lit., *belly* [a]1 Sam. 30:6; Ps. 18:4-6; 22:24; 120:1 [b]Ps. 18:5, 6; 86:13; 88:1–7
3 [1]Lit., *surrounded* [a]Ps. 69:1, 2, 14, 15; Lam. 3:54 [b]Ps. 42:7
4 [1]Lit., *before Thine eyes* [a]Ps. 31:22; Jer. 7:15 [b]1 Kin. 8:38; 2 Chr. 6:38; Ps. 5:7
5 [1]Lit., *soul* [2]Lit., *surrounded* [a]Lam. 3:54 [b]Ps. 69:1, 2
6 [1]Or, *corruption* [a]Ps. 18:5; 116:3 [b]Is. 38:10; Matt. 16:18 [c]Job 33:28; Ps. 16:10; 30:3; Is. 38:17
7 [1]Lit., *my soul . . . within me* [a]Ps. 142:3 [b]Ps. 77:10, 11; 143:5 [c]2 Chr. 30:27; Ps. 18:6 [d]Ps. 11:4; 65:4; Jon. 2:4; Mic. 1:2; Hab. 2:20
8 [1]Lit., *empty vanities* [a]2 Kin. 17:15; Ps. 31:6; Jer. 10:8
9 [a]Ps. 50:14, 23; Jer. 33:11; Hos. 14:2 [b]Job 22:27; Eccl. 5:4, 5 [c]Ps. 3:8; Is. 45:17
10 [a]Jon. 1:17

2 [a]Zeph. 2:13 [b]Jer. 1:17; Ezek. 2:7

3 So Jonah arose and went to Nineveh according to the word of the LORD.
Now Nineveh was [1]an [a]exceedingly
great city, a three days' walk.
4 Then Jonah began to go through
the city one day's walk; and he [a]cried
out and said, "Yet forty days and Nineveh will be overthrown."
5 Then the people of Nineveh believed in God; and they called a [a]fast
and put on sackcloth from the greatest
to the least of them.
6 When the word reached the king of
Nineveh, he arose from his throne, laid
aside his robe from him, [a]covered *himself*
with sackcloth, and sat on the [1]ashes.
7 And he issued a [a]proclamation and
it said, "In Nineveh by the decree of the
king and his nobles: Do not let man,
beast, herd, or flock taste a thing. Do not
let them eat or drink water.
8 "But both man and beast must be
covered with sackcloth; and let [1]men
[a]call on God earnestly that each may
[b]turn from his wicked way and from the
violence which is in [2]his hands.
9 "[a]Who knows, God may turn and
relent, and withdraw His burning anger
so that we shall not perish?"
10 When God saw their deeds, that
they [a]turned from their wicked way, then
[b]God relented concerning the calamity
which He had declared He would [1]bring
upon them. And He did not do *it.*

Jonah's Displeasure Rebuked

4 BUT it greatly displeased Jonah,
and he became [a]angry.
2 And he [a]prayed to the LORD and
said, "Please LORD, was not this [1]what I
said while I was still in my *own* country?
Therefore, [2]in order to forestall this I
[b]fled to Tarshish, for I knew that Thou
art a [c]gracious and compassionate God,
slow to anger and abundant in lovingkindness, and one who relents concerning calamity.
3 "Therefore now, O LORD, please
[a]take my [1]life from me, for death is
[b]better to me than life."
4 And the LORD said, "Do you have
good reason to be angry?"
5 Then Jonah went out from the city
and sat east of [1]it. There he made a
shelter for himself and [a]sat under it in
the shade until he could see what would
happen in the city.
6 So the LORD God appointed a
[1]plant and it grew up over Jonah to be a
shade over his head to deliver him from
his discomfort. And Jonah was [2]ex-
tremely happy about the [1]plant.
7 But God appointed a worm when
dawn came the next day, and it attacked
the plant and it [a]withered.
8 And it came about when the sun
came up that God appointed a scorching
[a]east wind, and the [b]sun beat down on
Jonah's head so that he became faint
and begged with *all* his soul to die,
saying, "[c]Death is better to me than
life."
9 Then God said to Jonah, "Do you
have good reason to be angry about the
plant?" And he said, "I have good
reason to be angry, even to death."
10 Then the LORD said, "You had
compassion on the plant for which you
did not work, and *which* you did not
cause to grow, which [1]came up overnight
and perished [2]overnight.
11 "And should I not [a]have compassion on Nineveh, the great city in which
there are more than 120,000 persons who
do not [b]know *the difference* between
their right and left hand, as well as many
[c]animals?"

4 [a]Matt. 12:41; Luke 11:32
5 [a]Dan. 9:3; Joel 1:14
6 [1]Or, *dust* [a]Esth. 4:1-4; Jer. 6:26; Ezek. 27:30, 31
7 [a]2 Chr. 20:3; Ezra 8:21; Jon. 3:5
8 [1]Lit., *them* [2]Lit., *their* [a]Ps. 130:1; Jon. 1:6, 14 [b]Is. 1:16-19; 55:6, 7; Jer. 18:11
9 [a]2 Sam. 12:22; Joel 2:14
10 [1]Lit., *do* [a]1 Kin. 21:27-29; Jer. 31:18 [b]Ex. 32:14; Jer. 18:8; Amos 7:3, 6

1 [a]Jon. 4:4, 9; Matt. 20:15; Luke 15:28
2 [1]Lit., *my word* [2]Lit., *I was beforehand in fleeing* [a]Jer. 20:7 [b]Jon. 1:3 [c]Ex. 34:6; Num. 14:18; Ps. 86:5, 15; Joel 2:13
3 [1]Lit., *soul* [a]1 Kin. 19:4; Job 6:8, 9 [b]Job 7:15, 16; Eccl. 7:1
5 [1]Lit., *the city* [a]1 Kin. 19:9, 13
6 [1]Probably a castor oil plant, and so in vv. 7, 9 and 10 [2]Lit., *greatly*
7 [a]Joel 1:12
8 [a]Ezek. 19:12; Hos. 13:15 [b]Ps. 121:6; Is. 49:10 [c]Jon. 4:3
10 [1]Lit., *was a son of a night* [2]Lit., *a son of a night*
11 [a]Jon. 3:10 [b]Deut. 1:39; Is. 7:16 [c]Ps. 36:6

THE BOOK OF
MICAH

Destruction in Israel and Judah

1 THE [a]word of the LORD which came *to* [b]Micah of Moresheth in the days of [c]Jotham, [d]Ahaz, *and* [e]Hezekiah, kings of Judah, which he saw concerning Samaria and Jerusalem.
2 Hear, O peoples, all of [1]you;
[a]Listen, O earth and [2]all it contains,
And let the Lord [3]GOD be a [b]witness against you,
The Lord from His holy temple.
3 For behold, the LORD is [a]coming forth from His place.
He will come down and [b]tread on the high places of the [1]earth.
4 [a]The mountains will melt under Him,
And the valleys will be split,
Like wax before the fire,
Like water poured down a steep place.
5 All this is for the rebellion of Jacob
And for the sins of the house of Israel.
What is the [a]rebellion of Jacob?
Is it not [b]Samaria?
What is the [c]high [1]place of Judah?
Is it not Jerusalem?
6 For I will make Samaria a [a]heap of ruins [1]in the open country,
[b]Planting places for a vineyard.
I will [c]pour her stones down into the valley,
And will [d]lay bare her foundations.
7 All of her [a]idols will be smashed,
All of her earnings will be burned with fire,
And all of her images I will make desolate,
For she collected *them* from a [b]harlot's earnings,
And to the earnings of a harlot they will return.

8 Because of this I must lament and wail,
I must go [a]barefoot and naked;
I must make a lament like the [b]jackals
And a mourning like the ostriches.
9 For her [1a]wound is incurable,
For [b]it has come to Judah;
It has reached the [c]gate of my people,
Even to Jerusalem.
10 [a]Tell it not in Gath,
Weep not at all.
At [1]Beth-le-aphrah roll yourself in the dust.
11 [1]Go on your way, inhabitant of [2]Shaphir, in [a]shameful nakedness.
The inhabitant of [3b]Zaanan does not [4]escape.
The lamentation of [5]Beth-ezel:
"He will take from you its [6]support."
12 For the inhabitant of [1]Maroth
Becomes weak [a]waiting for good,
Because a calamity has come down from the LORD
To the [b]gate of Jerusalem.
13 Harness the chariot to the team of horses,
O inhabitant of [a]Lachish—
She was the beginning of sin
To the daughter of Zion—
Because in you were found
The [b]rebellious acts of Israel.
14 Therefore, you will give parting [a]gifts
On behalf of Moresheth-gath;
The houses of [b]Achzib *will* become a [c]deception
To the kings of Israel.
15 Moreover, I will bring on you
The one who takes possession,
O inhabitant of [1a]Mareshah.
The glory of Israel will enter [b]Adullam.
16 Make yourself [a]bald and cut off your hair,
Because of the children of your delight;
Extend your baldness like the eagle,
For they will [b]go from you into exile.

Woe to Oppressors

2 WOE to those who [a]scheme iniquity,
Who work out evil on their beds!
[1b]When morning comes, they do it,
For it is in the [c]power of their hands.
2 They [a]covet fields and then [b]seize *them*,
And houses, and take *them* away.
They [1c]rob a man and his house,
A man and his inheritance.
3 Therefore, thus says the LORD,
"Behold, I am [a]planning against this [b]family a calamity
From which you [c]cannot remove your necks;
And you will not walk [d]haughtily,
For it will be an [e]evil time.
4 "On that day they will [a]take up against you a [1]taunt
And [2b]utter a bitter lamentation *and* say,
'We are completely [c]destroyed!
He exchanges the portion of my people;
How He removes it from me!
To the apostate He [d]apportions our fields.'
5 "Therefore, you will have no one [1a]stretching a measuring line
For you by lot in the assembly of the LORD.

6 '[a]Do not [1]speak out,' *so* they [1]speak out.
But if [2]they do [b]not [1]speak out concerning these things,
[c]Reproaches will not be turned back.

1 [a]2 Pet. 1:21 [b]Jer. 26:18 [c]2 Kin. 15:5, 32–38; 2 Chr. 27:1–9; Is. 1:1; Hos. 1:1 [d]2 Kin. 16:1–20; 2 Chr. 28:1–27; Is. 7:1–12 [e]2 Kin. 18:1–20; 2 Chr. 29:1–31
2 [1]Lit., *them* [2]Lit., *its fulness* [3]Heb., *YHWH*, usually rendered *LORD* [a]Jer. 6:19; 22:29 [b]Is. 50:7
3 [1]Or, *land* [a]Is. 26:21 [b]Amos 4:13
4 [a]Ps. 97:5; Is. 64:1, 2; Nah. 1:5
5 [1]Lit., *places* [a]Jer. 2:19 [b]Is. 7:9; Amos 8:14 [c]2 Chr. 34:3, 4
6 [1]Lit., *of the field* [a]2 Kin. 19:25; Mic. 3:12 [b]Jer. 31:5; Amos 5:11 [c]Lam. 4:1 [d]Ezek. 13:14
7 [a]Deut. 9:21; 2 Chr. 34:7 [b]Deut. 23:18; Is. 23:17
8 [a]Is. 32:11 [b]Is. 13:21, 22
9 [1]Lit., *wounds* [a]Is. 3:26; Jer. 30:12, 15 [b]2 Kin. 18:13; Is. 8:7, 8 [c]Mic. 1:12
10 [1]I.e., house of dust [a]2 Sam. 1:20
11 [1]I.e., Go into captivity [2]I.e., pleasantness [3]I.e., going out [4]Lit., *go out* [5]I.e., house of removal [6]Lit., *standing place* [a]Ezek. 23:29 [b]Josh. 15:37
12 [1]I.e., bitterness [a]Is. 59:9–11; Jer. 14:19 [b]Mic. 1:9
13 [a]Josh. 10:3; 2 Kin. 14:19; Is. 36:2 [b]Mic. 1:5
14 [a]2 Kin. 16:8 [b]Josh. 15:44 [c]Jer. 15:18
15 [1]I.e., possession [a]Josh. 15:44 [b]Josh. 12:15; 15:35; 2 Sam. 23:13
16 [a]Is. 22:12 [b]2 Kin. 17:6; Amos 7:11, 17

1 [1]Lit., *In the light of the morning* [a]Ps. 36:4; Is. 32:7; Nah. 1:11 [b]Hos. 7:6, 7 [c]Gen. 31:29; Deut. 28:32; Prov. 3:27
2 [1]Lit., *oppress* [a]Jer. 22:17; Amos 8:4 [b]Is. 5:8 [c]1 Kin. 21:1–15
3 [a]Deut. 28:48; Jer. 18:11 [b]Jer. 8:3; Amos 3:1, 2 [c]Lam. 1:14; 5:5 [d]Is. 2:11, 12 [e]Amos 5:13
4 [1]Or, *proverb* [2]Lit., *lament* [a]Hab. 2:6 [b]Jer. 9:10, 17–21; Mic. 1:8 [c]Is. 6:11; 24:3; Jer. 4:13 [d]Jer. 6:12; 8:10
5 [1]Lit., *casting* [a]Num. 34:13, 16–29; Deut. 32:8; Josh. 18:4, 10

6 [1]Lit., *flow* [2]I.e., God's prophets [a]Is. 30:10; Amos 2:12; 7:16 [b]Is. 29:10; Mic. 3:6 [c]Mic. 6:16

7"Is it being said, O house of Jacob:
'Is the Spirit of the LORD [a]impatient?
Are these His doings?'
Do not My words [b]do good
To the one [c]walking uprightly?
8"[1]Recently My people have arisen as an [a]enemy—
You [b]strip the [2]robe off the garment,
From [c]unsuspecting passers-by,
From those returned from war.
9"The women of My people you [a]evict,
Each *one* from her pleasant house.
From her children you take My [b]splendor forever.
10"Arise and go,
For this is no place [a]of rest
Because of the [b]uncleanness that brings on destruction,
A painful destruction.
11"If a man walking after wind and [a]falsehood
Had told lies *and said*,
'I will [1]speak out to you concerning [b]wine and liquor,'
He would be [2]spokesman to [c]this people.

12"I will surely [a]assemble all of you, Jacob,
I will surely gather the [b]remnant of Israel.
I will put them together like sheep in the fold;
Like a flock in the midst of its pasture
They will be noisy with men.
13"The breaker goes up before them;
They break out, pass through the gate, and go out by it.
So their king goes on before them,
And the LORD at their head."

Rulers Denounced

3 AND I said,
"[a]Hear now, heads of Jacob
And rulers of the house of Israel.
Is it not for you to [b]know justice?
2"You who hate good and love evil,
Who [a]tear off their skin from them
And their flesh from their bones,
3 And who [a]eat the flesh of my people,
Strip off their skin from them,
Break their bones,
And [b]chop *them* up as for the pot
And as meat in a kettle."
4 Then they will [a]cry out to the LORD,
But He will not answer them.
Instead, He will [b]hide His face from them at that time,
Because they have [c]practiced evil deeds.

5 Thus says the LORD concerning the prophets
Who [a]lead my people astray;
When they have *something* to bite with their teeth,
They [b]cry, "Peace,"
But against him who puts nothing in their mouths,
They declare holy war.
6 Therefore *it will be* [a]night for you—without vision,
And darkness for you—without divination.
The [b]sun will go down on the prophets,
And the day will become dark over them.
7 The seers will be [a]ashamed
And the [b]diviners will be embarrassed.
Indeed, they will all [c]cover *their* [1]mouths
Because there is [d]no answer from God.
8 On the other hand [a]I am filled with power—
With the Spirit of the LORD—
And with justice and courage
To [b]make known to Jacob his rebellious act,
Even to Israel his sin.
9 Now hear this, [a]heads of the house of Jacob
And rulers of the house of Israel,
Who [b]abhor justice
And twist everything that is straight,
10 Who [a]build Zion with bloodshed
And Jerusalem with violent injustice.
11 Her leaders pronounce [a]judgment for a bribe,
Her [b]priests instruct for a price,
And her prophets divine for money.
Yet they lean on the LORD saying,
"[c]Is not the LORD in our midst?
Calamity will not come upon us."
12 Therefore, on account of you,
[a]Zion will be plowed as a field,
[b]Jerusalem will become a heap of ruins,
And the [c]mountain of the [1]temple *will become* high places of a forest.

Peaceful Latter Days

4 AND it will come about in the [a]last days
That the [b]mountain of the house of the LORD
Will be established [1]as the chief of the mountains.
It will be raised above the hills,
And the [c]peoples will stream to it.
2 And [a]many nations will come and say,
"[b]Come and let us go up to the mountain of the LORD
And to the house of the God of Jacob,
That [c]He may teach us about His ways
And that we may walk in His paths."
For [d]from Zion will go forth the law,

7 [a]Is. 50:2; 59:1 [b]Ps. 119:65, 68, 116; Jer. 15:16 [c]Ps. 15:2; 84:11
8 [1]Lit., *And yesterday* [2]Or, *ornaments* [a]Jer. 12:8 [b]Mic. 3:2, 3; 7:2, 3 [c]Ps. 120:6, 7
9 [a]Jer. 10:20 [b]Ezek. 39:21; Hab. 2:14
10 [a]Deut. 12:9 [b]Ps. 106:38
11 [1]Lit., *flow* [2]Lit., *one who flows* oracles [a]Jer. 5:31 [b]Is. 28:7 [c]Is. 30:10, 11
12 [a]Mic. 4:6, 7 [b]Mic. 5:7, 8; 7:18
1 [a]Is. 1:10; Mic. 3:9 [b]Ps. 82:1-5; Jer. 5:5
2 [a]Ps. 53:4; Ezek. 22:27; Mic. 2:8; 7:2, 3
3 [a]Ps. 14:4; 27:2; Zeph. 3:3 [b]Ezek. 11:3, 6, 7
4 [a]Ps. 18:41; Prov. 1:28; Is. 1:15; Jer. 11:11 [b]Deut. 31:17; Is. 59:2 [c]Is. 3:11; Mic. 7:13
5 [a]Is. 3:12; 9:15, 16; Jer. 14:14, 15 [b]Jer. 6:14
6 [a]Is. 8:20-22; 29:10-12 [b]Is. 59:10
7 [1]Lit., *mustache* [a]Zech. 13:4 [b]Is. 44:25; 47:12-14 [c]Mic. 7:16 [d]1 Sam. 28:6; Mic. 3:4
8 [a]Is. 61:1, 2; Jer. 1:18 [b]Is. 58:1
9 [a]Mic. 1:1 [b]Ps. 58:1, 2; Is. 1:23
10 [a]Jer. 22:13, 17; Hab. 2:12
11 [a]Is. 1:23; Mic. 7:3 [b]Jer. 6:13 [c]Is. 48:2
12 [1]Lit., *house* [a]Jer. 26:18 [b]Ps. 79:1; Jer. 9:11 [c]Mic. 4:1
1 [1]Lit., *on* [a]Is. 2:2-4; Dan. 2:28; 10:14; Hos. 3:5 [b]Ezek. 43:12; Mic. 3:12; Zech. 8:3 [c]Ps. 22:27; 86:9; Jer. 3:17
2 [a]Zech. 2:11; 14:16 [b]Is. 2:3; Jer. 31:6 [c]Ps. 25:8, 9, 12; Is. 54:13 [d]Is. 42:1-4; Zech. 14:8, 9

Even the word of the LORD from Jerusalem.
3 And He will [a]judge between many peoples
And render decisions for mighty, [1]distant nations.
Then they will hammer their swords [b]into plowshares
And their spears into pruning hooks;
Nation will not lift up sword against nation,
And never again will they [2]train for war.
4 And each of them will [a]sit under his vine
And under his fig tree,
With [b]no one to make *them* afraid,
For the [c]mouth of the LORD of hosts has spoken.
5 Though all the peoples walk
Each in the [a]name of his god,
As for us, [b]we will walk
In the name of the [c]LORD our God forever and ever.

6 "In that day," declares the LORD,
"I will assemble the [a]lame,
And [b]gather the outcasts,
Even those whom I have afflicted.
7 "I will make the lame a [a]remnant,
And the outcasts a strong nation,
And the [b]LORD will reign over them in Mount Zion
From now on and forever.
8 "And as for you, [1][a]tower of the flock,
[2]Hill of the daughter of Zion,
To you it will come—
Even the [b]former dominion will come,
The kingdom of the daughter of Jerusalem.

9 "Now, why do you [a]cry out loudly?
Is there no king among you,
Or has your [b]counselor perished,
That agony has gripped you like a woman in childbirth?
10 "[a]Writhe and labor to give birth,
Daughter of Zion,
Like a woman in childbirth,
For now you will [b]go out of the city,
Dwell in the field,
And go to Babylon.
[c]There you will be rescued;
[d]There the LORD will redeem you
From the hand of your enemies.
11 "And now [a]many nations have been assembled against you
Who say, 'Let her be polluted,
And let our eyes [1]gloat over Zion.'
12 "But they do not [a]know the thoughts of the LORD,
And they do not understand His purpose;
For He has gathered them like sheaves to the threshing floor.
13 "Arise and [a]thresh, daughter of Zion,
For your horn I will make iron
And your hoofs I will make bronze,
That you may [b]pulverize many peoples,
That you may [c]devote to the LORD their unjust gain
And their wealth to the Lord of all the earth.

Birth of the King in Bethlehem

5 "[1]NOW muster yourselves in troops, daughter of troops;
[2]They have laid siege against us;
With a rod they will [a]smite the judge of Israel on the cheek.
2 "[1]But as for [a]you, Bethlehem Ephrathah,
Too little to be among the clans of Judah,
From [b]you One will go forth for Me to be [c]ruler in Israel.
[2]His goings forth are [d]from long ago,
From the days of eternity."
3 Therefore, He will [a]give them *up* until the time
When she [b]who is in labor has borne a child.
Then the [c]remainder of His brethren
Will return to the sons of Israel.
4 And He will arise and [a]shepherd *His flock*
In the strength of the LORD,
In the majesty of the name of the LORD His God.
And they will [1]remain,
Because [2]at that time He will be great
To the [b]ends of the earth.
5 And this One [a]will be *our* peace.

When the [b]Assyrian invades our land,
When he tramples on our [1]citadels,
Then we will raise against him
Seven shepherds and eight leaders of men.
6 And they will [a]shepherd the land of Assyria with the sword,
The land of [b]Nimrod at its entrances;
And He will [c]deliver *us* from the Assyrian
When he attacks our land
And when he tramples our territory.

7 Then the [a]remnant of Jacob
Will be among many peoples
Like [b]dew from the LORD,
Like [c]showers on vegetation
Which do not wait for man
Or delay for the sons of men.
8 And the remnant of Jacob
Will be among the nations,
Among many peoples
[a]Like a lion among the beasts of the forest,
Like a young lion among flocks of sheep,
Which, if he passes through,
[b]Tramples down and [c]tears,
And there is [d]none to rescue.

3 [1]Lit., *at a distance* [2]Lit., *learn* [a]Is. 2:4; 11:3-5 [b]Joel 3:10
4 [a]1 Kin. 4:25; Zech. 3:10 [b]Lev. 26:6; Jer. 30:10 [c]Is. 1:20; 40:5
5 [a]2 Kin. 17:29 [b]Zech. 10:12 [c]Josh. 24:15; Is. 26:8, 13
6 [a]Zeph. 3:19 [b]Ps. 147:2; Ezek. 34:13, 16; 37:21
7 [a]Mic. 5:7, 8; 7:18 [b]Is. 24:23
8 [1]Heb., *Migdal-eder* [2]Heb., *Ophel of* [a]Ps. 48:3, 12; 61:3; Mic. 2:12 [b]Is. 1:26; Zech. 9:10
9 [a]Jer. 8:19 [b]Is. 3:1-3
10 [a]Mic. 5:3 [b]2 Kin. 20:18; Hos. 2:14 [c]Is. 43:14; 45:13; Mic. 7:8-12 [d]Is. 48:20; 52:9-12
11 [1]Lit., *look on* [a]Is. 5:25-30; 17:12-14
12 [a]Ps. 147:19, 20
13 [a]Is. 41:15 [b]Jer. 51:20-23 [c]Is. 60:9
1 [1]Ch. 4:14 in Heb. [2]Lit., *He has* [a]1 Kin. 22:24; Job 16:10; Lam. 3:30
2 [1]Ch. 5:1 in Heb. [2]Or, *His appearances are from long ago, from days of old* [a]Gen. 35:19; 48:7; Ruth 4:11; Matt. 2:6 [b]Is. 11:1; Luke 2:4; John 7:42 [c]Jer. 30:21; Zech. 9:9 [d]Ps. 102:25; Prov. 8:22, 23
3 [a]Hos. 11:8; Mic. 4:10; 7:13 [b]Mic. 4:9, 10 [c]Is. 10:20-22; Mic. 5:7, 8
4 [1]Or, *live in safety* [2]Lit., *now* [a]Is. 40:11; 49:9; Ezek. 34:13-15, 23, 24; Mic. 7:14 [b]Is. 45:22; 52:10
5 [1]Or, *palaces* [a]Is. 9:6; Luke 2:14; Eph. 2:14; Col. 1:20 [b]Is. 8:7, 8; 10:24-27
6 [a]Nah. 2:11-13; Zeph. 2:13 [b]Gen. 10:8-11 [c]Is. 14:25; 37:36, 37
7 [a]Mic. 2:12; 4:7; 5:3; 7:18 [b]Deut. 32:2; Ps. 110:3; Hos. 14:5 [c]Ps. 72:6; Is. 44:3
8 [a]Gen. 49:9; Num. 24:9 [b]Ps. 44:5; Is. 41:15, 16; Mic. 4:13; Zech. 10:5 [c]Hos. 5:14 [d]Ps. 50:22

9 Your hand will be [a]lifted up against your adversaries,
And all your enemies will be cut off.

10 "And it will be in that day," declares the LORD,
"[a]That I will cut off your [b]horses from among you
And destroy your chariots.
11 "I will also cut off the [a]cities of your land
And tear down all your [b]fortifications.
12 "I will cut off [a]sorceries from your hand,
And you will have fortunetellers no more.
13 "[a]I will cut off your carved images
And your *sacred* pillars from among you,
So that you will no longer bow down
To the work of your hands.
14 "I will root out your [1a]Asherim from among you
And destroy your cities.
15 "And I will [a]execute vengeance in anger and wrath
On the nations which have not obeyed."

God's Indictment of His People

6 HEAR now what the LORD is saying,
"Arise, plead your case [1]before the mountains,
And let the hills hear your voice.
2 "Listen, you mountains, to the indictment of the LORD,
And you enduring [a]foundations of the earth,
Because the [b]LORD has a case against His people;
Even with Israel He will dispute.
3 "[a]My people, [b]what have I done to you,
And [c]how have I wearied you? Answer Me.
4 "Indeed, I [a]brought you up from the land of Egypt
And [b]ransomed you from the house of slavery,
And I sent before you [c]Moses, Aaron, and [d]Miriam.
5 "My people, remember now
What [a]Balak king of Moab counseled
And what Balaam son of Beor answered him,
And from [b]Shittim to [c]Gilgal,
In order [1]that you might know the [d]righteous acts of the LORD."

What God Requires of Man

6 [a]With what shall I come to the LORD
And bow myself before the God on high?
Shall I come to Him with [b]burnt offerings,
With yearling calves?
7 Does the LORD take delight in [a]thousands of rams,
In ten thousand rivers of oil?
Shall I present my [b]first-born *for* my rebellious acts,
The fruit of my body for the sin of my soul?
8 He has [a]told you, O man, what is good;
And [b]what does the LORD require of you
But to [c]do justice, to [d]love [1]kindness,
And to walk [2e]humbly with your God?

9 The voice of the LORD will call to the city—
And it is sound wisdom to fear Thy name:
"Hear, O tribe. Who has appointed [1]its time?
10 "Is there yet a man in the wicked house,
Along with treasures of [a]wickedness,
And a [1b]short measure *that is* cursed?
11 "Can I justify wicked [a]scales
And a bag of deceptive weights?
12 "For the rich men of *the* [1]city are full of [a]violence,
Her residents speak [b]lies,
And their [c]tongue is deceitful in their mouth.
13 "So also I will make *you* [a]sick, striking you down,
[b]Desolating *you* because of your sins.
14 "You will eat, but you will [a]not be satisfied,
And your [1]vileness will be in your midst.
You will *try to* remove *for safekeeping*,
But you will [b]not preserve *anything*,
And what you do preserve I will give to the sword.
15 "You will sow but you will [a]not reap.
You will tread the olive but will not anoint yourself with oil;
And the grapes, but you will [b]not drink wine.
16 "The statutes of [a]Omri
And all the works of the house of [b]Ahab are observed;
And in their devices you [c]walk.
Therefore, I will give you up for [d]destruction
And [1]your inhabitants for [e]derision,
And you will bear the [f]reproach of My people."

The Prophet Acknowledges

7 WOE is me! For I am
Like the fruit pickers and the [a]grape gatherers.
There is not a cluster of grapes to eat,
Or a [b]first-ripe fig *which* [1]I crave.

9 [a]Ps. 10:12; 21:8; Is. 26:11
10 [a]Zech. 9:10 [b]Deut. 17:16; Is. 2:7; Hos. 14:3
11 [a]Is. 1:7; 6:11 [b]Is. 2:12-17; Hos. 10:14; Amos 5:9
12 [a]Deut. 18:10-12; Is. 2:6; 8:19
13 [a]Is. 2:18; 17:8; Ezek. 6:9
14 [1]I.e., wooden symbols of a female deity [a]Ex. 34:13; Is. 17:8; 27:9
15 [a]Is. 1:24; 65:12
1 [1]Lit., *with*
2 [a]2 Sam. 22:16; Ps. 104:5 [b]Is. 1:18; Hos. 4:1; 12:2
3 [a]Ps. 50:7 [b]Jer. 2:5 [c]Is. 43:22, 23
4 [a]Ex. 12:51; 20:2 [b]Deut. 7:8 [c]Ex. 4:10-16; Ps. 77:20 [d]Ex. 15:20
5 [1]Lit., *to know* [a]Num. 22:5, 6 [b]Num. 25:1; Josh. 2:1; 3:1 [c]Josh. 4:19; 5:9, 10 [d]1 Sam. 12:7; Is. 1:27
6 [a]Ps. 40:6-8 [b]Ps. 51:16, 17
7 [a]Ps. 50:9; Is. 1:11; 40:16 [b]Lev. 18:21; 20:1-5; 2 Kin. 16:3; Jer. 7:31
8 [1]Or, *loyalty* [2]Or, *circumspectly* [a]Deut. 30:15 [b]Deut. 10:12 [c]Is. 56:1; Jer. 22:3 [d]Hos. 6:6 [e]Is. 57:15; 66:2
9 [1]Lit., *it*
10 [1]Lit., *shrunken ephah* [a]Jer. 5:26, 27; Amos 3:10 [b]Ezek. 45:9, 10; Amos 8:5
11 [a]Lev. 19:36; Hos. 12:7
12 [1]Lit., *her* [a]Is. 1:23; 5:7; Amos 6:3, 4; Mic. 2:1, 2 [b]Jer. 9:2-6, 8; Hos. 7:13; Amos 2:4 [c]Is. 3:8
13 [a]Mic. 1:9 [b]Is. 1:7; 6:11
14 [1]Or possibly, *garbage* or *excreta* [a]Is. 9:20 [b]Is. 30:6
15 [a]Deut. 28:38-40; Jer. 12:13 [b]Amos 5:11; Zeph. 1:13
16 [1]Lit., *her* [a]1 Kin. 16:25, 26 [b]1 Kin. 16:29-33 [c]Jer. 7:24 [d]Jer. 18:16; Mic. 6:13 [e]Jer. 19:8; 25:9, 18; 29:18 [f]Ps. 44:13; Jer. 51:51; Hos. 12:14
1 [1]Lit., *my soul* [a]Is. 24:13 [b]Is. 28:4; Hos. 9:10

2 The [1]godly person has [a]perished
from the land,
And there is no upright *person*
among men.
All of them lie in wait for [b]blood-
shed;
Each of them hunts the other with
a [c]net.
3 Concerning evil, both hands do it
[a]well.
The prince asks, also the judge, for
a [b]bribe,
And a great man speaks the desire
of his soul;
So they weave it together.
4 The best of them is like a [a]briar,
The most upright like a [b]thorn
hedge.
The day when you post a watchman,
Your [c]punishment will come.
Then their [d]confusion will occur.
5 Do not [a]trust in a neighbor;
Do not have confidence in a friend.
From her who lies in your bosom
Guard [1]your lips.
6 For [a]son treats father contemptu-
ously,
Daughter rises up against her
mother,
Daughter-in-law against her
mother-in-law;
[b]A man's enemies are the men of
his own household.

God Is the Source of Salvation and Light

7 But as for me, I will [a]watch expec-
tantly for the LORD;
I will [b]wait for the God of my
salvation.
My [c]God will hear me.
8 [a]Do not rejoice over me, O [b]my
enemy.
Though I fall I will [c]rise;
Though I dwell in darkness, the
LORD is a [d]light for me.

9 I will bear the indignation of the
LORD
Because I have sinned against Him,
Until He [a]pleads my case and ex-
ecutes justice for me.
He will bring me out to the [b]light,
And I will see His [1c]righteousness.
10 Then my enemy will see,
And shame will cover her who [a]said
to me,
"Where is the LORD your God?"
My eyes will look on her;
[1]At that time she will [2]be [b]tram-
pled down,
Like mire of the streets.

11 *It will be* a day for [a]building your
walls.
On that day will your boundary be
extended.
12 It *will be* a day when [1]they will
[a]come to you
From Assyria and the cities of
Egypt,
From Egypt even to the [2]Euphra-
tes,
Even from sea to sea and mountain
to mountain.
13 And the earth will become [a]deso-
late because of her inhabitants,
On account of the [b]fruit of their
deeds.

14 [a]Shepherd Thy people with Thy
[b]scepter,
The flock of Thy [1]possession
Which dwells by itself in the wood-
land,
In the midst of [2]a fruitful field.
Let them feed in [c]Bashan and Gilead
[d]As in the days of old.
15 "As in the days when you came out
from the land of Egypt,
I will show [1a]you miracles."
16 Nations [a]will see and be ashamed
Of all their might.
They will [b]put *their* hand on *their*
mouth,
Their ears will be deaf.
17 They will [a]lick the dust like a
serpent,
Like [b]reptiles of the earth.
They will come [c]trembling out of
their [1]fortresses;
To the LORD our God they will
come in [d]dread,
And they will be afraid before
Thee.
18 Who is a God like Thee, who [a]par-
dons iniquity
And passes over the rebellious act
of the [b]remnant of His [1]posses-
sion?
He does not [c]retain His anger forever,
Because He [d]delights in [2]unchang-
ing love.
19 He will again have compassion on
us;
[a]He will tread our iniquities under
foot.
Yes, Thou wilt [b]cast all [1]their sins
Into the depths of the sea.
20 Thou wilt give [1a]truth to Jacob
And [2]unchanging love to Abraham,
Which Thou didst [b]swear to our
forefathers
From the days of old.

2 [1]Or, *loyal* [a]Is. 57:1 [b]Is. 59:7; Mic. 3:10 [c]Jer. 5:26; Hos. 5:1
3 [a]Prov. 4:16, 17 [b]Amos 5:12; Mic. 3:11
4 [a]Ezek. 2:6; 28:24 [b]Nah. 1:10 [c]Is. 10:3; Hos. 9:7 [d]Is. 22:5
5 [1]Lit., *openings of your mouth* [a]Jer. 9:4
6 [a]Matt. 10:21, 35; Luke 12:53 [b]Matt. 10:36
7 [a]Hab. 2:1 [b]Ps. 130:5; Is. 25:9 [c]Ps. 4:3
8 [a]Prov. 24:17; Obad. 12 [b]Mic. 7:10 [c]Amos 9:11 [d]Is. 9:2
9 [1]I.e., right dealing [a]Jer. 50:34 [b]Ps. 37:6; Is. 42:7, 16 [c]Is. 46:13; 56:1
10 [1]Lit., *Now* [2]Lit., *become a trampled place* [a]Joel 2:17 [b]Is. 51:23; Zech. 10:5
11 [a]Is. 54:11; Amos 9:11
12 [1]Lit., *he* [2]Lit., *River* [a]Is. 19:23-25; 60:4, 9
13 [a]Jer. 25:11; Mic. 6:13 [b]Is. 3:10, 11; Mic. 3:4
14 [1]Or, *inheritance* [2]Or, *Carmel* [a]Ps. 95:7; Is. 40:11; 49:10; Mic. 5:4 [b]Lev. 27:32; Ps. 23:4 [c]Jer. 50:19 [d]Amos 9:11
15 [1]Lit., *him* [a]Ex. 3:20; 34:10; Ps. 78:12
16 [a]Is. 26:11 [b]Mic. 3:7
17 [1]Lit., *fastnesses* [a]Ps. 72:9; Is. 49:23 [b]Deut. 32:24 [c]Ps. 18:45 [d]Is. 25:3; 59:19
18 [1]Or, *inheritance* [2]Or, *lovingkindness* [a]Ex. 34:7, 9; Is. 43:25 [b]Mic. 2:12; 4:7; 5:7, 8 [c]Ps. 103:8, 9, 13 [d]Jer. 32:41
19 [1]Several ancient versions read *our* [a]Jer. 50:20 [b]Is. 38:17; 43:25; Jer. 31:34
20 [1]Or, *faithfulness* [2]Or, *lovingkindness* [a]Gen. 24:27; 32:10 [b]Deut. 7:8, 12

THE BOOK OF NAHUM

God Is Awesome

1 THE [1a]oracle of [b]Nineveh. The
book of the vision of Nahum the
Elkoshite.
2 A [a]jealous and avenging God is the
LORD;
The LORD is [b]avenging and [1]wrath-
ful.
The LORD takes [c]vengeance on His
adversaries,
And He reserves wrath for His
enemies.
3 The LORD is [a]slow to anger and
great in power,
And the LORD will by no means
leave *the guilty* unpunished.
In [b]whirlwind and storm is His
way,
And [c]clouds are the dust beneath
His feet.
4 He [a]rebukes the sea and makes it
dry;
He dries up all the rivers.
[b]Bashan and Carmel wither;
The blossoms of Lebanon wither.
5 Mountains [a]quake because of Him,
And the hills [b]dissolve;
Indeed the earth is [c]upheaved by
His presence,
The [d]world and all the inhabitants
in it.
6 [a]Who can stand before His indig-
nation?
Who can endure the [b]burning of
His anger?
His [c]wrath is poured out like fire,
And the [d]rocks are broken up by
Him.
7 The LORD is [a]good,
A stronghold in the day of trouble,
And [b]He knows those who take
refuge in Him.
8 But with an [a]overflowing flood
He will make a complete end of [1]its
site,
And will pursue His enemies into
[b]darkness.

9 Whatever you [a]devise against the
LORD,
He will make a [b]complete end of it.
Distress will not rise up twice.
10 Like tangled [a]thorns,
And like those who are [b]drunken
with their drink,
They are [c]consumed
As stubble completely withered.
11 From you has gone forth
One who [a]plotted evil against the
LORD,
A [1b]wicked counselor.
12 Thus says the LORD,
"Though they are at full *strength* and
likewise many,
Even so, they will be [a]cut off and
pass away.
Though I have afflicted you,
I will afflict you [b]no longer.
13 "So now, I will [a]break his yoke bar
from upon you,
And I will tear off your shackles."

14 The LORD has issued a command
concerning [1]you:
"[2]Your name will [a]no longer be
perpetuated.
I will cut off [3b]idol and [4]image
From the house of your gods.
I will prepare your [c]grave,
For you are contemptible."

15 [1]Behold, [a]on the mountains the feet
of him who brings good news,
Who announces peace!
[b]Celebrate your feasts, O Judah;
Pay your vows.
For [c]never again will the [2]wicked
one pass through you;
He is [d]cut off completely.

The Overthrow of Nineveh

2 [1]THE one who [a]scatters has come up
against [2]you.
Man the fortress, watch the road;
[3]Strengthen your back, [4]summon
all *your* strength.
2 For the LORD will restore the
[a]splendor of Jacob
[b]Like the splendor of Israel,
Even though devastators have devastated them
And [c]destroyed their vine
branches.

3 The shields of [1]his mighty men are
colored red,
The warriors are dressed in [a]scarlet,
The chariots are *enveloped* in [2]flash-
ing steel
[3]When he is prepared *to march*,
And the cypress [b]*spears* are bran-
dished.
4 The [a]chariots race madly in the
streets,
They rush wildly in the [1]squares,
Their appearance is like torches,
They dash to and fro like lightning
flashes.
5 He remembers his [a]nobles;
They [b]stumble in their march,
They hurry to her wall,
And the [1]mantelet is set up.
6 The gates of the rivers are opened,
And the palace is dissolved.
7 And it is fixed:
She is stripped, she is carried away,
And her handmaids are [a]moaning
like the sound of doves,
[b]Beating on their [1]breasts.

8 Though Nineveh *was* like a pool of
water throughout her days,
Now they are fleeing;
"Stop, stop,"
But [a]no one turns back.
9 Plunder the silver!
Plunder the [a]gold!
For there is no limit to the trea-
sure—
Wealth from every kind of desir-
able object.

1 [1]Or, *burden* [a]Is. 13:1; 19:1; Jer. 23:33, 34; Hab. 1:1; Zech. 9:1; Mal. 1:1 [b]2 Kin. 19:36; Jon. 1:2; Nah. 2:8; Zeph. 2:13
2 [1]Lit., *a possessor of wrath* [a]Ex. 20:5; Josh. 24:19 [b]Deut. 32:35, 41 [c]Ps. 94:1
3 [a]Ex. 34:6, 7; Neh. 9:17; Ps. 103:8 [b]Ex. 19:16; Is. 29:6 [c]Ps. 104:3; Is. 19:1
4 [a]Josh. 3:15, 16; Ps. 106:9; Is. 50:2; Matt. 8:26 [b]Is. 33:9
5 [a]Ex. 19:18; 2 Sam. 22:8; Ps. 18:7 [b]Mic. 1:4 [c]Is. 24:1, 20 [d]Ps. 98:7
6 [a]Jer. 10:10; Mal. 3:2 [b]Is. 13:13 [c]Is. 66:15 [d]1 Kin. 19:11
7 [a]Ps. 25:8; 37:39, 40; Jer. 33:11 [b]Ps. 1:6; John 10:14; 2 Tim. 2:19
8 [1]I.e., Nineveh's [a]Is. 28:2, 17f.; Amos 8:8 [b]Is. 13:9, 10
9 [a]Ps. 2:1; Nah. 1:11 [b]Is. 28:22
10 [a]2 Sam. 23:6; Mic. 7:4 [b]Is. 56:12; Nah. 3:11 [c]Is. 5:24; 10:17; Mal. 4:1
11 [1]Or, *worthless;* Heb., *Belial* [a]Is. 10:7-11; Nah. 1:9 [b]Ezek. 11:2
12 [a]Is. 10:16-19, 33, 34 [b]Lam. 3:31, 32
13 [a]Is. 9:4; 10:27; Jer. 2:20
14 [1]I.e., the king of Nineveh [2]Lit., *No more of your name will be sown* [3]Or, *a graven image* [4]Lit., *cast* metal *image* [a]Job 18:17; Ps. 109:13; Is. 14:22 [b]Is. 46:1, 2; Mic. 5:13, 14 [c]Ezek. 32:22, 23
15 [1]Ch. 2:1 in Heb. [2]Or, *worthless one;* Heb., *Belial* [a]Is. 40:9; 52:7; Rom. 10:15 [b]Lev. 23:2, 4 [c]Is. 52:1; Joel 3:17 [d]Is. 29:7, 8

1 [1]Ch. 2:2 in Heb. [2]Lit., *your face* [3]Lit., *Make strong your loins* [4]Lit., *strengthen power greatly* [a]Jer. 51:20-23
2 [a]Is. 60:15 [b]Ezek. 37:21-23 [c]Ps. 80:12, 13
3 [1]I.e., those attacking Nineveh [2]Lit., *fire of steel* [3]Lit., *On the day of his preparation* [a]Ezek. 23:14, 15 [b]Job 39:23
4 [1]Lit., *broad places* [a]Is. 66:15; Jer. 4:13; Ezek. 26:10; Nah. 3:2, 3
5 [1]Lit., *covering* used in a siege [a]Nah. 3:18 [b]Jer. 46:12

7 [1]Lit., *hearts* [a]Is. 38:14; 59:11 [b]Is. 32:12
8 [a]Jer. 46:5; 47:3
9 [a]Rev. 18:12, 16

10 She is [a]emptied! Yes, she is desolate and waste!
[b]Hearts are melting and knees knocking!
Also anguish is in [1]the whole body,
And all their [c]faces are grown pale!
11 Where is the den of the lions
And the feeding place of the [a]young lions,
Where the lion, lioness, and lion's cub prowled,
With nothing to disturb *them*?
12 The lion tore enough for his cubs,
[1]Killed *enough* for his lionesses,
And filled his lairs with prey
And his dens with torn flesh.
13 "Behold, [a]I am against you," declares the LORD of hosts. "I will [b]burn
up her chariots in smoke, a sword will
devour your young lions, I will [c]cut off
your prey from the land, and no longer
will the voice of your messengers be
heard."

Nineveh's Complete Ruin

3 [a]WOE to the bloody city, completely full of lies *and* pillage;
Her prey never departs.
2 The [a]noise of the whip,
The noise of the rattling of the wheel,
Galloping horses,
And [1]bounding chariots!
3 Horsemen charging,
Swords flashing, [a]spears gleaming,
[b]Many slain, a mass of corpses,
And [1c]countless dead bodies—
They stumble over [2]the dead bodies!
4 *All* because of the [a]many harlotries of the harlot,
The charming one, the [b]mistress of sorceries,
Who [c]sells nations by her harlotries
And families by her sorceries.
5 "Behold, [a]I am against you," declares the LORD of hosts;
"And I will [1b]lift up your skirts over your face,
And [c]show to the nations your nakedness
And to the kingdoms your disgrace.
6 "I will [a]throw [1]filth on you
And [b]make you vile,
And set you up as a [c]spectacle.
7 "And it will come about that all who see you
Will [1]shrink from you and say,
'Nineveh is devastated!
[a]Who will grieve for her?'
Where will I seek comforters for you?"

8 Are you better than [1a]No-amon,
Which was situated by the [b]waters of the Nile,
With water surrounding her,
Whose rampart *was* [2]the sea,
Whose wall *consisted* of [2]the sea?

10 [1]Lit., *all the loin* [a]Is. 24:1; 34:10-13; Nah. 2:2 [b]Ps. 22:14; Is. 13:7, 8; Ezek. 21:7 [c]Joel 2:6
11 [a]Is. 5:29
12 [1]Lit., *Strangled*
13 [a]Jer. 21:13; Ezek. 5:8; Nah. 3:5 [b]Josh. 11:6, 9; Ps. 46:9 [c]Is. 49:24, 25; Nah. 3:1
1 [a]Ezek. 24:6, 9
2 [1]Lit., *skipping* [a]Job 39:22-25; Jer. 47:3; Nah. 2:3, 4
3 [1]Lit., *there is no end to* [2]Lit., *their* [a]Hab. 3:11 [b]Is. 34:3; 66:16 [c]Is. 37:36; Ezek. 39:4
4 [a]Is. 23:17; Ezek. 16:25-29; Rev. 17:1, 2 [b]Is. 47:9, 12, 13 [c]Rev. 18:3
5 [1]Lit., *uncover your* [a]Jer. 50:31; Ezek. 26:3; Nah. 2:13 [b]Is. 47:2, 3; Jer. 13:26 [c]Ezek. 16:37
6 [1]Lit., *detestable things* [a]Job 9:31 [b]Job 30:8; Mal. 2:9 [c]Is. 14:16; Jer. 51:37
7 [1]Lit., *flee* [a]Is. 51:19; Jer. 15:5
8 [1]I.e., the city of Amon: Thebes [2]I.e., the Nile [a]Jer. 46:25; Ezek. 30:14-16 [b]Is. 19:6-8
9 [1]Lit., *your* [a]Is. 20:5 [b]Jer. 46:9; Ezek. 27:10; 30:5; 38:5 [c]2 Chr. 12:3; 16:8
10 [a]Is. 19:4; 20:4 [b]Ps. 137:9; Is. 13:16; Hos. 13:16 [c]Lam. 2:19 [d]Joel 3:3; Obad. 11
11 [a]Is. 49:26; Jer. 25:27; Nah. 1:10 [b]Is. 2:10, 19; Hos. 10:8
12 [1]Lit., *first fruits* [a]Rev. 6:13 [b]Is. 28:4
13 [a]Is. 19:16; Jer. 50:37; 51:30 [b]Is. 45:1, 2; Nah. 2:6
14 [a]2 Chr. 32:3, 4 [b]Nah. 2:1
15 [a]Is. 66:15, 16; Nah. 2:13; 3:13 [b]Joel 1:4
16 [1]I.e., strips vegetation; or, *molts* [a]Is. 23:8
17 [1]Or, *officials* [a]Rev. 9:7 [b]Jer. 51:27
18 [a]Ps. 76:5, 6; Is. 56:10; Jer. 51:57 [b]Jer. 50:18 [c]Nah. 2:5 [d]1 Kin. 22:17; Is. 13:14
19 [1]Lit., *your report* [a]Jer. 46:11; Mic. 1:9 [b]Jer. 30:12 [c]Job 27:23; Lam. 2:15

9 [a]Ethiopia was *her* might,
And Egypt too, without limits.
[b]Put and [c]Lubim were among [1]her helpers.
10 Yet she [a]became an exile,
She went into captivity;
Also her [b]small children were dashed to pieces
[c]At the head of every street;
They [d]cast lots for her honorable men,
And all her great men were bound with fetters.
11 You too will become [a]drunk,
You will be [b]hidden.
You too will search for a refuge from the enemy.
12 All your fortifications are [a]fig trees with [1b]ripe fruit—
When shaken, they fall into the eater's mouth.
13 Behold, your people are [a]women in your midst!
The gates of your land are [b]opened wide to your enemies;
Fire consumes your gate bars.
14 [a]Draw for yourself water for the siege!
[b]Strengthen your fortifications!
Go into the clay and tread the mortar!
Take hold of the brick mold!
15 There [a]fire will consume you,
The sword will cut you down;
It will [b]consume you as the locust *does*.

Multiply yourself like the creeping locust,
Multiply yourself like the swarming locust.
16 You have increased your [a]traders more than the stars of heaven—
The creeping locust [1]strips and flies away.
17 Your [1a]guardsmen are like the swarming locust.
Your [b]marshals are like hordes of grasshoppers
Settling in the stone walls on a cold day.
The sun rises and they flee,
And the place where they are is not known.
18 Your shepherds are [a]sleeping, O [b]king of Assyria;
Your [c]nobles are lying down.
Your people are [d]scattered on the mountains,
And there is no one to regather *them*.
19 There is [a]no relief for your breakdown,
Your [b]wound is incurable.
All who hear [1]about you
Will [c]clap *their* hands over you,
For on whom has not your evil passed continually?

THE BOOK OF
HABAKKUK

Chaldeans Used to Punish Judah

1 THE [1a]oracle which Habakkuk the prophet saw.
2 [a]How long, O LORD, will I call for help,
And Thou wilt not hear?
I cry out to Thee, "Violence!"
Yet Thou dost [b]not save.
3 Why dost Thou make me [a]see iniquity,
And cause *me* to look on wickedness?
Yes, [b]destruction and violence are before me;
[c]Strife exists and contention arises.
4 Therefore, the [a]law is [1]ignored
And justice [2]is never upheld.
For the wicked [b]surround the righteous;
Therefore, justice comes out [c]perverted.

5 "[a]Look among the nations! Observe!
Be astonished! [b]Wonder!
Because *I* am doing [c]something in your days—
You would not believe if [1]you were told.
6 "For behold, I am [a]raising up the Chaldeans,
That [1]fierce and impetuous people
Who march [2]throughout the earth
To [3b]seize dwelling places which are not theirs.
7 "They are dreaded and [a]feared.
Their [b]justice and [1]authority [2]originate with themselves.
8 "Their [a]horses are swifter than leopards
And [1]keener than [b]wolves in the evening.
Their [2]horsemen come galloping,
Their horsemen come from afar;
They fly like an [c]eagle swooping *down* to devour.
9 "All of them come for violence.
[1]Their horde of [a]faces *moves* forward.
They collect captives like sand.
10 "They [a]mock at kings,
And rulers are a laughing matter to them.
They [b]laugh at every fortress,
And [c]heap up rubble to capture it.
11 "Then they will sweep through *like* the [a]wind and pass on.
But they will be held [b]guilty,
They whose [c]strength is their god."

12 Art Thou not from [a]everlasting,
O LORD, my God, my Holy One?
We will not die.
Thou, O LORD, hast [b]appointed them to judge;
And Thou, O [c]Rock, hast established them to correct.
13 *Thine* eyes are too [a]pure to [1]approve evil,
And Thou canst not look on wickedness *with favor.*
Why dost Thou [b]look with favor
On those who deal [c]treacherously?
Why art Thou [d]silent when the wicked [e]swallow up
Those more righteous than they?
14 *Why* hast Thou made men like the fish of the sea,
Like creeping things without a ruler over them?
15 *The Chaldeans* [a]bring all of them up with a hook,
[b]Drag them away with their net,
And gather them together in their fishing net.
Therefore, they rejoice and are glad.
16 Therefore, they offer a sacrifice to their net.
And [1]burn incense to their fishing net;
Because through [a]these things their [2]catch is [3]large,
And their food is [4]plentiful.
17 Will they therefore empty their [a]net
And continually [b]slay nations without sparing?

God Answers the Prophet

2 I WILL [a]stand on my guard post
And station myself on the rampart;
And I will [b]keep watch to see [c]what He will speak to me,
And how I may reply [1]when I am reproved.
2 Then the LORD answered me and said,
"[a]Record the vision
And inscribe *it* on tablets,
That [1]the one who [2]reads it may run.
3 "For the vision is yet for the [a]appointed time;
It [1]hastens toward the goal, and it will not [2]fail.
Though it tarries, [b]wait for it;
For it will certainly come, it [c]will not delay.

4 "Behold, as for the [a]proud one,
His soul is not right within him;
But the [b]righteous will live by his [1]faith.
5 "Furthermore, [a]wine betrays the [b]haughty man,
So that he does not [c]stay at home.
He [d]enlarges his appetite like Sheol,
And he is like death, never satisfied.
He also gathers to himself all nations
And collects to himself all peoples.

6 "Will not all of these [a]take up a taunt-song against him,
Even mockery *and* insinuations against him,
And say, '[b]Woe to him who increases what is not his—
For how long—
And makes himself [1]rich with loans?'

---

1 [1]Or, *burden* [a]Is. 13:1; Nah. 1:1
2 [a]Ps. 13:1, 2; 22:1, 2 [b]Jer. 14:9
3 [a]Ps. 55:9-11; Jer. 20:18 [b]Jer. 20:8 [c]Jer. 15:10
4 [1]Or, *ineffective;* lit., *numbed* [2]Lit., *never goes forth* [a]Ps. 58:1, 2; 119:126; Is. 59:12-14 [b]Ps. 22:12; Is. 1:21-23 [c]Is. 5:20; Ezek. 9:9
5 [1]Lit., *it* [a]Acts 13:41 [b]Is. 29:9 [c]Is. 29:14; Ezek. 12:22-28
6 [1]Lit., *bitter* [2]Lit., *the breadth of* [3]Lit., *take possession of* [a]2 Kin. 24:2; Jer. 4:11-13 [b]Jer. 8:10
7 [1]Lit., *eminence* [2]Lit., *proceeds from* [a]Is. 18:2, 7 [b]Jer. 39:5-9
8 [1]Or, *more eager to attack* [2]Or, *steeds paw the ground* [a]Jer. 4:13 [b]Zeph. 3:3 [c]Ezek. 17:3; Hos. 8:1
9 [1]Or, *The eagerness of their faces* [a]2 Kin. 12:17; Dan. 11:17
10 [a]2 Chr. 36:6, 10; Is. 37:13 [b]Is. 10:9; 14:16 [c]Jer. 32:24; Ezek. 26:8
11 [a]Jer. 4:11, 12 [b]Jer. 2:3 [c]Dan. 4:30; Hab. 1:16
12 [a]Deut. 33:27; Ps. 90:2; Mal. 3:6 [b]Is. 10:5, 6; Mal. 3:5 [c]Deut. 32:4
13 [1]Lit., *look at* [a]Ps. 11:4-6; 34:15, 16 [b]Jer. 12:1, 2 [c]Is. 24:16 [d]Ps. 50:21 [e]Ps. 35:25
15 [a]Jer. 16:16; Amos 4:2 [b]Ps. 10:9
16 [1]Or, *sacrifice* [2]Lit., *portion* [3]Lit., *fat;* or, *plentiful* [4]Lit., *the fat portion* [a]Jer. 44:17
17 [a]Is. 19:8 [b]Is. 14:5, 6

1 [1]Lit., *upon my reproof* [a]Is. 21:8 [b]Ps. 5:3 [c]Ps. 85:8
2 [1]Or, *one may read it fluently* [2]Or, *is to proclaim it* [a]Deut. 27:8; Rom. 15:4; Rev. 1:19
3 [1]Lit., *pants* [2]Or, *lie* [a]Dan. 8:17, 19; 10:14 [b]Ps. 27:14 [c]Ezek. 12:25; Heb. 10:37
4 [1]Or, *faithfulness* [a]Ps. 49:18; Is. 13:11 [b]Rom. 1:17; Gal. 3:11; Heb. 10:38
5 [a]Prov. 20:1 [b]Prov. 21:24 [c]2 Kin. 14:10 [d]Prov. 27:20; 30:16; Is. 5:11-15
6 [1]Lit., *heavy* [a]Is. 14:4-10; Jer. 50:13 [b]Job 20:15-29; Hab. 2:12

7"Will not [1]your creditors [a]rise up suddenly,
And those who [2]collect from you awaken?
Indeed, you will become plunder for them.
8"Because you have [a]looted many nations,
All the remainder of the peoples will loot you—
Because of human bloodshed and violence [1]done to the land,
To the town and all its inhabitants.

9"Woe to him who gets [a]evil gain for his house
To [b]put his nest on high
To be delivered from the hand of calamity!
10"You have devised a [a]shameful thing for your house
By cutting off many peoples;
So you are [b]sinning against yourself.
11"Surely the [a]stone will cry out from the wall,
And the rafter will answer it from the [1]framework.

12"Woe to him who [a]builds a city with bloodshed
And founds a town with [1]violence!
13"Is it not indeed from the LORD of hosts
That peoples [a]toil for fire,
And nations grow weary for nothing?
14"For the earth will be [a]filled
With the knowledge of the glory of the LORD,
As the waters cover the sea.

15"Woe to you who make [1]your neighbors drink,
Who mix in your venom even to make *them* drunk
So as to look on their nakedness!
16"You will be filled with disgrace rather than honor.
Now you yourself [a]drink and [1]expose your *own* nakedness.
The [b]cup in the LORD's right hand will come around to you,
And [c]utter disgrace *will come* upon your glory.
17"For the [a]violence [1]done to Lebanon will [2]overwhelm you,
And the devastation of *its* beasts [3]by which you terrified them,
[b]Because of human bloodshed and [c]violence [4]done to the land,
To the town and all its inhabitants.

18"What [a]profit is the [1]idol when its maker has carved it,
Or [2]an image, a [b]teacher of falsehood?
For *its* maker [c]trusts in his *own* handiwork
When he fashions speechless idols.
19"Woe to him who [a]says to a *piece of* wood, '[b]Awake!'
To a dumb stone, 'Arise!'

7 [1]Lit., *those who bite you* [2]Lit., *violently shake you* [a]Prov. 29:1
8 [1]Lit., *of the land* [a]Is. 33:1; Jer. 27:7; Zech. 2:8
9 [a]Jer. 22:13; Ezek. 22:27 [b]Jer. 49:16
10 [a]2 Kin. 9:26; Nah. 1:14; Hab. 2:16 [b]Jer. 26:19
11 [1]Lit., *wood* [a]Josh. 24:27; Luke 19:40
12 [1]Or, *injustice* [a]Mic. 3:10; Nah. 3:1
13 [a]Is. 50:11; Jer. 51:58
14 [a]Ps. 22:27; Is. 11:9; Zech. 14:9
15 [1]Lit., *his neighbor*
16 [1]Lit., *show yourself uncircumcised;* or, *stagger;* so DSS and ancient versions [a]Lam. 4:21 [b]Jer. 25:15, 17 [c]Nah. 3:6
17 [1]Lit., *of Lebanon* [2]Lit., *cover* [3]Lit., which *terrified them* [4]Lit., *of the land* [a]Joel 3:19; Zech. 11:1 [b]Ps. 55:23; Hab. 2:8 [c]Jer. 51:35; Hab. 2:8
18 [1]Or, *a graven image* [2]Lit., a *cast* metal *image* [a]Is. 42:17; 44:9; Jer. 2:27, 28 [b]Jer. 10:8, 14; Zech. 10:2 [c]Ps. 115:4, 8
19 [a]Jer. 2:27, 28; 10:3 [b]1 Kin. 18:26-29 [c]Ps. 135:15-18; Jer. 10:4, 9, 14 [d]Ps. 135:17
20 [1]Lit., *Hush before Him, all the earth.* [a]Mic. 1:2 [b]Zeph. 1:7; Zech. 2:13

1 [1]I.e., a highly emotional poetic form
2 [1]Or, *Thy report* [2]Or, *I stand in awe of Thy work, O LORD; In the midst of the years revive it,* [3]Or, *compassion* [a]Job 42:5 [b]Ps. 119:120; Jer. 10:7 [c]Ps. 71:20; 85:6 [d]Ps. 44:1-8; Hab. 1:5 [e]Num. 14:19; 2 Sam. 24:15-17; Is. 54:8
3 [a]Jer. 49:7; Amos 1:12; Obad. 9 [b]Gen. 21:21; Deut. 33:2 [c]Ps. 113:4; 148:13 [d]Ps. 48:10
4 [a]Ps. 18:12 [b]Job 26:14
5 [1]Lit., *at His feet* [a]Ex. 12:29, 30; Num. 16:46-49 [b]Num. 11:1-3; Ps. 18:12, 13
6 [1]Lit., *bowed;* or, *sank down* [a]Job 21:18; Ps. 35:5 [b]Hab. 1:12
7 [a]Ex. 15:14-16 [b]Num. 31:7, 8; Judg. 7:24, 25; 8:12
8 [a]Ex. 7:19, 20; Josh. 3:16; Is. 50:2 [b]Ex. 14:16, 21; Ps. 114:3, 5 [c]Deut. 33:26; Ps. 18:10; Hab. 3:15 [d]Ps. 68:17

And that is *your* teacher?
Behold, it is overlaid with [c]gold and silver,
And there is [d]no breath at all inside it.
20"But the [a]LORD is in His holy temple.
[1]Let all the earth [b]be silent before Him."

God's Deliverance of His People

3 A PRAYER of Habakkuk the prophet, according to [1]Shigionoth.
2 LORD, I have [a]heard [1]the report about Thee *and* [2]I [b]fear.
O LORD, [c]revive [d]Thy work in the midst of the years,
In the midst of the years make it known;
In wrath remember [3][e]mercy.

3 God comes from [a]Teman,
And the Holy One from Mount [b]Paran. [Selah.
His [c]splendor covers the heavens,
And the [d]earth is full of His praise.
4 *His* [a]radiance is like the sunlight;
He has rays *flashing* from His hand,
And there is the hiding of His [b]power.
5 Before Him goes [a]pestilence,
And [b]plague comes [1]after Him.
6 He stood and surveyed the earth;
He looked and [a]startled the nations.
Yes, the perpetual mountains were shattered,
The ancient hills [1]collapsed.
His ways are [b]everlasting.
7 I saw the tents of Cushan under [a]distress,
The tent curtains of the land of [b]Midian were trembling.

8 Did the LORD rage against the [a]rivers,
Or *was* Thine anger against the rivers,
Or *was* Thy wrath against the [b]sea,
That Thou didst [c]ride on Thy horses,
On Thy [d]chariots of salvation?
9 Thy [a]bow was made bare,
The rods of [1]chastisement were sworn. [Selah.
Thou didst [b]cleave the earth with rivers.
10 The mountains saw Thee *and* quaked;
The downpour of waters swept by.
The deep [a]uttered forth its voice,
It lifted high its hands.
11 [a]Sun *and* moon stood in their places;
They went away at the [b]light of Thine arrows,
At the radiance of Thy gleaming spear.

9 [1]Lit., *word* [a]Ps. 7:12, 13; Hab. 3:11 [b]Ps. 78:16; 105:41
10 [a]Ps. 93:3; 98:7, 8
11 [a]Josh. 10:12-14 [b]Ps. 18:14

12 In indignation Thou didst [a]march through the earth;
In anger Thou didst [1b]trample the nations.
13 Thou didst go forth for the [a]salvation of Thy people,
For the salvation of Thine [b]anointed.
Thou didst strike the [c]head of the house of the evil
To lay him open from [1]thigh to neck. [Selah.
14 Thou didst pierce with his [a]own [1]spears
The head of his [2]throngs.
They [b]stormed in to scatter [3]us;
Their exultation *was* like those
Who [c]devour the oppressed in secret.
15 Thou didst [a]tread on the sea with Thy horses,
On the [b]surge of many waters.

16 I heard and my [1]inward parts [a]trembled,
At the sound my lips quivered.
Decay enters my [b]bones,
And in my place I tremble.
Because I must [c]wait quietly for the day of distress,
[2]For the [d]people to arise *who* will invade us.
17 Though the [a]fig tree should not blossom,
And there be no [1]fruit on the vines,
Though the yield of the [b]olive should fail,
And the fields produce no food,
Though the [c]flock should be cut off from the fold,
And there be [d]no cattle in the stalls,
18 Yet I will [a]exult in the LORD,
I will [b]rejoice in the [c]God of my salvation.
19 The Lord [1]GOD is my [a]strength,
And [b]He has made my feet like hinds' *feet,*
And makes me walk on my [c]high places.

For the choir director, on my stringed instruments.

12 [1]Or, *thresh* [a]Ps. 68:7 [b]Is. 41:15; Jer. 51:33; Mic. 4:13
13 [1]Lit., *foundation* [a]Ex. 15:2; 2 Sam. 5:20; Ps. 68:19, 20 [b]Ps. 20:6; 28:8 [c]Ps. 68:21; 110:6
14 [1]Lit., *shafts* [2]Or, *warriors* or *villagers* [3]Lit., *me* [a]Judg. 7:22 [b]Dan. 11:40; Zech. 9:14 [c]Ps. 10:8; 64:2-5
15 [a]Ps. 77:19; Hab. 3:8 [b]Ex. 15:8
16 [1]Lit., *belly* [2]Or, *To come upon the people* who will [a]Dan. 10:8; Hab. 3:2 [b]Job 30:17, 30; Jer. 23:9 [c]Luke 21:19 [d]Jer. 5:15
17 [1]Lit., *produce* [a]Joel 1:10-12; Amos 4:9; 2 Cor. 4:8, 9 [b]Mic. 6:15 [c]Joel 1:18 [d]Jer. 5:17
18 [a]Ex. 15:1, 2; Job 13:15; Is. 61:10; Rom. 5:2, 3 [b]Ps. 46:1-5; Phil. 4:4 [c]Ps. 25:5; 27:1; Is. 12:2
19 [1]Heb., *YHWH,* usually rendered *LORD* [a]Ps. 18:32, 33; 27:1; 46:1; Is. 45:24 [b]2 Sam. 22:34 [c]Deut. 33:29

THE BOOK OF ZEPHANIAH

Day of Judgment on Judah

1 THE word of the LORD which came to Zephaniah son of Cushi, son of Gedaliah, son of Amariah, son of Hezekiah, in the days of [a]Josiah son of [b]Amon, king of Judah,
2 "I will completely [a]remove all *things*
From the face of the [1]earth," declares the LORD.
3 "I will remove [a]man and beast;
I will remove the [b]birds of the sky
And the fish of the sea,
And the [1c]ruins along with the wicked;
And I will cut off man from the face of the [2]earth," declares the LORD.
4 "So I will [a]stretch out My hand against Judah
And against all the inhabitants of Jerusalem.
And I will [b]cut off the remnant of Baal from this place,
And the names of the [c]idolatrous priests along with the priests.
5 "And those who bow down on the [a]housetops to the host of heaven,
And those who bow down *and* [b]swear to the LORD and *yet* swear by [1c]Milcom,
6 And those who have [a]turned back from following the LORD,
And those who have [b]not sought the LORD or inquired of Him."
7 [1a]Be silent before the Lord [2]GOD!
For the [b]day of the LORD is near,
For the LORD has prepared a [c]sacrifice,
He has [d]consecrated His guests.
8 "Then it will come about on the day of the LORD's sacrifice,
That I will [a]punish the princes, the king's sons,
And all who clothe themselves with [b]foreign garments.
9 "And I will punish on that day all who leap on the *temple* threshold,
Who fill the house of their [1]lord with [a]violence and deceit.
10 "And on that day," declares the LORD,
"There will be the sound of a cry from the [a]Fish Gate,
A wail from the [1b]Second Quarter,
And a loud crash from the [c]hills.
11 "Wail, O inhabitants of the [1]Mortar,
For all the [2]people of [a]Canaan will be silenced;
All who weigh out [b]silver will be cut off.
12 "And it will come about at that time
That I will [a]search Jerusalem with lamps,
And I will punish the men

1 [a]2 Kin. 22:1, 2; 2 Chr. 34:1-33; Jer. 1:2; 22:11 [b]2 Kin. 21:18-26; 2 Chr. 33:20-25
2 [1]Lit., *ground* [a]Gen. 6:7; Jer. 7:20; Ezek. 33:27, 28
3 [1]Or, *stumbling blocks* [2]Lit., *ground* [a]Is. 6:11, 12 [b]Jer. 4:25; 9:10 [c]Ezek. 7:19; 14:3, 4, 8
4 [a]Jer. 6:12; Ezek. 6:14 [b]Mic. 5:13 [c]2 Kin. 23:5; Hos. 10:5
5 [1]Or, *their king;* M.T., *Malcam,* probably a variant spelling of Milcom [a]2 Kin. 23:12; Jer. 19:13 [b]Jer. 5:2, 7; 7:9, 10 [c]1 Kin. 11:5, 33; Jer. 49:1
6 [a]Is. 1:4; Hos. 7:10 [b]Is. 9:13
7 [1]Lit., *Hush* [2]Heb., *YHWH,* usually rendered *LORD* [a]Hab. 2:20; Zech. 2:13 [b]Zeph. 1:14 [c]Is. 34:6; Jer. 46:10 [d]1 Sam. 16:5; Is. 13:3
8 [a]Is. 24:21; Hab. 1:10 [b]Is. 2:6
9 [1]Or, *Lord* [a]Jer. 5:27; Amos 3:10
10 [1]I.e., a district of Jerusalem [a]2 Chr. 33:14; Neh. 3:3; 12:39 [b]2 Chr. 34:22 [c]Ezek. 6:13
11 [1]I.e., a district of Jerusalem [2]Or, *merchant people will* [a]Zeph. 2:5; Zech. 14:21 [b]Job 27:16, 17; Hos. 9:6
12 [a]Jer. 16:16, 17; Ezek. 9:4-11; Amos 9:1-3

Who are [1b]stagnant in spirit,
Who say in their hearts,
'The LORD will [c]not do good or evil!'
13 "Moreover, their wealth will become [a]plunder,
And their houses desolate;
Yes, [b]they will build houses but not inhabit *them*,
And plant vineyards but not drink their wine."

14 Near is the [a]great [b]day of the LORD,
Near and coming very quickly;
Listen, the day of the LORD!
[1]In it the warrior [c]cries out bitterly.
15 A day of wrath is that day,
A day of [a]trouble and distress,
A day of destruction and desolation,
A day of [b]darkness and gloom,
A day of clouds and thick darkness,
16 A day of [a]trumpet and battle cry,
Against the [b]fortified cities
And the high corner towers.
17 And I will bring [a]distress on men,
So that they will walk [b]like the blind,
Because they have sinned against the LORD;
And their [c]blood will be poured out like dust,
And their [d]flesh like dung.
18 Neither their [a]silver nor their gold
Will be able to deliver them
On the day of the LORD's wrath;
And [b]all the earth will be devoured
In the fire of His jealousy,
For He will [c]make a complete end,
Indeed a terrifying one,
Of all the inhabitants of the earth.

Judgments on Judah's Enemies

2 GATHER yourselves together, yes, [a]gather,
O nation [b]without [1]shame,
2 Before the decree [1]takes effect—
The day passes [a]like the chaff—
Before the [b]burning anger of the LORD comes upon you,
Before the [c]day of the LORD's anger comes upon you.
3 [a]Seek the LORD,
All you [b]humble of the [1]earth
Who have carried out His [2]ordinances;
[c]Seek righteousness, seek humility.
Perhaps you will be [d]hidden
In the day of the LORD's anger.

4 For [a]Gaza will be abandoned,
And Ashkelon a desolation;
[a]Ashdod will be driven out at noon,
And [a]Ekron will be uprooted.
5 Woe to the inhabitants of the seacoast,
The nation of the [1a]Cherethites!
The word of the LORD is [b]against you,
O [c]Canaan, land of the Philistines;
And I will [d]destroy you,
So that there will be [e]no inhabitant.
6 So the seacoast will be [a]pastures,
With [1]caves for shepherds and folds for flocks.
7 And the coast will be
For the [a]remnant of the house of Judah,
They will [b]pasture on it.
In the houses of Ashkelon they will lie down at evening;
For the LORD their God will [c]care for them
And [d]restore their fortune.

8 "I have heard the [1a]taunting of Moab
And the [b]revilings of the sons of Ammon,
With which they have [2]taunted My people
And [3c]become arrogant against their territory.
9 "Therefore, as I live," declares the LORD of hosts,
The God of Israel,
"Surely [a]Moab will be like [b]Sodom,
And the sons of [c]Ammon like [d]Gomorrah—
A place possessed by nettles and salt pits,
And a perpetual desolation.
The remnant of My people will [e]plunder them,
And the remainder of My nation will inherit them."
10 This they will have in return for
their [a]pride, because they have [1b]taunted
and [2]become arrogant against the people
of the LORD of hosts.
11 The LORD will be [a]terrifying to
them, for He will [1]starve [b]all the gods of
the earth; and all the [c]coastlands of the
nations will [d]bow down to Him, everyone from his *own* place.
12 "You also, O [a]Ethiopians, will be slain by My sword."
13 And He will [a]stretch out His hand against the north
And destroy [b]Assyria,
And He will make [c]Nineveh a desolation,
Parched like the wilderness.
14 And flocks will lie down in her midst,
[1]All beasts which range in herds;
Both the [2a]pelican and the hedgehog
Will lodge in [3]the tops of her pillars;
[4]Birds will sing in the window,
Desolation *will be* on the threshold;
For He has laid bare the cedar work.
15 This is the [a]exultant city
Which [b]dwells securely,
Who says in her heart,
"[c]I am, and there is no one besides me."
How she has become a [d]desolation,
A resting place for beasts!
[e]Everyone who passes by her will hiss
And wave his hand *in contempt.*

---

12 [1]Lit., *thickening on their lees* [b]Jer. 48:11; Amos 6:1 [c]Ezek. 8:12; 9:9
13 [a]Jer. 15:13; 17:3 [b]Amos 5:11; Mic. 6:15
14 [1]Lit., *There* [a]Jer. 30:7; Joel 2:11; Mal. 4:5 [b]Ezek. 7:7, 12; 30:3; Joel 1:15; 3:14; Zeph. 1:7 [c]Ezek. 7:16-18
15 [a]Is. 22:5 [b]Joel 2:2, 31; Amos 5:18-20
16 [a]Is. 27:13; Jer. 4:19 [b]Is. 2:12-15
17 [a]Jer. 10:18 [b]Deut. 28:29 [c]Ezek. 24:7, 8 [d]Jer. 8:2; 9:22
18 [a]Ezek. 7:19 [b]Zeph. 3:8 [c]Gen. 6:7; Ezek. 7:5-7

1 [1]Or, *longing* [a]2 Chr. 20:4; Joel 1:14 [b]Jer. 3:3; 6:15
2 [1]Lit., *is born* [a]Is. 17:13; Hos. 13:3 [b]Lam. 4:11; Nah. 1:6 [c]Zeph. 1:18
3 [1]Or, *land* [2]Or, *justice* [a]Ps. 105:4; Amos 5:6 [b]Ps. 22:26; Is. 11:4 [c]Amos 5:14, 15 [d]Ps. 57:1; Is. 26:20
4 [a]Amos 1:7, 8; Zech. 9:5-7
5 [1]I.e., a segment of the Philistines with roots in Crete [a]Ezek. 25:16 [b]Amos 3:1 [c]Zeph. 1:11 [d]Is. 14:29, 30 [e]Zeph. 3:6
6 [1]Or, *meadows* or *wells* [a]Is. 5:17; 7:25
7 [a]Is. 11:16 [b]Is. 32:14 [c]Ex. 4:31; Ps. 80:14 [d]Jer. 32:44; Zeph. 3:20
8 [1]Lit., *reproach* [2]Lit., *reproached* [3]Lit., *made themselves great* [a]Ezek. 25:8 [b]Ezek. 25:3 [c]Amos 1:13
9 [a]Is. 15:1-9; Jer. 48:1-47; Amos 2:1-3 [b]Gen. 19:24 [c]Jer. 49:1-6; Ezek. 25:1-10 [d]Deut. 29:23 [e]Is. 11:14
10 [1]Lit., *reproached* [2]Lit., *made themselves great* [a]Is. 16:6 [b]Zeph. 2:8
11 [1]Lit., *make lean* [a]Joel 2:11 [b]Zeph. 1:4 [c]Is. 24:15 [d]Ps. 72:8-11; Zeph. 3:9
12 [a]Is. 18:1-7; 20:4, 5; Ezek. 30:4-9
13 [a]Is. 14:26; Zeph. 1:4 [b]Is. 10:16; Mic. 5:6 [c]Nah. 3:7
14 [1]Or, *All* kinds of *beasts in crowds;* lit., *Every* kind of *beast of a nation* [2]Or, *owl* or *jackdaw* [3]Lit., *her capitals* [4]Lit., *A voice* [a]Is. 14:23; 34:11
15 [a]Is. 22:2 [b]Is. 32:9, 11; 47:8 [c]Is. 47:8; Ezek. 28:2, 9 [d]Is. 32:14 [e]Jer. 18:16; 19:8

Woe to Jerusalem and the Nations

3 WOE to her who is [a]rebellious and
[b]defiled,
The [c]tyrannical city!
2 She [a]heeded no voice;
She [b]accepted no instruction.
She did not [c]trust in the LORD;
She did not [d]draw near to her God.
3 Her [a]princes within her are roaring
lions,
Her judges are [b]wolves at evening;
They leave nothing for the morning.
4 Her prophets are [a]reckless, treacherous men;
Her [b]priests have profaned the
sanctuary.
They have done violence to the law.
5 The LORD is [a]righteous [b]within
her;
He will [c]do no injustice.
[d]Every morning He brings His justice to light;
He does not fail.
But the unjust [e]knows no shame.
6 "I have cut off nations;
Their corner towers are in ruins.
I have made their streets [a]desolate,
With no one passing by;
Their [b]cities are laid waste,
Without a man, [c]without an inhabitant.
7 "I said, 'Surely you will revere Me,
[a]Accept instruction.'
So her dwelling will [b]not be cut off
According to all that I have appointed concerning her.
But they were eager to [c]corrupt all
their deeds.

8 "Therefore, [a]wait for Me," declares
the LORD,
"For the day when I rise up to the
prey.
Indeed, My decision is to [b]gather
nations,
To assemble kingdoms,
To pour out on them My indignation,
All My burning anger;
For [c]all the earth will be devoured
By the fire of My zeal.
9 "For then I will [1]give to the peoples
[a]purified lips,
That all of them may [b]call on the
name of the LORD,
To serve Him [2]shoulder to shoulder.
10 "From beyond the rivers of [a]Ethiopia
My [1]worshipers, [2]My dispersed
ones,
Will [b]bring My offerings.
11 "In that day you will [a]feel no shame
Because of all your deeds
By which you have rebelled against
Me;
For then I will remove from your
midst
Your [b]proud, exulting ones,
And you will never again be
haughty
On My [c]holy mountain.

A Remnant of Israel

12 "But I will leave among you
A [a]humble and lowly people,
And they will [b]take refuge in the
name of the LORD.
13 "The [a]remnant of Israel will [b]do no
wrong
And [c]tell no lies,
Nor will a deceitful tongue
Be found in their mouths;
For they shall [d]feed and lie down
With no one to make them tremble."

14 Shout for joy, O daughter of Zion!
[a]Shout *in triumph,* O Israel!
Rejoice and exult with all *your*
heart,
O daughter of Jerusalem!
15 The LORD has taken away [a]*His*
judgments against you,
He has cleared away your enemies.
The King of Israel, the LORD, is [b]in
your midst;
You will [c]fear disaster no more.
16 [a]In that day it will be said to
Jerusalem:
"[b]Do not be afraid, O Zion;
[c]Do not let your hands fall limp.
17 "The LORD your God is [a]in your
midst,
A [1b]victorious warrior.
He will [c]exult over you with joy,
He will [2]be quiet in His love,
He will rejoice over you with shouts
of joy.
18 "I will gather those who [a]grieve
about the appointed feasts—
They [1]came from you, *O Zion;*
The reproach *of exile* is a burden on
[2]them.
19 "Behold, I am going to deal at that
time
With all your [a]oppressors,
I will save the [b]lame
And gather the outcast,
And I will turn their [c]shame into
[d]praise and renown
In all the earth.
20 "At that time I will [a]bring you in,
Even at the time when I gather you
together;
Indeed, I will give you [b]renown and
praise
Among all the peoples of the earth,
When I [c]restore your fortunes before your eyes,"
Says the LORD.

1 [a]Jer. 5:23 [b]Ezek. 23:30 [c]Jer. 6:6
2 [a]Jer. 7:23-28 [b]Jer. 2:30; 5:3; 2 Tim. 3:16 [c]Ps. 78:22; Jer. 13:25 [d]Ps. 73:28
3 [a]Ezek. 22:27 [b]Jer. 5:6; Hab. 1:8
4 [a]Judg. 9:4 [b]Ezek. 22:26; Mal. 2:7, 8
5 [a]Deut. 32:4 [b]Zeph. 3:15, 17 [c]Ps. 92:15 [d]Job 7:18 [e]Zeph. 2:1
6 [a]Jer. 9:12; Zech. 7:14; Matt. 23:38 [b]Lev. 26:31; Is. 6:11 [c]Zeph. 2:5
7 [a]Job 36:10; Ps. 32:8; 1 Tim. 1:5 [b]Jer. 7:7 [c]Hos. 9:9
8 [a]Ps. 27:14; Is. 30:18; Hab. 2:3 [b]Ezek. 38:14-23; Joel 3:2 [c]Zeph. 1:18
9 [1]Lit., *change* [2]Lit., *with one shoulder* [a]Is. 19:18; 57:19 [b]Ps. 22:27; 86:9; Hab. 2:14; Zeph. 2:11
10 [1]Or, *suppliants* [2]Lit., *the daughter of My dispersed ones* [a]Ps. 68:31; Is. 18:1 [b]Is. 60:6, 7
11 [a]Is. 45:17; 54:4; Joel 2:26, 27 [b]Is. 2:12; 5:15 [c]Is. 11:9; 56:7; Ezek. 20:40
12 [a]Is. 14:30 [b]Is. 14:32; 50:10; Nah. 1:7; Zech. 13:8, 9
13 [a]Is. 10:20-22; Mic. 4:7; Zeph. 2:7 [b]Ps. 119:3; Jer. 31:33; Zeph. 3:5 [c]Zech. 8:3, 16; Rev. 14:5 [d]Ezek. 34:13-15
14 [a]Zech. 9:9
15 [a]Ps. 19:9; John 5:30; Rev. 18:20 [b]Ezek. 37:26-28; Zeph. 3:5 [c]Is. 54:14
16 [a]Is. 25:9 [b]Is. 35:3, 4 [c]Job 4:3; Heb. 12:12
17 [1]Lit., *A warrior who saves* [2]Or, with some ancient versions, *renew* you *in* [a]Zeph. 3:5, 15 [b]Is. 63:1 [c]Is. 62:5
18 [1]Lit., *were* [2]Lit., *her* [a]Ps. 42:2-4; Ezek. 9:4
19 [a]Is. 60:14 [b]Ezek. 34:16; Mic. 4:6 [c]Ezek. 16:27, 57 [d]Is. 60:18; 62:7; Zech. 8:23
20 [a]Ezek. 37:12, 21 [b]Deut. 26:18, 19; Is. 56:5; 66:22 [c]Jer. 29:14; Joel 3:1; Zeph. 2:7

THE BOOK OF
HAGGAI

Haggai Begins Temple Building

1 IN the [a]second year of Darius the
king, on the first day of the sixth
month, the word of the LORD came by
the prophet [b]Haggai to [c]Zerubbabel the
son of Shealtiel, [d]governor of Judah, and
to [e]Joshua the son of Jehozadak, the
high priest saying,
2 "Thus says the LORD of [1]hosts, 'This
people says, "The time has not come,
even the time for the house of the LORD
to be rebuilt." ' "
3 Then the word of the LORD came
by Haggai the prophet saying,
4 "Is it time for you yourselves to
dwell in your paneled houses while this
house [a]*lies* desolate?"
5 Now therefore, thus says the LORD
of hosts, "[1]Consider your ways!
6 "You have [a]sown much, but [1]har-
vest little; *you* eat, but *there is* not
enough to be satisfied; *you* drink, but
there is [2]not *enough* to become drunk;
you put on clothing, but no one is warm
enough; and he who earns, earns wages
to put into a purse with holes."
7 Thus says the LORD of hosts,
"[1]Consider your ways!
8 "Go up to the [1]mountains, bring
wood and [a]rebuild the [2]temple, that I
may be [b]pleased with it and be [c]glori-
fied," says the LORD.
9 "[a]*You* look for much, but behold, *it*
comes to little; when you bring *it* home, I
[b]blow it *away.* Why?" declares the LORD
of hosts, "Because of My house which
[c]*lies* desolate, while each of you runs to
his own house.
10 "Therefore, because of you the [a]sky
has withheld [1]its dew, and the earth has
withheld its produce.
11 "And I called for a [a]drought on the
land, on the mountains, on the grain, on
the new wine, on the oil, on what the
ground produces, on [b]men, on cattle,
and on [c]all the labor of [1]your hands."
12 Then [a]Zerubbabel the son of Shealtiel, and [b]Joshua the son of Jehozadak,
the high priest, with all the remnant of
the people, [c]obeyed the voice of the
LORD their God and the words of Haggai the prophet, as the LORD their God
had sent him. And the people [1d]showed
reverence for the LORD.
13 Then Haggai, the [a]messenger of the
LORD, spoke [1]by the commission of the
LORD to the people saying, " '[b]I am with
you,' declares the LORD."
14 So the LORD stirred up the spirit of
[a]Zerubbabel the son of Shealtiel, [a]gover-
nor of Judah, and the spirit of Joshua
the son of Jehozadak, the high priest,
and the spirit of all the [b]remnant of the
people; and they came and [c]worked on
the house of the LORD of hosts, their
God,
15 on the twenty-fourth day of the
sixth month in the second year of Darius
the king.

1 [a]Ezra 4:24 [b]Ezra 5:1; 6:14; Hag. 1:3, 12, 13; 2:1, 10, 20 [c]Ezra 2:2; Neh. 7:7; Hag. 1:12, 14; Zech. 4:6; Matt. 1:12, 13 [d]1 Kin. 10:15; Ezra 5:3 [e]Zech. 6:11
2 [1]Lit., *hosts, saying*
4 [a]Jer. 33:10, 12; Hag. 1:9
5 [1]Lit., *Set your heart on*
6 [1]Lit., *bring in* [2]Lit., *not becoming drunk* [a]Deut. 28:38-40; Hos. 8:7; Hag. 1:9, 10; 2:16, 17
7 [1]Lit., *Set your heart on*
8 [1]Lit., *mountain* [2]Lit., *house* [a]1 Kin. 6:1 [b]Ps. 132:13, 14 [c]Hag. 2:7, 9
9 [a]Prov. 27:20; Eccl. 1:8 [b]Is. 40:7 [c]Hag. 1:4
10 [1]Lit., *from dew* [a]Deut. 28:23, 24; 1 Kin. 17:1; Joel 1:18-20
11 [1]Lit., *the palms* [a]Jer. 14:2-6; Mal. 3:9, 11 [b]Deut. 28:22 [c]Hag. 2:17
12 [1]Lit., *feared before* [a]Hag. 1:1 [b]Hag. 1:14; 2:2 [c]Is. 1:19; 1 Thess. 2:13 [d]Deut. 31:12, 13; Ps. 112:1; Is. 50:10
13 [1]Or, *the message* [a]Is. 44:26; Ezek. 3:17; Mal. 2:7; 3:1 [b]Ps. 46:11; Is. 41:10; 43:2
14 [a]Hag. 1:1; 2:2, 21 [b]Hag. 1:12 [c]Ezra 5:2; Neh. 4:6

1 [a]Hag. 1:1
2 [a]Hag. 1:1 [b]Hag. 1:12
3 [1]Lit., *house* [2]Lit., *in your eyes* [3]Lit., *like it* [a]Ezra 3:12 [b]Hag. 2:9
4 [1]Lit., *be strong* [a]Deut. 31:23; 1 Chr. 22:13; 28:20; Zech. 8:9; Eph. 6:10 [b]2 Sam. 5:10; Acts 7:9
5 [1]Lit., *word* [2]Lit., *cut with* [3]Or, *while . . . was standing* [a]Ex. 19:4-6; 29:45, 46; 33:12-14; 34:8-10 [b]Neh. 9:20; Is. 63:11, 14 [c]Is. 41:10, 13; Zech. 8:13
6 [1]Lit., *it is a little* [a]Heb. 12:26 [b]Is. 10:25; 29:17 [c]Hag. 2:21
7 [1]Or, *the desire of all nations will come* [a]Dan. 2:44; Joel 3:9, 16 [b]Is. 60:4-9 [c]1 Kin. 8:11; Is. 60:7
8 [a]1 Chr. 29:14, 16; Is. 60:17
9 [a]Zech. 2:5 [b]Hag. 2:3 [c]Is. 9:6, 7; 66:12
10 [a]Hag. 2:20
11 [1]Lit., *law* [a]Deut. 17:8-11; Mal. 2:7

The Builders Encouraged

2 ON the twenty-first of the seventh
month, the word of the LORD came
by [a]Haggai the prophet saying,
2 "Speak now to [a]Zerubbabel the son
of Shealtiel, [a]governor of Judah, and to
[a]Joshua the son of Jehozadak, the high
priest, and to the [b]remnant of the people
saying,
3 'Who is [a]left among you who saw
this [1]temple in its [b]former glory? And
how do you see it now? Does it not
[2]seem to you like nothing [3]in comparison?
4 'But now [1a]take courage, Zerubbabel,' declares the LORD, 'take courage
also, Joshua son of Jehozadak, the high
priest, and all you people of the land
take courage,' declares the LORD, 'and
work; for [b]I am with you,' says the LORD
of hosts.
5 'As for the [1a]promise which I [2]made
you when you came out of Egypt, [3]My
[b]Spirit is abiding in your midst; [c]do not
fear!'
6 "For thus says the LORD of hosts,
'[a]Once more [1]in a [b]little while, I am
going to [c]shake the heavens and the
earth, the sea also and the dry land.
7 'And I will shake [a]all the nations;
and [1]they will come with the [b]wealth of
all nations; and I will [c]fill this house
with glory,' says the LORD of hosts.
8 'The [a]silver is Mine, and the gold is
Mine,' declares the LORD of hosts.
9 'The latter [a]glory of this house will
be greater than the [b]former,' says the
LORD of hosts, 'and in this place I shall
give [c]peace,' declares the LORD of
hosts."
10 On the [a]twenty-fourth of the ninth
month, in the second year of Darius, the
word of the LORD came to Haggai the
prophet saying,
11 "Thus says the LORD of hosts, '[a]Ask
now the priests *for* a [1]ruling:
12 'If a man carries [a]holy meat in the
[1]fold of his garment, and touches bread
with [2]this fold, or cooked food, wine, oil,
or any *other* food, will it become holy?' "
And the priests answered and said,
"No."
13 Then Haggai said, "[a]If one who is
unclean from a [1]corpse touches any of
these, will *the latter* become unclean?"
And the priests answered and said, "It
will become unclean."
14 Then Haggai answered and said,
" '[a]So is this people. And so is this
nation before Me,' declares the LORD,
'and so is every work of their hands; and
what they offer there is unclean.
15 'But now, do [1a]consider from this
day [2]onward: before one [b]stone was

12 [1]Lit., *wing* [2]Lit., *his wing* [a]Ex. 29:37; Lev. 6:27, 29; 7:6; Ezek. 44:19; Matt. 23:19
13 [1]Lit., *soul* [a]Lev. 22:4-6; Num. 19:22
14 [a]Prov. 15:8; Is. 1:11-15
15 [1]Lit., *set your heart* [2]Or, *backward* [a]Hag. 1:5, 7; 2:18 [b]Ezra 3:10; 4:24

placed on another in the temple of the LORD,

16 [1]from that time *when* one came to a *grain* heap of twenty *measures,* there would be only ten; and *when* one came to the wine vat to draw fifty [2]measures, there would be *only* twenty.

17 'I smote you *and* every work of your hands with [a]blasting wind, mildew, and hail; [1]yet you *did* not *come back* to Me,' declares the LORD.

18 'Do [1a]consider from this day [2]onward, from the [b]twenty-fourth day of the ninth *month*; from the day when the temple of the LORD was [c]founded, [1]consider:

19 'Is the seed still in the barn? Even including the vine, the fig tree, the pomegranate, and the olive tree, it has not borne *fruit.* Yet from this day on I will [a]bless *you.*' "

16 [1]Lit., *since they were* [2]Or, *troughs full*
17 [1]Or, *but what did we have in common?* [a]Deut. 28:22; 1 Kin. 8:37; Amos 4:9
18 [1]Lit., *set your heart* [2]Or, *backward* [a]Deut. 32:29; Hag. 2:15 [b]Hag. 2:10 [c]Ezra 5:1, 2; Zech. 8:9, 12
19 [a]Ps. 128:1-6; Jer. 31:12, 14; Mal. 3:10
20 [a]Hag. 2:10
21 [a]Ezra 5:2; Hag. 1:1; Zech. 4:6-10 [b]Hag. 2:6; Heb. 12:26, 27
22 [1]Or, *Gentiles* [a]Ezek. 26:16; Zeph. 3:8 [b]Mic. 7:16 [c]Ps. 46:9; Ezek. 39:20; Mic. 5:10 [d]Amos 2:15 [e]Judg. 7:22; 2 Chr. 20:23

20 Then the word of the LORD came a second time to Haggai on the [a]twenty-fourth *day* of the month saying,

21 "Speak to [a]Zerubbabel governor of Judah saying, 'I am going to [b]shake the heavens and the earth.

22 'And I will [a]overthrow the thrones of kingdoms and destroy the [b]power of the kingdoms of the [1]nations; and I will [c]overthrow the chariots and their riders, and the [d]horses and their riders will go down, [e]everyone by the sword of another.'

23 'On that day,' declares the LORD of hosts, 'I will take you, Zerubbabel, son of Shealtiel, my servant,' declares the LORD, 'and I will make you like a [1a]signet *ring,* for [b]I have chosen you,' " declares the LORD of hosts.

23 [1]Or, *seal* [a]Song 8:6; Jer. 22:24 [b]Is. 42:1; 43:10

THE BOOK OF ZECHARIAH

A Call to Repentance

1 IN the eighth month of the second year of [a]Darius, the word of the LORD came to [b]Zechariah the prophet, the son of Berechiah, the son of [c]Iddo saying,

2 "The LORD was very [a]angry with your fathers.

3 "Therefore say to them, 'Thus says the LORD of hosts, "[a]Return to Me," declares the LORD of hosts, "that I may return to you," says the LORD of hosts.

4 "Do not be [a]like your fathers, to whom the [b]former prophets proclaimed, saying, 'Thus says the LORD of hosts, "[c]Return now from your evil ways and from your evil deeds." ' But they did [d]not listen or give heed to Me," declares the LORD.

5 "Your [a]fathers, where are they? And the [b]prophets, do they live forever?

6 "But did not My words and My statutes, which I commanded My servants the prophets, [a]overtake your fathers? Then they repented and said, '[b]As the LORD of hosts purposed to do to us in accordance with our ways and our deeds, so He has dealt with us.' " ' "

Patrol of the Earth

7 On the twenty-fourth day of the eleventh month, which is the month Shebat, in the second year of Darius, the word of the LORD came to Zechariah the prophet, the son of Berechiah, the son of Iddo, as follows:

8 I saw at night, and behold, a man was riding on a [a]red horse, and he was standing among the [b]myrtle trees which were in the ravine, with red, sorrel, and [c]white horses behind him.

9 Then I said, "My [a]lord, what are these?" And the [b]angel who was speaking with me said to me, "I will show you what these are."

10 And the man who was standing among the myrtle trees answered and said, "These are those whom the LORD has sent to [1a]patrol the earth."

11 So they answered the angel of the LORD who was [a]standing among the myrtle trees, and said, "We have [1]patrolled the earth, and behold, [b]all the earth is [2]peaceful and quiet."

12 Then the angel of the LORD answered and said, "O LORD of hosts, [a]how long wilt Thou [b]have no compassion for Jerusalem and the cities of Judah, with which Thou hast been [c]indignant these [d]seventy years?"

13 And the LORD answered the [a]angel who was speaking with me with [1]gracious words, [b]comforting words.

14 So the angel who was speaking with me said to me, "[a]Proclaim, saying, 'Thus says the LORD of hosts, "I am [b]exceedingly jealous for Jerusalem and Zion.

15 "But I am very [a]angry with the nations who are [b]at ease; for while I was only a little angry, they [1c]furthered the disaster."

16 'Therefore, thus says the LORD, "I will [a]return to Jerusalem with compassion; My [b]house will be built in it," declares the LORD of hosts, "and a measuring [c]line will be stretched over Jerusalem." '

17 "Again, proclaim, saying, 'Thus says the LORD of hosts, "My [a]cities will again overflow with prosperity, and the LORD will again [b]comfort Zion and again [c]choose Jerusalem." ' "

1 [a]Ezra 4:24; 6:15; Hag. 1:15; 2:10; Zech. 1:7; 7:1 [b]Ezra 5:1; 6:14; Zech. 7:1; Matt. 23:35; Luke 11:51 [c]Neh. 12:4, 16
2 [a]2 Chr. 36:16; Jer. 44:6; Ezek. 8:18; Zech. 1:15
3 [a]Is. 31:6; 44:22; Mal. 3:7
4 [a]Ps. 78:8; 106:6, 7 [b]2 Chr. 24:19; 36:15 [c]Is. 1:16-19; Jer. 4:1; Ezek. 33:11 [d]Jer. 6:17; 11:7, 8
5 [a]Lam. 5:7 [b]John 8:52
6 [a]Jer. 12:16, 17; 44:28, 29; Amos 9:10 [b]Lam. 2:17
8 [a]Zech. 6:2; Rev. 6:4 [b]Neh. 8:15; Is. 41:19; 55:13; Zech. 1:10, 11 [c]Zech. 6:3; Rev. 6:2
9 [a]Zech. 1:19; 4:4, 5, 13; 6:4 [b]Zech. 2:3; 5:5
10 [1]Lit., *walk about through* [a]Job 1:7; Zech. 1:11; 4:10; 6:5-8
11 [1]Lit., *walked about through* [2]Lit., *sitting* [a]Zech. 1:8, 10 [b]Is. 14:7
12 [a]Ps. 74:10; Jer. 12:4; Hab. 1:2 [b]Ps. 102:13; Jer. 30:18 [c]Ps. 102:10; Jer. 15:17 [d]Jer. 25:11; 29:10; Dan. 9:2; Zech. 7:5
13 [1]Lit., *good* [a]Zech. 1:9; 4:1 [b]Is. 40:1, 2; 57:18
14 [a]Is. 40:2, 6; Zech. 1:17 [b]Zech. 8:2
15 [1]Lit., *helped for evil* [a]Zech. 1:2 [b]Ps. 123:4; Jer. 48:11 [c]Amos 1:11
16 [a]Is. 54:8-10; Zech. 2:10, 11 [b]Ezra 6:14, 15; Zech. 4:9 [c]Jer. 31:39; Zech. 2:2, 4
17 [a]Is. 44:26; 61:4 [b]Is. 51:3 [c]Zech. 2:12

18 [1]Then I lifted up my eyes and
looked, and behold, *there were* four
horns.
19 So I said to the angel who was
speaking with me, "What are these?"
And he answered me, "These are the
[a]horns which have scattered Judah,
Israel, and Jerusalem."
20 Then the LORD showed me four
[a]craftsmen.
21 And I said, "What are these coming to do?" And he said, "These are the
[a]horns which have scattered Judah, so
that no man lifts up his head; but these
craftsmen have come to terrify them, to
[b]throw down the horns of the nations
who have lifted up *their* horns against
the land of Judah in order to scatter it."

God's Favor to Zion

2 1 THEN I lifted up my eyes and
looked, and behold, *there was* a man
with a [a]measuring line in his hand.
2 So I said, "Where are you going?"
And he said to me, "To [a]measure Jerusalem, to see how wide it is and how long it
is."
3 And behold, the [a]angel who was
speaking with me was going out, and
another angel was coming out to meet
him,
4 and said to him, "Run, speak to
that [a]young man, saying, '[b]Jerusalem
will be inhabited [1c]without walls, because of the [d]multitude of men and
cattle within it.
5 'For I,' declares the LORD, 'will be a
[a]wall of fire [1]around her, and I will be
the [b]glory in her midst.' "
6 "[1]Ho there! [a]Flee from the land of
the north," declares the LORD, "for I
have [b]dispersed you as the four winds of
the heavens," declares the LORD.
7 "Ho, Zion! [a]Escape, you who are
living with the daughter of Babylon."
8 For thus says the LORD of hosts,
"After [1a]glory He has sent me against
the nations which plunder you, for he
who touches you, touches the [2b]apple of
His eye.
9 "For behold, I will [a]wave My hand
over them, so that they will be [b]plunder
for their slaves. Then you will know that
the LORD of hosts has sent Me.
10 "[a]Sing for joy and be glad, O daughter of Zion; for behold I am coming and
I will [b]dwell in your midst," declares the
LORD.
11 "And [a]many nations will join themselves to the LORD in that day and will
become My people. Then I will [b]dwell in
your midst, and you will [c]know that the
LORD of hosts has sent Me to you.
12 "And the LORD will [1a]possess Judah
as His portion in the holy land, and will
again [b]choose Jerusalem.
13 "[1a]Be silent, all flesh, before the
LORD; for He is [b]aroused from His holy
habitation."

Joshua, the High Priest

3 THEN he showed me [a]Joshua the
high priest standing before the angel
of the LORD, and [1b]Satan standing at his
right hand to accuse him.
2 And the LORD said to Satan, "[a]The
LORD rebuke you, Satan! Indeed, the
LORD who has [b]chosen Jerusalem rebuke
you! Is this not a [c]brand plucked from
the fire?"
3 Now Joshua was clothed with
[a]filthy garments and standing before the
angel.
4 And he spoke and said to those
who were standing before him saying,
"[a]Remove the filthy garments from
him." Again he said to him, "See, I have
[b]taken your iniquity away from you and
[1]will [c]clothe you with festal robes."
5 Then I said, "Let them put a clean
[a]turban on his head." So they put a clean
turban on his head and clothed him with
garments, while the angel of the LORD
was standing by.
6 And the angel of the LORD admonished Joshua saying,
7 "Thus says the LORD of hosts, 'If
you will [a]walk in My ways, and if you
will perform My service, then you will
also [b]govern My house and also have
charge of My [c]courts, and I will grant
you [1]free access among these who are
standing *here.*

The Branch

8 'Now listen, Joshua the high priest,
you and your friends who are sitting in
front of you—indeed they are men who
are a [a]symbol, for behold, I am going to
bring in My servant the [1b]Branch.
9 'For behold, the stone that I have
set before Joshua; on one stone are
[a]seven eyes. Behold, I will engrave an
inscription on it,' declares the LORD of
hosts, 'and I will [b]remove the iniquity of
that land in one day.
10 'In that day,' declares the LORD of
hosts, 'every one of you will invite his
neighbor to *sit* under *his* [a]vine and under
his fig tree.' "

The Golden Lampstand and Olive Trees

4 THEN [a]the angel who was speaking
with me returned, and [b]roused me
as a man who is awakened from his
sleep.
2 And he said to me, "[a]What do you
see?" And I said, "I see, and behold, a
[b]lampstand all of gold with its bowl on
the top of it, and its [c]seven lamps on it
with seven spouts belonging to each of
the lamps which are on the top of it;
3 also [a]two olive trees by it, one on
the right side of the bowl and the other
on its left side."
4 Then I answered and said to the
angel who was speaking with me saying,
"What are these, [a]my lord?"
5 So [a]the angel who was speaking
with me answered and said to me, "[b]Do
you not know what these are?" And I
said, "No, my lord."

18 [1]Ch. 2:1 in Heb.
19 [a]1 Kin. 22:11; Ps. 75:4, 5; Amos 6:13 mg.
20 [a]Is. 44:12; 54:16
21 [a]Zech. 1:19 [b]Ps. 75:10

1 [1]Ch. 2:5 in Heb. [a]Jer. 31:39; Ezek. 40:3; 47:3; Zech. 1:16
2 [a]Jer. 31:39; Ezek. 40:3; Rev. 21:15-17
3 [a]Zech. 1:9
4 [1]Lit., like *unwalled villages;* or, like *open country* [a]Jer. 1:6; Dan. 1:4; 1 Tim. 4:12 [b]Zech. 1:17; 8:4 [c]Ezek. 38:11 [d]Is. 49:20; Jer. 30:19; 33:22
5 [1]Lit., *to her* [a]Is. 4:5; 26:1; 60:18 [b]Hag. 2:9; Zech. 2:10, 11
6 [1]Lit., *Ho! ho!* [a]Jer. 3:18 [b]Jer. 31:10; Ezek. 11:16
7 [a]Is. 48:20; Jer. 51:6
8 [1]Or, *the glory* [2]Lit., *pupil* [a]Is. 60:7-9 [b]Deut. 32:10; Ps. 17:8
9 [a]Is. 19:16 [b]Is. 14:2
10 [a]Is. 65:18, 19; Zech. 9:9 [b]Zech. 2:5; 8:3
11 [a]Mic. 4:2 [b]Zech. 2:5, 10 [c]Zech. 2:9
12 [1]Or, *inherit* [a]Deut. 32:9; Ps. 33:12; Jer. 10:16 [b]2 Chr. 6:6; Ps. 132:13, 14; Zech. 1:17
13 [1]Lit., *Hush* [a]Hab. 2:20; Zeph. 1:7 [b]Ps. 78:65; Is. 51:9

1 [1]Or, the *Adversary* or *Accuser* [a]Ezra 5:2; Hag. 1:1; Zech. 6:11 [b]1 Chr. 21:1; Job 1:6; Ps. 109:6; Rev. 12:10
2 [a]Mark 9:25; Jude 9 [b]Zech. 2:12 [c]Amos 4:11; Jude 23
3 [a]Ezra 9:15; Is. 4:4; 64:6
4 [1]Lit., *to clothe* [a]Is. 43:25; Ezek. 36:25 [b]Mic. 7:18, 19; Zech. 3:9 [c]Is. 52:1; 61:10
5 [a]Job 29:14; Is. 3:23
7 [1]Lit., *goings* [a]1 Kin. 3:14 [b]Deut. 17:9, 12 [c]Is. 62:9
8 [1]Lit., *Sprout* [a]Is. 8:18; 20:3; Ezek. 12:11 [b]Is. 11:1; 53:2; Jer. 23:5; 33:15; Zech. 6:12
9 [a]Zech. 4:10 [b]Jer. 31:34; 50:20; Zech. 3:4
10 [a]1 Kin. 4:25; Is. 36:16; Mic. 4:4

1 [a]Zech. 1:9 [b]1 Kin. 19:5-7; Jer. 31:26
2 [a]Jer. 1:13; Zech. 5:2 [b]Ex. 25:31, 37; Jer. 52:19 [c]Rev. 4:5
3 [a]Zech. 4:11; Rev. 11:4
4 [a]Zech. 1:9; 4:5, 13; 6:4
5 [a]Zech. 1:9; 4:1 [b]Zech. 4:13

6 Then he answered and [1]said to me, "This is the word of the LORD to [a]Zerubbabel saying, '[b]Not by might nor by power, but by My [c]Spirit,' says the LORD of hosts.

7 'What are you, O great [a]mountain? Before Zerubbabel *you will become* a plain; and he will bring forth the top stone with [b]shouts of "Grace, grace to it!" ' "

8 Also the word of the LORD came to me saying,

9 "The hands of Zerubbabel have [a]laid the foundation of this house, and his hands will [b]finish *it.* Then you will know that the LORD of hosts has sent me to [1]you.

10 "For who has despised the day of [a]small things? [1]But these [b]seven will be glad when they see the [2c]plumb line in the hand of Zerubbabel—*these are* the [d]eyes of the LORD which [e]range to and fro throughout the earth."

11 Then I answered and said to him, "What are these [a]two olive trees on the right of the lampstand and on its left?"

12 And I answered the second time and said to him, "What are the two olive [1]branches which are beside the two golden pipes, which empty the golden *oil* from themselves?"

13 So he answered me saying, "[a]Do you not know what these are?" And I said, "No, [b]my lord."

14 Then he said, "These are the two [1a]anointed ones, who are [b]standing by the [c]Lord of the whole earth."

The Flying Scroll

5 THEN I lifted up my eyes again and looked, and behold, *there was* a flying [a]scroll.

2 And he said to me, "[a]What do you see?" And I answered, "I see a flying scroll; its length is twenty [1]cubits and its width ten cubits."

3 Then he said to me, "This is the [a]curse that is going forth over the face of the whole [1]land; surely everyone who [b]steals will be purged away according to [2]the writing on one side, and everyone who [c]swears will be purged away according to [2]the writing on the other side.

4 "I will [a]make it go forth," declares the LORD of hosts, "and it will [b]enter the house of the [c]thief and the house of the one who swears falsely by My name; and it will spend the night within that house and [d]consume it with its timber and stones."

5 Then [a]the angel who was speaking with me went out, and said to me, "Lift up now your eyes, and see what this is, going forth."

6 And I said, "What is it?" And he said, "This is the [1a]ephah going forth." Again he said, "This is their [2]appearance in all the [3]land

7 (and behold, a lead cover was lifted up); and this is a woman sitting inside the ephah."

8 Then he said, "This is [a]Wickedness!" And he threw her down into the middle of the ephah and cast the lead weight on its [1]opening.

9 Then I lifted up my eyes and looked, and there two women were coming out with the wind in their wings; and they had wings like the wings of a [a]stork, and they lifted up the ephah between the earth and the heavens.

10 And I said to the angel who was speaking with me, "Where are they taking the ephah?"

11 Then he said to me, "To build a [1]temple for her in the land of [a]Shinar; and when it is prepared, she will be set there on her own pedestal."

The Four Chariots

6 NOW I lifted up my eyes again and looked, and behold, [a]four chariots were coming forth from between the two mountains; and the mountains *were* bronze mountains.

2 With the first chariot *were* [a]red horses, with the second chariot [b]black horses,

3 with the third chariot [a]white horses, and with the fourth chariot strong [b]dappled horses.

4 Then I spoke and said to the angel who was speaking with me, "[a]What are these, my lord?"

5 And the angel answered and said to me, "These are the [a]four spirits of heaven, going forth after standing before the Lord of all the earth,

6 with one of which the black horses are going forth to the [a]north country; and the white ones go forth after them, while the dappled ones go forth to the [b]south country.

7 "When the strong ones went out, they [1]were eager to go to [2a]patrol the earth." And He said, "Go, [2]patrol the earth." So they [3]patrolled the earth.

8 Then He cried out to me and spoke to me saying, "See, those who are going to the land of the north have [1a]appeased My wrath in the land of the north."

9 The [a]word of the LORD also came to me saying,

10 "[a]Take *an offering* from the exiles, from Heldai, Tobijah, and Jedaiah; and you go the same day and enter the house of Josiah the son of Zephaniah, where they have arrived from Babylon.

The Symbolic Crowns

11 "And take silver and gold, make an *ornate* [a]crown, and set *it* on the head of [b]Joshua the son of Jehozadak, the high priest.

12 "Then say to him, 'Thus says the LORD of hosts, "Behold, a man whose

4:6 [1]Lit., *said to me, saying* [a]Ezra 5:2; Hag. 2:4, 5 [b]Is. 11:2-4; 30:1; Hos. 1:7 [c]2 Chr. 32:7, 8; Eph. 6:17
7 [a]Ps. 114:4, 6; Is. 40:4; Jer. 51:25; Nah. 1:5; Zech. 14:4, 5 [b]Ezra 3:10, 11; Ps. 84:11
9 [1]Lit., *you* (plural) [a]Ezra 3:8-10; 5:16; Hag. 2:18 [b]Ezra 6:14, 15; Zech. 6:12, 13
10 [1]Or, *But they will rejoice when they see . . . Zerubbabel. These seven are the eyes of the* LORD [2]Lit., *plummet stone* [a]Neh. 4:2-4; Amos 7:2, 5; Hag. 2:3 [b]Zech. 3:9; Rev. 8:2 [c]Amos 7:7, 8 [d]2 Chr. 16:9; Prov. 15:3; Jer. 16:17 [e]Zech. 1:10; Rev. 5:6
11 [a]Zech. 4:3; Rev. 11:4
12 [1]Or, *clusters*
13 [a]Zech. 4:5 [b]Zech. 4:4, 5
14 [1]Lit., *sons of fresh oil* [a]Ex. 29:7; 40:15; 1 Sam. 16:1, 12, 13; Is. 61:1-3; Dan. 9:24-26 [b]Zech. 3:1-7 [c]Mic. 4:13

5:1 [a]Jer. 36:2; Ezek. 2:9; Rev. 5:1
2 [1]I.e., One cubit equals approx. 18 in. [a]Zech. 4:2
3 [1]Or, *earth* [2]Lit., *it* [a]Is. 24:6; 43:28; Jer. 26:6 [b]Ex. 20:15; Lev. 19:11; Mal. 3:8, 9 [c]Lev. 19:12; Is. 48:1; Jer. 5:2; Zech. 5:4
4 [a]Mal. 3:5 [b]Hos. 4:2, 3 [c]Jer. 2:26 [d]Lev. 14:34, 35; Job 18:15
5 [a]Zech. 1:9
6 [1]I.e., Approx. one bu. [2]Lit., *eye;* some ancient versions read *iniquity* [3]Or, *earth* [a]Lev. 19:36; Amos 8:5
8 [1]Lit., *mouth* [a]Hos. 12:7; Amos 8:5; Mic. 6:11
9 [a]Lev. 11:13, 19; Ps. 104:17; Jer. 8:7
11 [1]Lit., *house* [a]Gen. 10:10; 11:2; 14:1; Is. 11:11; Dan. 1:2

6:1 [a]Dan. 7:3; 8:22; Zech. 1:18; 6:5
2 [a]Zech. 1:8; Rev. 6:4 [b]Rev. 6:5
3 [a]Rev. 6:2 [b]Rev. 6:8
4 [a]Zech. 1:9
5 [a]Jer. 49:36; Ezek. 37:9; Dan. 7:2; 11:4; Matt. 24:31; Rev. 7:1
6 [a]Jer. 1:14, 15; 4:6; 6:1; 25:9; 46:10; Ezek. 1:4 [b]Is. 43:6; Dan. 11:5
7 [1]Lit., *sought to go* [2]Lit., *walk about through* [3]Lit., *walked about through* [a]Zech. 1:10
8 [1]Lit., *caused My spirit to rest in* [a]Ezek. 5:13; 24:13; Zech. 1:15
9 [a]Zech. 1:1; 7:1; 8:1
10 [a]Ezra 7:14-16; 8:26-30; Jer. 28:6
11 [a]2 Sam. 12:30; Ps. 21:3; Song 3:11 [b]Ezra 3:2; Hag. 1:1; Zech. 3:1

name is [1a]Branch, for He will [2b]branch
out from where He is; and He will [c]build
the temple of the LORD.
13"Yes, it is He who will build the
temple of the LORD, and He who will
[a]bear the honor and sit and [b]rule on His
throne. Thus, He will be a [c]priest on His
throne, and the counsel of peace will be
between the two [1]offices." '
14"Now the [a]crown will become a
reminder in the temple of the LORD to
Helem, Tobijah, [1]Jedaiah, and Hen the
son of Zephaniah.
15"And [a]those who are far off will
come and [1]build the temple of the
LORD." Then you will [b]know that the
LORD of hosts has sent me to you. And it
will take place, if you completely [c]obey
the LORD your God.

Hearts like Flint

7 THEN it came about in the fourth
year of King Darius, that the word
of the LORD came to Zechariah on the
fourth *day* of the ninth month, *which is*
[a]Chislev.
2 Now *the town of* Bethel had sent
Sharezer and Regemmelech and [1]their
men to [2a]seek the favor of the LORD,
3 speaking to the [a]priests who belong
to the house of the LORD of hosts, and to
the prophets saying, "Shall I weep in the
[b]fifth month [1]and abstain, as I have
done these many years?"
4 Then the word of the LORD of
hosts came to me saying,
5"Say to all the people of the land
and to the priests, 'When you fasted and
mourned in the fifth and seventh months
[1]these [a]seventy years, was it actually for
[b]Me that you fasted?
6 'And when you eat and drink, [1]do
you not eat for yourselves and do you
not drink for yourselves?
7 'Are not *these* the words which the
LORD [a]proclaimed by the former prophets, when Jerusalem was inhabited and
[1b]prosperous with its cities around it,
and the [2c]Negev and the [3]foothills were
inhabited?' "
8 Then the word of the LORD came
to Zechariah saying,
9"Thus has the LORD of hosts said,
'[a]Dispense true justice, and practice
[b]kindness and compassion each to his
brother;
10 and [a]do not oppress the widow or
the [1]orphan, the [2]stranger or the poor;
and do [b]not devise evil in your hearts
against one another.'
11"But they [a]refused to pay attention,
and [1b]turned a stubborn shoulder and
[2c]stopped their ears from hearing.
12"And they made their [a]hearts *like*
[1b]flint [2]so that they could not hear the
law and the [c]words which the LORD of
hosts had sent by His Spirit through the
[d]former prophets; therefore great [e]wrath
came from the LORD of hosts.
13"And it came about that just as [a]He
called and they would not listen, so
[b]they called and I would not listen," says
the LORD of hosts;
14"but I [1a]scattered them with a
[b]storm wind among all the nations
whom they have not known. Thus the
land is [c]desolated behind them, [2]so that
[d]no one went back and forth, for they
[e]made the pleasant land desolate."

The Coming Peace and Prosperity of Zion

8 THEN the word of the LORD of
hosts came saying,
2"Thus says the LORD of hosts, 'I am
[a]exceedingly jealous for Zion, yes, with
great wrath I am jealous for her.'
3"Thus says the LORD, 'I will return
to Zion and will [a]dwell in the midst of
Jerusalem. Then Jerusalem will be called
the City of [b]Truth, and the mountain of
the LORD of hosts *will be called* the Holy
Mountain.'
4"Thus says the LORD of hosts, '[a]Old
men and old women will again sit in the
[1]streets of Jerusalem, each man with his
staff in his hand because of [2]age.
5 'And the [1]streets of the city will be
filled with [a]boys and girls playing in its
[1]streets.'
6"Thus says the LORD of hosts, 'If it
is [1a]too difficult in the sight of the
remnant of this people in those days,
will it also be [1b]too difficult in My sight?'
declares the LORD of hosts.
7"Thus says the LORD of hosts, 'Behold, I am going to save My people from
the land of the [1a]east and from the land
of the [2]west;
8 and I will [a]bring them *back,* and
they will [b]live in the midst of Jerusalem,
and they will be [c]My people and I will
be their God in [1]truth and righteousness.'
9"Thus says the LORD of hosts, 'Let
your hands be [a]strong, you who are
listening in these days to these words
from the mouth of the [b]prophets, *those*
who *spoke* in the day that the foundation
of the house of the LORD of hosts was
laid, to the end that the temple might be
built.
10 'For before those days there was
[a]no wage for man or any wage for
animal; and for him who went out or
came in there was no [1b]peace because of
[2]his enemies, and I [c]set all men one
against another.
11 'But now I will [a]not [1]treat the
remnant of this people as in the former
days,' declares the LORD of hosts.
12 'For *there will be* [a]peace for the
seed: the vine will yield its fruit, the land
will yield its produce, and the heavens
will give their [b]dew; and I will cause the
remnant of this people to inherit [c]all
these *things.*

12 [1]Lit., *Sprout* [2]Lit., *sprout up* [a]Is. 4:2; 11:1; Jer. 23:5; 33:15; Zech. 3:8 [b]Is. 53:2 [c]Ezra 3:8, 10; Amos 9:11; Zech. 4:6-9
13 [1]Lit., *of them* [a]Is. 9:6; 11:10; 22:24; 49:5, 6 [b]Is. 9:7 [c]Ps. 110:1, 4
14 [1]I.e., Josiah [a]Zech. 6:11
15 [1]Lit., *build in* [a]Is. 56:6-8; 60:10 [b]Zech. 2:9-11; 4:9 [c]Is. 58:10-14; Jer. 7:23; Zech. 3:7

1 [a]Neh. 1:1
2 [1]Lit., *his* [2]Lit., *soften the face of* [a]1 Kin. 13:6; Jer. 26:19; Zech. 8:21
3 [1]Lit., *abstaining;* or, *dedicating myself* [a]Ezra 3:10-12 [b]Zech. 8:19
5 [1]Lit., *and these* [a]Zech. 1:12 [b]Is. 1:11, 12; 58:5
6 [1]Lit., *is it not you who eat and you who drink*
7 [1]Or, *at ease* [2]I.e., South country [3]Heb., *Shephelah* [a]Is. 1:16-20; Jer. 7:5, 23; Zech. 1:4 [b]Jer. 22:21 [c]Jer. 13:19; 32:44
9 [a]Ezek. 18:8; 45:9; Zech. 8:16 [b]2 Sam. 9:7; Job 6:14; Mic. 6:8
10 [1]Or, *fatherless* [2]Or, *resident alien* [a]Ex. 22:22; Ps. 72:4; Jer. 7:6 [b]Ps. 21:11; Mic. 2:1; Zech. 8:17
11 [1]Lit., *gave* [2]Lit., *made heavy* [a]Jer. 5:3; 8:5; 11:10 [b]Jer. 7:26; 17:23 [c]Ps. 58:4; Jer. 5:21
12 [1]Lit., *corundum* [2]Lit., *from hearing* [a]2 Chr. 36:13; Ezek. 2:4; 3:7-9 [b]Jer. 17:1; Ezek. 3:9 [c]Zech. 7:7 [d]Neh. 9:30 [e]2 Chr. 36:16; Dan. 9:11, 12
13 [a]Jer. 11:10, 14; 14:12 [b]Prov. 1:24-28; Is. 1:15
14 [1]Lit., *stormed them away upon all* [2]Lit., *from passing and from returning* [a]Deut. 4:27; 28:64 [b]Jer. 23:19 [c]Jer. 44:6 [d]Is. 60:15 [e]Jer. 12:10

2 [a]Zech. 1:14
3 [a]Zech. 2:10, 11 [b]Zech. 8:16, 19
4 [1]Or, *squares* [2]Lit., *the multitude of days* [a]Is. 65:20
5 [1]Or, *squares* [a]Jer. 30:19, 20; 31:12, 13
6 [1]Or, *wonderful* [a]Ps. 118:23; 126:1-3 [b]Jer. 32:17, 27
7 [1]Lit., *rising* [2]Lit., *setting sun* [a]Ps. 107:3; Is. 11:11; 27:12, 13; 43:5
8 [1]Or, *faithfulness* [a]Zeph. 3:20; Zech. 10:10 [b]Jer. 3:17; Ezek. 37:25 [c]Ezek. 11:20; 36:28; Zech. 2:11
9 [a]1 Chr. 22:13; Is. 35:4; Hag. 2:4 [b]Ezra 5:1; 6:14
10 [1]Or, *safety* [2]Lit., *the adversary* [a]Hag. 2:15-19 [b]2 Chr. 15:5 [c]Is. 19:2; Amos 3:6; 9:4
11 [1]Lit., *be to the* [a]Ps. 103:9; Is. 12:1; Hag. 2:19
12 [a]Lev. 26:3-6 [b]Gen. 27:28; Deut. 33:13, 28; Hos. 13:3 [c]Is. 61:7; Obad. 17

13 'And it will come about that just as
you were a [a]curse among the nations, O
house of Judah and house of Israel, so I
will save you that you may become a
[b]blessing. Do not fear; let your [c]hands
be strong.'
14 "For thus says the LORD of hosts,
'Just as I [a]purposed to do harm to you
when your fathers provoked Me to
wrath,' says the LORD of hosts, 'and I
have not [b]relented,
15 so I have again purposed in these
days to [a]do good to Jerusalem and to the
house of Judah. [b]Do not fear!
16 'These are the things which you
should do: speak the [a]truth to one
another; [b]judge with truth and judgment
for peace in your [1]gates.
17 'Also let none of you [a]devise evil in
your heart against another, and do not
love [1][b]perjury; for all these are what I
[c]hate,' declares the LORD."
18 Then the word of the LORD of
hosts came to me saying,
19 "Thus says the LORD of hosts, 'The
fast of the [a]fourth, the fast of the [b]fifth,
the fast of the [c]seventh, and the fast of
the [d]tenth *months* will become [e]joy,
gladness, and [1]cheerful feasts for the
house of Judah; so [f]love truth and
peace.'
20 "Thus says the LORD of hosts, '*It
will* yet *be* that [a]peoples will come, even
the inhabitants of many cities.
21 'And the inhabitants of one will go
to another saying, "Let us go at once to
[a]entreat the favor of the LORD, and to
seek the LORD of hosts; [1]I will also go."
22 'So [a]many peoples and mighty nations will come to seek the LORD of
hosts in Jerusalem and to [b]entreat the
favor of the LORD.'
23 "Thus says the LORD of hosts, 'In
those days ten men from all the [1]nations
will [2][a]grasp the [3]garment of a Jew saying, "Let us go with you, for we have
heard that God is with you." ' "

Prophecies against Neighboring Nations

9 THE [1]burden of the word of the LORD is against the land of Hadrach, with [a]Damascus as its resting place (for the eyes of men, especially of all the tribes of Israel, are toward the LORD),

2 And [a]Hamath also, which borders on it;
[b]Tyre and [c]Sidon, [1]though [2]they are [b]very wise.
3 For Tyre built herself a [a]fortress
And [b]piled up silver like dust,
And [c]gold like the mire of the streets.
4 Behold, the Lord will [a]dispossess her
And cast her wealth into the sea;
And she will be [b]consumed with fire.
5 Ashkelon will see *it* and be afraid.
Gaza too will writhe in great pain;
Also Ekron, for her expectation has been confounded.
Moreover, the king will perish from Gaza,
And Ashkelon will not be inhabited.
6 And a [1]mongrel race will dwell in [a]Ashdod,
And I will cut off the pride of the Philistines.
7 And I will remove their blood from their mouth,
And their detestable things from between their teeth.
Then they also will be a remnant for our God,
And be like a [1]clan in Judah,
And Ekron like a Jebusite.
8 But I will camp around My house [1]because of an army,
Because of [a]him who passes by and returns;
And [b]no oppressor will pass over them anymore,
For now I have seen with My eyes.
9 [a]Rejoice greatly, O daughter of Zion!
Shout *in triumph,* O daughter of Jerusalem!
Behold, your [b]king is coming to you;
He is [1][c]just and [d]endowed with salvation,
[e]Humble, and mounted on a donkey,
Even on a [f]colt, the [2]foal of a donkey.
10 And I will [a]cut off the chariot from Ephraim,
And the [b]horse from Jerusalem;
And the [c]bow of war will be cut off.
And He will speak [d]peace to the nations;
And His [e]dominion will be from sea to sea,
And from the [1]River to the ends of the earth.

Deliverance of Judah and Ephraim

11 As for you also, because of the [a]blood of *My* covenant with you,
I have set your [b]prisoners free from the [1]waterless pit.
12 Return to the [1][a]stronghold, O prisoners [2]who have the [b]hope;
This very day I am declaring that I will restore [c]double to you.
13 For I will [a]bend Judah [1]as My bow,
I will fill the bow with Ephraim.
And I will stir up your sons, O Zion, against your sons, O [b]Greece;
And I will make you like a [c]warrior's sword.

13 [a]Jer. 29:18; Dan. 9:11 [b]Ps. 72:17; Is. 19:24, 25; Ezek. 34:26; Zech. 14:11 [c]Zech. 8:9
14 [a]Jer. 31:28 [b]Jer. 4:28; Ezek. 24:14
15 [a]Jer. 29:11; Mic. 7:18-20 [b]Zech. 8:13
16 [1]I.e., the place where court was held
[a]Ps. 15:2; Prov. 12:17-19; Zech. 8:3; Eph. 4:25 [b]Is. 9:7; 11:4, 5; Zech. 7:9
17 [1]Lit., *false oath*
[a]Prov. 3:29; Jer. 4:14; Zech. 7:10 [b]Zech. 5:4; Mal. 3:5 [c]Prov. 6:16-19; Hab. 1:13
19 [1]Or, *goodly*
[a]2 Kin. 25:3, 4; Jer. 39:2 [b]Zech. 7:3, 5 [c]2 Kin. 25:25; Zech. 7:5 [d]Jer. 52:4 [e]Ps. 30:11; Is. 12:1 [f]Zech. 8:16; Luke 1:74, 75
20 [a]Ps. 117:1; Jer. 16:19; Mic. 4:2, 3; Zech. 2:11; 14:16
21 [1]Or, *let me go too*
[a]Zech. 7:2
22 [a]Is. 2:2, 3; 25:7; 49:6, 22, 23; 60:3-12 [b]Zech. 8:21
23 [1]Lit., *languages of the nations* [2]Lit., *grasp, and they will grasp* [3]Or, *corner of the garment*
[a]Is. 45:14, 24; 60:14

1 [1]Or, *oracle*
[a]Is. 17:1; Jer. 49:23-27; Amos 1:3-5
2 [1]Or, *because* [2]I.e., they think they are
[a]Jer. 49:23 [b]Ezek. 28:2-5, 12 [c]Ezek. 28:21
3 [a]Josh. 19:29; 2 Sam. 24:7 [b]Job 27:16; Ezek. 27:33; 28:4, 5 [c]1 Kin. 10:21, 27
4 [a]Ezek. 26:3-5 [b]Ezek. 28:18
6 [1]Lit., *bastard will*
[a]Amos 1:8; Zeph. 2:4
7 [1]Or, *chief*
8 [1]Or, *as a guard, so that none will go back and forth*
[a]Is. 52:1 [b]Is. 54:14; 60:18
9 [1]Or, *vindicated and victorious* [2]Lit., *son of a female donkey*
[a]Zeph. 3:14, 15; Zech. 2:10 [b]Ps. 110:1; Is. 9:6, 7; Jer. 23:5, 6; Matt. 21:5; John 12:15 [c]Zeph. 3:5 [d]Is. 43:3, 11 [e]Is. 57:15 [f]Judg. 10:4; Is. 30:6
10 [1]I.e., Euphrates
[a]Hos. 1:7 [b]Mic. 5:10 [c]Hos. 2:18 [d]Is. 57:19; Mic. 4:2-4 [e]Ps. 72:8; Is. 60:12
11 [1]Lit., *cistern in which there is no water*
[a]Ex. 24:8; Heb. 10:2 [b]Is. 24:22; 51:14

12 [1]Or, *Stronghold* [2]Lit., *of the hope* [a]Jer. 16:19; Joel 3:16 [b]Jer. 14:8; 17:13; Heb. 6:18, 19 [c]Is. 61:7
13 [1]Lit., *for Me* [a]Jer. 51:20 [b]Joel 3:6 [c]Ps. 45:3

14 Then the LORD will appear [a]over them,
And His [b]arrow will go forth like lightning;
And the Lord [1]GOD will blow the [c]trumpet,
And will march in the [d]storm winds of the south.
15 [a]The LORD of hosts will defend them.
And they will [b]devour, and trample on the [c]sling stones;
And they will drink, *and* be [d]boisterous as with wine;
And they will be filled like a *sacrificial* basin,
Drenched like the [e]corners of the altar.
16 And the LORD their God will [a]save them in that day
As the flock of His people;
For *they are as* the stones of a [b]crown,
[1]Sparkling in His land.
17 For what [1a]comeliness and [b]beauty *will be* [2]theirs!
Grain will make the young men flourish, and new wine the virgins.

God Will Bless Judah and Ephraim

10 ASK [a]rain from the LORD at the time of the spring rain—
The LORD who [b]makes the [1]storm clouds;
And He will give them [c]showers of rain, vegetation in the field to *each* man.
2 For the [a]teraphim speak [1]iniquity,
And the [b]diviners see [2]lying visions,
And tell [c]false dreams;
They comfort in vain.
Therefore *the people* [3]wander like [d]sheep,
They are afflicted, because there is no shepherd.
3 "My [a]anger is kindled against the shepherds,
And I will punish the [1]male goats;
For the LORD of hosts has [b]visited His flock, the house of Judah,
And will make them like His majestic horse in battle.
4 "From [1]them will come the [a]cornerstone,
From [1]them the tent peg,
From [1]them the bow of [b]battle,
From [1]them every [2]ruler, *all* of them together.
5 "And they will be as mighty men,
[a]Treading down *the enemy* in the mire of the streets in battle;
And they will fight, for the LORD *will be* with them;
And the [b]riders on horses will be put to shame.
6 "And I shall [a]strengthen the house of Judah,
And I shall [b]save the house of Joseph,
And I shall [1c]bring them back,
Because I have had [d]compassion on them;
And they will be as though I had [e]not rejected them,
For I am the LORD their God, and I will [f]answer them.
7 "And Ephraim will be like a mighty man,
And their heart will be glad as if *from* wine;
Indeed, their [a]children will see *it* and be glad,
[1]Their heart will rejoice in the LORD.
8 "I will [a]whistle for them to gather them together,
For I have redeemed them;
And they will be as [b]numerous as they [1c]were before.
9 "When I [1]scatter them among the peoples,
They will [a]remember Me in far countries,
And they with their children will live and come back.
10 "I will [a]bring them back from the land of Egypt,
And gather them from Assyria;
And I will bring them into the land of [b]Gilead and Lebanon,
[1]Until [c]no *room* can be found for them.
11 "And He will pass through the [a]sea *of* distress,
And strike the waves in the sea,
So that all the depths of the [b]Nile will dry up;
And the pride of [c]Assyria will be brought down,
And the scepter of [d]Egypt will depart.
12 "And I shall [a]strengthen them in the LORD,
And in His name [b]they will walk,"
declares the LORD.

The Doomed Flock

11 OPEN your doors, O Lebanon,
That a [a]fire may feed on your [b]cedars.
2 Wail, O [1]cypress, for the cedar has fallen,
Because the glorious *trees* have been destroyed;
Wail, O oaks of Bashan,
For the [2]impenetrable forest has come down.
3 There is a sound of the shepherds' [a]wail,
For their glory is ruined;
There is a [b]sound of the young lions' roar,
For the [1]pride of the Jordan is ruined.
4 Thus says the LORD my God, "Pasture the flock *doomed* to [a]slaughter.
5 "Those who buy them slay them and [1]go [a]unpunished, and *each of* those who sell them says, 'Blessed be the LORD, for [b]I have become rich!' And their [c]own shepherds have no pity on them.

14 [1]Heb., *YHWH,* usually rendered *LORD* [a]Is. 31:5; Zech. 2:5 [b]Ps. 18:14; Hab. 3:11 [c]Is. 27:13 [d]Is. 21:1; 66:15
15 [a]Is. 37:35; Zech. 12:8 [b]Zech. 12:6 [c]Job 41:28 [d]Ps. 78:65 [e]Ex. 27:2
16 [1]Or, *Displayed over* [a]Jer. 31:10, 11 [b]Is. 62:3
17 [1]Lit., *goodness* [2]Lit., *his* [a]Jer. 31:12, 14 [b]Ps. 27:4; Is. 33:17

1 [1]Or, *thunderbolts* [a]Joel 2:23 [b]Jer. 10:13 [c]Is. 30:23
2 [1]Or, *futility* [2]Lit., *a lie* [3]Lit., *journey* [a]Ezek. 21:21; Hos. 3:4 [b]Jer. 27:9 [c]Jer. 23:32 [d]Ezek. 34:5, 8; Matt. 9:36; Mark 6:34
3 [1]I.e., leaders [a]Jer. 25:34-36 [b]Ezek. 34:12
4 [1]Lit., *him* [2]Or, *oppressor* [a]Luke 20:17; Eph. 2:20; 1 Pet. 2:6 [b]Jer. 51:20; Zech. 9:10
5 [a]2 Sam. 22:43 [b]Amos 2:15; Hag. 2:22
6 [1]Or, *make them dwell* [a]Zech. 10:12 [b]Zech. 8:7; 9:16 [c]Zech. 8:8 [d]Is. 54:8; Zech. 1:16 [e]Is. 54:4 [f]Zech. 13:9
7 [1]Or, *Let their heart rejoice* [a]Is. 54:13; Ezek. 37:25
8 [1]Lit., *were numerous* [a]Is. 5:26; 7:18, 19 [b]Jer. 33:22; Rev. 7:9 [c]Jer. 30:20; Ezek. 36:11
9 [1]Lit., *sow* [a]1 Kin. 8:47, 48; Ezek. 6:9
10 [1]Lit., *And* [a]Is. 11:11 [b]Jer. 50:19 [c]Is. 49:19, 20
11 [a]Is. 51:9, 10 [b]Is. 19:5-7 [c]Zeph. 2:13 [d]Ezek. 30:13
12 [a]Zech. 10:6 [b]Mic. 4:5

1 [a]Jer. 22:6, 7 [b]Ezek. 31:3
2 [1]Or, *juniper* [2]Another reading is *forest of the vintage*
3 [1]Or, *jungle* [a]Jer. 25:34-36 [b]Jer. 2:15; 50:44
4 [a]Ps. 44:22; Zech. 11:7
5 [1]Lit., *are not held guilty* [a]Jer. 50:7 [b]Hos. 12:8; 1 Tim. 6:9 [c]Ezek. 34:2, 3

6"For I shall [a]no longer have pity on
the inhabitants of the land," declares the
LORD; "but behold, I shall [b]cause the
men to [1]fall, each into another's [2]power
and into the [2]power of his king; and they
will strike the land, and I shall [c]not
deliver *them* from their [2]power."
7 So I [a]pastured the flock *doomed* to
slaughter, [1]hence the [b]afflicted of the
flock. And I took for myself two [c]staffs:
the one I called [2d]Favor, and the other I
called [3e]Union; so I pastured the flock.
8 Then I annihilated the three shepherds in [a]one month, for my soul was
impatient with them, and their soul also
[1]was weary of me.
9 Then I said, "I will not pasture
you. What is to [a]die, [1]let it die, and what
is to be annihilated, [2]let it be annihilated; and [3]let those who are left eat one
another's flesh."
10 And I took my staff, [1a]Favor, and
cut it in pieces, to [2b]break my covenant
which I had made with all the peoples.
11 So it was [1]broken on that day, and
[2]thus the [a]afflicted of the flock who were
watching me realized that it was the
word of the LORD.
12 And I said to them, "If it is good in
your sight, give *me* my [a]wages; but if
not, [1]never mind!" So they weighed out
[b]thirty *shekels* of silver as my wages.
13 Then the LORD said to me, "Throw
it to the [a]potter, *that* magnificent price at
which I was valued by them." So I took
the thirty *shekels* of silver and threw
them to the potter in the house of the
LORD.
14 Then I cut my second staff,
[1a]Union, in pieces, to [b]break the brotherhood between Judah and Israel.
15 And the LORD said to me, "Take
again for yourself the equipment of a
[1a]foolish shepherd.
16"For behold, I am going to raise up
a shepherd in the land who will [a]not care
for the perishing, seek the scattered, heal
the broken, or sustain the one standing,
but will [b]devour the flesh of the fat *sheep*
and tear off their hoofs.
17 "[a]Woe to the worthless shepherd
Who leaves the flock!
A [b]sword will be on his arm
And on his right eye!
His [c]arm will be totally withered,
And his right eye will be [1]blind."

Jerusalem to Be Attacked

12 THE [1]burden of the word of the
LORD concerning Israel.
Thus declares the LORD who
[a]stretches out the heavens, [b]lays the
foundation of the earth, and [c]forms the
spirit of man within him,
2"Behold, I am going to make Jerusalem a [a]cup [1]that causes reeling to all the
peoples around; and when the siege is
against Jerusalem, it will also be against
[b]Judah.
3"And it will come about in that day
that I will make Jerusalem a heavy
[a]stone for all the peoples; all who lift it
will be [b]severely [1]injured. And all the
[c]nations of the earth will be gathered
against it.
4"In that day," declares the LORD, "I
will strike every horse with bewilderment, and his rider with madness. But I
will [1]watch over the house of Judah,
while I strike every horse of the peoples
with blindness.
5"Then the clans of Judah will say in
their hearts, '[1]A strong support for us
are the inhabitants of Jerusalem through
the LORD of hosts, their God.'
6"In that day I will make the clans of
Judah like a [a]firepot among pieces of
wood and a flaming torch among
sheaves, so they will consume on the
right hand and on the left all the surrounding peoples, while the [b]inhabitants
of Jerusalem again dwell on their own
sites in Jerusalem.
7"The LORD also will [a]save the tents
of Judah first in order that the glory of
the house of [b]David and the glory of the
inhabitants of Jerusalem may not be
magnified above Judah.
8"In that day the LORD will [a]defend
the inhabitants of Jerusalem, and the
one who [1b]is feeble among them in that
day will be like David, and the house of
David *will be* like [c]God, like the [d]angel
of the LORD before them.
9"And it will come about in that day
that I will [1a]set about to destroy all the
nations that come against Jerusalem.
10"And I will [a]pour out on the house
of David and on the inhabitants of
Jerusalem, [1]the Spirit of grace and of
supplication, so that they will look on
Me whom they have [b]pierced; and they
will mourn for Him, as one [c]mourns for
an only son, and they will weep bitterly
over Him, like the bitter weeping over a
first-born.
11"In that day there will be great
[a]mourning in Jerusalem, like the mourning of Hadadrimmon in the [1]plain of
[2]Megiddo.
12"And the land will mourn, every
family by itself; the family of the house
of David by itself, and their wives by
themselves; the family of the house of
Nathan by itself, and their wives by
themselves;
13 the family of the house of Levi by
itself, and their wives by themselves; the
family of the Shimeites by itself, and
their wives by themselves;
14 all the families that remain, every
family by itself, and their wives by
themselves.

False Prophets Ashamed

13 "IN that day a [a]fountain will be
opened for the house of David
and for the inhabitants of Jerusalem, for
[b]sin and for [c]impurity.

6 [1]Lit., *find* [2]Lit., *hand*
[a]Jer. 13:14 [b]Is. 9:19-21; Mic. 7:2-6; Zech. 14:13 [c]Ps. 50:22; Mic. 5:8
7 [1]Another reading is *for the sheep dealers* [2]Or, *Pleasantness* [3]Or, *Cords*
[a]Zech. 11:4 [b]Jer. 39:10; Zeph. 3:12 [c]Ezek. 37:16 [d]Ps. 27:4; 90:17; Zech. 11:10 [e]Ps. 133:1; Ezek. 37:16-23; Zech. 11:14
8 [1]Or, *detested*
[a]Hos. 5:7
9 [1]Or, *will die* [2]Or, *will be annihilated* [3]Or, *those . . . will eat*
[a]Jer. 15:2
10 [1]Or, *Pleasantness* [2]Or, *annul*
[a]Zech. 11:7 [b]Ps. 89:39; Jer. 14:21
11 [1]Or, *annulled* [2]Another reading is *the sheep dealers who*
[a]Zeph. 3:12
12 [1]Lit., *cease*
[a]1 Kin. 5:6; Mal. 3:5 [b]Gen. 37:28; Ex. 21:32; Matt. 26:15; 27:9, 10
13 [a]Matt. 27:3-10; Acts 1:18, 19
14 [1]Or, *Cords*
[a]Zech. 11:7 [b]Is. 9:21; Zech. 11:6
15 [1]Or, *useless*
[a]Is. 6:10-12; Zech. 11:17
16 [a]Jer. 23:2 [b]Ezek. 34:2-6
17 [1]Lit., *completely dimmed*
[a]Jer. 23:1; Zech. 10:2; 11:15 [b]Jer. 50:35-37 [c]Ezek. 30:21, 22

1 [1]Or, *oracle*
[a]Is. 42:5; 44:24; Jer. 51:15 [b]Job 26:7; Ps. 102:25, 26; Heb. 1:10-12 [c]Is. 57:16; Heb. 12:9
2 [1]Lit., *of reeling*
[a]Ps. 75:8; Is. 51:22, 23 [b]Zech. 14:14
3 [1]Lit., *scratched*
[a]Dan. 2:34, 35, 44, 45 [b]Matt. 21:44 [c]Zech. 14:2
4 [1]Lit., *open My eyes*
5 [1]Lit., *My strength is*
6 [a]Is. 10:17, 18; Obad. 18; Zech. 11:1 [b]Zech. 2:4; 8:3-5
7 [a]Jer. 30:18 [b]Amos 9:11
8 [1]Or, *stumbles*
[a]Joel 3:16; Zech. 9:14, 15 [b]Lev. 26:8; Josh. 23:10; Mic. 7:8 [c]Ps. 8:5; 82:6 [d]Ex. 14:19; 33:2
9 [1]Lit., *seek to*
[a]Zech. 14:2, 3
10 [1]Or, *a spirit*
[a]Is. 44:3; Ezek. 39:29; Joel 2:28, 29 [b]John 19:37; Rev. 1:7 [c]Jer. 6:26; Amos 8:10
11 [1]I.e., broad valley [2]Heb., *Megiddon*
[a]Matt. 24:30; Rev. 1:7

1 [a]Jer. 2:13; 17:13 [b]Ps. 51:2, 7; Is. 1:16-18; John 1:29 [c]Num. 19:17; Is. 4:4; Ezek. 36:25

2“And it will come about in that
day,” declares the LORD of hosts, “that I
will [a]cut off the names of the idols from
the land, and they will no longer be
remembered; and I will also remove the
[b]prophets and the [c]unclean spirit from
the land.
3“And it will come about that if
anyone still [a]prophesies, then his father
and mother who gave birth to him will
say to him, ‘You shall [b]not live, for you
have spoken [c]falsely in the name of the
LORD’; and his [d]father and mother who
gave birth to him will pierce him through
when he prophesies.
4“Also it will come about in that day
that the prophets will each be [a]ashamed
of his vision when he prophesies, and
they will not put on a [b]hairy robe in
order to deceive;
5 but he will say, ‘I am [a]not a
prophet; I am a tiller of the ground, for a
man [1]sold me as a slave in my youth.’
6“And one will say to him, ‘What are
these wounds [a]between your [1]arms?’
Then he will say, ‘*Those* with which I
was wounded in the house of [2]my
friends.’

7 “Awake, O [a]sword, against My [b]Shepherd,
And against the man, My [c]Associate,”
Declares the LORD of hosts.
“[d]Strike the Shepherd that the sheep may be scattered;
And I will [e]turn My hand [1]against the little ones.
8 “And it will come about in all the land,”
Declares the LORD,
“That [a]two parts in it will be cut off *and* perish;
But the third will be left in it.
9 “And I will bring the third part through the [a]fire,
Refine them as silver is refined,
And test them as gold is tested.
They will [b]call on My name,
And I will [c]answer them;
I will say, ‘They are [d]My people,’
And they will say, ‘The LORD is my God.’ ”

God Will Battle Jerusalem’s Foes

14 BEHOLD, a [a]day is coming for
the LORD when [b]the spoil taken
from you will be divided among you.
2 For I will [a]gather all the nations
against Jerusalem to battle, and the city
will be captured, the [b]houses plundered,
the women ravished, and half of the city
exiled, but the rest of the people will not
be cut off from the city.
3 Then the LORD will go forth and
[a]fight against those nations, as [1]when He
fights on a day of battle.
4 And in that day His feet will [a]stand
on the Mount of Olives, which is in front
of Jerusalem on the east; and the Mount
of Olives will be [b]split in its middle from
east to west by a very large valley, so
that half of the mountain will move
toward the north and the other half
toward the south.
5 And you will flee by the valley of
My mountains, for the valley of the
mountains will reach to Azel; yes, you
will flee just as you fled before the
[a]earthquake in the days of Uzziah king
of Judah. [b]Then the LORD, my God, will
come, *and* all the holy ones with [1]Him!
6 And it will come about in that day
that there will be [a]no light; the [1]luminar-
ies will dwindle.
7 For it will be [a]a unique day which
is [b]known to the LORD, neither day nor
night, but it will come about that at
[c]evening time there will be light.
8 And it will come about in that day
that [a]living waters will flow out of Jerusalem, half of them toward the eastern
sea and the other half toward the western sea; it will be in summer as well as in
winter.

God Will Be King over All

9 And the LORD will be [a]king over all
the earth; in that day the LORD will be
the only [b]one, and His name *the only* one.
10 All the land will be changed into a
plain from [a]Geba to [b]Rimmon south of
Jerusalem; but [1]Jerusalem will [c]rise and
[d]remain on its site from [e]Benjamin’s
Gate as far as the place of the First Gate
to the [f]Corner Gate, and from the
[g]Tower of Hananel to the king’s wine
presses.
11 And [1]people will live in it, and
there will be [a]no more curse, for Jerusalem will [b]dwell in security.
12 Now this will be the plague with
which the LORD will strike all the peoples who have gone to war against Jerusalem; their flesh will [a]rot while they
stand on their feet, and their eyes will rot
in their sockets, and their tongue will rot
in their mouth.
13 And it will come about in that day
that a great panic from the LORD will
[1]fall on them; and they will [a]seize one
another’s hand, and the hand of one will
[2]be lifted against the hand of another.
14 And [a]Judah also will fight at Jerusalem; and the [b]wealth of all the surrounding nations will be gathered, gold
and silver and garments in great abundance.
15 So also like this [a]plague, will be the
plague on the horse, the mule, the camel,
the donkey, and all the cattle that will be
in those camps.
16 Then it will come about that any
who are left of all the nations that went
against Jerusalem will [a]go up from year
to year to worship the King, the LORD of
hosts, and to celebrate the [b]Feast of
Booths.
17 And it will be that whichever of the
families of the earth does not go up to
Jerusalem to worship the [a]King, the
LORD of hosts, there will be [b]no rain on
them.

2 [a]Ex. 23:13; Hos. 2:17 [b]Jer. 23:14, 15 [c]1 Kin. 22:22; Ezek. 36:25, 29
3 [a]Jer. 23:34 [b]Deut. 18:20; Ezek. 14:9 [c]Jer. 23:25 [d]Deut. 13:6-11; Matt. 10:37
4 [a]Jer. 6:15; 8:9; Mic. 3:7 [b]2 Kin. 1:8; Is. 20:2; Matt. 3:4
5 [1]Lit., *caused another to buy me* [a]Amos 7:14
6 [1]Lit., *hands* [2]Lit., *those who love me* [a]2 Kin. 9:24
7 [1]Or, *upon* [a]Jer. 47:6; Ezek. 21:3-5 [b]Is. 40:11; Ezek. 34:23, 24; 37:24; Mic. 5:2, 4 [c]Ps. 2:2; Jer. 23:5, 6 [d]Is. 53:4, 5, 10; Matt. 26:31; Mark 14:27 [e]Is. 1:25
8 [a]Is. 6:13; Ezek. 5:2-4, 12
9 [a]Is. 48:10; Mal. 3:3 [b]Ps. 34:15-17; 50:15; Zech. 12:10 [c]Is. 58:9; 65:24; Jer. 29:11-13; Zech. 10:6 [d]Hos. 2:23

1 [a]Is. 13:6, 9; Joel 2:1; Mal. 4:1 [b]Zech. 14:14
2 [a]Zech. 12:2, 3 [b]Is. 13:16
3 [1]Lit., *His day of fighting* [a]Zech. 9:14, 15
4 [a]Ezek. 11:23 [b]Is. 64:1, 2; Ezek. 47:1-10; Mic. 1:3, 4; Hab. 3:6; Zech. 4:7; 14:8
5 [1]So the versions; Heb., *Thee* [a]Is. 29:6; Amos 1:1 [b]Ps. 96:13; Is. 66:15, 16; Matt. 16:27; 25:31
6 [1]Lit., *glorious ones will congeal* [a]Is. 13:10; Jer. 4:23; Ezek. 32:7, 8; Joel 2:30, 31; Acts 2:16, 19
7 [a]Jer. 30:7; Amos 8:9 [b]Is. 45:21; Acts 15:18 [c]Is. 58:10; Rev. 22:5
8 [a]Ezek. 47:1-12; Joel 3:18; John 7:38; Rev. 22:1, 2
9 [a]Is. 2:2-4; 45:23; Zech. 9:9; 14:16, 17 [b]Deut. 6:4; Is. 45:21-24
10 [1]Lit., *it* [a]1 Kin. 15:22 [b]Josh. 15:32; Judg. 20:45, 47 [c]Is. 2:2; Amos 9:11 [d]Jer. 30:18; Zech. 12:6 [e]Jer. 37:13; 38:7 [f]2 Kin. 14:13 [g]Jer. 31:38
11 [1]Lit., *they* [a]Zech. 8:13; Rev. 22:3 [b]Jer. 23:5, 6; Ezek. 34:25-28
12 [a]Lev. 26:16; Deut. 28:21, 22
13 [1]Lit., *be among* [2]Lit., *rise up against* [a]Zech. 11:6
14 [a]Zech. 12:2, 5 [b]Is. 23:18; Zech. 14:1
15 [a]Zech. 14:12
16 [a]Is. 60:6-9; 66:18-21, 23 [b]Lev. 23:34-44
17 [a]Zech. 14:9, 16 [b]Jer. 14:3-6; Amos 4:7

18 And if the family of Egypt does not
go up or enter, then no *rain will fall* on
them; it will be the [a]plague with which
the LORD smites the nations who do not
go up to celebrate the Feast of Booths.
19 This will be the [1]punishment of
Egypt, and the [1]punishment of all the
nations who do not go up to celebrate
the Feast of Booths.
20 In that day there will *be inscribed*
on the bells of the horses, "[a]HOLY TO
THE LORD." And the [b]cooking pots in
the LORD's house will be like the bowls
before the altar.
21 And every cooking pot in Jerusalem and in Judah will be [a]holy to the
LORD of hosts; and all who sacrifice will
come and take of them and boil in them.
And there will no longer be a [1b]Canaan-
ite in the house of the LORD of hosts in
that day.

18 aZech. 14:12, 15
19 1Lit., *sin*
20 aEx. 28:36-38 bEzek. 46:20
21 1Or, *merchant* aNeh. 8:10; Rom. 14:6, 7; 1 Cor. 10:31 bZeph. 1:11

THE BOOK OF MALACHI

God's Love for Jacob

1 THE [1a]oracle of the word of the
LORD to [b]Israel through [2]Malachi.
2"I have [a]loved you," says the LORD.
But you say, "How hast Thou loved us?"
"*Was* not Esau Jacob's brother?" declares the LORD. "Yet I [b]have loved
Jacob;
3 but I have hated Esau, and I have
[a]made his mountains a desolation, and
appointed his inheritance for the jackals
of the wilderness."
4 Though Edom says, "We have been
[a]beaten down, but we will [1b]return and
build up the ruins"; thus says the LORD
of hosts, "They may [c]build, but I will
tear down; and *men* will call them the
[2]wicked territory, and the people
[3]toward whom the LORD is indignant
[d]forever."
5 And your eyes will see this and you
will say, "[a]The LORD [1]be magnified
beyond the [2]border of Israel!"

Sin of the Priests

6"'A son [a]honors *his* father, and a
servant his master. Then if I am a
[b]father, where is My honor? And if I am
a master, where is My [1]respect?' says the
LORD of hosts to you, O [c]priests who
despise My name. But you say, 'How
have we despised Thy name?'
7"*You* are presenting [a]defiled [1b]food
upon My altar. But you say, 'How have
we defiled Thee?' In that you say, 'The
[c]table of the LORD is to be despised.'
8"But when you present the [a]blind
for sacrifice, is it not evil? And when you
present the lame and sick, is it not evil?
[1]Why not offer it to your [b]governor?
Would he be pleased with you? Or
would he receive you kindly?" says the
LORD of hosts.
9"But now [1]will you not [a]entreat
God's favor, that He may be gracious to
us? [2]With such an offering on your part,
will He [b]receive any of you kindly?" says
the LORD of hosts.
10"Oh that there were one among you
who would [a]shut the [1]gates, that you
might not uselessly kindle *fire on* My
altar! I am not pleased with you," says
the LORD of hosts, "[b]nor will I accept an
offering from [2]you.
11"For from the [a]rising of the sun,
even to its setting, [b]My name *will be*
[c]great among the nations, and in every
place [d]incense is going to be offered to
My name, and a grain offering *that is*
pure; for My name *will be* [e]great among
the nations," says the LORD of hosts.
12"But you are [a]profaning it, in that
you say, 'The table of the Lord is defiled,
and as for its fruit, its food is to be
despised.'
13"You also say, '[1]My, how [a]tiresome
it is!' And you disdainfully sniff at it,"
says the LORD of hosts, "and you bring
what was taken by [b]robbery, and *what is*
[c]lame or sick; so you bring the offering!
Should I [d]receive that from your hand?"
says the LORD.
14"But cursed be the [a]swindler who
has a male in his flock, and vows it, but
sacrifices a [b]blemished animal to the
Lord, for I am a great [c]King," says the
LORD of hosts, "and My name is
[1d]feared among the [2]nations."

Priests to Be Disciplined

2 "AND now, this commandment is
for you, O priests.
2"If you do [a]not listen, and if you do
not take it to heart to give honor to My
name," says the LORD of hosts, "then I
will send the [b]curse upon you, and I will
curse your blessings; and indeed, I have
[c]cursed them *already*, because you are
not taking *it* to heart.
3"Behold, I am going to [a]rebuke your
[1]offspring, and I will [b]spread [2]refuse on
your faces, the [2]refuse of your [c]feasts;
and you will be taken away [3]with it.
4"Then you will know that I have
sent this commandment to you, [1]that
My [a]covenant may [2]continue with Levi,"
says the LORD of hosts.
5"My covenant with him was *one of*
life and [a]peace, and I gave them to him
as an object of [1]reverence; so he [2b]re-
vered Me, and stood in awe of My name.

1 1Lit., *burden* 2Or, *My messenger* aIs. 13:1; Nah. 1:1; Hab. 1:1; Zech. 9:1 bMal. 2:11
2 aDeut. 4:37; 7:8; 23:5; Is. 41:8, 9; Jer. 31:3; John 15:12 bRom. 9:13
3 aJer. 49:10, 16-18; Ezek. 35:3, 4, 7, 8, 15
4 1Or, *rebuild the ruins* 2Lit., *border of wickedness* 3Or, *whom the LORD has cursed* aJer. 5:17 bIs. 9:9, 10 cAmos 3:15; 5:11; 6:11 dEzek. 35:9; Obad. 10
5 1Or, *will be great* 2Or, *territory* aPs. 35:27; Mic. 5:4
6 1Lit., *fear* aEx. 20:12; Prov. 30:11, 17 bDeut. 1:31; Is. 1:2; Jer. 3:4; Mal. 2:10 cZeph. 3:4; Mal. 2:1-9
7 1Lit., *bread* aMal. 1:8, 13 bLev. 3:11; 21:6, 8 cMal. 1:12
8 1Lit., *Offer it, please* aLev. 22:22; Deut. 15:21 bHag. 1:1
9 1Lit., *entreat, please* 2Lit., *This has been from your hand* aJer. 27:18; Joel 2:12-14 bAmos 5:22
10 1Or, *doors* 2Lit., *your hand* aIs. 1:13 bJer. 14:10, 12; Hos. 5:6
11 aIs. 45:6 bPs. 111:9 cIs. 66:18, 19 dIs. 60:6 eIs. 12:4, 5; 54:5; Jer. 10:6, 7
12 aMal. 1:7
13 1Lit., *Behold it is weariness* aIs. 43:22 bLev. 6:4; Is. 61:8 cMal. 1:8 dMal. 1:10
14 1Or, *revered* 2Or, *Gentiles* aActs 5:1-4 bLev. 22:18-20 cZech. 14:9 dZeph. 2:11

2 aLev. 26:14, 15; Deut. 28:15 bDeut. 28:16-20 cMal. 3:9
3 1Lit., *seed* 2Or, *vomit* 3Lit., *to* aLev. 26:16; Deut. 28:38 bNah. 3:6 cEx. 29:14
4 1Or, *to be My covenant with* 2Lit., *be* aNum. 3:11-13, 45; 18:21; Neh. 13:29; Mal. 3:1
5 1Or, *fear* 2Or, *feared* aNum. 25:12 bNum. 25:7, 8, 13

6"[1a]True instruction was in his mouth, and unrighteousness was not found on his lips; he walked [b]with Me in peace and uprightness, and he [c]turned many back from iniquity.

7"For the lips of a priest should preserve [a]knowledge, and [1]men should [b]seek [2]instruction from his mouth; for he is the [c]messenger of the LORD of hosts.

8"But as for you, you have turned aside from the way; you have caused many to [a]stumble [1]by the instruction; you have [2b]corrupted the covenant of Levi," says the LORD of hosts.

9"So [a]I also have made you despised and [b]abased [1]before all the people, just as you are not keeping My ways, but are showing [c]partiality in the [2]instruction.

Sin in the Family

10"Do we not all have [a]one father? [b]Has not one God created us? Why do we deal [c]treacherously each against his brother so as to profane the [d]covenant of our fathers?

11"Judah has dealt [a]treacherously, and an abomination has been committed in Israel and in Jerusalem; for Judah has [b]profaned the sanctuary of the LORD [1]which He loves, and has married the daughter of a foreign god.

12"*As* for the man who does this, may the [a]LORD cut off from the tents of Jacob *everyone* who awakes and answers, or who [b]presents [1]an offering to the LORD of hosts.

13"And this is [1]another thing you do: you cover the altar of the LORD with tears, with weeping and with groaning, because He [a]no longer regards the [2]offering or accepts *it with* favor from your hand.

14"Yet you say, 'For what reason?' Because the LORD has been a witness between you and the [a]wife of your youth, against whom you have dealt [b]treacherously, though she is your companion and your wife by covenant.

15"[1]But not one has [a]done *so* who has a remnant of the Spirit. And [2]what did *that* one *do* while he was seeking a [b]godly [3]offspring? Take heed then, to your spirit, and let no one deal [c]treacherously against the wife of your youth.

16"For [1]I hate [2a]divorce," says the LORD, the God of Israel, "and [3]him who covers his garment with [4b]wrong," says the LORD of hosts. "So take heed to your spirit, that you do not deal treacherously."

17 You have [a]wearied the LORD with your words. Yet you say, "How have we wearied *Him*?" In that you say, "[b]Everyone who does evil is good in the sight of the LORD, and He [c]delights in them," or, "[d]Where is the God of [e]justice?"

The Purifier

3 "[a]BEHOLD, I am going to send [b]My [1]messenger, and he will [2c]clear the way before Me. And the Lord, whom you seek, will suddenly come to His temple; [3]and the [1d]messenger of the covenant, in whom you delight, behold, He is coming," says the LORD of hosts.

2"But who can [a]endure the day of His coming? And who can stand when He appears? For He is like a [b]refiner's fire and like [1]fullers' soap.

3"And He will sit as a smelter and purifier of silver, and He will [a]purify the sons of Levi and refine them like gold and silver, so that they may [b]present to the LORD [1]offerings in righteousness.

4"Then the [1]offering of Judah and Jerusalem will be [a]pleasing to the LORD, as in the [b]days of old and as in former years.

5"Then I will draw near to you for judgment; and I will be a swift witness against the [a]sorcerers and against the [b]adulterers and against those who [c]swear falsely, and against those who oppress the [d]wage earner in his wages, the [e]widow and the [1]orphan, and those who turn aside the [2f]alien, and do not [3]fear Me," says the LORD of hosts.

6"For [1]I, the LORD, [a]do not change; therefore you, O sons of Jacob, [2]are not consumed.

7"From the [a]days of your fathers you have turned aside from My statutes, and have not kept *them*. [b]Return to Me, and I will return to you," says the LORD of hosts. "But you say, 'How shall we return?'

You Have Robbed God

8"Will a man [1]rob God? Yet you are robbing Me! But you say, 'How have we robbed Thee?' In [a]tithes and [2]offerings.

9"You are [a]cursed with a curse, for you are [1]robbing Me, the whole nation *of you*!

10"[a]Bring the whole tithe into the storehouse, so that there may be [1]food in My house, and test Me now in this," says the LORD of hosts, "if I will not [b]open for you the windows of heaven, and [c]pour out for you a blessing until [2d]it overflows.

11"Then I will rebuke the [a]devourer for you, so that it may not [1]destroy the fruits of the ground; nor will your vine in the field cast *its grapes*," says the LORD of hosts.

12"And [a]all the nations will call you blessed, for you shall be a [b]delightful land," says the LORD of hosts.

13"Your words have been [1]arrogant against Me," says the LORD. "Yet you say, 'What have we spoken against Thee?'

14"You have said, 'It is [a]vain to serve God; and what [b]profit is it that we have

6 [1]Or, *Law of truth* [a]Ps. 119:142, 151, 160 [b]Deut. 33:8, 9; Ps. 37:37 [c]Jer. 23:22
7 [1]Lit., *they* [2]Or, *law* [a]Lev. 10:11; Neh. 8:7 [b]Num. 27:21; Deut. 17:8-11; Jer. 18:18; Ezek. 7:26 [c]Hag. 1:13
8 [1]Or, *in the law* [2]Or, *violated* [a]Jer. 18:15 [b]Num. 25:12, 13; Neh. 13:29; Ezek. 44:10
9 [1]Lit., *to* [2]Or, *law* [a]Nah. 3:6 [b]Ezek. 7:26 [c]Deut. 1:17; Mic. 3:11
10 [a]Is. 63:16; 64:8; Jer. 31:9; 1 Cor. 8:6; Eph. 4:6 [b]Acts 17:24f. [c]Jer. 9:4, 5 [d]Ex. 19:4-6; 24:3, 7, 8
11 [1]Or, *in that he has loved and married* [a]Jer. 3:7-9 [b]Ezra 9:1, 2
12 [1]Or, *a grain offering* [a]Ezek. 24:21; Hos. 9:12 [b]Mal. 1:10, 13
13 [1]Lit., *second* [2]Or, *grain offering* [a]Jer. 11:14; 14:12
14 [a]Is. 54:6 [b]Jer. 9:2; Mal. 3:5
15 [1]Or, *Did He not make one, although He had the remnant* [2]Or, *why one? He sought a godly offspring* [3]Lit., *seed* [a]Gen. 2:24; Matt. 19:4, 5 [b]Ruth 4:12; 1 Sam. 2:20 [c]Ex. 20:14; Lev. 20:10
16 [1]Lit., *He hates* [2]Lit., *sending away* [3]Lit., *he covers* [4]Or, *violence* [a]Deut. 24:1; Matt. 5:31; 19:6-8 [b]Ps. 73:6; Is. 59:6
17 [a]Is. 43:22, 24 [b]Is. 5:20; Zeph. 1:12 [c]Job 9:24 [d]2 Pet. 3:4 [e]Is. 5:19; Jer. 17:15

1 [1]Or, *angel* [2]Or, *prepare* [3]Or, *even* [a]Matt. 11:10, 14; Mark 1:2; Luke 1:76; 7:27 [b]Hag. 1:13; John 1:6, 7 [c]Is. 40:3 [d]Is. 63:9
2 [1]Lit., *laundrymen's* [a]Is. 33:14; Ezek. 22:14; Rev. 6:17 [b]Zech. 13:9; Matt. 3:10-12; 1 Cor. 3:13-15
3 [1]Or, *grain offerings* [a]Is. 1:25; Dan. 12:10 [b]Ps. 4:5; 51:19
4 [1]Or, *grain offering* [a]Ps. 51:17-19 [b]2 Chr. 7:1-3, 12
5 [1]Or, *fatherless* [2]Or, *sojourner* [3]Or, *revere* [a]Deut. 18:10; Jer. 27:9, 10 [b]Ezek. 22:9-11 [c]Jer. 5:2; 7:9; Zech. 5:4 [d]Lev. 19:13 [e]Ex. 22:22-24 [f]Deut. 27:19

6 [1]Or, *I am the LORD; I do not* [2]Or, *have not come to an end* [a]Num. 23:19; James 1:17
7 [a]Jer. 7:25, 26; 16:11, 12 [b]Zech. 1:3
8 [1]Or, *defraud* [2]Or, *heave offerings* [a]Neh. 13:11, 12
9 [1]Or, *defrauding* [a]Mal. 2:2
10 [1]Lit., *prey* [2]Or, *there is not room enough* [a]Lev. 27:30; Num. 18:21-24; Deut. 12:6; 14:22-29; Neh. 13:12 [b]Ps. 78:23-29 [c]Ezek. 34:26 [d]Lev. 26:3-5
11 [1]Lit., *ruin* [a]Joel 1:4; 2:25
12 [a]Is. 61:9 [b]Is. 62:4
13 [1]Lit., *strong*
14 [a]Jer. 2:25; 18:12 [b]Is. 58:3

kept His charge, and that we have
walked in mourning before the LORD of
hosts?
15 'So now we [a]call the arrogant
blessed; not only are the doers of wickedness built up, but they also test God
and [b]escape.' "

The Book of Remembrance

16 Then those who [1]feared the LORD
spoke to one another, and the LORD
[a]gave attention and heard *it,* and a
[b]book of remembrance was written before Him for those who [1]fear the LORD
and who esteem His name.
17 "And they will be [a]Mine," says the
LORD of hosts, "on the [b]day that I
[1]prepare *My* [2c]own possession, and I will
[3]spare them as a man [3d]spares his own
son who serves him."
18 So you will again [a]distinguish between the righteous and the wicked,
between one who serves God and one
who does not serve Him.

Final Admonition

4 "[1]FOR behold, the day is coming,
[a]burning like a furnace; and all the
arrogant and every evildoer will be
[b]chaff; and the day that is coming will
[c]set them ablaze," says the LORD of
hosts, "so that it will leave them neither
root nor branch."
2 "But for you who [1]fear My name the
[a]sun of righteousness will rise with
[b]healing in its wings; and you will go
forth and [c]skip about like calves from
the stall.
3 "And you will [a]tread down the
wicked, for they shall be [b]ashes under
the soles of your feet [c]on the day [1]which
I am preparing," says the LORD of hosts.
4 "[1a]Remember the law of Moses My
servant, *even the* statutes and ordinances
which I commanded him in Horeb for
all Israel.
5 "Behold, I am going to send you
[a]Elijah the prophet before the coming of
the great and terrible day of the LORD.
6 "And he will [1a]restore the hearts of
the fathers to *their* children, and the
hearts of the children to their fathers,
lest I come and [b]smite the land with a
[2]curse."

15 [a]Is. 2:22; Mal. 4:1 [b]Jer. 7:10
16 [1]Or, *revere(d)* [a]Ps. 34:15; Jer. 31:18-20 [b]Is. 4:3; Dan. 12:1
17 [1]Lit., *make* [2]Or, *special treasure* [3]Or, *have (has) compassion on* [a]Is. 43:1 [b]Is. 4:2 [c]Ex. 19:5; Deut. 7:6; Is. 43:21; 1 Pet. 2:9 [d]Ps. 103:13
18 [a]Gen. 18:25; Amos 5:15

1 [1]Ch. 3:19 in Heb. [a]Ps. 21:9; Nah. 1:5, 6; Mal. 3:2, 3; 2 Pet. 3:7 [b]Is. 5:24; Obad. 18 [c]Is. 9:18, 19
2 [1]Or, *revere* [a]2 Sam. 23:4; Is. 30:26; 60:1 [b]Jer. 30:17; 33:6 [c]Is. 35:6
3 [1]Or, *when I act* [a]Job 40:12; Is. 26:6; Mic. 5:8 [b]Ezek. 28:18 [c]Mal. 3:17
4 [1]Ch. 3:22 in Heb. [a]Deut. 4:23; 8:11, 19
5 [a]Matt. 11:14; 17:10-13; Mark 9:11-13; Luke 1:17; John 1:21
6 [1]Or, *turn* [2]Or, *ban of destruction* [a]Luke 1:17 [b]Is. 11:4; Rev. 19:15

New Testament

THE GOSPEL
ACCORDING TO
MATTHEW

Genealogy of Jesus Christ

1 THE book of the genealogy of Jesus Christ, [a]the son of David, [b]the son of Abraham.

2 To Abraham was born Isaac; and to Isaac, Jacob; and to Jacob, [1]Judah and his brothers;

3 and to Judah were born Perez and Zerah by Tamar; and to [a]Perez was born Hezron; and to Hezron, [1]Ram;

4 and to Ram was born Amminadab; and to Amminadab, Nahshon; and to Nahshon, Salmon;

5 and to Salmon was born Boaz by Rahab; and to Boaz was born Obed by Ruth; and to Obed, Jesse;

6 and to Jesse was born David the king.

And to David [a]was born Solomon by her *who had been the wife* of Uriah;

7 and to Solomon [a]was born Rehoboam; and to Rehoboam, Abijah; and to Abijah, [1]Asa;

8 and to Asa was born Jehoshaphat; and to Jehoshaphat, [1]Joram; and to Joram, Uzziah;

9 and to Uzziah was born [1]Jotham; and to Jotham, Ahaz; and to Ahaz, Hezekiah;

10 and to Hezekiah was born Manasseh; and to Manasseh, [1]Amon; and to Amon, Josiah;

11 and to Josiah were born [1]Jeconiah and his brothers, at the time of the [a]deportation to Babylon.

12 And after the [a]deportation to Babylon, to Jeconiah was born [1]Shealtiel; and to Shealtiel, Zerubbabel;

13 and to Zerubbabel was born [1]Abiud; and to Abiud, Eliakim; and to Eliakim, Azor;

14 and to Azor was born Zadok; and to Zadok, Achim; and to Achim, Eliud;

15 and to Eliud was born Eleazar; and to Eleazar, Matthan; and to Matthan, Jacob;

16 and to Jacob was born Joseph the husband of Mary, by whom was born Jesus, [a]who is called [1]Christ.

17 Therefore all the generations from Abraham to David are fourteen generations; and from David to the [a]deportation to Babylon fourteen generations; and from the [a]deportation to Babylon to *the time of* [1]Christ fourteen generations.

Conception and Birth of Jesus

18 Now the birth of Jesus Christ was as follows. When His [a]mother Mary had been betrothed to Joseph, before they came together she was [b]found to be with child by the Holy Spirit.

19 And Joseph her husband, being a righteous man, and not wanting to disgrace her, desired [1a]to put her away secretly.

20 But when he had considered this, behold, an angel of the Lord appeared to him in a dream, saying, "[a]Joseph, son of David, do not be afraid to take Mary as your wife; for that which has been [1]conceived in her is of the Holy Spirit.

21 "And she will bear a Son; and [a]you shall call His name Jesus, for it is He who [b]will save His people from their sins."

22 Now all this [1]took place that what was [a]spoken by the Lord through the prophet might be fulfilled, saying,

23 "[a]BEHOLD, THE VIRGIN SHALL BE WITH [b]CHILD, AND SHALL BEAR A SON, AND THEY SHALL CALL HIS NAME [1]IMMANUEL," which translated means, "[c]GOD WITH US."

24 And Joseph arose from his sleep, and did as the angel of the Lord commanded him, and took *her* as his wife,

25 and [1]kept her a virgin until she [a]gave birth to a Son; and [b]he called His name Jesus.

Visit of the Wise Men

2 NOW after Jesus was [a]born in Bethlehem of Judea in the days of [b]Herod the king, behold, [1]magi from the east arrived in Jerusalem, saying,

2 "Where is He who has been born [a]King of the Jews? For we saw [b]His star in the east, and have come to worship Him."

3 And when Herod the king heard it, he was troubled, and all Jerusalem with him.

4 And gathering together all the chief priests and scribes of the people, he *began* to inquire of them where [1]the Christ was to be born.

5 And they said to him, "[a]In Bethlehem of Judea, for so it has been written [1]by the prophet,

6 '[a]AND YOU, BETHLEHEM, LAND OF JUDAH,
ARE BY NO MEANS LEAST AMONG THE LEADERS OF JUDAH;
FOR OUT OF YOU SHALL COME FORTH A RULER,
WHO WILL [b]SHEPHERD MY PEOPLE ISRAEL.' "

7 Then Herod secretly called the magi, and ascertained from them [1]the time [a]the star appeared.

8 And he sent them to Bethlehem, and said, "Go and make careful search for the Child; and when you have found *Him,* report to me, that I too may come and worship Him."

9 And having heard the king, they went their way; and lo, the star, which they had seen in the east, went on before them, until it came and stood over where the Child was.

10 And when they saw the star, they rejoiced exceedingly with great joy.

---

1 [a]2 Sam. 7:12-16; Ps. 89:3f.; 132:11; Is. 9:6f.; 11:1; Matt. 9:27; Luke 1:32, 69; John 7:42; Acts 13:23; Rom. 1:3; Rev. 22:16 [b]Matt. 1:1-6: *Luke 3:32-34;* Gen. 22:18; Gal. 3:16
2 [1]Gr., *Judas.* Names of Old Testament characters will be given in their Old Testament form.
3 [1]Gr., *Aram* [a]Ruth 4:18-22; 1 Chr. 2:1-15; Matt. 1:3-6
6 [a]2 Sam. 11:27; 12:24
7 [1]Gr., *Asaph* [a]1 Chr. 3:10ff.
8 [1]Gr., *Jehoram*
9 [1]Gr., *Joatham*
10 [1]Gr., *Amos*
11 [1]Or, *Jehoiachin* [a]2 Kin. 24:14f.; Jer. 27:20; Matt. 1:17
12 [1]Gr., *Salathiel* [a]2 Kin. 24:14f.; Jer. 27:20; Matt. 1:17
13 [1]Gr., *Abihud*
16 [1]I.e., the Messiah [a]Matt. 27:17, 22; Luke 2:11; John 4:25
17 [1]I.e., the Messiah [a]2 Kin. 24:14f.; Jer. 27:20; Matt. 1:11, 12
18 [a]Matt. 12:46; Luke 1:27 [b]Luke 1:35
19 [1]Or, *to divorce her* [a]Deut. 22:20-24; 24:1-4; John 8:4, 5
20 [1]Lit., *begotten* [a]Luke 2:4
21 [a]Luke 1:31; 2:21 [b]Luke 2:11; John 1:29; Acts 4:12; 5:31; 13:23, 38, 39; Col. 1:20-23
22 [1]Or, *has taken place* [a]Luke 24:44; Rom. 1:2-4
23 [1]Or, *Emmanuel* [a]Is. 7:14 [b]Is. 9:6, 7 [c]Is. 8:10
25 [1]Lit., *was not knowing her* [a]Luke 2:7 [b]Matt. 1:21; Luke 2:21

1 [1]Pronounced may-ji, a caste of wise men specializing in astrology, medicine and natural science [a]Mic. 5:2; Luke 2:4-7 [b]Luke 1:5
2 [a]Jer. 23:5; 30:9; Zech. 9:9; Matt. 27:11; Luke 19:38; 23:38; John 1:49 [b]Num. 24:17
4 [1]I.e., the Messiah
5 [1]Lit., *through* [a]John 7:42
6 [a]Mic. 5:2; John 7:42 [b]John 21:16
7 [1]Lit., *the time of the appearing star* [a]Num. 24:17

11 And they came into the house and saw the Child with [a]Mary His mother; and they fell down and [b]worshiped Him; and opening their treasures they presented to Him gifts of gold and frankincense and myrrh.

12 And having been [a]warned *by God* [b]in a dream not to return to Herod, they departed for their own country by another way.

The Flight to Egypt

13 Now when they had departed, behold, an [a]angel of the Lord *[b]appeared to Joseph in a dream, saying, "Arise and take the Child and His mother, and flee to Egypt, and remain there until I tell you; for Herod is going to search for the Child to destroy Him."

14 And he arose and took the Child and His mother by night, and departed for Egypt;

15 and was there until the death of Herod, that what was spoken by the Lord through the prophet might be fulfilled, saying, "[a]OUT OF EGYPT DID I CALL [b]MY SON."

Herod Slaughters Babies

16 Then when Herod saw that he had been tricked by [a]the magi, he became very enraged, and sent and [b]slew all the male children who were in Bethlehem and in all its environs, from two years old and under, according to the time which he had ascertained from the magi.

17 Then that which was spoken through Jeremiah the prophet was fulfilled, saying,

18 "[a]A VOICE WAS HEARD IN RAMAH,
WEEPING AND GREAT MOURNING,
RACHEL WEEPING FOR HER CHILDREN;
AND SHE REFUSED TO BE COMFORTED,
BECAUSE THEY WERE NO MORE."

19 But when Herod was dead, behold, an angel of the Lord *[a]appeared in a dream to Joseph in Egypt, saying,

20 "Arise and take the Child and His mother, and go into the land of Israel; for those who sought the Child's life are dead."

21 And he arose and took the Child and His mother, and came into the land of Israel.

22 But when he heard that Archelaus was reigning over Judea in place of his father Herod, he was afraid to go there. And being [a]warned *by God* in a dream, he departed for the regions of Galilee,

23 and came and resided in a city called [a]Nazareth, that what was spoken through the prophets might be fulfilled, "He shall be called a [b]Nazarene."

John the Baptist Preaches

3 NOW [a]in those days [b]John the Baptist *[1]came, [2]preaching in the [c]wilderness of Judea, saying,

2 "[a]Repent, for [b]the kingdom of [1]heaven [2]is at hand."

3 For this is the [a]one referred to [1]by Isaiah the prophet, saying,
"[b]THE VOICE OF ONE CRYING IN THE WILDERNESS,
'[c]MAKE READY THE WAY OF THE LORD,
MAKE HIS PATHS STRAIGHT!'"

4 Now John himself had [1a]a garment of camel's hair, and a leather belt about his waist; and his food was [b]locusts and wild honey.

5 Then Jerusalem [a]was going out to him, and all Judea, and all [b]the district around the Jordan;

6 and they were being [a]baptized by him in the Jordan River, as they confessed their sins.

7 But when he saw many of the [a]Pharisees and [b]Sadducees coming for baptism, he said to them, "You [c]brood of vipers, who warned you to flee from [d]the wrath to come?

8 "[a]Therefore bring forth fruit [b]in keeping with repentance;

9 and do not suppose that you can say to yourselves, '[a]We have Abraham for our father'; for I say to you, that God is able from these stones to raise up children to Abraham.

10 "And [a]the axe is already laid at the root of the trees; [b]every tree therefore that does not bear good fruit is cut down and thrown into the fire.

11 "As for me, [a]I baptize you [1]with water for repentance, but He who is coming after me is mightier than I, and I am not fit to remove His sandals; [b]He will baptize you [1]with the Holy Spirit and fire.

12 "And His [a]winnowing fork is in His hand, and He will thoroughly clear His threshing floor; and He will [b]gather His wheat into the barn, but He will burn up the [c]chaff with [d]unquenchable fire."

The Baptism of Jesus

13 [a]Then Jesus *arrived [b]from Galilee at the Jordan *coming* to John, to be baptized by him.

14 But John tried to prevent Him, saying, "I have need to be baptized by You, and do You come to me?"

15 But Jesus answering said to him, "Permit *it* at this time; for in this way it is fitting for us [a]to fulfill all righteousness." Then he *permitted Him.

16 And after being baptized, Jesus went up immediately from the water; and behold, the heavens were opened, and [1a]he saw the Spirit of God descending as a dove, *and* coming upon Him,

17 and behold, a voice out of the heavens, saying, "[a]This is [1]My beloved Son, in whom I am well-pleased."

---

11 [a]Matt. 1:18; 12:46 [b]Matt. 14:33
12 [a]Matt. 2:13, 19, 22; Luke 2:26; Acts 10:22; Heb. 8:5; 11:7 [b]Job 33:15, 16; Matt. 1:20
13 [a]Acts 5:19; 10:7; 12:7-11 [b]Matt. 2:12, 19
15 [a]Hos. 11:1; Num. 24:8 [b]Ex. 4:22f.
16 [a]Matt. 2:1 [b]Is. 59:7
18 [a]Jer. 31:15
19 [a]Matt. 1:20; 2:12, 13, 22
22 [a]Matt. 2:12, 13, 19
23 [a]Luke 1:26; 2:39; John 1:45, 46 [b]Mark 1:24; John 18:5, 7; 19:19

1 [1]Or, *arrived* [2]Or, *proclaiming as a herald* [a]Matt. 3:1-12: *Mark 1:3-8; Luke 3:2-17;* John 1:6-8, 19-28 [b]Matt. 11:11-14; 16:14 [c]Josh. 15:61; Judg. 1:16
2 [1]Lit., *the heavens* [2]Lit., *has come near* [a]Matt. 4:17 [b]Dan. 2:44; Matt. 4:17, 23; 6:10; 10:7; Mark 1:15; Luke 10:9f.; 11:20; 21:31
3 [1]Lit., *through* [a]Luke 1:17, 76 [b]Is. 40:3 [c]John 1:23
4 [1]Lit., *his garment* [a]2 Kin. 1:8; Zech. 13:4; Matt. 11:8; Mark 1:6 [b]Lev. 11:22
5 [a]Mark 1:5 [b]Luke 3:3
6 [a]Matt. 3:11, 13-16; Mark 1:5; John 1:25, 26; 3:23; Acts 1:5; 2:38-41; 10:37
7 [a]Matt. 16:1ff.; 23:13, 15 [b]Matt. 22:23; Acts 4:1; 5:17; 23:6ff. [c]Matt. 12:34; 23:33 [d]1 Thess. 1:10
8 [a]Luke 3:8; Eph. 5:8, 9 [b]Acts 26:20
9 [a]Luke 3:8; 16:24; John 8:33, 39, 53; Acts 13:26; Rom. 4:1; 9:7, 8; Gal. 3:29
10 [a]Luke 3:9 [b]Ps. 92:12-14; Matt. 7:19; John 15:2
11 [1]The Gr. here can be translated *in, with* or *by* [a]Mark 1:4, 8; Luke 3:16; John 1:26f.; Acts 1:5; 8:36, 38; 11:16 [b]John 1:33; Acts 2:3, 4; Titus 3:5
12 [a]Is. 30:24; 41:16; Jer. 15:7; 51:2; Luke 3:17 [b]Matt. 13:30 [c]Ps. 1:4 [d]Is. 66:24; Jer. 7:20; Matt. 13:41, 42; Mark 9:43, 48
13 [a]Matt. 3:13-17: *Mark 1:9-11; Luke 3:21, 22;* John 1:31-34 [b]Matt. 2:22
15 [a]Ps. 40:7, 8; John 4:34; 8:29

16 [1]Or, *He* [a]Mark 1:10; Luke 3:22; John 1:32; Acts 7:56
17 [1]Lit., *My Son, the Beloved* [a]Ps. 2:7; Is. 42:1; Matt. 12:18; 17:5; Mark 9:7; Luke 9:35; John 12:28

Temptation of Jesus

4 [a]THEN Jesus was led up by the Spirit into the wilderness [b]to be tempted by the devil.

2 And after He had [a]fasted forty days and forty nights, He [1]then became hungry.

3 And [a]the tempter came and said to Him, "If You are the [b]Son of God, command that these stones become [1]bread."

4 But He answered and said, "It is written, '[a]MAN SHALL NOT LIVE ON BREAD ALONE, BUT ON EVERY WORD THAT PROCEEDS OUT OF THE MOUTH OF GOD.'"

5 Then the devil *took Him into [a]the holy city; and he had Him stand on the pinnacle of the temple,

6 and *said to Him, "If You are the Son of God throw Yourself down; for it is written,

'[a]HE WILL GIVE HIS ANGELS CHARGE CONCERNING YOU';
and
'ON *their* HANDS THEY WILL BEAR YOU UP,
LEST YOU STRIKE YOUR FOOT AGAINST A STONE.'"

7 Jesus said to him, "[1]On the other hand, it is written, '[a]YOU SHALL NOT [2]PUT THE LORD YOUR GOD TO THE TEST.'"

8 [a]Again, the devil *took Him to a very high mountain, and *showed Him all the kingdoms of the world, and their glory;

9 and he said to Him, "[a]All these things will I give You, if You fall down and worship me."

10 Then Jesus *said to him, "Begone, Satan! For it is written, '[a]YOU SHALL WORSHIP THE LORD YOUR GOD, AND [1]SERVE HIM ONLY.'"

11 Then the devil *left Him; and behold, [a]angels came and *began* to minister to Him.

Jesus Begins His Ministry

12 Now when He heard that [a]John had [1]been taken into custody, [b]He withdrew into Galilee;

13 and leaving Nazareth, He came and [a]settled in Capernaum, which is by the sea, in the region of Zebulun and Naphtali.

14 *This was* to fulfill what was spoken through Isaiah the prophet, saying,

15 "[a]THE LAND OF ZEBULUN AND THE LAND OF NAPHTALI,
[1]BY THE WAY OF THE SEA, BEYOND THE JORDAN, GALILEE OF THE [2]GENTILES—

16 "[a]THE PEOPLE WHO WERE SITTING IN DARKNESS SAW A GREAT LIGHT,
AND TO THOSE WHO WERE SITTING IN THE LAND AND SHADOW OF DEATH,
UPON THEM A LIGHT DAWNED."

1 [a]Matt. 4:1-11: *Mark 1:12, 13; Luke 4:1-13* [b]Heb. 4:15; James 1:14
2 [1]Lit., *later, afterward* [a]Ex. 34:28; 1 Kin. 19:8
3 [1]Lit., *loaves* [a]1 Thess. 3:5 [b]Matt. 14:33; 26:63; Mark 3:11; 5:7; Luke 1:35; 4:41; John 1:34, 49; Acts 9:20
4 [a]Deut. 8:3
5 [a]Neh. 11:1, 18; Dan. 9:24; Matt. 27:53
6 [a]Ps. 91:11, 12
7 [1]Lit., *Again* [2]Or, *tempt . . . God* [a]Deut. 6:16
8 [a]Matt. 16:26; 1 John 2:15-17
9 [a]1 Cor. 10:20f.
10 [1]Or, *fulfill religious duty to Him* [a]Deut. 6:13; 10:20
11 [a]Matt. 26:53; Luke 22:43; Heb. 1:14
12 [1]Lit., *been delivered up* [a]Matt. 14:3; Mark 1:14; Luke 3:20; John 3:24 [b]Mark 1:14; Luke 4:14; John 1:43; 2:11
13 [a]Matt. 11:23; Mark 1:21; 2:1; Luke 4:23, 31; John 2:12; 4:46f.
15 [1]Or, *Toward the sea* [2]Or, *nations* [a]Is. 9:1
16 [a]Is. 9:2; 60:1-3; Luke 2:32
17 [1]Or, *proclaim* [a]Mark 1:14, 15 [b]Matt. 3:2
18 [a]Matt. 4:18-22: *Mark 1:16-20;* Luke 5:2-11; John 1:40-42 [b]Matt. 15:29; Mark 7:31; Luke 5:1; John 6:1 [c]Matt. 10:2; 16:18; John 1:40-42
19 [1]Lit., *Come here after Me*
21 [1]Or, *Jacob* [2]Gr., *Joannes,* Heb., *Johanan* [a]Matt. 10:2; 20:20
23 [1]Or, *good news* [a]Mark 1:39; Luke 4:14, 44 [b]Matt. 9:35; 13:54; Mark 1:21; 6:2; 10:1; Luke 4:15; 6:6; 13:10; John 6:59; 18:20 [c]Matt. 3:2; 9:35; 24:14; Mark 1:14; Luke 4:43; 8:1; 16:16; Acts 20:25; 28:31 [d]Matt. 8:16; 9:35; 14:14; 15:30; 19:2; 21:14; Mark 1:34; 3:10; Luke 4:40; 7:21; Acts 10:38
24 [1]Lit., *moon-smitten* [a]Mark 7:26; Luke 2:2; Acts 15:23; 18:18; 20:3; 21:3; Gal. 1:21 [b]Matt. 8:16, 28, 33; 9:32; 12:22; 15:22; Mark 1:32; 5:15, 16, 18; Luke 8:36; John 10:21 [c]Matt. 17:15 [d]Matt. 8:6; 9:2, 6; Mark 2:3, 5, 9; Luke 5:24
25 [a]Mark 3:7, 8; Luke 6:17 [b]Mark 5:20; 7:31 [c]Matt. 4:15

17 [a]From that time Jesus began to [1]preach and say, "[b]Repent, for the kingdom of heaven is at hand."

The First Disciples

18 [a]And walking by [b]the Sea of Galilee, He saw two brothers, [c]Simon who was called Peter, and Andrew his brother, casting a net into the sea; for they were fishermen.

19 And He *said to them, "[1]Follow Me, and I will make you fishers of men."

20 And they immediately left the nets, and followed Him.

21 And going on from there He saw two other brothers, [1a]James the *son* of Zebedee, and [2]John his brother, in the boat with Zebedee their father, mending their nets; and He called them.

22 And they immediately left the boat and their father, and followed Him.

Ministry in Galilee

23 And *Jesus* was going about [a]in all Galilee, [b]teaching in their synagogues, and [c]proclaiming the [1]gospel of the kingdom, and [d]healing every kind of disease and every kind of sickness among the people.

24 And the news about Him went out [a]into all Syria; and they brought to Him all who were ill, taken with various diseases and pains, [b]demoniacs, [1c]epileptics, [d]paralytics; and He healed them.

25 And great multitudes [a]followed Him from Galilee and [b]Decapolis and Jerusalem and Judea and *from* [c]beyond the Jordan.

The Sermon on the Mount
The Beatitudes

5 [a]AND when He saw the multitudes, He went up on [b]the [1]mountain; and after He sat down, His disciples came to Him.

2 And [a]opening His mouth He *began* to teach them, saying,

3 "[a]Blessed are the poor in spirit, for [b]theirs is the kingdom of heaven.

4 "Blessed are [a]those who mourn, for they shall be comforted.

5 "Blessed are [a]the [1]gentle, for they shall inherit the earth.

6 "Blessed are [a]those who hunger and thirst for righteousness, for they shall be satisfied.

7 "Blessed are [a]the merciful, for they shall receive mercy.

8 "Blessed are [a]the pure in heart, for [b]they shall see God.

9 "Blessed are the peacemakers, for [a]they shall be called sons of God.

1 [1]Or, *hill* [a]Matt. ch. 5-7; Luke 6:20-49 [b]Mark 3:13; Luke 6:17; 9:28; John 6:3, 15
2 [a]Matt. 13:35; Acts 8:35; 10:34; 18:14
3 [a]Matt. 5:3-12; Luke 6:20-23 [b]Matt. 5:10; 19:14; 25:34; Mark 10:14; Luke 6:20; 22:29f.
4 [a]Is. 61:2; John 16:20; Rev. 7:17
5 [1]Or, *humble, meek* [a]Ps. 37:11
6 [a]Is. 55:1, 2; John 4:14; 6:48ff.; 7:37
7 [a]Prov. 11:17; Matt. 6:14, 15; 18:33-35
8 [a]Ps. 24:4 [b]Heb. 12:14; 1 John 3:2; Rev. 22:4
9 [a]Matt. 5:45; Luke 6:35; Rom. 8:14

10“Blessed are those who have been
[a]persecuted for the sake of righteousness, for [b]theirs is the kingdom of
heaven.
11“Blessed are you when *men* [a]cast
insults at you, and persecute you, and
say all kinds of evil against you falsely,
on account of Me.
12“Rejoice, and be glad, for your
reward in heaven is great, for [a]so they
persecuted the prophets who were before
you.

Disciples and the World

13“You are the salt of the earth; but
[a]if the salt has become tasteless, how will
it be made salty *again*? It is good for
nothing anymore, except to be thrown
out and trampled under foot by men.
14“You are [a]the light of the world. A
city set on a [1]hill cannot be hidden.
15“[a]Nor do *men* light a lamp, and put
it under the peck-measure, but on the
lampstand; and it gives light to all who
are in the house.
16“Let your light shine before men in
such a way that they may [a]see your good
works, and [b]glorify your Father who is
in heaven.
17“Do not think that I came to abolish
the [a]Law or the Prophets; I did not come
to abolish, but to fulfill.
18“For truly I say to you, [a]until
heaven and earth pass away, not [1]the
smallest letter or stroke shall pass away
from the Law, until all is accomplished.
19“Whoever then annuls one of the
least of these commandments, and so
teaches [1]others, shall be called least [a]in
the kingdom of heaven; but whoever
[2]keeps and teaches *them,* he shall be
called great in the kingdom of heaven.
20“For I say to you, that unless your
[a]righteousness surpasses *that* of the
scribes and Pharisees, you shall not enter
the kingdom of heaven.

Personal Relationships

21“[a]You have heard that [1]the ancients
were told, ‘[b]YOU SHALL NOT COMMIT
MURDER’ and ‘Whoever commits murder
shall be [2]liable to [c]the court.’
22“But I say to you that everyone who
is angry with his brother[1] shall be [2]guilty
before [a]the court; and whoever shall say
to his brother, ‘[3]Raca,’ shall be [2]guilty
before [4b]the supreme court; and whoever shall say, ‘You fool,’ shall be [2]guilty
enough to go into the [5c]fiery hell.
23“If therefore you are [a]presenting
your [1]offering at the altar, and there
remember that your brother has something against you,
24 leave your [1]offering there before
the altar, and go your way; first be
[a]reconciled to your brother, and then
come and present your [1]offering.
25“[a]Make friends quickly with your
opponent at law while you are with him
on the way, in order that your opponent
may not deliver you to the judge, and the
judge to the officer, and you be thrown
into prison.
26“Truly I say to you, [a]you shall not
come out of there, until you have paid
up the last [1]cent.
27“[a]You have heard that it was said,
‘[b]YOU SHALL NOT COMMIT ADULTERY’;
28 but I say to you, that everyone who
looks on a woman [a]to lust for her has
committed adultery with her already in
his heart.
29“And [a]if your right eye makes you
[1]stumble, tear it out, and throw it from
you; for it is better for you that one of
the parts of your body perish, [2]than for
your whole body to be thrown into
[3b]hell.
30“And [a]if your right hand makes you
[1]stumble, cut it off, and throw it from
you; for it is better for you that one of
the parts of your body perish, [2]than for
your whole body to go into [3b]hell.
31“And it was said, ‘[a]WHOEVER SENDS
HIS WIFE AWAY, LET HIM GIVE HER A
CERTIFICATE OF DIVORCE’;
32 [a]but I say to you that everyone who
[1]divorces his wife, except for *the* cause of
unchastity, makes her commit adultery;
and whoever marries a [2]divorced woman
commits adultery.
33“Again, [a]you have heard that [1]the
ancients were told, ‘[2b]YOU SHALL NOT
[3]MAKE FALSE VOWS, BUT SHALL FULFILL
YOUR [4]VOWS TO THE LORD.’
34“But I say to you, [a]make no oath at
all, either by heaven, for it is [b]the throne
of God,
35 or by the earth, for it is the [a]foot-
stool of His feet, or [1]by Jerusalem, for it
is [b]THE CITY OF THE GREAT KING.
36“Nor shall you make an oath by
your head, for you cannot make one hair
white or black.
37“But let your statement be, ‘Yes,
yes’ *or* ‘No, no’; and anything beyond
these is [1]of [a]evil.
38“[a]You have heard that it was said,
‘[b]AN EYE FOR AN EYE, AND A TOOTH FOR
A TOOTH.’
39“But I say to you, do not resist him
who is evil; but [a]whoever slaps you on
your right cheek, turn to him the other
also.
40“And if anyone wants to sue you,
and take your [1]shirt, let him have your
[2]coat also.
41“And whoever shall force you to go
one mile, go with him two.

10 [a]1 Pet. 3:14 [b]Matt. 5:3; 19:14; 25:34; Mark 10:14; Luke 6:20; 22:29f.
11 [a]1 Pet. 4:14
12 [a]2 Chr. 36:16; Matt. 23:37; Acts 7:52; 1 Thess. 2:15; Heb. 11:33ff.; James 5:10
13 [a]Mark 9:50; Luke 14:34f.
14 [1]Or, *mountain* [a]Prov. 4:18; John 8:12; 9:5; 12:36
15 [a]Mark 4:21; Luke 8:16; 11:33; Phil. 2:15
16 [a]1 Pet. 2:12 [b]Matt. 9:8
17 [a]Matt. 7:12
18 [1]Lit., *one iota* (yodh) or *one projection of a letter* (serif) [a]Matt. 24:35; Luke 16:17
19 [1]Lit., *the men* [2]Lit., *does* [a]Matt. 11:11
20 [a]Luke 18:11, 12
21 [1]Lit., *it was said to the ancients* [2]Or, *guilty before* [a]Matt. 5:27, 33, 38, 43 [b]Ex. 20:13; Deut. 5:17 [c]Deut. 16:18; 2 Chr. 19:5f.
22 [1]Some mss. insert *without cause* [2]Or, *liable to* [3]Aram. for *empty-head* or *good for nothing* [4]Lit., *the Sanhedrin* [5]Lit., *Gehenna of fire* [a]Deut. 16:18; 2 Chr. 19:5f. [b]Matt. 10:17; 26:59; Mark 13:9; 14:55; 15:1; Luke 22:66; John 11:47; Acts 4:15; 5:21; 6:12; 22:30; 23:1; 24:20 [c]Matt. 5:29f.; 10:28; 18:9; 23:15, 33; Mark 9:43ff.; Luke 12:5; James 3:6
23 [1]Or, *gift* [a]Matt. 5:24
24 [1]Or, *gift* [a]Rom. 12:17, 18
25 [a]Prov. 25:8f.; Luke 12:58
26 [1]Lit., *quadrans* (equaling two lepta or mites); i.e., 1/64 of a denarius [a]Luke 12:59
27 [a]Matt. 5:21, 33, 38, 43 [b]Ex. 20:14; Deut. 5:18
28 [a]2 Sam. 11:2-5; Job 31:1; Matt. 15:19; James 1:14, 15
29 [1]I.e., cause to sin [2]Lit., *not your whole body* [3]Gr., *Gehenna* [a]Matt. 18:9; Mark 9:47 [b]Matt. 5:22
30 [1]I.e., cause to sin [2]Lit., *not your whole body* [3]Gr., *Gehenna* [a]Matt. 18:8; Mark 9:43 [b]Matt. 5:22
31 [a]Deut. 24:1, 3; Jer. 3:1; Matt. 19:7; Mark 10:4
32 [1]Or, *sends away* [2]Or, *sent away* [a]Matt. 19:9; Mark 10:11f.; Luke 16:18; 1 Cor. 7:11f.

33 [1]Lit., *it was said to the ancients* [2]*you* and *your* are singular here [3]Or, *break your vows* [4]Lit., *oaths* [a]Matt. 5:21, 27, 38, 43; 23:16ff. [b]Lev. 19:12; Num. 30:2; Deut. 23:21, 23
34 [a]James 5:12 [b]Is. 66:1; Matt. 23:22
35 [1]Or, *toward* [a]Is. 66:1; Acts 7:49 [b]Ps. 48:2
37 [1]Or, *from the evil one* [a]Matt. 6:13; 13:19, 38; John 17:15; 2 Thess. 3:3; 1 John 2:13f.; 3:12; 5:18f.
38 [a]Matt. 5:21, 27, 33, 43 [b]Ex. 21:24; Lev. 24:20; Deut. 19:21
39 [a]Matt. 5:39-42: *Luke 6:29, 30;* 1 Cor. 6:7
40 [1]Or, *tunic*; i.e., garment worn next to the body [2]Or, *cloak*; i.e., outer garment

42"[a]Give to him who asks of you, and
do not turn away from him who wants to
borrow from you.
43"[a]You have heard that it was said,
'[b]YOU SHALL LOVE YOUR NEIGHBOR,
[c]and hate your enemy.'
44"But I say to you, [a]love your enemies, and pray for those who persecute
you
45 in order that you may [1]be [a]sons of
your Father who is in heaven; for He
causes His sun to rise on *the* evil and *the*
good, and sends rain on *the* righteous
and *the* unrighteous.
46"For [a]if you love those who love
you, what reward have you? Do not even
the [1]tax-gatherers do the same?
47"And if you greet your brothers
only, what do you do more *than others*?
Do not even the Gentiles do the same?
48"Therefore [a]you are to be perfect, as
your heavenly Father is perfect.

Concerning Alms and Prayer

6 "BEWARE of practicing your righteousness before men [a]to be noticed
by them; otherwise you have no reward
with your Father who is in heaven.
2"When therefore you [1]give alms, do
not sound a trumpet before you, as the
hypocrites do in the synagogues and in
the streets, that they [a]may be honored by
men. [b]Truly I say to you, they have their
reward in full.
3"But when you give alms, do not let
your left hand know what your right
hand is doing
4 that your [1]alms may be in secret;
and [a]your Father who sees in secret will
repay you.
5"And when you pray, you are not to
be as the hypocrites; for they love to
[a]stand and pray in the synagogues and
on the street corners, [1b]in order to be
seen by men. [c]Truly I say to you, they
have their reward in full.
6"But you, when you pray, [a]go into
your inner room, and when you have
shut your door, pray to your Father who
is in secret, and [b]your Father who sees in
secret will repay you.
7"And when you are praying, do not
use meaningless repetition, as the Gentiles do, for they suppose that they will
be heard for their [a]many words.
8"Therefore do not be like them; for
[a]your Father knows what you need,
before you ask Him.
9"[a]Pray, then, in this way:
'Our Father who art in [1]heaven,
Hallowed be Thy name.
10 '[a]Thy kingdom come.
[b]Thy will be done,
On earth as it is in heaven.
11 '[a]Give us this day [1]our daily
bread.
12 'And [a]forgive us our debts, as we
also have forgiven our debtors.
13 'And do not lead us into temptation, but [a]deliver us from [1b]evil.

42 [a]Deut. 15:7-11; Luke 6:34f.; 1 Tim. 6:18
43 [a]Matt. 5:21, 27, 33, 38 [b]Lev. 19:18 [c]Deut. 23:3-6
44 [a]Luke 6:27f.; 23:34; Acts 7:60; Rom. 12:20
45 [1]Or, *show yourselves to be* [a]Matt. 5:9; Luke 6:35; Acts 14:17
46 [1]I.e., Collectors of Roman taxes for profit [a]Luke 6:32
48 [a]Lev. 19:2; Deut. 18:13; 2 Cor. 7:1; Phil. 3:12-15
1 [a]Matt. 6:5, 16; 23:5
2 [1]Or, *do an act of charity* [a]Matt. 6:5, 16; 23:5 [b]Matt. 6:5, 16; Luke 6:24
4 [1]Or, *deeds of charity* [a]Jer. 17:10; Matt. 6:6, 18; Heb. 4:13
5 [1]Lit., *to be apparent to men* [a]Mark 11:25; Luke 18:11, 13 [b]Matt. 6:1, 16 [c]Matt. 6:2, 16; Luke 6:24
6 [a]Is. 26:20; Matt. 26:36-39; Acts 9:40 [b]Matt. 6:4, 18
7 [a]1 Kin. 18:26f.
8 [a]Ps. 38:9; 69:17-19; Matt. 6:32; Luke 12:30
9 [1]Lit., *the heavens* [a]Matt. 6:9-13: *Luke 11:2-4*
10 [a]Matt. 3:2; 4:17 [b]Matt. 26:42; Luke 22:42; Acts 21:14
11 [1]Or, *our bread for the coming day* or *our needful bread* [a]Prov. 30:8; Is. 33:16; Luke 11:3
12 [a]Ex. 34:7; Ps. 32:1; 130:4; Matt. 9:2; 26:28; Eph. 1:7; 1 John 1:7-9
13 [1]Or, *the evil one* [2]This clause omitted in the earliest mss. [a]John 17:15; 1 Cor. 10:13; 2 Thess. 3:3; 2 Tim. 4:18; 2 Pet. 2:9; 1 John 5:18 [b]Matt. 5:37
14 [a]Matt. 7:2; Mark 11:25f.; Eph. 4:32; Col. 3:13
15 [a]Matt. 18:35
16 [1]Lit., *render their faces unrecognizable* [a]Is. 58:5 [b]Matt. 6:2
17 [a]Ruth 3:3; 2 Sam. 12:20
18 [a]Matt. 6:4, 6
19 [a]Prov. 23:4; Matt. 19:21; Luke 12:21, 33; 18:22; 1 Tim. 6:9, 10; Heb. 13:5; James 5:2
20 [a]Matt. 19:21; Luke 12:33; 1 Tim. 6:19
21 [a]Luke 12:34
22 [1]Or, *healthy* [a]Matt. 6:22, 23: *Luke 11:34, 35*
23 [a]Matt. 20:15; Mark 7:22

[2][For Thine is the kingdom, and
the power, and the glory, forever. Amen.']
14"[a]For if you forgive men for their
transgressions, your heavenly Father will
also forgive you.
15"But [a]if you do not forgive men,
then your Father will not forgive your
transgressions.

Concerning Fasting
True Treasure
Mammon

16"And [a]whenever you fast, do not put
on a gloomy face as the hypocrites *do,*
for they [1]neglect their appearance in
order to be seen fasting by men. [b]Truly I
say to you, they have their reward in full.
17"But you, when you fast, [a]anoint
your head, and wash your face
18 so that you may not be seen fasting
by men, but by your Father who is in
secret; and your [a]Father who sees in
secret will repay you.
19"[a]Do not lay up for yourselves
treasures upon earth, where moth and
rust destroy, and where thieves break in
and steal.
20"But lay up for yourselves [a]treasures
in heaven, where neither moth nor rust
destroys, and where thieves do not break
in or steal;
21 for [a]where your treasure is, there
will your heart be also.
22"[a]The lamp of the body is the eye; if
therefore your eye is [1]clear, your whole
body will be full of light.
23"But if [a]your eye is bad, your whole
body will be full of darkness. If therefore
the light that is in you is darkness, how
great is the darkness!
24"[a]No one can serve two masters; for
either he will hate the one and love the
other, or he will hold to one and despise
the other. You cannot serve God and
[1b]mammon.

The Cure for Anxiety

25"[a]For this reason I say to you, [1]do
not be [b]anxious for your life, *as to* what
you shall eat, or what you shall drink;
nor for your body, *as to* what you shall
put on. Is not life more than food, and
the body than clothing?
26"[a]Look at the birds of the [1]air, that
they do not sow, neither do they reap,
nor gather into barns, and *yet* your
heavenly Father feeds them. Are you not
worth much more than they?
27"And which of you by being [a]anx-
ious can [b]add a *single* [1]cubit to his [2]life's
span?

24 [1]Or, *riches* [a]1 Kin. 18:21; Luke 16:13; Gal. 1:10; James 4:4 [b]Luke 16:9, 11, 13
25 [1]Or, *stop being anxious* [a]Matt. 6:25-33: *Luke 12:22-31* [b]Matt. 6:27, 28, 31, 34; Luke 10:41; 12:11, 22; Phil. 4:6; 1 Pet. 5:7
26 [1]Lit., *heaven* [a]Job 35:11; 38:41; Ps. 104:27, 28; Matt. 10:29ff.; Luke 12:24
27 [1]I.e., One cubit equals approx. 18 in. [2]Or, *height* [a]Matt. 6:25, 28, 31, 34; Luke 10:41; 12:11, 22; Phil. 4:6; 1 Pet. 5:7 [b]Ps. 39:5

28 "And why are you [a]anxious about clothing? Observe how the lilies of the field grow; they do not toil nor do they spin,

29 yet I say to you that even [a]Solomon in all his glory did not clothe himself like one of these.

30 "But if God so arrays the [a]grass of the field, which is *alive* today and tomorrow is thrown into the furnace, *will He* not much more *do so for* you, [b]O men of little faith?

31 "Do not be [a]anxious then, saying, 'What shall we eat?' or 'What shall we drink?' or 'With what shall we clothe ourselves?'

32 "For all these things the Gentiles eagerly seek; for [a]your heavenly Father knows that you need all these things.

33 "But [1]seek first [2]His kingdom and His righteousness; and [a]all these things shall be [3]added to you.

34 "Therefore do not be [a]anxious for tomorrow; for tomorrow will [1]care for itself. *Each* day has enough trouble of its own.

Concerning Judging Others

7 "[a]DO not judge lest you be judged.

2 "For in the way you judge, you will be judged; and [1a]by your standard of measure, it will be measured to you.

3 "And why do you [a]look at the speck that is in your brother's eye, but do not notice the log that is in your own eye?

4 "[a]Or how [1]can you say to your brother, 'Let me take the speck out of your eye,' and behold, the log is in your own eye?

5 "You hypocrite, first take the log out of your own eye, and then you will see clearly to take the speck out of your brother's eye.

6 "[a]Do not give what is holy to dogs, and do not throw your pearls before swine, lest they trample them under their feet, and turn and tear you to pieces.

Encouragement to Pray

7 "[1a]Ask, and [b]it shall be given to you; [2]seek, and you shall find; [3]knock, and it shall be opened to you.

8 "For everyone who asks receives, and he who seeks finds, and to him who knocks it shall be opened.

9 "Or what man is there among you, [1]when his son shall ask him for a loaf, [2]will give him a stone?

10 "Or [1]if he shall ask for a fish, he will not give him a snake, will he?

11 "If you then, being evil, know how to give good gifts to your children, [a]how much more shall your Father who is in heaven give what is good to those who ask Him!

12 "[a]Therefore, however you want people to treat you, [1]so treat them, for [b]this is the Law and the Prophets.

Ways Contrasted
Fruits Contrasted

13 "[a]Enter by the narrow gate; for the gate is wide, and the way is broad that leads to destruction, and many are those who enter by it.

14 "For the gate is small, and the way is narrow that leads to life, and few are those who find it.

15 "Beware of the [a]false prophets, who come to you in sheep's clothing, but inwardly are [b]ravenous wolves.

16 "You will [1a]know them by their fruits. [2]Grapes are not gathered from thorn *bushes,* nor figs from thistles, are they?

17 "Even so, [a]every good tree bears good fruit; but the bad tree bears bad fruit.

18 "A good tree cannot produce bad fruit, nor can a bad tree produce good fruit.

19 "[a]Every tree that does not bear good fruit is cut down and thrown into the fire.

20 "So then, you will [1]know them [a]by their fruits.

21 "[a]Not everyone who says to Me, 'Lord, Lord,' will enter the kingdom of heaven; but he who does the will of My Father who is in heaven.

22 "[a]Many will say to Me on [b]that day, 'Lord, Lord, did we not prophesy in Your name, and in Your name cast out demons, and in Your name perform many [1]miracles?'

23 "And then I will declare to them, 'I never knew you; [a]DEPART FROM ME, YOU WHO PRACTICE LAWLESSNESS.'

The Two Foundations

24 "Therefore [a]everyone who hears these words of Mine, and [1]acts upon them, [2]may be compared to a wise man, who built his house upon the rock.

25 "And the rain descended, and the [1]floods came, and the winds blew, and burst against that house; and *yet* it did not fall, for it had been founded upon the rock.

26 "And everyone who hears these words of Mine, and does not [1]act upon them, will be like a foolish man, who built his house upon the sand.

27 "And the rain descended, and the [1]floods came, and the winds blew, and burst against that house; and it fell, and great was its fall."

28 [1a]The result was that when Jesus had finished these words, [b]the multitudes were amazed at His teaching;

29 for He was teaching them as *one* having authority, and not as their scribes.

28 [a]Matt. 6:25, 27, 31, 34; Luke 10:41; 12:11, 22; Phil. 4:6; 1 Pet. 5:7
29 [a]1 Kin. 10:4-7; 2 Chr. 9:4-6, 20-22
30 [a]James 1:10, 11; 1 Pet. 1:24 [b]Matt. 8:26; 14:31; 16:8
31 [a]Matt. 6:25, 27, 28, 34; Luke 10:41; 12:11, 22; Phil. 4:6; 1 Pet. 5:7
32 [a]Matt. 6:8; Phil. 4:19
33 [1]Or, *continually seek* [2]Or, *the kingdom* [3]Or, *provided* [a]Matt. 19:28; Mark 10:29f.; Luke 18:29f.; 1 Tim. 4:8
34 [1]Or, *will worry about itself* [a]Matt. 6:25, 27, 28, 31; Luke 10:41; 12:11, 22; Phil. 4:6; 1 Pet. 5:7
1 [a]Matt. 7:1-5: *Luke 6:37f., 41f.;* Rom. 14:10, 13
2 [1]Lit., *by what measure you measure* [a]Mark 4:24; Luke 6:38
3 [a]Rom. 2:1
4 [1]Lit., *will* [a]Luke 6:42
6 [a]Matt. 15:26
7 [1]Or, *Keep asking* [2]Or, *keep seeking* [3]Or, *keep knocking* [a]Matt. 7:7-11: *Luke 11:9-13* [b]Matt. 18:19; 21:22; Mark 11:24; John 14:13; 15:7, 16; 16:23f.; James 1:5f.; 1 John 3:22; 5:14f.
9 [1]Lit., *whom* [2]Lit., *he will not give him a stone, will he?*
10 [1]Lit., *also*
11 [a]Ps. 84:11; Is. 63:7; Rom. 8:32; James 1:17
12 [1]Or, *you, too, do so for* [a]Luke 6:31 [b]Matt. 22:40; Rom. 13:8ff.; Gal. 5:14
13 [a]Luke 13:24
15 [a]Matt. 24:11, 24; Mark 13:22; Luke 6:26; Acts 13:6; 2 Pet. 2:1; 1 John 4:1; Rev. 16:13; 19:20; 20:10 [b]Ezek. 22:27; John 10:12; Acts 20:29
16 [1]Or, *recognize* [2]Lit., *They do not gather* [a]Matt. 7:20; 12:33; Luke 6:44; James 3:12
17 [a]Matt. 12:33, 35
19 [a]Matt. 3:10; Luke 3:9; 13:7; John 15:2, 6
20 [1]Or, *recognize* [a]Matt. 7:16; 12:33; Luke 6:44; James 3:12
21 [a]Luke 6:46
22 [1]Or, *works of power* [a]Matt. 25:11f.; Luke 13:25ff. [b]Matt. 10:15
23 [a]Ps. 6:8; Matt. 25:41; Luke 13:27
24 [1]Lit., *does* [2]Lit., *will be compared to* [a]Matt. 7:24-27: *Luke 6:47-49;* Matt. 16:18; James 1:22-25
25 [1]Lit., *rivers*
26 [1]Lit., *do*
27 [1]Lit., *rivers*
28 [1]Lit., *And it came to pass* [a]Matt. 11:1; 13:53; 19:1; 26:1 [b]Matt. 13:54; 22:33; Mark 1:22; 6:2; 11:18; Luke 4:32; John 7:46

Jesus Cleanses a Leper
The Centurion's Faith

8 AND when He had come down from the mountain, great multitudes followed Him.

2 And behold, [a]a leper came to Him, and [1][b]bowed down to Him, saying, "Lord, if You are willing, You can make me clean."

3 And He stretched out His hand and touched him, saying, "I am willing; be cleansed." And immediately his [a]leprosy was cleansed.

4 And Jesus *said to him, "[a]See that you tell no one; but [b]go, [c]show yourself to the priest, and present the [1]offering that Moses commanded, for a testimony to them."

5 And [a]when He had entered Capernaum, a centurion came to Him, entreating Him,

6 and saying, "[1]Lord, my [2]servant is [3]lying [a]paralyzed at home, [4]suffering great pain."

7 And He *said to him, "I will come and heal him."

8 But the centurion answered and said, "[1]Lord, I am not worthy for You to come under my roof, but just [2]say the word, and my [3]servant will be healed.

9 "For I, too, am a man under [a]authority, with soldiers under me; and I say to this one, 'Go!' and he goes, and to another, 'Come!' and he comes, and to my slave, 'Do this!' and he does *it*."

10 Now when Jesus heard *this*, He marveled, and said to those who were following, "Truly I say to you, I have not found such great faith [1]with anyone in Israel.

11 "And I say to you, that many [a]shall come from east and west, and [1]recline *at the table* with Abraham, and Isaac, and Jacob, in the kingdom of heaven;

12 but [a]the sons of the kingdom shall be cast out into [b]the outer darkness; in that place [c]there shall be weeping and gnashing of teeth."

13 And Jesus said to the centurion, "Go your way; let it be done to you [a]as you have believed." And the [1]servant was healed that *very* hour.

Peter's Mother-in-law Healed
Many Healed

14 [a]And when Jesus had come to Peter's [1]home, He saw his mother-in-law lying sick in bed with a fever.

15 And He touched her hand, and the fever left her; and she arose, and [1]waited on Him.

16 And when evening had come, they brought to Him many [a]who were demon-possessed; and He cast out the spirits with a word, and [b]healed all who were ill

17 in order that what was spoken through Isaiah the prophet might be fulfilled, saying, "[a]HE HIMSELF TOOK OUR INFIRMITIES, AND [1]CARRIED AWAY OUR DISEASES."

Discipleship Tested

18 Now when Jesus saw a crowd around Him, [a]He gave orders to depart to the other side.

19 [a]And a certain scribe came and said to Him, "Teacher, I will follow You wherever You go."

20 And Jesus *said to him, "The foxes have holes, and the birds of the [1]air *have* [2]nests; but [a]the Son of Man has nowhere to lay His head."

21 And another of the disciples said to Him, "Lord, permit me first to go and bury my father."

22 But Jesus *said to him, "[a]Follow Me; and allow the dead to bury their own dead."

23 [a]And when He got into the boat, His disciples followed Him.

24 And behold, there arose [1]a great storm in the sea, so that the boat was covered with the waves; but He Himself was asleep.

25 And they came to *Him*, and awoke Him, saying, "[a]Save *us*, Lord; we are perishing!"

26 And He *said to them, "Why are you timid, [a]you men of little faith?" Then He arose, and rebuked the winds and the sea; and [1]it became perfectly calm.

27 And the men marveled, saying, "What kind of a man is this, that even the winds and the sea obey Him?"

Jesus Casts Out Demons

28 [a]And when He had come to the other side into the country of the Gadarenes, two men who were [b]demon-possessed met Him as they were coming out of the tombs; *they were* so exceedingly violent that no one could pass by that road.

29 And behold, they cried out, saying, "[a]What do we have to do with You, Son of God? Have You come here to torment us before [1]the time?"

30 Now there was at a distance from them a herd of many swine feeding.

31 And the demons *began* to entreat Him, saying, "If You are *going to* cast us out, send us into the herd of swine."

32 And He said to them, "Begone!" And they came out, and went into the swine, and behold, the whole herd rushed down the steep bank into the sea and perished in the waters.

2 [1]Or, *worshiped* [a]Matt. 8:2-4: *Mark 1:40-44; Luke 5:12-14* [b]Matt. 9:18; 15:25; 18:26; 20:20; John 9:38; Acts 10:25
3 [a]Matt. 11:5; Luke 4:27
4 [1]Or, *gift* [a]Matt. 9:30; 12:16; 17:9; Mark 1:44; 3:12; 5:43; 7:36; 8:30; 9:9; Luke 4:41; 8:56; 9:21 [b]Mark 1:44; Luke 5:14; 17:14 [c]Lev. 13:49; 14:2ff.
5 [a]Matt. 8:5-13: *Luke 7:1-10*
6 [1]Or, *Sir* [2]Lit., *boy* [3]Lit., *throwing* [4]Lit., *fearfully tormented* [a]Matt. 4:24
8 [1]Or, *Sir* [2]Lit., *say with a word* [3]Lit., *boy*
9 [a]Mark 1:27; Luke 9:1
10 [1]Some mss. read *not even in Israel*
11 [1]Or, *dine* [a]Is. 49:12; 59:19; Mal. 1:11; Luke 13:29
12 [a]Matt. 13:38 [b]Matt. 22:13; 25:30 [c]Matt. 13:42, 50; 22:13; 24:51; 25:30; Luke 13:28
13 [1]Lit., *boy* [a]Matt. 9:22, 29
14 [1]Or, *house* [a]Matt. 8:14-16: *Mark 1:29-34; Luke 4:38-41*
15 [1]Or, *served*
16 [a]Matt. 4:24 [b]Matt. 4:23; 8:33
17 [1]Or, *removed* [a]Is. 53:4
18 [a]Mark 4:35; Luke 8:22
19 [a]Matt. 8:19-22: *Luke 9:57-60*
20 [1]Or, *sky* [2]Or, *roosting places* [a]Dan. 7:13; Matt. 9:6; 12:8, 32, 40; 13:41; 16:13, 27f.; 17:9; 19:28; 26:64; Mark 8:38; Luke 12:8; 18:8; 21:36; John 1:51; 3:13f.; 6:27; 12:34; Acts 7:56
22 [a]Matt. 9:9; Mark 2:14; Luke 9:59, 60; John 1:43; 21:19
23 [a]Matt. 8:23-27: *Mark 4:36-41; Luke 8:22-25*
24 [1]Lit., *a shaking*
25 [a]Matt. 8:2; 9:18
26 [1]Lit., *a great calm occurred* [a]Matt. 6:30; 14:31; 16:8; 17:20
28 [a]Matt. 8:28-34: *Mark 5:1-17; Luke 8:26-37* [b]Matt. 4:24

29 [1]I.e., the appointed time of judgment [a]Judg. 11:12; 2 Sam. 16:10; 19:22; 1 Kin. 17:18; 2 Kin. 3:13; 2 Chr. 35:21; Mark 1:24; 5:7; Luke 4:34; 8:28; John 2:4

33 And the herdsmen ran away, and
went to the city, and reported everything, [1]including the *incident* of the
[a]demoniacs.
34 And behold, the whole city came
out to meet Jesus; and when they saw
Him, [a]they entreated *Him* to depart
from their region.

A Paralytic Cured

9 AND getting into a boat, He
crossed over, and came to [a]His own
city.
2 [a]And behold, they were bringing to
Him a [b]paralytic, lying on a bed; and
Jesus seeing their faith said to the paralytic, "[c]Take courage, My [1]son, [d]your
sins [2]are forgiven."
3 And behold, some of the scribes
said [1]to themselves, "This *fellow* [a]blas-
phemes."
4 And Jesus [a]knowing their thoughts
said, "Why are you thinking evil in your
hearts?
5 "For which is easier, to say, '[a]Your
sins [1]are forgiven,' or to say, 'Rise, and
walk'?
6 "But in order that you may know
that [a]the Son of Man has authority on
earth to forgive sins"—then He *said to
the [b]paralytic—"Rise, take up your bed,
and go home."
7 And he rose, and [1]went home.
8 But when the multitudes saw *this,*
they were [1]filled with awe, and [a]glorified
God, who had given such authority to
men.

Matthew Called

9 [a]And as Jesus passed on from
there, He saw a man, called [b]Matthew,
sitting [1]in the tax office; and He *said to
him, "[c]Follow Me!" And he rose, and
followed Him.
10 And it happened that as He was
reclining *at the table* in the house, behold
many [1]tax-gatherers and [2]sinners came
and [3]were dining with Jesus and His
disciples.
11 And when the Pharisees saw *this,*
they said to His disciples, "[a]Why is your
Teacher eating with the tax-gatherers
and sinners?"
12 But when He heard this, He said,
"*It is* not [a]those who are healthy who
need a physician, but those who are sick.
13 "But go and learn [a]what *this* means,
'[b]I DESIRE [1]COMPASSION, [2]AND NOT SAC-
RIFICE,' for [c]I did not come to call the
righteous, but sinners."
14 Then the disciples of John *came
to Him, saying, "Why do we and [a]the
Pharisees fast, but Your disciples do not
fast?"
15 And Jesus said to them, "The [1]at-
tendants of the bridegroom cannot
mourn as long as the bridegroom is with
them, can they? But the days will come
when the bridegroom is taken away from
them, and then they will fast.
16 "But no one puts [1]a patch of unshrunk cloth on an old garment; for [2]the
patch pulls away from the garment, and
a worse tear results.
17 "Nor do *men* put new wine into old
[1]wineskins; otherwise the wineskins
burst, and the wine pours out, and the
wineskins are ruined; but they put new
wine into fresh wineskins, and both are
preserved."

Miracles of Healing

18 [a]While He was saying these things
to them, behold, there came [1]a *synagogue* [2]official, and [3b]bowed down before Him, saying, "My daughter has just
died; but come and lay Your hand on
her, and she will live."
19 And Jesus rose and *began* to follow
him, and *so did* His disciples.
20 And behold, a woman who had
been suffering from a hemorrhage for
twelve years, came up behind Him and
touched [a]the fringe of His [1]cloak;
21 for she was saying [1]to herself, "If I
only [a]touch His garment, I shall [2]get
well."
22 But Jesus turning and seeing her
said, "Daughter, [a]take courage; [b]your
faith has [1]made you well." And [2]at once
the woman was [1]made well.
23 And when Jesus came into the
[1]official's house, and saw [a]the flute-
players, and the crowd in noisy disorder,
24 He *began* to say, "Depart; for the
girl [a]has not died, but is asleep." And
they *began* laughing at Him.
25 But [a]when the crowd had been put
out, He entered and [b]took her by the
hand; and the girl [1]arose.
26 And [a]this news went out into all
that land.
27 And as Jesus passed on from there,
two blind men followed Him, crying out,
and saying, "Have mercy on us, [a]Son of
David!"
28 And after He had come into the
house, the blind men came up to Him,
and Jesus *said to them, "Do you believe that I am able to do this?" They
*said to Him, "Yes, Lord."
29 Then He touched their eyes, saying,
"Be it done to you [a]according to your
faith."
30 And their eyes were opened. And
Jesus [a]sternly warned them, saying, "See
here, let no one know *about this!*"
31 But they went out, and [a]spread the
news about Him in all that land.
32 And as they were going out, behold, [a]a dumb man, [b]demon-possessed,
[1]was brought to Him.

33 [1]Lit., *and* [a]Matt. 4:24
34 [a]Amos 7:12; Acts 16:39

1 [a]Matt. 4:13; Mark 5:21
2 [1]Lit., *child* [2]Lit., *are being forgiven* [a]Matt. 9:2-8: *Mark 2:3-12; Luke 5:18-26* [b]Matt. 4:24; 9:6 [c]Matt. 9:22; 14:27; Mark 6:50; 10:49; John 16:33; Acts 23:11 [d]Mark 2:5, 9; Luke 5:20, 23; 7:48
3 [1]Lit., *among* [a]Mark 3:28, 29
4 [a]Matt. 12:25; Luke 6:8; 9:47
5 [1]Lit., *are being forgiven* [a]Matt. 9:2, 6; Mark 2:5, 9; Luke 5:20, 23; 7:48
6 [a]Matt. 8:20; John 5:27 [b]Matt. 4:24; 9:2
7 [1]Or, *departed*
8 [1]Or, *afraid* [a]Matt. 5:16; 15:31; Mark 2:12; Luke 2:20; 5:25, 26; 7:16; 13:13; 17:15; 23:47; John 15:8; Acts 4:21; 11:18; 21:20; 2 Cor. 9:13; Gal. 1:24
9 [1]Lit., *at the tax booth* [a]Matt. 9:9-17: *Mark 2:14-22; Luke 5:27-38* [b]Matt. 10:3; Mark 2:14; 3:18; Luke 6:15; Acts 1:13 [c]Matt. 8:22
10 [1]I.e., Collectors of Roman taxes for profit [2]I.e., irreligious Jews [3]Lit., *reclined with*
11 [a]Matt. 11:19; Mark 2:16; Luke 5:30; 15:2
12 [a]Mark 2:17; Luke 5:31
13 [1]Or, *mercy* [2]I.e., more than [a]Matt. 12:7 [b]Hos. 6:6 [c]Mark 2:17; Luke 5:32; 1 Tim. 1:15
14 [a]Luke 18:12
15 [1]Lit., *sons of the bridal-chamber*
16 [1]Lit., *that which is put on* [2]Lit., *that which fills up*
17 [1]I.e., skins used as bottles
18 [1]Or, *one* [2]Lit., *ruler* [3]Or, *worshiped* [a]Matt. 9:18-26: *Mark 5:22-43; Luke 8:41-56* [b]Matt. 8:2
20 [1]Or, *outer garment* [a]Num. 15:38; Deut. 22:12; Matt. 14:36; 23:5
21 [1]Lit., *in herself* [2]Lit., *be saved* [a]Matt. 14:36; Mark 3:10; Luke 6:19
22 [1]Lit., *saved you* [2]Lit., *from that hour* [a]Matt. 9:2 [b]Matt. 9:29; 15:28; Mark 5:34; 10:52; Luke 7:50; 8:48; 17:19; 18:42
23 [1]Lit., *ruler's* [a]2 Chr. 35:25; Jer. 9:17; 16:6; Ezek. 24:17
24 [a]John 11:13; Acts 20:10
25 [1]Or, *was raised up* [a]Acts 9:40 [b]Mark 9:27
26 [a]Matt. 4:24; 9:31; 14:1; Mark 1:28, 45; Luke 4:14, 37; 5:15; 7:17
27 [a]Matt. 1:1; 12:23; 15:22; 20:30, 31; 21:9, 15; 22:42; Mark 10:47, 48; 12:35; Luke 18:38, 39; 20:41f.
29 [a]Matt. 8:13; 9:22
30 [a]Matt. 8:4
31 [a]Matt. 4:24; 9:26; 14:1; Mark 1:28, 45; Luke 4:14, 37; 5:15; 7:17
32 [1]Lit., *they brought* [a]Matt. 12:22, 24 [b]Matt. 4:24

33 And after the demon was cast out,
the dumb man spoke; and the multitudes marveled, saying, "[a]Nothing like
this [1]was ever seen in Israel."
34 But the Pharisees were saying, "He
[a]casts out the demons by the ruler of the
demons."
35 And Jesus was going about all the
cities and the villages, [a]teaching in their
synagogues, and proclaiming the gospel
of the kingdom, and healing every kind
of disease and every kind of sickness.
36 And [a]seeing the multitudes, He felt
compassion for them, [b]because they
were [1]distressed and [2]downcast like
sheep [3]without a shepherd.
37 Then He *said to His disciples,
"[a]The harvest is plentiful, but the workers are few.
38 "Therefore beseech the Lord of the
harvest to send out workers into His
harvest."

The Twelve Disciples
Instructions for Service

10 AND [a]having summoned His
twelve disciples, He gave them
authority over unclean spirits, to cast
them out, and to [b]heal every kind of
disease and every kind of sickness.
2 [a]Now the names of the twelve
apostles are these: The first, [b]Simon,
who is called Peter, and [c]Andrew his
brother; and [1d]James the *son* of Zebedee, and [2]John his brother;
3 [a]Philip and [1]Bartholomew;
[b]Thomas and [c]Matthew the tax-
gatherer; [2d]James the *son* of Alphaeus,
and [e]Thaddaeus;
4 Simon the [1]Zealot, and [a]Judas
Iscariot, the one who betrayed Him.
5 [a]These twelve Jesus sent out after
instructing them, saying, "Do not [1]go in
the way of *the* Gentiles, and do not enter
any city of the [b]Samaritans;
6 but rather [1]go to [a]the lost sheep of
the house of Israel.
7 "And as you [1]go, [2]preach, saying,
'[a]The kingdom of heaven [3]is at hand.'
8 "Heal *the* sick, raise *the* dead,
cleanse *the* lepers, cast out demons;
freely you received, freely give.
9 "[a]Do not acquire gold, or silver, or
copper [1]for your money belts,
10 or a [1]bag for *your* journey, or even
two [2]tunics, or sandals, or a staff; for
[a]the worker is worthy of his [3]support.
11 "And into whatever city or village
you enter, inquire who is worthy in it;
and abide there until you go away.
12 "And as you enter the [1]house, [a]give
it your greeting.
13 "And if the house is worthy, let your
greeting of peace come upon it; but if it
is not worthy, let your *greeting of* peace
return to you.
14 "And whoever does not receive you,
nor heed your words, as you go out of
that house or that city, [a]shake off the
dust of your feet.

33 [1]Lit., *ever appeared* [a]Mark 2:12
34 [a]Matt. 12:24; Mark 3:22; Luke 11:15; John 7:20f.
35 [a]Matt. 4:23; Mark 1:14
36 [1]Or, *harassed* [2]Lit., *thrown down* [3]Lit., *not having* [a]Matt. 14:14; 15:32; Mark 6:34; 8:2 [b]Num. 27:17; Ezek. 34:5; Zech. 10:2; Mark 6:34
37 [a]Luke 10:2

1 [a]Mark 3:13-15; 6:7 [b]Matt. 9:35; Luke 9:1
2 [1]Or, *Jacob* [2]Gr., *Joannes,* Heb., *Johanan* [a]Matt. 10:2-4: *Mark 3:16-19; Luke 6:14-16; Acts 1:13* [b]Matt. 4:18 [c]Matt. 4:18 [d]Matt. 4:21
3 [1]I.e., son of Talmai (Aram.) [2]Or, *Jacob* [a]John 1:43ff. [b]John 11:16; 14:5; 20:24ff.; 21:2 [c]Matt. 9:9 [d]Mark 15:40 [e]Mark 3:18; Luke 6:16; Acts 1:13
4 [1]Or, *Cananaean* [a]Matt. 26:14; Luke 22:3; John 6:71; 13:2, 26
5 [1]Or, *go off to* [a]Mark 6:7; Luke 9:2 [b]2 Kin. 17:24ff.; Luke 9:52; 10:33; 17:16; John 4:9, 39f.; 8:48; Acts 8:25
6 [1]Or, *proceed* [a]Matt. 15:24
7 [1]Or, *proceed* [2]Or, *proclaim* [3]Lit., *has come near* [a]Matt. 3:2
9 [1]Lit., *into* [a]Matt. 10:9-15: *Mark 6:8-11; Luke 9:3-5; 10:4-12;* Luke 22:35
10 [1]Or, *knapsack or beggar's bag* [2]Or, *inner garments* [3]Lit., *nourishment* [a]1 Cor. 9:14; 1 Tim. 5:18
12 [1]Or, *household* [a]1 Sam. 25:6; Ps. 122:7, 8
14 [a]Acts 13:51
15 [a]Matt. 11:22, 24 [b]Matt. 11:24; 2 Pet. 2:6; Jude 7 [c]Matt. 7:22; 11:22, 24; 12:36; Acts 17:31; 1 Thess. 5:4; Heb. 10:25; 2 Pet. 2:9; 3:7; 1 John 4:17; Jude 6
16 [1]Or, *show yourselves to be* [a]Luke 10:3 [b]Gen. 3:1; Matt. 24:25; Rom. 16:19 [c]Hos. 7:11
17 [a]Matt. 5:22 [b]Matt. 23:34; Mark 13:9; Luke 12:11; Acts 5:40; 22:19; 26:11
19 [a]Matt. 10:19-22: *Mark 13:11-13; Luke 21:12-17* [b]Matt. 6:25; Luke 12:11, 12
20 [a]Luke 12:12; Acts 4:8; 13:9; 2 Cor. 13:3

15 "Truly I say to you, [a]it will be more
tolerable for *the* land of [b]Sodom and
Gomorrah in [c]the day of judgment, than
for that city.

A Hard Road before Them

16 "[a]Behold, I send you out as sheep in
the midst of wolves; therefore [1]be
[b]shrewd as serpents, and [c]innocent as
doves.
17 "But beware of men; for they will
deliver you up to *the* [a]courts, and
scourge you [b]in their synagogues;
18 and you shall even be brought
before governors and kings for My sake,
as a testimony to them and to the Gentiles.
19 "[a]But when they deliver you up, [b]do
not become anxious about how or what
you will speak; for it shall be given you
in that hour what you are to speak.
20 "For [a]it is not you who speak, but *it*
is the Spirit of your Father who speaks
in you.
21 "[a]And brother will deliver up
brother to death, and a father *his* child;
and [b]children will rise up against parents, and [1]cause them to be put to death.
22 "And [a]you will be hated by all on
account of My name, but [b]it is the one
who has endured to the end who will be
saved.
23 "But whenever they [a]persecute you
in this city, flee to [1]the next; for truly I
say to you, you shall not finish *going*
through the cities of Israel, [b]until the Son
of Man comes.

The Meaning of Discipleship

24 "[a]A [1]disciple is not above his
teacher, nor a slave above his master.
25 "It is enough for the disciple that he
become as his teacher, and the slave as
his master. [a]If they have called the head
of the house [1b]Beelzebul, how much
more the members of his household!
26 "Therefore do not [a]fear them, [b]for
there is nothing covered that will not be
revealed, and hidden that will not be
known.
27 "[a]What I tell you in the darkness,
speak in the light; and what you hear
whispered in *your* ear, proclaim [b]upon
the housetops.
28 "And do not fear those who kill the
body, but are unable to kill the soul; but
rather [a]fear Him who is able to destroy
both soul and body in [1b]hell.
29 "[a]Are not two sparrows sold for a
[1]cent? And *yet* not one of them will fall
to the ground apart from your Father.

21 [1]Or, *put them to death* [a]Matt. 10:35, 36; Mark 13:12 [b]Mic. 7:6
22 [a]Matt. 24:9; Luke 21:17; John 15:18ff. [b]Matt. 24:13; Mark 13:13
23 [1]Lit., *the other* [a]Matt. 23:34 [b]Matt. 16:27f.
24 [1]Or, *pupil* [a]Luke 6:40; John 13:16; 15:20
25 [1]Or, *Beezebul;* others read *Beelzebub* [a]Matt. 9:34 [b]2 Kin. 1:2; Matt. 12:24, 27; Mark 3:22; Luke 11:15, 18, 19
26 [a]Matt. 10:26-33: *Luke 12:2-9* [b]Mark 4:22; Luke 8:17; 12:2; 1 Cor. 4:5
27 [a]Luke 12:3 [b]Matt. 24:17; Acts 5:20
28 [1]Gr., *Gehenna* [a]Heb. 10:31 [b]Matt. 5:22; Luke 12:5
29 [1]Gr., *assarion,* the smallest copper coin [a]Luke 12:6

30 "But [a]the very hairs of your head are all numbered.

31 "Therefore do not fear; [a]you are of more value than many sparrows.

32 "[a]Everyone therefore who shall confess [1]Me before men, I will also confess [2]him before My Father who is in heaven.

33 "But [a]whoever shall deny Me before men, I will also deny him before My Father who is in heaven.

34 "[a]Do not think that I came to [1]bring peace on the earth; I did not come to bring peace, but a sword.

35 "For I came to [a]SET A MAN AGAINST HIS FATHER, AND A DAUGHTER AGAINST HER MOTHER, AND A DAUGHTER-IN-LAW AGAINST HER MOTHER-IN-LAW;

36 and [a]A MAN'S ENEMIES WILL BE THE MEMBERS OF HIS HOUSEHOLD.

37 "[a]He who loves father or mother more than Me is not worthy of Me; and he who loves son or daughter more than Me is not worthy of Me.

38 "And [a]he who does not take his cross and follow after Me is not worthy of Me.

39 "[a]He who has found his [1]life shall lose it, and he who has lost his [1]life for My sake shall find it.

40 "[a]He who receives you receives Me, and [b]he who receives Me receives Him who sent Me.

41 "[a]He who receives a prophet in *the* name of a prophet shall receive a prophet's reward; and he who receives a righteous man in the name of a righteous man shall receive a righteous man's reward.

42 "And [a]whoever in the name of a disciple gives to one of these [1]little ones even a cup of cold water to drink, truly I say to you he shall not lose his reward."

John's Questions

11 [a]AND it came about that when Jesus had finished [1]giving instructions to His twelve disciples, He departed from there [b]to teach and [2]preach in their cities.

2 [a]Now when [b]John in prison heard of the works of Christ, he sent *word* by his disciples,

3 and said to Him, "Are You [a]the [1]Expected One, or shall we look for someone else?"

4 And Jesus answered and said to them, "Go and report to John what you hear and see:

5 [a]*the* BLIND RECEIVE SIGHT and *the* lame walk, *the* lepers are cleansed and *the* deaf hear, and *the* dead are raised up, and *the* [b]POOR HAVE THE [1]GOSPEL PREACHED TO THEM.

6 "And blessed is he [1]who [a]keeps from [2]stumbling over Me."

Jesus' Tribute to John

7 And as these were going *away,* Jesus began to speak to the multitudes about John, "What did you go out into [a]the wilderness to look at? A reed shaken by the wind?

8 "[1]But what did you go out to see? A man dressed in soft *clothing*? Behold, those who wear soft *clothing* are in kings' [2]palaces.

9 "[1]But why did you go out? To see [a]a prophet? Yes, I say to you, and one who is more than a prophet.

10 "This is the one about whom it [1]is written,

'[a]BEHOLD, I SEND MY MESSENGER BEFORE YOUR FACE,
WHO WILL PREPARE YOUR WAY BEFORE YOU.'

11 "Truly, I say to you, among those born of women there has not arisen *anyone* greater than John the Baptist; yet he who is [1]least in the kingdom of heaven is greater than he.

12 "And [a]from the days of John the Baptist until now the kingdom of heaven [1]suffers violence, and violent men [2]take it by force.

13 "For all the prophets and the Law prophesied until John.

14 "And if you care to accept *it,* he himself is [a]Elijah, who [1]was to come.

15 "[a]He who has ears to hear, let him hear.

16 "But to what shall I compare this generation? It is like children sitting in the market places, who call out to the other *children,*

17 and say, 'We played the flute for you, and you did not dance; we sang a dirge, and you did not [1]mourn.'

18 "For John came neither [a]eating nor [b]drinking, and they say, '[c]He has a demon!'

19 "The Son of Man came eating and drinking, and they say, 'Behold, a gluttonous man and a [1]drunkard, [a]a friend of [2]tax-gatherers and sinners!' [3]Yet wisdom is vindicated by her deeds."

The Unrepenting Cities

20 Then He began to reproach the cities in which most of His [1a]miracles were done, because they did not repent.

21 "[a]Woe to you, Chorazin! Woe to you, [b]Bethsaida! For if the [1]miracles had occurred in [c]Tyre and [c]Sidon which occurred in you, they would have repented long ago in [d]sackcloth and ashes.

22 "Nevertheless I say to you, [a]it shall be more tolerable for Tyre and Sidon in [b]*the* day of judgment, than for you.

23 "And you, [a]Capernaum, will not be exalted to heaven, will you? You shall [1b]descend to [c]Hades; for if the [2]miracles had occurred in [d]Sodom which occurred

30 [a]1 Sam. 14:45; 2 Sam. 14:11; 1 Kin. 1:52; Luke 21:18; Acts 27:34
31 [a]Matt. 12:12
32 [1]Lit., *in Me* [2]Lit., *in him* [a]Luke 12:8; Rev. 3:5
33 [a]Mark 8:38; Luke 9:26; 2 Tim. 2:12
34 [1]Lit., *cast* [a]Matt. 10:34, 35: *Luke 12:51-53*
35 [a]Mic. 7:6; Matt. 10:21; Luke 12:53
36 [a]Mic. 7:6; Matt. 10:21
37 [a]Deut. 33:9; Luke 14:26
38 [a]Matt. 16:24; Mark 8:34; Luke 9:23; 14:27
39 [1]Or, *soul* [a]Matt. 16:25; Mark 8:35; Luke 9:24; 17:33; John 12:25
40 [a]Matt. 18:5; Luke 10:16; John 13:20; Gal. 4:14 [b]Mark 9:37; Luke 9:48; John 12:44
41 [a]Matt. 25:44, 45
42 [1]I.e., humble [a]Matt. 25:40; Mark 9:41

1 [1]Or, *commanding* [2]Or, *proclaim* [a]Matt. 7:28 [b]Matt. 9:35; Luke 23:5
2 [a]Matt. 11:2-19: *Luke 7:18-35;* Matt. 4:12 [b]Matt. 14:3; Mark 6:17; Luke 9:7ff.
3 [1]Lit., *Coming One* [a]Ps. 118:26; Matt. 11:10; John 6:14; 11:27; Heb. 10:37
5 [1]Or, *good news* [a]Is. 35:5f.; Matt. 8:3; 12:13 [b]Is. 61:1; Luke 4:18
6 [1]Lit., *whoever* [2]Or, *taking offense at* [a]Matt. 5:29; 13:57; 24:10; 26:31; Mark 6:3; John 6:61; 16:1
7 [a]Matt. 3:1
8 [1]Or, *Well then,* [2]Lit., *houses*
9 [1]Or, *Well then,* [a]Matt. 14:5; 21:26; Luke 1:76; 20:6
10 [1]Lit., *has been written* [a]Mal. 3:1; Mark 1:2
11 [1]Lit., *less*
12 [1]Or, *is forcibly entered* [2]Or, *seize it for themselves* [a]Luke 16:16
14 [1]Or, *is to come* [a]Mal. 4:5; Matt. 17:10-13; Mark 9:11-13; Luke 1:17; John 1:21
15 [a]Matt. 13:9, 43; Mark 4:9, 23; Luke 8:8; 14:35; Rev. 2:7, 11, 17, 29; 3:6, 13, 22; 13:9
17 [1]Lit., *beat the breast*
18 [a]Matt. 3:4 [b]Luke 1:15 [c]Matt. 9:34; John 7:20; 8:48f., 52; 10:20
19 [1]Or, *winedrinker* [2]I.e., Collectors of Roman taxes for profit [3]Lit., *And* [a]Matt. 9:11; Luke 5:29-32; 15:2

20 [1]Or, *works of power* [a]Luke 10:13-15
21 [1]Or, *works of power* [a]Matt. 11:21-23: *Luke 10:13-15* [b]Mark 6:45; 8:22; Luke 9:10; John 1:44; 12:21 [c]Matt. 11:22; 15:21; Mark 3:8; 7:24, 31; Luke 4:26; 6:17; Acts 12:20; 27:3 [d]Rev. 11:3
22 [a]Matt. 10:15; 11:24 [b]Matt. 10:15; 12:36; Rev. 20:11, 12
23 [1]Some mss. read *be brought down* [2]Or, *works of power* [a]Matt. 4:13 [b]Is. 14:13, 15; Ezek. 26:20; 31:14; 32:18, 24 [c]Matt. 16:18; Luke 10:15; 16:23; Acts 2:27, 31; Rev. 1:18; 6:8; 20:13f. [d]Matt. 10:15

in you, it would have remained to this
day."
24 "Nevertheless I say to you that [a]it
shall be more tolerable for the land of
[b]Sodom in *the* day of judgment, than for
you."

Come to Me

25 [a]At that [1]time Jesus answered and
said, "I [2]praise Thee, O [b]Father, Lord of
heaven and earth, that [c]Thou didst hide
these things from *the* wise and intelligent
and didst reveal them to babes.
26 "Yes, [a]Father, for thus it was well-
pleasing in Thy sight.
27 "[a]All things [1]have been handed over
to Me by My Father; and no one [2]knows
the Son, except the Father; nor does
anyone [2]know the Father, [b]except the
Son, and anyone to whom the Son wills
to reveal *Him.*
28 "[a]Come to Me, all [1]who are weary
and heavy-laden, and I will give you rest.
29 "Take My yoke upon you, and
[a]learn from Me, for I am gentle and
humble in heart; and [b]YOU SHALL FIND
REST FOR YOUR SOULS.
30 "For [a]My yoke is [1]easy, and My
load is light."

Sabbath Questions

12 [a]AT that [1]time Jesus went on the
Sabbath through the grainfields,
and His disciples became hungry and
began to [b]pick the heads *of grain* and
eat.
2 But when the Pharisees saw it, they
said to Him, "Behold, Your disciples do
what [a]is not lawful to do on a Sabbath."
3 But He said to them, "Have you
not read what David did, when he became hungry, he and his companions;
4 how he entered the house of God,
and [a]they ate the [1]consecrated bread,
which was not lawful for him to eat, nor
for those with him, but for the priests
alone?
5 "Or have you not read in the Law,
that on the Sabbath the priests in the
temple [1]break the Sabbath, and are
innocent?
6 "But I say to you, that something
[a]greater than the temple is here.
7 "But if you had known what this
[1]means, '[a]I DESIRE [2]COMPASSION, AND
NOT A SACRIFICE,' you would not have
condemned the innocent.

Lord of the Sabbath

8 "For [a]the Son of Man is Lord of the
Sabbath."
9 [a]And departing from there, He
went into their synagogue.
10 And behold, *there was* a man with a
withered hand. And they questioned
Him, saying, "[a]Is it lawful to heal on the
Sabbath?"—in order that they might
accuse Him.
11 And He said to them, "[a]What man
shall there be [1]among you, who shall
have one sheep, and if it falls into a pit

24 [a]Matt. 10:15; 11:22 [b]Matt. 10:15
25 [1]Or, *occasion* [2]Or, *acknowledge to Thy praise* [a]Matt. 11:25-27: *Luke 10:21, 22* [b]Luke 22:42; 23:34; John 11:41; 12:27, 28 [c]Ps. 8:2; 1 Cor. 1:26ff.
26 [a]Luke 22:42; 23:34; John 11:41; 12:27, 28
27 [1]Lit., *were given over* [2]Or, *perfectly know(s)* [a]Matt. 28:18; John 3:35; 13:3; 17:2 [b]John 7:29; 10:15; 17:25
28 [1]Or, *who work to exhaustion* [a]Jer. 31:25; John 7:37
29 [a]John 13:15; Eph. 4:20; Phil. 2:5; 1 Pet. 2:21; 1 John 2:6 [b]Jer. 6:16
30 [1]Or, *kindly* or *pleasant* [a]1 John 5:3

1 [1]Or, *occasion* [a]Matt. 12:1-8: *Mark 2:23-28; Luke 6:1-5* [b]Deut. 23:25
2 [a]Matt. 12:10; Luke 13:14; 14:3; John 5:10; 7:23; 9:16
4 [1]Or, *showbread;* lit., *loaves of presentation* [a]1 Sam. 21:6
5 [1]Or, *profane*
6 [a]2 Chr. 6:18; Is. 66:1, 2; Matt. 12:41, 42
7 [1]Lit., *is* [2]Or, *mercy* [a]Hos. 6:6; Matt. 9:13
8 [a]Matt. 8:20; 12:32, 40
9 [a]Matt. 12:9-14: *Mark 3:1-6; Luke 6:6-11*
10 [a]Matt. 12:2; Luke 13:14; 14:3; John 5:10; 7:23; 9:16
11 [1]Lit., *of* [a]Luke 14:5
12 [1]Lit., *well* [a]Matt. 10:31; Luke 14:1-6
13 [1]Lit., *health* [a]Matt. 8:3; Acts 28:8
14 [a]Matt. 26:4; Mark 14:1; Luke 22:2; John 7:30, 44; 8:59; 10:31, 39; 11:53
15 [1]Lit., *knowing* [a]Matt. 4:23
16 [1]Or, *reveal who He was* [a]Matt. 8:4; 9:30; 17:9
18 [1]Lit., *Child* [2]Lit., *chose* [3]Or, *took pleasure* [4]Or, *judgment* [5]Or, *nations* [a]Is. 42:1 [b]Matt. 3:17; 17:5 [c]Luke 4:18; John 3:34
19 [a]Is. 42:2
20 [1]Or, *puts forth* [2]Or, *judgment* [a]Is. 42:3
21 [1]Or, *nations* [a]Rom. 15:12

on the Sabbath, will he not take hold of
it, and lift it out?
12 "Of [a]how much more value then is a
man than a sheep! So then, it is lawful to
do [1]good on the Sabbath."
13 Then He *said to the man, "Stretch
out your hand!" And [a]he stretched it
out, and it was restored to [1]normal, like
the other.
14 But the Pharisees went out, and
[a]counseled together against Him, *as to*
how they might destroy Him.
15 But Jesus, [1]aware of *this,* withdrew
from there. And many followed Him,
and [a]He healed them all,
16 and [a]warned them not to [1]make
Him known,
17 in order that what was spoken
through Isaiah the prophet, might be
fulfilled, saying,
18 "[a]BEHOLD, MY [1]SERVANT WHOM I
[2]HAVE CHOSEN;
[b]MY BELOVED IN WHOM MY SOUL
[3]IS WELL-PLEASED;
[c]I WILL PUT MY SPIRIT UPON
HIM,
[a]AND HE SHALL PROCLAIM [4]JUS-
TICE TO THE [5]GENTILES.
19 "[a]HE WILL NOT QUARREL, NOR CRY
OUT;
NOR WILL ANYONE HEAR HIS
VOICE IN THE STREETS.
20 "[a]A BATTERED REED HE WILL NOT
BREAK OFF,
AND A SMOLDERING WICK HE
WILL NOT PUT OUT,
UNTIL HE [1]LEADS [2]JUSTICE TO
VICTORY.
21 "[a]AND IN HIS NAME THE [1]GEN-
TILES WILL HOPE."

The Pharisees Rebuked

22 [a]Then there was brought to Him a
[b]demon-possessed man *who was* blind
and dumb, and He healed him, so that
the dumb man spoke and saw.
23 And all the multitudes were
amazed, and *began* to say, "This *man*
cannot be the [a]Son of David, can he?"
24 But when the Pharisees heard it,
they said, "This man [a]casts out demons
only by [1]Beelzebul the ruler of the
demons."
25 [a]And [b]knowing their thoughts He
said to them, "[1]Any kingdom divided
against itself is laid waste; and [1]any city
or house divided against itself shall not
stand.
26 "And if [a]Satan casts out Satan, he
[1]is divided against himself; how then
shall his kingdom stand?
27 "And if I [a]by [1]Beelzebul cast out
demons, [b]by whom do your sons cast
them out? Consequently they shall be
your judges.

22 [a]Matt. 12:22, 24: *Luke 11:14, 15;* Matt. 9:32, 34 [b]Matt. 4:24; 2 Thess. 2:9
23 [a]Matt. 9:27
24 [1]Or, *Beezebul;* others read *Beelzebub* [a]Matt. 9:34
25 [1]Lit., *Every* [a]Matt. 12:25-29: *Mark 3:23-27; Luke 11:17-22* [b]Matt. 9:4
26 [1]Lit., *was* [a]Matt. 4:10; 13:19
27 [1]V. 24, note 1 [a]Matt. 9:34 [b]Acts 19:13

28"But [a]if I cast out demons by the Spirit of God, then the kingdom of God has come upon you.

29"Or how can anyone enter the strong man's house and carry off his property, unless he first binds the strong *man*? And then he will plunder his house.

The Unpardonable Sin

30"[a]He who is not with Me is against Me; and he who does not gather with Me scatters.

31"[a]Therefore I say to you, any sin and blasphemy shall be forgiven men, but blasphemy against the Spirit shall not be forgiven.

32"[a]And whoever shall speak a word against the Son of Man, it shall be forgiven him; but whoever shall speak against the Holy Spirit, it shall not be forgiven him, either in [b]this age, or in the *age* to come.

Words Reveal Character

33"Either make the tree good, and its fruit good; or make the tree bad, and its fruit bad; for [a]the tree is known by its fruit.

34"[a]You brood of vipers, how can you, being evil, speak [1]what is good? [b]For the mouth speaks out of that which fills the heart.

35"[a]The good man out of *his* good treasure brings forth [1]what is good; and the evil man out of *his* evil treasure brings forth [2]what is evil.

36"And I say to you, that every [1]careless word that men shall speak, they shall render account for it in [a]the day of judgment.

37"For [1]by your words you shall be justified, and [1]by your words you shall be condemned."

The Desire for Signs

38 Then some of the scribes and Pharisees answered Him, saying, "Teacher, [a]we want to see a [1]sign from You."

39 But He answered and said to them, "[a]An evil and adulterous generation craves for a [1]sign; and *yet* no [1]sign shall be given to it but the [1]sign of Jonah the prophet;

40 for just as [a]JONAH WAS THREE DAYS AND THREE NIGHTS IN THE BELLY OF THE SEA MONSTER, so shall [b]the Son of Man be [c]three days and three nights in the heart of the earth.

41"[a]The men of Nineveh shall stand up with this generation at the judgment, and shall condemn it because [b]they repented at the preaching of Jonah; and behold, [c]something greater than Jonah is here.

42"[a]*The* Queen of *the* South shall rise up with this generation at the judgment and shall condemn it, because she came from the ends of the earth to hear the wisdom of Solomon; and behold, [b]something greater than Solomon is here.

43"[a]Now when the unclean spirit goes out of a man, it passes through waterless places, seeking rest, and does not find *it*.

44"Then it says, 'I will return to my house from which I came'; and when it comes, it finds it unoccupied, swept, and put in order.

45"Then it goes, and takes along with it seven other spirits more wicked than itself, and they go in and live there; and [a]the last state of that man becomes worse than the first. That is the way it will also be with this evil generation."

Changed Relationships

46 [a]While He was still speaking to the multitudes, behold, His [b]mother and [c]brothers were standing outside, seeking to speak to Him.

47 And someone said to Him, "Behold, Your mother and Your brothers are standing outside seeking to speak to You."

48 But He answered the one who was telling Him and said, "Who is My mother and who are My brothers?"

49 And stretching out His hand toward His disciples, He said, "Behold, My mother and My brothers!

50"For whoever does the will of My Father who is in heaven, he is My brother and sister and mother."

Jesus Teaches in Parables

13 ON that day Jesus went out of [a]the house, and was sitting [b]by the sea.

2 And great multitudes gathered to Him, so that [a]He got into a boat and sat down, and the whole multitude was standing on the beach.

3 And He spoke many things to them in [a]parables, saying, "Behold, the sower went out to sow;

4 and as he sowed, some *seeds* fell beside the road, and the birds came and ate them up.

5"And others fell upon the rocky places, where they [1]did not have much soil; and immediately they sprang up, because they had no depth of soil.

6"But when the sun had risen, they were scorched; and because they had no root, they withered away.

7"And others fell [1]among the thorns, and the thorns came up and choked them out.

8"And others fell on the good soil, and *yielded a crop, some a [a]hundredfold, some sixty, and some thirty.

9"[a]He who has ears, let him hear."

An Explanation

10 And the disciples came and said to Him, "Why do You speak to them in parables?"

11 And He answered and said to them, "[a]To you it has been granted to

---

28 [a]1 John 3:8
30 [a]Mark 9:40; Luke 9:50; 11:23
31 [a]Matt. 12:31, 32; Mark 3:28-30; Luke 12:10
32 [a]Luke 12:10 [b]Matt. 13:22, 39; Mark 10:30; Luke 16:8; 18:30; 20:34, 35; Eph. 1:21; 1 Tim. 6:17; 2 Tim. 4:10; Titus 2:12; Heb. 6:5
33 [a]Matt. 7:16-18; Luke 6:43, 44; John 15:4-7
34 [1]Lit., *good things* [a]Matt. 3:7; 23:33; Luke 3:7 [b]1 Sam. 24:13; Is. 32:6; Matt. 12:34, 35; 15:18; Luke 6:45; Eph. 4:29; James 3:2-12
35 [1]Lit., *good things* [2]Lit., *evil things* [a]Prov. 10:20, 21; 25:11, 12; Matt. 13:52; Col. 4:6
36 [1]Or, *useless* [a]Matt. 10:15
37 [1]Or, *in accordance with*
38 [1]Or, *attesting miracle* [a]Matt. 16:1; Mark 8:11, 12; Luke 11:16; John 2:18; 6:30; 1 Cor. 1:22
39 [1]Or, *attesting miracle* [a]Matt. 12:39-42: *Luke 11:29-32;* Matt. 16:4
40 [a]Jon. 1:17 [b]Matt. 8:20 [c]Matt. 16:21
41 [a]Jon. 1:2 [b]Jon. 3:5 [c]Matt. 12:6, 42
42 [a]1 Kin. 10:1; 2 Chr. 9:1 [b]Matt. 12:6, 41
43 [a]Matt. 12:43-45: *Luke 11:24-26*
45 [a]Mark 5:9; Luke 11:26; Heb. 6:4-8; 2 Pet. 2:20
46 [a]Matt. 12:46-50: *Mark 3:31-35; Luke 8:19-21* [b]Matt. 1:18; 2:11ff.; 13:55; Luke 1:43; 2:33f., 48, 51; John 2:1, 5, 12; 19:25f.; Acts 1:14 [c]Matt. 13:55; Mark 6:3; John 2:12; 7:3, 5, 10; Acts 1:14; 1 Cor. 9:5; Gal. 1:19

1 [a]Matt. 9:28; 13:36 [b]Matt. 13:1-15: *Mark 4:1-12; Luke 8:4-10;* Mark 2:13
2 [a]Luke 5:3
3 [a]Matt. 13:10ff.; Mark 4:2ff.
5 [1]Lit., *were not having*
7 [1]Lit., *upon*
8 [a]Gen. 26:12; Matt. 13:23
9 [a]Matt. 11:15; Rev. 2:7, 11, 17, 29; 3:6, 13, 22
11 [a]Matt. 19:11; 20:23; John 6:65; 1 Cor. 2:10; Col. 1:27; 1 John 2:20, 27

know the mysteries of the kingdom of heaven, but to them it has not been granted.

12 "[a]For whoever has, to him shall *more* be given, and he shall have an abundance; but whoever does not have, even what he has shall be taken away from him.

13 "Therefore I speak to them in parables; because while [a]seeing they do not see, and while hearing they do not hear, nor do they understand.

14 "And [1]in their case the prophecy of Isaiah is being fulfilled, which says,

'[2][a]YOU WILL KEEP ON HEARING,
[3]BUT WILL NOT UNDERSTAND;
AND [4]YOU WILL KEEP ON SEEING,
BUT WILL NOT PERCEIVE;

15 [a]FOR THE HEART OF THIS PEOPLE
HAS BECOME DULL,
AND WITH THEIR EARS THEY
SCARCELY HEAR,
AND THEY HAVE CLOSED THEIR
EYES
LEST THEY SHOULD SEE WITH
THEIR EYES,
AND HEAR WITH THEIR EARS,
AND UNDERSTAND WITH THEIR
HEART AND RETURN,
AND I SHOULD HEAL THEM.'

16 "[a]But blessed are your eyes, because they see; and your ears, because they hear.

17 "For truly I say to you, that [a]many prophets and righteous men desired to see what you see, and did not see *it*; and to hear what you hear, and did not hear *it*.

The Sower Explained

18 "[a]Hear then the parable of the sower.

19 "When anyone hears [a]the word of the kingdom, and does not understand it, [b]the evil *one* comes and snatches away what has been sown in his heart. This is the one on whom seed was sown beside the road.

20 "And the one on whom seed was sown on the rocky places, this is the man who hears the word, and immediately receives it with joy;

21 yet he has no *firm* root in himself, but is *only* temporary, and when affliction or persecution arises because of the word, immediately he [1][a]falls away.

22 "And the one on whom seed was sown among the thorns, this is the man who hears the word, and the worry of [a]the [1]world, and the [b]deceitfulness of riches choke the word, and it becomes unfruitful.

23 "And the one on whom seed was sown on the good soil, this is the man who hears the word and understands it; who indeed bears fruit, and brings forth, some [a]a hundredfold, some sixty, and some thirty."

Tares among Wheat

24 He presented another parable to them, saying, "[a]The kingdom of heaven [1]may be compared to a man who sowed good seed in his field.

25 "But while men were sleeping, his enemy came and sowed [1]tares also among the wheat, and went away.

26 "But when the [1]wheat sprang up and bore grain, then the tares became evident also.

27 "And the slaves of the landowner came and said to him, 'Sir, did you not sow good seed in your field? [1]How then does it have tares?'

28 "And he said to them, 'An [1]enemy has done this!' And the slaves *said to him, 'Do you want us, then, to go and gather them up?'

29 "But he *said, 'No; lest while you are gathering up the tares, you may root up the wheat with them.

30 'Allow both to grow together until the harvest; and in the time of the harvest I will say to the reapers, "First gather up the tares and bind them in bundles to burn them up; but [a]gather the wheat into my barn." ' "

The Mustard Seed

31 He presented another parable to them, saying, "[a]The kingdom of heaven is like [b]a mustard seed, which a man took and sowed in his field;

32 and this is smaller than all *other* seeds; but when it is full grown, it is larger than the garden plants, and becomes a tree, so that [a]THE BIRDS OF THE [1]AIR come and NEST IN ITS BRANCHES."

The Leaven

33 He spoke another parable to them, "[a]The kingdom of heaven is like leaven, which a woman took, and hid in [b]three [1]pecks of meal, until it was all leavened."

34 All these things Jesus spoke to the multitudes in parables, and He did not speak to them [a]without a parable,

35 so that what was spoken through the prophet might be fulfilled, saying,

"[a]I WILL OPEN MY MOUTH IN PARABLES;
I WILL UTTER THINGS HIDDEN SINCE THE FOUNDATION OF THE WORLD."

The Tares Explained

36 Then He left the multitudes, and went into [a]the house. And His disciples came to Him, saying, "[b]Explain to us the parable of the [1]tares of the field."

37 And He answered and said, "The one who sows the good seed is [a]the Son of Man,

38 and the field is the world; and *as for* the good seed, these are [a]the sons of the kingdom; and the tares are [b]the sons of [c]the evil *one;*

39 and the enemy who sowed them is the devil, and the harvest is [a]the [1]end of the age; and the reapers are angels.

12 [a]Matt. 25:29; Mark 4:25; Luke 8:18; 19:26
13 [a]Deut. 29:4; Is. 42:19, 20; Jer. 5:21; Ezek. 12:2
14 [1]Lit., *for them* [2]Lit., *With a hearing you will hear* [3]Lit., *and* [4]Lit., *seeing you will see* [a]Is. 6:9; Mark 4:12; Luke 8:10; John 12:40; Acts 28:26, 27; Rom. 10:16; 11:8
15 [a]Is. 6:10; Ps. 119:70; Zech. 7:11; Luke 19:42; John 8:43, 44; 2 Tim. 4:4; Heb. 5:11
16 [a]Matt. 13:16, 17: *Luke 10:23, 24;* Matt. 16:17; John 20:29
17 [a]John 8:56; Heb. 11:13; 1 Pet. 1:10-12
18 [a]Matt. 13:18-23: *Mark 4:13-20; Luke 8:11-15*
19 [a]Matt. 4:23 [b]Matt. 5:37
21 [1]Lit., *is caused to stumble* [a]Matt. 11:6
22 [1]Or, *age* [a]Matt. 12:32; 13:39; Mark 4:19; Rom. 12:2; 1 Cor. 1:20; 2:6, 8; 3:18; 2 Cor. 4:4; Gal. 1:4; Eph. 2:2 [b]Matt. 19:23; 1 Tim. 6:9, 10, 17
23 [a]Matt. 13:8
24 [1]Lit., *was compared to* [a]Matt. 13:31, 33, 45, 47; 18:23; 20:1; 22:2; 25:1; Mark 4:26-30; Luke 13:18, 20
25 [1]Or, *darnel,* a weed resembling wheat
26 [1]Lit., *grass*
27 [1]Lit., *From where*
28 [1]Lit., *enemy man*
30 [a]Matt. 3:12
31 [a]Matt. 13:31, 32: *Mark 4:30-32; Luke 13:18, 19;* Matt. 13:24 [b]Matt. 17:20; Luke 17:6
32 [1]Or, *sky* [a]Ezek. 17:23; Ps. 104:12; Ezek. 31:6; Dan. 4:12
33 [1]Gr., *sata* [a]Matt. 13:33: *Luke 13:21;* Matt. 13:24 [b]Gen. 18:6; Judg. 6:19; 1 Sam. 1:24
34 [a]Mark 4:34; John 10:6; 16:25
35 [a]Ps. 78:2
36 [1]Or, *darnel,* a weed resembling wheat [a]Matt. 13:1 [b]Matt. 15:15
37 [a]Matt. 8:20
38 [a]Matt. 8:12 [b]John 8:44; Acts 13:10; 1 John 3:10 [c]Matt. 5:37
39 [1]Or, *consummation* [a]Matt. 12:32; 13:22, 40, 49; 24:3; 28:20; 1 Cor. 10:11; Heb. 9:26

40"Therefore just as the tares are
gathered up and burned with fire, so
shall it be at [a]the [1]end of the age.
41"[a]The Son of Man [b]will send forth
His angels, and they will gather out of
His kingdom [1]all [c]stumbling blocks, and
those who commit lawlessness,
42 and [a]will cast them into the furnace
of fire; in that place [b]there shall be
weeping and gnashing of teeth.
43"[a]Then THE RIGHTEOUS WILL SHINE
FORTH AS THE SUN in the kingdom of
their Father. [b]He who has ears, let him
hear.

Hidden Treasure

44"[a]The kingdom of heaven is like a
treasure hidden in the field, which a man
found and hid; and from joy over it he
goes and [b]sells all that he has, and buys
that field.

A Costly Pearl

45"Again, [a]the kingdom of heaven is
like a merchant seeking fine pearls,
46 and upon finding one pearl of great
value, he went and sold all that he had,
and bought it.

A Dragnet

47"Again, [a]the kingdom of heaven is
like a dragnet cast into the sea, and
gathering *fish* of every kind;
48 and when it was filled, they drew it
up on the beach; and they sat down, and
gathered the good *fish* into containers,
but the bad they threw away.
49"So it will be at [a]the [1]end of the age;
the angels shall come forth, and [2]take
out the wicked from among the righteous,
50 and [a]will cast them into the furnace
of fire; [b]there shall be weeping and
gnashing of teeth.
51"Have you understood all these
things?" They *said to Him, "Yes."
52 And He said to them, "Therefore
every scribe who has become a disciple
of the kingdom of heaven is like a head
of a household, who brings forth out of
his treasure things new and old."

Jesus Revisits Nazareth

53 [a]And it came about that when
Jesus had finished these parables, He
departed from there.
54 [a]And coming to [1]His home town
He [2b]*began* teaching them in their synagogue, so that [c]they became astonished,
and said, "Where *did* this man *get* this
wisdom, and *these* [3]miraculous powers?
55"Is not this the carpenter's son? Is
not [a]His mother called Mary, and His
[a]brothers, James and Joseph and Simon
and Judas?
56"And [a]His sisters, are they not all
with us? Where then *did* this man *get* all
these things?"
57 And they [1]took [a]offense at Him.
But Jesus said to them, "[b]A prophet is
not without honor except in his [2]home
town, and in his *own* household."
58 And He did not do many [1]miracles
there because of their unbelief.

John the Baptist Beheaded

14 [a]AT that [1]time [b]Herod the tetrarch heard the news about
Jesus,
2 and said to his servants, "[a]This is
John the Baptist; [1]he has risen from the
dead; and that is why miraculous powers
are at work in him."
3 For when [a]Herod had John arrested, he bound him, and put him [b]in
prison on account of [c]Herodias, the wife
of his brother Philip.
4 For John had been saying to him,
"[a]It is not lawful for you to have her."
5 And although he wanted to put
him to death, he feared the multitude,
because [1]they regarded him as [a]a
prophet.
6 But when Herod's birthday [1]came,
the daughter of [a]Herodias danced [2]be-
fore *them* and pleased [b]Herod.
7 Thereupon he promised with an
oath to give her whatever she asked.
8 And having been prompted by her
mother, she *said, "Give me here on a
platter the head of John the Baptist."
9 And although he was grieved, the
king commanded *it* to be given because
of his oaths, and because of [1]his dinner
guests.
10 And he sent and had John beheaded in the prison.
11 And his head was brought on a
platter and given to the girl; and she
brought *it* to her mother.
12 And his disciples came and took
away the body and buried [1]it; and they
went and reported to Jesus.

Five Thousand Fed

13 [a]Now when Jesus heard *it,* He
withdrew from there in a boat, to a
lonely place by Himself; and when the
multitudes heard *of this,* they followed
Him on foot from the cities.
14 And when He went [1]ashore, He
[a]saw a great multitude, and felt compassion for them, and [b]healed their sick.
15 And when it was evening, the disciples came to Him, saying, "The place is
desolate, and the time is already past; so
send the multitudes away, that they may
go into the villages and buy food for
themselves."
16 But Jesus said to them, "They do
not need to go away; you give them
something to eat!"
17 And they *said to Him, "We have
here only [a]five loaves and two fish."
18 And He said, "Bring them here to
Me."
19 And ordering the multitudes to
recline on the grass, He took the five
loaves and the two fish, and looking up
toward heaven, He [a]blessed *the food,* and

40 [1]Or, *consummation* [a]Matt. 12:32; 13:22, 39, 49; 24:3; 28:20; 1 Cor. 10:11; Heb. 9:26
41 [1]Or, *everything that is offensive* [a]Matt. 8:20 [b]Matt. 24:31 [c]Zeph. 1:3
42 [a]Matt. 13:50 [b]Matt. 8:12
43 [a]Dan. 12:3 [b]Matt. 11:15
44 [a]Matt. 13:24 [b]Matt. 13:46
45 [a]Matt. 13:24
47 [a]Matt. 13:44
49 [1]Or, *consummation* [2]Or, *separate* [a]Matt. 13:39, 40
50 [a]Matt. 13:42 [b]Matt. 8:12
53 [a]Matt. 7:28
54 [1]Or, *His own part of the country* [2]Or, *was teaching* [3]Or, *miracles* [a]Matt. 13:54-58: *Mark 6:1-6* [b]Matt. 4:23 [c]Matt. 7:28
55 [a]Matt. 12:46
56 [a]Mark 6:3
57 [1]Lit., *were being made to stumble* [2]Or, *own part of the country* [a]Matt. 11:6 [b]Mark 6:4; Luke 4:24; John 4:44
58 [1]Or, *works of power*
1 [1]Or, *occasion* [a]Matt. 14:1-12: *Mark 6:14-29;* Matt. 14:1, 2: *Luke 9:7-9* [b]Mark 8:15; Luke 3:1, 19; 8:3; 13:31; 23:7f., 11f., 15; Acts 4:27; 12:1
2 [1]Or, *he, himself* [a]Matt. 16:14; Mark 6:14; Luke 9:7
3 [a]Matt. 14:1-12: *Mark 6:14-29;* Mark 8:15; Luke 3:1, 19; 8:3; 13:31; 23:7f., 11f., 15; Acts 4:27; 12:1 [b]Matt. 4:12; 11:2 [c]Matt. 14:6; Mark 6:17, 19, 22; Luke 3:19f.
4 [a]Lev. 18:16; 20:21
5 [1]Lit., *they were holding* [a]Matt. 11:9
6 [1]Lit., *occurred* [2]Lit., *in the midst* [a]Matt. 14:3; Mark 6:17, 19, 22; Luke 3:19 [b]Matt. 14:1-12: *Mark 6:14-29;* Mark 8:15; Luke 3:1, 19; 8:3; 13:31; 23:7f., 11f., 15; Acts 4:27; 12:1
9 [1]Lit., *those who reclined at the table with him*
12 [1]Lit., *him*
13 [a]Matt. 14:13-21: *Mark 6:32-44; Luke 9:10-17; John 6:1-13;* Matt. 15:32-38
14 [1]Lit., *out* [a]Matt. 9:36 [b]Matt. 4:23
17 [a]Matt. 16:9
19 [a]1 Sam. 9:13; Matt. 15:36; 26:26; Mark 6:41; 8:7; 14:22; Luke 24:30; Acts 27:35; Rom. 14:6

breaking the loaves He gave them to the
disciples, and the disciples *gave* to the
multitudes,
20 and they all ate, and were satisfied.
And they picked up what was left over
of the broken pieces, twelve full [a]bas-
kets.
21 And there were about five thousand men who ate, aside from women
and children.

Jesus Walks on the Water

22 [a]And immediately He [1]made the
disciples get into the boat, and go ahead
of Him to the other side, while He sent
the multitudes away.
23 And after He had sent the multitudes away, [a]He went up to the mountain by Himself to pray; and when it was
evening, He was there alone.
24 But the boat was already many
[1]stadia away from the land, [2]battered by
the waves; for the wind was contrary.
25 And in [a]the [1]fourth watch of the
night He came to them, walking on the
sea.
26 And when the disciples saw Him
walking on the sea, they were [1]fright-
ened, saying, "It is [a]a ghost!" And they
cried out for fear.
27 But immediately Jesus spoke to
them, saying, "[a]Take courage, it is I; [b]do
not be afraid."
28 And Peter answered Him and said,
"Lord, if it is You, command me to
come to You on the water."
29 And He said, "Come!" And Peter
got out of the boat, and walked on the
water and came toward Jesus.
30 But seeing the wind, he became
afraid, and beginning to sink, he cried
out, saying, "Lord, save me!"
31 And immediately Jesus stretched
out His hand and took hold of him, and
*said to him, "[a]O you of little faith, why
did you doubt?"
32 And when they got into the boat,
the wind stopped.
33 And those who were in the boat
worshiped Him, saying, "You are certainly [a]God's Son!"
34 [a]And when they had crossed over,
they came to [1]land at [b]Gennesaret.
35 And when the men of that place
[1]recognized Him, they sent into all that
surrounding district and brought to Him
all who were sick;
36 and they *began* to entreat Him that
they might just touch [a]the fringe of His
cloak; and as many as [b]touched *it* were
cured.

Tradition and Commandment

15 [a]THEN some Pharisees and
scribes *came to Jesus [b]from
Jerusalem, saying,
2 "Why do Your disciples transgress
the tradition of the elders? For they [a]do
not wash their hands when they eat
bread."
3 And He answered and said to
them, "And why do [1]you yourselves
transgress the commandment of God for
the sake of your tradition?
4 "For God said, '[a]HONOR YOUR FA-
THER AND MOTHER,' and, '[b]HE WHO
SPEAKS EVIL OF FATHER OR MOTHER, LET
HIM [1]BE PUT TO DEATH.'
5 "But you say, 'Whoever shall say to
his father or mother, "Anything of mine
you might have been helped by has been
[1]given *to God,*"
6 he is not to honor his father [1]or his
mother[2].' And *thus* you invalidated the
[3]word of God for the sake of your
tradition.
7 "You hypocrites, rightly did Isaiah
prophesy of you, saying,
8 '[a]THIS PEOPLE HONORS ME WITH
THEIR LIPS,
BUT THEIR HEART IS FAR AWAY
FROM ME.
9 'BUT IN VAIN DO THEY WORSHIP
ME,
TEACHING AS [a]DOCTRINES THE
PRECEPTS OF MEN.' "
10 And after He called the multitude
to Him, He said to them, "Hear, and
understand.
11 "[a]Not what enters into the mouth
defiles the man, but what proceeds out
of the mouth, this defiles the man."
12 Then the disciples *came and *said
to Him, "Do You know that the Pharisees were [1]offended when they heard this
statement?"
13 But He answered and said, "[a]Every
plant which My heavenly Father did not
plant shall be rooted up.
14 "Let them alone; [a]they are blind
guides [1]of the blind. And [b]if a blind man
guides a blind man, both will fall into a
pit."

The Heart of Man

15 And Peter answered and said to
Him, "[a]Explain the parable to us."
16 And He said, "Are you still lacking
in understanding also?
17 "Do you not understand that everything that goes into the mouth passes
into the [1]stomach, and is [2]eliminated?
18 "But [a]the things that proceed out of
the mouth come from the heart, and
those defile the man.
19 "[a]For out of the heart come evil
thoughts, murders, adulteries, [1]fornica-
tions, thefts, false witness, slanders.
20 "These are the things which defile
the man; but to eat with unwashed
hands does not defile the man."

The Syrophoenician Woman

21 [a]And Jesus went away from there,
and withdrew into the district of [b]Tyre
and [b]Sidon.
22 And behold, a Canaanite woman
came out from that region, and *began* to
cry out, saying, "Have mercy on me, O
Lord, [a]Son of David; my daughter is
cruelly [b]demon-possessed."

20 [a]Matt. 16:9; Mark 6:43; 8:19; Luke 9:17; John 6:13
22 [1]Lit., *compelled* [a]Matt. 14:22-33: *Mark 6:45-51; John 6:15-21*
23 [a]Mark 6:46; Luke 6:12; 9:28; John 6:15
24 [1]A stadion was about 600 feet [2]Lit., *tormented*
25 [1]I.e., 3-6 a.m. [a]Matt. 24:43; Mark 13:35
26 [1]Or, *troubled* [a]Luke 24:37
27 [a]Matt. 9:2 [b]Matt. 17:7; 28:5, 10; Mark 6:50; Luke 1:13, 30; 2:10; 5:10; 12:32; John 6:20; Rev. 1:17
31 [a]Matt. 6:30; 8:26; 16:8
33 [a]Matt. 4:3
34 [1]Lit., *the land* [a]Matt. 14:34-36: *Mark 6:53-56;* John 6:24, 25 [b]Mark 6:53; Luke 5:1
35 [1]Or, *knew*
36 [a]Matt. 9:20 [b]Matt. 9:21; Mark 3:10; 6:56; 8:22; Luke 6:19

1 [a]Matt. 15:1-20: *Mark 7:1-23* [b]Mark 3:22; 7:1; John 1:19; Acts 25:7
2 [a]Luke 11:38
3 [1]Or, *you also*
4 [1]Lit., *die the death* [a]Ex. 20:12; Deut. 5:16 [b]Ex. 21:17; Lev. 20:9
5 [1]Or, *a gift, an offering*
6 [1]Many mss. do not contain *or his mother* [2]I.e., by supporting them with it [3]Some mss. read *law*
8 [a]Is. 29:13
9 [a]Col. 2:22
11 [a]Matt. 15:18; Acts 10:14, 15; 1 Tim. 4:3
12 [1]Lit., *caused to stumble*
13 [a]Is. 60:21; 61:3; John 15:2; 1 Cor. 3:9
14 [1]Some mss. do not contain *of the blind* [a]Matt. 23:16, 24 [b]Luke 6:39
15 [a]Matt. 13:36
17 [1]Lit., *belly* [2]Lit., *cast out into the latrine*
18 [a]Matt. 12:34; Mark 7:20
19 [1]I.e., sexual immorality [a]Gal. 5:19ff.
21 [a]Matt. 15:21-28: *Mark 7:24-30* [b]Matt. 11:21
22 [a]Matt. 9:27 [b]Matt. 4:24

23 But He did not answer her a word. And His disciples came to *Him* and kept asking Him, saying, "Send her away, for she is shouting out after us."

24 But He answered and said, "I was sent only to [a]the lost sheep of the house of Israel."

25 But she came and [a]*began* [1]to bow down before Him, saying, "Lord, help me!"

26 And He answered and said, "It is not [1]good to take the children's bread and throw it to the dogs."

27 But she said, "Yes, Lord; [1]but even the dogs feed on the crumbs which fall from their masters' table."

28 Then Jesus answered and said to her, "O woman, [a]your faith is great; be it done for you as you wish." And her daughter was healed [1]at once.

Healing Multitudes

29 [a]And departing from there, Jesus went along by [b]the Sea of Galilee, and having gone up to the mountain, He was sitting there.

30 And great multitudes came to Him, bringing with them *those who were* lame, crippled, blind, dumb, and many others, and they laid them down at His feet; and [a]He healed them,

31 so that the multitude marveled as they saw the dumb speaking, the crippled [1]restored, and the lame walking, and the blind seeing; and they [a]glorified the God of Israel.

Four Thousand Fed

32 [a]And Jesus called His disciples to Him, and said, "[b]I feel compassion for the multitude, because they [1]have remained with Me now three days and have nothing to eat; and I do not wish to send them away hungry, lest they faint on the way."

33 And the disciples *said to Him, "Where would we get so many loaves in a desolate place to satisfy such a great multitude?"

34 And Jesus *said to them, "How many loaves do you have?" And they said, "Seven, and a few small fish."

35 And He directed the multitude to [1]sit down on the ground;

36 and He took the seven loaves and the fish; and [a]giving thanks, He broke them and started giving them to the disciples, and the disciples *in turn*, to the multitudes.

37 And they all ate, and were satisfied, and they picked up what was left over of the broken pieces, seven large [a]baskets full.

38 And those who ate were four thousand men, besides women and children.

39 And sending away the multitudes, He got into [a]the boat, and came to the region of [b]Magadan.

Pharisees Test Jesus

16 [a]AND the [b]Pharisees and Sadducees came up, and testing Him [c]asked Him to show them a [1]sign from heaven.

2 But He answered and said to them, [1]"[a]When it is evening, you say, '*It will be* fair weather, for the sky is red.'

3 "And in the morning, '*There will be* a storm today, for the sky is red and threatening.' [a]Do you know how to discern the [1]appearance of the sky, but cannot *discern* the signs of the times?

4 "[a]An evil and adulterous generation seeks after a [1]sign; and a [1]sign will not be given it, except the sign of Jonah." And He left them, and went away.

5 And the disciples came to the other side and had forgotten to take bread.

6 And Jesus said to them, "Watch out and [a]beware of the [1]leaven of the [b]Pharisees and Sadducees."

7 And they began to discuss among themselves, saying, "*It is* because we took no bread."

8 But Jesus, aware of this, said, "[a]You men of little faith, why do you discuss among yourselves that you have no bread?

9 "Do you not yet understand or remember [a]the five loaves of the five thousand, and how many baskets you took up?

10 "Or [a]the seven loaves of the four thousand, and how many large baskets you took up?

11 "How is it that you do not understand that I did not speak to you concerning bread? But [a]beware of the [1]leaven of the [b]Pharisees and Sadducees."

12 Then they understood that He did not say to beware of the leaven of bread, but of the teaching of the [a]Pharisees and Sadducees.

Peter's Confession of Christ

13 [a]Now when Jesus came into the district of [b]Caesarea Philippi, He *began* asking His disciples, saying, "Who do people say that [c]the Son of Man is?"

14 And they said, "Some *say* [a]John the Baptist; and others, [1b]Elijah; but still others, [2]Jeremiah, or one of the prophets."

15 He *said to them, "But who do you say that I am?"

16 And Simon Peter answered and said, "Thou art [1a]the Christ, [b]the Son of [c]the living God."

17 And Jesus answered and said to him, "Blessed are you, [a]Simon [1]Barjona, because [b]flesh and blood did not reveal *this* to you, but My Father who is in heaven.

18 "And I also say to you that you are [1a]Peter, and upon this [2]rock I will build My church; and the gates of [b]Hades shall not overpower it.

---

24 [a]Matt. 10:6
25 [1]Or, *to worship* [a]Matt. 8:2
26 [1]Or, *proper*
27 [1]Lit., *for*
28 [1]Lit., *from that hour* [a]Matt. 9:22
29 [a]Matt. 15:29-31; Mark 7:31-37 [b]Matt. 4:18
30 [a]Matt. 4:23
31 [1]Or, *healthy* [a]Matt. 9:8
32 [1]Lit., *are remaining* [a]Matt. 15:32-39: *Mark 8:1-10;* Matt. 14:13-21 [b]Matt. 9:36
35 [1]Lit., *recline*
36 [a]Matt. 14:19; 26:27; Luke 22:17, 19; John 6:11, 23; Acts 27:35; Rom. 14:6
37 [a]Matt. 16:10; Mark 8:8, 20; Acts 9:25
39 [a]Mark 3:9 [b]Mark 8:10

1 [1]Or, *attesting miracle* [a]Matt. 16:1-12: *Mark 8:11-21* [b]Matt. 3:7; 16:6, 11, 12 [c]Matt. 12:38; Luke 11:16
2 [1]The earliest mss. do not contain the rest of v. 2 and v. 3. [a]Luke 12:54f.
3 [1]Lit., *face* [a]Luke 12:56
4 [1]Or, *attesting miracle* [a]Matt. 12:39; Luke 11:29
6 [1]Or, *yeast* [a]Mark 8:15; Luke 12:1 [b]Matt. 3:7
8 [a]Matt. 6:30; 8:26; 14:31
9 [a]Matt. 14:17-21
10 [a]Matt. 15:34-38
11 [1]Or, *yeast* [a]Matt. 16:6; Mark 8:15; Luke 12:1 [b]Matt. 3:7; 16:6, 12
12 [a]Matt. 3:7; 5:20
13 [a]Matt. 16:13-16: *Mark 8:27-29; Luke 9:18-20* [b]Mark 8:27 [c]Matt. 8:20; 16:27, 28
14 [1]Gr., *Elias* [2]Gr., *Jeremias* [a]Matt. 14:2 [b]Matt. 17:10; Mark 6:15; Luke 9:8; John 1:21
16 [1]I.e., the Messiah [a]Matt. 1:16; 16:20; John 11:27 [b]Matt. 4:3 [c]Ps. 42:2; Matt. 26:63; Acts 14:15; Rom. 9:26; 2 Cor. 3:3; 6:16; 1 Thess. 1:9; 1 Tim. 3:15; 4:10; Heb. 3:12; 9:14; 10:31; 12:22; Rev. 7:2
17 [1]I.e., son of Jonah [a]John 1:42; 21:15-17 [b]1 Cor. 15:50; Gal. 1:16; Eph. 6:12; Heb. 2:14
18 [1]Gr., *Petros*, a stone [2]Gr., *petra*, large rock, bed-rock [a]Matt. 4:18 [b]Matt. 11:23

19 "I will give you [a]the keys of the kingdom of heaven; and [b]whatever you shall bind on earth shall be bound in heaven, and whatever you shall loose on earth shall be loosed in heaven."

20 [a]Then He [1]warned the disciples that they should tell no one that He was [2b]the Christ.

Jesus Foretells His Death

21 [a]From that time Jesus Christ began to show His disciples that He must go to Jerusalem, and [b]suffer many things from the elders and chief priests and scribes, and be killed, and be raised up on the third day.

22 And Peter took Him aside and began to rebuke Him, saying, "[1]God forbid *it,* Lord! This shall never [2]happen to You."

23 But He turned and said to Peter, "Get behind Me, [a]Satan! You are a stumbling block to Me; for you are not setting your mind on [1]God's interests, but man's."

Discipleship Is Costly

24 Then Jesus said to His disciples, "If anyone wishes to come after Me, let him deny himself, and [a]take up his cross, and follow Me.

25 "For [a]whoever wishes to save his [1]life shall lose it; but whoever loses his [1]life for My sake shall find it.

26 "For what will a man be profited, if he gains the whole world, and forfeits his soul? Or what will a man give in exchange for his soul?

27 "For the [a]Son of Man [b]is going to come in the glory of His Father with His angels; and [c]WILL THEN RECOMPENSE EVERY MAN ACCORDING TO HIS [1]DEEDS.

28 "Truly I say to you, there are some of those who are standing here who shall not taste death until they see the [a]Son of Man [b]coming in His kingdom."

The Transfiguration

17 [a]AND six days later Jesus *took with Him [b]Peter and [1]James and John his brother, and *brought them up to a high mountain by themselves.

2 And He was transfigured before them; and His face shone like the sun, and His garments became as white as light.

3 And behold, Moses and Elijah appeared to them, talking with Him.

4 And Peter answered and said to Jesus, "Lord, it is good for us to be here; if You wish, [a]I will make three [1]tabernacles here, one for You, and one for Moses, and one for Elijah."

5 While he was still speaking, behold, a bright cloud overshadowed them; and behold, [a]a voice out of the cloud, saying, "[b]This is My beloved Son, with whom I am well-pleased; listen to Him!"

6 And when the disciples heard *this,* they fell on their faces and were much afraid.

7 And Jesus came to *them* and touched them and said, "Arise, and [a]do not be afraid."

8 And lifting up their eyes, they saw no one, except Jesus Himself alone.

9 [a]And as they were coming down from the mountain, Jesus commanded them, saying, "[b]Tell the vision to no one until [c]the Son of Man has [d]risen from the dead."

10 And His disciples asked Him, saying, "Why then do the scribes say that [a]Elijah must come first?"

11 And He answered and said, "Elijah is coming and will restore all things;

12 but I say to you, that Elijah already came, and they did not recognize him, but did [1]to him whatever they wished. So also [a]the Son of Man is going to suffer [2]at their hands."

13 Then the disciples understood that He had spoken to them about John the Baptist.

The Demoniac

14 [a]And when they came to the multitude, a man came up to Him, falling on his knees before Him, and saying,

15 "[1]Lord, have mercy on my son, for he is a [a]lunatic, and is very ill; for he often falls into the fire, and often into the water.

16 "And I brought him to Your disciples, and they could not cure him."

17 And Jesus answered and said, "O unbelieving and perverted generation, how long shall I be with you? How long shall I put up with you? Bring him here to Me."

18 And Jesus rebuked him, and the demon came out of him, and the boy was cured [1]at once.

19 Then the disciples came to Jesus privately and said, "Why could we not cast it out?"

20 And He *said to them, "Because of the littleness of your faith; for truly I say to you, [a]if you have faith as [b]a mustard seed, you shall say to [c]this mountain, 'Move from here to there,' and it shall move; and [d]nothing shall be impossible to you.

21 ["[1a]But this kind does not go out except by prayer and fasting."]

22 [a]And while they were gathering together in Galilee, Jesus said to them, "The Son of Man is going to be [1]delivered into the hands of men;

23 and [a]they will kill Him, and He will be raised on the third day." And they were deeply grieved.

19 [a]Is. 22:22; Rev. 1:18; 3:7 [b]Matt. 18:18; John 20:23
20 [1]Or, *strictly admonished* [2]I.e., the Messiah [a]Matt. 8:4; Mark 8:30; Luke 9:21 [b]Matt. 1:16; 16:16; John 11:27
21 [a]Matt. 16:21-28: *Mark 8:31-9:1; Luke 9:22-27* [b]Matt. 12:40; 17:9, 12, 22f.; 20:18f.; 27:63; Mark 9:12, 31; Luke 17:25; 18:32; 24:7; John 2:19
22 [1]Lit., (God be) *merciful to You* [2]Lit., *be*
23 [1]Lit., *the things of God* [a]Matt. 4:10
24 [a]Matt. 10:38; Luke 14:27
25 [1]Or, *soul* [a]Matt. 10:39
27 [1]Lit., *doing* [a]Matt. 8:20 [b]Matt. 10:23; 24:3, 27, 37, 39; 26:64; Mark 8:38; 13:26; Luke 21:27; John 21:22; Acts 1:11; 1 Cor. 15:23; 1 Thess. 1:10; 4:16; 2 Thess. 1:7, 10; 2:1, 8; James 5:7f.; 2 Pet. 1:16; 3:4, 12; 1 John 2:28; Rev. 1:7 [c]Ps. 62:12; Prov. 24:12; Rom. 2:6; 14:12; 1 Cor. 3:13; 2 Cor. 5:10; Eph. 6:8; Col. 3:25; Rev. 2:23; 20:12; 22:12
28 [a]Matt. 8:20 [b]Matt. 10:23; 24:3, 27, 37, 39; 26:64; Mark 8:38; 13:26; Luke 21:27; John 21:22; Acts 1:11; 1 Cor. 15:23; 1 Thess. 1:10; 4:16; 2 Thess. 1:7, 10; 2:1, 8; James 5:7f.; 2 Pet. 1:16; 3:4, 12; 1 John 2:28; Rev. 1:7

1 [1]Or, *Jacob* [a]Matt. 17:1-8: *Mark 9:2-8; Luke 9:28-36* [b]Matt. 26:37; Mark 5:37; 13:3
4 [1]Or, *sacred tents* [a]Mark 9:5; Luke 9:33
5 [a]Mark 1:11; Luke 3:22; 2 Pet. 1:17f. [b]Is. 42:1; Matt. 3:17; 12:18
7 [a]Matt. 14:27
9 [a]Matt. 17:9-13: *Mark 9:9-13* [b]Matt. 8:4 [c]Matt. 8:20; 17:12, 22 [d]Matt. 16:21
10 [a]Mal. 4:5; Matt. 11:14; 16:14
12 [1]Lit., *in him;* or, *in his case* [2]Lit., *by them* [a]Matt. 8:20; 17:9, 22
14 [a]Matt. 17:14-19: *Mark 9:14-28;* Matt. 17:14-18: *Luke 9:37-42*
15 [1]Or, *Sir* [a]Matt. 4:24
18 [1]Lit., *from that hour*

20 [a]Matt. 21:21f.; Mark 11:23f.; Luke 17:6 [b]Matt. 13:31; Luke 17:6 [c]Matt. 17:9; 1 Cor. 13:2 [d]Mark 9:23; John 11:40
21 [1]Many mss. do not contain this v. [a]Mark 9:29
22 [1]Or, *betrayed* [a]Matt. 17:22, 23: *Mark 9:30-32; Luke 9:44, 45*
23 [a]Matt. 16:21; 17:9

The Tribute Money

24 And when they had come to Capernaum, those who collected [a]the [1]two-drachma *tax* came to Peter, and said, "Does your teacher not pay [a]the [1]two-drachma *tax*?"

25 He *said, "Yes." And when he came into the house, Jesus [1]spoke to him first, saying, "What do you think, Simon? From whom do the kings of the earth collect [a]customs or [b]poll-tax, from their sons or from strangers?"

26 And upon his saying, "From strangers," Jesus said to him, "Consequently the sons are [1]exempt.

27 "But, lest we [1a]give them offense, go to the sea, and throw in a hook, and take the first fish that comes up; and when you open its mouth, you will find a [2]stater. Take that and give it to them for you and Me."

Rank in the Kingdom

18 [a]AT that [1]time the disciples came to Jesus, saying, "[b]Who then is [2]greatest in the kingdom of heaven?"

2 And He called a child to Himself and set him [1]before them,

3 and said, "Truly I say to you, unless you [1]are converted and [a]become like children, you shall not enter the kingdom of heaven.

4 "Whoever then humbles himself as this child, he is the greatest in the kingdom of heaven.

5 "And whoever receives one such child in My name receives Me;

6 but [a]whoever [b]causes one of these little ones who believe in Me to stumble, it is better for him that a [1]heavy millstone be hung around his neck, and that he be drowned in the depth of the sea.

Stumbling Blocks

7 "Woe to the world because of *its* stumbling blocks! For [a]it is inevitable that stumbling blocks come; but woe to that man through whom the stumbling block comes!

8 "And [a]if your hand or your foot causes you to stumble, cut it off and throw it from you; it is better for you to enter life crippled or lame, than having two hands or two feet, to be cast into the eternal fire.

9 "And [a]if your eye causes you to stumble, pluck it out, and throw it from you. It is better for you to enter life with one eye, than having two eyes, to be cast into the [1b]fiery hell.

10 "See that you do not despise one of these little ones, for I say to you, that [a]their angels in heaven continually behold the face of My Father who is in heaven.

11 ["[1a]For the Son of Man has come to save that which was lost.]

Ninety-nine Plus One

12 "What do you think? [a]If any man [1]has a hundred sheep, and one of them has gone astray, does he not leave the ninety-nine on the mountains and go and search for the one that is straying?

13 "And if it turns out that he finds it, truly I say to you, he rejoices over it more than over the ninety-nine which have not gone astray.

14 "Thus it is not *the* will [1]of your Father who is in heaven that one of these little ones perish.

Discipline and Prayer

15 "And [a]if your brother sins[1], go and reprove him [2]in private; if he listens to you, you have won your brother.

16 "But if he does not listen *to you,* take one or two more with you, so that [a]BY THE MOUTH OF TWO OR THREE WITNESSES EVERY [1]FACT MAY BE CONFIRMED.

17 "And if he refuses to listen to them, [a]tell it to the church; and if he refuses to listen even to the church, [b]let him be to you as [1]a Gentile and [1]a [2]tax-gatherer.

18 "Truly I say to you, [a]whatever you shall [1]bind on earth shall be bound in heaven; and whatever you [2]loose on earth shall be loosed in heaven.

19 "Again I say to you, that if two of you agree on earth about anything that they may ask, [a]it shall be done for them [1]by My Father who is in heaven.

20 "For where two or three have gathered together in My name, [a]there I am in their midst."

Forgiveness

21 Then Peter came and said to Him, "Lord, [a]how often shall my brother sin against me and I forgive him? Up to [b]seven times?"

22 Jesus *said to him, "I do not say to you, up to seven times, but up to [a]seventy times seven.

23 "For this reason [a]the kingdom of heaven may be compared to a certain king who wished to [b]settle accounts with his slaves.

24 "And when he had begun to settle *them,* there was brought to him one who owed him [1]ten thousand talents.

25 "But since he [1a]did not have *the means* to repay, his lord commanded him [b]to be sold, along with his wife and children and all that he had, and repayment to be made.

26 "The slave therefore falling down, [a]prostrated himself before him, saying, 'Have patience with me, and I will repay you everything.'

27 "And the lord of that slave felt compassion and released him and [a]forgave him the [1]debt.

28 "But that slave went out and found one of his fellow slaves who owed him a hundred [1]denarii; and he seized him and *began* to choke *him,* saying, 'Pay back what you owe.'

29 "So his fellow slave fell down and *began* to entreat him, saying, 'Have patience with me and I will repay you.'

24 [1]Equivalent to two denarii or two days' wages paid as a temple tax [a]Ex. 30:13; 38:26
25 [1]Or, *anticipated what he was going to say,* [a]Rom. 13:7 [b]Matt. 22:17, 19
26 [1]Or, *free*
27 [1]Lit., *cause them to stumble* [2]Or, *shekel,* worth four drachmas [a]Matt. 5:29, 30; 18:6, 8, 9; Mark 9:42, 43, 45, 47; Luke 17:2; John 6:61; 1 Cor. 8:13
1 [1]Lit., *hour* [2]Lit., *greater* [a]Matt. 18:1-5: *Mark 9:33-37; Luke 9:46-48* [b]Luke 22:24
2 [1]Lit., *in their midst*
3 [1]Lit., *are turned* [a]Matt. 19:14; Mark 10:15; Luke 18:17; 1 Cor. 14:20; 1 Pet. 2:2
6 [1]Lit., *millstone turned by a donkey* [a]Mark 9:42; Luke 17:2; 1 Cor. 8:12 [b]Matt. 17:27
7 [a]Luke 17:1; 1 Cor. 11:19; 1 Tim. 4:1
8 [a]Matt. 5:30; Mark 9:43
9 [1]Lit., *Gehenna of fire* [a]Matt. 5:29; Mark 9:47 [b]Matt. 5:22
10 [a]Luke 1:19; Acts 12:15; Rev. 8:2
11 [1]Most ancient mss. do not contain this v. [a]Luke 19:10
12 [1]Or, *comes to have* [a]Matt. 18:12-14: *Luke 15:4-7*
14 [1]Lit., *before*
15 [1]Many mss. add *against you* [2]Lit., *between you and him alone* [a]Lev. 19:17; Luke 17:3; Gal. 6:1; 2 Thess. 3:15; James 5:19
16 [1]Lit., *word* [a]Deut. 19:15; John 8:17; 2 Cor. 13:1; 1 Tim. 5:19; Heb. 10:28
17 [1]Lit., *the* [2]I.e., Collector of Roman taxes for profit [a]1 Cor. 6:1ff. [b]2 Thess. 3:6, 14f.
18 [1]Or, *forbid* [2]Or, *permit* [a]Matt. 16:19; John 20:23
19 [1]Lit., *from* [a]Matt. 7:7
20 [a]Matt. 28:20
21 [a]Matt. 18:15 [b]Luke 17:4
22 [a]Gen. 4:24
23 [a]Matt. 13:24 [b]Matt. 25:19
24 [1]About $10,000,000 in silver content but worth much more in buying power
25 [1]Or, *was unable to* [a]Luke 7:42 [b]Ex. 21:2; Lev. 25:39; 2 Kin. 4:1; Neh. 5:5
26 [a]Matt. 8:2

27 [1]Or, *loan* [a]Luke 7:42
28 [1]The denarius was equivalent to one day's wage

30"He was unwilling however, but
went and threw him in prison until he
should pay back what was owed.
31"So when his fellow slaves saw what
had happened, they were deeply grieved
and came and reported to their lord all
that had happened.
32"Then summoning him, his lord
*said to him, 'You wicked slave, I for-
gave you all that debt because you
entreated me.
33 '[a]Should you not also have had
mercy on your fellow slave, even as I had
mercy on you?'
34"And his lord, moved with anger,
handed him over to the torturers until he
should repay all that was owed him.
35"[a]So shall My heavenly Father also
do to you, if each of you does not forgive
his brother from [1]your heart."

Concerning Divorce

19 [a]AND it came about that when
Jesus had finished these words,
He departed from Galilee, and [b]came
into the region of Judea beyond the
Jordan;
2 and great multitudes followed
Him, and [a]He healed them there.
3 And *some* Pharisees came to Him,
testing Him, and saying, "[a]Is it lawful
for a man to [1]divorce his wife for any
cause at all?"
4 And He answered and said, "Have
you not read, [a]that He who created *them*
from the beginning MADE THEM MALE
AND FEMALE,
5 and said, '[a]FOR THIS CAUSE A MAN
SHALL LEAVE HIS FATHER AND MOTHER,
AND SHALL CLEAVE TO HIS WIFE; AND
[b]THE TWO SHALL BECOME ONE FLESH'?
6"Consequently they are no longer
two, but one flesh. What therefore God
has joined together, let no man separate."
7 They *said to Him, "[a]Why then did
Moses command to GIVE HER A CERTIFI-
CATE OF DIVORCE AND SEND *her* AWAY?"
8 He *said to them, "[1]Because of
your hardness of heart, Moses permitted
you to [2]divorce your wives; but from the
beginning it has not been this way.
9"And I say to you, [a]whoever [1]di-
vorces his wife, except for [2]immorality,
and marries another woman [3]commits
adultery[4]."
10 The disciples *said to Him, "If the
relationship of the man with his wife is
like this, it is better not to marry."
11 But He said to them, "[a]Not all men
can accept this statement, but [b]*only*
those to whom it has been given.
12"For there are eunuchs who were
born that way from their mother's
womb; and there are eunuchs who were
made eunuchs by men; and there are
also eunuchs who made themselves eunuchs for the sake of the kingdom of
heaven. He who is able to accept *this,* let
him accept *it.*"

Jesus Blesses Little Children

13 [a]Then *some* children were brought
to Him so that He might lay His hands
on them and pray; and the disciples
rebuked them.
14 But Jesus said, "[1a]Let the children
alone, and do not hinder them from
coming to Me; for [b]the kingdom of
heaven belongs to such as these."
15 And after laying His hands on
them, He departed from there.

The Rich Young Ruler

16 [a]And behold, one came to Him and
said, "Teacher, what good thing shall I
do that I may obtain [b]eternal life?"
17 And He said to him, "Why are you
asking Me about what is good? There is
only One who is good; but [a]if you wish
to enter into life, keep the commandments."
18 He *said to Him, "Which ones?"
And Jesus said, "[a]YOU SHALL NOT COM-
MIT MURDER; YOU SHALL NOT COMMIT
ADULTERY; YOU SHALL NOT STEAL; YOU
SHALL NOT BEAR FALSE WITNESS;
19 [a]HONOR YOUR FATHER AND
MOTHER; and [b]YOU SHALL LOVE YOUR
NEIGHBOR AS YOURSELF."
20 The young man *said to Him, "All
these things I have kept; what am I still
lacking?"
21 Jesus said to him, "If you wish to
be [1]complete, go *and* [a]sell your possessions and give to *the* poor, and you shall
have [b]treasure in heaven; and come,
follow Me."
22 But when the young man heard this
statement, he went away grieved; for he
was one who owned much property.
23 And Jesus said to His disciples,
"Truly I say to you, [a]it is hard for a rich
man to enter the kingdom of heaven.
24"And again I say to you, [a]it is easier
for a camel to go through the eye of a
needle, than for a rich man to enter the
kingdom of God."
25 And when the disciples heard *this,*
they were very astonished and said,
"Then who can be saved?"
26 And looking upon *them* Jesus said
to them, "[a]With men this is impossible,
but with God all things are possible."

The Disciples' Reward

27 Then Peter answered and said to
Him, "Behold, we have left everything
and followed You; what then will there
be for us?"
28 And Jesus said to them, "Truly I
say to you, that you who have followed
Me, in the regeneration when [a]the Son of
Man will sit on [1]His glorious throne,
[b]you also shall sit upon twelve thrones,
judging the twelve tribes of Israel.
29"And [a]everyone who has left houses
or brothers or sisters or father or
mother[1] or children or farms for My
name's sake, shall receive [2]many times
as much, and shall inherit eternal life.

33 [a]Matt. 6:12; Eph. 4:32
35 [1]Lit., *your hearts* [a]Matt. 6:14
1 [a]Matt. 7:28 [b]Matt. 19:1-9: *Mark 10:1-12*
2 [a]Matt. 4:23
3 [1]Or, *send away* [a]Matt. 5:31
4 [a]Gen. 1:27; 5:2
5 [a]Gen. 2:24; Eph. 5:31 [b]1 Cor. 6:16
7 [a]Deut. 24:1-4; Matt. 5:31
8 [1]Or, *With reference to* [2]Or, *send away*
9 [1]Or, *sends away* [2]I.e., sexual immorality [3]Some early mss. read *makes her commit adultery* [4]Some early mss. add *and he who marries a divorced woman commits adultery* [a]Matt. 5:32
11 [a]1 Cor. 7:7ff. [b]Matt. 13:11
13 [a]Matt. 19:13-15: *Mark 10:13-16; Luke 18:15-17*
14 [1]Or, *Permit the children* [a]Matt. 18:3; Mark 10:15; Luke 18:17; 1 Cor. 14:20; 1 Pet. 2:2 [b]Matt. 5:3
16 [a]Matt. 19:16-29: *Mark 10:17-30; Luke 18:18-30;* Luke 10:25-28 [b]Matt. 25:46
17 [a]Lev. 18:5; Neh. 9:29; Ezek. 20:21
18 [a]Ex. 20:13-16; Deut. 5:17-20
19 [a]Ex. 20:12; Deut. 5:16 [b]Lev. 19:18
21 [1]Or, *perfect* [a]Luke 12:33; 16:9; Acts 2:45; 4:34f. [b]Matt. 6:20
23 [a]Matt. 13:22; Mark 10:23f.; Luke 18:24
24 [a]Mark 10:25; Luke 18:25
26 [a]Gen. 18:14; Job 42:2; Jer. 32:17; Zech. 8:6; Mark 10:27; Luke 1:37; 18:27
28 [1]Lit., *the throne of His glory* [a]Matt. 25:31 [b]Luke 22:30; Rev. 3:21; 4:4; 11:16; 20:4
29 [1]Many mss. add *or wife* [2]Many mss. read *a hundredfold* [a]Matt. 6:33; Mark 10:29f.; Luke 18:29f.

30"[a]But many *who are* first will be last; and *the* last, first.

Laborers in the Vineyard

20 "FOR [a]the kingdom of heaven is like [1]a landowner who went out early in the morning to hire laborers [2]for his [b]vineyard.

2"And when he had agreed with the laborers for a [1]denarius for the day, he sent them into his vineyard.

3"And he went out about the [1]third hour and saw others standing idle in the market place;

4 and to those he said, 'You too go into the vineyard, and whatever is right I will give you.' And *so* they went.

5"Again he went out about the [1]sixth and the ninth hour, and did [2]the same thing.

6"And about the [1]eleventh *hour* he went out, and found others standing; and he *said to them, 'Why have you been standing here idle all day long?'

7"They *said to him, 'Because no one hired us.' He *said to them, 'You too go into the vineyard.'

8"And when [a]evening had come, the [1]owner of the vineyard *said to his [b]foreman, 'Call the laborers and pay them their wages, beginning with the last *group* to the first.'

9"And when those *hired* about the eleventh hour came, each one received a [1]denarius.

10"And when those *hired* first came, they thought that they would receive more; and they also received each one a denarius.

11"And when they received it, they grumbled at the landowner,

12 saying, 'These last men have worked *only* one hour, and you have made them equal to us who have borne the burden and the [a]scorching heat of the day.'

13"But he answered and said to one of them, '[a]Friend, I am doing you no wrong; did you not agree with me for a denarius?

14 'Take what is yours and go your way, but I wish to give to this last man the same as to you.

15 'Is it not lawful for me to do what I wish with what is my own? Or is your [a]eye [1]envious because I am [2]generous?'

16"Thus [a]the last shall be first, and the first last."

Death, Resurrection Foretold

17 [a]And as Jesus was about to go up to Jerusalem, He took the twelve *disciples* aside by themselves, and on the way He said to them,

18"Behold, we are going up to Jerusalem; and the Son of Man [a]will be [1]delivered to the chief priests and scribes, and they will condemn Him to death,

19 and [a]will deliver Him to the Gentiles to mock and scourge and crucify *Him,* and on [b]the third day He will be raised up."

Preferment Asked

20 [a]Then the mother of [b]the sons of Zebedee came to Him with her sons, [c]bowing down, and making a request of Him.

21 And He said to her, "What do you wish?" She *said to Him, "Command that in Your kingdom these two sons of mine [a]may sit, one on Your right and one on Your left."

22 But Jesus answered and said, "You do not know what you are asking for. Are you able [a]to drink the cup that I am about to drink?" They *said to Him, "We are able."

23 He *said to them, "[a]My cup you shall drink; but to sit on My right and on *My* left, this is not Mine to give, [b]but it is for those for whom it has been [c]prepared by My Father."

24 And hearing *this,* the ten became indignant with the two brothers.

25 [a]But Jesus called them to Himself, and said, "You know that the rulers of the Gentiles lord it over them, and *their* great men exercise authority over them.

26"It is not so among you, [a]but whoever wishes to become great among you shall be your servant,

27 and whoever wishes to be first among you shall be your slave;

28 just as [a]the Son of Man [b]did not come to be served, but to serve, and to give His [1]life a ransom for many."

Sight for the Blind

29 [a]And as they were going out from Jericho, a great multitude followed Him.

30 And behold, two blind men sitting by the road, hearing that Jesus was passing by, cried out, saying, "Lord, [a]have mercy on us, [b]Son of David!"

31 And the multitude sternly told them to be quiet; but they cried out all the more, saying, "Lord, have mercy on us, [a]Son of David!"

32 And Jesus stopped and called them, and said, "What do you want Me to do for you?"

33 They *said to Him, "Lord, *we want* our eyes to be opened."

34 And moved with compassion, Jesus touched their eyes; and immediately they regained their sight and followed Him.

The Triumphal Entry

21 [a]AND when they had approached Jerusalem and had come to Bethphage, to [b]the Mount of Olives, then Jesus sent two disciples,

2 saying to them, "Go into the village opposite you, and immediately you will find a donkey tied *there* and a colt with her; untie *them,* and bring *them* to Me.

3"And if anyone says something to you, you shall say, 'The Lord has need of

---

30 [a]Matt. 20:16; Mark 10:31; Luke 13:30

1 [1]Lit., *a man, a landowner* [2]Lit., *into* [a]Matt. 13:24 [b]Matt. 21:28, 33

2 [1]The denarius was equivalent to one day's wage

3 [1]I.e., 9 a.m.

5 [1]I.e., Noon and 3 p.m. [2]Lit., *similarly*

6 [1]I.e., 5 p.m.

8 [1]Or, *lord* [a]Lev. 19:13; Deut. 24:15 [b]Luke 8:3

9 [1]The denarius was equivalent to one day's wage

12 [a]Jon. 4:8; Luke 12:55; James 1:11

13 [a]Matt. 22:12; 26:50

15 [1]Lit., *evil* [2]Lit., *good* [a]Deut. 15:9; Matt. 6:23; Mark 7:22

16 [a]Matt. 19:30; Mark 10:31; Luke 13:30

17 [a]Matt. 20:17-19: *Mark 10:32-34; Luke 18:31-33*

18 [1]Or, *betrayed* [a]Matt. 16:21

19 [a]Matt. 27:2; Acts 2:23; 3:13; 4:27; 21:11 [b]Matt. 16:21; 17:23; Luke 18:32f.

20 [a]Matt. 20:20-28: *Mark 10:35-45* [b]Matt. 4:21; 10:2 [c]Matt. 8:2

21 [a]Matt. 19:28

22 [a]Is. 51:17, 22; Jer. 49:12; Matt. 26:39, 42; Luke 22:42; John 18:11

23 [a]Acts 12:2; Rev. 1:9 [b]Matt. 13:11 [c]Matt. 25:34

25 [a]Matt. 20:25-28; Luke 22:25-27

26 [a]Matt. 23:11; Mark 9:35; 10:43; Luke 22:26

28 [1]Or, *soul* [a]Matt. 8:20 [b]Matt. 26:28; John 13:13ff.; 2 Cor. 8:9; Phil. 2:7; 1 Tim. 2:6; Titus 2:14; Heb. 9:28; Rev. 1:5

29 [a]Matt. 20:29-34: *Mark 10:46-52; Luke 18:35-43;* Matt. 9:27-31

30 [a]Matt. 20:31 [b]Matt. 9:27

31 [a]Matt. 9:27

1 [a]Matt. 21:1-9: *Mark 11:1-10; Luke 19:29-38* [b]Matt. 24:3; 26:30; Mark 11:1; 13:3; 14:26; Luke 19:29, 37; 21:37; 22:39; John 8:1; Acts 1:12

them,' and immediately he will send them."

4 [a]Now this took place that what was spoken through the prophet might be fulfilled, saying,

5 "[a]SAY TO THE DAUGHTER OF ZION,
'BEHOLD YOUR KING IS COMING TO YOU,
GENTLE, AND MOUNTED ON A DONKEY,
EVEN ON A COLT, THE FOAL OF A BEAST OF BURDEN.'"

6 And the disciples went and did just as Jesus had directed them,

7 and brought the donkey and the colt, and laid on them their garments, [1]on which He sat.

8 And most of the multitude [a]spread their garments in the road, and others were cutting branches from the trees, and spreading them in the road.

9 And the multitudes going before Him, and those who followed after were crying out, saying,
"Hosanna to the [a]Son of David;
[b]BLESSED IS HE WHO COMES IN THE NAME OF THE LORD;
Hosanna [c]in the highest!"

10 And when He had entered Jerusalem, all the city was stirred, saying, "Who is this?"

11 And the multitudes were saying, "This is [a]the prophet Jesus, from [b]Nazareth in Galilee."

Cleansing the Temple

12 [a]And Jesus entered the temple and cast out all those who were buying and selling in the temple, and overturned the tables of the [b]moneychangers and the seats of those who were selling [1c]doves.

13 And He *said to them, "It is written, '[a]MY HOUSE SHALL BE CALLED A HOUSE OF PRAYER'; but you are making it a [b]ROBBERS' [1]DEN."

14 And *the* blind and *the* lame came to Him in the temple, and [a]He healed them.

15 But when the chief priests and the scribes saw the wonderful things that He had done, and the children who were crying out in the temple and saying, "Hosanna to the [a]Son of David," they became indignant,

16 and said to Him, "Do You hear what these are saying?" And Jesus *said to them, "Yes; have you never read, '[a]OUT OF THE MOUTH OF INFANTS AND NURSING BABES THOU HAST PREPARED PRAISE FOR THYSELF'?"

17 And He left them and went out of the city to [a]Bethany, and lodged there.

The Barren Fig Tree

18 [a]Now in the morning, when He returned to the city, He became hungry.

19 And seeing a lone [a]fig tree by the road, He came to it, and found nothing on it except leaves only; and He *said to it, "No longer shall there ever be *any* fruit from you." And at once the fig tree withered.

20 And seeing *this,* the disciples marveled, saying, "How did the fig tree wither at once?"

21 And Jesus answered and said to them, "Truly I say to you, [a]if you have faith, and do not doubt, you shall not only do what was done to the fig tree, but even if you say to this mountain, 'Be taken up and cast into the sea,' it shall happen.

22 "And [a]all things you ask in prayer, believing, you shall receive."

Authority Challenged

23 [a]And when He had come into the temple, the chief priests and the elders of the people came to Him [b]as He was teaching, and said, "By what authority are You doing these things, and who gave You this authority?"

24 And Jesus answered and said to them, "I will ask you one [1]thing too, which if you tell Me, I will also tell you by what authority I do these things.

25 "The baptism of John was from what *source,* from heaven or from men?" And they *began* reasoning among themselves, saying, "If we say, 'From heaven,' He will say to us, 'Then why did you not believe him?'

26 "But if we say, 'From men,' we fear the multitude; for they all hold John to be [a]a prophet."

27 And answering Jesus, they said, "We do not know." He also said to them, "Neither will I tell you by what authority I do these things.

Parable of Two Sons

28 "But what do you think? A man had two [1]sons, and he came to the first and said, '[2]Son, go work today in the [a]vineyard.'

29 "And he answered and said, '[1]I will, sir'; and he did not go.

30 "And he came to the second and said [1]the same thing. But he answered and said, '[2]I will not'; *yet* he afterward regretted *it* and went.

31 "Which of the two did the will of his father?" They *said, "The latter." Jesus *said to them, "Truly I say to you that [a]the [1]tax-gatherers and harlots [2]will get into the kingdom of God before you.

32 "For John came to you in the way of righteousness and you did not believe him; but [a]the tax-gatherers and harlots did believe him; and you, seeing this, did not even feel remorse afterward so as to believe him.

Parable of the Landowner

33 "Listen to another parable. [a]There was a [1]landowner who [b]PLANTED A [c]VINEYARD AND PUT A WALL AROUND IT AND DUG A WINE PRESS IN IT, AND BUILT A TOWER, and rented it out to [2]vine-growers, and [d]went on a journey.

---

4 [a]Matt. 21:4-9: *Mark 11:7-10; Luke 19:35-38; John 12:12-15*

5 [a]Is. 62:11; Zech. 9:9

7 [1]Lit., *on them*

8 [a]2 Kin. 9:13

9 [a]Matt. 9:27 [b]Ps. 118:26 [c]Luke 2:14

11 [a]Matt. 21:26; Mark 6:15; Luke 7:16, 39; 13:33; 24:19; John 1:21, 25; 4:19; 6:14; 7:40; 9:17; Acts 3:22f.; 7:37 [b]Matt. 2:23

12 [1]Lit., *the doves* [a]Matt. 21:12-16: *Mark 11:15-18; Luke 19:45-47;* Matt. 21:12, 13: *John 2:13-16* [b]Ex. 30:13 [c]Lev. 1:14; 5:7; 12:8

13 [1]Lit., *cave* [a]Is. 56:7 [b]Jer. 7:11

14 [a]Matt. 4:23

15 [a]Matt. 9:27

16 [a]Ps. 8:2; Matt. 11:25

17 [a]Matt. 26:6; Mark 11:1, 11, 12; 14:3; Luke 19:29; 24:50; John 11:1, 18; 12:1

18 [a]Matt. 21:18-22: *Mark 11:12-14, 20-24*

19 [a]Luke 13:6-9

21 [a]Matt. 17:20; Mark 11:23; Luke 17:6; James 1:6

22 [a]Matt. 7:7

23 [a]Matt. 21:23-27: *Mark 11:27-33; Luke 20:1-8* [b]Matt. 26:55

24 [1]Lit., *word*

26 [a]Matt. 11:9; Mark 6:20

28 [1]Lit., *children* [2]Lit., *Child* [a]Matt. 20:1; 21:33

29 [1]Some mss. read *'I will not'; yet he afterward regretted and went*

30 [1]Lit., *likewise* [2]Some mss. read *'I will'; and he did not go*

31 [1]I.e., Collectors of Roman taxes for profit [2]Or, *are getting into* [a]Luke 7:29, 37-50

32 [a]Luke 3:12; 7:29f.

33 [1]Lit., *a man, a householder* [2]Or, *tenant farmers,* also vv. 34, 35, 38, 40 [a]Matt. 21:33-46: *Mark 12:1-12; Luke 20:9-19* [b]Is. 5:1, 2 [c]Matt. 20:1; 21:28 [d]Matt. 25:14

34 "And when the [1]harvest time approached, he [a]sent his slaves to the vine-growers to receive his produce.

35 "And the vine-growers took his slaves and beat one, and killed another, and stoned a third.

36 "Again he [a]sent another group of slaves larger than the first; and they did [1]the same thing to them.

37 "But afterward he sent his son to them, saying, 'They will respect my son.'

38 "But when the vine-growers saw the son, they said among themselves, 'This is the heir; come, let us kill him, and seize his inheritance.'

39 "And they took him, and threw him out of the vineyard, and killed him.

40 "Therefore when the [1]owner of the vineyard comes, what will he do to those vine-growers?"

41 They *said to Him, "He will bring those wretches to a wretched end, and [a]will rent out the vineyard to other vine-growers, who will pay him the proceeds at the *proper* seasons."

42 Jesus *said to them, "Did you never read in the Scriptures,

'[a]THE STONE WHICH THE BUILDERS REJECTED,
THIS BECAME THE CHIEF CORNER *stone;*
THIS CAME ABOUT FROM THE LORD,
AND IT IS MARVELOUS IN OUR EYES'?

43 "Therefore I say to you, the kingdom of God will be taken away from you, and be given to a nation producing the fruit of it.

44 "And [a]he who falls on this stone will be broken to pieces; but on whomever it falls, it will scatter him like dust."

45 And when the chief priests and the Pharisees heard His parables, they understood that He was speaking about them.

46 And when they sought to seize Him, they [a]feared the multitudes, because they held Him to be a [b]prophet.

Parable of the Marriage Feast

22 AND Jesus answered and spoke to them again in parables, saying,

2 "[a]The kingdom of heaven may be compared to [1]a king, who [2]gave a [b]wedding feast for his son.

3 "And he [a]sent out his slaves to call those who had been invited to the wedding feast, and they were unwilling to come.

4 "Again he [a]sent out other slaves saying, 'Tell those who have been invited, "Behold, I have prepared my dinner; my oxen and my fattened livestock are *all* butchered and everything is ready; come to the wedding feast." '

5 "But they paid no attention and went their way, one to his own [1]farm, another to his business,

6 and the rest seized his slaves and mistreated them and killed them.

7 "But the king was enraged and sent his armies, and destroyed those murderers, and set their city on fire.

8 "Then he *said to his slaves, 'The wedding is ready, but those who were invited were not worthy.

9 'Go therefore to [a]the main highways, and as many as you find *there,* invite to the wedding feast.'

10 "And those slaves went out into the streets, and gathered together all they found, both evil and good; and the wedding hall was filled with [1]dinner guests.

11 "But when the king came in to look over the dinner guests, he saw there [a]a man not dressed in wedding clothes,

12 and he *said to him, '[a]Friend, how did you come in here [1]without wedding clothes?' And he was speechless.

13 "Then the king said to the servants, 'Bind him hand and foot, and cast him into [a]the outer darkness; in that place there shall be weeping and gnashing of teeth.'

14 "For many are [1a]called, but few *are* [a]chosen."

Tribute to Caesar

15 [a]Then the Pharisees went and counseled together how they might trap Him [1]in what He said.

16 And they *sent their disciples to Him, along with the [a]Herodians, saying, "Teacher, we know that You are truthful and teach the way of God in truth, and [1]defer to no one; for You are not partial to any.

17 "Tell us therefore, what do You think? Is it [1]lawful to give a [a]poll-tax to [b]Caesar, or not?"

18 But Jesus perceived their [1]malice, and said, "Why are you testing Me, you hypocrites?

19 "Show Me the [a]coin *used* for the poll-tax." And they brought Him a [1]denarius.

20 And He *said to them, "Whose likeness and inscription is this?"

21 They *said to Him, "Caesar's." Then He *said to them, "[a]Then render to Caesar the things that are Caesar's; and to God the things that are God's."

22 And hearing *this,* they marveled, and [a]leaving Him, they went away.

Jesus Answers the Sadducees

23 [a]On that day *some* [b]Sadducees (who say [c]there is no resurrection) came to Him and questioned Him,

24 saying, "Teacher, Moses said, '[a]IF A MAN DIES, HAVING NO CHILDREN, HIS BROTHER AS NEXT OF KIN SHALL MARRY HIS WIFE, AND RAISE UP AN OFFSPRING TO HIS BROTHER.'

25 "Now there were seven brothers with us; and the first married and died, and having no offspring left his wife to his brother;

26 so also the second, and the third, down to the seventh.

34 [1]Lit., *the season of the fruits* [a]Matt. 22:3
36 [1]Lit., *likewise* [a]Matt. 22:4
40 [1]Lit., *lord*
41 [a]Matt. 8:11f.; Acts 13:46; 18:6; 28:28
42 [a]Ps. 118:22f.; Acts 4:11; Rom. 9:33; 1 Pet. 2:7
44 [a]Is. 8:14, 15
46 [a]Matt. 21:26 [b]Matt. 21:11
2 [1]Lit., *a man, a king* [2]Lit., *made* [a]Matt. 13:24; 22:2-14; Luke 14:16-24 [b]Luke 12:36; John 2:2
3 [a]Matt. 21:34
4 [a]Matt. 21:36
5 [1]Or, *field*
9 [a]Ezek. 21:21; Obad. 14
10 [1]Lit., *those reclining at the table*
11 [a]2 Kin. 10:22; Zech. 3:3, 4
12 [1]Lit., *not having* [a]Matt. 20:13; 26:50
13 [a]Matt. 8:12; 25:30; Luke 13:28
14 [1]Or, *invited* [a]Matt. 24:22; 2 Pet. 1:10; Rev. 17:14
15 [1]Lit., *in word* [a]Matt. 22:15-22: *Mark 12:13-17; Luke 20:20-26*
16 [1]I.e., you court no man's favor [a]Mark 3:6; 8:15; 12:13
17 [1]Or, *permissible* [a]Matt. 17:25 [b]Luke 2:1; 3:1
18 [1]Or, *wickedness*
19 [1]The denarius was equivalent to one day's wage [a]Matt. 17:25
21 [a]Mark 12:17; Luke 20:25; Rom. 13:7
22 [a]Mark 12:12
23 [a]Matt. 22:23-33: *Mark 12:18-27; Luke 20:27-40* [b]Matt. 3:7 [c]Acts 23:8
24 [a]Deut. 25:5

NAMES

The name of God (*Yahweh* or *Jah*) was often incorporate into personal names. *Abijah* means *"God is his father"*; *Elijah* means *"my God is Yahweh"*; *Jonathan* means *"gift of Yahweh."* Other names remind people of birth. *Moses* means *"drawn forth"* because he was taken from the river Nile.

JESUS' CHILDHOOD

Luke 2:21-39. Mary and Joseph had Jesus circumcised on the eighth day. At the end of forty days they went up to Jerusalem (about four miles from Bethlehem) to offer the required sacrifices and to pay the redemption money (vv.22-24). It is clear that Mary and Joseph were extremely poor because they could afford only two birds. Immediately after this they returned to Nazareth with Jesus (v. 39). If the wise men arrived at the time when Jesus was approximately two years old (Matthew 2:16), then the wise men could have gone to Nazareth. The richness of the gifts (which had great symbolic value) must have been a fortune to Mary and Joseph. The gifts might have enabled them to set up a carpentry business and to look after Jesus and later a larger family.

BREAKING THE LAWS

Leviticus 18. The laws of Leviticus 18 were not always kept during Bible times. Sarah was Abraham's half sister (Genesis 20:12), and Amnon wanted to marry his half sister Tamar in 2 Samuel 13 (cf. Leviticus 18:11). Moses' parents were nephew and aunt (Exodus 6:20; cf. Leviticus 18:12-13). Jacob married two sisters (Genesis 29:16-30; cf. Leviticus 18:18).

FIDELITY

Proverbs 5. A man was exhorted to be faithful, and he was put to death if he violated a married woman (Leviticus 20:10). He was not punished if he violated an unmarried girl; he had to marry her (Deuteronomy 22:28). The married woman on the other hand was put to death if she had sexual relations with any man other than her husband, unless her husband forgave her. This was called the *"great sin."* This was because the woman was the fundamental center of the family, and for her to be unfaithful would be for her to destroy the family. This was not considered true of the man.

THE BURIAL OF JESUS

John 20. Because Jesus was wrapped in a cocoon, one can understand why it was that the disciples saw and *then* believed in the resurrection, and why it was that the body had not been stolen. Jesus' body had passed through the cocoon of spice-impregnated bandages, just as it did through the door of the upper room. Looking quickly through the doorway of the tomb, John thought that the body was still there because he could see the cocoon, and therefore he would not enter. Only when John and Peter went in and saw that there was a gap where the face should have been (the cap was separated) did they realize what had happened.

BEREAVEMENT

Psalm 119:136; Jeremiah 9:1. These verses reflect an extreme kind of grief, which was much the same as that felt at time of death. The psalmist wept rivers of water because he knew what would follow the breaking of the law.

SWEETER THAN HONEY

Psalm 19:9-10. When a boy first went to school in New Testament times, he went down to the synagogue while it was still dark to listen to the story of how Moses received the law. Then he was taken to the teacher's house for breakfast, where he received cakes with letters of the law written on them. In school, the boy received a slate with passages from the Scriptures written on it. The slate was smeared with honey. He had to trace the letters through the honey with his pen, and it was natural to lick the nib of the pen as he proceeded. The idea was that he would realize that the purpose of his going to school was to absorb the Scriptures. This learning practice seems to have been based on an old custom that David refers to in the psalm.

TEACHING BY ROTE

Isaiah 28:9-10. Here the people are complaining about the way the prophet is teaching them, for it is *"do and do...rule on rule...a little here, a little there."* It literally means, *"s after s, q after q"* and refers to the method of teaching by repetition. The master would say an s, and the scholars would have to repeat it.

"SCHOOLMASTER"?

Galatians 3:24 (KJV). The *"schoolmaster"* of this passage is not the teacher, but the slave whose job it was to take his master's sons to school and to stop them from getting into mischief. Paul says that Jesus is the real teacher; the Jewish law was simply the slave that took the pupils safely to school.

Mary - *surrendered to God*

Mary, the mother of Jesus, is the most honored and revered woman in history. Though being the mother of Christ would have entitled anyone to special recognition, it is because of who Mary herself was that she was chosen by God.

Mary was a young girl when God called her to be part of the miracle of Jesus's virgin birth. In doing so, God indicated He found her the most perfect woman in the world, yet she did not flaunt her holiness, nor was she overcome by pride. She did not brag to her friends of visits from angels. Even in the presence of angels, she behaved humbly and obediently.

Although God's will for Mary was a high honor, the situation is even today difficult to understand. When God told her the Holy Spirit would come upon her and she would give birth to the Son of God, she did not ask questions. Neither did she ask for a detailed plan, or say she needed time to think things over. She accepted what God said completely, surrendering her body and her life totally to God's will.

The social implications of Mary's pregnancy are staggering even in today's moral climate. Her very life was endangered by her conception outside of marriage. Yet she believed God would take care of her and protect her and her unborn son. She was not overwhelmed at the difficulties of her position. Rather she concentrated on the spiritual importance of what God was doing.

Throughout Jesus's upbringing, Mary showed great spiritual discernment. She was able to focus on the larger picture of what God wanted to do and see past what was happening in her own life.

Because of her acceptance of God's plan, she could encourage Jesus's ministry beginning at an early age. She was even able to bear the heartache as she remained with her son at the foot of the cross.

After Christ's Ascension into heaven, Mary was with the apostles in the Upper Room. Throughout her life, she was faithful to God's service and surrendered to God's will.

QUESTIONS

1. Many believe young people cannot be used effectively by God, but Mary's life disproves this. What ways can you find to serve God today?

2. Mary was willing to sacrifice her body, her reputation, her social acceptance, her own understanding—everything for God's use. Which areas of your life could you more fully surrender to God's will?

3. Mary's life centered on what God wanted to do for the world. What do you think God wants to do in the world today? How can you be a part of His work?

4. Mary's life stands out as an example of difference—she was willing, all her life—to be different. How can you be more willing to stand out as different in your own life for God?

27"And last of all, the woman died.
28"In the resurrection therefore whose
wife of the seven shall she be? For they
all had her."
29 But Jesus answered and said to
them, "You are mistaken, [a]not [1]under-
standing the Scriptures, or the power of
God.
30"For in the resurrection they neither
[a]marry, nor are given in marriage, but
are like angels[1] in heaven.
31"But regarding the resurrection of
the dead, have you not read that which
was spoken to you by God, saying,
32 '[a]I AM THE GOD OF ABRAHAM, AND
THE GOD OF ISAAC, AND THE GOD OF
JACOB'? He is not the God of the dead
but of the living."
33 And when the multitudes heard
this, [a]they were astonished at His teaching.
34 [a]But when the Pharisees heard that
He had put [b]the Sadducees to silence,
they gathered themselves together.
35 And one of them, [1a]a lawyer, asked
Him *a question,* testing Him,
36"Teacher, which is the great commandment in the Law?"
37 And He said to him, " '[a]YOU SHALL
LOVE THE LORD YOUR GOD WITH ALL
YOUR HEART, AND WITH ALL YOUR SOUL,
AND WITH ALL YOUR MIND.'
38"This is the great and [1]foremost
commandment.
39"The second is like it, '[a]YOU SHALL
LOVE YOUR NEIGHBOR AS YOURSELF.'
40"[a]On these two commandments depend the whole Law and the Prophets."
41 [a]Now while the Pharisees were
gathered together, Jesus asked them a
question,
42 saying, "What do you think about
[1]the Christ, whose son is He?" They
*said to Him, "[a]*The son* of David."
43 He *said to them, "Then how does
David [1a]in the Spirit call Him 'Lord,'
saying,
44 '[a]THE LORD SAID TO MY LORD,
"SIT AT MY RIGHT HAND,
UNTIL I PUT THINE ENEMIES BE-
NEATH THY FEET" '?
45"If David then calls Him 'Lord,'
how is He his son?"
46 And [a]no one was able to answer
Him a word, nor did anyone dare from
that day on to ask Him another question.

Pharisaism Exposed

23 [a]THEN Jesus spoke to the multitudes and to His disciples,
2 saying, "[a]The scribes and the
Pharisees have seated themselves in the
chair of Moses;
3 therefore all that they tell you, do
and observe, but do not do according to
their deeds; for they say *things,* and do
not do *them.*
4"And [a]they tie up heavy loads, and
lay them on men's shoulders; but they
themselves are unwilling to move them
with *so much as* a finger.
5"But they do all their deeds [a]to be
noticed by men; for they [b]broaden their
[1]phylacteries, and lengthen [c]the tassels
of their garments.
6"And they [a]love the place of honor
at banquets, and the chief seats in the
synagogues,
7 and respectful greetings in the
market places, and being called by men,
[a]Rabbi.
8"But [a]do not be called [b]Rabbi; for
One is your Teacher, and you are all
brothers.
9"And do not call *anyone* on earth
your father; for [a]One is your Father, He
who is in heaven.
10"And do not be called [1]leaders; for
One is your Leader, *that is,* Christ.
11"[a]But the greatest among you shall
be your servant.
12"And [a]whoever exalts himself shall
be humbled; and whoever humbles himself shall be exalted.

Seven Woes

13"[a]But woe to you, scribes and Pharisees, hypocrites, [b]because you shut off
the kingdom of heaven [1]from men; for
you do not enter in yourselves, nor do
you allow those who are entering to go
in.
14 ["[1]Woe to you, scribes and Pharisees, hypocrites, because [a]you devour
widows' houses, even while for a pretense you make long prayers; therefore
you shall receive greater condemnation.]
15"Woe to you, scribes and Pharisees,
hypocrites, because you travel about on
sea and land to make one [1a]proselyte;
and when he becomes one, you make
him twice as much a son of [2b]hell as
yourselves.
16"Woe to you, [a]blind guides, who
say, '[b]Whoever swears by the [1]temple,
that is nothing; but whoever swears by
the gold of the [1]temple, he is obligated.'
17"You fools and blind men; [a]which is
[1]more important, the gold, or the [2]tem-
ple that sanctified the gold?
18"And, 'Whoever swears by the altar,
that is nothing, but whoever swears by
the [1]offering upon it, he is obligated.'
19"You blind men, [a]which is [1]more
important, the [2]offering or the altar that
sanctifies the [2]offering?
20"Therefore he who swears, swears
both by the altar and by everything on it.
21"And he who swears by the [1]temple,
swears *both* by [2]the temple and by Him
who [a]dwells within it.
22"And he who swears by heaven,
[a]swears *both* by the throne of God and
by Him who sits upon it.

29 [1]Or, *knowing* [a]John 20:9
30 [1]Other mss. add *of God* [a]Matt. 24:38; Luke 17:27
32 [a]Ex. 3:6
33 [a]Matt. 7:28
34 [a]Matt. 22:34-40: *Mark 12:28-31;* Luke 10:25-37 [b]Matt. 3:7
35 [1]I.e., an expert in the Mosaic Law [a]Luke 7:30; 10:25; 11:45, 46, 52; 14:3; Titus 3:13
37 [a]Deut. 6:5
38 [1]Or, *first*
39 [a]Lev. 19:18; Matt. 19:19; Gal. 5:14
40 [a]Matt. 7:12
41 [a]Matt. 22:41-46: *Mark 12:35-37; Luke 20:41-44*
42 [1]I.e., the Messiah [a]Matt. 9:27
43 [1]Or, *by inspiration* [a]2 Sam. 23:2; Rev. 1:10; 4:2
44 [a]Ps. 110:1; Matt. 26:64; Mark 16:19; Acts 2:34f.; 1 Cor. 15:25; Heb. 1:13; 10:13
46 [a]Mark 12:34; Luke 14:6; 20:40

1 [a]Matt. 23:1-7: *Mark 12:38, 39; Luke 20:45, 46*
2 [a]Deut. 33:3f.; Ezra 7:6, 25; Neh. 8:4
4 [a]Luke 11:46; Acts 15:10
5 [1]I.e., small boxes containing Scripture texts worn for religious purposes [a]Matt. 6:1, 5, 16 [b]Ex. 13:9; Deut. 6:8; 11:18 [c]Matt. 9:20
6 [a]Luke 11:43; 14:7; 20:46
7 [a]Matt. 23:8; 26:25, 49; Mark 9:5; 10:51; 11:21; John 1:38, 49; 3:2, 26; 4:31; 6:25; 9:2; 11:8; 20:16
8 [a]James 3:1 [b]Matt. 23:7; 26:25, 49; Mark 9:5; 10:51; 11:21; 14:45; John 1:38, 49; 3:2, 26; 4:31; 6:25; 9:2; 11:8; 20:16
9 [a]Matt. 6:9; 7:11
10 [1]Or, *teachers*
11 [a]Matt. 20:26
12 [a]Luke 14:11; 18:14
13 [1]Lit., *in front of* [a]Matt. 23:15, 16, 23, 25, 27, 29 [b]Luke 11:52
14 [1]This v. not found in the earliest mss. [a]Mark 12:40; Luke 20:47
15 [1]Or, *convert* [2]Gr., *Gehenna* [a]Acts 2:10; 6:5; 13:43 [b]Matt. 5:22
16 [1]Or, *sanctuary* [a]Matt. 15:14; 23:24 [b]Matt. 5:33-35
17 [1]Lit., *greater* [2]Or, *sanctuary* [a]Ex. 30:29

18 [1]Or, *gift*
19 [1]Lit., *greater* [2]Or, *gift* [a]Ex. 29:37
21 [1]Or, *sanctuary* [2]Lit., *it* [a]1 Kin. 8:13; Ps. 26:8; 132:14
22 [a]Is. 66:1; Matt. 5:34

23“[a]Woe to you, scribes and Pharisees,
hypocrites! For you tithe the mint and dill
and [1]cummin, and have neglected the
weightier provisions of the law: justice
and mercy and faithfulness; but these
are the things you should have done
without neglecting the others.
24“You [a]blind guides, who strain out a
gnat and swallow a camel!
25“Woe to you, scribes and Pharisees,
hypocrites! For [a]you clean the outside of
the cup and of the dish, but inside they
are full [1]of robbery and self-indulgence.
26“You blind Pharisee, first [a]clean the
inside of the cup and of the dish, so that
the outside of it may become clean also.
27“[a]Woe to you, scribes and Pharisees,
hypocrites! For you are like whitewashed tombs which on the outside
appear beautiful, but inside they are full
of dead men’s bones and all uncleanness.
28“Even so you too outwardly appear
righteous to men, but inwardly you are
full of hypocrisy and lawlessness.
29“[a]Woe to you, scribes and Pharisees,
hypocrites! For you build the tombs of
the prophets and adorn the monuments
of the righteous,
30 and say, ‘If we had been *living* in
the days of our fathers, we would not
have been partners with them in *shedding* the blood of the prophets.’
31“Consequently you bear witness
against yourselves, that you [a]are [1]sons of
those who murdered the prophets.
32“[1]Fill up then the measure *of the
guilt* of your fathers.
33“You serpents, [a]you brood of vipers,
how shall you escape the [1]sentence of
[2b]hell?
34“[a]Therefore, behold, [b]I am sending
you prophets and wise men and scribes;
some of them you will kill and crucify,
and some of them you will [c]scourge in
your synagogues, and [d]persecute from
city to city,
35 that upon you may fall *the guilt of*
all the righteous blood shed on earth,
from the blood of righteous [a]Abel to the
blood of Zechariah, the [b]son of Berechiah, whom [c]you murdered between the
[1]temple and the altar.
36“Truly I say to you, all these things
shall come upon [a]this generation.

Lament over Jerusalem

37“[a]O Jerusalem, Jerusalem, who [b]kills
the prophets and stones those who are
sent to her! How often I wanted to
gather your children together, [c]the way a
hen gathers her chicks under her wings,
and you were unwilling.
38“Behold, [a]your house is being left to
you [1]desolate!
39“For I say to you, from now on you
shall not see Me until you say, ‘[a]BLESSED
IS HE WHO COMES IN THE NAME OF THE
LORD!’ ”

Signs of Christ’s Return

24 [a]AND Jesus [b]came out from the
temple and was going away
[1]when His disciples came up to point out
the temple buildings to Him.
2 And He answered and said to
them, “Do you not see all these things?
Truly I say to you, [a]not one stone here
shall be left upon another, which will not
be torn down.”
3 And as He was sitting on [a]the
Mount of Olives, the disciples came to
Him privately, saying, “Tell us, when
will these things be, and what *will be* the
sign of [b]Your coming, and of the [1]end of
the age?”
4 And Jesus answered and said to
them, “[a]See to it that no one misleads
you.
5“For [a]many will come in My name,
saying, ‘I am the [1]Christ,’ and will
mislead many.
6“And you will be hearing of [a]wars
and rumors of wars; see that you are not
frightened, for *those things* must take
place, but *that* is not yet the end.
7“For [a]nation will rise against nation,
and kingdom against kingdom, and in
various places there will be [b]famines and
earthquakes.
8“[a]But all these things are *merely* the
beginning of birth pangs.
9“[a]Then they will deliver you to
tribulation, and will kill you, and [b]you
will be hated by all nations on account
of My name.
10“And at that time many will [1a]fall
away and will deliver up one another
and hate one another.
11“And many [a]false prophets will
arise, and will mislead many.
12“And because lawlessness is increased, [1]most people’s love will grow
cold.
13“[a]But the one who endures to the
end, he shall be saved.
14“And this [a]gospel of the kingdom
[b]shall be preached in the whole [1c]world
for a witness to all the nations, and then
the end shall come.

Perilous Times

15“Therefore when you see the
[a]ABOMINATION OF DESOLATION which
was spoken of through Daniel the
prophet, standing in [b]the holy place ([c]let
the reader understand),
16 then let those who are in Judea flee
to the mountains;
17 let him who is on [a]the housetop not
go down to get the things out that are in
his house;
18 and let him who is in the field not
turn back to get his cloak.
19“But [a]woe to those who are with
child and to those who nurse babes in
those days!
20“But pray that your flight may not
be in the winter, or on a Sabbath;

23 [1]Similar to caraway seeds [a]Matt. 23:13; Luke 11:42
24 [a]Matt. 23:16
25 [1]Or, *as a result of* [a]Mark 7:4; Luke 11:39f.
26 [a]Mark 7:4; Luke 11:39f.
27 [a]Luke 11:44; Acts 23:3
29 [a]Luke 11:47f.
31 [1]Or, *descendants* [a]Matt. 23:34, 37; Acts 7:51f.
32 [1]Lit., *And fill up*
33 [1]Or, *judgment* [2]Gr., *Gehenna* [a]Matt. 3:7; Luke 3:7 [b]Matt. 5:22
34 [a]Matt. 23:34-36; Luke 11:49-51 [b]2 Chr. 36:15, 16 [c]Matt. 10:17 [d]Matt. 10:23
35 [1]Or, *sanctuary* [a]Gen. 4:8ff.; Heb. 11:4 [b]Zech. 1:1 [c]2 Chr. 24:21
36 [a]Matt. 10:23; 24:34
37 [a]Matt. 23:37-39: *Luke 13:34, 35* [b]Matt. 5:12 [c]Ruth 2:12
38 [1]Some mss. do not contain *desolate* [a]1 Kin. 9:7f.; Jer. 22:5
39 [a]Ps. 118:26; Matt. 21:9

1 [1]Lit., *and* [a]Matt. 24:1-51: *Mark 13; Luke 21:5-36* [b]Matt. 21:23
2 [a]Luke 19:44
3 [1]Or, *consummation* [a]Matt. 21:1 [b]Matt. 16:27f.; 24:27, 37, 39
4 [a]Jer. 29:8
5 [1]I.e., Messiah [a]Matt. 24:11, 24; Acts 5:36f.; 1 John 2:18; 4:3
6 [a]Rev. 6:4
7 [a]2 Chr. 15:6; Is. 19:2; Rev. 6:8, 12 [b]Acts 11:28; Rev. 6:5, 6
8 [a]Matt. 24:8-20; Luke 21:12-24
9 [a]Matt. 10:17; John 16:2 [b]Matt. 10:22; John 15:18ff.
10 [1]Lit., *be caused to stumble* [a]Matt. 11:6
11 [a]Matt. 7:15; 24:24
12 [1]Lit., *the love of many*
13 [a]Matt. 10:22
14 [1]Lit., *inhabited earth* [a]Matt. 4:23 [b]Rom. 10:18; Col. 1:6, 23 [c]Luke 2:1; 4:5; Acts 11:28; 17:6, 31; 19:27; Rom. 10:18; Heb. 1:6; 2:5; Rev. 3:10; 16:14
15 [a]Dan. 9:27; 11:31; 12:11 [b]Mark 13:14; Luke 21:20; John 11:48; Acts 6:13f.; 21:28 [c]Mark 13:14; Rev. 1:3
17 [a]1 Sam. 9:25; 2 Sam. 11:2; Matt. 10:27; Luke 5:19; 12:3; 17:31; Acts 10:9
19 [a]Luke 23:29

21 for then there will be a [a]great
tribulation, such as has not occurred
since the beginning of the world until
now, nor ever shall.
22"And unless those days had been cut
short, no [1]life would have been saved;
but for [a]the sake of the [2]elect those days
shall be cut short.
23"[a]Then if anyone says to you, 'Behold, here is the [1]Christ,' or '[2]There *He*
is,' do not believe *him.*
24"For false Christs and [a]false prophets will arise and will show great [1b]signs
and wonders, so as to mislead, if possible, even [c]the [2]elect.
25"Behold, I have told you in advance.
26"If therefore they say to you, 'Behold, He is in the wilderness,' do not go
forth, *or,* 'Behold, He is in the inner
rooms,' do not believe *them.*
27"[a]For just as the lightning comes
from the east, and flashes even to the
west, so shall the [b]coming of the [c]Son of
Man be.
28"[a]Wherever the corpse is, there the
[1]vultures will gather.

The Glorious Return

29"But immediately after the [a]tribula-
tion of those days [b]THE SUN WILL BE
DARKENED, AND THE MOON WILL NOT
GIVE ITS LIGHT, AND [c]THE STARS WILL
FALL from [1]the sky, and the powers of
[1]the heavens will be shaken,
30 and then [a]the sign of the Son of
Man will appear in the sky, and then all
the tribes of the earth will mourn, and
they will see [b]the SON OF MAN COMING
ON THE CLOUDS OF THE SKY with power
and great glory.
31"And [a]He will send forth His angels
with [b]A GREAT TRUMPET and THEY WILL
GATHER TOGETHER His [1c]elect from [d]the
four winds, from one end of the sky to
the other.

Parable of the Fig Tree

32"Now learn the parable from the fig
tree: when its branch has already become tender, and puts forth its leaves,
you know that summer is near;
33 even so you too, when you see all
these things, [1]recognize that [2]He is near,
right [a]at the [3]door.
34"Truly I say to you, [a]this [1]genera-
tion will not pass away until all these
things take place.
35"[a]Heaven and earth will pass away,
but My words shall not pass away.
36"But [a]of that day and hour no one
knows, not even the angels of heaven,
nor the Son, but the Father alone.
37"For [1]the [a]coming of the Son of
Man will be [b]just like the days of Noah.
38"For as in those days which were
before the flood they were eating and
drinking, they were [a]marrying and giving in marriage, until the day that [b]Noah
entered the ark,
39 and they did not [1]understand until
the flood came and took them all away;
so shall the [a]coming of the Son of Man
be.
40"Then there shall be two men in the
field; one [1]will be taken, and one [1]will be
left.
41"[a]Two women *will be* grinding at the
[1b]mill; one [2]will be taken, and one [2]will
be left.

Be Ready for His Coming

42"Therefore [a]be on the alert, for you
do not know which day your Lord is
coming.
43"But [1]be sure of this, that [a]if the
head of the house had known [b]at what
time of the night the thief was coming,
he would have been on the alert and
would not have allowed his house to be
[2]broken into.
44"For this reason [a]you be ready too;
for [b]the Son of Man is coming at an
hour when you do not think *He will.*
45"[a]Who then is the [b]faithful and
[c]sensible slave whom his [1]master [d]put in
charge of his household to give them
their food at the proper time?
46"Blessed is that slave whom his
[1]master finds so doing when he comes.
47"Truly I say to you, that [a]he will put
him in charge of all his possessions.
48"But if that evil slave says in his
heart, 'My [1]master [2]is not coming for a
long time,'
49 and shall begin to beat his fellow
slaves and eat and drink with [1]drunk-
ards;
50 the [1]master of that slave will come
on a day when he does not expect *him*
and at an hour which he does not know,
51 and shall [1]cut him in pieces and
[2]assign him a place with the hypocrites;
[a]weeping shall be there and the gnashing
of teeth.

Parable of Ten Virgins

25 "THEN [a]the kingdom of heaven
will be comparable to ten virgins,
who took their [b]lamps, and went out to
meet the bridegroom.
2"And five of them were foolish, and
five were [a]prudent.
3"For when the foolish took their
lamps, they took no oil with them,
4 but the [a]prudent took oil in flasks
along with their lamps.
5"Now while the bridegroom was
delaying, they all got drowsy and *began*
to sleep.
6"But at midnight there was a shout,
'Behold, the bridegroom! Come out to
meet *him.'*
7"Then all those virgins rose, and
trimmed their lamps.

21 [a]Dan. 12:1; Joel 2:2; Matt. 24:29
22 [1]Lit., *flesh* [2]Or, *chosen ones* [a]Matt. 22:14; 24:24, 31; Luke 18:7
23 [1]I.e., Messiah [2]Lit., *here* [a]Luke 17:23f.
24 [1]Or, *attesting miracles* [2]Or, *chosen ones* [a]Matt. 7:15; 24:11 [b]John 4:48; 2 Thess. 2:9 [c]Matt. 22:14; 24:22, 31; Luke 18:7
27 [a]Luke 17:24 [b]Matt. 24:3, 37, 39 [c]Matt. 8:20
28 [1]Or, *eagles* [a]Job 39:30; Ezek. 39:17; Hab. 1:8; Luke 17:37
29 [1]Or, *heaven* [a]Matt. 24:21 [b]Is. 13:10; 24:23; Ezek. 32:7; Joel 2:10, 31; 3:15f.; Amos 5:20; 8:9; Zeph. 1:15; Matt. 24:29-35; Acts 2:20; Rev. 6:12-17; 8:12 [c]Is. 34:4; Rev. 6:13
30 [a]Matt. 24:3; Rev. 1:7 [b]Dan. 7:13; Matt. 16:27; 24:3, 37, 39
31 [1]Or, *chosen ones* [a]Matt. 13:41 [b]Ex. 19:16; Deut. 30:4; Is. 27:13; Zech. 9:14; 1 Cor. 15:52; 1 Thess. 4:16; Heb. 12:19; Rev. 8:2; 11:15 [c]Matt. 24:22 [d]Dan. 7:2; Zech. 2:6; Rev. 7:1
33 [1]Lit., *know* [2]Or, *it* [3]Lit., *doors* [a]James 5:9; Rev. 3:20
34 [1]Or, *race* [a]Matt. 10:23; 16:28; 23:36
35 [a]Matt. 5:18; Mark 13:31; Luke 21:33
36 [a]Mark 13:32; Acts 1:7
37 [1]Lit., *just as . . . were the days* [a]Matt. 16:27; 24:3, 30, 39 [b]Gen. 6:5; 7:6-23; Luke 17:26f.
38 [a]Matt. 22:30 [b]Gen. 7:7
39 [1]Lit., *know* [a]Matt. 16:27; 24:3, 30, 37
40 [1]Lit., *is*
41 [1]I.e., handmill [2]Lit., *is* [a]Luke 17:35 [b]Ex. 11:5; Deut. 24:6; Is. 47:2
42 [a]Matt. 24:43, 44; 25:10, 13; Luke 12:39f.; 21:36
43 [1]Lit., *know this* [2]Lit., *dug through* [a]Matt. 24:42, 44; 25:10, 13; Luke 12:39f.; 21:36 [b]Matt. 14:25; Mark 6:48; 13:35; Luke 12:38
44 [a]Matt. 24:42, 43; 25:10, 13; Luke 12:39f.; 21:36 [b]Matt. 24:27
45 [1]Or, *lord* [a]Matt. 24:45-51: *Luke 12:42-46* [b]Matt. 25:21, 23; Luke 16:10 [c]Matt. 7:24; 10:16; 25:2ff. [d]Matt. 25:21, 23
46 [1]Or, *lord*
47 [a]Matt. 25:21, 23
48 [1]Or, *lord* [2]Lit., *lingers*
49 [1]Lit., *those who get drunk*
50 [1]Or, *lord*
51 [1]Or, *severely scourge him* [2]Lit., *appoint his portion* [a]Matt. 8:12

1 [a]Matt. 13:24 [b]John 18:3; Acts 20:8; Rev. 4:5; 8:10
2 [a]Matt. 7:24; 10:16; 25:2ff.
4 [a]Matt. 7:24; 10:16; 25:2ff.

8"And the foolish said to the prudent, 'Give us some of your oil, for our
lamps are going out.'
9"But the [a]prudent answered, saying,
'No, there will not be enough for us and
you *too;* go instead to the dealers and
buy *some* for yourselves.'
10"And while they were going away to
make the purchase, the bridegroom
came, and those who were [a]ready went
in with him to [b]the wedding feast; and
[c]the door was shut.
11"And later the other virgins also
came, saying, '[a]Lord, lord, open up for
us.'
12"But he answered and said, 'Truly I
say to you, I do not know you.'
13"[a]Be on the alert then, for you do
not know the day nor the hour.

Parable of the Talents

14"[a]For *it is* just like a man [b]*about* to
go on a journey, who called his own
slaves, and entrusted his possessions to
them.
15"And to one he gave five [1a]talents,
to another, two, and to another, one,
each according to his own ability; and
he [b]went on his journey.
16"Immediately the one who had received the five [a]talents went and traded
with them, and gained five more talents.
17"In the same manner the one who
had received the two *talents* gained two
more.
18"But he who received the one *talent*
went away and dug in the ground, and
hid his [1]master's money.
19"Now after a long time the master of
those slaves *came and *[a]settled accounts with them.
20"And the one who had received the
five [a]talents came up and brought five
more talents, saying, 'Master, you entrusted five talents to me; see, I have
gained five more talents.'
21"His master said to him, 'Well done,
good and [a]faithful slave; you were faithful with a few things, I will [b]put you in
charge of many things, enter into the joy
of your [1]master.'
22"The one also who *had received* the
two [a]talents came up and said, 'Master,
you entrusted to me two talents; see, I
have gained two more talents.'
23"His master said to him, 'Well done,
good and [a]faithful slave; you were faithful with a few things, I will put you in
charge of many things; enter into the joy
of your master.'
24"And the one also who had received
the one [a]talent came up and said, 'Master, I knew you to be a hard man,
reaping where you did not sow, and
gathering where you scattered no *seed.*
25'And I was afraid, and went away
and hid your talent in the ground; see,
you have what is yours.'
26"But his master answered and said
to him, 'You wicked, lazy slave, you
knew that I reap where I did not sow,
and gather where I scattered no *seed.*
27'Then you ought to have put my
money [1]in the bank, and on my arrival I
would have received my *money* back
with interest.
28'Therefore take away the talent
from him, and give it to the one who has
the ten talents.'
29"[a]For to everyone who has shall
more be given, and he shall have an
abundance; but from the one who does
not have, even what he does have shall
be taken away.
30"And cast out the worthless slave
into [a]the outer darkness; in that place
there shall be weeping and gnashing of
teeth.

The Judgment

31"But when [a]the Son of Man comes
in His glory, and all the angels with
Him, then [b]He will sit on His glorious
throne.
32"And all the nations will be [a]gath-
ered before Him; and He will separate
them from one another, [b]as the shepherd
separates the sheep from the goats;
33 and He will put the sheep [a]on His
right, and the goats [b]on the left.
34"Then the King will say to those on
His right, 'Come, you who are blessed of
My Father, [a]inherit the kingdom prepared for you [b]from the foundation of
the world.
35'For [a]I was hungry, and you gave
Me *something* to eat; I was thirsty, and
you gave Me drink; [b]I was a stranger,
and you invited Me in;
36 [a]naked, and you clothed Me; I was
sick, and you [b]visited Me; [c]I was in
prison, and you came to Me.'
37"Then the righteous will answer
Him, saying, 'Lord, when did we see
You hungry, and feed You, or thirsty,
and give You drink?
38'And when did we see You a stranger, and invite You in, or naked, and
clothe You?
39'And when did we see You sick, or
in prison, and come to You?'
40"And [a]the King will answer and say
to them, 'Truly I say to you, [b]to the
extent that you did it to one of these
brothers of Mine, *even* the least *of them,*
you did it to Me.'
41"Then He will also say to those on
His left, '[a]Depart from Me, accursed
ones, into the [b]eternal fire which has
been prepared for [c]the devil and his
angels;
42 for I was hungry, and you gave Me
nothing to eat; I was thirsty, and you
gave Me nothing to drink;
43 I was a stranger, and you did not
invite Me in; naked, and you did not
clothe Me; sick, and in prison, and you
did not visit Me.'
44"Then they themselves also will
answer, saying, 'Lord, when did we see
You hungry, or thirsty, or a stranger, or

9 [a]Matt. 7:24; 10:16; 25:2ff.

10 [a]Matt. 24:42ff. [b]Luke 12:35f. [c]Matt. 7:21ff.; Luke 13:25

11 [a]Matt. 7:21ff.; Luke 13:25

13 [a]Matt. 24:42ff.

14 [a]Matt. 25:14-30; Luke 19:12-27 [b]Matt. 21:33

15 [1]A talent was $1,000 in silver content, much more in buying power. [a]Matt. 18:24; Luke 19:13 [b]Matt. 21:33

16 [a]Matt. 18:24; Luke 19:13

18 [1]Or, *lord's*

19 [a]Matt. 18:23

20 [a]Matt. 18:24; Luke 19:13

21 [1]Or, *lord* [a]Matt. 24:45, 47; 25:23 [b]Luke 12:44; 22:29; Rev. 3:21; 21:7

22 [a]Matt. 18:24; Luke 19:13

23 [a]Matt. 24:45, 47; 25:21

24 [a]Matt. 18:24; Luke 19:13

27 [1]Lit., *to the bankers*

29 [a]Matt. 13:12; Mark 4:25; Luke 8:18; John 15:2

30 [a]Matt. 8:12; 22:13; Luke 13:28

31 [a]Matt. 16:27f.; 1 Thess. 4:16; 2 Thess. 1:7; Heb. 9:28; Jude 14; Rev. 1:7 [b]Matt. 19:28

32 [a]Matt. 13:49; 2 Cor. 5:10 [b]Ezek. 34:17, 20

33 [a]1 Kin. 2:19; Ps. 45:9 [b]Eccl. 10:2

34 [a]Matt. 5:3; 19:29; Luke 12:32; 1 Cor. 6:9; 15:50; Gal. 5:21; James 2:5 [b]Matt. 13:35; Luke 11:50; John 17:24; Eph. 1:4; Heb. 4:3; 9:26; 1 Pet. 1:20; Rev. 13:8; 17:8

35 [a]Is. 58:7; Ezek. 18:7, 16; James 2:15, 16 [b]Job 31:32; Heb. 13:2

36 [a]Is. 58:7; Ezek. 18:7, 16; James 2:15, 16 [b]James 1:27 [c]2 Tim. 1:16f.

40 [a]Matt. 25:34; Luke 19:38; Rev. 17:14; 19:16 [b]Prov. 19:17; Matt. 10:42; Heb. 6:10

41 [a]Matt. 7:23 [b]Mark 9:48; Luke 16:24; Jude 7 [c]Matt. 4:10; Rev. 12:9

naked, or sick, or in prison, and did not [1]take care of You?'

45 "Then He will answer them, saying, 'Truly I say to you, to the extent that you did not do it to one of the least of these, you did not do it to Me.'

46 "And these will go away into [a]eternal punishment, but the righteous into [b]eternal life."

The Plot to Kill Jesus

26 [a]AND it came about that when Jesus had finished all these words, He said to His disciples,

2 "[a]You know that after two days [b]the Passover is coming, and the Son of Man is *to be* [c]delivered up for crucifixion."

3 [a]Then the chief priests and the elders of the people were gathered together in [b]the court of the high priest, named [c]Caiaphas;

4 and they [a]plotted together to seize Jesus by stealth, and kill *Him.*

5 But they were saying, "Not during the festival, [a]lest a riot occur among the people."

The Precious Ointment

6 [a]Now when Jesus was in [b]Bethany, at the home of Simon the leper,

7 [a]a woman came to Him with an alabaster vial of very costly perfume, and she poured it upon His head as He reclined *at the table.*

8 But the disciples were indignant when they saw *this,* and said, "Why this waste?

9 "For this *perfume* might have been sold for a high price and *the money* given to the poor."

10 But Jesus, aware of this, said to them, "Why do you bother the woman? For she has done a good deed to Me.

11 "For [a]the poor you have with you always; but you do not always have Me.

12 "For when she poured this perfume upon My body, she did it [a]to prepare Me for burial.

13 "Truly I say to you, [a]wherever this gospel is preached in the whole world, what this woman has done shall also be spoken of in memory of her."

Judas' Bargain

14 [a]Then one of the twelve, named [b]Judas Iscariot, went to the chief priests,

15 and said, "What are you willing to give me [1]to [2a]deliver Him up to you?" And [b]they weighed out to him thirty [3]pieces of silver.

16 And from then on he *began* looking for a good opportunity to [1]betray Him.

17 [a]Now on the first *day* of [b]Unleavened Bread the disciples came to Jesus, saying, "Where do You want us to prepare for You to eat the Passover?"

18 And He said, "Go into the city to [a]a certain man, and say to him, 'The Teacher says, "[b]My time is at hand; I *am to* keep the Passover at your house with My disciples." ' "

19 And the disciples did as Jesus had directed them; and they prepared the Passover.

The Last Passover

20 [a]Now when evening had come, He was reclining *at the table* with the twelve disciples.

21 And as they were eating, He said, "[a]Truly I say to you that one of you will betray Me."

22 And being deeply grieved, they [1]each one began to say to Him, "Surely not I, Lord?"

23 And He answered and said, "[a]He who dipped his hand with Me in the bowl is the one who will betray Me.

24 "The Son of Man *is to* go, [a]just as it is written of Him; but woe to that man by whom the Son of Man is betrayed! [b]It would have been good [1]for that man if he had not been born."

25 And [a]Judas, who was betraying Him, answered and said, "Surely it is not I, [b]Rabbi?" He *said to him, "[c]You have said *it* yourself."

The Lord's Supper Instituted

26 [a]And while they were eating, Jesus took *some* bread, and [1b]after a blessing, He broke *it* and gave *it* to the disciples, and said, "Take, eat; this is My body."

27 And when He had taken a cup and given thanks, He gave *it* to them, saying, "Drink from it, all of you;

28 for [a]this is My blood of the covenant, which is poured out for [b]many for forgiveness of sins.

29 "But I say to you, I will not drink of this fruit of the vine from now on until that day when I drink it new with you in My Father's kingdom."

30 [a]And after singing a hymn, they went out to [b]the Mount of Olives.

31 Then Jesus *said to them, "You will all [1a]fall away because of Me this night, for it is written, '[b]I WILL STRIKE DOWN THE SHEPHERD, AND THE SHEEP OF THE FLOCK SHALL BE [c]SCATTERED.'

32 "But after I have been raised, [a]I will go before you to Galilee."

33 But Peter answered and said to Him, "*Even* though all may [1]fall away because of You, I will never fall away."

34 Jesus said to him, "[a]Truly I say to you that [b]this *very* night, before a cock crows, you shall deny Me three times."

35 Peter *said to Him, "[a]Even if I have to die with You, I will not deny You." All the disciples said the same thing too.

The Garden of Gethsemane

36 [a]Then Jesus *came with them to a place called [b]Gethsemane, and *said to His disciples, "Sit here while I go over there and pray."

44 [1]Or, *serve*
46 [a]Dan. 12:2; John 5:29; Acts 24:15 [b]Matt. 19:29; John 3:15f., 36; 5:24; 6:27, 40, 47, 54; 17:2f.; Acts 13:46, 48; Rom. 2:7; 5:21; 6:23; Gal. 6:8; 1 John 5:11

1 [a]Matt. 7:28
2 [a]Matt. 26:2-5: *Mark 14:1, 2; Luke 22:1, 2* [b]John 11:55; 13:1 [c]Matt. 10:4
3 [a]John 11:47 [b]Matt. 26:58, 69; 27:27; Mark 14:54, 66; 15:16; Luke 22:55; John 18:15 [c]Matt. 26:57; Luke 3:2; John 11:49; 18:13, 14, 24, 28; Acts 4:6
4 [a]Matt. 12:14
5 [a]Matt. 27:24
6 [a]Matt. 26:6-13: *Mark 14:3-9;* Luke 7:37-39; John 12:1-8 [b]Matt. 21:17
7 [a]Luke 7:37f.
11 [a]Deut. 15:11; Mark 14:7; John 12:8
12 [a]John 19:40
13 [a]Mark 14:9
14 [a]Matt. 26:14-16: *Mark 14:10, 11; Luke 22:3-6* [b]Matt. 10:4; 26:25, 47; 27:3; John 6:71; 12:4; 13:26; Acts 1:16
15 [1]Lit., *and I will* [2]Or, *betray* [3]Or, *silver shekels* [a]Matt. 10:4 [b]Ex. 21:32; Zech. 11:12
16 [1]Or, *deliver Him up*
17 [a]Matt. 26:17-19: *Mark 14:12-16; Luke 22:7-13* [b]Ex. 12:18-20
18 [a]Mark 14:13; Luke 22:10 [b]John 7:6, 8
20 [a]Matt. 26:20-24: *Mark 14:17-21*
21 [a]Luke 22:21-23; John 13:21f.
22 [1]Or, *one after another*
23 [a]Ps. 41:9; John 13:18, 26
24 [1]Lit., *for him if that man had not been born* [a]Matt. 26:31, 54, 56; Mark 9:12; Luke 24:25-27, 46; Acts 17:2f.; 26:22f.; 1 Cor. 15:3; 1 Pet. 1:10f. [b]Matt. 18:7; Mark 14:21
25 [a]Matt. 26:14 [b]Matt. 23:7; 26:49 [c]Matt. 26:64; 27:11; Luke 22:70
26 [1]Lit., *having blessed* [a]Matt. 26:26-29: *Mark 14:22-25; Luke 22:17-20; 1 Cor. 11:23-25;* 1 Cor. 10:16 [b]Matt. 14:19
28 [a]Ex. 24:8; Heb. 9:20 [b]Matt. 20:28
30 [a]Matt. 26:30-35: *Mark 14:26-31; Luke 22:31-34* [b]Matt. 21:1
31 [1]Or, *stumble* [a]Matt. 11:6 [b]Zech. 13:7 [c]John 16:32

32 [a]Matt. 28:7, 10, 16; Mark 16:7
33 [1]Or, *stumble*
34 [a]Matt. 26:75; John 13:38 [b]Mark 14:30
35 [a]John 13:37
36 [a]Matt. 26:36-46: *Mark 14:32-42; Luke 22:40-46* [b]Mark 14:32; Luke 22:39; John 18:1

37 And He took with Him [a]Peter and
the two sons of Zebedee, and began to
be grieved and distressed.
38 Then He *said to them, "[a]My soul
is deeply grieved, to the point of death;
remain here and [b]keep watch with Me."
39 And He went a little beyond *them,*
and fell on His face and prayed, saying,
"My Father, if it is possible, let [a]this cup
pass from Me; [b]yet not as I will, but as
Thou wilt."
40 And He *came to the disciples and
*found them sleeping, and *said to
Peter, "So, you *men* could not [a]keep
watch with Me for one hour?
41 "[a]Keep watching and praying, that
you may not enter into temptation; [b]the
spirit is willing, but the flesh is weak."
42 He went away again a second time
and prayed, saying, "My Father, if this
[a]cannot pass away unless I drink it, [b]Thy
will be done."
43 And again He came and found
them sleeping, for their eyes were heavy.
44 And He left them again, and went
away and prayed a third time, saying the
same thing once more.
45 Then He *came to the disciples,
and *said to them, "[1]Are you still sleeping and taking your rest? Behold, [a]the
hour is at hand and the Son of Man is
being betrayed into the hands of sinners.
46 "Arise, let us be going; behold, the
one who betrays Me is at hand!"

Jesus' Betrayal and Arrest

47 [a]And while He was still speaking,
behold, [b]Judas, one of the twelve, came
up, [1]accompanied by a great multitude
with swords and clubs, from the chief
priests and elders of the people.
48 Now he who was betraying Him
gave them a sign, saying, "Whomever I
shall kiss, He is the one; seize Him."
49 And immediately he went to Jesus
and said, "Hail, [a]Rabbi!" and kissed
Him.
50 And Jesus said to him, "[a]Friend, *do*
what you have come for." Then they
came and laid hands on Jesus and seized
Him.
51 And behold, [a]one of those who
were with Jesus [1]reached and drew out
his [b]sword, and struck the [c]slave of the
high priest, and [2]cut off his ear.
52 Then Jesus *said to him, "Put your
sword back into its place; for [a]all those
who take up the sword shall perish by
the sword.
53 "Or do you think that I cannot
appeal to My Father, and He will at
once put at My disposal more than
twelve [1a]legions of [b]angels?
54 "How then shall [a]the Scriptures be
fulfilled, that it must happen this way?"
55 At that time Jesus said to the
multitudes, "Have you come out with
swords and clubs to arrest Me as against
a robber? [a]Every day I used to sit in the
temple teaching and you did not seize
Me.
56 "But all this has taken place that
[a]the Scriptures of the prophets may be
fulfilled." Then all the disciples left Him
and fled.

Jesus before Caiaphas

57 [a]And those who had seized Jesus
led Him away to [b]Caiaphas, the high
priest, where the scribes and the elders
were gathered together.
58 But [a]Peter also was following Him
at a distance as far as the [b]courtyard of
the high priest, and entered in, and sat
down with the [1c]officers to see the outcome.
59 Now the chief priests and the
whole [1a]Council kept trying to obtain
false testimony against Jesus, in order
that they might put Him to death;
60 and they did not find *any,* even
though many false witnesses came forward. But later on [a]two came forward,
61 and said, "This man stated, '[a]I am
able to destroy the [1]temple of God and
to rebuild it [2]in three days.' "
62 And the high priest stood up and
said to Him, "Do You make no answer?
What is it that these men are testifying
against You?"
63 But [a]Jesus kept silent. [b]And the
high priest said to Him, "I [1c]adjure You
by [d]the living God, that You tell us
whether You are [2]the Christ, [e]the Son of
God."
64 Jesus *said to him, "[a]You have said
it *yourself*; nevertheless I tell you, [1]here-
after you shall see [b]THE SON OF MAN
SITTING AT THE RIGHT HAND OF POWER,
and [c]COMING ON THE CLOUDS OF
HEAVEN."
65 Then the high priest [a]tore his
[1]robes, saying, "He has blasphemed!
What further need do we have of witnesses? Behold, you have now heard the
blasphemy;
66 what do you think?" They answered and said, "[a]He is deserving of
death!"
67 [a]Then they [b]spat in His face and
beat Him with their fists; and others
[1]slapped Him,
68 and said, "[a]Prophesy to us, You
[1]Christ; who is the one who hit You?"

Peter's Denials

69 [a]Now Peter was sitting outside in
the [b]courtyard, and a certain servant-girl
came to him and said, "You too were
with Jesus the Galilean."
70 But he denied *it* before them all,
saying, "I do not know what you are
talking about."
71 And when he had gone out to the
gateway, another *servant-girl* saw him
and *said to those who were there, "This
man was with Jesus of Nazareth."
72 And again he denied *it* with an
oath, "I do not know the man."

37 [a]Matt. 4:21; 17:1; Mark 5:37
38 [a]John 12:27 [b]Matt. 26:40, 41
39 [a]Matt. 20:22 [b]Matt. 26:42; Mark 14:36; Luke 22:42; John 6:38
40 [a]Matt. 26:38
41 [a]Matt. 26:38 [b]Mark 14:38
42 [a]Matt. 20:22 [b]Matt. 26:39; Mark 14:36; Luke 22:42; John 6:38
45 [1]Or, *Keep on sleeping therefore* [a]Mark 14:41; John 12:27; 13:1
47 [1]Lit., *and with him* [a]Matt. 26:47-56: *Mark 14:43-50; Luke 22:47-53; John 18:3-11* [b]Matt. 26:14
49 [a]Matt. 23:7; 26:25
50 [a]Matt. 20:13; 22:12
51 [1]Lit., *extended the hand* [2]Lit., *took off* [a]Mark 14:47; Luke 22:50; John 18:10 [b]Luke 22:38 [c]Mark 14:47; Luke 22:50; John 18:10
52 [a]Gen. 9:6; Rev. 13:10
53 [1]A legion equaled 6,000 troops [a]Mark 5:9, 15; Luke 8:30 [b]Matt. 4:11
54 [a]Matt. 26:24
55 [a]Mark 12:35; 14:49; Luke 4:20; 19:47; 20:1; 21:37; John 7:14, 28; 8:2, 20; 18:20
56 [a]Matt. 26:24
57 [a]Matt. 26:57-68: *Mark 14:53-65; John 18:12f., 19-24* [b]Matt. 26:3
58 [1]Or, *servants* [a]John 18:15 [b]Matt. 26:3 [c]Matt. 5:25; John 7:32, 45f.; 19:6; Acts 5:22, 26
59 [1]Or, *Sanhedrin* [a]Matt. 5:22
60 [a]Deut. 19:15
61 [1]Or, *sanctuary* [2]Or, *after* [a]Matt. 27:40; Mark 14:58; 15:29; John 2:19; Acts 6:14
63 [1]Or, *charge You under oath* [2]I.e., the Messiah [a]Matt. 27:12, 14; John 19:9 [b]Matt. 26:63-66; Luke 22:67-71 [c]Lev. 5:1 [d]Matt. 16:16 [e]Matt. 4:3
64 [1]Or, *from now on* [a]Matt. 26:25 [b]Ps. 110:1; Mark 14:62 [c]Dan. 7:13; Matt. 16:27f.
65 [1]Or, *outer garments* [a]Num. 14:6; Mark 14:63; Acts 14:14
66 [a]Lev. 24:16; John 19:7
67 [1]Or possibly, *beat Him with rods* [a]Is. 50:6; Matt. 26:67, 68; Luke 22:63-65; John 18:22 [b]Matt. 27:30; Mark 10:34
68 [1]I.e., the Messiah [a]Mark 14:65; Luke 22:64
69 [a]Matt. 26:69-75: *Mark 14:66-72; Luke 22:55-62; John 18:16-18, 25-27* [b]Matt. 26:3

73 And a little later the bystanders
came up and said to Peter, "Surely you
too are *one* of them; [a]for the way you
talk [1]gives you away."
74 Then he began to curse and swear,
"I do not know the man!" And immediately a cock crowed.
75 And Peter remembered the word
which Jesus had said, "[a]Before a cock
crows, you will deny Me three times."
And he went out and wept bitterly.

Judas' Remorse

27 [a]NOW when morning had come,
all the chief priests and the elders
of the people took counsel against Jesus
to put Him to death;
2 and they bound Him, and led Him
away, and [a]delivered Him up to [b]Pilate
the governor.
3 Then when [a]Judas, who had betrayed Him, saw that He had been
condemned, he felt remorse and returned [b]the thirty [1]pieces of silver to the
chief priests and elders,
4 saying, "I have sinned by betraying
innocent blood." But they said, "What is
that to us? [a]See *to that* yourself!"
5 And he threw the pieces of silver
into [a]the sanctuary and departed; and
[b]he went away and hanged himself.
6 And the chief priests took the
pieces of silver and said, "It is not lawful
to put them into the temple treasury,
since it is the price of blood."
7 And they counseled together and
with [1]the money bought the Potter's
Field as a burial place for strangers.
8 [a]For this reason that field has been
called the Field of Blood to this day.
9 Then that which was spoken
through Jeremiah the prophet was fulfilled, saying, "[a]AND [1]THEY TOOK THE
THIRTY PIECES OF SILVER, THE PRICE OF
THE ONE WHOSE PRICE HAD BEEN SET by
the sons of Israel;
10 [a]AND [1]THEY GAVE THEM FOR THE
POTTER'S FIELD, AS THE LORD DIRECTED
ME."

Jesus before Pilate

11 [a]Now Jesus stood before the governor, and the governor questioned Him,
saying, "Are You the [b]King of the
Jews?" And Jesus said to him, "[c]*It is as*
you say."
12 And while He was being accused
by the chief priests and elders, [a]He made
no answer.
13 Then Pilate *said to Him, "Do You
not hear how many things they testify
against You?"
14 And [a]He did not answer him with
regard to even a *single* [1]charge, so that
the governor was quite amazed.
15 [a]Now at *the* feast the governor was
accustomed to release for the multitude
any one prisoner whom they wanted.
16 And they were holding at that time
a notorious prisoner, called Barabbas.
17 When therefore they were gathered
together, Pilate said to them, "Whom do
you want me to release for you? Barabbas, or Jesus [a]who is called Christ?"
18 For he knew that because of envy
they had delivered Him up.
19 And [a]while he was sitting on the
judgment seat, his wife sent to him,
saying, "Have nothing to do with that
[b]righteous Man; for [1]last night I suffered
greatly [c]in a dream because of Him."
20 But the chief priests and the elders
persuaded the multitudes to [a]ask for
Barabbas, and to put Jesus to death.
21 But the governor answered and
said to them, "Which of the two do you
want me to release for you?" And they
said, "Barabbas."
22 Pilate *said to them, "Then what
shall I do with Jesus [a]who is called
Christ?" They all *said, "Let Him be
crucified!"
23 And he said, "Why, what evil has
He done?" But they kept shouting all the
more, saying, "Let Him be crucified!"
24 And when Pilate saw that he was
accomplishing nothing, but rather that
[a]a riot was starting, he took water and
[b]washed his hands in front of the multitude, saying, "I am innocent of [1c]this
Man's blood; [d]see *to that* yourselves."
25 And all the people answered and
said, "[a]His blood *be* on us and on our
children!"
26 Then he released Barabbas [1]for
them; but after having Jesus [a]scourged,
he delivered Him to be crucified.

Jesus Is Mocked

27 [a]Then the soldiers of the governor
took Jesus into [b]the Praetorium and
gathered the whole *Roman* [1c]cohort
around Him.
28 And they stripped Him, and [a]put a
scarlet robe on Him.
29 [a]And after weaving a crown of
thorns, they put it on His head, and a
[1]reed in His right hand; and they
kneeled down before Him and mocked
Him, saying, "[b]Hail, King of the Jews!"
30 And [a]they spat on Him, and took
the reed and *began* to beat Him on the
head.
31 [a]And after they had mocked Him,
they took His robe off and put His
garments on Him, and led Him away to
crucify *Him*.
32 [a]And as they were coming out, they
found a man of [b]Cyrene named Simon,
[1]whom they pressed into service to bear
His cross.

The Crucifixion

33 [a]And when they had come to a
place called [b]Golgotha, which means
Place of a Skull,
34 [a]they gave Him [b]wine to drink
mingled with gall; and after tasting *it*,
He was unwilling to drink.

73 [1]Lit., *makes you evident* [a]Mark 14:70; Luke 22:59; John 18:26
75 [a]Matt. 26:34
1 [a]Mark 15:1; Luke 22:66; John 18:28
2 [a]Matt. 20:19 [b]Luke 3:1; 13:1; 23:12; Acts 3:13; 4:27; 1 Tim. 6:13
3 [1]Or, *silver shekels* [a]Matt. 26:14 [b]Matt. 26:15
4 [a]Matt. 27:24
5 [a]Matt. 26:61; Luke 1:9, 21 [b]Acts 1:18
7 [1]Lit., *them*
8 [a]Acts 1:19
9 [1]Some mss. read *I took* [a]Zech. 11:12
10 [1]Some mss. read *I gave* [a]Zech. 11:13
11 [a]Matt. 27:11-14: *Mark 15:2-5; Luke 23:2, 3; John 18:29-38* [b]Matt. 2:2 [c]Matt. 26:25
12 [a]Matt. 26:63; John 19:9
14 [1]Lit., *word* [a]Matt. 27:12; Mark 15:5; Luke 23:9; John 19:9
15 [a]Matt. 27:15-26: *Mark 15:6-15; Luke 23:[17]-25;* John 18:39-19:16
17 [a]Matt. 1:16; 27:22
19 [1]Lit., *today* [a]John 19:13; Acts 12:21; 18:12, 16f.; 25:6, 10, 17 [b]Matt. 27:24 [c]Gen. 20:6; 31:11; Num. 12:6; Job 33:15; Matt. 1:20; 2:12f., 19, 22
20 [a]Acts 3:14
22 [a]Matt. 1:16
24 [1]Many mss. read *the blood of this righteous Man* [a]Matt. 26:5 [b]Deut. 21:6-8 [c]Matt. 27:19 [d]Matt. 27:4
25 [a]Josh. 2:19; Acts 5:28
26 [1]Or, *to them* [a]Mark 15:15; Luke 23:16; John 19:1
27 [1]Or, *battalion* [a]Matt. 27:27-31: *Mark 15:16-20* [b]Matt. 26:3; John 18:28, 33; 19:9 [c]Acts 10:1
28 [a]Mark 15:17; John 19:2
29 [1]Or, *staff* (made of a reed) [a]Mark 15:17; John 19:2 [b]Mark 15:18; John 19:3
30 [a]Matt. 26:67; Mark 10:34; 14:65; 15:19
31 [a]Mark 15:20
32 [1]Lit., *this one* [a]Matt. 27:32: *Mark 15:21; Luke 23:26;* John 19:17 [b]Acts 2:10; 6:9; 11:20; 13:1
33 [a]Matt. 27:34-44: *Mark 15:22-32; Luke 23:33-43; John 19:17-24* [b]Luke 23:33; John 19:17
34 [a]Ps. 69:21 [b]Mark 15:23

35 And when they had crucified Him, [a]they divided up His garments among themselves, casting [1]lots;

36 and sitting down, they *began* to [a]keep watch over Him there.

37 And they put up above His head the charge against Him [1]which read, "[a]THIS IS JESUS THE KING OF THE JEWS."

38 At that time two robbers *were crucified with Him, one on the right and one on the left.

39 And those passing by were [1]hurling abuse at Him, [a]wagging their heads,

40 and saying, "[a]You who *are going to* destroy the temple and rebuild it in three days, save Yourself! [b]If You are the Son of God, come down from the cross."

41 In the same way the chief priests also, along with the scribes and elders, were mocking *Him*, and saying,

42 "[a]He saved others; [1]He cannot save Himself. [b]He is the King of Israel; let Him now come down from the cross, and we shall believe in Him.

43 "[a]HE TRUSTS IN GOD; LET HIM DELIVER *Him* now, IF HE TAKES PLEASURE IN HIM; for He said, 'I am the Son of God.' "

44 [a]And the robbers also who had been crucified with Him were casting the same insult at Him.

45 [a]Now from the [1]sixth hour darkness [2]fell upon all the land until the [3]ninth hour.

46 And about the ninth hour Jesus cried out with a loud voice, saying, "[a]ELI, ELI, LAMA SABACHTHANI?" that is, "MY GOD, MY GOD, WHY HAST THOU FORSAKEN ME?"

47 And some of those who were standing there, when they heard it, *began* saying, "This man is calling for Elijah."

48 And [a]immediately one of them ran, and taking a sponge, he filled it with sour wine, and put it on a reed, and gave Him a drink.

49 But the rest *of them* said, "[1]Let us see whether Elijah will come to save Him."[2]

50 And Jesus [a]cried out again with a loud voice, and yielded up *His* spirit.

51 [a]And behold, [b]the veil of the temple was torn in two from top to bottom, and [c]the earth shook; and the rocks were split,

52 and the tombs were opened; and many bodies of the [1]saints who had [a]fallen asleep were raised;

53 and coming out of the tombs after His resurrection they entered [a]the holy city and appeared to many.

54 [a]Now the centurion, and those who were with him [b]keeping guard over Jesus, when they saw [c]the earthquake and the things that were happening, became very frightened and said, "Truly this was [1d]the Son of God!"

55 [a]And many women were there looking on from a distance, who had followed Jesus from Galilee, [1b]ministering to Him,

56 among whom was [a]Mary Magdalene, *along with* Mary the mother of James and Joseph, and [b]the mother of the sons of Zebedee.

Jesus Is Buried

57 [a]And when it was evening, there came a rich man from Arimathea, named Joseph, who himself had also become a disciple of Jesus.

58 This man went to Pilate and asked for the body of Jesus. Then Pilate ordered *it* to be given over *to him.*

59 And Joseph took the body and wrapped it in a clean linen cloth,

60 and laid it in his own new tomb, which he had hewn out in the rock; and he rolled [a]a large stone against the entrance of the tomb and went away.

61 And [a]Mary Magdalene was there, and the other Mary, sitting opposite the grave.

62 Now on the next day, which is *the one* after [a]the preparation, the chief priests and the Pharisees gathered together with Pilate,

63 and said, "Sir, we remember that when He was still alive that deceiver said, '[a]After three days I *am to* rise again.'

64 "Therefore, give orders for the grave to be made secure until the third day, lest the disciples come and steal Him away and say to the people, 'He has risen from the dead,' and the last deception will be worse than the first."

65 Pilate said to them, "You have a [a]guard; go, make it *as* secure as you know how."

66 And they went and made the grave secure, and along with [a]the guard they set a [b]seal on [c]the stone.

Jesus Is Risen!

28 [a]NOW after the Sabbath, as it began to dawn toward the first *day* of the week, [b]Mary Magdalene and the other Mary came to look at the grave.

2 And behold, a severe earthquake had occurred, for [a]an angel of the Lord descended from heaven and came and rolled away [b]the stone and sat upon it.

3 And [a]his appearance was like lightning, and his garment as white as snow;

4 and the guards shook for fear of him, and became like dead men.

5 And the angel answered and said to the women, "[1a]Do not be afraid; for I know that you are looking for Jesus who has been crucified.

6 "He is not here, for He has risen, [a]just as He said. Come, see the place where He was lying.

7 "And go quickly and tell His disciples that He has risen from the dead;

35 [1]Lit., *a lot* [a]Ps. 22:18
36 [a]Matt. 27:54
37 [1]Lit., *written* [a]Mark 15:26; Luke 23:38; John 19:19
39 [1]Or, *blaspheming* [a]Job 16:4; Ps. 22:7; 109:25; Lam. 2:15; Mark 15:29
40 [a]Matt. 26:61; John 2:19 [b]Matt. 27:42
42 [1]Or, *can He not save Himself* [a]Mark 15:31; Luke 23:35 [b]Matt. 27:37; Luke 23:37; John 1:49; 12:13
43 [a]Ps. 22:8
44 [a]Luke 23:39-43
45 [1]I.e., noon [2]Or, *occurred* [3]I.e., 3 p.m. [a]Matt. 27:45-56: *Mark 15:33-41; Luke 23:44-49*
46 [a]Ps. 22:1
48 [a]Ps. 69:21; Mark 15:36; Luke 23:36; John 19:29
49 [1]Lit., *Permit that we see* [2]Some early mss. add *And another took a spear and pierced His side, and there came out water and blood.* (cf. John 19:34)
50 [a]Mark 15:37; Luke 23:46; John 19:30
51 [a]Matt. 27:51-56: *Mark 15:38-41;* Luke 23:47-49 [b]Ex. 26:31ff.; Mark 15:38; Luke 23:45; Heb. 9:3 [c]Matt. 27:54
52 [1]Or, *holy ones* [a]Acts 7:60
53 [a]Matt. 4:5
54 [1]Or possibly, *a son of God* or *a son of a god* [a]Mark 15:39; Luke 23:47 [b]Matt. 27:36 [c]Matt. 27:51 [d]Matt. 4:3; 27:43
55 [1]Or, *waiting on* [a]Mark 15:40f.; Luke 23:49; John 19:25 [b]Mark 15:41; Luke 8:2, 3
56 [a]Matt. 28:1; Mark 15:40, 47; 16:9; Luke 8:2; John 19:25; 20:1, 18 [b]Matt. 20:20
57 [a]Matt. 27:57-61: *Mark 15:42-47; Luke 23:50-56; John 19:38-42*
60 [a]Matt. 27:66; 28:2; Mark 16:4
61 [a]Matt. 27:56; 28:1
62 [a]Mark 15:42; Luke 23:54; John 19:14, 31, 42
63 [a]Matt. 16:21; 17:23; 20:19; Mark 8:31; 9:31; 10:34; Luke 9:22; 18:31-33
65 [a]Matt. 27:66; 28:11
66 [a]Matt. 27:65; 28:11 [b]Dan. 6:17 [c]Matt. 27:60; 28:2; Mark 16:4

1 [a]Matt. 28:1-8: *Mark 16:1-8; Luke 24:1-10;* John 20:1-8 [b]Matt. 27:56, 61
2 [a]Luke 24:4; John 20:12 [b]Matt. 27:66; Mark 16:4

3 [a]Dan. 7:9; 10:6; Mark 9:3; John 20:12; Acts 1:10
5 [1]Or, *Stop being afraid* [a]Matt. 14:27; 28:10; Rev. 1:17
6 [a]Matt. 12:40; 16:21; 27:63

and behold, He is going before you [a]into Galilee, there you will see Him; behold, I have told you."

8 And they departed quickly from the tomb with fear and great joy and ran to report it to His disciples.

9 And behold, Jesus met them [1]and greeted them. And they came up and took hold of His feet and worshiped Him.

10 Then Jesus *said to them, "[1][a]Do not be afraid; go and take word to [b]My brethren to leave [c]for Galilee, and there they shall see Me."

11 Now while they were on their way, behold, some of [a]the guard came into the city and reported to the chief priests all that had happened.

12 And when they had assembled with the elders and counseled together, they gave a large sum of money to the soldiers,

13 and said, "You are to say, 'His disciples came by night and stole Him away while we were asleep.'

14 "And if this should come to [a]the governor's ears, we will win him over and [1]keep you out of trouble."

15 And they took the money and did as they had been instructed; and this story was widely [a]spread among the Jews, *and is* [b]to this day.

The Great Commission

16 But the eleven disciples proceeded [a]to Galilee, to the mountain which Jesus had designated.

17 And when they saw Him, they worshiped *Him*; but [a]some were doubtful.

18 And Jesus came up and spoke to them, saying, "[a]All authority has been given to Me in heaven and on earth.

19 "[a]Go therefore and [b]make disciples of [c]all the nations, [d]baptizing them in the name of the Father and the Son and the Holy Spirit,

20 teaching them to observe all that I commanded you; and lo, [a]I am with you [1]always, even to [b]the end of the age."

7 [a]Matt. 26:32; 28:10, 16; Mark 16:7
9 [1]Lit., *saying hello*
10 [1]Or, *Stop being afraid* [a]Matt. 14:27; 28:5 [b]John 20:17; Rom. 8:29; Heb. 2:11f., 17 [c]Matt. 26:32; 28:7, 16
11 [a]Matt. 27:65, 66
14 [1]Lit., *make you free from care* [a]Matt. 27:2
15 [a]Matt. 9:31; Mark 1:45 [b]Matt. 27:8
16 [a]Matt. 26:32; 28:7, 10; Mark 15:41; 16:7
17 [a]Mark 16:11
18 [a]Dan. 7:13f.; Matt. 11:27; 26:64; Rom. 14:9; Eph. 1:20-22; Phil. 2:9f.; Col. 2:10; 1 Pet. 3:22
19 [a]Mark 16:15f. [b]Matt. 13:52; Acts 1:8; 14:21 [c]Matt. 25:32; Luke 24:47 [d]Acts 2:38; 8:16; Rom. 6:3; 1 Cor. 1:13, 15ff.; Gal. 3:27
20 [1]Lit., *all the days* [a]Matt. 18:20; Acts 18:10 [b]Matt. 13:39

THE GOSPEL ACCORDING TO MARK

Preaching of John the Baptist

1 THE beginning of the gospel of Jesus Christ, [1][a]the Son of God.

2 [a]As it is written in Isaiah the prophet,

"[b]BEHOLD, I SEND MY MESSENGER BEFORE YOUR FACE,
WHO WILL PREPARE YOUR WAY;

3 [a]THE VOICE OF ONE CRYING IN THE WILDERNESS,
'MAKE READY THE WAY OF THE LORD,
MAKE HIS PATHS STRAIGHT.' "

4 John the Baptist appeared in the wilderness [1][a]preaching a baptism of repentance for the [b]forgiveness of sins.

5 And all the country of Judea was going out to him, and all the people of Jerusalem; and they were being baptized by him in the Jordan River, confessing their sins.

6 And John was clothed with camel's hair and *wore* [a]a leather belt around his waist, and [1]his diet was locusts and wild honey.

7 And he was [1]preaching, and saying, "After me One is coming who is mightier than I, and I am not fit to stoop down and untie the thong of His sandals.

8 "I baptized you [1]with water; but He will baptize you [1]with the Holy Spirit."

The Baptism of Jesus

9 [a]And it came about in those days that Jesus [b]came from Nazareth in Galilee, and was baptized by John in the Jordan.

10 And immediately coming up out of the water, He saw the heavens [1]opening, and the Spirit like a dove descending upon Him;

11 and a voice came out of the heavens: "[a]Thou art My beloved Son, in Thee I am well-pleased."

12 [a]And immediately the Spirit *impelled Him *to go* out into the wilderness.

13 And He was in the wilderness forty days being tempted by [a]Satan; and He was with the wild beasts, and the angels were ministering to Him.

Jesus Preaches in Galilee

14 [a]And after John had been [1]taken into custody, Jesus came into Galilee, [2][b]preaching the gospel of God,

15 and saying, "[a]The time is fulfilled, and the kingdom of God is at hand; [b]repent and [1]believe in the gospel."

16 [a]And as He was going along by the Sea of Galilee, He saw Simon and Andrew, the brother of Simon, casting a net in the sea; for they were fishermen.

17 And Jesus said to them, "Follow Me, and I will make you become fishers of men."

18 And they immediately left the nets and followed Him.

19 And going on a little farther, He saw [1]James the *son* of Zebedee, and John his brother, who were also in the boat mending the nets.

20 And immediately He called them; and they left their father Zebedee in the

1 [1]Many mss. do not contain *the Son of God* [a]Matt. 4:3
2 [a]Mark 1:2-8: *Matt. 3:1-11; Luke 3:2-16* [b]Mal. 3:1; Matt. 11:10; Luke 7:27
3 [a]Is. 40:3; Matt. 3:3; Luke 3:4; John 1:23
4 [1]Or, *proclaiming* [a]Acts 13:24 [b]Luke 1:77
6 [1]Lit., *he was eating* [a]2 Kin. 1:8
7 [1]Or, *proclaiming*
8 [1]The Gr. here can be translated *in, with* or *by*
9 [a]Mark 1:9-11: *Matt. 3:13-17; Luke 3:21, 22* [b]Matt. 2:23; Luke 2:51
10 [1]Or, *being parted*
11 [a]Ps. 2:7; Is. 42:1; Matt. 3:17; 12:18; Mark 9:7; Luke 3:22
12 [a]Mark 1:12, 13: *Matt. 4:1-11; Luke 4:1-13*
13 [a]Matt. 4:10
14 [1]Lit., *delivered up* [2]Or, *proclaiming* [a]Matt. 4:12 [b]Matt. 4:23
15 [1]Or, *put your trust in* [a]Gal. 4:4; Eph. 1:10; 1 Tim. 2:6; Titus 1:3 [b]Matt. 3:2; Acts 20:21
16 [a]Mark 1:16-20: *Matt. 4:18-22;* Luke 5:2-11; John 1:40-42
19 [1]Or, *Jacob*

boat with the hired servants, and went away [1]to follow Him.

21 [a]And they *went into Capernaum; and immediately on the Sabbath [b]He entered the synagogue and *began* to teach.

22 And [a]they were amazed at His teaching; for He was teaching them as *one* having authority, and not as the scribes.

23 And just then there was in their synagogue a man with an unclean spirit; and he cried out,

24 saying, "[a]What do we have to do with You, Jesus [1]of [b]Nazareth? Have You come to destroy us? I know who You are—[c]the Holy One of God!"

25 And Jesus rebuked him, saying, "Be quiet, and come out of him!"

26 And throwing him into convulsions, the unclean spirit cried out with a loud voice, and came out of him.

27 And they were all [a]amazed, so that they debated among themselves, saying, "What is this? A new teaching with authority! He commands even the unclean spirits, and they obey Him."

28 And immediately the news about Him went out everywhere into all the surrounding district of Galilee.

Multitudes Healed

29 [a]And immediately [1]after they had come [b]out of the synagogue, they came into the house of Simon and Andrew, with [2]James and John.

30 Now Simon's mother-in-law was lying sick with a fever; and immediately they *spoke to Him about her.

31 And He came to her and raised her up, taking her by the hand, and the fever left her, and she [1]waited on them.

32 [a]And [b]when evening had come, [b]after the sun had set, they *began* bringing to Him all who were ill and those who were [c]demon-possessed.

33 And the whole [a]city had gathered at the door.

34 And He [a]healed many who were ill with various diseases, and cast out many demons; and He was not permitting the demons to speak, because they [1]knew who He was.

35 [a]And in the early morning, while it was still dark, He arose and went out and departed to a lonely place, and [b]was praying there.

36 And Simon and his companions hunted for Him;

37 and they found Him, and *said to Him, "Everyone is looking for You."

38 And He *said to them, "Let us go somewhere else to the towns nearby, in order that I may [1]preach there also; for that is what I came out for."

39 [a]And He went into their synagogues throughout all Galilee, [1]preaching and casting out the demons.

40 [a]And a leper *came to Him, beseeching Him and [b]falling on his knees before Him, and saying to Him, "If You are willing, You can make me clean."

41 And moved with compassion, He stretched out His hand, and touched him, and *said to him, "I am willing; be cleansed."

42 And immediately the leprosy left him and he was cleansed.

43 And He sternly warned him and immediately sent him away,

44 and He *said to him, "[a]See that you say nothing to anyone; but [b]go, show yourself to the priest and [c]offer for your cleansing what Moses commanded, for a testimony to them."

45 But he went out and began to [a]proclaim it freely and to [a]spread the news about, to such an extent that [1]Jesus could no longer publicly enter a city, but [2]stayed out in unpopulated areas; and [b]they were coming to Him from everywhere.

The Paralytic Healed

2 AND when He had come back to Capernaum several days afterward, it was heard that He was at home.

2 And [a]many were gathered together, so that there was no longer room, even near the door; and He was speaking the word to them.

3 [a]And they *came, bringing to Him a [b]paralytic, carried by four men.

4 And being unable to [1]get to Him because of the crowd, they [a]removed the roof [2]above Him; and when they had dug an opening, they let down the pallet on which the [b]paralytic was lying.

5 And Jesus seeing their faith *said to the paralytic, "My [1]son, [a]your sins are forgiven."

6 But there were some of the scribes sitting there and reasoning in their hearts,

7 "Why does this man speak that way? He is blaspheming; [a]who can forgive sins [1]but God alone?"

8 And immediately Jesus, aware [1]in His spirit that they were reasoning that way within themselves, *said to them, "Why are you reasoning about these things in your hearts?

9 "Which is easier, to say to the [a]paralytic, 'Your sins are forgiven'; or to say, 'Arise, and take up your pallet and walk'?

10 "But in order that you may know that the Son of Man has authority on earth to forgive sins"—He *said to the paralytic—

11 "I say to you, rise, take up your pallet and go home."

12 And he rose and immediately took up the pallet and went out in the sight of all; so that they were all amazed and [a]were glorifying God, saying, "[b]We have never seen anything like this."

13 And He went out again by the seashore; and [a]all the multitude were coming to Him, and He was teaching them.

20 [1]Lit., *after Him*

21 [a]Mark 1:21-28: *Luke 4:31-37* [b]Matt. 4:23; Mark 1:39; 10:1

22 [a]Matt. 7:28

24 [1]Lit., *the Nazarene* [a]Matt. 8:29 [b]Matt. 2:23; Mark 10:47; 14:67; 16:6; Luke 4:34; 24:19; Acts 24:5 [c]Luke 1:35; 4:34; John 6:69; Acts 3:14

27 [a]Mark 10:24, 32; 16:5, 6

29 [1]Some mss. read *after He had come out, He came* [2]Or, *Jacob* [a]Mark 1:29-31: *Matt. 8:14, 15; Luke 4:38, 39* [b]Mark 1:21, 23

31 [1]Or, *served*

32 [a]Mark 1:32-34: *Matt. 8:16, 17; Luke 4:40, 41* [b]Matt. 8:16; Luke 4:40 [c]Matt. 4:24

33 [a]Mark 1:21

34 [1]Some mss. read *knew Him to be Christ* [a]Matt. 4:23

35 [a]Mark 1:35-38: *Luke 4:42, 43* [b]Matt. 14:23; Luke 5:16

38 [1]Or, *proclaim*

39 [1]Or, *proclaiming* [a]Matt. 4:23; 9:35; Mark 1:23; 3:1

40 [a]Mark 1:40-44: *Matt. 8:2-4; Luke 5:12-14* [b]Matt. 8:2; Mark 10:17; Luke 5:12

44 [a]Matt. 8:4 [b]Matt. 8:4 [c]Lev. 14:1-32

45 [1]Lit., *He* [2]Lit., *was* [a]Matt. 28:15; Luke 5:15 [b]Mark 2:2, 13; 3:7; Luke 5:17; John 6:2

2 [a]Mark 1:45; 2:13

3 [a]Mark 2:3-12: *Matt. 9:2-8; Luke 5:18-26* [b]Matt. 4:24

4 [1]Lit., *bring to* [2]Lit., *where He was* [a]Luke 5:19 [b]Matt. 4:24

5 [1]Lit., *child* [a]Matt. 9:2

7 [1]Lit., *if not one, God* [a]Is. 43:25

8 [1]Lit., *by*

9 [a]Matt. 4:24

12 [a]Matt. 9:8 [b]Matt. 9:33

13 [a]Mark 1:45

Levi (Matthew) Called

14 [a]And as He passed by, He saw [b]Levi the *son* of Alphaeus sitting in the tax office, and He *said to him, "[c]Follow Me!" And he rose and followed Him.

15 And it [1]came about that He was reclining *at the table* in his house, and many [2]tax-gatherers and sinners [3]were dining with Jesus and His disciples; for there were many of them, and they were following Him.

16 And when [a]the scribes of the Pharisees saw that He was eating with the sinners and tax-gatherers, they *began* saying to His disciples, "[b]Why is He eating and drinking with tax-gatherers and sinners?"

17 And hearing this, Jesus *said to them, "[a]*It is* not those who are healthy who need a physician, but those who are sick; I did not come to call the righteous, but sinners."

18 [a]And John's disciples and the Pharisees were fasting; and they *came and *said to Him, "Why do John's disciples and the disciples of the Pharisees fast, but Your disciples do not fast?"

19 And Jesus said to them, "While the bridegroom is with them, [1]the attendants of the bridegroom do not fast, do they? So long as they have the bridegroom with them, they cannot fast.

20 "But the [a]days will come when the bridegroom is taken away from them, and then they will fast in that day.

21 "No one sews [1]a patch of unshrunk cloth on an old garment; otherwise [2]the patch pulls away from it, the new from the old, and a worse tear results.

22 "And no one puts new wine into old [1]wineskins; otherwise the wine will burst the skins, and the wine is lost, and the skins *as well;* but *one puts* new wine into fresh wineskins."

Question of the Sabbath

23 [a]And it came about that He was passing through the grainfields on the Sabbath, and His disciples began to make their way along while [b]picking the heads *of grain.*

24 And the Pharisees were saying to Him, "See here, [a]why are they doing what is not lawful on the Sabbath?"

25 And He *said to them, "Have you never read what David did when he was in need and became hungry, he and his companions:

26 how he entered the house of God in the time of [a]Abiathar *the* high priest, and ate the [1]consecrated bread, which [b]is not lawful for *anyone* to eat except the priests, and he gave *it* also to those who were with him?"

27 And He was saying to them, "[a]The Sabbath [1]was made [2]for man, and [b]not man [2]for the Sabbath.

28 "Consequently, the Son of Man is Lord even of the Sabbath."

Jesus Heals on the Sabbath

3 [a]AND He [b]entered again into a synagogue; and a man was there with a withered hand.

2 And [a]they were watching Him *to see* if He would heal him on the Sabbath, [b]in order that they might accuse Him.

3 And He *said to the man with the withered hand, "[1]Rise and *come* forward!"

4 And He *said to them, "Is it lawful on the Sabbath to do good or to do harm, to save a life or to kill?" But they kept silent.

5 And after [a]looking around at them with anger, grieved at their hardness of heart, He *said to the man, "Stretch out your hand." And he stretched it out, and his hand was restored.

6 And the Pharisees went out and immediately *began* [1]taking counsel with the [a]Herodians against Him, *as to* how they might destroy Him.

7 [a]And Jesus withdrew to the sea with His disciples; and [b]a great multitude from Galilee followed; and *also* from Judea,

8 and from Jerusalem, and from [a]Idumea, and beyond the Jordan, and the vicinity of [b]Tyre and Sidon, a great multitude heard of all that He was doing and came to Him.

9 [a]And He told His disciples that a boat should stand ready for Him because of the multitude, in order that they might not crowd Him;

10 for He had [a]healed many, with the result that all those who had [b]afflictions pressed about Him in order to [c]touch Him.

11 And whenever the unclean spirits beheld Him, they would fall down before Him and cry out, saying, "You are [a]the Son of God!"

12 And He [a]earnestly warned them not to [1]make Him known.

The Twelve Are Chosen

13 And He *went up to [a]the mountain and *[b]summoned those whom He Himself wanted, and they came to Him.

14 And He appointed twelve[1], that they might be with Him, and that He might send them out to preach,

15 and to have authority to cast out the demons.

16 And He appointed the twelve: [a]Simon (to whom He gave the name Peter),

17 and [1]James, the *son* of Zebedee, and John the brother of [1]James (to them He gave the name Boanerges, which means, "Sons of Thunder");

18 and Andrew, and Philip, and Bartholomew, and Matthew, and Thomas, and [1]James the *son* of Alphaeus, and Thaddaeus, and Simon the [2]Zealot;

19 and Judas Iscariot, who also betrayed Him.

---

14 [a]Mark 2:14-17: *Matt. 9:9-13; Luke 5:27-32* [b]Matt. 9:9 [c]Matt. 8:22
15 [1]Lit., *comes* [2]I.e., Collectors of Roman taxes for profit [3]Lit., *were reclining with*
16 [a]Luke 5:30; Acts 23:9 [b]Matt. 9:11
17 [a]Matt. 9:12, 13; Luke 5:31, 32
18 [a]Mark 2:18-22: *Matt. 9:14-17; Luke 5:33-38*
19 [1]Lit., *sons of the bridalchamber*
20 [a]Matt. 9:15; Luke 17:22
21 [1]Lit., *that which is put on* [2]Lit., *that which fills up*
22 [1]I.e., skins used as bottles
23 [a]Mark 2:23-28: *Matt. 12:1-8; Luke 6:1-5* [b]Deut. 23:25
24 [a]Matt. 12:2
26 [1]Or, *showbread;* lit., *loaves of presentation* [a]1 Sam. 21:1; 2 Sam. 8:17; 1 Chr. 24:6 [b]Lev. 24:9
27 [1]Or, *came into being* [2]Lit., *for the sake of* [a]Ex. 23:12; Deut. 5:14 [b]Col. 2:16

1 [a]Mark 3:1-6: *Matt. 12:9-14; Luke 6:6-11* [b]Mark 1:21, 39
2 [a]Luke 6:7; 14:1; 20:20 [b]Matt. 12:10; Luke 6:7; 11:54
3 [1]Lit., *Arise into the midst*
5 [a]Luke 6:10
6 [1]Lit., *giving* [a]Matt. 22:16; Mark 12:13
7 [a]Mark 3:7-12: *Matt. 12:15, 16; Luke 6:17-19* [b]Matt. 4:25; Luke 6:17
8 [a]Josh. 15:1, 21; Ezek. 35:15; 36:5 [b]Matt. 11:21
9 [a]Mark 4:1; Luke 5:1-3
10 [a]Matt. 4:23 [b]Mark 5:29, 34; Luke 7:21 [c]Matt. 9:21; 14:36; Mark 6:56; 8:22
11 [a]Matt. 4:3
12 [1]Or, *reveal who He was* [a]Matt. 8:4
13 [a]Matt. 5:1; Luke 6:12 [b]Matt. 10:1; Mark 6:7; Luke 9:1
14 [1]Some early mss. add *whom He named apostles*
16 [a]Mark 3:16-19: *Matt. 10:2-4; Luke 6:14-16;* Acts 1:13
17 [1]Or, *Jacob*
18 [1]Or, *Jacob* [2]Or, *Cananaean*

20 And He *came [1a]home, and the [b]multitude *gathered again, [c]to such an extent that they could not even eat [2]a meal.

21 And when [a]His own [1]people heard _of this,_ they went out to take custody of Him; for they were saying, "[b]He has lost His senses."

22 And the scribes who came down [a]from Jerusalem were saying, "He is possessed by [1b]Beelzebul," and "[c]He casts out the demons by the ruler of the demons."

23 [a]And He called them to Himself and began speaking to them in [b]parables, "How can [c]Satan cast out Satan?

24 "And if a kingdom is divided against itself, that kingdom cannot stand.

25 "And if a house is divided against itself, that house will not be able to stand.

26 "And if [a]Satan has risen up against himself and is divided, he cannot stand, but [1]he is finished!

27 "[a]But no one can enter the strong man's house and plunder his property unless he first binds the strong man, and then he will plunder his house.

28 "[a]Truly I say to you, all sins shall be forgiven the sons of men, and whatever blasphemies they utter;

29 but [a]whoever blasphemes against the Holy Spirit never has forgiveness, but is guilty of an eternal sin"—

30 because they were saying, "He has an unclean spirit."

31 [a]And His mother and His brothers *arrived, and standing outside they sent _word_ to Him, and called Him.

32 And a multitude was sitting around Him, and they *said to Him, "Behold, Your mother and Your brothers[1] are outside looking for You."

33 And answering them, He *said, "Who are My mother and My brothers?"

34 And looking about on those who were sitting around Him, He *said, "[a]Behold, My mother and My brothers!

35 "For whoever [a]does the will of God, he is My brother and sister and mother."

[a]_Parable of the Sower and Soils_

4 AND He began to teach again [b]by the sea. And such a very great multitude [1]gathered to Him that [c]He got into a boat in the sea and sat down; and the whole multitude was by the sea on the land.

2 And He was teaching them many things in [a]parables, and was saying to them in His teaching,

3 "Listen _to this_! Behold, the sower went out to sow;

4 and it came about that as he was sowing, some _seed_ fell beside the road, and the birds came and ate it up.

5 "And other _seed_ fell on the rocky _ground_ where it did not have much soil; and immediately it sprang up because it had no depth of soil.

20 [1]Lit., _into a house_ [2]Lit., _bread_ [a]Mark 2:1; 7:17; 9:28 [b]Mark 1:45; 3:7 [c]Mark 6:31

21 [1]Or, _kinsmen_ [a]Mark 3:31f. [b]John 10:20; Acts 26:24

22 [1]Or, _Beezebul;_ others read _Beelzebub_ [a]Matt. 15:1 [b]Matt. 10:25; 11:18 [c]Matt. 9:34

23 [a]Mark 3:23-27: _Matt. 12:25-29; Luke 11:17-22_ [b]Matt. 13:3ff.; Mark 4:2ff. [c]Matt. 4:10

26 [1]Lit., _he has an end_ [a]Matt. 4:10

27 [a]Is. 49:24, 25

28 [a]Matt. 12:31, 32; Mark 3:28-30; Luke 12:10

29 [a]Luke 12:10

31 [a]Mark 3:31-35: _Matt. 12:46-50; Luke 8:19-21_

32 [1]Later mss. add _and Your sisters_

34 [a]Matt. 12:49

35 [a]Eph. 6:6; Heb. 10:36; 1 Pet. 4:2; 1 John 2:17

1 [1]Lit., _is gathered_ [a]Mark 4:1-12: _Matt. 13:1-15; Luke 8:4-10_ [b]Mark 2:13; 3:7 [c]Luke 5:1-3

2 [a]Matt. 13:3ff.; Mark 3:23; 4:2ff.

9 [a]Matt. 11:15; Mark 4:23; Rev. 2:7, 11, 17, 29

10 [1]Lit., _those about Him_

11 [a]1 Cor. 5:12f.; Col. 4:5; 1 Thess. 4:12; 1 Tim. 3:7 [b]Mark 3:23; 4:2

12 [a]Is. 6:9f.; 43:8; Jer. 5:21; Ezek. 12:2; Matt. 13:14; Luke 8:10; John 12:40; Rom. 11:8

13 [a]Mark 4:13-20: _Matt. 13:18-23; Luke 8:11-15_

15 [a]Matt. 4:10f.; 1 Pet. 5:8; Rev. 20:2, 3, 7-10

17 [1]Lit., _are caused to stumble_

19 [1]Or, _age_ [a]Matt. 13:22; Rom. 12:2; Eph. 2:2; 6:12 [b]Prov. 23:4; 1 Tim. 6:9, 10, 17

20 [a]John 15:2ff.; Rom. 7:4

21 [a]Matt. 5:15; Luke 8:16; 11:33

22 [a]Matt. 10:26; Luke 8:17; 12:2

23 [a]Matt. 11:15; 13:9, 43; Mark 4:9; Luke 8:8; 14:35; Rev. 3:6, 13, 22; 13:9

24 [1]Lit., _By what measure you measure_ [a]Matt. 7:2; Luke 6:38

6 "And after the sun had risen, it was scorched; and because it had no root, it withered away.

7 "And other _seed_ fell among the thorns, and the thorns came up and choked it, and it yielded no crop.

8 "And other _seeds_ fell into the good soil and as they grew up and increased, they yielded a crop and produced thirty, sixty, and a hundredfold."

9 And He was saying, "[a]He who has ears to hear, let him hear."

10 And as soon as He was alone, [1]His followers, along with the twelve, _began_ asking Him _about_ the parables.

11 And He was saying to them, "To you has been given the mystery of the kingdom of God; but [a]those who are outside get everything [b]in parables,

12 in order that [a]WHILE SEEING, THEY MAY SEE AND NOT PERCEIVE; AND WHILE HEARING, THEY MAY HEAR AND NOT UNDERSTAND LEST THEY RETURN AND BE FORGIVEN."

Explanation

13 [a]And He *said to them, "Do you not understand this parable? And how will you understand all the parables?

14 "The sower sows the word.

15 "And these are the ones who are beside the road where the word is sown; and when they hear, immediately [a]Satan comes and takes away the word which has been sown in them.

16 "And in a similar way these are the ones on whom seed was sown on the rocky _places,_ who, when they hear the word, immediately receive it with joy;

17 and they have no _firm_ root in themselves, but are _only_ temporary; then, when affliction or persecution arises because of the word, immediately they [1]fall away.

18 "And others are the ones on whom seed was sown among the thorns; these are the ones who have heard the word,

19 and the worries of [a]the [1]world, and the [b]deceitfulness of riches, and the desires for other things enter in and choke the word, and it becomes unfruitful.

20 "And those are the ones on whom seed was sown on the good soil; and they hear the word and accept it, and [a]bear fruit, thirty, sixty, and a hundredfold."

21 And He was saying to them, "[a]A lamp is not brought to be put under a peck-measure, is it, or under a bed? Is it not _brought_ to be put on the lampstand?

22 "[a]For nothing is hidden, except to be revealed; nor has _anything_ been secret, but that it should come to light.

23 "[a]If any man has ears to hear, let him hear."

24 And He was saying to them, "Take care what you listen to. [1a]By your standard of measure it shall be measured to you; and more shall be given you besides.

25"[a]For whoever has, to him shall
more be given; and whoever does not
have, even what he has shall be taken
away from him."

Parable of the Seed

26 And He was saying, "The kingdom
of God is like a man who casts seed
upon the soil;
27 and goes to bed at night and gets
up by day, and the seed sprouts up and
grows—how, he himself does not know.
28"The soil produces crops by itself;
first the blade, then the head, then the
mature grain in the head.
29"But when the crop permits, he
immediately [1a]puts in the sickle, because
the harvest has come."

Parable of the Mustard Seed

30 [a]And He said, "How shall we
[1b]picture the kingdom of God, or by
what parable shall we present it?
31"*It is* like a mustard seed, which,
when sown upon the soil, though it is
smaller than all the seeds that are upon
the soil,
32 yet when it is sown, grows up and
becomes larger than all the garden
plants and forms large branches; so that
[a]THE BIRDS OF THE [1]AIR can NEST UNDER
ITS SHADE."
33 And with many such parables He
was speaking the word to them as they
were able to hear it;
34 and He did not speak to them
[a]without a parable; but He was [b]explaining
everything privately to His own
disciples.

Jesus Stills the Sea

35 [a]And on that day, when evening
had come, He *said to them, "Let us go
over to the other side."
36 And [1]leaving the multitude, they
*took Him along with them, just as He
was, [a]in the boat; and other boats were
with Him.
37 And there *arose a fierce gale of
wind, and the waves were breaking over
the boat so much that the boat was
already filling up.
38 And He Himself was in the stern,
asleep on the cushion; and they *awoke
Him and *said to Him, "Teacher, do
You not care that we are perishing?"
39 And being aroused, [a]He rebuked
the wind and said to the sea, "Hush, be
still." And the wind died down and [1]it
became perfectly calm.
40 And He said to them, "Why are
you so timid? [a]How is it that you have
no faith?"
41 And they became very much afraid
and said to one another, "Who then is
this, that even the wind and the sea obey
Him?"

The Gerasene Demoniac

5 [a]AND they came to the other side of
the sea, into the country of the
Gerasenes.
2 And when He had come out of [a]the
boat, immediately a man from the tombs
[b]with an unclean spirit met Him,
3 and he had his dwelling among the
tombs. And no one was able to bind him
anymore, even with a chain;
4 because he had often been bound
with shackles and chains, and the chains
had been torn apart by him, and the
shackles broken in pieces, and no one
was strong enough to subdue him.
5 And constantly night and day,
among the tombs and in the mountains,
he was crying out and gashing himself
with stones.
6 And seeing Jesus from a distance,
he ran up and bowed down before Him;
7 and crying out with a loud voice,
he *said, "[a]What do I have to do with
You, Jesus, [b]Son of [c]the Most High
God? I implore You by God, do not
torment me!"
8 For He had been saying to him,
"Come out of the man, you unclean
spirit!"
9 And He was asking him, "What is
your name?" And he *said to Him, "My
name is [a]Legion; for we are many."
10 And he *began* to entreat Him earnestly not to send them out of the
country.
11 Now there was a big herd of swine
feeding there on the mountain.
12 And *the demons* entreated Him,
saying, "Send us into the swine so that
we may enter them."
13 And He gave them permission.
And coming out, the unclean spirits
entered the swine; and the herd rushed
down the steep bank into the sea, about
two thousand *of them;* and they [1]were
drowned in the sea.
14 And their herdsmen ran away and
reported it in the city and *out* in the
country. And *the people* came to see
what it was that had happened.
15 And they *came to Jesus and *observed the man who had been [a]demon-
possessed sitting down, [b]clothed and [c]in
his right mind, the very man who had
had the "[d]legion"; and they became
frightened.
16 And those who had seen it described to them how it had happened to
the [a]demon-possessed man, and *all*
about the swine.
17 And they began to [a]entreat Him to
depart from their region.
18 [a]And as He was getting into the
boat, the man who had been [b]demon-
possessed was entreating Him that he
might [1]accompany Him.
19 And He did not let him, but He
*said to him, "[a]Go home to your people
and report to them [1]what great things
the Lord has done for you, and *how* He
had mercy on you."
20 And he went away and began to
[a]proclaim in [b]Decapolis [1]what great
things Jesus had done for him; and
everyone marveled.

25 [a]Matt. 13:12; 25:29; Luke 8:18; 19:26
29 [1]Lit., *sends forth* [a]Joel 3:13
30 [1]Lit., *compare* [a]Mark 4:30-32: *Matt. 13:31, 32; Luke 13:18, 19* [b]Matt. 13:24
32 [1]Or, *sky* [a]Ezek. 17:23; Ps. 104:12; Ezek. 31:6; Dan. 4:12
34 [a]Matt. 13:34; John 10:6; 16:25 [b]Luke 24:27
35 [a]Mark 4:35-41: *Matt. 8:18, 23-27; Luke 8:22, 25*
36 [1]Or, *sending away* [a]Mark 3:9; 4:1; 5:2, 21
39 [1]Lit., *a great calm occurred* [a]Ps. 65:7; 89:9; 107:29; Matt. 8:26; Luke 8:24
40 [a]Matt. 14:31; Luke 8:25
1 [a]Mark 5:1-17: *Matt. 8:28-34; Luke 8:26-37*
2 [a]Mark 3:9; 4:1, 36; 5:21 [b]Mark 1:23
7 [a]Matt. 8:29 [b]Matt. 4:3 [c]Luke 8:28; Acts 16:17; Heb. 7:1
9 [a]Matt. 26:53; Mark 5:15; Luke 8:30
13 [1]Lit., *were drowning*
15 [a]Matt. 4:24; Mark 5:16, 18 [b]Luke 8:27 [c]Luke 8:35 [d]Mark 5:9
16 [a]Matt. 4:24; Mark 5:15
17 [a]Matt. 8:34; Acts 16:39
18 [1]Lit., *be with Him* [a]Mark 5:18-20: *Luke 8:38, 39* [b]Matt. 4:24; Mark 5:15, 16
19 [1]Or, *everything that* [a]Luke 8:39
20 [1]Or, *everything that* [a]Ps. 66:16 [b]Matt. 4:25; Mark 7:31

Miracles and Healing

21 [a]And when Jesus had crossed over again in [b]the boat to the other side, a great multitude gathered about Him; and He [1]stayed [c]by the seashore.
22 [a]And one of [b]the synagogue [1]officials named Jairus *came up, and upon seeing Him, *fell at His feet,
23 and *entreated Him earnestly, saying, "My little daughter is at the point of death; *please* come and [a]lay Your hands on her, that she may [1]get well and live."
24 And He went off with him; and a great multitude was following Him and pressing in on Him.
25 And a woman who had had a hemorrhage for twelve years,
26 and had endured much at the hands of many physicians, and had spent all that she had and was not helped at all, but rather had grown worse,
27 after hearing about Jesus, came up in the crowd behind *Him,* and touched His [1]cloak.
28 For she [1]thought, "If I just touch His garments, I shall [2]get well."
29 And immediately the flow of her blood was dried up; and she felt in her body that she was healed of her [a]affliction.
30 And immediately Jesus, perceiving in Himself that [a]the power *proceeding* from Him had gone forth, turned around in the crowd and said, "Who touched My garments?"
31 And His disciples said to Him, "You see the multitude pressing in on You, and You say, 'Who touched Me?' "
32 And He looked around to see the woman who had done this.
33 But the woman fearing and trembling, aware of what had happened to her, came and fell down before Him, and told Him the whole truth.
34 And He said to her, "Daughter, [a]your faith has [1]made you well; [b]go in peace, and be healed of your [c]affliction."
35 While He was still speaking, they *came from the *house of* the [a]synagogue official, saying, "Your daughter has died; why trouble the Teacher anymore?"
36 But Jesus, overhearing what was being spoken, *said to the [a]synagogue official, "[b]Do not be afraid *any longer,* only [1]believe."
37 And He allowed no one to follow with Him, except [a]Peter and [1]James and John the brother of [1]James.
38 And they *came to the house of the [a]synagogue official; and He *beheld a commotion, and *people* loudly weeping and wailing.
39 And entering in, He *said to them, "Why make a commotion and weep? The child has not died, but is asleep."
40 And they *began* laughing at Him. But putting them all out, He *took along the child's father and mother and His own companions, and *entered *the room* where the child was.
41 And taking the child by the hand, He *said to her, "Talitha kum!" (which translated means, "Little girl, [a]I say to you, arise!").
42 And immediately the girl rose and *began* to walk; for she was twelve years old. And immediately they were completely astounded.
43 And He [a]gave them strict orders that no one should know about this; and He said that *something* should be given her to eat.

Teaching at Nazareth

6 [a]AND He went out from there, and He *came into [1b]His home town; and His disciples *followed Him.
2 And when the Sabbath had come, He began [a]to teach in the synagogue; and the [b]many listeners were astonished, saying, "Where did this man *get* these things, and what is *this* wisdom given to Him, and such [1]miracles as these performed by His hands?
3 "Is not this [a]the carpenter, [b]the son of Mary, and brother of [1]James, and Joses, and Judas, and Simon? Are not [c]His sisters here with us?" And they [2]took [d]offense at Him.
4 And Jesus said to them, "[a]A prophet is not without honor except in [1b]his home town and among his *own* relatives and in his *own* household."
5 And He could do no [1]miracle there except that He [a]laid His hands upon a few sick people and healed them.
6 And He wondered at their unbelief.
[a]And He was going around the villages teaching.

The Twelve Sent Out

7 [a]And [b]He *summoned the twelve and began to send them out [c]in pairs; and He was giving them authority over the unclean spirits;
8 [a]and He instructed them that they should take nothing for *their* journey, except a mere staff; no bread, no [1]bag, no money in their belt;
9 but [1]*to* wear sandals; and *He added,* "Do not put on two [2]tunics."
10 And He said to them, "Wherever you enter a house, stay there until you [1]leave town.
11 "And any place that does not receive you or listen to you, as you go out from there, [a]shake off the dust [1]from the soles of your feet for a testimony against them."
12 [a]And they went out and [1]preached that *men* should repent.
13 And they were casting out many demons and [a]were anointing with oil many sick people and healing them.

John's Fate Recalled

14 [a]And King Herod heard *of it,* for His name had become well known; and *people* were saying, "[b]John the Baptist

21 [1]Lit., *was* [a]Matt. 9:1; Luke 8:40 [b]Mark 4:36 [c]Mark 4:1
22 [1]Or, *rulers* [a]Mark 5:22-43: *Matt. 9:18-26; Luke 8:41-56* [b]Matt. 9:18; Mark 5:35, 36, 38; Luke 8:49; 13:14; Acts 13:15; 18:8, 17
23 [1]Lit., *be saved* [a]Mark 6:5; 7:32; 8:23; 16:18; Luke 4:40; 13:13; Acts 6:6; 9:17; 28:8
27 [1]Or, *outer garment*
28 [1]Lit., *was saying* [2]Lit., *be saved*
29 [a]Mark 3:10; 5:34
30 [a]Luke 5:17
34 [1]Lit., *saved you* [a]Matt. 9:22 [b]Luke 7:50; 8:48; Acts 16:36; James 2:16 [c]Mark 3:10; 5:29
35 [a]Mark 5:22
36 [1]Or, *keep on believing* [a]Mark 5:22 [b]Luke 8:50
37 [1]Or, *Jacob* [a]Matt. 17:1; 26:37
38 [a]Mark 5:22
41 [a]Luke 7:14; Acts 9:40
43 [a]Matt. 8:4

1 [1]Or, *His own part of the country* [a]Mark 6:1-6: *Matt. 13:54-58* [b]Matt. 13:54, 57; Luke 4:16, 23
2 [1]Or, *works of power* [a]Matt. 4:23; Mark 10:1 [b]Matt. 7:28
3 [1]Or, *Jacob* [2]Lit., *were being made to stumble* [a]Matt. 13:55 [b]Matt. 12:46 [c]Matt. 13:56 [d]Matt. 11:6
4 [1]Or, *his own part of the country* [a]Matt. 13:57; John 4:44 [b]Mark 6:1
5 [1]Or, *work of power* [a]Mark 5:23
6 [a]Matt. 9:35; Mark 1:39; 10:1; Luke 13:22
7 [a]Mark 6:7-11: *Matt. 10:1, 9-14; Luke 9:1, 3-5;* Luke 10:4-11 [b]Matt. 10:1, 5; Mark 3:13; Luke 9:1 [c]Luke 10:1
8 [1]Or, *knapsack or beggar's bag* [a]Matt. 10:10
9 [1]Lit., *being shod with* [2]Or, *inner garments*
10 [1]Lit., *go out from there*
11 [1]Lit., *under your feet* [a]Matt. 10:14; Acts 13:51
12 [1]Or, *proclaimed as a herald* [a]Matt. 11:1; Luke 9:6
13 [a]James 5:14
14 [a]Mark 6:14-29: *Matt. 14:1-12;* Mark 6:14-16: *Luke 9:7-9* [b]Matt. 14:2; Luke 9:19

has risen from the dead, and that is why
these miraculous powers are at work in
Him."
15 But others were saying, "He is
[a]Elijah." And others were saying, "*He is*
[b]a prophet, like one of the prophets *of*
old."
16 But when Herod heard *of it,* he
kept saying, "John, whom I beheaded,
has risen!"
17 For Herod himself had sent and
had John arrested and bound in prison
on account of [a]Herodias, the wife of his
brother Philip, because he had married
her.
18 For John had been saying to
Herod, "[a]It is not lawful for you to have
your brother's wife."
19 And [a]Herodias had a grudge
against him and wanted to put him to
death and could not *do so;*
20 for [a]Herod was afraid of John,
knowing that he was a righteous and
holy man, and kept him safe. And when
he heard him, he was very perplexed;
[1]but he [2]used to enjoy listening to him.
21 And a strategic day came when
Herod on his birthday [a]gave a banquet
for his lords and [1]military commanders
and the leading men [b]of Galilee;
22 and when the daughter of [a]Hero-
dias herself came in and danced, she
pleased Herod and [1]his dinner guests;
and the king said to the girl, "Ask me for
whatever you want and I will give it to
you."
23 And he swore to her, "Whatever
you ask of me, I will give it to you; up to
[a]half of my kingdom."
24 And she went out and said to her
mother, "What shall I ask for?" And she
said, "The head of John the Baptist."
25 And immediately she came in haste
before the king and asked, saying, "I
want you to give me right away the head
of John the Baptist on a platter."
26 And although the king was very
sorry, *yet* because of his oaths and
because of [1]his dinner guests, he was
unwilling to refuse her.
27 And immediately the king sent an
executioner and commanded *him* to
bring *back* his head. And he went and
had him beheaded in the prison,
28 and brought his head on a platter,
and gave it to the girl; and the girl gave
it to her mother.
29 And when his disciples heard *about*
this, they came and took away his body
and laid it in a tomb.
30 [a]And the [b]apostles *gathered together with Jesus; and they reported to
Him all that they had done and taught.
31 And He *said to them, "Come
away by yourselves to a lonely place and
rest a while." (For there were many
people coming and going, and [a]they did
not even have time to eat.)
32 [a]And they went away in [b]the boat
to a lonely place by themselves.

Five Thousand Fed

33 And *the people* saw them going,
and many recognized *them,* and they ran
there together on foot from all the cities,
and got there ahead of them.
34 And when He went [1]ashore, He
[a]saw a great multitude, and He felt
compassion for them because [b]they were
like sheep without a shepherd; and He
began to teach them many things.
35 And when it was already quite late,
His disciples came up to Him and *began*
saying, "The place is desolate and it is
already quite late;
36 send them away so that they may
go into the surrounding countryside and
villages and buy themselves [1]something
to eat."
37 But He answered and said to them,
"You give them *something* to eat!" [a]And
they *said to Him, "Shall we go and
spend two hundred [1b]denarii on bread
and give them *something* to eat?"
38 And He *said to them, "How many
loaves do you have? Go look!" And
when they found out, they *said, "Five
and two fish."
39 And He commanded them all to
recline by groups on the green grass.
40 And they reclined in companies of
hundreds and of fifties.
41 And He took the five loaves and
the two fish, and looking up toward
heaven, He [a]blessed *the food* and broke
the loaves and He kept giving *them* to
the disciples to set before them; and He
divided up the two fish among them all.
42 And they all ate and were satisfied.
43 And they picked up twelve full
[a]baskets of the broken pieces, and also
of the fish.
44 And there were [a]five thousand men
who ate the loaves.

Jesus Walks on the Water

45 [a]And immediately He made His
disciples get into [b]the boat and go ahead
of *Him* to the other side to [c]Bethsaida,
while He Himself was sending the multitude away.
46 And after [a]bidding them farewell,
He departed [b]to the mountain to pray.
47 And when it was evening, the boat
was in the midst of the sea, and He *was*
alone on the land.
48 And seeing them [1]straining at the
oars, for the wind was against them, at
about the [2a]fourth watch of the night,
He *came to them, walking on the sea;
and He intended to pass by them.
49 But when they saw Him walking on
the sea, they supposed that it was a
ghost, and cried out;
50 for they all saw Him and were
[1]frightened. But immediately He spoke
with them and *said to them, "[a]Take
courage; it is I, [b]do not be afraid."
51 And He got into [a]the boat with
them, and the wind stopped; and they
were greatly astonished,

15 [a]Matt. 16:14; Mark 8:28 [b]Matt. 21:11
17 [a]Matt. 14:3; Luke 3:19
18 [a]Matt. 14:4
19 [a]Matt. 14:3
20 [1]Lit., *and* [2]Lit., *was hearing him gladly* [a]Matt. 21:26
21 [1]I.e., chiliarchs, in command of a thousand troops [a]Esth. 1:3; 2:18 [b]Luke 3:1
22 [1]Lit., *those who reclined at the table with him* [a]Matt. 14:3
23 [a]Esth. 5:3, 6; 7:2
26 [1]Lit., *those reclining at the table*
30 [a]Luke 9:10 [b]Matt. 10:2; Mark 3:14; Luke 6:13; 9:10; 17:5; 22:14; 24:10; Acts 1:2, 26
31 [a]Mark 3:20
32 [a]Mark 6:32-44: *Matt. 14:13-21; Luke 9:10-17; John 6:5-13;* Mark 8:2-9 [b]Mark 3:9; 4:36; 6:45
34 [1]Lit., *out* [a]Matt. 9:36 [b]Num. 27:17; 1 Kin. 22:17; 2 Chr. 18:16; Zech. 10:2
36 [1]Lit., *what they may eat*
37 [1]The denarius was equivalent to one day's wage [a]John 6:7 [b]Matt. 18:28; Luke 7:41
41 [a]Matt. 14:19
43 [a]Matt. 14:20
44 [a]Matt. 14:21
45 [a]Mark 6:45-51: *Matt. 14:22-32; John 6:15-21* [b]Mark 6:32 [c]Matt. 11:21; Mark 8:22
46 [a]Acts 18:18, 21; 2 Cor. 2:13 [b]Matt. 14:23
48 [1]Lit., *harassed in rowing* [2]I.e., 3-6 a.m. [a]Matt. 24:43; Mark 13:35
50 [1]Or, *troubled* [a]Matt. 9:2 [b]Matt. 14:27
51 [a]Mark 6:32

52 for [a]they [1]had not gained any insight from the *incident of* the loaves, but [2]their heart [b]was hardened.

Healing at Gennesaret

53 [a]And when they had crossed over they came to land at Gennesaret, and moored to the shore.

54 And when they had come out of the boat, immediately *the people* recognized Him,

55 and ran about that whole country and began to carry about on their pallets those who were sick, to [1]the place they heard He was.

56 And wherever He entered villages, or cities, or countryside, they were laying the sick in the market places, and entreating Him that they might just [a]touch [b]the fringe of His cloak; and as many as touched it were being cured.

Followers of Tradition

7 [a]AND the Pharisees and some of the scribes gathered together around Him when they had come [b]from Jerusalem,

2 and had seen that some of His disciples were eating their bread with [a]impure hands, that is, unwashed.

3 (For the Pharisees and all the Jews do not eat unless they [1]carefully wash their hands, *thus* observing the [a]traditions of the elders;

4 and *when they come* from the market place, they do not eat unless they [1]cleanse themselves; and there are many other things which they have received in order to observe, such as the [2]washing of [a]cups and pitchers and copper pots.)

5 And the Pharisees and the scribes *asked Him, "Why do Your disciples not walk according to the [a]tradition of the elders, but eat their bread with [b]impure hands?"

6 And He said to them, "Rightly did Isaiah prophesy of you hypocrites, as it is written,

'[a]THIS PEOPLE HONORS ME WITH THEIR LIPS,
BUT THEIR HEART IS FAR AWAY FROM ME.

7 '[a]BUT IN VAIN DO THEY WORSHIP ME,
TEACHING AS DOCTRINES THE PRECEPTS OF MEN.'

8 "Neglecting the commandment of God, you hold to the [a]tradition of men."

9 He was also saying to them, "You nicely set aside the commandment of God in order to keep your [a]tradition.

10 "For Moses said, '[a]HONOR YOUR FATHER AND YOUR MOTHER'; and, '[b]HE WHO SPEAKS EVIL OF FATHER OR MOTHER, LET HIM [1]BE PUT TO DEATH';

11 but you say, 'If a man says to *his* father or *his* mother, anything of mine you might have been helped by is [a]Corban (that is to say, [1]given *to God*),'

12 you no longer permit him to do anything for *his* father or *his* mother;

52 [1]Lit., *had not understood on the basis of* [2]Or, *their mind was closed, made dull,* or *insensible* [a]Mark 8:17ff. [b]Rom. 11:7
53 [a]Mark 6:53-56: *Matt. 14:34-36;* John 6:24, 25
55 [1]Or, *where they were hearing that He was*
56 [a]Mark 3:10 [b]Matt. 9:20
1 [a]Mark 7:1-23: *Matt. 15:1-20* [b]Matt. 15:1
2 [a]Matt. 15:2; Mark 7:5; Luke 11:38; Acts 10:14, 28; 11:8; Rom. 14:14; Heb. 10:29; Rev. 21:27
3 [1]Lit., *with the fist* [a]Mark 7:5, 8, 9, 13; Gal. 1:14
4 [1]Or, *sprinkle* [2]Lit., *baptizing* [a]Matt. 23:25
5 [a]Mark 7:3, 8, 9, 13; Gal. 1:14 [b]Mark 7:2
6 [a]Is. 29:13
7 [a]Is. 29:13
8 [a]Mark 7:3, 5, 9, 13; Gal. 1:14
9 [a]Mark 7:3, 5, 8, 13; Gal. 1:14
10 [1]Lit., *die the death* [a]Ex. 20:12; Deut. 5:16 [b]Ex. 21:17; Lev. 20:9
11 [1]Or, *a gift, an offering* [a]Lev. 1:2; Matt. 27:6
13 [a]Mark 7:3, 5, 8, 9; Gal. 1:14
16 [1]Many mss. do not contain this verse
17 [a]Mark 2:1; 3:20; 9:28 [b]Matt. 15:15
19 [1]Lit., *goes out into the latrine* [a]Rom. 14:1-12; Col. 2:16 [b]Luke 11:41; Acts 10:15; 11:9
20 [a]Matt. 15:18; Mark 7:23
21 [1]I.e., acts of sexual immorality
22 [1]Lit., *an evil eye* [2]Or, *arrogance* [a]Matt. 6:23; 20:15
24 [1]Some early mss. add *and Sidon* [2]Lit., *and* [a]Mark 7:24-30: *Matt. 15:21-28* [b]Matt. 11:21; Mark 7:31
26 [1]Lit., *Greek*
27 [1]Or, *proper*
29 [1]Lit., *word*
30 [1]Lit., *thrown*
31 [a]Mark 7:31-37: *Matt. 15:29-31* [b]Matt. 11:21; Mark 7:24 [c]Matt. 4:18 [d]Matt. 4:25; Mark 5:20

13 *thus* invalidating the word of God by your [a]tradition which you have handed down; and you do many things such as that."

The Heart of Man

14 And after He called the multitude to Him again, He *began* saying to them, "Listen to Me, all of you, and understand:

15 there is nothing outside the man which going into him can defile him; but the things which proceed out of the man are what defile the man.

16 ["[1]If any man has ears to hear, let him hear."]

17 And when leaving the multitude, He had entered [a]the house, [b]His disciples questioned Him about the parable.

18 And He *said to them, "Are you so lacking in understanding also? Do you not understand that whatever goes into the man from outside cannot defile him;

19 because it does not go into his heart, but into his stomach, and [1]is eliminated?" (*Thus He* declared [a]all foods [b]clean.)

20 And He was saying, "[a]That which proceeds out of the man, that is what defiles the man.

21 "For from within, out of the heart of men, proceed the evil thoughts, [1]fornications, thefts, murders, adulteries,

22 deeds of coveting *and* wickedness, *as well as* deceit, sensuality, [1a]envy, slander, [2]pride *and* foolishness.

23 "All these evil things proceed from within and defile the man."

The Syrophoenician Woman

24 [a]And from there He arose and went away to the region of [b]Tyre[1]. And when He had entered a house, He wanted no one to know *of it;* [2]yet He could not escape notice.

25 But after hearing of Him, a woman whose little daughter had an unclean spirit, immediately came and fell at His feet.

26 Now the woman was a [1]Gentile, of the Syrophoenician race. And she kept asking Him to cast the demon out of her daughter.

27 And He was saying to her, "Let the children be satisfied first, for it is not [1]good to take the children's bread and throw it to the dogs."

28 But she answered and *said to Him, "Yes, Lord, *but* even the dogs under the table feed on the children's crumbs."

29 And He said to her, "Because of this [1]answer go your way; the demon has gone out of your daughter."

30 And going back to her home, she found the child [1]lying on the bed, the demon having departed.

31 [a]And again He went out from the region of [b]Tyre, and came through Sidon to [c]the Sea of Galilee, within the region of [d]Decapolis.

32 And they *brought to Him one who was deaf and spoke with difficulty, and they *entreated Him to [a]lay His hand upon him.

33 And [a]He took him aside from the multitude by himself, and put His fingers into his ears, and after [a]spitting, He touched his tongue *with the saliva;*

34 and looking up to heaven with a deep [a]sigh, He *said to him, "Ephphatha!" that is, "Be opened!"

35 And his ears were opened, and the [1]impediment of his tongue [2]was removed, and he *began* speaking plainly.

36 And [a]He gave them orders not to tell anyone; but the more He ordered them, the more widely they [b]continued to proclaim it.

37 And they were utterly astonished, saying, "He has done all things well; He makes even the deaf to hear, and the dumb to speak."

Four Thousand Fed

8 IN those days again, when there was a great multitude and they had nothing to eat, [a]He called His disciples and *said to them,

2 "[a]I feel compassion for the multitude because they have remained with Me now three days, and have nothing to eat;

3 and if I send them away hungry to their home, they will faint on the way; and some of them have come from a distance."

4 And His disciples answered Him, "Where will anyone be able to *find enough to* satisfy these men with [1]bread here in a desolate place?"

5 And He was asking them, "How many loaves do you have?" And they said, "Seven."

6 And He *directed the multitude to [1]sit down on the ground; and taking the seven loaves, He gave thanks and broke them, and started giving them to His disciples to [2]serve to them, and they served them to the multitude.

7 They also had a few small fish; and [a]after He had blessed them, He ordered these to be [1]served as well.

8 And they ate and were satisfied; and they picked up seven large [a]baskets full of what was left over of the broken pieces.

9 And about four thousand were *there;* and He sent them away.

10 And immediately He entered the boat with His disciples, and came to the district of [a]Dalmanutha.

11 [a]And the Pharisees came out and began to argue with Him, [b]seeking from Him a [1]sign from heaven, [2]to test Him.

12 And [a]sighing deeply [1]in His spirit, He *said, "Why does this generation seek for a [2]sign? Truly I say to you, [3][b]no [2]sign shall be given to this generation."

13 And leaving them, He again embarked and went away to the other side.

14 And they had forgotten to take bread; and [1]did not have more than one loaf in the boat with them.

15 And He was giving orders to them, saying, "[a]Watch out! Beware of the leaven of the Pharisees and the leaven of [b]Herod."

16 And they *began* to discuss with one another *the fact* that they had no bread.

17 And Jesus, aware of this, *said to them, "Why do you discuss *the fact* that you have no bread? [a]Do you not yet see or understand? Do you have a [1]hardened heart?

18 "[a]HAVING EYES, DO YOU NOT SEE? AND HAVING EARS, DO YOU NOT HEAR? And do you not remember,

19 when I broke [a]the five loaves for the five thousand, how many [b]baskets full of broken pieces you picked up?" They *said to Him, "Twelve."

20 "And when *I broke* [a]the seven for the four thousand, how many large [b]baskets full of broken pieces did you pick up?" And they *said to Him, "Seven."

21 And He was saying to them, "[a]Do you not yet understand?"

22 And they *came to [a]Bethsaida. And they *brought a blind man to Him, and *entreated Him to [b]touch him.

23 And taking the blind man by the hand, He [a]brought him out of the village; and after [a]spitting on his eyes, and [b]laying His hands upon him, He asked him, "Do you see anything?"

24 And he [1]looked up and said, "I see men, for [2]I am seeing *them* like trees, walking about."

25 Then again He laid His hands upon his eyes; and he looked intently and was restored, and *began* to see everything clearly.

26 And He sent him to his home, saying, "Do not even enter [a]the village."

Peter's Confession of Christ

27 [a]And Jesus went out, along with His disciples, to the villages of [b]Caesarea Philippi; and on the way He questioned His disciples, saying to them, "Who do people say that I am?"

28 [a]And they told Him, saying, "John the Baptist; and others *say* Elijah; but others, one of the prophets."

29 And He *continued* by questioning them, "But who do you say that I am?" [a]Peter *answered and *said to Him, "Thou art [1]the Christ."

30 And [a]He [1]warned them to tell no one about Him.

31 [a]And He began to teach them that [b]the Son of Man must suffer many things and be rejected by the elders and the chief priests and the scribes, and be killed, and after three days rise again.

32 And He was stating the matter [a]plainly. And Peter took Him aside and began to rebuke Him.

32 [a]Mark 5:23
33 [a]Mark 8:23
34 [a]Mark 8:12
35 [1]Or, *bond* [2]Lit., *was loosed*
36 [a]Matt. 8:4 [b]Mark 1:45
1 [a]Mark 8:1-9: *Matt. 15:32-39;* Mark 6:34-44
2 [a]Matt. 9:36; Mark 6:34
4 [1]Lit., *loaves*
6 [1]Lit., *recline* [2]Lit., *set before*
7 [1]Lit., *set before them* [a]Matt. 14:19
8 [a]Matt. 15:37; Mark 8:20
10 [a]Matt. 15:39
11 [1]Or, *attesting miracle* [2]Lit., *testing Him* [a]Mark 8:11-21: *Matt. 16:1-12* [b]Matt. 12:38
12 [1]Or, *to Himself* [2]Or, *attesting miracle* [3]Lit., *if a sign shall be given* [a]Mark 7:34 [b]Matt. 12:39
14 [1]Lit., *were not having*
15 [a]Matt. 16:6; Luke 12:1 [b]Matt. 14:1; 22:16
17 [1]Or, *dull, insensible* [a]Mark 6:52
18 [a]Jer. 5:21; Ezek. 12:2; Mark 4:12
19 [a]Mark 6:41-44 [b]Matt. 14:20
20 [a]Mark 8:6-9 [b]Mark 8:8
21 [a]Mark 6:52
22 [a]Matt. 11:21; Mark 6:45 [b]Mark 3:10
23 [a]Mark 7:33 [b]Mark 5:23
24 [1]Or, *gained sight* [2]Or, *they look to me*
26 [a]Mark 8:23
27 [a]Mark 8:27-29: *Matt. 16:13-16; Luke 9:18-20* [b]Matt. 16:13
28 [a]Mark 6:14; Luke 9:7, 8
29 [1]I.e., the Messiah [a]John 6:68, 69
30 [1]Or, *strictly admonished* [a]Matt. 8:4; 16:20; Luke 9:21
31 [a]Mark 8:31-9:1: *Matt. 16:21-28; Luke 9:22-27* [b]Matt. 16:21
32 [a]John 10:24; 11:14; 16:25, 29; 18:20

33 But turning around and seeing His
disciples, He rebuked Peter, and *said,
"Get behind Me, [a]Satan; for you are not
setting your mind on [1]God's interests,
but man's."
34 And He summoned the multitude
with His disciples, and said to them, "If
anyone wishes to come after Me, let him
deny himself, and [a]take up his cross, and
follow Me.
35 "For [a]whoever wishes to save his
[1]life shall lose it; but whoever loses his
[1]life for My sake and the gospel's shall
save it.
36 "For what does it profit a man to
gain the whole world, and forfeit his
soul?
37 "For what shall a man give in exchange for his soul?
38 "For [a]whoever is ashamed of Me
and My words in this adulterous and
sinful generation, [b]the Son of Man will
also be ashamed of him when He [c]comes
in the glory of His Father with the holy
angels."

The Transfiguration

9 AND He was saying to them,
"[a]Truly I say to you, there are some
of those who are standing here who shall
not taste death until they see the kingdom of God after it has come with
power."
2 [a]And six days later, Jesus *took
with Him [b]Peter and [1]James and John,
and *brought them up to a high mountain by themselves. And He was transfigured before them;
3 and [a]His garments became radiant
and exceedingly white, as no launderer
on earth can whiten them.
4 And Elijah appeared to them along
with Moses; and they were talking with
Jesus.
5 And Peter answered and *said to
Jesus, "[a]Rabbi, it is good for us to be
here; and [b]let us make three [1]taberna-
cles, one for You, and one for Moses,
and one for Elijah."
6 For he did not know what to answer; for they became terrified.
7 Then a cloud [1]formed, overshad-
owing them, and [a]a voice [1]came out of
the cloud, "[b]This is My beloved Son,
[2]listen to Him!"
8 And all at once they looked around
and saw no one with them anymore,
except Jesus alone.
9 [a]And as they were coming down
from the mountain, He [b]gave them
orders not to relate to anyone what they
had seen, [1]until the Son of Man should
rise from the dead.
10 And they [1]seized upon [2]that statement, discussing with one another [3]what
rising from the dead might mean.
11 And they asked Him, saying, "*Why
is it* that the scribes say that [a]Elijah must
come first?"
12 And He said to them, "Elijah does
first come and restore all things. And *yet*
how is it written of [a]the Son of Man that
[b]He should suffer many things and be
treated with contempt?
13 "But I say to you, that Elijah has
[1]indeed come, and they did to him
whatever they wished, just as it is written
of him."

All Things Possible

14 [a]And when they came *back* to the
disciples, they saw a large crowd around
them, and *some* scribes arguing with
them.
15 And immediately, when the entire
crowd saw Him, they were [a]amazed, and
began running up to greet Him.
16 And He asked them, "What are
you discussing with them?"
17 And one of the crowd answered
Him, "Teacher, I brought You my son,
possessed with a spirit which makes him
mute;
18 and [1]whenever it seizes him, it
[2]dashes him *to the ground* and he foams
at the mouth, and grinds his teeth, and
[3]stiffens out. And I told Your disciples
to cast it out, and they could not *do it.*"
19 And He *answered them and *said,
"O unbelieving generation, how long
shall I be with you? How long shall I put
up with you? Bring him to Me!"
20 And they brought [1]the boy to Him.
And when he saw Him, immediately the
spirit threw him into a convulsion, and
falling to the ground, he *began* rolling
about and foaming *at the mouth.*
21 And He asked his father, "How
long has this been happening to him?"
And he said, "From childhood.
22 "And it has often thrown him both
into the fire and into the water to destroy him. But if You can do anything,
take pity on us and help us!"
23 And Jesus said to him, " 'If You
can!' [a]All things are possible to him who
believes."
24 Immediately the boy's father cried
out and *began* saying, "I do believe; help
my unbelief."
25 And when Jesus saw that [a]a crowd
was [1]rapidly gathering, He rebuked the
unclean spirit, saying to it, "You deaf
and dumb spirit, I [2]command you, come
out of him and do not enter him [3]again."
26 And after crying out and throwing
him into terrible convulsions, it came
out; and *the boy* became so much like a
corpse that most *of them* said, "He is
dead!"
27 But Jesus took him by the hand
and raised him; and he got up.
28 And when He had come [a]into *the*
house, His disciples *began* questioning
Him privately, "Why could we not cast
it out?"
29 And He said to them, "This kind
cannot come out by anything but
prayer[1]."

33 [1]Lit., *the things of God* [a]Matt. 4:10

34 [a]Matt. 10:38; Luke 14:27

35 [1]Or, *soul* [a]Matt. 10:39; Luke 17:33; John 12:25

38 [a]Matt. 10:33; Luke 9:26; Heb. 11:16 [b]Matt. 8:20 [c]Matt. 16:27; Mark 13:26; Luke 9:26

1 [a]Matt. 16:28; Mark 13:26; Luke 9:27

2 [1]Or, *Jacob* [a]Mark 9:2-8: *Matt. 17:1-8; Luke 9:28-36* [b]Mark 5:37

3 [a]Matt. 28:3

5 [1]Or, *sacred tents* [a]Matt. 23:7 [b]Matt. 17:4; Luke 9:33

7 [1]Or, *occurred* [2]Or, *give constant heed* [a]2 Pet. 1:17f. [b]Matt. 3:17; Mark 1:11; Luke 3:22

9 [1]Lit., *except when* [a]Mark 9:9-13: *Matt. 17:9-13* [b]Matt. 8:4; Mark 5:43; 7:36; 8:30

10 [1]Or, *kept to themselves* [2]Lit., *the statement* [3]Lit., *what was the rising from the dead*

11 [a]Mal. 4:5; Matt. 11:14

12 [a]Mark 9:31 [b]Matt. 16:21; 26:24

13 [1]Lit., *also*

14 [a]Mark 9:14-28: *Matt. 17:14-19; Luke 9:37-42*

15 [a]Mark 14:33; 16:5, 6

18 [1]Or, *wherever* [2]Or, *tears him* [3]Or, *withers away*

20 [1]Lit., *him*

23 [a]Matt. 17:20; John 11:40

25 [1]Or, *running together* [2]Or, *I Myself command* [3]Or, *from now on* [a]Mark 9:15

28 [a]Mark 2:1; 7:17

29 [1]Many mss. add *and fasting*

Death and Resurrection Foretold

30 [a]And from there they went out and
began to go through Galilee, and He was
unwilling for anyone to know *about it.*
31 For He was teaching His disciples
and telling them, "[a]The Son of Man is to
be [1]delivered into the hands of men, and
they will kill Him; and when He has
been killed, He will rise three days
later."
32 But [a]they [1]did not understand *this*
statement, and they were afraid to ask
Him.
33 [a]And they came to Capernaum;
and when He [1]was in [b]the house, He
began to question them, "What were you
discussing on the way?"
34 But they kept silent, for on the way
[a]they had discussed with one another
which *of them was* the greatest.
35 And sitting down, He called the
twelve and *said to them, "[a]If anyone
wants to be first, [1]he shall be last of all,
and servant of all."
36 And taking a child, He set him
[1]before them, and taking him in His
arms, He said to them,
37 "[a]Whoever receives [1]one child like
this in My name receives Me; and whoever receives Me does not receive Me,
but Him who sent Me."

Dire Warnings

38 [a]John said to Him, "Teacher, we
saw someone casting out demons in
Your name, and [b]we tried to hinder him
because he was not following us."
39 But Jesus said, "Do not hinder
him, for there is no one who shall perform a miracle in My name, and be able
soon afterward to speak evil of Me.
40 "[a]For he who is not against us is [1]for
us.
41 "For [a]whoever gives you a cup of
water to drink [1]because of your name as
followers of Christ, truly I say to you, he
shall not lose his reward.
42 "And [a]whoever causes one of these
[1]little ones who believe to stumble, it
[2]would be better for him if, with a heavy
millstone hung around his neck, he [3]had
been cast into the sea.
43 "And [a]if your hand causes you to
stumble, cut it off; it is better for you to
enter life crippled, than having your two
hands, to go into [1b]hell, into the [c]un-
quenchable fire,
44 [[1]where THEIR WORM DOES NOT
DIE, AND THE FIRE IS NOT QUENCHED.]
45 "And if your foot causes you to
stumble, cut it off; it is better for you to
enter life lame, than having your two
feet, to be cast into [1a]hell,
46 [[1]where THEIR WORM DOES NOT
DIE, AND THE FIRE IS NOT QUENCHED.]
47 "And [a]if your eye causes you to
stumble, cast it out; it is better for you to
enter the kingdom of God with one eye,
than having two eyes, to be cast into
[1b]hell,
48 [a]where THEIR WORM DOES NOT DIE,
AND [b]THE FIRE IS NOT QUENCHED.
49 "For everyone will be salted with
fire.
50 "Salt is good; but [a]if the salt becomes unsalty, with what will you [1]make
it salty *again*? [b]Have salt in yourselves,
and [c]be at peace with one another."

Jesus' Teaching about Divorce

10 [a]AND rising up, He *went from
there to the region of Judea, and
beyond the Jordan; and crowds *gathered around Him again, and, [b]according
to His custom, He once more *began* to
teach them.
2 And *some* Pharisees came up to
Him, testing Him, and *began* to question
Him whether it was lawful for a man to
[1]divorce a wife.
3 And He answered and said to
them, "What did Moses command you?"
4 And they said, "[a]Moses permitted
a man TO WRITE A CERTIFICATE OF
DIVORCE AND [1]SEND *her* AWAY."
5 But Jesus said to them, "[1a]Because
of your hardness of heart he wrote you
this commandment.
6 "But [a]from the beginning of creation, *God* [b]MADE THEM MALE AND FE-
MALE.
7 "[a]FOR THIS CAUSE A MAN SHALL
LEAVE HIS FATHER AND MOTHER,[1]
8 [a]AND THE TWO SHALL BECOME ONE
FLESH; consequently they are no longer
two, but one flesh.
9 "What therefore God has joined
together, let no man separate."
10 And in the house the disciples
began questioning Him about this again.
11 And He *said to them, "[a]Whoever
[1]divorces his wife and marries another
woman commits adultery against her;
12 and [a]if she herself [1]divorces her
husband and marries another man, she is
committing adultery."

Jesus Blesses Little Children

13 [a]And they were bringing children
to Him so that He might touch them;
and the disciples rebuked them.
14 But when Jesus saw this, He was
indignant and said to them, "Permit the
children to come to Me; do not hinder
them; [a]for the kingdom of God belongs
to such as these.
15 "Truly I say to you, [a]whoever does
not receive the kingdom of God like a
child shall not enter it *at all.*"
16 And He [a]took them in His arms
and *began* blessing them, laying His
hands upon them.

30 [a]Mark 9:30-32: *Matt. 17:22, 23; Luke 9:43-45*
31 [1]Or, *betrayed* [a]Matt. 16:21; Mark 8:31; 9:12
32 [1]Lit., *were not knowing* [a]Luke 2:50; 9:45; 18:34; John 12:16
33 [1]Lit., *had come* [a]Mark 9:33-37: *Matt. 18:1-5; Luke 9:46-48* [b]Mark 3:19
34 [a]Matt. 18:4; Mark 9:50; Luke 22:24
35 [1]Or, *let him be* [a]Matt. 20:26; 23:11; Mark 10:43, 44; Luke 22:26
36 [1]Lit., *in their midst*
37 [1]Lit., *one of such children* [a]Matt. 10:40; Luke 10:16; John 13:20
38 [a]Mark 9:38-40: *Luke 9:49, 50* [b]Num. 11:27-29
40 [1]Or, *on our side* [a]Matt. 12:30; Luke 11:23
41 [1]Lit., *in a name that you are Christ's* [a]Matt. 10:42
42 [1]I.e., humble [2]Lit., *is better for him if a millstone turned by a donkey is hung* [3]Lit., *has been cast* [a]Matt. 18:6; Luke 17:2; 1 Cor. 8:12
43 [1]Gr., *Gehenna* [a]Matt. 5:30; 18:8 [b]Matt. 5:22 [c]Matt. 3:12; 25:41
44 [1]Vv. 44 and 46, which are identical with v. 48, are not found in the best ancient mss.
45 [1]Gr., *Gehenna* [a]Matt. 5:22
46 [1]V. 44, note 1
47 [1]Gr., *Gehenna* [a]Matt. 5:29; 18:9 [b]Matt. 5:22
48 [a]Is. 66:24 [b]Matt. 3:12; 25:41
50 [1]Lit., *season it* [a]Matt. 5:13; Luke 14:34f. [b]Col. 4:6 [c]Mark 9:34; Rom. 12:18; 2 Cor. 13:11;

1 [a]Mark 10:1-12: *Matt. 19:1-9* [b]Matt. 4:23; 26:55; Mark 1:21; 2:13; 4:2; 6:2, 6, 34; 12:35; 14:49
2 [1]Or, *send away*
4 [1]Or, *divorce* her [a]Deut. 24:1, 3; Matt. 5:31
5 [1]Or, *With reference to* [a]Matt. 19:8
6 [a]Mark 13:19; 2 Pet. 3:4 [b]Gen. 1:27; 5:2
7 [1]Some mss. add *and shall cleave to his wife* [a]Gen. 2:24
8 [a]Gen. 2:24
11 [1]Or, *sends away* [a]Matt. 5:32
12 [1]Or, *sends away* [a]1 Cor. 7:11, 13
13 [a]Mark 10:13-16: *Matt. 19:13-15; Luke 18:15-17*

14 [a]Matt. 5:3
15 [a]Matt. 18:3; 19:14; Luke 18:17; 1 Cor. 14:20; 1 Pet. 2:2
16 [a]Mark 9:36

The Rich Young Ruler

17 [a]And as He was setting out on a
journey, a man ran up to Him and [b]knelt
before Him, and *began* asking Him,
"Good Teacher, what shall I do to
[c]inherit eternal life?"
18 And Jesus said to him, "Why do
you call Me good? No one is good
except God alone.
19 "You know the commandments,
'[a]DO NOT MURDER, DO NOT COMMIT
ADULTERY, DO NOT STEAL, DO NOT BEAR
FALSE WITNESS, Do not defraud, HONOR
YOUR FATHER AND MOTHER.'"
20 And he said to Him, "Teacher, I
have kept [a]all these things from my
youth up."
21 And looking at him, Jesus felt a
love for him, and said to him, "One
thing you lack: go and sell all you
possess, and give to the poor, and you
shall have [a]treasure in heaven; and
come, follow Me."
22 But at these words [1]his face fell,
and he went away grieved, for he was
one who owned much property.
23 And Jesus, looking around, *said
to His disciples, "[a]How hard it will be
for those who are wealthy to enter the
kingdom of God!"
24 And the disciples [a]were amazed at
His words. But Jesus *answered again
and *said to them, "Children, how hard
it is [1]to enter the kingdom of God!
25 "[a]It is easier for a camel to go
through the eye of [1]a needle than for a
rich man to enter the kingdom of God."
26 And they were even more astonished and said [1]to Him, "[2]Then who can
be saved?"
27 Looking upon them, Jesus *said,
"[a]With men it is impossible, but not
with God; for all things are possible with
God."
28 [a]Peter began to say to Him, "Behold, we have left everything and followed You."
29 Jesus said, "Truly I say to you,
[a]there is no one who has left house or
brothers or sisters or mother or father or
children or farms, for My sake and for
the gospel's sake,
30 but that he shall receive a hundred
times as much now in [1]the present age,
houses and brothers and sisters and
mothers and children and farms, along
with persecutions; and in [a]the age to
come, eternal life.
31 "But [a]many *who are* first, will be
last; and the last, first."

Jesus' Sufferings Foretold

32 [a]And they were on the road, going
up to Jerusalem, and Jesus was walking
on ahead of them; and they [b]were
amazed, and those who followed were
fearful. And again He took the twelve
aside and began to tell them what was
going to happen to Him,
33 *saying,* "Behold, we are going up to
Jerusalem, and [a]the Son of Man will be
[1]delivered to the chief priests and the
scribes; and they will condemn Him to
death, and will [2]deliver Him to the
Gentiles.
34 "And they will mock Him and [a]spit
upon Him, and scourge Him, and kill
Him, and three days later He will rise
again."
35 [a]And [1]James and John, the two
sons of Zebedee, *came up to Him,
saying to Him, "Teacher, we want You
to do for us whatever we ask of You."
36 And He said to them, "What do
you want Me to do for you?"
37 And they said to Him, "[1]Grant
that we [a]may sit in Your glory, one on
Your right, and one on *Your* left."
38 But Jesus said to them, "You do
not know what you are asking for. Are
you able [a]to drink the cup that I drink,
or [b]to be baptized with the baptism with
which I am baptized?"
39 And they said to Him, "We are
able." And Jesus said to them, "The cup
that I drink [a]you shall drink; and you
shall be baptized with the baptism with
which I am baptized.
40 "But to sit on My right or on *My*
left, this is not Mine to give; [a]but it is for
those for whom it has been prepared."
41 [a]And hearing this, the ten began to
feel indignant with [1]James and John.
42 And calling them to Himself, Jesus
*said to them, "You know that those
who are recognized as rulers of the
Gentiles lord it over them; and their
great men exercise authority over them.
43 "But it is not so among you, [a]but
whoever wishes to become great among
you shall be your servant;
44 and whoever wishes to be first
among you shall be slave of all.
45 "For even the Son of Man [a]did not
come to be served, but to serve, and to
give His [1]life a ransom for many."

Bartimaeus Receives His Sight

46 [a]And they *came to Jericho. And
[b]as He was going out from Jericho with
His disciples and a great multitude, a
blind beggar *named* Bartimaeus, the son
of Timaeus, was sitting by the road.
47 And when he heard that it was
Jesus the [a]Nazarene, he began to cry out
and say, "Jesus, [b]Son of David, have
mercy on me!"
48 And many were sternly telling him
to be quiet, but he kept crying out all the
more, "[a]Son of David, have mercy on
me!"
49 And Jesus stopped and said, "Call
him *here.*" And they *called the blind
man, saying to him, "[a]Take courage,
arise! He is calling for you."
50 And casting aside his cloak, he
jumped up, and came to Jesus.
51 And answering him, Jesus said,
"What do you want Me to do for you?"
And the blind man said to Him, "[1][a]Rab-
boni, *I want* to regain my sight!"

17 [a]Mark 10:17-31: *Matt. 19:16-30; Luke 18:18-30* [b]Mark 1:40 [c]Matt. 25:34; Luke 10:25; 18:18; Acts 20:32; Eph. 1:18; 1 Pet. 1:4
19 [a]Ex. 20:12-16; Deut. 5:16-20
20 [a]Matt. 19:20
21 [a]Matt. 6:20
22 [1]Or, *he became gloomy*
23 [a]Matt. 19:23
24 [1]Later mss. insert *for those who trust in wealth* [a]Mark 1:27
25 [1]Lit., *the* [a]Matt. 19:24
26 [1]Later mss. read *to one another* [2]Lit., *And*
27 [a]Matt. 19:26
28 [a]Matt. 4:20-22
29 [a]Matt. 6:33; 19:29; Luke 18:29f.
30 [1]Lit., *this time* [a]Matt. 12:32
31 [a]Matt. 19:30; 20:16; Luke 13:30
32 [a]Mark 10:32-34: *Matt. 20:17-19; Luke 18:31-33* [b]Mark 1:27
33 [1]Or, *betrayed* [2]Or, *betray* [a]Mark 8:31; 9:12
34 [a]Matt. 16:21; 26:67; 27:30; Mark 9:31; 14:65
35 [1]Or, *Jacob* [a]Mark 10:35-45: *Matt. 20:20-28*
37 [1]Lit., *Give to us* [a]Matt. 19:28
38 [a]Matt. 20:22 [b]Luke 12:50
39 [a]Acts 12:2; Rev. 1:9
40 [a]Matt. 13:11
41 [1]Or, *Jacob* [a]Mark 10:42-45; Luke 22:25-27
43 [a]Matt. 20:26; 23:11; Mark 9:35; Luke 22:26
45 [1]Or, *soul* [a]Matt. 20:28
46 [a]Mark 10:46-52: *Matt. 20:29-34; Luke 18:35-43* [b]Luke 18:35; 19:1
47 [a]Mark 1:24 [b]Matt. 9:27
48 [a]Matt. 9:27
49 [a]Matt. 9:2
51 [1]I.e., My Master [a]Matt. 23:7; John 20:16

52 And Jesus said to him, "Go your
way; [a]your faith has [1]made you well."
And immediately he regained his sight
and *began* following Him on the road.

The Triumphal Entry

11 [a]AND as they *approached Jerusalem, at Bethphage and [b]Beth-
any, near [c]the Mount of Olives, He *sent
two of His disciples,
2 and *said to them, "Go into the
village opposite you, and immediately as
you enter it, you will find a colt tied
there, on which no one yet has ever sat;
untie it and bring it *here.*
3 "And if anyone says to you, 'Why
are you doing this?' you say, 'The Lord
has need of it'; and immediately he [1]will
send it back here."
4 And they went away and found a
colt tied at the door outside in the street;
and they *untied it.
5 And some of the bystanders were
saying to them, "What are you doing,
untying the colt?"
6 And they spoke to them just as
Jesus had told *them,* and they gave them
permission.
7 [a]And they *brought the colt to
Jesus and put their garments on it; and
He sat upon it.
8 And many spread their garments in
the road, and others *spread* leafy
branches which they had cut from the
fields.
9 And those who went before, and
those who followed after, were crying
out,
"Hosanna!
[a]BLESSED IS HE WHO COMES IN
THE NAME OF THE LORD;
10 Blessed *is* the coming kingdom of
our father David;
Hosanna [a]in the highest!"
11 And [a]He entered Jerusalem *and
came* into the temple; and after looking
all around, [b]He departed for Bethany
with the twelve, since it was already late.
12 [a]And on the next day, when they
had departed from Bethany, He became
hungry.
13 And seeing at a distance a fig tree
in leaf, He went *to see* if perhaps He
would find anything on it; and when He
came to it, He found nothing but leaves,
for it was not the season for figs.
14 And He answered and said to it,
"May no one ever eat fruit from you
again!" And His disciples were listening.

Jesus Drives Moneychangers from the Temple

15 [a]And they *came to Jerusalem.
And He entered the temple and began to
cast out those who were buying and
selling in the temple, and overturned the
tables of the moneychangers and the
seats of those who were selling [1]doves;
16 and He would not permit anyone
to carry [1]goods through the temple.
17 And He *began* to teach and say to
them, "Is it not written, '[a]MY HOUSE

52 [1]Lit., *saved you* [a]Matt. 9:22

1 [a]Mark 11:1-10: *Matt. 21:1-9; Luke 19:29-38* [b]Matt. 21:17 [c]Matt. 21:1

3 [1]Lit., *sends*

7 [a]Mark 11:7-10: *Matt. 21:4-9; Luke 19:35-38; John 12:12-15*

9 [a]Ps. 118:26; Matt. 21:9

10 [a]Matt. 21:9

11 [a]Matt. 21:12 [b]Matt. 21:17

12 [a]Mark 11:12-14, 20-24: *Matt. 21:18-22*

15 [1]Lit., *the doves* [a]Mark 11:15-18: *Matt. 21:12-16; Luke 19:45-47;* John 2:13-16

16 [1]Lit., *a vessel;* i.e., a receptacle or implement of any kind

17 [1]Lit., *cave* [a]Is. 56:7 [b]Jer. 7:11

18 [a]Matt. 21:46; Mark 12:12; Luke 20:19; John 7:1 [b]Matt. 7:28

19 [1]I.e., Jesus and His disciples [a]Matt. 21:17; Mark 11:11; Luke 21:37

20 [a]Mark 11:12-14, 20-24: *Matt. 21:19-22*

21 [a]Matt. 23:7

22 [a]Matt. 17:20; 21:21f.

23 [a]Matt. 17:20; 1 Cor. 13:2

24 [a]Matt. 7:7f.

25 [a]Matt. 6:5 [b]Matt. 6:14

26 [1]Many mss. do not contain this v. [a]Matt. 6:15; 18:35

27 [a]Mark 11:27-33: *Matt. 21:23-27; Luke 20:1-8*

32 [1]Or, *if we say*

33 [1]Lit., *do I tell*

1 [1]Or, *fence* [2]Or, *tenant farmers,* also vv. 2, 7, 9 [a]Mark 3:23; 4:2ff. [b]Mark 12:1-12: *Matt. 21:33-46; Luke 20:9-19* [c]Is. 5:1, 2

SHALL BE CALLED A HOUSE OF PRAYER
FOR ALL THE NATIONS'? [b]But you have
made it a ROBBERS' [1]DEN."
18 And the chief priests and the
scribes heard *this,* and [a]*began* seeking
how to destroy Him; for they were
afraid of Him, for [b]all the multitude was
astonished at His teaching.
19 And [a]whenever evening came,
[1]they would go out of the city.
20 [a]And as they were passing by in the
morning, they saw the fig tree withered
from the roots *up.*
21 And being reminded, Peter *said to
Him, "[a]Rabbi, behold, the fig tree which
You cursed has withered."
22 And Jesus *answered saying to
them, "[a]Have faith in God.
23 "[a]Truly I say to you, whoever says
to this mountain, 'Be taken up and cast
into the sea,' and does not doubt in his
heart, but believes that what he says is
going to happen, it shall be *granted* him.
24 "Therefore I say to you, [a]all things
for which you pray and ask, believe that
you have received them, and they shall
be *granted* you.
25 "And whenever you [a]stand praying,
[b]forgive, if you have anything against
anyone; so that your Father also who is
in heaven may forgive you your transgressions.
26 ["[1a]But if you do not forgive, neither will your Father who is in heaven
forgive your transgressions."]

Jesus' Authority Questioned

27 And they *came again to Jerusalem. [a]And as He was walking in the
temple, the chief priests, and scribes,
and elders *came to Him,
28 and *began* saying to Him, "By what
authority are You doing these things, or
who gave You this authority to do these
things?"
29 And Jesus said to them, "I will ask
you one question, and you answer Me,
and *then* I will tell you by what authority
I do these things.
30 "Was the baptism of John from
heaven, or from men? Answer Me."
31 And they *began* reasoning among
themselves, saying, "If we say, 'From
heaven,' He will say, 'Then why did you
not believe him?'
32 "But [1]shall we say, 'From men'?"—
they were afraid of the multitude, for all
considered John to have been a prophet
indeed.
33 And answering Jesus, they *said,
"We do not know." And Jesus *said to
them, "Neither [1]will I tell you by what
authority I do these things."

Parable of the Vine-growers

12 [a]AND He began to speak to them
in parables: "[b]A man [c]PLANTED A
VINEYARD, AND PUT A [1]WALL AROUND
IT, AND DUG A VAT UNDER THE WINE
PRESS, AND BUILT A TOWER, and rented it
out to [2]vine-growers and went on a
journey.

2"And at the *harvest* time he sent a
slave to the vine-growers, in order to
receive *some* of the produce of the vineyard from the vine-growers.
3"And they took him, and beat him,
and sent him away empty-handed.
4"And again he sent them another
slave, and they wounded him in the
head, and treated him shamefully.
5"And he sent another, and that one
they killed; and *so with* many others,
beating some, and killing others.
6"He had one more *to send*, a beloved
son; he sent him last *of all* to them,
saying, 'They will respect my son.'
7"But those vine-growers said to one
another, 'This is the heir; come, let us
kill him, and the inheritance will be
ours!'
8"And they took him, and killed him,
and threw him out of the vineyard.
9"What will the [1]owner of the vineyard do? He will come and destroy the
vine-growers, and will give the vineyard
to others.
10"Have you not even read this Scripture:

'[a]THE STONE WHICH THE BUILDERS REJECTED,
THIS BECAME THE CHIEF CORNER *stone*;
11 [a]THIS CAME ABOUT FROM THE LORD,
AND IT IS MARVELOUS IN OUR EYES'?"

12 And [a]they were seeking to seize
Him; and *yet* they feared the multitude;
for they understood that He spoke the
parable against them. And *so* [b]they left
Him, and went away.

Jesus Answers the Pharisees, Sadducees and Scribes

13 [a]And they *sent some of the Pharisees and [b]Herodians to Him, in order to
[c]trap Him in a statement.
14 And they *came and *said to Him,
"Teacher, we know that You are truthful, and [1]defer to no one; for You are
not partial to any, but teach the way of
God in truth. Is it [2]lawful to pay a poll-
tax to Caesar, or not?
15"Shall we pay, or shall we not pay?"
But He, knowing their hypocrisy, said to
them, "Why are you testing Me? Bring
Me a [1]denarius to look at."
16 And they brought *one*. And He
*said to them, "Whose likeness and
inscription is this?" And they said to
Him, "Caesar's."
17 And Jesus said to them, "[a]Render
to Caesar the things that are Caesar's,
and to God the things that are God's."
And they [1]were amazed at Him.
18 [a]And *some* Sadducees (who say
that there is no resurrection) *came to
Him, and *began* questioning Him, saying,
19"Teacher, Moses wrote for us that
[a]IF A MAN'S BROTHER DIES, and leaves
behind a wife, AND LEAVES NO CHILD,
HIS BROTHER SHOULD TAKE THE WIFE,
AND RAISE UP OFFSPRING TO HIS
BROTHER.
20"There were seven brothers; and the
first took a wife, and died, leaving no
offspring.
21"And the second one took her, and
died, leaving behind no offspring; and
the third likewise;
22 and *so* [1]all seven left no offspring.
Last of all the woman died also.
23"In the resurrection, [1]when they rise
again, which one's wife will she be? For
[2]all seven had her as wife."
24 Jesus said to them, "Is this not the
reason you are mistaken, that you do not
[1]understand the Scriptures, or the power
of God?
25"For when they rise from the dead,
they neither marry, nor are given in
marriage, but are like angels in heaven.
26"But [1]regarding the fact that the
dead rise again, have you not read in the
book of Moses, [a]in the *passage about the
burning* bush, how God spoke to him,
saying, '[b]I AM THE GOD OF ABRAHAM,
AND THE GOD OF ISAAC, AND THE GOD
OF JACOB'?
27"[a]He is not the God [1]of the dead,
but of the living; you are greatly mistaken."
28 [a]And one of the scribes came and
heard them arguing, and [b]recognizing
that He had answered them well, asked
Him, "What commandment is the [1]fore-
most of all?"
29 Jesus answered, "The foremost is,
'[a]HEAR, O ISRAEL! THE LORD OUR GOD
IS ONE LORD;
30 [a]AND YOU SHALL LOVE THE LORD
YOUR GOD WITH ALL YOUR HEART, AND
WITH ALL YOUR SOUL, AND WITH ALL
YOUR MIND, AND WITH ALL YOUR
STRENGTH.'
31"The second is this, '[a]YOU SHALL
LOVE YOUR NEIGHBOR AS YOURSELF.'
There is no other commandment greater
than these."
32 And the scribe said to Him, "Right,
Teacher, You have truly stated that [a]HE
IS ONE; AND THERE IS NO ONE ELSE
BESIDES HIM;
33 [a]AND TO LOVE HIM WITH ALL THE
HEART AND WITH ALL THE UNDERSTAND-
ING AND WITH ALL THE STRENGTH, AND
TO LOVE ONE'S NEIGHBOR AS HIMSELF, [b]is
much more than all burnt offerings and
sacrifices."
34 And when Jesus saw that he had
answered intelligently, He said to him,
"You are not far from the kingdom of
God." [a]And after that, no one would
venture to ask Him any more questions.
35 [a]And Jesus answering *began* to say,
as He [b]taught in the temple, "How *is it
that* the scribes say that [1]the Christ is the
[c]son of David?
36"David himself said [1]in the Holy
Spirit,

'[a]THE LORD SAID TO MY LORD,
"SIT AT MY RIGHT HAND,

9 [1]Lit., *lord*
10 [a]Ps. 118:22
11 [a]Ps. 118:23
12 [a]Mark 11:18 [b]Matt. 22:22
13 [a]Mark 12:13-17: *Matt. 22:15-22; Luke 20:20-26* [b]Matt. 22:16 [c]Luke 11:54
14 [1]Lit., *it is not a concern to You about anyone;* i.e., You court no man's favor [2]Or, *permissible*
15 [1]The denarius was equivalent to one day's wage
17 [1]Or, *were greatly marveling* [a]Matt. 22:21
18 [a]Mark 12:18-27: *Matt. 22:23-33; Luke 20:27-38;* Acts 23:8
19 [a]Deut. 25:5
22 [1]Lit., *the seven*
23 [1]Most ancient mss. do not contain *when they rise again* [2]Lit., *the seven*
24 [1]Or, *know*
26 [1]Lit., *concerning the dead, that they rise* [a]Luke 20:37; Rom. 11:2 [b]Ex. 3:6
27 [1]Or, *of corpses* [a]Matt. 22:32; Luke 20:38
28 [1]Or, *first* [a]Mark 12:28-34: *Matt. 22:34-40;* Luke 10:25-28; 20:39f. [b]Matt. 22:34; Luke 20:39
29 [a]Deut. 6:4
30 [a]Deut. 6:5
31 [a]Lev. 19:18
32 [a]Deut. 4:35
33 [a]Deut. 6:5 [b]1 Sam. 15:22; Hos. 6:6; Mic. 6:6-8; Matt. 9:13; 12:7
34 [a]Matt. 22:46
35 [1]I.e., the Messiah [a]Mark 12:35-37: *Matt. 22:41-46; Luke 20:41-44* [b]Matt. 26:55; Mark 10:1 [c]Matt. 9:27
36 [1]Or, *by* [a]Ps. 110:1

UNTIL I PUT THINE ENEMIES BE-
NEATH THY FEET." '
37"David himself calls Him 'Lord';
and *so* in what sense is He his son?" And
[a]the great crowd [1]enjoyed listening to
Him.
38 [a]And in His teaching He was saying: "Beware of the scribes who like to
walk around in long robes, and *like*
[b]respectful greetings in the market
places,
39 and chief seats in the synagogues,
and places of honor at banquets,
40 [a]who devour widows' houses, and
for appearance's sake offer long prayers;
these will receive greater condemnation."

The Widow's Mite

41 [a]And He sat down opposite [b]the
treasury, and *began* observing how the
multitude were [c]putting [1]money into
the treasury; and many rich people were
putting in large sums.
42 And a poor widow came and put in
two [1]small copper coins, which amount
to a [2]cent.
43 And calling His disciples to Him,
He said to them, "Truly I say to you, this
poor widow put in more than all [1]the
contributors to the treasury;
44 for they all put in out of their
[1]surplus, but she, out of her poverty, put
in all she owned, [2]all she had [a]to live
on."

Things to Come

13 [a]AND as He was going out of the
temple, one of His disciples *said
to Him, "Teacher, behold [1]what wonderful stones and [1]what wonderful buildings!"
2 And Jesus said to him, "Do you see
these great buildings? [a]Not one stone
shall be left upon another which will not
be torn down."
3 And as He was sitting on [a]the
Mount of Olives opposite the temple,
[b]Peter and [1]James and John and Andrew were questioning Him privately,
4"Tell us, when will these things be,
and what *will be* the [1]sign when all these
things are going to be fulfilled?"
5 And Jesus began to say to them,
"See to it that no one misleads you.
6"Many will come in My name, saying, '[a]I am *He!*' and will mislead many.
7"And when you hear of wars and
rumors of wars, do not be frightened;
those things must take place; but *that is*
not yet the end.
8"For nation will arise against nation, and kingdom against kingdom;
there will be earthquakes in various
places; there will *also* be famines. These
things are *merely* the beginning of birth
pangs.
9"But [1]be on your guard; for they
will [a]deliver you to *the* [2]courts, and you
will be flogged [b]in *the* synagogues, and
you will stand before governors and
kings for My sake, as a testimony to
them.
10"[a]And the gospel must first be
preached to all the nations.
11"[a]And when they [1]arrest you and
deliver you up, do not be anxious beforehand about what you are to say, but
say whatever is given you in that hour;
for it is not you who speak, but *it is* the
Holy Spirit.
12"And brother will deliver brother to
death, and a father *his* child; and children will rise up against parents and
[1]have them put to death.
13"And [a]you will be hated by all on
account of My name, but the one who
endures to the end, he shall be saved.
14"But [a]when you see the [b]ABOMINA-
TION OF DESOLATION standing where it
should not be (let the reader understand), then let those who are in Judea
flee to the mountains.
15"[a]And let him who is on the housetop not go down, or enter in, to get
anything out of his house;
16 and let him who is in the field not
turn back to get his cloak.
17"But woe to those who are with
child and to those who nurse babes in
those days!
18"But pray that it may not happen in
the winter.
19"For those days will be a *time of*
tribulation such as has not occurred
[a]since the beginning of the creation
which God created, until now, and never
shall.
20"And unless the Lord had shortened
those days, no [1]life would have been
saved; but for the sake of the [2]elect
whom He chose, He shortened the days.
21"And then if anyone says to you,
'Behold, here is [1]the Christ'; or, 'Behold,
He is there'; do not believe *him;*
22 for false Christs and [a]false prophets will arise, and will show [1b]signs and
[b]wonders, in order, if possible, to lead
the elect astray.
23"But take heed; behold, I have told
you everything in advance.

The Return of Christ

24"But in those days, after that tribulation, [a]THE SUN WILL BE DARKENED,
AND THE MOON WILL NOT GIVE ITS
LIGHT,
25 [a]AND THE STARS WILL BE FALLING
from heaven, and the powers that are in
[1]the heavens will be shaken.
26"And then they will see [a]THE SON OF
MAN [b]COMING IN CLOUDS with great
power and glory.
27"And then He will send forth the
angels, and [a]will gather together His
[1]elect from the four winds, [b]from the
farthest end of the earth, to the farthest
end of heaven.
28"Now learn the parable from the fig
tree: when its branch has already become tender, and puts forth its leaves,
you know that summer is near.

37 [1]Lit., *was gladly hearing Him* [a]John 12:9

38 [a]Mark 12:38-40: *Matt. 23:1-7; Luke 20:45-47* [b]Matt. 23:7; Luke 11:43

40 [a]Luke 20:47

41 [1]I.e., copper coins [a]Mark 12:41-44: *Luke 21:1-4* [b]John 8:20 [c]2 Kin. 12:9

42 [1]Gr., *lepta* [2]Gr., *quadrans;* i.e., 1/64 of a denarius

43 [1]Lit., *those who were putting in*

44 [1]Or, *abundance* [2]Lit., *her whole livelihood* [a]Luke 8:43; 15:12, 30; 21:4

1 [1]Lit., *how great* [a]Mark 13:1-37: *Matt. 24; Luke 21:5-36*

2 [a]Luke 19:44

3 [1]Or, *Jacob* [a]Matt. 21:1 [b]Matt. 17:1

4 [1]Or, *attesting miracle*

6 [a]John 8:24

9 [1]Lit., *look to yourselves* [2]Or, *Sanhedrin* or *council* [a]Matt. 10:17 [b]Matt. 10:17

10 [a]Matt. 24:14

11 [1]Lit., *lead* [a]Mark 13:11-13: *Matt. 10:19-22; Luke 21:12-17*

12 [1]Lit., *put them to death*

13 [a]Matt. 10:22; John 15:21

14 [a]Matt. 24:15f. [b]Dan. 9:27; 11:31; 12:11

15 [a]Luke 17:31

19 [a]Dan. 12:1; Mark 10:6

20 [1]Lit., *flesh* [2]Or, *chosen ones*

21 [1]I.e., the Messiah

22 [1]Or, *attesting miracles* [a]Matt. 7:15 [b]Matt. 24:24; John 4:48

24 [a]Is. 13:10; Ezek. 32:7; Joel 2:10, 31; 3:15; Rev. 6:12

25 [1]Or, *heaven* [a]Is. 34:4; Rev. 6:13

26 [a]Dan. 7:13; Rev. 1:7 [b]Matt. 16:27; Mark 8:38

27 [1]Or, *chosen ones* [a]Deut. 30:4 [b]Zech. 2:6

29 "Even so, you too, when you see these things happening, [1]recognize that [2]He is near, *right* at the [3]door.

30 "Truly I say to you, this [1]generation will not pass away until all these things take place.

31 "Heaven and earth will pass away, but My words will not pass away.

32 "[a]But of that day or hour no one knows, not even the angels in heaven, nor the Son, but the Father *alone.*

33 "Take heed, [a]keep on the alert; for you do not know when the *appointed* time is.

34 "[a]*It is* like a man, away on a journey, *who* upon leaving his house and [1]putting his slaves in charge, *assigning* to each one his task, also commanded the doorkeeper to stay on the alert.

35 "Therefore, [a]be on the alert—for you do not know when the [1]master of the house is coming, whether in the evening, at midnight, at [b]cockcrowing, or [c]in the morning—

36 lest he come suddenly and find you [a]asleep.

37 "And what I say to you I say to all, '[a]Be on the alert!' "

Death Plot and Anointing

14 [a]NOW [b]the Passover and Unleavened Bread was two days off; and the chief priests and the scribes [c]were seeking how to seize Him by stealth, and kill *Him;*

2 for they were saying, "Not during the festival, lest there be a riot of the people."

3 [a]And while He was in [b]Bethany at the home of Simon the leper, and reclining *at the table,* there came a woman with an alabaster vial of very [c]costly perfume of pure nard; *and* she broke the vial and poured it over His head.

4 But some were indignantly *remarking* to one another, "Why has this perfume been wasted?

5 "For this perfume might have been sold for over three hundred [1]denarii, and *the money* given to the poor." And they were scolding her.

6 But Jesus said, "Let her alone; why do you bother her? She has done a good deed to Me.

7 "For [a]the poor you always have with you, and whenever you wish, you can do them good; but you do not always have Me.

8 "She has done what she could; [a]she has anointed My body beforehand for the burial.

9 "And truly I say to you, [a]wherever the gospel is preached in the whole world, that also which this woman has done shall be spoken of in memory of her."

10 [a]And Judas Iscariot, [b]who was one of the twelve, went off to the chief priests, in order to [1]betray Him to them.

11 And they were glad when they heard *this,* and promised to give him money. And he *began* seeking how to betray Him at an opportune time.

The Last Passover

12 [a]And on the first day of [b]Unleavened Bread, when [1]the Passover *lamb* was being [c]sacrificed, His disciples *said to Him, "Where do You want us to go and prepare for You to eat the Passover?"

13 And He *sent two of His disciples, and *said to them, "Go into the city, and a man will meet you carrying a pitcher of water; follow him;

14 and wherever he enters, say to the owner of the house, 'The Teacher says, "Where is My [a]guest room in which I may eat the Passover with My disciples?" '

15 "And he himself will show you a large upper room furnished *and* ready; and prepare for us there."

16 And the disciples went out, and came to the city, and found *it* just as He had told them; and they prepared the Passover.

17 [a]And when it was evening He *came with the twelve.

18 And as they were reclining *at the table* and eating, Jesus said, "Truly I say to you that one of you will [1]betray Me—[2]one who is eating with Me."

19 They began to be grieved and to say to Him one by one, "Surely not I?"

20 And He said to them, "*It is* one of the twelve, [1]one who dips with Me in the bowl.

21 "For the Son of Man *is to* go, just as it is written of Him; but woe to that man [1]by whom the Son of Man is betrayed! *It would have been* good [2]for that man if he had not been born."

The Lord's Supper

22 [a]And while they were eating, He took *some* bread, and [1]after a [b]blessing He broke *it;* and gave *it* to them, and said, "Take *it;* this is My body."

23 And when He had taken a cup, *and* given thanks, He gave *it* to them; and they all drank from it.

24 And He said to them, "This is My [a]blood of the [b]covenant, which is poured out for many.

25 "Truly I say to you, I shall never again drink of the fruit of the vine until that day when I drink it new in the kingdom of God."

26 [a]And after singing a hymn, they went out to [b]the Mount of Olives.

27 [a]And Jesus *said to them, "You will all [1]fall away, because it is written, '[b]I WILL STRIKE DOWN THE SHEPHERD, AND THE SHEEP SHALL BE SCATTERED.'

28 "But after I have been raised, [a]I will go before you to Galilee."

29 But Peter said to Him, "*Even* though all may [1]fall away, yet I will not."

---

29 [1]Lit., *know* [2]Or, *it* [3]Lit., *doors*

30 [1]Or, *race*

32 [a]Matt. 24:36; Acts 1:7

33 [a]Eph. 6:18; Col. 4:2

34 [1]Lit., *giving the authority to* [a]Luke 12:36-38

35 [1]Lit., *lord* [a]Matt. 24:42; Mark 13:37 [b]Mark 14:30 [c]Matt. 14:25; Mark 6:48

36 [a]Rom. 13:11

37 [a]Matt. 24:42; Mark 13:35

1 [a]Mark 14:1, 2: *Matt. 26:2-5; Luke 22:1, 2* [b]Ex. 12:1-27; Mark 14:12; John 11:55; 13:1 [c]Matt. 12:14

3 [a]Mark 14:3-9: *Matt. 26:6-13;* Luke 7:37-39; John 12:1-8 [b]Matt. 21:17 [c]Matt. 26:6f.; John 12:3

5 [1]The denarius was equivalent to one day's wage

7 [a]Deut. 15:11; Matt. 26:11; John 12:8

8 [a]John 19:40

9 [a]Matt. 26:13

10 [1]Or, *deliver Him up* [a]Mark 14:10, 11: *Matt. 26:14-16; Luke 22:3-6* [b]John 6:71

12 [1]Lit., *they were sacrificing* [a]Mark 14:12-16: *Matt. 26:17-19; Luke 22:7-13* [b]Matt. 26:17 [c]Deut. 16:5; Mark 14:1; Luke 22:7; 1 Cor. 5:7

14 [a]Luke 22:11

17 [a]Mark 14:17-21: *Matt. 26:20-24; Luke 22:14, 21-23;* John 13:18ff.

18 [1]Or, *deliver Me up* [2]Or, *the one*

20 [1]Or, *the one*

21 [1]Or, *through* [2]Lit., *for him if that man had not been born*

22 [1]Lit., *having blessed* [a]Mark 14:22-25: *Matt. 26:26-29; Luke 22:17-20; 1 Cor. 11:23-25;* Mark 10:16 [b]Matt. 14:19

24 [a]Ex. 24:8 [b]Jer. 31:31-34

26 [a]Matt. 26:30 [b]Matt. 21:1

27 [1]Or, *stumble* [a]Mark 14:27-31: *Matt. 26:31-35* [b]Zech. 13:7

28 [a]Matt. 28:16

29 [1]Or, *stumble*

30 And Jesus *said to him, "Truly I
say to you, that you yourself [1a]this very
night, before [b]a cock crows twice, shall
three times deny Me."
31 But *Peter* kept saying insistently,
"*Even* if I have to die with You, I will
not deny You!" And they all were saying
the same thing, too.

Jesus in Gethsemane

32 [a]And they *came to a place named
Gethsemane; and He *said to His disciples, "Sit here until I have prayed."
33 And He *took with Him Peter and
[1]James and John, and began to be very
[a]distressed and troubled.
34 And He *said to them, "[a]My soul
is deeply grieved to the point of death;
remain here and keep watch."
35 And He went a little beyond *them,*
and [1]fell to the ground, and *began* to
pray that if it were possible, [a]the hour
might [2]pass Him by.
36 And He was saying, "[a]Abba! Father! All things are possible for Thee;
remove this cup from Me; [b]yet not what
I will, but what Thou wilt."
37 And He *came and *found them
sleeping, and *said to Peter, "Simon, are
you asleep? Could you not keep watch
for one hour?
38 "[a]Keep watching and praying, that
you may not come into temptation; the
spirit is willing, but the flesh is weak."
39 And again He went away and
prayed, saying the same [1]words.
40 And again He came and found
them sleeping, for their eyes were very
heavy; and they did not know what to
answer Him.
41 And He *came the third time, and
*said to them, "[1]Are you still sleeping
and taking your rest? It is enough; [a]the
hour has come; behold, the Son of Man
is being [2]betrayed into the hands of
sinners.
42 "Arise, let us be going; behold, the
one who betrays Me is at hand!"

Betrayal and Arrest

43 [a]And immediately while He was
still speaking, Judas, one of the twelve,
*came up, [1]accompanied by a multitude
with swords and clubs, from the chief
priests and the scribes and the elders.
44 Now he who was betraying Him
had given them a signal, saying,
"Whomever I shall kiss, He is the one;
seize Him, and lead Him away [1]under
guard."
45 And after coming, he immediately
went to Him, saying, "[a]Rabbi!" and
kissed Him.
46 And they laid hands on Him, and
seized Him.
47 But a certain one of those who
stood by drew his sword, and struck the
slave of the high priest, and [1]cut off his
ear.
48 And Jesus answered and said to
them, "Have you come out with swords
and clubs to arrest Me, as against a
robber?
49 "Every day I was with you [a]in the
temple teaching, and you did not seize
Me; but [1]*this has happened* that the
Scriptures might be fulfilled."
50 And they all left Him and fled.
51 And a certain young man was
following Him, wearing *nothing but* a
linen sheet over *his* naked *body;* and they
*seized him.
52 But he left the linen sheet behind,
and escaped naked.

Jesus before His Accusers

53 [a]And they led Jesus away to the
high priest; and all the chief priests and
the elders and the scribes *gathered
together.
54 And Peter had followed Him at a
distance, [a]right into [b]the courtyard of
the high priest; and he was sitting with
the [1]officers, and [c]warming himself at
the [2]fire.
55 Now the chief priests and the
whole [1a]Council kept trying to obtain
testimony against Jesus to put Him to
death; and they were not finding any.
56 For many were giving false testimony against Him, and *yet* their testimony was not consistent.
57 And some stood up and *began* to
give false testimony against Him, saying,
58 "We heard Him say, '[a]I will destroy
this [1]temple made with hands, and in
three days I will build another made
without hands.' "
59 And not even in this respect was
their testimony consistent.
60 And the high priest stood up *and
came* forward and questioned Jesus,
saying, "Do You make no answer?
[1]What is it that these men are testifying
against You?"
61 [a]But He kept silent, and made no
answer. [b]Again the high priest was questioning Him, and [1]saying to Him, "Are
You [2]the Christ, the Son of the Blessed
One?"
62 And Jesus said, "I am; and you
shall see [a]THE SON OF MAN SITTING AT
THE RIGHT HAND OF POWER, and [b]COM-
ING WITH THE CLOUDS OF HEAVEN."
63 And [a]tearing his clothes, the high
priest *said, "What further need do we
have of witnesses?
64 "You have heard the [a]blasphemy;
how does it seem to you?" And they all
condemned Him to be deserving of
death.
65 And some began to [a]spit at Him,
and [1b]to blindfold Him, and to beat
Him with their fists, and to say to Him,
"[c]Prophesy!" And the officers [2]received
Him with [3]slaps *in the face.*

Peter's Denials

66 [a]And as Peter was below in [b]the
courtyard, one of the servant-girls of the
high priest *came,

30 [1]Lit., *today, on this night* [a]Matt. 26:34 [b]Mark 14:68, 72; John 13:38

32 [a]Mark 14:32-42: *Matt. 26:36-46; Luke 22:40-46*

33 [1]Or, *Jacob* [a]Mark 9:15; 16:5, 6

34 [a]Matt. 26:38; John 12:27

35 [1]Lit., *was falling* [2]Lit., *pass from Him* [a]Matt. 26:45; Mark 14:41

36 [a]Rom. 8:15; Gal. 4:6 [b]Matt. 26:39

38 [a]Matt. 26:41

39 [1]Lit., *word*

41 [1]Or, *Keep on sleeping therefore* [2]Or, *delivered up* [a]Mark 14:35

43 [1]Lit., *and with him* [a]Mark 14:43-50: *Matt. 26:47-56; Luke 22:47-53; John 18:3-11*

44 [1]Lit., *safely*

45 [a]Matt. 23:7

47 [1]Lit., *took off*

49 [1]Or possibly, *let the Scriptures be fulfilled* [a]Mark 12:35; Luke 19:47; 21:37

53 [a]Mark 14:53-65: *Matt. 26:57-68; John 18:12f., 19-24*

54 [1]Or, *servants* [2]Lit., *light* [a]Mark 14:68 [b]Matt. 26:3 [c]Mark 14:67; John 18:18

55 [1]Or, *Sanhedrin* [a]Matt. 5:22

58 [1]Or, *sanctuary* [a]Matt. 26:61; Mark 15:29; John 2:19

60 [1]Or, *what do these testify?*

61 [1]Lit., *says* [2]I.e., the Messiah [a]Matt. 26:63 [b]Mark 14:61-63: *Matt. 26:63ff.; Luke 22:67-71*

62 [a]Ps. 110:1; Mark 13:26 [b]Dan. 7:13

63 [a]Num. 14:6; Matt. 26:65; Acts 14:14

64 [a]Lev. 24:16

65 [1]Or, *cover over His face* [2]Or, *treated* [3]Or possibly, *blows with rods* [a]Matt. 26:67; Mark 10:34 [b]Esth. 7:8 [c]Matt. 26:68; Luke 22:64

66 [a]Mark 14:66-72: *Matt. 26:69-75; Luke 22:56-62; John 18:16-18, 25-27* [b]Mark 14:54

67 and seeing Peter [a]warming himself, she looked at him, and *said, "You, too, were with Jesus the [b]Nazarene."

68 But he denied *it,* saying, "I neither know nor understand what you are talking about." And he [a]went out onto the [1]porch.[2]

69 And the maid saw him, and began once more to say to the bystanders, "This is *one* of them!"

70 But again [a]he was denying it. And after a little while the bystanders were again saying to Peter, "Surely you are *one* of them, [b]for you are a Galilean too."

71 But he began to [1]curse and swear, "I do not know this man you are talking about!"

72 And immediately a cock crowed a second time. And Peter remembered how Jesus had made the remark to him, "Before [a]a cock crows twice, you will deny Me three times." [1]And he began to weep.

Jesus before Pilate

15 [a]AND early in the morning the chief priests with the elders and scribes, and the whole [1b]Council, immediately held a consultation; and binding Jesus, they led Him away, and delivered Him up to Pilate.

2 [a]And Pilate questioned Him, "Are You the King of the Jews?" And answering He *said to him, "*It is as* you say."

3 And the chief priests *began* to accuse Him [1]harshly.

4 And Pilate was questioning Him again, saying, "Do You make no answer? See how many charges they bring against You!"

5 But Jesus [a]made no further answer; so that Pilate was amazed.

6 [a]Now at *the* feast he used to release for them *any* one prisoner whom they requested.

7 And the man named Barabbas had been imprisoned with the insurrectionists who had committed murder in the insurrection.

8 And the multitude went up and began asking him *to do* as he had been accustomed to do for them.

9 And Pilate answered them, saying, "Do you want me to release for you the King of the Jews?"

10 For he was aware that the chief priests had delivered Him up because of envy.

11 But the chief priests stirred up the multitude [a]*to ask* him to release Barabbas for them instead.

12 And answering again, Pilate was saying to them, "Then what shall I do with Him whom you call the King of the Jews?"

13 And they shouted [1]back, "Crucify Him!"

14 But Pilate was saying to them, "Why, what evil has He done?" But they shouted all the more, "Crucify Him!"

15 And wishing to satisfy the multitude, Pilate released Barabbas for them, and after having Jesus [a]scourged, he delivered *Him* to be crucified.

Jesus Is Mocked

16 [a]And the soldiers took Him away into [b]the [1]palace (that is, the Praetorium), and they *called together the whole *Roman* [2c]cohort.

17 And they *dressed Him up in [1]purple, and after weaving a crown of thorns, they put it on Him;

18 and they began to acclaim Him, "Hail, King of the Jews!"

19 And they kept beating His head with a [1]reed, and spitting at Him, and kneeling and bowing before Him.

20 And after they had mocked Him, they took the purple off Him, and put His garments on Him. And they *led Him out to crucify Him.

21 [a]And they *pressed into service a passer-by coming from the country, Simon of Cyrene (the father of Alexander and [b]Rufus), to bear His cross.

The Crucifixion

22 [a]And they *brought Him to the place [b]Golgotha, which is translated, Place of a Skull.

23 And they tried to give Him [a]wine mixed with myrrh; but He did not take it.

24 And they *crucified Him, and *[a]divided up His garments among themselves, casting [1]lots for them, *to decide* [2]what each should take.

25 And it was the [1a]third hour [2]when they crucified Him.

26 And the inscription of the charge against Him [1]read, "[a]THE KING OF THE JEWS."

27 And they *crucified two robbers with Him, one on His right and one on His left.

28 [[1]And the Scripture was fulfilled which says, "And He was numbered with transgressors."]

29 And those passing by were [1]hurling abuse at Him, [a]wagging their heads, and saying, "Ha! You who *are going to* [b]destroy the temple and rebuild it in three days,

30 save Yourself, and come down from the cross!"

31 In the same way the chief priests also, along with the scribes, were mocking *Him* among themselves and saying, "[a]He saved others; [1]He cannot save Himself.

32 "Let *this* Christ, [a]the King of Israel, now come down from the cross, so that we may see and believe!" And [b]those who were crucified with Him were casting the same insult at Him.

33 [a]And when the [1b]sixth hour had come, darkness [2]fell over the whole land until the [3b]ninth hour.

34 And at the [a]ninth hour Jesus cried out with a loud voice, "[b]ELOI, ELOI,

67 [a]Mark 14:54 [b]Mark 1:24
68 [1]Or, *forecourt, gateway* [2]Later mss. add *and a cock crowed* [a]Mark 14:54
70 [a]Mark 14:68 [b]Matt. 26:73; Luke 22:59
71 [1]Or, *put himself under a curse*
72 [1]Or, *Thinking of this, he began weeping* or *Rushing out, he began weeping* [a]Mark 14:30, 68

1 [1]Or, *Sanhedrin* [a]Matt. 27:1 [b]Matt. 5:22
2 [a]Mark 15:2-5: *Matt. 27:11-14; Luke 23:2, 3; John 18:29-38*
3 [1]Or, *of many things*
5 [a]Matt. 27:12
6 [a]Mark 15:6-15: *Matt. 27:15-26; Luke 23:18-25; John 18:39-19:16*
11 [a]Acts 3:14
13 [1]Or, *again*
15 [a]Matt. 27:26
16 [1]Or, *court* [2]Or, *battalion* [a]Mark 15:16-20: *Matt. 27:27-31* [b]Matt. 26:3; 27:27 [c]Acts 10:1
17 [1]A term for shades varying from rose to purple
19 [1]Or, *staff* (made of a reed)
21 [a]Mark 15:21: *Matt. 27:32; Luke 23:26* [b]Rom. 16:13
22 [a]Mark 15:22-32: *Matt. 27:33-44; Luke 23:33-43; John 19:17-24* [b]Luke 23:33; John 19:17
23 [a]Matt. 27:34
24 [1]Lit., *a lot upon* [2]Lit., *who should take what* [a]Ps. 22:18; John 19:24
25 [1]I.e., 9 a.m. [2]Lit., *and* [a]Mark 15:33
26 [1]Lit., *had been inscribed* [a]Matt. 27:37
28 [1]Many mss. do not contain this v.
29 [1]Or, *blaspheming* [a]Ps. 22:7; 109:25; Matt. 27:39 [b]Mark 14:58; John 2:19
31 [1]Or, *can He not save Himself?* [a]Matt. 27:42; Luke 23:35
32 [a]Matt. 27:42; Mark 15:26 [b]Matt. 27:44; Mark 15:27; Luke 23:39-43
33 [1]I.e., noon [2]Or, *occurred* [3]I.e., 3 p.m. [a]Mark 15:33-41: *Matt. 27:45-56; Luke 23:44-49* [b]Matt. 27:45f.; Mark 15:25; Luke 23:44
34 [a]Matt. 27:45f.; Mark 15:25; Luke 23:44 [b]Ps. 22:1; Matt. 27:46

LAMA SABACHTHANI?" which is translated, "MY GOD, MY GOD, WHY HAST THOU FORSAKEN ME?"

35 And when some of the bystanders heard it, they *began* saying, "Behold, He is calling for Elijah."

36 And someone ran and filled a sponge with sour wine, put it on a reed, and gave Him a drink, saying, "[1]Let us see whether Elijah will come to take Him down."

37 [a]And Jesus uttered a loud cry, and breathed His last.

38 [a]And the veil of the temple was torn in two from top to bottom.

39 [a]And when the centurion, who was standing [1]right in front of Him, saw [2]the way He breathed His last, he said, "Truly this man was [3]the Son of God!"

40 [a]And there were also *some* women looking on from a distance, among whom *were* Mary Magdalene, and Mary the mother of [1]James [b]the [2]Less and Joses, and [c]Salome.

41 And when He was in Galilee, they used to follow Him and [1a]minister to Him; and *there were* many other women who had come up with Him to Jerusalem.

Jesus Is Buried

42 [a]And when evening had already come, because it was [b]the preparation day, that is, the day before the Sabbath,

43 Joseph of Arimathea came, a [a]prominent member of the Council, who himself was [b]waiting for the kingdom of God; and he [c]gathered up courage and went in before Pilate, and asked for the body of Jesus.

44 And Pilate wondered if He was dead by this time, and summoning the centurion, he questioned him as to whether He was already dead.

45 And ascertaining this from [a]the centurion, he granted the body to Joseph.

46 And *Joseph* bought a linen cloth, took Him down, wrapped Him in the linen cloth, and laid Him in a tomb which had been hewn out in the rock; and he rolled a stone against the entrance of the tomb.

47 And [a]Mary Magdalene and Mary the *mother* of Joses were looking on *to see* where He was laid.

The Resurrection

16 [a]AND when the Sabbath was over, [b]Mary Magdalene, and Mary the *mother* of [1]James, and Salome, [c]bought spices, that they might come and anoint Him.

2 And very early on the first day of the week, they *came to the tomb when the sun had risen.

3 And they were saying to one another, "Who will roll away [a]the stone for us from the entrance of the tomb?"

4 And looking up, they *saw that the stone had been rolled away, [1]although it was extremely large.

5 And [a]entering the tomb, they saw a young man sitting at the right, wearing a white robe; and they [b]were amazed.

6 And he *said to them, "[a]Do not be amazed; you are looking for Jesus the [b]Nazarene, who has been crucified. [c]He has risen; He is not here; behold, *here is* the place where they laid Him.

7 "But go, tell His disciples and Peter, '[a]He is going before you into Galilee; there you will see Him, just as He said to you.' "

8 And they went out and fled from the tomb, for trembling and astonishment had gripped them; and they said nothing to anyone, for they were afraid.

9 [[1]Now after He had risen early on the first day of the week, He first appeared to [a]Mary Magdalene, from whom He had cast out seven demons.

10 [a]She went and reported to those who had been with Him, while they were mourning and weeping.

11 And when they heard that He was alive, and had been seen by her, [a]they refused to believe it.

12 And after that, [a]He appeared in a different form [b]to two of them, while they were walking along on their way to the country.

13 And they went away and reported it to the others, but they [a]did not believe them either.

The Disciples Commissioned

14 And afterward [a]He appeared [b]to the eleven themselves as they were reclining *at the table;* and He reproached them for their [c]unbelief and hardness of heart, because they had not believed those who had seen Him after He had risen.

15 And He said to them, "[a]Go into all the world and preach the gospel to all creation.

16 "[a]He who has believed and has been baptized shall be saved; but he who has disbelieved shall be condemned.

17 "And these [1]signs will accompany those who have believed: [a]in My name they will cast out demons, they will [b]speak with new tongues;

18 they will [a]pick up serpents, and if they drink any deadly *poison,* it shall not hurt them; they will [b]lay hands on the sick, and they will recover."

19 So then, when the Lord Jesus had [a]spoken to them, He [b]was received up into heaven, and [c]sat down at the right hand of God.

36 [1]Lit., *Permit that we see;* or, *Hold off, let us see*
37 [a]Matt. 27:50; Luke 23:46; John 19:30
38 [a]Ex. 26:31-33; Matt. 27:51; Luke 23:45
39 [1]Or, *opposite Him* [2]Lit., *that He thus* [3]Or possibly, *a son of God* or *son of a god* [a]Matt. 27:54; Mark 15:45; Luke 23:47
40 [1]Or, *Jacob* [2]Lit., *little* (either in stature or age) [a]Mark 15:40, 41: *Matt. 27:55f.;* Luke 23:49; John 19:25 [b]Luke 19:3 [c]Mark 16:1
41 [1]Or, *wait on* [a]Matt. 27:55f.
42 [a]Mark 15:42-47: *Matt. 27:57-61; Luke 23:50-56; John 19:38-42* [b]Matt. 27:62
43 [a]Matt. 27:57; Luke 23:50, 51; Acts 13:50; 17:12 [b]Matt. 27:57; Luke 2:25, 38; 23:51; John 19:38 [c]John 19:38
45 [a]Mark 15:39
47 [a]Matt. 27:56; Mark 15:40; 16:1

1 [1]Or, *Jacob* [a]Mark 16:1-8: *Matt. 28:1-8; Luke 24:1-10;* John 20:1-8 [b]Mark 15:47 [c]Luke 23:56; John 19:39f.
3 [a]Matt. 27:60; Mark 15:46; 16: 4
4 [1]Lit., *for*
5 [a]John 20:11, 12 [b]Mark 9:15
6 [a]Mark 9:15 [b]Mark 1:24 [c]Matt. 28:6; Luke 24:6
7 [a]Matt. 26:32; Mark 14:28
9 [1]Some of the oldest mss. do not contain vv. 9-20 [a]Matt. 27:56; John 20:14
10 [a]John 20:18
11 [a]Matt. 28:17; Mark 16:13, 14; Luke 24:11, 41; John 20:25
12 [a]Mark 16:14; John 21:1, 14 [b]Luke 24:13-35
13 [a]Matt. 28:17; Mark 16:11, 14; Luke 24:11, 41; John 20:25
14 [a]Mark 16:12; John 21:1, 14 [b]Luke 24:36; John 20:19, 26; 1 Cor. 15:5 [c]Matt. 28:17; Mark 16:11, 13; Luke 24:11, 41; John 20:25
15 [a]Matt. 28:19; Acts 1:8
16 [a]John 3:18, 36; Acts 16:31
17 [1]Or, *attesting miracles* [a]Mark 9:38; Luke 10:17; Acts 5:16; 8:7; 16:18; 19:12 [b]Acts 2:4; 10:46; 19:6; 1 Cor. 12:10, 28, 30; 13:1; 14:2
18 [a]Luke 10:19; Acts 28:3-5 [b]Mark 5:23
19 [a]Acts 1:3 [b]Luke 9:51; 24:51; John 6:62; 20:17; Acts 1:2, 9-11; 1 Tim. 3:16 [c]Ps. 110:1; Luke 22:69; Acts 7:55f.; Rom. 8:34; Eph. 1:20; Col. 3:1; Heb. 1:3; 8:1; 10:12; 12:2; 1 Pet. 3:22

20 And they went out and preached everywhere, while the Lord worked with them, and confirmed the word by the [1]signs that followed.[2]]

[[3]*And they promptly reported all these instructions to Peter and his companions. And after that, Jesus Himself sent out through them from east to west the sacred and imperishable proclamation of eternal salvation.*]

20 [1]Or, *attesting miracles* [2]Many mss. add *Amen* [3]A few later mss. and versions contain this paragraph, usually after v. 8; a few have it at the end of ch.

THE GOSPEL ACCORDING TO LUKE

Introduction

1 INASMUCH as many have undertaken to compile an account of the things [1a]accomplished among us,

2 just as those who [a]from the beginning [1]were [b]eyewitnesses and [2c]servants of [d]the [3]word have handed them down to us,

3 it seemed fitting for me as well, [a]having [1]investigated everything carefully from the beginning, to write *it* out for you [b]in consecutive order, [c]most excellent [d]Theophilus;

4 so that you might know the exact truth about the things you have been [1a]taught.

Birth of John the Baptist Foretold

5 [a]In the days of Herod, king of Judea, there [1]was a certain priest named [2]Zacharias, of the [b]division of [3]Abijah; and he had a wife [4]from the daughters of Aaron, and her name was Elizabeth.

6 And they were both [a]righteous in the sight of God, walking [b]blamelessly in all the commandments and requirements of the Lord.

7 And they had no child, because Elizabeth was barren, and they were both advanced in [1]years.

8 Now it came about, while [a]he was performing his priestly service before God in the *appointed* order of his division,

9 according to the custom of the priestly office, he was chosen by lot [a]to enter the temple of the Lord and burn incense.

10 And the whole multitude of the people were in prayer [a]outside at the hour of the incense offering.

11 And [a]an angel of the Lord appeared to him, standing to the right of the altar of incense.

12 And Zacharias was troubled when he saw *him,* and [a]fear [1]gripped him.

13 But the angel said to him, "[a]Do not be afraid, Zacharias, for your petition has been heard, and your wife Elizabeth will bear you a son, and [b]you will [1]give him the name John.

14 "And you will have joy and gladness, and many will rejoice at his birth.

15 "For he will be great in the sight of the Lord, and he will [a]drink no wine or liquor; and he will be filled with the Holy Spirit, [1]while yet in his mother's womb.

16 "And he will [a]turn back many of the sons of Israel to the Lord their God.

17 "And it is he who will [a]go *as a forerunner* before Him in the spirit and power of [b]Elijah, [c]TO TURN THE HEARTS OF THE FATHERS BACK TO THE CHILDREN, and the disobedient to the attitude of the righteous; so as to [a]make ready a people prepared for the Lord."

18 And Zacharias said to the angel, "How shall I know this *for certain*? For [a]I am an old man, and my wife is advanced in [1]years."

19 And the angel answered and said to him, "I am [a]Gabriel, who [1b]stands in the presence of God; and I have been sent to speak to you, and to bring you this good news.

20 "And behold, you shall be silent and unable to speak until the day when these things take place, because you did not believe my words, which shall be fulfilled in their proper time."

21 And the people were waiting for Zacharias, and were wondering at his delay in the temple.

22 But when he came out, he was unable to speak to them; and they realized that he had seen a vision in the temple; and he [a]kept [1]making signs to them, and remained mute.

23 And it came about, when the days of his priestly service were ended, that he went back home.

24 And after these days Elizabeth his wife became pregnant; and she [1]kept herself in seclusion for five months, saying,

25 "This is the way the Lord has dealt with me in the days when He looked *with favor* upon *me,* to [a]take away my disgrace among men."

Jesus' Birth Foretold

26 Now in the sixth month the angel [a]Gabriel was sent from God to a city in Galilee, called [b]Nazareth,

27 to [a]a virgin engaged to a man whose name was Joseph, [b]of the [1]descendants of David; and the virgin's name was Mary.

28 And coming in, he said to her, "Hail, [1]favored one! The Lord [2]*is* with you."[3]

1 [1]Or, *on which there is full conviction* [a]Rom. 4:21; 14:5; Col. 2:2; 4:12; 1 Thess. 1:5; 2 Tim. 4:17; Heb. 6:11; 10:22
2 [1]Lit., *became* [2]Or, *ministers* [3]I.e., gospel [a]John 15:27; Acts 1:21f. [b]2 Pet. 1:16; 1 John 1:1 [c]Acts 26:16; 1 Cor. 4:1; Heb. 2:3 [d]Mark 4:14; 16:20; Acts 8:4; 14:25; 16:6; 17:11
3 [1]Or, *followed* [a]1 Tim. 4:6 [b]Acts 11:4; 18:23 [c]Acts 23:26; 24:3; 26:25 [d]Acts 1:1
4 [1]Or, *orally instructed in* [a]Acts 18:25; Rom. 2:18; 1 Cor. 14:19; Gal. 6:6
5 [1]Lit., *came into being* [2]I.e., Zechariah [3]Gr., *Abia* [4]I.e., of priestly descent [a]Matt. 2:1 [b]1 Chr. 24:10
6 [a]Gen. 7:1; Acts 2:25; 8:21 [b]Phil. 2:15; 3:6; 1 Thess. 3:13
7 [1]Lit., *days*
8 [a]1 Chr. 24:19; 2 Chr. 8:14; 31:2
9 [a]Ex. 30:7f.
10 [a]Lev. 16:17
11 [a]Luke 2:9; Acts 5:19
12 [1]Or, *fell upon* [a]Luke 2:9
13 [1]Lit., *call his name* [a]Matt. 14:27; Luke 1:30 [b]Luke 1:60, 63
15 [1]Lit., *even from* [a]Num. 6:3; Judg. 13:4; Matt. 11:18; Luke 7:33
16 [a]Matt. 3:2, 6; Luke 3:3
17 [a]Luke 1:76 [b]Matt. 11:14 [c]Mal. 4:6
18 [1]Lit., *days* [a]Gen. 17:17
19 [1]Lit., *stand beside* [a]Dan. 8:16; 9:21; Luke 1:26 [b]Matt. 18:10
22 [1]Or, *beckoning to* or *nodding to* [a]Luke 1:62
24 [1]Lit., *was hidden*
25 [a]Gen. 30:23; Is. 4:1; 25:8
26 [a]Luke 1:19 [b]Matt. 2:23
27 [1]Lit., *house* [a]Matt. 1:18 [b]Matt. 1:16, 20; Luke 2:4

28 [1]Or, *O woman richly blessed* [2]Or, be [3]Later mss. add *you are blessed among women*

29 But she [a]was greatly troubled at
this statement, and kept pondering what
kind of salutation this might be.
30 And the angel said to her, "[a]Do not
be afraid, Mary; for you have found
favor with God.
31 "And behold, you will conceive in
your womb, and bear a son, and you
[a]shall name Him Jesus.
32 "He will be great, and will be called
the Son of [a]the Most High; and the Lord
God will give Him [b]the throne of His
father David;
33 [a]and He will reign over the house
of Jacob forever; [b]and His kingdom will
have no end."
34 And Mary said to the angel, "How
[1]can this be, since I [2]am a virgin?"
35 And the angel answered and said
to her, "[a]The Holy Spirit will come upon
you, and the power of [b]the Most High
will overshadow you; and for that reason
[c]the [1]holy offspring shall be called [d]the
Son of God.
36 "And behold, even your relative
Elizabeth has also conceived a son in her
old age; and [1]she who was called barren
is now in her sixth month.
37 "For [1a]nothing will be impossible
with God."
38 And [1]Mary said, "Behold, the
[2]bondslave of the Lord; be it done to me
according to your word." And the angel
departed from her.

Mary Visits Elizabeth

39 Now [1]at this time Mary arose and
went with haste to [a]the hill country, to a
city of Judah,
40 and entered the house of Zacharias
and greeted Elizabeth.
41 And it came about that when Elizabeth heard Mary's greeting, the baby
leaped in her womb; and Elizabeth was
[a]filled with the Holy Spirit.
42 And she cried out with a loud
voice, and said, "Blessed among women
are you, and blessed *is* the fruit of your
womb!
43 "And [1]how has it *happened* to me,
that the mother of [a]my Lord should
come to me?
44 "For behold, when the sound of
your greeting reached my ears, the baby
leaped in my womb for joy.
45 "And [a]blessed *is* she who believed
[1]that there would be a fulfillment of
what had been spoken to her [2]by the
Lord."

The Magnificat

46 And Mary said:
"[a]My soul [1b]exalts the Lord,
47 "And [a]my spirit has rejoiced in
[b]God my Savior.
48 "For [a]He has had regard for the
humble state of His [1]bondslave;
For behold, from this time on all
generations will count me
[b]blessed.
49 "For the Mighty One has done
great things for me;
And holy is His name.
50 "[a]AND HIS MERCY IS [1]UPON GEN-
ERATION AFTER GENERATION
TOWARD THOSE WHO FEAR HIM.
51 "[a]He has done [1]mighty deeds with
His arm;
He has scattered *those who were*
proud in the [2]thoughts of their
heart.
52 "He has brought down rulers from
their thrones,
And has [a]exalted those who were
humble.
53 "[a]HE HAS FILLED THE HUNGRY
WITH GOOD THINGS;
And sent away the rich empty-
handed.
54 "He has given help to Israel His
servant,
[1]In remembrance of His mercy,
55 [a]As He spoke to our fathers,
[b]To Abraham and his [1]offspring
forever."
56 And Mary stayed with her about
three months, and *then* returned to her
home.

John Is Born

57 Now the time [1]had come for Elizabeth to give birth, and she brought forth
a son.
58 And her neighbors and her relatives heard that the Lord had [1a]dis-
played His great mercy toward her; and
they were rejoicing with her.
59 And it came about that on [a]the
eighth day they came to circumcise the
child, and they were going to call him
Zacharias, [1]after his father.
60 And his mother answered and said,
"No indeed; but [a]he shall be called
John."
61 And they said to her, "There is no
one among your relatives who is called
by that name."
62 And they [a]made signs to his father,
as to what he wanted him called.
63 And he asked for a tablet, and
wrote as follows, "[a]His name is John."
And they were all astonished.
64 [a]And at once his mouth was
opened and his tongue *loosed,* and he
began to speak in praise of God.
65 And fear came on all those living
around them; and all these matters were
being talked about in all [a]the hill country of Judea.
66 And all who heard them kept them
in mind, saying, "What then will this
child *turn out to* be?" For [a]the hand of
the Lord was certainly with him.

Zacharias' Prophecy

67 And his father Zacharias [a]was filled
with the Holy Spirit, and [b]prophesied,
saying:

29 [a]Luke 1:12
30 [a]Matt. 14:27; Luke 1:13
31 [a]Is. 7:14; Matt. 1:21, 25; Luke 2:21
32 [a]Mark 5:7; Luke 1:35, 76; 6:35; Acts 7:48 [b]2 Sam. 7:12, 13, 16; Is. 9:7
33 [a]Matt. 1:1 [b]2 Sam. 7:13, 16; Ps. 89:36, 37; Dan. 2:44; 7:14, 18, 27; Matt. 28:18
34 [1]Lit., *shall* [2]Lit., *know no man*
35 [1]Lit., *the holy thing begotten* [a]Matt. 1:18 [b]Luke 1:32 [c]Mark 1:24 [d]Matt. 4:3; John 1:34, 49; 20:31
36 [1]Lit., *this is the sixth month to her who*
37 [1]Lit., *not any word* [a]Gen. 18:14; Jer. 32:17; Matt. 19:26
38 [1]Gr., *Mariam;* i.e., Miriam; so throughout Luke [2]I.e., female slave
39 [1]Lit., *in these days* [a]Josh. 20:7; 21:11; Luke 1:65
41 [a]Luke 1:67; Acts 2:4; 4:8; 9:17
43 [1]Lit., *whence this to me* [a]Luke 2:11
45 [1]Or possibly, *because there will be* [2]Lit., *from* [a]Luke 1:20, 48
46 [1]Lit., *makes great* [a]Luke 1:46-53: *1 Sam. 2:1-10* [b]Ps. 34:2f.
47 [a]Ps. 35:9; Hab. 3:18 [b]1 Tim. 1:1; 2:3; Titus 1:3; 2:10; 3:4; Jude 25
48 [1]I.e., female slave [a]Ps. 138:6 [b]Luke 1:45
50 [1]Lit., *unto generations and generations* [a]Ps. 103:17
51 [1]Lit., *might* [2]Lit., *thought, attitude* [a]Ps. 98:1; 118:15
52 [a]Job 5:11
53 [a]Ps. 107:9
54 [1]Lit., *So as to remember*
55 [1]Lit., *seed* [a]Gen. 17:19; Ps. 132:11; Gal. 3:16 [b]Gen. 17:7
57 [1]Lit., *was fulfilled*
58 [1]Lit., *magnified* [a]Gen. 19:19
59 [1]Lit., *after the name of* [a]Gen. 17:12; Lev. 12:3; Luke 2:21; Phil. 3:5
60 [a]Luke 1:13, 63
62 [a]Luke 1:22
63 [a]Luke 1:13, 60
64 [a]Luke 1:20
65 [a]Luke 1:39
66 [a]Acts 11:21
67 [a]Luke 1:41; Acts 2:4, 8; 9:17 [b]Joel 2:28

68 “[a]Blessed *be* the Lord God of
Israel,
For He has visited us and accomplished
[b]redemption for His
people,
69 And has raised up a [a]horn of
salvation for us
In the house of David [b]His servant—
70 [a]As He spoke by the mouth of His
holy prophets [b]from of old—
71 [1][a]Salvation [b]FROM OUR ENEMIES,
And FROM THE HAND OF ALL WHO
HATE US;
72 [a]To show mercy toward our fathers,
[b]And to remember His holy covenant,
73 [a]The oath which He swore to
Abraham our father,
74 To grant us that we, being delivered
from the hand of our enemies,
Might serve Him without fear,
75 [a]In holiness and righteousness
before Him all our days.
76 “And you, child, will be called the
[a]prophet of [b]the Most High;
For you will go on [c]BEFORE THE
LORD TO [d]PREPARE HIS WAYS;
77 To give to His people *the* knowledge
of salvation
[1]By [a]the forgiveness of their sins,
78 Because of the tender mercy of
our God,
With which [a]the Sunrise from on
high shall visit us,
79 [a]TO SHINE UPON THOSE WHO SIT
IN DARKNESS AND THE SHADOW
OF DEATH,
To guide our feet into the [b]way of
peace.”

80 [a]And the child continued to grow,
and to become strong in spirit, and he
lived in the deserts until the day of his
public appearance to Israel.

Jesus’ Birth in Bethlehem

2 NOW it came about in those days
that a decree went out from [a]Caesar
Augustus, that a census be taken of [b]all
[1]the inhabited earth.
2 [1]This was the first census taken
while [2]Quirinius was governor of [a]Syria.
3 And all were proceeding to register
for the census, everyone to his own city.
4 And Joseph also went up from
Galilee, from the city of Nazareth, to
Judea, to the city of David, which is
called Bethlehem, because [a]he was of the
house and family of David,
5 in order to register, along with
Mary, who was engaged to him, and was
with child.
6 And it came about that while they
were there, the days were completed for
her to give birth.
7 And she [a]gave birth to her firstborn
son; and she wrapped Him in
cloths, and laid Him in a [1]manger,
because there was no room for them in
the inn.
8 And in the same region there were
some shepherds staying out in the fields,
and keeping watch over their flock by
night.
9 And [a]an angel of the Lord suddenly
[b]stood before them, and the glory
of the Lord shone around them; and
they were terribly frightened.
10 And the angel said to them, “[a]Do
not be afraid; for behold, I bring you
good news of a great joy which shall be
for all the people;
11 for today in the city of David there
has been born for you a [a]Savior, who is
[1][b]Christ [c]the Lord.
12 “And [a]this *will be* a sign for you:
you will find a baby wrapped in cloths,
and lying in a [1]manger.”
13 And suddenly there appeared with
the angel a multitude of the heavenly
host praising God, and saying,
14 “[a]Glory to God in the highest,
And on earth peace among men
[1][b]with whom He is pleased.”
15 And it came about when the angels
had gone away from them into heaven,
that the shepherds *began* saying to one
another, “Let us go straight to Bethlehem
then, and see this thing that has
happened which the Lord has made
known to us.”
16 And they came in haste and found
their way to Mary and Joseph, and the
baby as He lay in the [1]manger.
17 And when they had seen this, they
made known the statement which had
been told them about this Child.
18 And all who heard it wondered at
the things which were told them by the
shepherds.
19 But Mary [a]treasured up all these
things, pondering them in her heart.
20 And the shepherds went back,
[a]glorifying and praising God for all that
they had heard and seen, just as had
been told them.

Jesus Presented at the Temple

21 And when [a]eight days were completed
[1]before His circumcision, [b]His
name was *then* called Jesus, the name
given by the angel before He was conceived
in the womb.
22 [a]And when the days for their purification
according to the law of Moses
were completed, they brought Him up to
Jerusalem to present Him to the Lord
23 (as it is written in the Law of the
Lord, “[a]EVERY *first-born* MALE THAT
OPENS THE WOMB SHALL BE CALLED
HOLY TO THE LORD”),
24 and to offer a sacrifice according to
what was said in the Law of the Lord,
“[a]A PAIR OF TURTLEDOVES, OR TWO
YOUNG PIGEONS.”
25 And behold, there was a man in
Jerusalem whose name was Simeon; and

68 [a]1 Kin. 1:48; Ps. 41:13; 72:18; 106:48 [b]Luke 1:71; 2:38; Heb. 9:12
69 [a]1 Sam. 2:1, 10; Ps. 18:2; 89:17; 132:17; Ezek. 29:21 [b]Matt. 1:1
70 [a]Rom. 1:2 [b]Acts 3:21
71 [1]Or, *Deliverance* [a]Luke 1:68 [b]Ps. 106:10
72 [a]Mic. 7:20 [b]Ps. 105:8f., 42; 106:45
73 [a]Gen. 22:16ff.; Heb. 6:13
75 [a]Eph. 4:24
76 [a]Matt. 11:9 [b]Luke 1:32 [c]Mal. 3:1; Matt. 11:10; Mark 1:2; Luke 7:27 [d]Luke 1:17
77 [1]Or, *Consisting in* [a]Jer. 31:34; Mark 1:4
78 [a]Mal. 4:2; Eph. 5:14; 2 Pet. 1:19
79 [a]Is. 9:2 [b]Is. 59:8; Matt. 4:16
80 [a]Luke 2:40
1 [1]I.e., the Roman empire [a]Matt. 22:17; Luke 3:1 [b]Matt. 24:14
2 [1]Or, *This took place as a first census* [2]Gr., *Kyrenios* [a]Matt. 4:24
4 [a]Luke 1:27
7 [1]Or, *feeding trough* [a]Matt. 1:25
9 [a]Luke 1:11; Acts 5:19 [b]Luke 24:4; Acts 12:7
10 [a]Matt. 14:27
11 [1]I.e., Messiah [a]Matt. 1:21; John 4:42; Acts 5:31 [b]Matt. 1:16; 16:16, 20; John 11:27 [c]Luke 1:43; Acts 2:36; 10:36
12 [1]Or, *feeding trough* [a]1 Sam. 2:34; 2 Kin. 19:29; 20:8f.; Is. 7:11, 14
14 [1]Lit., *of good pleasure;* or possibly, *of good will* [a]Matt. 21:9; Luke 19:38 [b]Luke 3:22; Eph. 1:9; Phil. 2:13
16 [1]Or, *feeding trough*
19 [a]Luke 2:51
20 [a]Matt. 9:8
21 [1]Lit., *so as to circumcise Him* [a]Gen. 17:12; Lev. 12:3; Luke 1:59 [b]Matt. 1:21, 25; Luke 1:31
22 [a]Lev. 12:6-8
23 [a]Ex. 13:2, 12; Num. 3:13; 8:17
24 [a]Lev. 5:11; 12:8

this man was [a]righteous and devout,
[b]looking for the consolation of Israel;
and the Holy Spirit was upon him.
26 And [a]it had been revealed to him
by the Holy Spirit that he would not [b]see
death before he had seen the Lord's
[1]Christ.
27 And he came in the Spirit into the
temple; and when the parents brought in
the child Jesus, [1a]to carry out for Him
the custom of the Law,
28 then he took Him into his arms,
and blessed God, and said,

29 "Now Lord, Thou dost let Thy
bond-servant depart
In peace, [a]according to Thy word;
30 For my eyes have [a]seen Thy salvation,
31 Which Thou hast prepared in the
presence of all peoples,
32 [a]A LIGHT [1]OF REVELATION TO THE
GENTILES,
And the glory of Thy people Israel."

33 And His father and [a]mother were
amazed at the things which were being
said about Him.
34 And Simeon blessed them, and said
to Mary [a]His mother, "Behold, this
Child is appointed for [b]the fall and [1]rise
of many in Israel, and for a sign to be
opposed—
35 and a sword will pierce even your
own soul—to the end that thoughts from
many hearts may be revealed."
36 And there was a [a]prophetess,
[1]Anna the daughter of Phanuel, of [b]the
tribe of Asher. She was advanced in
[2]years, [c]having lived with a husband
seven years after her [3]marriage,
37 and then as a widow to the age of
eighty-four. And she never left the temple,
serving night and day with [a]fastings
and prayers.
38 And at that very [1]moment she
came up and *began* giving thanks to
God, and continued to speak of Him to
all those who were [a]looking for the
redemption of Jerusalem.

Return to Nazareth

39 And when they had performed
everything according to the Law of the
Lord, they returned to Galilee, to [a]their
own city of Nazareth.
40 [a]And the Child continued to grow
and become strong, [1]increasing in wisdom;
and the grace of God was upon
Him.

Visit to Jerusalem

41 And His parents used to go to
Jerusalem every year at [a]the Feast of the
Passover.
42 And when He became twelve, they
went up *there* according to the custom of
the Feast;
43 and as they were returning, after
spending the [a]full number of days, the
boy Jesus stayed behind in Jerusalem.
And His parents were unaware of it,

25 [a]Luke 1:6 [b]Mark 15:43; Luke 2:38; 23:51
26 [1]I.e., Messiah [a]Matt. 2:12 [b]Ps. 89:48; John 8:51; Heb. 11:5
27 [1]Lit., *to do for Him according to* [a]Luke 2:22
29 [a]Luke 2:26
30 [a]Ps. 119:166, 174; Is. 52:10; Luke 3:6
32 [1]Or, *for* [a]Is. 9:2; 42:6; 49:6, 9; 51:4; 60:1-3; Matt. 4:16; Acts 13:47; 26:23
33 [a]Matt. 12:46
34 [1]Or, *resurrection* [a]Matt. 12:46 [b]Matt. 21:44; 1 Cor. 1:23; 2 Cor. 2:16; 1 Pet. 2:8
36 [1]Or, *Hannah* [2]Lit., *days* [3]Lit., *virginity* [a]Luke 2:38; Acts 21:9 [b]Josh. 19:24 [c]1 Tim. 5:9
37 [a]Luke 5:33; Acts 13:3; 14:23; 1 Tim. 5:5
38 [1]Lit., *hour* [a]Luke 1:68; 2:25
39 [a]Matt. 2:23; Luke 1:26; 2:51; 4:16
40 [1]Lit., *becoming full of* [a]Luke 1:80; 2:52
41 [a]Ex. 12:11; 23:15; Deut. 16:1-6
43 [a]Ex. 12:15
47 [a]Matt. 7:28; 13:54; 22:33; Mark 1:22; 6:2; 11:18; Luke 4:32; John 7:15
48 [1]Lit., *Child* [2]Lit., *are looking* [a]Matt. 12:46 [b]Luke 2:49; 3:23; 4:22
49 [1]Or, *affairs;* lit., *in the things of My Father* [a]John 4:34; 5:36
50 [1]Lit., *had spoken* [a]Mark 9:32; Luke 9:45; 18:34
51 [1]Lit., *was treasuring* [2]Lit., *words* [a]Luke 2:39 [b]Matt. 12:46 [c]Luke 2:19
52 [1]Or, *age* [a]Luke 2:40

1 [a]Matt. 27:2 [b]Matt. 14:1
2 [a]John 18:13, 24; Acts 4:6 [b]Matt. 26:3 [c]Luke 3:3-10: *Matt. 3:1-10; Mark 1:3-5*
3 [a]Matt. 3:5
4 [a]Is. 40:3
5 [1]Or, *leveled* [a]Is. 40:4
6 [1]Or, *mankind* [a]Is. 40:5 [b]Luke 2:30
7 [a]Matt. 12:34; 23:33

44 but supposed Him to be in the
caravan, and went a day's journey; and
they *began* looking for Him among their
relatives and acquaintances.
45 And when they did not find Him,
they returned to Jerusalem, looking for
Him.
46 And it came about that after three
days they found Him in the temple,
sitting in the midst of the teachers, both
listening to them, and asking them questions.
47 And all who heard Him [a]were
amazed at His understanding and His
answers.
48 And when they saw Him, they were
astonished; and [a]His mother said to
Him, "[1]Son, why have You treated us
this way? Behold, [b]Your father and I
[2]have been anxiously looking for You."
49 And He said to them, "Why is it
that you were looking for Me? Did you
not know that [a]I had to be in My
Father's [1]*house?*"
50 And [a]they did not understand the
statement which He [1]had made to them.
51 And He went down with them, and
came to [a]Nazareth; and He continued in
subjection to them; and [b]His mother
[1c]treasured all *these* [2]things in her heart.
52 And Jesus kept increasing in wisdom
and [1]stature, and in [a]favor with
God and men.

John the Baptist Preaches

3 NOW in the fifteenth year of the
reign of Tiberius Caesar, when
[a]Pontius Pilate was governor of Judea,
and [b]Herod was tetrarch of Galilee, and
his brother Philip was tetrarch of the
region of Ituraea and Trachonitis, and
Lysanias was tetrarch of Abilene,
2 in the high priesthood of [a]Annas
and [b]Caiaphas, [c]the word of God came
to John, the son of Zacharias, in the
wilderness.
3 And he came into all [a]the district
around the Jordan, preaching a baptism
of repentance for the forgiveness of sins;
4 as it is written in the book of the
words of Isaiah the prophet,

"[a]THE VOICE OF ONE CRYING IN
THE WILDERNESS,
'MAKE READY THE WAY OF THE
LORD,
MAKE HIS PATHS STRAIGHT.
5 '[a]EVERY RAVINE SHALL BE FILLED
UP,
AND EVERY MOUNTAIN AND HILL
SHALL BE [1]BROUGHT LOW;
AND THE CROOKED SHALL BECOME
STRAIGHT,
AND THE ROUGH ROADS SMOOTH;
6 [a]AND ALL [1]FLESH SHALL [b]SEE THE
SALVATION OF GOD.' "

7 He therefore *began* saying to the
multitudes who were going out to be
baptized by him, "[a]You brood of vipers,
who warned you to flee from the wrath
to come?

8 "Therefore bring forth fruits in keeping with repentance, and [a]do not begin to say [1]to yourselves, '[b]We have Abraham for our father,' for I say to you that God is able from these stones to raise up children to Abraham.

9 "And also the axe is already laid at the root of the trees; [a]every tree therefore that does not bear good fruit is cut down and thrown into the fire."

10 And the multitudes were questioning him, saying, "[a]Then what shall we do?"

11 And he would answer and say to them, "Let the man who has two tunics [a]share with him who has none; and let him who has food do likewise."

12 And *some* [1a]tax-gatherers also came to be baptized, and they said to him, "Teacher, what shall we do?"

13 And he said to them, "[1]Collect no more than what you have been ordered to."

14 And *some* [1]soldiers were questioning him, saying, "And *what about* us, what shall we do?" And he said to them, "Do not take money from anyone by force, or [a]accuse *anyone* falsely, and [b]be content with your wages."

15 Now while the people were in a state of expectation and all were [1]wondering in their hearts about John, [a]as to whether he might be [2]the Christ,

16 [a]John answered and said to them all, "As for me, I baptize you with water; but One is coming who is mightier than I, and I am not fit to untie the thong of His sandals; He will baptize you [1]with the Holy Spirit and fire.

17 "And His [a]winnowing fork is in His hand to thoroughly clear His threshing floor, and to gather the wheat into His barn; but He will burn up the chaff with [b]unquenchable fire."

18 So with many other exhortations also he preached the gospel to the people.

19 But when [a]Herod the tetrarch was reproved by him on account of [a]Herodias, his brother's wife, and on account of all the wicked things which [b]Herod had done,

20 he added this also to them all, that [a]he locked John up in prison.

Jesus Is Baptized

21 [a]Now it came about when all the people were baptized, that Jesus also was baptized, and while He was [b]praying, heaven was opened,

22 and the Holy Spirit descended upon Him in bodily form like a dove, and a voice came out of heaven, "[a]Thou art My beloved Son, in Thee I am well-pleased."

Genealogy of Jesus

23 And [a]when He began His ministry, Jesus Himself was about thirty years of age, [1]being supposedly *the* son of [b]Joseph, the *son* of [2]Eli,

24 the *son* of Matthat, the *son* of Levi, the *son* of Melchi, the *son* of Jannai, the *son* of Joseph,

25 the *son* of Mattathias, the *son* of Amos, the *son* of Nahum, the *son* of [1]Hesli, the *son* of Naggai,

26 the *son* of Maath, the *son* of Mattathias, the *son* of Semein, the *son* of Josech, the *son* of Joda,

27 the *son* of Joanan, the *son* of Rhesa, [a]the *son* of Zerubbabel, the *son* of [1]Shealtiel, the *son* of Neri,

28 the *son* of Melchi, the *son* of Addi, the *son* of Cosam, the *son* of Elmadam, the *son* of Er,

29 the *son* of [1]Joshua, the *son* of Eliezer, the *son* of Jorim, the *son* of Matthat, the *son* of Levi,

30 the *son* of Simeon, the *son* of [1]Judah, the *son* of Joseph, the *son* of Jonam, the *son* of Eliakim,

31 the *son* of Melea, the *son* of Menna, the *son* of Mattatha, the *son* of Nathan, the *son* of David,

32 [a]the *son* of Jesse, the *son* of Obed, the *son* of Boaz, the *son* of [1]Salmon, the *son* of [2]Nahshon,

33 the *son* of Amminadab, the *son* of Admin, the *son* of [1]Ram, the *son* of Hezron, the *son* of Perez, the *son* of Judah,

34 the *son* of Jacob, the *son* of Isaac, [a]the *son* of Abraham, the *son* of Terah, the *son* of Nahor,

35 the *son* of Serug, the *son* of [1]Reu, the *son* of Peleg, the *son* of [2]Heber, the *son* of Shelah,

36 the *son* of Cainan, the *son* of Arphaxad, the *son* of Shem, [a]the *son* of Noah, the *son* of Lamech,

37 the *son* of Methuselah, the *son* of Enoch, the *son* of Jared, the *son* of Mahalaleel, the *son* of Cainan,

38 the *son* of Enosh, the *son* of Seth, the *son* of Adam, the *son* of God.

The Temptation of Jesus

4 [a]AND Jesus, full of the Holy Spirit, [b]returned from the Jordan and was led about [1]by the Spirit in the wilderness

2 for [a]forty days, being tempted by the devil. And He ate nothing during those days; and when they had ended, He became hungry.

3 And the devil said to Him, "If You are the Son of God, tell this stone to become bread."

4 And Jesus answered him, "It is written, '[a]MAN SHALL NOT LIVE ON BREAD ALONE.' "

5 [a]And he led Him up and showed Him all the kingdoms of [1b]the world in a moment of time.

6 And the devil said to Him, "I will give You all this domain and [1]its glory; [a]for it has been handed over to me, and I give it to whomever I wish.

7 "Therefore if You [1]worship before me, it shall all be Yours."

---

8 [1]Or, *in* [a]Luke 5:21; 13:25, 26; 14:9 [b]John 8:33

9 [a]Matt. 7:19; Luke 13:6-9

10 [a]Luke 3:12, 14; Acts 2:37, 38

11 [a]Is. 58:7; 1 Tim. 6:17, 18; James 2:14-20

12 [1]I.e., Collectors of Roman taxes for profit [a]Luke 7:29

13 [1]Or, *Exact*

14 [1]I.e., men in active military service [a]Ex. 20:16; 23:1 [b]Phil. 4:11

15 [1]Or, *reasoning* or *debating* [2]I.e., the Messiah [a]John 1:19f.

16 [1]The Gr. here can be translated *in, with* or *by* [a]Luke 3:16, 17: *Matt. 3:11, 12; Mark 1:7, 8*

17 [a]Is. 30:24 [b]Mark 9:43, 48

19 [a]Matt. 14:3; Mark 6:17 [b]Matt. 14:1; Luke 3:1

20 [a]John 3:24

21 [a]Luke 3:21, 22: *Matt. 3:13-17; Mark 1:9-11* [b]Matt. 14:23; Luke 5:16; 9:18, 28f.

22 [a]Ps. 2:7; Is. 42:1; Matt. 3:17; 17:5; Mark 1:11; Luke 9:35; 2 Pet. 1:17

23 [1]Lit., *as it was being thought* [2]Also spelled *Heli* [a]Matt. 4:17; Acts 1:1 [b]Matt. 1:16; Luke 3:23-27

25 [1]Also spelled *Esli*

27 [1]Gr., *Salathiel* [a]Matt. 1:12

29 [1]Gr., *Jesus*

30 [1]Gr., *Judas*

32 [1]Gr., *Sala* [2]Gr., *Naasson* [a]Luke 3:32-34: *Matt. 1:1-6*

33 [1]Gr., *Arni*

34 [a]Luke 3:34-36: *Gen. 11:26-30; 1 Chr. 1:24-27*

35 [1]Gr., *Ragau* [2]Gr., *Eber*

36 [a]Luke 3:36-38: *Gen. 5:3-32; 1 Chr. 1:1-4*

1 [1]Or, *under the influence of;* lit., *in* [a]Luke 4:1-13: *Matt. 4:1-11; Mark 1:12, 13* [b]Luke 3:3

2 [a]Ex. 34:28; 1 Kin. 19:8

4 [a]Deut. 8:3

5 [1]Lit., *the inhabited earth* [a]Matt. 4:8-10 [b]Matt. 24:14

6 [1]Lit., *their* (referring to the kingdoms) [a]1 John 5:19

7 [1]Or, *bow down*

8 And Jesus answered and said to him, "It is written, '[a]YOU SHALL WORSHIP THE LORD YOUR GOD AND SERVE HIM ONLY.' "

9 [a]And he led Him to Jerusalem and had Him stand on the pinnacle of the temple, and said to Him, "If You are the Son of God, throw Yourself down from here;

10 for it is written,
'[a]HE WILL GIVE HIS ANGELS
CHARGE CONCERNING YOU TO
GUARD YOU,'
11 and,
'[a]ON *their* HANDS THEY WILL BEAR
YOU UP,
LEST YOU STRIKE YOUR FOOT
AGAINST A STONE.' "

12 And Jesus answered and said to him, "It is said, '[a]YOU SHALL NOT [1]PUT THE LORD YOUR GOD TO THE TEST.' "

13 And when the devil had finished every temptation, he departed from Him until an opportune time.

Jesus' Public Ministry

14 And [a]Jesus returned to Galilee in the power of the Spirit; and [b]news about Him spread through all the surrounding district.

15 And He *began* [a]teaching in their synagogues and was praised by all.

16 And He came to [a]Nazareth, where He had been brought up; and as was His custom, [b]He entered the synagogue on the Sabbath, and [c]stood up to read.

17 And the [1]book of the prophet Isaiah was handed to Him. And He opened the [1]book, and found the place where it was written,

18 "[a]THE SPIRIT OF THE LORD IS
UPON ME,
BECAUSE HE ANOINTED ME TO
PREACH THE GOSPEL TO THE
POOR.
HE HAS SENT ME TO PROCLAIM
RELEASE TO THE CAPTIVES,
AND RECOVERY OF SIGHT TO THE
BLIND,
TO SET FREE THOSE WHO ARE
DOWNTRODDEN,
19 [a]TO PROCLAIM THE FAVORABLE
YEAR OF THE LORD."

20 And He [a]closed the [1]book, and gave it back to the attendant, and [b]sat down; and the eyes of all in the synagogue were fixed upon Him.

21 And He began to say to them, "Today this Scripture has been fulfilled in your [1]hearing."

22 And all were [1]speaking well of Him, and wondering at the gracious words which [2]were falling from His lips; and they were saying, "[a]Is this not Joseph's son?"

23 And He said to them, "No doubt you will quote this proverb to Me, 'Physician, heal yourself! Whatever we heard was done [a]at Capernaum, do here in [b]your home town as well.' "

24 And He said, "Truly I say to you, [a]no prophet is welcome in his home town.

25 "But I say to you in truth, there were many widows in Israel [a]in the days of Elijah, when the sky was shut up for three years and six months, when a great famine came over all the land;

26 and yet Elijah was sent to none of them, but [a]only to [1]Zarephath, *in the land* of [b]Sidon, to a woman who was a widow.

27 "And there were many lepers in Israel in the time of Elisha the prophet; and none of them was cleansed, but [a]only Naaman the Syrian."

28 And all in the synagogue were filled with rage as they heard these things;

29 and they rose up and [a]cast Him out of the city, and led Him to the brow of the hill on which their city had been built, in order to throw Him down the cliff.

30 But [a]passing through their midst, He went His way.

31 And [a]He came down to [b]Capernaum, a city of Galilee. And He was teaching them on the Sabbath;

32 and [a]they were amazed at His teaching, for [b]His [1]message was with authority.

33 And there was a man in the synagogue [1]possessed by the spirit of an unclean demon, and he cried out with a loud voice,

34 "[1]Ha! [a]What do we have to do with You, Jesus [2]of [b]Nazareth? Have You come to destroy us? I know who You are—[b]the Holy One of God!"

35 And Jesus [a]rebuked him, saying, "Be quiet and come out of him!" And when the demon had thrown him down in *their* midst, he came out of him without doing him any harm.

36 And amazement came upon them all, and they *began* discussing with one another saying, "What is [1]this message? For [a]with authority and power He commands the unclean spirits, and they come out."

37 And [a]the report about Him was getting out into every locality in the surrounding district.

Many Are Healed

38 [a]And He arose and *left* the synagogue, and entered Simon's home. Now Simon's mother-in-law was [b]suffering from a high fever; and they made request of Him on her behalf.

39 And standing over her, He [a]rebuked the fever, and it left her; and she immediately arose and [1]waited on them.

40 [a]And while [b]the sun was setting, all who had any sick with various diseases brought them to Him; and [c]laying His hands on every one of them, He was [d]healing them.

8 [a]Deut. 6:13; 10:20; Matt. 4:10
9 [a]Matt. 4:5-7
10 [a]Ps. 91:11
11 [a]Ps. 91:12
12 [1]Or, *tempt . . . God* [a]Deut. 6:16
14 [a]Matt. 4:12 [b]Matt. 9:26; Luke 4:37
15 [a]Matt. 4:23
16 [a]Luke 2:39, 51 [b]Matt. 13:54; Mark 6:1f. [c]Acts 13:14-16
17 [1]Or, *scroll*
18 [a]Is. 61:1; Matt. 11:5; 12:18; John 3:34
19 [a]Is. 61:2; Lev. 25:10
20 [1]Or, *scroll* [a]Luke 4:17 [b]Matt. 26:55
21 [1]Lit., *ears*
22 [1]Or, *testifying* [2]Lit., *were proceeding out of His mouth* [a]Matt. 13:55; Mark 6:3; John 6:42
23 [a]Matt. 4:13; Mark 1:21ff.; 2:1ff.; Luke 4:35ff.; John 4:46ff. [b]Mark 6:1; Luke 2:39, 51; 4:16
24 [a]Matt. 13:57; Mark 6:4; John 4:44
25 [a]1 Kin. 17:1; 18:1; James 5:17
26 [1]Gr., *Sarepta* [a]1 Kin. 17:9 [b]Matt. 11:21
27 [a]2 Kin. 5:1-14
29 [a]Num. 15:35; Acts 7:58; Heb. 13:12
30 [a]John 10:39
31 [a]Luke 4:31-37: *Mark 1:21-28* [b]Matt. 4:13; Luke 4:23
32 [1]Lit., *word* [a]Matt. 7:28 [b]Luke 4:36; John 7:46
33 [1]Lit., *having a spirit*
34 [1]Or possibly, *Let us alone* [2]Lit., *the Nazarene* [a]Matt. 8:29 [b]Mark 1:24
35 [a]Matt. 8:26; Mark 4:39; Luke 4:39, 41; 8:24
36 [1]Or, *this word, that with authority . . . come out?* [a]Luke 4:32
37 [a]Luke 4:14
38 [a]Luke 4:38, 39: *Matt. 8:14, 15; Mark 1:29-31* [b]Matt. 4:24
39 [1]Or, *served* [a]Luke 4:35, 41
40 [a]Luke 4:40, 41: *Matt. 8:16, 17; Mark 1:32-34* [b]Mark 1:32 [c]Mark 5:23 [d]Matt. 4:23

41 And demons also were coming out of many, crying out and saying, "You are [a]the Son of God!" And [b]rebuking them, He would [c]not allow them to speak, because they knew Him to be [1]the Christ.

42 [a]And when day came, He departed and went to a lonely place; and the multitudes were searching for Him, and came to Him, and tried to keep Him from going away from them.

43 But He said to them, "I must preach the kingdom of God to the other cities also, [a]for I was sent for this purpose."

44 And He kept on preaching in the synagogues [a]of [1]Judea.

The First Disciples

5 [a]NOW it came about that while the multitude were pressing around Him and listening to the word of God, He was standing by [b]the lake of Gennesaret;

2 and He saw two boats lying at the edge of the lake; but the fishermen had gotten out of them, and were washing their nets.

3 And [a]He got into one of the boats, which was Simon's, and asked him to put out a little way from the land. And He sat down and *began* teaching the multitudes from the boat.

4 And when He had finished speaking, He said to Simon, "Put out into the deep water and [a]let down your nets for a catch."

5 And Simon answered and said, "[a]Master, [b]we worked hard all night and caught nothing, but at Your [1]bidding I will let down the nets."

6 And when they had done this, [a]they enclosed a great quantity of fish; and their nets *began* to break;

7 and they signaled to their partners in the other boat, for them to come and help them. And they came, and filled both of the boats, so that they began to sink.

8 But when Simon Peter saw *that,* he fell down at Jesus' [1]feet, saying, "Depart from me, for I am a sinful man, O Lord!"

9 For amazement had seized him and all his companions because of the catch of fish which they had taken;

10 and so also [1]James and John, sons of Zebedee, who were partners with Simon. And Jesus said to Simon, "[a]Do not fear, from now on you will be [b]catching men."

11 And when they had brought their boats to land, [a]they left everything and followed Him.

The Leper and the Paralytic

12 [a]And it came about that while He was in one of the cities, behold, *there was* a man full of leprosy; and when he saw Jesus, he fell on his face and implored Him, saying, "Lord, if You are willing, You can make me clean."

13 And He stretched out His hand, and touched him, saying, "I am willing; be cleansed." And immediately the leprosy left him.

14 And He ordered him to tell no one, "But go and [a]show yourself to the priest, and make an offering for your cleansing, just as Moses commanded, for a testimony to them."

15 But [a]the news about Him was spreading even farther, and great multitudes were gathering to hear *Him* and to be healed of their sicknesses.

16 But He Himself would *often* slip away [1]to the [2]wilderness and [a]pray.

17 And it came about [1]one day that He was teaching; and [a]there were *some* Pharisees and [b]teachers of the law sitting *there,* who had [c]come from every village of Galilee and Judea and *from* Jerusalem; and [d]the power of the Lord was *present* for Him to perform healing.

18 [a]And behold, *some* men *were* carrying on a [1]bed a man who was paralyzed; and they were trying to bring him in, and to set him down in front of Him.

19 And not finding any *way* to bring him in because of the crowd, they went up on [a]the roof and let him down [b]through the tiles with his stretcher, right in the center, in front of Jesus.

20 And seeing their faith, He said, "[1]Friend, [a]your sins are forgiven you."

21 And the scribes and the Pharisees [a]began to reason, saying, "[b]Who is this *man* who speaks blasphemies? [c]Who can forgive sins, but God alone?"

22 But Jesus, [1]aware of their reasonings, answered and said to them, "Why are you reasoning in your hearts?

23 "Which is easier, to say, 'Your sins have been forgiven you,' or to say, 'Rise and walk'?

24 "But in order that you may know that the Son of Man has authority on earth to forgive sins,"—He said to the [a]paralytic—"I say to you, rise, and take up your stretcher and go home."

25 And at once he rose up before them, and took up what he had been lying on, and went home, [a]glorifying God.

26 And they were all seized with astonishment and *began* [a]glorifying God; and they were filled [b]with fear, saying, "We have seen remarkable things today."

Call of Levi (Matthew)

27 [a]And after that He went out, and noticed a [1]tax-gatherer named [b]Levi, sitting in the tax office, and He said to him, "Follow Me."

28 And he [a]left everything behind, and rose and *began* to follow Him.

29 And [a]Levi gave a big [1]reception for Him in his house; and there was a great crowd of [b]tax-gatherers and other *people*

41 [1]I.e., the Messiah [a]Matt. 4:3 [b]Luke 4:35 [c]Matt. 8:16; Mark 1:34

42 [a]Luke 4:42, 43: *Mark 1:35-38*

43 [a]Mark 1:38

44 [1]I.e., the country of the Jews (including Galilee); some mss. read *Galilee* [a]Matt. 4:23

1 [a]Matt. 4:18-22; Mark 1:16-20; Luke 5:1-11; John 1:40-42 [b]Num. 34:11; Deut. 3:17; Josh. 12:3; 13:27; Matt. 4:18

3 [a]Matt. 13:2; Mark 3:9, 10; 4:1

4 [a]John 21:6

5 [1]Or, *word* [a]Luke 8:24; 9:33, 49; 17:13 [b]John 21:3

6 [a]John 21:6

8 [1]Lit., *knees*

10 [1]Or, *Jacob* [a]Matt. 14:27 [b]2 Tim. 2:26

11 [a]Matt. 4:20, 22; 19:29; Mark 1:18, 20; Luke 5:28

12 [a]Luke 5:12-14: *Matt. 8:2-4; Mark 1:40-44*

14 [a]Lev. 13:49; 14:2ff.

15 [a]Matt. 9:26

16 [1]Lit., *in* [2]Or, *lonely places* [a]Matt. 14:23; Mark 1:35; Luke 6:12

17 [1]Lit., *on one of the days* [a]Matt. 15:1 [b]Luke 2:46 [c]Mark 1:45 [d]Mark 5:30; Luke 6:19; 8:46

18 [1]Or, *stretcher* [a]Luke 5:18-26: *Matt. 9:2-8; Mark 2:3-12*

19 [a]Matt. 24:17 [b]Mark 2:4

20 [1]Lit., *Man* [a]Matt. 9:2

21 [a]Luke 3:8 [b]Luke 7:49 [c]Is. 43:25

22 [1]Or, *perceiving*

24 [a]Matt. 4:24

25 [a]Matt. 9:8

26 [a]Matt. 9:8 [b]Luke 1:65; 7:16

27 [1]I.e., Collector of Roman taxes for profit [a]Luke 5:27-39: *Matt. 9:9-17; Mark 2:14-22* [b]Matt. 9:9

28 [a]Luke 5:11

29 [1]Or, *banquet* [a]Matt. 9:9 [b]Luke 15:1

who were reclining *at the table* with
them.
30 And [a]the Pharisees and their
scribes *began* grumbling at His disciples,
saying, "Why do you eat and drink with
the tax-gatherers and sinners?"
31 And Jesus answered and said to
them, "[a]*It is* not those who are well who
need a physician, but those who are sick.
32 "I have not come to call the righteous but sinners to repentance."
33 And they said to Him, "[a]The disciples of John often fast and offer prayers;
the *disciples* of the Pharisees also do [1]the
same; but Yours eat and drink."
34 And Jesus said to them, "You
cannot make the [1]attendants of the
bridegroom fast while the bridegroom is
with them, can you?
35 "[a]But *the* days will come; and when
the bridegroom is taken away from
them, then they will fast in those days."
36 And He was also telling them a
parable: "No one tears a piece from a
new [1]garment and puts it on an old
[1]garment; otherwise he will both tear the
new, and the piece from the new will not
match the old.
37 "And no one puts new wine into old
[1]wineskins; otherwise the new wine will
burst the [1]skins, and it will be spilled
out, and the [1]skins will be ruined.
38 "But new wine must be put into
fresh wineskins.
39 "And no one, after drinking old *wine*
wishes for new; for he says, 'The old is
good *enough.*' "

Jesus Is Lord of the Sabbath

6 [a]NOW it came about that on a *cer-*
tain [1]Sabbath He was passing
through *some* grainfields; and His disciples [b]were picking and eating the heads
of grain, rubbing them in their hands.
2 But some of the Pharisees said,
"Why do you do what [a]is not lawful on
the Sabbath?"
3 And Jesus answering them said,
"Have you not even read [a]what David
did when he was hungry, he and those
who were with him,
4 how he entered the house of God,
and took and ate the [1]consecrated bread
which [a]is not lawful for any to eat except
the priests alone, and gave it to his
companions?"
5 And He was saying to them, "The
Son of Man is Lord of the Sabbath."
6 [a]And it came about [b]on another
Sabbath, that He entered [c]the synagogue
and was teaching; and there was a man
there [1]whose right hand was withered.
7 And the scribes and the Pharisees
[a]were watching Him closely, *to see* if He
healed on the Sabbath, in order that they
might find *reason* to accuse Him.
8 But He [a]knew [1]what they were
thinking, and He said to the man with
the withered hand, "Rise and [2]come
forward!" And he rose and [3]came forward.

30 [a]Mark 2:16; Luke 15:2; Acts 23:9
31 [a]Matt. 9:12, 13; Mark 2:17
33 [1]Or, *likewise* [a]Matt. 9:14; Mark 2:18
34 [1]Lit., *sons of the bridal-chamber*
35 [a]Matt. 9:15; Mark 2:20; Luke 17:22
36 [1]Or, *cloak*
37 [1]I.e., skins used as bottles

1 [1]Many mss. read *the second-first Sabbath;* i.e., the second Sabbath after the first [a]Luke 6:1-5: *Matt. 12:1-8; Mark 2:23-28* [b]Deut. 23:25
2 [a]Matt. 12:2
3 [a]1 Sam. 21:6
4 [1]Or, *showbread;* lit., *loaves of presentation* [a]Lev. 24:9
6 [1]Lit., *and his* [a]Luke 6:6-11: *Matt. 12:9-14; Mark 3:1-6* [b]Luke 6:1 [c]Matt. 4:23
7 [a]Mark 3:2
8 [1]Lit., *their thoughts* [2]Lit., *stand;* or, *stood into the midst* [3]Lit., *stood* [a]Matt. 9:4
10 [a]Mark 3:5
11 [1]Lit., *folly*
12 [1]Lit., *in these days* [a]Matt. 5:1 [b]Matt. 14:23; Luke 5:16; 9:18, 28
13 [a]Luke 6:13-16: *Matt. 10:2-4; Mark 3:16-19; Acts 1:13* [b]Mark 6:30
14 [1]Or, *Jacob,* also vv. 15 and 16
15 [a]Matt. 9:9
17 [a]Luke 6:12 [b]Matt. 4:25; Mark 3:7, 8 [c]Matt. 11:21
18 [1]Most English versions begin v. 18 with *and those who*
19 [a]Matt. 9:21; 14:36; Mark 3:10 [b]Luke 5:17
20 [a]Matt. 5:3-12; Luke 6:20-23 [b]Matt. 5:3
22 [a]1 Pet. 4:14 [b]John 9:22; 16:2
23 [1]Lit., *do to* [a]Mal. 4 [b]2 Chr. 36:16; Acts 7:52
24 [a]Luke 16:25; James 5:1 [b]Matt. 6:2
25 [1]Lit., *having been filled*
26 [1]Lit., *do to* [a]Matt. 7:15
27 [a]Matt. 5:44; Luke 6:35

9 And Jesus said to them, "I ask you,
is it lawful on the Sabbath to do good, or
to do harm, to save a life, or to destroy
it?"
10 And after [a]looking around at them
all, He said to him, "Stretch out your
hand!" And he did *so;* and his hand was
restored.
11 But they themselves were filled
with [1]rage, and discussed together what
they might do to Jesus.

Choosing the Twelve

12 And it was [1]at this time that He
went off to [a]the mountain to [b]pray, and
He spent the whole night in prayer to
God.
13 And when day came, [a]He called
His disciples to Him; and chose twelve
of them, whom He also named as [b]apos-
tles:
14 Simon, whom He also named Peter, and Andrew his brother; and [1]James
and John; and Philip and Bartholomew;
15 and [a]Matthew and Thomas; James
the son of Alphaeus, and Simon who was
called the Zealot;
16 Judas *the son* of James, and Judas
Iscariot, who became a traitor.
17 And He [a]descended with them, and
stood on a level place; and *there was* [b]a
great multitude of His disciples, and a
great throng of people from all Judea
and Jerusalem and the coastal region of
[c]Tyre and Sidon,
18 [1]who had come to hear Him, and
to be healed of their diseases; and those
who were troubled with unclean spirits
were being cured.
19 And all the multitude were trying
to [a]touch Him, for [b]power was coming
from Him and healing *them* all.

The Beatitudes

20 And turning His gaze on His disciples, He *began* to say, "[a]Blessed *are* you
who are poor, for [b]yours is the kingdom
of God.
21 "Blessed *are* you who hunger now,
for you shall be satisfied. Blessed *are* you
who weep now, for you shall laugh.
22 "[a]Blessed are you when men hate
you, and [b]ostracize you, and cast insults
at you, and spurn your name as evil, for
the sake of the Son of Man.
23 "Be glad in that day, and [a]leap *for*
joy, for behold, your reward is great in
heaven; for [b]in the same way their
fathers used to [1]treat the prophets.
24 "But woe to [a]you who are rich, for
[b]you are receiving your comfort in full.
25 "Woe to you who [1]are well-fed now,
for you shall be hungry. Woe *to you* who
laugh now, for you shall mourn and
weep.
26 "Woe *to you* when all men speak
well of you, for in the same way their
fathers used to [1]treat the [a]false prophets.
27 "But I say to you who hear, [a]love
your enemies, do good to those who hate
you,

28 bless those who curse you, [a]pray for those who [1]mistreat you.

29 "[a]Whoever hits you on the cheek, offer him the other also; and whoever takes away your [1]coat, do not withhold your [2]shirt from him either.

30 "Give to everyone who asks of you, and whoever takes away what is yours, do not demand it back.

31 "[a]And just as you want people to [1]treat you, [1]treat them in the same way.

32 "And [a]if you love those who love you, what credit is *that* to you? For even sinners love those who love them.

33 "And if you do good to those who do good to you, what credit is *that* to you? For even sinners do the same.

34 "[a]And if you lend to those from whom you expect to receive, what credit is *that* to you? Even sinners lend to sinners, in order to receive back the same *amount.*

35 "But [a]love your enemies, and do good, and lend, [1]expecting nothing in return; and your reward will be great, and you will be [b]sons of [c]the Most High; for He Himself is kind to ungrateful and evil *men.*

36 "[1]Be merciful, just as your Father is merciful.

37 "[a]And do not judge and you will not be judged; and do not condemn, and you will not be condemned; [1][b]pardon, and you will be pardoned.

38 "Give, and it will be given to you; [a]good measure, pressed down, shaken together, running over, they will pour [b]into your lap. For by your standard of measure it will be measured to you in return."

39 And He also spoke a parable to them: "[a]A blind man cannot guide a blind man, can he? Will they not both fall into a pit?

40 "[a]A [1]pupil is not above his teacher; but everyone, after he has been fully trained, will [2]be like his teacher.

41 "And why do you look at the speck that is in your brother's eye, but do not notice the log that is in your own eye?

42 "Or how can you say to your brother, 'Brother, let me take out the speck that is in your eye,' when you yourself do not see the log that is in your own eye? You hypocrite, first take the log out of your own eye, and then you will see clearly to take out the speck that is in your brother's eye.

43 "[a]For there is no good tree which produces bad fruit; nor, [1]on the other hand, a bad tree which produces good fruit.

44 "[a]For each tree is known by its own fruit. For men do not gather figs from thorns, nor do they pick grapes from a briar bush.

45 "[a]The good man out of the good [1]treasure of his heart brings forth what is good; and the evil *man* out of the evil *treasure* brings forth what is evil; [b]for his mouth speaks from [2]that which fills his heart.

Builders and Foundations

46 "And [a]why do you call Me, 'Lord, Lord,' and do not do what I say?

47 "[a]Everyone who comes to Me, and hears My words, and [1]acts upon them, I will show you whom he is like:

48 he is like a man building a house, who [1]dug deep and laid a foundation upon the rock; and when a flood rose, the [2]torrent burst against that house and could not shake it, because it had been well built.

49 "But the one who has heard, and has not acted *accordingly,* is like a man who built a house upon the ground without any foundation; and the [1]torrent burst against it and immediately it collapsed, and the ruin of that house was great."

Jesus Heals a Centurion's Servant

7 [a]WHEN He had completed all His discourse in the hearing of the people, [b]He went to Capernaum.

2 And a certain centurion's slave, [1]who was highly regarded by him, was sick and about to die.

3 And when he heard about Jesus, [a]he sent some [1]Jewish elders asking Him to come and [2]save the life of his slave.

4 And when they had come to Jesus, they earnestly entreated Him, saying, "He is worthy for You to grant this to him;

5 for he loves our nation, and it was he who built us our synagogue."

6 Now Jesus *started* on His way with them; and when He was already not far from the house, the centurion sent friends, saying to Him, "[1]Lord, do not trouble Yourself further, for I am not worthy for You to come under my roof;

7 for this reason I did not even consider myself worthy to come to You, but *just* [1]say the word, and my [2]servant will be healed.

8 "For I, too, am a man under authority, with soldiers under me; and I say to this one, 'Go!' and he goes; and to another, 'Come!' and he comes; and to my slave, 'Do this!' and he does it."

9 Now when Jesus heard this, He marveled at him, and turned and said to the multitude that was following Him, "I say to you, [a]not even in Israel have I found such great faith."

10 And when those who had been sent returned to the house, they found the slave in good health.

11 And it came about [1]soon afterwards, that He went to a city called Nain; and His disciples were going along with Him, [2]accompanied by a large multitude.

12 Now as He approached the gate of the city, behold, [1]a dead man was being carried out, the [2]only son of his mother, and she was a widow; and a sizeable crowd from the city was with her.

28 [1]Or, *revile* [a]Matt. 5:44; Luke 6:35

29 [1]Or, *cloak;* i.e., outer garment [2]Or, *tunic;* i.e., garment worn next to body [a]Luke 6:29, 30: *Matt. 5:39-42*

31 [1]Lit., *do to* [a]Matt. 7:12

32 [a]Matt. 5:46

34 [a]Matt. 5:42

35 [1]Or, *not despairing at all* [a]Luke 6:27 [b]Matt. 5:9 [c]Luke 1:32

36 [1]Or, *Become*

37 [1]Lit., *release* [a]Luke 6:37-42: *Matt. 7:1-5* [b]Matt. 6:14; Luke 23:16; Acts 3:13

38 [a]Mark 4:24 [b]Ps. 79:12; Is. 65:6, 7; Jer. 32:18

39 [a]Matt. 15:14

40 [1]Or, *disciple* [2]Or, *reach his teacher's level* [a]Matt. 10:24; John 13:16; 15:20

43 [1]Lit., *again* [a]Luke 6:43, 44: *Matt. 7:16, 18, 20*

44 [a]Matt. 7:16; 12:33

45 [1]Or, *treasury, storehouse* [2]Lit., *the abundance of* [a]Matt. 12:35 [b]Matt. 12:34

46 [a]Mal. 1:6; Matt. 7:21

47 [1]Lit., *does* [a]Luke 6:47-49: *Matt. 7:24-27;* James 1:22ff.

48 [1]Lit., *dug and went deep* [2]Lit., *river*

49 [1]Lit., *river*

1 [a]Matt. 7:28 [b]Luke 7:1-10: *Matt. 8:5-13*

2 [1]Lit., *to whom he was honorable*

3 [1]Lit., *elders of the Jews* [2]Lit., *bring safely through, rescue* [a]Matt. 8:5

6 [1]Or, *Sir*

7 [1]Lit., *say with a word* [2]Or, *boy*

9 [a]Matt. 8:10; Luke 7:50

11 [1]Some mss. read *on the next day* [2]Lit., *and*

12 [1]Lit., *one who had died* [2]Or, *only begotten*

13 And when [a]the Lord saw her, He
felt compassion for her, and said to her,
"[1]Do not weep."
14 And He came up and touched the
coffin; and the bearers came to a halt.
And He said, "Young man, I say to you,
arise!"
15 And the [1]dead man sat up, and
began to speak. And *Jesus* gave him
back to his mother.
16 And [a]fear gripped them all, and
they *began* [b]glorifying God, saying, "A
great [c]prophet has arisen among us!"
and, "God has [1]visited His people!"
17 [a]And this report concerning Him
went out all over Judea, and in all the
surrounding district.

A Deputation from John

18 [a]And the disciples of John reported
to him about all these things.
19 And summoning [1]two of his disciples, John sent them to [a]the Lord, saying, "Are You the [2]Expected One, or do
we look for [3]someone else?"
20 And when the men had come to
Him, they said, "John the Baptist has
sent us to You, saying, 'Are You the
[1]Expected One, or do we look for someone else?' "
21 At that [1]very time He [a]cured many
people of diseases and [b]afflictions and
evil spirits; and He granted sight to
many *who were* blind.
22 And He answered and said to
them, "Go and report to John what you
have seen and heard: *the* [a]BLIND RECEIVE
SIGHT, *the* lame walk, *the* lepers are
cleansed, and *the* deaf hear, *the* dead are
raised up, *the* [b]POOR HAVE THE GOSPEL
PREACHED TO THEM.
23 "And blessed is he [1]who keeps from
stumbling over Me."
24 And when the messengers of John
had left, He began to speak to the
multitudes about John, "What did you
go out into the wilderness to look at? A
reed shaken by the wind?
25 "[1]But what did you go out to see? A
man dressed in soft [2]clothing? Behold,
those who are splendidly clothed and
live in luxury are *found* in royal palaces.
26 "But what did you go out to see? A
prophet? Yes, I say to you, and one who
is more than a prophet.
27 "This is the one about whom it [1]is
written,

> '[a]BEHOLD, I SEND MY MESSENGER
> BEFORE YOUR FACE,
> WHO WILL PREPARE YOUR WAY
> BEFORE YOU.'

28 "I say to you, among those born of
women, there is no one greater than
John; yet he who is [1]least in the kingdom of God is greater than he."
29 And when all the people and the
[1]tax-gatherers heard *this,* they [2]acknowl-
edged [a]God's justice, [b]having been baptized with [c]the baptism of John.
30 But the Pharisees and the [1a]lawyers
rejected God's purpose for themselves,
not having been baptized by [2]John.
31 "To what then shall I compare the
men of this generation, and what are
they like?
32 "They are like children who sit in
the market place and call to one another; and they say, 'We played the flute
for you, and you did not dance; we sang
a dirge, and you did not weep.'
33 "For John the Baptist has come
[a]eating no bread and drinking no wine;
and you say, 'He has a demon!'
34 "The Son of Man has come eating
and drinking; and you say, 'Behold, a
gluttonous man, and a [1]drunkard, a
friend of [2]tax-gatherers and sinners!'
35 "[1]Yet wisdom [a]is vindicated by all
her children."
36 Now one of the Pharisees was
requesting Him to [1]dine with him. And
He entered the Pharisee's house, and
reclined *at the table.*
37 [a]And behold, there was a woman in
the city who was a [1]sinner; and when she
learned that He was reclining *at the table*
in the Pharisee's house, she brought an
alabaster vial of perfume,
38 and standing behind *Him* at His
feet, weeping, she began to wet His feet
with her tears, and kept wiping them
with the hair of her head, and kissing
His feet, and anointing them with the
perfume.
39 Now when the Pharisee who had
invited Him saw this, he said [1]to himself,
"If this man were [2a]a prophet He would
know who and what sort of person this
woman is who is touching Him, that she
is a [3]sinner."

Parable of Two Debtors

40 And Jesus answered and said to
him, "Simon, I have something to say to
you." And he [1]replied, "Say it, Teacher."
41 "A certain moneylender had two
debtors: one owed five hundred [1a]de-
narii, and the other fifty.
42 "When they [a]were unable to repay,
he graciously forgave them both. Which
of them therefore will love him more?"
43 Simon answered and said, "I suppose the one whom he forgave more."
And He said to him, "You have judged
correctly."
44 And turning toward the woman,
He said to Simon, "Do you see this
woman? I entered your house; you [a]gave
Me no water for My feet, but she has wet
My feet with her tears, and wiped them
with her hair.
45 "You [a]gave Me no kiss; but she,
since the time I came in, [1]has not ceased
to kiss My feet.
46 "[a]You did not anoint My head with
oil, but she anointed My feet with perfume.

13 [1]Or, *Stop weeping* [a]Luke 7:19; 10:1; 11:1, 39; 12:42; 13:15; 17:5, 6; 18:6; 19:8; 22:61; 24:34; John 4:1; 6:23; 11:2
15 [1]Or, *corpse*
16 [1]Or, *cared for* [a]Luke 5:26 [b]Matt. 9:8 [c]Matt. 21:11; Luke 7:39
17 [a]Matt. 9:26
18 [a]Luke 7:18-35: *Matt. 11:2-19*
19 [1]Lit., *a certain two* [2]Lit., *Coming One* [3]Some early mss. read *one who is different* [a]Luke 7:13; 10:1; 11:1, 39; 12:42; 13:15; 17:5, 6; 18:6; 19:8; 22:61; 24:34; John 4:1; 6:23; 11:2
20 [1]Lit., *Coming One*
21 [1]Lit., *hour* [a]Matt. 4:23 [b]Mark 3:10
22 [a]Is. 35:5 [b]Is. 61:1
23 [1]Lit., *whoever*
25 [1]Or, *Well then, what* [2]Or, *garments*
27 [1]Lit., *has been written* [a]Mal. 3:1; Matt. 11:10; Mark 1:2
28 [1]Lit., *less*
29 [1]I.e., Collectors of Roman taxes for profit [2]Or, *justified God* [a]Luke 7:35 [b]Matt. 21:32; Luke 3:12 [c]Acts 18:25; 19:3
30 [1]I.e., experts in the Mosaic Law [2]Lit., *him* [a]Matt. 22:35
33 [a]Luke 1:15
34 [1]Or, *wine-drinker* [2]I.e., Collectors of Roman taxes for profit
35 [1]Lit., *And* [a]Luke 7:29
36 [1]Lit., *eat*
37 [1]I.e., an immoral woman [a]Matt. 26:6-13; Mark 14:3-9; Luke 7:37-39; John 12:1-8
39 [1]Lit., *to himself, saying* [2]Some mss. read *the prophet* [3]I.e., an immoral woman [a]Luke 7:16; John 4:19
40 [1]Lit., *says*
41 [1]The denarius was equivalent to one day's wage [a]Matt. 18:28; Mark 6:37
42 [a]Matt. 18:25
44 [a]Gen. 18:4; 19:2; 43:24; Judg. 19:21; 1 Tim. 5:10
45 [1]Lit., *was not ceasing* [a]2 Sam. 15:5
46 [a]2 Sam. 12:20; Ps. 23:5; Eccl. 9:8; Dan. 10:3

47 "For this reason I say to you, her sins, which are many, have been forgiven, for she loved much; but he who is forgiven little, loves little."

48 And He said to her, "[a]Your sins have been forgiven."

49 And those who were reclining *at the table* with Him began to say [1]to themselves, "[a]Who is this *man* who even forgives sins?"

50 And He said to the woman, "[a]Your faith has saved you; [b]go in peace."

Ministering Women

8 AND it came about soon afterwards, that He *began* going about from one city and village to another, [a]proclaiming and preaching the kingdom of God; and the twelve were with Him,

2 and *also* [a]some women who had been healed of evil spirits and sicknesses: [b]Mary who was called Magdalene, from whom seven demons had gone out,

3 and Joanna the wife of Chuza, [a]Herod's [b]steward, and Susanna, and many others who were contributing to their support out of their private means.

Parable of the Sower

4 [a]And when a great multitude were coming together, and those from the various cities were journeying to Him, He spoke by way of a parable:

5 "The sower went out to sow his seed; and as he sowed, some fell beside the road; and it was trampled under foot, and the birds of the [1]air ate it up.

6 "And other *seed* fell on rocky *soil,* and as soon as it grew up, it withered away, because it had no moisture.

7 "And other *seed* fell among the thorns; and the thorns grew up with it, and choked it out.

8 "And other *seed* fell into the good soil, and grew up, and produced a crop a hundred times as great." As He said these things, He would call out, "[a]He who has ears to hear, let him hear."

9 [a]And His disciples *began* questioning Him as to what this parable might be.

10 And He said, "[a]To you it has been granted to know the mysteries of the kingdom of God, but to the rest *it is* in parables, in order that [b]SEEING THEY MAY NOT SEE, AND HEARING THEY MAY NOT UNDERSTAND.

11 "Now the parable is this: [a]the seed is the word of God.

12 "And those beside the road are those who have heard; then the devil comes and takes away the word from their heart, so that they may not believe and be saved.

13 "And those on the rocky *soil are* those who, when they hear, receive the word with joy; and these have no *firm* root; [1]they believe for a while, and in time of temptation fall away.

14 "And the *seed* which fell among the thorns, these are the ones who have heard, and as they go on their way they are choked with worries and riches and pleasures of *this* life, and bring no fruit to maturity.

15 "And the *seed* in the good soil, these are the ones who have heard the word in an honest and good heart, and hold it fast, and bear fruit with [1]perseverance.

Parable of the Lamp

16 "Now [a]no one after lighting a lamp covers it over with a container, or puts it under a bed; but he puts it on a lampstand, in order that those who come in may see the light.

17 "[a]For nothing is hidden that shall not become evident, nor *anything* secret that shall not be known and come to light.

18 "Therefore take care how you listen; [a]for whoever has, to him shall *more* be given; and whoever does not have, even what he [1]thinks he has shall be taken away from him."

19 [a]And His mother and brothers came to Him, and they were unable to get to Him because of the crowd.

20 And it was reported to Him, "Your mother and Your brothers are standing outside, wishing to see You."

21 But He answered and said to them, "My mother and My brothers are these [a]who hear the word of God and do it."

Jesus Stills the Sea

22 [a]Now it came about on one of *those* days, that He and His disciples got into a boat, and He said to them, "Let us go over to the other side of [b]the lake." And they launched out.

23 But as they were sailing along He fell asleep; and a fierce gale of wind descended upon [a]the lake, and they *began* to be swamped and to be in danger.

24 And they came to Him and woke Him up, saying, "[a]Master, Master, we are perishing!" And being aroused, He [b]rebuked the wind and the surging waves, and they stopped, and [1]it became calm.

25 And He said to them, "Where is your faith?" And they were fearful and amazed, saying to one another, "Who then is this, that He commands even the winds and the water, and they obey Him?"

The Demoniac Cured

26 [a]And they sailed to the country of the [1]Gerasenes, which is opposite Galilee.

27 And when He had come out onto the land, He was met by a certain man from the city who was possessed with demons; and who had not put on any clothing for a long time, and was not living in a house, but in the tombs.

---

48 [a]Matt. 9:2; Mark 2:5, 9; Luke 5:20, 23

49 [1]Or, *among* [a]Luke 5:21

50 [a]Matt. 9:22; Luke 17:19; 18:42 [b]Mark 5:34; Luke 8:48

1 [a]Matt. 4:23

2 [a]Matt. 27:55; Mark 15:40, 41; Luke 23:49, 55 [b]Matt. 27:56; Mark 16:9

3 [a]Matt. 14:1 [b]Matt. 20:8

4 [a]Luke 8:4-8: *Matt. 13:2-9; Mark 4:1-9*

5 [1]Lit., *heaven*

8 [a]Matt. 11:15; Mark 7:16; Luke 14:35; Rev. 2:7, 11, 17, 29; 3:6, 13, 22; 13:9

9 [a]Luke 8:9-15: *Matt. 13:10-23; Mark 4:10-20*

10 [a]Matt. 13:11 [b]Is. 6:9; Matt. 13:14; Acts 28:26

11 [a]1 Pet. 1:23

13 [1]Lit., *who believe*

15 [1]Or, *steadfastness*

16 [a]Matt. 5:15; Mark 4:21; Luke 11:33

17 [a]Matt. 10:26; Mark 4:22; Luke 12:2

18 [1]Or, *seems to have* [a]Matt. 13:12; 25:29; Luke 19:26

19 [a]Luke 8:19-21: *Matt. 12:46-50; Mark 3:31-35*

21 [a]Luke 11:28

22 [a]Luke 8:22-25: *Matt. 8:23-27; Mark 4:36-41* [b]Luke 5:1f.; 8:23

23 [a]Luke 5:1f.; 8:22

24 [1]Lit., *a calm occurred* [a]Luke 5:5 [b]Luke 4:39

26 [1]Other mss. read *Gergesenes* or *Gadarenes* [a]Luke 8:26-37: *Matt. 8:28-34; Mark 5:1-17*

28 And seeing Jesus, he cried out and
fell before Him, and said in a loud voice,
"[a]What do I have to do with You, Jesus,
Son of [b]the Most High God? I beg You,
do not torment me."
29 For He [1]had been commanding the
unclean spirit to come out of the man.
For it had seized him many times; and
he was bound with chains and shackles
and kept under guard; and *yet* he would
burst his fetters and be driven by the
demon into the desert.
30 And Jesus asked him, "What is
your name?" And he said, "[a]Legion";
for many demons had entered him.
31 And they were entreating Him not
to command them to depart into [a]the
abyss.
32 Now there was a herd of many
swine feeding there on the mountain;
and *the demons* entreated Him to permit
them to enter [1]the swine. And He gave
them permission.
33 And the demons came out from the
man and entered the swine; and the herd
rushed down the steep bank into [a]the
lake, and were drowned.
34 And when the herdsmen saw what
had happened, they ran away and reported it in the city and *out* in the
country.
35 And *the people* went out to see
what had happened; and they came to
Jesus, and found the man from whom
the demons had gone out, sitting down
[a]at the feet of Jesus, clothed and in his
right mind; and they became frightened.
36 And those who had seen it reported
to them how the man who was [a]demon-
possessed had been [1]made well.
37 And all the people of the country
of the [1]Gerasenes and the surrounding
district asked Him to depart from them;
for they were gripped with great fear;
and He got into a boat, and returned.
38 [a]But the man from whom the demons had gone out was begging Him
that he might [1]accompany Him; but He
sent him away, saying,
39 "Return to your house and describe
what great things God has done for
you." And he went away, proclaiming
throughout the whole city what great
things Jesus had done for him.

Miracles of Healing

40 [a]And as Jesus returned, the multitude welcomed Him, for they had all
been waiting for Him.
41 [a]And behold, there came a man
named Jairus, and he was an [1b]official of
the synagogue; and he fell at Jesus' feet,
and *began* to entreat Him to come to his
house;
42 for he had an [1]only daughter,
about twelve years old, and she was
dying. But as He went, the multitudes
were pressing against Him.
43 And a woman who had a hemorrhage for twelve years, [1]and could not be
healed by anyone,
44 came up behind Him, and touched
the fringe of His [1]cloak; and immediately her hemorrhage stopped.
45 And Jesus said, "Who is the one
who touched Me?" And while they were
all denying it, Peter said,[1] "[a]Master, the
multitudes are crowding and pressing
upon You."
46 But Jesus said, "Someone did
touch Me, for I was aware that [a]power
had gone out of Me."
47 And when the woman saw that she
had not escaped notice, she came trembling and fell down before Him, and
declared in the presence of all the people
the reason why she had touched Him,
and how she had been immediately
healed.
48 And He said to her, "Daughter,
[a]your faith has [1]made you well; [b]go in
peace."
49 While He was still speaking, someone *came from *the house of* [a]the synagogue official, saying, "Your daughter
has died; do not trouble the Teacher
anymore."
50 But when Jesus heard *this,* He
answered him, "[a]Do not be afraid *any
longer;* only believe, and she shall be
[1]made well."
51 And when He had come to the
house, He did not allow anyone to enter
with Him, except Peter and John and
James, and the girl's father and mother.
52 Now they were all weeping and
[a]lamenting for her; but He said, "Stop
weeping, for she has not died, but [b]is
asleep."
53 And they *began* laughing at Him,
knowing that she had died.
54 He, however, took her by the hand
and called, saying, "Child, arise!"
55 And her spirit returned, and she
rose immediately; and He gave orders
for *something* to be given her to eat.
56 And her parents were amazed; but
He [a]instructed them to tell no one what
had happened.

Ministry of the Twelve

9 [a]AND He called the twelve together,
and gave them power and authority
over all the demons, and to heal diseases.
2 And He sent them out to [a]proclaim
the kingdom of God, and [1]to perform
healing.
3 And He said to them, "[a]Take nothing for *your* journey, [b]neither a staff, nor
a [1]bag, nor bread, nor money; and do
not *even* have [2]two tunics apiece.
4 "And whatever house you enter,
stay there, and take your leave from
there.
5 "And as for those who do not receive you, as you go out from that city,
[a]shake off the dust from your feet as a
testimony against them."
6 And departing, they *began* going
about [1]among the villages, [a]preaching
the gospel, and healing everywhere.

28 [a]Matt. 8:29 [b]Mark 5:7

29 [1]Or, *was commanding*

30 [a]Matt. 26:53

31 [a]Rom. 10:7; Rev. 9:1f., 11; 11:7; 17:8; 20:1, 3

32 [1]Lit., *them*

33 [a]Luke 5:1f.; 8:22

35 [a]Luke 10:39

36 [1]Or, *saved* [a]Matt. 4:24

37 [1]Other mss. read *Gergesenes* or *Gadarenes*

38 [1]Lit., *be with* [a]Luke 8:38, 39: *Mark 5:18-20*

40 [a]Matt. 9:1; Mark 5:21

41 [1]Lit., *ruler* [a]Luke 8:41-56: *Matt. 9:18-26; Mark 5:22-43* [b]Mark 5:22; Luke 8:49

42 [1]Or, *only begotten*

43 [1]Some mss. add *who had spent all her living upon physicians*

44 [1]Or, *outer garment*

45 [1]Some early mss. add *and those with him* [a]Luke 5:5

46 [a]Luke 5:17

48 [1]Or, *saved you* [a]Matt. 9:22 [b]Mark 5:34; Luke 7:50

49 [a]Luke 8:41

50 [1]Or, *saved* [a]Mark 5:36

52 [a]Matt. 11:17; Luke 23:27 [b]John 11:13

56 [a]Matt. 8:4

1 [a]Matt. 10:5; Mark 6:7

2 [1]Some mss. read *to heal the sick* [a]Matt. 10:7

3 [1]Or, *knapsack or beggar's bag* [2]Or, *inner garment* [a]Luke 9:3-5: *Matt. 10:9-15; Mark 6:8-11;* Luke 10:4-12; 22:35 [b]Matt. 10:10; Mark 6:8; Luke 22:35f.

5 [a]Luke 10:11; Acts 13:51

6 [1]Or, *from village to village* [a]Mark 6:12; Luke 8:1

7 [a]Now [b]Herod the tetrarch heard of
all that was happening; and he was
greatly perplexed, because it was said by
some that [c]John had risen from the
dead,
8 and by some that [a]Elijah had appeared, and by others, that one of the
prophets of old had risen again.
9 And Herod said, "I myself had
John beheaded; but who is this man
about whom I hear such things?" And
[a]he kept trying to see Him.
10 [a]And when the apostles returned,
they gave an account to Him of all that
they had done. [b]And taking them with
Him, He withdrew by Himself to a city
called [c]Bethsaida.
11 But the multitudes were aware of
this and followed Him; and welcoming
them, He *began* speaking to them about
the kingdom of God and curing those
who had need of healing.

Five Thousand Fed

12 And the day began to decline, and
the twelve came and said to Him, "Send
the multitude away, that they may go
into the surrounding villages and countryside and find lodging and get [1]some-
thing to eat; for here we are in a desolate
place."
13 But He said to them, "You give
them *something* to eat!" And they said,
"We have no more than five loaves and
two fish, unless perhaps we go and buy
food for all these people."
14 (For there were about five thousand men.) And He said to His disciples,
"Have them recline *to eat* [a]in groups of
about fifty each."
15 And they did so, and had them all
recline.
16 And He took the five loaves and
the two fish, and looking up to heaven,
He blessed them, and broke *them,* and
kept giving *them* to the disciples to set
before the multitude.
17 And they all ate and were satisfied;
and [1]the broken pieces which they had
left over were picked up, twelve [a]baskets
full.
18 [a]And it came about that while He
was [b]praying alone, the disciples were
with Him, and He questioned them,
saying, "Who do the multitudes say that
I am?"
19 And they answered and said, "John
the Baptist, and others *say* Elijah; but
others, that one of the prophets of old
has risen again."
20 And He said to them, "But who do
you say that I am?" And Peter answered
and said, "[a]The [1]Christ of God."
21 But He [1a]warned them, and instructed *them* not to tell this to anyone,
22 [a]saying, "[b]The Son of Man must
suffer many things, and be rejected by
the elders and chief priests and scribes,
and be killed, and be raised up on the
third day."

23 And He was saying to *them* all, "[a]If
anyone wishes to come after Me, let him
deny himself, and take up his cross daily,
and follow Me.
24 "For [a]whoever wishes to save his
[1]life shall lose it, but whoever loses his
[1]life for My sake, he is the one who will
save it.
25 "For what is a man profited if he
gains the whole world, and [a]loses or
forfeits himself?
26 "[a]For whoever is ashamed of Me
and My words, of him will the Son of
Man be ashamed when He comes in His
glory, and *the glory* of the Father and of
the holy angels.
27 "But I say to you truthfully, [a]there
are some of those standing here who
shall not taste death until they see the
kingdom of God."

The Transfiguration

28 [a]And some eight days after these
sayings, it came about that He took
along [b]Peter and John and James, and
[c]went up to the mountain [d]to pray.
29 And while He was [a]praying, the
appearance of His face [b]became different, and His clothing *became* white *and*
[1]gleaming.
30 And behold, two men were talking
with Him; and they were Moses and
Elijah,
31 who, appearing in [1]glory, were
speaking of His [a]departure which He
was about to accomplish at Jerusalem.
32 Now Peter and his companions
[a]had been overcome with sleep; but
when they were fully awake, they saw
His glory and the two men standing with
Him.
33 And it came about, as [1]these were
parting from Him, Peter said to Jesus,
"[a]Master, it is good for us to be here;
and [b]let us make three [2]tabernacles: one
for You, and one for Moses, and one for
Elijah"—[c]not realizing what he was
saying.
34 And while he was saying this, a
cloud [1]formed and *began* to overshadow
them; and they were afraid as they
entered the cloud.
35 And [a]a voice came out of the cloud,
saying, "[b]This is My Son, *My* Chosen
One; listen to Him!"
36 And when the voice [1]had spoken,
Jesus was found alone. And [a]they kept
silent, and reported to no one in those
days any of the things which they had
seen.
37 [a]And it came about on the next
day, that when they had come down
from the mountain, a great multitude
met Him.
38 And behold, a man from the multitude shouted out, saying, "Teacher, I
beg You to look at my son, for he is my
[1]only *boy,*
39 and behold, a spirit seizes him, and
he suddenly screams, and it throws him
into a convulsion with foaming *at the*

7 [a]Luke 9:7-9: *Matt. 14:1, 2;* Mark 6:14f. [b]Matt. 14:1; Luke 3:1; 13:31; 23:7 [c]Matt. 14:2
8 [a]Matt. 16:14
9 [a]Luke 23:8
10 [a]Mark 6:30 [b]Luke 9:10-17: *Matt. 14:13-21; Mark 6:32-44; John 6:5-13* [c]Matt. 11:21
12 [1]Lit., *provisions*
14 [a]Mark 6:39
17 [1]Lit., *that which was left over to them of the broken pieces was* [a]Matt. 14:20
18 [a]Luke 9:18-20: *Matt. 16:13-16; Mark 8:27-29* [b]Matt. 14:23; Luke 6:12; 9:28
20 [1]I.e., Messiah [a]John 6:68f.
21 [1]Or, *strictly admonished* [a]Matt. 8:4; 16:20; Mark 8:30
22 [a]Luke 9:22-27: *Matt. 16:21-28; Mark 8:31-9:1* [b]Matt. 16:21; Luke 9:44
23 [a]Matt. 10:38; Luke 14:27
24 [1]Or, *soul* [a]Matt. 10:39; Luke 17:33; John 12:25
25 [a]Heb. 10:34
26 [a]Matt. 10:33; Luke 12:9
27 [a]Matt. 16:28
28 [a]Luke 9:28-36: *Matt. 17:1-8; Mark 9:2-8* [b]Matt. 17:1 [c]Matt. 5:1 [d]Luke 3:21; 5:16; 6:12; 9:18
29 [1]Lit., *flashing like lightning* [a]Luke 3:21; 5:16; 6:12; 9:18 [b]Mark 16:12
31 [1]Or, *splendor* [a]2 Pet. 1:15
32 [a]Matt. 26:43; Mark 14:40
33 [1]Lit., *they* [2]Or, *sacred tents* [a]Luke 5:5; 9:49 [b]Matt. 17:4; Mark 9:5 [c]Mark 9:6
34 [1]Or, *occurred*
35 [a]2 Pet. 1:17f. [b]Is. 42:1; Matt. 3:17; 12:18; Mark 1:11; Luke 3:22
36 [1]Lit., *occurred* [a]Matt. 17:9; Mark 9:9f.
37 [a]Luke 9:37-42: *Matt. 17:14-18; Mark 9:14-27*
38 [1]Or, *only begotten*

mouth, and as it mauls him, it scarcely
leaves him.
40 "And I begged Your disciples to cast
it out, and they could not."
41 And Jesus answered and said, "O
unbelieving and perverted generation,
how long shall I be with you, and put up
with you? Bring your son here."
42 And while he was still approaching,
the demon [1]dashed him *to the ground,*
and threw him into a convulsion. But
Jesus rebuked the unclean spirit, and
healed the boy, and gave him back to his
father.
43 And they were all amazed at the
[1a]greatness of God.
[b]But while everyone was marveling at
all that He was doing, He said to His
disciples,
44 "Let these words sink into your
ears; [a]for the Son of Man is going to be
[1]delivered into the hands of men."
45 But [a]they [1]did not understand this
statement, and it was concealed from
them so that they might not perceive it;
and they were afraid to ask Him about
this statement.

The Test of Greatness

46 [a]And an argument [1]arose among
them as to which of them might be the
greatest.
47 But Jesus, [a]knowing [1]what they
were thinking in their heart, took a child
and stood him by His side,
48 and said to them, "[a]Whoever receives this child in My name receives
Me; and whoever receives Me receives
Him who sent Me; [b]for he who is [1]least
among you, this is the one who is great."
49 [a]And John answered and said,
"[b]Master, we saw someone casting out
demons in Your name; and we tried to
hinder him because he does not follow
along with us."
50 But Jesus said to him, "Do not
hinder *him;* [a]for he who is not against
you is [1]for you."
51 And it came about, when the days
were approaching for [a]His [1]ascension,
that He resolutely set His face [b]to go to
Jerusalem;
52 and He sent messengers on ahead
of Him. And they went, and entered a
village of the [a]Samaritans, to [1]make
arrangements for Him.
53 And they did not receive Him,
[a]because [1]He was journeying with His
face toward Jerusalem.
54 And when His disciples [a]James and
John saw *this,* they said, "Lord, do You
want us to [b]command fire to come down
from heaven and consume them[1]?"
55 But He turned and rebuked them,
[[1]and said, "You do not know what kind
of spirit you are of;
56 for the Son of Man did not come to
destroy men's lives, but to save them."]
And they went on to another village.

Exacting Discipleship

57 And [a]as they were going along the
road, [b]someone said to Him, "I will
follow You wherever You go."
58 And Jesus said to him, "The foxes
have holes, and the birds of the [1]air *have*
[2]nests, but [a]the Son of Man has nowhere
to lay His head."
59 And He said to another, "[a]Follow
Me." But he said, "[1]Permit me first to go
and bury my father."
60 But He said to him, "Allow the
dead to bury their own dead; but as for
you, go and [a]proclaim everywhere the
kingdom of God."
61 And another also said, "I will
follow You, Lord; but [a]first permit me
to say good-bye to those at home."
62 But Jesus said to him, "[a]No one,
after putting his hand to the plow and
looking back, is fit for the kingdom of
God."

The Seventy Sent Out

10 NOW after this [a]the Lord appointed [1]seventy [b]others, and
sent them [c]two and two ahead of Him to
every city and place where He Himself
was going to come.
2 And He was saying to them, "[a]The
harvest is plentiful, but the laborers are
few; therefore beseech the Lord of the
harvest to send out laborers into His
harvest.
3 "Go your ways; [a]behold, I send you
out as lambs in the midst of wolves.
4 "[a]Carry no purse, no [1]bag, no shoes;
and greet no one on the way.
5 "And whatever house you enter, first
say, 'Peace *be* to this house.'
6 "And if a [1]man of peace is there,
your peace will rest upon him; but if not,
it will return to you.
7 "And stay in [1]that house, eating and
drinking [2]what they give you; for [a]the
laborer is worthy of his wages. Do not
keep moving from house to house.
8 "And whatever city you enter, and
they receive you, [a]eat what is set before
you;
9 and heal those in it who are sick,
and say to them, '[a]The kingdom of God
has come near to you.'
10 "But whatever city you enter and
they do not receive you, go out into its
streets and say,
11 '[a]Even the dust of your city which
clings to our feet, we wipe off *in protest*
against you; yet [1]be sure of this, that
[b]the kingdom of God has come near.'
12 "I say to you, [a]it will be more
tolerable in that day for [b]Sodom, than
for that city.
13 "[a]Woe to you, [b]Chorazin! Woe to
you, [b]Bethsaida! For if the [1]miracles had
been performed in [b]Tyre and Sidon
which occurred in you, they would have
repented long ago, sitting in [c]sackcloth
and ashes.

42 [1]Or, *tore him*
43 [1]Or, *majesty*
[a]2 Pet. 1:16 [b]Luke 9:43-45: *Matt. 17:22f.; Mark 9:30-32*
44 [1]Or, *betrayed*
[a]Luke 9:22
45 [1]Lit., *were not knowing*
[a]Mark 9:32
46 [1]Lit., *entered in*
[a]Luke 9:46-48: *Matt. 18:1-5; Mark 9:33-37;* Luke 22:24
47 [1]Lit., *the reasoning;* or, *argument*
[a]Matt. 9:4
48 [1]Or, *lowliest*
[a]Matt. 10:40; Luke 10:16; John 13:20
[b]Luke 22:26
49 [a]Luke 9:49, 50: *Mark 9:38-40* [b]Luke 5:5; 9:33
50 [1]Or, *on your side*
[a]Matt. 12:30; Luke 11:23
51 [1]Lit., *taking up*
[a]Mark 16:19 [b]Luke 13:22; 17:11; 18:31; 19:11, 28
52 [1]Or, *prepare*
[a]Matt. 10:5; Luke 10:33; 17:16; John 4:4
53 [1]Lit., *His face was proceeding toward*
[a]John 4:9
54 [1]Some mss. add *as Elijah did*
[a]Mark 3:17 [b]2 Kin. 1:9-16
55 [1]Many mss. do not contain bracketed portion
57 [a]Luke 9:51
[b]Luke 9:57-60: *Matt. 8:19-22*
58 [1]Or, *sky* [2]Or, *roosting-places*
[a]Matt. 8:20
59 [1]Some mss. add *Lord*
[a]Matt. 8:22
60 [a]Matt. 4:23
61 [a]1 Kin. 19:20
62 [a]Phil. 3:13

1 [1]Some mss. read *seventy-two*
[a]Luke 7:13 [b]Luke 9:1f., 52 [c]Mark 6:7
2 [a]Matt. 9:37, 38; John 4:35
3 [a]Matt. 10:16
4 [1]Or, *knapsack or beggar's bag*
[a]Matt. 10:9-14; Mark 6:8-11; Luke 9:3-5; 10:4-12
6 [1]Lit., *son*
7 [1]Or, *the house itself* [2]Lit., *the things from them*
[a]Matt. 10:10; 1 Cor. 9:14; 1 Tim. 5:18
8 [a]1 Cor. 10:27
9 [a]Matt. 3:2; 10:7; Luke 10:11
11 [1]Lit., *know*
[a]Matt. 10:14; Mark 6:11; Luke 9:5; Acts 13:51 [b]Matt. 3:2; 10:7; Luke 10:9
12 [a]Gen. 19:24-28; Matt. 10:15; 11:24
[b]Matt. 10:15
13 [1]Or, *works of power*
[a]Luke 10:13-15: *Matt. 11:21-23* [b]Is. 23:1-18; Ezek. 26:1-28:26; Joel 3:4-8; Matt. 11:21 [c]Rev. 11:3

14 "But it will be more tolerable for [a]Tyre and Sidon in the judgment, than for you.

15 "And you, [a]Capernaum, will not be exalted to heaven, will you? You will be brought down to Hades!

16 "[a]The one who listens to you listens to Me, and [b]the one who rejects you rejects Me; and he who rejects Me rejects the One who sent Me."

The Happy Results

17 And the [1]seventy returned with joy, saying, "Lord, even [a]the demons are subject to us in Your name."

18 And He said to them, "I was watching [a]Satan fall from heaven like lightning.

19 "Behold, I have given you authority to [a]tread upon serpents and scorpions, and over all the power of the enemy, and nothing shall injure you.

20 "Nevertheless do not rejoice in this, that the spirits are subject to you, but rejoice that [a]your names are recorded in heaven."

21 [a]At that very [1]time He rejoiced greatly in the Holy Spirit, and said, "I [2]praise Thee, O Father, Lord of heaven and earth, that Thou didst hide these things from *the* wise and intelligent and didst reveal them to babes. Yes, Father, for thus it was well-pleasing in Thy sight.

22 "[a]All things have been handed over to Me by My Father, and [b]no one knows who the Son is except the Father, and who the Father is except the Son, and anyone to whom the Son wills to reveal *Him.*"

23 [a]And turning to the disciples, He said privately, "Blessed *are* the eyes which see the things you see,

24 for I say to you, that many prophets and kings wished to see the things which you see, and did not see *them,* and to hear the things which you hear, and did not hear *them.*"

25 [a]And behold, a certain [1b]lawyer stood up and put Him to the test, saying, "Teacher, what shall I do to inherit eternal life?"

26 And He said to him, "What is written in the Law? How [1]does it read to you?"

27 And he answered and said, "[a]YOU SHALL LOVE THE LORD YOUR GOD WITH ALL YOUR HEART, AND WITH ALL YOUR SOUL, AND WITH ALL YOUR STRENGTH, AND WITH ALL YOUR MIND; AND YOUR NEIGHBOR AS YOURSELF."

28 And He said to him, "You have answered correctly; [a]DO THIS, AND YOU WILL LIVE."

29 But wishing [a]to justify himself, he said to Jesus, "And who is my neighbor?"

The Good Samaritan

30 Jesus replied and said, "A certain man was [a]going down from Jerusalem to Jericho; and he fell among robbers, and they stripped him and [1]beat him, and went off leaving him half dead.

31 "And by chance a certain priest was going down on that road, and when he saw him, he passed by on the other side.

32 "And likewise a Levite also, when he came to the place and saw him, passed by on the other side.

33 "But a certain [a]Samaritan, who was on a journey, came upon him; and when he saw him, he felt compassion,

34 and came to him, and bandaged up his wounds, pouring oil and wine on *them;* and he put him on his own beast, and brought him to an inn, and took care of him.

35 "And on the next day he took out two [1]denarii and gave them to the innkeeper and said, 'Take care of him; and whatever more you spend, when I return, I will repay you.'

36 "Which of these three do you think proved to be a neighbor to the man who fell into the robbers' *hands?*"

37 And he said, "The one who showed mercy toward him." And Jesus said to him, "Go and do [1]the same."

Martha and Mary

38 Now as they were traveling along, He entered a certain village; and a [1]woman named [a]Martha welcomed Him into her home.

39 And she had a sister called [a]Mary, who moreover was listening to the Lord's word, [b]seated at His feet.

40 But [a]Martha was distracted with [1]all her preparations; and she came up *to Him,* and said, "Lord, do You not care that my sister has left me to do all the serving alone? Then tell her to help me."

41 But the Lord answered and said to her, "[a]Martha, Martha, you are [b]worried and bothered about so many things;

42 [1a]but *only* a few things are necessary, [2]really *only* one, for [b]Mary has chosen the good part, which shall not be taken away from her."

Instruction about Prayer

11 AND it came about that while He was praying in a certain place, after He had finished, one of His disciples said to Him, "Lord, teach us to pray just as John also taught his disciples."

2 And He said to them, "[a]When you pray, say:

'[1]Father, hallowed be Thy name.
Thy kingdom come.
3 'Give us [a]each day our [1]daily bread.
4 'And forgive us our sins,
For we ourselves also forgive everyone who [a]is indebted to us.
And lead us not into temptation.' "

5 And He said to them, "[1]Suppose one of you shall have a friend, and shall go to him at midnight, and say to him, 'Friend, lend me three loaves;

14 [a]Matt. 11:21
15 [a]Is. 14:13-15; Matt. 4:13; 11:23
16 [a]Matt. 10:40; Mark 9:37; Luke 9:48; John 13:20; Gal. 4:14 [b]John 12:48; 1 Thess. 4:8
17 [1]Some mss. read *seventy-two* [a]Mark 16:17
18 [a]Matt. 4:10
19 [a]Ps. 91:13; Mark 16:18
20 [a]Ex. 32:32; Ps. 69:28; Is. 4:3; Ezek. 13:9; Dan. 12:1; Phil. 4:3; Heb. 12:23; Rev. 3:5; 13:8; 17:8; 20:12, 15; 21:27
21 [1]Lit., *hour* [2]Or, *acknowledge to Thy praise* [a]Luke 10:21, 22: *Matt. 11:25-27*
22 [a]John 3:35 [b]John 10:15
23 [a]Luke 10:23, 24: *Matt. 13:16, 17*
25 [1]I.e., an expert in the Mosaic Law [a]Luke 10:25-28: *Matt. 22:34-40; Mark 12:28-31;* Matt. 19:16-19 [b]Matt. 22:35
26 [1]Lit., *do you read?*
27 [a]Deut. 6:5; Lev. 19:18
28 [a]Lev. 18:5; Ezek. 20:11; Matt. 19:17
29 [a]Luke 16:15
30 [1]Lit., *laid blows upon* [a]Luke 18:31; 19:28
33 [a]Matt. 10:5; Luke 9:52
35 [1]The denarius was equivalent to one day's wage
37 [1]Or, *likewise*
38 [1]Lit., *certain woman* [a]Luke 10:40f.; John 11:1, 5, 19ff., 30, 39; 12:2
39 [a]Luke 10:42; John 11:1f., 19f., 28, 31f., 45; 12:3 [b]Luke 8:35; Acts 22:3
40 [1]Lit., *much service* [a]Luke 10:38, 41; John 11:1, 5, 19ff., 30, 39; 12:2
41 [a]Luke 10:38, 40; John 11:1, 5, 19ff., 30, 39; 12:2 [b]Matt. 6:25
42 [1]Some mss. read *but one thing is necessary* [2]Lit., *or* [a]Ps. 27:4; John 6:27 [b]Luke 10:39; John 11:1f., 19f., 28, 31f., 45; 12:3

2 [1]Some mss. insert phrases from Matt. 6:9-13 to make the two passages closely similar [a]Luke 11:2-4: *Matt. 6:9-13*
3 [1]Or, *bread for the coming day* or *needful bread* [a]Acts 17:11
4 [a]Luke 13:4 mg.
5 [1]Lit., *Which one of you*

6 for a friend of mine has come to me
from a journey, and I have nothing to set
before him';
7 and from inside he shall answer
and say, 'Do not bother me; the door
has already been shut and my children
[1]and I are in bed; I cannot get up and
give you *anything*.'
8 "I tell you, even though he will not
get up and give him *anything* because he
is his friend, yet [a]because of his [1]persis-
tence he will get up and give him as
much as he needs.
9 "And I say to you, [1a]ask, and it shall
be given to you; [2]seek, and you shall
find; [3]knock, and it shall be opened to
you.
10 "For everyone who asks, receives;
and he who seeks, finds; and to him who
knocks, it shall be opened.
11 "Now [1]suppose one of you fathers is
asked by his son for a [2]fish; he will not
give him a snake instead of a fish, will
he?
12 "Or *if* he is asked for an egg, he will
not give him a scorpion, will he?
13 "[a]If you then, being evil, know how
to give good gifts to your children, how
much more shall *your* [1]heavenly Father
give the Holy Spirit to those who ask
Him?"

Pharisees' Blasphemy

14 [a]And He was casting out a demon,
and it was dumb; and it came about that
when the demon had gone out, the dumb
man spoke; and the multitudes marveled.
15 But some of them said, "He casts
out demons [a]by [1b]Beelzebul, the ruler of
the demons."
16 And others, [1]to test *Him*, [a]were
demanding of Him a [2]sign from heaven.
17 [a]But He knew their thoughts, and
said to them, "[1]Any kingdom divided
against itself is laid waste; and a house
divided against [2]itself falls.
18 "And if [a]Satan also is divided
against himself, how shall his kingdom
stand? For you say that I cast out
demons by [b]Beelzebul.
19 "And if I by [a]Beelzebul cast out
demons, by whom do your sons cast
them out? Consequently they shall be
your judges.
20 "But if I cast out demons by the
[a]finger of God, then [b]the kingdom of
God has come upon you.
21 "When [1]a strong *man*, fully armed,
guards his own homestead, his possessions are [2]undisturbed;
22 but when someone stronger than he
attacks him and overpowers him, he
takes away from him all his armor on
which he had relied, and distributes his
plunder.
23 "[a]He who is not with Me is against
Me; and he who does not gather with
Me, scatters.
24 "[a]When the unclean spirit goes out
of [1]a man, it passes through waterless
places seeking rest, and not finding any,
it says, 'I will return to my house from
which I came.'
25 "And when it comes, it finds it
swept and put in order.
26 "Then it goes and takes *along* seven
other spirits more evil than itself, and
they go in and live there; and the last
state of that man becomes worse than
the first."
27 And it came about while He said
these things, one of the women in the
crowd raised her voice, and said to Him,
"[a]Blessed is the womb that bore You,
and the breasts at which You nursed."
28 But He said, "On the contrary,
blessed are [a]those who hear the word of
God, and observe it."

The Sign of Jonah

29 And as the crowds were increasing,
He began to say, "[a]This generation is a
wicked generation; it [b]seeks for a [1]sign,
and *yet* no [1]sign shall be given to it but
the [1]sign of Jonah.
30 "For just as [a]Jonah became a [1]sign
to the Ninevites, so shall the Son of Man
be to this generation.
31 "The [a]Queen of the South shall rise
up with the men of this generation at the
judgment and condemn them, because
she came from the ends of the earth to
hear the wisdom of Solomon; and behold, something greater than Solomon is
here.
32 "The men of Nineveh shall stand up
with this generation at the judgment and
condemn it, because [a]they repented at
the preaching of Jonah; and behold,
something greater than Jonah is here.
33 "[a]No one, after lighting a lamp, puts
it away in a cellar, nor under a peck-
measure, but on the lampstand, in order
that those who enter may see the light.
34 "[a]The lamp of your body is your
eye; when your eye is [1]clear, your whole
body also is full of light; but when it is
bad, your body also is full of darkness.
35 "Then watch out that the light in
you may not be darkness.
36 "If therefore your whole body is full
of light, with no dark part in it, it shall
be wholly illumined, as when the lamp
illumines you with its rays."

Woes upon the Pharisees

37 Now when He had spoken, a Pharisee *asked Him to have lunch with him;
and He went in, and reclined *at the table.*
38 And when the Pharisee saw it, he
was surprised that He had not first
[1a]ceremonially washed before the [2]meal.
39 But [a]the Lord said to him, "Now
[b]you Pharisees clean the outside of the
cup and of the platter; but [1]inside of
you, you are full of robbery and wickedness.
40 "[a]You foolish ones, did not He who
made the outside make the inside also?

7 [1]Lit., *with me*
8 [1]Or, *shamelessness* [a]Luke 18:1-5
9 [1]Or, *keep asking* [2]Or, *keep seeking* [3]Or, *keep knocking* [a]Luke 11:9-13: *Matt. 7:7-11*
11 [1]Lit., *which of you, a son, shall ask the father* [2]Some early mss. insert *loaf, he will not give him a stone, will he, or for a*
13 [1]Lit., *Father from heaven* [a]Matt. 7:11; Luke 18:7f.
14 [a]Luke 11:14, 15: *Matt. 12:22, 24;* Matt. 9:32-34
15 [1]Here and in vv. 18 and 19 some mss. read *Beezebul* [a]Matt. 9:34 [b]Matt. 10:25
16 [1]Lit., *were testing* [2]Or, *attesting miracle* [a]Matt. 12:38; 16:1; Mark 8:11
17 [1]Lit., *every* [2]Lit., *a house* [a]Luke 11:17-22: *Matt. 12:25-29; Mark 3:23-27*
18 [a]Matt. 4:10 [b]Matt. 10:25
19 [a]Matt. 10:25
20 [a]Ex. 8:19 [b]Matt. 3:2
21 [1]Lit., *the* [2]Lit., *in peace*
23 [a]Matt. 12:30; Mark 9:40
24 [1]Lit., *the* [a]Luke 11:24-26: *Matt. 12:43-45*
27 [a]Luke 23:29
28 [a]Luke 8:21
29 [1]Or, *attesting miracle* [a]Luke 11:29-32: *Matt. 12:39-42;* Matt. 16:4; Mark 8:12 [b]Matt. 12:38; Luke 11:16
30 [1]Or, *attesting miracle* [a]Jon. 3:4
31 [a]1 Kin. 10:1-10; 2 Chr. 9:1-12
32 [a]Jon. 3:5
33 [a]Matt. 5:15; Mark 4:21; Luke 8:16
34 [1]Or, *healthy* [a]Luke 11:34, 35: *Matt. 6:22, 23*
38 [1]Lit., *baptized* [2]Or, *lunch* [a]Matt. 15:2; Mark 7:3f.
39 [1]Lit., *your inside is full* [a]Luke 7:13 [b]Matt. 23:25f.
40 [a]Luke 12:20; 1 Cor. 15:36

41 "But [a]give that which is within as
charity, and [1]then all things are [b]clean
for you.
42 "[a]But woe to you Pharisees! For you
[b]pay tithe of mint and rue and every
kind of garden herb, and *yet* disregard
justice and the love of God; but these
are the things you should have done
without neglecting the others.
43 "Woe to you Pharisees! For you
[a]love the front seats in the synagogues,
and the respectful greetings in the market places.
44 "[a]Woe to you! For you are like
[1]concealed tombs, and the people who
walk over *them* are unaware *of it.*"
45 And one of the [1a]lawyers *said to
Him in reply, "Teacher, when You say
this, You insult us too."
46 But He said, "Woe to you [a]lawyers
as well! For [b]you weigh men down with
burdens hard to bear, [1]while you yourselves will not even touch the burdens
with one of your fingers.
47 "[a]Woe to you! For you build the
[1]tombs of the prophets, and *it was* your
fathers *who* killed them.
48 "Consequently, you are witnesses
and approve the deeds of your fathers;
because it was they who killed them, and
you build *their tombs.*
49 "For this reason also [a]the wisdom of
God said, '[b]I will send to them prophets
and apostles, and *some* of them they will
kill and *some* they will [1]persecute,
50 in order that the blood of all the
prophets, shed [a]since the foundation of
the world, may be [1]charged against this
generation,
51 from [a]the blood of Abel to [b]the
blood of Zechariah, who perished between the altar and the house *of God;*
yes, I tell you, it shall be [1]charged
against this generation.'
52 "Woe to you [1a]lawyers! For you
have taken away the key of knowledge;
[b]you did not enter in yourselves, and
those who were entering in you hindered."
53 And when He left there, the scribes
and the Pharisees began to be very
hostile and to question Him closely on
many subjects,
54 [a]plotting against Him, [b]to catch
[1]*Him* in something He might say.

God Knows and Cares

12 UNDER these circumstances,
after [1]so many thousands of the
multitude had gathered together that
they were stepping on one another, He
began saying to His disciples first *of all,*
"[a]Beware of the leaven of the Pharisees,
which is hypocrisy.
2 "[a]But there is nothing covered up
that will not be revealed, and hidden
that will not be known.
3 "Accordingly, whatever you have
said in the dark shall be heard in the
light, and what you have [1]whispered in

41 [1]Lit., *behold* [a]Luke 12:33; 16:9 [b]Mark 7:19; Titus 1:15
42 [a]Matt. 23:23 [b]Lev. 27:30; Luke 18:12
43 [a]Matt. 23:6f.; Mark 12:38f.; Luke 14:7; 20:46
44 [1]Or, *indistinct, unseen* [a]Matt. 23:27
45 [1]I.e., experts in the Mosaic Law [a]Matt. 22:35; Luke 11:46, 52
46 [1]Lit., *and* [a]Matt. 22:35; Luke 11:45, 52 [b]Matt. 23:4
47 [1]Or, *monuments to* [a]Matt. 23:29ff.
49 [1]Or, *drive out* [a]1 Cor. 1:24, 30; Col. 2:3 [b]Matt. 23:34-36
50 [1]Or, *required of* [a]Matt. 25:34
51 [1]Or, *required of* [a]Gen. 4:8 [b]2 Chr. 24:20, 21
52 [1]I.e., experts in the Mosaic Law [a]Matt. 22:35; Luke 11:45, 46 [b]Matt. 23:13
54 [1]Lit., *something out of His mouth* [a]Mark 3:2; Luke 20:20; Acts 23:21 [b]Mark 12:13

1 [1]Lit., *myriads* [a]Matt. 16:6, 11f.; Mark 8:15
2 [a]Luke 12:2-9: *Matt. 10:26-33;* Matt. 10:26; Mark 4:22; Luke 8:17
3 [1]Lit., *spoken in the ear* [a]Matt. 10:27; 24:17
4 [a]John 15:13-15
5 [1]Or, *show* [2]Gr., *Gehenna* [a]Heb. 10:31 [b]Matt. 5:22
6 [1]Gr., *assaria,* the smallest of copper coins [a]Matt. 10:29
7 [a]Matt. 10:30
8 [a]Matt. 10:32; Luke 15:10; Rom. 10:9
9 [a]Matt. 10:33; Luke 9:26 [b]Luke 15:10
10 [a]Matt. 12:31, 32; Mark 3:28-30
11 [a]Matt. 10:17 [b]Matt. 6:25; 10:19; Mark 13:11; Luke 12:22; 21:14
12 [a]Matt. 10:20; Luke 21:15
13 [1]Lit., *out of*
14 [a]Mic. 6:8; Rom. 2:1, 3; 9:20
15 [a]1 Tim. 6:6-10
19 [a]Eccl. 11:9
20 [1]Lit., *they are demanding your soul from you* [a]Jer. 17:11; Luke 11:40 [b]Job 27:8 [c]Ps. 39:6
21 [a]Luke 12:33

the inner rooms shall be proclaimed
upon [a]the housetops.
4 "And I say to you, [a]My friends, do
not be afraid of those who kill the body,
and after that have no more that they
can do.
5 "But I will [1]warn you whom to fear:
[a]fear the One who after He has killed has
authority to cast into [2b]hell; yes, I tell
you, fear Him!
6 "Are not [a]five sparrows sold for two
[1]cents? And *yet* not one of them is
forgotten before God.
7 "[a]Indeed, the very hairs of your
head are all numbered. Do not fear; you
are of more value than many sparrows.
8 "And I say to you, everyone who
[a]confesses Me before men, the Son of
Man shall confess him also before the
angels of God;
9 but [a]he who denies Me before men
shall be denied [b]before the angels of
God.
10 "[a]And everyone who will speak a
word against the Son of Man, it shall be
forgiven him; but he who blasphemes
against the Holy Spirit, it shall not be
forgiven him.
11 "And when they bring you before
[a]the synagogues and the rulers and the
authorities, do not become [b]anxious
about how or what you should speak in
your defense, or what you should say;
12 for [a]the Holy Spirit will teach you
in that very hour what you ought to
say."

Covetousness Denounced

13 And someone [1]in the crowd said to
Him, "Teacher, tell my brother to divide
the *family* inheritance with me."
14 But He said to him, "[a]Man, who
appointed Me a judge or arbiter over
you?"
15 And He said to them, "[a]Beware,
and be on your guard against every form
of greed; for not *even* when one has an
abundance does his life consist of his
possessions."
16 And He told them a parable, saying, "The land of a certain rich man was
very productive.
17 "And he began reasoning to himself,
saying, 'What shall I do, since I have no
place to store my crops?'
18 "And he said, 'This is what I will do:
I will tear down my barns and build
larger ones, and there I will store all my
grain and my goods.
19 'And I will say to my soul, "Soul,
[a]you have many goods laid up for many
years *to come;* take your ease, eat, drink
and be merry." '
20 "But God said to him, '[a]You fool!
This *very* night [1b]your soul is required of
you; and [c]*now* who will own what you
have prepared?'
21 "So is the man who [a]lays up treasure
for himself, and is not rich toward God."

22 And He said to His disciples, "[a]For
this reason I say to you, do not be
anxious for *your* [1]life, *as to* what you
shall eat; nor for your body, *as to* what
you shall put on.
23 "For life is more than food, and the
body than clothing.
24 "Consider the [a]ravens, for they
neither sow nor reap; and they have no
storeroom nor [b]barn; and *yet* God feeds
them; how much more valuable you are
than the birds!
25 "And which of you by being anxious
can add a *single* [1a]cubit to his [2]life's
span?
26 "If then you cannot do even a very
little thing, why are you anxious about
other matters?
27 "Consider the lilies, how [1]they grow;
they neither toil nor spin; but I tell you,
even [a]Solomon in all his glory did not
clothe himself like one of these.
28 "But if God so arrays the grass in
the field, which is *alive* today and tomorrow is thrown into the furnace, how
much more *will He clothe* you, [a]O men of
little faith!
29 "And do not seek what you shall eat,
and what you shall drink, and do not
[a]keep worrying.
30 "For [1]all these things the nations of
the world eagerly seek; but your Father
knows that you need these things.
31 "But seek for His kingdom, and
[a]these things shall be added to you.
32 "[a]Do not be afraid, [b]little flock, for
[c]your Father has chosen gladly to give
you the kingdom.
33 "[a]Sell your possessions and give to
charity; make yourselves purses which
do not wear out, [b]an unfailing treasure
in heaven, where no thief comes near,
nor moth destroys.
34 "For [a]where your treasure is, there
will your heart be also.

Be in Readiness

35 "[1a]Be dressed in [b]readiness, and
keep your lamps alight.
36 "And be like men who are waiting
for their master when he returns from
the wedding feast, so that they may
immediately open *the door* to him when
he comes and knocks.
37 "Blessed are those slaves whom the
master shall find [a]on the alert when he
comes; truly I say to you, that [b]he will
gird himself *to serve,* and have them
recline *at the table,* and will come up and
wait on them.
38 "[a]Whether he comes in the [1]second
watch, or even in the [2]third, and finds
them so, blessed are those *slaves.*
39 "[a]And [1]be sure of this, that if the
head of the house had known at what
hour the thief was coming, he would not
have allowed his house to be [2b]broken
into.
40 "[a]You too, be ready; for the Son of
Man is coming at an hour that you do
not [1]expect."

22 [1]Or, *soul* [a]Luke 12:22-31: *Matt. 6:25-33*
24 [a]Job 38:41 [b]Luke 12:18
25 [1]I.e., One cubit equals approx. 18 in. [2]Or, *height* [a]Ps. 39:5
27 [1]Some mss. omit *they grow* [a]1 Kin. 10:4-7; 2 Chr. 9:3-6
28 [a]Matt. 6:30
29 [a]Matt. 6:31
30 [1]Or, *these things all the nations of the world*
31 [a]Matt. 6:33
32 [a]Matt. 14:27 [b]John 21:15-17 [c]Eph. 1:5, 9
33 [a]Matt. 19:21; Luke 11:41; 18:22 [b]Matt. 6:20; Luke 12:21
34 [a]Matt. 6:21
35 [1]Lit., *Let your loins be girded* [a]Matt. 25:1ff. [b]Eph. 6:14; 1 Pet. 1:13
37 [a]Matt. 24:42 [b]Luke 17:8; John 13:4
38 [1]I.e., 9 p.m. to midnight [2]I.e., midnight to 3 a.m. [a]Matt. 24:43
39 [1]Lit., *know* [2]Lit., *dug through* [a]Luke 12:39, 40: *Matt. 24:43, 44* [b]Matt. 6:19
40 [1]Lit., *think, suppose* [a]Mark 13:33; Luke 21:36
41 [a]Luke 12:47, 48
42 [1]Lit., *service* [a]Luke 7:13 [b]Luke 12:42-46: *Matt. 24:45-51* [c]Matt. 24:45; Luke 16:1ff.
43 [1]Or, *lord* [a]Luke 12:42
45 [1]Lit., *is delaying to come*
47 [a]Deut. 25:2; James 4:17
48 [1]Lit., *blows* [a]Lev. 5:17; Num. 15:29f. [b]Matt. 13:12
49 [1]Or, *came* [2]Lit., *what do I wish if . . . ?*
50 [1]Lit., *be baptized with* [a]Mark 10:38
51 [a]Luke 12:51-53: *Matt. 10:34-36*
53 [a]Mic. 7:6; Matt. 10:21
54 [a]Matt. 16:2f.
55 [a]Matt. 20:12
56 [1]Lit., *how* [a]Matt. 16:3
57 [a]Luke 21:30
58 [1]Lit., *be released from him* [a]Luke 12:58, 59: *Matt. 5:25, 26*

41 And Peter said, "Lord, are You
addressing this parable to us, or [a]to
everyone *else* as well?"
42 And [a]the Lord said, "[b]Who then is
the faithful and sensible [c]steward, whom
his master will put in charge of his
[1]servants, to give them their rations at
the proper time?
43 "Blessed is that [a]slave whom his
[1]master finds so doing when he comes.
44 "Truly I say to you, that he will put
him in charge of all his possessions.
45 "But if that slave says in his heart,
'My master [1]will be a long time in
coming,' and begins to beat the slaves,
both men and women, and to eat and
drink and get drunk;
46 the master of that slave will come
on a day when he does not expect *him,*
and at an hour he does not know, and
will cut him in pieces, and assign him a
place with the unbelievers.
47 "And that slave who knew his master's will and did not get ready or act in
accord with his will, shall [a]receive many
lashes,
48 but the one who did not [a]know *it,*
and committed deeds worthy of [1]a flog-
ging, will receive but few. [b]And from
everyone who has been given much shall
much be required; and to whom they
entrusted much, of him they will ask all
the more.

Christ Divides Men

49 "I [1]have come to cast fire upon the
earth; and [2]how I wish it were already
kindled!
50 "But I have a [a]baptism to [1]undergo,
and how distressed I am until it is
accomplished!
51 "[a]Do you suppose that I came to
grant peace on earth? I tell you, no, but
rather division;
52 for from now on five *members* in
one household will be divided, three
against two, and two against three.
53 "They will be divided, [a]father
against son, and son against father;
mother against daughter, and daughter
against mother; mother-in-law against
daughter-in-law, and daughter-in-law
against mother-in-law."
54 And He was also saying to the
multitudes, "[a]When you see a cloud
rising in the west, immediately you say,
'A shower is coming,' and so it turns out.
55 "And when *you see* a south wind
blowing, you say, 'It will be a [a]hot day,'
and it turns out *that way.*
56 "You hypocrites! [a]You know how to
analyze the appearance of the earth and
the sky, but [1]why do you not analyze
this present time?
57 "And [a]why do you not even on your
own initiative judge what is right?
58 "For [a]while you are going with your
opponent to appear before the magis-
trate, on *your* way *there* make an effort
to [1]settle with him, in order that he may
not drag you before the judge, and the

judge turn you over to the constable, and
the constable throw you into prison.
59"I say to you, you shall not get out
of there until you have paid the very last
[1a]cent."

Call to Repent

13 NOW on the same occasion there
were some present who reported
to Him about the Galileans, whose
blood [a]Pilate had [1]mingled with their
sacrifices.
2 And He answered and said to
them, "[a]Do you suppose that these
Galileans were *greater* sinners than all
other Galileans, because they suffered
this *fate?*
3"I tell you, no, but, unless you
[1]repent, you will all likewise perish.
4"Or do you suppose that those
eighteen on whom the tower in [a]Siloam
fell and killed them, were *worse* [1b]cul-
prits than all the men who live in Jerusalem?
5"I tell you, no, but unless you repent, you will all likewise perish."
6 And He *began* telling this parable:
"A certain man had [a]a fig tree which had
been planted in his vineyard; and he
came looking for fruit on it, and did not
find any.
7"And he said to the vineyard-keeper,
'Behold, for three years I have come
looking for fruit on this fig tree [1]without
finding any. [a]Cut it down! Why does it
even use up the ground?'
8"And he answered and said to him,
'Let it alone, sir, for this year too, until I
dig around it and put in fertilizer;
9 and if it bears fruit next year, *fine;*
but if not, cut it down.' "

Healing on the Sabbath

10 And He was [a]teaching in one of the
synagogues on the Sabbath.
11 And behold, there was a woman
who for eighteen years had had [a]a sickness caused by a spirit; and she was bent
double, and could not straighten up at
all.
12 And when Jesus saw her, He called
her over and said to her, "Woman, you
are freed from your sickness."
13 And He [a]laid His hands upon her;
and immediately she was made erect
again, and *began* [b]glorifying God.
14 And [a]the synagogue official, indignant because Jesus [b]had healed on the
Sabbath, *began* saying to the multitude
in response, "[c]There are six days in
which work should be done; therefore
come during them and get healed, and
not on the Sabbath day."
15 But [a]the Lord answered him and
said, "You hypocrites, [b]does not each of
you on the Sabbath untie his ox or his
donkey from the stall, and lead him
away to water *him?*
16"And this woman, [a]a daughter of
Abraham as she is, whom [b]Satan has
bound for eighteen long years, should
she not have been released from this
bond on the Sabbath day?"
17 And as He said this, all His opponents were being humiliated; and [a]the
entire multitude was rejoicing over all
the glorious things being done by Him.

Parables of Mustard Seed and Leaven

18 Therefore [a]He was saying, "[b]What
is the kingdom of God like, and to what
shall I compare it?
19"It is like a mustard seed, which a
man took and threw into his own garden; and it grew and became a tree; and
[a]THE BIRDS OF THE [1]AIR NESTED IN ITS
BRANCHES."
20 And again He said, "[a]To what shall
I compare the kingdom of God?
21"[a]It is like leaven, which a woman
took and hid in [b]three [1]pecks of meal,
until it was all leavened."

Teaching in the Villages

22 And He was passing through from
one city and village to another, teaching,
and [a]proceeding on His way to Jerusalem.
23 And someone said to Him, "Lord,
are there *just* a few who are being
saved?" And He said to them,
24"[a]Strive to enter by the narrow
door; for many, I tell you, will seek to
enter and will not be [1]able.
25"Once the head of the house gets up
and [a]shuts the door, and you begin to
stand outside and knock on the door,
saying, '[b]Lord, open up to us!' [1]then He
will answer and say to you, '[c]I do not
know where you are from.'
26"Then you will [a]begin to say, 'We
ate and drank in Your presence, and
You taught in our streets';
27 and He will say, 'I tell you, [a]I do
not know where you are from; [b]DEPART
FROM ME, ALL YOU EVILDOERS.'
28"[a]There will be weeping and gnashing of teeth there when you see Abraham
and Isaac and Jacob and all the prophets
in the kingdom of God, but yourselves
being cast out.
29"And they [a]will come from east and
west, and from north and south, and will
recline *at the table* in the kingdom of
God.
30"And behold, [a]*some* are last who
will be first and *some* are first who will
be last."
31 Just at that time some Pharisees
came up, saying to Him, "Go away and
depart from here, for [a]Herod wants to
kill You."
32 And He said to them, "Go and tell
that fox, 'Behold, I cast out demons and
perform cures today and tomorrow, and
the third *day* I [1a]reach My goal.'
33"Nevertheless [a]I must journey on
today and tomorrow and the next *day;*
for it cannot be that a [b]prophet should
perish outside of Jerusalem.

59 [1]Gr., *lepton;* i.e., 1/128 of a denarius [a]Mark 12:42

1 [1]Or, *shed along with* [a]Matt. 27

2 [a]John 9:2f.

3 [1]Or, *are repentant*

4 [1]Lit., *debtors* [a]Neh. 3:15; Is. 8:6; John 9:7, 11 [b]Matt. 6:12; Luke 11:4

6 [a]Matt. 21:19

7 [1]Lit., *and I do not find* [a]Matt. 3:10; 7:19; Luke 3:9

10 [a]Matt. 4:23

11 [a]Luke 13:16

13 [a]Mark 5:23 [b]Matt. 9:8

14 [a]Mark 5:22 [b]Matt. 12:2; Luke 14:3 [c]Ex. 20:9; Deut. 5:13

15 [a]Luke 7:13 [b]Luke 14:5

16 [a]Luke 19:9 [b]Matt. 4:10; Luke 13:11

17 [a]Luke 18:43

18 [a]Luke 13:18, 19: *Matt. 13:31, 32; Mark 4:30-32* [b]Matt. 13:24; Luke 13:20

19 [1]Or, *sky* [a]Ezek. 17:23

20 [a]Matt. 13:24; Luke 13:18

21 [1]Gr., *sata* [a]Luke 13:20, 21: *Matt. 13:33* [b]Matt. 13:33

22 [a]Luke 9:51

24 [1]Or, *able, once* [a]Matt. 7:13

25 [1]Lit., *and* [a]Matt. 25:10 [b]Matt. 7:22; 25:11 [c]Matt. 7:23; 25:12; Luke 13:27

26 [a]Luke 3:8

27 [a]Luke 13:25 [b]Ps. 6:8; Matt. 25:41

28 [a]Matt. 8:12; 22:13; 25:30

29 [a]Matt. 8:11

30 [a]Matt. 19:30; 20:16; Mark 10:31

31 [a]Matt. 14:1; Luke 3:1; 9:7; 23:7

32 [1]Or possibly, *am perfected* [a]Heb. 2:10; 5:9; 7:28

33 [a]John 11:9 [b]Matt. 21:11

34"[a]O Jerusalem, Jerusalem, *the city*
that kills the prophets and stones those
sent to her! How often I wanted to
gather your children together, [b]just as a
hen *gathers* her brood under her wings,
and you would not *have it!*
35"Behold, your house is left to you
[1]*desolate;* and I say to you, you shall not
see Me until *the time* comes when you
say, '[a]BLESSED IS HE WHO COMES IN THE
NAME OF THE LORD!' "

Jesus Heals on the Sabbath

14 AND it came about when He
went into the house of one of the
[1]leaders of the Pharisees on *the* Sabbath
to eat bread, that [a]they were watching
Him closely.
2 And [1]there, in front of Him was a
certain man suffering from dropsy.
3 And Jesus answered and spoke to
the [1a]lawyers and Pharisees, saying, "[b]Is
it lawful to heal on the Sabbath, or not?"
4 But they kept silent. And He took
hold of him, and healed him, and sent
him away.
5 And He said to them, "[a]Which one
of you shall have a [1]son or an ox fall into
a well, and will not immediately pull him
out on a Sabbath day?"
6 [a]And they could make no reply to
this.

Parable of the Guests

7 And He *began* speaking a parable
to the invited guests when He noticed
how [a]they had been picking out the
places of honor *at the table;* saying to
them,
8"When you are invited by someone
to a wedding feast, [a]do not [1]take the
place of honor, lest someone more distinguished than you may have been
invited by him,
9 and he who invited you both shall
come and say to you, 'Give place to this
man,' and then [a]in disgrace you [1]proceed
to occupy the last place.
10"But when you are invited, go and
recline at the last place, so that when the
one who has invited you comes, he may
say to you, 'Friend, [a]move up higher';
then you will have honor in the sight of
all who [1]are at the table with you.
11"[a]For everyone who exalts himself
shall be humbled, and he who humbles
himself shall be exalted."
12 And He also went on to say to the
one who had invited Him, "When you
give a luncheon or a dinner, do not
invite your friends or your brothers or
your relatives or rich neighbors, lest they
also invite you in return, and repayment
come to you.
13"But when you give a [1]reception,
invite *the* poor, *the* crippled, *the* lame,
the blind,
14 and you will be [1]blessed, since they
[2]do not have *the means* to repay you; for
you will be repaid at [a]the resurrection of
the righteous."
15 And when one of those who were
reclining *at the table* with Him heard
this, he said to Him, "[a]Blessed is everyone who shall eat bread in the kingdom
of God!"

Parable of the Dinner

16 But He said to him, "[a]A certain
man was giving a big dinner, and he
invited many;
17 and at the dinner hour he sent his
slave to say to those who had been
invited, 'Come; for everything is ready
now.'
18"But they all alike began to make
excuses. The first one said to him, 'I have
bought a [1]piece of land and I need to go
out and look at it; [2]please consider me
excused.'
19"And another one said, 'I have
bought five yoke of oxen, and I am going
to try them out; [1]please consider me
excused.'
20"And another one said, '[a]I have
married a wife, and for that reason I
cannot come.'
21"And the slave came *back* and reported this to his master. Then the head
of the household became angry and said
to his slave, 'Go out at once into the
streets and lanes of the city and bring in
here the poor and crippled and blind
and lame.'
22"And the slave said, 'Master, what
you commanded has been done, and still
there is room.'
23"And the master said to the slave,
'Go out into the highways and along the
hedges, and compel *them* to come in,
that my house may be filled.
24 'For I tell you, none of those men
who were invited shall taste of my dinner.' "

Discipleship Tested

25 Now great multitudes were going
along with Him; and He turned and said
to them,
26"[a]If anyone comes to Me, and does
not [1]hate his own father and mother and
wife and children and brothers and
sisters, yes, and even his own life, he
cannot be My disciple.
27"Whoever does not [a]carry his own
cross and come after Me cannot be My
disciple.
28"For which one of you, when he
wants to build a tower, does not first sit
down and calculate the cost, to see if he
has enough to complete it?
29"Otherwise, when he has laid a
foundation, and is not able to finish, all
who observe it begin to ridicule him,
30 saying, 'This man began to build
and was not able to finish.'
31"Or what king, when he sets out to
meet another king in battle, will not first
sit down and take [a]counsel whether he is
strong enough with ten thousand *men* to
encounter the one coming against him
with twenty thousand?

34 [a]Luke 13:34, 35: *Matt. 23:37-39;* Luke 19:41 [b]Matt. 23:37

35 [1]Later mss. add *desolate* [a]Ps. 118:26; Matt. 21:9; Luke 19:38

1 [1]I.e., members of the Sanhedrin [a]Mark 3:2

2 [1]Lit., *behold*

3 [1]I.e., experts in Mosaic Law [a]Matt. 22:35 [b]Matt. 12:2; Luke 13:14

5 [1]Some ancient mss. read *donkey* [a]Matt. 12:11; Luke 13:15

6 [a]Matt. 22:46; Luke 20:40

7 [a]Matt. 23:6

8 [1]Lit., *recline at* [a]Prov. 25:6, 7

9 [1]Lit., *begin* [a]Luke 3:8

10 [1]Lit., *recline at the table* [a]Prov. 25:6, 7

11 [a]2 Sam. 22:28; Prov. 29:23; Matt. 23:12; Luke 1:52; 18:14; James 4:10

13 [1]Or, *banquet*

14 [1]Or, *happy* [2]Or, *are unable to* [a]John 5:29; Acts 24:15; Rev. 20:4, 5

15 [a]Rev. 19:9

16 [a]Matt. 22:2-14; Luke 14:16-24

18 [1]Or, *field* [2]Lit., *I request you*

19 [1]Lit., *I request you*

20 [a]Deut. 24:5; 1 Cor. 7:33

26 [1]I.e., by comparison of his love for Me [a]Matt. 10:37

27 [a]Matt. 10:38; 16:24; Mark 8:34; Luke 9:23

31 [a]Prov. 20:18

32"Or else, while the other is still far
away, he sends [1]a delegation and asks
terms of peace.
33"So therefore, no one of you can be
My disciple who [a]does not give up all his
own possessions.
34"Therefore, salt is good; but [a]if even
salt has become tasteless, with what will
it be seasoned?
35"It is useless either for the soil or for
the manure pile; [1]it is thrown out. [a]He
who has ears to hear, let him hear."

The Lost Sheep

15 NOW all the [1a]tax-gatherers and
the [2]sinners were coming near
Him to listen to Him.
2 And both the Pharisees and the
scribes *began* to [1]grumble, saying, "This
man receives sinners and [a]eats with
them."
3 And He told them this parable,
saying,
4"[a]What man among you, if he has a
hundred sheep and has lost one of them,
does not leave the ninety-nine in the
[1]open pasture, and go after the one
which is lost, until he finds it?
5"And when he has found it, he lays
it on his shoulders, rejoicing.
6"And when he comes home, he calls
together his friends and his neighbors,
saying to them, 'Rejoice with me, for I
have found my sheep which was lost!'
7"I tell you that in the same way,
there will be *more* joy in heaven over one
sinner who repents, than over ninety-
nine righteous persons who need no
repentance.

The Lost Coin

8"Or what woman, if she has ten
[1]silver coins and loses one coin, does not
light a lamp and sweep the house and
search carefully until she finds it?
9"And when she has found it, she
calls together her [1]friends and neighbors,
saying, 'Rejoice with me, for I have
found the coin which I had lost!'
10"In the same way, I tell you, there is
joy [a]in the presence of the angels of God
over one sinner who repents."

The Prodigal Son

11 And He said, "A certain man had
two sons;
12 and the younger of them said to his
father, 'Father, give me [a]the share of the
estate that falls to me.' And he divided
his [1b]wealth between them.
13"And not many days later, the younger son gathered everything together and
went on a journey into a distant country,
and there he squandered his estate with
loose living.
14"Now when he had spent everything, a severe famine occurred in that
country, and he began to be in need.
15"And he went and [1]attached himself
to one of the citizens of that country,
and he sent him into his fields to feed
swine.
16"And he was longing [1]to fill his
[2]stomach with the [3]pods that the swine
were eating, and no one was giving
anything to him.
17"But when he came to [1]his senses, he
said, 'How many of my father's hired
men have more than enough bread, but I
am dying here with hunger!
18 'I will get up and go to my father,
and will say to him, "Father, I have
sinned against heaven, and [1]in your
sight;
19 I am no longer worthy to be called
your son; make me as one of your hired
men." '
20"And he got up and came to [1]his
father. But while he was still a long way
off, his father saw him, and felt compassion *for him,* and ran and [2a]embraced
him, and [3]kissed him.
21"And the son said to him, 'Father, I
have sinned against heaven and in your
sight; I am no longer worthy to be called
your son.[1]'
22"But the father said to his slaves,
'Quickly bring out [a]the best robe and
put it on him, and [b]put a ring on his
hand and sandals on his feet;
23 and bring the fattened calf, kill it,
and let us eat and be merry;
24 for this son of mine was [a]dead, and
has come to life again; he was lost, and
has been found.' And they began to be
merry.
25"Now his older son was in the field,
and when he came and approached the
house, he heard music and dancing.
26"And he summoned one of the
servants and *began* inquiring what these
things might be.
27"And he said to him, 'Your brother
has come, and your father has killed the
fattened calf, because he has received
him back safe and sound.'
28"But he became angry, and was not
willing to go in; and his father came out
and *began* entreating him.
29"But he answered and said to his
father, 'Look! For so many years I have
been serving you, and I have never
[1]neglected a command of yours; and *yet*
you have never given me a [2]kid, that I
might be merry with my friends;
30 but when this son of yours came,
who has devoured your [1a]wealth with
harlots, you killed the fattened calf for
him.'
31"And he said to him, '*My* child, you
[1]have always been with me, and all that
is mine is yours.
32 'But [1]we had to be merry and rejoice, for this brother of yours was [a]dead
and *has begun* to live, and *was* lost and
has been found.' "

The Unrighteous Steward

16 NOW He was also saying to the
disciples, "There was a certain
rich man who had a steward, and this

32 [1]Or, *an embassy*

33 [a]Phil. 3:7; Heb. 11:26

34 [a]Matt. 5:13; Mark 9:50

35 [1]Lit., *they throw it out* [a]Matt. 11:15

1 [1]I.e., Collectors of Roman taxes for profit [2]I.e., irreligious or non-practicing Jews [a]Luke 5:29

2 [1]Lit., *grumble among themselves* [a]Matt. 9:11

4 [1]Lit., *wilderness* [a]Matt. 18:12-14; Luke 15:4-7

8 [1]Gr., *drachmas,* one drachma was equivalent to a day's wages

9 [1]Lit., *women friends and neighbors*

10 [a]Matt. 10:32; Luke 15:7

12 [1]Lit., *living* [a]Deut. 21:17 [b]Mark 12:44; Luke 15:30

15 [1]Lit., *was joined to*

16 [1]Some mss. read *to be satisfied with* [2]Lit., *belly* [3]I.e., of the carob tree

17 [1]Lit., *himself*

18 [1]Lit., *before you*

20 [1]Lit., *his own* [2]Lit., *fell on his neck* [3]Lit., *kissed him again and again* [a]Gen. 45:14; 46:29; Acts 20:37

21 [1]Some ancient mss. add *make me as one of your hired men*

22 [a]Zech. 3:4; Rev. 6:11 [b]Gen. 41:42

24 [a]Matt. 8:22; Luke 9:60; 15:32; Rom. 11:15; Eph. 2:1, 5; 5:14; Col. 2:13; 1 Tim. 5:6

29 [1]Or, *disobeyed* [2]Or, *young goat*

30 [1]Lit., *living* [a]Prov. 29:3; Luke 15:12

31 [1]Lit., *are always with me*

32 [1]Lit., *it was necessary* [a]Luke 15:24

steward was [1]reported to him as [a]squan-
dering his possessions.
2"And he called him and said to him,
'What is this I hear about you? Give an
account of your stewardship, for you can
no longer be steward.'
3"And the steward said to himself,
'What shall I do, since my [1]master is
taking the stewardship away from me? I
am not strong enough to dig; I am
ashamed to beg.
4'I [1]know what I shall do, so that
when I am removed from the stewardship, they will receive me into their
homes.'
5"And he summoned each one of his
[1]master's debtors, and he *began* saying
to the first, 'How much do you owe my
master?'
6"And he said, 'A hundred [1]measures
of oil.' And he said to him, 'Take your
bill, and sit down quickly and write
fifty.'
7"Then he said to another, 'And how
much do you owe?' And he said, 'A
hundred [1]measures of wheat.' He *said
to him, 'Take your bill, and write eighty.'
8"And his [1]master praised the unrighteous steward because he had acted
shrewdly; for the sons of [a]this age are
more shrewd in relation to their own
[2]kind than the [b]sons of light.
9"And I say to you, [a]make friends for
yourselves by means of the [1b]mammon
of unrighteousness; that when it fails,
[c]they may receive you into the eternal
dwellings.
10"[a]He who is faithful in a very little
thing is faithful also in much; and he
who is unrighteous in a very little thing
is unrighteous also in much.
11"If therefore you have not been
faithful in the *use of* unrighteous [1a]mam-
mon, who will entrust the true *riches* to
you?
12"And if you have not been faithful
in *the use of* that which is another's, who
will give you that which is [1]your own?
13"[a]No [1]servant can serve two masters; for either he will hate the one, and
love the other, or else he will hold to one,
and despise the other. You cannot serve
God and [2b]mammon."
14 Now the Pharisees, who were [a]lov-
ers of money, were listening to all these
things, and they [b]were scoffing at Him.
15 And He said to them, "You are
those who [a]justify yourselves [1]in the
sight of men, but [b]God knows your
hearts; for that which is [2]highly esteemed among men is detestable [3]in the
sight of God.
16"[a]The Law and the Prophets *were
proclaimed* until John; since then [b]the
gospel of the kingdom of God is
preached, and everyone is forcing his
way into it.
17"[a]But it is easier for heaven and
earth to pass away than for one [1]stroke
of a letter of the Law to fail.
18"[a]Everyone who [1]divorces his wife
and marries another commits adultery;
and he who marries one who is [2]divorced
from a husband commits adultery.

The Rich Man and Lazarus

19"Now there was a certain rich man,
and he habitually dressed in purple and
fine linen, gaily living in splendor every
day.
20"And a certain poor man named
Lazarus [a]was laid at his gate, covered
with sores,
21 and longing to be fed with the
crumbs which were falling from the rich
man's table; besides, even the dogs were
coming and licking his sores.
22"Now it came about that the poor
man died and he was carried away by
the angels to [a]Abraham's bosom; and
the rich man also died and was buried.
23"And in [a]Hades [1]he lifted up his
eyes, being in torment, and *saw Abraham far away, and Lazarus in his bosom.
24"And he cried out and said, '[a]Father
Abraham, have mercy on me, and send
Lazarus, that he may dip the tip of his
finger in water and cool off my tongue;
for I am in agony in [b]this flame.'
25"But Abraham said, 'Child, remember that [a]during your life you received
your good things, and likewise Lazarus
bad things; but now he is being comforted here, and you are in agony.
26'And [1]besides all this, between us
and you there is a great chasm fixed, in
order that those who wish to come over
from here to you may not be able, and
that none may cross over from there to
us.'
27"And he said, 'Then I beg you,
Father, that you send him to my father's
house—
28 for I have five brothers—that he
may [a]warn them, lest they also come to
this place of torment.'
29"But Abraham *said, 'They have
[a]Moses and the Prophets; let them hear
them.'
30"But he said, 'No, [a]Father Abraham,
but if someone goes to them from the
dead, they will repent!'
31"But he said to him, 'If they do not
listen to Moses and the Prophets, neither
will they be persuaded if someone rises
from the dead.'"

Instructions

17 AND He said to His disciples,
"[a]It is inevitable that [1]stumbling
blocks should come, but woe to him
through whom they come!
2"[a]It would be better for him if a
millstone were hung around his neck
and he were thrown into the sea, than
that he should cause one of these [1]little
ones to stumble.
3"[1]Be on your guard! [a]If your brother
sins, rebuke him; and if he repents,
forgive him.

1 [1]Or, *accused* [a]Luke 15:13
3 [1]Or, *lord*
4 [1]Lit., *have come to the knowledge of*
5 [1]Or, *lord's*
6 [1]Gr., *baths,* one bath equals between 8 and 9 gal.
7 [1]Gr., *kors,* one kor equals between 10 and 12 bu.
8 [1]Or, *lord* [2]Lit., *generation* [a]Matt. 12:32; Luke 20:34 [b]John 12:36; Eph. 5:8; 1 Thess. 5:5
9 [1]Or, *riches* [a]Matt. 19:21; Luke 11:41; 12:33 [b]Matt. 6:24; Luke 16:11, 13 [c]Luke 16:4
10 [a]Matt. 25:21, 23
11 [1]Or, *riches* [a]Luke 16:9
12 [1]Some mss. read *our own*
13 [1]Or, *house-servant* [2]Or, *riches* [a]Matt. 6:24 [b]Luke 16:9
14 [a]2 Tim. 3:2 [b]Luke 23:35
15 [1]Lit., *before men* [2]Lit., *high* [3]Lit., *before God* [a]Luke 10:29; 18:9, 14 [b]1 Sam. 16:7; Prov. 21:2; Acts 1:24; Rom. 8:27
16 [a]Matt. 11:12f. [b]Matt. 4:23
17 [1]I.e., projection of a letter (serif) [a]Matt. 5:18
18 [1]Or, *sends away* [2]Or, *sent away* [a]Matt. 5:32; 1 Cor. 7:10, 11
20 [a]Acts 3:2
22 [a]John 1:18; 13:23
23 [1]Lit., *having lifted up* [a]Matt. 11:23
24 [a]Luke 3:8; 16:30; 19:9 [b]Matt. 25:41
25 [a]Luke 6:24
26 [1]Lit., *in all these things*
28 [a]Acts 2:40; 8:25; 10:42; 18:5; 20:21ff.; 23:11; 28:23; Gal. 5:3; Eph. 4:17; 1 Thess. 2:11; 4:6
29 [a]Luke 4:17; John 5:45-47; Acts 15:21
30 [a]Luke 3:8; 16:24; 19:9

1 [1]Or, *temptations to sin* [a]Matt. 18:7; 1 Cor. 11:19; 1 Tim. 4:1
2 [1]I.e., humble [a]Matt. 18:6; Mark 9:42; 1 Cor. 8:12
3 [1]Lit., *Take heed to yourselves* [a]Matt. 18:15

4“And if he sins against you [a]seven
times a day, and returns to you seven
times, saying, ‘I repent,’ [1]forgive him.”
5 And [a]the apostles said to [b]the
Lord, “Increase our faith!”
6 And [a]the Lord said, “If you had
faith like [b]a mustard seed, you would say
to this [c]mulberry tree, ‘Be uprooted and
be planted in the sea’; and it would
[1]obey you.
7“But which of you, having a slave
plowing or tending sheep, will say to him
when he has come in from the field,
‘Come immediately and [1]sit down to
eat’?
8“But will he not say to him, ‘[a]Pre-
pare something for me to eat, and *properly* [1]clothe yourself and serve me until I
have eaten and drunk; and [2]afterward
you will eat and drink’?
9“He does not thank the slave because he did the things which were
commanded, does he?
10“So you too, when you do all the
things which are commanded you, say,
‘We are unworthy slaves; we have done
only that which we ought to have
done.’ ”

Ten Lepers Cleansed

11 And it came about while He was
[a]on the way to Jerusalem, that [b]He was
passing [1]between Samaria and Galilee.
12 And as He entered a certain village,
ten leprous men who [a]stood at a distance
met Him;
13 and they raised their voices, saying,
“Jesus, [a]Master, have mercy on us!”
14 And when He saw them, He said to
them, “[a]Go and show yourselves to the
priests.” And it came about that as they
were going, they were cleansed.
15 Now one of them, when he saw
that he had been healed, turned back,
[a]glorifying God with a loud voice,
16 and he fell on his face at His feet,
giving thanks to Him. And he was a
[a]Samaritan.
17 And Jesus answered and said,
“Were there not ten cleansed? But the
nine—where are they?
18“[1]Was no one found who turned
back to [a]give glory to God, except this
foreigner?”
19 And He said to him, “Rise, and go
your way; [a]your faith [1]has made you
well.”
20 Now having been questioned by
the Pharisees [a]as to when the kingdom of
God was coming, He answered them and
said, “The kingdom of God is not coming with [1b]signs to be observed;
21 nor will [a]they say, ‘Look, here *it
is!*’ or, ‘There *it is!*’ For behold, the
kingdom of God is [1]in your midst.”

Second Coming Foretold

22 And He said to the disciples, “[a]The
days shall come when you will long to
see one of the days of the Son of Man,
and you will not see it.
23“[a]And they will say to you, ‘Look
there! Look here!’ Do not go away, and
do not run after *them.*
24“[a]For just as the lightning, when it
flashes out of one part [1]of the sky, shines
to the other part [1]of the sky, so will the
Son of Man be in His day.
25“[a]But first He must suffer many
things and be rejected by this generation.
26“[a]And just as it happened [b]in the
days of Noah, so it shall be also in the
days of the Son of Man:
27 they were eating, they were drinking, they were marrying, they were being
given in marriage, until the day that
Noah entered the ark, and the flood
came and destroyed them all.
28“[1]It was the same as happened in
[a]the days of Lot: they were eating, they
were drinking, they were buying,
they were selling, they were planting,
they were building;
29 but on the day that Lot went out
from Sodom it rained fire and [1]brim-
stone from heaven and destroyed them
all.
30“It will be [1]just the same on the day
that the Son of Man [a]is revealed.
31“On that day, let not the one who is
[a]on the housetop and whose goods are in
the house go down to take them away;
and likewise let not the one who is in the
field turn back.
32“[a]Remember Lot’s wife.
33“[a]Whoever seeks to keep his [1]life
shall lose it, and whoever loses *his life*
shall preserve it.
34“I tell you, on that night there will
be two men in one bed; one will be
taken, and the other will be left.
35“[a]There will be two women grinding
at the same place; one will be taken, and
the other will be left.
36 [“[1a]Two men will be in the field;
one will be taken and the other will be
left.”]
37 And answering they *said to Him,
“Where, Lord?” And He said to them,
“[a]Where the body *is,* there also will the
[1]vultures be gathered.”

Parables on Prayer

18 NOW He was telling them a parable to show that at all times they
[a]ought to pray and not to [b]lose heart,
2 saying, “There was in a certain city
a judge who did not fear God, and did
not [a]respect man.
3“And there was a widow in that city,
and she kept coming to him, saying,
‘[1]Give me legal protection from my
opponent.’
4“And for a while he was unwilling;
but afterward he said to himself, ‘Even
though I do not fear God nor [a]respect
man,
5 yet [a]because this widow bothers
me, I will [1]give her legal protection, lest
by continually coming she [2b]wear me
out.’ ”

4 [1]Lit., *you shall forgive* [a]Matt. 18:21f.
5 [a]Mark 6:30 [b]Luke 7:13
6 [1]Or, *have obeyed* [a]Luke 7:13 [b]Matt. 13:31; 17:20; Mark 4:31; Luke 13:19 [c]Luke 19:4
7 [1]Lit., *recline*
8 [1]Lit., *gird* [2]Lit., *after these things* [a]Luke 12:37
11 [1]Lit., *through the midst of;* or, *along the borders of* [a]Luke 9:51 [b]Luke 9:52ff.; John 4:3f.
12 [a]Lev. 13:45f.
13 [a]Luke 5:5
14 [a]Lev. 14:1-32; Matt. 8:4; Luke 5:14
15 [a]Matt. 9:8
16 [a]Matt. 10:5
18 [1]Lit., *Were there not found those who* [a]Matt. 9:8
19 [1]Or, *has saved you* [a]Matt. 9:22; Luke 18:42
20 [1]Lit., *observation* [a]Luke 19:11; Acts 1:6 [b]Luke 14:1
21 [1]Or, *within you* [a]Luke 17:23
22 [a]Matt. 9:15; Mark 2:20; Luke 5:35
23 [a]Matt. 24:23; Mark 13:21; Luke 21:8
24 [1]Lit., *under heaven* [a]Matt. 24:27
25 [a]Matt. 16:21; Luke 9:22
26 [a]Luke 17:26, 27: *Matt. 24:37-39* [b]Gen. 6:5-8; 7
28 [1]Lit., *In the same way as* [a]Gen. 19
29 [1]Or, *sulphur*
30 [1]Lit., *according to the same things* [a]Matt. 16:27; 1 Cor. 1:7; Col. 3:4; 2 Thess. 1:7; 1 Pet. 1:7; 4:13; 1 John 2:28
31 [a]Matt. 24:17, 18; Mark 13:15f.; Luke 21:21
32 [a]Gen. 19:26
33 [1]Or, *soul* [a]Matt. 10:39
35 [a]Matt. 24:41
36 [1]Many mss. do not contain this v. [a]Matt. 24:40
37 [1]Or, *eagles* [a]Matt. 24:28

1 [a]Luke 11:5-10 [b]2 Cor. 4:1
2 [a]Luke 18:4; 20:13; Heb. 12:9
3 [1]Lit., *Do me justice*
4 [a]Luke 18:2; 20:13; Heb. 12:9
5 [1]Lit., *do her justice* [2]Lit., *hit me under the eye* [a]Luke 11:8 [b]1 Cor. 9:27

6 And [a]the Lord said, "Hear what the unrighteous judge *said;

7 now shall not God [a]bring about justice for His [b]elect, who cry to Him day and night, [1]and will He [c]delay long over them?

8 "I tell you that He will bring about justice for them speedily. However, when the Son of Man comes, [a]will He find [1]faith on the earth?"

The Pharisee and the Publican

9 And He also told this parable to certain ones who [a]trusted in themselves that they were righteous, and [b]viewed others with contempt:

10 "Two men [a]went up into the temple to pray, one a Pharisee, and the other a [1]tax-gatherer.

11 "The Pharisee [a]stood and was praying thus to himself, 'God, I thank Thee that I am not like other people: swindlers, unjust, adulterers, or even like this [1]tax-gatherer.

12 'I [a]fast twice a week; I [b]pay tithes of all that I get.'

13 "But the [1]tax-gatherer, [a]standing some distance away, [b]was even unwilling to lift up his eyes to heaven, but [c]was beating his breast, saying, 'God, be [2]merciful to me, the sinner!'

14 "I tell you, this man went down to his house justified rather than the other; [a]for everyone who exalts himself shall be humbled, but he who humbles himself shall be exalted."

15 [a]And they were bringing even their babies to Him so that He might touch them, but when the disciples saw it, they *began* rebuking them.

16 But Jesus called for them, saying, "Permit the children to come to Me, and do not hinder them, for the kingdom of God belongs to such as these.

17 "Truly I say to you, [a]whoever does not receive the kingdom of God like a child shall not enter it *at all.*"

The Rich Young Ruler

18 [a]And a certain ruler questioned Him, saying, "Good Teacher, what shall I do to inherit eternal life?"

19 And Jesus said to him, "Why do you call Me good? No one is good except God alone.

20 "You know the commandments, '[a]Do not commit adultery, Do not murder, Do not steal, Do not bear false witness, Honor your father and mother.' "

21 And he said, "All these things I have kept from *my* youth."

22 And when Jesus heard *this,* He said to him, "One thing you still lack; [a]sell all that you possess, and distribute it to the poor, and you shall have [b]treasure in heaven; and come, follow Me."

23 But when he had heard these things, he became very sad; for he was extremely rich.

24 And Jesus looked at him and said, "[a]How hard it is for those who are wealthy to enter the kingdom of God!

25 "For [a]it is easier for a camel to [1]go through the eye of a needle, than for a rich man to enter the kingdom of God."

26 And they who heard it said, "[1]Then who can be saved?"

27 But He said, "[a]The things impossible with men are possible with God."

28 And Peter said, "Behold, [a]we have left [1]our own *homes,* and followed You."

29 And He said to them, "Truly I say to you, [a]there is no one who has left house or wife or brothers or parents or children, for the sake of the kingdom of God,

30 who shall not receive many times as much at this time and in [a]the age to come, eternal life."

31 [a]And He took the twelve aside and said to them, "Behold, [b]we are going up to Jerusalem, and [c]all things which are written through the prophets about the Son of Man will be accomplished.

32 "[a]For He will be [1]delivered to the Gentiles, and will be mocked and mistreated and spit upon,

33 and after they have scourged Him, they will kill Him; and the third day He will rise again."

34 And [a]they understood none of these things, and this saying was hidden from them, and they did not comprehend the things that were said.

Bartimaeus Receives Sight

35 [a]And it came about that [b]as He was approaching Jericho, a certain blind man was sitting by the road, begging.

36 Now hearing a multitude going by, he *began* to inquire what this might be.

37 And they told him that Jesus of Nazareth was passing by.

38 And he called out, saying, "Jesus, [a]Son of David, have mercy on me!"

39 And those who led the way were sternly telling him to be quiet; but he kept crying out all the more, "[a]Son of David, have mercy on me!"

40 And Jesus [1]stopped and commanded that he be brought to Him; and when he had come near, He questioned him,

41 "What do you want Me to do for you?" And he said, "Lord, *I want* to regain my sight!"

42 And Jesus said to him, "[1]Receive your sight; [a]your faith has [2]made you well."

43 And immediately he regained his sight, and *began* following Him, [a]glorifying God; and when [b]all the people saw it, they gave praise to God.

Zaccheus Converted

19 AND He [a]entered and was passing through Jericho.

2 And behold, there was a man called by the name of Zaccheus; and he

6 [a]Luke 7:13
7 [1]Or, *and yet He is long-suffering over them* [a]Rev. 6:10 [b]Matt. 24:22; Rom. 8:33; Col. 3:12; 2 Tim. 2:10; Titus 1:1 [c]2 Pet. 3:9
8 [1]Lit., *the faith* [a]Luke 17:26ff.
9 [a]Luke 16:15 [b]Rom. 14:3, 10
10 [1]I.e., Collector of Roman taxes for profit [a]1 Kin. 10:5; 2 Kin. 20:5, 8; Acts 3:1
11 [1]V. 10, note 1 [a]Matt. 6:5; Mark 11:25; Luke 22:41
12 [a]Matt. 9:14 [b]Luke 11:42
13 [1]V. 10, note 1 [2]Or, *propitious* [a]Matt. 6:5; Mark 11:25; Luke 22:41 [b]Ezra 9:6 [c]Luke 23:48
14 [a]Matt. 23:12; Luke 14:11
15 [a]Luke 18:15-17: *Matt. 19:13-15; Mark 10:13-16*
17 [a]Matt. 18:3; 19:14; Mark 10:15; 1 Cor. 14:20; 1 Pet. 2:2
18 [a]Luke 18:18-30: *Matt. 19:16-29; Mark 10:17-30;* Luke 10:25-28
20 [a]Ex. 20:12-16; Deut. 5:16-20
22 [a]Matt. 19:21; Luke 12:33 [b]Matt. 6:20
24 [a]Matt. 19:23; Mark 10:23f.
25 [1]Lit., *enter* [a]Matt. 19:24; Mark 10:25
26 [1]Lit., *And*
27 [a]Matt. 19:26
28 [1]Lit., *our own things* [a]Luke 5:11
29 [a]Matt. 6:33; 19:29; Mark 10:29f.
30 [a]Matt. 12:32
31 [a]Luke 18:31-33: *Matt. 20:17-19; Mark 10:32-34* [b]Luke 9:51 [c]Ps. 22; Is. 53
32 [1]Or, *betrayed* [a]Matt. 16:21
34 [a]Mark 9:32; Luke 9:45
35 [a]Luke 18:35-43: *Matt. 20:29-34; Mark 10:46-52* [b]Matt. 20:29; Mark 10:46; Luke 19:1
38 [a]Matt. 9:27; Luke 18:39
39 [a]Luke 18:38
40 [1]Lit., *stood*
42 [1]Or, *Regain* [2]Or, *saved you* [a]Matt. 9:22
43 [a]Matt. 9:8 [b]Luke 9:43; 13:17; 19:37

1 [a]Luke 18:35

was a chief [1]tax-gatherer, and he was
rich.
3 And he was trying to see who Jesus
was, and he was unable because of the
crowd, for he was small in stature.
4 And he ran on ahead and climbed
up into a [1a]sycamore tree in order to see
Him, for He was about to pass through
that way.
5 And when Jesus came to the place,
He looked up and said to him, "Zaccheus, hurry and come down, for today I
must stay at your house."
6 And he hurried and came down,
and received Him [1]gladly.
7 And when they saw it, they all
began to [1]grumble, saying, "He has gone
[2]to be the guest of a man who is a
sinner."
8 And Zaccheus [1]stopped and said to
[a]the Lord, "Behold, Lord, half of my
possessions I will give to the poor, and if
I have [b]defrauded anyone of anything, I
will give back [c]four times as much."
9 And Jesus said to him, "Today
salvation has come to this house, because he, too, is [a]a son of Abraham.
10 "For [a]the Son of Man has come to
seek and to save that which was lost."

Parable of Money Usage

11 And while they were listening to
these things, He went on to tell a parable, because [a]He was near Jerusalem,
and they supposed that [b]the kingdom of
God was going to appear immediately.
12 He said therefore, "[a]A certain
nobleman went to a distant country to
receive a kingdom for himself, and *then*
return.
13 "And he called ten of his slaves, and
gave them ten [1]minas, and said to them,
'Do business *with this* [2]until I come
back.'
14 "But his citizens hated him, and sent
[1]a delegation after him, saying, 'We do
not want this man to reign over us.'
15 "And it came about that when he
returned, after receiving the kingdom,
he ordered that these slaves, to whom he
had given the money, be called to him in
order that he might know what business
they had done.
16 "And the first appeared, saying,
'[1]Master, your [2]mina has made ten
minas more.'
17 "And he said to him, 'Well done,
good slave, because you have been
[a]faithful in a very little thing, be in
authority over ten cities.'
18 "And the second came, saying,
'Your [1]mina, [2]master, has made five
minas.'
19 "And he said to him also, 'And you
are to be over five cities.'
20 "And another came, saying, 'Master,
behold your mina, which I kept put
away in a handkerchief;
21 for I was afraid of you, because you
are an exacting man; you take up what
you did not lay down, and reap what
you did not sow.'
22 "He *said to him, '[1]By your own
words I will judge you, you worthless
slave. Did you know that I am an exacting man, taking up what I did not lay
down, and reaping what I did not sow?
23 '[1]Then why did you not put the
money in the bank, and having come, I
would have collected it with interest?'
24 "And he said to the bystanders,
'Take the mina away from him, and give
it to the one who has the ten minas.'
25 "And they said to him, 'Master, he
has ten minas *already.*'
26 "[a]I tell you, that to everyone who
has shall *more* be given, but from the one
who does not have, even what he does
have shall be taken away.
27 "But [a]these enemies of mine, who
did not want me to reign over them,
bring them here and [b]slay them in my
presence."

Triumphal Entry

28 And after He had said these things,
He [a]was going on ahead, [b]ascending to
Jerusalem.
29 And it came about that [a]when He
approached Bethphage and [b]Bethany,
near the [1]mount that is called [2c]Olivet,
He sent two of the disciples,
30 saying, "Go into the village opposite *you,* in which as you enter you will
find a colt tied, on which no one yet has
ever sat; untie it, and bring it *here.*
31 "And if anyone asks you, 'Why are
you untying it?' thus shall you speak,
'The Lord has need of it.' "
32 And those who were sent went
away and found it just as He had told
them.
33 And as they were untying the colt,
its [1]owners said to them, "Why are you
untying the colt?"
34 And they said, "The Lord has need
of it."
35 And they brought it to Jesus, [a]and
they threw their garments on the colt,
and put Jesus *on it.*
36 And as He was going, they were
spreading their garments in the road.
37 And as He was now approaching,
near the descent of [a]the Mount of Olives, the whole multitude of the disciples
began to [b]praise God [1]joyfully with a
loud voice for all the [2]miracles which
they had seen,
38 saying,
"[a]BLESSED IS THE [b]King WHO
COMES IN THE NAME OF THE
LORD;
Peace in heaven and [c]glory in the
highest!"
39 [a]And some of the Pharisees [1]in the
multitude said to Him, "Teacher, rebuke
Your disciples."
40 And He answered and said, "I tell
you, if these become silent, [a]the stones
will cry out!"

2 [1]I.e., Collector of Roman taxes for profit

4 [1]I.e., fig-mulberry [a]1 Kin. 10:27; 1 Chr. 27:28; 2 Chr. 1:15; 9:27; Ps. 78:47; Is. 9:10; Luke 17:6

6 [1]Lit., *rejoicing*

7 [1]Lit., *grumble among themselves* [2]Or, *to find lodging*

8 [1]Lit., *stood* [a]Luke 7:13 [b]Luke 3:14 [c]Ex. 22:1; Lev. 6:5; Num. 5:7; 2 Sam. 12:6

9 [a]Luke 3:8; 13:16; Rom. 4:16; Gal. 3:7

10 [a]Matt. 18:11

11 [a]Luke 9:51 [b]Luke 17:20

12 [a]Matt. 25:14-30; Luke 19:12-27

13 [1]A mina is equal to about 100 days' wages [2]Lit., *while I am coming*

14 [1]Or, *an embassy*

16 [1]Lit., *Lord* [2]V. 13, note 1

17 [a]Luke 16:10

18 [1]V. 13, note 1 [2]Lit., *lord*

22 [1]Lit., *Out of your own mouth*

23 [1]Lit., *And*

26 [a]Matt. 13:12; Mark 4:25; Luke 8:18

27 [a]Luke 19:14 [b]Matt. 22:7; Luke 20:16

28 [a]Mark 10:32 [b]Luke 9:51

29 [1]Or, *hill* [2]Or, *Olive Grove* [a]Luke 19:29-38: *Matt. 21:1-9; Mark 11:1-10* [b]Matt. 21:17 [c]Luke 21:37; Acts 1:12

33 [1]Lit., *lords*

35 [a]Luke 19:35-38: *Matt. 21:4-9; Mark 11:7-10; John 12:12-15*

37 [1]Lit., *as they were rejoicing* [2]Or, *works of power* [a]Matt. 21:1; Luke 19:29 [b]Luke 18:43

38 [a]Ps. 118:26 [b]Matt. 2:2; 25:34 [c]Matt. 21:9; Luke 2:14

39 [1]Lit., *from* [a]Matt. 21:15f.

40 [a]Hab. 2:11

41 And when He approached, He saw
the city and [a]wept over it,
42 saying, "If you had known in this
day, even you, the things which make for
peace! But now they have been hidden
from your eyes.
43 "For the days shall come upon you
[1]when your enemies will [a]throw up a
[2]bank before you, and [b]surround you,
and hem you in on every side,
44 and will level you to the ground
and your children within you, and [a]they
will not leave in you one stone upon
another, because you did not recognize
[b]the time of your visitation."

Traders Driven from the Temple

45 [a]And He entered the temple and
began to cast out those who were selling,
46 saying to them, "It is written,
'[a]AND MY HOUSE SHALL BE A HOUSE OF
PRAYER,' [b]but you have made it a ROB-
BERS' [1]DEN."
47 And [a]He was teaching daily in the
temple; but the chief priests and the
scribes and the leading men among
the people [b]were trying to destroy Him,
48 and they could not find [1]anything
that they might do, for all the people
were hanging upon [2]His words.

Jesus' Authority Questioned

20 [a]AND it came about on one of the
days while [b]He was teaching the
people in the temple and [c]preaching
the gospel, that the chief priests and the
scribes with the elders [d]confronted *Him,*
2 and they spoke, saying to Him,
"Tell us by what authority You are
doing these things, or who is the one
who gave You this authority?"
3 And He answered and said to
them, "I shall also ask you a [1]question,
and you tell Me:
4 "Was the baptism of John from
heaven or from men?"
5 And they reasoned among themselves, saying, "If we say, 'From heaven,'
He will say, 'Why did you not believe
him?'
6 "But if we say, 'From men,' all the
people will stone us to death, for they
are convinced that John was a
[a]prophet."
7 And they answered that they did
not know where *it came* from.
8 And Jesus said to them, "Neither
[1]will I tell you by what authority I do
these things."

Parable of the Vine-growers

9 [a]And He began to tell the people
this parable: "A man planted a vineyard
and rented it out to [1]vine-growers, and
went on a journey for a long time.
10 "And at the *harvest* time he sent a
slave to the vine-growers, in order that
they might give him *some* of the produce
of the vineyard; but the vine-growers
beat him and sent him away empty-
handed.
11 "And he proceeded to send another
slave; and they beat him also and treated
him shamefully, and sent him away
empty-handed.
12 "And he proceeded to send a third;
and this one also they wounded and cast
out.
13 "And the [1]owner of the vineyard
said, 'What shall I do? I will send my
beloved son; perhaps they will [a]respect
him.'
14 "But when the vine-growers saw
him, they reasoned with one another,
saying, 'This is the heir; let us kill him
that the inheritance may be ours.'
15 "And they threw him out of the
vineyard and killed him. What, therefore, will the [1]owner of the vineyard do
to them?
16 "He will come and [a]destroy these
vine-growers and will give the vineyard
to others." And when they heard it, they
said, "[b]May it never be!"
17 But He looked at them and said,
"What then is this that is written,
'[a]THE STONE WHICH THE BUILDERS
REJECTED,
THIS BECAME [b]THE CHIEF CORNER
stone'?
18 "[a]Everyone who falls on that stone
will be broken to pieces; but on whomever it falls, it will scatter him like dust."

Tribute to Caesar

19 And the scribes and the chief
priests [a]tried to lay hands on Him that
very hour, and they feared the people;
for they understood that He spoke this
parable against them.
20 [a]And they watched Him, and sent
spies who [1]pretended to be righteous, in
order [b]that they might [2]catch Him in
some statement, so as to deliver Him up
to the rule and the authority of [c]the
governor.
21 And they questioned Him, saying,
"Teacher, we know that You speak and
teach correctly, and You [1]are not partial
to any, but teach the way of God in
truth.
22 "Is it [1]lawful for us [a]to pay taxes to
Caesar, or not?"
23 But He detected their trickery and
said to them,
24 "Show Me a [1]denarius. Whose [2]like-
ness and inscription does it have?" And
they said, "Caesar's."
25 And He said to them, "Then [a]ren-
der to Caesar the things that are Caesar's, and to God the things that are
God's."
26 And they were unable to [1a]catch
Him in a saying in the presence of the
people; and marveling at His answer,
they became silent.

Is There a Resurrection?

27 [a]Now there came to Him some of
the [b]Sadducees (who say that there is no
resurrection),

41 [a]Luke 13:34, 35
43 [1]Lit., *and* [2]I.e., a dirt wall or mound for siege purposes [a]Eccl. 9:14; Is. 29:3; 37:33; Jer. 6:6; Ezek. 4:2; 26:8 [b]Luke 21:20
44 [a]Matt. 24:2; Mark 13:2; Luke 21:6 [b]1 Pet. 2:12
45 [a]Luke 19:45, 46: *Matt. 21:12, 13; Mark 11:15-17;* John 2:13-16
46 [1]Lit., *cave* [a]Is. 56:7; Jer. 7:11; Matt. 21:13; Mark 11:17 [b]Jer. 7:11
47 [a]Matt. 26:55; Luke 21:37 [b]Luke 20:19
48 [1]Lit., *what they might do* [2]Lit., *Him, listening*
1 [a]Luke 20:1-8: *Matt. 21:23-27; Mark 11:27-33* [b]Matt. 26:55 [c]Luke 8:1 [d]Acts 4:1; 6:12
3 [1]Lit., *word*
6 [a]Matt. 11:9; Luke 7:29, 30
8 [1]Lit., *do I tell*
9 [1]Or, *tenant farmers,* also vv. 10, 14, 16 [a]Luke 20:9-19: *Matt. 21:33-46; Mark 12:1-12*
13 [1]Lit., *lord* [a]Luke 18:2
15 [1]Lit., *lord*
16 [a]Matt. 21:41; Mark 12:9; Luke 19:27 [b]Rom. 3:4, 6, 31; 6:2, 15; 7:7, 13; 9:14; 11:1, 11; 1 Cor. 6:15; Gal. 2:17; 3:21; 6:14
17 [a]Ps. 118:22 [b]Eph. 2:20; 1 Pet. 2:6
18 [a]Matt. 21:44
19 [a]Luke 19:47
20 [1]Lit., *feigned themselves* [2]Lit., *take hold of His word* [a]Luke 20:20-26: *Matt. 22:15-22; Mark 12:13-17;* Mark 3:2 [b]Luke 11:54; 20:26 [c]Matt. 27:2
21 [1]Lit., *do not receive a face*
22 [1]Or, *permissible* [a]Matt. 17:25; Luke 23:2
24 [1]The denarius was equivalent to one day's wage [2]Lit., *image*
25 [a]Matt. 22:21; Mark 12:17
26 [1]Lit., *take hold of His saying* [a]Luke 11:54
27 [a]Luke 20:27-40: *Matt. 22:23-33; Mark 12:18-27* [b]Acts 23:8

28 and they questioned Him, saying,
"Teacher, Moses wrote for us that [a]IF A
MAN'S BROTHER DIES, having a wife, AND
HE IS CHILDLESS, HIS BROTHER SHOULD
TAKE THE WIFE AND RAISE UP OFFSPRING
TO HIS BROTHER.
29 "Now there were seven brothers;
and the first took a wife, and died
childless;
30 and the second
31 and the third took her; and in the
same way [1]all seven [2]died, leaving no
children.
32 "Finally the woman died also.
33 "In the resurrection therefore, which
one's wife will she be? For [1]all seven had
her as wife."
34 And Jesus said to them, "The sons
of [a]this age marry and are given in
marriage,
35 but those who are considered worthy to attain to [a]that age and the resurrection from the dead, neither marry,
nor are given in marriage;
36 for neither can they die anymore,
for they are like angels, and are [a]sons of
God, being sons of the resurrection.
37 "But that the dead are raised, even
Moses showed, in [a]the *passage about the*
burning bush, where he calls the Lord
[b]THE GOD OF ABRAHAM, AND THE GOD
OF ISAAC, AND THE GOD OF JACOB.
38 "[a]Now He is not the God of the
dead, but of the living; for [b]all live to
Him."
39 And some of the scribes answered
and said, "Teacher, You have spoken
well."
40 For [a]they did not have courage to
question Him any longer about anything.
41 [a]And He said to them, "How *is it*
that they say [1]the Christ is [b]David's son?
42 "For David himself says in the book
of Psalms,

'[a]THE LORD SAID TO MY LORD,
"SIT AT MY RIGHT HAND,
43 [a]UNTIL I MAKE THINE ENEMIES A
FOOTSTOOL FOR THY FEET." '

44 "David therefore calls Him 'Lord,'
and how is He his son?"
45 [a]And while all the people were
listening, He said to the disciples,
46 "Beware of the scribes, [a]who like to
walk around in long robes, and love
respectful greetings in the market places,
and chief seats in the synagogues, and
places of honor at banquets,
47 who devour widows' houses, and
for appearance's sake offer long prayers;
these will receive greater condemnation."

The Widow's Gift

21 [a]AND He looked up and saw the
rich putting their gifts into the
treasury.
2 And He saw a certain poor widow
putting [1]in [a]two [2]small copper coins.
3 And He said, "Truly I say to you,
this poor widow put in more than all *of*
them;
4 for they all out of their [1]surplus put
into the [2]offering; but she out of her
poverty put in all [3]that she had [a]to live
on."
5 [a]And while some were talking
about the temple, that it was adorned
with beautiful stones and votive gifts, He
said,
6 "*As for* these things which you are
looking at, the days will come in which
[a]there will not be left one stone upon
another which will not be torn down."
7 And they questioned Him, saying,
"Teacher, when therefore will these
things be? And what *will be* the [1]sign
when these things are about to take
place?"
8 And He said, "See to it that you be
not misled; for many will come in My
name, saying, '[a]I am *He,*' and, 'The time
is at hand'; [b]do not go after them.
9 "And when you hear of wars and
disturbances, do not be terrified; for
these things must take place first, but the
end *does* not *follow* immediately."

Things to Come

10 Then He continued by saying to
them, "Nation will rise against nation,
and kingdom against kingdom,
11 and there will be great earthquakes,
and in various places plagues and famines; and there will be terrors and great
[1]signs from heaven.
12 "But before all these things, [a]they
will lay their hands on you and will
persecute you, delivering you to the
synagogues and prisons, [1]bringing you
before kings and governors for My
name's sake.
13 "[a]It will lead to [1]an opportunity for
your testimony.
14 "[a]So make up your minds not to
prepare beforehand to defend yourselves;
15 for [a]I will give you [1]utterance and
wisdom which none of your opponents
will be able to resist or refute.
16 "But you will be delivered up even
by parents and brothers and relatives
and friends, and they will put *some* of
you to death,
17 and you will be hated by all on
account of My name.
18 "Yet [a]not a hair of your head will
perish.
19 "[a]By your endurance you will gain
your [1]lives.
20 "But when you see Jerusalem [a]sur-
rounded by armies, then [1]recognize that
her desolation is at hand.
21 "Then let those who are in Judea
flee to the mountains, and let those who
are in the midst of [1]the city depart, and
[a]let not those who are in the country
enter [1]the city;

28 [a]Deut. 25:5
31 [1]Lit., *the seven also* [2]Lit., *left no children, and died*
33 [1]Lit., *the*
34 [a]Matt. 12:32; Luke 16:8
35 [a]Matt. 12:32; Luke 16:8
36 [a]Rom. 8:16f.; 1 John 3:1, 2
37 [a]Mark 12:26 [b]Ex. 3:6
38 [a]Matt. 22:32; Mark 12:27 [b]Rom. 14:8
40 [a]Matt. 22:46; Luke 14:6
41 [1]I.e., the Messiah [a]Luke 20:41-44: *Matt. 22:41-46; Mark 12:35-37* [b]Matt. 9:27
42 [a]Ps. 110:1
43 [a]Ps. 110:1
45 [a]Luke 20:45-47: *Matt. 23:1-7; Mark 12:38-40*
46 [a]Luke 11:43; 14:7
1 [a]Luke 21:1-4: *Mark 12:41-44*
2 [1]Or, *therein* [2]Gr., *lepta* [a]Mark 12:42
4 [1]Or, *abundance* [2]Lit., *gifts* [3]Lit., *the living that she had* [a]Mark 12:44
5 [a]Luke 21:5-36: *Matt. 24; Mark 13*
6 [a]Luke 19:44
7 [1]Or, *attesting miracle*
8 [a]John 8:24 [b]Luke 17:23
11 [1]Or, *attesting miracles*
12 [1]Lit., *being brought* [a]Luke 21:12-17: *Matt. 10:19-22; Mark 13:11-13*
13 [1]Lit., *a testimony for you* [a]Phil. 1:12
14 [a]Luke 12:11
15 [1]Lit., *a mouth* [a]Luke 12:12
18 [a]Matt. 10:30; Luke 12:7
19 [1]Or, *soul* [a]Matt. 10:22; 24:13; Rom. 2:7; 5:3f.; Heb. 10:36; James 1:3; 2 Pet. 1:6
20 [1]Lit., *know* [a]Luke 19:43
21 [1]Lit., *her* [a]Luke 17:31

22 because these are [a]days of vengeance, in order that all things which are
written may be fulfilled.
23"Woe to those who are with child
and to those who nurse babes in those
days; for [a]there will be great distress
upon the [1]land, and wrath to this people,
24 and they will fall by [a]the edge of
the sword, and will be led captive into all
the nations; and [b]Jerusalem will be
[c]trampled under foot by the Gentiles
until [d]the times of the Gentiles be fulfilled.

The Return of Christ

25"And there will be [1]signs in sun and
moon and stars, and upon the earth
dismay among nations, in perplexity at
the roaring of the sea and the waves,
26 men fainting from fear and the
expectation of the things which are
coming upon the [1]world; for the powers
of [2]the heavens will be shaken.
27"And [a]then they will see [b]THE SON
OF MAN COMING IN A CLOUD with power
and great glory.
28"But when these things begin to take
place, straighten up and lift up your
heads, because [a]your redemption is
drawing near."
29 And He told them a parable: "Behold the fig tree and all the trees;
30 as soon as they put forth *leaves,*
you see it and [a]know for yourselves that
summer is now near.
31"Even so you, too, when you see
these things happening, [1]recognize that
[a]the kingdom of God is near.
32"Truly I say to you, this [1]generation
will not pass away until all things take
place.
33"[a]Heaven and earth will pass away,
but My words will not pass away.
34"[a]Be on guard, that your hearts may
not be weighted down with dissipation
and drunkenness and the worries of life,
and that day come on you suddenly like
a trap;
35 for it will come upon all those who
dwell on the face of all the earth.
36"But [a]keep on the alert at all times,
praying in order that you may have
strength to escape all these things that
are about to take place, and to [b]stand
before the Son of Man."
37 Now [1]during the day He was
[a]teaching in the temple, but [2b]at evening
He would go out and spend the night on
[3c]the mount that is called [4]Olivet.
38 And all the people would get up
[a]early in the morning *to come* to Him in
the temple to listen to Him.

Preparing the Passover

22 [a]NOW the Feast of Unleavened
Bread, which is called the [b]Pass-
over, was approaching.
2 And the chief priests and the
scribes [a]were seeking how they might
put Him to death; for they were afraid
of the people.
3 [a]And [b]Satan entered into Judas
who was called Iscariot, [1]belonging to
the number of the twelve.
4 And he went away and discussed
with the chief priests and [a]officers how
he might betray Him to them.
5 And they were glad, and agreed to
give him money.
6 And he consented, and *began* seeking a good opportunity to betray Him to
them [1]apart from the multitude.
7 [a]Then came the *first* day of Unleavened Bread on which [b]the Passover *lamb*
had to be sacrificed.
8 And He sent [a]Peter and John,
saying, "Go and prepare the Passover
for us, that we may eat it."
9 And they said to Him, "Where do
You want us to prepare it?"
10 And He said to them, "Behold,
when you have entered the city, a man
will meet you carrying a pitcher of
water; follow him into the house that he
enters.
11"And you shall say to the owner of
the house, 'The Teacher says to you,
"Where is the guest room in which I may
eat the Passover with My disciples?"'
12"And he will show you a large,
furnished, upper room; prepare it
there."
13 And they departed and found
everything just as He had told them; and
they prepared the Passover.

The Lord's Supper

14 [a]And when the hour had come He
reclined *at the table,* and [b]the apostles
with Him.
15 And He said to them, "I have
earnestly desired to eat this Passover
with you before I suffer;
16 for I say to you, I shall never again
eat it [a]until it is fulfilled in the kingdom
of God."
17 [a]And when He had taken a cup *and*
[b]given thanks, He said, "Take this and
share it among yourselves;
18 for [a]I say to you, I will not drink of
the fruit of the vine from now on until
the kingdom of God comes."
19 And when He had taken *some*
bread *and* [a]given thanks, He broke *it,*
and gave *it* to them, saying, "This is My
body [1]which is given for you; do this in
remembrance of Me."
20 And in the same way *He took* the
cup after they had eaten, saying, "This
cup which is [a]poured out for you is the
[b]new covenant in My blood.
21"[a]But behold, the hand of the one
betraying Me is with Me on the table.
22"For indeed, the Son of Man is
going [a]as it has been determined; but
woe to that man by whom He is betrayed!"
23 And they began to discuss among
themselves which one of them it might
be who was going to do this thing.

22 [a]Is. 63:4; Dan. 9:24-27; Hos. 9:7
23 [1]Or, *earth* [a]Dan. 8:19; 1 Cor. 7:26
24 [a]Gen. 34:26; Ex. 17:13; Heb. 11:34 [b]Is. 63:18; Dan. 8:13 [c]Rev. 11:2 [d]Rom. 11:25
25 [1]Or, *attesting miracles*
26 [1]Lit., *inhabited earth* [2]Or, *heaven*
27 [a]Matt. 16:27; 24:30; 26:64; Mark 13:26 [b]Dan. 7:13; Rev. 1:7
28 [a]Luke 18:7
30 [a]Luke 12:57
31 [1]Lit., *know* [a]Matt. 3:2
32 [1]Or, *race*
33 [a]Matt. 5:18; Luke 16:17
34 [a]Matt. 24:42-44; Mark 4:19; Luke 12:40, 45; 1 Thess. 5:2ff.
36 [a]Mark 13:33; Luke 12:40 [b]Luke 1:19; Rev. 7:9; 8:2; 11:4
37 [1]Lit., *days* [2]Lit., *nights* [3]Or, *the hill* [4]Or, *Olive Grove* [a]Matt. 26:55; Luke 19:47 [b]Mark 11:19 [c]Matt. 21:1
38 [a]John 8:2

1 [a]Luke 22:1, 2: *Matt. 26:2-5; Mark 14:1, 2;* Ex. 12:1-27 [b]John 11:55; 13:1
2 [a]Matt. 12:14
3 [1]Lit., *being of* [a]Luke 22:3-6: *Matt. 26:14-16; Mark 14:10, 11* [b]Matt. 4:10; John 13:2, 27
4 [a]1 Chr. 9:11; Neh. 11:11; Luke 22:52; Acts 4:1; 5:24, 26
6 [1]Or, *without a disturbance*
7 [a]Luke 22:7-13: *Matt. 26:17-19; Mark 14:12-16* [b]Mark 14:12
8 [a]Acts 3:1, 11; 4:13, 19; 8:14; Gal. 2:9
14 [a]Matt. 26:20; Mark 14:17 [b]Mark 6:30
16 [a]Luke 14:15; 22:18, 30; Rev. 19:9
17 [a]Luke 22:17-20: *Matt. 26:26-29; Mark 14:22-25; 1 Cor. 11:23-25;* 1 Cor. 10:16 [b]Matt. 14:19
18 [a]Matt. 26:29; Mark 14:25
19 [1]Some ancient mss. do not contain the remainder of v. 19 nor any of v. 20 [a]Matt. 14:19
20 [a]Matt. 26:28; Mark 14:24 [b]Ex. 24:8; Jer. 31:31; 1 Cor. 11:25; 2 Cor. 3:6; Heb. 8:8, 13; 9:15
21 [a]Luke 22:21-23: *Matt. 26:21-24; Mark 14:18-21;* Ps. 41:9; John 13:18, 21, 22, 26
22 [a]Acts 2:23; 4:28; 10:42; 17:31

Who Is Greatest

24 And there arose also [a]a dispute among them *as to* which one of them was regarded to be greatest.

25 [a]And He said to them, "The kings of the Gentiles lord it over them; and those who have authority over them are called 'Benefactors.'

26 "But not so with you, [a]but let him who is the greatest among you become as [b]the youngest, and the leader as the servant.

27 "For [a]who is greater, the one who reclines *at the table,* or the one who serves? Is it not the one who reclines *at the table*? But [b]I am among you as the one who serves.

28 "And you are those who have stood by Me in My [a]trials;

29 and just as My Father has granted Me a [a]kingdom, I grant you

30 that you may [a]eat and drink at My table in My [b]kingdom, and [c]you will sit on thrones judging the twelve tribes of Israel.

31 "Simon, Simon, behold, [a]Satan has [1]demanded *permission* to [b]sift you like wheat;

32 but I [a]have prayed for you, that your faith may not fail; and you, when once you have turned again, [b]strengthen your brothers."

33 [a]And he said to Him, "Lord, with You I am ready to go both to prison and to death!"

34 And He said, "I say to you, Peter, the cock will not crow today until you have denied three times that you know Me."

35 And He said to them, "[a]When I sent you out without purse and bag and sandals, you did not lack anything, did you?" And they said, "*No,* nothing."

36 And He said to them, "But now, let him who has a purse take it along, likewise also a bag, and let him who has no sword sell his [1]robe and buy one.

37 "For I tell you, that this which is written must be fulfilled in Me, '[a]AND HE WAS NUMBERED WITH TRANSGRESSORS'; for [b]that which refers to Me has *its* fulfillment."

38 And they said, "Lord, look, here are two [a]swords." And He said to them, "It is enough."

The Garden of Gethsemane

39 [a]And He came out and proceeded [b]as was His custom to [c]the Mount of Olives; and the disciples also followed Him.

40 [a]And when He arrived at the place, He said to them, "[b]Pray that you may not enter into temptation."

41 And He withdrew from them about a stone's throw, and He [a]knelt down and *began* to pray,

42 saying, "Father, if Thou art willing, remove this [a]cup from Me; [b]yet not My will, but Thine be done."

43 [1]Now an [a]angel from heaven appeared to Him, strengthening Him.

44 And [a]being in agony He was praying very fervently; and His sweat became like drops of blood, falling down upon the ground.

45 And when He rose from prayer, He came to the disciples and found them sleeping from sorrow,

46 and said to them, "Why are you sleeping? Rise and [a]pray that you may not enter into temptation."

Jesus Betrayed by Judas

47 [a]While He was still speaking, behold, a multitude *came,* and the one called Judas, one of the twelve, was preceding them; and he approached Jesus to kiss Him.

48 But Jesus said to him, "Judas, are you betraying the Son of Man with a kiss?"

49 And when those who were around Him saw what was going to happen, they said, "Lord, shall we strike with the [a]sword?"

50 And a certain one of them struck the slave of the high priest and cut off his right ear.

51 But Jesus answered and said, "[1]Stop! No more of this." And He touched his ear and healed him.

52 And Jesus said to the chief priests and [a]officers of the temple and elders who had come against Him, "Have you come out with swords and clubs [b]as against a robber?

53 "While I was with you daily in the temple, you did not lay hands on Me; but [1]this hour and the power of darkness are yours."

Jesus' Arrest

54 [a]And having arrested Him, they led Him *away,* and brought Him to the house of the high priest; but [b]Peter was following at a distance.

55 [a]And after they had kindled a fire in the middle of [b]the courtyard and had sat down together, Peter was sitting among them.

56 And a certain servant-girl, seeing him as he sat in the firelight, and looking intently at him, said, "This man was with Him too."

57 But he denied *it,* saying, "Woman, I do not know Him."

58 And a little later, [a]another saw him and said, "You are *one* of them too!" But Peter said, "Man, I am not!"

59 And after about an hour had passed, another man *began* to insist, saying, "Certainly this man also was with Him, [a]for he is a Galilean too."

60 But Peter said, "Man, I do not know what you are talking about." And immediately, while he was still speaking, a cock crowed.

24 [a]Mark 9:34; Luke 9:46

25 [a]Luke 22:25-27: *Matt. 20:25-28; Mark 10:42-45*

26 [a]Matt. 23:11; Mark 9:35; Luke 9:48 [b]1 Pet. 5:5

27 [a]Luke 12:37 [b]Matt. 20:28; John 13:12-15

28 [a]Heb. 2:18; 4:15

29 [a]Matt. 5:3; 2 Tim. 2:12

30 [a]Luke 22:16 [b]Matt. 5:3; 2 Tim. 2:12 [c]Matt. 19:28

31 [1]Or, *obtained by asking* [a]Job 1:6-12; 2:1-6; Matt. 4:10 [b]Amos 9:9

32 [a]John 17:9, 15 [b]John 21:15-17

33 [a]Luke 22:33, 34: *Matt. 26:33-35; Mark 14:29-31; John 13:37, 38*

35 [a]Matt. 10:9f.; Mark 6:8; Luke 9:3ff.; 10:4

36 [1]Or, *outer garment*

37 [a]Is. 53:12 [b]John 17:4; 19:30

38 [a]Luke 22:36, 49

39 [a]Matt. 26:30; Mark 14:26; John 18:1 [b]Luke 21:37 [c]Matt. 21:1

40 [a]Luke 22:40-46: *Matt. 26:36-46; Mark 14:32-42* [b]Matt. 6:13; Luke 22:46

41 [a]Matt. 26:39; Mark 14:35; Luke 18:11

42 [a]Matt. 20:22 [b]Matt. 26:39

43 [1]Some ancient mss. do not contain vv. 43 and 44 [a]Matt. 4:11

44 [a]Heb. 5:7

46 [a]Luke 22:40

47 [a]Luke 22:47-53: *Matt. 26:47-56; Mark 14:43-50; John 18:3-11*

49 [a]Luke 22:38

51 [1]Or, *"Let Me at least do this," and He touched*

52 [a]Luke 22:4 [b]Luke 22:37

53 [1]Lit., *this is your hour and power of darkness*

54 [a]Matt. 26:57; Mark 14:53 [b]Matt. 26:58; Mark 14:54; John 18:15

55 [a]Luke 22:55-62: *Matt. 26:69-75; Mark 14:66-72; John 18:16-18, 25-27* [b]Matt. 26:3

58 [a]John 18:26

59 [a]Matt. 26:73; Mark 14:70

61 And [a]the Lord turned and looked
at Peter. And Peter remembered the
word of the Lord, how He had told him,
"[b]Before a cock crows today, you will
deny Me three times."
62 And he went out and wept bitterly.
63 [a]And the men who were holding
[1]Jesus in custody were mocking Him,
and beating Him,
64 and they blindfolded Him and
were asking Him, saying, "[a]Prophesy,
who is the one who hit You?"
65 And they were saying many other
things against Him, [a]blaspheming.

Jesus before the Sanhedrin

66 [a]And when it was day, [b]the [1]Coun-
cil of elders of the people assembled,
both chief priests and scribes, and they
led Him away to their [c]council *chamber,*
saying,
67 "[a]If You are the [1]Christ, tell us."
But He said to them, "If I tell you, you
will not believe;
68 and if I ask a question, you will not
answer.
69 "[a]But from now on [b]THE SON OF
MAN WILL BE SEATED AT THE RIGHT
HAND of the power OF GOD."
70 And they all said, "Are You [a]the
Son of God, then?" And He said to
them, "[1][b]Yes, I am."
71 And they said, "What further need
do we have of testimony? For we have
heard it ourselves from His own mouth."

Jesus before Pilate

23 THEN the whole body of them
arose and [a]brought Him before
Pilate.
2 [a]And they began to accuse Him,
saying, "We found this man [b]misleading
our nation and [c]forbidding to pay taxes
to Caesar, and saying that He Himself is
[1]Christ, a King."
3 And Pilate asked Him, saying,
"Are You the King of the Jews?" And
He answered him and said, "[a]*It is as* you
say."
4 And Pilate said to the chief priests
and the multitudes, "[a]I find no guilt in
this man."
5 But they kept on insisting, saying,
"He stirs up the people, teaching all over
Judea, [a]starting from Galilee, even as far
as this place."
6 But when Pilate heard it, he asked
whether the man was a Galilean.
7 And when he learned that He belonged to Herod's jurisdiction, he sent
Him to [a]Herod, who himself also was in
Jerusalem [1]at that time.

Jesus before Herod

8 Now Herod was very glad when he
saw Jesus; for [a]he had wanted to see
Him for a long time, because he had
been hearing about Him and was hoping
to see some [1]sign performed by Him.
9 And he questioned Him [1]at some
length; but [a]He answered him nothing.
10 And the chief priests and the
scribes were standing there, accusing
Him vehemently.
11 And Herod with his soldiers, after
treating Him with contempt and mocking Him, [a]dressed Him in a gorgeous
robe and sent Him back to Pilate.
12 Now [a]Herod and Pilate became
friends with one another that very day;
for before they had been at enmity with
each other.

Pilate Seeks Jesus' Release

13 And Pilate summoned the chief
priests and the [a]rulers and the people,
14 and said to them, "You brought
this man to me as one who [a]incites the
people to rebellion, and behold, having
examined Him before you, I [b]have found
no guilt in this man regarding the
charges which you make against Him.
15 "No, nor has [a]Herod, for he sent
Him back to us; and behold, nothing
deserving death has been done by Him.
16 "I will therefore [a]punish Him and
release Him."
17 [[1]Now he was obliged to release to
them at the feast one prisoner.]
18 But they cried out all together,
saying, "[a]Away with this man, and
release for us Barabbas!"
19 (He was one who had been thrown
into prison for a certain insurrection
made in the city, and for murder.)
20 And Pilate, wanting to release
Jesus, addressed them again,
21 but they kept on calling out, saying, "Crucify, crucify Him!"
22 And he said to them the third time,
"Why, what evil has this man done? I
have found in Him no guilt *demanding*
death; I will therefore [a]punish Him and
release Him."
23 But they were insistent, with loud
voices asking that He be crucified. And
their voices *began* to prevail.
24 And Pilate pronounced sentence
that their demand should be granted.
25 And he released the man they were
asking for who had been thrown into
prison for insurrection and murder, but
he delivered Jesus to their will.

Simon Bears the Cross

26 [a]And when they led Him away,
they laid hold of one Simon of [b]Cyrene,
coming in from the country, and placed
on him the cross to carry behind Jesus.
27 And there were following Him a
great multitude of the people, and of
women who were [1][a]mourning and lamenting Him.
28 But Jesus turning to them said,
"Daughters of Jerusalem, stop weeping
for Me, but weep for yourselves and for
your children.
29 "For behold, the days are coming
when they will say, '[a]Blessed are the

61 [a]Luke 7:13 [b]Luke 22:34
63 [1]Lit., *Him* [a]Matt. 26:67f.; Mark 14:65; John 18:22f.
64 [a]Matt. 26:68; Mark 14:65
65 [a]Matt. 27:39
66 [1]Or, *Sanhedrin* [a]Matt. 27:1f.; Mark 15:1; John 18:28 [b]Acts 22:5 [c]Matt. 5:22
67 [1]I.e., Messiah [a]Matt. 26:63-66; Mark 14:61-63; Luke 22:67-71; John 18:19-21
69 [a]Matt. 26:64; Mark 14:62; 16:19 [b]Ps. 110:1
70 [1]Lit., *You say that I am* [a]Matt. 4:3 [b]Matt. 26:64; 27:11; Luke 23:3

1 [a]Matt. 27:2; Mark 15:1; John 18:28
2 [1]I.e., Messiah [a]Luke 23:2, 3: *Matt. 27:11-14; Mark 15:2-5; John 18:29-37* [b]Luke 23:14 [c]Luke 20:22; John 18:33ff.; 19:12; Acts 17:7
3 [a]Luke 22:70
4 [a]Matt. 27:23; Mark 15:14; Luke 23:14, 22; John 18:38; 19:4, 6
5 [a]Matt. 4:12
7 [1]Lit., *in these days* [a]Matt. 14:1; Mark 6:14; Luke 3:1; 9:7; 13:31
8 [1]Or, *attesting miracle* [a]Luke 9:9
9 [1]Lit., *in many words* [a]Matt. 27:12, 14; Mark 15:5; John 19:9
11 [a]Matt. 27:28
12 [a]Acts 4:27
13 [a]Luke 23:35; John 7:26, 48; 12:42; Acts 3:17; 4:5, 8; 13:27
14 [a]Luke 23:2 [b]Luke 23:4
15 [a]Luke 9:9
16 [a]Matt. 27:26; Mark 15:15; Luke 23:22; John 19:1; Acts 16:37
17 [1]Many mss. do not contain this v.
18 [a]Luke 23:18-25: *Matt. 27:15-26; Mark 15:6-15;* John 18:39-19:16
22 [a]Luke 23:16
26 [a]Luke 23:26: *Matt. 27:32; Mark 15:21;* John 19:17 [b]Matt. 27:32
27 [1]Lit., *beating the breast* [a]Luke 8:52
29 [a]Matt. 24:19; Luke 11:27; 21:23

barren, and the wombs that never bore, and the breasts that never nursed.'

30 "Then they will begin TO [a]SAY TO THE MOUNTAINS, 'FALL ON US,' AND TO THE HILLS, 'COVER US.'

31 "For if they do these things in the green tree, what will happen in the dry?"

32 [a]And two others also, who were criminals, were being led away to be put to death with Him.

The Crucifixion

33 [a]And when they came to the place called [1]The Skull, there they crucified Him and the criminals, one on the right and the other on the left.

34 [1]But Jesus was saying, "[a]Father, forgive them; for they do not know what they are doing." [b]And they cast lots, dividing up His garments among themselves.

35 And the people stood by, looking on. And even the [a]rulers were sneering at Him, saying, "He saved others; [b]let Him save Himself if this is the [1]Christ of God, His Chosen One."

36 And the soldiers also mocked Him, coming up to Him, [a]offering Him sour wine,

37 and saying, "[a]If You are the King of the Jews, save Yourself!"

38 Now there was also an inscription above Him, "[a]THIS IS THE KING OF THE JEWS."

39 [a]And one of the criminals who were hanged *there* was [1]hurling abuse at Him, saying, "Are You not the [2]Christ? [b]Save Yourself and us!"

40 But the other answered, and rebuking him said, "Do you not even fear God, since you are under the same sentence of condemnation?

41 "And we indeed justly, for we are receiving [1]what we deserve for our deeds; but this man has done nothing wrong."

42 And he was saying, "Jesus, remember me when You come [1]in Your kingdom!"

43 And He said to him, "Truly I say to you, today you shall be with Me in [a]Paradise."

44 [a]And it was now about [1b]the sixth hour, and darkness [2]fell over the whole land until [3]the ninth hour,

45 the sun [1]being obscured; and [a]the veil of the temple was torn [2]in two.

46 And Jesus, [a]crying out with a loud voice, said, "Father, [b]INTO THY HANDS I COMMIT MY SPIRIT." And having said this, He breathed His last.

47 [a]Now when the centurion saw what had happened, he *began* [b]praising God, saying, "Certainly this man was [1]innocent."

48 And all the multitudes who came together for this spectacle, when they observed what had happened, *began* to return, [a]beating their breasts.

49 [a]And all His acquaintances and [a]the women who accompanied Him

30 [a]Hos. 10:8; Is. 2:19, 20; Rev. 6:16
32 [a]Matt. 27:38; Mark 15:27; John 19:18
33 [1]In Lat., *Calvarius;* or, *Calvary* [a]Luke 23:33-43: *Matt. 27:33-44; Mark 15:22-32; John 19:17-24*
34 [1]Some mss. do not contain *But Jesus was saying . . . doing.* [a]Matt. 11:25; Luke 22:42 [b]Ps. 22:18; John 19:24
35 [1]I.e., Messiah [a]Luke 23:13 [b]Matt. 27:43
36 [a]Matt. 27:48
37 [a]Matt. 27:43
38 [a]Matt. 27:37; Mark 15:26; John 19:19
39 [1]Or, *blaspheming* [2]I.e., Messiah [a]Matt. 27:44; Mark 15:32; Luke 23:39-43 [b]Luke 23:35, 37
41 [1]Lit., *things worthy of what we have done*
42 [1]Or, *into*
43 [a]2 Cor. 12:4; Rev. 2:7
44 [1]I.e., 12 noon [2]Or, *occurred* [3]I.e., 3 p.m. [a]Luke 23:44-49: *Matt. 27:45-56; Mark 15:33-41* [b]John 19:14
45 [1]Lit., *failing* [2]Lit., *in the middle* [a]Ex. 26:31-33; Matt. 27:51
46 [a]Matt. 27:50; Mark 15:37; John 19:30 [b]Ps. 31:5
47 [1]Lit., *righteous* [a]Matt. 27:54; Mark 15:39 [b]Matt. 9:8
48 [a]Luke 8:52; 18:13
49 [a]Matt. 27:55f.; Mark 15:40f.; Luke 8:2; John 19:25
50 [a]Luke 23:50-56: *Matt. 27:57-61; Mark 15:42-47; John 19:38-42* [b]Mark 15:43
51 [a]Mark 15:43; Luke 2:25
54 [1]Lit., *dawn* [a]Matt. 27:62; Mark 15:42
55 [a]Luke 23:49
56 [a]Mark 16:1; Luke 24:1 [b]Ex. 20:10f.; Deut. 5:14

1 [a]Luke 24:1-10: *Matt. 28:1-8; Mark 16:1-8;* John 20:1-8
3 [a]Luke 7:13; Acts 1:21
4 [a]John 20:12 [b]Luke 2:9; Acts 12:7
6 [1]Some ancient mss. do not contain *He is not here, but He has risen* [2]Or, *been raised* [a]Mark 16:6 [b]Matt. 17:22f.; Mark 9:30f.; Luke 9:44; 24:44
7 [a]Matt. 16:21; Luke 24:46
8 [a]John 2:22

from Galilee, were standing at a distance, seeing these things.

Jesus Is Buried

50 [a]And behold, a man named Joseph, who was a [b]member of the Council, a good and righteous man

51 (he had not consented to their plan and action), *a man* from Arimathea, a city of the Jews, who was [a]waiting for the kingdom of God;

52 this man went to Pilate and asked for the body of Jesus.

53 And he took it down and wrapped it in a linen cloth, and laid Him in a tomb cut into the rock, where no one had ever lain.

54 And it was [a]the preparation day, and the Sabbath was about to [1]begin.

55 Now [a]the women who had come with Him out of Galilee followed after, and saw the tomb and how His body was laid.

56 And they returned and [a]prepared spices and perfumes.

And [b]on the Sabbath they rested according to the commandment.

The Resurrection

24 [a]BUT on the first day of the week, at early dawn, they came to the tomb, bringing the spices which they had prepared.

2 And they found the stone rolled away from the tomb,

3 but when they entered, they did not find the body of [a]the Lord Jesus.

4 And it happened that while they were perplexed about this, behold, [a]two men suddenly [b]stood near them in dazzling apparel;

5 and as *the women* were terrified and bowed their faces to the ground, *the men* said to them, "Why do you seek the living One among the dead?

6 "[1]He is not here, but He [a]has [2]risen. Remember how He spoke to you [b]while He was still in Galilee,

7 saying that [a]the Son of Man must be delivered into the hands of sinful men, and be crucified, and the third day rise again."

8 And [a]they remembered His words,

9 and returned from the tomb and reported all these things to the eleven and to all the rest.

10 Now they were [a]Mary Magdalene and Joanna and Mary the *mother* of James; also the other women with them were telling these things to [b]the apostles.

11 And these words appeared [1]to them as nonsense, and they [a]would not believe them.

12 [[1]But Peter arose and [a]ran to the tomb; stooping and looking in, he *saw the linen wrappings [2]only; and he went away [b]to his home, marveling at that which had happened.]

10 [a]Matt. 27:56 [b]Mark 6:30
11 [1]Lit., *in their sight* [a]Mark 16:11
12 [1]Some ancient mss. do not contain v. 12 [2]Or, *by themselves* [a]John 20:3-6 [b]John 20:10

The Road to Emmaus

13 And behold, [a]two of them were
going that very day to a village named
Emmaus, which was [1]about seven miles
from Jerusalem.
14 And they were conversing with
each other about all these things which
had taken place.
15 And it came about that while they
were conversing and discussing, Jesus
Himself approached, and *began* traveling with them.
16 But [a]their eyes [1]were prevented
from recognizing Him.
17 And He said to them, "What are
these words that you are exchanging
with one another as you are walking?"
And they stood still, looking sad.
18 And one of them, named Cleopas,
answered and said to Him, "Are You
[1]the only one visiting Jerusalem and
unaware of the things which have happened here in these days?"
19 And He said to them, "What
things?" And they said to Him, "The
things about [a]Jesus the Nazarene, who
was a [b]prophet mighty in deed and word
in the sight of God and all the people,
20 and how the chief priests and our
[a]rulers delivered Him up to the sentence
of death, and crucified Him.
21 "But we were hoping that it was He
who was going to [a]redeem Israel. Indeed, besides all this, it is the third day
since these things happened.
22 "But also some women among us
amazed us. [a]When they were at the tomb
early in the morning,
23 and did not find His body, they
came, saying that they had also seen a
vision of angels, who said that He was
alive.
24 "And some of those who were with
us went to the tomb and found it just
exactly as the women also had said; but
Him they did not see."
25 And He said to them, "O foolish
men and slow of heart to believe in all
that [a]the prophets have spoken!
26 "[a]Was it not necessary for the
[1]Christ to suffer these things and to
enter into His glory?"
27 And beginning [1]with [a]Moses and
[1]with all the [b]prophets, He explained to
them the things concerning Himself in
all the Scriptures.
28 And they approached the village
where they were going, and [a]He acted as
though He would go farther.
29 And they urged Him, saying, "Stay
with us, for it is *getting* toward evening,
and the day [1]is now nearly over." And
He went in to stay with them.
30 And it came about that when He
had reclined *at the table* with them, He
took the bread and [a]blessed *it*, and
breaking *it*, He *began* giving *it* to them.
31 And their [a]eyes were opened and
they recognized Him; and He vanished
from [1]their sight.
32 And they said to one another,
"[1]Were not our hearts burning within us
while He was speaking to us on the road,
while He [a]was [2]explaining the Scriptures
to us?"
33 And they arose that very hour and
returned to Jerusalem, and [a]found gathered together the eleven and [b]those who
were with them,
34 saying, "[a]The Lord has really risen,
and [b]has appeared to Simon."
35 And they *began* to relate [1]their
experiences on the road and how [a]He
was recognized by them in the breaking
of the bread.

Other Appearances

36 And while they were telling these
things, [a]He Himself stood in their
midst.[1]
37 But they were startled and frightened and thought that they were seeing
[a]a spirit.
38 And He said to them, "Why are
you troubled, and why do doubts arise
in your [1]hearts?
39 "[a]See My hands and My feet, that it
is I Myself; [b]touch Me and see, for a
spirit does not have flesh and bones as
you see that I have."
40 [[1]And when He had said this, He
showed them His hands and His feet.]
41 And while they still [1a]could not
believe *it* for joy and were marveling, He
said to them, "[b]Have you anything here
to eat?"
42 And they gave Him a piece of a
broiled fish;
43 and He took it and [a]ate *it* before
them.
44 Now He said to them, "[a]These are
My words which I spoke to you while I
was still with you, that all things which
are written about Me in the [b]Law of
Moses and the Prophets and [c]the Psalms
must be fulfilled."
45 Then He [a]opened their [1]minds to
understand the Scriptures,
46 and He said to them, "[a]Thus it is
written, that the [1]Christ should suffer
and [b]rise again from the dead the third
day;
47 and that [a]repentance [1]for forgiveness of sins should be proclaimed [2]in His
name to [b]all the nations, beginning from
Jerusalem.
48 "You are [a]witnesses of these things.
49 "And behold, [a]I am sending forth
the promise of My Father upon you; but
[b]you are to stay in the city until you are
clothed with power from on high."

13 [1]I.e., 60 stadia, one stadion was about 600 ft. [a]Mark 16:12
16 [1]Lit., *were being prevented* [a]Luke 24:31; John 20:14; 21:4
18 [1]Or, *visiting Jerusalem alone*
19 [a]Mark 1:24 [b]Matt. 21:11
20 [a]Luke 23:13
21 [a]Luke 1:68
22 [a]Luke 24:1ff.
25 [a]Matt. 26:24
26 [1]I.e., Messiah [a]Luke 24:7, 44ff.; Heb. 2:10; 1 Pet. 1:11
27 [1]Lit., *from* [a]Gen. 3:15; 12:3; Num. 21:9 [John 3:14]; Deut. 18:15 [John 1:45]; John 5:46 [b]2 Sam. 7:12-16; Is. 7:14 [Matt. 1:23]; Is. 9:1f. [Matt. 4:15f.]; Is. 42:1 [Matt. 12:18ff.]; Is. 53:4 [Matt. 8:17; Luke 22:37]; Dan. 7:13 [Matt. 24:30]; Mic. 5:2 [Matt. 2:6]; Zech. 9:9 [Matt. 21:5]; Acts 13:27
28 [a]Mark 6:48
29 [1]Lit., *has now declined*
30 [a]Matt. 14:19
31 [1]Lit., *them* [a]Luke 24:16
32 [1]Lit., *Was not our heart* [2]Lit., *opening* [a]Luke 24:45
33 [a]Mark 16:13 [b]Acts 1:14
34 [a]Luke 24:6 [b]1 Cor. 15:5
35 [1]Lit., *the things* [a]Luke 24:30f.
36 [1]Some ancient mss. insert *And He says to them, "Peace be to you."* [a]Mark 16:14
37 [a]Matt. 14:26; Mark 6:49
38 [1]Lit., *heart*
39 [a]John 20:20, 27 [b]John 20:27; 1 John 1:1
40 [1]Many mss. do not contain this v.
41 [1]Lit., *were disbelieving* [a]Luke 24:11 [b]John 21:5
43 [a]Acts 10:41
44 [a]Luke 9:22, 44f.; 18:31-34; 22:37 [b]Luke 24:27 [c]Ps. 2:7ff. [Acts 13:33]; Ps. 16:10 [Acts 2:27]; Ps. 22:1-18 [Matt. 27:34-46]; Ps. 69:1-21 [John 19:28ff.]; Ps. 72; 110:1 [Matt. 22:43f.]; Ps. 118:22f. [Matt. 21:42]
45 [1]Lit., *mind* [a]Luke 24:32; Acts 16:14; 1 John 5:20
46 [1]I.e., Messiah [a]Luke 24:26, 44 [b]Luke 24:7
47 [1]Some mss. read *and forgiveness* [2]Or, *on the basis of* [a]Acts 5:31; 10:43; 13:38; 26:18 [b]Matt. 28:19
48 [a]Acts 1:8, 22; 2:32; 3:15; 4:33; 5:32; 10:39, 41; 13:31; 1 Pet. 5:1
49 [a]John 14:26 [b]Acts 1:4

The Ascension

50 And He led them out as far as [a]Bethany, and He lifted up His hands and blessed them.

51 And it came about that while He was blessing them, He parted from them.[1]

52 And they[1] returned to Jerusalem with great joy,

53 and were continually in the temple, [1]praising God.

50 [a]Matt. 21:17; Acts 1:12
51 [1]Some mss. add *and was carried up into heaven*
52 [1]Some mss. insert *worshiped Him, and*
53 [1]Lit., *blessing*

THE GOSPEL ACCORDING TO JOHN

The Deity of Jesus Christ

1 [a]IN the beginning was [b]the Word, and the Word was [c]with God, and [d]the Word was God.

2 [1]He was in the beginning with God.

3 [a]All things came into being [1]by Him, and apart from Him nothing came into being that has come into being.

4 [a]In Him was life, and the life was [b]the light of men.

5 And [a]the light shines in the darkness, and the darkness did not [1]comprehend it.

The Witness of John

6 There [1]came a man, sent from God, whose name was [a]John.

7 [1]He came [a]for a witness, that he might bear witness of the light, [b]that all might believe through him.

8 [1a]He was not the light, but *came* that he might bear witness of the light.

9 There was [a]the true light [1]which, coming into the world, enlightens every man.

10 He was in the world, and [a]the world was made through Him, and the world did not know Him.

11 He came to His [1]own, and those who were His own did not receive Him.

12 But as many as received Him, to them He gave the right to become [a]children of God, *even* [b]to those who believe in His name,

13 [a]who were [1]born not of [2]blood, nor of the will of the flesh, nor of the will of man, but of God.

The Word Made Flesh

14 And [a]the Word [b]became flesh, and [1c]dwelt among us, and [d]we beheld His glory, glory as of [2]the only begotten from the Father, full of [e]grace and [f]truth.

15 John *[a]bore witness of Him, and cried out, saying, "This was He of whom I said, '[b]He who comes after me [1]has a higher rank than I, [c]for He existed before me.' "

16 For of His [a]fulness [1]we have all received, and [2]grace upon grace.

17 For [a]the Law was given through Moses; [b]grace and [c]truth were realized through Jesus Christ.

18 [a]No man has seen God at any time; [b]the only begotten [1]God, who is [c]in the bosom of the Father, [d]He has explained *Him.*

The Testimony of John

19 And this is [a]the witness of John, when [b]the Jews sent to him priests and Levites [c]from Jerusalem to ask him, "Who are you?"

20 And he confessed, and did not deny, and he confessed, "[a]I am not [1]the Christ."

21 And they asked him, "What then? Are you [a]Elijah?" And he *said, "I am not." "Are you [b]the Prophet?" And he answered, "No."

22 They said then to him, "Who are you, so that we may give an answer to those who sent us? What do you say about yourself?"

23 He said, "I am [a]A VOICE OF ONE CRYING IN THE WILDERNESS, 'MAKE STRAIGHT THE WAY OF THE LORD,' as Isaiah the prophet said."

24 Now they had been sent from the Pharisees.

25 And they asked him, and said to him, "Why then are you baptizing, if you are not the [1]Christ, nor Elijah, nor [a]the Prophet?"

26 John answered them saying, "[a]I baptize [1]in water, *but* among you stands One whom you do not know.

27 "*It is* [a]He who comes after me, the [b]thong of whose sandal I am not worthy to untie."

28 These things took place in Bethany [a]beyond the Jordan, where John was baptizing.

29 The next day he *saw Jesus coming to him, and *said, "Behold, [a]the Lamb of God who [b]takes away the sin of the world!

1 [a]Gen. 1:1; Col. 1:17; 1 John 1:1 [b]John 1:14; Rev. 19:13 [c]John 17:5; 1 John 1:2 [d]Phil. 2:6
2 [1]Lit., *This one*
3 [1]Or, *through* [a]John 1:10; 1 Cor. 8:6; Col. 1:16; Heb. 1:2
4 [a]John 5:26; 11:25; 14:6 [b]John 8:12; 9:5; 12:46
5 [1]Or, *overpower* [a]John 3:19
6 [1]Or, *came into being* [a]Matt. 3:1
7 [1]Lit., *This one* [a]John 1:15, 19, 32; 3:26; 5:33 [b]John 1:12; Acts 19:4; Gal. 3:26
8 [1]Lit., *That one* [a]John 1:20
9 [1]Or, *which enlightens every man coming into the world* [a]1 John 2:8
10 [a]1 Cor. 8:6; Col. 1:16; Heb. 1:2
11 [1]Or, *own things, possessions, domain*
12 [a]John 11:52; Gal. 3:26 [b]John 1:7; 3:18; 1 John 3:23; 5:13
13 [1]Or, *begotten* [2]Lit., *bloods* [a]John 3:5f.; James 1:18; 1 Pet. 1:23; 1 John 2:29; 3:9
14 [1]Or, *tabernacled* [2]Or, *unique, only one of His kind* [a]Rev. 19:13 [b]Rom. 1:3; Gal. 4:4; Phil. 2:7f.; 1 Tim. 3:16; Heb. 2:14; 1 John 1:1f.; 4:2; 2 John 7 [c]Rev. 21:3 [d]Luke 9:32; John 2:11; 17:22, 24; 2 Pet. 1:16f.; 1 John 1:1 [e]John 1:17; Rom. 5:21; 6:14 [f]John 8:32; 14:6; 18:37
15 [1]Lit., *is become before me* [a]John 1:7 [b]Matt. 3:11; John 1:27, 30 [c]John 1:30
16 [1]Lit., *we all received* [2]Lit., *grace for grace* [a]Eph. 1:23; 3:19; 4:13; Col. 1:19; 2:9
17 [a]John 7:19 [b]John 1:14; Rom. 5:21; 6:14 [c]John 8:32; 14:6; 18:37
18 [1]Some later mss. read *Son* [a]Ex. 33:20; John 6:46; Col. 1:15; 1 Tim. 6:16; 1 John 4:12 [b]John 3:16, 18; 1 John 4:9 [c]Luke 16:22; John 13:23 [d]John 3:11

19 [a]John 1:7 [b]John 2:18, 20; 5:10, 15f., 18; 6:41, 52; 7:1, 11, 13, 15, 35; 8:22, 48, 52, 57; 9:18, 22; 10:24, 31, 33 [c]Matt. 15:1
20 [1]I.e., the Messiah [a]Luke 3:15f.; John 3:28
21 [a]Matt. 11:14; 16:14 [b]Deut. 18:15, 18; Matt. 21:11; John 1:25
23 [a]Is. 40:3; Matt. 3:3; Mark 1:3; Luke 3:4
25 [1]I.e., Messiah [a]Deut. 18:15, 18; Matt. 21:11; John 1:21
26 [1]The Gr. here can be translated *in, with* or *by* [a]Matt. 3:11; Mark 1:8; Luke 3:16; Acts 1:5
27 [a]Matt. 3:11; John 1:30 [b]Matt. 3:11; Mark 1:7; Luke 3:16
28 [a]John 3:26; 10:40
29 [a]Is. 53:7; John 1:36; Acts 8:32; 1 Pet. 1:19; Rev. 5:6, 8, 12f.; 6:1 [b]Matt. 1:21; 1 John 3:5

30"This is He on behalf of whom I
said, '[a]After me comes a Man who [1]has a
higher rank than I, [b]for He existed
before me.'
31"And I did not recognize [1]Him, but
in order that He might be manifested to
Israel, I came baptizing [2]in water."
32 And John [a]bore witness saying, "[b]I
have beheld the Spirit descending as a
dove out of heaven, and He remained
upon Him.
33"And I did not recognize [1]Him, but
He who sent me to baptize [2]in water said
to me, 'He upon whom you see the Spirit
descending and remaining upon Him,
[a]this is the one who baptizes [2]in the
Holy Spirit.'
34"And I have seen, and have borne
witness that this is [a]the Son of God."

Jesus' Public Ministry, First Converts

35 Again [a]the next day John was
standing [1]with two of his disciples,
36 and he looked upon Jesus as He
walked, and *said, "Behold, [a]the Lamb
of God!"
37 And the two disciples heard him
speak, and they followed Jesus.
38 And Jesus turned, and beheld them
following, and *said to them, "What do
you seek?" And they said to Him,
"[a]Rabbi (which translated means
Teacher), where are You staying?"
39 He *said to them, "Come, and you
will see." They came therefore and saw
where He was staying; and they stayed
with Him that day, for it was about the
[1]tenth hour.
40 [a]One of the two who heard John
speak, and followed Him, was Andrew,
Simon Peter's brother.
41 He *found first his own brother
Simon, and *said to him, "We have
found the [a]Messiah" (which translated
means [1]Christ).
42 He brought him to Jesus. Jesus
looked at him, and said, "You are Simon
the son of [1a]John; you shall be called
[b]Cephas" (which is translated [2c]Peter).
43 [a]The next day He purposed to go
forth into [b]Galilee, and He *found
[c]Philip. And Jesus *said to him, "[d]Fol-
low Me."
44 Now [a]Philip was from [b]Bethsaida,
of the city of Andrew and Peter.
45 [a]Philip *found [b]Nathanael and
*said to him, "We have found Him of
whom [c]Moses in the Law and *also* [c]the
Prophets wrote, Jesus of [d]Nazareth, [e]the
son of Joseph."
46 And Nathanael *said to him,
"[a]Can any good thing come out of
Nazareth?" [b]Philip *said to him, "Come
and see."
47 Jesus saw Nathanael coming to
Him, and *said of him, "Behold, an
[a]Israelite indeed, in whom is no guile!"
48 Nathanael *said to Him, "How do
You know me?" Jesus answered and said
to him, "Before [a]Philip called you, when
you were under the fig tree, I saw you."
49 Nathanael answered Him,
"[a]Rabbi, You are [b]the Son of God; You
are the [c]King of Israel."
50 Jesus answered and said to him,
"Because I said to you that I saw you
under the fig tree, do you believe? You
shall see greater things than these."
51 And He *said to him, "Truly, truly,
I say to you, you shall see [a]the heavens
opened, and [b]the angels of God ascending and descending on [c]the Son of
Man."

Miracle at Cana

2 AND on [a]the third day there was a
wedding in [b]Cana of Galilee, and
the [c]mother of Jesus was there;
2 and Jesus also was invited, and His
[a]disciples, to the wedding.
3 And when the wine gave out, the
mother of Jesus *said to Him, "They
have no wine."
4 And Jesus *said to her, "[a]Woman,
[1b]what do I have to do with you? [c]My
hour has not yet come."
5 His [a]mother *said to the servants,
"Whatever He says to you, do it."
6 Now there were six stone waterpots
set there [a]for the Jewish custom of
purification, containing [1]twenty or thirty
gallons each.
7 Jesus *said to them, "Fill the waterpots with water." And they filled
them up to the brim.
8 And He *said to them, "Draw *some*
out now, and take it to the [1]headwaiter."
And they took it *to him.*
9 And when the headwaiter tasted
the water [a]which had become wine, and
did not know where it came from (but
the servants who had drawn the water
knew), the headwaiter *called the bridegroom,
10 and *said to him, "Every man
serves the good wine first, and when *men*
[a]have [1]drunk freely, *then* that which is
poorer; you have kept the good wine
until now."
11 This beginning of *His* [1a]signs Jesus
did in Cana of [b]Galilee, and manifested
His [c]glory, and His disciples believed in
Him.
12 After this He went down to [a]Ca-
pernaum, He and His [b]mother, and *His*
[b]brothers, and His [c]disciples; and there
they stayed a few days.

30 [1]Lit., *has become before me* [a]Matt. 3:11; John 1:27 [b]John 1:15
31 [1]I.e., as the Messiah [2]The Gr. here can be translated *in, with* or *by*
32 [a]John 1:7 [b]Matt. 3:16; Mark 1:10; Luke 3:22
33 [1]I.e., as the Messiah [2]The Gr. here can be translated *in, with,* or *by* [a]Matt. 3:11; Mark 1:8; Luke 3:16; Acts 1:5
34 [a]Matt. 4:3; John 1:49
35 [1]Lit., *and* [a]John 1:29
36 [a]John 1:29
38 [a]Matt. 23:7f.; John 1:49
39 [1]Perhaps 10 a.m. (Roman time)
40 [a]Matt. 4:18-22; Mark 1:16-20; Luke 5:2-11; John 1:40-42
41 [1]Gr., *Anointed One* [a]Dan. 9:25; John 4:25
42 [1]Gr., *Joannes* [2]I.e., Rock or Stone [a]Matt. 16:17; John 21:15-17 [b]1 Cor. 1:12; 3:22; 9:5; 15:5; Gal. 1:18; 2:9, 11, 14 [c]Matt. 16:18
43 [a]John 1:29, 35 [b]Matt. 4:12; John 1:28; 2:11 [c]Matt. 10:3; John 1:44-48; 6:5, 7; 12:21f.; 14:8f. [d]Matt. 8:22
44 [a]Matt. 10:3; John 1:44-48; 6:5, 7; 12:21f.; 14:8f. [b]Matt. 11:21
45 [a]Matt. 10:3; John 1:44-48; 6:5, 7; 12:21f.; 14:8f. [b]John 1:46-49; 21:2 [c]Luke 24:27 [d]Matt. 2:23 [e]Luke 2:48; 3:23; 4:22; John 6:42
46 [a]John 7:41, 52 [b]Matt. 10:3; John 1:44-48; 6:5, 7; 12:21f.; 14:8f.
47 [a]Rom. 9:4
48 [a]Matt. 10:3; John 1:44-48; 6:5, 7; 12:21f.; 14:8f.
49 [a]John 1:38 [b]John 1:34 [c]Matt. 2:2; 27:42; Mark 15:32; John 12:13
51 [a]Ezek. 1:1; Matt. 3:16; Luke 3:21; Acts 7:56; 10:11; Rev. 19:11 [b]Gen. 28:12 [c]Matt. 8:20

1 [a]John 1:29, 35, 43 [b]John 2:11; 4:46; 21:2 [c]Matt. 12:46
2 [a]John 1:40-49; 2:12, 17, 22; 3:22; 4:2, 8, 27; 6:8, 12, 16, 22, 24, 60f., 66; 7:3; 8:31
4 [1]Lit., *what to Me and to you* (a Hebrew idiom) [a]John 19:26 [b]Matt. 8:29 [c]John 7:6, 8, 30; 8:20
5 [a]Matt. 12:46
6 [1]Two or three metretai [a]Mark 7:3f.; John 3:25

8 [1]Or, *steward*
9 [a]John 4:46
10 [1]Or, *have become drunk* [a]Matt. 24:49; Luke 12:45; Acts 2:15; 1 Cor. 11:21; Eph. 5:18; 1 Thess. 5:7; Rev. 17:2, 6
11 [1]Or, *attesting miracles*; i.e., one which points to the supernatural power of God in redeeming grace [a]John 2:23; 3:2; 4:54; 6:2, 14, 26, 30; 7:31; 9:16; 10:41; 11:47; 12:18, 37; 20:30 [b]John 1:43 [c]John 1:14
12 [a]Matt. 4:13 [b]Matt. 12:46 [c]John 2:2

First Passover—Cleansing the Temple

13 And [a]the Passover of the Jews was at hand, and Jesus [b]went up to Jerusalem.

14 [a]And He found in the temple those who were selling oxen and sheep and doves, and the moneychangers seated.

15 And He made a scourge of cords, and drove *them* all out of the temple, with the sheep and the oxen; and He poured out the coins of the moneychangers, and overturned their tables;

16 and to those who were selling [a]the doves He said, "Take these things away; stop making [b]My Father's house a house of merchandise."

17 His [a]disciples remembered that it was written, "[b]ZEAL FOR THY HOUSE WILL CONSUME ME."

18 [a]The Jews therefore answered and said to Him, "[b]What sign do You show to us, seeing that You do these things?"

19 Jesus answered and said to them, "[a]Destroy this [1]temple, and in three days I will raise it up."

20 [a]The Jews therefore said, "It took [b]forty-six years to build this [1]temple, and will You raise it up in three days?"

21 But He was speaking of [a]the [1]temple of His body.

22 When therefore He was raised from the dead, His [a]disciples [b]remembered that He said this; and they believed [c]the Scripture, and the word which Jesus had spoken.

23 Now when He was in Jerusalem at [a]the Passover, during the feast, many believed in His name, [b]beholding His signs which He was doing.

24 But Jesus, on His part, was not entrusting Himself to them, for [a]He knew all men,

25 and because He did not need anyone to bear witness concerning man [a]for He Himself knew what was in man.

The New Birth

3 NOW there was a man of the Pharisees, named [a]Nicodemus, a [b]ruler of the Jews;

2 this man came to Him by night, and said to Him, "[a]Rabbi, we know that You have come from God *as* a teacher; for no one can do these [1b]signs that You do unless [c]God is with him."

3 Jesus answered and said to him, "Truly, truly, I say to you, unless one [a]is born [1]again, he cannot see [b]the kingdom of God."

4 Nicodemus *said to Him, "How can a man be born when he is old? He cannot enter a second time into his mother's womb and be born, can he?"

5 Jesus answered, "Truly, truly, I say to you, unless one is born of [a]water and the Spirit, he cannot enter into [b]the kingdom of God.

6 "[a]That which is born of the flesh is flesh, and that which is born of the Spirit is spirit.

7 "Do not marvel that I said to you, 'You must be born [1]again.'

8 "[a]The wind blows where it wishes and you hear the sound of it, but do not know where it comes from and where it is going; so is everyone who is born of the Spirit."

9 Nicodemus answered and said to Him, "How can these things be?"

10 Jesus answered and said to him, "Are you [a]the teacher of Israel, and do not understand these things?

11 "Truly, truly, I say to you, [a]we speak that which we know, and [b]bear witness of that which we have seen; and [b]you do not receive our witness.

12 "If I told you earthly things and you do not believe, how shall you believe if I tell you heavenly things?

13 "And [a]no one has ascended into heaven, but [b]He who descended from heaven, *even* [c]the Son of Man.[1]

14 "And as [a]Moses lifted up the serpent in the wilderness, even so must [b]the Son of Man [c]be lifted up;

15 that whoever [1]believes may [a]in Him have eternal life.

16 "For God so [a]loved the world, that He [b]gave His [1c]only begotten Son, that whoever [d]believes in Him should not perish, but have eternal life.

17 "For God [a]did not send the Son into the world [b]to judge the world, but that the world should be saved through Him.

18 "[a]He who believes in Him is not judged; he who does not believe has been judged already, because he has not believed in the name of [b]the [1]only begotten Son of God.

19 "And this is the judgment, that [a]the light is come into the world, and men loved the darkness rather than the light; for [b]their deeds were evil.

20 "[a]For everyone who does evil hates the light, and does not come to the light, lest his deeds should be exposed.

21 "But he who [a]practices the truth comes to the light, that his deeds may be manifested as having been wrought in God."

John's Last Testimony

22 After these things Jesus and His [a]disciples came into the land of Judea, and there He was spending time with them and [b]baptizing.

13 [a]Deut. 16:1-6; John 5:1; 6:4; 11:55 [b]Luke 2:41; John 2:23
14 [a]John 2:14-16: *Matt. 21:12ff.; Mark 11:15, 17; Luke 19:45f.;* Mal. 3:1ff.
16 [a]Matt. 21:12 [b]Luke 2:49
17 [a]John 2:2 [b]Ps. 69:9
18 [a]John 1:19 [b]Matt. 12:38
19 [1]Or, *sanctuary* [a]Matt. 26:61; 27:40; Mark 14:58; 15:29; Acts 6:14
20 [1]Or, *sanctuary* [a]John 1:19 [b]Ezra 5:16
21 [1]Or, *sanctuary* [a]1 Cor. 6:19
22 [a]John 2:2 [b]Luke 24:8; John 2:17; 12:16; 14:26 [c]Ps. 16:10; Luke 24:26f.; John 20:9; Acts 13:33
23 [a]John 2:13 [b]John 2:11
24 [a]Acts 1:24; 15:8
25 [a]Matt. 9:4; John 1:42, 47; 6:61, 64; 13:11

1 [a]John 7:50; 19:39 [b]Luke 23:13; John 7:26, 48
2 [1]Or, *attesting miracles* [a]Matt. 23:7; John 3:26 [b]John 2:11 [c]John 9:33; 10:38; 14:10f.; Acts 2:22; 10:38
3 [1]Or, *from above* [a]2 Cor. 5:17; 1 Pet. 1:23 [b]Matt. 19:24; 21:31; Mark 9:47; 10:14f.; John 3:5
5 [a]Ezek. 36:25-27; Eph. 5:26; Titus 3:5 [b]Matt. 19:24; 21:31; Mark 9:47; 10:14f.; John 3:3
6 [a]John 1:13; 1 Cor. 15:50
7 [1]Or, *from above*
8 [a]Ps. 135:7; Eccl. 11:5; Ezek. 37:9
10 [a]Luke 2:46; 5:17; Acts 5:34
11 [a]John 1:18; 7:16f.; 8:26, 28; 12:49; 14:24 [b]John 3:32
13 [1]Later mss. add *who is in heaven* [a]Deut. 30:12; Prov. 30:4; Acts 2:34; Rom. 10:6; Eph. 4:9 [b]John 3:31; 6:38, 42 [c]Matt. 8:20
14 [a]Num. 21:9 [b]Matt. 8:20 [c]John 8:28; 12:34
15 [1]Some mss. read *believes in Him may have eternal life* [a]John 20:31; 1 John 5:11-13
16 [1]Or, *unique,* only one of His kind [a]Rom. 5:8; Eph. 2:4; 2 Thess. 2:16; 1 John 4:10; Rev. 1:5 [b]Rom. 8:32; 1 John 4:9 [c]John 1:18; 3:18; 1 John 4:9 [d]John 3:36; 6:40; 11:25f.
17 [a]John 3:34; 5:36, 38; 6:29, 38, 57; 7:29; 8:42; 10:36; 11:42; 17:3, 8, 18, 21, 23, 25; 20:21 [b]Luke 19:10; John 8:15; 12:47; 1 John 4:14
18 [1]Or, *unique,* only one of His kind [a]Mark 16:16; John 5:24 [b]John 1:18; 1 John 4:9
19 [a]John 1:4; 8:12; 9:5; 12:46 [b]John 7:7
20 [a]John 3:20, 21; Eph. 5:11, 13
21 [a]1 John 1:6
22 [a]John 2:2 [b]John 4:1, 2

23 And John also was baptizing in Aenon near Salim, because there was [1]much water there; and they were coming and were being baptized.

24 For [a]John had not yet been thrown into prison.

25 There arose therefore a discussion on the part of John's disciples with a Jew about [a]purification.

26 And they came to John and said to him, "[a]Rabbi, He who was with you [b]beyond the Jordan, to whom you [c]have borne witness, behold, He is baptizing, and all are coming to Him."

27 John answered and said, "[a]A man can receive nothing, unless it [b]has been given him from heaven.

28 "You yourselves bear me witness, that I said, '[a]I am not the [1]Christ,' but, 'I have been sent before Him.'

29 "He who has the bride is [a]the bridegroom; but the friend of the bridegroom, who stands and hears him, rejoices greatly because of the bridegroom's voice. And so this [b]joy of mine has been made full.

30 "He must increase, but I must decrease.

31 "[a]He who comes from above is above all, [b]he who is of the earth is from the earth and speaks of the earth. [a]He who comes from heaven is above all.

32 "What He has seen and heard, of that He [a]bears witness; and [a]no man receives His witness.

33 "He who has received His witness [a]has set his seal to *this,* that God is true.

34 "For He whom God has [a]sent speaks the words of God; [1b]for He gives the Spirit without measure.

35 "[a]The Father loves the Son, and [b]has given all things into His hand.

36 "He who [a]believes in the Son has eternal life; but he who [b]does not [1]obey the Son shall not see life, but the wrath of God abides on him."

Jesus Goes to Galilee

4 WHEN therefore [a]the Lord knew that the Pharisees had heard that Jesus was making and [b]baptizing more disciples than John

2 (although [a]Jesus Himself was not baptizing, but His [b]disciples were),

3 He left [a]Judea, and departed [b]again into Galilee.

4 And He had to pass through [a]Samaria.

5 So He *came to a city of [a]Samaria, called Sychar, near [b]the parcel of ground that [c]Jacob gave to his son Joseph;

6 and Jacob's well was there. Jesus therefore, being wearied from His journey, was sitting thus by the well. It was about [1]the sixth hour.

The Woman of Samaria

7 There *came a woman of Samaria to draw water. Jesus *said to her, "Give Me a drink."

8 For His [a]disciples had gone away into [b]the city to buy food.

9 The [a]Samaritan woman therefore *said to Him, "How is it that You, being a Jew, ask me for a drink since I am a Samaritan woman?" (For [b]Jews have no dealings with Samaritans.)

10 Jesus answered and said to her, "If you knew the gift of God, and who it is who says to you, 'Give Me a drink,' you would have asked Him, and He would have given you [a]living water."

11 She *said to Him, "[1]Sir, You have nothing to draw with and the well is deep; where then do You get that [a]living water?

12 "You are not greater than our father Jacob, are You, who [a]gave us the well, and drank of it himself, and his sons, and his cattle?"

13 Jesus answered and said to her, "Everyone who drinks of this water shall thirst again;

14 but whoever drinks of the water that I shall give him [a]shall never thirst; but the water that I shall give him shall become in him a well of water springing up to [b]eternal life."

15 The woman *said to Him, "[1]Sir, [a]give me this water, so I will not be thirsty, nor come all the way here to draw."

16 He *said to her, "Go, call your husband, and come here."

17 The woman answered and said, "I have no husband." Jesus *said to her, "You have well said, 'I have no husband';

18 for you have had five husbands, and the one whom you now have is not your husband; this you have said truly."

19 The woman *said to Him, "[1]Sir, I perceive that You are [a]a prophet.

20 "[a]Our fathers worshiped in [b]this mountain, and you *people* say that [c]in Jerusalem is the place where men ought to worship."

21 Jesus *said to her, "Woman, believe Me, [a]an hour is coming when [b]neither in this mountain, nor in Jerusalem, shall you worship the Father.

22 "[a]You worship that which you do not know; we worship that which we know, for [b]salvation is from the Jews.

23 "But [a]an hour is coming, and now is, when the true worshipers shall worship the Father [b]in spirit and truth; for such people the Father seeks to be His worshipers.

24 "God is [1]spirit, and those who worship Him must worship [a]in spirit and truth."

25 The woman *said to Him, "I know that [a]Messiah is coming ([b]He who is called Christ); when that One comes, He will declare all things to us."

23 [1]Lit., *many waters*
24 [a]Matt. 4:12; 14:3; Mark 6:17; Luke 3:20
25 [a]John 2:6
26 [a]Matt. 23:7; John 3:2 [b]John 1:28 [c]John 1:7
27 [a]1 Cor. 4:7; Heb. 5:4 [b]James 1:17
28 [1]I.e., Messiah [a]John 1:20, 23
29 [a]Matt. 9:15; 25:1 [b]John 15:11; 16:24; 17:13; Phil. 2:2; 1 John 1:4; 2 John 12
31 [a]Matt. 28:18; John 3:13; 8:23 [b]1 Cor. 15:47; 1 John 4:5
32 [a]John 3:11
33 [a]John 6:27; Rom. 4:11; 15:28; 1 Cor. 9:2; 2 Cor. 1:22; Eph. 1:13; 4:30; 2 Tim. 2:19; Rev. 7:3-8
34 [1]Lit., *for He does not give the Spirit by measure* [a]John 3:17 [b]Matt. 12:18; Luke 4:18; Acts 1:2; 10:38
35 [a]Matt. 28:18; John 5:20; 17:2 [b]Matt. 11:27; Luke 10:22
36 [1]Or, *believe* [a]John 3:16 [b]Acts 14:2; Heb. 3:18

1 [a]Luke 7:13 [b]John 3:22, 26; 1 Cor. 1:17
2 [a]John 3:22, 26; 1 Cor. 1:17 [b]John 2:2
3 [a]John 3:22 [b]John 2:11f.
4 [a]Luke 9:52
5 [a]Luke 9:52 [b]Gen. 33:19; Josh. 24:32 [c]Gen. 48:22; John 4:12
6 [1]Perhaps 6 p.m. (Roman time)
8 [a]John 2:2 [b]John 4:5, 39
9 [a]Luke 9:52 [b]Ezra 4:3-6, 11ff.; Matt. 10:5; John 8:48; Acts 10:28
10 [a]Jer. 2:13; John 4:14; 7:37f.; Rev. 7:17; 21:6; 22:1, 17
11 [1]Or, *Lord* [a]Jer. 2:13; John 4:14; 7:37f.; Rev. 7:17; 21:6; 22:1, 17
12 [a]John 4:6
14 [a]John 6:35; 7:38 [b]Matt. 25:46; John 6:27
15 [1]Or, *Lord* [a]John 6:35
19 [1]Or, *Lord* [a]Matt. 21:11; Luke 7:16, 39; 24:19; John 6:14; 7:40; 9:17
20 [a]Gen. 33:20; John 4:12 [b]Deut. 11:29; Josh. 8:33 [c]Luke 9:53
21 [a]John 4:23; 5:25, 28; 16:2, 32 [b]Mal. 1:11; 1 Tim. 2:8
22 [a]2 Kin. 17:28-41 [b]Is. 2:3; Rom. 3:1f.; 9:4f.
23 [a]John 4:21; 5:25, 28; 16:2, 32 [b]Phil. 3:3

24 [1]Or, *a Spirit* [a]Phil. 3:3
25 [a]Dan. 9:25; John 1:41 [b]Matt. 1:16; 27:17, 22; Luke 2:11

26 Jesus *said to her, "[a]I who speak to
you am *He.*"
27 And at this point His [a]disciples
came, and they marveled that He had
been speaking with a woman; yet no one
said, "What do You seek?" or, "Why do
You speak with her?"
28 So the woman left her waterpot,
and went into the city, and *said to the
men,
29 "Come, see a man [a]who told me all
the things that I *have* done; [b]this is not
[1]the Christ, is it?"
30 They went out of the city, and were
coming to Him.
31 In the meanwhile the disciples were
requesting Him, saying, "[a]Rabbi, eat."
32 But He said to them, "I have food
to eat that you do not know about."
33 The [a]disciples therefore were saying to one another, "No one brought
Him *anything* to eat, did he?"
34 Jesus *said to them, "My food is to
[a]do the will of Him who sent Me, and to
[b]accomplish His work.
35 "Do you not say, 'There are yet four
months, and *then* comes the harvest'?
Behold, I say to you, lift up your eyes,
and look on the fields, that they are
white [a]for harvest.
36 "Already he who reaps is receiving
[a]wages, and is gathering [b]fruit for [c]life
eternal; that he who sows and he who
reaps may rejoice together.
37 "For in this *case* the saying is true,
'[a]One sows, and another reaps.'
38 "I sent you to reap that for which
you have not labored; others have labored, and you have entered into their
labor."

The Samaritans

39 And from [a]that city many of the
Samaritans believed in Him because of
the word of the woman who testified,
"[b]He told me all the things that I *have*
done."
40 So when the Samaritans came to
Him, they were asking Him to stay with
them; and He stayed there two days.
41 And many more believed because
of His word;
42 and they were saying to the
woman, "It is no longer because of what
you said that we believe, for we have
heard for ourselves and know that this
One is indeed [a]the Savior of the world."
43 And after [a]the two days He went
forth from there into Galilee.
44 For Jesus Himself testified that [a]a
prophet has no honor in his own country.
45 So when He came to Galilee, the
Galileans received Him, [a]having seen all
the things that He did in Jerusalem at
the feast; for they themselves also went
to the feast.

Healing a Nobleman's Son

46 He came therefore again to [a]Cana
of Galilee [b]where He had made the
water wine. And there was a certain
royal official, whose son was sick at
[c]Capernaum.
47 When he heard that Jesus had
come [a]out of Judea into Galilee, he went
to Him, and was requesting *Him* to
come down and heal his son; for he was
at the point of death.
48 Jesus therefore said to him, "Unless you *people* see [1a]signs and [a]wonders,
you *simply* will not believe."
49 The royal official *said to Him,
"[1]Sir, come down before my child dies."
50 Jesus *said to him, "[a]Go your way;
your son lives." The man believed the
word that Jesus spoke to him, and he
started off.
51 And as he was now going down, *his*
slaves met him, saying that his [1]son was
living.
52 So he inquired of them the hour
when he began to get better. They said
therefore to him, "Yesterday at the
[1]seventh hour the fever left him."
53 So the father knew that *it was* at
that hour in which Jesus said to him,
"Your son lives"; and he himself believed, and [a]his whole household.
54 This is again a [a]second [1]sign that
Jesus performed, when He had [b]come
out of Judea into Galilee.

The Healing at Bethesda

5 AFTER these things there was [1a]a
feast of the Jews, and Jesus went up
to Jerusalem.
2 Now there is in Jerusalem by [a]the
sheep *gate* a pool, which is called [b]in
[1]Hebrew [2]Bethesda, having five porti-
coes.
3 In these lay a multitude of those
who were sick, blind, lame, and withered, [[1]waiting for the moving of the
waters;
4 for an angel of the Lord went down
at certain seasons into the pool, and
stirred up the water; whoever then first,
after the stirring up of the water, stepped
in was made well from whatever disease
with which he was afflicted.]
5 And a certain man was there, who
had been thirty-eight years in his sickness.
6 When Jesus saw him lying there,
and knew that he had already been a
long time *in that condition,* He *said to
him, "Do you wish to get well?"
7 The sick man answered Him, "Sir,
I have no man to put me into the pool
when [a]the water is stirred up, but while I
am coming, another steps down before
me."
8 Jesus *said to him, "[a]Arise, take up
your pallet, and walk."
9 And immediately the man became
well, and took up his pallet and *began* to
walk.
[a]Now it was the Sabbath on that day.

26 [a]John 8:24, 28, 58; 9:37; 13:19
27 [a]John 4:8
29 [1]I.e., the Messiah [a]John 4:17f. [b]Matt. 12:23; John 7:26, 31
31 [a]Matt. 23:7; 26:25, 49; Mark 9:5; 11:21; 14:45; John 1:38, 49; 3:2, 26; 6:25; 9:2; 11:8
33 [a]Luke 6:13-16; John 1:40-49; 2:2
34 [a]John 5:30; 6:38 [b]John 5:36; 17:4; 19:28, 30
35 [a]Matt. 9:37, 38; Luke 10:2
36 [a]Prov. 11:18; 1 Cor. 9:17f. [b]Rom. 1:13 [c]Matt. 19:29; John 3:36; 4:14; 5:24; Rom. 2:7; 6:23
37 [a]Job 31:8; Mic. 6:15
39 [a]John 4:5, 30 [b]John 4:29
42 [a]Matt. 1:21; Luke 2:11; John 1:29; Acts 5:31; 13:23; 1 Tim. 4:10; 1 John 4:14
43 [a]John 4:40
44 [a]Matt. 13:57; Mark 6:4; Luke 4:24
45 [a]John 2:23
46 [a]John 2:1 [b]John 2:9 [c]Luke 4:23; John 2:12
47 [a]John 4:3, 54
48 [1]Or, *attesting miracles* [a]Dan. 4:2f.; 6:27; Matt. 24:24; Mark 13:22; Acts 2:19, 22, 43; 4:30; 5:12; 6:8; 7:36; 14:3; 15:12; Rom. 15:19; 1 Cor. 1:22; 2 Cor. 12:12; 2 Thess. 2:9; Heb. 2:4
49 [1]Or, *Lord*
50 [a]Matt. 8:13
51 [1]Or, *boy*
52 [1]Perhaps 7 p.m. (Roman time)
53 [a]Acts 11:14
54 [1]Or, *attesting miracle* [a]John 2:11 [b]John 4:45f.

1 [1]Many mss. read *the feast*; i.e., the Passover [a]Deut. 16:1; John 2:13
2 [1]I.e., Jewish Aramaic [2]Many mss. read *Bethsaida* or *Bethzatha* [a]Neh. 3:1, 32; 12:39 [b]John 19:13, 17, 20; 20:16; Acts 21:40; Rev. 9:11; 16:16
3 [1]Many mss. do not contain the remainder of v. 3, nor v. 4
7 [a]John 5:4
8 [a]Matt. 9:6; Mark 2:11; Luke 5:24
9 [a]John 9:14

10 Therefore [a]the Jews were saying to him who was cured, "It is the Sabbath, and [b]it is not permissible for you to carry your pallet."

11 But he answered them, "He who made me well was the one who said to me, 'Take up your pallet and walk.'"

12 They asked him, "Who is the man who said to you, 'Take up *your pallet,* and walk'?"

13 But he who was healed did not know who it was; for Jesus had slipped away while there was a crowd in *that* place.

14 Afterward Jesus *found him in the temple, and said to him, "Behold, you have become well; do not [a]sin anymore, [b]so that nothing worse may befall you."

15 The man went away, and told [a]the Jews that it was Jesus who had made him well.

16 And for this reason [a]the Jews were persecuting Jesus, because He was doing these things on the Sabbath.

17 But He answered them, "My Father is working until now, and I Myself am working."

Jesus' Equality with God

18 For this cause therefore [a]the Jews [b]were seeking all the more to kill Him, because He not only was breaking the Sabbath, but also was calling God His own Father, [c]making Himself equal with God.

19 Jesus therefore answered and was saying to them, "Truly, truly, I say to you, [a]the Son can do nothing of Himself, unless *it is* something He sees the Father doing; for whatever *the Father* does, these things the Son also does in like manner.

20 "[a]For the Father loves the Son, and shows Him all things that He Himself is doing; and [b]greater works than these will He show Him, that you may marvel.

21 "For just as the Father raises the dead and [a]gives them life, even so [b]the Son also gives life to whom He wishes.

22 "For not even the Father judges anyone, but [a]He has given all judgment to the Son,

23 in order that all may honor the Son, even as they honor the Father. [a]He who does not honor the Son does not honor the Father who sent Him.

24 "Truly, truly, I say to you, he who hears My word, and [a]believes Him who sent Me, has eternal life, and [b]does not come into judgment, but has [c]passed out of death into life.

Two Resurrections

25 "Truly, truly, I say to you, [a]an hour is coming and now is, when [b]the dead shall hear the voice of the Son of God; and those who [c]hear shall live.

26 "For just as the Father has life in Himself, even so He [a]gave to the Son also to have life in Himself;

27 and He gave Him authority to [a]execute judgment, because He is [1]*the* Son of Man.

28 "Do not marvel at this; for [a]an hour is coming, in which [b]all who are in the tombs shall hear His voice,

29 and shall come forth; [a]those who did the good *deeds* to a resurrection of life, those who committed the evil *deeds* to a resurrection of judgment.

30 "[a]I can do nothing on My own initiative. As I hear, I judge; and [b]My judgment is just, because I do not seek My own will, but [c]the will of Him who sent Me.

31 "[a]If I *alone* bear witness of Myself, My testimony is not [1]true.

32 "There is [a]another who bears witness of Me, and I know that the testimony which He bears of Me is true.

Witness of John

33 "You have sent to John, and he [a]has borne witness to the truth.

34 "But [a]the witness which I receive is not from man, but I say these things that you may be saved.

35 "He was [a]the lamp that was burning and was shining and you [b]were willing to rejoice for a while in his light.

Witness of Works

36 "But the witness which I have is greater than *that of* John; for [a]the works which the Father has given Me [b]to accomplish, the very works that I do, bear witness of Me, that the Father [c]has sent Me.

Witness of the Father

37 "And the Father who sent Me, [a]He has borne witness of Me. You have neither heard His voice at any time, nor seen His form.

38 "And you do not have [a]His word abiding in you, for you do not believe Him whom He [b]sent.

Witness of the Scripture

39 "[1a]You search the Scriptures, because you think that in them you have eternal life; and it is [b]these that bear witness of Me;

40 and you are unwilling to come to Me, that you may have life.

41 "[a]I do not receive glory from men;

42 but I know you, that you do not have the love of God in yourselves.

43 "I have come in My Father's name, and you do not receive Me; [a]if another shall come in his own name, you will receive him.

44 "How can you believe, when you [a]receive [1]glory from one another, and you do not seek [b]the [1]glory that is from [c]the *one and* only God?

45 "Do not think that I will accuse you before the Father; the one who accuses you is [a]Moses, in whom you have set your hope.

10 [a]John 1:19; 5:15, 16, 18 [b]Neh. 13:19; Jer. 17:21f.; Matt. 12:2; Luke 6:2; John 7:23; 9:16
14 [a]Mark 2:5; John 8:11 [b]Ezra 9:14
15 [a]John 1:19; 5:16, 18
16 [a]John 1:19; 5:10, 15, 18
18 [a]John 1:19; 5:15, 16 [b]John 5:16; 7:1 [c]John 10:33; 19:7
19 [a]Matt. 26:39; John 5:30; 6:38; 8:28; 12:49; 14:10
20 [a]Matt. 3:17; John 3:35; 2 Pet. 1:17 [b]John 14:12
21 [a]Rom. 4:17; 8:11 [b]John 11:25
22 [a]John 5:27; 9:39; Acts 10:42; 17:31
23 [a]Luke 10:16; 1 John 2:23
24 [a]John 3:18; 12:44; 20:31; 1 John 5:13 [b]John 3:18 [c]1 John 3:14
25 [a]John 4:21, 23; 5:28 [b]Luke 15:24 [c]John 6:60; 8:43, 47; 9:27
26 [a]John 1:4; 6:57
27 [1]Or, *a son of man* [a]John 9:39; Acts 10:42; 17:31
28 [a]John 4:21 [b]John 11:24; 1 Cor. 15:52
29 [a]Dan. 12:2; Matt. 25:46; Acts 24:15
30 [a]John 5:19 [b]John 8:16 [c]John 4:34; 6:38
31 [1]I.e., admissible as legal evidence [a]John 8:14
32 [a]John 5:37
33 [a]John 1:7, 15, 19, 32; 3:26-30
34 [a]John 5:32; 1 John 5:9
35 [a]2 Sam. 21:17; 2 Pet. 1:19 [b]Mark 1:5
36 [a]Matt. 11:4; John 2:23; 10:25, 38; 14:11; 15:24 [b]John 4:34 [c]John 3:17
37 [a]Matt. 3:17; Mark 1:11; Luke 3:22; 24:27; John 8:18; 1 John 5:9
38 [a]1 John 2:14 [b]John 3:17
39 [1]Or, (a command) *Search the Scriptures!* [a]John 7:52; Rom. 2:17ff. [b]Luke 24:25, 27; Acts 13:27
41 [a]John 5:44; 7:18; 1 Thess. 2:6
43 [a]Matt. 24:5
44 [1]Or, *honor* or *fame* [a]John 5:41 [b]Rom. 2:29 [c]John 17:3; 1 Tim. 1:17
45 [a]John 9:28; Rom. 2:17ff.

46 "For if you believed Moses, you would believe Me; for [a]he wrote of Me.

47 "But [a]if you do not believe his writings, how will you believe My words?"

Five Thousand Fed

6 AFTER these things [a]Jesus went away to the other side of [b]the Sea of Galilee (or [c]Tiberias).

2 And a great multitude was following Him, because they were seeing the [1a]signs which He was performing on those who were sick.

3 And [a]Jesus went up on the mountain, and there He sat with His disciples.

4 Now [a]the Passover, the feast of the Jews, was at hand.

5 Jesus therefore lifting up His eyes, and seeing that a great multitude was coming to Him, *said to [a]Philip, "Where are we to buy bread, that these may eat?"

6 And this He was saying to [a]test him; for He Himself knew what He was intending to do.

7 [a]Philip answered Him, "[b]Two hundred [1]denarii worth of bread is not sufficient for them, for everyone to receive a little."

8 One of His [a]disciples, [b]Andrew, Simon Peter's brother, *said to Him,

9 "There is a lad here who has five barley loaves and two [a]fish, but what are these for so many people?"

10 Jesus said, "Have the people [1]sit down." Now there was [a]much grass in the place. So the men [1]sat down, in number about [b]five thousand.

11 Jesus therefore took the loaves; and [a]having given thanks, He distributed to those who were seated; likewise also of the [b]fish as much as they wanted.

12 And when they were filled, He *said to His [a]disciples, "Gather up the leftover fragments that nothing may be lost."

13 And so they gathered them up, and filled twelve [a]baskets with fragments from the five barley loaves, which were left over by those who had eaten.

14 When therefore the people saw the [1]sign which He had performed, they said, "This is of a truth the [a]Prophet who is to come into the world."

Jesus Walks on the Water

15 Jesus therefore perceiving that they were [1]intending to come and take Him by force, [a]to make Him king, [b]withdrew again to [c]the mountain by Himself alone.

16 Now when evening came, His [a]disciples went down to the sea,

17 and after getting into a boat, they *started to* cross the sea [a]to Capernaum. And it had already become dark, and Jesus had not yet come to them.

18 And the sea *began* to be stirred up because a strong wind was blowing.

19 When therefore they had rowed about [1]three or four miles, they *beheld Jesus walking on the sea and drawing near to the boat; and they were frightened.

20 But He *said to them, "It is I; [1a]do not be afraid."

21 They were willing therefore to receive Him into the boat; and immediately the boat was at the land to which they were going.

22 The next day [a]the multitude that stood on the other side of the sea saw that there was no other small boat there, except one, and that Jesus [b]had not entered with His disciples into the boat, but *that* His disciples had gone away alone.

23 There came other small boats from [a]Tiberias near to the place where they ate the bread after the [b]Lord [c]had given thanks.

24 When the multitude therefore saw that Jesus was not there, nor His disciples, they themselves got into the small boats, and [a]came to Capernaum, seeking Jesus.

25 And when they found Him on the other side of the sea, they said to Him, "[a]Rabbi, when did You get here?"

Words to the People

26 Jesus answered them and said, "Truly, truly, I say to you, you [a]seek Me, not because you saw [b]signs, but because you ate of the loaves, and were filled.

27 "Do not [a]work for the food which perishes, but for the food which endures to [b]eternal life, which [c]the Son of Man shall give to you, for on Him the Father, *even* God, [d]has set His seal."

28 They said therefore to Him, "What shall we do, that we may work the works of God?"

29 Jesus answered and said to them, "This is [a]the work of God, that you believe in Him whom He [b]has sent."

30 They said therefore to Him, "[a]What then do You do for a [b]sign, that we may see, and believe You? What work do You perform?

31 "[a]Our fathers ate the manna in the wilderness; as it is written, '[b]HE GAVE THEM BREAD OUT OF HEAVEN TO EAT.' "

32 Jesus therefore said to them, "Truly, truly, I say to you, it is not Moses who has given you the bread out of heaven, but it is My Father who gives you the true bread out of heaven.

33 "For the bread of God is [1]that which [a]comes down out of heaven, and gives life to the world."

34 They said therefore to Him, "Lord, evermore [a]give us this bread."

35 Jesus said to them, "[a]I am the bread of life; he who comes to Me shall not hunger, and he who believes in Me [b]shall never thirst.

36 "But [a]I said to you, that you have seen Me, and yet do not believe.

---

46 [a]Luke 24:27
47 [a]Luke 16:29, 31

1 [a]John 6:1-13: *Matt. 14:13-21; Mark 6:32-44; Luke 9:10-17* [b]Matt. 4:18; Luke 5:1 [c]John 6:23; 21:1
2 [1]Or, *attesting miracles* [a]John 2:11, 23; 3:2; 6:14, 30; 11:47; 12:18, 37; 20:30
3 [a]Matt. 5:1; Mark 3:13; Luke 6:12; 9:28; John 6:15
4 [a]Deut. 16:1; John 2:13
5 [a]John 1:43
6 [a]2 Cor. 13:5; Rev. 2:2
7 [1]The denarius was equivalent to one day's wage [a]John 1:43 [b]Mark 6:37
8 [a]John 2:2 [b]John 1:40
9 [a]John 6:11; 21:9, 10, 13
10 [1]Lit., *recline(d)* [a]Mark 6:39 [b]Matt. 14:21
11 [a]Matt. 15:36; John 6:23 [b]John 6:9; 21:9, 10, 13
12 [a]John 2:2
13 [a]Matt. 14:20
14 [1]Or, *attesting miracle* [a]Matt. 11:3; 21:11; John 1:21
15 [1]Or, *about* [a]John 18:36f. [b]John 6:15-21: *Matt. 14:22-33; Mark 6:45-51* [c]John 6:3
16 [a]John 2:2
17 [a]Mark 6:45; John 6:24, 59
19 [1]I.e., 25 or 30 stadia
20 [1]Or, *stop fearing* [a]Matt. 14:27
22 [a]John 6:2 [b]John 6:15ff.
23 [a]John 6:1 [b]Luke 7:13 [c]John 6:11
24 [a]Matt. 14:34; Mark 6:53; John 6:17, 59
25 [a]Matt. 23:7
26 [a]John 6:24 [b]John 6:2, 14, 30
27 [a]Is. 55:2 [b]John 3:15f.; 4:14; 6:40, 47, 54; 10:28; 17:2f. [c]Matt. 8:20; John 6:53, 62 [d]John 3:33
29 [a]1 Thess. 1:3; James 2:22; 1 John 3:23; Rev. 2:26 [b]John 3:17
30 [a]Matt. 12:38 [b]John 6:2, 14, 26
31 [a]Ex. 16:4, 15, 21; Num. 11:8; John 6:49, 58 [b]Ps. 78:24; Ex. 16:4, 15; Neh. 9:15; Ps. 105:40
33 [1]Or, *He who comes* [a]John 6:41, 50
34 [a]John 4:15
35 [a]John 6:48, 51 [b]John 4:14
36 [a]John 6:26

37“[a]All that the Father gives Me shall
come to Me, and the one who comes to
Me I will certainly not cast out.
38“For [a]I have come down from
heaven, [b]not to do My own will, but [c]the
will of Him who [d]sent Me.
39“And this is the will of Him who
sent Me, that of [a]all that He has given
Me I [b]lose nothing, but [c]raise it up on
the last day.
40“For this is the will of My Father,
that everyone who [a]beholds the Son and
[b]believes in Him, may have eternal life;
and I Myself will [c]raise him up on the
last day.”

Words to the Jews

41 [a]The Jews therefore were grumbling about Him, because He said, “I am
the bread that [b]came down out of
heaven.”
42 And they were saying, “[a]Is not this
Jesus, the son of Joseph, whose father
and mother [b]we know? How does He
now say, ‘[c]I have come down out of
heaven’?”
43 Jesus answered and said to them,
“Do not grumble among yourselves.
44“No one can come to Me, unless the
Father who sent Me [a]draws him; and I
will [b]raise him up on the last day.
45“It is written [a]in the prophets,
‘[b]AND THEY SHALL ALL BE [c]TAUGHT OF
GOD.’ Everyone who has heard and
learned from the Father, comes to Me.
46“[a]Not that any man has seen the
Father, except the One who is from
God; He has seen the Father.
47“Truly, truly, I say to you, he who
believes [a]has eternal life.
48“[a]I am the bread of life.
49“[a]Your fathers ate the manna in the
wilderness, and they died.
50“This is the bread which [a]comes
down out of heaven, so that one may eat
of it and [b]not die.
51“[a]I am the living bread that [b]came
down out of heaven; if anyone eats of
this bread, [c]he shall live forever; and the
bread also which I shall give [d]for the life
of the world is [e]My flesh.”
52 [a]The Jews therefore [b]*began* to argue with one another, saying, “How can
this man give us *His* flesh to eat?”
53 Jesus therefore said to them,
“Truly, truly, I say to you, unless you eat
the flesh of [a]the Son of Man and drink
His blood, you have no life in yourselves.
54“He who eats My flesh and drinks
My blood has eternal life, and I will
[a]raise him up on the last day.
55“For My flesh is true food, and My
blood is true drink.
56“He who eats My flesh and drinks
My blood [a]abides in Me, and I in him.
57“As the [a]living Father [b]sent Me, and
I live because of the Father, so he who
eats Me, he also shall live because of Me.
58“This is the bread which [a]came
down out of heaven; not as [b]the fathers
ate, and died, he who eats this bread
[c]shall live forever.”

Words to the Disciples

59 These things He said [a]in the synagogue, as He taught [b]in Capernaum.
60 Many therefore of His [a]disciples,
when they heard *this* said, “[b]This is a
difficult statement; who can listen to it?”
61 But Jesus, [a]conscious that His
disciples grumbled at this, said to them,
“Does this [b]cause you to stumble?
62“*What* then if you should behold
[a]the Son of Man [b]ascending where He
was before?
63“[a]It is the Spirit who gives life; the
flesh profits nothing; [b]the words that I
have spoken to you are spirit and are
life.
64“But there are [a]some of you who do
not believe.” For Jesus [b]knew from the
beginning who they were who did not
believe, and [c]who it was that would
[1]betray Him.
65 And He was saying, “For this
reason I have [a]said to you, that no one
can come to Me, unless [b]it has been
granted him from the Father.”

Peter's Confession of Faith

66 As a result of this many of His
[a]disciples [b]withdrew, and were not walking with Him anymore.
67 Jesus said therefore to [a]the twelve,
“You do not want to go away also, do
you?”
68 [a]Simon Peter answered Him,
“Lord, to whom shall we go? You have
[b]words of eternal life.
69“And we have believed and have
come to know that You are [a]the Holy
One of God.”
70 Jesus answered them, “[a]Did I Myself not choose you, [b]the twelve, and *yet*
one of you is [c]a devil?”
71 Now He meant Judas [a]*the son* of
Simon Iscariot, for he, [b]one of [c]the
twelve, [1]was going to betray Him.

Jesus Teaches at the Feast

7 AND after these things Jesus [a]was
walking in Galilee; for He was unwilling to walk in Judea, because [b]the
Jews [c]were seeking to kill Him.
2 Now the feast of the Jews, [a]the
Feast of Booths, was at hand.
3 His [a]brothers therefore said to
Him, “Depart from here, and go into
Judea, that Your [b]disciples also may
behold Your works which You are doing.
4“For no one does anything in secret,
[1]when he himself seeks to be *known*
publicly. If You do these things, show
Yourself to the world.”

37 [a]John 6:39; 17:2, 24
38 [a]John 3:13 [b]Matt. 26:39 [c]John 4:34; 5:30 [d]John 6:29
39 [a]John 6:37; 17:2, 24 [b]John 17:12; 18:9 [c]Matt. 10:15; John 6:40, 44, 54; 11:24
40 [a]John 12:45; 14:17, 19 [b]John 3:16 [c]Matt. 10:15; John 6:39, 44, 54; 11:24
41 [a]John 1:19; 6:52 [b]John 6:33, 51, 58
42 [a]Luke 4:22 [b]John 7:27f. [c]John 6:38, 62
44 [a]Jer. 31:3; Hos. 11:4; John 6:65; 12:32 [b]John 6:39
45 [a]Acts 7:42; 13:40; Heb. 8:11 [b]Is. 54:13; Jer. 31:34 [c]Phil. 3:15; 1 Thess. 4:9; 1 John 2:27
46 [a]John 1:18
47 [a]John 3:36; 5:24; 6:51, 58; 11:26
48 [a]John 6:35, 51
49 [a]John 6:31, 58
50 [a]John 6:33 [b]John 3:36; 5:24; 6:47, 51, 58; 11:26
51 [a]John 6:35, 48 [b]John 6:41, 58 [c]John 3:36; 5:24; 6:47, 58; 11:26 [d]John 1:29; 3:14f.; Heb. 10:10; 1 John 4:10 [e]John 6:53-56
52 [a]John 1:19; 6:41 [b]John 9:16; 10:19
53 [a]Matt. 8:20; John 6:27, 62
54 [a]John 6:39
56 [a]John 15:4f.; 17:23; 1 John 2:24; 3:24; 4:15f.
57 [a]Matt. 16:16; John 5:26 [b]John 3:17; 6:29, 38
58 [a]John 6:33, 41, 51 [b]John 6:31, 49 [c]John 3:36; 5:24; 6:47, 51; 11:26
59 [a]Matt. 4:23 [b]John 6:24
60 [a]John 2:2; 6:66; 7:3 [b]John 6:52
61 [a]John 6:64 [b]Matt. 11:6
62 [a]Matt. 8:20; John 6:27, 53 [b]Mark 16:19; John 3:13
63 [a]2 Cor. 3:6 [b]John 6:68
64 [1]Or, *deliver Him up* [a]John 6:60, 66 [b]John 2:25 [c]Matt. 10:4; John 6:71; 13:11
65 [a]John 6:37, 44 [b]Matt. 13:11; John 3:27
66 [a]John 2:2; 7:3 [b]John 6:60, 64
67 [a]Matt. 10:2; John 2:2; 6:70f.; 20:24
68 [a]Matt. 16:16 [b]John 6:63; 12:49f.; 17:8
69 [a]Mark 1:24; 8:29; Luke 9:20
70 [a]John 15:16, 19 [b]Matt. 10:2; John 2:2; 6:71; 20:24 [c]John 8:44; 13:2, 27; 17:12
71 [1]Or, *was intending to* [a]John 12:4; 13:2, 26 [b]Mark 14:10 [c]Matt. 10:2; John 2:2; 6:70; 20:24

1 [a]John 4:3; 6:1; 11:54 [b]John 1:19; 7:11, 13, 15, 35 [c]John 5:18; 7:19; 8:37, 40; 11:53
2 [a]Lev. 23:34; Deut. 16:13, 16; Zech. 14:16-19
3 [a]Matt. 12:46; Mark 3:21; John 7:5, 10 [b]John 6:60
4 [1]Lit., *and*

5 For not even His [a]brothers were believing in Him.

6 Jesus therefore *said to them, "[a]My time is not yet at hand, but your time is always opportune.

7 "[a]The world cannot hate you; but it hates Me because I testify of it, that [b]its deeds are evil.

8 "Go up to the feast yourselves; I do not go up[1] to this feast because [a]My time has not yet fully come."

9 And having said these things to them, He stayed in Galilee.

10 But when His [a]brothers had gone up to the feast, then He Himself also went up, not publicly, but as it were, in secret.

11 [a]The Jews therefore [b]were seeking Him at the feast, and were saying, "Where is He?"

12 And there was much grumbling among the multitudes concerning Him; [a]some were saying, "He is a good man"; others were saying, "No, on the contrary, He leads the multitude astray."

13 Yet no one was speaking openly of Him for [a]fear of the Jews.

14 But when it was now the midst of the feast Jesus went up into the temple, and *began to* [a]teach.

15 [a]The Jews therefore were marveling, saying, "How has this man [b]become learned, having never been educated?"

16 Jesus therefore answered them, and said, "[a]My teaching is not Mine, but His who sent Me.

17 "[a]If any man is willing to do His will, he shall know of the teaching, whether it is of God, or *whether* I speak from Myself.

18 "He who speaks from himself [a]seeks his own glory; but He who is seeking the glory of the one who sent Him, He is true, and there is no unrighteousness in Him.

19 "[a]Did not Moses give you the Law, and *yet* none of you carries out the Law? Why do you [b]seek to kill Me?"

20 The multitude answered, "[a]You [1]have a demon! Who seeks to kill You?"

21 Jesus answered and said to them, "I did [a]one [1]deed, and you all marvel.

22 "On this account [a]Moses has given you circumcision (not because it is from Moses, but from [b]the fathers), and on *the* Sabbath you circumcise a man.

23 "[a]If a man receives circumcision on *the* Sabbath that the Law of Moses may not be broken, are you angry with Me because I made an entire man well on *the* Sabbath?

24 "Do not [a]judge according to appearance, but [1]judge with righteous judgment."

25 Therefore some of the people of Jerusalem were saying, "Is this not the man whom they are seeking to kill?

26 "And look, He is speaking publicly, and they are saying nothing to Him. [a]The rulers do not really know that this is [1]the Christ, do they?

27 "However, [a]we know where this man is from; but whenever the Christ may come, no one knows where He is from."

28 Jesus therefore cried out in the temple, [a]teaching and saying, "[b]You both know Me and know where I am from; and [c]I have not come of Myself, but He who sent Me is true, whom you do not know.

29 "[a]I know Him; because [b]I am from Him, and [c]He sent Me."

30 They [a]were seeking therefore to seize Him; and no man laid his hand on Him, because His [b]hour had not yet come.

31 But [a]many of the multitude believed in Him; and they were saying, "[b]When [1]the Christ shall come, He will not perform more [2c]signs than those which this man has, will He?"

32 The Pharisees heard the multitude muttering these things about Him; and the chief priests and the Pharisees sent [a]officers to [b]seize Him.

33 Jesus therefore said, "[a]For a little while longer I am with you, then [b]I go to Him who sent Me.

34 "[a]You shall seek Me, and shall not find Me; and where I am, you cannot come."

35 [a]The Jews therefore said to one another, "[b]Where does this man intend to go that we shall not find Him? He is not intending to go to [c]the Dispersion among [d]the Greeks, and teach the Greeks, is He?

36 "What is this statement that He said, 'You will seek Me, and will not find Me; and where I am, you cannot come'?"

37 Now on [a]the last day, the great *day* of the feast, Jesus stood and cried out, saying, "[b]If any man is thirsty, [1]let him come to Me and drink.

38 "He who believes in Me, [a]as the Scripture said, 'From [1]his innermost being shall flow rivers of [b]living water.' "

39 But this He spoke [a]of the Spirit, whom those who believed in Him were to receive; [1]for [b]the Spirit was not yet *given,* because Jesus was not yet [c]glorified.

Division of People over Jesus

40 *Some* of the multitude therefore, when they heard these words, were saying, "This certainly is [a]the Prophet."

41 Others were saying, "This is [1]the Christ." Still others were saying, "[a]Surely [1]the Christ is not going to come from Galilee, is He?

5 [a]Matt. 12:46; Mark 3:21; John 7:3, 10
6 [a]Matt. 26:18; John 2:4; 7:8, 30
7 [a]John 15:18f. [b]John 3:19f.
8 [1]Some authorities add *yet* [a]John 7:6
10 [a]Matt. 12:46; Mark 3:21; John 7:3, 5
11 [a]John 7:13, 15, 35 [b]John 11:56
12 [a]John 7:40-43
13 [a]John 9:22; 12:42; 19:38; 20:19
14 [a]Matt. 26:55; John 7:28
15 [a]John 1:19; 7:11, 13, 35 [b]Acts 26:24
16 [a]John 3:11
17 [a]Ps. 25:9, 14; Prov. 3:32; Dan. 12:10; John 3:21; 8:43f.
18 [a]John 5:41; 8:50, 54; 12:43
19 [a]John 1:17 [b]Mark 11:18; John 7:1
20 [1]Or, *are demented* [a]Matt. 11:18; John 8:48f., 52; 10:20
21 [1]Or, *work* [a]John 5:2-9, 16; 7:23
22 [a]Lev. 12:3 [b]Gen. 17:10ff.; 21:4; Acts 7:8
23 [a]Matt. 12:2; John 5:9, 10
24 [1]Lit., *judge the righteous judgment* [a]Lev. 19:15; Is. 11:3; Zech. 7:9; John 8:15
26 [1]I.e., the Messiah [a]Luke 23:13; John 3:1
27 [a]John 6:42; 7:41f.; 9:29
28 [a]John 7:14 [b]John 6:42; 7:14f.; 9:29 [c]John 8:42
29 [a]Matt. 11:27; John 8:55; 17:25 [b]John 6:46 [c]John 3:17
30 [a]Matt. 21:46; John 7:32, 44; 10:39 [b]John 7:6; 8:20
31 [1]I.e., the Messiah [2]Or, *attesting miracles* [a]John 2:23; 8:30; 10:42; 11:45; 12:11, 42 [b]John 7:26 [c]John 2:11
32 [a]Matt. 26:58; John 7:45f. [b]Matt. 12:14
33 [a]John 12:35; 13:33; 14:19; 16:16-19 [b]John 14:12, 28; 16:5, 10, 17, 28; 20:17
34 [a]John 7:36; 8:21; 13:33
35 [a]John 7:1 [b]John 8:22 [c]Ps. 147:2; Is. 11:12; 56:8; Zeph. 3:10; James 1:1; 1 Pet. 1:1 [d]John 12:20; Acts 14:1; 17:4; 18:4; Rom. 1:16
36 [a]John 7:34; 8:21; 13:33

37 [1]I.e., let him keep coming to Me and let him keep drinking [a]Lev. 23:36; Num. 29:35; Neh. 8:18 [b]John 4:10, 14; 6:35
38 [1]Lit., *out of his belly* [a]Is. 44:3; 55:1; 58:11 [b]John 4:10
39 [1]Other mss. read *for the Holy Spirit was not yet given* [a]Joel 2:28; John 1:33 [b]John 20:22; Acts 1:4f.; 2:4, 33; 19:2 [c]John 12:16, 23; 13:31f.; 16:14; 17:1
40 [a]Matt. 21:11; John 1:21
41 [1]I.e., the Messiah [a]John 1:46; 7:52

42"Has not the Scripture said that the
Christ comes from [a]the offspring of
David, and from Bethlehem, the village
where David was?"
43 So [a]there arose a division in the
multitude because of Him.
44 And [a]some of them wanted to seize
Him, but no one laid hands on Him.
45 The [a]officers therefore came to the
chief priests and Pharisees, and they said
to them, "Why did you not bring Him?"
46 The [a]officers answered, "[b]Never
did a man speak the way this man
speaks."
47 The Pharisees therefore answered
them, "[a]You have not also been led
astray, have you?
48"[a]No one of [b]the rulers or Pharisees
has believed in Him, has he?
49"But this multitude which does not
know the Law is accursed."
50 [a]Nicodemus *said to them (he who
came to Him before, being one of them),
51"[a]Our Law does not judge a man,
unless it first hears from him and knows
what he is doing, does it?"
52 They answered and said to him,
"[a]You are not also from Galilee, are
you? Search, and see that no prophet
arises out of Galilee."
53 [[1]And everyone went to his home.

The Adulterous Woman

8 BUT Jesus went to [a]the Mount of
Olives.
2 And early in the morning He came
again into the temple, and all the people
were coming to Him; and [a]He sat down
and *began* to teach them.
3 And the scribes and the Pharisees
*brought a woman caught in adultery,
and having set her in the midst,
4 they *said to Him, "Teacher, this
woman has been caught in adultery, in
the very act.
5"Now in the Law [a]Moses commanded us to stone such women; what
then do You say?"
6 And they were saying this, [a]testing
Him, [b]in order that they might have
grounds for accusing Him. But Jesus
stooped down, and with His finger wrote
on the ground.
7 But when they persisted in asking
Him, [a]He straightened up, and said to
them, "[b]He who is without sin among
you, let him *be the* [c]first to throw a stone
at her."
8 And again He stooped down, and
wrote on the ground.
9 And when they heard it, they *began*
to go out one by one, beginning with the
older ones, and He was left alone, and
the woman, where she was, in the midst.
10 And [a]straightening up, Jesus said
to her, "Woman, where are they? Did no
one condemn you?"
11 And she said, "No one, [1]Lord."
And Jesus said, "[a]Neither do I condemn
you; go your way. From now on [b]sin no
more."

Jesus Is the Light of the World

12 Again therefore Jesus spoke to
them, saying, "[a]I am the light of the
world; [b]he who follows Me shall not
walk in the darkness, but shall have the
light of life."
13 The Pharisees therefore said to
Him, "[a]You are bearing witness of
Yourself; Your witness is not [1]true."
14 Jesus answered and said to them,
"[a]Even if I bear witness of Myself, My
witness is true; for I know [b]where I came
from, and where I am going; but [c]you do
not know where I come from, or where I
am going.
15"[a]You people judge [1]according to
the flesh; [b]I am not judging anyone.
16"But even [a]if I do judge, My judgment is true; for I am not alone *in it,* but
I and [1]He who sent Me.
17"Even in [a]your law it has been
written, that the testimony of [b]two men
is [1]true.
18"I am He who bears witness of
Myself, and [a]the Father who sent Me
bears witness of Me."
19 And so they were saying to Him,
"Where is Your Father?" Jesus answered, "You know neither Me, nor My
Father; [a]if you knew Me, you would
know My Father also."
20 These words He spoke in [a]the
treasury, as [b]He taught in the temple;
and no one seized Him, because [c]His
hour had not yet come.
21 He said therefore again to them, "I
go away, and [a]you shall seek Me, and
[b]shall die in your sin; where I am going,
you cannot come."
22 Therefore [a]the Jews were saying,
"Surely He will not kill Himself, will He,
since He says, '[b]Where I am going, you
cannot come'?"
23 And He was saying to them, "[a]You
are from below, I am from above; [b]you
are of this world, [c]I am not of this world.
24"I said therefore to you, that you
[a]shall die in your sins; for unless you
believe that [1b]I am *He,* [a]you shall die in
your sins."
25 And so they were saying to Him,
"Who are You?" Jesus said to them,
"[1]What have I been saying to you *from*
the beginning?
26"I have many things to speak and to
judge concerning you, but [a]He who sent
Me is true; and [b]the things which I
heard from Him, these I speak to the
world."
27 They did not realize that He had
been speaking to them about the Father.
28 Jesus therefore said, "When you
[a]lift up the Son of Man, then you will
know that [1b]I am *He,* and [c]I do nothing
on My own initiative, but I speak these
things as the Father taught Me.
29"And He who sent Me is with Me;
[a]He [1]has not left Me alone, for [b]I always
do the things that are pleasing to Him."

42 [a]Ps. 89:4; Mic. 5:2; Matt. 1:1; 2:5f.; Luke 2:4ff.
43 [a]John 9:16; 10:19
44 [a]John 7:30
45 [a]John 7:32
46 [a]John 7:32 [b]Matt. 7:28
47 [a]John 7:12
48 [a]John 12:42 [b]Luke 23:13; John 7:26
50 [a]John 3:1; 19:39
51 [a]Ex. 23:1; Deut. 17:6; 19:15; Prov. 18:13; Acts 23:3
52 [a]John 1:46; 7:41
53 [1]John 7:53-8:11 is not found in most of the old mss.

1 [a]Matt. 21:1
2 [a]Matt. 26:55; John 8:20
5 [a]Lev. 20:10; Deut. 22:22f.
6 [a]Matt. 16:1; 19:3; 22:18, 35; Mark 8:11; 10:2; 12:15; Luke 10:25; 11:16 [b]Mark 3:2
7 [a]John 8:10 [b]Matt. 7:1; Rom. 2:1 [c]Deut. 17:7
10 [a]John 8:7
11 [1]Or, *Sir* [a]John 3:17 [b]John 5:14
12 [a]John 1:4; 9:5; 12:35 [b]Matt. 5:14
13 [1]Or, *valid* [a]John 5:31
14 [a]John 18:37; Rev. 1:5; 3:14 [b]John 8:42; 13:3; 16:28 [c]John 7:28; 9:29
15 [1]I.e., a carnal standard [a]1 Sam. 16:7; John 7:24 [b]John 3:17
16 [1]Many ancient mss. read *the Father who sent Me* [a]John 5:30
17 [1]I.e., valid or admissible [a]Deut. 17:6; 19:15 [b]Matt. 18:16
18 [a]John 5:37; 1 John 5:9
19 [a]John 7:28; 8:55; 14:7, 9; 16:3
20 [a]Mark 12:41, 43; Luke 21:1 [b]John 7:14; 8:2 [c]John 7:30
21 [a]John 7:34 [b]John 8:24
22 [a]John 1:19; 8:48, 52, 57 [b]John 7:35
23 [a]John 3:31 [b]1 John 4:5 [c]John 17:14, 16
24 [1]Most authorities associate this with Ex. 3:14, *I AM WHO I AM* [a]John 8:21 [b]Matt. 24:5; Mark 13:6; Luke 21:8; John 4:26; 8:28, 58; 13:19
25 [1]Or, *That which I have been saying to you from the beginning.*
26 [a]John 3:33; 7:28 [b]John 8:40; 12:49; 15:15
28 [1]Lit., *I AM* (v. 24 note) [a]John 3:14; 12:32 [b]Matt. 24:5; Mark 13:6; Luke 21:8; John 4:26; 8:24, 58; 13:19 [c]John 3:11; 5:19

29 [1]Or, *did not leave* [a]John 8:16; 16:32 [b]John 4:34

30 As He spoke these things, [a]many came to believe in Him.

The Truth Shall Make You Free

31 Jesus therefore was saying to those Jews who had believed Him, "[a]If you abide in My word, *then* you are truly [b]disciples of Mine;

32 and [a]you shall know the truth, and [b]the truth shall make you free."

33 They answered Him, "[a]We are Abraham's offspring, and have never yet been enslaved to anyone; how is it that You say, 'You shall become free'?"

34 Jesus answered them, "Truly, truly, I say to you, [a]everyone who commits sin is the slave of sin.

35 "And [a]the slave does not remain in the house forever; [b]the son does remain forever.

36 "If therefore the Son [a]shall make you free, you shall be free indeed.

37 "I know that you are [a]Abraham's offspring; yet [b]you seek to kill Me, because My word [1]has no place in you.

38 "I speak the things which I have seen [1]with *My* Father; therefore you also do the things which you heard from [a]*your* father."

39 They answered and said to Him, "Abraham is [a]our father." Jesus *said to them, "[b]If you are Abraham's children, do the deeds of Abraham.

40 "But as it is, [a]you are seeking to kill Me, a man who has [b]told you the truth, which I heard from God; this Abraham did not do.

41 "You are doing the deeds of [a]your father." They said to Him, "We were not born of fornication; [b]we have one Father, *even* God."

42 Jesus said to them, "If God were your Father, [a]you would love Me; [b]for I proceeded forth and have come from God, for I have [c]not even come on My own initiative, but [1][d]He sent Me.

43 "Why do you not understand [1][a]what I am saying? *It is* because you cannot [b]hear My word.

44 "[a]You are of [b]*your* father the devil, and [c]you want to do the desires of your father. [d]He was a murderer from the beginning, and does not stand in the truth, because [e]there is no truth in him. Whenever he speaks [1]a lie, he [f]speaks from his own *nature;* for he is a liar, and the father of [2]lies.

45 "But because [a]I speak the truth, you do not believe Me.

46 "Which one of you convicts Me of sin? If [a]I speak truth, why do you not believe Me?

47 "[a]He who is of God hears the words of God; for this reason you do not hear *them,* because you are not of God."

48 [a]The Jews answered and said to Him, "Do we not say rightly that You are a [b]Samaritan and [c]have a demon?"

49 Jesus answered, "I do not [a]have a demon; but I honor My Father, and you dishonor Me.

50 "But [a]I do not seek My glory; there is One who seeks and judges.

51 "Truly, truly, I say to you, if anyone [a]keeps My word he shall never [b]see death."

52 [a]The Jews said to Him, "Now we know that You [b]have a demon. Abraham died, and the prophets *also;* and You say, 'If anyone [c]keeps My word, he shall never [d]taste of death.'

53 "Surely You [a]are not greater than our father Abraham, who died? The prophets died too; whom do You make Yourself out *to be?*"

54 Jesus answered, "[a]If I glorify Myself, My glory is nothing; [b]it is My Father who glorifies Me, of whom you say, 'He is our God';

55 and [a]you have not come to know Him, [b]but I know Him; and if I say that I do not know Him, I shall be [c]a liar like you, [b]but I do know Him, and [d]keep His word.

56 "[a]Your father Abraham [b]rejoiced [1]to see My day, and he saw *it* and was glad."

57 [a]The Jews therefore said to Him, "You are not yet fifty years old, and have You seen Abraham?"

58 Jesus said to them, "Truly, truly, I say to you, before Abraham [1]was born, [a]I am."

59 Therefore they [a]picked up stones to throw at Him; but Jesus [1][b]hid Himself, and went out of the temple[2].

Healing the Man Born Blind

9 AND as He passed by, He saw a man blind from birth.

2 And His disciples asked Him, saying, "[a]Rabbi, who sinned, [b]this man or his [c]parents, that he should be born blind?"

3 Jesus answered, "*It was* neither *that* this man sinned, nor his parents; but *it was* in order [a]that the works of God might be displayed in him.

4 "We must work the works of Him who sent Me, [a]as long as it is day; night is coming, when no man can work.

5 "While I am in the world, I am [a]the light of the world."

6 When He had said this, He [a]spat on the ground, and made clay of the spittle, and applied the clay to his eyes,

7 and said to him, "Go, wash in [a]the pool of Siloam" (which is translated, Sent). And so he went away and [b]washed, and [c]came *back* seeing.

8 The neighbors therefore, and those who previously saw him as a beggar, were saying, "Is not this the one who used to [a]sit and beg?"

9 Others were saying, "This is he," *still* others were saying, "No, but he is

30 [a]John 7:31
31 [a]John 15:7; 2 John 9 [b]John 2:2
32 [a]John 1:14, 17 [b]John 8:36; Rom. 8:2; 2 Cor. 3:17; Gal. 5:1, 13; James 2:12; 1 Pet. 2:16
33 [a]Matt. 3:9; Luke 3:8; John 8:37, 39
34 [a]Rom. 6:16; 2 Pet. 2:19
35 [a]Gen. 21:10; Gal. 4:30 [b]Luke 15:31
36 [a]John 8:32
37 [1]Or, *makes no progress* [a]Matt. 3:9; John 8:39 [b]John 7:1; 8:40
38 [1]Or, *in the presence of* [a]John 8:41, 44
39 [a]Matt. 3:9; John 8:37 [b]Rom. 9:7; Gal. 3:7
40 [a]John 7:1; 8:37 [b]John 8:26
41 [a]John 8:38, 44 [b]Deut. 32:6; Is. 63:16; 64:8
42 [1]Lit., *that One* [a]1 John 5:1 [b]John 13:3; 16:28, 30; 17:8 [c]John 7:28 [d]John 3:17
43 [1]Or, *My mode of speaking* [a]John 8:33, 39, 41 [b]John 5:25
44 [1]Lit., *the lie* [2]Lit., *it* [a]1 John 3:8 [b]John 8:38, 41 [c]John 7:17 [d]Gen. 3:4; 1 John 3:8, 15 [e]1 John 2:4 [f]Matt. 12:34
45 [a]John 18:37
46 [a]John 18:37
47 [a]1 John 4:6
48 [a]John 1:19 [b]Matt. 10:5; John 4:9 [c]John 7:20
49 [a]John 7:20
50 [a]John 5:41; 8:54
51 [a]John 8:55; 14:23; 15:20; 17:6 [b]Matt. 16:28; Luke 2:26; John 8:52; Heb. 2:9; 11:5
52 [a]John 1:19 [b]John 7:20 [c]John 8:55; 14:23; 15:20; 17:6 [d]John 8:51
53 [a]John 4:12
54 [a]John 8:50 [b]John 7:39
55 [a]John 8:19; 15:21 [b]John 7:29 [c]John 8:44 [d]John 8:51; 15:10
56 [1]Lit., *in order that he might see* [a]John 8:37, 39 [b]Matt. 13:17; Heb. 11:13
57 [a]John 1:19
58 [1]Lit., *came into being* [a]Ex. 3:14; John 1:1; 17:5, 24
59 [1]Lit., *was hidden* [2]Some mss. add *and going through the midst of them went His way and so passed by* [a]Matt. 12:14; John 10:31; 11:8 [b]John 12:36

2 [a]Matt. 23:7 [b]Luke 13:2; John 9:34; Acts 28:4 [c]Ex. 20:5
3 [a]John 11:4
4 [a]John 7:33; 11:9; 12:35; Gal. 6:10
5 [a]Matt. 5:14; John 1:4; 8:12; 12:46
6 [a]Mark 7:33; 8:23
7 [a]Neh. 3:15; Is. 8:6; Luke 13:4; John 9:11 [b]2 Kin. 5:13f. [c]Is. 29:18; 35:5; 42:7; Matt. 11:5; John 11:37
8 [a]Acts 3:2, 10

like him." He kept saying, "I am the one."
10 Therefore they were saying to him, "How then were your eyes opened?"
11 He answered, "The man who is called Jesus made clay, and anointed my eyes, and said to me, 'Go to [a]Siloam, and wash'; so I went away and washed, and I received sight."
12 And they said to him, "Where is He?" He *said, "I do not know."

Controversy over the Man

13 They *brought to the Pharisees him who was formerly blind.
14 [a]Now it was a Sabbath on the day when Jesus made the clay, and opened his eyes.
15 [a]Again, therefore, the Pharisees also were asking him how he received his sight. And he said to them, "He applied clay to my eyes, and I washed, and I see."
16 Therefore some of the Pharisees were saying, "This man is not from God, because He [a]does not keep the Sabbath." But others were saying, "How can a man who is a sinner perform such [1][b]signs?" And [c]there was a division among them.
17 They *said therefore to the blind man [a]again, "What do you say about Him, since He opened your eyes?" And he said, "He is a [b]prophet."
18 [a]The Jews therefore did not believe *it* of him, that he had been blind, and had received sight, until they called the parents of the very one who had received his sight,
19 and questioned them, saying, "Is this your son, who you say was born blind? Then how does he now see?"
20 His parents answered them and said, "We know that this is our son, and that he was born blind;
21 but how he now sees, we do not know; or who opened his eyes, we do not know. Ask him; he is of age, he shall speak for himself."
22 His parents said this because they [a]were afraid of the Jews; for the Jews [b]had already agreed, that if anyone should confess Him to be [1]Christ, [c]he should be put out of the synagogue.
23 For this reason his parents said, "[a]He is of age; ask him."
24 So a second time they called the man who had been blind, and said to him, "[a]Give glory to God; we know that [b]this man is a sinner."
25 He therefore answered, "Whether He is a sinner, I do not know; one thing I do know, that, whereas I was blind, now I see."
26 They said therefore to him, "What did He do to you? How did He open your eyes?"
27 He answered them, "[a]I told you already, and you did not [b]listen; why do you want to hear *it* again? You do not want to become His disciples too, do you?"
28 And they reviled him, and said, "You are His disciple, but [a]we are disciples of Moses.
29 "We know that God has spoken to Moses; but as for this man, [a]we do not know where He is from."
30 The man answered and said to them, "Well, here is an amazing thing, that you do not know where He is from, and *yet* He opened my eyes.
31 "We know that [a]God does not hear sinners; but if anyone is God-fearing, and does His will, He hears him.
32 "[1]Since the beginning of time it has never been heard that anyone opened the eyes of a person born blind.
33 "[a]If this man were not from God, He could do nothing."
34 They answered and said to him, "[a]You were born entirely in sins, and are you teaching us?" And they [b]put him out.

Jesus Affirms His Deity

35 Jesus heard that they had [a]put him out; and finding him, He said, "Do you believe in the [b]Son of Man?"
36 He answered and said, "And [a]who is He, [1]Lord, that I may believe in Him?"
37 Jesus said to him, "You have both seen Him, and [a]He is the one who is talking with you."
38 And he said, "Lord, I believe." And he [a]worshiped Him.
39 And Jesus said, "[a]For judgment I came into this world, that [b]those who do not see may see; and that [c]those who see may become blind."
40 Those of the Pharisees who were with Him heard these things, and said to Him, "[a]We are not blind too, are we?"
41 Jesus said to them, "[a]If you were blind, you would have no sin; but since you say, '[b]We see,' your sin remains.

Parable of the Good Shepherd

10 "TRULY, truly, I say to you, he who does not enter by the door into the fold of the sheep, but climbs up some other way, he is [a]a thief and a robber.
2 "But he who enters by the door is [a]a shepherd of the sheep.
3 "To him the doorkeeper opens, and the sheep hear [a]his voice, and he calls his own sheep by name, and [b]leads them out.
4 "When he puts forth all his own, he goes before them, and the sheep follow him because they know [a]his voice.
5 "And a stranger they simply will not follow, but will flee from him, because they do not know [a]the voice of strangers."
6 This [a]figure of speech Jesus spoke to them, but they did not understand what those things were which He had been saying to them.

11 [a]John 9:7
14 [a]John 5:9
15 [a]John 9:10
16 [1]Or, *attesting miracles* [a]Matt. 12:2; Luke 13:14; John 5:10; 7:23 [b]John 2:11 [c]John 6:52; 7:12, 43; 10:19
17 [a]John 9:15 [b]Deut. 18:15; Matt. 21:11
18 [a]John 1:19; 9:22
22 [1]I.e., the Messiah [a]John 7:13 [b]John 7:45-52 [c]Luke 6:22; John 12:42; 16:2
23 [a]John 9:21
24 [a]Josh. 7:19; Ezra 10:11; Rev. 11:13 [b]John 9:16
27 [a]John 9:15 [b]John 5:25
28 [a]John 5:45; Rom. 2:17
29 [a]John 8:14
31 [a]Job 27:8f.; 35:13; Ps. 34:15f.; 66:18; 145:19; Prov. 15:29; 28:9; Is. 1:15; James 5:16ff.
32 [1]Lit., *From antiquity it was not heard*
33 [a]John 3:2; 9:16
34 [a]John 9:2 [b]John 9:22, 35; 3 John 10
35 [a]John 9:22, 34; 3 John 10 [b]Matt. 4:3
36 [1]Or, *Sir* [a]Rom. 10:14
37 [a]John 4:26
38 [a]Matt. 8:2
39 [a]John 3:19; 5:22, 27 [b]Luke 4:18 [c]Matt. 13:13; 15:14
40 [a]Rom. 2:19
41 [a]John 15:22, 24 [b]Prov. 26:12
1 [a]John 10:8
2 [a]John 10:11f.
3 [a]John 10:4f., 16, 27 [b]John 10:9
4 [a]John 10:5, 16, 27
5 [a]John 10:4, 16, 27
6 [a]John 16:25, 29; 2 Pet. 2:22

7 Jesus therefore said to them again,
"Truly, truly, I say to you, I am [a]the
door of the sheep.
8 "All who came before Me are
[a]thieves and robbers, but the sheep did
not hear them.
9 "[a]I am the door; if anyone enters
through Me, he shall be saved, and shall
go in and out, and find pasture.
10 "The thief comes only to steal, and
kill, and destroy; I came that they
[a]might have life, and might [1]have *it*
abundantly.
11 "[a]I am the good shepherd; the good
shepherd [b]lays down His life for the
sheep.
12 "He who is a hireling, and not a
[a]shepherd, who is not the owner of the
sheep, beholds the wolf coming, and
leaves the sheep, and flees, and the wolf
snatches them, and scatters *them.*
13 "*He flees* because he is a hireling,
and is not concerned about the sheep.
14 "[a]I am the good shepherd; and [b]I
know My own, and My own know Me,
15 even as [a]the Father knows Me and
I know the Father; and [b]I lay down My
life for the sheep.
16 "And I have [a]other sheep, which are
not of this fold; I must bring them also,
and they shall hear My voice; and they
shall become [b]one flock *with* [c]one shepherd.
17 "For this reason the Father loves
Me, because I [a]lay down My life that I
may take it again.
18 "[a]No one [1]has taken it away from
Me, but I [b]lay it down on My own
initiative. I have authority to lay it
down, and I have authority to take it up
again. [c]This commandment I received
from My Father."
19 [a]There arose a division again
among the Jews because of these words.
20 And many of them were saying,
"He [a]has a demon and [b]is insane. Why
do you listen to Him?"
21 Others were saying, "These are not
the sayings of one [a]demon-possessed. [b]A
demon cannot open the eyes of the
blind, can he?"

Jesus Asserts His Deity

22 At that time the Feast of the Dedication took place at Jerusalem;
23 it was winter, and Jesus was walking in the temple in the portico of
[a]Solomon.
24 [a]The Jews therefore gathered
around Him, and were saying to Him,
"How long will You keep us in sus-
pense? If You are [1]the Christ, tell us
[b]plainly."
25 Jesus answered them, "[a]I told you,
and you do not believe; [b]the works that I
do in My Father's name, these bear
witness of Me.
26 "But you do not believe, because
[a]you are not of My sheep.
27 "My sheep [a]hear My voice, and [b]I
know them, and they follow Me;
28 and I give [a]eternal life to them, and
they shall never perish; and [b]no one
shall snatch them out of My hand.
29 "[1]My Father, who has given *them* to
Me, is greater than all; and no one is
able to snatch *them* out of the Father's
hand.
30 "[a]I and the Father are [1]one."
31 The Jews [a]took up stones again to
stone Him.
32 Jesus answered them, "I showed
you many good works from the Father;
for which of them are you stoning Me?"
33 The Jews answered Him, "For a
good work we do not stone You, but for
[a]blasphemy; and because You, being a
man, [b]make Yourself out *to be* God."
34 Jesus answered them, "Has it not
been written in [a]your [b]Law, '[c]I SAID,
YOU ARE GODS'?
35 "If he called them gods, to whom
the word of God came (and the Scripture cannot be broken),
36 do you say of Him, whom the
Father [a]sanctified and [b]sent into the
world, 'You are blaspheming,' because I
said, '[c]I am the Son of God'?
37 "[a]If I do not do the works of My
Father, do not believe Me;
38 but if I do them, though you do not
believe Me, believe [a]the works, that you
may [1]know and understand that [b]the
Father is in Me, and I in the Father."
39 Therefore [a]they were seeking again
to seize Him, and [b]He eluded their
grasp.
40 And He went away [a]again beyond
the Jordan to the place where John was
first baptizing, and He was staying there.
41 And many came to Him and were
saying, "While John performed no [a]sign,
yet [b]everything John said about this man
was true."
42 And [a]many believed in Him there.

The Death and Resurrection of Lazarus

11 NOW a certain man was sick,
Lazarus of [a]Bethany, the village
of Mary and her sister [b]Martha.
2 And it was the Mary who
[a]anointed [b]the Lord with ointment, and
wiped His feet with her hair, whose
brother Lazarus was sick.
3 The sisters therefore sent to Him,
saying, "[a]Lord, behold, [b]he whom You
love is sick."
4 But when Jesus heard it, He said,
"This sickness is not unto death, but for
[a]the glory of God, that the Son of God
may be glorified by it."
5 Now Jesus loved [a]Martha, and her
sister, and Lazarus.
6 When therefore He heard that he
was sick, He stayed then two days *longer*
in the place where He was.
7 Then after this He *said to the
disciples, "[a]Let us go to Judea again."

7 [a]John 10:1f., 9
8 [a]Jer. 23:1f.; Ezek. 34:2ff.; John 10:1
9 [a]John 10:1f., 9
10 [1]Or, *have abundance*
[a]John 5:40
11 [a]Is. 40:11; Ezek. 34:11-16, 23; John 10:14; Heb. 13:20; 1 Pet. 5:4; Rev. 7:17 [b]John 10:15, 17, 18; 15:13; 1 John 3:16
12 [a]John 10:2
14 [a]John 10:11 [b]John 10:27
15 [a]Matt. 11:27; Luke 10:22 [b]John 10:11, 17, 18
16 [a]Is. 56:8 [b]John 11:52; 17:20f.; Eph. 2:13-18; 1 Pet. 2:25 [c]Ezek. 34:23; 37:24
17 [a]John 10:11, 15, 18
18 [1]Many Gr. mss. read *takes* [a]Matt. 26:53; John 2:19; 5:26 [b]John 10:11, 15, 17 [c]John 14:31; 15:10; Phil. 2:8; Heb. 5:8
19 [a]John 7:43; 9:16
20 [a]John 7:20 [b]Mark 3:21
21 [a]Matt. 4:24 [b]Ex. 4:11; John 9:32f.
23 [a]Acts 3:11; 5:12
24 [1]I.e., the Messiah [a]John 1:19; 10:31, 33 [b]Luke 22:67; John 16:25
25 [a]John 8:56, 58 [b]John 5:36; 10:38
26 [a]John 8:47
27 [a]John 10:4, 16 [b]John 10:14
28 [a]John 17:2f.; 1 John 2:25; 5:11 [b]John 6:37, 39
29 [1]Some early mss. read *What My Father has given Me is greater than all*
30 [1]Lit., (neuter) *a unity;* or, *one essence* [a]John 17:21ff.
31 [a]John 8:59
33 [a]Lev. 24:16 [b]John 5:18
34 [a]John 8:17 [b]John 12:34; 15:25; Rom. 3:19; 1 Cor. 14:21 [c]Ps. 82:6
36 [a]Jer. 1:5; John 6:69 [b]John 3:17 [c]John 5:17f.; 10:30
37 [a]John 10:25; 15:24
38 [1]Lit., *know and continue knowing* [a]John 10:25; 14:11 [b]John 14:10f., 20; 17:21, 23
39 [a]John 7:30 [b]Luke 4:30; John 8:59
40 [a]John 1:28
41 [a]John 2:11 [b]John 1:27, 30, 34; 3:27-30
42 [a]John 7:31

1 [a]Matt. 21:17; John 11:18 [b]Luke 10:38; John 11:5, 19ff.
2 [a]Luke 7:38; John 12:3 [b]Luke 7:13; John 11:3, 21, 32; 13:13f.
3 [a]Luke 7:13; John 11:2, 21, 32; 13:13f. [b]John 11:5, 11, 36
4 [a]John 9:3; 10:38; 11:40
5 [a]John 11:1
7 [a]John 10:40

8 The disciples *said to Him, "[a]Rabbi, the Jews were just now seeking [b]to stone You, and are You going there again?"

9 Jesus answered, "[a]Are there not twelve hours in the day? If anyone walks in the day, he does not stumble, because he sees the light of this world.

10 "But if anyone walks in the night, he stumbles, because the light is not in him."

11 This He said, and after that He *said to them, "Our [a]friend Lazarus [b]has fallen asleep; but I go, that I may awaken him out of sleep."

12 The disciples therefore said to Him, "Lord, if he has fallen asleep, he will [1]recover."

13 Now [a]Jesus had spoken of his death, but they thought that He was speaking of [1]literal sleep.

14 Then Jesus therefore said to them plainly, "Lazarus is dead,

15 and I am glad for your sakes that I was not there, so that you may believe; but let us go to him."

16 [a]Thomas therefore, who is called [1b]Didymus, said to *his* fellow disciples, "Let us also go, that we may die with Him."

17 So when Jesus came, He found that he had already been in the tomb [a]four days.

18 Now [a]Bethany was near Jerusalem, about [1]two miles off;

19 and many of [a]the Jews had come to [b]Martha and Mary, [c]to console them concerning *their* brother.

20 [a]Martha therefore, when she heard that Jesus was coming, went to meet Him; but [a]Mary still sat in the house.

21 Martha therefore said to Jesus, "[a]Lord, [b]if You had been here, my brother would not have died.

22 "Even now I know that [a]whatever You ask of God, God will give You."

23 Jesus *said to her, "Your brother shall rise again."

24 Martha *said to Him, "[a]I know that he will rise again in the resurrection on the last day."

25 Jesus said to her, "[a]I am the resurrection and the life; he who believes in Me shall live even if he dies,

26 and everyone who lives and believes in Me [a]shall never die. Do you believe this?"

27 She *said to Him, "Yes, Lord; I have believed that You are [1a]the Christ, the Son of God, *even* [2b]He who comes into the world."

28 And when she had said this, she [a]went away, and called Mary her sister, saying secretly, "[b]The Teacher is here, and is calling for you."

29 And when she heard it, she *arose quickly, and was coming to Him.

30 Now Jesus had not yet come into the village, but [a]was still in the place where Martha met Him.

31 [a]The Jews then who were with her in the house, and [b]consoling her, when they saw that Mary rose up quickly and went out, followed her, supposing that she was going to the tomb to [1]weep there.

32 Therefore, when Mary came where Jesus was, she saw Him, and fell at His feet, saying to Him, "[a]Lord, [b]if You had been here, my brother would not have died."

33 When Jesus therefore saw her [1]weeping, and [a]the Jews who came with her, *also* [1]weeping, He [b]was deeply moved in spirit, and [2c]was troubled,

34 and said, "Where have you laid him?" They *said to Him, "Lord, come and see."

35 Jesus [a]wept.

36 And so [a]the Jews were saying, "Behold how He [1b]loved him!"

37 But some of them said, "Could not this man, who [a]opened the eyes of him who was blind, [1]have kept this man also from dying?"

38 Jesus therefore again being deeply moved within, *came to the tomb. Now it was a [a]cave, and a stone was lying against it.

39 Jesus *said, "Remove the stone." Martha, the sister of the deceased, *said to Him, "Lord, by this time [1]there will be a stench, for he has been *dead* [a]four days."

40 Jesus *said to her, "[a]Did I not say to you, if you believe, you will see the glory of God?"

41 And so they removed the [a]stone. And Jesus [b]raised His eyes, and said, "[c]Father, I thank Thee that Thou heardest Me.

42 "And I knew that Thou hearest Me always; but [a]because of the people standing around I said it, that they may believe that [b]Thou didst send Me."

43 And when He had said these things, He cried out with a loud voice, "Lazarus, come forth."

44 He who had died came forth, [a]bound hand and foot with wrappings; and [b]his face was wrapped around with a cloth. Jesus *said to them, "Unbind him, and let him go."

45 [a]Many therefore of the Jews, [b]who had come to Mary and [c]beheld what He had done, believed in Him.

46 But some of them went away to the [a]Pharisees, and told them the things which Jesus had done.

Conspiracy to Kill Jesus

47 Therefore [a]the chief priests and the Pharisees [b]convened a [c]council, and were saying, "What are we doing? For this man is performing many [1d]signs.

48 "If we let Him *go on* like this, all men will believe in Him, and the Romans will come and take away both our [a]place and our nation."

8 [a]Matt. 23:7 [b]John 8:59; 10:31
9 [a]Luke 13:33; John 9:4; 12:35
11 [a]John 11:3 [b]Matt. 27:52; Mark 5:39; John 11:13; Acts 7:60
12 [1]Lit., *be saved*
13 [1]Lit., *the slumber of sleep* [a]Matt. 9:24; Luke 8:52
16 [1]I.e., the Twin [a]Matt. 10:3; Mark 3:18; Luke 6:15; John 14:5; 20:26-28; Acts 1:13 [b]John 20:24; 21:2
17 [a]John 11:39
18 [1]I.e., 15 stadia (9,090 ft.) [a]John 11:1
19 [a]John 1:19; 11:8 [b]John 11:1 [c]1 Sam. 31:13; 1 Chr. 10:12; Job 2:11; John 11:31
20 [a]Luke 10:38-42
21 [a]John 11:2 [b]John 11:32, 37
22 [a]John 9:31; 11:41f.
24 [a]Dan. 12:2; John 5:28f.; Acts 24:15
25 [a]John 1:4; 5:26; 6:39f.; Rev. 1:18
26 [a]John 6:47, 50, 51; 8:51
27 [1]I.e., the Messiah [2]The Coming One was the Messianic title [a]Matt. 16:16; Luke 2:11 [b]John 6:14
28 [a]John 11:30 [b]Matt. 26:18; Mark 14:14; Luke 22:11; John 13:13
30 [a]John 11:20
31 [1]Lit., *wail* [a]John 11:19, 33 [b]John 11:19
32 [a]John 11:2 [b]John 11:21
33 [1]Lit., *wailing* [2]Lit., *troubled Himself* [a]John 11:19 [b]John 11:38 [c]John 12:27; 13:21
35 [a]Luke 19:41; John 11:33
36 [1]Lit., *was loving* [a]John 11:19 [b]John 11:3
37 [1]Lit., *have caused that this man also not die* [a]John 9:7
38 [a]Matt. 27:60; Mark 15:46; Luke 24:2; John 20:1
39 [1]Lit., *he stinks* [a]John 11:17
40 [a]John 11:4, 23ff.
41 [a]Matt. 27:60; Mark 15:46; Luke 24:2; John 20:1 [b]John 17:1; Acts 7:55 [c]Matt. 11:25
42 [a]John 12:30; 17:21 [b]John 3:17
44 [a]John 19:40 [b]John 20:7
45 [a]John 7:31 [b]John 11:19; 12:17f. [c]John 2:23
46 [a]John 7:32, 45; 11:57
47 [1]Or, *attesting miracles* [a]John 7:32, 45; 11:57 [b]Matt. 26:3 [c]Matt. 5:22 [d]John 2:11

49 But a certain one of them, [a]Caiaphas, [b]who was high priest that year, said to them, "You know nothing at all,
50 nor do you take into account that [a]it is expedient for you that one man should die for the people, and that the whole nation should not perish."
51 Now this he did not say [1]on his own initiative; but [a]being high priest that year, he prophesied that Jesus was going to die for the nation,
52 and not for the nation only, but that He might also [a]gather together into one the children of God who are scattered abroad.
53 So from that day on they [a]planned together to kill Him.
54 Jesus therefore [a]no longer continued to walk publicly among the Jews, but went away from there to the country near the wilderness, into a city called [b]Ephraim; and there He stayed with the disciples.
55 Now [a]the Passover of the Jews was at hand, and many went up to Jerusalem out of the country before the Passover, [b]to purify themselves.
56 Therefore they [a]were seeking for Jesus, and were saying to one another, as they stood in the temple, "What do you think; that He will not come to the feast at all?"
57 Now [a]the chief priests and the Pharisees had given orders that if anyone knew where He was, he should report it, that they might seize Him.

Mary Anoints Jesus

12 [a]JESUS, therefore, six days before [b]the Passover, came to [c]Bethany where Lazarus was, whom Jesus had raised from the dead.
2 So they made Him a supper there, and [a]Martha was serving; but Lazarus was one of those reclining *at the table* with Him.
3 [a]Mary therefore took a pound of very costly [b]perfume of pure nard, and anointed the feet of Jesus, and wiped His feet with her hair; and the house was filled with the fragrance of the perfume.
4 But [a]Judas Iscariot, one of His disciples, who was intending to [1]betray Him, *said,
5 "Why was this perfume not sold for [1]three hundred denarii, and given to poor *people*?"
6 Now he said this, not because he was concerned about the poor, but because he was a thief, and as he [a]had the money box, he used to pilfer [b]what was put into it.
7 Jesus therefore said, "Let her alone, in order that she may keep [1]it for [a]the day of My burial.
8 "[a]For the poor you always have with you, but you do not always have Me."
9 The [a]great multitude therefore of the Jews learned that He was there; and they came, not for Jesus' sake only, but that they might also see Lazarus, [b]whom He raised from the dead.
10 But the chief priests took counsel that they might put Lazarus to death also;
11 because [a]on account of him [b]many of the Jews were going away, and were believing in Jesus.

Jesus Enters Jerusalem

12 On the next day [1a]the great multitude who had come to [b]the feast, when they heard that Jesus was coming to Jerusalem,
13 took the branches of the palm trees, and went out to meet Him, and *began* to cry out, "[a]Hosanna! BLESSED IS HE WHO COMES IN THE NAME OF THE LORD, even the [b]King of Israel."
14 And Jesus, finding a young donkey, sat on it; as it is written,
15 "[a]FEAR NOT, DAUGHTER OF ZION; BEHOLD, YOUR KING IS COMING, SEATED ON A DONKEY'S COLT."
16 [a]These things His disciples did not understand at the first; but when Jesus [b]was glorified, then they remembered that these things were written of Him, and that they had done these things to Him.
17 And so [a]the multitude who were with Him when He called Lazarus out of the tomb, and raised him from the dead, were bearing Him witness.
18 [a]For this cause also the multitude went and met Him, [b]because they heard that He had performed this [1]sign.
19 The Pharisees therefore said to one another, "You see that you are not doing any good; look, the world has gone after Him."

Greeks Seek Jesus

20 Now there were certain [a]Greeks among those who were going up to worship at [b]the feast;
21 these therefore came to [a]Philip, who was from [b]Bethsaida of Galilee, and *began to* ask him, saying, "Sir, we wish to see Jesus."
22 Philip *came and *told [a]Andrew; Andrew and Philip *came, and they *told Jesus.
23 And Jesus *answered them, saying, "[a]The hour has come for the Son of Man to [b]be glorified.
24 "Truly, truly, I say to you, [a]unless a grain of wheat falls into the earth and dies, it remains by itself alone; but if it dies, it bears much fruit.
25 "[a]He who loves his [1]life loses it; and he who [b]hates his [1]life in this world shall keep it to life eternal.
26 "If anyone serves Me, let him follow Me; and [a]where I am, there shall My servant also be; if anyone serves Me, the Father will [b]honor him.

48 [a]Matt. 24:15
49 [a]Matt. 26:3 [b]John 11:51; 18:13
50 [a]John 18:14
51 [1]Lit., *from himself* [a]John 18:13
52 [a]John 10:16
53 [a]Matt. 26:4
54 [a]John 7:1 [b]2 Chr. 13:19 mg.
55 [a]Matt. 26:1f.; Mark 14:1; Luke 22:1; John 2:13; 12:1; 13:1 [b]Num. 9:10; 2 Chr. 30:17f.; John 18:28
56 [a]John 7:11
57 [a]John 11:47

1 [a]John 12:1-8: *Matt. 26:6-13; Mark 14:3-9; Luke 7:37-39* [b]John 11:55; 12:20 [c]Matt. 21:17; John 11:43f.
2 [a]Luke 10:38
3 [a]Luke 7:37f.; John 11:2 [b]Mark 14:3
4 [1]Or, *deliver Him up* [a]John 6:71
5 [1]Equivalent to 11 months' wages
6 [a]John 13:29 [b]Luke 8:3
7 [1]I.e., The custom of anointing for burial [a]John 19:40
8 [a]Deut. 15:11; Matt. 26:11; Mark 14:7
9 [a]Mark 12:37; John 12:12 mg. [b]John 11:43f.; 12:1, 17f.
11 [a]John 11:45f.; 12:18 [b]John 7:31; 11:42
12 [1]Or, *the common people* [a]John 12:12-15: *Matt. 21:4-9; Mark 11:7-10; Luke 19:35-38* [b]John 12:1
13 [a]Ps. 118:26 [b]John 1:49
15 [a]Zech. 9:9
16 [a]Mark 9:32; John 2:22; 14:26 [b]John 7:39; 12:23
17 [a]John 11:42
18 [1]Or, *attesting miracle* [a]Luke 19:37; John 12:12 [b]John 12:11
20 [a]John 7:35 [b]John 12:1
21 [a]John 1:44 [b]Matt. 11:21
22 [a]John 1:44
23 [a]Matt. 26:45; Mark 14:35, 41; John 13:1; 17:1 [b]John 7:39; 12:16; 13:32
24 [a]Rom. 14:9; 1 Cor. 15:36
25 [1]Or, *soul* [a]Matt. 10:39; 16:25; Mark 8:35; Luke 9:24; 17:33 [b]Luke 14:26
26 [a]John 14:3; 17:24; 2 Cor. 5:8; Phil. 1:23; 1 Thess. 4:17 [b]1 Sam. 2:30; Ps. 91:15; Luke 12:37

Jesus Foretells His Death

27 "[a]Now My soul has become troubled; and what shall I say, '[b]Father, save Me from [c]this hour'? But for this purpose I came to this hour.

28 "[a]Father, glorify Thy name." There came therefore a [b]voice out of heaven: "I have both glorified it, and will glorify it again."

29 The multitude therefore, who stood by and heard it, were saying that it had thundered; others were saying, "[a]An angel has spoken to Him."

30 Jesus answered and said, "[a]This voice has not come for My sake, but for your sakes.

31 "[a]Now judgment is upon this world; now [b]the ruler of this world shall be cast out.

32 "And I, if I [a]be lifted up from the earth, will [b]draw all men to Myself."

33 But He was saying this [a]to indicate the kind of death by which He was to die.

34 The multitude therefore answered Him, "We have heard out of [a]the Law that [1b]the Christ is to remain forever; and how can You say, 'The [c]Son of Man must be [d]lifted up'? Who is this [c]Son of Man?"

35 Jesus therefore said to them, "[a]For a little while longer [b]the light is among you. [c]Walk while you have the light, that darkness may not overtake you; he who [d]walks in the darkness does not know where he goes.

36 "While you have the light, [a]believe in the light, in order that you may become [b]sons of light."

These things Jesus spoke, and He departed and [1c]hid Himself from them.

37 But though He had performed so many [1]signs before them, *yet* they were not believing in Him;

38 that the word of Isaiah the prophet might be fulfilled, which he spoke, "[a]LORD, WHO HAS BELIEVED OUR REPORT? AND TO WHOM HAS THE ARM OF THE LORD BEEN REVEALED?"

39 For this cause they could not believe, for Isaiah said again,

40 "[a]HE HAS BLINDED THEIR EYES, AND HE [b]HARDENED THEIR HEART; LEST THEY SEE WITH THEIR EYES, AND PERCEIVE WITH THEIR HEART, AND [1]BE CONVERTED, AND I HEAL THEM."

41 These things Isaiah said, because [a]he saw His glory, and [b]he spoke of Him.

42 Nevertheless [a]many even of [b]the rulers believed in Him, but [c]because of the Pharisees they were not confessing *Him,* lest they should be [1d]put out of the synagogue;

43 [a]for they loved the approval of men rather than the approval of God.

44 And Jesus cried out and said, "[a]He who believes in Me does not believe in Me, but in Him who sent Me.

45 "And [a]he who beholds Me beholds the One who sent Me.

46 "[a]I have come *as* light into the world, that everyone who believes in Me may not remain in darkness.

47 "And if anyone hears My sayings, and does not keep them, I do not judge him; for [a]I did not come to judge the world, but to save the world.

48 "[a]He who rejects Me, and does not receive My sayings, has one who judges him; [b]the word I spoke is what will judge him at [c]the last day.

49 "[a]For I did not speak [1]on My own initiative, but the Father Himself who sent Me [b]has given Me commandment, what to say, and what to speak.

50 "And I know that [a]His commandment is eternal life; therefore the things I speak, I speak [b]just as the Father has told Me."

The Lord's Supper

13 NOW before the Feast of [a]the Passover, Jesus knowing that [b]His hour had come that He should depart out of this world [c]to the Father, having loved His own who were in the world, He loved them [1]to the end.

2 And during supper, [a]the devil having already put into the heart of [b]Judas Iscariot, *the son* of Simon, to betray Him,

3 *Jesus,* [a]knowing that the Father had given all things into His hands, and that [b]He had come forth from God, and was going back to God,

4 *rose from supper, and *laid aside His garments; and taking a towel, He [a]girded Himself about.

Jesus Washes the Disciples' Feet

5 Then He *poured water into the basin, and began to [a]wash the disciples' feet, and to wipe them with the towel with which He was girded.

6 And so He *came to Simon Peter. He *said to Him, "Lord, do You wash my feet?"

7 Jesus answered and said to him, "What I do you do not realize now, but you shall understand [a]hereafter."

8 Peter *said to Him, "Never shall You wash my feet!" Jesus answered him, "[a]If I do not wash you, [b]you have no part with Me."

9 Simon Peter *said to Him, "Lord, not my feet only, but also my hands and my head."

10 Jesus *said to him, "He who has bathed needs only to wash his feet, but is completely clean; and [a]you are clean, but not all *of you.*"

11 For [a]He knew the one who was betraying Him; for this reason He said, "Not all of you are clean."

12 And so when He had washed their feet, and [a]taken His garments, and

27 [a]Matt. 26:38; Mark 14:34; John 11:33 [b]Matt. 11:25 [c]John 12:23
28 [a]Matt. 11:25 [b]Matt. 3:17; 17:5; Mark 1:11; 9:7; Luke 3:22; 9:35
29 [a]Acts 23:9
30 [a]John 11:42
31 [a]John 3:19; 9:39; 16:11 [b]John 14:30; 16:11; 2 Cor. 4:4; Eph. 2:2; 6:12; 1 John 4:4; 5:19
32 [a]John 3:14; 8:28; 12:34 [b]John 6:44
33 [a]John 18:32; 21:19
34 [1]I.e., the Messiah [a]John 10:34 [b]Ps. 110:4; Is. 9:7; Ezek. 37:25; Dan. 7:14 [c]Matt. 8:20 [d]John 3:14; 8:28; 12:32
35 [a]John 7:33; 9:4 [b]John 12:46; 1 John 2:10 [c]Gal. 6:10; Eph. 5:8 [d]1 John 1:6; 2:11
36 [1]Lit., *was hidden* [a]John 12:46 [b]Luke 16:8; John 8:12 [c]John 8:59
37 [1]Or, *attesting miracles*
38 [a]Is. 53:1; Rom. 10:16
40 [1]Lit., *should be turned*; i.e., turn about [a]Is. 6:10; Matt. 13:14f. [b]Mark 6:52
41 [a]Is. 6:1ff. [b]Luke 24:27
42 [1]I.e., excommunicated [a]John 7:48; 12:11 [b]Luke 23:13 [c]John 7:13 [d]John 9:22
43 [a]John 5:41, 44
44 [a]Matt. 10:40; John 5:24
45 [a]John 14:9
46 [a]John 1:4; 3:19; 8:12; 9:5; 12:35f.
47 [a]John 3:17; 8:15f.
48 [a]Luke 10:16 [b]Deut. 18:18f.; John 5:45ff.; 8:47 [c]Matt. 10:15; John 6:39; Acts 17:31; 1 Pet. 1:5; 2 Pet. 3:3, 7; Heb. 10:25
49 [1]Lit., *of Myself* [a]John 3:11; 7:16; 8:26, 28, 38; 14:10, 24 [b]John 14:31; 17:8
50 [a]John 6:68 [b]John 5:19; 8:28

1 [1]Lit., *to the uttermost;* or, *eternally* [a]John 2:13; 11:55 [b]John 12:23 [c]John 13:3; 16:28
2 [a]John 6:70; 13:27 [b]John 6:71
3 [a]John 3:35 [b]John 8:42
4 [a]Luke 12:37; 17:8
5 [a]Gen. 18:4; 19:2; 43:24; Judg. 19:21; Luke 7:44; 1 Tim. 5:10
7 [a]John 13:12ff.
8 [a]Ps. 51:2, 7; Ezek. 36:25; Acts 22:16; 1 Cor. 6:11; Heb. 10:22 [b]Deut. 12:12; 2 Sam. 20:1; 1 Kin. 12:16
10 [a]John 15:3; Eph. 5:26
11 [a]John 6:64; 13:2
12 [a]John 13:4

reclined _at the table_ again, He said to
them, "Do you know what I have done
to you?
13"You call Me [a]Teacher and [b]Lord;
and [1]you are right, for _so_ I am.
14"If I then, [a]the Lord and the
Teacher, washed your feet, you also
ought to wash one another's feet.
15"For I gave you [a]an example that
you also should do as I did to you.
16"Truly, truly, I say to you, [a]a slave is
not greater than his master; neither _is_
[b]one who is sent greater than the one
who sent him.
17"If you know these things, you are
[a]blessed if you do them.
18"[a]I do not speak of all of you. I
know the ones I have [b]chosen; but _it is_
[c]that the Scripture may be fulfilled, '[d]HE
WHO EATS MY BREAD HAS LIFTED UP HIS
HEEL AGAINST ME.'
19"From now on [a]I am telling you
before _it_ comes to pass, so that when it
does occur, you may believe that [b]I am
_He._
20"Truly, truly, I say to you, [a]he who
receives whomever I send receives Me;
and he who receives Me receives Him
who sent Me."

Jesus Predicts His Betrayal

21 When Jesus had said this, He [a]be-
came troubled in spirit, and testified,
and said, "Truly, truly, I say to you, that
[b]one of you will [1]betray Me."
22 The disciples _began_ looking at one
another, [a]at a loss _to know_ of which one
He was speaking.
23 There was reclining on [a]Jesus'
breast one of His disciples, [b]whom Jesus
loved.
24 Simon Peter therefore *gestured to
him, and *said to him, "Tell _us_ who it is
of whom He is speaking."
25 He, [a]leaning back thus on Jesus'
breast, *said to Him, "Lord, who is it?"
26 Jesus therefore *answered, "That is
the one for whom I shall dip the morsel
and give it to him." So when He had
dipped the morsel, He *took and *gave
it to Judas, [a]_the son_ of Simon Iscariot.
27 And after the morsel, [a]Satan then
[b]entered into him. Jesus therefore *said
to him, "What you do, do quickly."
28 Now no one of those reclining _at
the table_ knew for what purpose He had
said this to him.
29 For some were supposing, because
Judas [a]had the money box, that Jesus
was saying to him, "Buy the things we
have need of [b]for the feast"; or else, that
he should [c]give something to the poor.
30 And so after receiving the morsel
he went out immediately; and [a]it was
night.
31 When therefore he had gone out,
Jesus *said, "Now [1]is [a]the Son of Man
[b]glorified, and [c]God [1]is glorified in Him;
32 [1]if God is glorified in Him, [a]God
will also glorify Him in Himself, and will
glorify Him immediately.
33"[a]Little children, I am with you [b]a
little while longer. [c]You shall seek Me;
and as I said to the Jews, I now say to
you also, 'Where I am going, you cannot
come.'
34"A [a]new commandment I give to
you, [b]that you love one another, [c]even as
I have loved you, that you also love one
another.
35"[a]By this all men will know that you
are My disciples, if you have love for one
another."
36 Simon Peter *said to Him, "Lord,
where are You going?" Jesus answered,
"[a]Where I go, you cannot follow Me
now; but [b]you shall follow later."
37 Peter *said to Him, "Lord, why can
I not follow You right now? [a]I will lay
down my life for You."
38 Jesus *answered, "Will you lay
down your life for Me? Truly, truly, I
say to you, [a]a cock shall not crow, until
you deny Me three times.

Jesus Comforts His Disciples

14 "[a]LET not your heart be troubled; [1]believe in God, believe
also in Me.
2"In My Father's house are many
dwelling places; if it were not so, I would
have told you; for [a]I go to prepare a
place for you.
3"And if I go and prepare a place for
you, [a]I will come again, and receive you
to Myself; that [b]where I am, _there_ you
may be also.
4"[1]And you know the way where I
am going."
5 [a]Thomas *said to Him, "Lord, we
do not know where You are going, how
do we know the way?"
6 Jesus *said to him, "I am [a]the way,
and [b]the truth, and [c]the life; no one
comes to the Father, but through Me.

Oneness with the Father

7"[a]If you had known Me, you would
have known My Father also; from now
on you [b]know Him, and have [c]seen
Him."
8 [a]Philip *said to Him, "Lord, show
us the Father, and it is enough for us."
9 Jesus *said to him, "Have I been so
long with you, and _yet_ you have not
come to know Me, Philip? [a]He who has
seen Me has seen the Father; how do
you say, 'Show us the Father'?
10"Do you not believe that [a]I am in
the Father, and the Father is in Me?
[b]The words that I say to you I do not
speak on My own initiative, but the
Father abiding in Me does His works.

13 [1]Lit., _you say well_
aJohn 11:28 bJohn 11:2; 1 Cor. 12:3; Phil. 2:11
14 aJohn 11:2; 1 Cor. 12:3; Phil. 2:11
15 a1 Pet. 5:3
16 aMatt. 10:24; Luke 6:40; John 15:20 b2 Cor. 8:23; Phil. 2:25
17 aMatt. 7:24ff.; Luke 11:28; James 1:25
18 aJohn 13:10f. bJohn 6:70; 15:16, 19 cJohn 15:25; 17:12; 18:32; 19:24, 36 dPs. 41:9; Matt. 26:21ff.; Mark 14:18f.; Luke 22:21ff.; John 13:21, 22, 26
19 aJohn 14:29; 16:4 bJohn 8:24
20 aMatt. 10:40; Mark 9:37; Luke 9:48; 10:16; Gal. 4:14
21 [1]Or, _deliver Me up_
aJohn 11:33 bMatt. 26:21f.; Mark 14:18ff.; Luke 22:21ff.; John 13:18, 22, 26
22 aMatt. 26:21ff.; Mark 14:18ff.; Luke 22:21ff.; John 13:18, 21, 26
23 aJohn 1:18 bJohn 19:26; 20:2; 21:7, 20
25 aJohn 21:20
26 aJohn 6:71
27 aMatt. 4:10 bLuke 22:3; John 13:2
29 aJohn 12:6 bJohn 13:1 cJohn 12:5
30 aLuke 22:53
31 [1]Or, _was_
aMatt. 8:20 bJohn 7:39 cJohn 14:13; 17:4; 1 Pet. 4:11
32 [1]Some ancient mss. do not contain this phrase
aJohn 17:1
33 a1 John 2:1 bJohn 7:33 cJohn 7:34
34 aJohn 15:12, 17; 1 John 2:7f.; 3:11, 23; 2 John 5 bLev. 19:18; Matt. 5:44; Gal. 5:14; 1 Thess. 4:9; Heb. 13:1; 1 Pet. 1:22; 1 John 4:7 cEph. 5:2; 1 John 4:10f.
35 a1 John 3:14; 4:20
36 aJohn 13:33; 14:2; 16:5 bJohn 21:18f.; 2 Pet. 1:14
37 aJohn 13:37, 38: _Matt. 26:33-35; Mark 14:29-31; Luke 22:33-34_
38 aMark 14:30; John 18:27

1 [1]Or, _you believe in God_
aJohn 14:27; 16:22, 24
2 aJohn 13:33, 36
3 aJohn 14:18, 28 bJohn 12:26
4 [1]Many ancient authorities read _And where I go you know, and the way you know_

5 aJohn 11:16
6 aJohn 10:9; Rom. 5:2; Eph. 2:18; Heb. 10:20 bJohn 1:14 cJohn 1:4; 11:25; 1 John 5:20
7 aJohn 8:19 b1 John 2:13 cJohn 6:46
8 aJohn 1:43
9 aJohn 1:14; 12:45; Col. 1:15; Heb. 1:3
10 aJohn 10:38; 14:11, 20 bJohn 5:19; 14:24

11 "Believe Me that [a]I am in the Father, and the Father in Me; otherwise
[b]believe on account of the works themselves.
12 "Truly, truly, I say to you, he who
believes in Me, the works that I do shall
he do also; and [a]greater *works* than these
shall he do; because [b]I go to the Father.
13 "And [a]whatever you ask in My
name, that will I do, that [b]the Father
may be glorified in the Son.
14 "If you ask Me anything [a]in My
name, I will do *it*.
15 "[a]If you love Me, you will keep My
commandments.

Role of the Spirit

16 "And I will ask the Father, and He
will give you another [1a]Helper, that He
may be with you forever;
17 *that is* [a]the Spirit of truth, [b]whom
the world cannot receive, because it does
not behold Him or know Him, *but* you
know Him because He abides with you,
and will be in you.
18 "I will not leave you as orphans; [a]I
will come to you.
19 "[1a]After a little while [b]the world will
behold Me no more; but you *will* behold
Me; [c]because I live, you shall live also.
20 "[a]In that day you shall know that [b]I
am in My Father, and you in Me, and I
in you.
21 "[a]He who has My commandments
and keeps them, he it is who loves Me;
and [b]he who loves Me shall be loved by
My Father, and I will love him, and will
[c]disclose Myself to him."
22 [a]Judas (not Iscariot) *said to Him,
"Lord, what then has happened [b]that
You are going to disclose Yourself to us,
and not to the world?"
23 Jesus answered and said to him,
"[a]If anyone loves Me, he will [b]keep My
word; and [c]My Father will love him, and
We [d]will come to him, and make Our
abode with him.
24 "He who does not love Me [a]does not
keep My words; and [b]the word which
you hear is not Mine, but the Father's
who sent Me.
25 "These things I have spoken to you,
while abiding with you.
26 "But the [a]Helper, the Holy Spirit,
[b]whom the Father will send in My name,
[c]He will teach you all things, and [d]bring
to your remembrance all that I said to
you.
27 "[a]Peace I leave with you; My peace
I give to you; not as the world gives, do
I give to you. [b]Let not your heart be
troubled, nor let it be fearful.
28 "[a]You heard that I said to you, 'I go
away, and [b]I will come to you.' If you
loved Me, you would have rejoiced,
because [c]I go to the Father; for [d]the
Father is greater than I.
29 "And now [a]I have told you before it
comes to pass, that when it comes to
pass, you may believe.
30 "I will not speak much more with
you, for [a]the ruler of the world is coming, and he has nothing in Me;
31 but that the world may know that I
love the Father, and as [a]the Father gave
Me commandment, even so I do. Arise,
[b]let us go from here.

Jesus Is the Vine—Followers Are Branches

15 "[a]I AM the true vine, and My
Father is the [b]vinedresser.
2 "Every branch in Me that does not
bear fruit, He takes away; and every
branch that bears fruit, He [1]prunes it,
that it may bear more fruit.
3 "[a]You are already clean because of
the word which I have spoken to you.
4 "[a]Abide in Me, and I in you. As the
branch cannot bear fruit of itself, unless
it abides in the vine, so neither *can* you,
unless you abide in Me.
5 "I am the vine, you are the
branches; he who abides in Me, and I in
him, he [a]bears much fruit; for apart
from Me you can do nothing.
6 "If anyone does not abide in Me, he
is [a]thrown away as a branch, and dries
up; and they gather them, and cast them
into the fire, and they are burned.
7 "If you abide in Me, and My words
abide in you, [a]ask whatever you wish,
and it shall be done for you.
8 "[a]By this is My Father glorified,
[1]that you bear much fruit, and *so* [b]prove
to be My disciples.
9 "Just as [a]the Father has loved Me, I
have also loved you; abide in My love.
10 "[a]If you keep My commandments,
you will abide in My love; just as [b]I have
kept My Father's commandments, and
abide in His love.
11 "[a]These things I have spoken to you,
that My joy may be in you, and *that*
your [b]joy may be made full.

Disciples' Relation to Each Other

12 "This is [a]My commandment, that
you love one another, just as I have
loved you.
13 "[a]Greater love has no one than this,
that one [b]lay down his life for his
friends.
14 "You are My [a]friends, if [b]you do
what I command you.
15 "No longer do I call you slaves, for
the slave does not know what his master
is doing; but I have called you friends,
for [a]all things that I have heard from My
Father I have made known to you.
16 "[a]You did not choose Me, but I
chose you, and appointed you, that you
should go and [b]bear fruit, and *that* your
fruit should remain, that [c]whatever you
ask of the Father in My name, He may
give to you.

11 [a]John 10:38; 14:10, 20 [b]John 5:36
12 [a]John 4:37f.; 5:20 [b]John 7:33; 14:28
13 [a]Matt. 7:7 [b]John 13:31
14 [a]John 15:16; 16:23f.
15 [a]John 14:21, 23; 15:10; 1 John 5:3; 2 John 6
16 [1]Gr., *Paracletos, one called alongside to help; or, Intercessor* [a]John 7:39; 14:26; 15:26; 16:7; Rom. 8:26; 1 John 2:1
17 [a]John 15:26; 16:13; 1 John 4:6; 5:7 [b]1 Cor. 2:14
18 [a]John 14:3, 28
19 [1]Lit., *Yet a little and the world* [a]John 7:33 [b]John 16:16, 22 [c]John 6:57
20 [a]John 16:23, 26 [b]John 10:38; 14:11
21 [a]John 14:15, 23; 15:10; 1 John 5:3; 2 John 6 [b]John 14:23; 16:27 [c]Ex. 33:18f.; Prov. 8:17
22 [a]Luke 6:16; Acts 1:13 [b]Acts 10:40, 41
23 [a]John 14:15, 21; 15:10; 1 John 5:3; 2 John 6 [b]John 8:51; 1 John 2:5 [c]John 14:21 [d]2 Cor. 6:16; Eph. 3:17; 1 John 2:24; Rev. 3:20; 21:3
24 [a]John 14:23 [b]John 7:16; 14:10
26 [a]John 14:16 [b]Luke 24:49; John 1:33; 15:26; 16:7; Acts 2:33 [c]John 16:13f.; 1 John 2:20, 27 [d]John 2:22
27 [a]John 16:33; 20:19; Phil. 4:7; Col. 3:15 [b]John 14:1
28 [a]John 14:2-4 [b]John 14:3, 18 [c]John 14:12 [d]John 10:29; Phil. 2:6
29 [a]John 13:19
30 [a]John 12:31
31 [a]John 10:18; 12:49 [b]John 13:1; 18:1

1 [a]Ps. 80:8ff.; Is. 5:1ff.; Ezek. 19:10ff.; Matt. 21:33ff. [b]Matt. 15:13; Rom. 11:17; 1 Cor. 3:9
2 [1]Lit., *cleanses*
3 [a]John 13:10; 17:17; Eph. 5:26
4 [a]John 6:56; 15:4-7; 1 John 2:6
5 [a]John 15:16
6 [a]John 15:2
7 [a]Matt. 7:7; John 15:16
8 [1]Another reading is *that you bear much fruit, and become My disciples* [a]Matt. 5:16 [b]John 8:31
9 [a]John 3:35; 17:23, 24, 26
10 [a]John 14:15 [b]John 8:29
11 [a]John 17:13 [b]John 3:29
12 [a]John 13:34; 15:17; 1 John 3:23; 2 John 5
13 [a]Rom. 5:7f. [b]John 10:11
14 [a]Luke 12:4 [b]Matt. 12:50
15 [a]John 8:26; 16:12
16 [a]John 6:70; 13:18; 15:19 [b]John 15:5 [c]John 14:13; 15:7; 16:23

17"This [a]I command you, that you
love one another.

Disciples' Relation to the World

18"[a]If the world hates you, [1]you know
that it has hated Me before *it hated* you.
19"If you were of the world, the world
would love its own; but because you are
not of the world, but [a]I chose you out of
the world, [b]therefore the world hates
you.
20"Remember the word that I said to
you, '[a]A slave is not greater than his
master.' If they persecuted Me, [b]they
will also persecute you; if they [c]kept My
word, they will keep yours also.
21"But all these things they will do to
you [a]for My name's sake, [b]because they
do not know the One who sent Me.
22"[a]If I had not come and spoken to
them, they would not have [1]sin, but now
they have no excuse for their sin.
23"He who hates Me hates My Father
also.
24"[a]If I had not done among them
[b]the works which no one else did, they
would not have [1]sin; but now they have
both seen and hated Me and My Father
as well.
25"But *they have done this* in order that
the word may be fulfilled that is written
in their [a]Law, '[b]THEY HATED ME WITH-
OUT A CAUSE.'
26"When the [1a]Helper comes, [b]whom
I will send to you from the Father, *that is*
[c]the Spirit of truth, who proceeds from
the Father, [d]He will bear witness of Me,
27 [1]and [a]you *will* bear witness also,
because you have been with Me [b]from
the beginning.

Jesus' Warning

16 "[a]THESE things I have spoken to
you, that you may be kept from
[b]stumbling.
2"[1]They will [a]make you outcasts from
the synagogue, but [b]an hour is coming
for everyone [c]who kills you to think that
he is offering service to God.
3"And these things they will do,
[a]because they have not known the Father, or Me.
4"But these things I have spoken to
you, [a]that when their hour comes, you
[1]may remember that I told you of them.
And these things I did not say to you [b]at
the beginning, because I was with you.

The Holy Spirit Promised

5"But now [a]I am going to Him who
sent Me; and none of you asks Me,
'[b]Where are You going?'
6"But because I have said these
things to you, [a]sorrow has filled your
heart.
7"But I tell you the truth, it is to your
advantage that I go away; for if I do not
go away, the [1a]Helper shall not come to
you; but if I go, [b]I will send Him to you.

17 [a]John 15:12
18 [1]Or, (imperative) *know that* [a]John 7:7; 1 John 3:13
19 [a]John 15:16 [b]Matt. 10:22; 24:9; John 17:14
20 [a]Matt. 10:24; John 13:16 [b]1 Cor. 4:12; 2 Cor. 4:9; 2 Tim. 3:12 [c]John 8:51
21 [a]Matt. 10:22; 24:9; Mark 13:13; Luke 21:12, 17; Acts 4:17; 5:41; 9:14; 26:9; 1 Pet. 4:14; Rev. 2:3 [b]John 8:19, 55; 16:3; 17:25; Acts 3:17; 1 John 3:1
22 [1]I.e., guilt [a]John 9:41; 15:24
24 [1]I.e., guilt [a]John 9:41; 15:21 [b]John 5:36; 10:37
25 [a]John 10:34 [b]Ps. 35:19; 69:4
26 [1]Gr., *Paracletos,* one called alongside to help; or, *Intercessor* [a]John 14:16 [b]John 14:26 [c]John 14:17 [d]1 John 5:7
27 [1]Or, (imperative) *and bear witness* [a]Luke 24:48; John 19:35; 21:24; 1 John 1:2; 4:14 [b]Luke 1:2

1 [a]John 15:18-27 [b]Matt. 11:6
2 [1]Or, *They will make you excommunicated* [a]John 9:22 [b]John 4:21; 16:25 [c]Is. 66:5; Acts 26:9-11; Rev. 6:9
3 [a]John 8:19, 55; 15:21; 17:25; Acts 3:17; 1 John 3:1
4 [1]Lit., *may remember them, that I told you* [a]John 13:19 [b]Luke 1:2
5 [a]John 7:33; 16:10, 17, 28 [b]John 13:36; 14:5
6 [a]John 14:1; 16:22
7 [1]Gr., *Paracletos,* one called alongside to help; or, *Intercessor* [a]John 14:16 [b]John 14:26
9 [a]John 15:22, 24
10 [a]Acts 3:14; 7:52; 17:31; 1 Pet. 3:18 [b]John 16:5
11 [a]John 12:31
13 [a]John 14:17 [b]John 14:26
14 [a]John 7:39
15 [a]John 17:10
16 [a]John 7:33 [b]John 14:18-24; 16:16-24 [c]John 16:22
17 [a]John 16:16 [b]John 16:5
19 [a]Mark 9:32; John 6:61
20 [a]Mark 16:10; Luke 23:27 [b]John 20:20
21 [1]Lit., *human being* [a]Is. 13:8; 21:3; 26:17; 66:7; Hos. 13:13; Mic. 4:9; 1 Thess. 5:3

8"And He, when He comes, will
convict the world concerning sin, and
righteousness, and judgment;
9 concerning sin, [a]because they do
not believe in Me;
10 and concerning [a]righteousness, because [b]I go to the Father, and you no
longer behold Me;
11 [a]and concerning judgment, because
the ruler of this world has been judged.
12"I have many more things to say to
you, but you cannot bear *them* now.
13"But when He, [a]the Spirit of truth,
comes, He will [b]guide you into all the
truth; for He will not speak on His own
initiative, but whatever He hears, He will
speak; and He will disclose to you what
is to come.
14"He shall [a]glorify Me; for He shall
take of Mine, and shall disclose *it* to you.
15"[a]All things that the Father has are
Mine; therefore I said, that He takes of
Mine, and will disclose *it* to you.

Jesus' Death and Resurrection Foretold

16"[a]A little while, and [b]you will no
longer behold Me; and again a little
while, and [c]you will see Me."
17 *Some* of His disciples therefore said
to one another, "What is this thing He is
telling us, '[a]A little while, and you will
not behold Me; and again a little while,
and you will see Me'; and, 'because [b]I go
to the Father'?"
18 And so they were saying, "What is
this that He says, 'A little while'? We do
not know what He is talking about."
19 [a]Jesus knew that they wished to
question Him, and He said to them,
"Are you deliberating together about
this, that I said, 'A little while, and you
will not behold Me, and again a little
while, and you will see Me'?
20"Truly, truly, I say to you, that [a]you
will weep and lament, but the world will
rejoice; you will be sorrowful, but [b]your
sorrow will be turned to joy.
21"[a]Whenever a woman is in travail
she has sorrow, because her hour has
come; but when she gives birth to the
child, she remembers the anguish no
more, for joy that a [1]child has been born
into the world.
22"Therefore [a]you too now have sorrow; but [b]I will see you again, and your
heart will rejoice, and no one takes your
joy away from you.

Prayer Promises

23"And [a]in that day [b]you will [1]ask Me
no question. Truly, truly, I say to you, [c]if
you shall ask the Father for anything,
He will give it to you in My name.
24"[a]Until now you have asked for
nothing in My name; ask, and you will
receive, that your [b]joy may be made full.

22 [a]John 16:6 [b]John 16:16
23 [1]Lit., *question Me nothing* [a]John 14:20; 16:26 [b]John 16:19, 30 [c]John 15:16
24 [a]John 14:14 [b]John 3:29; 15:11

25"These things I have spoken to you
in [1a]figurative language; [b]an hour is
coming when I will speak no more to
you in [1]figurative language, but will tell
you plainly of the Father.
26"[a]In that day [b]you will ask in My
name, and I do not say to you that I will
request the Father on your behalf;
27 for [a]the Father Himself loves you,
because you have loved Me, and [b]have
believed that [c]I came forth from the
Father.
28"[a]I came forth from the Father, and
have come into the world; I am leaving
the world again, and [b]going to the
Father."
29 His disciples *said, "Lo, now You
are speaking plainly, and are not using
[a]a [1]figure of speech.
30"Now we know that You know all
things, and have no need for anyone to
question You; by this we [a]believe that
You [b]came from God."
31 Jesus answered them, "Do you now
believe?
32"Behold, [a]an hour is coming, and
has *already* come, for [b]you to be scattered, each to [c]his own *home,* and to
leave Me alone; and *yet* [d]I am not alone,
because the Father is with Me.
33"These things I have spoken to you,
that [a]in Me you may have peace. [b]In the
world you have tribulation, but [c]take
courage; [d]I have overcome the world."

The High Priestly Prayer

17 THESE things Jesus spoke; and
[a]lifting up His eyes to heaven, He
said, "Father, the hour has come; [b]glo-
rify Thy Son, that the Son may glorify
Thee,
2 even as [a]Thou gavest Him authority over all [1]mankind, that [b]to [2]all whom
Thou hast given Him, [c]He may give
eternal life.
3"And this is eternal life, that they
may know Thee, [a]the only true God, and
Jesus Christ whom [b]Thou hast sent.
4"[a]I glorified Thee on the earth,
[b]having accomplished the work which
Thou hast given Me to do.
5"And now, [a]glorify Thou Me together with Thyself, Father, with the
glory which I had [b]with Thee before the
world was.
6"[a]I manifested Thy name to the men
whom [b]Thou gavest Me out of the
world; [c]Thine they were, and Thou
gavest them to Me, and they have [d]kept
Thy word.
7"Now they have come to know that
everything Thou hast given Me is from
Thee;
8 for [a]the words which Thou gavest
Me [b]I have given to them; and they
received *them,* and truly understood that
[c]I came forth from Thee, and they believed that [d]Thou didst send Me.
9"[a]I ask on their behalf; [b]I do not ask
on behalf of the world, but of those
whom [c]Thou hast given Me; for [d]they
are Thine;
10 and [a]all things that are Mine are
Thine, and Thine are Mine; and I have
been glorified in them.
11"And I am no more in the world;
and *yet* [a]they themselves are in the
world, and [b]I come to Thee. [c]Holy
Father, keep them in Thy name, *the
name* [d]which Thou hast given Me, that
[e]they may be one, even as We *are.*
12"While I was with them, I was
keeping them in Thy name [a]which Thou
hast given Me; and I guarded them, and
[b]not one of them perished but [c]the son
of perdition, that the [d]Scripture might be
fulfilled.

The Disciples in the World

13"But now [a]I come to Thee; and
[b]these things I speak in the world, that
they may have My [c]joy made full in
themselves.
14"I have given them Thy word; and
[a]the world has hated them, because
[b]they are not of the world, even as I am
not of the world.
15"I do not ask Thee to take them out
of the world, but to keep them [1]from
[2a]the evil *one.*
16"[a]They are not of the world, even as
I am not of the world.
17"[a]Sanctify them in the truth; Thy
word is truth.
18"As [a]Thou didst send Me into the
world, [b]I also have sent them into the
world.
19"And for their sakes I [a]sanctify
Myself, that they themselves also may be
[b]sanctified [c]in truth.
20"I do not ask in behalf of these
alone, but for those also who believe in
Me through their word;
21 that they may all be one; [a]even as
Thou, Father, *art* in Me, and I in Thee,
that they also may be in Us; [b]that the
world may [1]believe that [c]Thou didst
send Me.

Their Future Glory

22"And the [a]glory which Thou hast
given Me I have given to them; that they
may be one, just as We are one;
23 [a]I in them, and Thou in Me, that
they may be perfected [1]in unity, that the
world may [2]know that [b]Thou didst send
Me, and didst [c]love them, even as Thou
didst love Me.
24"Father, [1]I desire that [a]they also,
whom Thou hast given Me, [b]be with Me
where I am, in order that they may
behold My [c]glory, which Thou hast
given Me; for Thou didst love Me before
[d]the foundation of the world.

25 [1]Lit., *proverbs;* or, *figures of speech* [a]Matt. 13:34; John 10:6; 16:29 [b]John 16:2
26 [a]John 14:20; 16:23 [b]John 16:19, 30
27 [a]John 14:21, 23 [b]John 2:11; 16:30 [c]John 8:42
28 [a]John 8:42; 16:30 [b]John 13:1, 3; 16:5, 10, 17
29 [1]Lit., *proverb* [a]Matt. 13:34; John 10:6; 16:25
30 [a]John 2:11; 16:27 [b]John 8:42; 16:28
32 [a]John 4:23; 16:2, 25 [b]Zech. 13:7; Matt. 26:31 [c]John 19:27 [d]John 8:29
33 [a]John 14:27 [b]John 15:18ff. [c]Matt. 9:2 [d]Rom. 8:37; 2 Cor. 2:14; 4:7ff.; 6:4ff.; Rev. 3:21; 12:11

1 [a]John 11:41 [b]John 7:39; 13:31f.
2 [1]Lit., *flesh* [2]Lit., *all that which Thou hast given Him, to them He* [a]John 3:35 [b]John 6:37, 39; 17:6, 9, 24 [c]John 10:28
3 [a]John 5:44 [b]John 3:17; 17:8, 21, 23, 25
4 [a]John 13:31 [b]Luke 22:37; John 4:34
5 [a]John 17:1 [b]John 1:1; 8:58; 17:24; Phil. 2:6
6 [a]John 17:26 [b]John 6:37, 39; 17:2, 9, 24 [c]John 17:9 [d]John 8:51
8 [a]John 6:68; 12:49 [b]John 15:15; 17:14, 26 [c]John 8:42; 16:27, 30 [d]John 3:17; 17:18, 21, 23, 25
9 [a]Luke 22:32; John 14:16 [b]Luke 23:34; John 17:20f. [c]John 6:37, 39; 17:2, 6, 24 [d]John 17:6
10 [a]John 16:15
11 [a]John 13:1 [b]John 7:33; 17:13 [c]John 17:25 [d]John 17:6; Phil. 2:9; Rev. 19:12 [e]John 17:21f.; Rom. 12:5; Gal. 3:28
12 [a]John 17:6; Phil. 2:9; Rev. 19:12 [b]John 6:39; 18:9 [c]John 6:70 [d]Ps. 41:9; John 13:18
13 [a]John 7:33; 17:11 [b]John 15:11 [c]John 3:29
14 [a]John 15:19 [b]John 8:23; 17:16
15 [1]Or, *out of* the power of [2]Or, *evil* [a]Matt. 5:37
16 [a]John 17:14
17 [a]John 15:3
18 [a]John 3:17; 17:3, 8, 21, 23, 25 [b]Matt. 10:5; John 4:38; 20:21
19 [a]John 15:13 [b]John 15:3 [c]2 Cor. 7:14; Col. 1:6; 1 John 3:18

21 [1]Gr. tense indicates *continually believe* [a]John 10:38; 17:11, 23 [b]John 17:8 [c]John 3:17; 17:3, 8, 18, 23, 25
22 [a]John 1:14; 17:24
23 [1]Lit., *into a unit* [2]Gr. tense indicates *continually know* [a]John 10:38; 17:11, 21 [b]John 3:17; 17:3, 8, 18, 21, 25 [c]John 16:27
24 [1]Some mss. read *that which Thou hast given Me, I desire that where I am, they also may be with Me, that* [a]John 17:2 [b]John 12:26 [c]John 1:14; 17:22 [d]Matt. 25:34; John 17:5

25 "O [a]righteous Father, [1]although [b]the
world has not known Thee, [1]yet I have
known Thee; and these have known that
[c]Thou didst send Me;
26 and [a]I have made Thy name known
to them, and will make it known; that
[b]the love wherewith Thou didst love Me
may be in them, and I in them."

Judas Betrays Jesus

18 WHEN Jesus had spoken these
words, [a]He went forth with His
disciples over [b]the [1]ravine of the Kidron,
where there was [c]a garden, into which
He Himself entered, and His disciples.
2 Now Judas also, who was [1]betray-
ing Him, knew the place; for Jesus had
[a]often met there with His disciples.
3 [a]Judas then, having received [b]the
Roman [1]cohort, and [c]officers from the
chief priests and the Pharisees, *came
there with lanterns and [d]torches and
weapons.
4 Jesus therefore, [a]knowing all the
things that were coming upon Him, went
forth, and *said to them, "[b]Whom do
you seek?"
5 They answered Him, "Jesus the
Nazarene." He *said to them, "I am
He." And Judas also who was betraying
Him, was standing with them.
6 When therefore He said to them, "I
am *He,*" they drew back, and fell to the
ground.
7 Again therefore He asked them,
"[a]Whom do you seek?" And they said,
"Jesus the Nazarene."
8 Jesus answered, "I told you that I
am *He*; if therefore you seek Me, let
these go their way,"
9 that the word might be fulfilled
which He spoke, "[a]Of those whom Thou
hast given Me I lost not one."
10 Simon Peter therefore [a]having a
sword, drew it, and struck the high
priest's slave, and cut off his right ear;
and the slave's name was Malchus.
11 Jesus therefore said to Peter, "Put
the sword into the sheath; [a]the cup
which the Father has given Me, shall I
not drink it?"

Jesus before the Priests

12 [a]So [b]the *Roman* [1]cohort and the
[2]commander, and the [b]officers of the
Jews, arrested Jesus and bound Him,
13 and led Him to [a]Annas first; for he
was father-in-law of [b]Caiaphas, who was
high priest that year.
14 Now Caiaphas was the one who
had advised the Jews that [a]it was expedient for one man to die on behalf of the
people.
15 And [a]Simon Peter was following
Jesus, and *so was* another disciple. Now
that disciple was known to the high
priest, and entered with Jesus into [b]the
court of the high priest,
16 [a]but Peter was standing at the door
outside. So the other disciple, who was
known to the high priest, went out and
spoke to the doorkeeper, and brought in
Peter.
17 [a]The slave-girl therefore who kept
the door *said to Peter, "[b]You are not
also *one* of this man's disciples, are
you?" He *said, "I am not."
18 Now the slaves and the [a]officers
were standing *there,* having made [b]a
charcoal fire, for it was cold and they
were [c]warming themselves; and Peter
also was with them, standing and warming himself.
19 [a]The high priest therefore questioned Jesus about His disciples, and
about His teaching.
20 Jesus answered him, "I [a]have spoken openly to the world; I always
[b]taught in [1]synagogues, and [c]in the
temple, where all the Jews come together; and I spoke nothing in secret.
21 "Why do you question Me? Question those who have heard what I spoke
to them; behold, these know what I
said."
22 And when He had said this, one of
the [a]officers standing by [b]gave Jesus a
blow, saying, "Is that the way You
answer the high priest?"
23 [a]Jesus answered him, "If I have
spoken wrongly, bear witness of the
wrong; but if rightly, why do you strike
Me?"
24 [a]Annas therefore sent Him bound
to [a]Caiaphas the high priest.

Peter's Denial of Jesus

25 [a]Now [b]Simon Peter was standing
and warming himself. They said therefore to him, "[c]You are not also *one* of
His disciples, are you?" He denied *it,*
and said, "I am not."
26 One of the slaves of the high priest,
being a relative of the one [a]whose ear
Peter cut off, *said, "Did I not see you in
[b]the garden with Him?"
27 Peter therefore denied *it* again; and
immediately [a]a cock crowed.

Jesus before Pilate

28 [a]They *led Jesus therefore from
[b]Caiaphas into [c]the [1]Praetorium, and it
was early; and they themselves did not
enter into [c]the [1]Praetorium in order that
[d]they might not be defiled, but might eat
the Passover.
29 [a]Pilate therefore went out to them,
and *said, "What accusation do you
bring against this Man?"
30 They answered and said to him, "If
this Man were not an evildoer, we would
not have delivered Him up to you."
31 Pilate therefore said to them,
"Take Him yourselves, and judge Him
according to your law." The Jews said to
him, "We are not permitted to put
anyone to death,"
32 that [a]the word of Jesus might be
fulfilled, which He spoke, signifying by
what kind of death He was about to die.

25 [1]Lit., *and* [a]John 17:11; 1 John 1:9 [b]John 7:29; 15:21 [c]John 3:17; 17:3, 8, 18, 21, 23
26 [a]John 17:6 [b]John 15:9

1 [1]Lit., *winter-torrent* [a]Matt. 26:30, 36; Mark 14:26, 32; Luke 22:39 [b]2 Sam. 15:23; 1 Kin. 2:37; 15:13; 2 Kin. 23:4, 6, 12; 2 Chr. 15:16; 29:16; 30:14; Jer. 31:40 [c]Matt. 26:36; Mark 14:32; John 18:26
2 [1]Or, *delivering Him up* [a]Luke 21:37; 22:39
3 [1]Normally 600 men; *a battalion* [a]John 18:3-11: *Matt. 26:47-56; Mark 14:43-50; Luke 22:47-53* [b]John 18:12; Acts 10:1 [c]John 7:32; 18:12, 18 [d]Matt. 25:1
4 [a]John 6:64; 13:1, 11 [b]John 18:7
7 [a]John 18:4
9 [a]John 17:12
10 [a]Matt. 26:51; Mark 14:47
11 [a]Matt. 20:22; 26:39; Mark 14:36; Luke 22:42
12 [1]Or, *battalion* [2]I.e., chiliarch, in command of a thousand troops [a]John 18:12f.: *Matt. 26:57ff.* [b]John 18:3
13 [a]Luke 3:2; John 18:24 [b]Matt. 26:3; John 11:49, 51
14 [a]John 11:50
15 [a]Matt. 26:58; Mark 14:54; Luke 22:54 [b]Matt. 26:3; John 18:24, 28
16 [a]John 18:16-18: *Matt. 26:69f.; Mark 14:66-68; Luke 22:55-57*
17 [a]Acts 12:13 [b]John 18:25
18 [a]John 18:3 [b]John 21:9 [c]Mark 14:54, 67
19 [a]John 18:19-24: *Matt. 26:59-68; Mark 14:55-65; Luke 22:63-71*
20 [1]Lit., *the synagogue* [a]John 7:26; 8:26 [b]Matt. 4:23; John 6:59 [c]Matt. 26:55
22 [a]John 18:3 [b]John 19:3
23 [a]Matt. 5:39; Acts 23:2-5
24 [a]John 18:13
25 [a]John 18:25-27: *Matt. 26:71-75; Mark 14:69-72; Luke 22:58-62* [b]John 18:18 [c]John 18:17
26 [a]John 18:10 [b]John 18:1
27 [a]John 13:38
28 [1]I.e., governor's official residence [a]Matt. 27:2; Mark 15:1; Luke 23:1 [b]John 18:13 [c]Matt. 27:27; John 18:33; 19:9 [d]John 11:55; Acts 11:3
29 [a]John 18:29-38: *Matt. 27:11-14; Mark 15:2-5; Luke 23:2, 3*

32 [a]Matt. 20:19; 26:2; Mark 10:33f.; Luke 18:32f.; John 3:14; 8:28; 12:32f.

33 Pilate therefore [a]entered again into
the Praetorium, and summoned Jesus,
and said to Him, "[b]Are You the King of
the Jews?"
34 Jesus answered, "Are you saying
this [1]on your own initiative, or did
others tell you about Me?"
35 Pilate answered, "I am not a Jew,
am I? Your own nation and the chief
priests delivered You up to me; what
have You done?"
36 Jesus answered, "[a]My kingdom [1]is
not of this world. If My kingdom were of
this world, then My servants would be
fighting, that I might not be delivered up
to the Jews; but as it is, My kingdom is
not [2]of this realm."
37 Pilate therefore said to Him, "So
You are a king?" Jesus answered, "[a]You
say *correctly* that I am a king. For this I
have been born, and for this I have come
into the world, [b]to bear witness to the
truth. [c]Everyone who is of the truth
hears My voice."
38 Pilate *said to Him, "What is
truth?"
And when he had said this, he [a]went
out again to the Jews, and *said to them,
"[b]I find no guilt in Him.
39 "[a]But you have a custom, that I
should release someone [1]for you at the
Passover; do you wish then that I release
[1]for you the King of the Jews?"
40 Therefore they cried out again,
saying, "[a]Not this Man, but Barabbas."
Now Barabbas was a robber.

The Crown of Thorns

19 THEN Pilate therefore took
Jesus, and [1a]scourged Him.
2 [a]And the soldiers wove a crown of
thorns and put it on His head, and
arrayed Him in a purple robe;
3 and they *began* to come up to Him,
and say, "[a]Hail, King of the Jews!" and
to [b]give Him blows *in the face.*
4 And Pilate [a]came out again, and
*said to them, "Behold, I am bringing
Him out to you, that you may know that
[b]I find no guilt in Him."
5 Jesus therefore came out, [a]wearing
the crown of thorns and the purple robe.
And *Pilate* *said to them, "Behold, the
Man!"
6 When therefore the chief priests
and the [a]officers saw Him, they cried
out, saying, "Crucify, crucify!" Pilate
*said to them, "Take Him yourselves,
and crucify Him, for [b]I find no guilt in
Him."
7 The Jews answered him, "[a]We have
a law, and by that law He ought to die
because He [b]made Himself out *to be* the
Son of God."
8 When Pilate therefore heard this
statement, he was the more afraid;
9 and he [a]entered into the [1]Praeto-
rium again, and *said to Jesus, "Where
are You from?" But [b]Jesus gave him no
answer.
10 Pilate therefore *said to Him, "You
do not speak to me? Do You not know
that I have authority to release You, and
I have authority to crucify You?"
11 Jesus answered, "[a]You would have
no authority [1]over Me, unless it had
been given you from above; for this
reason [b]he who delivered Me up to you
has *the* greater sin."
12 As a result of this Pilate [1]made
efforts to release Him, but the Jews cried
out, saying, "[a]If you release this Man,
you are no friend of Caesar; everyone
who makes himself out *to be* a king
[2]opposes Caesar."
13 When Pilate therefore heard these
words, he brought Jesus out, and [a]sat
down on the judgment seat at a place
called [1]The Pavement, but [b]in [2]Hebrew,
Gabbatha.
14 Now it was [a]the day of preparation
for the Passover; it was about the [1b]sixth
hour. And he *said to the Jews, "Behold,
[c]your King!"
15 They therefore cried out, "[a]Away
with *Him,* away with *Him,* crucify
Him!" Pilate *said to them, "Shall I
crucify your King?" The chief priests
answered, "We have no king but Caesar."

The Crucifixion

16 So he then [a]delivered Him to them
to be crucified.
17 [a]They took Jesus therefore, and He
went out, [1b]bearing His own cross, to the
place called [c]the Place of a Skull, which
is called [d]in [2]Hebrew, Golgotha.
18 There they crucified Him, and with
Him [a]two other men, one on either side,
and Jesus in between.
19 And Pilate wrote an inscription
also, and put it on the cross. And it was
written, "[a]JESUS THE NAZARENE,
[b]THE KING OF THE JEWS."
20 Therefore this inscription many of
the Jews read, for the place where Jesus
was crucified was near the city; and it
was written [a]in [1]Hebrew, Latin, *and* in
Greek.
21 And so the chief priests of the Jews
were saying to Pilate, "Do not write,
'[a]The King of the Jews'; but that He
said, 'I am [a]King of the Jews.'"
22 Pilate answered, "[a]What I have
written I have written."
23 [a]The soldiers therefore, when they
had crucified Jesus, took His outer garments and made [b]four parts, a part to
every soldier and *also* the [1]tunic; now
the tunic was seamless, woven [2]in one
piece.
24 They said therefore to one another,
"[a]Let us not tear it, but cast [1]lots for it,
to decide whose it shall be"; [b]that the
Scripture might be fulfilled, "THEY [c]DI-
VIDED MY OUTER GARMENTS AMONG
THEM, AND FOR MY CLOTHING THEY
CAST [1]LOTS."

33 [a]John 18:28, 29; 19:9 [b]Luke 23:3; John 19:12
34 [1]Lit., *from yourself*
36 [1]Or, *is not derived from* [2]Lit., *from here* [a]Matt. 26:53; Luke 17:21; John 6:15
37 [a]Matt. 27:11; Mark 15:2; Luke 22:70; 23:3 [b]John 1:14; 3:32; 8:14 [c]John 8:47; 1 John 4:6
38 [a]John 18:33; 19:4 [b]Luke 23:4; John 19:4, 6
39 [1]Or, *to you* [a]John 18:39-19:16: *Matt. 27:15-26; Mark 15:6-15; Luke 23:18-25*
40 [a]Acts 3:14

1 [1]Or, *had Him scourged* [a]Matt. 27:26
2 [a]Matt. 27:27-30: *Mark 15:16-19*
3 [a]Matt. 27:29; Mark 15:18 [b]John 18:22
4 [a]John 18:33, 38 [b]Luke 23:4; John 18:38; 19:6
5 [a]John 19:2
6 [a]Matt. 26:58; John 18:3 [b]Luke 23:4; John 18:38; 19:4
7 [a]Lev. 24:16; Matt. 26:63-66 [b]John 5:18; 10:33
9 [1]I.e., governor's official residence [a]John 18:33 [b]Matt. 26:63; 27:12, 14; John 18:34-37
11 [1]Lit., *against* [a]Rom. 13:1 [b]John 18:13f., 28ff.; Acts 3:13
12 [1]Lit., *was seeking to* [2]Or, *speaks against* [a]Luke 23:2; John 18:33ff.
13 [1]Gr., *The Lithostrotos* [2]I.e., Jewish Aramaic [a]Matt. 27:19 [b]John 5:2; 19:17, 20
14 [1]Perhaps 6 a.m. (Roman time) [a]Matt. 27:62; John 19:31, 42 [b]Matt. 27:45; Mark 15:25 [c]John 19:19, 21
15 [a]Luke 23:18
16 [a]Matt. 27:26; Mark 15:15; Luke 23:25
17 [1]Lit., *bearing the cross for Himself* [2]I.e., Jewish Aramaic [a]John 19:17-24: *Matt. 27:33-44; Mark 15:22-32; Luke 23:33-43* [b]Matt. 27:32; Mark 15:21; Luke 14:27; 23:26 [c]Luke 23:33 [d]John 19:13
18 [a]Luke 23:32
19 [a]Matt. 27:37; Mark 15:26; Luke 23:38 [b]John 19:14, 21
20 [1]I.e., Jewish Aramaic [a]John 19:13
21 [a]John 19:14, 19
22 [a]Gen. 43:14; Esth. 4:16

23 [1]Gr., *khiton,* the garment worn next to the skin [2]Lit., *woven from the upper part through the whole* [a]Matt. 27:35; Mark 15:24; Luke 23:34 [b]Acts 12:4
24 [1]Lit., *a lot* [a]Ex. 28:32; Matt. 27:35; Mark 15:24; Luke 23:34 [b]John 19:28, 36f. [c]Ps. 22:18

25 Therefore the soldiers did these things. [a]But there were standing by the cross of Jesus [b]His mother, and His mother's sister, Mary the *wife* of [c]Clopas, and [d]Mary Magdalene.

26 When Jesus therefore saw His mother, and [a]the disciple whom He loved standing nearby, He *said to His mother, "[b]Woman, behold, your son!"

27 Then He *said to the disciple, "Behold, your mother!" And from that hour the disciple took her into [a]his own *household.*

28 After this, Jesus, [a]knowing that all things had already been accomplished, [b]in order that the Scripture might be fulfilled, *said, "[c]I am thirsty."

29 A jar full of sour wine was standing there; so [a]they put a sponge full of the sour wine upon *a branch of* hyssop, and brought it up to His mouth.

30 When Jesus therefore had received the sour wine, He said, "[a]It is finished!" And He bowed His head, and [b]gave up His spirit.

Care of the Body of Jesus

31 The Jews therefore, because it was [a]the day of preparation, so that [b]the bodies should not remain on the cross on the Sabbath ([1]for that Sabbath was a [c]high *day*), asked Pilate that their legs might be broken, and *that* they might be taken away.

32 The soldiers therefore came, and broke the legs of the first man, and of the other man who was [a]crucified with Him;

33 but coming to Jesus, when they saw that He was already dead, they did not break His legs;

34 but one of the soldiers pierced His side with a spear, and immediately there came out [a]blood and water.

35 And he who has seen has [a]borne witness, and his witness is true; and he knows that he is telling the truth, so that you also may believe.

36 For these things came to pass, [a]that the Scripture might be fulfilled, "[b]NOT A BONE OF HIM SHALL BE [1]BROKEN."

37 And again another Scripture says, "[a]THEY SHALL LOOK ON HIM WHOM THEY PIERCED."

38 [a]And after these things Joseph of Arimathea, being a disciple of Jesus, but a [b]secret *one,* for [c]fear of the Jews, asked Pilate that he might take away the body of Jesus; and Pilate granted permission. He came therefore, and took away His body.

39 And [a]Nicodemus came also, who had first come to Him by night; [b]bringing a [1]mixture of [c]myrrh and aloes, about a [d]hundred [2]pounds *weight.*

40 And so they took the body of Jesus, and [a]bound it in [b]linen wrappings with the spices, as is the burial custom of the Jews.

41 Now in the place where He was crucified there was a garden; and in the garden a [a]new tomb, [b]in which no one had yet been laid.

42 Therefore on account of the Jewish day of [a]preparation, because the tomb was [b]nearby, they laid Jesus there.

The Empty Tomb

20 [a]NOW on the first *day* of the week [b]Mary Magdalene *came early to the tomb, while it *was still dark, and *saw [c]the stone *already* taken away from the tomb.

2 And so she *ran and *came to Simon Peter, and to the other [a]disciple whom Jesus [1]loved, and *said to them, "[b]They have taken away the Lord out of the tomb, and we do not know where they have laid Him."

3 [a]Peter therefore went forth, and the other disciple, and they were going to the tomb.

4 And the two were running together; and the other disciple ran ahead faster than Peter, and came to the tomb first;

5 and [a]stooping and looking in, he *saw the [b]linen wrappings lying *there;* but he did not go in.

6 Simon Peter therefore also *came, following him, and entered the tomb; and he *beheld the linen wrappings lying *there,*

7 and [a]the face-cloth, which had been on His head, not lying with the [b]linen wrappings, but rolled up in a place by itself.

8 So the other disciple who [a]had first come to the tomb entered then also, and he saw and believed.

9 For as yet [a]they did not understand the Scripture, [b]that He must rise again from the dead.

10 So the disciples went away again [a]to their own homes.

11 [a]But Mary was standing outside the tomb weeping; and so, as she wept, she [b]stooped and looked into the tomb;

12 and she *beheld [a]two angels in white sitting, one at the head, and one at the feet, where the body of Jesus had been lying.

13 And they *said to her, "[a]Woman, why are you weeping?" She *said to them, "Because [b]they have taken away my Lord, and I do not know where they have laid Him."

14 When she had said this, she turned around, and *[a]beheld Jesus standing *there,* and [b]did not know that it was Jesus.

15 Jesus *said to her, "[a]Woman, why are you weeping? Whom are you seeking?" Supposing Him to be the gardener, she *said to Him, "Sir, if you have carried Him away, tell me where you have laid Him, and I will take Him away."

16 Jesus *said to her, "Mary!" She *turned and *said to Him [a]in [1]Hebrew, "[b]Rabboni!" (which means, Teacher).

---

25 [a]Matt. 27:55f.; Mark 15:40f.; Luke 23:49 [b]Matt. 12:46 [c]Luke 24:18 [d]Luke 8:2; John 20:1, 18
26 [a]John 13:23 [b]John 2:4
27 [a]Luke 18:28; John 1:11; 16:32; Acts 21:6
28 [a]John 13:1; 17:4 [b]John 19:24, 36f. [c]Ps. 69:21
29 [a]John 19:29, 30: *Matt. 27:48, 50; Mark 15:36f.; Luke 23:36*
30 [a]John 17:4 [b]Matt. 27:50; Mark 15:37; Luke 23:46
31 [1]Lit., *for the day of that Sabbath was great* [a]John 19:14, 42 [b]Deut. 21:23; Josh. 8:29; 10:26f. [c]Ex. 12:16
32 [a]John 19:18
34 [a]1 John 5:6, 8
35 [a]John 15:27; 21:24
36 [1]Or, *crushed* or *shattered* [a]John 19:24, 28 [b]Ex. 12:46; Num. 9:12; Ps. 34:20
37 [a]Zech. 12:10; Rev. 1:7
38 [a]John 19:38-42: *Matt. 27:57-61; Mark 15:42-47; Luke 23:50-56* [b]Mark 15:43 [c]John 7:13
39 [1]Another reading is *package of* [2]I.e., 100 litras (12 oz. each) [a]John 3:1 [b]Mark 16:1 [c]Ps. 45:8; Prov. 7:17; Song 4:14; Matt. 2:11 [d]John 12:3
40 [a]Matt. 26:12; Mark 14:8; John 11:44 [b]Luke 24:12; John 20:5, 7
41 [a]Matt. 27:60 [b]Luke 23:53
42 [a]John 19:14, 31 [b]John 19:20, 41

1 [a]John 20:1-8: *Matt. 28:1-8; Mark 16:1-8; Luke 24:1-10* [b]John 19:25; 20:18 [c]Matt. 27:60, 66; 28:2; Mark 15:46; 16:3f.; Luke 24:2; John 11:38
2 [1]Lit., *was loving* [a]John 13:23 [b]John 20:13
3 [a]Luke 24:12; John 20:3-10
5 [a]John 20:11 [b]John 19:40
7 [a]John 11:44 [b]John 19:40
8 [a]John 20:4
9 [a]Matt. 22:29; John 2:22 [b]Luke 24:26ff., 46
10 [a]Luke 24:12
11 [a]Mark 16:5 [b]John 20:5
12 [a]Matt. 28:2f.; Mark 16:5; Luke 24:4
13 [a]John 20:15 [b]John 20:2
14 [a]Matt. 28:9; Mark 16:9 [b]John 21:4
15 [a]John 20:13
16 [1]I.e., Jewish Aramaic [a]John 5:2 [b]Matt. 23:7; Mark 10:51

17 Jesus *said to her, "Stop clinging
to Me, for I have not yet ascended to the
Father; but go to [a]My brethren, and say
to them, 'I [b]ascend to My Father and
your Father, and My God and your
God.'"
18 [a]Mary Magdalene *came, [b]an-
nouncing to the disciples, "I have seen
the Lord," and *that* He had said these
things to her.

Jesus among His Disciples

19 When therefore it was evening, on
that day, the first *day* of the week, and
when the doors were shut where the
disciples were, for [a]fear of the Jews,
Jesus came and stood in their midst, and
*said to them, "[1b]Peace *be* with you."
20 And when He had said this, [a]He
showed them both His hands and His
side. The disciples therefore [b]rejoiced
when they saw the Lord.
21 Jesus therefore said to them again,
"[a]Peace *be* with you; [b]as the Father has
sent Me, I also send you."
22 And when He had said this, He
breathed on them, and *said to them,
"Receive the Holy Spirit.
23 "[a]If you forgive the sins of any, *their*
sins [1]have been forgiven them; if you
retain the *sins* of any, they have been
retained."
24 But [a]Thomas, one of [b]the twelve,
called [1a]Didymus, was not with them
when Jesus came.
25 The other disciples therefore were
saying to him, "We have seen the Lord!"
But he said to them, "Unless I shall see
in [a]His hands the imprint of the nails,
and put my finger into the place of the
nails, and put my hand into His side, [b]I
will not believe."
26 And [1]after eight days again His
disciples were inside, and Thomas with
them. Jesus *came, the doors having
been [2]shut, and stood in their midst, and
said, "[a]Peace *be* with you."
27 Then He *said to Thomas, "[a]Reach
here your finger, and see My hands; and
reach here your hand, and put it into My
side; and be not unbelieving, but believing."
28 Thomas answered and said to Him,
"My Lord and my God!"
29 Jesus *said to him, "Because you
have seen Me, have you believed?
[a]Blessed *are* they who did not see, and
yet believed."

Why This Gospel Was Written

30 [a]Many other [1b]signs therefore Jesus
also performed in the presence of the
disciples, which are not written in this
book;
31 but these have been written [a]that
you may believe that Jesus is [1]the Christ,
[b]the Son of God; and that [c]believing you
may have life in His name.

Jesus Appears at the Sea of Galilee

21 AFTER these things Jesus
[1a]manifested Himself [b]again to
the disciples at the [c]Sea of Tiberias, and
He manifested *Himself* in this way.
2 There were together Simon Peter,
and [a]Thomas called [1]Didymus, and
[b]Nathanael of [c]Cana in Galilee, and [d]the
sons of Zebedee, and two others of His
disciples.
3 Simon Peter *said to them, "I am
going fishing." They *said to him, "We
will also come with you." They went out,
and got into the boat; and [a]that night
they caught nothing.
4 But when the day was now breaking, Jesus stood on the beach; yet the
disciples did not [a]know that it was Jesus.
5 Jesus therefore *said to them,
"Children, [a]you do not have [1]any fish,
do you?" They answered Him, "No."
6 And He said to them, "[a]Cast the
net on the right-hand side of the boat,
and you will find *a catch.*" They cast
therefore, and then they were not able to
haul it in because of the great number of
fish.
7 [a]That disciple therefore whom
Jesus [1]loved *said to Peter, "It is the
Lord." And so when Simon Peter heard
that it was the Lord, he put his outer
garment on (for he was stripped *for*
work), and threw himself into the sea.
8 But the other disciples came in the
little boat, for they were not far from the
land, but about [1]one hundred yards
away, dragging the net *full* of fish.
9 And so when they got out upon the
land, they *saw a charcoal [a]fire *already*
laid, and [b]fish placed on it, and bread.
10 Jesus *said to them, "Bring some of
the [a]fish which you have now caught."
11 Simon Peter went up, and drew the
net to land, full of large fish, a hundred
and fifty-three; and although there were
so many, the net was not torn.

Jesus Provides

12 Jesus *said to them, "Come *and*
have [a]breakfast." None of the disciples
ventured to question Him, "Who are
You?" knowing that it was the Lord.
13 Jesus *came and *took [a]the bread,
and *gave them, and the [b]fish likewise.
14 This is now the [a]third time that
Jesus [1]was manifested to the disciples,
after He was raised from the dead.

The Love Motivation

15 So when they had [a]finished breakfast, Jesus *said to Simon Peter, "Simon,
[1]*son* of John, do you [2b]love Me more
than these?" He *said to Him, "Yes,
Lord; You know that I [3]love You." He
*said to him, "Tend [c]My lambs."
16 He *said to him again a second
time, "Simon, *son* of John, do you [1]love
Me?" He *said to Him, "Yes, Lord; You
know that I [2]love You." He *said to
him, "[a]Shepherd My sheep."

17 [a]Matt. 28:10 [b]Mark 12:26; 16:19; John 7:33
18 [a]John 20:1 [b]Mark 16:10; Luke 24:10, 23
19 [1]Lit., *Peace to you* [a]John 7:13 [b]Luke 24:36; John 14:27; 20:21, 26
20 [a]Luke 24:39, 40; John 19:34 [b]John 16:20, 22
21 [a]Luke 24:36; John 14:27; 20:19, 26 [b]John 17:18
23 [1]I.e., have previously been forgiven [a]Matt. 16:19; 18:18
24 [1]I.e., the Twin [a]John 11:16 [b]John 6:67
25 [a]John 20:20 [b]Mark 16:11
26 [1]Or, *a week later* [2]Or, *locked* [a]Luke 24:36; John 14:27; 20:19, 21
27 [a]Luke 24:40; John 20:25
29 [a]1 Pet. 1:8
30 [1]Or, *attesting miracles* [a]John 21:25 [b]John 2:11
31 [1]I.e., the Messiah [a]John 19:35 [b]Matt. 4:3 [c]John 3:15

1 [1]Or, *made Himself visible* [a]Mark 16:12; John 21:14 [b]John 20:19, 26 [c]John 6:1
2 [1]I.e., the Twin [a]John 11:16 [b]John 1:45ff. [c]John 2:1 [d]Matt. 4:21; Mark 1:19; Luke 5:10
3 [a]Luke 5:5
4 [a]Luke 24:16; John 20:14
5 [1]Lit., *something eaten with bread* [a]Luke 24:41
6 [a]Luke 5:4ff.
7 [1]Lit., *was loving* [a]John 13:23; 21:20
8 [1]Lit., *200 cubits*
9 [a]John 18:18 [b]John 6:9, 11; 21:10, 13
10 [a]John 6:9, 11; 21:9, 13
12 [a]John 21:15
13 [a]John 21:9 [b]John 6:9, 11; 21:9, 10
14 [1]Or, *made Himself visible* [a]John 20:19, 26
15 [1]Here and in vv. 16 and 17 some mss. read *son of Jonas* [2]Gr., *agapao* [3]Gr., *phileo* [a]John 21:12 [b]Matt. 26:33; Mark 14:29; John 13:37 [c]Luke 12:32
16 [1]Gr., *agapao* [2]Gr., *phileo* [a]Matt. 2:6; Acts 20:28; 1 Pet. 5:2; Rev. 7:17

17 He *said to him the third time,
"Simon, *son* of John, do you [1]love Me?"
Peter was grieved because He said to
him [a]the third time, "Do you [1]love Me?"
And he said to Him, "Lord, [b]You know
all things; You know that I [1]love You."
Jesus *said to him, "[c]Tend My sheep.

Our Times Are in His Hand

18 "Truly, truly, I say to you, when you
were younger, you used to gird yourself,
and walk wherever you wished; but
when you grow old, you will stretch out
your hands, and someone else will gird
you, and bring you where you do not
wish to *go.*"
19 Now this He said, [a]signifying by
[b]what kind of death he would glorify
God. And when He had spoken this, He
*said to him, "[c]Follow Me!"
20 Peter, turning around, *saw the
[a]disciple whom Jesus loved following
them; the one who also had [b]leaned back
on His breast at the supper, and said,
"Lord, who is the one who betrays
You?"
21 Peter therefore seeing him *said to
Jesus, "Lord, and what about this man?"
22 Jesus *said to him, "If I want him
to remain [a]until I come, what *is that* to
you? You [b]follow Me!"
23 This saying therefore went out
among [a]the brethren that that disciple
would not die; yet Jesus did not say to
him that he would not die, but *only,* "If I
want him to remain [b]until I come, what
is that to you?"
24 This is the disciple who [a]bears
witness of these things, and wrote these
things; and we know that his witness is
true.
25 And there are also [a]many other
things which Jesus did, which if they
*were written in detail, I suppose that
even the world itself *would not contain
the books which *were written.

17 [1]Gr., *phileo* [a]John 13:38 [b]John 16:30 [c]John 21:15, 16

19 [a]John 12:33; 18:32 [b]2 Pet. 1:14 [c]Matt. 8:22; 16:24; John 21:22

20 [a]John 21:7 [b]John 13:25

22 [a]Matt. 16:27f.; 1 Cor. 4:5; 11:26; James 5:7; Rev. 2:25 [b]Matt. 8:22; 16:24; John 21:19

23 [a]Acts 1:15 [b]Matt. 16:27f.; 1 Cor. 4:5; 11:26; James 5:7; Rev. 2:25

24 [a]John 15:27

25 [a]John 20:30

THE ACTS
OF THE APOSTLES

Introduction

1 THE first account I [1]composed,
[a]Theophilus, about all that Jesus
[b]began to do and teach,
2 until the day when He [a]was taken
up, after He [b]had [1]by the Holy Spirit
given orders to [c]the apostles whom He
had [d]chosen.
3 To [1]these [a]He also presented Himself alive, after His suffering, by many
convincing proofs, appearing to them
over *a period of* forty days, and speaking
of [b]the things concerning the kingdom of
God.
4 And [1]gathering them together, He
commanded them [a]not to leave Jerusalem, but to wait for [2b]what the Father
had promised, "Which," *He said,* "you
heard of from Me;
5 for [a]John baptized with water, but
you shall be baptized [1]with the Holy
Spirit [2b]not many days from now."
6 And so when they had come together, they were asking Him, saying,
"Lord, [a]is it at this time You are restoring the kingdom to Israel?"
7 He said to them, "It is not for you
to know times or epochs which [a]the
Father has fixed by His own authority;
8 but you shall receive power [a]when
the Holy Spirit has come upon you; and
you shall be [b]My witnesses both in
Jerusalem, and in all Judea and [c]Sa-
maria, and even to [d]the remotest part of
the earth."

The Ascension

9 And after He had said these things,
[a]He was lifted up while they were looking on, and a cloud received Him out of
their sight.
10 And as they were gazing intently
into [1]the sky while He was departing,
[2]behold, [a]two men in white clothing
stood beside them;
11 and they also said, "[a]Men of Galilee, why do you stand looking into [1]the
sky? This Jesus, who [b]has been taken up
from you into heaven, will [c]come in just
the same way as you have watched Him
go into heaven."

The Upper Room

12 Then they [a]returned to Jerusalem
from the [1b]mount called [2]Olivet, which
is near Jerusalem, a Sabbath day's journey away.
13 And when they had entered, they
went up to [a]the upper room, where they
were staying; [b]that is, Peter and John
and [1]James and Andrew, Philip and
Thomas, Bartholomew and Matthew,
[1]James *the son* of Alphaeus, and Simon
the Zealot, and [c]Judas *the* [2]*son* of
[1]James.
14 These all with one mind [a]were
continually devoting themselves to
prayer, along with [1b]*the* women, and
Mary the [c]mother of Jesus, and with His
[c]brothers.
15 And [1]at this time Peter stood up in
the midst of [a]the brethren (a gathering of

1 [1]Lit., *made* [a]Luke 1:3 [b]Luke 3:23
2 [1]Or, *through* [a]Mark 16:19; Acts 1:9, 11, 22 [b]Matt. 28:19f.; Mark 16:15; John 20:21f.; Acts 10:42 [c]Mark 6:30 [d]John 13:18; Acts 10:41
3 [1]Lit., *whom* [a]Matt. 28:17; Mark 16:12, 14; Luke 24:34, 36; John 20:19, 26; 21:1, 14; 1 Cor. 15:5-7 [b]Acts 8:12; 19:8; 28:23, 31
4 [1]Or, *eating with;* or possibly, *lodging with* [2]Lit., *the promise of the Father* [a]Luke 24:49 [b]John 14:16, 26; 15:26; Acts 2:33
5 [1]Or, *in* [2]Lit., *not long after these many days* [a]Matt. 3:11; Mark 1:8; Luke 3:16; John 1:33; Acts 11:16 [b]Acts 2:1-4
6 [a]Matt. 17:11; Mark 9:12; Luke 17:20; 19:11
7 [a]Matt. 24:36; Mark 13:32
8 [a]Acts 2:1-4 [b]Luke 24:48; John 15:27 [c]Acts 8:1, 5, 14 [d]Matt. 28:19; Mark 16:15; Rom. 10:18; Col. 1:23
9 [a]Luke 24:50, 51; Acts 1:2
10 [1]Or, *heaven* [2]Lit., *and behold* [a]Luke 24:4; John 20:12
11 [1]Or, *heaven* [a]Acts 2:7; 13:31 [b]Mark 16:19; Acts 1:9, 22 [c]Matt. 16:27f.; Acts 3:21

12 [1]Or, *hill* [2]Or, *Olive Grove* [a]Luke 24:52 [b]Matt. 21:1
13 [1]Or, *Jacob* [2]Or possibly, *brother* [a]Mark 14:15; Luke 22:12; Acts 9:37, 39; 20:8 [b]Acts 1:13: *Matt. 10:2-4; Mark 3:16-19; Luke 6:14-16* [c]John 14:22
14 [1]Or, *certain women* [a]Acts 2:42; 6:4; Rom. 12:12; Eph. 6:18; Col. 4:2 [b]Luke 8:2f. [c]Matt. 12:46
15 [1]Lit., *in these days* [2]Lit., *names* [a]John 21:23; Acts 6:3; 9:30; 10:23; 11:1, 12, 26, 29; 12:17; 14:2; 15:1, 3, 22, 23, 32f., 40; 16:2, 40; 17:6, 10, 14; 18:18, 27; 21:7, 17; 22:5; 28:14f.; Rom. 1:13

about one hundred and twenty [2]persons was there together), and said,

16 "Brethren, [a]the Scripture had to be fulfilled, which the Holy Spirit foretold by the mouth of David concerning Judas, [b]who became a guide to those who arrested Jesus.

17 "For he was [a]counted among us, and received his portion in [b]this ministry."

18 (Now this man [a]acquired a field with [b]the price of his wickedness; and falling headlong, he burst open in the middle and all his bowels gushed out.

19 And it became known to all who were living in Jerusalem; so that in [a]their own language that field was called [1]Hakeldama, that is, Field of Blood.)

20 "For it is written in the book of Psalms,

'[a]LET HIS HOMESTEAD BE MADE
DESOLATE,
AND LET NO MAN DWELL IN IT';
and,
'[b]HIS [1]OFFICE LET ANOTHER MAN
TAKE.'

21 "It is therefore necessary that of the men who have accompanied us all the time that [a]the Lord Jesus went in and out [1]among us—

22 [a]beginning [1]with the baptism of John, until the day that He [b]was taken up from us—one of these should become a [c]witness with us of His resurrection."

23 And they put forward two men, Joseph called Barsabbas (who was also called Justus), and [a]Matthias.

24 And they [a]prayed, and said, "Thou, Lord, [b]who knowest the hearts of all men, show which one of these two Thou hast chosen

25 to [1]occupy [a]this ministry and [b]apostleship from which Judas turned aside to go to his own place."

26 And they [1a]drew lots for them, and the lot fell [2]to [b]Matthias; and he was [3]numbered with [c]the eleven apostles.

The Day of Pentecost

2 AND when [a]the day of Pentecost [1]had come, they were all together in one place.

2 And suddenly there came from heaven a noise like a violent, rushing wind, and it filled [a]the whole house where they were sitting.

3 And there appeared to them tongues as of fire [1]distributing themselves, and [2]they [3]rested on each one of them.

4 And they were all [a]filled with the Holy Spirit and began to [b]speak with other tongues, as the Spirit was giving them [1]utterance.

5 Now there were Jews living in Jerusalem, [a]devout men, from every nation under heaven.

6 And when [a]this sound occurred, the multitude came together, and were bewildered, because they were each one hearing them speak in his own [1]language.

7 And [a]they were amazed and marveled, saying, "[1]Why, are not all these who are speaking [b]Galileans?

8 "And how is it that we each hear *them* in our own [1]language [2]to which we were born?

9 "Parthians and Medes and Elamites, and residents of Mesopotamia, Judea and [a]Cappadocia, [b]Pontus and [1c]Asia,

10 [a]Phrygia and [b]Pamphylia, Egypt and the districts of Libya around [c]Cyrene, and [1d]visitors from Rome, both Jews and [2e]proselytes,

11 Cretans and Arabs—we hear them in our *own* tongues speaking of the mighty deeds of God."

12 And [a]they all continued in amazement and great perplexity, saying to one another, "What does this mean?"

13 But others were mocking and saying, "[a]They are full of [1]sweet wine."

Peter's Sermon

14 But Peter, [1]taking his stand with [a]the eleven, raised his voice and declared to them: "Men of Judea, and all you who live in Jerusalem, let this be known to you, and give heed to my words.

15 "For these men are not drunk, as you suppose, [a]for it is *only* the [1]third hour of the day;

16 but this is what was spoken of through the prophet Joel:

17 '[a]AND IT SHALL BE IN THE LAST
DAYS,' God says,
'THAT I WILL POUR FORTH OF MY
SPIRIT UPON ALL [1]MANKIND;
AND YOUR SONS AND YOUR
DAUGHTERS SHALL PROPHESY,
AND YOUR YOUNG MEN SHALL SEE
VISIONS,
AND YOUR OLD MEN SHALL
DREAM DREAMS;
18 EVEN UPON MY BONDSLAVES,
BOTH MEN AND WOMEN,
I WILL IN THOSE DAYS POUR
FORTH OF MY SPIRIT
And they shall prophesy.
19 'AND I WILL GRANT WONDERS IN
THE SKY ABOVE,
AND SIGNS ON THE EARTH BENEATH,
BLOOD, AND FIRE, AND VAPOR OF
SMOKE.
20 'THE SUN SHALL BE TURNED INTO
DARKNESS,
AND THE MOON INTO BLOOD,
BEFORE THE GREAT AND GLORIOUS DAY OF THE LORD SHALL
COME.
21 'AND IT SHALL BE, THAT [a]EVERYONE WHO CALLS ON THE NAME
OF THE LORD SHALL BE SAVED.'

15 [2]Lit., *names*
16 [a]John 13:18; 17:12; Acts 1:20 [b]Matt. 26:47; Mark 14:43; Luke 22:47; John 18:3
17 [a]John 6:70f. [b]Acts 1:25; 20:24; 21:19
18 [a]Matt. 27:3-10 [b]Matt. 26:14f.
19 [1]Some early mss. read *Hakeldamach* [a]Matt. 27:8; Acts 21:40
20 [1]Lit., *position as overseer* [a]Ps. 69:25 [b]Ps. 109:8
21 [1]Lit., *to us* [a]Luke 24:3
22 [1]Lit., *from* [a]Matt. 3:16; Mark 1:1-4, 9; Luke 3:21 [b]Mark 16:19; Acts 1:2 [c]Acts 1:8; 2:32
23 [a]Acts 1:26
24 [a]Acts 6:6; 13:3; 14:23 [b]1 Sam. 16:7; Jer. 17:10; Acts 15:8; Rom. 8:27
25 [1]Lit., *take the place of* [a]Acts 1:17 [b]Rom. 1:5; 1 Cor. 9:2; Gal. 2:8
26 [1]Lit., *gave* [2]Or, *upon* [3]Lit., *chosen* [a]Lev. 16:8; Josh. 14:2; 1 Sam. 14:41f.; Neh. 10:34; 11:1; Prov. 16:33 [b]Acts 1:23 [c]Acts 2:14

1 [1]Lit., *was being fulfilled* [a]Lev. 23:15f.; Acts 20:16; 1 Cor. 16:8
2 [a]Acts 4:31
3 [1]Or, *being distributed* [2]Lit., *it* [3]Or, *sat*
4 [1]Or, *ability to speak out* [a]Matt. 10:20; Acts 1:5, 8; 4:8, 31; 6:3, 5; 7:55; 8:17; 9:17; 11:15; 13:9, 52 [b]Mark 16:17; 1 Cor. 12:10f.; 14:21
5 [a]Luke 2:25; Acts 8:2
6 [1]Or, *dialect* [a]Acts 2:2
7 [1]Lit., *Behold* [a]Acts 2:12 [b]Matt. 26:73; Acts 1:11
8 [1]Or, *dialect* [2]Lit., *in*
9 [1]I.e., west coast province of Asia Minor [a]1 Pet. 1:1 [b]Acts 18:2; 1 Pet. 1:1 [c]Acts 6:9; 16:6; 19:10; 20:4; 21:27; 24:18; 27:2; Rom. 16:5; 1 Cor. 16:19; 2 Cor. 1:8; 2 Tim. 1:15; Rev. 1:4
10 [1]Lit., *the sojourning Romans* [2]I.e., Gentile converts to Judaism [a]Acts 16:6; 18:23 [b]Acts 13:13; 14:24; 15:38; 27:5 [c]Matt. 27:32 [d]Acts 17:21 [e]Matt. 23:15
12 [a]Acts 2:7
13 [1]Or, *new wine* [a]1 Cor. 14:23
14 [1]Or, *being put forward as spokesman* [a]Acts 1:26

15 [1]I.e., 9 a.m. [a]1 Thess. 5:7
17 [1]Lit., *flesh* [a]Joel 2:28-32
21 [a]Rom. 10:13

22"Men of Israel, listen to these
words: [a]Jesus the Nazarene, [b]a man
[1]attested to you by God with [2]miracles
and [c]wonders and [3]signs which God
performed through Him in your midst,
just as you yourselves know—
23 this *Man*, delivered up by the [a]pre-
determined plan and foreknowledge of
God, [b]you nailed to a cross by the hands
of [1]godless men and put *Him* to death.
24"[1]And [a]God raised Him up again,
putting an end to the [2]agony of death,
since it [b]was impossible for Him to be
held in its power.
25"For David says of Him,
'[a]I WAS ALWAYS BEHOLDING THE
LORD IN MY PRESENCE;
FOR HE IS AT MY RIGHT HAND,
THAT I MAY NOT BE SHAKEN.
26 'THEREFORE MY HEART WAS GLAD
AND MY TONGUE EXULTED;
MOREOVER MY FLESH ALSO WILL
ABIDE IN HOPE;
27 BECAUSE THOU WILT NOT ABAN-
DON MY SOUL TO [a]HADES,
[b]NOR [1]ALLOW THY [2]HOLY ONE
TO [3]UNDERGO DECAY.
28 'THOU HAST MADE KNOWN TO ME
THE WAYS OF LIFE;
THOU WILT MAKE ME FULL OF
GLADNESS WITH THY PRESENCE.'
29"[1]Brethren, I may confidently say to
you regarding the [a]patriarch David that
he both [b]died and [c]was buried, and [d]his
tomb is [2]with us to this day.
30"And so, because he was [a]a prophet,
and knew that [b]GOD HAD SWORN TO HIM
WITH AN OATH TO SEAT *one* [1]OF HIS
DESCENDANTS UPON HIS THRONE,
31 he looked ahead and spoke of the
resurrection of [1]the Christ, that [a]HE WAS
NEITHER ABANDONED TO HADES, NOR
DID His flesh [2]SUFFER DECAY.
32"This Jesus [a]God raised up again, to
which we are all [b]witnesses.
33"Therefore having been exalted [1a]to
the right hand of God, and [b]having
received from the Father [c]the promise of
the Holy Spirit, He has [d]poured forth
this which you both see and hear.
34"For it was not David who ascended
into [1]heaven, but he himself says:
'[a]THE LORD SAID TO MY LORD,
"SIT AT MY RIGHT HAND,
35 UNTIL I MAKE THINE ENEMIES A
FOOTSTOOL FOR THY FEET." '
36"Therefore let all the [a]house of
Israel know for certain that God has
made Him both [b]Lord and [1]Christ—this
Jesus [c]whom you crucified."

The Ingathering

37 Now when they heard *this*, they
were [1]pierced to the heart, and said to
Peter and the rest of the apostles,
"[2]Brethren, [a]what shall we do?"
38 And Peter *said* to them, "[a]Repent,
and let each of you be [b]baptized in the
name of Jesus Christ for the forgiveness
of your sins; and you shall receive the
gift of the Holy Spirit.

22 [1]Or, *exhibited* or *accredited* [2]Or, *works of power* [3]Or, *attesting miracles* [a]Acts 3:6; 4:10; 10:38 [b]John 3:2 [c]John 4:48; Acts 2:19, 43
23 [1]Or, *men without the Law;* i.e., heathen [a]Luke 22:22; Acts 3:18; 4:28; 1 Pet. 1:20 [b]Matt. 27:35; Mark 15:24; Luke 23:33; 24:20; John 19:18; Acts 3:13
24 [1]Lit., *Whom God raised up* [2]Lit., *birth pangs* [a]Matt. 28:5, 6; Mark 16:6; Luke 24:5, 6; Acts 2:32; 3:15, 26; 4:10; 5:30; 10:40; 13:30, 33, 34, 37; 17:31; Rom. 4:24; 6:4; 8:11; 10:9; 1 Cor. 6:14; 15:15; 2 Cor. 4:14; Gal. 1:1; Eph. 1:20; Col. 2:12; 1 Thess. 1:10; Heb. 13:20; 1 Pet. 1:21 [b]John 20:9
25 [a]Ps. 16:8-11
27 [1]Lit., *give* [2]Or, *devout* or *pious* [3]Lit., *see corruption* [a]Matt. 11:23; Acts 2:31 [b]Acts 13:35
29 [1]Lit., *Men brothers* [2]Lit., *among* [a]Acts 7:8f.; Heb. 7:4 [b]Acts 13:36 [c]1 Kin. 2:10 [d]Neh. 3:16
30 [1]Lit., *of the fruit of his loins* [a]Matt. 22:43 [b]Ps. 132:11; 2 Sam. 7:12f.; Ps. 89:3f.
31 [1]I.e., the Messiah [2]Lit., *see corruption* [a]Matt. 11:23; Acts 2:27
32 [a]Acts 2:24; 3:15, 26; 4:10; 5:30; 10:40; 13:30, 33, 34, 37; 17:31; Rom. 4:24; 6:4; 8:11; 10:9; 1 Cor. 6:14; 15:15; 2 Cor. 4:14; Gal. 1:1; Eph. 1:20; Col. 2:12; 1 Thess. 1:10; Heb. 13:20; 1 Pet. 1:21 [b]Acts 1:8
33 [1]Or, *by* [a]Mark 16:19; Acts 5:31 [b]Acts 1:4 [c]John 7:39; Gal. 3:14 [d]Acts 2:17; 10:45
34 [1]Lit., *the heavens* [a]Ps. 110:1; Matt. 22:44f.
36 [1]I.e., Messiah [a]Ezek. 36:22, 32, 37; 45:6 [b]Luke 2:11 [c]Acts 2:23
37 [1]Or, *smitten in conscience* [2]Lit., *Men brothers* [a]Luke 3:10, 12, 14
38 [a]Mark 1:15; Luke 24:47; Acts 3:19; 5:31; 20:21 [b]Mark 16:16; Acts 8:12, 16; 22:16
39 [a]Is. 44:3; 54:13; 57:19; Joel 2:32; Rom. 9:4; Eph. 2:12 [b]Eph. 2:13, 17
40 [1]Or, *Escape* [a]Luke 16:28 [b]Deut. 32:5; Matt. 17:17; Phil. 2:15

39"For [a]the promise is for you and
your children, and for all who are [b]far
off, as many as the Lord our God shall
call to Himself."
40 And with many other words he
solemnly [a]testified and kept on exhorting them, saying, "[1]Be saved from this
[b]perverse generation!"
41 So then, those who had received his
word were baptized; and there were
added that day about three thousand
[1a]souls.
42 And they were [a]continually devoting themselves to the apostles' teaching
and to fellowship, to [b]the breaking of
bread and [1a]to prayer.
43 And [1]everyone kept feeling a sense
of awe; and many [a]wonders and [2]signs
were taking place through the apostles[3].
44 And all those who had believed
[1]were together, and [a]had all things in
common;
45 and they [a]*began* selling their property and possessions, and were sharing
them with all, as anyone might have
need.
46 [a]And day by day continuing with
one mind in the temple, and [b]breaking
bread [1]from house to house, they were
taking their [2]meals together with gladness and [3]sincerity of heart,
47 praising God, and [a]having favor
with all the people. And the Lord [b]was
adding [1]to their number day by day
[c]those who were being saved.

Healing the Lame Beggar

3 NOW [a]Peter and John were going
up to the temple at the [1]ninth *hour,*
[b]the hour of prayer.
2 And [a]a certain man who had been
lame from his mother's womb was being
carried along, whom they [b]used to set
down every day at the gate of the temple
which is called Beautiful, [c]in order to
beg [1]alms of those who were entering the
temple.
3 And when he saw [a]Peter and John
about to go into the temple, he *began*
asking to receive alms.
4 And Peter, along with John, [a]fixed
his gaze upon him and said, "Look at
us!"

41 [1]I.e., persons [a]Acts 3:23; 7:14; 27:37; Rom. 13:1; 1 Pet. 3:20; Rev. 16:3
42 [1]Lit., *the prayers* [a]Acts 1:14 [b]Luke 24:30; Acts 2:46; 20:7; 1 Cor. 10:16
43 [1]Lit., *fear was occurring to every soul* [2]Or, *attesting miracles* [3]Some ancient mss. add *in Jerusalem; and great fear was upon all* [a]Acts 2:22
44 [1]Some ancient mss. do not contain *were* [a]Acts 4:32, 37; 5:2
45 [a]Matt. 19:21; Acts 4:34
46 [1]Or, *in the various private homes* [2]Lit., *food* [3]Or, *simplicity* [a]Acts 5:42 [b]Luke 24:30; Acts 2:42; 20:7; 1 Cor. 10:16
47 [1]Lit., *together* [a]Acts 5:13 [b]Acts 2:41; 4:4; 5:14; 6:1, 7; 9:31, 35, 42; 11:21, 24; 14:1, 21; 16:5; 17:12 [c]1 Cor. 1:18

1 [1]I.e., 3 p.m. [a]Luke 22:8; Acts 3:3, 4, 11 [b]Ps. 55:17; Matt. 27:45; Acts 10:30
2 [1]Or, *a gift of charity* [a]Acts 14:8 [b]Luke 16:20 [c]John 9:8; Acts 3:10
3 [a]Luke 22:8; Acts 3:1, 4, 11
4 [a]Acts 10:4

5 And he *began* to give them his attention, expecting to receive something from them.
6 But Peter said, "I do not possess silver and gold, but what I do have I give to you: [a]In the name of Jesus Christ the Nazarene—walk!"
7 And seizing him by the right hand, he raised him up; and immediately his feet and his ankles were strengthened.
8 [a]And [1]with a leap, he stood upright and *began* to walk; and he entered the temple with them, walking and leaping and praising God.
9 And [a]all the people saw him walking and praising God;
10 and they were taking note of him as being the one who used to [a]sit at the Beautiful Gate of the temple to *beg* alms, and they were filled with wonder and amazement at what had happened to him.

Peter's Second Sermon

11 And while he was clinging to [a]Peter and John, all the people ran together to them at the so-called [1b]portico of Solomon, full of amazement.
12 But when Peter saw *this,* he replied to the people, "Men of Israel, why do you marvel at this, or why do you gaze at us, as if by our own power or piety we had made him walk?
13 "[a]The God of Abraham, Isaac, and Jacob, [b]the God of our fathers, has glorified His [1c]servant Jesus, *the one* whom [d]you delivered up, and disowned in the presence of [e]Pilate, when he had [f]decided to release Him.
14 "But you disowned [a]the Holy and Righteous One, and [b]asked for a murderer to be granted to you,
15 but put to death the [1a]Prince of life, *the one* whom [b]God raised from the dead, *a fact* to which we are [c]witnesses.
16 "And on the basis of faith [a]in His name, *it is* the name of [1]Jesus which has strengthened this man whom you see and know; and the faith which *comes* through Him has given him this perfect health in the presence of you all.
17 "And now, brethren, I know that you acted [a]in ignorance, just as your [b]rulers did also.
18 "But the things which [a]God announced beforehand by the mouth of all the prophets, [b]that His [1]Christ should suffer, He has thus fulfilled.
19 "[a]Repent therefore and return, that your sins may be wiped away, in order that [b]times of refreshing may come from the presence of the Lord;
20 and that He may send Jesus, the [1]Christ appointed for you,
21 [a]whom heaven must receive until *the* [1]period of [b]restoration of all things about which [c]God spoke by the mouth of His holy prophets from ancient time.
22 "Moses said, '[a]THE LORD GOD SHALL RAISE UP FOR YOU A PROPHET [1]LIKE ME FROM YOUR BRETHREN; TO HIM YOU SHALL GIVE HEED in everything He says to you.
23 '[a]And it shall be that every [b]soul that does not heed that prophet [c]shall be utterly destroyed from among the people.'
24 "And likewise, [a]all the prophets who have spoken, from Samuel and *his* successors onward, also announced these days.
25 "It is you who are [a]the sons of the prophets, and of the [b]covenant which God [1]made with your fathers, saying to Abraham, '[c]AND IN YOUR SEED ALL THE FAMILIES OF THE EARTH SHALL BE BLESSED.'
26 "For you [a]first, God [b]raised up His [1]Servant, and sent Him to bless you by turning every one *of you* from your wicked ways."

Peter and John Arrested

4 AND as they were speaking to the people, the priests and [a]the captain of the temple *guard,* and [b]the Sadducees, [c]came upon them,
2 being greatly disturbed because they were teaching the people and proclaiming [1a]in Jesus the resurrection from the dead.
3 And they laid hands on them, and [a]put them in jail until the next day, for it was already evening.
4 But many of those who had heard the [1]message believed; and [a]the number of the men came to be about five thousand.
5 And it came about on the next day, that their [a]rulers and elders and scribes were gathered together in Jerusalem;
6 and [a]Annas the high priest *was there,* and [b]Caiaphas and John and Alexander, and all who were of high-priestly descent.
7 And when they had placed them in the center, they *began to* inquire, "By what power, or in what name, have you done this?"
8 Then Peter, [1a]filled with the Holy Spirit, said to them, "[2b]Rulers and elders of the people,
9 if we are on trial today for [a]a benefit done to a sick man, [1]as to how this man has been made well,
10 let it be known to all of you, and to all the people of Israel, that [1a]by the name of Jesus Christ the Nazarene, whom you crucified, whom [b]God raised from the dead—[1]by [2]this *name* this man stands here before you in good health.
11 "[1a]He is the [b]STONE WHICH WAS [c]REJECTED by you, THE BUILDERS, *but* WHICH BECAME THE VERY CORNER *stone.*
12 "And there is salvation in [a]no one else; for there is no other name under heaven that has been given among men, by which we must be saved."

6 [a]Acts 2:22; 3:16; 4:10
8 [1]Lit., *leaping up* [a]Acts 14:10
9 [a]Acts 4:16, 21
10 [a]John 9:8; Acts 3:2
11 [1]Or, *colonnade* [a]Luke 22:8; Acts 3:3, 4 [b]John 10:23; Acts 5:12
13 [1]Or, *Child* [a]Matt. 22:32 [b]Ex. 3:13, 15; Acts 5:30; 7:32; 22:14 [c]Acts 3:26; 4:27, 30 [d]Matt. 20:19; John 19:11; Acts 2:23 [e]Matt. 27:2 [f]Luke 23:4
14 [a]Mark 1:24; Acts 4:27; 7:52; 2 Cor. 5:21 [b]Matt. 27:20; Mark 15:11; Luke 23:18, 25
15 [1]Or, *Author* [a]Acts 5:31; Heb. 2:10; 12:2 [b]Acts 2:24 [c]Luke 24:48
16 [1]Lit., *His* [a]Acts 3:6
17 [a]Luke 23:34; John 15:21; Acts 13:27; 26:9; Eph. 4:18 [b]Luke 23:13
18 [1]Or, *Anointed One;* i.e., Messiah [a]Acts 2:23 [b]Luke 24:27; Acts 17:3; 26:23
19 [a]Acts 2:38; 26:20 [b]2 Thess. 1:7; Heb. 4:1ff.
20 [1]Or, *Anointed One;* i.e., Messiah
21 [1]Lit., *periods, times* [a]Acts 1:11 [b]Matt. 17:11; Rom. 8:21 [c]Luke 1:70
22 [1]Or, *as* He raised up *me* [a]Deut. 18:15, 18; Acts 7:37
23 [a]Deut. 18:19 [b]Acts 2:41 [c]Lev. 23:29
24 [a]Luke 24:27; Acts 17:3; 26:23
25 [1]Lit., *covenanted* [a]Acts 2:39 [b]Rom. 9:4f. [c]Gen. 22:18
26 [1]Or, *Child* [a]Matt. 15:24; John 4:22; Acts 13:46; Rom. 1:16; 2:9f. [b]Acts 2:24

1 [a]Luke 22:4 [b]Matt. 3:7 [c]Luke 20:1; Acts 6:12
2 [1]Or, *in the case of* [a]Acts 3:15; 17:18
3 [a]Acts 5:18
4 [1]Or, *word* [a]Acts 2:41
5 [a]Luke 23:13; Acts 4:8
6 [a]Luke 3:2 [b]Matt. 26:3
8 [1]Or, *having* just *been filled* [2]Or, *Rulers of the people and elders* [a]Acts 2:4; 13:9 [b]Luke 23:13; Acts 4:5
9 [1]Or, *by whom* [a]Acts 3:7f.
10 [1]Or, *in* [2]Or, *him* [a]Acts 2:22; 3:6 [b]Acts 2:24
11 [1]Lit., *This One* [a]Matt. 21:42 [b]Ps. 118:22 [c]Mark 9:12
12 [a]Matt. 1:21; Acts 10:43; 1 Tim. 2:5

Threat and Release

13 Now as they observed the [a]confi-
dence of [b]Peter and John, and understood that they were uneducated and
untrained men, they were marveling, and
[c]*began* to recognize them [1]as having
been with Jesus.
14 And seeing the man who had been
healed standing with them, they had
nothing to say in reply.
15 But when they had ordered them to
go aside out of the [1a]Council, they *began*
to confer with one another,
16 saying, "[a]What shall we do with
these men? For the fact that a [b]notewor-
thy [1]miracle has taken place through
them is apparent to all who live in
Jerusalem, and we cannot deny it.
17 "But in order that it may not spread
any further among the people, let us
warn them to speak no more to any man
[a]in this name."
18 And when they had summoned
them, they [a]commanded them not to
speak or teach at all [1]in the name of
Jesus.
19 But [a]Peter and John answered and
said to them, "[b]Whether it is right in the
sight of God to give heed to you rather
than to God, you be the judge;
20 for [a]we cannot stop speaking what
we have seen and heard."
21 And when they had threatened
them further, they let them go (finding
no basis on which they might punish
them) [a]on account of the people, because
they were all [b]glorifying God for what
had happened;
22 for the man was more than forty
years old on whom this [1]miracle of
healing had been performed.
23 And when they had been released,
they went to their own *companions,* and
reported all that the chief priests and the
elders had said to them.
24 And when they heard *this,* they
lifted their voices to God with one
accord and said, "O [1]Lord, it is Thou
who [a]DIDST MAKE THE HEAVEN AND THE
EARTH AND THE SEA, AND ALL THAT IS IN
THEM,
25 who [a]by the Holy Spirit, *through*
the mouth of our father David Thy
servant, didst say,
'[b]WHY DID THE [1]GENTILES RAGE,
AND THE PEOPLES DEVISE FUTILE
THINGS?
26 '[a]THE KINGS OF THE EARTH [1]TOOK
THEIR STAND,
AND THE RULERS WERE GATHERED
TOGETHER
AGAINST THE LORD, AND AGAINST
HIS [2b]CHRIST.'
27 "For truly in this city there were
gathered together against Thy holy [1a]ser-
vant Jesus, whom Thou didst anoint,
both [b]Herod and [c]Pontius Pilate, along
with [d]the [2]Gentiles and the peoples of
Israel,
28 to do whatever Thy hand and [a]Thy
purpose predestined to occur.
29 "And [1]now, Lord, take note of their
threats, and grant that Thy bond-
servants may [a]speak Thy word with all
[b]confidence,
30 while Thou dost extend Thy hand
to heal, and [1a]signs and wonders take
place through the name of Thy holy
[2b]servant Jesus."
31 And when they had prayed, the
[a]place where they had gathered together
was shaken, and they were all [b]filled
with the Holy Spirit, and *began* to [c]speak
the word of God with [d]boldness.

Sharing among Believers

32 And the [1]congregation of those
who believed were of one heart and soul;
and not one *of them* [2]claimed that anything belonging to him was his own; but
[a]all things were common property to
them.
33 And [a]with great power the apostles
were giving [b]witness to the resurrection
of the Lord Jesus[1], and abundant grace
was upon them all.
34 For there was not a needy person
among them, for all who were owners of
land or houses [a]would sell them and
bring the [1]proceeds of the sales,
35 and [a]lay them at the apostles' feet;
and they would be [b]distributed to each,
as any had need.
36 And Joseph, a Levite of [a]Cyprian
birth, who was also called [b]Barnabas by
the apostles (which translated means,
Son of [1c]Encouragement),
37 and who owned a tract of land,
sold it and brought the money and [a]laid
it at the apostles' feet.

Fate of Ananias and Sapphira

5 BUT a certain man named Ananias,
with his wife Sapphira, sold a piece
of property,
2 and [a]kept back *some* of the price
for himself, with his wife's [1]full knowledge, and bringing a portion of it, he
[b]laid it at the apostles' feet.
3 But Peter said, "Ananias, why has
[a]Satan filled your heart to lie [b]to the
Holy Spirit, and to [c]keep back *some* of
the price of the land?
4 "While it remained *unsold,* did it not
remain your own? And after it was sold,
was it not [1]under your control? Why is it
that you have [2]conceived this deed in
your heart? You have not lied to men,
but [a]to God."
5 And as he heard these words, Ananias [a]fell down and breathed his last;
and [b]great fear came upon all who heard
of it.
6 And the [1]young men arose and
[a]covered him up, and after carrying him
out, they buried him.
7 Now there elapsed an interval of
about three hours, and his wife came in,
not knowing what had happened.

13 [1]Lit., *that they had been* [a]Acts 4:31 [b]Luke 22:8; Acts 4:19 [c]John 7:15
15 [1]Or, *Sanhedrin* [a]Matt. 5:22
16 [1]Or, *sign* [a]John 11:47 [b]Acts 3:7-10
17 [a]John 15:21
18 [1]Or, *on the basis of* [a]Acts 5:28f.
19 [a]Acts 4:13 [b]Acts 5:28f.
20 [a]I Cor. 9:16
21 [a]Acts 5:26 [b]Matt. 9:8
22 [1]Or, *sign*
24 [1]Or, *Master* [a]Ex. 20:11; Neh. 9:6; Ps. 146:6
25 [1]Or, *nations* [a]Acts 1:16 [b]Ps. 2:1
26 [1]Or, *approached* [2]Or, *Anointed One;* i.e., Messiah [a]Ps. 2:2 [b]Dan. 9:24f.; Luke 4:18; Acts 10:38; Heb. 1:9
27 [1]Or, *Child* [2]Or, *nations* [a]Acts 3:13; 4:30 [b]Matt. 14:1; Luke 23:7-11 [c]Matt. 27:2; Mark 15:1; Luke 23:1, 12; John 18:28, 29 [d]Matt. 20:19
28 [a]Acts 2:23
29 [1]Or, *as for the present situation* [a]Phil. 1:14 [b]Acts 4:13, 31; 14:3
30 [1]Or, *attesting miracles* [2]Or, *Child* [a]John 4:48 [b]Acts 3:13; 4:27
31 [a]Acts 2:1 [b]Acts 2:4 [c]Phil. 1:14 [d]Acts 4:13; 14:3
32 [1]Or, *multitude* [2]Lit., *was saying* [a]Acts 2:44
33 [1]Some mss. add *Christ* [a]Acts 1:8 [b]Luke 24:48
34 [1]Lit., *the prices of the things being sold* [a]Matt. 19:21
35 [a]Acts 4:37; 5:2 [b]Acts 2:45; 6:1
36 [1]Or, *Exhortation* or *Consolation* [a]Acts 11:19f.; 13:4; 15:39; 21:3, 16; 27:4 [b]Acts 9:27; 11:22, 30; 12:25; 13:1, 2, 7; 1 Cor. 9:6; Gal. 2:1, 9, 13; Col. 4:10 [c]Acts 2:40; 11:23; 13:15; 1 Cor. 14:3; 1 Thess. 2:3
37 [a]Acts 4:35; 5:2

2 [1]Or, *collusion* [a]Acts 5:3 [b]Acts 4:35, 37
3 [a]Matt. 4:10; Luke 22:3; John 13:2, 27 [b]Acts 5:4, 9 [c]Acts 5:2
4 [1]Or, *in your authority* [2]Or, *placed* [a]Acts 5:3, 9
5 [a]Ezek. 11:13; Acts 5:10 [b]Acts 2:43; 5:11
6 [1]Lit., *younger* [a]John 19:40

8 And Peter responded to her, "Tell
me whether you sold the land [1a]for such
and such a price?" And she said, "Yes,
[1]that was the price."
9 Then Peter *said* to her, "Why is it
that you have agreed together to [a]put
[b]the Spirit of the Lord to the test?
Behold, the feet of those who have
buried your husband are at the door,
and they shall carry you out *as well.*"
10 And she [a]fell immediately at his
feet, and breathed her last; and the
young men came in and found her dead,
and they carried her out and buried her
beside her husband.
11 And [a]great fear came upon the
whole church, and upon all who heard of
these things.
12 And [1]at the hands of the apostles
many [a]signs and wonders were taking
place among the people; and they were
all with one accord in [b]Solomon's portico.
13 But none of the rest dared to associate with them; however, [a]the people
[1]held them in high esteem.
14 And all the more [a]believers in the
Lord, multitudes of men and women,
were constantly [b]added to *their number*;
15 to such an extent that they even
carried the sick out into the streets, and
laid them on cots and pallets, so that
when Peter came by, [a]at least his shadow
might fall on any one of them.
16 And also the [1]people from the
cities in the vicinity of Jerusalem were
coming together, bringing people who
were sick [2]or afflicted with unclean
spirits; and they were all being healed.

Imprisonment and Release

17 But the high priest rose up, along
with all his associates (that is [a]the sect of
[b]the Sadducees), and they were filled
with jealousy;
18 and they laid hands on the apostles, and [a]put them in a public jail.
19 But [a]an angel of the Lord during
the night opened the gates of the prison,
and taking them out he said,
20 "Go your way, stand and [1]speak to
the people in the temple [2a]the whole
message of this Life."
21 And upon hearing *this,* they entered into the temple [a]about daybreak,
and *began* to teach. Now when [b]the high
priest and his associates had come, they
called [c]the [1]Council together, even all
the Senate of the sons of Israel, and sent
orders to the prison house for them to be
brought.
22 But [a]the officers who came did not
find them in the prison; and they returned, and reported back,
23 saying, "We found the prison
house locked quite securely and the
guards standing at the doors; but when
we had opened up, we found no one
inside."
24 Now when [a]the captain of the
temple *guard* and the chief priests heard
these words, they were greatly perplexed
about them as to what [1]would come of
this.
25 But someone came and reported to
them, "Behold, the men whom you put
in prison are standing in the temple and
teaching the people!"
26 Then [a]the captain went along with
[b]the officers and *proceeded* to bring them
back without violence (for [c]they were
afraid of the people, lest they should be
stoned).
27 And when they had brought them,
they stood them [1]before [a]the Council.
And the high priest questioned them,
28 saying, "We gave you [a]strict orders
not to continue teaching in this name,
and behold, you have filled Jerusalem
with your teaching, and [b]intend to bring
this man's blood upon us."
29 But Peter and the apostles answered and said, "[a]We must obey God
rather than men.
30 "[a]The God of our fathers [b]raised up
Jesus, [1]whom you had [c]put to death by
hanging Him on a [2]cross.
31 "[a]He is the one whom God exalted
[1]to His right hand as a [2b]Prince and a
[c]Savior, to grant [d]repentance to Israel,
and forgiveness of sins.
32 "And we are [a]witnesses[1] of these
things; and [b]*so is* the Holy Spirit, whom
God has given to those who obey Him."

Gamaliel's Counsel

33 But when they heard this, they
were [a]cut [1]to the quick and were intending to slay them.
34 But a certain Pharisee named [a]Ga-
maliel, a [b]teacher of the Law, respected
by all the people, stood up in [c]the
Council and gave orders to put the men
outside for a short time.
35 And he said to them, "Men of
Israel, take care what you propose to do
with these men.
36 "For some time ago Theudas rose
up, [a]claiming to be somebody; and a
group of about four hundred men joined
up with him. [1]And he was slain; and all
who [2]followed him were dispersed and
came to nothing.
37 "After this man Judas of Galilee
rose up in the days of [a]the census, and
drew away *some* people after him, he too
perished, and all those who [1]followed
him were scattered.
38 "And so in the present case, I say to
you, stay away from these men and let
them alone, for if this plan or [1]action
should [a]be of men, it will be overthrown;
39 but if it is of God, you will not be
able to overthrow them; or else you may
even be found [a]fighting against God."
40 And they [1]took his advice; and
after calling the apostles in, they
[a]flogged them and ordered them to
[2]speak no more in the name of Jesus,
and *then* released them.

8 [1]Lit., *for so much* [a]Acts 5:2
9 [a]Acts 15:10 [b]Acts 5:3, 4
10 [a]Ezek. 11:13; Acts 5:5
11 [a]Acts 2:43; 5:5
12 [1]Lit., *through* [a]John 4:48 [b]John 10:23; Acts 3:11
13 [1]Lit., *were holding* [a]Acts 2:47; 4:21
14 [a]2 Cor. 6:15 [b]Acts 2:47; 11:24
15 [a]Acts 19:12
16 [1]Lit., *multitude* [2]Lit., *and*
17 [a]Acts 15:5 [b]Matt. 3:7; Acts 4:1
18 [a]Acts 4:3
19 [a]Matt. 1:20, 24; 2:13, 19; 28:2; Luke 1:11; 2:9; Acts 8:26; 10:3; 12:7, 23; 27:23
20 [1]Or, *continue to speak* [2]Lit., *all the words* [a]John 6:63, 68
21 [1]Or, *Sanhedrin* [a]John 8:2 [b]Acts 4:6 [c]Matt. 5:22; Acts 5:27, 34, 41
22 [a]Matt. 26:58; Acts 5:26
24 [1]Lit., *this would become* [a]Acts 4:1; 5:26
26 [a]Acts 5:24 [b]Acts 5:22 [c]Acts 4:21; 5:13
27 [1]Lit., *in* [a]Matt. 5:22; Acts 5:21, 34, 41
28 [a]Acts 4:18 [b]Matt. 23:35; 27:25; Acts 2:23, 36; 3:14f.; 7:52
29 [a]Acts 4:19
30 [1]Or, *on whom you had laid violent hands* [2]Lit., *wood* [a]Acts 3:13 [b]Acts 2:24 [c]Acts 10:39; 13:29; Gal. 3:13; 1 Pet. 2:24
31 [1]Or, *by* [2]Or, *Leader* [a]Acts 2:33 [b]Acts 3:15 [c]Luke 2:11 [d]Luke 24:47; Acts 2:38
32 [1]Some mss. add *in Him,* or *of Him* [a]Luke 24:48 [b]John 15:26; Acts 15:28; Rom. 8:16; Heb. 2:4
33 [1]Lit., *in their hearts* [a]Acts 2:37; 7:54
34 [a]Acts 22:3 [b]Luke 2:46; 5:17 [c]Acts 5:21
36 [1]Lit., *Who was slain* [2]Lit., *were obeying* [a]Acts 8:9; Gal. 2:6; 6:3
37 [1]Lit., *were obeying* [a]Luke 2:2
38 [1]Or, *work* [a]Mark 11:30
39 [a]Prov. 21:30; Acts 11:17
40 [1]Lit., *were persuaded by him* [2]Lit., *not be speaking* [a]Matt. 10:17

41 So they went on their way from the presence of the [1][a]Council, [b]rejoicing that they had been considered worthy to suffer shame [c]for [2]*His* name.

42 [a]And every day, in the temple and [1]from house to house, they [2]kept right on teaching and [3][b]preaching Jesus *as* the [4]Christ.

Choosing of the Seven

6 NOW [1]at this time while the [a]disciples were [b]increasing *in number,* a complaint arose on the part of the [2][c]Hellenistic *Jews* against the *native* [d]Hebrews, because their [e]widows were being overlooked in [f]the daily serving *of food.*

2 And the twelve summoned the [1]congregation of the disciples and said, "It is not desirable for us to neglect the word of God in order to serve tables.

3 "But select from among you, [a]brethren, seven men of good reputation, [b]full of the Spirit and of wisdom, whom we may put in charge of this task.

4 "But we will [a]devote ourselves to prayer, and to the [1]ministry of the word."

5 And the statement found approval with the whole [1]congregation; and they chose [a]Stephen, a man [b]full of faith and of the Holy Spirit, and [c]Philip, Prochorus, Nicanor, Timon, Parmenas and [2]Nicolas, a [3][d]proselyte from [e]Antioch.

6 And these they brought before the apostles; and after [a]praying, they [b]laid their hands on them.

7 And [a]the word of God kept on spreading; and [b]the number of the disciples continued to increase greatly in Jerusalem, and a great many of the priests were becoming obedient to [c]the faith.

8 And Stephen, full of grace and power, was performing great [a]wonders and [1]signs among the people.

9 But some men from what was called the Synagogue of the Freedmen, *including* both [a]Cyrenians and [b]Alexandrians, and some from [c]Cilicia and [1][d]Asia, rose up and argued with Stephen.

10 And *yet* they were unable to cope with the wisdom and the Spirit with which he was speaking.

11 Then they secretly induced men [1]to say, "We have heard him speak blasphemous words against Moses and *against* God."

12 And they stirred up the people, the elders and the scribes, and they [a]came upon him and dragged him away, and brought him [1]before [b]the [2]Council.

13 And they put forward [a]false witnesses who said, "This man incessantly speaks against this [b]holy place, and the Law;

14 for we have heard him say that [a]this Nazarene, Jesus, will destroy this place and alter [b]the customs which Moses handed down to us."

15 And fixing their gaze on him, all who were sitting in the [1][a]Council saw his face like the face of an angel.

Stephen's Defense

7 AND the high priest said, "Are these things so?"

2 And he said, "Hear me, [a]brethren and fathers! [b]The God of glory [c]appeared to our father Abraham when he was in Mesopotamia, before he lived in [1]Haran,

3 and said to him, '[a]DEPART FROM YOUR COUNTRY AND YOUR RELATIVES, AND COME INTO THE LAND THAT I WILL SHOW YOU.'

4 "[a]Then he departed from the land of the Chaldeans, and settled in [1]Haran. And [b]from there, after his father died, *God* removed him into this country in which you are now living.

5 "And He gave him no inheritance in it, not even a foot of ground; and *yet,* even when he had no child, [a]He promised that HE WOULD GIVE IT TO HIM AS A POSSESSION, AND TO HIS OFFSPRING AFTER HIM.

6 "But [a]God spoke to this effect, that his OFFSPRING WOULD BE ALIENS IN A FOREIGN LAND, AND THAT THEY WOULD [1]BE ENSLAVED AND MISTREATED FOR FOUR HUNDRED YEARS.

7 " 'AND WHATEVER NATION TO WHICH THEY SHALL BE IN BONDAGE I MYSELF WILL JUDGE,' said God, 'AND [a]AFTER THAT THEY WILL COME OUT AND [1]SERVE ME IN THIS PLACE.'

8 "And He [a]gave him [1]the covenant of circumcision; and so [b]*Abraham* became the father of Isaac, and circumcised him on the eighth day; and [c]Isaac *became the father of* Jacob, and [d]Jacob *of* the twelve [e]patriarchs.

9 "And the patriarchs [a]became jealous of Joseph and sold him into Egypt. And *yet* God was with him,

10 and rescued him from all his afflictions, and [a]granted him favor and wisdom in the sight of Pharaoh, king of Egypt; and he made him governor over Egypt and all his household.

11 "Now [a]a famine came over all Egypt and Canaan, and great affliction *with it;* and our fathers [1]could find no [2]food.

12 "But [a]when Jacob heard that there was grain in Egypt, he sent our fathers *there* the first time.

13 "And on the second *visit* [a]Joseph [1]made himself known to his brothers, and [b]Joseph's family was disclosed to Pharaoh.

41 [1]Or, *Sanhedrin* [2]Lit., the *name* (par excellence) [a]Acts 5:21 [b]1 Pet. 4:14, 16 [c]John 15:21
42 [1]Or, *in the various private homes* [2]Lit., *were not ceasing to* [3]Or, *telling the good news of* [4]I.e., Messiah [a]Acts 2:46 [b]Acts 8:35; 11:20; 17:18; Gal. 1:16

1 [1]Lit., *in these days* [2]I.e., non-Palestinian Jews who normally spoke Greek [a]Acts 11:26 [b]Acts 2:47; 6:7 [c]Acts 9:29; 11:20 [d]2 Cor. 11:22; Phil. 3:5 [e]Acts 9:39, 41; 1 Tim. 5:3 [f]Acts 4:35; 11:29
2 [1]Or, *multitude*
3 [a]John 21:23; Acts 1:15 [b]Acts 2:4
4 [1]Or, *service* [a]Acts 1:14
5 [1]Lit., *multitude* [2]Gr., *Nikolaos* [3]I.e., a Gentile convert to Judaism [a]Acts 6:8ff.; 11:19; 22:20 [b]Acts 6:3; 11:24 [c]Acts 8:5ff.; 21:8 [d]Matt. 23:15 [e]Acts 11:19
6 [a]Acts 1:24 [b]Num. 8:10; 27:18; Deut. 34:9; Mark 5:23; Acts 8:17ff.; 9:17; 13:3; 19:6; 1 Tim. 4:14; 2 Tim. 1:6; Heb. 6:2
7 [a]Acts 12:24; 19:20 [b]Acts 6:1 [c]Acts 13:8; 14:22; Gal. 1:23; 6:10; Jude 3, 20
8 [1]Or, *attesting miracles* [a]John 4:48
9 [1]I.e., west coast province of Asia Minor [a]Matt. 27:32; Acts 2:10 [b]Acts 18:24 [c]Acts 15:23, 41; 21:39; 22:3; 23:34; 27:5; Gal. 1:21 [d]Acts 16:6; 19:10; 21:27; 24:18
11 [1]Lit., *saying*
12 [1]Lit., *into* [2]Or, *Sanhedrin* [a]Luke 20:1; Acts 4:1 [b]Matt. 5:22
13 [a]Matt. 26:59-61; Acts 7:58 [b]Matt. 24:15; Acts 21:28; 25:8
14 [a]Matt. 26:61 [b]Acts 15:1; 21:21; 26:3; 28:17
15 [1]Or, *Sanhedrin* [a]Matt. 5:22

2 [1]Gr., *Kharran* [a]Acts 22:1 [b]Ps. 29:3; 1 Cor. 2:8 [c]Gen. 11:31; 15:7
3 [a]Gen. 12:1
4 [1]Gr., *Kharran* [a]Gen. 11:31; 15:7 [b]Gen. 12:4, 5
5 [a]Gen. 12:7; 13:15; 15:18; 17:8
6 [1]Lit., *enslave them and mistreat them* [a]Gen. 15:13f.
7 [1]Or, *worship* [a]Ex. 3:12

8 [1]Or, *a* [a]Gen. 17:10ff. [b]Gen. 21:2-4 [c]Gen. 25:26 [d]Gen. 29:31ff.; 30:5ff.; 35:23ff. [e]Acts 2:29
9 [a]Gen. 37:11, 28; 39:2, 21f.; 45:4
10 [a]Gen. 39:21; 41:40-46; Ps. 105:21
11 [1]Lit., *were not finding* [2]Or, *fodder* [a]Gen. 41:54f.; 42:5
12 [a]Gen. 42:2
13 [1]Or, *was made known* [a]Gen. 45:1-4 [b]Gen. 45:16

14 "And [a]Joseph sent *word* and invited
Jacob his father and all his relatives to
come to him, [b]seventy-five [c]persons *in
all.*
15 "And [a]Jacob went down to Egypt
and *there* passed away, he and our
fathers.
16 "And *from there* they were removed
to [1a]Shechem, and laid in the tomb
which Abraham had purchased for a
sum of money from the sons of [2]Hamor
in [1]Shechem.
17 "But as the [a]time of the promise was
approaching which God had assured to
Abraham, [b]the people increased and
multiplied in Egypt,
18 until [a]THERE AROSE ANOTHER KING
OVER EGYPT WHO KNEW NOTHING
ABOUT JOSEPH.
19 "It was he who took [a]shrewd advantage of our race, and mistreated our
fathers so that they would [1b]expose their
infants and they would not survive.
20 "And it was at this time that [a]Moses
was born; and he was lovely [1]in the sight
of God; and he was nurtured three
months in his father's home.
21 "And after he had been [1]exposed,
[a]Pharaoh's daughter [2]took him away,
and nurtured him as her own son.
22 "And Moses was educated in all [a]the
learning of the Egyptians, and he was a
man of power in words and deeds.
23 "But when he was approaching the
age of forty, [a]it entered his [1]mind to visit
his brethren, the sons of Israel.
24 "And when he saw one *of them*
being treated unjustly, he defended him
and took vengeance for the oppressed by
striking down the Egyptian.
25 "And he [1]supposed that his brethren
understood that God was granting them
[2]deliverance [3]through him; but they did
not understand.
26 "[a]And on the following day he
appeared to them as they were fighting
together, and he tried to reconcile them
in peace, saying, 'Men, you are brethren,
why do you injure one another?'
27 "But the one who was injuring his
neighbor pushed him away, saying,
'[a]WHO MADE YOU A RULER AND JUDGE
OVER US?
28 '[a]YOU DO NOT MEAN TO KILL ME AS
YOU KILLED THE EGYPTIAN YESTERDAY,
DO YOU?'
29 "And at this remark [a]MOSES FLED,
AND BECAME AN ALIEN IN THE LAND OF
[1]MIDIAN, where he [b]became the father
of two sons.
30 "And after forty years had passed,
[a]AN ANGEL APPEARED TO HIM IN THE
WILDERNESS OF MOUNT Sinai, IN THE
FLAME OF A BURNING THORN BUSH.
31 "And when Moses saw it, he *began*
to marvel at the sight; and as he approached to look *more* closely, there
came the voice of the Lord:
32 '[a]I AM THE GOD OF YOUR FATHERS,
THE GOD OF ABRAHAM AND ISAAC AND
JACOB.' And Moses shook with fear and
would not venture to look.
33 "[a]BUT THE LORD SAID TO HIM,
'[b]TAKE OFF THE SANDALS FROM YOUR
FEET, FOR THE PLACE ON WHICH YOU ARE
STANDING IS HOLY GROUND.
34 '[a]I HAVE CERTAINLY SEEN THE OP-
PRESSION OF MY PEOPLE IN EGYPT, AND
HAVE HEARD THEIR GROANS, AND I HAVE
COME DOWN TO DELIVER THEM; [1b]COME
NOW, AND I WILL SEND YOU TO EGYPT.'
35 "This Moses whom they [a]disowned,
saying, 'WHO MADE YOU A RULER AND A
JUDGE?' is the one whom God [1]sent *to be*
both a ruler and a deliverer with the
[2]help of the angel who appeared to him
in the thorn bush.
36 "[a]This man led them out, performing [b]wonders and [1]signs in the land of
Egypt and in the Red Sea and in the
[c]wilderness for forty years.
37 "This is the Moses who said to the
sons of Israel, '[a]GOD SHALL RAISE UP
FOR YOU A PROPHET [1]LIKE ME FROM
YOUR BRETHREN.'
38 "This is the one who was in [a]the
[1]congregation in the wilderness together
with [b]the angel who was speaking to him
on Mount Sinai, and *who was* with our
fathers; and he received [c]living [d]oracles
to pass on to you.
39 "And our fathers were unwilling to
be obedient to him, but [a]repudiated him
and in their hearts turned back to Egypt,
40 [a]SAYING TO AARON, 'MAKE FOR US
GODS WHO WILL GO BEFORE US; FOR
THIS MOSES WHO LED US OUT OF THE
LAND OF EGYPT—WE DO NOT KNOW
WHAT HAPPENED TO HIM.'
41 "And [1]at that time [a]they made a
[2]calf and brought a sacrifice to the idol,
and were rejoicing in [b]the works of their
hands.
42 "But God [a]turned away and delivered them up to [1]serve the [2]host of
heaven; as it is written in the book of the
prophets, '[b]IT WAS NOT TO ME THAT YOU
OFFERED VICTIMS AND SACRIFICES
[c]FORTY YEARS IN THE WILDERNESS, WAS
IT, O HOUSE OF ISRAEL?
43 '[a]YOU ALSO TOOK ALONG THE TAB-
ERNACLE OF MOLOCH AND THE STAR OF
THE GOD [1]ROMPHA, THE IMAGES WHICH
YOU MADE TO WORSHIP THEM. I ALSO
WILL REMOVE YOU BEYOND BABYLON.'
44 "Our fathers had [a]the tabernacle of
testimony in the wilderness, just as He
who spoke to Moses directed *him* to
make it [b]according to the pattern which
he had seen.
45 "And having received it in their
turn, our fathers [a]brought it in with
[1]Joshua upon dispossessing the [2]nations
whom God drove out before our fathers,
until the time of David.
46 "And [a]*David* found favor in God's
sight, and [b]asked that he might find a
dwelling place for the [1]God of Jacob.

14 [a]Gen. 45:9, 10, 17, 18 [b]Gen. 46:26f.; Ex. 1:5; Deut. 10:22 [c]Acts 2:41
15 [a]Gen. 46:1-7; 49:33; Ex. 1:6
16 [1]Gr., *Sychem* [2]Gr., *Emmor* [a]Gen. 23:16; 33:19; 50:13; Josh. 24:32
17 [a]Gen. 15:13 [b]Ex. 1:7f.
18 [a]Ex. 1:8
19 [1]Or, *put out to die* [a]Ex. 1:10f., 16ff. [b]Ex. 1:22
20 [1]Lit., *to God* [a]Ex. 2:2; Heb. 11:23
21 [1]Or, *put out to die* [2]Or, *adopted him* [a]Ex. 2:5f., 10
22 [a]1 Kin. 4:30; Is. 19:11
23 [1]Lit., *heart* [a]Ex. 2:11f.; Heb. 11:24-26
25 [1]Lit., *was thinking* [2]Or, *salvation* [3]Lit., *through his hand*
26 [a]Ex. 2:13f.
27 [a]Ex. 2:14; Acts 7:35
28 [a]Ex. 2:14
29 [1]Gr., *Madiam* [a]Ex. 2:15, 22 [b]Ex. 18:3, 4
30 [a]Ex. 3:1f.; Is. 63:9
32 [a]Ex. 3:6; Matt. 22:32
33 [a]Ex. 3:5 [b]Josh. 5:15
34 [1]Lit., *and now hither!* [a]Ex. 3:7f. [b]Ex. 3:10
35 [1]Lit., *has sent* [2]Lit., *hand* [a]Ex. 2:14; Acts 7:27
36 [1]Or, *attesting miracles* [a]Ex. 12:41; 33:1; Heb. 8:9 [b]Ex. 7:3; 14:21; John 4:48 [c]Ex. 16:35; Num. 14:33; Ps. 95:8-10; Acts 7:42; 13:18; Heb. 3:8f.
37 [1]Or, *as* He raised up *me* [a]Deut. 18:15, 18; Acts 3:22
38 [1]Or, *church;* Gr., *ekklesia* [a]Ex. 19:17 [b]Acts 7:53 [c]Deut. 32:47; Heb. 4:12 [d]Rom. 3:2; Heb. 5:12; 1 Pet. 4:11
39 [a]Num. 14:3f.
40 [a]Ex. 32:1, 23
41 [1]Lit., *in those days* [2]Or, *young bull* [a]Ex. 32:4, 6 [b]Rev. 9:20
42 [1]Or, *worship* [2]I.e., heavenly bodies [a]Josh. 24:20; Is. 63:10; Jer. 19:13; Ezek. 20:39 [b]Amos 5:25 [c]Acts 7:36
43 [1]Other mss. spell it: *Romphan,* or *Rempham,* or *Raiphan,* or *Rephan* [a]Amos 5:26, 27
44 [a]Ex. 25:8, 9; 38:21 [b]Ex. 25:40
45 [1]Gr., *Jesus* [2]Or, *Gentiles* [a]Deut. 32:49; Josh. 3:14ff.; 18:1; 23:9; 24:18; Ps. 44:2f.

46 [1]The earliest mss. read *house* instead of *God;* the Septuagint reads *God* [a]2 Sam. 7:8ff.; Ps. 132:1-5; Acts 13:22 [b]2 Sam. 7:1-16; 1 Chr. 17:1-14

47"But it was [a]Solomon who built a
house for Him.
48"However, [a]the Most High does not
dwell in *houses* made by *human* hands;
as the prophet says:
49 '[a]HEAVEN IS MY THRONE,
AND EARTH IS THE FOOTSTOOL OF
MY FEET;
WHAT KIND OF HOUSE WILL YOU
BUILD FOR ME?' says the Lord;
'OR WHAT PLACE IS THERE FOR MY
REPOSE?
50 '[a]WAS IT NOT MY HAND WHICH
MADE ALL THESE THINGS?'
51"You men who are [a]stiff-necked and
uncircumcised in heart and ears are
always resisting the Holy Spirit; you are
doing just as your fathers did.
52"[a]Which one of the prophets did
your fathers not persecute? And they
killed those who had previously announced the coming of [b]the Righteous
One, whose betrayers and murderers
[c]you have now become;
53 you who received the law as [a]or-
dained by angels, and *yet* did not keep
it."

Stephen Put to Death

54 Now when they heard this, they
were [a]cut [1]to the quick, and they *began*
gnashing their teeth at him.
55 But being [a]full of the Holy Spirit,
he [b]gazed intently into heaven and saw
the glory of God, and Jesus standing [c]at
the right hand of God;
56 and he said, "Behold, I see the
[a]heavens opened up and [b]the Son of
Man standing at the right hand of God."
57 But they cried out with a loud
voice, and covered their ears, and they
rushed upon him with one impulse.
58 And when they had [a]driven him
out of the city, they *began* stoning *him,*
and [b]the witnesses [c]laid aside their robes
at the feet of [d]a young man named Saul.
59 And they went on stoning Stephen
as he [a]called upon *the Lord* and said,
"Lord Jesus, receive my spirit!"
60 And [a]falling on his knees, he cried
out with a loud voice, "Lord, [b]do not
hold this sin against them!" And having
said this, he [1c]fell asleep.

Saul Persecutes the Church

8 AND [a]Saul was in hearty agreement
with putting him to death.
And on that day a great persecution
arose against [b]the church in Jerusalem;
and they were all [c]scattered throughout
the regions of Judea and [d]Samaria,
except the apostles.
2 And *some* devout men buried Stephen, and made loud lamentation over
him.
3 But [a]Saul *began* ravaging the
church, entering house after house; and
[b]dragging off men and women, he would
put them in prison.

Philip in Samaria

4 Therefore, those [a]who had been
scattered went about [1b]preaching the
word.
5 And [a]Philip went down to the city
of Samaria and *began* proclaiming
[1]Christ to them.
6 And the multitudes with one accord were giving attention to what was
said by Philip, as they heard and saw the
[1]signs which he was performing.
7 For *in the case of* many who had
[a]unclean spirits, they were coming out *of*
them shouting with a loud voice; and
many who had been [b]paralyzed and
lame were healed.
8 And there was [a]much rejoicing in
that city.
9 Now there was a certain man
named Simon, who formerly was practicing [a]magic in the city, and astonishing
the people of Samaria, [b]claiming to be
someone great;
10 and they all, from smallest to greatest, were giving attention to him, saying,
"[a]This man is what is called the Great
Power of God."
11 And they were giving him attention
because he had for a long time astonished them with his [a]magic arts.
12 But when they believed Philip
[a]preaching the good news about the
kingdom of God and the name of Jesus
Christ, they were being [b]baptized, men
and women alike.
13 And even Simon himself believed;
and after being baptized, he continued
on with Philip; and as he observed [a]signs
and [b]great miracles taking place, he was
constantly amazed.
14 Now when [a]the apostles in Jerusalem heard that Samaria had received the
word of God, they sent them [b]Peter and
John,
15 who came down and prayed for
them, [a]that they might receive the Holy
Spirit.
16 For He had [a]not yet fallen upon
any of them; they had simply been
[b]baptized [1]in the name of the Lord
Jesus.
17 Then they [a]*began* laying their
hands on them, and they were [b]receiving
the Holy Spirit.
18 Now when Simon saw that the
Spirit was bestowed through the laying
on of the apostles' hands, he offered
them money,
19 saying, "Give this authority to me
as well, so that everyone on whom I lay
my hands may receive the Holy Spirit."
20 But Peter said to him, "May your
silver perish with you, because you
thought you could [a]obtain the gift of
God with money!
21"You have [a]no part or portion in
this [1]matter, for your heart is not [b]right
before God.
22"Therefore repent of this wickedness
of yours, and pray the Lord that [a]if

---

47 [a]1 Kin. 6:1-38; 8:20; 2 Chr. 3:1-17
48 [a]Luke 1:32
49 [a]Is. 66:1; Matt. 5:34f.
50 [a]Is. 66:2
51 [a]Ex. 32:9; 33:3, 5; Lev. 26:41; Num. 27:14; Is. 63:10; Jer. 6:10; 9:26
52 [a]2 Chr. 36:15f.; Matt. 5:12; 23:31, 37 [b]Acts 3:14; 22:14; 1 John 2:1 [c]Acts 3:14; 5:28
53 [a]Deut. 33:2; Acts 7:38; Gal. 3:19; Heb. 2:2
54 [1]Lit., *in their hearts* [a]Acts 5:33
55 [a]Acts 2:4 [b]John 11:41 [c]Mark 16:19
56 [a]John 1:51 [b]Matt. 8:20
58 [a]Lev. 24:14, 16; Luke 4:29 [b]Deut. 13:9f.; 17:7; Acts 6:13 [c]Acts 22:20 [d]Acts 8:1; 22:20; 26:10
59 [a]Acts 9:14, 21; 22:16; Rom. 10:12–14; 1 Cor. 1:2; 2 Tim. 2:22
60 [1]Or, *expired* [a]Luke 22:41 [b]Matt. 5:44; Luke 23:34 [c]Dan. 12:2; Matt. 27:52; John 11:11f.; Acts 13:36; 1 Cor. 15:6, 18, 20; 1 Thess. 4:13ff.; 2 Pet. 3:4

1 [a]Acts 7:58; 22:20; 26:10 [b]Acts 9:31 [c]Acts 8:4; 11:19 [d]Acts 1:8; 8:5, 14; 9:31
3 [a]Acts 9:1, 13, 21; 22:4, 19; 26:10f.; 1 Cor. 15:9; Gal. 1:13; Phil. 3:6; 1 Tim. 1:13 [b]James 2:6
4 [1]Or, *bringing the good tidings of* [a]Acts 8:1 [b]Acts 8:12; 15:35
5 [1]I.e., the Messiah [a]Acts 6:5; 8:26, 30
6 [1]Or, *attesting miracles*
7 [a]Mark 16:17 [b]Matt. 4:24
8 [a]John 4:40-42; Acts 8:39
9 [a]Acts 8:11; 13:6 [b]Acts 5:36
10 [a]Acts 14:11; 28:6
11 [a]Acts 8:9; 13:6
12 [a]Acts 1:3; 8:4 [b]Acts 2:38
13 [a]Acts 8:6 [b]Acts 19:11
14 [a]Acts 8:1 [b]Luke 22:8
15 [a]Acts 2:38; 19:2
16 [1]Lit., *into* [a]Matt. 28:19; Acts 19:2 [b]Acts 2:38; 10:48
17 [a]Mark 5:23; Acts 6:6 [b]Acts 2:4
20 [a]2 Kin. 5:16; Is. 55:1; Dan. 5:17; Matt. 10:8; Acts 2:38
21 [1]Or, *teaching;* lit., *word* [a]Deut. 10:9; 12:12; Eph. 5:5 [b]Ps. 78:37
22 [a]Is. 55:7

possible, the intention of your heart may be forgiven you.

23 "For I see that you are in the gall of bitterness and in [a]the [1]bondage of iniquity."

24 But Simon answered and said, "[a]Pray to the Lord for me yourselves, so that nothing of what you have said may come upon me."

An Ethiopian Receives Christ

25 And so, when they had solemnly [a]testified and spoken [b]the word of the Lord, they started back to Jerusalem, and were [c]preaching the gospel to many villages of the [d]Samaritans.

26 But [a]an angel of the Lord spoke to [b]Philip saying, "Arise and go south to the road that descends from Jerusalem to [c]Gaza." ([1]This is a desert *road*.)

27 And he arose and went; and behold, [a]there was an Ethiopian eunuch, a court official of Candace, queen of the Ethiopians, who was in charge of all her treasure; and he [b]had come to Jerusalem to worship.

28 And he was returning and sitting in his [1]chariot, and was reading the prophet Isaiah.

29 And [a]the Spirit said to Philip, "Go up and join this [1]chariot."

30 And when Philip had run up, he heard him reading Isaiah the prophet, and said, "Do you understand what you are reading?"

31 And he said, "Well, how could I, unless someone guides me?" And he invited Philip to come up and sit with him.

32 Now the passage of Scripture which he was reading was this:

"[a]HE WAS LED AS A SHEEP TO SLAUGHTER;
AND AS A LAMB BEFORE ITS SHEARER IS SILENT,
SO HE DOES NOT OPEN HIS MOUTH.

33 "[a]IN HUMILIATION HIS JUDGMENT WAS TAKEN AWAY;
WHO SHALL [1]RELATE HIS [2]GENERATION?
FOR HIS LIFE IS REMOVED FROM THE EARTH."

34 And the eunuch answered Philip and said, "Please *tell me*, of whom does the prophet say this? Of himself, or of someone else?"

35 And Philip [a]opened his mouth, and [b]beginning from this Scripture he [c]preached Jesus to him.

36 And as they went along the road they came to some water; and the eunuch *said, "Look! Water! [a]What prevents me from being baptized?"

37 [[1]And Philip said, "If you believe with all your heart, you may." And he answered and said, "I believe that Jesus Christ is the Son of God."]

38 And he ordered the [1]chariot to stop; and they both went down into the water, Philip as well as the eunuch; and he baptized him.

39 And when they came up out of the water, [a]the Spirit of the Lord snatched Philip away; and the eunuch saw him no more, but went on his way rejoicing.

40 But Philip [1]found himself at [2a]Azotus; and as he passed through he [b]kept preaching the gospel to all the cities, until he came to [c]Caesarea.

The Conversion of Saul

9 [a]NOW Saul, still [b]breathing [1]threats and murder against the disciples of the Lord, went to the high priest,

2 and asked for [a]letters from him to [b]the synagogues at [c]Damascus, so that if he found any belonging to [d]the Way, both men and women, he might bring them bound to Jerusalem.

3 And it came about that as he journeyed, he was approaching Damascus, and [a]suddenly a light from heaven flashed around him;

4 and [a]he fell to the ground, and heard a voice saying to him, "Saul, Saul, why are you persecuting Me?"

5 And he said, "Who art Thou, Lord?" And He *said*, "I am Jesus whom you are persecuting,

6 but rise, and enter the city, and [a]it shall be told you what you must do."

7 And the men who traveled with him [a]stood speechless, [b]hearing the [1]voice, but seeing no one.

8 And Saul got up from the ground, and [a]though his eyes were open, he [1]could see nothing; and leading him by the hand, they brought him into [b]Damascus.

9 And he was three days without sight, and neither ate nor drank.

10 Now there was a certain disciple at [a]Damascus, named [b]Ananias; and the Lord said to him in [c]a vision, "Ananias." And he said, "Behold, *here am* I, Lord."

11 And the Lord *said* to him, "Arise and go to the street called Straight, and inquire at the house of Judas for a man from [a]Tarsus named Saul, for behold, he is praying,

12 and he has seen [1]in a vision a man named Ananias come in and [a]lay his hands on him, so that he might regain his sight."

13 But Ananias answered, "Lord, I have heard from many about this man, [a]how much harm he did to [b]Thy [1]saints at Jerusalem;

14 and here he [a]has authority from the chief priests to bind all who [b]call upon Thy name."

15 But the Lord said to him, "Go, for [a]he is a chosen [1]instrument of Mine, to bear My name before [b]the Gentiles and [c]kings and the sons of Israel;

23 [1]Or, *fetter* [a]Is. 58:6
24 [a]Gen. 20:7; Ex. 8:8; Num. 21:7; James 5:16
25 [a]Luke 16:28 [b]Acts 13:12 [c]Acts 8:40 [d]Matt. 10:5
26 [1]Or, *This city is deserted* [a]Acts 5:19; 8:29 [b]Acts 8:5 [c]Gen. 10:19
27 [a]Ps. 68:31; 87:4; Is. 56:3ff. [b]1 Kin. 8:41f.; John 12:20
28 [1]Or, *carriage*
29 [1]Or, *carriage* [a]Acts 8:39; 10:19; 11:12; 13:2; 16:6, 7; 20:23; 21:11; 28:25; Heb. 3:7
32 [a]Is. 53:7
33 [1]Or, *describe* [2]Or, *family* or *origin* [a]Is. 53:8
35 [a]Matt. 5:2 [b]Luke 24:27; Acts 17:2; 18:28; 28:23 [c]Acts 5:42
36 [a]Acts 10:47
37 [1]Many mss. do not contain this v.
38 [1]Or, *carriage*
39 [a]1 Kin. 18:12; 2 Kin. 2:16; Ezek. 3:12, 14; 8:3; 11:1, 24; 43:5; 2 Cor. 12:2
40 [1]Or, *was found* [2]O.T.: Ashdod [a]Josh. 11:22; 1 Sam. 5:1 [b]Acts 8:25 [c]Acts 9:30; 10:1, 24; 11:11; 12:19; 18:22; 21:8, 16; 23:23, 33; 25:1, 4, 6, 13

1 [1]Lit., *threat* [a]Acts 9:1-22; 22:3-16; 26:9-18 [b]Acts 8:3; 9:13-21
2 [a]Acts 9:14, 21; 22:5; 26:10 [b]Matt. 10:17 [c]Gen. 14:15; 2 Cor. 11:32; Gal. 1:17 [d]John 14:6; Acts 18:25f.; 19:9, 23; 22:4; 24:14, 22
3 [a]1 Cor. 15:8
4 [a]Acts 22:7; 26:14
6 [a]Acts 9:16
7 [1]Or, *sound* [a]Acts 26:14 [b]John 12:29f.; Acts 22:9
8 [1]Lit., *was seeing* [a]Acts 9:18; 22:11 [b]Gen. 14:15; 2 Cor. 11:32; Gal. 1:17
10 [a]Gen. 14:15; 2 Cor. 11:32; Gal. 1:17 [b]Acts 22:12 [c]Acts 10:3, 17, 19; 11:5; 12:9; 16:9f.; 18:9
11 [a]Acts 9:30; 11:25; 21:39; 22:3
12 [1]Some mss. do not contain *in a vision* [a]Mark 5:23; Acts 6:6; 9:17
13 [1]Or, *holy ones* [a]Acts 8:3 [b]Acts 9:32, 41; 26:10; Rom. 1:7; 15:25, 26, 31; 16:2, 15; 1 Cor. 1:2
14 [a]Acts 9:2, 21 [b]Acts 7:59

15 [1]Or, *vessel* [a]Acts 13:2; Rom. 1:1; 9:23; Gal. 1:15; Eph. 3:7 [b]Acts 22:21; 26:17; Rom. 1:5; 11:13; 15:16; Gal. 1:16; 2:7ff.; Eph. 3:1, 8; 1 Tim. 2:7; 2 Tim. 4:17 [c]Acts 25:22f.; 26:1, 32; 2 Tim. 4:17

16 for [a]I will show him how much he
must suffer for My name's sake."
17 And Ananias departed and entered
the house, and after [a]laying his hands on
him said, "[b]Brother Saul, the Lord Jesus,
who appeared to you on the road by
which you were coming, has sent me so
that you may regain your sight, and be
[c]filled with the Holy Spirit."
18 And immediately there fell from
his eyes something like scales, and he
regained his sight, and he arose and was
baptized;
19 and he took food and was
strengthened.

Saul Begins to Preach Christ

Now [a]for several days he was with [b]the
disciples who were at Damascus,
20 and immediately he *began* to proclaim Jesus [a]in the synagogues, [1]saying,
"He is [b]the Son of God."
21 And all those hearing him continued to be amazed, and were saying, "Is
this not he who in Jerusalem [a]destroyed
those who [b]called on this name, and *who*
had come here for the purpose of bringing them bound before the chief
priests?"
22 But Saul kept increasing in
strength and confounding the Jews who
lived at Damascus by proving that this
Jesus is the [1]Christ.
23 And when [a]many days had elapsed,
[b]the Jews plotted together to do away
with him,
24 but [a]their plot became known to
Saul. And [b]they were also watching the
gates day and night so that they might
put him to death;
25 but his disciples took him by night,
and let him down through *an opening in*
the wall, lowering him in a large basket.
26 And [a]when he had come to Jerusalem, he was trying to associate with the
disciples; and they were all afraid of
him, not believing that he was a disciple.
27 But [a]Barnabas took hold of him
and brought him to the apostles and
described to them how he had [b]seen the
Lord on the road, and that He had
talked to him, and how [c]at Damascus he
had [d]spoken out boldly in the name of
Jesus.
28 And he was with them [1]moving
about freely in Jerusalem, [a]speaking out
boldly in the name of the Lord.
29 And he was talking and arguing
with the [a]Hellenistic *Jews;* but they were
attempting to put him to death.
30 But when [a]the brethren learned *of*
it, they brought him down to [b]Caesarea
and [c]sent him away to [d]Tarsus.
31 So [a]the church throughout all Judea and Galilee and Samaria [1]enjoyed
peace, being built up; and, going on in
the fear of the Lord and in the comfort
of the Holy Spirit, it continued to increase.

Peter's Ministry

32 Now it came about that as Peter
was traveling through all *those parts,* he
came down also to [a]the [1]saints who lived
at [2b]Lydda.
33 And there he found a certain man
named Aeneas, who had been bedridden
eight years, for he was paralyzed.
34 And Peter said to him, "Aeneas,
Jesus Christ heals you; arise, and make
your bed." And immediately he arose.
35 And all who lived at [1a]Lydda and
[b]Sharon saw him, and they [c]turned to
the Lord.
36 Now in [a]Joppa there was a certain
disciple named Tabitha (which translated *in Greek* is called [1]Dorcas); this
woman was abounding with deeds of
kindness and charity, which she continually did.
37 And it came about [1]at that time
that she fell sick and died; and when
they had washed her body, they laid it in
an [a]upper room.
38 And since Lydda was near [a]Joppa,
[b]the disciples, having heard that Peter
was there, sent two men to him, entreating him, "Do not delay to come to us."
39 And Peter arose and went with
them. And when he had come, they
brought him into the [a]upper room; and
all the [b]widows stood beside him weeping, and showing all the [1]tunics and
garments that Dorcas used to make
while she was with them.
40 But Peter [a]sent them all out and
[b]knelt down and prayed, and turning to
the body, he said, "[c]Tabitha, arise." And
she opened her eyes, and when she saw
Peter, she sat up.
41 And he gave her his hand and
raised her up; and calling [a]the [1]saints
and [b]widows, he presented her alive.
42 And it became known all over
[a]Joppa, and [b]many believed in the Lord.
43 And it came about that he stayed
many days in [a]Joppa with [b]a certain
tanner, Simon.

Cornelius' Vision

10 NOW *there was* a certain man at
[a]Caesarea named Cornelius, a
centurion of what was [b]called the Italian
[1]cohort,
2 a devout man, and [a]one who feared
God with all his household, and [b]gave
many [1]alms to the *Jewish* people, and
prayed to God continually.
3 About [a]the [1]ninth hour of the day
he clearly saw [b]in a vision [c]an angel of
God who had *just* come in to him, and
said to him, "Cornelius!"
4 And [a]fixing his gaze upon him and
being much alarmed, he said, "What is
it, Lord?" And he said to him, "Your
prayers and [1]alms [b]have ascended [c]as a
memorial before God.

16 [a]Acts 20:23; 21:4, 11, 13; 2 Cor. 6:4f.; 11:23-27; 1 Thess. 3:3
17 [a]Mark 5:23; Acts 6:6; 9:12 [b]Acts 22:13 [c]Acts 2:4
19 [a]Acts 26:20 [b]Acts 9:26, 38; 11:26
20 [1]Lit., *that* [a]Acts 13:5, 14; 14:1; 16:13; 17:2, 10; 18:4, 19; 19:8 [b]Matt. 4:3; Acts 9:22; 13:33
21 [a]Acts 8:3; 9:13; Gal. 1:13, 23 [b]Acts 9:14
22 [1]I.e., Messiah
23 [a]Gal. 1:17, 18 [b]1 Thess. 2:16
24 [a]Acts 20:3, 19; 23:12, 30; 25:3 [b]2 Cor. 11:32f.
26 [a]Acts 22:17-20; 26:20
27 [a]Acts 4:36 [b]Acts 9:3-6 [c]Acts 9:20, 22 [d]Acts 4:13, 29; 9:29
28 [1]Lit., *going in and going out* [a]Acts 4:13, 29; 9:29
29 [a]Acts 6:1
30 [a]Acts 1:15 [b]Acts 8:40 [c]Gal. 1:21 [d]Acts 9:11
31 [1]Lit., *was having* [a]Acts 5:11; 8:1; 16:5
32 [1]Or, *holy ones* [2]I.e., Lod [a]Acts 9:13 [b]1 Chr. 8:12; Ezra 2:33; Neh. 7:37; 11:35
35 [1]I.e., Lod [a]1 Chr. 8:12; Ezra 2:33; Neh. 7:37; 11:35 [b]1 Chr. 5:16; 27:29; Is. 33:9; 35:2; 65:10 [c]Acts 2:47; 9:42; 11:21
36 [1]Or, *Gazelle* [a]Josh. 19:46; 2 Chr. 2:16; Ezra 3:7; Jon. 1:3; Acts 9:38, 42f.; 10:5, 8, 23, 32; 11:5, 13
37 [1]Lit., *in those days* [a]Acts 1:13; 9:39
38 [a]Josh. 19:46; 2 Chr. 2:16; Ezra 3:7; Jon. 1:3; Acts 9:36, 42f.; 10:5, 8, 23, 32; 11:5, 13 [b]Acts 11:26
39 [1]Or, *inner garments* [a]Acts 1:13; 9:37 [b]Acts 6:1
40 [a]Matt. 9:25 [b]Luke 22:41; Acts 7:60 [c]Mark 5:41
41 [1]Or, *holy ones* [a]Acts 9:13, 32 [b]Acts 6:1
42 [a]Josh. 19:46; 2 Chr. 2:16; Jon. 1:3; Acts 9:38, 42f.; 10:5, 8, 23, 32; 11:5, 13 [b]Acts 9:35
43 [a]Josh. 19:46; 2 Chr. 2:16; Ezra 3:7; Jon. 1:3; Acts 9:38, 42f.; 10:5, 8, 23, 32; 11:13, 15 [b]Acts 10:6

1 [1]Or, *battalion* [a]Acts 8:40; 10:24 [b]Matt. 27:27; Mark 15:16; John 18:3, 12; Acts 21:31; 27:1
2 [1]Or, *gifts of charity* [a]Acts 10:22, 35; 13:16, 26 [b]Luke 7:4f.

3 [1]I.e., 3 p.m. [a]Acts 3:1 [b]Acts 9:10; 10:17, 19 [c]Acts 5:19
4 [1]Or, *deeds of charity* [a]Acts 3:4 [b]Rev. 8:4 [c]Matt. 26:13; Phil. 4:18; Heb. 6:10

5"And now dispatch *some* men to [a]Joppa, and send for a man *named* Simon, who is also called Peter;

6 he [1]is staying with a certain tanner *named* [a]Simon, whose house is by the sea."

7 And when the angel who was speaking to him had departed, he summoned two of his [1]servants and a devout soldier of those who were in constant attendance upon him,

8 and after he had explained everything to them, he sent them to [a]Joppa.

9 And on the next day, as they were on their way, and approaching the city, [a]Peter went up on [b]the housetop about [c]the [1]sixth hour to pray.

10 And he became hungry, and was desiring to eat; but while they were making preparations, he [a]fell into a trance;

11 and he *beheld [a]the [1]sky opened up, and a certain [2]object like a great sheet coming down, lowered by four corners to the ground,

12 and there were in it all *kinds of* four-footed animals and [1]crawling creatures of the earth and birds of the [2]air.

13 And a voice came to him, "Arise, Peter, [1]kill and eat!"

14 But Peter said, "By no means, [a]Lord, for [b]I have never eaten anything [1]unholy and unclean."

15 And again a voice *came* to him a second time, "[a]What God has cleansed, no *longer* consider [1]unholy."

16 And this happened three times; and immediately the [1]object was taken up into the [2]sky.

17 Now while Peter was greatly perplexed [1]in mind as to what [a]the vision which he had seen might be, behold, [b]the men who had been sent by Cornelius, having asked directions for Simon's house, appeared at the gate;

18 and calling out, they were asking whether Simon, who was also called Peter, was [1]staying there.

19 And while Peter was reflecting on [a]the vision, [b]the Spirit said to him, "Behold, [1]three men are looking for you.

20"But arise, go downstairs, and [a]accompany them [1]without misgivings; for I have sent them Myself."

21 And Peter went down to the men and said, "Behold, I am the one you are looking for; what is the reason for which you have come?"

22 And they said, "Cornelius, a centurion, a righteous and [a]God-fearing man well spoken of by the entire nation of the Jews, [b]was *divinely* directed by a [c]holy angel to send for you *to come* to his house and hear [1d]a message from you."

23 And so he invited them in and gave them lodging.

Peter at Caesarea

And on the next day he arose and went away with them, and [a]some of [b]the brethren from [c]Joppa accompanied him.

24 And on the following day he entered [a]Caesarea. Now Cornelius was waiting for them, and had called together his relatives and close friends.

25 And when it came about that Peter entered, Cornelius met him, and fell at his feet and [1a]worshiped *him.*

26 But Peter raised him up, saying, "[a]Stand up; I too am *just* a man."

27 And as he talked with him, he entered, and [1]found [a]many people assembled.

28 And he said to them, "You yourselves know how [a]unlawful it is for a man who is a Jew to associate with a foreigner or to visit him; and *yet* [b]God has shown me that I should not call any man [1]unholy or unclean.

29"That is why I came without even raising any objection when I was sent for. And so I ask for what reason you have sent for me."

30 And Cornelius said, "[a]Four days ago to this hour, I was praying in my house during [b]the [1]ninth hour; and behold, [c]a man stood before me in shining garments,

31 and he *said, 'Cornelius, your prayer has been heard and your [1]alms have been remembered before God.

32 'Send therefore to [a]Joppa and invite Simon, who is also called Peter, to come to you; he is [1]staying at the house of Simon *the* tanner by the sea.'

33"And so I sent to you immediately, and you have [1]been kind enough to come. Now then, we are all here present before God to hear all that you have been commanded by the Lord."

Gentiles Hear Good News

34 And [a]opening his mouth, Peter said:

"I most certainly understand *now* that [b]God is not one to show partiality,

35 but [a]in every nation the man who [1b]fears Him and [2]does what is right, is welcome to Him.

36"[1]The word which He sent to the sons of Israel, [a]preaching [2b]peace through Jesus Christ (He is [c]Lord of all)—

37 you yourselves know the thing which took place throughout all Judea, starting from Galilee, after the baptism which John proclaimed.

38"[1]*You know of* [a]Jesus of Nazareth, how God [b]anointed Him with the Holy Spirit and with power, [2c]and *how* He went about doing good, and healing all who were oppressed by the devil; for [d]God was with Him.

5 [a]Acts 9:36
6 [1]Or, *is lodging* [a]Acts 9:43
7 [1]Or, *household slaves*
8 [a]Acts 9:36
9 [1]I.e., noon [a]Acts 10:9-32; 11:5-14 [b]Jer. 19:13; 32:29; Zeph. 1:5; Matt. 24:17 [c]Ps. 55:17; Acts 10:3
10 [a]Acts 11:5; 22:17
11 [1]Or, *heaven* [2]Or, *vessel* [a]John 1:51
12 [1]Or possibly, *reptiles* [2]Or, *heaven*
13 [1]Or, *sacrifice*
14 [1]Or, *profane;* lit., *common* [a]Matt. 8:2ff.; John 4:11ff.; Acts 9:5; 22:8 [b]Lev. 11:20-25; Deut. 14:4-20; Ezek. 4:14; Dan. 1:8; Acts 10:28
15 [1]Lit., *common* [a]Matt. 15:11; Mark 7:19; Rom. 14:14; 1 Cor. 10:25ff.; 1 Tim. 4:4f.; Titus 1:15
16 [1]Or, *vessel* [2]Or, *heaven*
17 [1]Lit., *himself* [a]Acts 10:3 [b]Acts 10:8
18 [1]Or, *lodging*
19 [1]One early ms. reads *two* [a]Acts 10:3 [b]Acts 8:29
20 [1]Lit., *doubting nothing* [a]Acts 15:7-9
22 [1]Lit., *words* [a]Acts 10:2 [b]Matt. 2:12 [c]Mark 8:38; Luke 9:26; Rev. 14:10 [d]Acts 11:14
23 [a]Acts 10:45; 11:12 [b]Acts 1:15 [c]Acts 9:36
24 [a]Acts 8:40; 10:1
25 [1]Or, *prostrated himself in reverence* [a]Matt. 8:2
26 [a]Acts 14:15; Rev. 19:10; 22:8f.
27 [1]Lit., *finds* [a]Acts 10:24
28 [1]Or, *profane;* lit., *common* [a]John 4:9; 18:28; Acts 11:3 [b]Acts 10:14f., 35; 15:9
30 [1]I.e., 3 to 4 p.m. [a]Acts 10:9, 22f. [b]Acts 3:1; 10:3 [c]Acts 10:3-6, 30-32
31 [1]Or, *deeds of charity*
32 [1]Or, *lodging* [a]John 4:9; 18:28; Acts 11:3
33 [1]Lit., *done well in coming*
34 [a]Matt. 5:2 [b]Deut. 10:17; 2 Chr. 19:7; Rom. 2:11; Gal. 2:6; Eph. 6:9; Col. 3:25; 1 Pet. 1:17
35 [1]Or, *reverences* [2]Lit., *works righteousness* [a]Acts 10:28 [b]Acts 10:2

36 [1]Some mss. read *He sent the word to* [2]Or, *the gospel of peace* [a]Acts 13:32 [b]Luke 1:79; 2:14; Rom. 5:1; Eph. 2:17 [c]Matt. 28:18; Acts 2:36; Rom. 10:12
38 [1]Or possibly, *How God anointed Jesus of Nazareth* [2]Lit., *who went* [a]Acts 2:22 [b]Acts 4:26 [c]Matt. 4:23 [d]John 3:2

39"And we are [a]witnesses of all the
things He did both in the [1]land of the
Jews and in Jerusalem. And they also
[b]put Him to death by hanging Him on a
[2]cross.
40"[a]God raised Him up on the third
day, and granted that He should become
visible,
41 [a]not to all the people, but to [b]wit-
nesses who were chosen beforehand by
God, *that is,* to us, [c]who ate and drank
with Him after He arose from the dead.
42"And He [a]ordered us to [1]preach to
the people, and solemnly to [b]testify that
this is the One who has been [c]appointed
by God as [d]Judge of the living and the
dead.
43"Of Him [a]all the prophets bear
witness that through [b]His name everyone who believes in Him receives forgiveness of sins."
44 While Peter was still speaking these
words, [a]the Holy Spirit fell upon all
those who were listening to the [1]mes-
sage.
45 And [a]all the [1]circumcised believers
who had come with Peter were amazed,
because the gift of the Holy Spirit had
been [b]poured out upon the Gentiles also.
46 For they were hearing them [a]speak-
ing with tongues and exalting God. Then
Peter answered,
47"[a]Surely no one can refuse the water
for these to be baptized who [b]have
received the Holy Spirit just as we *did,*
can he?"
48 And he [a]ordered them to be baptized [b]in the name of Jesus Christ. Then
they asked him to stay on for a few days.

Peter Reports at Jerusalem

11 NOW the apostles and [a]the
brethren who were throughout
Judea heard that the Gentiles also had
received the word of God.
2 And when Peter came up to Jerusalem, [1a]those who were circumcised took
issue with him,
3 saying, "[a]You [1]went to uncircumcised men and ate with them."
4 But Peter began *speaking* and *proceeded* to explain to them [a]in orderly
sequence, saying,
5"[a]I was in the city of Joppa praying;
and in a trance I saw [b]a vision, a certain
[1]object coming down like a great sheet
lowered by four corners from [2]the sky;
and it came right down to me,
6 and when I had fixed my gaze upon
it and was observing it [1]I saw the four-
footed animals of the earth and the wild
beasts and the [2]crawling creatures and
the birds of the [3]air.
7"And I also heard a voice saying to
me, 'Arise, Peter; [1]kill and eat.'
8"But I said, 'By no means, Lord, for
nothing [1]unholy or unclean has ever
entered my mouth.'
9"But a voice from heaven answered
a second time, '[a]What God has cleansed,
no longer [1]consider unholy.'
10"And this happened three times, and
everything was drawn back up into [1]the
sky.
11"And behold, at that moment three
men appeared before the house in which
we were *staying,* having been sent to me
from [a]Caesarea.
12"And [a]the Spirit told me to go with
them [1b]without misgivings. And [c]these
six brethren also went with me, and we
entered the man's house.
13"And he reported to us how he had
seen the angel [1]standing in his house,
and saying, 'Send to Joppa, and have
Simon, who is also called Peter, brought
here;
14 and he shall speak [a]words to you
by which you will be saved, you and [b]all
your household.'
15"And as I began to speak, [a]the Holy
Spirit fell upon them, just [b]as *He did*
upon us at the beginning.
16"And I remembered the word of the
Lord, how He used to say, '[a]John baptized with water, but you shall be baptized [1]with the Holy Spirit.'
17"If [a]God therefore gave to them the
same gift as *He gave* to us also after
believing in the Lord Jesus Christ, [b]who
was I that I could [1]stand in God's way?"
18 And when they heard this, they
[1]quieted down, and [a]glorified God, saying, "Well then, God has granted to the
Gentiles also the [b]repentance *that leads*
to life."

The Church at Antioch

19 [a]So then those who were scattered
because of the [1]persecution that arose in
connection with Stephen made their way
[2]to [b]Phoenicia and [c]Cyprus and [d]Anti-
och, speaking the word to no one except
to Jews alone.
20 But there were some of them, men
of [a]Cyprus and [b]Cyrene, who came to
[c]Antioch and *began* speaking to the
[1d]Greeks also, [2e]preaching the Lord
Jesus.
21 And [a]the hand of the Lord was
with them, and [b]a large number who
believed turned to the Lord.
22 And the [1]news about them
[2]reached the ears of the church at Jerusalem, and they sent [a]Barnabas off [3]to
[b]Antioch.
23 Then when he had come and [1]wit-
nessed [a]the grace of God, he rejoiced
and *began* to encourage them all with
[2]resolute heart to remain *true* to the
Lord;

39 [1]Or, *countryside* [2]Lit., *wood* [a]Luke 24:48; Acts 10:41 [b]Acts 5:30
40 [a]Acts 2:24
41 [a]John 14:19, 22; 15:27 [b]Luke 24:48; Acts 10:39 [c]Luke 24:43; Acts 1:4 mg.
42 [1]Or, *proclaim* [a]Acts 1:2 [b]Luke 16:28 [c]Luke 22:22 [d]John 5:22, 27; Acts 17:31; 2 Tim. 4:1; 1 Pet. 4:5
43 [a]Acts 3:18 [b]Luke 24:47; Acts 2:38; 4:12
44 [1]Lit., *word* [a]Acts 11:15; 15:8
45 [1]Lit., *believers from among the circumcision;* i.e., Jewish Christians [a]Acts 10:23 [b]Acts 2:33, 38
46 [a]Mark 16:17; Acts 2:4; 19:6
47 [a]Acts 8:36 [b]Acts 2:4; 10:44f.; 11:17; 15:8
48 [a]1 Cor. 1:14-17 [b]Acts 2:38; 8:16; 19:5

1 [a]Acts 1:15
2 [1]Lit., *those of the circumcision;* i.e., Jewish Christians [a]Acts 10:45
3 [1]Or, *entered the house of* [a]Matt. 9:11; Acts 10:28; Gal. 2:12
4 [a]Luke 1:3
5 [1]Or, *vessel* [2]Or, *heaven* [a]Acts 10:9-32; 11:5-14 [b]Acts 9:10
6 [1]Lit., *and I saw* [2]Or possibly, *reptiles* [3]Or, *heaven*
7 [1]Or, *sacrifice*
8 [1]Or, *profane;* lit., *common*
9 [1]Lit., *make common* [a]Acts 10:15
10 [1]Or, *heaven*
11 [a]Acts 8:40
12 [1]Or, *without making any distinction* [a]Acts 8:29 [b]Acts 15:9; Rom. 3:22 [c]Acts 10:23
13 [1]Or, *after he had stood in his house and said*
14 [a]Acts 10:22 [b]John 4:53; Acts 10:2; 16:15, 31-34; 18:8; 1 Cor. 1:16
15 [a]Acts 10:44 [b]Acts 2:4
16 [1]Or, *in* [a]Acts 1:5
17 [1]Or, *prevent God* [a]Acts 10:45, 47 [b]Acts 5:39
18 [1]Lit., *became silent* [a]Matt. 9:8 [b]2 Cor. 7:10
19 [1]Or, *tribulation* [2]Lit., *as far as* [a]Acts 8:1, 4 [b]Acts 15:3; 21:2 [c]Acts 4:36 [d]Acts 6:5; 11:20, 22, 27; 13:1; 14:26; 15:22f., 30, 35; 18:22; Gal. 2:11

20 [1]Some mss. read *Greek-speaking Jews* [2]Or, *bringing the good news of* [a]Acts 4:36 [b]Matt. 27:32; Acts 2:10; 6:9; 13:1 [c]Acts 6:5; 11:19, 22, 27; 13:1; 14:26; 15:22f., 30, 35; 18:22; Gal. 2:11 [d]John 7:35 [e]Acts 5:42
21 [a]Luke 1:66 [b]Acts 2:47
22 [1]Lit., *word* [2]Lit., *was heard in* [3]Lit., *as far as* [a]Acts 4:36 [b]Acts 6:5; 11:19, 20, 27; 13:1; 18:22; Gal. 2:11
23 [1]Lit., *seen* [2]Lit., *purpose of heart* [a]Acts 13:43; 14:26; 15:40; 20:24, 32

PROPERTY RIGHTS

Matthew 13:44. As part of the laws of property, everything buried on the land belonged to the person who purchased it. This lies behind Jesus' illustration of the truth that it is sometimes worthwhile giving everything; you have for something supremely good. It was quite common to bury the family treasure in one's land in time of war or exile, which led to the common practice of digging for treasure (Job 3:20-21; Proverbs 2:3-5).

"HOME"

To a nomad, a home is not a place of possession because it is moved from place to place; rather it is a place of welcome. When the British government drew up the Balfour Declaration and said that Palestine was to be a *"homeland"* for the Jews, the Arab people understood it to mean a place where they would welcome their guests. The Jews, on the other hand, look upon home and land as a possession, and they therefore understood homeland in the Balfour Declaration to mean a place for possession. Much of the original Arab/Israeli misunderstanding was based upon these different understandings of the word *homeland.* The nomadic idea of a home as a shelter is reflected in passages that describe God as a shelter (Psalm 61:3-4; Isaiah 4:6, *"it will be a shelter and shade from the heat of the day, and a refuge and hiding-place from the storm and rain").*

THE OPEN DOOR

Revelation 3:8. *"I have placed before you an open door."* This refers to a house in the country. To have it shut would indicate that it was nighttime (compare Luke 11:7) or that people were not there. It therefore means that God is always available; it has nothing to do with opportunity.

LIGHT IN THE DARKNESS

Isaiah 42:3. Light in the dark peasant home was a necessity. To sleep without a light was a sign of utter poverty. The light indicated to all outside that there were sleepers present. For anyone to be put outside into the darkness was therefore a disaster (Job 18:6). For God to light one's lamp was a supreme blessing (Psalm 18:28). Therefore when Isaiah says that the Messiah will not put out a lamp if the flax is smoking, but will trim the wick and replenish the oil, it is a comforting picture of God's care for wayward followers.

CHARCOAL FIRES

John 18:18; 21:9. Charcoal has a particularly pungent smell. It is referred to only on these two occasions in the New Testament. At the first, Peter was warming his hands at a charcoal fire when he denied Jesus three times. Jesus made the second charcoal fire on the shore of

Galilee. It must have stirred up Peter's conscience!

HEALING THE PARALYTIC

Mark 2:4; Luke 5:19. It has often been assumed that the four friends who brought their paralytic friend to Jesus broke through the mud and brushwood roof to let him down. This assumes that the roof was easily repaired. The tiles Luke refers to would then be sun-baked mud. But Luke was writing to a Roman who knew about Roman tiling. It is therefore more likely that Jesus was talking under a colonnade/ veranda attached to the house, and that the friends, having gained access to the roof, stripped off some of the tiling of the colonnade.

SALT UNDER FOOT

Matthew 5:13. When salt was collected from the Dead Sea area, some of it was good for salting and cooking, but other salt had lost its saltiness. This salt was not thrown away, however. It was stored in the Jerusalem Temple, and when the winter rains made the marble courtyards slippery, it was spread on them to reduce the slipperiness. Hence salt that has lost its saltiness is trodden under foot of men.

LOCUSTS–OR LOCUST BEANS?

Matthew 3:4. It was perfectly all right under the food laws to eat locusts (Leviticus 11:22). It is much more likely, however, as locusts were not readily available all the time, and John the Baptist had to eat daily, that locust beans are being referred to. These beans (carob pods) are sweet and sticky. The prodigal son was also glad to eat the same food (Luke 15:16).

MEAT WITHOUT BLOOD

Acts 15:29. The first-century Christians were encouraged to follow the Jewish food laws concerning the draining of the blood from the animal. It is difficult to know for sure why the Jews were forbidden to eat blood. If might have been purely ritual because life and blood are identified and the life belongs to God (Leviticus 17:14); the blood was therefore used as a means of atonement with God.

The prohibition against eating blood might have been based on an earlier practice that was intensely cruel. Because meat would not keep, some tribespeople cut parts from an animal and then kept the animal alive until more meat was required. The draining of blood prevented such practices. The prohibition might have been a health law to prevent blood-borne infections and diseases.

TIMOTHY *- faithful*

Timothy was a teenager when he began working with Paul. Though it is unusual for such a young man to have been in such a position, he had proven he was faithful.

From the Bible, we know that Timothy's mother and grandmother were Christians. We also knew that Timothy was saved while a young boy and began studying the bible. He was developing the strength he would need later to serve God faithfully.

Paul returned to Lystra several years after Timothy was saved. By then, Timothy had a good reputation among his fellow believers. Paul wrote of him to the Philippians (Phil. 2:20) *"For I have no one else of kindred spirit who will genuinely be concerned for your welfare."* It is clear that Timothy's life centered not on himself, but on other people.

Timothy was chosen by Paul and Barnabas to accompany them on their mission trip, doing the menial tasks that allowed the ministry to function effectively. He replaced another young man, John Mark, who had returned home early. Apparently, John Mark had gone into God's service before he was completely prepared. However, later on he did indeed serve God mightily and wrote the book of Mark. But Timothy was ready to be a *"... soldier of Christ Jesus,"* as Paul called him in 2 Timothy 2:3. Timothy served the next twenty years with Paul, firmly devoted to God and effectively performing his duty.

Paul entrusted Timothy with the gospel, advising him to pass it on to trustworthy men who would continue to pass it on to others. Because of these faithful men, today we have the gospel and can pass it on.

Timothy was young, but he understood the importance of the message of Christ Jesus. Because he gave it the highest importance in his life, he was able to serve God from his youth until his death as a martyr for Christ.

QUESTIONS

1. Timothy developed spiritually from childhood. What are you doing now to train yourself for the service God has for you?

2. Timothy was focused on the importance of the Gospel of Christ and remained true to it. Are there times when your focus is on the things of this world? If so, what could you do to remain centered on Christ?

3. The true Word of God was what Timothy studied to grow in wisdom and knowledge. Have you ever gotten excited over an idea or philosophy, only to learn it was false knowledge. How can you guard yourself against false doctrine?

4. To live faithfully like Timothy, you must live what you believe. Do you ever violate your conscience with secret sin, believing no one will ever know? How can you deal with this to keep your heart from becoming divided?

24 for he was a good man, and [a]full of the Holy Spirit and of faith. And [b]considerable [1]numbers were [2]brought to the Lord.

25 And he left for [a]Tarsus to look for Saul;

26 and when he had found him, he brought him to [a]Antioch. And it came about that for an entire year they [1]met with the church, and taught considerable [2]numbers; and [b]the disciples were first called [c]Christians in [a]Antioch.

27 Now [1]at this time [a]some prophets came down from Jerusalem to [b]Antioch.

28 And one of them named [a]Agabus stood up and *began* to indicate [1]by the Spirit that there would certainly be a great famine [b]all over the [2]world. And this took place in the *reign* of [c]Claudius.

29 And in the proportion that any of [a]the disciples had means, each of them determined to send *a contribution* for the [1]relief of [b]the brethren living in Judea.

30 [a]And this they did, sending it [1]in charge of [b]Barnabas and Saul to the [c]elders.

Peter's Arrest and Deliverance

12 NOW about that time [1]Herod the king laid hands on some who belonged to the church, in order to mistreat them.

2 And he [a]had James the brother of John [b]put to death with a sword.

3 And when he saw that it [a]pleased the Jews, he proceeded to arrest Peter also. Now [1]it was during [b]the days of Unleavened Bread.

4 And when he had seized him, he put him in prison, delivering him to four [1a]squads of soldiers to guard him, intending after [b]the Passover to bring him out before the people.

5 So Peter was kept in the prison, but prayer for him was being made fervently by the church to God.

6 And on the very night when Herod was about to bring him forward, Peter was sleeping between two soldiers, [a]bound with two chains; and guards in front of the door were watching over the prison.

7 And behold, [a]an angel of the Lord suddenly [b]appeared, and a light shone in the cell; and he struck Peter's side and roused him, saying, "Get up quickly." And [c]his chains fell off his hands.

8 And the angel said to him, "Gird yourself and [1]put on your sandals." And he did so. And he *said to him, "Wrap your cloak around you and follow me."

9 And he went out and continued to follow, and he did not know that what was being done by the angel was real, but thought he was seeing [a]a vision.

10 And when they had passed the first and second guard, they came to the iron gate that leads into the city, which [a]opened for them by itself; and they went out and went along one street; and immediately the angel departed from him.

11 And when Peter [a]came to himself, he said, "Now I know for sure that [b]the Lord has sent forth His angel and rescued me from the hand of Herod and from all [1]that the Jewish people were expecting."

12 And when he realized *this,* he went to the house of Mary, the mother of [a]John who was also called Mark, where many were gathered together and [b]were praying.

13 And when he knocked at the door of the gate, [a]a servant-girl named Rhoda came to answer.

14 And when she recognized Peter's voice, [a]because of her joy she did not open the gate, but ran in and announced that Peter was standing in front of the gate.

15 And they said to her, "You are out of your mind!" But she kept insisting that it was so. And they kept saying, "It is [a]his angel."

16 But Peter continued knocking; and when they had opened *the door,* they saw him and were amazed.

17 But [a]motioning to them with his hand to be silent, he described to them how the Lord had led him out of the prison. And he said, "Report these things to [1b]James and [c]the brethren." And he departed and went to another place.

18 Now when day came, there was no small disturbance among the soldiers *as to* [1]what could have become of Peter.

19 And when Herod had searched for him and had not found him, he examined the guards and ordered that they [a]be led away *to execution.* And he went down from Judea to [b]Caesarea and was spending time there.

Death of Herod

20 Now he was very angry with the people of [a]Tyre and Sidon; and with one accord they came to him, and having won over Blastus the king's chamberlain, they were asking for peace, because [b]their country was fed by the king's country.

21 And on an appointed day Herod, having put on his royal apparel, took his seat on the [1]rostrum and *began* delivering an address to them.

22 And the people kept crying out, "The voice of a god and not of a man!"

23 And immediately [a]an angel of the Lord struck him because he did not give God the glory, and he was eaten by worms and [1]died.

24 But [a]the word of the Lord continued to grow and to be multiplied.

24 [1]Lit., *multitudes* [2]Lit., *added* [a]Acts 2:4 [b]Acts 2:47; 5:14; 11:21
25 [a]Acts 9:11
26 [1]Or, *were gathered together* [2]Lit., *multitude* [a]Acts 6:5; 11:20, 22, 27 [b]John 2:2; Acts 1:15 [c]Acts 26:28; 1 Pet. 4:16
27 [1]Lit., *in these days* [a]Luke 11:49; Acts 2:17; 13:1; 1 Cor. 12:10, 28f. [b]Acts 6:5; 11:20, 22, 26; 13:1; 14:26; 15:22f., 30, 35; 18:22; Gal. 2:11
28 [1]Or, *through* [2]Lit., *inhabited earth* [a]Acts 21:10 [b]Matt. 24:14 [c]Acts 18:2
29 [1]Lit., *service* [a]John 2:2; Acts 1:15; 6:1f.; 9:19, 25, 26, 38; 11:26; 13:52; 14:20, 22, 28 [b]Acts 11:1
30 [1]Lit., *through the hand of* [a]Acts 12:25 [b]Acts 4:36 [c]Acts 14:23; 15:2, 4, 6, 22f.; 16:4; 20:17; 21:18; 1 Tim. 5:17, 19; Titus 1:5; James 5:14; 1 Pet. 5:1; 2 John 1; 3 John 1

1 [1]I.e., Herod Agrippa I
2 [a]Matt. 4:21; 20:23 [b]Mark 10:39
3 [1]Lit., *they were the days* [a]Acts 24:27; 25:9 [b]Ex. 12:15; 23:15; Acts 20:6
4 [1]Lit., *quaternions;* one quaternion is composed of four soldiers [a]John 19:23 [b]Ex. 12:1-27; Mark 14:1; Acts 12:3
6 [a]Acts 21:33
7 [a]Acts 5:19 [b]Luke 2:9; 24:4 [c]Acts 16:26
8 [1]Lit., *bind*
9 [a]Acts 9:10
10 [a]Acts 5:19; 16:26
11 [1]Lit., *the expectation of the people of the Jews* [a]Luke 15:17 [b]Dan. 3:28; 6:22
12 [a]Acts 12:25; 13:5, 13; 15:37, 39; Col. 4:10; 2 Tim. 4:11; Philem. 24; 1 Pet. 5:13 [b]Acts 12:5
13 [a]John 18:16f.
14 [a]Luke 24:41
15 [a]Matt. 18:10
17 [1]Or, *Jacob* [a]Acts 13:16; 19:33; 21:40 [b]Mark 6:3; Acts 15:13; 21:18; 1 Cor. 15:7; Gal. 1:19; 2:9, 12 [c]Acts 1:15
18 [1]Lit., *what therefore had become*
19 [a]Acts 16:27; 27:42 [b]Acts 8:40
20 [a]Matt. 11:21 [b]1 Kin. 5:11; Ezra 3:7; Ezek. 27:17

21 [1]Or, *judgment seat*
23 [1]Lit., *breathed his last* [a]2 Sam. 24:16; 2 Kin. 19:35; Acts 5:19
24 [a]Acts 6:7; 19:20

25 And [a]Barnabas and [a]Saul returned [1]from Jerusalem [b]when they had fulfilled their [2]mission, taking along with *them* [c]John, who was also called Mark.

First Missionary Journey

13 NOW there were at [a]Antioch, in the [b]church that was *there*, [c]prophets and [d]teachers: [e]Barnabas, and Simeon who was called Niger, and Lucius of [f]Cyrene, and Manaen who had been brought up with [g]Herod the tetrarch, and Saul.

2 And while they were ministering to the Lord and fasting, [a]the Holy Spirit said, "Set apart for Me [b]Barnabas and Saul for [c]the work to which I have called them."

3 Then, when they had fasted and [a]prayed and [b]laid their hands on them, [c]they sent them away.

4 So, being [a]sent out by the Holy Spirit, they went down to Seleucia and from there they sailed to [b]Cyprus.

5 And when they reached Salamis, they *began* to proclaim the word of God in [a]the synagogues of the Jews; and they also had [b]John as their helper.

6 And when they had gone through the whole island as far as Paphos, they found a certain [a]magician, a Jewish [b]false prophet whose name was Bar-Jesus,

7 who was with the [a]proconsul, Sergius Paulus, a man of intelligence. This man summoned Barnabas and Saul and sought to hear the word of God.

8 But Elymas the [a]magician (for thus his name is translated) was opposing them, seeking to turn the [b]proconsul away from [c]the faith.

9 But Saul, who was also *known as* Paul, [1a]filled with the Holy Spirit, fixed his gaze upon him,

10 and said, "You who are full of all deceit and fraud, you [a]son of the devil, you enemy of all righteousness, will you not cease to make crooked [b]the straight ways of the Lord?

11 "And now, behold, [a]the hand of the Lord is upon you, and you will be blind and not see the sun for a time." And immediately a mist and a darkness fell upon him, and he went about seeking those who would lead him by the hand.

12 Then the [a]proconsul believed when he saw what had happened, being amazed at [b]the teaching of the Lord.

13 Now Paul and his companions put out to sea from [a]Paphos and came to [b]Perga in [c]Pamphylia; and [d]John left them and returned to Jerusalem.

14 But going on from Perga, they arrived at [a]Pisidian [b]Antioch, and on [c]the Sabbath day they went into [d]the synagogue and sat down.

15 And after [a]the reading of the Law and [b]the Prophets [c]the synagogue officials sent to them, saying, "Brethren, if you have any word of exhortation for the people, say it."

16 And Paul stood up, and [a]motioning with his hand, he said,

"Men of Israel, and [b]you who fear God, listen:

17 "The God of this people Israel [a]chose our fathers, and [1b]made the people great during their stay in the land of Egypt, and with an uplifted arm [c]He led them out from it.

18 "And for [a]a period of about forty years [b]He [1]put up with them in the wilderness.

19 "And [a]when He had destroyed [b]seven nations in the land of Canaan, He [c]distributed their land as an inheritance—*all of which took* [d]about four hundred and fifty years.

20 "And after these things He [a]gave *them* judges until [b]Samuel the prophet.

21 "And then they [a]asked for a king, and God gave them [b]Saul the son of Kish, a man of the tribe of Benjamin, for forty years.

22 "And after He had [a]removed him, He raised up David to be their king, concerning whom He also testified and said, '[b]I HAVE FOUND DAVID the son of Jesse, A MAN AFTER MY HEART, who will do all My [1]will.'

23 "[a]From the offspring of this man, [b]according to promise, God has brought to Israel [c]a Savior, Jesus,

24 after [a]John had proclaimed before [1]His coming a [b]baptism of repentance to all the people of Israel.

25 "And while John [a]was completing his course, [b]he kept saying, 'What do you suppose that I am? I am not *He*. But behold, one is coming after me the sandals of whose feet I am not worthy to untie.'

26 "Brethren, sons of Abraham's family, and those among you who fear God, to us the word of [a]this salvation is sent out.

27 "For those who live in Jerusalem, and their [a]rulers, [b]recognizing neither Him nor the [1]utterances of [c]the prophets which are [d]read every Sabbath, fulfilled *these* by condemning *Him*.

28 "And though they found no ground for *putting Him to* death, they [a]asked Pilate that He be [1]executed.

29 "And when they had [a]carried out all that was written concerning Him, [b]they took Him down from [c]the [1]cross and [d]laid Him in a tomb.

30 "But God [a]raised Him from the dead;

25 [1]Some ancient mss. read *to Jerusalem* [2]Lit., *ministry* [a]Acts 4:36; 13:1ff. [b]Acts 11:30 [c]Acts 12:12
1 [a]Acts 11:19 [b]Acts 11:26 [c]Acts 11:27; 15:32; 19:6; 21:9; 1 Cor. 11:4f.; 13:2, 8f.; 14:29, 32, 37 [d]Rom. 12:6f.; 1 Cor. 12:28f.; Eph. 4:11; James 3:1 [e]Acts 4:36 [f]Matt. 27:32; Acts 11:20 [g]Matt. 14:1
2 [a]Acts 8:29; 13:4 [b]Acts 4:36 [c]Acts 9:15
3 [a]Acts 1:24 [b]Acts 6:6 [c]Acts 13:4; 14:26
4 [a]Acts 13:2f. [b]Acts 4:36
5 [a]Acts 9:20; 13:14 [b]Acts 12:12
6 [a]Acts 8:9 [b]Matt. 7:15
7 [a]Acts 13:8, 12; 18:12; 19:38
8 [a]Acts 8:9 [b]Acts 13:7, 12; 18:12; 19:38 [c]Acts 6:7
9 [1]Or, *having just been filled* [a]Acts 2:4; 4:8
10 [a]Matt. 13:38; John 8:44 [b]Hos. 14:9; 2 Pet. 2:15
11 [a]Ex. 9:3; 1 Sam. 5:6f.; Job 19:21; Ps. 32:4; Heb. 10:31
12 [a]Acts 13:7, 8; 18:12; 19:38 [b]Acts 8:25; 13:49; 15:35f.; 19:10, 20
13 [a]Acts 13:6 [b]Acts 14:25 [c]Acts 2:10; 14:24; 15:38; 27:5 [d]Acts 12:12
14 [a]Acts 14:24 [b]Acts 14:19, 21; 2 Tim. 3:11 [c]Acts 13:42, 44; 16:13; 17:2; 18:4 [d]Acts 9:20; 13:5
15 [a]Acts 15:21; 2 Cor. 3:14f. [b]Acts 13:27 [c]Mark 5:22
16 [a]Acts 12:17 [b]Acts 10:2; 13:26
17 [1]Or, *exalted* [a]Ex. 6:1, 6; 13:14, 16; Deut. 7:6-8; Acts 7:17ff. [b]Ex. 1:7 [c]Ex. 12:51
18 [1]Some ancient mss. read *bore them up in His arms as a nurse in the wilderness* [a]Num. 14:34; Acts 7:36 [b]Deut. 1:31
19 [a]Acts 7:45 [b]Deut. 7:1 [c]Josh. 14:1; 19:51; Ps. 78:55 [d]Judg. 11:26; 1 Kin. 6:1
20 [a]Judg. 2:16 [b]1 Sam. 3:20; Acts 3:24
21 [a]1 Sam. 8:5 [b]1 Sam. 9:1f.; 10:1, 21
22 [1]Lit., *wills* [a]1 Sam. 15:23, 26, 28; 16:1, 13 [b]1 Sam. 13:14; Ps. 89:20; Acts 7:46
23 [a]Matt. 1:1 [b]Acts 13:32f. [c]Luke 2:11; John 4:42

24 [1]Lit., *the face of His entering* [a]Mark 1:1-4; Acts 1:22; 19:4 [b]Luke 3:3
25 [a]Acts 20:24 [b]Matt. 3:11; Mark 1:7; Luke 3:16; John 1:20, 27
26 [a]John 6:68; Acts 4:12; 5:20; 13:46; 28:28
27 [1]Lit., *voices* [a]Luke 23:13 [b]Acts 3:17 [c]Luke 24:27 [d]Acts 13:15
28 [1]Lit., *destroyed* [a]Matt. 27:22, 23; Mark 15:13, 14; Luke 23:21-23; John 19:15; Acts 3:14
29 [1]Lit., *wood* [a]Acts 26:22 [b]Luke 23:53 [c]Acts 5:30 [d]Matt. 27:57-61; Mark 15:42-47; Luke 23:50-56; John 19:38-42
30 [a]Acts 2:24; 13:33, 34, 37

31 and for many days [a]He appeared to
those who came up with Him from
Galilee to Jerusalem, the very ones who
are now [b]His witnesses to the people.
32 "And we [a]preach to you the good
news of [b]the promise made to the fathers,
33 that God has fulfilled this *promise*
[1]to our children in that He [a]raised up
Jesus, as it is also written in the second
Psalm, '[b]THOU ART MY SON; TODAY I
HAVE BEGOTTEN THEE.'
34 "*And as for the fact* that He [a]raised
Him up from the dead, no more to
return to decay, He has spoken in this
way: '[b]I WILL GIVE YOU THE HOLY *and*
SURE *blessings* OF DAVID.'
35 "Therefore He also says in another
Psalm, '[a]THOU WILT NOT [1]ALLOW THY
[2]HOLY ONE TO [3]UNDERGO DECAY.'
36 "For [a]David, after he had [1]served
[b]the purpose of God in his own generation, [c]fell asleep, and was laid among his
fathers, and [2]underwent decay;
37 but He whom God [a]raised did not
[1]undergo decay.
38 "Therefore let it be known to you,
brethren, that [a]through [1]Him forgiveness
of sins is proclaimed to you,
39 and through Him [a]everyone who
believes is [1]freed[2] from all things, from
which you could not be [1]freed through
the Law of Moses.
40 "Take heed therefore, so that the
thing spoken of [a]in the Prophets may
not come upon *you*:
41 '[a]BEHOLD, YOU SCOFFERS, AND
MARVEL, AND [1]PERISH;
FOR I AM ACCOMPLISHING A
WORK IN YOUR DAYS,
A WORK WHICH YOU WILL NEVER
BELIEVE, THOUGH SOMEONE
SHOULD DESCRIBE IT TO YOU.' "
42 And as [1]Paul and Barnabas were
going out, [2]the people kept begging that
these [3]things might be spoken to them
the next [a]Sabbath.
43 Now when *the meeting of* the synagogue had broken up, many of the Jews
and of the [a]God-fearing [1b]proselytes
followed Paul and Barnabas, who,
speaking to them, were urging them to
continue in [c]the grace of God.

Paul Turns to the Gentiles

44 And the next [a]Sabbath nearly the
whole city assembled to hear the word of
[1]God.
45 But when [a]the Jews saw the
crowds, they were filled with jealousy,
and *began* contradicting the things spoken by Paul, and were [1]blaspheming.
46 And Paul and Barnabas spoke out
boldly and said, "It was necessary that
the word of God should be spoken to
you [a]first; since you repudiate it, and
judge yourselves unworthy of eternal
life, behold, [b]we are turning to the
Gentiles.
47 "For thus the Lord has commanded
us,
'[a]I HAVE PLACED YOU AS A [b]LIGHT
FOR THE GENTILES,
THAT YOU SHOULD [1]BRING SAL-
VATION TO THE END OF THE
EARTH.' "
48 And when the Gentiles heard this,
they *began* rejoicing and glorifying [a]the
word of [1]the Lord; and as many as [b]had
been appointed to eternal life believed.
49 And [a]the word of the Lord was
being spread through the whole region.
50 But [a]the Jews aroused the [1b]devout
women [c]of prominence and the leading
men of the city, and instigated a persecution against Paul and Barnabas, and
drove them out of their [2]district.
51 But [a]they shook off the dust of
their feet *in protest* against them and
went to [b]Iconium.
52 And the disciples were continually
[a]filled with joy and with the Holy Spirit.

Acceptance and Opposition

14 AND it came about that in [a]Ico-
nium [b]they entered the synagogue of the Jews together, and spoke in
such a manner [c]that a great multitude
believed, both of Jews and of [d]Greeks.
2 But [a]the Jews who [1b]disbelieved
stirred up the [2]minds of the Gentiles,
and embittered them against [c]the brethren.
3 Therefore they spent a long time
there [a]speaking boldly *with reliance* upon
the Lord, who was bearing witness to the
word of His grace, granting that [1b]signs
and wonders be done by their hands.
4 [a]But the multitude of the city was
divided; and some [1]sided with [b]the Jews,
and some with [c]the apostles.
5 And when an attempt was made by
both the Gentiles and [a]the Jews with
their rulers, to mistreat and to [b]stone
them,
6 they became aware of it and fled to
the cities of [a]Lycaonia, [b]Lystra and
[c]Derbe, and the surrounding region;
7 and there they continued to
[a]preach the gospel.
8 And at [a]Lystra there was sitting [b]a
certain man, without strength in his feet,
lame from his mother's womb, who had
never walked.
9 This man was listening to Paul as
he spoke, who, [a]when he had fixed his
gaze upon him, and had seen that he had
[b]faith to be [1]made well,
10 said with a loud voice, "Stand
upright on your feet." [a]And he leaped up
and *began* to walk.

31 [a]Acts 1:3 [b]Luke 24:48
32 [a]Acts 5:42; 14:15 [b]Acts 13:23; 26:6; Rom. 1:2; 4:13; 9:4
33 [1]Some mss. read *to us their children* [a]Acts 2:24; 13:30, 34, 37 [b]Ps. 2:7
34 [a]Acts 2:24; 13:30, 33, 37 [b]Is. 55:3
35 [1]Lit., *give* [2]Or, *Devout* or *Pious* [3]Lit., *see corruption* [a]Ps. 16:10; Acts 2:27
36 [1]Or, *served his own generation by the purpose of God* [2]Lit., *saw corruption* [a]Acts 2:29 [b]Acts 13:22; 20:27 [c]1 Kin. 2:10; Acts 8:1
37 [1]Lit., *see corruption* [a]Acts 2:24; 13:30, 33, 34
38 [1]Lit., *this One* [a]Luke 24:47; Acts 2:38
39 [1]Lit., *justified* [2]In the Gr. text the remainder of this v. is part of v. 38 [a]Acts 10:43; Rom. 3:28; 10:4
40 [a]Luke 24:44; John 6:45; Acts 7:42
41 [1]Lit., *disappear* [a]Hab. 1:5
42 [1]Lit., *they were* [2]Lit., *they* [3]Lit., *words* [a]Acts 13:14
43 [1]I.e., Gentile converts to Judaism [a]Acts 13:50; 16:14; 17:4, 17; 18:7 [b]Matt. 23:15 [c]Acts 11:23
44 [1]Some ancient mss. read *the Lord* [a]Acts 13:14
45 [1]Or, *reviling* [a]Acts 13:50; 14:2, 4, 5, 19; 1 Thess. 2:16
46 [a]Acts 3:26; 9:20; 13:5, 14 [b]Acts 18:6; 19:9; 22:21; 26:20; 28:28
47 [1]Lit., *be for salvation* [a]Is. 42:6; 49:6 [b]Luke 2:32
48 [1]Some ancient mss. read *God* [a]Acts 13:12 [b]Rom. 8:28ff.; Eph. 1:4f., 11
49 [a]Acts 13:12
50 [1]Or, *worshiping* [2]Lit., *boundaries* [a]Acts 13:45; 14:2, 4, 5, 19; 1 Thess. 2:14ff. [b]Acts 13:43; 16:14; 17:4, 17; 18:7 [c]Mark 15:43
51 [a]Matt. 10:14; Mark 6:11; Luke 9:5; 10:11; Acts 18:6 [b]Acts 14:1, 19, 21; 16:2; 2 Tim. 3:11
52 [a]Acts 2:4

1 [a]Acts 13:51; 14:19, 21; 16:2; 2 Tim. 3:11 [b]Acts 13:5 [c]Acts 2:47 [d]John 7:35; Acts 18:4
2 [1]Or, *disobeyed* [2]Lit., *souls* [a]Acts 13:45, 50; 14:4, 5, 19; 1 Thess. 2:14ff. [b]John 3:36 [c]Acts 1:15
3 [1]Or, *attesting miracles* [a]Acts 4:29f.; 20:32; Heb. 2:4 [b]John 4:48
4 [1]Lit., *were* [a]Acts 17:4f.; 19:9; 28:24 [b]Acts 13:45, 50; 14:2, 5, 19; 1 Thess. 2:14ff. [c]Acts 14:14
5 [a]Acts 13:45, 50; 14:2, 4, 19; 1 Thess. 2:14ff. [b]Acts 14:19
6 [a]Acts 14:11 [b]Acts 14:8, 21; 16:1f.; 2 Tim. 3:11 [c]Acts 14:20; 16:1; 20:4
7 [a]Acts 14:15, 21; 16:10
8 [a]Acts 14:6, 21; 16:1f.; 2 Tim. 3:11 [b]Acts 3:2
9 [1]Lit., *saved* [a]Acts 3:4; 10:4 [b]Matt. 9:28
10 [a]Acts 3:8

11 And when the multitudes saw what
Paul had done, they raised their voice,
saying in the [a]Lycaonian language,
"[b]The gods have become like men and
have come down to us."
12 And they *began* calling Barnabas,
[1]Zeus, and Paul, [2]Hermes, because he
was [3]the chief speaker.
13 And the priest of Zeus, whose
temple was [1]just outside the city, brought
oxen and garlands to the gates, and
[a]wanted to offer sacrifice with the
crowds.
14 But when [a]the apostles, Barnabas
and Paul, heard of it, they [b]tore their
[1]robes and rushed out into the crowd,
crying out
15 and saying, "Men, why are you
doing these things? We are also [a]men of
the same nature as you, and [b]preach the
gospel to you in order that you should
turn from these [1c]vain things to a [d]living
God, [e]WHO MADE THE HEAVEN AND THE
EARTH AND THE SEA, AND ALL THAT IS IN
THEM.
16 "[1]And in the generations gone by
He [a]permitted all the [2]nations to [b]go
their own ways;
17 and yet [a]He did not leave Himself
without witness, in that He did good and
[b]gave you rains from heaven and fruitful
seasons, [1]satisfying your hearts with
food and gladness."
18 And *even* saying these things, they
with difficulty restrained the crowds
from offering sacrifice to them.
19 But [a]Jews came from [b]Antioch and
[c]Iconium, and having won over the
multitudes, they [d]stoned Paul and
[1]dragged him out of the city, supposing
him to be dead.
20 But while [a]the disciples stood
around him, he arose and entered the
city. And the next day he went away
with Barnabas to [b]Derbe.
21 And after they had [a]preached the
gospel to that city and had [b]made many
disciples, they returned to [c]Lystra and to
[d]Iconium and to [e]Antioch,
22 strengthening the souls of [a]the
disciples, encouraging them to continue
in [b]the faith, and *saying,* "[c]Through
many tribulations we must enter the
kingdom of God."
23 And when [a]they had appointed
[b]elders for them in every church, having
[c]prayed with fasting, they [d]commended
them to the Lord in whom they had
believed.
24 And they passed through [a]Pisidia
and came into [b]Pamphylia.
25 And when they had spoken the
word in [a]Perga, they went down to
Attalia;
26 and from there they sailed to [a]Anti-
och, from [b]which they had been [c]com-
mended to the grace of God for the work
that they had [1]accomplished.
27 And when they had arrived and
gathered the church together, they *began*
to [a]report all things that God had done
with them and [1]how He had opened a
[b]door of faith to the Gentiles.
28 And they spent [1]a long time with
[a]the disciples.

The Council at Jerusalem

15 AND [a]some men came down
from Judea and *began* teaching
[b]the brethren, "Unless you are [c]circum-
cised according to [d]the custom of Moses,
you cannot be saved."
2 And when Paul and Barnabas had
[1]great dissension and [a]debate with them,
[2b]*the brethren* determined that Paul and
Barnabas and certain others of them
should go up to Jerusalem to the [c]apos-
tles and elders concerning this issue.
3 Therefore, being [a]sent on their way
by the church, they were passing through
both [b]Phoenicia and Samaria, [c]describ-
ing in detail the conversion of the Gentiles, and were bringing great joy to all
[d]the brethren.
4 And when they arrived at Jerusalem, they were received by the church
and [a]the apostles and the elders, and
they [b]reported all that God had done
with them.
5 But certain ones of [a]the sect of the
[b]Pharisees who had believed, stood up,
saying, "It is necessary to [c]circumcise
them, and to direct them to observe the
Law of Moses."
6 And [a]the apostles and the elders
came together to [1]look into this [2]matter.
7 And after there had been much
[a]debate, Peter stood up and said to
them, "Brethren, you know that [1]in the
early days [b]God made a choice among
you, that by my mouth the Gentiles
should hear the word of [c]the gospel and
believe.
8 "And God, [a]who knows the heart,
bore witness to them, [b]giving them the
Holy Spirit, just as He also did to us;
9 and [a]He made no distinction between us and them, [b]cleansing their
hearts by faith.
10 "Now therefore why do you [a]put
God to the test by placing upon the neck
of the disciples a yoke which [b]neither
our fathers nor we have been able to
bear?
11 "But we believe that we are saved
through [a]the grace of the Lord Jesus, in
the same way as they also are."
12 And all the multitude kept silent,
and they were listening to Barnabas and
Paul as they were [a]relating what [b]signs
and wonders God had done through
them among the Gentiles.

11 [a]Acts 14:6 [b]Acts 8:10; 28:6
12 [1]Lat., *Jupiter* [2]Lat., *Mercurius* [3]Lit., *the leader of the speaking*
13 [1]Lit., *in front of* [a]Dan. 2:46
14 [1]Or, *outer garments* [a]Acts 14:4 [b]Num. 14:6; Matt. 26:65; Mark 14:63
15 [1]I.e., idols [a]Acts 10:26; James 5:17 [b]Acts 13:32; 14:7, 21 [c]Deut. 32:21; 1 Sam. 12:21; Jer. 8:19; 14:22; 1 Cor. 8:4 [d]Matt. 16:16 [e]Ex. 20:11; Ps. 146:6; Acts 4:24; 17:24; Rev. 14:7
16 [1]Lit., *Who in the generations gone by permitted* [2]Or, *Gentiles* [a]Acts 17:30 [b]Ps. 81:12; Mic. 4:5
17 [1]Lit., *filling* [a]Acts 17:26f.; Rom. 1:19f. [b]Deut. 11:14; Job 5:10; Ps. 65:10f.; Ezek. 34:26f.; Joel 2:23
19 [1]Lit., *were dragging* [a]Acts 13:45, 50; 14:2, 4, 5; 1 Thess. 2:14ff. [b]Acts 13:14; 14:21, 26 [c]Acts 13:51; 14:1, 21 [d]Acts 14:5; 2 Cor. 11:25; 2 Tim. 3:11
20 [a]Acts 11:26; 14:22, 28 [b]Acts 14:6
21 [a]Acts 14:7 [b]Acts 2:47 [c]Acts 14:6 [d]Acts 13:51; 14:1, 19 [e]Acts 13:14; 14:19, 26
22 [a]Acts 11:26; 14:28 [b]Acts 6:7 [c]Mark 10:30; John 15:18, 20; 16:33; Acts 9:16; 1 Thess. 3:3; 2 Tim. 3:12; 1 Pet. 2:21; Rev. 1:9
23 [a]2 Cor. 8:19; Titus 1:5 [b]Acts 11:30 [c]Acts 1:24; 13:3 [d]Acts 20:32
24 [a]Acts 13:14 [b]Acts 13:13
25 [a]Acts 13:13
26 [1]Lit., *fulfilled* [a]Acts 11:19 [b]Acts 13:3 [c]Acts 11:23; 15:40
27 [1]Lit., *that* [a]Acts 15:3, 4, 12; 21:19 [b]1 Cor. 16:9; 2 Cor. 2:12; Col. 4:3; Rev. 3:8
28 [1]Lit., *not a little* [a]Acts 11:26; 14:22

1 [a]Acts 15:24 [b]Acts 1:15; 15:3, 22, 32 [c]Lev. 12:3; Acts 15:5; 1 Cor. 7:18; Gal. 2:11, 14; 5:2f. [d]Acts 6:14
2 [1]Lit., *not a little* [2]Or, *it was determined* [a]Acts 15:7 [b]Gal. 2:2 [c]Acts 11:30; 15:4, 6, 22, 23; 16:4
3 [a]Acts 20:38; 21:5; Rom. 15:24; 1 Cor. 16:6, 11; 2 Cor. 1:16; Titus 3:13; 3 John 6 [b]Acts 11:19 [c]Acts 14:27; 15:4, 12 [d]Acts 1:15; 15:22, 32
4 [a]Acts 11:30; 15:6, 22, 23; 16:4 [b]Acts 14:27; 15:12
5 [a]Acts 5:17; 24:5, 14; 26:5; 28:22 [b]Matt. 3:7; Acts 26:5 [c]1 Cor. 7:18; Gal. 2:11, 14; 5:2f.
6 [1]Lit., *see about* [2]Lit., *word* [a]Acts 11:30; 15:4, 22, 23; 16:4
7 [1]Lit., *from days of old* [a]Acts 15:2 [b]Acts 10:19f. [c]Acts 20:24
8 [a]Acts 1:24 [b]Acts 2:4; 10:44, 47
9 [a]Acts 10:28, 34; 11:12 [b]Acts 10:43
10 [a]Acts 5:9 [b]Matt. 23:4; Gal. 5:1
11 [a]Rom. 3:24; 5:15; 2 Cor. 13:14; Eph. 2:5-8
12 [a]Acts 14:27; 15:3, 4 [b]John 4:48

James' Judgment

13 And after they had stopped speaking, [1a]James answered, saying, "Brethren, listen to me.
14 "[a]Simeon has related how God first
concerned Himself about taking from
among the Gentiles a people for His
name.
15 "And with this the words of [a]the
Prophets agree, just as it is written,
16 '[a]AFTER THESE THINGS [b]I will return,
AND I WILL REBUILD THE [1]TABER-
NACLE OF DAVID WHICH HAS
FALLEN,
AND I WILL REBUILD ITS RUINS,
AND I WILL RESTORE IT,
17 [a]IN ORDER THAT THE REST OF
[1]MANKIND MAY SEEK THE LORD,
AND ALL THE GENTILES [2b]WHO
ARE CALLED BY MY NAME,'
18 [a]SAYS THE LORD, WHO [1b]MAKES
THESE THINGS KNOWN FROM OF
OLD.
19 "Therefore it is [a]my judgment that
we do not trouble those who are turning
to God from among the Gentiles,
20 but that we write to them that they
abstain from [1a]things contaminated by
idols and from [b]fornication and from
[c]what is strangled and from blood.
21 "For [a]Moses from ancient generations has in every city those who preach
him, since he is read in the synagogues
every Sabbath."
22 Then it seemed good to [a]the apostles and the elders, with the whole
church, to choose men from among them
to send to [b]Antioch with Paul and
Barnabas—Judas called Barsabbas, and
[c]Silas, leading men among [d]the brethren,
23 and they [1]sent this letter by them,
"[a]The apostles and the brethren
who are elders, to [b]the brethren
in [c]Antioch and [d]Syria and
[e]Cilicia who are from the Gentiles, [f]greetings.
24 "Since we have heard that [a]some
[1]of our number to whom we
gave no instruction have [b]dis-
turbed you with *their* words,
unsettling your souls,
25 [a]it seemed good to us, having
[1]become of one mind, to select
men to send to you with our
beloved Barnabas and Paul,
26 men who have [1a]risked their
lives for the name of our Lord
Jesus Christ.
27 "Therefore we have sent [a]Judas
and [b]Silas, who themselves will
also report the same things by
word *of mouth*.
28 "For [a]it seemed good to [b]the
Holy Spirit and to [c]us to lay
upon you no greater burden
than these essentials:
29 that you abstain from [a]things
sacrificed to idols and from
[a]blood and from [a]things strangled and from [a]fornication; [1]if
you keep yourselves free from
such things, you will do well.
Farewell."
30 So, when they were sent away,
[a]they went down to Antioch; and having
gathered the [1]congregation together,
they delivered the letter.
31 And when they had read it, they
rejoiced because of its [1]encouragement.
32 And [a]Judas and [b]Silas, also being
[c]prophets themselves, [1]encouraged and
strengthened [d]the brethren with a
lengthy message.
33 And after they had spent time
there, they were sent away from the
brethren [a]in peace to those who had
[b]sent them out.
34 [[1]But it seemed good to Silas to
remain there.]
35 But [a]Paul and Barnabas stayed in
Antioch, teaching and [b]preaching, with
many others also, [c]the word of the Lord.

Second Missionary Journey

36 And after some days Paul said to
Barnabas, "Let us return and visit the
brethren in [a]every city in which we
proclaimed [b]the word of the Lord, *and*
see how they are."
37 And Barnabas was desirous of
taking [a]John, called Mark, along with
them also.
38 But Paul kept insisting that they
should not take him along who had
[a]deserted them [1]in Pamphylia and had
not gone with them to the work.
39 And there arose such a sharp disagreement that they separated from one
another, and Barnabas took [a]Mark with
him and sailed away to [b]Cyprus.
40 But Paul chose [a]Silas and departed,
being [b]committed by the brethren to the
grace of the Lord.
41 And he was traveling through
[a]Syria and [b]Cilicia, strengthening the
churches.

The Macedonian Vision

16 AND he came also to [a]Derbe and
to [a]Lystra. And behold, a certain
disciple was there, named [b]Timothy, the
son of a [c]Jewish woman who was a
believer, but his father was a Greek,
2 and he was well spoken of by [a]the
brethren who were in [b]Lystra and [c]Ico-
nium.
3 Paul wanted this man to [1]go with
him; and he [a]took him and circumcised
him because of the Jews who were in
those parts, for they all knew that his
father was a Greek.

13 [1]Or, *Jacob*
[a]Acts 12:17
14 [a]Acts 15:7; 2 Pet. 1:1
15 [a]Acts 13:40
16 [1]Or, *tent*
[a]Amos 9:11 [b]Jer. 12:15
17 [1]Lit., *men* [2]Lit., *upon whom My name is called*
[a]Amos 9:12 [b]Deut. 28:10; Is. 63:19; Jer. 14:9; Dan. 9:19; James 2:7
18 [1]Or, *does these things* which were *known*
[a]Amos 9:12 [b]Is. 45:21
19 [a]Acts 15:28; 21:25
20 [1]Lit., *the pollutions of*
[a]Ex. 34:15-17; Dan. 1:8; Acts 15:29; 1 Cor. 8:7, 13; 10:7f., 14-28; Rev. 2:14, 20 [b]Lev. 18:6-23 [c]Gen. 9:4; Lev. 3:17; 7:26; 17:10, 14; 19:26; Deut. 12:16, 23; 15:23; 1 Sam. 14:33
21 [a]Acts 13:15; 2 Cor. 3:14f.
22 [a]Acts 15:2 [b]Acts 11:20 [c]Acts 15:27, 32, 40; 16:19, 25, 29; 17:4, 10, 14f.; 18:5; 2 Cor. 1:19; 1 Thess. 1:1; 2 Thess. 1:1; 1 Pet. 5:12 [d]Acts 15:1
23 [1]Lit., *wrote by their hand*
[a]Acts 15:2 [b]Acts 15:1 [c]Acts 11:20 [d]Matt. 4:24; Acts 15:41; Gal. 1:21 [e]Acts 6:9 [f]Acts 23:26; James 1:1; 2 John 10f.
24 [1]Lit., *from us*
[a]Acts 15:1 [b]Gal. 1:7; 5:10
25 [1]Or, *met together*
[a]Acts 15:28
26 [1]Lit., *given over*
[a]Acts 9:23ff.; 14:19
27 [a]Acts 15:22, 32 [b]Acts 15:22
28 [a]Acts 15:25 [b]Acts 5:32; 15:8 [c]Acts 15:19, 25
29 [1]Lit., *from which keeping yourselves free*
[a]Acts 15:20
30 [1]Or, *multitude*
[a]Acts 15:22f.
31 [1]Or, *exhortation*
32 [1]Or, *exhorted*
[a]Acts 15:22, 27 [b]Acts 15:22 [c]Acts 13:1 [d]Acts 15:1
33 [a]Mark 5:34; Acts 16:36; 1 Cor. 16:11; Heb. 11:31 [b]Acts 15:22
34 [1]Many mss. do not contain this v.
35 [a]Acts 12:25 [b]Acts 8:4 [c]Acts 13:12
36 [a]Acts 13:4, 13, 14, 51; 14:6, 24f. [b]Acts 13:12
37 [a]Acts 12:12
38 [1]Lit., *from*
[a]Acts 13:13
39 [a]Acts 12:12; 15:37; Col. 4:10 [b]Acts 4:36
40 [a]Acts 15:22 [b]Acts 11:23; 14:26
41 [a]Matt. 4:24; Acts 15:23 [b]Acts 6:9

1 [a]Acts 14:6 [b]Acts 17:14f.; 18:5; 19:22; 20:4; Rom. 16:21; 1 Cor. 4:17; 16:10; 2 Cor. 1:1, 19; Phil. 1:1; 2:19; Col. 1:1; 1 Thess. 1:1; 3:2, 6; 2 Thess. 1:1; 1 Tim. 1:2, 18; 6:20; 2 Tim. 1:2; Philem. 1; Heb. 13:23 [c]2 Tim. 1:5; 3:15
2 [a]Acts 16:40 [b]Acts 14:6 [c]Acts 13:51
3 [1]Lit., *go out* [a]Gal. 2:3

4 Now while they were passing through the cities, they were delivering [a]the decrees, which had been decided upon by [b]the apostles and [c]elders who were in Jerusalem, for them to observe.

5 So [a]the churches were being strengthened [1]in the faith, and were [b]increasing in number daily.

6 And they passed through the [1a]Phrygian and [b]Galatian region, having been forbidden by the Holy Spirit to speak the word in [2c]Asia;

7 and when they had come to [a]Mysia, they were trying to go into [b]Bithynia, and the [c]Spirit of Jesus did not permit them;

8 and passing [1]by [a]Mysia, they came down to [b]Troas.

9 And [a]a vision appeared to Paul in the night: [1]a certain man of [b]Macedonia was standing and appealing to him, and saying, "Come over to Macedonia and help us."

10 And when he had seen [a]the vision, immediately [b]we sought to [1]go into Macedonia, concluding that God had called us to [c]preach the gospel to them.

11 [1]Therefore putting out to sea from [a]Troas, we ran [b]a straight course to Samothrace, and on the day following to Neapolis;

12 and from there to [a]Philippi, which is a leading city of the district of [b]Macedonia, [c]a *Roman* colony; and we were staying in this city for some days.

13 And on [a]the Sabbath day we went outside the gate to a riverside, where we were supposing that there would be a place of prayer; and we sat down and began speaking to the women who had assembled.

First Convert in Europe

14 And a certain woman named Lydia, from the city of [a]Thyatira, a seller of purple fabrics, [b]a worshiper of God, was listening; [1]and the Lord [c]opened her heart to respond to the things spoken by Paul.

15 And when she and [a]her household had been baptized, she urged us, saying, "If you have judged me to be faithful to the Lord, come into my house and stay." And she prevailed upon us.

16 And it happened that as we were going to [a]the place of prayer, a certain slave-girl having [b]a spirit of divination met us, who was bringing her masters much profit by fortunetelling.

17 Following after Paul and us, she kept crying out, saying, "These men are bond-servants of [a]the Most High God, who are proclaiming to you [1]the way of salvation."

18 And she continued doing this for many days. But Paul was greatly annoyed, and turned and said to the spirit, "I command you [a]in the name of Jesus Christ to come out of her!" And it came out at that very [1]moment.

19 But when her masters saw that their hope of [a]profit was [1]gone, they seized [b]Paul and Silas and [c]dragged them into the market place before the authorities,

20 and when they had brought them to the chief magistrates, they said, "These men are throwing our city into confusion, being Jews,

21 and [a]are proclaiming customs which it is not lawful for us to accept or to observe, being [b]Romans."

Paul and Silas Imprisoned

22 And the crowd rose up together against them, and the chief magistrates tore their [1]robes off them, and proceeded to order [2]*them* to be [a]beaten with rods.

23 And when they had inflicted many blows upon them, they threw them into prison, commanding [a]the jailer to guard them securely;

24 [1]and he, having received such a command, threw them into the inner prison, and fastened their feet in [a]the stocks.

25 But about midnight [a]Paul and Silas were praying and [b]singing hymns of praise to God, and the prisoners were listening to them;

26 and suddenly [a]there came a great earthquake, so that the foundations of the prison house were shaken; and immediately [b]all the doors were opened, and everyone's [c]chains were unfastened.

27 And when [a]the jailer had been roused out of sleep and had seen the prison doors opened, he drew his sword and was about [b]to kill himself, supposing that the prisoners had escaped.

28 But Paul cried out with a loud voice, saying, "Do yourself no harm, for we are all here!"

29 And he called for lights and rushed in and, trembling with fear, he fell down before [a]Paul and Silas,

30 and after he brought them out, he said, "Sirs, [a]what must I do to be saved?"

The Jailer Converted

31 And they said, "[a]Believe in the Lord Jesus, and you shall be saved, you and [b]your household."

32 And they spoke the word of [1]the Lord to him together with all who were in his house.

33 And he took them [a]that *very* hour of the night and washed their wounds, and immediately he was baptized, he and all his *household.*

34 And he brought them into his house and set [1]food before them, and rejoiced [2]greatly, having believed in God with [a]his whole household.

35 Now when day came, the chief magistrates sent their policemen, saying, "Release those men."

4 [a]Acts 15:28f. [b]Acts 15:2 [c]Acts 11:30
5 [1]Or, *in faith* [a]Acts 9:31 [b]Acts 2:47
6 [1]Or, *Phrygia and the Galatian region* [2]I.e., west coast province of Asia Minor [a]Acts 2:10; 18:23 [b]Acts 18:23; 1 Cor. 16:1; Gal. 1:2; 3:1; 2 Tim. 4:10; 1 Pet. 1:1 [c]Acts 2:9
7 [a]Acts 16:8 [b]1 Pet. 1:1 [c]Luke 24:49; Acts 8:29; Rom. 8:9; Gal. 4:6; Phil. 1:19; 1 Pet. 1:11
8 [1]Or, *through* [a]Acts 16:7 [b]Acts 16:11; 20:5f.; 2 Cor. 2:12; 2 Tim. 4:13
9 [1]Or, *A man* [a]Acts 9:10 [b]Acts 16:10, 12; 18:5; 19:21f., 29; 20:1, 3; 27:2; Rom. 15:26
10 [1]Lit., *go out* [a]Acts 9:10 [b][we] Acts 16:10-17; 20:5-15; 21:1-18; 27:1-28:16 [c]Acts 14:7
11 [1]Some ancient mss. read *And* [a]Acts 16:8; 20:5f.; 2 Cor. 2:12; 2 Tim. 4:13 [b]Acts 21:1
12 [a]Acts 20:6; Phil. 1:1; 1 Thess. 2:2 [b]Acts 16:9, 10; 18:5; 19:21f., 29; 20:1, 3; 27:2; Rom. 15:26 [c]Acts 16:21
13 [a]Acts 13:14
14 [1]Lit., *whose heart the Lord opened* [a]Rev. 1:11; 2:18, 24 [b]Acts 13:43; 18:7 [c]Luke 24:45
15 [a]Acts 11:14
16 [a]Acts 16:13 [b]Lev. 19:31; 20:6, 27; Deut. 18:11; 1 Sam. 28:3, 7; 2 Kin. 21:6; 1 Chr. 10:13; Is. 8:19
17 [1]Lit., *a way* [a]Mark 5:7
18 [1]Lit., *hour* [a]Mark 16:17
19 [1]Lit., *gone out* [a]Acts 16:16; 19:25f. [b]Acts 15:22, 40; 16:25, 29 [c]Acts 8:3; 17:6f.; 21:30; James 2:6
21 [a]Esth. 3:8 [b]Acts 16:12
22 [1]Or, *outer garments* [2]Lit., *to beat with rods* [a]2 Cor. 11:25; 1 Thess. 2:2
23 [a]Acts 16:27, 36
24 [1]Lit., *who, having received* [a]Job 13:27; 33:11; Jer. 20:2f.; 29:26
25 [a]Acts 16:19 [b]Eph. 5:19
26 [a]Acts 4:31 [b]Acts 12:10 [c]Acts 12:7
27 [a]Acts 16:23, 36 [b]Acts 12:19
29 [a]Acts 16:19
30 [a]Acts 2:37; 22:10
31 [a]Mark 16:16 [b]Acts 11:14; 16:15
32 [1]Some ancient mss. read *God*
33 [a]Acts 16:25

34 [1]Lit., *a table* [2]Or, *greatly with his whole household, having believed in God* [a]Acts 11:14; 16:15

36 And [a]the jailer reported these
words to Paul, *saying,* "The chief magistrates have sent to release you. Now
therefore, come out and go [b]in peace."
37 But Paul said to them, "They have
beaten us in public without trial, [a]men
who are Romans, and have thrown us
into prison; and now are they sending us
away secretly? No indeed! But let them
come themselves and bring us out."
38 And the policemen reported these
words to the chief magistrates. And
[a]they were afraid when they heard that
they were Romans,
39 and they came and appealed to
them, and when they had brought them
out, they kept begging them [a]to leave the
city.
40 And they went out of the prison
and entered *the house of* [a]Lydia, and
when they saw [b]the brethren, they [1]en-
couraged them and departed.

Paul at Thessalonica

17 NOW when they had traveled
through Amphipolis and Apollo-
nia, they came to [a]Thessalonica, where
there was a synagogue of the Jews.
2 And [a]according to Paul's custom,
he went to them, and for three [b]Sab-
baths reasoned with them from [c]the
Scriptures,
3 [1]explaining and [2]giving evidence
that the [3]Christ [a]had to suffer and [b]rise
again from the dead, and *saying,* "[c]This
Jesus whom I am proclaiming to you is
the [3]Christ."
4 [a]And some of them were persuaded
and joined [b]Paul and Silas, [1]along with a
great multitude of the [c]God-fearing
[d]Greeks and [2]a number of the [e]leading
women.
5 But [a]the Jews, becoming jealous
and taking along some wicked men from
the market place, formed a mob and set
the city in an uproar; and coming upon
the house of [b]Jason, they were seeking to
bring them out to the people.
6 And when they did not find them,
they *began* [a]dragging Jason and some
brethren before the city authorities,
shouting, "These men who have upset
[1b]the world have come here also;
7 [1]and Jason [a]has welcomed them,
and they all act [b]contrary to the decrees
of Caesar, saying that there is another
king, Jesus."
8 And they stirred up the crowd and
the city authorities who heard these
things.
9 And when they had received a
[1]pledge from [a]Jason and the others, they
released them.

Paul at Berea

10 And [a]the brethren immediately
sent [b]Paul and Silas away by night to
[c]Berea; [1]and when they arrived, they
went into [d]the synagogue of the Jews.
11 Now these were more noble-
minded than those in [a]Thessalonica, [1]for
they received the word with [2]great eagerness, examining the Scriptures daily, *to
see* whether these things were so.
12 [a]Many of them therefore believed,
[1]along with a number of [b]prominent
Greek [c]women and men.
13 But when the Jews of [a]Thessalonica
found out that the word of God had
been proclaimed by Paul in [b]Berea also,
they came there likewise, agitating and
stirring up the crowds.
14 And then immediately [a]the brethren sent Paul out to go as far as the sea;
and [b]Silas and [c]Timothy remained there.
15 Now [a]those who conducted Paul
brought him as far as [b]Athens; and
receiving a command for [c]Silas and
Timothy to [d]come to him as soon as
possible, they departed.

Paul at Athens

16 Now while Paul was waiting for
them at [a]Athens, his spirit was being
provoked within him as he was beholding the city full of idols.
17 So he was reasoning [a]in the synagogue with the Jews and [b]the God-
fearing *Gentiles,* and in the market place
every day with those who happened to
be present.
18 And also some of the Epicurean
and Stoic philosophers were [1]conversing
with him. And some were saying, "What
would [a]this [2]idle babbler wish to say?"
Others, "He seems to be a proclaimer of
strange [3]deities,"—because he was
preaching [b]Jesus and the resurrection.
19 And they [a]took him and brought
him [1]to the [2b]Areopagus, saying, "May
we know what [c]this new teaching is
[3]which you are proclaiming?
20 "For you are bringing some strange
things to our ears; we want to know
therefore what these things mean."
21 (Now all the Athenians and the
strangers [a]visiting there used to spend
their time in nothing other than telling
or hearing something new.)

Sermon on Mars Hill

22 And Paul stood in the midst of the
[1]Areopagus and said, "Men of [a]Athens,
I observe that you are very [b]religious in
all respects.
23 "For while I was passing through
and examining the [a]objects of your
worship, I also found an altar with this
inscription, 'TO AN UNKNOWN
GOD.' What therefore [b]you worship in
ignorance, this I proclaim to you.
24 "[a]The God who made the world and
all things in it, since He is [b]Lord of
heaven and earth, does not [c]dwell in
temples made with hands;
25 neither is He served by human
hands, [a]as though He needed anything,
since He Himself gives to all life and
breath and all things;

36 [a]Acts 16:27 [b]Acts 15:33
37 [a]Acts 22:25-29
38 [a]Acts 22:29
39 [a]Matt. 8:34
40 [1]Or, *exhorted* [a]Acts 16:14 [b]Acts 1:15; 16:2

1 [a]Acts 17:11, 13; 20:4; 27:2; Phil. 4:16; 1 Thess. 1:1; 2 Thess. 1:1; 2 Tim. 4:10
2 [a]Acts 9:20; 17:10, 17 [b]Acts 13:14 [c]Acts 8:35
3 [1]Lit., *opening* [2]Lit., *placing before* [3]I.e., Messiah [a]Acts 3:18 [b]John 20:9 [c]Acts 9:22; 18:5, 28
4 [1]Lit., *and a great* [2]Lit., *not a few* [a]Acts 14:4 [b]Acts 15:22, 40; 17:10, 14f. [c]Acts 13:43; 17:17 [d]John 7:35 [e]Acts 13:50
5 [a]Acts 17:13; 1 Thess. 2:14ff. [b]Acts 17:6, 7, 9; Rom. 16:21
6 [1]Lit., *the inhabited earth* [a]Acts 16:19f. [b]Matt. 24:14; Acts 17:31
7 [1]Lit., *whom Jason has welcomed* [a]Luke 10:38; James 2:25 [b]Luke 23:2
9 [1]Or, *bond* [a]Acts 17:5
10 [1]Lit., *who when . . . arrived went* [a]Acts 1:15; 17:6, 14f. [b]Acts 17:4 [c]Acts 17:13; 20:4 [d]Acts 17:1f.
11 [1]Lit., *who received* [2]Lit., *all* [a]Acts 17:1
12 [1]Lit., *and not a few* [a]Acts 2:47 [b]Mark 15:43 [c]Acts 13:50
13 [a]Acts 17:1 [b]Acts 17:10; 20:4
14 [a]Acts 1:15; 17:6, 10 [b]Acts 15:22; 17:4, 10 [c]Acts 16:1
15 [a]Acts 15:3 [b]Acts 17:16, 21f.; 18:1; 1 Thess. 3:1 [c]Acts 17:14 [d]Acts 18:5
16 [a]Acts 17:15, 21f.; 18:1; 1 Thess. 3:1
17 [a]Acts 9:20; 17:2 [b]Acts 17:4
18 [1]Or, *disputing* [2]I.e., one who makes his living by picking up scraps [3]Lit., *demons* [a]1 Cor. 1:20; 4:10 [b]Acts 4:2; 17:31f.
19 [1]Or, *before* [2]Or, *Hill of Ares,* god of war [3]Lit., *which is being spoken by you* [a]Acts 23:19 [b]Acts 17:22 [c]Mark 1:27
21 [a]Acts 2:10
22 [1]Or possibly, the Council of the Areopagus [a]Acts 17:15 [b]Acts 25:19
23 [a]2 Thess. 2:4 [b]John 4:22
24 [a]Is. 42:5; Acts 14:15 [b]Deut. 10:14; Ps. 115:16; Matt. 11:25 [c]1 Kin. 8:27; Acts 7:48

25 [a]Job 22:2; Ps. 50:10-12

26 and [a]He made from [1]one, every
nation of mankind to live on all the face
of the earth, having [b]determined *their*
appointed times, and the boundaries of
their habitation,
27 that they should seek God, if perhaps they might grope for Him and find
Him, [a]though He is not far from each
one of us;
28 for [a]in Him we live and move and
[1]exist, as even some of your own poets
have said, 'For we also are His offspring.'
29 "Being then the offspring of God,
we [a]ought not to think that the Divine
Nature is like gold or silver or stone, an
image formed by the art and thought of
man.
30 "Therefore having [a]overlooked [b]the
times of ignorance, God is [c]now declaring to men that all everywhere should
repent,
31 because He has fixed [a]a day in
which [b]He will judge [1c]the world in
righteousness through a Man whom He
has [d]appointed, having furnished proof
to all men [2]by [e]raising Him from the
dead."
32 Now when they heard of [a]the resurrection of the dead, some *began* to sneer,
but others said, "We shall hear you
[1]again concerning this."
33 So Paul went out of their midst.
34 But some men joined him and
believed, among whom also were Diony-
sius the [a]Areopagite and a woman
named Damaris and others with them.

Paul at Corinth

18 AFTER these things he left [a]Ath-
ens and went to [b]Corinth.
2 And he found a certain Jew named
[a]Aquila, a native of [b]Pontus, having
recently come from [c]Italy with his wife
[a]Priscilla, because [d]Claudius had commanded all the Jews to leave Rome. He
came to them,
3 and because he was of the same
trade, he stayed with them and [a]they
were working; for by trade they were
tent-makers.
4 And he was reasoning [a]in the synagogue every [b]Sabbath and trying to
persuade [c]Jews and Greeks.
5 But when [a]Silas and Timothy
[b]came down from [c]Macedonia, Paul
began devoting himself completely to the
word, solemnly [d]testifying to the Jews
that [e]Jesus was the [1]Christ.
6 And when they resisted and blasphemed, he [a]shook out his garments and
said to them, "Your [b]blood *be* upon
your own heads! I am clean. From now
on I shall go [c]to the Gentiles."
7 And he departed from there and
went to the house of a certain man
named [1]Titius Justus, [a]a worshiper of
God, whose house was next to the synagogue.
8 And [a]Crispus, [b]the leader of the
synagogue, believed in the Lord [c]with all
his household, and many of the [d]Corin-
thians when they heard were believing
and being baptized.
9 And the Lord said to Paul in the
night by [a]a vision, "Do not be afraid *any
longer*, but go on speaking and do not be
silent;
10 for I am with you, and no man will
attack you in order to harm you, for I
have many people in this city."
11 And he settled *there* a year and six
months, teaching the word of God
among them.
12 But while Gallio was [a]proconsul of
[b]Achaia, [c]the Jews with one accord rose
up against Paul and brought him before
[d]the judgment seat,
13 saying, "This man persuades men
to worship God contrary to [a]the law."
14 But when Paul was about to [a]open
his mouth, Gallio said to the Jews, "If it
were a matter of wrong or of vicious
crime, O Jews, it would be reasonable
for me to put up with you;
15 but if there are [a]questions about
words and names and your own law,
look after it yourselves; I am unwilling
to be a judge of these matters."
16 And he drove them away from [a]the
judgment seat.
17 And they all took hold of [a]Sosthe-
nes, [b]the leader of the synagogue, and
began beating him in front of [c]the judgment seat. And Gallio was not concerned about any of these things.
18 And Paul, having remained many
days longer, [a]took leave of [b]the brethren
and put out to sea for [c]Syria, and with
him were [d]Priscilla and [d]Aquila. In
[e]Cenchrea [1]he [f]had his hair cut, for he
was keeping a vow.
19 And they came to [a]Ephesus, and he
left them there. Now he himself entered
[b]the synagogue and reasoned with the
Jews.
20 And when they asked him to stay
for a longer time, he did not consent,
21 but [a]taking leave of them and
saying, "I will return to you again [b]if
God wills," he set sail from [c]Ephesus.
22 And when he had landed at [a]Caes-
area, he went up and greeted the church,
and went down to [b]Antioch.

Third Missionary Journey

23 And having spent some time *there*,
he departed and passed successively
through the [a]Galatian region and
Phrygia, strengthening all the disciples.

26 [1]Some later mss. read *one blood* [a]Mal. 2:10 [b]Deut. 32:8; Job 12:23
27 [a]Deut. 4:7; Jer. 23:23f.; Acts 14:17
28 [1]Lit., *are* [a]Job 12:10; Dan. 5:23
29 [a]Is. 40:18ff.; Rom. 1:23
30 [a]Acts 14:16; Rom. 3:25 [b]Acts 17:23 [c]Luke 24:47; Acts 26:20; Titus 2:11f.
31 [1]Lit., *the inhabited earth* [2]Or, *when He raised* [a]Matt. 10:15 [b]Ps. 9:8; 96:13; 98:9; John 5:22, 27; Acts 10:42 [c]Matt. 24:14; Acts 17:6 [d]Luke 22:22 [e]Acts 2:24
32 [1]Lit., *also again* [a]Acts 17:18, 31
34 [a]Acts 17:19, 22

1 [a]Acts 17:15 [b]Acts 18:8; 19:1; 1 Cor. 1:2; 2 Cor. 1:1, 23; 6:11; 2 Tim. 4:20
2 [a]Acts 18:18, 26; Rom. 16:3; 1 Cor. 16:19; 2 Tim. 4:19 [b]Acts 2:9 [c]Acts 27:1, 6; Heb. 13:24 [d]Acts 11:28
3 [a]Acts 20:34; 1 Cor. 4:12; 9:14f.; 2 Cor. 11:7; 12:13; 1 Thess. 2:9; 4:11; 2 Thess. 3:8
4 [a]Acts 9:20; 18:19 [b]Acts 13:14 [c]Acts 14:1
5 [1]I.e., Messiah [a]Acts 15:22; 16:1; 17:14 [b]Acts 17:15 [c]Acts 16:9 [d]Luke 16:28; Acts 20:21 [e]Acts 17:3; 18:28
6 [a]Neh. 5:13; Acts 13:51 [b]2 Sam. 1:16; 1 Kin. 2:33; Ezek. 18:13; 33:4, 6, 8; Matt. 27:25; Acts 20:26 [c]Acts 13:46
7 [1]Some ancient mss. read *Titus*, others omit it altogether [a]Acts 13:43; 16:14
8 [a]1 Cor. 1:14 [b]Mark 5:22 [c]Acts 11:14 [d]Acts 18:1; 19:1; 1 Cor. 1:2; 2 Cor. 1:1, 23; 6:11; 2 Tim. 4:20
9 [a]Acts 9:10
12 [a]Acts 13:7 [b]Acts 18:27; 19:21; Rom. 15:26; 1 Cor. 16:15; 2 Cor. 1:1; 9:2; 11:10; 1 Thess. 1:7f. [c]1 Thess. 2:14ff. [d]Matt. 27:19
13 [a]John 19:7; Acts 18:15
14 [a]Matt. 5:2
15 [a]Acts 23:29; 25:19
16 [a]Matt. 27:19
17 [a]1 Cor. 1:1 [b]Acts 18:8 [c]Matt. 27:19
18 [1]Lit., *having his hair cut* [a]Mark 6:46 [b]Acts 1:15; 18:27 [c]Matt. 4:24 [d]Acts 18:2, 26 [e]Rom. 16:1 [f]Num. 6:2, 5, 9, 18; Acts 21:24
19 [a]Acts 18:21, 24; 19:1, 17, 26, 28, 34f.; 20:16f.; 21:29; 1 Cor. 15:32; 16:8; Eph. 1:1; 1 Tim. 1:3; 2 Tim. 1:18; 4:12; Rev. 1:11; 2:1 [b]Acts 18:4
21 [a]Mark 6:46 [b]Rom. 1:10; 15:32; 1 Cor. 4:19; 16:7; Heb. 6:3; James 4:15; 1 Pet. 3:17 [c]Acts 18:19, 24; 19:1, 17, 26, 28, 34f.; 20:16f.; 21:29; 1 Cor. 15:32; 16:8; Eph. 1:1; 1 Tim. 1:3; 2 Tim. 1:18; 4:12; Rev. 1:11; 2:1
22 [a]Acts 8:40 [b]Acts 11:19
23 [a]Acts 16:6

24 Now a certain Jew named [a]Apollos, an [b]Alexandrian by birth, [1]an eloquent man, came to [c]Ephesus; and he was mighty in the Scriptures.

25 This man had been instructed in [a]the way of the Lord; and being fervent in spirit, he was speaking and teaching accurately the things concerning Jesus, being acquainted only with [b]the baptism of John;

26 and he began to speak out boldly in the synagogue. But when [a]Priscilla and Aquila heard him, they took him aside and explained to him [b]the way of God more accurately.

27 And when he wanted to go across to [a]Achaia, [b]the brethren encouraged him and wrote to [c]the disciples to welcome him; and when he had arrived, he [1]helped greatly those who had believed through grace;

28 for he powerfully refuted the Jews in public, demonstrating [a]by the Scriptures that [b]Jesus was the [1]Christ.

Paul at Ephesus

19 AND it came about that while [a]Apollos was at [b]Corinth, Paul having passed through the [c]upper country came to [d]Ephesus, and found some disciples,

2 and he said to them, "[a]Did you receive the Holy Spirit when you believed?" And they *said* to him, "No, [b]we have not even heard whether [1]there is a Holy Spirit."

3 And he said, "Into what then were you baptized?" And they said, "[a]Into John's baptism."

4 And Paul said, "[a]John baptized with the baptism of repentance, telling the people [b]to believe in Him who was coming after him, that is, in Jesus."

5 And when they heard this, they were [a]baptized [1]in the name of the Lord Jesus.

6 And when Paul had [a]laid his hands upon them, the Holy Spirit came on them, and they *began* [b]speaking with tongues and [c]prophesying.

7 And there were in all about twelve men.

8 And he entered [a]the synagogue and continued speaking out boldly for three months, reasoning and [1]persuading *them* [b]about the kingdom of God.

9 But when [a]some were becoming hardened and disobedient, speaking evil of [b]the Way before the multitude, he withdrew from them and took away [c]the disciples, reasoning daily in the school of Tyrannus.

10 And this took place for [a]two years, so that all who lived in [1b]Asia heard [c]the word of the Lord, both Jews and Greeks.

Miracles at Ephesus

11 And God was performing [a]extraordinary [1]miracles by the hands of Paul,

12 [a]so that handkerchiefs or aprons were even carried from his body to the sick, and the diseases left them and [b]the evil spirits went out.

13 But also some of the Jewish [a]exorcists, who went from place to place, attempted to name over those who had the evil spirits the name of the Lord Jesus, saying, "I adjure you by Jesus whom Paul preaches."

14 And seven sons of one Sceva, a Jewish chief priest, were doing this.

15 And the evil spirit answered and said to them, "I recognize Jesus, and I know about Paul, but who are you?"

16 And the man, in whom was the evil spirit, leaped on them and subdued all of them and overpowered them, so that they fled out of that house naked and wounded.

17 And this became known to all, both Jews and Greeks, who lived in [a]Ephesus; and fear fell upon them all and the name of the Lord Jesus was being magnified.

18 Many also of those who had believed kept coming, confessing and disclosing their practices.

19 And many of those who practiced magic brought their books together and *began* burning them in the sight of all; and they counted up the price of them and found it [1]fifty thousand [a]pieces of silver.

20 So [1a]the word of the Lord [b]was growing mightily and prevailing.

21 Now after these things were finished, Paul purposed in the [1]spirit to [a]go to Jerusalem [b]after he had passed through [c]Macedonia and [d]Achaia, saying, "After I have been there, [e]I must also see Rome."

22 And having sent into [a]Macedonia two of [b]those who ministered to him, [c]Timothy and [d]Erastus, he himself stayed in [1e]Asia for a while.

23 And about that time there arose no small disturbance concerning [a]the Way.

24 For a certain man named Demetrius, a silversmith, who made silver shrines of [1]Artemis, [a]was bringing no little [2]business to the craftsmen;

25 these he gathered together with the workmen of similar *trades,* and said, "Men, you know that our prosperity [1]depends upon this business.

26 "And you see and hear that not only in [a]Ephesus, but in almost all of [1b]Asia, this Paul has persuaded and turned away a considerable number of people, saying that [2c]gods made with hands are no gods *at all.*

27 "And not only is there danger that this trade of ours fall into disrepute, but also that the temple of the great goddess

24 [1]Or, *a learned man* [a]Acts 19:1; 1 Cor. 1:12; 3:5, 6, 22; 4:6; 16:12; Titus 3:13 [b]Acts 6:9 [c]Acts 18:19
25 [a]Acts 9:2; 18:26 [b]Luke 7:29; Acts 19:3
26 [a]Acts 18:2, 18 [b]Acts 18:25
27 [1]Or, *helped greatly through grace those who had believed* [a]Acts 18:12; 19:1 [b]Acts 18:18 [c]Acts 11:26
28 [1]I.e., Messiah [a]Acts 8:35 [b]Acts 18:5

1 [a]Acts 18:24; 1 Cor. 1:12; 3:5, 6, 22; 4:6; 16:12; Titus 3:13 [b]Acts 18:1 [c]Acts 18:23 [d]Acts 18:21, 24; 19:17, 26, 28, 34f.; 20:16f.; 21:29; 1 Cor. 15:32; 16:8; Eph. 1:1; 1 Tim. 1:3; 2 Tim. 1:18; 4:12; Rev. 1:11; 2:1
2 [1]Or, *the Holy Spirit has been* given [a]Acts 8:15f.; 11:16f. [b]John 7:39
3 [a]Luke 7:29; Acts 18:25
4 [a]Matt. 3:11; Mark 1:4, 7, 8; Luke 3:16; John 1:26, 27; Acts 13:24 [b]John 1:7
5 [1]Lit., *into* [a]Acts 8:12, 16; 10:48
6 [a]Acts 6:6; 8:17 [b]Mark 16:17; Acts 2:4; 10:46 [c]Acts 13:1
8 [1]Some ancient mss. read *persuading* as to *the things about* [a]Acts 9:20; 18:26 [b]Acts 1:3
9 [a]Acts 14:4 [b]Acts 9:2; 19:23 [c]Acts 11:26; 19:30
10 [1]I.e., west coast province of Asia Minor [a]Acts 19:8; 20:31 [b]Acts 16:6; 19:22, 26, 27 [c]Acts 13:12; 19:20
11 [1]Or, *works of power* [a]Acts 8:13
12 [a]Acts 5:15 [b]Mark 16:17
13 [a]Matt. 12:27; Luke 11:19
17 [a]Acts 18:19
19 [1]Or probably, fifty thousand Greek drachmas. A drachma approximated a day's wage. [a]Luke 15:8
20 [1]Or, *according to the power of the Lord the word was growing* [a]Acts 19:10 [b]Acts 6:7; 12:24
21 [1]Or, *Spirit* [a]Acts 20:16, 22; 21:15; Rom. 15:25; 2 Cor. 1:16 [b]Acts 20:1; 1 Cor. 16:5 [c]Acts 16:9; 19:22, 29; Rom. 15:26; 1 Thess. 1:7f. [d]Acts 18:12 [e]Acts 23:11; Rom. 15:24, 28

22 [1]I.e., west coast province of Asia Minor [a]Acts 16:9; 19:21, 29 [b]Acts 13:5; 19:29; 20:34; 2 Cor. 8:19 [c]Acts 16:1 [d]Rom. 16:23; 2 Tim. 4:20 [e]Acts 19:10
23 [a]Acts 19:9
24 [1]Lat., *Diana* [2]Or, *profit* [a]Acts 16:16, 19f.
25 [1]Lit., *is from*
26 [1]V. 22, note 1 [2]Lit., *those* [a]Acts 18:19 [b]Acts 19:10 [c]Deut. 4:28; Ps. 115:4; Is. 44:10-20; Jer. 10:3ff.; Acts 17:29; 1 Cor. 8:4; 10:19; Rev. 9:20

[1]Artemis be regarded as worthless and that she whom all of [2a]Asia and [b]the [3]world worship should even be dethroned from her magnificence."

28 And when they heard *this* and were filled with rage, they *began* crying out, saying, "Great is [1]Artemis of the [a]Ephesians!"

29 And the city was filled with the confusion, and they rushed with one accord into the theater, [1]dragging along [a]Gaius and [b]Aristarchus, Paul's traveling [c]companions from [d]Macedonia.

30 And when Paul wanted to go into the [1]assembly, [a]the disciples would not let him.

31 And also some of the [1]Asiarchs who were friends of his sent to him and repeatedly urged him not to [2]venture into the theater.

32 [a]So then, some were shouting one thing and some another, for the [1]assembly was in confusion, and the majority did not know [2]for what cause they had come together.

33 And some of the crowd [1]concluded *it was* Alexander, since the Jews had put him forward; and having [a]motioned with his hand, Alexander was intending to make a defense to the [2]assembly.

34 But when they recognized that he was a Jew, a *single* outcry arose from them all as they shouted for about two hours, "Great is [1]Artemis of the Ephesians!"

35 And after quieting the multitude, the town clerk *said, "Men of [a]Ephesus, what man is there after all who does not know that the city of the Ephesians is guardian of the temple of the great [1]Artemis, and of the *image* which fell down from [2]heaven?

36 "Since then these are undeniable facts, you ought to keep calm and to do nothing rash.

37 "For you have brought these men *here* who are neither [a]robbers of temples nor blasphemers of our goddess.

38 "So then, if Demetrius and the craftsmen who are with him have a complaint against any man, the courts are in session and [1a]proconsuls are *available*; let them bring charges against one another.

39 "But if you want anything beyond this, it shall be settled in the [1]lawful [2]assembly.

40 "For indeed we are in danger of being accused of a riot in connection with today's affair, since there is no *real* cause *for it*; and in this connection we shall be unable to account for this disorderly gathering."

41 And after saying this he dismissed the [1]assembly.

Paul in Macedonia and Greece

20 AND after the uproar had ceased, Paul sent for [a]the disciples and when he had exhorted them and taken his leave of them, he departed [b]to go to [c]Macedonia.

2 And when he had gone through those districts and had given them much exhortation, he came to Greece.

3 And *there* he spent three months, and when [a]a plot was formed against him by the Jews as he was about to set sail for [b]Syria, he determined to return through [c]Macedonia.

4 And [1]he was accompanied by Sopater of [a]Berea, *the son* of Pyrrhus; and by [b]Aristarchus and Secundus of the [c]Thessalonians; and [d]Gaius of [e]Derbe, and [f]Timothy; and [g]Tychicus and [h]Trophimus of [2i]Asia.

5 But these had gone on ahead and were waiting for [a]us at [b]Troas.

6 And [a]we sailed from [b]Philippi after [c]the days of Unleavened Bread, and came to them at [d]Troas within five days; and there we stayed seven days.

7 And on [a]the first day of the week, when [b]we were gathered together to [c]break bread, Paul *began* talking to them, intending to depart the next day, and he prolonged his [1]message until midnight.

8 And there were many [a]lamps in the [b]upper room where we were gathered together.

9 And there was a certain young man named Eutychus sitting [1]on the window sill, sinking into a deep sleep; and as Paul kept on talking, he was overcome by sleep and fell down from the third floor, and was picked up dead.

10 But Paul went down and [a]fell upon him and after embracing him, he [b]said, "[1]Do not be troubled, for his life is in him."

11 And when he had gone *back* up, and had [a]broken the bread and [1]eaten, he talked with them a long while, until daybreak, and so departed.

12 And they took away the boy alive, and were [1]greatly comforted.

Troas to Miletus

13 But [a]we, going ahead to the ship, set sail for Assos, intending from there to take Paul on board; for thus he had arranged it, intending himself to go [1]by land.

14 And when he met us at Assos, we took him on board and came to Mitylene.

15 And sailing from there, we arrived the following day opposite Chios; and the next day we crossed over to Samos; and [1]the day following we came to [a]Miletus.

16 For Paul had decided to sail past [a]Ephesus in order that he might not have to spend time in [1b]Asia; for he was hurrying [c]to be in Jerusalem, if possible, [d]on the day of Pentecost.

27 [1]Lat., *Diana* [2]V. 22, note 1 [3]Lit., *the inhabited earth* [a]Acts 19:10 [b]Matt. 24:14
28 [1]Lat., *Diana* [a]Acts 18:19
29 [1]Lit., *having dragged* [a]Acts 20:4 [b]Acts 20:4; 27:2; Col. 4:10; Philem. 24 [c]Acts 13:5; 19:22; 20:34; 2 Cor. 8:19 [d]Acts 16:9; 19:22
30 [1]Lit., *people* [a]Acts 19:9
31 [1]I.e., political or religious officials of the province of Asia [2]Lit., *give himself*
32 [1]Gr., *ekklesia* [2]Or, *on whose account* [a]Acts 21:34
33 [1]Or, *instructed Alexander* [2]Lit., *people* [a]Acts 12:17
34 [1]Lat., *Diana*
35 [1]Lat., *Diana* [2]Lit., *Zeus;* or, *Jupiter* [a]Acts 18:19
37 [a]Rom. 2:22
38 [1]Or, *provincial governors* [a]Acts 13:7
39 [1]Or, *regular* [2]Gr., *ekklesia*
41 [1]Gr., *ekklesia*

1 [a]Acts 11:26 [b]Acts 19:21 [c]Acts 16:9; 20:3
3 [a]Acts 9:23f.; 20:19 [b]Matt. 4:24 [c]Acts 16:9; 20:1
4 [1]Lit., *there accompanied him* [2]I.e., west coast province of Asia Minor [a]Acts 17:10 [b]Acts 19:29 [c]Acts 17:1 [d]Acts 19:29 [e]Acts 14:6 [f]Acts 16:1 [g]Eph. 6:21; Col. 4:7; 2 Tim. 4:12; Titus 3:12 [h]Acts 21:29; 2 Tim. 4:20 [i]Acts 16:6; 20:16, 18
5 [a]Acts 16:10; 20:5-15 [b]Acts 16:8
6 [a]Acts 16:10; 20:5-15 [b]Acts 16:12 [c]Acts 12:3 [d]Acts 16:8
7 [1]Lit., *word, speech* [a]1 Cor. 16:2; Rev. 1:10 [b]Acts 16:10; 20:5-15 [c]Acts 2:42; 20:11
8 [a]Matt. 25:1 [b]Acts 1:13
9 [1]Or, *at the window*
10 [1]Or, *Stop being troubled* [a]1 Kin. 17:21; 2 Kin. 4:34 [b]Matt. 9:23f.; Mark 5:39
11 [1]Lit., *tasted* [a]Acts 2:42; 20:7
12 [1]Lit., *not moderately*
13 [1]Or, *on foot* [a]Acts 16:10; 20:5-15
15 [1]Later mss. add *after staying at Trogyllium, the day following* [a]Acts 20:17; 2 Tim. 4:20

16 [1]I.e., west coast province of Asia Minor [a]Acts 18:19 [b]Acts 16:6; 20:4, 18 [c]Acts 19:21; 20:6, 22; 1 Cor. 16:8 [d]Acts 2:1

Farewell to Ephesus

17 And from Miletus he sent to [a]Ephesus and called to him [b]the elders of the church.
18 And when they had come to him, he said to them,
"You yourselves know, [a]from the first day that I set foot in [1]Asia, how I was with you the whole time,
19 serving the Lord with all humility and with tears and with trials which came upon me through [a]the plots of the Jews;
20 how I [a]did not shrink from declaring to you anything that was profitable, and teaching you publicly and [1]from house to house,
21 solemnly [a]testifying to both Jews and Greeks of [b]repentance toward God and [c]faith in our Lord Jesus Christ.
22 "And now, behold, bound in [1]spirit, [a]I am on my way to Jerusalem, not knowing what will happen to me there,
23 except that [a]the Holy Spirit solemnly [b]testifies to me in every city, saying that [c]bonds and afflictions await me.
24 "But [a]I do not consider my life of any account as dear to myself, in order that I may [b]finish my course, and [c]the ministry which I received from the Lord Jesus, to [d]testify solemnly of the gospel of [e]the grace of God.
25 "And now, behold, I know that all of you, among whom I went about [a]preaching the kingdom, will see my face no more.
26 "Therefore I [1]testify to you this day, that [a]I am [2]innocent of the blood of all men.
27 "For I [a]did not shrink from declaring to you the whole [b]purpose of God.
28 "Be on guard for yourselves and for all [a]the flock, among which the Holy Spirit has made you [1]overseers, to shepherd [b]the church of [2]God which [c]He [3]purchased with His own blood.
29 "I know that after my departure [a]savage wolves will come in among you, not sparing [b]the flock;
30 and from among your own selves men will arise, speaking perverse things, to draw away [a]the disciples after them.
31 "Therefore be on the alert, remembering that night and day for a period of [a]three years I did not cease to admonish each one [b]with tears.
32 "And now I [a]commend you to [1]God and to [b]the word of His grace, which is able to [c]build *you* up and to give *you* [d]the inheritance among all those who are sanctified.
33 "[a]I have coveted no one's silver or gold or clothes.
34 "You yourselves know that [a]these hands ministered to my *own* needs and to the [b]men who were with me.
35 "In everything I showed you that by working hard in this manner you must help the weak and remember the words of the Lord Jesus, that He Himself said, 'It is more blessed to give than to receive.' "
36 And when he had said these things, he [a]knelt down and prayed with them all.
37 And [1]they *began* to weep aloud and [2a]embraced Paul, and repeatedly kissed him,
38 [1]grieving especially over [a]the word which he had spoken, that they should see his face no more. And they were [b]accompanying him to the ship.

Paul Sails from Miletus

21 AND when it came about that [a]we had parted from them and had set sail, we ran [b]a straight course to Cos and the next day to Rhodes and from there to Patara;
2 and having found a ship crossing over to [a]Phoenicia, we went aboard and set sail.
3 And when we had come in sight of [a]Cyprus, leaving it on the left, we kept sailing to [b]Syria and landed at [c]Tyre; for [d]there the ship was to unload its cargo.
4 And after looking up [a]the disciples, we stayed there seven days; and they kept telling Paul [1b]through the Spirit not to set foot in Jerusalem.
5 And when it came about that [1]our days there were ended, we departed and started on our journey, while they all, with wives and children, [a]escorted us until *we were* out of the city. And after [b]kneeling down on the beach and praying, we said farewell to one another.
6 Then we went on board the ship, and they returned [a]home again.
7 And when we had finished the voyage from [a]Tyre, we arrived at Ptolemais; and after greeting [b]the brethren, we stayed with them for a day.
8 And on the next day we departed and came to [a]Caesarea; and entering the house of [b]Philip the [c]evangelist, who was [b]one of the seven, we stayed with him.
9 Now this man had four virgin daughters who were [a]prophetesses.
10 And as we were staying there for some days, a certain prophet named [a]Agabus came down from Judea.
11 And coming to us, he [a]took Paul's belt and bound his own feet and hands, and said, "This [b]is what the Holy Spirit says: 'In this way the Jews at Jerusalem will [c]bind the man who owns this belt and [d]deliver him into the hands of the Gentiles.' "
12 And when we had heard this, we as well as the local residents *began* begging him [a]not to go up to Jerusalem.

17 [a]Acts 18:19 [b]Acts 11:30
18 [1]V. 16, note 1 [a]Acts 18:19; 19:1, 10; 20:4, 16
19 [a]Acts 20:3
20 [1]Or, *in the various private homes* [a]Acts 20:27
21 [a]Luke 16:28; Acts 18:5; 20:23, 24 [b]Acts 2:38; 11:18; 26:20 [c]Acts 24:24; 26:18; Eph. 1:15; Col. 2:5; Philem. 5
22 [1]Or, *the Spirit* [a]Acts 17:16; 20:16
23 [a]Acts 8:29 [b]Luke 16:28; Acts 18:5; 20:21, 24 [c]Acts 9:16; 21:33
24 [a]Acts 21:13 [b]Acts 13:25; 2 Tim. 4:7 [c]Acts 1:17 [d]Luke 16:28; Acts 18:5; 20:21 [e]Acts 11:23; 20:32
25 [a]Matt. 4:23; Acts 28:31
26 [1]Or, *call you to witness* [2]Lit., *pure from* [a]Acts 18:6
27 [a]Acts 20:20 [b]Acts 13:36
28 [1]Or, *bishops* [2]Some ancient mss. read *the Lord* [3]Lit., *acquired* [a]Luke 12:32; John 21:15-17; Acts 20:29; 1 Pet. 5:2f. [b]Matt. 16:18; Rom. 16:16; 1 Cor. 10:32 [c]Eph. 1:7, 14; Titus 2:14; 1 Pet. 1:19; 2:9; Rev. 5:9
29 [a]Ezek. 22:27; Matt. 7:15 [b]Luke 12:32; John 21:15-17; Acts 20:28; 1 Pet. 5:2f.
30 [a]Acts 11:26
31 [a]Acts 19:8, 10; 24:17 [b]Acts 20:19
32 [1]One ancient mss. reads *the Lord* [a]Acts 14:23 [b]Acts 14:3; 20:24 [c]Acts 9:31 [d]Acts 26:18; Eph. 1:14; 5:5; Col. 1:12; 3:24; Heb. 9:15; 1 Pet. 1:4
33 [a]1 Cor. 9:4-18; 2 Cor. 11:7-12; 12:14-18; 1 Thess. 2:5f.
34 [a]Acts 18:3 [b]Acts 19:22
36 [a]Acts 9:40; 21:5; Luke 22:41
37 [1]Lit., *a considerable weeping of all occurred* [2]Lit., *fell on Paul's neck* [a]Luke 15:20
38 [1]Lit., *suffering pain* [a]Acts 20:25 [b]Acts 15:3

1 [a][we] Acts 16:10; 21:1-18 [b]Acts 16:11
2 [a]Acts 11:19; 21:3
3 [a]Acts 4:36; 21:16 [b]Matt. 4:24 [c]Acts 12:20; 21:7 [d]Acts 21:2
4 [1]I.e., because of impressions made by the Spirit [a]Acts 11:26; 21:16 [b]Acts 20:23; 21:11
5 [1]Lit., *we had completed the days* [a]Acts 15:3 [b]Luke 22:41; Acts 9:40; 20:36
6 [a]John 19:27
7 [a]Acts 12:20; 21:3 [b]Acts 1:15; 21:17
8 [a]Acts 8:40; 21:16 [b]Acts 6:5; 8:5 [c]Eph. 4:11; 2 Tim. 4:5
9 [a]Luke 2:36; Acts 13:1; 1 Cor. 11:5
10 [a]Acts 11:28
11 [a]1 Kin. 22:11; Is. 20:2; Jer. 13:1-11; 19:1, 11; John 18 [b]Acts 8:29 [c]Acts 9:16; 21:33 [d]Matt. 20:19
12 [a]Acts 21:15

13 Then Paul answered, "What are
you doing, weeping and breaking my
heart? For [a]I am ready not only to be
bound, but even to die at Jerusalem for
[b]the name of the Lord Jesus."
14 And since he would not be persuaded, we fell silent, remarking, "[a]The
will of the Lord be done!"

Paul at Jerusalem

15 And after these days we got ready
and [a]started on our way up to Jerusalem.
16 And *some* of [a]the disciples from
[b]Caesarea also came with us, taking us
to Mnason of [c]Cyprus, a [d]disciple of
long standing with whom we were to
lodge.
17 And when we had come to Jerusalem, [a]the brethren received us gladly.
18 And now the following day Paul
went in with us to [1a]James, and all [b]the
elders were present.
19 And after he had greeted them, he
[a]*began* to relate one by one the things
which God had done among the Gentiles through his [b]ministry.
20 And when they heard it they *began*
[a]glorifying God; and they said to him,
"You see, brother, how many [1]thou-
sands there are among the Jews of those
who have believed, and they are all
[b]zealous for the Law;
21 and they have been told about you,
that you are [a]teaching all the Jews who
are among the Gentiles to forsake Moses, telling them [b]not to circumcise their
children nor to walk according to [c]the
customs.
22 "What, then, is *to be done*? They will
certainly hear that you have come.
23 "Therefore do this that we tell you.
We have four men who [1a]are under a
vow;
24 take them and [a]purify yourself
along with them, and [1]pay their expenses
in order that they may [b]shave their
[2]heads; and all will know that there is
nothing to the things which they have
been told about you, but that you yourself also walk orderly, keeping the Law.
25 "But concerning the Gentiles who
have believed, we wrote, [a]having decided
that they should abstain from [1]meat
sacrificed to idols and from blood and
from what is strangled and from fornication."
26 Then Paul [1]took the men, and the
next day, [a]purifying himself along with
them, [b]went into the temple, giving
notice of the completion of the days of
purification, until the sacrifice was offered for each one of them.

Paul Seized in the Temple

27 And when [a]the seven days were
almost over, [b]the Jews from [1c]Asia, upon
seeing him in the temple, *began* to stir up
all the multitude and laid hands on him,
28 crying out, "Men of Israel, come to
our aid! [a]This is the man who preaches
to all men everywhere against our people, and the Law, and this place; and
besides he has even brought Greeks into
the temple and has [b]defiled this holy
place."
29 For they had previously seen [a]Tro-
phimus the [b]Ephesian in the city with
him, and they supposed that Paul had
brought him into the temple.
30 And all the city was aroused, and
[1]the people rushed together; and taking
hold of Paul, they [a]dragged him out of
the temple; and immediately the doors
were shut.
31 And while they were seeking to kill
him, a report came up to the [1]com-
mander of the [a]*Roman* [2]cohort that all
Jerusalem was in confusion.
32 And at once he [a]took along *some*
soldiers and centurions, and ran down to
them; and when they saw the [1]com-
mander and the soldiers, they stopped
beating Paul.
33 Then the [1]commander came up
and took hold of him, and ordered him
to be [a]bound with [b]two chains; and he
began asking who he was and what he
had done.
34 But among the crowd [a]some were
shouting one thing *and* some another,
and when he could not find out the
[1]facts on account of the uproar, he
ordered him to be brought into [b]the
barracks.
35 And when he got to [a]the stairs, it so
happened that he was carried by the
soldiers because of the violence of the
[1]mob;
36 for the multitude of the people kept
following behind, crying out, "[a]Away
with him!"
37 And as Paul was about to be
brought into [a]the barracks, he said to the
[1]commander, "May I say something to
you?" And he *said, "Do you know
Greek?
38 "Then you are not [a]the Egyptian
who some [1]time ago stirred up a revolt
and led the four thousand men of the
Assassins out [b]into the wilderness?"
39 But Paul said, "[a]I am a Jew of
Tarsus in [b]Cilicia, a citizen of no insignificant city; and I beg you, allow me to
speak to the people."
40 And when he had given him permission, Paul, standing on [a]the stairs,
[b]motioned to the people with his hand;
and when there [1]was a great hush, he
spoke to them in the [2c]Hebrew dialect,
saying,

Paul's Defense before the Jews

22 "[a]BRETHREN and fathers, hear
my defense which I now *offer* to
you."
2 And when they heard that he was
addressing them in the [1a]Hebrew dialect,
they became even more quiet; and he
*said,

13 [a]Acts 20:24 [b]Acts 5:41; 9:16
14 [a]Luke 22:42
15 [a]Acts 21:12
16 [a]Acts 21:4 [b]Acts 8:40 [c]Acts 4:36; 21:3 [d]Acts 15:7
17 [a]Acts 1:15; 21:7
18 [1]Or, *Jacob* [a]Acts 12:17 [b]Acts 11:30
19 [a]Acts 14:27 [b]Acts 1:17
20 [1]Lit., *ten thousands* [a]Matt. 9:8 [b]Acts 15:1; 22:3; Rom. 10:2; Gal. 1:14
21 [a]Acts 21:28 [b]Acts 15:19ff.; 1 Cor. 7:18f. [c]Acts 6:14
23 [1]Lit., *have a vow on them* [a]Num. 6:13-21; Acts 18:18
24 [1]Lit., *spend on them* [2]Lit., *head* [a]John 11:55; Acts 21:26; 24:18 [b]Acts 18:18
25 [1]Lit., *the thing* [a]Acts 15:19f., 29
26 [1]Or, *took the men the next day, and purifying himself* [a]John 11:55; Acts 21:24; 24:18 [b]Num. 6:13; Acts 24:18
27 [1]I.e., west coast province of Asia Minor [a]Num. 6:9, 13-20 [b]Acts 20:19; 24:18 [c]Acts 16:6
28 [a]Acts 6:13 [b]Matt. 24:15; Acts 6:13f.; 24:6
29 [a]Acts 20:4 [b]Acts 18:19
30 [1]Lit., *a running together of the people occurred* [a]2 Kin. 11:15; Acts 16:19; 26:21
31 [1]I.e., chiliarch, in command of one thousand troops [2]Or, *battalion* [a]Acts 10:1
32 [1]V. 31, note 1 [a]Acts 23:27
33 [1]V. 31, note 1 [a]Acts 20:23; 21:11; 22:29; 26:29; 28:20; Eph. 6:20; 2 Tim. 1:16; 2:9 [b]Acts 12:6
34 [1]Lit., *certainty* [a]Acts 19:32 [b]Acts 21:37; 22:24; 23:10, 16, 32
35 [1]Or, *multitude* [a]Acts 21:40
36 [a]Luke 23:18; John 19:15; Acts 22:22
37 [1]V. 31, note 1 [a]Acts 21:34; 22:24; 23:10, 16, 32
38 [1]Lit., *days* [a]Acts 5:36 [b]Matt. 24:26
39 [a]Acts 9:11; 22:3 [b]Acts 6:9
40 [1]Lit., *occurred* [2]I.e., Jewish Aramaic [a]Acts 21:35 [b]Acts 12:17 [c]John 5:2; Acts 1:19; 22:2; 26:14

1 [a]Acts 7:2
2 [1]I.e., Jewish Aramaic [a]Acts 21:40

3"[a]I am [b]a Jew, born in [c]Tarsus of
[d]Cilicia, but brought up in this city,
educated [1]under [e]Gamaliel, [2][f]strictly
according to the law of our fathers,
being zealous for God, just as [g]you all
are today.
4"And [a]I persecuted this [b]Way to the
death, binding and putting both men
and women into prisons,
5 as also [a]the high priest and all [b]the
Council of the elders [1]can testify. From
them I also [c]received letters to [d]the
brethren, and started off for [e]Damascus
in order to bring even those who were
there to Jerusalem [2]as prisoners to be
punished.
6"[a]And it came about that as I was
on my way, approaching Damascus
about noontime, a very bright light
suddenly flashed from heaven all around
me,
7 and I fell to the ground and heard a
voice saying to me, 'Saul, Saul, why are
you persecuting Me?'
8"And I answered, 'Who art Thou,
Lord?' And He said to me, 'I am [a]Jesus
the Nazarene, whom you are persecuting.'
9"And those who were with me [a]be-
held the light, to be sure, but [b]did not
[1]understand the voice of the One who
was speaking to me.
10"And I said, '[a]What shall I do,
Lord?' And the Lord said to me, 'Arise
and go on into Damascus; and there you
will be told of all that has been appointed for you to do.'
11"But since I [a]could not see because
of the [1]brightness of that light, I was led
by the hand by those who were with me,
and came into Damascus.
12"And a certain [a]Ananias, a man who
was devout by the standard of the Law,
and [b]well spoken of by all the Jews who
lived there,
13 came to me, and standing near said
to me, '[a]Brother Saul, receive your
sight!' And [1][b]at that very time I looked
up at him.
14"And he said, '[a]The God of our
fathers has [b]appointed you to know His
will, and to [c]see the [d]Righteous One, and
to hear an [1]utterance from His mouth.
15 'For you will be [a]a witness for Him
to all men of [b]what you have seen and
heard.
16 'And now why do you delay?
[a]Arise, and be baptized, and [b]wash away
your sins, [c]calling on His name.'
17"And it came about when I [a]re-
turned to Jerusalem and was praying in
the temple, that I [b]fell into a trance,
18 and I saw Him saying to me,
'[a]Make haste, and get out of Jerusalem
quickly, because they will not accept
your testimony about Me.'
19"And I said, 'Lord, they themselves
understand that in one synagogue after
another [a]I used to imprison and [b]beat
those who believed in Thee.
20 'And [a]when the blood of Thy witness Stephen was being shed, I also was
standing by approving, and watching
out for the cloaks of those who were
slaying him.'
21"And He said to me, 'Go! For I will
send you far away [a]to the Gentiles.' "
22 And they listened to him up to this
statement, and *then* they raised their
voices and said, "[a]Away with such a
fellow from the earth, for [b]he should not
be allowed to live!"
23 And as they were crying out and
[a]throwing off their cloaks and [b]tossing
dust into the air,
24 the [1]commander ordered him to be
brought into [a]the barracks, stating that
he should be [b]examined by scourging so
that he might find out the reason why
they were shouting against him that way.
25 And when they stretched him out
[1]with thongs, Paul said to the centurion
who was standing by, "Is it lawful for
you to scourge [a]a man who is a Roman
and uncondemned?"
26 And when the centurion heard *this,*
he went to the [1]commander and told
him, saying, "What are you about to do?
For this man is a Roman."
27 And the [1]commander came and
said to him, "Tell me, are you a Roman?" And he said, "Yes."
28 And the [1]commander answered, "I
acquired this citizenship with a large
sum of money." And Paul said, "But I
was actually born *a citizen.*"
29 Therefore those who were about to
[a]examine him immediately [1]let go of
him; and the [2]commander also [b]was
afraid when he found out that he was a
Roman, and because he had [3][c]put him in
chains.
30 But on the next day, [a]wishing to
know for certain why he had been accused by the Jews, he [b]released him and
ordered the chief priests and all [c]the
[1]Council to assemble, and brought Paul
down and set him before them.

Paul before the Council

23 AND Paul, looking intently at
[a]the [1]Council, said, "[b]Brethren, [c]I
have [2]lived my life with a perfectly good
conscience before God up to this day."
2 And the high priest [a]Ananias commanded those standing beside him [b]to
strike him on the mouth.
3 Then Paul said to him, "God is
going to strike you, [a]you whitewashed
wall! And do you [b]sit to try me according to the Law, and in violation of the
Law order me to be struck?"
4 But the bystanders said, "Do you
revile God's high priest?"
5 And Paul said, "I was not aware,
brethren, that he was high priest; for it is
written, '[a]YOU SHALL NOT SPEAK EVIL OF
A RULER OF YOUR PEOPLE.' "

3 [1]Lit., *at the feet of* [2]Lit., *according to the strictness of the ancestral law* [a]Acts 9:1-22; 22:3-16; 26:9-18 [b]Acts 21:39 [c]Acts 9:11 [d]Acts 6:9 [e]Acts 5:34 [f]Acts 23:6; 26:5; Phil. 3:6 [g]Acts 21:20
4 [a]Acts 8:3; 22:19f.; 26:9-11 [b]Acts 9:2
5 [1]Lit., *testifies for me* [2]Lit., *having been bound* [a]Acts 9:1 [b]Luke 22:66; Acts 5:21; 1 Tim. 4:14 [c]Acts 9:2 [d]Acts 2:29; 3:17; 13:26; 23:1; 28:17, 21; Rom. 9:3 [e]Acts 9:2
6 [a]Acts 22:6-11: *Acts 9:3-8; 26:12-18*
8 [a]Acts 26:9
9 [1]Or, *hear* (with comprehension) [a]Acts 26:13 [b]Acts 9:7
10 [a]Acts 16:30
11 [1]Or, *glory* [a]Acts 9:8
12 [a]Acts 9:10 [b]Acts 6:3; 10:22
13 [1]Or, *instantly;* lit., *at that very hour* [a]Acts 9:17 [b]Acts 9:18
14 [1]Or, *message;* lit., *voice* [a]Acts 3:13 [b]Acts 9:15; 26:16 [c]Acts 9:17; 26:16; 1 Cor. 9:1; 15:8 [d]Acts 7:52
15 [a]Acts 23:11; 26:16 [b]Acts 22:14
16 [a]Acts 9:18 [b]Acts 2:38; 1 Cor. 6:11; Eph. 5:26; Heb. 10:22 [c]Acts 7:59
17 [a]Acts 9:26; 26:20 [b]Acts 10:10
18 [a]Acts 9:29
19 [a]Acts 8:3; 22:4 [b]Matt. 10:17; Acts 26:11
20 [a]Acts 7:58f.; 8:1; 26:10
21 [a]Acts 9:15
22 [a]Acts 21:36; 1 Thess. 2:16 [b]Acts 25:24
23 [a]Acts 7:58 [b]2 Sam. 16:13
24 [1]I.e., chiliarch, in command of one thousand troops [a]Acts 21:34 [b]Acts 22:29
25 [1]Lit., *for the thongs* [a]Acts 16:37
26 [1]V. 24, note 1
27 [1]V. 24, note 1
28 [1]V. 24, note 1
29 [1]Or, *withdrew from* [2]V. 24, note 1 [3]Lit., *bound him* [a]Acts 22:24 [b]Acts 16:38 [c]Acts 21:33
30 [1]Or, *Sanhedrin* [a]Acts 23:28 [b]Acts 21:33 [c]Matt. 5:22

1 [1]Or, *Sanhedrin* [2]Or, *conducted myself as a citizen* [a]Acts 22:30; 23:6, 15, 20, 28 [b]Acts 22:5 [c]Acts 24:16; 2 Cor. 1:12; 2 Tim. 1:3
2 [a]Acts 24:1 [b]John 18:22
3 [a]Matt. 23:27 [b]Lev. 19:15; Deut. 25:2; John 7:51

5 [a]Ex. 22:28

6 But perceiving that one part were
[a]Sadducees and the other Pharisees, Paul
began crying out in [b]the [1]Council,
"[c]Brethren, [d]I am a Pharisee, a son of
Pharisees; I am on trial for [e]the hope
and resurrection of the dead!"
7 And as he said this, there arose a
dissension between the Pharisees and
Sadducees; and the assembly was divided.
8 For [a]the Sadducees say that there is
no resurrection, nor an angel, nor a
spirit; but the Pharisees acknowledge
them all.
9 And there arose a great uproar;
and some of [a]the scribes of the Pharisaic
party stood up and *began* to argue
heatedly, saying, "[b]We find nothing
wrong with this man; [c]suppose a spirit
or an angel has spoken to him?"
10 And as a great dissension was
developing, the [1]commander was afraid
Paul would be torn to pieces by them
and ordered the troops to go down and
take him away from them by force, and
bring him into [a]the barracks.
11 But on [a]the night *immediately* following, the Lord stood at his side and
said, "[b]Take courage; for [c]as you have
[d]solemnly witnessed to My cause at
Jerusalem, so you must witness at Rome
also."

A Conspiracy to Kill Paul

12 And when it was day, [a]the Jews
formed a [1]conspiracy and [b]bound themselves under an oath, saying that they
would neither eat nor drink until they
had killed Paul.
13 And there were more than forty
who formed this plot.
14 And they came to the chief priests
and the elders, and said, "We have
[a]bound ourselves under a solemn oath to
taste nothing until we have killed Paul.
15 "Now, therefore, you [1]and [a]the
[2]Council notify the [3]commander to
bring him down to you, as though you
were going to determine his case by a
more thorough investigation; and we for
our part are ready to slay him before he
comes near *the place.*"
16 But the son of Paul's sister heard of
their ambush, [1]and he came and entered
[a]the barracks and told Paul.
17 And Paul called one of the centurions to him and said, "Lead this young
man to the [1]commander, for he has
something to report to him."
18 So he took him and led him to the
[1]commander and *said, "Paul [a]the prisoner called me to him and asked me to
lead this young man to you since he has
something to tell you."
19 And the [1]commander took him by
the hand and stepping aside, *began* to
inquire of him privately, "What is it that
you have to report to me?"
20 And he said, "[a]The Jews have
agreed to ask you to bring Paul down
tomorrow to [b]the [1]Council, as though
they were going to inquire somewhat
more thoroughly about him.
21 "So do not [1]listen to them, for more
than forty of them are [a]lying in wait for
him who have [b]bound themselves under
a curse not to eat or drink until they slay
him; and now they are ready and waiting for the promise from you."
22 Therefore the [1]commander let the
young man go, instructing him, "Tell no
one that you have notified me of these
things."

Paul Moved to Caesarea

23 And he called to him two of the
centurions, and said, "Get two hundred
soldiers ready by [1]the third hour of the
night to proceed to [a]Caesarea, [2]with
seventy horsemen and two hundred
[3]spearmen."
24 *They were* also to provide mounts
to put Paul on and bring him safely to
[a]Felix the governor.
25 And he wrote a letter having this
form:
26 "Claudius Lysias, to the [a]most
excellent governor Felix,
[b]greetings.
27 "When this man was arrested by
the Jews and was about to be
slain by them, [a]I came upon
them with the troops and rescued him, [b]having learned that
he was a Roman.
28 "And [a]wanting to ascertain the
charge for which they were accusing him, I [b]brought him
down to their [1c]Council;
29 and I found him to be accused
over [a]questions about their
Law, but [1]under [b]no accusation
deserving death or [2]imprison-
ment.
30 "And when I was [a]informed that
there would be [b]a plot against
the man, I sent him to you at
once, also instructing [c]his accusers to [1]bring charges against
him before you.[2]"
31 So the soldiers, in accordance with
their orders, took Paul and brought him
by night to Antipatris.
32 But the next day, leaving [a]the
horsemen to go on with him, they returned to [b]the barracks.
33 And when these had come to
[a]Caesarea and delivered the letter to [b]the
governor, they also presented Paul to
him.
34 And when he had read it, he asked
from what [a]province he was; and when
he learned that [b]he was from Cilicia,
35 he said, "I will give you a hearing
after your [a]accusers arrive also," giving
orders for him to be [b]kept in Herod's
[1]Praetorium.

---

6 [1]Or, *Sanhedrin* [a]Matt. 3:7; 22:23 [b]Acts 22:30; 23:1, 15, 20, 28 [c]Acts 22:5 [d]Acts 26:5; Phil. 3:5 [e]Acts 24:15, 21; 26:8
8 [a]Matt. 22:23; Mark 12:18; Luke 20:27
9 [a]Mark 2:16; Luke 5:30 [b]Acts 23:29 [c]John 12:29; Acts 22:6ff.
10 [1]I.e., chiliarch, in command of one thousand troops [a]Acts 21:34; 23:16, 32
11 [a]Acts 18:9 [b]Matt. 9:2 [c]Acts 19:21 [d]Luke 16:28; Acts 28:23
12 [1]Or, *mob* [a]Acts 9:23; 23:30; 1 Thess. 2:16 [b]Acts 23:14, 21
14 [a]Acts 23:12, 21
15 [1]Lit., *with* [2]Or, *Sanhedrin* [3]V. 10, note 1 [a]Acts 22:30; 23:1, 6, 20, 28
16 [1]Or, *having been present* with them, *and he entered* [a]Acts 21:34; 23:10, 32
17 [1]V. 10, note 1
18 [1]V. 10, note 1 [a]Eph. 3:1
19 [1]V. 10, note 1
20 [1]Or, *Sanhedrin* [a]Acts 23:14f. [b]Acts 22:30; 23:1, 6, 15, 28
21 [1]Lit., *be persuaded by them* [a]Luke 11:54 [b]Acts 23:12, 14
22 [1]V. 10, note 1
23 [1]I.e., 9 p.m. [2]Lit., *and* [3]Or, *slingers* or *bowmen* [a]Acts 8:40; 23:33
24 [a]Acts 23:26, 33; 24:1, 3, 10; 25:14
26 [a]Luke 1:3; Acts 24:3; 26:25 [b]Acts 15:23
27 [a]Acts 21:32f. [b]Acts 22:25-29
28 [1]Or, *Sanhedrin* [a]Acts 22:30 [b]Acts 23:10 [c]Acts 23:1
29 [1]Lit., *having* [2]Lit., *bonds* [a]Acts 18:15; 25:19 [b]Acts 23:9; 25:25; 26:31; 28:18
30 [1]Lit., *speak against him* [2]Some mss. add *Farewell* [a]Acts 23:20f. [b]Acts 9:24; 23:12 [c]Acts 23:35; 24:19; 25:16
32 [a]Acts 23:23 [b]Acts 23:10
33 [a]Acts 8:40; 23:23 [b]Acts 23:24, 26; 24:1, 3, 10; 25:14
34 [a]Acts 25:1 [b]Acts 6:9; 21:39
35 [1]I.e., governor's official residence [a]Acts 23:30; 24:19; 25:16 [b]Acts 24:27

Paul before Felix

24 AND after [a]five days the high
priest [b]Ananias came down with
some elders, [1]with a certain [2]attorney
named Tertullus; and they [3]brought
charges to [c]the governor against Paul.
2 And after *Paul* had been summoned, Tertullus began to accuse him,
saying *to the governor*,
"Since we have through you attained
much peace, and since by your provi-
dence reforms are being carried out for
this nation,
3 we acknowledge *this* in every way
and everywhere, [a]most excellent Felix,
with all thankfulness.
4 "But, that I may not weary you any
further, I beg you [1]to grant us, by your
kindness, a brief hearing.
5 "For we have found this man a real
pest and a fellow who stirs up dissension
among all the Jews throughout [1]the
world, and a ringleader of the [a]sect of
the Nazarenes.
6 "And he even tried to [a]desecrate the
temple; and [1]then we arrested him.
[[2]And we wanted to judge him according
to our own Law.
7 "But Lysias the commander came
along, and with much violence took him
out of our hands,
8 ordering his accusers to come before you.] And by examining him yourself concerning all these matters, you
will be able to ascertain the things of
which we accuse him."
9 And [a]the Jews also joined in the
attack, asserting that these things were
so.
10 And when [a]the governor had
nodded for him to speak, Paul responded:
"Knowing that for many years you
have been a judge to this nation, I
cheerfully make my defense,
11 since you can take note of the fact
that no more than [a]twelve days ago I
went up to Jerusalem to worship.
12 "And [a]neither in the temple, nor in
the synagogues, nor in the city *itself* did
they find me carrying on a discussion
with anyone or [b]causing [1]a riot.
13 "[a]Nor can they prove to you *the
charges* of which they now accuse me.
14 "But this I admit to you, that according to [a]the Way which they call a
[b]sect I do serve [1c]the God of our fathers,
[d]believing everything that is in accordance with the Law, and that is written in
the Prophets;
15 having a hope in God, which [a]these
men cherish themselves, that there shall
certainly be a resurrection of both the
righteous and the wicked.
16 "In view of this, [a]I also [1]do my best
to maintain always a blameless conscience *both* before God and before men.
17 "Now [a]after several years I [b]came to
bring [1]alms to my nation and to present
offerings;
18 in which they found me *occupied* in
the temple, having been [a]purified, without *any* [b]crowd or uproar. But *there were*
certain [c]Jews from [1]Asia—
19 who ought to have been present
before you, and to [a]make accusation, if
they should have anything against me.
20 "Or else let these men themselves
tell what misdeed they found when I
stood before [a]the [1]Council,
21 other than for this one statement
which [a]I shouted out while standing
among them, 'For the resurrection of the
dead I am on trial before you today.' "
22 But Felix, having a more exact
knowledge about [a]the Way, put them
off, saying, "When Lysias the [1]com-
mander comes down, I will decide your
case."
23 And he gave orders to the centurion for him to be [a]kept in custody and
yet [b]have *some* freedom, and not to
prevent any of [c]his friends from ministering to him.
24 But some days later, Felix arrived
with Drusilla, his [1]wife who was a Jew-
ess, and sent for Paul, and heard him
speak about [a]faith in Christ Jesus.
25 And as he was discussing [a]right-
eousness, [b]self-control and [c]the judgment to come, Felix became frightened
and said, "Go away for the present, and
when I find time, I will summon you."
26 At the same time too, he was hoping that [a]money would be given him by
Paul; therefore he also used to send for
him quite often and converse with him.
27 But after two years had passed,
Felix [1]was succeeded by Porcius [a]Fes-
tus; and [b]wishing to do the Jews a favor,
Felix left Paul [c]imprisoned.

Paul before Festus

25 FESTUS therefore, having arrived in [a]the province, three days
later went up to Jerusalem from [b]Caesa-
rea.
2 And the chief priests and the leading men of the Jews [a]brought charges
against Paul; and they were urging him,
3 requesting a [1]concession against
[2]Paul, that he might [3]have him brought
to Jerusalem (*at the same time,* [a]setting
an ambush to kill him on the way).
4 Festus then [a]answered that Paul
[b]was being kept in custody at [c]Caesarea
and that he himself was about to leave
shortly.
5 "Therefore," he *said, "let the influ-
ential men among you [1]go there with me,
and if there is anything wrong [2]about the
man, let them [3]prosecute him."
6 And after he had spent not more
than eight or ten days among them, he
went down to [a]Caesarea; and on the
next day he took his seat on [b]the tribunal and ordered Paul to be brought.

1 [1]Lit., *and* [2]Lit., *orator* [3]Or, *presented their evidence* or *case* [a]Acts 24:11 [b]Acts 23:2 [c]Acts 23:24
3 [a]Acts 23:26; 26:25
4 [1]Lit., *to hear . . . briefly*
5 [1]Lit., *the inhabited earth* [a]Acts 15:5; 24:14
6 [1]Lit., *also* [2]Many mss. do not contain the remainder of v. 6, v. 7, nor the first part of v. 8 [a]Acts 21:28
9 [a]1 Thess. 2:16
10 [a]Acts 23:24
11 [a]Acts 21:18, 27; 24:1
12 [1]Lit., *an attack of a mob* [a]Acts 25:8 [b]Acts 24:18
13 [a]Acts 25:7
14 [1]Lit., *the ancestral god* [a]Acts 9:2; 24:22 [b]Acts 15:5; 24:5 [c]Acts 3:13 [d]Acts 25:8; 26:4ff., 22f.; 28:23
15 [a]Dan. 12:2; John 5:28f.; 11:24; Acts 23:6
16 [1]Lit., *practice myself* [a]Acts 23:1
17 [1]Or, *gifts to charity* [a]Acts 20:31 [b]Acts 11:29f.; Rom. 15:25-28; 1 Cor. 16:1-4; 2 Cor. 8:1-4; 9:1, 2, 12; Gal. 2:10
18 [1]I.e., west coast province of Asia Minor [a]Acts 21:26 [b]Acts 24:12 [c]Acts 21:27
19 [a]Acts 23:30
20 [1]Or, *Sanhedrin* [a]Matt. 5:22
21 [a]Acts 23:6; 24:15
22 [1]I.e., chiliarch, in command of one thousand troops [a]Acts 24:14
23 [a]Acts 23:35 [b]Acts 28:16 [c]Acts 23:16; 27:3
24 [1]Lit., *own wife* [a]Acts 20:21
25 [a]Titus 2:12 [b]Gal. 5:23; Titus 1:8; 2 Pet. 1:6 [c]Acts 10:42
26 [a]Acts 24:17
27 [1]Lit., *received a successor, Porcius Festus* [a]Acts 25:1, 4, 9, 12; 26:24f., 32 [b]Acts 12:3; 25:9 [c]Acts 23:35; 25:14

1 [a]Acts 23:34 [b]Acts 8:40; 25:4, 6, 13
2 [a]Acts 24:1; 25:15
3 [1]Or, *favor* [2]Lit., *him* [3]Lit., *send for him to Jerusalem* [a]Acts 9:24
4 [a]Acts 25:16 [b]Acts 24:23 [c]Acts 8:40; 25:1, 6, 13
5 [1]Lit., *go down* [2]Lit., *in* [3]Or, *accuse*
6 [a]Acts 8:40; 25:1, 4, 13 [b]Matt. 27:19; Acts 25:10, 17

7 And after he had arrived, the Jews
who had come down from Jerusalem
stood around him, bringing [a]many and
serious charges against him [b]which they
could not prove;
8 while Paul said in his own defense,
"[a]I have committed no offense either
against the Law of the Jews or against
the temple or against Caesar."
9 But Festus, [a]wishing to do the Jews
a favor, answered Paul and said, "[b]Are
you willing to go up to Jerusalem and
[1]stand trial before me on these *charges*?"
10 But Paul said, "I am standing
before Caesar's [a]tribunal, where I ought
to be tried. I have done no wrong to *the*
Jews, as you also very well know.
11 "If then I am a wrongdoer, and have
committed anything worthy of death, I
do not refuse to die; but if none of those
things is *true* of which these men accuse
me, no one can hand me over to them. I
[a]appeal to Caesar."
12 Then when Festus had conferred
with [1]his council, he answered, "You
have appealed to Caesar, to Caesar you
shall go."
13 Now when several days had
elapsed, King Agrippa and Bernice arrived at [a]Caesarea, [1]and paid their respects to Festus.
14 And while they were spending
many days there, Festus laid Paul's case
before the king, saying, "There is a
certain man [a]left a prisoner by Felix;
15 and when I was at Jerusalem, the
chief priests and the elders of the Jews
[a]brought charges against him, asking for
a sentence of condemnation upon him.
16 "And I [a]answered them that it is not
the custom of the Romans to hand over
any man before [b]the accused meets his
accusers face to face, and has an opportunity to make his defense against the
charges.
17 "And so after they had assembled
here, I made no delay, but on the next
day took my seat on [a]the tribunal, and
ordered the man to be brought.
18 "And when the accusers stood up,
they *began* bringing charges against him
not of such crimes as I was expecting;
19 but they *simply* had some [a]points of
disagreement with him about their own
[1b]religion and about a certain dead man,
Jesus, whom Paul asserted to be alive.
20 "And [a]being at a loss how to investigate [1]such matters, I asked whether he
was willing to go to Jerusalem and there
stand trial on these matters.
21 "But when Paul [a]appealed to be held
in custody for [1]the Emperor's decision, I
ordered him to be kept in custody until I
send him to Caesar."
22 And [a]Agrippa *said* to Festus, "I
also would like to hear the man myself."
"Tomorrow," he *said, "you shall hear
him."

Paul before Agrippa

23 And so, on the next day when
[a]Agrippa had come [1]together with [a]Ber-
nice, amid great pomp, and had entered
the auditorium [2]accompanied by the
[3]commanders and the prominent men of
the city, at the command of Festus, Paul
was brought in.
24 And Festus *said, "King Agrippa,
and all you gentlemen here present with
us, you behold this man about whom [a]all
the people of the Jews appealed to me,
both at Jerusalem and here, loudly declaring that [b]he ought not to live any
longer.
25 "But I found that he had committed
[a]nothing worthy of death; and since he
himself [b]appealed to [1]the Emperor, I
decided to send him.
26 "[1]Yet I have nothing definite about
him to write to my lord. Therefore I have
brought him before you *all* and especially before you, King Agrippa, so that
after the investigation has taken place, I
may have something to write.
27 "For it seems absurd to me in sending a prisoner, not to indicate also the
charges against him."

Paul's Defense before Agrippa

26 AND [a]Agrippa said to Paul,
"You are permitted to speak for
yourself." Then Paul stretched out his
hand and *proceeded* to make his defense:
2 "In regard to all the things of which
I am accused by the Jews, I consider
myself fortunate, King Agrippa, that I
am about to make my defense before
you today;
3 [1]especially because you are an
expert in all [a]customs and [2]questions
among *the* Jews; therefore I beg you to
listen to me patiently.
4 "So then, all Jews know [a]my manner
of life from my youth up, which from the
beginning was spent among my *own*
nation and at Jerusalem;
5 since they have known about me
for a long time previously, if they are
willing to testify, that I lived *as* a [a]Phari-
see [b]according to the strictest [c]sect of
our religion.
6 "And now I am [1]standing trial [a]for
the hope of [b]the promise made by God
to our fathers;
7 *the promise* [a]to which our twelve
tribes hope to attain, as they earnestly
serve *God* night and day. And for this
[b]hope, O King, I am being [c]accused by
Jews.
8 "Why is it considered incredible
among you *people* [a]if God does raise the
dead?
9 "So then, [a]I thought to myself that I
had to do many things hostile to [b]the
name of Jesus of Nazareth.
10 "And this is [1]just what I [a]did in
Jerusalem; not only did I lock up many
of the [2]saints in prisons, having [b]re-
ceived authority from the chief priests,
but also when they were being put to
death I [c]cast my vote against them.

7 [a]Acts 24:5f. [b]Acts 24:13
8 [a]Acts 6:13; 24:12; 28:17
9 [1]Lit., *be judged* [a]Acts 12:3; 24:27 [b]Acts 25:20
10 [a]Matt. 27:19; Acts 25:6, 17
11 [a]Acts 25:21, 25; 26:32; 28:19
12 [1]A different body from that mentioned in Acts 4:15 and 24:20
13 [1]Lit., *greeting Festus* [a]Acts 8:40; 25:1, 4, 6
14 [a]Acts 24:27
15 [a]Acts 24:1; 25:2
16 [a]Acts 25:4f. [b]Acts 23:30
17 [a]Matt. 27:19; Acts 25:6, 10
19 [1]Or, *superstition* [a]Acts 18:15; 23:29 [b]Acts 17:22
20 [1]Lit., *these* [a]Acts 25:9
21 [1]Lit., *the Augustus'* (in this case Nero) [a]Acts 25:11f.
22 [a]Acts 9:15
23 [1]Lit., *and Bernice* [2]Lit., *and with* [3]I.e., chiliarchs, in command of one thousand troops [a]Acts 25:13; 26:30
24 [a]Acts 25:2, 7 [b]Acts 22:22
25 [1]V. 21, note 1 [a]Luke 23:4; Acts 23:29 [b]Acts 25:11f.
26 [1]Lit., *About whom I have nothing definite*

1 [a]Acts 9:15
3 [1]Or, *because you are especially expert* [2]Or, *controversial issues* [a]Acts 6:14; 25:19; 26:7
4 [a]Gal. 1:13f.; Phil. 3:5
5 [a]Acts 23:6; Phil. 3:5 [b]Acts 22:3 [c]Acts 15:5
6 [1]Lit., *being tried* [a]Acts 24:15; 28:20 [b]Acts 13:32
7 [a]James 1:1 [b]Acts 24:15; 28:20 [c]Acts 26:2
8 [a]Acts 23:6
9 [a]John 16:2; 1 Tim. 1:13 [b]John 15:21
10 [1]Lit., *also* [2]Or, *holy ones* [a]Acts 8:3; 9:13 [b]Acts 9:1f. [c]Acts 22:20

11“And [a]as I punished them often in all the synagogues, I tried to force them to blaspheme; and being [b]furiously enraged at them, I kept pursuing them [c]even to [1]foreign cities.

12“[1]While thus engaged [a]as I was journeying to Damascus with the authority and commission of the chief priests,

13 at midday, O King, I saw on the way a light from heaven, [1]brighter than the sun, shining all around me and those who were journeying with me.

14“And when we had [a]all fallen to the ground, I heard a voice saying to me in the [1b]Hebrew dialect, ‘Saul, Saul, why are you persecuting Me? It is hard for you to kick against the goads.’

15“And I said, ‘Who art Thou, Lord?’ And the Lord said, ‘I am Jesus whom you are persecuting.

16 ‘But arise, and [a]stand on your feet; for this purpose I have appeared to you, to [b]appoint you a [c]minister and [d]a witness not only to the things which you have [1]seen, but also to the things in which I will appear to you;

17 [a]delivering you [b]from the *Jewish* people and from the Gentiles, to whom I am sending you,

18 to [a]open their eyes so that they may turn from [b]darkness to light and from the dominion of [c]Satan to God, in order that they may receive [d]forgiveness of sins and an [e]inheritance among those who have been sanctified by [f]faith in Me.’

19“Consequently, King Agrippa, I did not prove disobedient to the heavenly vision,

20 but *kept* declaring both [a]to those of Damascus first, and *also* [b]at Jerusalem and *then* throughout all the region of Judea, and *even* [c]to the Gentiles, that they should [d]repent and turn to God, performing deeds [e]appropriate to repentance.

21“For this reason *some* Jews [a]seized me in the temple and tried [b]to put me to death.

22“And so, having obtained help from God, I stand to this day [a]testifying both to small and great, stating nothing but what [b]the Prophets and Moses said was going to take place;

23 [1a]that [2]the Christ was [3]to suffer, *and* [1]that [b]by reason of *His* resurrection from the dead He should be the first to proclaim [c]light both to the *Jewish* people and to the Gentiles.”

24 And while *Paul* was saying this in his defense, Festus *said in a loud voice, “Paul, you are out of your mind! [1]*Your* great [a]learning is [2]driving you mad.”

25 But Paul *said, “I am not out of my mind, [a]most excellent Festus, but I utter words [1]of sober truth.

26“For the king [1a]knows about these matters, and I speak to him also with confidence, [2]since I am persuaded that none of these things escape his notice; for this has not been done in a corner.

27“King Agrippa, do you believe the Prophets? I know that you [1]do.”

28 And Agrippa *replied* to Paul, “[1]In a short time you [2]will persuade me to [3]become a [a]Christian.”

29 And Paul *said,* “[1]I would to God, that whether [2]in a short or long time, not only you, but also all who hear me this day, might become such as I am, except for these [a]chains.”

30 And [a]the king arose and the governor and Bernice, and those who were sitting with them,

31 and when they had drawn aside, they *began* talking to one another, saying, “[a]This man is not doing anything worthy of death or [1]imprisonment.”

32 And Agrippa said to Festus, “This man might have been [a]set free if he had not [b]appealed to Caesar.”

Paul Is Sent to Rome

27 AND when it was decided that [a]we [b]should sail for [c]Italy, they proceeded to deliver Paul and some other prisoners to a centurion of the Augustan [1d]cohort named Julius.

2 And embarking in an Adramyttian ship, which was about to sail to the regions along the coast of [1a]Asia, we put out to sea, accompanied by [b]Aristarchus, a [c]Macedonian of [d]Thessalonica.

3 And the next day we put in at [a]Sidon; and Julius [b]treated Paul with consideration and [c]allowed him to go to his friends and receive care.

4 And from there we put out to sea and sailed under the shelter of [a]Cyprus because [b]the winds were contrary.

5 And when we had sailed through the sea along the coast of [a]Cilicia and [b]Pamphylia, we landed at Myra in Lycia.

6 And there the centurion found an [a]Alexandrian ship sailing for [b]Italy, and he put us aboard it.

7 And when we had sailed slowly for a good many days, and with difficulty had arrived off Cnidus, [a]since the wind did not permit us *to go* farther, we sailed under the shelter of [b]Crete, off Salmone;

8 and with difficulty [a]sailing past it we came to a certain place called Fair Havens, near which was the city of Lasea.

9 And when considerable time had passed and the voyage was now dangerous, since even [a]the [1]fast was already over, Paul *began* to admonish them,

10 and said to them, “Men, I perceive that the voyage will certainly be *attended* with [a]damage and great loss, not only of the cargo and the ship, but also of our lives.”

11 [1]Or, *outlying* [a]Matt. 10:17; Acts 22:19 [b]Acts 9:1 [c]Acts 22:5
12 [1]Lit., *In which things* [a]Acts 26:12-18: *9:3-8; 22:6-11*
13 [1]Lit., *above the brightness of*
14 [1]I.e., Jewish Aramaic [a]Acts 9:7 [b]Acts 21:40
16 [1]Some early mss. read *seen Me* [a]Ezek. 2:1; Dan. 10:11 [b]Acts 22:14 [c]Luke 1:2 [d]Acts 22:15
17 [a]Jer. 1:8, 19 [b]1 Chr. 16:35; Acts 9:15
18 [a]Is. 35:5; 42:7, 16; Eph. 5:8; Col. 1:13; 1 Pet. 2:9 [b]John 1:5; Eph. 5:8; Col. 1:12f.; 1 Thess. 5:5; 1 Pet. 2:9 [c]Matt. 4:10 [d]Luke 24:47; Acts 2:38 [e]Acts 20:32 [f]Acts 20:21
20 [a]Acts 9:19ff. [b]Acts 9:26-29; 22:17-20 [c]Acts 9:15; 13:46 [d]Acts 3:19 [e]Matt. 3:8; Luke 3:8
21 [a]Acts 21:27, 30 [b]Acts 21:31
22 [a]Luke 16:28 [b]Acts 10:43; 24:14
23 [1]Lit., *whether* [2]I.e., the Messiah [3]Lit., *subject to suffering* [a]Matt. 26:24; Acts 3:18 [b]1 Cor. 15:20, 23; Col. 1:18; Rev. 1:5 [c]Is. 42:6; 49:6; Luke 2:32; 2 Cor. 4:4
24 [1]Lit., *The many letters* [2]Lit., *turning you to madness* [a]John 7:15; 2 Tim. 3:15
25 [1]Lit., *of truth and rationality* [a]Acts 23:26; 24:3
26 [1]Or, *understands* [2]Or, *for* [a]Acts 26:3
27 [1]Lit., *believe*
28 [1]Or, *With a little* [2]Or, *try to convince* [3]Lit., *make* [a]Acts 11:26
29 [1]Lit., *I would pray to* [2]Or, *with a little or with much* [a]Acts 21:33
30 [a]Acts 25:23
31 [1]Lit., *bonds* [a]Acts 23:29
32 [a]Acts 28:18 [b]Acts 25:11
1 [1]Or, *battalion* [a][we] Acts 16:10; 27:1-28 [b]Acts 25:12, 25 [c]Acts 18:2; 27:6 [d]Acts 10:1
2 [1]I.e., west coast province of Asia Minor [a]Acts 2:9 [b]Acts 19:29 [c]Acts 16:9 [d]Acts 17:1
3 [a]Matt. 11:21 [b]Acts 27:43 [c]Acts 24:23
4 [a]Acts 4:36 [b]Acts 27:7
5 [a]Acts 6:9 [b]Acts 13:13
6 [a]Acts 28:11 [b]Acts 18:2; 27:1
7 [a]Acts 27:4 [b]Acts 2:11; 27:12f., 21; Titus 1:5, 12
8 [a]Acts 27:13
9 [1]I.e., Day of Atonement in September or October [a]Lev. 16:29-31; 23:27-29; Num. 29:7
10 [a]Acts 27:21

11 But the centurion was more persuaded by the [a]pilot and the [1]captain of
the ship, than by what was being said by
Paul.
12 And because the harbor was not
suitable for wintering, the majority
reached a decision to put out to sea from
there, if somehow they could reach
Phoenix, a harbor of [a]Crete, facing
[1]southwest and northwest, and spend
the winter *there.*
13 And [1]when a moderate south wind
came up, supposing that they had gained
their purpose, they weighed anchor and
began [a]sailing along [b]Crete, close *in-*
shore.

Shipwreck

14 But before very long there [a]rushed
down from [1]the land a violent wind,
called [2]Euraquilo;
15 and when the ship was caught *in it,*
and could not face the wind, we gave
way *to it,* and let ourselves be driven
along.
16 And running under the shelter of a
small island called [1]Clauda, we were
scarcely able to get the *ship's* boat under
control.
17 And after they had hoisted it up,
they used [1]supporting cables in under-
girding the ship; and fearing that they
might [a]run aground on *the shallows* of
Syrtis, they let down the [2]sea anchor,
and so let themselves be driven along.
18 The next day as we were being
violently storm-tossed, [1]they began to
[a]jettison the cargo;
19 and on the third day they threw the
ship's tackle overboard with their own
hands.
20 And since neither sun nor stars
appeared for many days, and no small
storm was assailing *us,* from then on all
hope of our being saved was gradually
abandoned.
21 And [1]when they had gone a long
time without food, then Paul stood up in
their midst and said, "[a]Men, you ought
to have [2]followed my advice and not to
have set sail from [b]Crete, and [3]incurred
this [a]damage and loss.
22 "And *yet* now I urge you to [a]keep up
your courage, for there shall be no loss
of life among you, but *only* of the ship.
23 "For this very night [a]an angel of the
God to whom I belong and [b]whom I
serve [c]stood before me,
24 saying, 'Do not be afraid, Paul;
[a]you must stand before Caesar; and
behold, God has granted you [b]all those
who are sailing with you.'
25 "Therefore, [a]keep up your courage,
men, for I believe God, that [1]it will turn
out exactly as I have been told.
26 "But we must [a]run aground on a
certain [b]island."
27 But when the fourteenth night had
come, as we were being driven about in
the Adriatic Sea, about midnight the
sailors *began* to surmise that [1]they were
approaching some land.
28 And they took soundings, and
found *it to be* twenty fathoms; and a
little farther on they took another
sounding and found *it to be* fifteen
fathoms.
29 And fearing that we might [a]run
aground somewhere on the [1]rocks, they
cast four anchors from the stern and
[2]wished for daybreak.
30 And as the sailors were trying to
escape from the ship, and had let down
[a]the *ship's* boat into the sea, on the
pretense of intending to lay out anchors
from the bow,
31 Paul said to the centurion and to
the soldiers, "Unless these men remain
in the ship, you yourselves cannot be
saved."
32 Then the soldiers cut away the
[a]ropes of the *ship's* boat, and let it fall
away.
33 And until the day was about to
dawn, Paul was encouraging them all to
take some food, saying, "Today is the
fourteenth day that you have been constantly watching and going without
eating, having taken nothing.
34 "Therefore I encourage you to take
some food, for this is for your preservation; for [a]not a hair from the head of any
of you shall perish."
35 And having said this, he took bread
and [a]gave thanks to God in the presence
of all; and he broke it and began to eat.
36 And all [a]of them [1]were encouraged,
and they themselves also took food.
37 And all of us in the ship were two
hundred and seventy-six [1a]persons.
38 And when they had eaten enough,
they *began* to lighten the ship by [a]throw-
ing out the wheat into the sea.
39 And when day came, [a]they [1]could
not recognize the land; but they [2]did
observe a certain bay with a beach, and
they [3]resolved to [4]drive the ship onto it
if they could.
40 And casting off [a]the anchors, they
[1]left them in the sea while at the same
time they were loosening the ropes of the
rudders, and hoisting the foresail to the
wind, they were heading for the beach.
41 But striking a [1]reef where two seas
met, they ran the vessel aground; and
the prow stuck fast and remained immovable, but the stern *began* to be
broken up by the force *of the waves.*
42 And the soldiers' plan was to [a]kill
the prisoners, that none *of them* should
swim away and escape;
43 but the centurion, [a]wanting to
bring Paul safely through, kept them
from their intention, and commanded
that those who could swim should [1]jump
overboard first and get to land,
44 and the rest *should follow,* some on
planks, and others on various things
from the ship. And thus it happened that
[a]they all were brought safely to land.

11 [1]Or, *owner* [a]Rev. 18:17

12 [1]Or possibly, *northeast and southeast* [a]Acts 2:11; 27:13, 21; Titus 1:5, 12

13 [1]Lit., *a south wind having gently blown* [a]Acts 27:8 [b]Acts 2:11; 27:12f., 21; Titus 1:5, 12

14 [1]Lit., *it* [2]I.e., a northeaster [a]Mark 4:37

16 [1]Some ancient mss. read *Cauda*

17 [1]Lit., *helps* [2]Or possibly, *sail* [a]Acts 27:26, 29

18 [1]Lit., *they were doing a throwing out* [a]Jon. 1:5; Acts 27:38

21 [1]Lit., *there being much abstinence from food* [2]Lit., *obeyed me* [3]Lit., *gained* [a]Acts 27:10 [b]Acts 27:7

22 [a]Acts 27:25, 36

23 [a]Acts 5:19 [b]Rom. 1:9 [c]Acts 18:9; 23:11; 2 Tim. 4:17

24 [a]Acts 23:11 [b]Acts 27:31, 42, 44

25 [1]Lit., *it will be* [a]Acts 27:22, 36

26 [a]Acts 27:17, 29 [b]Acts 28:1

27 [1]Lit., *some land was approaching them*

29 [1]Lit., *rough places* [2]Lit., *they were praying for it to become day* [a]Acts 27:17, 26

30 [a]Acts 27:16

32 [a]John 2:15

34 [a]Matt. 10:30

35 [a]Matt. 14:19

36 [1]Lit., *became cheerful* [a]Acts 27:22, 25

37 [1]Lit., *souls* [a]Acts 2:41

38 [a]Jon. 1:5; Acts 27:18

39 [1]Or, *were not recognizing* [2]Or, *were observing* [3]Or, *were resolving* [4]Some ancient mss. read *bring the ship safely ashore* [a]Acts 28:1

40 [1]Or, *were leaving* [a]Acts 27:29

41 [1]Lit., *place*

42 [a]Acts 12:19

43 [1]Lit., *cast themselves* [a]Acts 27:3

44 [a]Acts 27:22, 31

Safe at Malta

28 AND when [a]they had been
brought safely through, [b]then we
found out that [c]the island was called
[1]Malta.
2 And [a]the [1]natives showed us
extraordinary kindness; for because of
the rain that had set in and because of
the cold, they kindled a fire and [b]re-
ceived us all.
3 But when Paul had gathered a
bundle of sticks and laid them on the
fire, a viper came out [1]because of the
heat, and fastened on his hand.
4 And when [a]the [1]natives saw the
creature hanging from his hand, they
began saying to one another, "[b]Un-
doubtedly this man is a murderer, and
though he has been saved from the sea,
[2]justice has not allowed him to live."
5 However [a]he shook the creature off
into the fire and suffered no harm.
6 But they were expecting that he
was about to swell up or suddenly fall
down dead. But after they had waited a
long time and had seen nothing unusual
happen to him, they changed their minds
and [a]*began* to say that he was a god.
7 Now in the neighborhood of that
place were lands belonging to the leading man of the island, named Publius,
who welcomed us and entertained us
courteously three days.
8 And it came about that the father
of Publius was lying *in bed* afflicted with
recurrent fever and dysentery; and Paul
went in *to see* him and after he had
[a]prayed, he [b]laid his hands on him and
healed him.
9 And after this had happened, the
rest of the people on the island who had
diseases were coming to him and getting
cured.
10 And they also honored us with
many [1]marks of respect; and when we
were setting sail, they [2]supplied *us* with
[3]all we needed.

Paul Arrives at Rome

11 And at the end of three months we
set sail on [a]an Alexandrian ship which
had wintered at the island, and which
had [1]the Twin Brothers for its figure-
head.
12 And after we put in at Syracuse, we
stayed there for three days.
13 And from there we [1]sailed around
and arrived at Rhegium, and a day later
a south wind sprang up, and on the
second day we came to Puteoli.
14 [1]There we found *some* [a]brethren,
and were invited to stay with them for
seven days; and thus we came to Rome.
15 And the [a]brethren, when they
heard about us, came from there as far
as the [1]Market of Appius and [2]Three
Inns to meet us; and when Paul saw
them, he thanked God and took courage.
16 And when we entered Rome, Paul
was [a]allowed to stay by himself, with the
soldier who was guarding him.
17 And it happened that after three
days he called together those who were
[a]the leading men of the Jews, and when
they had come together, he *began* saying
to them, "[b]Brethren, [c]though I had done
nothing against our people, or [d]the
customs of our [1]fathers, yet I was delivered prisoner from Jerusalem into the
hands of the Romans.
18 "And when they had [a]examined me,
they [b]were willing to release me because
there was [c]no ground [1]for putting me to
death.
19 "But when the Jews [1]objected, I was
forced to [a]appeal to Caesar; not that I
had any accusation against my nation.
20 "For this reason therefore, I [1]re-
quested to see you and to speak with
you, for I am wearing [a]this chain for [b]the
sake of the hope of Israel."
21 And they said to him, "We have
neither received letters from Judea concerning you, nor have any of [a]the brethren come here and reported or spoken
anything bad about you.
22 "But we desire to hear from you
what [1]your views are; for concerning this
[a]sect, it is known to us that [b]it is spoken
against everywhere."
23 And when they had set a day for
him, they came to him at [a]his lodging in
large numbers; and he was explaining to
them by solemnly [b]testifying about the
kingdom of God, and trying to persuade
them concerning Jesus, [c]from both the
Law of Moses and from the Prophets,
from morning until evening.
24 And [a]some were being persuaded
by the things spoken, but others would
not believe.
25 And when they did not agree with
one another, they *began* leaving after
Paul had spoken one *parting* word, "The
Holy Spirit rightly spoke through Isaiah
the prophet to your fathers,
26 saying,
'[a]GO TO THIS PEOPLE AND SAY,
"[1][b]YOU WILL KEEP ON HEARING,
[2]BUT WILL NOT UNDERSTAND;
AND [3]YOU WILL KEEP ON SEEING,
BUT WILL NOT PERCEIVE;
27 [a]FOR THE HEART OF THIS PEOPLE
HAS BECOME DULL,
AND WITH THEIR EARS THEY
SCARCELY HEAR,
AND THEY HAVE CLOSED THEIR
EYES;
LEST THEY SHOULD SEE WITH
THEIR EYES,
AND HEAR WITH THEIR EARS,
AND UNDERSTAND WITH THEIR
HEART AND RETURN,
AND I SHOULD HEAL THEM." '

1 [1]Or, *Melita.* Some mss. read *Melitene* [a][we] Acts 16:10; 27:1 [b]Acts 27:39 [c]Acts 27:26
2 [1]Lit., *barbarians* [a]Acts 28:4; Rom. 1:14; 1 Cor. 14:11; Col. 3:11 [b]Rom. 14:1
3 [1]Or, *from the heat*
4 [1]Lit., *barbarians* [2]I.e., personification of a goddess [a]Acts 28:2 [b]Luke 13:2, 4
5 [a]Mark 16:18
6 [a]Acts 14:11
8 [a]Acts 9:40; James 5:14f. [b]Matt. 9:18; Mark 5:23; 6:5
10 [1]Lit., *honors* [2]Or, *put on board* [3]Lit., *the things pertaining to the needs*
11 [1]Gr., the Dioscuri; i.e., Castor and Pollux, twin sons of Zeus [a]Acts 27:6
13 [1]Some early mss. read *weighed anchor*
14 [1]Lit., *where* [a]John 21:23; Acts 1:15; 6:3; 9:30; Rom. 1:13; 28:15
15 [1]Lat., *Appii Forum,* a station about 43 miles from Rome [2]Lat., *Tres Tabernae,* a station about 33 miles from Rome [a]Acts 1:15; 10:23; 11:1, 12, 29; 12:17
16 [a]Acts 24:23
17 [1]Or, *forefathers* [a]Acts 13:50; 25:2 [b]Acts 22:5 [c]Acts 25:8 [d]Acts 6:14
18 [1]Lit., *of death in me* [a]Acts 22:24 [b]Acts 26:32 [c]Acts 23:29; 25:25; 26:31
19 [1]Lit., *spoke against it* [a]Acts 25:11, 21, 25; 26:32
20 [1]Or, *invited you to see me and speak with me* [a]Acts 21:33 [b]Acts 26:6f.
21 [a]Acts 3:17; 22:5; 28:14; Rom. 9:3
22 [1]Lit., *you think* [a]Acts 24:14 [b]1 Pet. 2:12; 3:16; 4:14, 16
23 [a]Philem. 22 [b]Luke 16:28; Acts 1:3; 23:11 [c]Acts 8:35
24 [a]Acts 14:4
26 [1]Lit., *with a hearing* [2]Lit., *and* [3]Lit., *seeing you will see* [a]Is. 6:9 [b]Matt. 13:14f.
27 [a]Is. 6:10

28 "Let it be known to you therefore, that [a]this salvation of God has been sent [b]to the Gentiles; they will also listen."

29 [[1]And when he had spoken these words, the Jews departed, having a great dispute among themselves.]

30 And he stayed two full years [1]in his own rented quarters, and was welcoming all who came to him,

31 [1a]preaching the kingdom of God, and teaching concerning the Lord Jesus Christ [b]with all openness, unhindered.

28 [a]Ps. 98:3; Luke 2:30; Acts 13:26 [b]Acts 9:15; 13:46
29 [1]Many mss. do not contain this v.
30 [1]Or, *at his own expense*
31 [1]Or, *proclaiming* [a]Matt. 4:23; Acts 20:25; 28:23 [b]2 Tim. 2:9

THE EPISTLE OF PAUL TO THE ROMANS

The Gospel Exalted

1 PAUL, a bond-servant of Christ Jesus, [1a]called *as* an apostle, [b]set apart for [c]the gospel of God,

2 which He [a]promised beforehand through His [b]prophets in the holy Scriptures,

3 concerning His Son, who was born [a]of a [1]descendant of David [b]according to the flesh,

4 who was declared [a]the Son of God with power [1]by the resurrection from the dead, according to the [2]spirit of holiness, Jesus Christ our Lord,

5 through whom we have received grace and [a]apostleship [1]to bring about *the* [b]obedience of faith among [c]all the Gentiles, for His name's sake,

6 among whom you also are the [a]called of Jesus Christ;

7 to all who are [a]beloved of God in Rome, called *as* [1b]saints: [c]Grace to you and peace from God our Father and the Lord Jesus Christ.

8 First, [a]I thank my God through Jesus Christ for you all, because [b]your faith is being proclaimed throughout the whole world.

9 For [a]God, whom I [b]serve in my spirit in the *preaching of the* gospel of His Son, is my witness *as to* how unceasingly [c]I make mention of you,

10 always in my prayers making request, if perhaps now at last by [a]the will of God I may succeed in coming to you.

11 For [a]I long to see you in order that I may impart some spiritual gift to you, that you may be established;

12 that is, that I may be encouraged together with you *while* among you, each of us by the other's faith, both yours and mine.

13 And [a]I do not want you to be unaware, [b]brethren, that often I [c]have planned to come to you (and have been prevented thus far) in order that I might obtain some [d]fruit among you also, even as among the rest of the Gentiles.

14 [a]I am [1]under obligation both to Greeks and to [b]barbarians, both to the wise and to the foolish.

15 Thus, for my part, I am eager to [a]preach the gospel to you also who are in Rome.

1 [1]Lit., *a called apostle* [a]1 Cor. 1:1; 9:1; 2 Cor. 1:1 [b]Acts 9:15; 13:2; Gal. 1:15 [c]Mark 1:14; Rom. 15:16
2 [a]Titus 1:2 [b]Luke 1:70; Rom. 3:21; 16:26
3 [1]Lit., *seed* [a]Matt. 1:1 [b]John 1:14; Rom. 4:1; 9:3, 5; 1 Cor. 10:18
4 [1]Or, *as a result of* [2]Or, *spirit* [a]Matt. 4:3
5 [1]Lit., *for obedience* [a]Acts 1:25; Gal. 1:16 [b]Acts 6:7; Rom. 16:26 [c]Acts 9:15
6 [a]Jude 1; Rev. 17:14
7 [1]Or, *holy ones* [a]Rom. 5:5ff.; 8:39 [b]Acts 9:13; Rom. 8:28ff.; 1 Cor. 1:2, 24 [c]Num. 6:25f.; 1 Cor. 1:3; 2 Cor. 1:2; Gal. 1:3; Eph. 1:2; Phil. 1:2; Col. 1:2; 1 Thess. 1:1; 2 Thess. 1:2
8 [a]1 Cor. 1:4; Eph. 1:15f.; Phil. 1:3f.; Col. 1:3f.; 1 Thess. 1:2; 2:13 [b]Acts 28:22; Rom. 16:19
9 [a]Rom. 9:1 [b]Acts 24:14; 2 Tim. 1:3 [c]Eph. 1:16; Phil. 1:3f.
10 [a]Acts 18:21; Rom. 15:32
11 [a]Acts 19:21; Rom. 15:23
13 [a]Rom. 11:25; 1 Cor. 10:1; 12:1; 2 Cor. 1:8; 1 Thess. 4:13 [b]Acts 1:15; Rom. 7:1; 1 Cor. 1:10; 14:20, 26; Gal. 3:15 [c]Acts 19:21; Rom. 15:22f. [d]John 4:36; 15:16; Phil. 1:22; Col. 1:6
14 [1]Lit., *debtor* [a]1 Cor. 9:16 [b]Acts 28:2
15 [a]Rom. 15:20
16 [a]Mark 8:38; 2 Tim. 1:8, 12, 16 [b]1 Cor. 1:18, 24 [c]Acts 3:26; Rom. 2:9 [d]John 7:35
17 [1]Or, *by* [2]Or, *But he who is righteous by faith shall live.* [a]Rom. 3:21; 9:30; Phil. 3:9 [b]Hab. 2:4; Gal. 3:11; Heb. 10:38

16 For I am not [a]ashamed of the gospel, for [b]it is the power of God for salvation to everyone who believes, to the [c]Jew first and also to [d]the Greek.

17 For in it [a]*the* righteousness of God is revealed [1]from faith to faith; as it is written, "[2b]BUT THE RIGHTEOUS *man* SHALL LIVE BY FAITH."

Unbelief and Its Consequences

18 For [a]the wrath of God is revealed from heaven against all ungodliness and unrighteousness of men, who [b]suppress the truth [1]in unrighteousness,

19 because [a]that which is known about God is evident [1]within them; for God made it evident to them.

20 For [a]since the creation of the world His invisible attributes, His eternal power and divine nature, have been clearly seen, [b]being understood through what has been made, so that they are without excuse.

21 For even though they knew God, they did not [1]honor Him as God, or give thanks; but they became [a]futile in their speculations, and their foolish heart was darkened.

22 [a]Professing to be wise, they became fools,

23 and [a]exchanged the glory of the incorruptible God for an image in the form of corruptible man and of birds and four-footed animals and [1]crawling creatures.

24 Therefore [a]God gave them over in the lusts of their hearts to impurity, that their bodies might be [b]dishonored among them.

25 For they exchanged the truth of God for [1]a [a]lie, and worshiped and served the creature rather than the Creator, [b]who is blessed [2]forever. Amen.

26 For this reason [a]God gave them over to [b]degrading passions; for their women exchanged the natural function for that which is [1]unnatural,

18 [1]Or, *by* [a]Rom. 5:9; Eph. 5:6; Col. 3:6 [b]2 Thess. 2:6f.
19 [1]Or, *among* [a]Acts 14:17; 17:24ff.
20 [a]Mark 10:6 [b]Job 12:7-9; Ps. 19:1-6; Jer. 5:21f.
21 [1]Lit., *glorify* [a]2 Kin. 17:15; Jer. 2:5; Eph. 4:17f.
22 [a]Jer. 10:14; 1 Cor. 1:20
23 [1]Or possibly, *reptiles* [a]Deut. 4:16-18; Ps. 106:20; Jer. 2:11; Acts 17:29
24 [a]Rom. 1:26, 28; Eph. 4:19 [b]Eph. 2:3
25 [1]Lit., *the lie* [2]Lit., *unto the ages* [a]Is. 44:20; Jer. 10:14; 13:25; 16:19 [b]Rom. 9:5; 2 Cor. 11:31
26 [1]Lit., *against nature* [a]Rom. 1:24 [b]1 Thess. 4:5

27 and in the same way also the men
abandoned the natural function of the
woman and burned in their desire
toward one another, [a]men with men
committing [1]indecent acts and receiving
in [2]their own persons the due penalty of
their error.
28 And just as they did not see fit [1]to
acknowledge God any longer, [a]God gave
them over to a depraved mind, to do
those things which are not proper,
29 being filled with all unrighteousness, wickedness, greed, evil; full of
envy, murder, strife, deceit, malice; *they
are* [a]gossips,
30 slanderers, [1a]haters of God, insolent, arrogant, boastful, inventors of evil,
[b]disobedient to parents,
31 without understanding, untrustworthy, [a]unloving, unmerciful;
32 and, although they know the ordinance of God, that those who practice
such things are worthy of [a]death, they
not only do the same, but also [b]give
hearty approval to those who practice
them.

The Impartiality of God

2 THEREFORE you are [a]without excuse, [b]every man *of you* who passes
judgment, for in that [c]you judge another,
you condemn yourself; for you who
judge practice the same things.
2 And we know that the judgment of
God [1]rightly falls upon those who practice such things.
3 And do you suppose this, [a]O man,
[1]when you pass judgment upon those
who practice such things and do the
same *yourself,* that you will escape the
judgment of God?
4 Or do you think lightly of [a]the
riches of His [b]kindness and [c]forbearance
and [d]patience, not knowing that the
kindness of God leads you to repentance?
5 But [1]because of your stubbornness
and unrepentant heart [a]you are storing
up wrath for yourself [b]in the day of
wrath and revelation of the righteous
judgment of God,
6 [a]who WILL RENDER TO EVERY MAN
ACCORDING TO HIS DEEDS:
7 to those who by [a]perseverance in
doing good seek for [b]glory and honor
and [c]immortality, [d]eternal life;
8 but to those who are [a]selfishly
ambitious and [b]do not obey the truth,
but obey unrighteousness, wrath and
indignation.
9 *There will be* [a]tribulation and distress [1]for every soul of man who does
evil, of the Jew [b]first and also of the
Greek,
10 but [a]glory and honor and peace to
every man who does good, to the Jew
[b]first and also to the Greek.
11 For [a]there is no partiality with
God.
12 For all who have sinned [1a]without
the Law will also perish [1]without the
Law; and all who have sinned [2]under the
Law will be judged [3]by the Law;
13 for [a]not the hearers [1]of the Law are
[2]just before God, but the doers [1]of the
Law will be justified.
14 For when Gentiles who do not
have [1]the Law do [2a]instinctively the
things of the Law, these, not having [1]the
Law, are a law to themselves,
15 in that they show [a]the work of the
Law written in their hearts, their conscience bearing witness, and their
thoughts alternately accusing or else
defending them,
16 on the day when, [a]according to my
gospel, [b]God will judge the secrets of
men through Christ Jesus.

The Jew Is Condemned by the Law

17 But if you bear the name "Jew,"
and [a]rely [1]upon the Law, and boast in
God,
18 and know *His* will, and [1a]approve
the things that are essential, being instructed out of the Law,
19 and are confident that you yourself
are a guide to the blind, a light to those
who are in darkness,
20 a [1]corrector of the foolish, a
teacher of [2]the immature, having in the
Law [a]the embodiment of knowledge and
of the truth,
21 you, therefore, [a]who teach another,
do you not teach yourself? You who
[1]preach that one should not steal, do you
steal?
22 You who say that one should not
commit adultery, do you commit adultery? You who abhor idols, do you [a]rob
temples?
23 You who [a]boast [1]in the Law,
through your breaking the Law, do you
dishonor God?
24 For "[a]THE NAME OF GOD IS BLAS-
PHEMED AMONG THE GENTILES [b]BECAUSE
OF YOU," just as it is written.
25 For indeed circumcision is of value,
if you [a]practice [1]the Law; but if you are
a transgressor [2]of the Law, [b]your circumcision has become uncircumcision.
26 [a]If therefore [b]the [1]uncircumcised
man [c]keeps the requirements of the Law,
will not his uncircumcision be regarded
as circumcision?
27 And will not [a]he who is physically
uncircumcised, if he keeps the Law, will
he not [b]judge you who [1]though having
the letter *of the Law* and circumcision
are a transgressor [2]of the Law?

27 [1]Lit., *the shameless deed* [2]Lit., *themselves* [a]Lev. 18:22; 20:13; 1 Cor. 6:9
28 [1]Lit., *to have God in knowledge* [a]Rom. 1:24
29 [a]2 Cor. 12:20
30 [1]Or, *hateful to God* [a]Ps. 5:5 [b]2 Tim. 3:2
31 [a]2 Tim. 3:3
32 [a]Rom. 6:21 [b]Luke 11:48; Acts 8:1; 22:20

1 [a]Rom. 1:20 [b]Luke 12:14; Rom. 2:3; 9:20 [c]2 Sam. 12:5-7; Matt. 7:1; Luke 6:37; Rom. 14:22
2 [1]Lit., *is according to truth against*
3 [1]Lit., *who pass judgment* [a]Luke 12:14; Rom. 2:1; 9:20
4 [a]Rom. 9:23; 11:33; 2 Cor. 8:2; Eph. 1:7, 18; 2:7; Phil. 4:19; Col. 1:27; 2:2; Titus 3:6 [b]Rom. 11:22 [c]Rom. 3:25 [d]Ex. 34:6; Rom. 9:22; 1 Tim. 1:16; 1 Pet. 3:20; 2 Pet. 3:9, 15
5 [1]Or, *in accordance with* [a]Deut. 32:34f.; Prov. 1:18 [b]Ps. 110:5; 2 Cor. 5:10; 2 Thess. 1:5; Jude 6
6 [a]Ps. 62:12; Prov. 24:12; Matt. 16:27
7 [a]Luke 8:15; Heb. 10:36 [b]Rom. 2:10; Heb. 2:7; 1 Pet. 1:7 [c]1 Cor. 15:42, 50, 53f.; Eph. 6:24; 2 Tim. 1:10 [d]Matt. 25:46
8 [a]2 Cor. 12:20; Gal. 5:20; Phil. 1:17; 2:3; James 3:14, 16 [b]2 Thess. 2:12
9 [1]Lit., *upon* [a]Rom. 8:35 [b]Acts 3:26; Rom. 1:16; 1 Pet. 4:17
10 [a]Rom. 2:7; Heb. 2:7; 1 Pet. 1:7 [b]Rom. 2:9
11 [a]Deut. 10:17; Acts 10:34
12 [1]Or, *without law* [2]Or, *under law* [3]Or, *by law* [a]Acts 2:23; 1 Cor. 9:21
13 [1]Or, *of law* [2]Or, *righteous* [a]Matt. 7:21, 24ff.; John 13:17; James 1:22f., 25
14 [1]Or, *law* [2]Lit., *by nature* [a]Acts 10:35; Rom. 1:19; 2:15
15 [a]Rom. 2:14, 27
16 [a]Rom. 16:25; 1 Cor. 15:1; Gal. 1:11; 1 Tim. 1:11; 2 Tim. 2:8 [b]Acts 10:42; 17:31; Rom. 3:6; 14:10
17 [1]Or, *upon law* [a]Mic. 3:11; John 5:45; Rom. 2:23; 9:4

18 [1]Or, *distinguish between the things which differ* [a]Phil. 1:10
20 [1]Or, *instructor* [2]Lit., *infants* [a]Rom. 3:31; 2 Tim. 1:13
21 [1]Or, *proclaim* [a]Matt. 23:3ff.
22 [a]Acts 19:37
23 [1]Or, *in law* [a]Mic. 3:11; John 5:45; Rom. 2:17; 9:4
24 [a]Is. 52:5; Ezek. 36:20ff. [b]2 Pet. 2:2
25 [1]Or, *law* [2]Or, *of law* [a]Rom. 2:13f., 27 [b]Jer. 4:4; 9:25f.
26 [1]Lit., *uncircumcision* [a]1 Cor. 7:19 [b]Rom. 3:30; Eph. 2:11 [c]Rom. 2:25, 27; 8:4
27 [1]Lit., *through the letter* [2]Or, *of law* [a]Rom. 3:30; Eph. 2:11 [b]Matt. 12:41

28 For [a]he is not a Jew who is one
outwardly; neither is circumcision that
which is outward in the flesh.
29 But [a]he is a Jew who is one inwardly; and [b]circumcision is that which
is of the heart, by the [c]Spirit, not by the
letter; [d]and his praise is not from men,
but from God.

All the World Guilty

3 THEN what [1]advantage has the
Jew? Or what is the benefit of circumcision?
2 Great in every respect. First of all,
that [a]they were entrusted with the [b]ora-
cles of God.
3 What then? If [a]some [1]did not believe, their [2]unbelief will not nullify the
faithfulness of God, will it?
4 [a]May it never be! Rather, let God
be found true, though every man *be
found* [b]a liar, as it is written,
"[c]THAT THOU MIGHTEST BE JUSTI-
FIED IN THY WORDS,
AND MIGHTEST PREVAIL WHEN
THOU [1]ART JUDGED."
5 But if our unrighteousness [1a]dem-
onstrates the righteousness of God,
[b]what shall we say? The God who inflicts wrath is not unrighteous, is He? ([c]I
am speaking in human terms.)
6 [a]May it never be! For otherwise
how will [b]God judge the world?
7 But if through my lie [a]the truth of
God abounded to His glory, [b]why am I
also still being judged as a sinner?
8 And why not *say* (as we are slan-
derously reported and as some affirm
that we say), "[a]Let us do evil that good
may come"? [1]Their condemnation is
just.
9 What then? [1a]Are we better than
they? Not at all; for we have already
charged that both [b]Jews and [c]Greeks are
[d]all under sin;
10 as it is written,
"[a]THERE IS NONE RIGHTEOUS, NOT
EVEN ONE;
11 THERE IS NONE WHO UNDER-
STANDS,
THERE IS NONE WHO SEEKS FOR
GOD;
12 ALL HAVE TURNED ASIDE, TO-
GETHER THEY HAVE BECOME USE-
LESS;
THERE IS NONE WHO DOES GOOD,
THERE IS NOT EVEN ONE."
13 "[a]THEIR THROAT IS AN OPEN
GRAVE,
WITH THEIR TONGUES THEY KEEP
DECEIVING,"
"[b]THE POISON OF ASPS IS UNDER
THEIR LIPS";
14 "[a]WHOSE MOUTH IS FULL OF CURS-
ING AND BITTERNESS";
15 "[a]THEIR FEET ARE SWIFT TO SHED
BLOOD,
16 DESTRUCTION AND MISERY ARE IN
THEIR PATHS,
17 AND THE PATH OF PEACE HAVE
THEY NOT KNOWN."
18 "[a]THERE IS NO FEAR OF GOD BE-
FORE THEIR EYES."
19 Now we know that whatever the
[a]Law says, it speaks to [b]those who are
[1]under the Law, that every mouth may
be closed, and [c]all the world may become accountable to God;
20 because [a]by the works [1]of the Law
no flesh will be justified in His sight; for
[2b]through the Law *comes* the knowledge
of sin.

Justification by Faith

21 But now apart [1]from the Law [a]*the*
righteousness of God has been manifested, being [b]witnessed by the Law and
the Prophets,
22 even *the* [a]righteousness of God
through [b]faith [c]in Jesus Christ for [d]all
those who believe; for [e]there is no distinction;
23 for [1]all [a]have sinned and fall short
of the glory of God,
24 being justified as a gift [a]by His
grace through [b]the redemption which is
in Christ Jesus;
25 whom God displayed publicly as [a]a
[1]propitiation [2b]in His blood through
faith. *This was* to demonstrate His righteousness, [3]because in the [c]forbearance of
God He [d]passed over the sins previously
committed;
26 for the demonstration, *I say,* of His
righteousness at the present time, that
He might be just and the justifier of the
one who [1]has faith in Jesus.
27 Where then is [a]boasting? It is excluded. By [b]what kind of law? Of works?
No, but by a law of faith.
28 [1]For [a]we maintain that a man is
justified by faith apart from works [2]of
the Law.
29 Or [a]is God *the God* of Jews only? Is
He not *the God* of Gentiles also? Yes, of
Gentiles also,
30 since indeed [a]God [b]who will justify
the [1]circumcised [2]by faith and the [3]un-
circumcised through faith [c]is one.
31 Do we then nullify [1]the Law
through faith? [a]May it never be! On the
contrary, we [b]establish the Law.

Justification by Faith Evidenced in Old Testament

4 WHAT then shall we say that Abraham, [1]our forefather [a]according to
the flesh, has found?

28 [a]John 8:39; Rom. 2:17; 9:6; Gal. 6:15
29 [a]Phil. 3:3; Col. 2:11 [b]Deut. 30:6 [c]Rom. 2:27; 7:6; 2 Cor. 3:6 [d]John 5:44; 12:43; 1 Cor. 4:5; 2 Cor. 10:18
1 [1]Lit., *is the advantage of the Jew*
2 [a]Deut. 4:8; Ps. 147:19; Rom. 9:4 [b]Acts 7:38
3 [1]Or, *were unfaithful* [2]Or, *unfaithfulness* [a]Rom. 10:16; Heb. 4:2
4 [1]Or, *dost enter into judgment* [a]Luke 20:16; Rom. 3:6, 31 [b]Ps. 116:11; Rom. 3:7 [c]Ps. 51:4
5 [1]Or, *commends* [a]Rom. 5:8; 2 Cor. 6:4; 7:11 [b]Rom. 4:1; 7:7; 8:31; 9:14, 30 [c]Rom. 6:19; 1 Cor. 9:8; 15:32; Gal. 3:15
6 [a]Luke 20:16; Rom. 3:4, 31 [b]Rom. 2:16
7 [a]Rom. 3:4 [b]Rom. 9:19
8 [1]Lit., *Whose* [a]Rom. 6:1
9 [1]Or possibly, *Are we worse* [a]Rom. 3:1 [b]Rom. 2:1-29 [c]Rom. 1:18-32 [d]Rom. 3:19, 23; 11:32; Gal. 3:22
10 [a]Ps. 14:1-3; 53:1-3
13 [a]Ps. 5:9 [b]Ps. 140:3
14 [a]Ps. 10:7
15 [a]Is. 59:7f.
18 [a]Ps. 36:1
19 [1]Lit., *in* [a]John 10:34 [b]Rom. 2:12 [c]Rom. 3:9
20 [1]Or, *of law* [2]Or, *through law* [a]Ps. 143:2; Acts 13:39; Gal. 2:16 [b]Rom. 4:15; 5:13, 20; 7:7
21 [1]Or, *from law* [a]Rom. 1:17; 9:30 [b]Acts 10:43; Rom. 1:2
22 [a]Rom. 1:17; 9:30 [b]Rom. 4:5 [c]Acts 3:16; Gal. 2:16, 20; 3:22; Eph. 3:12 [d]Rom. 4:11, 16; 10:4 [e]Rom. 10:12; Gal. 3:28; Col. 3:11
23 [1]Or, *all sinned* [a]Rom. 3:9
24 [a]Rom. 4:4f., 16; Eph. 2:8 [b]1 Cor. 1:30; Eph. 1:7; Col. 1:14; Heb. 9:15

25 [1]Or, *a propitiatory sacrifice* [2]Or, *by* [3]Lit., *because of the passing over of the sins previously committed in the forbearance of God* [a]1 John 2:2; 4:10 [b]1 Cor. 5:7; Heb. 9:14, 28; 1 Pet. 1:19; Rev. 1:5 [c]Rom. 2:4 [d]Acts 14:16; 17:30
26 [1]Lit., *is of the faith of Jesus.*
27 [a]Rom. 2:17, 23; 4:2; 1 Cor. 1:29ff. [b]Rom. 9:31
28 [1]Some ancient mss. read *Therefore* [2]Or, *of law* [a]Acts 13:39; Rom. 3:20, 21; Eph. 2:9; James 2:20, 24, 26
29 [a]Acts 10:34f.; Rom. 9:24; 10:12; 15:9; Gal. 3:28
30 [1]Lit., *circumcision* [2]Lit., *out of* [3]Lit., *uncircumcision* [a]Rom. 10:12; Gal. 3:20 [b]Rom. 3:22; 4:11f., 16; Gal. 3:8 [c]Deut. 6:4
31 [1]Or, *law* [a]Luke 20:16; Rom. 3:4 [b]Matt. 5:17; Rom. 3:4, 6; 8:4

1 [1]Or, *our forefather, has found according to the flesh* [a]Rom. 1:3

2 For if Abraham was justified by works, he has something to boast about; but [a]not [1]before God.

3 For what does the Scripture say? "[a]AND ABRAHAM BELIEVED GOD, AND IT WAS RECKONED TO HIM AS RIGHTEOUSNESS."

4 Now to the one who [a]works, his wage is not reckoned as a favor, but as what is due.

5 But to the one who does not work, but [a]believes in Him who justifies the ungodly, his faith is reckoned as righteousness,

6 just as David also speaks of the blessing upon the man to whom God reckons righteousness apart from works:

7 "[a]BLESSED ARE THOSE WHOSE LAWLESS DEEDS HAVE BEEN FORGIVEN,
AND WHOSE SINS HAVE BEEN COVERED.

8 "[a]BLESSED IS THE MAN WHOSE SIN THE LORD WILL NOT [1b]TAKE INTO ACCOUNT."

9 Is this blessing then upon [1a]the circumcised, or upon [2]the uncircumcised also? For [b]we say, "[c]FAITH WAS RECKONED TO ABRAHAM AS RIGHTEOUSNESS."

10 How then was it reckoned? While he was [1]circumcised, or [2]uncircumcised? Not while [1]circumcised, but while [2]uncircumcised;

11 and he [a]received the sign of circumcision, [b]a seal of the righteousness of the faith which [1]he had while uncircumcised, that he might be [c]the father of [d]all who believe without being circumcised, that righteousness might be reckoned to them,

12 and the father of circumcision to those who not only are of the circumcision, but who also follow in the steps of the faith of our father Abraham which [1]he had while uncircumcised.

13 For [a]the promise to Abraham or to his [1]descendants [b]that he would be heir of the world was not [2]through the Law, but through the righteousness of faith.

14 For [a]if those who are [1]of the Law are heirs, faith is made void and the promise is nullified;

15 for [a]the Law brings about wrath, but [b]where there is no law, neither is there violation.

16 For this reason *it is* [1]by faith, that *it might be* in accordance with [a]grace, in order that the promise may be certain to [b]all the [2]descendants, not only to [3]those who are of the Law, but also to [3c]those who are of the faith of Abraham, who is [d]the father of us all,

17 (as it is written, "[a]A FATHER OF MANY NATIONS HAVE I MADE YOU") in the sight of Him whom he believed, *even* God, [b]who gives life to the dead and [1c]calls into being [d]that which does not exist.

18 In hope against hope he believed, in order that he might become [a]a father of many nations, according to that which had been spoken, "[b]SO SHALL YOUR [1]DESCENDANTS BE."

19 And without becoming weak in faith he contemplated his own body, now [a]as good as dead since [b]he was about a hundred years old, and [c]the deadness of Sarah's womb;

20 yet, with respect to the promise of God, he did not waver in unbelief, but grew strong in faith, [a]giving glory to God,

21 and [a]being fully assured that [b]what He had promised, He was able also to perform.

22 Therefore also [a]IT WAS RECKONED TO HIM AS RIGHTEOUSNESS.

23 Now [a]not for his sake only was it written, that it was reckoned to him,

24 but for our sake also, to whom it will be reckoned, as those [a]who believe in Him who [b]raised Jesus our Lord from the dead,

25 *He* who was [a]delivered up because of our transgressions, and was [b]raised because of our justification.

Results of Justification

5 [a]THEREFORE having been justified by faith, [1b]we have peace with God through our Lord Jesus Christ,

2 through whom also we have [a]obtained our introduction by faith into this grace [b]in which we stand; and [1]we exult in hope of the glory of God.

3 [a]And not only this, but [1]we also [b]exult in our tribulations, knowing that tribulation brings about [c]perseverance;

4 and [a]perseverance, [b]proven character; and proven character, hope;

5 and hope [a]does not disappoint, because the love of God has been [b]poured out within our hearts through the Holy Spirit who was given to us.

6 For while we were still [a]helpless, [b]at the right time [c]Christ died for the ungodly.

7 For one will hardly die for a righteous man; though perhaps for the good man someone would dare even to die.

8 But God [a]demonstrates [b]His own love toward us, in that while we were yet sinners, [c]Christ died for us.

9 Much more then, having now been justified [1a]by His blood, we shall be saved [b]from the wrath *of God* through Him.

10 For if while we were [a]enemies, we were reconciled to God through the death of His Son, much more, having been reconciled, we shall be saved [1b]by His life.

2 [1]Lit., *toward* [a]1 Cor. 1:31
3 [a]Gen. 15:6; Rom. 4:9, 22; Gal. 3:6; James 2:23
4 [a]Rom. 11:6
5 [a]John 6:29; Rom. 3:22
7 [a]Ps. 32:1
8 [1]Or, *reckon* [a]Ps. 32:2 [b]2 Cor. 5:19
9 [1]Lit., *circumcision* [2]Lit., *uncircumcision* [a]Rom. 3:30 [b]Rom. 4:3 [c]Gen. 15:6
10 [1]Lit., *in circumcision* [2]Lit., *in uncircumcision*
11 [1]Lit., *was in uncircumcision* [a]Gen. 17:10f. [b]John 3:33 [c]Luke 19:9; Rom. 4:16f. [d]Rom. 3:22; 4:16
12 [1]Lit., *was in uncircumcision*
13 [1]Lit., *seed* [2]Or, *through law* [a]Rom. 9:8; Gal. 3:16, 29 [b]Gen. 17:4-6; 22:17f.
14 [1]Or, *of law* [a]Gal. 3:18
15 [a]Rom. 7:7, 10-25; 1 Cor. 15:56; Gal. 3:10 [b]Rom. 3:20
16 [1]Or, *of* [2]Lit., *seed* [3]Lit., *that which is* [a]Rom. 3:24 [b]Rom. 4:11; 9:8; 15:8 [c]Gal. 3:7 [d]Luke 19:9; Rom. 4:11
17 [1]Lit., *calls the things which do not exist as existing* [a]Gen. 17:5 [b]John 5:21 [c]Is. 48:13; 51:2 [d]1 Cor. 1:28
18 [1]Lit., *seed* [a]Rom. 4:17 [b]Gen. 15:5
19 [a]Heb. 11:12 [b]Gen. 17:17 [c]Gen. 18:11
20 [a]Matt. 9:8
21 [a]Rom. 14:5 [b]Gen. 18:14; Heb. 11:19
22 [a]Gen. 15:6; Rom. 4:3
23 [a]Rom. 15:4; 1 Cor. 9:9f.; 10:11; 2 Tim. 3:16f.
24 [a]Rom. 10:9; 1 Pet. 1:21 [b]Acts 2:24
25 [a]Is. 53:4, 5; Rom. 5:6, 8; 8:32; Gal. 2:20; Eph. 5:2 [b]Rom. 5:18; 1 Cor. 15:17; 2 Cor. 5:15

1 [1]Some ancient mss. read *let us have* [a]Rom. 3:28 [b]Rom. 5:11
2 [1]Or, *let us exult* [a]Eph. 2:18; 3:12; Heb. 10:19f.; 1 Pet. 3:18 [b]1 Cor. 15:1
3 [1]Or, *let us also exult* [a]Rom. 5:11; 8:23; 9:10; 2 Cor. 8:19 [b]Matt. 5:12; James 1:2f. [c]Luke 21:19
4 [a]Luke 21:19 [b]Phil. 2:22; James 1:12
5 [a]Ps. 119:116; Rom. 9:33; Heb. 6:18f. [b]Acts 2:33; 10:45; Gal. 4:6; Titus 3:6
6 [a]Rom. 5:8, 10 [b]Gal. 4:4 [c]Rom. 4:25; 5:8; 8:32; Gal. 2:20; Eph. 5:2
8 [a]Rom. 3:5 [b]John 3:16; 15:13; Rom. 8:39 [c]Rom. 4:25; 5:6; 8:32; Gal. 2:20; Eph. 5:2
9 [1]Or, *in* [a]Rom. 3:25 [b]Rom. 1:18; 1 Thess. 1:10
10 [1]Or, *in* [a]Rom. 11:28; 2 Cor. 5:18f.; Eph. 2:3; Col. 1:21f. [b]Rom. 8:34; Heb. 7:25; 1 John 2:1

11 [a]And not only this, [1]but we also exult in God through our Lord Jesus Christ, through whom we have now received [b]the reconciliation.

12 Therefore, just as through [a]one man sin entered into the world, and [b]death through sin, and [c]so death spread to all men, because all sinned—

13 for [1]until the Law sin was in the world; but [a]sin is not imputed when there is no law.

14 Nevertheless death reigned from Adam until Moses, even over those who had not sinned [a]in the likeness of the offense of Adam, who is a [1b]type of Him who was to come.

15 But [1]the free gift is not like the transgression. For if by the transgression of [a]the one [b]the many died, much more did the grace of God and the gift by [c]the grace of the one Man, Jesus Christ, abound to the many.

16 And the gift is not like *that which came* through the one who sinned; for on the one hand [a]the judgment *arose* from one *transgression* [1]resulting in condemnation, but on the other hand the free gift *arose* from many transgressions [2]resulting in justification.

17 For if by the transgression of the one, death reigned [a]through the one, much more those who receive the abundance of grace and of the gift of righteousness will [b]reign in life through the One, Jesus Christ.

18 So then as through [a]one transgression [1]there resulted condemnation to all men, even so through one [b]act of righteousness [2]there resulted [c]justification of life to all men.

19 For as through the one man's disobedience [a]the many [b]were made sinners, even so through [c]the obedience of the One [a]the many will be made righteous.

20 And [1a]the Law came in that the transgression might increase; but where sin increased, [b]grace abounded all the more,

21 that, as [a]sin reigned in death, even so [b]grace might reign through righteousness to eternal life through Jesus Christ our Lord.

Believers Are Dead to Sin, Alive to God

6 [a]WHAT shall we say then? Are we to [b]continue in sin that grace might increase?

2 [a]May it never be! How shall we who [b]died to sin still live in it?

3 Or do you not know that all of us who have been [a]baptized into [b]Christ Jesus have been baptized into His death?

4 Therefore we have been [a]buried with Him through baptism into death, in order that as Christ was [b]raised from the dead through the [c]glory of the Father, so we too might walk in [d]newness of life.

5 For [a]if we have become [1]united with *Him* in the likeness of His death, certainly we shall be also [2]*in the likeness* of His resurrection,

6 knowing this, that our [a]old [1]self was [b]crucified with *Him,* that our [c]body of sin might be [2]done away with, that we should no longer be slaves to sin;

7 for [a]he who has died is [1]freed from sin.

8 Now [a]if we have died with Christ, we believe that we shall also live with Him,

9 knowing that Christ, having been [a]raised from the dead, is never to die again; [b]death no longer is master over Him.

10 For the death that He died, He died to sin, once for all; but the life that He lives, He lives to God.

11 Even so consider yourselves to be [a]dead to sin, but alive to God in Christ Jesus.

12 Therefore do not let sin [a]reign in your mortal body that you should obey its lusts,

13 and do not go on [a]presenting [1]the members of your body to sin *as* [2]instruments of unrighteousness; but [b]present yourselves to God as those alive from the dead, and your members *as* [2]instruments of righteousness to God.

14 For [a]sin shall not [b]be master over you, for [c]you are not under law, but [d]under grace.

15 What then? [a]Shall we sin because we are not under law but under grace? [b]May it never be!

16 Do you not [a]know that when you present yourselves to someone *as* [b]slaves for obedience, you are slaves of the one whom you obey, either of [c]sin [1]resulting in death, or of obedience [2]resulting in righteousness?

17 But [a]thanks be to God that [1]though you were slaves of sin, you became obedient from the heart to that [b]form of teaching to which you were committed,

18 and having been [a]freed from sin, you became slaves of righteousness.

19 [a]I am speaking in human terms because of the weakness of your flesh. For just [b]as you presented your members *as* slaves to impurity and to lawlessness, [1]resulting in *further* lawlessness, so now present your members *as* slaves to righteousness, [2]resulting in sanctification.

20 For [a]when you were slaves of sin, you were free in regard to righteousness.

---

11 [1]Lit., *but also exulting* [a]Rom. 5:3; 8:23; 9:10; 2 Cor. 8:19 [b]Rom. 5:10; 11:15; 2 Cor. 5:18f.
12 [a]Gen. 2:17; 3:6, 19; Rom. 5:15-17; 1 Cor. 15:21f. [b]Rom. 6:23; 1 Cor. 15:56; James 1:15 [c]Rom. 5:14, 19, 21; 1 Cor. 15:22
13 [1]Or, *until law* [a]Rom. 4:15
14 [1]Or, *foreshadowing* [a]Hos. 6:7 [b]1 Cor. 15:45
15 [1]Lit., *not as the trespass, so also is the free gift* [a]Rom. 5:12, 18, 19 [b]Rom. 5:19 [c]Acts 15:11
16 [1]Lit., *to condemnation* [2]Lit., *to an act of righteousness* [a]1 Cor. 11:32
17 [a]Gen. 2:17; 3:6, 19; Rom. 5:12, 15, 16; 1 Cor. 15:21f. [b]2 Tim. 2:12; Rev. 22:5
18 [1]Lit., *to condemnation* [2]Lit., *to justification* [a]Rom. 5:12, 15 [b]Rom. 3:25 [c]Rom. 4:25
19 [a]Rom. 5:15, 18 [b]Rom. 5:12; 11:32 [c]Phil. 2:8
20 [1]Or, *law* [a]Rom. 3:20; 7:7f.; Gal. 3:19 [b]Rom. 6:1; 1 Tim. 1:14
21 [a]Rom. 5:12, 14 [b]John 1:17; Rom. 6:23

1 [a]Rom. 3:5 [b]Rom. 3:8; 6:15
2 [a]Luke 20:16; Rom. 6:15 [b]Rom. 6:11; 7:4, 6; Gal. 2:19; Col. 2:20; 3:3; 1 Pet. 2:24
3 [a]Matt. 28:19 [b]Acts 2:38; 8:16; 19:5; Gal. 3:27
4 [a]Col. 2:12 [b]Acts 2:24; Rom. 6:9 [c]John 11:40; 2 Cor. 13:4 [d]Rom. 7:6; 2 Cor. 5:17; Gal. 6:15; Eph. 4:23f.; Col. 3:10
5 [1]Or, *united with the likeness* [2]Or, *with* [a]2 Cor. 4:10; Phil. 3:10f.; Col. 2:12; 3:1
6 [1]Lit., *man* [2]Or, *made powerless* [a]Eph. 4:22; Col. 3:9 [b]Gal. 2:20; 5:24; 6:14 [c]Rom. 7:24
7 [1]Or, *acquitted* [a]1 Pet. 4:1
8 [a]Rom. 6:4; 2 Cor. 4:10; 2 Tim. 2:11
9 [a]Acts 2:24; Rom. 6:4 [b]Rev. 1:18
11 [a]Rom. 6:2; 7:4, 6; Gal. 2:19; Col. 2:20; 3:3; 1 Pet. 2:24
12 [a]Rom. 6:14
13 [1]Lit., *your members to sin* [2]Or, *weapons* [a]Rom. 6:16, 19; 7:5; Col. 3:5 [b]Rom. 12:1; 2 Cor. 5:14f.; 1 Pet. 2:24

14 [a]Rom. 8:2, 12 [b]Rom. 6:12 [c]Rom. 5:18; 7:4, 6; Gal. 4:21 [d]Rom. 5:17, 21
15 [a]Rom. 6:1 [b]Luke 20:16; Rom. 6:2
16 [1]Lit., *to death* [2]Lit., *to righteousness* [a]Rom. 11:2; 1 Cor. 3:16; 5:6; 6:2, 3, 9, 15, 16, 19; 9:13, 24 [b]John 8:34; 2 Pet. 2:19 [c]Rom. 6:21, 23
17 [1]Lit., *you were slaves . . . but you became* [a]Rom. 1:8; 2 Cor. 2:14 [b]2 Tim. 1:13
18 [a]John 8:32; Rom. 6:22; 8:2
19 [1]Lit., *to lawlessness* [2]Lit., *to sanctification* [a]Rom. 3:5 [b]Rom. 6:13
20 [a]Matt. 6:24; Rom. 6:16

21 Therefore what [1a]benefit were you then [2]deriving [3]from the things of which you are now ashamed? For the outcome of those things is [b]death.

22 But now having been [a]freed from sin and [b]enslaved to God, you [1]derive your [2c]benefit, [3]resulting in sanctification, and [d]the outcome, eternal life.

23 For the wages of [a]sin is death, but the free gift of God is [b]eternal life in Christ Jesus our Lord.

Believers United to Christ

7 OR do you not know, [a]brethren (for I am speaking to those who know the law), that the law has jurisdiction over a person as long as he lives?

2 For [a]the married woman is bound by law to her husband while he is living; but if her husband dies, she is released from the law concerning the husband.

3 So then if, while her husband is living, she is joined to another man, she shall be called an adulteress; but if her husband dies, she is free from the law, so that she is not an adulteress, though she is joined to another man.

4 Therefore, my brethren, you also were [a]made to die [b]to the Law [c]through the body of Christ, that you might be joined to another, to Him who was raised from the dead, that we might bear fruit for God.

5 For while we were [a]in the flesh, the sinful passions, which were [b]*aroused* by the Law, were at work [c]in [1]the members of our body to bear fruit for death.

6 But now we have been [a]released from the Law, having [b]died to that by which we were bound, so that we serve in [c]newness of [d]the [1]Spirit and not in oldness of the letter.

7 [a]What shall we say then? Is the Law sin? [b]May it never be! On the contrary, [c]I would not have come to know sin except [1]through the Law; for I would not have known about [2]coveting if the Law had not said, "[d]YOU SHALL NOT [3]COVET."

8 But sin, [a]taking opportunity [b]through the commandment, produced in me [1]coveting of every kind; for [c]apart [2]from the Law sin *is* dead.

9 And I was once alive apart [1]from the Law; but when the commandment came, sin became alive, and I died;

10 and this commandment, which was [1a]to result in life, proved [2]to result in death for me;

11 for sin, [a]taking opportunity [b]through the commandment, [c]deceived me, and through it killed me.

12 [a]So then, the Law is holy, and the commandment is holy and righteous and good.

13 Therefore did that which is good become *a cause of* death for me? [a]May it never be! Rather it was sin, in order that it might be shown to be sin by effecting my death through that which is good,

6:21 [1]Lit., *fruit* [2]Lit., *having* [3]Lit., *in* [a]Jer. 12:13; Ezek. 16:63; Rom. 7:5 [b]Rom. 1:32; 5:12; 6:16, 23; 8:6, 13; Gal. 6:8
22 [1]Lit., *have* [2]Lit., *fruit* [3]Lit., *to sanctification* [a]John 8:32; Rom. 6:18; 8:2 [b]1 Cor. 7:22; 1 Pet. 2:16 [c]Rom. 7:4 [d]1 Pet. 1:9
23 [a]Rom. 1:32; 5:12; 6:16, 21; 8:6, 13; Gal. 6:8 [b]Matt. 25:46; Rom. 5:21; 8:38, 39

7:1 [a]Rom. 1:13
2 [a]1 Cor. 7:39
4 [a]Rom. 6:2; 7:6 [b]Rom. 8:2; Gal. 2:19; 5:18 [c]Col. 1:22
5 [1]Lit., *our members to bear* [a]Rom. 8:8f.; 2 Cor. 10:3 [b]Rom. 7:7f. [c]Rom. 6:13, 21, 23
6 [1]Or, *spirit* [a]Rom. 7:2 [b]Rom. 6:2 [c]Rom. 6:4 [d]Rom. 2:29
7 [1]Or, *through law* [2]Or, *lust* [3]Or, *lust* [a]Rom. 3:5 [b]Luke 20:16 [c]Rom. 3:20; 4:15; 5:20 [d]Ex. 20:17; Deut. 5:21
8 [1]Or, *lust* [2]Or, *from law* [a]Rom. 7:11 [b]Rom. 3:20; 7:11 [c]1 Cor. 15:56
9 [1]Or, *from law*
10 [1]Lit., *to life* [2]Lit., *to death* [a]Lev. 18:5; Luke 10:28; Rom. 10:5; Gal. 3:12
11 [a]Rom. 7:8 [b]Rom. 3:20; 7:8 [c]Gen. 3:13
12 [a]Rom. 7:16; 1 Tim. 1:8
13 [a]Luke 20:16
14 [1]Lit., *under sin* [a]1 Cor. 3:1 [b]1 Kin. 21:20, 25; 2 Kin. 17:17; Rom. 6:6; Gal. 4:3 [c]Rom. 3:9
15 [a]John 15:15 [b]Rom. 7:19; Gal. 5:17
16 [a]Rom. 7:12; 1 Tim. 1:8
17 [a]Rom. 7:20
18 [a]John 3:6; Rom. 7:25; 8:3
19 [a]Rom. 7:15
20 [a]Rom. 7:17
21 [1]Lit., *law* [a]Rom. 7:23, 25; 8:2
22 [1]Or, *concerning* [a]2 Cor. 4:16; Eph. 3:16; 1 Pet. 3:4
23 [1]Lit., *my members* [2]Lit., *in* [a]Rom. 6:19; Gal. 5:17; James 4:1; 1 Pet. 2:11 [b]Rom. 7:25 [c]Rom. 7:21, 25; 8:2
24 [1]Or, *this body of death* [a]Rom. 6:6; Col. 2:11 [b]Rom. 8:2
25 [a]1 Cor. 15:57 [b]Rom. 7:21, 23; 8:2

8:1 [a]Rom. 5:16; 8:34 [b]Rom. 8:9f. [c]Rom. 8:2, 11, 39; 16:3

that through the commandment sin might become utterly sinful.

The Conflict of Two Natures

14 For we know that the Law is [a]spiritual; but I am [a]of flesh, [b]sold [1c]into bondage to sin.

15 For that which I am doing, [a]I do not understand; for I am not practicing [b]what I *would* like to *do,* but I am doing the very thing I hate.

16 But if I do the very thing I do not wish *to do,* I agree with [a]the Law, *confessing* that it is good.

17 So now, [a]no longer am I the one doing it, but sin which indwells me.

18 For I know that nothing good dwells in me, that is, in my [a]flesh; for the wishing is present in me, but the doing of the good *is* not.

19 For [a]the good that I wish, I do not do; but I practice the very evil that I do not wish.

20 But if I am doing the very thing I do not wish, [a]I am no longer the one doing it, but sin which dwells in me.

21 I find then [a]the [1]principle that evil is present in me, the one who wishes to do good.

22 For I joyfully concur with the law of God [1]in [a]the inner man,

23 but I see [a]a different law in [1]the members of my body, waging war against the [b]law of my mind, and making me a prisoner [2]of [c]the law of sin which is in my members.

24 Wretched man that I am! Who will set me free from [1a]the body of this [b]death?

25 [a]Thanks be to God through Jesus Christ our Lord! So then, on the one hand I myself with my mind am serving the law of God, but on the other, with my flesh [b]the law of sin.

Deliverance from Bondage

8 THERE is therefore now no [a]condemnation for those who are [b]in [c]Christ Jesus.

2 For [a]the law of the Spirit of life [1]in [b]Christ Jesus [c]has set [2]you free from the law of sin and of death.

3 For [a]what the Law could not do, [1b]weak as it was through the flesh, God *did:* sending His own Son in [c]the likeness of [2]sinful flesh and *as an offering* for sin, He condemned sin in the flesh,

4 in order that the [a]requirement of the Law might be fulfilled in us, who [b]do not walk according to the flesh, but according to the Spirit.

5 For those who are according to the flesh set their minds on [a]the things of the flesh, but those who are according to the Spirit, [b]the things of the Spirit.

2 [1]Or, *has set you free in Christ Jesus* [2]Some ancient mss. read *me* [a]1 Cor. 15:45 [b]Rom. 8:1, 11, 39; 16:3 [c]John 8:32, 36; Rom. 6:14, 18; 7:4
3 [1]Lit., *wherein it was weak* [2]Lit., *flesh of sin* [a]Acts 13:39; Heb. 10:1ff. [b]Rom. 7:18f.; Heb. 7:18 [c]Phil. 2:7; Heb. 2:14, 17; 4:15
4 [a]Luke 1:6; Rom. 2:26 [b]Gal. 5:16, 25
5 [a]Gal. 5:19-21 [b]Gal. 5:22-25

6 [a]For the mind set on the flesh is
[b]death, but the mind set on the Spirit is
life and peace,
7 because the mind set on the flesh is
[a]hostile toward God; for it does not
subject itself to the law of God, for it is
not even able *to do so*;
8 and those who are [a]in the flesh
cannot please God.
9 However, you are not [a]in the flesh
but in the Spirit, if indeed the Spirit of
God [b]dwells in you. But [c]if anyone does
not have the Spirit of Christ, he does not
belong to Him.
10 And [a]if Christ is in you, though the
body is dead because of sin, yet the spirit
is [1]alive because of righteousness.
11 But if the Spirit of Him who [a]raised
Jesus from the dead dwells in you, [b]He
who raised [c]Christ Jesus from the dead
will also give life to your mortal bodies
[1]through His Spirit who indwells you.
12 So then, brethren, we are under
obligation, not to the flesh, to live according to the flesh—
13 for [a]if you are living according to
the flesh, you [1]must die; but if by the
Spirit you are [b]putting to death the
deeds of the body, you will live.
14 For all who are [a]being led by the
Spirit of God, these are [b]sons of God.
15 For you [a]have not received a spirit
of slavery [1]leading to fear again, but you
[b]have received [2]a spirit of adoption as
sons by which we cry out, "[c]Abba!
Father!"
16 The Spirit Himself [a]bears witness
with our spirit that we are [b]children of
God,
17 and if children, [a]heirs also, heirs of
God and fellow heirs with Christ, [b]if
indeed we suffer with *Him* in order that
we may also be glorified with *Him*.
18 For I consider that the sufferings of
this present time [a]are not worthy to be
compared with the [b]glory that is to be
revealed to us.
19 For the [a]anxious longing of the
creation waits eagerly for [b]the revealing
of the [c]sons of God.
20 For the creation [a]was subjected to
[b]futility, not of its own will, but [c]because
of Him who subjected it, [1]in hope
21 that [a]the creation itself also will be
set free from its slavery to corruption
into the freedom of the glory of the
children of God.
22 For we know that the whole creation [a]groans and suffers the pains of
childbirth together until now.
23 [a]And not only this, but also we
ourselves, having [b]the first fruits of the
Spirit, even we ourselves [c]groan within
ourselves, [d]waiting eagerly for *our* adoption as sons, [e]the redemption of our
body.
24 For [a]in hope we have been saved,
but [b]hope that is seen is not hope; for
[1]why does one also hope for what he
sees?
25 But [a]if we hope for what we do not
see, with perseverance we wait eagerly
for it.

Our Victory in Christ

26 And in the same way the Spirit also
helps our weakness; for [a]we do not know
how to pray as we should, but [b]the Spirit
Himself intercedes for *us* with groanings
too deep for words;
27 and [a]He who searches the hearts
knows what [b]the mind of the Spirit is,
because He [c]intercedes for the [1]saints
according to *the will of* God.
28 And we know that [1]God causes [a]all
things to work together for good to those
who love God, to those who are [b]called
according to *His* purpose.
29 For whom He [a]foreknew, He also
[b]predestined *to become* [c]conformed to
the image of His Son, that He might be
the [d]first-born among many brethren;
30 and whom He [a]predestined, these
He also [b]called; and whom He called,
these He also [c]justified; and whom He
justified, these He also [d]glorified.
31 [a]What then shall we say to these
things? [b]If God *is* for us, who *is* against
us?
32 He who [a]did not spare His own
Son, but [b]delivered Him up for us all,
how will He not also with Him freely
give us all things?
33 Who will bring a charge against
[a]God's elect? [b]God is the one who
justifies;
34 who is the one who [a]condemns?
Christ Jesus is He who [b]died, yes, rather
who was [1c]raised, who is [d]at the right
hand of God, who also [e]intercedes for
us.
35 Who shall separate us from [a]the
love of [1]Christ? Shall [b]tribulation, or
distress, or [c]persecution, or [c]famine, or
[c]nakedness, or [c]peril, or sword?
36 Just as it is written,
"[a]FOR THY SAKE WE ARE BEING
PUT TO DEATH ALL DAY LONG;
WE WERE CONSIDERED AS SHEEP
TO BE SLAUGHTERED."
37 But in all these things we over-
whelmingly [a]conquer through [b]Him who
loved us.
38 For I am convinced that neither

6 [a]Gal. 6:8 [b]Rom. 6:21; 8:13
7 [a]James 4:4
8 [a]Rom. 7:5
9 [a]Rom. 7:5 [b]John 14:23; Rom. 8:11; 1 Cor. 3:16; 6:19; 2 Cor. 6:16; Gal. 4:6; Phil. 1:19; 2 Tim. 1:14; 1 John 4:13 [c]John 14:17
10 [1]Lit., *life* [a]John 17:23; Gal. 2:20; Eph. 3:17; Col. 1:27
11 [1]Some ancient mss. read *because of* [a]Acts 2:24; Rom. 6:4 [b]John 5:21 [c]Rom. 8:1, 2, 39; 16:3
13 [1]Or, *are about to* [a]Rom. 8:6 [b]Col. 3:5
14 [a]Gal. 5:18 [b]Hos. 1:10; Matt. 5:9; John 1:12; Rom. 8:16, 19; 9:8, 26; 2 Cor. 6:18; Gal. 3:26; 1 John 3:1; Rev. 21:7
15 [1]Lit., *for fear again* [2]Or, *the Spirit* [a]2 Tim. 1:7; Heb. 2:15 [b]Rom. 8:23; Gal. 4:5f. [c]Mark 14:36; Gal. 4:6
16 [a]Acts 5:32 [b]Hos. 1:10; Matt. 5:9; John 1:12; Rom. 8:14, 19; 9:8, 26; 2 Cor. 6:18; Gal. 3:26; 1 John 3:1; Rev. 21:7
17 [a]Acts 20:32; Gal. 3:29; 4:7; Eph. 3:6; Titus 3:7; Heb. 1:14; Rev. 21:7 [b]2 Cor. 1:5, 7; Phil. 3:10; Col. 1:24; 2 Tim. 2:12; 1 Pet. 4:13
18 [a]2 Cor. 4:17; 1 Pet. 4:13 [b]Col. 3:4; Titus 2:13; 1 Pet. 1:5; 5:1
19 [a]Phil. 1:20 [b]Rom. 8:18; 1 Cor. 1:7f.; Col. 3:4; 1 Pet. 1:7, 13; 1 John 3:2 [c]Hos. 1:10; Matt. 5:9; John 1:12; Rom. 8:14, 16; 9:8, 26; 2 Cor. 6:18; Gal. 3:26; 1 John 3:1; Rev. 21:7
20 [1]Some ancient mss. read *in hope; because the creation* [a]Gen. 3:17-19 [b]Ps. 39:5f.; Eccl. 1:2 [c]Gen. 3:17; 5:29
21 [a]Acts 3:21; 2 Pet. 3:13; Rev. 21:1
22 [a]Jer. 12:4, 11
23 [a]Rom. 5:3 [b]Rom. 8:16; 2 Cor. 1:22 [c]2 Cor. 5:2, 4 [d]Rom. 8:15, 19, 25; Gal. 5:5 [e]Rom. 7:24
24 [1]Some ancient mss. read *who hopes for what he sees?* [a]Rom. 8:20; 1 Thess. 5:8; Titus 3:7 [b]Rom. 4:18; 2 Cor. 5:7; Heb. 11:1
25 [a]1 Thess. 1:3
26 [a]Matt. 20:22; 2 Cor. 12:8 [b]John 14:16; Rom. 8:15f.; Eph. 6:18
27 [1]Or, *holy ones* [a]Ps. 139:1f.; Luke 16:15; Acts 1:24; Rev. 2:23 [b]Rom. 8:6 [c]Rom. 8:34

28 [1]Some ancient mss. read *all things work together for good* [a]Rom. 8:32 [b]Rom. 8:30; 9:24; 11:29; 1 Cor. 1:9; Gal. 1:6, 15; 5:8; Eph. 1:11; 3:11; 2 Thess. 2:14; Heb. 9:15; 1 Pet. 2:9; 3:9
29 [a]Rom. 11:2; 1 Cor. 8:3; 2 Tim. 1:9; 1 Pet. 1:2, 20 [b]Rom. 9:23; 1 Cor. 2:7; Eph. 1:5, 11 [c]1 Cor. 15:49; Phil. 3:21 [d]Col. 1:18; Heb. 1:6
30 [a]Rom. 9:23; 11:29; 1 Cor. 2:7; Eph. 1:5, 11 [b]Rom. 8:28; 9:24; 1 Cor. 1:9; Gal. 1:6, 15; 5:8; Eph. 1:11; 3:11; 2 Thess. 2:14; Heb. 9:15; 1 Pet. 2:9; 3:9 [c]1 Cor. 6:11 [d]John 17:22; Rom. 8:21; 9:23
31 [a]Rom. 3:5; 4:1 [b]Ps. 118:6; Matt. 1:23
32 [a]John 3:16; Rom. 5:8 [b]Rom. 4:25
33 [a]Luke 18:7 [b]Is. 50:8f.
34 [1]Some ancient mss. read *raised from the dead* [a]Rom. 8:1 [b]Rom. 5:6f. [c]Acts 2:24 [d]Mark 16:19 [e]Rom. 8:27; Heb. 7:25
35 [1]Some ancient mss. read *God* [a]Rom. 8:37f. [b]Rom. 2:9; 2 Cor. 4:8 [c]1 Cor. 4:11; 2 Cor. 11:26f.
36 [a]Ps. 44:22; Acts 20:24; 1 Cor. 4:9; 15:30f.; 2 Cor. 1:9; 4:10f.; 6:9; 11:23
37 [a]John 16:33; 1 Cor. 15:57 [b]Gal. 2:20; Eph. 5:2; Rev. 1:5

[a]death, nor life, nor [b]angels, nor principalities, nor [c]things present, nor things
to come, nor powers,
39 nor height, nor depth, nor any
other created thing, shall be able to
separate us from [a]the love of God, which
is [b]in Christ Jesus our Lord.

Solicitude for Israel

9 [a]I AM telling the truth in Christ, I
am not lying, my conscience bearing
me witness in the Holy Spirit,
2 that I have great sorrow and unceasing grief in my heart.
3 For [a]I could [1]wish that I myself
were [b]accursed, *separated* from Christ
for the sake of my brethren, my kinsmen
[c]according to the flesh,
4 who are [a]Israelites, to whom belongs [b]the adoption as sons and [c]the
glory and [d]the covenants and [e]the giving
of the Law and [f]the *temple* service and
[g]the promises,
5 whose are [a]the fathers, and [b]from
whom is [1]the Christ according to the
flesh, [c]who is over all, [d]God [e]blessed
[2]forever. Amen.
6 But *it is* not as though [a]the word of
God has failed. [b]For they are not all
Israel who are *descended* from Israel;
7 neither are they all children [a]be-
cause they are Abraham's [1]descendants,
but: "[b]THROUGH ISAAC YOUR [1]DESCEND-
ANTS WILL BE NAMED."
8 That is, it is not the children of the
flesh who are [a]children of God, but the
[b]children of the promise are regarded as
[1]descendants.
9 For this is a word of promise: "[a]AT
THIS TIME I WILL COME, AND SARAH
SHALL HAVE A SON."
10 [a]And not only this, but there was
[b]Rebekah also, when she had conceived
twins by one man, our father Isaac;
11 for though *the twins* were not yet
born, and had not done anything good
or bad, in order that [a]God's purpose
according to *His* choice might stand, not
because of works, but because of Him
who calls,
12 it was said to her, "[a]THE OLDER
WILL SERVE THE YOUNGER."
13 Just as it is written, "[a]JACOB I
LOVED, BUT ESAU I HATED."
14 [a]What shall we say then? [b]There is
no injustice with God, is there? [c]May it
never be!
15 For He says to Moses, "[a]I WILL
HAVE MERCY ON WHOM I HAVE MERCY,
AND I WILL HAVE COMPASSION ON WHOM
I HAVE COMPASSION."
16 So then it *does* not *depend* on the
man who wills or the man who [a]runs,
but on [b]God who has mercy.
17 For the Scripture says to Pharaoh,
"[a]FOR THIS VERY PURPOSE I RAISED YOU
UP, TO DEMONSTRATE MY POWER IN
YOU, AND THAT MY NAME MIGHT BE
PROCLAIMED [1]THROUGHOUT THE WHOLE
EARTH."
18 So then He has mercy on whom He
desires, and He [a]hardens whom He
desires.
19 [a]You will say to me then, "[b]Why
does He still find fault? For [c]who resists
His will?"
20 On the contrary, who are you, [a]O
man, who [b]answers back to God? [c]The
thing molded will not say to the molder,
"Why did you make me like this," will
it?
21 Or does not the potter have a right
over the clay, to make from the same
lump one vessel [1]for honorable use, and
another [2]for common use?
22 What if God, although willing to
demonstrate His wrath and to make His
power known, endured with much [a]pa-
tience vessels of wrath [b]prepared for
destruction?
23 And *He did so* in order that He
might make known [a]the riches of His
glory upon [b]vessels of mercy, which He
[c]prepared beforehand for glory,
24 *even* us, whom He also [a]called, [b]not
from among Jews only, but also from
among Gentiles.
25 As He says also in Hosea,
"[a]I WILL CALL THOSE WHO WERE
NOT MY PEOPLE, 'MY PEOPLE,'
AND HER WHO WAS NOT BELOVED,
'BELOVED.'"
26 "[a]AND IT SHALL BE THAT IN THE
PLACE WHERE IT WAS SAID TO
THEM, 'YOU ARE NOT MY PEO-
PLE,'
THERE THEY SHALL BE CALLED
SONS OF [b]THE LIVING GOD."
27 And Isaiah cries out concerning
Israel, "[a]THOUGH THE NUMBER OF THE
SONS OF ISRAEL BE [b]AS THE SAND OF THE
SEA, IT IS [c]THE REMNANT THAT WILL BE
SAVED;
28 [a]FOR THE LORD WILL EXECUTE HIS
WORD UPON THE EARTH, [1]THOROUGHLY
AND [2]QUICKLY."
29 And just as Isaiah foretold,
"[a]EXCEPT [b]THE LORD OF [1]SABAOTH
HAD LEFT TO US A [2]POSTERITY,
[c]WE WOULD HAVE BECOME AS
SODOM, AND WOULD HAVE [3]RE-
SEMBLED GOMORRAH."
30 [a]What shall we say then? That
Gentiles, who did not pursue righteousness, attained righteousness, even [b]the
righteousness which is [1]by faith;
31 but Israel, [a]pursuing a law of righteousness, did not [b]arrive at *that* law.
32 Why? Because *they did* not *pursue it*
[1]by faith, but as though *it were* [1]by
works. They stumbled over [a]the stumbling stone,
33 just as it is written,

38 [a]1 Cor. 3:22 [b]1 Cor. 15:24; Eph. 1:21; 1 Pet. 3:22 [c]1 Cor. 3:22
39 [a]Rom. 5:8 [b]Rom. 8:1
1 [a]2 Cor. 11:10; Gal. 1:20; 1 Tim. 2:7
3 [1]Lit., *pray* [a]Ex. 32:32 [b]1 Cor. 12:3; 16:22; Gal. 1:8f. [c]Rom. 1:3; 11:14; Eph. 6:5
4 [a]Deut. 7:6; 14:1f.; Rom. 9:6 [b]Ex. 4:22; Rom. 8:15 [c]Ex. 40:34; 1 Kin. 8:11; Ezek. 1:28; Heb. 9:5 [d]Gen. 17:2; Deut. 29:14; Luke 1:72; Acts 3:25; Eph. 2:12 [e]Deut. 4:13f.; Ps. 147:19 [f]Heb. 9:1, 6 [g]Acts 2:39; 13:32; Eph. 2:12
5 [1]I.e., the Messiah [2]Lit., *unto the ages* [a]Acts 3:13; Rom. 11:28 [b]Matt. 1:1-16; Rom. 1:3 [c]Col. 1:16-19 [d]John 1:1 [e]Rom. 1:25
6 [a]Num. 23:19 [b]John 1:47; Rom. 2:28f.; Gal. 6:16
7 [1]Lit., *seed* [a]John 8:33, 39; Gal. 4:23 [b]Gen. 21:12; Heb. 11:18
8 [1]Lit., *seed* [a]Rom. 8:14 [b]Rom. 4:13, 16; Gal. 3:29; 4:28; Heb. 11:11
9 [a]Gen. 18:10
10 [a]Rom. 5:3 [b]Gen. 25:21
11 [a]Rom. 4:17; 8:28
12 [a]Gen. 25:23
13 [a]Mal. 1:2f.
14 [a]Rom. 3:5 [b]2 Chr. 19:7; Rom. 2:11 [c]Luke 20:16
15 [a]Ex. 33:19
16 [a]Gal. 2:2 [b]Eph. 2:8
17 [1]Lit., *in* [a]Ex. 9:16
18 [a]Ex. 4:21; 7:3; 9:12; 10:20, 27; 11:10; 14:4, 17; Deut. 2:30; Josh. 11:20; John 12:40; Rom. 11:7, 25
19 [a]Rom. 11:19; 1 Cor. 15:35; James 2:18 [b]Rom. 3:7 [c]2 Chr. 20:6; Job 9:12; Dan. 4:35
20 [a]Rom. 2:1 [b]Job 33:13 [c]Is. 29:16; 45:9; 64:8; Jer. 18:6; Rom. 9:22f.; 2 Tim. 2:20
21 [1]Lit., *for honor* [2]Lit., *for dishonor*
22 [a]Rom. 2:4 [b]Prov. 16:4; 1 Pet. 2:8
23 [a]Rom. 2:4; Eph. 3:16 [b]Acts 9:15 [c]Rom. 8:29f.
24 [a]Rom. 8:28 [b]Rom. 3:29
25 [a]Hos. 2:23; 1 Pet. 2:10
26 [a]Hos. 1:10 [b]Matt. 16:16
27 [a]Is. 10:22 [b]Gen. 22:17; Hos. 1:10 [c]Rom. 11:5
28 [1]Lit., *finishing it* [2]Lit., *cutting it short* [a]Is. 10:23

29 [1]I.e., Hosts [2]Lit., *seed* [3]Lit., *been made like* [a]Is. 1:9 [b]James 5:4 [c]Deut. 29:23; Is. 13:19; Jer. 49:18; 50:40; Amos 4:11
30 [1]Lit., *out of* [a]Rom. 9:14 [b]Rom. 1:17; 3:21f.; 10:6; Gal. 2:16; 3:24; Phil. 3:9; Heb. 11:7
31 [a]Is. 51:1; Rom. 9:30; 10:2f., 20; 11:7 [b]Gal. 5:4
32 [1]Lit., *out of* [a]Is. 8:14; 1 Pet. 2:6, 8

"[a]BEHOLD, I LAY IN ZION [b]A STONE
OF STUMBLING AND A ROCK OF
OFFENSE,
[c]AND HE WHO BELIEVES IN HIM
[d]WILL NOT BE [1]DISAPPOINTED."

The Word of Faith Brings Salvation

10 BRETHREN, my heart's desire
and my prayer to God for them is
for *their* salvation.
2 For I bear them witness that they
have [a]a zeal for God, but not in accordance with knowledge.
3 For not knowing about [a]God's
righteousness, and [b]seeking to establish
their own, they did not subject themselves to the righteousness of God.
4 For [a]Christ is the [1]end of the law
for righteousness to [b]everyone who believes.
5 For Moses writes that the man who
practices the righteousness which is
[1]based on law [a]shall live [2]by that righteousness.
6 But [a]the righteousness [1]based on
faith speaks thus, "[b]DO NOT SAY IN
YOUR HEART, 'WHO WILL ASCEND INTO
HEAVEN?' (that is, to bring Christ down),
7 or 'WHO WILL DESCEND INTO THE
[a]ABYSS?' (that is, to [b]bring Christ up
from the dead)."
8 But what does it say? "[a]THE WORD
IS NEAR YOU, IN YOUR MOUTH AND IN
YOUR HEART"—that is, the word of faith
which we are preaching,
9 [1]that [a]if you confess with your
mouth Jesus *as* Lord, and [b]believe in
your heart that [c]God raised Him from
the dead, you shall be saved;
10 for with the heart man believes,
[1]resulting in righteousness, and with the
mouth he confesses, [2]resulting in salvation.
11 For the Scripture says, "[a]WHOEVER
BELIEVES IN HIM WILL NOT BE [1]DISAP-
POINTED."
12 For [a]there is no distinction between Jew and Greek; for the same *Lord*
is [b]Lord of [c]all, abounding in riches for
all who call upon Him;
13 for "[a]WHOEVER WILL CALL UPON
THE NAME OF THE LORD WILL BE SAVED."
14 How then shall they call upon Him
in whom they have not believed? And
how shall they believe in Him [a]whom
they have not heard? And how shall they
hear without [b]a preacher?
15 And how shall they preach unless
they are sent? Just as it is written,
"[a]HOW BEAUTIFUL ARE THE FEET OF
THOSE WHO [1][b]BRING GLAD TIDINGS OF
GOOD THINGS!"
16 However, they [a]did not all heed the
[1]glad tidings; for Isaiah says, "[b]LORD,
WHO HAS BELIEVED OUR REPORT?"
17 So faith *comes* from [a]hearing, and
hearing by [b]the word [1]of Christ.
18 But I say, surely they have never
heard, have they? Indeed they have;
"[a]THEIR VOICE HAS GONE OUT INTO
ALL THE EARTH,
AND THEIR WORDS TO THE ENDS
OF THE [1]WORLD."
19 But I say, surely Israel did not
know, did they? At the first Moses says,
"[a]I WILL [b]MAKE YOU JEALOUS BY
THAT WHICH IS NOT A NATION,
BY A NATION WITHOUT UNDER-
STANDING WILL I ANGER YOU."
20 And Isaiah is very bold and says,
"[a]I WAS FOUND BY THOSE WHO
SOUGHT ME NOT,
I BECAME MANIFEST TO THOSE
WHO DID NOT ASK FOR ME."
21 But as for Israel He says, "[a]ALL
THE DAY LONG I HAVE STRETCHED OUT
MY HANDS TO A DISOBEDIENT AND OB-
STINATE PEOPLE."

Israel Is Not Cast Away

11 I SAY then, God has not [a]re-
jected His people, has He? [b]May
it never be! For [c]I too am an Israelite, [1]a
descendant of Abraham, of the tribe of
Benjamin.
2 God [a]has not rejected His people
whom He [b]foreknew. [c]Or do you not
know what the Scripture says in *the
passage about* Elijah, how he pleads with
God against Israel?
3 "Lord, [a]THEY HAVE KILLED THY
PROPHETS, THEY HAVE TORN DOWN
THINE ALTARS, AND I ALONE AM LEFT,
AND THEY ARE SEEKING MY LIFE."
4 But what [1]is the divine response to
him? "[a]I HAVE KEPT for Myself SEVEN
THOUSAND MEN WHO HAVE NOT BOWED
THE KNEE TO BAAL."
5 In the same way then, there has
also come to be at the present time [a]a
remnant according to *God's* [1]gracious
choice.
6 But [a]if it is by grace, it is no longer
on the basis of works, otherwise grace is
no longer grace.
7 What then? That which [a]Israel is
seeking for, it has not obtained, but
[1]those who were chosen obtained it, and
the rest were [b]hardened;
8 just as it is written,
"[a]GOD GAVE THEM A SPIRIT OF
STUPOR,
EYES TO SEE NOT AND EARS TO
HEAR NOT,
DOWN TO THIS VERY DAY."
9 And David says,
"[a]LET THEIR TABLE BECOME A
SNARE AND A TRAP,
AND A STUMBLING BLOCK AND A
RETRIBUTION TO THEM.
10 "[a]LET THEIR EYES BE DARKENED TO
SEE NOT,
AND BEND THEIR BACKS FOR-
EVER."
11 [a]I say then, they did not stumble so
as to fall, did they? [b]May it never be!
But by their transgression [c]salvation *has
come* to the Gentiles, to [d]make them
jealous.
12 Now if their transgression be riches
for the world and their failure be riches

---

33 [1]Lit., *put to shame* [a]Is. 28:16 [b]Is. 8:14 [c]Rom. 10:11 [d]Rom. 5:5

2 [a]Acts 21:20
3 [a]Rom. 1:17 [b]Is. 51:1; Rom. 10:2f., 20; 11:7
4 [1]Or, *goal* [a]Rom. 7:1-4; Gal. 3:24; 4:5 [b]Rom. 3:22
5 [1]Lit., *out of, from* [2]Lit., *by it* [a]Lev. 18:5; Neh. 9:29; Ezek. 20:11, 13, 21; Rom. 7:10
6 [1]Lit., *out of, from* [a]Rom. 9:30 [b]Deut. 30:12
7 [a]Luke 8:31 [b]Heb. 13:20
8 [a]Deut. 30:14
9 [1]Or, *because* [a]Matt. 10:32; Luke 12:8; Rom. 14:9; 1 Cor. 12:3; Phil. 2:11 [b]Acts 16:31; Rom. 4:24 [c]Acts 2:24
10 [1]Lit., *to righteousness* [2]Lit., *to salvation*
11 [1]Lit., *put to shame* [a]Is. 28:16; Rom. 9:33
12 [a]Rom. 3:22, 29 [b]Acts 10:36 [c]Rom. 3:29
13 [a]Joel 2:32; Acts 2:21
14 [a]Eph. 2:17; 4:21 [b]Acts 8:31; Titus 1:3
15 [1]Or, *preach the gospel* [a]Is. 52:7 [b]Rom. 1:15; 15:20
16 [1]Lit., *gospel* [a]Rom. 3:3 [b]Is. 53:1; John 12:38
17 [1]Or, *concerning Christ* [a]Gal. 3:2, 5 [b]Col. 3:16
18 [1]Or, *inhabited earth* [a]Ps. 19:4; Rom. 1:8; Col. 1:6, 23; 1 Thess. 1:8
19 [a]Deut. 32:21 [b]Rom. 11:11, 14
20 [a]Is. 65:1; Rom. 9:30
21 [a]Is. 65:2

1 [1]Lit., *of the seed of Abraham* [a]1 Sam. 12:22; Jer. 31:37; 33:24-26 [b]Luke 20:16 [c]2 Cor. 11:22; Phil. 3:5
2 [a]Ps. 94:14 [b]Rom. 8:29 [c]Rom. 6:16
3 [a]1 Kin. 19:10, 14
4 [1]Lit., *says* [a]1 Kin. 19:18
5 [1]Lit., *choice of grace* [a]2 Kin. 19:4; Rom. 9:27
6 [a]Rom. 4:4
7 [1]Lit., *the election* [a]Rom. 9:31 [b]Mark 6:52; Rom. 9:18; 11:25; 2 Cor. 3:14
8 [a]Deut. 29:4; Is. 29:10; Matt. 13:13f.
9 [a]Ps. 69:22
10 [a]Ps. 69:23
11 [a]Rom. 11:1 [b]Luke 20:16 [c]Acts 28:28 [d]Rom. 11:14

for the Gentiles, how much more will
their [1a]fulfillment be!
13 But I am speaking to you who are
Gentiles. Inasmuch then as [a]I am an
apostle of Gentiles, I magnify my ministry,
14 if somehow I might [a]move to jealousy [b]my [1]fellow countrymen and [c]save
some of them.
15 For if their rejection be the [a]rec-
onciliation of the world, what will *their*
acceptance be but [b]life from the dead?
16 And if the [a]first piece *of dough* be
holy, the lump is also; and if the root be
holy, the branches are too.
17 But if some of the [a]branches were
broken off, and [b]you, being a wild olive,
were grafted in among them and became
partaker with them of the [1]rich root of
the olive tree,
18 do not be arrogant toward the
branches; but if you are arrogant, *remember that* [a]it is not you who supports
the root, but the root *supports* you.
19 [a]You will say then, "Branches were
broken off so that I might be grafted in."
20 Quite right, they were broken off
for their unbelief, but you [a]stand by
your faith. [b]Do not be conceited, but
fear;
21 for if God did not spare the natural
branches, neither will He spare you.
22 Behold then the kindness and severity of God; to those who fell, severity,
but to you, God's [a]kindness, [b]if you
continue in His kindness; otherwise you
also [c]will be cut off.
23 And they also, [a]if they do not
continue in their unbelief, will be grafted
in; for God is able to graft them in
again.
24 For if you were cut off from what is
by nature a wild olive tree, and were
grafted contrary to nature into a cultivated olive tree, how much more shall
these who are the natural *branches* be
grafted into their own olive tree?
25 For [a]I do not want you, brethren,
to be uninformed of this [b]mystery, lest
you be [c]wise in your own estimation,
that a partial [d]hardening has happened
to Israel until the [e]fulness of the Gentiles
has come in;
26 and thus all Israel will be saved;
just as it is written,
"[a]THE DELIVERER WILL COME
FROM ZION,
HE WILL REMOVE UNGODLINESS
FROM JACOB."
27 "[a]AND THIS IS [1]MY COVENANT
WITH THEM,
[b]WHEN I TAKE AWAY THEIR SINS."
28 [1]From the standpoint of the gospel
they are [a]enemies for your sake, but
[2]from the standpoint of *God's* choice
they are beloved for [b]the sake of the
fathers;
29 for the gifts and the [a]calling of God
[b]are irrevocable.
30 For just as you once were disobedient to God, but now have been shown
mercy because of their disobedience,
31 so these also now have been disobedient, in order that because of the
mercy shown to you they also may now
be shown mercy.
32 For [a]God has shut up all in disobedience that He might show mercy to all.
33 Oh, the depth of [a]the riches [1]both
of the [b]wisdom and knowledge of God!
[c]How unsearchable are His judgments
and unfathomable His ways!
34 For [a]WHO HAS KNOWN THE MIND
OF THE LORD, OR WHO BECAME HIS
COUNSELOR?
35 Or [a]WHO HAS FIRST GIVEN TO HIM
[1]THAT IT MIGHT BE PAID BACK TO HIM
AGAIN?
36 For [a]from Him and through Him
and to Him are all things. [b]To Him *be*
the glory [1]forever. Amen.

Dedicated Service

12 [a]I URGE you therefore, brethren,
by the mercies of God, to [b]pre-
sent your bodies a living and holy sacrifice, [1]acceptable to God, *which is* your
[2]spiritual service of worship.
2 And do not [a]be conformed to [b]this
[1]world, but be transformed by the [c]re-
newing of your mind, that you may
[d]prove what the will of God is, that
which is good and [2]acceptable and perfect.
3 For through [a]the grace given to me
I say to every man among you [b]not to
think more highly of himself than he
ought to think; but to think so as to have
sound judgment, as God has allotted to
[c]each a measure of faith.
4 For [a]just as we have many members in one body and all the members do
not have the same function,
5 so we, [a]who are many, are [b]one
body in Christ, and individually members one of another.
6 And since we have gifts that [a]differ
according to the grace given to us, *let
each exercise them accordingly:* if
[b]prophecy, according to the proportion
of his faith;
7 if [1a]service, in his serving; or he
who [b]teaches, in his teaching;
8 or he who [a]exhorts, in his exhortation; he who gives, with [1b]liberality; [c]he
who [2]leads, with diligence; he who
shows mercy, with [d]cheerfulness.
9 Let [a]love be without hypocrisy.
[b]Abhor what is evil; cling to what is
good.

12 [1]Or, *fulness* [a]Rom. 11:25
13 [a]Acts 9:15
14 [1]Lit., *flesh* [a]Rom. 11:11 [b]Gen. 29:14; 2 Sam. 19:12f.; Rom. 9:3 [c]1 Cor. 1:21; 7:16; 9:22; 1 Tim. 1:15; 2:4; 2 Tim. 1:9; Titus 3:5
15 [a]Rom. 5:11 [b]Luke 15:24, 32
16 [a]Num. 15:18ff.; Neh. 10:37; Ezek. 44:30
17 [1]Lit., *root of the fatness* [a]Jer. 11:16; John 15:2 [b]Eph. 2:11ff.
18 [a]John 4:22
19 [a]Rom. 9:19
20 [a]Rom. 5:2; 1 Cor. 10:12; 2 Cor. 1:24 [b]Rom. 12:16; 1 Tim. 6:17; 1 Pet. 1:17
22 [a]Rom. 2:4 [b]1 Cor. 15:2; Heb. 3:6, 14 [c]John 15:2
23 [a]2 Cor. 3:16
25 [a]Rom. 1:13 [b]Matt. 13:11; Rom. 16:25; 1 Cor. 2:7-10; Eph. 3:3-5, 9 [c]Rom. 12:16 [d]Rom. 11:7 [e]Luke 21:24; John 10:16; Rom. 11:12
26 [a]Is. 59:20
27 [1]Lit., *the covenant from Me* [a]Is. 59:21; Jer. 31:33, 34; Heb. 8:10 [b]Is. 27:9; Heb. 8:12
28 [1]Lit., *According to the gospel* [2]Lit., *according to the election* [a]Rom. 5:10 [b]Deut. 7:8; 10:15; Rom. 9:5
29 [a]Rom. 8:28; 1 Cor. 1:26; Eph. 1:18; 4:1, 4; Phil. 3:14; 2 Thess. 1:11; 2 Tim. 1:9; Heb. 3:1; 2 Pet. 1:10 [b]Heb. 7:21
32 [a]Rom. 3:9; Gal. 3:22f.
33 [1]Or, *and the wisdom* [a]Rom. 2:4; Eph. 3:8 [b]Eph. 3:10; Col. 2:3 [c]Job 5:9; 11:7; 15:8
34 [a]Is. 40:13f.; 1 Cor. 2:16
35 [1]Lit., *and it will be paid back* [a]Job 35:7; 41:11
36 [1]Lit., *to the ages* [a]1 Cor. 8:6; 11:12; Col. 1:16; Heb. 2:10 [b]Rom. 16:27; Eph. 3:21; Phil. 4:20; 1 Tim. 1:17; 2 Tim. 4:18; 1 Pet. 4:11; 5:11; 2 Pet. 3:18; Jude 25; Rev. 1:6; 5:13; 7:12

1 [1]Or, *well-pleasing* [2]Or, *rational* [a]1 Cor. 1:10; 2 Cor. 10:1-4; Eph. 4:1; 1 Pet. 2:11 [b]Rom. 6:13, 16, 19; 1 Cor. 6:20; Heb. 13:15; 1 Pet. 2:5
2 [1]Or, *age* [2]Or, *well-pleasing* [a]1 Pet. 1:14 [b]Matt. 13:22; Gal. 1:4; 1 John 2:15 [c]Eph. 4:23; Titus 3:5 [d]Eph. 5:10, 17; Col. 1:9

3 [a]Rom. 1:5; 15:15; 1 Cor. 3:10; 15:10; Gal. 2:9; Eph. 3:7f. [b]Rom. 11:20; 12:16 [c]1 Cor. 7:17; 2 Cor. 10:13; Eph. 4:7; 1 Pet. 4:11
4 [a]1 Cor. 12:12-14; Eph. 4:4, 16
5 [a]1 Cor. 10:17, 33 [b]1 Cor. 12:20, 27; Eph. 4:12, 25
6 [a]Rom. 12:3; 1 Cor. 7:7; 12:4; 1 Pet. 4:10 [b]Acts 13:1; 1 Cor. 12:10
7 [1]Or, *office of service* [a]Acts 6:1; 1 Cor. 12:5, 28 [b]Acts 13:1; 1 Cor. 12:28; 14:26
8 [1]Or, *simplicity* [2]Or, *gives aid* [a]Acts 4:36; 11:23; 13:15 [b]2 Cor. 8:2; 9:11, 13 [c]1 Cor. 12:28; 1 Tim. 5:17 [d]2 Cor. 9:7
9 [a]2 Cor. 6:6; 1 Tim. 1:5 [b]1 Thess. 5:21f.

10 Be [a]devoted to one another in brotherly love; [1]give preference to one another [b]in honor;

11 not lagging behind in diligence, [a]fervent in spirit, [b]serving the Lord;

12 [a]rejoicing in hope, [b]persevering in tribulation, [c]devoted to prayer,

13 [a]contributing to the needs of the [1]saints, [2b]practicing hospitality.

14 [a]Bless those who persecute [1]you; bless and curse not.

15 [a]Rejoice with those who rejoice, and weep with those who weep.

16 [a]Be of the same mind toward one another; [b]do not be haughty in mind, but [1]associate with the lowly. [c]Do not be wise in your own estimation.

17 [a]Never pay back evil for evil to anyone. [1b]Respect what is right in the sight of all men.

18 If possible, [a]so far as it depends on you, [b]be at peace with all men.

19 [a]Never take your own revenge, beloved, but [1]leave room for the wrath *of God,* for it is written, "[b]VENGEANCE IS MINE, I WILL REPAY," says the Lord.

20 "[a]BUT IF YOUR ENEMY IS HUNGRY, FEED HIM, AND IF HE IS THIRSTY, GIVE HIM A DRINK; FOR IN SO DOING YOU WILL HEAP BURNING COALS UPON HIS HEAD."

21 Do not be overcome by evil, but overcome evil with good.

Be Subject to Government

13 LET every [1a]person be in [b]subjection to the governing authorities. For [c]there is no authority except [2]from God, and those which exist are established by God.

2 Therefore he who resists authority has opposed the ordinance of God; and they who have opposed will receive condemnation upon themselves.

3 For [a]rulers are not a cause of fear for [1]good behavior, but for evil. Do you want to have no fear of authority? Do what is good, and you will have praise from the same;

4 for it is a minister of God to you for good. But if you do what is evil, be afraid; for it does not bear the sword for nothing; for it is a minister of God, an [a]avenger who brings wrath upon the one who practices evil.

5 Wherefore it is necessary to be in subjection, not only because of wrath, but also [a]for conscience' sake.

6 For because of this you also pay taxes, for *rulers* are servants of God, devoting themselves to this very thing.

7 [a]Render to all what is due them: [b]tax to whom tax *is due;* [c]custom to whom custom; fear to whom fear; honor to whom honor.

8 Owe nothing to anyone except to love one another; for [a]he who loves [1]his neighbor has fulfilled *the* law.

9 For this, "[a]YOU SHALL NOT COMMIT ADULTERY, YOU SHALL NOT MURDER, YOU SHALL NOT STEAL, YOU SHALL NOT COVET," and if there is any other commandment, it is summed up in this saying, "[b]YOU SHALL LOVE YOUR NEIGHBOR AS YOURSELF."

10 Love [1]does no wrong to a neighbor; [a]love therefore is the fulfillment of *the* law.

11 And this *do,* knowing the time, that it is [a]already the hour for you to [b]awaken from sleep; for now [1]salvation is nearer to us than when we believed.

12 [a]The night is almost gone, and [b]the day is at hand. Let us therefore lay aside [c]the deeds of darkness and put on [d]the armor of light.

13 Let us [1a]behave properly as in the day, [b]not in carousing and drunkenness, not in sexual promiscuity and sensuality, not in strife and jealousy.

14 But [a]put on the Lord Jesus Christ, and make no provision for the flesh [b]in regard to *its* lusts.

Principles of Conscience

14 NOW [a]accept the one who is [b]weak in faith, *but* not for *the purpose of* passing judgment on his opinions.

2 [a]One man has faith that he may eat all things, but he who is [b]weak eats vegetables *only.*

3 Let not him who eats [a]regard with contempt him who does not eat, and let not him who does not eat [b]judge him who eats, for God has [c]accepted him.

4 [a]Who are you to judge the [1]servant of another? To his own [2]master he stands or falls; and stand he will, for the Lord is able to make him stand.

5 [a]One man [1]regards one day above another, another regards every day *alike.* Let each man be [b]fully convinced in his own mind.

6 He who observes the day, observes it for the Lord, and he who eats, [1]does so for the Lord, for he [a]gives thanks to God; and he who eats not, for the Lord he does not eat, and gives thanks to God.

7 For not one of us [a]lives for himself, and not one dies for himself;

8 for if we live, we live for the Lord, or if we die, we die for the Lord; therefore [a]whether we live or die, we are the Lord's.

10 [1]Or, *outdo one another in showing honor* [a]John 13:34; 1 Thess. 4:9; Heb. 13:1; 2 Pet. 1:7 [b]Rom. 13:7; Phil. 2:3; 1 Pet. 2:17
11 [a]Acts 18:25 [b]Acts 20:19
12 [a]Rom. 5:2 [b]Heb. 10:32, 36 [c]Acts 1:14
13 [1]Or, *holy ones* [2]Lit., *pursuing* [a]Rom. 15:25; 1 Cor. 16:15; 2 Cor. 9:1; Heb. 6:10 [b]Matt. 25:35; 1 Tim. 3:2
14 [1]Some ancient mss. do not contain *you* [a]Matt. 5:44; Luke 6:28; 1 Cor. 4:12
15 [a]Job 30:25; Heb. 13:3
16 [1]Or, *accommodate yourself to lowly things* [a]Rom. 15:5; 2 Cor. 13:11; Phil. 2:2; 4:2; 1 Pet. 3:8 [b]Rom. 11:20; 12:3 [c]Prov. 3:7; Rom. 11:25
17 [1]Lit., *Take thought for* [a]Prov. 20:22; 24:29; Rom. 12:19 [b]2 Cor. 8:21
18 [a]Rom. 1:15 [b]Mark 9:50; Rom. 14:19
19 [1]Lit., *give a place* [a]Prov. 20:22; 24:29; Rom. 12:17 [b]Deut. 32:35; Ps. 94:1; 1 Thess. 4:6; Heb. 10:30
20 [a]2 Kin. 6:22; Prov. 25:21f.; Matt. 5:44; Luke 6:27

1 [1]Or, *soul* [2]Lit., *by* [a]Acts 2:41 [b]Titus 3:1; 1 Pet. 2:13f. [c]Dan. 2:21; 4:17; John 19:11
3 [1]Lit., *good work* [a]1 Pet. 2:14
4 [a]1 Thess. 4:6
5 [a]Eccl. 8; 1 Pet. 2:13, 19
7 [a]Matt. 22:21; Mark 12:17; Luke 20:25 [b]Luke 20:22; 23:2 [c]Matt. 17:25
8 [1]Lit., *the other* [a]Matt. 7:12; 22:39f.; John 13:34; Rom. 13:10; Gal. 5:14; James 2:8
9 [a]Ex. 20:13ff.; Deut. 5:17ff. [b]Lev. 19:18; Matt. 19:19
10 [1]Lit., *works no evil* [a]Matt. 7:12; 22:39f.; John 13:34; Rom. 13:8; Gal. 5:14; James 2:8
11 [1]Or, *our salvation is nearer than when* [a]1 Cor. 7:29f.; 10:11; James 5:8; 1 Pet. 4:7; 2 Pet. 3:9, 11; 1 John 2:18; Rev. 1:3; 22:10 [b]Mark 13:37; 1 Cor. 15:34; Eph. 5:14; 1 Thess. 5:6
12 [a]1 Cor. 7:29f.; 10:11; James 5:8; 1 Pet. 4:7; 2 Pet. 3:9, 11; 1 John 2:18; Rev. 1:3; 22:10 [b]Heb. 10:25; 1 John 2:8; Rev. 1:3; 22:10 [c]Eph. 5:11 [d]2 Cor. 6:7; 10:4; Eph. 6:11, 13; 1 Thess. 5:8
13 [1]Lit., *walk* [a]1 Thess. 4:12 [b]Luke 21:34; Gal. 5:21; Eph. 5:18; 1 Pet. 4:3
14 [a]Job 29:14; Gal. 3:27; Eph. 4:24; Col. 3:10, 12 [b]Gal. 5:16; 1 Pet. 2:11

1 [a]Acts 28:2; Rom. 11:15; 14:3; 15:7 [b]Rom. 14:2; 15:1; 1 Cor. 8:9ff.; 9:22
2 [a]Rom. 14:14 [b]Rom. 14:1; 15:1; 1 Cor. 8:9ff.; 9:22
3 [a]Luke 18:9; Rom. 14:10 [b]Rom. 14:10, 13; Col. 2:16 [c]Acts 28:2; Rom. 11:15; 14:1; 15:7
4 [1]Or, *house-servant* [2]Lit., *lord* [a]Rom. 9:20; James 4:12
5 [1]Lit., *judges* [a]Gal. 4:10 [b]Luke 1:1; Rom. 4:21; 14:23
6 [1]Lit., *eats* [a]Matt. 14:19; 15:36; 1 Cor. 10:30; 1 Tim. 4:3f.
7 [a]Rom. 8:38f.; 2 Cor. 5:15; Gal. 2:20; Phil. 1:20f.
8 [a]Luke 20:38; Phil. 1:20; 1 Thess. 5:10; Rev. 14:13

9 For to this end [a]Christ died and
lived *again,* that He might be [b]Lord both
of the dead and of the living.
10 But you, why do you judge your
brother? Or you again, why do you
[a]regard your brother with contempt? For
[b]we shall all stand before the judgment
seat of God.
11 For it is written,
"[a]AS I LIVE, SAYS THE LORD, [b]EVERY KNEE SHALL BOW TO ME,
AND EVERY TONGUE SHALL [1]GIVE PRAISE TO GOD."
12 So then [a]each one of us shall give
account of himself to God.
13 Therefore let us not [a]judge one
another anymore, but rather determine
this—[b]not to put an obstacle or a stumbling block in a brother's way.
14 I know and am convinced in the
Lord Jesus that [a]nothing is unclean in
itself; but to him who [b]thinks anything
to be unclean, to him it is unclean.
15 For if because of food your brother
is hurt, you are no longer [a]walking
according to love. [b]Do not destroy with
your food him for whom Christ died.
16 Therefore [a]do not let what is for
you a good thing be [1]spoken of as evil;
17 for the kingdom of God [a]is not
eating and drinking, but righteousness
and [b]peace and [b]joy in the Holy Spirit.
18 For he who in this *way* [a]serves
Christ is [b]acceptable to God and approved by men.
19 So then [1]let us [a]pursue the things
which make for peace and the [b]building
up of one another.
20 [a]Do not tear down the work of
God for the sake of food. [b]All things
indeed are clean, but [c]they are evil for
the man who eats [1]and gives offense.
21 [a]It is good not to eat meat or to
drink wine, or *to do anything* by which
your brother stumbles.
22 The faith which you have, have [1]as
your own conviction before God. Happy
is he who [a]does not condemn himself in
what he approves.
23 But [a]he who doubts is condemned
if he eats, because *his eating is* not from
faith; and whatever is not from faith is
sin.

Self-denial on Behalf of Others

15 NOW we who are strong ought to
bear the weaknesses of [a]those
without strength and not *just* please
ourselves.
2 Let each of us [a]please his neighbor
[1]for his good, to his [b]edification.
3 For even [a]Christ did not please
Himself; but as it is written, "[b]THE
REPROACHES OF THOSE WHO REPROACHED THEE FELL UPON ME."
4 For [a]whatever was written in earlier times was written for our instruction,
that through perseverance and the encouragement of the Scriptures we might
have hope.
5 Now may the [a]God [1]who gives
perseverance and encouragement grant
you [b]to be of the same mind with one
another according to Christ Jesus;
6 that with one accord you may with
one [1]voice glorify [a]the God and Father
of our Lord Jesus Christ.
7 Wherefore, [a]accept one another,
just as Christ also accepted [1]us to the
glory of God.
8 For I say that Christ has become a
servant to [a]the circumcision on behalf of
the truth of God to confirm [b]the promises *given* to the fathers,
9 and for [a]the Gentiles to [b]glorify
God for His mercy; as it is written,
"[c]THEREFORE I WILL [1]GIVE PRAISE TO THEE AMONG THE GENTILES,
AND I WILL SING TO THY NAME."
10 And again he says,
"[a]REJOICE, O GENTILES, WITH HIS PEOPLE."
11 And again,
"[a]PRAISE THE LORD ALL YOU GENTILES,
AND LET ALL THE PEOPLES PRAISE HIM."
12 And again Isaiah says,
"[a]THERE SHALL COME [b]THE ROOT OF JESSE,
AND HE WHO ARISES TO RULE OVER THE GENTILES,
[c]IN HIM SHALL THE GENTILES HOPE."
13 Now may the God of hope fill you
with all [a]joy and peace in believing, that
you may abound in hope [b]by the power
of the Holy Spirit.
14 And concerning you, my brethren,
I myself also am convinced that you
yourselves are full of [a]goodness, filled
with [b]all knowledge, and able also to
admonish one another.
15 But I have written very boldly to
you on some points, so as to remind you
again, because of [a]the grace that was
given me [1]from God,
16 to be [a]a minister of Christ Jesus to
the Gentiles, ministering as a priest the
[b]gospel of God, that *my* [c]offering of the
Gentiles might become acceptable, sanctified by the Holy Spirit.
17 Therefore in Christ Jesus I have
found [a]reason for boasting in [b]things
pertaining to God.
18 For I will not presume to speak of
anything [1]except what [a]Christ has accomplished through me, [2]resulting in the
obedience of the Gentiles by word and
deed,
19 in the power of [1a]signs and wonders, [b]in the power of the Spirit; so that
[c]from Jerusalem and round about as [d]far
as Illyricum I have [2]fully preached the
gospel of Christ.

9 [a]Rev. 1:18; 2:8 [b]Matt. 28:18; John 12:24; Phil. 2:11; 1 Thess. 5:10
10 [a]Luke 18:9; Rom. 14:3 [b]Rom. 2:16; 2 Cor. 5:10
11 [1]Or, *confess* [a]Is. 45:23 [b]Phil. 2:10f.
12 [a]Matt. 12:36; 16:27; 1 Pet. 4:5
13 [a]Matt. 7:1; Rom. 14:3 [b]1 Cor. 8:13
14 [a]Acts 10:15; Rom. 14:2, 20 [b]1 Cor. 8:7
15 [a]Eph. 5:2 [b]Rom. 14:20; 1 Cor. 8:11
16 [1]Lit., *blasphemed* [a]1 Cor. 10:30; Titus 2:5
17 [a]1 Cor. 8:8 [b]Rom. 15:13; Gal. 5:22
18 [a]Rom. 16:18 [b]2 Cor. 8:21; Phil. 4:8; 1 Pet. 2:12
19 [1]Many ancient mss. read *we pursue* [a]Ps. 34:14; Rom. 12:18; 1 Cor. 7:15; 2 Tim. 2:22; Heb. 12:14 [b]Rom. 15:2; 1 Cor. 10:23; 14:3f., 26; 2 Cor. 12:19; Eph. 4:12, 29
20 [1]Lit., *with offense* [a]Rom. 14:15 [b]Acts 10:15; Rom. 14:2, 14 [c]1 Cor. 8:9-12
21 [a]1 Cor. 8:13
22 [1]Lit., *according to yourself* [a]1 John 3:21
23 [a]Rom. 14:5

1 [a]Rom. 14:1; Gal. 6:2; 1 Thess. 5:14
2 [1]Lit., *for what is good to edification* [a]1 Cor. 9:22; 10:24, 33; 2 Cor. 13:9 [b]Rom. 14:19; 1 Cor. 10:23; 14:3f., 26; 2 Cor. 12:19; Eph. 4:12, 29
3 [a]2 Cor. 8:9 [b]Ps. 69:9
4 [a]Rom. 4:23f.; 2 Tim. 3:16
5 [1]Lit., *of perseverance* [a]2 Cor. 1:3 [b]Rom. 12:16
6 [1]Lit., *mouth* [a]Rev. 1:6
7 [1]Some mss. read *you* [a]Rom. 14:1
8 [a]Matt. 15:24; Acts 3:26 [b]Rom. 4:16; 2 Cor. 1:20
9 [1]Or, *confess* [a]Rom. 3:29; 11:30f. [b]Matt. 9:8 [c]2 Sam. 22:50; Ps. 18:49
10 [a]Deut. 32:43
11 [a]Ps. 117:1
12 [a]Is. 11:10 [b]Rev. 5:5; 22:16 [c]Matt. 12:21
13 [a]Rom. 14:17 [b]Rom. 15:19; 1 Cor. 2:4; 1 Thess. 1:5
14 [a]Eph. 5:9; 2 Thess. 1:11 [b]1 Cor. 1:5; 8:1, 7, 10; 12:8; 13:2
15 [1]Some mss. read *by God* [a]Rom. 12:3
16 [a]Acts 9:15; Rom. 11:13 [b]Rom. 1:1; 15:19, 20 [c]Rom. 12:1; Eph. 5:2; Phil. 2:17
17 [a]Phil. 3:3 [b]Heb. 2:17; 5:1
18 [1]Or, *which Christ has not accomplished* [2]Lit., *to the obedience* [a]Acts 15:12; 21:19; Rom. 1:5; 2 Cor. 3:5
19 [1]Or, *attesting miracles* [2]Lit., *fulfilled* [a]John 4:48 [b]Rom. 15:13; 1 Cor. 2:4; 1 Thess. 1:5 [c]Acts 22:17-21 [d]Acts 20:1f.

20 And thus I aspired to [a]preach the gospel, not where Christ was *already* named, [b]that I might not build upon another man's foundation;

21 but as it is written,

"[a]THEY WHO HAD NO NEWS OF HIM SHALL SEE,
AND THEY WHO HAVE NOT HEARD SHALL UNDERSTAND."

22 For this reason [a]I have often been hindered from coming to you;

23 but now, with no further place for me in these regions, and since I [a]have had for many years a longing to come to you

24 whenever I [a]go to Spain—for I hope to see you in passing, and to be [b]helped on my way there by you, when I have first [c]enjoyed your company [1]for a while—

25 but now, [a]I am going to Jerusalem [b]serving the [1]saints.

26 For [a]Macedonia and [b]Achaia have been pleased to make a contribution for the poor among the [1]saints in Jerusalem.

27 Yes, they were pleased *to do so,* and they are indebted to them. For [a]if the Gentiles have shared in their spiritual things, they are indebted to minister to them also in material things.

28 Therefore, when I have finished this, and [a]have [1]put my seal on this fruit of theirs, I will [b]go on by way of you to Spain.

29 And I know that when [a]I come to you, I will come in the fulness of the blessing of Christ.

30 Now I urge you, brethren, by our Lord Jesus Christ and by [a]the love of the Spirit, to [b]strive together with me in your prayers to God for me,

31 that I may be [a]delivered from those who are disobedient in Judea, and *that* my [b]service for Jerusalem may prove acceptable to the [1c]saints;

32 so that [a]I may come to you in joy by [b]the will of God and find *refreshing* rest in your company.

33 Now [a]the God of peace be with you all. Amen.

Greetings and Love Expressed

16 I [a]COMMEND to you our sister Phoebe, who is a [1]servant of the church which is at [b]Cenchrea;

2 that you [a]receive her in the Lord in a manner worthy of the [1b]saints, and that you help her in whatever matter she may have need of you; for she herself has also been a helper of many, [2]and of myself as well.

3 Greet [a]Prisca and Aquila, my fellow workers [b]in [c]Christ Jesus,

4 who for my life risked their own necks, to whom not only do I give thanks, but also all the churches of the Gentiles;

5 also *greet* [a]the church that is in their house. Greet Epaenetus, my beloved, who is the [b]first convert to Christ from [1c]Asia.

6 Greet Mary, who has worked hard for you.

7 Greet Andronicus and [1]Junias, my [a]kinsmen, and my [b]fellow prisoners, who are outstanding among the apostles, who also were [c]in Christ before me.

8 Greet Ampliatus, my beloved in the Lord.

9 Greet Urbanus, our fellow worker [a]in Christ, and Stachys my beloved.

10 Greet Apelles, the approved [a]in Christ. Greet those who are of the *household* of Aristobulus.

11 Greet Herodion, my [a]kinsman. Greet those of the *household* of Narcissus, who are in the Lord.

12 Greet Tryphaena and Tryphosa, workers in the Lord. Greet Persis the beloved, who has worked hard in the Lord.

13 Greet [a]Rufus, a choice man in the Lord, also his mother and mine.

14 Greet Asyncritus, Phlegon, Hermes, Patrobas, Hermas and the brethren with them.

15 Greet Philologus and Julia, Nereus and his sister, and Olympas, and all [a]the [1]saints who are with them.

16 [a]Greet one another with a holy kiss. All the churches of Christ greet you.

17 Now I urge you, brethren, keep your eye on those who cause dissensions and [1]hindrances [a]contrary to the teaching which you learned, and [b]turn away from them.

18 For such men are [a]slaves, not of our Lord Christ but of [b]their own [1]appetites; and by their [c]smooth and flattering speech they deceive the hearts of the unsuspecting.

19 For the report of your obedience [a]has reached to all; therefore I am rejoicing over you, but [b]I want you to be wise in what is good, and innocent in what is evil.

20 And [a]the God of peace will soon crush [b]Satan under your feet.

[c]The grace of our Lord Jesus be with you.

21 [a]Timothy my fellow worker greets you, and *so do* [b]Lucius and [c]Jason and [d]Sosipater, my [e]kinsmen.

22 I, Tertius, who [a]write this letter, greet you in the Lord.

23 [a]Gaius, host to me and to the whole church, greets you. [b]Erastus, the city treasurer greets you, and Quartus, the brother.

---

20 [a]Rom. 1:15; 10:15; 15:16 [b]1 Cor. 3:10; 2 Cor. 10:15f.
21 [a]Is. 52:15
22 [a]Rom. 1:13; 1 Thess. 2:18
23 [a]Acts 19:21; Rom. 1:10f.; 15:29, 32
24 [1]Lit., *in part* [a]Rom. 15:28 [b]Acts 15:3 [c]Rom. 1:12
25 [1]Or, *holy ones* [a]Acts 19:21 [b]Acts 24:17
26 [1]V. 25, note 1 [a]Acts 16:9; 1 Cor. 16:5; 2 Cor. 1:16; 2:13; 7:5; 8:1; 9:2, 4; 11:9; Phil. 4:15; 1 Thess. 1:7f.; 4:10; 1 Tim. 1:3 [b]Acts 18:12; 19:21
27 [a]1 Cor. 9:11
28 [1]Lit., *sealed to them this fruit* [a]John 3:33 [b]Rom. 15:24
29 [a]Acts 19:21; Rom. 1:10f.; 15:23, 32
30 [a]Gal. 5:22; Col. 1:8 [b]2 Cor. 1:11; Col. 4:12
31 [1]V. 25, note 1 [a]2 Cor. 1:10; 2 Thess. 3:2; 2 Tim. 3:11; 4:17 [b]Rom. 15:25f.; 2 Cor. 8:4; 9:1 [c]Acts 9:13, 15
32 [a]Rom. 15:23 [b]Acts 18:21; Rom. 1:10
33 [a]Rom. 16:20; 2 Cor. 13:11; Phil. 4:9; 1 Thess. 5:23; 2 Thess. 3:16; Heb. 13:20

1 [1]Or, *deaconess* [a]2 Cor. 3:1 [b]Acts 18:18
2 [1]Or, *holy ones* [2]Lit., *and of me, myself* [a]Phil. 2:29 [b]Acts 9:13, 15
3 [a]Acts 18:2 [b]Rom. 8:1ff.; 16:7, 9, 10; 2 Cor. 5:17; 12:2; Gal. 1:22 [c]Rom. 8:1
5 [1]I.e., west coast province of Asia Minor [a]1 Cor. 16:19; Col. 4:15; Philem. 2 [b]1 Cor. 16:15 [c]Acts 16:6
7 [1]Or, *Junia* (fem.) [a]Rom. 9:3; 16:11, 21 [b]Col. 4:10; Philem. 23 [c]Rom. 8:1ff.; 16:3, 9, 10; 2 Cor. 5:17; 12:2; Gal. 1:22
9 [a]Rom. 8:1ff.; 16:3, 7, 10; 2 Cor. 5:17; 12:2; Gal. 1:22
10 [a]Rom. 8:1ff.; 16:3, 7, 9; 2 Cor. 5:17; 12:2; Gal. 1:22
11 [a]Rom. 9:3; 16:7, 21
13 [a]Mark 15:21
15 [1]V. 2, note 1 [a]Rom. 16:2, 14
16 [a]1 Cor. 16:20; 2 Cor. 13:12; 1 Thess. 5:26; 1 Pet. 5:14

17 [1]Lit., *occasions of stumbling* [a]1 Tim. 1:3; 6:3 [b]Matt. 7:15; Gal. 1:8f.; 2 Thess. 3:6, 14; Titus 3:10; 2 John 10
18 [1]Lit., *belly* [a]Rom. 14:18 [b]Phil. 3:19 [c]Col. 2:4; 2 Pet. 2:3
19 [a]Rom. 1:8 [b]Jer. 4:22; Matt. 10:16; 1 Cor. 14:20
20 [a]Rom. 15:33 [b]Matt. 4:10 [c]1 Cor. 16:23; 2 Cor. 13:14; Gal. 6:18; Phil. 4:23; 1 Thess. 5:28; 2 Thess. 3:18; Rev. 22:21
21 [a]Acts 16:1 [b]Acts 13:1 [?] [c]Acts 17:5 [?] [d]Acts 20:4 [?] [e]Rom. 9:3; 16:7, 11
22 [a]1 Cor. 16:21; Gal. 6:11; Col. 4:18; 2 Thess. 3:17; Philem. 19
23 [a]Acts 19:29; 20:4 [?]; 1 Cor. 1:14 [b]Acts 19:22; 2 Tim. 4:20

24 [[1]The grace of our Lord Jesus
Christ be with you all. Amen.]
25 [a]Now to Him who is able to establish you [b]according to my gospel and the
preaching of Jesus Christ, according to
the revelation of [c]the mystery which has
been kept secret for [d]long ages past,
26 but now is manifested, and by [a]the
Scriptures of the prophets, according to
the commandment of the eternal God,
has been made known to all the nations,
leading to [b]obedience of faith;
27 to the only wise God, through
Jesus Christ, [a]be the glory forever.
Amen.

24 [1]Many mss. do not contain this v.
25 [a]Eph. 3:20; Jude 24 [b]Rom. 2:16 [c]Matt. 13:35; Rom. 11:25; 1 Cor. 2:1, 7; 4:1; Eph. 1:9; 3:3, 9; 6:19; Col. 1:26f.; 2:2; 4:3; 1 Tim. 3:16 [d]2 Tim. 1:9; Titus 1:2
26 [a]Rom. 1:2 [b]Rom. 1:5
27 [a]Rom. 11:36

THE FIRST EPISTLE OF PAUL TO THE CORINTHIANS

Appeal to Unity

1 PAUL, [a]called *as* an apostle of Jesus
Christ [1]by [b]the will of God, and
[c]Sosthenes our [d]brother,
2 to [a]the church of God which is at
[b]Corinth, to those who have been sanctified in Christ Jesus, [1]saints [c]by calling,
with all who in every place [d]call upon
the name of our Lord Jesus Christ, their
Lord and ours:
3 [a]Grace to you and peace from God
our Father and the Lord Jesus Christ.
4 [a]I thank [1]my God always concerning you, for the grace of God which was
given you in Christ Jesus,
5 that in everything you were [a]en-
riched in Him, in all [b]speech and [b]all
knowledge,
6 even as [a]the testimony concerning
Christ was confirmed [1]in you,
7 so that you are not lacking in any
gift, [a]awaiting eagerly the revelation of
our Lord Jesus Christ,
8 [a]who shall also confirm you to the
end, blameless in [b]the day of our Lord
Jesus Christ.
9 [a]God is faithful, through whom
you were [b]called into [c]fellowship with
His Son, Jesus Christ our Lord.
10 Now [a]I exhort you, [b]brethren, by
the name of our Lord Jesus Christ, that
you all [1]agree, and there be no [2c]divi-
sions among you, but you be [3]made
complete in [d]the same mind and in the
same judgment.
11 For I have been informed concerning you, my brethren, by Chloe's *people,*
that there are quarrels among you.
12 Now I mean this, that [a]each one of
you is saying, "I am of Paul," and "I of
[b]Apollos," and "I of [c]Cephas," and "I of
Christ."
13 [1]Has Christ been divided? Paul was
not crucified for you, was he? Or were
you [a]baptized [2]in the name of Paul?
14 [1]I thank God that I [a]baptized none
of you except [a]Crispus and [b]Gaius,
15 that no man should say you were
baptized [1]in my name.
16 Now I did baptize also the [a]house-
hold of Stephanas; beyond that, I do not
know whether I baptized any other.
17 [a]For Christ did not send me to
baptize, but to preach the gospel, [b]not in
[1]cleverness of speech, that the cross of
Christ should not be made void.

The Wisdom of God

18 For the word of the cross is to
[a]those who [1]are perishing [b]foolishness,
but to us who [2]are being saved it is [c]the
power of God.
19 For it is written,

"[a]I WILL DESTROY THE WISDOM OF THE WISE,
AND THE CLEVERNESS OF THE CLEVER I WILL SET ASIDE."

20 [a]Where is the wise man? Where is
the scribe? Where is the debater of [b]this
age? Has not God [c]made foolish the
wisdom of [d]the world?
21 For since in the wisdom of God
[a]the world through its wisdom did not
come to know God, [b]God was well-
pleased through the [c]foolishness of the
[1]message preached to [d]save those who
believe.
22 For indeed [a]Jews ask for [1]signs,
and Greeks search for wisdom;
23 but we preach [1a]Christ crucified,
[b]to Jews a stumbling block, and to
Gentiles [c]foolishness,
24 but to those who are [a]the called,
both Jews and Greeks, Christ [b]the power
of God and [c]the wisdom of God.
25 Because the [a]foolishness of God is
wiser than men, and [b]the weakness of
God is stronger than men.
26 For [1]consider your [a]calling, brethren, that there were [b]not many wise
according to [2]the flesh, not many
mighty, not many noble;

1 [1]Lit., *through* [a]Rom. 1:1 [b]Rom. 1:10; 2 Tim. 1:1 [c]Acts 18:17 [d]Acts 1:15
2 [1]Or, *holy ones* [a]1 Cor. 10:32 [b]Acts 18:1 [c]Rom. 1:7; 8:28 [d]Acts 7:59
3 [a]Rom. 1:7
4 [1]Some ancient mss. do not contain *my* [a]Rom. 1:8
5 [a]2 Cor. 9:11 [b]Rom. 15:14; 2 Cor. 8:7
6 [1]Or, *among* [a]2 Thess. 1:10; 1 Tim. 2:6; 2 Tim. 1:8; Rev. 1:2
7 [a]Luke 17:30; Rom. 8:19, 23; Phil. 3:20; 2 Pet. 3:12
8 [a]Rom. 8:19; Phil. 1:6; Col. 2:7; 1 Thess. 3:13; 5:23 [b]Luke 17:24, 30; 1 Cor. 5:5; 2 Cor. 1:14; Phil. 1:6, 10; 2:16; 1 Thess. 5:2; 2 Thess. 2:2
9 [a]Deut. 7:9; Is. 49:7; 1 Cor. 10:13; 2 Cor. 1:18; 1 Thess. 5:24; 2 Thess. 3:3 [b]Rom. 8:28 [c]1 John 1:3
10 [1]Lit., *speak the same thing* [2]Lit., *schisms* [3]Or, *united* [a]Rom. 12:1 [b]Rom. 1:13 [c]1 Cor. 11:18 [d]Rom. 12:16; Phil. 1:27
12 [a]Matt. 23:8-10; 1 Cor. 3:4 [b]Acts 18:24; 1 Cor. 3:22 [c]John 1:42; 1 Cor. 3:22; 9:5; 15:5
13 [1]Or, *Christ has been divided!* or, *Christ is divided!* [2]Lit., *into* [a]Matt. 28:19; Acts 2:38
14 [1]Some ancient mss. read *I give thanks that* [a]Acts 18:8 [b]Rom. 16:23
15 [1]Lit., *into*
16 [a]1 Cor. 16:15, 17
17 [1]Lit., *wisdom* [a]John 4:2; Acts 10:48 [b]1 Cor. 2:1, 4, 13; 2 Cor. 10:10; 11:6

18 [1]Or, *perish* [2]Or, *are saved* [a]Acts 2:47; 2 Cor. 2:15; 4:3; 2 Thess. 2:10 [b]1 Cor. 1:21, 23, 25; 2:14; 4:10 [c]Rom. 1:16; 1 Cor. 1:24
19 [a]Is. 29:14
20 [a]Job 12:17; Is. 19:11f.; 33:18 [b]Matt. 13:22; 1 Cor. 2:6, 8; 3:18, 19 [c]Rom. 1:20ff. [d]John 12:31; 1 Cor. 1:27f.; 6:2; 11:32; James 4:4
21 [1]Lit., *preaching* [a]John 12:31; 1 Cor. 1:27f.; 6:2; 11:32; James 4:4 [b]Luke 12:32; Gal. 1:15; Col. 1:19 [c]1 Cor. 1:18, 23, 25; 2:14; 4:10 [d]Rom. 11:14; James 5:20
22 [1]Or, *attesting miracles* [a]Matt. 12:38
23 [1]I.e., Messiah [a]1 Cor. 2:2; Gal. 3:1; 5:11 [b]Luke 2:34; 1 Pet. 2:8 [c]1 Cor. 1:18, 21, 25; 2:14; 4:10
24 [a]Rom. 8:28 [b]Rom. 1:16; 1 Cor. 1:18 [c]Luke 11:49; 1 Cor. 1:30
25 [a]1 Cor. 1:18, 21, 23; 2:14; 4:10 [b]2 Cor. 13:4
26 [1]Lit., *see* [2]Or, *human standards* [a]Rom. 11:29 [b]Matt. 11:25; 1 Cor. 1:20; 2:8

27 but [a]God has chosen the foolish
things of [b]the world to shame the wise,
and God has chosen the weak things of
[b]the world to shame the things which are
strong,
28 and the base things of [a]the world
and the despised, God has chosen, [b]the
things that are not, that He might [c]nul-
lify the things that are,
29 that [a]no [1]man should boast before
God.
30 But [1]by His doing you are in
[a]Christ Jesus, who became to us [b]wis-
dom from God, [2]and [c]righteousness and
[d]sanctification, and [e]redemption,
31 that, just as it is written, "[a]LET HIM
WHO BOASTS, BOAST IN THE LORD."

Paul's Reliance upon the Spirit

2 AND when I came to you, brethren,
I [a]did not come with superiority of
speech or of wisdom, proclaiming to you
[b]the [1]testimony of God.
2 For I determined to know nothing
among you except [a]Jesus Christ, and
Him crucified.
3 And I was with you in [a]weakness
and in [b]fear and in much trembling.
4 And my [1]message and my preaching were [a]not in persuasive words of
wisdom, but in demonstration of [b]the
Spirit and of power,
5 that your faith should not [1]rest on
the wisdom of men, but on [a]the power of
God.
6 Yet we do speak wisdom among
those who are [a]mature; a wisdom, however, not of [b]this age, nor of the rulers of
[b]this age, who are [c]passing away;
7 but we speak God's wisdom in a
[a]mystery, the hidden *wisdom,* which God
[b]predestined before the [c]ages to our
glory;
8 *the wisdom* [a]which none of the
rulers of [b]this age has understood; for if
they had understood it, they would not
have crucified [c]the Lord of glory;
9 but just as it is written,
"[a]THINGS WHICH EYE HAS NOT
SEEN AND EAR HAS NOT HEARD,
AND *which* HAVE NOT ENTERED
THE HEART OF MAN,
ALL THAT GOD HAS PREPARED
FOR THOSE WHO LOVE HIM."
10 [1a]For to us God revealed *them*
[b]through the Spirit; for the Spirit
searches all things, even the [c]depths of
God.
11 For who among men knows the
thoughts of a man except the [a]spirit of
the man, which is in him? Even so the
thoughts of God no one knows except
the Spirit of God.
12 Now we [a]have received, not the
spirit of [b]the world, but the Spirit who is
from God, that we might know the
things freely given to us by God,
13 which things we also speak, [a]not in
words taught by human wisdom, but in
those taught by the Spirit, [1]combining
spiritual *thoughts* with spiritual *words.*

27 [a]James 2:5 [b]1 Cor. 1:20
28 [a]1 Cor. 1:20 [b]Rom. 4:17 [c]Job 34:19; 1 Cor. 2:6; 2 Thess. 2:8; Heb. 2:14
29 [1]Lit., *flesh* [a]Eph. 2:9
30 [1]Lit., *of Him* [2]Or, *both* [a]Rom. 8:1; 1 Cor. 4:15 [b]1 Cor. 1:24 [c]Jer. 23:5f.; 33:16; 2 Cor. 5:21; Phil. 3:9 [d]1 Cor. 1:2; 6:11; 1 Thess. 5:23 [e]Rom. 3:24; Eph. 1:7, 14; Col. 1:14
31 [a]Jer. 9:23f.; 2 Cor. 10:17
1 [1]Some ancient mss. read *mystery* [a]1 Cor. 1:17; 2:4, 13 [b]1 Cor. 2:7
2 [a]1 Cor. 1:23; Gal. 6:14
3 [a]1 Cor. 4:10; 2 Cor. 11:30; 12:5, 9f.; 13:9 [b]Is. 19:16; 2 Cor. 7:15; Eph. 6:5
4 [1]Lit., *word* [a]1 Cor. 1:17; 2:1, 13 [b]Rom. 15:19; 1 Cor. 4:20
5 [1]Lit., *be* [a]2 Cor. 4:7; 6:7; 12:9
6 [a]Eph. 4:13; Phil. 3:15; Heb. 5:14; 6:1 [b]Matt. 13:22; 1 Cor. 1:20 [c]1 Cor. 1:28
7 [a]Rom. 11:25; 16:25f.; 1 Cor. 2:1 [b]Rom. 8:29f. [c]Heb. 1:2; 11:3
8 [a]1 Cor. 1:26; 2:6 [b]Matt. 13:22; 1 Cor. 1:20 [c]Acts 7:2; James 2:1
9 [a]Is. 64:4; 65:17
10 [1]Some ancient mss. use *But* [a]Matt. 11:25; 13:11; 16:17; Gal. 1:12; Eph. 3:3, 5 [b]John 14:26 [c]Rom. 11:33ff.
11 [a]Prov. 20:27
12 [a]Rom. 8:15 [b]1 Cor. 1:27
13 [1]Or, *interpreting spiritual* things *to spiritual* men [a]1 Cor. 1:17; 2:1, 4
14 [1]Or, *an unspiritual* [2]Or, *examined* [a]1 Cor. 15:44, 46; James 3:15; Jude 19 mg. [b]John 14:17 [c]1 Cor. 1:18
15 [a]1 Cor. 3:1; 14:37; Gal. 6:1
16 [a]Is. 40:13; Rom. 11:34 [b]John 15:15
1 [a]1 Cor. 2:15; 14:37; Gal. 6:1 [b]Rom. 7:14; 1 Cor. 2:14 [c]1 Cor. 2:6; Eph. 4:14; Heb. 5:13
2 [a]Heb. 5:12f.; 1 Pet. 2:2 [b]John 16:12
3 [1]Lit., *according to man* [a]Rom. 13:13; 1 Cor. 1:10f.; 11:18 [b]1 Cor. 3:4
4 [a]1 Cor. 1:12 [b]1 Cor. 3:3
5 [a]Rom. 15:16; 2 Cor. 3:3, 6; 4:1; 5:18; 6:4; Eph. 3:7; Col. 1:25; 1 Tim. 1:12 [b]Rom. 12:6; 1 Cor. 3:10

14 But [1]a [a]natural man [b]does not
accept the things of the Spirit of God;
for they are [c]foolishness to him, and he
cannot understand them, because they
are spiritually [2]appraised.
15 But he who is [a]spiritual appraises
all things, yet he himself is appraised by
no man.
16 For [a]WHO HAS KNOWN THE MIND
OF THE LORD, THAT HE SHOULD IN-
STRUCT HIM? But [b]we have the mind of
Christ.

Foundations for Living

3 AND I, brethren, could not speak to
you as to [a]spiritual men, but as to
[b]men of flesh, as to [c]babes in Christ.
2 I gave you [a]milk to drink, not solid
food; for you [b]were not yet able *to*
receive it. Indeed, even now you are not
yet able,
3 for you are still fleshly. For since
there is [a]jealousy and strife among you,
are you not fleshly, and are you not
walking [1b]like mere men?
4 For when [a]one says, "I am of
Paul," and another, "I am of Apollos,"
are you not *mere* [b]men?
5 What then is Apollos? And what is
Paul? [a]Servants through whom you believed, even [b]as the Lord gave *opportu-*
nity to each one.
6 [a]I planted, [b]Apollos watered, but
[c]God was causing the growth.
7 So then neither the one who plants
nor the one who waters is anything, but
God who causes the growth.
8 Now he who plants and he who
waters are one; but each will [a]receive his
own [1]reward according to his own labor.
9 For we are God's [a]fellow workers;
you are God's [1b]field, God's [c]building.
10 According to [a]the grace of God
which was given to me, as a wise master
builder [b]I laid a foundation, and [c]an-
other is building upon it. But let each
man be careful how he builds upon it.
11 For no man can lay a [a]foundation
other than the one which is laid, which is
Jesus Christ.
12 Now if any man builds upon the
foundation with gold, silver, [1]precious
stones, wood, hay, straw,
13 [a]each man's work will become
evident; for [b]the day will show it, because it is *to be* revealed with fire; and
the fire itself will test [1]the quality of each
man's work.
14 If any man's work which he has
built upon it remains, he shall [a]receive a
reward.

6 [a]1 Cor. 4:15; 9:1; 15:1; 2 Cor. 10:14f. [b]Acts 18:24-27; 1 Cor. 1:12 [c]1 Cor. 15:10
8 [1]Or, *wages* [a]1 Cor. 3:14; 4:5; 9:17; Gal. 6:4
9 [1]Or, *cultivated land* [a]Mark 16:20; 2 Cor. 6:1 [b]Is. 61:3; Matt. 15:13 [c]1 Cor. 3:16; Eph. 2:20-22; Col. 2:7; 1 Pet. 2:5
10 [a]Rom. 12:3; 1 Cor. 15:10 [b]Rom. 15:20; 1 Cor. 3:11f. [c]1 Thess. 3:2
11 [a]Is. 28:16; Eph. 2:20; 1 Pet. 2:4ff.
12 [1]Or, *costly*
13 [1]Lit., *of what sort each man's work is* [a]1 Cor. 4:5 [b]Matt. 10:15; 1 Cor. 1:8; 2 Thess. 1:7-10; 2 Tim. 1:12, 18; 4:8
14 [a]1 Cor. 3:8; 4:5; 9:17; Gal. 6:4

15 If any man's work is burned up, he
shall suffer loss; but he himself shall be
saved, yet [a]so as through fire.
16 [a]Do you not know that [b]you are a
[1]temple of God, and *that* the Spirit of
God dwells in you?
17 If any man destroys the [1]temple of
God, God will destroy him, for the
[1]temple of God is holy, and [2]that is what
you are.
18 [a]Let no man deceive himself. [b]If
any man among you thinks that he is
wise in [c]this age, let him become foolish
that he may become wise.
19 For [a]the wisdom of this world is
foolishness before God. For it is written,
"*He is* [b]THE ONE WHO CATCHES THE WISE
IN THEIR CRAFTINESS";
20 and again, "[a]THE LORD KNOWS
THE REASONINGS of the wise, THAT THEY
ARE USELESS."
21 So then [a]let no one boast in men.
For [b]all things belong to you,
22 [a]whether Paul or Apollos or Cephas or the world or [b]life or death or
things present or things to come; all
things belong to you,
23 and [a]you belong to Christ; and
[b]Christ belongs to God.

Servants of Christ

4 LET a man regard us in this manner, as [a]servants of Christ, and
[b]stewards of [c]the mysteries of God.
2 In this case, moreover, it is required [1]of stewards that one be found
trustworthy.
3 But to me it is a very small thing
that I should be examined by you, or by
any human [1]court; in fact, I do not even
examine myself.
4 For I [a]am conscious of nothing
against myself, yet I am not by this
[b]acquitted; but the one who examines
me is the Lord.
5 Therefore [a]do not go on [1]passing
judgment before [2]the time, *but wait*
[b]until the Lord comes who will both
[c]bring to light the things hidden in the
darkness and disclose the motives of
men's hearts; and then each man's
[d]praise will come to him from God.
6 Now these things, brethren, I have
figuratively applied to myself and Apollos for your sakes, that in us you might
learn not to exceed [a]what is written, in
order that no one of you might [b]become
[1]arrogant [c]in behalf of one against the
other.
7 For who regards you as superior?
And [a]what do you have that you did not
receive? But if you did receive it, why do
you boast as if you had not received it?
8 You are [a]already filled, you have
already become rich, you have become
kings without us; and *I* would indeed
that you had become kings so that we
also might reign with you.
9 For, I think, God has exhibited us
apostles last of all, as men [a]condemned
to death; because we [b]have become a
spectacle to the world, [1]both to angels
and to men.
10 We are [a]fools for Christ's sake, but
[b]you are prudent in Christ; [c]we are
weak, but you are strong; you are distinguished, but we are without honor.
11 To this present hour we are both
[a]hungry and thirsty, and are poorly
clothed, and are roughly treated, and are
homeless;
12 and we toil, [a]working with our own
hands; when we are [b]reviled, we bless;
when we are [c]persecuted, we endure;
13 when we are slandered, we try to
[1]conciliate; we have [a]become as the
scum of the world, the dregs of all
things, *even* until now.
14 I do not write these things to
[a]shame you, but to admonish you as my
beloved [b]children.
15 For if you were to have countless
[a]tutors in Christ, yet *you would* not *have*
many fathers; for in [b]Christ Jesus I
[c]became your father through the [d]gospel.
16 I exhort you therefore, be [a]imita-
tors of me.
17 For this reason I [a]have sent to you
[b]Timothy, who is my [c]beloved and faithful child in the Lord, and he will remind
you of my ways which are in Christ,
[d]just as I teach everywhere in every
church.
18 Now some have become [1a]arro-
gant, as though I were not [b]coming to
you.
19 But I [a]will come to you soon, [b]if
the Lord wills, and I shall find out, not
the [1]words of those who are [c]arrogant,
but their power.
20 For the kingdom of God does [a]not
consist in [1]words, but in power.
21 What do you desire? [a]Shall I come
to you with a rod or with love and a
spirit of gentleness?

Immorality Rebuked

5 IT is actually reported that there is
immorality among you, and immorality of such a kind as does not exist
even among the Gentiles, that someone
has [a]his father's wife.
2 And [1]you [a]have become [2]arrogant,
and [3]have not [b]mourned instead, in
order that the one who had done this
deed might be [c]removed from your
midst.
3 For I, on my part, though [a]absent
in body but present in spirit, have already judged him who has so committed
this, as though I were present.
4 [a]In the name of our Lord Jesus,
when you are assembled, and [1]I with you
in spirit, [b]with the power of our Lord
Jesus,

15 [a]Job 23:10; Ps. 66:10, 12; Jude 23
16 [1]Or, *sanctuary* [a]Rom. 6:16 [b]Rom. 8:9; 1 Cor. 6:19; 2 Cor. 6:16; Eph. 2:21f.
17 [1]Or, *sanctuary* [2]Lit., *which you are*
18 [a]Is. 5:21 [b]1 Cor. 8:2; Gal. 6:3 [c]1 Cor. 1:20
19 [a]1 Cor. 1:20 [b]Job 5:13
20 [a]Ps. 94:11
21 [a]1 Cor. 4:6 [b]Rom. 8:32
22 [a]1 Cor. 1:12; 3:5, 6 [b]Rom. 8:38
23 [a]1 Cor. 15:23; 2 Cor. 10:7; Gal. 3:29 [b]1 Cor. 11:3; 15:28

1 [a]Luke 1:2 [b]1 Cor. 9:17; Titus 1:7; 1 Pet. 4:10 [c]Rom. 11:25; 16:25
2 [1]Lit., *in*
3 [1]Lit., *day*
4 [a]Acts 23:1; 2 Cor. 1:12 [b]Ps. 143:2; Rom. 2:13
5 [1]Lit., *judging anything* [2]I.e., the appointed time of judgment [a]Matt. 7:1; Rom. 2:1 [b]John 21:22; Rom. 2:16 [c]1 Cor. 3:13 [d]Rom. 2:29; 1 Cor. 3:8; 2 Cor. 10:18
6 [1]Lit., *puffed up* [a]1 Cor. 1:19, 31; 3:19f. [b]1 Cor. 4:18f.; 8:1; 13:4 [c]1 Cor. 1:12; 3:4
7 [a]John 3:27; Rom. 12:3, 6; 1 Pet. 4:10
8 [a]Rev. 3:17f.
9 [1]Or, *and to angels and to men* [a]Rom. 8:36; 1 Cor. 15:31; 2 Cor. 11:23 [b]Heb. 10:33
10 [a]Acts 17:18; 26:24; 1 Cor. 1:18 [b]1 Cor. 1:19f.; 3:18; 2 Cor. 11:19 [c]1 Cor. 2:3; 2 Cor. 13:9
11 [a]Rom. 8:35; 2 Cor. 11:23-27
12 [a]Acts 18:3 [b]1 Pet. 3:9 [c]John 15:20; Rom. 8:35
13 [1]Or, *console* [a]Lam. 3:45
14 [a]1 Cor. 6:5; 15:34 [b]2 Cor. 6:13; 12:14; 1 Thess. 2:11; 1 John 2:1; 3 John 4
15 [a]Gal. 3:24f. [b]1 Cor. 1:30; [c]Num. 11:12; 1 Cor. 3:8; Gal. 4:19; Philem. 10 [d]1 Cor. 9:12, 14, 18, 23; 15:1
16 [a]1 Cor. 11:1; Phil. 3:17; 4:9; 1 Thess. 1:6; 2 Thess. 3:9
17 [a]1 Cor. 16:10 [b]Acts 16:1 [c]1 Cor. 4:14; 1 Tim. 1:2, 18; 2 Tim. 1:2 [d]1 Cor. 7:17; 14:33; 16:1; Titus 1:5
18 [1]Lit., *puffed up* [a]1 Cor. 4:6 [b]1 Cor. 4:21
19 [1]Lit., *word* [a]Acts 19:21; 20:2; 1 Cor. 11:34; 16:5f.; 16:7-9; 2 Cor. 1:15f. [b]Acts 18:21 [c]1 Cor. 4:6

20 [1]Lit., *word* [a]1 Cor. 2:4
21 [a]2 Cor. 1:23; 2:1, 3; 12:20; 13:2, 10

1 [a]Lev. 18:8; Deut. 22:30; 27:20
2 [1]Or, *have you . . . ?* [2]Lit., *puffed up* [3]Or, *have you . . . ?* [a]1 Cor. 4:6 [b]2 Cor. 7:7-10 [c]1 Cor. 5:13
3 [a]Col. 2:5; 1 Thess. 2:17
4 [1]Lit., *my spirit, with the power* [a]2 Thess. 3:6 [b]John 20:23; 2 Cor. 2:10; 13:3, 10

5 *I have decided* to [a]deliver such a one to [b]Satan for the destruction of his flesh, that his spirit may be saved in [c]the day of the Lord [1]Jesus.

6 [a]Your boasting is not good. [b]Do you not know that [c]a little leaven leavens the whole lump *of dough*?

7 Clean out the old leaven, that you may be a new lump, just as you are *in fact* unleavened. For Christ our [a]Passover also has been sacrificed.

8 Let us therefore celebrate the feast, [a]not with old leaven, nor with the leaven of malice and wickedness, but with the unleavened bread of sincerity and truth.

9 I wrote you in my letter [a]not to associate with immoral people;

10 I *did* not at all *mean* with the immoral people of this world, or with the covetous and swindlers, or with [a]idolaters; for then you would have to go out of the world.

11 But [1]actually, I wrote to you not to associate [2]with any so-called [a]brother if he should be an immoral person, or covetous, or [b]an idolater, or a reviler, or a drunkard, or a swindler—not even to eat with such a one.

12 For what have I to do with judging [a]outsiders? [b]Do you not judge those who are within *the church*?

13 But those who are outside, God [1]judges. [a]REMOVE THE WICKED MAN FROM AMONG YOURSELVES.

Lawsuits Discouraged

6 DOES any one of you, when he has a [1]case against his neighbor, dare to go to law before the unrighteous, and [a]not before the [2]saints?

2 Or [a]do you not know that [b]the [1]saints will judge [c]the world? And if the world is judged by you, are you not competent *to* [2]*constitute* the smallest law courts?

3 [a]Do you not know that we shall judge angels? How much more, matters of this life?

4 If then you have law courts dealing with matters of this life, [1]do you appoint them as judges who are of no account in the church?

5 [a]I say *this* to your shame. *Is it* so, *that* there is not among you one wise man who will be able to decide between his [b]brethren,

6 but brother goes to law with brother, and that before [a]unbelievers?

7 Actually, then, it is already a defeat for you, that you have lawsuits with one another. [a]Why not rather be wronged? Why not rather be defrauded?

8 On the contrary, you yourselves wrong and defraud, and that *your* [a]brethren.

9 Or [a]do you not know that the unrighteous shall not [b]inherit the kingdom of God? [c]Do not be deceived; [d]neither fornicators, nor idolaters, nor adulterers, nor [1]effeminate, nor homosexuals,

10 nor thieves, nor *the* covetous, nor drunkards, nor revilers, nor swindlers, shall [a]inherit the kingdom of God.

11 And [a]such were some of you; but you were [b]washed, but you were [c]sanctified, but you were [d]justified in the name of the Lord Jesus Christ, and in the Spirit of our God.

The Body Is the Lord's

12 [a]All things are lawful for me, but not all things are profitable. All things are lawful for me, but I will not be mastered by anything.

13 [a]Food is for the [1]stomach, and the [1]stomach is for food; but God will [b]do away with both [2]of them. Yet the body is not for immorality, but [c]for the Lord; and [d]the Lord is for the body.

14 Now God has not only [a]raised the Lord, but [b]will also raise us up through His power.

15 [a]Do you not know that [b]your bodies are members of Christ? Shall I then take away the members of Christ and make them members of a harlot? [c]May it never be!

16 Or [a]do you not know that the one who joins himself to a harlot is one body *with her*? For He says, "[b]THE TWO WILL BECOME ONE FLESH."

17 But the one who joins himself to the Lord is [a]one spirit *with Him*.

18 [a]Flee immorality. Every *other* sin that a man commits is outside the body, but the [1]immoral man sins against his own body.

19 Or [a]do you not know that [b]your body is a [1]temple of the Holy Spirit who is in you, whom you have from [2]God, and that [c]you are not your own?

20 For [a]you have been bought with a price: therefore glorify God in [b]your body.

Advice on Marriage

7 NOW concerning the things about which you wrote, it is [a]good for a man not to touch a woman.

2 But because of immoralities, let each man have his own wife, and let each woman have her own husband.

3 Let the husband [1]fulfill his duty to his wife, and likewise also the wife to her husband.

4 The wife does not have authority over her own body, but the husband *does*; and likewise also the husband does not have authority over his own body, but the wife *does*.

5 [1]Some ancient mss. do not contain *Jesus* [a]Prov. 23:14; Luke 22:31; 1 Tim. 1:20 [b]Matt. 4:10 [c]1 Cor. 1:8
6 [a]1 Cor. 5:2; James 4:16 [b]Rom. 6:16 [c]Hos. 7:4; Matt. 16:6, 12; Gal. 5:9
7 [a]Mark 14:12; 1 Pet. 1:19
8 [a]Ex. 12:19; 13:7; Deut. 16:3
9 [a]2 Cor. 6:14; Eph. 5:11; 2 Thess. 3:6
10 [a]1 Cor. 10:27
11 [1]Or, *now I write* [2]Lit., *together if any man called a brother should be* [a]Acts 1:15; 2 Thess. 3:6 [b]1 Cor. 10:7, 14, 20f.
12 [a]Mark 4:11 [b]1 Cor. 5:3-5; 6:1-4
13 [1]Or, *will judge* [a]Deut. 13:5; 17:7, 12; 21:21; 22:21; 1 Cor. 5:2
1 [1]Lit., *matter* [2]Or, *holy ones* [a]Matt. 18:17
2 [1]V. 1, note 2 [2]Or, try *the trivial cases?* [a]Rom. 6:16 [b]Dan. 7:18, 22, 27; Matt. 19:28 [c]1 Cor. 1:20
3 [a]Rom. 6:16
4 [1]Or, *appoint them . . . church.*
5 [a]1 Cor. 4:14; 15:34 [b]Acts 1:15; 9:13; 1 Cor. 6:1
6 [a]2 Cor. 6:14f.; 1 Tim. 5:8
7 [a]Matt. 5:39f.
8 [a]1 Thess. 4:6
9 [1]I.e., effeminate by perversion [a]Rom. 6:16 [b]Acts 20:32; 1 Cor. 15:50; Gal. 5:21; Eph. 5:5 [c]Luke 21:8; 1 Cor. 15:33; Gal. 6:7; James 1:16; 1 John 3:7 [d]Rom. 13:13; 1 Cor. 5:11; Gal. 5:19-21; Eph. 5:5; 1 Tim. 1:10; Rev. 21:8; 22:15
10 [a]Acts 20:32; 1 Cor. 15:50; Gal. 5:21; Eph. 5:5
11 [a]1 Cor. 12:2; Eph. 2:2f.; Col. 3:5-7; Titus 3:3-7 [b]Acts 22:16; Eph. 5:26 [c]1 Cor. 1:2, 30 [d]Rom. 8:30
12 [a]1 Cor. 10:23
13 [1]Lit., *belly* [2]Lit., *it and them* [a]Matt. 15:17 [b]Col. 2:22 [c]1 Cor. 6:15, 19 [d]Gal. 5:24; Eph. 5:23
14 [a]Acts 2:24 [b]John 6:39f.; 1 Cor. 15:23
15 [a]1 Cor. 6:3 [b]Rom. 12:5; 1 Cor. 6:13; 12:27; Eph. 5:30 [c]Luke 20:16
16 [a]1 Cor. 6:3 [b]Gen. 2:24; Matt. 19:5; Mark 10:8; Eph. 5:31
17 [a]John 17:21-23; Rom. 8:9-11; 1 Cor. 6:15; Gal. 2:20
18 [1]Or, *one who practices immorality* [a]1 Cor. 6:9; 2 Cor. 12:21; Eph. 5:3; Col. 3:5; Heb. 13:4
19 [1]Or, *sanctuary* [2]Or, *God? And you . . . own* [a]1 Cor. 6:3 [b]John 2:21; 1 Cor. 3:16; 2 Cor. 6:16 [c]Rom. 14:7f.
20 [a]Acts 20:28; 1 Cor. 7:23; 1 Pet. 1:18f.; 2 Pet. 2:1; Rev. 5:9 [b]Rom. 12:1; Phil. 1:20

1 [a]1 Cor. 7:8, 26
3 [1]Lit., *render*

5 [a]Stop depriving one another, except by agreement for a time that you may devote yourselves to prayer, and [1]come together again lest [b]Satan tempt you because of your lack of self-control.

6 But this I say by way of concession, [a]not of command.

7 [1]Yet I wish that all men were [a]even as I myself am. However, [b]each man has his own gift from God, one in this manner, and another in that.

8 But I say to the unmarried and to widows that it is [a]good for them if they remain [b]even as I.

9 But if they do not have self-control, [a]let them marry; for it is better to marry than to [1]burn.

10 But to the married I give instructions, [a]not I, but the Lord, that the wife should not [1]leave her husband

11 (but if she does leave, let her remain unmarried, or else be reconciled to her husband), and that the husband should not [1]send his wife away.

12 But to the rest [a]I say, not the Lord, that if any brother has a wife who is an unbeliever, and she consents to live with him, let him not [1]send her away.

13 And a woman who has an unbelieving husband, and he consents to live with her, let her not [1]send her husband away.

14 For the unbelieving husband is sanctified through his wife, and the unbelieving wife is sanctified through [1]her believing husband; for otherwise your children are unclean, but now they are [a]holy.

15 Yet if the unbelieving one leaves, let him leave; the brother or the sister is not under bondage in such *cases,* but God has called [1]us [2a]to peace.

16 For how do you know, O wife, whether you will [a]save your husband? Or how do you know, O husband, whether you will save your wife?

17 Only, [a]as the Lord has assigned to each one, as God has called each, in this manner let him walk. And [b]thus I direct in [c]all the churches.

18 Was any man called *already* circumcised? Let him not become uncircumcised. Has anyone been called in uncircumcision? [a]Let him not be circumcised.

19 [a]Circumcision is nothing, and uncircumcision is nothing, but *what matters is* [b]the keeping of the commandments of God.

20 [a]Let each man remain in that [1]condition in which he was called.

21 Were you called while a slave? [1]Do not worry about it; but if you are able also to become free, rather [2]do that.

22 For he who was called in the Lord while a slave, is [a]the Lord's freedman; likewise he who was called while free, is [b]Christ's slave.

23 [a]You were bought with a price; do not become slaves of men.

5 [1]Lit., *be*
[a]Ex. 19:15; 1 Sam. 21:5 [b]Matt. 4:10
6 [a]2 Cor. 8:8
7 [1]Some ancient mss. read *For*
[a]1 Cor. 7:8; 9:5
[b]Matt. 19:11f.; Rom. 12:6; 1 Cor. 12:4, 11
8 [a]1 Cor. 7:1, 26
[b]1 Cor. 7:7; 9:5
9 [1]I.e., burn with passion
[a]1 Tim. 5:14
10 [1]Lit., *depart from*
[a]Mal. 2:16; Matt. 5:32; 19:3-9; Mark 10:2-12; Luke 16:18; 1 Cor. 7:6
11 [1]Or, *leave his wife*
12 [1]Or, *leave her*
[a]1 Cor. 7:6; 2 Cor. 11:17
13 [1]Or, *leave her husband*
14 [1]Lit., *the brother*
[a]Ezra 9:2; Mal. 2:15
15 [1]Some ancient mss. read *you* [2]Lit., *in*
[a]Rom. 14:19
16 [a]Rom. 11:14; 1 Pet. 3:1
17 [a]Rom. 12:3
[b]1 Cor. 4:17 [c]1 Cor. 11:16; 14:33; 2 Cor. 8:18; 11:28; Gal. 1:22; 1 Thess. 2:14; 2 Thess. 1:4
18 [a]Acts 15:1ff.
19 [a]Rom. 2:27, 29; Gal. 3:28; 5:6; 6:15; Col. 3:11 [b]Rom. 2:25
20 [1]Lit., *calling*
[a]1 Cor. 7:24
21 [1]Lit., *Let it not be a care to you* [2]Lit., *use*
22 [a]John 8:32, 36; Philem. 16 [b]Eph. 6:6; Col. 3:24; 1 Pet. 2:16
23 [a]1 Cor. 6:20
24 [a]1 Cor. 7:20
25 [1]Lit., *has had mercy shown on him by the Lord to be trustworthy*
[a]1 Cor. 7:6 [b]2 Cor. 4:1; 1 Tim. 1:13, 16
26 [1]Or, *impending* [2]Lit., *so to be*
[a]Luke 21:23; 2 Thess. 2:2 [b]1 Cor. 7:1, 8
28 [1]Lit., *tribulation in the flesh*
29 [a]Rom. 13:11f.; 1 Cor. 7:31
31 [a]1 Cor. 9:18
[b]1 Cor. 7:29; 1 John 2:17
32 [a]1 Tim. 5:5
33 [1]Some mss. read *wife. And there is a difference also between the wife and the virgin. One who is unmarried is concerned...*
35 [1]Lit., *for what is seemly*
36 [1]Lit., *them*
37 [1]Lit., *having no necessity* [2]Lit., *pertaining to*
39 [1]Lit., *has fallen asleep*
[a]Rom. 7:2 [b]2 Cor. 6:14
40 [a]1 Cor. 7:6, 25

24 Brethren, [a]let each man remain with God in that *condition* in which he was called.

25 Now concerning virgins I have [a]no command of the Lord, but I give an opinion as one who [1b]by the mercy of the Lord is trustworthy.

26 I think then that this is good in view of the [1]present [a]distress, that [b]it is good for a man [2]to remain as he is.

27 Are you bound to a wife? Do not seek to be released. Are you released from a wife? Do not seek a wife.

28 But if you should marry, you have not sinned; and if a virgin should marry, she has not sinned. Yet such will have [1]trouble in this life, and I am trying to spare you.

29 But this I say, brethren, [a]the time has been shortened, so that from now on those who have wives should be as though they had none;

30 and those who weep, as though they did not weep; and those who rejoice, as though they did not rejoice; and those who buy, as though they did not possess;

31 and those who use the world, as though they did not [a]make full use of it; for [b]the form of this world is passing away.

32 But I want you to be free from concern. One who is [a]unmarried is concerned about the things of the Lord, how he may please the Lord;

33 but one who is married is concerned about the things of the world, how he may please his [1]wife,

34 and *his interests* are divided. And the woman who is unmarried, and the virgin, is concerned about the things of the Lord, that she may be holy both in body and spirit; but one who is married is concerned about the things of the world, how she may please her husband.

35 And this I say for your own benefit; not to put a restraint upon you, but [1]to promote what is seemly, and *to secure* undistracted devotion to the Lord.

36 But if any man thinks that he is acting unbecomingly toward his virgin *daughter,* if she should be of full age, and if it must be so, let him do what he wishes, he does not sin; let [1]her marry.

37 But he who stands firm in his heart, [1]being under no constraint, but has authority [2]over his own will, and has decided this in his own heart, to keep his own virgin *daughter,* he will do well.

38 So then both he who gives his own virgin *daughter* in marriage does well, and he who does not give her in marriage will do better.

39 [a]A wife is bound as long as her husband lives; but if her husband [1]is dead, she is free to be married to whom she wishes, only [b]in the Lord.

40 But [a]in my opinion she is happier if she remains as she is; and I think that I also have the Spirit of God.

Take Care with Your Liberty

8 NOW concerning [a]things sacrificed
to idols, we know that we all have
[b]knowledge. Knowledge [1c]makes arrogant, but love [d]edifies.
2 [a]If anyone supposes that he knows
anything, he has not yet [b]known as he
ought to know;
3 but if anyone loves God, he [a]is
known by Him.
4 Therefore concerning the eating of
[a]things sacrificed to idols, we know that
[1]there is [b]no such thing as an idol in the
world, and that [c]there is no God but
one.
5 For even if [a]there are so-called
gods whether in heaven or on earth, as
indeed there are many gods and many
lords,
6 yet for us [a]there is *but* one God,
[b]the Father, [c]from whom are all things,
and we *exist* for Him; and [d]one Lord,
Jesus Christ, [e]by whom are all things,
and we *exist* through Him.
7 However not all men [a]have this
knowledge; but [b]some, being accustomed to the idol until now, eat *food* as if
it were sacrificed to an idol; and their
conscience being weak is defiled.
8 But [a]food will not [1]commend us to
God; we are neither [2]the worse if we do
not eat, nor [3]the better if we do eat.
9 But [a]take care lest this [1]liberty of
yours somehow become a stumbling
block to the [b]weak.
10 For if someone sees you, who have
[a]knowledge, dining in an idol's temple,
will not his conscience, if he is weak, be
strengthened to eat [b]things sacrificed to
idols?
11 For through [a]your knowledge he
who is weak [b]is ruined, the brother for
whose sake Christ died.
12 [a]And thus, by sinning against the
brethren and wounding their conscience
when it is weak, you sin [b]against Christ.
13 Therefore, [a]if food causes my
brother to stumble, I will never eat meat
again, that I might not cause my brother
to stumble.

Paul's Use of Liberty

9 AM I not [a]free? Am I not an [b]apos-
tle? Have I not [c]seen Jesus our
Lord? Are you not [d]my work in the
Lord?
2 If to others I am not an apostle, at
least I am to you; for you are the [a]seal of
my [b]apostleship in the Lord.
3 My defense to those who examine
me is this:
4 [1a]Do we not have a right to eat and
drink?
5 [1a]Do we not have a right to take
along a [2]believing wife, even as the rest
of the apostles, and the [b]brothers of the
Lord, and [c]Cephas?
6 Or do only [1a]Barnabas and I not
have a right to refrain from working?
7 Who at any time serves [a]as a soldier at his own expense? Who [b]plants a
vineyard, and does not eat the fruit of it?
Or who tends a flock and does not [1]use
the milk of the flock?
8 I am not speaking these things
[a]according to [1]human judgment, am I?
Or does not the Law also say these
things?
9 For it is written in the Law of
Moses, "[a]YOU SHALL NOT MUZZLE THE
OX WHILE HE IS THRESHING." God is not
concerned about [b]oxen, is He?
10 Or is He speaking altogether for
our sake? Yes, [a]for our sake it was
written, because [b]the plowman ought to
plow in hope, and the thresher *to thresh*
in hope of sharing *the crops.*
11 [a]If we sowed spiritual things in
you, is it too much if we should reap
material things from you?
12 If others share the right over you,
do we not more? Nevertheless, we [a]did
not use this right, but we endure all
things, [b]that we may cause no hindrance
to the [c]gospel of Christ.
13 [a]Do you not know that those who
[b]perform sacred services eat the *food* of
the temple, *and* those who attend regularly to the altar have their share with
the altar?
14 So also [a]the Lord directed those
who proclaim the [b]gospel to [c]get their
living from the gospel.
15 But I have [a]used none of these
things. And I am not writing these things
that it may be done so in my case; for it
would be better for me to die than have
any man make [b]my boast an empty one.
16 For if I preach the gospel, I have
nothing to boast of, for [a]I am under
compulsion; for woe is me if I do not
preach [b]the gospel.
17 For if I do this voluntarily, I have a
[a]reward; but if against my will, I have a
[b]stewardship entrusted to me.
18 What then is my [a]reward? That,
when I preach the gospel, I may offer the
gospel [b]without charge, so as [c]not to
make full use of my right in the gospel.
19 For though I am [a]free from all *men,*
I have made myself [b]a slave to all, that I
might [c]win the more.
20 And [a]to the Jews I became as a
Jew, that I might win Jews; to those who
are under [1]the Law, as under [1]the Law,
though [b]not being myself under [1]the
Law, that I might win those who are
under [1]the Law;

1 [1]Lit., *puffs up* [a]Acts 15:20; 1 Cor. 8:4, 7, 10 [b]Rom. 15:14; 1 Cor. 8:7, 10; 10:15 [c]1 Cor. 4:6 [d]Rom. 14:19
2 [a]1 Cor. 3:18 [b]1 Cor. 13:8-12; 1 Tim. 6:4
3 [a]Ps. 1:6; Jer. 1:5; Amos 3:2; Rom. 8:29; 11:2; Gal. 4:9
4 [1]I.e., has no real existence [a]Acts 15:20; 1 Cor. 8:1, 7, 10 [b]Acts 14:15; 1 Cor. 10:19; Gal. 4:8 [c]Deut. 4:35, 39; 6:4; 1 Cor. 8:6
5 [a]2 Thess. 2:4
6 [a]Deut. 4:35, 39; 6:4; Is. 46:9; Jer. 10:6, 7; 1 Cor. 8:4 [b]Mal. 2:10; Eph. 4:6 [c]Rom. 11:36 [d]John 13:13; 1 Cor. 1:2; Eph. 4:5; 1 Tim. 2:5 [e]John 1:3; Col. 1:16
7 [a]1 Cor. 8:4ff. [b]Rom. 14:14, 22f.
8 [1]Or, *present* [2]Lit., *lacking* [3]Lit., *abounding* [a]Rom. 14:17
9 [1]Lit., *right* [a]Rom. 14:13, 21; 1 Cor. 10:28; Gal. 5:13 [b]Rom. 14:1; 1 Cor. 8:10f.
10 [a]1 Cor. 8:4ff. [b]Acts 15:20; 1 Cor. 8:1, 4, 7
11 [a]1 Cor. 8:4ff. [b]Rom. 14:15, 20
12 [a]Matt. 18:6; Rom. 14:20 [b]Matt. 25:45
13 [a]Rom. 14:21; 1 Cor. 10:32; 2 Cor. 6:3; 11:29

1 [a]1 Cor. 9:19; 10:29 [b]Acts 14:14; Rom. 1:1; 2 Cor. 12:12; 1 Thess. 2:6; 1 Tim. 2:7; 2 Tim. 1:11 [c]Acts 9:3, 17; 18:9; 22:14, 18; 23:11; 1 Cor. 15:8 [d]1 Cor. 3:6; 4:15
2 [a]John 3:33; 2 Cor. 3:2f. [b]Acts 1:25
4 [1]Lit., *It is not that we have no right to eat and drink, is it?* [a]1 Cor. 9:14; 1 Thess. 2:6, 9; 2 Thess. 3:8f.
5 [1]Lit., *It is not that we have no right to take along . . . Cephas, is it?* [2]Lit., *sister, as wife* [a]1 Cor. 7:7f. [b]Matt. 12:46 [c]Matt. 8:14; John 1:42
6 [1]Lit., *I and Barnabas* [a]Acts 4:36
7 [1]Lit., *eat of* [a]2 Cor. 10:4; 1 Tim. 1:18; 2 Tim. 2:3f. [b]Deut. 20:6; Prov. 27:18; 1 Cor. 3:6, 8
8 [1]Lit., *man* [a]Rom. 3:5
9 [a]Deut. 25:4; 1 Tim. 5:18 [b]Deut. 22:1-4; Prov. 12:10
10 [a]Rom. 4:23f. [b]2 Tim. 2:6
11 [a]Rom. 15:27; 1 Cor. 9:14

12 [a]Acts 18:3; 20:33; 1 Cor. 9:15, 18 [b]2 Cor. 6:3; 11:12 [c]1 Cor. 4:15; 9:14, 16, 18, 23; 2 Cor. 2:12
13 [a]Rom. 6:16 [b]Lev. 6:16, 26; 7:6, 31ff.; Num. 5:9f.; 18:8-20, 31; Deut. 18:1
14 [a]Matt. 10:10; Luke 10:7; 1 Tim. 5:18 [b]1 Cor. 4:15; 9:12, 16, 18, 23; 2 Cor. 2:12 [c]Luke 10:8; 1 Cor. 9:4
15 [a]Acts 18:3; 20:33; 1 Cor. 9:12, 18 [b]2 Cor. 11:10
16 [a]Acts 9:15; Rom. 1:14 [b]1 Cor. 4:15; 9:12, 14, 18, 23; 2 Cor. 2:12
17 [a]John 4:36; 1 Cor. 3:8; 9:18 [b]1 Cor. 4:1; Gal. 2:7; Eph. 3:2; Phil. 1:16; Col. 1:25
18 [a]John 4:36; 1 Cor. 3:8; 9:17 [b]Acts 18:3; 2 Cor. 11:7; 12:13 [c]1 Cor. 7:31; 9:12
19 [a]1 Cor. 9:1 [b]2 Cor. 4:5; Gal. 5:13 [c]Matt. 18:15; 1 Pet. 3:1
20 [1]Or, *law* [a]Acts 16:3; 21:23-26; Rom. 11:14 [b]Gal. 2:19

21 to those who are [a]without law, [b]as
without law, though not being without
the law of God but [c]under the law of
Christ, that I might win those who are
without law.
22 To the [a]weak I became weak, that I
might win the weak; I have become [b]all
things to all men, [c]that I may by all
means save some.
23 And I do all things for the sake of
the gospel, that I may become a fellow
partaker of it.
24 [a]Do you not know that those who
run in a race all run, but *only* one
receives [b]the prize? [c]Run in such a way
that you may win.
25 And everyone who [a]competes in
the games exercises self-control in all
things. They then *do it* to receive a
perishable [b]wreath, but we an imperishable.
26 Therefore I [a]run in such a way, as
not without aim; I box in such a way, as
not [b]beating the air;
27 but I [1]buffet [a]my body and make it
my slave, lest possibly, after I have
preached to others, I myself should be
disqualified.

Avoid Israel's Mistakes

10 FOR [a]I do not want you to be
unaware, brethren, that our fathers were all [b]under the cloud, and all
[c]passed through the sea;
2 and all [1]were [a]baptized into Moses
in the cloud and in the sea;
3 and all [a]ate the same spiritual food;
4 and all [a]drank the same spiritual
drink, for they were drinking from a
spiritual rock which followed them; and
the rock was [1]Christ.
5 Nevertheless, with most of them
God was not well-pleased; for [a]they
were laid low in the wilderness.
6 Now these things happened as
[a]examples for us, that we should not
crave evil things, as [b]they also craved.
7 And do not be [a]idolaters, as some
of them were; as it is written, "[b]THE
PEOPLE SAT DOWN TO EAT AND DRINK,
AND STOOD UP TO [c]PLAY."
8 Nor let us act immorally, as [a]some
of them [1]did, and [b]twenty-three thousand fell in one day.
9 Nor let us try the Lord, as [a]some of
them [1]did, and were destroyed by the
serpents.
10 Nor [a]grumble, as some of them
[1]did, and [b]were [2]destroyed by the [c]de-
stroyer.
11 Now these things happened to
them as an [a]example, and [b]they were
written for our instruction, upon whom
[c]the ends of the ages have come.
12 Therefore let him who [a]thinks he
stands take heed lest he fall.
13 No temptation has overtaken you
but such as is common to man; and
[a]God is faithful, who will not allow you
to be [b]tempted beyond what you are
able, but with the temptation will provide the way of escape also, that you
may be able to endure it.
14 Therefore, my [a]beloved, flee from
[b]idolatry.
15 I speak as to wise men; you judge
what I say.
16 Is not the [a]cup of blessing which
we bless a sharing in the blood of Christ?
Is not the [1b]bread which we break a
sharing in the body of Christ?
17 Since there is one [1]bread, we [a]who
are many are one body; for we all
partake of the one [1]bread.
18 Look at [1]the nation [a]Israel; are not
those who [b]eat the sacrifices sharers in
the altar?
19 What do I mean then? That a thing
sacrificed to idols is anything, or [a]that an
idol is anything?
20 *No,* but *I say* that the things which
the Gentiles sacrifice, they [a]sacrifice to
demons, and not to God; and I do not
want you to become sharers in demons.
21 [a]You cannot drink the cup of the
Lord and the cup of demons; you cannot
partake of the table of the Lord and [b]the
table of demons.
22 Or do we [a]provoke the Lord to
jealousy? We are not [b]stronger than He,
are we?
23 [a]All things are lawful, but not all
things are profitable. All things are
lawful, but not all things [b]edify.
24 Let no one [a]seek his own *good,* but
that of his [1]neighbor.
25 [a]Eat anything that is sold in the
meat market, without asking questions
for conscience' sake;
26 [a]FOR THE EARTH IS THE LORD'S,
AND [1]ALL IT CONTAINS.
27 If [a]one of the unbelievers invites
you, and you wish to go, [b]eat anything
that is set before you, without asking
questions for conscience' sake.
28 But [a]if anyone should say to you,
"This is meat sacrificed to idols," do not
eat *it,* for the sake of the one who
informed *you,* and for conscience' sake;
29 I mean not your own conscience,
but the other *man's;* for [a]why is my
freedom judged by another's conscience?
30 If I partake with thankfulness,
[a]why am I slandered concerning that for
which I [b]give thanks?
31 Whether, then, you eat or drink or
[a]whatever you do, do all to the glory of
God.
32 [a]Give no offense either to Jews or
to Greeks or to [b]the church of God;

21 [a]Rom. 2:12, 14 [b]Gal. 2:3; 3:2 [c]1 Cor. 7:22; Gal. 6:2
22 [a]Rom. 14:1; 15:1; 2 Cor. 11:29 [b]1 Cor. 10:33 [c]Rom. 11:14
24 [a]1 Cor. 9:13 [b]Phil. 3:14; Col. 2:18 [c]Gal. 2:2; 2 Tim. 4:7; Heb. 12:1
25 [a]Eph. 6:12; 1 Tim. 6:12; 2 Tim. 2:5; 4:7 [b]2 Tim. 4:8; James 1:12; 1 Pet. 5:4; Rev. 2:10; 3:11
26 [a]Gal. 2:2; 2 Tim. 4:7; Heb. 12:1 [b]1 Cor. 14:9
27 [1]Lit., *bruise* [a]Rom. 8:13

1 [a]Rom. 1:13 [b]Ex. 13:21; Ps. 105:39 [c]Ex. 14:22, 29; Neh. 9:11; Ps. 66:6
2 [1]Some ancient mss. read *received baptism* [a]Rom. 6:3; 1 Cor. 1:13; Gal. 3:27
3 [a]Ex. 16:4, 35; Deut. 8:3; Neh. 9:15, 20; Ps. 78:24f.; John 6:31
4 [1]I.e., the Messiah [a]Ex. 17:6; Num. 20:11; Ps. 78:15
5 [a]Num. 14:29ff., 37; 26:65; Heb. 3:17; Jude 5
6 [a]1 Cor. 10:11 [b]Num. 11:4, 34; Ps. 106:14
7 [a]Ex. 32:4; 1 Cor. 5:11; 10:14 [b]Ex. 32:6 [c]Ex. 32:19
8 [1]Lit., *acted immorally* [a]Num. 25:1ff. [b]Num. 25:9
9 [1]Lit., *made trial* [a]Num. 21:5f.
10 [1]Lit., *grumbled* [2]Lit., *being destroyed* [a]Num. 16:41; 17:5, 10 [b]Num. 16:49 [c]Ex. 12:23; 2 Sam. 24:16; 1 Chr. 21:15; Heb. 11:28
11 [a]1 Cor. 10:6 [b]Rom. 4:23 [c]Rom. 13:11
12 [a]Rom. 11:20; 2 Pet. 3:17
13 [a]1 Cor. 1:9 [b]2 Pet. 2:9
14 [a]Heb. 6:9 [b]1 Cor. 10:7, 19f.; 1 John 5:21
16 [1]Lit., *loaf* [a]Matt. 26:27f.; Mark 14:23f.; Luke 22:20; 1 Cor. 11:25 [b]Matt. 26:26; Luke 22:19; Acts 2:42; 1 Cor. 11:23f.
17 [1]Lit., *loaf* [a]Rom. 12:5; 1 Cor. 12:12f., 27; Eph. 4:4, 16; Col. 3:15
18 [1]Lit., *Israel according to the flesh* [a]Rom. 1:3 [b]Lev. 7:6, 14f.; Deut. 12:17f.
19 [a]1 Cor. 8:4
20 [a]Deut. 32:17; Ps. 106:37; Gal. 4:8; Rev. 9:20
21 [a]2 Cor. 6:16 [b]Is. 65:11
22 [a]Deut. 32:21 [b]Eccl. 6:10; Is. 45:9
23 [a]1 Cor. 6:12 [b]Rom. 14:19

24 [1]Or, *the other* [a]Rom. 15:2; 1 Cor. 10:33; 13:5; 2 Cor. 12:14; Phil. 2:21
25 [a]Acts 10:15; 1 Cor. 8:7
26 [1]Lit., *its fulness* [a]Ps. 24:1; 50:12; 1 Tim. 4:4
27 [a]1 Cor. 5:10 [b]Luke 10:8
28 [a]1 Cor. 8:7, 10-12
29 [a]Rom. 14:16; 1 Cor. 9:19
30 [a]1 Cor. 9:1 [b]Rom. 14:6
31 [a]Col. 3:17; 1 Pet. 4:11
32 [a]Acts 24:16; 1 Cor. 8:13 [b]Acts 20:28; 1 Cor. 1:2; 7:17; 11:22; 15:9; 2 Cor. 1:1; Gal. 1:13; Phil. 3:6; 1 Tim. 3:5, 15

33 just as I also [a]please all men in all
things, [b]not seeking my own profit, but
the *profit* of the many, [c]that they may be
saved.

Christian Order

11 [a]BE imitators of me, just as I also
am of Christ.
2 Now [a]I praise you because you
[b]remember me in everything, and [c]hold
firmly to the traditions, just as I delivered them to you.
3 But I want you to understand that
[1]Christ is the [a]head of every man, and
[b]the man is the head of a woman, and
God is the [c]head of [1]Christ.
4 Every man who has *something* on
his head while praying or [a]prophesying,
disgraces his head.
5 But every [a]woman who has her
head uncovered while praying or prophesying, disgraces her head; for she is one
and the same with her [1]whose head is
[b]shaved.
6 For if a woman does not cover [1]her
head, let her also [2]have her hair cut off;
but if it is disgraceful for a woman to
[2]have her hair cut off or [1]her head
shaved, let her cover [1]her head.
7 For a man ought not to have his
head covered, since he is the [a]image and
glory of God; but the woman is the glory
of man.
8 For [a]man [1]does not originate from
woman, but woman from man;
9 for indeed man was not created for
the woman's sake, but [a]woman for the
man's sake.
10 Therefore the woman ought to
have *a symbol of* authority on her head,
because of the angels.
11 However, in the Lord, neither is
woman [1]independent of man, nor is man
[1]independent of woman.
12 For as the woman [1]originates from
the man, so also the man *has his birth*
through the woman; and [a]all things
[2]originate [b]from God.
13 [a]Judge [1]for yourselves: is it proper
for a woman to pray to God *with head*
uncovered?
14 Does not even nature itself teach
you that if a man has long hair, it is a
dishonor to him,
15 but if a woman has long hair, it is a
glory to her? For her hair is given to her
for a covering.
16 But if one is inclined to be contentious, [a]we have no [1]other practice, nor
have [b]the churches of God.
17 But in giving this instruction, [a]I do
not praise you, because you come together not for the better but for the
worse.
18 For, in the first place, when you
come together [1]as a church, I hear that
[2a]divisions exist among you; and in part,
I believe it.
19 For there [a]must also be factions
among you, [b]in order that those who are
approved may have become [1]evident
among you.
20 Therefore when you meet together,
it is not to eat the Lord's Supper,
21 for in your eating each one takes
his own supper first; and one is hungry
and [a]another is drunk.
22 What! Do you not have houses in
which to eat and drink? Or do you
despise the [a]church of God, and [b]shame
those who have nothing? What shall I
say to you? Shall [c]I praise you? In this I
will not praise you.

The Lord's Supper

23 For [a]I received from the Lord that
which I also delivered to you, that [b]the
Lord Jesus in the night in which He was
betrayed took bread;
24 and when He had given thanks, He
broke it, and said, "This is My body,
which [1]is for you; do this in remembrance of Me."
25 In the same way *He took* [a]the cup
also, after supper, saying, "This cup is
the [b]new covenant in My blood; do this,
as often as you drink *it*, in remembrance
of Me."
26 For as often as you eat this bread
and drink the cup, you proclaim the
Lord's death [a]until He comes.
27 Therefore whoever eats the bread
or drinks the cup of the Lord in an
unworthy manner, shall be [a]guilty of the
body and the blood of the Lord.
28 But let a man [a]examine himself,
and so let him eat of the bread and drink
of the cup.
29 For he who eats and drinks, eats
and drinks judgment to himself, if he
does not judge the body rightly.
30 For this reason many among you
are weak and sick, and a number [a]sleep.
31 But if we judged ourselves rightly,
we should not be judged.
32 But when we are judged, we are
[a]disciplined by the Lord in order that we
may not be condemned along with [b]the
world.
33 So then, my brethren, when you
come together to eat, wait for one another.
34 If anyone is [a]hungry, let him eat [b]at
home, so that you may not come together for judgment. And the remaining
matters I shall [c]arrange [d]when I come.

The Use of Spiritual Gifts

12 NOW concerning [a]spiritual *gifts*,
brethren, [b]I do not want you to
be unaware.
2 [a]You know that when you were
pagans, *you were* [b]led astray to the
[c]dumb idols, however you were led.
3 Therefore I make known to you,
that no one speaking [1a]by the Spirit of
God says, "Jesus is [2b]accursed"; and no
one can say, "Jesus is [c]Lord," except
[1a]by the Holy Spirit.

33 [a]Rom. 15:2; 1 Cor. 9:22; Gal. 1:10 [b]Rom. 15:2; 1 Cor. 13:5; 2 Cor. 12:14; Phil. 2:21 [c]Rom. 11:14; 1 Thess. 2:16
1 [a]1 Cor. 4:16; Phil. 3:17
2 [a]1 Cor. 11:17, 22 [b]1 Cor. 4:17; 15:2; 1 Thess. 1:6; 3:6 [c]2 Thess. 2:15; 3:6
3 [1]I.e., the Messiah [a]Eph. 1:22; 4:15; 5:23; Col. 1:18; 2:19 [b]Gen. 3:16; Eph. 5:23 [c]1 Cor. 3:23
4 [a]Acts 13:1; 1 Thess. 5:20
5 [1]Lit., *who is shaved* [a]Luke 2:36; Acts 21:9; 1 Cor. 14:34 [b]Deut. 21:12
6 [1]Lit., *herself* [2]Lit., *shear herself*
7 [a]Gen. 1:26; 5:1; 9:6; James 3:9
8 [1]Lit., *is not from* [a]Gen. 2:21-23; 1 Tim. 2:13
9 [a]Gen. 2:18
11 [1]Lit., *without*
12 [1]Lit., *is* [2]Lit., *are* [a]2 Cor. 5:18 [b]Rom. 11:36
13 [1]Lit., *in* [a]Luke 12:57
16 [1]Lit., *such* [a]1 Cor. 4:5; 9:1-3, 6 [b]1 Cor. 7:17
17 [a]1 Cor. 11:2, 22
18 [1]Lit., *in church* [2]Lit., *schisms* [a]1 Cor. 1:10; 3:3
19 [1]Or, *manifest* [a]Matt. 18:7; Luke 17:1; 1 Tim. 4:1; 2 Pet. 2:1 [b]Deut. 13:3; 1 John 2:19
21 [a]Jude 12
22 [a]1 Cor. 10:32 [b]James 2:6 [c]1 Cor. 11:2, 17
23 [a]1 Cor. 15:3; Gal. 1:12; Col. 3:24 [b]1 Cor. 11:23-25: *Matt. 26:26-28; Mark 14:22-24; Luke 22:17-20;* 1 Cor. 10:16
24 [1]Some ancient mss. read *is broken*
25 [a]1 Cor. 10:16 [b]Ex. 24:6-8; Luke 22:20; 2 Cor. 3:6
26 [a]John 21:22; 1 Cor. 4:5
27 [a]Heb. 10:29
28 [a]Matt. 26:22; 2 Cor. 13:5; Gal. 6:4
30 [a]Acts 7:60
32 [a]2 Sam. 7:14; Ps. 94:12; Heb. 12:7-10; Rev. 3:19 [b]1 Cor. 1:20
34 [a]1 Cor. 11:21 [b]1 Cor. 11:22 [c]1 Cor. 4:17; 7:17; 16:1 [d]1 Cor. 4:19
1 [a]1 Cor. 12:4; 14:1 [b]Rom. 1:13
2 [a]1 Cor. 6:11; Eph. 2:11f.; 1 Pet. 4:3 [b]1 Thess. 1:9 [c]Ps. 115:5; Is. 46:7; Jer. 10:5; Hab. 2:18f.
3 [1]Or, *in* [2]Gr., *anathema* [a]Matt. 22:43; 1 John 4:2f.; Rev. 1:10 [b]Rom. 9:3 [c]John 13:13; Rom. 10:9

4 Now there are [a]varieties of gifts, but the same Spirit.

5 And there are varieties of ministries, and the same Lord.

6 And there are varieties of effects, but the same [a]God who works all things in all *persons.*

7 But to each one is given the manifestation of the Spirit [a]for the common good.

8 For to one is given the word of [a]wisdom through the Spirit, and to another the word of [b]knowledge according to the same Spirit;

9 to another [a]faith [1]by the same Spirit, and to another [b]gifts of [2]healing [1]by the one Spirit,

10 and to another the [1]effecting of [2a]miracles, and to another [b]prophecy, and to another the [3c]distinguishing of spirits, to another *various* [d]kinds of tongues, and to another the [e]interpretation of tongues.

11 But one and the same Spirit works all these things, [a]distributing to each one individually just as He wills.

12 For even [a]as the body is one and *yet* has many members, and all the members of the body, though they are many, are one body, [b]so also is Christ.

13 For [1a]by one Spirit we were all baptized into one body, whether [b]Jews or Greeks, whether slaves or free, and we were all made to [c]drink of one Spirit.

14 For [a]the body is not one member, but many.

15 If the foot should say, "Because I am not a hand, I am not *a part* of the body," it is not for this reason [1]any the less *a part* of the body.

16 And if the ear should say, "Because I am not an eye, I am not *a part* of the body," it is not for this reason [1]any the less *a part* of the body.

17 If the whole body were an eye, where would the hearing be? If the whole were hearing, where would the sense of smell be?

18 But now God has [a]placed the members, each one of them, in the body, [b]just as He desired.

19 And if they were all one member, where would the body be?

20 But now [a]there are many members, but one body.

21 And the eye cannot say to the hand, "I have no need of you"; or again the head to the feet, "I have no need of you."

22 On the contrary, [1]it is much truer that the members of the body which seem to be weaker are necessary;

23 and those *members* of the body, which we [1]deem less honorable, [2]on these we bestow more abundant honor, and our unseemly *members come to* have more abundant seemliness,

24 whereas our seemly *members* have no need *of it.* But God has *so* composed the body, giving more abundant honor to that *member* which lacked,

25 that there should be no [1]division in the body, but *that* the members should have the same care for one another.

26 And if one member suffers, all the members suffer with it; if *one* member is [1]honored, all the members rejoice with it.

27 Now you are [a]Christ's body, and [b]individually members of it.

28 And God has [1a]appointed in [b]the church, first [c]apostles, second [d]prophets, third [e]teachers, then [2f]miracles, then [g]gifts of healings, helps, [h]administrations, *various* [i]kinds of tongues.

29 All are not apostles, are they? All are not prophets, are they? All are not teachers, are they? All are not *workers of* [1]miracles, are they?

30 All do not have gifts of healings, do they? All do not speak with tongues, do they? All do not [a]interpret, do they?

31 But [a]earnestly desire the greater gifts.

And I show you a still more excellent way.

The Excellence of Love

13 IF I speak with the [a]tongues of men and of [b]angels, but do not have love, I have become a noisy gong or a [c]clanging cymbal.

2 And if I have *the gift of* [a]prophecy, and know all [b]mysteries and all [c]knowledge; and if I have [d]all faith, so as to [e]remove mountains, but do not have love, I am nothing.

3 And if I [a]give all my possessions to feed *the poor,* and if I [b]deliver my body [1]to be burned, but do not have love, it profits me nothing.

4 Love [a]is patient, love is kind, *and* [b]is not jealous; love does not brag *and* is not [c]arrogant,

5 does not act unbecomingly; it [a]does not seek its own, is not provoked, [b]does not take into account a wrong *suffered,*

6 [a]does not rejoice in unrighteousness, but [b]rejoices with the truth;

7 [1a]bears all things, believes all things, hopes all things, endures all things.

8 Love never fails; but if *there are gifts of* [1a]prophecy, they will be done away; if *there are* [b]tongues, they will cease; if *there is* knowledge, it will be done away.

9 For we [a]know in part, and we prophesy in part;

10 but when the perfect comes, the partial will be done away.

11 When I was a child, I used to speak as a child, think as a child, reason as a child; when I became a man, I did away with childish things.

4 [a]Rom. 12:6f.; 1 Cor. 12:11; Eph. 4:4ff., 11; Heb. 2:4
6 [a]1 Cor. 15:28; Eph. 1:23; 4:6
7 [a]1 Cor. 12:12-30; 14:26; Eph. 4:12
8 [a]1 Cor. 2:6; 2 Cor. 1:12 [b]Rom. 15:14; 1 Cor. 2:11, 16; 2 Cor. 2:14; 4:6; 8:7; 11:6
9 [1]Or, *in* [2]Lit., *healings* [a]1 Cor. 13:2; 2 Cor. 4:13 [b]1 Cor. 12:28, 30
10 [1]Lit., *effects* [2]Or, *works of power* [3]Lit., *distinguishings* [a]1 Cor. 12:28f.; Gal. 3:5 [b]1 Cor. 11:4; 13:2, 8 [c]1 Cor. 14:29; 1 John 4:1 [d]Mark 16:17; 1 Cor. 12:28, 30; 13:1; 14:2ff. [e]1 Cor. 12:30; 14:26
11 [a]1 Cor. 12:4
12 [a]Rom. 12:4f.; 1 Cor. 10:17 [b]1 Cor. 12:27
13 [1]Or, *in* [a]Eph. 2:18 [b]Rom. 3:22; Gal. 3:28; Eph. 2:13-18; Col. 3:11 [c]John 7:37-39
14 [a]1 Cor. 12:20
15 [1]Lit., *not* a part
16 [1]Lit., *not* a part
18 [a]1 Cor. 12:28 [b]Rom. 12:6; 1 Cor. 12:11
20 [a]1 Cor. 12:12, 14
22 [1]Lit., *to a much greater degree the members*
23 [1]Or, *think to be* [2]Or, *these we clothe with*
25 [1]Lit., *schism*
26 [1]Lit., *glorified*
27 [a]1 Cor. 1:2; 12:12; Eph. 1:23; 4:12; Col. 1:18, 24; 2:19 [b]Rom. 12:5; Eph. 5:30
28 [1]Lit., *set some in* [2]Or, *works of power* [a]1 Cor. 12:18 [b]1 Cor. 10:32 [c]Eph. 4:11 [d]Acts 13:1; Eph. 2:20; 3:5 [e]Acts 13:1 [f]1 Cor. 12:10, 29 [g]1 Cor. 12:9, 30 [h]Rom. 12:8 [i]1 Cor. 12:10
29 [1]Or, *works of power*
30 [a]1 Cor. 12:10
31 [a]1 Cor. 14:1, 39

1 [a]1 Cor. 12:10 [b]2 Cor. 12:4; Rev. 14:2 [c]Ps. 150:5
2 [a]Matt. 7:22; Acts 13:1; 1 Cor. 11:4; 13:8; 14:1, 39 [b]1 Cor. 14:2; 15:51 [c]Rom. 15:14 [d]1 Cor. 12:9 [e]Matt. 17:20; 21:21; Mark 11:23
3 [1]Some ancient mss. read *that I may boast* [a]Matt. 6:2 [b]Dan. 3:28
4 [a]Prov. 10:12; 17:9; 1 Thess. 5:14; 1 Pet. 4:8 [b]Acts 7:9 [c]1 Cor. 4:6
5 [a]1 Cor. 10:24; Phil. 2:21 [b]2 Cor. 5:19
6 [a]2 Thess. 2:12 [b]2 John 4; 3 John 3f.
7 [1]Or, *covers* [a]1 Cor. 9:12

8 [1]Lit., *prophecies* [a]1 Cor. 13:2 [b]1 Cor. 13:1
9 [a]1 Cor. 8:2; 13:12

12 For now we [a]see in a mirror [1]dimly,
but then [b]face to face; now I know in
part, but then I shall know fully just as I
also [c]have been fully known.
13 But now abide faith, hope, love,
these three; but the [1]greatest of these is
[a]love.

Prophecy a Superior Gift

14 [a]PURSUE love, yet [b]desire earnestly [c]spiritual *gifts,* but especially that you may [d]prophesy.
2 For one who [a]speaks in a tongue
does not speak to men, but to God; for
no one [1]understands, but [2]in *his* spirit he
speaks [b]mysteries.
3 But one who prophesies speaks to
men for [a]edification and [b]exhortation
and consolation.
4 One who [a]speaks in a tongue [b]edi-
fies himself; but one who [c]prophesies
[b]edifies the church.
5 Now I wish that you all [a]spoke in
tongues, but [b]*even* more that you would
prophesy; and greater is one who prophesies than one who [a]speaks in tongues,
unless he interprets, so that the church
may receive [c]edifying.
6 But now, brethren, if I come to you
speaking in tongues, what shall I profit
you, unless I speak to you either by way
of [a]revelation or of [b]knowledge or of
[c]prophecy or of [d]teaching?
7 Yet *even* lifeless things, either flute
or harp, in producing a sound, if they do
not produce a distinction in the tones,
how will it be known what is played on
the flute or on the harp?
8 For if [a]the [1]bugle produces an
indistinct sound, who will prepare himself for battle?
9 So also you, unless you utter by the
tongue speech that is clear, how will it be
known what is spoken? For you will be
[a]speaking into the air.
10 There are, perhaps, a great many
kinds of [1]languages in the world, and no
kind is without meaning.
11 If then I do not know the meaning
of the language, I shall be to the one who
speaks a [1a]barbarian, and the one who
speaks will be a [1]barbarian [2]to me.
12 So also you, since you are zealous
of [1]spiritual *gifts,* seek to abound for the
[a]edification of the church.
13 Therefore let one who speaks in a
tongue pray that he may interpret.
14 For if I pray in a tongue, my spirit
prays, but my mind is unfruitful.
15 [a]What is *the outcome* then? I shall
pray with the spirit and I shall pray with
the mind also; I shall [b]sing with the
spirit and I shall sing with the mind also.
16 Otherwise if you bless [1]in the spirit
only, how will the one who fills the place
of the [2]ungifted say [a]the "Amen" at your
[b]giving of thanks, since he does not
know what you are saying?
17 For you are giving thanks well
enough, but the other man is not [a]edi-
fied.
18 I thank God, I speak in tongues
more than you all;
19 however, in the church I desire to
speak five words with my mind, that I
may instruct others also, rather than ten
thousand words in a tongue.

Instruction for the Church

20 [a]Brethren, [b]do not be children in
your thinking; yet in evil [c]be babes, but
in your thinking be mature.
21 In [a]the Law it is written, "[b]BY MEN
OF STRANGE TONGUES AND BY THE LIPS
OF STRANGERS I WILL SPEAK TO THIS
PEOPLE, AND EVEN SO THEY WILL NOT
LISTEN TO ME," says the Lord.
22 So then tongues are for a sign, not
to those who believe, but to unbelievers;
but [a]prophecy *is for a sign,* not to unbelievers, but to those who believe.
23 If therefore the whole church
should assemble together and all speak
in tongues, and [1]ungifted men or unbelievers enter, will they not say that [a]you
are mad?
24 But if all [a]prophesy, and an unbeliever or an [1]ungifted man enters, he is
[b]convicted by all, he is called to account
by all;
25 [a]the secrets of his heart are disclosed; and so he will [b]fall on his face
and worship God, [c]declaring that God is
certainly among you.
26 [a]What is *the outcome* then, [b]breth-
ren? When you assemble, [c]each one has
a [d]psalm, has a [e]teaching, has a [e]revela-
tion, has a [f]tongue, has an [g]interpreta-
tion. Let [h]all things be done for edification.
27 If anyone speaks in a [a]tongue, *it
should be* by two or at the most three,
and *each* in turn, and let one [b]interpret;
28 but if there is no interpreter, let
him keep silent in the church; and let
him speak to himself and to God.
29 And let two or three [a]prophets
speak, and let the others [b]pass judgment.
30 But if a revelation is made to
another who is seated, let the first keep
silent.
31 For you can all prophesy one by
one, so that all may learn and all may be
exhorted;
32 and the spirits of prophets are
subject to prophets;
33 for God is not *a God* of [a]confusion
but of [1]peace, as in [b]all the churches of
the [c]saints.
34 Let the women [a]keep silent in the
churches; for they are not permitted to
speak, but [b]let them subject themselves,
just as [c]the Law also says.
35 And if they desire to learn anything, let them ask their own husbands
at home; for it is [1]improper for a woman
to speak in church.

12 [1]Lit., *in a riddle* [a]2 Cor. 5:7; Phil. 3:12; James 1:23 [b]Gen. 32:30; Num. 12:8; 1 John 3:2 [c]1 Cor. 8:3
13 [1]Lit., *greater* [a]Gal. 5:6
1 [a]1 Cor. 16:14 [b]1 Cor. 12:31; 14:39 [c]1 Cor. 12:1 [d]1 Cor. 13:2
2 [1]Lit., *hears* [2]Or, *by the Spirit* [a]Mark 16:17; 1 Cor. 12:10, 28, 30; 13:1; 14:18ff. [b]1 Cor. 13:2
3 [a]Rom. 14:19; 1 Cor. 14:5, 12, 17, 26 [b]Acts 4:36
4 [a]Mark 16:17; 1 Cor. 12:10, 28, 30; 13:1; 14:18ff., 26f. [b]Rom. 14:19; 1 Cor. 14:5, 12, 17, 26 [c]1 Cor. 13:2
5 [a]Mark 16:17; 1 Cor. 12:10, 28, 30; 13:1; 14:18ff., 26f. [b]Num. 11:29 [c]Rom. 14:19; 1 Cor. 14:4, 12, 17, 26
6 [a]1 Cor. 14:26; Eph. 1:17 [b]1 Cor. 12:8 [c]1 Cor. 13:2 [d]Acts 2:42; Rom. 6:17; 1 Cor. 14:26
8 [1]Lit., *trumpet* [a]Num. 10:9; Jer. 4:19; Ezek. 33:3-6; Joel 2:1
9 [a]1 Cor. 9:26
10 [1]Lit., *voices*
11 [1]Or, *foreigner* [2]Or, *in my estimation* [a]Acts 28:2
12 [1]Lit., *spirits* [a]Rom. 14:19; 1 Cor. 14:4, 5, 17, 26
15 [a]Acts 21:22; 1 Cor. 14:26 [b]Eph. 5:19; Col. 3:16
16 [1]Or, *with the* [2]I.e., unversed in spiritual gifts [a]Deut. 27:15-26; 1 Chr. 16:36; Neh. 5:13; 8:6; Ps. 106:48; Jer. 11:5; 28:6; Rev. 5:14; 7:12 [b]Matt. 15:36
17 [a]Rom. 14:19; 1 Cor. 14:4, 5, 12, 26
20 [a]Rom. 1:13 [b]Eph. 4:14; Heb. 5:12f. [c]Ps. 131:2; Matt. 18:3; Rom. 16:19; 1 Pet. 2:2
21 [a]John 10:34; 1 Cor. 14:34 [b]Is. 28:11f.
22 [a]1 Cor. 14:1
23 [1]V. 16, note 2 [a]Acts 2:13
24 [1]V. 16, note 2 [a]1 Cor. 14:1 [b]John 16:8
25 [a]John 4:19 [b]Luke 17:16 [c]Is. 45:14; Dan. 2:47; Zech. 8:23; Acts 4:13
26 [a]1 Cor. 14:15 [b]Rom. 1:13 [c]1 Cor. 12:8-10 [d]Eph. 5:19 [e]1 Cor. 14:6 [f]1 Cor. 14:2 [g]1 Cor. 12:10; 14:5, 13, 27f. [h]Rom. 14:19
27 [a]1 Cor. 14:2 [b]1 Cor. 12:10; 14:5, 13, 26ff.
29 [a]1 Cor. 13:2; 14:32, 37 [b]1 Cor. 12:10

33 [1]Or, *peace. As in all . . . saints, let* [a]1 Cor. 14:40 [b]1 Cor. 4:17; 7:17 [c]Acts 9:13
34 [a]1 Cor. 11:5, 13 [b]1 Tim. 2:11f.; 1 Pet. 3:1 [c]1 Cor. 14:21
35 [1]Or, *disgraceful*

36 [1]Was it from you that the word of God *first* went forth? Or has it come to you only?

37 [a]If anyone thinks he is a prophet or [b]spiritual, let him recognize that the things which I write to you [c]are the Lord's commandment.

38 But if anyone [1]does not recognize *this*, he is not recognized.

39 Therefore, my brethren, [a]desire earnestly to [b]prophesy, and do not forbid to speak in tongues.

40 But [a]let all things be done properly and in an orderly manner.

The Fact of Christ's Resurrection

15 NOW [a]I make known to you, brethren, the [b]gospel which I preached to you, which also you received, [c]in which also you stand,

2 by which also you are saved, [a]if you hold fast [1]the word which I preached to you, [b]unless you believed in vain.

3 For [a]I delivered to you [1]as of first importance what I also received, that Christ died [b]for our sins [c]according to the Scriptures,

4 and that He was buried, and that He was [a]raised on the third day [b]according to the Scriptures,

5 and that [a]He appeared to [b]Cephas, then [c]to the twelve.

6 After that He appeared to more than five hundred brethren at one time, most of whom remain until now, but some [a]have fallen asleep;

7 then He appeared to [1a]James, then to [b]all the apostles;

8 and last of all, as it were [1]to one untimely born, [a]He appeared to me also.

9 For I am [a]the least of the apostles, who am not fit to be called an apostle, because I [b]persecuted the church of God.

10 But by [a]the grace of God I am what I am, and His grace toward me did not prove vain; but I [b]labored even more than all of them, yet [c]not I, but the grace of God with me.

11 Whether then *it was* I or they, so we preach and so you believed.

12 Now if Christ is preached, that He has been raised from the dead, how do some among you say that there [a]is no resurrection of the dead?

13 But if there is no resurrection of the dead, not even Christ has been raised;

14 and [a]if Christ has not been raised, then our preaching is vain, your faith also is vain.

15 Moreover we are even found *to be* false witnesses of God, because we witnessed [1]against God that He [a]raised [2]Christ, whom He did not raise, if in fact the dead are not raised.

16 For if the dead are not raised, not even Christ has been raised;

17 and if Christ has not been raised, your faith is worthless; [a]you are still in your sins.

18 Then those also who [a]have fallen asleep in Christ have perished.

19 If we have hoped in Christ in this life only, we are [a]of all men most to be pitied.

The Order of Resurrection

20 But now Christ [a]has been raised from the dead, the [b]first fruits of those who [c]are asleep.

21 For since [a]by a man *came* death, by a man also *came* the resurrection of the dead.

22 For [a]as in Adam all die, so also in [1]Christ all shall be made alive.

23 But each in his own order: Christ [a]the first fruits, after that [b]those who are Christ's at [c]His coming,

24 then *comes* the end, when He delivers up [a]the kingdom to the [b]God and Father, when He has abolished [c]all rule and all authority and power.

25 For He must reign [a]until He has put all His enemies under His feet.

26 The last enemy that will be [a]abolished is death.

27 For [a]HE HAS PUT ALL THINGS IN SUBJECTION UNDER HIS FEET. But when He says, "[b]All things are put in subjection," it is evident that He is excepted who put all things in subjection to Him.

28 And when [a]all things are subjected to Him, then the Son Himself also will be subjected to the One who subjected all things to Him, that [b]God may be all in all.

29 Otherwise, what will those do who are baptized for the dead? If the dead are not raised at all, why then are they baptized for them?

30 Why are we also [a]in danger every hour?

31 I protest, brethren, by the boasting in you, which I have in Christ Jesus our Lord, [a]I die daily.

32 If [1]from human motives I [a]fought with wild beasts at [b]Ephesus, what does it profit me? If the dead are not raised, [c]LET US EAT AND DRINK, FOR TOMORROW WE DIE.

33 [a]Do not be deceived: "Bad company corrupts good morals."

34 [a]Become sober-minded [1]as you ought, and stop sinning; for some have [b]no knowledge of God. [c]I speak *this* to your shame.

35 But [a]someone will say, "How are [b]the dead raised? And with what kind of body do they come?"

36 [a]You fool! That which you [b]sow does not come to life unless it dies;

37 and that which you sow, you do not sow the body which is to be, but a bare grain, perhaps of wheat or of [1]something else.

38 But God gives it a body just as He

36 [1]Lit., *Or was*
37 [a]2 Cor. 10:7 [b]1 Cor. 2:15 [c]1 John 4:6
38 [1]Some ancient mss. read *is ignorant, let him be ignorant*
39 [a]1 Cor. 12:31 [b]1 Cor. 13:2; 14:1
40 [a]1 Cor. 14:33

1 [a]Rom. 2:16; Gal. 1:11 [b]Rom. 2:16; 1 Cor. 3:6; 4:15 [c]Rom. 5:2; 11:20; 2 Cor. 1:24
2 [1]Lit., *to what word I* [a]Rom. 11:22 [b]Gal. 3:4
3 [1]Lit., *among the first* [a]1 Cor. 11:23 [b]John 1:29; Gal. 1:4; Heb. 5:1, 3; 1 Pet. 2:24 [c]Is. 53:5-12; Matt. 26:24; Luke 24:25-27; Acts 8:32f.; 17:2f.; 26:22
4 [a]Matt. 16:21; John 2:20ff.; Acts 2:24 [b]Ps. 16:8ff.; Acts 2:31; 26:22f.
5 [a]Luke 24:34 [b]1 Cor. 1:12 [c]Mark 16:14; Luke 24:36; John 20:19
6 [a]Acts 7:60; 1 Cor. 15:18, 20
7 [1]Or, *Jacob* [a]Acts 12:17 [b]Luke 24:33, 36f.; Acts 1:3f.
8 [1]Lit., *to an untimely birth* [a]Acts 9:3-8; 22:6-11; 26:12-18; 1 Cor. 9:1
9 [a]2 Cor. 12:11; Eph. 3:8; 1 Tim. 1:15 [b]Acts 8:3
10 [a]Rom. 12:3 [b]2 Cor. 11:23; Col. 1:29; 1 Tim. 4:10 [c]1 Cor. 3:6; 2 Cor. 3:5; Phil. 2:13
12 [a]Acts 17:32; 23:8; 2 Tim. 2:18
14 [a]1 Thess. 4:14
15 [1]Or, *concerning* [2]I.e., the Messiah [a]Acts 2:24
17 [a]Rom. 4:25
18 [a]1 Cor. 15:6; 1 Thess. 4:16; Rev. 14:13
19 [a]1 Cor. 4:9; 2 Tim. 3:12
20 [a]Acts 2:24; 1 Pet. 1:3 [b]Acts 26:23; 1 Cor. 15:23; Rev. 1:5 [c]1 Cor. 15:6; 1 Thess. 4:16; Rev. 14:13
21 [a]Rom. 5:12
22 [1]I.e., the Messiah [a]Rom. 5:14-18
23 [a]Acts 26:23; 1 Cor. 15:20; Rev. 1:5 [b]1 Cor. 6:14; 15:52; 1 Thess. 4:16 [c]1 Thess. 2:19
24 [a]Dan. 2:44; 7:14, 27; 2 Pet. 1:11 [b]Eph. 5:20 [c]Rom. 8:38
25 [a]Ps. 110:1; Matt. 22:44
26 [a]2 Tim. 1:10; Rev. 20:14; 21:4
27 [a]Ps. 8:6 [b]Matt. 11:27; 28:18; Eph. 1:22; Heb. 2:8
28 [a]Phil. 3:21 [b]1 Cor. 3:23; 12:6
30 [a]2 Cor. 11:26
31 [a]Rom. 8:36

32 [1]Lit., *according to man* [a]2 Cor. 1:8 [b]Acts 18:19; 1 Cor. 16:8 [c]Is. 22:13; 56:12; Luke 12:19
33 [a]1 Cor. 6:9
34 [1]Lit., *righteously* [a]Rom. 13:11 [b]Matt. 22:29; Acts 26:8 [c]1 Cor. 6:5
35 [a]Rom. 9:19 [b]Ezek. 37:3
36 [a]Luke 11:40 [b]John 12:24
37 [1]Lit., *some of the rest*

wished, and [a]to each of the seeds a body of its own.

39 All flesh is not the same flesh, but there is one *flesh* of men, and another flesh of beasts, and another flesh of birds, and another of fish.

40 There are also heavenly bodies and earthly bodies, but the glory of the heavenly is one, and the *glory* of the earthly is another.

41 There is one glory of the sun, and another glory of the moon, and another glory of the stars; for star differs from star in glory.

42 [a]So also is the resurrection of the dead. It is sown [1][b]a perishable *body*, it is raised [2][c]an imperishable *body*;

43 it is sown in dishonor, it is raised in [a]glory; it is sown in weakness, it is raised in power;

44 it is sown a [a]natural body, it is raised a [b]spiritual body. If there is a natural body, there is also a spiritual *body*.

45 So also it is written, "The first [a]MAN, Adam, BECAME A LIVING SOUL." The [b]last Adam *became* a [c]life-giving spirit.

46 However, the spiritual is not first, but the natural; then the spiritual.

47 The first man is [a]from the earth, [1][b]earthy; the second man is from heaven.

48 As is the earthy, so also are those who are earthy; and as is the heavenly, [a]so also are those who are heavenly.

49 And just as we have [a]borne the image of the earthy, [1]we [b]shall also bear the image of the heavenly.

The Mystery of Resurrection

50 Now I say this, brethren, that [a]flesh and blood cannot [b]inherit the kingdom of God; nor does [1]the perishable inherit [2][c]the imperishable.

51 Behold, I tell you a [a]mystery; we shall not all sleep, but we shall all be [b]changed,

52 in a moment, in the twinkling of an eye, at the last trumpet; for [a]the trumpet will sound, and [b]the dead will be raised [1]imperishable, and [c]we shall be changed.

53 For this [1]perishable must put on [2][a]the imperishable, and this [b]mortal must put on immortality.

54 But when this [1]perishable will have put on [2]the imperishable, and this mortal will have put on immortality, then will come about the saying that is written, "[a]DEATH IS SWALLOWED UP in victory.

55 "[a]O DEATH, WHERE IS YOUR VICTORY? O DEATH, WHERE IS YOUR STING?"

56 The sting of [a]death is sin, and [b]the power of sin is the law;

57 but [a]thanks be to God, who gives us the [b]victory through our Lord Jesus Christ.

58 [a]Therefore, my beloved brethren, be steadfast, immovable, always abounding in [b]the work of the Lord, knowing that your toil is not *in* vain in the Lord.

Instructions and Greetings

16 NOW concerning [a]the collection for [b]the saints, as [c]I directed the churches of [d]Galatia, so do you also.

2 On [a]the first day of every week let each one of you [1]put aside and save, as he may prosper, that [b]no collections be made when I come.

3 And when I arrive, [a]whomever you may approve, I shall send them with letters to carry your gift to Jerusalem;

4 and if it is fitting for me to go also, they will go with me.

5 But I [a]shall come to you after I go through [b]Macedonia, for I [c]am going through Macedonia;

6 and perhaps I shall stay with you, or even spend the winter, that you may [a]send me on my way wherever I may go.

7 For I do not wish to see you now [a]*just* in passing; for I hope to remain with you for some time, [b]if the Lord permits.

8 But I shall remain in [a]Ephesus until [b]Pentecost;

9 for a [a]wide door [1]for effective *service* has opened to me, and [b]there are many adversaries.

10 Now if [a]Timothy comes, see that he is with you without [1]cause to be afraid; for he is doing [b]the Lord's work, as I also am.

11 [a]Let no one therefore despise him. But [b]send him on his way [c]in peace, so that he may come to me; for I expect him with the brethren.

12 But concerning [a]Apollos our brother, I encouraged him greatly to come to you with the brethren; and it was not at all *his* desire to come now, but he will come when he has opportunity.

13 [a]Be on the alert, [b]stand firm in the faith, [c]act like men, [d]be strong.

14 Let all that you do be done [a]in love.

15 Now I urge you, brethren (you know the [a]household of Stephanas, that [1]they were the [b]first fruits of [c]Achaia, and that they have devoted themselves for [d]ministry to [e]the saints),

16 that [a]you also be in subjection to such men and to everyone who helps in the work and labors.

17 And I rejoice over the [1][a]coming of Stephanas and Fortunatus and Achaicus; because they have [2]supplied [b]what was lacking on your part.

18 For they [a]have refreshed my spirit and yours. Therefore [b]acknowledge such men.

38 [a]Gen. 1:11
42 [1]Lit., *in corruption* [2]Lit., *in incorruption* [a]Dan. 12:3; Matt. 13:43 [b]Rom. 8:21; 1 Cor. 15:50; Gal. 6:8 [c]Rom. 2:7
43 [a]Phil. 3:21; Col. 3:4
44 [a]1 Cor. 2:14 [b]1 Cor. 15:50
45 [a]Gen. 2:7 [b]Rom. 5:14 [c]John 5:21; 6:57f.; Rom. 8:2
47 [1]Lit., *made of dust* [a]John 3:31 [b]Gen. 2:7; 3:19
48 [a]Phil. 3:20f.
49 [1]Some ancient mss. read *let us also* [a]Gen. 5:3 [b]Rom. 8:29
50 [1]Lit., *corruption* [2]Lit., *incorruption* [a]Matt. 16:17; John 3:5f. [b]1 Cor. 6:9 [c]Rom. 2:7
51 [a]1 Cor. 13:2 [b]2 Cor. 5:2, 4
52 [1]Lit., *incorruptible* [a]Matt. 24:31 [b]John 5:28 [c]1 Thess. 4:15, 17
53 [1]Lit., *corruptible* [2]Lit., *incorruption* [a]Rom. 2:7 [b]2 Cor. 5:4
54 [1]V. 53, note 1 [2]V. 53, note 2 [a]Is. 25:8
55 [a]Hos. 13:14
56 [a]Rom. 5:12 [b]Rom. 3:20; 4:15; 7:8
57 [a]Rom. 7:25; 2 Cor. 2:14 [b]Rom. 8:37; Heb. 2:14f.; 1 John 5:4; Rev. 21:4
58 [a]2 Pet. 3:14 [b]1 Cor. 16:10

1 [a]Acts 24:17; Rom. 15:25f. [b]Acts 9:13 [c]1 Cor. 4:17 [d]Acts 16:6
2 [1]Lit., *put by himself* [a]Acts 20:7 [b]2 Cor. 9:4f.
3 [a]2 Cor. 3:1; 8:18f.
5 [a]1 Cor. 4:19 [b]Rom. 15:26 [c]Acts 19:21
6 [a]Acts 15:3; 1 Cor. 16:11
7 [a]2 Cor. 1:15f. [b]Acts 18:21
8 [a]Acts 18:19 [b]Acts 2:1
9 [1]Lit., *and* [a]Acts 14:27 [b]Acts 19:9
10 [1]Lit., *fear; for* [a]Acts 16:1; 1 Cor. 4:17; 2 Cor. 1:1 [b]1 Cor. 15:58
11 [a]1 Tim. 4:12; Titus 2:15 [b]Acts 15:3; 1 Cor. 16:6 [c]Acts 15:33
12 [a]Acts 18:24; 1 Cor. 1:12; 3:5f.
13 [a]Matt. 24:42 [b]1 Cor. 15:1; Gal. 5:1; Phil. 1:27; 4:1; 1 Thess. 3:8; 2 Thess. 2:15 [c]1 Sam. 4:9; 2 Sam. 10:12 [d]Ps. 31:24; Eph. 3:16; 6:10; Col. 1:11
14 [a]1 Cor. 14:1

15 [1]Lit., *it was* [a]1 Cor. 1:16 [b]Rom. 16:5 [c]Acts 18:12 [d]Rom. 15:31 [e]1 Cor. 16:1
16 [a]1 Thess. 5:12; Heb. 13:17
17 [1]Or, *presence* [2]Or, *made up for your absence* [a]2 Cor. 7:6f. [b]2 Cor. 11:9; Phil. 2:30
18 [a]2 Cor. 7:13; Philem. 7, 20 [b]Phil. 2:29; 1 Thess. 5:12

19 The churches of [a]Asia greet you. [b]Aquila and Prisca greet you heartily in the Lord, with [c]the church that is in their house.

20 All the brethren greet you. [a]Greet one another with a holy kiss.

21 The greeting is in [a]my own hand—[1]Paul.

19 [a]Acts 16:6 [b]Acts 18:2 [c]Rom. 16:5

20 [a]Rom. 16:16

21 [1]Lit., *Paul's* [a]Rom. 16:22; Gal. 6:11; Col. 4:18; 2 Thess. 3:17; Philem. 19

22 If anyone does not love the Lord, let him be [1a]accursed. [2b]Maranatha.

23 [a]The grace of the Lord Jesus be with you.

24 My love be with you all in Christ Jesus. Amen.

22 [1]Gr., *anathema* [2]I.e., O [our] Lord come! [a]Rom. 9:3 [b]Phil. 4:5; Rev. 22:20

23 [a]Rom. 16:20

THE SECOND EPISTLE OF PAUL TO THE CORINTHIANS

Introduction

1 PAUL, [a]an apostle of [b]Christ Jesus [c]by the will of God, and [d]Timothy *our* brother, to [e]the church of God which is at [f]Corinth with all the [1]saints who are throughout [g]Achaia:

2 [a]Grace to you and peace from God our Father and the Lord Jesus Christ.

3 [a]Blessed *be* the God and Father of our Lord Jesus Christ, the Father of mercies and [b]God of all comfort;

4 who [a]comforts us in all our affliction so that we may be able to comfort those who are in any affliction with the comfort with which we ourselves are comforted by God.

5 For just [a]as the sufferings of Christ are [1]ours in abundance, so also our comfort is abundant through Christ.

6 But if we are afflicted, it is [a]for your comfort and salvation; or if we are comforted, it is for your comfort, which is effective in the patient enduring of the same sufferings which we also suffer;

7 and our hope for you is firmly grounded, knowing that [a]as you are sharers of our sufferings, so also you are *sharers* of our comfort.

8 For [a]we do not want you to be unaware, brethren, of our [b]affliction which came *to us* in [1c]Asia, that we were burdened excessively, beyond our strength, so that we despaired even of life;

9 [1]indeed, we had the sentence of death within ourselves in order that we should not trust in ourselves, but in God who raises the dead;

10 who [a]delivered us from so great a *peril of* death, and will deliver *us,* [1]He [b]on whom we have set our hope. And He will yet deliver us,

11 you also joining in [a]helping us through your prayers, that thanks may be given by [b]many persons on our behalf for the favor bestowed upon us through *the prayers of* many.

Paul's Integrity

12 For our [1]proud confidence is this, the testimony of [a]our conscience, that in holiness and [b]godly sincerity, [c]not in fleshly wisdom but in the grace of God, we have conducted ourselves in the world, and especially toward you.

1 [1]Or, *holy ones* [a]Rom. 1:1; Gal. 1:1; Eph. 1:1; Col. 1:1; 2 Tim. 1:1; Titus 1:1 [b]Gal. 3:26 [c]1 Cor. 1:1 [d]Acts 16:1; 1 Cor. 16:10; 2 Cor. 1:19 [e]1 Cor. 10:32 [f]Acts 18:1 [g]Acts 18:12

2 [a]Rom. 1:7

3 [a]Eph. 1:3; 1 Pet. 1:3 [b]Rom. 15:5

4 [a]Is. 51:12; 66:13; 2 Cor. 7:6, 7, 13

5 [1]Lit., *to us* [a]2 Cor. 4:10; Phil. 3:10; Col. 1:24

6 [a]2 Cor. 4:15; 12:15; Eph. 3:1, 13; 2 Tim. 2:10

7 [a]Rom. 8:17

8 [1]I.e., west coast province of Asia Minor [a]Rom. 1:13 [b]Acts 19:23; 1 Cor. 15:32 [c]Acts 16:6

9 [1]Lit., *but we ourselves*

10 [1]Or, *on whom we have set our hope that He will also* [a]Rom. 15:31 [b]1 Tim. 4:10

11 [a]Rom. 15:30; Phil. 1:19; Philem. 22 [b]2 Cor. 4:15; 9:11f.

12 [1]Lit., *boasting* [a]Acts 23:1; 1 Thess. 2:10; Heb. 13:18 [b]2 Cor. 2:17 [c]1 Cor. 1:17; James 3:15

13 [a]1 Cor. 1:8

14 [a]1 Cor. 1:8

15 [1]Lit., *have a second grace* [2]Some ancient mss. read *joy* [a]1 Cor. 4:19 [b]Rom. 1:11; 15:29

16 [1]Lit., *and* [2]Lit., *through you into* [a]Acts 19:21; 1 Cor. 16:5-7 [b]Acts 19:21; Rom. 15:26 [c]Acts 15:3; 1 Cor. 16:6, 11

17 [a]2 Cor. 10:2f.; 11:18

18 [a]1 Cor. 1:9 [b]2 Cor. 2:17

19 [a]Matt. 4:3; 16:16; 26:63 [b]Acts 15:22; 1 Thess. 1:1; 2 Thess. 1:1; 1 Pet. 5:12 [c]Acts 18:5; 2 Cor. 1:1 [d]Heb. 13:8

20 [a]Rom. 15:8 [b]Heb. 13:8 [c]1 Cor. 14:16; Rev. 3:14

21 [a]1 Cor. 1:8 [b]1 John 2:20, 27

13 For we write nothing else to you than what you read and understand, and I hope you will understand [a]until the end;

14 just as you also partially did understand us, that we are your reason to be proud as you also are ours, in [a]the day of our Lord Jesus.

15 And in this confidence I intended at first to [a]come to you, that you might [1]twice receive a [2b]blessing;

16 [1]that is, to [a]pass [2]your way into [b]Macedonia, and again from Macedonia to come to you, and by you to be [c]helped on my journey to Judea.

17 Therefore, I was not vacillating when I intended to do this, was I? Or that which I purpose, do I purpose [a]according to the flesh, that with me there should be yes, yes and no, no *at the same time*?

18 But as [a]God is faithful, [b]our word to you is not yes and no.

19 For [a]the Son of God, Christ Jesus, who was preached among you by us—by me and [b]Silvanus and [c]Timothy—was not yes and no, but is yes [d]in Him.

20 For [a]as many as may be the promises of God, [b]in Him they are yes; wherefore also by Him is [c]our Amen to the glory of God through us.

21 Now He who [a]establishes us with you in Christ and [b]anointed us is God,

22 who also [a]sealed us and [b]gave *us* the Spirit in our hearts as a [1]pledge.

23 But [a]I call God as witness [1]to my soul, that [b]to spare you I came no more to [c]Corinth.

24 Not that we [a]lord it over your faith, but are workers with you for your joy; for in your faith you are [b]standing firm.

Reaffirm Your Love

2 BUT I determined this [1]for my own sake, that I [a]would not come to you in sorrow again.

22 [1]Or, *down payment* [a]John 3:33 [b]Rom. 8:16; 2 Cor. 5:5; Eph. 1:14

23 [1]Lit., *upon* [a]Rom. 1:9; Gal. 1:20 [b]1 Cor. 4:21; 2 Cor. 2:1, 3 [c]2 Cor. 1:1

24 [a]2 Cor. 4:5; 11:20; 1 Pet. 5:3 [b]Rom. 11:20; 1 Cor. 15:1

1 [1]Or, *as far as I am concerned* [a]1 Cor. 4:21; 2 Cor. 12:21

2 For if I [a]cause you sorrow, who
then makes me glad but the one whom I
made sorrowful?
3 And this is the very thing I [a]wrote
you, lest, [b]when I came, I should have
sorrow from those who ought to make
me rejoice; having [c]confidence in you all,
that my joy would be *the joy* of you all.
4 For out of much affliction and
anguish of heart I [a]wrote to you with
many tears; not that you should be made
sorrowful, but that you might know the
love which I have especially for you.
5 But [a]if any has caused sorrow, he
has caused sorrow not to me, but in
some degree—[1]in order not to say too
much—to all of you.
6 Sufficient for such a one is [a]this
punishment which was *inflicted by* the
majority,
7 so that on the contrary you should
rather [a]forgive and comfort *him*, lest
somehow such a one be overwhelmed by
excessive sorrow.
8 Wherefore I urge you to reaffirm
your love for him.
9 For to this end also [a]I wrote that I
might [1b]put you to the test, whether you
are [c]obedient in all things.
10 But whom you forgive anything, I
forgive also; for indeed what I have
forgiven, if I have forgiven anything, *I
did it* for your sakes [a]in the presence of
Christ,
11 in order that no advantage be
taken of us by [a]Satan; for [b]we are not
ignorant of his schemes.
12 Now when I came to [a]Troas for the
[b]gospel of Christ and when a [c]door was
opened for me in the Lord,
13 I [a]had no rest for my spirit, not
finding [b]Titus my brother; but [c]taking
my leave of them, I went on to [d]Macedo-
nia.
14 [a]But thanks be to God, who always
[b]leads us in His triumph in Christ, and
manifests through us the [c]sweet aroma
of the [d]knowledge of Him in every place.
15 For we are a [a]fragrance of Christ to
God among [b]those who are being saved
and among those who are perishing;
16 [a]to the one an aroma from death to
death, to the other an aroma from life to
life. And who is [b]adequate for these
things?
17 For we are not like many, [1a]ped-
dling the word of God, but [b]as from
sincerity, but as from God, we speak in
Christ [c]in the sight of God.

Ministers of a New Covenant

3 ARE we beginning to [a]commend
ourselves again? Or do we need, as
some, [b]letters of commendation to you
or from you?
2 [a]You are our letter, written in our
hearts, known and read by all men;
3 being manifested that you are a
letter of Christ, [1a]cared for by us, written
not with ink, but with the Spirit of [b]the
living God, not on [c]tablets of stone, but
on [d]tablets of [2e]human hearts.
4 And such [a]confidence we have
through Christ toward God.
5 Not that we are adequate in ourselves to consider anything as *coming*
from ourselves, but [a]our adequacy is
from God,
6 who also made us adequate *as*
[a]servants of a [b]new covenant, not of [c]the
letter, but of the Spirit; for the letter
kills, but [d]the Spirit gives life.
7 But if the [a]ministry of death, [b]in
letters engraved on stones, came [1]with
glory, [c]so that the sons of Israel could
not look intently at the face of Moses
because of the glory of his face, fading *as*
it was,
8 how shall the ministry of the Spirit
fail to be even more with glory?
9 For if [a]the ministry of condemnation has glory, much more does the
[b]ministry of righteousness abound in
glory.
10 For indeed what had glory, in this
case has no glory on account of the glory
that surpasses *it*.
11 For if that which fades away *was*
[1]with glory, much more that which
remains *is* in glory.
12 [a]Having therefore such a hope, [b]we
use great boldness in *our* speech,
13 and *are* not as Moses, [a]*who* used to
put a veil over his face that the sons of
Israel might not look intently at the end
of what was fading away.
14 But their minds were [a]hardened;
for until this very day at the [b]reading of
[c]the old covenant the same veil [1]remains
unlifted, because it is removed in Christ.
15 But to this day whenever Moses is
read, a veil lies over their heart;
16 [a]but whenever a man turns to the
Lord, the veil is taken away.
17 Now the Lord is the Spirit; and
where [a]the Spirit of the Lord is, [b]*there* is
liberty.
18 But we all, with unveiled face
[a]beholding as in a mirror the [b]glory of
the Lord, are being [c]transformed into
the same image from glory to glory, just
as from [d]the Lord, the Spirit.

Paul's Apostolic Ministry

4 THEREFORE, since we have this
[a]ministry, as we [b]received mercy, we
[c]do not lose heart,
2 but we have renounced the [a]things
hidden because of shame, not walking in
craftiness or [b]adulterating the word of
God, but by the manifestation of truth
[c]commending ourselves to every man's
conscience in the sight of God.

2 [a]2 Cor. 7:8
3 [a]2 Cor. 2:9; 7:8, 12 [b]1 Cor. 4:21; 2 Cor. 12:21 [c]Gal. 5:10; 2 Thess. 3:4; Philem. 21
4 [a]2 Cor. 2:9; 7:8, 12
5 [1]Lit., *that I be not burdensome* [a]1 Cor. 5:1f.
6 [a]1 Cor. 5:4f.; 2 Cor. 7:11
7 [a]Gal. 6:1; Eph. 4:32
9 [1]Lit., *know the proof of you* [a]2 Cor. 2:3f. [b]2 Cor. 8:2; Phil. 2:22 [c]2 Cor. 7:15; 10:6
10 [a]1 Cor. 5:4; 2 Cor. 4:6
11 [a]Matt. 4:10 [b]Luke 22:31; 2 Cor. 4:4; 1 Pet. 5:8
12 [a]Acts 16:8 [b]Rom. 1:1; 2 Cor. 4:3, 4; 8:18; 9:13; 10:14; 11:4, 7; 1 Thess. 3:2 [c]Acts 14:27
13 [a]2 Cor. 7:5 [b]2 Cor. 7:6, 13f.; 8:6, 16, 23; 12:18; Gal. 2:1, 3; 2 Tim. 4:10; Titus 1:4 [c]Mark 6:46 [d]Rom. 15:26
14 [a]Rom. 1:8; 6:17; 1 Cor. 15:57; 2 Cor. 8:16; 9:15 [b]Col. 2:15 [c]Song 1:3; Ezek. 20:41; Eph. 5:2; Phil. 4:18 [d]1 Cor. 12:8
15 [a]Song 1:3; Ezek. 20:41; Eph. 5:2; Phil. 4:18 [b]1 Cor. 1:18
16 [a]Luke 2:34; John 9:39; 1 Pet. 2:7f. [b]2 Cor. 3:5f.
17 [1]Or, *corrupting* [a]2 Cor. 4:2; Gal. 1:6-9 [b]1 Cor. 5:8; 2 Cor. 1:12; 1 Thess. 2:4; 1 Pet. 4:11 [c]2 Cor. 12:19

1 [a]2 Cor. 5:12; 10:12, 18; 12:11 [b]Acts 18:27; 1 Cor. 16:3
2 [a]1 Cor. 9:2
3 [1]Lit., *served* [2]Lit., *hearts of flesh* [a]2 Cor. 3:6 [b]Matt. 16:16 [c]Ex. 24:12; 31:18; 32:15f.; 2 Cor. 3:7 [d]Prov. 3:3; 7:3; Jer. 17:1 [e]Jer. 31:33; Ezek. 11:19; 36:26
4 [a]Eph. 3:12
5 [a]1 Cor. 15:10
6 [a]1 Cor. 3:5 [b]Jer. 31:31; Luke 22:20 [c]Rom. 2:29 [d]John 6:63; Rom. 7:6
7 [1]Or, *in glory* [a]Rom. 4:15; 5:20; 7:5f.; 2 Cor. 3:9; Gal. 3:10, 21f. [b]Ex. 24:12; 31:18; 32:15f.; 2 Cor. 3:3 [c]Ex. 34:29-35; 2 Cor. 3:13
9 [a]Deut. 27:26; 2 Cor. 3:7; Heb. 12:18-21 [b]Rom. 1:17; 3:21f.
11 [1]Lit., *through*
12 [a]2 Cor. 7:4 [b]Acts 4:13, 29; 2 Cor. 7:4; Eph. 6:19; 1 Thess. 2:2
13 [a]Ex. 34:33-35; 2 Cor. 3:7
14 [1]Or, *remains, it not being revealed that it is done away in Christ.* [a]Rom. 11:7; 2 Cor. 4:4 [b]Acts 13:15 [c]2 Cor. 3:6
16 [a]Ex. 34:34; Rom. 11:23
17 [a]Is. 61:1f.; Gal. 4:6 [b]John 8:32; Gal. 5:1, 13
18 [a]1 Cor. 13:12 [b]John 17:22, 24; 2 Cor. 4:4, 6 [c]Rom. 8:29 [d]2 Cor. 3:17

1 [a]1 Cor. 3:5 [b]1 Cor. 7:25 [c]Luke 18:1; 2 Cor. 4:16; Gal. 6:9; Eph. 3:13; 2 Thess. 3:13
2 [a]Rom. 6:21; 1 Cor. 4:5 [b]2 Cor. 2:17 [c]2 Cor. 5:11f.

3 And even if our [a]gospel is [b]veiled,
it is veiled [1]to [c]those who are perishing,
4 in whose case [a]the god of [b]this
[1]world has [c]blinded the minds of the
unbelieving, [2]that they might not see the
[d]light of the gospel of the [e]glory of
Christ, who is the [f]image of God.
5 For we [a]do not preach ourselves
but Christ Jesus as Lord, and ourselves
as your bond-servants [1]for Jesus' sake.
6 For God, who said, "[a]Light shall
shine out of darkness," is the One who
has [b]shone in our hearts to give the [c]light
of the knowledge of the glory of God in
the face of Christ.
7 But we have this treasure in
[a]earthen vessels, that the surpassing
greatness of [b]the power may be of God
and not from ourselves;
8 *we are* [a]afflicted in every way, but
not [b]crushed; [c]perplexed, but not despairing;
9 [a]persecuted, but not [b]forsaken;
[c]struck down, but not destroyed;
10 [a]always carrying about in the body
the dying of Jesus, that [b]the life of Jesus
also may be manifested in our body.
11 For we who live are constantly
being delivered over to death for Jesus'
sake, that the life of Jesus also may be
manifested in our mortal flesh.
12 So death works in us, but life in
you.
13 But having the same [a]spirit of faith,
according to what is written, "[b]I BE-
LIEVED, THEREFORE I SPOKE," we also
believe, therefore also we speak;
14 knowing that He who [a]raised the
Lord Jesus [b]will raise us also with Jesus
and will [c]present us with you.
15 For all things *are* [a]for your sakes,
that the grace which is [1b]spreading to
more and more people may cause the
giving of thanks to abound to the glory
of God.
16 Therefore we [a]do not lose heart,
but though our outer man is decaying,
yet our [b]inner man is [c]being renewed
day by day.
17 For momentary, [a]light affliction is
producing for us an eternal weight of
glory far beyond all comparison,
18 while we [a]look not at the things
which are seen, but at the things which
are not seen; for the things which are
seen are temporal, but the things which
are not seen are eternal.

The Temporal and Eternal

5 FOR we know that if [1]the [a]earthly
[b]tent which is our house is torn
down, we have a building from God, a
house [c]not made with hands, eternal in
the heavens.
2 For indeed in this *house* we [a]groan,
longing to be [b]clothed with our dwelling
from heaven;
3 inasmuch as we, having put it on,
shall not be found naked.
4 For indeed while we are in this
tent, we [a]groan, being burdened, because
we do not want to be unclothed, but to
be [b]clothed, in order that what is [c]mortal
may be swallowed up by life.
5 Now He who prepared us for this
very purpose is God, who [a]gave to us the
Spirit as a [1]pledge.
6 Therefore, being always of good
courage, and knowing that [a]while we are
at home in the body we are absent from
the Lord—
7 for [a]we walk by faith, not by
[1]sight—
8 we are of good courage, I say, and
[a]prefer rather to be absent from the
body and [b]to be at home with the Lord.
9 Therefore also we have as our
ambition, whether at home or absent, to
be [a]pleasing to Him.
10 For we must all appear before [a]the
judgment seat of Christ, that each one
may be recompensed for [1]his deeds in
the body, according to what he has done,
whether good or bad.
11 Therefore knowing the [a]fear of the
Lord, we persuade men, but we are
made manifest to God; and I hope that
we are [b]made manifest also in your
consciences.
12 We are not [a]again commending
ourselves to you but *are* giving you an
[b]occasion to be proud of us, that you
may have *an answer* for those who take
pride in appearance, and not in heart.
13 For if we [1]are [a]beside ourselves, it
is for God; if we are of sound mind, it is
for you.
14 For the love of Christ [a]controls us,
having concluded this, that [b]one died for
all, therefore all died;
15 and He died for all, that they who
live should no longer [a]live for themselves, but for Him who died and rose
again on their behalf.
16 Therefore from now on we recognize no man [1a]according to the flesh;
even though we have known Christ
[1]according to the flesh, yet now we know
Him thus no longer.
17 Therefore if any man is [a]in Christ,
[1]*he is* [b]a new creature; [c]the old things
passed away; behold, new things have
come.
18 Now [a]all *these* things are from
God, [b]who reconciled us to Himself
through Christ, and gave us the [c]minis-
try of reconciliation,
19 namely, that [a]God was in Christ
reconciling the world to Himself, [b]not
counting their trespasses against them,
and [1]He has [2]committed to us the word
of reconciliation.

3 [1]Lit., *in* [a]2 Cor. 2:12 [b]1 Cor. 2:6ff.; 2 Cor. 3:14 [c]1 Cor. 1:18; 2 Cor. 2:15
4 [1]Lit., *age* [2]Or, *that the light . . . image of God, should not dawn* upon them [a]John 12:31 [b]Matt. 13:22 [c]2 Cor. 3:14 [d]Acts 26:18; 2 Cor. 4:6 [e]2 Cor. 3:18; 4:6 [f]John 1:18; Phil. 2:6; Col. 1:15; Heb. 1:3
5 [1]Or, *through Jesus* [a]1 Cor. 4:15f.; 1 Thess. 2:6f.
6 [a]Gen. 1:3 [b]2 Pet. 1:19 [c]Acts 26:18; 2 Cor. 4:4
7 [a]Job 4:19; 10:9; 33:6; Lam. 4:2; 2 Cor. 5:1; 2 Tim. 2:20 [b]Judg. 7:2; 1 Cor. 2:5
8 [a]2 Cor. 1:8; 7:5 [b]2 Cor. 6:12 [c]Gal. 4:20
9 [a]John 15:20; Rom. 8:35f. [b]Ps. 129:2; Heb. 13:5 [c]Ps. 37:24; Prov. 24:16; Mic. 7:8
10 [a]Rom. 6:5; 8:36; Gal. 6:17 [b]Rom. 6:8
13 [a]1 Cor. 12:9 [b]Ps. 116:10
14 [a]Acts 2:24 [b]1 Thess. 4:14 [c]Luke 21:36; Eph. 5:27; Col. 1:22; Jude 24
15 [1]Lit., *being multiplied through the many* [a]Rom. 8:28; 2 Cor. 1:6 [b]1 Cor. 9:19; 2 Cor. 1:11
16 [a]2 Cor. 4:1 [b]Rom. 7:22 [c]Is. 40:29, 31; Col. 3:10
17 [a]Rom. 8:18
18 [a]Rom. 8:24; 2 Cor. 5:7; Heb. 11:1, 13

1 [1]Lit., *our earthly house of the tent* [a]Job 4:19; 1 Cor. 15:47; 2 Cor. 4:7 [b]2 Pet. 1:13f. [c]Mark 14:58; Acts 7:48; Heb. 9:11, 24
2 [a]Rom. 8:23; 2 Cor. 5:4 [b]1 Cor. 15:53f.; 2 Cor. 5:4
4 [a]2 Cor. 5:2 [b]1 Cor. 15:53f.; 2 Cor. 5:2 [c]1 Cor. 15:54
5 [1]Or, *down payment* [a]Rom. 8:23; 2 Cor. 1:22
6 [a]Heb. 11:13f.
7 [1]Or, *appearance* [a]1 Cor. 13:12; 2 Cor. 4:18
8 [a]Phil. 1:23 [b]John 12:26; Phil. 1:23
9 [a]Rom. 14:18; Col. 1:10; 1 Thess. 4:1
10 [1]Lit., *the things through the body* [a]Matt. 16:27; Acts 10:42; Rom. 2:16; 14:10, 12; Eph. 6:8
11 [a]Heb. 10:31; 12:29; Jude 23 [b]2 Cor. 4:2
12 [a]2 Cor. 3:1 [b]2 Cor. 1:14; Phil. 1:26
13 [1]Lit., *were* [a]Mark 3:21; 2 Cor. 11:1, 16ff.; 12:11
14 [a]Acts 18:5 [b]Rom. 5:15; 6:6f.; Gal. 2:20; Col. 3:3
15 [a]Rom. 14:7-9
16 [1]I.e., by what he is in the flesh [a]John 8:15; 2 Cor. 11:18; Phil. 3:4
17 [1]Or, there is *a new creation* [a]Rom. 16:7 [b]John 3:3; Rom. 6:4; Gal. 6:15 [c]Is. 43:18f.; 65:17; Eph. 4:24; Rev. 21:4f.
18 [a]1 Cor. 11:12 [b]Rom. 5:10; Col. 1:20 [c]1 Cor. 3:5
19 [1]Lit., *having* [2]Lit., *placed in us* [a]Col. 2:9 [b]Rom. 4:8; 1 Cor. 13:5

20 Therefore, we are [a]ambassadors for Christ, [b]as though God were entreating through us; we beg you on behalf of Christ, be [c]reconciled to God.
21 He made Him who [a]knew no sin *to be* [b]sin on our behalf, that we might become the [c]righteousness of God in Him.

Their Ministry Commended

6 AND [a]working together *with Him,* [b]we also urge you not to receive [c]the grace of God in vain—
2 for He says,
"[a]AT THE ACCEPTABLE TIME I LISTENED TO YOU,
AND ON THE DAY OF SALVATION I HELPED YOU";
behold, now is "THE ACCEPTABLE TIME," behold, now is "THE DAY OF SALVATION"—
3 [a]giving no cause for offense in anything, in order that the ministry be not discredited,
4 but in everything [a]commending ourselves as [1b]servants of God, [c]in much endurance, in afflictions, in hardships, in distresses,
5 in [a]beatings, in imprisonments, in [b]tumults, in labors, in sleeplessness, in [c]hunger,
6 in purity, in [a]knowledge, in [b]patience, in kindness, in the [c]Holy Spirit, in [d]genuine love,
7 in [a]the word of truth, in [b]the power of God; by [c]the weapons of righteousness for the right hand and the left,
8 by glory and [a]dishonor, by [b]evil report and good report; *regarded* as [c]deceivers and yet [d]true;
9 as unknown yet well-known, as [a]dying yet behold, [b]we live; as [1]punished yet not put to death,
10 as [a]sorrowful yet always [a]rejoicing, as [b]poor yet making many rich, as [c]having nothing yet possessing [d]all things.
11 [a]Our mouth [1]has spoken freely to you, O Corinthians, our [b]heart is opened wide.
12 You are not restrained [1]by us, but [a]you are restrained in your own [2]affections.
13 Now in a like [a]exchange—I speak as to [b]children—open wide *to us* also.
14 [a]Do not be [1]bound together with [b]unbelievers; for what [c]partnership have righteousness and lawlessness, or what fellowship has light with darkness?
15 Or what [a]harmony has Christ with [1]Belial, or [2]what has a [b]believer in common with an [c]unbeliever?
16 Or [a]what agreement has the temple of God with idols? For we are [b]the temple of [c]the living God; just as God said,
"[d]I WILL [e]DWELL IN THEM AND [f]WALK AMONG THEM;
AND I WILL BE THEIR GOD, AND THEY SHALL BE MY PEOPLE.

20 [a]Mal. 2:7; Eph. 6:20 [b]2 Cor. 6:1 [c]Rom. 5:10; Col. 1:20
21 [a]Acts 3:14; Heb. 4:15; 7:26; 1 Pet. 2:22; 1 John 3:5 [b]Rom. 3:25; 4:25; 8:3; Gal. 3:13 [c]Rom. 1:17; 3:21f.; 1 Cor. 1:30

1 [a]1 Cor. 3:9 [b]2 Cor. 5:20 [c]Acts 11:23
2 [a]Is. 49:8
3 [a]1 Cor. 8:9, 13; 9:12
4 [1]Or, *ministers* [a]Rom. 3:5 [b]1 Cor. 3:5; 2 Tim. 2:24f. [c]Acts 9:16; 2 Cor. 4:8-11; 6:4ff.; 11:23-27; 12:10
5 [a]Acts 16:23 [b]Acts 19:23ff. [c]1 Cor. 4:11
6 [a]1 Cor. 12:8; 2 Cor. 11:6 [b]2 Cor. 1:23; 2:10; 13:10 [c]1 Cor. 2:4; 1 Thess. 1:5 [d]Rom. 12:9
7 [a]2 Cor. 2:17; 4:2 [b]1 Cor. 2:5 [c]Rom. 13:12; 2 Cor. 10:4; Eph. 6:11ff.
8 [a]1 Cor. 4:10 [b]Rom. 3:8; 1 Cor. 4:13; 2 Cor. 12:16 [c]Matt. 27:63 [d]2 Cor. 1:18; 4:2; 1 Thess. 2:3f.
9 [1]Or, *disciplined* [a]Rom. 8:36 [b]2 Cor. 1:8, 10; 4:11
10 [a]John 16:22; 2 Cor. 7:4; Phil. 2:17; 4:4; Col. 1:24; 1 Thess. 1:6 [b]1 Cor. 1:5; 2 Cor. 8:9 [c]Acts 3:6 [d]Rom. 8:32; 1 Cor. 3:21
11 [1]Lit., *is open to you* [a]Ezek. 33:22; Eph. 6:19 [b]Is. 60:5; 2 Cor. 7:3
12 [1]Or, *in us* [2]Lit., *inward parts* [a]2 Cor. 7:2
13 [a]Gal. 4:12 [b]1 Cor. 4:14
14 [1]Lit., *unequally yoked* [a]Deut. 22:10; 1 Cor. 5:9f. [b]1 Cor. 6:6 [c]Eph. 5:7, 11; 1 John 1:6
15 [1]Gr., *Beliar* [2]Lit., *what part has a believer with an unbeliever* [a]1 Cor. 10:21 [b]Acts 5:14; 1 Pet. 1:21 [c]1 Cor. 6:6
16 [a]1 Cor. 10:21 [b]1 Cor. 3:16; 6:19 [c]Matt. 16:16 [d]Ex. 29:45; Lev. 26:12; Jer. 31:1; Ezek. 37:27 [e]Ex. 25:8; John 14:23 [f]Rev. 2:1
17 [a]Is. 52:11 [b]Rev. 18:4
18 [a]2 Sam. 7:14; 1 Chr. 17:13; Is. 43:6; Hos. 1:10 [b]Rom. 8:14

1 [a]Heb. 6:9 [b]1 Pet. 1:15f.
2 [a]2 Cor. 6:12f.; 12:15
3 [a]2 Cor. 6:11f. [b]Phil. 1:7

17 "[a]Therefore, [b]COME OUT FROM THEIR MIDST AND BE SEPARATE,"
says the Lord.
"AND DO NOT TOUCH WHAT IS UNCLEAN;
And I will welcome you.
18 "[a]And I will be a father to you,
And you shall be [b]sons and daughters to Me,"
Says the Lord Almighty.

Paul Reveals His Heart

7 THEREFORE, having these promises, [a]beloved, [b]let us cleanse ourselves from all defilement of flesh and spirit, perfecting holiness in the fear of God.
2 [a]Make room for us *in your hearts;* we wronged no one, we corrupted no one, we took advantage of no one.
3 I do not speak to condemn you; for I have said [a]before that you are [b]in our hearts to die together and to live together.
4 Great is my [a]confidence [1]in you, great is my [b]boasting on your behalf; I am filled with [c]comfort. I am overflowing with [d]joy in all our affliction.
5 For even when we came into [a]Macedonia our flesh had no rest, but we were [b]afflicted on every side: [c]conflicts without, fears within.
6 But [a]God, who comforts the [1]depressed, [b]comforted us by the coming of [c]Titus;
7 and not only by his coming, but also by the comfort with which he was comforted in you, as he reported to us your longing, your mourning, your zeal for me; so that I rejoiced even more.
8 For though I [a]caused you sorrow by my letter, I do not regret it; though I did regret it—*for* I see that that letter caused you sorrow, though only for a while—
9 I now rejoice, not that you were made sorrowful, but that you were made sorrowful to *the point of* repentance; for you were made sorrowful according to *the will of* God, in order that you might not suffer loss in anything through us.
10 For the sorrow that is according to *the will of* God produces a [a]repentance [1]without regret, *leading* to salvation; but the sorrow of the world produces death.
11 For behold what earnestness this very thing, this [1]godly sorrow, has produced in you: what vindication of yourselves, what indignation, what fear, what [a]longing, what zeal, what [b]avenging of wrong! In everything you [c]demonstrated yourselves to be innocent in the matter.

4 [1]Lit., *to* [a]2 Cor. 3:12 [b]2 Cor. 7:14; 8:24; 9:2f.; 10:8; Phil. 1:26; 2 Thess. 1:4 [c]2 Cor. 1:4 [d]2 Cor. 6:10
5 [a]Rom. 15:26; 2 Cor. 2:13 [b]2 Cor. 4:8 [c]Deut. 32:25
6 [1]Or, *humble* [a]2 Cor. 1:3f. [b]2 Cor. 7:13 [c]2 Cor. 2:13; 7:13f.
8 [a]2 Cor. 2:2
10 [1]Or, *leading to a salvation without regret* [a]Acts 11:18
11 [1]Lit., *sorrow according to God* [a]2 Cor. 7:7 [b]2 Cor. 2:6 [c]Rom. 3:5

12 So although [a]I wrote to you *it was* not for the sake of [b]the offender, nor for the sake of the one offended, but that your earnestness on our behalf might be made known to you in the sight of God.

13 For this reason we have been [a]comforted.

And besides our comfort, we rejoiced even much more for the joy of [b]Titus, because his [c]spirit has been refreshed by you all.

14 For if in anything I have [a]boasted to him about you, I was not put to shame; but as we spoke all things to you in truth, so also our boasting before [b]Titus proved to be *the* truth.

15 And his [1]affection abounds all the more toward you, as he remembers the [a]obedience of you all, how you received him with [b]fear and trembling.

16 I rejoice that in everything [a]I have confidence in you.

Great Generosity

8 NOW, brethren, we *wish to* make known to you the grace of God which has been [a]given in the churches of [b]Macedonia,

2 that in a great ordeal of affliction their abundance of joy and their deep poverty overflowed in the [a]wealth of their liberality.

3 For I testify that [a]according to their ability, and beyond their ability *they gave* of their own accord,

4 begging us with much entreaty for the [a]favor of participation in the [1b]support of the [2]saints,

5 and *this,* not as we had [1]expected, but they first [a]gave themselves to the Lord and to us by [b]the will of God.

6 Consequently we [a]urged [b]Titus that as he had previously [c]made a beginning, so he would also complete in you [d]this gracious work as well.

7 But just as you [a]abound [b]in everything, in faith and utterance and knowledge and in all earnestness and in the [1]love we inspired in you, *see* that you [a]abound in this gracious work also.

8 I [a]am not speaking *this* as a command, but as proving through the earnestness of others the sincerity of your love also.

9 For you know [a]the grace of our Lord Jesus Christ, that [b]though He was rich, yet for your sake He became poor, that you through His poverty might become rich.

10 And I [a]give *my* opinion in this matter, for this is to your advantage, who were the first to begin [b]a year ago not only to do *this,* but also to desire *to do it.*

11 But now finish [1]doing it also; that just as *there was* the [a]readiness to desire it, so *there may be* also the completion of it by your ability.

12 For if the readiness is present, it is acceptable [a]according to what *a man* has, not according to what he does not have.

13 For *this* is not for the ease of others *and* for your affliction, but by way of equality—

14 at this present time your abundance *being a supply* for [a]their want, that their abundance also may become *a supply* for [a]your want, that there may be equality;

15 as it is written, "[a]HE WHO *gathered* MUCH DID NOT HAVE TOO MUCH, AND HE WHO *gathered* LITTLE HAD NO LACK."

16 But [a]thanks be to God, who [b]puts the same earnestness on your behalf in the heart of [c]Titus.

17 For he not only accepted our [a]appeal, but being himself very earnest, he has gone to you of his own accord.

18 And we have sent along with him [a]the brother whose fame in *the things of* the [b]gospel *has spread* through [c]all the churches;

19 [a]and not only *this,* but he has also been [b]appointed by the churches to travel with us in [c]this gracious work, which is being administered by us for the glory of the Lord Himself, and *to show* our [d]readiness,

20 [1]taking precaution that no one should discredit us in our administration of this generous gift;

21 for we [a]have regard for what is honorable, not only in [b]the sight of the Lord, but also in the sight of men.

22 And we have sent with them our brother, whom we have often tested and found diligent in many things, but now even more diligent, because of *his* great confidence in you.

23 As for [a]Titus, *he is* my [b]partner and fellow worker [1]among you; as for our [c]brethren, *they are* [2d]messengers of the churches, [e]a glory to Christ.

24 Therefore [1]openly before the churches [2]show them the proof of your love and of our [a]reason for boasting about you.

God Gives Most

9 FOR [a]it is superfluous for me to write to you about this [b]ministry to the [1]saints;

2 for I know your readiness, of which I [a]boast about you to the [b]Macedonians, *namely,* that [c]Achaia has been prepared since [d]last year, and your zeal has stirred up most of them.

3 But I have sent the brethren, that our [a]boasting about you may not be made empty in this case, that, [b]as I was saying, you may be prepared;

4 lest if any [a]Macedonians come with me and find you unprepared, we (not to speak of you) should be put to shame by this confidence.

12 [a]2 Cor. 2:3, 9; 7:8 [b]1 Cor. 5:1f.
13 [a]2 Cor. 7:6 [b]2 Cor. 2:13; 7:6, 14 [c]1 Cor. 16:18
14 [a]2 Cor. 7:4; 8:24; 9:2f.; 10:8; Phil. 1:26; 2 Thess. 1:4 [b]2 Cor. 2:13; 7:6, 13
15 [1]Lit., *inward parts* [a]2 Cor. 2:9 [b]1 Cor. 2:3; Phil. 2:12
16 [a]2 Cor. 2:3
1 [a]2 Cor. 8:5 [b]Acts 16:9
2 [a]Rom. 2:4
3 [a]1 Cor. 16:2; 2 Cor. 8:11
4 [1]Lit., *service to the saints* [2]Or, *holy ones* [a]Acts 24:17; Rom. 15:25f. [b]Rom. 15:31; 2 Cor. 8:19f.; 9:1, 12f.
5 [1]Lit., *hoped* [a]2 Cor. 8:1 [b]1 Cor. 1:1
6 [a]2 Cor. 8:17; 12:18 [b]2 Cor. 2:13; 8:16, 23 [c]2 Cor. 8:10 [d]Acts 24:17; Rom. 15:25f.
7 [1]Lit., *love from us in you;* some ancient mss. read *your love for us* [a]2 Cor. 9:8 [b]Rom. 15:14; 1 Cor. 1:5; 12:8
8 [a]1 Cor. 7:6
9 [a]2 Cor. 13:14 [b]Matt. 20:28; 2 Cor. 6:10; Phil. 2:6f.
10 [a]1 Cor. 7:25, 40 [b]1 Cor. 16:2f.; 2 Cor. 9:2
11 [1]Lit., *the doing* [a]2 Cor. 8:12, 19; 9:2
12 [a]Mark 12:43f.; Luke 21:3, 4; 2 Cor. 9:7
14 [a]Acts 4:34; 2 Cor. 9:12
15 [a]Ex. 16:18
16 [a]2 Cor. 2:14 [b]Rev. 17:17 [c]2 Cor. 2:13; 8:6, 23
17 [a]2 Cor. 8:6; 12:18
18 [a]1 Cor. 16:3; 2 Cor. 12:18 [b]2 Cor. 2:12 [c]1 Cor. 4:17; 7:17
19 [a]Rom. 5:3 [b]Acts 14:23; 1 Cor. 16:3f. [c]2 Cor. 8:4, 6 [d]2 Cor. 8:11, 12; 9:2
20 [1]Lit., *avoiding this*
21 [a]Rom. 12:17 [b]Prov. 3:4; Rom. 14:18
23 [1]Lit., *for you* [2]Lit., *apostles* [a]2 Cor. 8:6 [b]Philem. 17 [c]2 Cor. 8:18, 22 [d]John 13:16; Phil. 2:25 [e]1 Cor. 11:7
24 [1]Lit., *in the face of the churches* [2]Or, *show the proof . . . for boasting to them about you* [a]2 Cor. 7:4
1 [1]Or, *holy ones* [a]1 Thess. 4:9 [b]2 Cor. 8:4
2 [a]2 Cor. 7:4 [b]Rom. 15:26 [c]Acts 18:12 [d]2 Cor. 8:10
3 [a]2 Cor. 7:4 [b]1 Cor. 16:2
4 [a]Rom. 15:26

5 So I thought it necessary to urge the [a]brethren that they would go on ahead to you and arrange beforehand your previously promised [1b]bountiful gift, that the same might be ready as a [1c]bountiful gift, and not [2d]affected by covetousness.

6 Now this *I say,* [a]he who sows sparingly shall also reap sparingly; and he who sows [1]bountifully shall also reap [1]bountifully.

7 Let each one *do* just as he has purposed in his heart; not [a]grudgingly or under compulsion; for [b]God loves a cheerful giver.

8 And [a]God is able to make all grace abound to you, that always having all sufficiency in everything, you may have an abundance for every good deed;

9 as it is written,

"[a]HE SCATTERED ABROAD, HE GAVE TO THE POOR,
HIS RIGHTEOUSNESS ABIDES FOREVER."

10 Now He who supplies [a]seed to the sower and bread for food, will supply and multiply your seed for sowing and [b]increase the harvest of your righteousness;

11 you will be [a]enriched in everything for all liberality, which through us is producing [b]thanksgiving to God.

12 For the ministry of this service is not only fully supplying [a]the needs of the [1]saints, but is also overflowing [b]through many thanksgivings to God.

13 Because of the proof given by this [a]ministry they will [b]glorify God for *your* obedience to your [c]confession of the [d]gospel of Christ, and for the liberality of your [1]contribution to them and to all,

14 while they also, by prayer on your behalf, yearn for you because of the surpassing grace of God in you.

15 [a]Thanks be to God for His indescribable [b]gift!

Paul Describes Himself

10 NOW [a]I, Paul, myself [b]urge you by the [c]meekness and gentleness of Christ—I who [d]am [1]meek when face to face with you, but bold toward you when absent!

2 I ask that [a]when I am present I may not be bold with the confidence with which I propose to be courageous against [b]some, who regard us as if we walked [c]according to the flesh.

3 For though we walk in the flesh, we do not war [a]according to the flesh,

4 for the [a]weapons of our warfare are not of the flesh, but [1]divinely powerful [b]for the destruction of fortresses.

5 *We are* destroying speculations and every [a]lofty thing raised up against the knowledge of God, and *we are* taking every thought captive to the [b]obedience of Christ,

6 and we are ready to punish all disobedience, whenever [a]your obedience is complete.

7 [1a]You are looking at [2]things as they are outwardly. [b]If anyone is confident in himself that he is Christ's, let him consider this again within himself, that just as he is Christ's, [c]so also are we.

8 For even if [a]I should boast somewhat [1]further about our [b]authority, which the Lord gave for building you up and not for destroying you, I shall not be put to shame,

9 [1]for I do not wish to seem as if I would terrify you by my letters.

10 For they say, "His letters are weighty and strong, but his [1]personal presence is [a]unimpressive, and [b]his speech contemptible."

11 Let such a person consider this, that what we are in word by letters when absent, such persons *we are* also in deed when present.

12 For we are not bold to class or compare ourselves with [1]some of those who [a]commend themselves; but when they measure themselves by themselves, and compare themselves with themselves, they are without understanding.

13 But we will not boast [a]beyond *our* measure, but [1b]within the measure of the sphere which God apportioned to us as a measure, to reach even as far as you.

14 For we are not overextending ourselves, as if we did not reach to you, for [a]we were the first to come even as far as you in the [b]gospel of Christ;

15 not boasting [a]beyond *our* measure, *that is,* in [b]other men's labors, but with the hope that as [c]your faith grows, we shall be, [1]within our sphere, [d]enlarged even more by you,

16 so as to [a]preach the gospel even to [b]the regions beyond you, *and* not to boast [1c]in what has been accomplished in the sphere of another.

17 But [a]HE WHO BOASTS, LET HIM BOAST IN THE LORD.

18 For not he who [a]commends himself is approved, but [b]whom the Lord commends.

Paul Defends His Apostleship

11 I WISH that you would [a]bear with me in a little [b]foolishness; but [1]indeed you are bearing with me.

2 For I am jealous for you with a godly jealousy; for I [a]betrothed you to one husband, that to Christ I might [b]present you *as* a pure virgin.

3 But I am afraid, lest as the [a]serpent deceived Eve by his craftiness, your minds should be led astray from the simplicity and purity *of devotion* to Christ.

---

5 [1]Lit., *blessing* [2]Lit., *as covetousness* [a]2 Cor. 9:3 [b]Gen. 33:11; Judg. 1:15; 2 Cor. 9:6 [c]Phil. 4:17 [d]2 Cor. 12:17f.
6 [1]Lit., *with blessings* [a]Prov. 11:24f.; 22:9; Gal. 6:7, 9
7 [a]Deut. 15:10; 1 Chr. 29:17; Rom. 12:8; 2 Cor. 8:12 [b]Ex. 25:2
8 [a]Eph. 3:20
9 [a]Ps. 112:9
10 [a]Is. 55:10 [b]Hos. 10:12
11 [a]1 Cor. 1:5 [b]2 Cor. 1:11
12 [1]Or, *holy ones* [a]2 Cor. 8:14 [b]2 Cor. 1:11
13 [1]Or, *sharing with them* [a]Rom. 15:31; 2 Cor. 8:4 [b]Matt. 9:8 [c]1 Tim. 6:12f.; Heb. 3:1; 4:14; 10:23 [d]2 Cor. 2:12
15 [a]2 Cor. 2:14 [b]Rom. 5:15f.

1 [1]Lit., *lowly* [a]Gal. 5:2; Eph. 3:1; Col. 1:23 [b]Rom. 12:1 [c]Matt. 11:29; 1 Cor. 4:21; Phil. 4:5 [d]1 Cor. 2:3f.; 2 Cor. 10:10
2 [a]1 Cor. 4:21; 2 Cor. 13:2, 10 [b]1 Cor. 4:18f. [c]Rom. 8:4; 2 Cor. 1:17
3 [a]Rom. 8:4; 2 Cor. 1:17
4 [1]Or, *mighty before God* [a]1 Cor. 9:7; 2 Cor. 6:7; 1 Tim. 1:18 [b]Jer. 1:10; 2 Cor. 10:8; 13:10
5 [a]Is. 2:11f. [b]2 Cor. 9:13
6 [a]2 Cor. 2:9
7 [1]Or, *Look at . . .* or *Do you look at . . . ?* [2]Lit., *what is before your face* [a]John 7:24; 2 Cor. 5:12 [b]1 Cor. 1:12; 14:37 [c]1 Cor. 9:1; 2 Cor. 11:23; Gal. 1:12
8 [1]Or, *more abundantly* [a]2 Cor. 7:4 [b]2 Cor. 13:10
9 [1]Lit., *that I may not seem*
10 [1]Lit., *bodily presence is weak* [a]1 Cor. 2:3; 2 Cor. 12:7; Gal. 4:13f. [b]1 Cor. 1:17; 2 Cor. 11:6
12 [1]Or, *any* [a]2 Cor. 3:1; 10:18
13 [1]Lit., *according to the measure* [a]2 Cor. 10:15 [b]Rom. 12:3; 2 Cor. 10:15f.
14 [a]1 Cor. 3:6 [b]2 Cor. 2:12
15 [1]Lit., *according to our sphere* [a]2 Cor. 10:13 [b]Rom. 15:20 [c]2 Thess. 1:3 [d]Acts 5:13
16 [1]Lit., *to the things prepared in the* [a]2 Cor. 11:7 [b]Acts 19:21 [c]Rom. 15:20
17 [a]Jer. 9:24; 1 Cor. 1:31
18 [a]2 Cor. 10:12 [b]Rom. 2:29; 1 Cor. 4:5

1 [1]Or, *do indeed bear with me* [a]Matt. 17:17; 2 Cor. 11:4, 16, 19f. [b]2 Cor. 5:13; 11:17, 21
2 [a]Hos. 2:19f.; Eph. 5:26f. [b]2 Cor. 4:14
3 [a]Gen. 3:4, 13; John 8:44; 1 Thess. 3:5; 1 Tim. 2:14; Rev. 12:9, 15

4 For if one comes and preaches
[a]another Jesus whom we have not
preached, or you receive a [b]different
spirit which you have not received, or a
[c]different gospel which you have not
accepted, you [d]bear *this* [e]beautifully.
5 For I consider myself [a]not in the
least inferior to the [1]most eminent apostles.
6 But even if I am [a]unskilled in
speech, yet I am not *so* in [b]knowledge; in
fact, in every way we have [c]made *this*
evident to you in all things.
7 Or [a]did I commit a sin in humbling
myself that you might be exalted, because I preached the [b]gospel of God to
you [c]without charge?
8 I robbed other churches, [a]taking
wages *from them* to serve you;
9 and when I was present with you
and was in need, I was [a]not a burden to
anyone; for when [b]the brethren came
from [c]Macedonia, they fully supplied my
need, and in everything I kept myself
from [a]being a burden to you, [1]and will
continue to do so.
10 [a]As the truth of Christ is in me,
[b]this boasting of mine will not be
stopped in the regions of [c]Achaia.
11 Why? [a]Because I do not love you?
[b]God knows *I do!*
12 But what I am doing, I will continue to do, [a]that I may cut off opportunity from those who desire an opportunity to be [1]regarded just as we are in the
matter about which they are boasting.
13 For such men are [a]false apostles,
[b]deceitful workers, disguising themselves
as apostles of Christ.
14 And no wonder, for even [a]Satan
disguises himself as an [b]angel of light.
15 Therefore it is not surprising if his
servants also disguise themselves as
servants of righteousness; [a]whose end
shall be according to their deeds.
16 [a]Again I say, let no one think me
foolish; but if *you do,* receive me even as
foolish, that I also may boast a little.
17 That which I am speaking, I am
not speaking [1a]as the Lord would, but as
[b]in foolishness, in this confidence of
boasting.
18 Since [a]many boast [b]according to
the flesh, I will boast also.
19 For you, [a]being *so* wise, bear with
the foolish gladly.
20 For you bear with anyone if he
[a]enslaves you, if he [b]devours you, if he
[c]takes advantage of you, if he [d]exalts
himself, if he [e]hits you in the face.
21 To *my* [a]shame I *must* say that we
have been [b]weak *by comparison.* But in
whatever respect anyone *else* [c]is bold (I
[d]speak in foolishness), I am just as bold
myself.
22 Are they [a]Hebrews? [b]So am I. Are
they [c]Israelites? [c]So am I. Are they
[1d]descendants of Abraham? [e]So am I.
23 Are they [a]servants of Christ? (I
speak as if insane) I more so; in [1b]far
more labors, in [1c]far more imprisonments, [2d]beaten times without number,
often in [e]danger of death.
24 Five times I received from the Jews
[a]thirty-nine *lashes.*
25 Three times I was [a]beaten with
rods, once I was [b]stoned, three times I
was shipwrecked, a night and a day I
have spent in the deep.
26 *I have been* on frequent journeys, in
dangers from rivers, dangers from robbers, dangers from *my* [a]countrymen,
dangers from the [b]Gentiles, dangers in
the [c]city, dangers in the wilderness,
dangers on the sea, dangers among [d]false
brethren;
27 *I have been* in [a]labor and hardship,
[1]through many sleepless nights, in [b]hun-
ger and thirst, often [c]without food, in
cold and [2d]exposure.
28 Apart from *such* [1]external things,
there is the daily pressure upon me *of*
concern for [a]all the churches.
29 Who is [a]weak without my being
weak? Who is [1]led into sin [2]without my
intense concern?
30 If I have to boast, I will boast of
what pertains to my [a]weakness.
31 The God and Father of the Lord
Jesus, [a]He who is blessed forever,
[b]knows that I am not lying.
32 In [a]Damascus the ethnarch under
Aretas the king was [b]guarding the city of
the Damascenes in order to seize me,
33 and I was let down in a basket
[a]through a window [1]in the wall, and *so*
escaped his hands.

Paul's Vision

12 [a]BOASTING is necessary, though
it is not profitable; but I will go
on to visions and [b]revelations [1]of the
Lord.
2 I know a man [a]in Christ who fourteen years ago—whether in the body I
do not know, or out of the body I do not
know, [b]God knows—such a man was
[c]caught up to the [d]third heaven.
3 And I know how such a man—
whether in the body or apart from the
body I do not know, [a]God knows—
4 was [a]caught up into [b]Paradise, and
heard inexpressible words, which a man
is not permitted to speak.
5 [a]On behalf of such a man will I
boast; but on my own behalf I will not
boast, except in regard to *my* [b]weak-
nesses.

4 [a]1 Cor. 3:11 [b]Rom. 8:15 [c]Gal. 1:6 [d]2 Cor. 11:1 [e]Mark 7:9
5 [1]Or, *super-apostles* [a]2 Cor. 12:11; Gal. 2:6
6 [a]1 Cor. 1:17 [b]1 Cor. 12:8; Eph. 3:4 [c]2 Cor. 4:2
7 [a]2 Cor. 12:13 [b]Rom. 1:1; 2 Cor. 2:12 [c]Acts 18:3; 1 Cor. 9:18
8 [a]1 Cor. 4:12; 9:6; Phil. 4:15, 18
9 [1]Lit., *and I will keep* [a]2 Cor. 12:13f., 16 [b]Acts 18:5 [c]Rom. 15:26; Phil. 4:15-18
10 [a]Rom. 1:9; 9:1; 2 Cor. 1:23; Gal. 2:20 [b]1 Cor. 9:15 [c]Acts 18:12
11 [a]2 Cor. 12:15 [b]Rom. 1:9; 2 Cor. 2:17; 11:31; 12:2f.
12 [1]Lit., *found* [a]1 Cor. 9:12
13 [a]Acts 20:30; Gal. 1:7; 2:4; Phil. 1:15; Titus 1:10f.; 2 Pet. 2:1; Rev. 2:2 [b]Phil. 3:2
14 [a]Matt. 4:10; Eph. 6:12; Col. 1:13 [b]Col. 1:12
15 [a]Rom. 2:6; 3:8
16 [a]2 Cor. 11:1
17 [1]Lit., *in accordance with the Lord* [a]1 Cor. 7:12, 25 [b]2 Cor. 11:21
18 [a]Phil. 3:3f. [b]2 Cor. 5:16
19 [a]1 Cor. 4:10
20 [a]2 Cor. 1:24; Gal. 2:4; 4:3, 9; 5:1 [b]Mark 12:40 [c]2 Cor. 11:3; 12:16 [d]2 Cor. 10:5 [e]1 Cor. 4:11
21 [a]2 Cor. 6:8 [b]2 Cor. 10:10 [c]2 Cor. 10:2 [d]2 Cor. 11:17
22 [1]Lit., *seed* [a]Acts 6:1 [b]Phil. 3:5 [c]Rom. 9:4 [d]Gal. 3:16 [e]Rom. 11:1
23 [1]Lit., *more abundant* [2]Lit., *exceedingly in stripes* [a]1 Cor. 3:5; 2 Cor. 3:6; 10:7 [b]1 Cor. 15:10 [c]2 Cor. 6:5 [d]Acts 16:23; 2 Cor. 6:5 [e]Rom. 8:36
24 [a]Deut. 25:3
25 [a]Acts 16:22 [b]Acts 14:19
26 [a]Acts 9:23; 13:45, 50; 14:5; 17:5, 13; 18:12; 20:3, 19; 21:27; 23:10, 12; 25:3; 1 Thess. 2:15 [b]Acts 14:5, 19; 19:23ff.; 27:42 [c]Acts 21:31 [d]Gal. 2:4
27 [1]Lit., *often in wakefulness* [2]Lit., *nakedness;* i.e., lack of clothing [a]1 Thess. 2:9; 2 Thess. 3:8 [b]1 Cor. 4:11; Phil. 4:12 [c]2 Cor. 6:5 [d]1 Cor. 4:11
28 [1]Or, *the things unmentioned* [a]1 Cor. 7:17
29 [1]Lit., *made to stumble* [2]Lit., *and I do not burn* [a]1 Cor. 8:9, 13; 9:22
30 [a]1 Cor. 2:3
31 [a]Rom. 1:25 [b]2 Cor. 11:11
32 [a]Acts 9:2 [b]Acts 9:24
33 [1]Lit., *through* [a]Acts 9:25

1 [1]Or possibly, *from* [a]2 Cor. 11:16, 18, 30; 12:5, 9 [b]1 Cor. 14:6; 2 Cor. 12:7; Gal. 1:12; 2:2; Eph. 3:3
2 [a]Rom. 16:7 [b]2 Cor. 11:11 [c]Ezek. 8:3; Acts 8:39; 2 Cor. 12:4; 1 Thess. 4:17; Rev. 12:5 [d]Deut. 10:14; Ps. 148:4; Eph. 4:10; Heb. 4:14
3 [a]2 Cor. 11:11
4 [a]Ezek. 8:3; Acts 8:39; 2 Cor. 12:2; 1 Thess. 4:17; Rev. 12:5 [b]Luke 23:43
5 [a]2 Cor. 12:1 [b]1 Cor. 2:3; 2 Cor. 12:9f.

6 For if I do wish to boast I shall not be [a]foolish, [b]for I shall be speaking the truth; but I refrain *from this,* so that no one may credit me with more than he sees *in* me or hears from me.

A Thorn in the Flesh

7 And because of the surpassing greatness of the [a]revelations, for this reason, to keep me from exalting myself, there was given me a [b]thorn in the flesh, a [c]messenger of Satan to buffet me—to keep me from exalting myself!

8 Concerning this I entreated the Lord [a]three times that it might depart from me.

9 And He has said to me, "My grace is sufficient for you, for [1a]power is perfected in weakness." Most gladly, therefore, I will rather [b]boast about my weaknesses, that the power of Christ may dwell in me.

10 Therefore [a]I am well content with weaknesses, with [1]insults, with [b]distresses, with [c]persecutions, with [b]difficulties, [d]for Christ's sake; for [e]when I am weak, then I am strong.

11 I have become [a]foolish; you yourselves compelled me. Actually I should have been commended by you, for [b]in no respect was I inferior to the [1]most eminent apostles, even though [c]I am a nobody.

12 The [1a]signs [2]of a true apostle were performed among you with all perseverance, by [1]signs and wonders and [3]miracles.

13 For in what respect were you treated as inferior to the rest of the churches, except that [a]I myself did not become a burden to you? Forgive me [b]this wrong!

14 Here [a]for this third time I am ready to come to you, and I [b]will not be a burden to you; for I [c]do not seek what is yours, but [d]you; for [e]children are not responsible to save up for *their* parents, but [f]parents for *their* children.

15 And I will [a]most gladly spend and be expended for your souls. If [b]I love you the more, am I to be loved the less?

16 But be that as it may, I [a]did not burden you myself; nevertheless, crafty fellow that I am, I [b]took you in by deceit.

17 [a]*Certainly* I have not taken advantage of you through any of those whom I have sent to you, have I?

18 I [a]urged [b]Titus *to go,* and sent [c]the brother with him. Titus did not take any advantage of you, did he? Did we not [1]conduct ourselves [2]in the same [d]spirit *and walk* [e]in the same steps?

19 All this time [1]you have been thinking that we are defending ourselves to you. *Actually,* [a]it is in the sight of God that we have been speaking in Christ; and [b]all for your upbuilding, [c]beloved.

20 For I am afraid that perhaps [a]when I come I may find you to be not what I wish and may be found by you to be not what you wish; that perhaps *there may be* [b]strife, jealousy, [c]angry tempers, [d]disputes, [e]slanders, [f]gossip, [g]arrogance, [h]disturbances;

21 I am afraid that when I come again my God may humiliate me before you, and I may mourn over many of those who have [a]sinned in the past and not repented of the [b]impurity, [1]immorality and sensuality which they have practiced.

Examine Yourselves

13 [a]THIS is the third time I am coming to you. [b]EVERY [1]FACT [2]IS TO BE CONFIRMED BY THE [3]TESTIMONY OF TWO OR THREE WITNESSES.

2 I have previously said when present the second time, and though now absent I say in advance to those who have [a]sinned in the past and to all the rest as well, that [b]if I come again, I will not [c]spare *anyone,*

3 since you are [a]seeking for proof of the [b]Christ who speaks in me, and who is not weak toward you, but [c]mighty in you.

4 For indeed He was [a]crucified because of weakness, yet He lives [b]because of the power of God. For we also are [c]weak [1]in Him, yet [d]we shall live with Him because of the power of God *directed* toward you.

5 [a]Test yourselves *to see* if you are in the faith; [b]examine yourselves! Or do you not recognize this about yourselves, that Jesus Christ is in you—unless indeed you [1c]fail the test?

6 But I trust that you will realize that we ourselves [1]do not fail the test.

7 Now we pray to God that you do no wrong; not that we ourselves may appear approved, but that you may do what is right, even though we should [1]appear unapproved.

8 For we can do nothing against the truth, but *only* for the truth.

9 For we rejoice when we ourselves are [a]weak but you are strong; this we also pray for, [1]that you be [b]made complete.

10 For this reason I am writing these things while absent, in order that when present [a]I may not use [b]severity, in accordance with the [c]authority which the Lord gave me, for building up and not for tearing down.

6 [a]2 Cor. 5:13; 11:16f.; 12:11 [b]2 Cor. 7:14
7 [a]2 Cor. 12:1 [b]Num. 33:55; Ezek. 28:24; Hos. 2:6 [c]Job 2:6; Matt. 4:10; 1 Cor. 5:5
8 [a]Matt. 26:44
9 [1]Later mss. read *My power* [a]1 Cor. 2:5; Eph. 3:16; Phil. 4:13 [b]1 Cor. 2:3; 2 Cor. 12:5
10 [1]Or, *mistreatment* [a]Rom. 5:3; 8:35 [b]2 Cor. 6:4 [c]2 Thess. 1:4; 2 Tim. 3:11 [d]2 Cor. 5:15, 20 [e]2 Cor. 13:4
11 [1]Or, *super-apostles* [a]2 Cor. 5:13; 11:16f.; 12:6 [b]1 Cor. 15:10; 2 Cor. 11:5 [c]1 Cor. 3:7; 13:2; 15:9
12 [1]Or, *attesting miracles* [2]Lit., *of the apostle* [3]Or, *works of power* [a]John 4:48; Rom. 15:19; 1 Cor. 9:1
13 [a]1 Cor. 9:12, 18; 2 Cor. 11:9; 12:14 [b]2 Cor. 11:7
14 [a]2 Cor. 1:15; 13:1, 2 [b]1 Cor. 9:12, 18; 2 Cor. 11:9; 12:13 [c]1 Cor. 10:24, 33 [d]1 Cor. 9:19 [e]1 Cor. 4:14f.; Gal. 4:19 [f]Prov. 19:14; Ezek. 34:2
15 [a]Rom. 9:3; 2 Cor. 1:6; Phil. 2:17; Col. 1:24; 1 Thess. 2:8; 2 Tim. 2:10 [b]2 Cor. 11:11
16 [a]2 Cor. 11:9 [b]2 Cor. 11:20
17 [a]2 Cor. 9:5
18 [1]Lit., *walk* [2]Or, *by the same Spirit* [a]2 Cor. 8:6 [b]2 Cor. 2:13 [c]2 Cor. 8:18 [d]1 Cor. 4:21 [e]Rom. 4:12
19 [1]Or, *have you been thinking . . . ?* [a]Rom. 9:1; 2 Cor. 2:17 [b]Rom. 14:19; 2 Cor. 10:8; 1 Thess. 5:11 [c]Heb. 6:9
20 [a]1 Cor. 4:21; 2 Cor. 2:1-4 [b]1 Cor. 1:11; 3:3 [c]Gal. 5:20 [d]Rom. 2:8; 1 Cor. 11:19 [e]Rom. 1:30; James 4:11; 1 Pet. 2:1 [f]Rom. 1:29 [g]1 Cor. 4:6, 18; 5:2 [h]1 Cor. 14:33
21 [1]I.e., sexual immorality [a]2 Cor. 13:2 [b]1 Cor. 6:9, 18; Gal. 5:19; Col. 3:5

1 [1]Lit., *word* [2]Lit., *will be* [3]Lit., *mouth* [a]2 Cor. 12:14 [b]Deut. 17:6; 19:15; Matt. 18:16
2 [a]2 Cor. 12:21 [b]1 Cor. 4:21; 2 Cor. 13:10 [c]2 Cor. 1:23; 10:11
3 [a]2 Cor. 10:1, 10 [b]Matt. 10:20; 1 Cor. 5:4; 7:40 [c]2 Cor. 9:8; 10:4
4 [1]Some early mss. read *with Him* [a]Phil. 2:7f.; 1 Pet. 3:18 [b]Rom. 1:4; 6:4; 1 Cor. 6:14 [c]1 Cor. 2:3; 2 Cor. 13:9 [d]Rom. 6:8
5 [1]Lit., *are unapproved* [a]John 6:6 [b]1 Cor. 11:28 [c]1 Cor. 9:27
6 [1]Lit., *are not unapproved*
7 [1]Lit., *be as*
9 [1]Lit., *your completion* [a]2 Cor. 12:10; 13:4 [b]1 Cor. 1:10; 2 Cor. 13:11; Eph. 4:12; 1 Thess. 3:10
10 [a]2 Cor. 2:3 [b]Titus 1:13 [c]1 Cor. 5:4; 2 Cor. 10:8

11 [a]Finally, brethren, [1]rejoice, [2][b]be
made complete, be comforted, [c]be like-
minded, [d]live in peace; and [e]the God of
love and peace shall be with you.
12 [a]Greet one another with a holy
kiss.
13 [a]All the [1]saints greet you.
14 [a]The grace of the Lord Jesus
Christ, and the [b]love of God, and the
[c]fellowship of the Holy Spirit, be with
you all.

11 [1]Or possibly, *farewell* [2]Or, *put yourselves in order* [a]1 Thess. 4:1; 2 Thess. 3:1 [b]1 Cor. 1:10; 2 Cor. 13:9; Eph. 4:12; 1 Thess. 3:10 [c]Rom. 12:16 [d]Mark 9:50 [e]Rom. 15:33; Eph. 6:23

12 [a]Rom. 16:16
13 [1]Or, *holy ones* [a]Phil. 4:22
14 [a]Rom. 16:20; 2 Cor. 8:9 [b]Rom. 5:5; Jude 21 [c]Phil. 2:1

THE EPISTLE OF PAUL TO THE GALATIANS

Introduction

1 PAUL, [a]an apostle ([b]not *sent* from
men, nor through the agency of
man, but [c]through Jesus Christ, and God
the Father, who [d]raised Him from the
dead),
2 and all [a]the brethren who are with
me, to [b]the churches of Galatia:
3 [a]Grace to you and peace from
[1]God our Father, and the Lord Jesus
Christ,
4 who [a]gave Himself for our sins,
that He might deliver us out of [b]this
present evil [1]age, according to the will of
[c]our God and Father,
5 [a]to whom *be* the glory forevermore.
Amen.

Perversion of the Gospel

6 I am amazed that you are so
quickly deserting [a]Him who called you
[1]by the grace of Christ, for a [b]different
gospel;
7 which is *really* not another; only
there are some who are [a]disturbing you,
and want to distort the gospel of Christ.
8 But even though we, or [a]an angel
from heaven, should preach to you a
gospel [1]contrary to that which we have
preached to you, let him be [2][b]accursed.
9 As we [a]have said before, so I say
again now, [b]if any man is preaching to
you a gospel [1]contrary to that which you
received, let him be [2][c]accursed.
10 For am I now [a]seeking the favor of
men, or of God? Or am I striving to
please men? If I were still trying to
please men, I would not be a [b]bond-
servant of Christ.

Paul Defends His Ministry

11 For [a]I would have you know,
brethren, that the gospel which was
preached by me is [b]not according to
man.
12 For [a]I neither received it from man,
nor was I taught it, but *I received it*
through a [b]revelation of Jesus Christ.
13 For you have heard of [a]my former
manner of life in Judaism, how I [b]used
to persecute [c]the church of God beyond
measure, and [d]tried to destroy it;
14 and I [a]was advancing in Judaism
beyond many of my contemporaries
among my [1]countrymen, being more
extremely zealous for my [b]ancestral
traditions.
15 But when He who had set me
apart, *even* from my mother's womb, and
[a]called me through His grace, was
pleased
16 to reveal His Son in me, that I
might [a]preach Him among the Gentiles,
[b]I did not immediately consult with
[1][c]flesh and blood,
17 [a]nor did I go up to Jerusalem to
those who were apostles before me; but I
went away to Arabia, and returned once
more to [b]Damascus.
18 Then [a]three years later I went up
[b]to Jerusalem to [1]become acquainted
with [c]Cephas, and stayed with him
fifteen days.
19 But I did not see any other of the
apostles except [1][a]James, the Lord's
brother.
20 (Now in what I am writing to you,
[1]I assure you [a]before God that I am not
lying.)
21 Then [a]I went into the regions of
[b]Syria and [c]Cilicia.
22 And I was *still* unknown by [1]sight
to [a]the churches of Judea which were [b]in
Christ;
23 but only, they kept hearing, "He
who once persecuted us is now preaching [a]the faith which he once [b]tried to
destroy."
24 And they [a]were glorifying God
[1]because of me.

The Council at Jerusalem

2 THEN after an interval of fourteen
years I [a]went up again to Jerusalem
with [b]Barnabas, taking [c]Titus along also.
2 And [1]it was because of a [a]revela-
tion that I went up; and I submitted to
them the [b]gospel which I preach among
the Gentiles, but *I did so* in private to
those who were of reputation, for fear
that I might be [c]running, or had run, in
vain.

1 [a]2 Cor. 1:1 [b]Gal. 1:11f. [c]Acts 9:15; Gal. 1:15f. [d]Acts 2:24
2 [a]Phil. 4:21 [b]Acts 16:6; 1 Cor. 16:1
3 [1]Some early mss. read *God the Father, and our Lord Jesus Christ* [a]Rom. 1:7
4 [1]Or, *world* [a]Gal. 2:20 [b]Matt. 13:22; Rom. 12:2; 2 Cor. 4:4 [c]Phil. 4:20
5 [a]Rom. 11:36
6 [1]Lit., *in* [a]Rom. 8:28; Gal. 1:15; 5:8 [b]2 Cor. 11:4; Gal. 1:7, 11; 2:2, 7; 5:14; 1 Tim. 1:3
7 [a]Acts 15:24; Gal. 5:10
8 [1]Or, *other than, more than* [2]Gr., *anathema* [a]2 Cor. 11:14 [b]Rom. 9:3
9 [1]Or, *other than, more than* [2]Gr., *anathema* [a]Acts 18:23 [b]Rom. 16:17 [c]Rom. 9:3
10 [a]1 Cor. 10:33; 1 Thess. 2:4 [b]Rom. 1:1; Phil. 1:1
11 [a]Rom. 2:16; 1 Cor. 15:1 [b]1 Cor. 3:4; 9:8
12 [a]1 Cor. 11:23; Gal. 1:1 [b]1 Cor. 2:10; 2 Cor. 12:1; Gal. 1:16; 2:2
13 [a]Acts 26:4f. [b]Acts 8:3; 22:4, 5 [c]1 Cor. 10:32 [d]Acts 9:21
14 [1]Lit., *race* [a]Acts 22:3 [b]Jer. 9:14; Matt. 15:2; Mark 7:3; Col. 2:8
15 [a]Is. 49:1, 5; Jer. 1:5; Acts 9:15; Rom. 1:1; Gal. 1:6
16 [1]I.e., human beings [a]Acts 9:15; Gal. 2:9 [b]Acts 9:20 [c]Matt. 16:17
17 [a]Acts 9:19-22 [b]Acts 9:2
18 [1]Or, *visit Cephas* [a]Acts 9:22f. [b]Acts 9:26 [c]John 1:42; Gal. 2:9, 11, 14
19 [1]Or, *Jacob* [a]Matt. 12:46; Acts 12:17
20 [1]Lit., *behold before God* [a]Rom. 9:1; 2 Cor. 1:23; 11:31
21 [a]Acts 9:30 [b]Acts 15:23, 41 [c]Acts 6:9

22 [1]Lit., *face* [a]1 Cor. 7:17; 1 Thess. 2:14 [b]Rom. 16:7
23 [a]Acts 6:7; Gal. 6:10 [b]Acts 9:21
24 [1]Lit., *in me* [a]Matt. 9:8

1 [a]Acts 15:2 [b]Acts 4:36; Gal. 2:9, 13 [c]2 Cor. 2:13; Gal. 2:3
2 [1]Lit., *according to revelation I went up* [a]Acts 15:2; Gal. 1:12 [b]Gal. 1:6 [c]Rom. 9:16; 1 Cor. 9:24ff.; Gal. 5:7; Phil. 2:16; 2 Tim. 4:7; Heb. 12:1

3 But not even [a]Titus who was with me, though he was a Greek, was [b]compelled to be circumcised.

4 But *it was* because of the [a]false brethren who [b]had sneaked in to spy out our [c]liberty which we have in Christ Jesus, in order to [d]bring us into bondage.

5 But we did not yield in subjection to them for even an hour, so that [a]the truth of the gospel might remain with you.

6 But from those who [1]were of high [a]reputation (what they were makes no difference to me; [b]God [2]shows no partiality)—well, those who were of reputation contributed nothing to me.

7 But on the contrary, seeing that I had been [a]entrusted with the [b]gospel [1]to the uncircumcised, just as [c]Peter *had been* [2]to the circumcised

8 (for He who effectually worked for Peter in *his* [a]apostleship [1]to the circumcised effectually worked for me also to the Gentiles),

9 and recognizing [a]the grace that had been given to me, [1b]James and [c]Cephas and John, who were [d]reputed to be [e]pillars, gave to me and [f]Barnabas the [g]right [2]hand of fellowship, that we *might* [h]*go* to the Gentiles, and they to the circumcised.

10 *They* only *asked* us to remember the poor—[a]the very thing I also was eager to do.

Peter (Cephas) Opposed by Paul

11 But when [a]Cephas came to [b]Antioch, I opposed him to his face, because he [1]stood condemned.

12 For prior to the coming of certain men from [1a]James, he used to [b]eat with the Gentiles; but when they came, he *began* to withdraw and hold himself aloof, [c]fearing [2]the party of the circumcision.

13 And the rest of the Jews joined him in hypocrisy, with the result that even [a]Barnabas was carried away by their hypocrisy.

14 But when I saw that they [a]were not [1]straightforward about [b]the truth of the gospel, I said to [c]Cephas in the presence of all, "If you, being a Jew, [d]live like the Gentiles and not like the Jews, how *is it that* you compel the Gentiles to live like Jews?[2]

15 "We *are* [a]Jews by nature, and not [b]sinners from among the Gentiles;

16 nevertheless knowing that [a]a man is not justified by the works of [1]the Law but through faith in Christ Jesus, even we have believed in Christ Jesus, that we may be justified by [b]faith in Christ, and not by the works of [1]the Law; since [c]by the works of [1]the Law shall no [2]flesh be justified.

17 "But if, while seeking to be justified in Christ, we ourselves have also been found [a]sinners, is Christ then a minister of sin? [b]May it never be!

18 "For if I rebuild what I have *once* destroyed, I [a]prove myself to be a transgressor.

19 "For through [1]the Law I [a]died to [1]the Law, that I might live to God.

20 "I have been [a]crucified with Christ; and it is no longer I who live, but [b]Christ lives in me; and [1]the *life* which I now live in the flesh I live by faith in [c]the Son of God, who [d]loved me, and [e]delivered Himself up for me.

21 "I do not nullify the grace of God; for [a]if righteousness *comes* through [1]the Law, then Christ died needlessly."

Faith Brings Righteousness

3 [1]YOU foolish [a]Galatians, who has bewitched you, before whose eyes Jesus Christ [b]was publicly portrayed *as* crucified?

2 This is the only thing I want to find out from you: did you receive the Spirit by the works of [1]the Law, or by [2a]hearing with faith?

3 Are you so foolish? Having begun [1]by the Spirit, are you now [2]being perfected by the flesh?

4 Did you suffer so many things in vain—[a]if indeed it was in vain?

5 Does He then, who [a]provides you with the Spirit and [b]works [1]miracles among you, do it by the works of [2]the Law, or by [3c]hearing with faith?

6 [1]Even so [a]Abraham [b]BELIEVED GOD, AND IT WAS RECKONED TO HIM AS RIGHTEOUSNESS.

7 Therefore, [1]be sure that [a]it is those who are of faith who are [b]sons of Abraham.

8 And the Scripture, foreseeing that God [1]would justify the [2]Gentiles by faith, preached the gospel beforehand to Abraham, *saying*, "[a]ALL THE NATIONS SHALL BE BLESSED IN YOU."

9 So then [a]those who are of faith are blessed with [1]Abraham, the believer.

10 For as many as are of the works of [1]the Law are under a curse; for it is written, "[a]CURSED IS EVERYONE WHO DOES NOT ABIDE BY ALL THINGS WRITTEN IN THE BOOK OF THE LAW, TO PERFORM THEM."

11 Now that [a]no one is justified [1]by [2]the Law before God is evident; for, "[3b]THE RIGHTEOUS MAN SHALL LIVE BY FAITH."

12 [1]However, the Law is not [2]of faith; on the contrary, "[a]HE WHO PRACTICES THEM SHALL LIVE [3]BY THEM."

3 [a]2 Cor. 2:13; Gal. 2:1 [b]Acts 16:3; 1 Cor. 9:21
4 [a]Acts 15:1, 24; 2 Cor. 11:13, 26; Gal. 1:7 [b]2 Pet. 2:1; Jude 4 [c]Gal. 5:1, 13; James 1:25 [d]Rom. 8:15; 2 Cor. 11:20
5 [a]Gal. 1:6; 2:14; Col. 1:5
6 [1]Lit., *seemed to be something* [2]Lit., *does not receive a face* [a]2 Cor. 11:5; 12:11; Gal. 2:9; 6:3 [b]Acts 10:34
7 [1]Lit., *of the uncircumcision* [2]Lit., *of the circumcision* [a]1 Cor. 9:17; 1 Thess. 2:4; 1 Tim. 1:11 [b]Acts 9:15; Gal. 1:16 [c]Gal. 1:18; 2:9, 11, 14
8 [1]Lit., *of the circumcision* [a]Acts 1:25
9 [1]Or, *Jacob* [2]Lit., *hands* [a]Rom. 12:3 [b]Acts 12:17; Gal. 2:12 [c]Luke 22:8; Gal. 1:18; 2:7, 11, 14 [d]2 Cor. 11:5; 12:11; Gal. 2:2, 6; 6:3 [e]1 Tim. 3:15; Rev. 3:12 [f]Acts 4:36; Gal. 2:1, 13 [g]2 Kin. 10:15 [h]Gal. 1:16
10 [a]Acts 24:17
11 [1]Or, *was to be condemned;* lit., *was one who was condemned,* or, *was self-condemned* [a]Gal. 1:18; 2:7, 9, 14 [b]Acts 11:19; 15:1
12 [1]Or, *Jacob* [2]Or, converts *from the circumcised;* lit., *those from the circumcision* [a]Acts 12:17; Gal. 2:9 [b]Acts 11:3 [c]Acts 11:2
13 [a]Acts 4:36; Gal. 2:1, 9
14 [1]Or, *progressing toward;* lit., *walking straightly* [2]Some close the direct quotation here, others extend it through v. 21 [a]Heb. 12:13 [b]Gal. 1:6; 2:5; Col. 1:5 [c]Gal. 1:18; 2:7, 9, 11 [d]Acts 10:28; Gal. 2:12
15 [a]Phil. 3:4f. [b]1 Sam. 15:18; Luke 24:7
16 [1]Or, *law* [2]Or, *mortal man* [a]Acts 13:39; Gal. 3:11 [b]Rom. 3:22; 9:30 [c]Ps. 143:2; Rom. 3:20
17 [a]Gal. 2:15 [b]Luke 20:16; Gal. 3:21
18 [a]Rom. 3:5
19 [1]Or, *law* [a]Rom. 6:2; 7:4; 1 Cor. 9:20
20 [1]Or, *insofar as I* [a]Rom. 6:6; Gal. 5:24; 6:14 [b]Rom. 8:10 [c]Matt. 4:3 [d]Rom. 8:37 [e]Gal. 1:4
21 [1]Or, *law* [a]Gal. 3:21

1 [1]Lit., *O* [a]Gal. 1:2 [b]1 Cor. 1:23; Gal. 5:11

2 [1]Or, *law* [2]Lit., *the hearing of faith* [a]Rom. 10:17
3 [1]Or, *with* [2]Or, *ending with*
4 [a]1 Cor. 15:2
5 [1]Or, *works of power* [2]Or, *law* [3]Lit., *the hearing of faith* [a]2 Cor. 9:10; Phil. 1:19 [b]1 Cor. 12:10 [c]Rom. 10:17
6 [1]Lit., *Just as* [a]Rom. 4:3 [b]Gen. 15:6
7 [1]Lit., *know* [a]Rom. 4:16; Gal. 3:9 [b]Luke 19:9; Gal. 6:16
8 [1]Lit., *justifies* [2]Lit., *nations* [a]Gen. 12:3
9 [1]Lit., *the believing Abraham* [a]Gal. 3:7
10 [1]Or, *law* [a]Deut. 27:26
11 [1]Or, *in* [2]Or, *law* [3]Or, *But he who is righteous by faith shall live.* [a]Gal. 2:16 [b]Hab. 2:4; Rom. 1:17; Heb. 10:38
12 [1]Or, *And* [2]Or, *based on* [3]Or, *in* [a]Lev. 18:5; Rom. 10:5

13 Christ [a]redeemed us from the curse
of the Law, having become a curse for
us—for it is written, "[b]CURSED IS EVERY-
ONE WHO HANGS ON [c]A [1]TREE"—
14 in order that [a]in Christ Jesus the
blessing of Abraham might [1]come to the
Gentiles, so that we [b]might receive
[c]the promise of the Spirit through faith.

Intent of the Law

15 [a]Brethren, [b]I speak [1]in terms of
human relations: [c]even though it is *only*
a man's [2]covenant, yet when it has been
ratified, no one sets it aside or adds
[3]conditions to it.
16 Now the promises were spoken [a]to
Abraham and to his seed. He does not
say, "And to seeds," as *referring* to
many, but *rather* to one, "[b]And to your
seed," that is, Christ.
17 What I am saying is this: the Law,
which came [a]four hundred and thirty
years later, does not invalidate a covenant previously ratified by God, so as
to nullify the promise.
18 For [a]if the inheritance is [1]based on
law, it is no longer [1]based on a promise;
but [b]God has granted it to Abraham by
means of a promise.
19 [a]Why the Law then? It was added
[1]because of transgressions, having been
[b]ordained through angels [c]by the
[2]agency of a mediator, until [d]the seed
should come to whom the promise had
been made.
20 Now [a]a mediator is not [1]for one
party only; whereas God is *only* one.
21 Is the Law then contrary to the
promises of God? [a]May it never be! For
[b]if a law had been given which was able
to impart life, then righteousness [1]would
indeed have been [2]based on law.
22 But the Scripture has [a]shut up all
[1]men under sin, that the promise by
faith in Jesus Christ might be given to
those who believe.
23 But before faith came, we were
kept in custody under the law, [a]being
shut up to the faith which was later to be
revealed.
24 Therefore the Law has become our
[1a]tutor *to lead us* to Christ, that [b]we may
be justified by faith.
25 But now that faith has come, we
are no longer under a [1a]tutor.
26 For you are all [a]sons of God
through faith in [b]Christ Jesus.
27 For all of you who were [a]baptized
into Christ have [b]clothed yourselves
with Christ.
28 [a]There is neither Jew nor Greek,
there is neither slave nor free man, there
is [1]neither male nor female; for [b]you are
all one in [c]Christ Jesus.
29 And if [a]you [1]belong to Christ, then
you are Abraham's [2]offspring, heirs
according to [b]promise.

Sonship in Christ

4 NOW I say, as long as the heir is a
[1]child, he does not differ at all from

13 [1]Or, *cross;* lit., *wood*
[a]Gal. 4:5 [b]Deut. 21:23 [c]Acts 5:30
14 [1]Or, *occur*
[a]Rom. 4:9, 16; Gal. 3:28 [b]Gal. 3:2 [c]Acts 2:33; Eph. 1:13
15 [1]Lit., *according to man* [2]Or, *will* or *testament* [3]Or, *a codicil*
[a]Acts 1:15; Rom. 1:13; Gal. 6:18 [b]Rom. 3:5 [c]Heb. 6:16
16 [a]Luke 1:55; Rom. 4:13, 16; 9:4 [b]Acts 3:25
17 [a]Gen. 15:13f.; Ex. 12:40; Acts 7:6
18 [1]Lit., *out of, from*
[a]Rom. 4:14 [b]Heb. 6:14
19 [1]Or, *for the sake of defining* [2]Lit., *hand*
[a]Rom. 5:20 [b]Acts 7:53 [c]Ex. 20:19; Deut. 5:5 [d]Gal. 3:16
20 [1]Lit., *of one*
[a]1 Tim. 2:5; Heb. 8:6; 9:15; 12:24
21 [1]Or, *would indeed be* [2]Lit., *out of, from*
[a]Luke 20:16; Gal. 2:17 [b]Gal. 2:21
22 [1]Lit., *things*
[a]Rom. 11:32
23 [a]Rom. 11:32
24 [1]Lit., *child-conductor*
[a]1 Cor. 4:15 [b]Gal. 2:16
25 [1]Lit., *child-conductor*
[a]1 Cor. 4:15
26 [a]Rom. 8:14; Gal. 4:5 [b]Rom. 8:1; Gal. 3:28; 4:14; 5:6, 24; Eph. 1:1; Phil. 1:1; Col. 1:4; 1 Tim. 1:12; 2 Tim. 1:1; Titus 1:4
27 [a]Matt. 28:19; Rom. 6:3; 1 Cor. 10:2 [b]Rom. 13:14
28 [1]Lit., *not male and female*
[a]Rom. 3:22; 1 Cor. 12:13; Col. 3:11 [b]John 17:11; Eph. 2:15 [c]Rom. 8:1; Gal. 3:26; 4:14; 5:6, 24; Eph. 1:1; Phil. 1:1; Col. 1:4; 1 Tim. 1:12; 2 Tim. 1:1; Titus 1:4
29 [1]Lit., *are Christ's* [2]Lit., *seed*
[a]Rom. 4:13; 1 Cor. 3:23 [b]Rom. 9:8; Gal. 3:18; 4:28

1 [1]Or, *minor* [2]Lit., *lord*
2 [1]Or, *stewards*
3 [1]Or, *rudimentary teachings* or *principles*
[a]Gal. 2:4; 4:8f., 24f. [b]Gal. 4:9; Col. 2:8, 20; Heb. 5:12
4 [1]Or, *law*
[a]Mark 1:15 [b]John 1:14; Rom. 1:3; 8:3; Phil. 2:7 [c]Luke 2:21f., 27
5 [1]Or, *law*
[a]Rom. 8:14; Gal. 3:26

a slave although he is [2]owner of everything,
2 but he is under guardians and
[1]managers until the date set by the
father.
3 So also we, while we were children,
were held [a]in bondage under the [1b]ele-
mental things of the world.
4 But when [a]the fulness of the time
came, God sent forth His Son, [b]born of
a woman, born [c]under [1]the Law,
5 in order that He might redeem
those who were under [1]the Law, that we
might receive the adoption as [a]sons.
6 And because you are sons, [a]God
has sent forth the Spirit of His Son into
our hearts, crying, "[b]Abba! Father!"
7 Therefore you are no longer a
slave, but a son; and [a]if a son, then an
heir [1]through God.
8 However at that time, [a]when you
did not know God, you were [b]slaves to
[c]those which by nature are no gods.
9 But now that you have come to
know God, or rather to be [a]known by
God, [b]how is it that you turn back again
to the weak and worthless [1c]elemental
things, to which you desire to be enslaved all over again?
10 You [a]observe days and months and
seasons and years.
11 I fear for you, that perhaps I have
labored [1]over you in vain.
12 I beg of you, [a]brethren, [b]become as
I *am*, for I also *have become* as you *are*.
You have done me no wrong;
13 but you know that it was because
of a [1]bodily illness that I preached the
gospel to you the [2]first time;
14 and that which was a [1]trial to you
in my [2]bodily condition you did not
despise or [3]loathe, but [a]you received me
as an angel of God, as [b]Christ Jesus
Himself.
15 Where then is [1]that sense of blessing you had? For I bear you witness, that
if possible, you would have plucked out
your eyes and given them to me.
16 Have I therefore become your
enemy [a]by [1]telling you the truth?
17 They eagerly seek you, not com-
mendably, but they wish to shut you out,
in order that you may seek them.
18 But it is good always to be eagerly
sought in a commendable manner, and
[a]not only when I am present with you.

6 [a]Acts 16:7; Rom. 5:5; 8:9, 16; 2 Cor. 3:17 [b]Mark 14:36; Rom. 8:15
7 [1]I.e., through the gracious act of [a]Rom. 8:17
8 [a]1 Cor. 1:21; Eph. 2:12; 1 Thess. 4:5; 2 Thess. 1:8 [b]Gal. 4:3 [c]2 Chr. 13:9; Is. 37:19; Jer. 2:11; 1 Cor. 8:4f.; 10:20
9 [1]Or, *rudimentary teachings* or *principles* [a]1 Cor. 8:3 [b]Col. 2:20 [c]Gal. 4:3
10 [a]Rom. 14:5; Col. 2:16
11 [1]Or, *for*
12 [a]Gal. 6:18 [b]2 Cor. 6:11, 13
13 [1]Lit., *weakness of the flesh* [2]Or, *former*
14 [1]Or, *temptation* [2]Lit., *flesh* [3]Lit., *spit out at* [a]Matt. 10:40; 1 Thess. 2:13 [b]Gal. 3:26
15 [1]Lit., *the congratulation of yourselves*
16 [1]Or, *dealing truthfully with you* [a]Amos 5:10
18 [a]Gal. 4:13f.

19 [a]My children, with whom [b]I am
again in labor until [c]Christ is formed in
you—
20 but I could wish to be present with
you now and to change my tone, for [a]I
am perplexed about you.

Bond and Free

21 Tell me, you who want to be under
law, do you not [a]listen to the law?
22 For it is written that Abraham had
two sons, [a]one by the bondwoman and
[b]one by the free woman.
23 But [a]the son by the bondwoman
was born according to the flesh, and [b]the
son by the free woman through the
promise.
24 [1a]This is allegorically speaking: for
these *women* are two covenants, one
proceeding from [b]Mount Sinai bearing
children [2]who are to be [c]slaves; [3]she is
Hagar.
25 Now this Hagar is Mount Sinai in
Arabia, and corresponds to the present
Jerusalem, for she is in slavery with her
children.
26 But [a]the Jerusalem above is free;
[1]she is our mother.
27 For it is written,
"[a]REJOICE, BARREN WOMAN WHO
DOES NOT BEAR;
BREAK FORTH AND SHOUT, YOU
WHO ARE NOT IN LABOR;
FOR MORE ARE THE CHILDREN OF
THE DESOLATE
THAN OF THE ONE WHO HAS A
HUSBAND."
28 And you brethren, [a]like Isaac, are
[b]children of promise.
29 But as at that time [a]he who was
born according to the flesh [b]persecuted
him *who was born* according to the
Spirit, [c]so it is now also.
30 But what does the Scripture say?
"[a]CAST OUT THE BONDWOMAN AND
HER SON,
FOR [b]THE SON OF THE BOND-
WOMAN SHALL NOT BE AN HEIR
WITH THE SON OF THE FREE
WOMAN."
31 So then, brethren, we are not children of a bondwoman, [1]but of the free
woman.

Walk by the Spirit

5 [1a]IT was for freedom that Christ set
us free; therefore [b]keep standing
firm and do not be subject again to a
[c]yoke of slavery.
2 Behold I, [a]Paul, say to you that if
you receive [b]circumcision, Christ will be
of no benefit to you.
3 And I [a]testify again to every man
who receives [b]circumcision, that he is
under obligation to [c]keep the whole
Law.
4 You have been severed from
Christ, you who [1]are seeking to be
justified by law; you have [a]fallen from
grace.
5 For we through the Spirit, by faith,
are [a]waiting for the hope of righteousness.
6 For in [a]Christ Jesus [b]neither circumcision nor uncircumcision means
anything, but [c]faith working through
love.
7 You were [a]running well; who hindered you from obeying the truth?
8 This persuasion *did* not *come* from
[a]Him who calls you.
9 [a]A little leaven leavens the whole
lump *of dough.*
10 [a]I have confidence [1]in you in the
Lord, that you [b]will adopt no other
view; but the one who is [c]disturbing you
shall bear his judgment, whoever he is.
11 But I, brethren, if I still preach
circumcision, why am I still [a]persecuted?
Then [b]the stumbling block of the cross
has been abolished.
12 Would that [a]those who are troubling you would even [1b]mutilate themselves.
13 For you were called to [a]freedom,
brethren; [b]only *do* not *turn* your freedom
into an opportunity for the flesh, but
through love [c]serve one another.
14 For [a]the whole Law is fulfilled in
one word, in the *statement*, "[b]YOU SHALL
LOVE YOUR NEIGHBOR AS YOURSELF."
15 But if you [a]bite and devour one
another, take care lest you be consumed
by one another.
16 But I say, [a]walk by the Spirit, and
you will not carry out [b]the desire of the
flesh.
17 For [a]the flesh [1]sets its desire
against the Spirit, and the Spirit against
the flesh; for these are in opposition to
one another, [b]so that you may not do the
things that you [2]please.
18 But if you are [a]led by the Spirit,
[b]you are not under the Law.
19 Now the deeds of the flesh are
evident, which are: [1a]immorality, impurity, sensuality,
20 idolatry, [a]sorcery, enmities, [b]strife,
jealousy, outbursts of anger, [c]disputes,
dissensions, [1d]factions,
21 envying, [a]drunkenness, carousing,
and things like these, of which I fore-
warn you just as I have forewarned you
that those who practice such things shall
not [b]inherit the kingdom of God.
22 But [a]the fruit of the Spirit is [b]love,
joy, peace, patience, kindness, goodness,
faithfulness,
23 gentleness, [a]self-control; against
such things [b]there is no law.
24 Now those who [1]belong to [a]Christ
Jesus have [b]crucified the flesh with its
passions and [c]desires.
25 If we live by the Spirit, let us also
[1]walk [a]by the Spirit.

19 [a]1 John 2:1 [b]1 Cor. 4:15 [c]Eph. 4:13
20 [a]2 Cor. 4:8
21 [a]Luke 16:29
22 [a]Gen. 16:15 [b]Gen. 21:2
23 [a]Rom. 9:7; Gal. 4:29 [b]Gen. 17:16ff.; 18:10ff.; 21:1; Gal. 4:28; Heb. 11:11
24 [1]Lit., *Which* [2]Lit., *into slavery* [3]Lit., *which* [a]1 Cor. 10:11 [b]Deut. 33:2 [c]Gal. 4:3
26 [1]Lit., *which* [a]Heb. 12:22; Rev. 3:12; 21:2, 10
27 [a]Is. 54:1
28 [a]Gal. 4:23 [b]Rom. 9:7ff.; Gal. 3:29
29 [a]Gal. 4:23 [b]Gen. 21:9 [c]Gal. 5:11
30 [a]Gen. 21:10, 12 [b]John 8:35
31 [1]V. 5:1, note 1

1 [1]Some authorities prefer to join with 4:31 and render *but with the freedom of the free woman Christ set us free* [a]John 8:32, 36; Rom. 8:15; 2 Cor. 3:17; Gal. 2:4; 5:13 [b]1 Cor. 16:13 [c]Acts 15:10; Gal. 2:4
2 [a]2 Cor. 10:1 [b]Acts 15:1; Gal. 5:3, 6, 11
3 [a]Luke 16:28 [b]Acts 15:1; Gal. 5:2, 6, 11 [c]Rom. 2:25
4 [1]Or, *would be* [a]Heb. 12:15; 2 Pet. 3:17
5 [a]Rom. 8:23; 1 Cor. 1:7
6 [a]Gal. 3:26 [b]1 Cor. 7:19; Gal. 6:15 [c]Col. 1:4f.; 1 Thess. 1:3; James 2:18, 20, 22
7 [a]Gal. 2:2
8 [a]Rom. 8:28; Gal. 1:6
9 [a]1 Cor. 5:6
10 [1]Lit., *toward* [a]2 Cor. 2:3 [b]Gal. 5:7; Phil. 3:15 [c]Gal. 1:7; 5:12
11 [a]Gal. 4:29; 6:12 [b]Rom. 9:33; 1 Cor. 1:23
12 [1]Or, *cut themselves off* [a]Gal. 2:4; 5:10 [b]Deut. 23:1
13 [a]Gal. 5:1 [b]1 Cor. 8:9; 1 Pet. 2:16 [c]1 Cor. 9:19; Eph. 5:21
14 [a]Matt. 7:12; 22:40; Rom. 13:8, 10; Gal. 6:2 [b]Lev. 19:18; Matt. 19:19; John 13:34
15 [a]Gal. 5:20; Phil. 3:2
16 [a]Rom. 8:4; 13:14; Gal. 5:24f. [b]Rom. 13:14; Eph. 2:3
17 [1]Lit., *lusts against* [2]Lit., *wish* [a]Rom. 7:18, 23; 8:5ff. [b]Rom. 7:15ff.
18 [a]Rom. 8:14 [b]Rom. 6:14; 7:4; 1 Tim. 1:9
19 [1]I.e., sexual immorality [a]1 Cor. 6:9, 18; 2 Cor. 12:21

20 [1]Or, *heresies* [a]Rev. 21:8 [b]2 Cor. 12:20 [c]Rom. 2:8; James 3:14ff. [d]1 Cor. 11:19
21 [a]Rom. 13:13 [b]1 Cor. 6:9
22 [a]Matt. 7:16ff.; Eph. 5:9 [b]Rom. 5:1-5; 1 Cor. 13:4; Col. 3:12-15
23 [a]Acts 24:25 [b]Gal. 5:18
24 [1]Lit., *are of Christ Jesus* [a]Gal. 3:26 [b]Rom. 6:6; Gal. 2:20; 6:14 [c]Gal. 5:16f.
25 [1]Or, *follow the Spirit* [a]Gal. 5:16

26 Let us not become [a]boastful, challenging one another, envying one another.

Bear One Another's Burdens

6 [a]BRETHREN, even if a man is caught in any trespass, you who are [b]spiritual, [c]restore such a one [d]in a spirit of gentleness; *each one* looking to yourself, lest you too be tempted.

2 [a]Bear one another's burdens, and thus fulfill [b]the law of Christ.

3 For [a]if anyone thinks he is something when he is nothing, he deceives himself.

4 But let each one [a]examine his own work, and then he will have *reason for* [b]boasting in regard to himself alone, and not in regard to another.

5 For [a]each one shall bear his own load.

6 And [a]let the one who is taught [b]the word share all good things with him who teaches.

7 [a]Do not be deceived, [b]God is not mocked; for [c]whatever a man sows, this he will also reap.

8 [a]For the one who sows to his own flesh shall from the flesh reap [b]corruption, but [c]the one who sows to the Spirit shall from the Spirit reap eternal life.

9 And [a]let us not lose heart in doing good, for in due time we shall reap if we [b]do not grow weary.

10 So then, [1a]while we have opportunity, let us do good to all men, and especially to those who are of the [b]household of [c]the faith.

11 See with what large letters I [1]am writing to you [a]with my own hand.

12 Those who desire [a]to make a good showing in the flesh try to [b]compel you to be circumcised, simply that they [c]may not be persecuted [1]for the cross of Christ.

13 For those who [1]are circumcised do not even [a]keep [2]the Law themselves, but they desire to have you circumcised, that they may [b]boast in your flesh.

14 But [a]may it never be that I should boast, [b]except in the cross of our Lord Jesus Christ, [c]through [1]which the world has been crucified to me, and [d]I to the world.

15 For [a]neither is circumcision anything, nor uncircumcision, but a [b]new [1]creation.

16 And those who will [1]walk by this rule, peace and mercy *be* upon them, and upon the [a]Israel of God.

17 From now on let no one cause trouble for me, for I bear on my body the [a]brand-marks of Jesus.

18 [a]The grace of our Lord Jesus Christ be [b]with your spirit, [c]brethren. Amen.

26 [a]Phil. 2:3
1 [a]Gal. 6:18; 1 Thess. 4:1 [b]1 Cor. 2:15 [c]2 Cor. 2:7; 2 Thess. 3:15; Heb. 12:13; James 5:19f. [d]1 Cor. 4:21
2 [a]Rom. 15:1 [b]Rom. 8:2; 1 Cor. 9:21; James 1:25; 2:12; 2 Pet. 3:2
3 [a]Acts 5:36; 1 Cor. 3:18; 2 Cor. 12:11
4 [a]1 Cor. 11:28 [b]Phil. 1:26
5 [a]Prov. 9:12; Rom. 14:12; 1 Cor. 3:8
6 [a]1 Cor. 9:11, 14 [b]2 Tim. 4:2
7 [a]1 Cor. 6:9 [b]Job 13:9 [c]2 Cor. 9:6
8 [a]Job 4:8; Hos. 8:7; Rom. 6:21 [b]1 Cor. 15:42 [c]Rom. 8:11; James 3:18
9 [a]1 Cor. 15:58; 2 Cor. 4:1 [b]Matt. 10:22; Heb. 12:3, 5; James 5:7f.
10 [1]Or, *as* [a]Prov. 3:27; John 12:35 [b]Eph. 2:19; Heb. 3:6; 1 Pet. 2:5; 4:17 [c]Acts 6:7; Gal. 1:23
11 [1]Or, *have written* [a]1 Cor. 16:21
12 [1]Or, *because of* [a]Matt. 23:27f. [b]Acts 15:1 [c]Gal. 5:11
13 [1]Some ancient mss. read *have been* [2]Or, *law* [a]Rom. 2:25 [b]Phil. 3:3

14 [1]Or, *whom* [a]Luke 20:16; Gal. 2:17; 3:21 [b]1 Cor. 2:2 [c]Gal. 2:20; Col. 2:20 [d]Rom. 6:2, 6; Gal. 2:19f.; 5:24
15 [1]Or, *creature* [a]Rom. 2:26, 28; 1 Cor. 7:19; Gal. 5:6 [b]2 Cor. 5:17; Eph. 2:10, 15; 4:24; Col. 3:10
16 [1]Or, *follow this rule* [a]Rom. 9:6; Gal. 3:7, 29; Phil. 3:3
17 [a]Is. 44:5; Ezek. 9:4; 2 Cor. 4:10; 11:23; Rev. 13:16
18 [a]Rom. 16:20 [b]2 Tim. 4:22 [c]Acts 1:15; Rom. 1:13; Gal. 3:15; 4:12, 28, 31

THE EPISTLE OF PAUL TO THE EPHESIANS

The Blessings of Redemption

1 PAUL, [a]an apostle of [b]Christ Jesus [1c]by the will of God, to the [2d]saints who are [3]at [e]Ephesus, and [f]*who are* faithful in [b]Christ Jesus:

2 [a]Grace to you and peace from God our Father and the Lord Jesus Christ.

3 [a]Blessed *be* the God and Father of our Lord Jesus Christ, who has blessed us with every spiritual blessing in [b]the heavenly *places* in Christ,

4 just as [a]He chose us in Him before [b]the foundation of the world, that we should be [c]holy and blameless before [1]Him. [d]In love

5 [1]He [a]predestined us to [b]adoption as sons through Jesus Christ to Himself, [c]according to the [2]kind intention of His will,

6 [a]to the praise of the glory of His grace, which He freely bestowed on us in [b]the Beloved.

7 [a]In [1]Him we have [b]redemption [c]through His blood, the [d]forgiveness of our trespasses, according to [e]the riches of His grace,

8 which He [1]lavished upon [2]us. In all wisdom and insight

9 He [1a]made known to us the mystery of His will, [b]according to His [2]kind intention which He [c]purposed in Him

10 with a view to an administration [1]suitable to [a]the fulness of the times, *that is,* [b]the summing up of all things in Christ, things [2]in the heavens and things upon the earth. In Him

11 [1]also we [2a]have obtained an inheritance, having been [b]predestined [c]according to His purpose who works all things [d]after the counsel of His will,

12 to the end that we who were the first to hope in [1]Christ should be [a]to the praise of His glory.

13 In [1]Him, you also, after listening to [a]the message of truth, the gospel of your salvation—having also [2]believed, you

1 [1]Lit., *through* [2]Or, *holy ones* [3]Some ancient mss. do not contain *at Ephesus* [a]2 Cor. 1:1 [b]Rom. 8:1 [c]1 Cor. 1:1 [d]Acts 9:13 [e]Acts 18:19 [f]Col. 1:2
2 [a]Rom. 1:7
3 [a]2 Cor. 1:3 [b]Eph. 1:20; 2:6; 3:10; 6:12
4 [1]Or, *Him, in love.* [a]Eph. 2:10; 2 Thess. 2:13f. [b]Matt. 25:34 [c]Eph. 5:27; Col. 1:22 [d]Eph. 4:2, 15, 16; 5:2
5 [1]Lit., *having predestined* [2]Lit., *good pleasure* [a]Acts 13:48; Rom. 8:29f. [b]Rom. 8:14ff. [c]Phil. 2:13; Col. 1:19
6 [a]Eph. 1:12, 14 [b]Matt. 3:17
7 [1]Lit., *whom* [a]Col. 1:14 [b]Rom. 3:24; 1 Cor. 1:30; Eph. 1:14 [c]Acts 20:28; Rom. 3:25 [d]Acts 2:38 [e]Rom. 2:4; Eph. 1:18; 2:7; 3:8, 16

8 [1]Lit., *made abundant toward* [2]Or, *us, in all wisdom and insight*
9 [1]Lit., *making known* [2]Lit., *good pleasure* [a]Rom. 11:25; Eph. 3:3 [b]1 Cor. 1:21; Gal. 1:15 [c]Rom. 8:28; Eph. 1:11
10 [1]Lit., *of* [2]Lit., *upon* [a]Mark 1:15 [b]Eph. 3:15; Phil. 2:9f.; Col. 1:16, 20
11 [1]Lit., *in whom also* [2]Or, *were made a heritage* [a]Deut. 4:20; Eph. 1:14; Titus 2:14 [b]Eph. 1:5 [c]Rom. 8:28f.; Eph. 3:11 [d]Rom. 9:11; Heb. 6:17
12 [1]I.e., the Messiah [a]Eph. 1:6, 14
13 [1]Lit., *whom* [2]Or, *believed in Him, you were sealed* [a]Eph. 4:21; Col. 1:5

were [b]sealed in [1]Him with [c]the Holy
Spirit of promise,
14 who is [1a]given as a pledge of [b]our
inheritance, with a view to the [c]redemp-
tion of [d]*God's own* possession, [e]to the
praise of His glory.
15 For this reason I too, [a]having heard
of the faith in the Lord Jesus which
exists among you, and [1]your love for [b]all
the [2]saints,
16 [a]do not cease giving thanks for you,
[b]while making mention *of you* in my
prayers;
17 that the [a]God of our Lord Jesus
Christ, [b]the Father of glory, may give to
you a spirit of [c]wisdom and of [d]revela-
tion in the [1]knowledge of Him.
18 *I pray that* [a]the eyes of your heart
[1]may be enlightened, so that you may
know what is the [b]hope of His [c]calling,
what are [d]the riches of the glory of [e]His
inheritance in [f]the [2]saints,
19 and what is the surpassing greatness of His power toward us who believe. [a]*These are* in accordance with the
working of the [b]strength of His might
20 which He brought about in Christ,
when He [a]raised Him from the dead,
and [b]seated Him at His right hand in
[c]the heavenly *places*,
21 far above [a]all rule and authority
and power and dominion, and every
[b]name that is named, not only in [c]this
age, but also in the one to come.
22 And He [a]put all things in subjection under His feet, and gave Him as
[b]head over all things to the church,
23 which is His [a]body, the [b]fulness of
Him who [c]fills [d]all in all.

Made Alive in Christ

2 AND you [1]were [a]dead [2]in your
trespasses and sins,
2 in which you [a]formerly walked
according to the [1]course of [b]this world,
according to [c]the prince of the power of
the air, of the spirit that is now working
in [d]the sons of disobedience.
3 Among them we too all [a]formerly
lived in [b]the lusts of our flesh, [1]indulging
the desires of the flesh and of the [2]mind,
and were [c]by nature [d]children of wrath,
[e]even as the rest.
4 But God, being [a]rich in mercy,
because of [b]His great love with which
He loved us,
5 even when we were [a]dead [1]in our
transgressions, made us alive together
[2]with Christ ([b]by grace you have been
saved),
6 and [a]raised us up with Him, and
[b]seated us with Him in [c]the heavenly
places, in [d]Christ Jesus,
7 in order that in the ages to come
He might show the surpassing [a]riches of
His grace in [b]kindness toward us in
Christ Jesus.

13 [1]Lit., *whom* [b]Eph. 4:30 [c]Acts 2:33

14 [1]Or, *a down payment* [a]2 Cor. 1:22 [b]Acts 20:32 [c]Eph. 1:7 [d]Eph. 1:11 [e]Eph. 1:6, 12

15 [1]Many ancient mss. do not contain *your love* [2]V. 1, note 2 [a]Col. 1:4; Philem. 5 [b]Eph. 1:1; 3:18

16 [a]Rom. 1:8f.; Col. 1:9 [b]Rom. 1:9

17 [1]Or, *true knowledge* [a]John 20:17; Rom. 15:6 [b]Acts 7:2; 1 Cor. 2:8 [c]Col. 1:9 [d]1 Cor. 14:6

18 [1]Lit., *being* [2]Or, *holy ones* [a]Acts 26:18; 2 Cor. 4:6; Heb. 6:4 [b]Eph. 4:4 [c]Rom. 11:29 [d]Eph. 1:7 [e]Eph. 1:11 [f]Col. 1:12

19 [a]Eph. 3:7; Col. 1:29 [b]Eph. 6:10

20 [a]Acts 2:24 [b]Mark 16:19 [c]Eph. 1:3

21 [a]Matt. 28:18; Col. 1:16 [b]Phil. 2:9; Rev. 19:12 [c]Matt. 12:32

22 [a]Ps. 8:6; 1 Cor. 15:27 [b]1 Cor. 11:3; Eph. 4:15; Col. 1:18

23 [a]1 Cor. 12:27; Eph. 4:12; Col. 1:18, 24 [b]John 1:16; Eph. 3:19 [c]Eph. 4:10 [d]Col. 3:11

1 [1]Lit., *being* [2]Or, *by reason of* [a]Eph. 2:5; Col. 2:13

2 [1]Lit., *age* [a]1 Cor. 6:11; Eph. 2:3 [b]Eph. 1:21 [c]John 12:31; Eph. 6:12 [d]Eph. 5:6

3 [1]Lit., *doing* [2]Lit., *thoughts* [a]Eph. 2:2 [b]Gal. 5:16f. [c]Rom. 2:14; Gal. 2:15 [d]Rom. 5:9; Col. 1:21; 2 Pet. 2:14 [e]Rom. 5:12

4 [a]Eph. 1:7 [b]John 3:16

5 [1]Or, *by reason of* [2]Some ancient mss. read *in Christ* [a]Eph. 2:1 [b]Acts 15:11

6 [a]Col. 2:12 [b]Eph. 1:20 [c]Eph. 1:3 [d]Eph. 1:1; 2:10, 13

7 [a]Rom. 2:4; Eph. 1:7 [b]Titus 3:4

8 [1]I.e., that salvation [a]Acts 15:11; Eph. 2:5 [b]1 Pet. 1:5 [c]John 4:10

9 [a]Rom. 3:28; 2 Tim. 1:9 [b]1 Cor. 1:29

10 [a]Eph. 2:15; 4:24; Col. 3:10 [b]Eph. 1:1; 2:6, 13 [c]Titus 2:14 [d]Eph. 1:4 [e]Eph. 4:1

11 [a]Eph. 2:2 [b]1 Cor. 12:2; Eph. 5:8 [c]Rom. 2:28f.; Col. 2:11

12 [1]Or, *alienated* [a]Rom. 9:4; Col. 1:21 [b]Gal. 3:17; Heb. 8:6 [c]1 Thess. 4:13 [d]Gal. 4:8; 1 Thess. 4:5

8 For [a]by grace you have been saved
[b]through faith; and [1]that not of yourselves, *it is* [c]the gift of God;
9 [a]not as a result of works, that [b]no
one should boast.
10 For we are His workmanship, [a]cre-
ated in [b]Christ Jesus for [c]good works,
which God [d]prepared beforehand, that
we should [e]walk in them.
11 Therefore remember, that [a]for-
merly [b]you, the Gentiles in the flesh,
who are called "[c]Uncircumcision" by the
so-called "[c]Circumcision," *which is* performed in the flesh by human hands—
12 *remember* that you were at that
time separate from Christ, [1a]excluded
from the commonwealth of Israel, and
strangers to [b]the covenants of promise,
having [c]no hope and [d]without God in
the world.
13 But now in [a]Christ Jesus you who
[b]formerly were [c]far off [1]have [c]been
brought near [2d]by the blood of Christ.
14 For He Himself is [a]our peace, [b]who
made both *groups into* one, and broke
down the [1]barrier of the dividing wall,
15 [1]by [a]abolishing in His flesh the
enmity, *which is* [b]the Law of commandments *contained* in ordinances, that in
Himself He might [2c]make the two into
[d]one new man, *thus* establishing [e]peace,
16 and might [a]reconcile them both in
[b]one body to God through the cross, [1]by
it having [c]put to death the enmity.
17 AND [a]HE CAME AND PREACHED
[b]PEACE TO YOU WHO WERE [c]FAR AWAY,
AND PEACE TO THOSE WHO WERE [c]NEAR;
18 for through Him we both have [a]our
access in [b]one Spirit to [c]the Father.
19 So then you are no longer [a]strang-
ers and aliens, but you are [b]fellow
citizens with the [1]saints, and are of
[c]God's household,
20 having been [a]built upon [b]the foundation of [c]the apostles and prophets,
[d]Christ Jesus Himself being the [e]corner
stone,
21 [a]in whom the whole building, being
fitted together is growing into [b]a holy
[1]temple in the Lord;
22 in whom you also are being [a]built
together into a [b]dwelling of God in the
Spirit.

13 [1]Lit., *became;* or, *were made* [2]Or, *in* [a]Eph. 1:1; 2:6 [b]Eph. 2:2 [c]Is. 57:19; Acts 2:39; Eph. 2:17 [d]Rom. 3:25; Col. 1:20

14 [1]Lit., *the dividing wall of the barrier* [a]Is. 9:6; Eph. 2:15; Col. 3:15 [b]1 Cor. 12:13; Gal. 3:28; Col. 3:11

15 [1]Or, *the enmity, by abolishing in His flesh the Law* [2]Lit., *create* [a]Eph. 2:16; Col. 1:21f. [b]Col. 2:14, 20 [c]Gal. 3:28; Eph. 2:10; Col. 3:10, 11 [d]Gal. 3:28; Col. 3:10f. [e]Is. 9:6; Eph. 2:14; Col. 3:15

16 [1]Or, *in Himself* [a]2 Cor. 5:18; Col. 1:20, 22 [b]1 Cor. 10:17; Eph. 4:4 [c]Eph. 2:15

17 [a]Is. 57:19; Rom. 10:14 [b]Acts 10:36; Eph. 2:14 [c]Eph. 2:13

18 [a]Rom. 5:2; Eph. 3:12 [b]1 Cor. 12:13; Eph. 4:4 [c]Col. 1:12

19 [1]Or, *holy ones* [a]Eph. 2:12; Heb. 11:13; 1 Pet. 2:11 [b]Phil. 3:20; Heb. 12:22f. [c]Gal. 6:10

20 [a]1 Cor. 3:9 [b]Matt. 16:18; 1 Cor. 3:10; Rev. 21:14 [c]1 Cor. 12:28; Eph. 3:5 [d]1 Cor. 3:11 [e]Ps. 118:22; Luke 20:17

21 [1]Or, *sanctuary* [a]Eph. 4:15f.; Col. 2:19 [b]1 Cor. 3:16f.

22 [a]1 Cor. 3:9, 16; 2 Cor. 6:16 [b]Eph. 3:17

Paul's Stewardship

3 FOR this reason I, Paul, [a]the prisoner of [b]Christ Jesus [c]for the sake of you [d]Gentiles—

2 if indeed you have heard of the [a]stewardship of God's grace which was given to me for you;

3 [a]that [b]by revelation there was [c]made known to me [d]the mystery, [e]as I wrote before in brief.

4 [1]And by referring to this, when you read you can understand [a]my insight [2]into the [b]mystery of Christ,

5 which in other generations was not made known to the sons of men, as it has now been revealed to His holy [a]apostles and prophets [1]in the Spirit;

6 *to be specific*, that the Gentiles are [a]fellow heirs and [b]fellow members of the body, and [c]fellow partakers of the promise in [d]Christ Jesus through the gospel,

7 [a]of which I was made a [b]minister, according to the gift of [c]God's grace which was given to me [d]according to the working of His power.

8 To me, [a]the very least of all [1]saints, this grace was given, to [b]preach to the Gentiles the unfathomable [c]riches of Christ,

9 and to [1]bring to light what is the administration of the [a]mystery which for ages has been [b]hidden in God, [c]who created all things;

10 in order that the manifold [a]wisdom of God might now be [b]made known through the church to the [c]rulers and the authorities in [d]the heavenly *places.*

11 *This was* in [a]accordance with the [1]eternal purpose which He [2]carried out in [b]Christ Jesus our Lord,

12 in whom we have boldness and [1a]confident [b]access through faith [2]in Him.

13 Therefore I ask [1]you not [a]to lose heart at my tribulations [b]on your behalf, [2]for they are your glory.

14 For this reason, I [a]bow my knees before the Father,

15 from whom [1]every family in heaven and on earth derives its name,

16 that He would grant you, according to [a]the riches of His glory, to be [b]strengthened with power through His Spirit in [c]the inner man;

17 so that [a]Christ may dwell in your hearts through faith; *and* that you, being [b]rooted and [c]grounded in love,

18 may be able to comprehend with [a]all the [1]saints what is [b]the breadth and length and height and depth,

19 and to know [a]the love of Christ which [b]surpasses knowledge, that you may be [c]filled up to all the [d]fulness of God.

20 [a]Now to Him who is [b]able to do exceeding abundantly beyond all that we ask or think, [c]according to the power that works within us,

21 [a]to Him *be* the glory in the church and in Christ Jesus to all generations [1]forever and ever. Amen.

1 [a]Acts 23:18; Eph. 4:1; 2 Tim. 1:8; Philem. 1, 9, 23 [b]Gal. 5:24 [c]2 Cor. 1:6; Eph. 3:13 [d]Eph. 3:8
2 [a]Eph. 1:10; 3:9; Col. 1:25; 1 Tim. 1:4
3 [a]Acts 22:17, 21; 26:16ff. [b]Gal. 1:12 [c]Eph. 1:9; 3:4, 6, 9 [d]Rom. 11:25; 16:25; Eph. 3:4, 9; 6:19; Col. 1:26f.; 4:3 [e]Eph. 1:9f.; Heb. 13:22; 1 Pet. 5:12
4 [1]Lit., *To which, when you read* [2]Lit., *in* [a]2 Cor. 11:6 [b]Rom. 11:25; 16:25; Eph. 3:3, 9; 6:19; Col. 1:26f.; 4:3
5 [1]Or, *by* [a]1 Cor. 12:28; Eph. 2:20
6 [a]Gal. 3:29 [b]Eph. 2:16 [c]Eph. 5:7 [d]Gal. 5:24
7 [a]Col. 1:23, 25 [b]1 Cor. 3:5 [c]Acts 9:15; Rom. 12:3; Eph. 3:2 [d]Eph. 1:19; 3:20
8 [1]Or, *holy ones* [a]1 Cor. 15:9 [b]Acts 9:15; Eph. 3:1f. [c]Rom. 2:4; Eph. 1:7; 3:16
9 [1]Some ancient mss. read *make all know* [a]Rom. 11:25; 16:25; Eph. 3:3, 4; 6:19; Col. 1:26f.; 4:3 [b]Col. 3:3 [c]Rev. 4:11
10 [a]Rom. 11:33; 1 Cor. 2:7 [b]Eph. 1:23; 1 Pet. 1:12 [c]Eph. 1:21; 6:12; Col. 2:10, 15 [d]Eph. 1:3
11 [1]Lit., *purpose of the ages* [2]Or, *formed* [a]Eph. 1:11 [b]Gal. 5:24; Eph. 3:1
12 [1]Lit., *access in confidence* [2]Lit., *of Him* [a]2 Cor. 3:4; Heb. 4:16; 10:19, 35; 1 John 2:28; 3:21 [b]Eph. 2:18
13 [1]Or, *that I may not lose* [2]Lit., *which are* [a]2 Cor. 4:1 [b]Eph. 3:1
14 [a]Phil. 2:10
15 [1]Or, *the whole*
16 [a]Eph. 1:18; 3:8 [b]1 Cor. 16:13; Phil. 4:13; Col. 1:11 [c]Rom. 7:22
17 [a]John 14:23; Rom. 8:9f.; 2 Cor. 13:5; Eph. 2:22 [b]1 Cor. 3:6; Col. 2:7 [c]Col. 1:23
18 [1]V. 8, note 1 [a]Eph. 1:15 [b]Job 11:8f.
19 [a]Rom. 8:35, 39 [b]Phil. 4:7 [c]Col. 2:10 [d]Eph. 1:23
20 [a]Rom. 16:25 [b]2 Cor. 9:8 [c]Eph. 3:7
21 [1]Lit., *of the age of the ages* [a]Rom. 11:36

1 [a]Eph. 3:1 [b]Rom. 12:1 [c]Eph. 2:10; Col. 1:10; 2:6; 1 Thess. 2:12 [d]Rom. 11:29 [e]Rom. 8:28f.

Unity of the Spirit

4 I, THEREFORE, [a]the prisoner of the Lord, [b]entreat you to [c]walk in a manner worthy of the [d]calling with which you have been [e]called,

2 with all [a]humility and gentleness, with patience, showing forbearance to one another [b]in love,

3 being diligent to preserve the unity of the Spirit in the [a]bond of peace.

4 *There is* [a]one body and one Spirit, just as also you were called in one [b]hope of your calling;

5 [a]one Lord, one faith, one baptism,

6 one God and Father of all [a]who is over all and through all and in all.

7 But [a]to each one of us [b]grace was given [c]according to the measure of Christ's gift.

8 Therefore [1]it says,

"[a]WHEN HE ASCENDED ON HIGH,
HE [b]LED CAPTIVE A HOST OF CAPTIVES,
AND HE GAVE GIFTS TO MEN."

9 (Now this *expression,* "He [a]ascended," what [1]does it mean except that He also [2]had descended into [b]the lower parts of the earth?

10 He who descended is Himself also He who ascended [a]far above all the heavens, that He might [b]fill all things.)

11 And He [a]gave [b]some *as* apostles, and some *as* prophets, and some *as* [c]evangelists, and some *as* pastors and [d]teachers,

12 [a]for the equipping of the [1]saints for the work of service, to the building up of [b]the body of Christ;

13 until we all attain to [a]the unity of the faith, and of the [1b]knowledge of the Son of God, to a [c]mature man, to the measure of the stature [2]which belongs to the [d]fulness of Christ.

14 [1]As a result, we are [a]no longer to be children, [b]tossed here and there by waves, and carried about by every wind of doctrine, by the trickery of men, by [c]craftiness [2]in [d]deceitful scheming;

15 but [1]speaking the truth [a]in love, we [2]are to [b]grow up in all *aspects* into Him, who is the [c]head, *even* Christ,

2 [a]Col. 3:12f. [b]Eph. 1:4
3 [a]Col. 3:14f.
4 [a]1 Cor. 12:4ff.; Eph. 2:16, 18 [b]Eph. 1:18
5 [a]1 Cor. 8:6
6 [a]Rom. 11:36
7 [a]1 Cor. 12:7, 11 [b]Eph. 3:2 [c]Rom. 12:3
8 [1]Or, *He* [a]Ps. 68:18 [b]Col. 2:15
9 [1]Lit., *is it except* [2]Some ancient mss. read *had first descended* [a]John 3:13 [b]Is. 44:23
10 [a]Eph. 1:20f.; Heb. 4:14; 7:26 [b]Eph. 1:23
11 [a]Eph. 4:8 [b]Acts 13:1; 1 Cor. 12:28 [c]Acts 21:8 [d]Acts 13:1
12 [1]Or, *holy ones* [a]2 Cor. 13:9 [b]1 Cor. 12:27; Eph. 1:23
13 [1]Or, *true knowledge* [2]Lit., *of the fulness* [a]Eph. 4:3, 5 [b]John 6:69; Eph. 1:17; Phil. 3:10 [c]1 Cor. 14:20; Col. 1:28; Heb. 5:14 [d]John 1:16; Eph. 1:23
14 [1]Lit., *that we may no longer be* [2]Lit., *with regard to the scheming of deceit* [a]1 Cor. 14:20 [b]James 1:6; Jude 12 [c]1 Cor. 3:19; 2 Cor. 4:2; 11:3 [d]Eph. 6:11
15 [1]Or, *holding to* or *walking in* [2]Lit., *may grow up* [a]Eph. 1:4 [b]Eph. 2:21 [c]Eph. 1:22

16 from whom [a]the whole body, being
fitted and held together [1]by that which
every joint supplies, according to the
[2]proper working of each individual part,
causes the growth of the body for the
building up of itself [b]in love.

The Christian's Walk

17 [a]This I say therefore, and affirm
together with the Lord, [b]that you walk
no longer just as the Gentiles also walk,
in the [c]futility of their mind,
18 being [a]darkened in their understanding, [1b]excluded from the life of
God, because of the [c]ignorance that is in
them, because of the [d]hardness of their
heart;
19 and they, having [a]become callous,
[b]have given themselves over to [c]sensual-
ity, [1]for the practice of every kind of
impurity with greediness.
20 But you did not [a]learn [1]Christ in
this way,
21 if indeed you [a]have heard Him and
have [b]been taught in Him, just as truth
is in Jesus,
22 that, in reference to your former
manner of life, you [a]lay aside the [b]old
[1]self, which is being corrupted in accordance with the [c]lusts of deceit,
23 and that you be [a]renewed in the
spirit of your mind,
24 and [a]put on the [b]new [1]self, which
[2c]in *the likeness of* God has been created
in righteousness and holiness of the
truth.
25 Therefore, [a]laying aside falsehood,
[b]SPEAK TRUTH, EACH ONE *of you,* WITH
HIS NEIGHBOR, for we are [c]members of
one another.
26 [a]BE ANGRY, AND *yet* DO NOT SIN;
do not let the sun go down on your
anger,
27 and do not [a]give the devil [1]an
opportunity.
28 Let him who steals steal no longer;
but rather [a]let him labor, [b]performing
with his own hands what is good, [c]in
order that he may have *something* to
share with him who has need.
29 Let no [1a]unwholesome word proceed from your mouth, but only such *a
word* as is good for [b]edification [2]accord-
ing to the need *of the moment,* that it
may give grace to those who hear.
30 And [a]do not grieve the Holy Spirit
of God, [1]by whom you were [b]sealed for
the day of redemption.
31 [a]Let all bitterness and wrath and
anger and clamor and slander be [b]put
away from you, along with all [c]malice.
32 And [a]be kind to one another,
tender-hearted, forgiving each other,
[b]just as God in Christ also has forgiven
[1]you.

Be Imitators of God

5 [a]THEREFORE be imitators of God,
as beloved children;
2 and [a]walk in love, just as Christ
also [b]loved [1]you, and [c]gave Himself up

16 [1]Lit., *through every joint of the supply* [2]Lit., *working in measure* [a]Rom. 12:4f.; Col. 2:19 [b]Eph. 1:4
17 [a]Col. 2:4 [b]Eph. 2:2; 4:22 [c]Rom. 1:21; Col. 2:18; 1 Pet. 1:18; 2 Pet. 2:18
18 [1]Or, *alienated* [a]Rom. 1:21 [b]Eph. 2:1, 12 [c]Acts 3:17; 17:30; 1 Cor. 2:8; Heb. 5:2; 9:7; 1 Pet. 1:14 [d]Mark 3:5; Rom. 11:7, 25; 2 Cor. 3:14
19 [1]Or, *greedy for the practice of every kind of impurity* [a]1 Tim. 4:2 [b]Rom. 1:24 [c]Col. 3:5
20 [1]I.e., the Messiah [a]Matt. 11:29
21 [a]Rom. 10:14; Eph. 1:13; 2:17; Col. 1:5 [b]Col. 2:7
22 [1]Lit., *man* [a]Eph. 4:25, 31; Col. 3:8; Heb. 12:1; James 1:21; 1 Pet. 2:1 [b]Rom. 6:6 [c]2 Cor. 11:3; Heb. 3:13
23 [a]Rom. 12:2
24 [1]Lit., *man* [2]Lit., *according to God* [a]Rom. 13:14 [b]Rom. 6:4; 7:6; 12:2; 2 Cor. 5:17; Col. 3:10 [c]Eph. 2:10
25 [a]Eph. 4:22, 31; Col. 3:8; Heb. 12:1; James 1:21; 1 Pet. 2:1 [b]Zech. 8:16; Eph. 4:15; Col. 3:9 [c]Rom. 12:5
26 [a]Ps. 4:4
27 [1]Lit., *a place* [a]Rom. 12:19; James 4:7
28 [a]Acts 20:35; 1 Cor. 4:12; Gal. 6:10 [b]1 Thess. 4:11; 2 Thess. 3:8, 11f.; Titus 3:8, 14 [c]Luke 3:11; 1 Thess. 4:12
29 [1]Lit., *rotten* [2]Lit., *of the need* [a]Matt. 12:34; Eph. 5:4; Col. 3:8 [b]Eccl. 10:12; Rom. 14:19; Col. 4:6
30 [1]Lit., *in* [a]Is. 63:10; 1 Thess. 5:19 [b]John 3:33; Eph. 1:13
31 [a]Rom. 3:14; Col. 3:8, 19 [b]Eph. 4:22 [c]1 Pet. 2:1
32 [1]Some ancient mss. read *us* [a]1 Cor. 13:4; Col. 3:12f.; 1 Pet. 3:8 [b]Matt. 6:14f.; 2 Cor. 2:10

1 [a]Matt. 5:48; Luke 6:36; Eph. 4:32
2 [1]Some ancient mss. read *us* [2]Lit., *for an odor of fragrance* [a]Rom. 14:15; Col. 3:14 [b]John 13:34; Rom. 8:37 [c]John 6:51; Rom. 4:25; Gal. 2:20; Eph. 5:25 [d]Heb. 7:27; 9:14; 10:10, 12 [e]Ex. 29:18, 25; 2 Cor. 2:14
3 [1]Lit., *and all* [2]Or, *holy ones* [a]Col. 3:5

for us, an [d]offering and a sacrifice to
God [2]as a [e]fragrant aroma.
3 But do not let [a]immorality [1]or any
impurity or greed even be named among
you, as is proper among [2]saints;
4 and *there must be no* [a]filthiness and
silly talk, or coarse jesting, which [b]are
not fitting, but rather [c]giving of thanks.
5 For this you know with certainty,
that [a]no [1]immoral or impure person or
covetous man, who is an idolater, has an
inheritance in the kingdom [b]of Christ
and God.
6 [a]Let no one deceive you with
empty words, for because of these things
[b]the wrath of God comes upon [c]the sons
of disobedience.
7 Therefore do not be [a]partakers
with them;
8 for [a]you were formerly [b]darkness,
but now you are light in the Lord; walk
as [c]children of light
9 (for [a]the fruit of the light *consists* in
all [b]goodness and righteousness and
truth),
10 [1a]trying to learn what is pleasing to
the Lord.
11 And [a]do not participate in the
unfruitful [b]deeds of [c]darkness, but instead even [1d]expose them;
12 for it is disgraceful even to speak of
the things which are done by them in
secret.
13 But all things become visible [a]when
they are [1]exposed by the light, for everything that becomes visible is light.
14 For this reason [1]it says,
"[a]Awake, sleeper,
And arise from [b]the dead,
And Christ [c]will shine on you."
15 Therefore [1]be careful how you
[a]walk, not [b]as unwise men, but as wise,
16 [1a]making the most of your time,
because [b]the days are evil.
17 So then do not be foolish, but
[a]understand what the will of the Lord is.
18 And [a]do not get drunk with wine,
[1]for that is [b]dissipation, but be [c]filled
with the Spirit,
19 [a]speaking to [1]one another in
[b]psalms and [c]hymns and spiritual
[d]songs, [e]singing and making melody
with your heart to the Lord;

4 [a]Matt. 12:34; Eph. 4:29; Col. 3:8 [b]Rom. 1:28 [c]Eph. 5:20
5 [1]I.e., one who commits sexual immorality [a]1 Cor. 6:9; Col. 3:5 [b]Col. 1:13
6 [a]Col. 2:8 [b]Rom. 1:18; Col. 3:6 [c]Eph. 2:2
7 [a]Eph. 3:6
8 [a]Eph. 2:2 [b]Acts 26:18; Col. 1:12f. [c]John 12:36; Rom. 13:12
9 [a]Gal. 5:22 [b]Rom. 15:14
10 [1]Lit., *proving what* [a]Rom. 12:2
11 [1]Or, *reprove* [a]1 Cor. 5:9; 2 Cor. 6:14 [b]Rom. 13:12 [c]Acts 26:18; Col. 1:12f. [d]1 Tim. 5:20
13 [1]Or, *reproved* [a]John 3:20f.
14 [1]Or, *He* [a]Is. 26:19; 51:17; 52:1; 60:1; Rom. 13:11 [b]Eph. 2:1 [c]Luke 1:78f.
15 [1]Lit., *look carefully* [a]Eph. 5:2 [b]Col. 4:5
16 [1]Lit., *redeeming the time* [a]Col. 4:5 [b]Gal. 1:4; Eph. 6:13
17 [a]Rom. 12:2; Col. 1:9; 1 Thess. 4:3
18 [1]Lit., *in which is* [a]Prov. 20:1; 23:31f.; Rom. 13:13; 1 Cor. 5:11; 1 Thess. 5:7 [b]Titus 1:6; 1 Pet. 4:4 [c]Luke 1:15
19 [1]Or, *yourselves* [a]Col. 3:16 [b]1 Cor. 14:26 [c]Acts 16:25 [d]Rev. 5:9 [e]1 Cor. 14:15

20 [a]always giving thanks for all things
in the name of our Lord Jesus Christ to
[1b]God, even the Father;
21 [1a]and be subject to one another in
the [2b]fear of Christ.

Marriage Like Christ and the Church

22 [a]Wives, [b]*be subject* to your own
husbands, [c]as to the Lord.
23 For [a]the husband is the head of the
wife, as Christ also is the [b]head of the
church, He Himself [c]*being* the Savior of
the body.
24 But as the church is subject to
Christ, so also the wives *ought to be* to
their husbands in everything.
25 [a]Husbands, love your wives, just as
Christ also loved the church and [b]gave
Himself up for her;
26 [a]that He might sanctify her, having
[b]cleansed her by the [c]washing of water
with [d]the word,
27 that He might [a]present to Himself
the church [1]in all her glory, having no
spot or wrinkle or any such thing; but
that she should be [b]holy and blameless.
28 So husbands ought also to [a]love
their own wives as their own bodies. He
who loves his own wife loves himself;
29 for no one ever hated his own flesh,
but nourishes and cherishes it, just as
Christ also *does* the church,
30 because we are [a]members of His
[b]body.
31 [a]FOR THIS CAUSE A MAN SHALL
LEAVE HIS FATHER AND MOTHER, AND
SHALL CLEAVE TO HIS WIFE; AND THE
TWO SHALL BECOME ONE FLESH.
32 This mystery is great; but I am
speaking with reference to Christ and
the church.
33 Nevertheless let each individual
among you also [a]love his own wife even
as himself; and *let* the wife *see to it* that
she [1b]respect her husband.

Family Relationships

6 [a]CHILDREN, obey your parents in
the Lord, for this is right.
2 [a]HONOR YOUR FATHER AND
MOTHER (which is the first commandment with a promise),
3 THAT IT MAY BE WELL WITH YOU,
AND THAT YOU MAY LIVE LONG ON THE
EARTH.
4 And, [a]fathers, do not provoke your
children to anger; but [b]bring them up in
the discipline and instruction of the
Lord.
5 [a]Slaves, be obedient to those who
are your [1]masters according to the flesh,
with [b]fear and trembling, in the sincerity
of your heart, [c]as to Christ;
6 [a]not [1]by way of eyeservice, as
[b]men-pleasers, but as [c]slaves of Christ,
[d]doing the will of God from the [2]heart.
7 With good will [1]render service, [a]as
to the Lord, and not to men,
8 [a]knowing that [b]whatever good
thing each one does, this he will receive
back from the Lord, [c]whether slave or
free.
9 And, masters, do the same things
to them, and [a]give up threatening, knowing that [b]both their Master and yours is
in heaven, and there is [c]no partiality
with Him.

The Armor of God

10 Finally, [a]be strong in the Lord, and
in [b]the strength of His might.
11 [a]Put on the full armor of God, that
you may be able to stand firm against
the [b]schemes of the devil.
12 For our [a]struggle is not against
[1b]flesh and blood, but [c]against the rulers,
against the powers, against the [d]world
forces of this [e]darkness, against the
[f]spiritual *forces* of wickedness in [g]the
heavenly *places*.
13 Therefore, take up [a]the full armor
of God, that you may be able to [b]resist
in [c]the evil day, and having done everything, to stand firm.
14 Stand firm therefore, [a]HAVING
GIRDED YOUR LOINS WITH TRUTH, and
HAVING [b]PUT ON THE BREASTPLATE OF
RIGHTEOUSNESS,
15 and having [a]shod YOUR FEET WITH
THE PREPARATION OF THE GOSPEL OF
PEACE;
16 [1]in addition to all, taking up the
[a]shield of faith with which you will be
able to extinguish all the [b]flaming mis-
siles of [c]the evil *one*.
17 And take [a]THE HELMET OF SALVA-
TION, and the [b]sword of the Spirit, which
is [c]the word of God.
18 With all [a]prayer and petition
[1b]pray at all times [c]in the Spirit, and
with this in view, [2d]be on the alert with
all [e]perseverance and [f]petition for all the
saints,
19 and [a]*pray* on my behalf, that utterance may be given to me [b]in the opening
of my mouth, to make known with
[c]boldness [d]the mystery of the gospel,
20 for which I am an [a]ambassador [b]in
[1]chains; that [2]in *proclaiming* it I may
speak [c]boldly, [d]as I ought to speak.
21 [a]But that you also may know about
my circumstances, how I am doing,
[b]Tychicus, [c]the beloved brother and

20 [1]Lit., *the God and Father* [a]Rom. 1:8; Eph. 5:4; Col. 3:17 [b]1 Cor. 15:24
21 [1]Lit., *being subject* [2]Or, *reverence* [a]Gal. 5:13; Phil. 2:3; 1 Pet. 5:5 [b]2 Cor. 5:11
22 [a]Eph. 5:22-6:9: *Col. 3:18-4:1* [b]1 Cor. 14:34f.; Titus 2:5; 1 Pet. 3:1 [c]Eph. 6:5
23 [a]1 Cor. 11:3 [b]Eph. 1:22 [c]1 Cor. 6:13
25 [a]Eph. 5:28, 33; Col. 3:19; 1 Pet. 3:7 [b]Eph. 5:2
26 [a]Titus 2:14; Heb. 10:10, 14, 29; 13:12 [b]2 Pet. 1:9 [c]Acts 22:16; 1 Cor. 6:11; Titus 3:5 [d]John 15:3; 17:17; Rom. 10:8f.; Eph. 6:17
27 [1]Lit., *glorious* [a]2 Cor. 4:14; 11:2; Col. 1:22 [b]Eph. 1:4
28 [a]Eph. 5:25, 33; 1 Pet. 3:7
30 [a]1 Cor. 6:15; 12:27 [b]Eph. 1:23
31 [a]Gen. 2:24; Matt. 19:5; Mark 10:7f.
33 [1]Lit., *fear* [a]Eph. 5:25, 28; 1 Pet. 3:7 [b]1 Pet. 3:2, 5f.

1 [a]Prov. 6:20; 23:22; Col. 3:20
2 [a]Ex. 20:12; Deut. 5:16
4 [a]Col. 3:21 [b]Gen. 18:19; Deut. 6:7; 11:19; Ps. 78:4; Prov. 22:6; 2 Tim. 3:15
5 [1]I.e., earthly masters, with fear [a]Col. 3:22; 1 Tim. 6:1; Titus 2:9 [b]1 Cor. 2:3 [c]Eph. 5:22
6 [1]Lit., *according to* [2]Lit., *soul* [a]Col. 3:22 [b]Gal. 1:10 [c]1 Cor. 7:22 [d]Mark 3:35
7 [1]Lit., *rendering* [a]Col. 3:23
8 [a]Col. 3:24 [b]Matt. 16:27; 2 Cor. 5:10; Col. 3:24f. [c]1 Cor. 12:13; Col. 3:11
9 [a]Lev. 25:43 [b]Job 31:13ff.; John 13:13; Col. 4:1 [c]Deut. 10:17; Acts 10:34; Col. 3:25
10 [a]1 Cor. 16:13; 2 Tim. 2:1 [b]Eph. 1:19
11 [a]Rom. 13:12; Eph. 6:13 [b]Eph. 4:14
12 [1]Lit., *blood and flesh* [a]1 Cor. 9:25 [b]Matt. 16:17 [c]Eph. 1:21; 2:2; 3:10 [d]John 12:31 [e]Acts 26:18; Col. 1:13 [f]Eph. 3:10 [g]Eph. 1:3
13 [a]Eph. 6:11 [b]James 4:7 [c]Eph. 5:16
14 [a]Is. 11:5; Luke 12:35; 1 Pet. 1:13 [b]Is. 59:17; Rom. 13:12; Eph. 6:13; 1 Thess. 5:8

15 [a]Is. 52:7; Rom. 10:15
16 [1]Lit., *in all* [a]1 Thess. 5:8 [b]Ps. 7:13; 120:4 [c]Matt. 5:37
17 [a]Is. 59:17 [b]Is. 49:2; Hos. 6:5; Heb. 4:12 [c]Eph. 5:26; Heb. 6:5
18 [1]Lit., *praying* [2]Lit., *being* [a]Phil. 4:6 [b]Luke 18:1; Col. 1:3; 4:2; 1 Thess. 5:17 [c]Rom. 8:26f. [d]Mark 13:33 [e]Acts 1:14 [f]1 Tim. 2:1
19 [a]Col. 4:3; 1 Thess. 5:25 [b]2 Cor. 6:11 [c]2 Cor. 3:12 [d]Eph. 3:3
20 [1]Lit., *a chain* [2]Some ancient mss. read *I may speak it boldly* [a]2 Cor. 5:20; Philem. 9 mg. [b]Acts 21:33; 28:20; Eph. 3:1; Phil. 1:7; Col. 4:3 [c]2 Cor. 3:12 [d]Col. 4:4
21 [a]Eph. 6:21, 22: *Col. 4:7-9* [b]Acts 20:4; 2 Tim. 4:12 [c]Col. 4:7

faithful minister in the Lord, will make
everything known to you.
22 [1]And [a]I have sent him to you for
this very purpose, so that you may know
[2]about us, and that he may [b]comfort
your hearts.
23 [a]Peace be to the brethren, and
[b]love with faith, from God the Father
and the Lord Jesus Christ.
24 Grace be with all those who love
our Lord Jesus Christ [1]with *a love* incorruptible.

22 [1]Lit., *Whom I have sent to you* [2]Lit., *the things about us* [a]Col. 4:8 [b]Col. 2:2; 4:8
23 [a]Rom. 15:33; Gal. 6:16; 2 Thess. 3:16; 1 Pet. 5:14 [b]Gal. 5:6; 1 Thess. 5:8
24 [1]Lit., *in incorruption*

THE EPISTLE OF PAUL TO THE **PHILIPPIANS**

Thanksgiving

1 [a]PAUL and [b]Timothy, [c]bond-ser-
vants of [d]Christ Jesus, to [e]all the
[1f]saints in Christ Jesus who are in [g]Phi-
lippi, including the [h]overseers and [i]dea-
cons:
2 [a]Grace to you and peace from God
our Father and the Lord Jesus Christ.
3 [a]I thank my God in all my remembrance of you,
4 always offering prayer with joy in
[a]my every prayer for you all,
5 in view of your [1a]participation in
the [b]gospel [c]from the first day until now.
6 *For I am* confident of this very
thing, that He who began a good work in
you will perfect it until [a]the day of
Christ Jesus.
7 [1]For [a]it is only right for me to feel
this way about you all, because I [b]have
you in my heart, since both in my [2c]im-
prisonment and in the [d]defense and
confirmation of the [e]gospel, you all are
partakers of grace with me.
8 For [a]God is my witness, how I long
for you all with the [1]affection of [b]Christ
Jesus.
9 And this I pray, that [a]your love
may abound still more and more in [b]real
knowledge and all discernment,
10 so that you may [1a]approve the
things that are excellent, in order to be
sincere and blameless [2]until [b]the day of
Christ;
11 having been filled with the [a]fruit of
righteousness which *comes* through Jesus
Christ, to the glory and praise of God.

The Gospel Is Preached

12 Now I want you to know, brethren,
that my circumstances [a]have turned out
for the greater progress of the [b]gospel,
13 so that my [1a]imprisonment in *the
cause of* Christ has become well known
throughout the whole [2]praetorian guard
and to [b]everyone else,
14 and that most of the [1]brethren,
trusting in the Lord because of my
[2a]imprisonment, have [b]far more courage
to speak the word of God without fear.
15 [a]Some, to be sure, are preaching
Christ even from envy and strife, but
some also from good will;
16 [1]the latter *do it* out of love, knowing that I am appointed for the defense
of the [a]gospel;
17 the former proclaim Christ [a]out of
selfish ambition, [1]rather than from pure
motives, thinking to cause me distress in
my [2b]imprisonment.
18 What then? Only that in every way,
whether in pretense or in truth, Christ is
proclaimed; and in this I rejoice, yes,
and I will rejoice.
19 For I know that this shall turn out
for my [1]deliverance [a]through your [2]pray-
ers and the provision of [b]the Spirit of
Jesus Christ,
20 according to my [a]earnest expectation and [b]hope, that I shall not be put to
shame in anything, but *that* with [c]all
boldness, Christ shall even now, as
always, be [d]exalted in my body,
[e]whether by life or by death.

To Live Is Christ

21 For to me, [a]to live is Christ, and to
die is gain.
22 [1]But if *I am* to live *on* in the flesh,
this *will mean* [a]fruitful labor for me; and
I do not know [2]which to choose.
23 But I am hard-pressed from both
directions, having the [a]desire to depart
and [b]be with Christ, for *that* is very
much better;
24 yet to remain on in the flesh is
more necessary for your sake.
25 And [a]convinced of this, I know
that I shall remain and continue with
you all for your progress and joy in the
faith,
26 so that your [a]proud confidence in
me may abound in Christ Jesus through
my coming to you again.
27 Only conduct yourselves in a manner [a]worthy of the [b]gospel of Christ; so
that whether I come and see you or
remain absent, I may hear of you that
you are [c]standing firm in [d]one spirit,
with one [1]mind [e]striving together for the
faith of the gospel;
28 in no way alarmed by *your* opponents—which is a [a]sign of destruction
for them, but of salvation for you, and
that *too,* from God.

1 [1]Or, *holy ones* [a]2 Cor. 1:1 [b]Acts 16:1 [c]Rom. 1:1; Gal. 1:10 [d]Gal. 3:26 [e]2 Cor. 1:1; Col. 1:2 [f]Acts 9:13 [g]Acts 16:12 [h]Acts 20:28; 1 Tim. 3:1f.; Titus 1:7 [i]1 Tim. 3:8ff.
2 [a]Rom. 1:7
3 [a]Rom. 1:8
4 [a]Rom. 1:9
5 [1]Or, *sharing in the preaching of the gospel* [a]Acts 2:42; Phil. 4:15 [b]Phil. 1:7; 2:22; 4:3, 15 [c]Acts 16:12-40; Phil. 2:12; 4:15
6 [a]1 Cor. 1:8; Phil. 1:10; 2:16
7 [1]Lit., *Just as it is right* [2]Lit., *bonds* [a]2 Pet. 1:13 [b]2 Cor. 7:3 [c]Acts 21:33; Eph. 6:20; Phil. 1:13f., 17 [d]Phil. 1:16 [e]Phil. 1:5, 12, 16, 27; 2:22; 4:3, 15
8 [1]Lit., *inward parts* [a]Rom. 1:9 [b]Gal. 3:26
9 [a]1 Thess. 3:12 [b]Col. 1:9
10 [1]Or, *distinguish between the things which differ* [2]Lit., *for* [a]Rom. 2:18 [b]1 Cor. 1:8; Phil. 1:6; 2:16
11 [a]James 3:18
12 [a]Luke 21:13 [b]Phil. 1:5, 7, 16, 27; 2:22; 4:3, 15
13 [1]Lit., *bonds* [2]Or, *governor's palace* [a]Phil. 1:7; 2 Tim. 2:9 [b]Acts 28:30
14 [1]Or, *brethren in the Lord, trusting because of my bonds* [2]Lit., *bonds* [a]Phil. 1:7; 2 Tim. 2:9 [b]Acts 4:31; 2 Cor. 3:12; 7:4; Phil. 1:20
15 [a]2 Cor. 11:13
16 [1]Some later mss. reverse the order of vv. 16 and 17 [a]Phil. 1:5, 7, 12, 27; 2:22; 4:3, 15
17 [1]Lit., *not sincerely* [2]Lit., *bonds* [a]Rom. 2:8; Phil. 2:3 [b]Phil. 1:7; 2 Tim. 2:9
19 [1]Or, *salvation* [2]Lit., *supplication* [a]2 Cor. 1:11 [b]Acts 16:7
20 [a]Rom. 8:19 [b]Rom. 5:5; 1 Pet. 4:16 [c]Acts 4:31; 2 Cor. 3:12; 7:4; Phil. 1:14 [d]1 Cor. 6:20 [e]Rom. 14:8

21 [a]Gal. 2:20
22 [1]Or, *But if to live in the flesh, this will be fruitful labor for me, then I* [2]Lit., *what I shall choose* [a]Rom. 1:13
23 [a]2 Cor. 5:8; 2 Tim. 4:6 [b]John 12:26
25 [a]Phil. 2:24
26 [a]2 Cor. 5:12; 7:4; Phil. 2:16
27 [1]Lit., *soul* [a]Eph. 4:1 [b]Phil. 1:5 [c]1 Cor. 16:13; Phil. 4:1 [d]Acts 4:32 [e]Jude 3
28 [a]2 Thess. 1:5

29 For to you [a]it has been granted for
Christ's sake, not only to believe in Him,
but also to [b]suffer for His sake,
30 experiencing the same [a]conflict
which [b]you saw in me, and now hear *to*
be in me.

Be Like Christ

2 IF therefore there is any encouragement in Christ, if there is any consolation of love, if there is any [a]fellowship
of the Spirit, if any [1b]affection and
compassion,
2 [a]make my joy complete [1]by [b]being
of the same mind, maintaining the same
love, united in spirit, intent on one
purpose.
3 Do nothing from [1a]selfishness or
[b]empty conceit, but with humility of
mind let [c]each of you regard one another
as more important than himself;
4 [a]do not *merely* look out for your
own personal interests, but also for the
interests of others.
5 [a]Have this attitude [1]in yourselves
which was also in [b]Christ Jesus,
6 who, although He [a]existed in the
[b]form of God, [c]did not regard equality
with God a thing to be grasped,
7 but [1a]emptied Himself, taking the
form of a [b]bond-servant, *and* [c]being
made in the likeness of men.
8 And being found in appearance as
a man, [a]He humbled Himself by becoming [b]obedient to the point of death, even
[c]death [1]on a cross.
9 [a]Therefore also God [b]highly exalted Him, and bestowed on Him [c]the
name which is above every name,
10 that at the name of Jesus [a]EVERY
KNEE SHOULD BOW, of [b]those who are in
heaven, and on earth, and under the
earth,
11 and that every tongue should confess that Jesus Christ is [a]Lord, to the
glory of God the Father.
12 So then, my beloved, [a]just as you
have always obeyed, not as in my presence only, but now much more in my
absence, work out your [b]salvation with
[c]fear and trembling;
13 for it is [a]God who is at work in
you, both to will and to work [b]for *His*
good pleasure.
14 Do all things without [a]grumbling
or disputing;
15 that you may [1]prove yourselves to
be [a]blameless and innocent, [b]children of
God above reproach in the midst of a
[c]crooked and perverse generation,
among whom you [2d]appear as [3]lights in
the world,
16 holding [1]fast the word of life, so
that in [a]the day of Christ I may have
cause to glory because I did not [b]run in
vain nor [c]toil in vain.
17 But even if I am being [a]poured out
as a drink offering upon [b]the sacrifice
and service of your faith, I rejoice and
share my joy with you all.

29 [a]Matt. 5:11, 12 [b]Acts 14:22
30 [a]Col. 1:29; 2:1; 1 Thess. 2:2; 1 Tim. 6:12; 2 Tim. 4:7; Heb. 10:32; 12:1 [b]Acts 16:19-40; Phil. 1:13

1 [1]Lit., *inward parts* [a]2 Cor. 13:14 [b]Col. 3:12
2 [1]Lit., *that you be* [a]John 3:29 [b]Rom. 12:16; Phil. 4:2
3 [1]Or, *contentiousness* [a]Rom. 2:8; Phil. 1:17 [b]Gal. 5:26 [c]Rom. 12:10; Eph. 5:21
4 [a]Rom. 15:1f.
5 [1]Or, *among* [a]Matt. 11:29; Rom. 15:3 [b]Phil. 1:1
6 [a]John 1:1 [b]2 Cor. 4:4 [c]John 5:18; 10:33; 14:28
7 [1]I.e., laid aside His privileges [a]2 Cor. 8:9 [b]Matt. 20:28 [c]John 1:14; Rom. 8:3; Gal. 4:4; Heb. 2:17
8 [1]Lit., *of* [a]2 Cor. 8:9 [b]Matt. 26:39; John 10:18; Rom. 5:19; Heb. 5:8 [c]Heb. 12:2
9 [a]Heb. 1:9 [b]Matt. 28:18; Acts 2:33; Heb. 2:9 [c]Eph. 1:21
10 [a]Is. 45:23; Rom. 14:11 [b]Eph. 1:10
11 [a]John 13:13; Rom. 10:9; 14:9
12 [a]Phil. 1:5, 6; 4:15 [b]Heb. 5:9 [c]2 Cor. 7:15
13 [a]Rom. 12:3; 1 Cor. 12:6; 15:10; Heb. 13:21 [b]Eph. 1:5
14 [a]1 Cor. 10:10; 1 Pet. 4:9
15 [1]Or, *become* [2]Or, *shine* [3]Or, *luminaries, stars* [a]Luke 1:6; Phil. 3:6 [b]Matt. 5:45; Eph. 5:1 [c]Deut. 32:5; Acts 2:40 [d]Matt. 5:14-16
16 [1]Or, *forth* [a]Phil. 1:6 [b]Gal. 2:2 [c]Is. 49:4; Gal. 4:11; 1 Thess. 3:5
17 [a]2 Cor. 12:15; 2 Tim. 4:6 [b]Num. 28:6, 7; Rom. 15:16
19 [1]Or, *trusting in* [a]Phil. 2:23 [b]Phil. 1:1
20 [a]1 Cor. 16:10; 2 Tim. 3:10
21 [a]1 Cor. 10:24; 13:5; Phil. 2:4
22 [a]Rom. 5:4; Acts 16:2 [b]Acts 16:3; 1 Cor. 16:10; 2 Tim. 3:10 [c]1 Cor. 4:17
23 [a]Phil. 2:19
24 [a]Phil. 1:25
25 [1]Lit., *apostle* [a]Phil. 4:18 [b]Rom. 16:3, 9, 21; Phil. 4:3; Philem. 1, 24 [c]Philem. 2 [d]John 13:16; 2 Cor. 8:23 [e]Phil. 4:18
26 [1]Some ancient mss. read *to see you all*
29 [a]Rom. 16:2 [b]1 Cor. 16:18

18 And you too, *I urge you,* rejoice in
the same way and share your joy with
me.

Timothy and Epaphroditus

19 But I hope [1]in the Lord Jesus to
[a]send [b]Timothy to you shortly, so that I
also may be encouraged when I learn of
your condition.
20 For I have no one *else* [a]of kindred
spirit who will genuinely be concerned
for your welfare.
21 For they all [a]seek after their own
interests, not those of Christ Jesus.
22 But you know [a]of his proven worth
that [b]he served with me in the further-
ance of the gospel [c]like a child *serving*
his father.
23 [a]Therefore I hope to send him
immediately, as soon as I see how things
go with me;
24 and [a]I trust in the Lord that I
myself also shall be coming shortly.
25 But I thought it necessary to send
to you [a]Epaphroditus, my brother and
[b]fellow worker and [c]fellow soldier, who
is also your [1d]messenger and [e]minister to
my need;
26 because he was longing [1]for you all
and was distressed because you had
heard that he was sick.
27 For indeed he was sick to the point
of death, but God had mercy on him,
and not on him only but also on me, lest
I should have sorrow upon sorrow.
28 Therefore I have sent him all the
more eagerly in order that when you see
him again you may rejoice and I may be
less concerned *about you.*
29 Therefore [a]receive him in the Lord
with all joy, and [b]hold men like him in
high regard;
30 because he came close to death [a]for
the work of Christ, risking his life to
[b]complete [1]what was deficient in your
service to me.

The Goal of Life

3 FINALLY, my brethren, [a]rejoice in
the Lord. To write the same things
again is no trouble to me, and it is a
safeguard for you.
2 Beware of the [a]dogs, beware of the
[b]evil workers, beware of the [1]false circumcision;
3 for [a]we are the *true* [1]circumcision,
who [b]worship in the Spirit of God and
[c]glory in [d]Christ Jesus and put no confidence in the flesh,
4 although [a]I myself might have
confidence even in the flesh. If anyone
else has a mind to put confidence in the
flesh, I far more:

30 [1]Lit., *your deficiency of service* [a]Acts 20:24 [b]1 Cor. 16:17; Phil. 4:10

1 [a]Phil. 2:18; 4:4
2 [1]Lit., *mutilation;* Gr., katatome [a]Ps. 22:16, 20; Gal. 5:15; Rev. 22:15 [b]2 Cor. 11:13
3 [1]Gr., peritomé [a]Rom. 2:29; 9:6; Gal. 6:15 [b]Gal. 5:25 [c]Rom. 15:17; Gal. 6:14 [d]Rom. 8:39; Phil. 1:1; 3:12
4 [a]2 Cor. 5:16; 11:18

5 [a]circumcised the eighth day, of the
[b]nation of Israel, of the [c]tribe of Benjamin, a [b]Hebrew of Hebrews; as to the
Law, [d]a Pharisee;
6 as to zeal, [a]a persecutor of the
church; as to the [b]righteousness which is
in the Law, found [c]blameless.
7 But [a]whatever things were gain to
me, those things I have counted as loss
for the sake of Christ.
8 More than that, I count all things
to be loss in view of the surpassing value
of [1a]knowing [b]Christ Jesus my Lord, for
whom I have suffered the loss of all
things, and count them but rubbish in
order that I may gain Christ,
9 and may be found in Him, not
having [a]a righteousness of my own derived from *the* Law, but that which is
through faith in Christ, [b]the righteousness which *comes* from God on the basis
of faith,
10 that I may [a]know Him, and [b]the
power of His resurrection and [1c]the
fellowship of His sufferings, being [d]con-
formed to His death;
11 [1]in order that I may [a]attain to the
resurrection from the dead.
12 Not that I have already [a]obtained
it, or have already [b]become perfect, but I
press on [1]in order that I may [c]lay hold of
that [2]for which also I [d]was laid hold of
by [e]Christ Jesus.
13 Brethren, I do not regard myself as
having laid hold of *it* yet; but one thing *I*
do: [a]forgetting what *lies* behind and
reaching forward to what *lies* ahead,
14 I [a]press on toward the goal for the
prize of the [b]upward call of God in
[c]Christ Jesus.
15 Let us therefore, as many as are
[1a]perfect, have this attitude; and if in
anything you have a [b]different attitude,
[c]God will reveal that also to you;
16 however, let us keep [1a]living by
that same *standard* to which we have
attained.
17 Brethren, [a]join in following my
example, and observe those who walk
according to the [b]pattern you have in us.
18 For [a]many walk, of whom I often
told you, and now tell you even [b]weep-
ing, *that they are* enemies of [c]the cross of
Christ,
19 whose end is destruction, whose
god is *their* [1a]appetite, and *whose* [b]glory
is in their shame, who [c]set their minds
on earthly things.
20 For [a]our [1]citizenship is in heaven,
from which also we eagerly [b]wait for a
Savior, the Lord Jesus Christ;
21 who will [a]transform [1]the body of
our humble state into [b]conformity with
[2]the [c]body of His glory, [d]by the exertion
of the power that He has even to [e]subject
all things to Himself.

Think of Excellence

4 THEREFORE, my beloved breth-
ren [1]whom I [a]long *to see*, my joy and
crown, so [b]stand firm in the Lord, my
beloved.
2 I urge Euodia and I urge Syntyche
to [1a]live in harmony in the Lord.
3 Indeed, true comrade, I ask you
also to help these women who have
shared my struggle in *the cause of* the
gospel, together with Clement also, and
the rest of my [a]fellow workers, whose
[b]names are in the book of life.
4 [a]Rejoice in the Lord always; again
I will say, rejoice!
5 Let your forbearing *spirit* be known
to all men. [a]The Lord is [1]near.
6 [a]Be anxious for nothing, but in
everything by [b]prayer and supplication
with thanksgiving let your requests be
made known to God.
7 And [a]the peace of God, which
surpasses all [1]comprehension, shall
[b]guard your hearts and your [c]minds in
[d]Christ Jesus.
8 Finally, brethren, [a]whatever is true,
whatever is honorable, whatever is
right, whatever is pure, whatever is
[1]lovely, whatever is [2]of good repute, if
there is any excellence and if anything
worthy of praise, [3]let your mind dwell
on these things.
9 The things you have learned and
received and heard and seen [a]in me,
practice these things; and [b]the God of
peace shall be with you.

God's Provisions

10 But I rejoiced in the Lord greatly,
that now at last [a]you have revived your
concern for me; indeed, you were concerned *before,* but you lacked opportunity.
11 Not that I speak [1]from want; for I
have learned to be [2a]content in whatever
circumstances I am.
12 I know how to get along with
humble means, and I also know how to
live in prosperity; in any and every
circumstance I have learned the secret of
being filled and going [a]hungry, both of
having abundance and [b]suffering need.
13 I can do all things [1]through Him
who [a]strengthens me.
14 Nevertheless, you have done well
to [a]share *with me* in my affliction.
15 And you yourselves also know,
Philippians, that at the [1a]first preaching
of the gospel, after I departed from
[b]Macedonia, no church [c]shared with me
in the matter of giving and receiving but
you alone;
16 for even in [a]Thessalonica you sent
a gift more than once for my needs.

5 [a]Luke 1:59 [b]Rom. 11:1; 2 Cor. 11:22 [c]Rom. 11:1 [d]Acts 22:3; 23:6; 26:5
6 [a]Acts 8:3; 22:4, 5; 26:9-11 [b]Phil. 3:9 [c]Phil. 2:15
7 [a]Luke 14:33
8 [1]Lit., *the knowledge of* [a]Jer. 9:23f.; John 17:3; Eph. 4:13; Phil. 3:10; 2 Pet. 1:3 [b]Rom. 8:39; Phil. 1:1; 3:12
9 [a]Rom. 10:5; Phil. 3:6 [b]Rom. 9:30; 1 Cor. 1:30
10 [1]Or, *participation in* [a]Jer. 9:23f.; John 17:3; Eph. 4:13; Phil. 3:8; 2 Pet. 1:13 [b]Rom. 6:5 [c]Rom. 8:17 [d]Rom. 6:5; 8:36; Gal. 6:17
11 [1]Lit., *if somehow* [a]Acts 26:7; 1 Cor. 15:23; Rev. 20:5f.
12 [1]Lit., *if I may even* [2]Or, *because also* [a]1 Cor. 9:24f.; 1 Tim. 6:12, 19 [b]1 Cor. 13:10 [c]1 Tim. 6:12, 19 [d]Acts 9:5f. [e]Rom. 8:39; Phil. 1:1; 3:3, 8
13 [a]Luke 9:62
14 [a]1 Cor. 9:24; Heb. 6:1 [b]Rom. 8:28; 11:29; 2 Tim. 1:9 [c]Phil. 3:3
15 [1]Or, *mature* [a]Matt. 5:48; 1 Cor. 2:6 [b]Gal. 5:10 [c]John 6:45; Eph. 1:17; 1 Thess. 4:9
16 [1]Lit., *following in line* [a]Gal. 6:16
17 [a]1 Cor. 4:16; 11:1; Phil. 4:9 [b]1 Pet. 5:3
18 [a]2 Cor. 11:13 [b]Acts 20:31 [c]Gal. 6:14
19 [1]Lit., *belly* [a]Rom. 16:18; Titus 1:12 [b]Rom. 6:21; Jude 13 [c]Rom. 8:5f.; Col. 3:2
20 [1]Lit., *common-wealth* [a]Eph. 2:19; Phil. 1:27; Col. 3:1; Heb. 12:22 [b]1 Cor. 1:7
21 [1]Or, *our lowly body* [2]Or, *His glorious body* [a]1 Cor. 15:43-53 [b]Rom. 8:29; Col. 3:4 [c]1 Cor. 15:43, 49 [d]Eph. 1:19 [e]1 Cor. 15:28

1 [1]Lit., *and longed for* [a]Phil. 1:8 [b]1 Cor. 16:13; Phil. 1:27
2 [1]Or, *be of the same mind* [a]Phil. 2:2
3 [a]Phil. 2:25 [b]Luke 10:20
4 [a]Phil. 3:1
5 [1]Or, *at hand* [a]1 Cor. 16:22 mg.; Heb. 10:37; James 5:8f.
6 [a]Matt. 6:25 [b]Eph. 6:18; 1 Tim. 2:1; 5:5

7 [1]Lit., *mind* [a]Is. 26:3; John 14:27; Phil. 4:9; Col. 3:15 [b]1 Pet. 1:5 [c]2 Cor. 10:5 [d]Phil. 1:1; 4:19, 21
8 [1]Or, *lovable and gracious* [2]Or, *attractive* [3]Lit., *ponder these things* [a]Rom. 14:18; 1 Pet. 2:12
9 [a]Phil. 3:17 [b]Rom. 15:33
10 [a]2 Cor. 11:9; Phil. 2:30
11 [1]Lit., *according to* [2]Or, *self-sufficient* [a]2 Cor. 9:8; 1 Tim. 6:6, 8; Heb. 13:5
12 [a]1 Cor. 4:11 [b]2 Cor. 11:9
13 [1]Lit., *in* [a]2 Cor. 12:9; Eph. 3:16; Col. 1:11
14 [a]Heb. 10:33; Rev. 1:9
15 [1]Lit., *beginning of* [a]Phil. 1:5 [b]Rom. 15:26 [c]2 Cor. 11:9
16 [a]Acts 17:1; 1 Thess. 2:9

17 [a]Not that I seek the gift itself, but I seek for the [1]profit which increases to your account.

18 But I have received everything in full, and have an abundance; I am [1]amply supplied, having received from [a]Epaphroditus [2]what you have sent, [3b]a fragrant aroma, an acceptable sacrifice, well-pleasing to God.

19 And [a]my God shall supply [1]all your needs according to His [b]riches in glory in Christ Jesus.

17 [1]Lit., *fruit*
[a]1 Cor. 9:11f.; 2 Cor. 9:5
18 [1]Lit., *made full* [2]Lit., *the things from you* [3]Lit., *an odor of fragrance*
[a]Phil. 2:25 [b]Ex. 29:18; 2 Cor. 2:14; Eph. 5:2
19 [1]Or, *every need of yours*
[a]2 Cor. 9:8 [b]Rom. 2:4
20 [1]Lit., *to the ages of the ages*
[a]Gal. 1:4 [b]Rom. 11:36

20 Now to [a]our God and Father [b]*be* the glory [1]forever and ever. Amen.

21 Greet every [1]saint in Christ Jesus. [a]The brethren who are with me greet you.

22 [a]All the [1b]saints greet you, especially those of Caesar's household.

23 [a]The grace of the Lord Jesus Christ [b]be with your spirit.

21 [1]Or, *holy one* [a]Gal. 1:2
22 [1]V. 21, note 1 [a]2 Cor. 13:13 [b]Acts 9:13
23 [a]Rom. 16:20 [b]2 Tim. 4:22

THE EPISTLE OF PAUL TO THE COLOSSIANS

Thankfulness for Spiritual Attainments

1 [a]PAUL, [b]an apostle of Jesus Christ [1c]by the will of God, and [d]Timothy [2]our brother,

2 to the [1a]saints and faithful brethren in Christ *who are* at Colossae: [b]Grace to you and peace from God our Father.

3 [a]We give thanks to God, [b]the Father of our Lord Jesus Christ, praying always for you,

4 [a]since we heard of your faith in Christ Jesus and the [b]love which you have [1]for [c]all the [2]saints;

5 because of the [a]hope [b]laid up for you in [1]heaven, of which you previously [c]heard in the word of truth, [2]the gospel,

6 which has come to you, just as [1a]in all the world also it is constantly bearing [b]fruit and [2]increasing, even as *it has been doing* in you also since the day you [c]heard *of it* and [3]understood the grace of God in truth;

7 just as you learned *it* from [a]Epaphras, our [b]beloved fellow bond-servant, who is a faithful servant of Christ on [1]our behalf,

8 and he also informed us of your [a]love in the Spirit.

9 For this reason also, [a]since the day we heard *of it*, [b]we have not ceased to pray for you and to ask that you may be filled with the [1c]knowledge of His will in all spiritual [d]wisdom and understanding,

10 so that you may [a]walk in a manner worthy of the Lord, [1b]to please *Him* in all respects, [c]bearing fruit in every good work and [2]increasing in the [3]knowledge of God;

11 [a]strengthened with all power, according to [1]His glorious might, [2]for the attaining of all steadfastness and [3]patience; [b]joyously

12 giving thanks to [a]the Father, who has qualified us [1]to share in [b]the inheritance of the [2]saints in [c]light.

The Incomparable Christ

13 For He delivered us from the [1a]domain of darkness, and transferred us to the kingdom of [2b]His beloved Son,

1 [1]Lit., *through* [2]Lit., *the*
[a]Phil. 1:1 [b]2 Cor. 1:1 [c]1 Cor. 1:1 [d]2 Cor. 1:1; 1 Thess. 3:2
2 [1]Or, *holy ones*
[a]Acts 9:13 [b]Rom. 1:7
3 [a]Rom. 1:8 [b]Rom. 15:6; 2 Cor. 1:3
4 [1]Or, *toward* [2]Or, *holy ones*
[a]Eph. 1:15 [b]Gal. 5:6 [c]Eph. 6:18
5 [1]Lit., *the heavens* [2]Or, *of the gospel*
[a]Acts 23:6 [b]2 Tim. 4:8 [c]Eph. 1:13
6 [1]Or, *it is in the world* [2]Or, *spreading abroad* [3]Or, *came really to know*
[a]Rom. 10:18 [b]Rom. 1:13 [c]Eph. 4:21
7 [1]Some later mss. read *your*
[a]Col. 4:12 [b]Col. 4:7
8 [a]Rom. 15:30
9 [1]Or, *real knowledge*
[a]Col. 1:4 [b]Eph. 1:16 [c]Phil. 1:9 [d]Eph. 1:17
10 [1]Lit., *unto all pleasing* [2]Or, *growing by the knowledge* [3]Or, *real knowledge*
[a]Eph. 4:1 [b]Eph. 5:10 [c]Rom. 1:13
11 [1]Lit., *the might of His glory* [2]Lit., *unto all* [3]Or, *patience with joy*
[a]1 Cor. 16:13 [b]Eph. 4:2
12 [1]Lit., *unto the portion of* [2]Or, *holy ones*
[a]Eph. 2:18 [b]Acts 20:32 [c]Acts 26:18
13 [1]Lit., *authority* [2]Lit., *the Son of His love*
[a]Eph. 6:12 [b]Eph. 1:6
14 [a]Rom. 3:24
15 [a]2 Cor. 4:4 [b]John 1:18; [c]Rom. 8:29
16 [1]Or, *in* [2]Or, *through*
[a]Eph. 1:10 [b]Eph. 1:20f.; Col. 2:15 [c]John 1:3 Rom. 11:36; 1 Cor. 8:6

14 [a]in whom we have redemption, the forgiveness of sins.

15 And He is the [a]image of the [b]invisible God, the [c]first-born of all creation.

16 For [1a]by Him all things were created, [a]*both* in the heavens and on earth, visible and invisible, whether [b]thrones or dominions or rulers or authorities—[c]all things have been created [2]by Him and for Him.

17 And He [1a]is before all things, and in Him all things [2]hold together.

18 He is also [a]head of [b]the body, the church; and He is [c]the beginning, [d]the first-born from the dead; so that He Himself might come to have first place in everything.

19 For [1]it was [a]the *Father's* good pleasure for all [b]the [2]fulness to dwell in Him,

20 and through Him to [a]reconcile all things to Himself, having made [b]peace through [c]the blood of His cross; through Him, *I say*, [d]whether things on earth or things in [1]heaven.

21 And although you were [a]formerly alienated and hostile in mind, *engaged* in evil deeds,

22 yet He has now [a]reconciled you in His fleshly [b]body through death, in order to [c]present you before Him [d]holy and blameless and beyond reproach—

23 if indeed you continue in [1]the faith firmly [a]established and steadfast, and not moved away from the [b]hope of the gospel that you have heard, which was

17 [1]Or, *has existed prior to* [2]Or, *endure* [a]John 1:1; 8:58
18 [a]Eph. 1:22 [b]Eph. 1:23; Col. 1:24; 2:19 [c]Rev. 3:14 [d]Acts 26:23
19 [1]Or, *all the fulness was pleased to dwell* [2]I.e., fulness of deity [a]Eph. 1:5 [b]John 1:16
20 [1]Lit., *the heavens* [a]2 Cor. 5:18; Eph. 2:16 [b]Rom. 5:1; Eph. 2:14 [c]Eph. 2:13 [d]Col. 1:16
21 [a]Rom. 5:10; Eph. 2:3, 12
22 [a]2 Cor. 5:18; Eph. 2:16 [b]Rom. 7:4 [c]Eph. 5:27; Col. 1:28 [d]Eph. 1:4
23 [1]Or omit, *the* [a]Eph. 3:17; Col. 2:7 [b]Col. 1:5

proclaimed [c]in all creation under
heaven, [d]and of which I, Paul, [2]was
made a [3e]minister.
24 [a]Now I rejoice in my sufferings for
your sake, and in my flesh [b]I [1]do my
share on behalf of [c]His body (which is
the church) in filling up that which is
lacking [2]in Christ's afflictions.
25 [a]Of *this church* I [1]was made a
minister according to the [b]stewardship
from God bestowed on me for your
benefit, that I might [2]fully carry out the
preaching of the word of God,
26 *that is,* [a]the mystery which has been
hidden from the *past* ages and generations; but has now been manifested to
His [1]saints,
27 to whom [a]God willed to make
known what is [b]the riches of the glory of
this mystery among the Gentiles, which
is [c]Christ in you, the [d]hope of glory.
28 And we proclaim Him, [a]admonish-
ing every man and teaching every man
[1]with all [b]wisdom, that we may [c]present
every man [2d]complete in Christ.
29 And for this purpose also I [a]labor,
[b]striving [c]according to His [1]power,
which [2]mightily works within me.

You Are Built Up in Christ

2 FOR I want you to know how great
a [a]struggle I have on your behalf,
and for those who are at [b]Laodicea, and
for all those who have not [1]personally
seen my face,
2 that their [a]hearts may be encouraged, having been [b]knit together in love,
and *attaining* to all [c]the wealth [1]that
comes from the full assurance of understanding, *resulting* in a [d]true knowledge
of [e]God's mystery, *that is,* Christ *Himself,*
3 in whom are hidden all [a]the treasures of wisdom and knowledge.
4 [a]I say this in order that no one may
delude you with [b]persuasive argument.
5 For even though I am [a]absent in
body, nevertheless I am with you in
spirit, rejoicing [1]to see [2]your [b]good
discipline and the [c]stability of your faith
in Christ.
6 As you therefore have received
[a]Christ Jesus the Lord, *so* [1b]walk in Him,
7 having been firmly [a]rooted *and now*
being [b]built up in Him and [c]established
[1]in your faith, just as you [d]were instructed, *and* overflowing [2]with gratitude.
8 [a]See to it that no one takes you
captive through [b]philosophy and empty
deception, according to the tradition of
men, according to the [c]elementary principles of the world, [1]rather than according to Christ.
9 For in Him all the [a]fulness of Deity
dwells in bodily form,
10 and in Him you have been [a]made
[1]complete, and [b]He is the head [2]over all
[c]rule and authority;
11 and in Him [a]you were also circumcised with a circumcision made without
hands, in the removal of [b]the body of the
flesh by the circumcision of Christ;
12 having been [a]buried with Him in
baptism, in which you were also [b]raised
up with Him through faith in the working of God, who [c]raised Him from the
dead.
13 And when you were [a]dead [1]in your
transgressions and the uncircumcision of
your flesh, He [b]made you alive together
with Him, having forgiven us all our
transgressions,
14 having canceled out [a]the certificate
of debt consisting of decrees against us
and which was hostile to us; and [b]He has
taken it out of the way, having nailed it
to the cross.
15 When He had [1a]disarmed the [b]rul-
ers and authorities, He [c]made a public
display of them, having [d]triumphed over
them through [2]Him.
16 Therefore let no one [1a]act as your
judge in regard to [b]food or [b]drink or in
respect to a [c]festival or a [d]new moon or a
[e]Sabbath [2]day—
17 things which are [a]a *mere* shadow of
what is to come; but the [1]substance
[2]belongs to Christ.
18 Let no one keep [1a]defrauding you
of your prize by [b]delighting in [2]self-
abasement and the worship of the angels, taking his stand on *visions* he has
seen, [c]inflated without cause by his
[d]fleshly mind,
19 and not holding fast to [a]the head,
from whom [b]the entire body, being
supplied and held together by the joints
and [1]ligaments, grows with a growth
[2]which is from God.
20 [a]If you have died with Christ [1]to
the [b]elementary principles of the world,
[c]why, as if you were living in the world,
do you submit yourself to [d]decrees, such
as,
21 "Do not handle, do not taste, do not
touch!"
22 (which all *refer* [a]*to* things destined
to perish [1]with the using)—in accordance with the [b]commandments and
teachings of men?
23 These are matters which have, to be
sure, the appearance of wisdom in [1a]self-
made religion and self-abasement and
[b]severe treatment of the body, *but are* of
no value against [c]fleshly indulgence.

23 [2]Lit., *became* [3]Or, *servant* [c]Mark 16:15; Acts 2:5; Col. 1:6 [d]Eph. 3:7; Col. 1:25 [e]1 Cor. 3:5
24 [1]Or, *representatively . . . fill up* [2]Lit., *of* [a]Rom. 8:17; 2 Cor. 1:5; 12:15; Phil. 2:17 [b]2 Tim. 1:8; 2:10 [c]Col. 1:18
25 [1]Lit., *became* [2]Lit., *make full the word of God* [a]Col. 1:23 [b]Eph. 3:2
26 [1]Or, *holy ones* [a]Rom. 16:25f.; Eph. 3:3f.; Col. 2:2; 4:3
27 [a]Matt. 13:11 [b]Eph. 1:7, 18; 3:16 [c]Rom. 8:10 [d]1 Tim. 1:1
28 [1]Lit., *in* [2]Or, *perfect* [a]Acts 20:31; Col. 3:16 [b]1 Cor. 2:6f.; Col. 2:3 [c]Col. 1:22 [d]Matt. 5:48; Eph. 4:13
29 [1]Lit., *working* [2]Lit., *in power* [a]1 Cor. 15:10 [b]Col. 2:1; 4:12 [c]Eph. 1:19; Col. 2:12

1 [1]Lit., *in the flesh* [a]Col. 1:29; 4:12 [b]Col. 4:13, 15f.; Rev. 1:11
2 [1]Lit., *of the full assurance* [a]1 Cor. 14:31; Eph. 6:22; Col. 4:8 [b]Col. 2:19 [c]Eph. 1:7, 18; 3:16 [d]Matt. 13:11 [e]Rom. 16:25f.; Eph. 3:3f.; Col. 1:26; 4:3
3 [a]Is. 11:2; Rom. 11:33
4 [a]Eph. 4:17 [b]Rom. 16:18
5 [1]Lit., *and seeing* [2]Or, *your ordered array* [a]1 Cor. 5:3 [b]1 Cor. 14:40 [c]1 Pet. 5:9
6 [1]Or, *lead your life* [a]Gal. 3:26 [b]Col. 1:10
7 [1]Or, *by* [2]Some mss. read *in it with* [a]Eph. 3:17 [b]1 Cor. 3:9; Eph. 2:20 [c]1 Cor. 1:8 [d]Eph. 4:21
8 [1]Lit., *and not* [a]1 Cor. 8:9; 10:12; Gal. 5:15; Heb. 3:12 [b]Eph. 5:6; Col. 2:23; 1 Tim. 6:20 [c]Gal. 4:3; Col. 2:20
9 [a]2 Cor. 5:19; Col. 1:19
10 [1]Or, *full* [2]Lit., *of* [a]Eph. 3:19 [b]Eph. 1:21f. [c]1 Cor. 15:24; Eph. 3:10; Col. 2:15
11 [a]Rom. 2:29; Eph. 2:11 [b]Rom. 6:6; 7:24; Gal. 5:24; Col. 3:5
12 [a]Rom. 6:4f. [b]Rom. 6:5; Eph. 2:6; Col. 2:13; 3:1 [c]Acts 2:24
13 [1]Or, *by reason of* [a]Eph. 2:1 [b]Eph. 2:5; Col. 2:12
14 [a]Eph. 2:15; Col. 2:20 [b]1 Pet. 2:24

15 [1]Or, *divested Himself of* [2]Or, *it;* i.e., the cross [a]Eph. 4:8 [b]John 12:31; 1 Cor. 15:24; Eph. 3:10; Col. 2:10 [c]Eph. 4:8 [d]2 Cor. 2:14
16 [1]Lit., *judge you* [2]Or, *days* [a]Rom. 14:3 [b]Mark 7:19; Rom. 14:17; Heb. 9:10 [c]Lev. 23:2; Rom. 14:5 [d]1 Chr. 23:31; 2 Chr. 31:3; Neh. 10:33 [e]Mark 2:27f.; Gal. 4:10
17 [1]Lit., *body* [2]Lit., *of Christ* [a]Heb. 8:5; 10:1
18 [1]Or, *giving judgment against you* [2]Or, *humility* [a]1 Cor. 9:24; Phil. 3:14 [b]Col. 2:23 [c]1 Cor. 4:6 [d]Rom. 8:7
19 [1]Lit., *bonds* [2]Lit., *of God* [a]Eph. 1:22 [b]Eph. 1:23; 4:16
20 [1]Lit., *from* [a]Rom. 6:2 [b]Col. 2:8 [c]Gal. 4:9 [d]Col. 2:14, 16
22 [1]Or, *by being consumed* [a]1 Cor. 6:13 [b]Is. 29:13; Matt. 15:9; Titus 1:14
23 [1]Or, *delight in religiousness* [a]Col. 2:18 [b]1 Tim. 4:3 [c]Rom. 13:14; 1 Tim. 4:8

Put On the New Self

3 IF then you have been [a]raised up
with Christ, keep seeking the things
above, where Christ is, [b]seated at the
right hand of God.
2 [1a]Set your mind on the things
above, not on the things that are on
earth.
3 For you have [a]died and your life is
hidden with Christ in God.
4 When Christ, [a]who is our life, is
revealed, [b]then you also will be revealed
with Him in glory.
5 [a]Therefore [1]consider [b]the members
of your earthly body as dead to [2c]immo-
rality, impurity, passion, evil desire, and
greed, which [3]amounts to idolatry.
6 For it is on account of these things
that [a]the wrath of God will come[1],
7 and [a]in them you also once walked,
when you were living in them.
8 But now you also, [a]put them all
aside: [b]anger, wrath, malice, slander,
and [c]abusive speech from your mouth.
9 [1a]Do not lie to one another, since
you [b]laid aside the old [2]self with its *evil*
practices,
10 and have [a]put on the new [1]self who
is being [2b]renewed to a true knowledge
[c]according to the image of the One who
[d]created him
11 —*a renewal* in which [a]there is no
distinction between Greek and Jew, [b]cir-
cumcised and uncircumcised, [c]barbar-
ian, Scythian, [d]slave and freeman, but
[e]Christ is all, and in all.
12 And so, as those who have been
[a]chosen of God, holy and beloved, [b]put
on a [c]heart of compassion, kindness,
[d]humility, gentleness and [1e]patience;
13 [a]bearing with one another, and
[b]forgiving each other, whoever has a
complaint against anyone; [b]just as the
Lord forgave you, so also should you.
14 And beyond all these things *put on*
love, which is [1a]the perfect bond of
[b]unity.
15 And let [a]the peace of Christ [1]rule
in your hearts, to which [2]indeed you
were called in [b]one body; and [3]be thankful.
16 Let [a]the word of [1]Christ richly
dwell within you, [2]with all wisdom
[b]teaching and admonishing one another
[c]with psalms *and* hymns *and* spiritual
songs, [d]singing [3]with thankfulness in
your hearts to God.
17 And [a]whatever you do in word or
deed, *do* all in the name of the Lord
Jesus, [b]giving thanks through Him to
God the Father.

Family Relations

18 [a]Wives, [b]be subject to your husbands, as is fitting in the Lord.
19 [a]Husbands, love your wives, and
do not be embittered against them.
20 [a]Children, be obedient to your
parents in all things, for this is well-
pleasing [1]to the Lord.
21 [a]Fathers, do not [1]exasperate your
children, that they may not lose heart.
22 [a]Slaves, in all things obey those
who are your masters [1]on earth, [b]not
with [2]external service, as those who
merely please men, but with sincerity of
heart, fearing the Lord.
23 Whatever you do, do your work
[1]heartily, [a]as for the Lord [2]rather than
for men;
24 [a]knowing that from the Lord you
will receive the reward [1]of [b]the inheritance. It is the Lord Christ whom you
[c]serve.
25 For [a]he who does wrong will receive the consequences of the wrong
which he has done, and [1b]that without
partiality.

Fellow Workers

4 MASTERS, grant to your slaves
justice and fairness, [a]knowing that
you too have a Master in heaven.
2 [a]Devote yourselves to prayer, keeping alert in it with *an attitude of* thanksgiving;
3 praying at the same time [a]for us as
well, that God may open up to us a
[b]door for [c]the word, so that we may
speak forth [d]the mystery of Christ, for
which I have also [e]been imprisoned;
4 in order that I may make it clear
[a]in the way I ought to speak.
5 [1a]Conduct yourselves with wisdom
toward [b]outsiders, [2c]making the most of
the opportunity.
6 [a]Let your speech always be [1]with
grace, seasoned, *as it were,* with [b]salt, so
that you may know how you should
[c]respond to each person.
7 [a]As to all my affairs, [b]Tychicus, *our*
[c]beloved brother and faithful servant
and fellow bond-servant in the Lord,
will bring you information.
8 [a]For I have sent him to you for this
very purpose, that you may know *about*
our circumstances and that he may
[b]encourage your hearts;
9 [1]and with him [a]Onesimus, *our*
faithful and [b]beloved brother, [c]who is
one of your *number.* They will inform
you about the whole situation here.

1 [a]Col. 2:12 [b]Ps. 110:1; Mark 16:19
2 [1]Or, *Be intent on* [a]Matt. 16:23; Phil. 3:19, 20
3 [a]Rom. 6:2; 2 Cor. 5:14; Col. 2:20
4 [a]John 11:25; Gal. 2:20 [b]1 Cor. 1:7; Phil. 3:21; 1 Pet. 1:13; 1 John 2:28; 3:2
5 [1]Lit., *put to death the members which are upon the earth* [2]Lit., *fornication* [3]Lit., *is* [a]Rom. 8:13 [b]Col. 2:11 [c]Mark 7:21f.; 1 Cor. 6:9f., 18; 2 Cor. 12:21; Gal. 5:19f.; Eph. 4:19; 5:3, 5
6 [1]Some early mss. add *upon the sons of disobedience* [a]Rom. 1:18; Eph. 5:6
7 [a]Eph. 2:2
8 [a]Eph. 4:22 [b]Eph. 4:31 [c]Eph. 4:29
9 [1]Or, *Stop lying* [2]Lit., *man* [a]Eph. 4:25 [b]Eph. 4:22
10 [1]Lit., *man* [2]Lit., *renovated* [a]Eph. 4:24 [b]Rom. 12:2; 2 Cor. 4:16; Eph. 4:23 [c]Gen. 1:26; Rom. 8:29 [d]Eph. 2:10
11 [a]Rom. 10:12; 1 Cor. 12:13; Gal. 3:28 [b]1 Cor. 7:19; Gal. 5:6 [c]Acts 28:2 [d]Eph. 6:8 [e]Eph. 1:23
12 [1]I.e., forbearance toward others [a]Luke 18:7 [b]Eph. 4:24 [c]Luke 1:78; Gal. 5:22f.; Phil. 2:1 [d]Eph. 4:2; Phil. 2:3 [e]1 Cor. 13:4; 2 Cor. 6:6
13 [a]Eph. 4:2 [b]Rom. 15:7; Eph. 4:32
14 [1]Lit., *the uniting bond of perfectness* [a]Eph. 4:3 [b]John 17:23; Heb. 6:1
15 [1]Or, *act as arbiter* [2]Lit., *also* [3]Or, *show yourselves thankful* [a]John 14:27 [b]Eph. 2:16
16 [1]Some mss. read *the Lord;* others read *God* [2]Or, *in* [3]Or, *by;* lit., *in His grace* [a]Rom. 10:17; Eph. 5:26; 1 Thess. 1:8 [b]Col. 1:28 [c]Eph. 5:19 [d]1 Cor. 14:15
17 [a]1 Cor. 10:31 [b]Eph. 5:20; Col. 3:15
18 [a]Col. 3:18-4:1: *Eph. 5:22-6:9* [b]Eph. 5:22
19 [a]Eph. 5:25; 1 Pet. 3:7
20 [1]Lit., *in* [a]Eph. 6:1
21 [1]Some early mss. read *provoke to anger* [a]Eph. 6:4
22 [1]Lit., *according to the flesh* [2]Lit., *eyeservice* [a]Eph. 6:5 [b]Eph. 6:6

23 [1]Lit., *from the soul* [2]Lit., *and not* [a]Eph. 6:7
24 [1]I.e., consisting of [a]Eph. 6:8 [b]Acts 20:32; 1 Pet. 1:4 [c]1 Cor. 7:22
25 [1]Lit., *there is no partiality* [a]Eph. 6:8 [b]Deut. 10:17; Acts 10:34; Eph. 6:9

1 [a]Eph. 6:9
2 [a]Acts 1:14; Eph. 6:18
3 [a]Eph. 6:19 [b]Acts 14:27 [c]2 Tim. 4:2 [d]Eph. 3:3, 4; 6:19 [e]Eph. 6:20
4 [a]Eph. 6:20
5 [1]Lit., *Walk* [2]Lit., *redeeming the time* [a]Eph. 5:15 [b]Mark 4:11 [c]Eph. 5:16
6 [1]Or, *gracious* [a]Eph. 4:29 [b]Mark 9:50 [c]1 Pet. 3:15
7 [a]Col. 4:7-9: *Eph. 6:21, 22* [b]Acts 20:4; 2 Tim. 4:12 [c]Eph. 6:21; Col. 1:7
8 [a]Eph. 6:22 [b]Col. 2:2
9 [1]Lit., *along with Onesimus* [a]Philem. 10 [b]Col. 1:7 [c]Col. 4:12

10 [a]Aristarchus, my [b]fellow prisoner,
sends you his greetings; and *also* [c]Barna-
bas' cousin Mark (about whom you
received [1]instructions: [d]if he comes to
you, welcome him);
11 and *also* Jesus who is called Justus;
these are the only [a]fellow workers for the
kingdom of God [b]who are from the
circumcision; and they have proved to
be an encouragement to me.
12 [a]Epaphras, [b]who is one of your
number, a bondslave of Jesus Christ,
sends you his greetings, always [c]laboring
earnestly for you in his prayers, that you
may [1]stand [2][d]perfect and [3]fully assured
in all the will of God.
13 For I bear him witness that he has
[1]a deep concern for you and for those
who are in [a]Laodicea and Hierapolis.

10 [1]Or, *orders* [a]Acts 19:29; 27:2; Philem. 24 [b]Rom. 16:7 [c]Acts 4:36; 12:12, 25; 15:37, 39 [d]2 Tim. 4:11
11 [a]Rom. 16:3 [b]Acts 11:2
12 [1]Or, *stand firm* [2]Or, *complete* or *mature* [3]Or, *made complete* [a]Col. 1:7; Philem. 23 [b]Col. 4:9 [c]Rom. 15:30 [d]Col. 1:28
13 [1]Or, *much toil* or *great pain* [a]Col. 2:1; 4:15f.
14 [a]2 Tim. 4:11; Philem. 24 [b]2 Tim. 4:10; Philem. 24
15 [1]Or, *Nymphas* (masc.) [2]Some ancient mss. read *their* [a]Col. 2:1; 4:13, 16 [b]Rom. 16:5

14 [a]Luke, the beloved physician, sends
you his greetings, and *also* [b]Demas.
15 Greet the brethren who are in
[a]Laodicea and also [1]Nympha and [b]the
church that is in [2]her house.
16 And [a]when [1]this letter is read
among you, have it also read in the
church of the Laodiceans; and you, for
your part [a]read [1]my letter *that is coming*
from [b]Laodicea.
17 And say to [a]Archippus, "Take heed
to the [b]ministry which you have received
in the Lord, that you may [1]fulfill it."
18 [1]I, Paul, [a]write this greeting with
my own hand. [b]Remember my [2][c]impris-
onment. [d]Grace be with you.

16 [1]Lit., *the* [a]1 Thess. 5:27; 2 Thess. 3:14 [b]Col. 2:1; 4:13, 15
17 [1]Or, *continually fulfill* [a]Philem. 2 [b]2 Tim. 4:5
18 [1]Lit., *The greeting by my hand of Paul* [2]Lit., *bonds* [a]1 Cor. 16:21 [b]Heb. 13:3 [c]Phil. 1:7; Col. 4:3 [d]1 Tim. 6:21; 2 Tim. 4:22; Titus 3:15; Heb. 13:25

THE FIRST EPISTLE OF PAUL TO THE THESSALONIANS

Thanksgiving for These Believers

1 [a]PAUL and [b]Silvanus and [c]Timothy
to the [d]church of the Thessalonians
in God the Father and the Lord Jesus
Christ: [e]Grace to you and peace.
2 [a]We give thanks to God always for
all of you, [b]making mention *of you* in
our prayers;
3 constantly bearing in mind your
[a]work of faith and labor of [b]love and
[1][c]steadfastness of hope [2]in our Lord
Jesus Christ in the presence of [d]our God
and Father,
4 knowing, [a]brethren beloved by
God, [b]*His* choice of you;
5 for our [a]gospel did not come to you
in word only, but also [b]in power and in
the Holy Spirit and with [c]full conviction; just as you know [d]what kind of
men we [1]proved to be among you for
your sake.
6 You also became [a]imitators of us
and of the Lord, [b]having received [c]the
word in much tribulation with the [d]joy
of the Holy Spirit,
7 so that you became an example to
all the believers in [a]Macedonia and in
[b]Achaia.
8 For [a]the word of the Lord has
[b]sounded forth from you, not only in
[c]Macedonia and [d]Achaia, but also [e]in
every place your faith toward God has
gone forth, so that we have no need to
say anything.
9 For they themselves report about
us what kind of a [1][a]reception we had
[2]with you, and how you [b]turned to God
[c]from [3]idols to serve [4][d]a living and true
God,
10 and to [a]wait for His Son from
[1]heaven, whom He [b]raised from the
dead, *that is* Jesus, who [c]delivers us from
[d]the wrath to come.

1 [a]2 Thess. 1:1 [b]2 Cor. 1:19 [c]Acts 16:1 [d]Acts 17:1 [e]Rom. 1:7
2 [a]Rom. 1:8; 2 Thess. 1:3 [b]Rom. 1:9
3 [1]Or, *perseverance* [2]Lit., *of* [a]John 6:29 [b]1 Cor. 13:13 [c]Rom. 8:25; 15:4 [d]Gal. 1:4
4 [a]Rom. 1:7; 2 Thess. 2:13 [b]2 Pet. 1:10
5 [1]Lit., *became* [a]1 Cor. 9:14 [b]Rom. 15:19 [c]Luke 1:1; Col. 2:2 [d]1 Thess. 2:10
6 [a]1 Cor. 4:16; 11:1f. [b]Acts 17:5-10 [c]2 Tim. 4:2 [d]Acts 13:52; 2 Cor. 6:10; Gal. 5:22
7 [a]Rom. 15:26 [b]Acts 18:12
8 [a]Col. 3:16; 2 Thess. 3:1 [b]Rom. 10:18 [c]Rom. 15:26 [d]Acts 18:12 [e]Rom. 1:8; 16:19; 2 Cor. 2:14
9 [1]Lit., *entrance* [2]Lit., *to* [3]Or, *the idols* [4]Or, *the* [a]1 Thess. 2:1 [b]Acts 14:15 [c]1 Cor. 12:2 [d]Matt. 16:16
10 [1]Lit., *the heavens* [a]Matt. 16:27f.; 1 Cor. 1:7 [b]Acts 2:24 [c]Rom. 5:9 [d]Matt. 3:7; 1 Thess. 2:16; 5:9

1 [1]Lit., *entrance* [a]1 Thess. 1:9 [b]2 Thess. 1:10
2 [1]Or, *struggle, conflict* [a]Acts 14:5; 16:19-24; Phil. 1:30 [b]Acts 16:22-24 [c]Acts 17:1-9 [d]Rom. 1:1 [e]Phil. 1:30

Paul's Ministry

2 FOR you yourselves know, brethren, that our [1][a]coming to you [b]was
not in vain,
2 but after we had already suffered
and been [a]mistreated in [b]Philippi, as you
know, we had the boldness in our God
[c]to speak to you the [d]gospel of God
amid much [1][e]opposition.
3 For our [a]exhortation does not *come*
from [b]error or [c]impurity or [1]by way of
[d]deceit;
4 [a]but just as we have been approved
by God to be [b]entrusted with the gospel,
so we speak, [c]not as pleasing men but
God, who [1][d]examines our hearts.
5 For we never came [1]with flattering
speech, as you know, nor with [a]a pretext
for greed—[b]God is witness—
6 nor did we [a]seek glory from men,
either from you or from others, even
though as [b]apostles of Christ we might
have [1]asserted our authority.
7 But we [1]proved to be [2][a]gentle
[3]among you, [b]as a nursing *mother* [4]ten-
derly cares for her own children.
8 Having thus a fond affection for
you, we were well-pleased to [a]impart to
you not only the [b]gospel of God but also
our own [1]lives, because you had become
[2]very dear to us.

3 [1]Lit., *in deceit* [a]Acts 13:15 [b]2 Thess. 2:11 [c]1 Thess. 4:7 [d]2 Cor. 4:2
4 [1]Or, *approves* [a]2 Cor. 2:17 [b]Gal. 2:7 [c]Gal. 1:10 [d]Rom. 8:27
5 [1]Lit., *in a word of flattery* [a]Acts 20:33; 2 Pet. 2:3 [b]Rom. 1:9; 1 Thess. 2:10
6 [1]Or, *been burdensome* [a]John 5:41, 44; 2 Cor. 4:5 [b]1 Cor. 9:1f.
7 [1]Lit., *became gentle* [2]Some ancient mss. read *babes* [3]Lit., *in the midst of you* [4]Or, *cherishes* [a]2 Tim. 2:24 [b]Gal. 4:19; 1 Thess. 2:11
8 [1]Or, *souls* [2]Lit., *beloved* [a]2 Cor. 12:15; 1 John 3:16 [b]Rom. 1:1

9 For you recall, brethren, our [a]labor
and hardship, *how* [b]working night and
day so as not to be a [c]burden to any of
you, we proclaimed to you the [d]gospel of
God.
10 You are witnesses, and *so is* [a]God,
[b]how devoutly and uprightly and blamelessly we [1]behaved toward you [2]believ-
ers;
11 just as you know how we *were*
[a]exhorting and encouraging and [1b]im-
ploring each one of you as [c]a father
would his own children,
12 so that you may [a]walk in a manner
worthy of the God who [b]calls you into
His own kingdom and [c]glory.
13 And for this reason we also constantly [a]thank God that when you received from us the [b]word of God's
message, you accepted *it* [c]not *as* the
word of men, but *for* what it really is, the
word of God, [d]which also performs its
work in you who believe.
14 For you, brethren, became [a]imita-
tors of [b]the churches of God in Christ
Jesus that are [c]in Judea, for [d]you also
endured the same sufferings at the hands
of your own countrymen, [e]even as they
did from the Jews,
15 [a]who both killed the Lord Jesus
and [b]the prophets, and [1]drove us out.
[2]They are not pleasing to God, [3]but
hostile to all men,
16 [a]hindering us from speaking to the
Gentiles [b]that they might be saved; with
the result that they always [c]fill up the
measure of their sins. But [d]wrath has
come upon them [1]to the utmost.
17 But we, brethren, having been bereft of you for a [1]short while—[a]in [2]per-
son, not in [3]spirit—were all the more
eager with great desire [b]to see your face.
18 [1]For [a]we wanted to come to you—
I, Paul, [2b]more than once—and *yet*
[c]Satan [d]thwarted us.
19 For who is our hope or [a]joy or
crown of exultation? Is it not even you,
in the presence of our Lord Jesus at His
[1b]coming?
20 For you are [a]our glory and joy.

Encouragement of Timothy's Visit

3 THEREFORE [a]when we could endure *it* no longer, we thought it best
to be left behind at [b]Athens alone;
2 and we sent [a]Timothy, our brother
and God's fellow worker in the gospel of
Christ, to strengthen and encourage you
as to your faith,
3 so that no man may be [1]disturbed
by these afflictions; for you yourselves
know that [a]we have been destined for
this.
4 For indeed when we were with you,
we *kept* telling you in advance that we
were going to suffer affliction; [1a]and so it
came to pass, [2]as you know.
5 For this reason, [a]when I could
endure *it* no longer, I also [b]sent to [1]find
out about your faith, for fear that [c]the

9 [a]Phil. 4:16; 2 Thess. 3:8 [b]Acts 18:3 [c]1 Cor. 9:4f.; 2 Cor. 11:9 [d]Rom. 1:1
10 [1]Lit., *became* [2]Or, who *believe* [a]1 Thess. 2:5 [b]2 Cor. 1:12; 1 Thess. 1:5
11 [1]Or, *testifying* [a]1 Thess. 5:14 [b]Luke 16:28; 1 Thess. 4:6 [c]1 Cor. 4:14; 1 Thess. 2:7
12 [a]Eph. 4:1 [b]Rom. 8:28; 1 Thess. 5:24; 2 Thess. 2:14 [c]2 Cor. 4:6; 1 Pet. 5:10
13 [a]Rom. 1:8; 1 Thess. 1:2 [b]Rom. 10:17; Heb. 4:2 [c]Matt. 10:20; Gal. 4:14 [d]Heb. 4:12
14 [a]1 Thess. 1:6 [b]1 Cor. 7:17; 10:32 [c]Gal. 1:22 [d]Acts 17:5; 1 Thess. 3:4; 2 Thess. 1:4f. [e]Heb. 10:33f.
15 [1]Or, *persecuted us* [2]Lit., *and* [3]Lit., *and* [a]Luke 24:20; Acts 2:23 [b]Matt. 5:12; Acts 7:52
16 [1]Or, *forever* or *altogether* [a]Acts 9:23; 13:45, 50; 14:2, 5, 19; 17:5, 13; 18:12; 21:21f., 27; 25:2, 7 [b]1 Cor. 10:33 [c]Gen. 15:16; Dan. 8:23; Matt. 23:32 [d]1 Thess. 1:10
17 [1]Lit., *occasion of an hour* [2]Lit., *face* [3]Lit., *heart* [a]1 Cor. 5:3 [b]1 Thess. 3:10
18 [1]Or, *Because* [2]Lit., *both once and twice* [a]Rom. 15:22 [b]Phil. 4:16 [c]Matt. 4:10 [d]Rom. 1:13; 15:22
19 [1]Or, *presence* [a]Phil. 4:1 [b]Matt. 16:27; Mark 8:38; John 21:22; 1 Thess. 3:13; 4:15; 5:23
20 [a]2 Cor. 1:14

1 [a]1 Thess. 3:5 [b]Acts 17:15f.
2 [a]2 Cor. 1:1; Col. 1:1
3 [1]Or, *deceived* [a]Acts 9:16; 14:22
4 [1]Lit., *just as* [2]Lit., *and* [a]1 Thess. 2:14
5 [1]Or, *to know, to ascertain* [a]Phil. 2:19; 1 Thess. 3:1 [b]1 Thess. 3:2 [c]Matt. 4:3 [d]2 Cor. 6:1; Phil. 2:16
6 [a]Acts 18:5 [b]1 Thess. 1:3 [c]1 Cor. 11:2
8 [a]1 Cor. 6:13
9 [a]1 Thess. 1:2
10 [a]2 Tim. 1:3 [b]1 Thess. 2:17 [c]2 Cor. 13:9
11 [a]2 Thess. 2:16 [b]Gal. 1:4; 1 Thess. 3:13 [c]1 Thess. 4:16; 5:23; 2 Thess. 2:16; 3:16; Rev. 21:3 [d]2 Thess. 3:5
12 [a]Phil. 1:9; 1 Thess. 4:1, 10; 2 Thess. 1:3

tempter might have tempted you, and
[d]our labor should be in vain.
6 But now that [a]Timothy has come
to us from you, and has brought us good
news of [b]your faith and love, and that
you always [c]think kindly of us, longing
to see us just as we also long to see you,
7 for this reason, brethren, in all our
distress and affliction we were comforted
about you through your faith;
8 for now we *really* live, if you [a]stand
firm in the Lord.
9 For [a]what thanks can we render to
God for you in return for all the joy with
which we rejoice before our God on your
account,
10 as we [a]night and day keep praying
most earnestly that we may [b]see your
face, and may [c]complete what is lacking
in your faith?
11 [a]Now may [b]our God and Father
[c]Himself and Jesus our Lord [d]direct our
way to you;
12 and may the Lord cause you to
increase and [a]abound in love for one
another, and for all men, just as we also
do for you;
13 so that He may [a]establish your
hearts [b]unblamable in holiness before
[c]our God and Father at the [1d]coming of
our Lord Jesus [e]with all His [2]saints.

Sanctification and Love

4 [a]FINALLY then, [b]brethren, we request and exhort you in the Lord
Jesus, that, as you received from us
instruction as to how you ought to [1c]walk
and [d]please God (just as you actually do
[1]walk), that you may [e]excel still more.
2 For you know what command-
ments we gave you [1]by *the authority of*
the Lord Jesus.
3 For this is the will of God, your
sanctification; *that is,* that you [a]abstain
from [1]sexual immorality;
4 that [a]each of you know how to
[1]possess his own [2b]vessel in sanctification and [c]honor,
5 not in [1a]lustful passion, like the
Gentiles who [b]do not know God;
6 *and* that no man transgress and
[a]defraud his brother [b]in the matter
because [c]the Lord is *the* avenger in all
these things, just as we also [d]told you
before and solemnly warned *you.*
7 For [a]God has not called us for [b]the
purpose of impurity, but [1]in sanctification.

13 [1]Or, *presence* [2]Or, *holy ones* [a]1 Cor. 1:8; 1 Thess. 3:2 [b]Luke 1:6 [c]Gal. 1:4; 1 Thess. 3:11 [d]1 Thess. 2:19 [e]Matt. 25:31; Mark 8:38; 1 Thess. 4:17; 2 Thess. 1:7

1 [1]Or, *conduct yourselves* [a]2 Cor. 13:11; 2 Thess. 3:1 [b]Gal. 6:1; 1 Thess. 5:12; 2 Thess. 1:3; 2:1; 3:1, 13 [c]Eph. 4:1 [d]2 Cor. 5:9 [e]Phil. 1:9; 1 Thess. 3:12; 4:10; 2 Thess. 1:3
2 [1]Lit., *through the Lord*
3 [1]Or, *fornication* [a]1 Cor. 6:18
4 [1]Or, *acquire* [2]I.e., body; or possibly, wife [a]1 Cor. 7:2, 9 [b]2 Cor. 4:7; 1 Pet. 3:7 [c]Rom. 1:24
5 [1]Lit., *passion of lust* [a]Rom. 1:26 [b]Gal. 4:8
6 [a]1 Cor. 6:8 [b]2 Cor. 7:11 [c]Rom. 12:19; 13:4; Heb. 13:4 [d]Luke 16:28; 1 Thess. 2:11; Heb. 2:6
7 [1]I.e., in the state or sphere of [a]1 Pet. 1:15 [b]1 Thess. 2:3

8 Consequently, he who rejects *this* is
not rejecting man but the God who
[a]gives His Holy Spirit to you.
9 Now as to the [a]love of the brethren,
you [b]have no need for *anyone* to write to
you, for you yourselves are [c]taught by
God to love one another;
10 for indeed [a]you do practice it
toward all the brethren who are in all
Macedonia. But we urge you, brethren,
to [b]excel still more,
11 and to make it your ambition [a]to
lead a quiet life and [b]attend to your own
business and [c]work with your hands, just
as we commanded you;
12 so that you may [1a]behave properly
toward [b]outsiders and [2c]not be in any
need.

Those Who Died in Christ

13 But [a]we do not want you to be
uninformed, brethren, about those who
[b]are asleep, that you may not grieve, as
do [c]the rest who have [d]no hope.
14 For if we believe that Jesus died
and rose again, [a]even so God will bring
with Him [b]those who have fallen asleep
[1]in Jesus.
15 For this we say to you [a]by the word
of the Lord, that [b]we who are alive, [1]and
remain until [c]the coming of the Lord,
shall not precede [d]those who have fallen
asleep.
16 For the Lord [a]Himself [b]will descend from heaven with a [1c]shout, with
the voice of [d]*the* archangel, and with the
[e]trumpet of God; and [f]the dead in Christ
shall rise first.
17 Then [a]we who are alive [1]and remain shall be [b]caught up together with
them [c]in the clouds to meet the Lord in
the air, and thus we shall always [d]be
with the Lord.
18 Therefore comfort one another
with these words.

The Day of the Lord

5 NOW as to the [a]times and the
epochs, brethren, you [b]have no need
of anything to be written to you.
2 For you yourselves know full well
that [a]the day of the Lord [1]will come
[b]just like a thief in the night.
3 While they are saying, "[a]Peace and
safety!" then [1b]destruction [2]will come
upon them suddenly like [c]birth pangs
upon a woman with child; and they shall
not escape.
4 But you, brethren, are not in [a]dark-
ness, that the day should overtake you
[1b]like a thief;
5 for you are all [a]sons of light and
sons of day. We are not of night nor of
[b]darkness;
6 so then let us not [a]sleep as [1b]others
do, but let us be alert and [2c]sober.
7 For those who sleep do their sleeping at night, and those who get drunk get
[a]drunk at night.
8 But since [a]we are of *the* day, let us
[b]be [1]sober, having put on the [c]breast-

8 [a]Rom. 5:5; 2 Cor. 1:22; Gal. 4:6; 1 John 3:24
9 [a]John 13:34; Rom. 12:10 [b]2 Cor. 9:1; 1 Thess. 5:1 [c]Jer. 31:33f.; John 6:45; 1 John 2:27
10 [a]1 Thess. 1:7 [b]1 Thess. 3:12
11 [a]2 Thess. 3:12 [b]1 Pet. 4:15 [c]Acts 18:3; Eph. 4:28; 2 Thess. 3:10-12
12 [1]Lit., *walk* [2]Lit., *have need of nothing* [a]Rom. 13:13; Col. 4:5 [b]Mark 4:11 [c]Eph. 4:28
13 [a]Rom. 1:13 [b]Acts 7:60 [c]Eph. 2:3; 1 Thess. 5:6 [d]Eph. 2:12
14 [1]Lit., *through* [a]Rom. 14:9; 2 Cor. 4:14 [b]1 Cor. 15:18; 1 Thess. 4:13
15 [1]Lit., *who* [a]1 Kin. 13:17f.; 20:35; 2 Cor. 12:1; Gal. 1:12 [b]1 Cor. 15:52; 1 Thess. 5:10 [c]1 Thess. 2:19 [d]1 Cor. 15:18; 1 Thess. 4:13
16 [1]Or, *cry of command* [a]1 Thess. 3:11 [b]1 Thess. 1:10; 2 Thess. 1:7 [c]Joel 2:11 [d]Jude 9 [e]Matt. 24:31 [f]1 Cor. 15:23; 2 Thess. 2:1; Rev. 14:13
17 [1]Lit., *who* [a]1 Cor. 15:52; 1 Thess. 5:10 [b]2 Cor. 12:2 [c]Dan. 7:13; Acts 1:9; Rev. 11:12 [d]John 12:26

1 [a]Acts 1:7 [b]1 Thess. 4:9
2 [1]Lit., *is coming* [a]1 Cor. 1:8 [b]Luke 21:34; 1 Thess. 5:4; 2 Pet. 3:10; Rev. 3:3; 16:15
3 [1]Or, *sudden destruction* [2]Lit., *is at hand* [a]Jer. 6:14; 8:11; Ezek. 13:10 [b]2 Thess. 1:9 [c]John 16:21
4 [1]Some early mss. read *like thieves* [a]Acts 26:18; 1 John 2:8 [b]Luke 21:34; 1 Thess. 5:2; 2 Pet. 3:10; Rev. 3:3; 16:15
5 [a]Luke 16:8 [b]Acts 26:18; 1 John 2:8
6 [1]Lit., *the remaining ones* [2]Or, *self-controlled* [a]Rom. 13:11; 1 Thess. 5:10 [b]Eph. 2:3; 1 Thess. 4:13 [c]1 Pet. 1:13
7 [a]Acts 2:15; 2 Pet. 2:13
8 [1]Or, *self-controlled* [a]1 Thess. 5:5 [b]1 Pet. 1:13 [c]Is. 59:17; Eph. 6:14 [d]Eph. 6:23 [e]Eph. 6:17 [f]Rom. 8:24
9 [a]1 Thess. 1:10 [b]2 Thess. 2:13f.
10 [a]Rom. 14:9
11 [1]Or, *comfort* [a]Eph. 4:29

plate of [d]faith and love, and as a [e]hel-
met, the [f] hope of salvation.
9 For God has not destined us for
[a]wrath, but for [b]obtaining salvation
through our Lord Jesus Christ,
10 [a]who died for us, that whether we
are awake or asleep, we may live together with Him.
11 Therefore [1]encourage one another,
and [a]build up one another, just as you
also are doing.

Christian Conduct

12 But we request of you, brethren,
that you [1a]appreciate those [b]who diligently labor among you, and [c]have
charge over you in the Lord and give you
[2]instruction,
13 and that you esteem them very
highly in love because of their work.
[a]Live in peace with one another.
14 And we urge you, brethren, admonish [a]the [1]unruly, encourage [b]the
fainthearted, help [c]the weak, be [d]patient
with all men.
15 See that [a]no one repays another
with evil for evil, but always [b]seek after
that which is good for one another and
for all men.
16 [a]Rejoice always;
17 [a]pray without ceasing;
18 in everything [a]give thanks; for this
is God's will for you in Christ Jesus.
19 [a]Do not quench the Spirit;
20 do not despise [a]prophetic [1]utter-
ances.
21 But [a]examine everything *carefully*;
[b]hold fast to that which is good;
22 abstain from every [1]form of evil.
23 Now [a]may the God of peace [b]Him-
self sanctify you entirely; and may your
[c]spirit and soul and body be preserved
complete, [d]without blame at [e]the coming
of our Lord Jesus Christ.
24 [a]Faithful is He who [b]calls you, and
He also will bring it to pass.
25 Brethren, [a]pray for us[1].
26 [a]Greet all the brethren with a holy
kiss.
27 I adjure you by the Lord to [a]have
this letter read to all the [b]brethren.
28 [a]The grace of our Lord Jesus Christ
be with you.

12 [1]Lit., *know* [2]Or, *admonition* [a]1 Cor. 16:18; 1 Tim. 5:17 [b]Rom. 16:6, 12; 1 Cor. 15:10; 16:16 [c]Heb. 13:17
13 [a]Mark 9:50
14 [1]Or, *undisciplined* [a]2 Thess. 3:6, 7, 11 [b]Is. 35:4 [c]Rom. 14:1f.; 1 Cor. 8:7ff.; Rom. 15:1 [d]1 Cor. 13:4
15 [a]Matt. 5:44; Rom. 12:17; 1 Pet. 3:9 [b]Rom. 12:9; Gal. 6:10; 1 Thess. 5:21
16 [a]Phil. 4:4
17 [a]Eph. 6:18
18 [a]Eph. 5:20
19 [a]Eph. 4:30
20 [1]Or, *gifts* [a]Acts 13:1; 1 Cor. 14:31
21 [a]1 Cor. 14:29; 1 John 4:1 [b]Rom. 12:9; Gal. 6:10; 1 Thess. 5:15
22 [1]Or, *appearance*
23 [a]Rom. 15:33 [b]1 Thess. 3:11 [c]Luke 1:46f.; Heb. 4:12 [d]James 1:4; 2 Pet. 3:14 [e]1 Thess. 2:19
24 [a]1 Cor. 1:9; 2 Thess. 3:3 [b]1 Thess. 2:12
25 [1]Some mss. add *also* [a]Eph. 6:19; 2 Thess. 3:1; Heb. 13:18
26 [a]Rom. 16:16
27 [a]Col. 4:16 [b]Acts 1:15
28 [a]Rom. 16:20; 2 Thess. 3:18

THE SECOND EPISTLE OF PAUL TO THE
THESSALONIANS

Thanksgiving for Faith and Perseverance

1 [a]PAUL and [b]Silvanus and [c]Timothy to the [d]church of the Thessalonians in God our Father and the Lord Jesus Christ:

2 [a]Grace to you and peace from God the Father and the Lord Jesus Christ.

3 We ought always [a]to give thanks to God for you, [b]brethren, as is *only* fitting, because your faith is greatly enlarged, and the [c]love of each one of you toward one another grows *ever* greater;

4 therefore, we ourselves [a]speak proudly of you among [b]the churches of God for your [1]perseverance and faith [b]in the midst of all your persecutions and afflictions which you endure.

5 *This is* a [a]plain indication of God's righteous judgment so that you may be [b]considered worthy of the kingdom of God, for which indeed you are suffering.

6 [1]For after all [a]it is *only* just [2]for God to repay with affliction those who afflict you,

7 and *to give* relief to you who are afflicted [1]and to us as well [2a]when the Lord Jesus shall be revealed [b]from heaven [c]with [3]His mighty angels [d]in flaming fire,

8 dealing out retribution to those who [a]do not know God and to those who [b]do not obey the gospel of our Lord Jesus.

9 And these will pay the penalty of [a]eternal destruction, [b]away from the presence of the Lord and from the glory of His power,

10 when He comes to be [a]glorified [1]in His [2]saints on that [b]day, and to be marveled at among all who have believed—for our [c]testimony to you was believed.

11 To this end also we [a]pray for you always that our God may [1b]count you worthy of your [c]calling, and fulfill every desire for [d]goodness and the [e]work of faith with power;

12 in order that the [a]name of our Lord Jesus may be glorified in you, and you in Him, according to the grace of our God and [1]the Lord Jesus Christ.

Man of Lawlessness

2 NOW we request you, [a]brethren, with regard to the [1b]coming of our Lord Jesus Christ, and our [c]gathering together to Him,

2 that you may not be quickly shaken from your [1]composure or be disturbed either by a [a]spirit or a [2b]message or a [c]letter as if from us, to the effect that [d]the day of the Lord [e]has come.

3 [a]Let no one in any way deceive you, for *it will not come* unless the [1b]apostasy comes first, and the [c]man of [2]lawlessness is revealed, the [d]son of destruction,

4 who opposes and exalts himself above [1a]every so-called god or object of worship, so that he takes his seat in the temple of God, [b]displaying himself as being God.

5 Do you not remember that [a]while I was still with you, I was telling you these things?

6 And you know [a]what restrains him now, so that in his time he may be revealed.

7 For [a]the mystery of lawlessness is already at work; only [b]he who now restrains *will do so* until he is taken out of the way.

8 And then that lawless one [a]will be revealed whom the Lord will slay [b]with the breath of His mouth and bring to an end by the [c]appearance of His [1]coming;

9 *that is,* the one whose [1]coming is in accord with the activity of [a]Satan, with all power and [2b]signs and false wonders,

10 and with [1]all the deception of wickedness for [a]those who perish, because they did not receive the love of [b]the truth so as to be saved.

11 And for this reason [a]God [1]will send upon them [2]a [b]deluding influence so that they might believe [3]what is false,

12 in order that they all may be [1]judged who [a]did not believe the truth, but [2b]took pleasure in wickedness.

13 [a]But we should always give thanks to God for you, [b]brethren beloved by the Lord, because [c]God has chosen you [1]from the beginning [d]for salvation [2e]through sanctification [3]by the Spirit and faith in the truth.

14 And it was for this He [a]called you through [b]our gospel, [1]that you may gain the glory of our Lord Jesus Christ.

15 So then, brethren, [a]stand firm and [b]hold to the traditions which you were taught, whether [c]by word *of mouth* or [c]by letter [1]from us.

16 [a]Now may our Lord Jesus Christ [b]Himself and God our Father, who has [c]loved us and given us eternal comfort and [d]good hope by grace,

17 [a]comfort and [b]strengthen your hearts in every good work and word.

---

1 [a]1 Thess. 1:1 [b]2 Cor. 1:19 [c]Acts 16:1 [d]Acts 17:1; 1 Thess. 1:1
2 [a]Rom. 1:7
3 [a]Rom. 1:8; Eph. 5:20; 1 Thess. 1:2; 2 Thess. 2:13 [b]1 Thess. 4:1; 2 Thess. 2:1 [c]1 Thess. 3:12
4 [1]Or, *steadfastness* [a]2 Cor. 7:4; 1 Thess. 2:19 [b]1 Cor. 7:17; 1 Thess. 2:14
5 [a]Phil. 1:28 [b]Luke 20:35; 2 Thess. 1:11
6 [1]Lit., *If indeed* [2]Or, *in the sight of* [a]Ex. 23:22; Col. 3:25; Heb. 6:10
7 [1]Lit., *along with us* [2]Lit., *at the revelation of the Lord Jesus* [3]Lit., *the angels of His power* [a]Luke 17:30 [b]1 Thess. 4:16 [c]Jude 14 [d]Ex. 3:2; 19:18; Is. 66:15; Ezek. 1:13; Dan. 7:9; Matt. 25:41; 1 Cor. 3:13; Heb. 10:27; 12:29; 2 Pet. 3:7; Jude 7; Rev. 14:10
8 [a]Gal. 4:8 [b]Rom. 2:8
9 [a]Phil. 3:19; 1 Thess. 5:3 [b]Is. 2:10, 19, 21; 2 Thess. 2:8
10 [1]Or, *in the persons of* [2]Or, *holy ones* [a]Is. 49:3; John 17:10; 1 Thess. 2:12 [b]Is. 2:11ff.; 1 Cor. 3:13 [c]1 Cor. 1:6; 1 Thess. 2:1
11 [1]Or, *make* [a]Col. 1:9 [b]2 Thess. 1:5 [c]Rom. 11:29 [d]Rom. 15:14 [e]1 Thess. 1:3
12 [1]Or omit, *the* [a]Is. 24:15; 66:5; Mal. 1:11; Phil. 2:9ff.

1 [1]Or, *presence* [a]2 Thess. 1:3 [b]1 Thess. 2:19 [c]Mark 13:27; 1 Thess. 4:15-17
2 [1]Lit., *mind* [2]Lit., *word* [a]1 Cor. 14:32; 1 John 4:1 [b]1 Thess. 5:2; 2 Thess. 2:15 [c]2 Thess. 3:17 [d]1 Cor. 1:8 [e]1 Cor. 7:26
3 [1]Or, *falling away* from the faith [2]Some early mss. read *sin* [a]Eph. 5:6 [b]1 Tim. 4:1 [c]Dan. 7:25; 8:25; 11:36; 2 Thess. 2:8; Rev. 13:5ff. [d]John 17:12
4 [1]Or, *all that is called God* [a]1 Cor. 8:5 [b]Is. 14:14; Ezek. 28:2
5 [a]1 Thess. 3:4
6 [a]2 Thess. 2:7
7 [a]Rev. 17:5, 7 [b]2 Thess. 2:6
8 [1]Or, *presence* [a]Dan. 7:25; 8:25; 11:36; 2 Thess. 2:3; Rev. 13:5ff. [b]Is. 11:4; Rev. 2:16; 19:15 [c]1 Tim. 6:14; 2 Tim. 1:10; 4:1, 8; Titus 2:13
9 [1]Or, *presence* [2]Or, *attesting miracles* [a]Matt. 4:10 [b]Matt. 24:24; John 4:48
10 [1]Or, *every deception* [a]1 Cor. 1:18 [b]2 Thess. 2:12, 13
11 [1]Lit., *sends* [2]Lit., *an activity of error* [3]Or, *the lie* [a]1 Kin. 22:22; Rom. 1:28 [b]1 Thess. 2:3; 2 Tim. 4:4
12 [1]Or, *condemned* [2]Or, *approved* [a]Rom. 2:8 [b]Rom. 1:32; 1 Cor. 13:6
13 [1]Some ancient mss. read *first fruits* [2]Lit., *in* [3]Lit., *of* [a]2 Thess. 1:3 [b]1 Thess. 1:4 [c]Eph. 1:4ff. [d]1 Cor. 1:21; 1 Thess. 2:12; 5:9; 1 Pet. 1:5 [e]1 Thess. 4:7; 1 Pet. 1:2
14 [1]Lit., *to the gaining of* [a]1 Thess. 2:12 [b]1 Thess. 1:5
15 [1]Lit., *of* [a]1 Cor. 16:13 [b]1 Cor. 11:2; 2 Thess. 3:6 [c]2 Thess. 2:2
16 [a]1 Thess. 3:11 [b]1 Thess. 3:11 [c]John 3:16 [d]Titus 3:7; 1 Pet. 1:3
17 [a]1 Thess. 3:2, 13 [b]2 Thess. 3:3

Exhortation

3 [a]FINALLY, brethren, [b]pray for us that [c]the word of the Lord may [1]spread rapidly and be glorified, just as *it did* also with you;

2 and that we may be [a]delivered from [1]perverse and evil men; for not all have [2]faith.

3 But [a]the Lord is faithful, and [1]He will strengthen and protect you [2]from [b]the evil *one.*

4 And we have [a]confidence in the Lord concerning you, that you [b]are doing and will *continue to* do what we command.

5 And may the Lord [a]direct your hearts into the love of God and into the steadfastness of Christ.

6 Now we command you, brethren, [a]in the name of our Lord Jesus Christ, that you [1b]keep aloof from every brother who [2]leads an [3c]unruly life and not according to [d]the tradition which [4]you received from us.

7 For you yourselves know how you ought to [1a]follow our example, because we did not act in an undisciplined manner among you,

8 nor did we [a]eat [1]anyone's bread [2]without paying for it, but with [b]labor and hardship we *kept* [c]working night and day so that we might not be a burden to any of you;

9 not because we do not have [a]the right *to this,* but in order to offer ourselves [b]as a model for you, that you might [1]follow our example.

10 For even [a]when we were with you, we used to give you this order: [b]if anyone will not work, neither let him eat.

11 For we hear that some among you are [a]leading an undisciplined life, doing no work at all, but acting like [b]busybodies.

12 Now such persons we command and [a]exhort in the Lord Jesus Christ to [b]work in quiet fashion and eat their own bread.

13 But as for you, [a]brethren, [b]do not grow weary of doing good.

14 And if anyone does not obey our [1]instruction [2a]in this letter, take special note of that man [3b]and do not associate with him, so that he may be [c]put to shame.

15 And *yet* [a]do not regard him as an enemy, but [1b]admonish him as a [c]brother.

16 Now [a]may the Lord of peace [b]Himself continually grant you peace in every [1]circumstance. [c]The Lord be with you all!

17 [1]I, Paul, write this greeting [a]with my own hand, and this is a distinguishing mark in every letter; this is the way I write.

18 [a]The grace of our Lord Jesus Christ be with you all.

1 [1]Lit., *run* [a]1 Thess. 4:1 [b]1 Thess. 5:25 [c]1 Thess. 1:8
2 [1]Lit., *improper* [2]Or, *the faith* [a]Rom. 15:31
3 [1]Lit., *will* [2]Or, *from evil* [a]1 Cor. 1:9; 1 Thess. 5:24 [b]Matt. 5:37
4 [a]2 Cor. 2:3 [b]1 Thess. 4:10
5 [a]1 Thess. 3:11
6 [1]Or, *avoid* [2]Lit., *walks disorderly* [3]Or, *undisciplined* [4]Many ancient mss. read *they* [a]1 Cor. 5:4 [b]Rom. 16:17; 1 Cor. 5:11; 2 Thess. 3:14 [c]1 Thess. 5:14; 2 Thess. 3:7, 11 [d]1 Cor. 11:2; 2 Thess. 2:15
7 [1]Lit., *imitate us* [a]1 Thess. 1:6; 2 Thess. 3:9
8 [1]Lit., *from anyone* [2]Lit., *freely* [a]1 Cor. 9:4 [b]1 Thess. 2:9 [c]Acts 18:3; Eph. 4:28
9 [1]Lit., *imitate us* [a]1 Cor. 9:4ff. [b]2 Thess. 3:7
10 [a]1 Thess. 3:4 [b]1 Thess. 4:11
11 [a]2 Thess. 3:6 [b]1 Tim. 5:13; 1 Pet. 4:15
12 [a]1 Thess. 4:1 [b]1 Thess. 4:11
13 [a]1 Thess. 4:1 [b]2 Cor. 4:1; Gal. 6:9
14 [1]Lit., *word* [2]Lit., *through* [3]Lit., *not to associate* [a]Col. 4:16 [b]2 Thess. 3:6 [c]1 Cor. 4:14
15 [1]Or, *keep admonishing* [a]Gal. 6:1 [b]1 Thess. 5:14 [c]2 Thess. 3:6, 13
16 [1]Lit., *way* [a]Rom. 15:33 [b]1 Thess. 3:11 [c]Ruth 2:4
17 [1]Lit., *The greeting by my hand of Paul* [a]1 Cor. 16:21
18 [a]Rom. 16:20; 1 Thess. 5:28

THE FIRST EPISTLE OF PAUL TO
TIMOTHY

Misleadings in Doctrine and Living

1 PAUL, [a]an apostle of [b]Christ Jesus
[c]according to the commandment of
[d]God our Savior, and of [b]Christ Jesus,
who is our [e]hope;
2 to [a]Timothy, [b]*my* true child in *the*
faith: [c]Grace, mercy *and* peace from
God the Father and [d]Christ Jesus our
Lord.
3 As I urged you [1]upon my departure
for [a]Macedonia, [2]remain on at [b]Ephesus,
in order that you may instruct certain
men not to [c]teach strange doctrines,
4 nor to [1]pay attention to [a]myths and
endless [b]genealogies, which give rise to
mere [c]speculation rather than [d]*furthering*
[2]the administration of God which is by
faith.
5 But the goal of our [1a]instruction is
love [b]from a pure heart and a [c]good
conscience and a sincere [d]faith.
6 For some men, straying from these
things, have turned aside to [a]fruitless
discussion,
7 [a]wanting to be [b]teachers of the
Law, even though they do not understand either what they are saying or the
matters about which they make confident assertions.
8 But we know that [a]the Law is good,
if one uses it lawfully,
9 realizing the fact that [a]law is not
made for a righteous man, but for those
who are lawless and [b]rebellious, for the
[c]ungodly and sinners, for the unholy and
[d]profane, for those who kill their fathers
or mothers, for murderers
10 [1]and [2a]immoral men [1]and [b]homo-
sexuals [1]and [c]kidnappers [1]and [d]liars
[1]and [e]perjurers, and whatever else is
contrary to [f]sound teaching,
11 according to [a]the glorious gospel of
[b]the blessed God, with which I have
been [c]entrusted.
12 I thank [a]Christ Jesus our Lord,
who has [b]strengthened me, because He
considered me faithful, [c]putting me into
service;
13 even though I was formerly a blas-
phemer and a [a]persecutor and a violent
aggressor. And yet I was [b]shown mercy,
because [c]I acted ignorantly in unbelief;
14 and the [a]grace of our Lord was
more than abundant, with the [b]faith and
love which are *found* in Christ Jesus.
15 [a]It is a trustworthy statement,
deserving full acceptance, that [b]Christ
Jesus came into the world to [c]save
sinners, among whom [d]I am foremost *of*
all.
16 And yet for this reason I [a]found
mercy, in order that in me as the foremost, Jesus Christ might [b]demonstrate
His perfect patience, as an example for
those [1]who would believe in Him for
eternal life.
17 Now to the [a]King [1]eternal, [b]im-
mortal, [c]invisible, the [d]only God, [e]*be*
honor and glory [2]forever and ever.
Amen.
18 This [a]command I entrust to you,
Timothy, [b]my [1]son, in accordance with
the [c]prophecies previously made concerning you, that by them you may
[d]fight the good fight,
19 keeping [a]faith and a good conscience, which some have rejected and
suffered shipwreck in regard to [1b]their
faith.
20 [1]Among these are [a]Hymenaeus and
[b]Alexander, whom I have [c]delivered over
to Satan, so that they may be [d]taught
not to blaspheme.

A Call to Prayer

2 FIRST of all, then, I urge that
[a]entreaties *and* prayers, petitions
and thanksgivings, be made on behalf of
all men,
2 [a]for kings and all who are in [1]au-
thority, in order that we may lead a
tranquil and quiet life in all godliness
and [2]dignity.
3 This is good and acceptable in the
sight of [a]God our Savior,
4 [a]who desires all men to be [b]saved
and to [c]come to the [1]knowledge of the
truth.
5 For there is [a]one God, *and* [b]one
mediator also between God and men, *the*
[c]man Christ Jesus,
6 who [a]gave Himself as a ransom for
all, the [b]testimony [1]*borne* at [2c]the proper
time.
7 [a]And for this I was appointed a
[1]preacher and [b]an apostle ([c]I am telling
the truth, I am not lying) as a teacher of
[d]the Gentiles in faith and truth.
8 Therefore [a]I want the men [b]in
every place to pray, [c]lifting up [d]holy
hands, without wrath and dissension.

Women Instructed

9 Likewise, *I want* [a]women to adorn
themselves with proper clothing, [1]mod-
estly and discreetly, not with braided
hair and gold or pearls or costly garments;

1 [a]2 Cor. 1:1 [b]1 Tim. 1:12 [c]Titus 1:3 [d]Titus 1:3 [e]Col. 1:27
2 [a]2 Tim. 1:2 [b]2 Tim. 1:2 [c]Rom. 1:7; 2 Tim. 1:2; Titus 1:4 [d]1 Tim. 1:12
3 [1]Lit., *while departing* [2]Lit., *to remain* [a]Rom. 15:26 [b]Acts 18:19 [c]Rom. 16:17; 2 Cor. 11:4; Gal. 1:6f.; 1 Tim. 6:3
4 [1]Or, *occupy themselves with* [2]Lit., *God's provision* [a]1 Tim. 4:7; 2 Tim. 4:4; Titus 1:14; 2 Pet. 1:16 [b]Titus 3:9 [c]2 Tim. 2:23 [d]Eph. 3:2
5 [1]Lit., *commandment* [a]1 Tim. 1:18 [b]2 Tim. 2:22 [c]1 Tim. 1:19; 3:9; 2 Tim. 1:3; 1 Pet. 3:16, 21 [d]2 Tim. 1:5
6 [a]Titus 1:10
7 [a]James 3:1 [b]Luke 2:46
8 [a]Rom. 7:12, 16
9 [a]Gal. 5:23 [b]Titus 1:6, 10 [c]1 Pet. 4:18; Jude 15 [d]1 Tim. 4:7; 6:20; Heb. 12:16
10 [1]Lit., *for* [2]Or, *fornicators* [a]1 Cor. 6:9 [b]Lev. 18:22 [c]Ex. 21:16; Rev. 18:13 [d]Rev. 21:8, 27; 22:15 [e]Matt. 5:33 [f]1 Tim. 4:6; 6:3; 2 Tim. 4:3; Titus 1:9, 13; 2:1, 2
11 [a]2 Cor. 4:4 [b]1 Tim. 6:15 [c]Gal. 2:7
12 [a]Gal. 3:26 [b]Acts 9:22; Phil. 4:13; 2 Tim. 4:17 [c]Acts 9:15
13 [a]Acts 8:3 [b]1 Cor. 7:25 [c]Acts 26:9
14 [a]Rom. 5:20; 1 Cor. 3:10; 2 Cor. 4:15; Gal. 1:13-16 [b]1 Thess. 1:3; 1 Tim. 2:15; 4:12; 6:11; 2 Tim. 1:13; 2:22; Titus 2:2
15 [a]1 Tim. 3:1; 4:9; 2 Tim. 2:11; Titus 3:8 [b]Mark 2:17; Luke 15:2ff.; 19:10 [c]Rom. 11:14 [d]1 Cor. 15:9; Eph. 3:8
16 [1]Or, *destined to* [a]1 Cor. 7:25; 1 Tim. 1:13 [b]Eph. 2:7
17 [1]Lit., *of the ages* [2]Lit., *to the ages of the ages* [a]Rev. 15:3 [b]1 Tim. 6:16 [c]Col. 1:15 [d]John 5:44; 1 Tim. 6:15; Jude 25 [e]Rom. 2:7, 10; 11:36; Heb. 2:7
18 [1]Lit., *child* [a]1 Tim. 1:5 [b]1 Tim. 1:2 [c]1 Tim. 4:14 [d]2 Cor. 10:4; 1 Tim. 6:12; 2 Tim. 2:3f.; 4:7
19 [1]Lit., *the* [a]1 Tim. 1:5 [b]1 Tim. 6:12, 21; 2 Tim. 2:18
20 [1]Lit., *Of* [a]2 Tim. 2:17 [b]2 Tim. 4:14 [c]1 Cor. 5:5 [d]1 Cor. 11:32; Heb. 12:5ff.

1 [a]Eph. 6:18
2 [1]Or, *a high position* [2]Or, *seriousness* [a]Ezra 6:10; Rom. 13:1
3 [a]Luke 1:47; 1 Tim. 1:1; 4:10
4 [1]Or, *recognition* [a]Ezek. 18:23, 32; John 3:17; 1 Tim. 4:10; Titus 2:11; 2 Pet. 3:9 [b]Rom. 11:14 [c]2 Tim. 2:25; 3:7; Titus 1:1; Heb. 10:26
5 [a]Rom. 3:30; 10:12; 1 Cor. 8:4 [b]1 Cor. 8:6; Gal. 3:20 [c]Matt. 1:1; Rom. 1:3
6 [1]Or, to be borne [2]Lit., *its own times* [a]Matt. 20:28; Gal. 1:4 [b]1 Cor. 1:6 [c]Mark 1:15; Gal. 4:4; 1 Tim. 6:15; Titus 1:3
7 [1]Or, *herald* [a]Eph. 3:8; 1 Tim. 1:11; 2 Tim. 1:11 [b]1 Cor. 9:1 [c]Rom. 9:1 [d]Acts 9:15
8 [a]Phil. 1:12; 1 Tim. 5:14; Titus 3:8 [b]John 4:21; 1 Cor. 1:2; 2 Cor. 2:14; 1 Thess. 1:8 [c]Ps. 63:4; Luke 24:50 [d]Ps. 24:4; James 4:8
9 [1]Lit., *with modesty* [a]1 Pet. 3:3

10 but rather by means of good works, as befits women making a claim to godliness.

11 [a]Let a woman quietly receive instruction with entire submissiveness.

12 [a]But I do not allow a woman to teach or exercise authority over a man, but to remain quiet.

13 [a]For it was Adam who was first [1]created, *and* then Eve.

14 And *it was* not Adam *who* was deceived, but [a]the woman being quite deceived, fell into transgression.

15 But *women* shall be [1]preserved through the bearing of children if they continue in [a]faith and love and sanctity with [2]self-restraint.

Overseers and Deacons

3 [a]IT is a trustworthy statement: if any man aspires to the [b]office of [1]overseer, it is a fine work he desires *to do.*

2 [1a]An overseer, then, must be above reproach, [b]the husband of one wife, [c]temperate, prudent, respectable, [d]hospitable, [e]able to teach,

3 [a]not addicted to wine [1]or pugnacious, but gentle, uncontentious, [b]free from the love of money.

4 *He must be* one who [a]manages his own household well, keeping his children under control with all dignity

5 (but if a man does not know how to manage his own household, how will he take care of [a]the church of God?);

6 *and* not a new convert, lest he become [a]conceited and fall into the [b]condemnation [1]incurred by the devil.

7 And he must [a]have a good reputation with [b]those outside *the church,* so that he may not fall into reproach and [c]the snare of the devil.

8 [a]Deacons likewise *must be* men of dignity, not [1]double-tongued, [2b]or addicted to much wine [2c]or fond of sordid gain,

9 [a]*but* holding to the mystery of the faith with a clear conscience.

10 And [a]let these also first be tested; then let them serve as deacons if they are beyond reproach.

11 [1]Women *must* likewise *be* dignified, [a]not malicious gossips, but [b]temperate, faithful in all things.

12 Let [a]deacons be [b]husbands of *only* one wife, *and* [1c]good managers of *their* children and their own households.

13 For those who have served well as deacons [a]obtain for themselves a [1]high standing and great confidence in the faith that is in Christ Jesus.

14 I am writing these things to you, hoping to come to you before long;

15 but [1]in case I am delayed, *I write* so that you may know how [2]one ought to conduct himself in [a]the household of God, which is the [b]church of [c]the living God, the [d]pillar and support of the truth.

16 And by common confession great is [a]the mystery of godliness:

[1]He who was [b]revealed in the flesh,
Was [2c]vindicated [3]in the Spirit,
[d]Beheld by angels,
[e]Proclaimed among the nations,
[f]Believed on in the world,
[g]Taken up in glory.

Apostasy

4 BUT [a]the Spirit explicitly says that [b]in later times some will fall away from the faith, paying attention to [c]deceitful spirits and [d]doctrines of demons,

2 by means of the hypocrisy of liars [a]seared in their own conscience as with a branding iron,

3 *men* who [a]forbid marriage *and advocate* [b]abstaining from foods, which [c]God has created to be [d]gratefully shared in by those who believe and know the truth.

4 For [a]everything created by God is good, and nothing is to be rejected, if it is [b]received with gratitude;

5 for it is sanctified by means of [a]the word of God and prayer.

A Good Minister's Discipline

6 In pointing out these things to [a]the brethren, you will be a good [b]servant of Christ Jesus, *constantly* nourished on the words of the faith and of the [1c]sound doctrine which you [d]have been following.

7 But have nothing to do with [a]worldly [b]fables fit only for old women. On the other hand, discipline yourself for the purpose of [c]godliness;

8 for [a]bodily discipline is only of little profit, but [b]godliness is profitable for all things, since it [c]holds promise for the [d]present life and *also* for the *life* to come.

9 [a]It is a trustworthy statement deserving full acceptance.

10 For it is for this we labor and strive, because we have fixed [a]our hope on [b]the living God, who is [c]the Savior of all men, especially of believers.

11 [1a]Prescribe and teach these things.

12 [a]Let no one look down on your youthfulness, but *rather* in speech, conduct, [b]love, faith *and* purity, show yourself [c]an example [1]of those who believe.

13 [a]Until I come, give attention to the *public* [b]reading *of Scripture,* to exhortation and teaching.

14 Do not neglect the spiritual gift within you, which was bestowed upon

11 [a]1 Cor. 14:34; Titus 2:5
12 [a]1 Cor. 14:34; Titus 2:5
13 [1]Or, *formed* [a]Gen. 2:7, 22; 3:16; 1 Cor. 11:8ff.
14 [a]Gen. 3:6, 13; 2 Cor. 11:3
15 [1]Lit., *saved* [2]Or, *discretion* [a]1 Tim. 1:14

1 [1]Or, *bishop* [a]1 Tim. 1:15 [b]Acts 20:28; Phil. 1:1
2 [1]Lit., *The* [a]1 Tim. 3:2-4; Titus 1:6-8 [b]Luke 2:36f.; 1 Tim. 5:9; Titus 1:6 [c]1 Tim. 3:8, 11; Titus 2:2 [d]Rom. 12:13; Titus 1:8; Heb. 13:2; 1 Pet. 4:9 [e]2 Tim. 2:24
3 [1]Lit., *not* [a]Titus 1:7 [b]1 Tim. 3:8; 6:10; Titus 1:7; Heb. 13:5
4 [a]1 Tim. 3:12
5 [a]1 Cor. 10:32; 1 Tim. 3:15
6 [1]Lit., *of the devil* [a]1 Tim. 6:4; 2 Tim. 3:4 [b]1 Tim. 3:7
7 [a]2 Cor. 8:21 [b]Mark 4:11 [c]1 Tim. 6:9; 2 Tim. 2:26
8 [1]Or, *given to double-talk* [2]Lit., *not* [a]Phil. 1:1; 1 Tim. 3:12 [b]1 Tim. 5:23; Titus 2:3 [c]1 Tim. 3:3; Titus 1:7; 1 Pet. 5:2
9 [a]1 Tim. 1:5, 19
10 [a]1 Tim. 5:22
11 [1]I.e., either deacons' wives or deaconesses [a]2 Tim. 3:3; Titus 2:3 [b]1 Tim. 3:2
12 [1]Lit., *managing well* [a]Phil. 1:1; 1 Tim. 3:8 [b]1 Tim. 3:2 [c]1 Tim. 3:4
13 [1]Lit., *good* [a]Matt. 25:21
15 [1]Lit., *if I delay* [2]Or, *you ought to conduct yourself* [a]1 Cor. 3:16; 2 Cor. 6:16; Eph. 2:21f.; 1 Pet. 2:5; 4:17 [b]1 Tim. 3:5 [c]Matt. 16:16; 1 Tim. 4:10 [d]Gal. 2:9; 2 Tim. 2:19
16 [1]Some later mss. read *God* [2]Or, *justified* [3]Or, *by* [a]Rom. 16:25 [b]John 1:14; 1 Pet. 1:20; 1 John 3:5, 8 [c]Rom. 3:4 [d]Luke 2:13; 24:4; 1 Pet. 1:12 [e]Rom. 16:26; 2 Cor. 1:19; Col. 1:23 [f]2 Thess. 1:10 [g]Mark 16:19; Acts

1 [a]John 16:13; Acts 20:23; 21:11; 1 Cor. 2:10f. [b]2 Thess. 2:3ff.; 2 Tim. 3:1; 2 Pet. 3:3; Jude 18 [c]1 John 4:6 [d]James 3:15
2 [a]Eph. 4:19
3 [a]Heb. 13:4 [b]Col. 2:16, 23 [c]Gen. 1:29; 9:3 [d]Rom. 14:6; 1 Cor. 10:30f.; 1 Tim. 4:4
4 [a]1 Cor. 10:26 [b]Rom. 14:6; 1 Cor. 10:30f.; 1 Tim. 4:3
5 [a]Gen. 1:25, 31; Heb. 11:3
6 [1]Lit., *good* [a]Acts 1:15 [b]2 Cor. 11:23 [c]1 Tim. 1:10 [d]Luke 1:3; Phil. 2:20, 22; 2 Tim. 3:10
7 [a]1 Tim. 1:9 [b]1 Tim. 1:4 [c]1 Tim. 4:8; 6:3, 5f.; 2 Tim. 3:5
8 [a]Col. 2:23 [b]1 Tim. 4:7; 6:3, 5f.; 2 Tim. 3:5 [c]Ps. 37:9, 11; Prov. 19:23; 22:4; Matt. 6:33 [d]Matt. 6:33; 12:32; Mark 10:30
9 [a]1 Tim. 1:15
10 [a]2 Cor. 1:10; 1 Tim. 6:17 [b]1 Tim. 3:15 [c]John 4:42; 1 Tim. 2:4
11 [1]Or, *Keep commanding and teaching* [a]1 Tim. 5:7; 6:2
12 [1]Or, *to* [a]1 Cor. 16:11; Titus 2:15 [b]1 Tim. 1:14 [c]Titus 2:7; 1 Pet. 5:3
13 [a]1 Tim. 3:14 [b]2 Tim. 3:15ff.

you through [a]prophetic utterance with [b]the laying on of hands by the [1c]presbytery.

15 Take pains with these things; be *absorbed* in them, so that your progress may be evident to all.

16 [a]Pay close attention to yourself and to your teaching; persevere in these things; for as you do this you will [1b]insure salvation both for yourself and for those who hear you.

Honor Widows

5 [a]DO not sharply rebuke an [b]older man, but *rather* appeal to *him* as a father, *to* [c]the younger men as brothers,

2 the older women as mothers, *and* the younger women as sisters, in all purity.

3 Honor widows who are [a]widows indeed;

4 but if any widow has children or grandchildren, [a]let them first learn to practice piety in regard to their own family, and to [1]make some return to their parents; for this is [b]acceptable in the sight of God.

5 Now she who is a [a]widow indeed, and who has been left alone [b]has fixed her hope on God, and continues in [c]entreaties and prayers night and day.

6 But she who [a]gives herself to wanton pleasure is [b]dead even while she lives.

7 [1a]Prescribe these things as well, so that they may be above reproach.

8 But if anyone does not provide for his own, and especially for those of his household, he has [a]denied the faith, and is worse than an unbeliever.

9 Let a widow be [a]put on the list only if she is not less than sixty years old, *having been* [b]the wife of one man,

10 having a reputation for [a]good works; *and* if she has brought up children, if she has [b]shown hospitality to strangers, if she [c]has washed the [1]saints' feet, if she has [d]assisted those in distress, *and* if she has devoted herself to every good work.

11 But refuse *to put* younger widows *on the list*, for when they feel [a]sensual desires in disregard of Christ, they want to get married,

12 *thus* incurring condemnation, because they have set aside their previous [1]pledge.

13 And at the same time they also learn *to be* idle, as they go around from house to house; and not merely idle, but also [a]gossips and [b]busybodies, talking about [c]things not proper *to mention*.

14 Therefore, I want younger *widows* to get [a]married, bear children, [b]keep house, *and* [c]give the enemy no occasion for reproach;

15 for some [a]have already turned aside to follow [b]Satan.

16 If any woman who is a believer [a]has *dependent* widows, let her [b]assist them, and let not the church be burdened, so that it may assist those who are [c]widows indeed.

Concerning Elders

17 Let [a]the elders who [b]rule well be considered worthy of double honor, especially those who [c]work hard [1]at preaching and teaching.

18 For the Scripture says, "[a]YOU SHALL NOT MUZZLE THE OX WHILE HE IS THRESHING," and "[b]The laborer is worthy of his wages."

19 Do not receive an accusation against an [a]elder except on the basis of [b]two or three witnesses.

20 Those who continue in sin, [a]rebuke in the presence of all, [b]so that the rest also may be fearful *of sinning*.

21 [a]I solemnly charge you in the presence of God and of Christ Jesus and of *His* chosen angels, to maintain these *principles* without bias, doing nothing in a *spirit of* partiality.

22 [a]Do not lay hands upon anyone *too* hastily and [1]thus share [b]*responsibility for* the sins of others; keep yourself [2]free from sin.

23 No longer drink water *exclusively*, but [a]use a little wine for the sake of your stomach and your frequent ailments.

24 The sins of some men are quite evident, going before them to judgment; for others, their *sins* [a]follow after.

25 Likewise also, deeds that are good are quite evident, and [a]those which are otherwise cannot be concealed.

Instructions to Those Who Minister

6 [a]LET all who are under the yoke as slaves regard their own masters as worthy of all honor so [b]that the name of God and *our* doctrine may not be spoken against.

2 And let those who have believers as their masters not be disrespectful to them because they are [a]brethren, but let them serve them all the more, because those who [1]partake of the benefit are believers and beloved. [b]Teach and [2]preach these *principles*.

3 If anyone [a]advocates a different doctrine, and does not [1]agree with [b]sound words, those of our Lord Jesus Christ, and with the doctrine [c]conforming to godliness,

4 he is [a]conceited *and* understands nothing; but he [1]has a morbid interest in [b]controversial questions and [c]disputes about words, out of which arise envy, strife, abusive language, evil suspicions,

5 and constant friction between [a]men of depraved mind and deprived of the truth, who [b]suppose that [1]godliness is a means of gain.

14 [1]Or, *board of elders* [a]1 Tim. 1:18 [b]Acts 6:6; 1 Tim. 5:22; 2 Tim. 1:6 [c]Acts 11:30
16 [1]Lit., *save both yourself and those* [a]Acts 20:28 [b]1 Cor. 1:21

1 [a]Lev. 19:32 [b]Titus 2:2 [c]Titus 2:6
3 [a]Acts 6:1; 9:39, 41; 1 Tim. 5:5, 16
4 [1]Lit., *give back recompenses* [a]Eph. 6:2 [b]1 Tim. 2:3
5 [a]Acts 6:1; 9:39, 41; 1 Tim. 5:3, 16 [b]1 Cor. 7:34; 1 Pet. 3:5 [c]Luke 2:37; 1 Tim. 2:1; 2 Tim. 1:3
6 [a]James 5:5 [b]Luke 15:24; 2 Tim. 3:6; Rev. 3:1
7 [1]Or, *Keep commanding* [a]1 Tim. 4:11
8 [a]2 Tim. 2:12; Titus 1:16; 2 Pet. 2:1; Jude 4
9 [a]1 Tim. 5:16 [b]1 Tim. 3:2
10 [1]Or, *holy ones* [a]Acts 9:36; 1 Tim. 6:18; Titus 2:7; 3:8; 1 Pet. 2:12 [b]1 Tim. 3:2 [c]Luke 7:44; John 13:14 [d]1 Tim. 5:16
11 [a]Rev. 18:7
12 [1]Lit., *faith*
13 [a]3 John 10 [b]2 Thess. 3:11 [c]Titus 1:11
14 [a]1 Cor. 7:9; 1 Tim. 4:3 [b]Titus 2:5 [c]1 Tim. 6:1
15 [a]1 Tim. 1:20 [b]Matt. 4:10
16 [a]1 Tim. 5:4 [b]1 Tim. 5:10 [c]1 Tim. 5:3
17 [1]Lit., *in word* [a]Acts 11:30; 1 Tim. 4:14; 5:19 [b]Rom. 12:8 [c]1 Thess. 5:12
18 [a]Deut. 25:4; 1 Cor. 9:9 [b]Lev. 19:13; Deut. 24:15; Matt. 10:10; Luke 10:7; 1 Cor. 9:14
19 [a]Acts 11:30; 1 Tim. 4:14; 5:17 [b]Deut. 17:6; 19:15; Matt. 18:16
20 [a]Gal. 2:14; Eph. 5:11; 2 Tim. 4:2 [b]2 Cor. 7:11
21 [a]Luke 9:26; 1 Tim. 6:13; 2 Tim. 2:14; 4:1
22 [1]Lit., *do not share* [2]Lit., *pure* [a]1 Tim. 3:10; 4:14 [b]Eph. 5:11; 1 Tim. 3:2-7
23 [a]1 Tim. 3:8
24 [a]Rev. 14:13
25 [a]Prov. 10:9

1 [a]Eph. 6:5; Titus 2:9; 1 Pet. 2:18 [b]Titus 2:5
2 [1]Or, *benefit by their service* [2]Lit., *exhort, urge* [a]Acts 1:15; Gal. 3:28; Philem. 16 [b]1 Tim. 4:11

3 [1]Lit., *come to;* or, *come with* [a]1 Tim. 1:3 [b]1 Tim. 1:10 [c]Titus 1:1
4 [1]Lit., *is sick about* [a]1 Tim. 3:6 [b]1 Tim. 1:4 [c]Acts 18:15; 2 Tim. 2:14
5 [1]Or, *religion* [a]2 Tim. 3:8; Titus 1:15 [b]Titus 1:11; 2 Pet. 2:3

6 [a]But godliness *actually* is a means
of [b]great gain, when accompanied by
[c]contentment.
7 For [a]we have brought nothing into
the world, [1]so we cannot take anything
out of it either.
8 And if we [a]have food and covering,
with these we shall be content.
9 [a]But those who want to get rich fall
into temptation and [b]a snare and many
foolish and harmful desires which
plunge men into ruin and destruction.
10 For [a]the love of money is a root of
all [1]sorts of evil, and some by longing for
it have [b]wandered away from the faith,
and pierced themselves with many a
pang.
11 But [a]flee from these things, you
[b]man of God; and pursue righteousness,
godliness, [c]faith, [d]love, [1]perseverance
and gentleness.
12 [a]Fight the good fight of [b]faith;
[c]take hold of the eternal life [d]to which
you were called, and you made the good
[e]confession in the presence of [f]many
witnesses.
13 [a]I charge you in the presence of
God, who [1]gives life to all things, and of
[b]Christ Jesus, who testified the [c]good
confession [d]before Pontius Pilate,
14 that you keep the commandment
without stain or reproach until the [a]ap-
pearing of our Lord Jesus Christ,
15 which He will [1]bring about at [a]the
proper time—He who is [b]the blessed
and [c]only Sovereign, [d]the King of [2]kings
and [e]Lord of [3]lords;
16 [a]who alone possesses immortality
and [b]dwells in unapproachable light;
[c]whom no man has seen or can see. [d]To
Him *be* honor and eternal dominion!
Amen.
17 Instruct those who are rich in [a]this
present world [b]not to be conceited or to
[c]fix their hope on the uncertainty of
riches, but on God, [d]who richly supplies
us with all things to enjoy.
18 *Instruct them* to do good, to be rich
in [a]good [1]works, [b]to be generous and
ready to share,
19 [a]storing up for themselves the treasure of a good foundation for the future,
so that they may [b]take hold of that
which is life indeed.
20 O [a]Timothy, guard [b]what has been
entrusted to you, avoiding [c]worldly *and*
empty chatter *and* the opposing arguments of what is falsely called "knowledge"—
21 which some have professed and
thus [a]gone astray [1]from [b]the faith.
[c]Grace be with you.

6 [a]Luke 12:15-21; 1 Tim. 6:6-10 [b]1 Tim. 4:8 [c]Phil. 4:11; Heb. 13:5
7 [1]Later mss. read *it is clear that* [a]Job 1:21; Eccl. 5:15
8 [a]Prov. 30:8
9 [a]Prov. 15:27; 23:4; 28:20; Luke 12:21; 1 Tim. 6:17 [b]1 Tim. 3:7
10 [1]Lit., *the evils* [a]Col. 3:5; 1 Tim. 3:3; 6:9 [b]James 5:19
11 [1]Or, *steadfastness* [a]2 Tim. 2:22 [b]2 Tim. 3:17 [c]1 Tim. 1:14 [d]2 Tim. 3:10
12 [a]1 Cor. 9:25f.; Phil. 1:30; 1 Tim. 1:18 [b]1 Tim. 1:19 [c]Phil. 3:12; 1 Tim. 6:19 [d]Col. 3:15 [e]2 Cor. 9:13; 1 Tim. 6:13 [f]1 Tim. 4:14; 2 Tim. 2:2
13 [1]Or, *preserves alive* [a]1 Tim. 5:21 [b]Gal. 3:26; 1 Tim. 1:12, 15; 2:5 [c]2 Cor. 9:13; 1 Tim. 6:12 [d]Matt. 27:2; John 18:37
14 [a]2 Thess. 2:8
15 [1]Lit., *show* [2]Lit., *those who reign as kings* [3]Lit., *those who rule as lords* [a]1 Tim. 2:6 [b]1 Tim. 1:11 [c]1 Tim. 1:17 [d]Deut. 10:17; Rev. 17:14; 19:16 [e]Ps. 136:3
16 [a]1 Tim. 1:17 [b]Ps. 104:2; James 1:17; 1 John 1:5 [c]John 1:18 [d]1 Tim. 1:17
17 [a]Matt. 12:32; 2 Tim. 4:10; Titus 2:12 [b]Ps. 62:10; Luke 12:20; Rom. 11:20; 1 Tim. 6:9 [c]1 Tim. 4:10 [d]Acts 14:17
18 [1]Or, *deeds* [a]1 Tim. 5:10 [b]Rom. 12:8; Eph. 4:28
19 [a]Matt. 6:20 [b]1 Tim. 6:12
20 [a]1 Tim. 1:2 [b]2 Tim. 1:12, 14 [c]1 Tim. 1:9; 2 Tim. 2:16
21 [1]Lit., *concerning* [a]2 Tim. 2:18 [b]1 Tim. 1:19 [c]Col. 4:18

THE SECOND EPISTLE OF PAUL TO TIMOTHY

Timothy Charged to Guard His Trust

1 PAUL, [a]an apostle of [b]Christ Jesus
[1c]by the will of God, according to
the promise of [d]life in Christ Jesus,
2 to [a]Timothy, my beloved [1b]son:
[c]Grace, mercy *and* peace from God the
Father and Christ Jesus our Lord.
3 [a]I thank God, whom I [b]serve with a
[c]clear conscience [1]the way my forefathers did, [d]as I constantly remember you
in my [2]prayers night and day,
4 [a]longing to see you, [b]even as I
recall your tears, so that I may be filled
with joy.
5 [1]For I am mindful of the [a]sincere
faith within you, which first dwelt in
your grandmother Lois, and [b]your
mother Eunice, and I am sure that *it is* in
you as well.
6 And for this reason I remind you to
kindle afresh [a]the gift of God which is in
you through [a]the laying on of my hands.
7 For God has not given us a [a]spirit
of timidity, but of power and love and
[1]discipline.
8 Therefore [a]do not be ashamed of
the [b]testimony of our Lord, or of me
[c]His prisoner; but join with *me* in [d]suf-
fering for the [e]gospel according to the
power of God,
9 who has [a]saved us, and [b]called us
with a holy [c]calling, [d]not according to
our works, but according to His own
[b]purpose and grace which was granted
us in [e]Christ Jesus from [f]all eternity,
10 but [a]now has been revealed by the
[b]appearing of our Savior [c]Christ Jesus,
who [d]abolished death, and brought life
and immortality to light through the
gospel,
11 [a]for which I was appointed a
preacher and an apostle and a teacher.
12 For this reason I also suffer these
things, but [a]I am not ashamed; for I
know [b]whom I have believed and I am
convinced that He is able to [c]guard what
I have entrusted to Him [1]until [d]that day.

1 [1]Lit., *through* [a]2 Cor. 1:1 [b]Gal. 3:26 [c]1 Cor. 1:1 [d]1 Tim. 6:19
2 [1]Lit., *child* [a]Acts 16:1; 1 Tim. 1:2 [b]1 Tim. 1:2; 2 Tim. 2:1; Titus 1:4 [c]Rom. 1:7
3 [1]Lit., *from my forefathers* [2]Or, *petitions* [a]Rom. 1:8 [b]Acts 24:14 [c]Acts 23:1; 24:16; 1 Tim. 1:5 [d]Rom. 1:9
4 [a]2 Tim. 4:9, 21 [b]Acts 20:37
5 [1]Lit., *Receiving remembrance of* [a]1 Tim. 1:5 [b]Acts 16:1; 2 Tim. 3:15
6 [a]1 Tim. 4:14
7 [1]Or, *sound judgment* [a]John 14:27; Rom. 8:15
8 [a]Mark 8:38; Rom. 1:16; 2 Tim. 1:12, 16 [b]1 Cor. 1:6 [c]Eph. 3:1; 2 Tim. 1:16 [d]2 Tim. 2:3, 9; 4:5 [e]2 Tim. 1:10; 2:8
9 [a]Rom. 11:14 [b]Rom. 8:28ff. [c]Rom. 11:29 [d]Eph. 2:9 [e]2 Tim. 1:1 [f]Rom. 16:25; Eph. 1:4; Titus 1:2
10 [a]Rom. 16:26 [b]2 Thess. 2:8; 2 Tim. 4:1, 8; Titus 2:11 [c]2 Tim. 1:1 [d]1 Cor. 15:26; Heb. 2:14f.
11 [a]1 Tim. 2:7
12 [1]Or, *for* [a]2 Tim. 1:8, 16 [b]Titus 3:8 [c]1 Tim. 6:20; 2 Tim. 1:14 [d]1 Cor. 1:8; 3:13; 2 Tim. 1:18; 4:8

13 [1a]Retain the [b]standard of [c]sound
words [d]which you have heard from me,
in the [e]faith and love which are in
[f]Christ Jesus.
14 Guard, through the Holy Spirit
who [a]dwells in us, the [1b]treasure which
has been entrusted to *you.*
15 You are aware of the fact that all
who are in [1a]Asia [b]turned away from
me, among whom are Phygelus and
Hermogenes.
16 The Lord grant mercy to [a]the
house of Onesiphorus for he often refreshed me, and [b]was not ashamed of my
[1c]chains;
17 but when he was in Rome, he
eagerly searched for me, and found
me—
18 the Lord grant to him to find mercy
from the Lord on [a]that day—and you
know very well what services he rendered at [b]Ephesus.

Be Strong

2 YOU therefore, my [1a]son, [b]be
strong in the grace that is in [c]Christ
Jesus.
2 And the things [a]which you have
heard from me in the presence of [b]many
witnesses, these [c]entrust to [d]faithful
men, who will be [e]able to teach others
also.
3 [a]Suffer hardship with *me,* as a good
[b]soldier of [c]Christ Jesus.
4 No soldier in active service [a]entan-
gles himself in the affairs of everyday
life, so that he may please the one who
enlisted him as a soldier.
5 And also if anyone [a]competes as an
athlete, he [1]does not win the prize unless
he competes according to the rules.
6 [a]The hard-working farmer ought to
be the first to receive his share of the
crops.
7 Consider what I say, for the Lord
will give you understanding in everything.
8 Remember Jesus Christ, [a]risen
from the dead, [b]descendant of David,
[c]according to my gospel,
9 [1]for which I [a]suffer hardship even
to [b]imprisonment as a [c]criminal; but
[d]the word of God [e]is not imprisoned.
10 For this reason [a]I endure all things
for [b]the sake of those who are chosen,
[c]that they also may obtain the [d]salvation
which is in [e]Christ Jesus *and* with *it*
[f]eternal glory.
11 [a]It is a trustworthy statement:
For [b]if we died with Him, we shall
also live with Him;
12 If we endure, [a]we shall also reign
with Him;
If we [1b]deny Him, He also will
deny us;
13 If we are faithless, [a]He remains
faithful; for [b]He cannot deny
Himself.

An Unashamed Workman

14 Remind *them* of these things, and
solemnly [a]charge *them* in the presence of
God not to [b]wrangle about words, which
is useless, *and leads* to the ruin of the
hearers.
15 Be diligent to [a]present yourself
approved to God as a workman who
does not need to be ashamed, handling
accurately [b]the word of truth.
16 But [a]avoid [b]worldly *and* empty
chatter, for [1]it will lead to further ungodliness,
17 and their [1]talk will spread like
[2]gangrene. Among them are [a]Hyme-
naeus and Philetus,
18 *men* who have gone astray from the
truth saying that [a]the resurrection has
already taken place, and thus they upset
[b]the faith of some.
19 Nevertheless, the [a]firm foundation
of God stands, having this [b]seal, "[c]The
Lord knows those who are His," and,
"[d]Let everyone who names the name of
the Lord abstain from wickedness."
20 Now in a large house there are not
only gold and silver vessels, but also
vessels of wood and of earthenware, and
[a]some to honor and some to dishonor.
21 Therefore, if a man cleanses himself from [a]these *things,* he will be a vessel
for honor, sanctified, useful to the Master, [b]prepared for every good work.
22 Now [a]flee from youthful lusts, and
pursue righteousness, [b]faith, love *and*
peace, with those who [c]call on the Lord
[d]from a pure heart.
23 But refuse foolish and ignorant
[a]speculations, knowing that they [b]pro-
duce [1]quarrels.
24 And [a]the Lord's bond-servant must
not be quarrelsome, but be kind to all,
[b]able to teach, patient when wronged,
25 [a]with gentleness correcting those
who are in opposition, [b]if perhaps God
may grant them repentance leading to
[c]the knowledge of the truth,
26 and they may come to their senses
and escape from [a]the snare of the devil,
having been [b]held captive [1]by him to do
his will.

"Difficult Times Will Come"

3 BUT realize this, that [a]in the last
days difficult times will come.
2 For men will be [a]lovers of self,
[b]lovers of money, [c]boastful, [c]arrogant,
[d]revilers, [c]disobedient to parents, [e]un-
grateful, [f]unholy,
3 [a]unloving, irreconcilable, [b]mali-
cious gossips, without self-control, brutal, [1c]haters of good,

13 [1]Or, *Hold the example* [a]2 Tim. 3:14; Titus 1:9 [b]Rom. 2:20; 6:17 [c]1 Tim. 1:10 [d]2 Tim. 2:2 [e]1 Tim. 1:14 [f]2 Tim. 1:1
14 [1]Lit., *good deposit* [a]Rom. 8:9 [b]1 Tim. 6:20; 2 Tim. 1:12
15 [1]I.e., the province of Asia [a]Acts 2:9 [b]2 Tim. 4:10, 11, 16
16 [1]Lit., *chain* [a]2 Tim. 4:19 [b]2 Tim. 1:8 [c]Eph. 6:20
18 [a]1 Cor. 1:8; 3:13; 2 Tim. 1:12; 4:8 [b]Acts 18:19; 1 Tim. 1:3

1 [1]Lit., *child* [a]2 Tim. 1:2 [b]Eph. 6:10 [c]2 Tim. 1:1
2 [a]2 Tim. 1:13 [b]1 Tim. 6:12 [c]1 Tim. 1:18 [d]1 Tim. 1:12 [e]2 Cor. 2:14ff.; 3:5
3 [a]2 Tim. 1:8 [b]1 Cor. 9:7; 1 Tim. 1:18 [c]2 Tim. 1:1
4 [a]2 Pet. 2:20
5 [1]Lit., *is not crowned* [a]1 Cor. 9:25
6 [a]1 Cor. 9:10
8 [a]Acts 2:24 [b]Matt. 1:1 [c]Rom. 2:16
9 [1]Lit., *in which* [a]2 Tim. 1:8; 2:3 [b]Phil. 1:7 [c]Luke 23:32 [d]1 Thess. 1:8 [e]Acts 28:31; 2 Tim. 4:17
10 [a]Col. 1:24 [b]Luke 18:7; Titus 1:1 [c]2 Cor. 1:6; 1 Thess. 5:9 [d]1 Cor. 1:21 [e]2 Tim. 1:1; 2:1, 3 [f]2 Cor. 4:17; 1 Pet. 5:10
11 [a]1 Tim. 1:15 [b]Rom. 6:8; 1 Thess. 5:10
12 [1]Lit., *shall deny* [a]Matt. 19:28; Luke 22:29; Rom. 5:17; 8:17 [b]Matt. 10:33; Luke 12:9; 1 Tim. 5:8
13 [a]Rom. 3:3; 1 Cor. 1:9 [b]Num. 23:19; Titus 1:2
14 [a]1 Tim. 5:21; 2 Tim. 4:1 [b]1 Tim. 6:4; 2 Tim. 2:23; Titus 3:9
15 [a]Rom. 6:13; James 1:12 [b]Eph. 1:13; James 1:18
16 [1]Lit., *they will make further progress in ungodliness* [a]Titus 3:9 [b]1 Tim. 1:9; 6:20
17 [1]Lit., *word* [2]Or, *cancer* [a]1 Tim. 1:20
18 [a]1 Cor. 15:12 [b]1 Tim. 1:19; Titus 1:11
19 [a]Is. 28:16f.; 1 Tim. 3:15 [b]John 3:33 [c]John 10:14; 1 Cor. 8:3 [d]Luke 13:27; 1 Cor. 1:2
20 [a]Rom. 9:21
21 [a]1 Tim. 6:11; 2 Tim. 2:16-18 [b]2 Cor. 9:8; Eph. 2:10; 2 Tim. 3:17
22 [a]1 Tim. 6:11 [b]1 Tim. 1:14 [c]Acts 7:59 [d]1 Tim. 1:5

23 [1]Lit., *fightings* [a]1 Tim. 6:4; 2 Tim. 2:14; Titus 3:9 [b]Titus 3:9; James 4:1
24 [a]1 Tim. 3:3; Titus 1:7 [b]1 Tim. 3:2
25 [a]Gal. 6:1; Titus 3:2; 1 Pet. 3:15 [b]Acts 8:22 [c]1 Tim. 2:4
26 [1]Or possibly, *by him, to do His will* [a]1 Tim. 3:7 [b]Luke 5:10

1 [a]1 Tim. 4:1
2 [a]Phil. 2:21 [b]Luke 16:14; 1 Tim. 3:3; 6:10 [c]Rom. 1:30 [d]2 Pet. 2:10-12 [e]Luke 6:35 [f]1 Tim. 1:9
3 [1]Lit., *not loving good* [a]Rom. 1:31 [b]1 Tim. 3:11 [c]Titus 1:8

4 [a]treacherous, [b]reckless, [c]conceited,
[d]lovers of pleasure rather than lovers of
God;
5 holding to a form of [1a]godliness,
although they have [b]denied its power;
and [c]avoid such men as these.
6 For among them are those who
[1a]enter into households and captivate
[b]weak women weighed down with sins,
led on by [c]various impulses,
7 always learning and never able to
[a]come to the [1]knowledge of the truth.
8 And just as [a]Jannes and Jambres
[b]opposed Moses, so these *men* also
oppose the truth, [c]men of depraved
mind, rejected as regards the faith.
9 But they will not make further
progress; for their [a]folly will be obvious
to all, [b]as also that of those *two* came to
be.
10 But you [a]followed my teaching,
conduct, purpose, faith, patience, [b]love,
[1]perseverance,
11 [a]persecutions, *and* [b]sufferings, such
as happened to me at [c]Antioch, at [d]Ico-
nium *and* at [e]Lystra; what [f]persecutions
I endured, and out of them all [g]the Lord
delivered me!
12 And indeed, all who desire to live
godly in Christ Jesus [a]will be persecuted.
13 But evil men and impostors [a]will
proceed *from bad* to worse, [b]deceiving
and being deceived.
14 You, however, [a]continue in the
things you have learned and become
convinced of, knowing from whom you
have learned *them*;
15 and that [a]from childhood you have
known [b]the sacred writings which are
able to [c]give you the wisdom that leads
to [d]salvation through faith which is in
[e]Christ Jesus.
16 [1a]All Scripture is [2]inspired by God
and profitable for teaching, for reproof,
for correction, for [3]training in righteousness;
17 that [a]the man of God may be
adequate, [b]equipped for every good
work.

"Preach the Word"

4 [a]I SOLEMNLY charge *you* in the
presence of God and of Christ Jesus,
who is to [b]judge the living and the dead,
and by His [c]appearing and His kingdom:
2 preach [a]the word; be ready in
season *and* out of season; [b]reprove,
rebuke, exhort, with [1]great [c]patience and
instruction.
3 For [a]the time will come when they
will not endure [b]sound doctrine; but
wanting to have their ears tickled, they
will accumulate for themselves teachers
in accordance to their own desires;
4 and [a]will turn away their ears from
the truth, and [b]will turn aside to myths.
5 But you, [a]be sober in all things,
[b]endure hardship, do the work of an
[c]evangelist, fulfill your [d]ministry.

4 [a]Acts 7:52 [b]Acts 19:36 [c]1 Tim. 3:6 [d]Phil. 3:19
5 [1]Or, *religion* [a]1 Tim. 4:7 [b]1 Tim. 5:8 [c]Matt. 7:15; 2 Thess. 3:6
6 [1]Or, *creep into* [a]Jude 4 [b]1 Tim. 5:6; Titus 3:3 [c]Titus 3:3
7 [1]Or, *recognition* [a]2 Tim. 2:25
8 [a]Ex. 7:11 [b]Acts 13:8 [c]1 Tim. 6:5
9 [a]Luke 6:11 [b]Ex. 7:11, 12; 8:18; 9:11
10 [1]Or, *steadfastness* [a]Phil. 2:20, 22; 1 Tim. 4:6 [b]1 Tim. 6:11
11 [a]2 Cor. 12:10 [b]2 Cor. 1:5, 7 [c]Acts 13:14, 45, 50 [d]Acts 14:1-7, 19 [e]Acts 14:8-20 [f]2 Cor. 11:23-27 [g]Rom. 15:31
12 [a]John 15:20; Acts 14:22; 2 Cor. 4:9f.
13 [a]2 Tim. 2:16 [b]Titus 3:3
14 [a]2 Tim. 1:13; Titus 1:9
15 [a]2 Tim. 1:5 [b]John 5:47; Rom. 2:27 [c]Ps. 119:98f. [d]1 Cor. 1:21 [e]2 Tim. 1:1
16 [1]Or possibly, *Every Scripture inspired by God is also profitable* [2]Lit., *God-breathed* [3]Lit., *training which is in* [a]Rom. 4:23f.; 15:4; 2 Pet. 1:20f.
17 [a]1 Tim. 6:11 [b]2 Tim. 2:21; Heb. 13:21

1 [a]1 Tim. 5:21; 2 Tim. 2:14 [b]Acts 10:42 [c]2 Thess. 2:8; 2 Tim. 1:10; 4:8
2 [1]Lit., *all* [a]Gal. 6:6; Col. 4:3; 1 Thess. 1:6 [b]1 Tim. 5:20; Titus 1:13; 2:15 [c]2 Tim. 3:10
3 [a]2 Tim. 3:1 [b]1 Tim. 1:10; 2 Tim. 1:13
4 [a]2 Thess. 2:11; Titus 1:14 [b]1 Tim. 1:4
5 [a]1 Pet. 1:13 [b]2 Tim. 1:8 [c]Acts 21:8 [d]Eph. 4:12; Col. 4:17
6 [a]Phil. 2:17 [b]Phil. 1:23; 2 Pet. 1:14
7 [a]1 Cor. 9:25f.; Phil. 1:30; 1 Tim. 1:18; 6:12 [b]Acts 20:24; 1 Cor. 9:24 [c]2 Tim. 3:10
8 [a]Col. 1:5; 1 Pet. 1:4 [b]1 Cor. 9:25; 2 Tim. 2:5; James 1:12 [c]2 Tim. 1:12 [d]Phil. 3:11 [e]2 Tim. 4:1
9 [a]2 Tim. 1:4; 4:21; Titus 3:12
10 [1]Or, *age* [2]Some ancient mss. read *Gaul* [a]Col. 4:14 [b]1 Tim. 6:17 [c]Acts 17:1 [d]Acts 16:6 [e]2 Cor. 2:13; 8:23; Gal. 2:3; Titus 1:4

6 For I am already being [a]poured out
as a drink offering, and the time of [b]my
departure has come.
7 [a]I have fought the good fight, I
have finished [b]the course, I have kept
[c]the faith;
8 in the future there [a]is laid up for
me [b]the crown of righteousness, which
the Lord, the righteous Judge, will award
to me on [c]that day; and not only to me,
but also to [d]all who have loved His
[e]appearing.

Personal Concerns

9 [a]Make every effort to come to me
soon;
10 for [a]Demas, having loved [b]this
present [1]world, has deserted me and
gone to [c]Thessalonica; Crescens *has
gone* to [2d]Galatia, [e]Titus to Dalmatia.
11 [a]Only [b]Luke is with me. Pick up
[c]Mark and bring him with you, [d]for he is
useful to me for service.
12 But [a]Tychicus I have sent to [b]Eph-
esus.
13 When you come bring the cloak
which I left at [a]Troas with Carpus, and
the books, especially the parchments.
14 [a]Alexander the coppersmith did me
much harm; [b]the Lord will repay him
according to his deeds.
15 Be on guard against him yourself,
for he vigorously opposed our [1]teaching.
16 At my first defense no one supported me, but all deserted me; [a]may it
not be counted against them.
17 But the Lord stood with me, and
[a]strengthened me, in order that through
me [b]the proclamation might [1]be [c]fully
accomplished, and that all [d]the Gentiles
might hear; and I was [e]delivered out of
[f]the lion's mouth.
18 The Lord will deliver me from
every evil deed, and will [1a]bring me
safely to His [b]heavenly kingdom; [c]to
[2]Him *be* the glory forever and ever.
Amen.
19 Greet Prisca and [a]Aquila, and [b]the
household of Onesiphorus.
20 [a]Erastus remained at [b]Corinth, but
[c]Trophimus I left sick at [d]Miletus.
21 [a]Make every effort to come before
[b]winter. Eubulus greets you, also Pudens
and Linus and Claudia and all the
brethren.
22 [a]The Lord be with your spirit.
[b]Grace be with you.

11 [a]2 Tim. 1:15 [b]Col. 4:14; Philem. 24 [c]Acts 12:12, 25; 15:37-39; Col. 4:10 [d]2 Tim. 2:21
12 [a]Acts 20:4; Eph. 6:21, 22; Col. 4:7f. [b]Acts 18:19
13 [a]Acts 16:8
14 [a]Acts 19:33; 1 Tim. 1:20 [b]Ps. 62:12; Rom. 2:6; 12:19
15 [1]Lit., *words*
16 [a]Acts 7:60; 1 Cor. 13:5
17 [1]Or, *be fulfilled* [a]1 Tim. 1:12; 2 Tim. 2:1 [b]Titus 1:3 [c]2 Tim. 4:5 [d]Acts 9:15; Phil. 1:12ff. [e]Rom. 15:31; 2 Tim. 3:11 [f]1 Sam. 17:37; Ps. 22:21
18 [1]Or, *save me for* [2]Lit., *Whom* [a]1 Cor. 1:21 [b]1 Cor. 15:50; 2 Tim. 4:1; Heb. 11:16; 12:22 [c]Rom. 11:36; 2 Pet. 3:18
19 [a]Acts 18:2 [b]2 Tim. 1:16
20 [a]Acts 19:22; Rom. 16:23 [b]Acts 18:1 [c]Acts 20:4; 21:29 [d]Acts 20:15
21 [a]2 Tim. 4:9 [b]Titus 3:12
22 [a]Gal. 6:18; Phil. 4:23; Philem. 25 [b]Col. 4:18

THE EPISTLE OF PAUL TO
TITUS

Salutation

1 PAUL, [a]a bond-servant of God, and
an [b]apostle of Jesus Christ, [1]for the
faith of those [c]chosen of God and [d]the
knowledge of the truth which is [e]accord-
ing to godliness,
2 in [a]the hope of eternal life, which
God, [b]who cannot lie, [c]promised [1d]long
ages ago,
3 but [a]at the proper time manifested,
even His word, in [b]the proclamation
[c]with which I was entrusted [d]according
to the commandment of [e]God our Savior;
4 to [a]Titus, [b]my true child [1]in a
[c]common faith: [d]Grace and peace from
God the Father and [e]Christ Jesus our
Savior.

Qualifications of Elders

5 For this reason I left you in [a]Crete,
that you might set in order what remains, and [b]appoint [c]elders in every city
as I directed you,
6 *namely,* [a]if any man be above reproach, the [b]husband of one wife, having
children who believe, not accused of
[c]dissipation or [d]rebellion.
7 For the [1a]overseer must be above
reproach as [b]God's steward, not [c]self-
willed, not quick-tempered, not [d]ad-
dicted to wine, not pugnacious, [e]not
fond of sordid gain,
8 but [a]hospitable, [b]loving what is
good, sensible, just, devout, self-
controlled,
9 [a]holding fast the faithful word
which is in accordance with the teaching,
that he may be able both to exhort in
[b]sound doctrine and to refute those who
contradict.
10 [a]For there are many [b]rebellious
men, [c]empty talkers and deceivers, especially [d]those of the circumcision,
11 who must be silenced because they
are upsetting [a]whole families, teaching
[b]things they should not *teach,* [c]for the
sake of sordid gain.
12 One of themselves, a prophet of
their own, said, "[a]Cretans are always
liars, evil beasts, lazy gluttons."
13 This testimony is true. For this
cause [a]reprove them [b]severely that they
may be [c]sound in the faith,
14 not paying attention to Jewish
[a]myths and [b]commandments of men
who [c]turn away from the truth.
15 [a]To the pure, all things are pure;
but [b]to those who are defiled and unbelieving, nothing is pure, but both their
[c]mind and their conscience are defiled.
16 [a]They profess to know God, but by
their deeds they [b]deny *Him,* being [c]de-
testable and [d]disobedient, and [e]worth-
less [f]for any good deed.

1 [1]Or, *according to* [a]Rom. 1:1; James 1:1; Rev. 1:1 [b]2 Cor. 1:1 [c]Luke 18:7 [d]1 Tim. 2:4 [e]1 Tim. 6:3
2 [1]Lit., *before times eternal* [a]2 Tim. 1:1; Titus 3:7 [b]2 Tim. 2:13; Heb. 6:18 [c]Rom. 1:2 [d]2 Tim. 1:9
3 [a]1 Tim. 2:6 [b]Rom. 16:25; 2 Tim. 4:17 [c]1 Tim. 1:11 [d]1 Tim. 1:1 [e]Luke 1:47; 1 Tim. 1:1; Titus 2:10; 3:4
4 [1]Lit., *according to* [a]2 Cor. 2:13; 8:23; Gal. 2:3; 2 Tim. 4:10 [b]2 Tim. 1:2 [c]2 Pet. 1:1 [d]Rom. 1:7 [e]1 Tim. 1:12; 2 Tim. 1:1
5 [a]Acts 27:7; Titus 1:12 [b]Acts 14:23 [c]Acts 11:30
6 [a]1 Tim. 3:2-4; Titus 1:6-8 [b]1 Tim. 3:2 [c]Eph. 5:18 [d]Titus 1:10
7 [1]Or, *bishop* [a]1 Tim. 3:2 [b]1 Cor. 4:1 [c]2 Pet. 2:10 [d]1 Tim. 3:3 [e]1 Tim. 3:3, 8
8 [a]1 Tim. 3:2 [b]2 Tim. 3:3
9 [a]2 Thess. 2:15; 1 Tim. 1:19; 2 Tim. 1:13 [b]1 Tim. 1:10; Titus 2:1
10 [a]2 Cor. 11:13 [b]Titus 1:6 [c]1 Tim. 1:6 [d]Acts 11:2
11 [a]1 Tim. 5:4; 2 Tim. 3:6 [b]1 Tim. 5:13 [c]1 Tim. 6:5
12 [a]Acts 2:11; 27:7
13 [a]1 Tim. 5:20; 2 Tim. 4:2; Titus 2:15 [b]2 Cor. 13:10 [c]Titus 2:2
14 [a]1 Tim. 1:4 [b]Col. 2:22 [c]2 Tim. 4:4
15 [a]Luke 11:41; Rom. 14:20 [b]Rom. 14:14, 23 [c]1 Tim. 6:5
16 [a]1 John 2:4 [b]1 Tim. 5:8 [c]Rev. 21:8 [d]Titus 3:3 [e]2 Tim. 3:8 [f]2 Tim. 3:17; Titus 3:1

1 [a]Titus 1:9
2 [1]Or, *steadfastness* [a]Philem. 9 [b]1 Tim. 3:2 [c]Titus 1:13 [d]1 Tim. 1:2, 14
3 [a]1 Tim. 3:11 [b]1 Tim. 3:8
4 [1]Or, *train*
5 [a]1 Tim. 5:14 [b]Eph. 5:22 [c]1 Tim. 6:1
6 [1]Or, *sensible in all things; show* [a]1 Tim. 5:1
7 [1]Or, *soundness;* lit., *uncorruptness* [a]1 Tim. 4:12
8 [a]2 Thess. 3:14; 1 Pet. 2:12
9 [1]Lit., *contradicting* [a]Eph. 6:5; 1 Tim. 6:1
10 [a]Titus 1:3

Duties of the Older and Younger

2 BUT as for you, speak the things
which are fitting for [a]sound doctrine.
2 [a]Older men are to be [b]temperate,
dignified, sensible, [c]sound [d]in faith, in
love, in [1]perseverance.
3 Older women likewise are to be
reverent in their behavior, [a]not malicious
gossips, nor [b]enslaved to much wine,
teaching what is good,
4 that they may [1]encourage the
young women to love their husbands, to
love their children,
5 *to be* sensible, pure, [a]workers at
home, kind, being [b]subject to their own
husbands, [c]that the word of God may
not be dishonored.
6 Likewise urge [a]the young men to
be [1]sensible;
7 in all things show yourself to be [a]an
example of good deeds, *with* [1]purity in
doctrine, dignified,
8 sound *in* speech which is beyond
reproach, in order [a]that the opponent
may be put to shame, having nothing
bad to say about us.
9 *Urge* [a]bondslaves to be subject to
their own masters in everything, to be
well-pleasing, not [1]argumentative,
10 not pilfering, but showing all good
faith that they may adorn the doctrine of
[a]God our Savior in every respect.
11 For the grace of God has [a]ap-
peared, [1b]bringing salvation to all men,
12 [1]instructing us to deny ungodliness
and [a]worldly desires and [b]to live sensi-
bly, righteously and godly [c]in the present age,
13 looking for the blessed hope and
the [a]appearing of the glory of [1]our great
God and Savior, Christ Jesus;
14 who [a]gave Himself for us, [b]that He
might redeem us from every lawless deed
and [c]purify for Himself a [d]people for
His own possession, [e]zealous for good
deeds.
15 These things speak and [a]exhort and
[a]reprove with all [1]authority. [b]Let no one
disregard you.

Godly Living

3 [a]REMIND them [b]to be subject to
rulers, to authorities, to be obedient,
to be [c]ready for every good deed,
2 to malign no one, [a]to be uncontentious, [a]gentle, [b]showing every consideration for all men.

11 [1]Or, *to all men, bringing* [a]2 Tim. 1:10; Titus 3:4 [b]1 Tim. 2:4
12 [1]Or, *disciplining* [a]1 Tim. 6:9; Titus 3:3 [b]2 Tim. 3:12 [c]1 Tim. 6:17
13 [1]Or, *the great God and our Savior* [a]2 Thess. 2:8 [b]1 Tim. 1:1; 2 Tim. 1:2; Titus 1:4; 2 Pet. 1:1
14 [a]1 Tim. 2:6 [b]Ps. 130:8; 1 Pet. 1:18f. [c]Ezek. 37:23; Heb. 1:3; 9:14; 1 John 1:7 [d]Ex. 19:5; Deut. 4:20; 7:6; 14:2; Eph. 1:11; 1 Pet. 2:9 [e]Eph. 2:10; Titus 3:8; 1 Pet. 3:13
15 [1]Lit., *command* [a]1 Tim. 4:13; 5:20; 2 Tim. 4:2 [b]1 Tim. 4:12

1 [a]2 Tim. 2:14 [b]Rom. 13:1 [c]2 Tim. 2:21
2 [a]1 Tim. 3:3; 1 Pet. 2:18 [b]2 Tim. 2:25

3 [a]For we also once were foolish ourselves, [b]disobedient, [c]deceived, [d]enslaved to [e]various lusts and pleasures, spending our life in [f]malice and [f]envy, hateful, hating one another.
4 But when the [a]kindness of [b]God our Savior and *His* love for mankind [c]appeared,
5 [a]He saved us, [b]not on the basis of deeds which we have done in righteousness, but [c]according to His mercy, by the [d]washing of regeneration and [e]renewing by the Holy Spirit,
6 [a]whom He poured out upon us [b]richly through Jesus Christ our Savior,
7 that being justified by His grace we might be made [a]heirs [1]according to *the* hope of eternal life.
8 [a]This is a trustworthy statement; and concerning these things I [b]want you to speak confidently, so that those who have [c]believed God may be careful to [d]engage in good deeds. These things are good and profitable for men.
9 But [a]shun [b]foolish controversies and [c]genealogies and strife and [d]disputes about the Law; for they are [e]unprofitable and worthless.
10 [a]Reject a [b]factious man [c]after a first and second warning,
11 knowing that such a man is [a]perverted and is sinning, being self-condemned.

Personal Concerns

12 When I send Artemas or [a]Tychicus to you, [b]make every effort to come to me at Nicopolis, for I have decided to [c]spend the winter there.
13 Diligently help Zenas the [a]lawyer and [b]Apollos on their way so that nothing is lacking for them.
14 And let [a]our *people* also learn to [b]engage in good [1]deeds to meet [c]pressing needs, that they may not be [d]unfruitful.
15 [a]All who are with me greet you. Greet those who love us [b]in *the* faith.
[c]Grace be with you all.

3 aRom. 11:30; Col. 3:7 bTitus 1:16 c2 Tim. 3:13 dRom. 6:6, 12 e2 Tim. 3:6; Titus 2:12 fRom. 1:29
4 aRom. 2:4; Eph. 2:7; 1 Pet. 2:3 bTitus 2:10 cTitus 2:11
5 aRom. 11:14; 2 Tim. 1:9 bEph. 2:9 cEph. 2:4; 1 Pet. 1:3 dJohn 3:5; Eph. 5:26; 1 Pet. 3:21 eRom. 12:2
6 aRom. 5:5 bRom. 2:4; 1 Tim. 6:17
7 1Or, *of eternal life according to hope* aMatt. 25:34; Mark 10:17; Rom. 8:17, 24; Titus 1:2
8 a1 Tim. 1:15 b1 Tim. 2:8 c2 Tim. 1:12 dTitus 2:7, 14; 3:14
9 a2 Tim. 2:16 b1 Tim. 1:4; 2 Tim. 2:23 c1 Tim. 1:4 dJames 4:1 e2 Tim. 2:14
10 a2 John 10 bRom. 16:17 cMatt. 18:15f.
11 aTitus 1:14
12 aActs 20:4; Eph. 6:21f.; Col. 4:7f.; 2 Tim. 4:12 b2 Tim. 4:9 c2 Tim. 4:21
13 aMatt. 22:35 bActs 18:24; 1 Cor. 16:12
14 1Or, *occupations* aTitus 2:8 bTitus 3:8 cRom. 12:13; Phil. 4:16 dMatt. 7:19; Phil. 1:11; Col. 1:10
15 aActs 20:34 b1 Tim. 1:2 cCol. 4:18

THE EPISTLE OF PAUL TO PHILEMON

Salutation

1 [a]PAUL, [b]a prisoner of [c]Christ Jesus, and [d]Timothy [1]our brother, to Philemon our beloved *brother* and [e]fellow worker,
2 and to Apphia [1a]our sister, and to [b]Archippus our [c]fellow soldier, and to [d]the church in your house:
3 [a]Grace to you and peace from God our Father and the Lord Jesus Christ.

Philemon's Love and Faith

4 [a]I thank my God always, making mention of you in my prayers,
5 because I [a]hear of your love, and of the faith which you have toward the Lord Jesus, and toward all the [1]saints;
6 *and I pray* that the fellowship of your faith may become effective [1]through the [a]knowledge of every good thing which is in [2]you [3]for Christ's sake.
7 For I have come to have much [a]joy and comfort in your love, because the [1]hearts of the [2]saints have been [b]refreshed through you, brother.
8 Therefore, [a]though I have [1]enough confidence in Christ to order you *to do* that which is [b]proper,
9 yet for love's sake I rather [a]appeal *to you*—since I am such a person as Paul, [1]the [b]aged, and now also [c]a prisoner of [d]Christ Jesus—

Plea for Onesimus, a Free Man

10 I [a]appeal to you for my [b]child, whom I have begotten in my [1]imprisonment, [2c]Onesimus,
11 who formerly was useless to you, but now is useful both to you and to me.
12 And I have sent him back to you in person, that is, *sending* my very heart,
13 whom I wished to keep with me, that in your behalf he might minister to me in my [1a]imprisonment for the gospel;
14 but without your consent I did not want to do anything, that your goodness should [a]not be as it were by compulsion, but of your own free will.
15 For perhaps [a]he was for this reason parted *from you* for a while, that you should have him back forever,
16 [a]no longer as a slave, but more than a slave, [b]a beloved brother, especially to me, but how much more to you, both [c]in the flesh and in the Lord.
17 If then you regard me a [a]partner, accept him as *you would* me.
18 But if he has wronged you in any way, or owes you anything, charge that to my account;
19 [a]I, Paul, am writing this with my own hand, I will repay it ([b]lest I should [1]mention to you that you owe to me even your own self as well).

1 1Lit., *the* aPhil. 1:1 bEph. 3:1 cGal. 3:26 d2 Cor. 1:1; Col. 1:1 ePhil. 2:25; Philem. 24
2 1Lit., *the* aRom. 16:1 bCol. 4:17 cPhil. 2:25; 2 Tim. 2:3 dRom. 16:5
3 aRom. 1:7
4 aRom. 1:8f.
5 1Or., *holy ones* aEph. 1:15; Col. 1:4; 1 Thess. 3:6
6 1Or, *in* 2Some ancient mss. read *us* 3Lit., *toward Christ* aPhil. 1:9; Col. 1:9; 3:10
7 1Lit., *inward parts* 2Or, *holy ones* a2 Cor. 7:4, 13 b1 Cor. 16:18; Philem. 20
8 1Lit., *much* a2 Cor. 3:12; 1 Thess. 2:6 bEph. 5:4
9 1Or, *an ambassador* aRom. 12:1 bTitus 2:2 cPhilem. 1 dGal. 3:26; 1 Tim. 1:12; Philem. 23
10 1Lit., *bonds* 2I.e., useful aRom. 12:1 b1 Cor. 4:14f. cCol. 4:9
13 1Lit., *bonds* aPhil. 1:7; Philem. 10
14 a2 Cor. 9:7; 1 Pet. 5:2
15 aGen. 45:5, 8
16 a1 Cor. 7:22 bMatt. 23:8; 1 Tim. 6:2 cEph. 6:5; Col. 3:22
17 a2 Cor. 8:23
19 1Lit., *say* a1 Cor. 16:21; 2 Cor. 10:1; Gal. 5:2 b2 Cor. 9:4

20 Yes, brother, let me benefit from
you in the Lord; [a]refresh my heart in
Christ.
21 [a]Having confidence in your obedience, I write to you, since I know that
you will do even more than what I say.
22 And at the same time also prepare
me a [a]lodging; for [b]I hope that through
[c]your prayers [d]I shall be given to you.

20 [a]Philem. 7
21 [a]2 Cor. 2:3
22 [a]Acts 28:23 [b]Phil. 1:25; 2:24 [c]2 Cor. 1:11 [d]Acts 27:24; Heb. 13:19
23 [a]Col. 1:7; 4:12 [b]Rom. 16:7; Philem. 1

23 [a]Epaphras, my [b]fellow prisoner in
Christ Jesus, greets you,
24 *as do* [a]Mark, [b]Aristarchus, [c]Demas,
[c]Luke, my [d]fellow workers.
25 [a]The grace of the Lord Jesus Christ
be [b]with your spirit.[1]

24 [a]Acts 12:12, 25; 15:37-39; Col. 4:10 [b]Acts 19:29; 27:2; Col. 4:10 [c]Col. 4:14; 2 Tim. 4:10f. [d]Philem. 1
25 [1]Some ancient mss. add *Amen* [a]Gal. 6:18 [b]2 Tim. 4:22

THE EPISTLE TO THE HEBREWS

God's Final Word in His Son

1 GOD, after He [a]spoke long ago to
the fathers in [b]the prophets in many
portions and [c]in many ways,
2 [1a]in these last days [b]has spoken to
us in [c]*His* Son, whom He appointed
[d]heir of all things, [e]through whom also
He made the [2f]world.
3 [1]And He is the radiance of His
glory and the exact [a]representation of
His nature, and [2b]upholds all things by
the word of His power. When He had
made [c]purification of sins, He [d]sat down
at the right hand of the [e]Majesty on
high;
4 having become as much better than
the angels, as He has inherited a more
excellent [a]name than they.
5 For to which of the angels did He
ever say,
"[a]THOU ART MY SON,
TODAY I HAVE BEGOTTEN THEE"?
And again,
"[b]I WILL BE A FATHER TO HIM,
AND HE SHALL BE A SON TO ME"?
6 And [1]when He again [a]brings the
first-born into [2b]the world, He says,
"[c]AND LET ALL THE ANGELS OF
GOD WORSHIP HIM."
7 And of the angels He says,
"[a]WHO MAKES HIS ANGELS WINDS,
AND HIS MINISTERS A FLAME OF
FIRE."
8 But of the Son *He says,*
"[a]THY THRONE, O GOD, IS FOR-
EVER AND EVER,
AND THE RIGHTEOUS SCEPTER IS
THE SCEPTER OF [1]HIS KINGDOM.
9 "[a]THOU HAST LOVED RIGHTEOUS-
NESS AND HATED LAWLESSNESS;
[b]THEREFORE GOD, THY GOD,
HATH [c]ANOINTED THEE
WITH THE OIL OF GLADNESS
ABOVE THY COMPANIONS."
10 And,
"[a]THOU, LORD, IN THE BEGINNING
DIDST LAY THE FOUNDATION OF
THE EARTH,
AND THE HEAVENS ARE THE
WORKS OF THY HANDS;
11 [a]THEY WILL PERISH, BUT THOU
REMAINEST;
[b]AND THEY ALL WILL BECOME
OLD AS A GARMENT,

1 [a]John 9:29; 16:13; Heb. 2:2f.; 3:5; 4:8; 5:5; 11:18; 12:25 [b]Acts 2:30; 3:21 [c]Num. 12:6, 8; Joel 2:28
2 [1]Or, *at the end of these days* [2]Lit., *ages* [a]Matt. 13:39; 1 Pet. 1:20 [b]John 9:29 [c]John 5:26, 27; Heb. 3:6; 5:8; 7:28 [d]Ps. 2:8; Matt. 28:18; Mark 12:7; Rom. 8:17; Heb. 2:8 [e]John 1:3; 1 Cor. 8:6; Col. 1:16 [f]1 Cor. 2:7; Heb. 11:3
3 [1]Lit., *Who being* [2]Lit., *upholding* [a]2 Cor. 4:4 [b]Col. 1:17 [c]Titus 2:14; Heb. 9:14 [d]Mark 16:19; Heb. 8:1; 10:12; 12:2 [e]2 Pet. 1:17
4 [a]Eph. 1:21
5 [a]Ps. 2:7; Acts 13:33; Heb. 5:5 [b]2 Sam. 7:14
6 [1]Or, *again when He brings* [2]Lit., *the inhabited earth* [a]Heb. 10:5 [b]Matt. 24:14 [c]Ps. 97:7
7 [a]Ps. 104:4
8 [1]Some mss. read *Thy* [a]Ps. 45:6
9 [a]Ps. 45:7 [b]John 10:17; Phil. 2:9; Heb. 2:9 [c]Is. 61:1, 3
10 [a]Ps. 102:25
11 [a]Ps. 102:26 [b]Is. 51:6; Heb. 8:13
12 [a]Ps. 102:26, 27 [b]Heb. 13:8
13 [a]Ps. 110:1; Matt. 22:44; Heb. 1:3 [b]Josh. 10:24; Heb. 10:13
14 [a]Ps. 103:20f.; Dan. 7:10 [b]Matt. 25:34; Mark 10:17; Titus 3:7; Heb. 6:12 [c]Rom. 11:14; 1 Cor. 1:21; Heb. 2:3; 5:9; 9:28

12 [a]AND AS A MANTLE THOU WILT
ROLL THEM UP;
AS A GARMENT THEY WILL ALSO
BE CHANGED.
BUT THOU ART [b]THE SAME,
AND THY YEARS WILL NOT COME
TO AN END."
13 But to which of the angels has He
ever said,
"[a]SIT AT MY RIGHT HAND,
[b]UNTIL I MAKE THINE ENEMIES
A FOOTSTOOL FOR THY FEET"?
14 Are they not all [a]ministering spirits, sent out to render service for the sake
of those who will [b]inherit [c]salvation?

Give Heed

2 FOR this reason we must pay much
closer attention to [1]what we have
heard, lest [a]we drift away *from it.*
2 For if the word [a]spoken through
[b]angels proved [1]unalterable, and [c]every
transgression and disobedience received
a just [d]recompense,
3 [a]how shall we escape if we neglect
so great a [b]salvation? [1]After it was at the
first [c]spoken through the Lord, it was
[d]confirmed to us by those who heard,
4 God also bearing witness with
them, both by [a]signs and wonders and
by [b]various [1]miracles and by [2c]gifts of
the Holy Spirit [d]according to His own
will.

Earth Subject to Man

5 For He did not subject to angels
[1a]the world to come, concerning which
we are speaking.
6 But one has testified [a]somewhere,
saying,
"[b]WHAT IS MAN, THAT THOU RE-
MEMBEREST HIM?
OR THE SON OF MAN, THAT THOU
ART CONCERNED ABOUT HIM?
7 "[a]THOU HAST MADE HIM [1]FOR A
LITTLE WHILE LOWER THAN THE
ANGELS;
THOU HAST CROWNED HIM WITH
GLORY AND HONOR,
[2]AND HAST APPOINTED HIM OVER
THE WORKS OF THY HANDS;

1 [1]Lit., *the things that have been heard* [a]Prov. 3:21
2 [1]Or, *steadfast* [a]Heb. 1:1 [b]Acts 7:53 [c]Heb. 10:28 [d]Heb. 10:35; 11:26
3 [1]Lit., *Which was* [a]Heb. 10:29; 12:25 [b]Rom. 11:14; 1 Cor. 1:21; Heb. 1:14; 5:9; 9:28 [c]Heb. 1:1 [d]Mark 16:20; Luke 1:2; 1 John 1:1

4 [1]Or, *works of power* [2]Lit., *distributions* [a]John 4:48 [b]Mark 6:14 [c]1 Cor. 12:4, 11; Eph. 4:7 [d]Eph. 1:5
5 [1]Lit., *the inhabited earth* [a]Matt. 24:14; Heb. 6:5
6 [a]Heb. 4:4 [b]Ps. 8:4
7 [1]Or, *a little lower* [2]Some ancient mss. do not contain *And . . . hands* [a]Ps. 8:5, 6

8 [a]THOU HAST PUT ALL THINGS IN SUBJECTION UNDER HIS FEET."
For in subjecting all things to him, He left nothing that is not subject to him. But now [b]we do not yet see all things subjected to him.

Jesus Briefly Humbled

9 But we do see Him who has been [a]made [1]for a little while lower than the angels, *namely,* Jesus, [b]because of the suffering of death [c]crowned with glory and honor, that [d]by the grace of God He might [e]taste death [f]for everyone.
10 For [a]it was fitting for Him, [b]for whom are all things, and through whom are all things, in bringing many sons to glory, to [c]perfect the [1d]author of their salvation through sufferings.
11 For both He who [a]sanctifies and those who [b]are [1]sanctified are all [c]from one *Father*; for which reason He is not ashamed to call them [d]brethren,
12 saying,
"[a]I WILL PROCLAIM THY NAME TO MY BRETHREN,
IN THE MIDST OF THE [1]CONGREGATION I WILL SING THY PRAISE."
13 And again,
"[a]I WILL PUT MY TRUST IN HIM."
And again,
"[b]BEHOLD, I AND THE CHILDREN WHOM GOD HAS GIVEN ME."
14 Since then the children share in [1a]flesh and blood, [b]He Himself likewise also partook of the same, that [c]through death He might render powerless [d]him who had the power of death, that is, the devil;
15 and might deliver those who through [a]fear of death were subject to slavery all their lives.
16 For assuredly He does not [1]give help to angels, but He gives help to the [2]descendant of Abraham.
17 Therefore, He [1]had [a]to be made like His brethren in all things, that He might [b]become a merciful and faithful [c]high priest in [d]things pertaining to God, to [e]make propitiation for the sins of the people.
18 For since He Himself was [a]tempted in that which He has suffered, He is able to come to the aid of those who are tempted.

Jesus Our High Priest

3 THEREFORE, [a]holy brethren, partakers of a [b]heavenly calling, consider Jesus, [c]the Apostle and [d]High Priest of our [e]confession.
2 [1]He was faithful to Him who [2]appointed Him, as [a]Moses also was in all His house.
3 [a]For He has been counted worthy of more glory than Moses, by just so much as the builder of the house has more honor than the house.
4 For every house is built by someone, but the builder of all things is God.
5 Now [a]Moses was faithful in all His house as [b]a servant, [c]for a testimony of those things [d]which were to be spoken later;
6 but Christ *was faithful* as [a]a Son over His house [b]whose house we are, [c]if we hold fast our [d]confidence and the boast of our [e]hope firm until the end.
7 Therefore, just as [a]the Holy Spirit says,
"[b]TODAY IF YOU HEAR HIS VOICE,
8 [a]DO NOT HARDEN YOUR HEARTS AS [1]WHEN THEY PROVOKED ME,
AS IN THE DAY OF TRIAL IN THE WILDERNESS,
9 [a]WHERE YOUR FATHERS TRIED *Me* BY TESTING *Me*,
AND SAW MY WORKS FOR [b]FORTY YEARS.
10 "[a]THEREFORE I WAS ANGRY WITH THIS GENERATION,
AND SAID, 'THEY ALWAYS GO ASTRAY IN THEIR HEART;
AND THEY DID NOT KNOW MY WAYS';
11 [a]AS I SWORE IN MY WRATH,
'THEY SHALL NOT ENTER MY REST.'"

The Peril of Unbelief

12 [a]Take care, brethren, lest there should be in any one of you an evil, unbelieving heart, in falling away from [b]the living God.
13 But [a]encourage one another day after day, as long as it is *still* called "Today," lest any one of you be hardened by the [b]deceitfulness of sin.
14 For we have become partakers of Christ, [a]if we hold fast the beginning of our [b]assurance firm until the end;
15 while it is said,
"[a]TODAY IF YOU HEAR HIS VOICE,
DO NOT HARDEN YOUR HEARTS, AS [1]WHEN THEY PROVOKED ME."
16 For who [a]provoked *Him* when they had heard? Indeed, [b]did not all those who came out of Egypt *led* by Moses?
17 And with whom was He angry for forty years? Was it not with those who sinned, [a]whose bodies fell in the wilderness?
18 And to whom did He swear [a]that they should not enter His rest, but to those who were [b]disobedient?
19 And *so* we see that they were not able to enter because of [a]unbelief.

The Believer's Rest

4 THEREFORE, let us fear lest, while a promise remains of entering His rest, any one of you should seem to have [a]come short of it.

8 [a]Ps. 8:6; 1 Cor. 15:27 [b]1 Cor. 15:25
9 [1]Or, *a little lower* [a]Heb. 2:7 [b]Phil. 2:9; Heb. 1:9 [c]Acts 2:33; 3:13; 1 Pet. 1:21 [d]John 3:16 [e]Matt. 16:28; John 8:52 [f]Heb. 7:25
10 [1]Or, *leader* [a]Luke 24:26 [b]Rom. 11:36 [c]Heb. 5:9; 7:28 [d]Acts 3:15; 5:31
11 [1]Or, *being sanctified* [a]Heb. 13:12 [b]Heb. 10:10 [c]Acts 17:28 [d]Matt. 25:40; Mark 3:34f.; John 20:17
12 [1]Lit., *church* [a]Ps. 22:22
13 [a]Is. 8:17 [b]Is. 8:18
14 [1]Lit., *blood and flesh* [a]Matt. 16:17 [b]John 1:14 [c]1 Cor. 15:54-57; 2 Tim. 1:10 [d]John 12:31; 1 John 3:8
15 [a]Rom. 8:15
16 [1]Lit., *take hold of angels, but He takes hold of* [2]Lit., *seed*
17 [1]Lit., *was obligated to be* [a]Phil. 2:7; Heb. 2:14 [b]Heb. 4:15f.; 5:2 [c]Heb. 3:1; 4:14f.; 5:5, 10; 6:20; 7:26, 28; 8:1, 3; 9:11; 10:21 [d]Rom. 15:17; Heb. 5:1 [e]Dan. 9:24; 1 John 2:2; 4:10
18 [a]Heb. 4:15

1 [a]Acts 1:15; Heb. 2:11; 3:12; 10:19; 13:22 [b]Phil. 3:14 [c]John 17:3 [d]Heb. 2:17; 4:14f.; 5:5, 10; 6:20; 7:26, 28; 8:1, 3; 9:11; 10:21 [e]2 Cor. 9:13; Heb. 4:14; 10:23
2 [1]Lit., *Being faithful* [2]Or, *made* [a]Ex. 40:16; Num. 12:7; Heb. 3:5
3 [a]2 Cor. 3:7-11
5 [a]Ex. 40:16; Num. 12:7; Heb. 3:2 [b]Ex. 14:31; Num. 12:7 [c]Deut. 18:18f. [d]Heb. 1:1
6 [a]Heb. 1:2 [b]1 Cor. 3:16; 1 Tim. 3:15 [c]Rom. 11:22; Heb. 3:14; 4:14 [d]Eph. 3:12; Heb. 4:16; 10:19, 35 [e]Heb. 6:11; 7:19; 10:23; 11:1; 1 Pet. 1:3
7 [a]Acts 28:25; Heb. 9:8; 10:15 [b]Ps. 95:7; Heb. 3:15; 4:7
8 [1]Lit., *in the provocation* [a]Ps. 95:8
9 [a]Ps. 95:9-11 [b]Acts 7:36
10 [a]Ps. 95:10
11 [a]Ps. 95:11; Heb. 4:3, 5
12 [a]Col. 2:8; Heb. 12:25 [b]Matt. 16:16; Heb. 9:14; 10:31; 12:22
13 [a]Heb. 10:24f. [b]Eph. 4:22
14 [a]Heb. 3:6 [b]Heb. 11:1
15 [1]Lit., *in the provocation* [a]Ps. 95:7f.; Heb. 3:7; 4:7
16 [a]Jer. 32:29; 44:3, 8 [b]Num. 14:2, 11, 30; Deut. 1:35, 36, 38
17 [a]Num. 14:29; 1 Cor. 10:5
18 [a]Num. 14:23; Deut. 1:34f.; Heb. 4:2 [b]Rom. 11:30-32; Heb. 4:6, 11
19 [a]John 3:18, 36; Rom. 11:23; Heb 3:12

1 [a]2 Cor. 6:1; Gal. 5:4; Heb. 12:15

2 For indeed we have had good news
preached to us, just as they also; but [a]the
word [1]they heard did not profit them,
because [2]it was not united by faith in
those who heard.
3 [1]For we who have believed enter
that rest, just as He has said,
"[a]AS I SWORE IN MY WRATH,
THEY SHALL NOT ENTER MY
REST,"
although His works were finished [b]from
the foundation of the world.
4 For He has thus said [a]somewhere
concerning the seventh *day*, "[b]AND GOD
[c]RESTED ON THE SEVENTH DAY FROM ALL
HIS WORKS";
5 and again in this *passage*, "[a]THEY
SHALL NOT ENTER MY REST."
6 Since therefore it remains for some
to enter it, and those who formerly had
good news preached to them failed to
enter because of [a]disobedience,
7 He again fixes a certain day, "Today," saying [1]through David after so
long a time just [a]as has been said before,
"[b]TODAY IF YOU HEAR HIS VOICE,
DO NOT HARDEN YOUR HEARTS."
8 For [a]if [1]Joshua had given them
rest, He would not have spoken of
another day after that.
9 There remains therefore a Sabbath
rest for the people of God.
10 For the one who has entered His
rest has himself also [a]rested from his
works, as [b]God did from His.
11 Let us therefore be diligent to enter
that rest, lest anyone fall through *following* the same [a]example of [b]disobedience.
12 For [a]the word of God is [b]living and
[c]active and sharper than any two-edged
[d]sword, and piercing as far as the division of [e]soul and [e]spirit, of both joints
and marrow, and [f]able to judge the
thoughts and intentions of the heart.
13 And [a]there is no creature hidden
from His sight, but all things are [b]open
and laid bare to the eyes of Him with
whom we have to do.
14 Since then we have a great [a]high
priest who has [b]passed through the
heavens, Jesus [c]the Son of God, let us
hold fast our [d]confession.
15 For we do not have [a]a high priest
who cannot sympathize with our weaknesses, but one who has been [b]tempted
in all things as *we are, yet* [c]without sin.
16 Let us therefore [a]draw near with
[b]confidence to the throne of grace, that
we may receive mercy and may find
grace to help in time of need.

The Perfect High Priest

5 FOR every high priest [a]taken from
among men is appointed on behalf
of men in [b]things pertaining to God, in
order to [c]offer both gifts and sacrifices
[d]for sins;
2 [1a]he can deal gently with the [b]igno-
rant and [c]misguided, since he himself
also is [2d]beset with weakness;
3 and because of it he is obligated to
offer *sacrifices* [a]for sins, [b]as for the
people, so also for himself.
4 And [a]no one takes the honor to
himself, but *receives it* when he is called
by God, even [b]as Aaron was.
5 So also Christ [a]did not glorify
Himself so as to become a [b]high priest,
but He who [c]said to Him,
"[d]THOU ART MY SON,
TODAY I HAVE BEGOTTEN THEE";
6 just as He says also in another
passage,
"[a]THOU ART A PRIEST FOREVER
ACCORDING TO [b]THE ORDER OF
MELCHIZEDEK."
7 In the days of His flesh, [1a]He
offered up both prayers and supplications with [b]loud crying and tears to the
One [c]able to save Him [2]from death, and
He [3]was heard because of His [d]piety.
8 Although He was [a]a Son, He
learned [b]obedience from the things
which He suffered.
9 And having been made [a]perfect,
He became to all those who obey Him
the source of eternal salvation,
10 being designated by God as [a]a high
priest according to [b]the order of Melchizedek.
11 Concerning [1]him we have much to
say, and *it is* hard to explain, since you
have become dull of hearing.
12 For though [1]by this time you ought
to be teachers, you have need again for
someone to teach you [a]the [2b]elementary
principles of the [c]oracles of God, and
you have come to need [d]milk and not
solid food.
13 For everyone who partakes *only* of
milk is not accustomed to the word of
righteousness, for he is a [a]babe.
14 But solid food is for [a]the mature,
who because of practice have their
senses [b]trained to [c]discern good and evil.

The Peril of Falling Away

6 THEREFORE [a]leaving [b]the [1]ele-
mentary teaching about the [2]Christ,
let us press on to [3c]maturity, not laying
again a foundation of repentance from
[d]dead works and of faith toward God,
2 of [a]instruction about washings, and
[b]laying on of hands, and the [c]resurrec-
tion of the dead, and [c]eternal judgment.
3 And this we shall do, [a]if God
permits.
4 For in the case of those who have
once been [a]enlightened and have tasted
of [b]the heavenly gift and have been
made [c]partakers of the Holy Spirit,
5 and [a]have tasted the good [b]word of
God and the powers of [c]the age to come,

2 [1]Lit., *of hearing* [2]Or, *they were. . .faith with those who heard* [a]Rom. 10:17; Gal. 3:2; 1 Thess. 2:13
3 [1]Some ancient mss. read *Therefore* [a]Ps. 95:11; Heb. 3:11 [b]Matt. 25:34
4 [a]Heb. 2:6 [b]Gen. 2:2 [c]Ex. 20:11; 31:17
5 [a]Ps. 95:11; Heb. 3:11
6 [a]Heb. 3:18; 4:11
7 [1]Or, *in* [a]Heb. 3:7f. [b]Ps. 95:7f.
8 [1]Gr., *Jesus* [a]Josh. 22:4
10 [a]Rev. 14:13 [b]Gen. 2:2; Heb. 4:4
11 [a]2 Pet. 2:6 [b]Heb. 3:18; 4:6
12 [a]Jer. 23:29; Eph. 5:26; Heb. 6:5; 1 Pet. 1:23 [b]Acts 7:38 [c]1 Thess. 2:13 [d]Eph. 6:17 [e]1 Thess. 5:23 [f]John 12:48; 1 Cor. 14:24f.
13 [a]2 Chr. 16:9; Ps. 33:13-15 [b]Job 26:6
14 [a]Heb. 2:17 [b]Eph. 4:10; Heb. 6:20; 8:1; 9:24 [c]Matt. 4:3; Heb. 1:2; 6:6; 7:3; 10:29 [d]Heb. 3:1
15 [a]Heb. 2:17 [b]Heb. 2:18 [c]2 Cor. 5:21; Heb. 7:26
16 [a]Heb. 7:19 [b]Heb. 3:6

1 [a]Ex. 28:1 [b]Heb. 2:17 [c]Heb. 7:27; 8:3f.; 9:9; 10:11 [d]1 Cor. 15:3; Heb. 7:27; 10:12
2 [1]Lit., *being able to* [2]Or, *subject to weakness* [a]Heb. 2:18; 4:15 [b]Eph. 4:18; Heb. 9:7 mg. [c]James 5:19; 1 Pet. 2:25 [d]Heb. 7:28
3 [a]1 Cor. 15:3; Heb. 7:27; 10:12 [b]Lev. 9:7; 16:6; Heb. 7:27; 9:7
4 [a]Num. 16:40; 18:7; 2 Chr. 26:18 [b]Ex. 28:1; 1 Chr. 23:13
5 [a]John 8:54 [b]Heb. 2:17; 5:10 [c]Heb. 1:1, 5 [d]Ps. 2:7
6 [a]Ps. 110:4; Heb. 7:17 [b]Heb. 5:10; 6:20; 7:11, 17
7 [1]Lit., *who having offered up* [2]Or, *out of* [3]Lit., *having been heard* [a]Matt. 26:39, 42, 44; Mark 14:36, 39; Luke 22:41, 44 [b]Matt. 27:46, 50; Mark 15:34, 37; Luke 23:46 [c]Mark 14:36 [d]Heb. 11:7; 12:28
8 [a]Heb. 1:2 [b]Phil. 2:8
9 [a]Heb. 2:10
10 [a]Heb. 2:17; 5:5 [b]Heb. 5:6
11 [1]Or, *Him* or *this*
12 [1]Lit., *because of the time* [2]Lit., *elements of the beginning* [a]Gal. 4:3 [b]Heb. 6:1 [c]Acts 7:38 [d]1 Cor. 3:2; 1 Pet. 2:2
13 [a]1 Cor. 3:1; 14:20; 1 Pet. 2:2
14 [a]1 Cor. 2:6; Eph. 4:13; Heb. 6:1 [b]1 Tim. 4:7 [c]Rom. 14:1ff.

1 [1]Lit., *word of the beginning* [2]I.e., Messiah [3]Or, *perfection* [a]Phil. 3:13f. [b]Heb. 5:12 [c]Heb. 5:14 [d]Heb. 9:14
2 [a]John 3:25; Acts 19:3f. [b]Acts 6:6 [c]Acts 17:31f.
3 [a]Acts 18:21
4 [a]2 Cor. 4:4, 6; Heb. 10:32 [b]John 4:10; Eph. 2:8 [c]Gal. 3:2; Heb. 2:4
5 [a]1 Pet. 2:3 [b]Eph. 6:17 [c]Heb. 2:5

6 and *then* have fallen away, it is [a]impossible to renew them again to repentance, [1b]since they again crucify to themselves the Son of God, and put Him to open shame.

7 For ground that drinks the rain which often [1]falls upon it and brings forth vegetation useful to those [a]for whose sake it is also tilled, receives a blessing from God;

8 but if it yields thorns and thistles, it is worthless and [a]close [1]to being cursed, and [2]it ends up being burned.

Better Things for You

9 But, [a]beloved, we are convinced of better things concerning you, and things that [1]accompany salvation, though we are speaking in this way.

10 For [a]God is not unjust so as to forget [b]your work and the love which you have shown toward His name, in having [c]ministered and in still ministering to the [1]saints.

11 And we desire that each one of you show the same diligence [1]so as to realize the [a]full assurance of [b]hope until the end,

12 that you may not be sluggish, but [a]imitators of those who through [b]faith and patience [c]inherit the promises.

13 For [a]when God made the promise to Abraham, since He could swear by no one greater, He [b]swore by Himself,

14 saying, "[a]I WILL SURELY BLESS YOU, AND I WILL SURELY MULTIPLY YOU."

15 And thus, [a]having patiently waited, he obtained the promise.

16 [a]For men swear by one greater *than themselves*, and with them [b]an oath *given* as confirmation is an end of every dispute.

17 [1]In the same way God, desiring even more to show to [a]the heirs of the promise [b]the unchangeableness of His purpose, [2]interposed with an oath,

18 in order that by two unchangeable things, in which [a]it is impossible for God to lie, we may have strong encouragement, we who have fled for refuge in laying hold of [b]the hope set before us.

19 [1]This [a]hope we have as an anchor of the soul, a *hope* both sure and steadfast and one which [b]enters [2]within the veil,

20 [a]where Jesus has entered as a forerunner for us, having become a [b]high priest forever according to the order of Melchizedek.

Melchizedek's Priesthood Like Christ's

7 FOR this [a]Melchizedek, king of Salem, priest of the [b]Most High God, who met Abraham as he was returning from the slaughter of the kings and blessed him,

2 to whom also Abraham apportioned a tenth part of all *the spoils*, was first of all, by the translation *of his name*, king of righteousness, and then also king of Salem, which is king of peace.

3 Without father, without mother, [a]without genealogy, having neither beginning of days nor end of life, but made like [b]the Son of God, he abides a priest perpetually.

4 Now observe how great this man was to whom Abraham, the [a]patriarch, [b]gave a tenth of the choicest spoils.

5 And those indeed of [a]the sons of Levi who receive the priest's office have commandment [1]in the Law to collect [2]a tenth from the people, that is, from their brethren, although these [3]are descended from Abraham.

6 But the one [a]whose genealogy is not traced from them [b]collected [1]a tenth from Abraham, and [b]blessed the one who [c]had the promises.

7 But without any dispute the lesser is blessed by the greater.

8 And in this case mortal men receive tithes, but in that case one *receives them*, [a]of whom it is witnessed that he lives on.

9 And, so to speak, through Abraham even Levi, who received tithes, paid tithes,

10 for he was still in the loins of his father when Melchizedek met him.

11 [a]Now if perfection was through the Levitical priesthood (for on the basis of it [b]the people received the Law), what further need *was there* for another priest to arise [c]according to the order of Melchizedek, and not be designated according to the order of Aaron?

12 For when the priesthood is changed, of necessity there takes place a change of law also.

13 For [a]the one concerning whom [b]these things are spoken belongs to another tribe, from which no one has officiated at the altar.

14 For it is evident that our Lord [1]was [a]descended from Judah, a tribe with reference to which Moses spoke nothing concerning priests.

15 And this is clearer still, if another priest arises according to the likeness of Melchizedek,

16 who has become *such* not on the basis of a law of [a]physical requirement, but according to the power of [b]an indestructible life.

17 For it is witnessed *of Him*,

"[a]THOU ART A PRIEST FOREVER
ACCORDING TO THE ORDER OF
MELCHIZEDEK."

18 For, on the one hand, there is a setting aside of a former commandment [a]because of its weakness and uselessness

6 [1]Or, *while* [a]Matt. 19:26; Heb. 10:26f.; 2 Pet. 2:21; 1 John 5:16 [b]Heb. 10:29
7 [1]Lit., *comes* [a]2 Tim. 2:6
8 [1]Lit., *to a curse* [2]Lit., *its end is for burning* [a]Gen. 3:17f.; Deut. 29:22ff.
9 [1]Or, *belong to* [a]1 Cor. 10:14; 2 Cor. 7:1; 12:19; 1 Pet. 2:11; 2 Pet. 3:1; 1 John 2:7; Jude 3
10 [1]Or, *holy ones* [a]Prov. 19:17; Matt. 10:42; 25:40; Acts 10:4 [b]1 Thess. 1:3 [c]Rom. 15:25; Heb. 10:32-34
11 [1]Lit., *to the full* [a]Heb. 10:22 [b]Heb. 3:6
12 [a]Heb. 13:7 [b]2 Thess. 1:4; James 1:3; Rev. 13:10 [c]Heb. 1:14
13 [a]Gal. 3:15, 18 [b]Gen. 22:16; Luke 1:73
14 [a]Gen. 22:17
15 [a]Gen. 12:4; 21:5
16 [a]Gal. 3:15 [b]Ex. 22:11
17 [1]Or, *Therefore God* [2]Or, *guaranteed* [a]Heb. 11:9 [b]Ps. 110:4; Prov. 19:21; Heb. 6:18
18 [a]Num. 23:19; Titus 1:2 [b]Heb. 3:6; 7:19
19 [1]Lit., *Which we have* [2]Or, *inside* [a]Ps. 39:7; 62:5; Acts 23:6; Rom. 4:18; 5:4, 5; 1 Cor. 13:13; Col. 1:27; 1 Pet. 1:3 [b]Lev. 16:2, 15; Heb. 9:3, 7
20 [a]John 14:2; Heb. 4:14 [b]Ps. 110:4; Heb. 2:17; 5:6
1 [a]Gen. 14:18-20; Heb. 7:6 [b]Mark 5:7
3 [a]Heb. 7:6 [b]Matt. 4:3; Heb. 7:1, 28
4 [a]Acts 2:29; 7:8f. [b]Gen. 14:20
5 [1]Lit., *according to* [2]Or, *tithes* [3]Lit., *have come out of the loins of* [a]Num. 18:21, 26; 2 Chr. 31:4f.

6 [1]Or, *tithes* [a]Heb. 7:3 [b]Heb. 7:1f. [c]Rom. 4:13
8 [a]Heb. 5:6; 6:20
11 [a]Heb. 7:18f.; 8:7 [b]Heb. 9:6; 10:1 [c]Heb. 5:6; 7:17
13 [a]Heb. 7:14 [b]Heb. 7:11
14 [1]Lit., *rose from* [a]Num. 24:17; Is. 11:1; Mic. 5:2; Matt. 2:6; Rev. 5:5
16 [a]Heb. 9:10 [b]Heb. 9:14
17 [a]Ps. 110:4; Heb. 5:6; 6:20; 7:21
18 [a]Rom. 8:3; Gal. 3:21; Heb. 7:11

19 (for [a]the Law made nothing perfect), and on the other hand there is a bringing in of a better [b]hope, through which we [c]draw near to God.
20 And inasmuch as *it was* not without an oath
21 (for they indeed became priests without an oath, but He with an oath through the One who said to Him,

"[a]THE LORD HAS SWORN
AND [b]WILL NOT CHANGE HIS MIND,
'THOU ART A PRIEST [c]FOREVER' ");

22 so much the more also Jesus has become the [a]guarantee of [b]a better covenant.
23 And the *former* priests, on the one hand, existed in greater numbers, because they were prevented by death from continuing,
24 but He, on the other hand, because He abides [a]forever, holds His priesthood permanently.
25 Hence, also, He is able to [a]save [1]forever those who [b]draw near to God through Him, since He always lives to [c]make intercession for them.
26 For it was fitting that we should have such a [a]high priest, [b]holy, [c]innocent, undefiled, separated from sinners and [d]exalted above the heavens;
27 who does not need daily, like those high priests, to [a]offer up sacrifices, [b]first for His own sins, and then for the *sins* of the people, because this He did [c]once for all when He [d]offered up Himself.
28 For the Law appoints men as high priests [a]who are weak, but the word of the oath, which came after the Law, *appoints* [b]a Son, [c]made perfect forever.

A Better Ministry

8 NOW the main point in what has been said *is this*: we have such a [a]high priest, who has taken His seat at [b]the right hand of the throne of the [b]Majesty in the heavens,
2 a [a]minister [1]in the sanctuary, and [1]in the [b]true [2]tabernacle, which the Lord [c]pitched, not man.
3 For every [a]high priest is appointed [b]to offer both gifts and sacrifices; hence it is necessary that this *high priest* also have something to offer.
4 Now if He were on earth, He would not be a priest at all, since there are those who [a]offer the gifts according to the Law;
5 who serve [a]a copy and [b]shadow of the heavenly things, just as Moses [1]was [c]warned *by God* when he was about to erect the [2]tabernacle; for, "[d]SEE," He says, "THAT YOU MAKE all things ACCORDING TO THE PATTERN WHICH WAS SHOWN YOU ON THE MOUNTAIN."
6 But now He has obtained a more excellent ministry, by as much as He is also the [a]mediator of [b]a better covenant, which has been enacted on better promises.

19 [a]Acts 13:39; Rom. 3:20; 7:7f.; Gal. 2:16; 3:21; Heb. 9:9; 10:1 [b]Heb. 3:6 [c]Lam. 3:57; Heb. 4:16; 7:25; 10:1, 22; James 4:8
21 [a]Ps. 110:4; Heb. 5:6; 7:17 [b]Num. 23:19; 1 Sam. 15:29; Rom. 11:29 [c]Heb. 7:23f., 28
22 [a]Ps. 119:122; Is. 38:14 [b]Heb. 8:6
24 [a]Is. 9:7; John 12:34; Rom. 9:5; Heb. 7:23f., 28
25 [1]Or, *completely* [a]1 Cor. 1:21 [b]Heb. 7:19 [c]Rom. 8:34; Heb. 9:24
26 [a]Heb. 2:17 [b]2 Cor. 5:21; Heb. 4:15 [c]1 Pet. 2:22 [d]Heb. 4:14
27 [a]Heb. 5:1 [b]Lev. 9:7; Heb. 5:3 [c]Heb. 9:12, 28; 10:10 [d]Eph. 5:2; Heb. 9:14, 28; 10:10, 12
28 [a]Heb. 5:2 [b]Heb. 1:2 [c]Heb. 2:10

1 [a]Col. 3:1; Heb. 2:17; 3:1 [b]Ps. 110:1; Heb. 1:3
2 [1]Or, *of* [2]Or, *sacred tent* [a]Heb. 10:11 [b]Heb. 9:11, 24 [c]Ex. 33:7
3 [a]Heb. 2:17 [b]Rom. 4:25; 5:6, 8; Gal. 2:20; Eph. 5:2; Heb. 5:1; 8:4
4 [a]Heb. 5:1; 7:27; 8:3; 9:9; 10:11
5 [1]Lit., *is* [2]Or, *sacred tent* [a]Heb. 9:23 [b]Col. 2:17; Heb. 10:1 [c]Matt. 2:12; Heb. 11:7; 12:25 [d]Ex. 25:40
6 [a]1 Tim. 2:5 [b]Luke 22:20; Heb. 7:22; 8:8; 9:15; 12:24
7 [a]Heb. 7:11
8 [1]Lit., *And* [a]Jer. 31:31 [b]Luke 22:20; 2 Cor. 3:6; Heb. 7:22; 8:6, 13; 9:15; 12:24
9 [a]Ex. 19:5; 24:6-8; Deut. 5:2, 3; Jer. 31:32
10 [a]Jer. 31:33; Rom. 11:27; Heb. 10:16 [b]2 Cor. 3:3
11 [a]Jer. 31:34 [b]Is. 54:13; John 6:45; 1 John 2:27
12 [a]Is. 43:25; Jer. 31:34; 50:20; Mic. 7:18, 19 [b]Heb. 10:17
13 [1]Or, *In His saying* [2]Or, *near* [a]Luke 22:20; 2 Cor. 3:6; Heb. 7:22; 8:6, 8; 9:15; 12:24 [b]2 Cor. 5:17; Heb. 1:11

1 [a]Heb. 9:10 [b]Ex. 25:8; Heb. 8:2; 9:11, 24
2 [1]Or, *sacred tent* [2]Lit., *first* [3]Lit., *loaves of presentation* [a]Ex. 25:8, 9; 26:1-30 [b]Ex. 25:31-39 [c]Ex. 25:23-29 [d]Ex. 25:30; Lev. 24:5ff.; Matt. 12:4
3 [1]Or, *sacred tent* [a]Ex. 26:31-33; 40:3 [b]Ex. 26:33

A New Covenant

7 For [a]if that first *covenant* had been faultless, there would have been no occasion sought for a second.
8 For finding fault with them, He says,

"[a]BEHOLD, DAYS ARE COMING, SAYS THE LORD,
[1]WHEN I WILL EFFECT [b]A NEW COVENANT
WITH THE HOUSE OF ISRAEL AND WITH THE HOUSE OF JUDAH;
9 [a]NOT LIKE THE COVENANT WHICH I MADE WITH THEIR FATHERS
ON THE DAY WHEN I TOOK THEM BY THE HAND
TO LEAD THEM OUT OF THE LAND OF EGYPT;
FOR THEY DID NOT CONTINUE IN MY COVENANT,
AND I DID NOT CARE FOR THEM, SAYS THE LORD.
10 "[a]FOR THIS IS THE COVENANT THAT I WILL MAKE WITH THE HOUSE OF ISRAEL
AFTER THOSE DAYS, SAYS THE LORD:
I WILL PUT MY LAWS INTO THEIR MINDS,
AND I WILL WRITE THEM [b]UPON THEIR HEARTS.
AND I WILL BE THEIR GOD,
AND THEY SHALL BE MY PEOPLE.
11 "[a]AND THEY SHALL NOT TEACH EVERYONE HIS FELLOW CITIZEN,
AND EVERYONE HIS BROTHER,
SAYING, 'KNOW THE LORD,'
FOR [b]ALL SHALL KNOW ME,
FROM THE LEAST TO THE GREATEST OF THEM.
12 "[a]FOR I WILL BE MERCIFUL TO THEIR INIQUITIES,
[b]AND I WILL REMEMBER THEIR SINS NO MORE."

13 [1]When He said, "[a]A new *covenant*," He has made the first obsolete. [b]But whatever is becoming obsolete and growing old is [2]ready to disappear.

The Old and the New

9 NOW even the first *covenant* had [a]regulations of divine worship and [b]the earthly sanctuary.
2 For there was [a]a [1]tabernacle prepared, the [2]outer one, in which *were* [b]the lampstand and [c]the table and [d]the [3]sacred bread; this is called the holy place.
3 And behind [a]the second veil, there was a [1]tabernacle which is called the [b]Holy of Holies,
4 having a golden [1a]altar of incense and [b]the ark of the covenant covered on all sides with gold, in which *was* [c]a golden jar holding the manna, and [d]Aaron's rod which budded, and [e]the tables of the covenant.

4 [1]Or, *censer* [a]Ex. 30:1-5; 37:25f. [b]Ex. 25:10ff.; 37:1ff. [c]Ex. 16:32f. [d]Num. 17:10 [e]Ex. 25:16; 31:18; 32:15; Deut. 9:9, 11, 15; 10:3-5

5 And above it *were* the [a]cherubim of
glory [b]overshadowing the mercy seat;
but of these things we cannot now speak
in detail.
6 Now when these things have been
thus prepared, the priests [a]are continually entering the [1]outer [2]tabernacle,
performing the divine worship,
7 but into [a]the second only [b]the high
priest *enters*, [c]once a year, [d]not without
taking blood, which he [e]offers for himself and for the [1][f]sins of the people
committed in ignorance.
8 [a]The Holy Spirit *is* signifying this,
[b]that the way into the holy place has not
yet been disclosed, while the [1]outer
tabernacle is still standing,
9 which *is* a symbol for the present
time. Accordingly [a]both gifts and sacrifices are offered which [b]cannot make the
worshiper perfect in conscience,
10 since they *relate* only to [a]food and
[b]drink and various [c]washings, [d]regula-
tions for the [1]body imposed until [e]a time
of reformation.
11 But when Christ appeared *as* a
[a]high priest of the [b]good things [1]to
come, *He entered* through [c]the greater
and more perfect [2]tabernacle, [d]not made
with hands, that is to say, [e]not of this
creation;
12 and not through [a]the blood of
goats and calves, but [b]through His own
blood, He [c]entered the holy place [d]once
for all, [1]having obtained [e]eternal redemption.
13 For if [a]the blood of goats and bulls
and [b]the ashes of a heifer sprinkling
those who have been defiled, sanctify for
the [1]cleansing of the flesh,
14 how much more will [a]the blood of
Christ, who through [1][b]the eternal Spirit
[c]offered Himself without blemish to
God, [d]cleanse [2]your conscience from
[e]dead works to serve [f]the living God?
15 And for this reason [a]He is the
[b]mediator of a [c]new covenant, in order
that since a death has taken place for the
redemption of the transgressions that
were *committed* under the first covenant,
those who have been [d]called may [e]re-
ceive the promise of [f]the eternal inheritance.
16 For where a [1]covenant is, there
must of necessity [2]be the death of the
one who made it.
17 For a [1]covenant is valid *only* when
[2]men are dead, [3]for it is never in force
while the one who made it lives.
18 Therefore even the first *covenant*
was not inaugurated without blood.
19 For when every commandment had
been [a]spoken by Moses to all the people
according to the Law, [b]he took the
[c]blood of the calves and the goats, with
[d]water and scarlet wool and hyssop, and
sprinkled both [e]the book itself and all
the people,
20 saying, "[a]THIS IS THE BLOOD OF
THE COVENANT WHICH GOD COM-
MANDED YOU."

5 [a]Ex. 25:18ff. [b]Ex. 25:17, 20; Lev. 16:2; 1 Kin. 8:7
6 [1]Lit., *first* [2]Or, *sacred tent* [a]Num. 18:2-6; 28:3
7 [1]Lit., *ignorance of the people* [a]Heb. 9:3 [b]Lev. 16:12ff. [c]Ex. 30:10; Lev. 16:34; Heb. 10:3 [d]Lev. 16:11, 14 [e]Heb. 5:3 [f]Num. 15:25; Heb. 5:2
8 [1]Lit., *first* [a]Heb. 3:7 [b]John 14:6; Heb. 10:20
9 [a]Heb. 5:1 [b]Heb. 7:19
10 [1]Lit., *flesh* [a]Lev. 11:2ff.; Col. 2:16 [b]Num. 6:3 [c]Lev. 11:25; Num. 19:13; Mark 7:4 [d]Heb. 7:16 [e]Heb. 7:12
11 [1]Some ancient mss. read *that have come* [2]Or, *sacred tent* [a]Heb. 2:17 [b]Heb. 10:1 [c]Heb. 8:2; 9:24 [d]Mark 14:58; 2 Cor. 5:1 [e]2 Cor. 4:18; Heb. 12:27; 13:14
12 [1]Or, *obtaining* [a]Lev. 4:3; 16:6, 15; Heb. 9:19 [b]Heb. 9:14; 13:12 [c]Heb. 9:24 [d]Heb. 7:27 [e]Heb. 5:9; 9:15
13 [1]Lit., *purity* [a]Lev. 16:15; Heb. 9:19; 10:4 [b]Num. 19:9, 17f.
14 [1]Or, His *eternal spirit* [2]Some ancient mss. read *our* [a]Heb. 9:12; 13:12 [b]1 Cor. 15:45; 1 Pet. 3:18 [c]Eph. 5:2; Heb. 7:27; 10:10, 12 [d]Acts 15:9; Titus 2:14; Heb. 1:3; 10:2, 22 [e]Heb. 6:1 [f]Matt. 16:16; Heb. 3:12
15 [a]Rom. 3:24 [b]1 Tim. 2:5; Heb. 8:6; 12:24 [c]Heb. 8:8 [d]Matt. 22:3ff.; Rom. 8:28f.; Heb. 3:1 [e]Heb. 6:15; 10:36; 11:39 [f]Acts 20:32
16 [1]Or, *testament* [2]Lit., *be brought*
17 [1]V. 16, note 1 [2]Lit., *over the dead* [3]Some ancient mss. read *for is it then . . . lives?*
19 [a]Heb. 1:1 [b]Ex. 24:6ff. [c]Heb. 9:12 [d]Lev. 14:4, 7; Num. 19:6, 18 [e]Ex. 24:7
20 [a]Ex. 24:8; Matt. 26:28
21 [1]Or, *sacred tent* [a]Ex. 24:6; 40:9; Lev. 8:15, 19; 16:14-16
22 [1]Or, *Law, almost all things* [a]Lev. 5:11f. [b]Lev. 17:11
23 [a]Heb. 8:5
24 [a]Heb. 4:14; 9:12 [b]Heb. 8:2 [c]Heb. 9:12 [d]Matt. 18:10; Heb. 7:25
25 [a]Heb. 9:7 [b]Heb. 9:2; 10:19
26 [1]Or, *by His sacrifice* [a]Matt. 25:34; Heb. 4:3 [b]Heb. 7:27; 9:12 [c]Matt. 13:39; Heb. 1:2 [d]1 John 3:5, 8 [e]Heb. 9:12, 14
27 [1]Lit., *laid up* [a]Gen. 3:19 [b]2 Cor. 5:10; 1 John 4:17

21 And in the same way he [a]sprinkled
both the [1]tabernacle and all the vessels
of the ministry with the blood.
22 And according to the [1]Law, *one
may* [a]almost *say*, all things are cleansed
with blood, and [b]without shedding of
blood there is no forgiveness.
23 Therefore it was necessary for the
[a]copies of the things in the heavens to be
cleansed with these, but [a]the heavenly
things themselves with better sacrifices
than these.
24 For Christ [a]did not enter a holy
place made with hands, a *mere* copy of
[b]the true one, but into [c]heaven itself,
now [d]to appear in the presence of God
for us;
25 nor was it that He should offer
Himself often, as [a]the high priest enters
[b]the holy place [a]year by year with blood
not his own.
26 Otherwise, He would have needed
to suffer often since [a]the foundation of
the world; but now [b]once at [c]the consummation of the ages He has been
[d]manifested to put away sin [1][e]by the
sacrifice of Himself.
27 And inasmuch as [a]it is [1]appointed
for men to die once and after this [b]*comes*
judgment,
28 so Christ also, having been [a]offered
once to [b]bear the sins of many, shall
appear [c]a second time for [d]salvation
[e]without *reference to* sin, to those who
[f]eagerly await Him.

One Sacrifice of Christ Is Sufficient

10 FOR the Law, since it has *only* [a]a
shadow of [b]the good things to
come *and* not the very [1]form of things,
[2]can [c]never by the same sacrifices year
by year, which they offer continually,
[d]make perfect those who draw near.
2 Otherwise, would they not have
ceased to be offered, because the worshipers, having once been cleansed,
would no longer have had [a]conscious-
ness of sins?
3 But [a]in [1]those *sacrifices* there is a
reminder of sins year by year.
4 For it is [a]impossible for the [b]blood
of bulls and goats to take away sins.
5 Therefore, [a]when He comes into
the world, He says,
"[b]SACRIFICE AND OFFERING THOU
HAST NOT DESIRED,
BUT [c]A BODY THOU HAST PRE-
PARED FOR ME;
6 [a]IN WHOLE BURNT OFFERINGS
AND *sacrifices* FOR SIN THOU
HAST TAKEN NO PLEASURE.

28 [a]Heb. 7:27 [b]Is. 53:12; 1 Pet. 2:24 [c]Acts 1:11 [d]Heb. 5:9 [e]Heb. 4:15 [f]1 Cor. 1:7; Titus 2:13

1 [1]Lit., *image* [2]Some ancient mss. read *they can* [a]Heb. 8:5 [b]Heb. 9:11 [c]Rom. 8:3; Heb. 9:9; 10:4, 11 [d]Heb. 7:19
2 [a]1 Pet. 2:19
3 [1]Lit., *them there is* [a]Heb. 9:7
4 [a]Heb. 10:1, 11 [b]Heb. 9:12f.
5 [a]Heb. 1:6 [b]Ps. 40:6 [c]Heb. 2:14; 5:7; 1 Pet. 2:24
6 [a]Ps. 40:6

7 "[a]THEN I SAID, 'BEHOLD, I HAVE
COME
(IN [b]THE ROLL OF THE BOOK IT IS
WRITTEN OF ME)
TO DO THY WILL, O GOD.' "
8 After saying above, "[a]SACRIFICES
AND OFFERINGS AND [b]WHOLE BURNT
OFFERINGS AND *sacrifices* [c]FOR SIN THOU
HAST NOT DESIRED, NOR HAST THOU
TAKEN PLEASURE *in them*" (which are
offered according to the Law),
9 then He said, "[a]BEHOLD, I HAVE
COME TO DO THY WILL." He takes away
the first in order to establish the second.
10 By [1]this will we have been [a]sancti-
fied through [b]the offering of [c]the body of
Jesus Christ [d]once for all.
11 And every priest stands daily ministering and [a]offering time after time the
same sacrifices, which [b]can never take
away sins;
12 but He, having offered one sacrifice
[a]for [1]sins [b]for all time, [c]SAT DOWN AT
THE RIGHT HAND OF GOD,
13 waiting from that time onward
[a]UNTIL HIS ENEMIES BE MADE A FOOT-
STOOL FOR HIS FEET.
14 For by one offering He has [a]per-
fected [b]for all time those who are [1]sanc-
tified.
15 And [a]the Holy Spirit also bears
witness to us; for after saying,
16 "[a]THIS IS THE COVENANT THAT I
WILL MAKE WITH THEM
AFTER THOSE DAYS, SAYS THE
LORD:
I WILL PUT MY LAWS UPON THEIR
HEART,
AND UPON THEIR MIND I WILL
WRITE THEM,"
He then says,
17 "[a]AND THEIR SINS AND THEIR LAW-
LESS DEEDS
I WILL REMEMBER NO MORE."
18 Now where there is forgiveness of
these things, there is no longer *any*
offering for sin.

A New and Living Way

19 Since therefore, brethren, we [a]have
confidence to [b]enter the holy place by
the blood of Jesus,
20 by [a]a new and living way which He
inaugurated for us through [b]the veil, that
is, His flesh,
21 and since *we have* [a]a great priest
[b]over the house of God,
22 let us [a]draw near with a [1]sincere
heart in [b]full assurance of faith, having
our hearts [c]sprinkled *clean* from an evil
conscience and our bodies [d]washed with
pure water.
23 Let us hold fast the [a]confession of
our [b]hope without wavering, for [c]He
who promised is faithful;
24 and let us consider how [a]to stimu-
late one another to love and [b]good
deeds,
25 not forsaking our own [a]assembling
together, as is the habit of some, but
[b]encouraging *one another*; and all the
more, as you see [c]the day drawing near.

Christ or Judgment

26 For if we go on [a]sinning willfully
after receiving [b]the knowledge of the
truth, there no longer remains a sacrifice
for sins,
27 but a certain terrifying expectation
of [a]judgment, and [b]THE FURY OF A FIRE
WHICH WILL CONSUME THE ADVERSAR-
IES.
28 [a]Anyone who has set aside the Law
of Moses dies without mercy on *the
testimony of* two or three witnesses.
29 [a]How much severer punishment do
you think he will deserve [b]who has
trampled under foot the Son of God,
and has regarded as unclean [c]the blood
of the covenant [d]by which he was sanctified, and has [e]insulted the Spirit of
grace?
30 For we know Him who said,
"[a]VENGEANCE IS MINE, I WILL REPAY."
And again, "[b]THE LORD WILL JUDGE
HIS PEOPLE."
31 It is a [a]terrifying thing to fall into
the hands of the [b]living God.
32 But remember [a]the former days,
[1]when, after being [b]enlightened, you
endured a great [c]conflict of sufferings,
33 partly, by being [a]made a public
spectacle through reproaches and tribulations, and partly by becoming [b]sharers
with those who were so treated.
34 For you [a]showed sympathy to the
prisoners, and accepted [b]joyfully the
seizure of your property, knowing that
you have for yourselves [c]a better possession and an abiding one.
35 Therefore, do not throw away your
[a]confidence, which has a great [b]reward.
36 For you have need of [a]endurance,
so that when you have [b]done the will of
God, you may [c]receive [1]what was promised.
37 [a]FOR YET IN A VERY LITTLE
WHILE,
[b]HE WHO IS COMING WILL COME,
AND WILL NOT DELAY.
38 [a]BUT MY RIGHTEOUS ONE SHALL
LIVE BY FAITH;
AND IF HE SHRINKS BACK, MY
SOUL HAS NO PLEASURE IN HIM.
39 But [1]we are not of those who
shrink back to destruction, but of those
who have faith to the [2]preserving of the
soul.

The Triumphs of Faith

11 NOW faith is the [1a]assurance of
things [b]hoped for, the [2]conviction
of [c]things not seen.

7 [a]Ps. 40:7, 8 [b]Ezra 6:2; Jer. 36:2; Ezek. 2:9; 3:1f.
8 [a]Ps. 40:6; Heb. 10:5f. [b]Mark 12:33 [c]Rom. 8:3
9 [a]Ps. 40:7, 8; Heb. 10:7
10 [1]Lit., *which* [a]John 17:19; Eph. 5:26; Heb. 2:11; 10:14, 29; 13:12 [b]John 6:51; Eph. 5:2; Heb. 7:27; 9:14, 28; 10:12 [c]Heb. 2:14; 5:7; 1 Pet. 2:24 [d]Heb. 7:27
11 [a]Heb. 5:1 [b]Mic. 6:6-8; Heb. 10:1, 4
12 [1]Or, *sins, forever sat down* [a]Heb. 5:1 [b]Heb. 10:14 [c]Ps. 110:1; Heb. 1:3
13 [a]Ps. 110:1; Heb. 1:13
14 [1]Or, *being sanctified* [a]Heb. 10:1 [b]Heb. 10:12
15 [a]Heb. 3:7
16 [a]Jer. 31:33; Heb. 8:10
17 [a]Jer. 31:34; Heb. 8:12
19 [a]Heb. 3:6; 10:35 [b]Heb. 9:25
20 [a]Heb. 9:8 [b]Heb. 6:19; 9:3
21 [a]Heb. 2:17 [b]1 Tim. 3:15; Heb. 3:6
22 [1]Lit., *true* [a]Heb. 7:19; 10:1 [b]Heb. 6:11 [c]Ezek. 36:25; Heb. 9:19; 12:24; 1 Pet. 1:2 [d]Acts 22:16; 1 Cor. 6:11; Eph. 5:26; Titus 3:5; 1 Pet. 3:21
23 [a]Heb. 3:1 [b]Heb. 3:6 [c]1 Cor. 1:9; 10:13; Heb. 11:11
24 [a]Heb. 13:1 [b]Titus 3:8
25 [a]Acts 2:42 [b]Heb. 3:13 [c]1 Cor. 3:13
26 [a]Num. 15:30; Heb. 6:4-8; 2 Pet. 2:20f. [b]1 Tim. 2:4
27 [a]John 5:29; Heb. 9:27 [b]Is. 26:11; 2 Thess. 1:7
28 [a]Deut. 17:2-6; 19:15; Matt. 18:16; Heb. 2:2
29 [a]Heb. 2:3 [b]Heb. 6:6 [c]Ex. 24:8; Matt. 26:28; Heb. 13:20 [d]Eph. 5:26; Heb. 9:13f.; Rev. 1:5 [e]1 Cor. 6:11; Eph. 4:30; Heb. 6:4
30 [a]Deut. 32:35; Rom. 12:19 [b]Deut. 32:36
31 [a]2 Cor. 5:11 [b]Matt. 16:16; Heb. 3:12
32 [1]Lit., *in which* [a]Heb. 5:12 [b]Heb. 6:4 [c]Phil. 1:30
33 [a]1 Cor. 4:9; Heb. 12:4 [b]Phil. 4:14; 1 Thess. 2:14
34 [a]Heb. 13:3 [b]Matt. 5:12 [c]Heb. 9:15; 11:16; 13:14; 1 Pet. 1:4f.
35 [a]Heb. 10:19 [b]Heb. 2:2
36 [1]Lit., *the promise* [a]Luke 21:19; Heb. 12:1 [b]Mark 3:35 [c]Heb. 9:15

37 [a]Hab. 2:3; Heb. 10:25; Rev. 22:20 [b]Matt. 11:3
38 [a]Hab. 2:4; Rom. 1:17; Gal. 3:11
39 [1]Lit., *we are not of shrinking back . . . but of faith* [2]Or, *possessing*

1 [1]Or, *substance* [2]Or, *evidence* [a]Heb. 3:14 [b]Heb. 3:6 [c]Rom. 8:24; 2 Cor. 4:18; 5:7; Heb. 11:7, 27

2 For by it the [a]men of old [1b]gained approval.

3 By faith we understand that the [1a]worlds were prepared [b]by the word of God, so that what is seen [c]was not made out of things which are visible.

4 By faith [a]Abel offered to God a better sacrifice than Cain, through which he [b]obtained the testimony that he was righteous, God testifying [1]about his [c]gifts, and through [2]faith, though [d]he is dead, he still speaks.

5 By faith [a]Enoch was taken up so that he should not [b]see death; AND HE WAS NOT FOUND BECAUSE GOD TOOK HIM UP; for he obtained the witness that before his being taken up he was pleasing to God.

6 And without faith it is impossible to please *Him*, for he who [a]comes to God must believe that He is, and *that* He is a rewarder of those who seek Him.

7 By faith [a]Noah, being [b]warned *by God* about [c]things not yet seen, [1d]in reverence [e]prepared an ark for the salvation of his household, by which he condemned the world, and became an heir of [f]the righteousness which is according to faith.

8 By faith [a]Abraham, when he was called, obeyed by going out to a place which he was to [b]receive for an inheritance; and he went out, not knowing where he was going.

9 By faith he lived as an alien in [a]the land of promise, as in a foreign *land*, [b]dwelling in tents with Isaac and Jacob, [c]fellow heirs of the same promise;

10 for he was looking for [a]the city which has [b]foundations, [c]whose architect and builder is God.

11 By faith even [a]Sarah herself received [1]ability to conceive, even beyond the proper time of life, since she considered Him [b]faithful who had promised;

12 therefore, also, there was born of one man, and [a]him as good as dead [1]at that, *as many descendants* [b]AS THE STARS OF HEAVEN IN NUMBER, AND INNUMERABLE AS THE SAND WHICH IS BY THE SEASHORE.

13 [a]All these died in faith, [b]without receiving the promises, but [c]having seen them and having welcomed them from a distance, and [d]having confessed that they were strangers and exiles on the earth.

14 For those who say such things make it clear that they are seeking a country of their own.

15 And indeed if they had been [1]thinking of that *country* from which they went out, [a]they would have had opportunity to return.

16 But as it is, they desire a better *country*, that is a [a]heavenly one. Therefore [b]God is not [1]ashamed to be [c]called their God; for [d]He has prepared a city for them.

17 By faith [a]Abraham, when he was tested, offered up Isaac; and he who had [b]received the promises was offering up his only begotten *son*;

18 *it was he* to whom it was said, "[a]IN ISAAC YOUR [1]DESCENDANTS SHALL BE CALLED."

19 [1]He considered that [a]God is able to raise *men* even from the dead; from which he also received him back [2]as a [b]type.

20 By faith [a]Isaac blessed Jacob and Esau, even regarding things to come.

21 By faith [a]Jacob, as he was dying, blessed each of the sons of Joseph, and [b]worshiped, *leaning* on the top of his staff.

22 By faith [a]Joseph, when he was dying, made mention of the exodus of the sons of Israel, and gave orders concerning his bones.

23 By faith [a]Moses, when he was born, was hidden for three months by his parents, because they saw he was a beautiful child; and they were not afraid of the [b]king's edict.

24 By faith Moses, [a]when he had grown up, refused to be called the son of Pharaoh's daughter;

25 choosing rather to [a]endure ill-treatment with the people of God, than to enjoy the passing pleasures of sin;

26 [a]considering the reproach of [1]Christ greater riches than the treasures of Egypt; for he was looking to the [b]reward.

27 By faith he [a]left Egypt, not [b]fearing the wrath of the king; for he endured, as [c]seeing Him who is unseen.

28 By faith he [a]kept the Passover and the sprinkling of the blood, so that [b]he who destroyed the first-born might not touch them.

29 By faith they [a]passed through the Red Sea as though *they were passing* through dry land; and the Egyptians, when they attempted it, were [1]drowned.

30 By faith [a]the walls of Jericho fell down, [b]after they had been encircled for seven days.

31 By faith [a]Rahab the harlot did not perish along with those who were disobedient, after she had welcomed the spies [1]in peace.

32 And what more shall I say? For time will fail me if I tell of [a]Gideon, [b]Barak, [c]Samson, [d]Jephthah, of [e]David and [f]Samuel and the prophets,

33 who by faith [a]conquered kingdoms, [b]performed *acts of* righteousness, [c]obtained promises, [d]shut the mouths of lions,

2 [1]Lit., *obtained a testimony* [a]Heb. 1:1 [b]Heb. 11:4, 39
3 [1]Lit., *ages* [a]John 1:3; Heb. 1:2 [b]Gen. ch. 1; Ps. 33:6, 9; Heb. 6:5; 2 Pet. 3:5 [c]Rom. 4:17
4 [1]I.e., by receiving his gifts [2]Lit., *it* [a]Gen. 4:4; Matt. 23:35; 1 John 3:12 [b]Heb. 11:2 [c]Heb. 5:1 [d]Gen. 4:8-10; Heb. 12:24
5 [a]Gen. 5:21-24 [b]Luke 2:26; John 8:51; Heb. 2:9
6 [a]Heb. 7:19
7 [1]Lit., *having become reverent* [a]Gen. 6:13-22 [b]Heb. 8:5 [c]Heb. 11:1 [d]Heb. 5:7 [e]1 Pet. 3:20 [f]Gen. 6:9; Ezek. 14:14, 20; Rom. 4:13; 9:30
8 [a]Gen. 12:1-4; Acts 7:2-4 [b]Gen. 12:7
9 [a]Acts 7:5 [b]Gen. 12:8; 13:3, 18; 18:1, 9 [c]Heb. 6:17
10 [a]Heb. 12:22; 13:14 [b]Rev. 21:14ff. [c]Heb. 11:16
11 [1]Lit., *power for the laying down of seed* [a]Gen. 17:19; 18:11-14; 21:2 [b]Heb. 10:23
12 [1]Lit., *in these things* [a]Rom. 4:19 [b]Gen. 15:5; 22:17; 32:12
13 [a]Matt. 13:17 [b]Heb. 11:39 [c]John 8:56; Heb. 11:27 [d]Gen. 23:4; 47:9; 1 Chr. 29:15; Ps. 39:12; Eph. 2:19; 1 Pet. 1:1; 2:11
15 [1]Or, *remembering* [a]Gen. 24:6-8
16 [1]Lit., *ashamed of them, to be* [a]2 Tim. 4:18 [b]Mark 8:38; Heb. 2:11 [c]Gen. 26:24; 28:13; Ex. 3:6, 15; 4:5 [d]Heb. 11:10; Rev. 21:2
17 [a]Gen. 22:1-10; James 2:21 [b]Heb. 11:13
18 [1]Lit., *seed* [a]Gen. 21:12; Rom. 9:7
19 [1]Lit., *Considering* [2]Or, *figuratively speaking;* lit., *in a parable* [a]Rom. 4:21 [b]Heb. 9:9
20 [a]Gen. 27:27-29, 39f.
21 [a]Gen. 48:1, 5, 16, 20 [b]Gen. 47:31; 1 Kin. 1:47
22 [a]Gen. 50:24f.; Ex. 13:19
23 [a]Ex. 2:2 [b]Ex. 1:16, 22
24 [a]Ex. 2:10, 11ff.
25 [a]Heb. 11:37
26 [1]I.e., the Messiah [a]Luke 14:33; Phil. 3:7f. [b]Heb. 2:2
27 [a]Ex. 2:15; 12:50f.; 13:17f. [b]Ex. 2:14; 10:28f. [c]Col. 1:15; Heb. 11:1, 13
28 [a]Ex. 12:21ff. [b]Ex. 12:23, 29f.; 1 Cor. 10:10
29 [1]Lit., *swallowed up* [a]Ex. 14:22-29
30 [a]Josh. 6:20 [b]Josh. 6:15f.
31 [1]Lit., *with* [a]Josh. 2:9ff.; 6:23; James 2:25
32 [a]Judg. ch. 6-8 [b]Judg. ch. 4, 5 [c]Judg. ch. 13-16 [d]Judg. ch. 11, 12 [e]1 Sam. 16:1, 13 [f]1 Sam. 1:20
33 [a]Judg. ch. 4, 7, 11, 14; 2 Sam. 5:17-20; 8:1f.; 10:12 [b]1 Sam. 12:4; 2 Sam. 8:15 [c]2 Sam. 7:11f. [d]Judg. 14:6; 1 Sam. 17:34ff.; Dan. 6:22

34 [a]quenched the power of fire, [b]es-
caped the edge of the sword, from weakness were made strong, [c]became mighty
in war, [c]put foreign armies to flight.
35 [a]Women received *back* their dead
by resurrection; and others were tor-
tured, not accepting their [1]release, in
order that they might obtain a better
resurrection;
36 and others [1]experienced mockings
and scourgings, yes, also [a]chains and
imprisonment.
37 They were [a]stoned, they were
[b]sawn in two, [1]they were tempted, they
were [c]put to death with the sword; they
went about [d]in sheepskins, in goatskins,
being destitute, afflicted, [e]ill-treated
38 (*men* of whom the world was not
worthy), [a]wandering in deserts and
mountains and caves and holes [1]in the
ground.
39 And all these, having [1a]gained
approval through their faith, [b]did not
receive [2]what was promised,
40 because God had [1]provided [a]some-
thing better for us, so that [b]apart from
us they should not be made perfect.

Jesus, the Example

12 THEREFORE, since we have so
great a cloud of witnesses surrounding us, let us also [a]lay aside every
encumbrance, and the sin which so
easily entangles us, and let us [b]run with
[c]endurance the race that is set before us,
2 [1]fixing our eyes on Jesus, the [2a]au-
thor and perfecter of faith, who for the
joy set before Him [b]endured the cross,
[c]despising the shame, and has [d]sat down
at the right hand of the throne of God.
3 For [a]consider Him who has endured such hostility by sinners against
Himself, so that you may not grow
weary [1b]and lose heart.

A Father's Discipline

4 [a]You have not yet resisted [1b]to the
point of shedding blood in your striving
against sin;
5 and you have forgotten the exhortation which is addressed to you as sons,
"[a]MY SON, DO NOT REGARD
LIGHTLY THE DISCIPLINE OF THE
LORD,
NOR [b]FAINT WHEN YOU ARE RE-
PROVED BY HIM;
6 [a]FOR THOSE [b]WHOM THE LORD
LOVES HE DISCIPLINES,
AND HE SCOURGES EVERY SON
WHOM HE RECEIVES."
7 It is for discipline that you endure;
[a]God deals with you as with sons; for
what son is there whom *his* father does
not discipline?
8 But if you are without discipline,
[a]of which all have become partakers,
then you are illegitimate children and
not sons.
9 Furthermore, we had [1]earthly fathers to discipline us, and we [a]respected
them; shall we not much rather be
subject to [b]the Father of [2]spirits, and
[c]live?
10 For they [1]disciplined us for a short
time as seemed best to them, but He
disciplines us for *our* good, [a]that we may
share His holiness.
11 All discipline [a]for the moment
seems not to be joyful, but sorrowful;
yet to those who have been trained by it,
afterwards it yields the [b]peaceful fruit of
righteousness.
12 Therefore, [1a]strengthen the hands
that are weak and the knees that are
feeble,
13 and [a]make straight paths for your
feet, so that *the limb* which is lame may
not be put out of joint, but rather [b]be
healed.
14 [a]Pursue peace with all men, and the
[b]sanctification without which no one will
[c]see the Lord.
15 See to it that no one [a]comes short
of the grace of God; that no [b]root of
bitterness springing up causes trouble,
and by it many be [c]defiled;
16 that *there be* no [a]immoral or [b]god-
less person like Esau, [c]who sold his own
birthright for a *single* meal.
17 For you know that even afterwards, [a]when he desired to inherit the
blessing, he was rejected, for he found
no place for repentance, though he
sought for it with tears.

Contrast of Sinai and Zion

18 [a]For you have not come to [b]*a
mountain* that may be touched and to a
blazing fire, and to darkness and gloom
and whirlwind,
19 and to the [a]blast of a trumpet and
the [b]sound of words which *sound was
such that* those who heard [c]begged that
no further word should be spoken to
them.
20 For they could not bear the command, "[a]IF EVEN A BEAST TOUCHES THE
MOUNTAIN, IT WILL BE STONED."
21 And so terrible was the sight, *that*
Moses said, "[a]I AM FULL OF FEAR and
trembling."
22 But [a]you have come to Mount Zion
and to [b]the city of [c]the living God, [d]the
heavenly Jerusalem, and to [e]myriads of
[1]angels,
23 to the general assembly and
[a]church of the first-born who [b]are enrolled in heaven, and to God, [c]the Judge
of all, and to the [d]spirits of righteous
men made perfect,

34 [a]Dan. 3:23ff. [b]Ex. 18:4; 1 Sam. 18:11; 19:10; 1 Kin. ch. 19; 2 Kin. ch. 6; Ps. 144:10 [c]Judg. 7:21; 15:8, 15f.; 1 Sam. 17:51f.; 2 Sam. 8:1-6; 10:15ff.
35 [1]Lit., *redemption* [a]1 Kin. 17:23; 2 Kin. 4:36f.
36 [1]Lit., *received the trial of* [a]Gen. 39:20; 1 Kin. 22:27; 2 Chr. 18:26; Jer. 20:2; 37:15
37 [1]Some mss. do not contain *they were tempted* [a]1 Kin. 21:13; 2 Chr. 24:21 [b]2 Sam. 12:31; 1 Chr. 20:3 [c]1 Kin. 19:10; Jer. 26:23 [d]1 Kin. 19:13, 19; 2 Kin. 2:8, 13f.; Zech. 13:4 [e]Heb. 11:25; 13:3
38 [1]Lit., *of* [a]1 Kin. 18:4, 13; 19:9
39 [1]Lit., *obtained a testimony* [2]Lit., *the promise* [a]Heb. 11:2 [b]Heb. 10:36; 11:13
40 [1]Or, *foreseen* [a]Heb. 11:16 [b]Rev. 6:11

1 [a]Rom. 13:12; Eph. 4:22 [b]1 Cor. 9:24; Gal. 2:2 [c]Heb. 10:36
2 [1]Lit., *looking to* [2]Or, *leader* [a]Heb. 2:10 [b]Phil. 2:8f.; Heb. 2:9 [c]1 Cor. 1:18, 23; Heb. 13:13 [d]Heb. 1:3
3 [1]Lit., *fainting in your souls* [a]Rev. 2:3 [b]Gal. 6:9; Heb. 12:5
4 [1]Lit., *as far as blood* [a]Heb. 10:32ff.; 13:13 [b]Phil. 2:8
5 [a]Job 5:17; Prov. 3:11 [b]Heb. 12:3
6 [a]Prov. 3:12 [b]Ps. 119:75; Rev. 3:19
7 [a]Deut. 8:5; 2 Sam. 7:14; Prov. 13:24; 19:18; 23:13f.
8 [a]1 Pet. 5:9
9 [1]Lit., *fathers of our flesh* [2]Or, *our spirits* [a]Luke 18:2 [b]Num. 16:22; 27:16; Rev. 22:6 [c]Is. 38:16
10 [1]Lit., *were disciplining* [a]2 Pet. 1:4
11 [a]1 Pet. 1:6 [b]Is. 32:17; 2 Tim. 4:8; James 3:17f.
12 [1]Lit., *make straight* [a]Is. 35:3
13 [a]Prov. 4:26; Gal. 2:14 [b]Gal. 6:1; James 5:16
14 [a]Rom. 14:19 [b]Rom. 6:22; Heb. 12:10 [c]Matt. 5:8; Heb. 9:28
15 [a]2 Cor. 6:1; Gal. 5:4; Heb. 4:1 [b]Deut. 29:18 [c]Titus 1:15
16 [a]Heb. 13:4 [b]1 Tim. 1:9 [c]Gen. 25:33f.
17 [a]Gen. 27:30-40

18 [a]2 Cor. 3:7-13; Heb. 12:18ff. [b]Ex. 19:12, 16ff.; 20:18; Deut. 4:11; 5:22
19 [a]Ex. 19:16, 19; 20:18; Matt. 24:31 [b]Ex. 19:19; Deut. 4:12 [c]Ex. 20:19; Deut. 5:25; 18:16
20 [a]Ex. 19:12f.
21 [a]Deut. 9:19
22 [1]Or, *angels in festal assembly, and to the church* [a]Rev. 14:1 [b]Eph. 2:19; Phil. 3:20; Heb. 11:10; Rev. 21:2 [c]Heb. 3:12 [d]Gal. 4:26; Heb. 11:16 [e]Rev. 5:11
23 [a]Ex. 4:22; Heb. 2:12 [b]Luke 10:20 [c]Gen. 18:25; Ps. 50:6; 94:2 [d]Heb. 11:40; Rev. 6:9, 11

24 and to Jesus, the [a]mediator of a new covenant, and to the [b]sprinkled blood, which speaks better than [c]*the blood* of Abel.

The Unshaken Kingdom

25 [a]See to it that you do not refuse Him who is [b]speaking. For [c]if those [1]did not escape when they [d]refused him who [e]warned *them* on earth, much [2]less *shall* we *escape* who turn away from Him who [e]*warns* from heaven.

26 And [a]His voice shook the earth then, but now He has promised, saying, "[b]YET ONCE MORE I WILL SHAKE NOT ONLY THE EARTH, BUT ALSO THE HEAVEN."

27 And this *expression*, "Yet once more," denotes [a]the removing of those things which can be shaken, as of created things, in order that those things which cannot be shaken may remain.

28 Therefore, since we receive a [a]kingdom which cannot be shaken, let us [1]show gratitude, by which we may [b]offer to God an acceptable service with reverence and awe;

29 for [a]our God is a consuming fire.

The Changeless Christ

13 LET [a]love of the brethren continue.

2 Do not neglect to [a]show hospitality to strangers, for by this some have [b]entertained angels without knowing it.

3 [a]Remember [b]the prisoners, as though in prison with them, and those who are ill-treated, since you yourselves also are in the body.

4 [a]*Let* marriage *be held* in honor among all, and let the *marriage* bed *be* undefiled; [b]for fornicators and adulterers God will judge.

5 Let your character be [a]free from the love of money, [b]being content with what you have; for He Himself has said, "[c]I WILL NEVER DESERT YOU, NOR WILL I EVER FORSAKE YOU,"

6 so that we confidently say,

"[a]THE LORD IS MY HELPER, I WILL NOT BE AFRAID.
WHAT SHALL MAN DO TO ME?"

7 Remember [a]those who led you, who spoke [b]the word of God to you; and considering the [1]result of their conduct, [c]imitate their faith.

8 [a]Jesus Christ *is* the same yesterday and today, *yes* and forever.

9 [a]Do not be carried away by varied and strange teachings; for it is good for the heart to [b]be strengthened by grace, not by [c]foods, [d]through which those who [1]were thus occupied were not benefited.

10 We have an altar, [a]from which those [b]who serve the [1]tabernacle have no right to eat.

24 [a]1 Tim. 2:5; Heb. 8:6; 9:15 [b]Heb. 9:19; 10:22; 1 Pet. 1:2 [c]Gen. 4:10; Heb. 11:4
25 [1]Lit., *were not escaping* [2]Lit., *more* [a]Heb. 3:12 [b]Heb. 1:1 [c]Heb. 2:2f.; 10:28f. [d]Heb. 12:19 [e]Ex. 20:22; Heb. 8:5; 11:7
26 [a]Ex. 19:18; Judg. 5:4f. [b]Hag. 2:6
27 [a]Is. 34:4; 54:10; 65:17; Rom. 8:19, 21; 1 Cor. 7:31; Heb. 1:10ff.
28 [1]Lit., *have* [a]Dan. 2:44 [b]Heb. 13:15, 21
29 [a]Deut. 4:24; 9:3; Is. 33:14; 2 Thess. 1:7; Heb. 10:27, 31

1 [a]Rom. 12:10; 1 Thess. 4:9; 1 Pet. 1:22
2 [a]Matt. 25:35; Rom. 12:13; 1 Pet. 4:9 [b]Gen. 18:1ff.; 19:1f.
3 [a]Col. 4:18 [b]Matt. 25:36; Heb. 10:34
4 [a]1 Cor. 7:38; 1 Tim. 4:3 [b]1 Cor. 6:9; Gal. 5:19, 21; 1 Thess. 4:6
5 [a]Eph. 5:3; Col. 3:5; 1 Tim. 3:3 [b]Phil. 4:11 [c]Deut. 31:6, 8; Josh. 1:5
6 [a]Ps. 118:6
7 [1]Or, *end of their life* [a]Heb. 13:17, 24 [b]Luke 5:1 [c]Heb. 6:12
8 [a]2 Cor. 1:19; Heb. 1:12
9 [1]Lit., *walked* [a]Eph. 4:14; 5:6; Jude 12 [b]2 Cor. 1:21; Col. 2:7 [c]Col. 2:16 [d]Heb. 9:10
10 [1]Or, *sacred tent* [a]1 Cor. 10:18 [b]Heb. 8:5
11 [a]Ex. 29:14; Lev. 4:12, 21; 9:11; 16:27; Num. 19:3, 7
12 [a]Eph. 5:26; Heb. 2:11 [b]Heb. 9:12 [c]John 19:17
13 [a]Luke 9:23; Heb. 11:26; 12:2
14 [a]Heb. 10:34; 12:27 [b]Eph. 2:19; Heb. 2:5; 11:10, 16; 12:22
15 [1]Lit., *confess* [a]1 Pet. 2:5 [b]Lev. 7:12 [c]Is. 57:19; Hos. 14:2
16 [a]Rom. 12:13 [b]Phil. 4:18
17 [1]Lit., *in order that they may do this* [2]Lit., *groaning* [a]1 Cor. 16:16; Heb. 13:7, 24 [b]Is. 62:6; Ezek. 3:17; Acts 20:28
18 [a]1 Thess. 5:25 [b]Acts 24:16; 1 Tim. 1:5
19 [a]Philem. 22

11 For [a]the bodies of those animals whose blood is brought into the holy place by the high priest *as an offering* for sin, are burned outside the camp.

12 Therefore Jesus also, [a]that He might sanctify the people [b]through His own blood, suffered [c]outside the gate.

13 Hence, let us go out to Him outside the camp, [a]bearing His reproach.

14 For here [a]we do not have a lasting city, but we are seeking [b]*the city* which is to come.

God-pleasing Sacrifices

15 [a]Through Him then, let us continually offer up a [b]sacrifice of praise to God, that is, [c]the fruit of lips that [1]give thanks to His name.

16 And do not neglect doing good and [a]sharing; for [b]with such sacrifices God is pleased.

17 [a]Obey your leaders, and submit *to them*; for [b]they keep watch over your souls, as those who will give an account. [1]Let them do this with joy and not [2]with grief, for this would be unprofitable for you.

18 [a]Pray for us, for we are sure that we have a [b]good conscience, desiring to conduct ourselves honorably in all things.

19 And I urge *you* all the more to do this, [a]that I may be restored to you the sooner.

Benediction

20 Now [a]the God of peace, who [b]brought up from the dead the [c]great Shepherd of the sheep [1]through [d]the blood of the [e]eternal covenant, *even* Jesus our Lord,

21 [a]equip you in every good thing to do His will, [b]working in us that [c]which is pleasing in His sight, through Jesus Christ, [d]to whom *be* the glory forever and ever. Amen.

22 But [a]I urge you, [b]brethren, [1]bear with [2]this [b]word of exhortation, for [c]I have written to you briefly.

23 Take notice that [a]our brother Timothy has been released, with whom, if he comes soon, I shall see you.

24 Greet [a]all of your leaders and all the [1][b]saints. Those from [c]Italy greet you.

25 [a]Grace be with you all.

20 [1]Or, *in* [a]Rom. 15:33 [b]Acts 2:24; Rom. 10:7 [c]Is. 63:11; John 10:11; 1 Pet. 2:25 [d]Zech. 9:11; Heb. 10:29 [e]Is. 55:3; Jer. 32:40; Ezek. 37:26
21 [a]1 Pet. 5:10 [b]Phil. 2:13 [c]Heb. 12:28; 1 John 3:22 [d]Rom. 11:36
22 [1]Or, *listen to* [2]Lit., *the* [a]Acts 13:15; Heb. 3:13; 10:25; 12:5; 13:19 [b]Heb. 3:1 [c]1 Pet. 5:12
23 [a]Acts 16:1; Col. 1:1
24 [1]Or, *holy ones* [a]1 Cor. 16:16; Heb. 13:7, 17 [b]Acts 9:13 [c]Acts 18:2
25 [a]Col. 4:18

THE EPISTLE OF
JAMES

Testing Your Faith

1 [1a]JAMES, a [b]bond-servant of God
and [c]of the Lord Jesus Christ, to
[d]the twelve tribes who are [2e]dispersed
abroad, [f]greetings.
2 [a]Consider it all joy, my brethren,
when you encounter [b]various [1]trials,
3 knowing that [a]the testing of your
[b]faith produces [1c]endurance.
4 And let [1a]endurance have *its* perfect [2]result, that you may be [3b]perfect
and complete, lacking in nothing.
5 But if any of you [a]lacks wisdom, let
him ask of God, who gives to all men
generously and [1]without reproach, and
[b]it will be given to him.
6 But let him [a]ask in faith [b]without
any doubting, for the one who doubts is
like the surf of the sea [c]driven and tossed
by the wind.
7 For let not that man expect that he
will receive anything from the Lord,
8 *being* a [1a]double-minded man, [b]un-
stable in all his ways.
9 [a]But let the [1]brother of humble
circumstances glory in his high position;
10 and *let* the rich man *glory* in his
humiliation, because [a]like [1]flowering
grass he will pass away.
11 For the sun rises with [1a]a scorching
wind, and [b]withers the grass; and its
flower falls off, and the beauty of its
appearance is destroyed; so too the rich
man in the midst of his pursuits will fade
away.
12 [a]Blessed is a man who perseveres
under trial; for once he has [1]been approved, he will receive [b]the crown of life,
which *the Lord* [c]has promised to those
who [d]love Him.
13 Let no one say when he is tempted,
"[a]I am being tempted [1]by God"; for
God cannot be tempted [2]by evil, and He
Himself does not tempt anyone.
14 But each one is tempted when he is
carried away and enticed by his own
lust.
15 Then [a]when lust has conceived, it
gives birth to sin; and when [b]sin is
accomplished, it brings forth death.
16 [a]Do not be deceived, [b]my beloved
brethren.
17 Every good thing bestowed and
every perfect gift is [a]from above, coming
down from [b]the Father of lights, [c]with
whom there is no variation, or [1]shifting
shadow.
18 In the exercise of [a]His will He
[b]brought us forth by [c]the word of truth,
so that we might be, [1]as it were, the [d]first
fruits [2]among His creatures.
19 [1]*This* [a]you know, [b]my beloved
brethren. But let everyone be quick to
hear, [c]slow to speak *and* [d]slow to anger;
20 for [a]the anger of man does not
achieve the righteousness of God.
21 Therefore [a]putting aside all filthiness and *all* [1]that remains of wickedness,
in [2]humility receive [b]the word implanted, which is able to save your souls.
22 [a]But prove yourselves doers of the
word, and not merely hearers who delude themselves.
23 For if anyone is a hearer of the
word and not a doer, he is like a man
who looks at his [1]natural face [a]in a
mirror;
24 for *once* he has looked at himself
and gone away, [1]he has immediately
forgotten what kind of person he was.
25 But one who looks intently at the
perfect law, [a]the *law* of liberty, and
abides by it, not having become a forget-
ful hearer but [1]an effectual doer, this
man shall be [b]blessed in [2]what he does.
26 If anyone thinks himself to be
religious, and yet does not [a]bridle his
tongue but deceives his *own* heart, this
man's religion is worthless.
27 This is pure and undefiled religion
[a]in the sight of *our* God and Father, to
[b]visit [c]orphans and widows in their
distress, *and* to keep oneself unstained
[1]by [d]the world.

The Sin of Partiality

2 [a]MY brethren, [b]do not hold your
faith in our [c]glorious Lord Jesus
Christ with *an attitude of* [d]personal
favoritism.
2 For if a man comes into your
[1]assembly with a gold ring and dressed
in [2a]fine clothes, and there also comes in
a poor man in [b]dirty clothes,
3 and you [1]pay special attention to
the one who is wearing the [a]fine clothes,
and say, "You sit here in a good place,"
and you say to the poor man, "You
stand over there, or sit down by my
footstool,"
4 have you not made distinctions
among yourselves, and become judges
[a]with evil [1]motives?
5 Listen, [a]my beloved brethren: did
not [b]God choose the poor [1]of this world
to be [c]rich in faith and [d]heirs of the
kingdom which He [e]promised to those
who love Him?
6 But you have dishonored the poor
man. Is it not the rich who oppress you
and [1]personally [a]drag you into [2]court?

1 [1]Or, *Jacob* [2]Lit., *in the Dispersion* [a]Acts 12:17 [b]Titus 1:1 [c]Rom. 1:1 [d]Luke 22:30 [e]John 7:35 [f]Acts 15:23
2 [1]Or, *temptations* [a]Matt. 5:12; James 1:12; 5:11 [b]1 Pet. 1:6
3 [1]Or, *steadfastness* [a]1 Pet. 1:7 [b]Heb. 6:12 [c]Luke 21:19
4 [1]V. 3, note 1 [2]Lit., *work* [3]Or, *mature* [a]Luke 21:19 [b]Matt. 5:48; Col. 4:12
5 [1]Lit., *does not reproach* [a]1 Kin. 3:9ff.; James 3:17 [b]Matt. 7:7
6 [a]Matt. 21:21 [b]Mark 11:23; Acts 10:20 [c]Matt. 14:28-31; Eph. 4:14
8 [1]Or, *doubting, hesitating* [a]James 4:8 [b]2 Pet. 2:14
9 [1]I.e., church member [a]Luke 14:11
10 [1]Lit., *the flower of the grass* [a]1 Cor. 7:31; 1 Pet. 1:24
11 [1]Lit., *the* [a]Matt. 20:12 [b]Ps. 102:4, 11; Is. 40:7f.
12 [1]Or, *passed the test* [a]Luke 6:22; James 5:11; 1 Pet. 3:14; 4:14 [b]1 Cor. 9:25 [c]Ex. 20:6; James 2:5 [d]1 Cor. 2:9; 8:3
13 [1]Lit., *from* [2]Lit., *of evil things* [a]Gen. 22:1
15 [a]Job 15:35; Ps. 7:14; Is. 59:4 [b]Rom. 5:12; 6:23
16 [a]1 Cor. 6:9 [b]Acts 1:15; James 1:2, 19; 2:1, 5, 14; 3:1, 10; 4:11; 5:12, 19
17 [1]Lit., *shadow of turning* [a]John 3:3; James 3:15, 17 [b]Ps. 136:7; 1 John 1:5 [c]Mal. 3:6
18 [1]Lit., *a certain first fruits* [2]Lit., *of* [a]John 1:13 [b]James 1:15; 1 Pet. 1:3, 23 [c]2 Cor. 6:7; Eph. 1:13; 2 Tim. 2:15 [d]Jer. 2:3; Rev. 14:4
19 [1]Or, *Know* this [a]1 John 2:21 [b]Acts 1:15; James 1:2, 16; 2:1, 5, 14; 3:1, 10; 4:11; 5:12, 19 [c]Prov. 10:19; 17:27 [d]Prov. 16:32; Eccl. 7:9
20 [a]Matt. 5:22; Eph. 4:26
21 [1]Lit., *abundance of malice* [2]Or, *gentleness* [a]Eph. 4:22; 1 Pet. 2:1 [b]Eph. 1:13; 1 Pet. 1:22f.
22 [a]Matt. 7:24-27; Luke 6:46-49; Rom. 2:13; James 1:22-25; 2:14-20
23 [1]Lit., *the face of his birth;* or, *nature* [a]1 Cor. 13:12
24 [1]Lit., *and he*

25 [1]Lit., *a doer of a work* [2]Lit., *his doing* [a]John 8:32; Rom. 8:2; Gal. 2:4; 6:2; James 2:12; 1 Pet. 2:16 [b]John 13:17
26 [a]Ps. 39:1; 141:3; James 3:2-12
27 [1]Lit., *from* [a]Rom. 2:13; Gal. 3:11 [b]Matt. 25:36 [c]Deut. 14:29; Job 31:16, 17, 21; Ps. 146:9; Is. 1:17, 23 [d]Matt. 12:32; Eph. 2:2; Titus 2:12; James 4:4; 2 Pet. 1:4; 2:20; 1 John 2:15-17

1 [a]James 1:16 [b]Heb. 12:2 [c]Acts 7:2; 1 Cor. 2:8 [d]Acts 10:34; James 2:9
2 [1]Or, *synagogue* [2]Or, *bright* [a]Luke 23:11; James 2:3 [b]Zech. 3:3f.
3 [1]Lit., *look upon* [a]Luke 23:11
4 [1]Lit., *reasonings* [a]Luke 18:6; John 7:24
5 [1]Lit., *to the* [a]James 1:16 [b]Job 34:19; 1 Cor. 1:27f. [c]Luke 12:21; Rev. 2:9 [d]Matt. 5:3; 25:34 [e]James 1:12
6 [1]Lit., *they themselves* [2]Lit., *courts* [a]Acts 8:3; 16:19

7 [a]Do they not blaspheme the fair name [1]by which you have been called?

8 If, however, you [a]are fulfilling the [1]royal law, according to the Scripture, "[b]YOU SHALL LOVE YOUR NEIGHBOR AS YOURSELF," you are doing well.

9 But if you [a]show partiality, you are committing sin *and* are convicted by the [1]law as transgressors.

10 For whoever keeps the whole [1]law and yet [a]stumbles in one *point,* he has become [b]guilty of all.

11 For He who said, "[a]DO NOT COMMIT ADULTERY," also said, "[b]DO NOT COMMIT MURDER." Now if you do not commit adultery, but do commit murder, you have become a transgressor of the [1]law.

12 So speak and so act, as those who are to be judged by [a]*the* law of liberty.

13 For [a]judgment *will be* merciless to one who has shown no mercy; mercy [1]triumphs over judgment.

Faith and Works

14 [a]What use is it, [b]my brethren, if a man says he has faith, but he has no works? Can [1]that faith save him?

15 [a]If a brother or sister is without clothing and in need of daily food,

16 and one of you says to them, "[a]Go in peace, be warmed and be filled," and yet you do not give them what is necessary for *their* body, what use is that?

17 Even so [a]faith, if it has no works, is dead, *being* by itself.

18 [a]But someone [1]may *well* say, "You have faith, and I have works; show me your [b]faith without the works, and I will [c]show you my faith [d]by my works."

19 You believe that [1a]God is one. [b]You do well; [c]the demons also believe, and shudder.

20 But are you willing to recognize, [a]you foolish fellow, that [b]faith without works is useless?

21 [a]Was not Abraham our father justified by works, when he offered up Isaac his son on the altar?

22 You see that [a]faith was working with his works, and [1]as a result of the [b]works, faith was [2]perfected;

23 and the Scripture was fulfilled which says, "[a]AND ABRAHAM BELIEVED GOD, AND IT WAS RECKONED TO HIM AS RIGHTEOUSNESS," and he was called [b]the friend of God.

24 You see that a man is justified by works, and not by faith alone.

25 And in the same way was not [a]Rahab the harlot also justified by works, [b]when she received the messengers and sent them out by another way?

26 For just as the body without *the* spirit is dead, so also [a]faith without works is dead.

The Tongue Is a Fire

3 [a]LET not many *of you* become teachers, [b]my brethren, knowing that as such we shall incur a [1]stricter judgment.

7 [1]Lit., *which has been called upon you* [a]Acts 11:26; 1 Pet. 4:16
8 [1]Or, *law of* our *King* [a]Matt. 7:12 [b]Lev. 19:18
9 [1]Or, *Law* [a]Acts 10:34; James 2:1
10 [1]Or, *Law* [a]James 3:2; 2 Pet. 1:10; Jude 24 [b]Matt. 5:19; Gal. 5:3
11 [1]Or, *Law* [a]Ex. 20:14; Deut. 5:18 [b]Ex. 20:13; Deut. 5:17
12 [a]James 1:25
13 [1]Lit., *boasts against* [a]Prov. 21:13; Matt. 5:7; 18:32-35; Luke 6:37f.
14 [1]Lit., *the* [a]James 1:22ff. [b]James 1:16
15 [a]Matt. 25:35f.; Luke 3:11
16 [a]1 John 3:17f.
17 [a]Gal. 5:6; James 2:20, 26
18 [1]Lit., *will* [a]Rom. 9:19 [b]Rom. 3:28; 4:6; Heb. 11:33 [c]James 3:13 [d]Matt. 7:16f.; Gal. 5:6
19 [1]Or, *there is one God* [a]Deut. 6:4; Mark 12:29 [b]James 2:8 [c]Matt. 8:29; Mark 1:24; 5:7; Luke 4:34; Acts 19:15
20 [a]Rom. 9:20; 1 Cor. 15:36 [b]Gal. 5:6; James 2:17, 26
21 [a]Gen. 22:9, 10, 12, 16-18
22 [1]Or, *by the deeds* [2]Or, *completed* [a]John 6:29; Heb. 11:17 [b]1 Thess. 1:3
23 [a]Gen. 15:6; Rom. 4:3 [b]2 Chr. 20:7; Is. 41:8
25 [a]Heb. 11:31 [b]Josh. 2:4, 6, 15
26 [a]Gal. 5:6; James 2:17, 20

1 [1]Or, *greater condemnation* [a]Matt. 23:8; Rom. 2:20f.; 1 Tim. 1:7 [b]James 1:16; 3:10
2 [1]Lit., *word* [a]James 2:10 [b]Matt. 12:34-37; James 3:2-12 [c]James 1:4 [d]James 1:26
3 [a]Ps. 32:9
5 [a]Ps. 12:3f.; 73:8f. [b]Prov. 26:20f.
6 [1]Or, *existence, origin* [2]Gr., *Gehenna* [a]Ps. 120:2, 3; Prov. 16:27 [b]Matt. 12:36f.; 15:11, 18f. [c]Matt. 5:22
7 [1]Lit., *nature*
8 [a]Ps. 140:3; Eccl. 10:11; Rom. 3:13
9 [a]James 1:27 [b]Gen. 1:26; 1 Cor. 11:7
11 [1]Lit., *sweet*
12 [1]V. 11, note 1 [a]Matt. 7:16
13 [a]James 2:18 [b]1 Pet. 2:12
14 [1]Or, *strife* [a]Rom. 2:8; 2 Cor. 12:20; James 3:16 [b]1 Tim. 2:4; James 1:18; 5:19

2 For we all [a]stumble in many *ways.* [b]If anyone does not stumble in [1]what he says, he is a [c]perfect man, able to [d]bridle the whole body as well.

3 Now [a]if we put the bits into the horses' mouths so that they may obey us, we direct their entire body as well.

4 Behold, the ships also, though they are so great and are driven by strong winds, are still directed by a very small rudder, wherever the inclination of the pilot desires.

5 So also the tongue is a small part of the body, and *yet* it [a]boasts of great things. [b]Behold, how great a forest is set aflame by such a small fire!

6 And [a]the tongue is a fire, the *very* world of iniquity; the tongue is set among our members as that which [b]defiles the entire body, and sets on fire the course of *our* [1]life, and is set on fire by [2c]hell.

7 For every [1]species of beasts and birds, of reptiles and creatures of the sea, is tamed, and has been tamed by the human [1]race.

8 But no one can tame the tongue; *it is* a restless evil *and* full of [a]deadly poison.

9 With it we bless [a]*our* Lord and Father; and with it we curse men, [b]who have been made in the likeness of God;

10 from the same mouth come *both* blessing and cursing. My brethren, these things ought not to be this way.

11 Does a fountain send out from the same opening *both* [1]fresh and bitter *water?*

12 [a]Can a fig tree, my brethren, produce olives, or a vine produce figs? Neither *can* salt water produce [1]fresh.

Wisdom from Above

13 Who among you is wise and understanding? [a]Let him show by his [b]good behavior his deeds in the gentleness of wisdom.

14 But if you have bitter [a]jealousy and [1]selfish ambition in your heart, do not be arrogant and *so* lie against [b]the truth.

15 This wisdom is not that which comes down [a]from above, but is [b]earthly, [1c]natural, [d]demonic.

16 For where [a]jealousy and [1]selfish ambition exist, there is disorder and every evil thing.

17 But the wisdom [a]from above is first [b]pure, then [c]peaceable, [d]gentle, [1]reasonable, [e]full of mercy and good fruits, [f]unwavering, without [g]hypocrisy.

18 And the [1a]seed whose fruit is righteousness is sown in peace [2]by those who make peace.

15 [1]Or, *unspiritual* [a]James 1:17 [b]1 Cor. 2:6; 3:19 [c]2 Cor. 1:12; Jude 19 [d]2 Thess. 2:9f.; 1 Tim. 4:1; Rev. 2:24
16 [1]V. 14, note 1 [a]Rom. 2:8; 2 Cor. 12:20; James 3:14
17 [1]Or, *willing to yield* [a]James 1:17 [b]2 Cor. 7:11; James 4:8 [c]Matt. 5:9; Heb. 12:11 [d]Titus 3:2 [e]Luke 6:36; James 2:13 [f]James 2:4 [g]Rom. 12:9; 2 Cor. 6:6
18 [1]Lit., *fruit of righteousness* [2]Or, *for* [a]Prov. 11:18; Is. 32:17; Hos. 10:12; Amos 6:12; Gal. 6:8; Phil. 1:11

Things to Avoid

4 WHAT is the source of quarrels and [1] [a]conflicts among you? [2]Is not the source your pleasures that wage [b]war in your members?

2 You lust and do not have; *so* you [a]commit murder. And you are envious and cannot obtain; *so* you fight and quarrel. You do not have because you do not ask.

3 You ask and [a]do not receive, because you ask [1]with wrong motives, so that you may spend *it* [2]on your pleasures.

4 You [a]adulteresses, do you not know that friendship with [b]the world is [c]hostility toward God? [d]Therefore whoever wishes to be a friend of the world makes himself an enemy of God.

5 Or do you think that the Scripture [a]speaks to no purpose: "[1]He [2]jealously desires [b]the Spirit which He has made to dwell in us"?

6 But [a]He gives a greater grace. Therefore *it* says, "[b]GOD IS OPPOSED TO THE PROUD, BUT GIVES GRACE TO THE HUMBLE."

7 [a]Submit therefore to God. [b]Resist the devil and he will flee from you.

8 [a]Draw near to God and He will draw near to you. [b]Cleanse your hands, you sinners; and [c]purify your hearts, you [d]double-minded.

9 [a]Be miserable and mourn and weep; let your laughter be turned into mourning, and your joy to gloom.

10 [a]Humble yourselves in the presence of the Lord, and He will exalt you.

11 [a]Do not speak against one another, [b]brethren. He who speaks against a brother, or [c]judges his brother, speaks against [d]the law, and judges the law; but if you judge the law, you are not [e]a doer of the law, but a judge *of it.*

12 There is *only* one [a]Lawgiver and Judge, the One who is [b]able to save and to destroy; but [c]who are you who judge your neighbor?

13 [a]Come now, you who say, "[b]Today or tomorrow, we shall go to such and such a city, and spend a year there and engage in business and make a profit."

14 [1]Yet you do not know [2]what your life will be like tomorrow. [a]You are *just* a vapor that appears for a little while and then vanishes away.

15 [1]Instead, *you ought* to say, "[a]If the Lord wills, we shall live and also do this or that."

16 But as it is, you boast in your [1]arrogance; [a]all such boasting is evil.

17 Therefore, [a]to one who knows *the* [1]right thing to do, and does not do it, to him it is sin.

Misuse of Riches

5 [a]COME now, [b]you rich, [c]weep and howl for your miseries which are coming upon you.

2 [a]Your riches have rotted and your garments have become moth-eaten.

3 Your gold and your silver have rusted; and their rust will be a witness against you and will consume your flesh like fire. It is [a]in the last days that you have stored up your treasure!

4 Behold, [a]the pay of the laborers who mowed your fields, *and* which has been withheld by you, cries out *against you*; and [b]the outcry of those who did the harvesting has reached the ears of [c]the Lord of [1]Sabaoth.

5 You have [a]lived luxuriously on the earth and led a life of wanton pleasure; you have [1]fattened your hearts in [b]a day of slaughter.

6 You have condemned and [1][a]put to death [b]the righteous *man;* he does not resist you.

Exhortation

7 Be patient, therefore, [a]brethren, [b]until the coming of the Lord. [c]Behold, the farmer waits for the precious produce of the soil, being patient about it, until [1]it gets [d]the early and late rains.

8 [a]You too be patient; [b]strengthen your hearts, for [c]the coming of the Lord is [d]at hand.

9 [a]Do not [1]complain, [b]brethren, against one another, that you yourselves may not be judged; behold, [c]the Judge is standing [2][d]right at the [3]door.

10 As an example, [a]brethren, of suffering and patience, take [b]the prophets who spoke in the name of the Lord.

11 Behold, we count those [a]blessed who endured. You have heard of [b]the [1]endurance of Job and have seen [c]the [2]outcome of the Lord's dealings, that [d]the Lord is full of compassion and *is* merciful.

12 But above all, [a]my brethren, [b]do not swear, either by heaven or by earth or with any other oath; but [1]let your yes be yes, and your no, no; so that you may not fall under judgment.

13 Is anyone among you [a]suffering? [b]Let him pray. Is anyone cheerful? Let him [c]sing praises.

14 Is anyone among you sick? Let him call for [a]the elders of the church, and let them pray over him, [1][b]anointing him with oil in the name of the Lord;

15 and the [a]prayer [1]offered in faith will [2][b]restore the one who is sick, and the Lord will [c]raise him up, and if he has committed sins, [3]they will be forgiven him.

---

1 [1]Lit., *Whence wars and whence fightings* [2]Lit., Are they *not hence,* from your [a]Titus 3:9 [b]Rom. 7:23
2 [a]James 5:6; 1 John 3:15
3 [1]Lit., *wickedly* [2]Lit., *in* [a]1 John 3:22; 5:14
4 [a]Jer. 2:2; Ezek. 16:32 [b]James 1:27 [c]Rom. 8:7; 1 John 2:15 [d]Matt. 6:24; John 15:19
5 [1]Or, *The Spirit which He has made to dwell in us jealously desires us* [2]Lit., *desires to jealousy* [a]Num. 23:19 [b]1 Cor. 6:19; 2 Cor. 6:16
6 [a]Is. 54:7f.; Matt. 13:12 [b]Ps. 138:6; Prov. 3:34; Matt. 23:12; 1 Pet. 5:5
7 [a]1 Pet. 5:6 [b]Eph. 4:27; 6:11f.; 1 Pet. 5:8f.
8 [a]2 Chr. 15:2; Zech. 1:3; Mal. 3:7; Heb. 7:19 [b]Job 17:9; Is. 1:16; 1 Tim. 2:8 [c]Jer. 4:14; James 3:17; 1 Pet. 1:22; 1 John 3:3 [d]James 1:8
9 [a]Neh. 8:9; Prov. 14:13; Luke 6:25
10 [a]Job 5:11; Ezek. 21:26; Luke 1:52; James 4:6
11 [a]2 Cor. 12:20; James 5:9; 1 Pet. 2:1 [b]James 1:16; 5:7, 9, 10 [c]Matt. 7:1; Rom. 14:4 [d]James 2:8 [e]James 1:22
12 [a]Is. 33:22; James 5:9 [b]Matt. 10:28 [c]Rom. 14:4
13 [a]James 5:1 [b]Prov. 27:1; Luke 12:18-20
14 [1]Lit., *Who do not* [2]Some mss. read *the morrow; for what kind of life is yours* [a]Job 7:7; Ps. 39:5; 102:3; 144:4
15 [1]Lit., *Instead of your saying* [a]Acts 18:21
16 [1]Or, *pretensions* [a]1 Cor. 5:6
17 [1]Or, *good* [a]Luke 12:47; John 9:41; 2 Pet. 2:21

1 [a]James 4:13 [b]Luke 6:24; 1 Tim. 6:9 [c]Is. 13:6; 15:3; Ezek. 30:2
2 [a]Job 13:28; Is. 50:9; Matt. 6:19f.
3 [a]James 5:7, 8
4 [1]I.e., Hosts [a]Lev. 19:13; Job 24:10f.; Jer. 22:13; Mal. 3:5 [b]Ex. 2:23; Deut. 24:15; Job 31:38f. [c]Rom. 9:29
5 [1]Lit., *nourished* [a]Ezek. 16:49; Luke 16:19; 1 Tim. 5:6; 2 Pet. 2:13 [b]Jer. 12:3; 25:34
6 [1]Or, *murdered* [a]James 4:2 [b]Heb. 10:38; 1 Pet. 4:18

7 [1]Or, *he* [a]James 4:11; 5:9, 10 [b]John 21:22; 1 Thess. 2:19 [c]Gal. 6:9 [d]Deut. 11:14; Jer. 5:24; Joel 2:23
8 [a]Luke 21:19 [b]1 Thess. 3:13 [c]John 21:22; 1 Thess. 2:19 [d]Rom. 13:11, 12; 1 Pet. 4:7
9 [1]Lit., *groan* [2]Lit., *before* [3]Lit., *doors* [a]James 4:11 [b]James 5:7, 10 [c]1 Cor. 4:5; James 4:12; 1 Pet. 4:5 [d]Matt. 24:33; Mark 13:29
10 [a]James 4:11; 5:7, 9 [b]Matt. 5:12
11 [1]Or, *steadfastness* [2]Lit., *end of the Lord* [a]Matt. 5:10; 1 Pet. 3:14 [b]Job 1:21f.; 2:10 [c]Job 42:10, 12 [d]Ex. 34:6; Ps. 103:8
12 [1]Lit., *let yours be the yes, yes, and the no, no* [a]James 1:16 [b]Matt. 5:34-37
13 [a]James 5:10 [b]Ps. 50:15 [c]1 Cor. 14:15; Col. 3:16
14 [1]Lit., *having anointed* [a]Acts 11:30 [b]Mark 6:13; 16:18
15 [1]Lit., *of* [2]Or, *save* [3]Lit., *it* [a]James 1:6 [b]1 Cor. 1:21; James 5:20 [c]John 6:39; 2 Cor. 4:14

16 Therefore, [a]confess your sins to one another, and pray for one another, so that you may be [b]healed. [c]The effective [1]prayer of a righteous man can accomplish much.

17 Elijah was [a]a man with a nature like ours, and [b]he prayed [1]earnestly that it might not rain; and it did not rain on the earth for [c]three years and six months.

18 And he [a]prayed again, and [b]the [1]sky [2]poured rain, and the earth produced its fruit.

19 My brethren, [a]if any among you strays from [b]the truth, and one turns him back,

20 let him know that he who turns a sinner from the error of his way will [a]save his soul from death, and will [b]cover a multitude of sins.

16 [1]Lit., *supplication* [a]Matt. 3:6; Mark 1:5; Acts 19:18 [b]Heb. 12:13; 1 Pet. 2:24 [c]Gen. 18:23-32; John 9:31
17 [1]Lit., *with prayer* [a]Acts 14:15 [b]1 Kin. 17:1; 18:1 [c]Luke 4:25
18 [1]Lit., *heaven* [2]Lit., *gave* [a]1 Kin. 18:42 [b]1 Kin. 18:45
19 [a]Matt. 18:15; Gal. 6:1 [b]James 3:14
20 [a]Rom. 11:14; 1 Cor. 1:21; James 1:21 [b]Prov. 10:12; 1 Pet. 4:8

THE FIRST EPISTLE OF PETER

A Living Hope, and a Sure Salvation

1 [a]PETER, an apostle of Jesus Christ, to those who reside as [b]aliens, [c]scattered throughout [d]Pontus, [e]Galatia, [d]Cappadocia, [d]Asia, and [f]Bithynia, [g]who are chosen

2 according to the [a]foreknowledge of God the Father, [b]by the sanctifying work of the Spirit, [1]that you may [c]obey Jesus Christ and be [d]sprinkled with His blood: [e]May grace and peace [2]be yours in fullest measure.

3 [a]Blessed be the God and Father of our Lord Jesus Christ, who [b]according to His great mercy [c]has caused us to be born again to [d]a living hope through the [e]resurrection of Jesus Christ from the dead,

4 to *obtain* an [a]inheritance *which is* imperishable and undefiled and [b]will not fade away, [c]reserved in heaven for you,

5 who are [a]protected by the power of God [b]through faith for [c]a salvation ready [d]to be revealed in the last time.

6 [a]In this you greatly rejoice, even though now [b]for a little while, [c]if necessary, you have been distressed by [d]various [1]trials,

7 that the [1a]proof of your faith, *being* more precious than gold which [2]is perishable, [b]even though tested by fire, [c]may be found to result in praise and glory and honor at [d]the revelation of Jesus Christ;

8 and [a]though you have not seen Him, you [b]love Him, and though you do not see Him now, but believe in Him, you greatly rejoice with joy inexpressible and [1]full of glory,

9 obtaining as [a]the outcome of your faith the salvation of [1]your souls.

10 [a]As to this salvation, the prophets who [b]prophesied of the [c]grace that *would come* to you made careful search and inquiry,

11 [1]seeking to know what person or time [a]the Spirit of Christ within them was indicating as He [b]predicted the sufferings of Christ and the glories [2]to follow.

12 It was revealed to them that they were not serving themselves, but you, in these things which now have been announced to you through those who [a]preached the gospel to you by [b]the Holy Spirit sent from heaven—things into which [c]angels long to [1]look.

13 Therefore, [a]gird [1]your minds for action, [2b]keep sober *in spirit,* fix your [c]hope completely on the [d]grace [3]to be brought to you at [e]the revelation of Jesus Christ.

14 As [1a]obedient children, do not [2b]be conformed to the former lusts *which were yours* in your [c]ignorance,

15 but [1a]like the Holy One who called you, [2b]be holy yourselves also [c]in all *your* behavior;

16 because it is written, "[a]YOU SHALL BE HOLY, FOR I AM HOLY."

17 And if you [a]address as Father the One who [b]impartially [c]judges according to each man's work, conduct yourselves [d]in fear during the time of your [e]stay *upon earth;*

18 knowing that you were not [1a]redeemed with perishable things like silver or gold from your [b]futile way of life inherited from your forefathers,

19 but with precious [a]blood, as of a [b]lamb unblemished and spotless, *the blood* of Christ.

20 For He was [a]foreknown before [b]the foundation of the world, but has [c]appeared [1]in these last times [d]for the sake of you

21 who through Him are [a]believers in God, who raised Him from the dead and [b]gave Him glory, so that your faith and [c]hope are in God.

1 [a]2 Pet. 1:1 [b]1 Pet. 2:11 [c]James 1:1 [d]Acts 2:9 [e]Acts 16:6 [f]Acts 16:7 [g]Matt. 24:22; Luke 18:7
2 [1]Lit., *unto obedience and sprinkling* [2]Lit., *be multiplied for you* [a]Rom. 8:29; 1 Pet. 1:20 [b]2 Thess. 2:13 [c]1 Pet. 1:14, 22 [d]Heb. 10:22; 12:24 [e]2 Pet. 1:2
3 [a]2 Cor. 1:3 [b]Gal. 6:16; Titus 3:5 [c]James 1:18; 1 Pet. 1:23 [d]1 Pet. 1:13, 21; 3:5, 15; 1 John 3:3 [e]1 Cor. 15:20; 1 Pet. 3:21
4 [a]Acts 20:32; Rom. 8:17; Col. 3:24 [b]1 Pet. 5:4 [c]2 Tim. 4:8
5 [a]John 10:28; Phil. 4:7 [b]Eph. 2:8 [c]1 Cor. 1:21; 2 Thess. 2:13 [d]1 Pet. 4:13; 5:1
6 [1]Or, *temptations* [a]Rom. 5:2 [b]1 Pet. 5:10 [c]1 Pet. 3:17 [d]James 1:2; 1 Pet. 4:12
7 [1]Or, *genuineness* [2]Lit., *perishes* [a]James 1:3 [b]1 Cor. 3:13 [c]Rom. 2:7 [d]Luke 17:30; 1 Pet. 1:13; 4:13
8 [1]Lit., *glorified* [a]John 20:29 [b]Eph. 3:19
9 [1]Some ancient mss. do not contain *your* [a]Rom. 6:22
10 [a]Matt. 13:17; Luke 10:24 [b]Matt. 26:24 [c]1 Pet. 1:13
11 [1]Lit., *inquiring* [2]Lit., *after these* [a]2 Pet. 1:21 [b]Matt. 26:24
12 [1]Or, *gain a clear glimpse* [a]1 Pet. 1:25; 4:6 [b]Acts 2:2-4 [c]1 Tim. 3:16
13 [1]Lit., *the loins of your mind* [2]Lit., *be sober* [3]Or, *which is announced* [a]Eph. 6:14 [b]1 Thess. 5:6, 8; 2 Tim. 4:5; 1 Pet. 4:7; 5:8 [c]1 Pet. 1:3 [d]1 Pet. 1:10 [e]1 Pet. 1:7
14 [1]Lit., *children of obedience* [2]Or, *conform yourselves* [a]1 Pet. 1:2 [b]Rom. 12:2; 1 Pet. 4:2f. [c]Eph. 4:18
15 [1]Lit., *according to* [2]Or, *become* [a]1 Thess. 4:7; 1 John 3:3 [b]2 Cor. 7:1 [c]James 3:13
16 [a]Lev. 11:44f.; 19:2; 20:7
17 [a]Ps. 89:26; Jer. 3:19; Matt. 6:9 [b]Acts 10:34 [c]Matt. 16:27 [d]2 Cor. 7:1; Heb. 12:28; 1 Pet. 3:15 [e]1 Pet. 2:11
18 [1]Or, *ransomed* [a]Is. 52:3; 1 Cor. 6:20; Titus 2:14; Heb. 9:12 [b]Eph. 4:17
19 [a]Acts 20:28; 1 Pet. 1:2 [b]John 1:29
20 [1]Lit., *at the end of the times* [a]Acts 2:23; Eph. 1:4; 1 Pet. 1:2; Rev. 13:8 [b]Matt. 25:34 [c]Heb. 9:26 [d]Heb. 2:14
21 [a]Rom. 4:24; 10:9 [b]John 17:5, 24; 1 Tim. 3:16; Heb. 2:9 [c]1 Pet. 1:3

22 Since you have [a]in obedience to the truth [b]purified your souls for a [1c]sincere love of the brethren, fervently love one another from [2]the heart,
23 for you have been [a]born again [b]not of seed which is perishable but imperishable, *that is,* through the living and abiding [c]word of God.
24 For,
"[a]ALL FLESH IS LIKE GRASS,
AND ALL ITS GLORY LIKE THE FLOWER OF GRASS.
THE GRASS WITHERS,
AND THE FLOWER FALLS OFF,
25 [a]BUT THE WORD OF THE LORD ABIDES FOREVER."
And this is [b]the word which was [1]preached to you.

As Newborn Babes

2 THEREFORE, [a]putting aside all [1]malice and all guile and [2]hypocrisy and [2]envy and all [2b]slander,
2 [a]like newborn babes, long for the [1b]pure [2]milk of the word, that by it you may [c]grow [3]in respect to salvation,
3 if you have [a]tasted [1b]the kindness of the Lord.

As Living Stones

4 And coming to Him as to a living stone, [a]rejected by men, but [1]choice and precious in the sight of God,
5 [a]you also, as living stones, [1]are being built up as a [b]spiritual house for a holy [c]priesthood, to [d]offer up spiritual sacrifices acceptable to God through Jesus Christ.
6 For *this* is contained in [1]Scripture:
"[a]BEHOLD I LAY IN ZION A CHOICE STONE, A [b]PRECIOUS CORNER *stone,*
AND HE WHO BELIEVES IN [2]HIM SHALL NOT BE [3]DISAPPOINTED."
7 [a]This precious value, then, is for you who believe. But for those who disbelieve,
"[b]THE STONE WHICH THE BUILDERS [c]REJECTED,
THIS BECAME THE VERY CORNER *stone,*"
8 and,
"[a]A STONE OF STUMBLING AND A ROCK OF OFFENSE";
[b]for they stumble because they are disobedient to the word, [c]and to this *doom* they were also appointed.
9 But you are [a]A CHOSEN RACE, A royal [b]PRIESTHOOD, A [c]HOLY NATION, [d]A PEOPLE FOR *God's* OWN POSSESSION, that you may proclaim the excellencies of Him who has called you [e]out of darkness into His marvelous light;
10 [a]for you once were NOT A PEOPLE, but now you are THE PEOPLE OF GOD; you had NOT RECEIVED MERCY, but now you have RECEIVED MERCY.
11 [a]Beloved, [b]I urge you as [c]aliens and strangers to abstain from [d]fleshly lusts, which wage [e]war against the soul.
12 [a]Keep your behavior excellent among the Gentiles, so that in the thing in which they [b]slander you as evildoers, they may [1]on account of your good deeds, as they observe *them,* [c]glorify God [d]in the day of [2]visitation.

Honor Authority

13 [a]Submit yourselves for the Lord's sake to every human institution, whether to a king as the one in authority,
14 or to governors as sent [1]by him [a]for the punishment of evildoers and the [b]praise of those who do right.
15 For [a]such is the will of God that by doing right you may [b]silence the ignorance of foolish men.
16 *Act* as [a]free men, and do not use your freedom as a covering for evil, but *use it* as [b]bondslaves of God.
17 [a]Honor all men; [b]love the brotherhood, [c]fear God, [d]honor the [1]king.
18 [a]Servants, be submissive to your masters with all respect, not only to those who are good and [b]gentle, but also to those who are [1]unreasonable.
19 For this *finds* [1]favor, if for the sake of [a]conscience toward God a man bears up under sorrows when suffering unjustly.
20 For what credit is there if, when you sin and are harshly treated, you endure it with patience? But if [a]when you do what is right and suffer *for it* you patiently endure it, this *finds* [1]favor with God.

Christ Is Our Example

21 For [a]you have been called for this purpose, [b]since Christ also suffered for you, leaving you [c]an example for you to follow in His steps,
22 WHO [a]COMMITTED NO SIN, NOR WAS ANY DECEIT FOUND IN HIS MOUTH;
23 [1]and while being [a]reviled, He [2]did not revile in return; while suffering, He uttered no threats, but kept entrusting *Himself* to Him who judges righteously;
24 and He Himself [1a]bore our sins in His body on the [2b]cross, that we [c]might die to [3]sin and live to righteousness; for [d]by His [4]wounds you were [e]healed.
25 For you were [a]continually straying like sheep, but now you have returned to the [b]Shepherd and [1]Guardian of your souls.

22 [1]Lit., *unhypocritical* [2]Some mss. read *a clean heart* [a]1 Pet. 1:2 [b]James 4:8 [c]John 13:34; Rom. 12:10; Heb. 13:1; 1 Pet. 2:17; 3:8
23 [a]John 3:3; 1 Pet. 1:3 [b]John 1:13 [c]Heb. 4:12
24 [a]Is. 40:6ff.; James 1:10f.
25 [1]Lit., *preached as good news to you* [a]Is. 40:8 [b]Heb. 6:5

1 [1]Or, *wickedness* [2]plural nouns [a]Eph. 4:22, 25, 31; James 1:21 [b]James 4:11
2 [1]Or, *unadulterated* [2]Or, *spiritual* (Gr., *logikos*) *milk* [3]Or, *up to salvation* [a]Matt. 18:3; 19:14; Mark 10:15; Luke 18:17; 1 Cor. 14:20 [b]1 Cor. 3:2 [c]Eph. 4:15f.
3 [1]Lit., *that the Lord is kind* [a]Heb. 6:5 [b]Ps. 34:8; Titus 3:4
4 [1]Lit., *chosen;* or, *elect* [a]1 Pet. 2:7
5 [1]Or, *allow yourselves to be built up* or *build yourselves up* [a]1 Cor. 3:9 [b]Gal. 6:10; 1 Tim. 3:15 [c]Is. 61:6; 66:21; 1 Pet. 2:9; Rev. 1:6 [d]Rom. 15:16; Heb. 13:15
6 [1]Or, *a scripture* [2]Or, *it* [3]Or, *put to shame* [a]Is. 28:16; Rom. 9:32, 33; 10:11; 1 Pet. 2:8 [b]Eph. 2:20
7 [a]2 Cor. 2:16; 1 Pet. 2:7, 8 [b]Ps. 118:22; Matt. 21:42; Luke 2:34 [c]1 Pet. 2:4
8 [a]Is. 8:14 [b]1 Cor. 1:23; Gal. 5:11 [c]Rom. 9:22
9 [a]Is. 43:20f.; Deut. 10:15 [b]Is. 61:6; 66:21; 1 Pet. 2:5; Rev. 1:6 [c]Ex. 19:6; Deut. 7:6 [d]Ex. 19:5; Deut. 4:20; 14:2; Titus 2:14 [e]Is. 9:2; 42:16; Acts 26:18; 2 Cor. 4:6
10 [a]Hos. 1:10; 2:23; Rom. 9:25; 10:19
11 [a]Heb. 6:9; 1 Pet. 4:12 [b]Rom. 12:1 [c]Lev. 25:23; Ps. 39:12; Eph. 2:19; Heb. 11:13; 1 Pet. 1:17 [d]Rom. 13:14; Gal. 5:16, 24 [e]James 4:1
12 [1]Or, *as a result of* [2]I.e., Christ's coming again in judgment [a]2 Cor. 8:21; Phil. 2:15; Titus 2:8; 1 Pet. 2:15; 3:16 [b]Acts 28:22 [c]Matt. 5:16; 9:8; John 13:31; 1 Pet. 4:11, 16 [d]Is. 10:3; Luke 19:44
13 [a]Rom. 13:1
14 [1]Lit., *through* [a]Rom. 13:4 [b]Rom. 13:3
15 [a]1 Pet. 3:17 [b]1 Pet. 2:12
16 [a]John 8:32; James 1:25 [b]Rom. 6:22; 1 Cor. 7:22
17 [1]Or, *emperor* [a]Rom. 12:10; 13:7 [b]1 Pet. 1:22 [c]Prov. 24:21 [d]Matt. 22:21; 1 Pet. 2:13
18 [1]Or, *perverse* [a]Eph. 6:5 [b]James 3:17
19 [1]Or, *grace* [a]Rom. 13:5; 1 Pet. 3:14, 16f.
20 [1]V. 19, note 1 [a]1 Pet. 3:17
21 [a]Acts 14:22; 1 Pet. 3:9 [b]1 Pet. 3:18; 4:1, 13 [c]Matt. 11:29; 16:24
22 [a]Is. 53:9; 2 Cor. 5:21
23 [1]Lit., *who* [2]Lit., *was not reviling* [a]Is. 53:7; Heb. 12:3; 1 Pet. 3:9
24 [1]Or, *carried . . . up to the cross* [2]Lit., *wood* [3]Lit., *sins* [4]Lit., *wound;* or, *welt* [a]Is. 53:4, 11; 1 Cor. 15:3; Heb. 9:28 [b]Acts 5:30 [c]Rom. 6:2, 13 [d]Is. 53:5 [e]Heb. 12:13; James 5:16
25 [1]Or, *Bishop, Overseer* [a]Is. 53:6 [b]John 10:11; 1 Pet. 5:4

Godly Living

3 [a]IN the same way, you wives, [b]be
submissive to your own husbands so
that even if any *of them* are disobedient
to the word, they may be [c]won without a
word by the behavior of their wives,
2 as they observe your chaste and
[1]respectful behavior.
3 [a]And let not your adornment be
merely external—braiding the hair, and
wearing gold jewelry, or putting on
dresses;
4 but *let it be* [a]the hidden person of
the heart, with the imperishable quality
of a gentle and quiet spirit, which is
precious in the sight of God.
5 For in this way in former times the
holy women also, [a]who hoped in God,
used to adorn themselves, being submissive to their own husbands.
6 Thus Sarah obeyed Abraham, [a]call-
ing him lord, and you have become her
children if you do what is right [1][b]with-
out being frightened by any fear.
7 [a]You husbands likewise, live with
your wives in an understanding way, as
with a weaker [b]vessel, since she is a
woman; and grant her honor as a fellow
heir of the grace of life, so that your
prayers may not be hindered.
8 [1]To sum up, [a]let all be harmonious,
sympathetic, [b]brotherly, [c]kindhearted,
and [d]humble in spirit;
9 [a]not returning evil for evil, or
[b]insult for insult, but [1]giving a [c]blessing
instead; for [d]you were called for the very
purpose that you might [e]inherit a blessing.
10 For,
"[a]LET HIM WHO MEANS TO LOVE
LIFE AND SEE GOOD DAYS
REFRAIN HIS TONGUE FROM EVIL
AND HIS LIPS FROM SPEAKING
GUILE.
11 "[a]AND LET HIM TURN AWAY FROM
EVIL AND DO GOOD;
LET HIM SEEK PEACE AND PURSUE
IT.
12 "[a]FOR THE EYES OF THE LORD ARE
UPON THE RIGHTEOUS,
AND HIS EARS ATTEND TO THEIR
PRAYER,
BUT THE FACE OF THE LORD IS
AGAINST THOSE WHO DO EVIL."
13 And [a]who is there to harm you if
you prove zealous for what is good?
14 But even if you should [a]suffer for
the sake of righteousness, [b]*you are*
blessed. [c]AND DO NOT FEAR THEIR [1]IN-
TIMIDATION, AND DO NOT BE TROUBLED,
15 but [1]sanctify [a]Christ as Lord in
your hearts, always *being* ready [b]to make
a defense to everyone who asks you to
give an account for the [c]hope that is in
you, yet [d]with gentleness and [2][e]rever-
ence;
16 [1]and keep a [a]good conscience so
that in the thing in which [b]you are
slandered, those who revile your good
behavior in Christ may be put to shame.
17 For [a]it is better, [b]if [1]God should
will it so, that you suffer for doing what
is right rather than for doing what is
wrong.
18 For [a]Christ also died for sins [b]once
for all, *the* just for *the* unjust, in order
that He might [c]bring us to God, having
been put to death [d]in the flesh, but made
alive [e]in the [1]spirit;
19 in [1]which also He went and [a]made
proclamation to the spirits *now* in
prison,
20 who once were disobedient, when
the [a]patience of God [b]kept waiting in
the days of Noah, during the construction of [c]the ark, in which a few, that is,
[d]eight [e]persons, were brought safely
through *the* water.
21 [a]And corresponding to that, baptism now saves you—[b]not the removal
of dirt from the flesh, but an appeal to
God for a [c]good conscience—through
[d]the resurrection of Jesus Christ,
22 [a]who is at the right hand of God,
[b]having gone into heaven, [c]after angels
and authorities and powers had been
subjected to Him.

Keep Fervent in Your Love

4 THEREFORE, since [a]Christ has
[1]suffered in the flesh, [b]arm yourselves also with the same purpose, because [c]he who has [1]suffered in the flesh
has ceased from sin,
2 [a]so as to live [b]the rest of the time in
the flesh no longer for the lusts of men,
but for the [c]will of God.
3 For [a]the time already past is sufficient *for you* to have carried out the
desire of the Gentiles, [b]having pursued a
course of sensuality, lusts, drunkenness,
carousals, drinking parties and [1]abomi-
nable idolatries.
4 And in *all* this, they are surprised
that you do not run with *them* into the
same excess of [a]dissipation, and they
[b]malign *you*;
5 but they shall give account to Him
who is ready to judge [a]the living and the
dead.
6 For [a]the gospel has for this purpose
been preached even to those who are
dead, that though they are judged in the
flesh as men, they may live in the spirit
according to *the will of* God.
7 [a]The end of all things [1]is at hand;
therefore, [b]be of sound judgment and
sober *spirit* for the purpose of [2]prayer.
8 Above all, [a]keep fervent in your
love for one another, because [b]love
covers a multitude of sins.
9 [a]Be hospitable to one another without [b]complaint.
10 [a]As each one has received a *special*
gift, employ it in serving one another, as
good [b]stewards of the manifold grace of
God.

1 [a]1 Pet. 3:7 [b]Eph. 5:22; Col. 3:18 [c]1 Cor. 9:19
2 [1]Lit., *with fear*
3 [a]Is. 3:18ff.; 1 Tim. 2:9
4 [a]Rom. 7:22
5 [a]1 Tim. 5:5; 1 Pet. 1:3
6 [1]Lit., *and are not* [a]Gen. 18:12 [b]1 Pet. 3:14
7 [a]Eph. 5:25; Col. 3:19 [b]1 Thess. 4:4
8 [1]Or, *Finally* [a]Rom. 12:16 [b]1 Pet. 1:22 [c]Eph. 4:32 [d]Eph. 4:2; Phil. 2:3; 1 Pet. 5:5
9 [1]Lit., *blessing instead* [a]Rom. 12:17; 1 Thess. 5:15 [b]1 Cor. 4:12; 1 Pet. 2:23 [c]Luke 6:28; Rom. 12:14; 1 Cor. 4:12 [d]1 Pet. 2:21 [e]Gal. 3:14; Heb. 6:14; 12:17
10 [a]Ps. 34:12, 13
11 [a]Ps. 34:14
12 [a]Ps. 34:15, 16
13 [a]Prov. 16:7
14 [1]Lit., *fear* [a]Matt. 5:10; 1 Pet. 2:19ff.; 4:15f. [b]James 5:11 [c]Is. 8:12f.; 1 Pet. 3:6
15 [1]I.e., set apart [2]Or, *fear* [a]1 Pet. 1:3 [b]Col. 4:6 [c]1 Pet. 1:3 [d]2 Tim. 2:25 [e]1 Pet. 1:17
16 [1]Lit., *having a good* [a]1 Tim. 1:5; Heb. 13:18; 1 Pet. 3:21 [b]1 Pet. 2:12, 15
17 [1]Lit., *the will of God* [a]1 Pet. 2:20; 4:15f. [b]Acts 18:21; 1 Pet. 1:6; 2:15; 4:19
18 [1]Or, *Spirit* [a]1 Pet. 2:21 [b]Heb. 9:26, 28; 10:10 [c]Rom. 5:2; Eph. 3:12 [d]Col. 1:22; 1 Pet. 4:1 [e]1 Pet. 4:6
19 [1]Or, *whom* [a]1 Pet. 4:6
20 [a]Rom. 2:4 [b]Gen. 6:3, 5, 13f. [c]Heb. 11:7 [d]Gen. 8:18; 2 Pet. 2:5 [e]Acts 2:41; 1 Pet. 1:9, 22; 2:25; 4:19
21 [a]Acts 16:33; Titus 3:5 [b]Heb. 9:14; 10:22 [c]1 Tim. 1:5; Heb. 13:18; 1 Pet. 3:16 [d]1 Pet. 1:3
22 [a]Mark 16:19 [b]Heb. 4:14; 6:20 [c]Rom. 8:38f.; Heb. 1:6

1 [1]I.e., suffered death [a]1 Pet. 2:21 [b]Eph. 6:13 [c]Rom. 6:7
2 [a]Rom. 6:2; Col. 3:3 [b]1 Pet. 1:14 [c]Mark 3:35
3 [1]Lit., *lawless* [a]1 Cor. 12:2 [b]Rom. 13:13; Eph. 2:2; 4:17ff.
4 [a]Eph. 5:18 [b]1 Pet. 3:16
5 [a]Acts 10:42; Rom. 14:9; 2 Tim. 4:1
6 [a]1 Pet. 1:12; 3:19
7 [1]Lit., *has come near* [2]Lit., *prayers* [a]Rom. 13:11; Heb. 9:26; James 5:8; 1 John 2:18 [b]1 Pet. 1:13
8 [a]1 Pet. 1:22 [b]Prov. 10:12; 1 Cor. 13:4ff.; James 5:20
9 [a]1 Tim. 3:2; Heb. 13:2 [b]Phil. 2:14
10 [a]Rom. 12:6f. [b]1 Cor. 4:1

11 [a]Whoever speaks, *let him speak,* as
it were, the [b]utterances of God; whoever
serves, *let him do so* as [1c]by the strength
which God supplies; so that [d]in all
things God may be glorified through
Jesus Christ, [e]to whom belongs the glory
and dominion forever and ever. Amen.

Share the Sufferings of Christ

12 [a]Beloved, do not be surprised at
the [b]fiery ordeal among you, which
comes upon you for your testing, as
though some strange thing were happening to you;
13 but to the degree that you [a]share
the sufferings of Christ, keep on rejoicing; so that also at the [b]revelation of His
glory, [c]you may rejoice with exultation.
14 If you are reviled [1a]for the name of
Christ, [b]you are blessed, [c]because the
Spirit of glory and of God rests upon
you.
15 By no means [a]let any of you suffer
as a murderer, or thief, or evildoer, or a
[1b]troublesome meddler;
16 but if *anyone suffers* as a [a]Christian,
let him not feel ashamed, but in that
name let him [b]glorify God.
17 For *it is* time for judgment [a]to
begin [1]with [b]the household of God; and
if *it* [c]*begins* with us first, what *will be* the
outcome for those [d]who do not obey the
[e]gospel of God?
18 [a]AND IF IT IS WITH DIFFICULTY
THAT THE RIGHTEOUS IS SAVED, [1]WHAT
WILL BECOME OF THE [b]GODLESS MAN
AND THE SINNER?
19 Therefore, let those also who suffer
according to [a]the will of God entrust
their souls to a faithful Creator in doing
what is right.

Serve God Willingly

5 [a]THEREFORE, I exhort the elders
among you, as *your* [b]fellow elder
and [c]witness of the sufferings of Christ,
and a [d]partaker also of the glory that is
to be revealed,
2 shepherd [a]the flock of God among
you, exercising oversight [b]not under
compulsion, but voluntarily, according
to *the will of* God; and [c]not for sordid
gain, but with eagerness;
3 nor yet as [a]lording it over [1]those

11 [1]Lit., *from* [a]1 Thess. 2:4; Titus 2:1, 15; Heb. 13:7 [b]Acts 7:38 [c]Eph. 1:19; 6:10 [d]1 Cor. 10:31; 1 Pet. 2:12 [e]Rom. 11:36; 1 Pet. 5:11; Rev. 1:6; 5:13
12 [a]1 Pet. 2:11 [b]1 Pet. 1:6f.
13 [a]Rom. 8:17; 2 Cor. 1:5; 4:10; Phil. 3:10 [b]1 Pet. 1:7; 5:1 [c]2 Tim. 2:12
14 [1]Lit., *in* [a]John 15:21; Heb. 11:26; 1 Pet. 4:16 [b]Matt. 5:11; Luke 6:22; Acts 5:41 [c]2 Cor. 4:10f., 16
15 [1]Lit., *one who oversees others' affairs* [a]1 Pet. 2:19f.; 3:17 [b]1 Thess. 4:11; 2 Thess. 3:11; 1 Tim. 5:13
16 [a]Acts 5:41; 28:22; James 2:7 [b]1 Pet. 4:11
17 [1]Lit., *from* [a]Jer. 25:29; Ezek. 9:6; Amos 3:2 [b]1 Tim. 3:15; Heb. 3:6; 1 Pet. 2:5 [c]Rom. 2:9 [d]2 Thess. 1:8 [e]Rom. 1:1
18 [1]Lit., *where will appear* [a]Prov. 11:31; Luke 23:31 [b]1 Tim. 1:9
19 [a]1 Pet. 3:17

1 [a]Acts 11:30 [b]2 John 1; 3 John 1 [c]Luke 24:48; Heb. 12:1 [d]1 Pet. 1:5, 7; 4:13; Rev. 1:9
2 [a]John 21:16; Acts 20:28 [b]Philem. 14 [c]1 Tim. 3:8
3 [1]Lit., *the allotments* [2]Or, *becoming* [a]Ezek. 34:4; Matt. 20:25f. [b]John 13:15; Phil. 3:17; 1 Thess. 1:7; 2 Thess. 3:9; 1 Tim. 4:12; Titus 2:7
4 [1]Lit., *wreath* [a]1 Pet. 2:25 [b]1 Pet. 1:4 [c]1 Cor. 9:25
5 [a]Luke 22:26; 1 Tim. 5:1 [b]Eph. 5:21 [c]1 Pet. 3:8 [d]Prov. 3:34; James 4:6

allotted to your charge, but [2]proving to
be [b]examples to the flock.
4 And when the Chief [a]Shepherd
appears, you will receive the [b]unfading
[1c]crown of glory.
5 [a]You younger men, likewise, [b]be
subject to your elders; and all of you,
clothe yourselves with [c]humility toward
one another, for [d]GOD IS OPPOSED TO
THE PROUD, BUT GIVES GRACE TO THE
HUMBLE.
6 [a]Humble yourselves, therefore, under the mighty hand of God, that He
may exalt you at the proper time,
7 casting all your [a]anxiety upon Him,
because He cares for you.
8 [a]Be of sober *spirit,* [b]be on the alert.
Your adversary, [c]the devil, prowls about
like a roaring [d]lion, seeking someone to
devour.
9 [1a]But resist him, [b]firm in *your* faith,
knowing that [c]the same experiences of
suffering are being accomplished by
your [2]brethren who are in the world.
10 And after you have suffered [a]for a
little while, the [b]God of all grace, who
[c]called you to His [d]eternal glory in
Christ, will Himself [e]perfect, [f]confirm,
strengthen *and* establish you.
11 [a]To Him *be* dominion forever and
ever. Amen.
12 Through [a]Silvanus, our faithful
brother [1](for so I regard *him*), [b]I have
written to you briefly, exhorting and
testifying that this is [c]the true grace of
God. [d]Stand firm in it!
13 [1]She who is in Babylon, chosen
together with you, sends you greetings,
and *so does* my son, [a]Mark.
14 [a]Greet one another with a kiss of
love.
[b]Peace be to you all who are in Christ.

6 [a]Matt. 23:12; Luke 14:11; 18:14; James 4:10
7 [a]Ps. 55:22; Matt. 6:25
8 [a]1 Pet. 1:13 [b]Matt. 24:42 [c]James 4:7 [d]2 Tim. 4:17
9 [1]Lit., *whom resist* [2]Lit., *brotherhood* [a]James 4:7 [b]Col. 2:5 [c]Acts 14:22
10 [a]1 Pet. 1:6 [b]1 Pet. 4:10 [c]1 Cor. 1:9; 1 Thess. 2:12 [d]2 Cor. 4:17; 2 Tim. 2:10 [e]1 Cor. 1:10; Heb. 13:21 [f]Rom. 16:25; 2 Thess. 2:17; 3:3
11 [a]Rom. 11:36; 1 Pet. 4:11
12 [1]Lit., *(as I consider)* [a]2 Cor. 1:19 [b]Heb. 13:22 [c]Acts 11:23; 1 Pet. 1:13; 4:10 [d]1 Cor. 15:1
13 [1]Some mss. read *The church which* [a]Acts 12:12, 25; 15:37, 39; Col. 4:10; Philem. 24
14 [a]Rom. 16:16 [b]Eph. 6:23

THE SECOND EPISTLE OF
PETER

Growth in Christian Virtue

1 [1]SIMON PETER, a [a]bond-servant and [b]apostle of Jesus Christ, to those who have received [c]a faith of the same [2]kind as ours, [3]by [d]the righteousness of [e]our God and Savior, Jesus Christ:

2 [a]Grace and peace be multiplied to you in [b]the knowledge of God and of Jesus our Lord;

3 seeing that His [a]divine power has granted to us everything pertaining to life and godliness, through the true [b]knowledge of Him who [c]called us [1]by His own glory and [2]excellence.

4 [1]For by these He has granted to us His precious and magnificent [a]promises, in order that by them you might become [b]partakers of *the* divine nature, having [c]escaped the [d]corruption that is in [e]the world by lust.

5 Now for this very reason also, applying all diligence, in your faith [a]supply [b]moral [1]excellence, and in *your* moral excellence, [c]knowledge;

6 and in *your* knowledge, [a]self-control, and in *your* self-control, [b]perseverance, and in *your* perseverance, [c]godliness;

7 and in *your* godliness, [a]brotherly kindness, and in *your* brotherly kindness, love.

8 For if these *qualities* are yours and are increasing, they render you neither useless nor [a]unfruitful in the true [b]knowledge of our Lord Jesus Christ.

9 For he who lacks these *qualities* is [a]blind *or* short-sighted, having forgotten *his* [b]purification from his former sins.

10 Therefore, brethren, be all the more diligent to make certain about His [a]calling and [b]choosing you; for as long as you practice these things, you will never [c]stumble;

11 for in this way the entrance into [a]the eternal kingdom of our [b]Lord and Savior Jesus Christ will be [c]abundantly [d]supplied to you.

12 Therefore, [a]I shall always be ready to remind you of these things, even though you *already* know *them*, and have been established in [b]the truth which is present with *you.*

13 And I consider it [a]right, as long as I am in [b]this *earthly* dwelling, to [c]stir you up by way of reminder,

14 knowing that [a]the laying aside of my *earthly* dwelling is imminent, [b]as also our Lord Jesus Christ has made clear to me.

15 And I will also be diligent that at any time after my [a]departure you may be able to call these things to mind.

Eyewitnesses

16 For we did not follow cleverly devised [a]tales when we made known to you the [b]power and coming of our Lord Jesus Christ, but we were [c]eyewitnesses of His majesty.

17 For when He received honor and glory from God the Father, such an [1]utterance as this was [2]made to Him by the [b]Majestic Glory, "This is My beloved Son with whom I am well-pleased"—

18 and we ourselves heard this [1]utterance made from heaven when we were with Him on the [a]holy mountain.

19 [1]And *so* we have [a]the prophetic word *made* more [b]sure, to which you do well to pay attention as to [c]a lamp shining in a dark place, until the [d]day dawns and the [e]morning star arises [f]in your hearts.

20 But [a]know this first of all, that [b]no prophecy of Scripture is *a matter* of one's own interpretation,

21 for [a]no prophecy was ever made by an act of human will, but men [b]moved by the Holy Spirit spoke from God.

The Rise of False Prophets

2 BUT [a]false prophets also arose among the people, just as there will also be [b]false teachers [c]among you, who will [d]secretly introduce [e]destructive heresies, even [f]denying the [g]Master who [h]bought them, bringing swift destruction upon themselves.

2 And many will follow their [a]sensuality, and because of them [b]the way of the truth will be [c]maligned;

3 and in *their* [a]greed they will [b]exploit you with [c]false words; [d]their judgment from long ago is not idle, and their destruction is not asleep.

4 For [a]if God did not spare angels when they sinned, but cast them into hell and [b]committed them to pits of darkness, reserved for judgment;

5 and did not spare [a]the ancient world, but preserved [b]Noah, a [1]preacher of righteousness, with seven others, when He brought a [c]flood upon the world of the ungodly;

6 and *if* He [a]condemned the cities of Sodom and Gomorrah to destruction by reducing *them* to ashes, having made them an [b]example to those who would [c]live ungodly thereafter;

7 and *if* He [a]rescued righteous Lot, oppressed by the [b]sensual conduct of [c]unprincipled men

8 (for by what he saw and heard *that* [a]righteous man, while living among

1 [1]Most early mss. read *Simeon* [2]Or, *value* [3]Or, *in* [a]Rom. 1:1; Phil. 1:1; James 1:1; Jude 1 [b]1 Pet. 1:1 [c]Rom. 1:12; 2 Cor. 4:13; Titus 1:4 [d]Rom. 3:21-26 [e]Titus 2:13

2 [a]Rom. 1:7; 1 Pet. 1:2 [b]John 17:3; Phil. 3:8; 2 Pet. 1:3, 8; 2:20; 3:18

3 [1]Or possibly, *to* [2]Or, *virtue* [a]1 Pet. 1:5 [b]John 17:3; Phil. 3:8; 2 Pet. 1:2, 8; 2:20; 3:18 [c]1 Thess. 2:12; 2 Thess. 2:14; 1 Pet. 5:10

4 [1]Lit., *Through which* (things) [a]2 Pet. 3:9, 13 [b]Eph. 4:13, 24; Heb. 12:10; 1 John 3:2 [c]2 Pet. 2:18, 20 [d]2 Pet. 2:19 [e]James 1:27

5 [1]Or, *virtue* [a]2 Pet. 1:11 [b]2 Pet. 1:3 [c]Col. 2:3; 2 Pet. 1:2

6 [a]Acts 24:25 [b]Luke 21:19 [c]2 Pet. 1:3

7 [a]Rom. 12:10; 1 Pet. 1:22

8 [a]Col. 1:10 [b]John 17:3; Phil. 3:8; 2 Pet. 1:2, 3; 2:20; 3:18

9 [a]1 John 2:11 [b]Eph. 5:26; Titus 2:14

10 [a]Matt. 22:14; Rom. 11:29; 2 Pet. 1:3 [b]1 Thess. 1:4 [c]James 2:10; 2 Pet. 3:17; Jude 24

11 [a]2 Tim. 4:18 [b]2 Pet. 2:20; 3:18 [c]Rom. 2:4; 1 Tim. 6:17 [d]2 Pet. 1:5

12 [a]Phil. 3:1; 1 John 2:21; Jude 5 [b]Col. 1:5f.; 2 John 2

13 [a]Phil. 1:7 [b]2 Cor. 5:1, 4; 2 Pet. 1:14 [c]2 Pet. 3:1

14 [a]2 Cor. 5:1; 2 Tim. 4:6 [b]John 13:36; 21:19

15 [a]Luke 9:31

16 [a]1 Tim. 1:4; 2 Pet. 2:3 [b]Mark 13:26; 14:62; 1 Thess. 2:19 [c]Matt. 17:1ff.; Mark 9:2ff.; Luke 9:28ff.

17 [1]Lit., *voice* [2]Lit., *borne* [a]Matt. 17:5; Mark 9:7; Luke 9:35 [b]Heb. 1:3

18 [1]Lit., *voice borne* [a]Ex. 3:5; Josh. 5:15

19 [1]Or, *And we have the even surer prophetic word* [a]1 Pet. 1:10f. [b]Heb. 2:2 [c]Ps. 119:105 [d]Luke 1:78 [e]Rev. 22:16 [f]2 Cor. 4:6

20 [a]2 Pet. 3:3 [b]Rom. 12:6

21 [a]Jer. 23:26; 2 Tim. 3:16 [b]2 Sam. 23:2; Luke 1:70; Acts 1:16; 3:18; 1 Pet. 1:11

1 [a]Deut. 13:1ff.; Jer. 6:13 [b]2 Cor. 11:13 [c]Matt. 7:15; 1 Tim. 4:1 [d]Gal. 2:4; Jude 4 [e]1 Cor. 11:19; Gal. 5:20 [f]Jude 4 [g]Rev. 6:10 [h]1 Cor. 6:20

2 [a]Gen. 19:5ff.; 2 Pet. 2:7, 18; Jude 4 [b]Acts 16:17; 22:4; 24:14 [c]Rom. 2:24

3 [a]1 Tim. 6:5; 2 Pet. 2:14; Jude 16 [b]2 Cor. 2:17; 1 Thess. 2:5 [c]Rom. 16:18; 2 Pet. 1:16 [d]Deut. 32:35

4 [a]Jude 6 [b]Rev. 20:1f.

5 [1]Or, *herald* [a]Ezek. 26:20; 2 Pet. 3:6 [b]Gen. 6:8, 9; 1 Pet. 3:20 [c]2 Pet. 3:6

6 [a]Gen. 19:24; Jude 7 [b]Is. 1:9; Matt. 10:15; 11:23; Rom. 9:29; Jude 7 [c]Jude 15

7 [a]Gen. 19:16, 29 [b]Gen. 19:5ff.; 2 Pet. 2:2, 18; Jude 4 [c]2 Pet. 3:17

8 [a]Heb. 11:4

them, felt *his* righteous soul tormented
day after day with *their* lawless deeds),
9 [a]*then* the Lord knows how to rescue
the godly from [1]temptation, and to keep
the unrighteous under punishment
for the [b]day of judgment,
10 and especially those who [1][a]indulge
the flesh in *its* corrupt desires and [b]de-
spise authority. Daring, [c]self-willed, they
do not tremble when they [b]revile angelic
[2]majesties,
11 [a]whereas angels who are greater in
might and power do not bring a reviling
judgment against them before the Lord.
12 But [a]these, like unreasoning animals, [b]born as creatures of instinct to be
captured and killed, reviling where they
have no knowledge, will in [1]the destruction of those creatures also be destroyed,
13 suffering wrong as [a]the wages of
doing wrong. They count it a pleasure to
[b]revel in the [c]daytime. They are stains
and blemishes, [b]reveling in their [1]decep-
tions, as they [d]carouse with you,
14 having eyes full of adultery and
that never cease from sin, [a]enticing
[b]unstable souls, having a heart trained in
[c]greed, [d]accursed children;
15 forsaking [a]the right way they have
gone astray, having followed [b]the way of
Balaam, the *son* of Beor, who loved [c]the
wages of unrighteousness,
16 but he received a rebuke for his
own transgression; [a]*for* a dumb donkey,
speaking with a voice of a man, restrained the madness of the prophet.
17 These are [a]springs without water,
and mists driven by a storm, [b]for whom
the [1]black darkness has been reserved.
18 For speaking out [a]arrogant *words*
of [b]vanity they [c]entice by fleshly desires,
by [d]sensuality, those who barely [e]escape
from the ones who live in error,
19 promising them freedom while they
themselves are slaves of corruption; for
[a]by what a man is overcome, by this he
is enslaved.
20 For if after they have [a]escaped the
defilements of the world by [b]the knowledge of the [c]Lord and Savior Jesus
Christ, they are again [d]entangled in
them and are overcome, [e]the last state
has become worse for them than the
first.
21 [a]For it would be better for them
not to have known the way of righteousness, than having known it, to turn away
from [b]the holy commandment [c]delivered
to them.
22 It has happened to them according
to the true proverb, "[a]A DOG RETURNS
TO ITS OWN VOMIT," and, "A sow, after
washing, *returns* to wallowing in the
mire."

Purpose of This Letter

3 THIS is now, [a]beloved, the second
letter I am writing to you in which I
am [b]stirring up your sincere mind by
way of reminder,
2 that you should [a]remember the
words spoken beforehand by [b]the holy
prophets and [c]the commandment of the
Lord and Savior *spoken* by your apostles.

The Coming Day of the Lord

3 [a]Know this first of all, that [b]in the
last days [c]mockers will come with *their*
mocking, [d]following after their own
lusts,
4 and saying, "[a]Where is the promise
of His [b]coming? For *ever* since the
fathers [c]fell asleep, all continues just as
it was [d]from the beginning of creation."
5 For [1]when they maintain this, it
escapes their notice that [a]by the word of
God *the* heavens existed long ago and
the earth was [b]formed out of water and
by water,
6 through which [a]the world at that
time was [b]destroyed, being flooded with
water.
7 But [a]the present heavens and earth
by His word are being reserved for [b]fire,
kept for [c]the day of judgment and destruction of ungodly men.
8 But do not let this one *fact* escape
your notice, [a]beloved, that with the Lord
one day is as a thousand years, and [b]a
thousand years as one day.
9 [a]The Lord is not slow about His
promise, as some count slowness, but [b]is
patient toward you, [c]not wishing for any
to perish but for all to come to repentance.

A New Heaven and Earth

10 But [a]the day of the Lord [b]will come
like a thief, in which [c]the heavens [d]will
pass away with a roar and the [e]elements
will be destroyed with intense heat, and
[f]the earth and [1]its works will be [2]burned
up.
11 Since all these things are to be
destroyed in this way, what sort of
people ought you to be in holy conduct
and godliness,
12 [a]looking for and hastening the
coming of the day of God, on account of
which [b]the heavens will be destroyed by
burning, and the [c]elements will melt
with intense heat!
13 But according to His [a]promise we
are looking for [b]new heavens and a new
earth, [c]in which righteousness dwells.
14 [a]Therefore, [b]beloved, since you
look for these things, be diligent to be
[c]found by Him in peace, [d]spotless and
blameless,

9 [1]Or, *trial* [a]1 Cor. 10:13; Rev. 3:10 [b]Matt. 10:15; Jude 6
10 [1]Lit., *go after* [2]Lit., *glories* [a]2 Pet. 3:3; Jude 16, 18 [b]Ex. 22:28; Jude 8 [c]Titus 1:7
11 [a]Jude 9
12 [1]Lit., *their destruction also* [a]Jude 10 [b]Jer. 12:3; Col. 2:22
13 [1]Some ancient mss. read *love feasts* [a]2 Pet. 2:15 [b]Rom. 13:13 [c]1 Thess. 5:7 [d]1 Cor. 11:21; Jude 12
14 [a]2 Pet. 2:18 [b]James 1:8; 2 Pet. 3:16 [c]2 Pet. 2:3 [d]Eph. 2:3
15 [a]Acts 13:10 [b]Num. 22:5, 7; Deut. 23:4; Neh. 13:2; Jude 11; Rev. 2:14 [c]2 Pet. 2:13
16 [a]Num. 22:21, 23, 28, 30ff.
17 [1]Lit., *blackness of darkness* [a]Jude 12 [b]Jude 13
18 [a]Jude 16 [b]Eph. 4:17 [c]2 Pet. 2:14 [d]2 Pet. 2:2 [e]2 Pet. 1:4; 2:20
19 [a]John 8:34; Rom. 6:16
20 [a]2 Pet. 2:18 [b]2 Pet. 1:2 [c]2 Pet. 1:11; 3:18 [d]2 Tim. 2:4 [e]Matt. 12:45; Luke 11:26
21 [a]Ezek. 18:24; Heb. 6:4ff.; 10:26f.; James 4:17 [b]Gal. 6:2; 1 Tim. 6:14; 2 Pet. 3:2 [c]Jude 3
22 [a]Prov. 26:11

1 [a]1 Pet. 2:11; 2 Pet. 3:8, 14, 17 [b]2 Pet. 1:13
2 [a]Jude 17 [b]Luke 1:70; Acts 3:21; Eph. 3:5 [c]Gal. 6:2; 1 Tim. 6:14; 2 Pet. 2:21
3 [a]2 Pet. 1:20 [b]1 Tim. 4:1; Heb. 1:2 [c]Jude 18 [d]2 Pet. 2:10
4 [a]Is. 5:19; Jer. 17:15; Ezek. 11:3; 12:22, 27; Mal. 2:17; Matt. 24:48 [b]1 Thess. 2:19; 2 Pet. 3:12 [c]Acts 7:60 [d]Mark 10:6
5 [1]Or, *they are willfully ignorant of this fact, that* [a]Gen. 1:6, 9; Heb. 11:3 [b]Ps. 24:2; 136:6
6 [a]2 Pet. 2:5 [b]Gen. 7:11, 12, 21f.
7 [a]2 Pet. 3:10, 12 [b]Is. 66:15; Dan. 7:9f.; 2 Thess. 1:7; Heb. 12:29 [c]Matt. 10:15; 1 Cor. 3:13; Jude 7
8 [a]2 Pet. 3:1 [b]Ps. 90:4
9 [a]Hab. 2:3; Rom. 13:11; Heb. 10:37 [b]Rom. 2:4; Rev. 2:21 [c]1 Tim. 2:4; Rev. 2:21

10 [1]Lit., *the works in it* [2]Some ancient mss. read *discovered* [a]1 Cor. 1:8 [b]Matt. 24:43; Luke 12:39; 1 Thess. 5:2; Rev. 3:3; 16:15 [c]Is. 34:4; 2 Pet. 3:7, 12 [d]Matt. 24:35; Rev. 21:1 [e]Is. 24:19; Mic. 1:4 [f]2 Pet. 3:7
12 [a]1 Cor. 1:7 [b]2 Pet. 3:7, 10 [c]Is. 24:19; 34:4; Mic. 1:4
13 [a]Is. 65:17; 66:22 [b]Rom. 8:21; Rev. 21:1 [c]Is. 60:21; 65:25; Rev. 21:27
14 [a]1 Cor. 15:58; 2 Pet. 1:10 [b]2 Pet. 3:1 [c]1 Pet. 1:7 [d]Phil. 2:15; 1 Thess. 5:23; 1 Tim. 6:14; James 1:27

15 and regard the [a]patience of our
Lord *to be* salvation; just as also [b]our
beloved brother Paul, [c]according to the
wisdom given him, wrote to you,
16 as also in all *his* letters, speaking in
them of [a]these things, [b]in which are
some things hard to understand, which
the untaught and [c]unstable distort, as
they do also [d]the rest of the Scriptures, to
their own destruction.

15 [a]2 Pet. 3:9 [b]Acts 9:17; 15:25; 2 Pet. 3:2 [c]1 Cor. 3:10; Eph. 3:3
16 [a]2 Pet. 3:14 [b]Heb. 5:11 [c]2 Pet. 2:14 [d]2 Pet. 3:2
17 [a]2 Pet. 3:1 [b]1 Cor. 10:12 [c]2 Pet. 2:18 [d]2 Pet. 2:7 [e]Rev. 2:5

17 You therefore, [a]beloved, knowing
this beforehand, [b]be on your guard lest,
being carried away by [c]the error of
[d]unprincipled men, you [e]fall from your
own steadfastness,
18 but grow in the grace and [a]knowl-
edge of our [b]Lord and Savior Jesus
Christ. [c]To Him *be* the glory, both now
and to the day of eternity. Amen.

18 [a]2 Pet. 1:2 [b]2 Pet. 1:11; 2:20 [c]Rom. 11:36; 2 Tim. 4:18; Rev. 1:6

THE FIRST EPISTLE OF JOHN

Introduction
The Incarnate Word

1 WHAT was [a]from the beginning,
what we have [b]heard, what we have
[c]seen with our eyes, what we [d]beheld
and our hands [e]handled, concerning the
[f]Word of Life—
2 and [a]the life was manifested, and
we have [b]seen and [c]bear witness and
proclaim to you [d]the eternal life, which
was [e]with the Father and was [a]mani-
fested to us—
3 what we have [a]seen and [b]heard we
proclaim to you also, that you also may
have fellowship with us; and indeed our
[c]fellowship is with the Father, and with
His Son Jesus Christ.
4 And [a]these things we write, so that
our [b]joy may be made complete.

God Is Light

5 And [a]this is the message we have
heard from Him and announce to you,
that [b]God is light, and in Him there is
no darkness at all.
6 [a]If we say that we have fellowship
with Him and *yet* walk in the darkness,
we [b]lie and [c]do not practice the truth;
7 but if we [a]walk in the light as [b]He
Himself is in the light, we have fellowship with one another, and [c]the blood of
Jesus His Son cleanses us from all sin.
8 [a]If we say that we have no sin, we
are deceiving ourselves, and the [b]truth is
not in us.
9 [a]If we confess our sins, He is faithful and righteous to forgive us our sins
and [b]to cleanse us from all unrighteousness.
10 [a]If we say that we have not sinned,
we [b]make Him a liar, and [c]His word is
not in us.

Christ Is Our Advocate

2 [a]MY little children, I am [b]writing
these things to you that you may not
sin. And if anyone sins, [c]we have an
[1d]Advocate with the Father, Jesus Christ
the righteous;
2 and He Himself is [a]the [1]propitia-
tion for our sins; and not for ours only,
but also [b]for *those of* the whole world.
3 And [a]by this we know that we have
come to [b]know Him, if we [c]keep His
commandments.
4 The one who says, "[a]I have come to
[b]know Him," and does not keep His
commandments, is a [c]liar, and [d]the truth
is not in him;
5 but whoever [a]keeps His word, in
him the [b]love of God has truly been
perfected. [c]By this we know that we are
in Him:
6 the one who says he [a]abides in Him
[b]ought himself to walk in the same
manner as He walked.
7 [a]Beloved, I am [b]not writing a new
commandment to you, but an old commandment which you [1]have had [c]from
the beginning; the old commandment is
the word which you have heard.
8 [1]On the other hand, I am writing [a]a
new commandment to you, which is true
in Him and in you, because [b]the darkness is passing away, and [c]the true light
is already shining.
9 The one who says he is in the light
and *yet* [a]hates his [b]brother is in the
darkness until now.
10 [a]The one who loves his brother
abides in the light and there is no cause
for stumbling in him.
11 But the one who [a]hates his brother
is in the darkness and [b]walks in the
darkness, and does not know where he is
going because the darkness has [c]blinded
his eyes.
12 I am writing to you, [a]little children,
because [b]your sins are forgiven you for
His name's sake.

1 [a]John 1:1f.; 1 John 2:13, 14 [b]Acts 4:20; 1 John 1:3 [c]John 19:35; 2 Pet. 1:16; 1 John 1:2 [d]John 1:14; 1 John 4:14 [e]Luke 24:39; John 20:27 [f]John 1:1, 4
2 [a]John 1:4; 1 John 3:5, 8; 5:20 [b]John 19:35; 1 John 1:1 [c]John 15:27; 1 John 4:14 [d]John 10:28; 17:3; 1 John 2:25; 5:11, 13, 20 [e]John 1:1
3 [a]John 19:35; 2 Pet. 1:16; 1 John 1:1 [b]Acts 4:20; 1 John 1:1 [c]John 17:3, 21; 1 Cor. 1:9
4 [a]1 John 2:1 [b]John 3:29
5 [a]John 1:19; 1 John 3:11 [b]1 Tim. 6:16; James 1:17
6 [a]John 8:12; 1 John 2:11 [b]John 8:55; 1 John 2:4; 4:20 [c]John 3:21
7 [a]Is. 2:5 [b]1 Tim. 6:16 [c]Titus 2:14
8 [a]Job 15:14; Prov. 20:9; Rom. 3:10ff.; James 3:2 [b]John 8:44; 1 John 2:4
9 [a]Ps. 32:5; Prov. 28:13 [b]Titus 2:14
10 [a]Job 15:14 [b]John 3:33; 1 John 5:10 [c]1 John 2:14

1 [1]Gr., *Paracletos,* one called alongside to help [a]John 13:33; Gal. 4:19; 1 John 2:12, 28; 3:7, 18; 4:4; 5:21 [b]1 John 1:4 [c]Rom. 8:34; 1 Tim. 2:5; Heb. 7:25; 9:24 [d]John 14:16
2 [1]Or, *satisfaction* [a]Rom. 3:25; Heb. 2:17; 1 John 4:10 [b]John 4:42; 11:51f.; 1 John 4:14
3 [a]1 John 2:5; 3:24; 4:13; 5:2 [b]1 John 2:4; 3:6; 4:7f. [c]John 14:15; 15:10; 1 John 3:22, 24; 5:3; Rev. 12:17; 14:12
4 [a]Titus 1:10 [b]1 John 3:6; 4:7f. [c]1 John 1:6 [d]1 John 1:8

5 [a]John 14:23 [b]1 John 4:12 [c]1 John 2:3; 3:24; 4:13; 5:2
6 [a]John 15:4 [b]John 13:15; 15:10; 1 Pet. 2:21
7 [1]Lit., *were having* [a]Heb. 6:9; 1 John 3:2, 21; 4:1, 7, 11 [b]John 13:34; 1 John 3:11, 23; 4:21; 2 John 5 [c]1 John 2:24; 3:11; 2 John 5, 6
8 [1]Lit., *Again* [a]John 13:34 [b]Rom. 13:12; Eph. 5:8; 1 Thess. 5:4f. [c]John 1:9
9 [a]1 John 2:11; 3:15; 4:20 [b]Acts 1:15; 1 John 3:10, 16; 4:20f.
10 [a]John 11:9; 1 John 2:10, 11
11 [a]1 John 2:9; 3:15; 4:20 [b]John 12:35; 1 John 1:6 [c]2 Cor. 4:4; 2 Pet. 1:9
12 [a]1 John 2:1 [b]Acts 13:38; 1 Cor. 6:11

13 I am writing to you, fathers, because you know Him [a]who has been
from the beginning. I am writing to you,
young men, because [b]you have overcome
[c]the evil one. I have written to you,
children, because [d]you know the Father.
14 I have written to you, fathers,
because you know Him [a]who has been
from the beginning. I have written to
you, young men, because you are
[b]strong, and the [c]word of God abides in
you, and [d]you have overcome the evil
one.

Do Not Love the World

15 Do not love [a]the world, nor the
things in the world. [b]If anyone loves the
world, the love of the Father is not in
him.
16 For all that is in the world, [a]the lust
of the flesh and [b]the lust of the eyes and
[c]the boastful pride of life, is not from the
Father, but is from the world.
17 And [a]the world is passing away,
and *also* its lusts; but the one who [b]does
the will of God abides forever.
18 Children, [a]it is the last hour; and
just as you heard that [b]antichrist is
coming, [c]even now many antichrists
have arisen; from this we know that it is
the last hour.
19 [a]They went out from us, but they
were not *really* of us; for if they had
been of us, they would have remained
with us; but *they went out,* [b]in order that
[1]it might be shown that they all are not
of us.
20 [1]But you have an [a]anointing from
[b]the Holy One, and [2c]you all know.
21 I have not written to you because
you do not know the truth, but [a]because
you do know it, and [1]because no lie is
[b]of the truth.
22 Who is the liar but [a]the one who
denies that Jesus is the [1]Christ? This is
[b]the antichrist, the one who denies the
Father and the Son.
23 [a]Whoever denies the Son does not
have the Father; the one who confesses
the Son has the Father also.
24 As for you, let that abide in you
which you heard [a]from the beginning. If
what you heard from the beginning
abides in you, you also [b]will abide in the
Son and in the Father.

The Promise Is Eternal Life

25 And [a]this is the promise which He
Himself [1]made to us: eternal life.
26 These things I have written to you
concerning those who are trying to
[a]deceive you.
27 And as for you, the [a]anointing
which you received from Him abides in
you, and you have no need for anyone to
teach you; but as His anointing [b]teaches
you about all things, and is [c]true and is
not a lie, and just as it has taught you,
[1]you abide in Him.
28 And now, [a]little children, abide in
Him, so that when He [b]appears, we may
have [c]confidence and [d]not [1]shrink away
from Him in shame [2]at His [e]coming.
29 If you know that [a]He is righteous,
you know that everyone also who practices righteousness [b]is [1]born of Him.

Children of God Love One Another

3 SEE [1a]how great a love the Father
has bestowed upon us, that we
should be called [b]children of God; and
such we are. For this reason the world
does not know us, because [c]it did not
know Him.
2 [a]Beloved, now we are [b]children of
God, and [c]it has not appeared as yet
what we shall be. We know that, when
He [d]appears, we shall be [e]like Him,
because we shall [f]see Him just as He is.
3 And everyone who has this [a]hope
fixed on Him [b]purifies himself, just as
He is pure.
4 Everyone who practices sin also
practices lawlessness; and [a]sin is lawlessness.
5 And you know that He [a]appeared
in order to [b]take away sins; and [c]in Him
there is no sin.
6 No one who abides in Him [a]sins;
no one who sins has seen Him or
[1b]knows Him.
7 [a]Little children, let no one [b]deceive
you; [c]the one who practices righteousness is righteous, just as He is righteous;
8 the one who practices sin is [a]of the
devil; for the devil [1]has sinned from the
beginning. [b]The Son of God [c]appeared
for this purpose, [d]that He might destroy
the works of the devil.
9 No one who is [1a]born of God
[b]practices sin, because His seed abides
in him; and he cannot sin, because he is
[1]born of God.
10 By this the [a]children of God and
the [b]children of the devil are obvious:
anyone who does not practice righteousness is not of God, nor the one who
[c]does not love his [d]brother.
11 [a]For this is the message [b]which you
have heard from the beginning, [c]that we
should love one another;
12 not as [a]Cain, *who* was of [b]the evil
one, and slew his brother. And for what
reason did he slay him? Because [c]his
deeds were evil, and his brother's were
righteous.
13 Do not marvel, brethren, if [a]the
world hates you.

13 [a]1 John 1:1 [b]John 16:33; 1 John 2:14; 4:4; 5:4f.; Rev. 2:7 [c]Matt. 5:37; 1 John 2:14; 3:12; 5:18f. [d]John 14:7; 1 John 2:3
14 [a]1 John 1:1 [b]Eph. 6:10 [c]John 5:38; 8:37; 1 John 1:10 [d]1 John 2:13
15 [a]Rom. 12:2; James 1:27 [b]James 4:4
16 [a]Rom. 13:14; Eph. 2:3; 1 Pet. 2:11 [b]Prov. 27:20 [c]James 4:16
17 [a]1 Cor. 7:31 [b]Mark 3:35
18 [a]Rom. 13:11; 1 Tim. 4:1; 1 Pet. 4:7 [b]Matt. 24:5, 24; 1 John 2:22; 4:3; 2 John 7 [c]Mark 13:22; 1 John 4:1, 3
19 [1]Lit., *they might be made manifest* [a]Acts 20:30 [b]1 Cor. 11:19
20 [1]Lit., *And* [2]Some ancient mss. read *you know all things* [a]2 Cor. 1:21; 1 John 2:27 [b]Mark 1:24; Acts 10:38 [c]Prov. 28:5; Matt. 13:11; John 14:26; 1 Cor. 2:15f.; 1 John 2:27
21 [1]Or, *know that* [a]James 1:19; 2 Pet. 1:12; Jude 5 [b]John 8:44; 18:37; 1 John 3:19
22 [1]I.e., Messiah [a]1 John 4:3; 2 John 7 [b]Matt. 24:5, 24; 1 John 2:18; 4:3; 2 John 7
23 [a]John 8:19; 16:3; 17:3; 1 John 4:15; 5:1; 2 John 9
24 [a]1 John 2:7 [b]John 14:23; 1 John 1:3; 2 John 9
25 [1]Lit., *promised us* [a]John 3:15; 6:40; 1 John 1:2
26 [a]1 John 3:7; 2 John 7
27 [1]Or, *abide in Him* [a]John 14:16; 1 John 2:20 [b]John 14:26; 1 Cor. 2:12; 1 Thess. 4:9 [c]John 14:17
28 [1]Lit., *be put to shame from Him* [2]Or, *in His presence* [a]1 John 2:1 [b]Luke 17:30; Col. 3:4; 1 John 3:2 [c]Eph. 3:12; 1 John 3:21; 4:17; 5:14 [d]Mark 8:38 [e]1 Thess. 2:19
29 [1]Or, *begotten* [a]John 7:18; 1 John 3:7 [b]John 1:13; 3:3; 1 John 3:9; 4:7; 5:1, 4, 18; 3 John 11

1 [1]Lit., *what kind of love* [a]John 3:16; 1 John 4:10 [b]John 1:12; 11:52; Rom. 8:16; 1 John 3:2, 10 [c]John 15:18, 21; 16:3
2 [a]1 John 2:7 [b]John 1:12; 11:52; Rom. 8:16; 1 John 3:1, 10 [c]Rom. 8:19, 23f. [d]Luke 17:30; Col. 3:4; 1 John 2:28 [e]Rom. 8:29; 2 Pet. 1:4 [f]John 17:24; 2 Cor. 3:18
3 [a]Rom. 15:12; 1 Pet. 1:3 [b]John 17:19; 2 Cor. 7:1; 2 Pet. 3:13f.; 1 John 2:6
4 [a]Rom. 4:15; 1 John 5:17
5 [a]1 John 1:2; 3:8 [b]John 1:29; 1 Pet. 1:18-20; 1 John 2:2 [c]2 Cor. 5:21; 1 John 2:29
6 [1]Or, *has known* [a]1 John 3:9 [b]1 John 2:3; 3 John 11
7 [a]1 John 2:1 [b]1 John 2:26 [c]1 John 2:29
8 [1]Lit., *sins* [a]Matt. 13:38; John 8:44; 1 John 3:10 [b]Matt. 4:3 [c]1 John 3:5 [d]John 12:31; 16:11
9 [1]Or, *begotten* [a]John 1:13; 3:3; 1 John 2:29; 4:7; 5:1, 4, 18; 3 John 11 [b]1 Pet. 1:23; 1 John 3:6; 5:18
10 [a]John 1:12; 11:52; Rom. 8:16; 1 John 3:1, 2 [b]Matt. 13:38; John 8:44; 1 John 3:8 [c]Rom. 13:8ff.; Col. 3:14; 1 Tim. 1:5; 1 John 4:8 [d]1 John 2:9
11 [a]1 John 1:5 [b]1 John 2:7 [c]John 13:34f.; 15:12; 1 John 4:7, 11f., 21; 2 John 5
12 [a]Gen. 4:8 [b]Matt. 5:37; 1 John 2:13f. [c]Ps. 38:20; Prov. 29:10; John 8:40, 41
13 [a]John 15:18; 17:14

14 We know that we have [a]passed out of death into life, [b]because we love the brethren. He who does not love abides in death.

15 Everyone who [a]hates his brother is a murderer; and you know that [b]no murderer has eternal life abiding in him.

16 We know love by this, that [a]He laid down His life for us; and [b]we ought to lay down our lives for the [c]brethren.

17 But [a]whoever has the world's goods, and beholds his brother in need and [b]closes his [1]heart [2]against him, [c]how does the love of God abide in him?

18 [a]Little children, let us not love with word or with tongue, but in deed and [b]truth.

19 We shall know by this that we are [a]of the truth, and shall [1]assure our heart [2]before Him,

20 in whatever our heart condemns us; for God is greater than our heart, and knows all things.

21 [a]Beloved, if our heart does not condemn us, we have [b]confidence [1]before God;

22 and [a]whatever we ask we receive from Him, because we [b]keep His commandments and do [c]the things that are pleasing in His sight.

23 And this is His commandment, that we [1a]believe in [b]the name of His Son Jesus Christ, and love one another, just as [c]He [2]commanded us.

24 And the one who [a]keeps His commandments [b]abides in Him, and He in him. And [c]we know by this that [d]He abides in us, by the Spirit whom He has given us.

Testing the Spirits

4 [a]BELOVED, do not believe every [b]spirit, but test the spirits to see whether they are from God; because [c]many false prophets have gone out into the world.

2 By this you know the Spirit of God: [a]every spirit that [b]confesses that [c]Jesus Christ has come in the flesh is from God;

3 and every spirit that [a]does not confess Jesus is not from God; and this is the *spirit* of the [b]antichrist, of which you have heard that it is coming, and [c]now it is already in the world.

4 You are from God, [a]little children, and [b]have overcome them; because [c]greater is He who is in you than [d]he who is in the world.

5 [a]They are from the world; therefore they speak *as* from the world, and the world listens to them.

6 [a]We are from God; [b]he who knows God listens to us; [c]he who is not from God does not listen to us. By this we know [d]the spirit of truth and [e]the spirit of error.

God Is Love

7 [a]Beloved, let us [b]love one another, for love is from God; and [c]everyone who loves is [1d]born of God and [e]knows God.

8 The one who does not love does not know God, for [a]God is love.

9 By this the love of God was manifested [1a]in us, that [b]God has sent His [2]only begotten Son into the world so that we might live through Him.

10 In this is love, [a]not that we [1]loved God, but that [b]He loved us and sent His Son *to be* [c]the propitiation for our sins.

11 [a]Beloved, if God so loved us, [b]we also ought to love one another.

12 [a]No one has beheld God at any time; if we love one another, God abides in us, and His [b]love is perfected in us.

13 [a]By this we know that we abide in Him and He in us, because He has given us of His Spirit.

14 And we have beheld and [a]bear witness that the Father has [b]sent the Son *to be* the Savior of the world.

15 [a]Whoever confesses that [b]Jesus is the Son of God, God [c]abides in him, and he in God.

16 And [a]we have come to know and have believed the love which God has [1b]for us. [c]God is love, and the one who [d]abides in love abides in God, and God abides in him.

17 By this, [a]love is perfected with us, that we may have [b]confidence in [c]the day of judgment; because [d]as He is, so also are we in this world.

18 There is no fear in love; but [a]perfect love casts out fear, because fear [1]involves punishment, and the one who fears is not [b]perfected in love.

19 [a]We love, because He first loved us.

20 [a]If someone says, "I love God," and [b]hates his brother, he is a [c]liar; for [d]the one who does not love his brother whom he has seen, [1e]cannot love God whom he has not seen.

21 And [a]this commandment we have from Him, that the one who loves God [b]should love his brother also.

Overcoming the World

5 [a]WHOEVER believes that Jesus is the [1]Christ is [2b]born of God; and whoever loves the [3]Father [c]loves the *child* [2]born of Him.

2 [a]By this we know that [b]we love the children of God, when we love God and [1]observe His commandments.

14 aJohn 5:24 bJohn 13:35; 1 John 2:10
15 aMatt. 5:21f.; John 8:44 bGal. 5:20f.; Rev. 21:8
16 aJohn 10:11; 15:13 bPhil. 2:17; 1 Thess. 2:8 c1 John 2:9
17 [1]Lit., *inward parts* [2]Lit., *from* aJames 2:15f. bDeut. 15:7 c1 John 4:20
18 a1 John 2:1; 3:7 b2 John 1; 3 John 1
19 [1]Or, *persuade* [2]Or, *before Him; because if our heart* a1 John 2:21
21 [1]Lit., *toward* a1 John 3:2 b1 John 2:28; 5:14
22 aJob 22:26f.; Matt. 7:7; 21:22; John 9:31 b1 John 2:3 cJohn 8:29; Heb. 13:21
23 [1]Or, *believe the name* [2]Or, *gave us a commandment* aJohn 6:29 bJohn 1:12; 2:23; 3:18 cJohn 13:34; 15:12; 1 John 2:8
24 a1 John 2:3 bJohn 6:56; 10:38; 1 John 2:6, 24; 4:15 cJohn 14:17; Rom. 8:9, 14, 16; 1 Thess. 4:8; 1 John 4:13 d1 John 2:5

1 a3 John 11 bJer. 29:8; 1 Cor. 12:10; 1 Thess. 5:20f.; 2 Thess. 2:2 cJer. 14:14; 2 Pet. 2:1; 1 John 2:18
2 a1 Cor. 12:3 b1 John 2:23 cJohn 1:14; 1 John 1:2
3 a1 John 2:22; 2 John 7 b1 John 2:18, 22 c2 Thess. 2:3-7; 1 John 2:18
4 a1 John 2:1 b1 John 2:13 cRom. 8:31; 1 John 3:20 dJohn 12:31
5 aJohn 15:19; 17:14, 16
6 aJohn 8:23; 1 John 4:4 bJohn 8:47; 10:3ff.; 18:37 c1 Cor. 14:37 dJohn 14:17 e1 Tim. 4:1
7 [1]Or, *begotten* a1 John 2:7 b1 John 3:11 c1 John 5:1 d1 John 2:29 e1 Cor. 8:3; 1 John 2:3
8 a1 John 4:7, 16
9 [1]Or, *in our case* [2]Or, *unique,* only one of His kind aJohn 9:3; 1 John 4:16 bJohn 3:16f.; 1 John 4:10; 5:11
10 [1]Some mss. read *had loved* aRom. 5:8, 10; 1 John 4:19 bJohn 3:16f.; 1 John 4:9; 5:11 c1 John 2:2
11 a1 John 2:7 b1 John 4:7
12 aJohn 1:18; 1 Tim. 6:16; 1 John 4:20 b1 John 2:5; 4:17f.
13 aRom. 8:9; 1 John 3:24
14 aJohn 15:27; 1 John 1:2 bJohn 3:17; 4:42; 1 John 2:2

15 a1 John 2:23 bRom. 10:9; 1 John 3:23; 4:2; 5:1, 5 c1 John 2:24; 3:24
16 [1]Lit., *in* aJohn 6:69 bJohn 9:3; 1 John 4:9 c1 John 4:7, 8 d1 John 4:12f.
17 a1 John 2:5; 4:12 b1 John 2:28 cMatt. 10:15 dJohn 17:22; 1 John 2:6; 3:1, 7, 16
18 [1]Lit., *has* aRom. 8:15 b1 John 4:12
19 a1 John 4:10
20 [1]Some mss. read *how can he love God . . . seen?* a1 John 1:6, 8, 10; 2:4 b1 John 2:9, 11 c1 John 1:6 d1 John 3:17 e1 Pet. 1:8; 1 John 4:12
21 aLev. 19:18; Matt. 5:43f.; 22:37ff.; John 13:34 b1 John 3:11

1 [1]I.e., Messiah [2]Or, *begotten* [3]Lit., *one who begets* a1 John 2:22f.; 4:2, 15 bJohn 1:3; 3:3; 1 John 2:29; 5:4, 18 cJohn 8:42
2 [1]Lit., *do* a1 John 2:5 b1 John 3:14

3 For [a]this is the love of God, that
we [b]keep His commandments; and [c]His
commandments are not burdensome.
4 For whatever is [1a]born of God
[b]overcomes the world; and this is the
victory that has overcome the world—
our faith.
5 And who is the one who overcomes
the world, but he who [a]believes that
Jesus is the Son of God?
6 This is the one who came [a]by water
and blood, Jesus Christ; not [1]with the
water only, but [1]with the water and
[1]with the blood.
7 And it is [a]the Spirit who bears
witness, because the Spirit is the truth.
8 For there are [a]three that bear witness, [1]the Spirit and the water and the
blood; and the three are [2]in agreement.
9 [a]If we receive the witness of men,
the witness of God is greater; for the
witness of God is this, that [b]He has
borne witness concerning His Son.
10 The one who believes in the Son of
God [a]has the witness in himself; the one
who does not believe God has [b]made
Him a liar, because he has not believed
in the witness that God has borne concerning His Son.
11 And the witness is this, that God
has given us [a]eternal life, and [b]this life is
in His Son.
12 [a]He who has the Son has the life;
he who does not have the Son of God
does not have the life.

This Is Written That You May Know

13 [a]These things I have written to you
who [b]believe in the name of the Son of
God, in order that you may know that
you have [c]eternal life.
14 And this is [a]the confidence which
we have [1]before Him, that, [b]if we ask
anything according to His will, He hears
us.
15 And if we know that He hears us *in*
whatever we ask, [a]we know that we have
the requests which we have asked from
Him.
16 If anyone sees his brother [1]commit-
ting a sin not *leading* to death, [a]he shall
ask and *God* will for him give life to
those who commit sin not *leading* to
death. [b]There is a sin *leading* to death; [c]I
do not say that he should make request
for this.
17 [a]All unrighteousness is sin, and
[b]there is a sin not *leading* to death.
18 [a]We know that [b]no one who is
[1]born of God sins; but He who was
[1]born of God [c]keeps him and [d]the evil
one does not [e]touch him.
19 [a]We know that [b]we are of God,
and [c]the whole world lies in *the power of*
the evil one.
20 And [a]we know that [b]the Son of
God has come, and has [c]given us understanding, in order that we might know
[d]Him who is true, and we [e]are in Him
who is true, in His Son Jesus Christ.
[f]This is the true God and [g]eternal life.
21 [a]Little children, guard yourselves
from [b]idols.

3 [a]John 14:15; 2 John 6 [b]1 John 2:3 [c]Matt. 11:30; 23:4
4 [1]Or, *begotten* [a]John 1:13; 3:3; 1 John 2:29; 5:1, 18 [b]1 John 2:13; 4:4
5 [a]1 John 4:15; 5:1
6 [1]Lit., *in* [a]John 19:34
7 [a]Matt. 3:16f.; John 15:26; 16:13-15
8 [1]A few late mss. read *in heaven, the Father, the Word, and the Holy Spirit, and these three are one. And there are three that bear witness on earth, the Spirit* [2]Lit., *for the one thing* [a]Matt. 18:16
9 [a]John 5:34, 37; 8:18 [b]Matt. 3:17; John 5:32, 37
10 [a]Rom. 8:16; Gal. 4:6; Rev. 12:17 [b]John 3:18, 33; 1 John 1:10
11 [a]John 3:36; 1 John 1:2; 2:25; 4:9; 5:13, 20 [b]John 1:4
12 [a]John 3:15f., 36
13 [a]John 20:31 [b]1 John 3:23 [c]1 John 1:2; 2:25; 4:9; 5:11, 20
14 [1]Lit., *toward* [a]1 John 2:28; 3:21f. [b]Matt. 7:7; John 14:13; 1 John 3:22
15 [a]1 John 5:18-20
16 [1]Lit., *sinning* [a]James 5:15 [b]Num. 15:30; Heb. 6:4-6; 10:26 [c]Jer. 7:16; 14:11
17 [a]1 John 3:4 [b]1 John 2:1f.; 5:16
18 [1]Or, *begotten* [a]1 John 5:15, 19, 20 [b]1 John 3:9 [c]James 1:27; Jude 21 [d]1 John 2:13 [e]John 14:30
19 [a]1 John 5:15, 18, 20 [b]1 John 4:6 [c]John 12:31; 17:15; Gal. 1:4
20 [a]1 John 5:15, 18, 19 [b]John 8:42; 1 John 5:5 [c]Luke 24:45 [d]John 17:3; Rev. 3:7 [e]John 1:18; 14:9; 1 John 2:23; Rev. 3:7 [f]1 John 1:2 [g]1 John 5:11
21 [a]1 John 2:1 [b]1 Cor. 10:7, 14; 1 Thess. 1:9

THE SECOND EPISTLE OF JOHN

Walk According to His Commandments

1 [a]THE elder to the [b]chosen [c]lady and her children, whom I [d]love in truth; and not only I, but also all who [e]know the truth,

2 for [a]the sake of the truth which abides [b]in us and will be [c]with us forever:

3 [a]Grace, mercy *and* peace will be with us, from God the Father and from Jesus Christ, the Son of the Father, in truth and love.

4 [a]I was very glad to find *some* of your children walking in truth, just as we have received commandment *to do* from the Father.

5 And now I ask you, lady, [a]not as writing to you a new commandment, but the one which we have had [a]from the beginning, that we [b]love one another.

6 And [a]this is love, that we walk according to His commandments. This is the commandment, [b]just as you have heard [c]from the beginning, that you should walk in it.

7 For [a]many deceivers have [b]gone out into the world, those who [c]do not acknowledge Jesus Christ *as* coming in the flesh. This is [a]the deceiver and the [d]antichrist.

8 [a]Watch yourselves, [b]that you might not lose what [1]we have accomplished, but that you may receive a full reward.

9 Anyone who [1]goes too far and [a]does not abide in the teaching of Christ, does not have God; the one who abides in the teaching, he has both the Father and the Son.

10 If anyone comes to you and does not bring this teaching, [a]do not receive him into *your* house, and do not give him a greeting;

11 for the one who gives him a greeting [a]participates in his evil deeds.

12 [a]Having many things to write to you, I do not want to *do so* with paper and ink; but I hope to come to you and speak face to face, that [1]your [b]joy may be made full.

13 The children of your [a]chosen sister greet you.

1 [a]Acts 11:30; 1 Pet. 5:1; 3 John 1 [b]Rom. 16:13; 1 Pet. 5:13; 2 John 13 [c]2 John 5 [d]1 John 3:18; 2 John 3; 3 John 1 [e]John 8:32; 1 Tim. 2:4
2 [a]2 Pet. 1:12 [b]1 John 1:8 [c]John 14:16
3 [a]Rom. 1:7; 1 Tim. 1:2
4 [a]3 John 3f.
5 [a]1 John 2:7 [b]John 13:34, 35; 15:12, 17; 1 John 3:11; 4:7, 11
6 [a]1 John 2:5; 5:3 [b]1 John 2:24 [c]1 John 2:7
7 [a]1 John 2:26 [b]1 John 2:19; 4:1 [c]1 John 4:2f. [d]1 John 2:18
8 [1]Some ancient mss. read *you* [a]Mark 13:9 [b]1 Cor. 3:8; Heb. 10:35
9 [1]Lit., *goes on ahead* [a]John 7:16; 8:31; 1 John 2:23
10 [a]1 Kin. 13:16f.; Rom. 16:17; 2 Thess. 3:6, 14; Titus 3:10
11 [a]Eph. 5:11; 1 Tim. 5:22; Jude 23
12 [1]Some ancient mss. read *our* [a]3 John 13, 14 [b]John 3:29; 1 John 1:4
13 [a]2 John 1

THE THIRD EPISTLE OF JOHN

You Walk in the Truth

1 [a]THE elder to the beloved [b]Gaius, whom I [c]love in truth.

2 Beloved, I pray that in all respects you may prosper and be in good health, just as your soul prospers.

3 For I [1a]was very glad when [b]brethren came and bore witness to your truth, *that is,* how you [a]are walking in truth.

4 I have no greater joy than [1]this, to hear of [a]my children [b]walking in the truth.

5 Beloved, you are acting faithfully in whatever you accomplish for the [a]brethren, and especially *when they are* [b]strangers;

6 and they bear witness to your love before the church; and you will do well to [a]send them on their way in a manner [b]worthy of God.

7 For they went out for the sake of [a]the Name, [b]accepting nothing from the Gentiles.

8 Therefore we ought to [1]support such men, that we may be fellow workers [2]with the truth.

9 I wrote something to the church; but Diotrephes, who loves to [a]be first among them, does not accept [1]what we say.

10 For this reason, [a]if I come, I will call attention to his deeds which he does, unjustly accusing us with wicked words; and not satisfied with this, neither does he himself [b]receive the [c]brethren, and he forbids those who desire *to do so,* and [d]puts *them* out of the church.

11 Beloved, [a]do not imitate what is evil, but what is good. [b]The one who does good is of God; [c]the one who does evil has not seen God.

12 Demetrius [a]has received a *good* testimony from everyone, and from the truth itself; and we also bear witness, and [b]you know that our witness is true.

13 [a]I had many things to write to you, but I am not willing to write *them* to you with pen and ink;

14 but I hope to see you shortly, and we shall speak face to face. [a]Peace *be* to you. The friends greet you. Greet the friends [b]by name.

1 [a]2 John 1 [b]Acts 19:29; 20:4; Rom. 16:23; 1 Cor. 1:14 [c]1 John 3:18; 2 John 1
3 [1]Or, *am very glad when brethren come and bear witness* [a]2 John 4 [b]Acts 1:15; Gal. 6:10; 3 John 5, 10
4 [1]Lit., *these things, that I hear* [a]1 Cor. 4:14f.; 2 Cor. 6:13; Gal. 4:19; 1 Thess. 2:11; 1 Tim. 1:2; 2 Tim. 1:2; Philem. 10; 1 John 2:1 [b]2 John 4
5 [a]Acts 1:15; Gal. 6:10; 3 John 3, 10 [b]Rom. 12:13; Heb. 13:2
6 [a]Acts 15:3; Titus 3:13 [b]Col. 1:10; 1 Thess. 2:12
7 [a]John 15:21; Acts 5:41; Phil. 2:9 [b]Acts 20:33, 35
8 [1]Or, *receive such men as guests* [2]Or, *for*
9 [1]Lit., *us* [a]2 John 9
10 [a]2 John 12 [b]2 John 10; 3 John 5 [c]Acts 1:15; Gal. 6:10; 3 John 3, 5 [d]John 9:34
11 [a]Ps. 34:14; 37:27 [b]1 John 2:29; 3:10 [c]1 John 3:6
12 [a]Acts 6:3; 1 Tim. 3:7 [b]John 19:35; 21:24
13 [a]2 John 12
14 [a]John 20:19, 21, 26; Eph. 6:23; 1 Pet. 5:14 [b]John 10:3

THE EPISTLE OF
JUDE

The Warnings of History to the Ungodly

1 [1a]JUDE, a [b]bond-servant of Jesus
Christ, and brother of [2]James, to
[c]those who are the called, beloved in
God the Father, and [d]kept for Jesus
Christ:
2 [a]May mercy and peace and love
[b]be multiplied to you.
3 [a]Beloved, while I was making every
effort to write you about our [b]common
salvation, I felt the necessity to write to
you appealing that you [c]contend earnestly for [d]the faith which was once for
all [e]delivered to [f]the [1]saints.
4 For certain persons have [a]crept in
unnoticed, those who were long beforehand [1b]marked out for this condemnation, ungodly persons who turn [c]the
grace of our God into [d]licentiousness
and [e]deny our only Master and Lord,
Jesus Christ.
5 Now I desire to [a]remind you,
though [b]you know all things once for all,
that [1]the Lord, [c]after saving a people out
of the land of Egypt, [2]subsequently
destroyed those who did not believe.
6 And [a]angels who did not keep their
own domain, but abandoned their
proper abode, He has [b]kept in eternal
bonds under darkness for the judgment
of the great day.
7 Just as [a]Sodom and Gomorrah and
the [b]cities around them, since they in the
same way as these indulged in gross
immorality and [c]went after strange flesh,
are exhibited as an [1d]example, in undergoing the [e]punishment of eternal fire.
8 Yet in the same manner these men,
also by dreaming, [a]defile the flesh, and
reject authority, and revile [1]angelic
majesties.
9 But [a]Michael [b]the archangel, when
he disputed with the devil and argued
about [c]the body of Moses, did not dare
pronounce against him a railing judgment, but said, "[d]The Lord rebuke you."
10 But [a]these men revile the things
which they do not understand; and [b]the
things which they know by instinct, [a]like
unreasoning animals, by these things
they are [1]destroyed.
11 Woe to them! For they have gone
[a]the way of Cain, and for pay [1]they have
rushed headlong into [b]the error of Balaam, and [c]perished in the rebellion of
Korah.
12 These men are those who are [1]hid-
den reefs [a]in your love feasts when they
feast with you [b]without fear, caring for
themselves; [c]clouds without water, [d]car-
ried along by winds; autumn trees without fruit, [2]doubly dead, [e]uprooted;
13 [a]wild waves of the sea, casting up
[b]their own [1]shame like foam; wandering
stars, [c]for whom the [2]black darkness has
been reserved forever.
14 And about these also [a]Enoch, *in*
the seventh *generation* from Adam,
prophesied, saying, "[b]Behold, the Lord
came with [1]many thousands of His holy
ones,
15 [a]to execute judgment upon all, and
to convict all the ungodly of all their
ungodly deeds which they have done in
an ungodly way, and of all the harsh
things which [b]ungodly sinners have
spoken against Him."
16 These are [a]grumblers, finding fault,
[b]following after their *own* lusts; [1]they
speak [c]arrogantly, flattering people [d]for
the sake of *gaining an* advantage.

Keep Yourselves in the Love of God

17 But you, [a]beloved, [b]ought to remember the words that were spoken
beforehand by [c]the apostles of our Lord
Jesus Christ,
18 that they were saying to you, "[a]In
the last time there shall be mockers,
[b]following after their own ungodly
lusts."
19 These are the ones who cause divisions, [1a]worldly-minded, [2]devoid of the
Spirit.
20 But you, [a]beloved, [b]building yourselves up on your most holy [a]faith;
[c]praying in the Holy Spirit;
21 keep yourselves in the love of God,
[a]waiting anxiously for the mercy of our
Lord Jesus Christ to eternal life.
22 And [1]have mercy on some, who are
doubting;
23 save others, [a]snatching them out of
the fire; and on some have mercy with
fear, [b]hating even the garment polluted
by the flesh.
24 [a]Now to Him who is able to keep
you from stumbling, and to [b]make you
stand in the presence of His glory blameless with [c]great joy,
25 to the [a]only [b]God our Savior,
through Jesus Christ our Lord, [c]*be* glory,
majesty, dominion and authority, [d]be-
fore all time and now and [1]forever.
Amen.

1 [1]Gr., *Judas* [2]Or, *Jacob* [a]Matt. 13:55; Mark 6:3; [Luke 6:16; John 14:22; Acts 1:13?] [b]Rom. 1:1 [c]Rom. 1:6f. [d]John 17:11f.; 1 Pet. 1:5; Jude 21

2 [a]Gal. 6:16; 1 Tim. 1:2 [b]1 Pet. 1:2; 2 Pet. 1:2

3 [1]Or, *holy ones* [a]Heb. 6:9; Jude 1, 17, 20 [b]Titus 1:4 [c]1 Tim. 6:12 [d]Acts 6:7; Jude 20 [e]2 Pet. 2:21 [f]Acts 9:13

4 [1]Or, *written about* [a]Gal. 2:4; 2 Tim. 3:6 [b]1 Pet. 2:8 [c]Acts 11:23 [d]2 Pet. 2:7 [e]2 Tim. 2:12; Titus 1:16; 2 Pet. 2:1; 1 John 2:22

5 [1]Some ancient mss. read *Jesus* [2]Lit., *the second time* [a]2 Pet. 1:12f.; 3:1f. [b]1 John 2:20 [c]Ex. 12:51; 1 Cor. 10:5-10; Heb. 3:16f.

6 [a]2 Pet. 2:4 [b]2 Pet. 2:9

7 [1]Or, *example of eternal fire, in undergoing punishment* [a]Gen. 19:24f.; 2 Pet. 2:6 [b]Deut. 29:23; Hos. 11:8 [c]2 Pet. 2:2 [d]2 Pet. 2:6 [e]Matt. 25:41; 2 Thess. 1:8f.; 2 Pet. 3:7

8 [1]Lit., *glories* [a]2 Pet. 2:10

9 [a]Dan. 10:13, 21; 12:1; Rev. 12:7 [b]1 Thess. 4:16; 2 Pet. 2:11 [c]Deut. 34:6 [d]Zech. 3:2

10 [1]Lit., *corrupted* [a]2 Pet. 2:12 [b]Phil. 3:19

11 [1]Lit., *they have poured themselves out* [a]Gen. 4:3-8; Heb. 11:4; 1 John 3:12 [b]Num. 31:16; 2 Pet. 2:15; Rev. 2:14 [c]Num. 16:1-3, 31-35

12 [1]Or, *stains* [2]Lit., *twice* [a]1 Cor. 11:20ff.; 2 Pet. 2:13 and mg. [b]Ezek. 34:2, 8, 10 [c]Prov. 25:14; 2 Pet. 2:17 [d]Eph. 4:14 [e]Matt. 15:13

13 [1]Or, *shameless deeds* [2]Lit., *blackness of darkness;* or, *nether gloom* [a]Is. 57:20 [b]Phil. 3:19 [c]2 Pet. 2:17; Jude 6

14 [1]Lit., *His holy ten thousands* [a]Gen. 5:18, 21ff. [b]Deut. 33:2; Dan. 7:10; Matt. 16:27; Heb. 12:22

15 [a]2 Pet. 2:6ff. [b]1 Tim. 1:9

16 [1]Lit., *their mouth speaks* [a]Num. 16:11, 41; 1 Cor. 10:10 [b]2 Pet. 2:10; Jude 18 [c]2 Pet. 2:18 [d]2 Pet. 2:3

17 [a]Jude 3 [b]2 Pet. 3:2 [c]Heb. 2:3

18 [a]Acts 20:29; 1 Tim. 4:1; 2 Tim. 3:1f.; 4:3; 2 Pet. 3:3 [b]Jude 4, 16

19 [1]Or, *merely natural* [2]Lit., *not having* [a]1 Cor. 2:14f.; James 3:15

20 [a]Jude 3 [b]Col. 2:7; 1 Thess. 5:11 [c]Eph. 6:18

21 [a]Titus 2:13; Heb. 9:28; 2 Pet. 3:12

22 [1]Some ancient mss. read *convince*

23 [a]Amos 4:11; Zech. 3:2; 1 Cor. 3:15 [b]Zech. 3:3f.; Rev. 3:4

24 [a]Rom. 16:25 [b]2 Cor. 4:14 [c]1 Pet. 4:13

25 [1]Lit., *to all the ages* [a]John 5:44; 1 Tim. 1:17 [b]Luke 1:47 [c]Rom. 11:36 [d]Heb. 13:8

THE REVELATION
TO JOHN

The Revelation of Jesus Christ

1 THE Revelation of Jesus Christ, which [a]God gave Him to [b]show to His bond-servants, [c]the things which must shortly take place; and He sent and [1]communicated *it* [d]by His angel to His bond-servant [e]John,

2 who bore witness to [a]the word of God and to [b]the testimony of Jesus Christ, *even* to all that he saw.

3 [a]Blessed is he who reads and those who hear the words of the prophecy, and [1]heed the things which are written in it; [b]for the time is near.

Message to the Seven Churches

4 [a]John to [b]the seven churches that are in [c]Asia: [d]Grace to you and peace, from [e]Him who is and who was and who is to come; and from [f]the seven Spirits who are before His throne;

5 and from Jesus Christ, [a]the faithful witness, the [b]first-born of the dead, and the [c]ruler of the kings of the earth. To Him who [d]loves us, and released us from our sins [1]by His blood,

6 and He has made us *to be* a [a]kingdom, [a]priests to [1b]His God and Father; [c]to Him *be* the glory and the dominion forever and ever. Amen.

7 [a]BEHOLD, HE IS COMING WITH THE CLOUDS, and [b]every eye will see Him, even those who pierced Him; and all the tribes of the earth will [c]mourn over Him. Even so. Amen.

8 "I am [a]the Alpha and the Omega," says the [b]Lord God, "[c]who is and who was and who is to come, the Almighty."

The Patmos Vision

9 [a]I, John, your [b]brother and [c]fellow partaker in the tribulation and [d]kingdom and [1e]perseverance *which are* in Jesus, was on the island called Patmos, [f] because of the word of God and the testimony of Jesus.

10 I was [1a]in the Spirit on [b]the Lord's day, and I heard behind me a loud voice [c]like *the sound* of a trumpet,

11 saying, "[a]Write in a [1]book what you see, and send *it* to the [b]seven churches: to [c]Ephesus and to [d]Smyrna and to [e]Pergamum and to [f]Thyatira and to [g]Sardis and to [h]Philadelphia and to [i]Laodicea."

12 And I turned to see the voice that was speaking with me. And having turned I saw [a]seven golden lampstands;

13 and [a]in the middle of the lampstands one [b]like [1]a son of man, [c]clothed in a robe reaching to the feet, and [d]girded across His breast with a golden girdle.

14 And His head and His [a]hair were white like white wool, like snow; and [b]His eyes were like a flame of fire;

15 and His [a]feet *were* like burnished bronze, when it has been caused to glow in a furnace, and His [b]voice *was* like the sound of many waters.

16 And in His right hand He held [a]seven stars; and out of His mouth came a [b]sharp two-edged sword; and His [c]face was like [d]the sun [1]shining in its strength.

17 And when I saw Him, I [a]fell at His feet as a dead man. And He [b]laid His right hand upon me, saying, "[c]Do not be afraid; [d]I am the first and the last,

18 and the [a]living One; and I [1b]was dead, and behold, I am alive forevermore, and I have [c]the keys of death and of Hades.

19 "[a]Write therefore [b]the things which you have seen, and the things which are, and the things which shall take place [c]after these things.

20 "As for the [a]mystery of the [b]seven stars which you saw in My right hand, and the [c]seven golden lampstands: the [b]seven stars are the angels of [d]the seven churches, and the seven [e]lampstands are the seven churches.

Message to Ephesus

2 "TO the angel of the church in [a]Ephesus write:

The One who holds [b]the seven stars in His right hand, the One who walks [1c]among the seven golden lampstands, says this:

2 '[a]I know your deeds and your toil and [1]perseverance, and that you cannot endure evil men, and you [b]put to the test those who call themselves [c]apostles, and they are not, and you found them *to be* false;

3 and you have [1]perseverance and have endured [a]for My name's sake, and have not grown weary.

4 'But I have *this* against you, that you have [a]left your first love.

5 'Remember therefore from where you have fallen, and [a]repent and [b]do the [1]deeds you did at first; or else I am coming to you, and will remove your [c]lampstand out of its place—unless you repent.

6 'Yet this you do have, that you hate the deeds of the [a]Nicolaitans, which I also hate.

1 [1]Or, *signified* [a]John 17:8; Rev. 5:7 [b]Rev. 22:6 [c]Dan. 2:28f.; Rev. 1:19 [d]Rev. 17:1; 19:9f.; 21:9; 22:16 [e]Rev. 1:4, 9; 22:8
2 [a]Rev. 1:9; 6:9; 12:17; 20:4 [b]1 Cor. 1:6; Rev. 12:17
3 [1]Or, *keep* [a]Luke 11:28; Rev. 22:7 [b]Rom. 13:11; Rev. 3:11; 22:7, 10, 12
4 [a]Rev. 1:1, 9; 22:8 [b]Rev. 1:11, 20 [c]Acts 2:9 [d]Rom. 1:7 [e]Rev. 1:8, 17; 4:8; 16:5 [f]Is. 11:2; Rev. 3:1; 4:5; 5:6; 8:2
5 [1]Or, *in* [a]Rev. 3:14; 19:11 [b]1 Cor. 15:20; Col. 1:18 [c]Rev. 17:14; 19:16 [d]Rom. 8:37
6 [1]Or, *God and His Father* [a]Rev. 5:10; 20:6 [b]Rom. 15:6 [c]Rom. 11:36
7 [a]Dan. 7:13; 1 Thess. 4:17 [b]Zech. 12:10-14; John 19:37 [c]Luke 23:28
8 [a]Is. 41:4; Rev. 21:6; 22:13 [b]Rev. 4:8; 11:17 [c]Rev. 1:4
9 [1]Or, *steadfastness* [a]Rev. 1:1 [b]Acts 1:15 [c]Matt. 20:23; Acts 14:22; 2 Cor. 1:7; Phil. 4:14 [d]2 Tim. 2:12; Rev. 1:6 [e]2 Thess. 3:5; Rev. 3:10 [f]Rev. 1:2
10 [1]Or, *in spirit* [a]Matt. 22:43; Rev. 4:2; 17:3; 21:10 [b]Acts 20:7 [c]Rev. 4:1
11 [1]Or, *scroll* [a]Rev. 1:2, 19 [b]Rev. 1:4, 20 [c]Rev. 2:1 [d]Rev. 2:8 [e]Rev. 2:12 [f]Acts 16:14; Rev. 2:18, 24 [g]Rev. 3:1, 4 [h]Rev. 3:7 [i]Col. 2:1; Rev. 3:14
12 [a]Ex. 25:37; 37:23; Zech. 4:2; Rev. 1:20; 2:1
13 [1]Or, *the Son of Man* [a]Rev. 2:1 [b]Ezek. 1:26; Dan. 7:13; 10:16; Rev. 14:14 [c]Dan. 10:5 [d]Rev. 15:6
14 [a]Dan. 7:9 [b]Dan. 7:9; 10:6; Rev. 2:18; 19:12
15 [a]Ezek. 1:7; Dan. 10:6; Rev. 2:18 [b]Ezek. 1:24; 43:2; Rev. 14:2; 19:6
16 [1]Lit., *shines* [a]Rev. 1:20; 2:1; 3:1 [b]Is. 49:2; Heb. 4:12; Rev. 2:12, 16; 19:15 [c]Matt. 17:2; Rev. 10:1 [d]Judg. 5:31
17 [a]Dan. 8:17; 10:9, 10, 15 [b]Dan. 8:18; 10:10, 12 [c]Matt. 14:27; 17:7 [d]Is. 41:4; 44:6; 48:12; Rev. 2:8; 22:13

18 [1]Lit., *became* [a]Luke 24:5; Rev. 4:9f. [b]Rom. 6:9; Rev. 2:8; 10:6; 15:7 [c]Job 38:17; Matt. 11:23; 16:19; Rev. 9:1; 20:1
19 [a]Rev. 1:11 [b]Rev. 1:12-16 [c]Rev. 4:1
20 [a]Rom. 11:25 [b]Rev. 1:16; 2:1; 3:1 [c]Ex. 25:37; 37:23; Zech. 4:2; Rev. 1:12; 2:1 [d]Rev. 1:4, 11 [e]Matt. 5:14f.

1 [1]Lit., *in the middle of* [a]Rev. 1:11 [b]Rev. 1:16 [c]Rev. 1:12f.
2 [1]Or, *steadfastness* [a]Rev. 2:19; 3:1, 8, 15 [b]John 6:6; 1 John 4:1 [c]2 Cor. 11:13
3 [1]V. 2, note 1 [a]John 15:21
4 [a]Jer. 2:2; Matt. 24:12
5 [1]Lit., *first deeds* [a]Rev. 2:16, 22; 3:3, 19 [b]Heb. 10:32; Rev. 2:2 [c]Matt. 5:14ff.; Phil. 2:15; Rev. 1:20
6 [a]Rev. 2:15

7 '[a]He who has an ear, let him hear
what the Spirit says to the churches. [b]To
him who overcomes, I will grant to eat of
[c]the tree of life, which is in the [d]Paradise
of God.'

Message to Smyrna

8 "And to the angel of the church in
[a]Smyrna write:
[b]The first and the last, who [1c]was
dead, and has come to life, says this:
9 'I know your [a]tribulation and your
[b]poverty (but you are [b]rich), and the
blasphemy by those who [c]say they are
Jews and are not, but are a synagogue of
[d]Satan.
10 'Do not fear what you are about to
suffer. Behold, the devil is about to cast
some of you into prison, that you may be
[a]tested, and you will have tribulation
[b]ten days. Be [c]faithful until death, and I
will give you [d]the crown of life.
11 '[a]He who has an ear, let him hear
what the Spirit says to the churches. [b]He
who overcomes shall not be hurt by the
[c]second death.'

Message to Pergamum

12 "And to the angel of the church in
[a]Pergamum write:
The One who has [b]the sharp two-
edged sword says this:
13 'I know where you dwell, where
[a]Satan's throne is; and you hold fast My
name, and did not deny [b]My faith, even
in the days of Antipas, My [c]witness, My
[d]faithful one, who was killed among you,
[e]where Satan dwells.
14 'But [a]I have a few things against
you, because you have there some who
hold the [b]teaching of Balaam, who kept
teaching Balak to put a stumbling block
before the sons of Israel, [c]to eat things
sacrificed to idols, and to commit *acts of*
immorality.
15 'Thus you also have some who in
the same way hold the teaching of the
[a]Nicolaitans.
16 '[a]Repent therefore; or else [b]I am
coming to you quickly, and I will make
war against them with [c]the sword of My
mouth.
17 '[a]He who has an ear, let him hear
what the Spirit says to the churches. [a]To
him who overcomes, to him I will give
some of the hidden [b]manna, and I will
give him a white stone, and a [c]new name
written on the stone [d]which no one
knows but he who receives it.'

Message to Thyatira

18 "And to the angel of the church in
[a]Thyatira write:
[b]The Son of God, [c]who has [1]eyes like
a flame of fire, and His feet are like
burnished bronze, says this:
19 '[a]I know your deeds, and your love
and faith and service and [1]perseverance,
and that your [2]deeds of late are greater
than [3]at first.
20 'But [a]I have *this* against you, that
you tolerate the woman [b]Jezebel, who
calls herself a prophetess, and she
teaches and leads My bond-servants
astray, so that they [c]commit *acts of*
immorality and eat things sacrificed to
idols.
21 'And [a]I gave her time to repent; and
she [b]does not want to repent of her
immorality.
22 'Behold, [1]I will cast her [2]upon a bed
of sickness, and those who [a]commit
adultery with her into great tribulation,
unless they repent of [3]her deeds.
23 'And I will kill her children with
[1]pestilence; and all the churches will
know that I am He who [a]searches the
[2]minds and hearts; and [b]I will give to
each one of you according to your deeds.
24 'But I say to you, the rest who are in
[a]Thyatira, who do not hold this teaching, who have not known the [b]deep
things of Satan, as they call them—I
[c]place no other burden on you.
25 'Nevertheless [a]what you have, hold
fast [b]until I come.
26 'And [a]he who overcomes, and he
who keeps My deeds [b]until the end, [c]TO
HIM I WILL GIVE AUTHORITY OVER THE
[1]NATIONS;
27 AND HE SHALL [1a]RULE THEM WITH A
ROD OF IRON, [b]AS THE VESSELS OF THE
POTTER ARE BROKEN TO PIECES, as I also
have received *authority* from My Father;
28 and I will give him [a]the morning
star.
29 '[a]He who has an ear, let him hear
what the Spirit says to the churches.'

Message to Sardis

3 "AND to the angel of the church in
[a]Sardis write:
He who has [b]the seven Spirits of God,
and [c]the seven stars, says this: '[d]I know
your deeds, that you have a name that
you are alive, but you are [e]dead.
2 'Wake up, and strengthen the things
that remain, which were about to die; for
I have not found your deeds completed
in the sight of My God.
3 '[a]Remember therefore [1]what you
have received and heard; and keep *it*,
and [a]repent. If therefore you will not
wake up, [b]I will come [c]like a thief, and
you will not know at [d]what hour I will
come upon you.
4 'But you have a few [1a]people in
[b]Sardis who have not [c]soiled their garments; and they will walk with Me [d]in
white; for they are worthy.

7 [a]Matt. 11:15; Rev. 2:11, 17; 3:6, 13, 22; 13:9 [b]Rev. 2:11, 17, 26; 3:5, 12, 21; 21:7 [c]Gen. 2:9; 3:22; Prov. 3:18; 11:30; 13:12; 15:4; Rev. 22:2, 14 [d]Ezek. 28:13; 31:8f.; Luke 23:43
8 [1]Lit., *became* [a]Rev. 1:11 [b]Is. 44:6; 48:12; Rev. 1:17; 22:13 [c]Rev. 1:18
9 [a]Rev. 1:9 [b]2 Cor. 6:10; 8:9; James 2:5 [c]Rev. 3:9 [d]Matt. 4:10; Rev. 2:13, 24
10 [a]Rev. 3:10; 13:14ff. [b]Dan. 1:12, 14 [c]Rev. 2:13; 12:11; 17:14 [d]1 Cor. 9:25; Rev. 3:11
11 [a]Matt. 11:15; Rev. 2:7, 17, 29; 3:6, 13, 22; 13:9 [b]Rev. 2:7, 17, 26; 3:5, 12, 21; 21:7 [c]Rev. 20:6, 14; 21:8
12 [a]Rev. 1:11 [b]Rev. 1:16; 2:16
13 [a]Matt. 4:10; Rev. 2:24 [b]1 Tim. 5:8; Rev. 14:12 [c]Acts 22:20; Rev. 1:5; 11:3; 17:6 [d]Rev. 2:10; 12:11; 17:14 [e]Rev. 2:9
14 [a]Rev. 2:20 [b]Num. 31:16; 2 Pet. 2:15 [c]Num. 25:1f.; Acts 15:29; 1 Cor. 10:20; Rev. 2:20
15 [a]Rev. 2:6
16 [a]Rev. 2:5 [b]Rev. 22:7, 20 [c]2 Thess. 2:8; Rev. 1:16
17 [a]Rev. 2:7 [b]Ex. 16:33; John 6:49f. [c]Is. 56:5; 62:2; 65:15 [d]Rev. 14:3; 19:12
18 [1]Lit., *His eyes* [a]Rev. 1:11; 2:24 [b]Matt. 4:3 [c]Rev. 1:14f.
19 [1]Or, *steadfastness* [2]Lit., *last deeds* [3]Lit., *the first* [a]Rev. 2:2
20 [a]Rev. 2:14 [b]1 Kin. 16:31; 21:25; 2 Kin. 9:7, 22, 30 [c]Acts 15:29; 1 Cor. 10:20; Rev. 2:14
21 [a]Rom. 2:4; 2 Pet. 3:9 [b]Rom. 2:5; Rev. 9:20f.; 16:9, 11
22 [1]Lit., *I cast* [2]Lit., *into* [3]Some mss. read *their* [a]Rev. 17:2; 18:9
23 [1]Or, *death* [2]Lit., *kidneys,* i.e., inner man [a]Ps. 7:9; 26:2; 139:1; Jer. 11:20; 17:10; Matt. 16:27; Luke 16:15; Acts 1:24; Rom. 8:27 [b]Ps. 62:12
24 [a]Rev. 2:18 [b]1 Cor. 2:10 [c]Acts 15:28
25 [a]Rev. 3:11 [b]John 21:22
26 [1]Or, *Gentiles* [a]Rev. 2:7 [b]Matt. 10:22; Heb. 3:6 [c]Ps. 2:8; Rev. 3:21; 20:4

27 [1]Or, *shepherd* [a]Ps. 2:9; Rev. 12:5; 19:15 [b]Is. 30:14; Jer. 19:11
28 [a]1 John 3:2; Rev. 22:16
29 [a]Rev. 2:7

1 [a]Rev. 1:11 [b]Rev. 1:4 [c]Rev. 1:16 [d]Rev. 2:2; 3:8, 15 [e]1 Tim. 5:6
3 [1]Lit., *how* [a]Rev. 2:5 [b]Rev. 2:5 [c]1 Thess. 5:2; 2 Pet. 3:10; Rev. 16:15 [d]Matt. 24:43; Luke 12:39f.
4 [1]Lit., *names* [a]Rev. 11:13 [b]Rev. 1:11 [c]Jude 23 [d]Eccl. 9:8; Rev. 3:5, 18; 4:4; 6:11; 7:9, 13f.; 19:8, 14

5 '[a]He who overcomes shall thus be
clothed in [b]white garments; and I will
not [c]erase his name from the book of
life, and [d]I will confess his name before
My Father, and before His angels.
6 '[a]He who has an ear, let him hear
what the Spirit says to the churches.'

Message to Philadelphia

7 "And to the angel of the church in
[a]Philadelphia write:
[b]He who is holy, [c]who is true, who has
[d]the key of David, who opens and no
one will shut, and who shuts and no one
opens, says this:
8 '[a]I know your [1]deeds. Behold, I
have put before you [b]an open door
which no one can shut, because you have
a little power, and have kept My word,
and [c]have not denied My name.
9 'Behold, I [1]will cause *those* of [a]the
synagogue of Satan, who say that they
are Jews, and are not, but lie—behold, I
will make them to [b]come and bow down
[2]at your feet, and to know that [c]I have
loved you.
10 'Because you have [a]kept the word of
[b]My [1]perseverance, [c]I also will keep you
from the hour of [2d]testing, that *hour*
which is about to come upon the whole
[3e]world, to [4]test [f]those who dwell upon
the earth.
11 '[a]I am coming quickly; [b]hold fast
what you have, in order that no one take
your [c]crown.
12 '[a]He who overcomes, I will make
him a [b]pillar in the temple of My God,
and he will not go out from it anymore;
and I will write upon him the [c]name of
My God, and [d]the name of the city of
My God, [e]the new Jerusalem, which
comes down out of heaven from My
God, and My [f]new name.
13 '[a]He who has an ear, let him hear
what the Spirit says to the churches.'

Message to Laodicea

14 "And to the angel of the church in
[a]Laodicea write:
[b]The Amen, [c]the faithful and true
Witness, [d]the [1]Beginning of the creation
of God, says this:
15 '[a]I know your deeds, that you are
neither cold nor hot; [b]I would that you
were cold or hot.
16 'So because you are lukewarm, and
neither hot nor cold, I will [1]spit you out
of My mouth.
17 'Because you say, "[a]I am rich, and
have become wealthy, and have need of
nothing," and you do not know that you
are wretched and miserable and poor
and blind and naked,
18 I advise you to [a]buy from Me [b]gold
refined by fire, that you may become
rich, and [c]white garments, that you may
clothe yourself, and *that* [d]the shame of
your nakedness may not be revealed;
and eye salve to anoint your eyes, that
you may see.
19 '[a]Those whom I love, I reprove and
discipline; be zealous therefore, and
[b]repent.
20 'Behold, I stand [a]at the door and
[b]knock; if anyone hears My voice and
opens the door, [c]I will come in to him,
and will dine with him, and he with Me.
21 '[a]He who overcomes, I will grant to
him [b]to sit down with Me on My throne,
as [c]I also overcame and sat down with
My Father on His throne.
22 '[a]He who has an ear, let him hear
what the Spirit says to the churches.'"

5 [a]Rev. 2:7 [b]Rev. 3:4 [c]Ex. 32:32f.; Ps. 69:28; Luke 10:20; Rev. 13:8; 17:8; 20:12, 15; 21:27 [d]Matt. 10:32; Luke 12:8
6 [a]Rev. 2:7
7 [a]Rev. 1:11 [b]Rev. 6:10 [c]1 John 5:20; Rev. 3:14; 19:11 [d]Job 12:14; Is. 22:22; Matt. 16:19; Rev. 1:18
8 [1]Or, *deeds (behold . . . shut), that you* [a]Rev. 3:1 [b]Acts 14:27 [c]Rev. 2:13
9 [1]Lit., *give* [2]Lit., *before* [a]Rev. 2:9 [b]Is. 45:14; 49:23; 60:14 [c]Is. 43:4; John 17:23
10 [1]Or, *steadfastness* [2]Or, *temptation* [3]Lit., *inhabited earth* [4]Or, *tempt* [a]John 17:6; Rev. 3:8 [b]Rev. 1:9 [c]2 Tim. 2:12; 2 Pet. 2:9 [d]Rev. 2:10 [e]Matt. 24:14; Rev. 16:14 [f]Rev. 6:10; 8:13; 11:10; 13:8, 14; 17:8
11 [a]Rev. 1:3; 22:7, 12, 20 [b]Rev. 2:25 [c]Rev. 2:10
12 [a]Rev. 3:5 [b]1 Kin. 7:21; Jer. 1:18; Gal. 2:9 [c]Rev. 14:1; 22:4 [d]Ezek. 48:35; Rev. 21:2 [e]Gal. 4:26; Heb. 13:14; Rev. 21:2, 10 [f]Is. 62:2; Rev. 2:17
13 [a]Rev. 3:6
14 [1]I.e., origin or source [a]Rev. 1:11 [b]2 Cor. 1:20 [c]Rev. 1:5; 3:7 [d]Gen. 49:3; Deut. 21:17; Prov. 8:22; John 1:3; Col. 1:18; Rev. 21:6; 22:13
15 [a]Rev. 3:1 [b]Rom. 12:11
16 [1]Lit., *vomit*
17 [a]Hos. 12:8; Zech. 11:5; Matt. 5:3; 1 Cor. 4:8
18 [a]Is. 55:1; Matt. 13:44 [b]1 Pet. 1:7 [c]Rev. 3:4 [d]Rev. 16:15
19 [a]Prov. 3:12; 1 Cor. 11:32; Heb. 12:6 [b]Rev. 2:5
20 [a]Matt. 24:33; James 5:9 [b]Luke 12:36; John 10:3 [c]John 14:23
21 [a]Rev. 2:7 [b]Matt. 19:28; 2 Tim. 2:12; Rev. 2:26; 20:4 [c]John 16:33; Rev. 5:5; 6:2; 17:14
22 [a]Rev. 2:7

Scene in Heaven

4 AFTER [a]these things I looked, and
behold, [b]a door *standing* open in
heaven, and the first voice which I had
heard, [c]like *the sound* of a trumpet
speaking with me, [1]said, "[d]Come up
here, and I will [e]show you what must
take place after these things."
2 Immediately I was [1a]in the Spirit;
and behold, [b]a throne was standing in
heaven, and [c]One sitting on the throne.
3 And He who was sitting *was* like a
[a]jasper stone and a [b]sardius in appearance; and *there was* a [1c]rainbow around
the throne, like an [d]emerald in appearance.
4 And [a]around the throne *were*
[b]twenty-four thrones; and upon the
thrones *I saw* [c]twenty-four elders [d]sit-
ting, clothed in [e]white garments, and
[f]golden crowns on their heads.

The Throne and Worship of the Creator

5 And from the throne proceed
[a]flashes of lightning and sounds and
peals of thunder. And *there were* [b]seven
lamps of fire burning before the throne,
which are [c]the seven Spirits of God;
6 and before the throne *there was*, as
it were, a [a]sea of glass like crystal; and in
the [1]center and [b]around the throne,
[c]four living creatures [d]full of eyes in
front and behind.
7 [a]And the first creature *was* like a
lion, and the second creature like a calf,
and the third creature had a face like
that of a man, and the fourth creature
was like a flying eagle.
8 And the [a]four living creatures, each
one of them having [b]six wings, are [c]full
of eyes around and within; and [d]day and
night [1]they do not cease to say,
"[e]HOLY, HOLY, HOLY, *is* THE [f]LORD
GOD, THE ALMIGHTY, [g]who was
and who is and who is to come."

1 [1]Lit., *saying* [a]Rev. 1:12ff., 19 [b]Ezek. 1:1; Rev. 19:11 [c]Rev. 1:10 [d]Rev. 11:12 [e]Rev. 1:19; 22:6
2 [1]Or, *in spirit* [a]Rev. 1:10 [b]1 Kin. 22:19; Is. 6:1; Ezek. 1:26; Dan. 7:9; Rev. 4:9f. [c]Rev. 4:9
3 [1]Or, *halo* [a]Rev. 21:11 [b]Rev. 21:20 [c]Ezek. 1:28; Rev. 10:1 [d]Rev. 21:19
4 [a]Rev. 4:6; 5:11; 7:11 [b]Rev. 11:16 [c]Rev. 4:10; 5:6, 8, 14; 19:4 [d]Matt. 19:28; Rev. 20:4 [e]Rev. 3:18 [f]Rev. 4:10
5 [a]Ex. 19:16; Rev. 8:5; 11:19; 16:18 [b]Ex. 25:37; Zech. 4:2 [c]Rev. 1:4
6 [1]Lit., *middle of the throne and around* [a]Ezek. 1:22; Rev. 15:2; 21:18, 21 [b]Rev. 4:4 [c]Ezek. 1:5; Rev. 4:8f.; 5:6; 6:1, 6; 7:11; 14:3; 15:7; 19:4 [d]Ezek. 1:18; 10:12
7 [a]Ezek. 1:10; 10:14
8 [1]Lit., *they have no rest, saying,* [a]Ezek. 1:5; Rev. 4:6, 9; 5:6; 6:1, 6; 7:11; 14:3; 15:7; 19:4 [b]Is. 6:2 [c]Ezek. 1:18; 10:12 [d]Rev. 14:11 [e]Is. 6:3 [f]Rev. 1:8 [g]Rev. 1:4

9 And when the living creatures give
glory and honor and thanks to Him who
[a]sits on the throne, to [b]Him who lives
forever and ever,
10 the [a]twenty-four elders will [b]fall
down before Him who [c]sits on the
throne, and will worship [d]Him who lives
forever and ever, and will cast their
[e]crowns before the throne, saying,
11 "[a]Worthy art Thou, our Lord and
our God, to receive glory and
honor and power; for Thou [b]didst
create all things, and because of
Thy will they [1]existed, and were
created."

The Book with Seven Seals

5 AND I saw [1]in the right hand of
Him who [a]sat on the throne a
[2b]book written inside and on the back,
[c]sealed up with seven seals.
2 And I saw a [a]strong angel proclaiming with a loud voice, "Who is
worthy to open the [1]book and to break
its seals?"
3 And no one [a]in heaven, or on the
earth, or under the earth, was able to
open the [1]book, or to look into it.
4 And I *began* to weep greatly, because no one was found worthy to open
the [1]book, or to look into it;
5 and one of the elders *said to me,
"Stop weeping; behold, the [a]Lion that is
[b]from the tribe of Judah, the [c]Root of
David, has overcome so as to open the
[1]book and its seven seals."
6 And I saw [1]between the throne
(with the four living creatures) and [a]the
elders a [b]Lamb standing, as if [c]slain,
having seven [d]horns and [e]seven eyes,
which are [f]the seven Spirits of God, sent
out into all the earth.
7 And He came, and He took [a]*it* out
of the right hand of Him who [a]sat on the
throne.
8 And when He had taken the [1]book,
the [a]four living creatures and the
[b]twenty-four elders [c]fell down before the
[d]Lamb, having each one a [e]harp, and
[f]golden bowls full of incense, which are
the [g]prayers of the [2]saints.
9 And they *sang a [a]new song, saying,
"[b]Worthy art Thou to take the
[1]book, and to break its seals; for
Thou wast [c]slain, and didst [d]pur-
chase for God with Thy blood
men from [e]every tribe and tongue
and people and nation.
10 "And Thou hast made them *to be* a
[a]kingdom and [a]priests to our
God; and they will [b]reign upon
the earth."

Angels Exalt the Lamb

11 And I looked, and I heard the voice
of many angels [a]around the throne and

9 [a]Ps. 47:8; Is. 6:1; Rev. 4:2 [b]Deut. 32:40; Dan. 4:34; 12:7; Rev. 10:6; 15:7
10 [a]Rev. 4:4 [b]Rev. 5:8, 14; 7:11; 11:16; 19:4 [c]Ps. 47:8; Is. 6:1; Rev. 4:2 [d]Deut. 32:40; Dan. 4:34; 12:7 [e]Rev. 4:4; 10:6; 15:7
11 [1]Lit., *were* [a]Rev. 1:6; 5:12 [b]Acts 14:15; Rev. 10:6; 14:7

1 [1]Lit., *upon* [2]Or, *scroll* [a]Rev. 4:9; 5:7, 13 [b]Ezek. 2:9, 10 [c]Is. 29:11; Dan. 12:4
2 [1]Or, *scroll* [a]Rev. 10:1; 18:21
3 [1]Or, *scroll* [a]Phil. 2:10; Rev. 5:13
4 [1]Or, *scroll*
5 [1]Or, *scroll* [a]Gen. 49:9 [b]Heb. 7:14 [c]Is. 11:1, 10; Rom. 15:12; Rev. 22:16
6 [1]Lit., *in the middle of the throne and of the four living creatures, and in the middle of the elders* [a]Rev. 4:4; 5:8, 14 [b]John 1:29; Rev. 5:8, 12f.; 13:8 [c]Rev. 5:9, 12; 13:8 [d]Dan. 8:3f. [e]Zech. 3:9; 4:10 [f]Rev. 1:4
7 [a]Rev. 5:1
8 [1]Or, *scroll* [2]Or, *holy ones* [a]Rev. 4:6; 5:6, 11, 14 [b]Rev. 4:4; 5:14 [c]Rev. 4:10 [d]John 1:29; Rev. 5:6, 12f.; 13:8 [e]Rev. 14:2; 15:2 [f]Rev. 15:7 [g]Ps. 141:2; Rev. 8:3f.
9 [1]Or, *scroll* [a]Ps. 33:3; 40:3; 98:1; 149:1; Is. 42:10; Rev. 14:3; 15:3 [b]Rev. 4:11 [c]Rev. 5:6, 12; 13:8 [d]1 Cor. 6:20; Rev. 14:3f. [e]Dan. 3:4; 5:19; Rev. 7:9; 10:11; 11:9; 13:7; 14:6; 17:15
10 [a]Rev. 1:6 [b]Rev. 3:21; 20:4
11 [a]Rev. 4:4 [b]Rev. 4:6; 5:6, 8, 14 [c]Rev. 4:4; 5:6, 14 [d]Dan. 7:10; Heb. 12:22; Jude 14; Rev. 9:16
12 [a]Rev. 1:6; 4:11; 5:9 [b]John 1:29; Rev. 5:6, 13; 13:8
13 [a]Phil. 2:10; Rev. 5:3 [b]Rev. 5:1 [c]John 1:29; Rev. 5:6, 12f.; 13:8 [d]Rom. 11:36; Rev. 1:6
14 [a]Rev. 4:6; 5:6, 8, 11 [b]1 Cor. 14:16; Rev. 7:12; 19:4 [c]Rev. 4:4; 5:6, 8 [d]Rev. 4:10

1 [1]Some mss. add *and see* [a]John 1:29; Rev. 5:6, 12f.; 13:8 [b]Rev. 5:1 [c]Rev. 4:6; 5:6, 8, 11, 14 [d]Rev. 14:2; 19:6

the [b]living creatures and the [c]elders; and
the number of them was [d]myriads of
myriads, and thousands of thousands,
12 saying with a loud voice,
"[a]Worthy is the [b]Lamb that was
[b]slain to receive power and riches
and wisdom and might and honor
and glory and blessing."
13 And [a]every created thing which is
in heaven and on the earth and under
the earth and on the sea, and all things
in them, I heard saying,
"To Him who [b]sits on the throne,
and to the [c]Lamb, [d]*be* blessing
and honor and glory and dominion forever and ever."
14 And the [a]four living creatures kept
saying, "[b]Amen." And the [c]elders [d]fell
down and worshiped.

The Book Opened
The First Seal—False Christ

6 AND I saw when the [a]Lamb broke
one of the [b]seven seals, and I heard
one of the [c]four living creatures saying
as with a [d]voice of thunder, "Come[1]."
2 And I looked, and behold, a [a]white
horse, and he who sat on it had a bow;
and [b]a crown was given to him; and he
went out [c]conquering, and to conquer.

The Second Seal—War

3 And when He broke the second
seal, I heard the [a]second living creature
saying, "Come[1]."
4 And another, [a]a red horse, went
out; and to him who sat on it, it was
granted to [b]take peace from the earth,
and that *men* should slay one another;
and a great sword was given to him.

The Third Seal—Famine

5 And when He broke the third seal,
I heard the [a]third living creature saying,
"Come[1]." And I looked, and behold, a
[b]black horse; and he who sat on it had a
[c]pair of scales in his hand.
6 And I heard as it were a voice in
the center of the [a]four living creatures
saying, "A [1]quart of wheat for a [2]denar-
ius, and three [1]quarts of barley for a
[2]denarius; and [b]do not harm the oil and
the wine."

The Fourth Seal—Death

7 And when He broke the fourth
seal, I heard the voice of the [a]fourth
living creature saying, "Come[1]."

2 [a]Zech. 1:8; 6:3f.; Rev. 19:11 [b]Zech. 6:11; Rev. 9:7; 14:14; 19:12 [c]Rev. 3:21
3 [1]Some mss. add *and see* [a]Rev. 4:7
4 [a]Zech. 1:8; 6:2 [b]Matt. 10:34
5 [1]Some mss. add *and see* [a]Rev. 4:7 [b]Zech. 6:2, 6 [c]Ezek. 4:16
6 [1]Gr., *choenix;* i.e., a dry measure almost equal to a qt. [2]The denarius was equivalent to one day's wage [a]Rev. 4:6f. [b]Rev. 7:3; 9:4
7 [1]Some mss. add *and see* [a]Rev. 4:7

8 And I looked, and behold, an
[1a]ashen horse; and he who sat on it had
the name [b]Death; and [b]Hades was following with him. And authority was
given to them over a fourth of the earth,
[c]to kill with sword and with famine and
with [2]pestilence and by the wild beasts
of the earth.

The Fifth Seal—Martyrs

9 And when He broke the fifth seal, I
saw [a]underneath the [b]altar the [c]souls of
those who had been slain [d]because of the
word of God, and because of the [e]testi-
mony which they had maintained;
10 and they cried out with a loud
voice, saying, "[a]How long, O [1b]Lord,
[c]holy and true, [2]wilt Thou refrain from
[d]judging and avenging our blood on
[e]those who dwell on the earth?"
11 And [a]there was given to each of
them a white robe; and they were told
that they should [b]rest for a little while
longer, [c]until *the number of* their fellow
servants and their brethren who were to
be killed even as they had been, should
be [d]completed also.

The Sixth Seal—Terror

12 And I looked when He broke the
sixth seal, and there was a great [a]earth-
quake; and the [b]sun became black as
[c]sackcloth *made* of hair, and the whole
moon became like blood;
13 and [a]the stars of the sky fell to the
earth, [b]as a fig tree casts its unripe figs
when shaken by a great wind.
14 And [a]the sky was split apart like a
scroll when it is rolled up; and [b]every
mountain and island were moved out of
their places.
15 And [a]the kings of the earth and the
great men and the [1]commanders and the
rich and the strong and every slave and
free man, hid themselves in the caves
and among the rocks of the mountains;
16 and they *[a]said to the mountains
and to the rocks, "Fall on us and hide us
from the [1]presence of Him [b]who sits on
the throne, and from the [c]wrath of the
Lamb;
17 for [a]the great day of their wrath has
come; and [b]who is able to stand?"

An Interlude

7 AFTER this I saw [a]four angels
standing at the [b]four corners of the
earth, holding back [c]the four winds of
the earth, [d]so that no wind should blow
on the earth or on the sea or on any tree.
2 And I saw another angel ascending
[a]from the rising of the sun, having the
[b]seal of [c]the living God; and he cried out
with a loud voice to the [d]four angels to
whom it was granted to harm the earth
and the sea,
3 saying, "[a]Do not harm the earth or
the sea or the trees, until we have [b]sealed
the bond-servants of our God on their
[c]foreheads."

A Remnant of Israel—144,000

4 And I heard the [a]number of those
who were sealed, [b]one hundred and
forty-four thousand sealed from every
tribe of the sons of Israel:
5 from the tribe of Judah, twelve
thousand *were* sealed, from the tribe of
Reuben twelve thousand, from the tribe
of Gad twelve thousand,
6 from the tribe of Asher twelve
thousand, from the tribe of Naphtali
twelve thousand, from the tribe of Manasseh twelve thousand,
7 from the tribe of Simeon twelve
thousand, from the tribe of Levi twelve
thousand, from the tribe of Issachar
twelve thousand,
8 from the tribe of Zebulun twelve
thousand, from the tribe of Joseph
twelve thousand, from the tribe of Benjamin, twelve thousand *were* sealed.

A Multitude from the Tribulation

9 After these things I looked, and
behold, a great multitude, which no one
could count, from [a]every nation and *all*
tribes and peoples and tongues, standing
[b]before the throne and [c]before the
Lamb, clothed in [d]white robes, and
[e]palm branches *were* in their hands;
10 and they cry out with a loud voice,
saying,
"[a]Salvation to our God [b]who sits on
the throne, and to the Lamb."
11 And all the angels were standing
[a]around the throne and *around* [a]the
elders and the [b]four living creatures; and
they [c]fell on their faces before the throne
and worshiped God,
12 saying,
"[a]Amen, [b]blessing and glory and wisdom and thanksgiving and honor and
power and might, *be* to our God forever
and ever. [a]Amen."
13 And one of the elders [a]answered,
saying to me, "These who are clothed in
the [b]white robes, who are they, and from
where have they come?"
14 And I [1]said to him, "My lord, you
know." And he said to me, "These are
the ones who come out of the [a]great
tribulation, and they have [b]washed their
robes and made them [c]white in the
[d]blood of the Lamb.
15 "For this reason, they are [a]before
the throne of God; and they [b]serve Him
day and night in His [1c]temple; and [d]He
who sits on the throne shall spread His
[e]tabernacle over them.
16 "[a]They shall hunger no more, neither thirst anymore; neither shall the sun
[1]beat down on them, nor any heat;

8 [1]Or, *sickly pale* [2]Or, *death* [a]Zech. 6:3 [b]Prov. 5:5; Hos. 13:14; Matt. 11:23; Rev. 1:18; 20:13f. [c]Jer. 14:12; 15:2f.; 24:10; 29:17f.; Ezek. 5:12, 17; 14:21; 29:5
9 [a]Ex. 29:12; Lev. 4:7; John 16:2 [b]Rev. 14:18; 16:7 [c]Rev. 20:4 [d]Rev. 1:2, 9 [e]Rev. 12:17
10 [1]Or, *Master* [2]Lit., *dost Thou not judge and avenge* [a]Zech. 1:12 [b]Luke 2:29; 2 Pet. 2:1 [c]Rev. 3:7 [d]Deut. 32:43; Ps. 79:10; Luke 18:7; Rev. 19:2 [e]Rev. 3:10
11 [a]Rev. 3:4, 5; 7:9 [b]2 Thess. 1:7; Heb. 4:10; Rev. 14:13 [c]Heb. 11:40 [d]Acts 20:24; 2 Tim. 4:7
12 [a]Matt. 24:7; Rev. 8:5; 11:13; 16:18 [b]Is. 13:10; Joel 2:10, 31; 3:15; Matt. 24:29; Mark 13:24 [c]Is. 50:3; Matt. 11:21
13 [a]Matt. 24:29; Mark 13:25; Rev. 8:10; 9:1 [b]Is. 34:4
14 [a]Is. 34:4; 2 Pet. 3:10; Rev. 20:11; 21:1 [b]Is. 54:10; Jer. 4:24; Ezek. 38:20; Nah. 1:5; Rev. 16:20
15 [1]I.e., chiliarchs, in command of one thousand troops [a]Is. 2:10f., 19, 21; 24:21; Rev. 19:18
16 [1]Lit., *face* [a]Hos. 10:8; Luke 23:30; Rev. 9:6 [b]Rev. 4:9; 5:1 [c]Mark 3:5
17 [a]Is. 63:4; Jer. 30:7; Joel 1:15; 2:1f., 11, 31; Zeph. 1:14f.; Rev. 16:14 [b]Ps. 76:7; Nah. 1:6; Mal. 3:2; Luke 21:36

1 [a]Rev. 9:14 [b]Is. 11:12; Ezek. 7:2; Rev. 20:8 [c]Jer. 49:36; Dan. 7:2; Zech. 6:5; Matt. 24:31 [d]Rev. 7:3; 8:7; 9:4
2 [a]Is. 41:2 [b]Rev. 7:3; 9:4 [c]Matt. 16:16 [d]Rev. 9:14
3 [a]Rev. 6:6 [b]John 3:33; Rev. 7:3-8 [c]Ezek. 9:4, 6; Rev. 13:16; 14:1, 9; 20:4; 22:4
4 [a]Rev. 9:16 [b]Rev. 14:1, 3
9 [a]Rev. 5:9 [b]Rev. 7:15 [c]Rev. 22:3 [d]Rev. 6:11; 7:14 [e]Lev. 23:40
10 [a]Ps. 3:8; Rev. 12:10; 19:1 [b]Rev. 22:3
11 [a]Rev. 4:4 [b]Rev. 4:6 [c]Rev. 4:10
12 [a]Rev. 5:14 [b]Rev. 5:12
13 [a]Acts 3:12 [b]Rev. 7:9

14 [1]Lit., *have said* [a]Dan. 12:1; Matt. 24:21; Mark 13:19 [b]Zech. 3:3-5; Rev. 22:14 [c]Rev. 6:11; 7:9 [d]Heb. 9:14; 1 John 1:7
15 [1]Or, *sanctuary* [a]Rev. 7:9 [b]Rev. 4:8f.; 22:3 [c]Rev. 11:19; 21:22 [d]Rev. 4:9 [e]Lev. 26:11; Ezek. 37:27; John 1:14; Rev. 21:3
16 [1]Lit., *fall* [a]Ps. 121:5f.; Is. 49:10

17 for the Lamb in the center of the
throne shall be their [a]shepherd, and shall
guide them to springs of the [1b]water of
life; and [c]God shall wipe every tear from
their eyes."

The Seventh Seal—the Trumpets

8 AND when He broke the [a]seventh
seal, there was silence in heaven for
about half an hour.
2 And I saw [a]the seven angels who
stand before God; and seven [b]trumpets
were given to them.
3 And [a]another angel came and
stood at the [b]altar, holding a [c]golden
censer; and much [d]incense was given to
him, that he might [1]add it to the [d]pray-
ers of all the [2]saints upon the [e]golden
altar which was before the throne.
4 And [a]the smoke of the incense,
[1]with the prayers of the [2]saints, went up
before God out of the angel's hand.
5 And the angel took the censer; and
he [a]filled it with the fire of the altar and
[b]threw it to the earth; and there followed
[c]peals of thunder and sounds and flashes
of lightning and an [d]earthquake.
6 [a]And the seven angels who had the
seven trumpets prepared themselves to
sound them.
7 And the first sounded, and there
came [a]hail and fire, mixed with blood,
and they were thrown to the earth; and
[b]a third of the earth was burned up, and
[b]a third of the [c]trees were burned up,
and all the green [c]grass was burned up.
8 And the second angel sounded, and
something like a great [a]mountain burning with fire was thrown into the sea;
and [b]a third of the [c]sea became blood;
9 and [a]a third of the creatures, which
were in the sea [1]and had life, died; and a
third of the [b]ships were destroyed.
10 And the third angel sounded, and a
great star [a]fell from heaven, burning like
a torch, and it fell on a [b]third of the
rivers and on the [c]springs of waters;
11 and the name of the star is called
Wormwood; and a [a]third of the waters
became [b]wormwood; and many men
died from the waters, because they were
made bitter.
12 And the fourth angel sounded, and
a [a]third of the [b]sun and a third of the
[b]moon and a [a]third of the [b]stars were
smitten, so that a [a]third of them might
be darkened and the day might not shine
for a [a]third of it, and the night in the
same way.
13 And I looked, and I heard [1]an
eagle flying in [a]midheaven, saying with a
loud voice, "[b]Woe, woe, woe, to [c]those
who dwell on the earth, because of the
remaining blasts of the trumpet of the
[d]three angels who are about to sound!"

The Fifth Trumpet—the Bottomless Pit

9 AND the [a]fifth angel sounded, and I
saw a [b]star from heaven which had
fallen to the earth; and the [c]key of the
[1d]bottomless pit was given to him.

17 [1]Lit., *waters* [a]Ps. 23:1f.; Matt. 2:6; John 10:11 [b]John 4:14; Rev. 21:6; 22:1 [c]Is. 25:8; Matt. 5:4; Rev. 21:4

1 [a]Rev. 5:1; 6:1, 3, 5, 7, 9, 12
2 [a]Rev. 1:4; 8:6-13; 9:1, 13; 11:15 [b]1 Cor. 15:52; 1 Thess. 4:16
3 [1]Lit., *give* [2]Or, *holy ones* [a]Rev. 7:2 [b]Amos 9:1; Rev. 6:9 [c]Heb. 9:4 [d]Ex. 30:1; Rev. 5:8 [e]Ex. 30:3; Num. 4:11; Rev. 8:5; 9:13
4 [1]Or, *for* [2]V. 3, note 2 [a]Ps. 141:2
5 [a]Lev. 16:12 [b]Ezek. 10:2 [c]Ex. 19:16; Rev. 4:5; 11:19; 16:18 [d]Rev. 6:12
6 [a]Rev. 8:2
7 [a]Ex. 9:23ff.; Is. 28:2; Ezek. 38:22; Joel 2:30 [b]Zech. 13:8, 9; Rev. 8:7-12; 9:15, 18; 12:4 [c]Rev. 9:4
8 [a]Jer. 51:25 [b]Zech. 13:8, 9; Rev. 8:7-12; 9:15, 18; 12:4 [c]Ex. 7:17ff.; Rev. 11:6; 16:3
9 [1]Lit., *those which had* [a]Zech. 13:8, 9; Rev. 8:7-12; 9:15, 18; 12:4 [b]Is. 2:16
10 [a]Is. 14:12; Rev. 6:13; 9:1 [b]Zech. 13:8, 9; Rev. 8:7-12; 9:15, 18; 12:4 [c]Rev. 14:7; 16:4
11 [a]Zech. 13:8, 9; Rev. 8:7-12; 9:15, 18; 12:4 [b]Jer. 9:15; 23:15
12 [a]Zech. 13:8, 9; Rev. 8:7-12; 9:15, 18; 12:4 [b]Ex. 10:21ff.; Is. 13:10; Ezek. 32:7; Joel 2:10, 31; 3:15; Rev. 6:12f.
13 [1]Lit., *one eagle* [a]Rev. 14:6; 19:17 [b]Rev. 9:12; 11:14; 12:12 [c]Rev. 3:10 [d]Rev. 8:2

1 [1]Lit., *shaft of the abyss* [a]Rev. 8:2 [b]Rev. 8:10 [c]Rev. 1:18 [d]Luke 8:31; Rev. 9:2, 11
2 [1]V. 1, note 1 [a]Gen. 19:28; Ex. 19:18 [b]Joel 2:2, 10
3 [1]Lit., *into* [a]Ex. 10:12-15; Rev. 9:7 [b]2 Chr. 10:11, 14; Ezek. 2:6; Rev. 9:5, 10
4 [a]Rev. 6:6 [b]Rev. 8:7 [c]Ezek. 9:4; Rev. 7:2, 3
5 [1]Lit., *it was given to them* [2]Lit., *them* [3]Lit., *strikes* [a]Rev. 9:10 [b]2 Chr. 10:11, 14; Ezek. 2:6; Rev. 9:3, 10
6 [a]Job 3:21; 7:15; Jer. 8:3; Rev. 6:16
7 [1]Lit., *appearances* [a]Joel 2:4
8 [a]Joel 1:6
9 [a]Jer. 47:3; Joel 2:5

2 And he opened the [1]bottomless pit;
and [a]smoke went up out of the pit, like
the smoke of a great furnace; and [b]the
sun and the air were darkened by the
smoke of the pit.
3 And out of the smoke came forth
[a]locusts [1]upon the earth; and power was
given them, as the [b]scorpions of the
earth have power.
4 And they were told that they
should not [a]hurt the [b]grass of the earth,
nor any green thing, nor any tree, but
only the men who do not have the [c]seal
of God on their foreheads.
5 And [1]they were not permitted to
kill [2]anyone, but to torment for [a]five
months; and their torment was like the
torment of a [b]scorpion when it [3]stings a
man.
6 And in those days [a]men will seek
death and will not find it; and they will
long to die and death flees from them.
7 And the [1a]appearance of the locusts was like horses prepared for battle;
and on their heads, as it were, crowns
like gold, and their faces were like the
faces of men.
8 And they had hair like the hair of
women, and their [a]teeth were like *the
teeth* of lions.
9 And they had breastplates like
breastplates of iron; and the [a]sound of
their wings was like the sound of chariots, of many horses rushing to battle.
10 And they have tails like [a]scorpions,
and stings; and in their [b]tails is their
power to hurt men for [c]five months.
11 They have as king over them, the
angel of the [a]abyss; his name in [b]He-
brew is [1c]Abaddon, and in the Greek he
has the name [2]Apollyon.
12 [a]The first woe is past; behold, two
woes are still coming after these things.

The Sixth Trumpet—Army from the East

13 And the sixth angel sounded, and I
heard [1]a voice from the [2]four [a]horns of
the [b]golden altar which is before God,
14 one saying to the sixth angel who
had the trumpet, "Release the [a]four
angels who are bound at the [b]great river
Euphrates."
15 And the four angels, who had been
prepared for the hour and day and
month and year, were [a]released, so that
they might kill a [b]third of [1]mankind.
16 And the number of the armies of
the horsemen was [a]two hundred million;
[b]I heard the number of them.

10 [a]2 Chr. 10:11, 14; Ezek. 2:6; Rev. 9:3, 5 [b]Rev. 9:19 [c]Rev. 9:5
11 [1]I.e., destruction [2]I.e., destroyer [a]Luke 8:31; Rev. 9:1, 2 [b]John 5:2; Rev. 16:16 [c]Job 26:6; 28:22; 31:12; Ps. 88:11 mg.; Prov. 15:11
12 [a]Rev. 8:13; 11:14
13 [1]Lit., *one voice* [2]Some ancient mss. do not contain *four* [a]Ex. 30:2f., 10 [b]Rev. 8:3
14 [a]Rev. 7:1 [b]Gen. 15:18; Deut. 1:7; Josh. 1:4; Rev. 16:12
15 [1]Lit., *men* [a]Rev. 20:7 [b]Rev. 8:7; 9:18
16 [a]Rev. 5:11 [b]Rev. 7:4

17 And [1]this is how I saw [a]in the vision the horses and those who sat on them: *the riders* had breastplates *the color* of fire and of hyacinth and of [2][b]brimstone; and the heads of the horses are like the heads of lions; and [c]out of their mouths proceed fire and smoke and [2][b]brimstone.

18 A [a]third of [1]mankind was killed by these three plagues, by the [b]fire and the smoke and the [2]brimstone, which proceeded out of their mouths.

19 For the power of the horses is in their mouths and in their tails; for their tails are like serpents and have heads; and with them they do harm.

20 And the rest of [1]mankind, who were not killed by these plagues, [a]did not repent of [b]the works of their hands, so as not to [c]worship demons, and [d]the idols of gold and of silver and of brass and of stone and of wood, which can neither see nor hear nor walk;

21 and they [a]did not repent of their murders nor of their [b]sorceries nor of their [c]immorality nor of their thefts.

The Angel and the Little Book

10 AND I saw another [a]strong angel [b]coming down out of heaven, clothed with a cloud; and the [c]rainbow was upon his head, and [d]his face was like the sun, and his [e]feet like pillars of fire;

2 and he had in his hand a [a]little book which was open. And he placed [b]his right foot on the sea and his left on the land;

3 and he cried out with a loud voice, [a]as when a lion roars; and when he had cried out, the [b]seven peals of thunder [1]uttered their voices.

4 And when the seven peals of thunder had spoken, [a]I was about to write; and I [b]heard a voice from heaven saying, "[c]Seal up the things which the seven peals of thunder have spoken, and do not write them."

5 And the angel whom I saw standing on the sea and on the land [a]lifted up his right hand to heaven,

6 [a]and swore by [b]Him who lives forever and ever, [c]WHO CREATED HEAVEN AND THE THINGS IN IT, AND THE EARTH AND THE THINGS IN IT, AND THE SEA AND THE THINGS IN IT, that [d]there shall be delay no longer,

7 but in the days of the voice of the [a]seventh angel, when he is about to sound, then [b]the mystery of God is finished, as He [1]preached to His servants the prophets.

8 And [a]the voice which I heard from heaven, *I heard* again speaking with me, and saying, "Go, take [b]the [1]book which is open in the hand of the angel who [b]stands on the sea and on the land."

9 And I went to the angel, telling him to give me the little book. And he *said to me, "[a]Take it, and eat it; and it will make your stomach bitter, but in your mouth it will be sweet as honey."

10 And I took the little book out of the angel's hand and ate it, and it was in my mouth sweet as honey; and when I had eaten it, my stomach was made bitter.

11 And [a]they *said to me, "You must [b]prophesy again concerning [c]many peoples and nations and tongues and [d]kings."

The Two Witnesses

11 AND there was given me a [1][a]measuring rod like a staff; [2]and [b]someone said, "Rise and measure the [3]temple of God, and the altar, and those who worship in it.

2 "And [1]leave out the [a]court which is outside the [2]temple, and do not measure it, for [b]it has been given to the nations; and they will [b]tread under foot [c]the holy city for [d]forty-two months.

3 "And I will grant *authority* to my two [a]witnesses, and they will prophesy for [b]twelve hundred and sixty days, clothed in [c]sackcloth."

4 These are the [a]two olive trees and the two lampstands that stand before the Lord of the earth.

5 And if anyone desires to harm them, [a]fire proceeds out of their mouth and devours their enemies; and if anyone would desire to harm them, [b]in this manner he must be killed.

6 These have the power to [a]shut up the sky, in order that rain may not fall during [b]the days of their prophesying; and they have power over the waters to [c]turn them into blood, and [d]to smite the earth with every plague, as often as they desire.

7 And when they have finished their testimony, [a]the beast that comes up out of the [b]abyss will [c]make war with them, and overcome them and kill them.

8 And their dead [1]bodies *will lie* in the street of the [a]great city which [2]mystically is called [b]Sodom and [c]Egypt, where also their Lord was crucified.

9 And those from [a]the peoples and tribes and tongues and nations *will* look at their dead [1]bodies for three and a half days, and [2][b]will not permit their dead bodies to be laid in a tomb.

10 And [a]those who dwell on the earth *will* rejoice over them and make merry; and they will [b]send gifts to one another, because these two prophets tormented [a]those who dwell on the earth.

11 And after the three and a half days [a]the breath of life from God came into them, and they stood on their feet; and

17 [1]Lit., *thus I saw* [2]Or, *sulphur* [a]Dan. 8:2; 9:21 [b]Rev. 9:18; 14:10; 19:20; 20:10; 21:8 [c]Rev. 11:5
18 [1]Lit., *men* [2]Or, *sulphur* [a]Rev. 8:7; 9:15 [b]Rev. 9:17
20 [1]Lit., *men* [a]Rev. 2:21 [b]Deut. 4:28; Jer. 1:16; Mic. 5:13; Acts 7:41 [c]1 Cor. 10:20 [d]Ps. 115:4-7; 135:15-17; Dan. 5:23
21 [a]Rev. 9:20 [b]Is. 47:9, 12; Rev. 18:23 [c]Rev. 17:2, 4, 5

1 [a]Rev. 5:2 [b]Rev. 18:1; 20:1 [c]Rev. 4:3 [d]Matt. 17:2; Rev. 1:16 [e]Rev. 1:15
2 [a]Rev. 5:1; 10:8-10 [b]Rev. 10:5, 8
3 [1]Or, *spoke* [a]Is. 31:4; Hos. 11:10 [b]Ps. 29:3-9; Rev. 4:5
4 [a]Rev. 1:11, 19 [b]Rev. 10:8 [c]Dan. 8:26; 12:4, 9; Rev. 22:10
5 [a]Deut. 32:40; Dan. 12:7
6 [a]Gen. 14:22; Ex. 6:8; Num. 14:30; Ezek. 20:5 [b]Rev. 4:9 [c]Ex. 20:11; Rev. 4:11 [d]Rev. 6:11; 12:12; 16:17; 21:6
7 [1]Lit., *preached the gospel* [a]Rev. 11:15 [b]Amos 3:7; Rom. 16:25
8 [1]Or, *scroll* [a]Rev. 10:4 [b]Rev. 10:2
9 [a]Jer. 15:16; Ezek. 2:8; 3:1-3
11 [a]Rev. 11:1 [b]Ezek. 37:4, 9 [c]Rev. 5:9 [d]Rev. 17:10, 12

1 [1]Lit., *reed* [2]Lit., *saying* [3]Or, *sanctuary* [a]Ezek. 40:3-42:20; Zech. 2:1; Rev. 21:15f. [b]Rev. 10:11
2 [1]Lit., *throw out* [2]Or, *sanctuary* [a]Ezek. 40:17, 20 [b]Luke 21:24 [c]Is. 52:1; Matt. 4:5; 27:53; Rev. 21:2, 10; 22:19 [d]Dan. 7:25; 12:7; Rev. 12:6; 13:5
3 [a]Rev. 1:5; 2:13 [b]Dan. 7:25; 12:7; Rev. 12:6; 13:5 [c]Gen. 37:34; 2 Sam. 3:31; 1 Kin. 21:27; 2 Kin. 19:1f.; Neh. 9:1; Esth. 4:1; Ps. 69:11; Joel 1:13; Jon. 3:5f., 8
4 [a]Ps. 52:8; Jer. 11:16; Zech. 4:3, 11, 14
5 [a]2 Kin. 1:10-12; Jer. 5:14; Rev. 9:17f. [b]Num. 16:29, 35
6 [a]1 Kin. 17:1; Luke 4:25 [b]Rev. 11:3 [c]Ex. 7:17ff.; Rev. 8:8 [d]1 Sam. 4:8
7 [a]Rev. 13:1ff.; 17:8 [b]Rev. 9:1 [c]Dan. 7:21; Rev. 13:7

8 [1]Some ancient mss. read *body* [2]Lit., *spiritually* [a]Rev. 14:8; 16:19; 17:18; 18:2, 10, 16, 18, 19, 21 [b]Is. 1:9, 10; 3:9; Jer. 23:14; Ezek. 16:46, 49 [c]Ezek. 23:3, 8, 19, 27
9 [1]Lit., *body* [2]Lit., *do not permit* [a]Rev. 5:9; 10:11 [b]1 Kin. 13:22; Ps. 79:2f.
10 [a]Rev. 3:10 [b]Neh. 8:10, 12; Esth. 9:19, 22
11 [a]Ezek. 37:5, 9, 10, 14

great fear fell upon those who were beholding them.

12 And they heard a loud voice from heaven saying to them, "[a]Come up here." And they [b]went up into heaven in the cloud, and their enemies beheld them.

13 And in that hour there was a great [a]earthquake, and a tenth of the city fell; and [1]seven thousand people were killed in the earthquake, and the rest were terrified and [b]gave glory to the [c]God of heaven.

14 The second [a]woe is past; behold, the third woe is coming quickly.

The Seventh Trumpet—Christ's Reign Foreseen

15 And the [a]seventh angel sounded; and there arose [b]loud voices in heaven, saying,

"[c]The kingdom of the world has become *the kingdom* of our Lord, and of [d]His [1]Christ; and [e]He will reign forever and ever."

16 And the twenty-four elders, who [a]sit on their thrones before God, [b]fell on their faces and worshiped God,

17 saying,

"We give Thee thanks, [a]O Lord God, the Almighty, who art and who wast, because Thou hast taken Thy great power and [1]hast begun to [b]reign.

18 "And [a]the nations were enraged, and [b]Thy wrath came, and [c]the time *came* for the dead to be judged, and *the time* to give their reward to Thy [d]bond-servants the prophets and to the [1]saints and to those who fear Thy name, [e]the small and the great, and to destroy those who destroy the earth."

19 And [a]the [1]temple of God which is in heaven was opened; and [b]the ark of His covenant appeared in His [1]temple, and there were flashes of [c]lightning and sounds and peals of thunder and an earthquake and a [d]great [2]hailstorm.

The Woman, Israel

12 AND a great [a]sign appeared [b]in heaven: [c]a woman [d]clothed with the sun, and the moon under her feet, and on her head a crown of twelve stars;

2 and she was with child; and she *[a]cried out, being in labor and in pain to give birth.

The Red Dragon, Satan

3 And [a]another sign appeared in heaven: and behold, a great red [b]dragon having [c]seven heads and [d]ten horns, and on his heads *were* [e]seven diadems.

4 And his tail *swept away a [a]third of the stars of heaven, and [b]threw them to the earth. And the [c]dragon stood before the woman who was about to give birth, so that when she gave birth [d]he might devour her child.

The Male Child, Christ

5 And [a]she gave birth to a son, a male *child,* who is to [1][b]rule all the [2]nations with a rod of iron; and her child was [c]caught up to God and to His throne.

6 And the woman fled into the wilderness where she *had a place prepared by God, so that there [1]she might be nourished for [a]one thousand two hundred and sixty days.

The Angel, Michael

7 And there was war in heaven, [a]Michael and his angels waging war with the [b]dragon. And the dragon and [c]his angels waged war,

8 and they were not strong enough, and there was no longer a place found for them in heaven.

9 And the great [a]dragon was thrown down, the [b]serpent of old who is called the devil and [c]Satan, who [d]deceives the whole [1]world; he was [e]thrown down to the earth, and his angels were thrown down with him.

10 And I heard [a]a loud voice in heaven, saying,

"Now the [b]salvation, and the power, and the [a]kingdom of our God and the authority of His Christ have come, for the [c]accuser of our brethren has been thrown down, who accuses them before our God day and night.

11 "And they [a]overcame him because of [b]the blood of the Lamb and because of [c]the word of their testimony, and they [d]did not love their life even to death.

12 "For this reason, [a]rejoice, O heavens and [b]you who [1]dwell in them. [c]Woe to the earth and the sea, because [d]the devil has come down to you, having great wrath, knowing that he has *only* [e]a short time."

13 And when the [a]dragon saw that he was thrown down to the earth, he persecuted [b]the woman who gave birth to the male *child.*

14 And the [a]two wings of the great eagle were given to the woman, in order that she might fly [b]into the wilderness to her place, where she *was nourished for [c]a time and times and half a time, from the [1]presence of the serpent.

15 And the [a]serpent [1]poured water like a river out of his mouth after the woman, so that he might cause her to be swept away with the flood.

16 And the earth helped the woman, and the earth opened its mouth and drank up the river which the dragon [1]poured out of his mouth.

12 [a]Rev. 4:1 [b]2 Kin. 2:11; Acts 1:9
13 [1]Lit., *names of men, seven thousand* [a]Rev. 6:12; 8:5; 11:19; 16:18 [b]John 9:24; Rev. 14:7; 16:9; 19:7 [c]Rev. 16:11
14 [a]Rev. 8:13; 9:12
15 [1]I.e., Messiah [a]Rev. 8:2; 10:7 [b]Rev. 16:17; 19:1 [c]Rev. 12:10 [d]Ps. 2:2; Acts 4:26 [e]Ex. 15:18; Dan. 2:44; 7:14, 27; Luke 1:33
16 [a]Matt. 19:28; Rev. 4:4 [b]Rev. 4:10
17 [1]Lit., *didst reign* [a]Rev. 1:8 [b]Rev. 19:6
18 [1]Or, *holy ones* [a]Ps. 2:1 [b]Ps. 2:5; 110:5 [c]Dan. 7:10; Rev. 20:12 [d]Rev. 10:7; 16:6 [e]Ps. 115:13; Rev. 13:16; 19:5
19 [1]Or, *sanctuary* [2]Lit., *hail* [a]Rev. 4:1; 15:5 [b]Heb. 9:4 [c]Rev. 4:5; 8:5; 16:18 [d]Rev. 16:21

1 [a]Matt. 24:30; Rev. 12:3 [b]Rev. 11:19 [c]Gal. 4:26 [d]Ps. 104:2; Song 6:10
2 [a]Is. 26:17; 66:6-9; Mic. 4:9f.
3 [a]Rev. 12:1; 15:1 [b]Is. 27:1; Rev. 12:4, 7, 9, 13, 16f.; 13:2, 4, 11; 16:13; 20:2 [c]Rev. 13:1; 17:3, 7, 9ff. [d]Dan. 7:7, 20, 24; Rev. 13:1; 17:12, 16 [e]Rev. 13:1; 19:12
4 [a]Rev. 8:7, 12 [b]Dan. 8:10 [c]Is. 27:1; Rev. 12:3, 7, 9, 13, 16f.; 13:2, 4, 11; 16:13; 20:2 [d]Matt. 2:16
5 [1]Or, *shepherd* [2]Or, *Gentiles* [a]Is. 66:7 [b]Ps. 2:9; Rev. 2:27 [c]2 Cor. 12:2ff.
6 [1]Lit., *they may nourish her for* [a]Rev. 11:3; 13:5
7 [a]Dan. 10:13, 21; 12:1; Jude 9 [b]Rev. 12:3 [c]Matt. 25:41
9 [1]Lit., *inhabited earth* [a]Rev. 12:3 [b]Gen. 3:1; 2 Cor. 11:3; Rev. 12:15; 20:2 [c]Matt. 4:10; 25:41 [d]Rev. 13:14; 20:3, 8, 10 [e]Luke 10:18; John 12:31
10 [a]Rev. 11:15 [b]Rev. 7:10 [c]Job 1:11; 2:5; Zech. 3:1; Luke 22:31; 1 Pet. 5:8
11 [a]John 16:33; 1 John 2:13; Rev. 15:2 [b]Rev. 7:14 [c]Rev. 6:9 [d]Luke 14:26; Rev. 2:10
12 [1]Or, *tabernacle* [a]Ps. 96:11; Is. 44:23; Rev. 18:20 [b]Rev. 13:6 [c]Rev. 8:13 [d]Rev. 12:9 [e]Rev. 10:6
13 [a]Rev. 12:3 [b]Rev. 12:5
14 [1]Lit., *face* [a]Ex. 19:4; Deut. 32:11; Is. 40:31 [b]Rev. 12:6 [c]Dan. 7:25; 12:7
15 [1]Lit., *threw* [a]Gen. 3:1; 2 Cor. 11:3; Rev. 12:9; 20:2
16 [1]Lit., *threw*

17 And the dragon was enraged with
the woman, and went off to [a]make war
with the rest of her [b]offspring, who [c]keep
the commandments of God and [d]hold to
the testimony of Jesus.

The Beast from the Sea

13 AND [1]he stood on the sand of
the [2]seashore.
And I saw a [a]beast coming up out of
the sea, having [b]ten horns and [b]seven
heads, and on his horns *were* [c]ten diadems, and on his heads *were* [d]blasphe-
mous names.
2 And the beast which I saw was
[a]like a leopard, and his feet were *like*
those of [b]a bear, and his mouth like the
mouth of [c]a lion. And the [d]dragon gave
him his power and his [e]throne and great
authority.
3 And *I saw* one of his heads as if it
had been [1]slain, and his [a]fatal wound
was healed. And the whole earth [b]was
amazed *and followed* after the beast;
4 and they worshiped the [a]dragon,
because he [a]gave his authority to the
beast; and they worshiped the beast,
saying, "[b]Who is like the beast, and who
is able to wage war with him?"
5 And there was given to him a
mouth [a]speaking [1]arrogant words and
blasphemies; and authority to [2]act for
[b]forty-two months was given to him.
6 And he opened his mouth in blasphemies against God, to blaspheme His
name and His tabernacle, *that is,* [a]those
who [1]dwell in heaven.
7 And it was given to him to [a]make
war with the [1]saints and to overcome
them; and authority over [b]every tribe
and people and tongue and nation was
given to him.
8 And all who [a]dwell on the earth
will worship him, *everyone* [b]whose name
has not been [1]written [c]from the foundation of the world in the [d]book of life of
[e]the Lamb who has been slain.
9 [a]If anyone has an ear, let him hear.
10 [a]If anyone [1]*is destined* for captivity,
to captivity he goes; [b]if anyone kills with
the sword, with the sword he must be
killed. Here is [c]the [2]perseverance and the
faith of the [3]saints.

The Beast from the Earth

11 And [a]I saw another beast coming
up out of the earth; and he [1]had [b]two
horns like a lamb, and he [2]spoke as a
[c]dragon.
12 And he [a]exercises all the authority
of the first beast [1][b]in his presence. And
he makes [c]the earth and those who dwell
in it to [d]worship the first beast, whose
[e]fatal wound was healed.
13 And he [a]performs great signs, so
that he even makes [b]fire come down out
of heaven to the earth in the presence of
men.
14 And he [a]deceives [b]those who dwell
on the earth because of [c]the signs which
it was given him to perform [1][d]in the
presence of the beast, telling those who
dwell on the earth to make an image to
the beast who *had the [e]wound of the
sword and has come to life.
15 And there was given to him to give
breath to the image of the beast, that the
image of the beast might even [1]speak
and cause [a]as many as do not [b]worship
the image of the beast to be killed.
16 And he causes all, [a]the small and
the great, and the rich and the poor, and
the free men and the slaves, [1]to be given
a [b]mark on their right hand, or on their
forehead,
17 and *he provides* that no one should
be able to buy or to sell, except the one
who has the [a]mark, *either* [b]the name of
the beast or [c]the number of his name.
18 [a]Here is wisdom. Let him who has
understanding calculate the number of
the beast, for the number is that [b]of a
man; and his number is [1]six hundred
and sixty-six.

The Lamb and the 144,000 on Mount Zion

14 AND I looked, and behold, [a]the
Lamb *was* standing on [b]Mount
Zion, and with Him [c]one hundred and
forty-four thousand, having [d]His name
and the [d]name of His Father written [e]on
their foreheads.
2 And I heard a voice from heaven,
like [a]the sound of many waters and like
the [b]sound of loud thunder, and the
voice which I heard *was* like *the sound* of
[c]harpists playing on their harps.
3 And they [1]*sang [a]a new song before the throne and before the [b]four
living creatures and the [c]elders; and [d]no
one could learn the song except the [e]one
hundred and forty-four thousand who
had been [a]purchased from the earth.
4 [a]These are the ones who have not
been defiled with women, for they [1]have
kept themselves chaste. These *are* the
ones who [b]follow the Lamb wherever He
goes. These have been [c]purchased from
among men [d]as first fruits to God and to
the Lamb.
5 And [a]no lie was found in their
mouth; they are [b]blameless.

Vision of the Angel with the Gospel

6 And I saw another angel flying in
[a]midheaven, having [b]an eternal gospel to
preach to [c]those who [1]live on the earth,
and to [d]every nation and tribe and
tongue and people;

17 [a]Rev. 11:7; 13:7 [b]Gen. 3:15 [c]1 John 2:3; Rev. 14:12 [d]Rev. 1:2; 6:9; 14:12; 19:10

1 [1]Some mss. read *I stood* [2]Lit., *sea* [a]Dan. 7:3; Rev. 11:7; 13:14, 15; 15:2; 16:13; 17:8 [b]Rev. 12:3 [c]Rev. 12:3; 17:12 [d]Dan. 7:8; 11:36; Rev. 17:3
2 [a]Dan. 7:6; Hos. 13:7f. [b]Dan. 7:5 [c]Dan. 7:4 [d]Rev. 12:3; 13:4, 12 [e]Rev. 2:13; 16:10
3 [1]Lit., *smitten to death* [a]Rev. 13:12, 14 [b]Rev. 17:8
4 [a]Rev. 12:3; 13:2, 12 [b]Ex. 15:11; Is. 46:5; Rev. 18:18
5 [1]Lit., *great things* [2]Lit., *do* [a]Dan. 7:8, 11, 20, 25; 11:36; 2 Thess. 2:3f. [b]Rev. 11:2
6 [1]Or, *tabernacle* [a]Rev. 7:15; 12:12
7 [1]Or, *holy ones* [a]Dan. 7:21; Rev. 11:7 [b]Rev. 5:9
8 [1]Or, *written in the book . . . slain from the foundation of the world* [a]Rev. 3:10; 13:12, 14 [b]Rev. 3:5 [c]Matt. 25:34; Rev. 17:8 [d]Ps. 69:28 [e]Rev. 5:6
9 [a]Rev. 2:7
10 [1]Or, leads *into captivity* [2]Or, *steadfastness* [3]Or, *holy ones* [a]Is. 33:1; Jer. 15:2; 43:11 [b]Gen. 9:6; Matt. 26:52; Rev. 11:18 [c]Heb. 6:12; Rev. 14:12
11 [1]Lit., *was having* [2]Lit., *was speaking* [a]Rev. 13:1; 16:13 [b]Dan. 8:3 [c]Rev. 13:4
12 [1]Or, *by his authority* [a]Rev. 13:4 [b]Rev. 13:14; 19:20 [c]Rev. 13:8 [d]Rev. 13:15; 14:9, 11; 16:2; 19:20; 20:4 [e]Rev. 13:3
13 [a]Matt. 24:24; Rev. 16:14; 19:20 [b]1 Kin. 18:38; Luke 9:54; Rev. 11:5; 20:9
14 [1]Or, *by the authority of* [a]Rev. 12:9 [b]Rev. 13:8 [c]2 Thess. 2:9f. [d]Rev. 13:12; 19:20 [e]Rev. 13:3
15 [1]Some ancient mss. read *speak, and he will cause* [a]Dan. 3:3ff. [b]Rev. 13:12; 14:9, 11; 16:2; 19:20; 20:4
16 [1]Lit., *that they give to them a mark* [a]Rev. 11:18; 19:5, 18 [b]Gal. 6:17; Rev. 7:3; 14:9; 20:4
17 [a]Gal. 6:17; Rev. 7:3; 14:9; 20:4 [b]Rev. 14:11 [c]Rev. 15:2
18 [1]Some mss. read 616 [a]Rev. 17:9 [b]Rev. 21:17

1 [a]Rev. 5:6 [b]Ps. 2:6; Heb. 12:22 [c]Rev. 7:4; 14:3 [d]Rev. 3:12 [e]Ezek. 9:4; Rev. 7:3
2 [a]Rev. 1:15 [b]Rev. 6:1 [c]Rev. 5:8
3 [1]Some ancient mss. read *sing, as it were, a new song* [a]Rev. 5:9 [b]Rev. 4:6 [c]Rev. 4:4 [d]Rev. 2:17 [e]Rev. 7:4; 14:1
4 [1]Lit., *are chaste men* [a]Matt. 19:12; 2 Cor. 11:2; Eph. 5:27; Rev. 3:4 [b]Rev. 3:4; 7:17; 17:14 [c]Rev. 5:9 [d]Heb. 12:23; James 1:18
5 [a]Ps. 32:2; Zeph. 3:13; Mal. 2:6; John 1:47; 1 Pet. 2:22 [b]Heb. 9:14; 1 Pet. 1:19; Jude 24
6 [1]Lit., *sit* [a]Rev. 8:13 [b]1 Pet. 1:25; Rev. 10:7 [c]Rev. 3:10 [d]Rev. 5:9

7 and he said with a loud voice,
"[a]Fear God, and [b]give Him glory, because the hour of His judgment has
come; and worship Him who [c]made the
heaven and the earth and sea and
[d]springs of waters."
8 And another angel, a second one,
followed, saying, "[a]Fallen, fallen is
[b]Babylon the great, she who has [c]made
all the nations drink of the [d]wine of the
[1]passion of her immorality."

Doom for Worshipers of the Beast

9 And another angel, a third one,
followed them, saying with a loud voice,
"If anyone [a]worships the beast and his
[b]image, and receives a [c]mark on his
forehead or upon his hand,
10 he also will drink of the [a]wine of
the wrath of God, which is mixed [1]in full
strength [b]in the cup of His anger; and he
will be tormented with [c]fire and brimstone in the presence of the [d]holy angels
and in the presence of the Lamb.
11 "And the [a]smoke of their torment
goes up forever and ever; and [b]they have
no rest day and night, those who [c]wor-
ship the beast and his [c]image, and whoever receives the [d]mark of his name."
12 Here is [a]the [1]perseverance of the
[2]saints who [b]keep the commandments of
God and [3c]their faith in Jesus.
13 And I heard a voice from heaven,
saying, "Write, '[a]Blessed are the dead
who [b]die in the Lord from now on!' "
"Yes," [c]says the Spirit, "that they may
[d]rest from their labors, for their [e]deeds
follow with them."

The Reapers

14 And I looked, and behold, a [a]white
cloud, and sitting on the cloud *was* one
[b]like [1]a son of man, having a golden
[c]crown on His head, and a sharp sickle
in His hand.
15 And another angel [a]came out of the
[1]temple, crying out with a loud voice to
Him who sat on the cloud, "[2b]Put in
your sickle and reap, because the hour to
reap has come, because the [c]harvest of
the earth [3]is ripe."
16 And He who sat on the cloud
[1]swung His sickle over the earth; and the
earth was reaped.
17 And another angel [a]came out of the
[1]temple which is in heaven, [2]and he also
had a sharp sickle.
18 And another angel, [a]the one who
has power over fire, came out from [b]the
altar; and he called with a loud voice to
him who had the sharp sickle, saying,
"[1c]Put in your sharp sickle, and gather
the clusters [2]from the vine of the earth,
[d]because her grapes are ripe."
19 And the angel [1]swung his sickle to
the earth, and gathered *the clusters from*
the vine of the earth, and threw them
into [a]the great wine press of the wrath of
God.

7 [a]Rev. 15:4 [b]Rev. 11:13 [c]Rev. 4:11 [d]Rev. 8:10
8 [1]Or, *wrath* [a]Is. 21:9; Jer. 51:8; Rev. 18:2 [b]Dan. 4:30; Rev. 16:19; 17:5; 18:10 [c]Jer. 51:7 [d]Rev. 17:2, 4; 18:3
9 [a]Rev. 13:12; 14:11 [b]Rev. 13:14f.; 14:11 [c]Rev. 13:16
10 [1]Lit., *unmixed* [a]Is. 51:17; Jer. 25:15f., 27; Rev. 16:19; 19:15 [b]Ps. 75:8; Rev. 18:6 [c]Gen. 19:24; Ezek. 38:22; 2 Thess. 1:7; Rev. 19:20; 20:10, 14f.; 21:8 [d]Mark 8:38
11 [a]Is. 34:8-10; Rev. 18:9, 18; 19:3 [b]Rev. 4:8 [c]Rev. 13:12; 14:9 [d]Rev. 13:17
12 [1]Or, *steadfastness* [2]Or, *holy ones* [3]Lit., *the faith of* [a]Rev. 13:10 [b]Rev. 12:17 [c]Rev. 2:13
13 [a]Rev. 20:6 [b]1 Cor. 15:18; 1 Thess. 4:16 [c]Rev. 2:7; 22:17 [d]Heb. 4:9ff.; Rev. 6:11 [e]1 Tim. 5:25
14 [1]Or, *the Son of Man* [a]Matt. 17:5 [b]Dan. 7:13; Rev. 1:13 [c]Ps. 21:3; Rev. 6:2
15 [1]Or, *sanctuary* [2]Lit., *Send forth* [3]Lit., *has become dry* [a]Rev. 11:19; 14:17; 15:6; 16:17 [b]Joel 3:13; Mark 4:29; Rev. 14:18 [c]Jer. 51:33; Matt. 13:39-41
16 [1]Lit., *cast*
17 [1]Or, *sanctuary* [2]Lit., *having himself also* [a]Rev. 11:19; 14:15; 15:6; 16:17
18 [1]Lit., *Send forth* [2]Lit., *of* [a]Rev. 16:8 [b]Rev. 6:9; 8:3 [c]Joel 3:13; Mark 4:29; Rev. 14:15 [d]Joel 3:13
19 [1]Lit., *cast* [a]Is. 63:2f.; Rev. 19:15
20 [1]Lit., *from two hundred miles* [2]Lit., *sixteen hundred stadia;* a stadion was approx. 600 ft. [a]Is. 63:3; Lam. 1:15; Rev. 19:15 [b]Heb. 13:12; Rev. 11:8 [c]Gen. 49:11; Deut. 32:14

1 [a]Rev. 12:1, 3 [b]Rev. 15:6-8; 16:1; 17:1; 21:9 [c]Lev. 26:21 [d]Rev. 9:20
2 [a]Rev. 4:6 [b]Rev. 12:11 [c]Rev. 13:1 [d]Rev. 13:14f. [e]Rev. 13:17 [f]Rev. 5:8
3 [1]Some ancient mss. read *ages* [a]Ex. 15:1ff. [b]Josh. 22:5; Heb. 3:5 [c]Rev. 5:9f., 12f. [d]Deut. 32:3f.; Ps. 111:2; 139:14 [e]Hos. 14:9; Rev. 1:8 [f]1 Tim. 1:17

20 And [a]the wine press was trodden
[b]outside the city, and [c]blood came out
from the wine press, up to the horses'
bridles, [1]for a distance of [2]two hundred
miles.

A Scene of Heaven

15 AND I saw [a]another sign in
heaven, great and marvelous,
[b]seven angels who had [c]seven plagues,
which are [d]the last, because in them the
wrath of God is finished.
2 And I saw, as it were, a [a]sea of
glass mixed with fire, and those who had
[b]come off victorious from the [c]beast and
from [d]his image and from the [e]number
of his name, standing on the [a]sea of
glass, holding [f]harps of God.
3 And they *sang the [a]song of Moses
[b]the bond-servant of God and the [c]song
of the Lamb, saying,

"[d]Great and marvelous are Thy
works,
[e]O Lord God, the Almighty;
Righteous and true are Thy ways,
Thou [f]King of the [1]nations.
4 "[a]Who will not fear, O Lord, and
glorify Thy name?
For Thou alone art holy;
For [b]ALL THE NATIONS WILL COME
AND WORSHIP BEFORE THEE,
For Thy [1c]righteous acts have
been revealed."

5 After these things I looked, and
[a]the [1]temple of the [b]tabernacle of testimony in heaven was opened,
6 and the [a]seven angels who had the
seven plagues [b]came out of the [1]temple,
clothed in [2]linen, clean *and* bright, and
[c]girded around their breasts with golden
girdles.
7 And one of the [a]four living creatures gave to the [b]seven angels seven
[c]golden bowls full of the [d]wrath of God,
who [e]lives forever and ever.
8 And the [1]temple was filled with
[a]smoke from the glory of God and from
His power; and no one was able to enter
the [1]temple until the seven plagues of
the seven angels were finished.

Six Bowls of Wrath

16 AND I heard a loud voice from
[a]the [1]temple, saying to the [b]seven
angels, "Go and [c]pour out the seven
bowls of the wrath of God into the
earth."

4 [1]Or, *judgments* [a]Jer. 10:7; Rev. 14:7 [b]Ps. 86:9; Is. 66:23 [c]Rev. 19:8
5 [1]Or, *sanctuary* [a]Rev. 11:19 [b]Ex. 38:21; Num. 1:50; Heb. 8:5; Rev. 13:6
6 [1]Or, *sanctuary* [2]Some mss. read *stone* [a]Rev. 15:1 [b]Rev. 14:15 [c]Rev. 1:13
7 [a]Rev. 4:6 [b]Rev. 15:1 [c]Rev. 5:8 [d]Rev. 14:10; 15:1 [e]Rev. 4:9
8 [1]Or, *sanctuary* [a]Ex. 19:18; 40:34f.; Lev. 16:2; 1 Kin. 8:10f.; 2 Chr. 5:13f.; Is. 6:4

1 [1]Or, *sanctuary* [a]Rev. 11:19 [b]Rev. 15:1 [c]Ps. 79:6; Jer. 10:25; Ezek. 22:31; Zeph. 3:8; Rev. 16:2ff.

2 And the first *angel* went and poured out his bowl [a]into the earth; and it became a loathsome and malignant [b]sore upon the men [c]who had the mark of the beast and who worshiped his image.

3 And the second *angel* poured out his bowl [a]into the sea, and it became blood like *that* of a dead man; and every living [1]thing in the sea died.

4 And the third *angel* poured out his bowl into the [a]rivers and the springs of waters; and [1]they [b]became blood.

5 And I heard the angel of the waters saying, "[a]Righteous art Thou, [b]who art and who wast, O [c]Holy One, because Thou didst [d]judge these things;

6 for they poured out [a]the blood of saints and prophets, and Thou hast given them [b]blood to drink. They [1]deserve it."

7 And I heard [a]the altar saying, "Yes, O [b]Lord God, the Almighty, [c]true and righteous are Thy judgments."

8 And the fourth *angel* poured out his bowl upon [a]the sun; [b]and it was given to it to scorch men with fire.

9 And men were scorched with [1]fierce heat; and they [a]blasphemed the name of God who has the power over these plagues; and they [b]did not repent, so as to [c]give Him glory.

10 And the fifth *angel* poured out his bowl upon the [a]throne of the beast; and his kingdom became [b]darkened; and they gnawed their tongues because of pain,

11 and they [a]blasphemed the [b]God of heaven because of their pains and their [c]sores; and they [d]did not repent of their deeds.

12 And the sixth *angel* poured out his bowl upon the [a]great river, the Euphrates; and [b]its water was dried up, that [c]the way might be prepared for the kings [d]from the [1]east.

Armageddon

13 And I saw *coming* out of the mouth of the [a]dragon and out of the mouth of the [b]beast and out of the mouth of the [c]false prophet, three [d]unclean spirits like [e]frogs;

14 for they are [a]spirits of demons, [b]performing signs, which go out to the kings of the [c]whole [1]world, to [d]gather them together for the war of the [e]great day of God, the Almighty.

15 ("Behold, [a]I am coming like a thief. [b]Blessed is the one who stays awake and keeps his garments, [c]lest he walk about naked and [1]men see his shame.")

16 And they [a]gathered them together to the place which [b]in Hebrew is called [1]Har-[c]Magedon.

Seventh Bowl of Wrath

17 And the seventh *angel* poured out his bowl upon [a]the air; and a [b]loud voice came out of the [1c]temple from the throne, saying, "[d]It is done."

18 And there were flashes of [a]lightning and sounds and peals of thunder; and there was [b]a great earthquake, [c]such as there had not been since man came to be upon the earth, so great an earthquake *was it, and* so mighty.

19 And [a]the great city was split into three parts, and the cities of the [1]nations fell. And [b]Babylon the great was [c]remembered before God, to give her [d]the cup of the wine of His fierce wrath.

20 And [a]every island fled away, and the mountains were not found.

21 And [a]huge [1]hailstones, about [2]one hundred pounds each, *came down from heaven upon men; and men [b]blasphemed God because of the [c]plague of the hail, because its plague *was extremely [3]severe.

The Doom of Babylon

17 [a]AND one of the [b]seven angels who had the [c]seven bowls came and spoke with me, saying, "Come here, I shall show you [d]the judgment of the [e]great harlot who [f]sits on many waters,

2 with whom [a]the kings of the earth committed *acts of* immorality, and [b]those who dwell on the earth were [c]made drunk with the wine of her immorality."

3 And [a]he carried me away [1b]in the Spirit [c]into a wilderness; and I saw a woman sitting on a [d]scarlet beast, full of [e]blasphemous names, having [f]seven heads and ten horns.

4 And the woman [a]was clothed in purple and scarlet, and [1]adorned with gold and precious [2]stones and pearls, having in her hand [b]a gold cup full of abominations and of the unclean things of her immorality,

5 and upon her forehead a name *was* written, a [a]mystery, "[b]BABYLON THE GREAT, THE MOTHER OF HARLOTS AND OF [c]THE ABOMINATIONS OF THE EARTH."

6 And I saw the woman drunk with [a]the blood of the [1]saints, and with the blood of the witnesses of Jesus. And when I saw her, I wondered [2]greatly.

7 And the angel said to me, "Why [1]do you wonder? I shall tell you the [a]mystery of the woman and of the beast that carries her, which has the [b]seven heads and the ten horns.

2 [a]Rev. 8:7 [b]Ex. 9:9-11; Deut. 28:35; Rev. 16:11 [c]Rev. 13:15-17; 14:9
3 [1]Lit., *soul.* Some ancient mss. read *thing, the things in the sea.* [a]Ex. 7:17-21; Rev. 8:8f.; 11:6
4 [1]Some ancient mss. read *it became* [a]Rev. 8:10 [b]Ex. 7:17-20; Ps. 78:44; Rev. 11:6
5 [a]John 17:25 [b]Rev. 11:17 [c]Rev. 15:4 [d]Rev. 6:10
6 [1]Lit., *are worthy* [a]Rev. 17:6; 18:24 [b]Is. 49:26; Luke 11:49-51
7 [a]Rev. 6:9; 14:18 [b]Rev. 1:8 [c]Rev. 15:3; 19:2
8 [a]Rev. 6:12 [b]Rev. 14:18
9 [1]Lit., *great* [a]Rev. 16:11, 21 [b]Rev. 2:21 [c]Rev. 11:13
10 [a]Rev. 13:2 [b]Ex. 10:21f.; Is. 8:22; Rev. 8:12; 9:2
11 [a]Rev. 16:9, 21 [b]Rev. 11:13 [c]Rev. 16:2 [d]Rev. 2:21
12 [1]Lit., *rising of the sun* [a]Rev. 9:14 [b]Is. 11:15f.; 44:27; Jer. 51:36 [c]Is. 41:2, 25; 46:11 [d]Rev. 7:2
13 [a]Rev. 12:3 [b]Rev. 13:1 [c]Rev. 13:11, 14; 19:20; 20:10 [d]Rev. 18:2 [e]Ex. 8:6
14 [1]Lit., *inhabited earth* [a]1 Tim. 4:1 [b]Rev. 13:13 [c]Rev. 3:10 [d]1 Kin. 22:21-23; Rev. 17:14; 19:19; 20:8 [e]Rev. 6:17
15 [1]Lit., *they* [a]Matt. 24:43f.; Luke 12:39f.; Rev. 3:3, 11 [b]Luke 12:37 [c]Rev. 3:18
16 [1]Some authorities read *Armageddon* [a]Rev. 19:19 [b]Rev. 9:11 [c]Judg. 5:19; 2 Kin. 23:29f.; 2 Chr. 35:22; Zech. 12:11
17 [1]Or, *sanctuary* [a]Eph. 2:2 [b]Rev. 11:15 [c]Rev. 14:15 [d]Rev. 10:6; 21:6
18 [a]Rev. 4:5 [b]Rev. 6:12 [c]Dan. 12:1; Matt. 24:21
19 [1]Or, *Gentiles* [a]Rev. 11:8; 17:18; 18:10, 18f., 21 [b]Rev. 14:8 [c]Rev. 18:5 [d]Rev. 14:10
20 [a]Rev. 6:14; 20:11
21 [1]Lit., *hail* [2]Lit., *the weight of a talent* [3]Lit., *great* [a]Rev. 8:7; 11:19 [b]Rev. 16:9, 11 [c]Ex. 9:18-25

1 [a]Rev. 1:1; 21:9 [b]Rev. 15:1 [c]Rev. 15:7 [d]Rev. 16:19 [e]Is. 1:21; Jer. 2:20; Nah. 3:4; Rev. 17:5, 15f.; 19:2 [f]Jer. 51:13; Rev. 17:15
2 [a]Rev. 2:22; 18:3, 9 [b]Rev. 3:10; 17:8 [c]Rev. 14:8

3 [1]Or, *in spirit* [a]Rev. 21:10 [b]Rev. 1:10 [c]Rev. 12:6, 14; 21:10 [d]Matt. 27:28; Rev. 18:12, 16 [e]Rev. 13:1 [f]Rev. 12:3; 17:7, 9, 12, 16
4 [1]Lit., *gilded* [2]Lit., *stone* [a]Ezek. 28:13; Rev. 18:12, 16 [b]Jer. 51:7; Rev. 18:6
5 [a]2 Thess. 2:7; Rev. 1:20; 17:7 [b]Rev. 14:8; 16:19 [c]Rev. 17:2
6 [1]Or, *holy ones* [2]Lit., *with great wonder* [a]Rev. 16:6
7 [1]Lit., *have you wondered* [a]2 Thess. 2:7; Rev. 1:20; 17:5 [b]Rev. 17:3

8"[a]The beast that you saw [b]was and
is not, and is about to [c]come up out of
the [d]abyss and [1]to [e]go to destruction.
And [f]those who dwell on the earth will
[g]wonder, [h]whose name has not been
written in the book of life [i]from the
foundation of the world, when they see
the beast, that he was and is not and will
come.
9"[a]Here is the mind which has wisdom. The [b]seven heads are seven mountains on which the woman sits,
10 and they are seven [a]kings; five have
fallen, one is, the other has not yet come;
and when he comes, he must remain a
little while.
11"And the beast which [a]was and is
not, is himself also an eighth, and is *one*
of the seven, and he [b]goes to destruction.
12"And the [a]ten horns which you saw
are ten kings, who have not yet received
a kingdom, but they receive authority as
kings with the beast [b]for one hour.
13"These have [a]one [1]purpose and they
give their power and authority to the
beast.

Victory for the Lamb

14"These will wage [a]war against the
Lamb, and the Lamb will [b]overcome
them, because He is [c]Lord of lords and
[c]King of kings, and [d]those who are with
Him *are the* [e]called and chosen and
faithful."
15 And he *said to me, "The [a]waters
which you saw where the harlot sits, are
[b]peoples and multitudes and nations and
tongues.
16"And the [a]ten horns which you
saw, and the beast, these will hate the
harlot and will make her [b]desolate and
[c]naked, and will [d]eat her flesh and will
[e]burn her up with fire.
17"For [a]God has put it in their hearts
to execute His [1]purpose [2]by [b]having a
common purpose, and by giving their
kingdom to the beast, until the [c]words of
God should be fulfilled.
18"And the woman whom you saw is
[a]the great city, which [1]reigns over the
kings of the earth."

Babylon Is Fallen

18 AFTER these things I saw another [a]angel [b]coming down from
heaven, having great authority, and the
earth was [c]illumined with his glory.
2 And he cried out with a mighty
voice, saying, "[a]Fallen, fallen is Babylon
the great! And she [b]has become a dwelling place of demons and a [1]prison of
every [c]unclean spirit, and a [1]prison of
every unclean and hateful bird.
3"For all the nations [1]have drunk of
the [a]wine of the [2]passion of her immorality, and [b]the kings of the earth have
committed *acts of* immorality with her,
and the [c]merchants of the earth have
become rich by the [3]wealth of her [4d]sen-
suality."

4 And I heard another voice from
heaven, saying, "[a]Come out of her, my
people, that you may not participate in
her sins and that you may not receive of
her plagues;
5 for her sins have [1a]piled up as high
as heaven, and God has [b]remembered
her iniquities.
6"[a]Pay her back even as she has paid,
and [1]give back *to her* double according
to her deeds; in the [b]cup which she has
mixed, mix twice as much for her.
7"[a]To the degree that she glorified
herself and [b]lived [1]sensuously, to the
same degree give her torment and
mourning; for she says in her heart, '[c]I
SIT *as* A QUEEN AND I AM NOT A WIDOW,
and will never see mourning.'
8"For this reason [a]in one day her
plagues will come, [1]pestilence and
mourning and famine, and she will be
[b]burned up with fire; for the Lord God
who judges her [c]is strong.

Lament for Babylon

9"And [a]the kings of the earth, who
committed *acts of* immorality and [b]lived
[1]sensuously with her, will [c]weep and
lament over her when they [d]see the
smoke of her burning,
10 [a]standing at a distance because of
the fear of her torment, saying, '[b]Woe,
woe, [c]the great city, Babylon, the strong
city! For in [d]one hour your judgment
has come.'
11"And the [a]merchants of the earth
[b]weep and mourn over her, because no
one buys their cargoes any more;
12 cargoes of [a]gold and silver and
precious [1]stones and pearls and fine
linen and purple and silk and scarlet,
and every *kind of* citron wood and every
article of ivory and every article *made*
from very costly wood and [2]bronze and
iron and marble,
13 and cinnamon and [1]spice and incense and perfume and frankincense and
wine and olive oil and fine flour and
wheat and cattle and sheep, and *cargoes*
of horses and chariots and [2]slaves and
[3a]human lives.
14"And the fruit [1]you long for has
gone from you, and all things that were
luxurious and splendid have passed
away from you and *men* will no longer
find them.
15"The [a]merchants of [b]these things,
who became rich from her, will [c]stand at
a distance because of the fear of her
torment, weeping and mourning,
16 saying, '[a]Woe, woe, [b]the great city,
she who [c]was clothed in fine linen and
purple and scarlet, and [1]adorned with
gold and precious [2]stones and pearls;

8 [1]Some ancient mss. read *he goes* [a]Dan. 7:7 [b]Rev. 13:3, 12, 14; 17:11 [c]Rev. 11:7; 13:1 [d]Rev. 9:1; 13:1 [e]Rev. 13:10; 17:11 [f]Rev. 3:10 [g]Rev. 13:3 [h]Ps. 69:28; Rev. 3:5 [i]Matt. 25:34; Rev. 13:8
9 [a]Rev. 13:18 [b]Rev. 17:3
10 [a]Rev. 10:11
11 [a]Rev. 13:3, 12, 14; 17:8 [b]Rev. 13:10; 17:8
12 [a]Dan. 7:24; Rev. 12:3; 13:1; 17:16 [b]Rev. 18:10, 17, 19
13 [1]Or, *mind* [a]Rev. 17:17
14 [a]Rev. 16:14 [b]Rev. 3:21 [c]1 Tim. 6:15; Rev. 19:16 [d]Rev. 2:10f. [e]Matt. 22:14
15 [a]Is. 8:7; Jer. 47:2; Rev. 17:1 [b]Rev. 5:9
16 [a]Rev. 17:12 [b]Rev. 18:17, 19 [c]Ezek. 16:37, 39 [d]Rev. 19:18 [e]Rev. 18:8
17 [1]Or, *mind* [2]Lit., *even to do one mind and to give* [a]2 Cor. 8:16 [b]Rev. 17:13 [c]Rev. 10:7
18 [1]Lit., *has a kingdom* [a]Rev. 11:8; 16:19

1 [a]Rev. 17:1, 7 [b]Rev. 10:1 [c]Ezek. 43:2
2 [1]Or, *haunt* [a]Is. 21:9; Jer. 51:8; Rev. 14:8 [b]Is. 13:21f.; 34:11, 13-15; Jer. 50:39; 51:37; Zeph. 2:14f. [c]Rev. 16:13
3 [1]Many ancient mss. read *have fallen by* [2]Lit., *wrath* [3]Lit., *power* [4]Or, *luxury* [a]Jer. 51:7; Rev. 14:8 [b]Rev. 17:2; 18:9 [c]Ezek. 27:9-25; Rev. 18:11, 15, 19, 23 [d]1 Tim. 5:11; Rev. 18:7, 9
4 [a]Is. 52:11; Jer. 50:8; 51:6, 9, 45; 2 Cor. 6:17
5 [1]Lit., *joined together* [a]Jer. 51:9 [b]Rev. 16:19
6 [1]Lit., *double* to her [a]Ps. 137:8; Jer. 50:15, 29 [b]Rev. 17:4
7 [1]Or, *luxuriously* [a]Ezek. 28:2-8 [b]1 Tim. 5:11; Rev. 18:3, 9 [c]Is. 47:7f.; Zeph. 2:15
8 [1]Or, *death* [a]Is. 47:9; Jer. 50:31f.; Rev. 18:10 [b]Rev. 17:16 [c]Jer. 50:34; Rev. 11:17f.
9 [1]Or, *luxuriously* [a]Rev. 17:2; 18:3 [b]1 Tim. 5:11; Rev. 18:3, 7 [c]Ezek. 26:16f.; 27:35 [d]Rev. 14:11; 18:18; 19:3
10 [a]Rev. 18:15, 17 [b]Rev. 18:16, 19 [c]Rev. 11:8; 16:19; 18:16, 18, 19, 21 [d]Rev. 17:12; 18:8, 17, 19

11 [a]Ezek. 27:9-25; Rev. 18:3, 15, 19, 23 [b]Ezek. 27:27-34
12 [1]Lit., *stone* [2]Or, *brass* [a]Ezek. 27:12-22; Rev. 17:4
13 [1]Gr., amomum [2]Lit., *bodies* [3]Lit., *souls of men* [a]1 Chr. 5:21; Ezek. 27:13; 1 Tim. 1:10
14 [1]Lit., *of your soul's desire*
15 [a]Rev. 18:3 [b]Rev. 18:12, 13 [c]Rev. 18:10
16 [1]Lit., *gilded* [2]Lit., *stone and pearl* [a]Rev. 18:10, 19 [b]Rev. 18:10, 18, 19, 21 [c]Rev. 17:4

17 for in [a]one hour such great wealth
has been laid [b]waste!' And [c]every ship-
master and every [1]passenger and sailor,
and as many as make their living by the
sea, [a]stood at a distance,

18 and were [a]crying out as they [b]saw
the smoke of her burning, saying, '[c]What
city is like [d]the great city?'

19 "And they threw [a]dust on their
heads and were crying out, weeping and
mourning, saying, '[b]Woe, woe, the great
city, in which all who had ships at sea
[c]became rich by her [1]wealth, for in [b]one
hour she has been laid [d]waste!'

20 "[a]Rejoice over her, O heaven, and
you [1]saints and [b]apostles and prophets,
because [c]God has [2]pronounced judgment for you against her."

21 And [1]a [a]strong angel [b]took up a
stone like a great millstone and threw it
into the sea, saying, "Thus will Babylon,
[c]the great city, be thrown down with
violence, and [d]will not be found any
longer.

22 "And [a]the sound of harpists and
musicians and flute-players and trumpeters will not be heard in you any
longer; and no craftsman of any craft
will be found in you any longer; and the
[b]sound of a mill will not be heard in you
any longer;

23 and the light of a lamp will not
shine in you any longer; and the [a]voice
of the bridegroom and bride will not be
heard in you any longer; for your [b]mer-
chants were the great men of the earth,
because all the nations were deceived
[c]by your sorcery.

24 "And in her was found the [a]blood of
prophets and of [1]saints and of [b]all who
have been slain on the earth."

The Fourfold Hallelujah

19 AFTER these things I heard, as
it were, a [a]loud voice of a great
multitude in heaven, saying,
"[b]Hallelujah! [c]Salvation and [d]glory
and power belong to our God;

2 [a]BECAUSE HIS [b]JUDGMENTS ARE
[c]TRUE AND RIGHTEOUS; for He has
judged the [d]great harlot who was corrupting the earth with her immorality,
and HE HAS [e]AVENGED THE BLOOD OF
HIS BOND-SERVANTS [1]ON HER."

3 And a second time they said,
"[a]Hallelujah! [b]HER SMOKE RISES UP
FOREVER AND EVER."

4 And the [a]twenty-four elders and
the [b]four living creatures [c]fell down and
worshiped God who sits on the throne
saying, "[d]Amen. [e]Hallelujah!"

5 And a voice came from the throne,
saying,
"[a]Give praise to our God, all you His
bond-servants, [b]you who fear Him, the
small and the great."

6 And I heard, as it were, [a]the voice
of a great multitude and as [b]the sound of
many waters and as the [c]sound of
mighty peals of thunder, saying,
"[a]Hallelujah! For the [d]Lord our God,
the Almighty, reigns.

Marriage of the Lamb

7 "Let us rejoice and be glad and [a]give
the glory to Him, for [b]the marriage of
the Lamb has come and His [1][c]bride has
made herself ready."

8 And it was given to her to clothe
herself in [a]fine linen, bright *and* clean;
for the fine linen is the [b]righteous acts of
the [1]saints.

9 And [a]he *said to me, "[b]Write,
'[c]Blessed are those who are invited to the
marriage supper of the Lamb.' " And he
*said to me, "[d]These are true words of
God."

10 And [a]I fell at his feet to worship
him. [b]And he *said to me, "Do not do
that; I am a [c]fellow servant of yours and
your brethren who [d]hold the testimony
of Jesus; worship God. For the testimony of Jesus is the spirit of prophecy."

The Coming of Christ

11 And I saw [a]heaven opened; and
behold, a [b]white horse, and He who sat
upon it *is* called [c]Faithful and True; and
in [d]righteousness He judges and wages
war.

12 And His [a]eyes *are* a flame of fire,
and upon His head *are* many [b]diadems;
and He has a [c]name written *upon Him*
which no one knows except Himself.

13 And *He is* clothed with a [a]robe
dipped in blood; and His name is called
[b]The Word of God.

14 And the armies which are in
heaven, clothed in [a]fine linen, [b]white *and*
clean, were following Him on white
horses.

15 And [a]from His mouth comes a
sharp sword, so that [b]with it He may
smite the nations; and He will [1][c]rule
them with a rod of iron; and [d]He treads
the [2]wine press of the fierce wrath of
God, the Almighty.

16 And on His robe and on His thigh
He has [a]a name written, "[b]KING OF
KINGS, AND LORD OF LORDS."

17 And I saw [1]an angel standing in
the sun; and he cried out with a loud
voice, saying to [a]all the birds which fly in
[b]midheaven, "[c]Come, assemble for the
great supper of God;

18 in order that you may [a]eat the flesh
of kings and the flesh of [1]commanders
and the flesh of mighty men and the
flesh of horses and of those who sit on
them and the flesh of all men, [b]both free
men and slaves, and [c]small and great."

17 [1]Lit., *one who sails anywhere* [a]Rev. 18:10 [b]Rev. 17:16; 18:19 [c]Ezek. 27:28f.
18 [a]Ezek. 27:30 [b]Rev. 18:9 [c]Ezek. 27:32; Rev. 13:4 [d]Rev. 18:10
19 [1]Lit., *costliness* [a]Josh. 7:6; Job 2:12; Lam. 2:10 [b]Rev. 18:10 [c]Rev. 18:3, 15 [d]Rev. 17:16; 18:17
20 [1]Or, *holy ones* [2]Lit., *judged your judgment of her* [a]Jer. 51:48; Rev. 12:12 [b]Luke 11:49f. [c]Rev. 6:10; 18:6ff.; 19:2
21 [1]Lit., *one* [a]Rev. 5:2; 10:1 [b]Jer. 51:63f. [c]Rev. 18:10 [d]Ezek. 26:21
22 [a]Is. 24:8; Ezek. 26:13; Matt. 9:23 [b]Eccl. 12:4; Jer. 25:10
23 [a]Jer. 7:34; 16:9 [b]Is. 23:8; Rev. 6:15; 18:3 [c]Nah. 3:4; Rev. 9:21
24 [1]Or, *holy ones* [a]Rev. 16:6; 17:6 [b]Matt. 23:35

1 [a]Jer. 51:48; Rev. 11:15; 19:6 [b]Ps. 104:35; Rev. 19:3, 4, 6 [c]Rev. 7:10 [d]Rev. 4:11
2 [1]Lit., *from her hand* [a]Ps. 19:9 [b]Rev. 6:10 [c]Rev. 16:7 [d]Rev. 17:1 [e]Deut. 32:43; 2 Kin. 9:7; Rev. 16:6; 18:20
3 [a]Ps. 104:35; Rev. 19:1, 4, 6 [b]Is. 34:10; Rev. 14:11
4 [a]Rev. 4:4, 10 [b]Rev. 4:6 [c]Rev. 4:10 [d]Ps. 106:48; Rev. 5:14 [e]Ps. 104:35; Rev. 19:3, 6
5 [a]Ps. 22:23; 115:13; 134:1; 135:1 [b]Rev. 11:18
6 [a]Jer. 51:48; Rev. 11:15; 19:1 [b]Ezek. 1:24; Rev. 1:15 [c]Rev. 6:1 [d]Ps. 93:1; 97:1; 99:1; Rev. 1:8
7 [1]Lit., *wife* [a]Rev. 11:13 [b]Matt. 22:2; 25:10; Luke 12:36; John 3:29; Eph. 5:23, 32; Rev. 19:9 [c]Matt. 1:20; Rev. 21:2, 9
8 [1]Or, *holy ones* [a]Rev. 15:6; 19:14 [b]Rev. 15:4
9 [a]Rev. 17:1; 19:10 [b]Rev. 1:19 [c]Matt. 22:2f.; Luke 14:15 [d]Rev. 17:17; 21:5; 22:6
10 [a]Rev. 22:8 [b]Acts 10:26; Rev. 22:9 [c]Rev. 1:1f. [d]Rev. 12:17
11 [a]Ezek. 1:1; John 1:51; Rev. 4:1 [b]Rev. 6:2; 19:19, 21 [c]Rev. 3:14 [d]Ps. 96:13; Is. 11:4
12 [a]Dan. 10:6; Rev. 1:14 [b]Rev. 6:2; 12:3 [c]Rev. 2:17; 19:16
13 [a]Is. 63:3 [b]John 1:1
14 [a]Rev. 19:8 [b]Rev. 3:4; 19:8
15 [1]Or, *shepherd* [2]Lit., *wine press of the wine of His fierce wrath* [a]Rev. 1:16; 19:21 [b]Is. 11:4; 2 Thess. 2:8 [c]Ps. 2:9; Rev. 2:27 [d]Is. 63:3; Joel 3:13; Rev. 14:19, 20
16 [a]Rev. 2:17; 19:12 [b]Rev. 17:14
17 [1]Lit., *one* [a]Rev. 19:21 [b]Rev. 8:13 [c]1 Sam. 17:44; Jer. 12:9; Ezek. 39:17
18 [1]I.e., chiliarchs, in command of one thousand troops [a]Ezek. 39:18-20 [b]Rev. 6:15 [c]Rev. 11:18; 13:16; 19:5

19 And I saw [a]the beast and [b]the
kings of the earth and their armies,
assembled to make war against Him who
[c]sat upon the horse, and against His
army.

Doom of the Beast and False Prophet

20 And the beast was seized, and with
him the [a]false prophet who [b]performed
the signs [1c]in his presence, by which he
[d]deceived those who had received the
[e]mark of the beast and those who [f]wor-
shiped his image; these two were thrown
alive into the [g]lake of [h]fire which burns
with brimstone.
21 And the rest were killed with the
sword which [a]came from the mouth of
Him who [b]sat upon the horse, and [c]all
the birds were filled with their flesh.

Satan Bound

20 AND I saw [a]an angel coming
down from heaven, having the
[b]key of the abyss and a great chain [1]in
his hand.
2 And he laid hold of the [a]dragon,
the serpent of old, who is the devil and
Satan, and [b]bound him for a thousand
years,
3 and threw him into the [a]abyss, and
shut *it* and [b]sealed *it* over him, so that he
should [c]not deceive the nations any
longer, until the thousand years were
completed; after these things he must be
released for a short time.
4 And I saw [a]thrones, and [b]they sat
upon them, and [c]judgment was given to
them. And I *saw* [d]the souls of those who
had been beheaded because of the [e]testi-
mony of Jesus and because of the word
of God, and those who had not [f]wor-
shiped the beast or his image, and had
not received the [g]mark upon their forehead and upon their hand; and they
[h]came to life and [i]reigned with Christ for
a thousand years.
5 The rest of the dead did not come
to life until the thousand years were
completed. [a]This is the first resurrection.
6 [a]Blessed and holy is the one who
has a part in the first resurrection; over
these the [b]second death has no power,
but they will be [c]priests of God and of
Christ and will [d]reign with Him for a
thousand years.

Satan Freed, Doomed

7 And when the thousand years are
completed, Satan will be [a]released from
his prison,
8 and will come out to [a]deceive the
nations which are in the [b]four corners of
the earth, [c]Gog and Magog, to [d]gather
them together for the war; the number
of them is like the [e]sand of the [1]seashore.
9 And they [a]came up on the [1]broad
plain of the earth and surrounded the
[b]camp of the [2]saints and the [c]beloved
city, and [d]fire came down from heaven
and devoured them.
10 And [a]the devil who [a]deceived them
was thrown into the [b]lake of fire and
brimstone, where the [c]beast and the
[c]false prophet are also; and they will be
[d]tormented day and night forever and
ever.

Judgment at the Throne of God

11 And I saw a great white [a]throne
and Him who sat upon it, from whose
[1]presence [b]earth and heaven fled away,
and [c]no place was found for them.
12 And I saw the dead, the [a]great and
the small, standing before the throne,
and [1b]books were opened; and another
[2]book was opened, which is [c]*the book* of
life; and the dead [d]were judged from the
things which were written in the [1]books,
[e]according to their deeds.
13 And the sea gave up the dead
which were in it, and [a]death and Hades
[b]gave up the dead which were in them;
and they were judged, every one *of them*
[c]according to their deeds.
14 And [a]death and Hades were
thrown into [b]the lake of fire. This is the
[c]second death, the lake of fire.
15 And if [1]anyone's name was not
found written in [a]the book of life, he was
thrown into the lake of fire.

The New Heaven and Earth

21 AND I saw [a]a new heaven and a
new earth; for [b]the first heaven
and the first earth passed away, and
there is no longer *any* sea.
2 And I saw [a]the holy city, [b]new
Jerusalem, [c]coming down out of heaven
from God, [d]made ready as a bride
adorned for her husband.
3 And I heard a loud voice from the
throne, saying, "Behold, [a]the tabernacle
of God is among men, and He shall
[1b]dwell among them, and they shall be
His people, and God Himself shall be
among them,[2]
4 and He shall [a]wipe away every tear
from their eyes; and [b]there shall no
longer be *any* death; [c]there shall no
longer be *any* mourning, or crying, or
pain; [d]the first things have passed
away."
5 And [a]He who sits on the throne
said, "Behold, I am [b]making all things
new." And He *said, "Write, for [c]these
words are faithful and true."
6 And He said to me, "[1a]It is done. I
am the [b]Alpha and the Omega, the
beginning and the end. [c]I will give to the
one who thirsts from the spring of the
[d]water of life without cost.

19 [a]Rev. 11:7; 13:1 [b]Rev. 16:14, 16 [c]Rev. 19:11, 21
20 [1]Or, *by his authority* [a]Rev. 16:13 [b]Rev. 13:13 [c]Rev. 13:12 [d]Rev. 13:14 [e]Rev. 13:16f. [f]Rev. 13:12, 15 [g]Rev. 20:10, 14f.; 21:8 [h]Is. 30:33; Dan. 7:11; Rev. 14:10
21 [a]Rev. 19:15 [b]Rev. 19:11, 19 [c]Rev. 19:17

1 [1]Lit., *upon* [a]Rev. 10:1 [b]Rev. 1:18; 9:1
2 [a]Gen. 3:1; Rev. 12:9 [b]Is. 24:22; 2 Pet. 2:4; Jude 6
3 [a]Rev. 20:1 [b]Dan. 6:17; Matt. 27:66 [c]Rev. 12:9; 20:8, 10
4 [a]Dan. 7:9 [b]Matt. 19:28; Rev. 3:21 [c]Dan. 7:22; 1 Cor. 6:2 [d]Rev. 6:9 [e]Rev. 1:9 [f]Rev. 13:12, 15 [g]Rev. 13:16f. [h]John 14:19 [i]Rev. 3:21; 5:10; 20:6; 22:5
5 [a]Luke 14:14; Phil. 3:11; 1 Thess. 4:16
6 [a]Rev. 14:13 [b]Rev. 2:11; 20:14 [c]Rev. 1:6 [d]Rev. 3:21; 5:10; 20:4; 22:5
7 [a]Rev. 20:2f.
8 [1]Lit., *sea* [a]Rev. 12:9; 20:3, 10 [b]Ezek. 7:2; Rev. 7:1 [c]Ezek. 38:2; 39:1, 6 [d]Rev. 16:14 [e]Heb. 11:12
9 [1]Lit., *breadth of the earth* [2]Or, *holy ones* [a]Ezek. 38:9, 16 [b]Deut. 23:14 [c]Ps. 87:2 [d]Ezek. 38:22; 39:6; Rev. 13:13
10 [a]Rev. 20:2f. [b]Rev. 19:20; 20:14, 15 [c]Rev. 16:13 [d]Rev. 14:10f.
11 [1]Lit., *face* [a]Rev. 4:2 [b]Rev. 6:14; 21:1 [c]Dan. 2:35; Rev. 12:8
12 [1]Or, *scrolls* [2]Or, *scroll* [a]Rev. 11:18 [b]Dan. 7:10 [c]Rev. 3:5; 20:15 [d]Rev. 11:18 [e]Matt. 16:27; Rev. 2:23; 20:13
13 [a]1 Cor. 15:26; Rev. 1:18; 6:8; 21:4 [b]Is. 26:19 [c]Matt. 16:27; Rev. 2:23; 20:12
14 [a]1 Cor. 15:26; Rev. 1:18; 6:8; 21:4 [b]Rev. 19:20; 20:10, 15 [c]Rev. 20:6
15 [1]Lit., *anyone was* [a]Rev. 3:5; 20:12

1 [a]Is. 65:17; 66:22; 2 Pet. 3:13 [b]2 Pet. 3:10; Rev. 20:11
2 [a]Is. 52:1; Rev. 11:2; 21:10; 22:19 [b]Rev. 3:12; 21:10 [c]Heb. 11:10, 16; Rev. 21:10 [d]Is. 61:10; Rev. 19:7; 21:9; 22:17

3 [1]Or, *tabernacle* [2]Some ancient mss. add, and be *their God* [a]Lev. 26:11f.; Ezek. 37:27; 48:35; Heb. 8:2; Rev. 7:15 [b]John 14:23; 2 Cor. 6:16
4 [a]Is. 25:8; Rev. 7:17 [b]1 Cor. 15:26; Rev. 20:14 [c]Is. 35:10; 51:11; 65:19 [d]2 Cor. 5:17; Heb. 12:27
5 [a]Rev. 4:9; 20:11 [b]2 Cor. 5:17; Heb. 12:27 [c]Rev. 19:9; 22:6
6 [1]Lit., *They are* [a]Rev. 10:6; 16:17 [b]Rev. 1:8; 22:13 [c]Is. 55:1; John 4:10; Rev. 7:17; 22:17 [d]Rev. 7:17

7 "[a]He who overcomes shall inherit these things, and [b]I will be his God and he will be My son.

8 "[a]But for the cowardly and [1]unbelieving and abominable and murderers and immoral persons and sorcerers and idolaters and all liars, their part *will be* in [b]the lake that burns with fire and brimstone, which is the [c]second death."

9 [a]And one of the seven angels who had the [b]seven bowls [1]full of the [c]seven last plagues, came and spoke with me, saying, "[d]Come here, I shall show you the [e]bride, the wife of the Lamb."

The New Jerusalem

10 And [a]he carried me away [1b]in the Spirit to a great and high mountain, and showed me [c]the holy city, Jerusalem, coming down out of heaven from God,

11 having [a]the glory of God. Her [1]brilliance was like a very costly stone, as a [b]stone of [c]crystal-clear jasper.

12 [1]It had a great and high wall, [1a]with twelve [b]gates, and at the gates twelve angels; and names *were* written on them, which are *those* of the twelve tribes of the sons of Israel.

13 *There were* three gates on the east and three gates on the north and three gates on the south and three gates on the west.

14 And the wall of the city had [a]twelve foundation stones, and on them *were* the twelve names of the [b]twelve apostles of the Lamb.

15 And the one who spoke with me had a [1]gold measuring [a]rod to measure the city, and its [b]gates and its wall.

16 And the city is laid out as a square, and its length is as great as the width; and he measured the city with the [1]rod, [2]fifteen hundred miles; its length and width and height are equal.

17 And he measured its wall, [1]seventy-two yards, *according to* [a]human [2]measurements, which are *also* [b]angelic *measurements.*

18 And the material of the wall was [a]jasper; and the city was [b]pure gold, like [1]clear [c]glass.

19 [a]The foundation stones of the city wall were adorned with every kind of precious stone. The first foundation stone was [b]jasper; the second, sapphire; the third, chalcedony; the fourth, [c]emerald;

20 the fifth, sardonyx; the sixth, [a]sardius; the seventh, chrysolite; the eighth, beryl; the ninth, topaz; the tenth, chrysoprase; the eleventh, jacinth; the twelfth, amethyst.

21 And the twelve [a]gates were twelve [b]pearls; each one of the gates was a single pearl. And the street of the city was [c]pure gold, like transparent [d]glass.

22 And I saw [a]no [1]temple in it, for the [b]Lord God, the Almighty, and the [c]Lamb, are its [1]temple.

23 And the city [a]has no need of the sun or of the moon to shine upon it, for [b]the glory of God has illumined it, and its lamp *is* the [c]Lamb.

24 And [a]the nations shall walk by its light, and the [b]kings of the earth [1]shall bring their glory into it.

25 And in the daytime (for [a]there shall be no night there) [b]its gates [c]shall never be closed;

26 and [a]they shall bring the glory and the honor of the nations into it;

27 and [a]nothing unclean and no one who practices abomination and lying, shall ever come into it, but only those [1]whose names are [b]written in the Lamb's book of life.

The River and the Tree of Life

22 AND [a]he showed me a [b]river of the [c]water of life, [1]clear [d]as crystal, coming from the throne of God and of [2]the Lamb,

2 in the middle of [a]its street. And [b]on either side of the river was [c]the tree of life, bearing twelve [1]*kinds of* fruit, yielding its fruit every month; and the leaves of the tree were for the healing of the nations.

3 And [a]there shall no longer be any curse; and [b]the throne of God and of the Lamb shall be in it, and His bond-servants shall [c]serve Him;

4 and they shall [a]see His face, and His [b]name *shall be* on their [c]foreheads.

5 And [a]there shall no longer be *any* night; and they [1]shall not have need [b]of the light of a lamp nor the light of the sun, because the Lord God shall illumine them; and they shall [c]reign forever and ever.

6 And [a]he said to me, "[b]These words are faithful and true"; and the Lord, the [c]God of the spirits of the prophets, [d]sent His angel to show to His bond-servants the things which must shortly take place.

7 "And behold, [a]I am coming quickly. [b]Blessed is he who [1]heeds [c]the words of the prophecy of this book."

8 And [a]I, John, am the one who heard and saw these things. And when I heard and saw, [b]I fell down to worship at the feet of the angel who showed me these things.

9 And [a]he *said to me, "Do not do that; I am a [b]fellow servant of yours and of your brethren the prophets and of those who [1]heed the words of [c]this book; worship God."

The Final Message

10 And he *said to me, "[a]Do not seal up [b]the words of the prophecy of this book, [c]for the time is near.

7 [a]Rev. 2:7 [b]2 Sam. 7:14; Ps. 89:26f.; 2 Cor. 6:16, 18; Rev. 21:3
8 [1]Or, *untrustworthy* [a]1 Cor. 6:9; Gal. 5:19-21; Rev. 9:21; 21:27; 22:15 [b]Rev. 19:20 [c]Rev. 2:11
9 [1]Lit., *who were full* [a]Rev. 17:1 [b]Rev. 15:7 [c]Rev. 15:1 [d]Rev. 17:1 [e]Rev. 19:7; 21:2
10 [1]Or, *in spirit* [a]Ezek. 40:2; Rev. 17:3 [b]Rev. 1:10 [c]Rev. 21:2
11 [1]Lit., *luminary* [a]Is. 60:1f.; Ezek. 43:2; Rev. 15:8; 21:23; 22:5 [b]Rev. 4:3; 21:18, 19 [c]Rev. 4:6
12 [1]Lit., *having* [a]Ezek. 48:31-34 [b]Rev. 21:15, 21, 25; 22:14
14 [a]Heb. 11:10 [b]Acts 1:26
15 [1]Lit., *measure, a gold reed* [a]Ezek. 40:3; Rev. 11:1 [b]Rev. 21:12, 21, 25
16 [1]Lit., *reed* [2]Lit., *twelve thousand stadia;* a stadion was approx. 600 ft.
17 [1]Lit., *one hundred forty-four cubits* [2]Lit., *measure* [a]Deut. 3:11; Rev. 13:18 [b]Rev. 21:9
18 [1]Lit., *pure* [a]Rev. 21:11 [b]Rev. 21:21 [c]Rev. 4:6
19 [a]Ex. 28:17-20; Is. 54:11f.; Ezek. 28:13 [b]Rev. 21:11 [c]Rev. 4:3
20 [a]Rev. 4:3
21 [a]Rev. 21:12, 15, 25 [b]Rev. 17:4 [c]Rev. 21:18 [d]Rev. 4:6
22 [1]Or, *sanctuary* [a]Matt. 24:2; John 4:21 [b]Rev. 1:8 [c]Rev. 5:6; 7:17; 14:4
23 [a]Is. 24:23; 60:19, 20; Rev. 21:25; 22:5 [b]Rev. 21:11 [c]Rev. 5:6; 7:17; 14:4
24 [1]Lit., *bring* [a]Is. 60:3, 5 [b]Ps. 72:10f.; Is. 49:23; 60:16; Rev. 21:26
25 [a]Zech. 14:7; Rev. 21:23; 22:5 [b]Rev. 21:12, 15 [c]Is. 60:11
26 [a]Ps. 72:10f.; Is. 49:23; 60:16
27 [1]Lit., *who are* [a]Is. 52:1; Ezek. 44:9; Zech. 14:21; Rev. 22:14f. [b]Rev. 3:5

1 [1]Lit., *bright* [2]Or, *the Lamb. In the middle of its street, and on either side of the river, was* [a]Rev. 1:1; 21:9; 22:6 [b]Ps. 46:4; Ezek. 47:1 [c]Zech. 14:8; Rev. 7:17; 22:17 [d]Rev. 4:6
2 [1]Or, crops of *fruit* [a]Rev. 21:21 [b]Ezek. 47:12 [c]Gen. 2:9; Rev. 2:7; 22:14, 19
3 [a]Zech. 14:11 [b]Rev. 21:3 [c]Rev. 7:15
4 [a]Ps. 17:15; 42:2; Matt. 5:8 [b]Rev. 14:1 [c]Rev. 7:3
5 [1]Lit., *do not have* [a]Zech. 14:7; Rev. 21:25 [b]Is. 60:19; Rev. 21:23 [c]Dan. 7:18, 27; Matt. 19:28; Rom. 5:17; Rev. 20:4
6 [a]Rev. 1:1; 21:9 [b]Rev. 19:9; 21:5 [c]1 Cor. 14:32; Heb. 12:9 [d]Rev. 1:1; 22:16
7 [1]Or, *keeps* [a]Rev. 1:3; 3:3, 11; 16:15; 22:12, 20 [b]Rev. 1:3; 16:15 [c]Rev. 1:11; 22:9, 10, 18f.
8 [a]Rev. 1:1 [b]Rev. 19:10
9 [1]Or, *keep* [a]Rev. 19:10 [b]Rev. 1:1 [c]Rev. 1:11; 22:10, 18f.
10 [a]Dan. 8:26; Rev. 10:4 [b]Rev. 1:11; 22:9, 18f. [c]Rev. 1:3

11 "[a]Let the one who does wrong, still
do wrong; and let the one who is filthy,
still be filthy; and let the one who is
righteous, still practice righteousness;
and let the one who is holy, still keep
himself holy."
12 "Behold, [a]I am coming quickly, and
My [b]reward *is* with Me, [c]to render to
every man [1]according to what he has
done.
13 "I am the [a]Alpha and the Omega,
[b]the first and the last, [c]the beginning and
the end."
14 Blessed are those who [a]wash their
robes, that they may have the right to
[b]the tree of life, and may [c]enter by the
[d]gates into the city.
15 [a]Outside are the [b]dogs and the
sorcerers and the immoral persons and
the murderers and the idolaters, and
everyone who loves and practices lying.
16 "[a]I, Jesus, have sent [b]My angel to
testify to you these things [1c]for the
churches. I am [d]the root and the [e]off-
spring of David, the bright [f]morning
star."

11 [a]Ezek. 3:27; Dan. 12:10

12 [1]Lit., *as his work is* [a]Rev. 22:7 [b]Is. 40:10; 62:11 [c]Ps. 28:4; Jer. 17:10; Matt. 16:27; Rev. 2:23

13 [a]Rev. 1:8 [b]Is. 44:6; 48:12; Rev. 1:17; 2:8 [c]Rev. 21:6

14 [a]Rev. 7:14 [b]Gen. 2:9; 3:22; Rev. 22:2 [c]Rev. 21:27 [d]Rev. 21:12

15 [a]Matt. 8:12; 1 Cor. 6:9f.; Gal. 5:19ff.; Rev. 21:8 [b]Deut. 23:18; Matt. 7:6; Phil. 3:2

16 [1]Or, *concerning* [a]Rev. 1:1 [b]Rev. 1:1; 22:6 [c]Rev. 1:4, 11; 3:22 [d]Rev. 5:5 [e]Matt. 1:1 [f]Matt. 2:2; Rev. 2:28

17 [a]Rev. 2:7; 14:13 [b]Rev. 21:2, 9 [c]Is. 55:1; Rev. 21:6 [d]Rev. 7:17; 22:1

17 And the [a]Spirit and the [b]bride say,
"Come." And let the one who hears say,
"Come." And [c]let the one who is thirsty
come; let the one who wishes take the
[d]water of life without cost.
18 I testify to everyone who hears [a]the
words of the prophecy of this book: if
anyone [b]adds to them, God shall add to
him [c]the plagues which are written in
[d]this book;
19 and if anyone [a]takes away from the
[b]words of the book of this prophecy,
God shall take away his part from [c]the
tree of life and [1]from the holy city,
[d]which are written in this book.
20 He who [a]testifies to these things
says, "Yes, [b]I am coming quickly."
Amen. [c]Come, Lord Jesus.
21 [a]The grace of the Lord Jesus be
with [1]all. Amen.

18 [a]Rev. 22:7 [b]Deut. 4:2; 12:32; Prov. 30:6 [c]Rev. 15:6-16:21 [d]Rev. 22:7
19 [1]Lit., *out of* [a]Deut. 4:2; 12:32; Prov. 30:6 [b]Rev. 22:7 [c]Rev. 22:2 [d]Rev. 21:10-22:5
20 [a]Rev. 1:2 [b]Rev. 22:7 [c]1 Cor. 16:22
21 [1]Some ancient mss. read *the saints* [a]Rom. 16:20

The New American Standard

CONCORDANCE

to the

Old and New Testaments

A collection of the principal common words with their most widely used examples in text and lesser usages in reference. Related words, or synonyms follow the key word. The key word is abbreviated in the text to its first letter, e.g., "abide" is "**a**". Variants add suffixes or prefixes, e.g., "abiding" appears as "**a-ing**".

A

ABANDON—*leave* Judg. 6:13, LORD has **a-ed** us
1 Sam. 12:22; Ps. 94:14, LORD . . . **a** His people
2 Kin. 21:14, I will **a** the remnant
Ps. 27:9, Do not **a** me nor forsake me
Jer. 23:33, I shall **a** you
Acts 2:27, Thou wilt not **a** my soul to
27:20, hope of our being saved . . . **a-ed**
Ps. 16:10; Prov. 17:14; Is. 2:6; Jer. 12:7; Ezek. 29:5

ABASE—*humble* Ezek. 21:26; Mal. 2:9

ABATE—*decrease* Gen. 8:8,11, water was **a-d**
Deut. 34:7, his vigor **a-d**

ABBA Mark 14:36, saying, **A**! Father
Rom. 8:15, by which we cry out, **A**! Father
Gal. 4:6, crying, **A**! Father

ABHOR—*despise, detest, loathe*
Rom. 12:9, **A** what is evil
Deut. 7:26; Job 19:19; Ps. 78:59; Prov. 24:24; Is. 49:7

ABIDE—*remain, stay* Ps. 9:7, the LORD **a-s** forever
Ps. 15:1, who may **a** in Thy tent
91:1, Will **a** in the shadow
102:12, LORD, dost **a** forever
John 3:36, wrath of God **a-s** on him
5:38, His word **a-ing** in you
8:31, you **a** in My word
14:25, while **a-ing** with you
15:4, **A** in Me . . . it **a-s** in the vine . . . you **a** in Me
15:6, If anyone does not **a** in Me
15:7, **a** in Me, and My words **a** in you
15:9, **a** in My love
15:10, you will **a** in My love . . . **a** in His love
1 Cor. 13:13, But now **a** faith, hope, love
Heb. 10:34, a better possession and an **a-ing** one
1 Pet. 1:23, living and **a-ing** word of God
1:25, BUT THE WORD OF THE LORD **A-S** FOREVER
1 John 3:17, how does the love of God **a** in him
4:12, God **a-s** in us

ABILITY—*strength* Ezra 2:69, according to . . . **a**
Dan. 1:4, who had **a** for serving
Matt. 25:15, according to his own **a**

ABLE—*adequate* 1 Sam. 6:20, Who is **a** to stand
Matt. 3:9, God is **a** from these stones
9:28, believe that I am **a** to do this
10:28, fear Him who is **a** to destroy
20:22, Are you **a** to drink the cup
John 10:29, no one is **a** to snatch them
Acts 6:10, they were **un-a** to cope with the wisdom
Rom. 8:39, shall be **a** to separate us
1 Cor. 10:13, tempted beyond what you are **a**
Eph. 3:18, may be **a** to comprehend
2 Tim. 2:2, who will be **a** to teach
James 4:12, the One who is **a** to save
Jude 24, Now to Him who is **a** to keep
1 Kin. 3:9; 2 Chr. 2:6; Rev. 5:3; 6:17

ABOARD Acts 21:2, went **a** and set sail

ABODE—*habitation* Jer. 31:23; Jude 6
John 14:23, and make Our **a** with him

ABOLISH—*destroy* Matt. 5:17, I did not come to **a**
Eph. 2:15, by **a-ing** in His flesh
2 Tim. 1:10, Christ Jesus, who **a-ed** death

ABOMINABLE—*detestable, rejected*
Jer. 44:4, do not do this **a** thing
Ezek. 16:25, made your beauty **a**
1 Pet. 4:3, drinking parties and **a** idolatries
Ps. 14:1; 53:1; Rev. 21:8

ABOMINATION—*detestable thing*
Ex. 8:26, an **a** to the Egyptians
Prov. 3:32, an **a** to the LORD
8:7, an **a** to my lips
Ezek. 33:29, because of all their **a-s**
Dan. 12:11, the **a** of desolation
Rev. 17:5, the **a-s** of the earth
Lev. 18:26; Deut. 7:26; 29:17

ABOUND—*excel, multiply*
Ex. 34:6, **a-ing** in lovingkindness and truth
Prov. 28:20, a faithful man will **a** with blessings
Dan. 4:1, May your peace **a**
Rom. 15:13, that you may **a** in hope
1 Cor. 15:58, always **a-ing** in the work of the
1 Cor. 14:12; 2 Cor. 7:15; 9:8

ABOVE—*over* Ex. 20:4, what is in heaven **a** or on
Ps. 8:1, Thy splendor **a** the heavens
Matt. 10:24, A disciple is not **a** his teacher
John 3:31, He who comes from **a** is **a** all
8:23, I am from **a**
Phil. 2:9, the name which is **a** every name
Col. 3:1; 2 Thess. 2:4; James 1:17

ABSENT Gen. 31:49, we are **a** one from the other
1 Cor. 5:3, though **a** in body, but present
2 Cor. 5:6, we are **a** from the Lord
5:8, **a** from the body and to be
10:1, but bold toward you when **a**

ABSTAIN—*depart, separate* Num. 6:3
Acts 15:20, that they **a** from things
1 Thess. 5:22, **a** from every form of evil
1 Tim. 4:3, **a-ing** from foods, which
2 Tim. 2:19, who names . . . the Lord **a** from wickedness
1 Pet. 2:11, strangers to **a** from fleshly lusts

ABUNDANCE—*surplus, plenty, full, plenteous*
Gen. 41:34, seven years of **a**
Ps. 52:7, the **a** of his riches
72:7, And **a** of peace till
Is. 55:2, delight yourself in **a**
Matt. 13:12, and he shall have an **a**
Luke 12:15, when one has an **a** does his life
Rom. 5:17, receive the **a** of grace
Phil. 4:18, everything in full, and have an **a**
Gen. 41:29; Deut. 28:47; Neh. 9:25; Ps. 36:8; 72:16; 73:10; Prov. 24:6; Eccles. 5:10; Phil. 4:12

ABUNDANT—*plenteous* Job 36:28; Ezek. 16:49
Gen. 41:47, land brought forth **a-ly**
Ps. 86:5, **a** in lovingkindness to all
2 Cor. 1:5, our comfort is **a** through Christ

ABUSE Judg. 19:25, **a-d** her all night
1 Chr. 10:4, lest these . . . come and **a** me
Matt. 27:39, passing by were hurling **a** at Him
ABUSIVE—*filthy* Col. 3:8, a speech from your mouth
ABYSS—*deep, depth* Rom. 10:7, DESCEND INTO THE A
Rev. 20:3, threw him into the **a**
Luke 8:31; Rev. 11:7; 17:8; 20:1
ACCEPT—*receive* Deut. 33:11, And **a** the work
Job 2:10, a good from God and not **a** adversity
Jer. 2:30, They **a-ed** no chastening
Mark 4:20, hear the word and **a** it
Rom. 15:7, **a** one another
1 Tim. 1:15, statement, deserving full **a-ance**
ACCEPTABLE—*favorable, pleasing* Ps. 69:13, at an **a** time
Rom. 15:31, may prove **a** to the saints
2 Cor. 6:2, At the **a** time . . . the **a** time
Phil. 4:18, an **a** sacrifice
1 Tim. 2:3, good and **a** in the sight
ACCESS Eph. 2:18, have our **a** in one Spirit
Eph. 3:12, confident **a** through faith in Him
ACCOMPLISH—*perform* 1 Kin. 5:9, you shall **a** my desire
Ps. 57:2, God who **a-es** *all things*
John 4:34, and to **a** His work
James 5:16, prayer of a righteous man can **a**
ACCOMPLISHED—*realized, wrought*
Neh. 6:16, work had been **a** . . . God
Luke 1:1, things **a** among us
John 17:4, having **a** the work
Rom. 15:18, what Christ has **a** through me
James 1:15, when sin is **a**
Luke 12:50; John 19:28; 1 Pet. 5:9
ACCORD—*unite* Josh. 9:2; Acts 5:12
Acts 4:24, voices to God with one **a**
8:6, the multitudes with one **a**
12:20, one **a** they came to him
18:12, one **a** rose up against Paul
19:29, rushed with one **a** into the
2 Cor. 8:17, gone to you of his own **a**
ACCORDING Gen. 30:34, be **a** to your word
Matt. 16:27; Rom. 2:6, **a** to his deeds
Rom. 8:28, **a** to *His* purpose
Gal. 3:29, heirs **a** to promise
Rev. 22:12, render to every man **a**
Job 34:11; Jer. 17:10; John 7:24; 18:31; Rom. 12:6; 16:25; 2 Cor. 8:12
ACCOUNT—*declaration, sake, tell*
Gen. 2:4, is the **a** of the heavens and the earth
8:21, curse the ground on **a** of man
Esth. 10:2, full **a** of the greatness of Mordecai
1 Sam. 12:22, on **a** of His great name
Matt. 5:11, evil . . . falsely on **a** of Me
Luke 1:1, compile an **a** of the things accomplished
Rom. 3:19, become **a-able** to God
Num. 12:11; Judg. 7:15
ACCUMULATE—*heap* 2 Tim. 4:3, **a** for themselves teachers
ACCURATE Job 31:6; Acts 18:25
ACCURSED Is. 65:20; Matt. 25:41
Josh. 6:18, make the camp of Israel **a**
Rom. 9:3, wish that I myself were **a**
1 Cor. 12:3, no one . . . says, Jesus is **a**
Gal. 1:8, let him be **a**
ACCUSATION—*charge* Ezra 4:6, wrote an **a** against
Dan. 6:4, find no ground of **a** or
John 18:29, What **a** do you bring against
Acts 28:19, had any **a** against my nation
1 Tim. 5:19, Do not receive an **a** against
ACCUSE—*testify* Matt. 27:12, while He was being **a-d**
John 5:45, I will **a** you before the Father
Acts 22:30, why he had been **a-d** by the Jews
Deut. 19:18; Titus 1:6
ACKNOWLEDGE—*confess* Ps. 32:5, I **a-d** my sin
Prov. 3:6, In all your ways **a** Him
Acts 23:8, Pharisees **a** them all
Rom. 1:28, see fit to **a** God
ACQUAINT Ps. 139:3, **a-ed** with all my ways
Is. 53:3, **a-ed** with grief
ACQUAINTANCE Ps. 88:8, removed my **a-s** far from me
Luke 23:49, all His **a-s** and the women
Job 19:13; Ps. 31:11; 88:18; Luke 2:44
ACQUIRE—*get, purchase* Ruth 4:10; Prov. 1:5; 18:15
Prov. 4:5, **A** wisdom! **A** understanding
4:7, with all your **a-ing**, get understanding
Matt. 10:9, Do not **a** gold, or silver
ACQUIT—*cleanse* Job 10:14; Ps. 19:12
ACT—*behave* Ps. 103:7, made known His . . . **a** to the
1 Cor. 16:13, **a** like men, be strong
John 8:4; 1 Cor. 13:5
A-s of Solomon, 1 Kin. 11:41
Jeroboam, 14:19
Rehoboam, 14:29
Abijam, 15:7
Asa, 15:23
Nadab, 15:31
Baasha, 16:5
Elah, 16:14
Zimri, 16:20
Omri, 16:27
Ahab, 22:39
Jehoshaphat, 22:45
Ahaziah, 2 Kin. 1:18
Joram, 8:23
Jehu, 10:34
Joash, 12:19
Jehoahaz, 13:8
Joash, 13:12
Jehoash, 14:15
Amaziah, 14:18
Jeroboam, 14:28
Azariah, 15:6
Zechariah, 15:11
Shallum, 15:15
Menahem, 15:21
Pekahiah, 15:26
Pekah, 15:31
Jotham, 15:36
Ahaz, 16:19
Hezekiah, 20:20
Manasseh, 21:17
Amon, 21:25
Josiah, 23:28
Jehoiakim, 24:5
David, 1 Chr. 29:29
Uzziah, 2 Chr. 26:22
ACTION—*deed, work* Acts 5:38, plan or **a** should be of men
1 Sam. 2:3; Dan. 11:28,32; Luke 23:51
ACTIVITY Eccles. 11:5, you do not know the **a** of God
2 Thess. 2:9, accord with the **a** of Satan
ADDER—*serpent, viper* Is. 59:5, They hatch **a-s**
ADJURE—*implore* 1 Kin. 22:16, many times must I **a**
Matt. 26:63, I **a** You by the living God
Acts 19:13, I **a** you by Jesus
ADMINISTRATION 1 Cor. 12:28, **a-s** . . . kinds of tongues
2 Cor. 8:20, in our **a** of this
Eph. 1:10, an **a** suitable to the fulness of the times
3:9, **a** of the mystery
ADMONISH—*warn* Acts 20:31, cease to **a** each one
Acts 27:9, Paul *began* to **a** them
Rom. 15:14, able also to **a** one another
1 Cor. 4:14, to **a** you as my . . . children
Col. 1:28, **a-ing** every man
3:16, **a-ing** one another with psalms
1 Thess. 5:14, **a** the unruly
2 Thess. 3:15, **a** him as a brother
ADOPTION Rom. 8:15, spirit of **a** as sons
Rom. 8:23, waiting eagerly for *our* **a** as sons
9:4, to whom belong the **a**
Gal. 4:5, receive the **a** as sons
Eph. 1:5, predestined us to **a**
ADORN—*clothe, array* 1 Tim. 2:9, women to **a** themselves

1 Pet. 3:3, let not your **a-ment**
Rev. 21:2, as a bride **a-ed** for her husband
Job 40:10; Is. 61:10; Ezek. 16:11; Matt. 23:29; Luke 21:5; Rev. 17:4; 18:16; 21:19

ADULTERATING 2 Cor. 4:2, not . . . **a** the word of God

ADULTERER Lev. 20:10; Ps. 50:18; Heb. 13:4

ADULTERESS—*strange woman* Prov. 22:14, mouth of an **a**

ADULTERY Ex. 20:14; Deut. 5:18; Matt. 5:27, 28; Luke 18:20; James 2:11; 2 Pet. 2:14

ADVANCE Gen. 24:1; Luke 1:7

ADVANTAGE—*profit* Prov. 21:5; 2 Cor. 2:11
Eccles. 1:3, What **a** does man have in all his work
7:12, the **a** of knowledge
John 16:7, to your **a** that I go away
2 Cor. 12:17, I have not taken **a** of you

ADVERSARY—*opponent, foe*
1 Cor. 16:9, and there are many **a-es**
Heb. 10:27, which will consume the **a-es**
1 Pet. 5:8, Your **a**, the devil
Ex. 23:22; 1 Kin. 11:14; Ps. 27:2; 89:23

ADVERSITY—*distress, privation* Deut. 30:15; Job 2:10
Ps. 10:6, I shall not be in **a**
94:13, relief from the days of **a**
Prov. 17:17, is born for **a**

ADVISE—*inform, counsel* Num. 24:14; Rev. 3:18

ADVOCATE—*witness* Job 16:19, my **a** is on high
1 John 2:1, we have an **A** with the Father

AFFAIRS 1 Chr. 26:32, all the **a** of God and . . . the king
2 Tim. 2:4, entangles himself in the **a**

AFFECTION—*devotion, passion*
2 Cor. 6:12, restrained in your own **a-s**
7:15, his **a** abounds
Deut. 10:15; Phil. 1:8; 2:1; 1 Thess. 2:8

AFFLICT—*oppress, distress, trouble*
Deut. 26:6, Egyptians . . . **a-ed** us
Judg. 16:5, we may bind him to **a** him
Ps. 82:3, justice to the **a-ed** and destitute
147:6, LORD supports the **a-ed**
Is. 61:1, bring good news to the **a-ed**
63:9, He was **a-ed**
Lam. 3:33, does not **a** willingly
2 Cor. 4:8, *we are* **a-ed** in every way
Ex. 1:11,12; 22:22,23; Num. 24:24; 2 Sam. 7:10; 1 Kin. 11:39; 2 Kin. 17:20; Ps. 105:18; Prov. 15:15; Nah. 1:12

AFFLICTION—*misery, oppression*
Deut. 16:3, the bread of **a**
Job 36:15, delivers the afflicted in their **a**
Ps. 25:18, Look upon my **a**
Mark 4:17, when **a** or persecution arises
5:29, she was healed of her **a**
2 Cor. 2:4, out of much **a** and anguish
8:2, in a great ordeal of **a**
2 Thess. 1:6, **a** those who afflict you
Gen. 29:32; 31:42; 41:52; Job 5:6; 30:16; Eccles. 6:2; Acts 20:23

AFRAID—*dread, fear* Ex. 3:6, **a** to look at God
Deut. 20:8, Who is the man that is **a**
Ps. 56:4, not be **a**. What can *mere* man
91:5, **a** of the terror by night
Is. 51:12, are **a** of man who dies
Matt. 14:27, do not be **a**
21:46, they became **a** of the multitudes
Luke 9:34, they were **a** as they entered
12:4, **a** of those who kill the body
Gen. 3:10; Ex. 20:20; Josh. 11:6; Judg. 7:3; Job 9:28; 19:29; Prov. 31:21; Eccles. 9:2; Matt. 1:20; Mark 4:41; 5:36; 9:32; 11:18; 11:32; Luke 12:32; 19:21; John 9:22; 2 Cor. 11:3; 12:20; Heb. 13:6

AFTER Acts 13:22, a man **a** My heart
Acts 24:17, **a** several years I came
Gal. 2:1, **a** an interval
Gen. 7:4; Judg. 16:22; Dan. 2:39

AFTERWARD—*later, after* Gen. 38:30, And **a** his brother came
Matt. 21:30, he **a** regretted *it*
Mark 16:14, And **a** He appeared

AGAINST Gen. 16:12, hand *will be* **a** everyone
Lev. 20:3, set My face **a** that man
Matt. 12:30, not with Me is **a** Me
Gal. 5:23, **a** such things there is no law
Rev. 2:4, have *this* **a** you
Gen. 4:8; Job 16:4; Luke 4:11; Acts 19:38; 1 Pet. 3:12

AGE—*world, generations, elder*
1 Chr. 23:1, Now when David reached old **a**
Job 12:12, Wisdom is with **a-d** men
Matt. 12:32, this **a**, or in the **a** to come
Luke 16:8, sons of this **a** are more shrewd
John 9:21, he is of **a**, he shall speak
Eph. 2:7, that in the **a-s** to come
Col. 1:26, hidden from the *past* **a-s**
Heb. 6:5, powers of the **a** to come
Job 15:10; 32:7; Jer. 6:11; John 9:23; Philem. 9

AGITATION Ps. 38:8, the **a** of my heart

AGONY Luke 22:44, being in **a** He was praying
Acts 2:24, putting an end to the **a** of death

AGREE—*consent* Matt. 18:19, if two of you **a** on earth
John 9:22, Jews had already **a-d**
Acts 5:9, Why is it that you have **a-d** together
15:15, words of the Prophets **a**
28:25, when they did not **a** with one another
Matt. 20:13; Acts 23:20; 1 Tim. 6:3

AGREEMENT Acts 8:1, Saul was in hearty **a**
2 Cor. 6:16, what **a** has the temple
1 John 5:8, the three are in **a**

AILMENT—*infirmity* 1 Tim. 5:23, and your frequent **a-s**

AIR 1 Cor. 9:26, not beating the **a**
Eph. 2:2, prince of the power of the **a**
1 Thess. 4:17, meet the Lord in the **a**
Job 41:16; 1 Cor. 14:9

ALARM Jer. 4:19, The **a** of war
Num. 10:5,6,7,9; Ps. 31:22; 116:11; Joel 2:1

ALAS—*woe* 2 Kin. 6:5, **A**, my master! For it was
Judg. 6:22; 11:35; Amos 5:16

ALERT—*watch* Matt. 24:42; Acts 20:31, be on the **a**
1 Cor. 16:13, Be on the **a**, stand firm
1 Thess. 5:6, let us be **a** and sober

ALIEN—*stranger, foreigner*
Deut. 10:19, show your love for the **a**
14:21, **a** who is in your town
Acts 7:6, A-S IN A FOREIGN LAND
Eph. 2:19, no longer strangers and **a-s**
2 Sam. 1:13; Ps. 69:8; Lam. 5:2

ALIENATED Col. 1:21, you were formerly **a**

ALIVE Num. 16:33; 2 Kin. 5:7; Ps. 55:15
Gen. 43:7; 45:3, Is your father still **a**
Acts 1:3, presented Himself **a**
Rom. 6:13, those **a** from the dead
1 Cor. 15:22, Christ . . . made **a**
Eph. 2:5, made us **a** together with Christ
1 Pet. 3:18, made **a** in the spirit
Rev. 1:18, I am **a** forevermore

ALL—*whatever* Jer. 1:7, And **a** that I command you
Matt. 6:32, **a** these things the Gentiles
Mark 16:15, Go into **a** the world and preach
Luke 2:10, great joy which shall be for **a** the people
3:6, A FLESH SHALL SEE THE SALVATION OF GOD
4:6, I will give you **a** this domain
Acts 2:1, **a** together in one place
1 Cor. 10:26, LORD'S, AND A IT CONTAINS

ALLEGORY Gal. 4:24, This contains an **a**

ALLIANCE 1 Kin. 3:1, Solomon . . . marriage **a** with Pharaoh

ALLIED 2 Chr. 18:1; Ps. 94:20

ALLOT Job 7:3, I **a-ed** months of vanity
Rom. 12:3, as God has **a-ed** to each a measure of faith

ALLOW Ex. 12:23, a the destroyer to come
Ps. 16:10, a Thy Holy One to see the pit
Acts 2:27, A THY HOLY ONE TO UNDERGO
22:22, not be **a-ed** to live
1 Cor. 10:13, not a you to be tempted
1 Tim. 2:12, do not a a woman to teach

ALLOWANCE 2 Kin. 25:30, for his **a**, a regular **a** was given
Jer. 52:34, a regular **a** was given him

ALLY Gen. 14:13, these were **a-es** with Abram

ALMIGHTY Gen. 17:1, I am God **A**
Ps. 91:1, shadow of the **A**
Rev. 4:8, *is* THE LORD GOD, THE **A**
11:17, the **A**, who art and who wast
Ex. 6:3; Job 11:7; 29:5; 37:23

ALMS—*charity* Matt. 6:2, therefore you give **a**
Matt. 6:4, your **a** may be in secret
Acts 10:2; 24:17

ALONE Gen. 2:18, not good for the man to be **a**
Matt. 4:4, MAN SHALL NOT LIVE ON BREAD A
Luke 9:18, He was praying **a**
John 8:16, I am not **a**
Job 7:16; Mark 14:6

ALREADY—*utterly* Eccles. 1:10, **A** it has existed for ages
Matt. 5:28, committed adultery with her **a**
John 3:18, who does not believe . . . judged **a**
9:27, He answered them, I told you **a**
11:17, had **a** been in the tomb four days
1 Cor. 5:3, I . . . have **a** judged him who
6:7, it is **a** a defeat for you
2 Thess. 2:7, mystery of lawlessness is **a** at work

ALTAR Ps. 43:4, I will go to the **a**
Ezek. 6:4, your **a-s** will become desolate
Matt. 5:23, your offering at the **a**
Rev. 9:13, four horns of the golden **a**
Gen. 8:20; Ex. 17:15; Lev. 6:9; Judg. 6:24; Matt. 23:19

ALWAYS—*forever, ever* Matt. 28:20, lo, I am with you **a**
Mark 14:7, you do not **a** have Me
Phil. 4:4, Rejoice in the Lord **a**
1 Thess. 4:17, thus we shall **a** be with the Lord
Deut. 14:23; 2 Tim. 3:7; Heb. 7:25

AM Ex. 3:14, I **A** WHO I **A**
Matt. 18:20, there I **a** in their midst
1 Cor. 15:10, grace of God I **a** what I **a**
Gal. 4:12, brethren, become as I **a**

AMASS—*heap* Ps. 39:6, He **a-es** *riches*

AMAZE—*astonish, astound*
Matt. 7:28, were **a-d** at His teaching
Luke 9:43, **a-d** at the greatness of God
Rev. 13:3, the whole earth was **a-d**
Mark 2:12; Luke 24:22; John 9:30

AMAZEMENT—*astonishment* Acts 3:10, with wonder and **a**

AMBITION 1 Thess. 4:11, make it your **a** to lead
James 3:14,16, bitter jealousy and selfish **a**

AMBUSH—*wait* Josh. 8:2, Set an **a** for the city
Josh. 8:4,7,12,14,19,21; Jer. 51:12

AMEN Num. 5:22, the woman shall say, **A. A**
Ps. 41:13; 72:19; 89:52, **A** and **A**
Matt. 6:13, *the glory, forever.* **A**
Rev. 3:14, The **A**, the faithful and true Witness

ANALYZE—*discern* Luke 12:56, **a** this present time

ANCIENT—*aged, everlasting, old*
Deut. 33:15, of the **a** mountains
1 Chr. 4:22, the records are **a**
Ps. 24:7, be lifted up, O **a** doors
Dan. 7:9,13,22, **A** of Days
Matt. 5:21, the **a-s** were told

ANGEL Matt. 4:6, GIVE HIS A-S CHARGE
Luke 20:36, for they are like **a-s**
22:43, an **a** from heaven appeared
John 20:12, beheld two **a-s** in white
2 Cor. 11:14, as an **a** of light
Col. 2:18, worship of the **a-s**
Gen. 24:7; Ps. 78:25; Is. 63:9; Matt. 1:20,24; 2:13; Acts 6:15; 23:8; Heb. 13:2; 2 Pet. 2:4; Rev. 2:1,8,12; 9:11

ANGER—*exasperation, wrath, indignation*
Ex. 32:19, Moses' **a** burned
Deut. 13:17, from His burning **a**
Job 5:2, And **a** kills the simple
Ps. 30:5, His **a** is but for a moment
Prov. 15:18, the slow to **a**
22:24, a man given to **a**
Eph. 4:26, sun go down on your **a**
James 1:19, slow to speak *and* slow to **a**
Gen. 39:19; 49:7; Ex. 22:24; Neh. 9:17; Job 9:13; Ps. 37:8; 38:1; Prov. 14:29; Eccles. 5:17; Is. 5:25; 51:17; 54:8; Gal. 5:20

ANGRY—*indignant, enraged*
Prov. 29:22, An **a** man stirs up strife
Is. 64:9, Do not be **a** beyond measure
Eph. 4:26, BE A . . . DO NOT SIN
Gen. 4:6; 18:30; Esth. 1:12; Jon. 4:4; Matt. 5:22; Heb. 3:10

ANGUISH—*distress, pain* Ps. 55:4; Is. 30:6; Jer. 6:24

ANIMAL—*beast, creature, cattle*
Gen. 6:7, from man to **a-s** to creeping things
7:8, Of clean **a-s** and **a-s** that are not
8:20, took of every clean **a** and
Acts 10:12, four-footed **a-s** and crawling creatures
2 Pet. 2:12, like unreasoning **a-s**
Ex. 22:19; Ps. 104:25; Jer. 27:6

ANNOUNCE—*proclaim* Is. 52:7, **a-s** peace . . . **a-s** salvation

ANNUAL 1 Sam. 7:16, used to go **a-ly** on circuit

ANOINT Matt. 6:17, fast, **a** your head
Mark 14:8, she has **a-ed** My body
16:1, they might come and **a**
Ex. 28:41; Ps. 23:5; 105:15; Luke 7:46; Acts 10:38; 2 Cor. 1:21; Rev. 3:18

ANSWER—*respond* Ps. 65:5, Thou dost **a** us
Prov. 15:1, **a** turns away wrath
Eccles. 10:19, money is the **a** to everything
Mic. 3:7, there is no **a** from God
Luke 2:47, amazed at . . . His **a-s**
Deut. 27:15; Ps. 55:19; Prov. 24:26; 26:4,5; Matt. 26:62; Mark 14:60; John 19:9; Acts 12:13

ANT Prov. 6:6, Go to the **a**, O sluggard
Prov. 30:25, The **a-s** are not a strong folk

ANTICHRIST 1 John 2:18, **a** is coming
2 John 7, the deceiver and the **a**
1 John 2:22; 4:3

ANXIETY—*sorrow* Ps. 38:18, full of **a** because of my sin
Jer. 49:23, There is **a** by the sea

ANXIOUS—*worry, concern, thought* Jer. 17:8
Matt. 6:25, do not be **a** for your life
6:27; Luke 12:25, being **a** can add a single
6:31, Do not be **a** then, saying
6:34, be **a** for tomorrow
10:19, **a** about how or what you will speak
Mark 13:11, do not be **a** beforehand about what
Luke 12:26, why are you **a** about other
Phil. 4:6, Be **a** for nothing

APART—*separate, without* Matt. 10:29, **a** from your Father
John 1:3, **a** from Him nothing came into being
Acts 13:2, Set **a** for Me Barnabas and
Rom. 3:28, justified by faith **a** from works

APOSTASY—*backsliding, faithlessness*
Hos. 14:4, I will heal their **a**
2 Thess. 2:3, *not come* unless the **a** comes first
Jer. 2:19; 5:6; 8:5; 14:7

APOSTLE Matt. 10:2, names of the twelve **a-s**
Rom. 1:1, called *as* an **a**
11:13, **a** of the Gentiles
Eph. 4:11, He gave some as **a-s**
Luke 11:49; 1 Cor. 15:9; 2 Cor. 12:11; Gal. 1:19; 1 Tim. 2:7; 2 Tim. 1:11

APPALL—*astound, amaze, astonish*
Job 17:8, upright shall be **a-ed**

Ps. 40:15, Let those be **a-ed** because of their shame
143:4, My heart is **a-ed** within me
Lev. 26:32; Jer. 2:12; Ezek. 4:17; Dan. 4:19

APPAREL—*garment* 2 Sam. 1:24, gold on your **a**
Is. 63:1, is majestic in His **a**
Luke 24:4, two men . . . in dazzling **a**
Acts 12:21, put on his royal **a**

APPEAL—*ask, beg, entreat* Acts 25:11, I **a** to Caesar
Acts 28:19, I was forced to **a** to Caesar
1 Tim. 5:1, **a** to him as a father
Philem. 9, for love's sake I rather **a** to you
Acts 25:12,21,25; 26:32

APPEAR—*be seen* Gen. 12:7, LORD **a-ed** to Abram
Ex. 3:2, **a-ed** to him in a blazing
Mal. 3:2, who can stand when He **a-s**
Acts 2:3, **a-ed** to them tongues as of
16:9, a vision **a-ed** to Paul in the
27:20, sun nor stars **a-ed** for many days
2 Cor. 5:10, we must all **a** before
Heb. 9:24, now to **a** in . . . of God for us
9:28, shall **a** a second time
1 Pet. 5:4, Chief Shepherd **a-s**
1 John 3:2, it has not **a-ed** . . . if He should **a**
Gen. 19:14; Num. 14:10; 2 Sam. 22:11; Matt. 1:20; 2:13; 27:53; Mark 16:9

APPEARANCE—*brightness, radiance, sight*
1 Sam. 16:7, man looks at the *outward* **a**
Matt. 6:16, for they neglect their **a**
28:3, his **a** was like lightning
Phil. 2:8, found in **a** as a man
2 Thess. 2:8, **a** of His coming
Num. 11:7; 1 Sam. 16:12; 2 Sam. 11:2; 14:27; Dan. 1:15; Nah. 2:4; Luke 9:29; Rev. 4:3

APPETITE—*stomach, desire* Prov. 23:2, man of *great* **a**
Phil. 3:19, whose god is *their* **a**
Num. 11:6; Job 38:39; Eccles. 6:7; Hab. 2:5; Rom. 16:18

APPLE Ps. 17:8, **a** of the eye
Prov. 25:11; Song 2:3,5

APPOINT—*name* Num. 3:10, you shall **a** Aaron
1 Chr. 17:9, I will **a** a place for My people
Jon. 1:17, **a-ed** a great fish to swallow
Mark 3:14, He **a-ed** twelve, that they
Heb. 9:27, **a-ed** for men to die
Gen. 4:15; Job 36:23; Jer. 49:19; John 15:16; 1 Tim. 2:7

APPORTION—*distribute* Josh. 13:7, **a** this land for an
Job 21:17, Does God **a** destruction
2 Cor. 10:13, sphere which God **a-ed** to us

APPRAISE—*discern*
1 Cor. 2:14, they are spiritually **a-d**

APPROACH Matt. 21:34, the harvest time **a-ed**
Luke 24:15, Jesus Himself **a-ed**
Lev. 18:14,19; Judg. 19:25

APPROPRIATE Eccles. 3:11, everything **a** in its time
Ezek. 36:5, **a-d** My land for themselves

APPROVAL Heb. 11:2, men of old gained **a**
Heb. 11:39, having gained **a** through

APPROVE—*attest* Rom. 14:18, and **a-d** by men
Rom. 16:10, **a-d** in Christ
2 Tim. 2:15, present yourself **a-d** to God

APRON Acts 19:12, handkerchiefs or **a-s**

ARCHANGEL 1 Thess. 4:16; Jude 9

ARGUE—*dispute, question* Mark 8:11
Prov. 25:8, out hastily to **a** *your case*
25:9, **A** your case with your neighbor
Mark 9:14, *some* scribes **a-ing** with them
Acts 9:29, talking and **a-ing** with Hellenistic Jews

ARGUMENT Job 23:4, fill my mouth with **a-s**
Ps. 38:14, whose mouth are no **a-s**

ARISE—*rise, stand* Gen. 31:13, **a**, leave this land
Job 31:14, do when God **a-s**
Ps. 27:3, war **a** against me
Dan. 11:2, three more kings are going to **a**
Matt. 11:11, has not **a-n** *anyone* greater
24:11, false prophets will **a**
Acts 10:13, **A**, Peter, kill and eat
Eph. 5:14, AND **A** FROM THE DEAD
2 Pet. 1:19, morning star **a-s** in your hearts
Deut. 9:12; Ps. 3:7; Song 2:13; Matt. 2:13,20; Acts 22:16

ARK Gen. 6:14, an **a** of gopher wood
Heb. 9:4, **a** of the covenant
Ex. 37:1; Matt. 24:38; Rev. 11:19

ARM (n.)—*hand, side* Deut. 33:27, the everlasting **a-s**
Ps. 37:17, **a-s** of the wicked . . . broken
Mark 10:16, took them in His **a-s**
Ex. 6:6; Job 26:2; Ps. 98:1; Song 8:6; Is. 60:4; Zech. 13:6

ARM (v.) Num. 31:3, **A** men from among you
Luke 11:21, a strong *man* fully **a-ed**
1 Pet. 4:1, **a** yourselves also

ARMOR—*weapon, harness* 1 Kin. 20:11; 22:34; Luke 11:22
Rom. 13:12, put on the **a** of light
Eph. 6:11,13, full **a** of God

ARMY—*host, war* Deut. 24:5; 1 Chr. 12:22; 2 Chr. 26:11

AROMA Gen. 8:21, LORD smelled the soothing **a**
2 Cor. 2:16, **a** from death . . . **a** from life

AROUSE—*raise, stir* Is. 42:13, He will **a** *His* zeal like
Acts 13:50, Jews **a-d** the devout women
Job 14:12; Is. 41:25; 45:13; Jer. 51:11

ARRAY—*adorn, clothe* Matt. 6:30, God so **a-s** the grass
Judg. 20:20; Luke 12:28

ARROGANCE—*pride* Prov. 8:13, Pride and **a** and the evil way
Is. 13:11, **a** of the proud
16:6, *Even* of his **a**, pride, and
Jer. 48:29, his **a** and his self-exaltation
49:16, **a** of your heart has deceived you

ARROGANT—*proud* Jer. 48:26, become **a** toward the LORD
Rom. 1:30, insolent, **a**, boastful
Jude 16, they speak **a-ly**
Rev. 13:5, **a** words and blasphemies
Jer. 50:32; Dan. 5:20; 2 Pet. 2:18

ARROW—*dart, missile* 1 Sam. 20:36, he shot an **a** past him
Job 6:4, **a-s** of the Almighty
Jer. 9:8, Their tongue is a deadly **a**
Job 41:28; Ps. 45:5; Prov. 7:23; Lam. 3:12

ART 2 Chr. 16:14, blended by the perfumers' **a**
Acts 17:29, image formed by the **a**

ASCEND Ps. 24:3, may **a** into the hill of
Ps. 139:8, If I **a** to heaven
John 3:13, no one has **a-ed**
6:62, behold the Son of Man **a-ing**
20:17, I **a** to My Father
Rom. 10:6, WHO WILL **A** INTO HEAVEN

ASH Gen. 18:27, am *but* dust and **a-es**
Job 13:12, sayings are proverbs of **a-es**
42:6, repent in dust and **a-es**
Ps. 102:9, eat **a-es** like bread
Is. 61:3, a garland instead of **a-es**
Matt. 11:21, repented . . . sackcloth and **a-es**
Luke 10:13, sitting in sackcloth and **a-es**
Lev. 6:11; Num. 19:17; 1 Sam. 2:8; 2 Sam. 13:19; 1 Kin. 13:3,5; Esth. 4:1; Job 2:8; 30:19; Ps. 147:16; Is. 44:20; 58:5; Jer. 6:26; Mal. 4:3; Heb. 9:13

ASHAMED—*confused* Ps. 71:1, me never be **a**
Mark 8:38, the Son of Man . . . **a** of him
Rom. 1:16, not **a** of the gospel
Heb. 11:16, not **a** to be called their God
Gen. 2:25; Ps. 25:2; Is. 24:23; 2 Tim. 1:8; 1 Pet. 4:16

ASHERAH, ASHERIM (pl.)
1 Kin. 15:13, made a . . . image as an **A**
Ex. 34:13; 2 Kin. 17:10; 2 Chr. 19:3; 33:19; Mic. 5:14

ASIDE 1 Sam. 8:3, turned **a** after dishonest gain
1 Pet. 2:1, putting **a** all malice

ASK—*appeal, beg, inquire* 1 Kin. 3:5, **A** what *you wish*
Ps. 27:4, One thing I have **a-ed** from the LORD
Prov. 30:7, Two things I **a-ed** of Thee
Jer. 6:16, **a** for the ancient paths
Matt. 5:42, Give to him who **a-s** of
7:7, **A**, and it shall be given to you
Mark 10:38, not know . . . **a-ing** for
John 4:40, they were **a-ing** Him to stay
14:16, I will **a** the Father
James 1:5, let him **a** of God
Ruth 3:11; Job 42:4; Ps. 2:8; Is. 7:11; Zech. 10:1; Matt. 21:22; Mark 10:35; 11:24; Luke 11:11; 1 Cor. 1:22; 10:25; Eph. 3:13; 1 John 5:15

ASLEEP Matt. 9:24, not dead, but **a**
Mark 4:38, was in the stern, **a**
13:36, come suddenly and find you **a**
John 11:11, Our friend Lazarus has fallen **a**
Acts 7:60, having said this, he fell **a**
1 Cor. 15:6, some have fallen **a**
1 Thess. 4:14, those who have fallen **a** in Jesus
5:10, whether . . . awake or **a**
Judg. 4:21; 1 Thess. 4:13,15

ASSEMBLE—*gather* 1 Chr. 13:5; 15:3, David **a-d** all Israel
Lev. 8:3; Num. 8:9; 20:8; Deut. 4:10; 31:12; Is. 43:9; Jer. 4:5; 8:14; Ezek. 11:17; Hos. 7:14; Amos 3:9

ASSEMBLY—*band, congregation, convocation*
Ps. 1:5, in the **a** of the righteous
Joel 1:14; 2:15, Proclaim a solemn **a**
Heb. 12:23, to the general **a** and church
Ex. 12:16; Lev. 23:36; Num. 20:10,12; Job 11:10; Ps. 26:5; 111:1; Acts 19:39

ASSERT Acts 25:19, whom Paul **a-ed** to be alive
1 Tim. 1:7, they make confident **a-ions**

ASSIGN—*distribute* 1 Cor. 7:17, Lord has **a-ed** to each

ASSOCIATE Rom. 12:16, but **a** with the lowly
Job 19:19; Ps. 50:18; Zech. 13:7; 2 Thess. 3:14

ASSURANCE—*confidence* Job 24:22, no one has **a** of life
Col. 2:2, full **a** of understanding
Heb. 6:11, full **a** of hope
10:22, full **a** of faith
11:1, faith . . . **a** of things hoped for

ASTONISH—*amaze, astound*
Matt. 13:54, so that they became **a-ed**
22:33, they were **a-ed** at His teaching
Mark 6:2, many listeners were **a-ed**
7:37, they were utterly **a-ed**
10:26, they were even more **a-ed**
11:18, all the multitude were **a-ed**
Job 21:5; Matt. 19:25; Luke 1:63

ASTOUND—*amaze, astonish* Jer. 4:9, prophets will be **a-ed**
Dan. 8:27, **a-ed** at the vision
Mark 5:42; 10:26

ASTRAY—*err* Ps. 119:176, gone **a** like a lost sheep
Is. 53:6, sheep have gone **a**
1 Tim. 6:21, gone **a** from the faith
Ps. 119:110; Prov. 10:17; Is. 3:12; 9:16; Matt. 18:13; Heb. 3:10

ATE—*eat* Jer. 15:16, words were found and I **a** them
1 Cor. 10:3, all **a** the same spiritual food
Luke 13:26; 24:43; Acts 9:9

ATONEMENT—*reconciliation* Lev. 23:27; 25:9, the day of **a**
Ex. 30:15; 2 Sam. 21:3

ATTAIN—*acquire* Rom. 9:30, **a-ed** righteousness
Phil. 3:11, **a** to the resurrection

ATTENTION—*heed, regard* Prov. 4:1, give **a** . . . gain understanding
16:20, who gives **a** to the word
Is. 5:12, not pay **a** to the deeds
Heb. 2:1, we must pay closer **a**
Ex. 5:9; Job 33:31; Prov. 29:12; 1 Tim. 1:4; 4:13

ATTEST Acts 2:22, a man **a-ed** to you by God

AUTHOR—*source* Heb. 12:2, the **a** and perfecter of faith

AUTHORITY Eccles. 8:8, **a** over the day of death
Matt. 7:29, teaching them as one having **a**
8:9, For I too am a man under **a**
9:6, **a** on earth to forgive
10:1, **a** over unclean spirits
21:23, By what **a** are You doing these things
28:18, **a** has been given to Me
Luke 5:24, Son of Man has **a** on earth to forgive
9:1, gave them power and **a**
19:17, be in **a** over ten cities
20:8, by what **a** I am doing these things
John 5:27, **a** to execute judgment
10:18, **a** to lay it down . . . **a** to take it up
17:2, Thou gavest Him **a** over all mankind
Acts 8:19, Give this **a** to me as well, so
Rom. 13:1, no **a** except from God
1 Cor. 15:24, all rule and all **a**
1 Tim. 2:12, to teach or exercise **a**
Titus 2:15, reprove with all **a**
2 Pet. 2:10, and despise **a**
Jude 25, majesty, dominion and **a**
Rev. 2:26, GIVE A OVER THE NATIONS
Num. 27:20; Is. 22:21; Hab. 1:7; Luke 10:19; 12:5

AVAIL—*profit* Jer. 7:8, deceptive words to no **a**

AVENGE—*vengeance, revenge* 1 Sam. 24:12
Jer. 5:9,29, Shall I not **a** Myself
2 Cor. 7:11, what zeal, what **a-ing** of wrong

AVOID—*refuse* Prov. 4:15, **A** it, do not pass by it
1 Tim. 6:20, **a-ing** worldly *and* empty chatter
2 Tim. 3:5, **a** such men as these

AWAIT—*wait* 1 Cor. 1:7, **a-ing** eagerly the revelation

AWAKE—*watch* Ps. 139:18, when I **a**, I am still with Thee
Eph. 5:14, **A**, SLEEPER
Rev. 16:15, Blessed is the one who stays **a**
Judg. 5:12; Ps. 17:15; Is. 51:9; John 11:11; Rom. 13:11

AWARE Luke 8:46, I was **a** that power had gone

AWE—*fear* Ps. 33:8, inhabitants . . . in **a** of Him
Ps. 119:161, stands in **a** of Thy words
Heb. 12:28, with reverence and **a**

AWESOME—*fearful* Gen. 28:17, How **a** is this place
Ex. 15:11, **A** in praises
Judg. 13:6, angel of God, very **a**
Neh. 1:5, the great and **a** God
Job 37:22, Around God is **a** majesty
Ps. 89:7, **a** above all those . . . around Him
Song 6:4, **a** as an army with banners
Joel 2:31, great and **a** day of the LORD

AXE—*hatchet* 2 Kin. 6:5, **a** head fell into the water
Matt. 3:10, **a** is already laid at the root
Luke 3:9, the **a** . . . root of the trees
1 Sam. 13:20; 1 Kin. 6:7

B

BABBLER Acts 17:18, this idle **b**

BABE—*immature* Matt. 11:25, reveal . . . to **b-s**
1 Cor. 3:1, to **b-s** in Christ
Heb. 5:13, for he is a **b**
1 Pet. 2:2, like newborn **b-s**
Ps. 8:2; 17:14; Matt. 21:16; Luke 10:21

BABY—*babe, immature* Luke 2:12; 2:16

BACK—*backward* Is. 38:17, sins behind Thy **b**
Num. 24:11; 1 Sam. 10:9; Neh. 9:26; Ezek. 2:10; Mark 13:16

BACKBITING—*slanders* Prov. 25:23, a **b** tongue

BACKSLIDE—*apostasy, faithless*
Prov. 14:14, **b-r** in heart will have his fill
Jer. 49:4, O **b-ing** daughter Who trusts

BACKWARD 2 Kin. 20:10, shadow turn **b** ten steps
Gen. 9:23; 49:17; Job 23:8; Jer. 7:24

BAD—*evil, wrong* Gen. 24:50; 31:24,29; Lev. 27:12,14,33; Num. 13:19; 24:13; 2 Sam. 13:22; 2 Cor. 5:10, good or **b**

Lev. 27:10, good for a **b**, or a **b** for a good
Matt. 7:18, good tree cannot produce **b** fruit
Gen. 43:6; Is. 3:11; Jer. 24:2,3; Matt. 13:48

BAG—*purse* Deut. 25:13; 1 Sam. 17:40
Job 14:17, My transgression is sealed up in a **b**
Matt. 10:10, or a **b** for *your* journey
2 Kin. 5:23; Prov. 7:20; 16:11; Mic. 6:11

BAGGAGE 1 Sam. 17:22, David left his **b**

BAKE Gen. 19:3; 40:17; Ex. 12:39; 16:23; Lev. 2:4; 24:5; 26:26; Num. 11:8; 1 Sam. 28:24; Is. 44:15

BAKER Gen. 40:1, **b** of the king of Egypt
Gen. 41:10; 1 Sam. 8:13; Jer. 37:21; Hos. 7:4

BALANCE—*scale* Lev. 19:36, shall have just **b-s**
Prov. 11:1, A false **b** is an abomination to the LORD
16:11, A just **b** and scales belong to the LORD
Job 6:2; Ps. 62:9; Is. 40:12; Ezek. 45:10; Hos. 12:7

BALD—*baldhead* Lev. 13:41, head becomes **b**
Jer. 48:37; Ezek. 29:18

BALDHEAD—*bald* 2 Kin. 2:23, Go up, you **b**

BALDNESS Mic. 1:16, **b** like an eagle
Lev. 21:5; Ezek. 7:18; Amos 8:10

BALM Jer. 8:22, no **b** in Gilead
Gen. 37:25; 43:11; Jer. 46:11; 51:8; Ezek. 27:17

BAND—*bond, chain, fetter* Ex. 27:10; 28:8; 38:10; Judg. 8:26; Ps. 107:14; Is. 58:6

BANISH 2 Sam. 14:13,14; Ezra 7:26

BANK—*mound* Gen. 41:17, **b** of the Nile
Matt. 25:27, put my money in the **b**
Gen. 41:3; Ex. 2:3; 7:15; Ezek. 47:7; Luke 19:23

BANNER—*standard* Ps. 20:5; 60:4
Song 2:4, his **b** over me is love
6:4, awesome as an army with **b-s**

BANQUET—*feast, supper*
Song 2:4; Dan. 5:10; Amos 6:7
Esth. 5:4, the **b** that I have prepared for him
Matt. 23:6; Mark 12:39; Luke 20:46, place of honor at **b-s**
Mark 6:21, Herod on his birthday gave a **b**

BAPTISM—*washing*
Matt. 3:7; Mark 10:38; 1 Pet. 3:21
Matt. 21:25; Mark 11:30; Luke 7:29, **b** of John
Luke 20:4; Acts 1:22; 18:25; 19:3, **b** of John
Mark 1:4; Luke 3:3; Acts 13:24; 19:4, **b** of repentance
Luke 12:50, I have a **b** to undergo
Rom. 6:4, buried with Him through **b**
Col. 2:12, buried with Him in **b**
Eph. 4:5, one Lord, one faith, one **b**

BAPTIZE Matt. 3:11, I **b** you in water
Matt. 3:14, I have need to be **b-d** by You
28:19, **b-ing** them in the name of the Father
Mark 1:8; Luke 3:16, **b** you with the Holy Sp.
John 3:22, He was . . . with them and **b-ing**
Acts 1:5, John **b-d** with water
2:41, those . . . were **b-d**
8:16, **b-d** in the name of the Lord Jesus
9:18, Saul . . . arose and was **b-d**
19:4, John **b-d** with the baptism
Rom. 6:3, **b-d** into Christ Jesus . . . **b-d** into His death
1 Cor. 1:13, were you **b-d** in the name of Paul
12:13, by one Spirit we were all **b-d**
Mark 16:16; Luke 3:7,12,21; 7:29; John 1:25,33; 4:1; Acts 2:38; 8:12,36; 10:47; 16:15,33; 18:8; 22:16; 1 Cor. 10:2; 15:29

BARBARIAN Rom. 1:14; 1 Cor. 14:11

BARBER Ezek. 5:1, use it as a **b-'s** razor

BARE—*naked* Is. 52:10; 1 Cor. 15:37; Heb. 4:13

BARK Ex. 11:7; Is. 56:10

BARLEY Ex. 9:31; Deut. 8:8; Ruth 1:22; John 6:9

BARN Matt. 6:26, nor gather into **b-s**
Luke 12:18, I will tear down my **b-s**
Joel 1:17; Hag. 2:19; Matt. 3:12; 13:30; Luke 12:24

BARRACKS Acts 21:34; 22:24

BARREN—*unfruitful* Gen. 11:30; 29:31; Ex. 23:26; Job 24:21; Is. 54:1; Luke 1:7,36; 23:29

BARS 1 Sam. 23:7; Ps. 107:16; Is. 45:2; Ezek. 38:11

BASE 1 Cor. 1:28, the **b** things of the world

BASIN Ex. 12:22; 1 Chr. 28:17; Jer. 52:19; John 13:5

BASKET Ex. 2:3; 29:23; Judg. 6:19; Jer. 24:2; Amos 8:1; Matt. 14:20; 15:37; 16:9; Mark 6:43; 8:8; 8:19; Luke 9:17; John 6:13

BAT Lev. 11:19; Deut. 14:18; Is. 2:20

BATH—*measure* 1 Kin. 7:26; 2 Chr. 2:10; Ezra 7:22; Is. 5:10

BATHE—*wash* Song 5:12, eyes . . . **b-d** in milk
Lev. 15:5,22; 17:16; Num. 19:7; 2 Sam. 11:2

BATTER—*bruise, crush*
Matt. 12:20, **B-ED REED . . . NOT BREAK**

BATTLE—*war* 1 Sam. 17:47, **b** is the LORD's
2 Chr. 20:15, the **b** is not yours
1 Sam. 17:20; 1 Chr. 5:20; Job 39:25; 41:8; Ps. 18:39; 55:18; 140:7; 144:1; Eccles. 9:11; Is. 21:15; Jer. 50:22; Luke 14:31

BEACH Matt. 13:2; John 21:4; Acts 21:5

BEAM—*log* 2 Kin. 6:2; Ps. 104:3

BEAR (n.) 1 Sam. 17:34; 2 Sam. 17:8; Prov. 17:12; Is. 11:7; 59:11; Hos. 13:8; Amos 5:19

BEAR (v.)—*carry, sustain* Gen. 43:9; 44:32
Gen. 4:13, punishment is too great to **b**
Ex. 20:16, You shall not **b** false witness
Ps. 91:12, They will **b** you up
Matt. 1:23, VIRGIN . . . **SHALL B A** SON
27:32, to **b** His cross
Mark 15:21, that he might **b** His cross
John 1:7, **b** witness of the light
16:12, you cannot **b** *them* now
Rom. 8:16, Spirit Himself **b-s** witness
1 Cor. 13:7, **b-s** all things
15:49, **b** the image of the heavenly
Gal. 6:2, **B** one another's burdens
6:5, each one shall **b** his own load
6:17, I **b** on my body
1 John 1:2, we have seen and **b** witness
Ex. 28:12; Lev. 24:15; Deut. 1:9; Prov. 18:14; Lam. 3:27; Ezek. 23:49; Matt. 1:21; Luke 11:46; John 5:31; 8:18; 15:27; Rom. 13:4; 15:1; Heb 9:28

BEARD Lev. 13:29; 1 Sam. 21:13; 2 Sam. 10:4; 20:9; 1 Chr. 19:5; Ps. 133:2; Ezek. 5:1

BEARING—*carrying* Rom. 2:15; Gal. 4:24
John 19:17, **b** His own cross
Col. 3:13, **b** with one another
Heb. 13:13, **b** His reproach

BEAST—*animal, creature* Lev. 26:22; Job 12:7; 18:3
Ps. 50:10, every **b** of the forest is Mine
147:9, He gives to the **b** its food
Eccles. 3:19, no advantage for man over **b**
1 Cor. 15:32, I fought with wild **b-s**
Ps. 49:12; 73:22; Prov. 12:10; James 3:7

BEAT—*flog, hammer* Judg. 6:11; Matt. 26:67
Prov. 23:14, **b** him with the rod
Joel 3:10, **B** your plowshares into swords
Luke 18:13, was **b-ing** his breast
1 Cor. 9:26, as not **b-ing** the air
2 Cor. 11:23, **b-en** times without number

BEAUTIFUL—*appropriate, lovely* Lev. 23:40
Gen. 6:2, daughters of men were **b**
12:11, you are a **b** woman
Is. 4:2, the Branch of the LORD will be **b**
64:11, Our holy and **b** house
Matt. 23:27, tombs which on the outside appear **b**
Acts 3:2, gate of the temple which is called **B**
Rom. 10:15, How **B ARE THE FEET**
Judg. 15:2; Ps. 48:2; Song 1:8; 6:4; Is. 52:1; Jer. 11:16; 13:20

BEAUTY 2 Sam. 1:19; Prov. 31:30; Is. 3:18; Zech. 9:17
Ps. 27:4, To behold the **b** of the LORD
50:2, Out of Zion, the perfection of **b**

BECAME Gen. 26:13, and the man **b** rich
Heb. 11:34, **b** mighty in war

BECOME Ps. 33:1, Praise is **b-ing** to the upright
Luke 2:40, Child . . . to grow and **b** strong

BED—*pallet* Ps. 63:6, remember Thee on my **b**
Matt. 9:6, Rise, take up your **b**

BED *(Continued)*
2 Kin. 4:10; Job 7:13; 33:15; Is. 28:20; Ezek. 17:10; Mark 4:21; Luke 8:16
BEES Deut. 1:44; Judg. 14:8; Ps. 118:12; Is. 7:18
BEFALL—*happen* Gen. 42:4; 49:1; Deut. 31:29
Gen. 44:29, harm **b-s** him
Ps. 91:10, No evil will **b** you
BEFIT—*proper, worthy* Ps. 93:5, Holiness **b-s**
1 Tim. 2:10, as **b-s** women making a claim to godliness
BEG—*appeal, ask* Ps. 37:25, his descendants **b-ing** bread
Luke 16:3, I am ashamed to **b**
18:35, blind man by the road, **b-ing**
John 9:8, the one who used to sit and **b**
Ps. 109:10; Prov. 20:4; Luke 9:38
BEGINNING 1 Sam. 3:12; Prov. 8:22,23
Gen. 1:1, In the **b** God created the heavens
Job 8:7, your **b** was insignificant
Ps. 111:10, **b** of wisdom
Prov. 1:7, **b** of knowledge
Eccles. 7:8, end . . . better than its **b**
Luke 24:47, **b** from Jerusalem
John 1:1, In the **b** was the Word
Rev. 21:6, the **b** and the end
Matt. 19:8; John 2:11; 2 Cor. 3:1; 8:6; Col. 1:18; Heb. 3:14; Rev. 22:13
BEGOTTEN—*born* Ps. 2:7, Today I have **b** Thee
Job 38:28; Acts 13:33; Philem. 10; Heb. 1:5; 5:5
BEHALF—*place, sake* Job 36:2, more . . . said in God's **b**
2 Cor. 1:11, thanks may be given . . . on our **b**
5:20, we beg you on **b** of Christ
BEHAVE—*act* 1 Sam. 18:30, David **b-d** himself more wisely
1 Thess. 2:10, how devoutly . . . we **b-d**
BEHAVIOR—*conduct* James 3:13, his good **b**
1 Pet. 1:15, holy . . . in all *your* **b**
2:12, keep your **b** excellent
BEHEAD Luke 9:9; Rev. 20:4
Matt. 14:10, had John **b-ed** in prison
Mark 6:16, John whom I **b-ed**
BEHOLD—*look* Num. 24:17; Ps. 37:37
Matt. 18:10, angels . . . **b** the face of My Father
John 17:24, that they may **b** My glory
2 Cor. 3:18, **b-ing** as in a mirror
BEING Gen. 2:7, man became a living **b**
Matt. 7:11, **b** evil, know how to give
12:34, **b** evil, speak . . . good
John 4:9, **b** a Jew, ask me
1 Cor. 8:7, conscience **b** weak
9:21, **b** without the law
Eph. 2:20, **b** the chief cornerstone
BELIEVE—*faith, trust* Ex. 4:5; Matt. 8:13; 9:28
Num. 14:11, how long will they not **b** in Me
Ps. 78:22, Because they did not **b** in God
Prov. 14:15, The naive **b-s** everything
Matt. 21:22, everything you ask . . . **b-ing** you
Mark 5:36, Do not be afraid . . . only **b**
9:23, All things are possible to him who **b-s**
Luke 8:13, they **b** for a while
24:25, slow of heart to **b**
John 2:22, they **b-d** the Scripture
7:5, not even His brothers were **b-ing** in Him
8:24, unless you **b** that I am He
10:38, though you do not **b** Me, **b** the works
11:26, everyone who . . . **b-s** in Me shall never die
11:27, Yes, Lord; I have **b-d**
11:48, all men will **b** in Him
17:21, that the world may **b** that Thou didst send Me
20:25, Unless I shall see . . . I will not **b**
20:29, Blessed *are* they who . . . yet **b-d**
Rom. 4:11, the father of all who **b**
Heb. 11:6, he who comes to God must **b** that
James 2:19, You **b** that God is one . . . the
1 Pet. 2:6, HE WHO B-S IN HIM SHALL NOT BE
Matt. 21:25; 27:42; Mark 11:24,31; 16:13; Luke 8:50; 24:41; John 1:7; 3:12; 5:44,47; 6:36; 7:48; 10:37; 11:15; 12:36; Acts 4:32; 9:26; 13:39,48; 16:34; Rom. 4:18; 9:33; 10:14; 2 Cor. 4:13; Gal. 3:22; 2 Thess. 1:10
BELLY—*stomach* Gen. 3:14, On your **b** shall you go
BELONG Luke 23:7, He **b-ed** to Herod's
1 Cor. 3:21, all things **b** to you
3:23, **b** to Christ . . . **b-s** to God
BELOVED—*chosen* Ps. 127:2, He gives to His **b**
Matt. 3:17; 17:5, This is My **b** Son
Eph. 1:6, bestowed on us in the **B**
5:1, be imitators of God, as **b** children
Col. 1:13, kingdom of His **b** Son
2 Tim. 1:2, to Timothy, my **b** son
Philem. 16, more than a slave, a **b** brother
Jude 1, **b** in God the Father
Deut. 33:12; Jer. 12:7; Mark 1:11; 9:7; Luke 3:22; Rom. 11:28; 12:19; 16:9; 1 Cor. 10:14; 2 Cor. 7:1; 12:19; Phil. 4:1; Col. 4:9; 1 Pet. 2:11; 2 Pet. 1:17
BELOW—*beneath* Gen. 1:9; Deut. 4:39; Prov. 15:24; Jer. 31:37; John 8:23
BELT—*girdle* Mark 1:6, John . . . a leather **b**
Acts 21:11, took Paul's **b** and bound his own feet
1 Sam. 18:4; 2 Sam. 18:11; 20:8; Ps. 109:19; Prov. 31:24; Is. 3:24; 5:27; 11:5; Ezek. 23:15; Matt. 3:4
BEND—*bow* Ps. 11:2, the wicked **b** the bow
BENEFACTOR Luke 22:25, those . . . called **B-s**
BENEFIT—*profit, blessing* Ps. 103:2, forget none of His **b-s**
Ps. 116:12, For all His **b-s** toward me
1 Tim. 6:2, those who partake of the **b**
2 Chr. 32:25; Is. 65:8; Rom. 3:1; 1 Tim. 6:2
BEREAVE—*deprive* Gen. 27:45; 42:36; Lev. 26:22; Jer. 15:7; Ezek. 5:17; 36:12
BESIDE Ps. 23:2, He leads me **b** quiet waters
Is. 43:11, there is no saviour **b-s** Me
44:6, there is no God **b-s** Me
Matt. 13:4, *seeds* fell **b** the road
2 Cor. 5:13, if we are **b** ourselves, it is for God
Deut. 11:30; Ruth 2:14; 2 Kin. 21:16; Is. 32:20
BESIEGE Deut. 20:19; 2 Sam. 11:1; 1 Kin. 16:17; Is. 1:8; Ezek. 4:3; 6:12
BEST Ps. 39:5, man at his **b** is a mere breath
Luke 15:22, bring out the **b** robe
Gen. 43:11; 1 Sam. 15:9,15; 2 Sam. 18:4
BESTOW—*grant* Ex. 32:29, He may **b** a blessing upon you
1 Chr. 29:25, **b-ed** on him royal majesty
1 Cor. 12:23, we **b** more abundant honor
1 John 3:1, love the Father has **b-ed** on us
BETRAY Matt. 27:4, I have sinned by **b-ing**
Mark 14:11, he *began* seeking how to **b** Him
Luke 22:21, the hand of the one **b-ing** Me
1 Cor. 11:23, the night . . . He was **b-ed**
Is. 16:3; Matt. 24:10; 26:16; Mark 14:18; Luke 22:22; John 6:64; 21:20
BETROTH Hos. 2:19,20, I will **b** you to Me
Jer. 2:2; Matt. 1:18; 2 Cor. 11:2
BETTER 1 Sam. 15:22, to obey is **b** than sacrifice
Ps. 63:3, Thy lovingkindness is **b** than life
Heb. 11:16, they desire a **b** country
2 Pet. 2:21, **b** for them not to have known the way
1 Kin. 19:4; Eccles. 2:24; 4:9; 7:10; Song 1:2; Heb. 1:4
BEWARE Deut. 8:11, **B**, lest you forget the LORD
Deut. 15:9, **B**, lest there is a base thought
Matt. 6:1, **B** of practicing your righteousness
10:17, But **b** of men
16:6, **b** of the leaven of the Pharisees
Mark 12:38, **B** of the scribes
Luke 12:15, **B**, and be on your guard against . . . greed
Ex. 19:12; Job 36:18; Mark 8:15; Luke 12:1; 20:46; Phil. 3:2
BEWITCHED Gal. 3:1, You foolish Galatians, who has **b**
BEYOND 2 Cor. 8:3, **b** their ability
Gal. 1:13, persecute the church of God **b** measure
Gen. 35:21; Deut. 3:20; John 3:26; Acts 7:43

BIER 2 Sam. 3:31, David walked behind the **b**
BILLOWS—*waves* Jon. 2:3, **b** passed over me
BIND—*wrap* Num. 30:2, an oath to **b** himself
Prov. 6:21, **B** them continually on your heart
Is. 61:1, **b** up the brokenhearted
Matt. 16:19, **b** on earth shall be bound in heaven
Job 38:31; Matt. 12:29; 18:18; Mark 3:27
BIRD—*fowl, swallow* Lev. 20:25, unclean **b**
Ps. 84:3, **b** also has found a house
124:7, Our soul has escaped as a **b**
Matt. 6:26, Look at the **b-s** of the air
8:20, **b-s** of the air *have* nests
Gen. 1:20; 6:7; 2 Sam. 21:10; Ps. 8:8; 11:1; Prov. 1:17; Eccles. 10:20; Jer. 9:10; 12:9; Hos. 9:8; Luke 9:58; Rev. 19:17
BIRTH Eccles. 7:1, better than the day of **b**
Matt. 1:18, **b** of Jesus Christ was
John 9:1, a man blind from **b**
Gen. 38:27; Is. 66:9; Luke 1:14
BIRTHRIGHT Gen. 25:31, First sell me your **b**
Gen. 27:36, Jacob . . . took away my **b**
Heb. 12:16, sold his own **b** for a single meal
BIT (n.) Ps. 32:9; James 3:3
BITE Prov. 23:32; Eccles. 10:8; Amos 5:19; 9:3; Mic. 3:5; Gal. 5:15
BITTER Ex. 1:14, **b** with hard labor
Ex. 12:8, unleavened bread and **b** herbs
15:23, waters of Marah . . . were **b**
2 Kin. 14:26, affliction of Israel . . . was very **b**
Is. 24:9, Strong drink is **b** to those who drink
Matt. 26:75, went out and wept **b-ly**
Job 21:25; Is. 5:20; Luke 22:62
BITTERNESS—*gall* Job 10:1, **b** of my soul
Prov. 14:10; 17:25, heart knows its own **b**
Eph. 4:31, Let all **b** and wrath . . . be put away
Heb. 12:15, no root of **b**
1 Sam. 15:32; Is. 38:15; Lam. 3:19; Rom. 3:14
BLACK Matt. 5:36, make one hair **b** or white
Jude 13, for whom the **b** darkness has been reserved
Rev. 6:5, behold a **b** horse
BLADE Judg. 3:22, fat closed over the **b**
Mark 4:28, first the **b**, then the head
BLAMELESS Ps. 119:80, May my heart be **b**
Prov. 11:20, **b** in their walk are His delight
Acts 24:16, maintain always a **b** conscience
1 Cor. 1:8, **b** in the day of our Lord Jesus Christ
Eph. 1:4, holy and **b** before Him
2 Sam. 22:26; Ps. 119:1; Phil. 1:10; 2:15; 3:6; Jude 24; Rev. 14:5
BLASPHEME—*spoke* Is. 52:5, My name is continually **b-d**
Matt. 9:3, This *fellow* **b-s**
26:65, He has **b-d**
Mark 3:29, **b-s** against the Holy Spirit
2 Sam. 12:14; Acts 26:11; Rom. 2:24; 1 Tim. 1:20; James 2:7
BLASPHEMY Matt. 12:31, **b** against the Spirit
Matt. 26:65, you have now heard the **b**
Mark 3:28, whatever **b-es** they utter
Rev. 2:9, the **b** by those who say they are Jews
13:5, arrogant words and **b-es**
Mark 14:64; Luke 5:21; John 10:33
BLEMISH—*spot* Heb. 9:14, offered Himself without **b**
Num. 19:2; Song 4:7; Ezek. 43:22; 45:18; 46:4
BLEND 2 Chr. 16:14, **b-ed** by the perfumers' art
BLESS—*happy* Josh. 17:14, LORD has . . . **b-ed**
Ps. 144:15, **b-ed** are the people whose God is the LORD
Prov. 3:13, **b-ed** is the man who finds wisdom
10:7, memory of the righteous is **b-ed**
Luke 6:28, **b** those who curse you
Acts 20:35, more **b-ed** to give than to receive
Titus 2:13, looking for **b-ed** hope
James 3:9, we **b** *our* Lord and Father
Rev. 14:13, Write, **B-ed** are the dead
Gen. 22:17; Deut. 28:3-6; 33:29; Judg. 5:2; 1 Chr. 4:10; Ps. 127:5; Prov. 28:14; Is. 32:20; 65:16; Hag. 2:19; Mal. 3:15; John 13:17; Rom. 12:14; 2 Cor. 11:31; Titus 2:13; James 5:11; 1 Pet. 3:14; 4:14
BLESSING—*benefit* Gen. 39:5, LORD's **b** was upon all
Prov. 10:22, **b** of the LORD that makes rich
28:20, faithful man will abound with **b-s**
Mal. 3:10, pour out for you a **b**
Rom. 15:29, the fulness of the **b** of Christ
1 Cor. 10:16, Is not the cup of **b**
Gen. 27:35; Deut. 11:26; 23:5; Neh. 13:2; Job 29:13; Mal. 2:2; 2 Cor. 1:15; James 3:10; Rev. 5:12
BLIND Ex. 23:8, bribe **b-s** the clear-sighted
Matt. 11:5, *the* B RECEIVE SIGHT
2 Cor. 4:4, **b-ed** the minds of the unbelieving
1 John 2:11, darkness has **b-ed** his eyes
Deut. 16:19; 1 Sam. 12:3
BLINDNESS Deut. 28:28; 2 Kin. 6:18; Zech. 12:4
BLOOD Gen. 9:6, Whoever sheds man's **b**, By man his **b**
Ps. 72:14, their **b** will be precious in his sight
Ezek. 9:9, the land is filled with **b**
Matt. 16:17, because flesh and **b** did not reveal
27:4, by betraying innocent **b**
Luke 22:20, new covenant in My **b**
22:44, His sweat became like drops of **b**
Acts 20:28, He purchased with His own **b**
21:25, abstain from meat . . . and from **b**
Rom. 3:25, a propitiation in His **b**
5:9, justified by His **b**
1 Cor. 10:16, sharing in the **b** of Christ
11:27, guilty of the body . . . **b** of the Lord
15:50, flesh and **b** cannot inherit the kingdom
Eph. 1:7, redemption through His **b**
Heb. 9:22, shedding of **b** there is no forgiveness
1 Pet. 1:19, the **b** of Christ
Rev. 12:11, the **b** of the Lamb
Gen. 9:4; Ex. 12:22; Lev. 3:17; Josh. 2:19; 1 Kin. 2:32; Is. 9:5; Ezek. 18:13; Matt. 27:25; Mark 14:24; John 1:13; 6:54,55,56; Acts 15:20; 1 Cor. 11:25; Heb. 10:29; Rev. 7:14
BLOSSOM Gen. 40:10; Eccles. 12:5; Is. 17:11; 27:6; 35:1; Hos. 14:5; Hab. 3:17
BLOT—*erase* Ex. 32:32, please **b** me from Thy book
Deut. 9:14, **b** out their name from heaven
Ps. 51:1, Thy compassion **b** out my transgressions
51:9, **b** out all my iniquities
69:28, May they be **b-ed** out of the book of life
Deut. 25:19; 29:20; 2 Kin. 14:27; Neh. 4:5; Ps. 109:13,14; Prov. 6:33; Jer. 18:23
BLOWS Prov. 19:29, **b** for the back of fools
BOAST—*glory, rejoice, talk* Ps. 34:2, soul . . . make its **b**
Ps. 49:6, **b** in the abundance of their riches
Prov. 27:1, do not **b** about tomorrow
Rom. 2:23, You who **b** in the Law
James 4:16, all such **b-ing** is evil
1 Sam. 2:3; 1 Kin. 20:11; 2 Chr. 25:19; Ps. 5:5; 75:4; Prov. 20:14; Rom. 2:17; 3:27; 1 Cor. 5:6; 2 Cor. 11:16; Gal. 5:26; Eph. 2:9; James 3:5; 4:16
BOAT Is. 33:21; John 6:22; Acts 27:16; 27:30
BODILY Luke 3:22, Holy Spirit descended . . . in **b** form
Col. 2:9, fulness of Deity dwells in **b** form
1 Tim. 4:8, **b** discipline is only little profit
BODY—*corpse, flesh* Matt. 6:22, whole **b** . . . full of light
Mark 5:29, she felt in her **b** that she was healed
6:29, his **b** and laid it in a tomb
Luke 12:22, do not be anxious . . . for your **b**
Acts 19:12, carried from his **b** to the sick
Rom. 6:6, that our **b** of sin might be done away
12:1, present your **b-es** a living . . . sacrifice
12:4, many members in one **b**
12:5, we . . . are one **b** in Christ
1 Cor. 9:27, but I buffet my **b**
13:3, if I deliver my **b** to be burned
2 Cor. 5:8, prefer to be absent from the **b**

BODY *(Continued)*
Gal. 6:17, I bear on my **b** the brand-marks of Jesus
1 Pet. 2:24, bore our sins in His **b**
Gen. 47:18; Eccles. 12:12; Matt. 5:29; 6:23; Luke 11:34; 17:37; John 2:21; Rom. 7:24; 1 Cor. 12:14; 2 Cor. 12:2; Phil. 3:21

BODYGUARD—*guard* Gen. 40:4; Jer. 39:9

BOISTEROUS—*clamor*
Prov. 9:13, woman of folly is **b**

BOLD Prov. 28:1, righteous are **b** as a lion
Acts 13:46, Paul and Barnabas spoke out **b-ly**
Ex. 14:8; Num. 33:3; Rom. 10:20; 2 Cor. 10:2; 10:12

BOLDNESS—*confidence* Acts 4:31, speak . . . with **b**
Eph. 3:12, we have **b** and confident access
Phil. 1:20, with all **b**, Christ . . . be exalted

BOND—*cord* Hos. 11:4, with **b-s** of love
Eph. 4:3, in the **b** of peace
Col. 3:14, perfect **b** of unity
Ezek. 20:37; Luke 13:16; Jude 6

BOND-SERVANT—*servant* Luke 2:29, let Thy **b** depart
Rom. 1:1, Paul, a **b** of Christ Jesus
Phil. 1:1, Paul and Timothy, **b-s** of Christ
Titus 1:1; James 1:1; 2 Pet. 1:1

BONE Ezek. 37:7, **b-s** came together, **b** to its **b**
Luke 24:39, spirit does not have flesh and **b-s**
John 19:36, NOT A **B** OF HIM SHALL BE BROKEN
Gen. 2:23; Ex. 12:46; Job 20:11; Ps. 51:8; Prov. 12:4; Matt. 23:27

BOOK Is. 34:16, Seek from the **b** of the LORD
Mal. 3:16, **b** of remembrance
John 21:25, world itself would not contain the **b-s**
Phil. 4:3, names are in the **b** of life
Ex. 17:14; Ezra 4:15; Job 19:23; Luke 4:17; Acts 19:19; 1 Tim. 4:13; Rev. 3:5; 13:8; 17:8; 20:12; 21:27; 22:19

BOOTHS Gen. 33:17; Lev. 23:42,43; Neh. 8:14

BOOTY—*plunder* Num. 31:32; Is. 53:12; Jer. 38:2; 49:32

BORDER Gen. 47:21, one end of Egypt's **b** to the other
Ex. 34:24, drive out nations . . . . . . **b-s**
Jer. 15:13, . . . within all your **b-s**
50:26, Come to her from the farthest **b**
Gen. 23:17; Num. 21:13; 34:3; 35:26; Deut. 3:17; Josh. 12:5; 2 Kin. 3:21; 1 Chr. 4:10; Ps. 147:14; Is. 19:19; 60:18; Ezek. 11:10

BORE—*bear, carry, pierce, yield*
Ex. 19:4, how I **b** you on eagles' wings
Is. 53:4, our griefs He Himself **b**
53:12, He Himself **b** the sin of many
1 Pet. 2:24, He Himself **b** our sins
Num. 17:8; 2 Kin. 12:9; Jer. 31:19

BORN—*begotten, forth* Job 5:7, man is **b** for trouble
Job 14:1, Man, who is **b** of woman
Is. 9:6, For a child will be **b** to us
66:8, Can a land be **b** in one day
John 1:13, who were **b** not of blood
3:3, unless one is **b** again
3:6,8, **b** of the Spirit
1 Cor. 15:8, one untimely **b**
1 Pet. 1:3, **b** again to a living hope
1 John 4:7, every one who loves is **b** of God
5:4, whatever is **b** of God overcomes the world
Job 3:3; 15:14; 25:4; Ps. 87:4; 90:2; Prov. 17:17; Matt. 11:11; 1 Pet. 1:23; 1 John 5:1

BORNE Is. 46:3, been **b** by Me from birth
Job 34:31; Lam. 5:7; Matt. 20:12

BORROW Deut. 28:12, you shall not **b**
Prov. 22:7, **b-er** *becomes* the lender's slave
Ex. 22:14; Deut. 15:6; 2 Kin. 4:3; Ps. 37:21; Matt. 5:42

BOSOM—*breast* Prov. 6:27, fire in his **b**
Is. 40:11, carry *them* in His **b**
Luke 16:22, carried . . . to Abraham's **b**
John 1:18, in the **b** of the Father
Ex. 4:6; Job 31:33; Ps. 35:13

BOTHER—*trouble* Matt. 26:10, do you **b** the woman

BOTTLE—*jug, wineskin* Judg. 4:19; Ps. 56:8

BOUGH—*branch* Ps. 80:10, cedars of God with its **b-s**
Gen. 49:22; Lev. 23:40; Deut. 24:20; Ps. 80:10; Is. 17:6; Ezek. 31:6

BOUGHT Luke 14:18, I have **b** a piece of land
1 Cor. 6:20, been **b** with a price
7:23, You were **b** with a price
2 Pet. 2:1, denying the Master who **b** them

BOUND—*gird, yoke* Prov. 22:15, Foolishness is **b** up in
Matt. 16:19, **b** in heaven
Acts 20:22, **b** in spirit, I am on my way to Jerusalem
1 Cor. 7:27, Are you **b** to a wife
2 Cor. 6:14, Do not be **b** together
Gen. 44:30; Mark 5:4

BOUNDARY Prov. 8:29, He set for the sea its **b**

BOUNTIFUL—*generous*
Ps. 13:6, He has dealt **b-ly** with me
116:7, the LORD has dealt **b-ly** with you
2 Cor. 9:6, he who sows **b-ly** . . . reap **b-ly**
Ps. 119:17; 2 Cor. 9:5

BOUNTY 1 Kin. 10:13, according to his royal **b**

BOW—*bend, worship* Is. 66:23, to **b** down
1 Sam. 2:36; Ps. 10:10; Is. 60:14

BOWL—*dish, pitcher* Eccles. 12:6, golden **b** is crushed
Matt. 26:23, who dipped his hand in the **b**
Num. 7:25; 1 Kin. 17:12; Amos 6:6; Zech. 4:2; Mark 14:20

BOY—*child* Is. 11:6, a little **b** will lead them
Joel 3:3, Traded a **b** for a harlot
Gen. 25:27; Zech. 8:5

BRACELET Gen. 24:22; 24:30; 24:47; Ex. 35:22; Num. 31:50; 2 Sam. 1:10; Is. 3:19; Ezek. 16:11; 23:42

BRAMBLE—*briar* Judg. 9:14, trees said to the **b**
Judg. 9:15, fire come out from the **b**

BRANCH—*bough* Jer. 23:5, raise up for David a righteous **B**
Matt. 13:32, THE BIRDS . . . NEST IN ITS **B-ES**
21:8, others were cutting **b-es**
John 15:2, every **b** that bears fruit
15:4, **b** cannot bear fruit of itself
15:5, I am the vine, you are the **b-es**
Judg. 9:48; Ezek. 31:3; Mark 11:8; Luke 13:19; John 12:13; 15:6; Rom. 11:16

BRAND—*torch* Zech. 3:2; 1 Tim. 4:2

BRAY Job 6:5, wild donkey **b** over *his* grass

BREACH Judg. 21:15, LORD had made a **b** in . . . Israel
Job 16:14, breaks through me with **b** after **b**
Gen. 38:29; Ex. 22:9; 1 Kin. 11:27; Neh. 4:7; 6:1; Ps. 60:2; 106:23; Is. 22:9; 30:13; 58:12; Amos 4:3; 9:11

BREAD—*food* Ex. 16:4, I will rain **b** from heaven
Deut. 8:3, man does not live by **b** alone
Job 22:7, you have withheld **b**
Ps. 132:15, satisfy her needy with **b**
Prov. 31:27, does not eat the **b** of idleness
Eccles. 11:1, Cast your **b** on the surface of the waters
Is. 55:2, spend money for what is not **b**
55:10, seed to the sower and **b** to the eater
Matt. 4:3, command these stones become **b**
6:11, Give us this day our daily **b**
Mark 7:27, take the children's **b**
Acts 2:42, the breaking of **b**
20:7, gathered together to break **b**
Ex. 23:25; Josh. 9:5; Judg. 7:13; 1 Kin. 17:6; Job 33:20; Prov. 9:17; 12:11; Matt. 4:4; Luke 4:3,4; 24:35; Acts 27:35; 2 Thess. 3:8

BREAK—*broke, profane* 2 Chr. 32:1, to **b** into them
Is. 42:3, reed He will not **b**
Luke 5:6, their nets began to **b**
24:30, He took the bread . . . and **b-ing** it
1 Cor. 10:16, bread which we **b** a sharing in . . . Christ

Job 19:10; Jer. 4:3; Hos. 10:12; Matt. 12:5,20; 14:19; Acts 21:13

BREASTPIECE Ex. 25:7; 28:4,15,22,23; 35:9,27; 39:8; Lev. 8:8

BREASTPLATE Is. 59:17, put on righteousness like a **b**
Eph. 6:14, PUT ON THE B OF RIGHTEOUSNESS
1 Thess. 5:8, put on the **b** of faith and love
Neh. 4:16; Rev. 9:9,17

BREATH—*spirit, wind* Gen. 2:7, **b** of life
Job 7:16, my days are *but* a **b**
12:10, the **b** of all mankind
27:3, **b** of God is in my nostrils
Ps. 150:6, Let everything that has **b** praise the LORD
Acts 17:25, He Himself gives to all life and **b**
Gen. 6:17; 7:15; Eccles. 3:21; Is. 2:22; Ezek. 37:5,10

BREATHE Gen. 2:7, **b-d** into his nostrils the breath
Ezek. 37:9, **b** on these slain
Acts 9:1, **b-ing** threats and murder
Deut. 20:16; Josh. 10:40; 11:11,14; Ps. 27:12; John 20:22

BRETHREN—*brother* Ps. 22:22, tell of Thy name to my **b**
Is. 66:20, all your **b** from all the nations
1 Cor. 14:39, my **b**, desire earnestly to prophesy
2 Cor. 11:26, dangers among false **b**
Gal. 1:2, all the **b** who are with me
2:4, because of false **b**
Eph. 6:23, Peace be to the **b**
Col. 1:2, saints and faithful **b** in Christ
1 Thess. 4:9, love of the **b**
1 Pet. 1:22, sincere love of the **b**
1 John 3:14, because we love the **b**
Mic. 5:3; Rom. 1:13; 7:1; 8:12; Heb. 13:1

BRIAR—*thistle* Luke 6:44, nor ... pick grapes from a **b**

BRIBE Ex. 23:8, not take a **b**, for a **b** blinds
Is. 1:23, Every one loves a **b**
5:23, justify the wicked for a **b**
Deut. 10:17; 27:25; 1 Sam. 8:3; 12:3; Ps. 26:10; Is. 33:15; Mic. 7:3

BRICK Gen. 11:3; Ex. 1:14; 5:7; Is. 9:10; 65:3

BRIDE Rev. 21:2, as a **b** adorned for her husband
21:9, the **b**, the wife of the Lamb
22:17, the Spirit and the **b** say, Come
Is. 49:18; 61:10; 62:5; Jer. 2:32; 7:34; 16:9; 25:10; 33:11; Joel 2:16; John 3:29; Rev. 18:23

BRIDEGROOM Jer. 7:34; 16:9; 25:10; 33:11
Matt. 25:1, virgins ... went out to meet the **b**
John 3:29, He who has the bride is the **b**
Rev. 18:23, voice of the **b**
Ex. 4:25; Ps. 19:5; Is. 61:10; 62:5; Joel 2:16; Matt. 9:15; Mark 2:19; John 2:9

BRIDLE—*guard* James 1:26, not **b** his tongue
2 Kin. 19:28; Prov. 26:3; Is. 37:29

BRIGHT Rev. 22:16, **b** morning star
Lev. 13:2; Job 37:21; Matt. 17:5

BRIGHTNESS—*radiance* Is. 60:3, kings to the **b** of your
Is. 62:1, righteousness goes forth like **b**

BRIMSTONE Gen. 19:24; Is. 30:33; Rev. 9:17; 14:10; 19:20

BRISTLE Job 4:15, hair ... **b-d** up

BROAD—*wide* Ps. 119:96, commandment is exceedingly **b**
Matt. 7:13, way is **b** that leads to destruction
1 Chr. 4:40; Ps. 104:25; Matt. 23:5

BROILED Luke 24:42, gave Him a piece of **b** fish

BROKE—*break* John 19:32, **b** the legs of the first man
Eph. 2:14, **b** down the barrier
1 Sam. 4:18; 2 Kin. 23:14; 2 Chr. 34:4; Matt. 15:36; 26:26; Mark 6:41

BROKEN—*loose, void* Job 17:1, My spirit is **b**
Ps. 51:17, a **b** spirit; A **b** and a contrite heart
69:20, Reproach has **b** my heart
119:126, have **b** Thy law
Eccles. 12:6, the silver cord is **b**
Jer. 2:13, **B** cisterns
John 10:35, Scripture cannot be **b**
19:36, NOT A BONE OF HIM SHALL BE B

BROKENHEARTED
Ps. 34:18, Lord is near to the **b**

BRONZE Deut. 28:23; 2 Sam. 22:35; Ezra 8:27; Jer. 15:12

BROOD Matt. 3:7, You **b** of vipers, who warned you
Luke 13:34, a hen *gathers* her **b**

BROOK 1 Sam. 17:40; Ps. 110:7
Ps. 42:1, deer pants for the water **b-s**

BROTHER—*brethren* Gen. 4:9, Am I my **b-'s** keeper
Prov. 18:24, friend who sticks closer than a **b**
Matt. 10:21, **b** will deliver up **b** to death
23:8, you are all **b-s**
Luke 18:29, no one who has left ... **b-s**
John 7:5, not even His **b-s** were
1 Cor. 6:6, **b** goes to law with **b**
Gen. 42:8; Prov. 17:17; 18:9,19; 19:7; Eccles. 4:8; Matt. 5:23; Mark 3:35; 10:29; 2 Thess. 3:15

BROTHERHOOD Amos 1:9, covenant of **b**

BROTHERLY Rom. 12:10, in **b** love
2 Pet. 1:7, *your* **b** kindness

BROUGHT—*escape* Matt. 10:18, shall ... be **b** before governors

BROW Luke 4:29, led Him to the **b** of the hill

BRUISE—*batter, crush* Gen. 3:15, shall **b** you
Is. 1:6, **b-s**, welts, and raw wounds
42:3, A **b-d** reed He will not break

BRUTAL—*senseless, stupid, fierce* Ezek. 21:31; 2 Tim. 3:3

BUCKET Num. 24:7, flow from his **b-s**
Is. 40:15, nations are like a drop from a **b**

BUD—*sprout* Num. 17:8; Is. 18:5

BUFFET—*beat* 2 Cor. 12:7, to **b** me

BUGLE—*trumpet* 1 Cor. 14:8, **b** produces an ... sound

BUILD 1 Chr. 17:12, He shall **b** for Me a house
Ps. 127:1, Unless the LORD **b-s** the house
Eccles. 3:3, a time to **b** up
1 Cor. 3:12, if any man **b-s** upon the foundation
2 Chr. 6:9; Luke 14:30; Acts 20:32; Rom. 15:20

BUILDER—*maker* Ps. 118:22, the **b-s** rejected
Heb. 11:10, whose architect and **b** is God
1 Pet. 2:7, STONE WHICH THE B-S REJECTED
1 Kin. 5:18; Ezra 3:10; Matt. 21:42; Mark 12:10; Luke 20:17; Acts 4:11

BUILDING 1 Cor. 3:9, you are ... God's **b**
2 Cor. 5:1, we have a **b** from God
Eph. 2:21, **b**, being fitted together

BUILT Eccles. 2:4, I **b** houses for myself
Matt. 7:24, **b** his house upon the rock
Eph. 2:22, **b** together into a dwelling of God

BULL Lev. 4:3, a **b** without defect

BULRUSHES Is. 19:7, **b** by the Nile

BUNDLE Gen. 42:35; Acts 28:3
1 Sam. 25:29, bound in the **b** of living
Matt. 13:30, bind them in **b-s** to burn

BURDEN—*load* Ps. 55:22, Cast your **b** upon the LORD
Matt. 20:12, borne the **b** and ... heat of the day
Luke 11:46, weigh men down with **b-s** hard to bear
Gal. 6:2, Bear one another's **b-s**
Acts 15:28; 2 Cor. 11:9; 12:16; 1 Thess. 2:9

BURIAL John 19:40, **b** custom of the Jews
Gen. 23:4; Eccles. 6:3; Jer. 22:19; Matt. 26:12

BURN—*kindle* Ex. 3:2, bush was **b-ing** with fire
Ps. 39:3, While I was musing the fire **b-ed**
Prov. 26:23, **b-ing** lips and a wicked heart
Is. 9:18, wickedness **b-s** like a fire
42:3, dimly **b-ing** wick He will not
Luke 3:17, He will **b** up the chaff
24:32, our hearts **b-ing** within us
John 5:35, He was the lamp that was **b-ing**
1 Cor. 13:3, deliver my body to be **b-ed**
Rev. 18:8, she will be **b-ed** up with fire

BURN *(Continued)*
Gen. 30:2; Ex. 32:12,19; Ps. 11:6; Is. 33:14; Mal. 4:1; Matt. 13:30; Rom. 12:20; Heb. 6:8; Rev. 4:5; 19:20
BURNT OFFERING Gen. 22:7; Lev. 1:4; 6:9; Is. 61:8
Ps. 40:6, **B** and sin offering Thou hast not required
Jer. 6:20, **b-s** are not acceptable
Hos. 6:6, knowledge of God rather than **b-s**
Mark 12:33, more than all **b-s** and sacrifices
BURST—*break* Job 32:19; Matt. 9:17; Mark 2:22; Luke 5:37
BURY Rom. 6:4, **b-ed** with Him through baptism
1 Cor. 15:4, and that he was **b-ed**
Gen. 23:4; 47:29; Matt. 8:21,22; 14:12; Luke 9:59,60; Acts 8:2; Col. 2:12
BUSHEL—*ephah* Amos 8:5, To make **b** smaller
BUSINESS—*matter* Ps. 107:23, Who do **b** on great waters
1 Thess. 4:11, attend to your own **b**
James 4:13, engage in **b** and make a profit
Gen. 24:33; Josh. 2:14; Matt. 22:5; Acts 19:25
BUSYBODIES—*meddler* 2 Thess. 3:11, acting like **b**
1 Tim. 5:13, also gossips and **b**
BUTTER—*curds* Job 29:6; Prov. 30:33
Ps. 55:21, His speech was smoother than **b**
BUY Is. 55:1, **b** and eat . . . **b** wine and milk
Matt. 13:44, sells all that he has and **b-s** that field
Rev. 3:18, **b** from Me gold refined by fire
13:17, no one should be able to **b** or to sell
Gen. 42:2; 47:19; Lev. 22:11; Ruth 4:4; Prov. 23:23; Matt. 25:9; John 4:8; Rev. 18:11
BUYER Is. 24:2; Ezek. 7:12
Prov. 20:14, Bad, bad, says the **b**
BYWORD—*taunt* Job 30:9
1 Kin. 9:7, Israel will become . . . a **b** among all peoples
2 Chr. 7:20, a **b** among all peoples
Job 17:6, a **b** of the people
Ps. 44:14, **b** among the nations

C

CAGE Jer. 5:27, a **c** full of birds
CAKE Gen. 18:6; 1 Kin. 17:13; 2 Kin. 20:7
CALAMITY—*destruction* Job 31:23, **c** from God is a terror
Prov. 1:27, **c** comes on like a whirlwind
2 Sam. 22:19; 24:16; 1 Chr. 21:15; Job 6:30; 21:17; 31:3; Ps. 18:18; Prov. 24:16; 27:10; Jon. 3:10; 4:2
CALCULATE—*count* Is. 40:12, **c-d** the dust of the earth
Luke 14:28, sit down and **c** the cost
CALF Luke 15:23, bring the fattened **c**
Heb. 9:12, blood of goats and **c-ves**
Gen. 18:7; Is. 11:6; Rev. 4:7
CALL—*address* Gen. 4:26, to **c** upon the name
Ps. 4:1, Answer me when I **c**
Is. 7:14, **c** His name Immanuel
Matt. 9:13, not come to **c** *the* righteous
Luke 6:46, why do you **c** Me, Lord, Lord
John 13:13, **c** Me Teacher, and Lord
1 Cor. 1:26, consider your **c**, brethren
1 Thess. 4:7, God has not **c-ed** us for . . . impurity
Deut. 4:26; Ruth 1:20; Ps. 18:3; Prov. 8:1; Is. 5:20; Jer. 3:19
CALLING—*summoning* Is. 1:13, the **c** of assemblies
Rom. 11:29, gifts and the **c** of God
2 Tim. 1:9, called us with a holy **c**
Heb. 3:1, partakers of a heavenly **c**
CALM—*still* Is. 7:4, be **c**, have no fear
Jon. 1:11, the sea may become **c**
Matt. 8:26, it became perfectly **c**
Acts 19:36, you ought to keep **c** . . . do nothing rash
CAMEL Gen. 24:64; Mark 1:6
Matt. 3:4, John . . . a garment of **c-'s** hair
19:24, easier for a **c** . . . eye of a needle
23:24, out a gnat and swallow a **c**
CAMP—*settle* Ex. 14:19, before the **c**
Deut. 23:14, God walks . . . your **c**
Gen. 32:2; Num. 31:19; Ps. 69:25; Is. 29:3; Zech. 9:8; Rev. 20:9
CANCEL—*blot, erase* Is. 28:18; Col. 2:14
CAPTIVE Luke 4:18, RELEASE TO THE C-S
Eph. 4:8, LED C A HOST OF C-S
Ps. 68:18; Jer. 13:17; Col. 2:8
CAPTIVITY Is. 46:2, have themselves gone into **c**
CAPTURE Job 5:13, **c-s** the wise
CARCASS—*corpse* Gen. 15:11; Judg. 14:8
CARE—*concern, worry*
Gen. 50:24, God . . . take **c** of you
Ps. 142:4, No one **c-s** for my soul
Ezek. 34:12, I will **c** for My sheep
Luke 10:34, to an inn, and took **c** of him
1 Tim. 3:5, take **c** of the church
1 Pet. 5:7, because He **c-s** for you
Ps. 8:4; Mark 4:38; 1 Cor. 12:25
CAREFUL—*guard, diligent* Luke 15:8
Prov. 23:1, Consider **c-ly** what is before you
Eph. 5:15, be **c** how you walk
CARELESS—*idle* Matt. 12:36, every **c** word
CARGO—*merchandise* Rev. 18:12, **c-es** of gold
CAROUSE Rom. 13:13, not in **c-ing** and drunkenness
CARPENTER—*craftsmen* 2 Sam. 5:11; 2 Kin. 22:6; Matt. 13:55; Mark 6:3
CARRIED—*wrought* Is. 53:4, our sorrows He **c**
Matt. 8:17, **c** away our diseases
Luke 16:22, was **c** away by the angels
Heb. 13:9, not be **c** away by . . . teachings
1 Pet. 4:3, **c** out the desire of the Gentiles
CARRY—*bear, wear* Luke 10:4, **c** no purse, no bag
23:26, placed on him the cross to **c**
2 Cor. 4:10, **c-ing** about in the body the dying of Jesus
Ex. 23:1; Num. 10:17; 11:14; Deut. 1:31; 1 Sam. 2:28; Ps. 126:6; Is. 40:11; 52:11; 63:9; Mark 14:13
CART 1 Sam. 6:8, ark of the LORD . . . on the **c**
1 Sam. 6:7,14; Is. 5:18; 28:28
CASE—*matter* Job 19:28; 37:19
Deut. 17:8, any **c** is too difficult for you
Mic. 6:2, the LORD has a **c** against His people
CASSIA Ex. 30:24; Ps. 45:8; Ezek. 27:19
CAST—*drive, throw, thrust*
Ps. 51:11, Do not **c** me away
Eccles. 11:1, **C** your bread on the . . . waters
Luke 4:29, **c** Him out of the city
12:49, **c** fire upon the earth
John 6:37, will certainly not **c** out
1 Pet. 5:7, **c-ing** all your anxiety upon Him
Josh. 18:10; Job 6:27; Mark 15:32
CATCH—*trap* Ps. 10:9; Prov. 6:25; Song 2:15; Luke 5:10
CATTLE—*herd* Ps. 50:10, **c** on a thousand hills
Ex. 12:29; 20:10; Lev. 22:19; Num. 31:28; Ps. 104:14; Hab. 3:17
CAUGHT—*seized* 2 Cor. 12:4, was **c** up into Paradise
Gal. 6:1, if a man is **c** in any trespass
Gen. 22:13; Ex. 22:7; Judg. 15:4; John 21:3
CAUSE—*purpose* Gen. 2:24, For this **c** a man shall leave
Ps. 67:1, **c** His face to shine upon us
Prov. 3:30, Do not contend . . . without **c**
Matt. 19:5, THIS C A MAN SHALL LEAVE
John 15:25, HATED ME WITHOUT A C
Ps. 112:5; Is. 45:7; Rom. 16:17; 1 Cor. 3:6
CAVE—*shelter* 1 Kin. 18:4; Zeph. 2:6; John 11:38; Heb. 11:38
CEASE Ex. 23:12, day you shall **c** *from labor*
Ps. 46:9, He makes wars to **c**
Luke 7:45, not **c-d** to kiss My feet
1 Cor. 13:8, *are* tongues, they will **c**
1 Thess. 5:17, pray without **c-ing**
Gen. 8:22; Deut. 15:11; Ps. 37:8; Prov. 23:4

CEDAR—*fir* 1 Kin. 5:6; 6:15; Job 40:17; Ps. 92:12
CENSER Ezek. 8:11; Rev. 8:3,5
CENSUS—*tax* Luke 2:1, a **c** . . . of all the inhabited earth
Acts 5:37, rose up in the days of the **c**
CENT Matt. 5:26, paid up the last **c**
Matt. 10:29, sparrows sold for a **c**
Mark 12:42, two small copper coins . . . a **c**
CERTAIN—*sure* 2 Pet. 1:10, make **c** about His calling
CERTIFICATE Matt. 5:31, A C OF DISMISSAL
CHAFF Ps. 1:4; Matt. 3:12
CHAIN—*band* Acts 12:7, **c-s** fell off his hands
Heb. 11:36, also **c-s** and imprisonment
Judg. 16:21; 1 Kin. 6:21; Eccles. 7:26; Mark 5:3; Luke 8:29; Rev. 20:1
CHALCEDONY Rev. 21:19, the third, **c**
CHAMBER—*room* Gen. 43:30; Judg. 3:20,24; 2 Kin. 4:10; Ps. 19:5; Joel 2:16
CHAMPION 1 Sam. 17:4,23
CHANCE—*happen* Eccles. 9:11, for time and **c** overtake
Luke 10:31, by **c** a certain priest
CHANGE—*transform* Ps. 46:2, earth should **c**
Jer. 13:23, the Ethiopian **c** his skin
Mal. 3:6, I, the LORD, do not **c**
1 Cor. 15:51, we shall all be **c-d**
Gen. 35:2; Job 14:14; Prov. 24:21; Dan. 2:21
CHANNEL Job 28:10, hews out **c-s**
CHARCOAL—*coal, soot* John 18:18; 21:9
CHARGE—*accusation, crime* Lev. 8:35, **c** of the LORD
2 Chr. 23:6, keep the **c** of the LORD
Ps. 91:11, give His angels **c** concerning
Matt. 24:45, master put in **c** of his household
Ex. 23:7; Matt. 4:6; 27:37; Acts 25:27; 1 Cor. 9:18; 1 Tim. 5:21; 1 Pet. 5:3
CHARIOT Ps. 20:7, Some boast in **c-s**
Ps. 104:3, makes the clouds his **c**
Acts 8:28, sitting in his **c** . . . reading
Gen. 46:29; 2 Kin. 2:11; Ps. 46:9
CHARITY—*alms* Luke 12:33, sell . . . give to **c**
CHARM—*favor* Prov. 31:30, **C** is deceitful
CHARMER—*babbler* Ps. 58:5; Eccles. 10:11
CHASE—*drive* Lev. 26:7,8; Deut. 32:30; Job 20:8
CHASTE—*pure* 1 Pet. 3:2, **c** and respectful behavior
CHASTEN—*discipline* Is. 53:5, **c-ing** for our well-being
Ps. 38:1; 94:12
CHATTER—*babbling* 1 Tim. 6:20; 2 Tim. 2:16
CHEAT—*deceive, mislead*
Gen. 31:7, father has **c-ed** me
CHEEK Job 16:10; Is. 50:6; Matt. 5:39
CHEER—*merry* Judg. 9:13; 1 Sam. 15:32; Prov. 15:13
Prov. 15:15, **c-ful** heart *has* a continual feast
2 Cor. 9:7, God loves a **c-ful** giver
James 5:13, Is anyone **c-ful**
CHEESE 1 Sam. 17:18; 2 Sam. 17:29; Job 10:10
CHICK Matt. 23:37, way a hen gathers her **c-s**
CHILD Prov. 22:6, Train up a **c** . . . should go
Prov. 23:13, hold back discipline from the **c**
Is. 9:6, a **c** will be born to us
Matt. 1:18, Mary . . . with **c** by the Holy Spirit
2:8, make careful search for the **C**
2:9, stood over where the **C** was
2:13,20, take the **C** and His mother
1 Cor. 13:11, When I was a **c**
Gen. 21:8; Jer. 31:20; Matt. 18:2; Mark 5:39; Luke 8:54
CHILDBIRTH Ps. 48:6; Rom. 8:22
CHILDHOOD Eccles. 11:9, during your **c**
2 Tim. 3:15, from **c** you have known
CHILDREN—*babes, immature* Gen. 3:16; 1 Sam. 16:11
Ps. 103:13, father has compassion on *his* **c**
Prov. 31:28, **c** rise up and bless her
Jer. 31:15, Rachel is weeping for her **c**
Ezek. 18:2, **c-'s** teeth are set on edge
Matt. 2:16, slew all the male **c**
2:18, RACHEL WEEPING FOR HER C
10:21, C WILL RISE UP AGAINST PARENTS
18:3, and become like **c**
Is. 3:4; 49:21; Matt. 3:9; 11:16; 19:14; 1 John 2:1; Rev. 2:23
CHOICE—*pleasant* 1 Sam. 9:2, **c** and handsome man
Rom. 9:11, God's purpose according to *His* **c**
1 Thess. 1:4, knowing . . . *His* **c** of you
Gen. 23:6; 2 Sam. 10:9; Song 4:16; Acts 15:7; Rom. 11:5,28
CHOKE Matt. 13:22, riches **c** the word
Mark 4:19, **c** the word
Luke 8:14, **c-d** with worries
CHOOSE—*take* Heb. 11:25, **c-ing** . . . endure ill treatment
2 Pet. 1:10, calling and **c-ing** you
Ex. 17:9; Deut. 1:13; Josh. 24:15; Is. 7:15
CHOSEN—*elect, beloved, esteemed, loved, choose*
Is. 65:9, My **c** ones shall inherit
Luke 9:35, This is My son, *My* **C** One
Col. 3:12, who have been **c** of God
2 Tim. 2:10, endure all things . . . who are **c**
1 Pet. 2:9, you are A C RACE
Deut. 7:6; Ps. 119:30; Is. 42:1; 45:4; Matt. 12:18; Rom. 11:7; 1 Tim. 5:21; 1 Pet. 1:1; 2 John 1
CHRIST—*Messiah, Lord* 2 Thess. 3:5; 2 John 9
Matt. 16:16, Thou art the **C**, the Son
Luke 24:46, the **C** should suffer
Acts 2:36, made Him both Lord and **C**
1 Cor. 1:23, we preach **C** crucified
Phil. 1:21, to live is **C**
Col. 3:4, **C**, who is our life
1 Thess. 4:16, the dead in **C** shall rise
CHRISTIAN Acts 11:26, first called **C-s** in Antioch
Acts 26:28, persuade me to become a **C**
1 Pet. 4:16, if *anyone suffers* as a **C**
CHURCH Matt. 16:18, rock I will build My **c**
Matt. 18:17, tell it to the **c**; refuses to listen . . . **c**
Acts 15:4, received by the **c**
1 Cor. 11:18, come together as a **c**
14:35, for a woman to speak in **c**
2 Cor. 11:8, robbed other **c-es**
Eph. 5:23, Christ . . . head of the **c**
1 Tim. 3:5, how will he take care of the **c**
Heb. 12:23, general assembly and **c**
CIRCULATE 1 Sam. 2:24, LORD's people **c-ing**
CIRCUMCISE Phil. 3:5, **c-d** the eighth day
Col. 2:11, in Him you were also **c-d**
Gen. 17:10; Deut. 30:6; Luke 1:59
CIRCUMSTANCE—*degree*
James 1:9, humble **c-s**
CISTERN—*dungeon* Eccles. 12:6, wheel at the **c** is crushed
Jer. 2:13, hew for themselves **c-s**, Broken **c-s**
Prov. 5:15; Jer. 38:6
CITIZEN—*free* Eph. 2:19, fellow-**c-s** with the saints
Luke 15:15; Acts 21:39; 22:28
CITY Num. 35:6; Josh. 15:59, **c** of refuge
Ps. 46:4, make glad the **c** of God
107:4, an inhabited **c**
127:1, Unless the LORD guards the **c**
Zech. 8:3, the **C** of Truth
Matt. 2:23, resided in a **c** called Nazareth
4:5, took Him into the holy **c**
5:14, a **c** set on a hill
10:11, whatever **c** or village you enter
21:10, all the **c** was stirred
Acts 8:8, much rejoicing in that **c**
Heb. 11:10, a **c** which has foundations
12:22, the **c** of the living God
Rev. 21:2, I saw the holy **c**
Gen. 4:17; 11:4; 2 Sam. 19:37; Eccles. 9:14; Is. 1:26; 19:18; 33:20; Matt. 10:14; 21:10; Luke 9:5; 24:49; Acts 7:58
CLAMOR—*boisterous* Eph. 4:31, anger and **c**

CLAN—*thousand* Is. 60:22, become a **c**
CLAP Ps. 47:1, O **c** your hands, all peoples
Is. 55:12, trees of the field will **c**
2 Kin. 11:12; Job 27:23; 34:37; Ps. 98:8; Lam. 2:15; Ezek. 25:6
CLASS—*reckon* Luke 22:37, HE WAS C-ED
CLAW—*hoof* Dan. 4:33, nails like birds' **c-s**
CLAY Job 4:19, who dwell in houses of **c**
Job 33:6, formed out of **c**
Jer. 18:6, **c** in the potter's hand
1 Kin. 7:46; Is. 64:8; Dan. 2:33; John 9:6; Rom. 9:21
CLEAN—*cleanse, acquit, purify*
Ps. 19:9, fear of the LORD is **c**
24:4, who has **c** hands
51:10, Create in me a **c** heart
Matt. 3:12, thoroughly **c** His threshing floor
Matt. 8:2; Mark 1:40; Luke 5:12, Thou canst make me **c**
John 15:3, **c** because of the word
1 Cor. 5:7, **C** out the old leaven
2 Kin. 5:12; Job 14:4; Is. 1:16; 52:11; Matt. 23:26; Luke 11:39,41; John 13:10
CLEANSE—*clean, purify, wash*
Matt. 8:3; 10:8; 11:5, I am willing; be **c-d**
Mark 7:4, not eat unless they **c** themselves
Acts 10:15; 11:9, What God has **c-d**
15:9, **c-ing** their hearts by faith
James 4:8, **C** your hands, you sinners
1 John 1:7, blood . . . **c-s** us from all sin
Prov. 20:9; Luke 4:27; 7:22; 17:17; 2 Cor. 7:1
CLEAR—*pure, plain* Is. 40:3, **C** the way for the LORD
Matt. 7:5, you will see **c-ly** *enough*
Rom. 1:20, have been **c-ly** seen
Rev. 22:1, water of life, **c** as crystal
Gen. 20:16; Num. 14:18; Job 26:13; Is. 32:4
CLEAVE—*cling* Gen. 2:24, shall **c** to his wife
Hab. 3:9, **c** the earth with rivers
Matt. 19:5; Eph. 5:31
CLEFT Song 2:14; Is. 2:21; Jer. 49:16
CLEVER—*skillful, wise* 1 Cor. 1:17, not in **c-ness**
1 Cor. 1:19, **c-ness** of the **c** I will set aside
2 Pet. 1:16, not follow **c-ly** devised tales
CLIMB 1 Sam. 14:13; Jer. 48:44; Luke 19:4; John 10:1
CLING Josh. 23:8, **c** to the LORD your God
Ps. 63:8, My soul **c-s** to Thee
102:5, My bones **c** to my flesh
John 20:17, Stop **c-ing** to Me
CLOAK—*mantle, coat* Ruth 3:15, Give me the **c** . . . on you
Is. 3:7; Matt. 9:20; Acts 12:8; 2 Tim. 4:13
CLOD—*crust* Job 21:33, **c-s** of the valley
CLOSE (adj.)—*intimate, near*
Prov. 18:24, a friend who sticks **c-r** than
Judg. 20:34; Ps. 41:9
CLOSE (v.)—*shut, stop* Gen. 7:16; 8:2, LORD **c-d** *it* behind
Num. 16:33, the earth **c-d** over them
Acts 28:27, THEY HAVE C-D THEIR EYES
Rom. 3:19, every mouth may be **c-d**
1 John 3:17, **c-s** his heart against him
Rev. 21:25, its gates shall never be **c-d**
Judg. 19:9
CLOTH 1 Sam. 21:9; Matt. 9:16; Luke 2:7; John 11:44
CLOTHE—*array, adorn, wrap* Job 10:11, **C** me with skin
Matt. 6:29, Solomon . . . not **c-d** like
25:36, naked, and you **c-d** Me
1 Pet. 5:5, **c** yourselves with humility
Rev. 7:13, are **c-d** in the white robes
1 Kin. 11:29; Job 40:10; Ps. 65:13; 93:1; Is. 52:1; Luke 24:49; Rev. 3:5
CLOTHES—*dress, garment* Matt. 22:11, not . . . in wedding **c**
James 2:3, one who is wearing the fine **c**
Deut. 29:5; Josh. 9:5; 1 Sam. 19:13; 2 Sam. 12:20; Mark 14:63; James 2:2
CLOTHING—*clothes, dress, raiment*
Matt. 6:25, food, and the body than **c**
7:15, come to you in sheep's **c**
1 Tim. 2:9, with proper **c**
Deut. 8:4; Job 24:10; Jer. 10:9
CLOUD—*darkness* Gen. 9:13, My bow in the **c**
Ex. 13:21, a pillar of **c** by day
20:21, Moses approached the thick **c**
24:15, **c** covered the mountain
Matt. 24:30, SON OF MAN COMING ON THE C-S
Mark 9:7, a **c** formed . . . voice came out of the **c**
Luke 12:54, see a **c** rising in the west
21:27, IN A C with power and great glory
Acts 1:9, a **c** received Him out of their sight
1 Thess. 4:17, caught up . . . in the **c-s**
Rev. 1:7, HE IS COMING WITH THE C-S
Ex. 14:24; 33:9; 1 Kin. 8:12; 2 Chr. 6:1; Ps. 99:7; 105:39; Ezek. 30:3; Jude 12
CLUSTER Is. 65:8, new wine is found in the **c**
Num. 13:23; Mic. 7:1; Rev. 14:18
COAL—*soot, charcoal* Prov. 6:28; Is. 6:6
Prov. 25:22, heap burning **c-s** on his head
Rom. 12:20, HEAP . . . C-S UPON HIS HEAD
COAST Acts 27:2, the regions along the **c**
COAT—*cloak* Matt. 5:40, let him have your **c** also
COBRA Job 20:16, He sucks the poison of **c-s**
Ps. 58:4, Like a deaf **c**
91:13, tread upon the lion and **c**
COCK Matt. 26:34,75, before a **c** crows
Mark 13:35, at **c**-crowing, or in the morning
COFFIN—*bier* Gen. 50:26; Luke 7:14
COIN—*money* Matt. 22:19, Show Me the **c** *used* for
Luke 15:8, woman . . . loses **c**
COLD Prov. 25:25, Like **c** water to a weary soul
Matt. 10:42, a cup of **c** water
24:12, love will grow **c**
Rev. 3:15, that you were **c** or hot
Gen. 8:22; Job 24:7; 37:9; Prov. 25:13; John 18:18; 2 Cor. 11:27
COLLAPSED—*fell* Luke 6:49, immediately it **c**
COLLECT—*exact* Luke 3:13, **C** no more
Luke 19:23, would have **c-ed** it with interest
COLLECTION 1 Cor. 16:1, the **c** for the saints
COLOR Ezek. 16:16, high places of various **c-s**
COLT—*foal* Zech. 9:9, a **c**, the foal of a donkey
Matt. 21:2, a donkey tied *there* and a **c** with her
John 12:15, KING COMES . . . ON A DONKEY'S C
COMBINE 1 Cor. 2:13, **c-ing** spiritual *thoughts* . . . *words*
COME—*enter, return* Ps. 95:6, **C**, let us worship
Zech. 9:9, your king is **c-ing** to you
Matt. 6:10, Thy kingdom **c**
11:28, **C** to Me, all who are weary
Mark 10:14, children to **c** to Me
Luke 21:27, SON OF MAN C-ING
John 17:1, Father, the hour has **c**
Rev. 22:20, I am **c-ing** quickly
Mark 14:38; Luke 19:23; 2 Thess. 2:2
COMFORT—*consolation, rest*
Ps. 23:4, Thy rod . . . they **c** me
Is. 61:2, To **c** all who mourn
Matt. 5:4, who mourn, for they shall be **c-ed**
Acts 9:31, in the **c** of the Holy Spirit
2 Cor. 1:3, God of all **c**
1:6, for your **c** and salvation
1 Thess. 4:18, **c** one another
2 Thess. 2:17, **c** and strengthen your hearts
Job 29:25; Ps. 77:2; Prov. 29:17; Eccles. 4:1; Is. 54:11; Lam. 1:21; Matt. 2:18; Luke 6:24; 16:25; 2 Cor. 7:4,13; 2 Thess. 2:16
COMFORTER—*helper* Job 16:2, Sorry **c-s** are you all
Ps. 69:20, looked for . . . **c-s**, but I found none
Nah. 3:7, Where will I seek **c-s** for you
COMING 2 Sam. 3:25, your going out and **c** in
Mal. 3:2, endure the day of His **c**

Matt. 11:3, Are You the **C** One
24:30, SON OF MAN **C**
26:64, **C** ON THE CLOUDS OF HEAVEN
John 5:25, an hour is **c** and now is
James 5:8, **c** of the Lord is at hand
2 Pet. 3:4, promise of His **c**

COMMAND—*declare, spoke* Gen. 18:19; Lev. 24:12; Deut. 2:37
Ps. 33:9, He **c-ed**, and it stood fast
Jon. 2:10, LORD **c-ed** the fish
Matt. 1:24, angel of the Lord **c-ed** him
4:3, Son of God, **c** that these stones
20:21, **C** that ... these two sons of mine
Luke 8:25, He **c-s** even the winds
9:54, **c** fire to come down from heaven
John 15:14, do what I **c** you

COMMANDER—*general* Judg. 5:9; 1 Chr. 27:34; Is. 55:4

COMMANDMENT—*instruction, duty*
Ex. 20:6, keep My **c-s**
34:28, tablets ... the Ten **C-s**
Ps. 19:8, **C** of the LORD is pure
Matt. 5:19, one of the least of these **c-s**
22:36, which is the great **c**
John 14:15, If you love Me ... keep My **c-s**
Prov. 6:20; Eccles. 12:13; Matt. 22:40; John 15:10

COMMEND—*praise* Eccles. 8:15, So I **c-ed** pleasure
Acts 20:32, I **c** you to God
1 Cor. 8:8; 2 Cor. 3:1

COMMISSION Acts 26:12, authority and **c** of ... priests

COMMIT—*entrust, practice, wrought*
Ex. 20:14, You shall not **c** adultery
Ps. 31:5, into Thy hand I **c** my spirit
37:5, **C** your way to the LORD
Luke 23:46, into Thy hands I **c** My spirit
John 8:34, every one who **c-s** sin
Ex. 32:30; Lev. 20:12; Prov. 16:3; Luke 18:20; 1 Pet. 2:22

COMMON—*prevalent* Lev. 4:27; Jer. 26:23
Acts 2:44, had all things in **c**
Titus 1:4, in a **c** faith
Jude 3, write you about our **c** salvation

COMMOTION—*disturbance* Jer. 10:22, great **c** out of ... land

COMPANION—*fellow* Prov. 13:20, **c** of fools will suffer
Heb. 1:9, OIL OF GLADNESS ABOVE THY **C-S**
Ex. 2:13; Job 30:29; Eccles. 4:10

COMPANY—*congregation*
Job 15:34, the **c** of the godless

COMPARE Prov. 3:15, nothing ... **c-s** with her
Matt. 11:16, to what shall I **c** this generation
Rom. 8:18, not worthy ... **c-d** with the glory

COMPARISON Judg. 8:2; Hag. 2:3

COMPASSION—*lovingkindness, mercy*
Ex. 33:19, **c** on whom I will show **c**
Ps. 25:6, Remember ... Thy **c**
72:13, **c** on the poor and needy
103:13, father has **c** on *his* children
111:4, LORD is gracious and **c-ate**
Col. 3:12, put on a heart of **c**
Matt. 9:36; 15:32; Luke 15:20; Rom. 9:15

COMPEL—*force, press* Luke 14:23, **c** *them* to come in

COMPETE—*strive* 1 Cor. 9:25, everyone who **c-s**
2 Tim. 2:5, **c-s** as an athlete

COMPLACENCY Prov. 1:32, **c** of fools shall destroy them

COMPLAIN James 5:9, Do not **c** ... against one another
Job 7:11; Ps. 55:17

COMPLAINING—*babbling*
Prov. 23:29, Who has **c**

COMPLAINT—*grudge* 1 Pet. 4:9 without **c**

COMPLETE—*fulfill, full, utterly*
Is. 2:18, idols will **c-ly** vanish
Col. 2:10, in Him ... made **c**
James 1:4, that you may be perfect and **c**
1 John 1:4, our joy may be **c**
Rev. 20:3, thousand years were **c-d**
Gen. 2:1; 29:27; Ex. 5:13; Num. 15:31; Esth. 1:5; 1 Cor. 1:10; Rev. 20:7

COMPOSE Job 16:4, I could **c** words against you

COMPOSURE Eccles. 10:4, **c** allays great offenses

COMPREHEND—*calculate*
Job 37:5, things ... cannot **c**
John 1:5, darkness did not **c** it

COMPREHENSION—*understanding*
Phil. 4:7, peace ... surpasses all **c**

COMPULSION—*constrain*
1 Pet. 5:2, not under **c**, but

CONCEAL—*cover, hide* Prov. 12:23; Is. 3:9; Jer. 50:2
Ps. 40:10, have not **c-ed** thy lovingkindness
Prov. 27:5, love that is **c-ed**

CONCEIT—*pride*
Phil. 2:3, nothing ... selfishness or empty **c**
1 Tim. 6:4, is **c-ed** *and* understands nothing

CONCEIVE Num. 11:12; Job 15:35; Ps. 51:5; Matt. 1:20; Acts 5:4; James 1:15

CONCERN—*care* Col. 4:13, he has a deep **c** for you
1 Sam. 1:16; Matt. 4:6; John 12:6; Rom. 1:3; 1 Cor. 7:32; 9:9; 12:1

CONCILIATE—*entreat*
1 Cor. 4:13, slandered, we try to **c**

CONCLUSION
Eccles. 12:13, The **c** when all has been heard

CONDEMN—*discredit, judge*
Is. 50:9, Who ... **c-s** Me
Mark 16:16, who has disbelieved shall be **c-ed**
Gal. 2:11, because he stood **c-ed**
1 John 3:20, in whatever our heart **c-s** us
Job 9:20; Prov. 12:2; Mark 10:33; Luke 6:37; Rom. 2:1; 14:23

CONDEMNATION—*judgment* Rom. 3:8, Their **c** is just
Rom. 8:1, no **c** for those who are in
Matt. 23:14; Mark 12:40; Luke 20:47; 23:40; Rom. 13:2

CONDUCT—*bring, behavior* Job 33:17; Ezek. 7:27; Acts 17:15
Col. 4:5, **C** yourselves with wisdom
2 Pet. 2:7, sensual **c** of unprincipled men

CONDUIT 2 Kin. 18:17; 20:20; Is. 7:3; 36:2

CONFER—*consult* Acts 4:15; 25:12

CONFESS—*acknowledge* Matt. 3:6, they **c-ed** their sins
Matt. 10:32, **c** Me before men ... **c** him before My Father
Mark 1:5, baptized ... **c-ing** their sins
Rom. 10:9, **c** with your mouth
James 5:16, **c** your sins to one another
1 John 1:9, If we **c** our sins, He is
Ps. 32:5; John 1:20; Rom. 10:10

CONFESSION 2 Cor. 9:13, your **c** of the gospel of Christ
1 Tim. 6:13; Heb. 10:23

CONFIDENCE—*boldness, trust* Prov. 3:26; Heb. 3:6
Job 31:24, have put my **c** in gold
Is. 32:17, quietness and **c** forever
2 Cor. 1:12, For our proud **c** is this
Phil. 1:26, your proud **c** in me
3:3, and put no **c** in the flesh
Heb. 4:16, draw near with **c** to the throne of grace
1 John 4:17, we may have **c** in the day of judgment

CONFIDENT Eph. 3:12, **c** access through faith in Him

CONFIRM—*establish* Ps. 90:17, **c** the work of our hands
Rom. 15:8, to **c** the promises *given* to the fathers
1 Cor. 1:8, also **c** you to the end
Matt. 18:16; Mark 16:20

CONFIRMATION Phil. 1:7, defense and **c** of the gospel
Heb. 6:16, an oath *given* as **c** is an end

CONFORM Rom. 8:29, *to become* **c-ed** to the image
Rom. 12:2, do not be **c-ed** to this world
Phil. 3:10, being **c-ed** to His death
CONFOUND Josh. 10:10; Is. 19:3
CONFUSE Gen. 11:7, **c** their language
CONFUSION—*disorder*
1 Sam. 14:20, *was* very great **c**
1 Cor. 14:33, not *a God* of **c**
CONGREGATION—*company, assembly*
Ex. 12:3, Speak to all the **c**
Ps. 82:1, His stand in His own **c**
149:1, **c** of the godly ones
CONQUER Rom. 8:37, **c** through Him
Rev. 6:2, went out **c-ing**, and to **c**
CONSCIENCE Acts 23:1, lived . . . good **c** before God
Rom. 13:5, also for **c** sake
1 Cor. 8:7, their **c** being weak
1 Tim. 3:9, faith with a clear **c**
4:2, **c** as with a branding iron
1 Pet. 3:16, keep a good **c**
Acts 24:16; Rom. 2:15; Heb. 9:14; 10:22
CONSECRATE—*sanctify*
Lev. 11:44, **C** yourselves
1 Sam. 21:4, there is **c-d** bread
Matt. 12:4, They ate **c-d** bread
Ex. 28:38,41; 29:1,21,29,35; 40:9; Lev. 12:4; 16:19; 25:10; Num. 6:11; 1 Sam. 21:6; 1 Kin. 8:64; 9:3,7; 2 Chr. 7:7
CONSENT—*agree* Prov. 1:10; Is. 1:19; Luke 23:51
CONSIDER—*notice, observe*
Ps. 41:1, blessed is he who **c-s** the helpless
Eccles. 7:14, in the day of adversity **c**
Luke 12:24, **C** the ravens, for they
Heb. 10:24, let us **c** . . . one another
11:26, **c-ing** the reproach of Christ
2 Sam. 19:19; Ps. 44:22; 48:13; 77:5
CONSIDERATION
Acts 27:3, Julius treated Paul with **c**
CONSIST Luke 12:15, his life **c** of his possessions
CONSOLATION—*comfort* Job 15:11, Are the **c-s** of God . . . small
Phil. 2:1, if there is any **c** of love
CONSPIRACY—*plot* 2 Sam. 15:12, the **c** was strong
CONSTRAIN—*persuade, urge* Job 32:18
CONSULT—*confer, counsel* 1 Kin. 12:6,8
Gal. 1:16, I did not . . . **c** with flesh and blood
CONSUME—*eat, devour*
Ex. 3:2, yet the bush was not **c-d**
Ex. 24:17; Is. 29:6; 30:27,30; 33:14, **c-ing** fire
Deut. 4:24, God is a **c-ing** fire
Ezek. 15:7, yet the fire will **c** them
Lev. 10:2; Deut. 5:25; 32:24; Ps. 39:11; 49:14; 69:9; 90:7; Eccles. 4:5; Luke 9:54; John 2:17; Gal. 5:15; James 5:3
CONSUMMATION—*end* Heb. 9:26, at the **c**
CONSUMPTION Lev. 26:16; Deut. 28:22
CONTAIN 1 Kin. 8:27; 1 Pet. 2:6
CONTAINER Luke 8:16, covers it over with a **c**
CONTEMPT Rom. 14:10, regard your brother with **c**
2 Cor. 10:10, his speech **c-ible**
Job 12:21; Prov. 18:3; Dan. 12:2
CONTEND—*strive* Is. 50:8, Who will **c** with Me
Is. 57:16, I will not **c** forever
Jude 3, **c** earnestly for the faith
Judg. 8:1; Job 40:2; Prov. 3:30; Is. 49:25; Jer. 2:9
CONTENT—*satisfy* Luke 3:14, be **c** with your wages
Phil. 4:11, I have learned to be **c**
1 Tim. 6:6, accompanied by **c-ment**
2 Cor. 12:10; Heb. 13:5
CONTENTIOUS Prov. 21:19; 25:24; 1 Cor. 11:16
CONTINUAL—*unceasing, constant* Num. 4:16; 28:24
Prov. 15:15, cheerful heart *has* a **c** feast
CONTINUALLY—*perpetual*
1 Chr. 16:11, Seek His face **c**
Ps. 34:1, praise shall **c** be in my mouth
Prov. 6:21; Luke 18:5
CONTINUE—*persevere*
Acts 13:43, **c** in the grace of God
Heb. 13:1, Let love of the brethren **c**
CONTRARY—*hostile*
Matt. 14:24, for the wind was **c**
Rom. 11:24, grafted **c** to nature
16:17, **c** to the teaching
2 Cor. 2:7, on the **c** . . . rather forgive
Gal. 2:7, on the **c**, seeing that I
1 Tim. 1:10, **c** to sound teaching
CONTRIBUTE Rom. 12:13, **c-ing** to the needs of the saints
CONTRIBUTION Rom. 15:26, make a **c** for the poor
CONTRITE—*crush* Ps. 51:17, broken and a **c** heart
Is. 66:2, humble and **c** of spirit
CONTROL—*rule* Prov. 25:28, no **c** over his spirit
2 Cor. 5:14, love of Christ **c-s** us
CONTROVERSY—*dispute*
Jer. 25:31, **c** with the nations
CONVERSE—*discuss*
Luke 24:15, while they were **c-ing**
Acts 17:18, philosophers were **c-ing** with him
CONVERSION Acts 15:3, **c** of the Gentiles
CONVERT—*restore*
Matt. 18:3, unless you are **c-ed**
CONVICT—*reprove*
John 8:46, Which one of you **c-s** Me
16:8, **c** the world concerning sin
Heb. 11:1, the **c-ion** of things not seen
CONVINCE—*persuade* Rom. 14:14, am **c-d** in the Lord Jesus
Heb. 6:9, **c-d** of better things
COOK 1 Sam. 8:13; 9:23,24
COOL Gen. 3:8; Luke 16:24
COPE Acts 6:10, unable to **c** with the wisdom
COPPER Deut. 8:9, you can dig **c**
Matt. 10:9, Do not acquire gold . . . or **c**
COPPERSMITH 2 Tim. 4:14, Alexander the **c**
COPY—*transcribe* Deut. 17:18; Josh. 8:32; Heb. 9:24
CORBAN Mark 7:11, have been helped by is **C**
CORD—*band, chain*
Ps. 18:4, **c-s** of death encompassed me
Prov. 5:22, held with the **c-s** of his sin
Eccles. 12:6, the silver **c** is broken
John 2:15, made a scourge of **c-s**
2 Sam. 22:6; Job 36:8; 38:31; 41:1; Is. 5:18
CORNER Prov. 7:12, lurks by every **c**
Matt. 6:5, synagogues and on the street **c-s**
Acts 10:11, lowered by four **c-s** to the ground
Rev. 7:1, at the four **c-s** of the earth
CORNERSTONE—*corner* Ps. 118:22, the chief **c**
Matt. 21:42, BECAME THE CHIEF C
Eph. 2:20, Christ . . . being the **c**
Job 38:6; Is. 28:16
CORPSE—*body* Is. 14:19; Nah. 3:3; Matt. 24:28
CORRECT—*reprove*
Prov. 29:17, **C** your son, and he will
Jer. 10:24, **C** me . . . but with justice
2 Tim. 3:16, profitable . . . for **c-ion**
CORRUPT—*depraved, rotten*
Gen. 6:11, the earth was **c**
Ps. 14:1, They are **c**, they have committed
1 Cor. 15:33, Bad company **c-s** good morals
Job 15:16; Is. 1:4; Jer. 6:28; 2 Cor. 7:2; Eph. 4:22
CORRUPTIBLE—*perish*
Rom. 1:23, in the form of **c** man
CORRUPTION—*decay* Lev. 22:25; Rom. 8:21; 2 Pet. 2:19
Gal. 6:8, shall from the flesh reap **c**
2 Pet. 1:4, the **c** that is in the world
COST—*wealth, price*
Ps. 49:8, redemption . . . soul is **c-ly**
Is. 55:1, Without money and without **c**
Matt. 26:7, vial of very **c-ly** perfume
2 Sam. 24:24; 1 Kin. 5:17; Ezra 6:4,8; John 12:3; 1 Tim. 2:9

COUCH—*pallet* Gen. 49:4,9
Ps. 6:6, dissolve my **c** with my tears
COUNCIL Mark 15:43; Luke 23:50
Jer. 23:18, stood in the **c** of the LORD
Acts 5:27, stood them before the **C**
6:12, brought Stephen before the **C**
COUNSEL—*advice, opinion*
Ps. 1:1, not walk in the **c**
33:11, **C** of the LORD stands
73:24, With Thy **c** . . . guide me
Prov. 13:10, those who receive **c**
19:20, Listen to **c** and accept
Is. 28:29, made *His* **c** wonderful
John 12:10, chief priests took **c**
Eph. 1:11, after the **c** of His will
Ex. 18:19; Judg. 19:30; 1 Kin. 12:6; 2 Chr. 10:9; Ezra 4:5; Ps. 32:8; 62:4; Matt. 22:15; Luke 14:31
COUNSELOR
Is. 9:6, will be called Wonderful **C**
Rom. 11:34, WHO BECAME HIS **C**
Job 12:17; Prov. 11:14; Mic. 4:9
COUNT—*consider, number* 2 Cor. 5:19; James 5:11
Gen. 15:5, **c** the stars, if you are able
Prov. 17:28, closes his lips . . . **c-ed** prudent
1 Cor. 4:15, have **c-less** tutors in Christ
Phil. 3:8, I **c** all things to be loss
2 Pet. 3:9, as some **c** slowness
COUNTENANCE Gen. 4:6, why has your **c** fallen
Num. 6:26, The LORD lift up His **c**
Ps. 4:6; 89:15, light of Thy **c**
COUNTRY—*region*
John 4:44, no honor in his own **c**
Gen. 12:1; Matt. 2:12; Luke 15:13
COURAGE—*cheer* 2 Chr. 15:7, strong and do not lose **c**
Ps. 27:14, let your heart take **c**
John 16:33, take **c**; I have overcome
Matt. 9:2,22; 14:27; Acts 23:11
COURAGEOUS Deut. 31:6; Josh. 1:7
COURSE Ps. 19:5, strong man to run his **c**
2 Tim. 4:7, have finished the **c**
James 3:6, sets on fire the **c** of our life
Judg. 5:20; Acts 20:24
COURT—*council* Ps. 84:10, a day in Thy **c-s**
Ex. 27:9; Ps. 135:2; Matt. 10:17
COURTEOUS Acts 28:7, entertained us **c-ly** three days
COVENANT Job 31:1; Acts 3:25; Gal. 4:24
Gen. 6:18, I will establish My **c**
Num. 10:33, ark of the **c** of the LORD
2 Kin. 23:2, book of the **c**
Ps. 25:10; 103:18, To those who keep His **c**
Matt. 26:28, My blood of the **c**
Luke 22:20, This cup . . . is the new **c**
2 Cor. 3:6, servants of a new **c**
3:14, reading of the old **c**
Heb. 7:22, Jesus . . . guarantee of a better **c**
8:6, mediator of a better **c**
13:20, blood of the eternal **c**
Rev. 11:19, the ark of His **c**
COVER—*hide* Ps. 32:1, Whose sin is **c-ed**
Ps. 91:4, **c** you with His pinions
Prov. 10:12, love **c-s** all transgressions
Matt. 10:26, nothing **c-ed** that will not be revealed
James 5:20, will **c** a multitude of sins
1 Pet. 4:8, love **c-s** a multitude of sins
Gen. 37:26; Ex. 2:3; Job 36:32; Is. 6:2; 50:6; Luke 23:30
COVERING—*raiment*
Ps. 105:39, spread a cloud for a **c**
1 Cor. 11:15, her hair is given . . . for a **c**
Gen. 3:7; 2 Sam. 17:19; Is. 50:3; 1 Tim. 6:8
COVET—*crave, desire* Mic. 2:2; Rom. 13:9
Ex. 20:17, You shall not **c**
Mark 7:22, deeds of **c-ing** *and* wickedness
Acts 20:33, have **c-ed** no one's silver
Rom. 7:8, produced in me **c-ing** of every kind

COW—*ox* Is. 11:7, the **c** and the bear will graze
Lev. 22:28; Job 21:10
COWARDLY—*fearful* Rev. 21:8, for the **c** and unbelieving
CRAFT—*deceit* Job 15:5, language of the **c-y**
Ex. 21:14; Is. 2:16; 2 Cor. 12:16
CRAFTINESS—*shrewd* 2 Cor. 4:2, walking in **c**
CRAFTSMEN 2 Kin. 24:14; Hos. 13:2; Zech. 1:20; Acts 19:24
CRANE—*thrush* Is. 38:14
CRASH Zeph. 1:10, a loud **c** from the hills
CRAVE—*desire, covet* Mic. 7:1
Prov. 13:4, soul of the sluggard **c-s** and gets nothing
21:26, All day long he is **c-ing**
CRAWL—*creep* Acts 10:12, **c-ing** creatures of the earth
CREATE—*form* Gen. 1:1, **c-d** the heavens and the earth
Ps. 51:10, **C** in me a clean heart
Is. 45:12, made the earth, and **c-d** man
Mal. 2:10, Has not one God **c-d** us
Eph. 2:10, **c-d** in Christ Jesus
4:24, God . . . **c-d** in righteousness
Col. 1:16, in Him all things were **c-d**
Is. 57:19; 65:17; Mark 13:19; Eph. 3:9; 1 Tim. 2:13
CREATION Mark 10:6, beginning of **c**, *God* MADE THEM
Mark 13:19, **c** which God created
16:15, preach the gospel to all **c**
Rom. 1:20, since the **c** of the world
8:22, whole **c** groans
2 Pet. 3:4, from the beginning of **c**
CREATOR Eccles. 12:1, Remember also your **C**
Is. 40:28, **c** of the ends of the earth
Rom. 1:25, the creature rather than the **C**
1 Pet. 4:19, to a faithful **C**
CREATURE—*animal, beast* Gen. 1:21, every living **c**
Lev. 11:47, the edible **c** and the **c** . . . not to be eaten
2 Cor. 5:17, *he is* a new **c**; the old things
Rom. 1:23; James 1:18
CREDIT—*thanks* Luke 6:32, what **c** is *that* to you
CREDITOR Ps. 109:11; Is. 50:1
Deut. 15:2, every **c** shall release what . . . loaned
CREEP Gen. 1:26; Ps. 148:10
CRESCENT Is. 3:18, will take away . . . **c** ornaments
CRIME Job 31:11; Ezek. 7:23
CRIMINAL 2 Tim. 2:9, suffer hardship . . . as a **c**
CRIMSON 2 Chr. 2:7, in purple, **c** and violet
Is. 1:18, like **c**, They will be like wool
CRIPPLE Matt. 18:8, better . . . to enter life **c-d**
Luke 14:21, bring in **c-d** and blind
CRITICIZE Is. 29:24, those who **c** . . . accept instruction
CROCUS Is. 35:1, blossom; Like the **c**
CROOKED—*perverse* Deut. 32:5; Prov. 21:8; Phil. 2:15
Ps. 125:5, turn aside to their **c** ways
Eccles. 1:15, **c** cannot be straightened
Luke 3:5, THE **C** SHALL BECOME STRAIGHT
CROP Lev. 1:16, take away its **c**
CROSS—*tree* Matt. 10:38, take his **c**
Matt. 27:40, come down from the **c**
John 19:17, went out, bearing His own **c**
19:25, standing by the **c** of Jesus
Acts 5:30, hanging Him on a **c**
1 Cor. 1:17, that the **c** of Christ should not
Gal. 6:14, except in the **c** of our Lord
Phil. 2:8, even death on a **c**
3:18, enemies of the **c** of Christ
Heb. 12:2, endured the **c**, despising
1 Kin. 1:6; 1 Cor. 1:18; Eph. 2:16; Col. 1:20
CROUCH—*bow* Job 38:40; Ps. 10:10
CROW Matt. 26:74, immediately a cock **c-ed**
Mark 14:72; Luke 22:34; 22:60

CROWD—*press*
Mark 2:4, unable to get to Him . . . **c**
5:27, in the **c** behind *Him,* and touched
CROWN—*wreath* Ps. 8:5, **c** him with glory
Ps. 103:4, **c-s** you with lovingkindness
Prov. 12:4, excellent wife is the **c** of
14:18, are **c-ed** with knowledge
14:24, **c** of the wise is their
16:31, gray head is a **c** of glory
17:6, grandchildren are the **c** of old men
Heb. 2:9, Jesus . . . **c-ed** with glory and honor
Gen. 49:26; Ps. 21:3; 65:11
CRUCIFIXION Matt. 26:2, delivered up for **c**
CRUCIFY Matt. 27:22, Let Him be **c-ed**
Matt. 28:5, Jesus who has been **c-ed**
Mark 15:13, shouted back, **C** Him
1 Cor. 1:23, we preach Christ **c-ed**
Gal. 2:20, I have been **c-ed** with Christ
6:14, world has been **c-ed** to me
Heb. 6:6, **c** to themselves the Son of God
Matt. 20:19; 27:35; 1 Cor. 1:13; 2 Cor. 13:4
CRUEL—*fierce* Prov. 11:17; Matt. 15:22
CRUMBS Matt. 15:27; Mark 7:28
CRUSH—*batter* Ps. 34:18, saves those . . . **c-ed** in spirit
Is. 53:5, **c-ed** for our iniquities
53:10, LORD was pleased to **c** Him
Amos 4:1, who **c** the needy
Rom. 16:20, **c** Satan under your feet
2 Cor. 4:8, but not **c-ed**
Lev. 22:24; 2 Kin. 18:21; Job 39:15; Jer. 17:18
CRUST Job 7:5, flesh is clothed . . . a **c** of dirt
CRY—*outcry*
Gen. 4:10, your brother's blood is **c-ing**
Ps. 9:12, the **c** of the afflicted
130:1, Out of the depths I have **c-ed**
Matt. 3:3, ONE C-ING IN THE WILDERNESS
Rev. 21:4, no . . . mourning, or **c-ing**
Ex. 2:6; 32:18; Lev. 13:45; Ps. 17:1; 27:7; Is. 42:2; Mark 15:37
CRYSTAL Ezek. 1:22; Rev. 4:6; 21:11
CUB 2 Sam. 17:8; Jer. 51:38; Nah. 2:11
CUBIT Gen. 6:15, length of the ark 300 **c-s**
Esth. 5:14, a gallows fifty **c-s** high
Matt. 6:27, add a single **c** to his life's span
Deut. 3:11; Ezek. 43:13
CUCUMBER Num. 11:5; Is. 1:8
CUD Lev. 11:3; Deut. 14:6
CULTIVATE—*till* Gen. 2:5, no man to **c** the ground
Ps. 37:3, Dwell in the land and **c** faithfulness
Gen. 2:15; Deut. 28:39; 2 Sam. 9:10; Ezek. 36:9
CUMMIN Matt. 23:23, and dill and **c**
CUP Ps. 23:5, My **c** overflows
Matt. 10:42, a **c** of cold water
20:22, able to drink the **c**
23:25, outside of the **c**
26:27, took a **c** and gave thanks
26:39, let this **c** pass from Me
Luke 22:20, **c** . . . is the new covenant
John 18:11, the **c** which the Father has given
1 Cor. 10:16, the **c** of blessing
Ps. 116:13; Prov. 23:31; Mark 7:4; 1 Cor. 10:21
CUPBEARER Gen. 40:1; 41:9; 1 Kin. 10:5; 2 Chr. 9:4; Neh. 1:11
CURDLE Job 10:10, and **c** me like cheese
CURDS—*butter* Judg. 5:25; Is. 7:15,22
CURE Luke 7:21, At that very time He **c-d** many
Luke 13:32, perform **c-s** today and tomorrow
CURSE—*oath* Ex. 22:28, You shall not **c** God
Mal. 4:6, smite the land with a **c**
Luke 6:28, bless those who **c** you
Rom. 3:14, WHOSE MOUTH IS FULL OF C-ING
Gal. 3:13, redeemed us from the **c**
Gen. 3:14; 12:3; 27:12; Lev. 19:14; 1 Sam. 3:13; Jer. 42:18; 44:12; Mic. 6:10; Zech. 14:11; Mark 14:71; Rom. 12:14; James 3:9
CURTAIN Ex. 26:1; Song 1:5; Is. 40:22
CUSHION Mark 4:38, asleep on the **c**
CUSTODY—*prison* Esth. 2:3,8,14; Matt. 4:12
CUSTOM—*manner* Luke 4:16, as was His **c**
Acts 16:21, **c-s** which are not lawful
Judg. 11:39; Ezra 4:13; John 18:39; 19:40; Acts 28:17; Rom. 13:7
CUT Matt. 3:10, not bear good fruit is **c** down
Matt. 21:8, others were **c-ing** branches
26:51, and **c** off his ear
Acts 7:54, they were **c** to the quick
Rom. 11:22, you also will be **c** off
Ex. 9:15; Judg. 1:6; Ps. 12:3; Prov. 10:31; Is. 45:2; Jer. 7:29; Matt. 5:30; 24:51
CYMBAL 2 Sam. 6:5; 1 Chr. 15:16; 16:5; Ps. 150:5; 1 Cor. 13:1

D

DAILY—*continual* Ps. 68:19, who **d** bears our burden
Prov. 8:30, I was **d** His delight
Matt. 6:11; Luke 11:3, Give us . . . our **d** bread
Luke 9:23, take up his cross **d**
Acts 16:5, churches . . . increasing in number **d**
17:11, examining the Scriptures **d**
1 Cor. 15:31, I die **d**
Dan. 1:5; Acts 6:1; James 2:15
DAINTY Gen. 49:20; Jer. 6:2
DAMAGE—*loss* Ezra 4:13,22; Acts 27:10
DANCE—*skip* 2 Sam. 6:14, David was **d-ing** before the LORD
Ps. 30:11, turned . . . mourning into **d-ing**
149:3, praise His name with **d-ing**
150:4, Praise Him with timbrel and **d-ing**
Eccles. 3:4, a time to **d**
Matt. 11:17, We played . . . you did not **d**
14:6, daughter of Herodias **d-d**
Ex. 32:19; Judg. 21:23; 1 Sam. 18:6; Jer. 31:13; Lam. 5:15; Mark 6:22; Luke 7:32
DANGER Acts 19:27; 27:9
DARE—*presume*
Acts 5:13, none . . . **d-d** to associate
Rom. 5:7, someone would **d** even to die
1 Cor. 6:1, **d** to go to law before the unrighteous
Job 41:10; Jude 9
DARK—*dim, shadow* Num. 12:8, not in **d** sayings
Joel 2:10, sun and the moon grow **d**
Luke 12:3, whatever you have said in the **d**
Gen. 15:17; Job 24:16; Is. 9:2; Lam. 4:1
DARKEN—*obscure*
Job 38:2, Who is this that **d-s** counsel
Eccles. 12:2, stars are **d-ed**
Matt. 24:29, THE SUN WILL BE D-ED
Rom. 1:21, their foolish heart was **d-ed**
11:10, LET THEIR EYES BE D-ED TO SEE NOT
Eph. 4:18, being **d-ed** in their understanding
Ex. 10:15; Mark 13:24; Rev. 16:10
DARKNESS—*cloud, gloom* Gen. 1:2, **d** was over the surface
Ex. 10:21, **d** over the land of Egypt . . . **d** which
2 Sam. 22:29, the LORD illumines my **d**
Ps. 91:6, pestilence that stalks in **d**
107:10, those who dwelt in **d**
112:4, Light arises in the **d**
Eccles. 2:13, as light excels **d**
2:14, the fool walks in **d**
Matt. 6:23, full of **d**, how great is the **d**
10:27, What I tell you in **d**, speak
22:13, cast him into the outer **d**
Luke 1:79, SHINE UPON THOSE WHO SIT IN D
John 1:5, light shines in the **d**
3:19, men loved the **d** rather than the light
12:35, **d** may not overtake
Acts 26:18, they may turn from **d** to light
Rom. 2:19, a light to those who are in **d**
2 Cor. 6:14, what fellowship has light with **d**
Eph. 5:11, unfruitful deeds of **d**
6:12, world forces of this **d**

1 Pet. 2:9, out of **d** into His marvelous light
1 John 1:5, in Him there is no **d** at all
2:9, hates his brother is in the **d**
Deut. 28:29; 1 Sam. 2:9; 2 Sam. 22:10; Job 3:5; 10:22; 12:25; 30:26; Ps. 18:9,28; 88:12; 97:2; 139:12; Prov. 20:20; Is. 58:10; Matt. 25:30; Luke 22:53; 23:44; Rom. 13:12; 1 Cor. 4:5; 2 Cor. 4:6; Col. 1:13; Heb. 12:18; 2 Pet. 2:4; 1 John 1:6

DART—*arrow, missile* Job 41:26, the **d** or the

DASH—*shatter* Is. 13:16, **d-ed** to pieces
Nah. 2:4, **d** to and fro like lightning
2 Kin. 8:12; Ps. 137:9; Jer. 13:14; Hos. 13:16

DATE—*time* Gal. 4:2, the **d** set by the father

DAUGHTER—Gen. 6:1, **d-s** were born to them
Num. 27:8, transfer his inheritance to his **d**
Prov. 31:29, Many **d-s** have done nobly
Eccles. 12:4, **d-s** of song will sing softly
Is. 22:4, destruction of the **d** of my people
Mic. 7:6, **D** rises up against her mother
Heb. 11:24, son of Pharaoh's **d**
Gen. 24:23,47; 27:46; Ex. 21:7; Deut. 28:53; Judg. 11:34; 2 Sam. 1:20; 12:3; Ps. 45:9; 144:12; Prov. 30:15; Jer. 8:21; 9:1; Lam. 2:11; 3:48; Matt. 10:35; Luke 8:42; 12:53; 13:16

DAWN—*light, morning* Deut. 33:2; Josh. 6:15; Judg. 19:26
Ps. 119:147, I rise before **d** and cry for help
139:9, take the wings of the **d**
2 Pet. 1:19, until the day **d-s**
Job 7:4; 38:12; Joel 2:2

DAY—*age, time* Gen. 1:5, God called the light **d**
1 Chr. 29:15, our **d-s** on the earth are like a shadow
Ps. 19:2, **D** to **d** pours forth speech
41:1, deliver him in a **d** of trouble
84:10, a **d** in Thy courts is better
118:24, This is the **d** which the LORD has made
Prov. 3:2, For length of **d-s** and years of life
27:1, you do not know what a **d** may bring
Eccles. 7:1, **d** of *one's* death is better than
12:1, **d-s** of your youth, before the evil **d-s**
Is. 2:12, LORD of hosts will have a **d** of reckoning
13:6, **d** of the LORD is near
58:5, an acceptable **d** to the LORD
Joel 2:11, **d** of the LORD is indeed great
Zech. 4:10, who has despised the **d** of small things
Mal. 3:2, who can endure the **d** of His coming
Matt. 6:11, this **d** our daily bread
24:36, But of that **d** and hour no one knows
John 6:39, raise it up on the last **d**
8:56, Your father Abraham rejoiced to see My **d**
9:4, We must work . . . as long as it is **d**
Rom. 14:5, One man regards one **d** above another
1 Cor. 3:13, the **d** will show it
2 Cor. 6:2, ON THE D OF SALVATION
Phil. 1:6, will perfect it until the **d** of Christ
1 Thess. 5:5, all sons of light and sons of **d**
2 Pet. 3:8, one **d** is as a thousand years
Gen. 27:2; Deut. 4:32; 1 Sam. 25:8; 2 Kin. 7:9; Neh. 4:2; Job 1:4; 7:1; 8:9; 14:6; 21:30; Ps. 77:5; Prov. 4:18; Is. 2:2; 10:3; 13:9; 27:3; 65:20; Joel 1:15; 2:1; Mic. 4:1; Zeph. 1:7,14; Zech. 14:1; Mal. 4:5; Matt. 7:22; 24:50; 25:13; Mark 13:32; Luke 12:46; 21:34; John 11:24; 12:48; Acts 2:17,20; 17:31; Rom. 2:5; 1 Thess. 5:2; 2 Tim. 3:1; Heb. 1:2; James 5:3; 2 Pet. 3:3,10; Rev. 6:17; 16:14; 20:10

DAZZLE—*shine* Song 5:10, My beloved is **d-ing**
Luke 24:4, men . . . in **d-ing** apparel

DEAD 1 Sam. 24:14; 2 Sam. 9:8; 16:9, **d** dog
Ps. 31:12, I am forgotten as a **d** man
Eccles. 9:4, a live dog is better than a **d** lion
Is. 26:19, Your **d** will live
Matt. 11:5, and *the* **d** are raised up
22:32, God is not *the God* of *the* **d**
23:27, full of **d** men's bones
John 5:25, **d** shall hear the voice of the Son of God
Acts 10:42, Judge of the living and the **d**
26:23, *His* resurrection from the **d**
Rom. 6:11, consider yourselves to be **d** to sin
14:9, Lord both of the **d** and of the living
1 Cor. 15:15, if in fact the **d** are not raised
2 Cor. 1:9, God who raises the **d**
Eph. 2:1, you were **d** in your trespasses and sins
1 Tim. 5:6, **d** even while she lives
Heb. 6:1, repentance from **d** works
James 2:17, faith, if it has no works, is **d**
2:26, body without the spirit is **d**
Rev. 1:18, I was **d**, and behold, I am alive
3:1, name that you are alive, and you are **d**
14:13, Blessed are the **d** who die in the Lord
Gen. 23:3; Ex. 12:30; Lev. 19:28; Ruth 1:8; Ps. 115:17; Prov. 9:18; Eccles. 4:2; 9:5; 10:1; Jer. 22:10; Matt. 2:19,20; 8:22; 9:24; 10:8; Mark 9:10,26; Luke 7:22; 15:24,32; 16:31; Rom. 7:4; 1 Cor. 15:35; Eph. 5:14; Col. 1:18; 2:13; 1 Thess. 4:16; 2 Tim. 4:1; Heb. 11:4; 13:20; 1 Pet. 4:6; Jude 12; Rev. 1:5; 20:5,12,13

DEADLY 1 Sam. 5:11; Ps. 17:9; Mark 16:18; James 3:8

DEAF Matt. 11:5, lepers are cleansed and *the* **d** hear
Ex. 4:11; Lev. 19:14; Ps. 58:4; Is. 29:18; 42:18; 43:8; Mark 7:37; 9:25; Luke 7:22

DEAL—*allot, treat* Prov. 12:22, those who **d** faithfully are
Ex. 1:10; Lev. 19:11; Ps. 25:3; Is. 21:2; 24:16; 26:10; Jer. 6:13; Hos. 5:7

DEALINGS Judg. 18:7, had no **d** with anyone
John 4:9, Jews have no **d** with Samaritans

DEAR—*beloved* Jer. 31:20, Is Ephraim My **d** son
Acts 20:24, I do not consider my life . . . as **d**
1 Thess. 2:8, you had become very **d** to us

DEATH—*grave* Num. 23:10; Judg. 16:16; 2 Sam. 22:5
Judg. 16:30, whom he killed at his **d** were more
Ruth 1:17, if *anything but* **d** parts you and me
1 Sam. 15:32, Surely the bitterness of **d** is past
2 Sam. 1:23, in their **d** they were not parted
Ps. 23:4, valley of the shadow of **d**
89:48, what man can live and not see **d**
107:10, darkness and in the shadow of **d**
116:15, Precious . . . Is the **d** of His godly ones
Song 8:6, love is as strong as **d**
Is. 25:8, He will swallow up **d** for all time
Ezek. 33:11, no pleasure in the **d** of the wicked
Matt. 2:15, there until the **d** of Herod
16:28; Mark 9:1; Luke 9:27, shall not taste **d**
26:38; Mark 14:34, to the point of **d**
John 5:24, has passed out of **d** into life
8:51, never see **d**
Acts 10:39, **d** by hanging Him on a cross
Rom. 6:23, the wages of sin is **d**
8:2, free from the law of sin and **d**
8:36, WE ARE BEING PUT TO D ALL DAY LONG
1 Cor. 11:26, proclaim the Lord's **d** until He comes
15:21, by a man *came* **d**
15:56, the sting of **d** is sin
2 Cor. 4:12, **d** works in us
Phil. 2:8, obedient to the point of **d**, even **d** on
Heb. 2:9, suffering of **d** . . . He might taste **d**
2:15, through fear of **d** were subject to slavery
James 1:15, sin . . . brings forth **d**
5:20, will save his soul from **d**
Rev. 1:18, I have the keys of **d** and of Hades
2:10, Be faithful until **d**
6:8, he who sat on it had the name **D**
9:6, men will seek **d** . . . and **d** flees from them
21:4, there shall no longer be *any* **d**
2 Chr. 25:4; Job 3:21; 7:15; 30:23; Ps. 6:5; 13:3; 18:4; 22:15; 49:14; 68:20; 102:20; 116:3; Prov. 7:27; 8:36; 14:12; 16:25; Is. 38:18; Jer. 8:3; Ezek. 18:32; Hos. 13:14; Jon. 4:3,8; Matt. 10:21; 15:4; Mark 7:10; Luke 2:26; 22:33; John 11:4; 12:33; 18:31,32; 21:19; Acts 2:24; Rom. 1:32; 5:10,14,17; 6:5,21; 1 Cor. 3:22; 15:55; 2 Cor. 1:9; 11:23; James 5:6; 1 John 3:14; 5:16; Rev. 2:11; 20:6

DEBATE—*dispute* Acts 15:2,7; 1 Cor. 1:20

DEBT Matt. 6:12, forgive us our **d-s**
1 Sam. 22:2; 2 Kin. 4:7; Neh. 10:31; Prov. 22:26; Matt. 18:27

DEBTOR—*obligation*
Ezek. 18:7, restores to the **d**
Matt. 6:12, as we also have forgiven our **d-s**
Luke 7:41, a certain money-lender had two **d-s**
16:5, summoned each of his master's **d-s**
DECAY—*corruption* Job 21:20, own eyes see his **d**
Acts 2:27, HOLY ONE TO UNDERGO D
DECEIT—*falsehood, deception* Ps. 32:2; 36:3; 50:19
Ps. 10:7, mouth full of curses and **d** and oppression
34:13, your lips from speaking **d**
55:23, Men of bloodshed and **d** will not live
Prov. 12:5, counsels of the wicked are **d-ful**
31:30, Charm is **d-ful** and beauty is vain
Jer. 17:9, heart is more **d-ful** than all else
2 Cor. 11:13, false apostles, **d-ful** workers
1 Pet. 2:22, NOR WAS ANY D FOUND
Prov. 27:6; Is. 57:4; Jer. 5:27; 48:10; Dan. 8:25; Hos. 11:12; Zeph. 1:9; Mark 7:22; 2 Cor. 12:16; Eph. 4:14,22
DECEITFUL—*false* Ps. 120:3, You **d** tongue
Ps. 17:1; 26:4
DECEITFULNESS—*deception*
Matt. 13:22; Mark 4:19, **d** of riches
DECEIVE—*cheat, mislead, steal* Gen. 31:20,27; Num. 25:18
Gen. 29:25, Why then have you **d-d** me
Jer. 42:20, you have *only* **d-d** yourselves
Matt. 27:63, we remember that ... that **d-r** said
Rom. 3:13, THEY KEEP D-ING
2 Cor. 6:8, *regarded* as **d-rs** and yet true
Eph. 5:6, 1 John 3:7, Let no one **d** you
1 John 1:8, If we say ... no sin, we are **d-ing**
2 John 7, many **d-rs** ... This is the **d-r** and the antichrist
Rev. 12:9, Satan, who **d-s** the whole world
Deut. 11:16; Josh. 7:11; 9:22; 1 Kin. 22:22; 2 Kin. 19:10; Is. 37:10; 44:20; Jer. 20:7; 37:9; Obad. 3; 1 Cor. 6:9; 15:33; Gal. 6:7; 2 Thess. 2:3; 1 Tim. 2:14; 2 Tim. 3:13; James 1:16; Rev. 19:20
DECEPTION—*deceit*
Jer. 3:10, return to Me ... in **d**
Matt. 27:64, last **d** will be worse than the first
Col. 2:8, philosophy and empty **d**
DECEPTIVE Mic. 6:11, a bag of **d** weights
DECIDE—*determine* 1 Sam. 20:7, he has **d-d** on evil
2 Chr. 2:1, Solomon **d-d** to build a house
Ex. 21:22; Acts 3:13; 1 Cor. 7:37
DECISION—*rebuke* Prov. 16:33, every **d** is from the LORD
Joel 3:14, day ... is near in the valley of **d**
Mic. 4:3; Zeph. 3:8
DECK Is. 61:10, As a bridegroom **d-s** himself
DECLARATION—*account*
Job 13:17, let my **d** *fill* your ears
DECLARE—*explain, relate* Ps. 75:9, I will **d** it forever
Ps. 92:2, To **d** Thy lovingkindness
145:4, shall **d** Thy mighty acts
Is. 43:21, Will **d** My praise
45:19, **D-ing** things that are upright
46:10, **D-ing** the end from the beginning
John 4:25, He will **d** all things to us
Acts 20:27, **d-ing** to you the whole purpose of God
Rom. 1:4, **d-d** with power *to be* the Son of God
Deut. 30:18; Job 31:37; Ps. 9:11; 30:9; 51:15; Is. 41:26; 45:21; 66:19; Acts 17:30
DECORATE—*deck* Jer. 4:30; 10:4
DECREASE—*abate, subside* Gen. 8:3, the water **d-d**
Ps. 107:38, He does not let their cattle **d**
John 3:30, He must increase, but I must **d**
DECREE—*decide, determine* Job 22:28; Ps. 94:20; 148:6
Dan. 11:36, that which is **d-d** will be done
Prov. 8:15; Dan. 2:9; 9:24; Acts 16:4; 17:7
DEDICATE—*devote*
Ex. 32:29, **D** yourselves today to the
1 Kin. 7:51, Solomon brought things **d-d**
8:63, sons of Israel **d-d** the house of the LORD
Deut. 20:5; Judg. 17:3; 1 Kin. 15:15; 1 Chr. 18:11; 26:27
DEED—*action, practice, work* Gen. 44:15; 2 Sam. 12:14
Ps. 9:1, committed abominable **d-s**
28:4, according to the **d-s** of their hands
Is. 1:16, Remove the evil of your **d-s**
59:18; Jer. 25:4, according to their **d-s**
Luke 24:19, prophet mighty in **d** and word
John 3:19, their **d-s** were evil
Acts 7:22, man of power in words and **d-s**
Gal. 5:19, **d-s** of the flesh are evident
Col. 3:17, whatever you do in word or **d**
Titus 3:1, ready for every good **d**
1 John 3:18, not love with word ... but in **d** and truth
Rev. 2:2, I know your **d-s** and your toil
14:13, for their **d-s** follow with them
Ezra 9:13; Neh. 13:14; Ps. 66:5; Prov. 20:11; Jer. 32:10,44; Luke 11:48; 23:41; John 8:41; Rom. 2:6
DEEP—*abyss, depth*
Gen. 7:11, fountains of the great **d**
Job 28:14, the **d** says, It is not with me
Ps. 36:6, Thy judgments are *like* a great **d**
42:7, **D** calls to **d**
Prov. 19:15, Laziness casts into a **d** sleep
Matt. 26:38; Mark 14:34, soul is **d-ly** grieved
Luke 5:4, Put out into **d** water
Rom. 8:26, groanings too **d** for words
Gen. 8:2; Deut. 33:13; Job 4:13; 38:30; Ps. 33:7; 77:16; 106:9; 107:24; Prov. 22:14; 23:27; Is. 7:11; Luke 6:48; John 4:11
DEER Ps. 42:1, **d** pants for the water brooks
Is. 35:6, lame will leap like a **d**
Deut. 12:15; 14:5; 1 Kin. 4:23
DEFEAT 1 Chr. 18:1, David **d-ed** the Philistines
Jer. 37:10, had **d-ed** the entire army
Gen. 14:15; 36:35; Num. 22:6; Josh. 10:33; 12:1,7; 1 Chr. 1:46; 14:11; 18:3; Jer. 46:2
DEFECT—*spot* Lev. 21:17; Deut. 15:21; 2 Sam. 14:25; Job 11:15; Dan. 1:4
DEFEND—*protect*
Zech. 9:15, LORD of hosts will **d** them
Acts 7:24; Rom. 2:15; 2 Cor. 12:19
DEFENSE Acts 19:33; 22:1
Phil. 1:7, in the **d** ... of the gospel
DEFICIENT—*want* Dan. 5:27, and found **d**
DEFILE—*pollute, profane* Lev. 21:4; Is. 59:3; Jer. 2:7
2 Kin. 23:13, high places ... the king **d-d**
Neh. 13:29, they have **d-d** the priesthood
Ps. 74:7, **d-d** the dwelling place of Thy name
79:1, **d-d** Thy holy temple
Matt. 15:11,18,20; Mark 7:15,20,23, **d** the man
Titus 1:15, to those who are **d-d** ... nothing is pure
Heb. 12:15, by it many are **d-d**
James 3:6, that which **d-s** the entire body
Jude 8, these men also by dreaming **d** the flesh
Ezek. 23:38; 36:17; Dan. 1:8; John 18:28; 1 Cor. 8:7
DEFILEMENT—*filth* 2 Cor. 7:1, from all **d**
DEFRAUD—*deprive, wrong*
1 Cor. 6:7,8; 1 Thess. 4:6, transgress and **d**
1 Sam. 12:3; Lam. 3:36; Mark 10:19
DEGENERATE Jer. 2:21, **d** shoots of a foreign vine
DEGRADE Rom. 1:26, gave them over to **d-ing** passions
DEGREE—*standing* 1 Chr. 17:17; Ps. 62:9
DEITY Col. 2:9, fulness of **D** ... bodily form
DELAY—*hinder, linger*
Ex. 32:1, the people saw that Moses **d-ed**
Deut. 23:21, shall not **d** to pay it
1 Tim. 3:15, in case I am **d-ed**
Rev. 10:6, there shall be **d** no longer
Gen. 24:56; Ex. 22:29; Acts 9:38; 25:17
DELEGATION—*messenger*
Luke 19:14, sent a **d** after him
DELICACY—*dainty, delicate* Ps. 141:4; Prov. 23:3; Lam. 4:5

DELICATE—*dainty* Deut. 28:54,56; Is. 47:1

DELIGHT (n.)—*affection, luxury, observe, pleasure*
2 Sam. 15:26, I have no **d** in you
Ps. 1:2, his **d** is in the law of the LORD
Prov. 8:31, *having* my **d** in the sons of men
11:1, a just weight is His **d**
12:22, those who deal faithfully are His **d**
Job 27:10; Ps. 16:3; 119:24,77,92,143,174; Prov. 8:30; 15:8; 16:13; Song 2:3; Is. 58:13; 62:4

DELIGHT (v.)—*desire*
Job 22:26, you will **d** in the Almighty
Ps. 37:4, **D** yourself in the LORD
37:11, **d** themselves in abundant prosperity
51:16, Thou dost not **d** in sacrifice
Eccles. 5:4, He takes no **d** in fools
Is. 42:1, My chosen one *in whom* My soul **d-s**
55:2, **d** yourself in abundance
Mic. 7:18, He **d-s** in unchanging love
1 Sam. 15:22; Neh. 1:11; Ps. 94:19; Prov. 1:22; 2:14; 18:2; 23:26; Is. 11:3; Hos. 6:6; Mal. 3:1

DELIGHTFUL Mal. 3:12, you shall be a **d** land

DELIVER—*rescue, save* Ex. 3:8; Num. 35:25; Deut. 32:39
Job 5:19, From six troubles He will **d** you
Ps. 56:13, **d-ed** my soul from death
Is. 43:13, none who can **d** out of My hand
50:2, have I no power to **d**
Matt. 6:13, **d** us from evil
10:17, they will **d** you up to *the* courts
10:21, brother will **d** up brother
Acts 2:23, **d-ed** up by the predetermined plan
Rom. 4:25, who was **d-ed** up because of our trangressions
2 Cor. 1:10, **d-ed** us from so great a *peril of* death
Gal. 1:4, He might **d** us out of this present evil age
Jude 3, faith which was . . . **d-ed** to the saints
Judg. 7:2; 1 Sam. 10:27; 2 Chr. 20:9; 32:13; Ps. 33:17; Prov. 24:11; Eccles. 9:15; Jer. 1:8; 39:17; Dan. 3:17; 6:14; Joel 2:32; Matt. 26:15; Acts 7:34; 2 Cor. 4:11; 2 Tim. 4:18

DELIVERANCE—*victory, salvation* Gen. 45:7, by a great **d**
Ps. 32:7, surround me with songs of **d**
68:20, God is . . . a God of **d-s**

DELUDE 2 Thess. 2:11, God will send . . . a **d-ing** influence

DEMON—*satyr* Matt. 8:31, **d-s** *began* to entreat Him
Mark 3:15, authority to cast out the **d-s**
James 2:19, **d-s** also believe and shudder
3:15, is earthly, natural, **d-ic**
Lev. 17:7; Deut. 32:17; Ps. 106:37; Matt. 10:8; 1 Cor. 10:20; Rev. 9:20

DEMONSTRATE—*show* Rom. 5:8, God **d-s** His own love
Rom. 9:22, willing to **d** His wrath

DEMONSTRATION 1 Cor. 2:4, in **d** of the Spirit and of power

DEN Jer. 7:11, Has this house . . . become a **d** of robbers
Dan. 6:7, shall be cast into the lions' **d**
Judg. 6:2; Job 37:8; Is. 11:8; Amos 3:4; Matt. 21:13; Mark 11:17

DENOUNCE—*slander* Jer. 20:10, **D** *him;* yes, let us **d** him

DENY—*conceal* Matt. 10:33, whoever shall **d** Me before men
1 Tim. 5:8, he has **d-ed** the faith
2 Tim. 2:13, for He cannot **d** Himself
3:5, they have **d-ed** its power
Titus 2:12, instructing us to **d** ungodliness
Josh. 24:27; Job 6:10; Prov. 30:9; Titus 1:16

DEPART Job 21:14, they say to God, **D** from us
Job 28:28, to **d** from evil is understanding
Ps. 6:8, **D** from me, all you who do iniquity
Prov. 22:6, when he is old he will not **d** from it
27:22, his folly will not **d** from him
Is. 26:14, **d-ed** spirits will not rise
John 13:1, hour had come that He should **d**
2 Cor. 12:8, entreated . . . that it might **d**
Phil. 1:23, desire to **d** and be with Christ
Gen. 49:10; Job 22:17; Ps. 18:21; 34:14; 37:27; 105:38; Matt. 2:13,22; 7:23; 25:41; Luke 2:29; 4:13; 13:27; 21:21; Acts 7:3

DEPARTURE—*death* Luke 9:13, His **d**
2 Tim. 4:6, the time of my **d** has come
2 Pet. 1:15, at any time after my **d**

DEPEND—*hang* Matt. 22:40, two commandments **d** . . . Law

DEPOSE Dan. 5:20, he was **d-d** from his royal throne

DEPRAVE Rom. 1:28, gave them over to a **d-d** mind
2 Tim. 3:8, men of **d-d** mind

DEPRIVE Is. 38:10, **d-d** of the rest of my years
1 Cor. 7:5, Stop **d-ing** one another
1 Tim. 6:5, **d-d** of the truth

DEPTH—*abyss, deep*
Ps. 95:4, In whose hand are the **d-s** of the earth
107:26, they went down to the **d-s**
Prov. 25:3, heavens for height . . . for **d**
Mic. 7:19, cast all their sins Into the **d-s** of the sea
Matt. 13:5, they had no **d** of soil
18:6, better . . . be drowned in the **d** of the sea
Mark 4:5, it sprang up because it had no **d** of soil
Rom. 8:39, nor height, nor **d** . . . separate us
11:33, **d** of the riches
1 Cor. 2:10, searches all things, even the **d-s** of God
Job 41:31, Ps. 86:13; Prov. 8:24; Is. 63:13

DEPUTY—*proconsul* 1 Kin. 22:47, a **d** was king

DERIDE—*mock, scoff, sneer* Ps. 119:51, utterly **d** me

DERISION—*laughingstock, shame* Ex. 32:25; Ps. 79:4
Ps. 44:13, a **d** to those around us
Jer. 20:8; Ezek. 23:32; 36:4; Hos. 7:16

DESCEND Gen. 28:12, angels of God . . . **d-ing**
Matt. 7:25,27, rain **d-ed**, and the floods came
Mark 1:10, Spirit like a dove **d-ing** upon Him
Rom. 10:7, WHO WILL D INTO THE ABYSS
Ps. 49:17; Prov. 30:4; Matt. 11:23; John 1:32,33; Eph. 4:10

DESCENDANT—*seed* Ps. 37:28, **d-s** of the wicked will be
Rom. 4:18, SO SHALL YOUR D-S BE

DESCENT Luke 19:37, near the **d** of the Mount

DESCRIPTION Josh. 18:4, write a **d** of it according to

DESERT—*wild* Ps. 78:40, grieved Him in the **d**
Is. 35:1, the **d** will be glad
40:3, in the **d** a highway for our God
43:19, Rivers in the **d**
51:3, her **d** like the garden of the LORD
Prov. 21:19; Jer. 17:6; 25:24; 50:39; Luke 1:80

DESERT—*leave, forsake* 2 Kin. 25:11, the **d-ers** who had
2 Tim. 4:16, but all **d-ed** me
Heb. 13:5, I WILL NEVER D YOU

DESERVE—*due, worthy*
Matt. 26:66, He is **d-ing** of death
Luke 23:41, receiving what we **d** for our deeds
1 Tim. 1:15, statement, **d-ing** full acceptance
Judg. 9:16; Ezra 9:13

DESIGN—*device, devise* Ex. 31:4; 35:32,35; 2 Chr. 2:14

DESIRABLE Ps. 19:10, more **d** than gold
Prov. 19:22, What is **d** in a man is his kindness
Ezek. 23:6,12,23, **d** young men
Gen. 3:6; Prov. 8:11

DESIRE (n.)—*appetite* Job 31:16; Ps. 10:3; 140:8; Prov. 13:12
Gen. 3:16, your **d** shall be for your husband
Ps. 21:2, given him his heart's **d**
37:4, He will give you the **d-s** of your heart
112:10, **d** of the wicked will perish
145:16, satisfy the **d** of every living thing
Prov. 10:24; 11:23, the **d** of the righteous
Mic. 7:3, great man speaks the **d** of his soul

DESIRE (n.) *(Continued)*
Rom. 10:1, my heart's **d** . . . is for *their* salvation
Eph. 2:3, **d-s** of the flesh and of the mind
Phil. 1:23, having the **d** to depart
Prov. 21:25; Ezek. 24:16,21,25; Mark 4:19; Col. 3:5

DESIRE (v.)—*want, wish, crave* Deut. 14:26; 1 Sam. 2:16
Ps. 34:12, Who is the man who **d-s** life
51:6, Thou dost **d** truth
73:25, besides Thee, I **d** nothing on earth
Luke 22:15, earnestly **d-d** to eat this Passover
1 Cor. 12:31, earnestly **d** the greater gifts
14:1, yet **d** earnestly spiritual *gifts*
Gal. 6:12, who **d** to make a good showing in the flesh
Heb. 11:16, they **d** a better *country*
Job 13:3; Ps. 40:6; 45:11; 107:30; Prov. 3:15, 23:3; Eccles. 2:10; Matt. 13:17; Gal. 4:9; 1 Tim. 3:1

DESOLATE—*lonely, waste* Lev. 26:31; Is. 54:1; 62:4
Matt. 23:38, your house is being left to you **d**
Jer. 2:12; 12:10; Ezek. 6:6; Joel 2:3; Zech. 7:14; Luke 13:35; Acts 1:20; Gal. 4:27

DESOLATION—*ruins, waste*
Jer. 25:9; Ezek. 35:9, an everlasting **d**
32:43, a **d** without man or beast
Dan. 9:26, there will be war; **d-s** are determined
11:31; 12:11, abomination of **d**
Zeph. 1:15, day of destruction and **d**
2 Kin. 22:19; Josh. 8:28; Ps. 46:8; Is. 61:4; Luke 21:20

DESPAIR—*faint, sorrow* 1 Sam. 27:1; Job 6:26; Eccles. 2:20
Deut. 28:65, failing of eyes, and **d** of soul
2 Cor. 4:8, perplexed, but not **d-ing**

DESPERATE Jer. 17:9, The heart . . . is **d-ly** sick

DESPISE—*reject, scorn, spurn* Gen. 16:4; Num. 15:31
Gen. 25:34, Esau **d-d** his birthright
Job 5:17, do not **d** the discipline of the Almighty
36:5, God is mighty but does not **d** *any*
Ps. 51:17, a contrite heart . . . Thou wilt not **d**
Prov. 1:7, Fools **d** wisdom and instruction
15:32, He who neglects discipline **d-s** himself
Eccles. 9:16, wisdom of the poor man is **d-d**
Zech. 4:10, who has **d-d** the day of small things
Matt. 6:24; Luke 16:13, hold to one and **d** the other
18:10, do not **d** one of these little ones
1 Cor. 1:28, base things . . . and the **d-d**
Heb. 12:2, endured the cross, **d-ing** the shame
1 Sam. 2:30; 2 Sam. 6:16; Neh. 4:4; Job 19:18; Ps. 73:20; 102:17; 119:163; Prov. 6:30; 13:13; 15:20; Is. 5:24; 49:7; Jer. 49:15; Ezek. 21:10; 22:8; Mal. 1:6; 1 Cor. 11:22; 16:11; 1 Thess. 5:20

DESPONDENCY—*anguish, distress*
Ex. 6:9, on account of *their* **d**

DESTINE—*appoint, name*
1 Thess. 5:9, God has not **d-d** us for wrath

DESTITUTE—*deprive* Ezek. 32:15
Ps. 102:17, regarded the prayer of the **d**
Heb. 11:37, being **d**, afflicted, ill-treated

DESTROY—*defile, pollute, abolish, ruin, waste*
2 Sam. 1:14, **d** the LORD's anointed
Ps. 40:14, seek my life to **d** it
Prov. 1:32, complacency of fools shall **d** them
Is. 23:14, your stronghold is **d-ed**
Matt. 2:13, search . . . to **d** Him
6:19, where moth and rust **d**
10:28, fear Him who is able to **d**
12:14; Mark 3:6, they might **d** Him
Mark 14:58, I will **d** this temple
Luke 6:9, is it lawful . . . to save a life or **d** it
17:27, flood came and **d-ed** them all
1 Cor. 3:17, If any man **d-s** the temple
Gal. 1:13, church of God . . . tried to **d** it
1:23, the faith which he once tried to **d**
2:18, if I rebuild what I *once* **d-ed**
2 Pet. 3:12, heavens will be **d-ed** by burning
1 John 3:8, **d** the works of the devil
Gen. 6:17; Ex. 22:20; Deut. 9:14; 1 Sam. 15:6; Job 10:8; Ps. 63:9; 145:20; Prov. 28:24; 31:3; Eccles. 9:18; Is. 10:7; 11:9; Jer. 13:14; 23:1; Ezek. 9:1; 22:27; Dan. 8:24; Matt. 22:7; Mark 1:24; 11:18; 12:9; 15:29; Luke 4:34; 20:16; John 2:19; Rom. 14:15; James 4:12; 2 Pet. 2:12; 3:11; Jude 5

DESTROYER—*robber* Judg. 16:24, Even the **d** of our country
Job 12:6; 15:21; Is. 49:17; Jer. 22:7

DESTRUCTION—*calamity, ruin* Ps. 35:8, Let **d** come upon him
Ps. 52:2, Your tongue devises **d**
91:6, **d** that lays waste at noon
Prov. 16:18, Pride goes before **d**
Is. 19:18, called the City of **D**
59:7, Devastation and **d** are in their highways
Lam. 2:11; 3:48; 4:10, **d** of the daughter of my people
Matt. 7:13, way is broad that leads to **d**
Rom. 9:22, vessels of wrath prepared for **d**
Phil. 3:19, whose end is **d**
1 Thess. 5:3, **d** will come upon them suddenly
1 Tim. 6:9, desires plunge to ruin and **d**
2 Chr. 22:4; Esth. 8:6; Job 21:17; Ps. 5:9; 57:1; 73:18; Prov. 17:19; 19:13; Is. 10:22; 14:23; 28:2; Jer. 17:18; 50:22; Hos. 13:9; Rom. 3:16; 2 Thess. 1:9; 2 Pet. 2:1,3; 3:16; Rev. 17:8

DESTRUCTIVE—*false* Prov. 17:4, a **d** tongue
2 Pet. 2:1, secretly introduce **d** heresies

DETAIN Judg. 13:15,16; 1 Sam. 21:7

DETERMINE—*decide* Job 14:5, his days are **d-d**
Luke 22:22, Son . . . as it has been **d-d**
Acts 17:26, having **d-d** *their* appointed times
1 Cor. 2:2, I **d-d** to know nothing

DETEST—*despise, loathe* Deut. 7:26; Jer. 4:1; Amos 6:8

DETESTABLE—*abominable*
Deut. 14:3, eat any **d** thing
Is. 66:17, swine's flesh, **d** things
Luke 16:15, is **d** in the sight of God
Job 15:16; Jer. 16:18; Ezek. 5:11; 7:20; 11:18; 37:23

DEVASTATE—*waste* Nah. 2:2; 3:7

DEVASTATION—*oppression*
Ps. 12:5, the **d** of the afflicted

DEVICE—*design, plan, scheme*
Prov. 1:31, satiated . . . own **d-s**

DEVIOUS—*perverse* Prov. 4:24, put **d** lips far from you

DEVISE—*design, plan, scheme, fashion*
Prov. 3:29, Do not **d** harm against your neighbor
6:14, **d-s** evil continually
14:22, will they not go astray who **d** evil
2 Pet. 1:16, cleverly **d-d** tales
Esth. 9:25; Ps. 2:1; 10:2; 21:11; 35:4; 41:7; 94:20; Prov. 6:18; 12:2; Is. 32:7,8; Zech. 7:10; Acts 4:25

DEVOTE—*dedicate* Rom. 12:10, Be **d-d** to one another
Col. 4:2, **D** yourselves to prayer
Num. 18:14; Ezek. 44:29

DEVOTION Eccles. 12:12, excessive **d** *to books* is wearying

DEVOUR—*consume, swallow*
2 Sam. 2:26, Shall the sword **d** forever
11:25, the sword **d-s** one as well as another
Zeph. 1:18; 3:8, all the earth will be **d-ed**
Matt. 13:4, birds came and **d-ed** them
23:14, you **d** widows' houses
Luke 15:30, son of yours . . . has **d-ed** your wealth
Gal. 5:15, if you bite and **d** one another
Gen. 37:20; 2 Sam. 18:8; 22:9; Job 18:13; Ps. 18:8; 50:3; 52:4; Prov. 30:14; Is. 1:7,20; Jer. 2:30; 30:16; Amos 4:9; Mal. 3:11; Mark 12:40; Luke 8:5; 2 Cor. 11:20

DEVOUT—*God-fearing*
Luke 2:25, Simeon . . . righteous and **d**
Acts 2:5; 8:2, **d** men
Acts 10:2; 13:50; 22:12

DEW Gen. 27:28, God give you of the **d** of heaven
Judg. 6:37, If there is **d** on the fleece only

2 Sam. 17:12, we will fall on him as the **d** falls
Prov. 3:20, the skies drip with **d**
Is. 18:4, Like a cloud of **d** in the heat of harvest
Dan. 4:15,23,25,33, drenched with the **d** of heaven
Ex. 16:13; Num. 11:9; Deut. 32:2; 33:13; 2 Sam. 1:21; 1 Kin. 17:1; Job 29:19; 38:28; Ps. 110:3; 133:3; Prov. 19:12; Is. 26:19; Hos. 6:4; 13:3; 14:5; Hag. 1:10

DIADEM—*turban* Is. 28:5; 62:3

DIAMOND Ex. 28:18; 39:11; Jer. 17:1; Ezek. 28:13

DID—*put* Gen. 6:22; Job 1:5
2 Chr. 18:23, How **d** the Spirit . . . pass
Matt. 13:58, He **d** not do many miracles
John 9:26, What **d** He do to you
15:24, works which no one else **d**
1 Cor. 13:11, **d** away with childish things

DIE—*depart* Gen. 2:17; 20:7; 1 Sam. 14:44; 22:16; 1 Kin. 2:37,42; Ezek. 3:18; 33:8, you shall surely **d**
Deut. 14:21, not eat anything which **d-s** of itself
Ruth 1:17, Where you **d**, I will **d**
1 Sam. 26:16, *all* of you must surely **d**
Job 2:9, his wife said . . . Curse God and **d**
3:11, Why did I not **d** at birth
14:14, If a man **d-s**, will he live *again*
21:23, One **d-s** in his full strength
Ps. 49:10, *even* wise men **d**
49:17, when he **d-s** he will carry nothing away
Prov. 10:21, fools **d** for lack of understanding
Eccles. 2:16, wise man and fool alike **d**
Ezek. 18:4, soul who sins will **d**
18:32, no pleasure in . . . who **d-s**
Matt. 26:35, Even if I must **d** with you
Luke 8:52, she has not **d-d**, but is asleep
16:22, poor man **d-d** . . . rich man also **d-d**
John 6:49, ate the manna . . . and they **d-d**
11:25, who believes . . . live even if he **d-s**
11:51, that Jesus was going to **d** for the nation
12:24, a grain of wheat falls . . . and **d-s**
Rom. 5:6, Christ **d-d** for the ungodly
5:7, one will hardly **d** for a righteous man
6:2, How shall we who **d-d** to sin
14:9, Christ **d-d** and lived *again*
14:15, him for whom Christ **d-d**
1 Cor. 15:31, I **d** daily
2 Cor. 5:14, one **d-d** for all, therefore all **d-d**
Phil. 1:21, to **d** is gain
Col. 2:20, If you have **d-d** with Christ
1 Thess. 4:14, we believe that Jesus **d-d** and rose
5:10, who **d-d** for us, that . . . we may live
Heb. 9:27, appointed for men to **d** once
11:13, All these **d-d** in faith
Gen. 3:3; 25:8; 27:4; 45:28; Lev. 10:6; Num. 18:32; Prov. 14:32; 30:7; Jer. 26:8; 27:13; Ezek. 18:20,31; 33:11,14; Matt. 22:25; Mark 5:39; John 11:44; 19:7; Acts 9:37; 21:13; Rom. 6:10; 7:9; 8:34; 14:7; 1 Cor. 8:11; 15:3,22; Gal. 2:19; 2 Tim. 2:11; 1 Pet. 2:24; Rev. 9:6; 14:13

DIFFER Rom. 12:6, we have gifts that **d**
1 Cor. 15:41, star **d-s** from star in glory
Deut. 25:13; Gal. 4:1

DIFFERENCE—*distinction* Ezek. 44:23

DIFFICULT—*hard* Jer. 32:27; Ezek. 3:5
Gen. 18:14, Is anything too **d** for the LORD
1 Kin. 10:1; 2 Chr. 9:1, test Solomon with **d** questions
Jer. 32:17, Nothing is too **d** for Thee
John 6:60, This is a **d** statement

DIG Ex. 21:33; Deut. 6:11; 8:9; Job 3:21; 24:16; Ezek. 12:5; Luke 13:8; 16:3

DIGNITY—*majesty* Gen. 49:3; Esth. 6:3; 1 Tim. 2:2

DILIGENCE—*effort, speed* Ezra 6:12, carried out with all **d**
Prov. 4:23, Watch over your heart with all **d**
Rom. 12:11, not lagging behind in **d**

DILIGENT—*careful, eager, thorough* Prov. 1:28; Heb. 4:11
Prov. 11:27, **d-ly** seeks good seeks favor
Eph. 4:3, **d** to preserve the unity
2 Tim. 2:15, Be **d** to present yourself approved
2 Pet. 1:15, I will also be **d**

DILL Is. 28:25,27

DILUTE—*mix* Is. 1:22, drink **d-d** with water

DIM—*dark* Job 17:7, My eye has also grown **d**
1 Cor. 13:12, see in a mirror **d-ly**
Gen. 27:1; 48:10; Deut. 34:7; 1 Sam. 3:2; Ps. 69:23; Eccles. 12:3

DIMINISH—*dwindle, reduce* Lev. 25:16; Ezek. 16:27

DINE—*eat* Gen. 43:16; Prov. 23:1

DINNER—*lunch, supper* Matt. 22:4; Luke 14:12
Luke 14:16, certain man was giving a big **d**

DIP 2 Kin. 5:14, **d-ed** *himself* seven times in the Jordan
Matt. 26:23, **d-ed** his hand with Me in the bowl
Luke 16:24, **d** the tip of his finger in water and
Rev. 19:13, clothed with a robe **d-ed** in blood
Gen. 37:31; Lev. 4:6; 9:9; Josh. 3:15; Ruth 2:14; 1 Sam. 14:27; Mark 14:20; John 13:26

DIRECT—*arrange, order* Is. 40:13; Jer. 10:23; 1 Thess. 3:11
Prov. 16:9, the LORD **d-s** his steps
23:19, **d** your heart in the way
2 Thess. 3:5, **d** your hearts into the love of God

DIRGE Matt. 11:17, we sang a **d**

DIRTY James 2:2, a poor man in **d** clothes

DISAPPOINT—*frustrate* Ps. 22:5, they trusted . . . not **d-ed**
1 Pet. 2:6, SHALL NOT BE D-ED

DISASTER—*evil* Jer. 17:17; Ezek. 7:5

DISCERN—*appraise, analyze, recognize*
1 Kin. 3:9, **d** between good and evil
Matt. 16:3, **d** the appearance of the sky
Heb. 5:14, senses trained to **d** good and evil
Gen. 41:33; Deut. 32:29; 2 Sam. 14:17; Job 4:16; 6:30; Prov. 7:7; 8:5

DISCERNING—*understanding*
Deut. 1:13, Choose wise and **d**
1 Kin. 3:12, a wise and **d** heart
Prov. 16:21, wise in heart will be called **d**

DISCERNMENT—*judgment*
Ps. 119:66, Teach me good **d**
Is. 27:11, not a people of **d**
1 Sam. 25:33; 1 Kin. 3:11

DISCIPLE—*pupil* Matt. 10:24, A **d** is not above his teacher
Matt. 12:2, Your **d-s** do what is not lawful
26:56, all the **d-s** left Him and fled
28:7, tell His **d-s** that He has risen
28:19, make **d-s** of all nations
Mark 14:14; Luke 22:11, Passover with My **d-s**
Luke 6:13, He called His **d-s** to Him
11:1, just as John also taught his **d-s**
14:26,27, cannot be My **d**
19:37, **d-s** began to praise God joyfully
19:39, Teacher, rebuke Your **d-s**
John 2:11, His **d-s** believed in Him
6:66, many of His **d-s** withdrew
13:5, began to wash the **d-s'** feet
13:35, all men will know you are My **d-s**
19:26, **d** whom He loved standing nearby
Acts 9:26, associate with the **d-s**
11:26, **d-s** were first called Christians
Is. 8:16; Matt. 10:1,42; 11:1; 15:2; 17:16; 19:13; 20:17; 22:16; 26:18,35; 28:13; Mark 2:18; 4:34; 7:2,5; 10:13; Luke 5:30,33; 6:20; 14:33; John 4:2; 6:22; 7:3; 8:31; 9:27,28; 15:8; 18:1,15,16,17,25; 19:38; 20:2,18,26; 21:7,20,23,24; Acts 9:1; 20:30; 21:16

DISCIPLINE—*chasten, exercise*
Job 5:17; Prov. 3:11, not despise **d** of the Almighty
Prov. 16:22, **d** of fools is folly
19:18, **D** your son while there is hope
1 Cor. 11:32, we are **d-d** by the Lord
1 Tim. 4:7, **d** yourself for the purpose of godliness
Heb. 12:6, THE LORD LOVES HE D-S
Deut. 4:36; 8:5; 1 Kin. 12:11; Heb. 12:8

DISCONTENTED 1 Sam. 22:2, everyone . . . **d**

DISCOURAGE—*dishearten* Num. 32:7,9

DISCOVER—*reveal, find* Job 11:7, **d** the depths of God
DISCREDIT—*condemn*
2 Cor. 6:3, the ministry be not **d-ed**
8:20, no one should **d** us
DISCRETION—*understanding, wisdom*
1 Chr. 22:12, LORD give you **d**
Prov. 11:22, beautiful woman who lacks **d**
DISCUSS—*converse, reason* Matt. 16:7; Mark 9:33; Luke 6:11; 24:15
DISDAIN 1 Sam. 17:42, he **d-ed** him (David)
Job 30:1, whose fathers I **d-ed**
DISEASE—*affliction* Ps. 103:3, heals all your **d-s**
Matt. 4:23, healing every kind of **d**
Luke 9:1, gave them power . . . to heal **d-s**
Ex. 15:26; Deut. 7:15; 28:60; 2 Chr. 16:12; Ezek. 34:4; Matt. 4:24; Acts 28:9
DISGRACE—*shame, reproach* Gen. 34:7; Lev. 20:17; Job 10:15; Prov. 6:33; 14:34; Jer. 14:21; 1 Cor. 11:4,5,6
DISGUISE—*pretend* 1 Sam. 21:13, David **d-d** his sanity
1 Sam. 28:8, Saul **d-d** himself
1 Kin. 22:30; 2 Chr. 18:29, king of Israel **d-d** himself
1 Kin. 14:2; 20:38; 2 Chr. 35:22; Job 24:15
DISGUST—*exclude, alienate* Ezek. 23:17, became **d-ed** with
DISH—*bowl* Gen. 27:4; 2 Kin. 21:13
DISHEARTEN Is. 42:4, will not be **d-ed** or crushed
DISHONEST Amos 8:5, cheat with **d** scales
DISHONOR—*disgrace, shame* Ezra 4:14; Ps. 35:26; 71:13
John 8:49, I honor My Father, and you **d** Me
1 Cor. 15:43, it is sown in **d**
2 Cor. 6:8, by glory and **d**
2 Tim. 2:20, some to honor and some to **d**
Ps. 83:16; Prov. 12:16; Rom. 1:24; 2:23; James 2:6
DISLOCATE—*joint*
Gen. 32:25, Jacob's thigh was **d-d**
DISMAY—*astound, discourage*
Deut. 1:21, Do not fear or be **d-ed**
Deut. 31:8; Josh. 1:9; 8:1; 10:25; 1 Sam. 17:11; 1 Chr. 22:13; 28:20; 2 Chr. 20:15,17; 32:7; Job 41:22; Jer. 1:17; 8:9,21; 17:18; 30:10; 46:27; Ezek. 2:6; 3:9; Obad. 9
DISMISS 2 Chr. 23:8; Acts 19:41
DISOBEDIENCE Rom. 5:19, one man's **d**
Eph. 2:2, spirit . . . working in the sons of **d**
5:6 wrath of God comes upon the sons of **d**
Heb. 2:2, **d** received a just recompense
DISOBEDIENT—*rebellious* Neh. 9:26; Luke 1:17; Titus 3:3
Acts 26:19, did not prove **d** to the heavenly vision
Rom. 1:30; 2 Tim. 3:2, **d** to parents
10:21, A D AND OBSTINATE PEOPLE
1 Pet. 3:20, spirits who once were **d**
DISOBEY 1 Kin. 13:26, **d-ed** the command of the LORD
DISORDER—*confusion* James 3:16, **d** and every evil thing
DISPERSE—*spread* Esth. 3:8; Is. 11:12; Ezek. 20:23; 36:19; Zeph. 3:10
DISPERSION Jer. 25:34; John 7:35
DISPLAY—*declare* Esth. 1:11; Ps. 60:4; Is. 3:9
Ps. 8:1, Who hast **d-ed** Thy splendor above
John 9:3, works of God might be **d-ed**
DISPLEASE Gen. 48:17; Num. 22:34; 1 Sam. 8:6; 18:8; Prov. 24:18; Is. 59:15; Jon. 4:1
DISPLEASURE—*anger, fury*
Deut. 9:19, anger and hot **d**
DISPOSSESS Num. 14:12; Deut. 7:17
DISPUTE—*contend, controversy, debate* Deut. 25:1; Heb. 7:7
Phil. 2:14, Do all things without . . . **d-ing**
Jude 9, when he **d-d** with the devil
DISREGARD—*despise* Titus 2:15, Let no one **d** you
DISSENSION—*division* Acts 23:7
Acts 15:2, Paul and Barnabas had great **d**
Rom. 16:17, keep your eye on those who cause **d-s**
1 Tim. 2:8, without wrath and **d**
DISSIPATION Eph. 5:18, wine, for that is **d**
Titus 1:6, accused of **d** or rebellion
DISSOLVE—*melt* Ps. 6:6, I **d** my couch with my tears
Job 30:22; Nah. 2:6
DISTAFF Prov. 31:19, her hands to the **d**
DISTANCE Gen. 22:4; Matt. 26:58
DISTANT—*far* Luke 15:13, into a **d** country
DISTILL—*drip* Deut. 32:2, My speech **d** as the dew
DISTINCTION—*difference* Ex. 11:7; Lev. 11:47; 20:25
Lev. 10:10, **d** between the holy and the profane
Rom. 3:22; 10:12; for there is no **d**
Ezek. 22:26; Acts 15:9; 1 Cor. 14:7
DISTINCTLY—*plain*
Deut. 27:8, all the words . . . **d**
DISTINGUISH—*discern* Ezra 3:13; 1 Cor. 12:10
2 Sam. 19:35, Can I **d** between good and bad
Mal. 3:18, **d** between the righteous and the wicked
DISTORT—*pervert* Gal. 1:7, **d** the gospel of Christ
DISTRACTED Luke 10:40, Martha was **d** with
DISTRESS—*adversity, privation* Gen. 35:3; Deut. 4:30
2 Chr. 20:9, cry to Thee in our **d**
Ps. 25:17, Bring me out of my **d-es**
Prov. 1:27, when **d** *and* anguish come on you
Mark 14:33, began to be very **d-ed**
1 Thess. 3:7, in all our **d** and affliction
James 1:27, orphans and widows in their **d**
Deut. 28:53; 1 Sam. 26:24; 2 Sam. 4:9; 24:14; 2 Kin. 19:3; 2 Chr. 33:12; Prov. 24:10; Is. 25:4; 29:2; 33:2; Jer. 16:19; Lam. 1:20; Zeph. 1:17; Luke 21:23; Rom. 2:9; 1 Cor. 7:26; Phil. 1:17; 1 Tim. 5:10
DISTRIBUTE—*apportion*
Luke 18:22, **d** it to the poor
John 6:11, He **d-d** to those who were seated
DISTURBANCES
Luke 21:9, when you hear of war and **d**
DISTURBED 1 Sam. 28:15, Why have you **d** me by bringing
Ps. 42:5; 43:5, Why have you become **d** within me
DIVIDE—*apportion* 1 Kin. 3:25, **D** the living child in two
Ps. 22:18, **d** my garments among them
Prov. 16:19, **d** the spoil with the proud
Luke 11:17, Any kingdom **d-d** against itself
Eph. 2:14, broke down the barrier of the **d-ing** wall
Is. 53:12; Dan. 2:41; Matt. 27:35; Luke 15:12
DIVINATION Acts 16:16, having a spirit of **d**
Num. 22:7; Jer. 14:14; Ezek. 13:6,9
DIVINE Heb. 9:1, regulations of **d** worship
2 Pet. 1:4, partakers of *the* **d** nature
Gen. 30:27; Mic. 3:11; Zech. 10:2
DIVISION—*dissension* Ex. 8:23, put a **d** between My people
1 Chr. 23:6, divided them into **d-s**
John 7:43, arose a **d** in the multitude
1 Cor. 1:10, and there be no **d-s** among you
DIVORCE Lev. 21:14, widow, or a **d-d** woman
Deut. 24:1,3, a certificate of **d**
Jer. 3:8, given her a writ of **d**
Matt. 5:31, WHOEVER D-S HIS WIFE
DO—*practice, work* Gen. 11:6; 30:31; 1 Kin. 2:6
Ex. 20:9, Six days . . . labor and **d** all your work
Ps. 1:3, in whatever he **d-es**, he prospers
34:14, Depart from evil and **d** good
Eccles. 3:14, everything God **d-es** will remain forever
Matt. 12:50, whoever shall **d** the will of My Father
John 7:17, If any man is willing to **d** His will
15:5, apart from Me you can **d** nothing
Acts 16:30, what must I **d** to be saved
Rom. 13:3, **D** what is good

1 Cor. 9:23, I **d** all things for the sake of the gospel
11:24, **d** this in remembrance of Me
Gal. 6:10, let us **d** good to all men
2 Tim. 4:5, **d** the work of an evangelist
Heb. 10:7, BEHOLD, I HAVE COME . . . TO **D** THY WILL
1 Pet. 3:11, TURN AWAY FROM EVIL AND **D** GOOD
Prov. 2:14; 24:29; Matt. 23:3; John 2:5; 5:30

DOCTRINE—*teaching*
Eph. 4:14, every wind of **d**
1 Tim. 4:6, of the faith and of the sound **d**
Titus 1:9, able both to exhort in sound **d**

DOER—*workmen* Rom. 2:13, the **d-s** of the Law will be justified
James 1:22, prove yourselves **d-s** of the word
4:11, you are not a **d** of the law

DOG Eccles. 9:4, a live **d** is better than a dead lion
1 Sam. 17:43; 2 Sam. 3:8; Ps. 22:16; 59:6; Is. 56:10; Luke 16:21; Phil. 3:2; Rev. 22:15

DOING—*deeds*
Acts 10:38, He went about **d** good
Rom. 2:7, perseverance in **d** good
Gal. 6:9, let us not lose heart in **d** good
Eph. 6:6, **d** the will of God from the heart
2 Thess. 3:13, do not grow weary of **d** good
2 Cor. 8:11; 1 Pet. 2:15; 3:17

DOMAIN—*estate* Jude 6, angels who did not keep their own **d**
Luke 4:6; Col. 1:13

DOMINION—*kingdom, rule*
Ps. 103:22, in all places of His **d**
Zech. 9:10, His **d** will be from sea to sea
Col. 1:16, thrones or **d-s** or rulers
1 Pet. 4:11, belongs the glory and **d** forever
1 Chr. 29:11; Job 25:2; Eph. 1:21; Rev. 1:6

DONE—*wrought* Matt. 6:10, Thy will be **d**
Matt. 18:19, shall be **d** for them by My Father
Mark 14:6, has **d** a good deed to Me
Gen. 20:9; Ex. 31:15; Eccles. 2:11

DONKEY Zech. 9:9, mounted on a **d**
Matt. 21:2, you will find a **d** tied *there*
Num. 22:30; Prov. 26:3; Jer. 22:19; Matt. 21:5; 2 Pet. 2:16

DOOMED—*silenced* Ps. 79:11, those who are **d** to die
Jer. 8:14, God has **d** us

DOOR—*entrance*
Gen. 4:7, sin is crouching at the **d**
Ex. 12:7, put it on the two **d-posts**
Ps. 141:3, Keep watch over the **d** of my lips
Matt. 6:6, WHEN YOU HAVE SHUT YOUR **D**, pray
John 10:9, I am the **d**
1 Cor. 16:9, a wide **d** for effective *service*
James 5:9, Judge is standing right at the **d**
Rev. 3:8, put before you an open **d**
Gen. 6:16; 18:1; Judg. 4:20; 2 Sam. 11:9; 2 Chr. 12:10; Job 31:9; Prov. 26:14; Ezek. 40:38; Matt. 25:10; John 18:16; Rev. 4:1

DOUBLE—*twice* Gen. 43:12; Ps. 12:2; 1 Tim. 5:17
2 Kin. 2:9, **d** portion of your spirit be upon me
Is. 40:2, **D** for all her sins
James 1:8, *being* a **d-minded** man
Jude 12, without fruit, **d-ly** dead

DOUBT—*misgiving* Matt. 14:31, you of little faith, why did you **d**
Matt. 21:21, if you have faith and do not **d**
28:17, but some were **d-ful**
Luke 24:38, why do **d-s** arise in your hearts
Rom. 14:23, he who **d-s** is condemned if he eats

DOUGH—*flour* 2 Sam. 13:8, Tamar took **d**, kneaded *it*

DOVE Ps. 55:6, O that I had wings like a **d**
Matt. 3:16, Spirit of God descending as a **d**
10:16, shrewd as serpents . . . innocent as **d-s**
Gen. 8:8; Song 1:15; Is. 38:14; John 1:32

DOWN Ps. 23:2, makes me lie **d** in green pastures
Matt. 4:6, Son of God throw Yourself **d**
8:32, whole herd rushed **d** the steep bank
Gen. 12:10; 2 Sam. 3:35; Eccles. 3:21; John 8:6

DRAG—*draw* James 2:6, the rich who . . . **d** you into court
Jer. 12:3; 15:3; Acts 8:3

DRAGON Is. 51:9; Rev. 20:2

DRANK—*drink* 1 Cor. 10:4, all **d** the same spiritual drink
Gen. 9:21; Dan. 1:5; Mark 14:23; John 4:12

DRAW Ps. 69:18, **d** near to my soul
Is. 12:3, **d** water from the springs of salvation
Jer. 31:3, I have **d-n** you with lovingkindness
Luke 21:28, your redemption is **d-ing** near
John 4:11, You have nothing to **d** with
12:32, if I be lifted up . . . will **d** all men to Myself
Heb. 10:22, let us **d** near with a sincere heart
James 4:8, **D** near to God . . . He will **d** near to you
Gen. 24:13; Judg. 3:22; 19:9; Prov. 20:5; Zeph. 3:2; Acts 11:10

DREAD—*fear* Ps. 27:1, Whom shall I **d**
Prov. 1:27, **d** comes like a storm
Deut. 28:66; Job 3:25; Ps. 14:5; Is. 7:16; 8:13

DREAM Gen. 28:12, he had a **d**, and behold, a ladder
Gen. 37:19, Here comes this **d-er**
Dan. 1:17, Daniel understood all . . . **d-s**
Joel 2:28, Your old men will **d** dreams
Matt. 2:12, warned *by God* in a **d**
2:13, appeared to Joseph in a **d**
Jude 8, these men also by **d-ing** defile the flesh
Gen. 20:3; Judg. 7:13; Job 20:8; Ps. 73:20; 126:1; Is. 29:7; Matt. 1:20; 2:19; 27:19; Acts 2:17

DRENCHED—*wet* Dan. 4:15, **d** with the dew of heaven

DRESS—*array, clothe* Mark 15:17; Luke 7:25; 1 Pet. 3:3
Matt. 11:8, A man **d-ed** in soft *clothing*

DREW Gen. 47:29; Matt. 26:51; Acts 5:37
Ex. 2:10, I **d** him out of the water
Acts 1:26, they **d** lots for them

DRIED—*parched, withered* Job 18:16; Jer. 23:10
Gen. 8:7, water was **d** up from the earth
Ps. 22:15, My strength is **d** up

DRIES Joel 1:12, rejoicing **d** up

DRINK—*libation* Lev. 10:9, Do not **d** wine or strong **d**
Job 21:20, **d** the wrath of the Almighty
Ps. 80:5, made them to **d** tears
Prov. 20:1, strong **d** a brawler
Is. 22:13, Let us eat and **d**, for tomorrow
Matt. 11:18, neither eating nor **d-ing**
25:35, I was thirsty and you gave Me **d**
26:27, **D** from it, all of you
26:29, day when I **d** it new with you
27:34, GAVE HIM WINE TO **D** MINGLED WITH GALL
1 Cor. 10:4, all drank the same spiritual **d**
10:21, You cannot **d** the cup of the Lord
11:25, as often as you **d** *it*
Num. 6:3; 1 Kin. 17:6; Prov. 5:15; 7:18; Eccles. 9:7; Is. 24:9; Joel 1:5; Luke 5:39; 17:27; John 6:55; 18:11; Rom. 12:20; Heb. 6:7

DRIP Prov. 27:15, constant **d-ing** on a day of steady rain
Job 36:28; Ps. 65:11; Song 4:11; Is. 45:8

DRIVE—*chase* Ps. 1:4, chaff which the wind **d-s** away
Gen. 4:14; 21:10; Judg. 11:7; 2 Kin. 9:20; Ps. 35:5; Is. 58:3

DROP—*leak, drip* Deut. 32:2; Job 36:27
Is. 40:15, nations are like a **d** from a bucket
Luke 22:44, His sweat became like **d-s** of blood

DROUGHT—*famine* Jer. 14:1, in regard to the **d**

DROVE John 2:15; Acts 13:50

DROWNED Ex. 15:4, his officers are **d** in the Red Sea
Matt. 18:6, **d** in the depth of the sea

DROWSY Matt. 25:5, got **d** and *began* to sleep

DRUNK—*drink* Eph. 5:18, do not get **d** with wine
Lev. 11:34; Deut. 32:42; Is. 29:9; 63:6; John 2:10; 1 Thess. 5:7

DRUNKARD Deut. 21:20; Ps. 69:12; Joel 1:5; 1 Cor. 5:11
DRUNKENNESS
Luke 21:34, weighted down with . . . **d**
Rom. 13:13, not in carousing and **d**
Gal. 5:21, envyings, **d**, carousings and things
DRY—*parch, scorch, wither*
Ezek. 37:4, O **d** bones, hear the word
Gen. 1:9; Ps. 63:1; Prov. 17:1; Ezek. 17:24; Luke 23:31
DUE—*deserve, owe* Gal. 6:9, in **d** time we shall reap
Lev. 10:13; Ps. 104:27
DUG Ps. 7:15; 57:6; Is. 51:1; Ezek. 8:8; Matt. 21:33; 25:18; Luke 6:48
DULL—*red* Gen. 49:12, eyes are **d** from wine
DUMB—*silent* Mark 7:37, deaf to hear, and **d** to speak
Ps. 31:18, Let the lying lips be **d**
Ex. 4:11; Ps. 39:2; Matt. 9:32; 1 Cor. 12:2; 2 Pet. 2:16
DUNGEON—*pit* Gen. 41:14, out of the **d**
DUST Gen. 2:7, LORD God formed man of **d**
Gen. 3:19, you are **d**, And to **d** you shall return
Ps. 103:14, He is mindful we are *but* **d**
Matt. 10:14, shake off the **d** of your feet
Gen. 3:14; 13:16; 1 Sam. 2:8; 2 Sam. 22:43; Job 30:19; 34:15; 42:6; Ps. 18:42; 30:9; 72:9; Is. 26:19; 40:15; 65:25; Dan. 12:2; Luke 10:11; Acts 22:23; Rev. 18:19
DWELL—*abide, remain, live*
Ps. 5:4, No evil **d-s** with Thee
15:1, Who may **d** on Thy holy hill
23:6, will **d** in the house of the LORD
24:1, world, and those who **d** in it
91:1, **d-s** in the shelter of the Most High
Prov. 3:33, He blesses the **d-ing** of the righteous
Luke 16:9, receive you into the eternal **d-ings**
2 Cor. 5:2, our **d-ing** from heaven
Eph. 2:22, **d-ing** of God in the Spirit
3:17, Christ may **d** in your hearts
Phil. 4:8, mind **d** on these things
Col. 1:19, for all the fulness to **d** in Him
1 Tim. 6:16, **d-s** in unapproachable light
2 Pet. 1:14, laying aside . . . *earthly* **d-ing**
Gen. 4:20; Deut. 12:11; 1 Chr. 17:1; Ezra 7:15; Ps. 33:14; Prov. 15:31; Is. 57:15; Luke 21:35
DWELT—*sat* Ps. 107:10, those who **d** in darkness
DWINDLE—*diminish*
Prov. 13:11, wealth . . . by fraud **d-s**

E

EACH Acts 17:27, not far from **e** one of us
Rom. 14:12, **e** one of us shall give account
Phil. 2:3, let **e** of you regard one another
2 Thess. 1:3, the love of **e** one of you
Ex. 18:7; Ps. 85:10; Is. 57:2; Ezek. 4:6; Acts 2:3
EAGER—*hasty* Ps. 17:12; Eccles. 7:9
EAGERLY—*fervently*
Rom. 8:19, creation waits **e** for
Gal. 4:17, They **e** seek you
2 Tim. 1:17, in Rome, he **e** searched for me
EAGLE Ps. 103:5, youth is renewed like the **e**
Is. 40:31, with wings like **e-s**
Ex. 19:4; Deut. 28:49; 2 Sam. 1:23; Job 9:26; 39:27; Ezek. 1:10; 17:3; Dan. 4:33; Obad. 4; Rev. 4:7; 12:14
EAR Prov. 20:12, The hearing **e** and the seeing eye
Prov. 25:12, a wise reprover to a listening **e**
Is. 55:3, Incline your **e** and come to Me
1 Cor. 2:9, EYE HAS NOT SEEN AND E HAS NOT HEARD
Rev. 2:7, He who has an **e**, let him hear
Neh. 1:6; Job 12:11; 29:11; 42:5; Ps. 45:10; 58:4; 78:1; 94:9; Prov. 15:31; 18:15; 22:17; Eccles. 1:8; Is. 48:8; 50:4; 59:1; Jer. 9:20; Amos 3:12; Matt. 11:15; 1 Cor. 12:16
EARLY Gen. 26:31; Song 7:12; Hos. 6:4; Mark 16:2; Luke 24:22; John 20:1; James 5:7

EARNEST—*pledge* 2 Cor. 8:8; Phil. 1:20
EARNESTLY—*diligently, fervently*
Ps. 63:1, seek Thee **e**
1 Cor. 12:31, But **e** desire the greater gifts
Col. 4:12, always laboring **e** for you
James 5:17, he prayed **e** that it might not rain
Jude 3, contend **e** for the faith
EARNS Hag. 1:6, he who **e**, **e** wages to put into a purse
EARS—*hearing* 2 Sam. 7:22, heard with our **e**
Job 15:21, Sounds of terror are in his **e**
28:22, With our **e** we have heard
Ps. 34:15, His **e** are open to their cry
115:6, They have **e**, but they cannot hear
Prov. 21:13, shuts his **e** to the cry of the poor
26:17, *Like* one who takes a dog by the **e**
Mark 8:18, HAVING E, DO YOU NOT HEAR
2 Tim. 4:3, wanting to have their **e** tickled
James 5:4, reached the **e** of the Lord
1 Pet. 3:12, HIS E ATTEND TO THEIR PRAYER
Ps. 135:17; Is. 6:10; Matt. 10:27; 11:15; 13:15,16; 26:51; 28:14; Mark 4:9; 7:33; 14:47; Acts 7:51; 17:20
EARTH—*ground, land, soil*
Gen. 18:25, Shall not the judge of all the **e** deal
Ex. 9:29, the **e** is the LORD's
Num. 14:21, all the **e** will be filled with the glory
Josh. 3:11; Zech. 6:5, Lord of all the **e**
Job 26:7, hangs the **e** on nothing
Ps. 8:1, Thy name in all **e**
24:1, The **e** is the LORD's
33:5, **e** is full of the lovingkindness of the LORD
46:6, raised His voice, the **e** melted
97:1, LORD reigns; let the **e** rejoice
104:5, He established the **e**
104:24, The **e** is full of Thy possessions
Eccles. 1:4, the **e** remains forever
Is. 11:9, **e** will be full of the knowledge
51:6, the **e** will wear out like a garment
66:1, the **e** is My footstool
Jer. 51:15, made the **e** by His power
Mic. 1:2, Listen, O **e** and all it contains
Hab. 2:14, **e** will be filled with the knowledge
3:3, the **e** is full of His praise
Zech. 4:10, eyes of the LORD . . . the **e**
Matt. 5:5, gentle, for they shall inherit the **e**
6:10, on **e** as it is in heaven
6:19, treasures upon **e**
16:19; 18:18, shall bind on **e**
Luke 2:14, on **e** peace
John 12:32, lifted up from the **e**
17:4, I glorified Thee on the **e**
1 Cor. 15:47, first man is from the **e**, **e-y**
15:48, As is the **e-y**, so also . . . who are **e-y**
Col. 3:2, not on the things that are on **e**
2 Pet. 3:13, new heavens and a new **e**
Rev. 20:11, from whose presence **e** and heaven fled
21:1, a new **e**
Gen. 1:1,11; 7:10; 8:22; 10:25; Deut. 32:1; Josh. 23:14; 1 Kin. 8:27; 2 Kin. 5:17; 2 Chr. 6:18; Job 9:24; 12:8; 19:25; 38:4; 41:33; Ps. 2:8; 16:3; 34:16; 41:2; 46:2,8,10; 47:9; 50:4; 57:5; 58:11; 63:9; 65:8,9; 67:6; 68:8; 71:20; 72:6,16; 73:25; 75:3; 83:18; 90:2; 97:9; 99:1; 102:25; 104:13; 108:5; 112:2; 115:16; 119:19,64,90; 146:4; 147:8; 148:13; Prov. 3:19; 8:23,26; 11:31; 25:3, 30:14,16,21,24; Eccles. 3:21; 12:7; Is. 4:2; 13:13; 14:16; 24:1,19; 26:9,21; 34:1; 40:22,28; 44:24; 45:22; 48:13; 49:13; 65:16; Jer. 31:22; Ezek. 34:27; 43:2; Hos. 2:22; Amos 8:9; Jon. 2:6; Mic. 6:2; 7:17; Nah. 1:5; Zeph. 3:8; Hag. 1:10; Matt. 5:35; 10:34; 23:9; Mark 4:28; 9:3; John 3:31; Acts 8:33; 22:22; Rom. 10:18; 1 Cor. 15:49; Heb. 8:4; 11:13; 12:25,26; James 3:15; 5:5,18; 2 Pet. 3:7,10; Rev. 5:10; 7:3; 18:1; 20:9
EARTHEN Jer. 19:1; Lam. 4:2
2 Cor. 4:7, have this treasure in **e** vessels
EARTHLY John 3:12, If I told you **e** things
2 Cor. 5:1, **e** tent which is our house

Phil. 3:19, set their minds on **e** things
James 3:15, wisdom . . . is **e**, natural, demonic
EARTHQUAKE 1 Kin. 19:11; Is. 29:6; Amos 1:1; Zech. 14:5; Matt. 24:7; 27:54; Acts 16:26; Rev. 6:12; 8:5; 11:13; 16:18
EASE—*rest, prosperity* Job 12:5, He who is at **e**
Amos 6:1, Woe to those who are at **e**
Zech. 1:15, nations who are at **e**
Matt. 19:24; Mark 10:25; Luke 18:25, **e-ier** for a camel
Luke 12:19, take your **e**
Heb. 12:1, sin which so **e-ily** entangles us
Ex. 18:22; Job 21:23; Is. 32:9,11
EAST Judg. 6:3; 7:12, 1 Kin. 4:30, sons of the **e**
Ps. 103:12, As far as the **e**
Matt. 2:1, magi from the **e**
2:2, His star in the **e**
Gen. 28:14; Ex. 10:13; Job 1:3; Ps. 48:7; 75:6; Is. 27:8; 43:5; Ezek. 8:16; 17:10; Hos. 12:1; Joel 2:20; Jon. 4:5; Zech. 8:7; 14:4; Matt. 8:11; 24:27; Luke 13:29; Rev. 16:12; 21:13
EASY Prov. 14:6, knowledge is **e** to him
Matt. 11:30, My yoke is **e**
EAT—*consume, dine, feast* Prov. 31:27, not **e** the bread
Is. 55:1, come, buy and **e**
Ezek. 3:1, **e** this scroll
Dan. 4:33, began **e-ing** grass like cattle
Matt. 6:25; Luke 12:22, what you shall **e**
11:19, Son of Man came **e-ing** and drinking
15:20, **e** with unwashed hands
26:26, Take, **e**; this is My body
Mark 2:16, He was **e-ing** with the sinners
Luke 12:19, **e**, drink *and* be merry
15:2, receives sinners and **e-s** with them
22:30, may **e** and drink at My table
John 4:32, food to **e** that you do not know about
Acts 12:23, **e-en** by worms and died
Rom. 14:17, kingdom of God is not **e-ing**
1 Cor. 11:29, **e-s** and drinks judgment to himself
2 Thess. 3:10, not work, neither let him **e**
Heb. 13:10, have no right to **e**
Rev. 2:7, **e** of the tree of life
Gen. 2:16; 3:17; 9:4; Lev. 19:26; Deut. 6:11; 8:10; 12:16; Josh. 5:12; 1 Kin. 19:5; 2 Kin. 6:28; Neh. 5:2; 8:10; Ps. 22:26; 80:13; Prov. 1:31; 24:13; 25:27; Eccles. 5:12; Is. 1:19; 3:10; 4:1; 7:15; 11:7; 65:13, 25; Jer. 24:2; 29:17; 31:29; Ezek. 18:2; Hos. 4:10; 10:13; Mic. 6:14; Hag. 1:6; Matt. 9:11; 12:1; 14:16; Mark 6:31,37; 11:14; Luke 9:13; 10:8; 15:23; John 6:53; Acts 10:13; Rom. 14:2; 1 Cor. 8:13; 9:4; 10:27,31; Rev. 10:10; 19:18
EDGE—*bank* Josh. 3:8; Eccles. 10:10; Jer. 31:30
Prov. 5:4, sharp as a **two-e-d** sword
EDICT—*word* Ezra 6:11, violates this **e**
EDIFICATION Rom. 15:2, please his neighbor . . . to his **e**
1 Cor. 14:3, speaks to men for **e**
14:26, all things be done for **e**
EDIFY—*encourage* 1 Cor. 8:1, but love **e-es**
1 Cor. 10:23, lawful, but not all things **e**
14:5, church may receive **e-ing**
EDUCATE Acts 22:3, **e-d** under Gamaliel
EFFECT—*wise* Acts 7:6, God spoke to this **e**
EFFECTIVE 1 Cor. 16:9, door for **e** *service*
James 5:16, The **e** prayer
EFFEMINATE 1 Cor. 6:9, Do not be deceived . . . nor **e**
EFFORT—*diligence* 2 Tim. 4:9; Jude 3
EGG Job 6:6; 39:14; Is. 59:5; Jer. 17:11
Luke 11:12, asked for an **e** . . . give him a scorpion
ELDERS—*older, aged* 1 Sam. 15:30; Job 12:20; 32:9
Matt. 15:2; Mark 7:3, tradition of the **e**
Acts 14:23, appointed **e** for them in every church
1 Tim. 5:17, Let the **e** who rule
James 5:14, call for the **e**
Prov. 31:23; Titus 1:5; 1 Pet. 5:1; Rev. 4:4; 7:13
ELECT—*chosen* Matt. 24:22; Mark 13:20, sake of the **e**
Matt. 24:24, mislead, if possible, even the **e**
Mark 13:22, to lead the **e** astray
Luke 18:7, God bring about justice for His **e**
Rom. 8:33, charge against God's **e**
ELEMENT Gal. 4:3, **e-al** things
2 Pet. 3:10, **e-s** will be destroyed
ELOQUENT—*skillful* Ex. 4:10, never been **e**
Acts 18:24, Jew named Apollos . . . an **e** man
ELUDE—*escape* John 10:39, He **e-d** their grasp
EMBITTERED Acts 14:2, **e** them against
EMBRACE 2 Kin. 4:16, Prov. 5:20; Song 2:6
Gen. 33:4, Esau ran . . . and **e-d** him
48:10, Joseph . . . and **e-d**
Eccles. 3:5, a time to **e** . . . to shun **e-ing**
Luke 15:20, ran and **e-d** him
EMBROIDER—*weave* Ex. 35:35; Ezek. 16:10,13; 27:7,16,24
EMERALD Ex. 28:17; Ezek. 28:13; Rev. 4:3; 21:19
EMINENT—*foremost* 2 Cor. 11:5, inferior . . . **e** apostles
EMPTINESS—*vanity* Is. 34:11, plumb line of **e**
Jer. 2:5, And walked after **e**
EMPTY—*vain, void* 2 Kin. 18:20, *they are* only **e** words
Is. 55:11, not return to Me **e**
Eph. 5:6, deceive you with **e** words
1 Tim. 6:20, worldly and **e** chatter
Gen. 31:42; Ex. 3:21; 23:15; Deut. 15:13; Judg. 7:16; Ruth 1:21; 2 Sam. 1:22; 2 Kin. 4:3; Job 22:9; 26:7; Mark 12:3; Luke 1:53; 20:10
ENCAMP Ps. 27:3; 34:7; 53:5; Jer. 50:29
ENCIRCLE Ps. 22:12, bulls of Bashan have **e-d** me
ENCLOSE Job 38:8; Ps. 139:5
ENCOUNTER James 1:2, when you **e** various trials
ENCOURAGE—*strengthen* 2 Chr. 35:2; Is. 41:7
Deut. 1:38; 3:28; 2 Sam. 11:25, **e** him
1 Sam. 23:16, **e-d** him in God
Ezra 6:22, to **e** them in the work
1 Thess. 5:11, Therefore **e** one another
Heb. 3:13, **e** one another
10:25, but **e-ing** *one another*
ENCOURAGEMENT—*consolation*
Acts 4:36, Son of **E**
Rom. 15:5, God who gives perseverance and **e**
Phil. 2:1, if . . . any **e** in Christ
Heb. 6:18, may have strong **e**
ENCUMBRANCE—*weight*
Heb. 12:1, also lay aside every **e**
END—*goal, outcome* Gen. 6:13, **e** of all flesh
Job 6:11, what is my **e**
Ps. 2:8, *very* **e-s** of the earth
7:9, wicked come to an **e**
39:4, LORD, make me to know my **e**
Prov. 14:12, **e** is the way of death
Eccles. 4:8, no **e** to all his labor
Is. 9:7, no **e** to the increase of *His* government
Jer. 8:20, Harvest is past, summer is **e-ed**
Ezek. 21:25; 35:5, punishment of the **e**
Matt. 10:22; Mark 13:13, endured to the **e**
13:39, harvest is the **e** of the age
28:20, with you always, even to the **e**
Luke 1:33, His kingdom will have no **e**
21:9, the **e** *does* not *follow* immediately
John 13:1, He loved them to the **e**
Rom. 10:4, Christ is the **e** of the law
Heb. 7:3, beginning of days, nor **e** of life
Rev. 21:6; 22:13, the beginning and the **e**
Num. 23:10; Ps. 9:6; 19:6; 73:17; 102:27; 107:27; Eccles. 7:8; Jer. 5:31; Lam 4:18; Ezek. 7:2; Dan. 11:45; 12:13; Matt. 24:6,13; Mark 13:7; Heb. 6:8
ENDLESS Eccles. 12:12, writing . . . books is **e**
1 Tim. 1:4, attention to myths and **e** genealogies
ENDOW—*clothe* Gen. 30:20; 2 Chr. 2:13

Heb. 11:34, **e-d** the edge of the sword
2 Pet. 1:4, **e-d** the corruption that is in the world
Gen. 19:17; Deut. 23:15; 1 Kin. 18:40; 2 Kin. 9:15; Esth. 4:13; Job 11:20; 19:20; Ps. 124:7; Obad. 17; Matt. 23:33; Mark 14:52; Luke 21:36; Heb. 11:34

ESSENTIAL—*excellent*
Rom. 2:18, approve . . . that are **e**

ESTABLISH—*confirm, direct, plant, strengthen*
Ps. 119:5, that my ways may be **e-ed**
119:38, **E** Thy word to Thy servant
Prov. 16:12, throne is **e-ed** on righteousness
Is. 16:5, A throne . . . **e-ed** in lovingkindness
Rom. 16:25, able to **e** you according to
1 Thess. 3:13, He may **e** your hearts
2 Pet. 1:12, been **e-ed** in the truth
Gen. 17:19; Job 37:15; Ps. 65:6; Prov. 3:19; Is. 51:16; Jer. 10:12; 51:15; Rom. 3:31; 10:3

ESTATE—*domain, standard* Ps. 136:23, low **e**
Luke 15:13, squandered his **e** with loose living

ESTEEM—*regard, consider*
Ps. 119:128, I **e** right . . . precepts
1 Thess. 5:13, you **e** them very highly in love

ESTEEMED—*beloved, chosen, loved* 1 Sam. 18:23; Dan. 9:23
1 Sam. 2:30, despise Me will be lightly **e**
Is. 53:4, we ourselves **e** Him stricken
Luke 16:15, highly **e** among men

ESTIMATION—*imagination*
Rom. 11:25, wise in your own **e**

ESTRANGE Job 19:13; Ps. 58:3; Ezek. 14:5

ETERNAL—*everlasting* Deut. 33:27; Matt. 18:8
Is. 9:6, name will be called . . . **E** Father
Matt. 19:16, I may obtain **e** life
19:29, shall inherit **e** life
25:46, righteous into **e** life
Mark 10:17; Luke 10:25, what . . . to inherit **e** life
10:30, in the world to come, **e** life
John 3:15, may in Him have **e** life
3:16, whoever believes . . . have **e** life
3:36, who believes in the Son has **e** life
5:39, search the Scriptures . . . have **e** life
6:68, You have words of **e** life
10:28, I give **e** life to them
12:25, hates his life . . . keep it to life **e**
17:3, **e** life, that they may know Thee
Rom. 2:7, seek for glory and honor . . . **e** life
5:21, righteousness to **e**
6:23, free gift of God is **e** life
2 Cor. 4:17, an **e** weight of glory
4:18, things which are not seen are **e**
5:1, house . . . **e** in the heavens
Gal. 6:8, from the Spirit reap **e** life
Eph. 3:11, in accordance with the **e** purpose
1 Tim. 1:17, Now to the King **e**, immortal
6:12, take hold of the **e** life
Titus 1:2, in the hope of **e** life
Heb. 5:9, source of **e** salvation
9:14, through the **e** Spirit
1 Pet. 5:10, called you to His **e** glory in Christ
1 John 2:25, promise . . . made to us, **e** life
5:11, God has given us **e** life
Rev. 14:6, having an **e** gospel to preach
Matt. 25:41,46; Mark 3:29; Luke 16:9; 18:18; John 4:14,36; 6:54; 12:50; 17:2; Acts 13:46,48; Rom. 6:22; 16:26; 2 Thess. 1:9; 2:16; Heb. 6:2; 9:12,15; 1 John 1:2; 3:15; 5:20; Jude 6,7

ETERNITY—*world*
Eccles. 3:11, set **e** in their heart
Mic. 5:2, goings forth . . . from the days of **e**

EUNUCH—*chamberlain, official* Esth. 1:10; Is. 56:3; Matt. 19:12; Acts 8:27

EVANGELIST Acts 21:8, Philip the **e**
Eph. 4:11, He gave some . . . *as* **e-s**
2 Tim. 4:5, do the work of an **e**

EVAPORATE—*fail, gone* Ex. 16:14; Job 14:11

EVENING—*close* Ps. 104:23, to his labor until **e**
Jer. 6:4, shadows of the **e** lengthen
Zech. 14:7, at **e** time there will be light
Luke 24:29, for it is *getting* toward **e**
Judg. 20:23; 1 Sam. 14:24; 1 Kin. 17:6; Ps. 55:17; 90:6; 141:2; Eccles. 11:6; Matt. 8:16; 14:23; Mark 1:32

EVER—*forever* Ps. 52:8; Matt. 21:19; Mark 11:14; Rev. 14:11
Ps. 48:14, Our God forever and **e**
51:3, my sin is **e** before me
Rev. 11:15, He will reign forever and **e**
22:5, they shall reign forever and **e**

EVERLASTING—*endure, eternal, ancient, perpetual*
Gen. 21:33; Is. 40:28, the **E** God
Deut. 33:27, underneath are the **e** arms
Ps. 90:2, from **e** to **e**, Thou art God
106:1; 107:1; 136:1, lovingkindness is **e**
139:24, lead me in the **e** way
Is. 26:4, in GOD . . . *have* an **e** Rock
35:10; 51:11; 61:7, **e** joy
Jer. 31:3, loved you with an **e** love
Gen. 9:16; Ps. 103:17; 119:142; 138:8; Prov. 8:23; 10:25; Is. 45:17; 54:8; 55:13; 56:5; 60:19,20; 63:12; Dan. 4:34; 7:14

EVERMORE—*ever, forever* Ps. 92:7; John 6:34

EVERY Gen. 6:5, **e** intent . . . of his heart was only evil
Ps. 119:101, restrained my feet from **e** evil way
119:104, I hate **e** false way
Prov. 30:5, **E** word of God is tested
Eccles. 3:1, a time for **e** event under heaven
Is. 45:23, **e** knee will bow
55:1, Ho! **E** one who thirsts
Jer. 25:5, Turn now **e** one from his evil way
Matt. 4:4, ON **E** WORD THAT PROCEEDS
7:8, For **e** one who asks receives
John 3:8, so is **e** one who is born of the Spirit
2 Cor. 10:5, taking **e** thought captive
Eph. 1:21, far above all rule . . . **e** name
2 Tim. 2:21, prepared for **e** good work
Heb. 12:1, lay aside **e** encumbrance
James 1:17, **E** good thing . . . **e** perfect gift
1 John 4:1, do not believe **e** spirit
Rev. 20:13, **e** one of them according to their deeds
22:12, **e** man according to what he has done
Deut. 4:4; Prov. 2:9; 7:12; John 18:37; Rom. 14:11; 1 Tim. 2:8; 2 Tim. 2:19

EVERYONE Ps. 32:6, **e** who is godly pray
Eccles. 10:3, demonstrates to **e** *that* he is a fool
Luke 11:10, For **e** who asks receives
19:26, to **e** who has shall *more* be given

EVERYTHING Prov. 14:15, The naive believes **e**
1 Tim. 4:4, **e** created by God is good

EVERYWHERE Mark 1:45; 16:20; Acts 17:30

EVIDENCE—*mouth* Deut. 17:6, the **e** of two witnesses

EVIDENT—*see* Gal. 3:11; Heb. 7:14

EVIL—*bad, wicked, reproach*
Gen. 38:7, **e** in the sight of the LORD
Deut. 23:9, keep yourself from every **e**
1 Kin. 21:25, sold himself to do **e**
Ps. 15:3, Nor does **e** to his neighbor
23:4, I fear no **e**
34:14; 37:27, Depart from **e**, and do good
91:10, No **e** will befall you
97:10, Hate **e**, you who love the LORD
Jer. 7:26, did **e** more than their fathers
Matt. 5:11, all kinds of **e** against you falsely
6:13, deliver us from **e**
7:11; Luke 11:13, If you then, being **e**
12:45, this **e** generation
27:23; Mark 15:14, what **e** has He done
Mark 9:39, speak **e** of Me
Luke 6:45, **e** *man* out of the **e** *treasure*
John 3:20, does **e** hates the light
Rom. 12:17, Never pay back **e** for **e** to anyone
12:21, overcome **e** with good
Eph. 5:16, because the days are **e**
1 Thess. 5:22, abstain from every form of **e**
1 Tim. 6:10, love of money is a root of all **e**
James 3:8, tongue; *it is* a restless **e**

F

FAMILY Gen. 12:3, all the **f-es** of the earth
Eph. 3:15, every **f** in heaven
Gen. 10:5; Deut. 29:18; Judg. 6:15; Job 31:34; Ps. 107:41; Jer. 3:14; 31:1

FAMINE—*drought* Gen. 12:10; 41:27,54; 42:19
Matt. 24:7, there will be **f-s** and earthquakes
Mark 13:8, will *also* be **f-s**
Luke 15:14, a severe **f** occurred in that country
Rom. 8:35, or **f**, or nakedness, or peril
2 Kin. 4:38; 1 Chr. 21:12; 2 Chr. 6:28; Neh. 5:3; Job 5:20; Ps. 33:19; Is. 14:30; Jer. 14:12; Amos 8:11; Acts 7:11; 11:28

FAMISH—*hunger* Gen. 41:55, Egypt was **f-ed**

FAMOUS 1 Chr. 5:24, men of valor, **f** men

FANG Joel 1:6, the **f-s** of a lioness

FAR—*distant* Ps. 22:11, Be not **f** from me
Ps. 103:12, As **f** as the east is from the west
119:155, Salvation is **f** from the wicked
Prov. 15:29, LORD is **f** from the wicked
Jer. 23:23, a God **f** off
Matt. 15:8, THEIR HEART IS **F** AWAY FROM ME
Mark 12:34, are not **f** from the kingdom
Acts 17:27, though He is not **f** from
2 Cor. 4:17, glory **f** beyond all comparison
Eph. 1:21, **f** above all rule
Gen. 18:25; Ex. 23:7; Deut. 13:7; Josh. 9:6; 2 Sam. 20:20; Ps. 97:9; Prov. 4:24; 27:10; Is. 60:4; Ezek. 11:15; John 21:8; Eph. 2:17

FARE Jon. 1:3, Tarshish, paid the **f**

FAREWELL Acts 15:29, you will do well. **F**

FARTHEST—*utmost* Mark 13:27, **F** END of the earth

FASHION—*appearance* Job 10:8, Thy hands **f-ed**
Ps. 33:15, He who **f-s** the hearts
1 Kin. 7:15; Job 31:15; Is. 44:12; Jer. 18:11

FAST Matt. 4:2, after He had **f-ed** forty days
Matt. 6:16, whenever you **f**, do not ... as the
6:17, when you **f**, anoint your head
Acts 13:3, when they had **f-ed** and prayed
Is. 58:3,4,5,6; Joel 1:14; Zech. 7:5; Mark 2:18,19; Luke 18:12

FASTING—*hungry* Ps. 109:24, weak from **f**
Matt. 6:16,18, seen **f** by men
Luke 2:37, serving ... with **f-s** and prayers
Acts 14:23, having prayed with **f**
Esth. 4:3; Ps. 35:13; Joel 2:12; Mark 2:18

FAT Prov. 13:4, soul of the diligent is made **f**
Prov. 15:30, Good news puts **f** on the bones
Luke 15:23, bring the **f-ned** calf
James 5:5, you have **f-ned** your hearts
Gen. 45:18; Judg. 3:17; Neh. 8:10; 9:25; Ps. 73:4; 119:70

FATE Eccles. 2:14; 9:2,3

FATHER Gen. 2:24, leave his **f** and his mother
Gen. 9:23, covered the nakedness of their **f**
17:4, **f** of a multitude of nations
Ex. 20:12, Honor your **f** and your mother
Job 29:16, I was a **f** to the needy
Ps. 22:4, In Thee our **f-s** trusted
103:13, as a **f** has compassion on his
Prov. 10:1, A wise son makes a **f** glad
17:6, glory of sons is their **f-s**
Is. 9:6, Eternal **F**, Prince of Peace
63:16, Thou art our **F**
Matt. 3:9, We have Abraham for our **f**
5:16, glorify your **F** who is in heaven
6:1, your **F** who is in heaven
6:4,6,18, your **F** who sees in secret
6:9, Our **F** who art in heaven
7:21, he who does the will of My **F**
10:35, SET A MAN AGAINST HIS **F**
11:25, I praise Thee O **F**, Lord of
11:27, knows the Son, except the **F**
28:19, baptizing ... name of the **F**
Mark 8:38, comes in the glory of His **F**
Luke 2:49, be in My **F-'s** *house*
11:2, **F**, hallowed be Thy name
23:34, Jesus was saying, **F** forgive them
23:46, **F** ... HANDS I COMMIT
John 2:16, stop making My **F-'s** house a
5:17, My **F** is working until now and
10:15, **F** knows me and I know the **F**
14:2, In My **F-'s** house are many
17:1, **F**, the hour has come; glorify
2 Cor. 1:3, **F** of mercies and God of all
Eph. 3:14, I bow my knees before the **F**
6:4, **f-s**, do not provoke your children
Phil. 2:11, to the glory of God the **F**
Heb. 1:5, I will be a **F** to Him
1 Pet. 1:3, Blessed be the God and **F**
2 Pet. 1:17, honor ... from God the **F**
Jude 1, are the called, beloved in God the **F**
Rev. 1:6, priests to His God and **F**
Gen. 4:20; 43:7; 48:17; Ex. 21:15; Deut. 5:9; 1 Sam. 17:34; 2 Sam. 7:12; Job 17:14; 38:28; Ps. 68:5; 89:26; Prov. 1:8; 6:20; Jer. 3:19; Mal. 2:10; Matt. 11:26; 26:29; Mark 14:36; Luke 10:21; 15:18; 24:49; 1 Cor. 4:15; Heb. 3:9; 1 John 2:13; 2 John 4

FATHERLESS—*orphan*
Prov. 23:10, the fields of the **f**

FATNESS—*abundance*
Ps. 65:11, Thy paths drip *with* **f**
Gen. 27:28; Judg. 9:9; Ps. 63:5; 73:7

FAULT—*offense* 1 Sam. 29:3; Ps. 19:12; Rom. 9:19

FAULTLESS—*blameless*
Heb. 8:7, *covenant* had been **f**

FAVOR—*beauty, charm, grace, pleasure, supplication*
Ps. 90:17, let the **f** of the Lord our God
Prov. 8:35; 12:2; 18:22, obtains **f** from the LORD
13:15, Good understanding produces **f**
Luke 2:52, increasing ... in **f** with God and men
Acts 2:47, having **f** with all the people
Gen. 6:8; 39:21; Ex. 3:21; 33:12; Deut. 33:23; 1 Sam. 13:12; Esth. 2:17; Ps. 5:12; 30:5; 51:18; 85:1; Prov. 14:35; 19:12; Eccles. 9:11; Dan. 1:9; Zech. 11:7

FAVORABLE—*acceptable*
Ps. 77:7, will He never be **f** again
Is. 61:2, proclaim the **f** year of the LORD

FEAR (n.)—*dread, awe, terror* Gen. 9:2; 20:11; Deut. 2:25
Ps. 19:9, the **f** of the LORD is clean
53:5, in great **f** *where* no **f** had been
111:10; Prov. 9:10, **f** ... is the beginning of wisdom
Prov. 1:7, **f** ... is the beginning of knowledge
10:27, **f** of the LORD prolongs life
14:26, **f** of the LORD there is strong confidence
14:27, **f** of the LORD is a fountain of life
15:16, better is a little with the **f** of the LORD
19:23, the **f** of the LORD *leads* to life
29:25, the **f** of man brings a snare
Luke 21:26, men fainting from **f**
John 7:13; 19:38; 20:19, for **f** of the Jews
Rom. 13:3, not a cause of **f** for good behavior
1 Cor. 2:3, in weakness and in **f**
2 Cor. 5:11, knowing the **f** of the Lord
7:5, conflicts without, **f-s** within
7:11, what **f**, what longing, what zeal
Eph. 6:5; Phil. 2:12, with **f** and trembling
Deut. 11:25; 1 Chr. 14:17; Job 4:6; 39:22; Ps. 34:11; 36:1; Prov. 3:25; Is. 8:12; Jer. 32:40; Matt. 14:26; Rom. 3:18; Heb. 2:15; Jude 12,23

FEAR (v.)—*be afraid, revere* Gen. 22:12; 42:18
1 Kin. 18:12, I ... have **f-ed** the LORD from my youth
Job 1:9, Job **f** God for nothing
Ps. 27:1, Whom shall I **f**
118:6, will not **f**; what can man do
Prov. 31:30, woman who **f-s** the LORD, she shall be praised
Eccles. 12:13, **f** God and keep His commandments
Matt. 10:26, Therefore do not **f** them
10:28, do not **f** those who kill the body
10:31, do not **f**; you are of ... value
Luke 23:40, Do you not even **f** God
Ex. 1:21; 14:13; 18:21; Deut. 4:10; 5:29; 28:58; Neh. 7:2; Job 11:15; Ps. 27:3; 31:19; 34:9; 66:16;

FIELD *(Continued)*
2 Sam. 14:6; 1 Kin. 11:29; Job 5:23; Ps. 96:12; Prov. 24:30; Is. 1:8; 5:8; Jer. 4:17; 26:18; 32:44; Lam. 4:9; Dan. 4:15; Hos. 2:12; Joel 1:20; James 5:4

FIERCE Rev. 19:15, f wrath of God the Almighty
Gen. 49:7; Num. 25:4; Job 41:10; Prov. 27:4; Is. 33:19

FIERY Num. 21:6; Deut. 28:22; Ps. 21:9; 1 Pet. 4:12

FIFTEEN Gen. 5:10; Judg. 8:10; Hos. 3:2; Gal. 1:18

FIFTH Gen. 1:23; Lev. 5:16; Neh. 6:5; Jer. 1:3; Rev. 6:9

FIFTY Lev. 25:10, consecrate the **f-eth** year
Gen. 6:15; Ex. 18:21; 26:5; Lev. 23:16; Esth. 5:14; Luke 9:14; John 8:57; Acts 13:19

FIG Gen. 3:7, they sewed f leaves together
Matt. 21:19, the f tree withered
Mark 13:28, the parable from the f tree
Luke 6:44, men do not gather **f-s** from thorns
James 3:12, Can a f tree . . . produce olives
Rev. 6:13, as a f tree casts its unripe **f-s**
Deut. 8:8; Judg. 9:11; Jer. 29:17; Matt. 7:16; Mark 11:13; John 1:48

FIGHT Ex. 14:14, The LORD will f for you
1 Tim. 1:18, you may f the good f
6:12, F the good f of faith
James 4:2, so you f and quarrel
Josh. 9:2; 1 Sam. 8:20; Neh. 4:20; Ps. 35:1

FIGURATIVE 1 Cor. 4:6, I have **f-ly** applied to myself

FIGURE—*graven* Lev. 26:1; Deut. 4:16

FILL Gen. 42:25, gave orders to f their bags
Jer. 23:24, f the heavens and the earth
Gen. 1:22; Job 41:7; Ps. 83:16; Prov. 7:18; Is. 8:8; 65:11; Mic. 3:8; Matt. 22:10

FILTH—*uncleanness*
Is. 4:4, LORD has washed away the f
64:6, deeds are like a **f-y** garment
James 1:21, putting aside all **f-iness**
Is. 28:8; Nah. 3:6

FIND—*discover* Gen. 18:26, If I f in Sodom fifty
Num. 32:23, be sure your sin will f you out
Deut. 4:29, you will f *Him* if you search
Prov. 8:35, he who **f-s** Me **f-s** life
18:22, he who **f-s** a wife **f-s** a good thing
Is. 35:10, They will f gladness and joy
Matt. 7:7, Seek, and you shall f
10:39, lost his life . . . shall f it
11:29, YOU SHALL F REST FOR YOUR SOULS
Mark 13:36, f you asleep
Luke 2:12, you will f a baby wrapped
15:8, search . . . until she **f-s** it
23:4, I f no guilt in this man
John 10:9, go in and out, and f pasture
Acts 7:46, f a dwelling place for the God of
Gen. 32:5; Ruth 1:9; 2 Sam. 15:25; 20:6; Prov. 1:13; 3:4; Song 3:1; 5:8; Matt. 21:2; Mark 11:2; Luke 11:9; John 18:38; Acts 23:9; 2 Cor. 9:4; Rev. 18:14

FINE—*good* Ps. 19:10, than much f gold; Sweeter
Matt. 13:45, merchant seeking f pearls
Luke 16:19, in purple and f linen
Rev. 19:14, clothed in f linen, white
Gen. 41:42; Ex. 16:14; 25:4; Ps. 81:16

FINGER John 8:6, Jesus . . . with His f wrote on the ground
John 20:25, put my f into the place of the nails
20:27, Reach here your f
Ex. 8:19; Lev. 4:6; Deut. 9:10; 2 Sam. 21:20; 1 Kin. 12:10; 1 Chr. 20:6; Prov. 6:13; Jer. 52:21; Mark 7:33; Luke 11:20; 16:24

FINISH—*end, spend* 2 Chr. 7:11, Solomon **f-ed** the house
John 19:30, said, It is **f-ed**
Acts 20:24, that I may f my course
Ex. 40:33; Ps. 90:9; Mark 3:26; 2 Cor. 8:11

FIR—*cedar* 2 Sam. 6:5; Ps. 104:17; Ezek. 27:5

FIRE—*flame, burn* Ex. 13:21, pillar of f by night
Num. 3:4, offered strange f before the LORD
1 Kin. 18:38, Then f of the LORD fell
Neh. 9:12, with a pillar of f by night
Ps. 105:39, f to illumine by night
Is. 66:15, the LORD will come in f
Dan. 3:25, walking *about* in the midst of the f
Matt. 3:11, baptize you . . . Holy Spirit and f
Mark 9:43, into the unquenchable f
Acts 2:3, tongues as of f
1 Cor. 3:13, *to be* revealed with f
Rev. 3:18, gold refined by f
21:8, lake that burns with f and brimstone
Gen. 19:24; 22:6; Ex. 3:2; 9:24; Lev. 6:13; Deut. 9:3; Job 18:5; Ps. 46:9; Jer. 23:29; Matt. 3:10,12; Luke 3:17; 12:49; Jude 7

FIREPAN Lev. 16:12, take a f full of coals

FIRM—*hard, steadfast* Josh. 3:17, LORD stood f on dry
Is. 22:23, *like* a peg in a f place
1 Cor. 7:37, stands f in his heart
2 Tim. 2:19, the f foundation of God stands
Heb. 3:6, hope f until the end
1 Pet. 5:9, resist him, f in *your* faith

FIRMAMENT—*expanse* Ps. 19:1, f is declaring the work of

FIRST—*leader, eminent, foremost* Gen. 38:28
Matt. 6:33, seek f His kingdom
7:5, f take the log out of
19:30, many *who are* f will be last
20:27, be f among you
28:1, the f *day* of the week
1 John 4:19, because He f loved us
Rev. 1:17, I am the f and the last
2:4, you have left your f love
21:4, the f things have passed away
22:13, Omega, the f and the last
Deut. 26:10; Prov. 3:9; 18:17; Hos. 2:7; Mark 3:27; 10:44; Acts 1:1

FIRST-BORN Luke 2:7, she gave birth to her f son
Heb. 12:23, church of the f
Gen. 10:15; 19:37; 27:19; Ex. 11:5

FIRST FRUITS Ex. 23:16, the f of your labors
Rom. 8:23, the f of the Spirit
James 1:18, the f among His creatures
Rev. 14:4, f to God and to the Lamb

FISH Matt. 14:17, five loaves and two f
Luke 5:6, a great quantity of f
11:11, asked by his son for a f
Gen. 1:26; Num. 11:5; 2 Chr. 33:14; Is. 50:2; Jon. 1:17; John 21:10

FISHERMEN Is. 19:8; Jer. 16:16

FISHERS—*fishermen* Matt. 4:19, I will make you f of men
Mark 1:17, I will make you become f of men

FIT—*ready, prepare, worthy*
Matt. 3:11, not . . . f to remove His sandals
Luke 9:62, f for the kingdom of God
Eph. 2:21, whole building, being **f-ed** together
4:16, whole body, being **f-ed** and held together

FITTING—*opportune* Matt. 3:15, it is f for us to fulfill
Eph. 5:4, jesting, which are not f
Col. 3:18, as is f in the Lord

FIVE 1 Sam. 17:40, f smooth stones from the brook
Matt. 14:17, f loaves and two fish
25:2, f of them were foolish . . . f
25:20, who had received the f talents
Gen. 5:6; Ex. 22:1; Lev. 26:8; 2 Chr. 4:2; 2 Cor. 11:24; Rev. 17:10

FIXED Luke 16:26, there is a great chasm f

FLAG Is. 30:17, a f on a mountain top

FLAME—*fire* Is. 4:5, of a **f-ing** fire by night
Rev. 19:12, eyes *are* a f of fire
Gen. 3:24; Judg. 13:20; Ps. 106:18; Song 8:6; Is. 5:24; 10:17; Ezek. 20:47; Dan. 7:9; 10:6; Joel 2:5; Acts 7:30; 2 Thess. 1:7

FLASH Job 15:12, why do your eyes f
Acts 22:6, bright light suddenly **f-ed** from heaven
Deut. 32:41; Ezek. 1:13; 21:10; Nah. 3:3

FLASK—*vessel* Matt. 25:4, took oil in **f-s**
FLAT Josh. 6:5,20, wall fell down **f**
FLATTER Job 32:21, Nor **f** *any* man
Ps. 5:9, They **f** with their tongue
Prov. 7:21, **f-ing** lips she seduces him
1 Thess. 2:5, we never came with **f-ing** speech
FLAX Ex. 9:31; Judg. 15:14; Ezek. 40:3
FLEA 1 Sam. 24:14; 26:20
FLED—*escape* Matt. 26:56, left Him and **f**
Mark 16:8, **f** from the tomb
Rev. 20:11, whose presence earth and heaven **f**
Gen. 14:10; 31:21; 39:18; Is. 22:3
FLEE—*wander* Lev. 26:17, **f** when no one is pursuing
Ps. 11:1, **F** *as* a bird to your mountain
139:7, I **f** from Thy presence
Prov. 28:1, wicked **f** when no one
Is. 16:2, like **f-ing** birds
Matt. 3:7, **f** from the wrath to come
1 Tim. 6:11, But **f** from these things, you man
2 Tim. 2:22, **f** from youthful lusts
Gen. 16:8; Is. 30:16; Matt. 2:13; Rev. 9:6
FLEECE—*shear* Judg. 6:37; Job 31:20
FLESH—*body, meat, life*
Gen. 2:24, they shall become one **f**
Ps. 84:2, **f** sing for joy to the living God
136:25, Who gives food to all **f**
Is. 40:6, All **f** is grass
Matt. 16:17, because **f** and blood did not reveal
26:41, but the **f** is weak
Luke 24:39, spirit does not have **f** and bones
John 1:14, the Word became **f**
3:6, which is born of the **f** is **f**
Rom. 8:6, mind set on the **f** is death
2 Cor. 1:17, according to the **f** . . . should be
10:4, weapons . . . not of the **f**
Gal. 6:8, **f** shall from the **f** reap
Eph. 2:3, indulging the desires of the **f**
5:31, TWO SHALL BECOME ONE **F**
6:12, struggle is not against **f**
1 Pet. 2:11, abstain from **f-ly** lusts
Gen. 2:23; 7:21; 37:27; Num. 16:22; Job 19:26; 41:23; Ps. 16:9; Rom. 9:8; Jude 23; Rev. 19:21
FLIES—*fly* Job 20:8; Ps. 78:45; Prov. 23:5; Eccles. 10:1
FLIGHT Amos 2:14, **F** will perish from the swift
Matt. 24:20, your **f** may not be in the winter
Heb. 11:34, put foreign armies to **f**
FLINT—*stone* Zech. 7:12, hearts like **f** so
Ex. 4:25; Deut. 8:15; 32:13; Ps. 114:8; Is. 5:28; Ezek. 3:9
FLOCK—*fold, sheep* Gen. 4:2,4; 29:2; 30:31,38
Is. 40:11, Like a shepherd He will tend His **f**
Jer. 23:2, scattered My **f** and driven
Matt. 26:31, SHEEP OF THE **F** SHALL BE SCATTERED
Luke 2:8, keeping watch over their **f** by night
12:32, Do not be afraid, little **f**
John 10:16, become one **f** *with* one Shepherd
1 Pet. 5:2, the **f** of God among you
Ex. 2:16; 10:9; Judg. 5:16; 1 Sam. 16:19; 17:34; 2 Chr. 32:28; Ps. 77:20; Prov. 27:23; Is. 13:20; Ezek. 45:15; Amos 6:4; Hab. 3:17
FLOG Mark 13:9, you will be **f-ed**
FLOOD Gen. 7:17, **f** came upon the earth
Gen. 9:15, never . . . the water become a **f**
Matt. 7:25, **f-s** came, and the winds blew
Luke 17:27, **f** came and destroyed them all
Gen. 6:17; Dan. 9:26
FLOODGATES Gen. 7:11, **f** of the sky were opened
FLOOR Gen. 50:11; Ruth 3:3; 1 Kin. 6:30; 7:7; Joel 2:24; Matt. 3:12
FLOUR—*dough* Ex. 29:2; Lev. 2:1; Ezek. 16:13; Rev. 18:13
FLOURISH—*blossom, green*
Ps. 72:7, may the righteous **f**
92:7, all who did iniquity **f-ed**
103:15, a flower . . . so he **f-es**
Prov. 11:28, will **f** like the *green* leaf
Ezek. 17:24, make the dry tree **f**
FLOW—*gush* Ex. 3:8, land **f-ing** with milk and honey
John 7:38, shall **f** rivers of living water
Job 20:28; Ps. 147:18; Jer. 9:18; Joel 3:18; Mark 5:29
FLOWER Ps. 103:15, As a **f** of the field, so he
1 Pet. 1:24, AND THE **F** FALLS OFF
Job 14:2; Song 2:12; Is. 28:1
FLUENTLY—*well* Ex. 4:14, he speaks **f**
FLUSH Job 16:16, My face is **f-ed** from weeping
FLUTE 1 Sam. 10:5; 1 Kin. 1:40; 1 Cor. 14:7; Rev. 18:22
FLY Job 5:7, As sparks **f** upward
Gen. 1:20; Is. 14:29; Rev. 8:13; 12:14; 19:17
FOAL—*colt* Job 11:12; Zech. 9:9
FOE—*enemy*
1 Chr. 21:12, swept away before your **f-s**
FOLD—*flock* Eccles. 4:5, The fool **f-s** his hands
John 10:16, sheep, which are not of this **f**
Num. 32:24; Ps. 50:9; Prov. 6:10
FOLLOW—*cling, imitate, pursue* Gen. 24:5; 44:4; Ex. 11:8
Ruth 1:16, turn back from **f-ing** you
Ps. 23:6, goodness and lovingkindness will **f** me
Matt. 4:19, He said to them, **F** Me
4:20, left the nets, and **f-ed** Him
8:19, **f** You wherever You go
12:15, And many **f-ed** Him
16:24, take up his cross, and **f** Me
19:21, and come, **f** Me
Luke 22:39, disciples also **f-ed** Him
John 10:27, I know them, and they **f** Me
Jude 16, **f-ing** after their *own* lusts
Rev. 14:4, the ones who **f** the Lamb
Num. 15:39; 1 Sam. 12:14; Ps. 119:150; Jer. 48:2; Mark 5:37; 14:54; Luke 22:10; John 18:15; Acts 5:36; Rev. 14:13
FOLLY—*foolishness*
Prov. 14:18, The naive inherit **f**
15:2, mouth of fools spouts **f**
24:9, devising of **f** is sin
Judg. 19:23; Prov. 15:21
FOND—*greedy* 1 Tim. 3:8, or **f** of sordid gain
FONDLE Is. 66:12, **f-d** on the knees
FOOD—*bread, meat* Ps. 69:21, gall for my **f**
Ps. 136:25, Who gives **f** to all flesh
Matt. 6:25, Is not life more than **f**
John 4:34, My **f** is to do the will of Him
6:55, My flesh is true **f**
1 Cor. 6:13, **F** is for the stomach
James 2:15, in need of daily **f**
Gen. 1:29; 2:9; 3:6; 43:2; Lev. 3:11; Deut. 10:18; Ruth 1:6; Job 38:41; Ps. 78:25; 145:15; Prov. 6:8; 20:13; 23:3; 28:19; 30:8; Is. 65:25; Matt. 3:4; 1 Tim. 6:8
FOOL—*foolish, unwise* Ps. 14:1, The **f** has said in his
Prov. 1:7, **F-s** despise wisdom and instruction
15:5, A **f** rejects his father's discipline
26:3, a rod for the back of **f-s**
29:11, A **f** always loses his temper
Eccles. 10:14, the **f** multiplies words
Rom. 1:22, wise, they became **f-s**
1 Cor. 4:10, We are **f-s** for Christ's sake
1 Sam. 26:21; 2 Sam. 3:33; Prov. 24:7; Hos. 9:7; Matt. 5:22; 23:17
FOOLISH—*fool, boastful, folly, unwise*
Prov. 14:17, quick-tempered man acts **f-ly**
Luke 24:25, O **f** men and slow of heart
Rom. 1:14, the wise and to the **f**
1 Cor. 3:18, let him become **f**
Eph. 5:17, then do not be **f**
Gen. 31:28; Deut. 32:6; Job 5:3; Lam. 2:14; Matt. 25:8; 1 Pet. 2:15
FOOLISHNESS—*folly* Prov. 14:24; Is. 9:17; 2 Cor. 11:21
FOOT Prov. 25:17, **f** rarely be in your neighbor's house

FOOT *(Continued)*
Matt. 4:6, LEST YOU STRIKE YOUR **F**
Luke 4:11, STRIKE YOUR **F** AGAINST A STONE
Rev. 10:2, placed his right **f** on the sea
Gen. 8:9; 41:44; Deut. 2:28; 33:24; Num. 11:21; Josh. 14:9; 2 Sam. 8:4; 21:20; 1 Chr. 20:6; Ps. 26:12; 91:12; 121:3; Prov. 3:23; 25:19; Jer. 12:5; Matt. 22:13

FOOTSTOOL—*feet* 1 Chr. 28:2, for the **f** of our God
Ps. 99:5, And worship at His **f**
110:1, Thine enemies a **f**
132:7, Let us worship at His **f**
Is. 66:1, the earth is My **f**
James 2:3, or sit down by my **f**

FORBEARANCE Eph. 4:2, showing **f** to one another
Prov. 25:15; Rom. 3:25

FORBID—*hinder* 1 Cor. 14:39, do not **f** to speak in tongues
1 Tim. 4:3, *men* who **f** marriage *and*
Num. 30:5,8,11; Luke 23:2

FORCE—*compel* Matt. 5:41, **f** you to go one mile
Luke 3:14, Do not take money . . . by **f**
Gen. 31:31; 1 Sam. 2:16; Job 30:18; 36:19; Dan. 11:10; Matt. 11:12; Heb. 9:17

FOREHEAD 1 Sam. 17:49, stone sank into his **f**
Rev. 9:4, seal of God on their **f-s**
17:5, upon her **f** a name *was* written
Ex. 28:38; Lev. 13:42; Is. 48:4; Jer. 3:3; Ezek. 3:8; 9:4

FOREIGN—*strange* Gen. 35:2, Put away the **f** gods
Ex. 2:22, a sojourner in a **f** land
1 Kin. 11:1, Solomon loved many **f** women
Ezra 10:2, have married **f** women
Ps. 137:4, LORD's song in a **f** land
Heb. 11:34, put **f** armies to flight

FOREIGNER—*alien, sojourner*
Ruth 2:10, since I am a **f**
Prov. 5:20, embrace the bosom of a **f**
Deut. 14:21; 15:3; Job 19:15; Obad. 11

FOREMOST—*first*
Matt. 22:38, great and **f** commandment
Mark 12:28, commandment is the **f** of all
1 Tim. 1:15, among whom I am **f** *of all*

FOREST—*wood* Ps. 50:10, every beast of the **f** is Mine
James 3:5, how great a **f** is set aflame
1 Sam. 22:5; 2 Sam. 18:8; 1 Kin. 7:2; 1 Chr. 16:33; Ps. 83:14; Is. 10:18; 44:14; 56:9; Jer. 5:6; 21:14; Ezek. 15:2; Amos 3:4

FOREVER—*always, evermore, utmost* Gen. 3:22; 6:3
1 Chr. 17:14, throne shall be established **f**
Ps. 9:7, the LORD abides **f**
16:11, there are pleasures **f**
23:6, in the house of the LORD **f**
29:10, the LORD sits as King **f**
33:11, counsel of the LORD stands **f**
86:12, will glorify Thy name **f**
89:52, Blessed be the LORD **f**
92:8, O LORD, art on high **f**
102:12, Thou, O LORD, dost abide **f**
119:89, **F**, O LORD, Thy word is settled
121:8, LORD will guard your going out . . . **f**
133:3, the blessing . . . life **f**
Prov. 27:24, riches are not **f**
Eccles. 3:14, everything God does . . . **f**
Is. 40:8, word of our God stands **f**
57:15, exalted One Who lives **f**
57:16, For I will not contend **f**
John 6:51, eats of this bread, he shall live **f**
12:34, the Christ is to remain **f**
14:16, Helper, that he may be with you **f**
Rom. 9:5, God blessed **f**
2 Cor. 11:31, Lord Jesus, He who is blessed **f**
Eph. 3:21, all generations **f** and ever
Heb. 7:25, He is able to save **f**
7:28, a Son, made perfect **f**
13:8, today, *yes* and **f**
Ex. 14:13; Deut. 5:29; 12:28; 32:40; Ps. 12:7; 23:6; 61:4; 73:26; 77:8; 113:2; 115:18; 132:14; 146:6; Prov. 21:28; Is. 26:4; 34:10; Lam. 3:31

FOREVERMORE Rev. 1:18, I am alive **f**

FORFEIT Dan 1:10, make me **f** my head to the king

FORGAVE Ps. 78:38, **f** their iniquity, and
Matt. 18:27, and **f** him the debt
Luke 7:42, he graciously **f** them both
7:43, the one whom he **f** more

FORGET—*neglect, forsake*
Deut. 6:12, lest you **f** the LORD
Ps. 9:17, all the nations who **f** God
13:1, Wilt Thou **f** me forever
74:23, Do not **f** the voice of Thine
88:12, in the land of **f-fulness**
119:176, I do not **f** Thy commandments
Prov. 3:1, My son, do not **f** my teaching
Heb. 6:10, **f** your work and the love
Gen. 27:45; 41:51; Deut. 4:9; Prov. 4:5; 31:5; Is. 54:4; Jer. 2:32; 23:27

FORGIVE—*forgave, pardon*
Ps. 86:5, good, and ready to **f**
99:8, a **f-ing** God to them
Matt. 6:12, **f** us our debts, as we
6:14, if you **f** men for
6:15, if you do not **f** men
9:5, Your sins are **f-n**
9:6, on earth to **f** sins
Mark 2:7, who can **f** sins but God alone
11:26, if you do not **f**
Luke 7:47, sins . . . many, have been **f-n**
23:34, Father **f** them
2 Cor. 2:10, whom you **f** anything, I **f** also
Eph. 4:32, **f-ing** each other
Col. 2:13, **f-n** us all our transgressions
1 John 1:9, righteous to **f** us our sins
Gen. 50:17; Ex. 32:32; Num. 30:5; Ps. 25:18; 79:9; Jer. 18:23

FORGIVENESS—*pardon*
Neh. 9:17, art a God of **f**
Ps. 130:4, there is **f** with Thee
Matt. 26:28, for **f** of sins
Mark 1:4; Luke 24:47, repentance for the **f** of sins
3:29, Holy Spirit never has **f**
Acts 10:43, has received **f** of sins
13:38, through Him **f** of sins is proclaimed
26:18, they may receive **f** of sins
Eph. 1:7, the **f** of our trespasses
Col. 1:14, redemption, the **f** of sins
Heb. 9:22, shedding of blood . . . no **f**

FORGOT Deut. 32:18, **f** the God who gave you birth

FORGOTTEN—*neglect* Job 19:14, friends have **f** me
Ps. 9:18, needy will not always be **f**
Ezek. 23:35, Because you have **f** Me
Matt. 16:5, had **f** to take bread
Luke 12:6, is **f** before God
James 1:24, **f** what kind of person
Gen. 41:30; Job 28:4; Ps. 31:12; 77:9; Jer. 2:32; Lam. 2:6

FORK 1 Sam. 2:13; Matt. 3:12

FORM—*fashion* Ps. 95:5, His hands **f-ed** the dry land
Is. 53:2, no *stately* **f** or majesty
Mark 4:32, **f-s** large branches
16:12, He appeared in a different **f**
1 Cor. 7:31, the **f** of this world is passing
Gal. 4:19, until Christ is **f-ed** in you
2 Pet. 3:5, earth was **f-ed** out of water
Gen. 1:2; 2:7; Job 4:16; 33:6; Song 2:14; Is. 43:1; 44:13; 45:7; Amos 4:13; 7:1; Acts 17:29

FORMER—*past* 1 Pet. 1:14, conformed to the **f** lusts
Gen. 40:13; Deut. 4:32; 24:4; Ruth 4:7; Is. 42:9; 46:9; 65:16; Ezek. 16:55

FORNICATION—*immorality* Matt. 15:19; John 8:41

FORSAKE—*fail, leave, reject* Job 6:14; Ps. 27:9; 38:21
Josh. 1:5, not fail you or **f** you
2 Chr. 15:2, **f** Him, He will **f** you
Ezra 9:9, our God has not **f-n** us
Ps. 22:1, God, why hast Thou **f-n** me
27:10, father and my mother have **f-n** me
Prov. 1:8, do not **f** your mother's teaching
9:6, **F** *your* folly and live

Is. 53:3, despised and **f-n** of men
55:7, Let the wicked **f** his way
Matt. 27:46, God, why hast Thou f-n Me
2 Cor. 4:9, persecuted, but not **f**
Heb. 13:5, nor will I ever f you
Jer. 5:7; Ezek. 9:9; 20:8; Mark 15:34; 2 Pet. 2:15

FORSOOK—*left, deserted* Deut. 32:15; 1 Kin. 12:8; 2 Chr. 12:1

FORTIFICATION—*stronghold*
Is. 25:12, unassailable **f-s** of

FORTIFY—*strengthen* Num. 32:17; Deut. 3:5; Josh. 10:20; 1 Sam. 6:18; 2 Kin. 3:19; Is. 34:13; Jer. 5:17; 51:53

FORTRESS—*stronghold, power*
2 Sam. 22:2, my rock and my **f**
Ps. 91:2, My refuge and my **f**
2 Sam. 22:33; Ps. 18:2; Dan. 11:19

FORTY Gen. 7:4, the earth **f** days and **f** nights
Ex. 16:35, Israel ate the manna **f** years
Matt. 4:2, fasted **f** days and **f** nights
Gen. 7:17; Ex. 34:28; Num. 33:38; Ps. 95:10; Mark 1:13

FORWARD—*further*
2 Kin. 20:9, shadow go **f** ten steps
Job 23:8; Is. 41:21; Jer. 7:24; Ezek. 1:9; Acts 19:33

FOUGHT—*waged war* Num. 21:1, then he **f** against Israel
Judg. 5:20, stars **f** from heaven
2 Chr. 20:29, the Lord had **f** against
1 Cor. 15:32, I **f** with wild beasts
2 Tim. 4:7, I have **f** the good fight

FOUL Ezek. 32:2; 34:19

FOUND—*caught, proved*
Judg. 14:18, not have **f** out my riddle
Jer. 15:16, Thy words were **f** and I
Dan. 5:27, weighed on the scales and **f** deficient
Matt. 8:10, not **f** such great faith
10:39, He who has **f** his life shall
Mark 14:37, **f** them sleeping
Luke 2:46, they **f** Him in the temple
15:6, I have **f** my sheep
24:2, **f** the stone rolled away
John 1:41, We have **f** the Messiah
Acts 13:22, I have **f** David the son of
1 Cor. 15:15, we are even **f** *to be* false witnesses
Phil. 2:8, being **f** in appearance
Gen. 2:20; 6:8; Lev. 6:3; Deut. 17:2; Ruth 2:10,13; Job 28:12; Ps. 84:3; Prov. 25:16; Eccles. 7:29; Is. 51:3; Dan. 6:11; Mal. 2:6; Matt. 27:32; Mark 11:4; 14:40; Rev. 18:24

FOUNDATION—*habitation, founded* 2 Sam. 22:8; Job 4:19
Ps. 89:14; 97:2, Right and justice are the **f**
Matt. 13:35, since the f of the world
Luke 6:48, laid a **f** upon the rock
Rom. 15:20, upon another man's **f**
2 Tim. 2:19, the firm **f** of God stands
Heb. 1:10, didst lay the f of the earth
6:1, a **f** of repentance
Ps. 87:1; 104:5; Prov. 10:25; Is. 28:16

FOUNDED Ps. 24:2, He has **f** it upon the seas
Prov. 3:19, by wisdom **f** the earth
Matt. 7:25, **f** upon the rock
Ex. 9:18; Amos 9:6

FOUNTAIN—*spring, well* Gen. 7:11, **f-s** of the great deep
Ps. 36:9, with Thee is the **f** of life
Prov. 14:27, fear of the Lord is a **f** of life

FOUR Mark 13:27, from the f winds
Luke 19:8, give back **f** times as much
Gen. 2:10; Ex. 25:12; 2 Kin. 7:3; Is. 11:12; Matt. 15:38; John 11:39

FOURTEEN Gen. 31:41; 2 Chr. 13:21; 30:15; Is. 36:1; Matt. 1:17; Acts 27:27; 2 Cor. 12:2

FOURTH Gen. 1:19; Ex. 20:5; Judg. 19:5; Matt. 14:25; Rev. 6:7

FOWL—*bird* 1 Kin. 4:23; Ps. 148:10

FOX Judg. 15:4; Neh. 4:3; Song 2:15; Ezek. 13:4; Matt. 8:20; Luke 13:32

FRAGMENT—*piece*
John 6:12, Gather up the left-over **f-s**

FRAGRANCE 2 Cor. 2:15, we are a **f** of Christ
Song 1:3; 2:13

FRANKINCENSE Ex. 30:34; 1 Chr. 9:29; Song 4:6; Matt. 2:11

FRAUD—*mischief*
Acts 13:10, full of all deceit and **f**

FREE Matt. 10:8, **f-ly** you received, **f-ly** give
John 8:32, the truth shall make you **f**
Rom. 6:7, he who has died is **f-d**
6:22, now having been **f-d** from sin
8:2, **f** from the law
Gal. 5:1, that Christ set us **f**
Gen. 2:16; Deut. 15:8; Josh. 2:20; Ps. 110:3; Is. 58:6; Eph. 6:8; Rev. 19:18

FREEDOM—*liberty* 1 Pet. 2:16, use your **f** as a
Rom. 8:21; Gal. 5:13

FREEWILL Lev. 22:18; Ezra 7:16; Ps. 119:108

FREQUENT 1 Tim. 5:23, your **f** ailments

FRESH Prov. 5:15, **f** water from your own well
James 3:11, *both* **f** and bitter water
Job 33:25; Ps. 92:10; James 3:12

FRET Prov. 24:19, Do not **f** yourself because of

FRICTION—*dispute*
1 Tim. 6:5, constant **f** between men

FRIEND Prov. 17:17, A **f** loves at all times
Prov. 18:24, a **f** who sticks closer
Matt. 11:19, a **f** of tax-gatherers and sinners
John 15:13, lay down his life for his **f-s**
Gen. 38:12; Ex. 33:11; Judg. 14:20; Job 16:20; Ps. 38:11; Mic. 7:5; Matt. 20:13

FRIENDSHIP James 4:4, do you not know that **f**

FROGS Ex. 8:2; Ps. 78:45; 105:30; Rev. 16:13

FRONT Ex. 28:27, ephod, on the **f** of it

FROST—*ice* Gen. 31:40; Ex. 16:14; Ps. 78:47; Jer. 36:30

FRUIT—*labor, produce* Ps. 1:3, yields its **f** in its season
Prov. 11:30, **f** of the righteous
Matt. 3:8, Therefore bring forth **f**
7:16, know them by their **f-s**
John 4:36, **f** for life eternal
Rom. 7:4, bear **f** for God
Col. 1:10, bearing **f** in every good work
James 3:17, full of mercy and good **f-s**
Gen. 1:11; 3:6; Lev. 27:30; Ps. 92:14; 128:2; Song 4:16; Jer. 2:7; 6:19

FRUSTRATE Ezra 4:5; Job 5:12; Prov. 15:22; Is. 14:27

FUEL Is. 9:5,19; Ezek. 15:4; 21:32

FUGITIVE Judg. 12:4; Is. 15:5; 52:12

FULFILL—*complete*
Matt. 2:15, prophet might be **f-ed**
2:17, prophet was **f-ed** saying
3:15, fitting for us to **f** all righteousness
5:17, not come to abolish, but to **f**
Luke 22:16, it is **f-ed** in the kingdom
1 Cor. 7:3, husband **f** his duty to his wife
Gal. 6:2, **f** the law of Christ
2 Tim. 4:5, **f** your ministry
1 Chr. 17:11; 2 Chr. 36:21; Ps. 20:5; 148:8; Matt. 1:22

FULL—*complete, whole* 1 Chr. 21:24; Ps. 92:14; Prov. 4:18
Ps. 33:5, earth is **f** of the lovingkindness
Is. 11:9, will be **f** of knowledge
Matt. 6:2,5,16, have their reward in **f**
14:20, twelve **f** baskets
23:27, **f** of dead men's bones
Luke 4:1, **f** of the Holy Spirit
11:34, body also is **f** of light
John 1:14, **f** of grace and truth
Eph. 6:11, the **f** armor of God
James 5:11, the Lord is **f** of compassion
Acts 2:13; 1 Cor. 7:36; Col. 1:25

FULLER—*launderer* 2 Kin. 18:17; Mal. 3:2

FUNCTION Rom. 12:4, members do not have the same **f**
FURIOUS 2 Kin. 9:20; Dan. 2:12
FURNACE—*oven* Ps. 12:6; Is. 31:9; Dan. 3:6,15; Matt. 13:42; Rev. 1:15
FURNISH Deut. 15:14; Mark 14:15
FURNITURE Ex. 31:7, all the **f** of the tent
FURROWS Job 31:38; Ps. 65:10; 129:3
FURTHER Ex. 21:22; Num. 22:26; 1 Sam. 10:3; Matt. 26:65; Acts 24:4; Heb. 12:9
FURY—*displeasure* Gen. 27:44; Ps. 2:5; Ezek. 19:12; Heb. 10:27
FUTILE—*vain* 1 Sam. 12:21, **f** things . . . because they are **f**
Acts 4:25, PEOPLES DEVISE F THINGS
Rom. 1:21, **f** in their speculations
FUTILITY—*vanity*
Rom. 8:20, creation was subjected to **f**
Eph. 4:17, walk, in the **f** of their mind
FUTURE—*end, reward*
Prov. 24:20, no **f** for the evil man
Deut. 32:29; Jer. 31:17

G

GAIN—*price, profit* Prov. 10:2, Ill-gotten **g-s** do not
Matt. 16:26; Luke 9:25, if he **g-s** the whole world
Phil. 3:8, that I may **g** Christ
1 Tim. 6:5, godliness . . . means of **g**
1 Pet. 5:2, not for sordid **g**
1 Sam. 8:3; Prov. 3:14; Is. 33:15; Ezek. 22:12,27
GALE Mark 4:37, arose a fierce **g** of wind
GALL Ps. 69:21, Matt. 27:34; Acts 8:23
GALLERY Ezek. 41:15; 42:3
GALLOWS Esth. 5:14; 7:10; 9:25
GANGRENE 2 Tim. 2:17, will spread like **g**
GARDEN—*field* Gen. 3:8, God walking in the **g**
John 18:1, where there was a **g**
19:41, in the **g** a new tomb
Gen. 2:8; 3:10; Deut. 11:10; Lam. 2:6; Joel 2:3; John 18:26; 20:15
GARMENT—*clothing, dress* Gen. 41:42, in **g-s** . . . linen
Ex. 28:2, make holy **g-s** for Aaron
Ps. 22:18, divide my **g-s** among them
102:26, wear out like a **g**
Matt. 27:35, DIVIDED UP HIS G-S . . . CASTING
28:3, his **g** as white as snow
Luke 23:34, DIVIDING UP HIS G-S
Heb. 1:11, BECOME OLD AS A G
Gen. 3:21; 25:25; 38:14; 39:12; Ex. 19:10; Esth. 8:15; Is. 59:17; 63:1; Ezek. 27:24; Joel 2:13; Matt. 3:4; Mark 5:28; John 21:7; Acts 10:30
GARNER—*barn* Ps. 144:13, *Let* our **g-s** be full
GARRISON—*pillars* 1 Sam. 10:5; 14:12; 1 Chr. 18:13
GASH—*cut* Mark 5:5, **g-ing** himself
GATE Gen. 28:17, this is the **g** of heaven
Ps. 24:7, Lift your heads, O **g-s**
100:4, Enter His **g-s** with
Matt. 7:13, Enter by the narrow **g**
16:18, **g-s** of Hades shall not
Gen. 22:17; Judg. 16:3; Is. 38:10; Acts 12:14
GATHER—*assemble* Is. 40:11, His arm . . . **g** the lambs
John 4:36, **g-ing** fruit for life
6:12, **G** up the . . . fragments
Gen. 1:10; 31:46; 37:7; 41:35; Ps. 33:7; Is. 66:18; Matt. 26:3; Acts 19:40; Rev. 14:19
GAVE—*provide* Gen. 2:20, Adam **g** names to all
Gen. 3:12, Thou **g-st** to *be* with me
Ps. 69:21, they **g** me vinegar to drink
Eccles. 12:7, return to God who **g** it
Mark 8:6, He **g** thanks and broke them
John 3:16, He **g** His only begotten Son
13:26, morsel . . . He . . . **g** it to Judas
19:30, bowed . . . **g** up His spirit
Rom. 1:28, **g** them over to a depraved mind
1 Tim. 2:6, who **g** Himself as a ransom
Is. 50:6; Matt. 10:1; 26:48; Luke 7:44; Eph. 1:22
GAZE Ex. 19:21; Job 31:1
GENEALOGY—*descent* Heb. 7:3,6
GENERAL Heb. 12:23, to the **g** assembly and church
GENERATION—*ages* Deut. 1:35; Luke 21:32; Eph. 3:5
Ps. 90:1, dwelling place in all **g-s**
100:5, His faithfulness to all **g-s**
Matt. 1:17, to David are fourteen **g-s**
24:34, this **g** will not pass away
Luke 1:48, all **g-s** will count me blessed
Eph. 3:21, all **g-s** forever and ever
Phil. 2:15, a crooked and perverse **g**
GENEROUS—*bountiful* Prov. 22:9; Is. 32:5
GENTILE—*nations* Matt. 6:7, as the **G-s** do
Luke 2:32, LIGHT OF REVELATION TO THE G-S
Acts 4:25, WHY DID THE G-S RAGE
14:2, stirred the minds of the **G-s**
Rom. 11:11, salvation *has come* to the **G-s**
Gal. 1:16, I might preach Him among the **G-s**
GENTLE—*compassionate*
1 Kin. 19:12, sound of a **g** blowing
Prov. 15:1, **g** answer turns away wrath
Matt. 5:5, Blessed are the **g**
1 Cor. 4:21, with love and a spirit of **g-ness**
2 Cor. 10:1, **g-ness** of Christ
Gal. 5:23, **g-ness**, self-control
Eph. 4:2, with all humility and **g-ness**
1 Thess. 2:7, we proved to be **g** among you
1 Tim. 6:11, love, perseverance *and* **g-ness**
Titus 3:2, to be uncontentious, **g**
1 Pet. 3:4, a **g** and quiet spirit
Ps. 18:35; Matt. 21:5; 1 Tim. 3:3; Heb. 5:2; 1 Pet. 2:18
GESTURE—*motion*
John 13:24, Simon Peter therefore **g-d**
GET—*acquire, take* Gen. 34:4; Judg. 11:5; 14:2
Prov. 4:7, with all your acquiring, **g** understanding
Matt. 16:23, **G** behind Me, Satan
Luke 18:12, tithes of all that I **g**
1 Kin. 17:10; Job 9:18; Is. 30:11; 56:12; Jer. 36:21
GIANT—*Rephaim* 1 Chr. 20:6, he . . . was descended from **g-s**
GIFT Gen. 25:6, Abraham gave **g-s** while he was
Ps. 68:18, hast received **g-s** among men
127:3, children are a **g** of the LORD
Prov. 18:16, A man's **g** makes room for him
21:14, A **g** in secret subdues anger
Matt. 2:11, presented to Him **g-s**
John 4:10, you knew the **g** of God
Acts 2:38, the **g** of the Holy Spirit
Rom. 6:23, **g** of God is eternal life
James 1:17, every perfect **g** is from above
GIRD—*bound* Ex. 29:5; Job 38:3; Ps. 45:3; John 13:5
John 21:18, when you were younger . . . **g** . . . will **g** you
Eph. 6:14, G-ED YOUR LOINS WITH TRUTH
Rev. 1:13, **g-ed** across His breast with a golden
GIRDLE—*belt, waistband* 2 Kin. 1:8; Rev. 1:13; 15:6, golden **g**
Job 12:18, binds their loins with a **g**
GIRL—*maiden, woman* Gen. 24:55; 34:4; Joel 3:3; Zech. 8:5; Matt. 14:11; 26:69; Mark 6:28; John 18:17; Acts 12:13; 16:16
GIVE Num. 6:26, on you, And **g** you peace
Ps. 21:4, He asked life . . . Thou didst **g** it
Prov. 26:16, seven men . . . **g** a . . . answer
Is. 9:6, a son will be **g-n** to us
Matt. 6:11, **G** us this day our daily
10:8, freely **g**
15:36, **g-ing** thanks, He broke them
16:19, **g** you the keys
26:9, **g-n** to the poor
28:18, All authority has been **g-n** to Me
Luke 6:38, **G**, and it will be **g-n** to you
11:9, ask, and it shall be **g-n** to you
22:19, My body which is **g-n** for you

John 5:22, has **g-n** all judgment
6:11, and having **g-n** thanks
14:27, My peace I **g** to you
Acts 3:6, what I do have I **g** to you
12:23, he did not **g** God the glory
20:35, more blessed to **g** than to
Rom. 12:20, IF HE IS THIRSTY, G HIM A DRINK
14:6, he **g-s** thanks to God
1 Cor. 3:10, grace of God which was **g-n**
2 Cor. 12:7, was **g-n** me a thorn in
Eph. 4:27, do not **g** the devil an opportunity
5:20, always **g-ing** thanks
James 4:6, But He **g-s** a greater grace . . . **G-S GRACE**
1 John 5:11, has **g-n** us eternal life
Gen. 1:29; Ex. 20:12; Ps. 29:11; 68:11; 80:1; 145:15; Luke 1:77; 19:8; Rev. 19:8

GLAD Ps. 32:11, Be **g** in the LORD
Ps. 100:2, Serve the LORD with **g-ness**
122:1, I was **g** when they said to me
Prov. 10:1, wise son makes a father **g**
Matt. 5:12, Rejoice and be **g**
Luke 1:14, you will have joy and **g-ness**
6:23, Be **g** in that day, and leap
12:32, Father has chosen **g-ly** to give
Acts 2:46, **g-ness** and sincerity of heart
2 Cor. 11:19, bear with the foolish **g-ly**
Ex. 4:14; Num. 10:10; Deut. 28:47; 1 Chr. 16:31; Ps. 16:9; Is. 16:10

GLASS—*crystal* Job 28:17; Rev. 4:6

GLEAMING—*glitter*
Nah. 3:3, Swords flashing, spears **g**

GLEAN Lev. 19:10; Ruth 2:8,15,17; Is. 17:6; Jer. 49:9

GLISTEN Ps. 104:15, make his face **g** with oil

GLOOM Deut. 5:22; Job 3:5
Matt. 6:16, **g-y** face as the hypocrites *do*
Heb. 12:18, darkness and **g** and whirlwind

GLORIFY—*honor* Ps. 86:12, will **g** Thy name forever
Is. 66:5, Let the LORD be **g-ed**
Matt. 5:16, **g** your Father who is in heaven
John 12:28, Father **g** Thy name
13:31, is the Son of Man **g-ed**
16:14, He shall **g** Me
17:1, **g** Thy Son . . . **g** Thee
Acts 13:48, **g-ing** the word of the Lord
1 Cor. 6:20, **g** God in your body
Heb. 5:5, Christ did not **g** Himself

GLORIOUS—*exalt, glory, honor*
Neh. 9:5, Thy **g** name
Ps. 87:3, **G** things are spoken of you
1 Tim. 1:11, the **g** gospel of the blessed God

GLORY—*honor, splendor* Ex. 16:7, see . . . **g** of the Lord
Ps. 24:7, the King of **g** may come in
Prov. 16:31, gray head is a crown of **g**
Is. 6:3, earth is full of His **g**
66:19, heard . . . nor seen My **g** . . . **g** among the nations
Matt. 6:13, power, and the **g**
6:29, Solomon in all his **g** did not clothe
Luke 2:9, **g** of the Lord shone around
2:14, **G** to God in the highest
17:18, turned back to give **g** to God
John 5:44, you receive **g** from one another
9:24, Give **g** to God
Rom. 2:7, in doing good seek for **g** and honor
3:23, fall short of the **g** of God
2 Cor. 4:4, gospel of the **g** of Christ
Phil. 3:21, with the body of His **g**
Heb. 2:7, THOU HAST CROWNED HIM WITH G AND HONOR
Jude 25, through Jesus Christ . . . *be* **g**
Ex. 33:18; 1 Chr. 16:24; 29:11; Job 29:20; Ps. 105:3; Is. 35:2; Jer. 13:16; Ezek. 10:4; Hos. 4:7; John 8:50; James 1:9

GLUTTON Prov. 23:20; Matt. 11:19

GNASH—*grind* Ps. 35:16; 37:12; 112:10; Lam. 2:16; Matt. 8:12

GNAT Matt. 23:24, who strain out a **g**

GNAWED Rev. 16:10, they **g** their tongues

GO Ex. 14:15, Tell the sons of Israel to **g** forward
Ex. 23:23, My angel will **g** before you
33:14, My presence shall **g** with you
Ruth 1:16, where you **g**, I will **g**
Ps. 139:7, Where can I **g** from
Matt. 5:41, force you to **g** one mile, **g** . . . two
6:6, when you pray, **G INTO YOUR INNER ROOM**
Luke 10:37, **G** and do the same
John 14:12, I **g** to the Father
Gen. 12:1; 32:26; Deut. 17:8; 23:23; Job 23:8; Ps. 42:4; Prov. 22:6; Hos. 2:7; Mic. 2:11; Matt. 21:29

GOAD Judg. 3:31; 1 Sam. 13:20,21
Eccles. 12:11, words of wise men are like **g-s**

GOAL Phil. 3:14, press on toward the **g**
1 Tim. 1:5, **g** of our instruction is love

GOAT Ex. 26:7; Lev. 3:12; Num. 15:27; 1 Sam. 19:13; Dan. 8:5; Matt. 25:32; Heb. 9:13

GODDESS 1 Kin. 11:5; Acts 19:27,37

GOD-FEARING Acts 10:22, Cornelius . . . a righteous and **G** man
Acts 17:17, reasoning . . . with the Jews and **G** *Gentiles*

GODLESS Job 8:13, hope of the **g** will perish
Job 15:34, company of the **g** is barren
Is. 9:17, every one is **g**
Acts 2:23, hands of **g** men and put Him to death

GODLINESS 1 Tim. 2:2, in all **g** and dignity
1 Tim. 3:16, great is the mystery of **g**
4:8, but **g** is profitable
6:6, **g** *actually* is a means . . . contentment
2 Tim. 3:5, holding to a form of **g**
2 Pet. 1:7, **g**, brotherly kindness

GODLY 1 Sam. 2:9, keeps the feet of His **g** ones
Ps. 12:1, for the **g** man ceaseth
37:28, not forsake His **g** ones
2 Cor. 1:12, in holiness and **g** sincerity
2 Pet. 2:9, rescue the **g** from temptation

GODS Ex. 20:3, have no other **g** before Me
Judg. 5:8, New **g** were chosen
Is. 37:12, **g** of those nations . . . deliver
Jer. 22:9, bowed down to other **g**
Dan. 2:47, your God is a God of **g**
Gal. 4:8, by nature are no **g**

GOING Ps. 121:8, guard your **g** out
Is. 20:2, **g** naked and barefoot
Matt. 25:8, our lamps are **g** out
Mark 1:16, He was **g** along by the sea of Galilee
10:32, road, **g** up to Jerusalem
John 14:5, not know where You are **g**
Gen. 15:12; Mic. 5:2; Matt. 26:46

GOLD Job 22:25, The Almighty will be your **g**
Ps. 19:10, more desirable than **g** . . . much fine **g**
Prov. 8:19, **g**, even pure **g**
Matt. 2:11, to Him gifts of **g**
Acts 3:6, Peter said . . . not possess silver and **g**
20:33, coveted no one's silver or **g**
1 Pet. 1:7, more precious than **g**
Rev. 3:18, buy from Me **g** refined
Gen. 2:12; 24:22; Ex. 3:22; Job 31:24; Ps. 72:15; Prov. 16:16; 25:11; Lam. 4:1; Zech. 9:3; Matt. 10:9; James 2:2; Rev. 21:15

GOLDEN Job 37:22, Out of the north comes **g** *splendor*
Lev. 8:9; 1 Sam. 6:18; Dan. 3:5; Rev. 1:12

GOLDSMITH Neh. 3:31,32; Is. 40:19; 46:6

GONE Judg. 19:11, the day was almost **g**
Ps. 19:4, line has **g** out through
Prov. 7:19, **g** on a long journey
Hos. 4:18, Their liquor **g**
Mark 5:30, power . . . had **g** forth
Rom. 13:12, The night is almost **g**
2 Pet. 2:15, they have **g** astray
Gen. 31:30; Song 2:11; Lam. 1:3

GOOD Gen. 1:4, that the light was **g**
Gen. 50:20, God meant it for **g**
2 Chr. 6:41, godly ones rejoice in what is **g**

GOOD *(Continued)*
Esth. 10:3, sought the **g** of his people
Ps. 106:1; 136:1, give thanks . . . for He is **g**
Prov. 22:1, A **g** name . . . more desired
Is. 1:17, Learn to do **g**
Jer. 33:11, For the LORD is **g**, For His lovingkindness
Jon. 4:4, Do you have **g** reason
Matt. 3:10, does not bear **g** fruit
19:16, what **g** thing shall I do
Mark 9:50, Salt is **g**, but if the salt
Luke 1:19, to bring you this **g** news
6:27, do **g** to those who hate you
10:42; Mary has chosen the **g** part
John 10:14, I am the **g** shepherd
Acts 23:1, lived my life . . . **g** conscience
Rom. 2:7, perseverance in doing **g**
2:10, every man who does **g**
12:21, overcome evil with **g**
Gal. 6:10, do **g** to all men
Phil. 4:8, whatever is of **g** repute
1 Tim. 6:12, Fight the **g** fight of faith
1 Pet. 3:11, TURN . . . FROM EVIL AND DO G
Gen. 15:15; Lev. 27:10; Job 7:7; Prov. 25:25; Is. 39:8; Jer. 24:3; Amos 5:14; Matt. 25:23; Luke 18:19; Acts 6:3; Gal. 6:12; 2 Thess. 2:16; James 1:17

GOODNESS Ex. 33:19; 2 Sam. 2:6; Ps. 25:7
Ps. 23:6, Surely **g** and lovingkindness will follow
31:19, How great is Thy **g**
Gal. 5:22, kindness, **g**, faithfulness
2 Thess. 1:11, fulfill every desire for **g**

GOODS—*possessions* Gen. 14:21; Ezek. 38:12; Luke 12:19

GORGEOUS Luke 23:11, dressed Him in a **g** robe

GOSPEL Matt. 4:23, the **g** of the kingdom
Matt. 11:5, HAVE THE G PREACHED
Mark 16:15, preach the **g** to all
Luke 4:18, PREACH THE G TO THE POOR
Rom. 1:16, I am not ashamed of the **g**
2 Cor. 10:14, in the **g** of Christ
11:4, or a different **g**
Gal. 1:7, distort the **g** of Christ
Eph. 1:13, **g** of your salvation
6:15, G OF PEACE
Phil. 1:5, participation in the **g**
Col. 1:23, from the hope of the **g**
Rev. 14:6, an eternal **g**

GOSSIP Rom. 1:29, malice; *they are* **g-s**
2 Cor. 12:20, **g**, arrogance, disturbances

GOVERN—*rule* Gen. 1:16, to **g** the day . . . **g** the night

GOVERNMENT—*authority* Is. 9:6, **g** will rest on His

GOVERNOR—*commander*
Matt. 27:11; Acts 7:10

GRACE—*favor* Ps. 45:2; 2 Thess. 2:16
Luke 2:40, the **g** of God was upon Him
John 1:16, received, and **g** upon **g**
Rom. 1:5, through whom we have received **g**
5:2, this **g** in which we stand
16:20, The **g** of our Lord Jesus be with you
2 Cor. 9:8, make all **g** abound
12:9, My **g** is sufficient
1 Thess. 1:1, **G** to you and peace
Philem. 25, **g** of the Lord Jesus Christ
Heb. 4:16, the throne of **g** . . . may find **g**
James 4:6, GIVES G TO THE HUMBLE
2 Pet. 3:18, grow in the **g**

GRACIOUS—*kind* Neh. 9:31, art a **g** and compassionate God
Ps. 6:2, Be **g** to me, O LORD
111:4, LORD is **g** and compassionate
Luke 4:22, wondering at the **g** words
Gen. 43:29; Ex. 33:19; Ps. 77:9; 112:4; 119:29; Prov. 19:17, 26:25; Amos 5:15

GRAFT Rom. 11:23, God is able to **g** them in
Rom. 11:24, **g-ed** contrary to nature . . . branches be **g-ed**

GRAIN—*kernel* John 12:24, unless a **g** of wheat falls
1 Cor. 15:37, a bare **g**, perhaps of wheat
Gen. 41:5; Lev. 2:14; 2 Sam. 17:19; 2 Kin. 4:42; Jer. 23:28; Amos 9:9; Matt. 12:1; Mark 4:28

GRANDCHILDREN Prov. 17:6, **G** . . . crown of old men

GRANDMOTHER 2 Tim. 1:5, in your **g** Lois

GRANT—*give, provide*
Job 10:12, Thou hast **g-ed** me life
Ps. 85:7, **g** us Thy salvation
Prov. 10:24, of the righteous will be **g-ed**
Mark 10:37, **G** that we may sit
Rev. 3:21, He who overcomes, I will **g** . . . to sit
Is. 63:7; Luke 22:29

GRAPE Num. 6:3; Deut. 32:14; Jer. 49:9; Matt. 7:16; Luke 6:44

GRASS—*vegetation*
Ps. 103:15, man, his days are like **g**
Is. 40:6, All flesh is **g**
40:7, the **g** withers, the flower
Matt. 6:30, if God so arrays the **g** of the field
1 Pet. 1:24, ALL FLESH IS LIKE G
Num. 22:4; 2 Sam. 23:4; 2 Kin. 19:26; Ps. 102:11; Prov. 27:25; Is. 5:24; 15:6; 37:27; Dan. 5:21

GRASSHOPPER—*caterpillar*
Num. 13:33, we became like **g-s**
Lev. 11:22; 2 Chr. 6:28; Is. 40:22

GRATITUDE 1 Tim. 4:4, is received with **g**

GRAVE—*tomb* Gen. 35:20; 2 Sam. 3:32; Ps. 5:9; Ezek. 37:12; Nah. 1:14

GRAY Gen. 42:38, bring my **g** hair down . . . in sorrow
1 Sam. 12:2, I am old and **g**
Deut. 32:25; Job 15:10; Ps. 71:18; Hos. 7:9

GRAZE—*feed* Is. 5:17; 11:7; 27:10; 65:25

GREAT—*excellent, big* Gen. 12:2; 15:1; Ex. 18:11; 32:30
Gen. 1:16, two **g** lights; the **g-er** light
Ps. 48:1, **G** is the LORD
Mal. 4:5, the **g** and terrible day
Matt. 2:10, rejoiced exceedingly, with **g** joy
4:16, DARKNESS SAW A G LIGHT
5:12, your reward in heaven is **g**
7:27, **g** was its fall
11:11, he who is least . . . is **g-er** than he
Luke 2:10, good news of a **g** joy
6:23, your reward is **g** in heaven
John 5:20, **g-er** works than these
15:13, **G-er** love has no one
1 Cor. 13:13, **g-est** of these is love
1 Tim. 6:6, godliness . . . a means of **g** gain
Jude 24, stand in the presence . . . **g** joy
Rev. 8:10, a **g** star fell from heaven
15:3, G AND MARVELOUS ARE THY WORKS
Deut. 1:17; 2 Sam. 5:10; 19:32; 1 Chr. 16:25; Neh. 9:27; Job 31:25; Ps. 57:10; Prov. 15:16; Jer. 9:19; Dan. 4:22; Zeph. 1:14; Matt. 15:28; Luke 5:6; Acts 11:5; 2 Cor. 3:12

GREATLY—*utterly*
Gen. 20:8, men were **g** frightened
John 3:29, rejoices **g** because of the
Phil. 4:10, I rejoiced in the Lord **g**
Gen. 3:16; Num. 14:39; 1 Sam. 28:5; Ps. 89:7; Zech. 9:9; Mark 12:27

GREATNESS—*magnitude* Ps. 51:1, **g** of Thy compassion
Luke 9:43, the **g** of God
2 Cor. 4:7, the surpassing **g** of the power
Eph. 1:19, surpassing **g** of His power toward us
1 Chr. 29:11; Neh. 13:22; Ps. 150:2; Is. 63:1

GREED Is. 56:11, the dogs are **g-y**
Luke 12:15, Beware . . . every form of **g**
1 Thess. 2:5, a pretext for **g**

GREEK Acts 16:1; 21:37; Rom. 2:9; 1 Cor. 12:13; Gal. 3:28; Rev. 9:11

GREEN—*luxuriant*
Ps. 23:2, lie down in **g** pastures
Gen. 1:30; Ps. 92:14; Jer. 17:2; Ezek. 17:24; Luke 23:31

H

HAND *(Continued)*
2 Cor. 5:1, a house not made with **h-s**
Heb. 10:31, fall into the **h-s** of the living God
James 4:8, Cleanse your **h-s**
1 Pet. 4:7, end of all things is at **h**
1 John 1:1, our **h-s** handled
Gen. 3:22; 16:12; 24:2; 47:29; Ex. 21:24; 33:22; Deut. 8:17; 19:21; 33:3; 1 Sam. 5:11; 12:3; 26:18; 2 Sam. 24:14; 1 Kin. 18:44; 2 Kin. 5:11; 1 Chr. 21:13; 29:14; Ezra 7:9; Neh. 2:8,18; Job 12:10; 19:21; 40:14; Ps. 68:31; 80:17; 139:10; Prov. 3:16; 10:4; 12:24; 19:24; 26:15; Eccles. 2:24; Is. 5:25; 9:12; 10:4; 14:27; 53:10; 56:2; Ezek. 7:17; 21:7; Dan. 4:35; Mic. 7:3; Hab. 2:9; Zeph. 3:16; Matt. 3:12; 6:3; 18:8; Mark 9:43; 14:41; Luke 3:17; 9:44; John 20:27; 1 Cor. 12:15; Col. 2:11; 1 Thess. 4:11; 1 Tim. 2:8

HANDBREADTH Ex. 25:25; 1 Kin. 7:26; 2 Chr. 4:5; Ezek. 40:5
Ps. 39:5, Thou hast made my days *as* **h-s**

HANDFUL—*hand* Lev. 2:2; 5:12; 1 Kin. 20:10
1 Kin. 17:12, only a **h** of flour in the bowl

HANDKERCHIEF Acts 19:12, **h-s** . . . carried from his body

HANDLE—*touch* Song 5:5; Jer. 2:8; Ezek. 27:29
2 Tim. 2:15, **h-ing** accurately the word of truth
1 John 1:1, our hands **h-d**, concerning the Word of Life

HANDMAID—*servant, slave* Ps. 86:16; 116:16

HANDSOME—*becoming* 1 Sam. 16:18, and a **h** man

HANG Deut. 21:23, who is **h-ed** is accursed of God
Job 26:7, He . . . **h-s** the earth on nothing
Matt. 27:5, Judas went away and **h-ed** himself
Gal. 3:13, CURSED IS EVERY ONE WHO H-S

HAPPEN—*befall* Lev. 10:19; Deut. 22:6; Judg. 6:13; Dan. 10:14

HAPPINESS—*joy* Deut. 24:5, shall give **h** to his wife
Eccles. 9:7, eat your bread in **h**

HAPPY—*bless* Job 5:17, **h** is the man whom God reproves
Prov. 14:21, **h** is he who is gracious to the poor
Rom. 14:22, **H** is he who does not condemn himself

HARASS Deut. 2:9, Do not **h** Moab

HARBOR—*haven* Acts 27:12, **h** was not suitable

HARD—*difficult, firm* Ex. 1:14; Num. 11:11; Deut. 1:17
Matt. 19:23, is **h** for a rich man to enter . . . heaven
25:24, I knew you to be a **h** man
Mark 10:24, **h** it is to enter the Kingdom of God
Acts 26:14, **h** for you to kick against the goads
2 Tim. 2:3, Suffer **h-ship** . . . as a good soldier
Deut. 15:18; 2 Kin. 2:10; Job 38:30; 41:24; Prov. 13:15; 18:19; Is. 8:21; Mark 10:23; Luke 18:24

HARDEN—*hardness* Job 38:38; Prov. 29:1
John 12:40, HE H-ED THEIR HEART
Rom. 9:18, He **h-s** whom He desires
Heb. 3:13, **h-ed** by deceitfulness of sin
3:15; 4:7, Do NOT H YOUR HEARTS

HARDNESS—*stubborn* Matt. 19:8; Mark 10:5, **h** of heart
Mark 3:5, grieved at their **h** of heart
16:14, He reproached . . . **h** of heart

HARLOT Matt. 21:31, **h-s** will get into the kingdom
Luke 15:30, devoured your wealth with **h-s**
Josh. 6:17; Prov. 7:10; 29:3; Is. 1:21; 23:17; Jer. 2:20; Ezek. 16:15; Joel 3:3; Rev. 17:5

HARM—*evil, hurt* Lev. 19:27; Judg. 15:3; 2 Kin. 4:41
1 Chr. 16:22; Ps. 105:15, do my prophets no **h**
Prov. 12:21, No **h** befalls the righteous
1 Pet. 3:13, who is there to **h** you
Prov. 3:30; Jer. 25:6; Acts 16:28; 28:5; Rev. 6:6

HARMONY 2 Cor. 6:15, what **h** has Christ with

HARNESS—*armor* Jer. 46:4, **H** the horses

HARP—*lyre, instrument* 1 Sam. 16:16; Ps. 33:2; 49:4; 57:8
Job 30:31, my **h** is turned to mourning
Ps. 137:2, Upon the willows . . . hung our **h-s**
Is. 5:12; 24:8; Amos 6:5; 1 Cor. 14:7; Rev. 5:8; 14:2

HARROW—*instrument* Job 39:10, will he **h** the valleys

HARRY Job 18:11, terrors . . . **h** him at every step

HARSH 1 Sam. 20:10, father answers you **h-ly**
Gen. 16:6; 1 Sam. 25:3; Prov. 15:1

HARVEST—*reap, ripe*
Gen. 8:22, Seedtime and **h** . . . cease
Job 4:8, who sow trouble **h** it
Jer. 8:20, **h** is past, summer is ended
Joel 3:13, the **h** is ripe
Matt. 9:37, **h** is plentiful
9:38; Luke 10:2, the Lord of the **h**
13:30, both to grow together until the **h**
13:39, **h** is the end of the age
Mark 4:29, puts in the sickle . . ., **h** has come
John 4:35, fields, that they are white for **h**
Rev. 14:15, the **h** of the earth is ripe
Ex. 22:29; 23:16; 34:22; Lev. 19:9; Deut. 24:19; 1 Sam. 12:17; Job 5:5; Prov. 6:8; 10:5; 25:13; 26:1; Is. 9:3; 16:9; 18:4; Jer. 5:17; 51:33

HASTE—*hurry, urgent*
Prov. 7:23, As a bird **h-ns** . . . snare
Prov. 28:22, evil eye **h-ns** after wealth
2 Pet. 3:12, **h-ning** the coming of the day of God
Ex. 12:11; Ps. 22:19; Eccles. 1:5; Is. 52:12; Mark 6:25

HASTILY—*hurried* Prov. 25:8, Do not go out **h** to argue
1 Tim. 5:22, lay hands upon any one *too* **h**

HASTY—*impetuous* Prov. 29:20, a man who is **h**
Eccles. 5:2, Do not be **h** in word

HATCH Jer. 17:11, As a partridge that **h-es** eggs

HATCHET—*axe, war-club* Ps. 74:6, smash with **h** and hammers

HATE Ps. 81:15, Those who **h** the LORD
Ps. 97:10, **H** evil, you who love the LORD
Prov. 6:16, six things which the LORD **h-s**
8:13, fear of the LORD is to **h** evil
13:24, who spares his rod **h-s** his son
15:10, He who **h-s** reproof will die
Eccles. 3:8, A time to love, and a time to **h**
Matt. 6:24, he will **h** the one and love the other
10:22, Mark 13:13; Luke 21:17, will be **h-d**
Luke 6:22, Blessed are you when men **h** you
6:27, do good to those who **h** you
14:26, not **h** his own father and mother
John 3:20, does evil **h-s** the light
12:25, he who **h-s** his life
15:18; 1 John 3:13, If the world **h-s** you
15:23, He who **h-s** Me **h-s** My Father also
Rom. 1:30, slanderers, **h-rs** of God
7:15, I am doing the very thing I **h**
Eph. 5:29, no one ever **h-d** his own flesh
Titus 3:3, hateful, **h-ing** one another
1 John 2:9; 3:15; 4:20, **h-s** his brother
Gen. 24:60; Lev. 19:17; 26:17; 1 Kin. 22:8; 2 Chr. 18:7; 19:2; Ps. 34:21; 36:2; 139:21; Prov. 1:22; Is. 1:14; 61:8; Ezek. 23:29; Amos 5:15; Mic. 3:2; Zech. 8:17; Mal. 1:3; John 7:7; Rom. 9:13

HAUGHTY—*proud, lofty, high*
Ps. 131:1, nor my eyes **h**
Prov. 16:18, **h** spirit before stumbling
Rom. 12:16, do not be **h** in mind
2 Sam. 22:28; Prov. 6:17; 21:24; Zeph. 3:11

HAUNT—*habitation* Is. 34:13, also be a **h** of jackals

HAVEN—*harbor* Gen. 49:13; Ps. 107:30

HAWK Lev. 11:16; Deut. 14:15; Job 39:26

HEAD—*chief* 2 Kin. 6:5, axe **h** fell into the water
Ps. 24:7, Lift up your **h-s**, O gates
Prov. 25:22, burning coals on his **h**
Eccles. 2:14, wise man's eyes are in his **h**
Matt. 14:8, Give me . . . **h** of John the Baptist
27:39, WAGGING THEIR H-S
Luke 21:18, not a hair of your **h** will perish
21:28, straighten up and lift up your **h-s**
John 13:9, also my hands and my **h**
1 Cor. 11:3, Christ is the **h** of every man

Eph. 1:22, Him as **h** over all things
5:23, Christ also is the **h** of the church
Col. 2:19, not holding fast to the **H**
Rev. 1:14, His **h** and His hair were white
Gen. 3:15; 1 Sam. 1:11; 9:22; 2 Kin. 4:19; Ps. 66:12; Is. 3:16; 59:17; Jer. 18:16; Dan. 2:38; 7:6; Matt. 5:36; 6:17; Acts 21:24

HEAL 2 Chr. 7:14, and will **h** their land
Ps. 147:3, He **h-s** the broken-hearted
Prov. 3:8, will be **h-ing** to your body
Is. 53:5, by His scourging we are **h-ed**
Jer. 3:22, I will **h** your faithlessness
Hos. 14:4, I will **h** their apostasy
Matt. 10:8, **H** *the* sick, raise *the* dead
Mark 3:2, He would **h** him on the Sabbath
Luke 4:23, Physician, **h** yourself
9:2, kingdom of God, and to perform **h-ing**
9:11, those who had need of **h-ing**
Acts 9:34, Jesus Christ **h-s** you
1 Cor. 12:9, gifts of **h-ing** by the one Spirit
James 5:16, pray . . . that you may be **h-ed**
Rev. 22:2, the **h-ing** of the nations
Ex. 15:26; Num. 12:13; Deut. 32:39; Job 5:18; Ps. 6:2; Prov. 13:17; Jer. 17:14; 30:13; Matt. 4:23

HEALTH Jer. 30:17, will restore you to **h**
3 John 2, prosper and be in good **h**

HEAP—*store* Prov. 25:22, **h** burning coals on his head
Is. 25:2, made a city into a **h**
Gen. 31:46; Ex. 15:8; Deut. 32:23; Josh. 3:13; Ps. 33:7; Ezek. 24:10; Hab. 1:10

HEAR Job 27:9, Will God **h** his cry
Ps. 4:1, O God . . . **h** my prayer
135:17, have ears, but they do not **h**
Is. 28:14, **h** the word of the LORD
Ezek. 37:4, dry bones, **h** the word of the LORD
Matt. 11:15, ears to **h**, let him **h**
13:13, while **h-ing** they do not **h**
15:10, **H** and understand
17:5, I am well pleased; **h** Him
Mark 7:37, He makes even the deaf to **h**
John 5:24, he who **h-s** My word
10:3, the sheep **h** his voice
12:47, if any one **h-s** My sayings
Acts 17:32, We shall **h** you again
James 1:19, let every one be quick to **h**
Rev. 3:20, if any one **h-s** My voice
Lev. 5:1; Deut. 6:4; 1 Sam. 15:14; 1 Kin. 8:30; Job 15:8; 26:14; Ps. 38:13; 65:2; Is. 1:2; Matt. 10:27; Rom. 11:8

HEARD Matt. 2:18, A VOICE WAS H IN RAMAH
Acts 4:4, who had **h** the message believed
19:10, lived in Asia **h** the word
1 Cor. 2:9, EYE HAS NOT SEEN AND EAR HAS NOT H
2 Cor. 12:4, **h** inexpressible words
Phil. 4:9, learned and received and **h**
Rev. 10:4, I **h** a voice from heaven
Gen. 3:10; Ps. 10:17; Eccles. 12:13; Song 2:12; Is. 65:19; Jer. 31:15; Ezek. 1:24; Matt. 6:7; Luke 1:13

HEARING—*ears* Prov. 20:12, The **h** ear
Prov. 23:9, Do not speak in the **h** of a fool
Matt. 24:6, you will be **h** of wars
Rom. 10:17, So faith *comes* from **h**
Heb. 5:11, since you have become dull of **h**

HEART—*desire, mind*
Gen. 8:21, intent of man's **h** is evil
1 Sam. 16:7, LORD looks at the **h**
1 Kin. 3:9, an understanding **h**
15:3, his **h** was not wholly devoted
1 Chr. 28:9, serve Him with a whole **h**
Ps. 19:14, the meditation of my **h**
44:21, He knows the secrets of the **h**
51:10, Create in me a clean **h**
51:17, broken and contrite **h**
119:11, Thy word I have treasured in my **h**
Prov. 4:23, Watch . . . **h** with all diligence
17:22, joyful **h** is good medicine
25:20, sings songs to a troubled **h**
Jer. 17:9, **h** is more deceitful than all else
17:10, I, the LORD search the **h**
Matt. 5:8, Blessed are the pure in **h**
5:28, committed adultery . . . in his **h**
6:21, treasure is, there will your **h** be
11:29, I am gentle and humble in **h**
15:8, THEIR H IS FAR AWAY FROM ME
19:8, Because of your hardness of **h**
Mark 12:30, LOVE THE LORD . . . YOUR H
Luke 2:19, pondering them in her **h**
2:51, treasured all *these* things in her **h**
24:25, slow of **h** to believe
John 14:1, Let not your **h** be troubled
Acts 2:37, they were pierced to the **h**
Rom. 8:27, He who searches the **h-s** knows
10:10, for with the **h** man believes
Eph. 3:17, Christ may dwell in your **h-s**
5:19, making melody with your **h**
6:5, in the sincerity of your **h**
Phil. 4:7, guard your **h-s** and your minds
Col. 3:22, but with sincerity of **h**
2 Thess. 3:5, Lord direct your **h-s** into
Heb. 4:12, thoughts and intentions of the **h**
10:22, draw near with a sincere **h**
James 1:26, deceives his *own* **h**
2 Pet. 1:19, morning star arises in your **h-s**
Ex. 4:21; 31:6; Num. 15:39; Deut. 28:65; Josh. 5:1; Judg. 5:16; 1 Sam. 10:9; 13:14; 2 Sam. 6:16; 2 Chr. 15:15; Job 23:16; 29:13; 41:24; Ps. 4:7; 9:1; 12:2; 15:2; 17:3; 22:14; 27:3; 38:10; 111:1; Prov. 12:20; 16:5; 23:7,26; Eccles. 8:5; 11:9; Song 8:6; Is. 35:4; 47:10; Jer. 11:20; 24:7; Ezek. 11:19; 18:31; 21:7; 44:7,9; Joel 2:13; Mal. 4:6; Matt. 12:34; 2 Cor. 3:3; 6:11; 9:7

HEAT—*outburst* Gen. 8:22; 18:1; Job 24:19; Is. 25:4
2 Pet. 3:10, be destroyed with intense **h**
Rev. 16:9, men were scorched with fierce **h**
Jer. 2:24; Hos. 7:4; Matt. 20:12

HEAVEN—*sky* Gen. 1:1, God created the **h-s**
Gen. 1:8, God called the expanse **h**
28:17, this is the gate of **h**
Ps. 19:1, **h-s** are telling . . . glory of God
103:11, high as the **h-s** are above the earth
Is. 65:17, new **h-s** and a new earth
Mal. 3:10, open for you the windows of **h**
Matt. 3:2, Repent . . . kingdom of **h** is
3:17, behold, a voice out of the **h-s**
5:3, Blessed . . . theirs is the kingdom of **h**
5:12, your reward in **h** is great
6:9, Our Father who art in **h**
6:10, On earth as it is in **h**
6:14, your **h-ly** Father will also forgive
10:7, kingdom of **h** is at hand
16:19, keys of the kingdom of **h**
Mark 13:31, **H** and earth will pass away
Luke 10:20, your names are recorded in **h**
15:18, have sinned against **h**
John 3:13, from **h**, *even* the Son of Man
1 Cor. 15:40, are also **h-ly** bodies
15:47, second man is from **h**
2 Cor. 5:1, eternal in the **h-s**
12:2, was caught up to the third **h**
Gal. 1:8, or an angel from **h**, should preach
Eph. 6:9, their Master and yours is in **h**
Phil. 3:20, our citizenship is in **h**
Heb. 11:12, AS THE STARS OF H
12:23, who are enrolled in **h**
James 5:12, do not swear, either by **h**
Rev. 4:1, a door *standing* open in **h**
21:1, I saw a new **h**
Ex. 20:22; Deut. 33:13; 1 Sam. 2:10; 1 Kin. 8:27; 2 Kin. 7:2; Job 11:8; 22:12,14; Eccles. 5:2; Is. 14:12; Jer. 7:18; 23:24; Ezek. 32:8; John 3:12; 1 Cor. 15:48

HEAVY Matt. 11:28, who are weary and **h** laden
Matt. 26:43, their eyes were **h**
Ex. 17:12; 2 Chr. 10:10,11; Ps. 38:4; Prov. 27:3; Zech. 12:3; Matt. 23:4

HEDGE Luke 14:23, highways and along the **h-s**
Job 1:10; Prov. 15:19; Mic. 7:4

HEED Ps. 17:1; 55:2; Jer. 2:31

HEEL Gen. 3:15; 25:26; 49:17; Ps. 41:9

HEIGHT Rom. 8:39, nor **h**, nor depth
Job 22:12; Prov. 25:3; Rev. 21:16

HEIR Rom. 8:17, **h-s** also, **h-s** of God
Gal. 4:7, an **h** through God
James 2:5, **h-s** of the kingdom
Gen. 15:3; Jer. 49:1; Matt. 21:38

HELD Ezek. 31:15, and **h** back its rivers

HELL Mark 9:47, to be cast into **h**
James 3:6, tongue . . . is set on fire by **h**
2 Pet. 2:4, angels . . . cast them into **h**
Matt. 5:22; 10:28; 23:15

HELMET 1 Sam. 17:5, had a bronze **h** on his head
Is. 59:17, **h** of salvation on His head
Eph. 6:17, take the **h** of salvation

HELP 1 Sam. 7:12, the LORD has **h-ed** us
Ps. 33:20, He is our **h** and our shield
42:11, The **h** of my countenance
46:1, very present **h** in trouble
121:1, whence shall my **h** come
Matt. 15:25, Lord, **h** me
Mark 9:24, **h** *me in* my unbelief
2 Cor. 1:11, **h-ing** us through your prayers
Heb. 4:16, grace to **h** in time of need
Job 5:16; 6:13; Is. 41:6,13; Mark 7:11

HELPER—*comforter*
Gen. 2:18, I will make him a **h**
Ps. 10:14, **h** of the orphan
30:10, O LORD, be Thou my **h**
54:4, Behold, God is my **h**
John 14:16, will give you another **H**
Heb. 13:6, THE LORD IS MY H

HEMORRHAGE—*blood* Matt. 9:20; Mark 5:25; Luke 8:43

HEMORRHOIDS Deut. 28:27; 1 Sam. 5:6; 6:4

HERB Luke 11:42, tithe . . . every garden **h**
2 Kin. 4:39; 19:26; Ps. 37:2; Prov. 27:25; Is. 37:27

HERD—*cattle* Gen. 13:5; Jon. 3:7; Matt. 8:30

HERITAGE—*gift, possession* Ps. 16:6, my **h** is beautiful
Job 20:29; Ps. 135:12; 136:21,22; Is. 49:8

HESITATE 1 Kin. 18:21, How long *will* you **h**

HID—*cover, secret* Gen. 3:8, man and his wife **h** themselves
Matt. 10:26, and **h-en** that will not be known
13:44, treasure **h-en** in the field
25:25, **h** your talent in the ground
Mark 4:22, For nothing is **h-en**
1 Cor. 2:7, **h-en** wisdom, which God predestined
Col. 3:3, your life is **h-en** with Christ
Deut. 33:19; Josh. 2:4; 1 Sam. 20:24; 2 Sam. 17:9; Job 40:13; Ps. 19:6,12; 69:5; Is. 45:3; Dan. 2:22; Luke 8:17; John 8:59; Heb. 11:23

HIDE—*conceal, cover* Gen. 18:17; Job 14:13; 20:12; Ps. 27:5,9; Is. 2:10; Jer. 38:14

HIGH—*rank* Ps. 103:11, **h** as the heavens are above . . . earth
Matt. 4:8, devil took Him to a very **h** mountain
Mark 5:7, Jesus, Son of the Most **H** God
11:10, HOSANNA in the **h-est**
Luke 2:14, Glory to God in the **h-est**
John 19:31, for that Sabbath was a **h** *day*
Heb. 3:1, Jesus, the Apostle and **H** Priest
Gen. 29:7; Job 11:8; 22:12; Ps. 49:2; 91:14; Prov. 24:7; Is. 32:15; Luke 1:78

HIGHWAY—*way*
Num. 20:17, go along the king's **h**
Is. 35:8, **h** . . . called the **h** of holiness
40:3, a **h** for our God
59:7, Devastation and . . . in their **h-s**
Deut. 2:27; Prov. 15:19; Is. 11:16; 19:23; 49:11; 62:10; Matt. 22:9; Luke 14:23

HILL—*mountains*
Ps. 24:3, Who may ascend into the **h**
50:10, cattle on a thousand **h-s**
Matt. 5:14, city set on a **h** cannot be hidden
Luke 4:29, led Him to the brow of the **h**
Gen. 49:26; Deut. 11:11; Ps. 15:1; Is. 5:1; Luke 23:30

HINDER—*delay, forbid, restrain*
Matt. 19:14, do not **h** them from coming to Me
Mark 9:39, But Jesus said, Do not **h** him
Gal. 5:7, who **h-ed** you from obeying
1 Pet. 3:7, your prayers may not be **h-ed**
Mark 9:38; Luke 11:52; 18:16

HINDRANCE 1 Cor. 9:12, cause no **h** to the gospel

HIRE Is. 7:20, shave with a razor, **h-d**
Matt. 20:1, went out early . . . to **h** laborers
20:7, Because no one **h-d** us
Luke 15:19, as one of your **h-d** men

HIT 2 Cor. 11:20, if he **h-s** you in the face

HOARD—*store* Amos 3:10, **h** up violence and devastation

HOLD—*keep, retain*
Prov. 4:13, Take **h** of instruction
Is. 4:1, seven women . . . **h** of one man
Matt. 6:24, he will **h** to one
Mark 7:8, **h** to the tradition of men
Luke 8:15, heard the word, and **h** it fast
Phil. 2:16, **h-ing** fast the word of life
1 Thess. 5:21, **h** fast to that which is good
Titus 1:9, **h-ing** fast the faithful word
Job 2:9; 27:6; Ps. 64:5; Prov. 4:4; Is. 33:15; Jer. 20:9; Acts 7:60; Phil. 2:29

HOLE—*opening* Matt. 8:20, foxes have **h-s**
2 Kin. 12:9; Is. 11:8; Ezek. 8:7; Hag. 1:6

HOLINESS—*holy, sanctity* Ex. 15:11
Ps. 93:5, **H** befits Thy house
Is. 35:8, be called the highway of **h**
2 Cor. 7:1, perfecting **h** in the fear of God
1 Thess. 3:13, hearts unblameable in **h**
Heb. 12:10, we may share His **h**

HOLY—*holiness, sacred, sanctify* Ex. 3:5; 28:36
Ex. 20:8, sabbath day, to keep it **h**
Deut. 5:12, Observe the sabbath . . . keep it **h**
7:6, you are a **h** people
1 Chr. 16:10, Glory in His **h** name
Ps. 11:4, LORD is in His **h** temple
16:10, allow Thy **H** One to see the pit
145:21, bless His **h** name forever
Is. 6:3, **H**, **H**, **H**, is the LORD of hosts
Hab. 2:20, LORD is in His **h** temple
Matt. 7:6, not give what is **h** to dogs
Luke 1:49, **h** is His name
4:34, the **H** One of God
John 17:11, **H** Father, keep them in Thy name
Acts 2:27, THY H ONE
Rom. 12:1, your bodies a living and **h** sacrifice
1 Cor. 3:17, the temple of God is **h**
7:34, **h** both in body and spirit
Eph. 1:4, be **h** and blameless before Him
Col. 1:22, **h** and blameless
1 Tim. 2:8, lifting up **h** hands
2 Tim. 1:9, called us with a **h** calling
Lev. 20:7; Deut. 33:2; 1 Sam. 2:2; 2 Kin. 4:9; 1 Chr. 16:29; Job 15:15; Ps. 47:8; 89:5; 99:9; Jer. 17:22,24,27; 31:23; Mark 6:20; Rom. 16:16

HOLY SPIRIT—*spirit*
Matt. 1:20, in her is of the **H**
Matt. 3:11, baptize you with the **H**
Luke 3:22, **H** descended upon Him in bodily
4:1, Jesus, full of the **H**
11:13, give the **H** to those
12:12, **H** will teach you
John 14:26, Helper, the **H**
20:22, Receive the **H**
Acts 2:4, all filled with the **H**
2:38, receive the gift of the **H**
7:51, always resisting the **H**
10:38, the **H** and with power
19:2, Did you receive the **H**
Rom. 9:1, witness in the **H**
Eph. 1:13, with the **H** of promise
4:30, do not grieve the **H** of God
1 Thess. 4:8, God who gives His **H** to you

HOME Eccles. 12:5, man goes to his eternal **h**
2 Cor. 5:6, are at **h** in the body
Titus 2:5, sensible, pure, workers at **h**

Lev. 18:9; Deut. 24:5; 1 Kin. 13:15; 2 Chr. 25:19; Prov. 7:19; Mark 5:19; 1 Cor. 11:34; 14:35

HOMESTEAD—*habitation* Luke 11:21; Acts 1:20

HONEST—*good, true* Gen. 42:11, we are **h** men
Luke 8:15, an **h** and good heart

HONOR—*splendor* Ex. 20:12, **H** your father and your mother
Lev. 19:32, **h** the aged
Prov. 15:33, before **h** *comes* humility
Matt. 6:2, that they may be **h-ed** by men
13:57, A prophet is not without **h**
15:8, H-S ME WITH THEIR LIPS
John 5:23, all may **h** the Son
Rom. 2:10, glory and **h** and peace
1 Tim. 6:16, To Him *be* **h** and eternal dominion
Heb. 13:4, *Let* marriage *be held* in **h**
1 Pet. 2:17, **H** all men . . . **h** the king
3:7, grant her **h** as a fellow-heir
Rev. 5:13, *be* blessing and **h** and glory
1 Sam. 2:30; 9:6; 1 Kin. 3:13; 1 Chr. 29:28; Job 19:9; Ps. 50:23; Eccles. 6:2; Is. 49:5; Matt. 15:4; Rom. 12:10; 13:7; 1 Tim. 5:17

HONORABLE—*noble* Is. 9:15; Nah. 3:10
Rom. 9:21, one vessel for **h** use . . . another for common
Phil. 4:8, brethren . . . whatever is **h**
Heb. 13:18, conduct ourselves **h-y** in all things

HOOF—*claw* Lev. 11:3,4,5,6,7,26, whatever divides a **h**
Deut. 14:6,7,8; Ps. 69:31; Is. 5:28; Jer. 47:3; Ezek. 32:13; Zech. 11:16

HOOK 2 Kin. 19:28; Is. 37:29, put My **h** in your nose
Job 41:2, pierce his jaw with a **h**
Ezek. 29:4; 38:4; Amos 4:2

HOPE—*comfort, expectation, confidence, trust*
Job 13:15, I will **h** in Him
Ps. 39:7, My **h** is in Thee
62:5, my **h** is from Him
Prov. 13:12, **H** deferred *makes* the heart sick
19:18, Discipline your son while there is **h**
Acts 2:26, MY FLESH ALSO WILL ABIDE IN H
23:6, **h** and resurrection of the dead
28:20, for the sake of the **h** of Israel
Rom. 4:18, **h** against **h** he believed
5:5, **h** does not disappoint
8:24, **h** that is seen is not **h**
12:12, rejoicing in **h**
15:4, Scriptures we might have **h**
1 Cor. 13:7, **h-s** all things
13:13, now abide faith, **h**, love
2 Cor. 3:12, Having therefore such a **h**
Gal. 5:5, waiting for the **h** of righteousness
Eph. 4:4, you were called in one **h**
Col. 1:23, away from the **h** of the gospel
1:27, Christ in you, the **h** of glory
1 Thess. 5:8, as a helmet, the **h** of salvation
1 Tim. 4:10, our **h** on the living God
Titus 3:7, *the* **h** of eternal life
Heb. 6:19, **h** we have as an anchor
11:1, assurance of *things* **h-d** for
1 Pet. 1:3, born again to a living **h**
Ruth 1:12; Job 7:6; Ps. 9:18; 71:5; Prov. 26:12; Eccles. 9:4; Is. 20:5; 57:10; Jer. 29:11; 1 Cor. 9:10; 2 Cor. 1:7; 2 Thess. 2:16

HORN—*trumpet* Gen. 22:13; Lev. 25:9; Josh. 6:5; 2 Sam. 22:3; 1 Chr. 15:28; Dan. 3:5; 7:7; Rev. 5:6

HORRIBLE Jer. 5:30; 23:14; Hos. 6:10

HORROR Ps. 55:5; Jer. 25:18

HORSE Ps. 33:17, A **h** is a false hope
Gen. 49:17; 1 Kin. 10:29; Job 39:19; Ps. 32:9; Prov. 26:3; Jer. 4:13; 46:4; Hos. 14:3

HOSPITABLE 1 Tim. 3:2, must be above reproach . . . **h**
Titus 1:8, but **h**, loving what is good
1 Pet. 4:9, Be **h** to one another

HOSPITALITY Rom. 12:13, practicing **h**

HOST—*army, camp, innkeeper*
Ps. 24:10, LORD of **h-s**, He is the King
Luke 2:13, multitude of the heavenly **h**
Deut. 4:19; Josh. 5:15; Ps. 27:3; Is. 48:2; Rom. 16:23

HOSTILE—*enmity, contrary* Lev. 26:21, you act with **h-ity**
Rom. 8:7, mind set on the flesh is **h**
1 Thess. 2:15, but **h** to all men
Heb. 12:3, endured such **h-ity** by sinners
James 4:4, friendship with the world is **h-ity**

HOT—*branding* Ps. 39:3, My heart was **h** within me
Rev. 3:15, are neither cold nor **h**
Ex. 16:21; Deut. 9:19; Job 6:17; Prov. 6:28

HOT-TEMPERED Prov. 29:22, a **h** man abounds

HOUR—*time* Matt. 20:12, men have worked *only* one **h**
Matt. 24:36, day and **h** no one knows
26:40, watch with Me for one **h**
Mark 15:34, ninth **h** Jesus cried out
Luke 22:59, about an **h** had passed
John 5:25, an **h** is coming and now is
12:27, Father, save Me from this **h**
17:1, Father, the **h** has come
Matt. 8:13; Mark 13:32; Luke 12:39; John 11:9; Acts 3:1; Rom. 13:11; Rev. 3:10

HOUSE—*temple* Ps. 23:6, dwell in the **h** of the LORD
Ps. 127:1, Unless the LORD builds the **h**
Prov. 9:1, Wisdom has built her **h**
Matt. 2:11, they came into the **h** and saw
7:25, winds blew, and burst against that **h**
10:12, enter the **h**, give it your greeting
12:25, city or **h** divided against itself
21:13, MY H SHALL BE CALLED A H
Luke 11:17, a **h** divided against itself falls
John 14:2, Father's **h** are many dwelling places
Acts 2:46, breaking bread from **h** to **h**
7:48, does not dwell in **h-s** . . . human hands
7:49, WHAT KIND OF H WILL YOU BUILD
Rom. 16:5, church that is in their **h**
2 Cor. 5:1, **h** not made with hands
1 Tim. 5:13, go around from **h** to **h**
1 Pet. 2:5, built up as a spiritual **h**
Gen. 15:3; Ex. 20:2,17; Deut. 8:12; 22:8; 2 Kin. 20:1; Neh. 13:11; Job 27:18; 30:23; Ps. 55:14; 84:3; 93:5; 102:7; Prov. 24:3; Eccles. 7:2; Is. 5:8; Matt. 23:38; Mark 12:40; Luke 10:7

HOUSEHOLD—*home* Prov. 31:27, ways of her **h**
Gal. 6:10, who are of the **h** of the faith
Eph. 2:19, and are of God's **h**
1 Tim. 3:4, manages his own **h** well
3:15, conduct himself in the **h** of God
Gen. 18:19; 26:14; Ex. 1:1; Matt. 10:36; 13:52; John 19:27; 2 Tim. 3:6

HUMBLE—*abase, gentle* Mic. 6:8, walk **h-ly** with your God
Matt. 11:29, I am gentle and **h** in heart
23:12, exalts . . . shall be **h-d**; and . . . **h-s** himself
Phil. 3:21, body of our **h** state
4:12, get along with **h** means
James 4:6, BUT GIVES GRACE TO THE H
1 Pet. 5:6, **H** yourselves under the mighty hand
Ex. 10:3; Num. 12:3; Deut. 8:2; 2 Chr. 34:27; Job 40:12; Ps. 35:13; 37:11; Prov. 6:3; 11:2; Dan. 4:37; Zech. 9:9

HUMILIATE 2 Cor. 12:21, my God may **h** me before you

HUMILIATION—*confusion* Is. 45:16; Jer. 3:25
Acts 8:33, in **h** His judgment was taken

HUMILITY—*humble, self-abasement*
Prov. 15:33, before honor comes **h**
18:12, **h** *goes* before honor
22:4, The reward of **h**
Phil. 2:3, with **h** of mind
Col. 3:12, put on a heart of . . . **h**
1 Pet. 5:5, clothe yourselves with **h**

HUNG Ps. 137:2, Upon the willows . . . we **h** our harps
Matt. 18:6; Mark 9:4; Luke 17:2, better . . . millstone be **h** around his neck

HUNGER Ps. 34:10, lions do lack and suffer **h**
Prov. 10:3, not allow the righteous to **h**
19:15, an idle man will suffer **h**

HUNGER *(Continued)*
Is. 49:10, They will not **h** or thirst
Matt. 5:6; Luke 6:21, Blessed are those who **h**
John 6:35, comes to Me shall not **h**
Deut. 28:48; Luke 6:25; 15:17
HUNGRY Ps. 146:7, Who gives food to the **h**
Prov. 25:21, If your enemy is **h**
Matt. 4:2, He then became **h**
12:1, His disciples became **h**
12:3, David did, when he became **h**
15:32, do not wish to send them away **h**
25:35, For I was **h**
Rom. 12:20, BUT IF YOUR ENEMY IS H
1 Cor. 11:34, If anyone is **h**
Deut. 8:3; 2 Sam. 17:29; Job 22:7; Ps. 50:12; Is. 29:8; Ezek. 18:7; 1 Cor. 11:21; Phil. 4:12
HUNT Gen. 10:9, a mighty **h-er** before the LORD
Gen. 27:5; 1 Sam. 26:20; Ps. 140:11; Ezek. 13:18; Mic. 7:2
HURRIED Prov. 20:21, inheritance gained **h-ly**
HURRY—*speed* 1 Sam. 20:38, **H**, be quick, do not stay
HURT—*harm* Ps. 15:4, He swears to his own **h**
Is. 11:9; Mark 16:18
HUSBAND—*bridegroom*
Prov. 12:4, wife is a crown of her **h**
John 4:16, Go, call your **h**
Rom. 7:2,3, if her **h** dies
1 Cor. 7:3, **h** fulfill his duty to his wife
Eph. 5:23, **h** is the head of the wife
5:25, **H-s**, love your wives
Rev. 21:2, bride adorned for her **h**
Gen. 3:16; 29:32; 30:20; Is. 54:5; Hos. 3:1; Mark 10:12; 1 Cor. 7:2; 2 Cor. 11:2
HUSH—*silence* Acts 21:40, there was a great **h**
HYMN Matt. 26:30, singing a **h**, they went out
Eph. 5:19, in psalms and **h-s** and spiritual songs
HYPOCRISY Matt. 23:28, you are full of **h**
Rom. 12:9, Let love be without **h**
1 Tim. 4:2, means of the **h** of liars
James 3:17, wisdom from above ... without **h**
HYPOCRITE—*godless* Matt. 6:2, as the **h-s** do ... synagogues
Matt. 6:5, not to be as the **h-s**
6:16, gloomy face as the **h-s** *do*
7:5, You **h**, first take the log
22:18, Why are you testing Me, you **h-s**
23:13, scribes and Pharisees, **h-s**
Luke 12:56, You **h-s**! You know how to analyze

I

ICE—*frost* Job 37:10, breath of God **i** is made
IDLE Prov. 19:15, an **i** man will suffer hunger
Prov. 31:27, not eat the bread of **i-ness**
Matt. 20:6, Why have you been standing ... **i**
1 Tim. 5:13, not merely **i**, but also gossips
IDOL—*image* Ex. 20:4, make for yourself an **i**
Acts 15:20, abstain from ... **i-s**
1 Cor. 10:7, do not be **i-aters**
1 John 5:21, guard yourselves from **i-s**
Lev. 19:4; 26:1; Is. 66:3; Jer. 50:38
IGNORANCE—*unintentionally*
Acts 17:23, What ... worship in **i**
17:30, overlooked the times of **i**
Eph. 4:18, because of the **i** that is in them
1 Pet. 2:15, silence the **i** of foolish men
IGNORANT 2 Cor. 2:11, not **i** of his schemes
2 Tim. 2:23, refuse foolish and **i** speculations
ILLEGITIMATE Deut. 23:2; Heb. 12:8
ILLNESS—*infirmity* Gal. 4:13, a bodily **i**
ILLUMINE Ps. 18:28, God **i-s** my darkness
IMAGE—*likeness* Gen. 1:26, make man in Our **i**
Gen. 9:6, **i** of God He made man
1 Cor. 11:7, **i** and glory of God
Col. 1:15, **i** of the invisible God
IMAGINATION—*estimation*
Prov. 18:11, wall in his own **i**
IMITATE—*follow* 3 John 11, do not **i** what is evil
IMITATORS—*followers* Eph. 5:1, be **i** of God
1 Thess. 2:14, become **i** of the churches of God
IMMATURE—*babes, children*
Rom. 2:20, teacher of the **i**
IMMEDIATELY Matt. 3:16, went up **i** from the water
Matt. 4:20, **i** left the nets
21:2, **i** you will find a donkey tied
26:74, And **i** a cock crowed
Mark 4:15, **i** Satan comes
Luke 12:54, **i** you say, A shower is coming
14:5, **i** pull him out ... Sabbath
21:9, the end does not *follow* **i**
John 5:9, **i** the man became well
19:34, **i** there came out blood and water
Acts 9:18, **i** there fell from his eyes
9:20, **i** he began to proclaim Jesus
21:30, **i** the doors were shut
Rev. 4:2, **i** I was in the Spirit
Matt. 13:21; 26:49; Mark 6:25; Luke 17:7; Acts 13:11
IMMORALITY—*fornication* Matt. 19:9, except for **i**
1 Cor. 6:18, Flee **i**
1 Thess. 4:3, abstain from sexual **i**
Rev. 2:20, they commit *acts of* **i**
17:2, the wine of her **i**
IMMORTALITY 1 Cor. 15:53, mortal ... put on **i**
1 Tim. 6:16, who alone possesses **i**
2 Tim. 1:10, brought life and **i**
IMPATIENT Num. 21:4, people became **i**
IMPEL—*drive* Mark 1:12, the Spirit **i-ed** Him
IMPERISHABLE 1 Cor. 9:25, perishable ... an **i**
1 Cor. 15:52, the dead will be raised **i**
1 Pet. 1:4, *obtain* an inheritance *which is* **i**
IMPETUOUS Hab. 1:6, Chaldeans, That fierce and **i** people
IMPLORE—*adjure* Job 8:5, **i** the compassion of the Almighty
Mark 5:7, I **i** you by God
IMPOSSIBLE Matt. 19:26, With men this is **i**
Luke 1:37, nothing will be **i** with God
Heb. 6:18, it is **i** for God to lie
11:6, without faith it is **i** to
IMPROPER 1 Cor. 14:35, **i** for a woman to speak
IMPROVISE Amos 6:5, Who **i** to the sound of the harp
IMPUTE—*reckon* Rom. 5:13, sin is not **i-d** when there is
INAUGURATED—*dedicated*
Heb. 9:18, first covenant ... not **i**
10:20, way which He **i** for us
INCITE Luke 23:14, one who **i-s** the people
INCLINE Josh. 24:23, **i** your hearts to the LORD
Ps. 119:36, I my heart to Thy
Is. 37:17, I Thine ear, O LORD
INCREASE—*multiply, produce* Job 31:12; Prov. 28:8
Ps. 62:10, riches **i**, do not set *your* heart
Eccles. 1:18, **i-ing** knowledge results in **i-ing** pain
Luke 2:52, **i-ing** in wisdom and stature
11:29, the crowds were **i-ing**
Col. 1:10, **i-ing** in the knowledge of God
INDEBTED Rom. 15:27, they are **i**
INDEED—*surely, truly* Gen. 3:1, **I**, has God said, You shall
Ex. 4:25, **i** a bridegroom of blood
Num. 14:21, but **i**, as I live
1 Kin. 8:27, God **i** dwell on the earth
2 Chr. 6:18, will God **i** dwell with mankind
John 8:36, you shall be free **i**
Rom. 14:20, All things **i** are clean
1 Tim. 5:5, she who is a widow, **i**
INDEPENDENT 1 Cor. 11:11, woman **i** of man ... man **i** ... woman
INDESTRUCTIBLE—*endless*
Heb. 7:16, power of an **i** life

INDIGNANT Matt. 20:24; Luke 13:14
INDIGNATION—*anger* Jer. 15:17; Nah. 1:6
Ps. 7:11, God who has **i** every day
69:24, Pour out Thine **i** on them
Is. 30:27, lips are filled with **i**
INEXPERIENCED—*tender*
1 Chr. 22:5, My son . . . young and **i**
INFECTION—*plague*
Lev. 13:2, becomes an **i** of leprosy
INFERIOR—*base* Is. 3:5, And the **i** against the honorable
INFIRMITIES—*sickness, weakness*
Matt. 8:17, HIMSELF TOOK OUR I
INFLICT Job 5:18, He **i-s** pain, and gives relief
INFORM—*speak* Ruth 4:4; 2 Sam. 15:28; Ezra 4:16
Job 17:5, who **i-s** against friends
INHABITANTS Gen. 34:30; Num. 13:32; Ps. 49:1; Joel 2:1
INHABITED—*habitation* Ps. 107:7,36, an **i** city
INHERIT—*possess, possession* Ex. 32:13, they shall **i** *it*
Ps. 37:11, humble will **i** the land
Prov. 3:35, The wise will **i** honor
14:18, The naive **i** folly
Matt. 5:5, gentle . . . **i** the earth
19:29, shall **i** eternal life
25:34, **i** the kingdom prepared
Luke 10:25, do to **i** eternal life
1 Cor. 6:9, shall not **i** the kingdom
15:50, perishable **i** the imperishable
Rev. 21:7, who overcomes shall **i** these things
INHERITANCE—*possession* Judg. 11:2; Ps. 28:9
Ps. 2:8, give the nations as Thine **i**
94:14, Nor will He forsake His **i**
Jer. 3:19, most beautiful **i** of the nations
Mark 12:7, the **i** will be ours
Acts 7:5, He gave him no **i**
Eph. 1:11, also we have obtained an **i**
1 Pet. 1:4, an **i** which is imperishable
Prov. 13:22; Eccles. 7:11; Jer. 12:7,8,9,15; Joel 2:17; Mic. 2:2; Mal. 1:3
INIQUITY—*injustice* Lev. 16:22; Job 4:8; 13:26
Deut. 5:9, visiting the **i** of the fathers
Ps. 25:11, Pardon my **i**, for it is great
51:9, blot out all my **i-es**
Is. 53:5, He was crushed for our **i-es**
James 3:6, tongue is . . . world of **i**
Ps. 32:5; 51:5; 79:8; Prov. 22:8; Is. 1:4; 31:2; Jer. 31:30; Ezek. 18:30; 33:8
INJUNCTION—*decree* Dan. 6:7,8
INJURE—*wrong* Acts 7:26, why do you **i** one
INJUSTICE—*iniquity* Lev. 19:15, do no **i**
Deut. 32:4, A God of faithfulness without **i**
INNER—*inward* Matt. 6:6, GO INTO YOUR I ROOM
2 Cor. 4:16, **i** man is being renewed day by day
INNERMOST—*inward*
Job 38:36, wisdom in the **i** being
INNKEEPER—*host* Luke 10:35, denarii . . . gave them to the **i**
INNOCENT—*blameless, righteous* Ex. 23:7
Is. 59:7, hasten to shed **i** blood
Matt. 27:4, have sinned by betraying **i** blood
27:24, I am **i** of this Man's blood
Luke 23:47, this man was **i**
Phil. 2:15, blameless and **i**, children of God
Heb. 7:26, holy, **i**, undefiled
2 Sam. 3:28; Job 4:7; 22:19; Prov. 6:17; Matt. 10:16; 12:5,7
INQUIRE—*ask* Judg. 18:5, **I** of God
Matt. 2:4, **i** of them where the Christ
INSANE—*mad* 1 Sam. 21:13, acted **i-ly** in their hands
John 10:20, has a demon, and is **i**
INSCRIBE Hab. 2:2, And **i** *it* on tablets
INSCRIPTION Dan. 5:8, could not read the **i**
INSECTS Ex. 8:21, I will send swarms of **i** on you
INSENSITIVE Is. 6:10, Render . . . this people **i**
INSIDE—*within* Gen. 9:21, uncovered himself **i** his tent
Matt. 23:26, Pharisee . . . clean the **i** of the cup
Acts 5:23, we found no one **i**
Rev. 5:1, throne a book written **i**
INSIGNIFICANT—*mean, small* 2 Sam. 7:19, **i** in Thine eyes
Job 8:7, your beginning was **i**
40:4, Behold, I am **i**; what can
Acts 21:39, citizen of no **i** city
INSOLENCE—*pride* 1 Sam. 17:28, I know your **i**
INSPIRE—*spiritual* Hos. 9:7, **i-d** man is demented
INSTANT—*moment* Num. 16:21, consume **i-ly**
INSTITUTION 1 Pet. 2:13, Submit . . . to every human **i**
INSTRUCT—*discipline*
Neh. 9:20, Thy good Spirit to **i**
Ps. 32:8, I will **i** you and teach you
Matt. 10:5, twelve Jesus sent . . . **i-ing** them
Rom. 2:18, being **i-ed** out of the Law
INSTRUCTION—*admonition*
Job 36:10, He opens . . . ear to **i**
Matt. 11:1, **i-s** to His twelve disciples
Rom. 15:4, was written for our **i**
1 Cor. 7:10, **i-s**, not I, but the Lord
10:11, written for our **i**
Eph. 6:4, discipline and **i** of the Lord
1 Tim. 1:5, goal of our **i** is love
Heb. 6:2, of **i** about washing and laying on of hands
INSTRUMENT—*object, vessel*
Acts 9:15, he is a chosen **i**
Rom. 6:13, as **i-s** of unrighteousness
2 Sam. 12:31; 1 Chr. 20:3; Ps. 150:4; Ezek. 33:32
INSULT—*reproach*
Job 19:3, ten times you have **i-ed** me
Luke 6:22, heap **i-s** upon you
INTEGRITY—*upright* Gen. 20:5; Job 2:3; Prov. 19:1
Ps. 15:2, He who walks with **i**
26:1, have walked in my **i**
Prov. 10:9, who walks in **i** walks securely
20:7, righteous man who walks in his **i**
INTELLIGENT—*prudent*
Matt. 11:25, hide . . . wise and **i**
Mark 12:34, Jesus saw that he had . . . **i-ly**
INTENSE 2 Pet. 3:10, destroyed with **i** heat
INTENT Gen. 8:21, **i** of man's heart is evil
Deut. 31:21, for I know their **i**
Acts 1:10, gazing **i-ly** into the sky
INTERCEDE 1 Sam. 2:25, who can **i**
Is. 53:12, **i-d** for the transgressors
Rom. 8:26, the Spirit Himself **i-s** for *us*
INTERCESSION—*petition*
Heb. 7:25, always lives to make **i**
INTEREST—*usury* Ex. 22:25, not charge him **i**
Deut. 23:20, You may charge **i** to a foreigner
Ps. 15:5, not put out his money at **i**
Matt. 25:27, my *money* back with **i**
Luke 19:23, collected it with **i**
INTERMARRY Ezra 9:14, and **i** with the peoples
INTERPRET—*understand*
Gen. 41:8, dreams . . . no one who could **i** them
1 Cor. 12:10, the **i-ation** of tongues
14:27, and let one **i**
2 Pet. 1:20, *a matter* of one's own **i-ation**
INTIMATE—*close* Job 19:14, my **i** friends have forgotten
Prov. 17:9, matter separates **i** friends
INTRODUCTION Rom. 5:2, obtained our **i** by faith
INVALIDATE Matt. 15:6, you **i-d** the word of God
Mark 7:13, *thus* **i-ing** the word of God
INVESTIGATE—*examine*
Ezra 10:16, convened . . . to **i**
INVESTIGATION Acts 25:26, after the **i** has taken place
INVOLVE—*exercise* Ps. 131:1, Nor do I **i** myself
INWARD—*within* Matt. 7:15, **i-ly** are wolves

IRON 2 Kin. 6:6, and made the **i** float
Job 19:24, with an **i** stylus and lead
Ps. 2:9, break them with a rod of **i**
1 Tim. 4:2, seared . . . as with a branding **i**
Gen. 4:22; Deut. 3:11; 8:9; 33:25; Judg. 1:19; Job 40:18; Prov. 27:17; Jer. 11:4

IRREVERENCE
2 Sam. 6:7, struck him down . . . for his **i**

IRRITATE—*fret* 1 Sam. 1:6, provoke . . . to **i** her

IVORY 1 Kin. 10:18; Song 7:4; Amos 6:4

J

JACKAL Job 30:29, a brother to **j-s**
Jer. 9:11, Jerusalem . . . haunt of **j-s**

JAR—*jug, pitcher, vessel* 1 Kin. 17:10, water in **j**
John 19:29, A **j** full of sour wine
Gen. 24:14; 1 Kin. 14:3; 19:6; 2 Kin. 2:20

JAVELIN—*spear* Josh. 8:18, Stretch out the **j**
Job 41:29, at the rattling of the **j**

JEALOUS—*envy, zealous*
Ex. 20:5, LORD your God, am a **j** God
1 Cor. 13:4, love is kind, *and* is not **j**
Gen. 30:1; 37:11; Ex. 34:14; Num. 11:29; 25:11; Josh. 24:19; Is. 11:13; Ezek. 31:9; Nah. 1:2; Acts 7:9; 17:5; Rom. 10:19; 2 Cor. 11:2

JEALOUSY—*envy, jealous* Num. 5:14; Prov. 6:34
Rom. 13:13, not in strife and **j**
1 Cor. 3:3, since there is **j** . . . among you
2 Cor. 12:20, *there may be* strife, **j**
James 3:14, if you have bitter **j**
3:16, where **j** and selfish ambition exist
Prov. 27:4; Song 8:6; Acts 13:45; Rom. 11:14; Gal. 5:20

JEOPARDIZE Ruth 4:6, **j** my own inheritance

JEWEL—*pearl* Prov. 3:15, more precious than **j-s**
Prov. 31:10, her worth is far above **j-s**

JOIN—*couple* Ex. 23:1; 26:6; Is. 5:8
Matt. 19:6, What . . . God has **j-ed** together
1 Cor. 6:17, one who **j-s** himself to the Lord

JOINT—*dislocate* Ps. 22:14, bones are out of **j**

JOURNEY—*walk, way*
Ezra 8:21, seek from Him a safe **j**
Mark 13:34, like a man, away on a **j**
Luke 9:3, Take nothing for your **j**
13:33, must **j** on today and tomorrow
15:13, a **j** into a distant country
Acts 9:3, **j-ed**, he was approaching Damascus
2 Cor. 11:26, I have been on frequent **j-s**
Gen. 33:12; Josh. 9:11; Neh. 2:6; Matt. 10:10; Acts 1:12

JOY Prov. 17:21, father of a fool has no **j**
Matt. 2:10, with great **j**
25:21, enter into the **j** of your master
Luke 15:7, **j** in heaven over one sinner
John 15:11, My **j** may be in you
Rom. 14:17, and **j** in the Holy Spirit
Gal. 5:22, fruit of the Spirit is love, **j**
Phil. 2:2, make my **j** complete
James 1:2, Consider it all **j** . . . encounter . . .
1 John 1:4, our **j** may be made complete
1 Chr. 15:16; Ezra 3:12; Job 29:13; 33:26

JOYFUL—*merry* Ps. 21:6; 66:1; Is. 52:9
Ps. 126:5, sow in tears . . . reap with **j** shouting
Prov. 17:22, **j** heart is good medicine

JUDGE Gen. 18:25, the **J** of all the earth
Matt. 7:1, not **j** lest you be **j-d**
John 3:17, God did not send the Son . . . to **j**
7:24, but **j** with righteous judgment
7:51, Our Law does not **j** a man
12:47, not come to **j** the world
Acts 10:42, **J** of the living and the dead
2 Thess. 2:12, all may be **j-d** who did not believe
Heb. 4:12, word of God . . . able to **j** the thoughts
12:23, God the **J** of all
13:4, adulterers God will **j**
Gen. 16:5; Matt. 7:2

JUDGMENT—*justice, sentence*
Ps. 1:5, wicked will not stand in the **j**
19:9, **j-s** of the LORD are true
Matt. 10:15, Gomorrah in the day of **j**
11:24, Sodom in *the* day of **j**
27:19, he was sitting on the **j**-seat
John 3:19, this is the **j**, that the light is
5:29, resurrection of **j**
5:30, judge; and My **j** is just
1 Cor. 11:29, eats and drinks **j** to himself
Heb. 9:27, after this *comes* **j**
10:27, terrifying expectation of **j**
James 3:1, shall incur a stricter **j**
5:12, may not fall under **j**
2 Pet. 3:7, kept for the day of **j**
1 John 4:17, confidence in the day of **j**
Jude 15, to execute **j** upon all
Rev. 18:20, God has pronounced **j** for you
19:2, HIS **J-S** ARE TRUE AND RIGHTEOUS
Ex. 12:12; Lev. 18:4; Deut. 1:17; Ezra 7:26; Ps. 112:5; 2 Pet. 2:11; Jude 9

JUG—*bottle, wineskin* 1 Sam. 1:24; 10:3; 16:20; 25:18; 26:16; 2 Sam. 16:1

JUST—*right* Job 25:4, can a man be **j** with God
John 5:30, My judgment is **j**
Heb. 2:2, received a **j** recompense
1 Pet. 3:18, Christ also died . . . *the* **j** for *the* **un-j**
Lev. 19:36; Ps. 17:1; Luke 23:41

JUSTICE—*right, righteousness*
Job 8:3, Does God pervert **j**
Ps. 89:14, Righteousness and **j** are the
Prov. 28:5, Evil men do not understand **j**
Amos 5:24, let **j** roll down like waters
Mic. 6:8, to do **j**, to love kindness
Gen. 18:19; Deut. 16:19; Job 8:3; 36:6; Prov. 21:3; Is. 59:14; Jer. 10:24

JUSTIFY—*clear, vindicate* Gen. 44:16; Ps. 51:4
Luke 10:29, wishing to **j** himself
Rom. 8:33, God is the one who **j-es**

K

KEEP—*hold, guide, preserve* Gen. 18:19
Ex. 20:6, love Me and **k** My commandments
20:8, sabbath day, to **k** it holy
Num. 6:24, Lord bless you, and **k** you
Ps. 17:8, **K** me as the apple of the eye
34:13, **K** your tongue from evil
Matt. 19:17, enter into life, **k** the commandments
Luke 3:8, fruits in **k-ing** with your repentance
John 8:51, if anyone **k-s** My word
12:25, shall **k** it to life eternal
14:23, If anyone loves Me, he will **k** My word
17:15, **k** them from the evil *one*
1 Tim. 1:19, **k-ing** faith and a good conscience
5:14, bear children, **k** house
5:22, **k** yourself free from sin
James 1:27, **k** oneself unstained by the world
Jude 21, **k** yourselves in the love of God
Lev. 23:32; Prov. 1:15; Eccles. 3:6; Matt. 26:18; 1 Cor. 14:28; 1 Tim. 6:12

KEEPER—*guard* Gen. 4:9, Am I my brother's **k**
Ps. 121:5, The LORD is your **k**

KEPT—*observed* Gen. 37:11, his father **k** the saying
Mark 10:20, Teacher I have **k** all these things
Jude 6, He has **k** in eternal bonds

KERNEL—*grain* Amos 9:9, not a **k** will fall to the ground

KEY Matt. 16:19, **k-s** of the kingdom of heaven
Luke 11:52, taken away the **k** of knowledge
Rev. 1:18, I have the **k-s** of death and of Hades
9:1, **k** of the bottomless pit

KIDNAP—*steal* Deut. 24:7, man is caught **k-ing**

KIDNEY Job 16:13, splits my **k-s** open

KILL 1 Sam. 17:50, Philistine and **k-ed** him
Matt. 10:28, **k** the body . . . unable to **k** the soul
Luke 9:22, **k-ed**, and be raised up . . . third day
15:23, bring the fattened calf, **k** it

John 5:18, Jews were seeking . . . to **k** Him
7:19, Why do you seek to **k** Me
10:10, comes only to steal, and **k**
Acts 11:7, Arise, Peter; **k** and eat
2 Cor. 3:6, the letter **k-s** . . . Spirit gives life
Gen. 4:8,14,23; Ex. 13:15; 21:14; Num. 31:8; 2 Kin. 5:7; Job 5:2; Ps. 10:8; Acts 10:13; 1 Tim. 1:9

KIND—*gentle, gracious* Matt. 5:11, say all **k-s** of evil
1 Cor. 13:4, Love is patient, love is **k**
Eph. 4:32, be **k** to one another
2 Tim. 2:24, but be **k** to all
Gen. 1:11; 6:19; 2 Chr. 10:7

KINDLE—*burn* Ex. 35:3; Prov. 26:21; Is. 50:11

KINDNESS—*goodness, loyalty*
Ruth 3:10, your last **k** to be
Prov. 31:26, teaching of **k** is on her tongue
Acts 24:4, grant us, by your **k**
Rom. 11:22, **k** and severity of God
2 Cor. 6:6, in patience, in **k**, in the Holy Spirit
Col. 3:12, put on a heart of compassion, **k**
1 Pet. 2:3, tasted the **k** of the Lord
2 Pet. 1:7, *your* godliness, brotherly **k**

KING 1 Sam. 8:5, appoint a **k** for us to judge us
1 Sam. 10:24, Long live the **k**
Ps. 5:2, my **K** and my God
24:8, Who is the **K** of glory
Jer. 10:7, fear Thee, O **K** of the nations
Matt. 2:2, who has been born **K** of the Jews
2:9, having heard the **k**
10:18, brought before governors and **k-s** for My sake
21:5, BEHOLD YOUR **K** IS COMING TO YOU
27:11, Are You the **K** of the Jews
Luke 23:2, that He Himself is Christ, a **K**
John 12:15, YOUR **K** COMES SITTING ON A . . . COLT
1 Tim. 6:15, **K** of kings and Lord of lords
1 Pet. 2:17, fear God, honor the **k**
Judg. 9:8; 17:6; Job 18:14; Prov. 8:15; 22:29; Eccles. 10:20; Is. 43:15

KINGDOM—*dominion* Ps. 22:28, For the **k** is the LORD'S
Ps. 145:13, Thy **k** is an everlasting **k**
Matt. 3:2, the **k** of heaven is at hand
4:23, the gospel of the **k**
6:10, Thy **k** come, Thy will be done
13:38, these are the sons of the **k**
16:19, give you the keys of the **k**
19:14, **k** of heaven belongs to such as these
26:29, in My Father's **k**
Mark 10:24, hard it is to enter the **k** of God
12:34, not far from the **k** of God
Luke 6:20, for yours is the **k** of God
12:32, to give you the **k**
22:29, as My Father has granted me a **k**
John 3:3, he cannot see the **k** of God
18:36, My **k** is not of this world
Rom. 14:17, the **k** of God is not eating and drinking
Col. 1:13, to the **k** of His beloved Son
2 Tim. 4:18, bring me safely to His heavenly **k**
James 2:5, heirs of the **k** which He promised
Ex. 19:6; Esth. 1:20; Obad. 21

KISS Matt. 26:48, Whomever I shall **k**
Luke 7:45, has not ceased to **k** My feet
15:20, embraced him and **k-ed** him
22:48, betraying the Son of Man with a **k**
Rom. 16:16, Greet one another with a holy **k**
1 Pet. 5:14, Greet one another with a **k** of love
Gen. 29:11; 2 Sam. 20:9; Song 1:2

KNEE Gen. 41:43, Bow the **k**
Rom. 14:11, EVERY **K** SHALL BOW TO ME
Phil. 2:10, at the name of Jesus every **k** should bow
Heb. 12:12, strengthen . . . the **k-s** that are feeble

KNEEL Gen. 24:11, made the camels **k** down
Ps. 95:6, Let us **k** before the LORD
Matt. 27:29, they **k-ed** down before Him
Luke 22:41, He **k-t** down and *began* to pray

KNEW Jer. 1:5, Before I formed you . . . I **k** you
Matt. 7:23, I will declare . . . I never **k** you
Luke 6:8, But He **k** what they were thinking
John 4:10, If you **k** the gift of God
2 Cor. 5:21, made Him who **k** no sin *to be* sin

KNIFE—*sword* Prov. 30:14, jaw teeth *like* **k-s**

KNOCK—*smite* Nah. 2:10, knees **k-ing**
Matt. 7:7, **k** and it shall be opened
Luke 13:25, stand outside and **k** on the door
Acts 12:13, when he **k-ed** at the door
Rev. 3:20, I stand at the door and **k**

KNOW—*discern, recognize, understand*
Ex. 1:8, new king . . . who did not **k** Joseph
Deut. 4:9, **k-n** to your sons and your grandsons
Job 19:25, I **k** that my Redeemer lives
Ps. 1:6, the LORD **k-s** the way of the righteous
46:10, **k** that I am God
56:9, This I **k**, that God is for me
Prov. 27:1, do not **k** what a day may bring
Eccles. 8:5, wise heart **k-s** the proper time
Is. 59:8, They do not **k** the way of peace
Matt. 6:3, left hand **k** what your right hand
7:11, **k** how to give good gifts
7:20, you will **k** them by their fruits
25:12, I do not **k** you
Luke 10:22, no one **k-s** who the Son is
19:42, If you had **k-n** in this day
22:57, Woman, I do not **k** Him
John 8:32, you shall **k** the truth
10:14, I **k** My own, and My own **k** Me
14:7, If you had **k-n** Me . . . **k-n** My Father
21:17, You **k** all things; You **k** that I love You
Acts 1:7, not for you to **k** the times
1 Cor. 1:21, did not *come to* **k** God
13:2, and **k** all mysteries
13:9, we **k** in part and we prophesy
13:12, **k** in part, but then I shall **k** fully
2 Cor. 12:2, **k** a man in Christ . . . caught up
Eph. 3:19, to **k** the love of Christ
2 Tim. 3:15, **k-n** the sacred writings
1 John 3:2, We **k** that, if He should appear
3 John 12, you **k** that our witness is true
Rev. 2:2, I **k** your deeds
19:12, name written . . . no one **k-s** except Himself
Gen. 3:22; 28:16; Deut. 29:4; 1 Sam. 3:7; Job 13:18; Ps. 81:5; Eccles. 9:5; Is. 7:15; Hos. 6:3; Jon. 4:11; Matt. 9:30; 12:33; Mark 1:24; 13:33; Acts 19:15

KNOWLEDGE Gen. 2:9, tree of the **k** of good and evil
Ps. 19:2, night to night reveals **k**
139:6, *Such* **k** is too wonderful for me
Prov. 1:7, fear of the LORD the beginning of **k**
10:14, Wise men store up **k**
17:27, who restrains his words has **k**
Is. 11:9, full of the **k** of the LORD
Acts 24:22, more exact **k** about the Way
Rom. 10:2, but not in accordance with **k**
11:33, wisdom and **k** of God
1 Cor. 8:1, **K** makes arrogant, but love edifies
13:8, if *there is* **k**, it will be done away
15:34, some have no **k** of God
Eph. 3:19, love of Christ which surpasses **k**
Col. 2:3, treasures of wisdom and **k**
1 Tim. 2:4, come to the **k** of the truth
2 Pet. 1:5, in *your* moral excellence, **k** 1:6, in *your* **k,** self-control
3:18, grow in the grace and **k** of our LORD
Deut. 1:39; 1 Sam. 2:3; 2 Chr. 1:10; Job 10:7; 21:22; Eccles. 1:18; Is. 28:9; Hos. 4:6; Luke 11:52

L

LABOR—*fruit, toil, tribute, weary*
Ex. 20:9, Six days you shall **l**
Ps. 127:1, They **l** in vain who build it
Prov. 14:23, In all **l** there is profit
Eccles. 2:22, what does a man get in all his **l**
Is. 42:14, like a woman in **l** I will groan
1 Cor. 15:10, I **l-ed** even more than all of them
Gal. 4:11, perhaps I have **l-ed** over you in vain
4:19, again in **l** until Christ

LABOR *(Continued)*
Eph. 4:28, rather let him l, performing
Phil. 1:22, this *will mean* fruitful l
1 Thess. 1:3, work of faith and l of love
2 Thess. 3:8, with l and hardship we *kept*
Rev. 12:2, cried out, being in l and in pain
Gen. 49:15; Job 7:1; Ps. 78:46; Prov. 12:24; Eccles. 4:9; 2 Cor. 11:27

LABORER 1 Kin. 9:21, Solomon ... forced **l-s**

LACK—*need, void, want* Deut. 28:48, in the l of all things
Deut. 32:28, a nation **l-ing** in counsel
Judg. 18:10, place where there is no l
Prov. 7:7, young man **l-ing** sense
10:21, fools die for l of understanding
Is. 34:16, None will l its mate
Matt. 19:20, what am I still **l-ing**
Mark 10:21, One thing you l
James 1:4, **l-ing** in nothing
1:5, if any of you **l-s** wisdom
Deut. 8:9; 1 Kin. 8:25; Prov. 6:32; Eccles. 10:3

LADY 2 John 1, to the chosen l

LAGGING Rom. 12:11, not l behind in diligence

LAID Mark 6:5, He l His hands upon a few sick
Luke 12:19, many goods l up for many years
John 11:34, Where have you l him
2 Tim. 4:8, l up for me the crown of righteousness
1 John 3:16, He l down His life for us
1 Kin. 17:19; Job 6:2; 38:6

LAIR Job 38:40, lie in wait in *their* l

LAMB Gen. 22:8, God will provide ... the l
Is. 40:11, In His arm He will gather the **l-s**
53:7, Like a l that is led to slaughter
65:25, wolf and the l shall graze together
Hos. 4:16, Like a l in a large field
Luke 10:3, send you out as **l-s**
John 1:29, Behold the **L** of God
21:15, Tend My **l-s**
Acts 8:32, AS A L BEFORE ITS SHEARER IS SILENT
1 Pet. 1:19, a l unblemished and spotless

LAME Job 29:15, feet to the l
Matt. 11:5, and *the* l walk
Mark 9:45, better for you to enter life l
2 Sam. 9:13; Zeph. 3:19; Matt. 15:31; Acts 14:8

LAMENT—*mourn* Luke 8:52; 23:27; Rev. 18:9

LAMP—*light* Ps. 18:28, Thou dost light my l
Ps. 119:105, Thy word is a l to my feet
Matt. 5:15, light a l, and put it under
6:22, l of the body is the eye
25:8, our **l-s** are going out
Rev. 22:5, light of l nor ... of sun
1 Sam. 3:3; 2 Sam. 22:29; Job 18:6; Prov. 20:27; Zeph. 1:12; Rev. 4:5

LAMPSTAND Ex. 25:31; 1 Kin. 7:49; 2 Kin. 4:10; Luke 8:16

LAND—*country, earth, ground*
Gen. 1:9, let the dry l appear
Deut. 6:3, l flowing with milk and honey
Ps. 37:29, righteous will inherit the l
88:12, in the l of forgetfulness
Is. 66:8, Can a l be born in one day
Jer. 22:29, O l, l, l, Hear the word of the LORD
Matt. 2:6, AND YOU, BETHLEHEM, L OF JUDAH
27:45, darkness fell upon all the l
Luke 14:18, have bought a piece of l
23:44, darkness fell over the whole l
Heb. 11:29, Red Sea as ... through dry l
Gen. 15:18; Ex. 1:7; Deut. 8:8; 1 Sam. 6:5; Job 28:13; Ps. 25:13; 37:9,11,22; 60:2; Prov. 25:25; Eccles. 5:9; Is. 2:7; Jer. 15:10; Ezek. 9:9; Mic. 7:2; Mal. 4:6; Acts 4:37

LANGUAGE—*word, voice*
Gen. 10:5, one according to his l
11:1, whole earth used the same l
Ezek. 3:5,6, unintelligible speech or difficult l
Acts 2:6, hearing them speak in his own l
1 Cor. 14:10, many kinds of **l-s**

LANGUISH—*faint* Ps. 119:81, My soul **l-es** for Thy salvation

LAPIS LAZULI—*sapphire* Ezek. 28:13, The l, the turquoise

LARGE—*vast* Ps. 31:8; Matt. 28:12; Luke 22:12; Gal. 6:11

LASHES Luke 12:47, shall receive many l

LAST—*utmost* Ps. 30:5, weeping may l for the night
Is. 44:6, I am the first and I am the l
Matt. 5:26, have paid up the l cent
12:45, the l state of that man
19:30, first will be l; and *the* l, first
John 6:39, raise it up on the l day
1 Cor. 15:45, The l Adam *became* a life-giving spirit
15:52, at the l trumpet
1 Pet. 1:5, revealed in the l time
Rev. 1:17, I am the first and the l
Is. 7:9; Luke 11:26

LATER—*afterward* John 13:36, you shall follow l

LATTICE—*window*
Is. 60:8, like the doves to their **l-s**

LAUGH—*mock* Gen. 18:13, Why did Sarah l
Job 8:21, fill your mouth with **l-ter**
Prov. 14:13, Even in **l-ter** the heart ... in pain
Eccles. 3:4, time to weep, and a time to l
Matt. 9:24, they were **l-ing** at Him
Luke 6:25, Woe *to you* who l now
James 4:9, let your **l-ter** be turned

LAUGHINGSTOCK—*derision*
Jer. 20:7, a l all day long

LAUNDERER—*fuller* Mark 9:3, no l ... can whiten them

LAW—*teaching* Ps. 19:7, l of the LORD is perfect
Prov. 29:18, happy is he who keeps the l
Matt. 5:17, came to abolish the **L**
7:12, this is the **L** and the Prophets
12:2, disciples do what is not **l-ful**
12:4, bread ... not **l-ful** for him to eat
John 7:51, Our **L** does not judge a man
Rom. 13:10, love ... fulfillment of *the* l
Gal. 3:24, **L** has become our tutor
5:23, against such things there is no l
6:2, thus fulfill the l of Christ
Heb. 7:19, **L** made nothing perfect
James 1:25, the perfect l, the l of liberty
Ex. 12:49; Josh. 1:8; 2 Kin. 22:8; Prov. 28:7; John 19:7; Rom. 2:14; 4:15; 1 Cor. 6:2,7; Titus 3:9

LAWLESS—*wicked* 2 Thess. 2:8, l one will be revealed

LAWLESSNESS—*iniquity*
Matt. 24:12, because l is increased
2 Cor. 6:14, righteousness and l
1 John 3:4, and sin is l

LAY Ps. 3:5, I l down and slept
Matt. 6:19, Do not l up for yourselves treasures
John 10:11, good shepherd **l-s** down His life
10:15, I l down My life for the sheep
Rom. 13:12, l aside the deeds of darkness

LAZY—*idle, slothful* Ex. 5:8,17
Matt. 25:26, You wicked, l slave
Titus 1:12, evil beasts, l gluttons

LEAD—*guide* 2 Chr. 23:13; Ps. 25:9; 27:11; Is. 40:11
Ex. 13:21, cloud by day to l them on the way
Ps. 23:2, He **l-s** me beside quiet waters
25:5, **L** me in Thy truth
Is. 11:6, a little boy will l them
Matt. 6:13, do not l us into temptation
John 10:3, calls his own sheep ... **l-s** them out
1 Tim. 2:2, may l a tranquil and quiet life

LEADER—*first, head* Num. 16:2; Luke 22:26
Matt. 2:6, AMONG THE L-S OF JUDAH

LEAK—*drop* Eccles. 10:18, the house **l-s**

LEARN—*instruction* Deut. 31:13; Is. 1:17
Prov. 1:5, wise man will ... increase in **l-ing**
Is. 2:4, never again will they l war
Matt. 11:29, l from Me
Acts 26:24, great **l-ing** is driving you mad
Eph. 4:20, you did not l Christ

2 Tim. 3:7, always **l-ing**
Heb. 5:8, He **l-ed** obedience
LEAST—*young* 2 Kin. 18:24, l of my master's servants
Matt. 2:6, NO MEANS L AMONG THE LEADERS
5:19, called l in the kingdom of heaven
11:11, he who is l ... is greater
1 Cor. 15:9, I am the l of the apostles
Eph. 3:8, To me, the very l of all saints
LEATHER—*skin* Matt. 3:4, John ... l belt about his waist
Mark 1:6, *wore* a l belt around his waist
LEAVE—*abandon, desert, forsake* Ex. 20:7; Job 9:27
Gen. 2:24, man shall l his father ... mother
Ruth 1:16, Do not urge me to l you
Ps. 49:10, l their wealth to others
Matt. 18:12, does he not l the ninety-nine
19:5, MAN SHALL L HIS FATHER AND MOTHER
John 14:27, Peace I l with you
16:28, I am **l-ing** the world again
Prov. 2:17; 3:3
LEAVEN Ex. 12:19; Lev. 6:17
Matt. 13:33, kingdom of heaven is like l
16:6, beware of the l of the Pharisees
Luke 13:21, It is like l
1 Cor. 5:6, a little l **l-s** the whole lump
5:7, Clean out the old l
LEFT—*remain* Matt. 19:27, l everything and followed You
Matt. 26:56, disciples l Him and fled
Mark 1:18, l the nets and followed Him
Luke 5:11, l everything and followed Him
Heb. 11:27, By faith he l Egypt
Gen. 7:23; Matt. 14:20
LEND—*loan* Deut. 15:6; Neh. 5:10; Luke 11:5
Prov. 22:7, borrower *becomes* the **l-er's** slave
Luke 6:34, Even sinners l to sinners
LENGTH—*long* Prov. 3:2; Ezek. 31:7; Eph. 3:18
LENGTHEN Matt. 23:5, l the tassels of *their garments*
LEOPARD Jer. 13:23, Or the l his spots
Rev. 13:2, beast ... was like a l
Is. 11:6; Hos. 13:7
LEPER Matt. 10:8, cleanse *the* **l-s**
Matt. 11:5, *the* **l-s** are cleansed
Lev. 13:51; 2 Chr. 26:21; Matt. 8:2; Mark 14:3
LEPROUS Lev. 13:51, the mark is a l malignancy
LESS Gen. 1:16, **l-er** light to govern the night
Is. 40:17, regarded by Him as l than nothing
2 Cor. 12:15, am I to be loved the l
LET—*suffer* Matt. 19:14, **L** the children alone, and
LETTER 2 Cor. 3:2, You are our l
2 Cor. 3:3, you are a l of Christ
2 Pet. 3:16, as also in all *his* **l-s**
2 Chr. 2:11; Acts 15:30; Rom. 16:22; 2 Cor. 7:8; Col. 4:16; 2 Thess. 2:15; 3:14
LEVEL—*plain* Ps. 27:11, lead me in a l path
Luke 19:44, will l you to the ground
LEVY—*collection* 2 Chr. 24:6, the l *fixed by* Moses
LIAR Job 24:25; John 8:55
Rom. 3:4, every man ... a l
1 Tim. 4:2, by means of the hypocrisy of **l-s**
1 John 5:10, God has made Him a l
LIBATION—*drink* Gen. 35:14, poured out a l
LIBERTY Ps. 119:45, I will walk at l
Is. 61:1, proclaim l to the captives
2 Cor. 3:17, where the Spirit ... is, *there* is l
Gal. 2:4, to spy out our l
James 1:25, perfect law, the *law* of l
LICK 1 Kin. 21:19; Ps. 72:9; Luke 16:21
LIE—*guile, lay, sleep, vain* Deut. 19:11; 31:16
Ps. 4:8, In peace I will both l down
23:2, makes me l down in green pastures
Rom. 1:25, exchanged the truth of God for a l
Col. 3:9, Do not l to one another
Heb. 6:18, impossible for God to l
Rev. 14:5, no l was found in their mouth
Job 7:21; 34:6; 40:21; Ps. 119:69; Eccles. 4:11; Song 1:7; Jer. 8:8; Acts 5:3
LIFE—*flesh, living, soul* Ex. 21:23; Deut. 30:19
Gen. 2:7, into his nostrils the breath of l
Ps. 16:11, make known to me the path of l
36:9, with Thee is the fountain of l
89:47, Remember what my span of l is
133:3, LORD commanded ... l forever
Prov. 3:16, Long l is in her right hand
8:35, he who finds me finds l
Matt. 6:25, do not be anxious for your l
6:27, cubit to his **l-'s** span
10:39, who has lost his l for My sake
16:25, whoever wishes to save his l
19:16, that I may obtain eternal l
20:28, give His l a ransom for many
Mark 8:35, wishes to save his l shall lose it
10:17, shall I do to inherit eternal l
13:20, no l would have been saved
Luke 12:23, l is more than food
18:30, in the age to come, eternal l
John 4:36, gathering fruit for l eternal
5:21, Son also gives l to whom He wishes
5:24, passed out of death into l
6:35, I am the bread of l
10:11, shepherd lays down His l
11:25, I am the resurrection and the l
12:25, who loves his l loses it
14:6, the way, the truth, and the l
15:13, lay down his l for his friends
17:3, this is eternal l
20:31, you may have l in His name
Acts 3:15, put to death the Prince of l
Rom. 6:4, walk in newness of l
6:23, gift of God is eternal l
8:11, give l to your mortal bodies
2 Cor. 3:6, but the Spirit gives l
Gal. 6:8, from the Spirit reap eternal l
Phil. 2:16, holding fast the word of l
4:3, names are in the book of l
Col. 3:4, Christ, who is our l
1 Tim. 2:2, a tranquil and quiet l
Titus 3:7, hope of eternal l
James 1:12, receive the crown of l
1 John 1:1, concerning the Word of **L**
5:12, who has the Son has l
Rev. 2:10, give you the crown of l
13:8, not been written ... book of l of the Lamb
Deut. 32:39; Josh. 2:14; 1 Sam. 25:29; Job 10:1; Ps. 22:20; 35:17; Prov. 4:13,23; Jer. 21:8; 31:12; 38:16; Ezek. 18:27; Dan. 12:2; Luke 12:15; 15:24; Titus 3:3; Rev. 7:17
LIFT—*exalt, set, take* Num. 6:26, LORD l up ... countenance
Ps. 3:3, the One who **l-s** my head
24:7, **L** up your heads, O gates
116:13, l up the cup of salvation
121:1, l up my eyes to the mountains
Is. 2:4, Nation will not l up sword
John 3:14, Moses **l-ed** up the serpent
Acts 1:9, He was **l-ed** up
Gen. 13:14; Ex. 14:16; Job 38:34; Ps. 134:2; Is. 5:26; 11:12; 13:2; 40:4; Luke 18:13
LIGHT—*dawn, lamp* Ex. 10:23; Job 18:5; 38:19
Gen. 1:3, Let there be l; and there was l
Ps. 4:6, l of Thy countenance upon us
27:1, my l and my salvation
119:105, a l to my path
Is. 2:5, let us walk in the l of the LORD
60:1, Arise, shine; for your l has come
Matt. 5:14, You are the l of the world
5:15, Nor do men l a lamp
6:22, whole body will be full of l
11:30, My load is l
Luke 2:32, L OF REVELATION TO THE GENTILES
16:8, more shrewd ... than the sons of l
John 1:7, bear witness of the l
1:9, There was the true l
8:12, I am the l of the world
12:35, Walk while you have the l

LIGHT *(Continued)*
1 Cor. 4:5, bring to **l** the things hidden
2 Cor. 4:4, **l** of the gospel of glory
Eph. 5:8, walk as the children of **l**
1 John 1:7, if we walk in the **l** as He
Prov. 4:18; Eccles. 11:7; Is. 5:20; Jer. 31:35; Mic. 7:9; Matt. 10:27

LIKE—*desire* Luke 20:36,46

LIKENESS—*image* Ex. 20:4; Deut. 4:16; Matt. 22:20
Gen. 1:26, in Our image, according to Our **l**
Rom. 8:3, in the **l** of sinful flesh
Phil. 2:7, made in the **l** of men

LILY Song 2:1, **l** of the valleys
Hos. 14:5, He will blossom like the **l**
Matt. 6:28, Observe how the **l-es** of the field

LIMIT—*short* Num. 11:23, LORD's power **l-ed**
Job 15:8, **l** wisdom to yourself

LINE Joel 2:7, they each march in **l**

LINEN Gen. 41:42; Prov. 31:24; Jer. 13:1; Mark 15:46; John 20:5; Rev. 19:14

LINGER 2 Sam. 1:9; Prov. 23:30

LINTEL Ex. 12:7, on the **l** of the houses

LION
1 Pet. 5:8, devil, prowls about like a roaring **l**
Gen. 49:9; 1 Sam. 17:34; 1 Chr. 11:22; Job 10:16; Ps. 7:2; 57:4; Prov. 28:1; Eccles. 9:4; Rev. 9:8

LISTEN—*hear* Mark 4:3, **L** *to this* . . . sower
Mark 4:24, Take care what you **l** to
John 6:60, who can **l** to it
Eph. 1:13, **l-ing** to the message of truth
Gen. 4:23; Ex. 18:19; 20:19; Deut. 4:30; 11:27; Job 13:17; 35:13; 37:14; Prov. 23:22; 25:12; Eccles. 5:1; Dan. 9:19; Amos 5:23

LIT—*enlighten* Ps. 97:4, His lightnings **l** up the world

LITTLE—*small* Ps. 8:5, a **l** lower than God
Ps. 37:16, Better is the **l** of the righteous
Prov. 6:10, **l** sleep, a **l** slumber, A **l** folding
15:16, a **l** with the fear of the LORD
16:8, Better is a **l** with righteousness
Is. 11:6, a **l** boy will lead them
Matt. 6:30, O men of **l** faith
Luke 7:47, he who is forgiven **l**, loves **l**
12:32, Do not be afraid, **l** flock
John 7:33, For a **l** while longer I am with you
1 Cor. 5:6, a **l** leaven leavens the whole lump
Heb. 2:7, FOR A L WHILE LOWER THAN THE
Gen. 18:4; Judg. 4:19; 1 Sam. 2:19; Eccles. 5:12; Song 2:15; Is. 28:10

LIVE—*abide, reside, stay* Gen. 3:22; 42:18; Deut. 4:26
Deut. 8:3, man does not **l** by bread alone
Job 19:25, my Redeemer **l-s**
Prov. 21:9, better to **l** in a corner of a roof
Hab. 2:4, righteous will **l** by his faith
Matt. 4:4, MAN SHALL NOT L ON BREAD ALONE
Mark 12:44, put in . . . all she had to **l** on
Luke 10:28, DO THIS, AND YOU WILL L
20:38, for all **l** to Him
John 11:25, who believes in Me shall **l** even if he dies
Rom. 1:17, RIGHTEOUS *man* SHALL L BY FAITH
8:12, to **l** according to the flesh
14:8, if we **l**, we **l** for the Lord
14:9, Christ died and **l-d** again
2 Cor. 5:15, no longer **l** for themselves
Gal. 2:20, no longer I who **l**, but Christ **l-s** in me
Phil. 1:21, to me, to **l** is Christ
James 4:15, If the Lord wills, we shall **l**
Job 7:16; Ps. 119:175; Is. 55:3; Jer. 49:18; Ezek. 5:11; Matt. 12:45

LIVING Gen. 2:7, man became a **l** being
1 Kin. 3:25, Divide the **l** child in two
Matt. 16:16, Son of the **l** God
John 4:10, He would have given you **l** water
6:51, I am the **l** bread
7:38, rivers of **l** water
Acts 10:42, Judge of the **l** and the dead
Rom. 12:1, your bodies a **l** . . . sacrifice
1 Cor. 15:45, Adam, BECAME A L SOUL
2 Cor. 6:16, temple of the **l** God
Heb. 4:12, word of God is **l**
Num. 16:48; Deut. 5:26; Job 28:13; Eccles. 7:2; Dan. 6:26; 2 Pet. 2:8

LOAD—*burden* Matt. 11:30, My **l** is light
Matt. 23:4, they tie up heavy **l-s**

LOAN—*lend*
Deut. 23:19, *or* anything that may be **l-ed**

LOATHE Ps. 95:10; Amos 6:8

LOATHSOME Gen. 46:34, every shepherd is **l** to . . . Egyptians
Job 6:7, are like **l** food to me

LOAVES 1 Sam. 10:3, carrying three **l** of bread
Matt. 14:17, five **l** and two fish
Mark 6:52, the *incident of* the **l**

LOBE Ex. 29:13; Lev. 3:4,10,15

LOCK—*shut* Deut. 33:25; Judg. 16:13; Ezek. 44:20
Acts 5:23, prison-house **l-ed** quite securely

LOCUST—*grasshopper* Ex. 10:13; Lev. 11:22; Judg. 6:5; 1 Kin. 8:37; Job 39:20; Prov. 30:27; Joel 2:25; Nah. 3:17; Matt. 3:4

LODGE Job 19:4; 41:22
Ruth 1:16, where you **l**, I will **l**

LOFTY Is. 10:33, **l** will be abased

LOG—*beam* Eccles. 10:9; Luke 6:42
Matt. 7:5, first take the **l** out of your own eye

LOINS—*waist* Ex. 12:11; 2 Kin. 4:29
Eph. 6:14, GIRDED YOUR L WITH TRUTH

LONELY Ps. 25:16, be gracious . . . For I am **l**

LONG—*length* Ex. 2:3; 2 Sam. 3:1; Prov. 3:16
Matt. 23:14, for a pretense you make **l** prayers
1 Cor. 11:14, if a man has **l** hair
Eph. 6:3, LIVE L ON THE EARTH
Rev. 6:10, How **l**, O Lord

LONG (v.)—*desire* Job 3:21; Ps. 84:2
Luke 16:21, **l-ing** to be fed with the *crumbs*
Rom. 8:19, anxious **l-ing** of the creation
2 Cor. 5:2, **l-ing** to be clothed with our dwelling
1 Tim. 6:10, by **l-ing** for it have wandered away
1 Pet. 1:12, things into which angels **l** to look
2:2, like newborn babes, **l** for the pure milk

LOOK—*see* Ex. 3:6, he was afraid to **l** at God
Ps. 84:9, **l** upon the face of Thine anointed
Matt. 11:3, shall we **l** for someone else
14:19, and **l-ing** up toward heaven
Luke 2:38, **l-ing** for the redemption of Jerusalem
2:44, began **l-ing** for Him among their
9:62, hand to the plow and **l-ing** back
John 4:35, **l** on the fields
Acts 3:4, Peter . . . said, **L** at us
10:21, I am the one you are **l-ing** for
Gal. 6:1, **l-ing** to yourself, lest you
Phil. 2:4, do not . . . **l** out for your . . . interests
2 Pet. 3:13, **l-ing** for new heavens
Rev. 14:1, I **l-ed**, and behold, the Lamb
Gen. 19:17; Ex. 3:2; Job 35:5; Ps. 91:8; 114:3; Prov. 23:31; Eccles. 12:3; Is. 17:7; Luke 17:23

LOOM Judg. 16:14, pulled out the pin of the **l**

LOOSE—*release* Job 38:31, **l** the cords of Orion
Ps. 116:16, Thou hast **l-d** my bonds
Matt. 16:19, **l** on earth . . . **l-d** in heaven
Luke 15:13, his estate with **l** living

LORD 2 Cor. 1:24, Not that we **l** it over your faith
2 Thess. 2:2, day of the **L** has come

LOSE Joel 2:10, stars **l** their brightness
Matt. 10:39, who has found his life shall **l** it
16:25, save his life shall **l** it
Mark 9:41, he shall not **l** his reward

LOSS—*damage* Dan. 6:2; Acts 27:10
2 Cor. 7:9, you might not suffer **l**

LOST—*perish* Lev. 6:3; Ps. 119:176
Matt. 10:6, go to the **l** sheep of . . . Israel
18:11, come to save that which was **l**
Luke 15:24, he was **l** and has been found
John 6:12, fragments that nothing may be **l**

LOT—*portion* Lev. 16:8; Num. 26:55
Ps. 22:18, for my clothing they cast **l-s**

Prov. 1:14, Throw in your **l** with us
Jon. 1:7, cast **l-s** and the **l** fell on Jonah
John 19:24, Let us not tear it, but cast **l-s** for it
Acts 1:26, the **l** fell to Matthias

LOUD—*great* Rev. 21:3, I heard a **l** voice from the throne

LOVE (v.) Ex. 20:6; Neh. 13:26; Ps. 31:23; Zech. 8:17
Lev. 19:18, you shall **l** your neighbor as yourself
Deut. 6:5, **l** the LORD your God with all
Prov. 3:12, whom the LORD **l-s** He reproves
8:17, I **l** those who **l** me
12:1, whoever **l-s** discipline **l-s** knowledge
17:17, friend **l-s** at all times
20:13, Do not **l** sleep
Eccles. 3:8, time to **l**, and a time to hate
Amos 5:15, Hate evil, **l** good
Matt. 5:44, **l** your enemies
6:5, for they **l** to stand
6:24, hate the one and **l** the other
22:39, L YOUR NEIGHBOR AS YOURSELF
Luke 6:27, **l** your enemies
John 3:16, God so **l-d** the world
2 Cor. 9:7, God **l-s** a cheerful giver
Eph. 5:2, walk in **l**, just as Christ **l-d** you
Col. 3:19, Husbands, **l** your wives
Titus 2:4, **l** their husbands, to **l** their children
James 2:8, L YOUR NEIGHBOR AS YOURSELF
1 John 4:7, let us **l** one another . . . every one who **l-s**

LOVE (n.) Prov. 10:12, **l** covers all transgressions
Matt. 24:12, most people's **l** will grow cold
John 13:35, if you have **l** for one another
15:13, Greater **l** has no one than this
Rom. 12:9, Let **l** be without hypocrisy
1 Cor. 13:1, do not have **l**
14:1, Pursue **l**
Gal. 5:13, through **l** serve one another
Col. 3:14, beyond . . . *put on* **l**
1 Tim. 1:5, our instruction is **l**
6:10, **l** of money is a root of . . . evil
2 Tim. 2:22, righteousness, faith, **l**
Heb. 13:1, Let **l** of the brethren continue
1 Pet. 4:8, **l** covers a multitude of sins
2 Pet. 1:7, brotherly kindness, Christian **l**
1 John 4:7, **l** is from God
3 John 6, your **l** before the church
Jude 21, keep yourselves in the **l** of God
Rev. 2:4, you have left your first **l**
Gen. 29:20; 2 Sam. 1:26

LOVELY—*beautiful* Song 1:5, I am black but **l**
Is. 52:7, How **l** on the mountains

LOVINGKINDNESS—*compassion, mercy*
Ezra 3:11, His **l** is upon Israel forever
Ps. 86:15, a God . . . abundant in **l**
89:1, I will sing of the **l** of the LORD
117:2, His **l** is great toward us

LOW 1 Sam. 2:7, He brings **l**, He also exalts
Ps. 8:5, hast made him a little **l-er** than God
Jer. 9:10, **l-ing** of the cattle

LOWLIEST Dan. 4:17, And sets it over the **l** of men

LOWLY Job 5:11; Ps. 138:6
Rom. 12:16, associate with the **l**

LOYALTY 2 Sam. 16:17; Prov. 20:6

LUMP—*cake* Rom. 11:16, *dough* be holy, the **l** is also
1 Cor. 5:6, leavens the whole **l** of *dough*
5:7, that you may be a new **l**

LUNCH—*dinner* Luke 11:37, Pharisee asked Him to have **l**

LURK Prov. 7:12, And **l-s** by every corner

LUST—*desire* Matt. 5:28, looks on a woman to **l** for her
Rom. 13:14, no provision . . . regard to *its* **l-s**
James 4:2, You **l** and do not have
1 John 2:16, **l** of the flesh . . . **l** of the eyes
Jude 16, following after their own **l-s**

LUXURIANT Ps. 37:35; Hos. 10:1

LUXURIOUS James 5:5, lived **l-ly** on the earth

LUXURY Prov. 19:10, **L** is not fitting for a fool
Luke 7:25, live in **l** are *found* in royal palaces

LYING Prov. 6:17, Haughty eyes, a **l** tongue
Prov. 12:22, **L** lips are an abomination

LYRE—*harp* Gen. 4:21; Ps. 57:8; Is. 5:12

M

MAD—*insane* Eccles. 2:2, It is **m-ness**
Acts 26:24, learning is driving you **m**

MADE Gen. 1:7, God **m** the expanse
Ps. 8:5, **m** him a little lower than God
119:73, Thy hands **m** me
Eccles. 7:29, that God **m** men upright
Matt. 9:22, your faith has **m** you well
2 Cor. 5:21, **m** Him who knew no sin *to be* sin
Eph. 3:7, of which I was **m** a minister
Heb. 6:4, **m** partakers of the Holy Spirit
Ex. 4:11; Job 4:14; 17:6

MAGI—*wise* Matt. 2:1, **m** from the east arrived
Matt. 2:7, Herod secretly called the **m**
2:16, been tricked by the **m**

MAGIC Acts 19:19, those who practiced **m**

MAGNIFICENT—*gorgeous*
Ezek. 23:12, **m-ly** dressed, horsemen

MAGNIFY Ps. 34:3, O **m** the LORD with me
Acts 19:17, name . . . Jesus was being **m-ed**
Rom. 11:13, I **m** my ministry
2 Sam. 7:26; Job 7:17; Eccles. 1:16

MAGNITUDE—*greatness*
Jer. 13:22, the **m** of your iniquity

MAID Prov. 30:19, way of a man with a **m**
Gen. 16:6; Ruth 2:8; 3:9

MAIDEN Judg. 5:30; Job 41:5; Ps. 68:25

MAINTAIN Rom. 3:28, we **m** that a man is justified

MAJESTIC—*excellent* Ps. 8:1, Lord, How **m** is Thy name
Ps. 16:3; 2 Pet. 1:17

MAJESTY—*dignity, excellence*
Ps. 93:1, He is clothed with **m**
Is. 53:2, no *stately* form or **m**
Heb. 1:3, right hand of the **M** on high
Jude 25, glory, **m**, dominion and authority
Job 37:22; Is. 35:2; 2 Pet. 2:10; Jude 8

MAKE Gen. 1:26, Let Us **m** man in Our image
Gen. 2:18, **m** him a helper suitable for him
Ps. 25:4, **M** me know Thy ways, O LORD
Jer. 18:3, he was, **m-ing** something on the wheel
Matt. 3:3, **M** READY THE WAY OF THE LORD
4:19, I will **m** you fishers of men
5:34, **m** no oath at all
John 1:23, **M** STRAIGHT THE WAY OF THE LORD
James 4:13, engage in business and **m** a profit
2 Pet. 1:10, **m** certain about His calling and
Ex. 20:4,25; Deut. 8:18; Job 17:12; Luke 12:33; Rom. 10:19

MAKER Job 4:17; 35:10; Is. 17:7; 54:5; Jer. 10:16

MALE Gen. 5:2, He created them **m** and female
Matt. 2:16, slew all the **m** children
19:4, MADE THEM M AND FEMALE
Gen. 34:25; Deut. 4:16; Gal. 3:28

MALICE—*wickedness*
Matt. 22:18, Jesus perceived their **m**
1 Pet. 2:1, putting aside all **m**
1 Cor. 5:8; Eph. 4:31; Col. 3:8

MALICIOUS—*false* Ex. 23:1, to be a **m** witness
2 Tim. 3:3, **m** gossips, without

MALIGN—*speak* Titus 3:2, to **m** no one

MAN—*fellow, person, self* Gen. 1:26; 4:23
Gen. 3:22, the **m** has become like one of Us
Job 5:7, For **m** is born for trouble
Ps. 1:1, blessed is the **m** who does not walk in the
Matt. 4:4, **M** SHALL NOT LIVE ON BREAD ALONE
8:20, Son of **M** has nowhere to lay
26:61, This **m** stated, I am able to destroy
26:71, This **m** was with Jesus

MAN *(Continued)*
Mark 2:27, not **m** for the Sabbath
10:25, for a rich **m** to enter
Luke 6:45, The good **m** . . . the evil **m**
9:22, The Son of **M** must suffer
22:59, this **m** also was with Him
23:2, found this **m** misleading our nation
John 1:6, a **m**, sent from God
3:4, How can a **m** be born when
19:5, Behold, the **M**
1 Cor. 13:11, when I became a **m**
15:21, by a **m** *came* death
Eph. 4:13, to a mature **m**
James 1:8, a double-minded **m**, unstable in
Lev. 16:21; Num. 12:3; 1 Sam. 16:17; 1 Kin. 2:2; 2 Kin. 5:8; Job 14:1; 25:6; 33:12; Ps. 19:5; 37:37; Prov. 3:4; Eccles. 4:8; Is. 2:22; Matt. 26:2; John 7:12; 9:29; 2 Cor. 12:2
MANAGE—*rule* 1 Tim. 3:5, how to **m** his own household
MANGER Job 39:9; Prov. 14:4; Is. 1:3
MANIFEST—*reveal* John 17:6; Rom. 10:20; Col. 1:26
MANIFOLD—*various* Eph. 3:10, the **m** wisdom of God
1 Pet. 4:10, the **m** grace of God
MANKIND 2 Chr. 6:18; Job 4:17
MANNER Gen. 31:35, **m** of women is upon me
MANTLE—*garment* Heb. 1:12, AS A **M** THOU WILT ROLL THEM UP
1 Kin. 19:19; Is. 59:17
MANURE—*refuse*
Luke 14:35, for the soil or for the **m** pile
MANY—*multitude* Ps. 104:24, how **m** are Thy works
Song 8:7, **M** waters cannot quench love
Jer. 14:7, our apostasies have been **m**
Matt. 7:22, **M** will say to Me on that day
22:14, **m** are called, but few
Luke 7:47, her sins, which are **m**
21:8, **m** will come in My name
John 14:2, house are **m** dwelling places
Acts 2:43, **m** wonders and signs
Rom. 12:4, **m** members in one body
1 Cor. 11:30, **m** . . . are weak . . . a number sleep
James 3:1, **m** *of you* become teachers
Jude 14, **m** thousands of His holy ones
Rev. 1:15, sound of **m** waters
Gen. 16:10; 1 Kin. 11:1; Job 13:23; Ps. 71:7; Prov. 14:20
MARCH—*walk* Joel 2:8, **m** every one in his path
Nah. 2:5, stumble in their **m**
MARK Ps. 37:37, **M** the blameless
2 Thess. 3:17, a distinguishing **m** in every letter
Rev. 14:9, receives a **m** on his forehead
19:20, **m** of the beast
MARKET PLACES
Matt. 11:16, like children sitting in the **m**
Mark 6:56, laying the sick in the **m**
MARRIAGE Matt. 22:30, marry, are given in **m**
Heb. 13:4, Let **m** *be held* in honor
Rev. 19:7, **m** of the Lamb has come
MARRY Matt. 5:32, whoever **m-es** a divorced woman
Matt. 19:9, **m-es** another commits adultery
19:10, it is better not to **m**
Mark 12:25, they neither **m**, nor
Luke 20:34, sons of this age **m**
1 Cor. 7:9, better to **m** than to burn
1 Tim. 5:11, widows . . . want to get **m-ed**
MARVEL—*wonder* Ps. 71:7, I have become a **m** to many
Matt. 8:10, when Jesus heard *this*, He **m-ed**
15:31, the multitude **m-ed**
Mark 5:20, and everyone **m-ed**
John 3:7, Do not **m** that I said to you
1 Pet. 2:9, out of darkness into His **m-ous** light
Rev. 15:3, GREAT AND **M-OUS** ARE THY WORKS
MASSAH—*temptation* Ps. 95:8, in the day of **M**
MASTER—*dominion, teacher* Job 3:19; Eph. 6:5
Matt. 6:24, No one can serve two **m-s**
10:24, nor a slave above his **m**
Rom. 6:9, death no longer is **m** over Him
1 Cor. 3:10, as a wise **m-builder** I laid
MATERIAL Deut. 22:11, not wear a **m** mixed . . . together
1 Cor. 9:11, we should reap **m** things
MATTER Gen. 21:17; 30:15; 1 Sam. 11:5; 21:8
MEAN—*thought* Gen. 50:20, **m-t** evil against me
Ex. 34:7, by no **m-s** leave *the guilty* unpunished
Matt. 9:13, go and learn what this **m-s**
Acts 17:20, know . . . what these things **m**
1 Cor. 14:11, do not know the **m-ing** of the language
Gal. 5:6, neither circumcision . . . **m-s** anything
MEANINGLESS—*vain*
Matt. 6:7, do not use **m** repetition
MEASURE Eph. 4:7, according to the **m** of Christ's gift
Rev. 21:16, **m-d** the city with the rod
Gen. 18:6; Deut. 25:15; 2 Kin. 7:1; Ps. 80:5; Matt. 7:2
MEAT—*flesh* Ex. 16:3; Deut. 12:20
MEDDLER—*busybody*
1 Pet. 4:15, troublesome **m**
MEDIATOR Gal. 3:19, by the agency of a **m**
Gal. 3:20, a **m** is not for one *party*
1 Tim. 2:5, one **m** also between God and men
Heb. 8:6, **m** of a better covenant
12:24, to Jesus the **m** of a new covenant
MEDITATE Gen. 24:63, Isaac went out to **m**
Ps. 1:2, in His law he **m-s** day and night
19:14, **m-ion** of my heart
MEDIUM Lev. 19:31; 1 Sam. 28:7
MEETING—*congregation* Acts 13:43, **m** of the synagogue had
MELODY Is. 51:3, sound of a **m**
Eph. 5:19, making **m** with your heart
MELT—*dissolve* Josh. 2:11; Ps. 46:6; 75:3; 97:5; Is. 14:31
MEMBER Matt. 10:25, how much more the **m-s** . . . household
1 Cor. 6:15, your bodies are **m-s** of Christ
12:12, the body . . . has many **m-s**
12:14, body is not one **m**, but many
MEMORIAL Ex. 3:15; 17:14; Josh. 4:7; Acts 10:4
MEMORY Prov. 10:7, **m** of the righteous is blessed
Matt. 26:13, spoken of in **m** of her
Job 18:17; Ps. 9:6; 109:15
MEN Ps. 116:11, All **m** are liars
Mark 1:17, I will make you . . . fishers of **m**
Luke 20:4, from heaven or from **m**
1 Thess. 2:4, not as pleasing **m** but God
Gen. 6:1; 1 Sam 4:9; Job 11:3; Ps. 26:4; 82:7; Matt. 10:17; Mark 6:21; Acts 17:5
MENTION Ps. 71:16; Is. 63:7; Rom. 1:9,10
MERCHANDISE John 2:16, My Father's house a house of **m**
MERCHANT 1 Kin. 10:28; Hos. 12:7; Rev. 18:3
MERCY—*compassion*
2 Sam. 24:14, for His **m-es** are great
Matt. 5:7, for they shall receive **m**
18:33, I had **m** on you
Rom. 9:15, **M** ON WHOM I HAVE **M**
12:1, by the **m-es** of God
1 Cor. 7:25, as one who by the **m** of the LORD
Eph. 2:4, God, being rich in **m**
James 5:11, full of compassion and *is* **m-ful**
MERRY—*joyful* Eccles. 8:15, drink and be **m**
Luke 12:19, eat, drink *and* be **m**
15:29, might be **m** with my friends
MESSAGE—*tidings, word, report, speech*
Luke 4:32, His **m** was with authority
Acts 20:7, his **m** until midnight
Judg. 3:19,20; Jer. 49:14; Is. 53:1; Luke 4:36
MESSENGER Matt. 11:10, MY **M** BEFORE YOUR FACE
2 Cor. 12:7, a **m** of Satan
2 Kin. 6:32; Hag. 1:13
MESSIAH—*Lord, Christ* John 1:41, found the **M**
MIDDLE Josh. 12:2; Ruth 3:8; Prov. 30:19

MIDNIGHT Ps. 119:6; Matt. 25:6; Acts 16:25; 20:7
MIDST—*middle, within*
Matt. 10:16, sheep in the **m** of
18:20, there I am in their **m**
Luke 17:21, kingdom of God is in your **m**
24:36, He Himself stood in their **m**
John 20:26, Jesus . . . stood in their **m**
MIGHT Job 39:19, give the horse *his* **m**
Zech. 4:6, Not by **m** or by power
Acts 19:20, word . . . was growing **m-ily**
Eph. 1:19, working of the strength of His **m**
Col. 1:29, which **m-ily** works within me
Gen. 49:3; Deut. 6:5; Judg. 5:31; 2 Sam. 6:14; Eccles. 9:10; Jer. 9:23
MIGHTY 2 Sam. 1:19, How have the **m** fallen
Ps. 24:8, strong and **m** . . . **m** in battle
89:13, Thy hand is **m**
Jer. 48:17, How has the **m** scepter been broken
Joel 3:10, weak say, I am a **m** man
Mic. 4:3, decisions for **m**, distant nations
Luke 24:19, prophet **m** in deed and word
Acts 2:11, the **m** deeds of God
18:24, **m** in the Scriptures
2 Cor. 13:3, but **m** in you
1 Pet. 5:6, the **m** hand of God
Gen. 6:4; 10:9; Deut. 10:17; Is. 19:4; 63:1; Jer. 32:18
MILE Luke 24:13; John 11:18; Rev. 14:20
MILK Ex. 3:8, land flowing with **m** and honey
1 Cor. 3:2, I gave you **m** to drink
Heb. 5:12, you have come to need **m**
1 Pet. 2:2, pure **m** of the word
Gen. 49:12; Judg. 4:19; Job 10:10; Prov. 30:33
MIND—*heart* Ps. 7:9, tries the hearts and **m-s**
Mark 5:15, and in his right **m**
Acts 28:6, changed their **m-s**
Rom. 1:28, over to a depraved **m**
8:7, **m** set on the flesh is hostile
1 Cor. 1:10, complete in the same **m**
2 Cor. 13:11, be **like-m-ed**, live in peace
Phil. 2:2, being of the same **m**
2:3, with humility of **m** let each
Col. 3:2, Set your **m** on
James 1:8, a **double-m-ed** man
1 Pet. 1:13, gird your **m-s** for action
Gen. 40:14; Ps. 31:12; Is. 46:8; Jer. 17:10; Dan. 4:16; Rom. 14:5; 1 Tim. 6:5; 2 Pet. 1:15
MINISTER Is. 61:6; Eph. 3:7
MINISTRY—*service* 1 Cor. 12:5; 2 Cor. 9:12
Acts 6:4, to the **m** of the word
2 Cor. 5:18, **m** of reconciliation
Col. 4:17, Take heed to the **m**
2 Tim. 4:5, fulfill your **m**
Heb. 8:6, obtained a more excellent **m**
MIRACLE—*marvel, sign, mighty*
Matt. 11:21, if the **m-s** had occurred in Tyre
Ex. 34:10; Mark 6:5; 1 Cor. 12:10
MIRROR 1 Cor. 13:12, we see in a **m** dimly
James 1:23, his natural face in a **m**
Ex. 38:8; Job 37:18; Is. 3:23
MISCARRIAGE Ex. 21:22, so that she has a **m**
MISCARRY—*young* Ex. 23:26, no one **m-ing**
MISCHIEF Job 15:35, They conceive **m**
MISERY Job 10:15; Rom. 3:16
MISGIVING Acts 10:20, accompany them without **m-s**
MISGUIDE Heb. 5:2, deal gently with the ignorant and **m-d**
MISLEAD Deut. 27:18, **m-s** a blind person
Job 12:16, misled and the **m-er** belong to Him
Matt. 24:24, so as to **m** . . . even the elect
MISSILE Eph. 6:16, flaming **m-s** of the evil one
MISTAKE Eccles. 5:6; Matt. 22:29; Mark 12:24
MISTREAT—*wrong* Jer. 22:3, do not **m** *or* do violence
Matt. 22:6; Luke 18:32; Acts 7:19
MIX Deut. 22:11; Prov. 23:30; Dan. 2:41; Rev. 18:6
MOCK Prov. 14:9, Fools **m** at sin
Prov. 20:1, Wine is a **m-er**
Gal. 6:7, God is not **m-ed**
2 Kin. 2:23; Job 21:3; 30:1; Hab. 1:10; Matt. 27:29
MODE Judg. 13:12, shall be the boy's **m** of life
MODEL 2 Thess. 3:9, offer ourselves as a **m**
MOMENT—*instant* Ps. 30:5, His anger is for a **m**
Job 34:20, In a **m** they die
1 Cor. 15:52, in a **m**, in the twinkling of an
MONEY—*gain* Gen. 43:12; Deut. 21:14
Eccles. 5:10, who loves **m** will not be satisfied
10:19, **m** is the answer to everything
Matt. 21:12, tables of the **m-changers**
Mark 6:8, no **m** in their belt
Luke 19:23, why . . . not put the **m** . . . bank
1 Tim. 3:3, free from the love of **m**
6:10, love of **m** is a root . . . of evil
2 Kin. 5:26; Eccles. 7:12; Jer. 32:25; Amos 2:6
MONEYLENDER—*creditor*
Luke 7:41, certain **m** had two
MONGREL Zech. 9:6, a **m** race
MONSTER Gen. 1:21, created the great sea **m-s**
Job 7:12, sea, or the sea **m**
Ezek. 32:2, **m** in the seas
MOON—*crescent* Matt. 24:29, M WILL NOT GIVE ITS LIGHT
Luke 21:25, signs in the sun and **m**
Gen. 37:9; Josh. 10:12; 1 Sam. 20:5; Job 31:26; Ps. 136:9; Song 6:10; Is. 1:13; Joel 2:31; Acts 2:20
MORALS 1 Cor. 15:33, Bad company corrupts good **m**
MORNING—*early* Job 38:7, **m** stars sang together
2 Pet. 1:19, the **m** star arises in your hearts
Rev. 22:16, the bright **m** star
Gen. 19:15; Ex. 8:20; Deut. 28:67; Ps. 55:17; Eccles. 11:6
MORSEL—*piece* Job 31:17; Prov 17:1
MORTAL Rom. 6:12, sin reign in your **m** body
Rom. 8:11, give life to your **m** bodies
1 Cor. 15:53, **m** . . . put on immortality
2 Cor. 4:11, manifested in our **m** flesh
MOST—*many, very* Matt. 24:12, **m** people's love will grow
2 Cor. 11:5, least inferior to the **m** eminent
MOTHER Gen. 2:24, leave his father . . . **m**
Ex. 20:12, Honor your father and your **m**
Matt. 1:18, When His **m** Mary . . . betrothed
2:11, Child with Mary His **m**
2:13, **m** and flee to Egypt
19:19, HONOR YOUR FATHER AND M
John 19:27, the disciple, Behold, your **m**
Heb. 7:3, Without father, without **m**
Gen. 3:20; Ex. 22:30; Lev. 22:27; Deut. 22:6; Job 17:14; Ezek. 16:44; Hos. 2:2; Matt. 12:48
MOTION Ex. 15:16; Acts 12:17
MOTIVES—*thought* 1 Cor. 4:5, **m** of men's hearts
James 2:4, judges with evil **m**
MOUND—*bank* 2 Sam. 20:15, a **m** against the city
MOUNTAINS Ps. 121:1, will lift up my eyes to the **m**
Is. 5:25; Mic. 1:4
MOUNTED Zech. 9:9, **m** on a donkey
Matt. 21:5, GENTLE, AND M UPON A DONKEY
MOURN—*weep, wail*
Is. 61:2, To comfort all who **m**
Matt. 2:18, WEEPING AND GREAT M-ING
5:4, Blessed are those who **m**
Luke 6:25, for you shall **m** and weep
James 4:9, laughter be turned into **m-ing**
Rev. 1:7, TRIBES . . . M OVER HIM
Gen. 37:35; Deut. 21:13; Jer. 9:17; 15:5; 2 Cor. 12:21
MOUTH—*speech* Ps. 19:14, the words of my **m**
Ps. 39:1, guard my **m** as with a muzzle
Prov. 13:3, who guards his **m** preserves
Song 4:3, your **m** is lovely
Matt. 4:4, PROCEEDS OUT OF THE M OF GOD
13:35, OPEN MY M IN PARABLES
Acts 3:21, **m** of His holy prophets

MOUTH *(Continued)*
James 3:3, put the bits . . . horses' **m-s**
Ex. 4:11; Judg. 7:6; Job 8:21; 15:6; Ps. 8:2; 71:15; Prov. 4:24
MOVE 2 Chr. 16:9, eyes of the LORD **m**
Mark 1:41, **m-d** with compassion, He stretched
Acts 17:28, in Him we live and **m**
2 Pet. 1:21, **m-d** by the Holy Spirit
Gen. 1:2; Deut. 19:14; 1 Sam. 1:13; Jer. 4:24
MUCH Prov. 25:27, not good to eat **m** honey
Prov. 29:1, hardens his neck after **m** reproof
Eccles. 1:18, in **m** wisdom there is **m** grief
Luke 7:47, for she loved **m**
16:10, faithful also in **m**
MULTIPLY Gen. 1:22; Ex. 32:13; Deut. 6:3
MULTITUDE Matt. 14:15, send the **m-s** away
Luke 23:27, following Him a great **m**
James 5:20, cover a **m** of sins
1 Pet. 4:8, love covers a **m** of sins
Gen. 17:4; Ex. 23:2; Deut. 1:10
MURDER Ex. 20:13, You shall not **m**
Rom. 1:29, full of envy, **m**, strife
Matt. 5:21; 19:18
MURDERER Num. 35:16; John 8:44; Acts 28:4; 1 John 3:15
MURMUR Ps. 55:17, I will complain and **m**
MUSIC 1 Sam. 18:6; Luke 15:25
MUST—*ought* Acts 5:29, We **m** obey God
MUZZLE Deut. 25:4, not **m** the ox while
1 Cor. 9:9, 1 Tim. 5:18, NOT M THE OX WHILE
MYRRH Matt. 2:11, frankincense and **m**
John 19:39, mixture of **m** and aloes
Gen. 43:11; Ps. 45:8; Song 5:13
MYSTERY—*secret* Dan. 4:9, no **m** baffles you
Matt. 13:11, **m-es** of the kingdom
1 Cor. 2:7, God's wisdom in a **m**
4:1, stewards of the **m-es**
13:2, know all **m-es** . . . knowledge
Eph. 3:9, administration of the **m**
6:19, the **m** of the gospel
1 Tim. 3:9, the **m** of the faith
MYTHS—*fables* 1 Tim. 1:4, pay attention to **m**
Titus 1:14, paying attention to Jewish **m**

N

NAILS John 20:25, in His hands the imprint of **n**
Deut. 21:12; Dan. 4:33
NAIVE—*simple* Prov. 14:15, **n** believes everything
NAKED—*bare* Gen. 2:25; Job 1:21; 26:6; Matt. 25:36
NAME—*appoint* Job 1:21, Blessed be the **n** of the LORD
Ps. 8:1, How majestic is Thy **n**
18:49, sing praises to Thy **n**
72:17, his **n** endure forever . . . **n** increase
102:15, nations will fear the **n** of the LORD
111:9, Holy and awesome is His **n**
Prov. 22:1, good **n** is to be more desired
Matt. 6:9, Hallowed be Thy **n**
10:2, **n-s** of the twelve apostles are
18:5, one such child in My **n**
Mark 5:9, My **n** is Legion; for we are many
Luke 21:8, many will come in My **n**
John 15:16, you ask of the Father in My **n**
Acts 3:16, on the basis of faith in His **n**
4:12, no other **n** under heaven
Phil. 2:9, **n** which is above every **n**
4:3, whose **n-s** are in the book of life
Gen. 3:20; 30:28; Ex. 20:7; Deut. 29:20; Neh. 9:10; Prov. 30:9; Is. 42:8; 48:2; 57:15; Matt. 10:22; Eph. 1:21; 3 John 14
NARROW—*strait* Matt. 7:13, Enter by the **n** gate
NATION—*generation, Gentile*
Ps. 33:12, Blessed is the **n** whose God
Prov. 14:34, Righteousness exalts a **n**
Is. 2:4, **N** will not lift up sword against **n**
Matt. 24:7, **n** will rise against **n**
28:19, Go . . . make disciples of all the **n-s**
Acts 2:5, devout men, from every **n**
Gal. 3:8, ALL THE N-S SHALL BE BLESSED
Rev. 5:9, and tongue and people and **n**
Gen. 12:2; 20:4; Ex. 19:6; Lev. 26:33; Ps. 2:1; 102:15; Is. 18:2; 52:15; 66:19; Jer. 51:58; John 11:50; Rev. 11:2
NATIVE Acts 28:2,4
NATURAL Rom. 1:26, exchanged the **n** function
1 Cor. 15:44, it is sown a **n** body
NATURE 1 Cor. 11:14, Does not even **n** itself teach
2 Pet. 1:4, partakers of the divine **n**
NEAR—*close* Ps. 34:18, **n** to the brokenhearted
Ps. 145:18, **n** to all who call upon Him
Mark 13:28, you know that the summer is **n**
Eph. 2:13, brought **n** by the blood of Christ
Phil. 4:5, The Lord is **n**
Heb. 10:22, draw **n** with a sincere heart
James 4:8, Draw **n** to God and He will draw **n**
Ex. 19:22; Deut. 4:7; Ps. 22:11; Prov. 27:10; Joel 3:14
NECESSARY—*need*
Luke 10:42, *only* a few things are **n**
24:26, Was it not **n** for the Christ to suffer
NECK Gen. 27:16; Ex. 13:13; Deut. 28:48; Prov. 3:3; Matt. 18:6
NEED—*want* Prov. 25:16, Eat *only* what you **n**
Matt. 6:8, your Father knows what you **n**
9:12, not . . . healthy who **n** a physician
21:3, The Lord has **n** of them
Luke 15:14, he began to be in **n**
Phil. 4:19, God shall supply all your **n-s**
Heb. 4:16, help in time of **n**
1 John 3:17, beholds his brother in **n**
Rev. 3:17, have **n** of nothing
1 Cor. 12:21; 1 Thess. 4:12
NEEDLESS Gal. 2:21, then Christ died **n-ly**
NEEDY Ps. 9:18, **n** will not always be forgotten
Ps. 72:13, compassion on the poor and **n**
Is. 14:30, **n** will lie down in security
Ex. 23:6; Deut. 15:11; Job 29:16; Ps. 40:17; 69:33
NEGLECT—*forget*
Matt. 6:16, they **n** their appearance
Luke 15:29, I have never **n-ed** a command
Heb. 13:2,16
NEGLIGENCE—*error* Dan. 6:4, no **n** or corruption was *to be*
NEGLIGENT Prov. 10:4, works with a **n** hand
NEIGHBOR—*fellow-citizen*
Lev. 19:18, you shall love your **n**
Prov. 3:29, Do not devise harm against your **n**
27:10, Better is a **n** who is near
Hab. 2:15, who make your **n-s** drink
Matt. 5:43, YOU SHALL LOVE YOUR N
Luke 10:29, who is my **n**
NEST—*lodge* Matt. 8:20, birds have **n-s**
Luke 13:19, birds . . . **n-ed** in its branches
Num. 24:21; Deut. 32:11; Jer. 49:16; Obad. 4
NET Job 19:6; Ps. 57:6; Is. 51:20; Matt. 13:47
NEVER Matt. 7:23, I **n** knew you
John 4:14, of the water . . . shall **n** thirst
7:46, **N** did a man speak the way
8:51, he shall **n** see death
Heb. 13:5, I WILL N DESERT YOU
Deut. 15:11; Job 3:16; Ps. 31:1
NEW Lev. 23:14, roasted grain nor **n** growth
Ps. 33:3, Sing to Him a **n** song
Eccles. 1:9, nothing **n** under the sun
Is. 65:17, create **n** heavens and a **n** earth
Ezek. 11:19, put a **n** spirit within them
John 13:34, A **n** commandment I give to you
2 Cor. 5:17, a **n** creature . . . **n** things have come
Eph. 4:24, put on the **n** self
Rev. 21:1, a **n** heaven and a **n** earth
NEWS—*tidings* Gen. 29:13, heard the **n** of Jacob
2 Kin. 7:9, day is a day of good **n**
Is. 52:7, feet of him who brings good **n**
Luke 2:10, good **n** of a great joy
1 Thess. 3:6, good **n** of your faith
Prov. 15:30; Matt. 14:1; Mark 1:28,45

NIGHT Ex. 13:21, a pillar of fire by **n**
Ps. 19:2, **n** to **n** reveals knowledge
91:5, not be afraid of the terror by **n**
Is. 21:11, Watchman, how far gone is the **n**
Luke 2:8, watch over their flock by **n**
John 9:4, **n** is coming, when no man can work
Rom. 13:12, **n** is almost gone
2 Cor. 11:27, through many sleepless **n-s**
1 Thess. 5:2, like a thief in the **n**
Gen. 1:5; Josh. 1:8; Job 17:12

NOBLE Ps. 45:9; Prov. 8:6

NOISE—*sound* Is. 22:2, You who were full of **n**
Jer. 50:22, **n** of the battle is in the land
Acts 2:2, came from heaven a **n**
1 Cor. 13:1, have become a **n-y** gong

NONSENSE Luke 24:11, words appeared . . . as **n**

NOSTRIL Ezek. 16:12, put a ring in your **n**

NOTHING Job 26:7, hangs the earth on **n**
Ps. 49:17, he will carry **n** away
Prov. 13:7, pretends to be rich, but has **n**
John 15:5, apart from Me you can do **n**
1 Cor. 4:4, conscious of **n** against myself
Gal. 6:3, thinks he is something when he is **n**
Phil. 4:6, Be anxious for **n**
1 Tim. 4:7, have **n** to do with worldly fables
James 1:4, perfect and complete, lacking in **n**
Ex. 21:11; Lam. 1:12; Luke 6:35

NOTICE—*visit* Jer. 15:15, Remember me, take **n** of me
Matt. 6:1, righteousness . . . to be **n-d** by them
Matt. 7:3; Luke 6:41

NOURISH 1 Tim. 4:6, **n-ed** on the words of the faith

NULLIFY Rom. 3:3; 4:14; Gal. 2:21; 3:17

NUMBER—*measure, count* Num. 1:3; Job 14:16; Ps. 139:18; Matt. 10:30; 2 Cor. 11:23

NURSE Gen. 35:8; Ex. 2:7; Num. 11:12; 1 Thess. 2:7

O

OAK 2 Sam. 18:10; Is. 1:30; Amos 2:9

OATH—*vow* Gen. 26:3; Josh. 2:20; Acts 23:12

OBEDIENCE Rom. 16:26, to **o** of faith
2 Cor. 10:5, to the **o** of Christ
Heb. 5:8, He learned **o** from the things

OBEDIENT 2 Cor. 2:9, whether you are **o** in all things
Phil. 2:8, **o** to the point of death
1 Pet. 1:14, As **o** children

OBEY—*follow* Ps. 103:20, **O-ing** the voice of His word
Matt. 8:27, the winds and the sea **o** Him
Acts 5:29, **o** God rather than men
Eph. 6:1, Children, **o** your parents
Heb. 11:8, By faith Abraham . . . **o-ed**
13:17, **O** your leaders
1 Pet. 1:2, that you may **o** Jesus Christ
Ex. 19:5; Josh. 1:17; 1 Sam. 15:22; Is. 1:19

OBLIGATE Matt. 23:16, whoever swears by the gold . . . **o-d**

OBLIGATION Num. 32:22, be free of **o** toward the LORD
Rom. 1:14, I am under **o** both to Greeks
8:12, we are under **o**, not to the flesh
Gal. 5:3, he is under **o** to keep the whole Law

OBSCURE Prov. 22:29; Luke 23:45

OBSERVE—*keep* Deut. 5:15, to **o** the sabbath day
Prov. 6:6, **O** her ways and be wise
Matt. 6:28, **O** how the lilies of the field
28:20, teaching them to **o** all that I commanded
Luke 11:28, hear the word of God, and **o** it
Rom. 14:6, He who **o-s** the day, **o-s** it for the Lord
Prov. 5:2; 6:20; Jer. 2:10; Gal. 4:10

OBSOLETE Heb. 8:13, He has made the first **o**

OBSTACLE Rom. 14:13, not to put an **o** . . . in a brother's

OBTAIN—*purchase* Prov. 8:35, **o-s** favor from the LORD
1 Thess. 5:9, for **o-ing** salvation through our Lord
Heb. 11:35, that they might **o** a better resurrection
Gen. 16:2; Acts 8:20

OCCASION 1 Tim. 5:14, give the enemy no **o** for reproach

ODIOUS Ex. 5:21; 1 Sam. 13:4

OFFEND Ex. 2:13, he said to the **o-er**
Job 34:31, I will not **o** *any more*

OFFENSE—*strange* Job 19:17, breath is **o-ive** to my wife
1 Cor. 10:32, Give no **o**
1 Pet. 2:8, AND A ROCK OF **O**
Gen. 41:9; Eccles. 10:4; Jer. 23:13

OFFER—*present* Ps. 50:14, **O** to God a sacrifice
Mal. 1:8, Why not **o** it to your governor
Matt. 5:23, presenting your **o-ing** at the altar
5:24, come and present your **o-ing**
Luke 6:29, **o** him the other also
Heb. 9:14, **o-ed** Himself without blemish

OFFICE Judg. 5:14; Ps. 109:8; 1 Tim. 3:1; Heb. 7:5

OFFICER—*governor*
Jer. 20:1, chief **o** in the house . . . LORD

OFFICIAL 2 Kin. 20:18; 23:11; Is. 39:7; Dan. 1:9; Matt. 9:18

OFFSPRING Deut. 28:53; Is. 65:9

OFTEN Luke 13:34, How **o** I wanted to gather
1 Cor. 11:26, as **o** as you eat this bread

OIL Matt. 25:8, Give us some of your **o**
Luke 10:34, pouring **o** and wine on them
Rev. 6:6, harm the **o** and the wine
Ex. 25:6; Job 29:6; Ps. 23:5; 45:7; 55:21; 104:15; 133:2; Prov. 5:3; Luke 7:46

OINTMENT Job 41:31; John 12:5

OLD Matt. 9:17, new wine into **o** wineskins
John 3:4, man be born when he is **o**
Rom. 6:6, our **o** self was crucified
1 Cor. 5:7, Clean out the **o** leaven
2 Cor. 3:14, reading of the **o** covenant
5:17, the **o** things passed away
Col. 3:9, laid aside the **o** self
Rev. 12:9, serpent of **o** who is called the devil
Gen. 15:15; 44:20; Ruth 1:12; 1 Sam. 12:2; Job 42:17; Prov. 20:29; Matt. 9:16; Heb. 11:2

OLDER—*aged*
Job 32:4, waited . . . because they were . . . **o**
Titus 2:2,3, **O** men are to be temperate

ONCE—*soon* 1 Sam. 9:13, you will find him at **o**
Matt. 15:28, daughter was healed at **o**
21:20, did the fig tree wither at **o**
Rom. 6:10, died to sin, **o** for all
Heb. 9:28, offered **o** to bear the sins
Gen. 18:32; Is. 66:8

ONE Matt. 6:24, No **o** can serve two masters
Matt. 19:5, TWO SHALL BECOME **O** FLESH
John 10:30, I and the Father are **O**
17:21, that they may all be **o**
Gal. 6:4, let each **o** examine his own work
Eph. 4:4, **o** body and **o** Spirit . . . **o** hope
1 Tim. 2:5, **o** God, *and* **o** mediator
James 4:12, only **o** Lawgiver and Judge
Gen. 1:5; Deut. 6:4; 1 Sam. 21:15; 2 Sam. 6:20; Job 33:23; Mark 8:30; John 19:41

ONLY Gen. 6:5, thoughts of his heart . . . **o** evil
Ps. 62:2, He **o** is my rock . . . salvation
Luke 24:18, You the **o** one visiting
Rom. 16:27, **o** wise God . . . glory forever
Heb. 11:17, his **o** begotten *son*
Jude 25, **o** God . . . our Lord, *be* glory

OPEN—*explain, wide*
Matt. 7:7, knock and it shall be **o-ed**
20:33, we want our eyes to be **o-ed**
John 1:51, you shall see the heavens **o-ed**
Rev. 4:1, a door *standing* **o** in heaven
5:2, Who is worthy to **o** the book
Gen. 3:5; Job 29:23; Ps. 5:9; 51:15; Prov. 27:5; Is. 26:2; 42:7; Ezek. 16:63; Luke 13:25

OPENING Prov. 8:3; Song 5:4

OPINION—*counsel* 2 Cor. 8:10, give my **o** in this matter
OPPONENT—*adversary* Matt. 5:25; Luke 18:3; Phil. 1:28
OPPORTUNE Mark 14:11, betray Him at an **o** time
OPPORTUNITY—*occasion*
Gal. 5:13, turn your freedom ... **o**
Eph. 4:27, do not give the devil an **o**
OPPOSE—*resist* Ezra 10:15, Jahzeiah ... **o-d** this
Rom. 13:2, he who resists authority has **o-d**
James 4:6, GOD IS O-D TO THE PROUD
OPPOSITION Num. 14:34; Gal. 5:17
OPPRESS—*afflict*
Acts 10:38, healing all who were **o-ed**
James 2:6, Is it not the rich who **o** you
Gen. 15:13; Lev. 19:13; 1 Sam. 1:15; Job 5:4; Hos. 12:7
OPPRESSION—*affliction*
Ps. 62:10, Do not trust in **o**
Eccles. 7:7, **o** makes a wise man mad
Is. 30:20; Ezek. 22:12
ORCHARD—*garden* Song 6:11, down to the **o** of nut trees
ORDAIN Ex. 29:29,35; Ps. 8:3; Acts 7:53
ORDER 2 Kin. 20:1; Ps. 5:3; Mark 5:43; Luke 5:14; Titus 1:5; Philem. 8; Heb. 5:6
ORDINANCE—*statute* Job 38:33; Rom. 13:2; Eph. 2:15
ORPHAN—*fatherless*
Ex. 22:22, not afflict any widow or **o**
James 1:27, visit **o-s** and widows
Deut. 10:18; 14:29; 24:17; Job 31:17; Ps. 10:14; Is. 1:23; 10:2; Jer. 49:11; Hos. 14:3; Mal. 3:5
OTHER Ex. 22:20; Mark 16:13
OUGHT John 4:20, place where men **o** to worship
Heb. 5:12, you **o** to be teachers
James 3:10, these things **o** not to be
OUT Ex. 3:10, bring My people ... **o** of Egypt
Ex. 7:5, when I stretch **o** My hand
Num. 32:23, your sin will find you **o**
Prov. 31:20, she stretches **o** her hands to
Matt. 12:13, Stretch **o** your hand
12:34, **o** of that which fills the heart
13:3, the sower went **o** to sow
Mark 1:41, He stretched **o** His hand and touched
7:26, cast the demon **o** of her daughter
2 Tim. 4:2, in season *and* **o** of season
Gen. 8:7,8,18; 19:10; 24:45; Ex. 3:11; Judg. 20:25; 1 Sam. 30:21; 2 Sam. 19:7; Is. 37:36; Jer. 32:21
OUTBURST—*heat*
Deut. 29:24, Why this great **o** of anger
OUTCOME—*end* Rom. 6:21, the **o** of those things is death
Rom. 6:22, the **o**, eternal life
Heb. 13:7, the **o** of their way of life
James 5:11, seen the **o** of the Lord's dealings
1 Pet. 1:9, obtaining as the **o** of your faith
4:17, what will be the **o**
OUTCRY Gen. 18:21; Ps. 144:14
OUTER—*outward*
2 Cor. 4:16, **o** man is decaying
OUTSIDE—*without* Deut. 32:25, **O** the sword
Rev. 22:15, **O** are the dogs
OUTWARD Rom. 2:28, **o** in the flesh
OVEN Gen. 15:17, smoking **o** and a flaming torch
OVER—*spent* Luke 24:29, day is now nearly **o**
Eph. 4:6, who is **o** all
OVERCOME Luke 9:32, companions had been **o** with sleep
John 16:33, I have **o** the world
Rom. 12:21, Do not be **o** by evil
1 John 2:13, you have **o** the evil one
Jer. 20:7; 23:9
OVEREXTENDING—*stretching*
2 Cor. 10:14, we are not **o**
OVERFLOW 2 Cor. 7:4, I am **o-ing** with joy
Ps. 23:5; Prov. 3:10; Song 8:7
OVERLAID 2 Chr. 3:5, he **o** the main room with cypress
OVERPOWER—*prevail*
Matt. 16:18, gates of Hades shall not **o** it
OVERSEER Phil. 1:1, including the **o-s** and deacons
1 Tim. 3:1, aspires to the office of **o**
Titus 1:7, **o** must be above reproach
OVERTAKE Amos 9:10; 1 Thess. 5:4
OVERTHROW Ex. 23:24; Acts 5:39
OVERWHELM Ex. 17:13, Joshua **o-ed** Amalek
OWE—*due* Matt. 18:28, Pay back what you **o**
18:34, repay all that was **o-d** him
Rom. 13:8, **O** nothing to anyone
Philem. 19, you **o** to me even your own self
OWN Prov. 14:10, heart knows its **o** bitterness
John 1:11, came to His **o** ... **o** did not receive
10:3, calls his **o** sheep by name
Acts 2:6, speak in his **o** language
1 Tim. 5:8, does not provide for his **o**
2 Pet. 3:3, following after their **o** lusts
OX—*cow* Prov. 7:22, as an **o** goes to the slaughter
1 Tim. 5:18, MUZZLE THE O WHILE HE IS THRESHING
Lev. 22:28; Job 6:5; Prov. 15:17

P

PACT Is. 28:15, we have made a **p**
PAIN—*sorrow, torment, grief* Gen. 3:16, multiply Your **p**
1 Chr. 4:9, Because I bore *him* with **p**
Job 6:10, I rejoice in unsparing **p**
Ps. 127:2, eat the bread of **p-ful** labors
Eccles. 1:18, knowledge results in increasing **p**
Is. 14:3, gives you rest from your **p**
Jer. 30:15, Your **p** is incurable
Lam. 1:12, any **p** like my **p**
Matt. 8:6, home, suffering great **p**
Job 2:13; 15:20; Ps. 73:4; Lam. 3:51; Rev. 21:4
PAIR Judg. 19:3; Is. 21:7
PALATE—*mouth*
Job 29:10, their tongue stuck to their **p**
PALLET Mark 2:9, take up your **p** and walk
John 5:11; Acts 5:15
PALPITATING Is. 35:4, to those with **p** heart fear not
PANEL Jer. 22:14; Hag. 1:4
PANGS—*sorrow* Mark 13:8, beginning birth **p**
PANIC—*trouble* Is. 22:5, has a day of **p**
PANT Job 7:2, a slave who **p-s** for the shade
PAPYRUS Is. 18:2, in **p** vessels
PARAPET Deut. 22:8, a **p** for your roof
PARCH—*dried* Ps. 69:3; Is. 53:2
PARDON Is. 55:7 He will abundantly **p**
Luke 6:37, **p**, and you will be **p-ed**
Ex. 23:21; 2 Chr. 30:18; Ps. 25:11
PARENTS Matt. 10:21, CHILDREN WILL RISE UP AGAINST P
Luke 2:41, His **p** used to go to Jerusalem
18:29, left house ... or **p**
John 9:2, who sinned, this man, or his **p**
Rom. 1:30, disobedient to **p**
2 Cor. 12:14, for *their* **p**, but **p** for *their* children
Eph. 6:1, Children obey your **p**
2 Tim. 3:2, disobedient to **p**, ungrateful
PART Num. 18:20, nor own any **p** among them
Matt. 5:29, one of the **p-s** of your body perish
Luke 10:42, Mary has chosen the good **p**
John 13:8, you have no **p** with Me
Acts 8:21, You have no **p** or portion
1 Cor. 13:9, we know in **p**
PARTAKERS—*partners* Eph. 5:7, do not be **p** with them
Heb. 3:1, **p** of a heavenly calling
3:14, **p** of Christ
6:4, **p** of the Holy Spirit
2 Pet. 1:4, **p** of *the* divine nature

PARTIAL Prov. 28:21, To show **p-ity** is not good
Matt. 22:16, for You are not **p** to any
Acts 10:34, God is not one to show **p-ity**
Rom. 2:11, no **p-ity** with God
Lev. 19:15; Deut. 1:17
PARTICIPATE Eph. 5:11, do not **p** in the unfruitful deeds
PARTNERS Matt. 23:30, not have been **p** with them
PASS Matt. 26:39, let this cup **p** from Me
John 5:24, **p-ed** out of death into life
2 Cor. 5:17, old things **p-ed** away
Heb. 11:25, enjoy the **p-ing** pleasures of sin
Rev. 21:1, first earth **p-ed** away
Gen. 15:17; Ps. 109:23; Prov. 4:15; Is. 16:8; Acts 7:30
PASSION Prov. 14:30, But **p** is rottenness to the bone
Rom. 1:26, gave them over to degrading **p-s**
Col. 3:5, as dead to . . . **p**
1 Thess. 4:5, not in lustful **p**
PASSOVER Ex. 12:11, it is the LORD's **P**
Matt. 26:17, prepare for You to eat the **P**
Luke 22:15, desired to eat this **P**
John 18:39, release someone for you at the **P**
Acts 12:4, intending after the **P**
1 Cor. 5:7, Christ our **P** also has been sacrificed
PAST Song 2:11, the winter is **p**, The rain
Jer. 8:20, Harvest is **p**, summer is ended
PASTOR—*shepherd* Eph. 4:11, some *as* **p-s** and teachers
PASTURE—*feed* Song 1:7; Is. 61:5; Jer. 6:3; Zech. 11:4
PATCH—*piece* Matt. 9:16, puts a **p** of unshrunk cloth
PATH—*way* Job 12:24, makes them wander in a **p-less** waste
Ps. 16:11, make known to me the **p** of life
119:105, a light to my **p**
Prov. 4:18, **p** of the righteous is like the light
Eccles. 11:5, the **p** of the wind
Matt. 3:3, MAKE HIS P-S STRAIGHT
Rom. 3:17, P OF PEACE . . . NOT KNOWN
Gen. 49:17; Job 28:7; Ps. 27:11
PATIENCE Matt. 18:26, Have **p** with me
2 Cor. 6:6, in **p**, in kindness
Col. 1:11, steadfastness and **p**
2 Tim. 4:2, with great **p** and instruction
PATIENT—*gentle* 1 Cor. 13:4, Love is **p**, love is kind
James 5:8, You too be **p**
2 Pet. 3:9, is **p** toward you
PATTERN—*example* Phil. 3:17, according to **p**
PAY Matt. 18:28, **P** back what you owe
Gen. 50:15; Ex. 22:7; Deut. 23:21; Job 22:27; Mark 12:15
PEACE Num. 6:26, give you **p**
Ps. 34:14, Seek **p**, and pursue it
37:37, man of **p** will have a posterity
119:165, who love Thy law have great **p**
Eccles. 3:8, time for war, and a time for **p**
Is. 9:6, Eternal Father, Prince of **P**
Matt. 10:13, let your *greeting of* **p**
10:34, I did not come to bring **p**
Mark 9:50, be at **p** with one another
Luke 1:79, guide our feet . . . way of **p**
2:14, on earth **p** among men
John 14:27, **P** I leave you; My **p**
20:19, **P** *be* with you
Acts 24:2, we have through you attained **p**
Rom. 15:33, the God of **p** be with you
1 Cor. 7:15, God has called us to **p**
Gal. 5:22, fruit of the Spirit is . . . **p**
Eph. 2:14, He Himself is our **p**
Phil. 4:7, **p** of God, which surpasses all
1 Thess. 5:13, Live in **p** with one another
5:23, may the God of **P** . . . sanctify
2 Thess. 3:16, Lord of **p** . . . grant you **p**
Heb. 12:14, Pursue **p** with all men
James 2:16, Go in **p**
1 Pet. 5:14, **P** be to you all
Gen. 15:15; Lev. 26:6; 2 Kin. 9:17; Job 15:21; Ps. 4:8; 147:14; Prov. 3:17; 16:7; Is. 36:16; 52:7; 57:19; Jer. 6:14
PEARLS—*jewel*
Job 28:18, acquisition of wisdom . . . **p**
PECK Matt. 13:33, hid in three **p-s** of meal
PECK-MEASURE Matt. 5:15; Mark 4:21
PEG—*nail* Judg. 4:21; Is. 22:23
PENALTY 2 Thess. 1:9, pay the **p** of eternal destruction
PEOPLE Ps. 100:3, *We are* His **p** and the sheep
Prov. 11:14, no guidance, the **p** fall
29:18, no vision, the **p** are unrestrained
Matt. 1:21, save His **p** from their sins
Mark 7:6, P HONORS ME WITH THEIR LIPS
John 11:50, man should die for the **p**
Jude 16, flattering **p** for . . . advantage
Ex. 6:7; Ruth 1:16; Ps. 2:1; Mark 6:5; Acts 5:16
PERCEIVING Mark 2:8, Jesus, **p** in His spirit
PERDITION John 17:12, the son of **p**
PERFECT Deut. 32:4, The Rock! His work is **p**
Ps. 19:7, law of the LORD is **p**
Matt. 5:48, Therefore you are to be **p**
1 Cor. 13:10, but when the **p** comes
2 Cor. 12:9, power is **p-ed** in weakness
Phil. 1:6, **p** it until the day of Christ Jesus
James 1:4, endurance have *its* **p** result
1:25, **p** law, the *law* of liberty
1 John 4:17, love is **p-ed** with us
PERFECTER Heb. 12:2, author and **p** of faith
PERFORM—*wrought* Is. 26:12, **p-ed** for us all our works
Ps. 103:6; Luke 1:8; Rom. 4:21
PERFUME Is. 3:24, instead of sweet **p**
Matt. 26:7; Luke 7:46
PERFUMERS 1 Sam. 8:13, daughters for **p**
PERHAPS Mark 11:13; Acts 17:27; 1 Cor. 15:37
PERISH—*fail* Ps. 1:6, way of the wicked will **p**
Matt. 8:25, Save us, Lord; we are **p-ing**
18:14, one of these little ones **p**
John 6:27, work for the food which **p-s**
1 Cor. 9:25, *do it* to receive a **p-able** wreath
15:42, It is sown a **p-able** body
15:53, this **p-able** must put on
2 Cor. 4:3, veiled to those who are **p-ing**
1 Pet. 1:23, not of seed which is **p-able**
2 Pet. 3:9, not wishing for any to **p**
Num. 17:12; 2 Sam. 1:27; Job 34:15; Prov. 22:8; Ezek. 37:11
PERJURY Zech. 8:17, do not love **p**
PERMISSION Mark 5:13, And He gave them **p**
PERMIT—*suffer* Matt. 3:15, **P** *it* at this time
PERPETUAL Ex. 40:15; Num. 25:13, a **p** priesthood
Heb. 7:3, abides a priest **p-ly**
Ex. 31:16; Ps. 9:6; Jer. 15:18; 51:39; Hab. 3:6
PERSECUTE Matt. 5:11, when *men* revile you, and **p** you
5:44, pray for those who **p** you
10:23, they **p** you in this city, flee
John 15:20, If they **p-d** Me, they will also **p**
Acts 9:4, Saul, why are you **p-ing** Me
1 Cor. 4:12, when we are **p-d**, we endure
2 Cor. 4:9, **p-d**, but not forsaken
Job 19:22; Ps. 143:3
PERSEVERANCE Luke 21:19, By your **p** you will win
Rom. 2:7, by **p** in doing good
5:3, tribulation brings about **p**
15:4, **p** and the encouragement of the Scriptures
2 Thess. 1:4, for your **p** and faith
PERSEVERE Rom. 12:12, hope, **p-ing** in tribulation
James 1:12, Blessed is a man who **p-s** under trial
PERSON—*soul* Lev. 4:2, If a **p** sins unintentionally
Eccles. 12:13, this *applies to* every **p**
Is. 32:6, keep the hungry **p** unsatisfied

PERSON *(Continued)*
Rom. 13:1, Let every **p** be in subjection
Jude 4, certain **p-s** have crept in unnoticed
PERSUADE 2 Kin. 4:8, she **p-d** him to eat food
Prov. 25:15, a ruler may be **p-d**
Acts 26:28, you will **p** me
PERSUASIVE 1 Cor. 2:4, were not in **p** words
Col. 2:4, delude you with **p** argument
PERVERSE Acts 20:30, speaking **p** things
Phil. 2:15, a crooked and **p** generation
Deut. 32:5,20; Ps. 101:4; Prov. 23:33
PERVERSION Lev. 18:23, it is a **p**
PERVERT Deut. 16:19; 2 Sam. 22:27; Job 8:3; Prov. 10:31
PETITION Ps. 20:5, the LORD fulfill all your **p-s**
1 Tim. 2:1, prayers, **p-s** and thanksgivings
1 Sam. 1:17; Dan. 6:7,13
PHYSICIAN Jer. 8:22, Is there no **p** there
Matt. 9:12, not ... healthy who need a **p**
Luke 4:23, **P**, heal yourself
Col. 4:14, Luke, the beloved **p**
PICK Mark 16:18, they will **p** up serpents
Gen. 8:11; Mark 2:23
PIECE Matt. 14:20, left over of the broken **p-s**
Mark 6:43, twelve full baskets of broken **p-s**
Gen. 18:5; Ruth 2:14; 1 Sam. 2:36; Luke 24:42
PIERCE—*wound* Judg. 5:26, shattered and **p-d** his temple
Ps. 22:16, They **p-d** my hands ... feet
Is. 53:5, **p-d** through for our transgressions
Zech. 12:10, on Me whom they have **p-d**
Luke 2:35, **p** even your own soul
John 19:34, soldiers **p-d** His side
PIETY 1 Tim. 5:4, practice **p** in regard
PILES Job 27:16, he **p** up silver like dust
PILLAGE Nah. 3:1, city, ... full of lies *and* **p**
PILLAR Gen. 19:26, she became a **p** of salt
Job 26:11, The **p-s** of heaven tremble
Gal. 2:9, John, who were reputed to be **p-s**
1 Tim. 3:15, **p** and support of the truth
Prov. 9:1; Ezek. 26:11
PILOT James 3:4, inclination of the **p** desires
PIT—*destruction, dungeon*
Gen. 14:10, Siddim ... tar **p-s**
37:20, throw him into one of the **p-s**
Ex. 21:33, a man opens a **p**, or digs a **p**
Job 17:14, I call to the **p**, You are my father
33:18, his soul from the **p**
Ps. 16:10, Holy One to see the **p**
103:4, redeems your life from the **p**
Prov. 23:27, a harlot is a deep **p**
Lam. 3:53, they have silenced me in the **p**
Matt. 15:14, both will fall into a **p**
PITCH Gen. 6:14, cover it ... with **p**
Gen. 33:19, where he had **p-ed** his tent
Ex. 2:3, covered it over with tar and **p**
PITCHER—*bowl, jar*
Judg. 7:16, put trumpets and empty **p-s**
1 Kin. 18:33, fill four **p-s**
Eccles. 12:6, the **p** by the well is shattered
Mark 14:13, man ... carrying a **p** of water
PITY—*compassion* Ex. 2:6; Deut. 7:16; Job 19:21
PLACE—*room* Deut. 33:27, eternal God is a dwelling **p**
Ps. 31:8, set my feet in a large **p**
Prov. 15:3, eyes ... LORD ... in every **p**
Matt. 23:6, love the **p** of honor at banquets
24:51, **p** with the hypocrites
26:36, a **p** called Gethsemane
27:33, a **p** called Golgotha ... **P** of a Skull
28:6, **p** where He was lying
Luke 4:17, **p** where it was written
14:8, do not take the **p** of honor
John 14:2, go to prepare a **p** for you
Acts 13:47, I HAVE P-D YOU AS A LIGHT FOR
1 Cor. 14:16, fills the **p** of the ungifted
2 Pet. 1:19, lamp shining in a dark **p**
Rev. 20:11, no **p** was found for them
Gen. 1:9; 30:2; Ex. 3:5; 21:13; Num. 32:14; Deut. 2:23; 34:6; Judg. 18:10; Job 9:6; 16:4; Ps. 24:3; Is. 49:20; Jer. 51:51; Dan. 8:14; Hab. 3:11; Luke 14:9; John 18:2
PLAGUE Gen. 12:17; Rev. 16:21; 21:9
PLAIN—*distinct, clear* Is. 40:4; Mark 7:35; John 16:25
PLAN—*devise* Ps. 36:4, He **p-s** wickedness upon his bed
Prov. 16:9, mind of a man **p-s** his way
19:21, Many are the **p-s** in a man's heart
2 Sam. 14:14; Prov. 15:22; Jer. 18:12
PLANT Gen. 3:18, you shall eat the **p-s** of the field
Ps. 1:3, tree ... **p-ed** by streams
Eccles. 3:2, A time to **p**, and a time to
Matt. 13:32; Mark 4:32, larger than ... the garden **p-s**
15:13, **p** ... Father did not **p**
Mark 12:1, A man P-ED A VINEYARD
Luke 17:6, be **p-ed** in the sea
1 Cor. 3:6, I **p-ed**, Apollos watered
Gen. 1:29,30; 2:5,8; 9:3; Ex. 9:22,25; 10:12,15; Deut. 6:11; 2 Kin. 19:29; Job 14:9; Ps. 92:13
PLASTER Ezek. 13:10, **p** it over with whitewash
PLAY Gen. 4:21; Ex. 32:6; 1 Sam. 16:17; 1 Kin. 1:40; Job 41:5; Ps. 33:3; Is. 11:8; Matt. 11:17; 1 Cor. 14:7
PLEAD Gen. 42:21; Deut. 3:23; 1 Sam. 12:7; Ps. 43:1; Is. 1:17
PLEASANT—*smooth, sweet*
Ps. 16:6, lines have fallen ... **p**
133:1, how good and how **p** it is
Eccles. 5:12, sleep of the working man is **p**
2 Sam. 1:23; Prov. 9:17; 16:24; Is. 30:10
PLEASE Matt. 3:17, Son, in whom I am well **p-d**
Rom. 15:1, not *just* **p** ourselves
15:3, Christ did not **p** Himself
1 Cor. 7:33, how he may **p** his wife
7:34, how she may **p** her husband
10:5, God was not well **p-d**
Heb. 13:16, sacrifices God is **p-d**
PLEASING—*acceptable*
Prov. 16:7, man's ways ... **p** ... LORD
Matt. 11:26, it was **well-p** in Thy sight
John 8:29, things that are **p** to Him
2 Cor. 5:9, to be **p** to Him
Eph. 5:10, what is **p** to the Lord
Gen. 2:9; 1 Kin. 3:10
PLEASURE Ps. 16:11, there are **p-s** forever
Ps. 149:4, LORD takes **p** in His people
Luke 8:14, worries and riches and **p-s**
Phil. 2:13, to work for *His* good **p**
Heb. 11:25, the passing **p-s** of sin
Gen. 18:12; Job 36:11; Prov. 21:17; Is. 53:10
PLEDGE Prov. 22:26, among those who give **p-s**
2 Cor. 1:22, the Spirit in our hearts as a **p**
5:5, gave to us the Spirit as a **p**
Eph. 1:14, given as a **p** of our inheritance
1 Tim. 5:12, set aside their previous **p**
PLENTEOUS Is. 30:23, it will be rich and **p**
PLENTIFUL Ps. 68:9, didst shed abroad a **p** rain
Matt. 9:37, harvest is **p**
PLENTY Gen. 33:9; Prov. 3:10; 12:11; Joel 2:26
PLOT Prov. 30:32, if you have **p-ed** evil
Matt. 26:4; Acts 9:23; 23:13
PLOW Is. 2:4, their swords into **p-shares**
Joel 3:10, **p-shares** into swords
Luke 9:62, putting his hand to the **p**
1 Cor. 9:10, to **p** in hope
Deut. 22:10; Job 4:8; Prov. 20:4
PLUCK Ps. 25:15; Ezek. 17:22
PLUMAGE Job 39:13, pinion and **p** of love
PLUNDER (n.)—*booty* Judg. 5:19; Hab. 2:7; Zeph. 1:13
PLUNDER (v.)—*spoil* Matt. 12:29, he will **p** his house
Ex. 3:22; Ps. 76:5; Is. 42:22
PLUNGE 1 Tim. 6:9, desires which **p** men into ruin

POINT Jer. 17:1; Mark 5:23; James 2:10
POISON Ps. 140:3; Jer. 8:14; Amos 6:12; Mark 16:18
POLE—*staff* Num. 13:23, carried it on a **p** between two
POLLUTE—*spot* Num. 35:33; Jer. 16:18; Jude 23
POMP Is. 14:11, Your **p** *and* the music
PONDER Prov. 5:6, **p** the path of life
Luke 2:19, **p-ing** them in her heart
POOR Prov. 13:7, *Another* pretends to be **p**
Prov. 20:13, lest you become **p**
Amos 5:11, impose heavy rent upon the **p**
Matt. 5:3, Blessed are the **p** in
11:5, *the* **P** HAVE THE GOSPEL PREACHED
26:11, **p** you have with you always
Mark 10:21, and give *it* to the **p**
12:42, And a **p** widow came
Luke 4:18, PREACH THE GOSPEL TO THE **P**
19:8, my possessions I will give to the **p**
2 Cor. 8:9, for your sake He became **p**
James 2:5, God choose the **p** of this
1 Sam. 2:8; 2 Sam. 12:4; Prov. 22:22; Is. 3:15; 1 Cor. 13:3
PORPOISE SKINS Ex. 25:5; 26:14
PORTION Deut. 32:9, LORD's **p** is His people
2 Kin. 2:9, double **p** of your spirit
Ps. 119:57, The LORD is my **p**
Gen. 31:14; 2 Chr. 10:16; Eccles. 11:2; Acts 8:21
POSSESS Gen. 15:7; 24:60; Ps. 44:3; Is. 54:3; 2 Cor. 6:10
POSSESSION—*property, treasure* Gen. 17:8
Matt. 24:47, in charge of all his **p-s**
Luke 19:8, half of my **p-s** I will give to the
Ex. 6:8; 19:5; 21:16; 34:9; Deut. 4:20; Ps. 104:24; Acts 2:45
POSSIBLE Matt. 19:26, with God all things **p**
Matt. 26:39, **p**, let this cup pass
Luke 18:27, are **p** with God
Rom. 12:18, If **p**, so far as it depends
POT Ex. 16:3; 2 Kin. 4:40; Job 41:31; Jer. 1:13
POUR Eccles. 11:3, clouds are full, they **p** out rain
Joel 2:28, **p** out My Spirit on all mankind
Matt. 26:7, **p-ed** it upon His head
Luke 22:20, cup which is **p-ed** ... covenant in My blood
John 2:15, **p-ed** out the coins
Acts 10:45, gift of the Holy Spirit ... **p-ed** out
Rom. 5:5, love of God **p-ed** out within our hearts
Phil. 2:17, if I am being **p-ed** out as
Rev. 16:2, **p-ed** out his bowl
1 Sam. 1:15; Job 10:10; 29:6; Is. 44:3; Matt. 9:17
POVERTY Prov. 23:21, glutton will come to **p**
Prov. 30:8, neither **p** nor riches
2 Cor. 8:9, through His **p**
POWER—*authority, strength*
Deut. 8:18, you **p** to make wealth
1 Chr. 29:11, the **p** and the glory
Is. 40:29, *who* lacks might He increases **p**
Matt. 6:13, kingdom, and the **p**, and
Mark 5:30, **p** ... from Him had gone forth
9:1, kingdom of God ... come with **p**
13:26, IN CLOUDS with great **p**
14:62, AT THE RIGHT HAND OF **P**
Luke 1:35, **p** of the Most High will overshadow
4:14, in the **p** of the Spirit
22:69, RIGHT HAND of the **p** OF GOD
Acts 1:8, you shall receive **p** when
8:10, called the Great **P** of God
Rom. 1:4, with **p** to be the Son of God
1:16, the **p** of God for salvation
1 Cor. 1:24, Christ the **p** of God
15:56, the **p** of sin is the law
2 Cor. 12:9, **p** is perfected in weakness
Eph. 1:21, authority and **p** and dominion
2:2, prince of the **p** of the air
Phil. 3:21, exertion of the **p**
Heb. 1:3, by the word of His **p**
11:34, quenched the **p** of fire
Ex. 15:6; Judg. 7:2; Job 40:16; Ps. 49:15; Prov. 3:27; Jer. 18:21; 1 Cor. 5:4; 1 Pet. 3:22
PRACTICE Ps. 28:4, evil of their **p-s**
Matt. 6:1, Beware of **p-ing** your righteousness
Acts 19:18, disclosing their **p-s**
1 Cor. 11:16, we have no other **p**
Col. 3:9, laid aside the old self with its *evil* **p-s**
1 Tim. 5:4, **p** piety in regard to their own family
1 John 1:6, we lie and do not **p** the truth
3:8, the one who **p-s** sin is of the
PRAETORIUM Matt. 27:27, soldiers ... took Jesus into the **P**
Mark 15:16, took Him ... into the palace (that is, the **P**)
John 18:28, led Jesus ... into the **P**
18:33, Pilate ... entered ... into the **P**
PRAISE—*bless, commend*
Ex. 15:11, Awesome in **p-s**
Ps. 89:5, heavens will **p** Thy wonders
Prov. 27:21, man *is tested* by the **p**
Matt. 11:25, I **p** Thee, O Father
Luke 16:8, his master **p-d** the unrighteous steward
Rom. 2:29, his **p** is not from men
Phil. 4:8, if anything worthy of **p**
James 5:13, Let him sing **p-s**
Deut. 10:21; 1 Chr. 16:9; Neh. 12:46; Ps. 22:25; Prov. 12:8; Is. 38:18
PRAY—*ask* Is. 45:20, And **p** to a god who cannot save
Matt. 5:44, **p** for those who persecute
6:5, And when you **p**
6:6, **p** to your Father ... in secret
6:7, **p-ing**, do not use meaningless
14:23, mountain by Himself to **p**
26:41, Keep watching and **p-ing**, that
Mark 11:24, you **p** and ask, believe
Luke 11:1, Lord, teach us to **p** just
18:1, they ought to **p** and not
22:40, **P** that you may not ... temptation
1 Cor. 11:13, for a woman to **p** to God
14:14, if I **p** in a tongue
Col. 1:9, not ceased to **p** for you
1 Thess. 5:17, **p** without ceasing
James 5:13, suffering? Let him **p**
5:16, and **p** for one another
Gen. 20:7; Ex. 33:18; 1 Sam. 7:5; 12:23; Jon. 1:14
PRAYER Ps. 55:1, Give ear to my **p**, O God
Is. 56:7, called a house of **p**
Matt. 17:21, out except by **p** and fasting
21:22, everything ... in **p**, believing
Luke 6:12, whole night in **p**
19:46, A HOUSE OF **P**
Acts 3:1, the hour of **p**
Rom. 1:10, in my **p-s** making request
12:12, devoted to **p**
1 Cor. 7:5; Col. 4:2, devote yourselves to **p**
1 Pet. 3:7, your **p-s** may not be hindered
1 Kin. 8:45; Neh. 11:17; Ps. 4:1
PREACH—*declare, exhort, proclaim*
Matt. 4:17, that time Jesus began to **p**
10:7, go, **p**, saying ... kingdom ... is at hand
11:1, and **p** in their cities
11:5, POOR ... GOSPEL **P-ED** to them
Mark 13:10, gospel ... **p-ed** to all the nations
16:15, **p** the gospel to all
Luke 4:43, **p** the kingdom of God
Acts 13:32, we **p** to you the good news of the promise
1 Cor. 1:17, not ... to baptize, but to **p**
1:23, we **p** Christ crucified
2 Cor. 4:5, we do not **p** ourselves
1 Tim. 6:2, Teach and **p** these *principles*
2 Tim. 4:2, **p** the word, be ready
PREACHER Eccles. 1:1, words of the **P**
Rom. 10:14, how shall they hear without a **p**
1 Tim. 2:7, I was appointed a **p**
2 Pet. 2:5, Noah, a **p** of righteousness
PREACHING—*talk, word* Matt. 3:1, John ... **p**
Mark 1:4, **p** a baptism of repentance
1:39, **p** and casting out the demons

PREACHING *(Continued)*
Acts 5:42, teaching and **p** Jesus
8:4, scattered went about **p** the word
Rom. 16:25, **p** of Jesus Christ
1 Cor. 15:14, then our **p** is vain
PRECEDE 1 Thess. 4:15, **p** those who have fallen asleep
PRECEPT—*statute* Ps. 19:8, **p-s** of the LORD are right
PRECIOUS—*excellent* Ps. 36:7, How **p** is Thy lovingkindness
Ps. 116:15, **P** in the sight of the LORD
Prov. 3:15, more **p** than jewels
Is. 44:9, their **p** things are of no profit
1 Pet. 1:7, more **p** than gold which
1:19, but with **p** blood . . . of Christ
PREDETERMINE Acts 2:23, **p-d** plan and foreknowledge of God
PREEMINENT—*excellence*
Gen. 49:3, **P** in dignity and **p** in
PREPARATION—*serve*
Luke 10:40, distracted with all her **p-s**
PREPARE—*fashion, furnish, ready* Gen. 18:6
Ps. 23:5, dost **p** a table before me
78:19, God **p** a table in the
Matt. 11:10, WHO WILL P YOUR WAY
25:34, the kingdom **p-d** for you
John 14:2, I go to **p** a place for you
1 Cor. 2:9, P-D FOR THOSE WHO LOVE HIM
Heb. 11:3, worlds were **p-d** by the word
Lev. 7:9; Job 12:5; Ps. 57:6; Rom. 9:22
PRESCRIBE—*command*
1 Tim. 4:11, **P** and teach these things
PRESENCE Ex. 33:14, My **p** shall go *with you*
Ps. 23:5, **p** of my enemies
44:3, light of Thy **p**
95:2, before His **p** with thanksgiving
Is. 64:2, nations may tremble at Thy **p**
Luke 13:26, ate and drank in Your **p**
Jude 24, **p** of His glory blameless
Rev. 14:10, in the **p** of the Lamb
PRESENT—*offer, yield*
Gen. 43:11, to the man as a **p**
Ps. 46:1, A very **p** help in trouble
Mal. 1:8, **p** the blind . . . **p** the lame and
Luke 2:22, to **p** Him to the Lord
Rom. 6:13, **p-ing** the members of your body to sin
12:1, **p** your bodies a living sacrifice
1 Cor. 5:3, but **p** in spirit
Col. 1:22, **p** you before Him holy and blameless
2 Tim. 2:15, **p** yourself approved to God
4:10, loved this **p** world
PRESERVATION—*health*
Acts 27:34, food . . . for your **p**
PRESERVE—*guard, keep*
2 Sam. 18:18, no son to **p** my name
Ps. 16:1, **P** me, O God, for I take refuge
86:2, **p** my soul, for I am a godly man
Prov. 14:3, lips of the wise will **p** them
Luke 17:33, loses *his life* shall **p** it
Eph. 4:3, diligent to **p** the unity of the Spirit
1 Thess. 5:23, soul and body be **p-d** complete
PRESS Matt. 27:32, they **p-ed** . . . to bear His cross
Luke 6:38, good measure **p-ed** down
Phil. 3:14, I **p** on toward the goal
PRESUME—*dare* Rom. 15:18, I will not **p** to speak
PRESUMPTION Prov. 13:10, Through **p** comes nothing
PRETEND—*disguise* 2 Sam. 14:2, **p** to be a mourner
1 Kin. 14:5,6, **p** to be another woman
Luke 20:20, sent spies who **p-ed** to be righteous
PRETTY Jer. 46:20, Egypt is a **p** heifer
PREVAIL Gen. 7:20, water **p-ed** fifteen cubits higher
1 Sam. 2:9, not by might shall a man **p**
Ps. 65:3; Jer. 20:7
PREVALENT Eccles. 6:1, an evil . . . it is **p**
PREVENT Matt. 3:14, John tried to **p** Him,
PREY Ps. 76:4; Ezek. 22:25

PRICE Acts 1:18, field with the **p** of his wickedness
5:2, kept back *some* of the **p**
1 Cor. 6:20, you have been bought with a **p**
Lev. 25:16; Dan. 11:39; Mic. 3:11
PRIDE Prov. 16:18, **P** *goes* before destruction
Mark 7:22, slander, **p** *and* foolishness
1 John 2:16, the boastful **p** of life
Prov. 8:13; Is. 13:19; 60:15; Ezek. 32:12
PRIEST Gen. 14:18, **p** of God Most High
Ex. 19:6, shall be to Me a kingdom of **p-s**
1 Sam. 2:35, raise up for Myself a faithful **p**
Ps. 110:4, **p** forever . . . order of Melchizedek
Ezek. 44:21, Nor shall any of the **p-s** drink wine
Matt. 2:4, together all the chief **p-s**
8:4, SHOW YOURSELF TO THE P
Heb. 2:17, faithful high **p**
3:1, High **P** of our confession
5:6, P FOREVER . . . ORDER OF MELCHIZEDEK
2 Chr. 15:3; Is. 24:2
PRIME—*flower* 1 Sam. 2:33, will die in the **p** of life
PRINCE—*ruler* Ex. 2:14, Who made you a **p** or a judge
2 Sam. 3:38, **p** and a great man has fallen
Is. 9:6, **P** of Peace
Acts 3:15, put to death the **P** of life
5:31, as a **P** and a Saviour
Eph. 2:2, **p** of the power of the air
PRINCESS—*lady* Judg. 5:29, Her wise **p-es** would answer
PRINCIPALITY Rom. 8:38, nor **p-es** . . . nor powers
PRISON Judg. 16:21, he was a grinder in the **p**
Ps. 142:7, Bring my soul out of **p**
Matt. 14:10, had John beheaded in the **p**
Acts 5:19, Lord . . . opened the gates of the **p**
16:27, jailer . . . had seen the **p** doors opened
1 Kin. 22:27; Rev. 18:2
PRISONER Ps. 102:20, groaning of the **p**
Ps. 146:7, the LORD sets the **p-s** free
Matt. 27:15, release for the multitude *any* one **p**
Rom. 7:23, making me a **p** of the law
Eph. 3:1, Paul, the **p** of Christ Jesus
2 Tim. 1:8, ashamed . . . or of me His **p**
PRIVATION—*adversity, distress*
Is. 30:20, given you bread of **p**
PRIZE Col. 2:18, defrauding you of your **p**
PROCEED Deut. 8:3, everything that **p-s** out of the mouth
Jer. 9:3, **p** from evil to evil
Matt. 4:4, WORD THAT P-S OUT OF THE MOUTH
Mark 7:21, heart of men, **p** the evil thoughts
John 15:26, who **p-s** from the Father
2 Tim. 3:13, imposters will **p** . . . to worse
PROCLAIM—*declare, tell*
Ex. 33:19; Deut. 32:3, **p** the name of the LORD
Is. 61:1, **p** liberty to the captives
61:2, **p** the favorable year of the LORD
Jer. 34:15, **p-ing** release to his neighbor
Matt. 10:27; Luke 12:3, **p-ed** upon the housetops
Acts 17:3, Jesus whom I am **p-ing** to you
17:23, you worship in ignorance, this I **p** to
26:23, **p** light both to the *Jewish* and
1 Pet. 3:19, made **p-ation** to the spirits
1 John 1:3, what we have seen and heard we **p**
PROCONSUL—*deputy* Acts 13:7; 18:12; 19:38
PRODUCE—*yield* Deut. 14:22, tithe all the **p**
Ps. 67:6, the earth has yielded its **p**
2 Tim. 2:23, knowing that they **p** quarrels
James 3:12, Neither can salt water **p** fresh
Lev. 25:19; Hos. 10:1
PRODUCTIVE Luke 12:16, land . . . was **p**
PROFANE—*defile, pollute* Lev. 21:7,23; Ezek. 22:8
Ex. 31:14, Everyone who **p-s** it . . . put to death
Lev. 20:3, to **p** My holy name
Ezek. 23:38, have **p-d** My sabbaths
1 Tim. 1:9, law . . . for the unholy and **p**
PROFESS—*confession* Rom. 1:22, **P-ing** to be wise
Titus 1:16, They **p** to know God

PROFIT Job 15:3, words which are not **p-able**
Prov. 14:23, In all labor there is **p**
15:27, who **p-s** illicitly troubles his own
Matt. 16:26; Luke 9:25, will a man be **p-ed**
John 6:63, the flesh **p-s** nothing
Acts 16:19; hope of **p** was gone
1 Cor. 6:12; 10:23, not all things are **p-able**
13:3, not have love, it **p-s** me nothing
1 Tim. 4:8, bodily discipline is only of little **p**
2 Tim. 3:16, Scripture ... **p-able** for teaching
James 4:13, engage in business and make a **p**
Gen. 37:26; Prov. 3:14; Is. 48:17; Jer. 16:19

PROGRESS Phil. 1:12, greater **p** of the gospel

PROLONG Prov. 10:27, fear of the Lord **p-s** life

PROMINENCE Acts 13:50, devout women of **p**

PROMINENT Mark 15:43, Joseph ... **p** member

PROMISCUITY Rom. 13:13, not in sexual **p** and sensuality

PROMISE Acts 2:33, **p** of the Holy Spirit
Acts 26:6, hope of the **p** made by God
Rom. 4:14, **p** is nullified
9:8, children of the **p**
Gal. 3:14, might receive the **p** of the Spirit
Eph. 6:2, first commandment with a **p**
2 Tim. 1:1, **p** of life in Christ Jesus
Titus 1:2, **p-d** long ages ago
Heb. 10:23, for He who **p-d** is faithful
2 Pet. 1:4, His precious and magnificent **p-s**

PROMOTE Esth. 5:11; Ps. 140:8

PRONOUNCE—*utter* Jer. 1:16, I will **p** My judgments
Luke 23:24, Pilate **p-d** sentence

PROOF Acts 17:31, furnished **p** to all men
2 Cor. 8:24, show them the **p** of your love
13:3, **p** of the Christ who speaks in me

PROPER Rom. 13:13, Let us behave **p-ly** as in the day
1 Cor. 11:13, is it **p** for a woman to pray
14:40, let all things be done **p-ly**
Eph. 5:3, as is **p** among saints
1 Thess. 4:12, you may behave **p-ly** toward outsiders
1 Tim. 2:6, testimony *borne* at the **p** time

PROPERTY—*goods*
Gen. 34:10, and acquire **p** in it
Matt. 12:29, carry off his **p**
19:22, one who owned much **p**
Acts 2:45, selling their **p** and possessions

PROPHECY Dan. 9:24, seal up vision and **p**
1 Cor. 13:2, if I have the gift of **p**
2 Pet. 1:21, no **p** was ever made by ... human will
Rev. 19:10, testimony ... is the spirit of **p**

PROPHESY 1 Sam. 10:11, he **p-ed** now with the prophets
Is. 30:10, not **p** to us what is right
Matt. 7:22, did we not **p** in Your name
26:68, **P** to us, You Christ
1 Cor. 13:9, know in part, and we **p** in part
1 Chr. 25:3; Jer. 14:14; Ezek. 37:4; Joel 2:28

PROPHET Matt. 1:22, spoken ... through the **p**
Matt. 2:5, it had been written by the **p**
2:15, through the **p** might be fulfilled
2:17, Jeremiah the **p**
5:12, so they persecuted the **p-s**
10:41, **p** shall receive a **p-'s** reward
11:9, one who is more than a **p**
11:13, all the **p-s** and the Law
13:57, **p** is not without honor
21:11, the **p** Jesus, from Nazareth
Luke 4:24, no **p** is welcome in his home town
6:23, their fathers used to treat the **p-s**
John 1:21, Are you the **P**
4:19, perceive that You are a **p**
7:52, see that no **p** arises out of Galilee
Acts 13:15, reading of the Law and the **P-s**
1 Cor. 14:37, If anyone thinks he is a **p**
Eph. 4:11, some *as* apostles, and some *as* **p-s**
Heb. 1:1, to the fathers in the **p-s**
Gen. 20:7; Deut. 13:1; 18:18; Judg. 4:4; 1 Sam. 9:9; 1 Kin. 20:35; Is. 9:15; Jer. 23:11; Ezek. 13:3; Hos. 12:10; Amos 7:14; Acts 13:6

PROPHETIC 1 Thess. 5:20, do not despise **p** utterances
2 Pet. 1:19, the **p** word made more sure

PROSELYTE Matt. 23:15, make one **p**
Acts 2:10, both Jews and **p-s**
13:43, God-fearing **p-s** followed Paul

PROSPER 1 Sam. 18:14, David was **p-ing**
Ps. 10:5, His ways **p** at all times
Prov. 28:13, his transgressions will not **p**
1 Cor. 16:2, save, as he may **p**
Gen. 39:3; 1 Sam. 18:5

PROSPERITY—*wealth*
Ezra 9:12, never seek ... their **p**
Job 21:13, spend their days in **p**
Ps. 25:13, His soul will abide in **p**
73:3, saw the **p** of the wicked
Acts 19:25, our **p** depends upon this business

PROSPEROUS
Prov. 11:25, generous man will be **p**

PROSTITUTES
Hos. 4:14, offer sacrifices with temple **p**

PROSTRATE 2 Sam. 9:6, fell on his face and **p-d** himself
Job 14:10, man dies and lies **p**

PROTECT Is. 31:5, He will **p** and deliver it

PROTECTION Num. 14:9, Their **p** has been removed
Eccles. 7:12, wisdom is **p** *just as* money is **p**

PROUD—*arrogant, conceited*
Ps. 94:2, recompense to the **p**
Luke 1:51, **p** in the thoughts of their heart
James 4:6, GOD IS OPPOSED TO THE **P**
Is. 3:16; 13:11

PROVE—*test* Prov. 30:6; 2 Cor. 8:8
Acts 9:22, **p-ing** that this *Jesus* is the Christ
Rom. 12:2, **p** what the will of God is

PROVERB 1 Kin. 4:32, He also spoke 3,000 **p-s**
1 Kin. 9:7, Israel will become a **p** and a byword
Deut. 28:37; Jer. 24:9; 2 Pet. 2:22

PROVIDE—*gave* Gen. 22:8, God will **p** for Himself the Lamb
Neh. 9:15, didst **p** bread from heaven
1 Tim. 5:8, if any one does not **p** for his own
Lev. 25:24; 1 Sam. 16:17

PROVISION Josh. 9:5, bread of their **p** was dry
Ps. 132:15, abundantly bless her **p**
Rom. 13:14, make no **p** for the flesh

PROVOKE Prov. 20:2, who **p-s** him to anger
1 Cor. 13:5, is not **p-d**
Eph. 6:4, do not **p** your children to anger
2 Chr. 25:19; Job 12:6

PROW Acts 27:41, the **p** stuck fast and remained

PROWL—*walk* Ps. 104:20, beast of the forest **p**
1 Pet. 5:8, devil, **p-s** about like a roaring lion

PRUDENT Prov. 12:16, **p** man conceals dishonor
Prov. 19:14, a **p** wife is from the LORD
Jer. 49:7, good counsel been lost to the **p**

PSALMS Ps. 95:2, shout joyfully to Him with **p**
Luke 20:42, David ... says in the book of **P**
24:44, the **P** must be fulfilled
Eph. 5:19, speaking to one another in **p**

PUGNACIOUS 1 Tim. 3:3, addicted to wine or **p**

PULL Ps. 31:4, **p** me out of the net
Luke 14:5, **p** him out on a Sabbath day

PULVERIZE Mic. 4:13, That you may **p** many peoples

PUNISH—*visit* Lev. 26:18,28, will **p** you seven times
Is. 13:11, **p** the world for its evil
Lam. 4:22, He will **p** your iniquity
2 Cor. 10:6, to **p** all disobedience
Prov. 22:3; Luke 23:16; Acts 26:11

PUNISHMENT Gen. 4:13, **p** is too great to bear
Job 19:29, the **p** of the sword
Matt. 25:46, go away into eternal **p**
2 Cor. 2:6, Sufficient ... is this **p**

PUNISHMENT *(Continued)*
1 John 4:18, because fear involves **p**
Jude 7, the **p** of eternal fire
PUPIL Deut. 32:10, **p** of His eye
Luke 6:40, a **p** is not above his teacher
PURCHASE Gen. 49:32, field ... **p-d** from
Acts 20:28, He **p-d** with His own blood
Rev. 5:9, **p** for God with Thy blood
PURE Ps. 12:6, words of the LORD are **p** words
Ps. 19:8, commandment of the LORD is **p**
24:4, clean hands and a **p** heart
Matt. 5:8, Blessed are the **p** in heart
2 Cor. 11:2, present you *as* a **p** virgin
Phil. 4:8, whatever is **p**
1 Tim. 1:5, love from a **p** heart
Titus 1:15, To the **p**, all things are **p**
2:5, *be* sensible, **p**
James 1:27, **p** and undefiled religion
2 Sam. 22:27; Job 4:17; 11:4; 15:15; Song 6:10; Dan. 7:9
PURGE Dan. 12:10, Many will be **p-d**, purified, refined
PURIFY Ps. 51:7, **P** me with hyssop
1 Pet. 1:22, obedience ... **p-ed** your souls
2 Pet. 1:9, **p-cation** from his former sins
2 Kin. 2:21; Dan. 12:10
PURPOSE—*cause, devise, reason*
Jer. 49:20, **p-s** which He has **p-d**
Lam. 2:17, The LORD has done what He **p-d**
Ezek. 22:9, **p** of shedding blood
Luke 7:30, rejected God's **p**
Acts 26:16, for this **p** I have appeared to you
Rom. 8:28, called according to His **p**
Eph. 3:11, in accordance with the eternal **p**
6:22, for this very **p**
Heb. 6:17, unchangeableness of His **p**
1 Pet. 4:6, has for this **p** been preached
PURSE Is. 46:6; Hag. 1:6; Luke 12:33
PURSUE—*follow, persecute, sought* Gen. 31:36
Ps. 34:14, Seek peace, and **p** it
Prov. 21:21, who **p-s** righteousness and loyalty
Heb. 12:14, **P** peace with all men
1 Pet. 3:11, SEEK PEACE AND **P** IT
Lev. 26:17; Judg. 3:28; 2 Sam. 1:6; Job 30:15; Ps. 7:1; Is. 5:11
PUSH—*thrust* Ps. 118:13, **p-ed** me violently
PUT Gen. 3:15, I will **p** enmity Between you and
Ex. 9:15, now I had **p** forth My hand
Ps. 40:3, **p** a new song in my mouth
Matt. 1:19, desired to **p** her away secretly
12:18, I WILL **P** MY SPIRIT UPON HIM
26:52, **P** your sword back into its place
Mark 12:42, widow came ... **p** in two
Luke 9:62, **p-ing** his hand to the plow
John 19:2, crown of thorns ... **p** it on His head
20:27, hand, and **p** it into My side
Rom. 13:14, **p** on the Lord Jesus Christ
1 Cor. 15:53, **p** on the imperishable, **p** on immortality
Eph. 4:24, **p** on the new self
6:11, **P** on the full armor of God
1 Pet. 2:1, **p-ing** aside all malice
Rev. 14:15, **P** in your sickle
Josh. 1:18; 2 Chr. 18:22; Job 31:24; 38:36; Song 8:6; Mark 4:21; John 21:7

Q

QUAKE—*tremble, shake*
Judg. 5:4, The earth **q-d**, the heavens
Judg. 5:5; Ps. 68:8
QUARREL—*contend, war*
Ex. 21:18, if men have a **q**
James 4:1, source of **q-s** and conflicts
Ex. 17:2; Prov. 20:3; 1 Cor. 1:11
QUEEN 1 Kin. 10:1, the **q** of Sheba
Is. 47:5, the **q** of kingdoms
Matt. 12:42, **Q** of *the* South shall rise
Esth. 1:9; Is. 47:7; Jer. 7:18; Acts 8:27
QUENCH 1 Thess. 5:19, Do not **q** the Spirit
Ps. 104:11; Song 8:7
QUESTION 1 Kin. 10:1, test with difficult **q-s**
Mark 11:29, I will ask you one **q**
22:35, a lawyer, asked Him a **q**
Acts 18:15, **q-s** about words and names
1 Cor. 10:25, without asking **q-s** for conscience' sake
1 Tim. 6:4, **q-s** and disputes about words
QUICK—*swift, soon* Acts 7:54, cut to the **q**
Titus 1:7, not **q-tempered**, not addicted to
James 1:19, every one be **q** to hear
Judg. 2:23; John 11:31
QUICKLY—*shortly, suddenly*
Matt. 5:25, Make friends **q** with your opponent
John 13:27, what you do, do **q**
Rom. 9:28, EXECUTE HIS WORD ... **Q**
Rev. 3:11; 22:20, I am coming **q**
Gen. 18:6; Deut. 7:4; Ps. 31:2; Eccles. 4:12; 2 Thess. 2:2
QUICK-TEMPERED Prov. 14:17; 14:29; Titus 1:7
QUIET Job 20:20, he knew no **q** within him
Ps. 23:2, beside **q** waters
1 Thess. 4:11, your ambition to lead a **q** life
1 Tim. 2:2, lead a tranquil and **q** life
Prov. 17:1; Eccles. 9:17; Amos 6:10
QUILT 1 Sam. 19:13, put a **q** of goats' *hair*
QUOTA Ex. 5:18, deliver the **q** of bricks

R

RABBI Matt. 26:25; Mark 9:5
RABBIT Lev. 11:6; Deut. 14:7
RACE Eccles. 9:11, **r** is not to the swift
Nah. 2:4, chariots **r** madly in the streets
1 Cor. 9:24, those who run in a **r** all run
1 Pet. 2:9, A CHOSEN **R**, A ROYAL
RADIANCE Heb. 1:3, **r** of His glory
RADIANT Jer. 31:12, **r** over the bounty of the LORD
RAFTER Hab. 2:11, the **r** will answer it
RAGES—*frets* Prov. 19:3, his heart **r** against
RAID Gen. 49:19, raiders shall **r** him ... **r** at their heels
RAIMENT—*clothing* Is. 63:3, I stained all My **r**
RAIN Gen. 7:12, **r** fell upon the earth for forty days
Ex. 16:4, will **r** bread from heaven for you
Matt. 5:45, **r** on *the* righteous ... unrighteous
7:25, and the **r** descended
Heb. 6:7, ground that drinks the **r**
Lev. 26:4; Deut. 32:2; Job 24:8; Prov. 25:14; 25:23; Song 2:11
RAISE Matt. 20:19, third day He ... **r-d** up
John 2:19, in three days I will **r** it up
6:39, **r** it up on the last day
1 Cor. 15:13, not even Christ ... **r-d**
15:35, How are the dead **r-d**
15:42, it is **r-d**
15:44, **r-d** a spiritual body
Eph. 2:6, **r-d** us up with Him
Col. 3:1, If ... been **r-d** up with Christ
Heb. 11:19, God is able to **r** *men* from
Deut. 18:18; Judg. 2:16; Is. 2:2; Dan. 12:7; Hos. 6:2; Mic. 4:1; Luke 3:8
RAISIN 2 Sam. 6:19; Song 2:5; Hos. 3:1
RAMPARTS—*siege works* Ps. 48:13; Is. 26:1
RAN—*fled* Luke 8:34, they **r** away and reported
RANK—*high* Ps. 62:9, men of **r** are a lie
RANSOM Matt. 20:28, give His life a **r** for many
1 Tim. 2:6, gave Himself as a **r** for all
Ex. 30:12; Prov. 6:35
RAPID—*swift* Prov. 6:18, Feet that run **r-ly** to evil
RARE—*precious*
1 Sam. 3:1, word from the LORD was **r**
RASH Job 6:3, my words have been **r**
RATION—*provision* Dan. 1:5; Luke 12:42
RAVAGE Gen. 41:30; 1 Sam. 6:5; Acts 8:3

RAVINE—*valley* Luke 3:5, EVERY **R** SHALL BE
RAYS Hab. 3:4, He has **r** *flashing* from His hand
READ Hab. 2:2, one who **r-s** it may run
Luke 4:16, stood up to **r**
Acts 8:28, was **r-ing** the prophet Isaiah
2 Cor. 3:14, at the **r-ing** of the old covenant
1 Tim. 4:13, give attention to the public **r-ing**
Rev. 1:3, Blessed is he who **r-s**
Ex. 24:7; Is. 34:16; Dan. 5:8
READINESS 2 Cor. 8:12, if the **r** is present
READY 1 Chr. 7:11; Ps. 86:5; Prov. 24:27
REALIZED Prov. 13:19, Desire **r** is sweet
REALLY—*indeed* Luke 24:34, The Lord has **r** risen
REAP—*harvest* Hos. 8:7, they **r** the whirlwind
Matt. 6:26, neither do they **r**, nor
25:26, **r** where I did not sow
Luke 12:24, ravens . . . neither sow nor **r**
2 Cor. 9:6, shall also **r** sparingly
Gal. 6:7, this he will also **r**
6:8, flesh **r** corruption
6:9, in due time we shall **r**
Lev. 19:9; Ps. 126:5; Prov. 22:8; Rev. 14:16
REASON—*thought*
Job 23:7, the upright would **r** with Him
Is. 1:18, let us **r** together
Luke 5:22, Why are you **r-ing** in your hearts
Acts 17:17, he was **r-ing** in the synagogue
1 Cor. 3:20, KNOWS THE **R-INGS** of the wise
1 Tim. 1:16, for this **r** I found mercy
James 3:17, gentle, **r-able**, full of mercy
REBEL Ps. 107:11, **r-ed** against the words of God
Is. 63:10, **r-ed** . . . grieved His Holy Spirit
Num. 14:9; 1 Sam. 12:15; Ezek. 20:21
REBELLION—*transgression* 1 Sam. 24:11; Job 13:23
REBELLIOUS—*disobedient*
1 Tim. 1:9, those who are lawless and **r**
Ex. 23:21; Deut. 9:7; Ps. 66:7; 78:8; Jer. 5:23
REBUILD Is. 58:12, **r** the ancient ruins
REBUKE—*reprove, reproof*
Matt. 8:26, **r-d** the winds and
17:18, Jesus **r-d** him, and the demon
Mark 9:25, **r-d** the unclean spirit
Luke 4:39, He **r-d** the fever, and it left
1 Tim. 5:1, not sharply **r** an older man
Job 26:11; Ps. 38:1; Prov. 27:5; Zech. 3:2
RECEIVE—*accept* Prov. 1:3, **r** instruction in wise
Matt. 10:8, freely you **r-d**, freely give
10:14, whoever does not **r** you
10:40, who **r-s** you **r-s** Me
10:41, who **r-s** a prophet in *the* name of
11:5, BLIND **R** SIGHT
18:5, **r-s** one such child
25:27, **r-d** my money back with interest
Mark 16:19, **r-d** up into heaven
Luke 15:2, This man **r-s** sinners
20:47, **r** greater condemnation
John 1:11, His own did not **r** Him
5:44, **r** glory from one another
14:3, **r** you to Myself
20:22, **R** the Holy Spirit
Acts 20:35, blessed to give than to **r**
Rom. 5:17, **r** the abundance of grace
8:15, **r-d** a spirit of adoption
1 Cor. 3:8, will **r** his own reward
9:24, one **r-s** the prize
Gal. 4:5, **r** the adoption as sons
1 Thess. 1:6, **r-d** the word in much
2 Thess. 2:10, did not **r** the love of the
Heb. 2:2, **r-d** a just recompense
James 1:12, **r** the crown of life
Job 3:12; Is. 40:2
RECEPTION—*feast* Luke 14:13, you give a **r**
RECKLESS 2 Tim. 3:4, treacherous, **r** . . . lovers of pleasure
RECKON—*impute* Rom. 4:4, his wage is not **r-ed**
Rom. 4:6, God **r-s** righteousness
RECLINE—*sat* Matt. 9:10; 26:20, He was **r-ing**

RECOGNIZE—*know* Acts 19:15, I **r** Jesus
Gen. 27:23; 1 Cor. 14:38
RECOMPENSE—*reward*
Ps. 94:2, Render **r** to the proud
Heb. 2:2, received a just **r**
Ps. 28:4; Jer. 51:6
RECONCILE Matt. 5:24, be **r-d** to your brother
1 Cor. 7:11, be **r-d** to her husband
2 Cor. 5:20, be **r-d** to God
Col. 1:20, **r** all things to Himself
RECONCILIATION
Rom. 5:11, we have now received the **r**
RECORD—*write* Hab. 2:2, **R** the vision
RECOVERY—*health* Is. 58:8, your **r** will speedily spring
RED—*dull* Gen. 25:25, first came forth **r**, all over
Ex. 10:19, drove them into the **R** Sea
Prov. 23:31, on the wine when it is **r**
Is. 1:18, they are **r** like crimson
Zech. 1:8, man was riding on a **r** horse
Matt. 16:2, fair weather . . . sky is **r**
Rev. 6:4, another, a **r** horse, went out
REDEEM—*purchase*
Ex. 6:6, **r** you with an outstretched arm
Ps. 26:11, **R** me, and be gracious
49:15, God will **r** my soul
Gal. 3:13, **r-ed** us from the curse
Titus 2:14, **R** US FROM EVERY . . . DEED
Ruth 4:4; 2 Sam. 4:9
REDEEMER Job 19:25, know that my **R** lives
Ps. 19:14, my rock and my **r**
Is. 63:16, our Father, Our **R**
Jer. 50:34, Their **R** is strong
REDEMPTION Ps. 130:7, with Him is abundant **r**
Luke 21:28, your **r** is drawing near
Rom. 3:24, **r** which is in Christ Jesus
Eph. 1:7, **r** through His blood
4:30, sealed for the day of **r**
REDUCE—*diminish* Ex. 5:8, you are not to **r** any of it
REED—*bulrushes, rod*
Ex. 2:3, set it among the **r-s** by
Is. 42:3, bruised **r** He will not break
Matt. 27:30, **r** and *began* to beat Him
27:48, wine, and put it on a **r**
Is. 36:6; Matt. 11:7
REEF Jude 12, hidden **r-s** in your love-feasts
REEL Is. 28:7, these also **r** with wine
REFINE—*purify, try* Ps. 12:6, silver . . . **r-d** seven times
Rev. 3:18, gold **r-d** by fire
REFORM Acts 24:2, **r-s** are being carried out
REFRAIN 1 Pet. 3:10, **R** HIS TONGUE FROM EVIL
Ex. 23:5; Job 30:10; 1 Cor. 9:6; 2 Cor. 12:6
REFRESH—*comfort* 1 Cor. 16:18, **r-ed** my spirit and yours
Gen. 18:5; Ex. 23:12; 31:17; Song 2:5
REFUGE—*defense, strength, trust*
2 Sam. 22:3, God, my rock, in whom I take **r**
Ps. 46:1, God is our **r** and strength
Is. 17:10, remembered the rock of your **r**
33:16, His **r** will be the impregnable rock
Judg. 9:15; Ps. 55:8; Is. 28:17; Jer. 16:19
REFUSE (n.) Ex. 29:14; Judg. 3:22; Is. 57:20
REFUSE (v.) Gen. 23:6, none . . . will **r** you his grave
Prov. 21:25, his hands **r** to work
Matt. 2:18, SHE **R-D** TO BE COMFORTED
Acts 10:47, no one can **r** the water for these
2 Tim. 2:23, **r** foolish and ignorant speculations
Jer. 13:10; Heb. 12:25
REFUTE Job 32:12; Titus 1:9
REGARD Rom. 14:5, **r-s** one day above another
Phil. 2:3, you **r** one another as more important
Gen. 4:4; Job 18:3; 41:27; Prov. 15:5; Is. 17:7; Lam. 4:2; Luke 7:2

REGION Matt. 2:22, he departed for the **r-s** of Galilee
Mark 5:17; Luke 2:8; Acts 27:2
REGISTER—*number, written* Num. 11:26; 2 Sam. 24:4
REGRET 1 Sam. 15:35, the LORD **r-ed** that
2 Cor. 7:10, produces a repentance without **r**
REGULAR Dan. 8:11; 11:31; 12:11, **r** sacrifice
REIGN—*rule* Ex. 15:18, LORD shall **r** forever and
Luke 19:14, not want this man to **r** over
1 Cor. 15:25, must **r** until He has put
2 Tim. 2:12, we shall also **r** with Him
Rev. 20:6, **r** with Him for a thousand years
Gen. 37:8; Judg. 9:8; Prov. 8:15; Is. 32:1
REJECT Prov. 3:11, do not **r** the discipline of the LORD
Prov. 15:5, A fool **r-s** his father's discipline
Matt. 21:42, STONE . . . BUILDERS **R-ED**
Luke 10:16, the one who **r-s** you **r-s** Me
17:25, **r-ed** by this generation
John 12:48, He who **r-s** Me
1 Thess. 4:8, who **r-s** *this* is not **r-ing** man but God
2 Tim. 3:8, **r-ed** as regards the faith
1 Pet. 2:4, **r-ed** by men
2:7; Ps. 118:22, STONE . . . BUILDERS **R-ED**
Num. 11:20; Ps. 53:5; Is. 14:19; 30:12; 33:15; Jer. 6:30; Ezek. 20:13,16; Hos. 4:6; Amos 2:4
REJOICE Prov. 5:18, **r** in the wife of your youth
Matt. 2:10, they **r-d** exceedingly
5:12, **R**, and be glad
John 14:28, loved Me, you would have **r-d**
Rom. 12:15, **R** with those who **r**
1 Cor. 13:6, not **r** in unrighteousness
Phil. 3:1, brethren, **r** in the Lord
4:4, **R** in the Lord always
1 Thess. 5:16, **R** always
1 Pet. 1:8, **r** with joy inexpressible
Job 21:12; Eccles. 11:9; Is. 60:5; Luke 10:21; 1 Thess. 3:9
REJOICING Ps. 19:8, LORD are right, **r** the heart
Ps. 65:12, hills gird themselves with **r**
Joel 1:12, **r** dries up
Acts 5:41, **r** . . . been considered worthy
8:39, went on his way **r**
Rom. 12:12, **r** in hope, persevering
2 Cor. 6:10, sorrowful yet always **r**
RELATE Acts 8:33, WHO SHALL **R** HIS GENERATION
RELATIONSHIP
Matt. 19:10, **r** of the man with his wife
RELATIVE Luke 1:36,58
RELEASE—*deliverance, liberty*
Lev. 25:10, proclaim a **r** through the land
Matt. 27:26, Then he **r-d** Barabbas
Mark 15:9, **r** for you the King . . . Jews
Luke 4:18, PROCLAIM **R** TO THE CAPTIVES
23:20, Pilate, wanting to **r** Jesus
John 19:12, Pilate made efforts to **r** Him
Rom. 7:6, we have been **r-d** from the Law
1 Cor. 7:27, Are you **r-d** from a wife
Heb. 11:35, not accepting their **r**
Rev. 1:5, **r-d** us from our sins
RELIEF Job 32:20, speak that I may get **r**
RELIEVED Ps. 4:1, Thou hast **r** me in my distress
REMAIN—*abide, live, reside*
Gen. 8:22, While the earth **r-s**
Eccles. 1:4, But the earth **r-s** forever
Matt. 2:13, **r** there until I tell
11:23, **r-ed** to this day
26:38, **r** here and keep watch
John 1:32, He **r-ed** upon Him
19:31, not **r** on the cross
21:22, want him to **r** until I come
1 Cor. 3:14, If any man's work . . . **r-s**
7:8, they **r** even as I
7:11, let her **r** unmarried
Gal. 2:5, gospel might **r** with you
1 Thess. 4:15, **r** until the coming of
Titus 1:5, set in order what **r-s**
Rev. 3:2, strengthen the things that **r**
Ex. 16:29; Deut. 9:9; 1 Sam. 5:7; 16:11; Job 14:2; 21:34; John 8:35
REMARKABLE—*strange*
Luke 5:26, seen **r** things today
REMEMBER Gen. 9:15, I will **r** My covenant
Ex. 20:8, **R** the sabbath day
Job 7:7, **R** that my life is *but* breath
11:16, As waters . . . passed by . . . **r** *it*
Ps. 25:7, not **r** the sins of my youth
Eccles. 12:1, **R** also your Creator
Jer. 31:34, their sin I will **r** no more
Matt. 26:75, Peter **r-ed** the word which Jesus
27:63, **r** . . . that deceiver said
Luke 17:32, **R** Lot's wife
23:42, **r** me when You come in
John 15:20, **R** the word that I said
Acts 20:35, **r** the words of the Lord
Gal. 2:10, us to **r** the poor
Heb. 13:7, **R** those who led you
Rev. 2:5, **R** . . . from where you have fallen
Deut. 5:15; 32:7; 1 Chr. 16:12; Ps. 63:6; 105:42; Is. 46:8; Jer. 15:15; Lam. 3:20; Ezek. 21:32; Acts 10:31; Heb. 13:3
REMEMBRANCE Mal. 3:16, a book of **r** was written
Luke 22:19, do this in **r** of Me
1 Cor. 11:25, drink *it*, in **r** of Me
Eccles. 1:11; Is. 26:14; 43:26
REMNANT Rom. 11:5, **r** according to *God's* gracious choice
Deut. 3:11; Jer. 6:9; 23:3; Mal. 2:15
REMOTE—*utmost* Neh. 1:9, most **r** part of the heavens
REMOVE Gen. 8:13, Noah **r-d** the covering of the ark
Ex. 3:5, **r** your sandals from your feet
1 Kin. 15:12, **r-d** all the idols
2 Kin. 17:23, LORD **r-d** Israel from His sight
Ps. 103:12, **r-d** our transgressions
Is. 29:13, **r** their hearts far from
Ezek. 36:26, **r** the heart of stone
Matt. 3:11, not *even* fit to **r** His sandals
Luke 22:42, **r** this cup from Me
John 11:39, **R** the stone
1 Cor. 13:2, so as to **r** mountains
Ruth 4:8; 2 Kin. 18:4; Job 24:2
REND 1 Kin. 19:11; Is. 64:1; Joel 2:13
RENDER—*repay* Matt. 22:21, **r** to Caesar the things that
Rom. 13:7, **R** to all . . . due them
Deut. 32:41; Ps. 94:2; Prov. 24:12
RENEW Ps. 51:10, **r** a steadfast spirit within
Ps. 103:5, youth is **r-ed** like the
Lam. 5:21, **R** our days as of old
Rom. 12:2, **r-ing** of your mind
2 Cor. 4:16, inner man is being **r-ed** day by day
Col. 3:10, **r-ed** to a true knowledge
Titus 3:5, **r-ing** by the Holy Spirit
REPAY—*recompense* Gen. 44:4, **r-d** evil for good
Matt. 6:4,6,18, in secret will **r** you
Luke 10:35, return, I will **r** you
Rom. 12:19, I WILL **R**, SAYS THE LORD
1 Thess. 5:15, no one **r-s** . . . evil for evil
Philem. 19, own hand, I will **r** it
Heb. 10:30, VENGEANCE IS MINE, I WILL **R**
Deut. 7:10; 32:6; 2 Sam. 3:39; Jer. 18:20; 51:56; Luke 14:14
REPENT Job 42:6, **r** in dust and ashes
Matt. 3:2, **R**, for the kingdom of
11:21, **r-ed** long ago in sackcloth
Mark 1:15, **r** and believe in the gospel
6:12, preached that *men* should **r**
Luke 13:3, unless you **r**, you will all
15:7, one sinner who **r-s**
Acts 2:38, **R**, and . . . be baptized
3:19, **R** therefore and return
26:20, **r** and turn to God
Num. 23:19; Ezek. 18:30

REPENTANCE Matt. 3:8, fruit ... with *your* **r**
Matt. 3:11, in water for **r**
Mark 1:4, a baptism of **r**
Luke 24:47, **r** for forgiveness of sins
Acts 26:20, performing deeds ... to **r**
2 Cor. 7:10, God produces a **r** without regret
Heb. 6:1, laying ... foundation of **r**
2 Pet. 3:9, all to come to **r**

REPHAIM—*giant*
Deut. 3:13, it is called the land of **R**

REPORT Matt. 2:8, have found *Him,* **r** to me
Matt. 11:4, Go and **r** to John the things
Luke 7:17, this **r** concerning Him
John 12:38, WHO HAS BELIEVED OUR **R**

REPROACH Jer. 29:18, a hissing and a **r**
Ezek. 5:14, a **r** among the nations
Matt. 11:20, He began to **r** the cities
1 Tim. 3:7, fall into **r** and the snare of
Titus 2:8, speech which is beyond **r**
Heb. 11:26, considering the **r** of Christ
Gen. 30:23; Job 27:6; Ps. 4:2; 44:13; 119:39; Is. 51:7; Jer. 24:9; Hos. 12:14; Rom. 15:3

REPROBATE Ps. 15:4, a **r** is despised

REPROOF Prov. 15:10, who hates **r** will die
2 Tim. 3:16, for teaching, for **r**, for correction
Prov. 1:30; 10:17; 15:5; 29:1,15

REPROVE—*correct*
Job 5:17, the man whom God **r-s**
Prov. 3:12, whom the LORD loves He **r-s**
Matt. 18:15, **r** him in private
2 Tim. 4:2, **r**, rebuke, exhort, with ... patience
Rev. 3:19, I love, I **r** and discipline
Lev. 19:17; Job 13:10; 40:2; Prov. 9:8; Jer. 2:19

REPUTATION—*report*
Acts 6:3, seven men of good **r**
1 Tim. 5:10, having a **r** for good works

REPUTE—*report* Phil. 4:8, whatever is of good **r**

REQUEST—*desire*
Rom. 1:10, in my prayers making **r**
Phil. 4:6, let your **r-s** be made known
Judg. 8:24; 1 Kin. 2:16; Neh. 2:4; Job 6:8; Mark 15:6

REQUIRE Mic. 6:8, what does the Lord **r** of you
Luke 12:20, night your soul is **r-d** of you
1 Cor. 4:2, it is **r-d** of stewards
Gen. 9:5; Deut. 10:12; Ezra 3:4; Ps. 10:13; Is. 1:12

RESCUE Ps. 144:10; 2 Pet. 2:7

RESERVED 1 Pet. 1:4, **r** in heaven for you
2 Pet. 3:7, are being **r** for fire
Gen. 27:36; Job 21:30

RESIDE Matt. 2:23, **r-d** in a city called Nazareth
Lev. 19:34; Eccles. 7:9; Jer. 49:18

RESIST Matt. 5:39, do not **r** him who is evil
Luke 21:15, opponents will be able to **r** or
Acts 7:51, are always **r-ing** the Holy Spirit
Rom. 13:2, he who **r-s** authority has opposed
Heb. 12:4, not yet **r-ed** to the point of shedding
James 4:7, **R** the devil, and he

RESOLUTELY—*steadfastly*
1 Chr. 28:7, **r** performs My
Luke 9:51, He **r** set His face to go

RESPECT Matt. 21:37, They will **r** my son
Luke 18:2, and did not **r** man
Eph. 5:33, let the wife ... **r** her husband
1 Pet. 3:2, chaste and **r-ful** behavior
Gen. 34:19; Mal. 1:6; 1 Pet. 2:18

RESPOND Is. 19:22, LORD, and He will **r** to them
Col. 4:6, how you should **r** to each person

RESPONSE 2 Kin. 4:31, was neither sound nor **r**

REST—*stand* Josh. 1:13, God gives you **r**
Josh. 14:15, the land had **r** from war
Ps. 37:7, **R** in the LORD and wait
116:7, Return to your **r**, O my soul
Prov. 14:33, Wisdom **r-s** in the heart
Is. 11:2, Spirit of the LORD will **r** upon Him
11:10, His **r-ing** place will be glorious
Jer. 6:16, find **r** for your souls
Matt. 11:28, and I will give you **r**
11:29, **R** FOR YOUR SOULS
Luke 11:24, waterless places seeking **r**
1 Cor. 2:5, **r** on the wisdom of men
2 Cor. 2:13, I had no **r** for my spirit
Heb. 3:11, THEY SHALL NOT ENTER MY **R**
1 Pet. 4:2, live the **r** of the time in
Gen. 5:29; 8:9; 49:15; Ex. 10:5; Deut. 28:65; Ruth 1:9; 2 Sam. 4:5; Job 3:17; 11:18; Prov. 19:20; Eccles. 4:6; Is. 14:3; 38:10; 57:2; Lam. 5:5; Matt. 22:6; Rev. 19:21

RESTED Gen. 2:2, and He **r** on the seventh day
Ex. 24:16, glory of the LORD **r**
Acts 2:3, tongues of fire ... **r** on each one

RESTITUTION Lev. 6:5; 2 Sam. 12:6

RESTORE—*turn* Ps. 19:7, perfect **r-ing** the soul
Ps. 23:3, He **r-s** my soul; He guides
Matt. 17:11, is coming, and will **r** all things
Mark 3:5, his hand was **r-d**
James 5:15, prayer ... will **r** the one who is sick
Gen. 20:7; Neh. 3:8; 4:2; Ps. 80:3; Jer. 30:17

RESTRAIN Prov. 10:19, who **r-s** his lips is wise
Acts 14:18, they with difficulty **r-ed** the crowds
2 Cor. 6:12, You are not **r-ed** by us, but
Gen. 8:2; Job 7:11; 11:10; Jer. 31:16; 2 Pet. 2:16

RESTRICT Jer. 36:5, I am **r-ed**; I cannot go

RESULT—*work* Eph. 4:14, As a **r** ... no longer
James 1:4, endurance have *its* perfect **r**

RESURRECTION Matt. 22:23, say there is no **r**
Matt. 22:30, **r** they neither marry, nor
Luke 14:14, at the **r** of the righteous
20:27, who say that there is no **r**
20:36, being sons of the **r**
John 5:29, **r** of life ... **r** of judgment
11:25, the **r**, and the life
Acts 24:15, **r** of both the righteous and the
24:21, For the **r** of the dead
1 Cor. 15:13, if there is no **r**
Phil. 3:11, attain to the **r**
Heb. 11:35, might obtain a better **r**
1 Pet. 1:3, living hope through the **r**
Rev. 20:5, This is the first **r**

RETAIN John 20:23, **r** the sins of any ... **r-ed**

RETIRE Ps. 127:2, To **r** late

RETRIBUTION Hos. 9:7, days of **r** have come
Rom. 11:9, STUMBLING BLOCK ... A **R**

RETURN—*turn back*
Gen. 43:18, money ... **r-ed** in our sacks
Deut. 30:2, **r** to the LORD your God
Eccles. 4:9, a good **r** for their labor
Mal. 3:7, **R** to Me, and I will **r** to you
Matt. 10:13, let your ... peace **r** to you
Luke 2:39, they **r-ed** to Galilee
4:14, **r-ed** ... in the power of the Spirit
10:17, the seventy **r-ed** with joy
24:9, **r-ed** from the tomb
Acts 3:19, Repent therefore and **r**
1 Tim. 5:4, make some **r** to their parents
1 Pet. 2:25, now you have **r-ed** to the
3:9, not **r-ing** evil for evil
Gen. 3:19; 32:9; Ex. 14:28; Ruth 1:12; 1 Sam. 7:3; 25:21; 2 Sam. 1:22; 1 Kin. 22:17; Job 1:21; 10:21; 33:25; Eccles. 12:2,7; Is. 10:22; 55:11; Jer. 3:22; 4:1; Ezek. 16:55; Dan. 4:36; Matt. 12:44; Acts 13:34

REVEAL—*manifest* Job 20:27, will **r** his iniquity
Is. 40:5, glory of the LORD will be **r-ed**
53:1, arm of the LORD been **r-ed**
Matt. 11:25, didst **r** them to babes
16:17, blood did not **r** *this* to you
Luke 17:30, the Son of Man is **r-ed**
Rom. 8:18, glory that is to be **r-ed** to us
8:19, **r-ing** of the sons of God
1 Cor. 3:13, it is *to be* **r-ed** with fire
Gal. 1:16, to **r** His Son in me
Eph. 3:5, **r-ed** to His holy apostles
2 Thess. 2:3, man of lawlessness is **r-ed**
2:8, lawless one will be **r-ed**
1 Pet. 1:5, be **r-ed** in the last time
1 Sam. 14:8,11; Job 12:22; Prov. 11:13; 25:9; Is. 26:21; Dan. 2:47

REVEL 2 Pet. 2:13, to **r** in the daytime
REVELATION Rom. 16:25, the **r** of the mystery
1 Cor. 1:7, awaiting eagerly the **r**
14:6, speak . . . by way of **r**
Gal. 1:12, through a **r** of Jesus Christ
2:2, because of a **r** that I went up
Eph. 1:17, spirit of wisdom and **r**
Rev. 1:1, The **R** of Jesus Christ
REVENGE Jer. 20:10, take our **r** on him
Rom. 12:19, Never take your own **r**
REVERE Lev. 19:30; Zeph. 3:7
REVERENCE—*fear*
Ps. 2:11, Worship the LORD with **r**
5:7, bow in **r** for Thee
Heb. 11:7, in **r** prepared an ark
12:28, service with **r** and awe
Job 15:4; Is. 29:13
REVILE Ps. 74:10, long, will the adversary **r**
Matt. 5:11, when *men* **r** you
Acts 23:4, Do you **r** God's high priest
1 Cor. 4:12, when we are **r-d,** we bless
1 Pet. 2:23, being **r-d**, He did not **r**
4:14, **r-d** for the name of Christ
REVIVE Ps. 119:88, **R** me . . . Thy lovingkindness
REWARD—*recompense*
Job 15:31, emptiness will be his **r**
Ps. 58:11, a **r** for the righteous
Prov. 11:18, righteousness *gets* a true **r**
Is. 62:11, His **r** is with Him
Matt. 5:12, your **r** in heaven is great
6:1, no **r** with your Father who
6:2,5,16, have their **r** in full
10:42, shall not lose his **r**
1 Cor. 3:8, will receive his own **r**
Heb. 11:26, he was looking to the **r**
2 John 8, that you may receive a full **r**
Rev. 22:12, My **r** is with Me
Gen. 15:1; Ruth 2:12; Prov. 11:31; Is. 1:23; 45:13
RICH Gen. 13:2, Abram was very **r** in livestock
Jer. 9:23, **r** man boast of his riches
Matt. 19:23, hard for a **r** man to enter
Luke 1:53, sent away the **r** empty-handed
6:24, woe to you who are **r**
16:1, There was a certain **r** man
16:21, *crumbs* . . . falling from the **r** man's table
18:23, for he was extremely **r**
1 Cor. 4:8, filled, you have already become **r**
Eph. 2:4, God, being **r** in mercy
Col. 3:16, word of Christ **r-ly** dwell within
1 Tim. 6:18, to be **r** in good works
James 1:11, **r** man . . . will fade away
2:6, Is it not the **r** who oppress you
Rev. 13:16, **r** and the poor, and the free
Gen. 49:20; Ex. 30:15; 1 Sam. 2:7; Ps. 49:2; Prov. 10:4; 18:23; Eccles. 10:20
RICHES—*possessions* Prov. 11:4, **R** do not profit in the day
Prov. 22:1, more desired than great **r**
30:8, neither poverty nor **r**
Matt. 13:22, deceitfulness of **r**
Luke 8:14, choked with worries and **r**
Rom. 10:12, abounding in **r** for all who call
Eph. 1:7, **r** of His grace
3:8, unfathomable **r** of Christ
1 Tim. 6:17, hope on the uncertainty of **r**
James 5:2, Your **r** are rotted
1 Kin. 3:11; Job 20:15; 36:19; Ps. 62:10; Prov. 3:16; Jer. 9:23
RIDE 1 Kin. 1:33; Is. 19:1; Ezek. 23:12
RIGHT—*justice, just*
Judg. 17:6, man did what was **r**
Ps. 19:8, precepts of the LORD are **r**
Prov. 14:12, a way *which seems* **r**
Hos. 14:9, ways of the LORD are **r**
Matt. 5:29, **r** eye makes you stumble
22:44, SIT AT MY **R** HAND
26:64, AT THE **R** HAND OF POWER
Mark 5:15, and in his **r** mind
16:19, SAT DOWN AT THE **R** HAND OF GOD
Luke 22:50, cut off his **r** ear
John 1:12, the **r** to become children of God
Acts 8:21, your heart is not **r**
Rom. 9:21, potter have a **r** over the clay
12:17, **r** in the sight of all men
1 Cor. 9:18, full use of my **r** in the
2 Cor. 13:7, you may do what is **r**
Gal. 2:9, **r** hand of fellowship
Phil. 4:8, whatever is **r**
2 Pet. 2:15, forsaking the **r** way
Rev. 22:14, **r** to the tree of life
Gen. 24:48; Ex. 21:10; Deut. 12:25; 21:17; 2 Kin. 10:15; Job 9:2; 34:6; Prov. 24:26; Is. 41:13; Jer. 40:4; Ezek. 18:25,29; 33:17,20
RIGHTEOUS Gen. 6:9, Noah was a **r** man
Ps. 7:9, establish the **r**
Prov. 10:30, **r** will never be shaken
11:28, **r** will flourish
Jer. 23:5, David a **r** Branch
Hab. 2:4, the **r** will live by his faith
Matt. 5:45, rain on *the* **r** and *the* unrighteous
9:13, not come to call *the* **r**
10:41, a **r** man's reward
13:43, **R** WILL SHINE FORTH
25:46, **r** into eternal life
Luke 15:7, ninety-nine **r** persons
23:50, Joseph . . . a good and **r** man
John 7:24, with **r** judgment
Acts 7:52, the coming of the **R** One
Rom. 1:17, THE **R** *man* SHALL LIVE BY FAITH
3:10, NONE **R**, NOT EVEN
1 Tim. 1:9, Law . . . for a **r** man
James 5:16, prayer of a **r** man can
1 Pet. 4:18, THAT THE **R** IS SAVED
1 John 1:9, **r** to forgive us our sins
2:1, Jesus Christ the **r**
Gen. 18:23; Ex. 9:27; 23:7; 1 Sam. 24:17; Job 9:20; Ps. 1:5; 11:5; 33:1; 37:16; 55:22; 119:75,137; Prov. 2:20; 3:33; 4:18; 13:5; 16:13; 24:16; 28:1; Eccles. 3:17; 7:16; Is. 26:7; 32:1; 53:11; Jer. 33:15; Ezek. 13:22; Dan. 9:14; Amos 2:6
RIGHTEOUSNESS—*judgment, justice*
Ps. 23:3, in the paths of **r**
96:13, judge the world in **r**
97:6, heavens declare His **r**
111:3, His **r** endures forever
Prov. 14:34, **R** exalts a nation
16:8, Better is a little with **r**
Jer. 22:13, builds his house without **r**
23:6, The LORD our **r**
Dan. 12:3, lead the many to **r**
Matt. 3:15, fitting for us to fulfill all **r**
5:6, hunger and thirst for **r**
5:10, persecuted . . . sake of **r**
5:20, your **r** surpasses *that*
6:1, your **r** before men
6:33, seek first . . . and His **r**
Luke 1:75, holiness and **r** before Him
Rom. 4:3,22; Gal. 3:6, RECKONED TO HIM AS **R**
5:18, through one act of **r**
8:10, spirit is alive . . . **r**
2 Cor. 6:14, what partnership have **r** and
Gal. 2:21, if **r** *comes* through Law
Eph. 4:24, created in **r**
6:14, BREASTPLATE OF **R**
1 Tim. 6:11, pursue **r**
2 Tim. 4:8, the crown of **r**
Heb. 7:2, king of **r**
12:11, peaceful fruit of **r**
James 1:20, anger . . . not achieve the **r**
1 Pet. 3:14, for the sake of **r**
1 John 3:10, does not practice **r** is not
Gen. 15:6; 18:19; 1 Sam. 26:23; Job 27:6; 29:14; 36:3; Ps. 17:15; 48:10; Prov. 10:2; 11:19; Is. 45:8; 48:18; 51:5; 59:17; 60:17; Jer. 31:23; Ezek. 18:5; 33:13; Hos. 10:12; Mal. 4:2; Acts 13:10
RIPE Gen. 40:10; Jer. 24:2; Joel 3:13; Rev. 14:15,18
RISE Prov. 31:15, She **r-s** also while
Matt. 24:7, nation . . . **r** against nation
27:63, I *am* to **r** again

Mark 12:25, when they **r** from the dead
13:12, children will **r** up against parents
16:6, He has **r-n**, He is not here
Luke 5:23, **R** and walk
11:31, Queen of the South shall **r**
12:54, cloud **r-ing** in the west
22:46, **R** and pray that
24:34, Lord has really **r-n**
1 Thess. 4:16, dead in Christ shall **r**
Gen. 19:2; Lev. 19:32; Num. 24:17; Josh. 12:1; Ps. 35:11; 86:14; 113:3; Is. 32:9; 60:1; Jer. 47:2; Matt. 14:2; Luke 16:31

RIVER—*water* Ps. 46:4, a **r** whose streams make glad
Eccles. 1:7, All the **r-s** flow into the sea
Mark 1:5, baptized by him in the Jordan **R**
John 7:38, shall flow **r-s** of living water
2 Cor. 11:26, in dangers from **r-s**
Rev. 22:1, a **r** of the water of life
Gen. 2:10; Josh. 1:4; 24:2; Job 40:23; Ps. 24:2; 66:6; 137:1; Is. 11:15; Lam. 2:18; Ezek. 47:5

ROAD—*way* Luke 19:36, garments in the **r**
Acts 9:27, seen the Lord on the **r**

ROAM Job 1:7, From **r-ing** about on the earth

ROAR 1 Pet. 5:8, devil prowls about like a **r-ing** lion
2 Pet. 3:10, heavens pass away with a **r**
1 Chr. 16:32; Job 4:10; 37:4; Ps. 96:11; Jer. 25:30

ROAST Lev. 2:14, grain **r-ed** in the fire

ROB Prov. 22:22, Do not **r** the poor
Mal. 3:8, Will a man **r** God
2 Cor. 11:8, I **r-ed** other churches
Judg. 9:25; Prov. 17:12; 28:24; Is. 10:2

ROBBER Jer. 7:11, become a den of **r-s**
Matt. 21:13, making it a **r-s'** den
Mark 15:27, crucified two **r-s** with Him
Luke 10:30, he fell among **r-s**
22:52, come out . . . as against a **r**
John 10:1, he is a thief and a **r**
18:40, Now Barabbas was a **r**
Acts 19:37, neither **r-s** of temples

ROBBERY Ps. 62:10, do not vainly hope in **r**
Matt. 23:25, full of **r** and self-indulgence
Luke 11:39, full of **r** and wickedness

ROBE—*garment* Is. 61:10, with a **r** of righteousness
Matt. 27:28, put a scarlet **r** on Him
Mark 12:38, walk around in long **r-s**
16:5, young man . . . wearing a white **r**
Luke 15:22, bring out the best **r**
20:46, like to walk around in long **r-s**
John 19:2, arrayed Him in a purple **r**
Rev. 1:13, a **r** reaching to the feet
7:14, have washed their **r-s**
19:16, on His **r** and on His thigh
1 Sam. 24:4; Job 1:20; 29:14

ROCK—*stone, strength* Num. 20:11, struck the **r** twice
Ps. 19:14, LORD, my **r** and my redeemer
31:3, Thou art my **r** and my fortress
Matt. 7:24, built his house upon the **r**
13:5, fell upon the **r-y** places
16:18, upon this **r** I will build My church
Mark 15:46, tomb . . . hewn out in the **r**
Luke 8:6, other seed fell on **r-y** *soil*
Rom. 9:33, A **R** OF OFFENSE
1 Cor. 10:4, were drinking from a spiritual **r**
Ex. 17:6; 33:22; Deut. 32:4,13; 1 Sam. 2:2; 2 Sam. 22:2; Job 19:24; 28:2; 29:6; Ps. 18:2; 27:5; Prov. 30:19; Is. 8:14; 26:4; 51:1; Jer. 5:3

ROD Ps. 2:9, break them with a **r** of iron
Ps. 23:4, Thy **r** and Thy staff, they comfort
Prov. 13:24, spares his **r** hates his son
2 Cor. 11:25, Three times . . . beaten with **r-s**
Heb. 9:4, Aaron's **r** which budded
Rev. 19:15, rule them with a **r** of iron
Gen. 30:37; Num. 17:8; 2 Sam. 7:14; Prov. 26:3; Is. 10:5; Ezek. 20:37; 40:5; 41:8

ROGUE Is. 32:5, **r** be spoken of *as* generous

ROLL Is. 34:4, sky will be **r-ed** up
Matt. 27:60, he **r-ed** a large stone against
28:2, came and **r-ed** away the stone
Is. 22:18; Mark 16:3; Heb. 1:12

ROOF Gen. 19:8; Josh. 2:6; 2 Sam. 11:2; Matt. 8:8; Mark 2:4

ROOM Jer. 22:14, build myself a **r-y** house
Matt. 6:6, GO INTO YOUR INNER **R**
Mark 14:15, large upper **r** furnished
Luke 2:7, no **r** for them in the inn
Acts 1:13, went up to the upper **r**
Gen. 6:14; Judg. 3:24; Prov. 18:16; Matt. 24:26; Rom. 12:19

ROOT Matt. 3:10, axe . . . laid at the **r** of the trees
Mark 4:6, it had no **r**, it withered
Rom. 11:16, if the **r** be holy
Eph. 3:17, being **r-ed** and grounded in love
1 Tim. 6:10, money is a **r** of all sorts of evil
Deut. 29:18; Job 5:3; Ps. 80:9; Is. 5:24; 53:2; Jer. 12:2

ROPE Is. 3:24, Instead of a belt, a **r**

ROSE (n.) Song 2:1, I am the **r** of Sharon

ROSE (v.) Josh. 3:16, waters . . . **r** up in one heap

ROT—*wither* Is. 19:6, reeds and rushes will **r**
Zech. 14:12, tongue will **r** in their mouth
James 5:2, Your riches have **r-ed**

ROTTEN Matt. 7:17, **r** tree bears bad fruit

ROUND Lev. 19:27, not **r** off the side-growth

ROUGH Prov. 18:23; Is. 40:4

ROUT Judg. 4:15; 8:12; 2 Sam. 22:15; Ps. 18:14

RUBBISH Phil. 3:8, count them but **r**

RUIN—*destruction*
Ex. 9:31, flax . . . barley were **r-ed**
Prov. 10:15, **r** of the poor is their poverty
18:7, fool's mouth is his **r**
26:28, flattering mouth works **r**
Song 2:15, foxes that are **r-ing** the vineyards
Luke 6:49, **r** of that house was great
Acts 15:16, WILL REBUILD ITS **R-S**
Job 2:3; Ps. 74:3; Prov. 10:14,29; 14:28; Is. 23:13; 61:4; Lam. 2:13

RULE Judg. 8:22, **R** over us
Job 34:30, godless men should not **r**
Rom. 15:12, TO **R** OVER THE GENTILES
Gal. 6:16, will walk by this **r**
Eph. 1:21, far above all **r** and authority
Col. 3:15, peace of Christ **r** in your hearts
Rev. 2:27, **R** THEM WITH A ROD OF IRON
Gen. 1:26; Ps. 8:6; 49:14; Prov. 8:16; 16:32; Is. 3:12; 26:13

RULER Ex. 22:28, nor curse a **r** of your people
Matt. 2:6, SHALL COME FORTH A **R**, WHO WILL SHEPHERD
9:34, **r** of the demons
Mark 10:42, **r-s** of the Gentiles
John 3:1, Nicodemus, a **r** of the Jews
12:31, **r** of this world shall be cast out
Acts 7:27, WHO MADE YOU A **R** AND JUDGE
Eph. 6:12, struggle is . . . against the **r-s**
Titus 3:1, Remind them to be subject to **r-s**
Gen. 42:6; Ps. 2:2; Prov. 6:7; 29:12; Is. 22:3

RUMOR Matt. 24:6, wars and **r-s** of wars
Ex. 23:1; Ezek. 7:26

RUN Prov. 1:16, their feet **r** to evil
Is. 40:31, **r** and not get tired
1 Cor. 9:24, those who **r** in a race all **r**
Gal. 5:7, You were **r-ing** well
Heb. 12:1, let us **r** with endurance the race
Gen. 49:22; Lev. 15:13; 2 Kin. 4:22; Ps. 18:29; 19:5; Prov. 6:18; Ezek. 32:14; Gal. 2:2

RUSH Matt. 8:32, herd **r-ed** down the steep
Rev. 9:9, many horses **r-ing** to battle

RUSHES—*reeds* Job 8:11; Is. 19:6

RUST Matt. 6:19, moth and **r** destroy
James 5:3, Your gold and your silver have **r-ed**

RUTHLESS—*terrible*
Ezek. 28:7, most **r** of the nations

S

SABBATH Ex. 20:8, Remember the **s** day
Lev. 25:8, count off seven **s-s** of years
Matt. 12:8, is Lord of the **S**
28:1, Now late on the **S**
Mark 2:27, **S** was made for man
3:4, on the **S** to do good
John 19:31, that **S** was a high *day*
Acts 1:12, a **S** day's journey away
Ex. 16:26; 20:11; 31:15; 35:3; Lev. 26:2; Num. 15:32; Deut. 5:12; 2 Kin. 4:23

SACKCLOTH Matt. 11:21, repented . . . in **s**
Rev. 6:12, sun became black as **s** *made* of hair
Esth. 4:1; Job 16:15; Dan. 9:3

SACRED 2 Kin. 12:18, Joash . . . took all the **s** things
2 Tim. 3:15, have known the **s** writings

SACRIFICE Ps. 51:17, **s-s** of God are a broken
Matt. 9:13, COMPASSION, AND NOT S
Rom. 12:1, bodies a living and holy **s**
1 Cor. 8:1, things **s-d** to idols
10:20, they **s** to demons
Phil. 4:18, an acceptable **s**, well pleasing
Heb. 9:26, put away sin by the **s** of
11:4, a better **s** than Cain
13:16, such **s-s** God is pleased
Gen. 31:54; Ex. 12:27; Prov. 15:8; Is. 43:23; Dan. 11:31; Hos. 6:6; Acts 7:41

SAD—*sore* Prov. 15:13, when the heart is **s**
Is. 59:11, And moan **s-ly** like doves
Neh. 2:2; Luke 24:17

SADDLE Gen. 31:34, the camel's **s**

SAFE Job 21:9, houses are **s** from fear
Luke 15:27, received him back **s** and sound
Acts 27:43, centurion . . . bring Paul **s-ly**
Phil. 3:1, it is a **s-guard** for you

SAFETY Ezek. 39:6, inhabit the coastlands in **s**

SAIL Acts 28:13, from there we **s-ed** around

SAINT Matt. 27:52, bodies of the **s-s** . . . were raised
Acts 26:10, lock up . . . **s-s** in prisons
Rom. 1:7, called *as* **s-s**
8:27, He intercedes for the **s-s**
1 Cor. 6:2, **s-s** will judge the world
Eph. 2:19, fellow-citizens with the **s-s**
Phil. 1:1, all the **s-s** in Christ Jesus
1 Thess. 3:13, Lord Jesus with all His **s-s**
Rev. 14:12, perseverance of the **s-s**
20:9, the camp of the **s-s**

SAKE Ps. 23:3, For His name's **s**
Ps. 44:22, for Thy **s** we are killed
Is. 42:21, for His righteousness' **s**
Matt. 16:25, loses his life for My **s**
Mark 13:20, for the **s** of the elect
Luke 6:22, the **s** of the Son of Man
18:29, for the **s** of the kingdom of God
Rom. 8:36, THY S WE ARE . . . PUT TO DEATH
13:5, for conscience' **s**
1 Cor. 9:23, for the **s** of the gospel
2 Cor. 8:9, for your **s** He became poor
Phil. 1:29, for Christ's **s** . . . suffer for his **s**
1 Tim. 5:23, wine for the **s** of your stomach
Titus 1:11, for the **s** of sordid gain
2 John 2, for the **s** of the truth

SALT Gen. 19:26, became a pillar of **s**
Matt. 5:13, You are the **s** of the earth
Mark 9:50, **S** is good
Col. 4:6, seasoned, *as it were*, with **s**
James 3:12, *can* **s** water produce fresh
Judg. 9:45; Job 6:6

SALVATION Ps. 3:8, **S** belongs to the LORD
Ps. 27:1, LORD is my light and my **s**
62:1, From Him is my **s**
85:9, **s** is near to those who fear Him
98:3, seen the **s** of our God
Is. 59:17, helmet of **s** on His head
Luke 1:71, S FROM OUR ENEMIES
2:30, mine eyes have seen Thy **s**
3:6, FLESH SHALL SEE THE S OF GOD
19:9, **s** has come to this house
Acts 4:12, is **s** in no one else
13:26, word of this **s** is sent out
16:17, proclaiming to you the way of **s**
Rom. 1:16, power of God for **s**
11:11, **s** *has come* to the Gentiles
2 Cor. 6:2, ON THE DAY OF S
7:10, repentance . . . *leading* to **s**
Eph. 6:17, take the helmet of **s**
Phil. 2:12, work out your **s** with fear
1 Thess. 5:9, obtaining **s** through our Lord
2 Tim. 3:15, wisdom that leads to **s**
Titus 2:11, grace of God . . . bringing **s**
Heb. 1:14, who will inherit **s**
2:3, if we neglect so great a **s**
9:28, not to bear sin . . . for **s**
1 Pet. 1:5, through faith for a **s**
2 Pet. 3:15, patience of our Lord *to be* **s**
Rev. 7:10, **S** to our God who sits
12:10, Now the **s**, and the power
Gen. 49:18; Ex. 15:2; Deut. 32:15; Job 13:16; Ps. 116:13; 119:155; Is. 12:3; 33:2; 49:6; 51:6; 52:7; 56:1; Jon. 2:9; Zech. 9:9

SAME Ps. 102:27, But Thou art the **s**
Matt. 5:46, even the tax gatherers do the **s**
Luke 2:8, in the **s** region . . . shepherds
23:40, under the **s** sentence of
Rom. 10:12, **s** *Lord* is Lord of all
1 Cor. 12:4, of gifts, but the **s** Spirit
Heb. 13:8, Christ . . . **s** yesterday and today

SANCTIFY Lev. 22:32, I am the LORD who **s-es**
John 10:36, whom the Father **s-ed**
17:17, **S** them in the truth
Rom. 15:16, **s-ed** by the Holy Spirit
1 Cor. 6:11, washed, but you were **s-ed**
7:14, wife is **s-ed** . . . believing husband
1 Thess. 5:23, God of peace . . . **s** you entirely
Heb. 2:11, who **s-es** and those who are **s-ed**
Gen. 2:3; Ex. 13:2; Is. 29:23; Ezek. 20:20; 44:24

SANCTITY 1 Tim. 2:15, faith and love and **s**

SANCTUARY Ps. 150:1, Praise God in His **s**
Is. 60:13, beautify the place of My **s**
Heb. 8:2, a minister in the **s**
Ex. 25:8; Lev. 19:30; Ps. 73:17; Amos 7:13

SAND Gen. 32:12, descendants as the **s** of the sea
Matt. 7:26, built his house upon the **s**
Heb. 11:12, S . . . BY THE SEASHORE
Deut. 33:19; Job 29:18; Prov. 27:3

SANDAL Matt. 3:11, fit to remove His **s-s**
Matt. 10:10, tunics, or **s-s**, or
Ex. 12:11; Deut. 29:5; Amos 2:6; Mark 1:7; Acts 7:33

SANK Gen. 42:28, their hearts **s**

SAPPHIRE—*lapis lazuli* Ex. 28:18; Song 5:14; Rev. 21:19

SASH Ex. 28:40; 29:9

SAT Mark 16:19, S DOWN AT THE RIGHT HAND OF GOD
Luke 7:15, the dead man **s** up
Ex. 2:15; 16:3; Jon. 4:5; Mark 11:2

SATAN Matt. 4:10, Begone, **S**
Matt. 12:26, **S** casts out **S**
16:23, Get behind Me, **S**
Mark 1:13, forty days being tempted by **S**
Luke 10:18, watching **S** fall from heaven
22:3, **S** entered into Judas
Acts 5:3, why has **S** filled your heart
Rom. 16:20, crush **S** under your feet
2 Cor. 2:11, no advantage . . . of us by **S**
1 Thess. 2:18, *yet* **S** thwarted us
1 Tim. 1:20, I have delivered over to **S**
Rev. 3:9, *those* of the synagogue of **S**
12:9, called the Devil and **S**
20:7, **S** . . . released from his prison
Job 1:6; Zech. 3:2

SATIATE Is. 34:5, My sword is **s-d**

SATISFY Ps. 22:26, afflicted shall eat and be **s-ed**
Ps. 91:16, with long life I will **s** him
Mark 8:4, **s** these men with bread

Gen. 25:8; Lev. 26:26; Esth. 5:13; Job 21:23; 27:14; 38:27; Ps. 78:30; Prov. 6:30; 27:20; Is. 29:8; Joel 2:26; Mark 15:15

SATYR—*demon* 2 Chr. 11:15, he set up priests . . . for the **s-s**

SAVE—*deliver, escape, except*
Ps. 6:4, **S** me because of Thy lovingkindness
86:2, **s** Thy servant who trusts in Thee
Is. 35:4, God will come . . . He will **s** you
45:22, Turn to Me, and be **s-d**
63:1, mighty to **s**
Jer. 8:20, summer is ended . . . we are not **s-d**
Matt. 1:21, **s** His people from their sins
10:22, who has endured . . . will be **s-d**
16:25, **s** his life shall lose it
18:11, come to **s** that which is lost
19:25, Then who can be **s-d**
Mark 3:4, to **s** a life or to kill
13:13, one who has endured . . . will be **s-d**
16:16, been baptized shall be **s-d**
Luke 7:50, Your faith has **s-d** you; go in peace
23:35, let Him **s** Himself if . . . the Christ
John 3:17, world should be **s-d** through Him
10:9, enters through Me, he shall be **s-d**
12:27, Father, **s** Me from this hour
Acts 4:12, by which we must be **s-d**
16:30, what must I do to be **s-d**
Rom. 5:10, we shall be **s-d** by His life
8:24, in hope we have been **s-d**
1 Cor. 7:16, **s** your husband . . . **s** your wife
16:2, each . . . put aside and **s**
Eph. 2:5, by grace you have been **s-d**
1 Tim. 1:15, into the world to **s** sinners
2 Tim. 1:9, who has **s-d** us, and called us
James 1:21, able to **s** your souls
4:12, able to **s** and to destroy
1 Pet. 4:18, WITH DIFFICULTY . . . RIGHTEOUS **S-D**
Deut. 28:29; 33:29; 1 Sam. 14:6; Job 22:29; Ps. 28:9; 44:7; 60:5; Prov. 20:22; Jer. 30:10; 42:11; Ezek. 18:27; Amos 2:14; Acts 28:4

SAVIOR 2 Sam. 22:3, My **s**, Thou dost save me
Ps. 106:21, forgot God their **S**
Is. 19:20, He will send them a **S**
43:11, there is no **s** besides Me
45:21, a righteous God and a **S**
49:26, know that I, the LORD, am your **S**
Luke 2:11, a **S**, who is Christ the Lord
John 4:42, One is indeed the **S** of the world
Acts 5:31, as a Prince and a **S**
Eph. 5:23, He Himself *being* the **S** of the body
1 Tim. 4:10, God, who is the **S** of all men
2 Tim. 1:10, appearing of our **S** Christ Jesus
Titus 2:13, God and **S**, Christ Jesus
2 Pet. 1:11, our Lord and **S** Jesus Christ
1 John 4:14, sent the Son *to be* the **S**

SAW Gen. 1:4, God **s** that the light was good
Matt. 2:2, **s** His star in the east
2:11, **s** the Child with Mary
Mark 1:10, **s** the heavens opening
John 1:48, under the fig tree, I **s** you
Num. 22:23; Job 29:11; Eccles. 2:13; Is. 59:16; Dan. 4:5

SAY—*speak* Ps. 106:48, let all the people **s**,
Matt. 7:22, Many will **s** to Me on that day
16:13, Who do people **s** . . . Son of Man is
Luke 7:40, Simon, I have something to **s** to you
17:21, nor will they **s**, Look, here *it is*
1 John 1:8, If we **s** that we have no sin
Rev. 22:17, Spirit and the bride **s**, Come
Gen. 20:13; Ex. 3:13; Deut. 9:4; Job 33:32; 37:19; Prov. 3:28; 30:15; Is.58:9

SAYING Gen. 37:11; Ps. 78:2; Luke 18:34

SCALE Prov. 20:23, a false **s** is not good
Is. 40:15, as a speck of dust on the **s-s**
Amos 8:5, to cheat with dishonest **s-s**
Mic. 6:11, Can I justify wicked **s-s**
Rev. 6:5, a pair of **s-s** in his hand
Job 31:6; Is. 40:12; 46:6; Jer. 32:10

SCALE-ARMOR Jer. 46:4; 51:3

SCARCE—*want*
Ezek. 4:17, bread and water will be **s**
Is. 13:12; Luke 9:39

SCARLET Is. 1:18, Though your sins are as **s**
Matt. 27:28, put a **s** robe on Him
Rev. 17:3, woman sitting on a **s** beast
Gen. 38:28; Ex. 25:4; Josh. 2:18; Song 4:3; Jer. 4:30; Nah. 2:3

SCATTER
Ps. 92:9, All who do iniquity will be **s-ed**
Matt. 21:44, it will **s** him like dust
26:31, the flock shall be **s-ed**
Lev. 26:33; Job 18:15; 38:24; Ps. 141:7; Prov. 11:24; Is. 41:16; Jer. 23:1

SCENT Job 39:25, he **s-s** the battle from afar

SCHEME Esth. 8:3; Job 5:5; Ps. 37:7; Dan. 11:24,25; Mic. 2:1; 2 Cor. 2:11

SCOFF Ps. 2:4, The Lord **s-s** at them
Luke 16:14, the Pharisees . . . were **s-ing** at Him

SCOFFER Acts 13:41, BEHOLD, YOU **S-S**, AND MARVEL

SCORCH Jer. 4:11, A **s-ing** wind from the bare heights

SCORN Deut. 32:15; Prov. 30:17; Ezek. 25:6,15; 36:5

SCOURGE Job 5:21, hidden from the **s** of the tongue
Matt. 10:17, **s** you in their synagogues
20:19, mock and **s** and crucify Him
27:26, but Jesus he **s-d**
John 2:15, He made a **s** of cords
Heb. 12:6, **S-S** EVERY SON WHOM HE RECEIVES

SCRIBE Matt. 2:4, chief priests and **s-s** of the people
Matt. 23:13, Woe to you, **s-s** and Pharisees
Mark 1:22, authority, and not as **s-s**
12:38, Beware of the **s-s**
1 Cor. 1:20, Where is the **s**
Neh. 8:4; Jer. 8:8

SCRIPTURE(S), *writing*
Matt. 21:42, Did you never read in the **S-s**
22:29, not understanding the **S-s**
Mark 14:49, that the **S-s** might be fulfilled
Luke 4:21, Today this **S** has been fulfilled
24:32, He was explaining the **S-s** to us
John 5:39, You search the **S-s**
10:35, the **S** cannot be broken
20:9, they did not understand the **S**
Acts 18:24, he was mighty in the **S-s**
Rom. 4:3, For what does the **S** say
15:4, encouragement of the **S-s**
2 Tim. 3:16, All **S** is inspired by God

SCROLL—*roll* Jer. 36:2, Take a **s** and write
Ezek. 3:1, eat this **s**, and go
Zech. 5:1, behold, *there was* a flying **s**

SEA Gen. 1:10, He called **s-s**
Gen. 1:26, rule over the fish of the **s**
Ex. 10:19, drove them into the Red **S**
Ps. 24:2, founded it upon the **s-s**
107:23, down to the **s** in ships
146:6, The **s** and all that is in them
Is. 57:20, wicked are like the tossing **s**
Matt. 8:26, rebuked the winds and the **s**
14:26, saw Him walking on the **s**
Rev. 4:6, **s** of glass like crystal
21:1, There is no longer *any* **s**
2 Sam. 17:11; Job 7:12; 38:8; Ps. 65:5; Is. 11:9; Jer. 25:22; Nah. 1:4; 2 Cor. 11:26

SEAL—*shut* Dan. 12:4, **s** up the book . . . end of time
Rom. 4:11, **s** of the righteous of the faith
2 Cor. 1:22, who also **s-ed** us
Eph. 1:13, **s-ed** in Him with the Holy Spirit
Rev. 5:1, **s-ed** up with seven **s-s**
9:4, **s** of God on their foreheads
1 Kin. 21:8; Job 14:17; Song 4:12; 8:6; Is. 29:11; Jer. 32:10; Dan. 9:24; 12:4

SEA MONSTER Ps. 148:7; Matt. 12:40

SEARCH 1 Chr. 28:9, LORD **s-es** all hearts
Job 28:3, to the farthest limit he **s-es** out
Ps. 139:23, **S** me . . . know my heart

SEARCH *(Continued)*
Prov. 20:27, **S-ing** all the innermost parts
Jer. 17:10, I, the LORD, **s** the heart
Matt. 2:8, make careful **s** for the Child
2:13, Herod is going to **s**
John 5:39, You **s** the Scriptures, because
7:52, **S**, and see that no prophet arises
2 Tim. 1:17, he eagerly **s-ed** for me
Judg. 5:16; 1 Sam. 26:20; 1 Kin. 1:3

SEASON—*times* Ps. 1:3, yields its fruit in its **s**
Ps. 104:27, their food in due **s**
Luke 14:34, with what will it be **s-ed**
Gal. 4:10, observe days ... **s-s** and years
Col. 4:6, with grace, **s-ed**, *as it were*, with salt
2 Tim. 4:2, ready in **s** *and* out of **s**
Gen. 1:14; Lev. 26:4; Job 5:26

SEAT—*sat* Ps. 1:1, Nor sit in the **s** of the scoffers
Matt. 23:6, chief **s-s** in the synagogues
27:19, sitting on the judgment **s**
Luke 10:39, Mary ... **s-ed** at His feet
Rom. 14:10, the judgment **s** of God
Ex. 25:17; 1 Sam. 4:18; Ezek. 28:2

SECOND Matt. 22:39, And a **s** is like it
1 Cor. 15:47, the **s** man is from heaven
Rev. 2:11, not be hurt by the **s** death
Gen. 1:8; Ezek. 10:14

SECRET Ps. 44:21, knows the **s-s** of the heart
Prov. 9:17, bread *eaten* in **s** is pleasant
21:14, gift in **s** subdues anger
Matt. 6:4, your alms may be in **s**
6:6,18, your Father who is in **s**
Rom. 2:16, God will judge the **s-s**
16:25, kept **s** for long ages past
Deut. 27:15; Job 11:6; 15:8; Song 2:14; Is. 45:3,19; Hab. 3:14

SECRETLY Josh. 2:1, two men as spies **s**
Judg. 4:21, went **s** to him
Matt. 1:19, Joseph ... put her away **s**
2:7, Then Herod **s** called the
John 11:28, called Mary her sister, saying **s**
Deut. 13:6; Job 13:10; 31:27

SECURE—*sure* Prov. 3:23, walk in your way **s-ly**
Matt. 27:66, made the grave **s**
Acts 16:23, the jailer to guard them **s-ly**
Lev. 26:5; Ezek. 34:27

SECURITY Judg. 18:7, living in **s**

SEDUCES—*entice* Ex. 22:16, if a man **s** a virgin

SEE—*perceive* Ex. 33:20, no man can **s** Me and live
Job 19:26, without my flesh I shall **s** God
Ps. 16:10, allow Thy Holy One to **s** the pit
34:8, **s** that the LORD is good
66:5, Come and **s** the works of God
115:5, eyes, but they cannot **s**
Is. 35:2, **s** the glory of the LORD
62:2, nations will **s** your righteousness
Joel 2:28, young men will **s** visions
Matt. 5:16, may **s** your good works
11:8, what did you go out to **s**
16:28, **s** the Son of Man coming
Luke 2:26, would not **s** death before
8:10, **S-ING** THEY MAY NOT **S**
John 4:29, **s** a man who told me
7:52, Search, and **s** that no prophet
12:19, **s** that you are not doing any good
16:16, little while, and you will **s** Me
1 Cor. 13:12, now we **s** in a mirror dimly
Heb. 12:14, no one will **s** the Lord
1 John 3:2, we shall **s** Him just as He is
Ex. 10:23; Num 14:23; 24:17; Job 6:28; 9:11; 24:15; 34:32; Ps. 36:9; 49:19; Eccles. 6:9; Song 7:12; Is. 29:18; Ezek. 12:2

SEED—*descendant, offspring*
Gen. 8:22, **S-time** and harvest
Matt. 13:22, **s** was sown among the thorns
13:31, heaven is like a mustard **s**
Luke 8:5, sower went out to sow his **s**
8:11, the **s** is the word of God
1 Pet. 1:23, not of **s** which is perishable
Gen. 1:11; Lev. 19:19; 26:16; Eccles. 11:6; Is. 55:10; Hag. 2:19

SEEK—*desire, search* 2 Chr. 7:14, pray, and **s** My face
Ps. 24:6, generation of those who **s** Him
34:14, **S** peace and pursue it
63:1, I shall **s** Thee earnestly
119:2, **s** Him with all *their* heart
Prov. 8:17, who diligently **s** me will find me
Is. 55:6, **S** the LORD while He may be found
Jer. 29:13, you will **s** Me and find *Me*
Amos 5:4, **S** Me that you may live
Matt. 6:33, **s** first His kingdom
7:7, **s**, and you shall find
12:46, His brothers were ... **s-ing** to speak
Mark 8:12, this generation **s** for a sign
Luke 11:10, he who **s-s** finds
John 1:38, What do you **s**
5:30, I do not **s** My own will
8:50, One who **s-s** and judges
1 Cor. 10:24, Let no one **s** his own *good*
13:5, it does not **s** its own
Phil. 4:17, Not that I **s** the gift ... I **s** for the profit
Col. 3:1, keep **s-ing** the things above
Deut. 4:29; 2 Chr. 16:12; Job 7:21; Eccles. 7:25; Is. 34:16; Ezek. 7:25; 34:16; Dan. 9:3; Hos. 10:12; Amos 5:14; Gal. 1:10

SEEM—*appear* Gen. 29:20; Prov. 14:12

SEEN—*appeared* Gen. 9:14, bow shall be **s** in the cloud
Is. 6:5, my eyes have **s** the King
Luke 2:30, eyes have **s** Thy salvation
John 1:18, no man has **s** God at any time
Rom. 8:24, hope that is not **s** is not hope
1 Cor. 2:9, EYE HAS NOT **S**
Heb. 11:1, conviction of things not **s**
Gen. 32:30; Job 5:3; 38:22

SEIZE—*take* John 7:30, seeking ... to **s** Him
Jer. 50:24; Mic. 2:2

SELECT Acts 6:3, **s** from among you ... seven men

SELF Rom. 6:6, our old **s** was crucified
Col. 3:9, laid aside the old **s**

SELF-ABASEMENT Col. 2:18, delighting in **s**
Col. 2:23, wisdom in self-made religion and **s**

SELF-CONTROL Acts 24:25, righteousness, **s**, and the judgment
Gal. 5:23, gentleness, **s**

SELFISH Phil. 2:3, do nothing from **s-ness**
James 3:14,16, jealousy and **s** ambition

SELL Prov. 23:23, Buy truth, and do not **s** *it*
Matt. 19:21, go *and* **s** your possessions
Gen. 25:31; Lev. 25:29; Deut. 2:28; 2 Kin. 4:7

SEND—*cast* Is. 6:8, Whom shall I **s** ... Here
Matt. 5:45, **s-s** rain on *the* righteous
9:38, **s** out workers into His harvest
1 Cor. 7:13, let her not **s** her husband away
16:11, **s** him on his way in peace
2 Thess. 2:11, **s** ... a deluding influence
Gen. 7:4; 24:7; Num. 13:2; Job 5:10; 38:35

SENSELESS—*stupid* Ps. 49:10, stupid and the **s** alike perish
Ps. 92:6, **s** man has no knowledge

SENSIBLE Tit. 2:5, *to be* **s**, pure, workers at home

SENSUAL Ezek. 33:32, like a **s** song

SENSUALITY Eph. 4:19, given ... over to **s**
Rev. 18:3, rich by the wealth of her **s**

SENSUOUS Rev. 18:7, she ... lived **s-ly**

SENT Is. 61:1, He has **s** me to bind up the brokenhearted
Matt. 10:5, These twelve Jesus **s** out after
Luke 4:18, He has **s** Me to proclaim release
Acts 13:4, So, being **s** out by the Holy Spirit
Gal. 4:4, God **s** forth His Son
1 Pet. 1:12, Holy Spirit **s** from heaven
1 John 4:9, that God has **s** His only begotten
Gen. 8:7,8; Is. 48:16

SENTENCE—*condemnation*
Matt. 23:33, escape the **s** of hell

SEPARATE—*divide* Gen. 1:4, God **s-d** the light
Prov. 16:28, a slanderer **s-s** intimate friends

Matt. 19:6, let no man **s**
25:32, He will **s** them from one another
Rom. 8:35, Who shall **s** us from the love
Gen. 13:9; Lev. 20:24; Job 41:17; Ps. 22:7
SERIOUS Acts 25:7, **s** charges against him
SERPENT Gen. 3:1, Now the **s** was more crafty
Num. 21:9, Moses made a bronze **s**
Ps. 58:4, venom of a **s**
Matt. 10:16, be shrewd as **s-s**
Mark 16:18, they will pick up **s-s**
John 3:14, Moses lifted up the **s** in the wilderness
2 Cor. 11:3, lest as the **s** deceived Eve
Rev. 12:9, the **s** of old who is called the devil
Gen. 49:17; Ex. 7:12; Deut. 32:33; Ps. 91:13; Prov. 23:32; Is. 30:6; Jer. 8:17
SERVANT—*minister* Job 1:8, have you considered My **s** Job
Ps. 31:16, face to shine upon Thy **s**
Matt. 20:26, shall be your **s**
Luke 1:2, and **s-s** of the Word
2 Cor. 3:6, **s-s** of a new covenant
11:23, Are they **s-s** of Christ
1 Tim. 4:6, be a good **s** of Christ Jesus
Gen. 9:25; Ex. 14:31; Ruth 2:9; 1 Sam. 3:9; Ezra 7:24; Job 4:18; Prov. 11:29; Joel 2:29
SERVE—*worship, minister*
Ps. 100:2, **S** the LORD with gladness
Matt. 4:10, GOD, AND **S** HIM ONLY
6:24, No one can **s** two masters
20:28, not come to be **s-d**, but to **s**
John 12:26, If any one **s-s** Me, let him
Acts 24:14, I do **s** the God of our fathers
Rom. 7:6, so that we **s** in newness of the Spirit
12:11, fervent in spirit, **s-ing** the Lord
Gal. 5:13, through love **s** one another
1 Tim. 3:10, let them **s** as deacons
Josh. 22:5; 1 Chr. 6:10; 24:2; Jer. 5:19
SERVICE—*ministry*
Rom. 12:1, *which* is your spiritual **s**
Eph. 4:12, for the work of **s**
Phil. 2:30, was deficient in your **s** to me
Heb. 12:28, offer to God an acceptable **s**
Is. 32:17; Jer. 22:13
SET Gen. 9:13, I **s** my bow in the cloud
Ex. 2:3, she . . . **s** it among the reeds
Deut. 30:19, I have **s** before you life and death
Ps. 40:2, He **s** my feet upon a rock
Matt. 5:14, A city **s** on a hill cannot
Col. 3:2, **S** your mind on the things above
James 3:6, and is **s** on fire by hell
Lev. 17:10; Prov. 9:2; Eccles. 10:6; Is. 3:24; 38:1; Jer. 5:26; Ezek. 2:2
SETTING Prov. 25:11, apples of gold in **s-s** of silver
SETTLE—*reckon* Matt. 25:19, came and **s-d** accounts with them
Deut. 21:5; Nah. 3:17
SEVEN Gen. 29:20, Jacob served **s** years for Rachel
Ps. 119:164, **S** times a day I praise Thee
Is. 4:1, For **s** women will take hold of one man
Matt. 12:45, along with it **s** other spirits
18:21, forgive him? Up to **s** times
Acts 6:3, **s** men of good reputation
Rev. 1:4, John to the **s** churches
1:12, I saw **s** golden lampstands
3:1, He who has the **s** Spirits of God
15:1, **s** angels who had **s** plagues
Gen. 21:29; Prov. 9:1; Eccles. 11:2; Dan. 9:25; Zech. 4:2
SEVERE—*great* Matt. 28:2, a **s** earthquake
Song 8:6; Ezek. 34:4
SHACK Is. 24:20, it totters like a **s**
SHACKLES Mark 5:4, the **s** broken in pieces
SHADOW 2 Kin. 20:11, **s** on the stairway back ten steps
Ps. 17:8, Hide me in the **s** of Thy wings
23:4, valley of the **s** of death
91:1, abide in the **s** of the Almighty
Col. 2:17, a *mere* **s** of what is to come
Heb. 8:5, copy and **s** of the heavenly things
James 1:17, no variation, or shifting **s**
1 Chr. 29:15; Song 2:17
SHAKE—*tremble*
Prov. 10:30, righteous . . . never be **s-n**
Is. 13:13, earth . . . **s-n** from its place
Matt. 10:14, **s** off the dust of your feet
11:7, A reed **s-n** by the wind
Luke 6:38, pressed down, **s-n** together
Job 4:14; 16:4; Ps. 109:23
SHAME Acts 5:41, worthy to suffer **s**
2 Cor. 4:2, things hidden because of **s**
Phil. 3:19, glory is in their **s**
1 John 2:28, not shrink . . . Him in **s**
Prov. 19:26; Is. 54:4; Zeph. 3:5
SHARE—*portion* Luke 15:12, **s** of the estate
1 Cor. 10:16, a **s-ing** in the blood of Christ
10:20, to become **s-rs** in demons
Gal. 6:6, **s** . . . with him who teaches
1 Tim. 6:18, ready to **s**
Heb. 13:16, doing good and **s-ing**
SHARP Deut. 32:41, **s-en** My flashing sword
Ps. 57:4, tongue a **s** sword
64:3, **s-ened** their tongue
Prov. 5:4, **S** as a two-edged sword
27:17, Iron **s-ens** iron
Eccles. 10:10, does not **s-en** *its* edge
Heb. 4:12, **s-er** than any two-edged sword
SHATTER Ex. 15:6; Ps. 2:9
SHAVE Gen. 41:14; Judg. 16:19; 2 Sam. 10:4; Is. 7:20; 1 Cor. 11:6
SHEAR Deut. 18:4, first **s-ing** of your sheep
SHED—*pour* Matt. 26:28, My blood . . . **s** on behalf of many
Rom. 3:15, feet are swift to **s** blood
Gen. 9:6; Prov. 1:16
SHEEP—*flock* Ps. 44:22, a **s** to be slaughtered
Ps. 100:3, the **s** of his pasture
119:176, astray like a lost **s**
Is. 53:6, All of us like **s** have gone astray
53:7, **s** . . . silent before its shearers
Matt. 9:36, **s** without a shepherd
10:16, I send you out as **s**
15:24, lost **s** of the house of Israel
25:32, separates the **s** from the goats
26:31, **s** of the flock . . . scattered
Luke 15:6, found my **s** which was lost
John 10:3, calls his own **s** by name
10:7, I am the door of the **s**
10:27, My **s** hear My voice
21:16, Shepherd My **s**
Heb. 13:20, great Shepherd of the **s**
1 Pet. 2:25, straying like **s**
Gen. 29:9; Num. 27:17; 1 Sam. 15:14; Job 31:20; Jer. 12:3; 50:6
SHEKELS—*piece* Gen. 23:16; Zech. 11:12
SHELTER Ps. 5:11, mayest Thou **s** them
Ps. 61:4, refuge in the **s** of Thy wings
Gen. 19:8; Is. 1:8; 4:6; 32:2; Jon. 4:5
SHEOL Deut. 32:22, burns to the lowest . . . of **S**
Job 17:13, look for **S** as my home
26:6, Naked is **S** before Him
Ps. 16:10, not abandon my soul to **S**
30:3, brought up my soul from **S**
49:15, redeem . . . from the power of **S**
86:13, my soul from the depths of **S**
139:8, If I make my bed in **S**
Prov. 5:5, Her steps lay hold of **S**
Ezek. 32:21, speak . . . from the midst of **S**
Amos 9:2, Though they dig into **S**
Jon. 2:2, help from the depth of **S**
2 Sam. 22:6; Prov. 27:20; Song 8:6; Hab. 2:5
SHEPHERD (n.)—*pastor*
Ps. 23:1, The LORD is my **s**
28:9, Be their **s** also
Is. 40:11, Like a **s** He will tend His flock
Jer. 3:15, I will give you **s-s**
23:1, **s-s** who are destroying . . . the sheep
Zech. 11:16, I am going to raise up a **s**

SHEPHERD (n.) *(Continued)*
Matt. 9:36, like sheep without a **s**
26:31, I will strike down the **s**
Luke 2:8, **s-s** staying out in the fields
John 10:11, I am the good **s**
Heb. 13:20, the great **S** of the sheep
1 Pet. 2:25, returned to the **S** and Guardian
5:4, when the Chief **S** appears
Rev. 7:17, the Lamb . . . shall be their **s**
Gen. 46:34; 48:15; Num. 27:17; 1 Sam. 17:40; Jer. 10:21; Ezek. 34:5; 37:24; Zeph. 2:6

SHEPHERD (v.)—*fed* Ps. 78:72, David **s-ed**
Matt. 2:6, WHO WILL S MY PEOPLE
John 21:16, **S** My sheep
Acts 20:28, to **s** the church of God
1 Pet. 5:2, **s** the flock of God

SHIELD Ps. 18:2, My **s** and the horn of my salvation
Ps. 28:7, my strength and my **s**
91:4, His faithfulness is a **s**
Eph. 6:16, taking up the **s** of faith
Gen. 15:1; 2 Sam. 22:3,31; Ps. 7:10; 89:18; Prov. 2:7

SHINE Num. 6:25, make His face **s** on you
Job 9:7, sun not to **s**
41:32, Behind him . . . a wake to **s**
Prov. 4:18, **s-s** brighter and brighter
Is. 60:1, Arise, **s**; for your light has come
Matt. 5:16, Let your light **s** before men
13:43, RIGHTEOUS WILL S FORTH
John 1:5, light **s-s** in the darkness
2 Pet. 1:19, a lamp **s-ing** in a dark place
1 John 2:8, true light is already **s-ing**

SHOCK Deut. 1:29, Do not be **s-ed**, nor fear them

SHONE Luke 2:9, glory of the Lord **s** around
Ex. 34:29; 2 Kin. 3:22

SHOOK Neh. 5:13, also **s** out . . . my garment
Acts 28:5, he **s** the creature off
Heb. 12:26, His voice **s** the earth

SHOOT Is. 11:1, a **s** will spring from . . . Jesse
Is. 53:2, grew up . . . like a tender **s**
1 Sam. 20:20; Ps. 11:2; 64:4

SHORT Rom. 3:23, fall **s** of the glory of God
1 Cor. 7:29, time has been **s-ened**

SHOT 1 Sam. 20:20, as though I **s** at a target

SHOULD Matt. 23:23, these . . . things you **s** have done

SHOUT Josh. 6:16, Joshua said . . . **S**
Ps. 47:5, God has ascended with a **s**
66:1, **S** joyfully to God
Matt. 25:6, at midnight . . . a **s**
1 Thess. 4:16, descend from heaven with a **s**

SHOW—*demonstrate*
Matt. 22:19, **S** Me the coin
John 14:8, Lord, **s** us the Father
1 Cor. 3:13, for the day will **s** it
Gal. 6:12, make a good **s-ing** in the flesh
Gen. 12:1; Ex. 33:18; Deut. 5:10; 2 Sam. 10:12; 1 Chr. 19:13; Job 11:6

SHOWER 1 Kin. 18:41; Ps. 65:10; Jer. 14:22; Luke 12:54

SHREWD—*wise*
Job 5:13, wise by their own **s-ness**
Matt. 10:16, be **s** as serpents

SHRINE Ezek. 16:24,31,39

SHRINK—*draw* Heb. 10:38, IF HE S-S BACK, MY SOUL HAS NO PLEASURE

SHUDDER Jer. 2:12, and **s**, be very desolate
James 2:19, demons also believe, and **s**

SHUN—*refrain* Eccles. 3:5, time to **s** embracing

SHUT—*close* Matt. 6:6, WHEN YOU HAVE S YOUR DOOR
Matt. 23:13, **s** off the kingdom of heaven
Gal. 3:23, being **s** up to the faith
Job 5:16; Prov. 21:13; Dan. 6:22

SICK Prov. 13:12, Hope . . . *makes* the heart **s**
Matt. 10:8, Heal *the* **s**, raise
25:36, I was **s**, and you visited Me
Mark 1:30, Simon's mother-in-law . . . lying **s**
2:17, physician, but those who are **s**
Luke 7:2, and **s** and about to die
John 11:2, brother Lazarus was **s**
James 5:14, Is anyone among you **s**
5:15, prayer . . . restore the one who is **s**
Ps. 41:3; Song 2:5

SICKLE Deut. 16:9, put the **s** to the standing grain
Joel 3:13, Put in the **s** . . . harvest is ripe
Rev. 14:15, Put in your **s** and reap

SICKLINESS Is. 17:11, a day of **s** and incurable pain

SICKNESS Matt. 4:23, healing every kind of **s**
Matt. 10:1, authority . . . to heal . . . **s**
Luke 13:12, are freed from your **s**
John 5:5, thirty-eight years in his **s**
11:4, This **s** is not unto death
Deut. 7:15; 2 Kin. 1:2; 8:8,9

SIDE Ezek. 36:3, crushed you from every **s**
John 19:34, pierced His **s** with a spear
20:20, showed . . . His hands and His **s**

SIEGEWORKS Deut. 20:20; Eccles. 9:14

SIGHT Ps. 19:14, acceptable in Thy **s**
Ps. 90:4, thousand years in Thy **s**
Matt. 11:5, BLIND RECEIVE S
20:34, they received their **s**
Luke 4:18, RECOVERY OF S TO THE BLIND
Acts 9:9, three days without **s**
22:13, Saul, receive your **s**
2 Cor. 5:7, walk by faith, not by **s**
Gen. 2:9; 18:3; Ruth 2:13; Job 19:15

SIGN—*signal, witness, wonder*
Gen. 9:12, the **s** of the covenant
Ex. 3:12, this shall be a **s** to you
12:13, blood shall be a **s** . . . on the houses
Ps. 86:17, Show me a **s** for good
Matt. 12:38, we want a **s** from You
16:3, cannot *discern* the **s-s** of the times
24:3, *will be* the **s** of Your coming
Mark 13:22, show **s-s** and wonders
16:20, confirmed the word by the **s-s**
Luke 1:22, he kept making **s-s** to them
21:25, will be **s-s** in sun
23:8, hoping to see some **s** performed
John 2:11, beginning of *His* **s-s** Jesus did
10:41, John performed no **s**
11:47, this man is performing many **s-s**
Acts 5:12, many **s-s** and wonders were taking place
1 Cor. 1:22, Jews ask for **s-s**
Phil. 1:28, a **s** of destruction
2 Thess. 2:9, all power and **s-s**
Rev. 12:1, a great **s** appeared in heaven
15:1, saw another **s** in heaven
Gen. 4:15; Ex. 31:13; Is. 7:11,14; 55:13; Ezek. 14:8

SIGNAL Mark 14:44, had given them a **s**
Is. 11:10; 30:17

SILENCE Ps. 62:1, My soul *waits* in **s** for God
Titus 1:11, who must be **s-d**
Rev. 8:1, there was **s** in heaven

SILENT Eccles. 3:7, A time to be **s**
Matt. 26:63, But Jesus kept **s**
Luke 1:20, you shall be **s** and unable to speak
9:36, they kept **s**, and reported to no one
Acts 18:9, go on speaking . . . not be **s**
1 Cor. 14:28, keep **s** in the church
14:34, Let the women keep **s**
Judg. 18:19; Esth. 7:4; Job 6:24; 13:13

SILVER Matt. 10:9, Do not acquire gold, or **s**
Matt. 26:15, thirty pieces of **s**
Acts 3:6, I do not possess **s** and gold
8:20, May your **s** perish with you
20:33, coveted no one's **s**
James 5:3, gold and **s** have rusted
Gen. 13:2; Job 27:16; Prov. 16:16; 25:11; Is. 1:22; 39:2; Jer. 6:30; Zech. 11:12

SIMPLE—*naive* Ps. 19:7, making wise the **s**
Ps. 116:6, LORD preserves the **s**

SIN—*transgression* Ps. 25:7, remember the **s-s**
Ps. 51:3, my **s** is ever before me
Prov. 14:9, Fools mock at **s**
Is. 1:18, your **s-s** are as scarlet

Matt. 1:21, save His people from their **s-s**
3:6, as they confessed their **s-s**
12:31, **s** and blasphemy . . . forgiven men
18:15, if your brother **s-s**
18:21, brother **s** against me
26:28, for forgiveness of **s-s**
Mark 2:7, forgive **s-s** but God alone
Luke 11:4, forgive us our **s-s**
John 1:29, Lamb . . . takes away **s** of the world
8:7, He who is without **s**
8:11, go your way . . . **s** no more
15:22, they have no excuse for their **s**
16:8, convict the world concerning **s**
Acts 22:16, wash away your **s-s**
26:18, receive forgiveness of **s-s**
Rom. 5:12, **s** entered into the world
6:23, wages of **s** is death
14:23, whatever is not from faith is **s**
1 Cor. 15:3, Christ died for our **s-s**
15:56, sting of death is **s**
2 Cor. 5:21, Him who knew no **s** *to be* **s** on our behalf
Heb. 9:7, for the **s-s** of the people
11:25, enjoy the . . . pleasures of **s**
James 5:16, confess your **s-s** to one another
5:20, cover a multitude of **s-s**
1 Pet. 2:22, WHO COMMITTED NO **S**
1 John 1:8, If we say we have no **s**
1:9, If we confess our **s-s**
2:1, If anyone **s-s**, we have an Advocate
3:4, **s** is lawlessness
5:16, there is a **s** leading to death
5:17, All unrighteousness is **s**
Rev. 1:5, released us from our **s-s**
Gen. 4:7; 18:20; Ex. 10:17; 32:30; Job 1:22; 2:10; Ps. 51:2; 79:9; Is. 30:1; Mic. 6:7

SINCE Matt. 18:25, **s** he did not have *the means* to repay
1 Cor. 11:7, **s** he is the image and glory
Heb. 2:14, **S** then the children share
Gen. 41:39; Deut. 12:12

SINFUL Mark 8:38, **s** generation
Luke 5:8, I am a **s** man, O Lord
Rom. 8:3, the likeness of **s** flesh
Num. 32:14; Is. 1:4

SING—*shout, utter* Ps. 5:11, Let them ever **s** for joy
Ps. 33:3, **S** to Him a new song
100:2, Come before Him with joyful **s-ing**
1 Cor. 14:15, I shall **s** with the spirit
Col. 3:16, **s-ing** with thankfulness
James 5:13, cheerful? Let him **s** praises
Ex. 15:1; Judg. 5:12; 2 Sam. 22:50; 1 Chr. 16:23; 2 Chr. 23:13; Job 29:13; Prov. 29:6; Is. 5:1; Rev. 5:9

SINK Prov. 2:18, her house **s-s** down to death

SINNED Ps. 41:4, I have **s** against Thee
Ps. 51:4, Thee only, I have **s**
Luke 15:18, **s** against heaven
Rom. 3:23, **s**, and fall short of the glory
5:12, spread to all men, because all **s**
1 John 1:10, If we say that we have not **s**
Lev. 5:16; Deut. 1:41; Dan. 9:15

SINNER Ps. 1:1, stand in the path of **s-s**
Matt. 9:10, tax-gatherers and **s-s**
9:13, call *the* righteous, but **s-s**
11:19, a friend of . . . **s-s**
Mark 2:17, to call *the* righteous, but **s-s**
14:41, into the hands of **s-s**
Luke 6:34, Even **s-s** lend to **s-s**
15:7, *more* joy in heaven over one **s**
18:13, be merciful to me, the **s**
John 9:31, God does not hear **s-s**
Rom. 5:8, while we were yet **s-s**
1 Tim. 1:15, Jesus came . . . to save **s-s**
James 4:8, Cleanse your hands, you **s-s**
Prov. 1:10; 13:21; 23:17; Eccles. 9:18

SISTER Job 17:14, my mother, and my **s**
Matt. 12:50, is My brother and **s**
Luke 10:39, had a **s** called Mary
Gen. 12:13; Prov. 7:4; Song 8:8; Rom. 16:1

SIT Ps. 1:1, **S** in the seat of scoffers
Ps. 26:4, not **s** with deceitful men
110:1, **S** at My right hand
Matt. 4:16, WERE **S-ING** IN DARKNESS
9:9, Matthew, **s-ing** in the tax office
26:36, **S** here while I go
27:61, Mary, **s-ing** opposite the grave
Luke 2:46, temple, **s-ing** . . . midst of the teachers
8:35, **s-ing** down at the feet of Jesus
John 12:15, **S-ING** ON A DONKEY'S COLT
Acts 8:28, **s-ing** in his chariot
Gen. 18:1; 1 Kin. 22:19; Job 2:8; Ezek. 28:2

SITUATE Ps. 144:15, people who are so **s-d**

SIZE—*stature* Num. 13:32, are men of *great* **s**

SKILL Ps. 137:5, my right hand forget her **s**

SKILLFUL Gen. 25:27; Ex. 28:8; 1 Sam. 16:16; Ps. 139:15; Is. 3:3

SKIN Ex. 34:29, the **s** of his face shone
Job 2:4, **S** for **s**
10:11, Clothe me with **s** and flesh
Jer. 13:23, Ethiopian change his **s**
Job 19:20; 30:30

SKIP Job 21:11, children **s** about

SKULL Judg. 9:53, Abimelech's head, crushing his **s**
Matt. 27:33, which means Place of a **S**

SKY Ps. 36:5, faithfulness *reaches* to the **s-s**
Matt. 16:2,3, for the **s** is red
Luke 12:56, analyze the appearance . . . the **s**
Gen. 1:26,28; Deut. 4:17; 2 Sam. 21:10; Job 37:18; Prov. 30:19; James 5:18

SLACK Prov. 18:9, who is **s** in his work

SLAIN 1 Sam. 18:7; 29:5, Saul has **s** his thousands
Rev. 5:12, Worthy . . . Lamb that was **s**

SLANDER Ps. 15:3, He does not **s**
Prov. 30:10, Do not **s** a slave to his master
1 Cor. 4:13, when we are **s-ed**, we try to conciliate
2 Cor. 12:20, disputes, **s-s**, gossip
Eph. 4:31, and **s** be put away from you

SLANDERER—*whisperer*
Prov. 16:28, **s** separates . . . friends
Rom. 1:30, **s-s**, haters of God

SLAP Job 16:10, **s-ed** me on the cheek
Matt. 5:39, **s-s** you on your right cheek

SLAUGHTER—*sacrifice*
Ps. 44:22, as sheep to be **s-ed**
Is. 53:7, lamb that is led to **s**
Rom. 8:36, AS SHEEP TO BE **S-ED**
James 5:5, in a day of **s**
Prov. 7:22; Jer. 46:10

SLAVE Prov. 22:7, borrower becomes the lender's **s**
Matt. 25:21, Well done . . . faithful **s**
1 Cor. 7:21, Were you called while a **s**
9:27, body and make it my **s**
Gal. 4:7, no longer a **s**, but a son
Ex. 23:12; Lev. 19:20; 25:39,44; Deut. 15:15; 16:12; 24:18; Col. 3:22

SLAVERY—*bondage* Rom. 8:15, a spirit of **s**
Gal. 5:1, subject again to a yoke of **s**
Heb. 2:15, subject to **s** all their lives

SLAY—*destroy* Job 5:2, vexation **s-s** the foolish man
Job 13:15, Though He **s** me, I will hope
Ps. 34:21, Evil shall **s** the wicked
2 Thess. 2:8, the Lord will **s** with the breath of

SLEDGE Is. 41:15, a new, sharp threshing **s**

SLEEP Gen. 2:21, deep **s** to fall upon the man
Ps. 13:3, **s** the *sleep of* death
Prov. 6:10, A little **s**, a little slumber
Eccles. 5:12, **s** of the working man
Matt. 1:24, Joseph arose from his **s**
26:40,43, found them **s-ing**
26:45, Are you still **s-ing** and taking
Acts 20:9, sinking into a deep **s**
1 Cor. 15:51, we shall not all **s**
1 Thess. 5:7, those who **s** do their **s-ing** at night
Ps. 76:6; Prov. 3:24; 20:13; Jer. 31:26; Mark 14:40

SLEW Matt. 2:16, **s** all the male children

SLING 1 Sam. 17:40, his **s** was in his hand
Judg. 20:16; 1 Sam. 25:29

SLOTHFUL Prov. 12:27, **s** man does not roast
SLOW Ex. 4:10, **s** of speech and **s** of tongue
Ps. 103:8, **S** to anger and abounding
Prov. 16:32, He who is **s** to anger
Luke 24:25, foolish men and **s** of heart
James 1:19, **s** to speak *and* **s** to anger
2 Pet. 3:9, The Lord is not **s**
SLUGGISH Heb. 6:12, that you may not be **s**
SLUMBER Ps. 121:3, who keeps you will not **s**
Prov. 6:10, A little sleep, a little **s**
Job 33:15; Ps. 132:4; Is. 5:27; 56:10
SMALL—*little* Prov. 30:24, Four things are **s** on the earth
Mark 8:7, They also had a few **s** fish
James 3:4, directed by a very **s** rudder
3:5, tongue is a **s** part of the body
Num. 26:56; 35:8; Deut. 25:13; Is. 10:19
SMEAR Ezek. 22:28, prophets have **s-ed** whitewash
SMELL Gen. 27:27; Deut. 4:28; Ps. 115:6
SMELT Is. 1:25, **s** away your dross with lye
SMOKE Gen. 15:17; Job 41:20; Ps. 102:3; Prov. 10:26; Is. 6:4
SMOLDERING Matt. 12:20, **S** WICK HE WILL
SMOOTH Ps. 55:21, speech was **s-er** than butter
Prov. 5:3, **s-er** than oil is her speech
Is. 45:13, I will make all his ways **s**
Luke 3:5, THE ROUGH ROADS **S**
Gen. 27:11,16; 1 Sam. 17:40; Prov. 6:24; 11:5; Is. 40:3
SNAKE Matt. 7:10, he will not . . . a **s**, will he
SNARE—*web* Prov. 7:23, bird hastens to the **s**
Rom. 11:9, THEIR TABLE BECOME A **S**
2 Tim. 2:26, *escape* from the **s** of the devil
Ex. 10:7; Job 34:30; Ps. 91:3; Eccles. 7:26
SNATCH—*pluck* John 10:12, the wolf **s-es** them
John 10:28, **s** them out of My hand
Jude 23, **s-ing** them out of the fire
SNEER—*scoff* Luke 23:35, the rulers were **s-ing**
SNOW Ps. 51:7, I shall be whiter than **s**
Prov. 26:1, Like **s** in summer
Is. 1:18, scarlet . . . be as white as **s**
Matt. 28:3, his garment as white as **s**
Rev. 1:14, white like white wool, like **s**
Num. 12:10; Job 9:30; 38:22; Prov. 25:13
SOBER—*watch* Acts 26:25, utter words of **s** truth
1 Thess. 5:6, let us be alert and **s**
2 Tim. 4:5, be **s** in all things
1 Pet. 4:7, **s** *spirit* . . . purpose of prayer
5:8, Be of **s** *spirit*
SOFT Matt. 11:8, who wear **s** *clothing* are in
Ps. 65:10; Prov. 25:15
SOIL—*earth, ground*
Ezek. 17:5, planted it in fertile **s**
Matt. 13:5; Mark 4:5, did not have much **s**
13:8, others fell on the good **s**
James 5:7, the precious produce of the **s**
Rev. 3:4, few . . . who have not **s-ed** their garments
SOJOURN Gen. 26:3; Ex. 12:48
SOJOURNER—*foreigner, alien* Ex. 2:22; 12:45; 18:3; 20:10
SOLD Gen. 25:33, **s** his birthright
Gen. 45:4, brother Joseph, whom you **s** into
Matt. 10:29, two sparrows **s** for a cent
13:46, went and **s** all that he had
Acts 5:1, his wife Sapphira, **s** a piece of
Rom. 7:14, of flesh, **s** into bondage to sin
Lev. 25:23; 1 Kin. 21:20; Joel 3:3
SOLDIER Mark 15:16, the **s-s** took Him away
Luke 23:36, the **s-s** also mocked Him
John 19:23, four parts, a part to every **s**
Acts 28:16, with the **s** who was guarding
2 Tim. 2:3, as a good **s** of Christ Jesus
SOLVE—*dissolve*
Dan. 5:12, **s-ing** of difficult problems
5:16, give interpretations and **s** difficult
SOMEBODY Acts 5:36, Theudas rose up, claiming to be **s**
SOMEONE Luke 8:46, **S** did touch Me
SOMETHING—*this* 1 Kin. 2:14, have **s** *to say* to you
Hab. 1:5, *I* am doing **s** in your days
Luke 7:40, I have **s** to say to you
Acts 25:26, I may have **s** to write
SON 2 Sam. 13:37, *David* mourned for his **s**
Ps. 2:7, Thou art My **S**
8:4, **s** of man, that Thou dost care
Prov. 10:1, A wise **s** makes a father glad
17:25, A foolish **s** is a grief
Is. 7:14, a virgin will . . . bear a **s**
14:12, O star of the morning . . . **s** of
60:4, Your **s-s** will come from afar
Dan. 7:13, One like a **S** of Man
Hos. 11:1, out of Egypt I called My **s**
Matt. 1:25, virgin until she gave birth to a **S**
2:15, OUT OF EGYPT . . . CALL MY **S**
3:17, This is My beloved **S**
11:27, No one knows the **S**
13:55, Is not this the carpenter's **s**
16:16, the **S** of the living God
22:42, Christ, whose **s** is He
26:63, are the Christ, the **S** of God
27:43, I am the **S** of God
Mark 5:7, Jesus, **S** of the Most High God
12:6, one more *to send*, a . . . **s**
14:61, the **S** of the Blessed *One*
Luke 1:31, bear a **s**, and you shall name
2:7, birth to her first-born **s**
4:22, Is this not Joseph's **s**
15:11, A certain man had two **s-s**
15:24, this **s** of mine was dead
John 4:50, Go your way, your **s** lives
5:21, the **S** also gives life
6:42, this Jesus, the **s** of Joseph
12:36, may become **s-s** of light
14:13, may be glorified in the **S**
19:26, Woman, behold, your **s**
Acts 4:36, translated . . . **S** of Encouragement
Rom. 8:32, did not spare His own **S**
Gal. 4:7, but a **s**; and if a **s**
2 Thess. 2:3, revealed, the **s** of destruction
Heb. 6:6, again crucify . . . the **S** of God
1 John 2:22, denies the Father and the **S**
Rev. 21:7, be his God . . . will be My **s**
Gen. 6:2; 22:2; 37:33; Ex. 20:10; Deut. 8:5; 2 Kin. 2:3; Job 5:4; Eccles. 4:8; Is. 30:9; Ezek. 2:1; Mal. 3:17
SONG—*music, taunt*
Ex. 15:2, LORD is my strength and **s**
Judg. 5:12, Awake, awake, sing a **s**
Job 35:10, gives **s-s** in the night
Ps. 33:3, Sing to Him a new **s**
137:4, How . . . sing the LORD's **s**
Prov. 25:20, Sings **s-s** to a troubled heart
Eccles. 12:4, the daughters of **s**
Song 1:1, The **S** of **S-s**
Eph. 5:19, hymns and spiritual **s-s**
Is. 5:1; 23:16; 24:9; Ezek. 33:32
SOON—*shortly* Ex. 2:18, you come *back* so **s**
Job 32:22, Maker would **s** take me away
Heb. 13:23, if he comes **s**
SOOT Lam. 4:8, appearance is blacker than **s**
SOOTHE Gen. 8:21, LORD smelled a **s-ing** aroma
SORDID Titus 1:11, for the sake of **s** gain
SORE Luke 16:21, dogs . . . licking his **s-s**
SORROW Gen. 42:38, bring . . . down . . . in **s**
Ps. 31:10, my life is spent with **s**
Eccles. 7:3, **S** is better than laughter
Is. 35:10, **s** and sighing will flee away
53:3, A man of **s-s**
Jer. 8:18, My **s** is beyond healing
John 16:20, be **s-ful**, but your **s**
2 Cor. 2:2, For if I cause you **s**
2:5, he has caused **s** not to me
2:7, overwhelmed by excessive **s**
7:9, made **s-ful** according to *the will* of God
7:10, **s** . . . produces a repentance
Jer. 45:3; Luke 22:45

SORRY Gen. 6:6, the LORD was **s** . . . made man
Jer. 13:14, I will not show pity nor be **s**
SOUGHT—*seek, visit* Is. 26:16, they **s** Thee in distress
Matt. 2:20, who **s** the Child's life
21:46, they **s** to seize Him
Gal. 4:18, to be eagerly **s**
Ex. 33:7; Eccles. 7:29
SOUL—*life, person*
Deut. 4:29, with all your heart . . . **s**
1 Sam. 1:26, As your **s** lives
Job 33:30, bring back his **s** from the pit
Ps. 16:10, not abandon my **s** to Sheol
19:7, LORD is perfect, restoring the **s**
23:3, He restores my **s**
24:4, not lifted up his **s** to falsehood
42:1, So my **s** pants for Thee
62:1, My **s** *waits* in silence for God
63:1, My **s** thirsts for Thee
103:1, Bless the LORD, O my **s**
107:9, satisfied the thirsty **s**
Prov. 24:12, who keeps your **s**
25:25, cold water to a weary **s**
Ezek. 18:4, **s** who sins will die
Matt. 10:28, unable to kill the **s**
11:29, FIND REST FOR YOUR **S-S**
16:26, world, and forfeits his **s**
26:38, My **s** is deeply grieved
Luke 1:46, My **s** exalts the Lord
12:19, say to my **s**, **S** you have many
John 12:27, My **s** has become troubled
Acts 4:32, were of one heart and **s**
1 Thess. 5:23, your spirit and **s** and body
Heb. 4:12, division of **s** and spirit
6:19, as an anchor of the **s**
10:39, to the preserving of the **s**
James 1:21, is able to save your **s-s**
5:20, save his **s** from death
1 Pet. 2:11, which wage war against the **s**
2 Pet. 2:14, enticing unstable **s-s**
Deut. 4:9; Judg. 16:16; 1 Sam. 18:1; Job 3:20; 10:1
SOUND—*roar, shout, voice* Ex. 32:17; Lev. 26:36
Gen. 3:8, heard the **s** of the LORD God
Prov. 3:21, Keep **s** wisdom
Luke 15:27, received him back safe and **s**
1 Tim. 1:10, contrary to **s** teaching
2 Tim. 1:13, Retain . . . standard of **s** words
Titus 1:13, may be **s** in the faith
Rev. 1:15, **s** of many waters
8:7, And the first **s-ed**
Judg. 4:21; 1 Kin. 18:41; 19:12; Job 15:21; 33:15; Prov. 2:7; Eccles. 12:4; Jer. 25:10; Joel 2:1
SOUR Jer. 31:29, fathers have eaten **s** grapes
SOURCE Heb. 5:9, the **s** of eternal salvation
SOUTH Matt. 12:42, Queen of *the* **S**
Luke 12:55, *see* a **s** wind blowing
Acts 27:13, when a moderate **s** wind came up
Job 37:9,17; Eccles. 11:3
SOW Job 4:8, those who **s** trouble harvest it
Ps. 126:5, **s** in tears shall reap
Prov. 22:8, who **s-s** iniquity . . . reap vanity
Is. 55:10, furnishing seed to the **s-er**
Matt. 6:26, birds . . . they do not **s**
13:3, **s-er** went out to **s**
Luke 12:24, neither **s** nor reap
19:21, reap what you did not **s**
John 4:36, he who **s-s** and he who reaps
1 Cor. 9:11, **s-ed** spiritual things in you
15:42, **s-n** a perishable body
15:44, **s-n** a natural body
2 Cor. 9:6, he who **s-s** sparingly
Gal. 6:7, whatever a man **s-s**
James 3:18, is **s-n** in peace
Gen. 47:23; Lev. 26:16; Deut. 22:9; Job 31:8; Eccles. 11:4,6; Is. 32:20; Jer. 4:3; Hos. 8:7
SPACE—*time* Lev. 25:30, the **s** of a full year
SPACIOUS—*large* Ex. 3:8, to a good and **s** land
SPARE Ps. 78:50, **s** their soul from death
Prov. 13:24, **s-s** his rod hates his son
Acts 20:29, not **s-ing** the flock
Rom. 8:32, did not **s** His own Son
11:21, not **s** the natural branches
2 Cor. 9:6, who sows **s-ingly**
13:2, I come again, I will not **s**
2 Pet. 2:4, God did not **s** angels
Is. 9:19; Jer. 50:14; Mal. 3:17
SPARKLE Prov. 23:31, When it **s-s** in the cup
SPEAK—*tell, utter* Ps. 135:16, but they do not **s**
Prov. 23:9, Do not **s** . . . hearing of a fool
Eccles. 3:7, silent, and a time to **s**
Is. 32:4, stammerers will hasten to **s** clearly
Matt. 10:19, how or what you will **s**
10:20, Spirit of your Father who **s-s**
Mark 16:17, will **s** with new tongues
Luke 1:20, silent and unable to **s**
6:26, all men **s** well of you
John 3:11, we **s** that which we know
7:46, Never did a man **s** . . . this man **s-s**
8:45, because I **s** the truth
16:13, not **s** on His own initiative
Acts 2:4, began to **s** with other tongues
18:9, not be afraid . . . but go on **s-ing**
19:6, they began **s-ing** with tongues
Rom. 3:5, I am **s-ing** in human terms
1 Cor. 2:7, we **s** God's wisdom
13:1, I **s** with the tongues of men
13:11, I used to **s** as a child
2 Cor. 12:4, a man is not permitted to **s**
Eph. 5:19, **s-ing** to one another
6:20, **s** boldly, as I ought to **s**
Titus 3:8, I want you to **s** confidently
James 1:19, slow to **s** *and* slow to anger
2:12, so **s** and so act
4:11, not **s** against one another
1 Pet. 4:11, Whoever **s-s**, *let him* **S**
2 Pet. 2:18, **s-ing** out arrogant *words*
Gen. 18:32; Ex. 4:14; Lev. 1:2; Num. 22:35; Deut. 5:24; 1 Kin. 12:7; Job 2:13; 11:5; 33:14; 41:3; Ps. 28:3; 41:5; 101:7; Is. 29:4; 40:2; Mark 13:11; John 12:49; 2 Cor. 12:6
SPEAR 1 Sam. 26:7, his **s** stuck in the ground
2 Sam. 1:6, Saul was leaning on his **s**
Ps. 46:9, cuts the **s** in two
Is. 2:4, their **s-s** into pruning hooks
Joel 3:10, pruning hooks into **s-s**
John 19:34, pierced His side with a **s**
SPECIFICALLY 1 Sam. 20:21, If I **s** say to the lad
SPECULATIONS—*question*
Rom. 1:21, futile in their **s**
2 Cor. 10:5, *We are* destroying **s**
2 Tim. 2:23, foolish and ignorant **s**
SPED—*fly* Ps. 18:10, He **s** upon the wings of the wind
SPEECH—*message, word* Ex. 4:10, slow of **s**
Rom. 16:18, by their smooth and flattering **s**
1 Cor. 1:17, not in cleverness of **s**
2 Cor. 11:6, even if I am unskilled in **s**
Col. 4:6, **s** always be with grace
Deut. 32:2; Job 13:17; Prov. 17:7; Is. 33:19; Ezek. 3:5
SPEED—*quickly* Is. 5:19, Let Him make **s**
Luke 18:8, bring about justice . . . **s-ily**
SPELT Ezek. 4:9, beans, lentils, millet and **s**
SPEND Is. 55:2, Why do you **s** money
2 Cor. 12:15, I will most gladly **s** and
Gen. 19:2; Num. 22:8; Job 21:13
SPENT Gen. 47:15, money was all **s**
Ps. 31:10, my life is **s** with sorrow
Mark 5:26, **s** all that she had
SPICE Ex. 35:28; Song 8:2; Ezek. 24:10; John 19:40
SPIES Gen. 42:9, You are **s**
Josh. 6:23, young men who were **s**
Luke 20:20, sent **s** who pretended
Heb. 11:31, she had welcomed the **s**
SPIRIT Gen. 1:2, the **S** of God was moving
Ps. 31:5, Into Thy hand I commit my **s**
51:10, renew a steadfast **s** within me
Eccles. 12:7, the **s** will return to God

SPIRIT *(Continued)*
Is. 11:2, **s** of wisdom . . . understanding
32:15, Until the **S** is poured
61:1, **S** of the Lord GOD is upon
Joel 2:28, pour out My **S** on all mankind
Matt. 1:18, with child by the Holy **S**
3:16, **S** of God descending
5:3, Blessed are the poor in **s**
10:1, authority over unclean **s-s**
10:20, **S** of your Father who speaks
12:18, PUT MY **S** UPON HIM
12:31, blasphemy against the **S**
12:45, seven other **s-s** more
27:50, cried . . . yielded up *His* **s**
28:19, Son and the Holy **S**
Mark 1:8, baptize you with the Holy **S**
1:10, **S** like a dove descending
14:38, **s** is willing, but
Luke 1:15, be filled with the Holy **S**
4:18, **S** OF THE LORD IS UPON ME
11:13, give the Holy **S** to those
24:37, thought . . . seeing a **s**
24:39, **s** does not have flesh
John 3:5, is born of water . . . **s**
4:24, God is **s**
14:17, *that is* the **S** of truth
Acts 2:4, all filled with the Holy **S**
18:25, being fervent in **s**
Rom. 2:29, by the **S**, not by
8:6, mind set on the **S** is life
15:19, in the power of the **S**
1 Cor. 2:10, the **S** searches all things
2:13, taught by the **S**
3:16, **S** of God dwells in you
5:3, absent . . . present in **s**
12:4, gifts, but the same **S**
14:15, I shall pray with the **s**
2 Cor. 3:6, of the letter, but of the **S**
13:14, fellowship of the Holy **S**
Gal. 4:6, sent forth the **S** of His Son
5:16, walk by the **S**
5:22, fruit of the **S** is love
Eph. 1:13, with the Holy **S** of promise
2:18, access in one **S** to
4:4, body and one **S**
4:30, not grieve the Holy **S** of
Phil. 1:27, standing firm in one **s**
1 Thess. 5:19, Do not quench the **S**
Heb. 4:12, division of soul and **s**
James 2:26, body without *the* **s** is dead
1 Pet. 4:6, in the **s** according . . . *will of* God
1 John 4:1, not believe every **s**
5:7, **S** who bears witness
5:8, the **S** and the water . . . blood
Rev. 1:10, in the **S** on the Lord's
14:13, Yes, says the **S**
22:17, **S** and the bride say
Ex. 31:3; Judg. 9:23; 2 Kin. 2:9; Eccles. 7:8; Is. 42:1; 57:15; Ezek. 11:19; Acts 2:17

SPIRITIST Lev. 20:27; 2 Kin. 23:24

SPIRITUAL Rom. 15:27, shared in their **s** things
1 Cor. 10:3, ate the same **s** food
14:1, desire . . . **s** *gifts*
15:44, raised a **s** body
Eph. 1:3, blessed us . . . every **s** blessing
5:19, hymns and **s** songs
1 Pet. 2:5, built up as a **s** house

SPIT Job 30:10, refrain from **s-ing** . . . face
Matt. 26:67, they **s** in His face
27:30, they **s** on Him
Mark 8:23, after **s-ing** on his eyes
14:65, some began to **s** at Him
John 9:6, made clay of the **s-tle**

SPLENDID—*gorgeous* Luke 7:25, who are **s-ly** clothed

SPLENDOR—*glory, honor*
Ps. 8:1, hast displayed Thy **s**
96:6, **S** and majesty are before Him

SPLIT Lev. 11:3,7,26

SPOIL—*plunder* Gen. 49:27; Prov. 16:19; Is. 10:2; Ezek. 25:7

SPOKE—*declared, told* Gen. 8:15, God **s** to Noah
Ps. 33:9, He **s**, and it was done
40:10, I have **s-n** of Thy faithfulness
62:11, Once God has **s-n**
78:19, they **s** against God
87:3, Glorious things are **s-n** of you
Prov. 25:11, word **s-n** in right circumstances
Matt. 13:34, Jesus **s** . . . in parables
Mark 14:9, be **s-n** of in memory
Rom. 14:16, thing be **s-n** of as evil
1 Cor. 14:5, that you all **s** in tongues
Heb. 1:2, last days has **s-n** to us
2 Pet. 1:21, men . . . **s** from God
Mal. 3:16; Mark 7:32

SPOT—*blemish, defect*
Gen. 30:32, speckled and **s-ed** sheep
Jer. 13:23, Or the leopard his **s-s**
Eph. 5:27, having no **s** or wrinkle
1 Pet. 1:19, lamb unblemished and **s-less**

SPREAD—*disperse*
Prov. 15:7, lips . . . wise **s** knowledge
Matt. 21:8, multitude **s** their garments
Ex. 1:12; 9:29; Job 29:19; 37:18; Prov. 7:16; 29:5; Is. 19:8; 33:23; Ezek. 12:15; 16:8; Joel 2:2; Luke 19:36

SPRING—*well* Ps. 85:11, Truth **s-s** from the earth
Is. 45:8, righteousness **s** up with it
58:11, like a **s** of water
John 4:14, well of water **s-ing** up
Heb. 12:15, root of bitterness **s-ing**
Rev. 7:17, **s-s** of the water of life
21:6, thirsts from the **s** of the water
Gen. 16:7; 2 Kin. 3:19; Prov. 5:16; 25:26; Song 4:12; Is. 11:1

SPROUT—*grow* Gen. 1:11; Ex. 10:5; Ps. 90:5; 92:7; Is. 61:11

SPURNED—*despised* Ps. 10:13; 107:11; Prov. 1:30; 5:12

SPY Judg. 1:23, house of Joseph **s-ed** out Bethel

SQUANDERED—*wasted* Luke 15:13, **s** his estate

SQUARE Gen. 19:2; Ex. 27:1; Judg. 19:20; Rev. 21:16

STABILITY Col. 2:5, **s** of your faith

STAFF Gen. 38:18, your **s** that is in your hand
Ex. 7:12, Aaron's **s** swallowed up
Ps. 23:4, Thy rod and Thy **s**
Matt. 10:10, sandals, or a **s**
Ex. 4:4; Judg. 6:21; 2 Kin. 4:29; Is. 14:5; Ezek. 4:16; Zech. 11:10; Mark 6:8

STAIN 1 Tim. 6:14, commandment without **s**
2 Pet. 2:13, They are **s-s** and blemishes

STAIRWAY
2 Kin. 20:11, brought the shadow on the **s** back
Is. 38:8, shadow on the **s** . . . sun on the **s** of

STAND—*arise, form, rest, stood* Gen. 18:2
Ps. 1:5, will not **s** in the judgment
130:3, O Lord, who could **s**
Is. 40:8, word of our God **s-s** forever
Matt. 6:5, love to **s** and pray
12:25, house divided . . . shall not **s**
20:3, **s-ing** idle in the market place
Mark 11:25, whenever you **s** praying forgive
John 1:26, among you **s-s** One
19:25, were **s-ing** by the cross
20:11, Mary was **s-ing** outside
Acts 1:11, why do you **s** looking into
7:33, PLACE ON WHICH YOU ARE **S-ING** IS HOLY
21:40, Paul, **s-ing** on the stairs
Rom. 5:2, this grace in which we **s**
14:4, Lord is able to make him **s**
1 Cor. 16:13, **s** firm in the faith
2 Cor. 1:24, in your faith you are **s-ing** firm
Eph. 6:14, **S** firm . . . HAVING GIRDED YOUR LOINS
1 Tim. 3:13, obtain . . . a high **s-ing**
2 Tim. 2:19, foundation of God **s-s**
Rev. 3:20, Behold I **s** at the door
5:6, Lamb **s-ing**, as if slain
20:12, dead **s-ing** before the throne

Ex. 14:13; Num. 22:22; Josh. 10:12; Job 8:15; Prov. 22:29; 27:4; Is. 50:8; Jer. 6:16; 35:19; Ezek. 2:1; 13:5; Amos 7:7; Nah. 1:6

STANDARD—*banner*
Ps. 74:4, set up their own **s-s** for signs
Is. 13:2, Lift up a **s**
1 Chr. 17:17; Is. 5:26; 18:3; 31:9

STAR Gen. 1:16, *He made* the **s-s** also
Num. 24:17, A **s** shall come forth . . . Jacob
Job 38:7, morning **s-s** sang together
Ps. 147:4, counts the number of the **s-s**
Matt. 2:2, saw His **s** in the east
2:7, ascertained . . . time the **s** appeared
2:10, when they saw the **s**
24:29, **S-S** WILL FALL from the sky
1 Cor. 15:41, for **s** differs from **s**
2 Pet. 1:19, **s** arises in your hearts
Jude 13, wandering **s-s**, for whom
Rev. 1:16, right hand He held seven **s-s**
8:10, great **s** fell from heaven
8:11, **s** is called Wormwood
22:16, the bright morning **s**
Job 22:12; Ps. 136:9; Jer. 31:35

STARE Song 1:6, Do not **s** at me

STARVE Zeph. 2:11, He will **s** all the gods

STATE—*declare* Josh. 20:4; Luke 1:48

STATEMENT Matt. 5:37, your **s** be, Yes, yes
John 6:60, This is a difficult **s**
1 Tim. 1:15, It is a trustworthy **s**

STATURE—*size* 1 Sam. 16:7, the height of his **s**
Luke 2:52, increasing in wisdom and **s**
19:3, he was small in **s**

STATUTE—*precept*
Ps. 119:12, Teach me Thy **s-s**
Mal. 3:7, turned aside from My **s-s**
Gen. 26:5; Ex. 29:9; Lev. 18:5; Num. 35:29; Is. 10:1; Ezek. 5:7

STAY—*lodge, remain* Luke 2:8, shepherds **s-ing**
Luke 19:5, today I must **s** at your house
24:29, **S** with us . . . over. And . . . **s** with them
John 1:38, Rabbi . . . where are you **s-ing**
2:12, there they **s-ed** a few days
Acts 10:6, **s-ing** with a . . . tanner *named* Simon
1 Pet. 1:17, time of your **s** *upon earth*
Gen. 19:17; Ruth 2:8; 1 Sam. 20:38; 22:23; Ps. 18:18; Hos. 3:3; Luke 1:56; John 1:39; Acts 18:3

STEADFAST—*resolute*
Job 11:15, you would be **s**
Ps. 51:10, renew a **s** spirit within me
57:7, My heart is **s**, O God, my
112:7, His heart is **s**, trusting
1 Cor. 15:58, brethren, be **s**
Col. 1:11, all **s-ness** and patience
2 Thess. 3:5, into the **s-ness** of Christ

STEAL—*deceive* Matt. 6:19, break in and **s**
Matt. 19:18, YOU SHALL NOT **S**
Ex. 20:15; Lev. 19:11; Deut. 5:19; 2 Sam. 19:3; Prov. 30:9; Mark 10:19; Eph. 4:28

STEALTH—*craft* Mark 14:1, to seize Him by **s**

STEED 1 Kin. 4:28; Esth. 8:10

STEP Job 18:8, he **s-s** on the webbing
Rom. 4:12, follow in the **s-s** of the faith
1 Pet. 2:21, you to follow in His **s-s**
1 Kin. 10:19; Job 14:16; 29:6; Prov. 5:5

STERN Eccles. 8:1, causes his **s** face to beam

STEWARD Gen. 43:19, near to Joseph's house **s**
Luke 12:42, faithful and sensible **s**
1 Cor. 4:1, **s-s** of the mysteries of God
4:2, it is required of **s-s**

STEWARDSHIP Luke 16:2, an account of your **s**
1 Cor. 9:17, I have a **s** entrusted to me
Eph. 3:2, the **s** of God's grace
Col. 1:25, according to the **s** from God

STICK Prov. 18:24, friend who **s-s**
Num. 22:27; 2 Kin. 6:6; Job 33:21; 38:38; Ezek. 37:16,19

STILL Lev. 5:17, **s** he is guilty
Judg. 7:4, people are **s** too many
Dan. 11:35, **s** *to come* . . . appointed time
Matt. 19:20, what am I **s** lacking
Luke 24:44, while I was **s** with you
Rom. 5:6, while we were **s** helpless
Josh. 10:12; Ps. 65:7; 107:29; Jer. 8:14; Mark 4:39

STING 1 Cor. 15:55, O DEATH . . . YOUR **S**
1 Cor. 15:56, **s** of death is sin
Prov. 23:32; Rev. 9:10

STINKWEED Job 31:40, And **s** instead of barley

STIR Deut. 32:11, eagle that **s-s** up its nest
Ps. 35:23, **S** up Thyself, and awake
Prov. 10:12, Hatred **s-s** up strife
15:1, harsh word **s-s** up anger
28:25, arrogant man **s-s** up strife
29:22, angry man **s-s** up strife
Acts 14:2, Jews who disbelieved **s-ed** up
2 Pet. 3:1, I am **s-ing** up your

STOCKS Job 13:27; Acts 16:24

STOLE Gen. 31:19; 2 Sam. 15:6; Prov. 9:17

STOMACH Mark 7:19, but into his **s**

STONE Ex. 34:1, Cut out . . . two **s** tablets
Deut. 9:9, the tablets of **s**
1 Sam. 17:49, from it a **s** and slung
Ps. 118:22, **s** which the builders rejected
Ezek. 20:32, serving wood and **s**
Dan. 2:34, a **s** was cut out without
Matt. 3:9, God is able from these **s-s**
4:3, command . . . **s-s** become bread
4:6, YOUR FOOT AGAINST A **S**
7:9, will give him a **s**
21:42, **S** WHICH THE BUILDERS REJECTED
27:60, large **s** against the entrance
28:2, rolled away the **s** and sat
Luke 19:44, one **s** upon another
John 2:6, six **s** waterpots
8:7, first to throw a **s** at her
11:39, Jesus said, Remove the **s**
Acts 7:59, went on **s-ing** Stephen
2 Cor. 3:3, not on tablets of **s**
1 Pet. 2:5, also, as living **s-s**
2:8, **S** OF STUMBLING
Gen. 11:3; 29:3; Ex. 15:16; 20:25; Lev. 20:2; Num. 15:35; Deut. 8:9; 2 Sam. 17:13; 1 Kin. 6:18; 2 Kin. 12:12; 2 Chr. 34:11; Job 14:19; 41:24; Ps. 18:12; 91:12; Prov. 26:27; 27:3; Is. 28:16; 54:11; 57:6; Ezek. 11:19; Amos 5:11; Hab. 2:11; Luke 22:41; Rev. 2:17

STOOD Deut. 31:15, pillar of cloud **s** at
Josh. 10:13, So the sun **s** still
Matt. 2:9, came and **s** over where
4:5, devil . . . **s** Him on the pinnacle
Luke 4:16, and **s** up to read
24:36, He Himself **s** in their midst
John 21:4, Jesus **s** on the beach
Rev. 13:1, he **s** on the sand

STOP 1 Kin. 18:44; Ps. 63:11; 2 Cor. 11:10

STORE Prov. 10:14, Wise men **s** up knowledge
Luke 12:17, I have no place to **s** my crops
1 Tim. 6:19, **s-ing** up treasure
James 5:3, have **s-d** up your treasure

STOREHOUSE—*treasure* Deut. 28:12; Job 38:22

STORM—*tempest, whirlwind* Jon. 1:4, a great **s**
Jon. 1:12, this great **s** *has come* upon you
Matt. 16:3, *There will be* a **s** today
Acts 27:18, we were being violently **s-tossed**
2 Pet. 2:17, mists driven by a **s**
Job 21:18; 37:9; Ps. 55:8; 107:25; Is. 25:4; Ezek. 38:9

STRAIGHT—*equity* Matt. 3:3, MAKE PATHS **S**
Luke 3:5, CROOKED SHALL BECOME **S**
John 1:23, MAKE **S** THE WAY OF THE LORD
Acts 9:11, street called **S**
Heb. 12:13, make **s** paths for your feet
1 Sam. 6:12, Ps. 5:8; Eccles. 1:15; Mic. 3:9

STRAIGHTFORWARD Gal. 2:14, not **s** about the truth

STRAIT—*narrow* 1 Sam. 13:6, they were in a **s**

STRANGE Heb. 13:9, varied and **s** teachings
1 Pet. 4:12, some **s** thing were happening
Jude 7, went after **s** flesh

STRANGER—*alien, sojourner*
Gen. 23:4, I am a s and
Matt. 25:35, I was a s, and you invited
27:7, Potter's Field . . . for **s-s**
John 10:5, do not know the voice of **s-s**
Eph. 2:19, you are no longer **s-s** and aliens
Heb. 13:2, show hospitality to **s-s**
Gen. 15:13; Ex. 22:21; Is. 1:7; Jer. 22:3
STRATEGIC Mark 6:21, a s day came when Herod
STRAW Gen. 24:25; Ex. 5:7; 1 Kin. 4:28; Job 41:27; Is. 11:7
STRAY Prov. 7:25, not s into her paths
James 5:19, any among you **s-s** from the truth
1 Pet. 2:25, **s-ing** like sheep
STREAM—*river* Ps. 1:3, planted by the **s-s** of water
Is. 32:2, **s-s** of water in a dry country
STREET—*square*
Prov. 1:20, Wisdom shouts in the s
Is. 59:14, truth has stumbled in the s
Matt. 6:2, **s-s**, that they may be honored
6:5, pray . . . on the s corners
Acts 9:11, s called Straight
Rev. 21:21, s of the city was pure gold
2 Sam. 1:20; 22:43; Jer. 37:21; Nah. 2:4
STRENGTH Ex. 15:2, the LORD is my s and song
Ps. 28:7, LORD is my s and my shield
46:1, God is our refuge and s
Prov. 20:29, glory of young men . . . s
Is. 40:29, He gives s to the weary
Mark 12:30, MIND, AND WITH ALL YOUR S
1 Pet. 4:11, by the s which God supplies
Rev. 1:16, sun shining in its s
Gen. 4:12; Judg. 6:14; 8:21; 16:6; 1 Sam. 28:20; Job 6:12; 21:23; Ps. 84:7; Prov. 31:3; Eccles. 9:16; Is. 41:1; Hab. 3:19
STRENGTHEN—*fortify* 1 Sam. 30:6, David **s-ed**
Is. 35:3, s the feeble
Luke 22:32, s your brothers
Col. 1:11, **s-ed** with all power
2 Thess. 2:17, s your hearts in every
1 Tim. 1:12, who has **s-ed** me
Heb. 13:9, heart to be **s-ed** by grace
James 5:8, s your hearts, for the coming
1 Pet. 5:10, confirm, s *and* establish you
Deut. 3:28; Judg. 16:28; 2 Chr. 11:11; Job 4:3; Is. 35:3; Ezek. 34:16; Nah. 3:14
STRETCH Ps. 68:31, s out her hands to God
Ps. 104:2, **s-ing** out heaven like
Is. 28:20, too short . . . to s out
Job 30:24; 38:5; Jer. 10:12
STRETCHER
Luke 5:19, let him down . . . with his s
STRICKEN Is. 53:4, we . . . esteemed Him s
Is. 1:5; Jer. 14:19
STRICT Acts 26:5, the **s-est** sect of our religion
STRIFE—*quarrel*
Prov. 16:28, perverse man spreads s
18:6, fool's lips bring s
Rom. 13:13, not in s and jealousy
1 Cor. 3:3, jealousy and s among you
Gal. 5:20, enmities, s, jealousy
Titus 3:9, foolish controversies . . . and s
Gen. 13:7; Prov. 6:14,19; 10:12; 13:10; 20:3; Is. 58:4
STRIKE Ex. 7:17, I will s the water
Ex. 12:12, s down all the first-born
Ps. 91:12; Matt. 4:6; Luke 4:11, s your foot
Matt. 26:31, I WILL S DOWN THE SHEPHERD
Acts 23:3, God is going to s you
Gen. 4:23; Prov. 17:26; 19:25; Is. 49:10; Jer. 18:18
STRING Ps. 11:2; 33:2; Hab. 3:19
STRIP Ps. 29:9, **s-s** the forests bare
STRIPES Deut. 25:3, beat him with s
STRIVE Gen. 6:3, Spirit shall not s with man
Ps. 103:9, not always s *with us*
Luke 13:24, S to enter by the narrow door
STRONG—*courage* 2 Sam. 22:33, God is my s fortress
Ps. 24:8, the LORD s and mighty
Prov. 20:1, s drink a brawler
Jer. 50:34, Their Redeemer is s
Luke 2:40, Child . . . grow and become s
1 Cor. 4:10, we are weak, but you are s
2 Cor. 12:10, when I am weak, then I am s
Eph. 6:10, be s in the Lord
Heb. 11:34, from weakness were made s
James 3:4, ships . . . driven by s winds
Gen. 49:14; Ex. 10:19; 14:21; Lev. 10:9; Deut. 31:6; Judg. 14:18; Job 17:9; Ps. 19:5; Prov. 31:6; Song 8:6; Is. 5:11; 41:6; Ezek. 30:21; Luke 14:31
STRONGHOLD—*fortress, refuge*
Ps. 9:9, s in times of trouble
59:9,17, For God is my s
94:22, the LORD has been my s
2 Sam. 5:9; 22:3; 1 Chr. 11:5,7; Ps. 62:2; Prov. 10:29; Ezek. 33:27
STRUCK—*touched*
Job 19:21, hand of God has s me
Ex. 7:20; Num. 20:11; 22:23; Acts 12:23
STRUGGLE Col. 2:1, how great a s I have
STUBBORN Rom. 2:5, **s-ness** and unrepentant heart
Jer. 3:17; Hos. 4:16
STUMBLE—*fall*
Matt. 5:29, right eye makes you s
11:6, blessed . . . keeps from **s-ing** over
Luke 17:2, cause one of these . . . to s
James 3:2, For we all s in many *ways*
1 Pet. 2:8, s because they are disobedient
2 Pet. 1:10, you will never s
Prov. 3:23; Is. 8:14; 40:30; Jer. 50:32; Dan. 11:19
STUMBLING BLOCK—*ruin*
Ezek. 18:30, not become a s
Matt. 16:23, Satan! You are a s to Me
18:7, Woe . . . because of its **s-s**
Gal. 5:11, the s of the cross
STUPID—*senseless* Ps. 49:10; Prov. 30:2; Jer. 10:8,21
STUPOR Rom. 11:8, gave them a spirit of s
SUBJECT Luke 2:51, He continued in **s-ion** to them
Rom. 8:20, was **s-ed** to futility
Eph. 5:24, church is s to Christ
Titus 2:5, s to their own husbands
Heb. 2:8, PUT ALL THINGS IN **S-ION** UNDER
12:9, s to the Father
1 Pet. 3:22, and powers had been **s-ed** to Him
5:5, be s to your elders
SUBMISSIVE 1 Tim. 2:11, instruction with . . . **s-ness**
1 Pet. 2:18, be s to your masters
3:1, be s to your own husbands
SUBSIDED Judg. 8:3, their anger . . . s
SUBSTANCE Deut. 33:11, O LORD, bless his s
SUCCESS Gen. 24:12, grant me s today
SUDDENLY Mark 13:36, come s and find
Luke 21:34, come on you s like a trap
Acts 2:2, s there came from heaven
Job 21:13; Is. 29:5
SUFFER Job 3:20, light given to him who **s-s**
Ps. 34:10, lions do lack and s hunger
Mark 8:31, Son of Man must s many
Luke 24:46, Christ should s and rise again
Acts 28:5, into the fire and **s-ed** no harm
2 Tim. 2:3, S hardship with *me*
James 5:13, Is anyone among you **s-ing**
1 Pet. 2:21, Christ also **s-ed** for you
4:13, you share the **s-ings** of Christ
SUFFICIENT Ex. 36:7, material they had was s
Lev. 25:47, means of a stranger . . . becomes s
John 6:7, denarii worth of bread is not s
2 Cor. 12:9, My grace is s for you
SUIT Gen. 2:18; 2 Sam. 15:2
SULLEN 1 Kin. 21:5, your spirit is so s
SUM 1 Pet. 3:8, To s up, let all be harmonious
SUMMER Jer. 8:20, past, s is ended
Matt. 24:32, you know that s is near
Gen. 8:22; Ps. 74:17; Prov. 26:1; Zech. 14:8
SUMMON—*call* Num. 10:2, use them for **s-ing**
Job 9:19, who can s Him

SUN Eccles. 1:9, nothing new under the s
Is. 38:8 s-'s shadow went back ten steps
Matt. 5:45, causes His s to rise
13:43, RIGHTEOUS . . . SHINE FORTH AS THE S
Luke 21:25, will be signs in s
1 Cor. 15:41, There is one glory of the s
Eph. 4:26, s go down on your anger
Rev. 12:1, woman clothed with the s
22:5, nor the light of the s
Gen. 15:12; Ex. 16:21; Lev. 22:7; Josh. 10:12; Ps. 72:5; 84:11; 104:19; 121:6; Song. 6:10; Is. 60:19; Ezek. 32:7; Amos 8:9

SUNK Ps. 38:2, Thine arrows have s deep

SUNRISE Luke 1:78, the S from on high shall visit us

SUNSHINE 2 Sam. 23:4, Through s after rain

SUPERIORITY 1 Cor. 2:1, not come with s of speech

SUPPER John 13:4, rose from s and laid aside
1 Cor. 11:20, not to eat the Lord's S
Rev. 19:9, marriage s of the Lamb

SUPPLANTS Prov. 30:23, maidservant . . . s her mistress

SUPPLICATION Ex. 9:28, Make s to the LORD
Ps. 28:2, Hear the voice of my s-s
Dan. 9:3, seek *Him by* prayer and s-s

SUPPLY Is. 3:1, s of bread . . . s of water

SUPPORT Matt. 10:10, worker is worthy of his s
Ex. 17:12; 2 Tim. 4:16

SURE—*trust* Num. 32:23, be s your sin will find you out
Ps. 19:7, testimony of the LORD is s
Heb. 13:18, s that we have a good conscience
2 Pet. 1:19, prophetic word made more s

SURELY Gen. 2:17, eat from it you shall s die
Gen. 28:16, S the LORD is in this place
Deut. 14:22, s tithe all the produce
Ps. 23:6, S goodness and lovingkindness
Is. 53:4, S our griefs He . . . bore
Mark 14:70 S you are *one* of them
Heb. 6:14, S BLESS YOU . . . S MULTIPLY YOU
Ex. 31:13; 2 Sam. 17:11; Job 35:13; Jer. 23:39

SURFACE Gen. 1:2; 7:18; Job 38:30

SURMISE Acts 27:27, sailors *began* to s

SURPASS 2 Chr. 9:6, You s the report I heard
Eph. 1:19, the s-ing greatness of His power
2:7, the s-ing riches of His grace

SURPLUS Mark 12:44, put in out of their s

SURPRISE 1 Pet. 4:12, do not be s-d . . . fiery ordeal

SURROUND Ps. 18:5, cords of Sheol s-ed me
Luke 19:43, your enemies . . . and s you

SUSTAIN Gen. 13:6; 36:7; Song 2:5

SWALLOW Matt. 23:24, gnat and s a camel
1 Cor. 15:54, DEATH IS S-ED UP IN VICTORY
Gen. 41:7,24; Num. 16:34; Job 20:15; Is. 25:8; Jon. 1:17; Hab. 1:13

SWEAR Gen. 50:5; Lev. 19:12; Is. 45:23; Zech. 5:3; Matt. 23:18; 26:74; Mark 14:71; James 5:12

SWEET 2 Sam. 23:1, the s psalmist of Israel
Ps. 55:14, had s fellowship together
Prov. 3:24, your sleep will be s
9:17, Stolen water is s
Is. 5:20; 43:24; Jer. 6:20

SWELL—*bulge* Num. 5:21,22; Deut. 8:4

SWIFT Job 7:6, My days are s-er than
Eccles. 9:11, race is not to the s
Rom. 3:15, FEET ARE S TO SHED BLOOD

SWINDLER Luke 18:11, 1 Cor. 5:11, 6:10

SWINE Prov. 11:22, ring of gold in a s-'s snout
Matt. 7:6, throw your pearls before s
Mark 5:11, big herd of s feeding there
Luke 15:15, into his fields to feed s

SWOOP Job 9:26, eagle that s-s on its prey

SWORD Gen. 3:24, flaming s which turned
Gen. 27:40, by your s you shall live
Ps. 57:4, their tongue a sharp s
64:3, sharpened their tongue like a s
Prov. 5:4, Sharp as a two-edged s
Is. 2:4; Mic. 4:3, hammer their s-s into plowshares
Hos. 2:18, abolish the bow, the s, and war
Matt. 10:34, not . . . peace, but a s
26:51, drew out his s and struck the slave
26:52, take up the s shall perish by the s
Eph. 6:17, s of the Spirit
Rev. 1:16, mouth became a sharp . . . s
Ex. 5:3; Deut. 32:25; Judg. 3:16,21,22; 2 Sam. 2:26; Is. 2:4; Jer. 15:2; Hos. 1:7

SYNAGOGUE Matt. 6:2, the s-s and in the streets
Matt. 6:5, pray in the s-s and on
12:9, He went into their s
13:54, teaching them in their s
John 16:2, make you outcasts from the s
18:20, I always taught in s-s
Acts 9:20, proclaim Jesus in the s-s
Rev. 2:9, but are a s of Satan

T

TABERNACLE Ex. 26:1, t with ten curtains
Matt. 17:4, make three t-s here
Rev. 21:3, t of God is among men

TABLE Is. 21:5, They set the t
Matt. 21:12, t-s of the money-changers
Mark 7:28, dogs under the t feed
John 2:15, overturned their t-s
Acts 6:2, word of God . . . to serve t-s
1 Cor. 10:21, partake of the t of the Lord
Lev. 24:6; Judg. 1:7; 2 Kin. 4:10; Ps. 23:5

TABLET Ex. 24:12, give you the stone t-s
Ex. 31:18, two t-s of the testimony
Luke 1:63, asked for a t
2 Cor. 3:3, on t-s of human hearts
Is. 8:1; Jer. 17:1

TAKE Ex. 20:7, not t the name of the LORD
Ex. 34:9, t us as Thine own possession
Prov. 4:13, T hold of instruction
Is. 4:1, seven women will t hold of
Matt. 5:40, t your shirt
7:5, first t the log out . . . eye
11:29, T My yoke upon you
26:26, T, eat; this is My body
Mark 2:9, Arise, and t up your pallet
13:33, T heed, keep on the alert
Luke 9:3, T nothing for your journey
John 1:29, t-s away the sin of the world
20:2, have t-n away the Lord
Acts 1:20, HIS OFFICE LET ANOTHER MAN T
Eph. 6:16, t-ing up the shield of faith
Rev. 10:9, T it, and eat it
Gen. 3:22; 12:19; 22:2; Num. 30:2; Judg. 21:22; 1 Sam. 4:3; Ezek. 18:17; 37:19; Hos. 1:2; Mic. 2:4; Matt. 21:21; 1 Cor. 13:5

TALE 2 Pet. 1:16, cleverly devised t-s

TALK Acts 20:9, as Paul kept on t-ing
Eph. 5:4, *no* filthiness and silly t
Titus 1:10, empty t-ers and deceivers
Job 11:2; 15:3; Prov. 24:2; Luke 1:65

TARGET—*mark* 1 Sam. 20:20; Lam. 3:12

TASK Eccles. 2:26, sinner He has given the t

TASTE Ex. 16:31, t was like wafers
Ps. 34:8, t and see that the LORD is good
Matt. 16:28, shall not t death
Acts 23:14, t nothing until we have killed Paul
Heb. 2:9, t death for every one
6:4, t-d of the heavenly gift
Job 6:6; 34:3; Prov. 24:13; Dan. 10:3

TAUGHT Ps. 71:17, hast t me from my youth
Is. 54:13, sons will be t of the LORD
John 8:28, I speak . . . as the Father t Me
Gal. 1:12, nor was I t it
1 Thess. 4:9, t by God to love one another

TAUNT Deut. 28:37; Job 30:9

TAX—*tribute* Num. 31:28, levy a t for the LORD
Matt. 17:24, teacher not pay the . . . t
22:19, coin *used* for the poll-t

TAX *(Continued)*
Luke 20:22, pay **t-es** to Caesar
Rom. 13:7, **t** to whom **t** is *due*
2 Kin. 23:35; Matt. 9:9

TAX-GATHERER Matt. 5:46, even the **t-s** do the same
Matt. 10:3, Matthew the **t**
Luke 18:13, **t**, standing some distance away

TEACH Ps. 25:4, **T** me Thy paths
Ps. 27:11, **T** me Thy way, O LORD
143:10, **T** me to do Thy will
Prov. 1:8, do not forsake your mother's **t-ing**
Matt. 7:29, **t-ing** them as *one* having authority
11:1, **t** and preach in their cities
15:9, **T-ing** AS THEIR DOCTRINES
Mark 1:22, they were amazed at His **t-ing**
4:2, **t-ing** them ... in parables
Luke 11:1, Lord, **t** us to pray
19:47, **t-ing** daily in the temple
John 7:16, My **t-ing** is not Mine, but His
14:26, He will **t** you all things
Acts 1:1, Jesus began to do and **t**
2:42, devoting ... to the apostles' **t-ing**
15:35, **t-ing** and preaching
Rom. 2:21, **t** another, do you not **t** yourself
16:17, contrary to the **t-ing** which you learned
1 Cor. 11:14, nature itself **t** you
Col. 2:22, commandments and **t-ings** of men
3:16, **t-ing** and admonishing
1 Tim. 1:3, not to **t** strange doctrines
2:12, do not allow a woman to **t**
2 Tim. 3:10, you followed my **t-ing**
Titus 2:3, **t-ing** what is good
Heb. 8:11, NOT **T** EVERY ONE HIS FELLOW
Rev. 2:20, **t-es** and leads my bond-servants
2:24, the rest ... who do not hold this **t-ing**
Ex. 4:12; Deut. 32:2; 1 Kin. 8:36; Job 11:4; 15:5; 21:22; 37:19; Prov. 4:2; Is. 28:9

TEACHER Matt. 8:19, **T**, I will follow You
Matt. 10:24, disciple is not above his **t**
17:24, Does your **t** not pay
23:8, for One is your **T**
Mark 5:35, why trouble the **T** any more
Luke 2:46, in the midst of the **t-s**
5:17, Pharisees and **t-s** of the law
John 3:2, come from God *as* a **t**
3:10, Are you the **t** of Israel
13:13, You call Me **T** and Lord
Acts 5:34, Gamaliel, a **t** of the Law
Rom. 2:20, a **t** of the immature
1 Cor. 12:29, All are not **t-s**
Eph. 4:11, some *as* pastors and **t-s**
1 Tim. 2:7, **t** of the Gentiles in faith
2 Tim. 4:3, accumulate for themselves **t-s**
James 3:1, Let not many *of you* become **t-s**
2 Pet. 2:1, be false **t-s** among you
1 Chr. 25:8; Prov. 5:13

TEAR—*rend* Eccles. 3:7, time to **t** apart
Matt. 5:29, makes you stumble, **t** it out
7:6, turn and **t** you to pieces
Luke 12:18, I will **t** down my barns
John 19:24, Let us not **t** it, but cast
Lev. 10:6; Job 18:4; Ps. 7:2; Prov. 14:1; Ezek. 13:20

TEAR—*weep* Ps. 80:5, fed them ... bread of **t-s**
Ps. 126:5, sow in **t-s** shall reap with joyful shouting
Is. 25:8, God will wipe **t-s** away
Luke 7:38, wet His feet with her **t-s**
2 Tim. 1:4, even as I recall your **t-s**
Rev. 7:17, God shall wipe away every **t**
21:4, He shall wipe away every **t**
2 Kin. 20:5; Ps. 56:8; Eccles. 4:1; Is. 16:9; Jer. 9:1; Lam. 1:2; 2:18

TEETH Gen. 49:12; Job 13:14; 19:20; 41:14; Ps. 57:4; Prov. 10:26; Jer. 31:29; Amos 4:6; Matt. 8:12

TELL 1 Chr. 16:24; Ps. 96:3, **T** of His glory among
Ps. 19:1, heavens are **t-ing** of the glory of God
66:16, I will **t** of what He has done for my soul
118:17, **t** of the works of the LORD
Matt. 8:4, See that you **t** no one
26:63, **t** us whether You are the Christ
Luke 13:32, Go and **t** that fox
John 18:34, did others **t** you about Me
Ex. 19:3; Lev. 5:1; Judg. 14:14; Ps. 2:7; Eccles. 10:14; Dan. 2:2,36; Joel 1:3; Zeph. 3:13

TEMPER Prov. 29:11, A fool ... loses his **t**

TEMPERATE Titus 2:2, Older men are to be **t**

TEMPEST Job 9:17; Ps. 55:8; Is. 28:2; Amos 1:14

TEMPLE—*house* 2 Sam. 22:7, from His **t** He heard my voice
Ps. 11:4, LORD is in His holy **t**
Is. 6:4, **t** was filling with smoke
Jer. 7:4, **t** of the LORD, the **t** of the LORD
Matt. 4:5, pinnacle of the **t**
12:6, something greater than the **t**
Mark 14:58, destroy this **t** made with hands
Luke 23:45, veil of the **t** was torn
John 2:19, Destroy this **t** ... I will raise it
2:21, speaking of the **t** of His body
1 Cor. 3:17, **t** of God is holy ... what you are
2 Cor. 6:16, we are the **t** of the living God
2 Thess. 2:4, takes his seat in the **t** of God
Rev. 21:22, God ... and the Lamb are its **t**
1 Sam. 1:9; 1 Chr. 29:1; Neh. 6:11

TEMPT—*test* Matt. 4:1, Jesus ... **t-ed** by the devil
Matt. 4:3, **t-er** came and said to Him
Luke 4:2, forty days while **t-ed** by the devil
1 Cor. 10:13, not allow you to be **t-ed**
1 Thess. 3:5, tempter might have **t-ed** you
Heb. 4:15, **t-ed** in all things as *we are*
James 1:13, God cannot be **t-ed** by evil

TEMPTATION—*trial*
Matt. 6:13, do not lead us into **t**
26:41, you may not enter into **t**
Luke 8:13, time of **t** fall away
1 Cor. 10:13, No **t** has overtaken you
2 Pet. 2:9, rescue the godly from **t**

TEN Deut. 10:4, the **T** Commandments
Ps. 91:7, **t** thousand at your right hand
Matt. 25:1, comparable to **t** virgins
Luke 15:8, if she has **t** silver coins
17:17, Were there not **t** cleansed
Gen. 31:7; Num. 14:22; Job 19:3; Ps. 33:2; Song 5:10; Is. 38:8; Ezek. 45:14; Dan. 1:14; 7:7

TEND John 21:15,17

TENDER Is. 53:2, He grew up ... like a **t** shoot
Matt. 24:32, branch has already become **t**
Luke 1:78, **t** mercy of our God
Eph. 4:32, **t-hearted**, forgiving each other
Gen. 18:7; 2 Sam. 23:4; 2 Kin. 22:19

TENT—*tabernacle* 1 Kin. 12:16, To your **t-s**, O Israel
Ps. 15:1, who may abide in Thy **t**
61:4, dwell in Thy **t** forever
84:10, in the **t-s** of wickedness
Is. 38:12, Like a shepherd's **t**
Gen. 4:20; 18:1; 24:67; 25:27; Num. 24:5; Job 12:6; Song 1:8; Jer. 10:20

TENTH—*tithe* Gen. 14:20, he gave him a **t** of all
Heb. 7:2, Abraham apportioned a **t** part
7:5, to collect a **t** from the people
Rev. 11:13, a **t** of the city fell

TERMS Gal. 3:15, Speak in **t** of human relations

TERRIBLE—*dread*
Deut. 8:15, great and **t** wilderness
Mal. 4:5, the great and **t** day of the LORD
Mark 9:26, throwing him into **t** convulsions

TERRIFYING Is. 21:1, wilderness, from a **t** land
Heb. 10:27, **t** expectation of judgment
10:31, **t** thing to fall into the hands of

TERROR—*fear, dread* Ps. 91:5, afraid of the **t** by night
Luke 21:11, **t-s** and great signs
Lev. 26:16; Deut. 32:25; Job 15:21; 24:17; 41:14; Ps. 116:3; Eccles. 12:5; Is. 33:18

TEST—*try* Gen. 22:1, God **t-ed** Abraham
Ex. 17:2, Why do you **t** the LORD
Deut. 6:16, shall not put the LORD ... to the **t**
2 Sam. 22:31, word of the LORD is **t-ed**
Job 12:11, Does not the ear **t** words
Ps. 26:2, **T** my mind and my heart

Prov. 30:5, Every word of God is **t-ed**
Is. 28:16, a **t-ed** stone . . . costly
Matt. 22:18, Why are you **t-ing** Me
Acts 5:9, put the Spirit . . . to the **t**
1 Cor. 3:13, fire itself will **t** . . . man's work
2 Cor. 13:5, **T** yourselves *to see* if you are
James 1:3, **t-ing** of your faith
1 Pet. 1:7, even though **t-ed** by fire
4:12, fiery ordeal . . . for your **t-ing**
1 John 4:1, **t** the spirits to see
Ex. 20:20; 1 Kin. 10:1

TESTIFY
Acts 2:40, many other words he . . . **t-ed**
20:24, to **t** solemnly of the gospel
26:22, **t-ing** both to small and great
Gal. 5:3, **t** again to every man
1 Pet. 5:12, **t-ing** that this is the true
Ex. 23:2; 2 Sam. 1:16; 1 Kin. 21:10; Job 15:6; Is. 59:12

TESTIMONY—*witness* Ps. 19:7, **t** of the LORD is sure
Ps. 119:46, speak of Thy **t-s** before kings
Matt. 8:4, the offering . . . for a **t**
Luke 22:71, need do we have of **t**
John 8:17, the **t** of two men is true
1 Cor. 1:6, **t** concerning Christ was confirmed
2 Tim. 1:8, ashamed of the **t** of our Lord
Titus 1:13, This **t** is true
Rev. 19:10, **t** of Jesus is the spirit
Ex. 16:34; 25:16; 31:18; Lev. 16:13; Num. 35:30; Is. 8:16

THANK 1 Chr. 16:7, to give **t-s** to the LORD
1 Chr. 16:34, O give **t-s** to the LORD
Ps. 92:1, good to give **t-s** to the LORD
100:4, Give **t-s** to Him
Matt. 15:36, giving **t-s**, He broke *them*
26:27, took a cup and gave **t-s**
Luke 18:11, God, I **t** Thee that I am not
22:19, when He had given **t-s**, He broke
Rom. 6:17, But **t-s** be to God
14:6, he gives **t-s** to God
1 Cor. 14:16, Amen at your giving of **t-s**
15:57, but **t-s** be to God
Eph. 1:16, do not cease giving **t-s** for you
5:20, always giving **t-s** for all things
1 Thess. 3:9, what **t-s** can we render to God
5:18, in everything give **t-s**
2 Thess. 1:3, always to give **t-s** to God

THANKSGIVING—*gratitude*
Ps. 26:7, with the voice of **t**
95:2, before His presence with **t**
100:4, Enter His gates with **t**
Phil. 4:6, supplication with **t**
Rev. 7:12, and **t** and honor and power
Lev. 7:12; Neh. 11:17

THEIR Gen. 15:13, a land that is not **t-s**
Matt. 5:3, **t-s** is the kingdom of heaven
1 Cor. 1:2, Christ, **t** *Lord* and ours

THEN—*therefore* Gen. 4:26, **T** *men* began to call
Ex. 15:1, **T** Moses . . . sang this song
Matt. 6:9, Pray, **t**, in this way
24:14, **t** the end shall come
Mark 4:28, first the blade, **t** the head
13:26, T THEY SHALL SEE THE SON
Luke 20:25, **T** render to Caesar
Rom. 3:9, What **t**? Are we better
1 Cor. 13:12, but **t** face to face
2 Cor. 12:10, **t** I am strong

THERE Gen. 1:3, Let **t** be light; and **t** was
Lev. 7:7, **t** is one law for them
Matt. 2:13, remain **t** until I tell you
24:23, Behold, here is Christ or **t** *He is*
Luke 8:32, **t** was a herd of many swine
Rev. 21:25, **t** shall be no night **t**

THEREFORE 1 Pet. 4:1, **T**, since Christ has suffered
1 Pet. 4:7, **t**, be of sound judgment

THICK Ex. 10:22; Deut. 32:15; Joel 2:2

THIEF Matt. 6:19, **t-s** break in and steal
John 10:10, **t** comes only to steal
1 Cor. 6:10, nor **t-s**, nor covetous
1 Thess. 5:2, just like a **t** in the night
Deut. 24:7; Job 24:14; Ps. 50:18; Prov. 29:24; Is. 1:23; Joel 2:9

THINE Luke 22:42, not My will, but **T** be done
John 17:10, Mine are **T**, and **T** are Mine

THING Ps. 8:6, put all **t-s** under his feet
Eccles. 3:1, appointed time for **every-t**
Matt. 19:20, All these **t-s** I have kept
19:26, with God all **t-s** are possible
21:24, I will ask you one **t**
Mark 9:23, All **t-s** are possible to him
10:21, One **t** you lack
Luke 2:19, Mary treasured . . . these **t-s**
10:42, *only* a few **t-s** are necessary
John 14:14, ask Me **any-t** in My name
Acts 2:44, had all **t-s** in common
Phil. 3:13, but one **t** *I do*
4:8, let your mind dwell on these **t-s**
1 Tim. 4:15, Take pains with these **t-s**
James 3:10, **t-s** ought not to be this way
Rev. 16:3, every living **t** in the sea died
Gen. 7:23; 15:1; Ex. 20:17; Job 42:2; Ps. 2:1; Eccles. 9:5; Is. 7:13; 12:5; Ezek. 8:17

THINK—*esteem, thought* Prov. 23:7, as he **t-s**
Matt. 5:17, not **t** that I came to abolish
22:42, do you **t** about the Christ
John 5:39, you **t** that in them . . . life
Rom. 12:3, but to **t** so as . . . sound
14:14, to him who **t-s** anything to be unclean
1 Cor. 13:11, child, **t** as a child
14:20, do not be children in your **t-ing**
2 Cor. 11:16, no one **t** me foolish
Gal. 6:3, anyone **t-s** he is something
James 1:26, **t-s** himself to be religious

THIRD Ex. 20:5, **t** and fourth *generations*
Matt. 16:21, raised up on the **t** day
Luke 24:21, is the **t** day since
John 21:17, said to him the **t** time
1 Cor. 15:4, raised on the **t** day
2 Cor. 12:2, caught up to the **t** heaven

THIRST Ps. 42:2, My soul **t-s** for God
Matt. 5:6, **t** for righteousness
25:35, I was **t-y**, and you gave
John 4:13, drinks of this water shall **t**
6:35, believes . . . shall never **t**
19:28, said, I am **t-y**
Rom. 12:20, IF HE IS T-Y, GIVE HIM
2 Cor. 11:27, in hunger and **t**
Ex. 17:3; Judg. 15:18; Job 24:11; Ps. 69:21; 104:11; Is. 29:8; 41:17; 49:10; 65:13; Lam. 4:4

THIRTY Matt. 26:15, to him **t** pieces of silver
Ex. 21:32; Num. 20:29; Judg. 10:4; 12:9; 14:12; Zech. 11:12; Luke 3:23

THIRTY-NINE
2 Cor. 11:24, received . . . **t** *lashes*

THIS—*something* Rev. 2:4, I have **t** against you

THISTLE Is. 34:13, Nettles and **t-s** in its fortified cities

THORN—*hook* Prov. 15:19, as a hedge of **t-s**
Prov. 26:9, *Like* a **t** . . . into the hand of
Is. 55:13, Instead of the **t** bush the cypress
Jer. 4:3, not sow among **t-s**
12:13, sown wheat . . . reaped **t-s**
Matt. 7:16, Grapes . . . from **t** bushes
13:7, others fell among the **t-s**
27:29, weaving a crown of **t-s**
John 19:5, wearing the crown of **t-s**
2 Cor. 12:7, a **t** in the flesh
Gen. 3:18; Num. 33:55; Judg. 8:7; Eccles. 7:6; Song 2:2

THOROUGH—*diligent*
Deut. 19:18, judges shall investigate **t-ly**

THOUGHT—*reason, motive, plot*
Gen. 6:5, **t-s** of his heart
1 Chr. 28:9, every intent of the **t-s**
Job 21:27, I know your **t-s**
Ps. 94:11, know the **t-s** of man
Is. 55:8, My **t-s** are not your **t-s**

THOUGHT *(Continued)*
Matt. 9:4, Jesus knowing their **t-s**
15:19, heart come evil **t-s**
THOUSAND—*countless, clan*
1 Sam. 18:7, slain his **t-s** ... David his ten **t-s**
Job 9:3, answer Him ... a **t** *times*
Ps. 84:10, a day in Thy ... better than ... **t**
91:7, **t** may fall ... ten **t** at your right
Eccles. 7:28, found one man among a **t**
Mark 6:44, five **t** men who ate
8:9, about four **t** were *there*
1 Cor. 14:19, ten **t** words in a tongue
2 Pet. 3:8, **t** years as one day
Jude 14, came with many **t-s** of His
Lev. 26:8; Eccles. 6:6
Song 4:4; Is. 30:17; Jer. 32:18; Dan. 7:10; Rev. 5:11
THRASH Judg. 8:7, **t** your bodies with the thorns
THREE Job 2:11, Job's **t** friends heard
Prov. 30:15, **t** things ... not be satisfied
30:18, **t** things ... too wonderful
30:21, **t** things ... earth quakes
30:29, **t** things ... are stately
Dan. 6:10, knees **t** times a day
Jon. 1:17, fish **t** days and **t** nights
Matt. 12:40, JONAH WAS T DAYS AND T NIGHTS
17:4, make **t** tabernacles here
18:20, two or **t** have gathered
26:34, deny Me **t** times
27:63, After **t** days I *am*
Luke 2:46, after **t** days they found Him
10:36, Which of these **t** ... a neighbor
John 2:19, in **t** days I will raise it
Acts 2:41, about **t** thousand souls
9:9, **t** days without sight
1 Cor. 13:13, faith, hope, love, these **t**
Gen. 6:10; Ex. 34:23; Eccles. 4:12; Luke 12:52; 2 Cor. 11:25; 12:8
THRESH—*tread, beat, trample*
Deut. 25:4; 2 Sam. 24:21; 1 Chr. 21:20; Is. 21:10; 1 Tim. 5:18
THRESHING FLOOR
Matt. 3:12, thoroughly clean His **t**
THRESHOLD—*door* Ps. 84:10, stand at the **t** of the house
THREW—*toss, put*
2 Sam. 16:13, cast stones and **t** dust
2 Kin. 9:33, So they **t** her down
Luke 9:42, **t** him ... convulsion
19:35, they **t** their garments on the colt
THRIVE Job 8:16, He **t-s** before the sun
THROAT Ps. 69:3, crying; my **t** is parched
Rom. 3:13, T IS AN OPEN GRAVE
Ps. 5:9; 115:7; Prov. 23:2
THRONE Ps. 11:4, LORD's **t** is in heaven
Ps. 93:2, **t** is established from of old
Is. 66:1, Heaven is My **t**
Matt. 5:34, for it is THE T OF GOD
19:28, sit upon twelve **t-s**
Acts 7:49, HEAVEN IS MY T
Heb. 1:8, THY T ... IS FOREVER AND EVER
4:16, with confidence to the **t** of grace
Rev. 4:2, **t** was standing in heaven
20:11, I saw a great white **t**
Gen. 41:40; Ex. 11:5; 1 Kin. 22:19
THRONG Ps. 55:14, in the house of God in the **t**
THROUGH Is. 43:2, **t** the waters ... **t** the fire
Matt. 19:24, camel ... **t** the eye of a needle
Luke 6:1, passing **t** *some* grainfields
John 3:17, world should be saved **t** Him
Acts 10:43, bear witness that **t** His name
Rom. 1:8, thank my God **t** Jesus Christ
Gal. 4:7, then an heir **t** God
Eph. 2:8, you have been saved **t** faith
Phil. 4:13, do all things **t** Him
1 John 4:9, we might live **t** Him
Gen. 12:6; Ex. 14:16; Eccles. 10:18; Is. 62:10
THROW Gen. 37:20, **t** him into one of the pits
Eccles. 3:6, time to keep ... time to **t** away
Luke 9:39, **t-s** him into a convulsion
THRUSH Jer. 8:7, the swift and the **t**

THRUST—*cast, push* Josh. 23:5; Prov. 12:18; 18:5
THUNDER Mark 3:17, Boanerges ... Sons of **T**
John 12:29, multitude ... saying that it had **t-ed**
Rev. 14:2, voice ... like the sound of loud **t**
Ex. 9:23; 1 Sam. 2:10; 2 Sam. 22:14; Job 26:14; Ps. 81:7; Is. 29:6
THWART 2 Sam. 15:34; 17:14; 1 Thess. 2:18
TIDINGS—*message, news*
Ps. 112:7, He will not fear evil **t**
Rom. 10:15, BRING GLAD T OF GOOD THINGS
TILL—*cultivate* Jer. 27:11; Heb. 6:7
TIMBER—*wood*
2 Chr. 2:16, cut whatever **t** you need
TIME—*season, day, hour* Gen. 4:3; Judg. 15:1; Prov. 25:13
Job 22:16, snatched away before their **t**
Eccles. 3:1–8, appointed **t** for everything
9:12, man does not know his **t**
Is. 25:8, will swallow up death for all **t**
Dan. 12:7, for a **t**, **t-s**, and half a **t**
Hos. 10:12, it is **t** to seek the LORD
Matt. 2:7, ascertained from them the **t**
24:45, give them their food ... proper **t**
26:18, My **t** is at hand
John 7:6, My **t** is not yet at hand
1 Cor. 7:29, the **t** has been shortened
Gal. 6:9, in due **t** we shall reap
1 Tim. 2:6, testimony *borne* at the proper **t**
Jude 18, In the last **t** there shall be mockers
Rev. 1:3, for the **t** is near
2:21, I gave her **t** to repent
Eccles. 7:17; Song 2:12; Amos 5:13; Hag. 1:2; Zech. 14:7; Matt. 13:30; 24:43; Acts 5:34
TIMELY Prov. 15:23, how delightful is a **t** word
TIMES—*season*
1 Chr. 12:32, men who understood the **t**
Job 24:1, **t** not stored up by the Almighty
Ps. 9:9, stronghold in **t** of trouble
31:15, My **t** are in Thy hand
Dan. 2:21, changes the **t** and epochs
Matt. 16:3, *discern* the signs of the **t**
Acts 1:7, not for you to know **t**
Rev. 12:14, time and **t** and half a time
TIMID—*fearful* Matt. 8:26; Mark 4:40
TINGLE 1 Sam. 3:11; 2 Kin. 21:12; Jer. 19:3
TIP Job 38:37, Or **t** the water jars of the heavens
TIRED Gen. 27:46, I am **t** of living
TITHE—*tenth* Lev. 27:30, all the **t** of the land
Num. 18:26, take from ... Israel the **t**
18:28, offering to the LORD from your **t-s**
Deut. 12:17, the **t** of your grain
14:22, **t** all the produce
Matt. 23:23, you **t** mint and dill
Luke 18:12, pay **t-s** of all that I get
Heb. 7:8, mortal men receive **t-s**
TODAY—*age, day, life* Gen. 41:9, mention **t** of my own offenses
Ps. 2:7, **T** I have begotten Thee
Luke 23:43, **t** you shall be with Me in Paradise
Acts 13:33; Heb. 1:5, T I HAVE BEGOTTEN THEE
Heb. 13:8, Jesus Christ *is* the same ... **t**
TOIL—*labor, work, trouble*
Gen. 5:29, the **t** of our hands
31:42, and the **t** of my hands
Job 9:29, Why then should I **t** in vain
Matt. 6:28, do not **t** nor do they spin
1 Cor. 15:58, knowing that your **t** is not *in* vain
TOLD Matt. 24:25, I have **t** you in advance
Mark 3:9, He **t** His disciples
Luke 2:18, **t** them by the shepherds
John 4:39, **t** me all the things that I *have* done
14:2, not so, I would have **t** you
TOMB—*grave, place*
Is. 22:16, you have hewn a **t** for
Matt. 23:27, like whitewashed **t-s**
27:52, the **t-s** were opened
John 11:17, been in the **t** four days
12:17, Lazarus out of the **t**

19:41, in the garden a new **t**, in which
20:11, standing outside the **t** weeping
Rev. 11:9, bodies to be laid in a **t**

TOMORROW Prov. 27:1, Do not boast about **t**
Is. 22:13, drink, for **t** we may die
Matt. 6:34, do not be anxious for **t**
James 4:14, not know . . . life will be like **t**

TONE—*voice* Gal. 4:20, and to change my **t**

TONGUE—*language*
Ex. 4:10, speech and slow of **t**
Job 5:21, hidden from the scourge of the **t**
Ps. 5:9, They flatter with their **t**
34:13, keep your **t** from evil
57:4, their **t** a sharp sword
64:3, sharpened their **t** like a sword
140:3, sharpen their **t-s** as a serpent
Prov. 12:18, **t** of the wise brings healing
15:4, soothing **t** is a tree of life
25:15, soft **t** breaks the bone
Is. 30:27, His **t** is like a consuming fire
Mark 7:35, impediment of his **t** was removed
16:17, they will speak with new **t-s**
Luke 16:24, in water and cool off my **t**
Acts 2:4, began to speak with other **t-s**
Rom. 14:11, EVERY T SHALL GIVE PRAISE
1 Cor. 13:1, with the **t-s** of men and of
14:4, who speaks in a **t** edifies himself
14:5, that you all spoke in **t-s**
14:14, if I pray in a **t**
14:39, do not forbid to speak in **t-s**
Phil. 2:11, every **t** should confess . . . Jesus
James 3:5, **t** is a small part
3:8, no one can tame the **t**
1 Pet. 3:10, REFRAIN HIS T FROM EVIL
Rev. 5:9, *men* from every tribe and **t**
Job 6:30; 20:12; 29:10; Prov. 6:17; Is. 50:4; Jer. 9:8

TOOK Gen. 8:9, **t** her, and brought her into the ark
Ex. 4:7, **t** it out of his bosom

TOOTH Ex. 21:24; Lev. 24:20
Deut. 19:21, eye, **t** for **t**
Prov. 25:19, like a bad **t**
Matt. 5:38, EYE FOR AN EYE, AND A T FOR A T

TOP Gen. 28:12, **t** reaching to heaven
Ex. 19:20, to the **t** of the mountain
2 Kin. 19:26, as grass on the house **t-s**
Matt. 27:51, veil . . . torn . . . from **t** to bottom
Heb. 11:21, leaning on the **t** of his staff

TORCH Gen. 15:17, a flaming **t** which passed
Judg. 15:5, set fire to the **t-es**
Dan. 10:6, his eyes were like flaming **t-es**

TORE Matt. 26:65, high priest **t** his robes
2 Sam. 13:19; 1 Kin. 11:30; Job 1:20

TORMENT Job 19:2, How long will you **t** me
Luke 8:28, do not **t** me
16:23, Hades . . . being in **t**
16:28, to this place of **t**
2 Pet. 2:8, felt *his* righteous soul **t-ed**
Rev. 9:5, **t** was like the **t** of a scorpion

TORN Gen. 37:33, Joseph . . . been **t** to pieces
Josh. 9:4, wineskins, worn-out and **t**
Job 18:14, is **t** from the security
Matt. 27:51, veil of the temple was **t**

TOSS—*shake* Job 7:4, I am continually **t-ing**
Is. 54:11, **storm-t-ed**, and not comforted
Acts 22:23, **t-ing** dust into the air
Eph. 4:14, **t-ed** here and there by waves
James 1:6, driven and **t-ed** by the wind

TOTTER Is. 24:20; 28:7

TOUCH—*handle* Gen. 3:3, not eat from it or **t** it
Ps. 105:15, Do not **t** My anointed ones
Matt. 9:21, If I only **t** His garment
Mark 5:30, Who **t-ed** My garments
Luke 24:39, it is I Myself; **t** Me and see
1 Cor. 7:1, not to **t** a woman
Col. 2:21, do not taste, do not **t**
Ex. 19:12; Lev. 5:2; Job 5:19

TOWARD—*against* Rom. 8:7, is hostile **t** God

TOWER—*stronghold*
Prov. 18:10, name . . . is a strong **t**
Matt. 21:33, AND BUILT A T
Gen. 11:4; Ps. 48:12; Mic. 4:8

TRADE—*craft* Acts 18:3, he was of the same **t**
Acts 19:25, with the workmen of similar **t-s**

TRADER 2 Chr. 9:14, the **t-s** and merchants

TRAIN—*fit, instruct* 1 Chr. 12:8, men **t-ed** for war
2 Tim. 3:16, for **t-ing** in righteousness
Heb. 5:14, senses **t-ed** to discern good and evil
12:11, to those who have been **t-ed**

TRAMPLE Job 9:8, **t-s** down the waves
Prov. 25:26, *Like* a **t-d** spring
Hab. 3:12, didst **t** the nations

TRANSCRIBE
Prov. 25:1, proverbs . . . king of Judah, **t-d**

TRANSFORM—*change*
Rom. 12:2, **t-ed** by the renewing of
Phil. 3:21, who will **t** the body

TRANSGRESS Num. 14:41; Josh. 7:11; Jer. 2:8

TRANSGRESSION—*trespass, sin*
Job 14:17, My **t** is sealed up
33:9, pure without **t**
Ps. 32:1, he whose **t** is forgiven
39:8, Deliver me from all my **t-s**
51:3, I know my **t-s**
103:12, removed our **t-s** from us
Matt. 6:14, forgive men for their **t-s**
Col. 2:13, forgiven us all our **t-s**
Gen. 31:36; Ex. 34:7; Num. 14:18; Josh. 24:19; Prov. 10:12; 29:6; Is. 53:5; Ezek. 18:30; Matt. 6:15

TRANSGRESSOR
Ps. 37:38, **t-s** will be . . . destroyed
51:13, I will teach **t-s** Thy ways
Is. 53:12, numbered with the **t-s**
Mark 15:28, reckoned with **t-s**
James 2:11, become a **t** of the law

TRANSLATE Ezra 4:18, has been **t-d** and read
John 1:42, which **t-d** means Peter

TRAP—*entangle*
Matt. 22:15, how they might **t**
Mark 12:13, to **t** Him in a statement

TREACHEROUS
Prov. 2:22, the **t** will be uprooted
13:15, way of the **t** is hard
2 Sam. 18:13; Prov. 22:12; Is. 21:2; 24:16; Jer. 3:20; Lam. 1:2; Hos. 5:7; Mal. 2:10

TREAD—*trample* Luke 10:19, **t** upon serpents
Rev. 19:15, **t-s** the wine press
Job 24:11; Is. 16:10; 41:25; Jer. 25:30

TREASURE—*possession, gain*
Gen. 43:23, given you **t** in your
Is. 33:6, fear of the LORD is his **t**
Matt. 2:11, opening their **t-s** they presented
6:21, where your **t** is, there will
12:35, out of his good **t** brings
13:44, **t** hidden in the field
19:21, you shall have **t** in heaven
Col. 2:3, hidden all the **t-s** of wisdom
James 5:3, stored up your **t**
Deut. 33:19; Job 3:21; 23:12; Prov. 21:20

TREAT Mark 12:4, **t-ed** him shamefully
Luke 2:48, why have You **t-ed** us this way

TREE—*grove, cross* Gen. 1:11, fruit **t-s** bearing
Gen. 2:9, **t** of life . . . knowledge
3:8, God among the **t-s**
Ps. 1:3, **t** firmly planted by streams
37:35, like a luxuriant **t**
104:16, **t-s** of the LORD drink their fill
Prov. 3:18, She is a **t** of life
Is. 55:12, **t-s** . . . will clap *their* hands
Matt. 3:10, every **t** . . . not bear good fruit
7:17, good **t** bears good fruit
12:33, **t** is known by its fruit
Mark 8:24, see men . . . like **t-s**
Luke 19:4, climbed up into a sycamore **t**
John 1:50, saw you under the fig **t**
Jude 12, autumn **t-s** without fruit

TREE *(Continued)*
Rev. 2:7, eat of the **t** of life
Gen. 18:4; 21:33; Deut. 20:19; 21:22; Judg. 9:8; Prov. 27:18; Song 8:5; Is. 40:20; Mic. 4:4

TREMBLE—*fear*
1 Chr. 16:30; Ps. 96:9, **T** before Him . . . earth
Job 26:11, pillars of heaven **t**
Ps. 4:4, **T**, and do not sin
Is. 13:13, make the heavens **t**, and the earth
Mark 5:33, woman fearing and **t-ing**
Phil. 2:12, with fear and **t-ing**
2 Pet. 2:10, do not **t** when they revile
Lev. 26:6; Deut. 20:3; Ps. 2:11

TRENCH 2 Kin. 3:16, valley full of **t-es**

TRESPASS—*fault*
Gal. 6:1, if a man is caught in any **t**
Eph. 2:1, dead in your **t-s** and sins

TRIAL Deut. 7:19, great **t-s** which your eyes saw
Acts 4:9, if we are on **t** today
Gal. 4:14, a **t** to you in my bodily condition
James 1:12, a man who perseveres under **t**

TRIBE Gen. 49:28, these are the twelve **t-s**
Num. 1:4, a man of each **t**
Ps. 122:4, even the **t-s** of the LORD
Matt. 24:30, all the **t-s** of the earth
Luke 22:30, judging the twelve **t-s**

TRIBULATION—*affliction*
Matt. 24:21, will be a great **t**
John 16:33, world you have **t**
Rom. 5:3, **t** brings about perseverance
12:12, persevering in **t**
Eph. 3:13, not to lose heart at my **t-s**

TRIBUNAL—*judgment*
Acts 25:10, standing before Caesar's **t**

TRIBUTE—*tax* Ezra 7:24, impose tax, **t** or toll

TRICK—*craftiness* Matt. 2:16, Herod . . . **t-ed** by the magi
Luke 20:23, He detected their **t-ery**

TRIED Ex. 2:15, Pharaoh . . . **t** to kill Moses
Ps. 12:6, As silver **t** in a furnace

TRIM Ex. 30:7, when he **t-s** the lamps

TRIUMPH Ex. 32:18, sound of the cry of **t**

TROUBLE—*distress, affliction, pain*
1 Kin. 20:7, see how this man is looking for **t**
Job 4:8, plow iniquity . . . who sow **t** harvest it
5:6, does **t** sprout from the ground
5:7, man is born for **t**
Ps. 9:9, A stronghold in times of **t**
25:18, my affliction and my **t**
27:5, day of **t** He will conceal
41:1, deliver him in a day of **t**
Prov. 10:10, who winks the eye causes **t**
25:20, sings songs to a **t-d** heart
31:7, remember his **t** no more
Eccles. 8:6, a man's **t** is heavy
Matt. 2:3, Herod . . . heard it, he was **t-d**
Luke 6:18, **t-d** with unclean spirits
24:38, Why are you **t-d**
John 12:27, My soul has become **t-d**
Acts 20:10, Do not be **t-d**
1 Pet. 3:14, DO NOT BE T-D
Gen. 41:51; Ps. 77:4; 138:7; Is. 65:16; Ezek. 32:9

TRUE—*sure*
Prov. 11:18, sows righteousness . . . **t** reward
Luke 16:11, entrust the **t** *riches*
John 1:9, There was the **t** light
6:32, gives you the **t** bread
6:55, My flesh is **t** food . . . is **t** drink
7:28, He who sent Me is **t**
8:17, testimony of two men is **t**
Rom. 3:4, let God be found **t**
Phil. 4:8, whatever is **t**
Titus 1:13, This testimony is **t**
1 Pet. 5:12, the **t** grace of God
Rev. 3:14, faithful and **t** Witness

TRULY—*indeed* Josh. 7:20, **T**, I have sinned
Is. 45:15, **T**, Thou art a God who
Matt. 5:18, For **t** I say to you
John 1:51, **T**, **t**, I say to you
Gen. 24:49; 2 Sam. 14:5

TRUMPET—*horn* Is. 27:13, great **t** will be blown
Matt. 6:2, alms, do not sound a **t**
Ex. 19:16; Judg. 7:16

TRUST—*faith, confidence*
2 Chr. 20:20, **t** in the LORD . . . **t**
Job 8:14, whose **t** a spider's web
Ps. 4:5, And **t** in the LORD
118:8, Than to **t** in man
Prov. 11:28, **t-s** in his riches will fall
31:11, husband **t-s** in her
Is. 26:4, **T** in the LORD forever
Jer. 7:4, Do not **t** in deceptive words
20:10, All my **t-ed** friends
Mic. 7:5, Do not **t** in a neighbor
2 Cor. 1:9, should not **t** in ourselves
Heb. 2:13, I WILL PUT MY T IN HIM

TRUSTWORTHY—*true*
Prov. 20:6, who can find a **t** man
1 Tim. 3:1; 4:9, It is a **t** statement

TRUTH 1 Kin. 2:4, walk before Me in **t**
Ps. 15:2, speaks **t** in his heart
119:160, Thy word is **t**
Prov. 3:3, not let kindness and **t** leave you
23:23, Buy **t**, and do not sell *it*
Matt. 22:16, we know that You are **t-ful**
Luke 4:25, But I say to you in **t**
John 1:14, full of grace and **t**
8:32, **t** shall make you free
14:6, way, and the **t**, and the life
Rom. 1:25, **t** of God for a lie
Gal. 2:5, **t** of the gospel might remain
Phil. 1:18, in pretense or in **t**
1 Tim. 3:15, pillar and support of the **t**
2 Tim. 2:15, handling . . . the word of **t**
1 John 1:8, the **t** is not in us
Gen. 42:16; 1 Kin. 22:16; Is. 39:8; Zech. 8:16

TRY—*prove* Luke 14:19, oxen . . . going to **t** them
Luke 19:3, **t-ing** to see who Jesus was
Deut. 4:34; Is. 22:4; Acts 9:26

TUNIC—*garment, coat* Gen. 37:3; Lev. 16:4; Matt. 10:10; Luke 9:3

TURBAN—*diadem* Job 29:14; Ezek. 21:26

TURMOIL—*trouble* Prov. 15:16; Jer. 50:34

TURN 2 Kin. 20:10, shadow **t** backward ten steps
2 Chr. 34:2, did not **t** aside to the right or to the left
Job 23:11, kept His way and not **t-ed** aside
Ps. 119:157, I do not **t** aside from Thy
Prov. 7:25, Do not let your heart **t** aside
Is. 45:22, **T** to Me, and be saved
53:6, Each . . . has **t-ed** to his own way
Jer. 26:3, everyone will **t** from his evil way
Hos. 11:7, My people are bent on **t-ing** from Me
Joel 2:31, sun will be **t-ed** into darkness
Matt. 5:39, cheek, **t** to him the other
Acts 1:25, from which Judas **t-ed** aside
1 Tim. 5:15, **t-ed** aside to follow Satan
James 5:20, who **t-s** a sinner from the error
1 Pet. 3:11, T AWAY FROM EVIL
Ex. 23:2; Deut. 17:11; Ruth 1:16; 1 Kin. 20:26; 2 Kin. 17:13; Job 1:1; 2:3; 23:13; 36:21; Ps. 80:14; 119:51; Prov. 4:5; Is. 1:4; Jer. 23:20; Joel 2:14

TUTOR—*instruct* 1 Cor. 4:15, have countless **t-s** in Christ

TWELVE Gen. 17:20, become the father of **t** princes
Gen. 35:22, there were **t** sons of Jacob
Matt. 10:1, summoned His **t** disciples
Mark 3:14, He appointed **t**
Luke 2:42, when He became **t**
John 11:9, **t** hours in the day
Rev. 12:1, a crown of **t** stars

TWICE—*doubly*
Gen. 41:32, repeating . . . dream to Pharaoh **t**
Num. 20:11, struck the rock **t**
1 Sam. 18:11, David escaped . . . **t**

UNRIGHTEOUS *(Continued)*
Luke 16:10, **u** in . . . little thing is **u** also in much
16:11, faithful in the *use of* **u** Mammon
Rom. 3:5, God who inflicts wrath is not **u**
1 Cor. 6:9, **u** shall not inherit the kingdom
2 Pet. 2:9, keep the **u** under punishment
UNRIGHTEOUSNESS
1 Cor. 13:6, not rejoice in **u**
1 John 5:17, All **u** is sin
UNRULY 1 Thess. 5:14, admonish the **u**
2 Thess. 3:6, who leads an **u** life
UNSETTLING Acts 15:24, **u** your souls
UNSTEADY Prov. 25:19, and an **u** foot
UNSUSPECTING Rom. 16:18, hearts of the **u**
UNTAUGHT—*uneducated*
2 Pet. 3:16, **u** and unstable distort
UNTIE Luke 19:30, a colt . . . **u** it and bring it
UNTIL John 5:17, My Father is working **u** now
UNTIMELY 1 Cor. 15:8, to one **u** born
UNTRAINED Acts 4:13, uneducated and **u** men
UNWISE Deut. 32:6, O foolish and **u** people
Eph. 5:15, walk, not as **u** men
UNWORTHY
Gen. 32:10, **u** of all the lovingkindness
Luke 17:10, We are **u** slaves
UP Ex. 15:8, flowing waters stood **u** like a heap
UPHOLD Ps. 119:117, **U** me that I may be safe
Is. 41:13, God, who **u-s** your right hand
UPPER 2 Sam. 11:21, woman throw an **u** millstone
Luke 22:12, large, furnished, **u** room
Acts 1:13, they went up to the **u** room
19:1, Paul . . . passed through the **u** country
UPRIGHT Deut. 32:4, Righteous and **u** is He
Prov. 4:11, led you in **u** paths
Eccles. 7:29, God made men **u**
Mic. 7:2, is no **u** person among men
Acts 14:10, Stand **u** on your feet
1 Thess. 2:10, devoutly and **u-ly** and blamelessly
Num. 23:10; Job 1:8; 4:7
UPRIGHTNESS Prov. 17:26; Is. 59:14; Mal. 2:6
UPROAR 1 Kin. 1:41, city making such an **u**
Ps. 2:1, Why are the nations in an **u**
UPROOTJob 19:10, has **u-ed** my hope
Luke 17:6, Be **u-ed** and be planted
UPSET—*turn* 2 Sam. 6:6, oxen nearly **u** *it*
Acts 17:6, men . . . **u** the world have come here
2 Tim. 2:18, **u** the faith of some
Titus 1:11, **u-ing** whole families
UPWARD Phil. 3:14, prize of the **u** call
URGE—*constrain* Ruth 1:16, Do not **u** me to leave you
Prov. 16:26, his hunger **u-s** him *on*
Luke 24:29, And they **u-d** Him, saying
Rom. 12:1, I **u** you therefore, brethren
URGENT 1 Sam. 21:8, king's matter was **u**
USE Gen. 21:15; Deut. 32:23
1 Chr. 12:2, **u-ing** both the right hand and
2 Cor. 3:12, **u** great boldness in *our* speech
1 Tim. 5:23, **u** a little wine for the sake
USELESS Lev. 26:16, sow your seed **u-ly**
Rom. 3:12, TOGETHER THEY HAVE BECOME U
USURIOUS Lev. 25:36, not take **u** interest from him
USURY—*interest* Neh. 5:10, leave off this **u**
Prov. 28:8, increases his wealth by . . . **u**
UTENSILS Ex. 31:8, the table also and its **u**
UTMOST—*remote*
1 Thess. 2:16, wrath has come . . . to the **u**
UTTER—*speak* Ps. 119:171, Let my lips **u** praise
Acts 26:25, I **u** words of sober truth
1 Cor. 14:9, **u** by the tongue speech
UTTERANCE Luke 21:15, give you **u** and wisdom
Acts 2:4, Spirit was giving them **u**
2 Cor. 8:7, in faith and **u** and knowledge
Eph. 6:19, **u** may be given to me
UTTERLY—*greatly* Is. 42:17, be **u** put to shame
Rom. 7:13, sin might become **u** sinful

V

VAGRANT Gen. 4:12, a **v** and a wanderer
VAIN—*empty, futile* Ps. 2:1, peoples devising a **v** thing
Prov. 12:11, he who pursues **v** *things*
1 Cor. 15:14, then our preaching is **v**
VALLEY—*ravine*
Ps. 23:4, through the **v** of the shadow
Song 2:1, The lily of the **v-s**
Jer. 31:40, the whole **v** of the dead bodies
Ezek. 37:1, **v**; and it was full of bones
Joel 3:14, the **v** of decision
Gen. 14:17; 19:17; Josh. 10:12; 2 Sam. 18:18; 1 Kin. 20:28; 2 Kin. 3:16
VALUATION Lev. 5:15, according to your **v** in silver
Lev. 27:25, Every **v** of yours
Num. 18:16, redeem them, by your **v**
VALUE—*price* Matt. 10:31, you are of more **v** than
Matt. 12:12, how much more **v** is a man than a sheep
13:46, one pearl of great **v**
VANITY—*breath, emptiness, futility*
Prov. 22:8, sows iniquity will reap **v**
Eccles. 1:2, **V** of **v-es**! All is **v**
2 Pet. 2:18, arrogant *words* of **v**
VARICOLORED—*colored*
Gen. 37:3, made him a **v** tunic
Gen. 37:23,32
VARIETY 1 Cor. 12:4, there are **v-es** of gifts
VARIOUS—*manifold*
Matt. 4:24, taken with **v** diseases
24:7, in **v** places there will be famines
2 Tim. 3:6, led on by **v** impulses
James 1:2, when you encounter **v** trials
1 Pet. 1:6, distressed by **v** trials
VAST—*large* Is. 22:18, *To be cast* into a **v**
VAULT Job 22:14, walks on the **v** of heaven
VEGETABLES Deut. 11:10; 1 Kin. 21:2
Prov. 15:17, better is a dish of **v** where love is
Rom. 14:2, he who is weak eats **v** *only*
VEGETATION—*grass* Gen. 1:11, earth sprout **v**
Ps. 104:14, **v** for the labor of man
Gen. 1:12; Ps. 105:35; Is. 42:15; Jer. 12:4
VEIL Is. 25:7, **v** . . . stretched over all nations
Matt. 27:51, **v** of the temple was torn
2 Cor. 3:13, put a **v** over his face
Heb. 6:19, which enters within the **v**
9:3, behind the second **v**
Gen. 24:65; Ex. 34:33; Lev. 4:6; Song 4:1; Is. 47:2
VENGEANCE—*revenge*
Lev. 19:18, You shall not take **v**
Deut. 32:35, **V** is Mine
Ps. 94:1, O LORD, God of **v**
Is. 34:8, the LORD has a day of **v**
Heb. 10:30, **V** IS MINE
Gen. 4:15; 2 Sam. 22:48; Ps. 18:47; Jer. 15:15; Nah. 1:2
VENOM—*poison*
Deut. 32:24, **v** of crawling things
32:33, wine is the **v** of serpents
Job 20:14, the **v** of cobras
VENTURE Job 4:2, one **v-s** a word with you
VERY Gen. 1:31, behold, it was **v** good
Num. 12:3, Moses was **v** humble
Judg. 3:17, Eglon was a **v** fat man
1 Sam. 5:11, hand of God was **v** heavy
Ps. 46:1, A **v** present help in trouble
Matt. 17:15, an epileptic, and is **v** ill
Mark 16:2, **v** early on the first day
Luke 12:7, the **v** hairs of your head
Ex. 14:10; Mark 6:26
VESSEL Num. 5:17, holy water in . . . **v**
Ps. 31:12, I am like a broken **v**
Rom. 9:22, **v-s** of wrath
2 Cor. 4:7, treasure in earthen **v-s**
2 Tim. 2:21, will be a **v** for honor

1 Pet. 3:7, as with a weaker **v**
Rev. 2:27, AS THE V-S OF THE POTTER
Ex. 7:19; 2 Kin. 4:3; Is. 22:24; Jer. 48:11
VEXATION—*wrath* Prov. 12:16, fool's **v** is known
VICTORIOUS Rev. 15:2, come off **v** from the beast
VICTORY—*deliverance*
2 Sam. 23:10, LORD brought ... great **v**
2 Kin. 5:1, had given **v** to Syria
1 Chr. 11:14, the LORD saved them by a great **v**
29:11, the glory and the **v**
Ps. 98:1, holy arm have gained the **v**
Matt. 12:20, HE LEADS JUSTICE TO V
1 Cor. 15:54, DEATH IS SWALLOWED UP IN V
15:55, DEATH, WHERE IS YOUR V
1 John 5:4, **v** that has overcome the world
VIGOR Deut. 34:7, Moses ... nor his **v** abated
VINDICATE Ps. 82:3, **V** the weak and fatherless
Matt. 11:19, wisdom is **v-d** by her deeds
VINE Matt. 26:29, drink ... fruit of the **v**
John 15:1, I am the true **v**
Gen. 40:9; Judg. 9:12; 1 Kin. 4:25; Ps. 128:3; Song 2:13; Is. 36:16; Jer. 2:21; Ezek. 19:10; Joel 1:12; Mal. 3:11
VINEGAR Ruth 2:14; Ps. 69:21; Prov. 10:26
VINEYARD 1 Cor. 9:7, Who plants a **v**, and does not eat
Gen. 9:20; Lev. 19:10; 1 Kin. 21:1; Song 1:6; 2:15; Is. 1:8; Jer. 12:10; Matt. 20:4
VIOLATE 2 Sam. 13:12, do not **v** me
Rom. 4:15, law, neither is there **v-ion**
VIOLENCE Gen. 6:11, earth was filled with **v**
Ps. 55:9, **v** and strife in the city
Prov. 4:17, drink the wine of **v**
16:29, man of **v** entices his neighbor
Is. 53:9, He had done no **v**
Matt. 11:12, kingdom of heaven suffers **v**
Gen. 49:5; Job 5:21; Ps. 27:12; Prov. 26:6; Is. 60:18; Jer. 22:3
VIOLENT Ps. 18:48, rescue me from the **v** man
Ps. 37:35, seen a **v**, wicked man
Prov. 11:16, **v** men attain riches
Matt. 8:28, so exceedingly **v** that no one
VIPER—*adder, serpent* Job 20:16, **v-'s** tongue
Matt. 3:7, You brood of **v-s**
Acts 28:3, a **v** came out because of the heat
Is. 11:8; 14:29; 30:6
VIRGIN—*maid, maiden*
Matt. 1:23, V SHALL BE WITH CHILD
1:25, kept her a **v**
25:1, comparable to ten **v-s**
Luke 1:27, **v-'s** name was Mary
1 Cor. 7:28, if a **v** should marry
2 Cor. 11:2, to Christ ... a pure **v**
Gen. 24:16; Ex. 22:16,17; Judg. 19:24; Job 31:1; Ps. 148:12; Jer. 2:32; 31:13
VISIBLE Eph. 5:13, **v** when ... exposed by the light
VISION Prov. 29:18, Where there is no **v**
Is. 22:1, concerning the valley of **v**
Joel 2:28, young men will see **v-s**
Hab. 2:2, Record the **v** And inscribe *it*
Matt. 17:9, Tell the **v** to no one
Acts 2:17, YOUNG MEN SHALL SEE V-S
2 Cor. 12:1, to **v-s** and revelations
Gen. 15:1; 1 Sam. 3:1; Job 20:8; Lam. 2:9; Dan. 2:19
VISIT Ex. 20:5, **v-ing** the iniquity of
Matt. 25:36, sick, and you **v-ed** Me
Luke 1:68, **v-ed** us ... redemption for His people
James 1:27, **v** orphans and widows
VOICE—*sound* Ps. 19:3, Their **v** is not heard
Prov. 5:13, the **v** of my teachers
Eccles. 5:3, the **v** of a fool
Song 2:12, **v** of the turtledove
Is. 28:23, Give ear and hear my **v**
Matt. 2:18, V WAS HEARD IN RAMAH
3:3, V OF ONE CRYING
3:17, behold, a **v** out of the heavens
Mark 9:7, **v** came out of the cloud
Luke 3:4, **v** of one crying ... wilderness
John 5:25, **v** of the Son of God
Acts 10:13, **v** came to him, Arise, Peter
Rom. 10:18, V HAS GONE OUT INTO ALL
1 Thess. 4:16, **v** of *the* archangel
Heb. 12:26, His **v** shook the earth
2 Pet. 2:16, dumb donkey ... **v** of a man
Rev. 3:20, if any one hears My **v**
5:11, heard the **v** of many angels
Deut. 4:30; Josh. 6:10; 2 Sam. 19:35; Job 4:10; Is. 40:3; Jer. 7:34; Dan. 4:31; Rev. 6:1
VOID—*empty*
Gen. 1:2, earth was formless and **v**
Jer. 19:7, make **v** the counsel
Rom. 4:14, faith is made **v**
VOLUNTARILY—*willing* 1 Cor. 9:17, I do this **v**
VOLUNTEER Judg. 5:2, That the people **v-ed**
VOMIT Job 20:15, will **v** them up
Prov. 26:11, dog that returns to its **v**
Is. 19:14, staggers in his **v**
Jon. 2:10, fish ... **v-ed** Jonah up
2 Pet. 2:22, DOG RETURNS TO ITS OWN V
VOTIVE—*vow* Lev. 7:16, his offering is a **v**
VOW—*oath, votive* Gen. 28:20, Jacob made a **v**
Deut. 23:22, if you refrain from **v-ing**
Judg. 11:30, Jephthah made a **v**
2 Sam. 15:7, let me go and pay my **v**
Ps. 22:25, I shall pay my **v-s**
Eccles. 5:5, not **v** ... **v** and not pay
Matt. 5:33, MAKE FALSE V-S ... FULFILL YOUR V-S
Acts 18:18, he was keeping a **v**
VULTURES Matt. 24:28, the **v** will gather
Luke 17:37, will the **v** be gathered

W

WAGED—*fought*
Rev. 12:7, dragon and his angels **w** war
WAGES—*hire* Gen. 30:18, God has given me **w**
Deut. 23:18, the **w** of a dog
Job 7:2, hired man ... waits for his **w**
Luke 3:14, be content with your **w**
10:7; 1 Tim. 5:18, laborer is worthy ... **w**
John 4:36, who reaps is receiving **w**
2 Pet. 2:13, **w** of doing wrong
2:15, **w** of unrighteousness
Gen. 29:15; Ex. 2:9; Lev. 19:13; Deut. 24:15; Prov. 11:18; Jer. 22:13; Hag. 1:6; Zech. 8:10; 11:12; Mal. 3:5
WAIL—*mourn, weep* Jer. 9:19, voice of **w-ing** is heard
Mark 5:38, loudly weeping and **w-ing**
Esth. 4:3; Mic. 1:8
WAIST Matt. 3:4, leather belt about his **w**
WAISTBAND Jer. 13:1, Go and buy ... a linen **w**
WAIT Gen. 49:18, For Thy salvation I **w**
Ps. 25:5, For Thee I **w** all day
27:14; 37:34, **W** for the LORD
119:81, I **w** for Thy word
Prov. 1:18, **w** for their own blood
Is. 26:8, have **w-ed** for Thee eagerly
30:18, He **w-s** on high
Mark 15:43, **w-ing** for the kingdom
Luke 12:36, men who are **w-ing**
Rom. 8:23, **w-ing** eagerly for *our* adoption
Gal. 5:5, **w-ing** for the hope of
Phil. 3:20, we ... **w** for a Savior
Ruth 3:18; 2 Kin. 5:2; Job 14:14; Lam. 3:10; Dan. 12:12; Hos. 6:9; Mic. 7:2; Hab. 2:3; 3:16
WALK—*follow, journey* Gen. 3:8, God **w-ing** in the garden
Gen. 5:24, Enoch **w-ed** with God
Ex. 14:29, Israel **w-ed** on dry land
Lev. 26:3, If you **w** in My statutes
Josh. 18:8, Go and **w** through the land
1 Sam. 2:30, **w** before Me forever
Job 22:14, **w-s** on the vault of
Ps. 1:1, not **w** in the counsel of
15:2, He who **w-s** with integrity

Job 8:11; 11:16; Ps. 22:14; 46:3; Prov. 5:15; 20:5; Song 5:12; Is. 19:5; 32:2; Jer. 8:14; Lam. 1:16; Ezek. 4:11; 7:17; Dan. 1:12; 2 Pet. 3:5

WATERLESS Matt. 12:43, unclean spirit . . . passes through **w**

WAVE Ps. 42:7, Thy **w-s** have rolled over me
Is. 48:18, righteousness like the **w-s**
Matt. 8:24, covered with the **w-s**
Mark 4:37, **w-s** were breaking over the boat
Jude 13, wild **w-s** of the sea
2 Sam. 22:5; Job 9:8; Zech. 2:9

WAX Ps. 22:14, My heart is like **w**

WAY—*journey, manner, path, road*
Gen. 3:24, **w** to the tree of life
Josh. 23:14, the **w** of all the earth
Job 3:23, a man whose **w** is hidden
Ps. 1:6, the **w** of the righteous
18:30, His **w** is blameless
25:8, instructs sinners in the **w**
Is. 30:21, This is the **w**, walk in it
Jer. 12:1, **w** of the wicked prospered
Ezek. 3:18, wicked from his wicked **w**
Matt. 2:12, departed . . . by another **w**
3:3, READY THE **W** OF THE LORD
6:9, Pray, then, in this **w**
7:13, the **w** is broad
15:32, lest they faint on the **w**
Mark 1:3, MAKE READY THE **W** OF THE LORD
9:33, What were you discussing on the **w**
Luke 1:79, into the **w** of peace
John 1:23, STRAIGHT THE **W** OF THE LORD
14:6, I am the **w**, and the truth, and
Acts 9:2, found any belonging to the **W**
1 Cor. 12:31, a still more excellent **w**
2 Cor. 4:8, afflicted in every **w**
Heb. 10:20, by a new and living **w**
James 5:20, from the error of his **w**
2 Pet. 2:2, **w** of the truth will be maligned
2:15, forsaking the right **w**
Jude 11, gone the **w** of Cain
1 Sam. 12:23; 2 Sam. 22:33; Neh. 9:19; Ps. 50:23; Prov. 7:27; 12:15; Is. 26:7; 40:3; Jer. 2:36; 6:16; Nah. 1:3; Mal. 3:1

WAYS Deut. 8:6, to walk in His **w**
2 Kin. 17:13, Turn from your evil **w**
Prov. 6:6, ant . . . Observe her **w**
Is. 2:3, teach us concerning His **w**
Hab. 3:6, His **w** are everlasting
Rom. 11:33, unfathomable His **w**
1 Cor. 4:17, **w** which are in Christ
James 1:8, unstable in all his **w**
Judg. 5:6; Prov. 3:17; Lam. 3:40; Ezek. 7:3

WEAK—*unimpressive*
Matt. 26:41; Mark 14:38, but the flesh is **w**
Acts 20:35, you must help the **w**
Rom. 4:19, without becoming **w** in faith
1 Cor. 1:27, **w** things of the world
4:10, we are **w** , but you are strong
1 Thess. 5:14, help the **w**
Num. 13:18; Judg. 16:17; Is. 14:10; Joel 3:10

WEAKNESS—*infirmity*
Rom. 15:1, bear the **w-es** of those
1 Cor. 1:25, **w** of God is stronger than
2:3, with you in **w** and in fear
15:43, it is sown in **w**
2 Cor. 12:9, power is perfected in **w**
13:4, crucified because of **w**
Heb. 4:15, sympathize with our **w-es**
11:34, from **w** were made strong

WEALTH—*substance, prosperity* Gen. 31:1
Deut. 8:18, giving you power to make **w**
2 Chr. 1:11, not ask for riches, **w**
Job 5:5, schemer is eager for their **w**
Ps. 49:6, those who trust in their **w**
Prov. 3:9, Honor the LORD from your **w**
13:7, poor, but has great **w**
13:11, **W** *obtained* by fraud
Eccles. 5:19, given riches and **w**
Is. 45:3, hidden **w** of secret places
Hag. 2:7, come with the **w** of all nations
2 Cor. 8:2, **w** of their liberality
Rev. 3:17, rich, and have become **w-y**
18:19, became rich by her **w**
Ruth 2:1; Job 20:10; Prov. 23:4; Is. 5:17

WEAPONS—*armor*
Eccles. 9:18, Wisdom is better than **w**
Jer. 21:4, turn back the **w** of war
Ezek. 32:27, down to Sheol with their **w**
2 Cor. 6:7, **w** of righteousness
10:4, **w** of our warfare
Deut. 1:41; 1 Sam. 31:9; 2 Chr. 23:10; Neh. 4:17; Job 20:24

WEAR Deut. 22:5, woman shall not **w** man's clothing
Job 14:19, Water **w-s** away stones
John 19:5, Jesus . . . **w-ing** the crown of
James 2:3, who is **w-ing** the fine clothes
1 Pet. 3:3, and **w-ing** gold jewelry
Ex. 18:18; Deut. 8:4; Is. 50:9; Dan. 7:25; Matt. 11:8

WEARY—*faint, exhaust*
Job 3:17, there the **w** are at rest
Prov. 23:4, Do not **w** yourself to gain riches
25:25, cold water to a **w** soul
Eccles. 12:12, **w-ing** to the body
Is. 5:27, No one in it is **w** or stumbles
40:29, strength to the **w**
40:31, They will walk and not become **w**
50:4, sustain the **w** one with a word
Hab. 2:13, nations grow **w** for nothing
Matt. 11:28, Come to Me, all who are **w**
John 4:6, **w-ed** from His journey
Gal. 6:9, if we do not grow **w**
2 Sam. 17:2; Ps. 69:3; Prov. 25:17; Jer. 6:11

WEATHER—*day* Matt. 16:2, *will be* fair **w**

WEAVE—*embroider* Ex. 28:39; 38:23

WEB Job 18:8, he steps on the **w-ing**

WEDDING—*marriage* Song 3:11, day of his **w**
John 2:1, there was a **w** in Cana

WEEK Gen. 29:27, Complete the bridal **w**
Ex. 34:22, celebrate the Feast of **W-s**
Dan. 9:24, Seventy **w-s** have been decreed
Matt. 28:1, first *day* of the **w**
Luke 18:12, I fast twice a **w**

WEEP 1 Sam. 1:8, Hannah, why do you **w**
Neh. 8:9, do not mourn or **w**
Job 16:16, face is flushed from **w-ing**
16:20, My eye **w-s** to God
Eccles. 3:4, A time to **w**, and a time to laugh
Matt. 2:18, RACHEL **W-ING** FOR HER
13:42, **w-ing** and gnashing of
Mark 5:39, Why make a commotion and **w**
Luke 6:21, Blessed *are* you who **w** now
7:32, you did not **w**
John 11:31, to the tomb to **w** there
Acts 9:39, widows stood beside him **w-ing**
Rom. 12:15, who rejoice, and **w** with
James 4:9, miserable and mourn and **w**
Rev. 5:4, I *began* to **w** greatly
5:5, Stop **w-ing**; behold, the Lion
Gen. 43:30; Num. 11:13; Deut. 34:8; Judg. 11:37; Ps. 6:8; Is. 22:4; Jer. 9:1; Joel 1:5

WEIGH Prov. 16:2, the LORD **w-s** the motives
Dan. 5:27, you have been **w-ed** on the scales
Gen. 23:16; 24:22; 1 Sam. 2:3; Job 6:2; Ps. 58:2

WEIGHT Lev. 19:36, just balances, just **w-s**
Prov. 11:1, a just **w** is His delight
Ezek. 4:16, will eat bread by **w**
2 Cor. 4:17, eternal **w** of glory
Deut. 25:15; Job 28:25; Mic. 6:11

WELFARE 1 Sam. 17:18, the **w** of your brothers

WELL—*health, whole* Gen. 43:28, father is **w**
Deut. 4:40, that it may go **w** with you
1 Sam. 9:10, **W** said; come
2 Sam. 18:29, Is it **w** with the young man
Eccles. 12:6, pitcher by the **w** is shattered
Matt. 3:17, whom I am **w** pleased
Mark 7:37, has done all things **w**
Luke 5:31, not . . . **w** who need a physician
6:26, men speak **w** of you

WELL *(Continued)*
John 4:6, Jacob's **w** was there
5:6, Do you wish to get **w**
Gal. 5:7, You were running **w**
1 Tim. 3:4, his own household **w**
Gen. 4:7; Lev. 24:16; 2 Sam. 17:21; 20:9; 1 Chr. 11:17; Prov. 5:15; Eccles. 8:13; Song 4:15; Acts 15:29

WENT Is. 38:8, sun's *shadow* **w** back ten steps
Mark 1:28, news about Him **w** out
Jude 7, **w** after strange flesh

WEPT—*weep* Gen. 50:17, Joseph **w** when they
Matt. 26:75, went out and **w** bitterly
Luke 19:41, city and **w** over it
John 11:35, Jesus **w**

WEST Gen. 12:8, with Bethel on the **w**
Ex. 10:19, a very strong **w** wind
Ps. 107:3, east and from the **w**
Dan. 8:4, saw the ram butting **w-ward**

WET—*drench* Job 24:8, **w** with the mountain rains
Luke 7:44, **w** My feet with her tears

WHATEVER—*all* Ps. 1:3, in **w** he does, he prospers
Eccles. 9:10, **W** your hand finds to do
Matt. 7:12, **w** you want others to do for you
Luke 12:3, **w** you have said in the dark
John 11:22, **w** You ask of God
Rom. 14:23, **w** is not from faith is sin
1 Cor. 10:31, eat or drink or **w** you do
Gal. 6:7, for **w** a man sows
Eph. 6:8, **w** good things each one does
Phil. 4:8, **w** is true, **w** is honorable
Col. 3:17, **w** you do in word or deed
Gen. 31:16; Job 37:12

WHEAT—*kernel* Matt. 3:12, gather His **w** into the barn
Luke 22:31, to sift you like **w**
John 12:24, unless a grain of **w** falls
Rev. 6:6, quart of **w** for a denarius
Gen. 30:14; Ex. 34:22; Deut. 8:8; Judg. 6:11; 1 Sam. 12:17; Job 31:40

WHEEL—*whirl* Eccles. 12:6, **w** at the cistern is crushed
Is. 5:28, **w-s** like a whirlwind
Ezek. 1:16, one **w** were within another
1 Kin. 7:33; Prov. 20:26; Dan. 7:9; Nah. 3:2

WHELP Gen. 49:9; Deut. 33:22

WHERE Gen. 3:9, **W** are you
Ruth 1:17, **W** you die, I will die
Job 28:12, **w** can wisdom be found
Ps. 42:3, **W** is your God
139:7, **W** can I go from Thy Spirit
Prov. 29:18, **W** there is no vision
Is. 19:12, **w** are your wise men
Matt. 2:2, **W** is He who has been born
Luke 8:25, **W** is your faith
John 8:19, **W** is Your Father
8:21, **w** I am going, you cannot come
11:34, **W** have you laid him
Rom. 4:15, **w** there is no law
Gen. 28:15; 1 Sam. 27:10; 1 Cor. 1:20

WHILE—*moment* Is. 26:20, Hide for a little **w**
John 5:35, willing to rejoice for a **w**

WHIP 1 Kin. 12:11, disciplined you with **w-s**
Prov. 26:3, A **w** is for the horse
Nah. 3:2, The noise of the **w**

WHIRL Ps. 83:13, God, make them ... **w-ing** dust

WHIRLWIND—*storm, wind*
2 Kin. 2:1, Elijah by a **w** to
Ps. 58:9, sweep them away with a **w**
Prov. 1:27, calamity comes on ... **w**
Jer. 4:13; Hos. 8:7

WHISPER Ps. 41:7, hate me **w** together

WHITE Gen. 49:12, teeth **w** from milk
Ps. 51:7, I shall be **w-r** than snow
Is. 1:18, They will be as **w** as snow
Matt. 5:36, make one hair **w** or black
Luke 9:29, clothing *became* **w** *and* gleaming
John 4:35, they are **w** for harvest
Acts 23:3, you **w-washed** wall
Rev. 6:2, and behold, a **w** horse
Num. 12:10; Job 6:6; Dan. 7:9

WHOLE Gen. 2:6, water the **w** surface
Matt. 6:22, **w** body will be full of light
1 Cor. 5:6, leavens the **w** lump
1 John 2:2, *those of* the **w** world

WICK—*flax* Matt. 12:20, SMOLDERING **W** HE WILL NOT PUT OUT

WICKED—*evil, lawless, ungodly* Ex. 23:1
Ps. 1:1, not walk in the counsel of the **w**
Prov. 4:19, way of the **w** is like darkness
10:30, **w** will not dwell in the land
11:7, When a **w** man dies
13:9, lamp of the **w** goes out
Is. 53:9, His grave ... with **w** men
Acts 17:5, taking along some **w** men from the
24:15, both the righteous and the **w**
Job 8:22; 10:15; 11:20; Ps. 10:13; 12:8; 17:13; Eccles. 7:17; Ezek. 3:18; Dan. 12:10

WICKEDNESS—*evil* Gen. 6:5, the **w** of man was great
Ps. 10:7, Under his tongue is ... **w**
Prov. 4:17, they eat the bread of **w**
Is. 9:18, **w** burns like a fire
32:6, his heart inclines toward **w**
Acts 8:22, repent of this **w** of yours
Eph. 6:12, spiritual *forces* of **w** in the heavenly
Judg. 20:3; Jer. 14:20; Ezek. 3:19; Hos. 10:13

WIDE Nah. 3:13, gates of your land are opened **w**
Matt. 7:13, for the gate is **w**
28:15, story was **w-ly** spread

WIDOW Matt. 23:14, you devour **w-s** houses
Mark 12:43, **w** put in more than all
Luke 18:5, this **w** bothers me
1 Tim. 5:3, Honor **w-s** who are **w-s** indeed
Gen. 38:11; Ex. 22:22; Lev. 21:14; 2 Sam. 14:5; Job 22:9; Ps. 68:5; Is. 1:17

WIELD Judg. 5:14, those who **w** the staff of office

WIFE Gen. 2:24, shall cleave to his **w**
Ex. 20:17, not covet your neighbor's **w**
Prov. 12:4, excellent **w** ... crown of her husband
18:22, finds a **w** finds a good thing
Matt. 5:31, WHOEVER DIVORCES HIS **W**
Luke 17:32, Remember Lot's **w**
1 Cor. 7:2, each man have his own **w**
Eph. 5:23, husband ... head of the **w**
1 Tim. 3:2, husband of one **w**
Lev. 18:15; Job 31:10; Ps. 128:3

WILD Gen. 37:20,33, **w** beast devoured him
Mark 1:6, John ... diet was locusts and **w** honey
Gen. 16:12; Job 11:12; Ps. 104:11

WILDERNESS—*desert*
Deut. 29:5, forty years in the **w**
Is. 35:6, waters will break forth in the **w**
40:3, Clear the way ... LORD in the **w**
43:19, make a roadway in the **w**
Matt. 3:1, preaching ... **w** of Judea
3:3, VOICE ... CRYING IN THE **W**
4:1, led ... into the **w** to be tempted
24:26, Behold, He is in the **w**
Mark 1:13, He was in the **w** forty days
John 6:31, Our fathers ate manna in the **w**
1 Cor. 10:5, laid low in the **w**
Heb. 3:8, DAY OF TRIAL IN THE **W**
Rev. 12:6, woman fled into the **w**
Gen. 16:7; Ex. 5:3; 14:11; 19:2; Lev. 7:38; Ps. 65:12; 102:6; Is. 51:3; Jer. 2:6; 17:6

WILL Ps. 40:8, delight to do Thy **w**
Matt. 6:10, Thy **w** be done
7:21, who does the **w** of My Father
Mark 3:35, whoever does the **w** of God
Luke 22:42, not My **w**, but Thine be done
John 1:13, **w** of the flesh ... **w** of man
4:34, **w** of Him who sent Me
Acts 21:14, **w** of the Lord be done
Rom. 12:2, may prove what the **w** of God is
1 Cor. 4:19, if the Lord **w-s**
Eph. 5:17, what the **w** of the Lord is
Phil. 2:13, both to **w** and to work

Heb. 10:9, HAVE COME TO DO THY **W**
James 4:15, If the Lord **w-s**, we shall live
WILLING Ps. 51:12, with a **w** spirit
Matt. 26:41, spirit is **w** . . . flesh is weak
Luke 22:42, Father, if Thou art **w**
Gen. 24:5; Ex. 35:5; 1 Chr. 28:9
WIN—*gain* Prov. 11:30, he who is wise **w-s** souls
Matt. 28:14, we will **w** him over and keep
Luke 21:19, perseverance you will **w** . . . souls
1 Cor. 9:20, that I might **w** the Jews
9:24, Run in such a way that you may **w**
WIND—*breath, whirlwind*
Job 16:3, no limit to **w-y** words
Ps. 1:4, chaff which the **w** drives
Is. 17:13, like the chaff . . . before the **w**
Matt. 7:25, floods came, and the **w-s** blew
11:7, reed shaken by the **w**
Mark 4:41, **w** and the sea obey Him
Luke 8:24, He rebuked the **w**
John 3:8, **w** blows where it wishes
Acts 2:2, noise like a violent, rushing **w**
Eph. 4:14, every **w** of doctrine
Heb. 1:7, MAKES HIS ANGELS **W-S**
James 3:4, are driven by strong **w-s**
Jude 12, carried along by **w-s**
Gen. 8:1; 1 Kin. 19:11; 2 Kin. 3:17; Prov. 11:29; Eccles. 5:16; Song 4:16; Is. 7:2; Jer. 22:22; Ezek. 37:9; Hos. 8:7; Rev. 6:13
WINDOW Josh. 2:15, by a rope through the **w**
Acts 20:9, sitting on the **w-sill**
2 Cor. 11:33, through a **w** in the wall
Judg. 5:28; 2 Kin. 7:2; Jer. 9:21; Joel 2:9
WINE—*vinegar* Lev. 10:9, Do not drink **w**
Ps. 60:3, Thou hast given us **w** to drink
Jer. 35:6, We will not drink **w**
Matt. 9:17, new **w** into old wineskins
27:48, sponge, he filled it with sour **w**
Mark 15:23, give Him **w** mixed with myrrh
Luke 10:34, pouring oil and **w** on *them*
John 2:3, when the **w** gave out
2:9, water which had become **w**
19:29, A jar full of sour **w**
Acts 2:13, are full of sweet **w**
Eph. 5:18, do not get drunk with **w**
1 Tim. 3:3, not addicted to **w**
Rev. 6:6, not harm the oil and the **w**
Gen. 9:24; 1 Sam. 1:14; 2 Sam. 13:28; Prov. 3:10; Eccles. 9:7; Song 1:2; Is. 5:22
WINESKIN—*jug* Job 32:19, Like new **w-s** it is
Ps. 119:83, like a **w** in the smoke
Matt. 9:17; Mark 2:22, new wine . . . fresh **w-s**
Josh. 9:13; Luke 5:37
WINGS—*feathers* Job 39:13, ostriches' **w** flap
Ps. 17:8, in the shadow of Thy **w**
91:4, under His **w** you may seek refuge
Prov. 23:5, *wealth* certainly makes itself **w**
Mal. 4:2, with healing in its **w**
Matt. 23:37, chicks under her **w**
Luke 13:34, her brood under her **w**
Ex. 19:4; Lev. 1:17; Deut. 32:11; Ruth 2:12; 2 Sam. 22:11; Is. 6:2; Jer. 48:9; Ezek. 1:6; Zech. 5:9
WINK Ps. 35:19; Prov. 6:13
WINNOW Is. 30:24; 41:16; Matt. 3:12
WINTER Gen. 8:22; Song 2:11; 1 Cor. 16:6
WIPE—*blot, erase* Is. 25:8, God will **w** tears
Is. 44:22, **w-d** out your transgressions
John 11:2, **w-d** His feet with her hair
Acts 3:19, Repent . . . sins may be **w-ed** away
Rev. 21:4, He shall **w** away every tear
WISDOM Ex. 28:3, endowed with the spirit of **w**
1 Kin. 2:6, act according to your **w**
2 Chr. 1:10, Give me now **w**
Job 12:2, with you **w** will die
Ps. 51:6, make me know **w**
Prov. 1:7, Fools despise **w** and instruction
4:5, Acquire **w**! Acquire understanding
24:3, By **w** a house is built
Eccles. 1:18, in much **w** there is much grief
7:12, **w** preserves the lives
Jer. 9:23, wise man boast of his **w**
Mic. 6:9, it is sound **w** to fear Thy name
Matt. 11:19, **w** is vindicated by her deeds
Luke 2:52, Jesus kept increasing in **w** and stature
21:15, give you utterance and **w**
2 Cor. 1:12, not in fleshly **w**
2 Tim. 3:15, **w** that leads to salvation
James 1:5, if any of you lacks **w**
Rev. 13:18, Here is **w**
WISE—*shrewd* Gen. 3:6, tree . . . to make one **w**
Job 17:10, I do not find a **w** man
Ps. 19:7, making **w** the simple
Prov. 3:7, not be **w** in your own eyes
Luke 10:21, hide these things from *the* **w**
Rom. 1:14, the **w** and to the foolish
1 Cor. 1:19, DESTROY THE WISDOM OF THE **W**
3:18, that he may become **w**
Eph. 5:15, not as unwise men, but as **w**
James 3:13, Who . . . is **w** and understanding
Is. 19:12; Hos. 13:13
WISH—*desire*
Luke 5:39, drinking old *wine* **w-es** for new
Luke 8:20, brothers are . . . **w-ing**
10:24, prophets and kings **w-ed** to see
John 16:19, Jesus knew they **w-ed** to question
1 Cor. 10:27, If one . . . invites you, and you **w**
2 Pet. 3:9, not **w-ing** for any to perish
WITHDRAW Josh. 8:26; 1 Sam. 14:19
WITHER Ps. 1:3, leaf does not **w**
Ps. 37:2, **w** quickly like the grass
102:11, I **w** away like grass
Is. 34:4, As a leaf **w-s** from the vine
64:6, **w** like a leaf
Jer. 8:13, the leaf shall **w**
Zech. 11:17, His arm will be totally **w-ed**
Matt. 13:6, had no root, they **w-ed**
Mark 3:1, man . . . with a **w-ed** hand
11:20, fig tree **w-ed** from the roots up
James 1:11, **w-s** the grass
WITHHELD Job 22:7, from the hungry you . . . **w** bread
Hag. 1:10, sky has **w** its dew
WITHHOLD Prov. 11:24,26
WITHIN Ps. 51:10, renew a steadfast spirit **w** me
Jer. 31:33, put My law **w** them
Mark 7:23, evil things proceed from **w**
1 Cor. 5:12, not judge those who are **w** *the church*
2 Cor. 7:5, conflicts without, fears **w**
Prov. 22:18; Ezek. 11:19
WITHOUT 2 Chr. 15:3, Israel was **w** the true God
Is. 52:3, redeemed **w** money
Matt. 13:57, prophet is not **w** honor
Mark 14:58, made **w** hands
John 8:7, He who is **w** sin
Rom. 12:9, love be **w** hypocrisy
2 Cor. 7:5, conflicts **w**, fears within
Eph. 2:12, no hope and **w** God in the world
1 Thess. 5:17, pray **w** ceasing
1 Tim. 6:14, commandment **w** stain
Heb. 7:3, **W** father, **w** mother, **w** genealogy
13:2, entertained angels **w** knowing it
James 2:20, faith **w** works is useless
2 Pet. 2:17, are springs **w** water
Jude 12, **w** fear . . . **w** water . . . **w** fruit
Job 5:9; 8:11; Hos. 7:11; Col. 2:11
WITNESS—*advocate, testimony*
Ex. 4:8, **w** of the last sign
20:16, shall not bear false **w**
Judg. 11:10, LORD is **w** between us
Job 21:29, do you not recognize their **w**
Ps. 89:37, **w** in the sky is faithful
Matt. 19:18; Mark 10:19, NOT BEAR FALSE **W**
John 1:7, he might bear **w** of the light
1:32, John bore **w** saying, I have
3:11, bear **w** . . . do not receive our **w**
5:39, these that bear **w** of Me
8:14, **w** of Myself, My **w** is true
21:24, we know his **w** is true
1 Cor. 15:15, found *to be* false **w-es** of God

WITNESS *(Continued)*
2 Cor. 1:23, God as **w** to my soul
Phil. 1:8, For God is my **w**
Heb. 10:15, Holy Spirit also bears **w**
1 John 5:8, three that bear **w**
5:9, If we receive the **w** of men
Rev. 1:5, Christ, the faithful **w**
Gen. 31:48; Deut. 4:26; Job 16:19; Prov. 6:19; Is. 19:20

WIVES Deut. 17:17, Neither shall he multiply **w**
Eph. 5:22, **W** *be subject* to . . . husbands
1 Pet. 3:1, you **w**, be submissive
3:7, husbands, live with your **w**

WOE Prov. 23:29, Who has **w**?
Mark 14:21, **w** to that man by whom
Rev. 8:13, **W**, **w**, **w** . . . who dwell on the earth
18:10,16,19, **W**, **w**, the great city
Num. 21:29; Job 10:15; Ps. 120:5; Is. 6:5; Jer. 4:13; 44:11; Matt. 11:21

WOLF Is. 65:25, **w** and the lamb shall graze
Matt. 7:15, inwardly are ravenous **w-s**
10:16, sheep in the midst of **w-s**
Gen. 49:27; Jer. 5:6

WOMAN Gen. 2:23, She shall be called **W**
Ex. 2:9, **w** took the child
Deut. 22:5, **w** shall not wear man's clothing
Ruth 2:5, Whose young **w** is this
3:11, you are a **w** of excellence
Job 14:1, Man, who is born of **w**
Prov. 11:16, gracious **w** attains honor
Is. 49:15, **w** forget her nursing child
Matt. 5:28, looks on a **w** to lust for her
15:28, O **w**, your faith is great
Luke 7:44, said to Simon, Do you see this **w**
10:38, a **w** named Martha
John 4:7, **w** of Samaria to draw water
8:4, **w** has been caught in adultery
Acts 9:36, **w** abounding with deeds of kindness
1 Cor. 7:1, a man not to touch a **w**
7:2, each **w** have her own husband
14:35, a **w** to speak in church
Gal. 4:4, His Son, born of a **w**
1 Tim. 2:11, Let a **w** quietly receive instruction
Rev. 12:1, **w** clothed with the sun
Judg. 11:2; 1 Sam. 1:15; Eccles. 9:9

WOMB Gen. 25:23, Two nations are in your **w**
Ex. 13:2, first offspring of every **w**
Job 1:21, Naked . . . from my mother's **w**
Luke 1:41, baby leaped in her **w**
John 3:4, enter . . . into his mother's **w**
Acts 3:2, lame from his mother's **w**
Num. 12:12; Deut. 7:13; Ruth 1:11; Ps. 110:3; Prov. 30:16; Is. 44:2

WOMEN 2 Sam. 1:26, Than the love of **w**
1 Kin. 11:1, loved many foreign **w**
Ezra 10:2, have married foreign **w**
Prov. 31:3, not your strength to **w**
Is. 4:1, seven **w** will take hold of one man
Matt. 24:41, Two **w** *will be* grinding
Mark 15:40, *some* **w** looking on from afar
Acts 17:4, and a number of the leading **w**
1 Tim. 2:9, **w** to adorn themselves in proper
4:7, fables fit only for old **w**
2 Tim. 3:6, weak **w** weighed down with sins
Titus 2:4, young **w** to love their husbands
1 Pet. 3:5, the holy **w** also
Gen. 31:35; Judg. 5:24; Song 1:8; Jer. 50:37

WON Matt. 18:15, you have **w** your brother

WONDER—*marvel, sign*
1 Chr. 16:9, Speak of all His **w-s**
Job 37:14, consider the **w-s** of God
Ps. 9:1, I will tell of all Thy **w-s**
72:18, Who alone works **w-s**
78:12, He wrought **w-s** before their fathers
Is. 9:6, name will be called **W-ful** Counselor
Joel 2:30, display **w-s** in the sky
Rom. 15:19, power of signs and **w-s**
2 Thess. 2:9, signs and false **w-s**
Deut. 4:34; Dan. 6:27

WONDROUS—*marvelous* Job 9:10, **w** works
Job 37:5, God thunders . . . **w-ly**
Ps. 17:7, **W-ly** show Thy lovingkindness
71:17, I still declare Thy **w** deeds
Joel 2:26, dealt **w-ly** with you

WOOD Gen. 6:14, an ark of gopher **w**
1 Cor. 3:12, stones, **w**, hay, straw
Rev. 18:12, *made* from very costly **w**
Deut. 19:5; 2 Kin. 2:24; 2 Chr. 27:4; Neh. 8:4; Job 41:27; Prov. 26:20; Jer. 7:18; Lam. 5:4; Ezek. 24:10

WOOL Ps. 147:16, He gives snow like **w**
Is. 1:18, They will be like **w**
Heb. 9:19, scarlet **w** and hyssop
Rev. 1:14, His hair . . . white like white **w**
Deut. 22:11; Judg. 6:37; Ezek. 44:17; Dan. 7:9

WORD—*edict, message, speech* Gen. 15:1
Gen. 11:1, same language . . . same **w-s**
Ps. 12:6, **w-s** of the Lord are pure **w-s**
19:3, There is no speech, nor are there **w-s**
19:14, Let the **w-s** of my mouth
Prov. 15:1, a harsh **w** stirs up anger
15:23, how delightful is a timely **w**
Is. 5:24, despised the **w** of the Holy One
29:11, **w-s** of a sealed book
Matt. 4:4, on every **w** that proceeds
6:7, for their many **w-s**
7:24, every one who hears these **w-s**
8:8, but just say the **w**
10:14, nor heed your **w-s**
12:36, every careless **w** that men . . . speak
Mark 4:14, The sower sows the **w**
4:18, ones who have heard the **w**
7:13, invalidating the **w** of God
Luke 1:2, eyewitnesses and servants of the **W**
John 1:1, the beginning was the **W**
1:14, the **W** became flesh
6:68, **w-s** of eternal life
8:51, if anyone keeps My **w**
Acts 2:41, received his **w** were baptized
6:7, **w** of God kept on spreading
Rom. 10:8, **W** IS NEAR YOU . . . **w** of faith
1 Cor. 1:17, kingdom of God . . . in **w-s**
1:18, the **w** of the cross is to those
2 Cor. 4:2, not . . . adulterating the **w** of God
Gal. 5:14, Law is fulfilled in one **w**
Eph. 4:29, Let no unwholesome **w** proceed . . . mouth
5:6, deceive you with empty **w-s**
Phil. 2:16, holding fast the **w** of life
Col. 3:16, Let the **w** of Christ . . . dwell within you
4:3, open up to us a door for the **w**
1 Thess. 1:5, gospel did not come . . . in **w** only
2 Thess. 2:17, in every good work and **w**
1 Tim. 4:5, sanctified by the **w** of God
2 Tim. 2:15, handling accurately the **w** of truth
Titus 1:9, holding fast the faithful **w**
Heb. 2:2, **w** spoken through angels
4:12, **w** of God is living
James 1:21, receive the **w** implanted
1:22, prove yourselves doers of the **w**
1 Pet. 1:23, living and abiding **w** of God
2 Pet. 1:19, prophetic **w** *made* more sure
1 John 1:1, concerning the **W** of life
Rev. 19:13, name is called The **W** of God
Gen. 30:34; Ex. 20:1; Lev. 10:7; Num. 30:2; Deut. 5:5; Josh. 24:26; Judg. 13:12; 1 Sam. 3:1; 2 Kin. 9:5; 18:36; 1 Chr. 21:19; 2 Chr. 6:17; Job 2:13; 6:25; 12:11; Ps. 49:13; 55:21; Eccles. 5:2; Jer. 5:13; Mal. 1:1

WORK—*deed, labor, toil*
Gen. 2:2, God completed His **w**
Ex. 20:9, Six days . . . do all your **w**
30:25, the **w** of a perfumer
Lev. 23:3, For six days **w** may be done
1 Sam. 14:45, he has **w-ed** with God this day
Neh. 4:6, the people had a mind to **w**
Ps. 19:1, declaring the **w** of His hands
62:12, a man according to his **w**
Prov. 16:3, Commit your **w-s** to the LORD

Eccles. 5:12, sleep of the **w-ing** man
7:13, Consider the **w** of God
10:12, LORD has completed all His **w**
Matt. 5:16, may see your good **w-s**
11:2, John . . . heard of the **w-s** of Christ
20:12, last men have **w-ed** *only* one hour
Mark 16:20, the Lord **w-ed** with them
Luke 5:5, we **w-ed** hard all night
13:14, six days in which **w** should be
John 5:17, **w-ing** until now, and I
6:27, Do not **w** for the food which
6:28, may **w** the **w-s** of God
9:4, **w** the **w-s** of Him who sent Me
Acts 18:3, they were **w-ing**
Rom. 2:15, show the **w** of the Law
3:20, by the **w-s** of the Law no flesh
3:28, justified by faith apart from **w-s** of the Law
8:28, all things to **w** together for good
16:12, who has **w-ed** hard in the Lord
1 Cor. 3:13, man's **w** will become evident
3:14, If any man's **w** . . . remains
4:12, **w-ing** with our own hands
2 Cor. 6:1, **w-ing** together *with Him*
Gal. 2:8, effectually **w-ed** for Peter
Eph. 2:9, not as a result of **w-s**
4:12, saints for the **w** of service
Phil. 2:12, **w** out your salvation
2:13, both to will and to **w**
Col. 1:10, bearing fruit in every good **w**
2 Thess. 3:8, labor and hardship we *kept* **w-ing**
3:10, If anyone will not **w**
1 Tim. 6:18, be rich in good **w-s**
2 Tim. 4:5, do the **w** of an evangelist
Heb. 6:1, repentance from dead **w-s**
James 2:18, show you my faith by my **w-s**
1 John 3:8, destroy the **w-s** of the devil
Deut. 4:28; 1 Sam. 14:6; 1 Chr. 23:4; 2 Chr. 15:7; Is. 5:19; Ezek. 46:1

WORKER Ps. 52:2, O **w** of deceit
Prov. 10:29, **w-s** of iniquity
Matt. 10:10, **w** is worthy of his support
1 Cor. 12:29, are not **w-s** of miracles
Phil. 3:2, beware of the evil **w-s**
Titus 2:5, sensible, pure, **w-s** at home

WORKMAN Eph. 2:10, For we are His **w-ship**
Ex. 38:23; 2 Kin. 22:5

WORLD—*age* 2 Sam. 22:16, foundations of **w**
2 Chr. 16:30, **w** is firmly established
Job 34:13, laid *on Him* the whole **w**
Ps. 17:14, From men of the **w**
Prov. 8:26, first dust of the **w**
Is. 14:21, fill . . . the **w** with cities
Matt. 5:14, You are the light of the **w**
13:38, the field is the **w**
Mark 10:30, **w** to come, eternal life
John 1:10, **w** was made through Him
3:16, God so loved the **w**
4:42, Savior of the **w**
6:33, gives light to the **w**
7:7, **w** cannot hate you
8:12, I am the light of the **w**
Acts 17:6, men who have upset the **w**
Rom. 5:12, sin entered into the **w**
1 Cor. 1:28, base things of the **w**
2:12, not the spirit of the **w**
2 Cor. 7:10, sorrow of the **w** produces death
1 Tim. 6:17, rich in this present **w**
James 1:27, unstained by the **w**
2 Pet. 2:5, did not spare the ancient **w**
1 John 2:15, Do not love the **w**
2:17, the **w** is passing away

WORLDLY—*profane* 1 Tim. 4:7, **w** fables fit only for old
2 Tim. 2:16, avoid **w** *and* empty chatter

WORM Ex. 16:20, it bred **w-s** and became foul
Job 7:5, My flesh is clothed with **w-s**
Ps. 22:6, But I am a **w**
Is. 14:11, And **w-s** are your covering
Mark 9:48, where THEIR **W** DOES NOT DIE
Acts 12:23, he was eaten by **w-s**
Job 24:20; Jon. 4:7

WORMWOOD
Deut. 29:18, poisonous fruit and **w**
Prov. 5:4, she is bitter as **w**
Jer. 23:15, feed them **w**
Amos 5:7, turn justice into **w**
Rev. 8:11, star is called **W**

WORN—*old* Deut. 29:5, sandal has not **w** out

WORRY Luke 8:14, choked with **w-es** and riches
Luke 10:41, you are **w-ed** and bothered
12:29, do not keep **w-ing**

WORSE Matt. 9:16, a **w** tear results
John 5:14, nothing **w** may befall you
1 Cor. 11:17, better but for the **w**
2 Tim. 3:13, proceed *from bad* to **w**

WORSHIP—*bow, serve*
Ex. 34:14, shall not **w** any other
Ps. 2:11, **W** the LORD with reverence
29:2, **W** the LORD in holy array
Matt. 2:2, and have come to **w** Him
2:8, come and **w** Him
2:11, fell down and **w-ed** Him
4:10, SHALL **W** THE LORD YOUR GOD
John 4:20, place where men ought to **w**
4:22, we **w** that which we know
Phil. 3:3, **w** in the Spirit of God
Heb. 9:6, performing the divine **w**
Rev. 4:10, **w** Him who lives forever
Gen. 22:5; Deut. 6:13; 2 Chr. 29:28

WORTH—*price* Prov. 31:10, her **w** is far above jewels

WORTHLESS—*ungodly* Prov. 16:27, A **w** man
Matt. 25:30, cast out the **w** slave
Gal. 4:9, **w** elemental things
Titus 1:16, **w** for any good deed
James 1:26, this man's religion is **w**
Judg. 9:4; Is. 5:2

WORTHY—*befit, deserving, fit*
1 Kin. 1:52, If he will be a **w** man
Matt. 10:10, worker is **w** of his support
10:11, enter, inquire who is **w** in it
10:13, if the house is **w**
10:37, who loves father more . . . not **w** of Me
Luke 10:7, laborer is **w** of his wages
Rom. 16:2, a manner **w** of the saints
Phil. 1:27, a manner **w** of the gospel
Eph. 4:1, manner **w** of the calling
1 Thess. 2:12, walk in a manner **w** of God
Heb. 11:38, the world was not **w**
Rev. 5:2, Who is **w** to open the book

WOUND—*bruise, pierce*
Luke 10:34, bandaged up his **w-s**
Acts 19:16, fled . . . naked and **w-ed**
1 Pet. 2:24, by His **w-s** you were healed
Gen. 4:23; Ex. 21:25; Deut. 32:39; Job 34:6; Ps. 147:3; Prov. 23:29; Jer. 30:12,17; Nah. 3:19; Mark 12:4

WRANGLE 2 Tim. 2:14, not to **w** about words

WRAPPED Matt. 27:59, **w** it in a clean linen
Mark 15:46, **w** Him in the linen sheet
Luke 2:7, she **w** Him in cloths
Gen. 38:14; 1 Kin. 19:13; Job 26:8; Is. 59:17; Ezek. 16:10; 21:15

WRAPPINGS—*cloth* John 11:44; 20:7

WRATH—*anger, indignation* Deut. 29:28
Ps. 6:1, Nor chasten me in Thy **w**
Matt. 3:7, flee from the **w** to come
John 3:36, **w** of God abides on him
Rom. 2:5, **w** for yourself in the day of **w**
3:5, God who inflicts **w** is not unrighteous
Eph. 2:3, by nature children of **w**
Col. 3:6, **w** of God will come
1 Thess. 5:9, has not destined us for **w**
Heb. 3:11, I swore in My **w**
Rev. 6:16, from the **w** of the Lamb
Ps. 37:8; 89:38; Is. 27:4; Jer. 4:4; 6:11; 30:23; Ezek. 5:13; 23:25; Mic. 5:15; Nah. 1:2

WREATH—*crown*
1 Cor. 9:25, to receive a perishable **w**
WRITE—*record* Ex. 17:14; Is. 8:1
Prov. 3:3, **w** them on the tablet of your heart
Mark 10:4, **w** a certificate of divorce
John 19:21, Do not **w**, The King of the Jews
Rom. 16:22, I, Tertius, who **w** this letter
Heb. 10:16, UPON THEIR MIND I WILL **W** THEM
2 John 12, **w** . . . not . . . with paper and ink
Rev. 14:13, **W**, Blessed are the dead
WRITING—*inscription, letter*
Eccles. 12:12, the **w** of many books is endless
John 5:47, if you do not believe his **w-s**
1 Tim. 3:14, I am **w** these things to you
2 Tim. 3:15, you have known the sacred **w-s**
Philem. 19, **w** this with my own hand
1 John 2:8, **w** a new commandment
2 John 5, **w** . . . a new commandment
Ex. 32:16; 1 Chr. 28:19; Dan. 10:21
WRITTEN Ex. 31:18, **w** by the finger of God
Job 19:23, that my words were **w**
Mal. 3:16, book of remembrance was **w**
Matt. 2:5, been **w** by the prophet
4:4, It is **w**, MAN SHALL NOT LIVE
4:6, for it is **w**, HE WILL GIVE
11:10, one about whom it was **w**
John 19:22, What I have **w** I have **w**
Acts 1:20, **w** in the book of Psalms
Rom. 2:15, Law **w** in their hearts
Rev. 13:8, not been **w** . . . in the book of life
17:5, forehead a name *was* **w**
WRONG—*defraud, wicked* Ex. 22:21, not **w** a stranger
Lev. 25:14, you shall not **w** one another
2 Sam. 24:17, I who have done **w**
Matt. 20:13, Friend, I am doing you no **w**
John 18:23, If I have spoken **w-ly**
Rom. 13:10, Love does no **w**
1 Cor. 6:7, Why not rather be **w-ed**
2 Cor. 7:2, we **w-ed** no one
Rev. 22:11, Let the one who does **w**, still do **w**
Gen. 16:5; 1 Chr. 12:17; Esth. 1:16
WRONGDOER—*unrighteous* Ps. 71:4, the **w** and
WROTE Ex. 24:4, Moses **w** down all the words
Jer. 36:18, **w** them with ink on the
Mark 12:19, Teacher, Moses **w**
Luke 1:63, he asked for a tablet and **w**
John 8:6, finger **w** on the ground
3 John 9, I **w** something to the church
WROUGHT—*accomplished* John 3:21, been **w** in

X, Y, Z

YEAR—*annual* Gen. 1:14, for seasons . . . **y-s**
Ps. 90:4, thousand **y-s** in Thy sight
90:9, finished our **y-s** like a sigh
Prov. 4:10, **y-s** of your life will be many
Is. 61:2, favorable **y** of the LORD
Luke 3:23, was about thirty **y-s** of age
Gal. 4:10, months and season and **y-s**
Rev. 9:15, day and month and **y**
Gen. 7:11; Ex. 13:10; Lev. 16:34; Num. 14:34; 2 Sam. 14:26; 1 Kin. 17:1; 2 Chr. 14:6; Job 10:5; Jer. 11:23; Joel 2:25; Matt. 2:16
YEARN—*faint* Ps. 84:2, longed and even **y-ed**
YESTERDAY Ex. 5:14, **y** or today in making brick
Job 8:9, For we are *only* of **y**
Ps. 90:4, in Thy sight Are like **y**
Acts 7:28, KILLED THE EGYPTIAN **Y**
Heb. 13:8, the same **y** and today
YET—*still* Ps. 37:10, **Y** a little while
John 2:4, My hour has not **y** come
Heb. 11:7, things not **y** seen
1 John 3:2, appeared as **y** what we shall be
Deut. 9:29; Jon. 3:4
YIELD—*bear, produce* Ps. 1:3, Which **y-s** its fruit in
Ps. 67:6, earth has **y-ed** its produce
Heb. 12:11, **y-s** the peaceful fruit
YIELDING—*bearing* Gen. 1:11,29; Mark 4:8
YOKE Matt. 11:29, Take My **y** upon you
Matt. 11:30, For My **y** is easy
Gal. 5:1, to a **y** of slavery
1 Tim. 6:1, under the **y** as slaves
Gen. 27:40; Lev. 26:13; Deut. 28:48; 1 Kin. 12:4; Is. 9:4; Jer. 27:2; Lam. 1:14
YOUNG Ps. 37:25, been **y**, and now I am old
Prov. 20:29, glory of **y** men is their
Eccles. 11:9, Rejoice, **y** man, during your
Is. 11:7, Their **y** will lie down together
Acts 2:17, **Y** MEN SHALL SEE VISIONS
Titus 2:4, **y** women to love . . . husbands
1 John 2:13, I am writing . . . **y** men
Deut. 32:11; Judg. 6:15; 1 Sam. 8:16; Job 19:18; Ezek. 17:4
YOUNGER Luke 15:13, **y** son gathered
John 21:18, when you were **y**
1 Tim. 5:11, refuse *to put* **y** widows
1 Pet. 5:5, You **y** men, likewise
Gen. 25:23; Judg. 15:2
YOUR—*Thine* Gen. 22:2, **y** son, **y** only son
Ex. 4:4, Stretch out **y** hand and grasp *it*
2 Chr. 20:15, battle is not **y-s** but God's
Luke 6:20, **y-s** is the kingdom of God
15:31, all that is mine is **y-s**
John 15:20, they will keep **y-s** also
2 Cor. 12:14, I do not seek what is **y-s**
Gen. 45:20; Josh. 2:14; 1 Kin. 20:4; Jer. 5:19
YOURSELVES
Matt. 6:19, Do not lay . . . **y** treasures
Mark 9:50, Have salt in **y**
Luke 12:33, make **y** purses
Rom. 6:13, present **y** to God
2 Cor. 13:5, recognize . . . **y**
1 John 5:21, guard **y** from idols
Jude 21, keep **y** in the love of God
Gen. 18:4; Lev. 11:44; Deut. 4:16; Josh. 24:22; 2 Chr. 29:31; Jer. 37:9
YOUTH—*childhood* Acts 26:4, life from my **y** up
1 Tim. 4:12, look down on your **y-fulness**
2 Tim. 2:22, flee from **y-ful** lusts
Gen. 8:21; Num. 30:16; Judg. 8:20; Job 33:25; Ps. 25:7; Prov. 5:18; Is. 40:30; Jer. 3:4; 31:19
ZEAL—*concern* 2 Kin. 10:16, see my **z** for the LORD
Ps. 119:139, My **z** has consumed me
John 2:17, **Z** FOR THY HOUSE WILL
Rom. 10:2, have a **z** for God
2 Cor. 7:7, your **z** for me
7:11, what longing, what **z**
Phil. 3:6, as to **z**
2 Sam. 21:2; Eccles. 9:6; Is. 26:11; 59:17
ZEALOUS—*eager* 1 Kin. 19:10, very **z** for the LORD
Acts 21:20, all **z** for the law
1 Cor. 14:12, **z** of spiritual *gifts*
Titus 2:14, **z** for good deeds
Rev. 3:19, be **z** therefore, and repent

TURNING SCRIPTURE INTO PRAYER

Many times you may wonder how you should pray. The Lord's Prayer found in Matthew 6 is a great outline to follow when you pray. In addition to this, you may discover as you read God's Word, certain passages that describe how we should live or act or even think.

At times like that it is often good to write out that Scripture in the form of a specific first-person prayer. One good example of that is found in the first chapter of James:

"James, a bond-servant of God and of the Lord Jesus Christ, to the twelve tribes who are dispersed abroad, greetings. Consider it all joy, my brethren, when you encounter various trials, knowing that the testing of your faith produces endurance. And let endurance have its perfect result, that you may be perfect and complete, lacking in nothing. But if any of you lacks wisdom, let him ask of God, who gives to all men generously and without reproach, and it will be given to him. But let him ask in faith without any doubting, for he one who doubts is like the surf of the sea driven and tossed by the wind. For let not that man expect that he will receive anything from the Lord, being a double-minded man, unstable in all his ways."

Now compare this first-person prayer to the above passage.

"Father, I thank You that James was Your servant as well as the servant of the Lord Jesus Christ. Thank You for using James to send greetings to the twelve dispersed tribes. Lord, I also want to be known as one of Your servants. Please help me to bring Your good news to other people. When I face trials of many kinds, help me consider it pure joy. Help me to realize in such times that the testing of my faith develops perseverance. Please help me to let perseverance finish its work so I may be mature and complete, not lacking anything. Dear Father, when I lack wisdom, remind me to ask You. Thank You that You give generously to me without finding fault. Please help me to believe and not doubt when I ask You for help and wisdom with my problems and decisions. I don't want to be like a wave of the sea, blown and tossed by the wind. I want to receive what I ask from You. I don't want to be a double-minded man who is unstable in all he does. In the name of Jesus. Amen."

Note how restating God's Word as a personal prayer brings its truths out of the ancient world right into our lives.

TOUGH QUESTIONS FACING THE 90'S GENERATION

The questions selected in this section cover a wide range of important topics, and much research was put into the listing of Bible references given. However, due to limited space considerations only two or three verses per question were actually quoted in full.

The other references shown are listed in a specially arranged order to convey a flow of thought that will help you better understand the answer to the question.

- QUESTIONS ABOUT SEX -

What about sex before marriage—if we're really in love?

1 Corinthians 7:8-9. But I say to the unmarried and to widows that it is good for them if they remain even as I. But if they do not have self-control, let them marry; for it is better to marry than to burn.

1 Corinthians 7:1-2; 1 Timothy 5:22; Hebrews 13:4; 1 Corinthians 13:4-5.

How far is too far?

1 Corinthians 6:18-20. Flee immorality. Every other sin that a man commits is outside the body, but the immoral man sins against his own body. Or do you not know that your body is a temple of the Holy Spirit who is in you, whom you have from God, and that you are not your own? For you have been bought with a price: therefore glorify God in your body.

1 Thessalonians 4:3-5. For this is the will of God, your sanctification; that is, that you abstain from sexual immorality; that each of you know how to possess his own vessel in sanctification and honor, not in lustful passion, like the Gentiles who do not know God.

Romans 13:14; 1 Corinthians 6:18; 1 Corinthians 6:13; Ephesians 5:3; Galatians 5:24; Colossians 3:5-6; Proverbs 6:23-29.

I've gone too far—what should I do?

Revelation 3:19. Those whom I love I reprove and discipline; be zealous therefore and repent.

1 John 1:9. If we confess our sins He is faithful and righteous to forgive us our sins and to cleanse us from all unrighteousness.

Ezekiel 33:11; 2 Chronicles 7:14; Psalm 32:5; Psalm 38:18; Psalm 51:2; Psalm 32:1.

How do I overcome sexual temptations?

Colossians 3:1-3. If then you have been raised up with Christ, keep seeking the things above, where Christ is, seated at the right hand of God. Set your mind on the things above, not on the things that are on earth. For you have died and your life is hidden with Christ in God.

Galatians 5:16; Matthew 26:41; 1 Corinthians 10:12-13; 1 Corinthians 7:1-2; 1 Corinthians 6:18; Romans 13:12; Ephesians 5:8; Romans 13:14; Galatians 5:24; James 1:13-15; James 4:7-8; 2 Peter 2:9; Hebrews 4:14-16; Proverbs 7:4-5; Proverbs 6:23-24; Proverbs 7:25-27; 1 John 2:17; Philippians 4:8; Genesis 39:1-21.

Is there anything wrong with just looking?

1 John 2:16. For all that is in the world, the lust of the flesh and the lust of the eyes and the boastful pride of life, is not from the Father, but is from the world.

Matthew 5:27-28. "You have heard that it was said, 'YOU SHALL NOT COMMIT ADULTERY'; but I say to you, that everyone who looks on a woman to lust for her has committed adultery with her already in his heart.

Job 31:1; Job 31:4; Matthew 15:19-20; 1 Thessalonians 4:7; 1 Corinthians 6:20; Ephesians 5:1-3; Ephesians 5:5-6; 2 Peter 2:14; James 4:4; Proverbs 5:20-21; Proverbs 6:25-26.

If sex isn't love, what is?

1 Corinthians 13:4-8. Love is patient, love is kind, and is not jealous; love does not brag and is not arrogant, does not act unbecomingly; it does not seek its own, is not provoked, does not take into account a wrong suffered, does not rejoice in unrighteousness, but rejoices with the truth; bears all things, believes all things, hopes all things, endures all things. Love never fails.

1 John 5:3; John 14:21; 1 John 3:18; John 15:13; 1 John 3:16; 1 John 4:10; 1 John 4:11; 1 John 4:12; Matthew 22:37, 39; Psalm 97:10; Luke 6:27; Luke 6:32-38; 1 John 4:20; Hebrews 13:1; Proverbs 10:12; Romans 12:9-10; Romans 13:8; 1 Corinthians 8:1; 1 Corinthians 13:13; 1 Corinthians 14:1; Colossians 3:14; 1 Timothy 1:5; 1 Peter 4:8.

Is the homosexual lifestyle offensive to God?

Jude 1:7-8. Just as Sodom and Gomorrah and the cities around them, since they in the same way as these indulged in gross immorality and went after strange flesh, are exhibited as an example, in undergoing the punishment of eternal fire. Yet in the same matter these men, also by dreaming, defile the flesh, and reject authority, and revile angelic majesties.

Leviticus 18:22; Leviticus 20:13; Deuteronomy 23:17-18.

Does God hate homosexuals?

Romans 5:8. But God demonstrates His own love toward us, in that while we were yet sinners, Christ died for us.

Leviticus 18:22; John 3:16-17; 1 Corinthians 6:9-10; 1 Corinthians 6:11.

I've been sexually abused—can God heal my hurt?

Psalm 34:18. The Lord is near to the broken hearted, and saves those who are crushed in spirit.

Psalm 147:3. He heals the brokenhearted and binds up their wounds.

Isaiah 49:15-16; Luke 4:18; Isaiah 61:1; Psalm 27:10; Deuteronomy 4:31; Psalm 94:14; Hebrews 13:5; Matthew 28:20; Psalm 43:5; Isaiah 51:11-12; 2 Corinthians 1:4; Psalm 9:10; Isaiah 43:2; Romans 8:38-39; Psalm 119:50; Isaiah 41:10.

I am being sexually abused—what can I do?

Psalm 18:6. In my distress I called upon the Lord, and cried to my God for help; He heard my voice out of His temple, and my cry for help before Him came to His ears.

Psalm 46:1. God is our refuge and strength, a very present help in trouble.

Psalm 124:8; Psalm 18:10; Psalm 61:2; Psalm 27:7; Psalm 34:17; Psalm 56:9; Colossians 3:25; Psalm 72:4; Psalm 10:18; Psalm 40:17; Psalm 38:22; Psalm 17:7-9; Psalm 22:19; Isaiah 50:7.

I got my girlfriend pregnant—what should I do?

Proverbs 28:13. He who conceals his transgressions will not prosper, but he who confesses and forsakes them will find compassion

Acts 26:20; Revelation 3:17-19; Psalm 69:5; Psalm 90:8; Numbers 32:23; Psalm 25:7; Psalm 25:18; Psalm 51:9; Psalm 86:15; Psalm 61:2; Psalm 31:3; Psalm 73:24; Psalm 33:11; Proverbs 11:14; Proverbs 12:15; Proverbs 19:21; Deuteronomy 6:18; 1 Corinthians 13:7-8.

My boyfriend got me pregnant—is abortion ok?

Psalm 139: 13-19. For thou didst form my inward parts; Thou didst weave me in my mother's womb. I will give thanks to Thee, for I am fearfully and wonderfully made; Wonderful are thy works, and my soul knows it very well. My frame was not hidden from Thee, when I was made in secret, and skillfully wrought in the depths of the earth. Thine eyes have seen my unformed substance; and in thy book they were all written, the days that were ordained for me, when as yet there was not one of them. How precious also are thy thoughts to me O God! How vast is the sum of them! If I should count them, they would outnumber the sand. When I awake I am still with Thee. O that Thou wouldst slay the wicked, O God; Depart from me, therefore, men of bloodshed.

Job 31:15; Deuteronomy 32:18; Isaiah 43:7; Ecclesiastes 11:5; Proverbs 16:25; Exodus 20:13; Hebrews 12:1-4; James 4:17; Psalm 10:4-8; Isaiah 49:1; John 10:10.

I've had an abortion—can God still love me?

1 John 1:9-10. If we confess our sins, he is faithful and righteous to forgive us our sins and to cleanse us from all unrighteousness. If we say that we have not sinned, we make Him a liar and His word is not in us.

Psalm 51:14; Psalm 51:9-13; Psalm 86:15; Psalm 103:8; Ephesians 1:7; Psalm 130:4; James 5:16; Psalm 51:16-17; John 3:16-17; Ephesians 3:19; Romans 5:8; 1 Corinthians 2:9; John 14:23; John 15:10.

- QUESTIONS ABOUT DRUGS AND ALCOHOL -

Is there anything wrong with drinking?

Proverbs 20:1. Wine is a mocker, strong drink a brawler, and whoever is intoxicated by it is not wise.

Romans 13:13. Let us behave properly as in the day, not in carousing and drunkenness, not in sexual promiscuity and sensuality, not in strife and jealousy.

Isaiah 5:11; Isaiah 5:22; Proverbs 23:21; Ephesians 5:18-20; Proverbs 23:29-35; Luke 21:34; Galatians 5:19-21; Romans 14:21.

If I'm not hurting anyone, does it matter if I take drugs?

1 Corinthians 6:19-20. Or do you not know that your body is the

temple of the Holy Spirit who is in you, whom you have from God, and that you are not your own? For you have been bought with a price: therefore glorify God in your body.

Ephesians 5:17-20; 1 Peter 2:12; Matthew 5:16; 1 Corinthians 7:23; James 1:22; Numbers 32:23; Proverbs 23:21; 1 Corinthians 6:9-10; Luke 21:34; Ecclesiastes 12:1; 2 Corinthians 13:5; Romans 13:13-14.

I'm hooked on drugs and alcohol—can God help me?

1 Corinthians 10:13. No temptation has overtaken you but such as is common to man; and God is faithful, who will not allow you to be tempted beyond what you are able, but with the temptation will provide the way of escape also, that you may be able to endure it.

Colossians 1:9-11; Psalm 72:12; Isaiah 50:2; 2 Peter 2:9; John 8:31-32; John 8:34; John 8:36; Romans 6:17-19; Galatians 5:1; Galatians 5:25; Galatians 5:16; James 4:10; James 4:6; James 4:7; 1 Peter 5:8-9; Psalm 124:8; Psalm 121:2; Psalm 119:9.

I'm a druggie—will God forgive me?

Daniel 9:9. To the Lord our God belong compassion and forgiveness, for we have rebelled against Him.

Psalm 130:4. But there is forgiveness with Thee, That Thou mayest be feared.

Psalm 86:5. For Thou, Lord, art good, and ready to forgive, and abundant in lovingkindness to all who call upon Thee.

Psalm 119:9; Psalm 103:2-5; Acts 26:18; Ephesians 1:7; 1 John 1:9; 2 Chronicles 7:14; Psalm 32:5; Psalm 32:1-2.

I'm an alcoholic—is there any hope for me?

Hebrews 4:14-16. Since then we have a great high priest who has passed through the heavens, Jesus the Son of God, let us hold fast our confession. For we do not have a high priest who cannot sympathize with our weaknesses, but one who has been tempted in all things as we are, yet without sin. Let us therefore draw near with confidence to the throne of grace, that we may receive mercy and may find grace to help in the time of need.

Psalm 31:24; Psalm 33:18; Psalm 119:116; Philippians 4:13; Romans 12:21; 2 Peter 2:19; Galatians 5:16; Galatians 6:8; 1 Corinthians 10:13; 2 Peter 2:9; James 1:12; Mark 14:38; James 4:7; Romans 8:37; Micah 7:8; Proverbs 24:16; Romans 15:13; Psalm 54:4; Psalm 72:12.

Is there anything wrong with smoking?

1 Corinthians 9:27. But I buffet my body and make it my slave, lest possibly, after I have preached to others, I myself should be disqualified.

3 John 1:2. Beloved I pray that in all respects you may prosper and be in good health, just as your soul prospers.

1 Corinthians 6:19-20; 1 Corinthians 7:23; 1 Timothy 4:8; Romans 6:12-13.

- QUESTIONS ABOUT MUSIC -

Does God like music?

Psalm 95:2. Let us come before his presence with thanksgiving; Let us shout joyfully to Him with psalms.

Jeremiah 31:7. For thus says the Lord, Sing aloud with gladness for Jacob, and shout among the chiefs of the nations; Proclaim, give praise, and say, O Lord, save thy people, the remnant of Israel.

Psalms 147:1. Praise the Lord! For it is good to sing praises to our God; For it is pleasant and praise is becoming.

Psalm 92:1-3; Psalm 150:6; Proverbs 29:6; Isaiah 12:5; Isaiah 52:9; Psalm 33:3; Psalm 9:11; Psalm 21:13; Psalm 30:4; Psalm 66:2; James 5:13; Psalm 100:2; Zephaniah 3:17; 1 Corinthians 14:15; Ephesians 5:19; Colossians 3:16; 1 Chronicles 16:9; Proverbs 17:22; Proverbs 15:15.

What kind of music does God like?

Psalm 98:4-5. Shout joyfully to the Lord all the earth; Break forth and sing for joy and sing praises. Sing praises to the Lord with the lyre; With the lyre and the sound of melody.

Psalm 95:2. Let us come before His presence with thanksgiving; Let us shout joyfully to Him with psalms.

Psalm 33:3; Psalm 22:3; 2 Chronicles 5:13-14; Ephesians 5:19; Zephaniah 3:17; Psalm 150:1-3, 5-6.

Does it matter what kind of music I listen to?

1 Corinthians 10:23. All things are lawful, but not all things are profitable. All things are lawful, but not all things edify.

1 Corinthians 6:20. For you have been bought with a price, therefore glorify God in your body.

Psalm 95:1-2; Psalm 98:1; Psalm 147:1; Colossians 1:10;

Romans 14:19; 1 Thessalonians 5:11; Matthew 5:16; Psalm 86:12; Romans 15:6; Romans 8:8.

- QUESTIONS ON MY MIND -

What happens when I die?

Romans 2:5-8. But because of your stubbornness and unrepentant heart you are storing up wrath for yourself in the day of wrath and revelation of the righteous judgement of God, who will render to every man according to his deeds: to those who by perseverance in doing good seek for glory and honor and immortality, eternal life; but to those who are selfishly ambitious and do not obey the truth, but obey unrighteousness, wrath and indignation.

Hebrews 9:27; John 5:28-29; Romans 2:11; Romans 6:23; Matthew 25:31-46; Titus 1:2.

Is there really life after death?

John 11:25. Jesus said to her, "I am the resurrection and the life; he who believes in Me shall live even if He dies."

John 5:24. "Truly, Truly, I say to you, he who hears My word, and believes Him who sent Me, has eternal life, and does not come into judgement, but has passed out of death into life."

1 Corinthians 15:12-14, 16-20, 22, 51-52; John 3:16; 1 Corinthians 6:12.

Is suicide really a solution?

Psalm 90:12. So teach us to number our days, that we may present to Thee a heart of wisdom.

Exodus 20:13. You shall not murder.

Isaiah 38:18. "For Sheol cannot thank Thee, Death cannot praise Thee; Those who go down to the pit cannot hope for Thy faithfulness."

Psalm 6:5; Isaiah 38:19; Ecclesiastes 9:4-6, 10.

I don't want to live anymore—can God help me?

2 Corinthians 1:3-4. Blessed be the God and Father of our Lord Jesus Christ, the Father of mercies and God of all comfort; who comforts us in all our affliction so that we may be able to comfort those who are in any affliction with the comfort with which we ourselves are comforted by God.

Psalm 119:49-50; Proverbs 4:23; Proverbs 8:35; Psalm 36:9;

Psalm 103:4; Psalm 16:11; Psalm 94:14; Deuteronomy 4:31; Isaiah 41:10, Psalm 30:5; Psalm 27:14; 1 Peter 4:12; 2 Corinthians 4:17; 1 Thessalonians 5:18; Micah 7:8; 1 John 4:4; Philippians 4:13; Hebrews 13:5; Matthew 28:20; Acts 14:22; James 1:3-4.

Nobody loves me—why should I go on living?

Jeremiah 29: 11-13. For I know the plans that I have for you, declares the Lord, 'plans for welfare and not for calamity to give you a future and a hope. Then you will call upon Me and come and pray to Me, and I will listen to you. And you will seek Me and find Me, when you search for me with all your heart.

Isaiah 49:15-16; Ephesians 5:17; Ephesians 1:18; 2 Peter 1:10; 2 Timothy 1:9; Romans 8:29; Proverbs 3:5-6, Psalm 37:4-5; Psalm 37:7-10; Romans 8:31-32; Philippians 3:13-14.

Does it matter what kind of language I use?

Matthew 12:36-37. And I say to you, that every careless word that men shall speak, they shall render account for it in the day of judgement. For by words you shall be justified, and by your words you shall be condemned.

Proverbs 15:1. A gentle answer turns away wrath, but a harsh word stirs up anger.

Psalm 34:13; Psalm 139:4; James 3:2, 5-12. Psalm 19:14; Luke 6:45; Proverbs 18:8,21; Proverbs 6:2; Ecclesiastes 5:2-3; Proverbs 17:27; Proverbs 10:19; Ecclesiastes 10:12-13; Proverbs 15:26; Ephesians 4:15,31; Ephesians 5:4; Hebrews 10:23; Joel 3:10.

Is it okay to be rich?

3 John 1:2. Beloved, I pray that in all respects you may prosper and be in good health, just as your soul prospers.

Psalm 62:10. Do not trust in oppression, and do not vainly hope in robbery; If riches increase, do not set your heart upon them.

1 Timothy 6:7-11; Proverbs 22:4; Proverbs 27:24; Proverbs 11:28; Proverbs 23:4; Ecclesiastes 5:12; Proverbs 28:20, 22; Proverbs 11:16; Proverbs 21:5; Proverbs 10:4; Proverbs 13:22; Ecclesiastes 2:26; Joshua 1:8; Psalm 35:27; Jeremiah 9:23-24; Matthew 6:9-21; Matthew 6:24; Proverbs 23:5; Mark 10:24; 1 Samuel 2:7.

Does it matter what clothes we wear?

Luke 12:23. For life is more than food, and the body than clothing.

1 Timothy 6:8. And if we have food and covering, with these we shall be content.

John 7:24. Do not judge according to appearance, but judge with righteous judgement.

Matthew 6:25, 28-29, 30-33. Deuteronomy 22:5; 1 Timothy 2:9-10; 1 Peter 3:3-4.

Does everyone go to heaven when they die?

John 3:5. Jesus answered, "Truly, truly, I say to you, unless one is born of water and the Spirit, he cannot enter into the kingdom of God."

John 5:24. "Truly, truly, I say to you, he who hears My word, and believes Him who sent Me, has eternal life, and does not come into judgement, but has passed out of death into life."

Revelation 2:7; Revelation 3:5; Revelation 20: 12-15; Matthew 7:21; Matthew 18:3; John 3:5; John 5:24, 28-29.

Does God have a plan for my life?

2 Timothy 1:9. Who has saved us, and called us with a holy calling, not according to our works, but according to His own purpose and grace which was granted us in Christ Jesus from all eternity.

Ephesians 5:17; Ephesians 1:18; 2 Peter 1:10; Romans 11:29; 1 Corinthians 7:20; Acts 17:30; Luke 18:1; Romans 12:1-2; Micah 6:8; Deuteronomy 10:12-13; Proverbs 11:23; Proverbs 10:24; Psalm 145:19; Psalm 37:4; Jeremiah 29:11-13; Matthew 6:33; Proverbs 3:6; Proverbs 16:3; Ecclesiastes 3:1; Proverbs 20:18; Ephesians 5:15-16.

Am I supposed to obey the law?

Proverbs 28:7. He who keeps the law is a discerning son, But he who is a companion of gluttons humiliates his father.

1 Peter 2:12. Keep your behavior excellent among the Gentiles, so that in the thing in which they slander you as evildoers, they may on account of your good deeds, as they observe them, glorify God in the day of visitation.

Romans 13:1-7; 1 Peter 2:13-17; Exodus 1:15-21; Daniel 3:3-28; Acts 5:28-29.

How do I improve my thought life?

Philippians 4:8. Finally, brethren, whatever is true, whatever is honorable, whatever is right, whatever is pure, whatever is lovely, whatever is of good repute, if there is any excellence and if anything worthy of praise, let your mind dwell on these things.

Romans 12:2; 2 Corinthians 10:3-5; 1 Corinthians 13:11; 1 Corinthians 2:16; Ephesians 4:23; Philippians 2:5-8; Matthew 6:32-33; Luke 6:45; Mark 7:21-23; Psalm 51:10; Joshua 1:8; Psalm 143:5; Psalm 77:12; Psalm 19:14.

Will God help me choose my career?

Psalm 37:4-5. Delight yourself in the Lord; And He will give you the desires of your heart. Commit your way to the Lord, trust also in Him, and He will do it.

Philippians 3:14. I press toward the goal for the prize of the upward call of God in Christ Jesus.

James 1:5-7; Isaiah 48:17; Isaiah 58:11; Romans 8:26-27; John 16:13; Proverbs 3:5-7; Psalm 119:105; Psalm 32:8; Isaiah 30:21; Psalm 37:23-24; Psalm 145:19; Proverbs 20:18; Nehemiah 9:20.

Is an occasional lie any big deal?

Proverbs 6:16-19. There are six things which the Lord hates, Yes, seven which are an abomination to Him: Haughty eyes, a lying tongue, and hands that shed innocent blood, a heart that devises wicked plans, Feet that run rapidly to evil, A false witness who utters lies, and one who spreads strife among brothers.

Proverbs 13:5; Proverbs 12:22; Ephesians 4:25; Colossians 3:9; Psalm 31:18; Psalm 101:7; Proverbs 19:9; Revelation 21:8; Romans 12:17; 2 Corinthians 8:21; 1 Thessalonians 4:12.

- QUESTIONS ON MY HEART -

How can I get free from guilt?

Psalm 86:5. For thou, Lord, art good, and ready to forgive, and abundant in lovingkindness to all who call upon Thee.

Romans 2:4. Or do you think lightly of the riches of His kindness and forbearance and patience, not knowing that the kindness of God leads you to repentance?

Acts 17:30; Acts 26:20; Acts 2:38; Revelation 3:19; Revelation 2:5; 1 John 1:9; 2 Corinthians 7:10; Acts 3:19; John 8:31-32, 36; Romans 6:18, 22; Romans 8:2; Galatians 5:1.

How can I stop being depressed?

Psalm 42:11. Why are you in despair, O my soul? And why have you become disturbed within me? Hope in God, for I shall yet praise Him, the help of my countenance, and my God.

James 1:2-4. Consider it all joy, my brethren, when you encounter various trials, knowing that the testing of your faith produces endurance.

Psalm 42:6; Psalm 40:17, Psalm 147:3; Philippians 1:6; John 14:1, 27; Philippians 2:13; Psalm 5:11, Psalm 16:11; Ecclesiastes 11:10; Psalm 30:5; Psalm 126:5; 1 Thessalonians 5:18; 2 Corinthians 4:17; Philippians 4:4; 2 Corinthians 1:3-4; Isaiah 52:9; Isaiah 61:3; Habakkuk 3:17-18; Psalm 32:11; Nehemiah 8:10; Philippians 4:8.

Sometimes I am so afraid—how can I conquer fear?

Joshua 1:9. Have I not commanded you? Be strong and courageous! Do not tremble or be dismayed, for the Lord your God is with you wherever you go.

Psalms 27:5. For in the day of trouble He will conceal me in His tabernacle; In the secret place of His tent He will hide me; He will lift me up on a rock.

John 14:27; Psalm 27:3; Isaiah 43:2; Hebrews 10:35; Isaiah 51:7; Matthew 10:28; Psalm 3:6; 2 Kings 19:6; Hebrews 13:6; Luke 12:32; Psalm 46:1-3; Isaiah 41:10; Isaiah 43:1; Isaiah 35:4; Deuteronomy 31:8; Deuteronomy 20:3-4; Philippians 4:13; Philippians 1:6; Psalm 112:7; Romans 8:15; 2 Timothy 1:7; 1 John 4:18.

I get so angry I want to scream—what can I do?

Ephesians 4:31-32. Let all bitterness and wrath and anger and clamor and slander be put away from you, along with all malice. And be kind one to another, tender-hearted, forgiving each other, just as God in Christ also has forgiven you.

Ephesians 4:26. Be angry and yet do not sin; do not let the sun go down on your anger.

Romans 12:19-21; Proverbs 25:22; James 1:19-20; Proverbs 14:29; Proverbs 12:16; Proverbs 15:1; Ecclesiastes 7:9; Colossians 3:8; Proverbs 14:17; Proverbs 29:22; Psalm 37:8; Proverbs 16:32; Proverbs 19:11, 19; Proverbs 19:19; Matthew 5:22; Mark 11:25-26; Proverbs 22:4; Proverbs 27:4.

Things aren't going right—how do I stay patient?

Isaiah 40:31. Yet those who wait for the Lord will gain new strength; They will mount up with wings like eagles, they will run and not get tired, They will walk and not become weary.

Ecclesiastes 7:8. The end of a matter is better than its beginning; Patience of spirit is better than haughtiness of spirit.

Psalm 37:7, 34; Psalm 27:14; Romans 12:12; Romans 5:3-5; Romans 15:4; Hebrews 6:12; 2 Peter 1:5-8, 10-11; Hebrews 10:36; 1 Timothy 6:11; 1 Thessalonians 5:14; James 1:3-4; James 5:8.

I feel so lonely—can God help me?

Hebrews 10:25. Not forsaking our own assembling together, as is the habit of some, but encouraging one another; and all the more, as you see the day drawing near.

Hebrews 13:5. Let your character be free from the love of money, being content with what you have; for He Himself has said," I will never leave you or forsake you."

Romans 12:10; Colossians 3:16; Ephesians 3:17, 19; John 14:16-23; John 15:4-5; Amos 5:14; 2 Chronicles 13:12; Revelation 3:20; Psalm 140:13; 1 John 4:12, 15-16; Ecclesiastes 11:10; John 14:1; Philippians 2:13; Nehemiah 8:10; 1 Corinthians 2:9.

I am afraid of failing—does God promise success?

Deuteronomy 8:18. But you shall remember the Lord your God, for it He who is giving you power to make wealth, that He may confirm His covenant which He swore to your fathers, as it is this day.

Micah 7:8. Do not rejoice over me, O my enemy. Though I fall I will rise; Though I dwell in darkness, the Lord is light for me.

Luke 1:37; Hebrews 13:5; John 14:27; 2 Corinthians 13:11; Joshua 1:7-8; 1 John 5:4; Deuteronomy 31:6; Isaiah 41:13-14; Matthew 28:20; Romans 8:37; Philippians 4:13; Proverbs 24:16; Habakkuk 3:17-19.

I am insecure with low self esteem—can I change?

1 John 3:20-21. In whatever our heart condemns us; for God is greater than our heart, and knows all things. Beloved, if our heart does not condemn us, we have confidence before God.

Proverbs 3:26. For the Lord will be your confidence, and will keep your foot from being caught.

Romans 8:37; Psalm 145:19; Ephesians 3:11-12; Hebrews 10:19, 22-23; Hebrews 4:16; Proverbs 14:26; 1 John 5:14-15; Philippians 3:13-14; Romans 8:29; Romans 12:1-2; Psalm 37:4; 1 Thessalonians 5:24; Zechariah 4:6; John 14:12-13; Isaiah 43:2; 1 John 4:4; John 5:19; John 15:5; Psalm 18:29; Philippians 4:13; Psalm 116:8; Psalm 40:2; 1 Corinthians 2:9.

How do you handle big disappointments in life?

1 Thessalonians 5:17-19. Pray without ceasing; in everything give thanks; for this is God's will for you in Christ Jesus. Do not quench the Spirit;

Psalm 23:4. Even though I walk through the valley of the shadow of death, I fear no evil; for Thou art with me; Thy rod and Thy staff, they comfort me.

2 Corinthians 9:8; Galatians 6:9; Psalm 33:18; Psalm 147:11; Philippians 1:6; Psalm 138:7; Psalm 37:23-24; Psalm 145:14; Proverbs 24:16; 1 Peter 4:12-13; 1 Peter 1:7; 2 Corinthians 4:8-9; Hebrews 10:35-36; Philippians 4:4; 1 Thessalonians 5:16; Isaiah 41:10; Deuteronomy 31:8; Job 17:9; Habakkuk 3:17.

I'm so worried all the time—can I have peace?

Philippians 4:6-7. Be anxious for nothing, but in everything by prayer and supplication with thanksgiving let your requests be made known to God. And the peace of God, which surpasses all comprehension, shall guard your hearts and your minds in Christ Jesus.

Romans 5:1. Therefore having been justified by faith, we have peace with God through our Lord Jesus Christ.

1 Thessalonians 5:16-18; Romans 8:6; Romans 14:17, 19; Isaiah 26:3; John 14:1-3, 27; Psalm 4:8; Psalm 91:1, 3-10; Joshua 1:9; 1 Corinthians 7:15; Colossians 3:15; Psalm 34:14; Psalm 29:11; Psalm 119:165; 2 Thessalonians 3:16.

How do I get wisdom?

James 1:5-8. But if any of you lacks wisdom, let him ask of God, who gives to all men generously and without reproach, and it will be given to him. But let him ask in faith without any doubting, for the one who doubts is like the surf of the sea driven and tossed by the wind. For let not that man expect that he will receive anything from the Lord, being a double minded man, unstable in all his ways.

Hebrews 11:6; Proverbs 4:6-8; Proverbs 9:9-10; Psalm 111:10;

Psalm 90:12; Proverbs 13:20; Proverbs 29:15; Proverbs 19:20; Ecclesiastes 7:12; Proverbs 2:2; Proverbs 16:16; James 3:17; Colossians 1:9; Colossians 2:3; Matthew 7:7-8.

- QUESTIONS ABOUT DATING -

Should a Christian date an unbeliever?

2 Corinthians 6:14-17. Do not be bound together with unbelievers; for what partnership have righteousness with lawlessness, or what fellowship has light with darkness? Or what harmony has Christ with Belial, or what has a believer in common with an unbeliever? Or what agreement has the temple of God with idols? For we are the temple of the living God; just as God said, "I will dwell in them and walk among them; and I will be their God, and they shall be my people. Therefore, come out from their midst and be separate," says the Lord.

Amos 3:3; 1 Corinthians 1:10; 1 John 1:3, 6-7; Ephesians 5:11; James 4:4.

Nobody seems to like me—what should I do?

Proverbs 18:24. A man of many friends comes to ruin, but there is a friend who sticks closer than a brother.

Romans 12:14-16. Bless those who persecute you; bless and curse not. Rejoice with those who rejoice, and weep with those who weep. Be of the same mind toward one another; do not be haughty in mind, but associate with the lowly. Do not be wise in your own estimation.

Proverbs 17:17; Romans 12:9-10, 21; Matthew 5:44-45; Hebrews 13:1; 1 John 3:16; 1 John 4:7; Romans 8:38-39.

What is real love?

1 John 4:10. In this is love, not that we loved God, but that He loved us and sent His Son to be the propitiation for our sins.

1 John 15:13. Greater love hath no man than this, that one lay down his life for his friends.

1 Corinthians 8:1; 1 Corinthians 13:2, 4-13; Romans 12:9; Romans 13:10; Colossians 3:14; 1 Peter 4:8; 1 Peter 1:22; 1 John 4:7-8, 18, 21; 1 John 3:17-18; 1 John 5:3; Galatians 5:13.

How do I overcome rejection?

Psalm 30:5. For His anger is but for a moment, His favor is for a lifetime; Weeping may last for the night, but a shout of joy comes in the morning.

Psalm 126:5. Those who sow in tears shall reap with joyful shouting.

Mark 12:10, Romans 12:21; Luke 6:21; Isaiah 61:3; Proverbs 12:25; Psalm 119:28, 52, 162; Isaiah 51:3, 12; Isaiah 49:15-16; Psalm 40:17; Psalm 43:5; Psalm 16:11; Ecclesiastes 11:10; Luke 10:20; Psalm 5:11; Nehemiah 8:10; James 1:9; Philippians 1:6.

- QUESTIONS ABOUT FAMILY LIFE -

What does the Bible say about divorce?

Malachi 2:13-16. And this is another thing you do: you cover the altar of the Lord with tears, with weeping and with groaning, because he no longer regards the offering or accepts it with favor from your hand. "Yet you say, 'For what reason?' Because the Lord has been a witness between you and the wife of your youth, against whom you have dealt treacherously, though she is your companion and your wife by covenant. "For I hate divorce," says the Lord, the God of Israel, "and him who covers his garment with wrong," says the Lord of hosts. "So take heed to your spirit, that you do not deal treacherously." You have wearied the Lord with your words. Yet you say, "How have I wearied Him?" In that you say "Everyone who does evil is good in the sight of the Lord and He delights in them," or, "Where is the God of justice?"

Deuteronomy 24:1-4; Matthew 5:28, 31-32; Mark 10:6,8; Matthew19:5-6, 8; 1 Corinthians 7:10, 12-28.

My parents aren't Christians—do I still have to obey them?

Acts 5:29. But Peter and the apostles answered and said, "We must obey God rather than man."

Deuteronomy 5:16. Honor your father and your mother, as the Lord your God has commanded you, that your days may be prolonged, and that it may go well with you on the land which the Lord your God gives you.

Colossians 3:23. Whatever you do, do your work heartily, as for the Lord rather than for men;

Ephesians 6:1-3; Colossians 3:20-21; Proverbs 30:17; 1 Timothy 5:4.

- QUESTIONS ABOUT MY FRIENDS -

Does it really matter what kind of friends I choose?

Proverbs 13:20. He who walks with wise men will be wise, but the companion of fools will suffer harm.

Psalm 1:1. How blessed is the man who does not walk in the counsel of the wicked, nor stand in the path of sinners, nor sit in the seat of scoffers.

Proverbs 1:10-19; Ephesians 5:8, 10-12, 15; 2 Corinthians 6:14; 1 John 1:7; 2 Timothy 3:1-5; 1 Corinthians 5:11; James 4:4.

What do I do when my friends want me to do something wrong?

Ephesians 5:11-12. And do not participate in the unfruitful deeds of darkness, but instead even expose them; for it is disgraceful even to speak of the things which are done by them in secret.

Psalm 1:6. For the Lord knows the way of the righteous, but the way of the wicked will perish.

1 Peter 4:15-16; James 4:7; 1 Peter 5:8-9; Ephesians 6:11-12; Psalm 26:11; Colossians 3:2-3; 1 John 2:15-17; Proverbs 24:1-2; Proverbs 23:17-18.

How do I deal with enemies?

Luke 6:27-35. "But I say to you who hear, love your enemies, do good to those who hate you, bless those who curse you, pray for those who mistreat you. Whoever hits you on the cheek, offer him the other also; and whoever takes away your coat, do not withhold your shirt from him either. Give to everyone who asks of you and whoever takes away what is yours, do not demand it back. And just as you want people to treat you, treat them in the same way. And if you love those who love you, what credit is that to you? For even sinners love those who love them. And if you do good to those who do good to you, what credit is that to you? For even sinners do the same. And if you lend to those from whom you expect to receive, what credit is that to you? Even sinners lend to sinners, in order to receive back the same amount. But love your enemies, and do good, and lend, expecting nothing in return; and your reward will be great and you will be sons of the Most High; for He Himself is kind to ungrateful and evil men.

Romans 2:4; Proverbs 24:17-18; Proverbs 25:21-22; Psalm 18:3; Psalm 25:2; Psalm 27:11; Proverbs 16:7; Isaiah 59:19.

Is it possible to have eternal life with God?

John 3:16-18. For God so loved the world, that He gave his only begotten Son, that whoever believes in Him should not perish, but have eternal life. For God did not send the Son into the world to judge the world, but that the world should be saved through Him. He who believes in Him is not judged; but he who does not believe has been judged all ready, because he has not believed in the name of the only begotten Son of God.

John 3:3, 5-7; John 17:3; John 6:37, 44, 47; 2 Peter 3:9; Isaiah 53:6; Romans 3:23; Isaiah 64:6; James 1:15; Romans 6:23; Romans 5:8; John 5:24; Romans 10:9-10; John 1:12; Matthew 10:32-33; Luke 9:26.

Does God hear and answer prayer?

1 John 5:14-15. And this is the confidence which we have before Him, that, if we ask anything according to His will, He hears us. And if we know that He hears us in whatever we ask, we know that we have the requests which we have asked from Him.

Psalm 102:17. He has regarded the prayer of the destitute, and has not despised their prayer.

Proverbs 15:29; James 1:6-8; 2 Chronicles 7:14; Proverbs 15:8; 1 Peter 3:12; Luke 11:9-10; John 14:14; Mark 11:24; Matthew 18:18-20; Luke 12:29-31; Jude 20; James 5:16-18.

What is the Holy Spirit for?

1 Corinthians 2:11-12. For who among men knows the thoughts of a man except the spirit of the man, which is in him? Even so the thoughts of God no one knows except the Spirit of God. No, we have received, not the spirit of the world, but the Spirit who is from God, that we might know the things freely given to us by God.

Romans 8:15-16. For you have not received a spirit of slavery leading to fear again, but you have received a spirit of adoption as sons by which we cry out, "Abba! Father!" The Spirit Himself bears witness with our spirit that we are children of God...

John 16:13; John 14:16-17, 26; Acts 2:38; John 7:38-39; Acts 1:8; Jude 20; 1 Corinthians 6:19; Ephesians 4:30; 1 Thessalonians 4:8; Ephesians 1:14; Luke 11:13; Ephesians 5:18.

What do angels do?

Psalm 91:11-12. For He will give His angels charge concerning you, to guard you in all your ways. They will bear you up in their hands, Lest you strike your foot against the stone.

Psalm 34:7. The angel of the Lord encamps around those who fear Him and rescues them.

Psalm 103:20; Hebrews 1:14; 2 Peter 2:11; Jude 6; Matthew 13:41, 49; Matthew 24:31; Matthew 18:10.

Does it matter if I go to church?

Hebrews 10:25. Not forsaking our own assembling together, as is the habit of some, but encouraging one another; and all the more , as you see the day drawing near.

Ecclesiastes 4:9-10. Two are better than one because they have good return for their labor. For if either of them falls, the one will lift up his companion. But woe to the one who falls when there is not another to lift him up.

1 John 1:7; Ephesians 5:19-21; Acts 2:46; 1 Corinthians 14:26; 1 Corinthians 11:18; Acts 4:31; Colossians 2:19.

What does the Bible say about pride?

Proverbs 16:18. Pride goes before destruction, and a haughty spirit before stumbling.

Proverbs 18:12. Before destruction the heart of man is haughty, but humility goes before honor.

Proverbs 16:5, 19; Proverbs 15:25; Proverbs 6:16-17; Proverbs 21:4; Proverbs 28:25; Proverbs 13:10; Proverbs 11:2; Proverbs 29:23; Psalm 73:6; Obadiah 1:3; Daniel 4:37; 1 John 2:16; Proverbs 8:13; Psalm 12:3; Psalm 31:23; Psalm 40:4; Psalm 138:6; Ecclesiastes 7:8; 2 Samuel 22:28; James 4:6.

HOW TO SHARE CHRIST WITH A FRIEND

God desires for everyone to enter into the life that He offers, and share with others how they may also enter into that life. Many times as Christians we feel inadequately prepared to show the way to salvation to our friends.

Here are some general pointers along with Scripture that will help you share Christ with a friend.

1) **Explain that we all have sinned.**
Isaiah 53:6: *All of us like sheep have gone astray, each one has turned to his own way; But the Lord has caused the iniquity of us all to fall on Him.*
Romans 3:23: *For all have sinned and fall short of the glory of God.*

2) **Point out the end result of sin.**
James 1:15: *Then when lust has conceived, it gives birth to sin; and when sin is accomplished, it brings forth death.*
Romans 6:23: *For the wages of sin is death, but the free gift of God is eternal life in Christ Jesus our Lord.*

3) **Tell them what God did about it.**
John 3:16: *For God so loved the world, that He gave His only begotten Son, that whoever believes in Him should not perish, but have eternal life.*
Romans 5:8: *But God demonstrated His own love toward us, in that while we were yet sinners, Christ died for us.*

4) **Tell them how they can respond to God's offer.**
Romans 10:9-10: *That if you confess with your mouth Jesus as Lord, and believe in your heart that God raised Him from the dead, you shall be saved. For with the heart man believes, resulting in righteousness, and with the mouth he confesses, resulting in salvation.*
John 1:1-2: *But as many as received Him, to them He gave the right to become the children of God, even to those who believe in His name.*

5) **Give them God's assurance.**
Romans 8:38-39: *For I am convinced that neither death, nor life, nor angels, nor principalities, nor things present, nor things to come, nor powers, nor height, nor depth, nor any other created thing, shall be able to separate us from the love of God, which is in Christ Jesus our Lord.*
Hebrews 13:5: *Let your character be free from the love of*

money, being content with what you have; for He Himself has said, "I will never desert you, nor will I ever forsake you."

Matthew 28:20: *"Teaching them to observe all that I commanded you; and lo, I am with you always, even to the end of the age."*

6) **Show them how to walk.**

Romans 12:1-2: *I urge you therefore, brethren, by the mercies of God, to present your bodies a living and holy sacrifice, acceptable to God, which is your spiritual service of worship. And do not be conformed to this world, but be transformed by the renewing of your mind, that you may prove that the will of God is, that which is good and acceptable and perfect.*

7) **Give them one final piece of wisdom.**

Mark 12:30: *And you shall love the Lord your God with all your heart, and with all your soul and with all your mind, and with all your strength.*

Finally, a simple prayer that acknowledges one's sinful condition and expresses a sincere desire to be forgiven and to share in eternal life should be prayed.

It could go like this:

Father God,

I acknowledge that I have sinned and fallen short of your glory.

All my good works to obtain righteousness are as filthy rags.

I believe that Jesus died for me and that you raised Him from the dead to live forever.

I ask you to forgive me all my sins and to give me this free gift of eternal life through Jesus Christ.

Amen.

YOUTH AND MINISTRY ORGANIZATIONS

ABUSE

LIFE AFTER ASSAULT LEAGUE INC.
1336 W. Lindbergh
Appleton, WI 54914
414-739-4489
Provides free victim-to-victim counseling through the mail, by phone or one on one for those who are sexually abused.

AIDS MINISTRIES

AIDS INFORMATION MINISTRIES
PO Box 136116
Fort Worth, TX 76136
817-237-0230
Provides AIDS ministry and information to churches and schools.

LOVE & ACTION
3 Church Circle
Annapolis, MD 21401
301-268-3442
Volunteer ministry serving people with AIDS, their families, friends and churches. Provides an AIDS education program for churches. Brochures and educational materials available.

ALCOHOLISM/DRUG INTERVENTION

ALCOHOLICS FOR CHRIST
1316 N. Campbell Road
Royal Oak, MI 48067
1-800-441-7877
Nondenominational, non-profit, evangelical fellowship for substance abusers and their families.

EPHESIANS 5:18 LIFE MINISTRIES
1620 Elton Road, Suite 204
Silver Spring, MD 2090
301-439-7191
Provides a 12-step program, testing and clinical group work for substance abusers and their families.

NATIONAL TEEN CHALLENGE
1525 N. Campbell Avenue
Springfield, MO 65803
417-862-6969
Offers drug and alcohol treatment programs.

NATIONAL WOMEN'S CHRISTIAN TEMPERANCE UNION
Evanston, IL 60201
708-864-1396
Nonprofit, nonpartisan, interdenominational organization dedicated to educating people, especially youth on the harmful effects of alcohol and drugs on the body and society.

NEW LIFE MINISTRIES
7900 Plaza Blvd. #188, Suite 140
Mentor, OH 44060-5517
216-946-7037 or 216-257-7103
Nonprofit organization offering retreats, workshops, support groups and seminars on drug and alcohol abuse, codependency and related issues.

NEW LIFE TREATMENT CENTERS, INC.
570 Glenneyre, #107
Laguna Beach, CA 92651
800-227-LIFE
800-332-TEEN (Hotlines)
714-494-8383 (Office)
Offers Christian psychiatric health care to individuals dealing with eating disorders, chemical dependency, compulsive sexual behavior and depression.

OVERCOMERS OUTREACH, INC.
2290 W. Whittier Blvd., Suite A-D
La Habra, CA 90631
213-697-3994
Nonprofit ministry of support groups to chemically dependent people, their family members and friends.

WALTER HOVING HOME FOR WOMEN
PO Box 194
Garrison, NY 10524
914-424-3674
A one-year school promoting Christian growth for substance-abusing women 18 to 55.

CAMPUS OUTREACH

CAMPUS CRUSADE FOR CHRIST
Arrowhead Springs
San Bernardino, CA 92414
714-886-5224
Interdenominational ministry focusing on worldwide evangelism and discipleship.

CALEB CAMPAIGN
Rt. 4, Box 274
W. Frankfort, IL 62896
618-937-2348
Support and materials for teens witnessing in public schools.

FELLOWSHIP OF CHRISTIAN ATHLETES
8701 Leeds Road
Kansas City, MO 64129
816-921-0909
Christ-centered, Bible-based and athletically-focused ministry for coaches and student athletes.

INTERVARSITY CHRISTIAN FELLOWSHIP
PO Box 7895
Madison, WI 53707-7895
608-274-9001

THE NAVIGATORS
PO Box 6000
Colorado Springs, CO 80934
719-598-1212
Campus ministries focusing on evangelism and discipleship.

SPORTS WORLD MINISTRIES, INC.
Box 500, 104 Main Street
New Tazewell, TN 37825
615-626-8291
1-800-832-6546
Ministers through professional athletes to America's students and workforce in schools, offices and churches around the country.

YOUNG LIFE
PO Box 520
Colorado Springs, CO 80901
719-473-4262
Junior and senior high school relational ministry. Sponsors school-year meetings, week-long summer camps and seminary-level Institute for Youth Ministries.

YOUTH WITH A MISSION
Box 30
Elm Springs, AK 72728
501-248-7236

ABORTION ALTERNATIVES

ABORTION ALTERNATIVES OF THE NORTHEAST, INC.
25 John Street
Greenwich, NY 12834
518-692-7298 (collect calls accepted)
Offers free pregnancy testing, counseling, clothing, nursery furniture and follow-up visits. Educational materials available.

BETHANY CHRISTIAN SERVICES
901 Eastern Ave., NE
Grand Rapids, MI 49503
1-800-BETHANY (hotline)
616-459-6273 (office)
Offers 24-hour lifeline pregnancy counseling, full adoption services (domestic and international), interim care for infants, and foster care for children who are older and/or have special needs.

BIRTHRIGHT INTERNATIONAL
777 Coxwell Avenue
Toronto, Canada M4C 3C6
1-800-328-LOVE
Operates nearly 600 crisis pregnancy centers in the U.S. and Canada. Offers alternatives to abortion.

OPEN ARMS
PO Box 1056
Columbia, MO 65205
314-449-7672
Helps those suffering from the emotional and spiritual aftermath of abortion.

TROUBLED YOUTH

YOUTH FOR CHRIST
Youth Guidance Division
360 Main Place
Carol Stream, IL 60188
Nation's largest evangelical outreach to juvenile offenders. Works with juvenile courts, probation departments and police. Will help set up local chapter and train full-time staff.

FURTHER READING

Becker, Verne. *The Campus Life Guide to Surviving High School.* Grand Rapids: Zondervan, 1984.

Davis, Ken. *How to Live with Your Parents Without Losing Your Mind.* Grand Rapids: Zondervan, 1988.

Eble, Diane. *The Campus Life Guide to Dating.* Grand Rapids: Zondervan, 1990.

Hurnard, Hanna. *Hinds Feet on High Places.* Wheaton, IL: Tyndale, 1975.

Little, Paul. *How to Give Away Your Faith.* Downers Grove, IL: Intervarsity Press, 1988.

Lucado, Max. *No Wonder They Call Him the Savior.* Portland: Multnomah, 1986.

Lutes, Chris and Kris Bears. *The Campus Life Guide to Making and Keeping Friends.* Grand Rapids: Zondervan, 1984.

McDowell, Josh and Dr. Norm Wakefield. *Friend of the Lonely Heart: How to Overcome Feelings of Loneliness.* Dallas: Word, 1979.

McGinnis, Alan Loy. *The Friendship Factor.* Minneapolis: Augsburg, 1979.

Miller, Calvin. *The Singer Trilogy.* Downers Grove, IL: Intervarsity Press, 1990.

Moody, Dwight L. *Prevailing Prayer.* Chicago: Moody Press, 1979.

Morrison, Jan. *A Safe Place: Beyond Sexual Abuse.* Wheaton, IL: Harold Shaw, 1990.

Peterson, Lorraine. *Dying of Embarrassment... & Living to Tell About It.* Minneapolis, MN: Bethany, 1988.

Peterson, Lorraine. *Falling off Cloud Nine and Other High Places.* Minneapolis, MN: Bethany, 1981.

Pink, Michael. *Tough Questions Straight Answers.* Chicago: Moody Press, 1991.

Ryrie, Charles. *Biblical Answers to Contemporary Issues.* Chicago: Moody Press, 1991.

Sciacca, Fran. *To Walk and Not Grow Weary: Renewing Your Strength in Depressing Circumstances.* Colorado Springs: NavPress, 1984.

Sheldon, Charles M. *In His Steps.* Grand Rapids: Zondervan, 1967.

Speck, Greg. *Living for Jesus When the Party's Over.* Chicago: Moody Press, 1991.

Speck, Greg. *Sex: It's Worth Waiting For.* Chicago: Moody Press, 1989.

Taylor, Dr. and Mrs. Howard. *Hudson Taylor's Spiritual Secret.* Chicago: Moody Press, 1989.

Thoene, Bodie. *Jerusalem Interlude.* Minneapolis: Bethany House, 1990.

Tirabassi, Becky and Gregg Lewis. *The Life of the Party: A True Story of Teenage Alcoholism.* Grand Rapids: Zondervan, 1991.

Tozer, A.W. *The Pursuit of God.* Camp Hill, PA: Christian Publications, Inc., 1982.

Yancey, Philip. *Disappointment with God.* Grand Rapids: Zondervan, 1988.

TOOLS FOR BIBLE STUDY

(Recommended Books to Acquire)

BIBLE DICTIONARY - Bible Dictionaries (such as the *Unger's Bible Dictionary* [Moody] are mini-encyclopedias, giving facts and background information about the 2,930 people, 1,551 places and hundreds of perplexing terms mentioned in Scripture. A you encounter an unusual word in your Bible study, take a few moments to look up that item in your Bible dictionary. Bible dictionaries also assist in the pronunciation of difficult names.

CONCORDANCE - Another worthwhile tool is a complete concordance, which lists every word in the Bible alphabetically and indicates every passage in which it is used. Some, such as *Strong's* (for King James Version words) or *The New American Standard Exhaustive Concordances*, provide definitions from the original Greek or Hebrew for every English Bible word.

TOPICAL BIBLE - A topical Bible (such as *Nave's Topical Bible* [Moody]) arranges Bible passages under subject headings (not necessarily the same word, but the same concept).

BIBLE HANDBOOK - A Bible handbook (such as *The New Unger's Bible Handbook* [Moody]) is a mini-commentary that will take you through the Bible by book and chapter, giving summaries and interpretational help en route.

BIBLE ATLAS - A Bible atlas (such as *The Moody Atlas of Bible Lands* [Moody]) gives maps, photographs, and historical information about Bible places (more than a Bible dictionary gives).

COMMENTARIES - Bible commentaries give interpretations of others on Bible passages. One of the best one-volume commentaries on the whole Bible is *The Wycliffe Bible Commentary* (Moody).

BIBLE CUSTOMS - Bible culture books (such as *The New Manners and Customs of Bible Times* by R. Gower [Moody]) offer more depth on such subjects as Bible occupations and everyday life than a Bible dictionary can.

Excellent tools are available to aid the Bible student, but they're of little value unless secured–and used!

Choose a passage and locate key words in whatever available tools you have–even if nothing more than an English dictionary. Begin today to experience some of the wonder built into the world of Bible words!